TITAN BOOKS

in association with

PRICE GUIDE PRODUCTIONS

presents

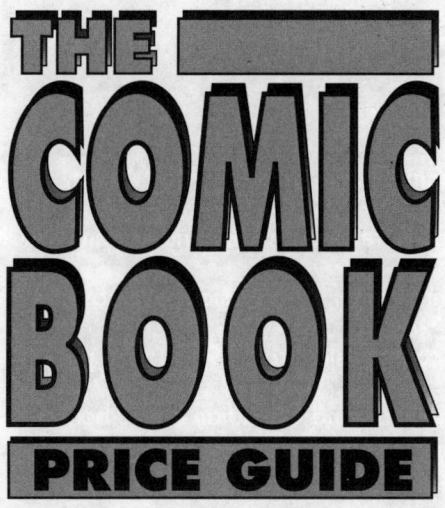

THE COMIC BOOK PRICE GUIDE

1996/97 EDITION

by DUNCAN McALPINE
(COMPILER AND EDITOR)

with John Skoulides

Editor (British Section)
STEVE HOLLAND

Honorary Editor
ALAN AUSTIN

The Comic Book Price Guide Hall of Fame
BOB OVERSTREET

The indispensable reference companion for British fans, collectors and dealers

"If you are reading this you will appreciate the value of some of the rarest and most sought after comics, the complexities of collecting and the need for such an authoritative catalogue"

— Colin Baker

- Based on the original 1983 guide by Alan Austin, Justin Ebbs and Gary Fox

- Completely updated, revised and expanded from the UK Price Guide #6

- Fully illustrated throughout with classic comic covers

- DC and Marvel comics listed from 1938 to the present

- Independent, American and Canadian comic books

- Graphic novels and trade paperbacks

- British comics and annuals

- Features on the grading, preservation, storage and handling of comics

- Collectors' information for Marvel, DC and Independents

- Prices for each comic in three grades in both $US and £UK, plus the differing formats, page-counts, rarity and distribution

- Major artists' and writers' work, back-ups, reprints, secondary features

- First appearances index plus cross-overs and tie-ins

- Sixteen page colour section featuring selected classic first appearances

- Top 50 rarest comics in the world

- Top 100 comics and titles for DC, Marvel and Independents

- New revised Trading and Bubble Gum Card guide

EDITOR'S FOREWORD

It's been a hell of a year. It's been a hell of a last two years. I was sad when it reached the point of not being able to do a Price Guide in 1995. But seeing one's business collapse in circumstances beyond one's control is bad enough. There are no winners in a liquidation. Only the company that administrates the process and takes its cut. To see it all happen again from afar after having left East Barnet Road was an experience I would not want to put my worst enemy through. All one can do is pick up the pieces and start again.

This new Price Guide has been very therapeutic for me. A new Publisher. A new Database System. A new Dual Price Format. It's been like writing two whole new books as it has been such a long time since the last U.K. Guide (July 1994). John Skoulides has been great. We delight in arguing over prices and dreaming of the day when the book will be what we want it to be. That can only be done with your help. There is a new Editorial Address. Don't wait to be asked or cajoled or begged. We're tired of doing that. The Price Guide should be a platform for everybody to have their say. So write. Anytime.

My thanks list is important. Louise, my better half, for all her help and encouragement. My children Benjamin and Ella for scribbling all over my computer printouts. And John Skoulides, without whom this book would not have been possible (he in turn would like to say "thank you" to his better half Sue and to Rick Appleby for constant research help).

A very special mention must be reserved for David Dupont and Helen Sawyer for their type-setting and design and a thousand other little jobs that you don't see and they receive no recognition for (like rescuing advertisers from major disasters with their copy).

Major thanks also to Steve Holland, compiler of the British section which is now looking somewhere near what we both dream about. It is surely the best British listing ever produced.

The roll call of thanks goes on to all the main and other contributors and market reporters who are credited elsewhere in this book. I look forward to the day when that contributors' listing runs into many pages.

The people at Titan Books cannot go without recognition. My thanks to Nick Landau, Katy Wild, Simon Furman, Ruth and Siobhan and anybody else who has been involved in the production of this book including Beverley at Marot.

Howard Hughes, Colin Clarke, Kelvin, Brian and all at Commercial Colour Press know they have my thanks and it has been a pleasure doing a sixth book with them.

While Alan Austin never seeks the limelight, I once again acknowledge him as the founding father of price guides in this country and his rightful place as "The Guvnor".

I seem to spend so much of my time mentioning Bob Overstreet as the author of the very first price guide for comic books. And rightly so for all he has done for this industry.

Penultimate thanks to Tony Petrou for all his work on the computing side. We're up, we're down, we agree, we disagree. But ultimately I acknowledge the amount of work he has done to make this book the best it can possibly be. And thanks also to his better half Demi for her hospitality when we're working late into the night.

My final thanks are reserved for the cover artist Gary Frank and especially the foreword writer Colin Baker who went out of his way for me.

Read and enjoy.

Duncan McAlpine

DUNCAN McALPINE
This book is as ever dedicated to my family Louise, Benjamin and Ella. Wouldn't mind another one...

CONTRIBUTORS TO THE 1996/97 EDITION

MAIN CONTRIBUTORS TO THE 1996/97 EDITION
RON HALL • DARRYL JONES • DAN MALAN • DUNCAN McMILLAN • JOHN PIRES • BARRIE RONESS • GRANT RYMER

MARKET REPORTERS TO THE 1996/97 EDITION
ANTHONY ADDISON & SHEILA ANN DUXBURY • MANNY AMARIO • RICK & STEVE APPLEBY • DAVID BRAYSHER • JULES BURT & GEORGE LESSITER
IVOR DAVIS • RICHARD EMMS • DAVE FINN & SUSAN FOORD • MARTIN GOLD • DARRYL JONES • ALAN SCOTT

OTHER CONTRIBUTORS TO THE 1996/97 EDITION
ALEX ALEXANDER • LARRY ALI • ROB BARROW (Fantasy Trading Card Company) • COLIN CAMPBELL (Comics Warehouse)
IAN HOLMES • DUNCAN McMILLAN • DANIEL MOKADES • TREVOR NORRIS • TIM O'DONNELL • IDHAM RAMADI
STANLEY RIIKS • PAUL SASSIENIE • STEPHEN SENNITT • MICHAEL STANWYCK • DEZ SKINN (Comics International) • GEOFF WEST (Conquistador)

Administrator: LOUISE CRAVEN
Computer Consultant: TONY PETROU
Design Consultants: XENDO

ABOUT THE COVER
In keeping with asking Britain's top artists to provide a cover, I was encouraged by Steve Holland to ask Mr Gary Frank whose work I have known for some time.
I have been particularly impressed with his work on *The Incredible Hulk*. As he was doing a *Sabretooth* one-shot comic at the time of asking and as Marvel Comics
have always been very helpful in clearing cover images quickly and efficiently for me, I thought that the least I could do was publicise one of their characters.
Illustration of *Sabretooth* by Gary Frank. Copyright © 1996 Marvel Entertainment Group, Inc.

DISCLAIMER
The views expressed by the contributors are not necessarily those of the Publishers. Every care is taken to ensure that the contents of this book are accurate but the
Publishers assume no responsibility for errors whatsoever. Whilst extreme care and prior conditions acceptance are used when accepting and publishing
advertisements, the Publishers cannot accept any responsibilty whatsoever for copyright infringement and plagiarism. All illustrations reproduced within the pages of
The Comic Book Price Guide for Great Britain remain the property of their respective copyright holders and are used in an information, news and comparative capacity.
No infringement of copyright is intended.

THE COMIC BOOK PRICE GUIDE 1996/97
ISBN 1 85286 675 6

Published by Titan Books
42–44 Dolben Street, London SE1 0UP

First Edition April 1996
10 9 8 7 6 5 4 3 2 1

WARNING
IN ORDER TO HELP PREVENT THE UNLAWFUL COPYING AND REPRODUCTION OF ANY SECTION OF THE PRICE GUIDE LISTINGS,
INFORMATIONAL DEVICES HAVE BEEN PLACED THROUGHOUT THE TEXT KNOWN ONLY TO THE EDITOR. THESE DEVICES ARE NOT
INTENTIONALLY MISLEADING, NOR DO THEY AFFECT THE VALUE OF ANY GIVEN COMIC. THEY ARE HOWEVER INSTANTLY
RECOGNISABLE SHOULD THE NEED AND OCCASION ARISE.

CORRESPONDENCE
PLEASE ADDRESS ALL COMMUNICATIONS TO THE FOLLOWING ADDRESS:
PRICE GUIDE PRODUCTIONS,
PO BOX 10793
LONDON N10 3NF

DESIGN AND TYPESETTING
XENDO, 167 FERNHEAD ROAD, LONDON W9 3ED

PRINTING
COMMERCIAL COLOUR PRESS, 116-118 WOODGRANGE ROAD, FOREST GATE, LONDON E7 0EW. TEL: (0181) 519 1919

Foreword by
COLIN BAKER

The word "comics" conjures for me memories of Rochdale Covered Market where I used to spend my hard-earned pocket-money on my favourite cowboy comics – *Tom Mix*, *Hopalong Cassidy* and *Lash Larue*. I also remember being enthralled by the adventures of young Billy Batson who with one magic word – *"SHAZAM!"* – transformed himself into Captain Marvel, the world's mightiest mortal. Then these new boys, Superman and Batman came along...

When I played Doctor Who in his sixth incarnation, I enjoyed a strange experience for any actor, that of seeing himself in comic-strip form. Some versions were flattering, though some of the better artists drew me a little too well! I have even contributed to the genre myself and wrote *Age of Chaos*, a Doctor Who graphic novel, for Marvel Comics and at the risk of the accusation of unsubtlety I'd be delighted to repeat the experience. I'm so glad to see the good Doctor making a comeback. Paul McGann is a very fine actor and will realise very quickly, as I did, that it's a peach of a part. I'm also glad that a new generation of children – like my four, the eldest of whom is ten – will now have a Doctor of their very own.

If you are reading this you will appreciate the value of some of the rarest and most sought after comics, the complexities of collecting and the need for such an authoritative catalogue. And remembering the Classic Comics series I used to buy forty years ago, like *Black Beauty* and *Lorna Doone*, at the very least it's a great way of getting kids into the world of fiction and story-telling and the worlds of the imagination in time and space.

CONTENTS

ADVERTISEMENTS

ABBREVIATIONS AND TERMINOLOGY USED IN THIS GUIDE

Arrival Date	pencil markings on the cover of a comic that indicate when that comic was received by the distributor or news-stand dealer to be sold on the news-stand. The date is usually two months prior to the cover date. Much more of a U.S. market phenomenon and concern
Ashcan	a prototype comic put together by a publisher to secure title and format copyright. Usually new black and white covers stapled around an existing comic
Baxter	a type of high quality heavier stock white paper
B&W	Black and White artwork
Bi-Monthly	published every two months
Bi-Weekly	published every two weeks
Bondage cover	usually shows a glamorous female bound and/or gagged
Bookshelf Format	Marvel's equivalent of DC's Prestige Format: a special edition of a comic that approaches a graphic novel
Bronze Age	generally accepted to be the period of comics from 1970-1980. More widely used in America than the U.K.
Cameo	a brief appearance by a character (comic book or real) in a comic story. Usually defined as being 2 or 3 panels only.
(c)or(cy)	the copyright date or copyright year on an otherwise undated publication
CCA	The Comics Code Authority that issued a Seal of Approval on most mainstream comics from April 1955
Digest	a paperback collected edition, smaller than regular comic size, most usually reprints. 4" x 6"
DS	double size: an issue with twice the number of pages than a normal size comic ie. 64 pages
Dust Shadow	when an edge of a comic, front or back cover, is exposed to a layer of dust over the years, leaving a dark shadow
Embossed	when a pattern is pressed into a cover to form a raised surface
Film	a film adaptation or a comic based on concepts from a film.
1st	first appearance, of a character or of a character in that title. Can also be used for objects, places etc.
flashback	a sequence injected into a story either by the narrators or a character remembering or re-telling the story in some part
Foil cover	a special coloured cover on card-stock paper with a "metallic" sheen
Foxing	tiny red-brown or red-orange spores in paper caused by damp. This is most prevalent on Golden Age and some Silver Age material
GA	Golden Age, commonly accepted to be 1938–1945.
Graphic Novel	paperback or hardback special edition of a comic, high production value text, art and reproduction. Term first coined by Will Eisner in the late 1970s. Usually 8" x 11" in size.
holo-grafix cover	a silver-shard printed effect on a cover that produces different colours radiating outward as the cover is rolled around in a light source
intro	introducing (usually a character)
JLA	Justice League of America
JLI	Justice League International
JSA	Justice Society of America
Late Golden Age	the period of comics from 1945-1949
Late Silver Age	the period of comics from 1966-1969
LD	Limited Distribution in the UK. Applies mainly to post 1970 comics. More recently denotes the fact that a high demand item has sold quickly and is scarce in its availability
less common	a term that is still being tested referring to a noticeable scarcity of a comic that was previously thought not to be scarce
LSH	Legion of Super-Heroes
Mag	Magazine format or size
Mando	a type of high-quality paper
Marvel Chipping	a defect peculiar to Marvel comics of the 1950's and 1960's in the trimming process that resulted in chips out of the right edge of the cover
Mature Readers	a comic labelled for Mature Readers; not intended for children
Modern Age	generally accepted to be from 1980 to the present day
MS	Mini or Maxi-series: an intentionally finite series
Mylar	inert plastic protective sleeve, stiffer and safer for storage purposes than an ordinary plastic bag
ND	Not Distributed in the UK
nn	No number: an unnumbered issue
OS	one-shot: a single issue, not part of a series
Pre Golden Age	the period of comics from 1933-1938
Pre Silver Age	the period of comics from 1950 -1955
Prestige Format	DC's equivalent of Marvel's Bookshelf Format: a special edition of a comic approaching a graphic novel

Printing defect	faults with a comic as a result of the production process. These include spine and cover wrinkles, extra paper "tags" on pages folded back in, pages still joined at top/bottom edges etc. While these still affect the grade of the comic, they are different from Grading Defects which occur as a result of wear and tear
Quarterly	published every three months
Rare	comics that are seldom seen in collections that come to light or are offered for sale in shops or on lists. Rarity may be due to original distribution or production circumstances. Applies readily to both new and old comics
re-done	a story re-told with new artwork
SA	Silver Age, 1956-1965
Scarce	a comic that is generally harder to obtain than most owing to original distribution circumstances. Applies mostly to pre 1970s comics
Scarcer	a comic that is noticeably not around for no apparent reason. Usually applied to newer comics and is a term that is still being tested like "less common"
Splash page	usually the first story art page, one single panel
Squarebound	a comic glue-bound with a square spined cover
sub crease	a vertical crease caused when a comic was folded in half for subscription mailing
3-D comic	comic produced in two colour tinted layers which produces a three-dimensional effect when viewed through special glasses
Toy	a comic title based on a toy product
Trade paperback	a 7"x10" paperback collection of a series of chosen stories, usually reprints
TV	a comic based on a Television show
Very Scarce	a comic that is harder to obtain than a Scarce issue, usually as a result of a production fault like a lost shipment or distribution inequality between US and UK. Also factors of high collector interest. Applies more readily to pre 1970 comics but can occasionally be used for newer comics
Very Rare	a comic that almost never turns up owing to original distribution or production reasons coupled with original and subsequent high collector interest resulting in many copies staying in collections for years away from the general circulation
X-over	Cross-over, when a character appears in another character's title so that the narrative directly continues. These occasions are usually multi-part stories and all parts are necessary to enjoy the full narrative

EXAMPLES OF USAGE

Neal Adams, Wrightson art	contains artwork by Adams and Wrightson, but not on the same strip
Neal Adams/Wrightson art	Neal Adams pencils, inked by Wrightson
Superman,Batman in 24	both appear in issue 24 in different stories
Superman/Batman in 24	both co-star in a story in issue 24
FEATURES	new stories, previously unpublished
REPRINT FEATURES	stories, often back-ups, which have been previously published elsewhere

ERRORS AND FURTHER INFORMATION

Although assembled directly from personal observations wherever possible, a project of this complexity will inevitably contain errors.
If you find any inaccuracies or omissions in the body of the text or in any of the featured articles, please write and tell us,
so that corrections can be made; any contributions will be credited in the next edition.

**FOR THOSE SENDING A SUBSTANTIAL BODY OF INFORMATION, THE BEST 5 WILL RECEIVE
A SPECIAL SIGNED AND NUMBERED COPY OF THE GUIDE. THESE 5 COPIES WILL BE UNIQUE.**

Have we omitted an artist whose work you feel should be noted, or ignored a title of collector interest?
With your suggestions and help, the 1997/8 edition can be more complete and comprehensive.
We would also like to hear from you if you have a particular field of knowledge;
Canadian comics or British reprints of American material, for instance.

PLEASE WRITE WITH ANY COMMENTS OR SUGGESTIONS TO:
Price Guide Productions,

PO Box 10793,

LONDON N10 3NF.

Always check the editorial address before sending any form of correspondence.

WELCOME to the 7th edition of the Comic Book Price Guide. This is in more ways than one a completely new book, having been re-designed to accommodate its most important new feature of dual-pricing for both the British and American markets.

For those not familiar with the history of the British Guide, particularly American dealers and collectors who may be seeing this book for the first time, this is how it went. The British Price Guide assumes its pedigree from the very fine pioneering work done by British dealer and fanzine editor Alan Austin (still in my opinion "The Guv'nor"), Justin Ebbs and Gary Fox, the 4th edition of which was released in 1982. In 1989, the 5th edition was released when myself and Lance Rickman assumed the agony and the ecstasy of production. We achieved what they said could not be done and moved the Guide into a new stage of professional packaging and widespread exposure.

Much experience was gained and after having taken over the sole responsibility of producing the Guide, the 6th Edition came out in April 1990 with a new look, a new format (professionally typeset) and a more comprehensive listing. Just to confuse matters I decided to establish a numbering sequence for this and future Guides, settling on a Number 2 as it was the second one that I had done. Number 3 came out in April 1991 with 30% more back-issue information and listings extended even further back into the early Silver Age. Numbers 4, 5 and 6 followed and this book is number 7.

This Guide, as with every other Guide that we have done, must be seen very much as a work-in-progress, a basis upon which to build for the future.

Where The Guide used to be divided into 4 sections of D.C., MARVEL, INDEPENDENTS and BRITISH with a general introduction to each, it was decided that this time around that all the American comics would be listed alpha-numerically with the section on British comics remaining separate at the end.

The British section is compiled by Mr. Steve Holland with help from a number of his associates and overseen by me.

It is necessarily a selection of the most sought after material though a definitive encyclopaedia and price guide of British comics is in development.

The British section dates largely from the beginning of the 20th Century and concentrates on that particularly area of science fiction and TV related material starting with The Eagle in 1950. This listing has also been expanded to include more British publications than ever before and once again a special Classics Illustrated section from Mr. Dan Malan, the foremost collector and historian of such material.

The pricing rationale for so vast and complex a subject is continually evolving as is more fully explained under the section PRICING STRUCTURE. Where the mechanics of the mathematics might necessarily break down, particularly with reference to more recent comics, a certain amount of judgement and common sense must be used. The more recent the comic, the less the margin between the near-mint and mint, to the point where they become more or less the same. And where the mathematics used to produce unsightly values like £13.20 or £3.60, we have devised a rounding up and rounding down formula to make for whole numbers in the Good and Fine columns.

As shall no doubt be repeated elsewhere, **IF A COMIC IS GRADED ACCURATELY AND FAIRLY, THE INFORMATION IN THIS BOOK WILL PROVIDE EXACTLY WHAT IT INTENDS – A GUIDE.**

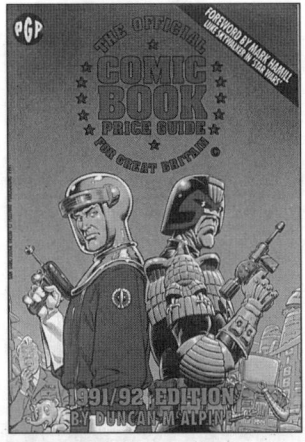

COLLECTING COMIC BOOKS

The collecting of comic books (or PANELOLOGY, to use the more scientific term) is at once fascinating and frustrating, exhaustive and rewarding, both creatively and often financially. Many people rediscover their interest in comics in later years (wishing Mother hadn't "thrown that pile of comics out, dear...") while others start collecting young and carry on building up their collections. This General Introduction highlights certain points worth remembering when buying new or old comics either on a regular basis or for the first time. This introduction is also written with the British market very much in mind though most of its points are universally applicable.

COMIC SHOPS AND SHOP ETIQUETTE

Brand new comics at the Newsagent or in specialist shops are not necessarily in MINT condition. They are more likely to be so at the comics shops rather than news-stands or newsagents as most comic shops now individually bag their new comics but they should still be checked for proper cut and trim, no creases or corners folded over, no ink stains inside or any other defects that may arise from packaging and delivery. When handling a shop's back-issue stock, a certain amount of care should be exercised. Individual comics are usually in alphabetical and numerical order in back-issue boxes and should not be shuffled around. Don't bend comics backwards to see the covers or thrust them carelessly back into place as you could be causing damage far in excess of the amount you will eventually spend. Comics should not be removed from bags without first checking with a member of staff as some dealers prefer to open and re-seal the bags themselves. Thoughtless customers soon become unpopular in any shop while careful browsers are universally welcomed.

BUYING NEW COMICS and BACK ISSUES

When buying back issues it is worth making a detailed "wants list" of a defined area of collecting, be it titles or characters, themes or artists. ABOVE ALL ELSE, IT PAYS TO SHOP AROUND as prices can vary tremendously and with patience a good deal can be obtained. Having said that it is also worthwhile concentrating on one shop or one dealer to build up a rapport and relationship that may lead to more personal service and better deals. It is also a good idea to budget strictly and collect within one's means though this often proves to be the greatest point of frustration and even more so if one chooses to collect higher condition (and therefore higher priced) comics. Collectors are becoming more and more aware of grading and condition and many set a minimum acceptable grade or improve the general condition of a collection by gradual replacement (upgrading). As ever it is all a matter of personal choice as some prefer to collect entire runs of high-grade comics and others just want to read the comics and stories whatever their condition.

PROFIT OR FUN?

As in any other dealing there is a certain element of financial speculation in the market where current fashions, hyped-up demand and limited supplies can realise quick profits for the well-informed investor. Recent market reports in American publications indicate that more and more businessmen are treating Golden Age comics especially as an easily-negotiable and high-return investment.

A personal collection, however, that is seen only in terms of capital investment is all too easy to mismanage. Potential profit can become actual loss and the pleasure of collecting and dealing can often turn to disappointment. **ABOVE ALL ELSE, I BELIEVE THAT COMICS ARE MEANT PRIMARILY FOR FUN AND ENJOYMENT,** to be read and appreciated for what they are and to be collected and dealt in on that basis. Any financial gain is purely a bonus and a reassurance that money can be well invested if so desired.

SELLING YOUR COLLECTION

When it comes to selling, a vendor has two courses of action – sell to a dealer or sell the comics yourself. Selling to a shop or dealer cuts out a lot of time and hassle but with their overheads and profit margins to consider, only a certain percentage – often around half and sometimes less – of a comic's market value will be given. Some may take comics in trade against purchase of other items but again percentages will be lower as any comics they take still have to be processed and sold. Selling comics yourself can be time consuming and involve certain costs but may realise higher gains.

Advertisements in fan publications and stalls at comic marts and conventions are the usual way of reaching potential customers. The disadvantage is that the rarer or the most popular comics will sell quite quickly, leaving you with a less saleable collection of low-interest titles.

STARTING A BUSINESS

(see also the article written by Suresh Tolat further on in this book)

With the continued growth of comics in this country as an industry it is tempting for a novice collector to start up in business, assuming that all dealers make huge profits and keep the best items for themselves. All too often a prized collection is used to start up a fledgling business with the best of intentions only to see it frittered away and wasted.

If there is an intention to turn collecting into a business or just start one having observed from the outside, it is essential to seek professional advice. Banks will provide all the information you need on finances and distribution companies will help you (or should do!) with stock control. Either way, a few points to bear in mind may help. These points are fairly obvious to most people but worth re-iterating nonetheless.

1) Have a very clear idea of your intended target-market and the size of your operation.
2) Have a very clear and professional business plan set out for at least 18 months ahead.
3) Have a very clear idea of your intended image or logo design and how you are going to advertise yourself. There is an awful lot of competition out there! You need to get your name known.
4) Be sure that you are well versed in the current state of the market. There are a number of magazines and books that are essential reading such as Comics International, Previews, Overstreet's Fan and Krause Publications' Comic Buyers Guide.
5) Be sure that you can afford the proper amount of time to your business, no matter how small or side-line. All dealers will tell you that everything takes longer than one might think. Be prepared for some long hours!
6) Seek advice from dealers, particularly those who have been established for some time but realise that they are not going to give away their trade secrets that they may have learned after years of hard work.
7) Try to find a new way of doing things, offering a level of service that makes you stand out from the rest.
8) Be approachable from other dealers in terms of doing business as things often come about after a chance meeting or conversation.
9) If employing others, make sure you are definite and clear in your relationship with them. Too often friends can fall out, particularly over money!
10) Above all else, approach your business with common sense and if in doubt, talk to someone.

These are by no means hard and fast rules to easy success but they are obvious considerations worth stating here. As such there is no formal training to be a comics dealer though a knowledge of financial matters coupled with expertise in a particular field is obviously advantageous.

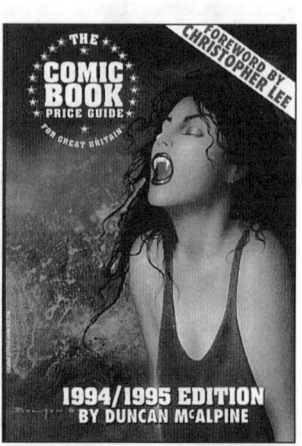

THE DISTRIBUTION AND SCARCITY OF COMICS

The relative scarcity of certain comics owing to original production factors or distribution patterns are denoted throughout the Guide very carefully. While it is impossible to ascribe actual numbers to the various terms that are used, every effort through consultation and comparison has been made to be accurate though the scarcity and distribution of some issues remains contentious. Below is a list of generally accepted terms in the U.K. market in order of degree of scarcity.

L.D.

LIMITED OR LOW DISTRIBUTION IN THE U.K.

This is a term for the purposes of this book that applies to the U.K. market and should be noted by American dealers and collectors. A good example of **L.D.** would be D.C.'s Crisis on Infinite Earths #1 which had a generally lower than usual distribution around the U.K. and as it didn't turn up in all the Newsagents it was a little harder to get in some areas. **L.D.** is a term that generally applies to comics after 1970 or thereabouts.

Please note however that owing to the number of specialist shops throughout the UK, ever growing distribution companies and more U.K. dealers bringing back quantities of material from U.S. conventions, the concept of Low Distribution of a comic through all the normal outlets has lost much of its meaning in the last few years. The term **L.D.** is now more often applied to a high-demand item that sells out very quickly, is therefore immediately sought after by fans and collectors and does not often turn up in collections bought by dealers a few months later.

N.D.

NON OR NOT DISTRIBUTED IN THE U.K.

to the usual network to Newsagents. These comics are thus harder to obtain than Low Distributed comics. This term is most traditionally applicable to certain 1970's comics. American dealers and collectors will note throughout this book that there are quite a few comics with this **N.D.** accreditation. There have, however, always been **N.D.** comics as far as the U.K. market is concerned in fluctuating degrees as prior to the mid 1970s there were no large-scale distributors of comics so an **N.D** comic then was considerably harder to obtain. More recently with an increase in the distribution of the **N.D** issues to the specialist shops, they have become a little easier to obtain so the concept of **NON DISTRIBUTED** has increasingly less meaning but because they are still imported on a comparatively limited basis, generally by air freight or mail order by dealers and collectors, they still remain scarce in the general circulation. An example in the U.K. market would be the run of Amazing Spiderman #121-214 which were not distributed in the U.K at the time of publication in order not to clash with the Marvel U.K reprints of the original U.S. Spiderman stories that began in 1972 (see Mighty World of Marvel and Spiderman Comics Weekly in the British section).

SCARCE IN THE U.K.

A TERM GENERALLY APPLIED TO PRE 1970s COMICS

as those being harder to come by than most. Actual numbers of a particular issue are difficult to determine. The problem with applying the term is deciding whether a comic is scarce owing to original circumstances (like missing shipments to the U.K. of American Flagg #19) or to popularity and demand and therefore collectors sitting on copies leaving fewer in circulation. I believe that both reasons make the use of the term valid. It may be noted that the terms **L.D.** and **SCARCE** are virtually inter-changeable as they both mean more or less the same thing. I prefer to use **SCARCE** for older items

Daredevil #2 – Scarce in the U.K.

Strange Tales #130 – Very Scarce in the U.K.

Amazing Spiderman #19 – Rare in the U.K.

such as Fantastic Four #51 (i.e. pre 1970) and **L.D.** for more recent ones such as Fantastic Four #286 (i.e. post 1970) as concerns and awareness of limited distribution and indeed the coining of the term are more recent phenomena. In some instances a comic can however be **SCARCE** as well as **N.D.** in the U.K. market and as such may also be called **VERY SCARCE.**

VERY SCARCE IN THE U.K.

HARDER TO OBTAIN THAN SCARCE AND MAY BE VIRTUALLY INTER-CHANGEABLE WITH THE LATER TERM N.D. SCARCE.

Once again the use of the term **VERY SCARCE** would be for older items, that is, pre 1970s comics. An indication of this particular degree comes when back issue collections are bought by shops or dealers and the same recurring numbers of certain titles are missing for one reason or another. Silver Surfer (1st Series) #4 is a good example. Being a thicker issue at 68 pages than a regular comic with a cross-over

appearance of Thor and considered a collectible even cult title, Silver Surfer #4 is a comic that is generally deemed **VERY SCARCE** in the U.K. market. A newer comic that I would rather call **N.D. SCARCE** in the U.K. market would be Captain America King Size Annual #4, not distributed to UK newsagents and scarce even over in America owing perhaps to a production problem or high demand/lower print run at the time.

RARE IN THE U.K.

HARDER STILL TO OBTAIN THAN ANY OF THE ABOVE.

These comics do not often turn up in bought collections in the U.K. or seen for sale in comics shops or on Mailing lists. Classic examples in the U.K. market would be Avengers #9, Fantastic Four #7, Spiderman #18, X-Men #8. It is a term that, owing to its minimal use, may be applied to older as well as newer comics.

VERY RARE IN THE U.K.

ALMOST IMPOSSIBLE TO OBTAIN AND NOT EVEN SEEN BY THE MAJORITY OF PEOPLE IN ANY CONDITION.

Once again it is a term that may be applied to any comic regardless of its age so newer example may be the G.I. Joe Treasury Edition and older examples would be issues of certain esoteric romance or humour titles. In particular it would refer to Golden Age comics, some examples can be counted in tens and twenties on both sides of the Atlantic (see The Top 50 Rarest Section). Whatever contentions and arguments remain, all the terms from **SCARCE** to **VERY RARE** must be used with extreme caution in order to preserve their meaning. **THE INDISCRIMINATE AND UNINFORMED USE OF THE TERMS RENDERS THEM WORTHLESS** as it must be remembered that any degrees of scarcity of any comic must take into consideration the picture of the market as a whole and not the local absence of something in any one area.

Journey Into Mystery #109 – Very Rare in the U.K.

Iron Man #67 – ND in the U.K.

Amazing Spiderman #251 – LD in the U.K.

CENTS OR PENCE?

The majority of comics in circulation in the U.K. have cover prices in old (that is pre-1971 decimalisation examples like 9d or 10d) or new pence (that is post 1971 decimalisation examples like 6p or 15p) either imprinted in the top left or right-hand corners or ink-stamped somewhere on the cover. Comics distributed in America always have their prices in cents. Over the last few years comics set for distribution in the U.K. have both sets of prices. Some collectors prefer to have cents copies of comics as a mark of a kind of purism. Other collectors prefer to have pence copies because that is what they may remember reading as children. Comic dealers in this country generally do not distinguish between the two although in the case of earlier or more sought-after issues cents copies are sought after/valued more. It is in the case of RARE or KEY books that this difference becomes more marked. A genuinely near-mint copy of Incredible Hulk #1 for example is listed in this guide at £6,000. A near-mint cents copy of the same comic would be valued more highly. One reason for this is that the American market does not very highly regard pence copies of comics though this varies tremendously from dealer to dealer. Indeed it has been noticed particularly in the last year that more and more British priced copies of Silver Age material are appearing on American dealers lists with anything from about a 25% less price tag to actual parity with a presumably cents copy of the same comic.

It would be a fallacy to say that the one comic is inferior to the other. **BOTH ARE ESSENTIALLY EXACTLY THE SAME**, appearing on the same paper printed at the same time on the same machine on the same day. A pence-priced (or black) plate would have been substituted towards the end of the print run of each comic to print up the overseas-market issues for distribution. One cannot be said to be an inferior reprint of the other (for more expansion on this matter, see the article dealing with the differences between the U.K. and U.S. markets to be found further on in this book).

Broadly speaking the question of cents or pence does not matter for the vast majority of comics. It is only really of importance on rare or key issues and even then only on older items and there seems to be a traditional 20-25% difference in price although this is very approximate: as has been already indicated American dealers generally regard pence copies as inferior and will not trade in them or if they do they will offer very low percentages. Whether this situation will change depends on the usual factors of supply and demand. If unrestored, high grade copies of key issues are demanded, where else can American dealers go apart from pence copies if the supply of unrestored cents copies is drying up?

KEY ISSUES

The term **KEY ISSUE** means a comic that features an important event like the first appearance of a character, the origin story of a character or an issue that is historically important as the first of its type. Very often it is the first issue of a character's title. The term originated in America and as such American dealers and collectors have found an almost innumerable number of Keys, particularly in recent years. At times it seems that any excuse is found to make an individual comic that much more valuable, particularly one that was not selling in any great number before! An example would be issues of DC's Omega Men featuring the first appearances of a character called Lobo which for years were consigned to the depths of bargain boxes. The situation is such that the terms "Major Keys" and "Minor Keys" has become prevalent. This Guide's position is that where possible it draws attention to these issues but takes this opportunity to urge caution with any comics that appear to be artificially inflated for no apparent reason. It is difficult to know where to draw the line at calling a comic a "key issue" and how far one should go in paying for a desired

item. Once again it is a matter of personal choice. If new to collecting comics it would be wise to seek expert advice.

Those Key issues that have been established as such for some time however may be prized as items of great interest. Showcase #4 as the comic that reintroduced the Golden Age hero The Flash in a new, or Silver Age, incarnation and the first appearances of The Fantastic Four, Spiderman, The Hulk and Thor or even a more modern instance of the first appearance of the new X-Men in Giant Size X-Men #1 for example are all well established Key issues and in top condition are able to command multiples of Guide.

MULTIPLES OF GUIDE

The concept of "multiples of Guide" again originated in America when a particular collection called the Mile High Collection (later renamed, and rightly so, The Edgar Church Collection) came to light in 1977. A collection of 22,000 comics from the late 1930s to the early 1950s was discovered in Denver, Colorado. The overall condition of these comics was of an unprecedented high grade owing to the very favourable storage conditions and the fact that they were all part of the same collection, bought as new and ageing together, gave these comics a unique feel rather than a collection assimilated over the years of varying grades and degrees of deterioration (for more information on this and

other pedigree collections, see The Photo-Journal Guide to Comic Books Volume 1 by Ernie Gerber, an excellent and breath-taking set of books). The comics were immediately sold at twice the listed price in the then edition of the American Overstreet Guide. They changed hands over the years at ever spiralling multiples. One American dealer/collector sold a large number to another at four times Guide across the board, no matter what the comic or condition. In this way the Mile High Collection assumed a certain pedigree. Other notable high grade collections have since been discovered – The San Francisco, The Larsen, The Denver and The Allentown are considered to be the next best in roughly that order and in most cases (but not all) the Key issues such as Detective Comics #27 (featuring the first appearance of Batman) or Batman #1 and Superman #1 etc. have been of the highest order in terms of condition. These collections often come with a certificate of authentication or are easily identifiable by certain characteristics or markings and as such represent some of the best copies available of a particular issue on the world market and as such have excellent investment potential. They are all for the most part Golden Age collections, that is, featuring comics from the Golden Age of comic book heroes from the late 1930s to the late 1940s.

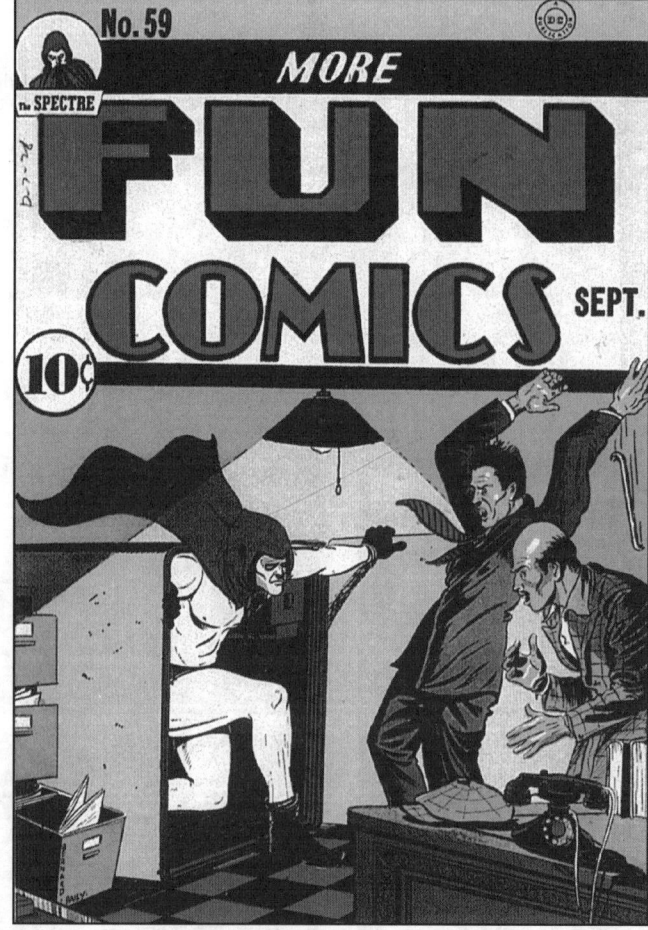

More Fun Comics #59 from the Edgar Church Collection.
Note the detail of "D-7-28" marked in distributor's crayon pencil top left of the cover. Most comics from this collection have variations on this coding and as such this is the identifying mark.

The most significant collection of recent years has been the White Mountain Collection of high grade Silver Age comics, much of which was sold at a San Diego Comicon. Key issues from this such as Spiderman #1 and Showcase #22 (1st Silver Age Green Lantern) have commanded multiples of Guide prices.

What this has meant for the discerning collector has been an increased awareness and valuation of comics that are in unusually nice condition, genuinely Very Fine or Near Mint. While comics in pedigree collections may command prices at three and four times the listed Guide price, comics that turn up individually in very high grade may vary as widely in price and as such more and more research is being done for this Guide to draw attention to particular issues. Key issues that are offered in unusually high grade but may not be from a pedigree collection may command prices over and above the listed Guide price (say Guide and a quarter or Guide and a half) though not in the accepted levels of 2 to 5 times Guide that the top pedigree collections can command. Outstanding examples of "multiples of Guide" are seven times Guide for a More Fun #52 (1st appearance of The Spectre) one particular year and more recently eight times Guide for an All Star Comics #8 (1st Wonder Woman).

A very noticeable distinction between the U.K. and U.S. markets is that in the former there is a marked resistance to the concept of multiples of Guide. This has been particularly true in the last couple of years. This point is discussed further in the article on the U.K. and U.S. markets and also under PRICING STRUCTURES.

Having taken all the above into consideration above all else this Guide advises those who are new to the field of collecting comics that it is essential to seek out professional advice before parting with large sums of money.

Inevitably where vast amounts of money are concerned, the problem of fakes and forgeries come into their own, particularly as the technology for the repair and restoration of comics gains in expertise and capability every year. It is unlikely that Silver and Golden Age forgeries can be created from scratch though there have been instances over the years of File Copies of key issues being created with elaborate stamps and approval ticks and signatures. Much of this is the subject of debate and speculation. Where possible and where known, details are given of forged comics that have appeared such as the counterfeit Cerebus the Aardvark #1 or Teenage Mutant Ninja Turtles #1. No value is given to these comics, as is the case quite rightly so with American guides.

THE REPAIR AND RESTORATION OF COMIC BOOKS

The repair and upgrading of comic books is still in its infancy in the U.K. That is to say that while it is a multi-million dollar industry in America, the full-time professional repair of comic books in this country is almost unheard of. The healthy market in America for Golden Age comics particularly from 1938-1948 means that there is a demand for repairing and effectively upgrading poorer condition copies of comics, very much more so for origin, first appearance or key issues. Comics purchased for hundreds of dollars and repaired for hundreds could be sold for thousands. This has led to a marked back-lash against restoration from time to time in the U.S. and a definite air of suspicion in the U.K. and certainly on both sides of the Atlantic against unskilled hack-jobs that even detract from the value of the comic in its original if poor condition. There is now a very definite distinction between comics that have been repaired by an amateur (often abbreviated in American catalogues by **rep.**) and those that have been professionally restored (often abbreviated as **rest.**). It is worthwhile for U.K. collectors and dealers for that matter getting hold of American catalogues and listings for examples of grading terminology and indications of restoration.

It is the intention of this Guide to produce in the near future a Restoration Guide for key issues in Heavy, Moderate and Light Restoration. Watch this space!

The more skilled and recognised work of the person who pioneered the restoration of comics Bill Sarrill, and today people like Susan Ciccione, Mark Wilson, Matt Wilson and Jef Hinds is generally held in esteem (as far as this author is concerned anyway). An argument for controlled restoration is that it may enhance and preserve an otherwise deteriorating comic for future appreciation and historical value. For example, if a comic has severe staple rust, should those staples be removed and the paper around that general area be restored to order to prevent further deterioration? An excellent publication that goes into greater depth on the subject is The Grading Guide by Bob Overstreet and is fully recommended by this publication.

an illustration of Susan Ciccone's work - a before and after of the same comic side by side - a landscape picture box across the bottom of the page?

All of this is not to say that restored comic books are in any way fakes or counterfeits. It merely depends on the amount of restoration and more importantly that both buyer and seller are fully aware and honest about the extent. It would be fair to say that American collectors are more experienced in recognising and understanding restoration than British collectors are. But British

collectors are becoming more aware of the situation as there is more documentation available and there are increasing numbers of British attendees at American conventions. Either way it is important when buying or selling special Gold and Silver Age comics, particularly for those people located in the U.K. market, to be aware of the restoration industry in general and to recognise what to look for.

For those unsure what to look for in a repaired or restored comic, these are some of the more common areas:

STAPLE REINFORCEMENT –

White Typex-like or transparent glue around the staples, usually on the inside front cover. The cover itself may have a certain stiff feeling when being opened and closed.

COLOUR TOUCHING –

Difficult to detect if done by a professional. Look at colour differences in the darker areas of the cover and particularly the spine. If any touch-ups have been done with a felt tip pen, these will show through on the inside of the cover. This Guide very much takes the attitude that if you have a comic with a worn spine or cover creases, DO NOT use felt tip pens! Leave well alone. You will only make the comic less attractive.

TEAR REPAIR –

The closing of tears in covers and pages using paper fibres or glue. Professional tear repair can be almost undetectable to the naked eye. Amateur attempts using glue or tiny pieces of magic tape can be easily spotted with careful inspection.

TRIMMING –

Where edges have been trimmed to even them up and lessen or hide original Marvel Chipping. This is considered to be a very serious defect and once again this Guide urges that if you have a comic that has even a tiny amount of Marvel chipping, even removing one or two millimetres from any edge of the covers will ultimately detract from that comic. Leave well alone.

DEACIDIFYING –

Where browning pages have been lightened or even whitened with chemicals. A slight chemical smell usually gives the game away though techniques have become very sophisticated and some would argue that controlled deacidification can benefit the long term life of a comic. Either way, such restoration should be thoroughly researched by a prospective client and only carried out by

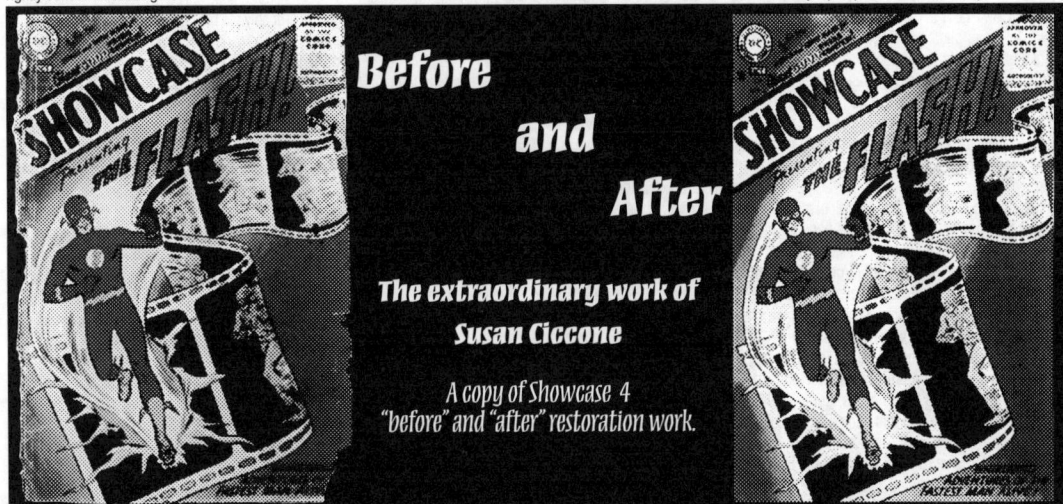

Before and After

The extraordinary work of Susan Ciccone

A copy of Showcase 4 "before" and "after" restoration work.

a professional. U.K. collectors should talk to people like Bill Cole of Bill Cole Enterprises in America for more information.

BLEACHING –

Where covers are lightened to give an almost unnatural white appearance. Generally considered to be more risky and less desirable than deacidifying as bleach physically weakens paper fibres. Again thorough information should be sought before embarking on this course of action.

SPINE REINFORCEMENT –

Where there was once a spine roll and it has been pressed out and weaker paper has had to be reinforced with acrylic and/or paper often giving a much stiffer feel to the covers. There are arguments for and against such a course of action if a comic is falling apart and deemed worth preserving. Once again, professional advice should be sought.

The number of restored comic books in circulation in the U.K. market is very low so this information is not meant to be alarmist. It simply means that one should exercise caution if buying a key issue for a lot of money. Again one should seek professional advice if one is unsure or unused to spotting restoration. This question of restoration only really applies to Golden and Silver Age comics. There would be little point in spending a fortune on restoring a £10 or $15 copy of X-Men. Thus an informed buyer can buy with confidence and the informed collector or dealer always has the choice of preserving certain comic books if so desired.

This Guide does not encourage amateur restoration using such things as felt tips and glue, magic tape and paper whatsoever. It also fully condemns the practice of restoration carried out for purely financial purposes, a "get rich quick" mentality, and the practice of deliberately ignoring or under-stating degrees of restoration by both dealers and collectors

STORAGE OF COMIC BOOKS

Storing and preserving a collection becomes more difficult the larger it becomes but a small amount of care is worthwhile in the long run. Many shops and dealers at marts and conventions sell their new comics and back issues in plastic bags and this is the most simple method of preservation. Plastic bags for all sizes of comics can now be bought, quite cheaply, for all sizes from Digest to Treasury. The best type to use is 250 gauge with a 1 inch flap at the top which provides an almost air-tight seal. THE SEAL SHOULD NOT BE COMPLETELY AIR-TIGHT as this has been known to cause chemical reactions among the inks and acids in comic book pages. A plastic bag will afford good protection from the usual effects of dust, dirt, wear and tear but they should be changed every two or three years as certain polymers can react with the acids, inks and paper. One should avoid the use of freezer bags bought from supermarkets and food stores.

A more ideal solution, and particularly for more valuable comics, is the use of Mylar bags which are chemically inert, stiff, clear plastic sleeves, some with flaps at the top. They are available from certain comic shops and come in three basic sizes for Marvel, DC and Golden Age comic books but they can be prohibitively expensive for collections running into thousands. A lighter and cheaper version called Mylites is available for bulk storage. There are a number of U.K. and U.S. suppliers, some of which can be found advertising in this book. Backing boards can also be used to help store comics but these should be of the acid-free variety and ordinary cardboard should be avoided at all costs. Please note

that there are many different types of backing boards available today so it is important to check that they are acid-free if claimed to be so. Ideally the board should be double-sided white or of food-board quality that companies like Birds Eye might use to package their food products. Avoid any boards with obvious wood-chips in them as this is commonly called box-board and is not acid-free. As ever, professional advice should be sought. Several comic shops sell custom-made comic boxes which are easily transportable, store around 150 bagged comics and can be stacked easily. There are also longer "coffin boxes" which can store up to 300 bagged comics. For the most part both types of boxes are not completely acid-free.

Other alternatives are ring binders with clear plastic sleeves may be used to store more valuable items (which themselves should be in Mylar bags) and bulk collections can be stored in wooden boxes or on wooden shelving units, again avoiding cardboard boxes at all times as the acids in these will react with the paper over a period of time. Ideally comics should be stored vertically in Mylars with acid-free backing boards in wooden or acid-free boxes. They may be stacked individually in horizontal piles but without the stiffness of Mylars or backing boards the top ones will tend to curl over and spine rolls may develop. Comics should also be kept in a dark, cool atmosphere with a reasonable amount of humidity. A dry atmosphere or too much sunlight can turn comics brown and then brittle in a comparatively short space of time. With careful storage comics will keep their freshness and colour for years to come. Careful storage is the key but remember that Mylars and acid-free backing boards are an aid to collecting, not an absolute necessity. Common sense can be just as valuable in the long term (and much cheaper in the short!)

As mentioned above in SOME RESTORATION TERMS, comics can be de-acidified but it is a complex and often expensive business (though Bill Cole Enterprises in America is constantly researching much cheaper and effective methods of de-acidification) that involves soaking the individual pages or hanging each page for spraying with specially prepared solutions. Covers of comics pose a special problem owing to the varied composition of the papers used. SUCH PROCEDURES SHOULD BE LEFT TO EXPERTS.

PRICING STRUCTURES

The question I most often get asked (not unreasonably) if how do you work out the prices? Most of those who ask realise that it is not just a matter of making them up out of the blue or taking last year's book and adding 10 percent (wish it was sometimes!)

As a GUIDE only, all the prices contained herein are necessarily approximations based on observations in comic shops and marts all over the country, mail order lists and catalogues (many thanks to those who send theirs such as Justin Ebbs of Just Comics and David Hern of Wonderworld for example), the collective knowledge of a great number of authoritative people who advise me every year and my own experience of twenty-five years as a collector.

The process of deciding prices has very much developed into an on-going situation all year round with detailed scrutiny before any publication.

The actual process of pricing is quite simple. Myself and my Assistant Editor John Skoulides go through the entire Guide from A to Z and discuss each and every price where possible. Obviously there are some one-shots and titles that just do not change in value year after year. But they still get a glance – it's amazing how a typo can creep in one year or an issue be lost another when it's been quite alright before. The

35 megabytes of data get manipulated around and transferred from machine to machine so many times and moved back and forth in the type-setting so often that it's inevitable one record of segment of a record is altered or lost. Necessarily there are other titles that need hours of discussion and it has not been unknown to spend a ludicrous amount of time discussing one issue! After an eight hour session with both our machines side by side, we both feel like never doing another Price Guide ever again. But then we arrange to meet again on Tuesday and do it all over again on another small section...

Our ambition is to have a regular Board of Advisors both from the U.K and U.S. and regular questionnaires to have maximum dealer and collector involvement in putting together an annual U.K. Price Guide. All this takes time and money and probably a larger set up than just we two. It is hoped with Titan Books taking over the packaging and administration of this book, more time can be spent on research and true national input.

The rationale behind pricing is a little more complex than the process itself. We have been helped enormously this time around by the decision to print prices in both pounds and dollars. We can see immediately the context of every issue which is exactly what a Guide is all about - context and thereby a rough guide to values.

There is no doubt in our minds that prices for Golden Age material in the U.K. are dictated by the American market. The Overstreet Price Guide has been long established and the market for Golden Age comics in the U.S. seems to be as healthy as it's always been. The market in the U.K. is quite small (and is possibly growing smaller?) as every year more and more Golden Age comics go up in value and thus in the higher grades out of most people's price ranges particularly in the U.K. If a British collector wants to purchase a Golden Age comic and more precisely a high grade key or pedigree issue, then they will probably have to pay American market rates. For the purposes of this book, we have used our judgement to estimate current American market values based on as many written, verbal and professional sources at our disposal and arrived by conversion at a British value. Whether comics would actually sell at these values and indeed sell on a regular basis is another matter, another book. But it is a starting point. A Guide price.

Some would argue that it should be more difficult to buy Golden Age comic in the U.K. than in the U.S and by and large that is probably true. Does it therefore follow that the British value of most Golden Age comics should be that much more than the American market value owing to factors of rarity, popularity and availability? The answer again is probably yes but one must also take into account the size of the market for Golden Age comics in this country, of a size that may negate the rarity/popularity/availability factor. The old adage of a comic's value being that which someone is prepared to pay for it comes very much into play. Thus this book's very general rationale for Golden Age material is a reasonable parity of prices with some of the more straightforward titles and issues, a lesser U.K. value after dollar/pound conversion on some of the more lesser titles and issues and a greater U.K. value on some of the most popular titles and issues after conversion (all the above assumes exact parity in grading which is another question entirely and yet another book!). Within these very general parameters there are going to be exceptions owing to character and creator considerations.

The same sort of rationale is used for Silver Age comics up to official distribution in the U.K. from the November 1959 cover date. Thereafter the question of cents priced U.S. copies and pence priced U.K. copies of the same comic come into play. For many collectors in the U.K. the cents/pence distinction as we have already stated does not matter. But for some it does. And particularly for American dealers and collectors considering British pence priced copies. And particularly on key issues.

Our rationale changes with comics in the 70's where so many Marvels were officially Not Distributed in the U.K. at the time. Or with how War and Romance comics are generally valued in the U.K. as opposed to the U.S. Or how "hot book" trends may happen in the U.S. first, peak higher and faster there than in the U.K. or how the trend may last longer in the U.K. than in the U.S.

Our rationale therefore has to be flexible from decade to decade, trend to trend, title to title, comic to comic. It may be noticed throughout this book that in our judgement, some British pound values are over a converted American dollar prices when there are factors of popularity and/or rarity. On the other hand there are many instances of the British pound price being half the converted American dollar price. These cases have been judged individually and can be found by studying the prices carefully. The overall conclusion that this book has come to is that at present American market values are generally higher across the board than British market values.

It may be noticed that many of the ratios between Good, Fine and Near Mint have changed (anything from a 1:3:5 right up to a 1:3:16). Each one has been judged

individually and they will keep altering and evolving as we observe the general prices between lower and higher grades. The overall effect of our ratio changes is that prices on Good and Fine material in the U.K. market have remained largely static since the last U.K. price guide whilst the values on Near Mint material have risen. We will have to monitor the situation to see if this trend continues.

The most complex part of pricing rationale but often the most enjoyable is discussing and establishing relationships between characters, issues and titles. For example, there is a year on year relationship between Flash, Green Lantern and Justice League of America from DC Comics where generally speaking, one title traditionally sells better in back-issue terms than another in the U.K. A character like the Hobgoblin may be more highly valued for a time and for whatever reason in the U.S. than in the U.K. or issues like the Silver Surfer Moebius series may be valued more highly in the U.K. than in the U.S. as it seems to be much harder to find in shops and collections in the U.K.

It is for these reasons, and many more besides, that we feel our Price Guide for American Comic Books should have prices in both pounds and dollars. We welcome any correspondence on the subject at the editorial address.

There are obviously design considerations when

dealing with so many more figures and we have tried to make the book as clear and user-friendly as possible. Again we welcome any comments on the subject.

THE BRITISH SECTION

The British section is compiled by Mr. Steve Holland as has already been noted. The production process requires many telephone calls as he sends me a disk/printout which then passes back and forth as I amend from my own collecting experiences. Steve himself calls upon a large number of people at his end. It is hoped to restrict the British section in future Guides to TV, film and sci-fi/comics related material and to list everything in a more comprehensive stand alone British Comics Guide.

It must be noted that collectors of British comics do not use precisely the same system of grading as used for American material and few British comics of any significant age survive in exceptionally high grade. In view of this, British comics' collectors tend to use a hybrid of terms that are used for books and paperbacks as well as American comics. For further information, see the introduction to the British section. For the purposes of this book, a single Near Mint price in pounds sterling is listed and a percentage chart can be used to work out prices on lower grades. In future Guides, there may be opportunities for a dollar price to be added as and when a regular U.S. market price can be established.

Showcase # 94 – price ratio 1:3:5

Showcase # 50 – price ratio 1:3:7

Showcase # 3 – price ratio 1:3:8

Showcase # 30 – price ratio 1:3:9

Showcase # 1 – price ratio 1:3:10

Showcase # 8 – price ratio 1:3:16

AN INTRODUCTION TO GRADING

The most difficult, contentious and eternally frustrating aspect of comic-book collecting is grading. For collector and dealer alike it is essential to grade the condition of a comic book fairly and accurately in order to determine its true value and worth. As the collecting trend in today's market seems to be more and more discerning as fandom becomes more and more knowledgeable, accuracy on the higher grades becomes even more essential.

As grading is very much a subjective exercise it is all to easy for the novice (and indeed the experienced collector) to allow wishful thinking and optimism to influence the appearance of a comic book and make it better than it really is. One man's idea of mint may be very different from another's! The stricter and harder one becomes, even to the point of under-grading, the more secure one can feel in selling comics and the happier one can be in collecting. It is worth re-evaluating one's grading criteria from time to time in order to become the more expert. Accurate and consistent grading only comes with experience. One exercise the novice may undertake could be to take a comic from each of the recognised grades and lay them side by side in order to appreciate more fully and put into perspective the varying degrees of wear and tear.

THE PROCESS OF GRADING

1) Open the comic and grade from the inside out. Lie it on a flat surface or hold it in the cup of the hand. Do not bend back or flatten out. Check the centrefold is there and attached by both staples. Check for missing pages, panels or coupons cut, tears in pages, writing or stains. Check outer edges of pages for browning/ brittleness. One may check the comic smell for signs of dampness or acidity.

2) Check inside front and back covers, particularly turning the cover to see how it strains against the staples and may have torn. Older comics in particular often have staples slightly out of line. They also tended not to use stainless steel staples so rust is more prevalent. Check for unusual whiteness as against the page colour which may indicate cover-bleaching and stain removal. Check for any staple reinforcement.

3) Check back cover for tears and/or pieces out. Check wear or any soiling along the spine.

4) Check front cover. This is the most important part of the comic as it is most seen when displayed and liable to the most wear. The areas of most common wear are around the staples and at the corners. Check for any cracks of chipping along the right hand edge. Hold it up to the light and check for cover gloss and any indentations. Check dark blue/black areas for any signs of colour touch-up.

5) Finally assess the overall appearance of the comic, checking for tightness and squareness of trim. Many comics were off-cut or had off-centre staples where the cover art wraps a little round to the back cover. Eye appeal is what can often influence an initial grading but is also vitally important as a final assessment.

These steps should be adhered to generally to treat all comics with respect but need only be exhaustively followed on more important items.

If one feels that grading is important or not, above all read and enjoy.

GRADING FOR BEGINNERS

Having been through the process of examining your comic book, the hard part comes with arriving at an accurate grade. Every comic has an accurate grade which can be arrived at by asking the right questions. As a beginner you might find yourself being a little vague and saying It's about VG or a Fine/NM copy. Spot-on grading only comes with practice. If you are just starting out it is worth getting these approximations in your head to give an overall picture:

MINT	Perfect
NEAR MINT	Nearly perfect
VERY FINE	Very nice condition
FINE	Above average
VERY GOOD	Average
GOOD	Below average
FAIR	Well worn
POOR	Very tatty

Practising with a stack of comics and sorting them out into these eight different piles is a very useful exercise and one that experts should do from time to time.

THE GRADING DEFINITIONS

Having got used to rough approximations, the next step is exact definition. The accepted grades of condition for comic books and their fuller definitions are as follows:

MINT (M)

Perfect and as new, REGARDLESS OF AGE, with full cover gloss and lustre and white, crisp pages. No printing or cutting defects, off-centre covers or staples. No marks on the cover whatsoever, not even an official distributors stamp, even if it is neatly done (note American Guides seem to allow this – why?)

As with coins or stamps, MINT really means uncirculated or untouched and as such the only MINT comics would be those kept on file at the various comic companies (and not all of these are untouched - quite the reverse!) or those comics issued in plastic bags and unopened. Either way a comic would have to be in quite spectacular condition to qualify for this grade. Even new comics on the rack at news-stands or comic shops are not necessarily Mint. They have been handled, transported, stacked and handled again even before they reach the shelves. Please note that there is no such grade as NEAR MINT/MINT or MINT–. A comic is either mint or it isn't. The true rarity of this grade cannot be emphasised enough.

PERMISSIBLE FAULTS:
None

NEAR MINT (NM)

Almost perfect and as new. White pages. Tight, flat and clean with only extremely light stress marks at a staple or staples or the smallest of creases at a corner or on the spine. No marks on cover except perhaps an official distributors stamp or mark in pencil and even then very neatly done. Please note that this is still an extremely high and very scarce grade.

PERMISSIBLE FAULTS:
You have to look very carefully and even then there should be no more than one, perhaps two very minor defects. Among the most common are
Extremely light stress around the staples.
The smallest corner crease.

NOT PERMISSIBLE FAULTS:
Any page discolouration
Anything missing
Anything added
Any degree of spine roll
Any writing anywhere apart from very neat arrival date (preferably in pencil)
Even within these strict confines, a spectacular copy may be referred to as a NM+ (a NM++ is taking things a bit far) and a comic that is very nice but just not quite up to being a Near Mint may be referred to as a Near Mint– (similarly NM— stretches the point beyond being a useful grading term)

VERY FINE (VF OR VFN)

Very slight wear beginning to show owing to an accumulation of very minor defects. This is a comic that has been read carefully a few times and stored away with due care and attention. Most of the cover lustre remaining and still clean, flat and tight with only the tiniest spine wear or perhaps nick at top and bottom. No major cover marks or creases. A light crease up to about half an inch. Pages may be off-white but in no way yellowing or beginning to brown. Very Fine means a copy with excellent eye appeal.

PERMISSIBLE FAULTS:
Minimal wear is apparent at first sight. One or two very minor faults are allowed. Some of the most common permissible defects are
A light cover crease up to about half an inch
Off white pages
Slight staple discolouration (but no rust)
One or two corners with slight rounding
Some minimal cover surface wear

NOT PERMISSIBLE FAULTS:
Yellowing pages or any worse than that
Staple rust
Any writing apart from neat arrival date or some other such small neat initial/figure
Anything missing apart from a slight nick in the spine top or bottom
Spine roll although "white spine" where the comic is still absolutely flat but the printing process has wrapped the cover around so that a slight edge of the cover illustration shows on the right edge of the back cover or a white edge has wrapped around from the back cover to show on the left edge of the front cover
Within these quite strict confines, a nice looking comic may be referred to as a VFN+ and one that is quite sharp but may have a noticeable defect that starts to offend the eye may be referred to as a VFN-.

FINE (FN)

The basic minimum for most collectors, a comic with wear showing on edges, slight spine creases or stress around the staples. Still clean and flat with no major marks major or writing on cover or inside. Some cover gloss or lustre remaining. Pages may be yellowing slightly but not browning or brown edges. Above-average, read quite a few times and stored away with some concern though not necessarily in ideal conditions. This is the most widely used (and abused) grade.

PERMISSIBLE FAULTS:
No major defects but an accumulation of a few minor defects instantly apparent. Some of the permissible faults are
A couple of cover creases or one or up to an inch or so
Some small spine creases
Pages may have a yellow tinge to them but in no way tanning
Small neat writing or name
Staple discolouration but not rusty
Tiniest piece chip may be out of a page or the cover
Slightest spine roll
Slight corner knock or impact

NOT PERMISSIBLE FAULTS:
Heavy creases
Any tanning of pages or worse
Very noticeable writing
Coupon or puzzle completing
Staple rust
Piece out of page or cover bigger than a chip
Anything other than the slightest spine roll
Any water mark/ripple/damage
Anything other than a slight stain either to the cover or inside
Big corner crunch or book crease
No tape of any description or size
There is obviously a lot more room for manoeuvre in this grade than with any of the above as far as combinations of minor defects goes, but the overall eye appeal of the comic must be above average with a good amount of gloss or lustre left on the cover.

VERY GOOD (VG)

An average, second-hand, obviously read copy with marks and minor defects. Printing lustre almost gone but not soiled or stained. Worn along spine with possible spine-roll or slightly loose staples. Pages may be yellowing with signs of browning around the edges. The cover could have minor tear or crease or there could be a loose centre-fold. NO PAGES OR PARTS MISSING. No coupons or panels cut

PERMISSIBLE FAULTS:

An average used comic which many collectors regard as the bare minimum as nothing major is actually missing. An accumulation of defects, one or two moderate. Some accepted defects in this grade are

- Moderate cover creasing
- Tanning or slightly browning pages
- Some cover writing but not scribble
- Rust spots on staple
- Cover detached from one staple
- Small piece out of page or cover, fingernail sized
- Moderate spine roll
- Water stain but not rippling
- Corner crunch or small book crease
- Small tape repair evident
- Some tape removal evident
- Coupon or small puzzle completed
- Centrefold loose

NOT PERMISSIBLE FAULTS:

- Heavy cover creasing
- Brown pages
- Cover or interior scribble, especially with a felt tip
- Rusty staples
- Cover detached
- Any piece out bigger than a fingernail size
- Heavy spine roll
- Water rippling or water damage
- Heavy book crease
- Moderate tape evident
- Major tape removal
- Major amateur colouring in
- Centrefold missing, panels or coupons cut

GOOD (G)

A well read copy with minor tears or splits, soiled and marked, rolled spine and creases. Tape repairs to the staples or spine but STILL COMPLETE and acceptable. Collectible mostly as a reading copy only. Please note that this grade is very misleading – "good" is basically a very low grade. Please also note that it is the condition in which the large majority of 50's and 60's collections that come out of attic rooms and old boxes. They would not have been consciously stored away in plastic bags and the damper climate of some areas in the U.K. and indeed the U.S. generally often results in rusty staples and a damp, musty smell to the comic and very often browning pages.

PERMISSIBLE FAULTS:

An accumulation of defects, one or two quite major ones. Some of the accepted defects in this grade are

- Generally heavy creasing
- Browning (but not brittle) pages
- General writing (but not heavy scribble or grafitti)
- Rusty staples (but not staining the immediate paper area)
- Piece out of cover or page about thumb-nail size
- Heavy spine roll
- Light water rippling (but not damage)
- Subscription crease
- Moderate tape evident
- Major tape removal (but only leaving stain, no tears or print removed)

NOT PERMISSIBLE FAULTS:

- Panels or coupons cut
- Anything worse than the above lists of faults

It must be stressed again that while a Good comic may have lots of faults and one or two quite major, there is NOTHING SUBSTANTIAL MISSING. The pages may

even be quite discoloured and may have lost their suppleness but in no way are they brittle.

FAIR (F) OR FAIRLY GOOD (FG)

Very worn and soiled with possible small chunks out of spine or cover. Some tears and heavy creases and marks or writing on cover/inside. A couple of extra staples as cover was detached at some time. No pages out but a panel and/or a coupon may be out or clipped. The pages are brown and bordering on the brittle.

NOT PERMISSIBLE FAULTS:

- Brittleness
- Page(s) out
- Coverless
- Lots of extra staples
- Heavy brown tape

This grade of comic is basically a mess and is only really collectible as a rare item because no better one exists or as a filler to complete a run until something better comes along which shouldn't be too hard.

POOR (P)

Well damaged and heavily soiled. Not collectible unless it is something very rare or very special. Very worn, torn, brittle, water-damaged, heavily brown-taped spine, absolute mess and may be incomplete – watch out for coupons cut out or pin-up pages missing, no centrefold or no back cover

Please note that A MISSING PAGE IS A VERY SERIOUS DEFECT, PARTICULARLY A STORY PAGE AND EVEN IF THE REST OF THE COMIC APPEARS TO BE ANYTHING FROM NEAR MINT DOWNWARDS, THIS DEFECT DEVALUES IT DRASTICALLY.

COVERLESS(C)

These turn up regularly, particularly as older comics but they have little value beyond reading copies, even if the interior is white and clean which it usually isn't. Only collectible as extremely rare or only curiosity items or research material. Having said that some people love them. Having a coverless Batman #1 in your collection may be the only way you'll ever afford one. It's great for pure reading value. While it is difficult to ascribe a universally held valuation formula, they may be offered at about one quarter to one sixth of the good price.

With the advances in restoration, coverless copies do have an added attraction in that it is sometimes possible to match up covers and coverless copies. I remember an advert where the covers of Batman #1 were advertised for $500 and that was some time ago.

PERCENTAGE CHART

For quick calculation of values other than the GOOD:FINE: NEAR MINT columns in this book, a percentage chart is offered for use. Percentage charts have been used by dealers for years and recently made more public by the work people like Gary Ochiltree (Board Member) of Krypton Komics in particular.

This is only a rough guide to the percentage breakdowns between the main grades so that Poors, Fairs and in-between plus and minus grades may be calculated.

PLEASE NOTE THAT PARTICULARLY IN GRADING RARE OR KEY ISSUES, PLUS AND MINUS SIGNS ALONG WITH THE GRADES IS ACCEPTABLE as it may more closely define that grade as being a Very Fine- copy or a Fine+ and these have been built into this chart. Obviously the difference is minimal but enough to make a difference to the experienced eye and more particularly when there are large sums of money involved. There is no such thing (in my opinion) as Very Fine++ or any other such excesses. POOR and FAIR are not usually given the distinction of being either plus or minus. It would be absurd to distinguish between a Poor+ and a Fair-, even on the most

expensive and sought after comics.

The established top grade for the purpose of Guide values is Near Mint or a figure of 100% from which the other grades can be calculated.

GRADE	Percentage of Near Mint Guide Price
MINT	120-200%+
NEAR MINT+	110%
NEAR MINT	100%
NEAR MINT-	90%
VERY FINE+	80%
VERY FINE	75%
VERY FINE-	70%
FINE+	65%
FINE	60%
FINE-	50%
VERY GOOD+	40%
VERY GOOD	35%
VERY GOOD-	30%
GOOD+	25%
GOOD	20%
GOOD-	15%
FAIR	10%
POOR	5%
COVERLESS	3.75%

FOR CENTS COPIES OF LONG-ESTABLISHED KEY ISSUES ADD 20-25% ONLY IF IN VERY HIGH GRADE (VF+ or better) (and see Multiples of Guide section)

This is a ROUGH GUIDE only and allows only for working with newer comics (in a ratio of 1:3:5) published for the most part from 1980 or so onwards. As many collectors and most new collectors nowadays concentrate on these comics, particularly at the beginning of their collecting, it is a useful chart with which to practice.

Other percentages charts for other ratios would need to be calculated if exact figures are needed. For example, comics in a 1:3:9 ratio would have Poor as 2.5% of Near Mint, not 5%.

Rather than write out all percentage charts for all ratios used in this book and beyond (a 1:3:20 ratio can't be far away), one may use The Hundred Scale which is favoured by many collectors and dealers, particularly in America. The very rough percentages can be used as follows for all comic books generally:

- MINT = ... 100%
- NEAR MINT (inc. +/-) = ... 90-99%
- VERY FINE (inc. +/-)= 75-89%
- FINE (inc. +/-) = ... 55-74%
- VERY GOOD (inc. +/-)= 35-54%
- GOOD (inc. +/-) =. 15-34%
- FAIR = ... 5-14%
- POOR = ... 1-4%

While these percentages are useful for rough calculations, on major issues where considerable sums are involved, differences of hundreds and even thousands of pounds or dollars could result from approximation. This Guide would advise accuracy and that means working out the ratio and calculating the exact percentage for the exact grade accordingly.

DEFECTS CHART

This is more difficult to quantify as the whole area of grading is at best subjective and can vary tremendously with the type, number and cumulative effect of the various defects common to most comics.

As a ROUGH GUIDE (with thanks to David Hern of Wonderworld for pioneering work) the following twelve tables demonstrate the most common areas of defect that a comic is likely to have and the varying degrees of that defect and how those degrees account for a final grade.

A drop of a FULL GRADE would be from say VERY FINE to FINE+.

A drop of a half a grade would be from say VERY FINE- to FINE+

1 PAGE COLOUR

PAGE COLOUR	PENALTY	GRADE
White	–	NM
Off White	6	NM-
Cream	16	VF+
Slight Yellowing	28	VF-
Yellowing and/or Shaded Edges	33	FN+
Light Tan and /or Darker Edges	38	FN
Light Brown and/or Brown Edges	56	VG+
Generally Brown	63	VG
Very Brown	78	G
Brittle	88	FR
Very Brittle	93	PR

e.g A brittle comic should not be graded more than FAIR even if it appears NM at first glance.

3 TEAR(S) COVER(S)/INTERIOR

TEAR(S) COVER(S)/INTERIOR	PENALTY	GRADE
No tears		NM
Tiny Tear – no more than 2mm	6	NM-
Small Tear(s) – totalling 3-10mm	28	VF-
Tear(s) – totalling 11-20mm	33	FN+
Larger Tear(s) – totalling 21-30mm	46	FN-
Major Tear(s) – totalling 31-50mm	63	VG
Torn generally – Covers	78	G
Torn generally – Covers and Interior	88	FR
Ripped through Comic	93	PR

e.g. A comic even with two small tears anywhere and no more than 10mm each should not grade above VF-

5 COVER(S) DEFECTS – GENERAL

COVER(S) DEFECTS – GENERAL	PENALTY	GRADE
Unmarked	–	NM
Small Writing – Neat up to 5x20 mm - Cover/Interior	28	VF-
Larger Writing – Neat up to 5x50 mm - Cover Interior	46	FN-
Some Scrawl: Felt Tip/Marker Pen	63	VG
Major Scrawl: Felt Tip/Marker Pen	78	G
Stain - less than 10 mm diameter	28	VF-
Stain – 11-50 mm diameter	38	FN
Stain – more than 50mm diameter	63+	VG or less
Non-Removable Sticky Label	23	VF
Label Stain/Discolouration	28	VF-
Foxing – Light	28	VF-
Foxing – Heavy	46	FN-

Grade Scale (centre column)

GRADE	RANGE
NM	(100)
NM-	(90-99)
VF+	(80-89)
VF	(75-79)
VF-	(70-74)
FN+	(65-69)
FN	(60-64)
FN-	(50-59)
VG+	(40-49)
VG	(35-39)
VG-	(30-34)
G+	(25-29)
G	(20-24)
G-	(15-19)
FR	(10-14)
PR	(5-9)
PR and/or COVER-LESS	(1-4)(and any minus values)

2 SPINE WEAR

SPINE WEAR	PENALTY	GRADE
None	–	NM
1/2 Tiny Creases	16	VF+
Very Light Wear/Creases	28	VF-
Medium Wear/Creases	38	FN
Heavy Wear/Creases	63	VG
Very Slight Spine Roll	28	VF-
Spine Roll	38	FN
Heavy Spine Roll	63	VG
Tiny Spine Tear Top and/or Bottom	23	VF
Spine Split Top and/or Bottom	38	FN
Half Spine Split	63	VG
Major Spine Split	78	G

e.g. A comic with a heavy spine roll should not be graded more than a VG even if otherwise perfect.

4 PIECES MISSING COVER/INTERIOR

PIECES MISSING COVER/INTERIOR	PENALTY	GRADE
Nothing Missing	–	NM
Tiny Chip – but less than 2mm square	23	VF
Small Chip – 3-5 mm square	23	VF
Chip – 6-9 mm square	28	VF-
Half Thumbnail Size – 10x10 mm	33	FN+
Thumbnail Size – 20x20 mm	38	FN
Chunk from Cover/Coupon Clipped	63	VG
Ad Page/Pin Up Page Missing	88	FR
Story Page/Back Cover Missing	93	PR
Covers Missing	98	Coverless!
Marvel Chipping – 1 edge	38	FN
Heavy Marvel Chipping – 2/3 Edges	63	VG

e.g. A comic with a coupon or panel cut out should grade no more than a VG even if otherwise perfect.

6 STAPLE DEFECTS

STAPLE DEFECTS	PENALTY	GRADE
Perfectly Centred/New Staples	–	NM
One Staple Missing	16	VF+
One Staple Detached	28	VF-
Both Staples Detached/Loose Cover	63	VG
Light Rust on Staple(s)	38	FN
Rust/Rust Stain Spine/Interior	63	VG
Heavy Rust/Staining	78	G
Staples Off-centre from Spine – 2 mm into Back or Front Cover	23	VF
Re-stapled correctly	28	VF-
Re-stapled incorrectly	38	FN
Extra Staples in Spine	46	FN-
Extra Staples through Spine	68	VG-

7 COVER CREASE(S)

	PENALTY	GRADE
No Crease(s)	–	NM
Tiny Crease(s) – totalling 10 mm or less	6	NM-
Light Crease(s) – totalling 11-20 mm	23	VF
Crease(s) – totalling 21-50 mm	33	FN+
Heavier Crease(s) – totalling 51-100mm	38	FN
General Crease(s) – 101-249 mm	46	FN-
Subscription Crease (250 mm) – unflattened	56	VG+
Heavy Subscription Crease – flattened	68	VG-
Subscription Crease – unflattened	78	G
Heavy Subscription Crease – unflattened	93	PR

e.g. A comic with a subscription crease, even if flattened out affects the whole comic \ no more than VG+

9 TAPE DEFECTS

	PENALTY	GRADE
No Tape	-	NM
Tiny Piece – 10 mm or less	28	VF-
Small Piece – 11 to 50 mm	38	FN
Larger Piece – 51 to 100 mm	56	VG+
Taped Spine – Scotch or Magic Tape	73	G+
Taped Spine – Sellotape	83	G-
Taped Spine + Edges Cover	88	FR
Taped Spine + Edges Yellowed/Brown	93	PR
Tiny Patch Torn Off by Tape	46	FN-
Patch Torn Off by Tape	63	VG
Large Patch Torn Off by Tape	88	FR
Glue Patch After Tape Removal	38	FN

e.g. A comic with a part taped spine (say 100 mm) should not grade more than a VG+ at best

11 MISCELLANEOUS DEFECTS (2)

	PENALTY	GRADE
Rubber Stamp – ink smudged	23	VF
Popular Book Centre Stamp	28	VF-
Popular Book Centre Stamps	46	FN-
Cover Off Centre ("white spine")	23	VF
Centre Fold Missing	93	PR
Slight Drawing/Colouring In	46	FN-
Drawing/Colouring In on figures etc	68	VG-
Much Drawing and Graffiti	83	G-
Spine Glue Stain – tape removed	56	VG+
General Indentations – held up to the light	46	FN-
General Soiling/Dirt – usually worst on back cover	46	FN-

Grade Scale (centre column)

GRADE	RANGE
NM	(100)
NM-	(90-99)
VF+	(80-89)
VF	(75-79)
VF-	(70-74)
FN+	(65-69)
FN	(60-64)
FN-	(50-59)
VG+	(40-49)
VG	(35-39)
VG-	(30-34)
G+	(25-29)
G	(20-24)
G-	(15-19)
FR	(10-14)
PR	(5-9)
PR and/or COVER-LESS	(1-4)(and any minus values)

8 COVER COLOURS/GLOSS

	PENALTY	GRADE
Full Colour/Full Gloss	–	NM
Most Gloss Remaining (75%)	6	NM-
Half Gloss Remaining (50%)	28	VF-
Some Gloss Remaining (25%)	33	FN+
Gloss Obviously Gone (particularly early 1960s)	46	FN-
Slightly Fading Colours (sun damage)	28	VF-
Fading Colours (sun damage)	38	FN
Extreme Fading Colours	63	VG
Colour Flakes Off at Staple	23	VF
Colour Flakes Off along Spine	28	VF-
Cover Re-glossed – Professionally	38	FN
Cover Bleached – Professionally	38	FN

e.g. If a comic has a very faded cover, it should not grade above a VG. Sun damage causes brittleness.

10 MISCELLANEOUS DEFECTS

	PENALTY	GRADE
Edge with Ink Spots (Usually red or blue)	28	VF-
Ink Staining along one edge	33	FN+
Heavy Ink Staining/Onto Cover	46	FN-
Slightly Trimmed Edge – usually top	63	VG
Heavily Trimmed Edges	88	FR
Slight Water Mark	33	FN+
Water Stain (Brown-edged)	46	FN-
Water Soak (slightly crinkled)	68	VG-
Water Soaked (rippled)	88	FR
Sun/Dust Shadow Cover(s) – slight	28	VF-
Sun/Dust Shadow Cover(s) – medium	38	FN
Sun/Dust Shadow Cover(s) – heavy	68	VG-

e.g. A comic with its edges trimmed, usually to hide severe chipping, affects the whole comic \ no better than FAIR. Some Golden Age are trimmed by 5 mm.

12 RESTORATION (see Section)

	PENALTY	GRADE
Restored to appear NM (Professional)	Assume ½ grade less	NM-
Restored to appear VF (Professional)	"	VF-
Restored to appear FN (Professional)	Assume 1 grade less	VG+
Restored to appear VG (Professional)	"	G+
Amateur Repair – felt tip colour touch	46 or +	FN- or less
Amateur Repair – tear mending	46 or +	FN- or less
Amateur Repair – trimming	63 or +	VG or less
Amateur Repair – re-stapling	28 or +	VF- or less
Amateur Repair – tape removal	46 or +	FN-or less
Amateur Repair - different back cover	78 or +	G- or less
Amateur Repair - pages from different comics	78 or +	G or less

The problem with any grading assessment whether using charts or not is the cumulative effects of the problem areas on a comic. It is easier to grade a comic with minimal damage (say a tiny crease at one corner making a Near Mint comic a Near Mint Minus) than a comic with multiple wounds (is a spine rolled comic with white pages and a tiny piece of tape inside better or worse than a comic with a light subscription crease, light white pages and a small piece out of the back cover?)

It is suggested that the tables may be reasonably used thus:

IF A COMIC HAS ONLY ONE NOTICEABLE DEFECT:

Find the degree of that defect and read across the page to find the grade.(e.g. if there is only a tiny chip = deduct 6 points = NM-)

IF THE COMIC HAS TWO OR THREE MINOR DEFECTS:

Add up the penalties and refer to the middle column and read off the grade there.(e.g. the comic has off white pages and a slight spine roll which means 6 + 28 = 34 deducted from 100 = 66 = FN+)

IF THE COMIC HAS MULTIPLE DEFECTS:

Take the one most serious penalty and read across the page to find the grade.(e.g. the comic is brittle with light rust on the staples and small tears and large writing. Penalties are 88 + 38 + 28 + 46 = 200. A brittle penalty makes it no better than a FAIR to start with and the other defects would probably push it into the POOR category therefore.)

THESE TABLES MAY BE USED PURELY FOR PRACTISING AND RECOGNISING THE NUMBER OF FAULTS A COMIC MAY HAVE, THEIR RELATIVE SEVERITY AND HOW THAT AFFECTS THE OVERALL FINAL GRADE. DON'T WORRY TOO MUCH IF YOU END UP WITH HUGE MINUS NUMBERS AND THEREFORE NO GRADE TO READ OFF. AT LEAST PRACTICE IN GRADING IS BEING ACQUIRED.

Once an assessment of the defect (if any) and thus grade has been made, then by using this book sensibly, a true Price Guide price or Price Guide value may be arrived at.

These are by no means hard and fast rules but do give some idea of the relative degrees of seriousness of damage that a comic may suffer over the years and the complexity that grading has reached now that there are comics in the hundreds of thousands of pounds and dollars. These charts are meant not just for the benefit of dealers new and old but also for fans and collectors.

Remember that it is the whole book that needs to be graded and not just the front cover. More and more attention is being paid to the interior whiteness and freshness of comic books. It also it cannot be stressed enough that MINT MEANS MINT, REGARDLESS OF AGE. New comics bought at shops or the newsagents are not necessarily mint. Older comics should not be more lightly graded because of the fact that they are simply older no matter how tempting it may be. Thus an Action Comics #1 should be graded as one would an Action Comics #701. The scarcity of an old or rare comic is reflected in its value or price. At the end of the day a comic is only really worth what someone is prepared to pay for it and as such

any formal prices are merely arbitrary. Guide prices serve to be just that: a guide to pricing and valuing a comic once the conditions of the certain recognised grades have been examined.

Some last grading points to remember as stressed in the above tables:

1) The term Pristine Mint occasionally arises and seems more popular in America than in the U.K. This would mean something that is unusually mint and could only really apply to a file copy that has hardly if ever been opened. As such comics of this sort hardly ever appear on the market and I would tend to disregard this grade.

2) Comics that appear to be of a high grade but have very brown or brittle pages should not be graded above fair. A comic is brittle if flakes of paper fall easily from

it or if a corner can be folded over and it comes away with little or no effort. See the section on the storage of comic books.3) A comic that has at one time been water-soaked (usually owing to being brought across on a ship as ballast) cannot be graded above fair condition, possibly very good minus if the damage is very slight.

4) Subscription copies (where a comic has been folded lengthways for mailing) should be noted even though after a period of time they may have been flattened out.

5) Finally, a comic should only be graded after careful consideration of the whole book, not just at first glance. Ideally, a second opinion should be sought on rare or important issues.

Superboy # 49 –
an example of FAIR condition

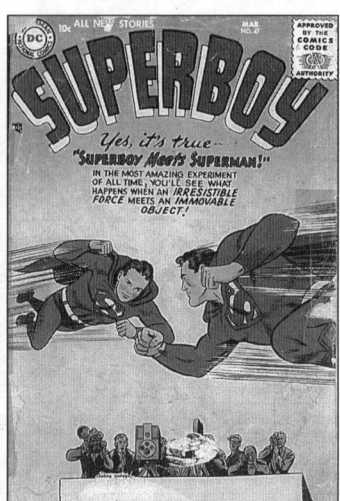

Superboy# 47 –
an example of POOR condition

SPECIFICATIONS

FOR THE SERIOUS STATISTICS & TRIVIA FREAKS ONLY

	£	$
Total number of DC comics	20,498	
Total number of Marvel comics	19,382	
Total number of Independent comics	30,288	
Total number of DC/Marvel comics	39,880	
Total number of DC/Marvel/Independent comics	70,170	
Total number of DC titles	1,101	
Total number of Marvel titles	1,353	
Total number of Independent titles	3,842	
Total number of DC/Marvel titles	2,454	
Total number of DC/Marvel/Independent titles	6,296	
Total value of DC comics	£2,239,227.30	$3,365,100.33
Total value of Marvel comics	£566,790.90	$888,593.16
Total value of Independent comics	£486,164.70	$730,176.28
Total value of DC/Marvel comics	£2,806,018.20	$4,253,693.49
TOTAL VALUE OF DC/MARVEL/ INDEPENDENT COMICS	**£3,292,185.90**	**$4,983,874.27**

THE BRITISH and AMERICAN MARKET
A Comparison

IT IS OFTEN SAID, more so here on the British side of the Atlantic than on the American, that the British comics scene, market and latterly industry is a mirror-image of America only on a smaller scale. As a certain Asgardian might quoth *"I say thee nay!"* or at least I hope to show throughout the course of this article that our green and sceptr'd isle has its own unique historical traditions, distribution patterns and consequently collecting habits. Where once it might have been thought that the British and American markets were gradually converging, the gap between the two markets is in the process of ever-widening in terms of speculative interest, pricing resistance and ultimately marketplace structure as I also hope to show.

One of the most fundamental differences between the U.K. and U.S. markets is that of comics history and traditions. In Great Britain we did not have a "Golden Age" (apart from the historical one of Queen Elizabeth I, Shakespeare and Raleigh, Drake and the Armada). The Golden Age of American comics (1938-1945) is almost completely unknown to and even ignored by many U.K. collectors. It is almost completely unknown to the general population who have their own memories of the comics they read as children back in the 1930s and 1940s. In fact Great Britain only just caught on to the next phase of American comic development, the Silver Age, after it had been well underway. As is generally regarded, Showcase #4 cover-dated September/October 1956 ushered in the Silver Age of American comics wherein Golden Age heroes were updated for a new generation of readers and super-heroes with super-powers became once more the dominant genre. It may not be widely known to American collectors and dealers but American comic books were not officially distributed in Great Britain until as late as the first couple of months of 1960 (issues cover-dated November 1959), mostly DCs with some Atlas, Archies, Charltons, Harveys and ACGs. There was some limited distribution of romance, war and funny animal titles from late 1957, presumably as market-testers, the most popular of those being Charlton war titles catering to a market stimulated in part by the

pocket sized War Picture Library and Battle Picture Library by Fleetway, publisher of today's 2000 AD comic.

While the transatlantic time-lag between actual distribution of American comics is more than twenty years, happily the same cannot be said for the establishment of a back-issue market. It may have begun in the United States before it did in the U.K. but thanks to certain pioneering individuals, the basis for markets that could at least be compared was established. There were isolated collectors up and down the U.K. who began to correspond and to trade comics with each other in the early 1960s as had begun in the States in the late 1950s. The establishment of fanzines were only a few years apart if one compares Jerry Bails' Alter Ego #1 in 1960 and in the U.K. Frank Dobson's Fantasy Advertiser #1 and Dez Skinn's interestingly-named Derinn Comicollector #1 in 1965. Comic book conventions seemed to have started at around the same time with Phil Seuling's New York convention in 1968 and Phil Clark's convention in Birmingham in the same year. When Bob Overstreet started his Comic Book Price Guide in 1970, British collector and dealer Alan Austin produced his first price guide in 1975, researched at source from his own massive collection and painstakingly typed out by hand with addenda at the back for titles he missed out along the way – no luxuries like a computer or word processor here! Alan's book represents an important pedigree of U.K. price guides that this present Guide is directly descended from. As such, the general pattern seemed to be that events in the awareness of the collectibility of back issues that happened in the States were mirrored over in the U.K. after some increasingly short time delay but the advantage in America was the much broader range and age of back issues available. By the mid 1960s, these isolated British collectors had five or six years' worth of distributed American comics to consider: their U.S. counterparts had more than twenty five. The beauty for collectors of American comics in the U.K. was that sets were entirely possible to put together, at least of Marvel comics. A DC comics fan was faced with the prospect of some very high numbers with the

first distributed issues of Action Comics at #258 and Detective Comics at #272 for example. British comics were equally daunting with 52 issues a year rather than twelve and generally being larger in size and even then being available in a wide variety of sizes, there were (and still are!) inevitable storage problems. It is no wonder that the collecting of American comics in general and some especially caught on so well in the U.K., presaged by the black and white album and comic reprints throughout the 1940s and 1950s.

Back-issue collecting of American comics had the perfect platform in the 1950s. In October 1951 the first Superman Annual from Atlas Publishing appeared. This collected the first six Australian issues that had appeared from July to December 1950 published by K.G. Murray for distribution by Atlas. The reprints from National Periodical Publications were black and white only and took their content from issues of late 1940s Superman, Action and World's Finest Comics. The cover was taken from the famous origin issue of Superman #53. Batman, Superboy and SuperAdventure Annuals followed along with monthly comics of the same titles. One hundred page reprint comics also appeared such as All Favourites, Hundred Comics and Superman Supacomics. By the end of the 1950s, there were not many National Periodical/DC comics characters that British youngsters had not seen. More importantly it got regular buyers into the habit of the monthly comic book so that when the originals arrived at the newsagents at the beginning of 1960, now they could read the adventures of familiar characters in full colour. Not surprisingly these British and Australian reprints are fast becoming very sought after for their unusual reprints and many original covers. Interestingly the process was reversed in the 1960s for Marvel comics as the colour originals were reprinted in black and white form by Alan Class titles like Astounding Stories and Secrets of the Unknown and Odhams Press titles like Pow! and Smash!

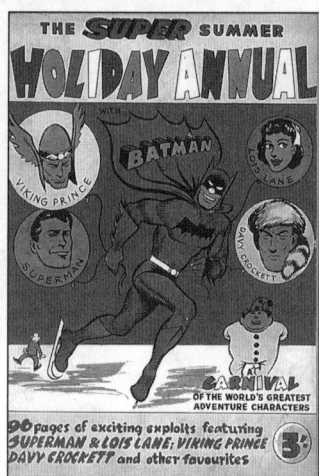

The Super Summer Holiday Annual

Five Score Comic Monthly #69

Mighty Comic #41

Superman #105

Superboy # 67

Batman #18

Super Adventure Comic #99

Super Adventure Annual 1958-59 (1st)

Superman Annual #1 (1951)

A selection of Atlas comics and annuals, available in the U.K. throughout the 1950s and the early 1960s
with a wide variety of reprint material before the "real thing" began to be distributed with cover date November 1959

The second fundamental difference is the weekly format established from the very beginning by British comics and the monthly magazine format favoured in America. One obvious reason must be the relative sizes of the countries. For America to base a comic distribution service on a weekly basis would have meant an extremely sophisticated distribution network in those early days. And on a more basic economic level, a shelf-life of a month (or more) was more attractive than a week, given the number of days it would take to get comics out to the furthest parts of the country by road. It is interesting to consider that though the British invented the very word itself when it first appeared in dictionaries in the 1780s as "comick" meaning satirical broadsheet paper with amusing stories and caricature illustrations, aimed at an adult audience and it was the British who developed the comic for a younger audience in the 1890s with Comic Cuts and the like, it was the Americans who took the genre and made it their own in the late 1920s when a month's worth of Sunday Funnies could be collected together and bound with cardboard covers. And there the American comic stayed and flourished right through the Thirties, Forties and Fifties while the British tradition carried on as it had done, almost unchanged during the same period.

Up until official distribution at the beginning of 1960, the staple diet of every school-boy (not discounting publications like June, Girl and Schoolfriend for the school-girl market) were weekly comics like The Dandy (first issue 14th December 1937 and still going today) or The Beano (first issue 30th July 1938 and likewise still going strong) which are even today still very much in the tradition of the finite one page jolly jape story. There were very few continuing dramatic stories with developing characters in this type of comic from the 1930s to the 1950s though the 1960s saw the rise and (some British collectors would argue) peak of this phenomenon, possibly owing to American influence. The other alternative was the generic term "Boys Papers" like The Rover or The Wizard, mostly text stories with illustrations dealing with stories based on school dormitory antics and castaways on desert islands, war hero exploits or tales of the athletes and other sportsmen. The outstanding exception to all this was The Eagle comic (first issue dated 14th April 1950) featuring Dan Dare Pilot of the Future as drawn in full colour by Frank Hampson. With its rocket ships and ray guns, futuristic cityscapes and the dreaded Mekon as principal foe, the Dan Dare strip freely borrowed from the American tradition of dashing heroes and outer space exploits though his firm square-set jaw and very British exclamations ("Cheerio!" and "Great Heavens!") planted him solidly in the British Royal Air Force world and vocabulary of the Second World War. Not a super power or a flapping cape to be seen. The brightly-costumed hero was relegated to decidedly second-raters like Electroman and Masterman though the one major exception to this was Marvelman, produced by Mick Anglo and Roy Parker from their tiny studio in Gower Street in London from 1954 to 1963 though the character, it could be argued, was an obvious derivative of Fawcett's Captain Marvel.

It was against this background that the American monthly comic book appeared, first in dribs and drabs and then in official distribution.

Their full colour glossy covers and colour interiors were a sharp contrast to the duller newsprint quality of virtually all British weeklies, most of which were black and white interiors or at best occasional spot colour.

Distribution of American comics, even when it was official, was patchy at first and very often the sea-side towns of Brighton and Bournemouth, Blackpool and Southend had ample supplies for holidaying youngsters with extra pocket money to spend, supplies that tended to get no further inland. Distribution to Scotland, however, has always been somewhat better from the start and as DCs seemed to be in the greatest supply, the marked fondness for mainstay characters like Superman and Batman still survives today in those areas.

While it was mentioned earlier that no Golden Age comics were distributed in Great Britain on an official scale, it is certain that some found their way over with visiting friends or relatives from the U.S. and indeed many thousands of comics came with the arrival of G.I.s stationed in Britain during the War. Areas where there are U.S.A.F. bases such as Norwich in the county of Norfolk north-east of London are generally good for turning up older, pre-distribution issues as these have been gradually disseminated throughout the county since the War. I myself have seen a copy of Action Comics #1 with an old sixpence stamp on it. It is highly unlikely that there is anything vaguely approaching a treasure trove of Golden Age comics to be found in this country, certainly not on the pedigree scale of some of the American finds such as The Edgar Church Collection. The dream of finding a box of Detective 27s in an old lady's attic will have to remain, as Charles Dickens would be wont to say, "..charming food for contemplation".

A number of early (pre-distribution) Batman and Detective Comics have been known with Popular Book Centre Stamps on the front cover for example. These PBC shops were more prevalent in the late 1940s and 1950s though the chain still survives today. The mainstay of their stock was cheap paperbacks and pornographic magazines and thus the inclusion of American comics associated them with literature that was liable to corrupt, a stigma attached to the American comic for a very long time. This attitude was not helped by the appearance in unusually large quantities of EC comics in the early 1950s, the first occasion of anything like mass-exposure to the American comic. Though short-lived in Britain, these comics were quickly banned, leading to the Children and Young Person (Harmful Publications) Act of 1955 and found themselves consigned to the same pornographic shelves in adult corner bookshops. The Popular Book Centre stamp is usually a very large diamond shape in the middle of the cover with the re-sale price, usually threepence or sixpence (these coins are no longer in circulation and then would have been worth about 4 cents and 7 cents respectively) scrawled in biro or felt tip pen in the box provided. These Popular Bookshop Centre-stamped copies were the scourge of those early collectors in Britain in the 1960s. Great for reading value but not so great for those interested in high grade copies.

The first American comic books to be distributed usually had the English price of ninepence stamped anywhere on the front cover. This stamp was done in ink and could often be in a neat circle on an unobtrusive part of the cover. More infuriatingly, it could be very heavy, even smudged and right on the face of a leading character or right in the middle of a clear expanse of cover so as to be all the more obvious. Occasionally the inking would be so heavy as to bleed through to the inside front cover.

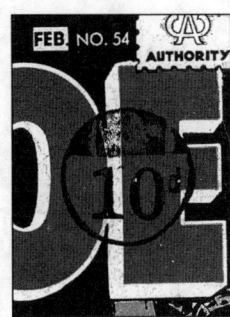

A pence stamp in detail.
A fairly typical example although there were many variations.

The very early Marvels more sensibly had the English price printed where the cents price would have been, ninepence from 1961 to mid 1964, tenpence from 1965 to 1967 and one shilling until decimalization in 1971 when it became six new pence or "6p". This gradually rose up to 15p until the practice of dual-pricing in the early 1980s. More confusing still, the "sell-by" month was removed for these exported copies as by the time they arrived on the British news-stands, it was already the actual month (and sometimes later) that was printed inside the comic. Nervous distributors felt that it would give a very limited shelf-life to a publication if the cover month was left on. Classic examples of this would be a Fantastic Four #1 with the "NOV" missing from a British-priced pence copy or the "AUG" missing from a British-priced Amazing Fantasy #15. Interestingly, the earliest distributed westerns, romance and war titles had the U.S. indicia removed inside and in its place had emblazoned "Exclusively distributed in the U.K. by Thorpe and Porter".

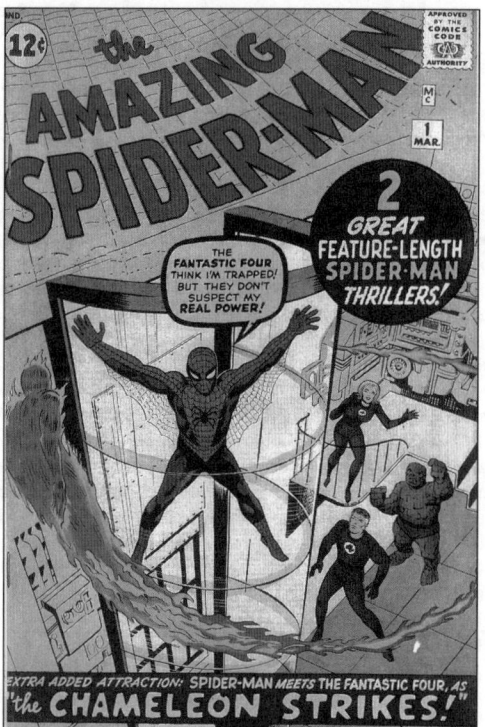

Amazing Spiderman #1 –
Cents copy of Amazing Spiderman compared to a Pence copy (see below).
Note that the covers are identical apart from the "9d" in place of the "12¢"
and the cover month of "MAR" missing under the number 1.

This has lead to the question of cents copies versus pence copies for collectors in the U.K. Many collectors feel that as American comics they should have the original American price while others, content in their nostalgia, prefer the pence pricing as that is what they remember as children. The debate still continues as a matter of personal

choice but for those who wish to invest their money in higher grade copies, particularly of key issues, only cents will do. For lower grade ordinary issues with no key significance, the cents/pence distinction becomes negligible. In a sense the pence copies are much rarer than cents copies as only a small fraction of the entire print run (2%?), usually at the end when the black cover plates were changed, were set aside for foreign distribution. Some would claim that this meant lesser clarity of printing quality as the inks became faded and the plates would start to show wear and as such a non-cents copy is necessarily of inferior production quality. Recent ideas have suggested that at the beginning of official distribution in early 1960, the pence-priced copies were produced first as there was a set number ordered by cautious British wholesalers, unsure as how how these new-fangled American comics would sell against the British weeklies which were cheaper (The Dandy and The Beano were 2 old/pre-decimalization pence at the time or just under 3 cents as opposed to 10 cents cover price for American comics to give some price perspective). It is possible therefore that mid Silver Age DCs and the very first Marvel comics are of a better quality of printing than the American cents-priced copies.

The actual process of printing renders these ideas doubtful as it would mean restarting the printing presses after an initial short run-time.

Either way, in this current age of collecting cover variants, American collectors and dealers may care to consider the possibilities of The British Cover Variant Edition of, say, an Amazing Spiderman #1 or a Superman Annual #1. They are certainly much rarer and the early Marvels do have these interesting printing variations. Most collectors in the U.K. cannot understand why most Americans consider these pence copies as inferior reprints. They were printed on the same day, in the same place, on the same paper using the same original artwork. When the finite resource of very high grade cent copies key issues runs out, if it hasn't done so already, where else can collectors turn in order to buy unrestored high grades? Surely the condition of the comic is more important? There is an argument for the attraction and genuine rarity value of a Near Mint unrestored pence copy of Amazing Fantasy #15 in the marketplace if only Fine and Very Fine cents copies are otherwise available. More and more pence-priced copies of Silver Age Marvels seem to be appearing on American dealers' mail order lists and are priced at about 75% of a similar grade cents copy. It would be interesting to find out how well they sell. It is still a remarkable fact of luck or foresight that a key issue survives in perfect condition whether it be a cents or pence copy, perhaps more so for "British copies" as there were far fewer pence copies produced in the first place.

Even today in Great Britain there is necessarily a greater supply of pence copies of Silver Age/1960s material in spite of the increasing amounts cents copies brought over by British dealers visiting American conventions in recent years. It will be some time, if ever, before there are equal amounts of cents and pence copies of Silver Age books in the U.K.

Tales of Suspense #59
An example of a comic made Scarce in the U.K. by a quirk of distribution at the time

Distribution throughout the 1960s and 1970s was handled by a company called Thorpe and Porter and the T & P stamp or later on the white sticker with the T & P in the symbol of an indian tent (or teepee – get it?) became what most British collectors fondly remember. While gaining in frequency and reliability, occasionally hiccups in distribution occurred. A national dock strike at the beginning of 1965 meant that for at least two (and possibly three) months Marvels in particular only came over in very limited quantities as most were turned away to be delivered to other parts of the Commonwealth, mostly South Africa and Australia. Issues across all the Marvel titles starting with cover-date Oct 1964 (in one instance Sept 1964, that of Two-Gun Kid #71) and ending with cover-date Jan 1965 are in generally short supply with cover date Dec 1964 being what seems to be the height of the dock strike as most of those issues are traditionally rare. As the dock strike gradually lessened so the issue numbers became very scarce or scarce and issues cover-dated Feb and Mar 1965 are increasingly found to be less common that otherwise thought. Issues of note affected by this dock strike in the U.K. market are: **Amazing Spiderman #18,#19** and to a lesser extent **#20**; **Avengers #9-11** and to a lesser extent **#12**; **Daredevil #4,5**; **Fantastic Four #32,#33** and to a lesser extent **#34**; **Journey into Mystery #109-112**; **Kid Colt, Outlaw #119, 120**; **Rawhide Kid #43**; **Sgt. Fury #11-13**; **Strange Tales #126,#127** and to a lesser extent **#128**; **Tales of Suspense #58-60**; **Tales to Astonish #60-63**; **Two-Gun Kid #71-73**; **X-Men #8,9**. DCs of the same cover-dates do not seem to be as unusually rare or scarce.

1,000 print run, an innocuous white cover and sold for $5. The first edition sold out and a second print run of 800 with a blue cover soon followed. The book did two very important things: it immediately established a market value for American comics the moment that prices were seen in black and white and thereby sowed the seed for speculative interest in the buying and selling of comics. It also, and perhaps more importantly, established a pricing structure centred around the three grades of Good, Fine and Mint. The ratios between the three were roughly 1 to 1.5 to 2 (a little different to some of today's ratios of 1 to 3 to 15!). The concept of the condition being the major factor of value was now set in stone. In 1982, Bob Overstreet with Jon Warren brought out a Price Update as a supplement to the Comic Book Price Guide #12 and the structure of the American market was complete. Dealers and collectors alike could look forward to a regular price increase in most cases (decreases some of the time) and report on the constant shifting state of the back issue industry. In the years that have followed, some would argue that such a system leads to a healthy and sustainable growth in the market year on year while others would make accusations of unnecessary hype and ever spiralling multiples of Guide. Either way, it is clear that the structure of the American market is more sophisticated in certain areas.

The first Overstreet Price Guide in 1970.
(Special note: Cover © Copyright Overstreet Publications)

The first Overstreet Update in 1982.
(Special note: Cover © Copyright Overstreet Publications)

There is another peculiarity to Marvel comics in the U.K. market. As the majority of issues in the 1960s and early 1970s were shipped by sea, very often bundles of them got water-stained and at worst completely water-soaked. Though sea-shipping still continues today, there must have been an unusually high proportion of un-seaworthy vessels in the early 1970s as Marvels in particular suffer from this severe fault. Amazing Spidermans from #105 to 110 and later on from #120-129 and Iron Mans from #42 to 44 are notoriously regular sufferers when they surface in indigenous collections. One wonders how many hundreds even thousands of copies have been rendered completely uncollectible in this way.

It is perhaps the history and establishment of Price Guides that cause the markets in the U.K. and U.S. to differ most significantly. In my opinion, one of the most important books about comics ever written appeared in 1970. Two hundred and twenty eight pages long with a handful of adverts at the back, typed out rather than type-set, a few mistakes like Batman #46 being the famous origin cover and story rather than #47 and with what were then ground-breaking prices like Action Comics #1 at $300 in Mint, Detective #27 at $275 and Showcase #4 at $12! The first Comic Book Price Guide by Bob Overstreet had a

Twenty six years later, the Overstreet Guide is still going strong when other American guides have come and gone. While values are set and shown to evolve every year for the American market, it is becoming increasingly clear that those same prices cannot be applied issue for issue to the British market. Different traditions. Different distribution patterns. Different character popularity. Different size of collector interest. Different general awareness. And different attitude to realistic levels of prices.

When Alan Austin produced his first Price Guide in 1975, the current Overstreet Guide of the time was number 4 with number 5 just about to come out. Interesting examples of price comparison would be X-Men #1 priced at $10 in Mint and Fantastic Four #1 priced at $70. Alan adopted more or less the same ratio splits as Overstreet between Good, Fine and Mint (which would seem logical at the time) and his pricing seems very consistent. He priced X-Men #1 at £3.50 (when $10 converted at the then exchange rate of 2.40 would have been £4.16) and Fantastic Four #1 at £25 ($70 converted at 2.40 being £29.16). It would not surprise me in the least if Alan had completely ignored the Overstreet price and came up with those values independently. He just knew the market rate for comics like that in this country. In his introduction he wrote about seeing "a trend back towards more reasonable prices" and twenty one years later I hope that this Guide will echo that same sentiment.

IT'S A QUESTION OF CULTURE
(by Alan Scott of Adventure Into Comics Inc.)

I WOULD LIKE to start by thanking Duncan McAlpine for inviting me to contribute this article about the differences in the UK and American market.

Over the years, we have seen dramatic changes in the comic industry with the influx of new, young artists which have taken comics and the industry in a new direction. To assess the differences between ourselves and our friends across the Atlantic, we must first look at what I deem to be the most important single factor—Culture. Americans being nurtured and weaned on Super Heroes, Hollywood, Rock & Roll and its paraphernalia.

Since the early 20s and 30s, the Americans were raised on super-heroes before the advent of TV by radio, Pulp Magazines and Newspaper strips. More so to the present. American publishers used comic book characters as part of their propaganda machine during the Second World War while we here at home still indulged in our Dandys and Beanos.

The American dream of super-heroes, baseball and football have been an integrated part of American culture from the time of conception. Therefore generation after generation have been subjected to super-heroes as an everyday form of entertainment.

During my trips to and from the USA, these differences become more and more apparent with my association with my colleagues across the Atlantic. It is an everyday occurrence to walk into any comic store in the USA and see grandfather, son and grandson all purchasing their favourite super-heroes. With the development of the multi media and licensing, it would be part of an everyday occurrence as well to see many of the super-heroes on everyday

products in and out of stores and supermarkets throughout the US from cereal packets to tins of beans.

Other areas of major differences are licensing on a big scale throughout large corporate bodies such as Universal Studios extending their theme parks to incorporate an X-Men Mutant Ride and all the merchandise; Burger King with their special deals and kids meals incorporating licensed super-hero products; toy companies producing all major super-hero figures; card companies producing a wide range of cards covering super-heroes to TV shows. Other media such as television, especially the Fox network screening new animated cartoon series (Spiderman, X-Men, Batman, Maxx, Ultraforce). The new TV special Generation X recently shown in the US helps strengthen the US awareness of products available to the public, which are seen as major investment and marketing by US companies; for example all major comic companies pushing their titles at comic marts with artists appearing, signings at stores and comic distributors sponsoring comic conventions.

Unfortunately none of the aforementioned are common to the UK market (take note publishers and distributors!).

As such, this fact of comic book culture being integrated into everyday living highlights the major differences between our two markets. In the UK, the comic book industry is still frowned upon and seen by many as adults playing with kids' books.

On many occasions, when asked by people what my profession is, when I tell them I sell comic books they look at me in dismay which then brings us on to one major factor in the two markets, and that

is product awareness.

As in New York and San Diego and in most major US cities, it is fairly commonplace to find people of professional standing such as lawyers, accountants and doctors regularly visiting their local comic store in search of rare and collectible books for investment. Comics being one of the top investment commodities in the US stock market over the last few years, older books have distinctly increased in value on a regular basis. It would not be an unusual occurrence for someone to approach a financial institution to request a loan to invest in comic books. On the other hand, if you were to ask an English bank, you would be taken away by men in white coats.

This is the basis of why there is such a large scale investment of rare and collectible books in the USA. We have seen many recent examples of such speculation in the last few years where books of notable interest have sold 4–5 times the value of its counterpart here at home.

Bearing this in mind, we would be hard pushed to compete in such an open and virile market. Such a difference can be seen in one key area and that is golden age books as the availability of such is virtually non existent here in the UK.

Therefore it is my personal belief that these differences could never really be bridged and we must therefore be thankful to our friends across the Atlantic for exposing us to this medium which has kept many of us from boys to men telling us of what things there are to come.

In memory of Jerry Siegel, creator of Superman (17 Oct 1914 –28 Jan 1996)

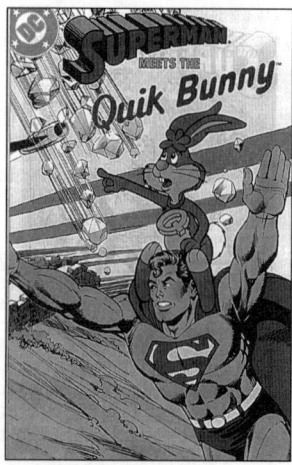

Superman Meets the Quik Bunny –
A super-hero association with a line of children's milk drinks

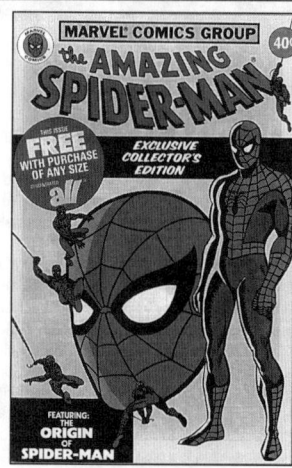

The Amazing Spiderman meets a household detergent

FIRST APPEARANCE INDEX

Below is the latest version of our First Appearance Index, a feature first brought to you by this publication. If there are any corrections or omissions please feel free to contact the Editorial address.

A.I.M.
STRANGE TALES #146..................................JULY 1966
ABEL
HOUSE OF SECRETS #61............JULY/AUGUST 1963
ABIGAIL ARCANE
SWAMP THING #2.............................FEBRUARY 1973
ABOMINATION
TALES TO ASTONISH #90..........................APRIL 1967
ABRA KADABRA
FLASH (1st Series) #128..............................MAY 1962
ABSORBING MAN
JOURNEY INTO MYSTERY #114............MARCH 1965
ADAM STRANGE
SHOWCASE #17..............................DECEMBER 1958
ADAMANTIUM
AVENGERS #66...JULY 1969
ADRIAN CHASE (Vigilante)
NEW TEEN TITANS, THE
(1st Series) #23................................SEPTEMBER 1982
ADULT LEGION
SUPERMAN #147.....................................AUGUST 1961
AGATHA HARKNESS
FANTASTIC FOUR #94.......................JANUARY 1970
AGENT 13
TALES OF SUSPENSE #75.....................MARCH 1966
AGENT LIBERTY
SUPERMAN (2nd Series) #60.............OCTOBER 1991
AGON
THOR #148..JANUARY 1968
AGUILA
POWER MAN AND IRON FIST #58.......AUGUST 1979
AIR WAVE (Golden Age)
DETECTIVE COMICS #60.................FEBRUARY 1942

AIR WAVE (Modern)
GREEN LANTERN #100......................JANUARY 1978
AIREO
FANTASTIC FOUR #47......................FEBRUARY 1966
AIRWALKER
FANTASTIC FOUR #120.........................MARCH 1972
ALCHEMIST
LEGION OF SUPER-HEROES #24....DECEMBER 1991
ALFRED
BATMAN #16.................................APRIL/MAY 1942
ALICIA MASTERS
FANTASTIC FOUR #8......................NOVEMBER 1962
ALL STAR SQUADRON
ALL STAR SQUADRON #1.............SEPTEMBER 1981
ALL WINNERS SQUAD
ALL WINNERS COMICS #19...............AUTUMN 1946
ALLATOU
MARVEL SPOTLIGHT #18.........................APRIL 1974
ALPHA FLIGHT
X-MEN, THE UNCANNY #120..................APRIL 1979
ALPHA PRIMITIVES
FANTASTIC FOUR #47......................FEBRUARY 1966
AMAZING MAN
ALL STAR SQUADRON #23.........................JULY 1983
AMAZO
BRAVE AND THE BOLD, THE #30..............JULY 1960
AMBUSH BUG
DC COMICS PRESENTS #52..........DECEMBER 1992
AMERICAN EAGLE
MARVEL TWO IN ONE ANNUAL #6.....................1981
AMERICAN SCREAM
SHADE, THE CHANGING MAN
(2nd Series) #1...JUNE 1990

AMETHYST
LEGION OF SUPER-HEROES
(1st Series) #298..APRIL 1983
AMPHIBIAN
AVENGERS #145.................................MARCH 1976
ANACONDA
MARVEL TWO IN ONE #64........................JUNE 1980
ANCIENT ONE
STRANGE TALES #111........................AUGUST 1963
ANDROMEDA (DC)
LEGION OF SUPER-HEROES..........DECEMBER 1991
ANDROMEDA (Marvel)
DEFENDERS #146...............................AUGUST 1985
ANGAR THE SCREAMER
DAREDEVIL #100....................................JUNE 1973
ANGEL (Archangel)
X-MEN, THE UNCANNY #1............SEPTEMBER 1963
ANGEL (Golden Age)
MARVEL COMICS #1...........................OCT/NOV 1939
ANGEL AND THE APE
SHOWCASE #77...................................AUGUST 1968
ANGLE MAN
WONDER WOMAN #70..................NOVEMBER 1954
ANIMAL MAN
STRANGE ADVENTURES #180.......SEPTEMBER 1965
ANNIHILUS
FANTASTIC FOUR ANNUAL #6.......NOVEMBER 1968
ANT BOY
ANT BOY #1...1984
ANT MAN
TALES TO ASTONISH #27.................JANUARY 1962
ANT MAN II
MARVEL PREMIERE #47...........................APRIL 1981

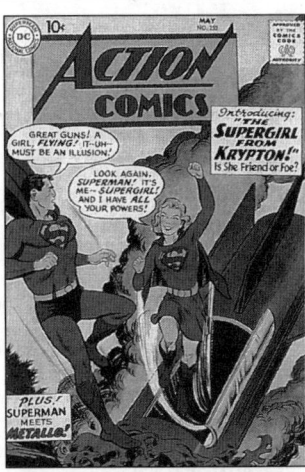

Action Comics # 252 – 1st appearance Supergirl

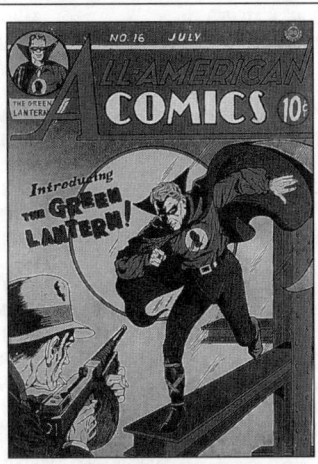

All America Comics # 16 –
1st appearance Golden Age Green Lantern

ANTHRO
SHOWCASE #74..MAY 1968
ANTON ARCANE
SWAMP THING #2......................FEBRUARY 1973
APARITION
LEGION OF SUPER-HEROES #25 ....DECEMBER 1991
APOCALYPSE
X-FACTOR #5...JUNE 1986
APOKOLIPS
NEW GODS, THE #1 ....FEB/MAR 1971
APOLLO
THOR #301...................................NOVEMBER 1980
AQUABOY
SUPERBOY #171............................JANUARY 1971
AQUAGIRL
AQUAMAN #33...JUNE 1967
AQUALAD
ADVENTURE COMICS #269............FEBRUARY 1960
AQUAMAN (Golden Age)
MORE FUN COMICS #73................NOVEMBER 1941
AQUAMAN (Silver Age)
ADVENTURE COMICS #260.......................MAY 1959
AQUARIAN
ADVENTURE INTO FEAR #17.............OCTOBER 1973
ARABIAN KNIGHT
INCREDIBLE HULK #257.......................MARCH 1981
ARAK
WARLORD #48...AUGUST 1981
ARCADE
MARVEL TEAM UP #65 ....JANUARY 1978
ARCHANGEL
X-FACTOR #24.............................JANUARY 1988
ARCHER & ARMSTRONG
ARCHER & ARMSTRONG #0......................JUNE 1992
ARCHIE
PEP COMICS #22.............................DECEMBER 1941
ARES
THOR #129...JUNE 1966
ARION
WARLORD #55...............................MARCH 1982
ARKON
AVENGERS #75................................APRIL 1970
ARMADILLO
CAPTAIN AMERICA #308.....................AUGUST 1985
ARMORINES
X-O MANOWAR #25........................NOVEMBER 1993
ARON THE ROGUE WATCHER
CAPTAIN MARVEL #39....................FEBRUARY 1975
ARTEMIS
THOR #129...JUNE 1966
ASGARD
JOURNEY INTO MYSTERY #85 ....OCTOBER 1962
ASMODEUS
FANTASTIC FOUR #117 ....DECEMBER 1971
ASP
CAPTAIN AMERICA #309 ....SEPTEMBER 1985
ASTRA
X-MEN, THE UNCANNY #107 ....NOVEMBER 1977
ASTROBOY
SHONEN MAGAZINE (Japan) #1..........................1951
ASTRONOMER
SILVER SURFER (3rd Series) #4..........OCTOBER 1987
ATARI FORCE
NEW TEEN TITANS, THE
(1st Series) #27..JANUARY 1983
ATHENA
THOR #164...MAY 1969

ATOM (Golden Age)
ALL AMERICAN COMICS #19 ....OCTOBER 1940
ATOM (Silver Age)
SHOWCASE #34...........................OCTOBER 1961
ATOMIC KNIGHTS
STRANGE ADVENTURES #117.................JUNE 1960
ATOMIC SKULL
SUPERMAN #323...MAY 1978
ATTILAN
FANTASTIC FOUR #47 ....FEBRUARY 1966
ATTUMA
FANTASTIC FOUR #33..................DECEMBER 1964
AUNT AGATHA
BATMAN #89.................................FEBRUARY 1955
AURON
GREEN LANTERN #141.............................JUNE 1981
AURORA
X-MEN, THE UNCANNY #120 ....APRIL 1979
AVALANCHE
X-MEN, THE UNCANNY #141............JANUARY 1981
AVENGERS
AVENGERS #1.............................SEPTEMBER 1963
AVENGERS MANSION
AVENGERS #2.................................NOVEMBER 1963
AVIUS
FANTASTIC FOUR #129 ....DECEMBER 1972
AWESOME ANDROID
FANTASTIC FOUR #15 ....JUNE 1963
AZRAEL (Jean Paul Valley)
BATMAN: SWORD OF AZRAEL #1......OCTOBER 1992
AZREAL
NEW TEEN TITANS, THE
(1st Series) #52..MAY 1985
BABE
ATARI FORCE #1.............................JANUARY 1984
BABY HUEY
CASPER #1 ....SEPTEMBER 1949
BADGER
BADGER #1....................................OCTOBER 1983
BALDER
JOURNEY INTO MYSTERY #85 ....OCTOBER 1962
BANE
VENGEANCE OF BANE SPECIAL ....JANUARY 1993
BANSHEE
X-MEN, THE UNCANNY #28 ....JANUARY 1967
BAPHOMET
MARVEL SPOTLIGHT #15 ....JANUARY 1974
BARBARUS
X-MEN, THE UNCANNY #62 ....NOVEMBER 1969
BARON BEDLAM
BATMAN AND THE OUTSIDERS #1......AUGUST 1983
BARON BLITZKRIEG
WORLD'S FINEST #246 ....AUGUST 1977
BARON BLOOD
INVADERS #7...JULY 1976
BARON EARTH
WARLORD #55...............................MARCH 1982
BARON MORDO
STRANGE TALES #111 ....AUGUST 1963
BARON STRUCKER
SGT. FURY AND HIS HOWLING
COMMANDOS #5 ....JANUARY 1964
BARON ZEMO I
AVENGERS #4 ....MARCH 1964
BARON ZEMO II
CAPTAIN AMERICA #168 ....DECEMBER 1973
BAT LASH
SHOWCASE #76 ....JULY 1968

BATGIRL (New)
DETECTIVE COMICS #359..................JANUARY 1967
BATGIRL (Old)
BATMAN #139...APRIL 1961
BAT-GYRO
DETECTIVE COMICS #31 ....SEPTEMBER 1939
BAT-HOUND
BATMAN #92...JUNE 1955
BATMAN (Golden Age)
DETECTIVE COMICS #27.........................MAY 1939
BATMAN (Silver Age)
DETECTIVE COMICS #327 ....MAY 1964
(Note: DC's official line debatable however)
BATMAN AND THE OUTSIDERS
BRAVE AND THE BOLD, THE #200 ....JULY 1983
BAT-MITE
DETECTIVE COMICS #267 ....MAY 1959
BATMOBILE
BATMAN #5...SPRING 1941
BATROC THE LEAPER
TALES OF SUSPENSE #76.......................APRIL 1966
BAT-SUBMARINE
BATMAN #86...............................SEPTEMBER 1954
BATTALION
TEAM TITANS #2 ....OCTOBER 1992
BATTLESTAR
CAPTAIN AMERICA #341 ....MAY 1988
BATWOMAN
DETECTIVE COMICS #233 ....JULY 1956
BEAST
X-MEN, THE UNCANNY #1 ....SEPTEMBER 1963
BEAST BOY
DOOM PATROL #99 ....NOVEMBER 1965
BEETLE
STRANGE TALES #123 ....AUGUST 1964
BELASCO
KA-ZAR THE SAVAGE #11 ....FEBRUARY 1982
BELATHAUZER
DEFENDERS #59...MAY 1978
BEL-DANN
X-MEN, THE UNCANNY #137 ....SEPTEMBER 1980
BELIT
GIANT SIZE CONAN #1 ....SEPTEMBER 1974
BETA RAY BILL
THOR #337...................................NOVEMBER 1983
BEYONDER
SECRET WARS II #1 ....JULY 1985
BIG BARDA
MISTER MIRACLE #4 ....SEPT/OCT 1971
BIG BERTHA
WEST COAST AVENGERS #46..................JULY 1988
BIG MAN AND THE ENFORCERS
AMAZING SPIDERMAN #10 ....MARCH 1964
BIG SIR
FLASH (1st Series) #338 ....OCTOBER 1984
BINARY
X-MEN, THE UNCANNY #164 ....DECEMBER 1982
BISHOP
X-MEN, THE UNCANNY #282 ....NOVEMBER 1992
BIZARRO (Modern)
MAN OF STEEL #5................................AUGUST 1986
BIZARRO (Silver Age)
SUPERBOY #68 ....OCTOBER 1956
BIZARRO BATMAN
WORLD'S FINEST #156 ....MARCH 1966
BIZARRO FLASH
LOIS LANE, SUPERMAN'S
GIRLFRIEND #74...MAY 1967

Amazing Spiderman # 2
1st appearance The Vulture

Avengers # 57
1st appearance The Vision

BOMBA
BOMBA, THE JUNGLE BOY #1 ....SEPT/OCT 1967

BOOMER
SECRET WARS II #5 ....NOVEMBER 1985

BOOMERANG
TALES TO ASTONISH #81 ....JULY 1966

BOOSTER GOLD
BOOSTER GOLD #1 ....FEBRUARY 1986

BOUNCING BOY
ACTION COMICS #276 ....MAY 1961

BOY COMMANDOS
DETECTIVE COMICS #64 ....JUNE 1942

BRAIN DRAIN
ALPHA FLIGHT #109..................................JUNE 1992

BRAINIAC (Silver Age)
ACTION COMICS #242................................JULY 1958

BRAINIAC (Modern)
SUPERMAN, THE ADVENTURES OF #438 .JULY 1988

BRAINIAC 5 (Silver Age)
ACTION COMICS #276 ....MAY 1961

BRAINIAC 5 (Modern)
LEGION OF SUPER-HEROES #24 ....DECEMBER 1991

BRAINSTORM
JUSTICE LEAGUE OF
AMERICA #32 ....DECEMBER 1964

BRONZE TIGER
RICHARD DRAGON, KUNG FU
FIGHTER #1 ....APRIL/MAY 1975

BROOD
X-MEN, THE UNCANNY #155................MARCH 1982

BROTHER BLOOD
NEW TEEN TITANS, THE
(1st Series) #21................................JULY 1982

BROTHER POWER
BROTHER POWER THE GEEK #1 ....SEP/OCT 1968

BROTHER VOODOO
STRANGE TALES #173...............................APRIL 1974

BROTHERS GRIMM
IRON MAN #188 ....NOVEMBER 1984

BUCKY
CAPTAIN AMERICA COMICS #1............MARCH 1941

BUCKY II
MARVEL PREMIERE #30............................JUNE 1976

BUDAN
MARVEL TWO-IN-ONE #71................JANUARY 1981

BULLDOZER
DEFENDERS #17 ....NOVEMBER 1974

BULLET
DAREDEVIL #250.............................JANUARY 1988

BULLSEYE
NICK FURY, AGENT OF
SHIELD #15................................NOVEMBER 1969

BUMBLEBEE
TEEN TITANS #48 ....JUNE 1977

BUN-DALL
CAPTAIN MARVEL #45 ....JULY 1976

BUSHMASTER
CAPTAIN AMERICA #310 ....OCTOBER 1985

BUSHWACKER
DAREDEVIL #249....................DECEMBER 1987

BUTCHER
BUTCHER #1..MAY 1990

B'WANA BEAST
SHOWCASE #66 ....JAN/FEB 1967

CABLE
NEW MUTANTS #87 ....MARCH 1990

CAIN
HOUSE OF MYSTERY #175..........JULY/AUGUST 196

CALIBAN
X-MEN, THE UNCANNY #148..............AUGUST 1981

CALLISTO
X-MEN, THE UNCANNY #169 ....MAY 1983

CALYPSO
AMAZING SPIDERMAN #209 ....OCTOBER 1980

CANNONBALL
MARVEL GRAPHIC NOVEL #4 1982

CAPTAIN AMERICA (Golden Age)
CAPTAIN AMERICA COMICS #1...........MARCH 1941

CAPTAIN AMERICA (Silver Age)
AVENGERS #4 ....MARCH 1964

CAPTAIN ATLAS
QUASAR #10...MAY 1990

CAPTAIN ATOM (Charlton)
SPACE ADVENTURES #33 ....MARCH 1960

CAPTAIN ATOM (DC)
CAPTAIN ATOM #1.............................MARCH 1987

CAPTAIN BOOMERANG
FLASH (1st Series) #117 ....DECEMBER 1960

CAPTAIN BRITAIN
CAPTAIN BRITAIN #1 ....OCTOBER 13TH 1976
(American Guides note!)

CAPTAIN BRITAIN
(1st US appearance)
MARVEL TEAM UP #66 ....FEBRUARY 1978

CAPTAIN CARROT
NEW TEEN TITANS, THE
(1st Series) #16 ....FEBRUARY 1982

CAPTAIN COLD
SHOWCASE #8..JUNE 1957

CAPTAIN COMET
STRANGE ADVENTURES #9 ....JUNE 1951

CAPTAIN COMMANDO
PEP COMICS #30..................................AUGUST 1942

CAPTAIN FREEDOM (Golden Age)
SPEED COMICS #13 ....MAY 1941

CAPTAIN FREEDOM (Modern)
AMERICOMICS #1...........................JANUARY 1983

CAPTAIN GEORGE STACY
AMAZING SPIDERMAN #56 ....JANUARY 1968

CAPTAIN MARVEL (Female)
AMAZING SPIDERMAN ANNUAL #16.................1982

CAPTAIN MARVEL (Kree)
MARVEL SUPER-HEROES #12 ....DECEMBER 1967

CAPTAIN MARVEL (M.F. Enterprises)
CAPTAIN MARVEL #1 ....APRIL 1966

CAPTAIN MARVEL (Modern)
SHAZAM, A NEW BEGINNING #1.............APRIL 1987

CAPTAIN MARVEL (Shazam)
WHIZ COMICS #2............................FEBRUARY 1940

CAPTAIN MARVEL Jnr
WHIZ COMICS #25...........................DECEMBER 1941

CAPTAIN PARAGON
BILL BLACK'S FUN COMICS #1 ......DECEMBER 1982

CAPTAIN SAVAGE
SGT. FURY AND HIS HOWLING
COMMANDOS #10 ....NOVEMBER 1964

CAPTAIN STORM
CAPTAIN STORM #1 ....MAY/JUN 1964

CAPTAIN STRONG
ACTION COMICS #421....................MARCH 1973

CAPTAIN THUNDER
FLASH COMICS (Fawcett) #1 ....JANUARY 1940

CAPTAIN UNIVERSE
MICRONAUTS #8....................................AUGUST 1979

CARDIAC
AMAZING SPIDERMAN #344...........FEBRUARY 1991

CARNAGE
AMAZING SPIDERMAN #361 ....APRIL 1992

CARRION
SPECTACULAR SPIDERMAN #25 ...DECEMBER 1978

CAT
THE CAT #1 ....NOVEMBER 1972

CATHERINE COBERT
JUSTICE LEAGUE EUROPE #1 ....APRIL 1989

CAT-MAN
DAREDEVIL #10 ....OCTOBER 1965

CATMAN
DETECTIVE COMICS #311 ....JANUARY 1963

CAT-MAN II
DAREDEVIL #157.................................MARCH 1979

CATSEYE
NEW MUTANTS #16....................................JUNE 1984

CATSPAW
LEGION OF SUPER-HEROES
#33 ....SEPTEMBER 1992

CATWOMAN
(Golden Age) called The Cat
BATMAN #1 ....SPRING 1940

CATWOMAN (Silver Age)
LOIS LANE, SUPERMAN'S
GIRLFRIEND #70 ....NOVEMBER 1966

CATWOMAN (Modern)
BATMAN #406 ....APRIL 1987

CAVALIER
DETECTIVE COMICS #81 ....NOVEMBER 1943

CAVE CARSON
BRAVE AND THE BOLD, THE
#31 ....SEPTEMBER 1960

CELESTIAL –
ARISHEM THE JUDGE
ETERNALS, THE #2..............................AUGUST 1976

CELESTIAL –
ESON THE SEARCHER
ETERNALS, THE #9 ....MARCH 1977

CELESTIAL –
GAMMENON THE GATHERER
ETERNALS, THE #4...........................OCTOBER 1976

CELESTIAL –
HARGEN THE MEASURER
ETERNALS, THE #9 ....MARCH 1977

CELESTIAL –
JEMIAH THE ANALYZER
ETERNALS, THE #7 ....JANUARY 1977

CELESTIAL –
NEZARR THE CALCULATOR
ETERNALS, THE #9 ....MARCH 1977

CELESTIAL –
ONE ABOVE ALL
ETERNALS, THE #7 ....JANUARY 1977

CELESTIAL –
ONEG THE PROBER
ETERNALS, THE #9 ....MARCH 1977

CELESTIAL –
TEFRAL THE SURVEYOR
ETERNALS, THE #7 ....JANUARY 1977

CELESTIAL –
ZIRAN THE TESTER
ETERNALS, THE #18......................DECEMBER 1977

CERBERUS
SUPERMAN: THE MAN OF STEEL #1 ....JULY 1991

CEREBRO
X-MEN, THE UNCANNY #7 ....SEPTEMBER 1964

CEREBUS THE AARDVARK
CEREBUS #1 ....DECEMBER 1977

CERISE
EXCALIBUR #47 ....FEBRUARY 1992
CHALLENGERS OF THE UNKNOWN
SHOWCASE #6 ....FEBRUARY 1957
CHAMELEON
AMAZING SPIDERMAN #1 ....MARCH 1963
CHAMELEON BOY
ACTION COMICS #267 ....AUGUST 1960
CHAMPION
MARVEL TWO IN ONE ANNUAL #7 1982
CHAMPIONS
CHAMPIONS #1 ....OCTOBER 1975
CHANGELING
X-MEN, THE UNCANNY #36 ....SEPTEMBER 1967
CHANGELING
(formerly Beast Boy)
NEW TEEN TITANS #1 ....NOVEMBER 1980
CHARLIE 27
MARVEL SUPER-HEROES #18 ....JANUARY 1969
CHECKMATE
ACTION COMICS #598.....................MARCH 1988
CHEETAH (Marvel)
CAPTAIN MARVEL #48.....................JANUARY 1977
CHEETAH I
WONDER WOMAN #6 ....AUTUMN 1943
CHEETAH II
WONDER WOMAN #274 ....JANUARY 1981
CHEETAH III
WONDER WOMAN #9 ....OCTOBER 1987
CHEMICAL KING
ADVENTURE COMICS #354..................MARCH 1967
CHEMO
SHOWCASE #39 ....JULY/AUG 1962
CHIRON
FANTASTIC FOUR #129 ....DECEMBER 1972
CHLOROPHYLL KID
ADVENTURE COMICS #306.................MARCH 1963
CHOD
X-MEN, THE UNCANNY #107 ....NOVEMBER 1977
CHOP-CHOP
MILITARY COMICS #3 ....OCTOBER 1941
CHRONOS
ATOM, THE #3 ....OCT/NOV 1962
CHTHON
AVENGERS #187 ....SEPTEMBER 1979
CIRCUS OF CRIME
DAREDEVIL #118 ....FEBRUARY 1975
CITADEL
GREEN LANTERN #136.....................JANUARY 1981
CLAW
CLAW THE UNCONQUERED #1 ....MAY/JUN 1975
CLAYFACE I
DETECTIVE COMICS #40 ....JUNE 1940
CLAYFACE II
DETECTIVE COMICS #298..............DECEMBER 1961
CLAYFACE III
DETECTIVE COMICS #478.........JULY/AUGUST 1978
CLAYFACE IV
OUTSIDERS #21 ....JULY 1987
CLEA
STRANGE TALES #126...................NOVEMBER 1964
CLETUS KASADY
AMAZING SPIDERMAN #345................MARCH 1991
CLIFF STEELE (Robotman)
MY GREATEST ADVENTURE #80 ....OCTOBER 1963
CLOAK AND DAGGER
PETER PARKER, THE SPECTACULAR
SPIDERMAN #64...........................MARCH 1982

CLOCK KING
WORLD'S FINEST COMICS #111 ....AUGUST 1960
COBRA
JOURNEY INTO MYSTERY #98 ....NOVEMBER 1963
COLLECTOR
AVENGERS #28...............................MAY 1966
COLLEEN WING
MARVEL PREMIERE #14 ....MARCH 1974
COLOSSAL BOY
ACTION COMICS #267 ....AUGUST 1960
COLOSSUS
X-MEN GIANT-SIZE #1 ....SUMMER 1975
COLOUR KID
ADVENTURE COMICS #342..................MARCH 1966
COMBAT KELLY
COMBAT KELLY #1............................JUNE 1967
COMET
ACTION COMICS #347......................MARCH 1967
COMMANDER KRAKEN
SUB-MARINER #27..............................JULY 1970
COMMISSIONER GORDON
DETECTIVE COMICS #27......................MAY 1939
COMPOSITE SUPERMAN
WORLD'S FINEST #142.........................JUNE 1964
COMPUTO (Silver Age)
ADVENTURE COMICS #340..............JANUARY 1966
COMPUTO (Modern)
LEGION OF SUPER-HEROES ANNUAL #1 1982
CONAN THE BARBARIAN
CONAN THE BARBARIAN #1.............OCTOBER 1970
CONCRETE
DARK HORSE PRESENTS #1...................JULY 1986
CONGO BILL
ACTION COMICS #37 ....JUNE 1941
CONGORILLA
ACTION COMICS #248......................JANUARY 1959
CONSTRICTOR
INCREDIBLE HULK #212 ....JUNE 1977
CONTEMPLATOR
MARVEL TREASURY SPECIAL #1 1974
CONTROLLER
IRON MAN #12 ....APRIL 1969
COPPERHEAD (DC)
BRAVE AND THE BOLD, THE #78.....JUNE/JULY 1968
COPPERHEAD (Marvel)
CAPTAIN AMERICA #337 ....JANUARY 1988
CORONA
SPECTACULAR SPIDERMAN #176 ....MAY 1991
CORRUPTOR
NOVA, THE MAN CALLED #4 ....DECEMBER 1976
CORSAIR
X-MEN, THE UNCANNY #107 ....NOVEMBER 1977
COSMIC BOY
ADVENTURE COMICS #247 ....APRIL 1958
COSMIC CUBE
TALES OF SUSPENSE #79........................JULY 1966
COTTONMOUTH
CAPTAIN AMERICA #310 ....OCTOBER 1985
COUGAR
COUGAR, THE #1 ....APRIL 1975
COUNT NEFARIA
AVENGERS #13 ....FEBRUARY 1965
COUNT VIRTIGO
WORLD'S FINEST #251......................JUNE/JULY 1978
CRAZY NATE
- GUARDIANS OF THE GALAXY #17.....OCTOBER 1991
CREATURE COMMANDOES
WEIRD WAR TALES #93.................NOVEMBER 1980

CREEPER
SHOWCASE #73 ....MAR/APRIL 1968
CRIME-BUSTER
NOVA, THE MAN CALLED #13 ....DECEMBER 1977
CRIMEMASTER
AMAZING SPIDERMAN #26 ....JULY 1965
CRIMSON
X-FACTOR #54 ....MAY 1990
CRIMSON AVENGER
DETECTIVE COMICS #20...................OCTOBER 1938
CRIMSON COMMANDO
X-MEN, THE UNCANNY #215............MARCH 1987
CRIMSON DYNAMO
TALES OF SUSPENSE #46 ....OCTOBER 1963
CRIMSON DYNAMO II
TALES OF SUSPENSE #52.....................APRIL 1964
CRIMSON DYNAMO III
IRON MAN #21...............................JANUARY 1970
CRIMSON DYNAMO IV
CHAMPIONS, THE #8..........................OCTOBER 1976
CRIMSON DYNAMO V
IRON MAN #109...............................APRIL 1978
CRIMSON FOX
JUSTICE LEAGUE EUROPE #6 ....SEPTEMBER 1989
CROSSBONES
CAPTAIN AMERICA #360...................OCTOBER 1989
CROSSFIRE
DNAGENTS #10 ....MARCH 1984
CROSSFIRE (Marvel)
MARVEL TWO IN ONE #52 ....JUNE 1979
CRUSADER
THOR #330 ....MARCH 1983
CRUSADER
(Formerly old Marvel Boy)
FANTASTIC FOUR #164 ....NOVEMBER 1975
CRUSADERS
INVADERS #14 ....MARCH 1977
CRYSTAL
FANTASTIC FOUR #45....................DECEMBER 1965
CRYSTAR
CRYSTAR, SAGA OF #1 ....MAY 1983
CUTTHROAT
MARVEL TEAM UP #89 ....JANUARY 1980
CYBELE
ETERNALS, THE (Limited Series) #1 ...OCTOBER 1985
CYBER
MARVEL COMICS PRESENTS #85 1991
CYBORG
DC COMICS PRESENTS #26 ....OCTOBER 1980
CYBORG SUPERMAN
(Hank Henshaw)
ADVENTURES OF SUPERMAN #465 ....MAY 1990
CYCLONE
AMAZING SPIDERMAN #143 ....APRIL 1975
CYCLOPS
X-MEN, THE UNCANNY #1 ....SEPTEMBER 1963
CYPHER
NEW MUTANTS #13 ....MARCH 1984
DAGOTH
MARVEL PREMIERE #7 ....MARCH 1973
DAILY BUGLE
AMAZING SPIDERMAN #1 ....MARCH 1963
DAILY PLANET
ACTION COMICS #23 ....APRIL 1940
DAIMON HELLSTROM
(see Son of Satan)
DAREDEVIL
DAREDEVIL #1..............................APRIL 1964

INTRODUCTION 33

Daredevil # 3
1st appearance The Owl

Fantastic Four # 4
1st appearance Sub-Mariner (in Silver Age)

GUARDIANS OF THE GALAXY
MARVEL SUPER-HEROES #18 ....JANUARY 1969
GUARDIANS OF THE UNIVERSE
GREEN LANTERN #1 ....JULY/AUGUST 1960
GUARDSMAN
IRON MAN #43.............................DECEMBER 1971
GUARDSMAN II
IRON MAN #97 ....APRIL 1977
GULLIVAR JONES
CREATURES ON THE LOOSE #16 ....MARCH 1972
GUNNER & SARGE
ALL AMERICAN MEN OF WAR #67 1958
GUY GARDNER
GREEN LANTERN #59 ....MARCH 1968
GWEN STACY
AMAZING SPIDERMAN #31...........DECEMBER 1965
GYPSY MOTH
SPIDERWOMAN #10 ....JANUARY 1979
H.A.R.D. CORPS
HARBINGER #10.............................OCTOBER 1992
HACKER
HACKER FILES #1.............................AUGUST 1992
HALO
BATMAN & THE OUTSIDER #1 ....AUGUST 1983
HAMMER & ANVIL
INCREDIBLE HULK #182.................DECEMBER 1974
HAMMERHEAD
AMAZING SPIDERMAN #113 ....OCTOBER 1972
HANGMAN
WEREWOLF BY NIGHT #11 ....NOVEMBER 1973
HANNIBAL KING
TOMB OF DRACULA #25 ....OCTOBER 1974
HARBINGER
HARBINGER #1...............................JANUARY 1992
HARLEQUIN (Golden Age)
ALL AMERICAN COMICS #89........SEPTEMBER 1947
HARLEQUIN
TEEN TITANS #48 ....JUNE 1977
HATEMONGER I
FANTASTIC FOUR #21 ....DECEMBER 1963
HAVOK
X-MEN, THE UNCANNY #56......................MAY 1969
HAWK AND DOVE (Silver Age)
HAWK AND DOVE
MINI SERIES #1 ....OCTOBER 1988
HAWK AND DOVE (Modern)
SHOWCASE #75.....................................JUNE 1968
HAWKEYE
TALES OF SUSPENSE #57..............SEPTEMBER 1964
HAWKGIRL (Golden Age)
ALL STAR COMICS #5......................JUN/JUL 1941
HAWKGIRL (Silver Age)
BRAVE AND THE BOLD, THE #34 ....MARCH 1961
HAWKMAN (Golden Age)
FLASH COMICS #1............................JANUARY 1940
HAWKWOMAN (Modern)
HAWKWORLD (Limited Series) #1 1989
HEATWAVE
FLASH (1st Series) #140 ....NOVEMBER 1963
HECKLER
HECKLER #1...............................SEPTEMBER 1992
HECTOR HAMMOND
GREEN LANTERN #5 ....APRIL 1961
HEIMDALL
JOURNEY INTO MYSTERY #85 ....OCTOBER 1962
HELA
JOURNEY INTO MYSTERY #102............MARCH 1964

HELIO
MARVEL TWO IN ONE #71 ....JANUARY 1981
HELLBLAZER
(John Constantine)
SWAMP THING #37 ....JUNE 1985
HELLCAT
(Formerly The Cat)
AVENGERS #144 ....FEBRUARY 1976
HELLFIRE CLUB
X-MEN, THE UNCANNY #129 ....JANUARY 1980
HELLGRAMITE
ACTION COMICS #673.......................JANUARY 1992
HELLSTORM
AVENGERS WEST COAST #14 ....NOVEMBER 1986
HENRY PETER GYRICH
AVENGERS #168 ....FEBRUARY 1978
HENRY PYM
TALES TO ASTONISH #27 ....JANUARY 1962
HEPHAESTUS
THOR ANNUAL #5 1976
HER
MARVEL TWO IN ONE #61 ....MARCH 1980
HERA
THOR #129...JUNE 1966
HERBIE
FORBIDDEN WORLDS #73..................JAN/FEB 1957
HERBIE THE ROBOT
FANTASTIC FOUR #209......................AUGUST 1979
HERCULES
JOURNEY INTO MYSTERY ANNUAL #1..............1965
HERMES
THOR #129...JUNE 1966
HIGH EVOLUTIONARY
THOR #134................................NOVEMBER 1966
HIM
FANTASTIC FOUR #67 ....OCTOBER 1967
HIPPOLYTE
ALL STAR COMICS #8......................DEC/JAN 1941
HOBGOBLIN
AMAZING SPIDERMAN #238 ....MARCH 1983
HOBGOBLIN II
AMAZING SPIDERMAN #289 ....JUNE 1987
HOCUS & POCUS
ACTION COMICS #83 ....APRIL 1945
HOGUN THE GRIM
JOURNEY INTO MYSTERY #119 ....AUGUST 1965
HOP HARRIGAN
ALL AMERICAN COMICS #1 ....APRIL 1939
HORUS
THOR #240...............................OCTOBER 1975
HOUNGAN
NEW TEEN TITANS, THE
(1st Series) #14 ....DECEMBER 1981
HOURMAN (Golden Age)
ADVENTURE COMICS #48..................MARCH 1940
HOURMAN (Silver Age)
JUSTICE SOCIETY OF
AMERICA #21.................................AUGUST 1963
HOURMAN (Modern)
INFINITY INC. #20 ....NOVEMBER 1985
HOWARD THE DUCK
FEAR #19.....................................DECEMBER 1973
HULK (Green)
INCREDIBLE HULK #2........................JULY 1962
HULK (Grey)
INCREDIBLE HULK #1........................MAY 1962
HULK (Modern Green Skin)
INCREDIBLE HULK #377 ....JANUARY 1991

HULK (Modern Grey Skin)
INCREDIBLE HULK #324.....................OCTOBER 1986
HULK 2099
2099 UNLIMITED #1 ....SEPTEMBER 1993
HULKBUSTERS
INCREDIBLE HULK #317 ....MARCH 1985
HUMAN TARGET
ACTION COMICS #419 ....DECEMBER 1972
HUMAN TOP
TALES TO ASTONISH #50 ....DECEMBER 1963
HUMAN TORCH (Golden Age)
MARVEL COMICS #1....................OCT/NOV 1939
HUMAN TORCH (Silver Age)
FANTASTIC FOUR #1 ....NOVEMBER 1961
HUNTRESS (Marvel)
MARVEL SUPER ACTION #1.....................MAY 1977
HUNTRESS (Golden Age)
SENSATION COMICS #68................AUGUST 1947
HUNTRESS (Modern)
ALL STAR COMICS #69.................NOV/DEC 1978
HUSSAR
X-MEN, THE UNCANNY #137 ....SEPTEMBER 1980
HYDRA
STRANGE TALES #135.......................AUGUST 1965
HYDROMAN
AMAZING SPIDERMAN #212.............JANUARY 1981
HYENA
FIRESTORM #4 ....AUG/SEPT 1978
HYPERION
AVENGERS #85 ....FEBRUARY 1971
IBIS THE INVINCIBLE
WHIZ COMICS #1.......................FEBRUARY 1940
ICE
SUPER FRIENDS #9 ....JANUARY 1977
ICE CREAM SOLDIER
OUR ARMY AT WAR #85 ....AUGUST 1959
ICE MAN
LEGION #32.....................................OCTOBER 1991
ICEMAN
X-MEN, THE UNCANNY #1 ....SEPTEMBER 1963
IG'NEA
LEGION #30......................................AUGUST 1991
IKARIS
ETERNALS, THE #1 ....JULY 1976
IKTHALON
MARVEL SPOTLIGHT #14...............DECEMBER 1973
ILLUSION
VISION AND SCARLET WITCH
(2nd Series) #4 ....JANUARY 1986
IMMORTUS
AVENGERS #10...............................NOVEMBER 1964
IMPERIAL GUARD
X-MEN, THE UNCANNY #107 ....NOVEMBER 1977
IMPOSSIBLE MAN
FANTASTIC FOUR #11.....................FEBRAURY 1963
IMPOSSIBLE WOMAN
MARVEL TWO IN ONE #60..............FEBRUARY 1980
IMPULSE
X-MEN, THE UNCANNY #107 ....NOVEMBER 1977
IN-BETWEENER
WARLOCK #10................................DECEMBER 1975
INFERIOR FIVE
SHOWCASE #62 ....MAY/JUNE 1966
INFERNO
LEGION OF SUPER-HEROES #24 ....DECEMBER 1991
INFINITY GAUNTLET
THANOS QUEST #2 ....OCTOBER 1990

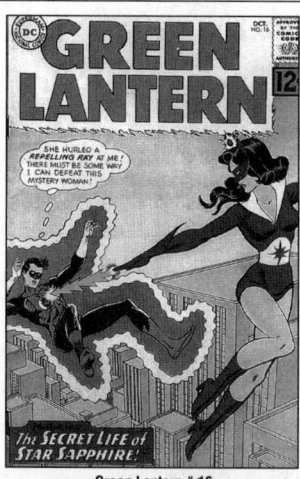

Green Lantern # 16
1st appearance Star Sapphire

Journey Into Mystery # 85
1st appearance Loki and Odin

LOKI
JOURNEY INTO MYSTERY #85 ....OCTOBER 1962

LONGSHOT
LONGSHOT #1 ....SEPTEMBER 1985

LOOTER
AMAZING SPIDERMAN #36...............MAY 1966

LORD CHAOS (Marvel)
MARVEL TWO IN ONE
ANNUAL #2 ....FEBRUARY 1977

LORD CHAOS (DC)
NEW TEEN TITANS
ANNUAL (2nd Series) #7 1991

LORD SATANIS
ACTION COMICS #527 ....JANUARY 1982

LORD SATANUS
ADVENTURES OF
SUPERMAN #493 ....AUGUST 1992

LORELEI
THOR #339 ....JANUARY 1984

LORI LEMARIS
SUPERMAN #127 ....FEBRUARY 1959

LOSERS
G.I. COMBAT #138 ....OCTOBER/NOVEMBER 1969

LUCIFER
X-MEN, THE UNCANNY #9 ....JANUARY 1965

LUDI
DOCTOR STRANGE (2nd Series) #35........JUNE 1979

LUKE CAGE
LUKE CAGE, HERO FOR HIRE #1 ....JUNE 1972

LUNA
FANTASTIC FOUR #240.......................MARCH 1982

LUNATIK
DEFENDERS #56 ....FEBRUARY 1978

LUPO
X-MEN, THE UNCANNY #62 ....NOVEMBER 1969

MARVEL FAMILY
CAPTAIN MARVEL
ADVENTURES #18 ....DECEMBER 1942

MACE
LUKE CAGE, HERO FOR HIRE #3........OCTOBER 1972

MACHETE
CAPTAIN AMERICA #302 ....FEBRUARY 1985

MACHINE MAN
2001: A SPACE ODYSSEY #8......................JULY 1977

MACHINESMITH
MARVEL TWO IN ONE #47 ....JANUARY 1979

MAC-RONN
CAPTAIN MARVEL #49 ....MARCH 1977

MAD DOG
DEFENDERS #125 ....NOVEMBER 1983

MAD HATTER (Golden Age)
BATMAN #49 ....OCT/NOV 1948

MAD HATTER (Silver Age)
DETECTIVE COMICS #230 ....APRIL 1956

MAD THINKER
FANTASTIC FOUR #15 ....JUNE 1963

MADAME MASQUE
IRON MAN #17 ....SEPTEMBER 1969

MADAME WEB
AMAZING SPIDERMAN #210 ....NOVEMBER 1980

MADCAP
CAPTAIN AMERICA #307 ....JULY 1985

MAD-DOG
DEFENDERS #125 ....NOVEMBER 1983

MADISON JEFFRIES
ALPHA FLIGHT #16 ....NOVEMBER 1984

MADMAN
BLUE BEETLE #3...........................AUGUST 1986

MAELSTROM
MARVEL TWO IN ONE #71 ....JANUARY 1981

MAELSTROM'S MINIONS
MARVEL TWO IN ONE #71 ....JANUARY 1981

MAGE
GRENDEL #16 ....JANUARY 1988

MAGIC
X-MEN, THE UNCANNY #107 ....NOVEMBER 1977

MAGMA
NEW MUTANTS #8 ....OCTOBER 1983

MAGNETO
X-MEN, THE UNCANNY #1 ....SEPTEMBER 1963

MAGNUS ROBOT FIGHTER
MAGNUS, ROBOT FIGHTER #1........FEBRUARY 1963

MAGPIE
MAN OF STEEL #3 ....JULY 1986

MAGUS
NEW MUTANTS #18 ....AUGUST 1984

MAHA YOGI
X-MEN, THE UNCANNY #47 ....AUGUST 1968

MAJOR MAPLE LEAF
ALPHA FLIGHT #106 ....MARCH 1992

MAJOR MYNAH
ATOM #37 ....JUN/JUL 1968

MAJOR VICTORY
GUARDIANS OF THE GALAXY #20 .....JANUARY 1992

MAKKARI
ETERNALS, THE #5 ....NOVEMBER 1976

MAKOTH
THOR #148 ....JANUARY 1968

MALEVOLENCE (Mephisto's Daughter)
GUARDIANS OF THE
GALAXY #7 ....DECEMBER 1990

MAN APE
AVENGERS #62 ....MARCH 1969

MAN BAT
DETECTIVE COMICS #400 ....JUNE 1970

MAN WOLF
AMAZING SPIDERMAN #124 ....SEPTEMBER 1973

MAN-BEAST
THOR #134....................................NOVEMBER 1966

MANDARIN
TALES OF SUSPENSE #50 ....FEBRUARY 1964

MANDRAKE THE MAGICIAN
KING COMICS #1 ....APRIL 1936

MANDRILL
SHANNA THE SHE-DEVIL #4....................JUNE 1973

MANDROID
AVENGERS #94 ....NOVEMBR 1971

MANGA KHAN
JUSTICE LEAGUE
INTERNATIONAL #14 ....JUNE 1988

MANHUNTER (Golden Age)
ADVENTURE COMICS #73 ....APRIL 1942

MANHUNTER (Modern)
DETECTIVE COMICS #437 ....OCT/NOV 1973

MANHUNTER II (Golden Age)
POLICE COMICS #8 ....MARCH 1942

MANHUNTER II (Modern)
MANHUNTER #1 ....JULY 1988

MANHUNTERS
FIRST ISSUE SPECIAL #5 ....AUGUST 1975

MANO
ADVENTURE COMICS #352................JANUARY 1967

MANSLAUGHTER
DEFENDERS #134 ....AUGUST 1984

MANTA
X-MEN, THE UNCANNY #137 ....SEPTEMBER 1980

MAN-THING
SAVAGE TALES #1 ....MAY 1971

MANTIS
AVENGERS #112 ....JUNE 1973

MANTRA
MANTRA #1 ....JULY 1993

MARAK
FANTASTIC FOUR #240.......................MARCH 1982

MARINNA
ALPHA FLIGHT #1 ....AUGUST 1983

MARK MERLIN
HOUSE OF SECRETS #23 ....AUGUST 1958

MARSHAL LAW
MARSHAL LAW #1 ....OCTOBER 1987

MARTIAN MANHUNTER
DETECTIVE COMICS #225 ....NOVEMBER 1955

MARTINEX
MARVEL SUPER-HEROES #18 ....JANUARY 1969

MARVEL GIRL
X-MEN, THE UNCANNY #1 ....SEPTEMBER 1963

MARVEL MAN (later Quasar)
CAPTAIN AMERICA #217 ....JANUARY 1978

MARY JANE WATSON
AMAZING SPIDERMAN #42 ....NOVEMBER 1966

MARY MARVEL
CAPTAIN MARVEL
ADVENTURES #18 ....DECEMBER 1942

MASS MASTER
POWER PACK #1 ....AUGUST 1984

MASTER
ALPHA FLIGHT #2............................SEPTEMBER 1983

MASTER D'ARQUE
SHADOWMAN #8 ....DECEMBER 1992

MASTER OF KUNG FU
MARVEL SPECIAL EDITION #15 ....JANUARY 1974

MASTER ORDER
MARVEL TWO IN ONE ANNUAL #2 ..FEBRUARY 1977

MASTER PANDEMONIUM
AVENGERS WEST COAST #4 ....JANUARY 1986

MASTERMIND
X-MEN, THE UNCANNY #4 ....MARCH 1964

MASTERS OF EVIL
AVENGERS #272................................NOVEMBER 1986

MATTER EATER LAD
ADVENTURE COMICS #303 ....DECEMBER 1962

MAVERICK
X-MEN (2nd Series) #5 ....FEBRUARY 1992

MAXIE ZEUS
DETECTIVE COMICS #483 ....APRIL 1979

MAXIMA
ACTION COMICS #645......................SEPTEMBER 1989

MAXIMUS
FANTASTIC FOUR #47 ....FEBRUARY 1966

MAYHEM
CLOAK AND DAGGER, THE MUTANT
MISADVENTURES OF #5...........................JULY 1989

MEDUSA
FANTASTIC FOUR #36 ....MARCH 1965

MEGGAN
NEW MUTANTS ANNUAL #2 ....OCTOBER 1986

MELTER
TALES OF SUSPENSE #47 ....NOVEMBER 1963

MENTALLO
STRANGE TALES #141 ....FEBRUARY 1966

MENTO
DOOM PATROL #91 ....DECEMBER 1964

MENTOR
IRON MAN #5 ....SEPTEMBER 1968

MEPHISTO
SILVER SURFER (1st Series) #3 ....OCTOBER 1968
MERA
AQUAMAN #11 ....SEPT/OCT 1963
MERBOY
WONDER WOMAN #107 ....APRIL 1959
MERCENARIES
G.I. COMBAT #244...1981
MESMERO
X-MEN, THE UNCANNY #49.............OCTOBER 1968
METAL MEN
SHOWCASE #37...APRIL 1962
METALLO (Silver Age)
ACTION COMICS #252 ....MAY 1959
METALLO (1970s)
SUPERMAN #310...APRIL 1977
METAMORPHO
BRAVE AND THE BOLD,
THE #57 ....DECEMBER 1964
METRON
NEW GODS, THE #1 ....FEB/MAR 1971
MEVERICK
X-MEN (2nd Series) #6 ....MARCH 1992
MIDAS
IRON MAN #17 ....SEPTEMBER 1969
MIDGARD SERPENT
THOR #127...APRIL 1966
MIDGET
X-MEN, THE UNCANNY #107 ....NOVEMBER 1977
MIDNIGHT SUN
SILVER SURFER (3rd Series) #29 ....NOVEMBER 1989
MIGHTY CRUSADERS
MIGHTY CRUSADERS #1 ....NOVEMBER 1965
MILLIE THE MODEL
MILLIE THE MODEL #1?.......................WINTER 1945
MIME
BATMAN #412 ....OCTOBER 1987
MIMIC
X-MEN, THE UNCANNY #19 ....APRIL 1986
MINERVA
CAPTAIN MARVEL #49 ....MARCH 1977
MIRAGE (DC)
NEW TEEN TITANS ANNUAL #7 1991
MIRAGE (Marvel)
MARVEL GRAPHIC NOVEL #4 1982
MIRROR MASTER
FLASH (1st Series) #105 ....FEB/MARCH 1955
MISS AMERICA
AVENGERS GIANT-SIZE #1 ....AUGUST 1974
MISSING LINK
INCREDIBLE HULK #105 ....JULY 1968
MISTER FANTASTIC
FANTASTIC FOUR #1 ....NOVEMBER 1961
MISTER FEAR I
DAREDEVIL #6 ....FEBRUARY 1965
MISTER FEAR II
DAREDEVIL #54 ....JULY 1969
MISTER FEAR III
DAREDEVIL #91 ....SEPTEMBER 1972
MISTER FEAR IV
MARVEL TEAM UP #92 ....APRIL 1980
MISTER HYDE
JOURNEY INTO MYSTERY #99 ....DECEMBER 1963
MISTER MIRACLE
MISTER MIRACLE #1 ....MAR/APRIL 1971
MISTER MIRACLE II
MISTER MIRACLE (2nd Series) #15 ....MAY 1990

MISTER SINISTER
X-MEN, THE UNCANNY #221 ....SEPTEMBER 1987
MISTY KNIGHT
MARVEL PREMIERE #20 ....FEBRUARY 1975
MOCKINGBIRD
MARVEL TEAM UP #95 ....JULY 1980
MODAM
QUASAR #9.......................................APRIL 1990
MODOK
TALES OF SUSPENSE #94 ....OCTOBER 1967
MODRED THE MYSTIC
MARVEL CHILLERS #1...................OCTOBER 1975
MODRED THE MYSTIC (re-introduced)
DARKOLD #3...............................DECEMBER 1992
MOJO
LONGSHOT #3...........................NOVEMBER 1985
MOJO II
X-MEN ANNUAL (2nd Series) #1 1992
MOLE MAN
FANTASTIC FOUR #1 ....NOVEMBER 1961
MOLECULE MAN
FANTASTIC FOUR #20 ....NOVEMBER 1963
MOLTEN MAN
AMAZING SPIDERMAN #28 ....SEPTEMBER 1965
MONARCH
ARMAGEDDON 2001 #1 ....MAY 1991
MON-EL (VALOR)
SUPERBOY #89 ....JUNE 1961
MONGOOSE
THOR #391..MAY 1988
MONGUL (Modern)
ADVENTURES OF SUPERMAN #454 ....MAY 1989
MONITOR
NEW TEEN TITANS, THE
(1st Series) #21.................................JULY 1982
MOON KNIGHT
WEREWOLF BY NIGHT #32 ....MAY 1976
MOONBOY
DEVIL DINOSAUR #1 ....APRIL 1978
MOONDRAGON
IRON MAN #54 ....JANUARY 1973
MOONSTONE
INCREDIBLE HULK #228....................OCTOBER 1978
MORAG
AVENGERS #133...............................MARCH 1975
MORBIUS
AMAZING SPIDERMAN #101 ....DECEMBER 1970
MORDRU
ADVENTURE COMICS #369.....................JUNE 1968
MORGAN EDGE
JIMMY OLSEN #133 ....OCTOBER 1970
MORGAN LE FAY
SPIDERWOMAN #2 ....MAY 1978
MOTHER NIGHT
CAPTAIN AMERICA #123 ....MARCH 1970
MR. AMERICA
ACTION COMICS #33.....................FEBRUARY 1941
MR. BONES
INFINITY INC. #16 ....JULY 1985
MR. ELEMENT
SHOWCASE #13....................................APRIL 1958
MR. HYDE
JOURNEY INTO MYSTERY #99 ....DECEMBER 1963
MR. MIND
CAPTAIN MARVEL
ADVENTURES #22 ....MARCH 1943
MR. MIND (Modern)
SHAZAM #2..APRIL 1973

MR. MONSTER
VANGUARD ILLUSTRATED #7 1984
MR. MXYZPTLK (Golden Age)
SUPERMAN #30.................................SEP/OCT 1944
MR. MXYZPTLK (Silver Age)
SUPERMAN #131.............................AUGUST 1959
MR. MXYZPTLK (Modern)
SUPERMAN (2nd Series) #11 ....NOVEMBER 1987
MR. TERRIFIC
SENSATION COMICS #1 ....JANUARY 1942
MR. X
VORTEX #2..1983
MR. Z
SUPERMAN #51...........................JANUARY 1991
MS. MARVEL
MS. MARVEL #1 ....JANUARY 1977
MS. MARVEL II
THING, THE #35....................................MAY 1986
MULTIPLE MAN
FANTASTIC FOUR GIANT
SIZE #4....................................FEBRUARY 1975
MYSTERIO
AMAZING SPIDERMAN #13 ....MARCH 1964
MYSTIQUE
MS. MARVEL #18 ....JULY 1978
NADAR
MARVEL TWO IN ONE #71 ....JANUARY 1981
NAMORA
MARVEL MYSTERY COMICS #82.............MAY 1947
NAMORITA
SUB-MARINER #50 ....JUNE 1972
N'ASTIRH
X-FACTOR #32 ....SEPTEMBER 1988
NEBULA
AVENGERS #257 ....AUGUST 1985
NEBULO
INCREDIBLE HULK ANNUAL #1 ....OCTOBER 1968
NEBULON
DEFENDERS #13..................................MAY 1974
NECROM
EXCALIBUR #45............................DECEMBER 1991
NED LEEDS
AMAZING SPIDERMAN #18..................AUGUST 1964
NEEDLE
SPIDERWOMAN #9 ....DECEMBER 1978
NEGATIVE MAN
MY GREATEST ADVENTURE #80 ....JUNE 1963
NEKRA
SHANNA THE SHE-DEVIL #4.....................JUNE 1973
NEMESIS KID
ADVENTURE COMICS #346.....................JULY 1966
NEPTUNE
TALES TO ASTONISH #70 ....AUGUST 1965
NEW GODS
NEW GODS, THE #1 ....FEB/MAR 1971
NEW MUTANTS
MARVEL GRAPHIC NOVEL #4 1982
NEW TEEN TITANS
DC COMICS PRESENTS #26 ....OCTOBER 1981
NEW WARRIORS
THOR #411.....................................NOVEMBER 1989
NEWSBOY LEGION (Golden Age)
STAR SPANGLED COMICS #7 ....APRIL 1942
NEWSBOY LEGION (Silver Age)
JIMMY OLSEN, SUPERMAN'S
PAL #133....................................OCTOBER 1969
NEXT MEN
DARK HORSE PRESENTS #54........SEPTEMBER 1991

NICK FURY
SGT. FURY AND HIS HOWLING
COMMANDOS #1........................MAY 1963
NICK FURY (As Agent of SHIELD)
STRANGE TALES #135........................AUGUST 1965
NIGHT THRASHER
THOR #411........................NOVEMBER 1989
NIGHTCRAWLER
X-MEN GIANT-SIZE #1........................SUMMER 1975
NIGHTGIRL
ADVENTURE COMICS #306...............MARCH 1963
NIGHTHAWK
AVENGERS #69........................OCTOBER 1969
NIGHTHAWK II
AVENGERS #85........................FEBRUARY 1971
NIGHTMAN
THE STRANGERS #1........................JUNE 1993
NIGHTMARE
STRANGE TALES #110........................JULY 1963
NIGHTMASTER
SHOWCASE #82........................MAY 1969
NIGHTRIDER
NEW TEEN TITANS ANNUAL #7...............1991
NIGHTSHADE (Marvel)
CAPTAIN AMERICA #164.................AUGUST 1973
NIGHTSHADE
CAPTAIN ATOM (Charlton) #82......SEPTEMBER 1966
NIGHTWING
(Dick Grayson)
NEW TEEN TITANS, THE
(1st Series) #43........................JUNE 1984
NIGHTWING (Superman)
SUPERMAN #158........................DECEMBER 1962
NIKKI
MARVEL PRESENTS #4........................APRIL 1976
NIMBUS
ADVENTURE COMICS #67................OCTOBER 1941
NIMROD
X-MEN, THE UNCANNY #191.............MARCH 1985
NINGAL
CHAMBER OF CHILLS #4..............DECEMBER 1951
NINJAK (as Colin King)
BLOODSHOT #6........................JULY 1993
NITRO
CAPTAIN MARVEL #34.................SEPTEMBER 1974
NOMAD I
CAPTAIN AMERICA #180...............DECEMBER 1974
NOMAD II
CAPTAIN AMERICA #261.............SEPTEMBER 1981
NOMAN
THUNDER AGENTS #1...............NOVEMBER 1965
NORMAN OSBORN
AMAZING SPIDERMAN #37.................JUNE 1966
NORTHSTAR
X-MEN, THE UNCANNY #120.................APRIL 1979
NORTHWIND
ALL STAR SQUADRON #25...........SEPTEMBER 1983
NOVA
THE MAN CALLED NOVA #1........SEPTEMBER 1976
NOVA II
FANTASTIC FOUR #244........................JULY 1982
NTH MAN
MARVEL COMICS PRESENTS #25......AUGUST 1989
NUKE
DEFENDERS #112........................OCTOBER 1982
NUKLO
AVENGERS GIANT SIZE #1.................AUGUST 1974

NUKLON
ALL STAR SQUADRON #25...........SEPTEMBER 1983
NULL THE LIVING DARKNESS
DEFENDERS #103........................JANUARY 1982
NUT
THOR #241........................NOVEMBER 1975
OBSIDIAN
ALL STAR SQUADRON #25...........SEPTEMBER 1983
OCEAN MASTER
AQUAMAN #29........................SEP/OCT 1966
ODDBALL
HAWKEYE #3........................NOVEMBER 1983
ODIN
JOURNEY INTO MYSTERY #85..........OCTOBER 1962
OLYMPIA
ETERNALS, THE #5........................NOVEMBER 1976
OLYMPUS
THOR ANNUAL #1........................1965
OMAC
OMAC #1........................SEP/OCT 1974
OMEGA
OMEGA THE UNKNOWN #1.................MARCH 1976
OMEGA FLIGHT
ALPHA FLIGHT #11........................JUNE 1984
OMEGA MEN
GREEN LANTERN #141........................JUNE 1981
OMEGA RED
X-MEN (2nd Series) #4........................JANUARY 1992
ORACLE
X-MEN, THE UNCANNY #107........NOVEMBER 1977
ORION
NEW GODS, THE #1........................FEB/MAR 1971
ORKA
SUB-MARINER #23........................MARCH 1970
OSIRIS
THOR #240........................OCTOBER 1975
OSWALD THE RABBIT
NEW FUN COMICS #1........................FEBRUARY 1935
OUTLAW KID
OUTLAW KID #1........................SEPTEMBER 1954
OUTSIDER
DETECTIVE COMICS #334..............DECEMBER 1964
OVERMIND
FANTASTIC FOUR #111........................JUNE 1971
OWL
DAREDEVIL #3........................AUGUST 1964
PALADIN
DAREDEVIL #150........................JANUARY 1978
PANTHA
NEW TITANS #73........................FEBRUARY 1991
PARASITE I
ACTION COMICS #340........................AUGUST 1966
PARASITE II
FIRESTORM THE NUCLEAR MAN,
THE FURY OF #58........................APRIL 1987
PATCHWORK MAN
SWAMP THING #2........................FEBRUARY 1973
PEACEMAKER
FIGHTIN' 5 #40........................DECEMBER 1966
PENGUIN (Golden Age)
DETECTIVE COMICS #58..............DECEMBER 1941
PENGUIN (Silver Age)
BATMAN #155........................MAY 1963
PEREGRINE
CONTEST OF CHAMPIONS #1.................JUNE 1982
PERRY WHITE
SUPERMAN #7........................NOV/DEC 1940

PERSUADER
ADVENTURE COMICS #352................JANUARY 1967
PESTILENCE
ALPHA FLIGHT #36........................JULY 1986
PETE ROSS
SUPERBOY #86........................JANUARY 1961
PHAEDER
MARVEL TWO IN ONE #71.................JANUARY 1981
PHANTOM
KING COMICS #61........................MAY 1941
PHANTOM EAGLE
MARVEL SUPER-HEROES #16.......SEPTEMBER 1968
PHANTOM GIRL
ACTION COMICS #276........................MAY 1961
PHANTOM LADY
POLICE COMICS #1........................AUGUST 1941
PHANTOM STRANGER (Golden Age)
PHANTOM STRANGER #1.................AUG/SEPT 1952
PHANTOM ZONE
ADVENTURE COMICS #283...................APRIL 1961
PHASTOS
ETERNALS, THE
(Limited Series) #1........................OCTOBER 1985
PHOBIA
NEW TEEN TITANS, THE
(1st Series) #14........................DECEMBER 1981
PHOBIUS
MARVEL TWO IN ONE #71.................JANUARY 1981
PHOENIX
(Jean Grey)
X-MEN, THE UNCANNY #101...........OCTOBER 1976
PHOENIX
(Rachel Summers)
X-MEN, THE UNCANNY #141...........JANUARY 1981
PIED PIPER
FLASH (1st Series) #106........................MAY 1959
PIEFACE
GREEN LANTERN #2........................OCTOBER 1960
PILEDRIVER
DEFENDERS #17........................NOVEMBER 1974
PINYON
FANTASTIC FOUR #129.................DECEMBER 1972
PIP THE TROLL
STRANGE TALES #179........................APRIL 1975
PIPER
X-MEN, THE UNCANNY #62..........NOVEMBER 1969
PISKAS
FANTASTIC FOUR #131...................FEBRUARY 1973
PLANTMAN
STRANGE TALES #113........................OCTOBER 1963
PLANTMASTER
ATOM #1........................JUNE/JULY 1962
PLASMUS
NEW TEEN TITANS, THE
(1st Series) #14........................DECEMBER 1981
PLASTIC MAN (Golden Age)
POLICE COMICS #1........................AUGUST 1941
PLASTIC MAN (Silver Age)
PLASTIC MAN #1........NOVEMBER/DECEMBER 1966
PLASTIC MAN (Modern)
PLASTIC MAN (2nd Series) #1.......NOVEMBER 1988
PLUNDERER
DAREDEVIL #12........................JANUARY 1966
PLUTO
THOR #127........................APRIL 1966
POISON IVY
BATMAN #181........................JUNE 1966

My Greatest Adventure # 80
1st appearance Doom Patrol

Sgt. Fury # 1
1st appearance Sgt. Fury and His Howling Commandos

RA'S AL G'HUL
BATMAN #232 ....APRIL 1971
RATTLER
CAPTAIN AMERICA #310 ....OCTOBER 1985
RAVEN
DC COMICS PRESENTS #26 ....OCTOBER 1980
RAWHIDE KID
RAWHIDE KID #1 ....MARCH 1955
RAY, THE
THE RAY #1 ....FEBRUARY 1992
RAZORBACK
SPECTACULAR SPIDERMAN #13 ...DECEMBER 1977
RAZOR-FIST
MASTER OF KUNG FU #29 ....JUNE 1975
REAPER
BATMAN #237 ....DECEMBER 1971
RED BEE
HIT COMICS #1 ....JULY 1940
RED GHOST
FANTASTIC FOUR #13 ....APRIL 1963
RED GUARDIAN
AVENGERS #43 ....AUGUST 1968
RED RAVEN (Golden Age)
RED RAVEN COMICS #1 ....AUGUST 1940
RED RAVEN (Modern)
X-MEN, THE UNCANNY #44 ....MAY 1968
RED RONIN
GODZILLA #7 ....FEBRUARY 1973
RED SKULL (Golden Age)
CAPTAIN AMERICA COMICS #1 ....MARCH 1941
RED SKULL (Silver Age)
TALES OF SUSPENSE #65 ....MAY 1965
RED SONJA
CONAN THE BARBARIAN #23 ....MARCH 1973
RED SOPHIA
CEREBUS #3 ....APRIL 1978
RED STAR
TEEN TITANS #18 ....DECEMBER 1968
RED TORNADO (Golden Age)
ALL AMERICAN COMICS #20 ....NOVEMBER 1940
RED TORNADO (Silver Age)
JUSTICE LEAGUE OF
AMERICA #64 ....AUGUST 1968
RED TORNADO (Modern)
JUSTICE LEAGUE OF
AMERICA #3 1985
RED WOLF I
MARVEL SPOTLIGHT #1 ....NOVEMBER 1971
RED WOLF II
AVENGERS #80 ....SEPTEMBER 1970
REDSTONE
SQUADRON SUPREME #9 ....MAY 1986
REDWING
NEW TEEN TITANS ANNUAL #7 1991
REJECT
ETERNALS, THE #8 ....FEBRUARY 1977
REX THE WONDER DOG
REX THE WONDER DOG #1 ....JAN/FEB 1952
RHINO
AMAZING SPIDERMAN #41 ....OCTOBER 1966
RICHIE RICH
LITTLE DOT #1 ....SEPTEMBER 1953
RICK JONES
INCREDIBLE HULK #1 ....MAY 1962
RIDDLER (Golden Age)
DETECTIVE COMICS #140 ....OCTOBER 1948
RIDDLER (Silver Age)
BATMAN #171 ....MAY 1965

RINGER
DEFENDERS #51 ....SEPTEMBER 1977
RINGMASTER
CAPTAIN AMERICA COMICS #5 ....AUGUST 1941
RINTRAH
DOCTOR STRANGE
(2nd Series) #81 ....FEBRUARY 1987
RIP HUNTER
SHOWCASE #20 ....JUNE 1959
ROBIN
(Carrie Kelly)
BATMAN THE DARK KNIGHT
RETURNS #2 ....APRIL 1986
ROBIN
(Dick Grayson)
DETECTIVE COMICS #38 ....APRIL 1940
ROBIN
(Jason Todd)
BATMAN #369 ....FEBRUARY 1984
ROBIN
(Timothy Drake)
BATMAN #442 ....DECEMBER 1989
ROBOCOP
ROBOCOP #1 ....OCTOBER 1987
ROBOTMAN (Golden Age)
STAR SPANGLED COMICS #7 ....APRIL 1942
ROBOTMAN (Silver Age)
MY GREATEST ADVENTURE #80 ....JUNE 1963
ROBOTMAN (Modern)
SHOWCASE #94 ....AUGUST/SEPTEMBER 1977
ROCK PYTHON
CAPTAIN AMERICA #342 ....JUNE 1988
ROCKET RACCOON
MARVEL PREVIEW #7 1975
ROCKET RACER
AMAZING SPIDERMAN #172 ....SEPTEMBER 1977
ROCKET RED
GREEN LANTERN CORPS #209 ....FEBRUARY 1987
ROCKETEER
STARSLAYER #1 ....FEBRUARY 1982
ROGUE
AVENGERS ANNUAL #10 1981
ROGUE'S GALLERY
FLASH (1st Series) #155 ....FEBRUARY 1965
ROH KAR
BATMAN #78 ....AUGUST/SEPTEMBER 1953
ROM
ROM #1 ....DECEMBER 1979
ROMA
X-MEN, THE UNCANNY #225 ....JANUARY 1988
ROMNAR
INCREDIBLE HULK ANNUAL #1 ....OCTOBER 1968
RONAN THE ACCUSER
FANTASTIC FOUR #65 ....AUGUST 1967
ROND VIDAR
ADVENTURE COMICS #349 ....OCTOBER 1966
ROSE
AMAZING SPIDERMAN #253 ....JUNE 1984
ROSE AND THORN
LOIS LANE, SUPERMAN'S
GIRLFRIEND #105 ....OCTOBER 1970
ROULETTE
NEW MUTANTS #16 ....JUNE 1984
ROY RAYMOND
DETECTIVE COMICS #153 ....NOVEMBER 1949
ROYAL FLUSH GANG
JUSTICE LEAGUE OF AMERICA #43 1966

RUNNER
DEFENDERS #143 ....MAY 1985
RYNDA
THOR #148 ....JANUARY 1968
SABRA
INCREDIBLE HULK #256 ....FEBRUARY 1981
SABRETOOTH
IRON FIST #14 ....APRIL 1977
SANDMAN (1970s)
SANDMAN #1 ....WINTER 1974
SANDMAN DC (Golden Age)
ADVENTURE COMICS #40 ....JULY 1939
SANDMAN DC (Golden Age in Silver Age)
JUSTICE LEAGUE OF
AMERICA #46 ....AUGUST 1966
SANDMAN (DC Modern)
SANDMAN (2nd Series) #1 ....JANUARY 1989
SANDMAN
(former Marvel villain)
AMAZING SPIDERMAN #4 ....JUNE 1963
SANDY
ADVENTURE COMICS #69 ....DECEMBER 1941
SARACEN
PUNISHER WAR JOURNAL #25 ......DECEMBER 1990
SARGON THE SORCERER
ALL AMERICAN COMICS #26 ....MAY 1941
SASQUATCH
X-MEN, THE UNCANNY #120 ....APRIL 1979
SATANNA
VAMPIRE TALES #2 ....DECEMBER 1973
SATANNISH
DOCTOR STRANGE
(1st Series) #174 ....NOVEMBER 1968
SATURN GIRL
ADVENTURE COMICS #247 ....APRIL 1958
SATURNINE
GHOST RIDER #76 ....JANUARY 1983
SAURON
X-MEN, THE UNCANNY #60 ....AUGUST 1969
SAVAGE DRAGON
MEGATON #3 1983
SCALPHUNTER
WEIRD WESTERN TALES #39 .....MARCH/APRIL 1977
SCARECROW (DC)
WORLD'S FINEST #3 ....AUTUMN 1941
SCARECROW (Marvel)
TALES OF SUSPENSE #51 ....MARCH 1964
SCARLET WITCH
X-MEN, THE UNCANNY #4 ....MARCH 1964
SCHEMER
AMAZING SPIDERMAN #83 ....APRIL 1970
SCORPION
AMAZING SPIDERMAN #20 ....OCTOBER 1964
SCOURGE
IRON MAN #194 ....MAY 1985
SEA DEVILS
SHOWCASE #27 ....AUGUST 1960
SEBASTIAN SHAW
X-MEN, THE UNCANNY #129 ....JANUARY 1980
SECRET SIX
SECRET SIX #1 ....APRIL/MAY 1968
SECRET SOCIETY OF SUPER-VILLAINS
SECRET SOCIETY OF
SUPER-VILLAINS #1 ....MAY/JUNE 1976
SEEKER
FANTASTIC FOUR #46 ....JANUARY 1966
SELENE
NEW MUTANTS #9 ....NOVEMBER 1983

SENSOR GIRL
LEGION OF SUPER-HEROES
(2nd Series) #14 ....SEPTEMBER 1985
SENTINELS
X-MEN, THE UNCANNY #14 ....NOVEMBER 1965
SENTRY
FANTASTIC FOUR #64 ....JULY 1967
SERPENT SOCIETY
CAPTAIN AMERICA #310 ....OCTOBER 1985
SERSI
STRANGE TALES #109 ....JUNE 1963
SET
CONAN THE BARBARIAN #7 ....JULY 1971
SETH
THOR #240 ....OCTOBER 1975
SEVEN SOLDIERS OF VICTORY
LEADING COMICS #1 ....WINTER 1941
SGT. BILKO
SGT. BILKO #1 ....MAY/JUNE 1957
SGT. BULLET & THE BRAVOS
G.I. COMBAT #264 ....APRIL 1984
SGT. FURY
SGT. FURY AND HIS HOWLING
COMMANDOS #1 ....MAY 1963
SGT. ROCK
OUR ARMY AT WAR #81 ....APRIL 1959
SHADE, THE CHANGING MAN
SHADE, THE CHANGING MAN #1 ......JUN/JULY 1977
SHADOW (DC)
SHADOW, THE #1 ....OCT/NOV 1973
SHADOW KING
X-MEN, THE UNCANNY #117 ....JANUARY 1979
SHADOW LASS
ADVENTURE COMICS #366 ....MARCH 1968
SHADOW THIEF
HAWKWORLD #5 ....OCTOBER 1990
SHADOWCAT
X-MEN, THE UNCANNY #129 ....JANUARY 1980
SHADOWHAWK
YOUNGBLOOD #2 ....AUGUST 1992
SHADOWMAN
X-O MANOWAR #4 ....APRIL 1992
SHANNA THE SHE-DEVIL
SHANNA THE SHE-DEVIL #1 ....DECEMBER 1972
SHAPER OF WORLDS
INCREDIBLE HULK #155 ....SEPTEMBER 1972
SHARK
GREEN LANTERN #24 ....OCTOBER 1963
SHARON CARTER
TALES OF SUSPENSE #75 ....MARCH 1966
SHATTERSTAR
INHUMANS #3 ....FEBRUARY 1976
SHAZAM
SHAZAM #1 ....FEBRUARY 1973
SHE HULK
SHE HULK, THE SAVAGE #1 ....FEBRUARY 1980
SHI'AR
X-MEN, THE UNCANNY #97 ....JANUARY 1976
SHIELD (organization)
STRANGE TALES #135 ....AUGUST 1965
SHIELD (Silver Age)
ADVENTURES OF THE FLY #8........SEPTEMBER 1960
SHINING KNIGHT
ADVENTURE COMICS #66............SEPTEMBER 1941
SHIVA
WOLVERINE #50................................JANUARY 1992
SHOCK
DAREDEVIL #315.......................................APRIL 1993

SHOCKER
AMAZING SPIDERMAN #46 ....MARCH 1967
SHOOTING STAR
INCREDIBLE HULK #265 ....NOVEMBER 1981
SHRINKING VIOLET
ACTION COMICS #276 ....MAY 1961
SHROUD
SUPER-VILLAIN TEAM-UP #5...................APRIL 1976
SIDEWINDER
MARVEL TWO IN ONE #64 ....JUNE 1980
SIF
JOURNEY INTO MYSTERY #102............MARCH 1964
SIGNALMAN
BATMAN #112..DECEMBER 1957
SILENT KNIGHT
BRAVE AND THE BOLD, THE #1 ....AUG/SEPT 1955
SILVER BANSHEE
ACTION COMICS #595 ....DECEMBER 1987
SILVER SABLE
AMAZING SPIDERMAN #265 ....JUNE 1985
SILVER SAMURAI
DAREDEVIL #111 ....JULY 1974
SILVER SHADE
FIRESTORM THE NUCLEAR MAN,
THE FURY OF #53 ....NOVEMBER 1986
SILVER SURFER
FANTASTIC FOUR #48 ....MARCH 1966
SILVER SWAN
WONDER WOMAN (2nd Series) #15.........APRIL 1988
SILVERMANE
AMAZING SPIDERMAN #73 ....JUNE 1969
SINESTRO
GREEN LANTERN #7 ....JUL/AUG 1961
SINISTER SIX
AMAZING SPIDERMAN ANNUAL #1 1963
SIRYN
SPIDERWOMAN #37 ....APRIL 1981
SIVANA
WHIZ COMICS #1 ....FEBRUARY 1940
SKIDS
X-FACTOR #7 ....AUGUST 1986
SKRULLS
FANTASTIC FOUR #2 ....JANUARY 1962
SKULL THE SALAYER
SKULL THE SLAYER #1 ....AUGUST 1975
SKY PIRATE
GREEN LANTERN #27 .....AUGUST/SEPTEMBER 1947
SLEEPWALKER
SLEEPWALKER #1...JUNE 1991
SLIGGUTH
MARVEL PREMIERE #5....................NOVEMBER 1972
SLUDGE
SLUDGE #1 ....OCTOBER 1993
SLUG
CAPTAIN AMERICA #325 ....JANUARY 1987
SLYDE
AMAZING SPIDERMAN #272.............JANUARY 1986
SMART ALEC
ALPHA FLIGHT #7............................FEBRUARY 1984
SMASHER
X-MEN, THE UNCANNY #107 ....NOVEMBER 1977
SMUGGLER
SPECTACULAR
SPIDERMAN #49 ....DECEMBER 1980
SNAPPER CARR
BRAVE AND THE
BOLD #28 ....FEBRUARY/MARCH 1960

SOLOMUN GRUNDY
ALL AMERICAN COMICS #59.....................JULY 1944
SON OF SATAN
MARVEL SPOTLIGHT #12.................OCTOBER 1973
SONAR
GREEN LANTERN #14 ....JULY 1962
SONS OF THE TIGER
DEADLY HANDS OF KUNG-FU #1 ....APRIL 1974
SOVIET SUPER-SOLDIERS
INCREDIBLE HULK #258 ....APRIL 1981
SPACE CABBIE
MYSTERY IN SPACE #26 ....JUNE/JULY 1955
SPACE PHANTOM
AVENGERS #2.................................NOVEMBER 1963
SPACE RANGER
SHOWCASE #15 ....AUGUST 1958
SPACENIGHTS
ROM #1 ....DECEMBER 1979
SPAWN
SPAWN #1 ....MAY 1992
SPECTRE (Golden Age)
MORE FUN COMICS #52 ....FEBRUARY 1940
SPECTRE (Silver Age)
SHOWCASE #60 ....JAN/FEB 1966
SPEED DEMON
AMAZING SPIDERMAN #222 ....NOVEMBER 1981
SPEED RACER
DAI KAMIKAZE #1 ....JUNE 1987
SPEEDBALL
AMAZING SPIDERMAN
ANNUAL #22 1988
SPEEDY
MORE FUN COMICS #73................NOVEMBER 1941
SPHINX
NOVA, THE MAN CALLED #6...........FEBRUARY 1977
SPIDERMAN
AMAZING FANTASY #15 ....AUGUST 1962
SPIDERMAN
(Black Costumed)
AMAZING SPIDERMAN #252 ....MAY 1984
SPIDERMAN
(Cosmic Powered)
SPECTACULAR
SPIDERMAN #158 ....DECEMBER 1989
SPIDERMAN 2099
AMAZING SPIDERMAN #365.............AUGUST 1992
SPIDERWOMAN
MARVEL SPOTLIGHT #32 ....FEBRUARY 1977
SPIDERWOMAN II
SECRET WARS #7 ....NOVEMBER 1984
SPIRAL
LONGSHOT #1 ....SEPTEMBER 1985
SPIRIT OF '76
INVADERS #14 ....MARCH 1977
SPITFIRE
INVADERS #12 ....JANUARY 1977
SPYMASTER
IRON MAN #33 ....JANUARY 1971
SQUADRON SUPREME
AVENGERS #85 ....FEBRUARY 1971
STARJAMMERS
UNCANNY X-MEN #104 ....APRIL 1977
SRO-HIMM
CAPTAIN MARVEL #37..................DECEMBER 1974
STALKER
STALKER #1 ....JUNE/JULY 1975
STALLIOR
INCREDIBLE HULK ANNUAL #1 ....OCTOBER 1968

Showcase # 37
1st appearance Metal Men

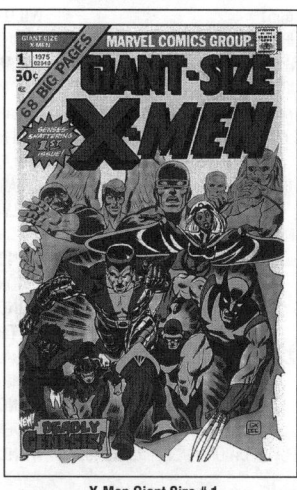

X-Men Giant Size # 1
1st appearance new X-Men

VANGUARD
IRON MAN #109 ....APRIL 1978
VANISHER
X-MEN, THE UNCANNY #2 ....NOVEMBER 1963
VELVET TIGER
DETECTIVE COMICS #518.............SEPTEMBER 1982
VENOM
AMAZING SPIDERMAN #300 ....MAY 1987
VENUS
SUB-MARINER #57..........................JANUARY 1973
VERMIN
CAPTAIN AMERICA #272 ....AUGUST 1982
VESTA
THOR #301.................................NOVEMBER 1980
VICKI VALE
BATMAN #45 ....FEBRUARY/MARCH 1948
VIGILANTE (Golden Age)
ACTION COMICS #42 ....NOVEMBER 1941
VIGILANTE II (Modern)
NEW TEEN TITANS ANNUAL
(1st Series) #2 1982
VIGILANTE III (female)
DEATHSTROKE THE
TERMINATOR #10.........................MAY 1992
VIKING PRINCE
BRAVE AND THE BOLD, THE #1 ....AUG/SEPT 1955
VINDICATOR
UNCANNY X-MEN #120 ....APRIL 1979
VINDICATOR II
ALPHA FLIGHT #32.........................MARCH 1986
VIPER
CAPTAIN AMERICA #110 ....FEBRUARY 1969
VISHANTI
MARVEL PREMIERE #5........NOVEMBER 1972
VISION
AVENGERS #57....................................OCTOBER 1968
VIXEN
ACTION COMICS #521.........................JULY 1981
VOLCANA
SECRET WARS #3 ....JULY 1984
VRIL DOX
INVASION! #1 ....FEBRUARY 1989
VULTURE I
AMAZING SPIDERMAN #2 ....APRIL 1963
WANDERERS
ADVENTURE COMICS #375 ....DECEMBER 1968
WARLOCK (Cocoon)
FANTASTIC FOUR #66 ....SEPTEMBER 1967
WARLOCK (Him)
FANTASTIC FOUR #67......................OCTOBER 1967
WARLOCK (New Mutants)
NEW MUTANTS #18 ....AUGUST 1984
WARLORD
FIRST ISSUE SPECIAL #8 ....NOVEMBER 1975
WARP
NEW TEEN TITANS, THE
(1st Series) #14 ....DECEMBER 1981
WARPATH
NEW MUTANTS #16...........................JUNE 1984
WARSTAR
X-MEN, THE UNCANNY #137 ....SEPTEMBER 1980
WARSTRIKE
MANTRA #1.......................................JULY 1993
WARWOLVES
EXCALIBUR SPECIAL EDITION #1 1987
WASP
TALES TO ASTONISH #44.........................JUNE 1963

WATCHER
FANTASTIC FOUR #13 ....APRIL 1963
WAVERIDER
ARMAGEDDON 2001 #1 ....MAY 1991
WEAPON ALPHA
(becomes Vindicator)
UNCANNY X-MEN #109..................FEBRUARY 1978
WEAPON OMEGA
ALPHA FLIGHT #102.......................NOVEMBER 1991
WEATHER WIZARD
FLASH (1st Series) #110..................JANUARY 1960
WEB, THE
FLYMAN #36 ....MARCH 1966
WENDIGO
INCREDIBLE HULK #162 ....APRIL 1973
WEREWOLF
MARVEL SPOTLIGHT #2 ....DECEMBER 1971
WHIPLASH
TALES OF SUSPENSE #97 ....JANUARY 1968
WHIPLASH II
MARVEL COMICS PRESENTS #49 1990
WHIRLWIND
AVENGERS #46...............................NOVEMBER 1968
WHIRLYBATS
DETECTIVE COMICS #257 ....JULY 1958
WHITE BISHOP
X-MEN, THE UNCANNY #129.............JANUARY 1980
WHITE KRYPTONITE
ADVENTURE COMICS #279 ....DECEMBER 1960
WHITE QUEEN
X-MEN, THE UNCANNY #129.............JANUARY 1980
WHITE WITCH
ADVENTURE COMICS #351 ....DECEMBER 1966
WHIZZER (Golden Age)
USA COMICS #1..................................AUGUST 1941
WHIZZER (Modern)
AVENGERS GIANT-SIZE #1 ....AUGUST 1974
WIDGET
EXCALIBUR #1 ....OCTOBER 1988
WILDCAT
SENSATION COMICS #1 ....JANUARY 1941
WILDCAT II (female)
CRISIS ON INFINITE
EARTHS #6 ....SEPTEMBER 1985
WILDCHILD
ALPHA FLIGHT #11 ....JUNE 1984
WILD DOG
WILD DOG #1 ....SEPTEMBER 1987
WIZARD
STRANGE TALES #102....................NOVEMBER 1962
WIZARD WORLD
WARLORD #28.................................DECEMBER 1979
WOLFSBANE
MARVEL GRAPHIC NOVEL #4 1982
WOLVERINE
INCREDIBLE HULK #180..................OCTOBER 1974
WONDER GIRL
WONDER WOMAN #107 ....JULY 1961
WONDER GIRL
(as Teen Titan)
BRAVE AND THE BOLD,
THE #60.....................................JUNE/JULY 1965
WONDER MAN
AVENGERS #9....................................OCTOBER 1964
WONDER TOT
WONDER WOMAN #122............................MAY 1961
WONDER WOMAN (Golden Age)
ALL STAR COMICS #8.........................DEC/JAN 1941

WONDER WOMAN (Silver Age)
WONDER WOMAN #105.......................APRIL 1959
WONDER WOMAN (Modern)
WONDER WOMAN
(2nd Series) #1 ....FEBRUARY 1987
WONG
STRANGE TALES #110.........................JULY 1963
WOODGOD
MARVEL PREMIERE #31........AUGUST 1976
WRECKER
THOR #148 ....JANUARY 1968
WYATT WINGFOOT
FANTASTIC FOUR #50..............................MAY 1966
X
DARK HORSE COMICS #8 ....MARCH 1993
XEMNU
JOURNEY INTO MYSTERY #62 ....NOVEMBER 1959
X-FACTOR
AVENGERS #263.............................JANUARY 1986
X-FORCE
NEW MUTANTS #100..............................APRIL 1991
X-KRYPTONITE
ACTION COMICS #261.....................FEBRUARY 1960
X-MEN
UNCANNY X-MEN #1 ....SEPTEMBER 1963
X-O MANOWAR
X-O MANOWAR #1 ....FEBRUARY 1992
X-RAY VISION
ACTION COMICS #18 ....NOVEMBER 1939
X-TERMINATORS
X-TERMINATORS #1 ....OCTOBER 1988
YELLOW CLAW
CAPTAIN AMERICA #165 ....SEPTEMBER 1973
YELLOWJACKET
AVENGERS #59.............................DECEMBER 1968
YELLOWJACKET II
AVENGERS #264.................................MARCH 1986
Y'GARON
DRACULA GIANT SIZE #2..............SEPTEMBER 1974
YON-ROGG
MARVEL SUPER-HEROES #12 ....DECEMBER 1967
YOUNG ALLIES
YOUNG ALLIES #1 ....SUMMER 1941
YOUNGBLOOD
MEGATON EXPLOSION............................JUNE 1987
ZARAN
MASTER OF KUNG FU #77 ....JUNE 1979
ZARATHOS
MARVEL SPOTLIGHT #5 ....MARCH 1972
ZAREK
MARVEL SUPER-HEROES #12 ....DECEMBER 1967
ZATANNA
HAWKMAN #4 ....OCT/NOV 1964
ZATARA
ACTION COMICS #1 ....JUNE 1938
ZODIAC
AVENGERS #72.................................JANUARY 1970
ZOM
STRANGE TALES #156 ....MAY 1967
ZURAS
ETERNALS, THE #5 ....NOVEMBER 1976
ZZAXX
INCREDIBLE HULK #166....................AUGUST 1973

ORIGINS INDEX

(Foundation work by ANDY KYTHREOTIS)

Below is a work-in-progress listing of the first and/or most detailed origins of selected characters. Very often the origin of a character comes along with his or her first appearance but that is not always the case. Indeed comic publishers often delight in producing a more detailed "secret origin" story years later. While there are many characters missing from our list, at least it gives some idea and where to look to read up on your favourites.

We hope to expand this feature in a number of ways. Our first objective is to give first origin story and most detailed origin story to every character that appears in the First Appearance Index. Our second objective is to list all subsequent origin retellings for major characters like Batman, Superman and Spiderman for example. Any volunteers?

Any further information may be sent to the editorial address.

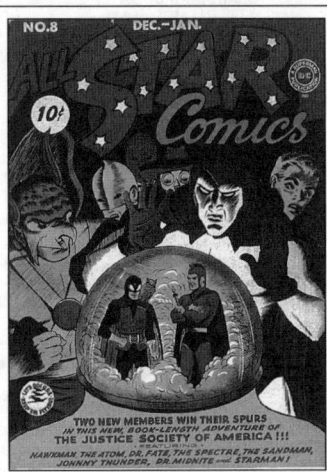

All Star Comics # 8
Origin Wonder Woman

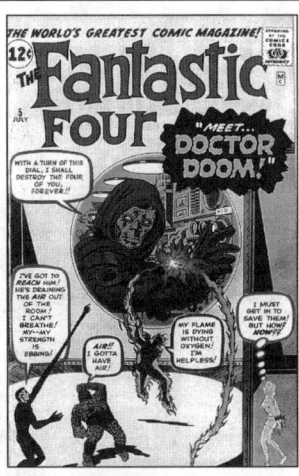

Fantastic Four # 5
Origin Dr. Doom

BOOMER
SECRET WARS II #5.................NOVEMBER 1985
BOOMERANG
TALES TO ASTONISH #81...............JULY 1966
BOOSTER GOLD
BOOSTER GOLD #6.....................JULY 1986
BOUNCING BOY
ADVENTURE COMICS #301 ....OCTOBER 1962
BOY COMMANDOES
DETECTIVE COMICS #64 ....JUNE 1942
BRAINIAC (Silver Age)
ACTION COMICS #242 ....JULY 1958
SUPERMAN #167...................FEBRUARY 1964
BROTHER VOODOO
STRANGE TALES #169 ....SEPTEMBER 1973
BROTHERS GRIMM
IRON MAN #187......................OCTOBER 1984
BULLSEYE
DAREDEVIL #131......................JUNE 1976
BUSHMASTER
CAPTAIN AMERICA ANNUAL #10...................1991
CANNONBALL
MARVEL GRAPHIC NOVEL #4.................1982
CAPTAIN AMERICA (Golden Age)
CAPTAIN AMERICA COMICS #1.........MARCH 1941
CAPTAIN AMERICA (Silver Age)
TALES OF SUSPENSE #63............MARCH 1965
CAPTAIN AMERICA #109...........JANUARY 1969
CAPTAIN ATOM
CAPTAIN ATOM #1....................MARCH 1987
CAPTAIN BOOMERANG
FLASH (1st Series) #117.............DECEMBER 1960
CAPTAIN BRITAIN (US)
MARVEL TEAM UP #65................JANUARY 1978
CAPTAIN COLD
SHOWCASE #8........................JUNE 1957
CAPTAIN COMET
STRANGE ADVENTURES #9............JUNE 1951
CAPTAIN MARVEL (Kree)
MARVEL SUPER-HEROES #18........JANUARY 1969
CAPTAIN STORM
CAPTAIN STORM #1.................MAY/JUN 1964
CARRION
SPECTACULAR SPIDERMAN #31 ....MAY 1979
CATWOMAN (Golden Age)
BATMAN #62........................DEC/JAN 1951
CATWOMAN (Modern)
BATMAN #404-406..................FEB/APR 1987
CHALLENGERS OF THE UNKNOWN
SHOWCASE #6.....................FEBRUARY 1957
CHAMELEON
AMAZING SPIDERMAN #307.......DECEMBER 1987
CHAMPIONS
CHAMPIONS, THE #1 ....OCTOBER 1975
CHIEF
DOOM PATROL #88....................JUNE 1964
CLAYFACE I
DETECTIVE COMICS #40..............JUNE 1940
SECRET ORIGINS
[2nd Series] #44 ....SEPTEMBER 1989
CLAYFACE II
DETECTIVE COMICS #298...........DECEMBER 1961
CLEA
DOCTOR STRANGE
(2nd Series) #8-9....................APRIL 1975
CLOAK AND DAGGER
CLOAK AND DAGGER
(Limited series) #4 ....JANUARY 1984
COBRA
JOURNEY INTO MYSTERY #98 ....NOVEMBER 1963
COLOSSUS
X-MEN, THE UNCANNY #122.................JUNE 1979
COMET THE SUPER-HORSE
ACTION COMICS #293 ....OCTOBER 1962
CONAN
CONAN THE BARBARIAN #1............OCTOBER 1970
CONCRETE
CONCRETE #3........................JULY 1987
CONGO BILL
ACTION COMICS #37 ....JUNE 1941
CORSAIR
X-MEN, THE UNCANNY #156.................APRIL 1982

CREEPER
SHOWCASE #73.......................APRIL 1968
CRUSADER
THOR #330.........................MARCH 1983
CYBORG
NEW TEEN TITANS, THE (1st Series) #7....MAY 1981
CYCLOPS
X-MEN, THE UNCANNY #38 ....NOVEMBER 1967
DAREDEVIL
DAREDEVIL #1.......................APRIL 1964
DAREDEVIL #53.......................JUNE 1969
DARKHAWK
DARKHAWK #1.......................MARCH 1991
DARKSTAR
INCREDIBLE HULK (2nd) #259 ....MAY 1981
DAZZLER
DAZZLER #1.........................JULY 1981
DEADMAN
STRANGE ADVENTURES #205....SEPTEMBER 1967
DEATHLOK
ASTONISHING TALES #25 ....AUGUST 1974
DEATHSTROKE THE TERMINATOR
NEW TEEN TITANS, THE
(1st Series) #44 ....JULY 1984
DEFENDERS
MARVEL FEATURE #1 ....DECEMBER 1971
DEMON
DEMON #1 ....AUG/SEPT 1978
DESPERO
JUSTICE LEAGUE OF AMERICA
(1st)#1...........................OCT/NOV 1960
DON BLAKE
THOR #158........................NOVEMBER 1968
DOOM PATROL
DOOM PATROL #86.....................MARCH 1964
DOOM PATROL
MY GREATEST ADVENTURE #80.....OCTOBER 1963
DORMAMMU
DOCTOR STRANGE (2nd Series) #71.....APRIL 1986
DR. DOOM
FANTASTIC FOUR #5 ....JULY 1962
FANTASTIC FOUR ANNUAL #2 1964
DR DROOM
AMAZING ADVENTURES #1..................JUNE 1961
DR. DESTINY
JUSTICE LEAGUE OF AMERICA #5 ....JULY 1961
DR. DOOM
FANTASTIC FOUR ANNUAL #2 1964
DR. FATE (Golden Age)
MORE FUN COMICS #67 ....MAY 1941
DR. OCTOPUS
AMAZING SPIDERMAN #3 ....MAY 1963
DR. POLARIS
GREEN LANTERN #21 ....JUNE 1963
DR. SOLAR
DR. SOLAR, MAN OF
THE ATOM #1................OCTOBER 1962
DR. STRANGE
STRANGE TALES #115.............DECEMBER 1963
DOCTOR STRANGE #169 ....JUNE 1968
DRAX THE DESTROYER
IRON MAN #55.....................FEBRUARY 1972
DREAM QUEEN
ALPHA FLIGHT #67....................FEBRUARY 1989
ELECTRO
AMAZING SPIDERMAN #9 ....NOVEMBER 1963
ELEKTRA
DAREDEVIL #168.....................JANUARY 1981
ELONGATED MAN
FLASH ANNUAL (1st Series) #1 1963
EXCALIBUR
EXCALIBUR SPECIAL EDITION #1 1987
FALCON
CAPTAIN AMERICA #117 ....SEPTEMBER 1969
FANTASTIC FOUR
FANTASTIC FOUR #1 ....NOVEMBER 1961
FIN FANG FOOM
STRANGE TALES #89..................OCTOBER 1961
FIRELORD
THOR #306.........................APRIL 1981
FIRESTAR
FIRESTAR #1-4 ....MARCH 1986

FIRESTORM
FIRESTORM #1.......................MARCH 1978
FLASH (Golden Age)
FLASH COMICS #1 ....JANUARY 1940
FLASH (Silver Age)
SHOWCASE #4......................SEPT/OCT 1956
FLASH (Modern Age)
FLASH #110......................DEC/JAN 1960
FOOLKILLER I
MAN THING (1st Series) #3.........MARCH 1974
FOOLKILLER II
OMEGA THE UNKOWN #8.....................MAY 1977
GAEA
THOR ANNUAL #10................................1982
GALACTUS
THOR #162.........................MARCH 1969
THOR #168/169...................SEPT/OCT 1969
GARGOYLE
DEFENDERS #95......................MAY 1981
GEE
POWER PACK #1....................AUGUST 1984
GHOST RIDER I
MARVEL SPOTLIGHT
(1st Series) #5 ....MARCH 1972
GIANT MAN II
LUKE CAGE, POWER MAN #24............APRIL 1975
GLORIAN
INCREDIBLE HULK #267.................JANUARY 1982
GREEN ARROW (Silver Age)
ADVENTURE COMICS #256............JANUARY 1959
SECRET ORIGINS
[2nd Series] #38 ....MARCH 1989
GREEN GOBLIN I
AMAZING SPIDERMAN #40 ....SEPTEMBER 1966
GREEN GOBLIN II
AMAZING SPIDERMAN #126 ....NOVEMBER 1974
GREEN GOBLIN III
AMAZING SPIDERMAN #176.........JANUARY 1978
GREEN LANTERN (Golden Age)
ALL-AMERICAN COMICS #16................JULY 1940
GREEN LANTERN (Silver Age)
SHOWCASE #22......................SEPT/OCT 1959
GREEN LANTERN
(John Stewart)
GREEN LANTERN #185 ....FEBRUARY 1985
GREEN LANTERN
(Kyle Rayner)
GREEN LANTERN [2nd Series] #50.... MARCH 1994
GREMLIN
ROM #44 ....JULY 1983
GRENDEL
COMICO PRIMER #2 1982
GUARDIAN
ALPHA FLIGHT #2 ....SEPTEMBER 1983
GUARDIAND OF OA
GREEN LANTERN #40...............OCTOBER 1965
GUARDIANS OF THE GALAXY
MARVEL SUPER-HEROES #18........JANUARY 1969
GYPSY MOTH
SPIDERWOMAN #48....................JUNE 1982
HANNIBAL KING
TOMB OF DRACULA #25.............OCTOBER 1974
HAVOK
X-MEN #54 ....MARCH 1969
HAWKEYE
AVENGERS #19 ....AUGUST 1965
HAWKMAN (Golden Age)
FLASH COMICS #1 ....JANUARY 1940
HAWKMAN (Silver Age)
BRAVE AND THE BOLD #34 ....MARCH 1961
HOBGOBLIN
SPECTACULAR
SPIDERMAN #85...................DECEMBER 1983
HOBGOBLIN II
WEB OF SPIDERMAN #48...............MARCH 1989
HOURMAN (Golden Age)
ADVENTURE COMICS #48.............MARCH 1940
HOWLING COMMANDOS
SGT. FURY AND HIS
HOWLING COMMANDOS #34 ....SEPTEMBER 1966
HULK
INCREDIBLE HULK (1st) #1 ....MAY 1962

Incredible Hulk # 1
Origin Hulk

Thor # 337
Origin new Thor (Beta Ray Bill)

DEATH INDEX

(Foundation work by Andy Kythreotis)

Below is a work-in-progress listing of the first deaths of selected characters *(Note: Some of these characters have since been resurrected)*. We hope to expand this feature to include subsequent rebirths/new incarnations in future editions. Any further information may be sent to the editorial address.

ADAM CRAY
SUICIDE SQUAD #62 ....FEBRUARY 1992
AGATHA HARKNESS
VISION & SCARLET WITCH (2nd Series) #3 ....DECEMBER 1985
AIRWALKER
THOR #306 ....APRIL 1981
AMAHL FAROUK
X-MEN, THE UNCANNY #117 ....JANUARY 1979
ANCIENT ONE
MARVEL PREMIERE #10 ....SEPTEMBER 1973
ANGLE-MAN
CRISIS ON INFINITE EARTHS #11 ....FEBRUARY 1986
AQUABABY
AQUAMAN 57 ....AUGUST/SEPT 1977
AQUAGIRL
CRISIS ON INFINTE EARTHS #10 ....JANUARY 1986
ARTEMIS
WONDER WOMAN [2nd Series] #100 ....JULY 1995
AUNT MAY
AMAZING SPIDERMAN #400...APRIL 1995
AURON
SUPERMAN #509...FEBRUARY 1994
BALDER
THOR #274 ....AUGUST 1978
BANDIT
CRISIS ON INFINITE EARTHS #12 ....MARCH 1986
BARON BLOOD
CAPTAIN AMERICA #254...FEBRUARY 1981
BARON STRUCKER
STRANGE TALES #158...JULY 1967

BARON ZEMO I
AVENGERS #15 ....APRIL 1965
BASILISK
FANTASTIC FOUR #289 ....APRIL 1986
BATMAN (Earth 2)
ADVENTURE COMICS #462 ....OCTOBER 1979
BATWOMAN
DETECTIVE COMICS #485...JUNE 1979
BELIT
CONAN THE BARBARIAN #100 ....JULY 1979
BEN PARKER
AMAZING FANTASY #15...AUGUST 1962
BEYONDER
SECRET WARS II #9..MARCH 1986
BIG MAN
AMAZING SPIDERMAN #52.....................................SEPTEMBER 1967
BLACK KNIGHT I
MARVEL SUPER HEROES #17 ....NOVEMBER 1968
BLACK KNIGHT II
AVENGERS #47 ....DECEMBER 1968
BLACK OUT
AVENGERS #277 ....APRIL 1987
BLIZZARD
AMAZING SPIDERMAN ANNUAL #20................................NOVEMBER 1986
BLOOD STONE
RAMPAGING HULK #8..AUGUST 1977
BLUE STREAK
CAPTAIN AMERICA #318...JUNE 1986
BUCKY
AVENGERS #4 ....MARCH 1964

Amazing Spiderman # 122
Death of Green Goblin I

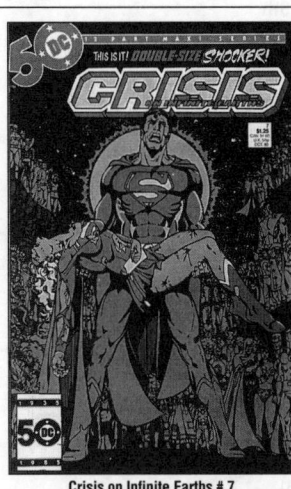

Crisis on Infinite Earths # 7
Death of Supergirl

Flash #243
Death of The Top

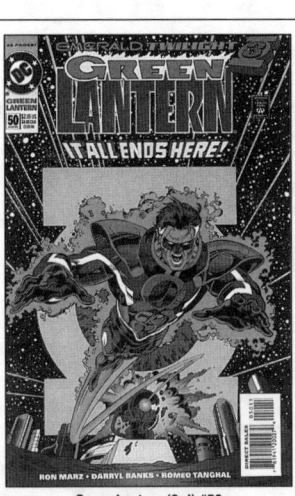

Green Lantern (3rd) #50
Death of Sinestro

REPRINT INDEX

(compiled by the author while sifting through his collection one day)

Below is a list-in-progress of key issues that can be found reprinted elsewhere and usually at much less cost to the collector. This index is designed with budgeting in mind, as very often collectors may wish to own an original first issue or appearance but it proves financially impossible. Many of the classic stories have been reprinted at some time or another and for the novice it is a valuable way of learning about the great heroes and villains and their backgrounds. Happy reading!

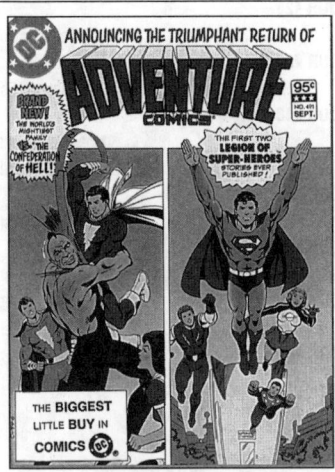

Adventure Comics # 491
reprints Adventure Comics #247, #267

Batman # 213
reprints Batman #16, Detective Comics #38,

Marvel Tales Annual # 2
Reprints Avengers #1, Strange Tales #110
and X-Men #1

Secret Origins (2nd) # 5
Reprints More Fun Comics #52 and #53

50 HOTTEST BABES PAST TO PRESENT

The 'Hot Babe' phenomenon of recent times is not necessarily a modern fad or fashion.
Below is a list of what in our opinion are the most popular 'Hot Babes' to be found in comics over the last 35 years, that is since American Comic Books were distributed in the UK. Obviously this is a very subjective feature but as with any article any further information is greatly appreciated (please submit any further information to the Editorial address given on the inside front page).

1 **ANGELA**
1st appearance Spawn #9

2 **AURORA**
1st appearance X-Men, The Uncanny #120

3 **AVENGELYNE**
1st appearance Avengelyne #1

4 **BARBI TWINS**
1st appearance Barbi Twins #1

5 **BLACK CANARY (SILVER AGE)**
1st appearance Justice League of America #75

6 **CATWOMAN (MODERN)**
1st appearance Batman #406

7 **DAWN**
1st appearance Continum #1

8 **DOLPHIN**
1st appearance Showcase #79

9 **DOUBLE IMPACT LADIES**
1st appearance Double Impact #1

10 **DONNA TROY**
(originally Wonder Girl, later a Darkstar)
1st appearance Brave and the Bold #60

11 **DREAM GIRL**
1st appearance Adventure Comics #317

12 **ENCHANTRESS**
1st appearance Journey Into Mystery #103

13 **FAIRCHILD**
1st appearance Deathmate Black

14 **FIRE (JUSTICE LEAGUE MEMBER)**
1st appearance Super Friends #25

15 **JEAN GREY**
(originally Marvel Girl, later Phoenix)
1st appearance X-Men, The Uncanny #1

16 **GHOST**
1st appearance Comics' Greatest World Arcadia
Week 3

17 **GLORY**
1st appearance Youngbood: Stryke File #1

18 **GWEN STACY**
1st appearance Amazing Spiderman #31

19 **INVISIBLE WOMAN**
1st appearance Fantastic Four #1

20 **LADY DEATH**
1st appearance Evil Ernie #1

21 **LIGHTNING LASS**
(later became Light Lass)
1st appearance Adventure Comics #308

22 **MARY JANE WATSON**
1st appearance Amazing Spiderman #42

23 **MERA**
1st appearance Aquaman (1st series) #11

24 **NAMORITA**
1st appearance Sub Mariner #50

25 **PHANTOM GIRL**
1st appearance Action Comics #276

26 **POISON**
1st appearance Razor #1/2

27 **POLARIS**
1st appearance X-Men, The Uncanny #49

28 **POWER GIRL**
1st appearance All Star Comics
(2nd series) #58

29 **PSYLOCKE**
1st appearance New Mutants Annual #2

30 **PURGATORY**
1st appearance Lady Death II:
Between Heavan and Hell #2

31 **RAINMAKER**
1st appearance Stormwatch #8

32 **RAZOR**
1st appearance Razor #0

33 **RIPTIDE**
1st appearance Youngblood #1

34 **ROGUE**
1st appearance Avengers Annual #10

35 **SCARLET WITCH**
1st appearance X-Men, The Uncanny #4

36 **SHE-HULK**
1st appearance She-Hulk, The Savage #1

37 **SHI**
1st appearance Razor Annual #1

38 **SIF**
1st appearance Journey Into Mystery #102

39 **STARFIRE**
1st appearance DC Comics Presents #26

40 **STORM**
1st appearance X-Men Giant Size #1

41 **STRYKE**
1st appearance Razor #1

42 **SUPERGIRL**
1st appearance Action Comics #252

43 **TITANIA**
1st appearance Marvel Super-Heroes
Secret Wars #3

44 **TOMOE**
1st appearance Shi: The Way of The Warrior #4

45 **VAMPIRELLA**
1st appearance Vampirella #1

46 **WASP**
1st appearance Tales to Astonish
(1st series) #44

47 **WHITE QUEEN**
1st appearance X-Men, The Uncanny #129

48 **WITCHBLADE**
1st appearance Witchblade #1

49 **WONDER WOMAN (SILVER AGE)**
1st appearance Wonder Woman #105

50 **ZATANA**
1st appearance Hawkman (1st series) #4

Lady Death II #2 – 1st appearance of Purgatory

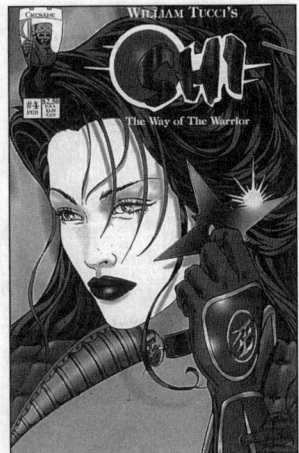

Shi #4 – 1st appearance of Tomoe

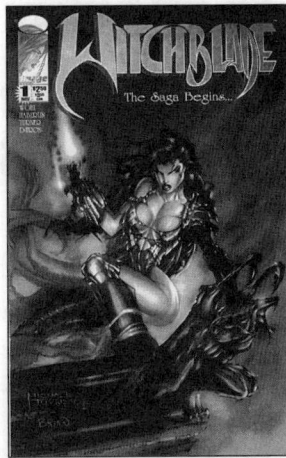

Witchblade #1 – 1st appearance of Witchblade

VARIANT COVERS-A SMALL LISTING

Below is a small listing of some of the Variant Covers/Editions that are contained within this guide, it is by no means complete but more a listing of the more popular or well known variants. As the level of variant/alternate covers increases, so shall the difficulty in cataloguing all of them. Any and all additions to this listing would be welcomed (please submit any further information to the editiorial address on the inside front page).

ALLIANCE #1
Variant Cover
ALLIANCE #2
Variant Cover
ALLIANCE #3
Variant Cover
ALLIANCE #4
Variant Cover
AMAZING SPIDERMAN #400
White Cover Variant
ANIMAL MYSTIC #1
Variant Cover
ASH #4
Gold Fahrenheit Edition
ASH #4
Red Fahrenheit Edition
ASH #4
White Fahrenheit Edition
ASH #5
Variant Cover
ASH #6
Variant Cover
ASTER #3
Variant Cover
AVENGELYNE #3
Variant Cover
AVENGELYNE: POWER #2
Variant Cover
AVENGELYNE: POWER #3
Photo Cover Variant - Holding Sword
AVENGELYNE: POWER #3
Photo Cover Variant - Holding Mini Crossbow
AVENGELYNE/GLORY #1
Variant Cover
BADROCK #1
Cover A - C

BERZERKERS #1
Variant Cover
BLACK FLAG (2ND SERIES) #2
Variant Cover
BLACK FLAG (2ND SERIES) #4
Variant Cover
BLOODFIRE/HELLINA #1
Variant Cover
BRIGADE (2ND SERIES) #20
Variant Cover
CATFIGHT: DREAM WARRIOR #1
Variant Cover
CAULDRON #1
Variant Cover
CHAPEL #1
Variant Cover
CHAPEL (2ND SERIES) #1
Variant Cover
CREED (2ND SERIES) #1
Variant Cover
CYBLADE/SHI SPECIAL-THE BATTLE FOR INDEPENDENCE #1
Variant Cover
DAWN #1
Black Light Edition
DAWN #1
Look Sharp Edition
DAWN #1
White Trash Edition
DEATHBLOW #5
Variant Cover
DOUBLE IMPACT #3
Variant Cover
DOUBLE IMPACT #5
Variant Cover
DOOM'S IV #1
Variant Cover

Creed 2nd Series #1 (variant cover)

Shi #5 (variant cover)

Vampirella Strikes #1 (variant cover)

EVIL ERNIE #0
    Platinum Edition
EVIL ERNIE: THE RESSURECTION #1
    Gold Edition
EXILES, THE ALL NEW #1
    Variant Cover
EXILES, THE ALL NEW #1
    E.T.M. Variant
EXILES: INFINITY NN
    Variant Cover
FUNNYTIME FEATURES #7
    Variant Cover
FUNNYTIME FEATURES #7
    Gold Variant Cover
GEN 13 #5
    Variant Cover
GEN 13 (2ND SERIES) #1
    Variant Covers A - M
GLORY #1
    Variant Cover
GLORY #4
    Variant Cover
GLORY/AVENGELYNE #1
    Variant Cover
HELLINA: KISS OF DEATH #1
    Variant Cover
HELLINA: WICKED WAYS #1
    Variant Cover
INVISIBLES #5
    Cover A - Cover D
KINDRED #3
    Variant Cover
KNIGHTMARE #4
    Variant Cover
LADY DEATH #1/2
    Gold Edition
LADY DEATH #1/2
    Red Velvet Edition
LADY DEATH II: BETWEEN HEAVEN & HELL #1
    Black Velvet Edition
LADY DEATH II: BETWEEN HEAVEN & HELL #4
    Variant Cover
LADY DEATH: IN LINGERIE #1
    Leather Edition
LADY DEATH: SWIMSUIT EDITION #1
    Red Velvet Edition
LEOPARD #1
    Signed Variant Edition
MANTRA: INFINITY NN
    Variant Cover
MANTRA (2ND SERIES) #1
    Variant Cover
MAXX #1
    Blue Variant
NIGHT MAN: INFINITY NN
    Variant Cover
NIGHT MAN (2ND SERIES) #1
    Variant Cover
PRIME: INFINITY NN
    Variant Cover
PRIME (2ND SERIES) #1
    Variant Cover
RAZOR #2
    Platinum Edition
RAZOR #2
    Limited Edition – Blue and Red Variants
RAZOR #5
    Platinum Edition
RAZOR #8
    Variant Cover
RAZOR AND SHI SPECIAL #1
    Platinum Edition
RAZOR ANNUAL #1
    Gold Edition
RAZOR: BURN #2
    Platinum Edition

RUNE: INFINITY NN
    Variant Cover
RUNE (2ND SERIES) #1
    Variant Cover
SAVAGE DRAGON #1
    Four Cover Variants
SHI/CYBLADE SPECIAL-THE BATTLE FOR INDEPENDENCE NN
    Variant Cover
SHI: SENRYAKU #1
    Variant Cover
SHI: THE WAY OF THE WARRIOR #1
    Fan Appreciation Edition
SHI: THE WAY OF THE WARRIOR #1
    Gold Fan Appreciation Edition
SHI: THE WAY OF THE WARRIOR #5
    Variant Cover
SHOTGUN MARY #1
    Variant Cover
SIREN #1
    Variant Cover
SIREN: INFINITY NN
    Variant Cover
STORMWATCH #10
    Variant Cover
STRYKE #0
    Variant Cover
SUPREME #28
    Variant Cover
TEAM 7 #1
    Variant Cover
TOMOE #0
    Variant Cover
ULTRAFORCE #2
    Variant Cover
ULTRAFORCE (2ND SERIES) #1
    Variant Cover
ULTRAFORCE: INFINITY NN
    Variant Cover
UNION #0
    Variant Cover
VAMPIRELLA STRIKES #1
    Variant Cover
VAMPIRELLA, VENGEANCE OF #14
    Variant Cover
VAMPIRELLA, VENGEANCE OF #15
    Variant Cover
VAMPIRELLA, VENGEANCE OF #16
    Variant Cover
VAMPIRELLA, VENGEANCE OF #17
    Variant Cover
VAMPIRELLA, VENGEANCE OF #18
    Variant Cover
VAMPIRELLA, VENGEANCE OF #19
    Variant Cover
WETWORKS #2
    Variant Cover
WILDC.A.T.S. #1
    Gold Embossed Cover Variant
WILDC.A.T.S. #11
    Variant Cover
X-FORCE #50
    Variant Cover
X-MEN #11
    Variant Cover
X-MEN #25
    Black and White Cover Variant
X-MEN: OMEGA #1
    Gold Variant Cover
X-O MANOWAR #1/2
    Gold Edition
X-O MANOWAR #0
    Gold Edition
X-O MANOWAR #15
    Pink Logo Variant

SUCCEEDING IN BUSINESS
SURESH TOLAT OF CASSON BECKMAN

Over the last 10 years, the comic industry has continued to grow with many new businesses starting up. In many cases, it is the enthusiastic collector who has started up using his own collection as his initial stock. Often these businesses fail so I set out below the main points that should be considered before taking the step of setting up your own business:-

1   Consider whether to start a full time business or initially trade on a part-time basis with a view to eventually going full-time. You must be sure that you have sufficient time to devote to your business.

2   Prepare a business plan which should cover the following:-

    a.   Target Market.

    b.   Site of business/Mail Order.

    c.   Cashflow forecasts.

    d.   Sources of capital.

    e.   Division of profits (if applicable).

    f.   Promotion methods/Advertising

3   Consider whether to be self-employed (or a partnership) or to set up a limited company. Self-employment has its advantages with regard to expenses but a Limited Company gives more protection. If setting up a partnership there should be a formal partnership agreement which sets out the specific duties of each partner and their profit share.

4   Ensure that you have a good knowledge of the current state of the market and that you read all the relevant trade magazines. In addition, establish that you have good contacts amongst other dealers who can often give practical advice.

5   Ensure that proper bookkeeping records are kept so that accounts can be prepared. With the advent of self-assessment, it will become even more essential (see note below).

6   Ensure that you have proper professional advice at the outset from your bank manager/accountant/solicitor - rather than when problems are encountered.

Once you have decided to commence the business, the following should be informed as soon as possible:-

    1.   **The Inland Revenue**
    They will require to know of your change of status and you should write to your own Tax District advising them of this. If you have no Tax District, then you should write to your local Tax District. They will then send you the appropriate forms for completion to enable them to set up the appropriate records

    In addition, if you have not done so before, you will have to submit a Tax Return detailing your income and claim for allowances to your Inspector of Taxes on an annual basis. The appropriate Tax Return form will be forwarded to you once you have notified them of your change in status.

    2.   **The Department of Social Security**
    This Government Office is responsible for dealing with National Insurance Contributions and you are required to notify them when you start a business. This will enable them to calculate the contributions that should be paid. If you are self-employed, you will normally have to pay the flat rate Class 2 National Insurance Contributions. In addition, Class 4 National Insurance Contributions have to be paid on your profits between certain defined limits.

    3.   **The Customs & Excise**
    Normally you only have to register for VAT once your turnover reaches a certain level (which is at present £47,000). However, as comics are zero rated for Value Added Tax purposes, it is advantageous to voluntarily register as this means that the VAT on most expenses incurred can be reclaimed from the Customs & Excise.

SELF ASSESSMENT AND THE SELF EMPLOYED
Many of you will have heard of "self assessment" either from the advertisements in the press or on television. However, although the Revenue have tried to emphasize their helpful side, they have not pointed out the more sinister side which will affect all small businesses, especially those that are in the main cash businesses. It is certain that the new system places a greater responsibility on small businesses which, to begin with, will mean extra work.

As the first new style Tax Return will not be issued until April 1997, it does mean that all individuals should be properly prepared from 6th April 1996. Everyone affected by the changes will find it much easier to cope if their tax affairs are up to date before the new system is introduced. Some of the main points that have not been highlighted in great detail during the Revenue's advertising campaign are the following:-

a.   The new Tax Return is in itself much larger than before. The basic return comprises of only six foolscap pages but there may be a number of additional schedules that need to be completed. Although the first new Tax Returns will be issued in April 1997, if you wish the Revenue to calculate your tax liability, they must be submitted by 30th September 1997. However, if the individual wishes to do the calculation himself, the deadline is 31st January 1998.

b.   If a tax return is not submitted by 31st January, there will be an automatic penalty of £100 (even if once the Tax Return is submitted there is no additional tax liability). If the Return is still outstanding six months later, the Inspector of Taxes may even seek a penalty of up to £60 for every day's delay in sending in the Return.

c.   At present if tax is paid late, interest will be charged. The Collector of Taxes will in future be entitled to make surcharges.

d.   From 6th April 1996, it will be necessary for taxpayers to retain records to back up their Tax Return for at least five years after it has been filed. Failure to comply with this will result in a penalty of up to £3,000. Whilst it has always been necessary for records to be retained, this is the first time that you can be fined for non-compliance.

e.   The Revenue are now allocating more resources to tax investigations and cash businesses will become likely targets. With self-assessment, the Inspector of Taxes no longer has to have reasonable grounds for opening up an investigation into an individual's affairs and may now challenge returns entirely at random.

f.   Employers face an extra burden as they will be given fixed dates by which they must provide their employees with certain specific information about their pay, benefits and tax liability.

Obviously the above is not intended to be an exhaustive list of points as each individual's circumstances should be considered on its own merits.

Casson Beckman is a medium sized firm of Chartered Accountants and Business Advisers who have a specialist department dealing with the Entertainment Industry.

Suresh Tolat qualified as a Chartered Accountant in 1982. He is an assistant manager in our tax division and being a keen comic collector himself, has a specialist knowledge of this industry. For a further discussion of your needs, why not telephone Suresh on 0171-387-2888. He will be pleased to discuss your requirements with no obligation whatsoever.

HOT COMICS
A Personal Opinion by
STANLEY RIIKS

LAST YEAR'S biggest TV hit was adapted in the hottest comic of the year. **X-Files #1** was an under-ordered comic and at the first mart after the launch the comic was already selling for double its price and was working its way up to the £5.00 mark. Within a month issue #2 came out and it just wasn't seen at normal cover price. Orders for this issue were far less than for #1 and it disappeared even more quickly. And issue #1 was selling for around £15.00.

Issue #2 soon caught up with its predecessor and the series had continued to increase in price, the second issue now out-stripping the first and reaching upwards of £20.00. Issue #3 was the last issue of the first story arc and is now worth somewhere in the region of £5.00 in most areas of the U.K. But I have seen it for over a tenner and at the relatively cheap price of £4.00, both at the same mart.

Orders rose significantly for issue #4 and subsequent issues but those X-philes continue to grab up copies in the hope of speculative gain. The second story arc in issue #4 has long since moved at above the cover price but the rapid increase in sales means that later issues are in good supply and not so collectible. The series will no doubt continue with its success for the near future anyway.

Charlie Adlard's artwork is suitably moody and dark. The characters are recognisable but only just. The stories are the strong point of the comic as with the series and packaged beautifully with some great covers by Kim. The general disdain for the comic from most reviewers hasn't stopped the price rising and does seem a bit envious. The comic is not great and doesn't really deserve the amount of speculative attention it has received but with the various reprints available the early issues are quite easily accessible at reasonable prices and well-deserving of your cash. Just don't splash out on those first printings expecting to get a great comic! But the quality of both artwork and writing is improving. The current price for X-Files #1 seems to be up to about £30.00 in the U.K. and about $50.00 in the U.S.

Other hot titles of the past year with an X in the title include Marvel's X-family. The whole series of titles went through a major revamp-type cross-over with the **After Xavier: The Age of Apocalypse** storyline. The first book of this huge summer cross-over was selling over its cover price the day it was shipped! **X-Men Alpha** has steadily increased in price since it came out and now reaches in excess of £5.00. Almost the entire cross-over series is seeing increases. The Alpha issue is highly sought after and continued increases are expected due to availability of the title. At the UK Comic Art Convention '95 there were only three copies on sale in the Dealer's Room.

The cross-over series produced what will probably be the top selling book of 1995 with the final chapter in the story: **X-Men Omega**. These books owe their success much more to hype and dedicated X-fans than quality or significance of story: after it was all over not a great deal had really changed as the alternative X-universe returned to virtual normality and Xavier was alive again. Probably the most blown out of proportion cross-over in history (so far!)

Also the **Generation X** book seems to have got the attention of comic fans everywhere, voted the second best book by the reviewers of Comics International. As drawn by hot artist Chris Bachalo, the book is beginning a slow but steady price rise and this is a book to watch in 1996. The best of the X-titles without a doubt, this is a book that deserves a little more interest than the others and is beginning to get it.

The success of that huge cross-over also spawned an increase in back-issue sales of the **X-Men** titles after a slump in all back-issue sales. The only other back-issues moving were **Spawn** and **Spiderman**. The latter's back-issue sales were bumped into action by the Clone storyline. This was a story revealing that Peter Parker hasn't been Spiderman since the first appearance of the Clone way back in **Amazing Spiderman #149** and many feel that more upheavals in the Spider-family will confuse continuity even more. The price of the early appearances of the Clone rose quickly, peaking at up to £100 for **Amazing Spiderman #149** but have since dropped just as dramatically to settle at about £50.00.

Spawn however did not lose the price increase it gained and its first spin-off, **Angela**, written by our very own Neil Gaiman, is rapidly increasing in price and this will almost certainly continue. The ongoing series of **Spawn**, the toy collection and numerous other Spawn projects will keep the popularity of the character and related characters in the Top 10.

Spawn had two spin-off mini-series in 1995 with the Alan Moore written **Violator** and **Badrock and Spawn: Bloodfeud**. Good sales for both have been instrumental in the price increase in early issues of the ongoing series but as yet no movement in the later mini-series. Watch them for the coming year though!

Another Gaiman-written project, **The Sandman**, is coming to an end with issue #75 and Vertigo's top-selling title – and probably the most acclaimed in comics history – has been steadily increasing in price and will continue to do so. The first issue varies tremendously in price and has been seen for as much as £30.00. And such success will probably continue as Gaiman says he will be working on **Sandman** one-shots and a second **Death** mini-series is in the works. The Sandman is one of the best comics to come out for many years and its back-issues are relatively cheap for such quality. Highly recommended are issue #19's **Midsummer Night's Dream** story and the **Seasons of Mist** storyline from issues #21-28.

Talking of **Death**, the mini-series has been increasing along with the Sandman on-going series. With the issues reaching as much as £7.00 in some areas of the U.K., it's one to watch.

Another Vertigo title that has proved to be a big hit is the brilliantly written and drawn **Preacher** by Garth Ennis and Steve Dillon. This is one of the best comics to appear since **Sandman** and is the logical successor at the top of Vertigo's line-up. Sales are picking up for this title and prices on the first four issues are constantly on the move with the first issue being regularly seen for £8.00. The comic is going to increase in price for a while as long as the quality is maintained and more acclaim is likely to follow as and when graphic novels and trade paperback collections of the series are produced.

Babe comics have been hot in the last year: **Vampirella**, **Shi** and **Lady Death** have all been increasing in value and will continue to do so for as long as this current fad will last. First issues of **Vampirella** are reaching the £20.00 mark, **Shi #1** as much as £25.00 and the first issue of the first **Lady Death** mini-series has been seen at £50.00.

Glory, a reasonably good babe book from Image in the capable hands of Mike Deodato, is another hot book with the alternative cover version of issue #1 selling for about £5.00. Dark Horse's **Ghost** by Adam Hughes is another of the better babe books around. This will be moving in the future and is one to watch. But some of the worst comics in the last year have been following the current craze and producing rip-offs like **Double Impact** and the **Barbi Twins**. If this at best mediocre material continues to find an outlet, it will be the most significant factor in the ultimate demise of the genre.

Glory artist Mike Deodato's run on **Wonder Woman** is increasing in price as he becomes more of a "hot" artist although his story-telling abilities have been called into question. The first issue of his run, #88, is particularly sought after and is seeing sale prices of £5.00. His run on the title has established the character as a force to be reckoned with in the DC universe after years of poor sales.

1994's **Gen 13** mini-series has given rise to a very successful on-going series with issue #1 of the mini-series fetching up to £30.00 and all the other issues increasing in price right up there behind it. The thirteen alternative covers of issue #1 from the ongoing series were a nightmare for collectors and a positive boon for dealers with all the rarer alternative covers reaching prices of between £15.00 and £20.00 in a fairly short space of time. The on-going series **Gen 13 #2** is also fast rising in price as it was part of the **Wildstorm Rising** storyline.

The alternative or variant cover trend continues with most examples immediately bringing a price of £5.00 or thereabouts. And there seems to be no sign of collector's reluctance to part with their cash.

The last year has been mixed with regard to back-issue sales largely owing to the interest in new material (and some exorbitant cover prices) – there is just not enough money to go round. Prices have remained static on lower grade issues and even gone down. Increases are generally only on the top grades. There is some hope for back issues with publishers now cutting back some of their lesser titles and putting some proper thought and arranging good creative teams on even standard titles. Perhaps then hot books will be created for the right reasons – not gimmick covers or bikini babes with big guns but the simplest formula of all: good stories told well.

Extremes of Violet #1

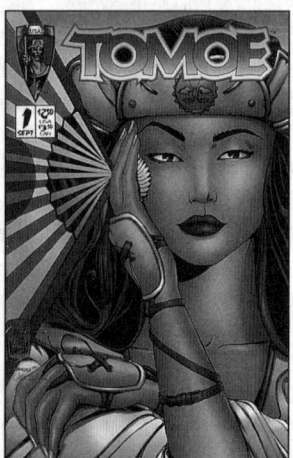

Tomoe #1

REFLECTIONS OF A COMIC COLLECTOR
by Ian G. Holmes

IT'S A LONG TIME since November 1959, a date that's of great historical importance to many comic collectors in the U.K. Some would refer to it as the birth of the Silver Age in this country.

My introduction to the hobby of comic collecting was some 18 months later thanks to a school friend who had the June 1961 issues of **Action**, **Adventure**, **Lois Lane**, **Jimmy Olsen** and **Superman**.

Within days of this first encounter **Superman** became my reason for living and Clark Kent had the job that I was going to relieve him of when I left school. I quickly extracted from my friend the source of these little gems and the mad rush was on to get to the market stall newsagents as soon as the Saturday morning matinee credits began to roll.

The fact that my mum gave me more pocket money than his mum gave him, coupled with his craving for pop-corn, ice-cream and chocolate during the interval definitely gave me the edge when it came to buying power. Within a few months you can imagine the scene of a little 10 year old proto-comic book dealer supplying his school mates in the playground although in those days we all referred to it as "swaps" (one to him, two for me was my particular angle). I must admit though that when he picked up a **Superman Annual #4** from the second-hand comics stall (sorry, "back-issue") it blew me away so much that I actually gave him 5 comics for it!

I noticed that it didn't have a thick cardboard cover like my **Dandy** and **Beano** annuals and I saw for the first time the actual covers of the stories within on the back cover. I could spend hours looking at these classic covers of issues that I thought at the time I could never hope to own. The one where **Superman** has a mysterious new power radiating from his finger-tips, where a knight in armour had wounded him and Superman's arm was bandaged or Superman's future wife where her head was blanked out

and you had to guess who it could possibly be (it could only be Lois). DC were very good at provocative covers depicting a situation that could not possibly happen if you knew the circumstances and powers of the heroes and the relationships of the supporting cast concerned. The company also had a habit of listing partial covers and story headlines inside in a feature called Coming Attractions and invariably there was always one that you couldn't get. A couple of years after my first Superfamily encounters (this would be early 1962), my newsagent's pile got noticeably bigger. It seemed there was a second bunch of books from another company called Marvel sitting next to the regular pile of DCs. At first I would just flick past these and pay no attention whatsoever (I have a recurring nightmare of the issues of **Fantastic Four #1** and **Amazing Spiderman #1** that I must have passed up in my quest to find my favourites. Come to think of it I remember trading back some odds 'n sods like **Amazing Fantasy #15** and **Hulk #3**, not realising they were Marvels…). But one day I thought "I'm feeling flush, let's go check out these **Avengers** and **X-Men**. After all they must be worth reading for only 9d each". The rest, as they say, is history. Everything in sight was purchased. Saturday became a day of hunting for those missing issues (I biked for miles), reading them in the safety of my room and reflecting on what it might be like to be one of the super heroes. Many years later, pressure from my friends stating that 20 year olds don't read comics and the fact that it's now 1971 and distribution of current titles seemed to have dried up made me put the lid on my hobby and also on the chest that I stored them in until early 1989.

All of a sudden **Superman**, **Batman**, **Spiderman** and the **Hulk** are characters that everyone has heard of. There were articles about them in the daily newspapers and they even had their own TV programmes and movies.

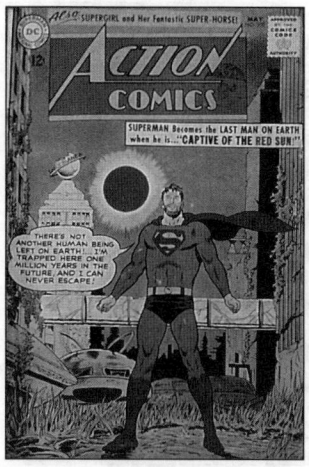

Action Comics # 300
(A favourite!)

Superman # 141
(Another favourite!)

Time to visit the loft and lift that lid I thought. You often see a seasoned Silver Age collector sniffing a comic. Well I got 10 years worth all in one go. A touch of acid in the odd issue but what a rush!

After a bit of investigative digging and delving I was soon the owner of a Steve Rock Grading Guide, a Justin Ebbs sales catalogue and a Duncan McAlpine British Price Guide, the one with Batman on the cover.

The next choice was very difficult and I'm sure it's one that other collectors have faced when they re-discover their old comics. Do I try and fill in the many gaps in my collection at the overwhelming prices before my very eyes (I mean, **Showcase #4** was a whopping £750!) or do I sell the lot for a percentage of the same? After all none of the 1500+ books in my collection had cost me more than 10d each.

During the pondering period a friend of mine who was aware of my dilemma mentioned that he knew of a shop that actually sold nothing but comics and it was only 30 minutes drive away. Within four months I was an equal partner in this comic retail store and owned half of an inventory of twenty five thousand books. Most items from 1971 to 1989 that I never knew existed were all of a sudden there to be read. A new trade paper called Comics International had recently been published and comic marts were being advertised around the country. At that time I thought to attend each of the 5 or 6 venues on offer throughout the whole year would be quite a workload but worth the effort if it meant that the shop would make a profit and I could sell some of my comics quickly.

The first one in Birmingham was a real eye opener. I carefully blue-tacked my **Avengers #1** and **Daredevil #1** to the back wall and sold both within 10 minutes for £85 and £95 respectively. Both had suffered grade wise from poor storage and multiple readings but I still felt guilty at the fact that I had just made £179.90 clear profit. An observant dealer opposite assured me that it's perfectly okay to buy books, sit on them for 25 years and sell them for guide price. He then commented "You actually read them?" I didn't get the joke at the time.

Alas the speculator boom quickly educated me to the fact that even this wonderful hobby of ours had its darker side.

Mart dealers who had already forked out for their tables (prices rising as marts became more popular) appeared to be forced into displaying these so called "hot items" as these were what seemed to be selling. The multiple purchasing of some speculators left supplies short resulting in the poor old customer who was actually buying the book to read paying over cover price for it. Back issue sales suffered as a consequence. Dealers were buying from dealers and all because profit was the name of the game at the end of the day.

Without wishing to go into great detail as this is neither the time nor the place, I myself could speak as a victim of what I have come to regard as the appalling word and concept called "speculation". As a dealer and collector I found that when such speculation was at its height both shop and marts sales suffered equally. This along with the continual feeling in my head of wanting everything that came into the store for myself forced me to sell my half to avoid a clash of interests. It turned out to be a wise choice as like so many aspiring outlets no profits means no store hence it now ceases to exist. Some good came out of it though by way of an observation of the behaviour amongst dealers. As part of "the gang" in some instances I saw and heard some dreadful back-biting and gutter-press politics. Yet at other times there seemed to be an unwritten law and an unquestioned trust within the ranks. If a book was reported stolen the entire network would act as one to identify the item if offered for sale to enable a safe return to their fellow dealer so he was not out of pocket for too long.

Eventually, books are sometimes offered to you for approval prior to payment. Likewise, dealers are trusted with customers books to sell on consignment and everyone can work together. This scenario may be idealistic but it exists.

The suggestion of obtaining a second opinion prior to finalising a purchase is something I would highly recommend in my experience. This will clearly benefit the highly respected dealers and send the less considerate ones to the back of the queue. On the other hand when you hear of a collector who is ready to sell his books to (hopefully) make a profit and he's told that "This book has been restored" or "This has been trimmed" and that old favourite "There's a colour touch and new staples in this one"...All well and good if he and the buyer knew all this from the onset and the collector paid accordingly and is willing to accurately report these grade considerations on to a prospective purchaser. Not quite such good news if original collector and potential purchaser discover something after close inspection. Such situations can either make or break friendships, make or break dealer/customer relations. With so many key books coming from the States purchased through the mail or as a last minute trade at the end of a mart, a weary head and a tired eye can sometimes lead to a lapse in concentration and book scrutiny. I am of the opinion that there are more restored books in the U.K. market than most people realise.

I can only end this personal trip down memory lane in perhaps the way I should have started it. We have all purchased this price guide because we have a common interest—comic books. If you are spending or thinking of spending considerable sums of money on the hobby you love, read price guides, seek professional opinions, do your homework and learn as much as you can about grading and prices, restoration techniques and the way local and global markets work. Everyone at one time or another has made a bad deal or suffered one. It's when it keeps happening that the love of your hobby becomes extinguished.

Showcase #4 – £750 in 1989

Avengers #1 – sold for £85!

SIGNED & NUMBERED LIMITED EDITIONS

BY GRANT RYMER
With a grateful assist from Geoff West of Conquistador

WELCOME AGAIN to the most unique section of the U.K. Price Guide and especially to all the new American readers.

The editions listed here are not of the kind currently being produced by certain American companies which are ordinary copies of the comics except for the signature and a Certificate of Authenticity. Rather, the editions listed here are those which have been specifically printed in order to be signed. There is a strictly limited print run, most commonly between one and two thousand copies. Many have new covers, a new art plate for the signature and new editorials.

The books in this Signed and Numbered Limited Edition Hardbacks section are also different from their respective trade paperback or previous hardback editions. Almost all have a new plate set in the frontispiece and in some cases a slipcase, expanded stories, sketch pages and text pages by the artist and author respectively. The plate is usually a unique piece of art with spaces specifically for signatures, the number of the copy and the total number of copies printed.

Currently, the two main publishers of Signed and Limited Editions are Graphitti Designs and Dark Horse Publishing. Dark Horse only publish editions from work already previously published by themselves either in comic or trade paperback format. Graphitti on the other hand publish a wide variety of material from companies ranging from DC to Epic, Pacific Comics to First Publishing. Graphitti publish no comics in their own right.

In the past a significant number of editions were also published by Eclipse and Kitchen Sink.

The Signed and Numbered Limited Edition Hardback represents the very pinnacle of production in the comics industry. They are produced very much for the connoisseur and in general feature the finest material the comics medium has to offer.

As investments they are not for the recent breed of "comics speculator". They tend to hold their value well but owing to the high initial cost and with few exceptions they tend to appreciate slowly. That said, once sold out from the publisher, prices can vary greatly owing to what some fans will pay for an edition they particularly want.

Also included in this section are Signed and Numbered Limited Edition trading cards, portfolios, trade paperbacks and prints. Both the prints and portfolios sections should be regarded as only a small sample of what is a vast body of work.

MARKET OVERVIEW
During the time since the last U.K. Guide (just over a year and a half ago at the time of writing) the comics indistry has suffered something of an implosion, greatly affecting the output of most companies.

However the highly specialised production of Signed and Numbered Limited Edition hardbacks has suffered relatively little with both the major players (Graphitti and Dark Horse) producing new material and even Marvel entering the high priced hardback market with its Marvel Limited Books. The Marvel Books will not be listed in this section however as they chose not to do them as signed editions.

Hardbacks
Fairly static although the retail price of new editions is increasing dramatically.

Prints & Portfolios
Very static. Virtually nothing of interest produced outside the big names such as Olivia.

Trading Cards
The trading cards market is generally very strong but there seems to be very few signed and numbered ones around. Any information would be greatly appreciated.

Comics
There are still very few companies producing truly worthwhile signed editions. However, any Cry For Dawn signed and numbered limited editions are on fire!

General rule of thumb – buy only what you really like. See you next time.

GRAPHITTI EDITIONS

Number/Title		Print Run	Value
1.	THE ROCKETEER	1,000	£175.00
2.	NEXUS	1,000	£ 90.00
3.	ELRIC OF MELNIBONE	2,000	£ 35.00
4.	GRENDEL: DEVIL BY THE DEED	2,000	£150.00
5.	THE RETURN OF MR. X	1,500	£ 35.00
6.	ELRIC: SAILOR ON THE SEAS OF FATE	1,800	£ 35.00
7.	AMERICAN FLAGG! SOUTHERN COMFORT	2,000	£ 35.00
8.	RIO	1,500	£ 25.00
9.	NIGHT AND THE ENEMY	1,500	£ 25.00
10.	AMERICAN FLAGG! HARD TIMES	1,800	£ 30.00
11.	GRENDEL: DEVIL'S LEGACY	2,000	£ 60.00
12.	MOEBIUS 1	1,500	£ 35.00
13.	MOEBIUS 2	1,500	£ 35.00
14.	MOEBIUS 3	1,500	£ 45.00
15.	SOMEPLACE STRANGE	1,200	£ 30.00
16.	ELEKTRA ASSASSIN	2,000	£ 75.00
17.	AMERICAN FLAGG! STATE OF THE UNION	1,800	£ 35.00
18.	MOONSHADOW	1,200	£ 75.00
19.	GRENDEL: THE DEVIL INSIDE	1,200	£ 75.00
20.	THE GROO CHRONICLES	1,500	£ 35.00
21.	HELLRAISER 1	1,500	£ 30.00
	HELLRAISER 1	500	£ 55.00
22.	MOEBIUS 4: BLUEBERRY	1,500	£ 35.00
23.	MOEBIUS 5: BLUEBERRY	1,500	£ 35.00
24.	MOEBIUS 6: YOUNG BLUEBERRY	1,500	£ 35.00

25.	MARSHALL LAW	1,500	£ 35.00
26.	PLASTIC FORKS	1,200	£ 35.00
27.	STRANGE ADVENTURES		
	(due for release late Oct. 1994)		
28.	MELTDOWN: HAVOC AND WOLVERINE	2,000	£ 35.00
29.	ELEKTRA LIVES AGAIN	2,500	£ 30.00
30.	STRAY TOASTERS (not yet released)		
31.	ELRIC: THE WEIRD OF THE WHITE WOLF	1,200	£ 35.00
32.	HELLRAISER II	1,500	£ 30.00
	HELLRAISER II	500	£ 55.00
33.	AKIRA BOOK 1 (not signed)	1,500	£ 35.00
34.	THE CROW		
	(just out at time of going to press. Details to follow)		
35.	MOEBIUS 7	1,500	£ 30.00
36.	MOEBIUS 8	1,500	£ 35.00
37.	MOEBIUS 9	1,500	£ 35.00
38.	HELLRAISER III	1,000	£ 30.00
	HELLRAISER III	500	£ 55.00
39.	AKIRA BOOK 2 (not signed)	1,500	£ 35.00
40.	CHAOS & METALLIC DREAMS (working title)		
	(not yet released)		
41.	HELLRAISER IV		
	(may be cancelled)		
42.	AKIRA BOOK 3 (not signed)	1,500	£ 35.00
NN	MYTHOLOGY OF AN ABANDONED CITY	500	£ 40.00
44.	AKIRA BOOK 4 (not signed)	1,500	£ 35.00
45.	AKIRA BOOK 5 (not signed)	1.500	£35.00
46.	AKIRA BOOK 6 (not signed)		
	(was due for release Summer 1994)		
47.	MARVELS	8,500	£40.00
48.	MADMAN (Two Volumes, slipcased)	1,500	£60.00
49.	MOEBIUS 10 (no release date as yet)		

NOTES ON THE GRAPHITTI SECTION

1) All of the Hellraiser volumes have two versions. Version 1 is signed by various creators who worked on the series and is limited to 1,500 copies (except Volume III which is 1,000 copies). Version 2 is signed by various of the creators plus Clive Barker. It is leather-bound and is limited to 500 copies.

2) Although all volumes of Akira are officially listed as unsigned, there are very limited quantities (between 12 and 15 copies) of Books 1-3 which are signed. Apparently Otomo did not want to get involved in the "commercialism" of signing all the copies.

3) Strange Adventures was delayed owing to the death of Harvey Kurtzman and although he has not signed all the copies, Graphitti say that he has signed "enough" and it should have been released in late 1994.

4) Stray Toasters has been indefinitely delayed and, as yet, no release date has been announced.

5) Graphitti's first ever edition The Rocketeer had a "sub-set"; as well as the books numbered 1 - 1,000 there were 26 additional copies numbered A - Z. These were created as artists' proofs and gifts for people involved in the production of the book.

6) Mythology of an Abandoned City is Graphitti's 43rd edition, however the number does not actually appear anywhere in the book. It is a boxed set which, as well as containing the book, comes with a CD featuring music composed by artist Jon J. Muth to accompany the story.

GRAPHITTI/DC CO-PRODUCTIONS

Number/Title	Print Run	Value
(NN) BATMAN: THE DARK KNIGHT RETURNS	4,000	£225.00

(NN) HISTORY OF THE DC UNIVERSE	2,000	£ 25.00
(NN) ENEMY ACE: WAR IDYLL	1,000	£ 50.00

NOTES ON THE GRAPHITTI/DC SECTION

1) Although the plates in Enemy Ace: War Idyll are numbered to 2,000 a last minute decision was taken to produce only 1,000 copies. It is also of note that the volume itself is designed to be a replica of the diary kept by the main character of the story.

2) Batman: The Dark Knight Returns also has a "sub-set" which again is numbered A – Z. These copies are additionally signed by Lynn Varley and Klaus Janson.

GRAPHITTI/IMAGE CO-PRODUCTIONS

Number/Title	Print Run	Value
1. SHADOWHAWK	5,000	£ 45.00
2. SAVAGE DRAGON	5,000	£ 45.00

NOTES ON THE GRAPHITTI/IMAGE SECTION

1) Owing to the splintered nature of the various studios publishing under the Image Comics banner, there is no "official" agreement between the two companies. It does however seem likely that there will be more editions following the two already released.

DARK HORSE EDITIONS

Title	Print Run	Value
ALIENS: VOLUME 1 (Slipcase)	1,500	£100.00
ALIENS: VOLUME 2	2,500	£ 45.00
ALIENS: EARTH WAR	2,000	£ 30.00
ALIENS Vs. PREDATOR (Slipcase)	1,000	£ 55.00
BOOK OF THE NIGHT (Slipcase)	500	£ 40.00
CONCRETE: SHORT STORIES	2,000	£ 30.00
DON MARTIN'S DROLL BOOK	500	£ 40.00
PREDATOR: VOLUME 1	2,500	£ 40.00
SIN CITY (Slipcase)	1,000	£ 60.00
STAR WARS: DARK EMPIRE (Slipcase)	1,000	£105.00
TERMINATOR: TEMPEST (Slipcase)	1,500	£ 50.00
THE COMPLETE ALIENS	500	£200.00
HELLBOY	2,000	£75.00
HARD BOILED	2,000	£80.00
SIN CITY (Big Fat Kill and A Dame To Kill For)	1,000	£75.00
GIVE ME LIBERTY	2,000	£80.00
ALIENS: TRIBES	1,200	£50.00

ECLIPSE EDITIONS

Title	Print Run	Value
ALEX TOTH'S ZORRO	350	£ 50.00
APPLESEED BOOK 1: THE PROMETHEAN CHALLENGE	230	£ 50.00
APPLESEED BOOK 2: PROMETHEUS UNBOUND	300	£ 40.00
APPLESEED BOOK 3: THE SCALES OF PROMETHEUS	300	£ 40.00
ARIANE AND BLUEBEARD	300	£ 25.00
BOB KANE'S BATMAN	2,500	£ 80.00
CLIVE BARKER, ILLUSTRATOR	1,000	£ 40.00
DIRTY PAIR: BIOHAZARDS	850	£ 35.00
DIRTY PAIR: DANGEROUS ACQUAINTANCES	850	£ 35.00

Title	Print Run	Value
DR. WATCHSTOP: ADVENTURES IN TIME & SPACE	350	£ 25.00
FUN WITH REID FLEMING	300	£ 55.00
THE HOBBIT	600	£100.00
JACK KIRBY TREASURY VOLUME 2	500	£ 60.00
LARRY MARDER'S BEANWORLD	300	£ 25.00
OPERA	300	£ 25.00
PANDEMONIUM	350	£ 20.00
PIGEONS FROM HELL	1,000	£ 25.00
SABRE (10TH ANNIVERSARY EDITION)	500	£ 30.00
THE SACRED AND THE PROFANE	500	£ 30.00
SCOUT: THE FOUR MONSTERS	1,750	£ 30.00
SCOUT: MOUNT FIRE	750	£ 30.00
SILVERHEELS	750	£ 25.00
THE SISTERHOOD OF STEEL	300	£ 20.00
SOMERSET HOLMES	750	£ 25.00
SWORDSMEN AND SAURIANS	175	£200.00
TECUMSEH!	250	£ 40.00
TOADSWART D'AMPLESTONE	250	£ 20.00
VALKYRIE: PRISONER OF THE PAST	250	£ 20.00
VALKYRIE: THE RETURN OF THE VALKYRIE	250	£ 20.00
ZOT!	450	£ 30.00

NOTES ON THE ECLIPSE SECTION

1) Some of the above limitations have yet to be verified so the above list should not be taken as 100% accurate. The majority of Eclipse's signed editions are clothbound.
2) Alex Toth's Zorro is a two volume set in one slipcase.
3) The Hobbit volume comes boxed.

KITCHEN SINK EDITIONS

Title	Print Run	Value
A CONTRACT WITH GOD (Eisner. 1st print)	600	£ 50.00
A CONTRACT WITH GOD (2nd Print)	600	£ 25.00
A LIFE FORCE (Eisner)	1,250	£ 20.00
BILL SIENKIEWICZ SKETCHBOOK	2,000	£ 25.00
CADILLACS AND DINOSAURS	1,500	£ 30.00
CITY PEOPLE (Eisner)	1,500	£ 20.00
CURSE OF THE MOLEMEN	1,000	£ 20.00
DINOSAUR SHAMEN	1,500	£ 20.00
DREAMER (Eisner)	750	£ 20.00
FLASH GORDON	750	£ 35.00
FROM AARGH TO ZAP	1,250	£ 40.00
HYPNOTIC TALES	250	£ 30.00
SPIRIT CASEBOOK (Eisner)	1,750	£ 25.00
STEVE RUDE SKETCHBOOK	1,200	£ 30.00
THE ART OF WILL EISNER	1,000	£ 40.00
THE BUILDING (Eisner)	750	£ 25.00
THE CITY (Eisner)	600	£ 30.00
THE HEART OF THE STORM (Eisner)	900	£ 25.00
WILL EISNER READER	600	£ 25.00
WILL EISNER SKETCHBOOK	1,000	£30.00

NOTES ON KITCHEN SINK SECTION

1) As can be seen from the above Kitchen Sink's limited editions have concentrated on the talents of Will Eisner. Of the 19 books listed above, 11 of them are Eisner editions.

EDITIONS BY OTHER COMPANIES

Title	Print Run	Publisher	Value
ART OF JACK DAVIS	750	Starburst	£ 26.00
ART OF JACK KIRBY	1,000	Blue Rose Press	£ 75.00
ART OF MOEBIUS	100	Byron Press	£ 85.00
BERNIE WRIGHTSON: A LOOK BACK			
(Original)	250	Land of Enchantment	£350.00
(Reprint)	250	Land of Enchantment	£195.00
[both the above with slipcase]			
BRAT PACK	1,000	King Hell/Tundra	£ 35.00
COMICS AND STORIES (Slipcase)	750	?	£ 65.00
COMPLETE ELFQUEST (Pini)	1,000	Warp Graphics	£150.00
COMPLETE ROBERT CRUMB #1-9	400	Fantagraphics	£ 55.00
COMPLETE STAR WARS			
(Williamson/Goodwin)	2,500	Russ Cochran	£140.00
CYCLE OF THE WEREWOLF	150	?	£300.00
DANCING NEKKID WITH ANGELS (Cruse)	1,250	?	£ 25.00
DONALD DUCK: 50 YEARS OF			
HAPPY FRUSTRATION	700	3 Ducks	£ 80.00
DRACULA (J.J. Muth)	1,000	NBM	£ 40.00
DRAWINGS & MONOTYPES			
(Kent Williams)	1,000	Tundra	£ 35.00
E. R. BURROUGHS LIBRARY			
OF ILLUSTRATION	2,000	Russ Cochran	£250.00
[above edition with slipcase]			
ELFQUEST #1 (Pini)	1,500	Warp Graphics	£ 80.00
ELFQUEST #2-4 (Pini)	1,500	Warp Graphics	£ 45.00
THE FINE ART OF WALT DISNEY'S			
DONALD DUCK (Barks)	1,850	Another Rainbow	£1000.00
[half the print run were burgundy bound, half were blue bound]			
[above edition with slipcase]			
FOEMINA (Manara)	1,200	Glittering Images	£ 95.00
FOREVER WAR #1,2,3 (Slipcase)			
(Marvano)	300	NBM	£100.00
FRANKENSTEIN (Wrightson/King)	250	?	£300.00
FUTURE DAY (Gene Day)	530	?	£ 25.00
GINGER FOX (O'Connell)	1,200	Comico	£ 25.00
GOLDEN AGE OF TARZAN (Hogarth)	2,000	Chelsea House	£180.00
HERNANDEZ BROTHERS			
SKETCHBOOK #1	750	Fantagraphics	£ 35.00
HERNANDEZ BROTHERS			
SKETCHBOOK #2	1,000	Fantagraphics	£ 25.00
HYPNOTIC TALES	250	?	£ 30.00
ILLUSTRATED HARLAN ELLISON	3,000	?	£ 35.00
INDIAN SUMMER (Manara)	500	Catalan	£ 50.00
JUST TEASING (Dave Stevens)	1,500	?	£ 50.00
LAW & CHAOS (Pini)	1,000	Warp Graphics	£ 30.00
LIGHTSHIP (Jim Burns)	250	?	£ 25.00
LORD OF THE RINGS (1 volume)	250	Unwin/Allen	£195.00
LORD OF THE RINGS (3 volume set)	250	Unwin/Allen	£250.00
LOVE & ROCKETS Volumes 1-3			
(1st print) each	400	Fantagraphics	£ 50.00
(2nd print) each	600	Fantagraphics	£ 30.00
Volumes 4-8 each	600	Fantagraphics	£ 40.00
MAGE VOLUME #1	1,500	Donning	£100.00
MAGE VOLUME #2	1,500	Donning	£ 60.00
MAGE VOLUME #3	1,500	Donning	£ 60.00
[the above three volumes with slipcase]			
MAUS 1,2 (Slipcase) (Spiegelman)	300	Pantheon	£150.00
MELTING POT	500	?	£35.00
METROPOLIS (Kaluta)	1,000	Donning	£ 40.00

MICKEY MOUSE IN COLOUR			
(Barks and Gottfredson)	2,500	Another Rainbow	£175.00
MOCKBA (Moebius)	1,500	Stardom	£ 60.00
NO MAN'S LAND	500	Tundra	£ 40.00
PHOTO JOURNAL GUIDE TO COMICS			
Vol 1,2 each	900	Gerber	£145.00
Vol 3,4 each	2,500	Gerber	£ 75.00
PRIME	5,000	Malibu	£30.00
QUADRANT	1,000	Malibu Graphics	£ 40.00
RAY BRADBURY CHRONICLES			
Vol 1-5 each	1,200	NBM	£ 35.00
REAPER OF LOVE (Wrightson)	1,200	Fantagraphics	£ 30.00
ROBERT CRUMB SKETCHBOOK #1	400	Fantagraphics	£ 55.00
ROBERT CRUMB SKETCHBOOK #2	400	Fantagraphics	£ 55.00
ROBERT CRUMB SKETCHBOOK #3	400	Fantagraphics	£ 55.00
SATAN'S TEARS	1,000	?	£ 30.00
SPACEHAWK	250	Archival	£ 40.00
THIEF OF BAGDAD (Russell)	1,000	Donning	£ 35.00
UNCLE SCROOGE McDUCK (Barks)	5,000	Celestial Arts	£250.00
VAMPIRE LESTAT	2,000	Innovation	£ 40.00
VIAMOUR (Moebius)	200	L'Atelier	£200.00

NOTES ON OTHER COMPANIES SECTION

1) The Complete Robert Crumb is an on-going series and the ten volumes published so far cover his work up to the mid 1970s.

2) The remarkable thing about the Ray Bradbury Chronicles is that as well as being signed by Mr. Bradbury himself, barring death, the five volumes are each signed by every creator who ever worked on them.

3) No Man's Land is a companion volume to Graphitti's Enemy Ace book, containing the research, background material and sketches produced by writer/artist George Pratt in the making of Enemy Ace: War Idyll.

4) There are two different signed and numbered editions of Quadrant.

5) Geof Darrow's Comics & Stories is a French edition and there is very little text. It also contains a magazine.

SIGNED AND NUMBERED LIMITED EDITION TRADE PAPERBACKS

Title	Print run	Publisher	Value
CEREBUS: FLIGHT	?	Aardvark	£ 20.00
CEREBUS: JAKA'S STORY	435	Aardvark	£ 20.00
CEREBUS: MOTHERS AND DAUGHTERS I	?	Aardvark	£ 17.00
CEREBUS: MOTHERS AND DAUGHTERS II	?	Aardvark	£ 17.00
FROM THE DARKNESS	300	Malibu Graphics	£ 20.00
SABRE	?	Eclipse	£ 15.00

SIGNED AND NUMBERED LIMITED EDITION TRADING CARDS

Title	Print run	Publisher	Value
FAUST (Vigil & Quinn) Gold Hologram	1,000	Rebel Studios	£ 20.00

SIGNED AND NUMBERED LIMITED EDITION PRINTS

Title	Print run	Value
A BAD NIGHT FOR NINJAS (2 prints - Jim Lee)	2,500	£ 75.00
ALIEN (John Bolton)	1,500	£ 75.00
ALIEN VS. PREDATOR (Dave Dorman)	1,500	£ 75.00
ANGEL (Bill Sienkiewicz)	201	£135.00

Title	Print run	Value
AVIATOR (Moebius)	150	£125.00
BETTY BATH (Dave Stevens)	395	£170.00
BLIND NARCISSUS (Jones)	1,000	£200.00
DARK MISTS (Richard Corben)	200	£ 20.00
DEVIL'S FOOD (Olivia)	250	£595.00
DINOSAUR (Mark Schultz)	250	£125.00
DOC SAVAGE: SQUEAKING GOBLIN (Bama)	150	£ 60.00
WORLD'S FAIR GOBLIN (Bama)	150	£ 60.00
PIRATE OF THE PACIFIC (Bama)	150	£ 60.00
SEA ANGEL (Bama)	150	£ 60.00
MYSTIC MULLAH (Bama)	150	£ 60.00
RED SNOW (Bama)	150	£ 60.00
DRACULA (Jon J. Muth)	200	£ 75.00
DRAGON SLAYER (Jones)	275	£ 45.00
DREAMS OF AN ANCIENT WORLD (Corben)	500	£ 30.00
FRANKENSTEIN 1. THE MONSTER (Wrightson)	300	£ 20.00
FRANKENSTEIN 2. THE BED (Wrightson)	300	£ 20.00
FRANKENSTEIN 3. THE BOAT (Wrightson)	300	£ 20.00
FRANKENSTEIN 4. THE WINDOW (Wrightson)	300	£ 20.00
FRANKENSTEIN 5. THE RAIN (Wrightson)	300	£ 20.00
FRANKENSTEIN 6. THE CLIFF (Wrightson)	300	£ 20.00
FRANKENSTEIN Embossed 1 (Wrightson)	275	£ 45.00
FRANKENSTEIN Embossed 2 (Wrightson)	275	£ 45.00
FREDER'S DREAMS (Mike Kaluta)	450	£ 40.00
GREEN HORNET (Jim Steranko)	1,500	£ 55.00
GRENDEL: WAR CHILD (Matt Wagner)	1,000	£ 30.00
HARD BOILED 1 (Darrow, Miller, Legris)	100	£ 55.00
HARD BOILED 2 (Darrow, Miller)	400	£ 95.00
KING KONG (Dave Stevens)	1,000	£ 85.00
LABYRINTH (Richard Corben)	250	£ 30.00
LADIES AND GENTLEMEN...MIMI RODAN (Dave Stevens)	850	£ 75.00
LA FEMME ET FELINE (Olivia)	40	£150.00
MAD (Harvey Kurtzman)	750	£195.00
MITRAS (Barry Windsor Smith)	350	£130.00
MIDNIGHT GROVE (Charles Vess)	75	£ 75.00
MIDNIGHT READER (Howard Chaykin)	325	£ 45.00
MEMENTOS (Bernie Wrightson)	600	£ 40.00
MISTER X (Dean Motter)	295	£ 55.00
NIMUE THE ENCHANTRESS (B. Windsor Smith)	100	£300.00
ODE TO A SCOTTISH PRAYER (Wrightson)	450	£ 50.00
PHARAGONESIA (Moebius)	50	£ 75.00
PYSCHE (Barry Windsor Smith)	1,000	£ 75.00
PURRFECT MEMORIES (Spiderman, 2 prints.Charles Vess)	2,500	£ 55.00
RETURN OF VALKYRIE (Jim Steranko)	1,500	£ 45.00
RUINS (George Pratt)	300	£ 20.00
SCORCHER (Dave Stevens)	750	£ 95.00
SIBYL (Barry Windsor Smith)	850	£ 95.00
SMOOTHIES (Olivia)	255	£350.00
SONNET (Jon J. Muth)	200	£ 50.00
STEALER OF SOULS (Mike Kaluta)	300	£ 40.00
STREET CASINO (Will Eisner)	800	£ 35.00
THE ACTRESS AND THE BISHOP (B. Bolland)	500	£ 65.00
THE BOOK OF SAMOTHRACE (B.W. Smith)	1,000	£ 65.00
THE CRYSTAL GATE (Moebius)	300	£125.00
THE DESIRE (Moebius)	150	£ 75.00
THE EMISSARY (Mike Kaluta)	100	£ 80.00
THE GHOUL (Edwards)	990	£ 20.00
THE GUN (Moebius)	200	£ 60.00
THE LAST ATLANTEAN (B. Windsor Smith)	960	£ 40.00
THE LATE TRAIN (Will Eisner)	800	£ 35.00
THE MAMMOTH (Arthur Suydam)	450	£ 50.00
THE SHADOW ABLAZE (Mike Kaluta)	2,500	£ 35.00
THE STREET (Moebius, Darrow)	100	£100.00

THE UNDYING WIZARD (Jones)	275	£ 45.00
THE VOLCANO (Moebius)	200	£ 85.00
THREE WOMEN (Dave Stevens)	850	£ 80.00
TURF WAR (Will Eisner)	800	£ 35.00
VAMPIRELLA (Dave Stevens)	850	£ 85.00
VIRTUE TRIUMPHANT (John Bolton)	500	£ 20.00
WEREWOLF (John Bolton)	1,000	£ 20.00
WHISPER (Dave McKean)	201	£135.00
WIZARD'S DREAMS (Richard Corben)	500	£ 25.00
YAQUI (Moebius)	175	£ 90.00

NOTES ON THE PRINTS SECTION

1) Purrfect Memories are two complimentary prints featuring Spiderman and Black Cat. There are 2,500 copies of each print but the value as listed is for the set of two.

2) A Bad Night for Ninjas is also a two print set, this time featuring Punisher and Wolverine. There are 2,500 copies of each print but the value as listed is for the set of two.

SIGNED AND NUMBERED LIMITED PORTFOLIOS

Title	Plates	Print Run	Value
BLUEBERRY PORTFOLIO (Moebius)	15 (c)	800	£ 75.00
BRIAN BOLLAND PORTFOLIO	6 (b&w)	666	£ 35.00
CITY OF FIRE (Moebius/Darrow)	11 (c)	950	£300.00
CRY FOR DAWN 1 (Linsner)	8 (b&w)	1,500	£ 40.00
EDGAR ALLEN POE (Wrightson)	8 (c)	2,000	£ 50.00
FANTASTIC ISLANDS (B.W. Smith)	4 (b&w)	1,000	£ 85.00
FRANKENSTEIN (Wrightson)	6 (b&w)	1,000	£100.00
FRANKENSTEIN II (Wrightson)	6 (b&w)	2,000	£ 60.00
FRANKENSTEIN III	6 (b&w)	1,000	£ 50.00
INDIAN SUMMER (Milo Manara)	2 (c)	999	£165.00
JEFF JONES FANTASY COLLECTION	8 (c)	275	£ 55.00
JOHN BOLTON PORTFOLIO	6 (b&w)	888	£ 20.00
KUBLA KHAN (Frank Frazetta)	5 (b&w)	1,500	£ 95.00
PUNISHER PORTFOLIO 1 (Zeck)	6 (b&w)	600	£ 85.00
PUNISHER PORTFOLIO 2 (Zeck)	6 (b&w)	600	£ 25.00
ROBERT E. HOWARD (B.W.S)	5 (c)	920	£125.00
SANDRA PORTFOLIO (Milo Manara)	8 (c)	600	£ 95.00
SIBYLA (Barry Windsor Smith)	5 (c)	1,000	£ 75.00
STARSTRUCK PORTFOLIO (Kaluta)	6 (b&w)	1,000	£ 20.00
THE CITY PORTFOLIO (Eisner)	6 (t/t)	1,200	£ 55.00
DRAWINGS OF BARRY WINDSOR SMITH	8 (b&w)	750	£ 95.00
THE FOUR AGES (B. Windsor Smith)	4 (b/i)	1,000	£ 85.00
THE PIN-UP COLLECTION (Olivia)	12 (c)	4,000	£200.00
THE SPIRIT PORTFOLIO (Eisner)	11 (c)	1,500	£ 95.00
THE STAND PORTFOLIO (Wrightson)	12 (b&w)	1,200	£ 50.00
TOUR DU MONDE (Moebius)	48 (c)	300	£235.00
TUPENNY CONAN (B.W. Smith)	6 (b&w)	1,000	£175.00
WATCHMEN (Gibbons, Moore)	12 (c)	2,000	£ 75.00
WOMEN OF THE AGES (Frazetta)	6 (b&w)	1,500	£ 95.00
7 WONDERS OF THE ANCIENT WORLD(Krenkel)	7 (c)	1,000	£ 60.00

NOTES ON THE PORTFOLIO SECTION

KEY: (c) colour (b&w) black and white (b/i) black on ivory (t/t) two tone

1) Of the 4,000 copies of Olivia's The Pin Up Collection, half were sold to Japan leaving only 2,000 copies for Europe and the U.S.A.
2) Tour Du Monde comes in a deluxe rubber-covered folder.

3) The five plates in the Robert E. Howard Portfolio feature: Conan, Toth Amon, Red Sonja, Bran Mak Morn and Soloman Kane.
4) The Stand Portfolio comes in a black and gold embossed folder and the Drawings of Barry Windsor Smith comes in a deluxe box folder.
5) Both of the Punisher Portfolios are French editions, one of which was later reprinted by Marvel in an unsigned, colour format.
6) Many of the above portfolios come in either an illustrated folder or an illustrated envelope. As previously stated, the above list covers only a fraction of the signed and numbered portfolios produced.
7) The City of Fire Portfolio is one of the most important portfolios of the 1980s. It comes in a hardcover, deluxe box folder which is embossed in yellow and red.

SIGNED AND NUMBERED LIMITED EDITION COMICS

Title/Number	Print Run	Publisher	Value
ACHILLES STORM #4	999	Aja Blue	£ 4.95
CRY FOR DAWN #4	1,500	C.F.D.	£ 25.00
CRY FOR DAWN #5	1,500	C.F.D	£ 25.00
CRY FOR DAWN #6	1,500	C.F.D	£ 25.00
CRY FOR DAWN #7	2,000	C.F.D	£ 20.00
CRY FOR DAWN #8	2,000	C.F.D.	£ 30.00
CRY FOR DAWN #9	2,000	C.F.D.	£ 20.00
DAWN #1 (Look Sharp)	1,000	Sirius	£25.00
DAWN #1 (White Trash)	1,000	Sirius	£25.00
DAWN #2	5,000	Sirius	£25.00
DAWN #3	1,500	Sirius	£25.00
DRAMA #1	2,000	Sirius	£25.00
EO #1	2,000	Rebel Studios	£ 40.00
FAUST #1	1,900	Northstar	£ 60.00
FAUST #6	1,900	Northstar	£ 50.00
THE MAXX ASHCAN #1	?	Image	£ 10.00
NIGHT VISIONS #1	3,000	Rebel Studios	£ 3.95
NORTHSTAR #1	1,000	Northstar	£ 70.00
OMEGA #1	1,900	Northstar	£ 50.00
PITT ASHCAN #1	5,500	Image	£ 10.00
PITT ASHCAN OLIVE #2	1,800	Image	£ 12.95
PITT ASHCAN BLACK #2	1,800	Image	£ 10.00
PITT ASHCAN PLATINUM #2	1,800	Image	£ 10.00
VAMPIRE LESTAT #1-12	1,000	Innovation	£ 45.00

NOTES ON THE COMICS SECTION

1) Cry for Dawn #8 is the "fan club" edition, available only through the fan club and almost impossible to find in this country. Cry for Dawn #6 is the only issue of the title, in both the regular and signed & numbered editions not to feature Dawn on the cover.

2) Copies of Omega #1 were recalled and destroyed by Northstar following threatened legal action by Marvel Comics over copyright infringement. The initial print run was 1,900 but it is unknown how many of these survived. The comic eventually reappeared as The Omen.

3) All of the Image ashcans are "mini" comics with coloured card covers and black and white interiors.

4) The twelve issues of Vampire Lestat come in a slipcase which also contains The Vampiré Companion #1 and 2.

5) Dawn is in a signed envelope with a sketch on it. Both editions of Dawn #1 are signed on certificates but have totally new covers.

EARLY WORKS OF ARTISTS

Below is a Work-in-progress list of the early works of 16 of the hottest artists currently working in the comics industry. The first five entries for all the artists have been placed in chronological order with the remaining entries in ALPHABETICAL ORDER ONLY. When time permits all will be put into order to illustrate their developing technique.

1 JOHN BYRNE

#	Title	Issue
1	**FLINTSTONES 2nd series ....37 1st Professional Work**	
2	**E-MAN 1st series 6,7**	
3	**DRACULA GIANT SIZE ....5 1st Work for Marvel**	
4	**E-MAN 1st series 9**	
5	**DOOMSDAY PLUS ONE 1**	
6	ACTION COMICS	584-600
7	ALPHA FLIGHT	1-28
8	ART OF JOHN BYRNE	nn
9	ATOM, POWER OF THE	6
10	AVENGERS, THE	164-166,181-191,233
11	AVENGERS ANNUAL, THE	13 (inks)
12	BATMAN	400 (1 page only)
13	BATMAN 3-D GRAPHIC ALBUM	nn
14	BATMAN: UNTOLD LEGEND OF THE	1
15	BIG BYRNE BOOK	nn
16	BIZZARE ADVENTURES	31
17	CAPTAIN AMERICA	247-255,350
18	CHRISTMAS WITH THE SUPER-HEROES	2
19	CHAMPIONS, THE	11-15, 17 (inks)
20	CHARLTON BULLSEYE	1,2,4,5
21	CLASSIC X-MEN	15-47
22	CRAZY 2nd series	88
23	CRITICAL ERROR	1
24	DAREDEVIL	138
25	DARK HORSE PRESENTS	54-57
26	DANGER UNLIMITED	1-4
27	DOOMSDAY PLUS ONE	2-12
28	DOOMSDAY SQUAD	1-7
29	E-MAN 1st series	10
30	E-MAN 2nd series	1 (1 page Byrne)
31	EMERGENCY 2nd series	1
32	FANTASTIC FOUR	209-218,220,221,232-293,358 (Pin-up)
33	FANTASTIC FOUR ANNUAL	17-19
34	FANTASTIC FOUR ROAST	1
35	FANTASTIC FOUR SPECIAL EDITION	1
36	FLINTSTONES 2nd series	42
37	GHOST RIDER 1st series	20
38	GREEN LANTERN CORPS ANNUAL	3
39	GREEN LANTERN: GANTHET'S TALE	1
40	HERBIE 2nd series	2-5
41	HEROES FOR HOPE STARRING THE X-MEN	nn
42	HOT AND COLD HEROES	1
43	HOWARD THE DUCK 2nd series	7 (1 page Byrne)
44	HULK 2nd series ....314-319,393-contains Byrne Hulk in flashback	
45	HULK ANNUAL 2nd series	7
46	INDIANA JONES, FURTHER ADVENTURES OF	1,2
47	IRON FIST	1-15
48	IRON MAN	118
49	IRON MAN ANNUAL	10 (Pin-up)
50	JOHN BYRNE'S 2112 GRAPHIC NOVEL	nn
51	JUDGE DREDD'S CRIME FILES	1
52	LEGENDS (limited series)	1-6
53	MAN OF STEEL	1-6
54	MARVEL CHILLERS	6
55	MARVEL COMICS PRESENTS	18,79
56	MARVEL FANFARE	29,45(Pin up),48
57	MARVEL PREMIERE	25,47,48
58	MARVEL PREVIEW	11
59	MARVEL SAGA, THE	3
60	MARVEL TALES	193-198,201-208
61	MARVEL TEAM UP	53-55,59-70,75,79,100
62	MARVEL TWO-IN-ONE	43,50,53-55
63	MARVEL YEAR IN REVIEW	2
64	NAMOR, THE SUB-MARINER	1-25
65	NEW MUTANTS	75
66	NEW TEEN TITANS ANNUAL 2nd series	2
67	NEXT MEN	0 -present
68	OMAC 2nd series	1-4
69	OUTSIDERS, THE	11
70	PHOENIX - THE UNTOLD STORY	1
71	POWERMAN	48-50
72	PREVIEWS 3rd series	1 -present
73	ROG 2000, THE COMPLETE	nn
74	ROM	74 (inks)
75	SAN DIEGO CONVENTION COMIC ART	1992 nn
76	SECRET ORIGINS ANNUAL	1
77	SHE HULK, THE SENSATION	1-8,31-46,48-50
78	SHE HULK TRADE PAPERBACK	nn
79	SILVER SURFER 2nd series	1
80	SPACE 1999	3-7
81	SPECTACULAR SPIDERMAN	58
82	SPIDERMAN, THE AMAZING	189,190,206
83	SPIDERMAN, THE AMAZING ANNUAL	13
84	SPIRIT MAGAZINE, THE	30
85	STAR BRAND, THE	10-19
86	STARLORD, THE SPECIAL EDITION	1
87	SUPERMAN 1st series	400 (1 page only)
88	SUPERMAN 2nd series	1-17,19-22,50 (Co-artist)
89	SUPERMAN ANNUAL 2nd series	2
90	SUPERMAN ANNUAL, THE ADVENTURES OF	2
91	SUPER VILLAIN CLASSICS	1
92	THING, THE	2 (inks),7
93	WEST COAST AVENGERS	42-57

THE HISTORICAL AGES OF COMIC BOOKS

With the wide variety of comics available, this Guide has a listing that is necessarily selective in its starting points as collecting markets determine the viability of exactly what to spend time according values to. Throughout the American comics section, reference is made to titles and comics outside the listing scope of this book for the time being, particularly those comics of the Golden Age which have a vastly greater functioning market in America than in this country. It is hoped that in the not too distant future a complete main title Golden Age listing will be possible. For a more complete listing of Golden Age material, we recommend the Overstreet Guide currently in its 26th year.

A S WITH MOST OTHER HISTORICAL LEISURE INTEREST HOBBIES, comic book collecting has its own set of generally accepted ages that separate different groups of comics to give some sort of historical perspective. British comics are generally referred to in time spans governed by actual dates and/or decades which need little explanation of the actual terms involved. Victorian, Edwardian, Twenties, Pre-War, War, Post-War, Fifties, Sixties, Seventies, Eighties and Nineties mean what they say though it is hoped to explore what exactly appeared when in a future article, as there are certain periods which are more complex than others. But American comic books have their own set of distinctive terms and phrases which are used in preference to simply naming the decade.

THESE HISTORICAL AGES ARE BY NO MEANS SET IN STONE AND INDEED VERY OFTEN OVERLAP.

Significant dates prior to the establishment of the American comic book are as follows:

1876 – Humorous story and political cartoon magazines "Puck" and "Judge" appear.

1895 – The Yellow Kid by R.F. Outcault appeared as a regular cartoon in the New York Sunday World and The Sunday Journal, reprinted as a collection of strips in 1897.

1911 – The Chicago American newspaper issues a number of books containing reprints of Sunday newspaper cartoon characters such as Mutt and Jeff. The print run was about 50,000.

1929 – The Dell Publishing Company issues a newspaper size collection of comic and cartoon strips called "The Funnies", reprinting material from what was affectionately known as The Funny Pages being a specific section inside the Sunday papers of the 1920s. "The Funnies" ran for 13 issues and most of the strips were four-colour rather than black and white or red on white.

1933 – Small, squat, hardcover books appeared called Big Little Books featuring characters from The Funny Pages newspaper sections and more significantly from film and film serials such as Tarzan and Flash Gordon. The format consisted of a full page of text next to a full page illustration alternating throughout the entire book.

At this point the established terms of American comic book collecting come into play.

Thus for the purposes of easy classification, the history and evolution of American comic books from 1933 on may be broken down into these ages:

1933-1937 THE PRE GOLDEN AGE

Sometimes referred to as the "antediluvian" era, it dates from the first recognisable comic book, **Funnies on Parade**. This was given away as a sales or radio premium. **Famous Funnies #1** was the first comic book to be sold on the news-stands in the early part of 1934. It sold for 10 cents and had 100 pages of strips, puzzles and games. Only by issue #7 did it make money for the Dell Publishing Company and thus the comic book industry had begun. This age is characterised by non-costumed heroes, usually police, secret agents and adventurers towards the latter half of the age with funny animals and slapstick characters in the earlier part. 1935 saw a number of other companies and products come to prominence: King Comics produced by King Features, Tip Top Comics by United Features and Popular Comics by M.C. Gaines to name three of the most influential. 1936/37 saw the rise of Centaur Comics which produced Funny Picture Stories and Detective Picture Stories. The publishing group went on to produce much super-hero material in the 1940's as Quality Comics.

One publisher in particular went on to become the most well established.

In February 1935, **New Fun #1** was produced by Donenfield and Co. in a format measuring 10" x 12", larger than the more standard format that the company went on to produce in comics like NEW FUN, MORE FUN, ADVENTURE and DETECTIVE COMICS, the latter from which the renamed National Periodical Publications took their modern intials DC Comics that today publish two of the most well-known comic book characters, Superman and Batman. Most of these comics are very scarce and very rare in the U.K. and very rare worldwide in anything approaching high grade condition. It is thought that less than 1% of comics published in this age remain today in any condition.

The rarest published comics are thought to be **New Fun #2** (March 1935) which was the 2nd DC comic published and **New (Adventure) Comics #7** (February 1937) also from DC. There may be fewer 6 copies in existence though these figures are difficult to verify. The most valuable comic from this period is **Detective Comics #1** and its current U.S and estimated U.K. value may be checked on the Top 50 Rarest Comics table elsewhere in this book.

The Funnies #1

1938-1945 THE GOLDEN AGE

Traditionally dating from **Action Comics #1** which saw the first appearance of the archetypal costumed hero Superman and coinciding with the end of the Second World War, this was the age of the most famous costumed super-heroes of today. Batman (1939), Sub-Mariner (1939), Human Torch (1939), Wonder Woman (1940), Flash (1940), Robin (1940), Green Lantern (1940), Captain Marvel (1940), The Spirit (1940) and Captain America (1941) all came to prominence during this period along with a host of successful and unsuccessful imitators. Some of these early comics may have come over to this country with the establishment of the G.I.'s and U.S.A.F. bases but they were not generally distributed and available. They are prized among collectors today as the most valuable items in terms of financial worth and historical significance. The two most valuable would be **Action Comics #1** from June 1938 and **Detective Comics #27** from May 1939 featuring the first appearance of Batman. A copy of Detective #27 sold in 1994 for $135,000 (or £90,000 depending on which side of the Atlantic you stand) and though relatively high grade, it was by no means the best copy available. Superman #1 came out in the summer of 1939 and reprinted the first four Superman stories from Action Comics #1-4 in this one volume with some extra introductory pages. It is a comic that is thought to have been shipped over to the British mainland in an effort to test the viability of the market as there seems to be more copies of this comic in British collectors' hands than other significant late 1930's comics. The massive paper drives of 1941 and particularly 1942 in America destroyed millions of comic books for the War Effort and comics dated before this time are generally in much scarcer supply than all others.

Action Comics #25

1946-1949 THE LATE GOLDEN AGE

This period saw the beginning of a decline in the popularity of the super-hero and the establishment of a much wider variety of genres from movie and television comics to crime, horror and mystery titles. For example, 1947 saw Timely (later to become Atlas then Marvel) introduce its first crime comic called JUSTICE which prided itself on the fact that the stories were based on fact while 1948 saw TWO GUN KID from the same publisher as the first all Western comic. The exception to this variation from the super-hero genre was the phenomenally successful story of Fawcett's CAPTAIN MARVEL which saw sales recorded in the millions per month rather than the hundred thousands. Encouraged by this and the steady sales of SUPERMAN at around the one million mark per month, **Superboy #1** was published in 1949 though the same year saw SUB-MARINER COMICS falter with #32 and the great MARVEL MYSTERY COMICS end with #92 to become MARVEL TALES.

1950-1954 THE PRE SILVER AGE

More comic titles were published at the beginning of this period than at any other time (estimated to be a staggering 74 million individual copies per month at its height) though in one sense these years are often thought of by some as "The Dark Ages" of comics as paper quality and paper rationing meant slimmer comics which do survive today in the best of condition but in much smaller relative percentages. For sheer depth in diversity, this period is unparalleled. One

comics' historian has noted that there were over 50 horror titles per month published between 1951 and 1954. While genre comics flourished, super-heroes like Sub-Mariner and Captain America finally saw the sunset. The rise of the horror comic and in particular the line published by EC Comics lead to a series of Congressional Hearings in 1954 which sought to prove a direct correlation between comics and rising juvenile delinquency. The net result was the establishment of The Comics Code Authority in 1955 to which all comics were morally obliged to subject themselves. In many cases this established a generally safe formulaic approach to story and character. A notable exception are the "monster" comics like Journey into Mystery, Strange Tales, Tales of Suspense and Tales to Astonish with the bold art styles of Steve Ditko and Jack Kirby to name but two. Concerns with a post nuclear age, global divide and faltering exploration of space became characterised in the mid and late 1950's by an array of fantastic monsters with names and story titles to match the best B-movie cliches: "Groot, The Monster from Planet X", "Fin Fang Foom" and "Gigantus, The Monster That Walked Like A Man".

1955-1965 THE SILVER AGE

The Silver Age relates to the Golden Age in that this period saw the re-launch of a number of costumed heroes in an up-dated form. Traditionally dating from **Detective Comics #225** (Nov 1955) which introduced the first significant new hero The Manhunter from Mars for some years (since Captain Comet in **Strange Adventures #9** in June 1951), it has since become more widely associated with **Showcase #4** which introduced a new realisation (though essentially a revival) of The Flash. The mid point of this age saw a panoply of successful remodellings from a new Green Lantern in **Showcase #22** (Sep/Oct 1959) through Aquaman in **Showcase #30** (Feb 1961), Hawkman in **Brave and the Bold #34** (Mar 1961) to Atom in **Showcase #34** (October 1961). More significantly however was the appearance of **Fantastic Four #1** in November 1961 which ushered in what has become known as "The Marvel Age" which saw the rapid introduction of Spiderman, Hulk, a re-discovered Sub-Mariner and Captain America and, not ashamed of besprinkling their epithets, the"mighty" Thor. For many collectors in this country, this sub-age is the most revered and fondly remembered, particularly because most Marvel comics were officially distributed in this country and continued to be distributed in generally good supply. Thus complete sets were possible from first issues and fan involvement meant that there was more scope for having one's name mentioned or even a full letter to the Editor in print (look for the many letters submitted by U.K. though U.S. born radio DJ Paul Gambaccini when he was a young fan in **Fantastic Four #7** for example). The Silver Age will continue to expand as it includes comics that are roughly 25 years old or more.

Showcase #22

1966-1969 THE LATE SILVER AGE

This period is gradually being swallowed up by the advance of the Silver Age. Some collectors and dealers already accept the Silver Age as lasting right up to 1969, particularly in America. However, what characterises and makes this small period unique is a flourish of re-launched characters in their own titles, particularly from Marvel Comics. **Hulk #102** (April 1968) continued the numbering from the anthology title TALES TO ASTONISH while **Captain America #100** (April 1968) continued from TALES OF SUSPENSE. **Iron Man #1** shortly followed in May 1968 and perhaps the most important mainstream publishing event came in August 1968 with **Silver Surfer #1**. At DC Comics there was a short-lived attempt to cash in on the energy of the hip and groovy youth with TEEN BEAT in December 1967 and BROTHER POWER, THE GEEK in October 1968. A chequered design ("go-go checks") found its way along the top edge of DC comic titles from February 1966 to July 1967 that sought to identify the company with a zappier image as well as being a marketing aid to find the comics more easily in the news-stand racks. Perhaps the most significant example of colourful camp came with the Batman television series that lasted three seasons from 1966 to 1969. Well remembered are those famous fight-scenes with pop-art word sound-effects splattered across the screen which found their way into the comic.

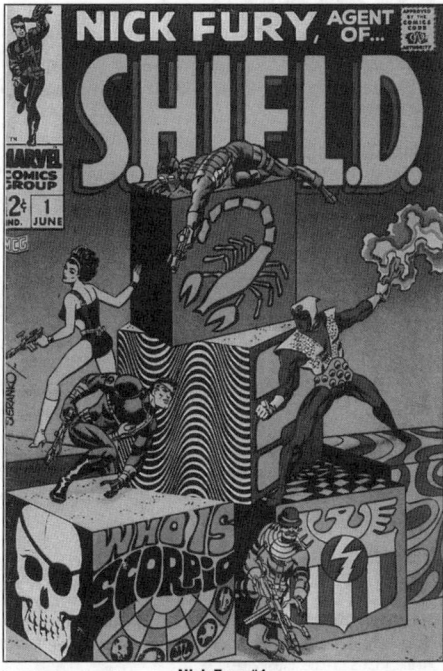

Nick Fury #1

1970-1979 THE SEVENTIES

This period is now becoming recognised in its own right as it is now twenty years removed and had a particular feel about it. In some cases that meant change with a re-vamp for Superman who had remained largely unchanged for over three decades. Clark Kent became a television reporter and that gruesome green chunk of rock called kryptonite transmuted to harmless lead. Supergirl got a wide variety of less than flattering costumes and Jack Kirby established his own unique art style in his "Fourth World" series including NEW GODS, FOREVER PEOPLE and giving Superman's pal Jimmy Olsen a few things to think about. Marvel Comics introduced Giant Size comics and multi-cross over annuals, some interesting characters like Killraven and Howard the Duck and hard, calculated market manipulation with endless reprint titles. For the first time, significant amounts of Marvel and a few DC comics were Non Distributed in the U.K. at the time of publication, leading to price differentials and new business opportunities for U.K. dealers. An air of uncertainty as to where comics were going lead (partly) to the DC Implosion of 1978 in which titles were cut back or cancelled after a period of steady exploration and the unquestioned establishment of Marvel as market leaders. Characters such as Deathlok and Wolverine, Ghost Rider and Punisher were all established in this period without any huge effect at the time but once re-introduced to modern audiences in new forms and formats, they enjoyed something of a renaissance through to the mid 1990's. In the current market, even these once extremely popular characters are subject to intense scrutiny for story quality and can easily become out of favour virtually overnight. This age is also referred to by some (mostly American dealers/collectors rather than U.K. ones) as "The Bronze Age" and traditionally it takes as its starting point the comic **Green**

Lantern #76 which featured new dynamic art by Neal Adams and a more down-to-earth and human story-line by Denny O'Neill. Quite when this Bronze Age is supposed to finish is unclear, so much so that the term "Lead Age of Comics" has been known to crop up on U.D. dealer lists which is perhaps the jaundiced view by some older dealers and collectors on today's output of material. The Bronze Age may be established more fully in time but for now the use of the actual decades will suffice.

Indeed The Seventies may well prove to be an important era of character-rediscovery and potential financial investment as prices are still within most people's reach as Golden and Silver Age prices continue to soar.

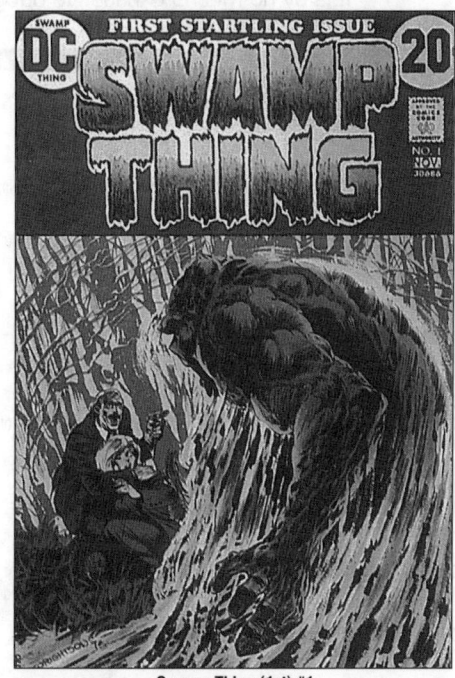

Swamp Thing (1st) #1

1980-PRESENT THE MODERN AGE

Never before has the medium of comic books gained so much widespread exposure through film and television. Films like Batman, Dick Tracy, The Teenage Mutant Ninja Turtles and Judge Dredd have grossed hundreds of millions of dollars at the box office in the last 15 years and plagued youth market pockets with their merchandising. Television has yet to find its own comic book hero but Star Trek - Voyager, Deep Space Nine and Babylon 5 may at least herald a new wave. There are something like 150 comic and cartoon characters under developmental consideration so the staple diet of screen entertainment for the next few years is not hard to fathom. Comic companies have been at once bold and bland in their efforts to cash in on such media awareness. The Independent Explosion in the early 80's saw hundreds of small presses spring up to produce some interesting material, champion creator rights and artist royalty payments but sadly the duopoly of Marvel and DC has all but re-established itself as cold hard economics count in the world of comics. The graphic novel became an accepted art form and concomitant catchword to be pilloried. While the age may be characterised by new formats/high-production value packages, media exposure as to the literacy and ultimate worth of comics has seen the inevitable backlash. Somewhere along the line someone forgot to mention that comics are still at root an escapist form of entertainment foremost with skillfully rendered art and fine story-telling making the most of the genre that for many still has its best potential to be realised. In spite of a world-wide market recession at the start of this decade, the future looks very bright for comics. More titles than ever before are being published with new experiments in story, art and subject. British artists and writers are held in the highest esteem on both sides of the Atlantic which is something that cannot be said of many industries in this country. Back issue collecting has never been more popular and record prices are being realised for comics in the best condition possible. Already several comics have passed the $100,000 mark and another is rumoured to be available soon at an unprecedented $200,000. But the real pleasure of the hobby is in the constant reading enjoyment and stimulus for thought that comics can bring, whether reading the latest in sociopolitical observations or fondly remembering a tale from one's childhood. After over 60 years of the American comic (and well over a hundred of the English variety), the genre is only now being recognised as something more than "kid's stuff".

SELECTED FURTHER READING

Below is a list of reference works on comics for general reading.
It is by no means exhaustive but gives some idea of the material available.

REFERENCE

THE BRITISH COMIC CATALOGUE
by Denis Gifford (Mansell 1975).

CANUCK COMICS
edited by John Bell (Matrix Books 1986): guide to Canadian comics, with price guide.

THE CHILDREN'S ANNUAL: A HISTORY AND COLLECTOR'S GUIDE
by Alan Clark (Boxtree 1988): the story of British annuals, with selected price guide.

THE COMIC BOOK
by Paul Sassienie (Ebury Press. 1994): Excellent.

THE COMIC BOOK IN AMERICA
by Mike Benton (Taylor Publishing. USA. 1989): chronological history of comics, publishers and genres.

COMIX: A HISTORY OF COMIC BOOKS IN AMERICA
by Les Daniels (Wildwood House 1971,1973): the history of American comics, with selected reprints.

THE COMPLETE CATALOGUE OF BRITISH COMICS
by Denis Gifford (Webb & Bower 1985). With (an out of date) Price Guide

THE DANDY MONSTER INDEX
Vol 1 & 2 by Ray Moore (BCW 1985)

DC COMICS: Sixty Years of the World's Favourite Comic Book Heroes
by Les Daniels (Virgin Books. 1995): an indispensable overview of DC comics with many excellent illustrations

ENCYCLOPAEDIA OF COMIC CHARACTERS
by Denis Gifford (Longman 1987): alphabetical listing of 1200 British characters.

THE GREAT COMIC BOOK HEROES
by Jules Feiffer (Penguin Press 1965, 1967): a short history of the Golden Age American heroes, with selected reprints.

HAPPY DAYS: A CENTURY OF COMICS
by Denis Gifford (Jupiter 1975): a guide to British comics.

HORROR COMICS: THE ILLUSTRATED HISTORY
by Mike Benton (Taylor Publishing 1991): an overview of the horror comic genre from the 1940's to present.

THE HOTSPUR - A CATALOGUE: 1933 to 1959
by D.J. Adley & W.O.G. Lofts (Cadwallender).

IDENTIFICATION GUIDE TO THE UNDATED D.C.THOMSON & JOHN LENG CHILDREN'S ANNUALS 1921-1965
by D.J. Adley & W.O.G. Lofts (Cadwallender 1982): cover descriptions and dates of 300+ annuals.

THE INTERNATIONAL BOOK OF COMICS
by Denis Gifford (W.H. Smith 1984): an introduction to comics, heavily illustrated.

AN INTRODUCTION TO CANADIAN COMIC BOOKS
by Dan Threaker (Aurora 1986): short history of Canadian-published comics, with price guide.

THE LYLE PRICE GUIDE TO PRINTED COLLECTIBLES
(Lyle 1984).

THE MAGIC INDEX
by Ray Moore (BCW 1988).

MARVEL: FIVE FABULOUS DECADES
by Les Daniels (Virgin Books. 1991): excellent overview of Marvel's output over the years, lavishly illustrated.

NOSTALGIA ABOUT COMICS
by Phil Clarke and Mike Higgs (Pegasus Publishing): a look at British albums and comics of the 1940s and 1950s. Also Australian, Canadian and some American material.

THE OFFICIAL COMIC BOOK PRICE GUIDE
by Robert M. Overstreet (House of Collectibles, annually): comprehensive listing of all American comic books from 1900-present, with American prices. The industry standard in America for many years now.

OVERSTREET'S FAN
by Robert M. Overstreet & Michael Renegar (Gemstone Publishing): monthly supplement to the above that replaced Overstreet's Comic Book Marketplace.

THE OFFICIAL UNDERGROUND AND NEWAVE COMIX PRICE GUIDE
by Jay Kennedy (Boatner Norton 1982): history of the Undergrounds, with price guide.

THE PENGUIN BOOK OF COMICS
by George Perry & Alan Aldridge (Penguin 1967, revised 1971): offers an overview of British and American comic books and newspaper strips. Soon to be re-issued by Paul Gravett?

THE ROVER INDEX
by Colin Morgan (Cadwallender).

SCIENCE FICTION COMICS: THE ILLUSTRATED HISTORY
by Mike Benton (Taylor Publishing. 1992): an overview of sci-fi comics from the 1920's to date. Illustrated.

A SMITHSONIAN BOOK OF COMIC-BOOK COMICS
edited by Michael Barrier & Martin Williams (Smithsonian Institution Press/Harry N. Abrams Inc. 1981): selected history and reprints.

STAP ME! THE BRITISH NEWSPAPER STRIP
by Denis Gifford (Shire 1971).

THE STERANKO HISTORY OF COMICS Vol 1 & 2
(Supergraphics 1970, 1972): comprehensive history of the early days of American comics.

SUPER-HERO COMICS OF THE GOLDEN AGE:THE ILLUSTRATED HISTORY
by Mike Benton (Taylor Publishing, 1992): an overview of the Golden Age period of American comics from the 1930s to 1950s. Illustrated.

SUPER-HERO COMICS OF THE SILVER AGE: THE ILLUSTRATED HISTORY
by Mike Benton (Taylor Publishing. 1991): an overview of the Silver Age period of American comics from mid 1950 to mid 1960. Illustrated.

TWO DECADES OF COMICS: A REVIEW
by David Cutler, Frank Plowright, Adrian Snowdon, Steve Whitaker & Hassan Yusuf (Slings & Arrows 1981).

VICTORIAN COMICS

by Denis Gifford (Allen & Unwin 1976).

THE WORLD ENCYCLOPAEDIA OF COMICS

edited by Maurice Horn (Chelsea House, New English Library 1976): massive work listing comic-book and newspaper strip characters, creators and publications.

Note: some of these publications may now be out of print and only available from specialist shops and libraries.

ABOUT COMIC ART AND ARTISTS

THE ART OF JACK DAVIS

by Hank Harrison (Stabur 1987).

THE BEST OF EAGLE

edited by Marcus Morris (Michael Joseph/Edbury Press 1977): short history and selected reprints.

CARL BARKS AND THE ART OF THE COMIC BOOK

by Michael Barrier (M. Lilien 1981).

COMICS AND SEQUENTIAL ART

by Will Eisner (Poorhouse/Eclipse 1985,1986, 1987): detailed guide to the execution and interpretation of comic art. Seminal work and essential reading.

A VERY FUNNY BUSINESS

by Leo Baxendale (Duckworth 1978).

THE COMIC ART OF REG PARLETT

by Alan Clark & David Ashford (Golden Fun 1986).

THE COMIC ART OF ROY WILSON

by Alan Clark & David Ashford (Midas 1983).

THE MAN WHO DREW TOMORROW

by Alistair Crompton (Who Dares 1985): the story of Frank Hampson's work on Dan Dare.

SUPERMAN AT FIFTY: THE PERSISTENCE OF A LEGEND

edited by Dennis Dooley and Gary Engle (Octavia Press 1987).

TIMEVIEW: THE COMPLETE DR. WHO ILLUSTRATIONS OF FRANK BELLAMY

(Who Dares 1985).

Note: some of these publications may now be out of print and only available at specialist shops and libraries.

BRITISH MAGAZINES AND NEWSPAPERS

ARK

(Titan bi-monthly): British and American comics interviews and articles. Now available as back-issues only.

BRITISH COMICS WORLD

(Alan & David Coates): British comics articles. Back issues now.

COMIC COLLECTOR

(Aceville Publications, monthly): news and features magazine on American and British comics with retailer ads. Re-titled Comics World before its cancellation in 1995. Real shame. Back issues only.

COMICS INTERNATIONAL

(Dez Skinn, monthly): trade journal/newspaper plus reviews of British and American comics. Comic shop and news-stand distribution. Still going strong.

COMICS SPECULATOR NEWS

(Jaspal S. Dale, monthly): trade journal that tended towards the speculator market as the title implies. Back issues only now.

ESCAPE

(Titan, bi-monthly): articles and reviews of mainly British and European comics and media, plus comics material. Now available as back issues only.

FANTASY ADVERTISER

(30th Century, quarterly): British and American comics information, news, reviews and articles. Available as back issues only.

GOLDEN FUN

(Alan & Laurel Clark): Golden Age British comics articles. Back issues only.

SPEAKEASY

(Acme Press, monthly): British and American comics information, news, reviews and articles. Amalgamated into a new magazine called BLAST. Cancelled so both are available as back issues only.

AMERICAN MAGAZINES AND NEWSPAPERS

ADVANCE COMICS

(Capital Distributors, monthly): A fully comprehensive listing of up and coming comics, merchandise, posters, books, portfolios, games and toys with descriptions and reviews.

AMAZING HEROES

(Fantagraphics, bi-weekly): news, reviews and articles on mainly American comics.

AMAZING HEROES PREVIEW SPECIAL

(Fantagraphics, semi-annually): special oversized editions of the above, listing the majority of coming American comics.

COMICS BUYER'S GUIDE

(Krause Publications, weekly): News and articles on mainly new and coming American comics. Essential reading.

COMIC BUYER'S GUIDE PRICE GUIDE

(Krause Publications, quarterly): Price guide update with some features/articles geared towards the speculator market.

COMICS INTERVIEW

(Fictioneer, monthly): interviews with American comic creators.

THE COMICS JOURNAL

(Fantagraphics, monthly): Articles, news and criticism of American and foreign comics.

COMIC VALUES MONTHLY

(Attic Books Ltd, monthly): Price guide update with better-than-average Independents listing. Back issues now.

PREVIEWS

(Diamond Distributors, monthly): A fully comprehensive listing of up and coming comics, merchandise, posters, books, portfolios, games and toys with reviews and descriptions.

WIZARD: THE GUIDE TO COMICS

(Wizard Press Ltd, monthly): Glossy covered price guide update with design-oriented articles and features that have surprising breadth. Least comprehensive comics listing but includes cards and toys. Very good on "hot" artists and with Jon Warren's influence, pricing is very sensible now.

THE COMIC BOOK PRICE GUIDE INVESTMENT GUIDE

TO INVEST OR NOT TO INVEST, THAT IS THE QUESTION

by

DARRYL JONES (Silver Acre Comics)

EVERY MONTH it seems new comics are being shipped out and within weeks are selling for £5.00 to £10.00 or more, usually owing to "hot" artists, writers or characters. Then only a couple of months later they are back selling at or just above cover price again. Most collectors would have paid the inflated value for the one month old comic because they believed they were buying an investment, certain to appreciate in value. Let us face the fact that most comics with very few exceptions are produced in the hundreds of thousands and even millions of copies. As such they are unlikely to bring you a high return for your money for many years, if ever. In order to substantiate the chances of investment potential in a comic, I suggest investing in books which are at least 20 years old or more. An "un-hyped" 20 year old comic will very rarely, possibly if ever, drop in value. When buying new issues, buy them for the enjoyment of reading and if they go up in value, consider it a bonus.

The following are personal suggestions in no particular order of merit of comics to keep a close watch on as particularly undervalued comics at the present time in this country and reasons why they may prove to be good investments:

GOLDEN AGE PRE-1950

1 **ACTION COMICS #23**
   (1st Lex Luthor, 1st Daily Planet)
2 **SUSPENSE COMICS #3**
   (classic L.B. Cole)
3 **CAPTAIN AMERICA #74, #75**
   (Rare high demand Weird War tales)
4 **DETECTIVE COMICS #26**
   (1st appearance of Batman in advert)
5 **MORE FUN #101**
   (1st appearance Superboy)
6 **BATMAN #47**
   (1st detailed origin)

SILVER AGE 1950-1969

1 **WONDER WOMAN #105**
   (rare origin issue)
2 **BATMAN #181**
   (1st Poison Ivy – look for the centrefold pin-up of Batman and Robin)
3 **GOLD KEY MOVIE TITLES**
   (great investment potential)
4 **AVENGERS #57**
   (1st Vision. Major character)
5 **METAL MEN #1**
   (scarce in VFN or better)
6 **SGT. FURY #1**
   (stupidly cheap)
7 **MARVEL TALES ANNUAL #1**
   (scarce in the U.K. and over-looked)
8 **OUR ARMY AT WAR #81**
   (1st Sgt. Rock)
9 **STAR SPANGLED WAR STORIES #90–137**
   (dinosaur covers are red hot)
10 **SHOWCASE #60**
   (1st Silver Age Spectre)
11 **STRANGE TALES #1**
   (try finding a copy)
12 **SUPERBOY #68**
   (1st Bizarro – a classic!)

Action Comics # 23

Azrael # 1

Batman# 47

Detective Comics # 26

Showcase # 60

Phoenix – The Untold Story

UNDER-VALUED COMICS

by JOHN PIRES of VAULT COMICS

Below is a list of Silver Age comics that I consider to be under-valued in today's U.K. market and concomitant reasons. The comics are not placed in any particular order other than alphabetical/numerical. Any comments are invited via the new editorial address.

AMAZING SPIDERMAN ANNUAL #1 Marvel 1964

Very scarce in high grade. Copies that have perfectly bound square spines are almost impossible to find, particularly in the U.K.

ATOM #1 DC 1963

Under-rated early Hawkman appearance as well as the first team-up with Atom. Great cover by Murphy Anderson

AVENGERS #1 Gold Key 1968

Rare TV related comic. Being a British comic (a one shot) generates higher interest in this country than in the States. However, seldom seen in either country.

AVENGERS #3 Marvel 1964

X-Men appear, same cover-date as X-Men #3. Dark cover.

BATMAN #171 DC 1965

1st Silver Age Riddler. Pink cover that tends to fade. Scarce in NM.

BATMAN #179 DC 1965

2nd Silver Age Riddler. Rare in almost any grade. Black cover makes it even tougher in NM.

BLACKHAWK #108 DC 1957

With popularity in war comics on the increase in the U.K., this 1st DC issue is rarely seen and considering it came out at the same time as Showcase #6, it seems comparatively cheap.

CAPTAIN AMERICA #111 Marvel 1969

Classic Captain America cover by Jim Steranko. Most copies have off-white rather than pure white cover. NM copies very difficult to find.

DAREDEVIL #1 Marvel 1964

Still greatly undervalued in NM. Cover must be white not off-white or translucent. Top left corner a rich, dark green.

DAREDEVIL #37 Marvel 1968

Black cover featuring Dr. Doom. Copies in NM are scarcely found.

DELL GIANT #48 Dell 1961

1st Flinstones appearance is fast becoming the one to look for as the movie gets underway. Unfortunately, this is easier said than done. Note: not listed in this Guide until actually studied by the author

DETECTIVE COMICS #327 DC 1964

Undervalued and very scarce minor key. Cover must be white in NM.

DOUBLE LIFE OF PRIVATE STRONG Archie 1959

Kirby collectors are constantly on the lookout for this one. An extremely difficult key issue to find containing the origin of The Shield and actual 1st appearance of The Fly (1/2 a page)

FANTASTIC FOUR #25 Marvel 1964

Key issue featuring Thing vs. Hulk. Over-looked as the 2nd Silver Age appearance of Captain America. Dark cover making high grade copies hard to find.

Avengers # 3

Batman # 179

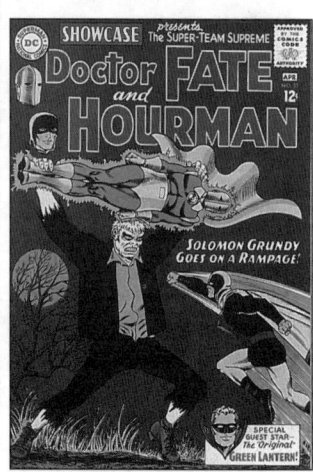

Showcase # 55

FANTASTIC FOUR #52 Marvel 1966

The 1st appearance of The Black Panther - 1st black super-hero. Interest and speculation is rising in this issue on both sides of the Atlantic and the dark cover will make it hard to find in high grade (VF+ or better)

FANTASTIC FOUR #112 Marvel 1971

Scarce comic. Black cover makes it tough to find without even the slightest stress marks along the spine.

FIGHTING AMERICAN #1 Prize 1954

An extremely scarce 1st issue in the U.K. from a run of 7. Most of these issues are found on plenty of Kirby fans wants lists but not at marts or on dealers sales lists.

GREEN LANTERN #8 DC 1961

One of the best Silver Age DC grey-tone covers. Very hard to get in VF or better. This cover stands out well from all the surrounding issues of the title and should do so in price as well.

HOUSE OF SECRETS #92 DC 1971

Greatly undervalued in NM. 1st Swamp Thing. Classic Bernie Wrigtson grey-tone cover.

IRON MAN #1 Marvel 1968

Although common, even in VFN+, a true NM copy with no stress marks and perfect corners is very scarce.

JUSTICE LEAGUE OF AMERICA #3 DC 1961

Probably the most difficult early issue to obtain from this title in any grade. A black cover makes it even harder to obtain in top shape.

MAGNUS ROBOT FIGHTER #1 Gold Key 1963

The first appearance of Magnus and with its dark, beautiful painted cover, it's a comic that's still defying collector's in high grade.

MILLIE THE MODEL ANNUAL #1 Marvel 1962

A very undervalued early Marvel annual. Strange Tales Annual #1 has always been thought of as the first Marvel annual. Millie came out in the same year and is by far more rare than S.T. Annual #1 in any grade, particularly in the U.K.

MYSTERY IN SPACE #55 DC 1959

A very sought after painted (grey-tone) cover of Adam Strange which is hard to find above a Fine. A NM copy should bring around 1.75 times Guide, even in the U.K.

NICK FURY AGENT OF SHIELD #1 Marvel 1968

A great Steranko cover makes it a must for all who admire his art. Highly sought after but not often offered for sale in true NM in the U.K.

NICK FURY AGENT OF SHIELD #5 Marvel 1968

As with Captain America #111, even high grade copies copies tend to have off-white covers. A true NM is hard to come by.

SGT. FURY #1 Marvel 1963

Nick Fury has been around now for 33 years! His recent death highlights this issue even more. This issue contains his first ever appearance and actually pre-dates the first Daredevil, Dr. Strange and X-Men. Rarely seen for sale in any grade in the U.K.

SHOWCASE #64 DC 1964

This is the 3rd Silver Age appearance of The Spectre and possibly the most scarce. It has a deep purple cover which shows up all the typical stress marks. Copies in NM are near impossible to find.

SHOWCASE #55 DC 1965

Rarely offered for sale in the U.K. Dark purple cover makes it a true rarity in high grade.

SHOWCASE #57 DC 1965

Black Joe Kubert Enemy Ace cover. Very scarce in the U.K., rare in NM.

SPECTACULAR SPIDERMAN MAG #1 Marvel 1968

Larger size format than #1, makes it tough to keep let alone get in top shape. It has a black and white interior printed on a darker, lower quality paper. Although not as desirable as #2, still undervalued and scarcer than the 2nd issue.

SPECTACULAR SPIDERMAN MAG #2 Marvel 1968

A greatly undervalued late Silver Age comic. Colour. Original Green Goblin story. This magazine size square-bound comic makes it very difficult to find in NM.

SUB-MARINER #8 Marvel 1968

As with F.F. #112, this comic has a black cover making it very scarce in anything better than a VFN.

SUPERMAN #200 DC 1967

Rarely found in collections. This issue is nearly 30 years old and still cheap at U.K. Guide prices - if you can find one!

TALES OF SUSPENSE #32 Marvel 1962

"The Man in the Beehive". Issued 7 months after "The Man in the Ant- Hill" (Tales to Astonish #27) and 1 month before the first costumed Ant-Man. Could this have been the 1st "Bee-Man"? As with most dark cover pre-hero comics, this issue is scarcely seen and undervalued in high grade.

TALES OF SUSPENSE #49 Marvel 1964

Immensely undervalued early Avengers and X-Men appearance (same date as X-Men #3) has made this issue rise in demand but supply is low.

TALES TO ASTONISH #60 Marvel 1964

This is the first Steve Ditko Hulk since the original Hulk series. It is often overlooked and overshadowed by the battle issue of #59.

TIME TUNNEL #1 Gold Key 1967

A very under-rated TV series (the 1960s version of "Quantum Leap"). This first issue (of 2) is not easy to locate and extremely scarce in high grade owing to its black cover.

X-MEN #18 Marvel 1966

A classic "floating heads" cover featuring Magneto. High grade copies are very difficult to locate owing to the dark cover.

THE TOP 50 RAREST COMICS

Below is an excercise that I carried out to determine the Top 50 rarest comic books. It is based on personal observation with some advice from a few friends and collectors. The numbers are "best guesses" at the time of going to press. I recently noticed another Action Comics ashcan advertised by Pacific Comics Exchange, citing only three copies in existence.

Therefore more information, particularly from American dealers, would be most welcome.

POS./TITLE/NUMBER	DATE	COPIES KNOWN

1) AMAZING MYSTERY FUNNIES   **1940?**   **1**
Discovered by Mark Wilson in America, it has the same cover as Amazing Man #23 from Centaur Comics but it has no number. The reason is unclear.

1) ALL STAR COMICS (ASH CAN)   **1940**   **1**
This comic was discovered by Jon Warren in America. It is an "ash can" copy or a publisher's in-house facsimile of a proposed new title and used to secure the name and design of the title. Most ash can comics have black and white covers stapled to an already existing coverless comic. Some ash cans are completely black and white throughout. This particular ash can shows what was to be the cover for DC's Flash Comics #1 (January 1940).

1) BLOOD IS THE HARVEST   **1950**   **1**
This was issued by the Cathetical Guild as less than a comic and more of an illustrated pamphlet against Communism. It is known in three forms and this is the black and white un-trimmed version.

[4) IS THIS TOMORROW?   **1947**   **2]**
Issued by the Cathetical Guild, a forerunner to Blood is the Harvest and the theme of Communists taking over America. This is the black and white advance copy. It is more of an educational pamphlet than a recognized comic book.

5) ACTION COMICS ASHCAN   **1938**   **3**
This is the black and white ash can comic that was used to secure the title and design of Action Comics that was to feature the first appearance of Superman. The cover shows a pirate type figure in head and shoulders close up brandishing a cutlass. This cover was eventually used in full colour for Action Comics #3, August 1938. A copy was on view for sale at the 1991 San Diego Comicon.

5) SYNDICATE COMICS FEATURES   **1937**   **3**
Discovered by Mark Wilson in 1990, this comic was designed to promote the character Dan Hastings to all the newspaper comic sections. Dated November 1937, this 4 page comic has artwork by Fred Guardineer who did much work for other major companies. Look for his cover art on early issues of Action Comics.

The front is done in green and red ink, the interior is black and white. The size is much larger than normal comic size at 17" by 11". All three known copies are in VG condition.

5) THRILL COMICS   **1939**   **3**
Fawcett Publications came up with an idea for a comic called Flash Comics starring Captain Thunder in 1939. The race was on to secure copyright. DC Comics (or National Periodical Publications as they were then known) beat Fawcett to it by publishing their own Flash Comics #1 cover dated January 1940. This Thrill Comics is an in-house ash can comic, re-titled from a second ash can Fawcett Flash Comics (same cover illustration of Captain Thunder snapping free from chains – see 19) to try and salvage the character of Captain Thunder. Unfortunately in December 1939 Better/Nedor Publications filed for a title which was to appear cover dated February 1940 called Thrilling Comics so Fawcett had to change to Whiz Comics which eventually came out in February 1940 as well.

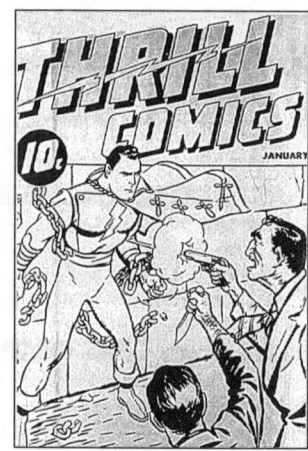

5) FEATURE BOOK (POPEYE)   **1937**   **3**
Issued by David McKay Publications, this hundred page comic had no number on the cover but was later issued as number 3, same interior but a different cover. It featured black and white newspaper reprints but unlike the ash cans, it is more of a recognized, proper comic. of the three known copies in existence, one is high grade and the other two are much lower grade.

9) SLAM BANG COMICS   **1940**   **3 TO 4**
An ash can black and white produced by Fawcett to secure the title which appeared in 1940 (cover dated March). There is no cover illustration but the announcement "Featuring the episode adventures of Ibis the Invincible..". Estimated number of copies is difficult to confirm. The 1st Sotheby's catalogue for the sale dated Wednesday December 18th 1991 had an example on offer and claimed it was the only copy in existence which seems unlikely. Further research is obviously needed though it does seem to be the rarest of this type of ash-can.

10) IF THE DEVIL WOULD TALK   1958   4

Issued by the Cathetical Guild, it treats of the threat of worldly temptations. This is a black and white, small size version of the original colour version. More of a pamphlet than a comic.

11) FLASH COMICS VOL 1 1   1939   4 TO 5

This was the black and white ash can copy produced by DC to secure the title in the race with Fawcett (see 5). It is cover dated December 1939 and reprints the cover from DC's Adventure Comics #41 with an underwater scene of a shark attacking a drowning man.

11) FLASH COMICS   1939   4 TO 5

This was the first (of three) black and white ash can copy produced by Fawcett in the race to secure the title (see 5 and 8). The cover has no illustration but rather the announcement "..featuring the episode adventures of Golden Arrow..". A copy was offered for sale at the 1st Sotheby's auction in December 1991. Other characters included Captain Thunder, Ibis and Dan Dare (not the British one!).

11) FIVE CENT COMICS   1940   4 TO 5

An ash can black and white produced by Fawcett cover dated February to secure a title which appeared in May 1940 as Nickel Comics featuring Bulletman. This copy has no cover illustration, only the announcement "Featuring the episode adventures of Dan Dare, brilliant young free-lance detective..". A copy was offered for sale in the 1st Sotheby's auction in December 1991.

11) NICKEL COMICS   1940   4 TO 5

An ash can black and white copy produced by Fawcett to secure the idea of comics sold at 5 cents and indeed that title (see 10). There is no cover illustration but an announcement of "Featuring the episode adventures of Scoop Smith, daring young newspaper reporter..". A copy was offered for sale in the 1st Sotheby's auction in December 1991.

11) WORLD'S BEST   1939   4 TO 5

This is another ash can comic cover dated February 1941 in order to secure copyright for the title of World's Best Comics which appeared in Spring 1941 and became World's Finest Comics with issue 2. The cover is a black and white reprint of Action Comics #29 showing Superman rescuing a bound and gagged Lois Lane from the back of a gangster's car. The interior is also made up from stock reprints from DC's inventory at the time.

16) WOW (1ST SERIES) 2   1936   4 TO 7

Sub-titled What a Magazine, this 52 page comic is magazine size and features characters like Fu Manchu and Popeye and artwork elsewhere featured is by Will Eisner. All copies of this four issue series are very rare but this is the rarest.

17) BLOOD IS THE HARVEST   1950   5

Issued by the Cathetical Guild announcing the impending threat of Communism, this is the black and white version of the original colour issue. More of a pamphlet than a comic. One of these has surfaced in un-trimmed condition (see entry #2).

18) DOUBLE ACTION COMICS   1940   5 TO 7

Dated January 1940 with a black and white interior, the colour cover is a reprint of Adventure Comics #37. It is not an ash can comic ie. it was distributed on the news-stands though issue 1 is thought to exist as an ash can as an experiment for Action Comics #1 that appeared in June 1938 (see Action Funnies - entry No. 5 above). The style of the words "Action" and "Comics" is very similar to what actually appeared on the comic that launched Superman.

19) FLASH COMICS   1939   8

This was the second (of three) black and white ash can copy produced by Fawcett in the race for the title (see entries 5,11,11). Thinking that they had secured the title, a cover illustration of Captain Thunder was drawn, snapping free from chains whilst being attacked by two thugs. When the existence of DC's own ash can Flash became known (see entry 11), Fawcett hastily re-drew the title to Thrill Comics (see entry 5). A copy was offered for sale at the 1st Sotheby's auction in December 1991. A copy was also sold in the U.K. in early 1994 for £18,000 in a cash and trade deal. It was apparently the best surviving copy.

20) MARVEL MYSTERY COMICS   1943/44   9

This 128 page comic was published during the classic Marvel Mystery Comics run which ended at issue 92 in June 1949. The interior is black and white, reprinting two Captain America stories and two other Marvel Mystery stock stories. It has the colour cover of Marvel Mystery Comics #33. It was possibly an experiment to produce some kind of annual to accompany the series cover priced at 25 cents. One estimate of known copies puts it as low as three.

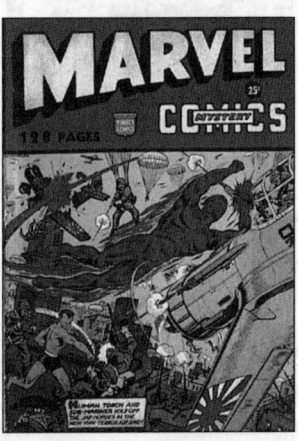

20) FEATURE BOOK (DICK TRACY)   **1937**   **9**

Like the other no number Feature Book with Popeye (see no. 5), this was later reprinted as Feature Book #4 with a new cover dated August 1937. It is 100 pages long.

22) ALL NEW 15   **1947**   **9/10**

Smaller than standard comic size, it was distributed through the mail only (see Stuntman #3). Joe Palooka and Black Cat appear. Black and white cover and interior. Estimates vary between 4 and 15 copies in existence.

23) FAMOUS FUNNIES (SERIES 1) 1   **1933**   **10**

This was the first recognisable comic book sold. Funnies On Parade and Famous Funnies A Carnival of Comics were given away. It was reprinted from a combination of these latter two comics and historians estimate about 35,000-40,000 were printed to be sold in chain stores throughout the U.S. Estimates vary between 8 and 12 copies in existence with 1 in strict NM condition which would bring at least 50% more than Guide values.

23) COMICS MAGAZINE 1   **1936**   **10**

Cover dated May 1936 this much under-rated comic contains Dr. Mystic, The Occult Detective by Siegel and Shuster as the inventory for this comic was sold by DC Comics from the pages of their magazine More Fun Comics. This first ever origin of a super-hero continues in the pages of DC's More Fun Comics #14. Dr. Mystic is a Superman prototype as his costume resembles Superman's and he can fly. Even though Superman appeared in 1938, the idea had been evolving as early as 1934.

23) NEW COMICS 2   **1936**   **10**

Cover dated January this comic is thought to be one of the rarest DC comics though others would disagree citing anything from 21 to 50 copies. Federal Men by Siegel and Shuster begins, a strip that went on to feature in Comics Magazine.

23) NEW FUN 2   **1935**   **10**

Cover dated March this is the second DC comic published and it is thought to be the rarest; certainly it has the tradition of being the hardest to find.

23) STUNTMAN 3   **1946**   **10**

This comic is smaller than standard comic size at 5" by 8". It was distributed through the mail only rather than sold on news-stands. It was only discovered to exist a few years ago.

23) DANGER TRAIL 3   **1950**   **10**

Cover dated November/December this comic is only very recently thought to be the rarest pre-Silver Age comic. The whole short-lived title (5 issues) is hard to come by in any condition. It is unusual for being the most recent comic book in this listing.

23) FAMOUS FUNNIES 2   **1934**   **10**

Published by Eastern Colour Printing Company, these comics contain all reprints from the Sunday funny pages like Mutt and Jeff and Joe Palooka.

23) FAMOUS FUNNIES 9   **1935**   **10**

Same as above. All these early Famous Funnies are very difficult to come by in any grade, let alone anything approaching high grade.

31) COMICS MAGAZINE 2   **1936**   **10 TO 12**

Cover dated June 1936 this comic features Federal Men by Siegel and Shuster. It is thought to be as rare as issue #1 but unlikely. These are only educated guesses by those that know.

32) MORE FUN 9   **1936**   **12**

This is the first comic sized issue of the title as the previous issues 7 and 8 were a slightly larger 8" by 10". Issues 1-6 were New Fun Comics before title changed with issue 7. Cover dated March.

33) BLOOD IS THE HARVEST   **1950**   **13**

This is the original educational pamphlet as published by the Cathetical Guild. A black and white version became available (see entry No. 17) and un untrimmed version as well (see entry No. 1).

33) DETECTIVE COMICS 3   **1937**   **13**

Considered the rarest of the pre-Batman Detective Comics (#1-26), this is cover-dated May, exactly two years before the first appearance of Batman. Lovely cover by Creig Flessel of an escaped convict caught in a yellow search-light. Estimated copies vary from a lower value of 6 to an upper value of 20.

35) BIG BOOK OF FUN COMICS   **1936**   **14**

The 1st ever DC annual dated Spring 1936. Estimates very from as little as 5 copies to 23 copies which goes to show how difficult it is to calculate exactly the number of extant copies of any of these books. 1 is known in strict NM condition which would bring at least 50% in addition to the estimated value given here.

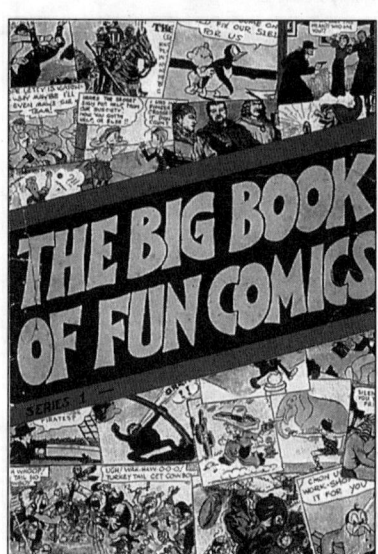

36) NEW FUN 6   **1935**   **15**

Cover-dated October, this is the first appearance of the Superman prototype Dr. Occult by Siegel and Shuster.

37) GREEN GIANT 1   **1940**   **16**

An experimental comic published by Moreau Publications to utilize a printing press of theirs. With no price on the cover it probably never got as far as the distribution stage. Estimates vary from 12 to 20 copies in existence. 3 are known in strict NM condition which would bring at least 50% more than any Guide values.

37) NEW FUN 1   **1935**   **17**

Cover-dated February, this is the first DC comic ever published. The title became More Fun with issue 7. Estimates of copies in existence run between 10 and 24 hence the average value of 17. There is one (1) known copy in Very Fine to Near Mint condition and it could bring double the current Guide value.

37) WOW COMICS 1   **1936**   **17**

Dated July, this is the magazine format from Henle Publishing sub-titled What a Magazine! (see No. 16). Estimated extant copies vary but only slightly from a lower limit of 15 to an upper limit of 20. The tightness of the range suggests that this comic is fairly well documented in its rarity value.

40) MORE FUN 8   **1936**   **18**

A slightly larger than standard comic (as was More Fun 7) at 10" by 12". Estimates of rarity vary from 15 to 20 copies but with another report citing parameters 21 to 50 though this is thought to be questionable. More information is obviously needed.

41) WOW COMICS 3   **1936**   **20**

Another in the short-lived magazine format series sub-titled What a Magazine!. The only reliable estimate at the moment suggests 20 copies though further research is needed.

42) DETECTIVE PICTURE STORIES 1   **1936**   **22**

One of the experts asked cites this as an extremely important comic as The Comics Magazine Co. and DC Comics raced to publish a comic devoted to a single theme. An ad appeared in New Comics #11 (December 1936) that Detective Comics #1 was appearing but it actually appeared three months after Detective Picture Stories #1, dated December 1936. Estimates vary from 15 to 30 copies in existence from three sources while another source seems way off the mark citing anywhere between 50 and 200 copies.

43) DETECTIVE COMICS 2   **1937**   **23**

Dated April 1937, another very rare pre-Batman Detective comic. Very distinctive cover illustration of a ugly thug's face in close up. Estimates of rarity vary tremendously from as few as 6 up to 35 copies though both of these seem extreme. A middle ground figure has been chosen.

44) NEW ADVENTURE COMICS 13   **1937**   **25**

One reliable source puts this at about 25 copies and this is the figure chosen for now. Another source claims it to be much rarer at under 5 copies but this seems a little extreme.

44) IF THE DEVIL WOULD TALK   **1950**   **25**

Educational pamphlet rather than really a comic book from the Cathedral Guild. Estimates run from between 20 to 30 copies so 25 has been chosen. The 1958 version is much rarer at 6 known copies and the black and white at 4 known copies.

46) MORE FUN 7   **1936**   **26**

Slightly over-sized comic at 10" by 12" as was More Fun #8. Estimated copies from as low as 7 to as high as 45. One estimate went as high as 50 but in view of one estimate of 7 and one of 10, the figure of 50 is discounted for now. 2 copies are known to exist in strict Near Mint and would bring at least 50% more above the suggested value here. Title was previously New Fun Comics #1-6.

47) BOY EXPLORERS 2   **1946**   **27**

Like Stuntman #3 and All New #15, this was a small size black and white comic distributed through the mail only and not on sale at news-stands. The only estimates available ranged between 20 and 35 copies so a middle figure has been chosen.

48) DETECTIVE COMICS 1   **1937**   **30**

The comic that gave DC its initials and in the race for the first comic with one theme (see entry No. 42). Estimates from sources said 20,25,30 and 35 copies respectively with one not so committal at 21-50 copies. A mid range value of 30 has been chosen for now. Sporting a beautiful Fu Manchu chinaman cover, probably by Creig Flessel, only one (1) known copy exists in Near Mint condition and could bring double the current Guide value. One more copy in this country came to the author's attention at the end of 1993, though the total estimated number has been left alone.

48) FAMOUS FUNNIES 1   **1934**   **30**

Not to be confused with Famous Funnies (Series 1) #1. This comic was the first regular monthly news-stand comic as number 2 came out one month later and so on. Two sources independently agreed on 30 extant copies while another went as low and as vague as 6 to 10 copies. For the moment the figure of 30 has been chosen. Two (2) copies are known to exist in Near Mint condition and would bring at least 50% above the current Guide value.

48) FUNNY PICTURE STORIES 1   1936   30
From The Comics Magazine Company a funnies anthology that was taken over by Centaur Publications with issue 6. Two estimates put extant copies from 25 to 35 copies so 30 was chosen. A third unconfirmed estimate suggests 21 to 50 copies.

OTHER RAREST COMIC BOOKS JUST OUTSIDE THE TOP 50 ARE:

DETECTIVE COMICS 4
has been suggested from 11-20 copies

FLASH GORDON 5
at about 30-40 copies as it was distributed through the mail like Stuntman #3, Boy Explorers #2 and All New #15

NEW FUN 3
which could be anywhere between 11 and 45 copies

NEW FUN 4
could be anywhere between 21 and 50 copies

MORE FUN 11, 15, 22 AND 23
may have anywhere between 11 and 50 copies

NEW COMICS 3, 6, 11

AND
NEW ADVENTURE COMICS 12, 14, 16, 18, 19, 22 AND 23
have been suggested by one source at 11-20 copies

CAPTAIN MARVEL THRILL BOOK
has been cited at 25 copies but as yet unconfirmed

NEW BOOK OF COMICS 2
at a possible 35 copies

NEW BOOK OF COMICS 1
at about 42 copies

JUMBO COMICS 1, CENTURY OF COMICS AND WOW COMICS 4
at a possible 40 copies each

FAMOUS FUNNIES (CARNIVAL OF COMICS), JUMBO COMICS 7 AND NEW COMICS 1
at a possible 50 copies each

ALL AMERICAN COMICS 16
at about 50–60 copies.

All the above information is at best mostly speculation based on observation by myself, what I have in my own collection, what I know for a fact are in other people's collections both here and in the America and informed guesses by a number of top American dealers, all of whom I credit and thank for their participation. No doubt when more information becomes available, positions in the Top 50 will alter.

THOSE AMERICAN DEALERS WHO ASSISTED IN THIS SURVEY WERE:

GARY CARTER, STEPHEN FISHLER, ERNST GERBER (and his invaluable Photo-Journals), **SEAN LINKENBACK, JAMES PAYETTE, JON WARREN** and **MARK WILSON** and a special mention for **BOB OVERSTREET** and his excellent Price Guide which pioneered the work of cataloguing the rarest comics in the world.

Even though many of the comics are very rare items indeed it does not necessarily make them the most valuable comics. Indeed only two (Detective Comics #1 and New Fun #1) feature in the Top 50 Rarest and Top 20 Most Valuable. The Top 20 most valuable comics in the U.K. market are valued according to those known to have been sold or offered for sale. A Near Mint price has been calculated on extant copies, known popularity of the characters and comics and educated guesses. Please note that the order may differ from that generally accepted in America as certain characters are less popular here than there. The values may be subject to variations of up to 20% either way.

Very high grade copies (Very Fine or better) of this Top Ten from "named" collections (Note: these are the only fully recognised and well documented "named" or "pedigree" collections: Mile High, San Francisco, Larsen, Allentown, Denver, Kansas City) may bring up to 50% more. Unrestored Near Mint copies from named collections may bring 100% more. Thus if ever the Mile High Action #1 or the Larsen Detective #27 ever came on the market, a genuine six figure sum in cash could easily be achieved. The continued success of the most recent Sotheby's and Christie's auctions in New York reinforce this belief.

Market Reports

Greetings and hello from Wales.

MARVEL RECENT

The **X-Men: Age of Apocalypse** story was Marvel's success of 1995 for us and still is, to date, one of our best sellers with high demand across the complete collector board. **Maximum Carnage/Clonage** sell well and **Wolverine**'s regular series is HOT! HOT! HOT! Keep an eye on issue #82...?

DC RECENT

As back issues, all of the **Superman** titles sell well if priced cheaply. The real DC movement is in the Vertigo titles especially **Sandman**, **Hellblazer** and **Shade**. Wizard Price Guide #53 at the beginning of 1996 listed **Sandman** #1 at $68.00! But in the U.K. it sells slow (for me) at £14.95.

INDEPENDENTS

I tend not to deal in the hot recent books. **Gen 13** did not work for me. **Spawn**, **Miracleman**, **Grendel**, Dark Horse **Star Wars** and old **Classics Illustrated** are all selling well at present and yes, **Aliens** is still asked for on a regular basis. Gold Key movie related titles are in great demand and we can sell **Four Colors** in any grade as soon as they come in.

1970s

Anything from the 1970s in high grade is in demand. All of Jack Kirby's work is hot especially **New Gods**, **Forever People** and **Mister Miracle**. **Avengers** issues between #87 and #185 have always sold well but now better than ever. Also, keep an eye on DC horror and ghost titles: an increased interest is noticeable. And be warned – prices on **Giant Size X-Men** #1, **X-Men** #94 and **Hulk** #181 are soaring in the States. Buy now or regret later.

SILVER AGE MARVEL AND DC

1995 was a fantastic year for us in this field. We have always been a major force in the buying and selling of high grade Silver Age books but in May of 1995 we reached new heights by managing to outbid fierce American competition on two of the highest grade collections sold that year. Issues in the collections included NM/NM- copies of **Amazing Spiderman** #1, #3, #5, #6, #7, #9, #10, #12, #13, #14, #16, #18, #19, #21 and **X-Men** #1-20 in grades between NM- and Mint excluding #17 which was a VFN. There was a very large selection of other issues which graded between VF- and upwards, averaging VF/NM. These issues sold very well at and above U.K. Guide. A small sample of recent sales would include: **Avengers** #1 in VF+ at £995.00, #1 Fair- at £39.95, #4 NM- at £1,400.00, **Amazing Spiderman** #1 in NM at £9,000.00, #1 in Good at £565, **Amazing Fantasy** #15 in FN+ for £2,700.00, 3 copies in varying VG-ish grades for between £800.00 and £950.00 and multiples of most other Silver Age issues in mixtures of grades. Expensive keys in very low grade were in high demand.

GOLDEN AGE

Demand for Golden Age issues is growing in the U.K. but it is still in its infancy compared to America. 75% of our sales are made to American collectors who have placed Wants Lists with us. Recent sales in the U.K. include: **Captain America** #59 in Fine at £600.00, #75 in FN+ at £525.00, **Detective Comics** #19 in Fine- at a stupid £650.00 - why did I do it? **More Fun** #102 in FN+ at £452.00, **Batman** #1 VG restored at £5,500.00, **Superman** #23 in VF+ at £450.00. Recent purchases include **Detective Comics** #1 and an unbelievable run of **More Fun** Comics including issues #8, #14, #52, #54, #57, #59, #61, #62, #63 and #65 in nice shape.

INTERESTING SALE OF THE YEAR

In 1995 I came across an original **Superman** colour press proof from 1941 in as new condition. It was signed by and came from Jerry Siegel's personal collection. This sold within 24 hours of purchasing it.

Well that's about it for another year. I would like to thank Duncan and John for giving me this chance to contribute and Melloney for her hard work and dedication.

All the best for now anyway.

Welcome to the new Price Guide. Firstly let me introduce myself, Alan Scott of Adventureland Inc. (Adventure into Comics Inc. USA).

Established over ten years ago in Florida we have been trading in the U.K. market for some seven years covering mail order, comic marts and retailing through our store. What we are covering in this report should give you an average guide to sales the past year. General sales have been good overall with all the major publishing houses pushing new lines and titles.

MARVEL

Marvel's line of comics has grown again this year with a range of old characters being re-launched i.e. **Captain Marvel** and **Doc Samson** plus a poor range of new titles i.e. **Green Goblin**, **Genesis 2099** etc.

General sales of Marvel have been steady on most regular titles. Noted sales have been the **Spiderman** Clone saga crossing all **Spiderman** titles as well as the Age of Apocalypse storyline and **Generation X** (in fact all mutant titles).

DC

Distinct improvement in DC sales this year with good quality writing and improved artwork on most major titles. Vertigo line of books - steady sales maintained throughout the year. **Superman/Batman** sales as strong as ever, some improvement in **Justice League of America**, **Green Lantern** and **Flash**. Some interesting comics in the pipeline with the World's End mini-series.

Generally good performance from DC this last year – very encouraging.

INDEPENDENTS

Again, generally good year for most Independents: Image, Dark Horse, Harris, Tekno, Crusader. Dramatic increase in sales of Image with the introduction of many new titles this last year. Noted sales are the very popular **Gen 13** series, good sales on **Spawn** (also back-issues!), **Pitt** and **WildC.A.T.S.**

Good year for the smaller companies with the popularity of Bad Girl books. Improved regular sales of new and back issues of **Dawn**, **Vampirella**, **Shi**, **Lady Death**, **Angela** and **Razor**. For books in high demand reflected in their market prices, look at all Dark Horse's **Star Wars** books.

DC/Marvel cross-overs this year were awaited with great anticipation. Generally good sales in DC vs. Marvel and the Amalgam line of books.

Slight improvement in the Silver Age market, especially **Spiderman** and **X-Men**. Key Silver Age Marvel books are still in demand in high grade (and cents copies too).

The comic market as a whole still seems unsettled as people wait too see the full implications of the Marvelution and a corporate mentality in the marketplace. This has caused retailers to become very conservative in their ordering with an agenda aimed at selling out. Such tactics have caused a very buoyant recent back issue market. This situation is most extreme with Marvel books as poor reordering methods leave their most popular titles, such as **X-Men** and Spider books, in high demand.

The main hot titles of the moment seem to be **Preacher**, **Wonder Woman** (Mike Deodato), **X-Men**, **DC vs. Marvel**, **X-Files**, **Gen 13**, **WildC.A.T.S.** and **Spawn**. One gets the impression from the comic marts that the profiteer has left the scene and that comics are once again being bought to read by people who really want them.

Things that are not hot must be lead by Acclaim; it's surely only a matter of time before they give up the ghost. The same could be said for Big Entertainment (Tekno Comix). As back issues I find these comics almost unsellable. No new mainstream titles from DC or Marvel seem to be setting the world on fire and fans appear to be sticking to old favourites. However sales of both **Superman** and **Batman** families seem to have dipped owing to a lack of direction in the books although **Robin** and **Catwoman** are holding their own. Image books do very well with the exception of the Extreme Studios line which is poor. Dark Horse continues to sell on its **Aliens**, **Legends** and **Star Wars** material but little else. Not much this year from the Indies but **Stray Bullets** and **Cerebus** are much asked after.

If you want something to watch, keep an eye on **Thor** and maybe **Supergirl** and **Dreaming** when they come out. In summary, look for quality comics which I'm glad to say finally seem to be sought after. Even if they're not worth anything, at least you can enjoy reading them.

RICHARD EMMS – CHAOS CITY COMICS

Over the past four and a half years that we have been in business, I have never seen this market to be as stable and as encouraging as others I have encountered.

SILVER AND BRONZE AGE

Over the past year of so we have sold an amazing amount of key silver and bronze age books in mid to high grades.

It seems that as soon as we get an **X-Men** #1, it will be snapped up within a few weeks. In the last few months we have sold three **X-Men** #1s: FN £1250.00, FN- £1150.00, VG/FN £1050.00. It seems with the **X-Men** film just around the corner, fans want these books more than before.

Other books that have sold over the past year or so include Giant **X-Men** #1 (VFN) £200.00, **X-Men** #94 (VFN) £200.00, **Daredevil** #1 (FN) £300.00 and (G+) £150.00. **Detective Comics** #45 (VFN) £995.00, **Conan the Barbarian** #1 (VFN) £80.00 and others too many to mention.

It seems that although the silver age market is quite volatile at present there are buyers out there who want key books and are prepared to pay decent money for them.

NEW COMICS

What can we say? Too much competition has made new product pretty poor when it comes to quality. Too much hype, too many variant covers spoil what I think should be readable and most of all enjoyable. But hey, those Bad Girl "nude covers" don't half sell well!

MARVEL

Marvel's books sell particularly well. The top books at present being the **X-Men** family (apart from Excalibur), **Captain America**, **Daredevil**, **Avengers** and the **Spidey** titles.

X-Men is by far the best selling group in the shop and need no promotion to sell off the shelf, although the quality has started to dip in the artwork and story-telling. **Wolverine** #100 was a bit of a let down with not even a hint about the return of the Adamantium Skeleton.

Spiderman seems to be in ever decreasing circles with the question of "Is it the real one or not?" looming over the book's head.

MARVEL & DC

It has to be said that Marvel vs DC was one of the biggest let- downs of all time. The Amalgam series had its ups and downs, but a few of the books were what I would call amazing.

It goes to show how big companies can sell large amounts of rubbish. But I'm afraid it was the same old case of "they sold well" scenario which I can't groan about after all I do own the shop.

DC – THE STEP FORWARD FOR COMICS.

The books that DC produce are still the best around when it comes to storytelling. **Batman** and the related books are far better than they have ever been.

Vertigo has to be the best thing that has ever happened to DC in a long while. Books such as **Preacher**, **Invisibles** and **Death** are simply milestones whenever produced.

And the new books that this company produces seem to be a bit more daring then any other publisher has ever produced.

IMAGE COMICS

Forget **Extreme** and Rob Liefeld – they are doomed. Not even Stephen Platt could save him and his dire comics. But when any **Top Cow**, **Wildstorm** and McFarlane related books hit the shelves they are sure to sell out.

21 #1 was massive and **Weapon Zero** even bigger. And books like Witchblade and Blackops seem to be picking up more readers every month.

Still at the top slot is **Spawn** but even this comic has started to lose a bit of momentum with readers but still it sells like hot cakes with readers and so do the spin-off titles such as **Spawn/WildC.A.T.S.** and **Angela** etc.

INDEPENDENTS

Remember those days when **Magnus the Robot Fighter** #12 was selling for thirty quid. Remember when **Harbinger** #1 was at an astonishing sixty quid (or sometimes more if you had the coupons still attached). What a shame about our Valiant. Fancy selling a pretty average comics publisher for 60 million dollars? They did. And what do they publish now? About two of the surviving comics namely **X-O Manowar** and **Solar Man of the Atom**.

Acclaim seem to be putting on a brave face offering comic related versions of **Magic The Gathering** character cards – which are not bad when you get a free rare card inside the package as well. Apart from the Magic series, Acclaim do not offer much in the way of readable material – let's hope **Sliders** does well for them.

Independents in general seemed to have picked up more readers than ever before. Titles such as **Dawn from Sirius** and David Lapham's **Stray Bullets** seem to have great reader potential as well.

MAGIC THE GATHERING AND OTHER CARD GAMES

It has to be said that these card games are amazing sellers. Magic The Gathering and its expansions were the first popular game to lift off but now it surprises even me the amount we sell.

The most popular card game so far this year has been the **Star Wars** Premiere Edition of which we have sold cases. In fact in January we sold more **Star Wars** cards than we did all other comics put together. If you are a retailer who is still wondering about the above all I can say is get them in quick!

Anyway I am going to draw a close to my words of wisdom. I would like to say a few thanks to a few people who make this industry worth being in…so thanks to Dave Gibbons, Derek Watson, Duncan McAlpine, John Skoulides, Duncan McMillan and all the Chaos staff.

All the best for 1996.

JOHN, MARTIN, DUNCAN, ALEX, PETER, PAUL, JON, ANDREA – MIGHTY WORLD OF COMICANA LTD

It is a great pleasure to be asked to contribute to this year's Price Guide as we have just settled into our new shop and offices and look forward to the next year with tremendous anticipation.

Another strange year in the industry, (aren't they all?) so let's start with…

NEW PRODUCT

From Bad Girl to Worse Girl, it has been the year of the Lady. Yes **Lady Death**, **Lady Rawhide**, **Vampirella**, **Double Impact**, **Shi**, **Angela**, **Dawn**, **Avengelyne** and many more. Hey what about all those Nude editions, rude editions, lewd editions. Naked lady with sword cover A or of course Big breasted girl with axe, includes foil cover and coupon to get your free velvet cover for only £30.00. What do mean cynical, who me? Look if you like it we will supply it and if you think the story quality is good then you at least bought an unbagged copy. Seriously though, a lot of high quality material surfaced in amongst the dross, Tucci, Linsner etc. **Preacher** is great and did you like **Ash**? And how about **Gen 13**? The award for most sought after and hottest title? **X-Files** comics of course. We like most of our competitors were CULT out by the demand (very little joke).

The most pleasing thing was the attention and availability of the new product lines, so keep up the good work Diamond.

I suppose I can't let the New Product year pass by without making reference to **Amalgam**. Yes, Marvel and D.C working together to make the world a safer place. Nuff said.

GOLDEN AGE, SILVER AGE AND OLD AGE

I am not going to bore you with all the big sales we made this year like the near mint **Daredevil** 1#, the **Batman** 1# etc as you already know that we are the best for back issues and make more effort than most to offer the keenest grading and pricing. I want to ask you to look very carefully at the Golden Age and Silver Age market and look for trends. Find the trends and find the bargains. Watch out this year for **Wonder Woman** and **Batman**. Also X-books will continue to be hot. It was again the year of low and high grade book sales with middle grades falling between the devil and the deep blue sea. Very few restored books surfaced this year. Look for more Movie titles and watch out for Archie Comics as you the reading public have finally noticed that they are **Wolverine** free.

SUMMARY
Just a brief summary as I don't want to disturb your sleep any longer. We can look towards a similar year as far as new material is concerned with numerous new titles and several artists and writers growing in popularity. Back issues will return to their former glories if you can find fair and honest traders who understand how to grade and more importantly understand the difference between the American and U.K markets.

For us as a company it has been an interesting year, what with moving into the old Stateside building and employing some of their staff.

I hope that we have been able to help some of their old customers and we are going to try some new and exciting things in future and hope that you will enjoy a great year. Thanks to the old grey one for allowing us this time and space and in the words of Alfred E Neuman, what me worry?

DAVE FINN AND SUSAN FOORD – INCOGNITO COMICS
Once again I would like to thank Duncan for letting me vent my spleen upon the comic world once more. It seems such a long time since our last market report for the UK guide, and so much water has passed under the bridge in the world of the four colour comic book, that I'm almost at a loss as to where to start.

As I write this report, its early 1996, and the comic world remains in turmoil.

Anyhow, here's how it is with us.

THE GOLDEN AGE
The UK Golden Age market, has really taken an upturn in the last couple of years. Many collectors, especially DC Silver Age collectors are reaching further back in time than ever to expand their collections. Most books from the late forties and early fifties are a lot more affordable than the majority of the DC Silver Age key books, and this is reflected in the increased popularity of comics such as **Batman** 50-100, **Superman** 60-130 and **Worlds Finest** 60-110. Availability is much more of a problem with these books than affordability though.

The biggest increase in demand has definitely been for **Golden Age Timelys**. Copies of **Captain America** Comics, **Sub-Mariner** and **Marvel Mystery Comics** are particularly hard to keep in stock. This of course, affects the prices of these books. Compare the prices in this, the new UK guide, with the prices in the last one, and see. Life would be a lot easier for a lot of us, if more of these books were available in the UK. Now as in the past, most of our Timely issues have to be purchased from collectors and dealers in the States.

Copies of **Timelys** are selling in almost every grade. Even very low grade copies of relatively scarce books are selling well.

Sales of Golden Age comics include; **Superman** #1 (1939) in VG+ restored; £7000. **Submariner** #1 (Timely) VF- £3200. **Submariner** #3 VG+, £600. **Captain America** Comics #2, VF, colour touched £2900. **Amazing Man** #5 (Centaur) VF, light restoration, £4000. **Marvel Mystery Comics** #15, Fine, £450.

SILVER AGE
The Silver Age comic book market, has remained one of he most consistent, since the last British Price Guide was published. Interest is still strong in most titles, but the main Marvel and DC titles are still the most popular, especially **Amazing Spider-Man**, **Avengers** and **X-Men**. All grades are selling well, especially very high grade books, as has been the case for as long as I can remember. Low grade key books also sell extremely well, at the right price. Recent sales of these books include **Tales Of Suspense** #39 (Fair), £100 and **Avengers** #1 (Fair), £75. There has also been a noticeable rise in interest in mid-grade books, particularly the key ones – if the price is right. We are selling more VG to Fine comics than ever before, which is surprising in that there is certainly a lot more mid grade collections surfacing, and there has never been so many on the market.

Sales of note, include Incredible **Hulk** #1, VF, trimmed, £3200; 1, Good, £495. **Amazing Fantasy** #15, Good, £995. **Amazing Spider-Man** #1, VG, £1495; 1, Good+, £650; 2, Fine+, £695; 3, VF-, £425; 4, VF, £450; 14, VF, £350. **Avengers** #1 VG+, £340. **Fantastic Four** #1, VF-, £3200; 3, VG, £395; 4, VG, £425. **X-Men** #1, Good+, £275. **Tales Of Suspense** #39, VG, £495. **Showcase** #13, VF-, £1200, 17, VF-, £450. **Action Comics** #252,VG, £175.

Showcase #22, VG+, £525. **Green Lantern** 1, Fine +,£550. **Flash** #105, Fine+, £795. **Justice League of America** #1, VG, £395.

Since the last UK guide, we have sold copies of almost every single Marvel and DC Silver Age key book, in one grade or another

RESTORATION
The professional restoration and the amateur repair of comic books, has never been so commonplace. The number of excellent restorers in the USA has increased over the last few years, as has, consequently, the number of restored books in circulation. It becomes increasingly more difficult to spot really professional work, though the more restored books handled, the easier it becomes to spot the restoration. A friendly word of advice – always check that the book that you are buying is really what you think it is? Amateur restoration is much easier to spot, but still, care must be taken when buying.

CENTS VERSUS PENCE
As this is the first UK price guide to include US prices, I thought it appropriate that I might mention the great Cents versus Pence debate.

Over the years, there has been much discussion over the American Cents copies of comics being much more desirable than the UK priced Pence copies, or the Cents priced books with the Thorpe and Porter "TP" ink stamp. Yes, it is nigh on impossible to sell a Pence book anywhere outside the UK, but collectors in the UK each have their own personal preferences. I have just as many customers for Pence/Stamped copies of Silver Age comics as I have for Cents unstamped copies. Not surprisingly almost all of the Cents copies are sold to collectors who look for high grade copies.

Collecting should always be a personal thing. If you are happy with a Pence or stamped copy, that is your prerogative. After all, it is your collection, not anybody else's. Why should you be told which version of a comic to collect? Just enjoy!

BRONZE AGE/1970s
The seventies have always been a bit of a doldrums for back-issues. Every now and then, there is a flurry of interest for a while, and then it quietens down again. When the Silver Age market became too expensive, some collectors decided to concentrate on the cheaper 70s comics. It was generally thought that this exodus would cause a rise in prices. This has happened, but not at the alarming rate that many thought. As in everything, there are exceptions. Most ND comics from the early to mid seventies are indeed very popular, especially the key first appearance issues (Hulk #181, **X-Men** #94 and **Giant Size X-Men** #1). Most early issues of the Marvel comic runs, also sell very well. There are some surprisingly hard to find comics from this time period – **Defenders** #10, and copies of **Avengers** #93 (without sticker damage) are good examples.

Notable sales from this period include Incredible **Hulk** #181, VF+, £265; 181 Fine, £150. **X-Men** #94, VF+, £185; 94, Fine+, £125. **Giant Size X-Men** #1, VF, £170. **House Of Secrets** #92, VF, £195. Other notable sellers include the ND **Amazing Spider-Man** issues, especially #121 and #122. **Spidey** #129 (first **Punisher**) along with the clone issues #149 and #150 have gone off the boil though. One small word of warning. Marvel had the annoying habit in the seventies of sticking their Marvel "Value" stamps in some very key issues. These value stamps were to be cut out of the comic and could be redeemed for various goodies. Incredible **Hulk** #181, the first full **Wolverine** story is one good example. When buying a copy, always check that the value stamp is still intact. Most of the stamps are on editorial pages, which are sometimes totally removed, to further confuse. Once again, let the buyer beware.

MODERN COMICS
I could use this report as a soapbox to comment on the lamentable state of the Direct Market, but I think I'll leave that to everyone else – mostly... The Buyouts and Exclusives. The Distributor Wars and Title Cancellations. Does our industry really need all this upheaval? All businesses must adapt to survive. Can our industry react fast enough to all this change without collapsing in on itself? In America, the market for new comics appears to be shrinking drastically, while the American economy appears to have taken a general upturn. On a recent visit to Florida, one of the local comic shop owners told me that the new edition of his local Yellow Pages had just been published. In the last edition approximately 35 shops were listed. In the new one – just 18! Ouch. This doesn't appear to be happening in the UK – at the moment. In the last year, shops have opened, and shops have closed, but the number appears to be reasonably stable.

Very few Publishers have expanding markets. Those that have bucked the trend are generally speculator driven (yes, there are a few left) and a few have held their own. How long before publishers begin to fold. Collectors are a lot more discerning these days. With the huge increases in cover pricing, few can collect everything that they would like, so titles are being cut by the customers. Shops then amend their orders, as do the distributors. Sales drop, and titles are cut. Some publishers just cannot survive.

I hope and pray that the comics industry survives these troubled times, and that we're all here to tell the tale.

What can I say... Always look on the bright side of life.

JULES BURT/GEORGE LESSITER – PURPLE HAZE

Hello from the West Country! Well, what a year. After outgrowing our old shop we have had to move to a new one, this time with even more space. We've had a definite upturn in business with more and more Standing Orders from new customers. This can only be healthy and we hope that it's a similar story for everyone else. New readers are the lifeblood of the hobby and without them the back issue market would be in a very sorry state. Let's hope it continues.

CURRENT TITLES/YEAR IN REVIEW

MARVEL

X-books have continued to dominate throughout the last year. The "Age of Apocalypse" storyline creating various mini-series spin-offs was a huge success with most books selling out almost immediately. The **Alpha/Omega Prime** books were an instant success and are still in demand.

X-Men, **Uncanny X-Men**, **X-Force**, **X-Factor** and **Generation X** continue to sell in vast quantities. The exceptions in X-books seem to be **X-Men Adventures** and the dreadful **Professor X and the X-Men**. The latter rehashing old **X-Men** adventures in a 1990s style doesn't really work. Check out the reprints of the original Lee/Kirby stories – they're still a much better read.

Wolverine remains one of our hottest sellers and **Cable** along with the new **X-Man** title have gained further ground with back issues being constantly sought out. **Storm** and **Askani's Son** mini-series are selling well.

Sales of the **Spiderman** family have remained healthy despite the ongoing Clone storyline which has stretched the patience of even the most ardent Spidey fans. Marvel have come up with this idea that the last 250+ issues of **Amazing Spiderman**, 200+ issues of **Spectacular Spiderman** and the entire run of **Web of Spiderman** have all been about a completely different character!! Come to think of it that also includes all the Marvel Team-Up stories and every appearance since around 1975. Hah! Still, Peter Parker, Ben Reilly AKA Scarlet Spider or whoever, these books have sold well throughout the past year. The **Scarlet Spider** spin-off series sold moderately well although nowhere in the same proportion as the **X-Men** mini-series. Other Spidey mini-series have fared well.

Spiderman Adventures has done well owing to the excellent animated TV series shown on Saturday mornings. **Amazing Spiderman** #400 with its tombstone cover must rate as one of the worst gimmick covers ever. It was almost impossible to tell what the book was!

Integrating the New Warriors title into the **Spiderman** family of books has not helped it. Sales of this title have always been lousy and it will no doubt soon be joining **Force Works**, **War Machine** and various 2099 titles in that great bargain box in the sky.

Venom mini-series have continued to do well with extremely healthy back issue sales. **Amazing Spiderman** #300 (1st Venom appearance) continued to be in demand and easily sells for £30 around here. Watch out for early Carnage appearances as these are now being steadily sought after.

Other Marvel titles? Well the recently re-vamped Warren Ellis/Mike Deodato **Thor** was just what this title needed. Many fans missed these when they first came out and #491 and up are now creating a minor stir and being snapped up. Hopefully the rumours abounding that this title is shortly to be cancelled after 34 years will not come true.

2099 titles – **X-Men 2099**, **Spiderman 2099** and **Doom 2099** sell okay. All the others are a waste of shelf space and do not sell.

Punisher books have taken a massive downturn. Interest in the latest series has waned after the first few issues. The only Punisher books that still seem to be of interest are the original mini-series and the first few issues of the second series. Even so these are only fetching around 50% of last year's Guide prices.

The same goes for **Ghost Rider** with the current and original series

having lost a great deal of interest.

Poor old **Conan**! This once great 1970s book is still not selling, even after various face-lifts and regenerations. Maybe it's time Marvel put this one out of its misery once and for all.

Some books which have picked up in sales recently are **The Avengers** and **Captain America**. The Timeslide storyline in **Avengers** #395 with the death of Tony Stark (Iron Man) and replacing him with a younger version has sparked further interest in the **Avengers** and given a fresh input into the **Iron Man** title which had become rather stale and jaded in recent months. **Captain America** is now being picked up once more by former fans who had dropped this title previously.

Daredevil remains a constant seller as do the **Fantastic Four**. Peter David's **Hulk** continues to attract a strong following with strong monthly sales. The forthcoming Lee/Liefeld take-over of certain Marvel books seems to be causing more apprehension than excitement. Time will tell.

Humour books such as **Ren & Stimpy** and **Beavis & Butt-Head** have slowed down during the year.

Marvel vs. DC has been a huge success with #1 being a complete sell out. The initial batch of **Amalgam** comics have just arrived and are selling like hot cakes!

ULTRAVERSE – the integration of the Malibu/Marvel Universes has produced two sets of books. Modest sales on those books with X-character appearances being picked up by **X-Men** fans and very poor sales on all other books with characters such as Mantra, Night Man etc. The only exception here is Rune.

Malibu's **Deep Space Nine** continued to sell well until Marvel stopped all UK imports.

DC

Superman and **Batman** titles have slowed a little during the past year. When DC come up with a good storyline like "Death of.." or "Knightfall" then there's no stopping these books. "Contagion" and "Underworld Unleashed" have hardly set the world on fire. Spin-offs, however, such as **Azrael**, **Catwoman** and **Robin** have sold steadily.

JLA and related characters such as **Flash** and **Green Lantern** have showed no dramatic increases during the year.

Starman was an unexpected hit and the Ostrander/Mandrake **Spectre** remains a classy but neglected-by-fans book.

Good solid sales on **Star Trek** and related books.

VERTIGO

As always **Sandman** leads the pack with strong healthy back issue and current sales. Shame that it's ending. **Hellblazer**, after going through a short slump, seems to be picking up again.

Sandman Mystery Theatre and **Swamp Thing** have shown steady sales.

Back issues of **Preacher** and **Invisibles** are hot and in demand and the new **Death – Time of Your Life** mini-series is selling like crazy!

IMAGE

Spawn remains our current biggest seller now closely being challenged by **Gen 13**. All **Gen 13** back issues are hot especially the first series and the 13 cover variations of the second series.

Astro City was a huge hit and sold extremely well. Sad to see Sergio Aragones **Groo** title finally bite the dust after all these years. It's one of the finest humour books on the market and will be missed around here.

"Babe" books such as **Avengelyne**, **Glory** and **Witchblade** have all sold well, mainly to adolescent (and a few older!) males.

Maxx and Pitt books have remained steady throughout the year. However many Image books have taken a sharp downturn over the past twelve months with some fans giving up on them altogether.

DARK HORSE

All **Alien** and **Predator** back issues continue to sell well. **Big Boy** and **Rusty the Boy Robot** was an unexpected gem. With its large format it caught many people's attention. Check out Geoff Darrow's detailed artwork on this one. Superb!

Star Wars mini-series remain extremely hot. **The Mask** sold initially but interest seems to have petered out. **G.I. Joe** was a complete flop.

VALIANT/ACCLAIM

What can we say? The only books left that sell in any small quantity are the former Gold Key characters **Magnus**, **Solar** and **Turok**. All back issues are extremely slow moving to stagnant. The days when a **Harbinger** #1 had a £50 price tag on it are long gone. Dealers are struggling to get a tenner on this one now. Titles such as **Archer & Armstrong**, **X-O Manowar** and **Bloodshot** are stone dead. To be honest we can't really see this company surviving in the long run.

TOPPS

X-Files #1. What more needs to be said. The biggest comic hit in the last couple of years. Topps' low print run and the astronomical demand for this book sent it spiralling to around the £50 mark in no time. We have sold around a dozen issues at this price and could sell more if we could get hold of them. Later issues are also heavily in demand with #2 fetching around £30 and #3 around £20. These books have certainly not peaked as yet.

Mars Attacks, the cult card classic, continues to gain ground and is attracting a firm following. The forthcoming Tim Burton film will either make or break this series. We shall have to wait and see.

TEKNO COMIX

Don't sell at all. Straight into the 25p back issue racks with these!

OTHERS

The "Bad Girl" books are hot, hot, hot! Chaos Comics' **Lady Death**, Harris' **Vampirella**, Sirius' **Dawn** and Crusade's **Shi** are what the fan boys want. Early issues of all these are rocketing with demand outstripping supply.

Bongo Comics' **Simpsons** remains a firm fan favourite. A great fun read. And as always we have to mention Knockabout's **Fabulous Furry Freak Brothers**. They just keep selling and selling.

U.K. MARKET

2000AD, once a superb seller, has taken somewhat of a downturn over the past year. The Judge Dredd film, which in the end was a bit of a let down, seems to have done more damage than good. Many former fans have given up buying this comic completely. Back issues are plentiful with little demand for them. The only ones of interest seem to be pre prog 100. Early issues with free gifts are still in demand by more serious collectors. Our #1 with Space Spinner recently went for £50. Low sales on other Dredd related comics.

Likewise with **Tank Girl**. The appalling film seems to have killed off whatever cult interest there had been in her previously.

U.K. **X-Files** editions are red hot. Many fans are picking this one up alongside their U.S. editions. As with the U.S. copies, the earlier ones are in demand. Our #1 with free badge gift has just sold for £35.

Marvel's **Essential X-Men** and **Astonishing Spiderman** are very popular with these magazine again being picked up alongside the U.S. editions.

Viz, once one of our best sellers, seems to have been in a tailspin for the last couple of years. Not as popular as it used to be. Perhaps the jokes are beginning to wear a bit thin.

Steady sales on U.K. edition **Manga** comics.

BACK ISSUES

MARVEL

All back issues of mutant related books sell well, **Uncanny X-Men** still being the most popular. **Wolverine** is proving to be a title which we have trouble keeping in stock – all issues and particularly the original mini-series are hot. Back issue **Cable**, **X-Force** and **Generation X** books still shift easily. Early issues of **New Mutants** have slowed however the later Cable related books, post #87, have picked up again during the past year.

Amazing **Spiderman** is as hot as ever, by far the most popular of the **Spiderman** family of books. Average sales on Spectacular and Web books. All gimmick/hologram covers are still selling extremely well.

Hulk sales are on the up with the McFarlane and Keown issues still going well.

Steady back issue sales on **Fantastic Four**, **Daredevil**, **Avengers** and **Thor**. Slow back issue sales on **Iron Man** and **Captain America**.

The original series of **Silver Surfer** remains heavily in demand with no signs of slowing down. Our #1 (VFN) and our #4 (VFN) both recently sold for £240 each.

Many once popular 1970s books have slowed down or become stagnant. A good example of these would be the **Astonishing Tales Deathlok** books or

Marvel Presents Guardians of the Galaxy which now only fetch a small fraction of their former guide prices. **Ghost Rider**, **Punisher**, **Sub-Mariner** and **Shield** books are virtually at a standstill. All early Silver Age Marvels from the 1962/63 period are still shifting well in any grade.

DC

Silver Age: Mid grade copies of most Silver Age books are selling very well. **Batman**, **Detective**, **Action** and **J.L.A.** being the best. Very high grade copies are slow movers. Recent sales include **J.L.A.** #34 (VFN) for £25 and **Swamp Thing** #1 (1st series) (VFN+) at £35.

Current titles fare much better in the back issues sales market. Most Vertigo titles are selling well with the exception of **Animal Man** – £12 for #1 seems way too high. **Sandman** and **Hellblazer** lead the pack. Recent sales include **Sandman** #1 (NM) at £30 and **Hellblazer** #1 (NM) at £20. All other issues at above previous U.K. guide price. Recent **Batman** issues are pretty slow with fans having enough trouble keeping up with new product let alone back issues. Generally not much action on the main super-hero lines. **Babylon 5** #1 was a definite sleeper and now commands at least £5. **Invisibles** #1 is impossible to keep in stock as are all issues of **Preacher**.

INDEPENDENTS

Silver Age: the only thing selling are Gold Key comics. High grade copies are not turning up but when they do they'll sell at any price. Recent sales include **Star Trek** #1 (VFN) for £200.

Modern comics: **Spawn** leads the way closely followed by The **X-Files**. Other Indies that move are **Gen 13**, **Razor**, **Star Wars**, **Ghost** and **Sin City**. Recent sales include **Spawn** #4 (with coupon. NM) for £11 and **Star Wars: Dark Empire** #1 (NM) for £20. Early copies of "Bad Girl" comics are still much in demand.

TRADING CARDS

Another busy year with these. Massive demand for The **X-Files** series 1 & 2 as well as all **Star Wars** cards. **Star Trek** cards have slowed down a little however the gaming cards are as hot as ever. Recent film tie-in sets have fared poorly this year, the best being **Batman Forever**. Comic related series are not so hot with the best being the **Shi Chromium**. The **Marvel Overpower** card game started well but has now petered out. Generally gaming cards are selling reasonably well with the best being **Star Wars**.

MERCHANDISE

Current action figures available in the U.K. are selling okay. New figures from the States that aren't going to be released over here are red hot. Examples are **Star Trek**, **Spiderman** The Animated Series and certain **Star Wars** figures. The U.K. action figure market is growing with more and more collectors getting into the hobby. However trying to sell a rare figure at American prices is very difficult. Most figures sell at about three quarters of the U.S. price.

Older figures sell a lot more easily. All **Star Wars** figures and accessories sell well in any condition, loose or boxed. Minimal interest in older **Star Trek** figures. Most other lines (**Black Hole**, **Battlestar Galactica**, **Indiana Jones** etc) are stagnant with virtually no collector interest.

Well there you have it for another year. See you in twelve months!

IVOR DAVIS – RED HOT COMICS

Hello again. Two years have flown by since the last Price Guide and although it's difficult to cover all that's been happening, I'll try to cover some of the important trends.

First off, I do not run a shop but rather a mail-order business which brings me into contact with customers the length and breadth of Britain as well as Ireland and Europe too. I regularly take stalls at marts in Newcastle, Manchester and Liverpool as well as Glasgow and I feel this gives me a good perspective to talk in general terms about the market we operate in. Over and above my Advance Import Service most of the stock which I deal with is 1970s to modern day, increasingly Independents.

MARVEL

Still the market leader in terms of overall sales and Market Share but no longer the House of Ideas. Marvel have reaped a terrible harvest from the speculator seeds they sowed in '92-94. I think the galling thing for people as I write this, however, is that just when my customers were beginning to say complimentary things about Marvel and buy more comics, Marvel have not only moved the goal posts but relaid the turf as well. By that I mean Thor and **Captain America** for example went from selling 1 or 2 copies each a year ago to 15 or 20 now. The **Avengers** has increased from about 4 copies to 12 or 16. Fans were enjoying the writing and the art – I've heard Mark Waid's stint on **Captain America** compared favourably with Steve Englehart's run on Cap in the 1970s – and who is taking over the reins this summer? Rob Liefeld. However, all is not yet lost. Bob Harras seems to know where he is going. In the short term, Lee and Liefeld's tenure on various Marvel books will at least maintain orders at current levels but I'm not sure that the quality will be sufficient to launch the new era that Calabrese and Co. hoped for.

The best selling new books that Marvel have launched in the last couple of years are both X-books: **Generation X** and **X-Man**. The "Phalanx Covenant" storyline and the "Age of Apocalypse" from last year were both extremely good sellers and **Generation X** and **X-Man** seem to have maintained a high quality of writing and artwork since then. Sadly the "Send in the Clones" shenanigans in the Spidey books has resulted in a downturn in orders in all the **Spiderman** family with the exception of **Untold Tales** which has to be one of the best buys around just now. Marvel's revamping of the **Ultraverse** was keenly anticipated and the Infinity issues, including the variant covers, flew off the shelves but sadly the books were already directionless before Black Wednesday signalled the end was nigh.

Hindsight is a wonderful thing and if I was to pick out a couple of Marvel books which I wish I'd over-ordered on at the time then I guess it would have to be Warren Ellis' **Ruins** from last year and **Star Trek: Deep Space Nine** #30-32 though for different, distributive reasons.

DC

Of all the major publishers DC seem to have come through the maelstrom of the past couple of years in the best shape. I've seen healthy increases in orders and on back issues sales for **Batman**, **Superman**, **Flash** and **Green Lantern** titles. However the most spectacular difference has been in orders and sales on Vertigo books. **Sandman** has continued to be a very good seller but it's the "new wave" of Vertigo titles – **Preacher** and **The Invisibles** – which appear to have caught the imagination. **Preacher** sells higher for me than all the **Batman** titles and runs the top three **X-Men** titles close. Not to be outdone the new Gaiman/Bachalo **Death** mini-series topped my chart with orders on #2 exceeding 50 copies. The most puzzling DC event of last year was the cancellation of the **Babylon 5** comic. After a slow start sales steadily picked up and orders for the final issue were higher than **Superman**. Wherever **Babylon 5** comics appear next, the publishers will have a sure-fire hit on their hands. (Hey, how about a **Hulk/Babylon 5** cross-over – get Rob Liefeld to do it. He's done such a good job with **Battlestar Galactica** don't you think?!). As I write this **Hitman** #1 has just come in and sold out. Methinks fans are going to scour the country looking for his appearance in **Batman Chronicles** #4.

IMAGE

The best selling Image books are **Spawn**, **Gen 13** and **WildC.A.T.S.** in that order. Remember that hindsight thing I mentioned a couple of paragraphs back? The **Gen 13** mini-series has been one of the sales phenomena of the last couple of years. The last #1 sold for £27.95 and as for the 13 variant covers...! Just when you think interest is cooling down in **Spawn**, along comes a customer who demands that you find him the first 10 issues of the series oh and **Angela** too while you're about it. And what would you like for an encore, sir? The **Gen 13** mini-series perhaps?

DARK HORSE

Orders for **Concrete**, **Sin City**, **Hellboy** and **Madman** have all steadily increased over the past couple of years – Dark Horse seems like a natural home for the Legends creators. **Star Wars** titles too have thrived and Dark Horse's sensitivity to the market was confirmed a few months ago when they announced that there would be no more than three titles solicited each month so as not to saturate the market (and fleece the loyal fan – Marvel take note). Back issues of **Ghost** and the various **Manga** titles sell well for us with **Appleseed**, **Ghost in the Shell** and **Dominion** growing in demand all the time.

TOPPS

The truth is in here! Little did we know when Topps released #1 of The **X-Files** just over a year ago how strong a seller it was going to be. #1 has been selling for us recently at £45 and orders for numbers #13-17 stand at 50 to 60 copies. We also managed to get copies of the Topps Edition of the magazine and they

have been flying off the wall boards at marts in the North of England. Although the title is one of the most erratically published there's no sign of this phenomenon abating. The fun is trying to predict what's going to take off next (**Independence Day** – that's my tip!)

INDIES

The market is so diverse that it's difficult to lump everything together as if it was an homogenous group. Amongst the true gems of the last couple of years are **Stray Bullets**, **Bone** (doing well with Image now), **Strangers in Paradise**, **Poison Elves**, **Strangehaven** and **Tyrant**. We pride ourselves on keeping a very large stock of Indies and it's books such as these that fans are hunting for at marts. Worthy of a mention for frenetic sales activity too are **Lady Death**, **Shi** (will #7 ever come out?), **Verotika**, **Satanika** and **Penthouse Comix**. There was a real boom in the sales of "bad girl" comics for several months but it's showing signs of slowing down now even though the number of Lingerie and Nude editions being solicited seems to be on the increase! Indies which I'm most asked about are first prints of **Stray Bullets** and early **Poison Elves** although **Dawn** manages to (ahem) hold her own with #1 selling out at £5.00.

SUMMARY

Although there's no doubt that the industry as a whole has gone through a very difficult period in the last 18 months, my business has gone from strength to strength enabling me to devote myself full-time to it now. As primarily a mail-order business I find that there are an awful lot of fans and collectors out there who for various reasons do not go into comic shops or attend marts and conventions. Despite hefty price increases too (which we have managed to mitigate) over the past year or so, support for the core titles from Marvel and DC remain strong and there is a growing readership for many of the self-published works and the more innovative titles produced by Dark Horse, for example. With a positive attitude, sound marketing and comics which are well written and drawn (which we're getting back to!) the industry can recover to former heights. See you next Guide.

A big hello to everyone from sunny Bradford! Firstly we would like to thank John and Duncan for inviting us to write our first market report. For those not familiar with our name we attend nearly all the major marts up and down the country and we also offer a friendly mail order service.

GOLDEN AGE

There is definitely a strong following for these books at the moment, especially the main super-hero lines. Recently we acquired a large collection of Golden Age and we have had some good sales throughout the last two months. Recent sales include **Superman** #3, **All Star Comics** #4,12,18 and 36, **Batman** #62 plus a Near Mint **Batman** #4.

SILVER AGE MARVEL AND DC

Massive! Demand for high grade VF+ and above unstamped cents copies with some key books selling at U.K. Guide and a half, double in some instances. There's still a healthy demand for lower grades but not at Guide. We're constantly fighting to keep certain issues in stock especially high grade **Spiderman**'s and all 10 cent DC copies. Recent sales include **Avengers** #1-10 (FN), **X-Men** #1 (VG+), **Fantastic Four** #5 (FN), Tales of Suspense #50-66 all being Near Mint, **Flash** #105 (VG), **Superman** #100 (FN+) and a whole host of **Spiderman**'s.

1970s

This era is selling very well at the moment. All ND issues are flying out of stock. A few surprises over the last few months with sales on titles like **Eternals**, **Jungle Action**, **Ghost Rider**, **Nova** and **Werewolf By Night**, comics that you could find in most dealers' cheap boxes a few years ago. **Bat** titles are very popular at the moment; Neal Adams issues are always in demand. Biggest scare of recent times has been the jump in price and demand for **Giant Size X-Men** #1 and **X-Men** #94, especially in high grade.

RECENT DC

Over the last six months we have seen a large leap in sales on quite a few titles. This has been most noticeable on all Vertigo titles, **The Flash**, **Impulse**, **Green Lantern**, **Hawkman** and all the **Superman** titles and one pleasant surprise was **Batman Adventures** becoming very popular.

RECENT MARVEL

We tend to sell a lot of Marvel, right across the range of titles, with anything X-title outselling everything else! Issues always in demand: **X-Men** #266, **Wolverine** #1,#10 and #75 and **Spiderman** #300. With Incredible **Hulk** picking up as well, **Hulk** #340 has been disappearing from boxes.

IMAGE

Can this company do no wrong? **Gen 13** (both series) always sell well, **Spawn** still as popular as ever including all spin-off titles. **Cyberforce** is picking up again but pick of the moment has to be **Witchblade** #1 with an excellent cover and the variant covers seem too be going if sensibly priced.

INDEPENDENTS

X-Files, Shi, Razor, Cry For Dawn, Double Impact, Creed, Lady Death, Avengelyne and **Ash** – just a selection of titles that have emerged through 1995/96, these seem as popular as the X-titles. Bad Girl books are in heavy demand, notably the early issues of **Cry For Dawn**. **Shi** is always selling, even more so with the introduction of the Tomoe character. All variants and special editions sell well.

The biggest hit this last year has to be **X-Files**. We are constantly selling out of all issues and at the time of writing we have just received the very elusive **X-Files** 1/2. Given the notoriety of Wizard's comic book productions and irrespective of any low print runs we can foresee demand far outstripping supply. Indeed the few copies we managed to acquire are already fetching prices around £25.00. How long will it be before this comic fetches more money than **X-Files** #1 which at the moment is hard enough to keep in stock at £34.95?

Once again thanks to John and Duncan and all our customers. We hope to hear from more of you soon.

MANNY AMARIO – WHATEVER COMICS

It's been two years since my last Market Report and what a busy two years it's been. We have now opened our second retail store in Maidstone and I am happy to say it is doing very well. All in all we seem to be very healthy in a shaky climate. Now, on with the report…

MARVEL

Marvel titles continue to sell. I have however noticed a slight drop in sales on X-titles but an increase in all **Spiderman** titles. The **Spiderman-Batman** team-up sold very well when you consider the $5.95 cover price. In fact all the Marvel/DC crossovers have sold well. The **Hulk** holds its own as does The **Avengers, Silver Surfer, Captain America** and The **Fantastic Four**. The 2099 line does well with the best being **Spiderman** 2099 and **X-Men** 2099. The new **X-Nation** 2099 sales look good too. The new 99 cents line sells well with the best being **Spiderman: The Untold Tales** which is a fine little comic. Low sales reported in both stores on **Ghost Rider, Conan, Dr. Strange** and **Ultraverse** titles. One little gem that I have read lately is the **T2** Comics which are very good. While on the subject of Marvel, what bright spark thought of giving **Captain America** to Liefeld? Cap's been around since 1941 and deserves to be treated with respect. Mark Waid's writing on this comic has made it a very readable title and sales have increased steadily over the months. I really don't see how Liefeld's outfit can improve on that.

DC

All **Batman** and related titles continue to do well such as **Robin, Catwoman** and **Azrael**. I have noticed a slight decrease in sales on **Superman** titles. Most other DC super-hero titles are selling steadily. Low sales recorded on **Firebrand, Green Arrow** and **Milestone** titles. Vertigo titles continue to do well with the best being **Sandman, Hellblazer, The Invisibles, Books of Magic** and **Preacher**. The Horrorist sold very well for me boosted by the signing hosted at my Canterbury store by Jamie Delano and David Lloyd who were great and signed anything and everything that was put in front of them. Thanks chaps.

Goddess has done well as has **Egypt** but **Chiaroscuro** is faltering. **Death II** has just arrived and looks great. Sales on **Swamp Thing** are down.

IMAGE

Most Image titles sell well, the best being **Gen 13, Spawn, WildC.A.T.S., Cyberforce** and **Witchblade**. The best new titles have been Weapon Zero and 21. The **Spawn** and **WildC.A.T.S.** mini-series has done very well while comics like **Casual Heroes** and **Crush** have flopped. Image seem to be putting

out a lot of new titles, some of which are good and some of which are not. On the company cross-over front, **Spawn Batman/Batman Spawn** sold very well indeed and continues to sell and sell. The **Cyblade/Shi** team-up also did very well as did the **Avengelyne/Glory** team-up. It seems that the different company cross-overs always do well and we have had a few to be getting on with over the last year or so.

DARK HORSE

The Dark Horse licensed titles on **Star Wars** continue to do very well, the best being Heir to the Empire and Empire's End. Also the **Boba Fett Bounty Hunter** one-shot sold very well but sales on **Jabba the Hutt** and **Droids** are slightly down. The Dark Horse **Manga** titles have a loyal following with **Oh My Goddess, Dirty Pair** and **Gunsmith Cats** doing well. Also **3x3 Eyes** and **Legend of Mother Sarah** are good sellers. The Legend line still shows promise with **Sin City** always selling well and **Martha Washington** not far behind. The **Big Guy** and **Rusty the Robot** sold well even if the comic was the size of a house. The Dark Horse heroes line does okay, the best being **Ghost**, the worst being **Mask**.

TOPPS

What can I say about **X-Files**? A huge hit with both Topps and U.K. editions selling well and making money. **Star Wars Galaxy Mag** does well and **Jason and Leatherface** was a surprise hit.

MAXIMUM PRESS

Both **Avengelyne** and **Battlestar Galactica** have been huge hits for me.

BROADWAY COMICS

All titles doing very poorly. I don't think I'll be ordering these for much longer.

OTHER INDEPENDENTS

The **Dawn** mini-series has been a huge hit with all issues selling fast, **Dawn** #1 already selling for £5.00. **Lady Death** and **Evil Ernie** comics seem to do well as do **Double Impact** and **Hellina**. Bongo Comics are holding their own and **Strangers in Paradise** is a gem - read it! Titles like **Eightball** and **Hate** have a very solid audience and the **Crow Deadtime** sold out. Tekno titles sell poorly as do all Valiant/Acclaim titles with the exception of Magic comics.

COLLECTIBLE CARD GAMES

Not strictly comics I know but we have seen a rise in the sale of these card games. The latest **Star Wars** card game has been a huge hit with record sales reported from both stores. **Star Trek Next Generation** continues to sell and all the Magic cards are doing well with the best being Ice Age.

BACK ISSUES

Sales on back issues have not been too bad with **Spiderman, X-Men, Batman, Spawn** and **Vertigo** being constant. Older comics picking up with recorded sales on **Conan** #1 in VFN at £90.00, **Tomb of Dracula** #1 in NM at £35.00, several copies of **Wolverine** #1 in NM at £12.00, loads of early **Spiderman**s between #3 and #100 with #3 is a very solid FN+ pence copy selling for £450.00. Some very early issues of **Fantastic Four**, too many to list here, have been selling at U.K. Guide prices. Other comics of note have been many pre-Code horror titles and some pre super-hero Marvels. We have also sold many pieces of original art ranging from #£35.00 to £250.00. Some other items have been **Star Wars** U.K. edition #1 with gift at three times U.K. Guide and also #2 in NM with gift at three times Guide.

1970s Kirby comics seem to be in demand with sales on **New Gods** and **Forever People** back issues on the up. **Batman** #155-181 have been sold as well as **Detective Comics** #387-410.

TRADING CARDS

Sales on trading cards have been good with popular sets like **X-Files** and **Star Wars** doing the best.

All in all the last year has not been too bad for us. The industry has seen many shake-ups but we seem to survive as long as the product finds its way into the store in a timely fashion – the customer is then happy and I'm happy.

Well this is the end of my report and if you've read it all, I thank you for your time. I would also like to thank everyone in the industry that makes it happen – publishers, distributors, artists, writers, creators and most of all the customers.

See you later.

Top 100 Best Selling Comics 1995

1	DC VS MARVEL #1	51	X-CALIBRE #3
2	X-MEN OMEGA	52	CYBLADE/SHI SPECIAL: BATTLE FOR INDEPENDENTS
3	SPAWN #37	53	SPAWN #30
4	MUTANTS: THE AMAZING X-MEN #4	54	MUTANTS: GENERATION NEXT #1
5	SPAWN #32	55	UNCANNY X-MEN #323
6	MUTANTS: THE ASTONISHING X-MEN #4	56	SPAWN #29
7	MUTANTS: THE AMAZING X-MEN #3	57	WOLVERINE #91
8	SPAWN #38	58	GEN 13 #2 - DIRECT MARKET
9	WEAPON X #4	59	SPAWN: BLOOD FEUD #3
10	MUTANTS: THE ASTONISHING X-MEN #3	60	SPAWN: BLOOD FEUD #4
11	MUTANTS: THE AMAZING X-MEN #2	61	FACTOR X #2
12	MUTANTS: GENERATION NEXT #4	62	X-MAN #2
13	GEN 13 #6	63	X-CALIBRE #2
14	MUTANTS: THE ASTONISHING X-MEN #2	64	VIOLATOR/BADROCK #2
15	SPAWN #36	65	X-UNIVERSE #1
16	MUTANTS: THE AMAZING X-MEN #1	66	GAMBIT & THE X-TERNALS #1
17	WEAPON X #3	67	SHI/CYBLADE SPECIAL #1
18	SPAWN #34	68	X-UNIVERSE #2
19	GAMBIT & THE X-TERNALS #4	69	FACTOR X #1
20	WEAPON X #2	70	GENERATION X #6
21	GEN 13 #1	71	SUPERMAN: THE MAN OF STEEL #50
22	SPAWN #35	72	GENERATION X #5
23	MUTANTS: NEXT GENERATION #3	73	SOVEREIGN SEVEN #1
24	MUTANTS: THE ASTONISHING X-MEN #1	74	X-MAN #5
25	SPAWN: BLOOD FEUD #1	75	X-MAN #1
26	GAMBIT & THE X-TERNALS #3	76	X-MAN #6
27	X-MEN #42	77	AMAZING SPIDERMAN #400 ENHANCED
28	FACTOR X #4	78	X-MEN CHRONICLES #1
29	X-MAN #4	79	WITCHBLADE #1
30	SPAWN #27	80	SUPERMAN #106
31	X-MEN #43	81	ADVENTURES OF SUPERMAN #529
32	WEAPON X #1	82	X-CALIBRE #1
33	GEN 13 #5	83	BATMAN #525
34	BATMAN: MAN-BAT #1	84	ANGELA #2
35	SPAWN #33	85	BATMAN #524
36	UNCANNY X-MEN #322	86	SUPERMAN #107
37	GEN 13 #4	87	SOVEREIGN SEVEN #3
38	GAMBIT & THE X-TERNALS #2	88	ACTION COMICS #715
39	FACTOR X #3	89	LADY DEATH II #1
40	MUTANTS: GENERATION NEXT #2	90	ADVENTURES OF SUPERMAN #530
41	SUPERMAN #100 COLLECTORS' EDITION	91	ACTION COMICS #716
42	X-MEN CHRONICLES #2	92	GREEN LANTERN/SILVER SURFER
43	X-MEN PRIME #1	93	X-FORCE #44
44	LADY DEATH: IN LINGERIE #1	94	SUPERMAN: THE MAN OF STEEL #51
45	SPAWN #31	95	SPIDERMAN #61
46	X-MAN #3	96	GLORY/AVENGELYNE #1
47	SPAWN #28	97	BATMAN #526
48	GEN 13 #3	98	DAWN #1
49	SPAWN: BLOOD FEUD #2	99	X-FACTOR #112
50	X-CALIBRE #4	100	DETECTIVE COMICS #691

Top 100 U.K. DC Comics

#	Title	Price
1	DETECTIVE COMICS #27	£95000.00
2	ACTION COMICS #1	£90000.00
3	SUPERMAN (1st Series) #1	£65000.00
4	DETECTIVE COMICS #1	£50000.00
5	ALL-AMERICAN COMICS #16	£40000.00
6	BATMAN #1	£36000.00
7	NEW FUN COMICS #1	£32000.00
8	MORE FUN COMICS #52	£30000.00
9	FLASH COMICS #1	£27500.00
10	ADVENTURE COMICS #40	£22000.00
	ALL STAR COMICS #3	£22000.00
12	MORE FUN COMICS #53	£20000.00
13	DETECTIVE COMICS #33	£17500.00
	DETECTIVE COMICS #38	£17500.00
	SHOWCASE #4	£17500.00
16	NEW FUN COMICS #6	£15000.00
	NEW YORK WORLD'S FAIR #1	£15000.00
18	DETECTIVE COMICS #29	£14250.00
19	DETECTIVE COMICS #31	£14000.00
	GREEN LANTERN (1st Series) #1	£14000.00
21	SENSATION COMICS #1	£13000.00
22	NEW FUN COMICS #2	£12000.00
23	NEW COMICS #1	£11500.00
24	ADVENTURE COMICS #48	£11000.00
25	ALL STAR COMICS #8	£10000.00
	WONDER WOMAN #1	£10000.00
27	SHOWCASE #8	£9750.00
28	DETECTIVE COMICS #28	£8750.00
29	DETECTIVE COMICS #2	£8500.00
	NEW YORK WORLD'S FAIR #2	£8500.00
	WORLD'S BEST COMICS #1	£8500.00
32	ACTION COMICS #2	£8300.00
33	ALL-AMERICAN COMICS #17	£7500.00
	ALL-AMERICAN COMICS #19	£7500.00
	DETECTIVE COMICS #3	£7500.00
36	ALL STAR COMICS #1	£7250.00
	MORE FUN COMICS #55	£7250.00
38	NEW FUN COMICS #3	£7000.00
	MORE FUN COMICS #14	£7000.00
40	NEW FUN COMICS #4	£6750.00
	NEW FUN COMICS #5	£6750.00
42	ALL-FLASH #1	£6500.00
	MORE FUN COMICS #73	£6500.00
44	ACTION COMICS #3	£6250.00
	BATMAN #2	£6250.00
46	ADVENTURE COMICS #61	£6000.00
	SUPERMAN (1st Series) #2	£6000.00
48	NEW COMICS #2	£5750.00
	ADVENTURE COMICS #73	£5750.00
50	ADVENTURE COMICS #72	£5500.00
51	ACTION COMICS #7	£5200.00
52	ALL-AMERICAN COMICS #18	£5000.00
53	ALL-AMERICAN COMICS #25	£4750.00
	MORE FUN COMICS #54	£4750.00
55	ACTION COMICS #10	£4700.00
56	COMIC CAVALCADE #1	£4500.00
	MORE FUN COMICS #101	£4500.00
58	BATMAN #3	£4250.00
	DETECTIVE COMICS #35	£4250.00
60	SUPERMAN (1st Series) #3	£4000.00
61	ACTION COMICS #6	£3850.00
	DETECTIVE COMICS #40	£3850.00
63	ACTION COMICS #4	£3750.00
	ACTION COMICS #5	£3750.00
	SUPERBOY #1	£3750.00
66	BATMAN #4	£3500.00
	BATMAN #11	£3500.00
	DETECTIVE COMICS #30	£3500.00
	DETECTIVE COMICS #32	£3500.00
	MORE FUN COMICS #9	£3500.00
	MORE FUN COMICS #67	£3500.00
72	BRAVE AND THE BOLD, THE #28	£3400.00
73	DETECTIVE COMICS #4	£3350.00
	DETECTIVE COMICS #5	£3350.00
75	FLASH COMICS #104	£3300.00
76	DETECTIVE COMICS #8	£3250.00
	MORE FUN COMICS #7	£3250.00
	SHOWCASE #9	£3250.00
79	ACTION COMICS #8	£3200.00
	ACTION COMICS #9	£3200.00
81	ACTION COMICS #23	£3150.00
82	BATMAN #16	£3000.00
	DETECTIVE COMICS #36	£3000.00
	DETECTIVE COMICS #39	£3000.00
	DETECTIVE COMICS #225	£3000.00
	FLASH COMICS #2	£3000.00
	GREEN LANTERN (1st Series) #2	£3000.00
	MORE FUN COMICS #8	£3000.00
	MORE FUN COMICS #15	£3000.00
	MORE FUN COMICS #71	£3000.00
	SHOWCASE #22	£3000.00
	SUPERMAN (1st Series) #4	£3000.00
93	NEW COMICS #3	£2950.00
	NEW COMICS #4	£2950.00
	NEW COMICS #5	£2950.00
96	ADVENTURE COMICS #42	£2900.00
	FLASH (1st Series) #105	£2900.00
	MORE FUN COMICS #16	£2900.00
	MORE FUN COMICS #17	£2900.00
100	ALL STAR COMICS #2	£2850.00

Top 100 U.S. DC Comics

1	DETECTIVE COMICS #27	$140000.00
2	ACTION COMICS #1	$135000.00
3	SUPERMAN (1st Series) #1	$97500.00
4	DETECTIVE COMICS #1	$75000.00
5	ALL-AMERICAN COMICS #16	$60000.00
6	BATMAN #1	$50000.00
7	NEW FUN COMICS #1	$47500.00
8	MORE FUN COMICS #52	$45000.00
9	FLASH COMICS #1	$41500.00
10	ADVENTURE COMICS #40	$30000.00
	ALL STAR COMICS #3	$30000.00
	MORE FUN COMICS #53	$30000.00
13	DETECTIVE COMICS #33	$26500.00
14	DETECTIVE COMICS #38	$25000.00
	SHOWCASE #4	$25000.00
16	NEW FUN COMICS #6	$22500.00
	NEW YORK WORLD'S FAIR #1	$22500.00
18	GREEN LANTERN (1st Series) #1	$21000.00
19	DETECTIVE COMICS #29	$20000.00
	DETECTIVE COMICS #31	$20000.00
21	SENSATION COMICS #1	$19500.00
22	NEW FUN COMICS #2	$17500.00
23	ADVENTURE COMICS #48	$16000.00
	DETECTIVE COMICS #2	$16000.00
25	ALL STAR COMICS #8	$15000.00
	NEW COMICS #1	$15000.00
	WONDER WOMAN #1	$15000.00
28	SHOWCASE #8	$14500.00
29	DETECTIVE COMICS #28	$13000.00
30	ACTION COMICS #2	$12500.00
	NEW YORK WORLD'S FAIR #2	$12500.00
32	WORLD'S BEST COMICS #1	$12000.00
33	ALL-AMERICAN COMICS #17	$11250.00
	ALL-AMERICAN COMICS #19	$11250.00
	DETECTIVE COMICS #3	$11250.00
36	MORE FUN COMICS #55	$11000.00
37	NEW FUN COMICS #3	$10500.00
38	MORE FUN COMICS #14	$10250.00
39	MORE FUN COMICS #73	$10000.00
	NEW FUN COMICS #4	$10000.00
	NEW FUN COMICS #5	$10000.00
42	ALL-FLASH #1	$9750.00
	ALL STAR COMICS #1	$9750.00
44	ACTION COMICS #3	$9500.00
	BATMAN #2	$9500.00
46	ADVENTURE COMICS #61	$9000.00
	SUPERMAN (1st Series) #2	$9000.00
48	ACTION COMICS #7	$7750.00
49	ADVENTURE COMICS #72	$7500.00

	ADVENTURE COMICS #73	$7500.00
	NEW COMICS #2	$7500.00
52	ALL-AMERICAN COMICS #18	$7400.00
53	ALL-AMERICAN COMICS #25	$7250.00
	MORE FUN COMICS #54	$7250.00
55	ACTION COMICS #10	$7000.00
56	COMIC CAVALCADE #1	$6750.00
	MORE FUN COMICS #101	$6750.00
58	BATMAN #3	$6700.00
59	DETECTIVE COMICS #35	$6500.00
60	SUPERMAN (1st Series) #3	$6000.00
61	ACTION COMICS #6	$5750.00
62	ACTION COMICS #4	$5500.00
	ACTION COMICS #5	$5500.00
	MORE FUN COMICS #9	$5500.00
	MORE FUN COMICS #67	$5500.00
	SUPERBOY #1	$5500.00
67	DETECTIVE COMICS #40	$5400.00
68	BATMAN #11	$5250.00
69	BATMAN #4	$5250.00
70	DETECTIVE COMICS #4	$5000.00
	DETECTIVE COMICS #5	$5000.00
	DETECTIVE COMICS #30	$5000.00
	DETECTIVE COMICS #32	$5000.00
	FLASH (1st Series) #105	$5000.00
	MORE FUN COMICS #7	$5000.00
	MORE FUN COMICS #8	$5000.00
77	ACTION COMICS #8	$4750.00
	ACTION COMICS #9	$4750.00
	ACTION COMICS #23	$4750.00
	BRAVE AND THE BOLD, THE #28	$4750.00
	DETECTIVE COMICS #8	$4750.00
	SHOWCASE #9	$4750.00
83	GREEN LANTERN (1st Series) #2	$4650.00
84	FLASH COMICS #2	$4600.00
	FLASH COMICS #104	$4600.00
86	BATMAN #16	$4500.00
	DETECTIVE COMICS #36	$4500.00
	DETECTIVE COMICS #39	$4500.00
	DETECTIVE COMICS #225	$4500.00
	MORE FUN COMICS #15	$4500.00
	MORE FUN COMICS #16	$4500.00
	MORE FUN COMICS #17	$4500.00
	MORE FUN COMICS #71	$4500.00
	SUPERMAN (1st Series) #4	$4500.00
95	NEW COMICS #3	$4400.00
	NEW COMICS #4	$4400.00
	NEW COMICS #5	$4400.00
	NEW COMICS #6	$4400.00
	SHOWCASE #22	$4400.00
100	DETECTIVE COMICS #37	$4300.00

Top 100 U.K. Marvel Comics

1	MARVEL COMICS #1	£60000.00
2	CAPTAIN AMERICA COMICS #1	£35000.00
3	AMAZING FANTASY #15	£14000.00
4	HUMAN TORCH (1st Series) #2	£12500.00
5	SUB-MARINER (1st) COMICS #1	£11500.00
6	MARVEL COMICS #2	£11000.00
7	AMAZING SPIDERMAN, THE #1	£10000.00
8	FANTASTIC FOUR #1	£9000.00
9	CAPTAIN AMERICA COMICS #22	£8500.00
	MARVEL COMICS #9	£8500.00
11	MARVEL COMICS #5	£8000.00
12	INCREDIBLE HULK (1st Series) #1	£6000.00
13	CAPTAIN AMERICA COMICS #2	£5700.00
14	RED RAVEN COMICS #1	£5500.00
15	MARVEL COMICS #3	£4500.00
16	CAPTAIN AMERICA COMICS #3	£4300.00
17	MARVEL COMICS #4	£3750.00
18	CAPTAIN AMERICA COMICS #4	£2850.00
19	MARVEL COMICS #8	£2750.00
	SUB-MARINER (1st) COMICS #2	£2750.00
	X-MEN, THE UNCANNY #1	£2750.00
22	CAPTAIN AMERICA COMICS #5	£2600.00
23	HUMAN TORCH (1st Series) #3	£2500.00
	JOURNEY INTO MYSTERY #83	£2500.00
25	CAPTAIN AMERICA COMICS #7	£2400.00
26	MARVEL COMICS #6	£2250.00
	MARVEL COMICS #7	£2250.00
28	CAPTAIN AMERICA COMICS #6	£2200.00
	HUMAN TORCH (1st Series) #5	£2200.00
	TALES OF SUSPENSE #39	£2200.00
31	TALES TO ASTONISH #27	£2000.00
32	FANTASTIC FOUR #2	£1950.00
33	HUMAN TORCH (1st Series) #4	£1900.00
	MARVEL COMICS #10	£1900.00
35	CAPTAIN AMERICA COMICS #8	£1850.00
	CAPTAIN AMERICA COMICS #9	£1850.00
	CAPTAIN AMERICA COMICS #10	£1850.00
38	SUB-MARINER (1st) COMICS #3	£1750.00
39	CAPTAIN AMERICA COMICS #16	£1675.00
40	AMAZING SPIDERMAN, THE #2	£1600.00
	FANTASTIC FOUR #5	£1600.00
	MARVEL COMICS #13	£1600.00
43	CAPTAIN AMERICA COMICS #11	£1550.00
44	FANTASTIC FOUR #4	£1500.00
	MARVEL COMICS #11	£1500.00
46	AVENGERS #1	£1450.00
	CAPTAIN AMERICA COMICS #12	£1450.00
	CAPTAIN AMERICA COMICS #13	£1450.00
	CAPTAIN AMERICA COMICS #14	£1450.00
	CAPTAIN AMERICA COMICS #15	£1450.00
51	CAPTAIN AMERICA COMICS #74	£1400.00
	DAREDEVIL #1	£1400.00
	INCREDIBLE HULK (1st Series) #2	£1400.00
	HUMAN TORCH (1st Series) #5	£1400.00
	HUMAN TORCH (1st Series) #8	£1400.00
	MARVEL COMICS #12	£1400.00
	SUB-MARINER (1st) COMICS #4	£1400.00
58	JOURNEY INTO MYSTERY #1	£1350.00
	STRANGE TALES #1	£1350.00
60	CAPTAIN AMERICA COMICS #17	£1275.00
61	FANTASTIC FOUR #3	£1250.00
62	CAPTAIN AMERICA COMICS #59	£1200.00
63	CAPTAIN AMERICA COMICS #36	£1100.00
64	HUMAN TORCH (1st Series) #10	£1050.00
65	AMAZING SPIDERMAN, THE #3	£1000.00
	CAPTAIN AMERICA COMICS #18	£1000.00
	CAPTAIN AMERICA COMICS #19	£1000.00
	CAPTAIN AMERICA COMICS #20	£1000.00
	MARVEL COMICS #17	£1000.00
	SUB-MARINER (1st) COMICS #5	£1000.00
71	CAPTAIN AMERICA COMICS #21	£950.00
	CAPTAIN AMERICA COMICS #22	£950.00
	CAPTAIN AMERICA COMICS #23	£950.00
	CAPTAIN AMERICA COMICS #24	£950.00
	CAPTAIN AMERICA COMICS #25	£950.00
	MARVEL COMICS #92	£950.00
	TALES OF SUSPENSE #1	£950.00
	TALES TO ASTONISH #1	£950.00
79	INCREDIBLE HULK (1st Series) #6	£900.00
80	CAPTAIN AMERICA COMICS #61	£850.00
	MARVEL COMICS #14	£850.00
	MARVEL COMICS #15	£850.00
	MARVEL COMICS #16	£850.00
	MARVEL COMICS #18	£850.00
	MARVEL COMICS #19	£850.00
	MARVEL COMICS #20	£850.00
87	CAPTAIN AMERICA COMICS #26	£825.00
	CAPTAIN AMERICA COMICS #27	£825.00
	CAPTAIN AMERICA COMICS #28	£825.00
	CAPTAIN AMERICA COMICS #29	£825.00
	CAPTAIN AMERICA COMICS #30	£825.00
	HUMAN TORCH (1st Series) #6	£825.00
	HUMAN TORCH (1st Series) #7	£825.00
	HUMAN TORCH (1st Series) #9	£825.00
95	AMAZING SPIDERMAN, THE #4	£800.00
	CAPTAIN AMERICA COMICS #37	£800.00
	FANTASTIC FOUR #6	£800.00
	INCREDIBLE HULK (1st Series) #3	£800.00
	MARVEL COMICS #21	£800.00
	MARVEL COMICS #82	£800.00

Top 100 U.S. Marvel Comics

1	MARVEL COMICS #1	$90000.00
2	CAPTAIN AMERICA COMICS #1	$50000.00
3	AMAZING FANTASY #15	$25000.00
4	AMAZING SPIDERMAN, THE #1	$19000.00
5	HUMAN TORCH (1st Series) #2	$18500.00
6	FANTASTIC FOUR #1	$18000.00
7	SUB-MARINER (1st) COMICS #1	$17000.00
8	CAPTAIN AMERICA COMICS #22	$16000.00
	MARVEL COMICS #2	$16000.00
10	MARVEL COMICS #9	$12500.00
11	MARVEL COMICS #5	$12000.00
12	INCREDIBLE HULK (1st Series) #1	$10000.00
13	CAPTAIN AMERICA COMICS #2	$8500.00
	RED RAVEN COMICS #1	$8500.00
15	MARVEL COMICS #3	$7000.00
16	CAPTAIN AMERICA COMICS #3	$6500.00
17	MARVEL COMICS #4	$5500.00
18	X-MEN, THE UNCANNY #1	$4600.00
19	JOURNEY INTO MYSTERY #83	$4500.00
20	CAPTAIN AMERICA COMICS #4	$4300.00
21	MARVEL COMICS #8	$4250.00
22	SUB-MARINER (1st) COMICS #2	$4000.00
23	CAPTAIN AMERICA COMICS #5	$3800.00
24	HUMAN TORCH (1st Series) #3	$3750.00
25	CAPTAIN AMERICA COMICS #7	$3600.00
26	MARVEL COMICS #6	$3500.00
	MARVEL COMICS #7	$3500.00
28	HUMAN TORCH (1st Series) #5	$3350.00
	TALES OF SUSPENSE #39	$3350.00
30	CAPTAIN AMERICA COMICS #6	$3300.00
31	FANTASTIC FOUR #2	$3250.00
32	INCREDIBLE HULK (1st Series) #2	$3000.00
	TALES TO ASTONISH #27	$3000.00
34	AMAZING SPIDERMAN, THE #2	$2850.00
35	HUMAN TORCH (1st Series) #4	$2800.00
	MARVEL COMICS #10	$2800.00
37	CAPTAIN AMERICA COMICS #8	$2750.00
	CAPTAIN AMERICA COMICS #9	$2750.00
	CAPTAIN AMERICA COMICS #10	$2750.00
40	FANTASTIC FOUR #5	$2700.00
41	FANTASTIC FOUR #4	$2600.00
42	CAPTAIN AMERICA COMICS #16	$2500.00
	SUB-MARINER (1st) COMICS #3	$2500.00
44	MARVEL COMICS #13	$2400.00
45	CAPTAIN AMERICA COMICS #11	$2350.00
46	AVENGERS #1	$2250.00
	MARVEL COMICS #11	$2250.00
48	CAPTAIN AMERICA COMICS #12	$2150.00
	CAPTAIN AMERICA COMICS #13	$2150.00
	CAPTAIN AMERICA COMICS #14	$2150.00
	CAPTAIN AMERICA COMICS #15	$2150.00
52	CAPTAIN AMERICA COMICS #74	$2100.00
	HUMAN TORCH (1st Series) #5	$2100.00
	HUMAN TORCH (1st Series) #8	$2100.00
	FANTASTIC FOUR #3	$2100.00
	MARVEL COMICS #12	$2100.00
	SUB-MARINER (1st) COMICS #4	$2100.00
58	STRANGE TALES #1	$2000.00
59	CAPTAIN AMERICA COMICS #17	$1900.00
	INCREDIBLE HULK (1st Series) #6	$1900.00
61	DAREDEVIL #1	$1850.00
62	JOURNEY INTO MYSTERY #1	$1800.00
63	AMAZING SPIDERMAN, THE #3	$1750.00
	CAPTAIN AMERICA COMICS #59	$1750.00
65	CAPTAIN AMERICA COMICS #36	$1600.00
66	HUMAN TORCH (1st Series) #10	$1575.00
67	CAPTAIN AMERICA COMICS #18	$1500.00
	CAPTAIN AMERICA COMICS #19	$1500.00
	CAPTAIN AMERICA COMICS #20	$1500.00
	FANTASTIC FOUR #6	$1500.00
	INCREDIBLE HULK (1st Series) #3	$1500.00
	MARVEL COMICS #17	$1500.00
	SUB-MARINER (1st) COMICS #5	$1500.00
74	AMAZING SPIDERMAN, THE #4	$1400.00
	AMAZING SPIDERMAN, THE #14	$1400.00
	AVENGERS #4	$1400.00
	CAPTAIN AMERICA COMICS #21	$1400.00
	CAPTAIN AMERICA COMICS #22	$1400.00
	CAPTAIN AMERICA COMICS #23	$1400.00
	CAPTAIN AMERICA COMICS #24	$1400.00
	CAPTAIN AMERICA COMICS #25	$1400.00
	MARVEL COMICS #92	$1400.00
83	TALES TO ASTONISH #35	$1375.00
84	AMAZING SPIDERMAN, THE #5	$1350.00
	INCREDIBLE HULK (1st Series) #4	$1350.00
	INCREDIBLE HULK (1st Series) #5	$1350.00
	TALES TO ASTONISH #1	$1350.00
	TALES OF SUSPENSE #1	$1350.00
	X-MEN, THE UNCANNY #2	$1350.00
90	MARVEL COMICS #14	$1300.00
	MARVEL COMICS #15	$1300.00
	MARVEL COMICS #16	$1300.00
93	CAPTAIN AMERICA COMICS #61	$1275.00
	MARVEL COMICS #18	$1275.00
	MARVEL COMICS #19	$1275.00
	MARVEL COMICS #20	$1275.00
97	HUMAN TORCH (1st Series) #6	$1250.00
	HUMAN TORCH (1st Series) #7	$1250.00
	HUMAN TORCH (1st Series) #9	$1250.00
	TALES OF SUSPENSE #40	$1250.00

Top 100 U.K. Independent Comics

1	WHIZ COMICS #1	£36000.00
2	CAPTAIN MARVEL ADVENTURES #1	£16500.00
3	WALT DISNEY'S COMICS AND STORIES #1	£9000.00
4	FOUR COLOR (Series I) #16	£6930.00
5	FOUR COLOR (Series I) #4	£5775.00
6	FOUR COLOR (Series II) #9	£5500.00
7	FOUR COLOR (Series II) #29	£4350.00
8	FOUR COLOR (Series I) #1	£4000.00
9	WALT DISNEY'S COMICS AND STORIES #2	£3600.00
10	MAD MAGAZINE #1	£3000.00
11	WHIZ COMICS #2	£2500.00
12	WHIZ COMICS #25	£2400.00
13	VAULT OF HORROR #12	£2250.00
14	WALT DISNEY'S COMICS AND STORIES #31	£1975.00
15	CAPTAIN MARVEL ADVENTURES #2	£1750.00
16	WHIZ COMICS #3	£1500.00
17	WALT DISNEY'S COMICS AND STORIES #3	£1280.00
18	WHIZ COMICS #4	£1250.00
19	HAUNT OF FEAR #1	£1175.00
20	CAPTAIN MARVEL ADVENTURES #3	£1150.00
21	FOUR COLOR (Series II) #62	£1075.00
22	FOUR COLOR (Series I) #17	£1015.00
23	WHIZ COMICS #5	£975.00
24	WALT DISNEY'S COMICS AND STORIES #4	£880.00
25	WALT DISNEY'S COMICS AND STORIES #32	£875.00
	WEIRD SCIENCE-FANTASY ANNUAL #1	£875.00
27	FOUR COLOR (Series I) #13	£840.00
	FOUR COLOR (Series II) #108	£840.00
29	CAPTAIN MARVEL ADVENTURES #4	£750.00
	WHIZ COMICS #6	£750.00
	WHIZ COMICS #7	£750.00
	WHIZ COMICS #8	£750.00
	WHIZ COMICS #9	£750.00
	WHIZ COMICS #10	£750.00
35	FOUR COLOR (Series I) #2	£700.00
	FOUR COLOR (Series I) #6	£700.00
	FOUR COLOR (Series II) #79	£700.00
	FOUR COLOR (Series II) #386	£700.00
	RICHIE RICH #1	£700.00
40	WALT DISNEY'S COMICS AND STORIES #5	£680.00
41	FOUR COLOR (Series II) #38	£650.00
	FOUR COLOR (Series II) #48	£650.00
43	EERIE #1	£625.00
44	WALT DISNEY'S COMICS AND STORIES #33	£615.00
45	WEIRD FANTASY #1	£600.00
	WEIRD SCIENCE #1	£600.00
	WHIZ COMICS #15	£600.00
48	FOUR COLOR (Series II) #74	£580.00
49	MAD MAGAZINE #2	£575.00
50	ADVENTURES INTO THE UNKNOWN #1	£550.00
	CAPTAIN MARVEL ADVENTURES #5	£550.00
	MAD MAGAZINE #5	£550.00
	TALES FROM THE CRYPT #20	£550.00
	TARZAN #1	£550.00
	WHIZ COMICS #11	£550.00
	WHIZ COMICS #12	£550.00
	WHIZ COMICS #13	£550.00
	WHIZ COMICS #14	£550.00
	WHIZ COMICS #16	£550.00
	WHIZ COMICS #17	£550.00
	WHIZ COMICS #18	£550.00
	WHIZ COMICS #19	£550.00
	WHIZ COMICS #20	£550.00
64	FOUR COLOR (Series II) #178	£540.00
65	WALT DISNEY'S COMICS AND STORIES #6	£535.00
	WALT DISNEY'S COMICS AND STORIES #7	£535.00
	WALT DISNEY'S COMICS AND STORIES #8	£535.00
	WALT DISNEY'S COMICS AND STORIES #9	£535.00
	WALT DISNEY'S COMICS AND STORIES #10	£535.00
	WALT DISNEY'S COMICS AND STORIES #34	£535.00
71	CAPTAIN MARVEL ADVENTURES #18	£525.00
72	FOUR COLOR (Series II) #27	£510.00
	FOUR COLOR (Series II) #71	£510.00
	FOUR COLOR (Series II) #147	£510.00
75	HAUNT OF FEAR #3	£500.00
	WEIRD SCIENCE-FANTASY ANNUAL #2	£500.00
77	WALT DISNEY'S COMICS AND STORIES #11	£480.00
78	MAD MAGAZINE #24	£475.00
	VAULT OF HORROR #13	£475.00
80	HAUNT OF FEAR #2	£470.00
81	WALT DISNEY'S COMICS AND STORIES #35	£470.00
	WALT DISNEY'S COMICS AND STORIES #36	£470.00
83	FOUR COLOR (Series I) #25	£455.00
	WALT DISNEY'S COMICS AND STORIES #12	£455.00
	WALT DISNEY'S COMICS AND STORIES #13	£455.00
	WALT DISNEY'S COMICS AND STORIES #14	£455.00
87	CRIME SUSPENSTORIES #1	£450.00
88	FOUR COLOR (Series II) #16	£445.00
	FOUR COLOR (Series II) #92	£445.00
	FOUR COLOR (Series II) #159	£445.00
	FOUR COLOR (Series II) #189	£445.00
92	WALT DISNEY'S COMICS AND STORIES #15	£440.00
	WALT DISNEY'S COMICS AND STORIES #16	£440.00
	WALT DISNEY'S COMICS AND STORIES #17	£440.00
95	FOUR COLOR (Series II) #199	£435.00
	TALES FROM THE CRYPT #21	£435.00
97	CAPTAIN MARVEL ADVENTURES #7	£425.00
	CAPTAIN MARVEL ADVENTURES #8	£425.00
	CAPTAIN MARVEL ADVENTURES #9	£425.00
	CAPTAIN MARVEL ADVENTURES #10	£425.00

Top 100 U.S. Independent Comics

1	WHIZ COMICS #1	$54000.00
2	CAPTAIN MARVEL ADVENTURES #0	$22500.00
3	WALT DISNEY'S COMICS AND STORIES #1	$13500.00
4	FOUR COLOR (Series I) #16	$9900.00
5	FOUR COLOR (Series I) #4	$8500.00
6	FOUR COLOR (Series II) #9	$7500.00
7	FOUR COLOR (Series II) #29	$6500.00
8	FOUR COLOR (Series I) #1	$6000.00
9	WALT DISNEY'S COMICS AND STORIES #2	$5400.00
10	MAD MAGAZINE #1	$4500.00
11	WHIZ COMICS #2	$3750.00
12	WHIZ COMICS #25	$3650.00
13	VAULT OF HORROR #12	$3400.00
14	WALT DISNEY'S COMICS AND STORIES #31	$2950.00
15	CAPTAIN MARVEL ADVENTURES #2	$2650.00
16	WHIZ COMICS #3	$2250.00
17	WALT DISNEY'S COMICS AND STORIES #3	$1880.00
18	WHIZ COMICS #4	$1850.00
19	CAPTAIN MARVEL ADVENTURES #3	$1750.00
	HAUNT OF FEAR #1	$1750.00
21	FOUR COLOR (Series II) #62	$1610.00
22	FOUR COLOR (Series I) #17	$1505.00
23	WHIZ COMICS #5	$1450.00
24	WALT DISNEY'S COMICS AND STORIES #32	$1325.00
25	WALT DISNEY'S COMICS AND STORIES #4	$1320.00
26	FOUR COLOR (Series I) #13	$1260.00
	FOUR COLOR (Series II) #108	$1260.00
28	WEIRD SCIENCE-FANTASY ANNUAL #1	$1250.00
29	WHIZ COMICS #6	$1100.00
	WHIZ COMICS #7	$1100.00
	WHIZ COMICS #8	$1100.00
	WHIZ COMICS #9	$1100.00
	WHIZ COMICS #10	$1100.00
34	CAPTAIN MARVEL ADVENTURES #4	$1050.00
	FOUR COLOR (Series II) #2	$1050.00
	FOUR COLOR (Series II) #6	$1050.00
	FOUR COLOR (Series I) #79	$1050.00
	FOUR COLOR (Series I) #386	$1050.00
	RICHIE RICH #1	$1050.00
40	WALT DISNEY'S COMICS AND STORIES #5	$1000.00
41	FOUR COLOR (Series II) #38	$980.00
	FOUR COLOR (Series II) #48	$980.00
43	EERIE #1	$950.00
44	WALT DISNEY'S COMICS AND STORIES #33	$925.00
45	MAD MAGAZINE #2	$900.00
	WEIRD SCIENCE #1	$900.00
	WHIZ COMICS #15	$900.00
48	FOUR COLOR (Series II) #74	$875.00
	WEIRD FANTASY #1	$875.00
50	CAPTAIN MARVEL ADVENTURES #5	$850.00
	MAD MAGAZINE #5	$850.00
	TARZAN #1	$850.00
53	TALES FROM THE CRYPT #20	$825.00
54	FOUR COLOR (Series II) #178	$805.00
55	ADVENTURES INTO THE UNKNOWN #1	$800.00
	WALT DISNEY'S COMICS AND STORIES #6	$800.00
	WALT DISNEY'S COMICS AND STORIES #7	$800.00
	WALT DISNEY'S COMICS AND STORIES #8	$800.00
	WALT DISNEY'S COMICS AND STORIES #9	$800.00
	WALT DISNEY'S COMICS AND STORIES #10	$800.00
	WALT DISNEY'S COMICS AND STORIES #34	$800.00
	WHIZ COMICS #11	$800.00
	WHIZ COMICS #12	$800.00
	WHIZ COMICS #13	$800.00
	WHIZ COMICS #14	$800.00
	WHIZ COMICS #16	$800.00
	WHIZ COMICS #17	$800.00
	WHIZ COMICS #18	$800.00
	WHIZ COMICS #19	$800.00
	WHIZ COMICS #20	$800.00
71	CAPTAIN MARVEL ADVENTURES #18	$775.00
72	FOUR COLOR (Series II) #27	$770.00
	FOUR COLOR (Series II) #71	$770.00
	FOUR COLOR (Series II) #147	$770.00
75	HAUNT OF FEAR #3	$750.00
76	MAD MAGAZINE #24	$725.00
	WEIRD SCIENCE-FANTASY ANNUAL #2	$725.00
78	WALT DISNEY'S COMICS AND STORIES #11	$720.00
79	HAUNT OF FEAR #2	$700.00
	VAULT OF HORROR #13	$700.00
	WALT DISNEY'S COMICS AND STORIES #35	$700.00
	WALT DISNEY'S COMICS AND STORIES #36	$700.00
83	WALT DISNEY'S COMICS AND STORIES #12	$680.00
	WALT DISNEY'S COMICS AND STORIES #13	$680.00
	WALT DISNEY'S COMICS AND STORIES #14	$680.00
86	FOUR COLOR (Series II) #16	$665.00
	FOUR COLOR (Series II) #25	$665.00
	FOUR COLOR (Series II) #92	$665.00
	FOUR COLOR (Series II) #159	$665.00
	FOUR COLOR (Series I) #189	$665.00
91	FOUR COLOR (Series II) #199	$655.00
92	CRIME SUSPENSTORIES #1	$650.00
	FAMOUS MONSTERS OF FILMLAND #1	$650.00
	LITTLE DOT #1	$650.00
	TALES FROM THE CRYPT #21	$650.00
96	WALT DISNEY'S COMICS AND STORIES #15	$640.00
	WALT DISNEY'S COMICS AND STORIES #16	$640.00
	WALT DISNEY'S COMICS AND STORIES #17	$640.00
99	FOUR COLOR (Series I) #3	$630.00
	FOUR COLOR (Series II) #105	$630.00

Top 100 U.K. DC Titles

#	Title	Price	#	Title	Price
1	DETECTIVE COMICS	£407046.60	51	EIGHTY PAGE GIANT MAGAZINE	£1725.00
2	MORE FUN COMICS	£267080.00	52	HEART THROBS	£1719.00
3	ADVENTURE COMICS	£224312.80	53	FALLING IN LOVE	£1675.00
4	ACTION COMICS	£216173.70		RIP HUNTER TIME MASTER	£1675.00
5	SUPERMAN (1st Series) (ADVENTURES OF SUPERMAN)	£134851.75	55	SEA DEVILS	£1635.00
6	BATMAN	£120058.70	56	AQUAMAN	£1504.50
7	ALL-AMERICAN COMICS	£114905.00	57	SUPERMAN (1st Series) ANNUAL	£1405.50
8	FLASH COMICS	£95530.00	58	DOOM PATROL	£1277.00
9	ALL STAR COMICS	£88400.00	59	MANY LOVES OF DOBIE GILLIS	£1215.00
10	SHOWCASE	£60058.60	60	FLIPPITY AND FLOP	£1210.00
11	WORLD'S FINEST COMICS	£46826.50	61	METAL MEN	£1137.50
12	GREEN LANTERN (1st Series)	£41870.00	62	JERRY LEWIS, THE ADVENTURES OF	£1127.50
13	SENSATION COMICS	£39630.00	63	FRONTIER FIGHTERS	£1125.00
14	WONDER WOMAN	£33358.75	64	CHARLIE CHAN, THE NEW ADVENTURES OF	£1025.00
15	NEW YORK WORLD'S FAIR	£23500.00	65	HAWKMAN	£1012.50
16	COMIC CAVALCADE	£20537.50	66	SECRET HEARTS	£994.00
17	STRANGE ADVENTURES	£20303.50	67	ROBIN HOOD TALES	£990.00
18	ALL-FLASH	£18750.00	68	TOMAHAWK	£913.00
19	SUPERBOY	£18626.75	69	SGT. BILKO'S PVT. DOBERMAN	£880.00
20	BRAVE AND THE BOLD, THE	£18560.10	70	BATMAN ANNUAL	£819.25
21	MYSTERY IN SPACE	£15479.00	71	PAT BOONE	£775.00
22	OUR ARMY AT WAR	£14388.00	72	TEEN TITANS	£711.00
23	HOUSE OF MYSTERY	£11389.50	73	BATMAN 3-D	£675.00
24	FLASH (1st Series)	£10098.50	74	FOX AND THE CROW	£652.00
25	STAR-SPANGLED WAR STORIES	£10004.50	75	YOUNG ROMANCE COMICS	£451.50
26	TALES OF THE UNEXPECTED	£9160.00	76	YOUNG LOVE	£439.50
27	JIMMY OLSEN, SUPERMAN'S PAL	£8932.50	77	TV SCREEN CARTOONS	£360.00
28	LEADING COMICS	£8721.00	78	SANDMAN (2nd Series)	£358.50
29	JUSTICE LEAGUE OF AMERICA	£7539.50	79	METAMORPHO	£340.00
30	MY GREATEST ADVENTURE	£7477.50	80	SWAMP THING (2nd Series)	£333.75
31	ALL-AMERICAN MEN OF WAR	£6729.00	81	UNEXPECTED, THE	£302.00
32	GREEN LANTERN (2nd Series)	£6571.25	82	WESTERN COMICS	£280.00
33	CHALLENGERS OF THE UNKNOWN	£6322.75	83	PHANTOM STRANGER	£263.50
34	LOIS LANE, SUPERMAN'S GIRLFRIEND	£6140.75	84	JONAH HEX	£253.50
35	BOB HOPE, THE ADVENTURES OF	£5563.50	85	SGT. ROCK	£250.50
36	HOUSE OF SECRETS	£5156.75	86	SECRET ORIGINS (1st Series)	£250.00
37	OUR FIGHTING FORCES	£4973.00	87	SPECTRE, THE	£249.00
38	SUGAR AND SPIKE	£4010.75	88	FLASH (1st Series) ANNUAL	£225.00
39	G.I. COMBAT	£3547.50	89	HELLBLAZER	£205.00
40	REX THE WONDER DOG	£3365.00	90	PLASTIC MAN	£198.50
41	BLACKHAWK	£3310.50	91	LOIS LANE ANNUAL, SUPERMAN'S GIRLFRIEND	£185.00
42	GIRL'S LOVE STORIES	£3149.00	92	SWING WITH SCOOTER	£183.50
43	GIRL'S ROMANCES	£2919.50		TARZAN	£183.50
44	ALL-STAR WESTERN	£2807.50	94	SUPERMAN (2nd Series)	£182.00
45	ALL-AMERICAN WESTERN	£2620.00	95	WEIRD WAR TALES	£179.25
46	SERGEANT BILKO	£2440.00	96	SWAMP THING	£160.00
47	BIG TOWN	£2075.00	97	WARLORD	£152.25
48	DANGER TRAIL	£1925.00	98	WITCHING HOUR	£151.75
49	ATOM, THE	£1808.50	99	ANIMAL MAN	£150.25
50	CONGO BILL	£1790.00	100	SUPERMAN ARCHIVES	£150.00

DETECTIVE COMICS #27 (MAY 1939) –
THE MOST VALUABLE COMIC IN THE WORLD AT $140,000/£95,000

ACTION COMICS #1 (JUNE 1938) – ARGUABLY THE MOST IMPORTANT COMIC BOOK EVER PUBLISHED
AS MOST SUPER-HEROES ADOPTED SOME OF THE ELEMENTS ESTABLISHED BY SUPERMAN

Top 100 U.S. DC Titles

#	Title	Price	#	Title	Price
1	DETECTIVE COMICS	$607762.75	51	DANGER TRAIL	$2850.00
2	MORE FUN COMICS	$402095.00	52	HEART THROBS	$2780.00
3	ADVENTURE COMICS	$324400.50	53	METAL MEN	$2720.00
4	ACTION COMICS	$324144.50	54	FALLING IN LOVE	$2663.00
5	SUPERMAN (1st Series) (ADVENTURES OF SUPERMAN)	$202102.75	55	EIGHTY PAGE GIANT MAGAZINE	$2650.00
6	BATMAN	$179928.50	56	RIP HUNTER TIME MASTER	$2515.00
7	ALL-AMERICAN COMICS	$171800.00	57	SEA DEVILS	$2460.00
8	FLASH COMICS	$141565.00	58	HAWKMAN	$2355.00
9	ALL STAR COMICS	$129350.00	59	JERRY LEWIS, THE ADVENTURES OF	$2199.00
10	SHOWCASE	$89973.75	60	SUPERMAN (1st Series) ANNUAL	$2105.00
11	WORLD'S FINEST COMICS	$70002.00	61	DOOM PATROL	$1985.00
12	GREEN LANTERN (1st Series)	$62350.00	62	FLIPPITY AND FLOP	$1982.50
13	SENSATION COMICS	$59115.00	63	FRONTIER FIGHTERS	$1950.00
14	WONDER WOMAN	$49819.50	64	MANY LOVES OF DOBIE GILLIS	$1840.00
15	NEW YORK WORLD'S FAIR	$35000.00	65	CHARLIE CHAN, THE NEW ADVENTURES OF	$1560.00
16	STRANGE ADVENTURES	$32676.00	66	SECRET HEARTS	$1549.50
17	COMIC CAVALCADE	$30520.00	67	ROBIN HOOD TALES	$1485.00
18	BRAVE AND THE BOLD, THE	$28017.25	68	BATMAN ANNUAL	$1431.00
19	ALL-FLASH	$28000.00	69	TOMAHAWK	$1389.00
20	SUPERBOY	$27877.75	70	SGT. BILKO'S PVT. DOBERMAN	$1335.00
21	MYSTERY IN SPACE	$23912.00	71	TEEN TITANS	$1307.50
22	OUR ARMY AT WAR	$22137.00	72	PAT BOONE	$1175.00
23	HOUSE OF MYSTERY	$19196.50	73	BATMAN 3-D	$1010.00
24	FLASH (1st Series)	$18064.60	74	FOX AND THE CROW	$1005.00
25	STAR-SPANGLED WAR STORIES	$15023.50	75	SANDMAN (2nd Series)	$948.00
26	TALES OF THE UNEXPECTED	$14300.00	76	YOUNG ROMANCE COMICS	$691.00
27	JIMMY OLSEN, SUPERMAN'S PAL	$13981.00	77	YOUNG LOVE	$670.50
28	LEADING COMICS	$13205.00	78	SGT. ROCK	$635.50
29	GREEN LANTERN (2nd Series)	$13158.25	79	METAMORPHO	$630.00
30	JUSTICE LEAGUE OF AMERICA	$12020.50	80	SPECTRE, THE	$555.00
31	MY GREATEST ADVENTURE	$11520.00	81	TV SCREEN CARTOONS	$520.00
32	LOIS LANE, SUPERMAN'S GIRLFRIEND	$10996.00	82	SECRET ORIGINS (1st Series)	$475.00
33	ALL-AMERICAN MEN OF WAR	$9927.50	83	UNEXPECTED, THE	$471.75
34	CHALLENGERS OF THE UNKNOWN	$9430.50	84	JONAH HEX	$447.00
35	HOUSE OF SECRETS	$8624.75	85	SWAMP THING (2nd Series)	$441.50
36	BOB HOPE, THE ADVENTURES OF	$8292.50	86	TARZAN	$409.00
37	OUR FIGHTING FORCES	$6901.80	87	PHANTOM STRANGER	$405.00
38	G.I. COMBAT	$6325.50	88	WESTERN COMICS	$400.00
39	SUGAR AND SPIKE	$6231.25	89	KAMANDI THE LAST BOY ON EARTH	$395.50
40	GIRL'S LOVE STORIES	$5485.00	90	FLASH (1st Series) ANNUAL	$325.00
41	BLACKHAWK	$5080.25	91	HELLBLAZER	$317.25
42	REX THE WONDER DOG	$5005.00	92	PLASTIC MAN	$302.50
43	GIRL'S ROMANCES	$4625.00	93	FOREVER PEOPLE	$287.50
44	ALL-STAR WESTERN	$4155.00	94	SWING WITH SCOOTER	$286.00
45	ATOM, THE	$4100.00	95	SWAMP THING	$278.50
46	ALL-AMERICAN WESTERN	$3890.00		WEIRD WAR TALES	$278.50
47	AQUAMAN	$3867.00	97	SUPERMAN (2nd Series)	$276.25
48	SERGEANT BILKO	$3655.00	98	LOIS LANE ANNUAL, SUPERMAN'S GIRLFRIEND	$275.00
49	BIG TOWN	$3115.00	99	NEW GODS, THE	$272.50
50	CONGO BILL	$2850.00	100	JUSTICE LEAGUE	$262.50

Top 100 U.K. Marvel Titles

1	MARVEL COMICS	£153650.00
2	CAPTAIN AMERICA COMICS	£122377.50
3	HUMAN TORCH (1st Series)	£38665.00
4	SUB-MARINER (1st) COMICS	£36650.00
5	AMAZING SPIDERMAN, THE	£26400.00
6	FANTASTIC FOUR	£25098.25
7	JOURNEY INTO MYSTERY	£17482.50
8	STRANGE TALES	£16688.50
9	AMAZING FANTASY	£14009.50
10	TALES OF SUSPENSE	£12877.00
11	TALES TO ASTONISH	£12272.50
12	INCREDIBLE HULK (1st Series)	£10551.50
13	X-MEN, THE UNCANNY	£9155.50
14	AVENGERS	£6351.25
15	RED RAVEN COMICS	£5500.00
16	DAREDEVIL	£4701.80
17	SGT. FURY AND HIS HOWLING COMMANDOS	£2991.50
18	AMAZING ADULT FANTASY	£2050.00
19	AMAZING ADVENTURES	£1800.00
20	RAWHIDE KID	£1779.50
21	THOR	£1603.00
22	INCREDIBLE HULK (2nd Series)	£1602.75
23	IRON MAN	£1549.50
24	CAPTAIN AMERICA	£1424.00
25	MILLIE THE MODEL	£1300.00
26	SILVER SURFER (1st Series)	£1297.50
27	CONAN THE BARBARIAN	£979.50
28	FANTASTIC FOUR ANNUAL	£848.15
29	GUNSMOKE WESTERN	£749.00
30	PATSY WALKER	£725.00
31	MARVEL MASTERWORKS	£690.00
32	AMAZING SPIDERMAN, THE ANNUAL	£663.50
33	STAR WARS	£656.00
34	MILLIE, MODELLING WITH	£625.00
	STRANGE TALES ANNUAL	£625.00
36	SPECTACULAR SPIDERMAN	£588.00
37	CONAN, SAVAGE SWORD OF	£583.00
38	SUB-MARINER (2nd Series)	£536.50
39	MARVEL TEAM-UP	£501.50
40	MARVEL TALES	£469.25
41	KID COLT OUTLAW	£455.25
42	DEFENDERS	£427.00
43	MILLIE THE MODEL ANNUAL	£422.50
44	TWO-GUN KID	£414.00
45	DOCTOR STRANGE (1st Series)	£396.00
46	CAPTAIN MARVEL	£394.50
47	MARVEL SUPER-HEROES	£382.75
48	TOMB OF DRACULA	£349.00
49	GHOST RIDER	£335.50
50	SPIDERMAN (2nd Series)	£288.00
51	MILLIE, A DATE WITH	£280.00
52	MARVEL PREMIERE	£273.75
53	MARVEL SPOTLIGHT	£261.00
54	MILLIE, LIFE WITH	£255.00
55	X-MEN GIANT SIZE	£253.00
56	PATSY AND HEDY CAREER GIRLS	£246.00
57	MARVEL COLLECTOR'S ITEM CLASSICS	£242.50
58	WOLVERINE	£238.75
59	WEB OF SPIDERMAN, THE	£231.00
60	G.I. JOE	£224.25
61	GROO THE WANDERER	£222.50
62	MARVEL COMICS PRESENTS	£218.75
63	MARVEL TWO-IN-ONE	£218.00
64	MILLIE, MAD ABOUT	£215.00
65	NEW MUTANTS	£214.50
	X-FACTOR	£214.50
67	FOOM	£200.00
68	IRON FIST	£199.85
69	MARVEL TALES ANNUAL	£195.00
70	MARVEL SUPER SPECIAL	£192.00
71	POWERMAN	£191.75
72	ALPHA FLIGHT	£190.50
73	DOCTOR STRANGE (2nd Series)	£185.75
74	MASTER OF KUNG FU	£185.00
	WEREWOLF BY NIGHT	£185.00
76	NICK FURY, AGENT OF SHIELD	£179.00
77	ASTONISHING TALES	£177.50
78	AKIRA	£168.00
79	SILVER SURFER (3rd Series)	£165.50
80	SGT. FURY ANNUAL	£160.00
81	EXCALIBUR	£157.50
82	SAVAGE TALES	£151.00
83	PUNISHER	£150.00
84	CONAN SAGA	£148.50
85	AVENGERS ANNUAL, THE	£145.75
86	WHAT IF...?	£142.50
87	BATTLE	£141.50
88	MARVEL FEATURE	£140.00
89	AMAZING ADVENTURES (2nd Series)	£134.00
90	CLASSIC X-MEN	£130.50
91	X-MEN, THE UNCANNY ANNUAL	£128.50
92	PUNISHER WAR JOURNAL	£128.25
93	CRAZY (2nd Series)	£125.00
94	GHOST RIDER (2nd Series)	£124.00
95	X-MEN	£118.25
96	NOT BRAND ECHH	£117.50
97	WARLOCK (1st Series)	£115.50
98	MARVEL'S GREATEST COMICS	£114.50
	WEST COAST AVENGERS	£114.50
100	FEAR, ADVENTURE INTO	£113.50

Top 100 U.S. Marvel Titles

1	MARVEL COMICS	$230125.00	51	MARVEL PREMIERE	$452.00
2	CAPTAIN AMERICA COMICS	$184349.00	52	SPIDERMAN (2nd Series)	$451.25
3	HUMAN TORCH (1st Series)	$58005.00	53	WOLVERINE	$447.00
4	SUB-MARINER (1st) COMICS	$54250.00	54	MILLIE, A DATE WITH	$420.00
5	AMAZING SPIDERMAN, THE	$48698.75	55	WEB OF SPIDERMAN, THE	$403.50
6	FANTASTIC FOUR	$44694.75	56	X-MEN GIANT SIZE	$394.50
7	JOURNEY INTO MYSTERY	$27460.00	57	MARVEL SPOTLIGHT	$391.50
8	STRANGE TALES	$25964.50	58	WEREWOLF BY NIGHT	$384.00
9	AMAZING FANTASY	$25015.00	59	MARVEL COMICS PRESENTS	$383.25
10	TALES OF SUSPENSE	$20898.00	60	MASTER OF KUNG FU	$377.00
11	TALES TO ASTONISH	$19995.00	61	MILLIE, LIFE WITH	$375.00
12	INCREDIBLE HULK (1st Series)	$19102.50	62	PATSY AND HEDY CAREER GIRLS	$369.00
13	X-MEN, THE UNCANNY	$16593.25	63	MARVEL TWO-IN-ONE	$362.00
14	AVENGERS	$10170.25	64	X-FACTOR	$351.25
15	RED RAVEN COMICS	$8500.00	65	G.I. JOE	$348.50
16	DAREDEVIL	$7207.25	66	NEW MUTANTS	$343.50
17	SGT. FURY AND HIS HOWLING COMMANDOS	$4692.00	67	MARVEL TALES ANNUAL	$340.00
18	AMAZING ADVENTURES	$2950.00	68	IRON FIST	$337.75
19	THOR	$2881.25	69	MILLIE, MAD ABOUT	$337.50
20	INCREDIBLE HULK (2nd Series)	$2881.00	70	FOOM	$299.98
21	RAWHIDE KID	$2766.00	71	ALPHA FLIGHT	$294.50
22	IRON MAN	$2742.95	72	NICK FURY, AGENT OF SHIELD	$292.00
23	AMAZING ADULT FANTASY	$2550.00	73	POWERMAN	$291.25
24	CAPTAIN AMERICA	$2459.45	74	MARVEL SUPER SPECIAL	$289.50
25	SILVER SURFER (1st Series)	$1965.00	75	ASTONISHING TALES	$287.50
26	MILLIE THE MODEL	$1947.00	76	DOCTOR STRANGE (2nd Series)	$282.00
27	CONAN THE BARBARIAN	$1902.50	77	GROO THE WANDERER	$279.00
28	FANTASTIC FOUR ANNUAL	$1402.00	78	SAVAGE TALES	$274.00
29	AMAZING SPIDERMAN, THE ANNUAL	$1286.00	79	SILVER SURFER (3rd Series)	$260.00
30	CONAN, SAVAGE SWORD OF	$1218.25	80	AKIRA	$253.00
31	GUNSMOKE WESTERN	$1123.50	81	AVENGERS ANNUAL, THE	$247.00
32	STAR WARS	$1062.50	82	EXCALIBUR	$244.25
33	PATSY WALKER	$1043.50	83	FANTASY MASTERPIECES	$239.50
34	MARVEL MASTERWORKS	$1042.50	84	WHAT IF..?	$238.00
35	SUB-MARINER (2nd Series)	$1004.00	85	PUNISHER	$233.75
36	MILLIE, MODELLING WITH	$955.00	86	SGT. FURY ANNUAL	$227.50
37	SPECTACULAR SPIDERMAN	$948.50	87	CONAN SAGA	$223.00
38	STRANGE TALES ANNUAL	$850.00	88	AMAZING ADVENTURES (2nd Series)	$220.50
39	MARVEL TEAM-UP	$799.50	89	NOT BRAND ECHH	$212.50
40	TOMB OF DRACULA	$745.00	90	MARVEL FEATURE	$211.00
41	MARVEL TALES	$737.00	91	PUNISHER WAR JOURNAL	$208.00
42	DOCTOR STRANGE (1st Series)	$730.00	92	X-MEN, THE UNCANNY ANNUAL	$206.50
43	GHOST RIDER	$709.50	93	CLASSIC X-MEN	$205.50
44	DEFENDERS	$704.00	94	BATTLE	$203.00
45	KID COLT OUTLAW	$692.35	95	X-MEN	$200.50
46	MILLIE THE MODEL ANNUAL	$615.00	96	FEAR, ADVENTURE INTO	$199.50
47	CAPTAIN MARVEL	$605.50	97	GHOST RIDER (2nd Series)	$199.00
48	MARVEL SUPER-HEROES	$601.50	98	CRAZY (2nd Series)	$198.00
49	TWO-GUN KID	$587.00	99	INVADERS, THE	$192.50
50	MARVEL COLLECTOR'S ITEM CLASSICS	$480.00	100	WARLOCK (1st Series)	$185.00

Top 100 U.K. Independent Titles

1	FOUR COLOR (Series II)	£96333.00	51	BILLY THE KID	£891.50
2	WHIZ COMICS	£68805.00	52	DOCTOR SOLAR, MAN OF THE ATOM	£862.50
3	WALT DISNEY'S COMICS AND STORIES	£48385.00	53	SPACE FAMILY ROBINSON	£862.50
4	CAPTAIN MARVEL ADVENTURES	£40465.00	54	SPACE WAR	£855.50
5	FOUR COLOR (Series I)	£24825.00	55	LASH LARUE WESTERN	£805.00
6	MAD MAGAZINE	£13667.50		STRANGE WORLDS	£805.00
7	TARZAN	£7958.00	57	CEREBUS THE AARDVARK	£803.25
8	VAULT OF HORROR	£7255.00	58	FORBIDDEN WORLDS (1st Series)	£782.50
9	ADVENTURES INTO THE UNKNOWN	£7205.50	59	ARCHIE'S MADHOUSE	£769.00
10	TALES FROM THE CRYPT	£6300.00	60	KONGA	£768.00
11	HAUNT OF FEAR	£5820.00	61	PHANTOM, THE	£758.50
12	WEIRD SCIENCE	£4590.00	62	SAD SACK LAUGH SPECIAL	£730.00
13	STRANGE SUSPENSE STORIES	£4245.00	63	EERIE (Magazine)	£726.50
14	WEIRD FANTASY	£4195.00	64	GORGO	£682.50
15	RICHIE RICH	£4094.25	65	MUNSTERS, THE	£665.00
16	TUROK SON OF STONE	£3868.00	66	TWILIGHT ZONE	£657.00
17	SPACE ADVENTURES	£3473.50	67	CREEPY	£634.50
18	CRIME SUSPENSTORIES	£3422.50	68	INCREDIBLE SCIENCE FICTION	£625.00
19	ARCHIE'S JOKE BOOK MAGAZINE	£2957.50		TWO-FISTED ANNUAL	£625.00
20	STAR TREK	£2802.50	70	FIGHTIN' MARINES	£621.00
21	EERIE	£2785.00	71	HERBIE	£620.00
22	LITTLE DOT	£2651.00	72	MAN FROM U.N.C.L.E., THE	£600.00
23	TWO-FISTED TALES	£2640.00	73	FIGHTIN' ARMY	£581.50
24	SHOCK SUSPENSTORIES (1st Series)	£2525.00	74	CHEYENNE	£580.00
25	FAMOUS MONSTERS OF FILMLAND	£2269.50	75	CHEYENNE KID	£539.50
26	VAMPIRELLA	£1995.00	76	MONKEES, THE	£537.50
27	TALES OF THE MYSTERIOUS TRAVELLER	£1682.50	77	WYATT EARP, FRONTIER MARSHAL	£513.00
28	MYSTERIES OF UNEXPLORED WORLDS	£1587.50	78	OUTLAWS OF THE WEST	£501.00
29	FRONTLINE COMBAT	£1483.00	79	DOUBLE LIFE OF PRIVATE STRONG, THE	£500.00
30	UNUSUAL TALES	£1482.50		WIN A PRIZE COMICS	£500.00
31	SPOOKY	£1416.25	81	BORIS KARLOFF TALES OF MYSTERY	£495.25
32	WEIRD SCIENCE-FANTASY ANNUAL	£1375.00	82	FANGORIA	£481.25
33	THREE STOOGES, THE	£1345.00	83	BONE	£449.50
34	MAGNUS ROBOT FIGHTER	£1337.00	84	THUNDER AGENTS	£442.50
35	FLY, ADVENTURES OF THE	£1270.00	85	OUTER SPACE	£440.00
36	JETSONS, THE	£1255.00	86	I LOVE YOU	£402.00
37	UNKNOWN WORLDS	£1182.50	87	RIPLEY'S BELIEVE IT OR NOT	£390.00
38	OUT OF THIS WORLD	£1180.00	88	SUPERCAR	£385.00
39	WEIRD SCIENCE-FANTASY	£1150.00	89	CRY FOR DAWN	£366.50
40	SIX-GUN HEROES	£1145.00	90	HAVE GUN WILL TRAVEL	£366.00
41	BLACK RIDER	£1117.50	91	JAGUAR, ADVENTURES OF THE	£363.00
42	MY LITTLE MARGIE	£1085.00	92	BRENDA STARR, REPORTER	£360.00
43	RIFLEMAN, THE	£1080.00	93	BEATLES LIFE STORY, THE	£350.00
44	BABY HUEY, THE BABY GIANT	£1024.50	94	WAGON TRAIN	£337.50
45	DARK SHADOWS	£985.00	95	SUBMARINE ATTACK	£329.00
46	ROMANTIC STORY	£965.50	96	L'IL GENIUS	£328.70
47	ROCKY LANE WESTERN	£965.00	97	HANNA-BARBERA SUPER TV HEROES	£325.00
48	SAD SACK AND THE SARGE	£960.50	98	ATOMIC RABBIT	£322.50
49	FLINTSTONES, THE	£947.50	99	SAD SACK ARMY LIFE (PARADE/TODAY)	£320.25
50	CASPER, THE FRIENDLY GHOST	£940.15	100	TEENAGE MUTANT NINJA TURTLES	£320.00

Top 100 U.S. Independent Titles

1	FOUR COLOR (Series II)	$143765.50
2	WHIZ COMICS	$103160.00
3	WALT DISNEY'S COMICS AND STORIES	$72155.25
4	CAPTAIN MARVEL ADVENTURES	$58242.50
5	FOUR COLOR (Series I)	$36531.00
6	MAD MAGAZINE	$20525.00
7	TARZAN	$11987.50
8	VAULT OF HORROR	$10750.00
9	ADVENTURES INTO THE UNKNOWN	$10677.50
10	TALES FROM THE CRYPT	$9400.00
11	HAUNT OF FEAR	$8655.00
12	WEIRD SCIENCE	$6865.00
13	STRANGE SUSPENSE STORIES	$6390.00
14	WEIRD FANTASY	$6230.00
15	RICHIE RICH	$6071.25
16	TUROK SON OF STONE	$6020.00
17	SPACE ADVENTURES	$5084.00
18	CRIME SUSPENSTORIES	$5010.00
19	ARCHIE'S JOKE BOOK MAGAZINE	$4417.00
20	STAR TREK	$4151.25
21	EERIE	$4150.00
22	LITTLE DOT	$3952.50
23	TWO-FISTED TALES	$3920.00
24	SHOCK SUSPENSTORIES (1st Series)	$3720.00
25	FAMOUS MONSTERS OF FILMLAND	$3470.50
26	VAMPIRELLA	$3425.00
27	TALES OF THE MYSTERIOUS TRAVELLER	$2494.00
28	MYSTERIES OF UNEXPLORED WORLDS	$2410.00
29	UNUSUAL TALES	$2290.00
30	FRONTLINE COMBAT	$2215.00
31	JETSONS, THE	$2110.00
32	SPOOKY	$2087.00
33	MAGNUS ROBOT FIGHTER	$2011.00
34	FLY, ADVENTURES OF THE	$1982.50
35	WEIRD SCIENCE-FANTASY ANNUAL	$1975.00
36	THREE STOOGES, THE	$1945.00
37	UNKNOWN WORLDS	$1835.00
38	OUT OF THIS WORLD	$1770.00
39	WEIRD SCIENCE-FANTASY	$1725.00
40	SIX-GUN HEROES	$1717.50
41	BLACK RIDER	$1715.00
42	RIFLEMAN, THE	$1660.00
43	MY LITTLE MARGIE	$1647.50
44	EERIE (Magazine)	$1633.00
45	BABY HUEY, THE BABY GIANT	$1569.00
46	DARK SHADOWS	$1542.50
47	SAD SACK AND THE SARGE	$1506.00
48	ROCKY LANE WESTERN	$1477.50
49	ROMANTIC STORY	$1435.00
50	FLINTSTONES, THE	$1425.00
51	CASPER, THE FRIENDLY GHOST	$1422.35
52	DOCTOR SOLAR, MAN OF THE ATOM	$1373.00
53	FORBIDDEN WORLDS (1st Series)	$1355.00
54	BILLY THE KID	$1316.25
55	SPACE WAR	$1284.50
56	SPACE FAMILY ROBINSON	$1280.00
57	CEREBUS THE AARDVARK	$1208.50
58	LASH LARUE WESTERN	$1207.50
59	STRANGE WORLDS	$1205.00
60	CREEPY	$1165.00
61	KONGA	$1152.00
62	GORGO	$1145.00
63	PHANTOM, THE	$1130.50
64	ARCHIE'S MADHOUSE	$1110.50
65	SAD SACK LAUGH SPECIAL	$1091.00
66	FIGHTIN' ARMY	$1015.00
67	TWILIGHT ZONE	$1003.50
68	FIGHTIN' MARINES	$994.50
69	CHEYENNE	$990.00
70	HERBIE	$983.75
71	INCREDIBLE SCIENCE FICTION	$975.00
72	MUNSTERS, THE	$970.00
73	TWO-FISTED ANNUAL	$925.00
74	MAN FROM U.N.C.L.E., THE	$910.00
75	CHEYENNE KID	$838.50
76	CRY FOR DAWN	$830.00
77	MONKEES, THE	$807.50
78	OUTLAWS OF THE WEST	$762.50
79	DOUBLE LIFE OF PRIVATE STRONG, THE	$750.00
80	WIN A PRIZE COMICS	$750.00
81	FANGORIA	$745.50
82	BORIS KARLOFF TALES OF MYSTERY	$741.00
83	WYATT EARP, FRONTIER MARSHAL	$737.50
84	BONE	$733.50
85	OUTER SPACE	$670.00
86	THUNDER AGENTS	$655.00
87	I LOVE YOU	$605.50
88	FIGHTIN' AIR FORCE	$605.00
89	EVIL ERNIE	$587.50
90	SUPERCAR	$565.00
91	RIPLEY'S BELIEVE IT OR NOT	$561.50
92	HAVE GUN WILL TRAVEL	$549.00
93	HANNA-BARBERA SUPER TV HEROES	$545.00
94	JAGUAR, ADVENTURES OF THE	$544.50
95	BRENDA STARR, REPORTER	$540.00
96	BEATLES LIFE STORY, THE	$525.00
97	TEENAGE MUTANT NINJA TURTLES	$497.00
98	WAGON TRAIN	$496.50
99	L'IL GENIUS	$493.05
100	WILD, WILD WEST, THE	$490.00

Top 100 U.K. Titles

#	Title	Price
1	DETECTIVE COMICS	£407046.60
2	MORE FUN COMICS	£267080.00
3	ADVENTURE COMICS	£224312.80
4	ACTION COMICS	£216173.70
5	MARVEL COMICS	£153650.00
6	SUPERMAN (1st Series) (ADVENTURES OF SUPERMAN)	£134851.75
7	CAPTAIN AMERICA COMICS	£122377.50
8	BATMAN	£120058.70
9	ALL-AMERICAN COMICS	£114905.00
10	FOUR COLOR (Series II)	£96333.00
11	FLASH COMICS	£95530.00
12	ALL STAR COMICS	£88400.00
13	WHIZ COMICS	£68805.00
14	SHOWCASE	£60058.60
15	WALT DISNEY'S COMICS AND STORIES	£48385.00
16	WORLD'S FINEST COMICS	£46826.50
17	GREEN LANTERN (1st Series)	£41870.00
18	CAPTAIN MARVEL ADVENTURES	£40465.00
19	SENSATION COMICS	£39630.00
20	HUMAN TORCH (1st Series)	£38665.00
21	SUB-MARINER (1st) COMICS	£36650.00
22	WONDER WOMAN	£33358.75
23	AMAZING SPIDERMAN, THE	£26400.00
24	FANTASTIC FOUR	£25098.25
25	FOUR COLOR (Series I)	£24825.00
26	NEW YORK WORLD'S FAIR	£23500.00
27	COMIC CAVALCADE	£20537.50
28	STRANGE ADVENTURES	£20303.50
29	ALL-FLASH	£18750.00
30	SUPERBOY	£18626.75
31	BRAVE AND THE BOLD, THE	£18560.10
32	JOURNEY INTO MYSTERY	£17482.50
33	STRANGE TALES	£16688.50
34	MYSTERY IN SPACE	£15479.00
35	OUR ARMY AT WAR	£14388.00
36	AMAZING FANTASY	£14009.50
37	MAD MAGAZINE	£13667.50
38	TALES OF SUSPENSE	£12877.00
39	TALES TO ASTONISH	£12272.50
40	HOUSE OF MYSTERY	£11389.50
41	INCREDIBLE HULK (1st Series)	£10551.50
42	FLASH (1st Series)	£10098.50
43	STAR-SPANGLED WAR STORIES	£10004.50
44	TALES OF THE UNEXPECTED	£9160.00
45	X-MEN, THE UNCANNY	£9155.50
46	JIMMY OLSEN, SUPERMAN'S PAL	£8932.50
47	LEADING COMICS	£8721.00
48	TARZAN	£7958.00
49	JUSTICE LEAGUE OF AMERICA	£7539.50
50	MY GREATEST ADVENTURE	£7477.50
51	VAULT OF HORROR	£7255.00
52	ADVENTURES INTO THE UNKNOWN	£7205.50
53	ALL-AMERICAN MEN OF WAR	£6729.00
54	GREEN LANTERN (2nd Series)	£6571.25
55	AVENGERS	£6351.25
56	CHALLENGERS OF THE UNKNOWN	£6322.75
57	TALES FROM THE CRYPT	£6300.00
58	LOIS LANE, SUPERMAN'S GIRLFRIEND	£6140.75
59	HAUNT OF FEAR	£5820.00
60	BOB HOPE, THE ADVENTURES OF	£5563.50
61	RED RAVEN COMICS	£5500.00
62	HOUSE OF SECRETS	£5156.75
63	OUR FIGHTING FORCES	£4973.00
64	DAREDEVIL	£4701.80
65	WEIRD SCIENCE	£4590.00
66	STRANGE SUSPENSE STORIES	£4245.00
67	WEIRD FANTASY	£4195.00
68	RICHIE RICH	£4094.25
69	SUGAR AND SPIKE	£4010.75
70	TUROK SON OF STONE	£3868.00
71	G.I. COMBAT	£3547.50
72	SPACE ADVENTURES	£3473.50
73	CRIME SUSPENSTORIES	£3422.50
74	REX THE WONDER DOG	£3365.00
75	BLACKHAWK	£3310.50
76	GIRL'S LOVE STORIES	£3149.00
77	SGT. FURY AND HIS HOWLING COMMANDOS	£2991.50
78	ARCHIE'S JOKE BOOK MAGAZINE	£2957.50
79	GIRL'S ROMANCES	£2919.50
80	ALL-STAR WESTERN	£2807.50
81	STAR TREK	£2802.50
82	EERIE	£2785.00
83	LITTLE DOT	£2651.00
84	TWO-FISTED TALES	£2640.00
85	ALL-AMERICAN WESTERN	£2620.00
86	SHOCK SUSPENSTORIES (1st Series)	£2525.00
87	SERGEANT BILKO	£2440.00
88	FAMOUS MONSTERS OF FILMLAND	£2269.50
89	BIG TOWN	£2075.00
90	AMAZING ADULT FANTASY	£2050.00
91	VAMPIRELLA	£1995.00
92	DANGER TRAIL	£1925.00
93	ATOM, THE	£1808.50
94	AMAZING ADVENTURES	£1800.00
95	CONGO BILL	£1790.00
96	RAWHIDE KID	£1779.50
97	EIGHTY PAGE GIANT MAGAZINE	£1725.00
98	HEART THROBS	£1719.00
99	TALES OF THE MYSTERIOUS TRAVELLER	£1682.50
100	FALLING IN LOVE	£1675.00

Top 100 U.S. Titles

#	Title	Price
1	DETECTIVE COMICS	$607762.73
2	MORE FUN COMICS	$402095.00
3	ADVENTURE COMICS	$324400.50
4	ACTION COMICS	$324144.50
5	MARVEL COMICS	$230125.00
6	SUPERMAN (1st Series) (ADVENTURES OF SUPERMAN)	$202102.75
7	CAPTAIN AMERICA COMICS	$184349.00
8	BATMAN	$179928.50
9	ALL-AMERICAN COMICS	$171800.00
10	FOUR COLOR (Series II)	$143765.50
11	FLASH COMICS	$141565.00
12	ALL STAR COMICS	$129350.00
13	WHIZ COMICS	$103160.00
14	SHOWCASE	$89973.75
15	WALT DISNEY'S COMICS AND STORIES	$72155.25
16	WORLD'S FINEST COMICS	$70002.00
17	GREEN LANTERN (1st Series)	$62350.00
18	SENSATION COMICS	$59115.00
19	CAPTAIN MARVEL ADVENTURES	$58242.50
20	HUMAN TORCH (1st Series)	$58005.00
21	SUB-MARINER (1st) COMICS	$54250.00
22	WONDER WOMAN	$49819.50
23	AMAZING SPIDERMAN, THE	$48698.75
24	FANTASTIC FOUR	$44694.75
25	FOUR COLOR (Series I)	$36531.00
26	NEW YORK WORLD'S FAIR	$35000.00
27	STRANGE ADVENTURES	$32676.00
28	COMIC CAVALCADE	$30520.00
29	BRAVE AND THE BOLD, THE	$28017.25
30	ALL-FLASH	$28000.00
31	SUPERBOY	$27877.75
32	JOURNEY INTO MYSTERY	$27460.00
33	STRANGE TALES	$25964.50
34	AMAZING FANTASY	$25015.00
35	MYSTERY IN SPACE	$23912.00
36	OUR ARMY AT WAR	$22137.00
37	TALES OF SUSPENSE	$20898.00
38	MAD MAGAZINE	$20525.00
39	TALES TO ASTONISH	$19995.00
40	HOUSE OF MYSTERY	$19196.50
41	INCREDIBLE HULK (1st Series)	$19102.50
42	FLASH (1st Series)	$18064.62
43	X-MEN, THE UNCANNY	$16593.25
44	STAR-SPANGLED WAR STORIES	$15023.50
45	TALES OF THE UNEXPECTED	$14300.00
46	JIMMY OLSEN, SUPERMAN'S PAL	$13981.00
47	LEADING COMICS	$13205.00
48	GREEN LANTERN (2nd Series)	$13158.25
49	JUSTICE LEAGUE OF AMERICA	$12020.50
50	TARZAN	$11987.50
51	MY GREATEST ADVENTURE	$11520.00
52	LOIS LANE, SUPERMAN'S GIRLFRIEND	$10996.00
53	VAULT OF HORROR	$10750.00
54	ADVENTURES INTO THE UNKNOWN	$10677.50
55	AVENGERS	$10170.25
56	ALL-AMERICAN MEN OF WAR	$9927.50
57	CHALLENGERS OF THE UNKNOWN	$9430.50
58	TALES FROM THE CRYPT	$9400.00
59	HAUNT OF FEAR	$8655.00
60	HOUSE OF SECRETS	$8624.75
61	RED RAVEN COMICS	$8500.00
62	BOB HOPE, THE ADVENTURES OF	$8292.50
63	DAREDEVIL	$7207.25
64	OUR FIGHTING FORCES	$6901.80
65	WEIRD SCIENCE	$6865.00
66	STRANGE SUSPENSE STORIES	$6390.00
67	G.I. COMBAT	$6325.50
68	SUGAR AND SPIKE	$6231.25
69	WEIRD FANTASY	$6230.00
70	RICHIE RICH	$6071.25
71	TUROK SON OF STONE	$6020.00
72	GIRL'S LOVE STORIES	$5485.00
73	SPACE ADVENTURES	$5084.00
74	BLACKHAWK	$5080.25
75	CRIME SUSPENSTORIES	$5010.00
76	REX THE WONDER DOG	$5005.00
77	SGT. FURY AND HIS HOWLING COMMANDOS	$4692.00
78	GIRL'S ROMANCES	$4625.00
79	ARCHIE'S JOKE BOOK MAGAZINE	$4417.00
80	ALL-STAR WESTERN	$4155.00
81	STAR TREK	$4151.25
82	EERIE	$4150.00
83	ATOM, THE	$4100.00
84	LITTLE DOT	$3952.50
85	TWO-FISTED TALES	$3920.00
86	ALL-AMERICAN WESTERN	$3890.00
87	AQUAMAN	$3867.00
88	SHOCK SUSPENSTORIES (1st Series)	$3720.00
89	SERGEANT BILKO	$3655.00
90	FAMOUS MONSTERS OF FILMLAND	$3470.50
91	VAMPIRELLA	$3425.00
92	BIG TOWN	$3115.00
93	AMAZING ADVENTURES	$2950.00
94	THOR	$2881.25
95	INCREDIBLE HULK (2nd Series)	$2881.00
96	CONGO BILL	$2850.00
	DANGER TRAIL	$2850.00
98	HEART THROBS	$2780.00
99	RAWHIDE KID	$2766.00
100	IRON MAN	$2742.95

Top 100 U.K. Comics

1	DETECTIVE COMICS #27	£95000.00
2	ACTION COMICS #1	£90000.00
3	SUPERMAN (1st Series) #1	£65000.00
4	MARVEL COMICS #1	£60000.00
5	DETECTIVE COMICS #1	£50000.00
6	ALL-AMERICAN COMICS #16	£40000.00
7	BATMAN #1	£36000.00
	WHIZ COMICS #1	£36000.00
9	CAPTAIN AMERICA COMICS #1	£35000.00
10	NEW FUN COMICS #1	£32000.00
11	MORE FUN COMICS #52	£30000.00
12	FLASH COMICS #1	£27500.00
13	ADVENTURE COMICS #40	£22000.00
	ALL STAR COMICS #3	£22000.00
15	MORE FUN COMICS #53	£20000.00
16	DETECTIVE COMICS #33	£17500.00
	DETECTIVE COMICS #38	£17500.00
	SHOWCASE #4	£17500.00
19	CAPTAIN MARVEL ADVENTURES #1	£16500.00
20	NEW FUN COMICS #6	£15000.00
	NEW YORK WORLD'S FAIR #1	£15000.00
22	DETECTIVE COMICS #29	£14250.00
23	AMAZING FANTASY #15	£14000.00
	DETECTIVE COMICS #31	£14000.00
	GREEN LANTERN (1st Series) #1	£14000.00
26	SENSATION COMICS #1	£13000.00
27	HUMAN TORCH (1st Series) #2	£12500.00
28	NEW FUN COMICS #2	£12000.00
29	NEW COMICS #1	£11500.00
	SUB-MARINER (1st) COMICS #1	£11500.00
31	ADVENTURE COMICS #48	£11000.00
	MARVEL COMICS #2	£11000.00
33	ALL STAR COMICS #8	£10000.00
	AMAZING SPIDERMAN, THE #1	£10000.00
	WONDER WOMAN #1	£10000.00
36	SHOWCASE #8	£9750.00
37	FANTASTIC FOUR #1	£9000.00
	WALT DISNEY'S COMICS AND STORIES #1	£9000.00
39	DETECTIVE COMICS #28	£8750.00
40	CAPTAIN AMERICA COMICS #22	£8500.00
	DETECTIVE COMICS #2	£8500.00
	MARVEL COMICS #9	£8500.00
	NEW YORK WORLD'S FAIR #2	£8500.00
	WORLD'S FINEST COMICS #1	£8500.00
45	ACTION COMICS #2	£8300.00
46	MARVEL COMICS #5	£8000.00
47	ALL-AMERICAN COMICS #17	£7500.00
	ALL-AMERICAN COMICS #19	£7500.00
	DETECTIVE COMICS #3	£7500.00
50	ALL STAR COMICS #1	£7250.00
	MORE FUN COMICS #55	£7250.00
52	MORE FUN COMICS #14	£7000.00
	NEW FUN COMICS #3	£7000.00
54	FOUR COLOR (Series I) #16	£6930.00
55	NEW FUN COMICS #4	£6750.00
	NEW FUN COMICS #5	£6750.00
57	ALL-FLASH #1	£6500.00
	MORE FUN COMICS #73	£6500.00
59	ACTION COMICS #3	£6250.00
	BATMAN #2	£6250.00
61	ADVENTURE COMICS #61	£6000.00
	INCREDIBLE HULK (1st Series) #1	£6000.00
	SUPERMAN (1st Series) #2	£6000.00
64	FOUR COLOR (Series I) #4	£5775.00
65	ADVENTURE COMICS #73	£5750.00
	NEW COMICS #2	£5750.00
67	CAPTAIN AMERICA COMICS #2	£5700.00
68	ADVENTURE COMICS #72	£5500.00
	FOUR COLOR (Series II) #9	£5500.00
	RED RAVEN COMICS #1	£5500.00
71	ACTION COMICS #7	£5200.00
72	ALL-AMERICAN COMICS #18	£5000.00
73	ALL-AMERICAN COMICS #25	£4750.00
	MORE FUN COMICS #54	£4750.00
75	ACTION COMICS #10	£4700.00
76	COMIC CAVALCADE #1	£4500.00
	MARVEL COMICS #3	£4500.00
	MORE FUN COMICS #101	£4500.00
79	FOUR COLOR (Series II) #29	£4350.00
80	CAPTAIN AMERICA COMICS #3	£4300.00
81	BATMAN #3	£4250.00
	DETECTIVE COMICS #35	£4250.00
83	FOUR COLOR (Series I) #1	£4000.00
	SUPERMAN (1st Series) #3	£4000.00
85	ACTION COMICS #6	£3850.00
	DETECTIVE COMICS #40	£3850.00
87	ACTION COMICS #4	£3750.00
	ACTION COMICS #5	£3750.00
	MARVEL COMICS #4	£3750.00
	SUPERBOY #1	£3750.00
91	WALT DISNEY'S COMICS AND STORIES #2	£3600.00
92	BATMAN #4	£3500.00
	BATMAN #11	£3500.00
	DETECTIVE COMICS #30	£3500.00
	DETECTIVE COMICS #32	£3500.00
	MORE FUN COMICS #9	£3500.00
	MORE FUN COMICS #67	£3500.00
98	BRAVE AND THE BOLD, THE #28	£3400.00
99	DETECTIVE COMICS #4	£3350.00
	DETECTIVE COMICS #5	£3350.00

Top 100 U.S. Comics

1	DETECTIVE COMICS #27	$140000.00
2	ACTION COMICS #1	$135000.00
3	SUPERMAN (1st Series) #1	$97500.00
4	MARVEL COMICS #1	$90000.00
5	DETECTIVE COMICS #1	$75000.00
6	ALL-AMERICAN COMICS #16	$60000.00
7	WHIZ COMICS #1	$54000.00
8	BATMAN #1	$50000.00
	CAPTAIN AMERICA COMICS #1	$50000.00
10	NEW FUN COMICS #1	$47500.00
11	MORE FUN COMICS #52	$45000.00
12	FLASH COMICS #1	$41500.00
13	ADVENTURE COMICS #40	$30000.00
	ALL STAR COMICS #3	$30000.00
	MORE FUN COMICS #53	$30000.00
16	DETECTIVE COMICS #33	$26500.00
17	AMAZING FANTASY #15	$25000.00
	DETECTIVE COMICS #38	$25000.00
	SHOWCASE #4	$25000.00
20	CAPTAIN MARVEL ADVENTURES nn (#1)	$22500.00
	NEW FUN COMICS #6	$22500.00
	NEW YORK WORLD'S FAIR #1	$22500.00
23	GREEN LANTERN (1st Series) #1	$21000.00
24	DETECTIVE COMICS #29	$20000.00
	DETECTIVE COMICS #31	$20000.00
26	SENSATION COMICS #1	$19500.00
27	AMAZING SPIDERMAN, THE #1	$19000.00
28	HUMAN TORCH (1st Series) #2	$18500.00
29	FANTASTIC FOUR #1	$18000.00
30	NEW FUN COMICS #2	$17500.00
31	SUB-MARINER (1st) COMICS #1	$17000.00
32	ADVENTURE COMICS #48	$16000.00
	CAPTAIN AMERICA COMICS #22	$16000.00
	DETECTIVE COMICS #2	$16000.00
	MARVEL COMICS #2	$16000.00
36	ALL STAR COMICS #8	$15000.00
	NEW COMICS #1	$15000.00
	WONDER WOMAN #1	$15000.00
39	SHOWCASE #8	$14500.00
40	WALT DISNEY'S COMICS AND STORIES #1	$13500.00
41	DETECTIVE COMICS #28	$13000.00
42	ACTION COMICS #2	$12500.00
	MARVEL COMICS #9	$12500.00
	NEW YORK WORLD'S FAIR #2	$12500.00
45	MARVEL COMICS #5	$12000.00
	WORLD'S BEST COMICS #1	$12000.00
47	ALL-AMERICAN COMICS #17	$11250.00
	ALL-AMERICAN COMICS #19	$11250.00
	DETECTIVE COMICS #3	$11250.00
50	MORE FUN COMICS #55	$11000.00
51	MORE FUN COMICS #3	$10500.00
52	MORE FUN COMICS #14	$10250.00
53	INCREDIBLE HULK (1st Series) #1	$10000.00
	MORE FUN COMICS #73	$10000.00
	NEW FUN COMICS #4	$10000.00
	NEW FUN COMICS #5	$10000.00
57	FOUR COLOR (Series I) #16	$9900.00
58	ALL-FLASH #1	$9750.00
	ALL STAR COMICS #1	$9750.00
60	ACTION COMICS #3	$9500.00
	BATMAN #2	$9500.00
62	ADVENTURE COMICS #61	$9000.00
	SUPERMAN (1st Series) #2	$9000.00
64	CAPTAIN AMERICA COMICS #2	$8500.00
	FOUR COLOR (Series I) #4	$8500.00
	RED RAVEN COMICS #1	$8500.00
67	ACTION COMICS #7	$7750.00
68	ADVENTURE COMICS #72	$7500.00
	ADVENTURE COMICS #73	$7500.00
	FOUR COLOR (Series II) #9	$7500.00
	NEW COMICS #2	$7500.00
72	ALL-AMERICAN COMICS #18	$7400.00
73	ALL-AMERICAN COMICS #25	$7250.00
	MORE FUN COMICS #54	$7250.00
75	ACTION COMICS #10	$7000.00
	MARVEL COMICS #3	$7000.00
77	COMIC CAVALCADE #1	$6750.00
	MORE FUN COMICS #101	$6750.00
79	BATMAN #3	$6700.00
80	CAPTAIN AMERICA COMICS #3	$6500.00
	DETECTIVE COMICS #35	$6500.00
	FOUR COLOR (Series II) #29	$6500.00
83	FOUR COLOR (Series I) #1	$6000.00
	SUPERMAN (1st Series) #3	$6000.00
85	ACTION COMICS #6	$5750.00
86	ACTION COMICS #4	$5500.00
	ACTION COMICS #5	$5500.00
	MARVEL COMICS #4	$5500.00
	MORE FUN COMICS #67	$5500.00
	MORE FUN COMICS #9	$5500.00
	SUPERBOY #1	$5500.00
92	DETECTIVE COMICS #40	$5400.00
	WALT DISNEY'S COMICS AND STORIES #2	$5400.00
94	BATMAN #4	$5250.00
	BATMAN #11	$5250.00
96	DETECTIVE COMICS #4	$5000.00
	DETECTIVE COMICS #5	$5000.00
	FLASH (1st Series) #105	$5000.00
	MORE FUN COMICS #7	$5000.00
	MORE FUN COMICS #8	$5000.00

Differential Examples

Percentages quoted below are not hard and fast but at least give some idea of
relative differences in value between the US and UK markets

Ms Marvel #18 – 555% greater value
in the US Market than in the UK Market

The Man Called Nova #25 – 166% greater
value in the UK Market than in the US Market

Showcase #88 – 381% greater value
in the US Market than in the UK Market

Kitty Pryde & Wolverine #6 – 111% greater
value in the UK Market than in the US Market

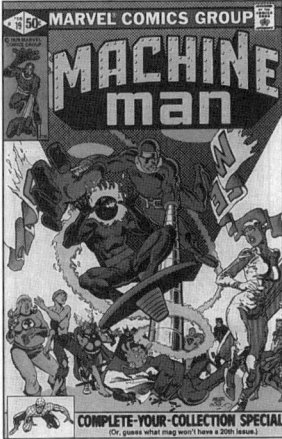

Machine Man #19 – 400% greater value
in the US Market than in the UK Market

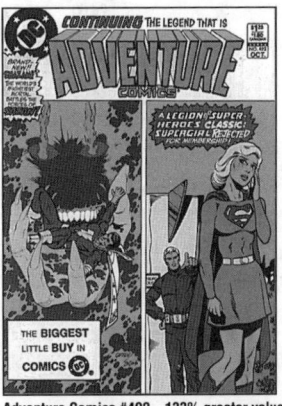

Adventure Comics #492 – 133% greater value
in the UK Market than in the US Market

Top 100
Differential DC Comics
and ranges £ to $

Below are listed comics valued in pounds sterling on the U.K. market and their equivalent guide value in dollars on the U.S. market. Rather than list simply individual comics when there may be a run of ten or twenty all the same price/percentage, ranges are included.

#	Comic	£	$	%
1	Strange Adventures #201	£5.00	$35.00	466%
2	Showcase #88-90	£3.50	$20.00	381%
3	Sandman (2nd Series) #8	£9.00	$50.00	370%
4	Green Lantern #116	£5.00	$27.50	366%
5	House of Mystery #301-321	£0.75	$4.00	355%
6	Action Comics #583	£2.00	$10.00	333%
7	Dark Mansion of Forbidden Love #1	£3.00	$15.00	333%
8	Dark Mansion of Forbidden Love #2-4	£2.00	$10.00	333%
9	Green Lantern #194	£1.00	$5.00	333%
10	House of Mystery #283-300	£1.00	$5.00	333%
11	Sandman #3	£7.00	$35.00	333%
12	Sandman #4,5	£6.00	$30.00	333%
13	Sandman #6,7	£5.00	$25.00	333%
14	Green Lantern #66-69	£7.50	$35.00	311%
15	Atom #31-35,37,38	£10.00	$45.00	300%
16	Aquaman #36-40	£12.50	$55.00	293%
17	Sandman (2nd Series) #11-13	£3.50	$15.00	285%
18	Flash #191-195,197-199	£6.00	$25.00	277%
19	Kamandi #6-10	£3.00	$12.50	277%
20	Lois Lane #76,78	£6.00	$25.00	277%
21	Lois Lane #87,88,90-92,94	£3.00	$12.50	277%
22	Atom #41,42,45	£8.50	$35.00	274%
23	Aquaman #41-49	£7.50	$30.00	266%
24	Green Lantern #195	£2.50	$10.00	266%
25	Green Lantern #112,123	£1.50	$6.00	266%
26	House of Mystery #281	£1.25	$5.00	266%
27	Jimmy Olsen #90,91,93,94,96-98	£5.00	$20.00	266%
28	Jimmy Olsen #121,123-130	£2.50	$10.00	266%
29	Sandman (2nd Series) #2	£10.00	$40.00	266%
30	Superman #499	£0.75	$3.00	266%
31	Atom #43,44	£9.00	$35.00	259%
32	Lois Lane #62-67,69	£9.00	$35.00	259%
33	Strange Adventures #132	£9.00	$35.00	259%
34	Adventure Comics #381	£4.00	$15.00	250%
35	Aquaman #53-56	£4.00	$15.00	250%
36	Demon #6	£4.00	$15.00	250%
37	Metal Men ##50-56	£4.00	$15.00	250%
38	Sandman #1	£20.00	$75.00	250%
39	Sandman #9,10,14,22	£4.00	$15.00	250%
40	Aquaman #31,32,34,35	£15.00	$55.00	244%
41	Batman #169	£30.00	$110.00	244%
42	Green Lantern #56-58	£15.00	$55.00	244%
43	Justice League of America #57	£7.50	$27.50	244%
44	Justice League of America #68-70	£6.00	$22.00	244%
45	Action Comics #683	£1.25	$4.50	240%
46	Lois Lane #56	£12.50	$45.00	240%
47	Flash #201-204,206,207	£3.50	$12.50	238%
48	Jimmy Olsen #85,88	£7.00	$25.00	238%
49	Lois Lane #89,93	£3.50	$12.50	238%
50	Action Comics #426-436,438,439	£2.00	$7.00	233%
51	Aquaman #33	£20.00	$70.00	233%
52	Atom #39,40	£10.00	$35.00	233%
53	Batman #189	£10.00	$35.00	233%
54	Green lantern #60,62-65	£10.00	$35.00	233%
55	Justice League of America #56	£10.00	$35.00	233%
56	Kamandi #3,4,5	£5.00	$17.50	233%
57	Lois Lane #74	£10.00	$35.00	233%
58	Showcase #67	£10.00	$35.00	233%
59	Strange Adventures #171-179	£10.00	$35.00	233%
60	Kamandi #2	£8.00	$27.50	229%
61	Aquaman #62,63	£1.75	$6.00	228%
62	Demon #11-16	£3.50	$12.00	228%
63	Adventure Comics #404-408	£1.50	$5.00	222%
64	Brave and the Bold #61,62	£30.00	$100.00	222%
65	Demon #8	£4.50	$15.00	222%
66	Flash #181-186,188-190,200	£7.50	$25.00	222%
67	Flash #208-210,212,213	£3.75	$12.50	222%
68	G.I. Combat #155-160	£3.00	$10.00	222%
69	Green Lantern (2nd) #70-74	£6.00	$20.00	222%
70	House of Mystery #263-282	£1.50	$5.00	222%
71	Jimmy Olsen #71,74,75,77-80	£7.50	$25.00	222%
72	Jimmy Olsen #81-84,86,89,92,99	£6.00	$20.00	222%
73	Jimmy Olsen #112,114-120	£3.00	$10.00	222%
74	Jimmy Olsen #133	£6.00	$20.00	222%
75	Jimmy Olsen #134	£9.00	$30.00	222%
76	Lois Lane #72,73,75	£7.50	$25.00	222%
77	Our Army at War #271-274,276-280, 281-289,292-301	£1.50	$5.00	222%
78	Sandman #15-20,23-25	£3.00	$10.00	222%
79	Showcase #85-87	£7.50	$25.00	222%
80	Strange Adventures #141,144,147	£22.50	$75.00	222%
81	Strange Sports Stories #2-6	£1.50	$5.00	222%
82	Forever People #3-5	£10.00	$32.00	216%
83	Hot Wheels #3	£10.00	$32.00	216%
84	Action Comics #421-424	£2.50	$8.00	213%
85	Aquaman #50-52	£12.50	$40.00	213%
86	Flash #176,177,179,180,196	£12.50	$40.00	213%
87	Green Lantern (2nd) #61	£12.50	$40.00	213%
88	House of Mystery #131-142	£12.50	$40.00	213%
89	Lois Lane #51-55,57-61	£12.50	$40.00	213%
90	Mystery in Space #112,117	£1.25	$4.00	213%
91	Sgt. Rock #401-422	£1.25	$4.00	213%
92	Aquaman #21-28,30	£17.50	$55.00	209%
93	Atom #36	£17.50	$55.00	209%
94	Justice League of America #61,62,65,66	£7.00	$22.00	209%
95	Lois Lane #41-46,48,49	£17.50	$55.00	209%
96	Green Lantern (2nd) #40	£150.00	$475.00	209%
97	Lois Lane #81-85	£4.00	$12.50	208%
98	Justice League of America #64	£8.00	$25.00	208%
99	Green Lantern (2nd) #75	£6.50	$20.00	205%
100	Strange Sports Stories #1	£2.50	$7.50	200%

Top 100
Differential DC Comics
and ranges $ to £

Below are listed comics valued in pounds sterling on the U.K market and their equivalent guide value in dollars on the U.S market after conversion. Rather than list simply individual comics when there may be a run of ten or twenty all the same price/percentage, ranges are included.

#	Title	$	£	%
1	Adventure Comics #491	$2.50	£6.00	160%
2	Adventure Comics #500	$2.50	£6.00	160%
3	Adventure Comics #492-499,501-503	$2.50	£5.00	133%
4	Superboy #211	$2.50	£5.00	133%
5	Swamp Thing (2nd) #15,16	$2.00	£4.00	133%
6	Batman & The Outsiders #1	$2.00	£3.50	116%
7	Superboy #227	$2.00	£3.50	116%
8	Justice League of America #150	$3.50	£6.00	114%
9	Batman Pizza Hut Giveaway	$3.00	£5.00	111%
10	Batman Family #19,20	$4.00	£6.00	100%
11	Batman: Shadow of the Bat #2-5	$4.00	£6.00	100%
12	Superboy #221-226,230	$2.00	£3.00	100%
13	Swamp Thing (2nd) #17-19	$2.00	£3.00	100%
14	Shadow of the Batman #1	$5.00	£7.00	93%
15	Justice League of America #159	$2.50	£3.50	93%
16	Superboy #212,213,218	$2.50	£3.50	93%
17	Batman Family #7,8	$4.00	£5.50	91%
18	Batman & The Outsiders #2	$1.50	£2.00	88%
19	Beowulf #4,6	$0.75	£1.00	88%
20	Vigilante #50	$1.50	£2.00	88%
21	Batman Family #5	$5.00	£6.50	86%
22	Swamp Thing (2nd) #26,27	$5.00	£6.50	86%
23	Justice League of America #143,145	$3.50	£4.50	85%
24	Batman Family #14,15,18	$4.00	£5.00	83%
25	Super-Team Family #2	$2.00	£2.50	83%
26	Superboy #232,235	$2.00	£2.50	83%
27	Swamp Thing (2nd) #11-14	$2.00	£2.50	83%
28	Batman #180	$50.00	£60.00	80%
29	Batman Family #2-4,17	$5.00	£6.00	80%
30	Batman Spectacular #15	$5.00	£6.00	80%
31	Justice League of America #160	$2.50	£3.00	80%
32	Superboy 198,199	$5.00	£6.00	80%
33	Superboy 219,220	$2.50	£3.00	80%
34	Wonder Woman #202	$2.50	£3.00	80%
35	Batman Family #6	$5.50	£6.50	78%
36	Fury of Firestorm #61 (Test)	$30.00	£35.00	77%
37	The Joker #9	$6.00	£7.00	77%
38	Justice League of America #122,151	$3.00	£3.50	77%
39	Super-Team Family #12-15	$1.50	£1.75	77%
40	Superman Family #182	$3.00	£3.50	77%
41	Justice League of America #141,146-148	$3.50	£4.00	76%
42	Green Lantern (3rd) #50	$4.00	£4.50	75%
43	Death: High Cost of Living #2	$2.25	£2.50	74%
44	Batman Family #11-13	$5.00	£5.50	73%
45	Swamp Thing (2nd) #28-30	$5.00	£5.50	73%
46	Detective Comics #480	$6.00	£6.50	72%
47	Justice League of America #110-116	$6.00	£6.50	72%
48	Green Lantern (2nd) #99	$2.75	£3.00	72%
49	Action Comics #544	$2.50	£2.50	66%
50	Action Comics #665,666	$1.00	£1.00	66%
51	Babylon 5 #1,2	$4.00	£4.00	66%
52	Babylon 5 #3	$3.00	£3.00	66%
53	Babylon 5 #4,5	$2.00	£2.00	66%
54	Batman and thenOutsiders #3-5	$1.50	£1.50	66%
55	Batman Family #9	$5.00	£5.00	66%
56	Batman Family #10,16	$4.00	£4.00	66%
57	Batman: Dark Knight Returns #1 (2nd)	$4.00	£4.00	66%
58	Batman: Dark Knight Returns #1 (2nd)	$4.00	£4.00	66%
59	Batman: Dark Knight Returns #1 (3rd)	$3.00	£3.00	66%
60	Batman: Dark Knight Returns #2 (2nd)	$3.00	£3.00	66%
61	Batman: Dark Knight Returns #2 (3rd)	$2.50	£2.50	66%
62	Batman: Dark Knight Returns #3 (2nd)	$2.50	£2.50	66%
63	Brave and the Bold #120	$3.50	£3.50	66%
64	DC Comics Presents #2,3	$1.50	£1.50	66%
65	DC Special #28,29	$5.00	£5.00	66%
66	DC Blue Ribbon Digest #1-24	$2.50	£2.50	66%
67	Detective Comics #472	$15.00	£15.00	66%
68	Dragonlance Comics #1	$2.50	£2.50	66%
69	First Issue Special #8	$5.00	£5.00	66%
70	Freedom Fighters #2,3	$2.00	£2.00	66%
71	Freedom Fighters #4	$1.50	£1.50	66%
72	Green Lantern (2nd) #224	$1.50	£1.50	66%
73	Adventures of Jerry Lewis #118-124	$6.00	£6.00	66%
74	The Joker #8	$6.00	£6.00	66%
75	Judge Dredd #1	$3.00	£3.00	66%
76	Justice League of America #121,123-126, 132-134,137,138	$3.00	£3.00	66%
77	Justice League of America #139,140,142,144,149	$3.50	£3.50	66%
78	Justice League of America #158	$3.00	£3.00	66%
79	Justice League of America #200	$4.00	£4.00	66%
80	Karate Kid #1	$3.00	£3.00	66%
81	Karate Kid #2,3	$2.00	£2.00	66%
82	Karate Kid #4,5,8	$1.50	£1.50	66%
83	Legion of Super-Heroes (2nd) #38	$10.00	£10.00	66%
84	Legion of Super-Heroes Annual (1st) #1	$2.00	£2.00	66%
85	Lois Lane #86	$9.00	£9.00	66%
86	New Teen Titans (1st) #13	$2.50	£2.50	66%
87	Super DC Giant #19,25	$4.00	£4.00	66%
88	Super-Team Family #1	$3.00	£3.00	66%
89	Super-Team Family #3,5	$2.00	£2.00	66%
90	Super-Team Family #6	$1.50	£1.50	66%
91	Superboy #190,191,193,195,201	$3.00	£3.00	66%
92	Superboy #202	$5.00	£5.00	66%
93	Superboy Spectacular #1	$2.00	£2.00	66%
94	Superman Family #176,194	$3.00	£3.00	66%
95	Swamp Thing (2nd) #22	$10.00	£10.00	66%
96	Swamp Thing (2nd) #23-25	$7.50	£7.50	66%
97	Who's Who #2	$1.50	£1.50	66%
98	Wonder Woman #214	$3.00	£3.00	66%
99	Wonder Woman #220	$2.50	£2.50	66%
100	Wonder Woman #228,247	$2.00	£2.00	66%

Top 100
Differential Marvel Comics and ranges £ to $

Below are listed comics valued in pounds sterling on the U.K. market and their equivalent guide value in dollars on the U.S. market after conversion. Rather than list simply individual comics when there may be a run of ten or twenty all the same price/percentage, ranges are included.

#	Title	£	$	%		#	Title	£	$	%
1	Ms. Marvel #18	£1.50	$12.50	555%		51	Incredible Hulk #368	£3.00	$10.00	222%
2	Amazing Spiderman #332	£1.75	$12.00	457%		52	Iron Man #191,244	£1.50	$5.00	222%
3	Amazing Spiderman #333	£1.75	$12.00	457%		53	New Mutants #87	£7.50	$25.00	222%
4	Uncanny X-Men #244	£3.00	$20.00	444%		54	Uncanny X-Men #96	£15.00	$50.00	222%
5	Machine Man #19	£2.00	$12.00	400%		55	Uncanny X-Men #98,99 (30 cents)	£15.00	$50.00	222%
6	Spectacular Spiderman #147	£3.50	$20.00	381%		56	Uncanny X-Men #201	£7.50	$25.00	222%
7	Amazing Spiderman #259,260	£2.00	$10.00	333%		57	Uncanny X-Men #246,247	£1.50	$5.00	222%
8	Ms. Marvel #17	£1.50	$7.50	333%		58	Uncanny X-Men #282	£3.00	$10.00	222%
9	Team America #11	£0.60	$3.00	333%		59	Venom: Lethal Protector (Black)	£30.00	$100.00	222%
10	Fantastic Four #244	£1.25	$6.00	320%		60	Web of Spiderman #48	£4.50	$15.00	222%
11	Amazing Spiderman Annual #26	£1.75	$8.00	304%		61	Tales of Suspense #80	£20.00	$65.00	216%
12	Uncanny X-Men #248	£5.00	$22.50	300%		62	Amazing Spiderman #200	£10.00	$32.00	213%
13	Amazing Spiderman #312	£6.00	$25.00	277%		63	Amazing Spiderman #240-248	£2.50	$8.00	213%
14	Amazing Spiderman #252	£9.00	$37.50	277%		64	Amazing Spiderman Annual #17-19,23	£2.50	$8.00	213%
15	Amazing Adventures #11	£7.50	$30.00	266%		65	Fantastic Four #237,238,242,245-248, 251-258,273	£1.25	$4.00	213%
16	Amazing Spiderman #247	£2.50	$10.00	266%		66	Invaders #31-40	£1.25	$4.00	213%
17	Amazing Spiderman #283	£2.50	$10.00	266%		67	Marvel Comics Presents #54-62	£1.25	$4.00	213%
18	Amazing Spiderman #276,281	£3.00	$12.00	266%		68	Uncanny X-Men #129	£7.50	$24.00	213%
19	Amazing Spiderman #262	£2.50	$10.00	266%		69	Uncanny X-Men #151-157	£2.50	$8.00	213%
20	Amazing Spiderman #315-317	£5.00	$20.00	266%		70	Uncanny X-Men #266	£12.50	$40.00	213%
21	Amazing Spiderman Annual #22	£2.00	$8.00	266%		71	Tales of Suspense #76-79	£17.50	$55.00	209%
22	Uncanny X-Men #139	£7.50	$30.00	266%		72	Conan the Barbarian #22	£8.00	$25.00	208%
23	Uncanny X-Men #216-218,220,221	£1.50	$6.00	266%		73	Incredible Hulk #200	£8.00	$25.00	208%
24	Uncanny X-Men #240	£2.00	$8.00	266%		74	Incredible Hulk #372	£4.00	$12.50	208%
25	Uncanny X-Men #283	£3.00	$12.00	266%		75	Uncanny X-Men #158	£4.00	$12.50	208%
26	Werewolf By Night #33	£7.50	$30.00	266%		76	Uncanny X-Men #225,227	£3.25	$10.00	205%
27	Amazing Spiderman #137	£12.00	$45.00	250%		77	Amazing Spiderman #239	£15.00	$45.00	200%
28	Amazing Spiderman #245,275	£4.00	$15.00	250%		78	Amazing Spiderman #260,261	£4.00	$12.00	200%
29	Amazing Spiderman #300	£20.00	$75.00	250%		79	Amazing Spiderman #263,264,295-297	£2.00	$6.00	200%
30	Ms. Marvel #16	£2.00	$7.50	250%		80	Amazing Spiderman #304-311,313,314	£4.00	$12.00	200%
31	Uncanny X-Men #110,111	£6.00	$22.50	250%		81	Amazing Spiderman #324	£5.00	$15.00	200%
32	Uncanny X-Men #222	£4.00	$15.00	250%		82	Amazing Spiderman #326,327	£1.50	$4.50	200%
33	Uncanny X-Men #98,98	£13.50	$50.00	246%		83	Amazing Spiderman #328	£4.00	$12.00	200%
34	Amazing Spiderman #361	£6.00	$22.50	244%		84	Amazing Spiderman #344	£2.00	$6.00	200%
35	Uncanny X-Men #100	£15.00	$55.00	244%		85	Amazing Spiderman #345	£5.00	$15.00	200%
36	Uncanny X-Men #131,132,134,135	£5.00	$18.00	240%		86	Amazing Spiderman Annual 21	£3.00	$9.00	200%
37	Amazing Spiderman #289	£7.00	$25.00	238%		87	Amazing Spiderman Annual 25	£4.00	$12.00	200%
38	Uncanny X-Men #101	£13.50	$47.50	234%		88	Master of Kung Fu #76-99	£1.00	$3.00	200%
39	Amazing Spiderman #244,257,258	£3.50	$12.00	228%		89	Spectacular Spiderman #160	£2.00	$6.00	200%
40	Iron Man #169	£3.50	$12.00	228%		90	Strange Tales #148	£20.00	$60.00	200%
41	Uncanny X-Men #235-238,241	£1.75	$6.00	228%		91	Uncanny X-Men #97,108	£15.00	$45.00	200%
42	Uncanny X-Men #140	£8.00	$27.00	225%		92	Uncanny X-Men #109	£12.00	$36.00	200%
43	Amazing Spiderman #249-251	£4.50	$15.00	222%		93	Uncanny X-Men #112-119,123-128	£6.00	$18.00	200%
44	Amazing Spiderman #288	£3.00	$10.00	222%		94	Uncanny X-Men #136	£5.00	$15.00	200%
45	Avengers #326	£1.50	$5.00	222%		95	Uncanny X-Men #141,144-150	£3.00	$9.00	200%
46	Avengers Annual #10	£7.50	$25.00	222%		96	Uncanny X-Men #162	£4.00	$12.00	200%
47	Captain America #323,339,340	£1.50	$5.00	222%		97	Uncanny X-Men #219,223,228,229-232,234,239	£2.00	$6.00	200%
48	Captain America Annual #9	£1.50	$5.00	222%		98	Werewolf by Night #32	£15.00	$45.00	200%
49	Fantastic Four #349	£1.50	$5.00	222%		99	Wolverine #2	£5.00	$15.00	200%
50	Fantasy Masterpieces #10,11	£6.00	$20.00	222%		100	X-Men (2nd Series) #11 (variant)	£5.00	$15.00	200%

Top 100
Differential Marvel Comics
and ranges $ to £

Below are listed comics valued in pounds sterling on the U.K. market and their equivalent guide value in dollars on the U.S. market after conversion. Rather than list simply individual comics when there may be a run of ten or twenty all the same price/percentage, ranges are included.

#	Title	$	£	%	#	Title	$	£	%
1	Nova #25	$2.00	£5.00	166%	51	Black Dragon #2-6	$1.50	£1.50	66%
2	Epic Illustrated #34	$2.50	£6.00	160%	52	Captain America #286	$3.00	£3.00	66%
3	Kitty Pryde and Wolverine #6	$3.00	£5.00	111%	53	Captain America #306	$2.00	£2.00	66%
4	Epic Illustrated #26,29,33	$2.50	£4.00	106%	54	Captain America Annual #3	$3.50	£3.50	66%
5	Daredevil #161	$10.00	£15.00	100%	55	Conan the Barbarian #17,18	$12.00	£12.00	66%
6	Groo the Wanderer #7	$5.00	£7.50	100%	56	Conan the Barbarian Annual #4,5	$2.00	£2.00	66%
7	Epic Illustrated #15	$2.50	£3.50	93%	57	Daredevil #150	$5.00	£5.00	66%
8	Groo the Wanderer #3,5,6	$5.00	£7.00	93%	58	Daredevil #160	$10.00	£10.00	66%
9	Magik: Storm & Illyana #4	$2.50	£3.50	93%	59	Daredevil #190	$3.00	£3.00	66%
10	Crazy #1-3	$1.50	£2.00	88%	60	Daredevil #218,219	$2.00	£2.00	66%
11	Daredevil #226	$3.00	£4.00	88%	61	Daredevil #228,230-233	$2.50	£2.50	66%
12	Groo the Wanderer #2	$6.00	£8.00	88%	62	Daredevil #250,251,253	$2.00	£2.00	66%
13	Groo the Wanderer #11,12	$3.00	£4.00	88%	63	Dracula Lives! #4	$2.50	£2.50	66%
14	Hawkeye #2	$1.50	£2.00	88%	64	Epic Illustrated #7	$3.00	£3.00	66%
15	Kitty Pryde and Wolverine #5	£4.00	£3.00	88%	65	Epic Illustrated #12-14,17-20	$2.50	£2.50	66%
16	Powerman #122-124	$1.50	£2.00	88%	66	Fantastic Four #320,347 (2nd)	$2.00	£2.00	66%
17	Bizarre Adventures #25,26,29	$2.00	£2.50	83%	67	Generation X #2	$3.00	£3.00	66%
18	Daredevil #169	$10.00	£12.50	83%	68	Groo the Wanderer #1	$12.50	£12.50	66%
19	Epic Illustrated #1	$4.00	£5.00	83%	69	Groo the Wanderer #8-10	$5.00	£5.00	66%
20	Generation X Collector's Preview	$2.00	£2.50	83%	70	Guardians of the Galaxy #1	$4.00	£4.00	66%
21	Incredible Hulk #153	$6.00	£7.50	83%	71	Guardians of the Galaxy #2,3	$2.50	£2.50	66%
22	New Warriors #1	$6.00	£7.50	83%	72	Guardians of the Galaxy #4-10	$2.00	£2.00	66%
23	Nick Fury, Agent of Shield #17,18	$4.00	£5.00	83%	73	Guardians of the Galaxy #11-15	$1.50	£1.50	66%
24	Ren & Stimpy #1	$10.00	£12.50	83%	74	Haunt of Horror (2nd) #5	$4.00	£4.00	66%
25	West Coast Avengers #3	$2.00	£2.50	83%	75	Hawkeye #1	$2.00	£2.00	66%
26	X-Men at the State Fair of Texas	$20.00	£25.00	83%	76	Hawkeye #3,4	$1.50	£1.50	66%
27	Captain America Annual #4	$5.00	£6.00	80%	77	Incredible Hulk #152	$6.00	£6.00	66%
28	Daredevil #229	$2.50	£3.00	80%	78	Incredible Hulk #171	$7.50	£7.50	66%
29	Epic Illustrated #11,16,27,28,30-32	$2.50	£3.00	80%	79	Inhumans #10,11	$3.00	£3.00	66%
30	G.I. Joe #2	$5.00	£6.00	80%	80	Iron Man #121	$3.00	£3.00	66%
31	Groo the Wanderer #4	$5.00	£6.00	80%	81	Iron Man #291	$1.25	£1.25	66%
32	Powerman #125	$2.50	£3.00	80%	82	Iron Man Annual #5,8	$3.00	£3.00	66%
33	West Coast Avengers #1	$2.50	£3.00	80%	83	Iron Manual #1	$1.50	£1.50	66%
34	Avengers #200	$3.00	£3.50	77%	84	Journey into Mystery (2nd) #19	$1.50	£1.50	66%
35	Bizarre Adventures #27,28	$3.00	£3.50	77%	85	Kitty Pryde and Wolverine #2-4	$3.00	£3.00	66%
36	Daredevil #252	$3.00	£3.50	77%	86	Magik: Storm & Illyana #3	$2.50	£2.50	66%
37	Incredible Hulk vs. Venom #1	$6.00	£7.00	77%	87	Marvel Adventure #1	$1.50	£1.50	66%
38	Inhumans #12	$3.00	£3.50	77%	88	Marvel Team-Up #38	$4.50	£4.50	66%
39	West Coast Avengers #101	$3.00	£3.50	77%	89	Marvel Team-Up #81	$2.50	£2.50	66%
40	Ren & Stimpy #4,5	$3.50	£4.00	76%	90	Marvel Triple Action Giant Size #1	$4.00	£4.00	66%
41	Nick Fury, Agent of Shield #16	$4.00	£4.50	75%	91	Marvel Triple Action Giant Size #2	$3.50	£3.50	66%
42	Monster of Frankenstein #11	$2.25	£2.50	74%	92	Moon Knight #37,38	$1.50	£1.50	66%
43	Incredible Hulk #176	$5.00	£5.50	73%	93	New Warriors #2	$5.00	£5.00	66%
44	Avengers #131	$8.00	£8.50	70%	94	New Warriors #3	$4.00	£4.00	66%
45	Amazing Adventures (2nd) #23-25	$3.00	£3.00	66%	95	Powerman #118-121	$1.50	£1.50	66%
46	Avengers #181	$3.00	£3.00	66%	96	Ren & Stimpy #3	$5.00	£5.00	66%
47	Avengers #183	$3.00	£3.00	66%	97	Ringo Kid #3	$2.00	£2.00	66%
48	Avengers #302	$2.50	£2.50	66%	98	Rom #4-7	$1.50	£1.50	66%
49	Avengers #368	$1.50	£1.50	66%	99	Secret Wars II #1,9	$1.25	£1.25	66%
50	Battlestar Galactica #3-5	$1.00	£1.00	66%	100	Spectacular Spiderman #17	$7.50	£7.50	66%

Top 100
Differential Independent Comics
and ranges £ to $

Below are listed comics valued in pounds sterling on the U.K. market and their equivalent guide value in dollars on the U.S. market after conversion. Rather than list simply individual comics when there may be a run of ten or twenty all the same price/percentage, ranges are included. For Independent Comics read all publishers other than Marvel and DC.

#	Title	£	$	%	#	Title	£	$	%
1	Eerie (Magazine) #66-80	£2.00	$8.00	266%	51	Jetsons #4,5	£10.00	$25.00	166%
2	Mickey & Donald #1	£1.00	$4.00	266%	52	Lord Pumpkin #0 (Signed)	£5.00	$12.50	166%
3	Mickey Mouse #219	£1.00	$4.00	266%	53	Mickey and Donald #17,18	£1.00	$2.50	166%
4	Vampirella #101-112	£5.00	$20.00	266%	54	Mickey Mouse #255,256	£1.00	$2.50	166%
5	Eerie (Magazine) #81-139	£1.50	$5.00	222%	55	Prototype #1 (Ultra Limited)	£5.00	$12.50	166%
6	Harbinger #0 (blue)	£1.50	$5.00	222%	56	Cry For Dawn #1	£75.00	$185.00	164%
7	Uncle Scrooge #212-218	£3.00	$10.00	222%	57	Cages #2	£2.50	$6.00	160%
8	Cry For Dawn #1 (3rd)	£20.00	$60.00	200%	58	Evil Ernie: Ressurection #2,3	£5.00	$12.00	160%
9	Eerie (Magazine) #21-25	£5.00	$15.00	200%	59	Prototype #1 (Gold hologram)	£8.50	$20.00	156%
10	Elfquest #1 (2nd)	£5.00	$15.00	200%	60	Dracula (Dell) #1	£15.00	$35.00	155%
11	Frankenstein #2	£5.00	$15.00	200%	61	Freex #15	£1.50	$3.50	155%
12	Jetsons #11-20	£5.00	$15.00	200%	62	Lady Death #1	£30.00	$70.00	155%
13	Mickey and Donald #2,3	£1.00	$3.00	200%	63	Underdog #4-10	£15.00	$35.00	155%
14	Mickey Mouse #220-225	£1.00	$3.00	200%	64	Eerie (Magazine) #41-64	£3.50	$8.00	152%
15	Uncle Scrooge #210,219	£5.00	$15.00	200%	65	Fightin' Air Force #22-30	£5.50	$12.50	151%
16	Vampirella #100	£10.00	$30.00	200%	66	Archer & Armstrong #10-25	£1.00	$2.25	150%
17	Frankenstein #1	£12.00	$35.00	194%	67	Creepy #2	£20.00	$45.00	150%
18	Eerie (Magazine) #34,38	£3.50	$10.00	190%	68	Cry For Dawn #6	£20.00	$45.00	150%
19	Frankenstein #3,4	£3.50	$10.00	190%	69	Underdog #1	£20.00	$45.00	150%
20	Uncle Scrooge #211	£3.50	$10.00	190%	70	Creepy #4-8	£9.00	$20.00	148%
21	Cry For Dawn #2 (2nd)	£12.50	$35.00	186%	71	Land of the Giants #1	£22.50	$50.00	148%
22	Creepy #14	£9.00	$25.00	185%	72	Charlton Bullseye #2,5	£5.00	$11.00	146%
23	Star Wars: Dark Empire #1,2	£10.00	$27.50	183%	73	Drag-Strip Hotrodders #5-10	£5.00	$11.00	146%
24	The Tick #2	£10.00	$27.50	183%	74	Cry For Dawn #2	£55.00	$120.00	145%
25	Cry For Dawn #1 (2nd)	£35.00	$95.00	180%	75	Cry For Dawn #5-8 (2nd print)	£3.50	$7.50	142%
26	Cages #1	£3.00	$8.00	177%	76	Deathmate #4	£3.50	$7.50	142%
27	Caliber Presents #15	£7.50	$20.00	177%	77	Eerie (Magazine) #11,15,17,18	£7.00	$15.00	142%
28	Dr. Graves, The Many Ghosts of #4-10	£1.50	$4.00	177%	78	Eerie Annual #1	£7.00	$15.00	142%
29	Eerie (Magazine) #62,65	£3.00	$8.00	177%	79	Evil Ernie #3	£75.00	$35.00	142%
30	Elfquest #4,5	£7.50	$20.00	177%	80	Hellina #1 (Signed)	£7.00	$15.00	142%
31	Jetsons #6-10	£7.50	$20.00	177%	81	Hellina #1 (Commemorative)	£7.00	$15.00	142%
32	1963 #1 (Gold)	£7.50	$20.00	177%	82	Pitt #1	£3.50	$7.50	142%
33	Evil Ernie #4,5	£25.00	$65.00	173%	83	Zorro #3	£7.00	$15.00	142%
34	Lady Death 1/2 Gold	£17.50	$45.00	171%	84	Creepy #1	£40.00	$85.00	141%
35	Captain Canuck #4 (1st print)	£10.00	$25.00	166%	85	Blip and the C.C.A.D.S	£0.60	$1.25	138%
36	Captain Canuck #4 (2nd print)	£5.00	$12.50	166%	86	Fightin' Air Force #12-21	£6.00	$12.50	138%
37	Creepy #113	£10.00	$25.00	166%	87	Fightin' Army #31-50	£6.00	$12.50	138%
38	Dr Graves, The Many Ghosts of #3	£2.00	$5.00	166%	88	Gen 13 #5 (Variant)	£12.00	$25.00	138%
39	Dracula #3,4	£4.00	$10.00	166%	89	Spawn #3	£6.00	$12.50	138%
40	Drag-Strip Hotrodders #11-16	£4.00	$10.00	166%	90	Turok: Dinosaur Hunter (Limited)	£6.00	$12.50	138%
41	Eerie (Magazine) #6-10	£10.00	$25.00	166%	91	Turok: Dinosaur Hunter (Signed)	£6.00	$12.50	138%
42	Eerie (Magazine) #12-14,16,19,20	£6.00	$15.00	166%	92	Hellboy: The Wolves of St August	£2.50	$5.00	133%
43	Eerie (Magazine) #30-33,35-37,39,40,54,55,58,60	£4.00	$10.00	166%	93	Primortals: Origins #1	£1.50	$3.00	133%
44	Elfquest #3	£10.00	$25.00	166%	94	Vampirella #71-99	£5.00	$10.00	133%
45	Evil Ernie #1	£60.00	$150.00	166%	95	Vampirella (3rd) #0 Gold	£20.00	$40.00	133%
46	Evil Ernie: Ressurection #4	£4.00	$10.00	166%	96	WildC.A.T.S #1	£3.00	$6.00	133%
47	Fightin' Army #161-172	£1.00	$2.50	166%	97	WildC.A.T.S #3,4	£2.00	$4.00	133%
48	Forbidden Worlds #94	£20.00	$50.00	166%	98	X-Files #3	£7.50	$15.00	133%
49	Frankenstein #1 (number on cover)	£8.00	$20.00	166%	99	X-O Manowar #0 (Limited)	£7.50	$15.00	133%
50	Hellina: Kiss of Death #1 (variant)	£3.00	$7.50	166%	100	X-O Manowar (Signed)	£7.50	$15.00	133%

Top 100
Differential Independent Comics
and ranges $ to £

Below are listed comics valued in pounds sterling on the U.K market and their equivalent guide value in dollars on the U.S market. Rather than list simply individual comics when there may be a run of ten or twenty all the same price/percentage, ranges are included. For Independent Comics read all publishers other than Marvel and DC.

#	Title	$	£	%	#	Title	$	£	%
1	Supreme #30	$2.50	£7.50	200%	51	Critters #1	$3.00	£3.00	66%
2	Deathblow #5	$2.25	£6.00	177%	52	Deathblow #5 (variant)	$10.00	£10.00	66%
3	Quantum Leap #3	$3.50	£7.50	142%	53	Elementals #1	$5.00	£5.00	66%
4	Quantum Leap #2	$5.00	£10.00	133%	54	Elementals #2	$3.00	£3.00	66%
5	Quantum Leap #4,5	$2.50	£5.00	133%	55	Elric: Sailor on the Seas of Fate #1	$2.00	£2.00	66%
6	Stray Bullets #1	$10.00	£20.00	133%	56	Elven #1 (Limited)	$2.50	£2.50	66%
7	Terminator: Burning Earth #2	$3.00	£4.00	133%	57	Famous Monsters of Filmland #32	$25.00	£25.00	66%
8	Quantum Leap #1	$10.00	£17.50	116%	58	Famous Monsters of Filmland #115-139	$3.50	£3.50	66%
9	Famous Monsters of Filmland #56	$15.00	£25.00	111%	59	Famous Monsters of Filmland #143-160	$3.00	£3.00	66%
10	Spawn #15,16	$3.00	£5.00	111%	60	Faust #4	$5.00	£5.00	66%
11	Stray Bullets #2	$7.50	£12.50	111%	61	Faust #5	$4.00	£4.00	66%
12	Terminator: Burning Earth #1	$3.00	£5.00	111%	62	Funnytime Features #7	$5.00	£5.00	66%
13	Quantum Leap #6-10	$2.50	£4.00	106%	63	Green Hornet #1	$4.00	£4.00	66%
14	Quantum Leap Time & Space Special #1	$2.50	£4.00	106%	64	Madhouse #97	$1.50	£1.50	66%
15	Anything Goes #2,5	$2.00	£3.00	100%	65	Mage #1	$10.00	£10.00	66%
16	Destroyer Duck #1	$4.00	£6.00	100%	66	Married with Children #3-7	$1.50	£1.50	66%
17	Donald Duck #246	$2.00	£3.00	100%	67	Miracleman #17	$2.00	£2.00	66%
18	Elflord (1st Series) #1	$2.00	£3.00	100%	68	Miracleman 3-D Special #1	$2.00	£2.00	66%
19	Famous Monsters of Filmland #95	$10.00	£15.00	100%	69	Nexus (1st) #1	$10.00	£10.00	66%
20	Miracleman #12	$2.00	£3.00	100%	70	Nexus (1st) #2	$7.50	£7.50	66%
21	Star Trek Dynabrite Comics #11357/58	$5.00	£7.50	100%	71	Nexus (1st) #3	$5.00	£5.00	66%
22	Termianator: Burning Earth #3-5	$2.00	£3.00	100%	72	Nexus (2nd) #3	$2.50	£2.50	66%
23	Shi: Way of the Warrior #6	$3.50	£5.00	95%	73	Primer #6	$5.00	£5.00	66%
24	Mr. Monster (1st Series) #3	$2.50	£3.50	93%	74	Quadrant #2	$2.50	£2.50	66%
25	Quantum Leap #11,12	$2.50	£3.50	93%	75	Queen of the Damned #1	$2.50	£2.50	66%
26	Anything Goes #1	$3.00	£4.00	88%	76	Roachmill #1	$2.50	£2.50	66%
27	Blood Sword #2,3	$1.50	£2.00	88%	77	Roachmill #2-6	$1.50	£1.50	66%
28	Blood Sword Dynasty #2-5	$1.50	£2.00	88%	78	Roachmill (2nd) #1	$2.00	£2.00	66%
29	Elflord (1st Series) #2	£2.00	$1.50	88%	79	Satanika #3	$4.00	£4.00	66%
30	Emergency #1	$3.00	£4.00	88%	80	Six Million Dollar Man (Mag) #1	$3.00	£3.00	66%
31	Spawn #17	$3.00	£4.00	88%	81	Six Million Dollar Man (Mag) #2-8	$2.00	£2.00	66%
32	Blood Sword #1	$2.00	£2.50	83%	82	Southern Knights #2	$2.00	£2.00	66%
33	Emergency #2-4	$2.00	£2.50	83%	83	Southern Knight #3-7	$1.50	£1.50	66%
34	Man From UNCLE (2nd) #5	$2.00	£2.50	83%	84	Spirit Magazine #2	$4.00	£4.00	66%
35	Quantum Leap: Second Childhood #1-3	$2.00	£2.00	83%	85	Spirit Magazine #3-5	$3.00	£3.00	66%
36	Warlock 5 #1,3	$2.00	£2.50	83%	86	Spirit Magazine #6-10	$2.50	£2.50	66%
37	Heap #1	$5.00	£6.00	80%	87	Spirit Special	$5.00	£5.00	66%
38	Quantum Leap #1 (special ed.)	$2.50	£3.00	80%	88	Stig's Inferno #1	$2.00	£2.00	66%
39	Spirit Magazine #18	$2.50	£3.00	80%	89	Stray Bullets #3	$6.00	£6.00	66%
40	Tomoe #1	$5.00	£6.00	80%	90	Supreme #28 (variant)	$3.00	£3.00	66%
41	Miracleman 3-D Special #1 (non 3-D)	$3.00	£3.50	77%	91	Tragg and the Sky Gods #9	$1.50	£1.50	66%
42	Famous Monsters of Filmland #140-142	$3.50	£4.00	76%	92	Vampirella (3rd) #5	$10.00	£10.00	66%
43	Creed #1,2	$35.00	£40.00	76%	93	Vogue #1 (variant)	$5.00	£5.00	66%
44	Asylum #3	$2.25	£2.50	74%	94	Warlock 5 #2-9	$2.00	£2.00	66%
45	Animal Mystic #3	$7.50	£7.50	66%	95	X-Files #1 (2nd)	$5.00	£5.00	66%
46	Animal Mystic #4	$5.00	£5.00	66%	96	X-Files #2 (2nd)	$3.00	£3.00	66%
47	Avengelyne #1	$5.00	£5.00	66%	97	X-Files #4	$5.00	£5.00	66%
48	Blood Sword #4-10	$1.50	£1.50	66%	98	X-O Manowar 1/2	$5.00	£5.00	66%
49	Blood Sword Dynasty #1,6-10	$1.50	£1.50	66%	99	X-O Manowar 1/2 Gold	$7.50	£7.50	66%
50	Creed (1st Series) #1	$7.50	£7.50	66%	100	Yummy Fur #9	$2.50	£2.50	66%

Top 100
Differential Comics
and ranges £ to $

Below are listed comics valued in pounds sterling on the U.K. market and their equivalent guide value in dollars on the U.S. market. Rather than list simply individual comics when there may be a run of ten or twenty all the same price/percentage, ranges are included.

1	Ms. Marvel #18	£1.50	$12.50	555%	51	Amazing Spiderman Annual #22	£2.00	$8.00	266%
2	Strange Adventures #201	£5.00	$35.00	466%	52	Superman #499	£0.75	$3.00	266%
3	Amazing Spiderman #332,333	£1.75	$12.00	457%	53	Vampirella #101-112	£5.00	$20.00	266%
4	Uncanny X-Men #244	£3.00	$20.00	444%	54	Werewolf By Night #33	£7.50	$30.00	266%
5	Machine Man #19	£2.00	$12.00	400%	55	Uncanny X-Men #139	£7.50	$30.00	266%
6	Showcase #88-90	£3.50	$20.00	381%	56	Uncanny X-Men #216-218,220,221	£1.50	$6.00	266%
7	Spectacular Spiderman #147	£3.50	$20.00	381%	57	Uncanny X-Men #240	£2.00	$8.00	266%
8	Sandman (2nd Series) #8	£9.00	$50.00	370%	58	Uncanny X-Men #283	£3.00	$12.00	266%
9	Green Lantern #116	£5.00	$27.50	366%	59	Atom #43,44	£9.00	$35.00	259%
10	House of Mystery #301-321	£0.75	$4.00	355%	60	Lois Lane #62-67,69	£9.00	$35.00	259%
11	Action Comics #583	£2.00	$10.00	333%	61	Strange Adventures #132	£9.00	$35.00	259%
12	Amazing Spiderman #259	£5.00	$25.00	333%	62	Adventure Comics #381	£4.00	$15.00	250%
13	Amazing Spiderman #360	£2.00	$10.00	333%	63	Aquaman #53-56	£4.00	$15.00	250%
14	Dark Mansion of Forbidden Love #1	£3.00	$15.00	333%	64	Demon #6	£4.00	$15.00	250%
15	Dark Mansion of Forbidden Love #2-4	£2.00	$10.00	333%	65	Metal Men ##50-56	£4.00	$15.00	250%
16	Green Lantern #194	£1.00	$5.00	333%	66	Ms. Marvel #16	£2.00	$7.50	250%
17	House of Mystery #283-300	£1.00	$5.00	333%	67	Sandman #1	£20.00	$75.00	250%
18	Ms. Marvel #17	£1.50	$7.50	333%	68	Sandman #9,10,14,22	£4.00	$15.00	250%
19	Sandman #3	£7.00	$35.00	333%	69	Uncanny X-Men #98,99	£13.50	$50.00	246%
20	Sandman #4,5	£6.00	$30.00	333%	70	Aquaman #31,32,34,35	£15.00	$55.00	244%
21	Sandman #6,7	£5.00	$25.00	333%	71	Batman #169	£30.00	$110.00	244%
22	Team America #11	£0.60	$3.00	333%	72	Green Lantern #56-58	£15.00	$55.00	244%
23	Green Lantern #66-69	£7.50	$35.00	311%	73	Justice League of America #57	£7.50	$27.50	244%
24	Fantastic Four #244	£1.25	$6.00	311%	74	Justice League of America #68-70	£6.00	$22.00	244%
25	Amazing Spiderman Annual #26	£1.75	$8.00	304%	75	Amazing Spiderman #361	£6.00	$22.00	244%
26	Atom #31-35,37,38	£10.00	$45.00	300%	76	Uncanny X-Men #100	£15.00	$55.00	244%
27	Uncanny X-Men #248	£5.00	$22.50	300%	77	Action Comics #683	£1.25	$4.50	240%
28	Aquaman #36-40	£12.50	$55.00	293%	78	Lois Lane #56	£12.50	$45.00	240%
29	Sandman (2nd Series) #11-13	£3.50	$15.00	285%	79	Uncanny X-Men #131,132,134,135	£5.00	$18.00	240%
30	Flash #191-195,197-199	£6.00	$25.00	277%	80	Flash #201-204,206,207	£3.50	$12.50	238%
31	Kamandi #6-10	£3.00	$12.50	277%	81	Jimmy Olsen #85,88	£7.00	$25.00	238%
32	Lois Lane #76,78	£6.00	$25.00	277%	82	Lois Lane #89,93	£3.50	$12.50	238%
33	Lois Lane #87,88,90-92,94	£3.00	$12.50	277%	83	Uncanny X-Men #101	£13.50	$47.50	234%
34	Amazing Spiderman #252	£9.00	$37.50	277%	84	Action Comics #426-436,438,439	£2.00	$7.00	233%
35	Amazing Spiderman #312	£6.00	$25.00	277%	85	Aquaman #33	£20.00	$70.00	233%
36	Atom #41,42,45	£8.50	$35.00	274%	86	Atom #39,40	£10.00	$35.00	233%
37	Amazing Adventures (2nd) #11	£7.50	$30.00	266%	87	Batman #189	£10.00	$35.00	233%
38	Aquaman #41-49	£7.50	$30.00	266%	88	Green lantern #60,62-65	£10.00	$35.00	233%
39	Eerie (Magazine) #66-80	£2.00	$8.00	266%	89	Justice League of America #56	£10.00	$35.00	233%
40	Green Lantern #112,123	£1.50	$6.00	266%	90	Kamandi #3,4,5	£5.00	$17.50	233%
41	Green Lantern #195	£2.50	$10.00	266%	91	Lois Lane #74	£10.00	$35.00	233%
42	House of Mystery #281	£1.25	$5.00	266%	92	Showcase #67	£10.00	$35.00	233%
43	Jimmy Olsen #90,91,93,94,96-98	£5.00	$20.00	266%	93	Strange Adventures #171-179	£10.00	$35.00	233%
44	Jimmy Olsen #121,123-130	£2.50	$10.00	266%	94	Kamandi #2	£8.00	$27.50	229%
45	Mickey and Donald #1	£1.00	$4.00	266%	95	Aquaman #62,63	£1.75	$6.00	228%
46	Mickey Mouse #219	£1.00	$4.00	266%	96	Demon #11-16	£3.50	$12.00	228%
47	Sandman (2nd Series) #2	£10.00	$40.00	266%	97	Iron Man #169	£3.50	$12.00	228%
48	Amazing Spiderman #262	£2.50	$10.00	266%	98	Amazing Spiderman #244,257,258	£3.50	$12.00	228%
49	Amazing Spiderman #276,281,283,347	£3.00	$12.00	266%	99	Uncanny X-Men #235-238,241	£1.75	$6.00	228%
50	Amazing Spiderman #315-317	£5.00	$20.00	266%	100	Uncanny X-Men #140	£8.00	$27.00	225

Top 100
Differential Comics
and ranges $ to £

Below are listed comics valued in pounds sterling on the U.K. market and their equivalent guide value in dollars on the U.S. market. Rather than list simply individual comics when there may be a run of ten or twenty all the same price/percentage, ranges are included.

#	Title	$	£	%		#	Title	$	£	%
1	Supreme #30	$2.50	£7.50	200%		51	Anything Goes #1	$3.00	£4.00	88%
2	Deathblow #5	$2.25	£6.00	177%		52	Batman & The Outsiders #2	$1.50	£2.00	88%
3	Nova #25	$2.00	£5.00	166%		53	Beowulf #4,6	$ .75	£1.00	88%
4	Adventure Comics #491	$2.50	£6.00	160%		54	Blood Sword #2,3	$1.50	£2.00	88%
5	Adventure Comics #500	$2.50	£6.00	160%		55	Blood Sword Dynasty #2-5	$1.50	£2.00	88%
6	Epic Illustrated #34	$2.50	£6.00	160%		56	Crazy #1-3	$1.50	£2.00	88%
7	Quantum Leap #3	$3.50	£7.50	142%		57	Daredevil #226	$3.00	£4.00	88%
8	Adventure Comics #492-499,501-503	$2.50	£5.00	133%		58	Elflord (1st) #2	$1.50	£2.00	88%
9	Quantum Leap #2	$5.00	£10.00	133%		59	Emergency #1	$3.00	£4.00	88%
10	Quantum Leap #4,5	$2.50	£5.00	133%		60	Groo the Wanderer #2	$6.00	£8.00	88%
11	Superboy #211	$2.50	£5.00	133%		61	Groo the Wanderer #11,12	$3.00	£4.00	88%
12	Swamp Thing (2nd) #15,16	$2.00	£4.00	133%		62	Hawkeye #2	$1.50	£2.00	88%
13	Stray Bullets #1	$10.00	£20.00	133%		63	Kitty Pryde and Wolverine #5	$3.00	£4.00	88%
14	Terminator: Burning Earth #2	$2.00	£4.00	133%		64	Powerman #122-124	$1.50	£2.00	88%
15	Batman & The Outsiders #1	$2.00	£3.50	116%		65	Spawn #17	$3.00	£4.00	88%
16	Quantum Leap #1	$10.00	£17.50	116%		66	Vigilante #50	$1.50	£2.00	88%
17	Superboy #227	$2.00	£3.50	116%		67	Batman Family #5	$5.00	£6.50	86%
18	Justice League of America #150	$3.50	£6.00	114%		68	Swamp Thing (2nd) #26,27	$5.00	£6.50	86%
19	Batman Pizza Hut Giveaway	$3.00	£5.00	111%		69	Justice League of America #143,145	$3.50	£4.50	85%
20	Famous Monsters of Filmland #56	$15.00	£25.00	111%		70	Batman Family #14,15,18	$4.00	£5.00	83%
21	Kitty Pryde and Wolverine #6	$3.00	£5.00	111%		71	Bizarre Adventures #25,26,29	$2.00	£2.50	83%
22	Spawn #15,16	$3.00	£5.00	111%		72	Blood Sword #1	$2.00	£2.50	83%
23	Terminator: Burning Earth #1	$3.00	£5.00	111%		73	Daredevil #169	$10.00	£12.50	83%
24	Stray Bullets #2	$7.50	£12.50	111%		74	Emergency #2-4	$2.00	£2.50	83%
25	Epic Illustrated #26,29,33	$2.50	£4.00	106%		75	Epic Illustrated #1	$4.00	£5.00	83%
26	Quantum Leap #6-10	$2.50	£4.00	106%		76	Generation X Collector's Preview	$2.00	£2.50	83%
27	Quantum Leap Time & Space Special #1	$2.50	£4.00	106%		77	Incredible Hulk #153	$6.00	£7.50	83%
28	Anything Goes #2,5	$2.00	£3.00	100%		78	Man From UNCLE (2nd) #5	$2.00	£2.50	83%
29	Batman Family #19,20	$4.00	£6.00	100%		79	New Warriors #1	$6.00	£7.50	83%
30	Batman: Shadow of the Bat #2-5	$4.00	£6.00	100%		80	Nick Fury, Agent of Shield #17,18	$4.00	£5.00	83%
31	Daredevil #161	$10.00	£15.00	100%		81	Quantum Leap: Second Childhood #1-3	$2.00	£2.50	83%
32	Destroyer Duck #1	$4.00	£6.00	100%		82	Ren & Stimpy #1	$10.00	£12.50	83%
33	Donald Duck #246	$2.00	£3.00	100%		83	Super-Team Family #2	$2.00	£2.50	83%
34	Elflord (1st) #1	$2.00	£3.00	100%		84	Superboy #232,235	$2.00	£2.50	83%
35	Famous Monsters of Filmland #95	$10.00	£15.00	100%		85	Swamp Thing (2nd) #11-14	$2.00	£2.50	83%
36	Groo the Wanderer #7	$5.00	£7.50	100%		86	Warlock 5 #1,3	$2.00	£2.50	83%
37	Miracleman #12	$2.00	£3.00	100%		87	West Coast Avengers #3	$2.00	£2.50	83%
38	Star Trek Dynabrite Comics #11357/58	$5.00	£7.50	100%		88	X-Men at the State Fair of Texas	$20.00	£25.00	83%
39	Superboy #221-226,230	$2.00	£3.00	100%		89	Batman #180	$50.00	£60.00	80%
40	Swamp Thing (2nd) #17-19	$2.00	£3.00	100%		90	Batman Family #2-4,17	$5.00	£6.00	80%
41	Terminator: Burning Earth #3-5	$2.00	£3.00	100%		91	Batman Spectacular #15	$5.00	£6.00	80%
42	Shi: Way of the Warrior #6	$3.50	£5.00	95%		92	Captain America Annual #4	$5.00	£6.00	80%
43	Shadow of the Batman #1	$5.00	£7.00	93%		93	Daredevil #229	$2.50	£3.00	80%
44	Epic Illustrated #15	$2.50	£3.50	93%		94	Epic Illustrated #11,16,27,28,30-32	$2.50	£3.00	80%
45	Groo the Wanderer	$5.00	£7.00	93%		95	G.I. Joe #2	$5.00	£6.00	80%
46	Justice League of America #159	$2.50	£3.50	93%		96	Groo the Wanderer #4	$5.00	£6.00	80%
47	Magik: Storm & Illyana #4	$2.50	£3.50	93%		97	The Heap	$5.00	£6.00	80%
48	Mr. Monster (1st) #3	$2.50	£3.50	93%		98	Justice League of America #160	$2.50	£3.00	80%
49	Quantum Leap #11,12	$2.50	£3.50	93%		99	Powerman #125	$2.50	£3.00	80%
50	Superboy #212,213,218	$2.50	£3.50	93%		100	Quantum Leap #1 (Special Edition)	$2.50	£2.50	80%

THE TOP 20 MOST VALUABLE COMICS

Estimated values are guide prices only. Please note that copies from named collections and copies sold at auction MAY command multiples of Guide.

RANK	COMIC/NUMBER	ESTIMATED TOTAL COPIES KNOWN	COPIES KNOWN IN U.K.	ESTIMATED U.K. VALUE IN UNRESTORED NEAR MINT
1	DETECTIVE COMICS #27	5-125 with 3 NM	7 (in varying grades, 2 heavily restored)	£80,000 to £95,000
2	ACTION COMICS #1	100-125 with 4 NM	6 (in varying grades)	£75,000 to £90,000
3	SUPERMAN #1	175-225 with 3 NM	12 (in varying grades, 3 heavily restored)	£50,000 to £65,000
4	MARVEL COMICS #1	75-125 with 4 NM	3(in varying grades)	£45,000 to £60,000
5	DETECTIVE COMICS #1	25-35 with 1 NM	4 (in varying grades)	£35,000 to £50,000
6	ALL AMERICAN #16	50-60 with 3 NM	2 (in lower grades)	£30,000 to £40,000
7	BATMAN #1	275-350 with 15 NM1	0 (in varying grades)	£25,000 to £36,000
7	WHIZ COMICS #1	125-175 with 3 NM	2 (in lower grades)	£26,000 to £36,000
9	CAPTAIN AMERICA #1	150-200 with 8 NM	5 (in varying grades)	£25,000 to £35,000
10	NEW FUN #1	10-25 with 1 VF/NM	None known in U.K.	£20,000 to £32,000
11	MORE FUN COMICS #52	60-70 with 3 NM	2 (1 grade not known, the other VG range)	£20,000 to £30,000
12	FLASH COMICS #1	125-150 with 7 NM 4	(2 in higher grades, 1 very low grade, 1 heavily restored)	£17,500 to £27,500
13	ADVENTURE COMICS #40	50-60 with 1 NM	2 (in varying grades)	£15,000 to £22,000
13	ALL STAR COMICS #3	150-175 with 6 NM	5 (2 in high grade, 2 restored and 1 in low grade)	£15,000 to £22,000
15	MORE FUN COMICS #53	60-70 with 3 NM	2 (1 in high grade,1 in low grade)	£12.500 to £20,000
16	DETECTIVE COMICS #33	75-100 with 7 NM	3 (all high grade)	£12,500 to £17,500
16	DETECTIVE COMICS #38	80-100 with 9 NM	5 (in varying grades)	£12,500 to £17,500
18	CAPTAIN MARVEL ADVENTURES #1	130-150 with 3 NM	1 (grade not known)	£10,000 to £16,500
19	Detective Comics #29	75-100 with 6 NM	2 (both grades not known)	£9,000 to £14,250
20	Detective Comics #31	75-100 with 6 NM	5 (2 in high grade, 3 not known)	£9,000 to £14,000

It will be noticed that the value range is very generous with an upper limit of the Guide price in this book. While it is very likely that an individual may reasonably expect to pay more than the Guide price stated, one must take into consideration the size of the market in the U.K. for this sort of material and that deals and discounts would be expected by a purchaser with serious money. The market in the U.K. for these books is almost exclusively driven by the U.S market and as such the popularity of books may differ. For example, Adventure Comics #40 is not such a popular Wants List item in the U.K. as it may be in the U.S. so it's actual market value in the U.K. may be less than the figure stated.

Please note that the numbers of copies known in the U.K. are known to myself personally. There may be others around yet to be documented. The high grade copies known to me are a mixture of unrestored and restored copies. THE VALUES GIVEN ARE FOR UNRESTORED COPIES ONLY. RESTORED COPIES WOULD BE LESS VALUABLE, DEPENDING ON THE AMOUNT OF RESTORATION AND (INCREASINGLY NOW) THE PERSON RESPONSIBLE FOR THAT RESTORATION AND THE DOCUMENTATION THAT GOES WITH THE COMIC. A RESTORED COMIC WITHOUT DOCUMENTATION WOULD OBVIOUSLY BE LESS VALUABLE.

We are in the process of putting together a Restoration Guide for key books which will feature in the next U.K. Price Guide.

It is important to remember that values are calculated on the basis of known availability should anyone suddenly decide to invest that sort of money and the very rare actual sale in the U.K. Necessarily there are very few known collectors aspiring to such heights at this present time so such prices may be treated with due consideration.

With the number of these key Golden Age comics being professionally (and unprofessionally!) restored, the unrestored comic will advance into a super-league of its own.

This goes to show that what makes a comic valuable apart from condition is the factor of the fame of the character coupled with rarity as secondary. Detective #27 shows that comics do not necessarily need to be first issues though this is a contributory factor. In any event such comics are highly prized as remarkable pieces of popular art and cultural consciousness and one hopes that they will be duly looked after for future generations to enjoy.

ALL AMERICAN MEN OF WAR #82
(1st appearance Johnny Cloud)

X-MEN GIANT SIZE #1
(1st appearance new X-Men)

FUNNIES ON PARADE
(the very first comic book)

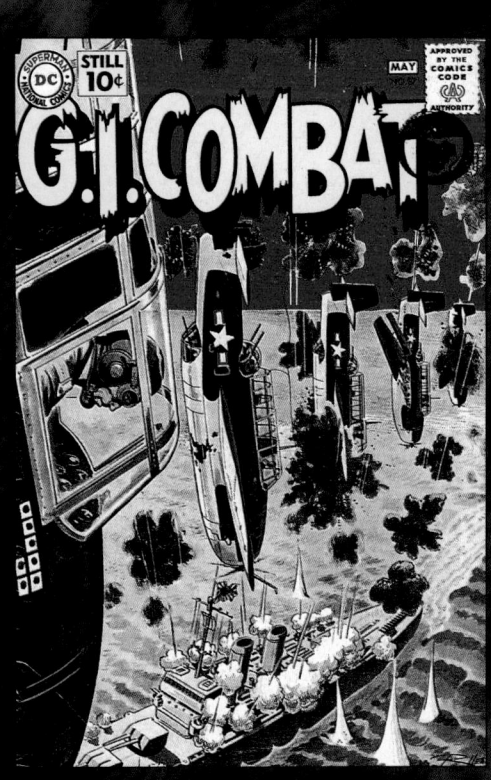

G.I. COMBAT #87
(1st appearance Haunted Tank)

AMAZING ADVENTURES (2nd) #11
(1st appearance The Beast in mutated form)

WONDER WOMAN (2nd) #85
(1st Mike Deodato Wonder Woman)

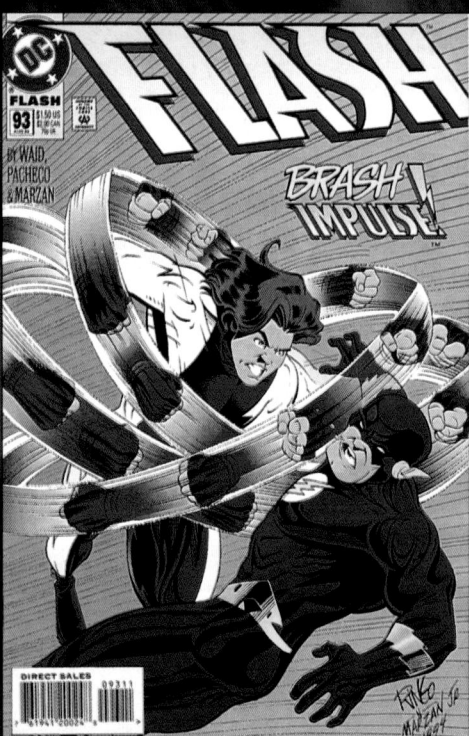

FLASH (2nd) #93
(1st full appearance Impulse)

HOUSE OF MYSTERY #143
(1st of Martian Manhunter series)

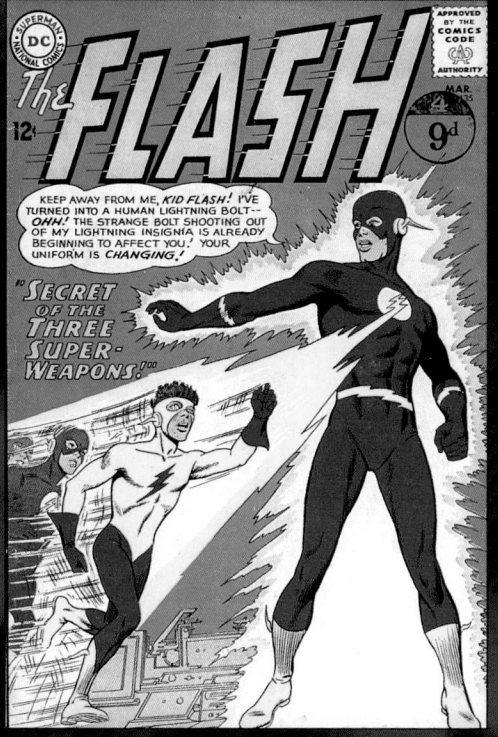

FLASH #135
(1st appearance new Kid Flash)

HOUSE OF SECRETS #61
(1st appearance Eclipso)

MARVEL PREMIERE #15
(1st appearance Iron Fist)

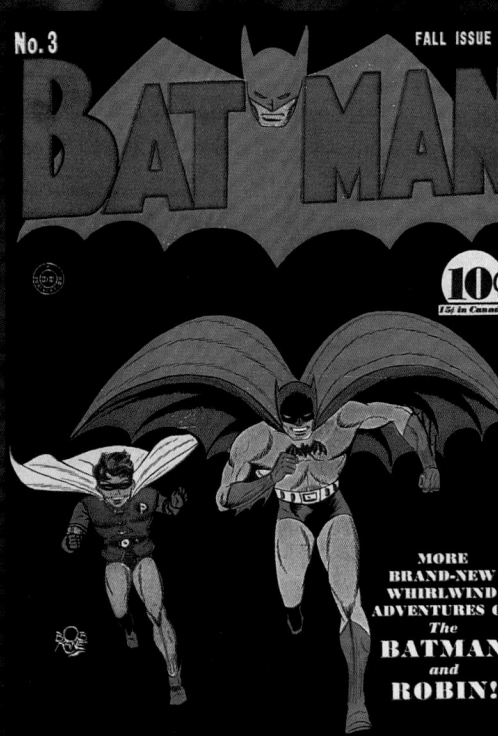

BATMAN #3
(1st Catwoman in costume)

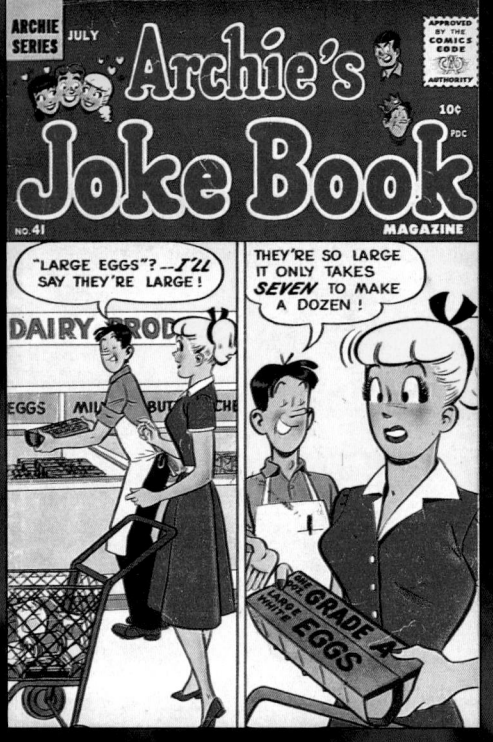

ARCHIE'S JOKEBOOK #41
(1st Neal adams art)

WONDER WOMAN (1st) #178
(1st new look Wonder Woman)

SUPERMAN #57
(1st Lois Lane as Superwoman)

AVENGERS #4
(1st appearance Captain America in Silver Age)

BATMAN #181
(1st appearance Poison Ivy)

STRANGE ADVENTURES #205
(1st appearance Deadman)

DETECTIVE COMICS #230
(1st appearance Silver Age Mad Hatter)

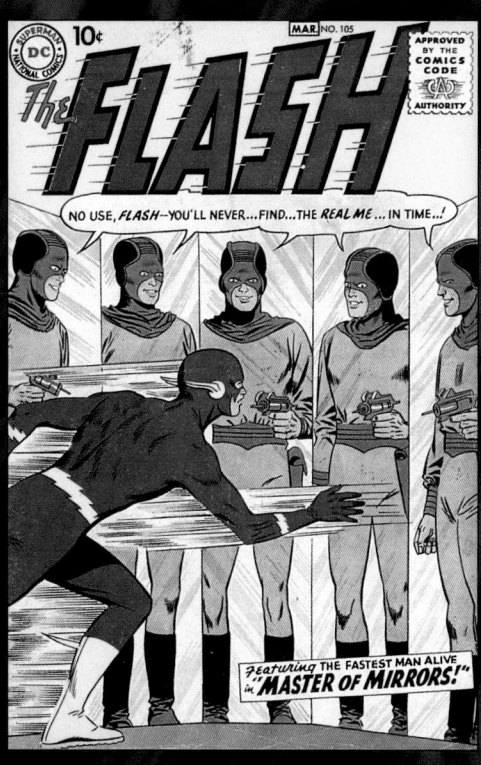

FLASH #105
(1st of regular Silver Age Flash series)

TITAN BOOKS

The Leading Publisher
of Graphic Novels
in the UK

Aliens

Babylon 5

Batman

Beavis & Butt-Head

Judge Dredd

The Mask

Ren & Stimpy

Sandman

The Simpsons

Sin City

Star Trek

Superman

BRAVE AND THE BOLD #30
(1st appearance Amazo)

SPECIAL MARVEL EDITION #15
(1st appearance Master of Kung Fu)

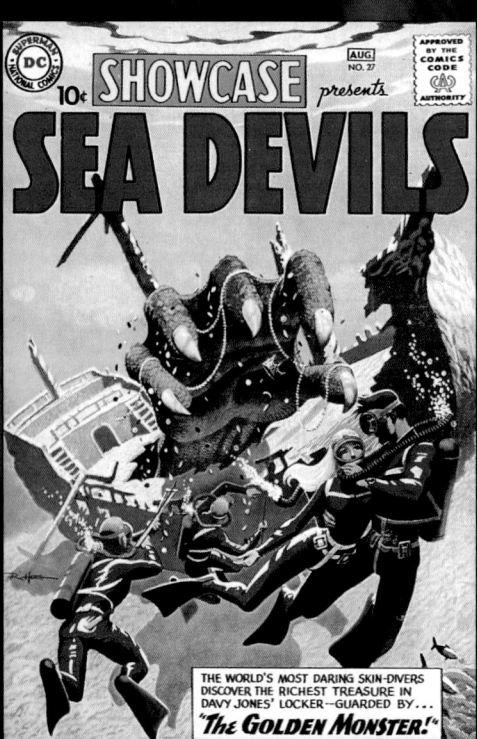

SHOWCASE #27
(1st appearance Sea Devils)

INCREDIBLE HULK #181
(1st appearance Wolverine)

DC HAS WHAT YOU'RE LOOKING FOR!

Can't find those rare, expensive back issues of your favorite DC Comics and Vertigo titles?

Many of our most famous sagas are available in affordable, convenient trade paperback collections. To find them, just ask your local comics retailer.

WORTH READING!
WORTH KEEPING!

All Vertigo titles are suggested for mature readers.

FANTASTIC FOUR #4
(1st appearance Sub-Mariner in the Silver Age)

BRAVE AND THE BOLD #34
(1st appearance Silver Age Hawkman)

SHOWCASE #20
(1st appearance Rip Hunter)

COMICO PRIMER #2
(1st appearance Grendel)

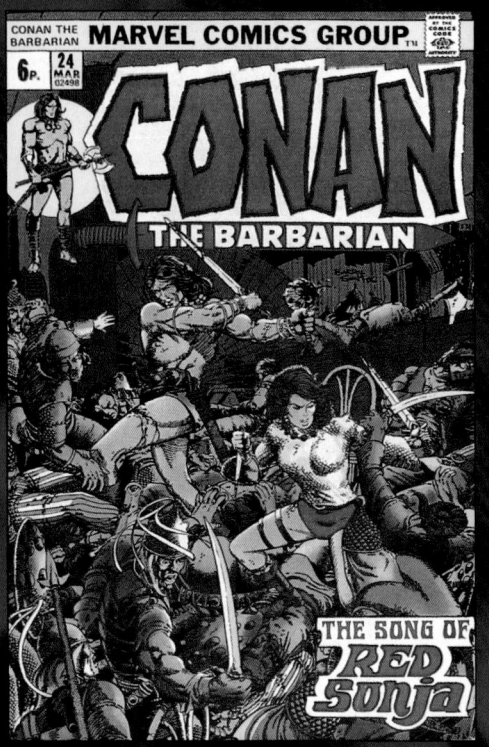

CONAN THE BARBARIAN #24
(1st appearance Red Sonja)

SHOWCASE #15
(1st appearance Space Ranger)

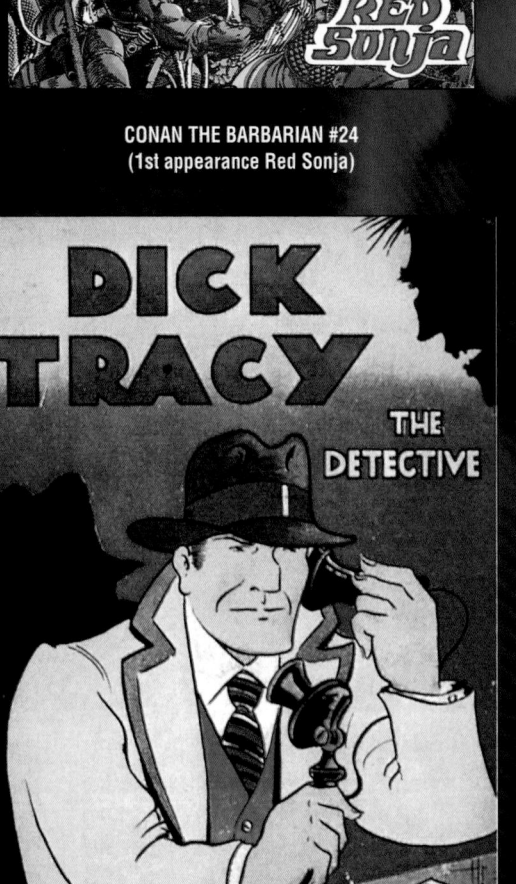

DICK TRACY NO NUMBER FEATURE BOOK
(1st appearance Dick Tracy in comics)

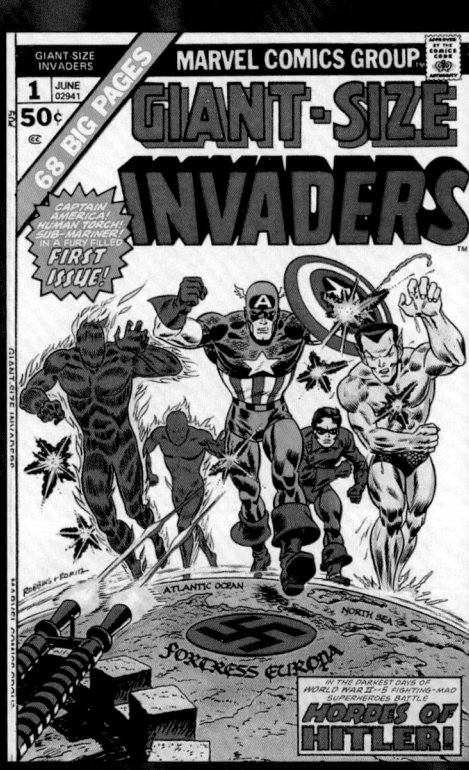

INVADERS GIANT SIZE #1
(1st appearance The Invaders)

DAREDEVIL #254
(1st appearance Typhoid Mary)

SENSATION COMICS #1
(1st solo Wonder Woman comic)

DETECTIVE COMICS #1
(1st widely successful anthology with detective themes)

SHOWCASE #9
(1st solo Lois Lane comic)

NIGHT NURSE #1
(1st appearance Night Nurse)

DETECTIVE COMICS #22
(1st Crimson Avenger cover)

JIMMY OLSEN #134
(1st appearance Darkseid)

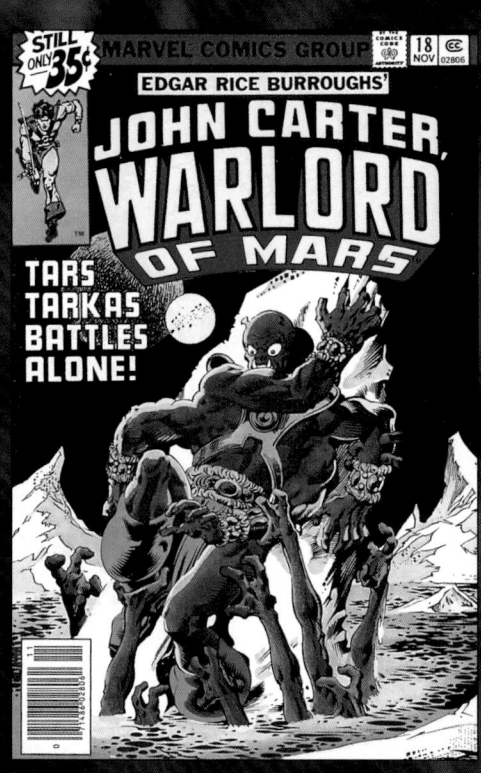

JOHN CARTER, WARLORD OF MARS
(1st Frank Miller art)

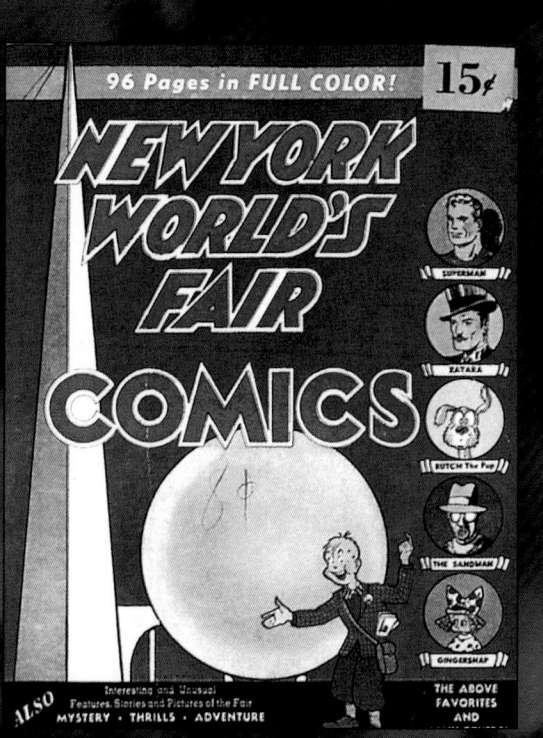

NEW YORK WORLD'S FAIR 1939
(1st published Golden Age Sandman)

DETECTIVE COMICS #225
(1st appearance Martian Manhunter)

MARVEL SUPER-HEROES #12
(1st appearance Captain Marvel)

TALES TO ASTONISH #27
(1st appearance Ant-Man – not in costume)

TRADING CARDS

The name Topps is synonymous with trading cards of the highest quality on the hottest themes around.

Now there's no need to look around to find them. X-Files, Star Wars, Barb Wire, ID4, Mars Attacks – there's one place to turn to:

Topps European head office here in the UK.

Contact Rod Pearson or Lisa Darby in our marketing department for the lowdown on the Topps universe.

Merlin Publishing (*a division of the Topps Company Inc.*)

18 Vincent Avenue, Crownhill, Milton Keynes MK8 0AW.   **Tel: 01908 561588   Fax: 01908 565773**

THE TRADING CARD GUIDE

(original foundation by BARRIE RONESS of PALAN DISTRIBUTION
with Rob Barrow & The Fantasy Domain Trading Card Company) (Further notes by Ron Hall of First Choice cards)
We have expanded a number of entries with a view to a more complete listing in future editions. Any additional information may be sent to the editorial address. We are also pleased to list selected sets from Merlin Publishing Ltd, the UK's only large-scale indigenous producer of trading cards.

ADDAMS FAMILY
PRODUCER:	TOPPS U.S.
ISSUE YEAR:	1991
CARD SET:	99 CARDS
SPECIAL CARDS:	11 STICKERS
COMPLETE SET:	£8.00
SINGLE CARDS:	5p - 15p
SINGLE SPECIAL CARDS:	20p

Important Notes: These sets broke badly from their boxes. In many cases more than one box of cards was required to complete a set.

ADVANCE COMICS PROMOTIONAL HOLOGRAM
Venom: £3.00
Issued free with Advance Comics magazine Spring 1992
DIAMOND U.S. PREVIEWS
Uncut promo sheet: £3.00
Issued free with Diamond Previews magazine

ADVENTURES OF BATMAN & ROBIN
PRODUCER:	SKYBOX
ISSUE YEAR:	1995
CARD SET:	90 CARDS
SPECIAL CARDS:	3 CARD DARK KNIGHT SET
	9 CARD FOIL SET
	12 CARD POP UP SET
COMPLETE SET:	£5.00
SINGLE CARDS:	10p

AKIRA MASTER SET
PRODUCER:	CORNERSTONE
ISSUE YEAR:	1994
CARD SET:	100 CARDS
SPECIAL CARDS:	3 CHROMIUM CARDS, 1
	PRISM (1 PER CASE)
COMPLETE SET:	£20.00
SINGLE CARDS:	20p
SINGLE SPECIAL CARDS (Chromium):	£1.00
SINGLE SPECIAL CARDS (Prism):	£20.00

ALADDIN
PRODUCER:	SKYBOX
ISSUE YEAR:	1993
CARD SET:	90 CARDS
SPECIAL CARDS:	3 SPECTRA CARDS
COMPLETE SET:	£8.00
SINGLE CARDS:	10p
SINGLE SPECIAL CARDS:	£5.00

ALF I
PRODUCER:	TOPPS U.S.
ISSUE YEAR:	1987
CARD SET:	69 CARDS
SPECIAL CARDS:	18 STICKERS
COMPLETE SET:	£8.00
SINGLE CARDS:	10p-15p
SINGLE SPECIAL CARDS:	20p

Important Notes: There are two different trading card sets, both of which are based on the hit American television series about a friendly alien.

ALF II
PRODUCER:	TOPPS U.S.
ISSUE YEAR:	1988
CARD SET:	66 CARDS
SPECIAL CARDS:	18 STICKERS
COMPLETE SET:	£6.00
SINGLE CARDS:	5p - 10p
SINGLE SPECIAL CARDS:	15p

Important Notes: See also Alf series I

ALIEN I
PRODUCER:	TOPPS U.S.
ISSUE YEAR:	1979
CARD SET:	84 CARDS
SPECIAL CARDS:	22 STICKERS
COMPLETE SET: (without stickers)	£30.00
COMPLETE SET (with stickers):	£45.00
SINGLE CARDS:	30p
SINGLE SPECIAL CARDS:	£1.00

Important Notes: Upon release of the Dark Horse Alien 3 trading card set, demand for the original set has risen making this set now even harder to locate. The complete set with stickers is very rare.

ALIEN 3
PRODUCER:	STAR PICS
ISSUE YEAR:	1992
CARD SET:	80 CARDS
SPECIAL CARDS:	8 DARK HORSE COMICS CARDS
COMPLETE SET:	£8.00
SINGLE CARDS:	10p
SINGLE SPECIAL CARDS:	15p

Important Notes: Widely sold throughout U.K. specialist comic shops, prices vary on this particular set.

ALIEN NATION
PRODUCER:	FTCC
ISSUE YEAR:	1990
CARD SET:	60 CARDS
SPECIAL CARDS:	No special cards
COMPLETE SET:	£10.00
SINGLE CARDS:	10p

ALIENS/PREDATOR UNIVERSE
PRODUCER:	TOPPS U.S.
ISSUE YEAR:	1995
CARD SET:	72 CARDS
SUB-SET CARDS:	15
SPECIAL CARDS:	6 CHASE CARDS
COMPLETE SET:	£8.00
SINGLE CARDS:	15p
SUB-SET CARD:	£1.00
SINGLE SPECIAL CARDS:	£5.00

Important Notes: The sub-set cards are numbered A1-A15 and should be included when considering the actual complete set

AMERICAN GLADIATORS
PRODUCER:	TOPPS U.S.
ISSUE YEAR:	1992
CARD SET:	88 CARDS
SPECIAL CARDS:	11 STICKERS
COMPLETE SET:	£7.00
SINGLE CARDS:	5p - 15p

AN AMERICAN TAIL II
PRODUCER:	TOPPS U.S.
ISSUE YEAR:	1991
CARD SET:	150 CARDS
SPECIAL CARDS:	5 HOLOGRAMS
COMPLETE SET:	£35.00
SINGLE CARDS:	15p
SINGLE SPECIAL CARDS:	£6.00

Important Notes: Scarce set, rarely seen in the U.K.

Batman Master Series #86

Comics Greatest World #32

Evil Ernie #81

ARCHIE COMIC CARDS
PRODUCER:	SKYBOX
ISSUE YEAR:	1992
CARD SET:	120 CARDS
SPECIAL CARDS:	5 HOLOGRAMS
COMPLETE SET:	£30.00
CARD SET ONLY:	£12.00
SINGLE CARDS:	10p
SINGLE SPECIAL CARDS:	£4.00

Important Notes: Generally unavailable in the U.K. This set will be difficult to locate due to its limited collector U.K. following.

ARTHUR ADAMS
PRODUCER:	COMIC IMAGES
ISSUE YEAR:	1989
CARD SET:	45 CARDS
SPECIAL CARDS:	No special cards
COMPLETE SET:	£10.00
SINGLE CARDS:	15p

A-TEAM
PRODUCER:	TOPPS U.S.
ISSUE YEAR:	1983
CARD SET:	66 CARDS
SPECIAL CARDS:	12 STICKERS
COMPLETE SET:	£8.00
SINGLE CARDS:	10p
SINGLE SPECIAL CARDS:	25p

Important Notes: Never sold in England

AVENGERS (BLACK + WHITE)
PRODUCER:	TOPPS U.S.
ISSUE YEAR:	1992
CARD SET:	81 CARDS
COMPLETE SET:	£15.00
SINGLE CARDS:	15p

AVENGERS (COLOUR)
PRODUCER:	TOPPS U.S.
ISSUE YEAR:	1993
CARD SET:	100 CARDS
COMPLETE SET:	£15.00
SINGLE CARDS:	15p

BABY
PRODUCER:	TOPPS U.S.
ISSUE YEAR:	1984
CARD SET:	66 CARDS
CARD SET:	11 STICKERS
COMPLETE SET:	£5.00
SINGLE CARDS:	15p

BABYLON 5
PRODUCER:	FLEER
ISSUE YEAR:	1995
CARD SET:	120 CARDS
SPECIAL CARDS:	8 CARD HOLOGRAM SET
	8 CARD SPACE GALLERY SET
	8 CARD PRISMATIC SET
COMPLETE SET:	£10.00
SINGLE CARDS:	10p

BACK TO THE FUTURE II MOVIE
PRODUCER:	TOPPS U.S.
ISSUE YEAR:	1989
CARD SET:	88 CARDS
SPECIAL CARDS:	11 STICKERS
COMPLETE SET:	£7.00
SINGLE CARDS:	10p
SINGLE SPECIAL CARDS:	20p

BARBIE
PRODUCER:	MATTELL TOY COMPANY
ISSUE YEAR:	1990
CARD SET:	300 CARDS
SPECIAL CARDS:	No special cards
COMPLETE SET:	£20.00
SINGLE CARDS:	10p

BARBIE 2
PRODUCER:	MATTELL TOY COMPANY
ISSUE YEAR:	1991
CARD SET:	300 CARDS
SPECIAL CARDS:	No special cards
COMPLETE SET:	£20.00
SINGLE CARDS:	20p

BATMAN ANIMATED
PRODUCER:	TOPPS U.S.
ISSUE YEAR:	1993
CARD SET:	100 CARDS
SPECIAL CARDS:	6 CARD CEL SET
COMPLETE SET:	£63.00
CARD SET ONLY:	£15.00
CEL CARDS:	£8.00
SINGLE CARDS:	15p

BATMAN ANIMATED II
PRODUCER:	TOPPS U.S.
ISSUE YEAR:	1994
CARD SET:	90 CARDS
SPECIAL CARDS:	4 CARD CEL SET
COMPLETE SET:	£47.00
CARD SET ONLY:	£15.00
SINGLE CARDS:	15p
CEL CARDS:	£8.00

BATMAN FOREVER FLEER ULTRA
PRODUCER:	FLEER
ISSUE YEAR:	1995
CARD SET:	120 CARDS
SPECIAL CARDS:	10 ANIMACTION CARDS
COMPLETE SET:	£12.00
SINGLE CARDS:	10p
SPECIAL SINGLE CARDS:	£2.50
HOLOGRAM SET (36):	£35.00

BATMAN FOREVER METAL
PRODUCER:	FLEER
ISSUE YEAR:	1995
CARD SET:	100 CARDS
SPECIAL CARDS:	8 MOVIE PREVIEW CARDS
COMPLETE SET:	£25.00
SINGLE CARDS:	25p
SPECIAL SINGLE CARDS:	
HOLOGRAM SET (4):	£30.00

BATMAN MOVIE SERIES I (U.S.)
PRODUCER:	TOPPS U.S.
ISSUE YEAR:	1989
CARD SET:	132
SPECIAL CARDS:	22 STICKERS
COMPLETE SET:	£12.00
SINGLE CARDS:	15p
SINGLE SPECIAL CARDS:	50p

Important Notes: There is a smaller British set available which are virtually identical, except in size.

BATMAN MOVIE SERIES II (U.S.)
PRODUCER:	TOPPS U.S.
ISSUE YEAR:	1989
CARD SET:	132
SPECIAL CARDS:	22 STICKERS
COMPLETE SET:	£12.00
SINGLE CARDS:	15p
SINGLE SPECIAL CARDS:	50p

Important Notes: There was not a British set of this set produced by Topps.

BATMAN MOVIE I U.K.
PRODUCER:	TOPPS U.K.
ISSUE YEAR:	1989
CARD SET:	132
SPECIAL CARDS:	22 STICKERS
COMPLETE SET:	£6.00
SINGLE CARDS:	10p
SINGLE SPECIAL CARDS:	25p

Important Notes: There was a slightly larger Topps U.S. set produced. Please see revelant section for further information.

BATMAN MOVIE DELUXE I U.S.
PRODUCER:	TOPPS U.S.
ISSUE YEAR:	1989
CARD SET:	132 CARDS
SPECIAL CARDS:	22 STICKERS
COMPLETE FACTORY SET:	£15.00

BATMAN MOVIE DELUXE II U.S.
PRODUCER:	TOPPS U.S.
ISSUE YEAR:	1989
CARD SET:	132
SPECIAL CARDS:	22 STICKERS
COMPLETE FACTORY SET:	£12.00

BATMAN RETURNS]
PRODUCER:	TOPPS U.S.
ISSUE YEAR:	1992
CARD SET:	88 CARDS
SPECIAL CARDS:	10 STADIUM CLUB CARDS
COMPLETE SET:	£9.00
SINGLE CARDS:	10p
SINGLE SPECIAL CARDS:	25p

Important Notes: Stadium club card sub set cards are all lettered A-J (Complete Subset £3.00)

BATMAN RETURNS STADIUM CLUB EDITION
PRODUCER:	TOPPS U.S.
ISSUE YEAR:	1992
CARD SET:	100 CARDS
COMPLETE SET:	£15.00
SINGLE CARDS:	20p

Important Notes: This second set of Batman Returns cards were produced with a very high quality gloss finish with gold embossed Batman Returns logo on each card.

BATMAN RETURNS CANADIAN
PRODUCER:	ZELLER
ISSUE YEAR:	1992
CARD SET:	24 CARDS
SPECIAL CARDS:	No special cards
COMPLETE SET:	£4.00
SINGLE CARDS:	25p

BATMAN, SAGA OF THE DARK KNIGHT
PRODUCER:	SKYBOX
ISSUE YEAR:	1994
CARD SET:	100 CARDS
SPECIAL CARDS:	
5 SPECTRA ETCH FOIL CARDS	£8 EACH
SKYDISC -(Rare)	£50.00
SKYDISC C.D. RETAILER GIVEAWAY	£80.00
COMPLETE SET:	£55.00
CARD SET ONLY:	£150.00
SINGLE CARDS:	15p

BATTLE CARDS - UK EDITION
PRODUCER:	MERLIN PUBLISHING LTD
ISSUE YEAR:	1993
CARD SET:	150
COMPLETE SET:	£20.00
SINGLE CARDS:	15p
SPECIAL CARDS:	TREASURE CARDS

Important Notes: A special card #150 Emperor of Vangoria was only obtainable from the publisher by solving a special quest on the other cards.

BATTLE CARDS - US EDITION
PRODUCER:	MERLIN PUBLISHING LTD
ISSUE YEAR:	1994
CARD SET:	140
COMPLETE SET:	£20.00
SINGLE CARDS:	15p
SPECIAL CARDS:	TREASURE CARDS

Important Notes: A special card #140 Emperor of Vangor was only obtainable from the publisher in the US by solving all the quests.

BATTLESTAR GALACTICA
PRODUCER:	TOPPS U.S.
ISSUE YEAR:	1978
CARD SET:	132 CARDS
SPECIAL CARDS:	22 STICKERS
COMPLETE SET:	£25.00
SINGLE CARDS:	20p
SPECIAL SINGLE CARDS:	75p

Important Notes: this set may gain in popularity in the U.K. with the TV series showing on the Sci-Fi Channel

BEAUTY AND THE BEAST
PRODUCER:	SKYBOX
ISSUE YEAR:	1992
CARD SET:	75 CARDS
SPECIAL CARDS:	20 ACTIVITY CARDS
COMPLETE SET:	£12.00
SINGLE CARDS:	15p
SPECIAL SINGLE CARDS:	25p

Important Notes: Following the success of the movie and subsequent video in the U.K., this card set picked up in popularity.

BEATLES COLLECTION
PRODUCER:	RIVER GROUP
ISSUE YEAR:	1993
CARD SET:	220 CARDS
COMPLETE SET:	£35.00
SINGLE CARDS:	15p

BEAVIS & BUTT-HEAD
PRODUCER:	FLEER ULTRA
ISSUE YEAR:	1994
CARD SET:	150 CARDS
COMPLETE SET:	£18.00
SPECIAL CARDS:	10 SCRATCH 'N' SNIFF SET
SINGLE CARDS:	15p
SPECIAL SINGLE CARDS:	£1.00

BENCHWARMERS
PRODUCER:	BENCHWARMER
ISSUE YEAR:	1992
CARD SET:	120 CARDS
COMPLETE SET:	£20.00
SINGLE CARDS:	15p

BENCHWARMERS MAIL IN PRISM SET
PRODUCER:	BENCHWARMER
ISSUE YEAR:	1992
CARD SET:	4 CARDS
SPECIAL CARDS:	No special cards
COMPLETE SET:	£15.00
SINGLE CARDS:	N/A

BERNI WRIGTSON
PRODUCER:	FPG
ISSUE YEAR:	1993
CARD SET:	135 CARDS
SPECIAL CARDS:	No special cards
COMPLETE SET:	£20.00
SINGLE CARDS:	15p

BEVERLY HILLS 90210
PRODUCER:	TOPPS U.S.
ISSUE YEAR:	1992
CARD SET:	88 CARDS
SPECIAL CARDS:	11 STICKERS
COMPLETE SET:	£8.00
SINGLE CARDS:	10p
SINGLE SPECIAL CARDS:	25p

Important Notes: Scarce in the U.K.

BILL AND TED'S EXCELLENT COLLECTOR CARDS
PRODUCER:	MERLIN PUBLISHING LTD
ISSUE YEAR:	1993
CARD SET:	128
COMPLETE SET:	£15.00
SINGLE CARDS:	5p

Important Notes: Photography provided by the film studio meant that this series was similar to the US published Pro-Set Bill and Ted series. Certain key cards were changed when the UK edition was produced.

BILL AND TED'S MOST ATYPICAL ADVENTURE
PRODUCER:	PRO SET
ISSUE YEAR:	1991
CARD SET:	100 CARDS
SPECIAL CARDS:	No special cards issued
COMPLETE SET:	£8.00
SINGLE CARDS:	10p

Important Notes: The Bill & Ted movie success, led to the now infamous production ideas on which Wayne's World was based.

BINGO THE DOG MOVIE
PRODUCER:	PACIFIC
ISSUE YEAR:	1991
CARD SET:	110 CARDS
SPECIAL CARDS:	No special cards
COMPLETE SET:	£5.00
SINGLE CARDS:	10p

BLACK HOLE
PRODUCER:	TOPPS U.S.
ISSUE YEAR:	1979
CARD SET:	88 CARDS
SPECIAL CARDS:	22 STICKERS
COMPLETE SET:	£12.00
SINGLE CARDS:	15p
SINGLE SPECIAL CARDS:	30p

Important Notes: Based on the Disney movie of the same name

BLUE CHIPS (SHAQUILLE O'NEAL MOVIE)
PRODUCER:	SKYBOX
ISSUE YEAR:	1994
CARD SET:	90 CARDS
SPECIAL CARDS:	5 FOIL CARDS
CARD SET:	£15.00
SINGLE CARDS:	15p
SINGLE SPECIAL CARDS:	£5.00-£10.00 EACH

BONE
PRODUCER:	COMIC IMAGES
ISSUE YEAR:	1994
CARD SET:	90 CARDS
SPECIAL CARDS:	6 FOIL CARDS
COMPLETE SET:	£9.00
SINGLE CARDS:	10p
SPECIAL SINGLE CARDS:	£5.00

BONE ALL CHROMIUM SERIES
PRODUCER:	COMIC IMAGES
CARD SET:	90 CARDS
SPECIAL CARDS:	6 MAGNACHROME CARDS
COMPLETE SET:	£15.00
SINGLE CARDS:	15p
SPECIAL SINGLE CARDS:	£5.00

BORIS I
PRODUCER:	COMIC IMAGES
ISSUE YEAR:	1991
CARD SET:	90 CARDS
SPECIAL CARDS:	No special cards
COMPLETE SET:	£13.00
SINGLE CARDS:	15p

BORIS II
PRODUCER:	COMIC IMAGES
ISSUE YEAR:	1992
CARD SET:	90 CARDS
SPECIAL CARDS:	6 PRISM CARDS
COMPLETE SET:	£45.00
CARD SET ONLY:	£10.00
SINGLE CARDS:	10p
SINGLE SPECIAL CARDS:	£7.00

BORIS III, ALL PRISM
PRODUCER:	COMIC IMAGES
ISSUE YEAR:	1993
CARD SET:	90 CARDS
SPECIAL CARDS:	6 CHROMIUM CARDS
COMPLETE SET:	£80.00
CARD SET ONLY:	£20.00
SINGLE CARDS:	20p
SINGLE SPECIAL CARDS:	£10.00 EACH

BORIS IV
PRODUCER:	COMIC IMAGES
ISSUE YEAR:	1994
CARD SET:	90 CARDS
SPECIAL CARDS:	6 FOIL CHASE CARDS
COMPLETE SET:	£7.50
SINGLE CARDS:	10p
SINGLE SPECIAL CARDS:	£5.00

BORIS, BEST OF (All Chrome Set)
PRODUCER:	COMIC IMAGES
ISSUE YEAR:	1995
CARD SET:	90 CARDS
SPECIAL CARDS:	6 OMNICHROME CARDS
COMPLETE SET:	£20.00
SINGLE CARDS:	20p
SINGLE SPECIAL CARDS:	£6.00

BUCK ROGERS IN THE 25TH CENTURY
PRODUCER:	TOPPS U.S.
ISSUE YEAR:	1979
CARD SET:	88 CARDS
SPECIAL CARDS:	22 STICKERS
COMPLETE SET:	£12.00
SINGLE CARDS:	20p
SINGLE SPECIAL CARDS:	30p

CALENDER GIRLS – GIL ELVGREN
PRODUCER:	COMIC IMAGES
ISSUE YEAR:	1993
CARD SET:	90 CARDS
SPECIAL CARDS:	6 CHASE CARDS (3 Spectra and 3 Chrome thought to exist. More information needed)
COMPLETE SET:	£20.00
SINGLE CARDS:	15p

Important Notes: a set that is becoming increasingly scarce

CALENDAR GIRLS – GIL ELVGREN II
PRODUCER:	COMIC IMAGES
ISSUE YEAR:	1994
CARD SET:	90 CARDS
SPECIAL CARDS:	6 CHASE CARDS
COMPLETE SET:	£10.00
SINGLE CARDS:	15p
SINGLE SPECIAL CARDS:	£5.00

CAPTAIN AMERICA 50TH ANNIVERSARY
PRODUCER:	COMIC IMAGES
ISSUE YEAR:	1990
CARD SET:	45 CARDS
SPECIAL CARDS:	No special cards
COMPLETE SET:	£12.00
SINGLE CARDS:	25p

CASPER ULTRA
PRODUCER:	FLEER
CARD SET:	119 CARDS
SPECIAL CARDS:	15 PRISMATIC FOIL CARDS
COMPLETE SET:	£12.00
SINGLE CARDS:	10p
SPECIAL SINGLE CARDS:	£1.00

Important Notes: the odd number of the set arises from the fact that numbers #13 and #77 were not printed for legal reasons and a Promo card was withdrawn. A duplicate #12 replaced the original #13 and a duplicate #69 replaced the original #77.

CHARLIE'S ANGELS SERIES I
PRODUCER:	TOPPS U.S.
ISSUE YEAR:	1977
CARD SET:	55
SPECIAL CARDS:	11 STICKERS
COMPLETE SET:	£15.00
SINGLE CARD:	25p
SPECIAL SINGLE CARD:	£2.00

CHARLIE'S ANGELS SERIES II
PRODUCER:	TOPPS U.S.
ISSUE YEAR:	1977
CARD SET:	66 CARDS
SPECIAL CARDS:	11 STICKERS
COMPLETE SET:	£10.00
SINGLE CARDS:	15p
SPECIAL SINGLE CARDS:	75p

CHARLIE'S ANGELS SERIES III
PRODUCER:	TOPPS U.S.
ISSUE YEAR:	1978
CARD SET:	66 CARDS
SPECIAL CARDS:	11 STICKERS
COMPLETE SET:	£10.00
SINGLE CARDS:	15p
SPECIAL SINGLE CARDS:	75p

CHARLIE'S ANGELS SERIES IV
PRODUCER:	TOPPS U.S.
ISSUE YEAR:	1978
CARD SET:	66 CARDS
SPECIAL CARDS:	11 STICKERS
COMPLETE SET:	£7.00
SINGLE CARDS:	10p
SPECIAL SINGLE CARDS:	50p

CINDERELLA
PRODUCER:	SKYBOX
ISSUE YEAR:	1995
CARD SET:	90 CARDS
SPECIAL CARDS:	5 FOIL CARD SET 2 TRANSFORMATION CARD SET
COMPLETE SET:	£9.00
SINGLE CARDS:	10p

CLOSE ENCOUNTERS OF THE THIRD KIND
PRODUCER:	TOPPS U.S.
ISSUE YEAR:	1978
CARD SET:	66 CARDS
SPECIAL CARDS:	11 STICKERS
COMPLETE SET:	£12.00
SINGLE CARDS:	20p
SINGLE SPECIAL CARDS:	30p

COMICS' GREATEST WORLD
PRODUCER:	TOPPS U.S.
ISSUE YEAR:	1994
CARD SET:	100 CARDS
SPECIAL CARDS:	6 MATRIX CARDS
COMPLETE SET:	£10.00
SINGLE CARDS:	10p
SPECIAL SINGLE CARDS:	£2.50

CONAN COLLECTORS CARDS
PRODUCER:	COMIC IMAGES
ISSUE YEAR:	1993
CARD SET (Chromium):	90 CARDS
CARD SET (Holochrome):	90 CARDS
SPECIAL CARDS:	10 COLOUR VARIATIONS FOR EACH SET
PRISM CARDS:	6
COMPLETE SET (Chromium):	£25.00
COMPLETE SET (Holochrome):	?
SINGLE CARDS (Chromium):	25p
SINGLE CARDS (Holochrome):	?
SPECIAL SINGLE CARDS:	£10.00

Important Notes: there is one holochrome card per box

CONAN II (Chromium)
PRODUCER:	COMIC IMAGES
ISSUE YEAR:	1994
CARD SET:	90 CARDS
SPECIAL CARDS:	6 GALAXY PRISM CARDS
COMPLETE SET:	£20.00
SINGLE CARDS:	20p
SPECIAL SINGLE CARDS:	£4.00

CREATORS MASTER SERIES
PRODUCER:	FLEER/SKYBOX
ISSUE YEAR:	1995
CARD SET:	90 CARDS
SPECIAL CARDS:	5 SPECTRA-ETCH CARD SET
SKYBOX CARD COMPLETE SET:	£12.00
SINGLE CARDS:	15p

CROW, THE
PRODUCER:	KITCHEN SINK
ISSUE YEAR:	1994
CARD SET:	100 CARDS
SPECIAL CARDS:	10 CROW VISION CARDS
COMPLETE SET:	£12.00
SINGLE CARDS:	15p
SPECIAL SINGLE CARDS:	£3.50

CYBERFORCE
PRODUCER:	TOPPS
ISSUE YEAR:	1995
CARD SET:	72 CARDS
SPECIAL CARDS:	18 CYBER OPTICS CARD SET
	3 CLEAR CHROME CARD SET
	6 MATRIX CARD SET
COMPLETE SET:	£8.00
SINGLE CARDS:	10p

DAWN AND BEYOND
PRODUCER:	COMIC IMAGES
ISSUE YEAR:	1995
CARD SET:	90 CARDS
SPECIAL CARDS:	6 CARD UNCUT SHEET
	6 MAGNACHROME CARD SET
	3 RARE ART CARD SET
COMPLETE SET:	£10.00
SINGLE CARDS:	10p

DC BLOODLINES
PRODUCER:	SKYBOX
ISSUE YEAR:	1993
CARD SET:	81 CARDS
SPECIAL CARDS:	4 SUPERMAN EMBOSSED
	CARD SET
SUPERMAN REDEMPTIONAL CARD	
COMPLETE SET:	£5.00
SINGLE CARDS:	5p

DC COSMIC CARDS I
PRODUCER:	IMPEL
ISSUE YEAR:	1992
CARD SET:	180 CARDS
SPECIAL CARDS:	10 HOLOGRAM CARDS
COMPLETE SET:	£30.00
SINGLE CARDS:	5p-10p
SINGLE SPECIAL CARDS:	£3.00

DC COSMIC TEAMS
PRODUCER:	SKYBOX
ISSUE YEAR:	1993
CARD SET:	120 CARDS
SPECIAL CARDS:	6 HOLOGRAM CARDS
COMPLETE SET:	£25.00
SINGLE CARDS:	10p
SINGLE SPECIAL CARDS:	£4.00

Important Notes: as there are certain cards that are more difficult to get than others, a complete set is more difficult to put together than one would expect

DC MASTER SERIES
PRODUCER:	SKYBOX
ISSUE YEAR:	1994
CARD SET:	90 CARDS
SPECIAL CARDS:	SUPERMAN SKYDISC
	4 FOIL CARDS SET
	5 SPECTRA-FOIL CARD SET
COMPLETE SET:	£7.00
SINGLE CARDS:	10p

DC MILESTONE MEDIA
PRODUCER:	SKYBOX
ISSUE YEAR:	1993
CARD SET:	100 CARDS
SPECIAL CARDS:	2 FOIL-EMBOSSED CARD SET
COMPLETE SET:	£4.00
SINGLE CARDS:	5p

DC VERTIGO
PRODUCER:	SKYBOX
ISSUE YEAR:	1995
CARD SET:	90 CARDS
SPECIAL CARDS:	DEATH SKYDISC
	6 GOLD FOIL CARD SET
COMPLETE SET:	£9.00
SINGLE CARDS:	15p

DC VILLAINS
PRODUCER:	FLEER/SKYBOX
ISSUE YEAR:	1995
CARD SET:	90 CARDS
SPECIAL CARDS:	SKYMOTION REDEMPTION
	CARD
	3 FOIL EMBOSSED CARD SET
	9 SPECTRA-ETCH CARD SET
COMPLETE SET:	£10.00
SINGLE CARDS:	15p

DARK CRYSTAL
PRODUCER:	DONRUSS
ISSUE YEAR:	1982
CARD SET:	78 CARDS
SPECIAL CARDS:	No special cards
COMPLETE SET:	£9.00
SINGLE CARDS:	20p

DEATHMATE
PRODUCER:	UPPER DECK
ISSUE YEAR:	1993
CARD SET:	110 CARDS
SPECIAL CARDS:	18 (Gold Foil Embossed,
	9 Foil)
COMPLETE SET:	£12.50
SINGLE CARDS:	10p
SPECIAL SINGLE CARDS	
(Gold Embossed):	£2.00
(Foil):	£5.00

DEATHWATCH 2000
PRODUCER:	CLASSIC/CONTINUITY
ISSUE YEAR:	1993
CARD SET:	100 CARDS
SPECIAL CARDS:	7 HYBRID CARDS
COMPLETE SET:	£14.00
SINGLE CARDS:	10p
SPECIAL SINGLE CARDS:	£6.00

DESERT STORM I
PRODUCER:	TOPPS U.S.
ISSUE YEAR:	1991
CARD SET:	88 CARDS
SPECIAL CARDS:	22 STICKERS
COMPLETE SET:	£10.00
SINGLE CARDS:	5p-10p
SINGLE SPECIAL CARDS:	15p

DESERT STORM I DELUXE EDITION
PRODUCER:	TOPPS U.S.
ISSUE YEAR:	1991
CARD SET:	88 CARDS
SPECIAL CARDS:	22 STICKERS
COMPLETE FACTORY SET:	£13.00

DESERT STORM II - VICTORY
PRODUCER:	TOPPS U.S.
ISSUE YEAR:	1991
CARD SET:	66 CARDS
SPECIAL CARDS:	11 STICKERS
COMPLETE SET:	£5.00
SINGLE CARDS:	5p
SINGLE SPECIAL CARDS:	15p

DESERT STORM III - HOMECOMING
PRODUCER:	TOPPS U.S.
ISSUE YEAR:	1991
CARD SET:	66 CARDS
SPECIAL CARDS:	11 STICKERS
COMPLETE SET:	£5.00
SINGLE CARDS:	5p
SINGLE SPECIAL CARDS:	15p

DINOSAURS, TV SERIES
PRODUCER:	PRO SET
ISSUE YEAR:	1992
CARD SET:	65 CARDS
COMPLETE CARD SET:	£6.00
SINGLE CARDS:	10p

DINOSAURS ATTACK
PRODUCER:	TOPPS U.S.
ISSUE YEAR:	1988
CARD SET:	55 CARDS
SPECIAL CARDS:	11 STICKERS
COMPLETE SET:	£8.00
SINGLE CARDS:	20p
SINGLE SPECIAL CARDS:	40p

Important Notes: this set was a send up of the Mars Attacks series, famous for its gory artwork

DISNEY PREMIUM
PRODUCER:	SKYBOX
ISSUE YEAR:	1995
CARD SET:	80 CARDS
SPECIAL CARDS:	
2 HOLOBOSSED CARD SET	£7.50
9 SILVERSCREEN CARD SET	£15.00
COMPLETE SET:	£12.00
SINGLE CARDS:	15p

DISNEY SERIES I
PRODUCER:	IMPEL
ISSUE YEAR:	1991
CARD SET:	200 CARDS
SPECIAL CARDS:	2 HOLOGRAMS
COMPLETE SET:	£55.00
CARD SET ONLY:	£15.00
SINGLE CARDS:	10p
SINGLE SPECIAL CARDS:	£20.00

Important Notes: The two holograms in this set are very scarce. They are the first double sided holograms to be produced for a trading card set.

DRACULA MOVIE
PRODUCER:	TOPPS
ISSUE YEAR:	1992
CARD SET:	100 CARDS
SPECIAL CARDS:	No special cards
COMPLETE SET:	£15.00
SINGLE CARDS:	15p

DR. WHO SERIES I
PRODUCER:	CORNERSTONE
ISSUE YEAR:	1994
CARD SET:	110 CARDS
SPECIAL CARDS:	7 DOCTOR'S FOIL CARDS
COMPLETE SET:	£12.50
FACTORY SET (with Dalek Prism card):	
	£20.00
GOLD FACTORY SET (with 7 Prism cards and	
1 gold ink autographed card):	£50.00?
SINGLE CARDS:	5p
SINGLE SPECIAL CARDS:	£8.00. CARD;#2 £15.00 (Rare)

DR. WHO SERIES II
PRODUCER:	CORNERSTONE
ISSUE YEAR:	1995
CARD SET:	110 CARDS
SPECIAL CARDS:	6 FOIL CHASE CARDS
COMPLETE SET:	£12.50
FACTORY SET:	£30.00
SINGLE CARDS:	15p
SPECIAL SINGLE CARDS:	£5.00

Important Notes: The Factory Set was UV COATED and came with a Davros foil card #7. This set without the card would be about £20.00. The numbering starts at #111.

EMPIRE STRIKES BACK SERIES I
PRODUCER:	TOPPS U.S.
ISSUE YEAR:	1980
CARD SET:	132 CARDS
SPECIAL CARDS:	33 STICKERS
COMPLETE SET:	£40.00
SINGLE CARDS:	30p
SPECIAL SINGLE CARDS:	£1.00

EMPIRE STRIKES BACK SERIES II
PRODUCER:	TOPPS U.S.
ISSUE YEAR:	1980
CARD SET:	132 CARDS
SPECIAL CARDS:	33 STICKERS
COMPLETE SET:	£30.00
SINGLE CARDS:	25p
SPECIAL SINGLE CARDS:	£1.00

EMPIRE STRIKES BACK SERIES III
PRODUCER:	TOPPS U.S.
ISSUE YEAR:	1980
CARDS SET:	88 CARDS
SPECIAL CARDS:	22 STICKERS
COMPLETE SET:	£15.00
SINGLE CARDS:	15p
SPECIAL SINGLE CARDS:	50p

EMPIRE STRIKES BACK WIDEVISION
PRODUCER:	TOPPS U.S.
ISSUE YEAR:	1995
CARD SET:	144 CARDS
SPECIAL CARDS:	7 PROMO CARDS
COMPLETE SET:	£20.00
SINGLE CARDS:	15p
SPECIAL SINGLE CARDS:	£3.00

Important Notes: the Promo Cards were numbered from #0 to #6 and were available in different magazines such as Combo and Wizard. Card #5 seems much scarcer and would be valued at £6.00

E.T. THE EXTRA TERRESTRIAL MOVIE
PRODUCER:	TOPPS U.S.
ISSUE YEAR:	1982
CARD SET:	87 CARDS
SPECIAL CARDS:	12 STICKERS
COMPLETE SET:	£20.00
SINGLE CARDS:	20p
SINGLE SPECIAL CARDS:	40p

EVIL ERNIE
PRODUCER:	KROME PRODUCTIONS
ISSUE YEAR:	1994
CARD SET:	100 CARDS
SPECIAL CARDS:	6 KROME CARDS
COMPLETE SET:	£12.50
FACTORY SET:	55 CARDS (all chrome)
COMPLETE FACTORY SET:	£40.00
SINGLE CARDS:	15p
SPECIAL SINGLE CARDS:	£6.00
SIGNED KROME CARD:	£20.00
SIGNED & NUMBERED KROME CARD:	£30.00

Important Notes: there were two signed Krome cards per case and one signed and numbered Krome card per case

EVIL ERNIE CHROMIUM
PRODUCER:	KROME PRODUCTIONS
ISSUE YEAR:	1995
CARD SET:	100 CARDS
SPECIAL CARDS:	5 SUPER PREMIUM CARDS
COMPLETE SET:	£20.00
SINGLE CARDS:	20p
SPECIAL SINGLE CARDS:	£6.00

Important Notes: special cards signed by Brian Pulido and Steven Hughes are about £40 each

FAMOUS COMICBOOK CREATORS
PRODUCER:	ECLIPSE
ISSUE YEAR:	1992
CARD SET:	110 CARDS
SPECIAL CARDS:	No special cards
COMPLETE SET:	£15.00
SINGLE CARDS:	10p

FIEVEL GOES WEST
PRODUCER:	IMPEL
ISSUE YEAR:	1991
CARD SET:	150 CARDS
SPECIAL CARDS:	5 HOLOGRAM CARDS
COMPLETE SET:	£20.00
CARD SET ONLY:	£10.00
SINGLE CARDS:	10p
SINGLE SPECIAL CARDS:	£3.00

FLAIR MARVEL
PRODUCER:	FLEER
ISSUE YEAR:	1994
CARD SET:	150 CARDS
SPECIAL CARDS:	
18 POWER BLASTS CARD SET	£50.00
COMPLETE SET:	£30.00
SINGLE CARDS:	20p
SINGLE SPECIAL CARDS:	£3.00-£4.50

FLAIR MARVEL ANNUAL
PRODUCER:	FLEER
ISSUE YEAR:	1995
CARD SET:	150 CARDS
SPECIAL CARDS:	
24 POWER BLASTS CARD SET	£16.00
12 CHROMIUM CARDS SET	£14.00
12 HOLOBLAST CARDS SET	£28.00
3 DUO-BLAST CARD SET	£6.00
COMPLETE SET:	£25.50
SINGLE CARDS:	15p
SINGLE SPECIAL CARDS:	£2.00-£3.50

FLINTSTONES MOVIE CARDS
PRODUCER:	TOPPS U.S.
ISSUE YEAR:	1994
CARD SET:	88 CARDS
SPECIAL CARDS:	11 STICKERS
COMPLETE SET:	£8.00
SINGLE CARDS:	10p
SPECIAL SINGLE CARDS:	75p

Important Notes: Factory Sets were heavily remaindered in the U.S.

FREE WILLY 2
PRODUCER:	SKYBOX
ISSUE YEAR:	1995
CARD SET:	90 CARDS
SPECIAL CARDS:	9 SPECTRA CARDS
COMPLETE SET:	£10.00
SINGLE CARDS:	10p
SPECIAL SINGLE CARDS:	£2.50

Important Notes: two holograms are available at approximately £10.00 each

FRIGHT FLICKS
PRODUCER:	TOPPS U.S.
ISSUE YEAR:	1988
CARD SET:	90 CARDS
SPECIAL CARDS:	11 STICKERS
COMPLETE SET:	£9.00
SINGLE CARDS:	15p
SINGLE SPECIAL CARDS:	20p

Important Notes: the sticker set is hard to find and the cards and stickers would be valued at around £15.00

FRAZETTA
PRODUCER:	COMIC IMAGES
ISSUE YEAR:	1991
CARD SET:	90 CARDS
SPECIAL CARDS:	No special cards
COMPLETE SET:	£10.00
SINGLE CARDS:	15p

FRAZETTA II
PRODUCER:	COMIC IMAGES
ISSUE YEAR:	1993
CARD SET:	90 CARDS
SPECIAL CARDS:	3 SPECTROSCOPE/3 CHROME
COMPLETE SET:	£9.00
SINGLE CARDS:	10p
SPECIAL SINGLE CARDS:	£5.00

GARFIELD THE CAT
PRODUCER:	SKYBOX
ISSUE YEAR:	1992
CARD SET:	100 CARDS
SPECIAL CARDS:	9 TATTOOS, 5 HOLOGRAMS
COMPLETE SET:	£35.00
SINGLE CARDS:	10p
SINGLE SPECIAL CARDS:	
TATTOOS	50p,
HOLOGRAMS	£5.00

Important Notes: Very scarce in the U.K.

GEN 13
PRODUCER:	WILDSTORM
ISSUE YEAR:	1995
CARD SET:	107 CARDS
SPECIAL CARDS:	
SINGLE REFRACTOR CARD	£6.00
9 GLOW-IN-THE-DARK CARD SET	
	£58.00
9 GEN-ACTIVE CARD SET	£70.00
COMPLETE SET:	£15.00
SINGLE CARDS:	15p
SINGLE SPECIAL CARDS:	£6.00-£15.00

GHOSTBUSTERS II MOVIE
PRODUCER:	TOPPS U.S.
ISSUE YEAR:	1989
CARD SET:	88 CARDS
SPECIAL CARDS:	11 STICKERS
COMPLETE SET:	£6.00
SINGLE CARDS:	10p
SINGLE SPECIAL CARDS:	25p

Important Notes: There were no trading cards produced for the first Ghostbusters movie.

GHOST RIDER I
PRODUCER:	COMIC IMAGES
ISSUE YEAR:	1990
CARD SET:	45 CARDS
SPECIAL CARDS:	No special cards
COMPLETE SET:	£8.00
SINGLE CARDS:	25p

Important Notes: This first set of Ghost Rider trading cards was only produced in limited quantities.

GHOST RIDER II
PRODUCER:	COMIC IMAGES
ISSUE YEAR:	1992
CARD SET:	80 CARDS
SPECIAL CARDS:	10 GLOW IN THE DARK CARDS
COMPLETE SET:	£7.00
SINGLE CARDS:	10p
SINGLE SPECIAL CARDS:	30p

Important Notes: There was one glow in dark special card contained within each packet of Ghost Rider II trading cards, so they are not scarce.

G.I.JOE
PRODUCER:	IMPEL
ISSUE YEAR:	1991
CARD SET:	200 CARDS
SPECIAL CARDS:	No special cards
COMPLETE SET:	£15.00
SINGLE CARDS:	10p

GLADIATORS
PRODUCER:	MERLIN PUBLISHING LTD
ISSUE YEAR:	1993
CARD SET:	32
COMPLETE SET:	£5.00
SINGLE CARDS:	5p

Important Notes: These cards were sold as a sub-set of the 1993 sticker collection and were never available separately.

GOLDEN AGE OF COMICS CHROMIUM
PRODUCER:	COMIC IMAGES
ISSUE YEAR:	1995
CARD SET:	90
SPECIAL CARDS:	
3 MAGNACHROME ART SET	£15.00
6 MAGNACHROME COVER SET	£25.00
6 MINI PROMO SHEET CARD SET	£10.00
MEDALLION CARD	£13.00
SIGNED CARD	£25.00
COMPLETE SET:	£13.00
SINGLE CARDS:	15p

Fleer Ultra X-Men #6

Incredible Hulk #80

Judge Dredd #26

GOLDENEYE

PRODUCER:	GRAFFITTI.
ISSUE YEAR:	1995
CARD SET:	90 CARDS
SPECIAL CARDS:3 PUZZLE SET	£18.00
6 GADGETS SET	£18.00
9 BOND COMPOSITE SET	£18.00
COMPLETE SET:	£7.00
SINGLE CARDS:	10p

GOONIES

PRODUCER:	TOPPS U.S.
ISSUE YEAR:	1986
CARD SET:	86 CARDS
SPECIAL CARDS:	22 STICKERS
COMPLETE SET:	£7.00
SINGLE CARDS:	10p
SINGLE SPECIAL CARDS:	25p

GREMLINS I MOVIE

PRODUCER:	TOPPS
ISSUE YEAR:	1984
CARD SET:	82 CARDS
SPECIAL CARDS:	11 STICKERS
COMPLETE SET:	£12.00
SINGLE CARDS:	15p
SINGLE SPECIAL CARDS:	25p

GREMLINS II MOVIE

PRODUCER:	TOPPS
ISSUE YEAR:	1992
CARD SET:	88 CARDS
SPECIAL CARDS:	11 STICKERS
COMPLETE SET:	£6.00
SINGLE CARDS:	10p
SINGLE SPECIAL CARDS:	20p

GROWING PAINS (US TV SERIES)

PRODUCER:	TOPPS US
ISSUE YEAR:	1988
CARD SET:	66
COMPLETE SET:	£4.00
SINGLE ACRDS:	10p
SPECIAL CARDS:	11 STICKERS
SINGLE SPECIAL CARDS:	15p

HARRY AND THE HENDERSONS MOVIE

PRODUCER:	TOPPS U.S.
ISSUE YEAR:	1987
CARD SET:	77 CARDS
SPECIAL CARDS:	22 STICKERS
COMPLETE SET:	£6.00
SINGLE CARDS:	10p
SINGLE SPECIAL CARDS:	15p

HELLRAISER (FIRST 3 MOVIES)

PRODUCER:	ECLIPSE
ISSUE YEAR:	1992
CARD SET:	110 CARDS
SPECIAL CARDS:	2 SILVER HOLOGRAMS/
	2 GOLD HOLOGRAMS
	(Pinhead and Cube)
COMPLETE SET:	£40.00
CARD SET ONLY	£10.00
SINGLE CARDS:	10p
SINGLE SPECIAL CARDS:	£20.00

Important Notes: Gold holograms were given to retailers with csaes of cards, the silver were randomly inserted

HILDEBRANDT I

PRODUCER:	COMIC IMAGES
ISSUE YEAR:	1992
CARD SET:	90 CARDS
SPECIAL CARDS:	6 CHROME CHASE CARDS
COMPLETE SET:	£10.00
SINGLE CARDS:	10p
SINGLE SPECIAL CARDS:	£5.00

HILDEBRANDT II

PRODUCER:	COMIC IMAGES
ISSUE YEAR:	1993
CARD SET:	90 CARDS
COMPLETE SET:	£9.00
SINGLE CARDS:	10p

HILDEBRANDT BROS.

PRODUCER:	COMIC IMAGES
ISSUE YEAR:	1994
CARD SET:	90 CARDS
SPECIAL CARDS:	6 FOIL EMBOSSED CHROME
COMPLETE SET:	£9.00
SINGLE CARDS:	10p
SPECIAL SINGLE CARDS:	£4.00

HILDEBRANDT CHROME

PRODUCER:	COMIC IMAGES
ISSUE YEAR:	1995
CARDS SET:	90 CARDS
SPECIAL CARDS:	6 FOIL EMBOSSED CHROME
COMPLETE SET:	£20.00
SINGLE CARDS:	20p
SPECIAL SINGLE CARDS:	£4.00

HOME ALONE 2 - LOST IN NEW YORK MOVIE

PRODUCER:	TOPPS U.S.
ISSUE YEAR:	1992
CARD SET:	66 CARDS
SPECIAL CARDS:	11 STICKERS
COMPLETE SET:	£8.00
SINGLE CARDS:	15p
SINGLE SPECIAL CARDS:	25p

HOOK MOVIE

PRODUCER:	TOPPS U.S.
ISSUE YEAR:	1991
CARD SET:	99 CARDS
SPECIAL CARDS:	11 STICKERS
COMPLETE SET:	£9.00
SINGLE CARDS:	10p - 20p
SINGLE SPECIAL CARDS:	25p

Important Notes: These sets broke badly from their boxes. In many cases more than one box of cards was required to complete a set.

HOWARD THE DUCK MOVIE

PRODUCER:	TOPPS
ISSUE YEAR:	1986
CARD SET:	77 CARDS
SPECIAL CARDS:	22 STICKERS
COMPLETE SET:	£10.00
SINGLE CARDS:	10p
SINGLE SPECIAL CARDS:	20p

IMAGE UNIVERSE

PRODUCER:	TOPPS
ISSUE YEAR:	1995
CARD SET:	90 CARDS
SPECIAL CARDS:	
6 CLEAR ZONE SET	£24.00
6 "I" HOLOCHROME SET	£24.00
6 "D" HOLOCHROME SET	£24.00
COMPLETE SET:	£30.00
SINGLE CARDS:	35p

IMAGES OF SHADOWHAWK

PRODUCER:	IMAGE
ISSUE YEAR:	1994
CARD SET:	100 CARDS
SPECIAL CARDS:	7 FOIL CARDS
COMPLETE SET:	£10.00
SINGLE CARDS:	10p
SPECIAL SINGLE CARDS:	£4.00

INCREDIBLE HULK

PRODUCER:	COMIC IMAGES
ISSUE YEAR:	1991
CARD SET:	90 CARDS
SPECIAL CARDS:	No special cards
COMPLETE SET:	£12.00
SINGLE CARDS:	10p

Important Notes: See also other set produced by Topps.

INCREDIBLE HULK TV PILOT MOVIE

PRODUCER:	TOPPS U.S.
ISSUE YEAR:	1979
CARD SET:	88 CARDS
SPECIAL CARDS:	22 STICKERS
COMPLETE SET:	£15.00
SINGLE CARDS:	20p
SINGLE SPECIAL CARDS:	30p

Important Notes: There was also a set produced by Comic Images in 1991.

INDIANA JONES AND THE TEMPLE OF DOOM MOVIE

PRODUCER:	TOPPS U.S.
ISSUE YEAR:	1984
CARD SET:	88 CARDS
SPECIAL CARDS:	11 STICKERS
COMPLETE SET:	£10.00
SINGLE CARDS:	15p
SINGLE SPECIAL CARDS:	20p

INSIDE COMICS (RARE ISSUE)

PRODUCER:	DOUBLE BARREL
	PRODUCTIONS
ISSUE YEAR:	1992
CARD SET:	3 CARDS
SPECIAL CARDS:	No special cards
COMPLETE SET:	£6.00
SINGLE CARDS:	£2.00

Important Notes: Card One: WILD C.A.T.S. by Jim Lee; Card Two: Youngblood by Rob Liefeld; Card Three: Spawn by Todd McFarlane. This set of three cards was originally intended as a giveaway with Inside Comics #3. The magazine was cancelled and the cards withdrawn after Image Comics issued a writ, claiming that the cards were produced without the correct licensing agreement. The magazines with their cards are now believed to have been destroyed, but a limited of sets came over to the U.K.

JACK KIRBY, THE COMIC ART TRIBUTE TO JOE SIMON AND

PRODUCER:	21ST CENTURY
ISSUE YEAR:	1995
CARD SET:	50 CARDS
SPECIAL CARDS:	5 K INSERT CARDS
COMPLETE SET:	£8.00
SINGLE CARDS:	15p
SINGLE SPECIAL CARDS:	£3.00

JACK KIRBY'S UNPUBLISHED ARCHIVES

PRODUCER:	COMIC IMAGES
ISSUE YEAR:	1994
CARD SET:	90 CARDS
SPECIAL CARDS:	6 CHROMIUM CARDS
COMPLETE SET:	£9.00
SINGLE CARDS:	10p
SINGLE SPECIAL CARDS:	£4.00

JAMES BOND

PRODUCER:	ECLIPSE
ISSUE YEAR:	1993
CARD SET:	110 CARDS (gold border)
SPECIAL CARDS:	2 HOLOGRAMS
COMPLETE SET:	£15.00
SINGLE CARDS:	15p
SINGLE SPECIAL CARDS:	£8.00

Important Notes: Boxes withdrawn from U.K. sale because Eclipse, only had production rights for th U.S. and Canada.

JAMES BOND II

PRODUCER:	ECLIPSE
ISSUE YEAR:	1994
CARD SET:	110 CARDS
SPECIAL CARDS:	6 BOND GIRL CHASE CARDS
COMPLETE SET:	£15.00
SINGLE CARDS:	15p
SINGLE SPECIAL CARDS:	£4.00

Important Notes: same set as before but with silver border

JAWS II

PRODUCER:	TOPPS U.S.
ISSUE YEAR:	1978
CARD SET:	59 CARDS
SPECIAL CARDS:	11 STICKERS
COMPLETE SET:	£7.00
SINGLE CARDS:	10p
SINGLE SPECIAL CARDS:	20p

JAWS 3D

PRODUCER:	TOPPS U.S.
ISSUE YEAR:	1983
CARD SET:	44 CARDS
SPECIAL CARDS:	No special cards
COMPLETE SET:	£5.00
SINGLE CARDS:	10p

JEFFREY JONES

PRODUCER:	FPG
ISSUE YEAR:	1993
CARD SET:	90 CARDS
SPECIAL CARDS:	3 HOLOGRAM CHASE CARDS
COMPLETE SET:	£12.00
SINGLE CARDS:	10p
SINGLE SPECIAL CARDS:	£5.00

JIM WARREN - BEYOND BIZARRE

PRODUCER:	COMIC IMAGES
ISSUE YEAR:	1993
CARD SET:	90 CARDS
SPECIAL CARDS:	3 SPECTRA/
	3 OPTI-PRISM CARDS
COMPLETE SET:	£9.00
SINGLE CARDS:	10p
SINGLE SPECIAL CARDS:	£5.00

JIM WARREN II - MORE BEYOND BIZARRE

PRODUCER:	COMIC IMAGES
ISSUE YEAR:	1994
CARD SET:	90 CARDS
SPECIAL CARDS:	6 PRISM CARDS
COMPLETE SET:	£9.00
SINGLE CARDS:	10p
SINGLE SPECIAL CARDS:	£5.00

JOE JUSKO'S EDGAR RICE BURROUGHS I

PRODUCER:	FPG
ISSUE YEAR:	1994
CARDS SET:	60 CARDS
SPECIAL CARDS:	6 METALLIC STORM CARDS
COMPLETE SET:	£15.00
SINGLE CARDS:	25p
SINGLE SPECIAL CARDS:	£5.00

JOE JUSKO'S EDGAR RICE BURROUGHS II

PRODUCER:	FPG
ISSUE YEAR:	1995
CARD SET:	60 CARDS
SPECIAL CARDS:	6 METALLIC STORM CARDS
COMPLETE SET:	£15.00
SINGLE CARDS:	25p
SINGLE SPECIAL CARDS:	£5.00

JOHN BERKEY - SPACE ART

PRODUCER:	COMIC IMAGES
ISSUE YEAR:	1994
CARD SET:	90 CARDS
SPECIAL CARDS:	5 METAL STORM CHASE CARDS
CARD SET	£12.00
SINGLE CARDS:	10p
SINGLE SPECIAL CARDS:	£6.00

JUDGE DREDD

PRODUCER:	EDGE
ISSUE YEAR:	1995
CARD SET:	90 CARDS
SPECIAL CARDS:	
3 MOVIE CARD SET	£7.00
4 DEATH DIMENSION 1 CARD SET	£30.00
4 DEATH DIMENSION 2 CARD SET	£30.00
9 SLEEP CARD SET	£10.00
13 LEGENDS CARD SET	£30.00
COMPLETE SET:	£6.00
SINGLE CARDS:	10p

JURASSIC PARK

PRODUCER:	TOPPS U.S.
ISSUE YEAR:	1993
CARD SET:	88 CARDS
SPECIAL CARDS:	11 STICKERS
COMPLETE SET:	£10.00
SINGLE CARDS:	10p
SINGLE SPECIAL CARDS:	20p

JURASSIC PARK II

PRODUCER:	TOPPS U.S.
ISSUE YEAR:	1993
CARD SET:	88 CARDS
SPECIAL CARDS:	11 STICKERS
COMPLETE SET:	£12.00
SINGLE CARDS:	10p
SINGLE SPECIAL CARDS:	20p

JURASSIC PARK GOLD

PRODUCER:	TOPPS U.S.
ISSUE YEAR:	1993
CARD SET:	88 CARDS
SPECIAL CARDS:	10 ART CARDS
COMPLETE SET:	£15.00
SINGLE CARDS:	20p
SINGLE SPECIAL CARDS:	50p

KEITH PARKINSON - FANTASY ART

PRODUCER:	FPG
ISSUE YEAR:	1994
CARD SET:	90 CARDS
SPECIAL CARDS:	5 METALLIC STORM CARDS
COMPLETE SET:	£12.00
SINGLE CARDS:	10p
SINGLE SPECIAL CARDS:	£6.00

KEN BARR - THE BEAST WITHIN

PRODUCER:	COMIC IMAGES
ISSUE YEAR:	1994
CARD SET:	90 CARDS
SPECIAL CARDS:	6 FOIL EMBOSSED CHASE CARDS
COMPLETE SET:	£8.00
SINGLE CARDS:	15p
SINGLE SPECIAL CARDS:	£4.50

KEN KELLY

PRODUCER:	FPG
ISSUE YEAR:	1993
CARD SET:	90 CARDS
SPECIAL CARDS:	3 HOLOGRAMS
CARD SET:	£12.00
SINGLE CARDS:	15p
SINGLE SPECIAL CARDS:	£6.00

KING KONG

PRODUCER:	TOPPS U.S.
ISSUE YEAR:	1976
CARD SET:	55 CARDS
SPECIAL CARDS:	11 STICKERS
COMPLETE SET:	£9.00
SINGLE CARDS:	15p
SINGLE SPECIAL CARDS:	£1.00

KING KONG II

PRODUCER:	ECLIPSE
ISSUE YEAR:	1993
CARD SET:	110 CARDS
SPECIAL CARD:	1 EMBOSSED
COMPLETE SET:	£10.00
SINGLE CARD:	10p
SINLGE SPECIAL CARD:	£10.00

KNIGHT RIDER

PRODUCER:	DONRUSS
ISSUE YEAR:	1983
CARD SET:	55 CARDS
SPECIAL CARDS:	No special cards
COMPLETE SET:	£5.00
SINGLE CARDS:	15p

LADY DEATH

PRODUCER:	KROME PRODUCTIONS
ISSUE YEAR:	1994
CARD SET:	90 CARDS
SPECIAL CARDS:	5 HOLOGRAM CARDS
COMPLETE SET:	£25.00
SINGLE CARD:	25p
SINGLE SPECIAL CARD:	£7.50

LADY DEATH SERIES 2

PRODUCER:	KROME PRODUCTIONS
ISSUE YEAR:	1995
CARD SET:	100 CARDS
SPECIAL CARDS:	
3 TRYPTIC CARD SET	£18.00
5 CHROMIUM CARD SET	£18.00
MYSTERY CARD	£10.00
PULIDO/HUGHES SIGNED CARD	£25.00
CHROMIUM (7"x9") CARD	£15.00
FULL CHROMIUM STICKER SET (100)	£55.00
COMPLETE SET:	£25.00
SINGLE CARD: 25p	

LION KING

PRODUCER:	SKY BOX
ISSUE YEAR:	1994
CARD SET:	90 CARDS
SPECIAL CARDS:	9 EMBOSSED FOIL CARDS
OTHER SPECIAL CARDS:	5 POP-UP CARDS
COMPLETE SET:	£10.00
SINGLE CARDS:	10p
SINGLE SPECIAL CARDS:	£6.00
OTHER SINGLE SPECIAL CARDS:	£3.00
FACTORY SET IN TIN:	£40.00

LION KING II

PRODUCER:	SKYBOX
ISSUE YEAR:	1994
CARD SET:	80 CARDS
SPECIAL CARDS:	9 THERMOGRAPH CARDS
COMPLETE SET:	£10.00
SINGLE CARDS:	10p
SINGLE SPECIAL CARDS:	£4.00

Important Notes: other Special Cards include 5 Pop-Up cards at £3.00 each and 2 Foil-Border Art cards at £15.00 each. Numbering runs from #91-170

LITTLE MERMAID - FACTORY SET

PRODUCER:	PRO SET
ISSUE YEAR:	1993
CARD SET:	127 CARDS
SPECIAL CARDS:	VARIOUS NOVELTY ITEMS
COMPLETE SET:	£17.50

Important Notes: Novelty items consist of 15 stand up cards, 15 colour in cards, 6 character sponges and 7 static sticks.

LOIS & CLARK

PRODUCER:	SKYBOX
ISSUE YEAR:	1995
CARD SET:	90 CARDS
SPECIAL CARDS:	6 HOLO-CHIP FOIL/ 9 DIFFUSER FOIL CARDS
COMPLETE SET:	£10.00
SINGLE CARDS:	10p
SINGLE SPECIAL CARDS:	£5.00

LUIS ROYO

PRODUCER:	COMIC IMAGES
ISSUE YEAR:	1993
CARD SET:	90 CARDS
SPECIAL CARDS:	6 PRISM CARDS
COMPLETE SET:	£8.00
SINGLE CARDS:	10p
SINGLE SPECIAL CARDS:	£5.00

LUIS ROYO II

PRODUCER:	COMIC IMAGES
ISSUE YEAR:	1994
CARD SET:	90 CARDS
SPECIAL CARDS:	6 PRISM CARDS
COMPLETE SET:	£8.00
SINGLE CARDS:	10p
SINGLE SPECIAL CARDS:	£5.00

LUIS ROYO CHROMIUM, THE BEST OF

PRODUCER:	COMIC IMAGES
ISSUE YEAR:	1995
CARD SET:	90 CARDS (all chrome)
SPECIAL CARDS:	6 MAGNACHROME CARDS
COMPLETE SET:	£20.00
SINGLE CARDS:	25p
SINGLE SPECIAL CARDS:	£5.00

MAD MAGAZINE I

PRODUCER:	LIME ROCK
ISSUE YEAR:	1992
CARD SET:	50 CARDS
SPECIAL CARDS:	1 HOLOGRAM
COMPLETE SET:	£15.00
CARD SET ONLY	£5.00
SINGLE CARDS:	15p
SINGLE SPECIAL CARDS:	£10.00

MAD MAGAZINE II

PRODUCER:	LIME ROCK
ISSUE YEAR:	1992
CARD SET:	50 CARDS
SPECIAL CARDS:	1 Hologram
COMPLETE SET:	£15.00
CARD SET ONLY	£5.00
SINGLE CARDS:	15p
SINGLE SPECIAL CARDS:	£10.00

MAGNUM P.I.

PRODUCER:	DONRUSS
ISSUE YEAR:	1983
CARD SET:	66 CARDS
SPECIAL CARDS:	No special cards
COMPLETE SET:	£15.00
SINGLE CARDS:	15p

Important Notes: Based on the US television series

MALIBU ULTRAVERSE

PRODUCER:	SKYBOX
ISSUE YEAR:	1993
CARD SET:	100 CARDS
SPECIAL CARDS:	
9 ROOKIES CARD SET	£7.00
4 FOIL-STAMPED CARD SET	£8.00
2 ULTRAVERSE ULTRA CARD SET	£10.00
COMPLETE SET:	£5.00
SINGLE CARDS:	5p

MALIBU ULTRAVERSE SERIES 2

PRODUCER:	SKYBOX
ISSUE YEAR:	1993
CARD SET:	90 CARDS
SPECIAL CARDS:	
2 ULTRAVERSE ULTRA CARD SE	£10.00
7 PAINTED ART CARD SET	£20.00
COMPLETE SET:	£5.00
SINGLE CARDS:	5p

MALIBU ULTRAVERSE MASTER SERIES

PRODUCER:	SKYBOX
ISSUE YEAR:	1993
CARD SET:	90 CARDS
SPECIAL CARDS:	
2 HOLITHOGRAM SET CARD SET	£10.00
5 ULTRA CARD SET	£10.00
COMPLETE SET:	£5.00
SINGLE CARDS:	5p

MARILYN MONROE

PRODUCER:	SPORTS TIME CARD COMPANY
ISSUE YEAR:	1993
CARD SET:	100 CARDS
SPECIAL CARDS:	10 CHROMIUM CARDS
COMPLETE SET:	£15.00
SINGLE CARDS:	15p
SINGLE SPECIAL CARDS:	£6.00

Important Notes: there was also a Diamond Distributors special Redemption Card (1 per case) which is rare in the U.K. and valued at approximately £75.00

MARILYN MONROE II

PRODUCER:	SPORTS TIME CARD COMPANY
ISSUE YEAR:	1995
CARD SET:	100 CARDS
SPECIAL CARDS:	10 HOLOCHROME CARDS
COMPLETE SET	£15.00
SINGLE CARDS:	15p
SINGLE SPECIAL CARDS:	£5.00

MARS ATTACKS

PRODUCER:	TOPPS U.S.
ISSUE YEAR:	1994
CARD SET:	100 CARDS
SPECIAL CARDS:	4 MATRIX CARDS
COMPLETE SET:	£15.00
SINGLE CARDS:	15p
SINGLE SPECIAL CARDS:	£6.00

MARVEL 1ST ISSUE COVERS I

PRODUCER:	FTCC
ISSUE YEAR:	1984
CARD SET:	60 CARDS
SPECIAL CARDS:	No special cards
COMPLETE SET:	£18.00
SINGLE CARDS:	25p

MARVEL 1ST ISSUE COVERS II

PRODUCER:	COMIC IMAGES
ISSUE YEAR:	1991
CARD SET:	90 CARDS
CARD SET:	£10.00
SINGLE CARDS:	15p

MARVEL FLAIR ANNUAL '95

PRODUCER:	FLEER
ISSUE YEAR:	1995
CARD SET:	100 CARDS
SPECIAL CARDS:	3 DUOBLAST/9 POWERBLAST/
	9 HOLOBLAST CARDS
COMPLETE SET:	£30.00
SINGLE CARDS:	25p
SINGLE SPECIAL CARDS:	£4.00 (Duoblast)
	£2.00 (Powerblast)
	£4.00 (Holoblast)

Important Notes: printed on extra thick stock

MARVEL FLAIR UNIVERSE DELUXE

PRODUCER:	FLEER
ISSUE YEAR:	1994
CARD SET:	150 CARDS
SPECIAL CARDS:	18 POWERBLAST CARDS
COMPLETE SET:	£35.00
SINGLE CARDS:	25p
SINGLE SPECIAL CARDS:	£6.00

Important Notes: printed on extra thick stock

MARVEL MASTERPIECES I

PRODUCER:	SKYBOX
ISSUE YEAR:	1992
CARD SET:	100 CARDS
SPECIAL CARDS:	5 SPECTRA-ETCH CARDS
COMPLETE SET:	£40.00
CARD SET ONLY	£18.00
SINGLE CARDS:	15p
SINGLE SPECIAL CARDS:	£10.00

Important Notes: there were 5 Limited Cards available only in the Factory Set. Prices on these vary from £15.00 to £25.00

MARVEL MASTERPIECES II

PRODUCER:	SKYBOX
ISSUE YEAR:	1993
CARD SET:	90 CARDS
SPECIAL CARDS:	8 DYNA-ETCH FOIL CARDS
COMPLETE SET:	£60.00
CARD SET ONLY	£15.00
SINGLE CARDS:	15p
SINGLE SPECIAL CARDS:	£5.00

MARVEL MASTERPIECES III

PRODUCER:	SKYBOX
ISSUE YEAR:	1994
CARD SET:	150 CARDS
SPECIAL CARDS:	9 POWERBLAST CARDS
	10 HOLOFOIL CARDS
COMPLETE SET:	£15.00
SINGLE CARDS:	10p

Important Notes: Powerblast Cards at £3.00 each, Holoblast Cards at £2.00 each. There are also 150 Parallel Signature cards at about 50p each.

MARVEL MASTERPIECES IV

PRODUCER:	SKYBOX
ISSUE YEAR:	1995
CARD SET:	150 CARDS
SPECIAL CARDS:	9 HOLOFOIL CARDS
COMPLETE SET:	£20.00
SINGLE CARDS:	15p
SINGLE SPECIAL CARDS:	£6.00

Important Notes: There are 2 Lenticular chase cards which are very rare in the U.K. priced at about £50.00 each. There are also 150 Parallel Signature Cards at about 50p each and 22 Canvas chase cards at about £2.00 each.

MARVEL MASTERPIECES

PRODUCER:	FLEER
ISSUE YEAR:	1995
CARD SET:	150 CARDS
FULL E-MOTION SET (150)	£65.00
SPECIAL CARDS:	
2 MIRAGE CARD SET	£40.00
8 HOLOFLASH CARD SET	£30.00
24 CANVAS CARD SET	£25.00
COMPLETE SET:	£20.00
SINGLE CARDS:	15p

MARVEL METAL

PRODUCER:	FLEER
ISSUE YEAR:	1995
CARD SET:	100 CARDS
SPECIAL CARDS:	18 GOLD BLASTER
	18 SILVER BLASTER
COMPLETE SET:	£20.00
SINGLE CARDS:	25p
SINGLE SPECIAL CARDS	£2-£3 (Gold)
	£1-£2 (Silver)

MARVEL TRADING CARD TREATS

PRODUCER:	IMPEL
ISSUE YEAR:	1992
CARD SET:	36 CARD SET
COMPLETE SET:	£6.00
SINGLE CARDS:	20p

MARVEL UNIVERSE I

PRODUCER:	IMPEL
ISSUE YEAR:	1990
CARD SET:	162 CARDS
SPECIAL CARDS:	5 HOLOGRAM
COMPLETE SET:	£85.00
CARD SET ONLY	£35.00
SINGLE CARDS:	30p
SINGLE SPECIAL CARDS:	£12.00
FACTORY TIN COLLECTORS SET	£150.00

MARVEL UNIVERSE II

PRODUCER:	IMPEL
ISSUE YEAR:	1991
CARD SET:	162 CARDS
SPECIAL CARDS:	5 HOLOGRAM CARDS
COMPLETE SET:	£50.00
CARD SET ONLY	£18.00
SINGLE CARDS:	20p
SINGLE SPECIAL CARDS:	£7.00

Important Notes: Factory Tin Collectors set £85.00

MARVEL UNIVERSE III

PRODUCER:	SKYBOX
ISSUE YEAR:	1992
CARD SET:	200 CARDS
SPECIAL CARDS:	5 HOLOGRAM CARDS
COMPLETE SET:	£30.00
CARD SET ONLY	£12.50
SINGLE CARDS:	10p
SINGLE SPECIAL CARDS:	£4.00

Important Notes: Factory Tin Collectors set £60.00

MARVEL UNIVERSE IV

PRODUCER:	SKYBOX
ISSUE YEAR:	1993
CARD SET:	180 CARDS
SPECIAL CARDS:	9 FOIL CARDS + H-IV
	HOLOGRAM CARD
COMPLETE SET:	£60.00
CARD SET ONLY	£10.00
SINGLE CARDS:	10p
SINGLE SPECIAL CARDS:	£4.00
SPIDEY/VENOM HOLOGRAM:	£35.00

MELTING POT CHROMIUM

PRODUCER:	COMIC IMAGES
ISSUE YEAR:	1993
CARD SET:	100 CARDS
SPECIAL CARDS:	No Special cards
COMPLETE SET:	£25.00
SINGLE CARDS:	25p

MICHAEL JACKSON

PRODUCER:	TOPPS U.S.
ISSUE YEAR:	1984
CARD SET:	33 CARDS
SPECIAL CARDS:	33 STICKERS
COMPLETE SET:	£5.00
SINGLE CARDS:	15p
SINGLE SPECIAL CARDS:	50p

MICHAEL WHELAN - ADVENTURES IN FANTASY

PRODUCER:	COMIC IMAGES
ISSUE YEAR:	1993
CARD SET:	90 CARDS
SPECIAL CARDS:	3 SPECTRA/3 OPTI-PRISM CARDS
COMPLETE SET:	£8.00
SINGLE CARDS:	10p
SINGLE SPECIAL CARDS:	£5.00

MICHAEL WHELAN II

PRODUCER:	COMIC IMAGES
ISSUE YEAR:	1994
CARD SET:	90 CARDS
SPECIAL CARDS:	6 CHASE CARDS
COMPLETE SET:	£8.00
SINGLE CARDS:	10p
SINGLE SPECIAL CARDS:	£5.00

MIKE ZECK

PRODUCER:	COMIC IMAGES
ISSUE YEAR:	1991
CARD SET:	45 CARD SET
SPECIAL CARDS:	No special cards
COMPLETE SET:	£9.00
SINGLE CARDS:	20p

MILESTONE - THE DAKOTA UNIVERSE

PRODUCER:	SKYBOX
ISSUE YEAR:	1993
CARD SET:	100 CARDS
SPECIAL CARDS:	2 FOIL EMBOSSED CHASE CARDS
COMPLETE SET:	£10.00
SINGLE CARDS:	10p
SINGLE SPECIAL CARDS:	£8.00

MINNIE AND ME

PRODUCER:	IMPEL
ISSUE YEAR:	1991
CARD SET:	160 CARDS
SPECIAL CARDS:	No special cards
COMPLETE SET:	£10.00
SINGLE CARDS:	10p

MOEBIUS

PRODUCER:	COMIC IMAGES
ISSUE YEAR:	1993
CARD SET:	90 CARDS
SPECIAL CARDS:	6 CHROMIUM CARDS
COMPLETE SET:	£9.00
SINGLE CARDS:	10p
SINGLE SPECIAL CARDS:	£5.00

MONTY PYTHON'S FLYING CIRCUS

PRODUCER:	CORNERSTONE
ISSUE YEAR:	1995
CARD SET:	108 CARDS
SPECIAL CARDS:	4 FOIL CARDS
COMPLETE SET:	£18.00
SINGLE CARDS:	10p
SINGLE SPECIAL CARDS:	£6.00

Important Notes: there was also a Fake Scratch and Listen card, rare in the U.K. and valued at approximately £40.00

MOONRAKER MOVIE

PRODUCER:	TOPPS U.S.
ISSUE YEAR:	1979
CARD SET:	99 CARDS
SPECIAL CARDS:	22 STICKERS
COMPLETE SET:	£15.00
SINGLE CARDS:	15p
SINGLE SPECIAL CARDS:	25p

MORK AND MINDY TV

PRODUCER:	TOPPS U.S.
ISSUE YEAR:	1978
CARD SET:	99 CARDS
SPECIAL CARDS:	22 STICKERS
COMPLETE SET:	£10.00
SINGLE CARDS:	15p
SINGLE SPECIAL CARDS:	30p

MORTAL KOMBAT

PRODUCER:	CLASSIC
ISSUE YEAR:	1994
CARD SET:	100 CARDS
SPECIAL CARDS:	5 CHASE CARDS
COMPLETE SET:	£10.00
SINGLE CARDS:	10p
SINGLE SPECIAL CARDS:	£2.00

NEW KIDS ON THE BLOCK

PRODUCER:	TOPPS U.S.
ISSUE YEAR:	1989
CARD SET:	90 CARDS
SPECIAL CARDS:	11 STICKERS
COMPLETE SET:	£6.00
SINGLE CARDS:	10p
SINGLE SPECIAL CARDS:	30p

NIGHTMARE BEFORE CHRISTMAS
PRODUCER:	SKYBOX
ISSUE YEAR:	1993
CARD SET:	90 CARDS
SPECIAL CARDS:	4 SPECTRA CARDS
COMPLETE SET:	£10.00
SINGLE CARDS:	10p
SINGLE SPECIAL CARDS:	£4.00

Important Notes: based on Tim Burton film

NIGHTMARE ON ELM STREET FACTORY SET
PRODUCER:	IMPEL
ISSUE YEAR:	1991
CARD SET:	118 CARDS
SPECIAL CARDS:	2 HOLOGRAM CARDS
COMPLETE SET:	£25.00

NORMAN ROCKWELL
PRODUCER:	COMIC IMAGES
ISSUE YEAR:	1993
CARD SET:	90 CARDS
SPECIAL CARDS:	6 WOODGRAIN CHASE CARDS
COMPLETE SET:	£7.00
SINGLE CARDS:	10p
SINGLE SPECIAL CARDS:	£5.00

NORMAN ROCKWELL II
PRODUCER:	COMICS IMAGES
ISSUE YEAR:	1995
CARD SET:	90 CARDS
SPECIAL CARDS:	6 SANTA CHROME CHASE CARDS
COMPLETE SET:	£8.00
SINGLE CARDS:	10p
SINGLE SPECIAL CARDS:	£6.00

OLIVIA I
PRODUCER:	COMIC IMAGES
ISSUE YEAR:	1992
CARD SET:	90 CARDS
SPECIAL CARDS:	6 PRISM CARDS
COMPLETE SET:	£40.00
CARD SET ONLY	£ 12.50
SINGLE CARDS:	15p
SINGLE SPECIAL CARDS:	£8.00

OLIVIA II ALL PRISM SET
PRODUCER:	COMIC IMAGES
ISSUE YEAR:	1993
CARD SET:	72 PRISM CARDS
SPECIAL CARDS:	6 CHROMIUM CARDS
COMPLETE SET:	£20.00
SINGLE CARDS:	25p
SINGLE SPECIAL CARDS:	£8.00-£10.00

OLIVIA III - LADIES, LEATHER & LACE
PRODUCER:	COMIC IMAGES
ISSUE YEAR:	1994
CARD SET:	90 CARDS
SPECIAL CARDS:	6 CHROMIUM CARDS
COMPLETE SET:	£40.00
CARD SET ONLY	£7.50
SINGLE CARDS:	15p
SINGLE SPECIAL CARDS:	£8.00

OLIVIA CHROME, BEST OF
PRODUCER:	COMIC IMAGES
ISSUE YEAR:	1994
CARD SET:	90 CARDS
SPECIAL CARDS:	6 OMNICHROME CARDS
COMPLETE SET:	£20.00
SINGLE CARDS:	25p
SINGLE SPECIAL CARDS:	£6.00

OLIVIA SENSUALITY CHROME II
PRODUCER:	COMIC IMAGES
ISSUE YEAR:	1995
CARD SET:	90 CARDS
SPECIAL CARDS:	6 FOIL EMBOSSED CARDS
COMPLETE SET:	£16-£20
SINGLE CARDS:	25p
SINGLE SPECIAL CARDS:	£8.00

PHANTOM, THE
PRODUCER:	COMIC IMAGES
ISSUE YEAR:	1995
CARD SET:	90 CARDS
SPECIAL CARDS:	6 CHROMIUM CARDS
COMPLETE SET:	£10.00
SINGLE CARDS:	10p
SINGLE SPECIAL CARDS:	£4.00

PLANET OF THE APES
PRODUCER:	TOPPS U.S.
ISSUE YEAR:	1975
CARD SET:	66 CARDS
SPECIAL CARDS:	NO SPECIAL CARDS
COMPLETE SET:	£12.00
SINGLE CARDS:	20p

PORTFOLIO 92 - SWIMSUITS
PRODUCER:	PORTFOLIO
ISSUE YEAR:	1992
CARD SET:	50 CARDS
SPECIAL CARDS:	
COMPLETE SET:	£5.00
SINGLE CARDS:	10p

PORTFOLIO 93 - SWIMSUITS
PRODUCER:	PORTFOLIO
ISSUE YEAR:	1993
CARD SET:	50 CARDS
SPECIAL CARDS:	BONUS CARDS 101-108
CARD SET:	£5.00
SINGLE CARDS:	10p
SPECIAL SINGLE CARDS:	£5.00

Important Notes: Cards Numbered 51-100 see Portfolio 92 for cards #1-50

PRO CHEERLEADERS
PRODUCER:	LIME ROCK
ISSUE YEAR:	1992
CARD SET:	41 CARDS
SPECIAL CARDS:	No Special Cards
COMPLETE SET:	£4.00
SINGLE CARDS:	10p

PRO CHEERLEADERS II
PRODUCER:	LIME ROCK
ISSUE YEAR:	1992
CARD SET:	150 CARDS
SPECIAL CARDS:	No Special Cards
COMPLETE SET:	£15.00
SINGLE CARDS:	10p

PUNISHER I
PRODUCER:	COMIC IMAGES
ISSUE YEAR:	1988
CARD SET:	50 CARDS
SPECIAL CARDS:	No special cards
COMPETE SET	£12.00
SINGLE CARDS:	20p

PUNISHER II
PRODUCER:	COMIC IMAGES
ISSUE YEAR:	1992
CARD SET:	90 CARDS
SPECIAL CARDS:	3 PRISM & 3 SCRATCH N' SNIFF
COMPLETE SET:	£25.00
CARD SET ONLY	£ 5.00
SINGLE CARDS:	10p
SINGLE SPECIAL CARDS:	Prism cards £4.00
SCRATCH N' SNIFF CARDS:	£3.00

Important Notes: When buying separate Scratch n' sniff cards, look carefully for damaged surface scratch marks. Imperfect cards are worth 50%-75% less than guide price.

RAIDERS OF THE LOST ARK
PRODUCER:	TOPPS U.S.
ISSUE YEAR:	1981
CARD SET:	88 CARDS
SPECIAL CARDS:	No special cards
COMPLETE SET:	£15.00
SINGLE CARDS:	15p

RAMBO - FIRST BLOOD II MOVIE
PRODUCER:	TOPPS
ISSUE YEAR:	1985
CARD SET:	66 CARDS
SPECIAL CARDS:	11 STICKERS
COMPLETE SET:	£10.00
SINGLE CARDS:	10p
SINGLE SPECIAL CARDS:	20p

RETURN OF THE JEDI 1 - MOVIE
PRODUCER:	TOPPS U.S.
ISSUE YEAR:	1983
CARD SET:	132 CARDS
SPECIAL CARDS:	33 STICKERS
COMPLETE SET:	£25.00
COMPLETE SET (with stickers):	£40.00
SINGLE CARDS:	15p
SINGLE SPECIAL CARDS:	25p

Punisher #7

Marvel Universe Series 1 #145

Skybox Master Series Creators Edition
(Prototype Card)

RETURN OF THE JEDI II - MOVIE
PRODUCER:	TOPPS U.S.
ISSUE YEAR:	1982
CARD SET:	88 CARDS
SPECIAL CARDS:	22 STICKERS
COMPLETE SET:	£20.00
COMPLETE SET (with stickers):	£35.00
SINGLE CARDS:	15p
SINGLE SPECIAL CARDS:	25p

ROBIN HOOD, PRINCE OF THIEVES MOVIE
PRODUCER:	TOPPS U.S.
ISSUE YEAR:	1991
CARD SET:	88 CARDS
SPECIAL CARDS:	9 STICKERS
COMPLETE SET:	£10.00
SINGLE CARDS:	15p
SINGLE SPECIAL CARDS:	30p

Important Notes: Based on the movie of the same name starring Kevin Costner. RARE SET (called the Mistake Set in the U.S.)

ROBIN HOOD, PRINCE OF THIEVES MOVIE
PRODUCER:	TOPPS U.S.
ISSUE YEAR:	1991
CARD SET:	55 CARDS
SPECIAL CARDS:	9 STICKERS
COMPLETE SET:	£5.00
SINGLE CARDS:	10p
SINGLE SPECIAL CARDS:	15p

ROBOCOP II MOVIE
PRODUCER:	TOPPS U.S.
ISSUE YEAR:	1990
CARD SET:	88 CARDS
SPECIAL CARDS:	11 STICKERS
COMPLETE SET:	£5.00
SINGLE CARDS:	10p
SINGLE SPECIAL CARDS:	25p

ROCKETEER MOVIE
PRODUCER:	TOPPS U.S.
ISSUE YEAR:	1991
CARD SET:	99 CARDS
SPECIAL CARDS:	11 STICKERS
COMPLETE SET:	£7.00
SINGLE CARDS:	15p
SINGLE SPECIAL CARDS:	30p

Important Notes: A very high quality and highly desirable set of trading cards and stickers.

ROCKY II MOVIE
PRODUCER:	TOPPS U.S.
ISSUE YEAR:	1979
CARD SET:	99 CARDS
SPECIAL CARDS:	11 STICKERS
COMPLETE SET:	£10.00
SINGLE CARDS:	15p
SINGLE SPECIAL CARDS:	25p

ROCKY IV MOVIE
PRODUCER:	TOPPS U.S.
ISSUE YEAR:	1985
CARD SET:	66 CARDS
SPECIAL CARDS:	11 STICKERS
COMPLETE SET:	£7.00
SINGLE CARDS:	15p
SINGLE SPECIAL CARDS:	25p

ROCKY HORROR PICTURE SHOW MOVIE
PRODUCER:	FTCC
ISSUE YEAR:	1980
CARD SET:	60 CARDS
SPECIAL CARDS:	No special cards
COMPLETE SET:	£12.00
SINGLE CARDS:	25p

ROCKY HORROR PICTURE SHOW II
PRODUCER:	COMIC IMAGES
ISSUE YEAR:	1995
CARD SET:	90 CARDS
SPECIAL CARDS:	6 CHROME CHASE CARDS
COMPLETE SET:	£8.00
SINGLE CARDS:	10p
SINGLE SPECIAL CARDS:	£5.00

ROGER DEAN
PRODUCER:	FPG
ISSUE YEAR:	1993
CARD SET:	90 CARDS
SPECIAL CARDSL	5 METALLIC STORM CARDS
COMPLETE SET	£10.00
SINGLE CARDS:	15p
SINGLE SPECIAL CARDS:	£5.00

ROGER RABBIT, WHO FRAMED MOVIE
PRODUCER:	TOPPS U.S.
ISSUE YEAR:	1990
CARD SET:	132 CARDS
SPECIAL CARDS:	22 STICKERS
COMPLETE SET:	£12.00
SINGLE CARDS:	10p
SINGLE SPECIAL CARDS:	25p

RON MILLER'S FIREBRANDS
PRODUCER:	COMIC IMAGES
ISSUE YEAR:	1994
CARD SET:	90 CARDS
SPECIAL CARDS:	6 GALAXY PRISM CARDS
COMPLETE SET:	£9.00
SINGLE CARDS:	10p
SINGLE SPECIAL CARDS:	£5.00

ROWENA
PRODUCER:	FPG
ISSUE YEAR:	1993
CARD SET:	90 CARDS
SPECIAL CARDS:	3 HOLOGRAMS
COMPLETE SET	£10.00
SINGLE CARDS:	15p
SINGLE SPECIAL CARDS:	£5.00

SANDMAN
PRODUCER:	SKYBOX
ISSUE YEAR:	1994
CARD SET:	90 CARDS
SPECIAL CARDS:	7 ENDLESS GALLERY BONUS CARDS
COMPLETE SET:	£90.00
CARD SET ONLY	£20.00
SINGLE CARDS:	15p
SINGLE SPECIAL CARDS:	£15.00

Important Notes: Morpheus Hologram woulkd be about £40.00

SANJULIAN COLLECTION
PRODUCER:	FPG
ISSUE YEAR:	1994
CARD SET:	90 CARDS
SPECIAL CARDS:	5 METALLIC STORM CARDS
COMPLETE SET	£10.00
SINGLE CARDS:	15p
SINGLE SPECIAL CARDS:	£5.00

SAVAGE DRAGON
PRODUCER:	COMIC IMAGES
ISSUE YEAR:	1992
CARD SET:	90 CARDS
SPECIAL CARDS:	6 PRISM CARDS
COMPLETE SET:	£30.00
CARD SET ONLY	£5.00
SINGLE CARDS:	10p
SINGLE SPECIAL CARDS:	£4.00

Important Notes: Generally the quality of the image series trading cards are quite poor and only the prism cards are impressive to view.

SEAQUEST DSV
PRODUCER:	SKYBOX
ISSUE YEAR:	1994
CARD SET:	100 CARDS
SPECIAL ACRDS:	4 FOIL CARDS
COMPLETE SET:	£10.00
SINGLE CARDS:	10p
SINGLE SPECIAL CARDS:	£5.00

SHADOW HAWK
PRODUCER:	COMIC IMAGES
ISSUE YEAR:	1992
CARD SET:	90 CARDS
SPECIAL CARDS:	6 PRISM CARDS
COMPLETE SET:	£35.00
SINGLE CARDS:	10p
SINGLE SPECIAL CARDS:	£5.00

SHI
PRODUCER:	COMIC IMAGES
ISSUE YEAR:	1995
CARD SET:	90 CARDS
SPECIAL CARDS:	
3 MAGNACHROME CARD SET	£22.00
6 MAGNACHROME CARD SET	£30.00
6 CARD UNCUT SHEET	£10.00
COMPLETE SET ALL-CHROMIUM:	£18.00
SINGLE CARDS:	25p

SILVER SURFER ALL PRISM SERIES
PRODUCER:	COMIC IMAGES
ISSUE YEAR:	1992
CARD SET:	72 ALL PRISM SET
SPECIAL CARDS:	No special cards
COMPLETE SET:	£20.00
SINGLE CARDS:	30p

SIMPSONS
PRODUCER:	TOPPS
ISSUE YEAR:	1990
CARD SET:	88 CARDS
SPECIAL CARDS:	22 STICKERS
COMPLETE SET:	£12.00
SINGLE CARDS:	10p
SINGLE SPECIAL CARDS:	20p

SIMPSONS
PRODUCER:	SKYBOX
ISSUE YEAR:	1994
CARD SET:	70 CARDS
SPECIAL CARDS:	4 GLOW IN THE DARK CARDS
COMPLETE SET:	£10.00
SINGLE CARDS:	15p
SINGLE SPECIAL CARDS:	£6.00

SNOW WHITE AND THE SEVEN DWARFS
PRODUCER:	SKYBOX
ISSUE YEAR:	1993
CARD SET:	90 CARDS
SPECIAL CARDS:	4 SPECTRA CARDS
COMPLETE SET:	£10.00
SINGLE CARDS:	10p
SINGLE SPECIAL CARDS:	£3.00

SNOW WHITE AND THE SEVEN DWARFS II
PRODUCER:	SKYBOX
ISSUE YEAR:	1994
CARD SET:	90 CARDS
SPECIAL CARDS:	4 FOIL EMBOSSED CARDS
COMPLETE SET:	£10.00
SINGLE CARDS:	10p
SINGLE SPECIAL CARDS:	£5.00

SONIC THE HEDGEHOG
PRODUCER:	TOPPS U.S.
ISSUE YEAR:	1993
CARD SET:	33 CARDS
SPECIAL CARDS:	33 STICKERS
COMPLETE SET	£5.00
SINGLE CARDS:	15p

SORAYAMA - SEXY ROBOTS
PRODUCER:	COMIC IMAGES
ISSUE YEAR:	1993
CARD SET:	90 CARDS
SPECIAL CARDS:	6 CHROMIUM CARDS
COMPLETE SET	£8.00
SINGLE CARDS:	15p
SINGLE SPECIAL CARDS:	£4.00

SORAYAMA II - CHROMIUM CREATURES
PRODUCER:	COMIC IMAGES
ISSUE YEAR:	1994
CARD SET:	100 CARDS
SPECIAL CARDS:	6 FOIL CARDS
COMPLETE SET	£25.00
SINGLE CARDS:	25p
SINGLE SPECIAL CARDS:	£5.00

SPAWN
PRODUCER:	WILDSTORM
ISSUE YEAR:	1995
CARD SET:	150 CARDS
SPECIAL CARDS:	12 PAINTED/ 6 TODD TOY CARDS
COMPLETE SET	£15.00
SINGLE CARD:	10p
SINGLE SPECIAL CARDS:	£3.00

SPIDERMAN FLEER ULTRA
PRODUCER:	FLEER
ISSUE YEAR:	1995
CARD SET:	150 CARDS
SPECIAL CARDS:	10 CLEARZONE CHASE/ 9 GOLD WEB CHASE/ 9 MONSTER CHASE CARDS
COMPLETE SET:	£18.00
SINGLE CARDS:	15p
SINGLE SPECIAL CARDS:	£5.00 (Clearzone) £3.00 (Gold Web and Monster)
GOLD SIGNATURE CARD SET:	£75.00
GOLD SIGNATURE SINGLE CARD:	50p

SPIDERMAN, 30TH ANNIVERSARY
PRODUCER:	COMIC IMAGES
ISSUE YEAR:	1992
CARD SET:	90 CARDS
SPECIAL CARDS:	6 PRISM CARDS
COMPLETE SET:	£35.00
CARD SET ONLY	£5.00
SINGLE CARDS:	10p
SINGLE SPECIAL CARDS:	£6.00

SPIDERMAN, TODD MCFARLANE

PRODUCER:	COMIC IMAGES
ISSUE YEAR:	1992
CARD SET:	90 CARDS
SPECIAL CARDS:	6 PRISM CARDS
CARD SET ONLY	£9.00
SINGLE CARDS:	15p
SINGLE SPECIAL CARDS:	£10.00

SPIDERMAN

PRODUCER	FLEER/MARVEL CARDS
ISSUE YEAR:	1994
CARD SET:	150 CARDS
SPECIAL CARDS:	4 HOLOGRAM CARDS &
	12 ANIMATION CARDS
COMPLETE SET:	£80.00
CARD SET ONLY	£18.00
SINGLE CARDS:	15p
SINGLE HOLOGRAM CARDS:	£8.00
SINGLE ANIMATION CARDS:	£4.00

STARLOG COVERS COLLECTION

PRODUCER:	TOPPS
ISSUE YEAR:	1993
CARD SET:	100 CARDS
SPECIAL CARDS:	4 + 1 HOLO?
COMPLETE SET	£25.00
SINGLE CARDS:	15p

STAR TREK

PRODUCER:	TOPPS U.S.
ISSUE YEAR:	1976
CARD SET:	88 CARDS
COMPLETE SET:	£150.00
SPECIAL CARDS:	22 STICKERS
SINGLE CARD:	£2.00
SINGLE SPECIAL CARDS:	£3.50

STAR TREK

PRODUCER:	TOPPS U.S.
ISSUE YEAR:	1979
CARD SET:	88 CARDS
COMPLETE SET:	£35.00
SPECIAL CARDS:	22 STICKERS
SINGLE CARDS:	50p
SINGLE SPECIAL CARDS:	£1.00

STAR TREK II

PRODUCER:	FTCC
ISSUE YEAR:	1983
CARD SET:	30 CARDS
SPECIAL CARDS:	No Special Cards
COMPLETE SET:	£40.00
SINGLE CARDS:	£1.50

Important Notes: scarce set inthe U.K.

STAR TREK III

PRODUCER:	FTCC
ISSUE YEAR:	1985
CARD SET:	80 CARDS
SPECIAL CARDS:	No Special Cards
COMPLETE SET:	£35.00
SINGLE CARDS:	50p

STAR TREK IV

PRODUVER:	FTCC
ISSUE YEAR:	1987
CARD SET:	60 CARDS
SPECIAL CARDS:	No Special Cards
COMPLETE SET:	£25.00
SINGLE CARDS:	40p

STAR TREK COLLECTORS TIN

PRODUCER:	IMPEL
ISSUE YEAR:	1992
CARD SET:	312 CARDS
SPECIAL CARDS:	4 HOLOGRAMS
COMPLETE FACTORY SET:	£75.00

Important Notes: Released in limited quanities, with no British retailer being allowed to order more than two tins.

STAR TREK - DEEP SPACE NINE

PRODUCER:	SKYBOX
ISSUE YEAR:	1994
CARD SET:	100 CARDS
SPECIAL CARDS:	5 SPECTRA CARDS
COMPLETE SET:	£15.00
SINGLE CARDS:	15p
SINGLE SPECIAL CARDS:	£6.00

STAR TREK GENERATIONS CINEMA CARDS

PRODUCER:	SKYBOX
ISSUE YEAR:	1995
CARD SET:	72 CARDS
SPECIAL CARDS:	3 SPECTRA (Captains)
	3 FOIL (Villains)
COMPLETE SET:	£15.00
SINGLE CARDS:	15p

SINGLE SPECIAL CARDS:	£7.50

Important Notes: there was a SkyMotion card available to US collectors through a wrapper offer. Rare in the U.K. and valued at approximately £50.00

STAR TREK - MASTERWORKS

PRODUCER:	SKYBOX
ISSUE YEAR:	1993
CARD SET:	90 CARDS
SPECIAL CARDS:	5 SPECTRA ETCH CARDS
CARD SET	£12.00
SINGLE CARDS:	15p
SINGLE SPECIAL CARDS:	£6.00

STAR TREK - MASTERWORKS II

PRODUCER:	SKYBOX
ISSUE YEAR:	1994
CARD SET:	90 CARDS
SPECIAL CARDS:	9 FOIL EMBOSSED (3 with
	artist signature)
COMPLETE SET:	£10.00
SINGLE CARDS:	15p
SINGLE SPECIAL CARDS:	£4.00

STAR TREK, 25TH ANNIVERSARY I

PRODUCER:	IMPEL
ISSUE YEAR:	1991
CARD SET:	160 CARDS
SPECIAL CARDS:	2 HOLOGRAM CARDS
COMPLETE SET:	£45.00
SINGLE CARDS:	10p
SINGLE SPECIAL CARDS:	£10.00

Important Notes: Large quantities of theses holograms have recently appeared on the market and the price has halved within the last year. The price has also depreciated due to Impel's release of the Collectors Tin. Note also that odd number cards feature Star Trek and even number cards feature Next Generation

STAR TREK, 25TH ANNIVERSARY II

PRODUCER:	IMPEL
ISSUE YEAR:	1991
CARD SET:	150 CARDS
SPECIAL CARDS:	2 HOLOGRAMS
COMPLETE SET:	£45.00
SINGLE CARDS:	10p
SINGLE SPECIAL CARDS:	£10.00

Important Notes: See Series One for important information on Star Trek 25th Anniversary holograms.

STAR TREK, THE NEXT GENERATION

PRODUCER:	IMPEL
ISSUE YEAR:	1992
CARD SET:	120 CARDS
	5 LANGUAGE CARDS
SPECIAL CARDS:	4 HOLOGRAMS
	1 "MAIL-IN" HOLO
COMPLETE SET:	£60.00
SINGLE CARDS:	10p,
LANGUAGE CARDS	£2.00
SINGLE SPECIAL CARDS:	£5.00
"MAIL-IN" HOLO	£20.00

Important Notes: The special "mail-in" hologram was only available to American collectors by post.

STAR TREK, THE NEXT GENERATION, BEHIND THE SCENES

PRODUCER:	SKYBOX
ISSUE YEAR:	1993
CARD SET:	39 CARDS
SPECIAL CARDS:	No special cards
COMPETE FACTORY SET:	£12.00

STAR TREK, THE NEXT GENERATION, THE MAKING OF

PRODUCER:	SKYBOX
ISSUE YEAR:	1994
CARD SET:	100 CARDS
COMPLETE SET:	£30.00
SINLE CARDS:	30p

Important Notes: the same set of 100 cards was available in a Gold Edition (set value approximately £50.00) and a Platinum Edition (set value approximately £70.00)

STAR TREK, THE NEXT GENERATION SEASON I

PRODUCER:	SKYBOX
ISSUE YEAR:	1994
CARD SET:	108 CARDS
COMPLETE SET:	£20.00
SPECIAL CARDS:	6 FOIL EMBOSSED/2 HOLOGRAMS
	(very scarce in the U.K.)
SINGLE CARDS:	15p
SINGLE SPECIAL CARDS:	£6.00 (Foil)
	£50.00 (Hologram)

Important Notes: this series is getting harder to obtain in the U.K.

STAR TREK, THE NEXT GENERATION SEASON II

PRODUCER:	SKYBOX
ISSUE YEAR:	1995
CARD SET:	96 CARDS
SPECIAL CARDS:	6 FOIL EMBOSSED/
	2 HOLOGRAMS
COMPLETE SET:	£10.00
SINGLE CARDS:	10-15p
SINGLE SPECIAL CARDS:	£6.00 (Foil),
	£50.00 (Hologram)

Important Notes: number on cards continues from #109–#204

STAR TREK, THE NEXT GENERATION SEASON III

PRODUCER:	SKYBOX
ISSUE YEAR:	1995
CARD SET:	106 CARDS
SPECIAL CARDS:	6 FOIL EMBOSSED/
	2 HOLOGRAMS
COMPLETE SET:	£10.00
SINGLE CARDS:	10p
SINGLE SPECIAL CARDS:	£6.00 (Foil),
	£50.00 (Hologram)

Important Notes: numbering on cards continues #205–#310. Note also that each of the above three sets contains a Survey Card which varies greatly in price in the U.K. but in fact is scarcer thatn the embossed cards

STAR TREK VOYAGER

PRODUCER:	SKYBOX
ISSUE YEAR:	1995
CARD SET:	101 CARDS
SPECIAL CARDS:	9 SPECTRA CARDS
COMPLETE SET:	£15.00
SINGLE CARDS:	15p
SINGLE SPECIAL CARDS:	£4.00

STAR TREK VOYAGER SERIES 2

PRODUCER:	FLEER/SKYBOX
ISSUE YEAR:	1995
CARD SET W/TATTOO:	90 CARDS
SPECIAL CARDS:	
6 RECEIPE CARDS	£15.00
9 SPECTRA FOIL CARD SET	£40.00
SKYMOTION: CAPT. JANEWAY	£35.00
SUPERSIZE SKYMOTION JANEMOTION	
	£30.00
COLLECTORS' ALBUM	£10.00
COMPLETE SET:	£7.00
SINGLE CARDS:	10p

STAR WARS GALAXY

PRODUCER:	SKYBOX
ISSUE YEAR:	1993
CARD SET:	140 CARDS
SPECIAL CARDS:	6 FOIL CARDS
CARD SET	£18.00
SINGLE CARDS:	10p-15p
SINGLE SPECIAL CARDS	£8.00

STAR WARS GALAXY II

PRODUCER:	TOPPS U.S.
ISSUE YEAR:	1994
CARD SET:	135 CARDS
SPECIAL CARDS:	6 FOIL ETCHED CARDS
COMPLETE SET:	£15.00
SINGLE CARDS:	15p
SINGLE SPECIAL CARDS:	£6.00
FACTORY SET:	£50.00

Important Notes: the factory set consists of 135 foil-stamped cards, 6 foil-etched cards, 3-D hologram, WideVision and Preview cards

STAR WARS WIDEVISION

PRODUCER:	TOPPS U.S.
ISSUE YEAR:	1995
CARD SET:	120 CARDS
SPECIAL CARDS:	10 CHASE CARDS
COMPLETE SET:	£15.00
SINGLE CARDS:	15p
SINGLE SPECIAL CARDS:	£7.00

STARS OF BOLLYWOOD (ASIAN CINEMA)

PRODUCER:	MERLIN PUBLISHING LTD
ISSUE YEAR:	1993
CARD SET:	144
COMPLETE SET:	£20.00
SINGLE CARDS:	5p

STREET FIGHTER

PRODUCER:	UPPER DECK
ISSUE YEAR:	1995
CARD SET:	90 CARDS
SPECIAL CARDS:	10 FX CARDS
COMPLETE SET:	£10.00
SINGLE CARDS:	10p
SINGLE SPECIAL CARDS:	£5.00

STREET FIGHTER II

PRODUCER:	TOPPS U.S.
ISSUE YEAR:	1993
CARD SET:	88 CARDS
SPECIAL CARDS:	11 STICKERS/4 HOLOFOIL CARDS
COMPLETE SET:	£8.00
SINGLE CARDS:	10p
SINGLE SPECIAL CARDS:	£1.00 (Stickers)
	£4.00 (Holofoil)

SUPERGIRL MOVIE

PRODUCER:	TOPPS
ISSUE YEAR:	1985
CARD SET:	44 STICKERS
SPECIAL CARDS:	No special cards
COMPLETE SET:	£3.00
SINGLE CARDS:	15p

SUPERMAN: THE MOVIE

PRODUCER:	TOPPS U.S.
ISSUE YEAR:	1978
CARD SET:	77 CARDS
SPECIAL CARDS:	6 REGULAR STICKERS/6 FOIL STICKERS
COMPLETE SET:	£10.00
SINGLE CARDS:	15p
SINGLE SPECIAL CARDS:	50p (regular)
	£2.00 (foil)

SUPERMAN II MOVIE

PRODUCER:	TOPPS U.S.
ISSUE YEAR:	1981
CARD SET:	88 CARDS
SPECIAL CARDS:	22 STICKERS
COMPLETE SET:	£12.00
SINGLE CARDS:	15p
SINGLE SPECIAL CARDS:	25p

SUPERMAN III MOVIE

PRODUCER:	TOPPS U.S.
ISSUE YEAR:	1983
CARD SET:	99 CARDS
SPECIAL CARDS:	22 STICKERS
COMPLETE SET:	£9.00
SINGLE CARDS:	15p
SINGLE SPECIAL CARDS:	20p

SUPERMAN: DOOMSDAY

PRODUCER:	SKYBOX
ISSUE YEAR:	1992
CARD SET:	100 CARDS
CARD SET ONLY:	£18.00
SPECIAL CARDS:	4 SPECTRA CARDS/2 FOIL CARDS
COMPLETE SET:	£100.00
SINGLE CARDS:	15p
SINGLE SPECIAL CARDS:	£15.00
FOIL CARDS:	£12.50

SUPERMAN: THE MAN OF STEEL COLLECTORS EDITION

PRODUCER:	SKYBOX
ISSUE YEAR:	1994
CARD SET:	90 CARDS
SPECIAL CARDS:	6 SPECTRA-ETCHED CARDS
COMPLETE SET:	£10.00
SINGLE CARDS:	10p
SINGLE SPECIAL CARDS:	£4.00

SUPERMAN: THE MAN OF STEEL PREMIUM EDITION

PRODUCER:	SKYBOX
ISSUE YEAR:	1994
CARD SET:	90 CARDS
SPECIAL CARDS:	4 SILVER/4 GOLD
COMPLETE SET:	£25.00
SINGLE CARDS:	25p
SINGLE SPECIAL CARDS:	£20.00 (Silver)
	£35.00 (Gold)

SUPER MARIO BROS.

PRODUCER:	SKYBOX
ISSUE YEAR:	1993
CARD SET:	100 CARDS
SPECIAL CARDS:	3 HOLOGRAMS
CARD SET	£10.00
SINGLE CARDS:	10p
SINGLE SPECIAL CARDS	£10.00

TANK GIRL

PRODUCER:	COMIC IMAGES
ISSUE YEAR:	1995
CARD SET:	90 CARDS
SPECIAL CARDS:	6 MAGNACHROME CARDS
COMPLETE SET:	£9.00
SINGLE CARDS:	10p
SINGLE SPECIAL CARDS:	£4.00

TEENAGE MUTANT NINJA TURTLES TV 1

PRODUCER:	TOPPS
ISSUE YEAR:	1989
CARD SET:	88 CARDS
SPECIAL CARDS:	11 STICKERS
COMPLETE SET:	£12.00
SINGLE CARDS:	15p
SINGLE SPECIAL CARDS:	25p

TEENAGE MUTANT NINJA TURTLES TV II

PRODUCER:	TOPPS U.S.
ISSUE YEAR:	1989
CARD SET:	88 CARDS
SPECIAL CARDS:	11 STICKERS
COMPLETE SET:	£10.00
SINGLE CARDS:	10p
SINGLE SPECIAL CARDS:	20p

TEENAGE MUTANT NINJA TURTLES MOVIE I

PRODUCER:	TOPPS U.S.
ISSUE YEAR:	1990
CARD SET:	132 CARDS
SPECIAL CARDS:	11 STICKERS
COMPLETE SET:	£12.00
SINGLE CARDS:	10p
SINGLE SPECIAL CARDS:	25p

TEENAGE MUTANT NINJA TURTLES SECRET OF THE OOZE, MOVIE 2

PRODUCER:	TOPPS U.S.
ISSUE YEAR:	1990
CARD SET:	99 CARDS
SPECIAL CARDS:	11 STICKERS
COMPLETE SET:	£12.00
SINGLE CARDS:	10p
SINGLE SPECIAL CARDS:	25p

TEK WORLD

PRODUCER:	CARDZ
ISSUE YEAR:	1994
CARD SET:	100 CARDS
SPECIAL CARDS:	4 TEKCHROME CARDS
COMPLETE SET:	£15.00
SINGLE CARDS:	15p
SINGLE SPECIAL CARDS:	£6.00

TERMINATOR 2

PRODUCER:	IMPEL
ISSUE YEAR:	1991
CARD SET:	140 CARDS
SPECIAL CARDS:	No special cards
COMPLETE SET:	£15.00
SINGLE CARDS:	10p - 20p

Important Notes: See also Impel factory set and Topps set.

TERMINATOR 2 - FACTORY SET

PRODUCER:	IMPEL
ISSUE YEAR:	1992
CARD SET:	141 CARDS
SPECIAL CARDS:	1 HOLOGRAM CARD
COMPLETE SET:	£30.00

Important Notes: Sold only as a complete set. Look for sets missing the hologram.

T2 (TERMINATOR 2)

PRODUCER:	TOPPS
ISSUE YEAR:	1991
CARD SET:	44 ALL STICKER SET
SPECIAL CARDS:	No special cards
COMPLETE SET:	£4.00
SINGLE CARDS:	10p

THE MAXX

PRODUCER:	TOPPS U.S.
ISSUE YEAR:	1994
CARD SET:	100 CARDS
SPECIAL CARDS:	7 FOIL ACRDS:
COMPLETE SET:	£10.00
SINGLE CARDS:	10p
SINGLE SPECIAL CARDS:	£4.00

THUNDERBIRDS ARE GO

PRODUCER:	PRO SET U.K.
ISSUE YEAR:	1992
CARD SET:	100 CARD SET
SPECIAL CARDS:	No special cards
COMPLETE SET:	£12.00
SINGLE CARDS:	10p

TIM HILDERBRANDT'S FLIGHTS OF FANTASY

PRODUCER:	COMIC IMAGES
ISSUE YEAR:	1994
CARD SET:	90 CARDS
SPECIAL CARDS:	6 CHASE CARDS
COMPLETE SET	£7.00
SINGLE CARDS:	15p
SINGLE SPECIAL CARDS:	£4.00

TOM & JERRY

PRODUCER:	CARDZ
ISSUE YEAR:	1994
CARD SET:	60 CARDS
SPECIAL CARDS:	3 HOLOGRAMS
COMPLETE SET	£6.00
SINGLE CARDS:	10p
SINGLE SPECIAL CARDS:	£5.00

TOON WORLD

PRODUCER:	UPPER DECK
ISSUE YEAR:	1993
CARD SET:	90 CARDS
SPECIAL CARDS:	5 HOLOGRAMS AND 5 INSERT CARDS
COMPLETE SET	£13.00
CARD SET ONLY	£ 5.00
SINGLE CARDS:	5p-10p

TOY STORY

PRODUCER:	FLEER/SKYBOX
ISSUE YEAR:	1995
CARD SET:	90 CARDS
SPECIAL CARDS:	
2 3-D LENTICULAR CARD SET	£20.00
9 FOIL EMBOSSED CARD SET	£40.00
COMPLETE SET	£10.00
SINGLE CARDS:	15p

TOTAL RECALL - FACTORY SET

PRODUCER:	PACIFIC
ISSUE YEAR:	1990
CARD SET:	110 CARDS
SPECIAL CARDS:	VARIOUS NOVELTY ITEMS
COMPLETE SET:	£15.00

TOXIC CRUSADERS - RARE TEST ISSUE

PRODUCER:	TOPPS
ISSUE YEAR:	1992
CARD SET:	88 CARDS
SPECIAL CARDS:	8 HOLOGRAMS
COMPLETE SET	£12.50
SINGLE CARDS:	15p
SINGLE SPECIAL CARDS:	£2.50

TOXIC HIGH SCHOOL

PRODUCER:	TOPPS
ISSUE YEAR:	1992
CARD SET:	88 STICKERS
SPECIAL CARDS:	No special cards
COMPLETE SET:	£4.00
SINGLE CARDS:	5p

TRANSFORMERS

PRODUCER:	HASBRO
ISSUE YEAR:	1985
CARD SET:	192 CARDS
SPECIAL CARDS:	24 STICKERS
COMPLETE SET:	£30.00
SINGLE CARDS:	15p
SINGLE SPECIAL CARDS:	25p

TRON MOVIE

PRODUCER:	DONRUSS
ISSUE YEAR:	1982
CARD SET:	66 CARDS
SPECIAL CARDS:	8 STICKERS
COMPLETE SET:	£10.00
SINGLE CARDS:	20p
SINGLE SPECIAL CARDS:	50p

UJENA - SWIMWEAR ILLUSTRATED GIRLS

PRODUCER:	COMIC IMAGES
ISSUE YEAR:	1993
CARD SET:	90 CARDS
SPECIAL CARDS:	6 CHASE CARDS
COMPLETE SET:	£8.50
SINGLE CARDS:	10p
SINGLE SPECIAL CARDS:	£5.00

UJENA II

PRODUCER:	COMIC IMAGES
ISSUE YEAR:	1994
CARD SET:	90 CARDS
SPECIAL CARDS:	6 EMBOSSED CHASE CARDS
COMPLETE SET:	£9.00
SINGLE CARDS:	10p
SINGLE SPECIAL CARDS:	£4.00

ULTRA X-MEN

PRODUCER:	FLEER ULTRA
ISSUE YEAR:	1994
CARD SET:	150 CARDS
SPECIAL CARDS:	
6 FATAL ATTRACTIONS CARD SET	£25.00
6 GREATEST BATTLES CARD SET	£25.00
9 PORTRAITS CARD SET	£22.50
6 RED-FOIL BONUS CARD SET	£22.50
6 SILVER X-OVERS	£40.00
5 ULTRAPRINTS	£8.00
COMPLETE SET:	£20.00
SINGLE CARDS:	15p

ULTRA X-MEN SERIES 2

PRODUCER:	FLEER ULTRA
ISSUE YEAR:	1994
CARD SET:	150 CARDS
SPECIAL CARDS:	
10 SINISTER OBSERVATIONS	
CHROMIUM CARD SET	£45.00
9 HUNTERS AND STALKERS CARD SET	
	£15.00
10 SUSPENDED ANIMATION CARD SET	
	£20.00
COMPLETE SET:	£12.00
SINGLE CARDS:	10p

ULTRAVERSE I

PRODUCER:	SKYBOX
ISSUE YEAR:	1993
CARD SET:	100 CARDS
SPECIAL CARDS:	9 ROOKIE/4 ULTIMATE
	ROOKIE CARDS
COMPLETE SET:	£10.00
SINGLE CARDS:	10p
SINGLE SPECIAL CARDS:	£1.50 (Rookie)
	£2.50 (Ultimate)

ULTRAVERSE 2

PRODUCER:	SKYBOX
ISSUE YEAR:	1994
CARD SET:	90 CARDS
SPECIAL CARDS:	9 BONUS CARDS
COMPLETE SET:	£40.00
CARD SET ONLY	£10.00
SINGLE CARDS:	10p
SINGLE SPECIAL CARDS	£5.00

ULTRAVERSE MASTER SERIES

PRODUCER:	SKYBOX
ISSUE YEAR:	1994
CARD SET:	90 CARDS
SPECIAL CARDS:	8 FOIL CARDS
COMPLETE SET:	£15.00
SINGLE CARDS:	15p
SINGLE SPECIAL CARDS:	£5.00

UNCANNY X MEN COVERS I

PRODUCER:	COMIC IMAGES
ISSUE YEAR:	1990
CARD SET:	90 CARD SET
SPECIAL CARDS:	No special cards
COMPLETE SET:	£12.00
SINGLE CARDS:	15p

UNCANNY X MEN COVERS II

PRODUCER:	COMIC IMAGES
ISSUE YEAR:	1991
CARD SET:	45 CARDS
SPECIAL CARDS:	No special cards
COMPLETE SET:	£9.00
SINGLE CARDS:	15p

UNITY

PRODUCER:	COMIC IMAGES
ISSUE YEAR:	1992
CARD SET:	90 CARDS
SPECIAL CARDS:	6 CHROMIUM CARDS
COMPLETE SET:	£40.00
CARD SET ONLY	£7.50
SINGLE CARDS:	15p
SINGLE SPECIAL CARDS:	£6.00

Important Notes: Promo Chromium Card £7.50

UNIVERSAL MONSTERS

PRODUCER:	TOPPS U.S.
ISSUE YEAR:	1994
CARD SET:	100 CARDS
SPECIAL CARDS:	10 MONSTERCHROME/
	4 HORRORGLOW
COMPLETE SET:	£15.00
SINGLE CARDS:	15p
SINGLE SPECIAL CARDS:	£5.00 (Monsterchrome)
	£15.00 (Horrorglow)

VAMPIRELLA

PRODUCER:	TOPPS U.S.
ISSUE YEAR:	1995
CARD SET:	90 CARDS (Red Foil)
SPECIAL CARDS:	6 HORRORGLOW CARDS
COMPLETE SET:	£15.00
SINGLE CARDS:	15p
SINGLE SPECIAL CARDS:	£6.00

Important Notes: a Gold Foil set of the 100 cards was available and is valued at approximately £75.00

VERTIGO, DC

PRODUCER:	SKYBOX
ISSUE YEAR:	1994
CARD SET:	90 CARDS
SPECIAL CARDS:	6 FOIL ENHANCED CARDS
COMPLETE SET:	£15.00
SINGLE CARDS:	15p
SINGLE SPECIAL CARDS:	£10.00

WAYNE BARLOWE, THE ALIEN WORLD OF

PRODUCER:	COMIC IMAGES
ISSUE YEAR:	1994
CARD SET:	90 CARDS
SPECIAL CARDS:	6 PRISM CARDS
COMPLETE SET:	£8.00
SINGLE CARDS:	10p
SINGLE SPECIAL CARDS:	£4.00

WCW WRESTLING - YELLOW BORDER

PRODUCER:	IMPEL
ISSUE YEAR:	1991
CARD SET:	160 CARDS
SPECIAL CARDS:	No special cards
COMPLETE SET:	£6.00
SINGLE CARDS:	10p

WCW WRESTLING - BLACK BORDER

PRODUCER:	IMPEL
ISSUE YEAR:	1991
CARD SET:	110 CARDS
SPECIAL CARDS:	No special cards
COMPLETE SET:	£9.00
SINGLE CARDS:	15p

WILDC.A.T.S

PRODUCER:	TOPPS U.S.
ISSUE YEAR:	1993
CARD SET:	100 CARDS
CARD SET:	6 PRISM CARDS
CARD SET:	£12.50
SINGLE CARDS:	15p
SINGLE SPECIAL CARDS	£15.00

WILDC.A.T.S. ANIMATED

PRODUCER:	WILDSTORM
ISSUE YEAR:	1995
CARD SET:	135 CARDS
SPECIAL CARDS:	9 ANIMATION CEL
	9 FOIL ETCHED CARDS
COMPLETE SET:	£17.00
SINGLE CARDS:	15p
SINGLE SPECIAL CARDS:	£3.00

WILDC.A.T.S. CHROMIUM

PRODUCER:	IMAGE
ISSUE YEAR:	1994
CARD SET:	96 CARDS
SPECIAL CARDS:	
5 CHROME CAP SET	£30.00
6 DOUBLE-SIDED CARD SET	£20.00
12 PAINTED CARD SET	£50.00
COMPLETE SET:	£14.00
SINGLE CARDS:	15p

WILDSTORM

PRODUCER:	WILDSTORM
ISSUE YEAR:	1994
CARD SET:	100 (Chromium) CARDS
SPECIAL CARDS:	9 HOLOCHROME CARDS
COMPLETE SET:	£30.00
SINGLE CARDS:	30p
SINGLE SPECIAL CARDS:	£6.00

WILDSTORM ARCHIVES

PRODUCER:	WILDSTORM
ISSUE YEAR:	1995
CARD SET:	99 (Chromium) CARDS
SPECIAL CARDS:	11 GEN 13 HOLO-FOIL CARDS
COMPLETE SET:	£20.00
SINGLE CARDS:	20p
SINGLE SPECIAL CARDS:	£5.00

WILDSTORM GALLERY

PRODUCER:	WILDSTORM
ISSUE YEAR:	1995
CARD SET:	126 CARDS
SPECIAL CARDS:	12 FAMOUS BATTLE/
	6 WILDSTORM CHARACTER
	CARDS
COMPLETE SET:	£20.00
SINGLE CARDS:	15p
SINGLE SPECIAL CARDS:	£2.00 (Battles)
	£5.00 (Characters)

WILLIAM STOUT

PRODUCER:	COMIC IMAGES
ISSUE YEAR:	1993
CARD SET:	90 CARDS
CARD SET:	£8.00
SINGLE CARDS:	10p

Vampirella Gallery #31

WildC.A.T.S. (Jim Lee's) #38

Jim Lee's X-Men Series 1 #94

WILLIAM STOUT II

PRODUCER:	COMIC IMAGES
ISSUE YEAR:	1994
CARD SET:	90 CARDS
SPECIAL CARDS:	6 CHROME CHASE CARDS
COMPLETE SET:	£7.50
SINGLE CARDS:	10p
SINGLE SPECIAL CARDS:	£6.00

WIZARD, THE GUIDE TO COMICS PROMOTIONAL GIVEAWAY CARDS

PRODUCER:	WIZARD
ISSUE YEAR:	1992
CARD SET:	ON-GOING SERIES

CARD NO/DESCRIPTION	VALUE
#0] Youngblood (Prism border) Issued Wizard #11	£3.50
#1] Spawn (Prism border) Issued Wizard #12	£3.50
#1] gold*	£15.00
#2] Shadowhawk (Prism border) Issued Wizard #13	£3.50
#2] gold*	£15.00
#3] Savage Dragon (Prism border) Issued Wizard #14	£3.50
#3] gold*	£15.00
#4] Savage Dragon, Youngblood, Cyberforce, WildC.A.T.S. (Prism border) Issued Wizard #15	£3.50
#4] gold*	£15.00
#5] Spawn, Wetworks, Shadowhawk (Prism border) Issued Wizard #16	£3.50
#5] gold*	£15.00
#6] Cyberforce (Prism border) Issued Wizard #17	£3.50
#6] gold*	£15.00
#7] Jim Lee's WildC.A.T.S. (Prism border) Issued Wizard #18	£3.50
#7] gold*	£15.00
#8] Wetworks (Prism border) Issued Wizard #19	£3.50
The Spirit by Will Eisner], Issued with 100 Most Collectible Comics]	£2.00

* sealed in plastic cases

WOLVERINE: FROM THEN 'TIL NOW I

PRODUCER:	COMIC IMAGES
ISSUE YEAR:	1988
CARD SET:	45 CARDS
SPECIAL CARDS:	No special cards
COMPLETE SET:	£12.00
SINGLE CARDS:	25p

Important Notes: card #50 is scarcer than the rest and sells for about £2.00

WOLVERINE: FROM THEN 'TIL NOW II

PRODUCER:	COMIC IMAGES
ISSUE YEAR:	1992
CARD SET:	90 CARDS
SPECIAL CARDS:	6 PRISM CARDS
COMPLETE SET:	£40.00
SINGLE CARDS:	10p
SINGLE SPECIAL CARDS:	£7.00

WWF BLACK SERIES - ENGLISH

PRODUCER:	MERLIN PUBLISHING LTD
ISSUE YEAR:	1992
CARD SET:	150
COMPLETE SET:	£20.00
SINGLE CARDS:	15p

Important Notes: The English language version of this series was only distributed in blister packs of 25 cards each through a limited number of retailers - WH Smith, John Menzies, Woolworth, Toys 'r Us.

WWF BLACK SERIES - GERMAN

PRODUCER:	MERLIN PUBLISHING LTD
ISSUE YEAR:	1992
CARD SET:	150
COMPLETE SET:	£25.00
SINGLE CARDS:	20p

WWF BLACK SERIES - ITALIAN

PRODUCER:	MERLIN PUBLISHING LTD
ISSUE YEAR:	1992
CARD SET:	150
COMPLETE SET:	£25.00
SINGLE CARDS:	20p

WWF "BRET HART" SERIES

PRODUCER:	MERLIN PUBLISHING LTD
ISSUE YEAR:	1993
CARD SET:	92
COMPLETE SET:	£30.00
SINGLE CARDS:	20p

Important Notes: German language only

WWF CLASSIC SERIES

PRODUCER:	MERLIN PUBLISHING LTD
ISSUE YEAR:	1991
CARD SET:	150
COMPLETE SET:	£20.00
SINGLE CARDS:	15p

Important Notes: First ever European WWF series. Produced as a co-edition from material originated by Classic cards in USA.

WWF GOLD SERIES PARTS 1 & 2

PRODUCER:	MERLIN PUBLISHING LTD
ISSUE YEAR:	1992
CARD SET:	96 + 96
COMPLETE SET:	£30.00
SINGLE CARDS:	20p

Important Notes: The series was split into two parts to allow part publication prior to SummerSlam '92, a live event which filled Wembley Stadium with 85,000 fans. Part 2 contained some photographs of action from SummerSlam.

WWF WRESTLEMANIA III

PRODUCER:	TOPPS U.S.
ISSUE YEAR:	1987
CARD SET:	75 CARDS
SPECIAL CARDS:	22 STICKERS
COMPLETE SET:	£7.00
SINGLE CARDS:	10p
SINGLE SPECIAL CARDS:	15p

X-CUTIONERS SONG

PRODUCER:	MARVEL/IMPEL
ISSUE YEAR:	1992
CARD SET:	12 CARDS
SPECIAL CARDS:	No special cards
COMPLETE SET:	£8.00
SINGLE CARDS:	50p

All cards issued free with the following comic books:

Card 1]	X MEN #294	XAVIER
Card 2]	X FACTOR #84	CALIBAN
Card 3]	X MEN #14	APOCALYPSE
Card 4]	X FORCE #16	CABLE
Card 5]	X MEN #295	WOLVERINE/BISHOP
Card 6]	X FACTOR #85	HAVOK/POLARIS
Card 7]	X MEN #15	MUTANT LIBERATION
Card 8]	X FORCE #17	MR SINISTER
Card 9]	X MEN 296	JEAN GREY/CYCLOPS
Card 10]	X FACTOR #86	MOONBOY
Card 11]	X MEN #16	ARCHANGEL
Card 12]	X FORCE #18	STRYFE/CABLE

X-FILES

PRODUCER:	TOPPS
ISSUE YEAR:	1995
CARD SET:	72 CARDS
SPECIAL CARDS:	
4 TOPPS FINEST CARD SET	£25.00
6 COMIC COVER CARD SET	£24.00
DELUXE BINDER W/INSERT CARD	£9.00
COMPLETE SET:	£8.00
SINGLE CARDS:	15p

X FORCE

PRODUCER:	COMIC IMAGES
ISSUE YEAR:	1991
CARD SET:	90 CARDS
SPECIAL CARDS:	No special cards
COMPLETE SET:	£8.00
SINGLE CARDS:	10p

X FORCE MINI SET

PRODUCER:	MARVEL/COMIC IMAGES
ISSUE YEAR:	1991
CARD SET:	5 CARDS
SPECIAL CARDS:	No special cards
COMPLETE SET:	£3.00
SINGLE CARDS:	50p / Cable card £1.00

Important Notes: These cards were issued within copies of X Force comic #1 1st printing.

X MEN - JIM LEE

PRODUCER:	COMIC IMAGES
ISSUE YEAR:	1991
CARD SET:	90 CARDS
COMPLETE SET:	£8.00
SINGLE CARDS:	10p

X MEN - JIM LEE

PRODUCER:	IMPEL
ISSUE YEAR:	1992
CARD SET:	100 CARDS
SPECIAL CARDS:	5 HOLOGRAMS
COMPLETE SET:	£30.00
CARD SET ONLY:	£12.50
SINGLE CARDS:	15p-35p
SINGLE SPECIAL CARDS:	H1, H2-£5.00
	H3, H4-£4.00

X-MEN '95

PRODUCER:	FLEER ULTRA
CARD SET:	150 CARDS
SPECIAL CARDS:	9 POWERBLAST/10 CHROMIUM
COMPLETE SET:	£17.50
SINGLE CARDS:	15p
SINGLE SPECIAL CARDS:	£2.00 (Powerblast)
	£5.00 (Chromium)

X MEN, PREMIERE SERIES

PRODUCER:	FLEER ULTRA
ISSUE YEAR:	1994
CARD SET:	150 CARDS
SPECIAL CARDS:	6 FATAL ATTRACTIONS CARDS AND 9 PORTRAITS CARDS
COMPLETE SET:	£90.00
CARD SET ONLY:	£20.00
SINGLE CARDS:	10p-30p
SINGLE FATAL CARDS:	£6.00
SINGLE PORTRAITS CARDS:	£4.00

X MEN II

PRODUCER:	SKYBOX
ISSUE YEAR:	1993
CARD SET:	100 CARDS
SPECIAL CARDS:	3 COLOUR HOLOGRAMS 9 FOIL STAMPED CARDS AND 1 H-X 3D WOLVERINE HOLOGRAM
COMPLETE SET:	£80.00
CARD SET ONLY:	£12.00
SINGLE CARDS:	10p-20p
COLOUR HOLOGRAMS:	£8.00
FOIL STAMPED CARDS:	£2.00
WOLVERINE H-X HOLOGRAM:	£30.00
TIN SET:	£40.00

X MEN ULTRA PRINTS

PRODUCER:	FLEER
ISSUE YEAR:	1994
CARD SET:	5 PRINTS
SPECIAL CARDS:	SEE ABOVE
COMPLETE SET:	£10.00
SINGLE CARDS:	N/A

Important Notes: One set of X Men Ultra prints were included free in each full case of Fleer Card boxes.

YO! RAPS - MTV

PRODUCER:	PRO SET U.S.
ISSUE YEAR:	1992
CARD SET:	150 CARDS
SPECIAL CARDS:	No special cards
COMPLETE SET:	£7.00
SINGLE CARDS:	10p

YOUNGBLOOD

PRODUCER:	COMIC IMAGES
ISSUE YEAR:	1992
CARD SET:	90 CARDS
SPECIAL CARDS:	6 PRISM CARDS
COMPLETE SET:	£30.00
CARD SET ONLY:	£5.00
SINGLE CARDS:	10p
SINGLE SPECIAL CARDS:	£5.00

Important Notes: Image's first set of trading cards were produced on rather poor quality card and were simply pictures taken straight out of it's comic book appearances. Prism cards are quite impressive.

YOUNGBLOOD

PRODUCER:	SKYBOX
ISSUE YEAR:	1995
CARD SET:	90 CARDS
SPECIAL CARDS:	9 STICKERS
COMPLETE SET:	£10.00
SINGLE CARDS:	10p
SINGLE SPECIAL CARDS:	£1.00

YOUNG INDIANA JONES CHRONICLES

PRODUCER:	PRO-SET
ISSUE YEAR:	1992
CARD SET:	114 CARDS
COMPLETE SET:	£15.00
SINGLE CARDS:	10p

Important Notes: the set breakdown is as follows: 95 TV Cards, 8 Hidden Treasure Crads, 10 3-D Cards and 1 Viewer Card.

BUBBLE GUM CARDS

(with grateful thanks to Ron Hall of First Choice Trading Cards for the extended information
First Choice Trading Cards 11 Keith Avenue Liverpool L4 5FL Tel (0831) 765 811).

INTRODUCTION

Bubble Gum cards are usually manufactured in 2 sizes 88mm x 63mm and 80mm x 55mm. The most prolific company in the 1960's was American and British Chewing Gum Ltd (A & BC GUM), owned by Topps Gum Inc., USA. Broadly speaking, US equivalent sets copyrighted Topps have a higher value. Other gum card companies included: Anglo Chewing Gum Ltd, Bubbles Inc. Chewing Gum (a subsidiary of A & BC Gum), Donruss (USA), Monty Gum (a Dutch company mainly active in the 1970's) and Somportex Ltd UK.

Sweet cigarette cards are normally, as tobacco cards, manufactured to the regimental size of 35mm x 65mm. An example of an exception to this rule is (Fireball) XL5 by Como. Companies that have issued popular sets include Barratt & Co. Ltd, Cadet Sweets, Como Confectionery Products Ltd and Primrose Confectionery Co. Ltd. A point to mention is that in this politically correct age, "Sweet Cigarettes" is now not allowed to be used as product terminology. On the occasions a product appears now, they are called "Candy Sticks".

Some sets, in particular A & BC Gum cards, vary in "finishing" ie. matt or shiny fronts. In normal circumstances this is of no consequence to collectors as differences are slight. However some sets do have obvious differences to their backs with strong distinction on colour. This is more important so colour matching sets are the order of the day!

Most card sets were/are manufactured in 2 separate sheets. Uncut sheets can command high prices although they are generally not in great demand. Cards that have been cut off-centre eg. wide border at the top of the card and picture pushed to the bottom edge of the card can detract from the price. Any card that has the picture incomplete with an adjacent card illustration showing is of very low value (note the difference to printing errors on comic books which can have a much higher value sometimes).

A first and foremost…you read it here! Also included here is a Price Guide to individual wrappers and packets that the cards were sold in. Bubble gum cards were usually sold in "wax packs" (an average of 6-8 in a packet) and a pack could be opened without damaging the wrapper. However, Somportex for example did issue most card sets in paper wrappers that were sealed at the edges so the packet had to be torn to remove that cards. A mint wrapper would therefore have to be an unopened pack! This would command a price 2-4 times that stated.

Sweet cigarette packets contained 1 card. Today's packets have the card printed on the box itself - no comment!

A few sets had an album exclusively produced. Prices stated for these is for Mint and Unused. The value of an exclusive album with the card set stuck down can vary widely depending on desirability of the set, the neatness of the sticking and personal choice. Cards that have been adhered to anything else or show clear signs of having once been, are of low value. It should be noted that card dealers usually charge double for Mint end numbers eg. Champions #1 and #45 at £4.00 each. This is because a large number of cards collected would be kept in number order with the end numbers being handled constantly and usually the cards were held together with an elastic band thus putting a strain on the edges.

Finally, the years stated are, where available, copyright dated on the card or packaging. Values for cards and sets are for those graded in EXCELLENT condition or NEAR MINT condition, that is, cards without any creases, dents, marks or rounded corners, nearly perfect in every way.

While some sets (Stingray (Cadet Sweets) or UFO (Barratt)) turn up in MINT condition fairly regularly, most of the sets listed below (and particularly the older ones) can command more than the listed price should they be found in genuine MINT condition.

ADDAMS FAMILY

PRODUCER:	DONRUSS
ISSUE YEAR:	1964
CARD SET:	66
COMPLETE SET:	£250.00
SINGLE CARDS:	£3.50
WRAPPER:	£35.00

Important Notes: With the success of the Addams Family movies, this rare set is now sought after. Issued in USA only. Fronts are black and white photos and backs are photo composites.

BATMAN (Pink Back, Fan Club Panel)

PRODUCER:	A & BC GUM
ISSUE YEAR:	1966
CARD SET:	55
COMPLETE SET:	£80.00
SINGLE CARDS:	£1.50
WRAPPER:	£25.00

BATMAN (Pink Back, no Fan Club Panel)

PRODUCER:	A & BC GUM
ISSUE YEAR:	1966
CARD SET:	55
COMPLETE SET:	£55.00
SINGLE CARDS:	£1.00
WRAPPER:	£25.00

BATMAN A SET

PRODUCER:	A & BC GUM
ISSUE YEAR:	1966
CARD SET:	44
COMPLETE SET:	£55.00
SINGLE CARDS:	£1.25
WRAPPER:	£25.00

Important Notes: the letter A appears after the number on the back which, like the B set, makes up a larger jigsaw picture of Batman, Robin and other characters.

BATMAN B SET

PRODUCER:	A & BC GUM
ISSUE YEAR:	1966
CARD SET:	44
COMPLETE SET:	£110.00
SINGLE CARDS:	£2.50
WRAPPER:	£25.00

Important Notes: This B set is much scarcer than the A set. Backs also make up a larger picture composite.

BATMAN (Black Back)

PRODUCER:	A & BC GUM
ISSUE YEAR:	1966
CARD SET:	38
COMPLETE SET:	£75.00
SINGLE CARDS:	£2.00

Important Notes: A secret decoder was included in each packet, used to decipher the Riddlers Riddles on the back. These are very rare and can fetch £10-£12 each for an excellent condition example. The fronts show colour photos from the 1966 feature film.

BATMAN (Black Back, Dutch)

PRODUCER:	A & BC GUM
ISSUE YEAR:	1966
CARD SET:	38
COMPLETE SET:	£115.00
SINGLE CARDS:	£3.00

Important Notes: As with the above, the cards featured scenes from the feature film. Backs of cards different to UK issue (different Riddler drawing, no Decoder message).

BATMAN (Number on front)

PRODUCER:	A & BC GUM
ISSUE YEAR:	1966
CARD SET:	55
COMPLETE SET:	£110.00
SINGLE CARDS:	£2.00
WRAPPER:	£30.00

Important Notes: These cards show scenes from the Batman TV series and the Batman 1966 movie including the famous rubber shark and anti-Bat shark repellent! Backs comprise of separate picture composites. The printing on this set often shows colour imperfections. Note also a BATMAN ALBUM which could house any of the above Batman sets, valued at about £40.00 in Near Mint unused condition.

BATTLE

PRODUCER:	A & BC GUM
ISSUE YEAR:	1966
CARD SET:	73
COMPLETE SET:	£75.00
SINGLE CARDS:	£1.00
WRAPPER:	£20.00

Important Notes: As with the Civil War News set, these were particularly violent and occasionally brutal cards and are highly collectible. This set had a check card which listed all the numbers of the set and they are often filled in or ticked off. Unmarked check cards are very scarce and would add £10 to the value of the set. There are two variations of the check cardas #32, 39, 42 and 44 were eventually withdrawn owing to excessive torture and violence. There are 2 variations of backs, the common being dark brown borders, the scarcer being light brown. Backs contain Headline Reports.

Note also:
MILITARY EMBLEMS. Set of 24 stickers (card size), one available in each packet.
COMPLETE SET: £60.00

BATTLE OF BRITAIN

PRODUCER:	A & BC GUM
ISSUE YEAR:	1969
CARD SET:	66
COMPLETE SET:	£82.50
SINGLE CARDS:	£1.25
WRAPPER:	£20.00

Important Notes: fronts show colour photos from the 1969 film. Backs contain Daily Mirror newspaper reports from 1940.

BEATLES (Black & white)

PRODUCER:	A & BC GUM
ISSUE YEAR:	1964
CARD SET:	60
COMPLETE SET:	£150.00
SINGLE CARDS:	£2.50
WRAPPER:	£35.00

Important Notes: black and white photos with individual signatures. Although this set was produced in large quantities, mint sets are not common.

BEATLES (2nd Series)

PRODUCER:	A & BC GUM
ISSUE YEAR:	1965
CARD SET:	45
COMPLETE SET:	£225.00
SINGLE CARDS:	£5.00
WRAPPER:	£45.00

Important Notes: This set carried on the numbering from the 1st Series as card numbers 61-105.

BEATLES (Colour)

PRODUCER:	A & BC GUM
ISSUE YEAR:	1965
CARD SET:	40
COMPLETE SET:	£200.00
SINGLE CARDS:	£5.00
WRAPPER:	£45.00

Important Notes: new series of colour photographs. Odds are not to be confused with the Top Pop Stars set of 50 from 1964 which includes 1-22 of The Beatles which state "in a series of 50 photos".

BEATLES (Yellow Submarine)

PRODUCER:	ANGLO CONFECTIONERY LTD
ISSUE YEAR:	1968
CARD SET:	66
COMPLETE SET:	£420.00
SINGLE CARDS:	£6.25
WRAPPER:	£60.00

Important Notes: Picture back composite. A very rare and collectible cult set, particularly as it was unissued in the USA.

BEATLES (Yellow Submarine)

PRODUCER:	PRIMROSE CONFECTIONERY LTD
ISSUE YEAR:	1968
CARDS SET:	50
COMPLETE SET:	£115.00
SINGLE CARDS:	£2.25
PACKET:	£35.00

Important Notes: sweet cigarettes set. Variation on the above gum card set, backs of cards containing a storyline.

CAPTAIN SCARLET & THE MYSTERONS

PRODUCER:	ANGLO CONFECTIONERY LTD
ISSUE YEAR:	1967
CARD SET:	66
COMPLETE SET:	£115.00
SINGLE CARDS:	£1.75
WRAPPER:	£20.00

Important Notes: This set is becoming more and more collectible with the current screening of the TV series. The cards are a mixture of scenes from the series and line drawings. The backs of the cards made up a giant collage picture of all the characters and machines. This composite picture could be obtained as a poster made of card via mail order. It is very rare and valued at £70.00.

CAPTAIN SCARLET

PRODUCER:	BARRATT & CO. LTD
ISSUE YEAR:	1967
CARD SET:	50
COMPLETE SET:	£55.00
SINGLE CARDS:	£1.10
PACKET:	£15.00

Important Notes: a sweet cigarette set which is rising rapidly in price.

CAPTAIN SCARLET

PRODUCER:	EDWARD SHARP & SONS
ISSUE YEAR:	1970
CARD SET:	20
COMPLETE SET:	£75.00
SINGLE CARDS:	£3.75

Important Notes: Re-issue of the character photos taken from the Barratt set. Also include 5 vehicle cards which are drawings which are not so sharp unlike the producer! 3 sides of the card are serrated as these were given out separately from the toffee. Although a scarce set, it is for completists only.

CHAMPIONS

PRODUCER:	A & BC GUM
ISSUE YEAR:	1969
CARD SET:	45
COMPLETE SET:	£90.00
SINGLE CARDS:	£2.00
WRAPPER:	£25.00

Important Notes: These cards show colour photos from the TV series. The female star Alexander Bastedo adds to the desirability of this set. As with the Batman Black Backs, each pack had a secret decoder in order to answer the general knowledge questions on the back. Slightly different, these are harder to find and in top shape can fetch £20 or add £20 to the value of the set.

CIVIL WAR NEWS

PRODUCER:	A & BC GUM
ISSUE YEAR:	1965
CARD SET:	88
COMPLETE SET:	£110.00
SINGLE CARDS:	£1.25
WRAPPER:	£20.00

Important Notes: As these cards were particularly gory, they were banned in some parts of the UK.
The backs contain headline reports from 1861 –1865. One of 15 Civil War Bank notes were also available in certain packets and these fetch £3.00 each. The denominations were as follows: 2 x $1.00, 2 x $2.00, 2 x $5.00, 2 x $10.00, 2 x $20.00, 2 x $50.00, 1 x $100.00, 1 x $500.00 and 1 x $1,000.00.

CLIFF RICHARD

PRODUCER:	LEAF SALES CONFECTIONERY LTD
ISSUE YEAR:	1960
CARD SET:	£50.00
COMPLETE SET:	£115.00
SINGLE CARDS:	£2.25
PACKET:	No price available

Important Notes: Black and white photos. Company and copyright not stated on the cards.

COMIC BOOK FOLDEES

PRODUCER:	A & BC GUM
ISSUE YEAR:	1968
CARD SET:	43
COMPLETE SET:	£65.00
SINGLE CARDS:	£1.50
WRAPPER:	£25.00

Important Notes: Originally produced as a 44 issue set, one featuring the Queen was banned but it occasionally turns up. This one fetches up to £20. They were not cards as such but two comedy pictures and one DC Super-hero and each outer picture folded in half with the third to form weird and wonderful combinations. Near Mint condition would mean that they would have to be unfolded and completely flat. Also, the original display box tends to turn up with reasonable frequency, some think after a quantity warehouse find.

COMBAT

PRODUCER:	SELMUR
ISSUE YEAR:	1963
CARD SET:	66
COMPLETE SET:	£100.00
SINGLE CARDS:	£1.50
WRAPPER:	£20.00

Important Notes: Black and white photos from TV series. Issued in the USA only. A 2nd series in the same year was also produced.

DANGER MAN, JOHN DRAKE

PRODUCER:	SOMPORTEX LTD
ISSUE YEAR:	1966
CARD SET:	72
COMPLETE SET:	£180.00
SINGLE CARDS:	£2.50
WRAPPER:	£20.00

Important Notes: A very scarce set with scenes from the TV series starring Patrick McGoohan. Black and white.

DOCTOR WHO ADVENTURE

PRODUCER:	T. WALL & SON
ISSUE YEAR:	1966
CARD SET:	36
COMPLETE SET:	£65.00
SINGLE CARDS:	£1.75
WRAPPER (Ice lolly):	£65.00
ALBUM:	£75.00

Important Notes: Colour art. This set was being produced at the time of Patrick Troughton taking over from William Hartnell in the TV series. The drawings of Hartnell on the front were changed at the last minute but the backs with Hartnell headers are unchanged!

DOCTOR WHO AND THE DALEKS

PRODUCER:	CADET SWEETS
ISSUE YEAR:	1965
CARD SET:	50
COMPLETE SET:	£125.00
SINGLE CARDS:	£2.50
PACKET:	£45.00

Important Notes: Although this set does not depict William Hartnell but rather a non-descript grey-haired character, the superb artwork which is compatible with the subject makes this set very desirable so expect a steady increase.

DOCTOR WHO AND THE DALEKS

PRODUCER:	GOODIES LTD
ISSUE YEAR:	1968
CARD SET:	50
COMPLETE SET:	£200.00
SINGLE CARDS:	£4.00
PACKET:	No price available.

Important Notes: Much scarcer re-issue set of the Cadet Sweets series.

DOCTOR WHO

PRODUCER:	WEETABIX
ISSUE YEAR:	1977
CARD SET:	24
COMPLETE SET	£48.00
SINGLE CARDS:	£1.50
SOURCE:	issued inside the cereal packets

Important Notes: Double-sided: colour photographs/art.

DOCTOR WHO, THE AMAZING WORLD OF

PRODUCER:	TYPHOO TEA
ISSUE UEAR:	1976
CARD SET:	12
COMPLETE SET:	24
SINGLE CARDS:	£2.00

Important Notes: Colour photo portraits of Doctor Who and assorted villains. The cards were hexagonal! Reprint imitations have been known.

ELVIS PRESLEY

PRODUCER:	A & BC GUM
ISSUE YEAR:	1959
CARD SET:	66
COMPLETE SET:	£630.00
SINGLE CARDS:	£9.50
WRAPPER:	£100.00

Important Notes: Hand coloured photographs.

FIREBALL XL5

PRODUCER:	COMO CONFECTIONERY PRODUCTS LTD
ISSUE YEAR:	1964
CARD SET:	26
COMPLETE SET:	£260.00
SINGLE CARDS:	£10.00
PACKET:	£35.00

Important Notes: Square cards measuring 65mm x 65mm. The cards were titled simply "XL5" while the packets were fully titled "Fireball XL5".

FIREBALL XL5

PRODUCER:	COMO CONFECTIONERY PRODUCTS LTD
ISSUE YEAR:	1965
CARDS SET:	26
COMPLETE SET:	£290.00
SINGLE CARDS:	£11.00
ALBUM:	£100.00

Important Notes: Very scarce, especially as a set. The numbering continued from the 1st series as #27-52. The format size is the same as the above. XL5 was not a big seller as the cards were issued after the initial screening of the TV series thus all the XL5 cards are very scarce. Note also: a smaller card of the above two series was issued in bags of "dolly mixture" type sweets. They are very scarce and single cards and sets would be valued at approximately 10%-15% more than the sweet cigarette prices.

GIRL FROM U.N.C.L.E., THE

PRODUCER:	A & BC GUM
ISSUE YEAR:	1967
CARD SET:	25
COMPLETE SET:	£50.00
SINGLE CARDS:	£2.00
WRAPPER:	£25.00

Important Notes: colour photos. Titled cards (un-numbered)

GREEN HORNET

PRODUCER:	DONRUSS
ISSUE YEAR:	1966
CARD SET:	44
COMPLETE SET:	£132.00
SINGLE CARDS:	£3.00
WRAPPER:	£45.00

Important Notes: Colour photos. Issued in USA only.

HIGH CHAPARRAL, THE

PRODUCER:	A & BC GUM
ISSUE YEAR:	1969
CARD SET:	36
COMPLETE SET:	£30.00
SINGLE CARDS:	85p
WRAPPER:	£15.00

Important Notes: Colour photos. Composite picture backs.

HUCK FINN

PRODUCER:	A & BC GUM
ISSUE YEAR:	1969
CARD SET:	55
COMPLETE SET:	£25.00
SINGLE CARDS:	45p
WRAPPER:	£15.00

Important Notes: Colour photos/art. 2 different copyrights stated: ILAMI 1968 and 1968 HANNA-BARBERA PRODUCTIONS INC.

JAMES BOND (Film Scene Series)

PRODUCER:	SOMPORTEX LTD
ISSUE YEAR:	1965
CARD SET:	60
COMPLETE SET:	£150.00
SINGLE CARDS:	£2.50
WRAPPER:	£25.00

Important Notes: Black and white photos depicting mainly scantily clad females!

JAMES BOND (Thunderball)

PRODUCER:	SOMPORTEX LTD
ISSUE YEAR:	1967
CARD SET:	72
COMPLETE SET:	£75.00
SINGLE CARDS:	£1.00
WRAPPER (Paper):	£25.00

Important Notes: These cards feature black & white scenes from the 4th Bond film Thunderball. There are five numbers that were issued with two different photos including numbers 15, 24 and 51. Number 24 was withdrawn as it depicted Bond about to punch a girl but it is not too difficult to obtain.

JAMES BOND, THE EXCITING WORLD OF

PRODUCER:	SOMPORTEX LTD
ISSUE YEAR:	1966
CARD SET:	50
COMPLETE SET:	£137.50
SINGLE CARDS:	£2.75
WRAPPER:	£35.00

Important Notes: Black and white photos.

BATMAN (Number on Front Series) #10

Captain Scarlet #64

James Bond (Thunderball) #14

JAMES BOND - YOU ONLY LIVE TWICE

PRODUCER:	SOMPORTEX LTD
ISSUE YEAR:	1969
SLIDE SET:	26
COMPLETE SET	£210.00
SLIDE STRIP:	£8.00
WRAPPER (Paper)	£18.00

Important Notes: Not cards but small colour film slides joined in strips of three individually numbered #1-72. Individual mounts were available by sending away a postal order for 1 shilling (5p) and Special Agent 007 Viewers by sending a postal order for 3 shillings and sixpence (17.5p). In order to mount and view the slides, the strips of three had to be cut. The price quoted is for un-cut strips.

JAMES BOND - THE NEW JAMES BOND 007: O.H.M.S.S.

PRODUCER:	ANGLO CONFECTIONERY LTD
ISSUE YEAR:	1969
CARD SET:	56
COMPLETE SET	£170.00
SINGLE CARDS:	£3.00
WRAPPER:	£30.00

Important Notes: Unlike previous the Somportex sets featuring Sean Connery, this series featutres George Lazenby (and Diana Rigg).

JOE 90

PRODUCER:	ANGLO CONFECTIONERY LTD
ISSUE YEAR:	1968
CARD SET:	66
COMPLETE SET	£115.00
SINGLE CARDS:	£1.75
WRAPPER:	£20.00

Important Notes: Colour photos/art. A scarce set that may rise in value as the TV series is now being repeated on cable/satellite. The composite picture on the backs of the cards like the Captain Scarlet set by Anglo could be purchased as a poster made of card and is similarly valued at £70.00.

JOE 90

PRODUCER:	PRIMROSE CONFECTIONERY LTD
ISSUE YEAR:	1968
CARD SET:	50
COMPLETE SET	£45.00
SINGLE CARDS:	90p
PACKET:	£20.00

Important Notes: Sets produced on paper-thin card are much more common than the standard thickness cards. These inferior sets were probably produced after the initial release.

KUNG FU

PRODUCER:	A & BC GUM
ISSUE YEAR:	1974
CARD SET:	60.00
COMPLETE SET:	£33.00
SINGLE CARDS:	55p
WRAPPER:	£6.00

Important Notes: Colour photos of David Carradine series which may experience renewed interest with the updated new TV series in USA about to air in the U.K.. Nos. 1-44 have two different composite pictures: Picture A and Picture B. Other backs have the history of Kung Fu, references to the TV series and diagrams on the art of Kung Fu which state: "CAUTION: Do not use Caine's combat techniques without professional training".

LAND OF THE GIANTS

PRODUCER:	A & BC GUM
ISSUE YEAR:	1969
CARD SET:	55
COMPLETE SET:	£165.00
SINGLE CARDS:	£3.00
WRAPPER:	£25.00

Important Notes: A scarce set that has risen in value owing to the recent screening of the TV series on cable/satellite. The check card is often marked or ticked and an unmarked one is vakued more highly. The backs depict a small cartoon strip and a small composite picture.

LEGEND OF CUSTER, THE

PRODUCER:	A & BC GUM
ISSUE YEAR:	1965
CARD SET:	54
COMPLETE SET:	£40.00
SINGLE CARDS:	75p
WRAPPER:	£12.00

Important Notes: Colour photos from TV series. The first 22 backs have spaces for colour, drawn Indian Chief Stamps, one included in each pack. Set of 22 unused stamps: £60.00.

MAN FROM U.N.C.L.E., THE (see U.N.C.L.E.)

PRODUCER:	A & BC GUM
ISSUE YEAR:	1966
CARD SET:	55
COMPLETE SET:	£55.00
SINGLE CARDS:	£1.00
WRAPPER:	£20.00

Important Notes: This set features black & white scenes and publicity stills from the series, "signed" by Robert Vaughan and David McCallum on the front. Composite picture backs. These cards were produced on 2 different types of card: one was more yellowy, giving an "aged" look and one was white, giving a "fresher" look. The yellower cards would be valued as a set at about £40.00.

MARS ATTACKS

PRODUCER:	BUBBLES INC
ISSUE YEAR:	1965
CARD SET:	55
COMPLETE SET:	£825.00
SINGLE CARDS:	£15.00
WRAPPER:	£175.00
REPRINT SET	(copyright TOPPS): £30.00

Important Notes: A very rare set and infamous in the 1960s for being particularly gory and consequently banned. The check card is often filled in. An untouched one would make the complete set worth in the region of £850.00.

MONKEES, THE

PRODUCER:	A & BC GUM
ISSUE YEAR:	1967
CARD SET:	55
COMPLETE SET:	£50.00
SINGLE CARDS:	£.90
WRAPPER:	£20.00

Important Notes: A particularly cult set based on the TV series. There is a colour set with different photographs available though with no discernible difference in price. Both sets have composite picture backs.

MONKEES HIT SONGS, THE

PRODUCER:	A & BC GUM
ISSUE YEAR:	1967
CARD SET:	30
COMPLTETE SET:	£37.50
SINGLE CARDS:	£1.25
WRAPPER:	£25.00

Important Notes: Colour photographs.Each card back has the lyrics to a Monkees song. Also stated on the back, including #27-30, is "Collect all 26"!

MONKEES, THE (1st Series)

PRODUCER:	GOODIES LTD
ISSUE YEAR:	1967
CARD SET:	25
COMPLETE SET:	£19.00
SINGLE CARDS:	75p
PACKET:	£25.00

Important Notes: Black and white photos.

MONKEES, THE (2nd Series)

PRODUCER:	GOODIES LTD
IISUE YEAR:	1968
CARD SET:	25
COMPLETE SET:	£62.50
SINGLE CARDS:	£2.50
PACKET:	£25.00

Important Notes: A scarcer set of black and white photos.

MUNSTERS, THE

PRODUCER:	DONRUSS
ISSUE YEAR:	1964
CARD SET:	72
COMPLETE SET:	£215.00
SINGLE CARDS:	£3.00
WRAPPER:	£35.00

Important Notes: Corney captions below photographs from the TV series.

OUTER LIMITS, THE

PRODUCER:	A & BC GUM
ISSUE YEAR:	1966
CARD SET:	50
COMPLETE SET:	£125.00
SINGLE CARDS:	£2.50
WRAPPER:	£50.00

Important Notes: Based on the TV series, these feature weird and wonderful schlock horror monsters.

PARTRIDGE FAMILY, THE

PRODUCER:	A & BC GUM
ISSUE YEAR:	1971
CARD SET:	55
COMPLETE SET:	£22.00
SINGLE CARDS:	40p
WRAPPER:	£8.00

Important Notes: Colour photos with composite picture backs.

PLANET OF THE APES

PRODUCER:	A & BC GUM
ISSUE YEAR:	1968
CARD SET:	44
COMPLETE SET:	£82.50
SINGLE CARDS:	£1.50
WRAPPER:	£20.00

Important Notes: Colour photos from first film. Backs contain storyline.

PLANET OF THE APES

PRODUCER:	TOPPS
ISSUE YEAR:	1974
CARD SET:	66
COMPLETE SET:	£33.00
SINGLE CARDS:	50p
WRAPPER:	£8.00

Important Notes: Colour photos from TV series (recently shown on cable/satellite TV). Backs contain story and separate composite pictures.

ROBIN HOOD – A BOMBSHELL FOR THE SHERRIFF

PRODUCER:	MASTER VENDING CO.
ISSUE YEAR:	1959
CARD SET:	25
COMPLETE SET:	£22.50
SINGLE CARDS:	90p
WRAPPER:	£15.00

Important Notes: Colour art. 2 different backs: dark grey and beige.

ROLLING STONES

PRODUCER:	A & BC GUM
ISSUE YEAR:	1965
CARD SET:	40
COMPLETE SET:	£250.00
SINGLE CARDS:	£6.00
WRAPPER:	£45.00

Important Notes: Colour photos. Unissued in USA. Backs state: "..in a series of 40 photos". This therefore should not be confused with TOP POP STARS series of 40 as there are no Stones cards in that particular set.

QUICK DRAW McGRAW

PRODUCER:	PRIMROSE CONFECTIONERY LTD
ISSUE YEAR:	1965
CARD SET (Q1):	50
COMPLETE SET:	£15.00
SINGLE CARDS:	30p
PACKET:	£12.00
ALBUM:	£40.00

Important Notes: Based on Hanna Barbera cartoon.

THE SAINT

PRODUCER:	SOMPORTEX LTD
ISSUE YEAR:	1967
CARD SET:	72
COMPLETE SET:	£220.00
SINGLE CARDS:	£3.00
WRAPPER (Paper):	£25.00

Important Notes: One of the rarest 60s gum card sets. Black and white photos.

SEA HUNT, T.V's

PRODUCER:	BARRATT & CO. LTD
ISSUE YEAR:	1961
CARD SET:	35
COMPLETE SET:	£65.00
SINGLE CARDS:	£1.80
PACKET:	£12.00
ALBUM:	£20.00

Important Notes: Colour art of TV series.

SECRET SERVICE

PRODUCER:	BARRATT & CO. LTD
ISSSUE YEAR:	1970
CARD SET:	50
COMPLETE SET:	£45.00
SINGLE CARDS:	90p
PACKET:	£25.00

Important Notes: Colour photos from Gerry Anderson puppet/live action TV series. Rarely seen on television, a screening would do much to popularise this set.

SPACE 1999

PRODUCER:	BASSETT
ISSUE YEAR:	1975
CARD SET:	50
COMPLETE SET:	£30.00
SINGLE CARDS:	40p
CARD NO. 42:	£10.00
PACKET:	£12.00

Important Notes: Card No. 42 was given a low distribution owing to the fact that it displayed face disfigurement. It was eventually withdrawn. Set without #42: £25.00

SPACE 1999

PRODUCER:	LYONS MAID
ISSUE YEAR:	1975
CARD SET:	25
COMPLETE SET:	£37.50
SINGLE CARDS:	£1.50
WRAPPER (Ice lolly):	£20.00

Important Notes: Colour art.

SPACE 1999

PRODUCER:	DONRUSS
ISSUE YEAR:	1976
CARD SET:	66
COMPLETE SET:	£36.00
SINGLE CARDS:	55p
WRAPPER:	£4.00

Important Notes: Colour photos with picture composite backs.

SPACE ALPHA 1999

PRODUCER:	MONTY GUM (Dutch)
ISSUE YEAR:	1976
CARD SET:	64
COMPLETE SET:	£20.00
SINGLE CARDS:	30p
WRAPPER:	£8.00

Important Notes: Small gum cards with colour photos dominated by title.

SPACE COSMO 1999

PRODUCER:	MONTY GUM (Dutch)
ISSUE YEAR:	1976
CARD SET:	64
COMPLETE SET:	£20.00
SINGLE CARDS:	30p
WRAPPER:	£8.00

Important Notes: Same format as "Alpha" set.

SPACE 1999

PRODUCER:	SUNICREST (New Zealand)
ISSUE YEAR:	1974
CARD SET:	50
COMPLETE SET:	£87.50
SINGLE CARDS:	£1.75

Important Notes: Issued in Australia/New Zealand only from bread packets.

STAR TREK

PRODUCER:	A & BC GUM
ISSUE YEAR:	1969
CARD SET:	55
COMPLETE SET:	£330.00
SINGLE CARDS:	£6.00
WRAPPER:	£35.00

Important Notes: Scenes from the TV series make this a particularly popular set, especially with all the recent Star Trek sets to come out in the wake of the 30th Anniversary.

STAR TREK

PRODUCER:	LYONS MAID
ISSUE YEAR:	1979
CARD SET:	25
COMPLETE SET:	£65.00
SINGLE CARDS:	£2.50
WRAPPER (Ice lolly):	£15.00
CHART (folded):	£10.00

Important Notes: Colour photos from first Star Trek film.

STAR TREK

PRODUCER:	WEETABIX
ISSUE YEAR:	1979
CARD SET:	18
COMPLETE SET:	£36.00

Important Notes: Double-sided: colour photos from the first film with art. Came in the cereal packet. 3 x 6 cards to a strip. £12.00 per strip. Separated cards at 50p each.

STINGRAY

PRODUCER:	CADET SWEETS
ISSUE YEAR:	1964
CARD SET:	50
COMPLETE SET:	£30.00
SINGLE CARDS:	60p
PACKET:	£15.00
ALBUM:	£85.00

Important Notes: Colour art though many feel the drawings are only average.

SUPERCAR (1st Series)

PRODUCER:	COMO CONFECTIONERY PRODUCTS LTD
ISSUE YEAR:	1962
CARD SET:	25
COMPLETE SET:	£87.50
SINGLE CARDS:	£3.50
PACKET:	£40.00

Important Notes: Colour photos and art - some combined.

SUPERCAR (2nd Series)

PRODUCER:	COMO CONFECTIONERY PRODUCTS LTD
ISSUE YEAR:	1962
CARD SET:	25
COMPLETE SET:	£62.50
SINGLE CARDS:	£2.50

Important Notes: Colour art only, numbered 26-50.

SUPERMAN IN THE JUNGLE

PRODUCER:	A & BC GUM
ISSUE YEAR:	1968
CARD SET:	66
COMPLETE SET:	£82.50
SINGLE CARDS:	£1.25
WRAPPER:	£30.00

Important Notes: Selected packs contained jig-saw pieces. There were 16 in all and made up a picture of Superman wrestling with a lion. These pieces are very rare and fetch up to £3.00 each.

TARZAN

PRODUCER:	ANGLO CONFECTIONERY LTD
ISSUE YEAR:	1966
CARD SET:	66
COMPLETE SET:	£33.00
SINGLE CARDS:	£0.50
WRAPPER:	£20.00

Important Notes: Cards 15 & 16 are unusually scarce. Don't know why! The artwork is fairly primitive, based on the Ron Ely TV series. Backs make up a single composite picture of Tarzan and family.

THUNDERBIRDS (Black & white)

PRODUCER:	SOMPORTEX LTD
ISSUE YEAR:	1966
CARD SET:	72
COMPLETE SET:	£165.00
SINGLE CARDS:	£2.25
WRAPPER:	£20.00

Important Notes: Card size 88mm x 63mm. Black and white photos, composite picture backs. Although not scarce, this set rarely turns up in truly mint condition.

THUNDERBIRDS (Black and White)

PRODUCER:	SOMPORTEX LTD
ISSUE YEAR:	1966
CARD SET:	72
COMPLETE SET:	£180.00
SINGLE CARDS:	£2.50
WRAPPER:	£30.00

Important Notes: Same series as above but card size is 76mm x 57mm (varying) and photos are grainy (dot matrix).

THUNDERBIRDS (Colour)

PRODUCER:	SOMPORTEX LTD
ISSUE YEAR:	1967
CARD SET:	73 (strange number?!)
COMPLETE SET:	£200.00
SINGLE CARDS:	£2.75
WRAPPER:	£25.00

Important Notes: These cards were slightly smaller than the black & white set. They are sometimes assumed to have been trimmed when directly compared.

THUNDERBIRDS

PRODUCER:	BARRATT & CO. LTD
ISSUE YEAR:	1965
CARD SET:	50
COMPLETE SET:	£125.00
SINGLE CARDS:	£2.50
PACKET:	£20.00

Important Notes: Colour art.

THUNDERBIRDS

PRODUCER:	BARRATT & CO. LTD
ISSUE YEAR:	1966
CARD SET:	50
COMPLETE SET:	£45.00
SINGLE CARDS:	90p
PACKET:	£20.00
ALBUM:	£90.00

Important Notes: Colour photos. Although not as scarce, this set should increase more in line with the first series owing to popularity and the fact the set shows scenes from the TV series. Time will tell.

TOP POP STARS

PRODUCER:	A & BC GUM
ISSUE YEAR:	1964
CARD SET:	50
COMPLETE SET:	£125.00
SINGLE CARDS:	BEATLES: £2.75
OTHERS:	£2.25
WRAPPER:	£35.00

Important Notes: Colour photos. Most cards have colour print errors (out of sync.)

TOP POP STARS

PRODUCER:	A & BC GUM
ISSUE YEAR:	40
COMPLETE SET:	£100.00
SINGLE CARDS:	£2.50
WRAPPER:	£40.00

Important Notes: Colour photos. Different to the above. A scarce set.

TV WESTERNS

PRODUCER:	A & BC GUM
ISSUE YEAR:	1958
CARD SET:	56
COMPLETE SET:	£84.00
SINGLE CARDS:	£1.50
WRAPPER:	£45.00

Important Notes: Colour photos. Most have colour print imperfections. Stars featured include Robert Horton, Dale Robertson, John Payne (not Wayne!), Steve McQueen etc. The are two different backs: light grey and dark grey.

U.F.O.

PRODUCER:	ANGLO CONFECTIONERY LTD
ISSUE YEAR:	1970
CARD SET:	64
COMPLETE SET:	£50.00
SINGLE CARDS:	£0.75
WRAPPER:	£25.00

Important Notes: These cards are a mixture of scenes from the Gerry Anderson TV series and line drawings. The backs make up a large collage picture of U.F.O. characters and machines. As with Captain Scarlet and Joe 90, this picture could be purchased as a poster made of card via mail order offer. It is scarcer/more sought after and would be valued at £125.00.

U.F.O.

PRODUCER:	BARRATT & CO. LTD
ISSUE YEAR:	1970
CARD SET:	70
COMPLETE SET:	£45.00
SINGLE CARDS:	65p
PACKET:	£15.00

Important Notes: Colour photographs.

U.F.O.

PRODUCER:	BASSETT
ISSUE YEAR:	1975
CARD SET:	70
COMPLETE SET:	£14.00
SINGLE CARDS:	20p
PACKET:	£15.00

Important Notes: Re-issue of Barratt set. Not usually sold in odds as there are a quantity of mint sets in circulation.

U.N.C.L.E.

PRODUCER:	CADET SWEETS
ISSUE YEAR:	1966
CARD SET:	50
COMPLETE SET:	£50.00
SINGLE CARDS:	90p
PACKET:	£18.00

Important Notes: Colour photos. There is also a colour art set by the same company and same number of cards. Card Set: £112.50, Single Cards: £2.25.

VOYAGE TO THE BOTTOM OF THE SEA

PRODUCER:	DONRUSS
ISSUE YEAR:	1964
CARD SET:	66
COMPLETE SET:	£100.00
SINGLE CARDS:	£1.25
WRAPPER:	£25.00

Important Notes: Black and white photos with blue backs. There is a reprint set with black and white backs. The photos are of poor quality.

WAR BULLETIN

PRODUCER:	P.C.G.C.
ISSUE YEAR:	1965
CARD SET:	88
COMPLETE SET:	£110.00
SINGLE CARDS:	£1.25
WRAPPER:	£35.00

Important Notes: Black and white action photographs from World War 2. Backs contain war headlines.

YOGI BEAR, T.V's

PRODUCER:	BARRATT & CO. LTD
ISSUE YEAR:	1968
CARD SET:	35
COMPLETE SET:	£70.00
SINGLE CARDS:	£2.00
PACKET:	£15.00

Important Notes: Black/yellow/white drawings, including Huckleberry Hound.

ZORRO

PRODUCER:	TOPPS
ISSUE YEAR:	1958
CARD SET:	88
COMPLETE SET:	£220.00
SINGLE CARDS:	£2.50
WRAPPER:	£65.00

Important Notes: Issued in the USA. There is also a Canadian set with photos produced with different backs.

A & BC GUM UNIVERSAL ALBUMS:

Blue/Grey:	£6.00
Red/Orange:	£12.00

These can house up to 96 cards. The spaces have slots so adhesive is not used. There is also a Red/Grey version, housing 80 cards at £5.00.

BARRATT/GOODIES LTD UNIVERSAL ALBUMS

These can house up to 80 cards and would be valued in Near Mint at £5.00.

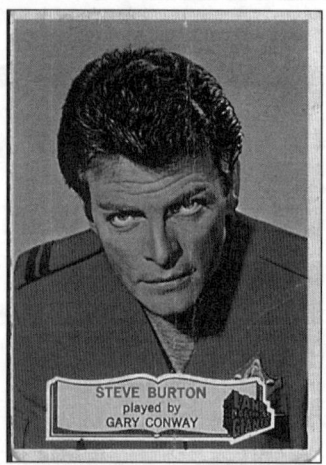

Land of the Giants #9

Kung Fu #51

Outer Limits #38

American Comics Guide

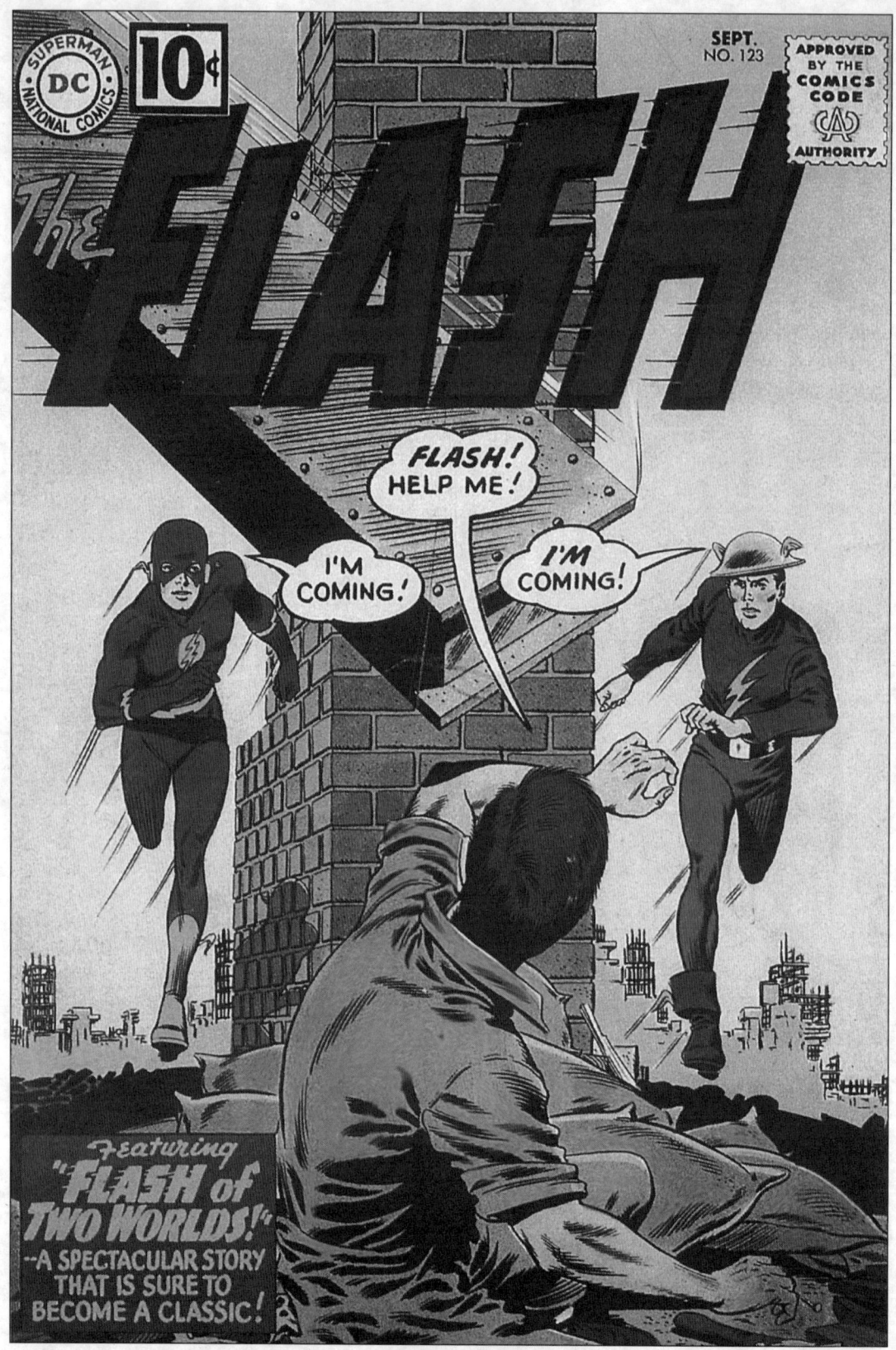

Flash #123 – The comic that introduced the concept of "Earth 2" to the DC Universe

An Introduction to
DC COMICS

DC **COMICS** have been published and distributed in America since February 1935 with **New Fun Comics #1**. For many years, the company was known as National Periodical Publications until it changed simply to D.C. at the beginning of 1977, the letters traditionally taken from the long running (since 1937) Batman title, Detective Comics. The Golden Age that saw the appearance of the main characters Superman in **Action Comics #1** in June 1938 and Batman in **Detective Comics #27**, May 1939, technically runs up to 1955 but the high point which saw the great plethora of costumed heroes ran from 1938 to 1942. What is known as the Silver Age runs from about January 1955 up to about 1965, in which a second age of costume heroes began more officially with an updated version of The Flash in **Showcase #4**, cover dated Sept/Oct 1956. There are many who cite the Martian Manhunter in **Detective #225**, November 1955, as the first significant costumed hero within the correct dates (some affectionately remember and would claim for Captain Comet from **Strange Adventures #9**, June 1951). In any event, many characters from the 1940s were updated and revamped by the then Editor, Julius Schwartz, like Hawkman, Atom and Green Lantern. D.C. Silver Age comics are in great demand in the current market, especially 10 cents cover-priced issues and especially in high grade.

In 1955, the Comics Code Authority was formed in response to Dr. Frederick Wertham's book "The Seduction of the Innocent" that decried the moral and sexual downslide of some comics that were available at the time; most notably the horror and mystery titles from E.C. (or Educational Comics) and its many, usually inferior, imitators. Although Code approval is not compulsory, most D.C. comics are still submitted for approval by the C.C.A. in order to ensure the widest distribution. Some comics have been submitted in the past but failed to gain Code acceptance; where applicable and of importance, this has been noted in the Guide. The introduction of the C.A.A. is another indication of the start of D.C.'s Silver Age.

Official distribution of D.C. comics in the U.K. began in very early 1960 with cover-dated issues November 1959, although there was some extremely limited distribution of romance and funny titles and the occasional super-hero title before this date. D.C. comics in the 1960s and 1970s were distributed through Thorpe and Porter who ink-stamped the front cover with their price. As they were not imported on a sale or return basis, any excess copies were further shipped abroad, resulting in an intrinsic scarcity of early 1960s D.C.s in this country. D.C.s (and especially Marvels) often came across on ships as ballast, so many issues have emerged as being water-damaged in some way; the varying degrees of damage greatly and proportionately devaluing a comic.

As they had remained unchanged since the late 1930s, D.C. tended to rest on its laurels in spite of producing some excellent super-heroes stories and science fiction art up to the late 1950s. When Marvel Comics appeared in November 1961, with **Fantastic Four #1**, their rapid success meant that for the first time in 25 years, D.C. could no longer rest on its laurels. They did seem, however, to be quite content with their position and in January 1962, did what seemed to be the unthinkable of putting the cover price up from 10 cents to 12, compounded by a letter of apology in their comics explaining rising paper costs. However, top D.C. titles continued to out-sell Marvel comics throughout the

1960s with Superman reaching sales of 800,000 and Batman at one point close to a million.

In May 1964, Batman and Detective Comics were revamped with a new look at art by Carmine Infantino and stories that did not pit the Caped Crusader against pink or green aliens. Batman reached new heights of popularity with the screening of the networked T.V. show in 1966 and another sign of the swinging Sixties was the appearance of the "Go Go Checks" at the top edge of the covers. This collectible quirk appeared from February 1966 to July 1967, but the story and art content of some D.C titles were at an all time low.

June 1969 saw another cover price rise to 15 cents and in January 1971, Superman had his first update in over thirty years. All Kryptonite was turned to harmless lead and Clark Kent became a T.V. news reporter and anchorman rather than the Daily Planet's ace newshound. Superman also lost about a third of his powers as it was felt that he was getting too omnipotent, but he gradually returned to normal without anybody noticing throughout the 1970s. In August 1971, the cover price went to 25 cents and the pages from 32 to 48. D.C. reprinted much classic 40s and 50s material in this expansion but it only lasted until June 1972 when comics reverted to normal page count but were up to 20 cents. "All New Stories Best in Comics", it said.

D.C. giants had always been popular since the first Superman Annual in 1960. Thereafter, annuals and 80 page giants featuring mainly reprints of the Superman and Batman family of stories, appeared with increasing frequency. As they were thicker comics, fewer were sent over to the U.K. in the regular packets, so they are generally scarcer. Very often the spines are crinkled owing to the way the glue dried, so perfectly flat and therefore near mint or mint copies are very rare. D.C. comics of the 1960s are generally of a higher quality than comparative Marvel comics in the paper stock they used, although it may be noticed that Marvel comics often retain the whiteness of their pages better and particularly their cover gloss owing to the composition of the papers used. Marvel comics from about 1964 onwards are in generally greater supply than D.C.s. Media coverage in America meant that dealers went around buying up vast stocks for a ready-made back issue market and it was also noticed that Marvel comic readers tended to save their comics more as stories and often referred back to previous incidents and characters, so there was more of an idea of a set of comics. Indeed, sets were more possible to collect as the numbers were not so astronomically high as D.C. titles seemed to be.

In 1973, a comic fan and dealer, Theo Holstein, paid $1,800 for a good copy of **Action Comics #1** and as news spread across America over the next year, the emergence of rare comics and the upward spiral of the sums they commanded began. The publication in 1970 of the Overstreet Comic Book Price Guide and its rapid acceptance as a monitor of market values contributed to public awareness of the potential value of comic books. The 1973 Overstreet mint price for **Action Comics #1** jumped from $1,000 to $2,800 in 1974. Such a percentage rise would be unthinkable today. D.C. reprinted a number of "Famous First Editions" facsimiles in an oversized format which further popularised the appeal of the top comics like **Action #1**, **Detective #27**, **Sensation #1**, **Whiz #2**, **Batman #1**, **Wonder Woman #1**, **All Star #3** and **Flash Comics #1**. In that same year, D.C.s went up to 25 cents and in August 1975, the unprecedented collaboration between Marvel and D.C. brought

M.G.M.'s Marvelous Wizard of Oz. There followed in 1976, the confrontation between Superman and Spiderman which was the same year that Jenette Kahn was appointed Publisher after having edited such magazines as "Smash" and "Dyna Mite". D.C. were, however, steadily declining in the face of the unstoppable, untoppable Marvel. Just as there had been a set-back to expansion in 1971, in 1978 came the "D.C. Implosion". Warner Brothers Communications who had taken over D.C. drastically cut back the number of monthly titles by 40% in an effort to halt declining sales. After only three months, the new 50 cents/44 pages format was cut back to 32 pages for 40 cents and most of the newer titles were cancelled. Among the casualties were All Star Comics, Black Lightning, Kamandi, Firestorm, Steel, the relaunched Showcase and The Witching Hour. New comics like The Vixen and The Deserter never saw print at all. The official reason was a revamped distribution process which sold larger quantities of proven sellers rather than risk and bombard the retailers with newer unknown titles. Marvel were at their strongest, still holding out on a 35 cent cover price and Spiderman being a runaway best-seller with the revamped X-Men not far behind.

In 1980/81, the advent of "Direct Sale" comics revolutionised the whole structure. Some comics were distributed only to specialist shops and the publishers who got their orders direct from the Direct Sale distributor were able to print a more exact number of the copies they needed with no unprofitable over-print runs. As more comic shops open, so the Direct Sale market expands. However, In 1981, increased paper costs and the fuel crisis forced the cover price of D.C. comics to 60 cents but in November of that year, D.C. followed the lead from the Independent comics group, Pacific, and offered royalty payments to artists and writers on the basis of sales (back dated to July). Marvel were soon to follow suit. D.C. underwent a steady period of growth with quality products like George Perez's New Teen Titans and Crisis on Infinite Earths which simplified and re-defined the D.C. Universe. They celebrated their 50th year in 1985 by introducing a "Superman for the 80s" in a six part mini-series called The Man of Steel, by the British-born John Byrne. Wonder Woman was similarly updated by George Perez.

In 1986 there occurred a piece of comics and publishing history with Frank Miller's apocryphal Batman tale, The Dark Knight Returns, which set new standards of excellence in story and art and introduced comics to a far wider range of people than ever before. It remained on the New York Times Best Seller list for 38 weeks. With Alan Moore's revitalised Swamp Thing, Howard Chaykin and Bill Seinkiewicz on The Shadow, and Alan Moore and Dave Gibbons on The Watchmen, D.C. went on to regain the lead of the comic market share from Marvel in early 1988 for the first time in more than 10 years but this was very much in terms of revenue earned rather than volume sold and it only lasted for a couple of months.

In 1987, D.C. announced a labelling policy which would display "For Mature Readers Only" on comics that were deemed to be unsuitable for universal readership. Many artists and writers felt this to be a judgement constraint akin to censorship and their disagreements became resignations, most notably Alan Moore and Frank Miller. While labelling still occurs, all other disagreements seem to have been ironed out.

The dating of comic books has long been the system of advance where the cover date is three months ahead of sale. This was thought to give a comic a longer shelf-life in comic shops and in newsagents. Towards the end of 1988, D.C. announced that they would suspend cover-dating for three months from October to December and either simply put "Winter", "Holiday" or nothing at all. Then in January 1989, the cover date would match the real date at which it was on sale. It was felt that this would be less confusing and more in keeping with other magazines available on the shelf, so that people would know it was "this month's".

1989 was also remarkable for the unprecedented media and cultural phenomenon surrounding the long-awaited release of the Batman movie starring Michael Keaton and Jack Nicholson. Shattering all previous box-office records the film has taken over $300 million worldwide to date. Although something of a backlash necessarily developed, this was almost entirely against the merchandising over-kill. The values of Batman and Batman-related comic books sky-rocketed. It seems that the Chinese menagerie has been added to with what has become "The Year of the Bat".

The end of the decade saw the continuation of quality products like Batman, The Cult, The Killing Joke and The Prisoner and other comics like Invasion, Black Orchid, Catwoman, Gotham by Gaslight, Hawkworld and the Arkham Asylum hardcover graphic novel. D.C.'s policy of revamped titles, high quality formats and mass-market trade paperbacks seemed designed less to wrest the existing market-share lead from Marvel Comics than to attract a larger market from outside the usual comics readership.

The Batman boom dissipated during 1990 as was seen by the luke-warm reception given to Batman: Digital Justice which boasted a new era of computer-generated graphics and a colour palette of over sixteen million combinations. Traditional comics are best it seems. Interest was kept alive by the new Robin, Tim Drake and his own mini-series and Batman celebrated his 600th appearance in **Detective Comics #627** featuring a painted cover by Norm Breyfogle based on the original back in 1939. Flash celebrated his fiftieth year in 1990 with a number of specials including a hardcover collection of "The Greatest Flash Stories Ever Told". Coupled with the success of the Flash TV series on CBS-Fox in America, **Showcase #4** featuring the first appearance of the Silver Age Flash consolidated its position as the most valuable Silver Age comic. Superman titles generally received a new injection of interest with Lois Lane finally getting her man after 52 years of courtship while Superman's arch foe, Lex Luthor, "died" in a plane crash, re-emerged as an Australian, died of kryptonite poisoning and has lately made a remarkable recovery!

For the start of 1991, comeback seemed to be the operative word with the return of the cult duo Angel and the Ape, the 1st super team in comics The Justice Society of America, the Challengers of the Unknown and a little-known Golden Age character called Kid Eternity given the Grant Morrison writing treatment though this and Bryan Talbot's The Nazz suffered from production delays which plagued D.C. even more towards the end of 1991. A follow up to the successful Green Lantern: Emerald Dawn mini-series epitomised D.C.'s attempts to launch a two-pronged attack of commercially successful projects and more specialised high-quality packages on the runaway success that Marvel Comics have enjoyed in recent times. However, D.C. slumped at one point in the latter half of 1991 to a market share of less than 20% while Marvel peaked at 68% largely through the marketing success of X-Men and other mutant titles. D.C.'s answer to all of this was another Robin mini-series in more permutations than one could imagine and the release of a line of comics based on old Archie Comics heroes like The Web, The Jaguar, The Fly and The Shield. It was greeted with cynicism from the retailers and little enthusiasm from the fans. The line was cancelled in 1992.

The last couple of years have seen mixed fortunes of the company off-set with the occasional flashes of

brilliance. Much hope was pinned on there being a repeat of the Batmania of 1989 with the release of the second film in 1991 but back-issue and current issue sales barely blipped. The absolute nadir for D.C. Comics came with the news in 1992 of their market share falling to an all-time low of 18%, in third place behind Marvel Comics and the new young upstart Valiant – new and forbidding territory for the giant publisher knocking 58 years old at the time.

The flashes of brilliance have been there more increasingly however. Some would say the most cynical of marketing ploys but others would argue one of the most successful for D.C. was the Death of Superman which recorded sales of 4 million for the issue of **Superman #75**. True to comic book fashion, he's back but it all showed that he was missed. More creatively, D.C. collected their horror and mystery titles under the generic banner of Vertigo with its own look and promotional push. Given that Swamp Thing, Hellblazer, Sandman, Shade and Animal Man feature some of the best in (British!) writing and drawing talent, it is a very strong base from which to launch spin-offs and one-shots which they have duly done.

D.C. had a good year in 1993 with the interest in Superman and Batman surprisingly catapulting these characters into some of the top-selling comics slots. In 1993/94 D.C. increasingly took the lead in innovative ideas with re-vamps for Superman and Batman followed by one for Green Lantern in issue #50 of his 2nd series. The 1994 mini-series Zero Hour tidied up many inconsistencies and loose ends much in the same way as Crisis on Infinite Earths did and has supposedly established one consistent timeline for the company. No doubt there will be another revision in ten year's time.

1995 saw the release of Batman Forever which critics hated but audiences loved. Judge Dredd did not fare so well at the box office and D.C. cancelled both their Judge Dredd titles. And fans everywhere mourned the horrific accident that befell Superman actor Christopher Reeve that left him paralysed from the neck down. An ironic mirroring of the Death of Clark Kent storyline that ran for a while throughout the Superman titles. At the end of the year, **D.C. Vs. Marvel #1** appeared, pitting selected heroes from one company against another in fights that fans could vote on the outcome. Such inter-company co-operation was extended by a series of Amalgam Comics featuring amalgamated D.C. and Marvel characters like Spider-Boy and Dr. Strange-Fate.

DC COMICS MARKET REPORT
This Market Report for D.C. comics examines the last twelve months or so of activity, looking particularly at value trends and reasons for increased or decreased collector interest. It is very generalized and regional variations should be taken into account. For titles and comics not mentioned, one may assume relatively stable values and collector interest not significantly differing from the last Guide.

ACTION COMICS
The listing starts from issue #1 to include those classic Golden Age comics and information. Though the market is small in the U.K. for these earlier comics owing to their generally being over the £500 mark, it is growing slowly as the fashion is often to possess at least one comic from Superman's hey-day of the 1930s and 1940s though probably in lower grade condition. Calculating values for these issues in the U.K. becomes virtually instinctive as copies of really early Action Comics are rarely offered for sale in the British market but if someone wanted to invest in them, they couldn't go far wrong with unrestored mid to high grades. It has been increasingly noticed at comic marts that lower grade copies of comics over 40 years old are popular sellers.

Reasonable increase on #242 again, increases on early Legion appearances (not around in high grade) and increases as ever on the 80pg giants (#334, #347 and

#360 in particular) and annuals which are generally snapped up as good reading value for those that like early '60s reprints. Action Comics Weekly continues to occupy the bargain bins and will probably do so forever more. While interest in the Death of Superman and Reign of the Supermen issues stabilized owing to the Trade paperback versions becoming available (and rattling good reads they are too), Superman as a character has surprised many dealers in the U.K. by sustaining sales in the last couple of years. One reason for this may be the "Lois & Clark" Superman TV series screened on a more prime time Saturday evening slot in the U.K. and also that there are now five Superman titles continuing to interweave their soap opera-like storylines very successfully.

ADVENTURE COMICS
The listing starts from #1 when it was known as New Comics to give more information on these rare Golden Age issues. In some cases they are so rare that existing copies in any condition worldwide can be counted in tens. While there is a very small (if any) market in the U.K. as yet for this material, in low grades it is quite possible to purchase some of these antediluvian comics, to see how it all began. Interesting to think that New Comics #1 was the first ever comic published by D.C. Could they have had any inkling what it would lead to? Other early Golden Age classics include the first Sandman in #40, the first Hourman in #48, the first Starman in #61 and some great Simon and Kirby Golden Age Sandman material from #72-91: crying out for reprinting (D.C. take note..).

The first appearance of the Legion in #247 saw a modest increase again but now that this issue is beyond the reach of most collectors in high grade (if you can find one!), the market interest for such a book in the U.K. necessarily shrinks. Time was it was the issue to get but it seems when this and other issues like it reach that £1,000+ barrier, the interest may still be there but sales are fewer and fewer.

The Legion issues from #300-380 are still in steady demand and a high grade run of these issues is becoming very difficult to put together. Many low grades have been reported sold as the stories are still a fun read. Issues #412, #414, #415, #420 and #421 have long ago been picked up by those who can't afford the original Animal appearances and they are a part of the general Silver Age Animal Man malaise so values are stagnant. The killers to find are those last Digest size issues – numbers #491 to #503. Drives completists wild. Others of interest are The Spectre issues #431-440, gaining in popularity on the back of the Spectre series by Tom Mandrake. They both evoke the "avenging spirit" of the character in the 1940s.

ALL AMERICAN COMICS/ALL FLASH/ALL STAR COMICS
The market in the U.K. for these Golden Age titles is quite small but issues can be picked up in average grades comparatively cheaply just to see what they are all about. For about forty pounds you could have a comic that is nearly 50 years old. All Star Comics have some great covers and lots of heroes for your money.

ALL STAR WESTERN
Worth mentioning for the first and early Jonah Hex stories. #10 is very hard to come by in any grade and is fast becoming something of a minor key issue.
1993 NM Price: £15.00
1994 NM Price: £30.00
1996 NM Price: £50.00

ANIMAL MAN
Animal Man underwent a period of revitalization under the Vertigo banner of titles with excellent scripting begun by Jamie Delano and experienced something of a comeback to fan popularity of yore. But now that the series has been cancelled, early issues (#1-10) are hardly

in demand though the excellent Trade paperback reprints these and is a great read with a fab Brian Bolland cover.

AQUAMAN
Back-issues sales of the 1960s issues are still slow in the U.K. market though the latest series (how many times have D.C. tried to launch this character?) has finally proved to be a winner with its "no more Mr. Nice Guy" approach. Still can't understand why the prices of the Silver Age material in America seem to be, if not ablaze, then at least very healthily warm, particularly on early issues. Every other Overstreet Fan Magazine has them coloured in red. Why? Love to know who's buying them over there. Aquaman #1 is still a reasonable key issue and tough to find in high grade. Issues #50-52 are sought after by Neal Adams completists even though the artwork is on the Deadman back-up strip. For the best in Aquaman entertainment, check out the back-up stories in early 1960s Adventure Comics. Octopi with boxing gloves, swordfish cutting through chains and Aquaman launching himself into the fray on a whale-spout. Great stuff.

ATOM
Still attractive as a set to complete for some collectors but like Aquaman not as popular here in the U.K. as he seems to be in America. General back issue buyers are just not interested in The Atom. Funny how it too goes up in value in one monthly Update magazine or other to the point of ridicule. Issue #1 is still a reasonable D.C. Silver Age first issue, particularly with the comic exceeding the 30 years old barrier. Issues #29 and #36 continue to be more highly valued in the States than in the U.K. but they are getting noticeably harder to find. The Atom & Hawkman issues of #39-45 are a little harder to find as print runs were lower. They also have some nice moody covers by Joe Kubert.

BATMAN
Although still regarded as D.C.s most popular character, Batman has never quite attained the dizzy heights it did in the summer of 1989 when the first movie opened in a blaze of publicity. In recent times, Batman has a mixed reception from fans in the U.K. The Knightfall issues of Batman and Detective seem to be in demand once more. The "breaking" of Batman issue #497 slackened in demand as the issue seems very common at marts and conventions in the U.K. now. Back issues are still raided from comic-shop bins, particularly any issues before #300. Even those in the 300s are in shorter supply than they were. Either way, 1996 should prove to be an interesting year for the Dark Knight Detective as he squares up against Captain America in the D.C. vs. Marvel series and a fourth Batman film with Poison Ivy and Mr. Freeze will be released.

The listing starts from #1 to give more information on some of these classic issues featuring some of the most classic Golden Age comics of all (perhaps a little bias comes into play here...) Low grade copies of these issues are excellent value for reading and enjoying the artwork of Bob Kane, Jerry Robinson, George Roussos, Dick Sprang and Charles Paris. As a general rule, this Guide has adopted a parity between the values of Golden Age Batman in the U.K. and the U.S. though in theory earlier issues of Batman, in common with virtually all Golden Age comics, are harder to get in the U.K. than in the U.S. Though they may be harder to obtain, the size of the market for them in the U.K. must be taken into account. #100 has taken another leap in value to become a serious back issue.

1993 NM Price: £690.00
1994 NM Price: £875.00
1996 NM Price: £1,100
It is very tough to find in high grade. #155 featuring the first Silver Age appearance of the Penguin has crept up only slightly.
1993 NM Price: £120.00

1994 NM Price: £140.00
1996 NM Price: £150.00
#171 featuring the first Silver Age Riddler took a leap in 1991 but has proved to be a fairly common book with many copies in lower grades appearing on Mart walls. Admittedly, the pink cover colour is prone to fading so very high grade copies are hard to come by. For this reason it still sky-rockets in the States. Historically however it is the 3rd ever appearance of this major Batman villain, made popular by Frank Gorshin on the Batman TV series. With Jim Carrey playing The Riddler in Batman Forever, much was done to popularise the character but prices only really rose in America on this comic so that the differential between values in the U.K. and U.S markets is increasing. The 80pg giants continue to be hard to find in high grade (#176 and #198 in particular) and with their reprints going back to the 1940s, they are excellent reading material. #200 is another very common issue in some areas of the U.K. It has always been much sought after in America as many collectors traditionally start their runs at anniversary numbers. #200 sports fine Neal Adams Batman and Robin figures set against a collage cover but the story and artwork (not by Adams) are less than breath-taking and values have stuck in the last year. #234 features the first modern appearance of Two Face as delineated by Neal Adams — amazing to think that such a major character never appeared right throughout the Silver Age. It is, however, an issue that turns up regularly on mart walls. #238 has become sought after as a giant issue with a dark cover that shows all the wear and tear. The 1st Doom Patrol reprint also helps. The 100 pagers from #254 to 261 continue to fly out of dealers boxes though #260 seems way higher in value on the American market. The run from #270 to #290 generally is as hard as ever to find.

Year One and Ten Nights of the Beast continue to drop in value and Death in the Family has dropped quite considerably in demand. There are still a lot of copies in circulation from this period of Batman and unless the fourth film catches fire, supplies should meet demand. Watch out for #181 with the first appearance of Poison Ivy.

One other footnote: Catwoman appearances will continue to be watched with interest as speculators wonder if the Catwoman film (if it's ever made!) will do anything like what it did for the Batman character.

BATMAN ANNUAL
Earlier issues elude in high grade. #1 in particular is becoming something of a major key issue, very hard to find in high grade with its darker cover. Lower grades always sell (Batman in various bizarre forms and roles — the Zebra Batman a particular favourite of mine). Try finding any of these issues in shop back-issue bins or on the walls..

BATMAN FAMILY
One of the more impossible sets to put together from recent times. Those that want one are continually frustrated. Keep looking. Values are steady in the U.K. market and still very reasonable on the U.S. market. The differential between the two is still quite high with "for-dollar-write-pound" prices.

BATMAN: LEGENDS OF THE DARK KNIGHT
One of D.C.'s continued best-sellers. The "Venom" story from #16-20 is a particular favourite making #16 and #17 tough to find in the U.K. The Destroyer story was well received at the time as it crossed into the Batman and Detective titles. The Prey and Gothic storylines from earlier issues continue to be sought after. "Mask" by Bryan Talbot was well received and sold well. #50 with its stunning Brian Bolland cover is still sought after. Other general issues, particularly the earlier issues, have fallen slightly in price from Guide #6.

BATMAN: SWORD OF AZRAEL
This mini-series continues to drop in value in the U.K. with prices almost double in the U.S. The stunning Joe Quesada artwork and covers are probably the only reason why this title does not slide more than it has. Production values on the current Azrael series continue to be high and its recent involvement in the Contagion storyline has brought in new readers.

BATMAN: THE DARK KNIGHT RETURNS
The mini-series that started it all for Batman in 1986. It has reached a point of stasis as a back-issue seller as The Cult did in 1991 (and that is now a relatively poor seller). It was thought at the time that these two series would continue to sky-rocket but only goes to show how dangerous it is to predict prices in the world of comics. Far better to reflect prices in a Guide. The value on #1 has fallen dramatically in the U.K. over the last couple of years. £30-£35 at one time, now about half that at £15. For those that have never read it or are hard-core Marvel-ites, this is one to pick up and read if only to love it or loathe it.

BATMAN VS. PREDATOR
A reasonable back-issue market has developed for this title but only really worth a mention for its marketing from D.C. and Dark Horse, the script by Dave Gibbons (who continues to grow in stature as a writer) and art by the Kuberts. The Prestige and Standard formats of each number smack a little of the Big Companies Game but nonetheless no harm done to the Batman character. One complaint however was the very dark reproduction in the Prestige Format issues, making it difficult to read.

BEST OF DC DIGEST
Worth mentioning as issues of these, let alone sets, just do not turn up. Or if they do they are not in any great shape as their Digest size makes them more difficult to store so they tend to get squeezed into book-shelves or get buried in dealers' boxes. Excellent reading value and some nice early Silver Age reprints. Not everyone's cup of tea owing to their smaller size but a title to watch. By the way, anyone got a #57?

BLACKHAWK
A title much more highly rated in the U.S. market than in the U.K. market. Early issues in high grade are very hard to find in the U.K. though the customer base for them is very small. Sixties issues in low grade sell quite well as do issues around #230. These issues with the Blackhawks as super-heroes have achieved something of a cult status for epitomising the era.

BRAVE AND THE BOLD
Another big increase for #28 as it assumes it's rightful place as one of the main D.C. key issues. This sells very well in poor and fair grades just for the sake of having one. #29 and #30 are deservedly recognised as minor key issues. #25 is as rare in the U.K. as it ever was and is impossible to find in any grade (has Brian Bolland still got his? Want it!). Issues before this occasionally appear on mart walls in the U.K. and in spite of great Kubert art, there is little interest in Robin Hood, Viking Prince or Silent Knight. It would take a blood and guts, slice 'em dice 'em mini-series featuring all three of these characters to stir the interest. One of the big movers again is #34, the first Silver Age Hawkman.
1993 NM Price: £510.00
1994 NM Price: £1,050.00
1996 NM Price: £1,200.00
It is very scarce in high grade and delights in a classic Kubert cover. The other Hawkman appearances in #35, #36, #42-44 have risen nicely in value. #54 continues to rise as it is proving hard to find though more research is being done on its scarcity in the U.K. Those other issues from #55 to #59 are also undervalued in many people's opinion. The Neal Adams issues from #79 to #86 have

picked up a little in interest. The 100pg issues from #112-117 are always missing from back-issue boxes which must tell you something though later issues from #150 onwards are in plentiful supply apart from #191 which annoys completists.

CHALLENGERS OF THE UNKNOWN
Back issues of this title have remained static. Shame. The Swamp Thing appearances in #82-87 again picked up as they are harder to find than ever. And the late reprint issues that ran the early Showcase appearances in all their glory are far cheaper than the originals and sport some nice Joe Kubert covers!

CRISIS ON INFINITE EARTHS
A check-list has been included for those after the cross-over issues. It still remains D.C.'s most successful mini-series. Amazing that there hasn't been a trade paperback version which would be of great benefit to those that missed it first time around. The Zero Hour mini-series of 1994 was not exactly regarded by many as "Crisis II" and it remains to see how long it will be before there is a "Crisis III".

DC COMICS SPECIAL
A much under-rated title that put together some nice classic collections for those who don't know a lot about where D.C. is coming from but would like to get a taste. Only 29 issues but it covers everything from super-hero to humour, horror to medieval. Reasonable parity of prices between the U.S. and U.K. markets. Notable exceptions are the last two issues which are scarce in the U.K.

DEMON
The Kirby series from the 1970s continues to be sought after with price increases in the U.K. market on the early issues. Great covers – a fab monster in issue #2 (check it out – Fin Fang Foom's cousin?). The 16 issues are difficult to put together as a run in a hurry. The Lobo cross-overs in the 2nd series are about the only thing worth mentioning, now cancelled.

DETECTIVE COMICS
The 2nd string Batman title has been extended back into the mists of time to #1 and includes of course the classic comics Detective #27-38 that would need a mortgage to buy. There is a small market for the very early issues of this title in the U.K. though copies sold are usually low grade. A small cachet of early issues was discovered in the U.K. about three years ago though some had missing pages. Still interesting is #168 with the first origin of The Joker though he had already been around for a dozen years or so but this issue has fallen back in value. Detective #225 saw a very healthy increase in value in the last year – it really is tough to find in high grade with its bright yellow cover and at one time it had been helped by some interest in the Martian Manhunter and his role in Justice League Task Force. That may change slightly with Justice League Task Force rumoured to be cancelled. #233 saw a smaller increase though it is thought to be much scarcer.

Issues around #235-239 are virtually never seen in the U.K. #327 is fast becoming a minor key issue at around £45 in the U.K. #387 is sought after for its cover and reprinting the first Batman appearance in Detective #27 (May 1939). It is regularly missing from collections bought in the U.K. The Marshall Rogers issues in the #470s picked up slightly with their classic renditions of Batman and particularly the Joker. The new Robin appearances in #524, #525 and #535 remain static. #599 and #600 fell slightly again as there seem to be a lot of copies hoarded by collectors. #627 with its tribute to #27 remains an attractive issue but in good supply. The conclusion to The Destroyer story proved very popular. Covers on issues #654-660 by Sam Kieth have been real eye-catchers but some fans may feel disappointed that such

artwork is not carried on once the book is opened.

#691's new Spellbinder was quite a hit with some fans, cashing in on the fad for "hot babes".

DOOM PATROL
Fortunes were revived for this title for a time under the Vertigo banner and scripting by Rachel Pollack but back-issue sales seem to have fallen off dramatically as the title was cancelled in early 1995. Back issues from #19 are still reasonably in demand for the stunning Simon Bisley covers and for the Grant Morrison scripts that remain as thought-provoking as ever. The original series has not fared too well with hardly any increases at all in the Good and Fine grades and copies sticking on Mart walls, even at 50% off. Only strict Near Mint copies are in demand. Seems that no-one is really that interested in the likes of Arnold Drake's bizarre scripts or Bruno Premiani artwork. #121 continues its something of a cult status book. Readers, it's up to you. You decide if the Doom Patrol lives or dies. Well, the readers decided alright as that was the last issue! The only real activity has been the trade in Erik Larsen issues (#6-15) of the 2nd series because they remain cheap and they are in plentiful supply.

ECLIPSO
His first appearances in House of Secrets are still in demand but more so in the U.S. and tough to find in high grade. No interest in his own series.

EIGHTY PAGE GIANT
This series has shown more interest as people realise what excellent reprints are to be found in there at a fraction of the cost of the originals. Having said that, the phenomenal interest in this title in the States keeps forcing up the price. This Guide is reflecting the availability and consequent static nature of prices in Good and Fine grades, but for those that want very high grade copies, reasonable parity of U.S. and U.K. prices comes into play. Of particular interest are #4 with the early Flash reprints, #8 for the origin stories and #14/#15 for their scarcity. #7 is still classified as rare in the U.K. as it does not seem to turn up in any grade.

FLASH
Still one of the biggest success stories as far as Silver Age D.C. back-issues go. All the early issues are in demand in the U.K. Flash #105 is proving to be one of the top D.C. key issues.
1993 NM Price: £1,350.00
1994 NM Price: £1,995.00
1996 NM Price: £2,900
A big jump also for #110, a mere skip #123 and no change in the U.K. for #175. The 80pg giants are much in demand for their reprints, indeed all the early issues can be found in reprint somewhere (see the Reprint Index). The 2nd series continues to sell, particularly the later issues with the introduction of Impulse, the Terminal Velocity and Dead Heat storylines and Mark Waid's writing.

GREEN LANTERN
#1 sees another healthy increase from £1,400 to £1,950 from Guides #6 to #7. Still very tough to find in unrestored NM. Early issues generally have seen healthy increases though #40 still remains a mystery. It is highly regarded in America and priced as such but according to observations and Questionnaires in this country it would be valued at around half current American prices. Indeed in the Guide we have priced it at less than half the U.S. value. #45 has remained static, #59 has gone down as has #116. #76 still seems to be undervalued for its historical importance and its package as a very attractive comic book. Emerald Dawn I continues to sell but II is proving less successful. The Golden Age Green Lantern market seems very slow in the U.K. This Guide has adopted a parity of pricing between U.S. and U.K. prices though in theory Golden Age issues are harder to get in

the U.K. and should be more expensive.

HARDWARE
It was erroneously reported in the last U.K. Guide that the Milestone imprint was being cancelled. Sorry about that. Hardware, Static and Icon seem to be going strong. Not so good for Xombi, Shadow Cabinet and Blood Syndicate. Doing occasional issues at 99 cents cover price seems to have proved useful for the Milestone group of titles. Time will tell.

HAWK AND DOVE
The 1988 mini-series with Image favourite artist Rob Liefeld has seen a drop in price from the last U.K. Guide. No interest.

HAWKMAN
Early issues continue to rise steadily in the U.S. but that is only reflected in the U.K. in the highest grades on the earliest issues. Good and Fine prices have gone down substantially in the U.K. as there seems to be a plentiful supply in most comic shops, at marts and on dealers' lists. Funny how all grades keep going up in American guides (see Aquaman and Atom!).

HEART THROBS
Mentioning these only as part of the D.C. Romance titles which are an under-collected genre in the U.K. Perhaps not to everyone's taste but they do have some great story titles, some nice grey-tone covers and their rarity drives D.C. completists wild.

HECKLER
Always worth mentioning for the Giffin art and the fun read.

HELLBLAZER
Always worth a mention as one of D.C.'s fan-favourites. Early issues are still in demand though prices in the U.K. have dropped slightly from the last Guide. From there on in the prices are static as sets keep turning up from fans cashing in their collections. Garth Ennis successfully took up the reigns of Jamie Delano and kept this title right on track along with Sean Phillips excellent art. There are stories that make you laugh out loud. Excellent. It is seen very much as a companion title to Sandman and collectors of one usually collect the other.

HOUSE OF MYSTERY
There has been a marked swing away from the earlier horror/mystery issues which have fallen in value. They are still hard to find in high grade though and low grade copies are an excellent read. #143 has risen in value and healthy rises for #178 and #179. Some lovely moody covers around here.

HOUSE OF SECRETS
Very early issues collected for their Jack Kirby art. The Eclipso run from #61 to #80 find it collectors. #92 continues to defy best efforts to find it in NM and interest in it has surged as sales have been reported consistently over the psychological £200 barrier.
1993 NM Price: £95.00
1994 NM Price: £160.00
1996 NM Price: £250.00

IMPULSE
A fan favourite on both sides of the Atlantic. Supplies seem to be reaching the fairly plentiful in the U.K. as #1 went up to £5.00 and slipped back to about half that. A fun read.

INFINITY INC.
#49 and #50 may be ones to watch with the appearance of Lyta that ties into the modern Sandman title. Otherwise this title is a cheap read and of great interest if you want a taste of Golden Age heroes and their off-spring.

INVISIBLES

Another Vertigo success story and the Britpack show the way in comics yet again. Lots of copies around so go read, though there are reports of scarcity in some areas of the U.K., particularly the West Country.

JIMMY OLSEN

Does #1 exist in high grade outside the U.S? A genuinely hard book to find in any grade. A title that appeals to thirty-somethings only these days. Probably true in the U.S. as well. Current collectors have no interest in Superman signal watches (prizes for anyone who can remember the sound it made?) and hoax stories involving kryptonite. Legion collectors pick up Legion appearances, the 80 page giants are hard to find as in any other title and most interest lies in issues #133-135 with the first appearances of Darkseid.

JONAH HEX

This 92 issue series has come on leaps and bounds in the U.K. in the last couple of years. Hard to believe that a #1 can fetch up to £30.00. More Price Guide prizes on offer here – can you find the issue with my (poetic but embarrassing) letter in it?

JUSTICE LEAGUE

#3 test cover has slipped again in interest. Hard to believe that this was once a £100 comic. £20 now if you're lucky. The Justice League family of titles have slipped badly in the past couple of years to the point of Justice League Europe and Justice League Quarterly being cancelled whereas in 1992/3 interest was very high. The alternative Justice League storyline of recent times where they break people's arms and kick in heads got great fan reaction. Recent storylines like Aftershocks, Judgement Day and Way of the Warrior have done their best to involve other characters in cross-over opportunities. One hopes for long-range plans of a big re-launch.

JUSTICE LEAGUE OF AMERICA

#1 is on the verge of cracking the £2,500 mark and #2 has risen well, having been under-rated before now. As for #3 with its black cover, this issue is notoriously hard to find in any decent shape. Big jump for #9, little jumps for #21 and #22. Issue #39 still in demand with its excellent reprints. Issues from #60-100 are getting scarcer in the U.K., particularly the Neal Adams cover issues in the #80s and #90s. The 100 pagers (#110-116) are always missing from back-issue boxes and #122-150 continue to drive JLA completists mad. Were more than just a few copies of #150 ever printed? This title is a steady back issue seller and gains new fans all the time even if the current Justice League incarnation has varied.

KAMANDI

Still an under-rated title in the U.K. It's just not to everyone's taste. Not the easiest of sets to complete but possible as prices remain static. A few shades of Kirby at his Fourth World best.

L.E.G.I.O.N.

Lobo's presence used to ensure that this book sold consistently though this seems to be a particularly regional creature – hot seller in some areas of the U.K., distinctly cool in others. Cancelled in late 1994 and back issue sales have suffered accordingly.

LEGION OF SUPER-HEROES

Throughout the history of the Legion of Super-Heroes, each incarnation has brought re-vamps and change but there is the feeling that the huge popularity gained by the first 25 issues of the 2nd series in the mid 1980s has never been regained since. The Quiet Darkness storyline towards the end of 1991 did something to improve the ratings. The destruction of the planet Earth went down very well which gave rise to a popular spin-off The

Legionnaires – the spirit of the Legion as they first were back in the very early 1960s, all about 14 years old and ready to take on the world. But though this title remains a decent seller, there just does not seem to be the interest in team books that there once was. Back-issue prices in the current Legion series have dropped to a general £1.00/£1.25 mark.

LOBO

Still one of D.C.'s most popular characters. The first mini-series continues to sell but supplies seem adequate for demand. Prices have dropped slightly from Guide #6.

Subsequent mini-series have done quite well and Lobo guest-appearances in other titles are a useful stand-by to help to halt flagging sales in lesser titles so that says something of the character's overall status in the D.C. universe. His first appearance in Omega Men #3 still hasn't taken off as any sort of key issue however (no matter how hard Darryl Jones tries!)

LOIS LANE

As with Jimmy Olsen, #1 is very hard to find in high grade though does turn up in the U.K. in lower grades fairly regularly. As with Jimmy Olsen, only a certain section of collectors bother with this title. Stories about Lois tricking Superman into revealing his identity belong to a different era. #70 is still quite big news in America, not so much in the U.K. and that is reflected in the price difference. One or two issues in the early '70s are sought after for Darkseid appearances and the last few issues can be quite scarce in the U.K. for completists.

MISTER MIRACLE

Sadly cancelled in 1991 after only 28 issues. The original Jack Kirby series continues to attract fans keen to collect The Fourth World of Kirby but having no current series to keep the interest going has affected back-issue sales. New Gods, also having been cancelled, interest in the original series from the early 1970s has been less affected and it does remain the most popular Fourth World series.

METAL MEN/METAMORPHO

Very static as back issues and reaching the stage of U.K. prices being half that of U.S. values.

MORE FUN COMICS

A monster of a title, many a classic has passed through its numbers. First appearances of the Spectre, Dr. Fate and Aquaman but demand is strictly limited to those that can afford them. Later issues in lower grades are fairly common and worth picking up. The very first few issues are very popular in America but sales are unheard of in the U.K. Will that ever change? About time more American dealers took a chance and came over to the U.K. with some interesting material at realistic prices. They may be pleasantly surprised.

MY GREATEST ADVENTURE

Some lovely covers on early issues. Notable for #80 being the first appearance of Doom Patrol. Hard to find in high grade with its black cover but these Doom Patrol issues are slow sellers and almost non-existent as far as sales go in mid grades.

MYSTERY IN SPACE

Much under-rated in the U.K. All that lovely Infantino artwork and some lovely covers on issues between #53 and about #90. Issue #75 continues to elude British collectors and #55 with its grey-tone cover is a genuine rarity in the U.K. #53 is sought after but only in lower grades as far as we can tell.

THE NEW TITANS

Like the Legion of Super-Heroes, this is one of those titles that enjoyed a high profile and popularity in the mid 1980s but saw years of decline and final cancellation in

early 1996. The New Titans title was helped in 1990 with the Batman/Tim Drake Robin cross-over and again in 1991 with Deathstroke appearances, his relationship with Jericho, a death here and there and a line-up change. The Titans Sell Out storyline was quite well received at the time. Back issues will probably remain static for some time to come.

NEW YORK WORLD'S FAIR

Unbelievably hard to find but to devoted Golden Age collectors covet these comics like very few others. The Guide can only adopt reasonable parity between U.S. and U.K. values. Theoretically it would be much harder for a U.K. collector to find and buy one of these issues without going to America himself/herself. Very low grade copies would sell in the U.K. with some regularity if they could be supplied. Noted for the only appearance of Superman with blond hair.

OMEGA MEN

The first Lobo appearances seem to be very static with little or no change from last year. Seems odd that Lobo is a major character in the D.C. universe and yet his 1st appearance commands nothing like the attention and value that it should. Maybe because it isn't really like the Lobo that the character has evolved into.

OUR ARMY AT WAR/OUR FIGHTING FORCES

The war comic genre is generally under-rated in the U.K. which is a shame as there are some lovely grey-tone covers and some great Russ Heath and Joe Kubert art to be sampled. The market on these is very U.S. driven and the U.K. Guide can only reflect the constantly rising prices in the U.S. with a conversion back-to-pounds-less-a-bit. The same can be said for All American Men of War, G.I. Combat and Star Spangled War Stories. Our Army at War #81 is big in the States. I can think of maybe two people over here that would be interested/could afford £1,000 or thereabouts for a Near Mint copy. An example of the difference of the size of markets.

PREACHER

One of the hottest (how I detest that word!) new series around, Preacher has caught everyone by surprise on both sides of the Atlantic. Prices are generally more here in the U.K. but it won't be long before the dollar price goes up and beyond. Well done Garth Ennis and Steve Dillon. Price on #1 about the £7.50 mark at the time of writing.

RAY

Early issues featuring Joe Quesada still sell. Shame he didn't do more of them. The new on-going series has yet to set the world alight although the cover of the first issue was impressive.

SANDMAN

What is there to say that hasn't been already? Still D.C's most popular series and award-winner (worth re-iterating that #19 won an international award for Best Short Story, significantly without there having to be a special category because it's a comic) is still a good read. Some over-criticise in the fan press, some over-intellectualise but it still demonstrates some of the best qualities about comics. The release of the trade paperbacks collecting the first 69 issues (ie. virtually all of them) has proved very popular over the last few years. #8 is still in demand as the first appearance of Death and the variant issue has been recorded as selling consistently in America for over $150 with a few recorded sales in this country at £100. Not sure that this will continue as the market for any kind of premium or special variant issue is virtually dead now. The Season of Mists storyline beginning in #21/#22 excited some interest in 1991 while the more recent Game of You and Brief Lives storylines continue the excellence. Issue #69, the conclusion of "The Kindly

Ones", is one to watch where Sandman/Morpheus dies. The most recent storyline of "The Wake" has provoked much interest, mainly because the title will be cancelled at issue #75 and I won't have a reason for living.

SECRET ORIGINS ANNUAL
Big book in high grade now. We have kept the prices on Good and Fine grades static as that is probably a true reflection in the U.K. market but the issue is quite hard find in any grade.

SENSATION COMICS
Worth mentioning only because we were so gobsmacked to hear about the phenomenal price rises in the States. Can it really double in price from one year to the next? Is #1 in particular that sought after? Not here in the U.K. And this is our constant problem. The U.K. Guide has to adopt some sort of parity on these issues as someone wishing to buy could reasonably be expected to pay at least the going U.S. rate and probably more without dealers' discounts if you go over to America yourself and with dealers' profit margins if you rely on a U.K. dealer bringing something back for you.

SHADE
Another British affair. This title began with a bang and promptly fizzled out in 1990. 1991 saw a steady improvement and the painted covers by Jamie Hewlett were well received. Improvement continued and steadied with the storyline of Shade the Changing Woman and then the Birth Pains storyline under the Vertigo banner by scripter Garth Ennis so finally people were beginning to pick it up along with their Sandmans and Hellblazers. Interest continued as the title reached its 50th issue but recently it has proved static, so much so that back issue prices on early issues have fallen. Good read though. I'll always champion the reading of comics. There is no interest it seems in the original late 1970s series featuring Steve Ditko artwork. Perhaps because the characters are completely different. Maybe for that reason alone, it is worth picking them up for comparison.

SHOWCASE
The title that requires a mortgage to acquire is rapidly seeing the same steps needed for single issues. It seems a pity that this title is pricing itself out of the reach of almost all collectors on both sides of the Atlantic. There are very few people in the U.K. right now saying to themselves "Right, I'm going to start collecting a set of Showcase". There are probably not many more saying "Well, I'll forget the first 20 or so". Showcase #4 widened the gap with its nearest rivals in the "most valuable" stakes.

1993 NM Price: £6,000.00
1994 NM Price: £9,000.00
1996 NM Price: £17,500.00
There seems to be no stopping this book. Some American guides value it even higher than this fabulous figure. Price variations on this comic are huge. Several high grade issues have sold in America in the last two years at up to $30,000 and one sold for a staggering $29,000 cash alone! One was very recently offered at $50,000 in an auction system of buying. As incredible as all that may seem, a relatively conservative value has been chosen for this British guide but bear in mind that this is one of those comics that genuinely sell for multiples of guide in high grades. Showcase #8 went much the same way:
1993 NM Price: £1,950.00
1994 NM Price: £4,000.00
1996 NM Price: £9750.00
It is very hard to find in Fine or above let alone Very Fine or better. As Showcase #4 rises, this 2nd appearance of Flash must also. #13 and #14 continue to climb (#14 is definitely harder to find). #15 took another jump. Space

Ranger may not be a major character (a Space Ranger mini-series is still on its way) but it is a notoriously hard issue to find, particularly with its black cover that usually hides someone's attempts at colour-touching with a felt tip pen. Other issues with significant value increases: #17, #22, #27, #34, #37, #45, #55, #59, #60-#62. And the whole set will put you back about 50 or 60 grand. Bargain. A series crying out for careful reprinting.

Showcase '93 was a nice idea but executed pretty poorly apart from issues #7 and #8. Showcase '94-'96 looked a lot better. Decide for yourself.

SPECTRE
This 3rd series has really caught on with many people. Back issue prices are still very reasonable but supplies of the first few numbers are drying up. The first series has always been popular in the States and has dragged that British market price along with it, not to parity levels but bubbling just under. #1 with its black cover is hard to find in high grade.

STAR TREK: THE NEXT GENERATION
Now that the series is regularly shown on terrestrial and satellite TV in the U.K., the comic book is bound to be a good, consistent seller. Star Trek in general is faring well after the media attention of the 25th anniversary and then the 30th anniversary this year will do no harm whatsoever. There is a healthy back-issue market for all D.C., Marvel and Gold Key Star Trek series though the prices on the early Gold key series are getting beyond the reach of most U.K. collectors.

STARMAN
The new series is pretty cool. Back issue prices are not high but £2 and £3 are not uncommon for the first couple of issues. Have a read if you are not familiar.

STRANGE ADVENTURES
The Animal Man issues (#180, #184, #190, #195, #201) are well dead. #117 (1st Atomic Knights) seems a more interesting book though its appeal is for the dedicated few. Excellent reading value as quirky sci-fi was one area that D.C. excelled in and didn't always rely on fabulous monsters that threatened the Earth etc. Some nice art by Gil Kane and Carmine Infantino too. The Deadman run from #205 to #216 with Neal Adams art in most has enjoyed a slight price increase at the front end, static city for the rest of the run.

SUPERBOY
Issue #100 was always a biggie in the States and the British equivalent price creeps a bit closer to parity. Silver Age collectors in the U.K. still like #86 and #89 and for my money #147 is a hard comic to find with its new Legion origin story. Interest remains in the increasingly difficult issues #197-#202 (Legion). All the 80pg giants with their value-for-money reprints are hard to find in back-issue boxes. Late Golden Age issues (ie. the first 20 or so) have a minority following but then they don't exactly turn up in cartloads.

SUPER FRIENDS
Something of a cult follows this title. Very cheap (when you can find them) and a must for D.C. completists.

SUPERMAN
The listing starts from #1 to take in some of those early classics. Even though the Golden Age market is relatively small in the U.K., Superman comics always sell, particularly in lower grades. Get a load, if you can, of such classic covers as #14 and #24. Note also undervalued keys like #61 and #76. #100 is as hard to find in any grade as ever. Back-issue sales on the 1960s material is steady: once again the 80pg giants are snapped up and some becoming noticeably scarcer

(#193 and #202 for example). Issue #200 is one that doesn't seem to turn up and it is getting on for 30 years old! #233 is an undervalued issue as all Kryptonite is turned to harmless lead. Issues in the 300s and 400s are in good supply but still don't stay long in back issue bins as they are still relatively cheap. As with Action Comics, interest in the Death and Rebirth issues of Superman is steady and sales of the current issues are healthy with storylines such as The Death of Clark Kent and The Trial of Superman. Latest storylines point to a break-up between Superman and Lois Lane. Watch this space...

SWAMP THING
Renewed interest in the first series. Some excellent Bernie Wrightson art and Len Wein scripts. £35 for a Near Mint #1 is not unreasonable. The last five issue of this series are hard to find in the U.K.

WEIRD WESTERN TALES
Jonah Hex appearances in #12 and #13 are especially sought after in the U.K. as is the rest of the series up to #38 before Jonah Hex graduated on to his own series.

WITCHING HOUR
This long-standing mystery title is being picked up in the U.K. for the Wrightson and Neal Adams art in the early issues and are good reading value for money.

WONDER WOMAN
Listing from #1 on the first series to take in some of those early classics though there is hardly any interest in these very early issues in the U.K.

Mid Golden Age issues on low to mid grades do sell however. The Animal Man appearances in #267/268 have long died in interest. War of the Gods, which was centred very much around the second series but to no great acclaim, has did nothing as back issues shortly after the time and still don't. The Brian Bolland covers on recent issues were up to his usual excellent standard. The title enjoyed a new lease of life with artwork by Mike Deodato but sadly his tenure was short-lived. Much was expected of John Byrne taking over the reins but fan reaction has been mixed. Issues #85 and #90 are still in demand.

WORLD'S FINEST
Listing starts at #1 to include the very scarce and rare issues with cardboard covers that obviously hardly ever turn up in great shape. Unfortunately the demand for early issues of this title is quite low in the U.K. and looks set to remain so. The absurdity of the stories remain the chief delight of this title. How else could you team the world's mightiest hero with a mere mortal man (even if it was Batman?). By using a healthy dose of magic and monsters, role reversal and powerlessness. Silver Age issues in general are quite sought after and there is that very tough-to-find late Golden Age/early Silver Age range from about #65-85. The 80pg and 100pg giants seem to be the best sellers along with #198/#199's Superman/Flash race part 3. #71 is still an undervalued issue and under-rated for its historical importance of being the first of regular Superman/Batman stories.

ZERO HOUR
The mini-series that removed the 25th and 30th Centuries from D.C. continuity but didn't set the back-issue world alight. #4 is slightly harder to find in the U.K. as the series caught many shops and dealers on the hop. The time-line chart is quite groovy.

Conan the Barbarian #1 – Hailed at the time as a ground-breaking comic book, helping to usher in the Bronze Age of Comics

An Introduction to
MARVEL COMICS

MARVEL COMICS (also known as Timely Comics in the 1940s and Atlas Comics in the 1950s) have been published and distributed in America since 1939. Offcial distribution in the U.K. began in July 1960, although there may have been sporadic trial distribution before this date. The first years of the original Marvel Bullpen fronted by Stan Lee, Jack Kirby, Steve Ditko and Dick Ayers produced Fantastic Four in November 1961, followed by The Incredible Hulk in May 1962 and Spiderman in **Amazing Fantasy #15** in August 1962, Sgt. Fury in May 1963, The Mighty Thor in August, The Avengers and The X-Men in September and Daredevil in April 1964. It was an impressive and enduring output.

The Marvel style was very much more dynamic than that of the more well established but by that time somewhat staid-in-some-areas D.C. Their heroes were younger and created a new kind of rapport with their readers. Heroes like the impetuous Human Torch, the misunderstood Hulk and the has-trouble-with-the-girls-gets-bullied-at-college Spiderman. The Marvel universe was very much more integrated from the start with characters crossing over into each other's territories and every permutation of team-up. This was very different from the D.C. Universe of more hermetically sealed characters and stories. Also, the use of a tight stable of artists and Stan Lee writing virtually everything made the feel and look of the Marvel Universe more coherent. Marvel very much led the way with the potential of team books like The Avengers, X-Men and Fantastic Four and later The Champions, The Defenders, Alpha Flight, Squadron Supreme, The New Mutants and Power Pack, although ironically, D.C. Comics had the first super-hero team of all in the Justice Society of America. Marvel also gave a kind of value for money by having composite books – The Hulk and Giant Man in Tales to Astonish and Captain America and Iron Man in Tales of Suspense. Perhaps where Marvel scored most of all was with the different kind of intimacy between creators and public. "Smiling" Stan Lee used his editorials and letters pages to add to the Marvel bandwagon and soon True Believers earned their 'No Prizes' for spotting mistakes in stories, enroled in the Merry Marching Marvel Society, became Quite 'Nuff Sayers if their letters got printed and read their own fanzine FOOM (Friends of Ol' Marvel). No wonder Stan Lee was smiling.

In the D.C. manner, Marvel went in for revivals. In **Avengers #4**, January 1964, Captain America was revived from being frozen in a block of ice, his first appearance since the hey-day of the 1940s and his slide into oblivion in the early 1950s. The Sub-Mariner had also been found wandering about as a down-and-out in the pages of The Fantastic Four and thus the origins of Marvel comics found their way to the forefront of their second age. While team-ups and confrontations abounded with the much heralded punch-ups between The Thing and The Hulk, the disadvantage of the Marvel formula was that it became well tried too quickly. When two heroes met it seemed the only way to fight a villain was to fight it out with each other first. Mountains moved, fights became more preposterous and the Marvel

style gloried in their majesty. Jack Kirby's four-square style did much to enhance splash-page spectacle in the early to mid 1960s.

Much more so than D.C., Marvel were quick to reprint even relatively recent material in King Size Annuals and anthologies like Marvel Collector's Item Classics and Marvel Tales. British reprints like Fantastic and Terrific and later the Mighty World of Marvel did much to popularize the early Marvel style in the U.K. Reprinting reached its peak in the mid 1970s and one expected to see new titles like Marvel Old Reprints Again and Marvel Marvel Marvel.

More recently, Marvel have reprinted the first 10 or 20 of their main line titles in coffee table format Marvel Masterworks. With such marketing and their zappier in-house style, Marvel have earned their place as the market leaders, virtually uninterrupted, for the last 10 years.

Marvel suffered from a patchy distribution network in this country and it was often easier to get DC comics at the newsagents, particularly in the North and Scotland. In the early part of 1964, however, a dock strike at the major ports of the U.K. meant that for two months, Marvels were strictly limited in distribution and across the whole line cover-dated November and December 1964, these issues are either SCARCE or RARE as noted in this guide (for more information on this, see the Comparison Between the U.S. and U.K. Markets article).

This situation may also have been aggravated by a change over of contracts for distribution. A bold experiment to expand to 52 pages across the range of titles in October and November 1971, lead to a limited distribution as less copies of these thicker issues came over in the regular size packets.

The experiment was a short-lived one. It may be noticed that many of these comics are ink-stained along the edges. This occurred when batches marked for return were splattered with ink, sometimes very heavily. Comics like **Conan the Barbarian #11** are extremely hard to find without such staining.

This practice continued well into the 1970s and ink stained comics must be considered damaged by at least a full grade. Another defect peculiar to Marvel comics is that of "Marvel Chipping". Many early Marvels suffer from little chips out of the right hand side of the cover, particularly **X-Men #1**, **Spiderman #2**, **Hulk #3**, and **Fantastic Four #4**. This can vary from tiny surface cracks to major raggedness. The reason for this is, according to legend, one of the then Editors of the Marvel Bullpen would not invest in a new sharp guillotine machine. When bundles of comics were cut and trimmed in post-production, the top copies were strained under the blunt blade and suffered the chipping damage. Whether this story is true or not, the defect is a serious one and would detract from the value of a comic by at least a full grade if noticeable, 2 full grades at least if the damage is heavy (see the Defects Chart for more information).

In August 1968, there debuted a character that more than any other captured the spirit of the times – The Silver Surfer. With his incredible powers first seen in the pages of the Fantastic Four

as the herald of an almighty power called Galactus, his later stranding on Earth, suffering and penance, many believe this to be Stan Lee's personal vision of Jesus Christ, Son of the Father. Appropriately enough, the character returned to preach to a new generation when his adventures were reprinted in a second series of Fantasy Masterpieces beginning in December 1979 and born again under the auspices of Steve Englehart and Marshall Rogers in July 1987.

In October 1970, Marvel introduced Robert. E. Howard's Conan the Barbarian under the pencils of Barry Smith. Although nearly cancelled, the character grew to achieve early cult status. The Barbarian was first tried out in April 1970 in **Chamber of Darkness #4**, an example of Marvel showcasing a character before trying an on-going series which was much more of a D.C. tradition.

The mid to late 1970s were the biggest crisis for Marvel when many of the lesser titles were cancelled like, Amazing Adventures, Astonishing Tales, Skull the Slayer, Doc Savage, Marvel Chillers, Tomb of Darkness and most horror/fantasy reprint titles. This was followed hard on the heels of the collapse of the quarterly Giant Size issues that were introduced in May 1974 in the Fantastic Four title. It was a case of too much too soon as fans had to buy to keep up. Rising paper costs affected all companies including D.C. who also cancelled many new titles like Justice Inc., The Stalker, Kong and Claw, leading to their "Implosion" of 1978. From August 1974 to mid 1980, Marvel comics in this country were denoted by the banner "Marvel All Colour Comics" at the top of the cover instead of "Marvel Comics Group", resulting in a confusion over British reprints. The confusion was added to as Marvel had four different price/number codes on the top left of the cover. The diamond shape with the number on the left and the cents price on the right denotes copies for direct sale/no return to American comic shops. The diamond shape with the cents price on the left, pence price on the right and number underneath, denotes copies for direct sale/no return to overseas (i.e U.K.) comic shops. The square shape with the cents price on the left and the number on the right is for the American news-stands and the square shape with pence price right and number left is for overseas and U.K. newsagents. There is no evidence to suggest that any one is a reprint of another. All comics were produced at the same time on the same machine on the same paper. It is possible that the overseas issues were produced towards the end of the print run with the usual substitution of pricing/code plates. This lasted until September 1982 when Marvel then rationalised their systems.

May 1979 saw **Daredevil #158** which brought artist and then writer, Frank Miller to the fore. His run on Daredevil until issue #191 and a second stint from #227 to #233 brought new heights and maturity of story and art working as an organic whole. March 1982 saw the first slick format regular comic book Marvel Fanfare whose higher production values and presentation lead to the current trend of D.C.'s New and Deluxe format and Marvel's on-going Epic Line. Marvel took the opportunity to combine the new slick process with reprints to produce in 1983 the Special Editions of Avengers and X-Men, Moon Knight and Micronauts to name but a few. These were high quality reprints and in some ways the pre-cursor to the now ubiquitous and it seems obligatory Trade Paperback. The early Eighties saw an expansion of the mini and maxi series with further permutations of team-ups and spin-offs to reach the plethora of X-Men progeny from Kitty Pryde/Wolverine and Iceman to Excalibur and the X-Babies. Coupled with this was the advent of the Direct Sales market which saw the unprecedented sale of 400,000 copies of **Dazzler #1** in May 1981 which was bettered still by **Marvel Super Heroes Secret Wars** in May 1984.

To celebrate their 25th anniversary in 1986, Marvel created a line of titles called New Universe which were all set in a Universe separate from the regular Marvel titles. With the exception of Star Brand and D.P. 7 they were not well received and the line all but disappeared in the first year with only sporadic appearances scheduled for the future. Another marketing ploy from Marvel was to produce their top three titles Spiderman, G.I.Joe and the X-Men twice monthly during the summer of 1988, summer being the peak sales period. Thus the cover dates would read "early" or "late" whatever the month.

In the same way that Walt Simonson breathed new life into (what had become a flagging title) **Thor #337**, Todd McFarlane similarly invigorated the traditionally slow-selling title Hulk, with issue #330. McFarlane's depiction of Spiderman has also proved to be very popular and his recent departure from that title will ensure their collectibility. The end of the decade saw the mutant titles like Excalibur, illustrated by British artists Alan Davis and Paul Neary proving to be extremely successful as other recent developments including a new-style Captain America, on-going titles for Wolverine and She-Hulk, constant line-up changes for the Avengers and the Fantastic Four and the return of the anthology title with Solo Avengers and Marvel Comics Presents. **Spectacular Spiderman #158** had Spiderman acquired "cosmic powers" from another Marvel character Captain Universe which met with much fan interest and the fact that The Punisher, Wolverine and Sabretooth, three of Marvel's ostensibly most violent characters also proving to be the most popular, is an interesting indicator of fashion, particularly with Sabretooth meeting a suitably bloody demise most recently.

Probably the appeal of Marvel comics has always been their intricate continuity and it is probably because of this that they have dominated the recent back-issue market for so many years. The inter-locking structure of the main group of titles, the proven loyalty of Marvel readers and the company's traditional alacrity to take advantage of current buying trends are all indications of Marvel's strong customer-base; there seems no reason to believe that Marvel back-issue sales shouldn't continue to make up a healthy percentage of every dealer's business though this may fluctuate from time to time. Big sellers in the cross-story stakes have been Lifeform, Atlantis Attacks, Acts of Vengeance, Inferno and Spidey's Totally Tiny Adventure all of which are detailed in the Guide. Another was the very popular X-Tinction Agenda storyline sought to resolve some of the loose plot threads and unnecessary complications that had built up in the X-Men and other mutant titles over the last two years. The arrival of artist Jim Lee has consolidated the X-Men's position as the biggest selling monthly comic.

The biggest selling individual comic of 1990

was the phenomenon of the latest Spiderman series from writer/artist Todd McFarlane. The first issue in its many variations sold over 2.5 million copies with a special Platinum version of 10,000 copies for retailers only. At best it is a carefully executed marketing ploy and at worst it is a speculator's nightmare. A printing error made an unspecified number of the first edition have a blue instead of green Lizard character on three pages. Isolated copies sold at premium prices all over the U.K. at the time. Printing mistakes have happened throughout comics history but a special importance has been attached to this particular issue. Collectors have been told that others may exist in their sealed bags but to open one in the hope of a gold mine reduces the value of that sealed-bag copy. Collectors have been told that these bags may not be acid-free and in an air-sealed environment the comic may deteriorate faster than a regular unbagged copy. Little mention is made of story content and art as the debate raged. While individuals are free to choose how much value and importance they place on this particular comic, the overall situation saw the uglier side of the industry come to the fore.

As 1991 developed, Marvel continued to consolidate their market-share lead with the promotion of the new Ghost Rider appearing in just about every other title, the new intelligent green Hulk with fine draughtsmanship by Dale Keown to match, a new detailed origin for Wolverine in a 13 part serial called "Weapon X", the New Mutants disbanding to form "X-Force" later on in the year, which itself became a record in volume sales. The new X-Men title was launched in 5 cover variations and a staggering 8 million copies printed. Speculators who stocked up with case-fulls for a rainy day may have a long time to wait. Through this extended marketing push Marvel gained an unprecedented 68% share of the market towards the latter half of 1991. No wonder Marvel's Editor-in-Chief Tom DeFalco claimed that 1991 was The Year of the Mutant.

In the last few years, Marvel have seen their fortunes rise to the dizzy heights of an unprecedented 68% market share followed by a falling off in sales in the face of the up and coming Independent companies Image and Valiant.

Marvel had much to celebrate and use to their advantage with 30th anniversaries being achieved by all of their major characters who started in the years 1961–1963. The X-Men was perhaps the most widely publicised and marketed milestone. Where Marvel experienced some back-lash however has been in the realm of "gimmick" covers. There was a time when if a title reaches double figures it's a cause for celebration and so the answer was to slap a foil cover on it. Or a holo-grafix one or an embossed one or a hologram one or a mirror finish one. As these are more expensive to produce so they cost more to the collector who has to let lesser titles go by the by as money can only stretch so far. The situation was not helped by Marvel's compulsive drive to produce as many new titles as they possibly can making it a nightmare for retailers who order blind three months ahead and fans who face the dilemma of missing certain regular titles to pick up the specials and the mini-series.

Marvel launched their 2099 Universe in 1992 with Doom, Spiderman, Punisher and Ravage and contrary to popular expectation, it wasn't another New Universe. But sales on the entire line have continued to slip with Ravage 2099 being the worst. Whereas once Marvel were credited as "The House of Ideas" it now seems that they observe more from the sidelines to see what DC will do

next, learn from any mistakes and then bring out their own version. A good example of this would be DC's Death of Superman storyline followed more recently by Marvel's plans to kill off Mr. Fantastic of the Fantastic Four. Or not. Mr. Fantastic and Dr. Doom duly returned. 1994 saw the demise of Marvel UK which many found sad but others rejoiced. A case of too much similar product was blamed.

In recent times, Marvel have sought to catch fan attention with The Age of Apocalypse storyline where all the X-titles were put on hiatus for new titles to appear – a nightmare for anyone writing Price Guides! Fans were mixed in their reaction to the news that Peter Parker as Spiderman has in fact been a clone for the last five years and the real Spiderman is in fact Ben Reilly. Only a matter of time to see how long that lasts.

The last year or so has seen a major upheavals for Marvel Comics. In a bid to make the company more profitable and to please their shareholders, major characters are being farmed out on license to other companies like Image. Marvel also went into direct distribution of their product through Heroes World, Marvel acquired Malibu Comics and their Ultraverse characters and many creative staff were lost in a reorganisation and streamlining. Time will tell as to how solid Marvel's creativity is and what they can do to dominate as they did so strongly at the start of the decade.

MARVEL COMICS MARKET REPORT
This Market Report for Marvel comics examines the last twelve months or so of activity, looking particularly at value trends and reasons for increased or decreased collector interest. It is very generalized and as such, regional variations should be taken into account. This is also purely a comparison with Guide #6 prices by way of on-going information. For titles and comics not mentioned one may assume relatively stable values and collector interest not significantly differing from last time. See the Market Reports from selected dealers around the country for more information.

AKIRA
Still a title in demand but not helped by the uncertainty of the publication of the last few issues – interest is easily lost on a title if there is a sudden and extended delay in the shipping of issues. And these last issues are expensive at a $6.95 cover price. Early numbers still hold their values and the series as a whole has only dropped marginally. Not as popular in the U.K. as it used to be.

ALPHA FLIGHT
Even though the series finished in March 1994, it is still a stable title with issues across the board having dropped by about 20%. Issue #51 (1st Jim Lee) has some demand but has dropped in value. Issue #106 having been hyped as the first homosexuality in comics (unbelievably – goes to show how hermetically sealed comics can occasionally be from real life and current concerns) has now dropped from a high in the U.K. of about £5.00 to half that.

AMAZING FANTASY
It's been on then off, off and on again. News of director Jim "Terminator" Cameron's live-action Spiderman film has experienced about four and a half years of frustration and rumour but seems to have done nothing to dampen the enthusiasm of fans and collectors for this title. The first

appearance of arguably Marvel's most famous character has once again gained incredibly in value, thanks largely to the hype in the States of the White Mountain copy selling for $39,100 (or 26 grand in real money!) a little while ago. There is a noticeably good supply of Amazing Fantasy #15's around in the U.K. but very few in very high grade and even fewer in an unrestored state. Beware heavy browning pages, even if the exterior looks glossy. A common fault. Must be something to do with the original paper composition. Beware also copies with amateur brown felt tip touching in around the top of the cover.

1993 NM Price: £4,250.00
1994 NM Price: £8,100.00
1996 NM Price: £14,000.00

U.S. dealers and collectors should take note of the fact that pence copies of this comic are exactly the same as the cents version apart from printed cover price and the cover month being removed. It could be regarded as a rare cover variant!

AMAZING SPIDERMAN

Listing Spiderman under "Amazing Spiderman" for the first time. Grudgingly. After all, why not "M" for Mighty Thor? I bow to our American cousins on this one.

McFarlane Mania isn't what it used to be on issues #298–#315. Prices in the U.K. have generally dropped on these. #300 in particular has established itself as a minor key book but with a big difference in prices between the dollar and the pound. Carnage and Venom appearances continue to be in some demand but not quite at the pitch they were.

The general consensus of opinion seems to be that this Spiderman-clone-thing has made the title into a kind of X-Men at its most complicated and there are reports of fans dropping the title in droves. Time will tell. The fact remains that should the Spiderman film ever get off the ground, the general audience are going to be more familiar with Peter Parker and the traditional costume, very valuable from a merchandising point of view. There will certainly be a conclusion to the clone saga.

The Spiderman 2nd Series continues with healthy sales. The various permutations of issue #1, bagged and un-bagged, signed and unsigned, continue to sell but as they were produced in such vast quantities and as collectors bought and saved multiple copies, long term investment value is very long term indeed. The phenomenon of the Platinum Spiderman edition seems to be dying a death (remember the Dark Knight Returns Signed/Limited Edition in 1986 – selling for £700 at one point and today can be picked up for around £150–200). All those who want copies have got copies and one more often sees a copy held up for auction with proceeds going to charitable causes which is no bad thing. All this is not to say that the Platinum Spiderman is worthless: it has settled on an average price at the moment and may see some movement if Spiderman hype surrounds a new film. But rather than play the predictive game, better to enjoy the comic as a high production value package of a very successful comic. The only other Spiderman variant worth mentioning is the "Blue Lizard" phenomenon of 1990 (an unknown quantity of the silver ink/black cover editions of #1 which had a blue rather than green coloured Lizard character in a number of panels) which waned rather in 1992 and 1993 and though copies still change hands today at whatever the purchaser is prepared to pay should he or she so desire one, there is still no firm proof as to exact numbers of this comic that is essentially a printing error (and how many of those have been there throughout comics' history?)

Amazing Spiderman back-issues of great interest are those from #100–#150 or so. Some very tough issues to find and some important changes for the Spiderman character though some of these issues are prone to volatile changes. #101 and #102 are prime examples of a once hot character (Morbius) peaking and now remaining static, even if they are difficult to find in high grade. #129 was very static for a time but there are signs of a pick up. There seem to be a lot of copies around but not many in strict NM. Many copies have a few millimetres of white area on the left of cover ("white spine") where the copy has been mis-cut slightly. Perfectly square-cut covers are difficult to find. The U.K.Guide remains cautious on this comic showing only a slight increase and still under the U.S. equivalent price. #149 sky-rocketed but now seems to have settled down at the £50.00 mark in the U.K. Hobgoblin appearances seem to be big news in American price guides but not in the U.K. #238 at $85 in the States translates to around £56—no way!

ASTONISHING TALES

As little a while ago as 1992 it was all Deathlok and Astonishing Tales #25. It still seems to be such a case over in America with their Guides, if not going crazy on the price, values are still holding. But over here, Deathlok may as well be dead. Copies just do not seem to be shifting. Copies are in plentiful supply, particularly in lower grades. Perhaps yet another mini-series is needed to kick-start this title. Or not.

AVENGERS

As 1993 was the 30th anniversary year of The Avengers, there was a welcome and now continued turn-around in the fortunes of this title, against the then general backlash towards team books. #360's bronze-foil cover was a real eye-catcher. #1 has now reached £1,450 though this is still fairly low relative to the other Marvel #1s as high grade copies of Avengers #1 are surprisingly common in both the U.S. and the U.K. Issues #3 and #5 with their darker covers have become increasingly harder to obtain in higher grades. There's new interest in #57/58 and #93 is still in demand and harder than ever to find without any label damage in the top left hand corner. #183, #204 and #205 seem noticeably scarcer in the general circulation in the U.K. Recent storylines involving teaming with Ultraforce have kept this title on track rather than set it ablaze.

BEAVIS & BUTT-HEAD

A palpable hit, owing much to its screening on late night satellite TV in the U.K. Find the first issue if you can. U.K. prices are keeping up with U.S. prices and #1 would see around £3.00. However, most recently there has been a noticeable decline in the popularity of humour comics in some areas of the U.K.

CAPTAIN AMERICA

After a fairly stable couple of years for the good Captain though there was much interest in the Operation Rebirth story courtesy of that man Mark Waid (see Impulse in the DC Market Report). #100 has seen a slight drop in value – very common in lower grades and while an absolute top grade copy is hard to find, high grade copies do seem to turn up in the U.K. #117 is still a tough issue to find too – very annoying for completists one would imagine. The Mike Zeck and Ron Lim issues continue to be reasonably sought after. #241 has slumped from £20.00 in the last U.K. Guide to

£14.00 in this one. The Golden Age title has something of a following here in the U.K. but the days of owning a Good copy of even the cheapest issue of the run for under £50.00 may be over. If you can find the slipcase set of Captain America The Classic Years that reprints issues #1–10, grab it and enjoy.

CAPTAIN MARVEL

No longer regarded as one of those seemingly junk titles from the 1970s with gains in U.K. Guide #6, still attractive as a run, not impossible to put together at 62 issues but increasingly harder. Interest in this title is mixed however, and that is reflected in the static nature of #1 and yet price rises on some earlier issues which do not seem to be around. The 2nd appearance of Thanos at #26 and indeed the other Starlin art issues have seen slight drops or no change. Time will tell what effect the new Captain Marvel series will have.

CONAN THE BARBARIAN

It was sad enough to see this title cancelled after nearly 24 years in 1993. A re-launch as Conan the Adventurer stuttered to a halt after 14 issues. Another re-launch as Conan in August 1995 and guess what, another cancellation. In this age of hi-tech mutants, maybe barbarians have had their day. Early issues still sell well and for #1 in top shape, a price of £200 has not been unknown in the U.K.

DAREDEVIL

Still one of the most undervalued titles of the early Marvel out-put. People forget that #1 only came out 7 months after X-Men #1; 1964 is over 30 years ago! Daredevil #1 in NM is very hard to find. The cover should be pure white and not the off-white/yellowing that often occurs.

1994 NM Price: £1,200.00
1996 NM Price: £1,400.00

Other early issues of note: #4 which still maintains its "rare in the U.K." status though copies do seem to be surfacing at marts so status will be monitored, #7 (still hard to find in high grade with that dark blue cover), #81 and particularly #82 definitely very scarce in the U.K. (particularly in high grade), the Miller issues from #158 showing a slight decrease for #158 and no change for the rest of the run. #227–#230 have had similar slight decreases and the first appearance of Typhoid Mary in #254 is static. #257 has dropped considerably (as has its counter-part Punisher #10). #319 was the shot in the arm that the title needed at the time and this issue peaked in the U.K. at about £10.00 but has slipped back to the £5.00 to £7.50 mark. That whole story arc has dropped slightly as supply seems to have met demand. Recent celebrations surrounding the 350th issue suggest that the title is quite strong.

DARKHAWK

One of the genuine surprises of 1992/93, this title has crashed. While issues #1–5 are generally not around in either the U.K. or the U.S., everyone who wants them seems to have them. Issue #1 was at £6.00 in U.K. Guide #6 and now struggles to £1.50. Now that the series has been cancelled, back-issue sales will be affected to the point of this title appearing more and more in the 50p bins at marts.

DEFENDERS

With issue #1 nearly 25 years old (is it possible?) and with those appearances of the Silver Surfer in the early numbers, this title has maintained interest. The Thor vs. Hulk #10 is a genuinely very scarce book in the U.K. and continues to defy many collections though the price seems to have reached a peak. Either that or there are so few sales that information is hard to come by. The Guardians of the Galaxy appearances that were once snapped up along with Son of Satan appearances between #92 and #109 in times past are no longer. Giant Size issues are static. The return of The (Secret) Defenders promised much but failed to deliver. The title was cancelled in March 1995.

DOCTOR STRANGE
Steady increases on the first series but they do tend to turn up in the U.K. in high grade quite frequently. The title value for the second series has risen by all of a pound so that must say something. Prices on the early issues of the third series have dropped though his new "hippie" look at issue #76 went down well with a lot of fans. Recent scripts by Warren Ellis and J.M. DeMatteis have kept this title alive.

DOCTOR WHO
With renewed interest in the character and a highly collectible series (of reprints admittedly) that are 10 years old, watch this space…

EPIC ILLUSTRATED
While there have been no price increases on this title, it is one to watch out for. A highly collectible set with some great art (Paul Gulacy, Neal Adams, John Bolton, Barry Windsor-Smith, John Byrne etc.) and some great stories (featuring Silver Surfer, Galactus and Dreadstar etc.). Good reading value if you can find them at marts and conventions. Forget the gimmicks. Forget the fads and fashions. Read!

EXCALIBUR
The title has dropped in value generally by about 10% pointing to a plentiful supply of issues in the U.K. marketplace. Mutant Genesis issues are still popular but no change in prices.

FANTASTIC FOUR
Big increases on early issues thanks to ever-spiralling rises in American guides.
1994 NM Price: £6,200.00
1996 NM Price: £9,000.00
Having said that it will be noticed that prices on Good and Fine issues have been kept static as this is a true reflection of the U.K. marketplace. Average grades are just not selling at the moment. How long this trend will last is hard to say. People seem to snap up very low grade copies to complete their runs and one or two who can afford it are prepared to pay for top quality. F.F. #48 is not unknown at $1,000 in the States. The rise in price by £100 from Guide #6 values has taken this reluctantly into account but the ceiling on this issue in the U.K. must have been reached. As far as other earlier issues go, there is less interest in #66 and #67 as the first appearances of "Him", later Warlock, though it's still hard to believe that people will pay such big money for basically a non-appearance. This is purely as a result of hype in America and too much regarding of America price guides. One hopes that fans and collectors will get wise to this. The U.K. Guide has had to follow U.S. prices to a certain extent but refuses to consider parity. If you want a Near Mint cents copy of these issues, be prepared to pay silly money. #80 seems finally to have lost its traditional rare/scarce status in the U.K. – so many have been brought over to this country from the States by dealers that it generally shows up in collections now. #100 is still as hard as ever to find for those completists and though dollar prices seem to keep

rising, even less-than-dollar/pound-translation forty pounds for this issue does seem a lot of money. The John Byrne issues (ranging between #209 and #293) are picking up in sales again after a lull. Current storylines are as complex as ever. Reed Richards and Dr. Doom are back (surprise, surprise!) and love triangles abound. More soap-opera than ever before, fans just may tire of increasingly higher percentages of issues being taken up with flashbacks, re-caps and the-story-so-far stuff.

FEAR, ADVENTURE INTO
One of the biggest 1970s titles of recent times with the Morbius appearances has plummeted in interest in the last 12 months. While #20 is genuinely hard to find in high grade on both sides of the Atlantic with its black-bordered cover, even in the States the price has dropped from around $50 to about half that.
1993 NM Price: £10.00
1994 NM Price: £15.00
1996 NM Price: £12.00
 The problem in the U.K. is that lots of copies turn up with some sort of inking stains on them, usually along the top edge in blue. All part of the same batch marked for return all those years ago. So one could expect to pay more than the Guide price stated for a genuinely Near Mint copy, especially as only cents copies are available. A decent read but forget whole words like "investment" or "speculation".

FRANKENSTEIN
Completely static both in the U.S. and U.K. However, the Mike Ploog art captures the mood of the subject quite well and there is something of a collectors' challenge to put a set together.

GHOST RIDER (1970s)
Prices on the early issues have come down in the U.K. though #1 is still quite hard to find in top grades. Formerly one of the hottest of the '70s Marvel series that everyone wanted to collect. The current series initially did much to hype its predecessor and elevated it to a status it perhaps didn't deserve. This was borne out by the fact that people begun to realise that the two Ghost Rider characters were different and separate and sales did begin to wane. Interest was temporarily renewed thanks largely to a few obscure panels showing Daimon Hellstrom (otherwise Son of Satan) getting dressed! But now that even the Son of Satan has cooled as a character, these first few issues have little to commend them to back-issue collectors. As ever, the genuine scarcity of the last few issues (#72-81 in particular) when the title was on its last legs makes this a difficult set to complete and may sustain collector interest.

GHOST RIDER (NEW)
Big drop in value on issue #1 on both sides of the Atlantic. The early issues have almost halved in value from the last U.K. Guide. The status as one of, if not the, hottest Marvel characters around at one time experienced a distinct resurgence of interest with the Rise of the Midnight Sons storyline, #28 being particularly in demand. The inclusion of other magic/horror-related characters like Morbius and Dr. Strange helped the situation. But this resurgence of interest was not sustained. The 20th anniversary issue #25 with its pop-up centre-spread is more or less back to cover price. The recent inclusion of guest-stars like Gambit has helped keep the title alive. The future looks uncertain.

GROO
Early issues of this title are always in demand with #1 at a very healthy £12.50. Prices of back-issues in the U.K. are slightly static as they rose so fast in the last two or three years. Great read. Sad to see the character finally cancelled after all these years

GUARDIANS OF THE GALAXY
Early issues of this title are generally not around in the U.K. and some very great price variations have been noticed at comic marts. Prices on early issues have slipped and there is no interest in issues #17–19 as there once was. Now that the title has been cancelled it would seem that back-issue sales are going to slip further as fan interest wanes.

HULK, THE INCREDIBLE
Prices on the first series are getting well out of most people's reach on both sides of the Atlantic, particularly looking at American guides (but we don't do that, do we?). The all Steve Ditko issue #6 is edging towards a £1,000 comic in the U.K. but if one does a direct translation from the American guides, one would be looking at over £1,250! Is this book so superior to #3, #4 and #5? The time has come now that these issues are lovely to look at but are difficult to sell now that they all top the £500.00 mark. Delighted to be proved wrong, however. Renewed interest in #181 as it doesn't seem to be around in NM shape. Even so the U.K. Guide strikes a note of caution by being under the American equivalent. The 30th anniversary issue #393 still sells well and the 2nd print grey cover seems to be harder to find in some areas of the U.K. #400 sported a dazzling holo-grafix cover and the great Dale Keown passed on from the book. Britain's own Gary Frank took on the unenviable task of following in his foot-steps but with Peter David scripts of a consistently high standard, this comic is still a firm fan favourite. Shame that it seems destined for cancellation/renewal in another guise under Marvel's plans for the future. Wait and see. A valuable Marvel asset won't be wasted.

INVADERS
Healthy increases in price for this title. Always quite highly valued in America, sets of these do not often turn up in the U.K. as #1, #2 and #41 are getting harder to find.

IRON FIST
As we all know it's a highly attractive 1970s set with only 15 issues, all Byrne art and all Non-Distributed in the U.K. Though issues have been brought over by dealers over the years it is still not the easiest set to complete, some claiming that #2 is impossible to find. #14 and the first appearance of Sabretooth was the Marvel back-issue for the greater part of the last three years. It is still tough to find in Very Fine+ or better.
1994 NM Price: £50.00
1996 NM Price: £70.00

IRON MAN
30th anniversary time for this character in 1993 and with Tony Stark being cryogenically frozen and brought back to life, with zappy new armour and Iron Man's struggles with The Avengers, it's been no more than a decent couple of years for old Tin Head but nothing special, indeed stagnant in some U.K. areas. Fans and collectors often talk about how great Armour Wars was but what about the 200 or so issues before that? Tons to look at with many odd issues to look out for. #101 with Frankenstein is often over-looked, a Thanos appearance in #88, Tony Stark's alcohol struggle in

#123–128, the great Barry Smith origin issue #47, some Jim Starlin art, John Romita Jnr's 1st work..all fab stuff. Demand for the fabled issue #55 has slackened off to the point of itself being cryogenically frozen.

1994 NM Price: £40.00
1996 NM Price: £30.00

There is slightly more demand for the 20 cents version (rather than the British 6p one) but it is nowhere near the key issue it used to be.

JOURNEY INTO MYSTERY
A mention for back issues of this late, great title. Catch Jack (still The King) Kirby at his quintessential best from #100–125. And issues #83 to #99 are not easy to come by in high grade, especially #84 with its dark brown cover. #112 is becoming a tough one to find but the size of the market after it is equally tough to estimate.

LUKE CAGE
The first 16 issues of this 1970's title are still hard to find being Non Distributed in the U.K. and #1 with its black-border cover is still very hard to find in anything approaching high grade. Historically an interesting title as one of the major black super-heroes (not too many of those around). Note that prices are unchanged frrom the last U.K. Guide reflecting its static status.

MARVEL COMICS
A mention for this Golden Age title if only to say that U.K. prices have to be calculated on the basis of U.S. guide values. The market in the U.K. for this title is small but could grow if more lower grade copies were brought over for people to try.

MARVEL CLASSICS COMICS
A mention for this much underrated set. Great reading for those who haven't tunnelled through several feet of college and university reading lists (I remember having to "do Dickens in a week"!) Issues #9 and #20 have decent Dracula and Frankenstein adaptations and a complete set is hard to come by.

MARVEL PREMIERE
One of the most attractive sets to collect for character and artist variation. #1 and #2 have Warlock-as-superhero for the first time, #3 sees the start of the Dr. Strange run by Barry Smith and Frank Brunner, #15 has the first Iron Fist (continuing to rise in value) and later issues have a variety of characters (Ant-Man, Man-Wolf) and a variety of artists (Chaykin, Byrne, Perez). Many issues are Non Distributed in the U.K. which makes collecting all 61 not the easiest task in the world. Keep an eye on #57-60, the Doctor Who issues…

MARVEL SPOTLIGHT
This title is very similar to Marvel Premiere as it introduced Werewolf By Night in #2, Ghost Rider in #5 (increasingly hard to find in top shape with its black cover) and a wide variety of characters in later issues (Son of Satan, Spiderwoman, Deathlok, Moon Knight, Sub-Mariner). The Ghost Rider run from #5 to #11 is hard to find without ink-staining along one or more edges. Prices are generally static and in one or two instances, issue #12 for example, have halved in value. Some good reading value here though.

MARVEL TALES
A series that represents remarkably good value as far as classic reprints go (and the same also applies to Marvel Collectors Item Classics). #1

may be beyond many people's pockets but later issues, particularly in low grade, provide the opportunity to read the very early issues of Spiderman, Fantastic Four, Tales to Astonish and Journey Into Mystery. Issues in the 100's reprint many classics like Spiderman #1 and Amazing Fantasy #15 and issues in the 200's reprint many 70's classics like Marvel Team Up #4. Some new covers by Todd McFarlane make for attractive packaging. This series deserves more attention, particularly as prices have fallen slightly so now's the time to buy.

MARVEL TEAM UP
With early issues now reaching nearly 25 years old, this series is coming into its own more and more. The first 23 issues are Non Distributed in the U.K. and feature most main Marvel characters teaming with Spiderman. They are all becoming harder to find in NM. Later issues with John Byrne art are still asked for and the greater part of the series is in enough supply to be very affordable and thus collectible. #1 with its black-border cover is notoriously hard to find in very high grade.

1993 NM Price: £35.00
1994 NM Price: £45.00
1996 NM Price: £50.00

Issue #150 has come down in price in the U.K.

MARVELS
Hailed as the best mini-series that Marvel (or perhaps anyone) has ever produced. A cracking read. A short-term goldmine but issues are in plentiful supply so don't over-pay. £4-£5 for #1. Plans are afoot for Marvels II. Can't wait.

MOON KNIGHT
Prices on the Stephen Platt issues are steady in both the U.S and U.K. Not much interest in other Moon Knight back issues as the last series was cancelled in early 1994.

MS. MARVEL
Worth mentioning for issue #18. £1.50 in the U.K., $12.50 in the U.S. Go Figure…

NAMOR
The label of "hot" artist is becoming increasingly more volatile. Jae Lee is not held in as high regard as of yore and consequently #26 has taken another tumble from £4 to £3. Cross-overs with Fantastic Four recently have helped as long time fans remember the attraction between Namor and Sue Richards (Invisible Woman). Prices on early issues are also down.

NEW MUTANTS
A title that was all the rage at the start of the '90s but now seems to have died somewhere along the line. Interest in #87 is very low now).

1993 NM Price: £25.00
1994 NM Price: £15.00
1996 NM Price: £7.50

Issues in the 90s seem to be steady in demand with 1st appearances of Deadpool and Feral and the 1st print of #100 is still popular but the title as a whole has lost about 15%.

NEW WARRIORS
Launched in 1990 this title was initially under-ordered by dealers, gained a fan-following after a year or so and thus early issues went up in value. This trend has now reversed with #1 slipping down from a U.K. Guide #6 value of £12.50 to £7.50. Recent storylines involving the Scarlet Spider have helped this title but time will tell.

NICK FURY
Brave of Marvel to kill off a character that's been around for over 30 years. It will be interesting to see what effect that will have on back issues of all Fury's various series. Probably negative.

NOVA
A title that did little to excite when it appeared from 1976 to 1979 but at only 25 issues and fuelled by the success of his appearances in New Warriors, this became an attractive title in the early 1990s. Completists have been known to go mad trying to find that elusive last issue which has been given a "very scarce in the U.K." status pending more information. The new on-going series started well with a (yet another!) gimmick cover. Prices have fallen ever so slightly on the first series.

POWERMAN
The Luke Cage – Hero for Hire title quickly metamorphosed into Powerman, added Iron Fist and has now produced a title of some collector interest. This was also helped by the appearances of Sabretooth in issues #66, #78 and #84. The appearance in #78 is, though highly suspect, most probably Sabretooth. For those that don't know/don't care (delete where applicable), there is one panel that shows a claw like Sabretooth's appearing from under a cloak and otherwise the mystery character wears a sack over his head. There is no mention by the name of Sabretooth but rather as "The Slasher". Prices are static. The last few issues of the run are the hardest to find and a completists nightmare though again prices are static.

PUNISHER
This once the hottest of all Marvel characters experienced an all-time low in 1995 when the long-running title was cancelled. Demand for the first series of 5 issues has slackened off to the point where the title value is about half the U.K. Guide #6 listing. The character achieved some notoriety by killing off Nick Fury and has been re-launched once more. Time will tell.

REN & STIMPY
Like Beavis & Butt Head, a cult favourite cartoon. Issue #1 has risen from £7.50 in U.K. Guide #6 to £12.50 now. All early issues are up and as long as the series continues and fan interest remains, prepare for more price rises.

SGT. FURY
Worth a mention to say that early issues are not around and #1 is rarely offered for sale in the U.K. It's a Marvel #1 that always gets over-looked. Surprising to think that it came out before Daredevil! A Near Mint #1 still seems very reasonable at £450 but the size of the market in the U.K. that wants one must be taken into consideration. U.S. prices seem to value this key issue more at around $800 or £533 at a rough conversion.

SILVER SURFER
As much a cult character as ever he was, the Silver Surfer continued to enjoy much success in the early 1990s. The first series remains much in demand, helped by the publication of the excellent Marvel Masterworks edition of reprinting #1–18. A pleasure to read. #4 over-took #1 in value for its rarity status around 1993 but now the situation has reversed and #1 has assumed precedence over #4 in importance and value. The John Byrne one-shot series remains in high demand though there are copies about in the U.K. so prices have remained

largely unchanged. Surprisingly the Moebius two-issue mini-series has dropped in value. Also watch out for the one-shot graphic novel The Ultimate Cosmic Experience. An all-new Stan Lee/Jack Kirby book which is very hard to find, let alone in high grade. £100.00 has been seen at recent marts. It has been noted that a number of mis-print copies came over to this country in varying degrees of the silver foil flaking off. Most look rather ugly and soiled but ones that have a pure-white Surfer and logo look very attractive indeed and the few that have sold have gone for a wide variety of prices. It remains to be seen how many there are of this curious mis-print and indeed how to judge an accurate market value in the U.K.
U.S. price guides make no mention of it.

SPIDEY SUPER STORIES
One to watch, I kid you not. Not around, a set is impossible and some interesting villains appear to appeal to completists. And cheap.

STAR WARS
Definitely a title to watch. News abounds at the possible start date of filming the next trilogy and this under-rated title has some nice Simonson art with the last few issues becoming increasingly hard to find. Issue #107 (the last) is a monster of a comic to find in the U.K. and a £20.00 price tag takes some getting used to if you were lucky enough to pick it up at cover price when it came out.

STRANGE TALES
Issues to watch as ever are #114, #115 and #135. #135 does not seem to be around in NM and the recent death of Nick Fury may add to its appeal. The Warlock issues #178–181 are static in value as they seem to be around in the U.K. in plentiful supply.

TALES OF SUSPENSE
Issues between #57 and #66 continue to grow in desirability and are genuinely hard to find in top grades. Price rises are slight however as the market in the U.K. for these sorts of books seems to be shrinking for the time being. As a general rule of thumb in the U.K. market, later issues of Tales of Suspense do not turn up in higher grades any more whereas comparative issues of Tales to Astonish do. Prices are generally static though. #39 is in demand but very common in lower grades. True NM copies are impossible to find but demand in the U.K. seems to be low. Pre super-hero issues are not often offered for sale which is a pity as there is some lovely artwork and great covers. Low grade copies would sell well in the U.K. if some enterprising dealer from the States brought them over.

TALES TO ASTONISH
Just as with Strange Tales #101 and #110, Astonish #35 is more sought after than #27. The first Ant Man in costume is deemed more important than a man-in-an-ant-hill fantasy type story though #27 remains the hardest early Marvel key issue to get in very high grade with Hulk #1 a close second. Astonish #57 is much sought after on both sides of the Atlantic as an early Spiderman appearance (1964), there's some interest in #59 as a battle issue, #60 as hard-to-find-in-high-grade and #61 as the first Ditko Hulk since Hulk #6 back in March 1963. Issues #92 and #93 are must-haves for all Silver Surfer fans being his 4th and 5th appearances. As commented above, later issues of this title do seem to turn up in higher grades and are very common in lower grades in the U.K.

THOR
Another better year for this title than recent times with the short run from #491–#494 attracting some interest. Nice Mike Deodato artwork and crisp Warren Ellis writing injected new enthusiasm for this title. Though prices are generally static, older back issue interest continues to focus on #134 with the 1st High Evolutionary, #158 for origin facts and a great cover, #165 and #166 in which "Him" appears, not yet called Warlock and issues in the #220's with Galactus and Firelord. #193 remains tough to find in high grade and like Avengers #93, Fantastic Four #116 and Daredevil #81 can suffer from label damage in the top left-hand corner. #126 is said by many to be under-rated as it is technically the first issue of Thor as a title. The Simonson issues beginning with #337 have enjoyed a new lease of interest as a rattling good read and more attention has been focused on the first and much under-rated Simonson run from #259-271. The planned re-launch of Thor with Image has caused concern rather than excitement.

TOMB OF DRACULA
Tomb of Dracula does very well as one of the best 1970s titles with its moody Gene Colan artwork and Marv Wolfman scripts. #1–6 are increasingly hard to find in top shape though #10 with Blade the Vampire Slayer hasn't taken off as well as some thought it might. #18 and #50 are worth looking out for and the last issue (#70) is always one to defeat the completists. Check out the availability Dracula Giant Sizes as well and be surprised at their scarcity in the U.K.

WARLOCK
This character gained a huge following in the early 1990s and this short-lived series that ran 15 issues between 1972 and 1976 became much sought after. The "Thanos factor", with appearances in #9,#10,#11 and #15, did much to fuel prices though these have showed yet more signs of slowing, certainly falling behind American excesses. Issues #10 and #11 have dropped in price in the U.K. Another example of a title rescued from bargain bins of a few years ago, hyped beyond all belief and now settling back to some reasonable, affordable levels. Expect the trend to continue.

WEB OF SPIDERMAN
Worth mentioning as it is was cancelled in late 1995. The value of #1 seems to have slipped but early issues generally are up a little. #29 and #30 have slipped. #48 is $15.00 in the States, about £4.00 over here in the U.K.

WEREWOLF BY NIGHT
And yet another example of bargain bins of yesteryear now wall books of many a comic shop. Not quite in the same league as Dracula or Frankenstein but still an attractive set at 43 issues, some common as dirt, others ND and very scarce in the U.K. This title does not seem to have suffered as much as other horror titles in falling back issue sales and the title value is up by about £30 on U.K. Guide #6.

WHAT IF
The first series is approaching 20 years old incredibly and is one to watch. #1 is becoming harder to find in the U.K. and the title value as a whole is up by about 15% or so.

WOLVERINE
Still as popular as ever, early issues of his main title are difficult to keep in constant stock in U.K.

shops. #50 still seems to be in plentiful supply (speculators beware) and Sabretooth keeps cropping up to fuel fan interest Interest in the Charleston Chew Bar Wolverine giveaway comic with Sam Kieth cover and art featured has fallen away in price from £10.00 in U.K. Guide #6 to £6.00 here. The Limited series seems to be in as much demand as ever before.

X-FACTOR
Early issues of X-Factor continue to hold in value. #24 is down slightly. #40 is static. #60 is up slightly.

X-FORCE
As a more than abundant supply of copies abound, the first issue will almost definitely remain static for some time. The preference for the issue #1 with the Cable trading card and thus selling for more in the U.K. marketplace no longer applies. Rather than being the poor relation to the established and new X-Men titles, sales are just as strong, even stronger in some areas of the U.K.

X-MEN
Still number one in just about every category, the X-Men just cannot be ignored as far as volume sales go. Looking back through the 1990s, 1991 was a great year with an incredible 8 million copies supposedly printed of the first issue with its five cover variations, dealers ordered heavily and some sold out, some got stung. There is no doubt that there will be enough copies to supply demand for some considerable time to come. The first issue was well distributed to the U.K. newsagents though they suffer from a large and ugly bar-code label stuck on the front cover which is very difficult to remove (not advised!). It is not yet fully established whether all distributed copies have these labels but it is thought highly likely. 1992 was also a good year for the X-Men with the build-up to #300 and the 30th anniversary celebrations neatly falling into place. Gimmick covers again but quite tastefully done on #300. Having Deluxe and Regular editions from #316 to #321 As far as earlier back issues go on the X-Men title, #1 is deservedly over the psychological £2,500 barrier as #94 and Giant Size #1 are likewise over the £200 barrier. These two are very important milestones as far as back issues go. #94 is as difficult as ever to find in Near Mint with that dark/black cover showing the tiniest crease. The Neal Adams issues from #56–#63 and #65 have shown a lot of increased interest. #201 with the first appearance of Cyclops' son Nathan (who becomes Cable) has slackened off in demand but that does not mean it turns up with any more frequency. Prices have dropped on this from about £10.00 to £7.50. #248 with the first Jim Lee art on X-Men was in huge demand but slackened off as there seems to be a reasonable supply. £7.00 in U.K. Guide #6, £5.00 here and now. #268 is in demand for its striking cover as are all Jim Lee and Whilce Portacio art issues. The return of Magneto, the marriage of Scott and Jean and the most recent Age of Apocalypse storyline has kept interest in this title high. There is still the general fan complaint that the sub-plots are too complicated and new fans have trouble just getting into the title though Marvel seem to be addressing this situation. Ones to watch out for though are #150–200, always in demand and supply could be exhausted to dangerous levels in the U.K. soon. Issues in the #210–250 range seem fairly common in the U.K. and issues #212 and #213 have come down. Expect further falls.

Cerebus the Aardvark #1 – self-published by Dave Sim, this comic helped to usher in the Independents boom of the late 70s & early 80s

Variety is the spice of life
– or a layman's guide to Variant covers !
by Rick Appleby

Variant a. different -n. difference in form; alternative form of reading

THE ABOVE DEFINITION is courtesy of my pocket dictionary. In comic terms, however the meaning can be somewhat more, especially to the ardent collector.

The "variant cover" theme was arguably kick-started with a different than standard cover on the Image Comics title "Prophet" Volume 1, #4. This variant cover was drawn by the (then) hot artist Stephen Platt. Image in their infinite wisdom decided unannounced to issue this variant cover comic on a basis of 1 copy of the variant cover issue for every 4 copies of the standard issue ordered by your friendly retailer. This had the effect of catching everybody (including myself) totally unaware and the demand for this book led to some amazing price increases.

Under the popular misconception "that there are only 1 in 4 copies of this comic, so it must be rare" the demand and hence the asking price went sky high. The standard cover comic could be bought for around £1.50 whilst the variant cover hit a peak of around £20.00 !!

Image (no doubt encouraged by the commotion and publicity caused by this event) then began to produce more variant covers, again drawn by "hot" artists. Whilce Portacio drew some variant covers which when joined together formed a much larger "poster" of the Wildstorm characters. Again fandom responded to the cause, helped by the fact that most of the titles concerned were more readily available as the ratio was on average about 1:4 (that is one variant for every 4 standard covers). On a side note, it is worth noting that of these Wildstorm cover variants the Deathblow #5 is probably the hardest one to track down. This book still had a variant ratio of 1:4, but unfortunately the U.K did not receive its full delivery of this book. The normal book retails at £3.00 upwards, and the variant can go for anything from £10.00 upwards.

Suddenly, more and more comics were having variant covers produced. Publishers were actively promoting through the main distributors the fact that this or that book has a variant cover and in some cases even cited the ratios! Naturally, the beleaguered dealer, perhaps encouraged by the sales he or she was realising on the more popular variants ordered accordingly. More comics were printed and made available and regrettably to some extent still remain sitting on dealers shelves.

The irony of all this is that variant covers are NOT NEW !! A detailed examination of the listings in this guide will show that there are variant "test" covers for Justice League #3 and Firestorm #61 !!

In order to generate yet more sales on a particular title/issue it even reached the ludicrous stage whereby it was not uncommon to have a variant ratio of 1:1. The thinking behind this idea being that the fan would buy "both" covers. Who is say which is the standard issue and which is the variant - if indeed one exists !! Does an American "newstand edition" (with UPC barcode) count as a variant ?

I discussed this subject with a close friend who also happens to be an American dealer and he told me that his definition of a "variant cover" was in the instance where there is a distinct "plus one" ratio. That is to say, where a ratio of more than 1:2 + exists. Using this philosophy, the multi covers used on the 2nd series X-MEN #1 would not count as variants, particularly given the huge print run on this (these ?) books.

On the subject of print runs, a 1 in 25 ratio does not necessarily mean that a book is rare, not if it's print run is 500,000 !! In this instance there exists 20,000 copies of the variant cover ! That said, demand dictates price, and even then 20,000 might not be enough.

All of this and I haven't even mentioned the specially produced retailer "thank-you" editions (e.g. Spiderman Platinum) colloquially know as "premiums". There are even examples of retailers producing their own "specials" sometimes for a charitable cause but more often as an "exclusive" offer only available through them. Then there are the American convention "specials" - do these count as variants ?

Taking the issue one step further and referring back to my opening definition, it could be argued that the 60's Marvel 64 page issues (Thor #193) or the 70's Marvel Two-in-One issue drawn sideways on could be variants in their own rights. What about the anniversary issues ? They were not the normal standard, often having larger page counts and / or glow-in-the-dark / hologram / fifth ink cover which may or may not be polybagged with / without trading card etc. Then there's the old cents vs. pence argument - are the 60's Marvel and D.C comics with pence indicas variants, or not ? It's all starting to get somewhat complicated isn't it ? Perhaps, the cruellest irony of all, is that underneath the cover most of the variant cover books have exactly the same story as their "standard" issues!

Each weeks shipment of new comics invariably brings a new variant in one form or another, the popularity of which lasting maybe just as long. At the beginning of this article, I mentioned Prophet #4A from Image Comics with a peak selling price of £20.00. I have two copies of this book on my wall at comic marts at £12.00 each. No-one is interested !! It seems that one mans' variant cover is another mans' poison - or something like that !!

Those of you particularly using this guide for details of variant covers should be aware that because of the time delay between submitting the guide to the printers and retailing to yourselves (2 months), will inevitably result in some variant cover comics not being detailed. It is hoped that these ill be included in future updates. However if there are any books which have escaped notice or you feel deserve mention I am sure the authors would be pleased to hear about them. In conclusion, with some variant cover comic books realising prices of £30.00 upwards and many an argument about whether or not it is better to "invest" your money in Silver/Golden age books, it certainly is a case of variety being the spice of life !!

Avengelyne/Glory #1
(variant cover)

Deathblow #85
(variant cover)

The Night Man #1
(variant cover)

DC, MARVEL, INDEPENDENT COMICS
POINTS TO REMEMBER

- THIS BOOK IS ONLY A GUIDE AND SHOULD BE TREATED AS ONLY A GUIDE.

- COMICS SHOULD BE VERY STRICTLY GRADED, EVEN UNDER-GRADED, TO ENSURE CORRECT VALUATION.

- WHEN GRADING A COMIC, THE WHOLE COMIC MUST BE GRADED, NOT JUST THE COVER. START FROM THE INSIDE AND WORK OUT.

- MINT CONDITION MEANS MINT CONDITION. IT IS A VERY RARE GRADE.

- PRICES OF COMICS ARE CALCULATED AND SET AT TIME OF GOING TO PRESS ONLY. PLEASE ALLOW FOR A PERCENTAGE INCREASE AT LEAST IN LINE WITH INFLATION THROUGHOUT THE YEAR. THIS PERCENTAGE MAY BE MUCH HIGHER FOR OLDER, SCARCER OR IMPORTANT ISSUES.

- PRICES MAY VARY WIDELY ON VERY HIGH GRADE OR VERY "HOT" COMIC BOOKS.

- THE PRICING STRUCTURE FOR THE AMERICAN COMICS SECTION IS IN A NUMBER OF DIFFERENT RATIOS RANGING FROM 1:3:5 UP TO 1:3:16 IN EXCEPTIONAL CIRCUMSTANCES (USUALLY MAJOR KEY ISSUES). PLEASE REFER TO THE DIFFERENT PERCENTAGE CHARTS AT THE BOTTOM OF EACH PAGE FOR FURTHER CLARIFICATION.

- SOME DEALERS AND SOME COLLECTORS MAKE A DISTINCTION BETWEEN CENTS AND PENCE COPIES THOUGH THIS IS MAINLY ON RARE OR "KEY" ISSUES. IT IS AN INDIVIDUAL CHOICE.

- SOME COMICS, PARTICULARLY RARE AND "KEY" ISSUES, MAY FETCH PREMIUM PRICES IN HIGH GRADE CONDITION, THAT IS, VERY FINE PLUS OR BETTER. THESE MAY BE CALCULATED IN MULTIPLES OF GUIDE (1.25, 1.5, 2.0 TIMES GUIDE - SEE RELEVANT SECTION IN THE INTRODUCTION). FOR THOSE NEW TO COLLECTING, IT IS ADVISED TO SEEK PROFESSIONAL OPINIONS.

- ON COMICS FROM THE LAST 5 YEARS OR SO, THE NEAR MINT PRICE MAY BE TAKEN AS THE MINT PRICE.

- SCARCE, RARE AND VERY RARE HAVE BEEN USED SPARINGLY. THEY MUST NOT BE OVER-USED OR USED CASUALLY.

- THIS BOOK MUST AT ALL TIMES BE USED WITH COMMON SENSE AND FLEXIBILITY OF INTERPRETATION WITH REGARD TO PRICES.

	$Good	$Fine	$N.Mint	£Good	£Fine	£N.Mint

A

A PLUS
Megaton Publications; 1 1977-5 1978

	$Good	$Fine	$N.Mint	£Good	£Fine	£N.Mint
1-5 ND 68pgs, sci-fi anthology	$0.25	$0.75	$1.25	£0.15	£0.45	£0.80
Title Value:	$1.25	$3.75	$6.25	£0.75	£2.25	£4.00

Note: quarterly frequency

A-1
Marvel Comics Group/Epic,MS; 1 Dec 1992-4 Mar 1993
(see British section)

	$Good	$Fine	$N.Mint	£Good	£Fine	£N.Mint
1 ND 48pgs, squarebound, anthology featuring work by P. Craig Russell and Scott Hampton, Fabry cover	$1.00	$3.00	$5.00	£0.70	£2.10	£3.50
2 ND 48pgs, squarebound, anthology featuring work by George Pratt and Roger Langridge, Hunt Emerson cover	$1.00	$3.00	$5.00	£0.70	£2.10	£3.50
3 ND 48pgs, squarebound, anthology featuring work by Kent Williams, Dave Dorman, cover by Simon Bisley	$1.00	$3.00	$5.00	£0.70	£2.10	£3.50
4 ND 48pgs, squarebound, anthology featuring work by Jamie Hewlett and Colin McNeil	$1.00	$3.00	$5.00	£0.70	£2.10	£3.50
Title Value:	$4.00	$12.00	$20.00	£2.80	£8.40	£14.00

A-TEAM, THE
Marvel Comics Group,MS TV; 1 Mar 1984

	$Good	$Fine	$N.Mint	£Good	£Fine	£N.Mint
1-3 ND	$0.15	$0.45	$0.75	£0.10	£0.35	£0.60
Title Value:	$0.45	$1.35	$2.25	£0.30	£1.05	£1.80

A-V IN 3-D
Aardvark-Vanaheim,OS; 1 Dec 1984

	$Good	$Fine	$N.Mint	£Good	£Fine	£N.Mint
1 ND scarce in the U.K. Cerebus, Flaming Carrot, Ms.Tree, Journey, Neil the Horse, Normalman appear; with bound-in 3-D glasses (25% less if without glasses)	$1.50	$4.50	$7.50	£1.00	£3.00	£5.00
Title Value:	$1.50	$4.50	$7.50	£1.00	£3.00	£5.00

A.R.M.
Adventure,MS; 1 Sep 1990-3 Dec 1990

	$Good	$Fine	$N.Mint	£Good	£Fine	£N.Mint
1-3 ND based on story by Larry Niven	$0.40	$1.20	$2.00	£0.25	£0.75	£1.25
Title Value:	$1.20	$3.60	$6.00	£0.75	£2.25	£3.75

ABRAHAM STONE
Marvel Comics Group,MS; 1 Jul 1995-2 Aug 1995

	$Good	$Fine	$N.Mint	£Good	£Fine	£N.Mint
1-2 ND 48pgs, Joe Kubert script and art	$1.40	$4.20	$7.00	£0.90	£2.70	£4.50
Title Value:	$2.80	$8.40	$14.00	£1.80	£5.40	£9.00

Note: originally presented in graphic novel format by Malibu Comics

ABSOLUTE VERTIGO
DC Comics,OS; nn Mar 1995

	$Good	$Fine	$N.Mint	£Good	£Fine	£N.Mint
1 ND promotional sampler previewing Vertigo titles with an original 6pg Invisibles story; 1st appearance Preacher	$0.50	$1.50	$2.50	£0.50	£1.50	£2.50
Title Value:	$0.50	$1.50	$2.50	£0.50	£1.50	£2.50

ABSOLUTE ZERO
Antarctic Press; 1 1995-present

	$Good	$Fine	$N.Mint	£Good	£Fine	£N.Mint
1-4 ND 40pgs, anthology; black and white	$0.70	$2.10	$3.50	£0.50	£1.50	£2.50
Title Value:	$2.80	$8.40	$14.00	£2.00	£6.00	£10.00

ABYSS, THE
Dark Horse; 1,2 1989

	$Good	$Fine	$N.Mint	£Good	£Fine	£N.Mint
1 ND Mike Kaluta art begins, colour	$0.90	$2.70	$4.50	£0.60	£1.80	£3.00
2 ND scarce	$0.60	$1.80	$3.00	£0.40	£1.20	£2.00
Title Value:	$1.50	$4.50	$7.50	£1.00	£3.00	£5.00
Trade paperback				£1.20	£3.60	£6.00

Note: all adaptations of film

AC ANNUAL
AC Comics; 1 1991-present

	$Good	$Fine	$N.Mint	£Good	£Fine	£N.Mint
1 ND 64pgs	$0.80	$2.40	$4.00	£0.50	£1.50	£2.50
2 ND 64pgs, Femforce	$0.80	$2.40	$4.00	£0.50	£1.50	£2.50
3 ND 48pgs	$0.70	$2.10	$3.50	£0.45	£1.35	£2.25
4 ND 48pgs, Femforce X-over	$0.70	$2.10	$3.50	£0.45	£1.35	£2.25
Title Value:	$3.00	$9.00	$15.00	£1.90	£5.70	£9.50

ACCIDENT MAN
Dark Horse,MS; 1 May 1993-3 Aug 1993

	$Good	$Fine	$N.Mint	£Good	£Fine	£N.Mint
1-3 ND Howard Chaykin covers	$0.45	$1.35	$2.25	£0.30	£0.90	£1.50
Title Value:	$1.35	$4.05	$6.75	£0.90	£2.70	£4.50

ACE COMICS PRESENTS
Ace; 1 May 1987-4 1987

	$Good	$Fine	$N.Mint	£Good	£Fine	£N.Mint
1 ND Jack Cole reprints	$0.30	$0.90	$1.50	£0.20	£0.60	£1.00
2 ND Jack Bradbury reprints	$0.30	$0.90	$1.50	£0.20	£0.60	£1.00
3-4 ND Lou Fine reprints	$0.30	$0.90	$1.50	£0.20	£0.60	£1.00
Title Value:	$1.20	$3.60	$6.00	£0.80	£2.40	£4.00

ACES
(see British section)

ACES HIGH
Gladstone; nn 1990

	$Good	$Fine	$N.Mint	£Good	£Fine	£N.Mint
nn ND Hardcover, reprints E.C.'s Aces High #1-5	$3.00	$9.00	$15.00	£2.00	£6.00	£10.00
Title Value:	$3.00	$9.00	$15.00	£2.00	£6.00	£10.00

ACHILLES STORM
Aja Blu Comix; 1 Oct 1990

	$Good	$Fine	$N.Mint	£Good	£Fine	£N.Mint
1 ND Sandra Chang and Mark Beachum art; black and white	$0.30	$0.90	$1.50	£0.20	£0.60	£1.00
Title Value:	$0.30	$0.90	$1.50	£0.20	£0.60	£1.00

ACK THE BARBARIAN
Innovation,OS; 1 1991

	$Good	$Fine	$N.Mint	£Good	£Fine	£N.Mint
1 ND black and white	$0.40	$1.20	$2.00	£0.25	£0.75	£1.25
Title Value:	$0.40	$1.20	$2.00	£0.25	£0.75	£1.25

ACTION COMICS
DC Comics; 0 Oct 1994; 1 Jun 1938-642 Mar 1989; 643 Jul 1989-present
(Becomes Action Comics Weekly #601-642)

	$Good	$Fine	$N.Mint	£Good	£Fine	£N.Mint
0 (Oct 1994) Zero Hour X-over, origin retold; continued from Adventures of Superman #0	$0.40	$1.20	$2.00	£0.25	£0.75	£1.25
1 origin and 1st appearance Superman, 1st appearance Lois Lane and Zatara the Magician; arguably the most important comic ever published; probably no more than 100 extant copies	$13500.00	$40500.00	$135000.00	£9000.00	£27000.00	£90000.00
[Prices may vary widely on this comic]						
2	$1375.00	$4150.00	$12500.00	£920.00	£2750.00	£8300.00
3 scarce in the U.S., very scarce in the U.K. cover used in black and white as comic called "Action Funnies" to secure the "Action Comics" title and logo design	$1050.00	$3150.00	$9500.00	£690.00	£2075.00	£6250.00
4-5	$610.00	$1825.00	$5500.00	£415.00	£1250.00	£3750.00
6 1st appearance Jimmy Olsen (as office boy - see Superman #13)	$710.00	$2150.00	$5750.00	£480.00	£1425.00	£3850.00
7 2nd ever Superman cover	$960.00	$2900.00	$7750.00	£650.00	£1950.00	£5200.00
8 (Jan 1939)	$590.00	$1775.00	$4750.00	£400.00	£1200.00	£3200.00
9	$590.00	$1775.00	$4750.00	£400.00	£1200.00	£3200.00
10 3rd ever Superman cover						

Action Comics #12

Action Comics #29

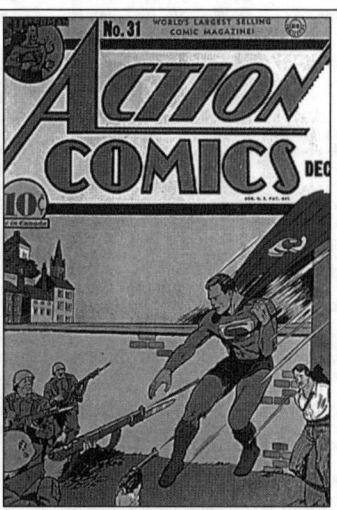
Action Comics #31

	$Good	$Fine	$N.Mint	£Good	£Fine	£N.Mint
	$870.00	$2600.00	$7000.00	£580.00	£1750.00	£4700.00
[please note that the above are approximate values only as copies very rarely come onto the UK market]						
11	$280.00	$840.00	$2250.00	£185.00	£560.00	£1500.00
12 classic science-fiction cover featuring Zatara and a rocketship blasted from a cannon; Detective Comics #27 advertised inside						
	$290.00	$880.00	$2350.00	£195.00	£590.00	£1575.00
13 4th ever Superman cover						
	$465.00	$1400.00	$3750.00	£310.00	£930.00	£2500.00
14	$275.00	$820.00	$2200.00	£180.00	£540.00	£1450.00
15 5th ever Superman cover						
	$350.00	$1050.00	$2800.00	£235.00	£710.00	£1900.00
16	$210.00	$630.00	$1700.00	£135.00	£410.00	£1100.00
17 6th ever Superman cover						
	$315.00	$950.00	$2550.00	£205.00	£610.00	£1650.00
18 last non-Superman cover, 1st mention of X-Ray vision						
	$210.00	$630.00	$1700.00	£135.00	£410.00	£1100.00
19 1st regular Superman cover						
	$265.00	$800.00	$2150.00	£180.00	£540.00	£1450.00
20 (Jan 1940), 1st mention of "The Daily Star" (later "The Daily Planet")						
	$250.00	$750.00	$2000.00	£165.00	£495.00	£1325.00
21	$175.00	$520.00	$1400.00	£115.00	£355.00	£950.00
22	$150.00	$450.00	$1200.00	£100.00	£300.00	£800.00
23 1st appearance Lex Luthor (red hair, not bald), 1st Black Pirate, 1st mention of The Daily Planet newspaper						
	$590.00	$1775.00	$4750.00	£390.00	£1175.00	£3150.00
24-28	$135.00	$410.00	$1100.00	£92.50	£280.00	£750.00
29 1st appearance of Lois Lane on cover; the cover was also used in a black and white version for "World's Best Comics" ash-can (see Top 50 Rarest Comics section)						
	$135.00	$410.00	$1100.00	£92.50	£280.00	£750.00
30	$135.00	$410.00	$1100.00	£92.50	£280.00	£750.00
(Note: all of these early issues are at least scarce in the U.K.)						
31	$105.00	$315.00	$850.00	£70.00	£215.00	£575.00
32 (Jan 1941)	$105.00	$315.00	$850.00	£70.00	£215.00	£575.00
33 origin Mr. America						
	$110.00	$335.00	$900.00	£75.00	£225.00	£600.00
34-35	$95.00	$290.00	$775.00	£65.00	£195.00	£520.00
36 robot cover	$95.00	$290.00	$775.00	£65.00	£195.00	£520.00
37 origin Congo Bill						
	$95.00	$290.00	$775.00	£65.00	£195.00	£520.00
38-39	$95.00	$290.00	$775.00	£65.00	£195.00	£520.00
40 1st appearance Star Spangled Kid						
	$95.00	$290.00	$775.00	£65.00	£195.00	£520.00
41	$95.00	$290.00	$775.00	£62.50	£185.00	£500.00
42 origin and 1st appearance Vigilante; Lex Luthor appears						
	$125.00	$375.00	$1000.00	£80.00	£240.00	£650.00
43	$92.50	$280.00	$750.00	£62.50	£185.00	£500.00
44 (Jan 1942)	$92.50	$280.00	$750.00	£62.50	£185.00	£500.00
45-46	$92.50	$280.00	$750.00	£62.50	£185.00	£500.00
47 1st Lex Luthor (bald) cover in title; Luthor acquires super-powers for the 1st time (see Superman #17) with the aid of the Powerstone (see also Superman #252)						
	$105.00	$325.00	$875.00	£72.50	£215.00	£580.00
48-50	$87.50	$260.00	$700.00	£55.00	£165.00	£450.00
51 1st appearance The Prankster						
	$95.00	$290.00	$775.00	£65.00	£195.00	£525.00
52 1st Americommandoes (Fatman and Mr. America), classic cover						
	$92.50	$280.00	$750.00	£62.50	£185.00	£500.00
53-55	$62.50	$185.00	$500.00	£44.00	£130.00	£350.00
56 (Jan 1943)	$55.00	$165.00	$450.00	£44.00	£130.00	£350.00
57 Prankster cover						
	$55.00	$165.00	$450.00	£44.00	£130.00	£350.00
58 "You Can Slap A Jap" patriotic war cover						
	$55.00	$165.00	$450.00	£44.00	£130.00	£350.00
59	$55.00	$165.00	$450.00	£44.00	£130.00	£350.00
60 1st appearance Lois Lane as Superwoman (see Superman #45)						
	$65.00	$195.00	$525.00	£46.00	£135.00	£365.00
61-63	$52.50	$155.00	$420.00	£35.00	£105.00	£280.00
64 1st appearance The Toyman, 1st Toyman cover						
	$65.00	$195.00	$525.00	£44.00	£130.00	£350.00
65-67	$52.50	$155.00	$425.00	£36.00	£105.00	£285.00
68 (Jan 1944)	$52.50	$155.00	$425.00	£36.00	£105.00	£285.00
69 Prankster cover and story						
	$52.50	$155.00	$425.00	£36.00	£105.00	£285.00
70	$52.50	$155.00	$425.00	£36.00	£105.00	£285.00
71-76	$48.00	$140.00	$385.00	£31.00	£92.50	£250.00
77 Prankster cover and story						
	$48.00	$140.00	$385.00	£31.00	£92.50	£250.00
78-79	$48.00	$140.00	$385.00	£31.00	£92.50	£250.00
80 (Jan 1945), 2nd appearance Mr. Myxyztplk (see Superman #30), 1st cover appearance						
	$75.00	$225.00	$600.00	£50.00	£150.00	£400.00
80 very scarce in the U.K., scarce in the U.S. giveaway issue with the banner "Special Edition - US Navy" across the top of cover						
	$95.00	$285.00	$675.00	£62.50	£190.00	£450.00
81	$47.00	$140.00	$375.00	£31.00	£92.50	£250.00
81 very scarce in the U.K., scarce in the U.S. giveaway issue with "Special Edition - US Navy" banner across the top of cover						
	$52.50	$155.00	$425.00	£38.00	£110.00	£300.00
82	$47.00	$140.00	$375.00	£31.00	£92.50	£250.00
83 1st appearance Hocus and Pocus						
	$50.00	$150.00	$400.00	£33.00	£97.50	£265.00
84-87	$47.00	$140.00	$375.00	£31.00	£92.50	£250.00
88 Hocus and Pocus appear						
	$47.00	$140.00	$375.00	£31.00	£92.50	£250.00
89-90	$47.00	$140.00	$375.00	£31.00	£92.50	£250.00
91	$44.00	$130.00	$350.00	£29.00	£87.50	£235.00
92 (Jan 1946)	$44.00	$130.00	$350.00	£29.00	£87.50	£235.00
93-94	$44.00	$130.00	$350.00	£29.00	£87.50	£235.00
95 Prankster cover and story						
	$44.00	$130.00	$350.00	£29.00	£87.50	£235.00
96	$44.00	$130.00	$350.00	£29.00	£87.50	£235.00
97 Hocus and Pocus appear						
	$44.00	$130.00	$350.00	£29.00	£87.50	£235.00
98	$44.00	$130.00	$350.00	£29.00	£87.50	£235.00
99 1st smaller logo on cover						
	$44.00	$130.00	$350.00	£29.00	£87.50	£235.00
100	$100.00	$305.00	$825.00	£67.50	£205.00	£550.00
101 nuclear explosion cover; cover-dated October 1946 and out on the news-stands around August of that year, therefore almost exactly a year after Hiroshima (deliberate anniversary?)						
	$85.00	$255.00	$600.00	£55.00	£170.00	£400.00
102 Mr. Mxyzptlk cover and story (the "t" and "p" were reversed in spelling in the Silver Age)						
	$52.50	$160.00	$375.00	£34.00	£100.00	£235.00
103	$52.50	$160.00	$375.00	£34.00	£100.00	£235.00
104 (Jan 1947), Prankster cover and story						
	$52.50	$160.00	$375.00	£34.00	£100.00	£235.00
105 Christmas cover						
	$52.50	$160.00	$375.00	£34.00	£100.00	£235.00
106-108	$50.00	$150.00	$350.00	£32.00	£95.00	£225.00
109 Prankster cover and story						
	$52.50	$160.00	$375.00	£34.00	£100.00	£235.00
110-111	$50.00	$150.00	$350.00	£32.00	£95.00	£225.00
112 Mr. Mxyztplk cover and story						
	$52.50	$160.00	$375.00	£34.00	£100.00	£235.00
113-115	$50.00	$150.00	$350.00	£32.00	£95.00	£225.00
116 (Jan 1948)	$50.00	$150.00	$350.00	£32.00	£95.00	£225.00
117 Christmas cover						
	$52.50	$160.00	$375.00	£34.00	£100.00	£235.00
118-120	$50.00	$150.00	$350.00	£32.00	£95.00	£225.00
121 Superman vs. Atlas						
	$49.00	$145.00	$340.00	£31.00	£92.50	£220.00
122-124	$49.00	$145.00	$340.00	£31.00	£92.50	£220.00
125 scarce in the U.K.						
	$50.00	$150.00	$350.00	£32.00	£95.00	£225.00
126	$49.00	$145.00	$340.00	£31.00	£92.50	£220.00
127 Tommy Tomorrow feature begins, Vigilante by Kubert						
	$55.00	$170.00	$400.00	£37.00	£110.00	£260.00
128 (Jan 1949)	$49.00	$145.00	$340.00	£31.00	£92.50	£220.00
129-130	$49.00	$145.00	$340.00	£31.00	£92.50	£220.00
131 Lex Luthor cover and story						
	$50.00	$150.00	$350.00	£32.00	£95.00	£225.00
132-137	$49.00	$145.00	$340.00	£31.00	£92.50	£220.00
138 nuclear bomb-carrying "flying wing" aeroplane cover						
	$50.00	$150.00	$350.00	£32.00	£95.00	£225.00
139	$49.00	$145.00	$340.00	£31.00	£92.50	£220.00
140 (Jan 1950)	$49.00	$145.00	$340.00	£31.00	£92.50	£220.00
141 Lex Luthor cover and story						
	$46.00	$135.00	$325.00	£31.00	£92.50	£220.00
142-145	$45.00	$135.00	$315.00	£30.00	£90.00	£210.00
146 cover based on Action Comics #20						
	$45.00	$135.00	$315.00	£30.00	£90.00	£210.00
147-150	$45.00	$135.00	$315.00	£30.00	£90.00	£210.00
151 Luthor, Prankster, Mr. Mxyzptlk appear						
	$45.00	$135.00	$315.00	£30.00	£90.00	£210.00
152 (Jan 1951)	$43.00	$125.00	$300.00	£29.00	£85.00	£200.00
153-155	$43.00	$125.00	$300.00	£29.00	£85.00	£200.00
156 Lois Lane as The Girl of Steel; the blonde wig makes this a much more direct Supergirl try-out than the brunette in Superman #123						
	$43.00	$125.00	$300.00	£30.00	£90.00	£210.00
157	$43.00	$125.00	$300.00	£29.00	£85.00	£200.00
158 Superman's origin retold						
	$87.50	$265.00	$625.00	£60.00	£180.00	£425.00
159-160	$43.00	$125.00	$300.00	£29.00	£85.00	£200.00
161-163	$39.00	$115.00	$275.00	£26.00	£77.50	£185.00
164 (Jan 1952)	$39.00	$115.00	$275.00	£26.00	£77.50	£185.00
165-170	$39.00	$115.00	$275.00	£26.00	£77.50	£185.00
171-175	$36.00	$105.00	$250.00	£23.50	£70.00	£165.00
176 (Jan 1953)	$36.00	$105.00	$250.00	£23.50	£70.00	£165.00
177-180	$36.00	$105.00	$250.00	£23.50	£70.00	£165.00
181	$34.00	$100.00	$250.00	£22.50	£67.50	£160.00
182 The Return of Planet Krypton story						
	$34.00	$100.00	$240.00	£22.50	£67.50	£160.00
183-187	$34.00	$100.00	$240.00	£22.50	£67.50	£160.00
188 (Jan 1954)	$34.00	$100.00	$240.00	£22.50	£67.50	£160.00
189-193	$34.00	$100.00	$240.00	£22.50	£67.50	£160.00
194 Return of the Foes from Krypton (see Superman #65)						
	$34.00	$100.00	$240.00	£22.50	£67.50	£160.00
195-199	$34.00	$100.00	$240.00	£22.50	£67.50	£160.00
200 very scarce in the U.K., scarce in the U.S						
	$39.00	$115.00	$275.00	£28.00	£82.50	£195.00
201-209 very scarce in the U.K., scarce in the U.S						
	$31.00	$90.00	$215.00	£22.00	£65.00	£155.00
210-211	$31.00	$90.00	$215.00	£20.50	£60.00	£145.00
212 (Jan 1956), 1956 Superman calendar included						
	$31.00	$90.00	$215.00	£20.50	£60.00	£145.00
213-217	$31.00	$90.00	$215.00	£20.50	£60.00	£145.00
218 Super-Ape from Krypton (pre Titano)						

Issue / Note	$Good	$Fine	$N.Mint	£Good	£Fine	£N.Mint
	$30.00	$90.00	$210.00	£20.50	£60.00	£145.00
219-220	$30.00	$90.00	$210.00	£20.50	£60.00	£145.00
221-222	$25.00	$75.00	$175.00	£17.50	£52.50	£122.50
223 scarce in the U.K. Jor-El as "Superman" on Krypton						
	$25.00	$75.00	$175.00	£20.00	£60.00	£140.00
224 (Jan 1957)	$25.00	$75.00	$175.00	£17.50	£52.50	£122.50
225-231	$25.00	$75.00	$175.00	£17.50	£52.50	£122.50
232 1st Curt Swan cover						
	$25.00	$75.00	$175.00	£17.50	£52.50	£122.50
233-234	$25.00	$75.00	$175.00	£17.50	£52.50	£122.50
235 scarce in the U.K.						
	$25.00	$75.00	$175.00	£20.00	£60.00	£140.00
236 scarce in the U.K. (Jan 1958)						
	$25.00	$75.00	$175.00	£20.00	£60.00	£140.00
237 scarce in the U.K.						
	$25.00	$75.00	$175.00	£20.00	£60.00	£140.00
238-240	$25.00	$75.00	$175.00	£17.50	£52.50	£122.50
241 Batman appears						
	$30.00	$90.00	$210.00	£20.00	£60.00	£140.00
242 origin and 1st appearance Brainiac, 1st mention of bottle-city of Kandor						
	$110.00	$335.00	$900.00	£80.00	£240.00	£650.00
[Rare in high grade - Very Fine+ or better]						
243-247	$20.00	$60.00	$140.00	£14.00	£43.00	£100.00
248 (Jan 1959), 1st appearance Congorilla (formerly Golden Gorilla, whose 1st appearance was in #224)						
	$20.00	$60.00	$140.00	£14.00	£43.00	£100.00
249-250	$20.00	$60.00	$140.00	£14.00	£43.00	£100.00
251 last Tommy Tomorrow						
	$20.00	$60.00	$140.00	£14.00	£43.00	£100.00
252 origin and 1st appearance Supergirl, Metallo appears						
	$150.00	$450.00	$1200.00	£100.00	£305.00	£825.00
252 ND Silver Age Classic reprint (Mar 1992)						
	$0.25	$0.75	$1.25	£0.15	£0.45	£0.80
253 2nd appearance Supergirl						
	$35.00	$105.00	$245.00	£23.50	£70.00	£165.00
254 Bizarro and Superman 1st meeting						
	$35.00	$105.00	$245.00	£21.00	£62.50	£150.00
255 1st appearance Bizarro Lois and making of Bizarro World						
	$25.00	$75.00	$175.00	£17.00	£50.00	£120.00
256	$15.00	$45.00	$105.00	£10.00	£30.00	£70.00
257 copies known with distribution stamps						
	$15.00	$45.00	$105.00	£10.00	£30.00	£70.00
1st official distribution in the U.K.						
258-259	$15.00	$45.00	$105.00	£10.00	£30.00	£70.00
260 (Jan 1960)	$15.00	$45.00	$105.00	£10.00	£30.00	£70.00
261 1st appearance X-Kryptonite, origin Streaky the Super-Cat						
	$16.00	$49.00	$115.00	£10.50	£32.00	£75.00
262	$12.50	$39.00	$90.00	£8.50	£26.00	£60.00
263 origin of the Bizarro World; Superman becomes a Bizarro						
	$12.50	$39.00	$90.00	£8.50	£26.00	£60.00
264 Superman as Bizarro						
	$12.50	$39.00	$90.00	£8.50	£26.00	£60.00
265-266	$12.50	$39.00	$90.00	£8.50	£26.00	£60.00
267 3rd appearance of Legion (Superboy story); 1st Invisible Kid, Chameleon Boy, Colossal Boy						
	$45.00	$135.00	$360.00	£30.00	£90.00	£240.00
268-270	$12.50	$39.00	$90.00	£8.50	£26.00	£60.00
271	$10.50	$32.00	$75.00	£7.00	£21.00	£50.00
272 (Jan 1961)	$10.50	$32.00	$75.00	£7.00	£21.00	£50.00
273-275	$10.50	$32.00	$75.00	£7.00	£21.00	£50.00
276 6th appearance of Legion (Supergirl story); 1st Brainiac 5, Bouncing Boy, Sun Boy, Shrinking Violet, Triplicate Girl, Phantom Girl						
	$21.50	$65.00	$175.00	£15.00	£45.00	£120.00
277-280	$10.50	$32.00	$75.00	£7.00	£21.00	£50.00
281	$10.50	$32.00	$75.00	£6.25	£19.00	£45.00
282 last 10 cents issue						
	$10.50	$32.00	$75.00	£6.25	£19.00	£45.00
283 Legion of Super-Villains appear; 1st 12 cents issue						
	$10.50	$32.00	$75.00	£7.00	£21.00	£50.00
284 (Jan 1962), Mon-El appearance						
	$10.50	$32.00	$75.00	£7.00	£21.00	£50.00
285 12th appearance of Legion; Supergirl's existence revealed to the world						
	$10.50	$32.00	$75.00	£7.00	£21.00	£50.00
286 Legion of Super-Villains appear						
	$7.75	$23.50	$55.00	£5.00	£15.00	£35.00
287 15th appearance of Legion (Supergirl story)						
	$7.75	$23.50	$55.00	£5.00	£15.00	£35.00
288 Mon-El appearance						
	$7.75	$23.50	$55.00	£5.00	£15.00	£35.00
289 17th appearance of Legion, as adults (Supergirl story)						
	$7.75	$23.50	$55.00	£5.00	£15.00	£35.00
290 18th appearance of Legion, 3 panels (Supergirl story)						
	$7.75	$23.50	$55.00	£5.00	£15.00	£35.00
291-292	$6.25	$19.00	$45.00	£3.55	£10.50	£25.00
293 origin Comet, the Super-Horse						
	$12.00	$36.00	$85.00	£6.25	£19.00	£45.00
294-295	$6.25	$19.00	$45.00	£3.55	£10.50	£25.00
296 (Jan 1963)	$6.25	$19.00	$45.00	£3.55	£10.50	£25.00
297-299	$6.25	$19.00	$45.00	£3.55	£10.50	£25.00
300 classic cover - "Superman Under a Red Sun" (highly rated by historian Ian G. Holmes)						
	$7.75	$23.50	$55.00	£5.00	£15.00	£35.00
301-303	$4.25	$12.50	$30.00	£2.50	£7.50	£17.50
304 1st appearance Black Flame						
	$4.25	$12.50	$30.00	£2.50	£7.50	£17.50

Issue / Note	$Good	$Fine	$N.Mint	£Good	£Fine	£N.Mint
305-307	$4.25	$12.50	$30.00	£2.50	£7.50	£17.50
308 (Jan 1964)	$4.25	$12.50	$30.00	£2.50	£7.50	£17.50
309 Batman and Legion appear						
	$4.25	$12.50	$30.00	£2.85	£8.50	£20.00
310 1st appearance Jewel Kryptonite						
	$4.25	$12.50	$30.00	£2.50	£7.50	£17.50
311-312	$3.55	$10.50	$25.00	£1.75	£5.25	£12.50
313 Batman appears; Lena Thorul learns she's Luthor's sister						
	$3.55	$10.50	$25.00	£1.75	£5.25	£12.50
314 Justice League of America X-over (Flash, Aquaman, Batman and Green Lantern)						
	$3.55	$10.50	$25.00	£1.75	£5.25	£12.50
315-319	$3.55	$10.50	$25.00	£1.75	£5.25	£12.50
320 (Jan 1965)	$3.55	$10.50	$25.00	£1.75	£5.25	£12.50
321-330	$3.30	$10.00	$20.00	£1.65	£5.00	£10.00
331 last Silver Age issue cover-dated Dec 1965						
	$3.30	$10.00	$20.00	£1.30	£4.00	£8.00
332 (Jan 1966)	$3.30	$10.00	$20.00	£1.30	£4.00	£8.00
333	$3.30	$10.00	$20.00	£1.30	£4.00	£8.00
334 scarce in the U.K. 80pgs, Giant G-20, reprints Supergirl origin from #252 and 3rd Legion from #267						
	$6.50	$20.00	$40.00	£4.15	£12.50	£25.00
335-339	$3.30	$10.00	$20.00	£1.65	£5.00	£10.00
340 1st appearance Parasite						
	$4.15	$12.50	$25.00	£2.05	£6.25	£12.50
341-344	$2.50	$7.50	$15.00	£1.05	£3.25	£6.50
345 (Jan 1967)	$2.50	$7.50	$15.00	£1.05	£3.25	£6.50
346	$2.50	$7.50	$15.00	£1.05	£3.25	£6.50
347 scarce in the U.K. 80pgs, Giant G-33						
	$4.15	$12.50	$25.00	£2.90	£8.75	£17.50
348-350	$2.50	$7.50	$15.00	£1.00	£3.00	£6.00
351 Captain Marvel inspired "Zha-Vam" story						
	$2.50	$7.50	$15.00	£1.00	£3.00	£6.00
352-357	$2.50	$7.50	$15.00	£1.00	£3.00	£6.00
358 (Jan 1968), Neal Adams cover						
	$2.50	$7.50	$15.00	£1.00	£3.00	£6.00
359 Neal Adams cover						
	$2.50	$7.50	$15.00	£1.00	£3.00	£6.00
360 scarce in the U.K. 80pgs, Giant G-45, full length Supergirl story from back-up reprints						
	$4.15	$12.50	$25.00	£2.90	£8.75	£17.50
361-365	$1.65	$5.00	$10.00	£0.75	£2.25	£4.50
366 Justice League of America appears						
	$1.65	$5.00	$10.00	£0.75	£2.25	£4.50
367 Neal Adams cover						
	$1.65	$5.00	$10.00	£0.75	£2.25	£4.50
368-369	$1.65	$5.00	$10.00	£0.75	£2.25	£4.50
370 Neal Adams cover						
	$1.65	$5.00	$10.00	£0.75	£2.25	£4.50
371 (Jan 1969), Neal Adams cover						
	$1.65	$5.00	$10.00	£0.75	£2.25	£4.50
372 Neal Adams cover						
	$1.65	$5.00	$10.00	£0.75	£2.25	£4.50
373 68pgs, Giant G-57						
	$4.15	$12.50	$25.00	£2.05	£6.25	£12.50
374 Neal Adams cover						
	$1.65	$5.00	$10.00	£0.75	£2.25	£4.50
375-376	$1.65	$5.00	$10.00	£0.75	£2.25	£4.50
377-379 Legion back-up						
	$1.65	$5.00	$10.00	£0.80	£2.50	£5.00
380 Legion back-up						
	$1.65	$5.00	$10.00	£0.80	£2.50	£5.00
381-383 Legion back-up						
	$1.30	$4.00	$8.00	£0.80	£2.50	£5.00
384 (Jan 1970), Legion back-up						
	$1.30	$4.00	$8.00	£0.80	£2.50	£5.00
385-391 Legion back-up						
	$1.30	$4.00	$8.00	£0.80	£2.50	£5.00
392 Legion back-up						
	$1.30	$4.00	$8.00	£0.80	£2.50	£5.00
393-395	$1.30	$4.00	$8.00	£0.55	£1.75	£3.50
396 (Jan 1971)	$1.30	$4.00	$8.00	£0.55	£1.75	£3.50
397	$1.30	$4.00	$8.00	£0.55	£1.75	£3.50
398-400 Neal Adams cover						
	$1.30	$4.00	$8.00	£0.55	£1.75	£3.50
401	$1.40	$4.20	$7.00	£0.70	£2.10	£3.50
402 Neal Adams cover						
	$1.40	$4.20	$7.00	£0.70	£2.10	£3.50
403-407 48pgs	$1.60	$4.80	$8.00	£0.80	£2.40	£4.00
408 48pgs, (Jan 1972)	$1.60	$4.80	$8.00	£0.80	£2.40	£4.00
409-410 48pgs	$1.60	$4.80	$8.00	£0.80	£2.40	£4.00
411 48pgs, Eclipso origin reprinted						
	$1.60	$4.80	$8.00	£0.80	£2.40	£4.00
412 48pgs	$1.60	$4.80	$8.00	£0.80	£2.40	£4.00
413 48pgs, Metamorpho begins, ends #418						
	$1.60	$4.80	$8.00	£0.80	£2.40	£4.00
414 scarce in the U.K.						
	$1.60	$4.80	$8.00	£0.80	£2.40	£4.00
415-418	$1.60	$4.80	$8.00	£0.60	£1.80	£3.00
419 scarce in the U.K. photo cover						
	$1.60	$4.80	$8.00	£0.70	£2.10	£3.50
420 (Jan 1973)	$1.60	$4.80	$8.00	£0.60	£1.80	£3.00
421 Green Arrow begins						
	$1.60	$4.80	$8.00	£0.50	£1.50	£2.50

Issue / Notes	$Good	$Fine	$N.Mint	£Good	£Fine	£N.Mint
422-424	$1.60	$4.80	$8.00	£0.50	£1.50	£2.50
425 Neal Adams art, Atom back-up begins						
	$3.00	$9.00	$15.00	£1.20	£3.60	£6.00
426-430	$1.40	$4.20	$7.00	£0.40	£1.20	£2.00
431 (Jan 1974)	$1.40	$4.20	$7.00	£0.40	£1.20	£2.00
432-436	$1.40	$4.20	$7.00	£0.40	£1.20	£2.00
437 LD in the U.K. 100pgs, reprints Sea Devils #1						
	$2.40	$7.00	$12.00	£0.80	£2.40	£4.00
438-439	$1.40	$4.20	$7.00	£0.40	£1.20	£2.00
440 1st Mike Grell Green Arrow						
	$1.20	$3.60	$6.00	£0.80	£2.40	£4.00
441 Grell Green Arrow						
	$1.20	$3.60	$6.00	£0.60	£1.80	£2.00
442	$0.80	$2.40		£0.40	£1.20	£2.00
443 LD in the U.K. 100pgs, (Jan 1975), Justice League appears						
	$2.40	$7.00	$12.00	£0.80	£2.40	£4.00
444-448	$0.80	$2.40	$4.00	£0.40	£1.20	£2.00
449 LD in the U.K. 68pgs						
	$0.80	$2.40	$4.00	£0.60	£1.80	£3.00
450	$0.80	$2.40	$4.00	£0.40	£1.20	£2.00
451-454 scarce in the U.K.						
	$0.80	$2.40	$4.00	£0.40	£1.50	£2.50
455 (Jan 1976)	$0.80	$2.40	$4.00	£0.40	£1.20	£2.00
456-457	$0.80	$2.40	$4.00	£0.40	£1.20	£2.00
458 last Green Arrow back-up						
	$0.80	$2.40	$4.00	£0.40	£1.20	
459 scarce in the U.K.						
	$0.80	$2.40	$4.00	£0.50	£1.50	£2.50
460	$0.80	$2.40	$4.00	£0.40	£1.20	£2.00
461 ND	$0.70	$2.10	$3.50	£0.60	£1.80	£3.00
462-465 scarce in the U.K.						
	$0.70	$2.10	$3.50	£0.40	£1.20	£2.00
466 scarce in the U.K. Neal Adams cover						
	$0.70	$2.10	$3.50	£0.40	£1.20	£2.00
467 scarce in the U.K. (Jan 1977)						
	$0.70	$2.10	$3.50	£0.40	£1.20	£2.00
468 scarce in the U.K. Neal Adams cover						
	$0.70	$2.10	$3.50	£0.40	£1.20	£2.00
469-472 scarce in the U.K.						
	$0.70	$2.10	$3.50	£0.40	£1.20	£2.00
473 scarce in the U.K. Neal Adams cover						
	$0.70	$2.10	$3.50	£0.40	£1.20	£2.00
474-478 scarce in the U.K.						
	$0.70	$2.10	$3.50	£0.40	£1.20	£2.00
479 scarce in the U.K. (Jan 1978)						
	$0.70	$2.10	$3.50	£0.40	£1.20	£2.00
480	$0.70	$2.10	$3.50	£0.30	£0.90	£1.50
481 1st Supermobile						
	$0.70	$2.10	$3.50	£0.30	£0.90	£1.50
482-483	$0.70	$2.10	$3.50	£0.30	£0.90	£1.50
484 40th anniversary, Earth-2 Superman weds						
	$0.70	$2.10	$3.50	£0.40	£1.20	£2.00
485 Neal Adams cover						
	$0.70	$2.10	$3.50	£0.30	£0.90	£1.50
486	$0.70	$2.10	$3.50	£0.30	£0.90	£1.50
487 scarce in the U.K. 44pgs, origin Atom retold						
	$0.70	$2.10	$3.50	£0.50	£1.50	£2.50
488-489 ND	$0.70	$2.10	$3.50	£0.60	£1.80	£3.00
490	$0.70	$2.10	$3.50	£0.30	£0.90	£1.50
491 (Jan 1979)	$0.70	$2.10	$3.50	£0.30	£0.90	£1.50
492-499	$0.70	$2.10	$3.50	£0.30	£0.90	£1.50
500 ND 68pgs, Superman's life story						
	$1.00	$3.00	$5.00	£0.60	£1.80	£3.00
501-502	$0.40	$1.20	$2.00	£0.25	£0.75	£1.25
503 (Jan 1980)	$0.40	$1.20	$2.00	£0.25	£0.75	£1.25
504-508	$0.40	$1.20	$2.00	£0.25	£0.75	£1.25
509 58pgs, Jim Starlin art on 28pg Superman insert "The Computer That Saved Metropolis" (later issued as a giveaway)						
	$0.40	$1.20	$2.00	£0.30	£0.90	£1.50
510-514	$0.40	$1.20	$2.00	£0.25	£0.75	£1.25
515 (Jan 1981)	$0.40	$1.20	$2.00	£0.25	£0.75	£1.25
516-520	$0.40	$1.20	$2.00	£0.25	£0.75	£1.25
521 1st appearance The Vixen						
	$0.40	$1.20	$2.00	£0.25	£0.75	£1.25
522 Teen Titans cameo						
	$0.40	$1.20	$2.00	£0.25	£0.75	£1.25
523-526	$0.40	$1.20	$2.00	£0.25	£0.75	£1.25
527 (Jan 1982), 1st appearance Lord Satanis						
	$0.40	$1.20	$2.00	£0.25	£0.75	£1.25
528	$0.40	$1.20	$2.00	£0.25	£0.75	£1.25
529 George Perez cover						
	$0.40	$1.20	$2.00	£0.25	£0.75	£1.25
530-534	$0.40	$1.20	$2.00	£0.25	£0.75	£1.25
535-536 Omega Men appear						
	$0.40	$1.20	$2.00	£0.25	£0.75	£1.25
537-538	$0.40	$1.20	$2.00	£0.25	£0.75	£1.25
539 (Jan 1983), Keith Giffen cover						
	$0.40	$1.20	$2.00	£0.25	£0.75	£1.25
540-543	$0.40	$1.20	$2.00	£0.25	£0.75	£1.25
544 LD in the U.K. 68pgs, 45th anniversary, origins new Brainiac and Luthor						
	$0.50	$1.50	$2.50	£0.50	£1.50	£2.50
545	$0.40	$1.20	$2.00	£0.25	£0.75	£1.25

Issue / Notes	$Good	$Fine	$N.Mint	£Good	£Fine	£N.Mint
546 Justice League of America, Teen Titans X-over						
	$0.40	$1.20	$2.00	£0.25	£0.75	£1.25
547	$0.40	$1.20	$2.00	£0.25	£0.75	£1.25
548 Jewel Kryptonite returns (see #310)						
	$0.40	$1.20	$2.00	£0.25	£0.75	£1.25
549-550	$0.40	$1.20	$2.00	£0.25	£0.75	£1.25
551 (Jan 1984)	$0.40	$1.20	$2.00	£0.25	£0.75	£1.25
552-553 Animal Man story/cover						
	$0.80	$2.40	$4.00	£0.30	£0.90	£1.50
554-559	$0.40	$1.20	$2.00	£0.25	£0.75	£1.25
560 Keith Giffen Ambush Bug						
	$0.40	$1.20	$2.00	£0.25	£0.75	£1.25
561-562	$0.40	$1.20	$2.00	£0.25	£0.75	£1.25
563 (Jan 1985), Ambush Bug						
	$0.40	$1.20	$2.00	£0.25	£0.75	£1.25
564	$0.40	$1.20	$2.00	£0.25	£0.75	£1.25
565 Ambush Bug	$0.40	$1.20	$2.00	£0.25	£0.75	£1.25
566-574	$0.40	$1.20	$2.00	£0.25	£0.75	£1.25
575 (Jan 1986)	$0.40	$1.20	$2.00	£0.25	£0.75	£1.25
576-578	$0.40	$1.20	$2.00	£0.25	£0.75	£1.25
579 unofficial Asterix X-over, Giffen art						
	$0.40	$1.20	$2.00	£0.25	£0.75	£1.25
580-582	$0.40	$1.20	$2.00	£0.25	£0.75	£1.25
583 Alan Moore script, "Last Superman story" (see Superman #423)						
	$2.00	$6.00	$10.00	£0.40	£1.20	£2.00
584 (Jan 1987), John Byrne art begins, New Teen Titans appear						
	$0.40	$1.20	$2.00	£0.25	£0.75	£1.25
585 John Byrne art, Phantom Stranger appears						
	$0.30	$0.90	$1.50	£0.20	£0.60	£1.00
586 John Byrne art, New Gods appear						
	$0.30	$0.90	$1.50	£0.20	£0.60	£1.00
587 John Byrne art, The Demon appears						
	$0.30	$0.90	$1.50	£0.20	£0.60	£1.00
588 John Byrne art, Hawkman appears						
	$0.30	$0.90	$1.50	£0.20	£0.60	£1.00
589 John Byrne art, Green Lantern Corps appear						
	$0.30	$0.90	$1.50	£0.20	£0.60	£1.00
590 John Byrne art, Metal Men appear						
	$0.30	$0.90	$1.50	£0.20	£0.60	£1.00
591 John Byrne art, Superboy, Legion appears; Superboy's existence explained Post-Crisis (see Legion #37/38, Superman #8)						
	$0.30	$0.90	$1.50	£0.25	£0.75	£1.25
592 John Byrne art, Big Barda appears						
	$0.30	$0.90	$1.50	£0.20	£0.60	£1.00
593 John Byrne art, Mister Miracle appears						
	$0.30	$0.90	$1.50	£0.20	£0.60	£1.00
594 John Byrne art, Booster Gold appears						
	$0.30	$0.90	$1.50	£0.20	£0.60	£1.00
595 John Byrne art, Martian Manhunter appears						
	$0.30	$0.90	$1.50	£0.20	£0.60	£1.00
596 (Jan 1988), John Byrne art, The Spectre appears; unofficial Millennium X-over						
	$0.30	$0.90	$1.50	£0.20	£0.60	£1.00
597 John Byrne art, Lois Lane & Lana Lang appear						
	$0.30	$0.90	$1.50	£0.20	£0.60	£1.00
598 John Byrne art, 1st appearance of Checkmate						
	$0.30	$0.90	$1.50	£0.20	£0.60	£1.00
599 John Byrne art, Metal Men appear						
	$0.30	$0.90	$1.50	£0.20	£0.60	£1.00
600 LD in the U.K. 80pgs, Giant, Golden anniversary, John Byrne, George Perez, Curt Swan & Mike Mignola art featured, Wonder Woman and Darkseid appear						
	$1.00	$3.00	$5.00	£0.50	£1.50	£2.50
601 Blackhawk, Deadman, Secret Six, Green Lantern, Superman, Wild Dog begin (5/6 features rotate around Superman until #642)						
	$0.35	$1.05	$1.75	£0.15	£0.45	£0.75
602-608	$0.35	$1.05	$1.75	£0.15	£0.45	£0.75
609 Bolland cover	$0.35	$1.05	$1.75	£0.15	£0.45	£0.75
610	$0.35	$1.05	$1.75	£0.15	£0.45	£0.75
611-614 Catwoman appears						
	$0.35	$1.05	$1.75	£0.15	£0.45	£0.75
615-625	$0.35	$1.05	$1.75	£0.10	£0.35	£0.60
626 Paul Chadwick cover						
	$0.35	$1.05	$1.75	£0.10	£0.35	£0.60
627 Gil Kane cover	$0.35	$1.05	$1.75	£0.10	£0.35	£0.60
628 (Jan 1989)	$0.35	$1.05	$1.75	£0.10	£0.35	£0.60
629-634	$0.35	$1.05	$1.75	£0.15	£0.45	£0.75
635 X-over story; Green Lantern, Superman, Black Canary, Blackhawk & Batman appear						
	$0.35	$1.05	$1.75	£0.15	£0.45	£0.75
636 intro new Phantom Lady, Demon begins written by Alan Grant (ends #641)						
	$0.35	$1.05	$1.75	£0.15	£0.45	£0.75
637	$0.35	$1.05	$1.75	£0.15	£0.45	£0.75
638 Jack Kirby cover (Demon)						
	$0.35	$1.05	$1.75	£0.15	£0.45	£0.75
639 Bolland cover	$0.35	$1.05	$1.75	£0.15	£0.45	£0.75
640	$0.35	$1.05	$1.75	£0.15	£0.45	£0.75
641 Superman cover based on Action #13						
	$0.35	$1.05	$1.75	£0.15	£0.45	£0.75
642 full length story, featuring art by Bob Kane/Steve Ditko/Curt Swan/Infantino/Nowlan						
	$0.35	$1.05	$1.75	£0.15	£0.45	£0.75
643 George Perez art; cover based on Superman #1						
	$0.20	$0.60	$1.00	£0.15	£0.45	£0.75
644-645 George Perez art						
	$0.20	$0.60	$1.00	£0.15	£0.45	£0.75

	$Good	$Fine	$N.Mint	£Good	£Fine	£N.Mint
646 Giffen art	$0.20	$0.60	$1.00	£0.15	£0.45	£0.75
647-648 George Perez art; Braniac Trilogy	$0.20	$0.60	$1.00	£0.15	£0.45	£0.75
649 (Jan 1990), George Perez art; Braniac Trilogy	$0.20	$0.60	$1.00	£0.15	£0.45	£0.75
650 48pgs, features Jerry Ordway, Curt Swan, George Perez art; Justice League International appear; Lobo cameo	$0.30	$0.90	$1.50	£0.25	£0.75	£1.25
651 George Perez lay-out art	$0.20	$0.60	$1.00	£0.15	£0.45	£0.75
652 X-over with Superman #42/Adventures of Superman #465; George Perez lay-out art	$0.20	$0.60	$1.00	£0.15	£0.45	£0.75
653	$0.20	$0.60	$1.00	£0.15	£0.45	£0.75
654 continues from Superman #44/Adventures of Superman #467; Batman appears, George Perez cover	$0.20	$0.60	$1.00	£0.15	£0.45	£0.75
655 free 8 page insert	$0.20	$0.60	$1.00	£0.15	£0.45	£0.75
656 X-over with Superman #47/Adventures of Superman #470	$0.20	$0.60	$1.00	£0.15	£0.45	£0.75
657 Toyman appears	$0.20	$0.60	$1.00	£0.15	£0.45	£0.75
658 The Sinbad Contract part 3	$0.20	$0.60	$1.00	£0.15	£0.45	£0.75
659 Krisis of the Krimson Kryptonite part 3, X-over Superman #50	$0.20	$0.60	$1.00	£0.15	£0.45	£0.75
660 Lex Luthor "dies"	$0.20	$0.60	$1.00	£0.15	£0.45	£0.75
661 (Jan 1991), Plastic Man appears	$0.20	$0.60	$1.00	£0.15	£0.45	£0.75
662 Superman's identity revealed to Lois Lane, story continued in Superman #53	$0.75	$2.25	$3.75	£0.25	£0.75	£1.25
663 Time and Time Again part 2, continues in Superman #54	$0.20	$0.60	$1.00	£0.15	£0.45	£0.75
664 Time and Time Again part 5	$0.20	$0.60	$1.00	£0.15	£0.45	£0.75
665 LD in the U.K.	$0.20	$0.60	$1.00	£0.20	£0.60	£1.00
666 LD in the U.K. The Red Glass Trilogy part 3	$0.20	$0.60	$1.00	£0.20	£0.60	£1.00
667 48pgs, Revenge of the Krypton Man part 4	$0.20	$0.60	$1.00	£0.15	£0.45	£0.75
668-669	$0.20	$0.60	$1.00	£0.15	£0.45	£0.75
670 Armageddon: 2001 tie-in	$0.20	$0.60	$1.00	£0.15	£0.45	£0.75
671 Blackout part 2	$0.20	$0.60	$1.00	£0.15	£0.45	£0.75
672	$0.20	$0.60	$1.00	£0.15	£0.45	£0.75
673 (Jan 1992)	$0.20	$0.60	$1.00	£0.15	£0.45	£0.75
674 Supergirl (Matrix) returns	$0.20	$0.60	$1.00	£0.15	£0.45	£0.75
675 Panic in the Sky part 4	$0.20	$0.60	$1.00	£0.15	£0.45	£0.75
676 Art Thibert cover	$0.20	$0.60	$1.00	£0.15	£0.45	£0.75
677 Superman vs. Supergirl, Art Thibert cover	$0.20	$0.60	$1.00	£0.15	£0.45	£0.75
678 Art Thibert cover	$0.20	$0.60	$1.00	£0.15	£0.45	£0.75
679 $1.25 cover begins, Art Thibert cover	$0.25	$0.75	$1.25	£0.15	£0.45	£0.80
680 The Blaze/Satanus War part 2, continued in Superman Man of Steel #15, Art Thibert cover	$0.25	$0.75	$1.25	£0.15	£0.45	£0.80
681 Art Thibert cover	$0.25	$0.75	$1.25	£0.15	£0.45	£0.80

	$Good	$Fine	$N.Mint	£Good	£Fine	£N.Mint
682	$0.25	$0.75	$1.25	£0.15	£0.45	£0.80
683 Robin appears and Doomsday cameo	$0.90	$2.70	$4.50	£0.25	£0.75	£1.25
683 2nd/3rd print	$0.25	$0.75	$1.25	£0.20	£0.60	£1.00
684 Superman: Doomsday part 4, continued in Superman: Man of Steel #19	$0.90	$2.70	$4.50	£0.30	£0.90	£1.50
685 (Jan 1993), Funeral for a Friend part 2, continued in Superman: Man of Steel #20; cover showing Supergirl smashing car overhead is based on Action Comics #1	$0.40	$1.20	$2.00	£0.25	£0.75	£1.25
685 2nd printing, (II in number/date box)	$0.30	$0.90	$1.50	£0.20	£0.60	£1.00
685 3rd printing	$0.25	$0.75	$1.25	£0.15	£0.45	£0.80
686 Funeral for a Friend part 6, continued in Superman: Man of Steel #21	$0.40	$1.20	$2.00	£0.20	£0.60	£1.00
687 Reign of the Supermen part 1	$0.30	$0.90	$1.50	£0.25	£0.75	£1.25
687 ND Reign of the Supermen part 1, die-cut outer cover and bound-in mini-poster	$0.40	$1.20	$2.00	£0.30	£0.90	£1.50
687 ND Dynamic Forces Edition, signed by Stern and Guice; 10,000 copies	$3.00	$9.00	$15.00	£1.50	£4.50	£7.50
688 Reign of the Supermen part 5	$0.30	$0.90	$1.50	£0.20	£0.60	£1.00
689 Reign of the Supermen part 9	$0.30	$0.90	$1.50	£0.20	£0.60	£1.00
690 Reign of the Supermen part 13, continued in Superman: The Man of Steel #25	$0.30	$0.90	$1.50	£0.20	£0.60	£1.00
691 Reign of the Supermen part 17, continued in Superman: The Man of Steel #26	$0.30	$0.90	$1.50	£0.15	£0.45	£0.80
692-693	$0.30	$0.90	$1.50	£0.15	£0.45	£0.80
694 continued from Superman #507, continued in Superman: The Man of Steel #29	$0.30	$0.90	$1.50	£0.15	£0.45	£0.80
695 (Jan 1994), Lobo cameo	$0.30	$0.90	$1.50	£0.15	£0.45	£0.80
695 ND Collector's Edition - silver foil embossed cover	$0.45	$1.35	$2.25	£0.30	£0.90	£1.50
696	$0.30	$0.90	$1.50	£0.15	£0.45	£0.80
697 Bizarro appears, continued in Superman: The Man of Steel #32	$0.30	$0.90	$1.50	£0.15	£0.45	£0.80
698-699	$0.30	$0.90	$1.50	£0.15	£0.45	£0.80
700 64pgs, The Fall of Metropolis story; Lex Luthor revealed as a villain	$0.60	$1.80	$3.00	£0.40	£1.20	£2.00
701 Fall of Metropolis concludes	$0.25	$0.75	$1.25	£0.15	£0.45	£0.80
702 David Michelinie scripts begin	$0.25	$0.75	$1.25	£0.15	£0.45	£0.80
703 Zero Hour X-over	$0.25	$0.75	$1.25	£0.15	£0.45	£0.80
704 Outsiders appear	$0.25	$0.75	$1.25	£0.15	£0.45	£0.80
705	$0.25	$0.75	$1.25	£0.15	£0.45	£0.80
706 (Jan 1995)	$0.25	$0.75	$1.25	£0.15	£0.45	£0.80
707	$0.25	$0.75	$1.25	£0.15	£0.45	£0.80
708 Mister Miracle appears	$0.25	$0.75	$1.25	£0.15	£0.45	£0.80
709 Guy Gardner appears, story continues in Guy Gardner #30	$0.25	$0.75	$1.25	£0.15	£0.45	£0.80
710 The Death of Clark Kent part 3, continued in Superman: The Man of Steel #45; upgraded coated paper stock (Miraweb Format) begins	$0.40	$1.20	$2.00	£0.25	£0.75	£1.25
711 The Death of Clark Kent part 7 (conclusion)	$0.40	$1.20	$2.00	£0.25	£0.75	£1.25

Action Comics #200

Action Comics #700

New Adventure Comics #36

MINT = 100% / NEAR MINT (inc. +/-) = 90-99% / VERY FINE (inc. +/-) = 75-89% / FINE (inc. +/-) = 55-74%
VERY GOOD (inc. +/-) = 35-54% / GOOD (inc. +/-) = 15-34% / FAIR = 5-14% / POOR = 1-4%

187

	$Good	$Fine	$N.Mint	£Good	£Fine	£N.Mint
712-713	$0.40	$1.20	$2.00	£0.25	£0.75	£1.25
714 Joker appears	$0.40	$1.20	$2.00	£0.25	£0.75	£1.25
715 the new Parasite appears						
	$0.40	$1.20	$2.00	£0.25	£0.75	£1.25
716 The Trial of Superman, continued in Superman: The Man of Steel #51						
	$0.40	$1.20	$2.00	£0.25	£0.75	£1.25
717 (Jan 1996), The Trial of Superman, continued in Superman: The Man of Steel #52						
	$0.40	$1.20	$2.00	£0.25	£0.75	£1.25
718	$0.40	$1.20	$2.00	£0.25	£0.75	£1.25
719 Batman guest-stars						
	$0.40	$1.20	$2.00	£0.25	£0.75	£1.25
Title Value:	$37453.25	$112291.30	$324144.50	£24957.20	£74811.75	£216173.70

NEW FEATURES

Air Wave in 488, 511, 512, 525, 526, 534, 535. Air Wave/ Atom in 513, 514, 524, 533. Air Wave/Aquaman in 527. Atom in 425, 427, 430, 433, 435, 438, 439, 442, 447, 448, 453, 454, 487, 489, 515, 516, 522, 523, 531, 532. Atom/Aquaman in 521, 530. Aquaman in 517-520, 528, 529, 536-540. Black Canary in 609-614, 624-635. Blackhawk in 601-608, 615-622, 628-635. Catwoman in 611-614. Clark Kent in 459, 464, 469, 471, 474, 477. Congorilla in 258-261. Deadman in 601-612, 618-621, 623-626, 642 Demon in 636-641. Green Arrow in 421, 424, 426, 431, 434, 436, 440, 441. Green Arrow/Black Canary in 428, 444-446, 450-452, 456-458. Green Lantern in 601-635, 642. Hero Hotline in 637-641. Jimmy Olsen in 599. Krypto in 462, 467. Legion of Super-Heroes in 378-387, 389-392. Lex Luthor in 486. Lori Lemaris in 475. Metamorpho in 413-418. Morgan Edge in 468. Mr Mxyzptlk in 460. Nightwing in 613-617, 627-631. Night-Wing/Speedy in 618, 632-635. Perry White in 461. Phantom Lady in 636-641. Phantom Stranger in 610, 613, 614, 617, 623, 631-635. Secret Six in 601-612 619-630. Shazam in 623-626. Speedy in 636-641. Starman in 622. Steve Lombard in 465, 472. Supergirl in 252-333, 335-346, 348-359, 361-372, 374-376. Superman in 1-333, 335-359, 361-372, 374-483, 486-642; Earth-2 Superman in 484. Wild Dog in 601-609, 615-622, 636-641.

REPRINT FEATURES

Aquaman, Vigilante in 405. Atom in 408. Atom, Aquaman in 404. Atom/Flash in 406, 407. Atom, Green Arrow in 449. Eclipso in 411-413. Legion of Super-Heroes in 377, 388. Supergirl in 334. Adam Strange, Doll Man, Sea Devils in 443. Sea Devils, Matt Savage, Hawkman, Adam Strange, Black Pirate in 443. Supergirl, Superman in 347. Supergirl, Superman/Supergirl in 360. Superboy, Vigilante in 403. Superman in 409, 410. Teen Titans in 409, 410.

ACTION COMICS ANNUAL

DC Comics; 1 Aug 1987-present

	$Good	$Fine	$N.Mint	£Good	£Fine	£N.Mint
1 LD in the U.K. Art Adams art; Batman co-stars						
	$1.20	$3.60	$6.00	£0.50	£1.50	£2.50
2 64pgs, squarebound, ties in with Superman #32; Curt Swan, Mike Mignola, Jerry Ordway, George Perez art						
	$0.45	$1.35	$2.25	£0.30	£0.90	£1.50
3 64pgs, squarebound, Armageddon: 2001 tie-in						
	$0.55	$1.65	$2.75	£0.30	£0.90	£1.50
Title Value:	$2.20	$6.60	$11.00	£1.10	£3.30	£5.50

ACTION COMICS NUMBER ONE

DC Comics; nn 1976

nn ND 16pgs, reprint of the first Superman story (Action Comics #1, June 1939), paper cover; inside front cover is a pin-up by original artist Joe Shuster though this is not to be found in the original comic

	$Good	$Fine	$N.Mint	£Good	£Fine	£N.Mint
	$0.50	$1.50	$2.50	£0.30	£0.90	£1.50
Title Value:	$0.50	$1.50	$2.50	£0.30	£0.90	£1.50

ACTION COMICS NUMBER ONE (2ND SERIES)

DC Comics; nn Jun 1988

nn ND 16pgs, reprint of the first Superman story (Action Comics #1, June 1938), glossy cover; celebrates Superman's 50th anniversary. The cover is not an exact reprint of the original

	$Good	$Fine	$N.Mint	£Good	£Fine	£N.Mint
	$0.25	$0.75	$1.25	£0.15	£0.45	£0.75
Title Value:	$0.25	$0.75	$1.25	£0.15	£0.45	£0.75

ACTS OF VENGEANCE

1990

Marvel cross-over series running throughout the issues listed in order below. Those in bold type are "core titles", others are simply related.

Avengers Spotlight	#26
Amazing Spiderman	#326
Avengers	#311
Incredible Hulk	#363
Iron Man	#250
Thor	#411
Fantastic Four	#334
Damage Control II	#1
Doctor Strange (3rd Series)	#11
Marc Spector: Moon Knight	#8
Spectacular Spiderman	#158
Punisher War Journal	#12
Avengers West Coast	#53
Captain America	#365
Uncanny X-Men	#256
Web of Spiderman	#59
Daredevil	#275
Avengers Spotlight	#27
Quasar	#5
Amazing Spiderman	#327
Alpha Flight	#79
New Mutants	#84
Wolverine	#19
Avengers	#312
Punisher	#28
Iron Man	#251
Thor	#412
Fantastic Four	#335
Damage Control II	#2
Mutant Misadventures of Cloak and Dagger	#9
Marc Spector:Moon Knight	#9
Punisher War Journal	#13
Spectacular Spiderman	#159
X-Factor	#49
Doctor Strange (3rd Series)	#12

Avengers West Coast	#54
Captain America	#366
Daredevil	#276
Uncanny X-Men	#257
Web of Spiderman	#60
Avengers Spotlight	#28
Quasar	#6
Amazing Spiderman	#328
Alpha Flight	#80
New Mutants	#85
Wolverine	#20
Avengers	#313
Power Pack	#53
Punisher	#29
Iron Man	#252
Fantastic Four	#336
Damage Control II	#3
Doctor Strange (3rd Series)	#13
Marc Spector: Moon Knight	#10
Spectacular Spiderman	#160
Thor	#413
X-Factor	#50
Avengers West Coast	#55
Captain America	#367
Web of Spiderman	#61
Uncanny X-Men	#258
Damage Control II	#4
What The-?! (parody)	#6
Avengers Spotlight (Epilogue)	#29

ADAM & EVE A.D.

BAM Productions; 1 Sep 1985-8 1986

	$Good	$Fine	$N.Mint	£Good	£Fine	£N.Mint
1-2 ND Jerry Ordway covers; black and white begins						
	$0.40	$1.20	$2.00	£0.25	£0.75	£1.25
3-8 ND	$0.30	$0.90	$1.50	£0.20	£0.60	£1.00
Title Value:	$2.60	$7.80	$13.00	£1.70	£5.10	£8.50

ADAM STRANGE

DC Comics, MS; 1 Mar 1990-3 May 1990

(see Brave and the Bold, DC Presents, Mystery in Space, Showcase)

	$Good	$Fine	$N.Mint	£Good	£Fine	£N.Mint
1-3 ND 48pgs	$0.80	$2.40	$4.00	£0.40	£1.20	£2.00
Title Value:	$2.40	$7.20	$12.00	£1.20	£3.60	£6.00

ADOLESCENT RADIOACTIVE BLACKBELT HAMSTERS

Eclipse; 1 1986-9 Feb 1988

(see Clint,Laffin' Gas, Target Airboy)

	$Good	$Fine	$N.Mint	£Good	£Fine	£N.Mint
1 ND scarce in the U.K. red/black cover						
	$1.05	$3.15	$5.25	£0.70	£2.10	£3.50
1 2nd printing, ND pink/black cover						
	$0.45	$1.35	$2.25	£0.30	£0.90	£1.50
2-3 ND	$0.55	$1.65	$2.75	£0.35	£1.05	£1.75
4-5 ND	$0.45	$1.35	$2.25	£0.30	£0.90	£1.50
6-9 ND	$0.40	$1.20	$2.00	£0.25	£0.75	£1.25
Title Value:	$5.10	$15.30	$25.50	£3.30	£9.90	£16.50
Limited Edition (Oct 1990),						
reprints 3 early tales. Signed and numbered Hardcover				£3.50	£10.50	£17.50
America The Beautiful Trade paperback				£1.10	£3.30	£5.50

ADOLESCENT RADIOACTIVE BLACKBELT HAMSTERS IN 3-D

Eclipse; 1 Jul 1986-4 Dec 1986

	$Good	$Fine	$N.Mint	£Good	£Fine	£N.Mint
1 ND all with bound-in 3-D glasses (25% less if without glasses)						
	$0.45	$1.35	$2.25	£0.30	£0.90	£1.50
1 ND scarce in the U.K. non 3-D						
	$0.90	$2.70	$4.50	£0.60	£1.80	£3.00
2 ND	$0.45	$1.35	$2.25	£0.30	£0.90	£1.50
2 ND non 3-D issue	$0.45	$1.35	$2.25	£0.30	£0.90	£1.50
3 ND (Eclipse 3-D Series #13)						
	$0.45	$1.35	$2.25	£0.30	£0.90	£1.50
3 ND non-3-D issue	$0.45	$1.35	$2.25	£0.30	£0.90	£1.50
4 ND (Eclipse 3-D series #14)						
	$0.45	$1.35	$2.25	£0.30	£0.90	£1.50
4 ND non-3-D issue	$0.45	$1.35	$2.25	£0.30	£0.90	£1.50
Title Value:	$4.05	$12.15	$20.25	£2.70	£8.10	£13.50
...Massacre The Japanese Invasion (1989)			£0.30		£0.90	£1.50

ADVANCED DUNGEONS AND DRAGONS

DC Comics, Game; 1 Dec 1988-36 Dec 1991

	$Good	$Fine	$N.Mint	£Good	£Fine	£N.Mint
1 ND based on the Advanced Dungeons and Dragons Role Playing Game						
	$1.10	$3.30	$5.50	£0.70	£2.10	£3.50
2 ND	$0.75	$2.25	$3.75	£0.50	£1.50	£2.50
3 ND	$0.60	$1.80	$3.00	£0.40	£1.20	£2.00
4-5 ND	$0.45	$1.35	$2.25	£0.30	£0.90	£1.50
6-11 ND	$0.40	$1.20	$2.00	£0.25	£0.75	£1.25
12-18 ND	$0.30	$0.90	$1.50	£0.20	£0.60	£1.00
19-22 ND Lunatics story						
	$0.30	$0.90	$1.50	£0.20	£0.60	£1.00
23 ND	$0.30	$0.90	$1.50	£0.20	£0.60	£1.00
24-26 ND Scavengers story						
	$0.30	$0.90	$1.50	£0.20	£0.60	£1.00
27-36 ND	$0.30	$0.90	$1.50	£0.20	£0.60	£1.00
Title Value:	$13.25	$39.75	$66.25	£8.70	£26.10	£43.50

Note: All New Format

ADVANCED DUNGEONS AND DRAGONS ANNUAL

DC Comics; 1 Sep 1990

	$Good	$Fine	$N.Mint	£Good	£Fine	£N.Mint
1 ND 64pgs	$0.45	$1.35	$2.25	£0.30	£0.90	£1.50
Title Value:	$0.45	$1.35	$2.25	£0.30	£0.90	£1.50

ADVENTURE COMICS

National Periodical Publications/DC Comics; 1 Dec 1935-11 Dec 1936; 12 Jan 1937-31 Oct 1938; 32 Nov 1938-490 Feb 1982; 491 Sep 1982-503 Sep 1983
(Formerly New Comics #1-11, becomes New Adventure Comics #12-32)
(Becomes Adventure Comics Presents Dial H For Hero #479-490)

	$Good	$Fine	$N.Mint	£Good	£Fine	£N.Mint
1 very rare in the U.K. 80pgs, probably less than 50 extant copies, the 1st comic ever published by DC (then known as National Periodical Publications)	$1650.00	$5000.00	$15000.00	£1275.00	£3800.00	£11500.00
2 very rare in the U.K. 80pgs, (Jan 1936), almost certainly less than 50 extant copies, could be as few as 10	$930.00	$2800.00	$7500.00	£710.00	£2150.00	£5750.00
3-5 rare in the U.K., 80pgs	$550.00	$1650.00	$4400.00	£365.00	£1100.00	£2950.00
6-10 rare in the U.K.	$550.00	$1650.00	$4400.00	£300.00	£900.00	£2400.00
11 rare in the U.K., last New Comics title	$550.00	$1650.00	$4400.00	£300.00	£900.00	£2400.00

(please note that the above are approximate values as far as the British market is concerned as copies very rarely become available. Also note that the Near Mint values are theoretical projections only in the event of any true Near Mint copies being discovered)

	$Good	$Fine	$N.Mint	£Good	£Fine	£N.Mint
12 rare in the U.K. (Jan 1937), titled New Adventure Comics for 1st time; contents shift away from purely funny animal and naughty kids material	$435.00	$1300.00	$3500.00	£310.00	£930.00	£2500.00
13 very rare in the U.K. probably no more than 25 extant copies (see Top 50 Rarest section)	$400.00	$1200.00	$3200.00	£335.00	£1000.00	£2700.00
14 rare in the U.K.	$375.00	$1125.00	$3000.00	£250.00	£750.00	£2000.00
15 rare in the U.K., 1st time the more familiar "Adventure" logo appears	$375.00	$1125.00	$3000.00	£250.00	£750.00	£2000.00
16-17 rare in the U.K.	$375.00	$1125.00	$3000.00	£250.00	£750.00	£2000.00
18 rare in the U.K. (Jan 1938)	$375.00	$1125.00	$3000.00	£250.00	£750.00	£2000.00
19-20 rare in the U.K.	$375.00	$1125.00	$3000.00	£250.00	£750.00	£2000.00
21-22 very scarce in the U.K.	$285.00	$860.00	$2300.00	£200.00	£600.00	£1600.00
23 very scarce in the U.K. 1st "Adventure" theme cover; begins a line of classic covers of man vs. beast or the elements	$285.00	$860.00	$2300.00	£200.00	£600.00	£1600.00
24-25 very scarce in the U.K.	$285.00	$860.00	$2300.00	£200.00	£600.00	£1600.00
26 very scarce in the U.K.	$275.00	$820.00	$2200.00	£185.00	£560.00	£1500.00
27 very scarce in the U.K., carries advertisement for Action Comics #1 (1st Superman)	$275.00	$820.00	$2200.00	£185.00	£560.00	£1500.00
28-30 very scarce in the U.K.	$275.00	$820.00	$2200.00	£185.00	£560.00	£1500.00
31 very scarce in the U.K. last New Adventure Comics	$275.00	$820.00	$2200.00	£185.00	£560.00	£1500.00
32 very scarce in the U.K. title becomes simply Adventure Comics for 1st time	$310.00	$930.00	$2500.00	£215.00	£650.00	£1750.00
33 very scarce in the U.K.	$150.00	$455.00	$1225.00	£105.00	£315.00	£850.00
34 very scarce in the U.K. (Jan 1939)	$150.00	$455.00	$1225.00	£105.00	£315.00	£850.00
35-36 very scarce in the U.K.	$150.00	$455.00	$1225.00	£105.00	£315.00	£850.00
37 very scarce in the U.K. cover used for Double Action Comics #2	$150.00	$455.00	$1225.00	£105.00	£315.00	£850.00
38-39 very scarce in the U.K.	$150.00	$455.00	$1225.00	£105.00	£315.00	£850.00
40 very rare in the U.K. Sandman series begins, probably less than 50 extant copies	$3000.00	$9000.00	$30000.00	£2200.00	£6600.00	£22000.00

[Rare in high grade - Very Fine+ or better]

	$Good	$Fine	$N.Mint	£Good	£Fine	£N.Mint
41 very scarce in the U.K. 2nd appearance Sandman	$375.00	$1125.00	$3000.00	£275.00	£820.00	£2200.00
42 very scarce in the U.K. 3rd appearance Sandman, Sandman cover	$500.00	$1500.00	$4000.00	£360.00	£1075.00	£2900.00
43 very scarce in the U.K.	$250.00	$750.00	$2000.00	£175.00	£520.00	£1400.00
44 very scarce in the U.K. Sandman cover	$450.00	$1350.00	$3600.00	£310.00	£930.00	£2500.00
45 very scarce in the U.K.	$250.00	$750.00	$2000.00	£175.00	£520.00	£1400.00
46 very scarce in the U.K. (Jan 1940), Sandman cover	$350.00	$1050.00	$2800.00	£235.00	£710.00	£1900.00
47 very scarce in the U.K. Sandman cover	$350.00	$1050.00	$2800.00	£235.00	£710.00	£1900.00
48 rare in the U.K., origin and 1st appearance Hourman, Hourman cover	$1600.00	$4800.00	$16000.00	£1100.00	£3300.00	£11000.00

[Scarce in high grade - Very Fine+ or better]

	$Good	$Fine	$N.Mint	£Good	£Fine	£N.Mint
49 scarce in the U.K. 2nd appearance Hourman	$225.00	$670.00	$1800.00	£155.00	£465.00	£1250.00
50 scarce in the U.K. 3rd appearance Hourman, Hourman cover	$190.00	$580.00	$1550.00	£130.00	£390.00	£1050.00
51 Sandman cover	$215.00	$650.00	$1750.00	£145.00	£440.00	£1175.00
52-57 Hourman cover	$140.00	$430.00	$1150.00	£95.00	£290.00	£775.00
58 (Jan 1941), Hourman cover	$140.00	$430.00	$1150.00	£95.00	£290.00	£775.00
59 Hourman cover	$140.00	$430.00	$1150.00	£95.00	£290.00	£775.00
60 Sandman cover	$195.00	$590.00	$1575.00	£130.00	£390.00	£1050.00
61 very scarce in the U.K. origin and 1st appearance Starman, classic cover	$900.00	$2700.00	$9000.00	£600.00	£1800.00	£6000.00
62 2nd appearance Starman	$200.00	$600.00	$1600.00	£130.00	£400.00	£1075.00
63 3rd appearance Starman	$150.00	$450.00	$1200.00	£100.00	£300.00	£800.00
64-65	$130.00	$390.00	$1050.00	£87.50	£260.00	£700.00
66 origin and 1st appearance The Shining Knight	$155.00	$475.00	$1275.00	£105.00	£315.00	£850.00
67-68	$130.00	$390.00	$1050.00	£87.50	£260.00	£700.00
69 1st appearance Sandy, new Sandman costume	$150.00	$450.00	$1200.00	£100.00	£300.00	£800.00
70 (Jan 1942)	$130.00	$390.00	$1050.00	£87.50	£260.00	£700.00
71 1st Miracle Ray machine used by Hourman	$105.00	$325.00	$875.00	£70.00	£215.00	£575.00
72 very scarce in the U.K. 1st Sandman by Joe Simon and Jack Kirby	$750.00	$2250.00	$7500.00	£550.00	£1650.00	£5500.00
73 rare in the U.K., origin Manhunter by Joe Simon and Jack Kirby, classic cover	$750.00	$2250.00	$7500.00	£570.00	£1725.00	£5750.00
74 2nd Manhunter by Joe Simon and Jack Kirby	$175.00	$520.00	$1400.00	£115.00	£345.00	£925.00
75	$150.00	$455.00	$1225.00	£100.00	£305.00	£825.00
76 scarce in the U.K.	$165.00	$495.00	$1325.00	£110.00	£335.00	£900.00
77-78	$150.00	$455.00	$1225.00	£100.00	£305.00	£825.00
79 classic cover, Manhunter stalks Nazi Raiders	$150.00	$455.00	$1225.00	£100.00	£305.00	£825.00
80 last Manhunter by Joe Simon and Jack Kirby	$150.00	$455.00	$1225.00	£100.00	£305.00	£825.00
81	$100.00	$300.00	$800.00	£65.00	£195.00	£525.00
82 (Jan 1943)	$100.00	$300.00	$800.00	£65.00	£195.00	£525.00
83-86	$100.00	$300.00	$800.00	£65.00	£195.00	£525.00
87 scarce in the U.K.	$105.00	$325.00	$875.00	£75.00	£225.00	£600.00
88	$100.00	$300.00	$800.00	£65.00	£195.00	£525.00
89 (Dec/Jan 1944)	$100.00	$300.00	$800.00	£65.00	£195.00	£525.00
90	$100.00	$300.00	$800.00	£65.00	£195.00	£525.00
91 last Sandman by Joe Simon and Jack Kirby	$82.50	$250.00	$675.00	£55.00	£165.00	£450.00
92-93	$65.00	$195.00	$525.00	£44.00	£130.00	£350.00
94 scarce in the U.K.	$70.00	$210.00	$560.00	£49.00	£145.00	£395.00
95 (Dec/Jan 1945)	$65.00	$195.00	$525.00	£44.00	£130.00	£350.00
96-99	$65.00	$195.00	$525.00	£44.00	£130.00	£350.00
100	$105.00	$325.00	$850.00	£70.00	£215.00	£575.00

[Note: most issues pre #100 are at least scarce in the U.K.]

	$Good	$Fine	$N.Mint	£Good	£Fine	£N.Mint
101 (Dec/Jan 1946)	$70.00	$210.00	$500.00	£49.00	£145.00	£340.00
102 last Sandman and Starman, last Sandman cover	$70.00	$210.00	$500.00	£49.00	£145.00	£340.00
103 scarce in the U.K. 1st small logo, Superboy covers and stories begin	$220.00	$660.00	$2000.00	£165.00	£500.00	£1500.00

[Scarce in high grade - Very Fine+ or better]

	$Good	$Fine	$N.Mint	£Good	£Fine	£N.Mint
104 2nd Superboy in title	$110.00	$330.00	$775.00	£75.00	£225.00	£525.00
105-110	$70.00	$210.00	$500.00	£46.00	£135.00	£325.00
111	$62.50	$190.00	$450.00	£43.00	£125.00	£300.00
112 (Jan 1947)	$62.50	$190.00	$450.00	£43.00	£125.00	£300.00
113 Christmas cover	$62.50	$190.00	$450.00	£43.00	£125.00	£300.00
114-120	$62.50	$190.00	$450.00	£43.00	£125.00	£300.00
121-123	$60.00	$180.00	$425.00	£41.00	£120.00	£285.00
124 (Jan 1948)	$60.00	$180.00	$425.00	£41.00	£120.00	£285.00
125-127	$60.00	$180.00	$425.00	£41.00	£120.00	£285.00
128 1st time Superboy meets a young Lois Lane - classic story	$70.00	$210.00	$490.00	£46.00	£135.00	£325.00
129-130	$60.00	$180.00	$425.00	£41.00	£120.00	£285.00
131	$50.00	$150.00	$350.00	£34.00	£100.00	£235.00
132 "The Aquagirl" appears in Aquaman back-up story	$50.00	$150.00	$350.00	£34.00	£100.00	£235.00
133-135	$50.00	$150.00	$350.00	£34.00	£100.00	£235.00
136 (Jan 1949)	$50.00	$150.00	$350.00	£34.00	£100.00	£235.00
137-147	$50.00	$150.00	$350.00	£34.00	£100.00	£235.00
148 (Jan 1950)	$50.00	$150.00	$350.00	£34.00	£100.00	£235.00
149	$50.00	$150.00	$350.00	£34.00	£100.00	£235.00
150-151 Shining Knight, Frank Frazetta art	$55.00	$165.00	$385.00	£36.00	£105.00	£250.00
152	$45.00	$135.00	$315.00	£30.00	£90.00	£210.00
153 Shining Knight, Frank Frazetta art	$55.00	$165.00	$385.00	£36.00	£105.00	£250.00
154	$45.00	$135.00	$315.00	£30.00	£90.00	£210.00
155 Shining Knight, Frank Frazetta art	$55.00	$165.00	$385.00	£36.00	£105.00	£250.00
156	$45.00	$135.00	$315.00	£30.00	£90.00	£210.00
157 Shining Knight, Frank Frazetta art	$55.00	$165.00	$385.00	£36.00	£105.00	£250.00

	$Good	$Fine	$N.Mint	£Good	£Fine	£N.Mint
158	$45.00	$135.00	$315.00	£30.00	£90.00	£210.00
159 Shining Knight, Frank Frazetta art, origin Johnny Quick	$55.00	$165.00	$385.00	£36.00	£105.00	£250.00
160 (Jan 1951)	$45.00	$135.00	$315.00	£30.00	£90.00	£210.00
161 Shining Knight, Frank Frazetta art	$50.00	$150.00	$350.00	£34.00	£100.00	£235.00
162	$43.00	$125.00	$300.00	£29.00	£85.00	£200.00
163 Shining Knight, Frank Frazetta art	$50.00	$150.00	$350.00	£34.00	£100.00	£235.00
164-166	$43.00	$125.00	$300.00	£29.00	£85.00	£200.00
167 Lana Lang: Super-Girl story	$45.00	$135.00	$315.00	£30.00	£90.00	£210.00
168 last 52pg issue	$39.00	$115.00	$275.00	£26.00	£77.50	£185.00
169-170	$39.00	$115.00	$275.00	£26.00	£77.50	£185.00
171	$34.00	$100.00	$240.00	£22.50	£67.50	£160.00
172 (Jan 1952)	$34.00	$100.00	$240.00	£22.50	£67.50	£160.00
173-180	$34.00	$100.00	$240.00	£22.50	£67.50	£160.00
181-183	$34.00	$100.00	$240.00	£21.00	£62.50	£150.00
184 (Jan 1953)	$34.00	$100.00	$240.00	£21.00	£62.50	£150.00
185-188	$34.00	$100.00	$240.00	£21.00	£62.50	£150.00
189 Lana Lang as The Girl of Steel	$37.00	$110.00	$260.00	£25.00	£75.00	£175.00
190-195	$34.00	$100.00	$240.00	£21.00	£62.50	£150.00
196 (Jan 1954)	$34.00	$100.00	$240.00	£21.00	£62.50	£150.00
197-198	$34.00	$100.00	$240.00	£21.00	£62.50	£150.00
199 Superboy meets Superlad	$37.00	$110.00	$260.00	£25.00	£75.00	£175.00
200 scarce in the U.K.	$60.00	$180.00	$425.00	£43.00	£125.00	£300.00
201-207	$40.00	$120.00	$280.00	£26.00	£77.50	£185.00
208 (Jan 1955)	$40.00	$120.00	$280.00	£26.00	£77.50	£185.00
209	$40.00	$120.00	$280.00	£26.00	£77.50	£185.00
210 very scarce in the U.K. 1st appearance of Krypto the Wonder dog	$250.00	$750.00	$2500.00	£175.00	£520.00	£1750.00
[Scarce in high grade - Very Fine+ or better]						
211 young Lois Lane appears	$30.00	$90.00	$210.00	£20.00	£60.00	£140.00
212-213	$30.00	$90.00	$210.00	£20.00	£60.00	£140.00
214 2nd appearance Krypto	$50.00	$150.00	$350.00	£35.00	£105.00	£245.00
215-216	$30.00	$90.00	$210.00	£20.00	£60.00	£140.00
217-218 classic two part story; Jor-El and Lara return for Superboy	$30.00	$90.00	$210.00	£20.00	£60.00	£140.00
219	$30.00	$90.00	$210.00	£20.00	£60.00	£140.00
220 (Jan 1956), 3rd appearance Krypto	$35.00	$105.00	$245.00	£25.00	£75.00	£175.00
221-230	$28.00	$82.50	$195.00	£18.50	£55.00	£130.00
231	$25.00	$75.00	$175.00	£17.50	£52.50	£122.50
232 (Jan 1957)	$25.00	$75.00	$175.00	£17.50	£52.50	£122.50
233-234	$25.00	$75.00	$175.00	£17.50	£52.50	£122.50
235-236 scarce in the U.K.	$25.00	$75.00	$175.00	£20.00	£60.00	£140.00
237 1st appearance Intergalactic Vigilante Squadron, possible Legion prototype	$25.00	$75.00	$175.00	£17.50	£52.50	£122.50
238-243	$25.00	$75.00	$175.00	£17.50	£52.50	£122.50
244 (Jan 1958)	$25.00	$75.00	$175.00	£17.50	£52.50	£122.50
245	$25.00	$75.00	$175.00	£17.50	£52.50	£122.50
246 scarce in the U.K.	$25.00	$75.00	$175.00	£20.00	£60.00	£140.00
247 1st appearance of Legion of Super Heroes (Superboy story), Green Arrow by Jack Kirby	$400.00	$1200.00	$4000.00	£265.00	£790.00	£2650.00
[Prices may vary widely on this comic]						
247 ND Silver Age Classic reprint (Mar 1992)	$0.25	$0.75	$1.25	£0.15	£0.45	£0.80
248 scarce in the U.K.	$20.00	$60.00	$140.00	£15.00	£45.00	£105.00
249	$20.00	$60.00	$140.00	£13.50	£41.00	£95.00
250 Jack Kirby art on Green Arrow	$20.00	$60.00	$140.00	£13.50	£41.00	£95.00
251 Jack Kirby art on Green Arrow, 1st appearance Superboy robot	$20.00	$60.00	$140.00	£13.50	£41.00	£95.00
252 Jack Kirby art on Green Arrow, 1st mention of Red Kryptonite	$20.00	$60.00	$140.00	£13.50	£41.00	£95.00
253 Jack Kirby art on Green Arrow, Superboy meets Robin	$20.00	$60.00	$140.00	£15.00	£45.00	£105.00
254 Jack Kirby art on Green Arrow	$20.00	$60.00	$140.00	£13.50	£41.00	£95.00
255 Jack Kirby art on Green Arrow, 1st Red Kryptonite effect	$20.00	$60.00	$140.00	£13.50	£41.00	£95.00
256 (Jan 1959), Jack Kirby art, origin Green Arrow retold (1st time since Golden Age)	$62.50	$185.00	$500.00	£35.00	£105.00	£280.00
257	$17.50	$52.50	$125.00	£11.50	£35.00	£82.50
258 Superboy meets young Green Arrow	$17.50	$52.50	$125.00	£11.50	£35.00	£82.50
259 part origin Krypto	$17.50	$52.50	$125.00	£11.50	£35.00	£82.50
260 origin and 1st Silver Age appearance of Aquaman (see Showcase #30)	$70.00	$210.00	$560.00	£43.00	£125.00	£340.00
261 young Lois Lane appears	$15.00	$45.00	$105.00	£10.00	£30.00	£70.00
262-264	$15.00	$45.00	$105.00	£10.00	£30.00	£70.00
265 1st appearance Superman robot	$15.00	$45.00	$105.00	£10.00	£30.00	£70.00
1st official distribution in the U.K.						
266 1st appearance prototype Aquagirl (see Aquaman #33)	$15.00	$45.00	$105.00	£10.00	£30.00	£70.00
267 2nd appearance of Legion of Super-Heroes (Superboy story)	$85.00	$255.00	$680.00	£60.00	£180.00	£480.00
268 (Jan 1960)	$15.00	$45.00	$105.00	£10.00	£30.00	£70.00
269 1st appearance Aqualad	$30.00	$90.00	$210.00	£20.00	£60.00	£140.00
270	$15.00	$45.00	$105.00	£10.00	£30.00	£70.00
271 1st Silver Age appearance Lex Luthor, origin retold	$30.00	$90.00	$210.00	£20.00	£60.00	£140.00
272-274	$13.50	$41.00	$95.00	£8.50	£26.00	£60.00
275 Superman/Batman team origin retold	$23.50	$70.00	$165.00	£15.50	£47.00	£110.00
276-278	$13.50	$41.00	$95.00	£8.50	£26.00	£60.00
279 1st appearance White Kryptonite	$13.50	$41.00	$95.00	£8.50	£26.00	£60.00
280 (Jan 1961), Superboy meets young Lori Lemaris	$13.50	$41.00	$95.00	£8.50	£26.00	£60.00
281	$13.50	$41.00	$95.00	£8.50	£26.00	£60.00
282 5th appearance of Legion (Superboy story), origin and 1st appearance Star Boy	$21.00	$62.50	$150.00	£15.50	£47.00	£110.00
283 1st appearance of the Phantom Zone	$22.50	$67.50	$160.00	£13.50	£41.00	£95.00
284	$13.50	$41.00	$95.00	£8.50	£26.00	£60.00
285 Bizarro World series begins, classic cover (series ends #299)	$17.50	$52.50	$125.00	£12.00	£36.00	£84.00
286 1st appearance Bizarro Mr. Mxyzptlk	$15.00	$45.00	$105.00	£10.00	£30.00	£70.00
287-288	$12.50	$39.00	$90.00	£7.75	£23.50	£55.00
289 8th appearance of Legion (one panel, as statuettes only thus highly debateable as an official appearance)	$12.50	$39.00	$90.00	£10.00	£30.00	£70.00
290 9th appearance of Legion (Superboy story), 1st appearance Sunboy	$21.00	$62.50	$150.00	£15.50	£47.00	£110.00
291	$7.75	$23.50	$55.00	£5.00	£15.00	£35.00
292 (Jan 1962)	$7.75	$23.50	$55.00	£5.00	£15.00	£35.00
293 14th appearance of Legion (Superboy story), 1st Legion of Super-Pets	$13.50	$41.00	$95.00	£8.50	£26.00	£60.00
294 Bizarro Marilyn Monroe and President Kennedy; classic cover	$15.00	$45.00	$105.00	£7.00	£21.00	£50.00
295-298	$7.75	$23.50	$55.00	£5.00	£15.00	£35.00
299 1st Gold Kryptonite (more significant than White or Blue as it removes super-powers permanently)	$9.25	$28.00	$65.00	£5.50	£17.00	£40.00
300 1st of Legion series, ends #380	$44.00	$130.00	$350.00	£29.00	£85.00	£230.00
301 origin Bouncing Boy	$17.00	$50.00	$120.00	£11.00	£34.00	£80.00
302-303	$12.00	$36.00	$85.00	£7.75	£23.50	£55.00
304 (Jan 1963), death of Lightning Lad (returns #312)	$12.00	$36.00	$85.00	£7.75	£23.50	£55.00
305 Mon-El cured from lead poisoning	$12.00	$36.00	$85.00	£7.75	£23.50	£55.00
306 1st appearance Legion of Substitute Heroes	$9.25	$28.00	$65.00	£5.50	£17.00	£40.00
307 1st appearance Element Lad	$9.25	$28.00	$65.00	£5.50	£17.00	£40.00
308 1st appearance Lightning Lass	$9.25	$28.00	$65.00	£5.50	£17.00	£40.00
309-310	$9.25	$28.00	$65.00	£5.00	£15.00	£35.00
311-315	$7.00	$21.00	$50.00	£4.25	£12.50	£30.00
316 (Jan 1964)	$7.00	$21.00	$50.00	£3.90	£11.50	£27.50
317 1st appearance Dream Girl; Lightning Lass becomes Light Lass	$7.00	$21.00	$50.00	£4.25	£12.50	£30.00
318-320	$7.00	$21.00	$50.00	£3.90	£11.50	£27.50
321 1st appearance Time Trapper (see Crisis on Infinite Earths)	$7.50	$22.50	$45.00	£4.15	£12.50	£25.00
322-324	$5.75	$17.50	$35.00	£3.30	£10.00	£20.00
325 Lex Luthor appears	$5.75	$17.50	$35.00	£3.30	£10.00	£20.00
326	$5.75	$17.50	$35.00	£3.30	£10.00	£20.00
327 1st appearance Timber Wolf (initially called Lone Wolf)	$5.75	$17.50	$35.00	£3.75	£11.00	£22.50
328 (Jan 1965)	$5.75	$17.50	$35.00	£3.30	£10.00	£20.00
329 1st Bizarro Legion	$5.75	$17.50	$35.00	£3.30	£10.00	£20.00
330	$5.75	$17.50	$35.00	£3.30	£10.00	£20.00
331-335	$5.75	$17.50	$35.00	£2.90	£8.75	£17.50
336-339	$5.75	$17.50	$35.00	£2.50	£7.50	£15.00
340 (Jan 1966)	$5.75	$17.50	$35.00	£2.50	£7.50	£15.00
341 Triplicate Girl becomes Duo Damsel (1st appearance)	$5.00	$15.00	$30.00	£2.90	£8.75	£17.50
342-345	$3.30	$10.00	$20.00	£2.05	£6.25	£12.50
346 1st appearance Princess Projectra, Nemesis Kid, Karate Kid, Ferro Lad	$4.15	$12.50	$25.00	£2.50	£7.50	£15.00
347	$3.30	$10.00	$20.00	£2.05	£6.25	£12.50
348 origin Sunboy	$3.30	$10.00	$20.00	£2.05	£6.25	£12.50
349-350	$3.30	$10.00	$20.00	£2.05	£6.25	£12.50
351	$2.50	$7.50	$15.00	£1.50	£4.50	£9.00
352 (Jan 1967), classic Sun-Eater story begins	$2.50	$7.50	$15.00	£1.50	£4.50	£9.00

	$Good	$Fine	$N.Mint	£Good	£Fine	£N.Mint
353 Ferro Lad dies destroying Sun-Eater						
	$3.30	$10.00	$20.00	£2.05	£6.25	£12.50
354-360	$2.50	$7.50	$15.00	£1.50	£4.50	£9.00
361-363	$2.00	$6.00	$12.00	£1.00	£3.00	£6.00
364 (Jan 1968)	$2.00	$6.00	$12.00	£1.00	£3.00	£6.00
365	$2.00	$6.00	$12.00	£1.00	£3.00	£6.00
366 1st appearance Shadow Lass						
	$2.00	$6.00	$12.00	£1.15	£3.50	£7.00
367-374	$2.00	$6.00	$12.00	£1.00	£3.00	£6.00
375 1st appearance Quantum Queen and The Wanderers						
	$2.00	$6.00	$12.00	£1.15	£3.50	£7.00
376 (Jan 1969)	$2.00	$6.00	$12.00	£1.00	£3.00	£6.00
377-379	$2.00	$6.00	$12.00	£1.00	£3.00	£6.00
380 last of Legion series - moves to back-ups in Action Comics; text feature on Detective Comics #27						
	$2.00	$6.00	$12.00	£1.00	£3.00	£6.00
381 Supergirl series begins (continued from Action Comics #376; series ends #424)						
	$3.00	$9.00	$15.00	£0.80	£2.40	£4.00
382-383 Neal Adams cover						
	$1.00	$3.00	$5.00	£0.50	£1.50	£2.50
384-387	$1.00	$3.00	$5.00	£0.50	£1.50	£2.50
388 (Jan 1970)	$1.00	$3.00	$5.00	£0.50	£1.50	£2.50
389	$1.00	$3.00	$5.00	£0.50	£1.50	£2.50
390 68pgs, Giant G-69, all romance issue						
	$3.00	$9.00	$15.00	£1.00	£3.00	£5.00
391-396	$1.00	$3.00	$5.00	£0.40	£1.20	£2.00
397 Supergirl's new costume						
	$1.00	$3.00	$5.00	£0.40	£1.20	£2.00
398-399 scarce in the U.K.						
	$1.00	$3.00	$5.00	£0.40	£1.20	£2.00
400 scarce in the U.K.						
	$0.70	$2.10	$3.50	£0.45	£1.35	£2.25
401 (Jan 1971)	$1.00	$3.00	$5.00	£0.35	£1.05	£1.75
402	$1.00	$3.00	$5.00	£0.35	£1.05	£1.75
403 68pgs, Giant G-81, all Legion reprints including classic death/rebirth Lightning Lad						
	$2.40	$7.00	$12.00	£1.20	£3.60	£6.00
404-408	$1.00	$3.00	$5.00	£0.30	£0.90	£1.50
409-411 48pgs	$1.00	$3.00	$5.00	£0.35	£1.05	£1.75
412 48pgs, reprints origin Animal Man from Strange Adventures #180						
	$0.80	$2.40	$4.00	£0.50	£1.50	£2.50
413 48pgs	$0.55	$1.65	$2.75	£0.35	£1.05	£1.75
414 48pgs, (Jan 1972), 2nd Animal Man reprint from Strange Adventures #184						
	$0.70	$2.10	$3.50	£0.45	£1.35	£2.25
415 48pgs, 1st Animal Man in costume reprint from Strange Adventures #190						
	$0.70	$2.10	$3.50	£0.45	£1.35	£2.25
416 100pgs, DC-100pg Super Spectacular #10						
	$0.80	$2.40	$4.00	£0.50	£1.50	£2.50
417 48pgs, Frazetta reprint						
	$0.55	$1.65	$2.75	£0.35	£1.05	£1.75
418-419 48pgs	$0.55	$1.65	$2.75	£0.35	£1.05	£1.75
420 48pgs, Animal Man reprint from Strange Adventures #195						
	$0.55	$1.65	$2.75	£0.35	£1.05	£1.75
421 scarce in the U.K. Animal Man reprint from Strange Adventures #201						
	$0.60	$1.80	$3.00	£0.40	£1.20	£2.00
422	$0.45	$1.35	$2.25	£0.30	£0.90	£1.50
423 Justice League of America appear						
	$0.60	$1.80	$3.00	£0.40	£1.20	£2.00
424 scarce in the U.K.						
	$0.55	$1.65	$2.75	£0.35	£1.05	£1.75
425 (Jan 1973), Alex Toth, Gil Kane art, Kaluta cover; title becomes mystery orientated						
	$0.45	$1.35	$2.25	£0.30	£0.90	£1.50
426-427	$0.45	$1.35	$2.25	£0.30	£0.90	£1.50

	$Good	$Fine	$N.Mint	£Good	£Fine	£N.Mint
428 1st appearance Black Orchid						
	$1.50	$4.50	$7.50	£1.00	£3.00	£5.00
429 2nd appearance Black Orchid						
	$0.90	$2.70	$4.50	£0.60	£1.80	£3.00
430 3rd appearance Black Orchid						
	$0.70	$2.10	$3.50	£0.45	£1.35	£2.25
431 (Feb 1974), Spectre series begins by Fleischer and Aparo (reprinted in Wrath of the Spectre); a return to the Golden Age avenging spirit						
	$1.20	$3.60	$6.00	£0.50	£1.50	£2.50
432	$0.60	$1.80	$3.00	£0.40	£1.20	£2.00
433 Spectre, cover titled "Weird Adventure Comics" (ends #437)						
	$0.55	$1.65	$2.75	£0.35	£1.05	£1.75
434 Spectre	$0.55	$1.65	$2.75	£0.35	£1.05	£1.75
435 Spectre, Mike Grell's 1st pro work on back-up Aquaman story						
	$0.55	$1.65	$2.75	£0.40	£1.20	£2.00
436 Spectre	$0.55	$1.65	$2.75	£0.35	£1.05	£1.75
437 (Feb 1975), Spectre						
	$0.55	$1.65	$2.75	£0.35	£1.05	£1.75
438 Spectre; Shining Knight back-up by Chaykin						
	$0.55	$1.65	$2.75	£0.35	£1.05	£1.75
439 Spectre	$0.55	$1.65	$2.75	£0.35	£1.05	£1.75
440 Spectre, origin retold						
	$0.55	$1.65	$2.75	£0.35	£1.05	£1.75
441 1st of Aquaman series						
	$0.45	$1.35	$2.25	£0.30	£0.90	£1.50
442	$0.40	$1.20	$2.00	£0.25	£0.75	£1.25
443 (Feb 1976)	$0.40	$1.20	$2.00	£0.25	£0.75	£1.25
444-445	$0.40	$1.20	$2.00	£0.25	£0.75	£1.25
446-448 scarce in the U.K.						
	$0.45	$1.35	$2.25	£0.30	£0.90	£1.50
449 scarce in the U.K. (Jan 1977)						
	$0.45	$1.35	$2.25	£0.30	£0.90	£1.50
450 scarce in the U.K.						
	$0.45	$1.35	$2.25	£0.30	£0.90	£1.50
451-452	$0.40	$1.20	$2.00	£0.25	£0.75	£1.25
453 Batgirl appears						
	$0.40	$1.20	$2.00	£0.25	£0.75	£1.25
454	$0.40	$1.20	$2.00	£0.25	£0.75	£1.25
455 (Jan 1978)	$0.40	$1.20	$2.00	£0.25	£0.75	£1.25
456	$0.40	$1.20	$2.00	£0.25	£0.75	£1.25
457-458 Eclipso appears						
	$0.45	$1.35	$2.25	£0.30	£0.90	£1.50
459-460 scarce in the U.K. 68pgs, Darkseid, New Gods appear; story continued from New Gods #19						
	$0.70	$2.10	$3.50	£0.40	£1.20	£2.00
461 ND 68pgs, (Jan 1979)						
	$1.00	$3.00	$5.00	£0.40	£1.20	£2.00
462 ND very scarce in the U.K. 68pgs, Earth-2 Batman dies						
	$1.50	$4.50	$7.50	£1.00	£3.00	£5.00
463-464 scarce in the U.K. 68pgs						
	$0.45	$1.35	$2.25	£0.30	£0.90	£1.50
465 ND 68pgs	$0.45	$1.35	$2.25	£0.30	£1.20	£2.00
466 scarce in the U.K. 68pgs						
	$0.45	$1.35	$2.25	£0.30	£0.90	£1.50
467 ND (Jan 1980), Starman appears (an 80s version by Steve Ditko; see First Issue Special #12)						
	$0.40	$1.20	$2.00	£0.25	£0.75	£1.25
468-472 ND	$0.40	$1.20	$2.00	£0.25	£0.75	£1.25
473-474	$0.30	$0.90	$1.50	£0.20	£0.60	£1.00
475 Bolland cover	$0.30	$0.90	$1.50	£0.20	£0.60	£1.00
476-478	$0.30	$0.90	$1.50	£0.20	£0.60	£1.00
479 (Mar 1981), Dial H for Hero begins						
	$0.30	$0.90	$1.50	£0.20	£0.60	£1.00

Adventure Comics #211

Adventure Comics #500

Adventures on the Planet of the Apes #1

EXTREMELY HIGH GRADE COPIES MAY COMMAND MULTIPLES OF GUIDE ALTHOUGH THIS IS MORE PREVALENT IN THE US THAN IN THE UK

	$Good	$Fine	$N.Mint	£Good	£Fine	£N.Mint
480-483	$0.30	$0.90	$1.50	£0.20	£0.60	£1.00
484-486 George Perez cover	$0.30	$0.90	$1.50	£0.20	£0.60	£1.00
487-488	$0.30	$0.90	$1.50	£0.20	£0.60	£1.00
489 (Jan 1982)	$0.30	$0.90	$1.50	£0.20	£0.60	£1.00
490 George Perez cover	$0.30	$0.90	$1.50	£0.20	£0.60	£1.00
491 very scarce in the U.K. 1st of digest size (all 100pgs), reprints Adventure #247 and #267	$0.50	$1.50	$2.50	£1.20	£3.60	£6.00
492 scarce in the U.K.	$0.50	$1.50	$2.50	£1.00	£3.00	£5.00
493 scarce in the U.K. new origin story Challengers of the Unknown	$0.50	$1.50	$2.50	£1.00	£3.00	£5.00
494 scarce in the U.K.	$0.50	$1.50	$2.50	£1.00	£3.00	£5.00
495 scarce in the U.K. (Jan 1983), Neal Adams reprint, Toth art	$0.50	$1.50	$2.50	£1.00	£3.00	£5.00
496 scarce in the U.K. Neal Adams reprint, Toth, Cockrum art	$0.50	$1.50	$2.50	£1.00	£3.00	£5.00
497 scarce in the U.K. Neal Adams reprint, Toth art	$0.50	$1.50	$2.50	£1.00	£3.00	£5.00
498 scarce in the U.K. Neal Adams reprint	$0.50	$1.50	$2.50	£1.00	£3.00	£5.00
499 scarce in the U.K.	$0.50	$1.50	$2.50	£1.00	£3.00	£5.00
500 very scarce in the U.K. 144pgs	$0.50	$1.50	$2.50	£1.20	£3.60	£6.00
501 scarce in the U.K.	$0.50	$1.50	$2.50	£1.00	£3.00	£5.00
502-503 scarce in the U.K. Morrow reprints	$0.50	$1.50	$2.50	£1.00	£3.00	£5.00
Title Value:	$39756.65	$119445.95	$324400.50	£27011.70	£80968.20	£224312.80

ARTISTS

Ditko in 467-478. Nasser in 466. Nino in 425-427, 429, 432, 433.

NEW FEATURES

Adventurer's Club in 426, 427, 430. Aquaman in 260-280, 282, 284, 435-437, 441-452, 460-466, 475-478. Aqualad in 453-455. Bizarro World in 285-299. Black Canary in 399, 418, 419. Black Orchid in 428-430. Captain Fear in 425-427, 429, 432, 433. Capt. Marvel in 49, 492, 499. Capt.Marvel/Mary Marvel in 498. Capt. Marvel Jr. in 496. Challengers of the Unknown in 493-497. Congorilla in 270-281, 283. Creeper in 445-447. Deadman in 459-466. Dr Mid-Nite in 418. Dr.13 in 428. Eclipso in 457, 458. Elongated Man in 459. Flash in 459-466. Green Arrow in 266-269. Green Lantern in 459, 460. Justice Society in 461-466. Legion of Super-Heroes in 300-380. Martian Manhunter in 449-451. New Gods in 459, 460. Phantom Stranger in 467-478, 498, 499. Seven Soldiers of Victory in 438-443. Starman in 467-478. Superboy in 103-315, 453-458. Supergirl in 381-389, 391-402, 404-415, 417-424. Tracy Thompson in 410, 402. Vigilante in 417, 422, 426, 427. Wonder Woman in 459-464. Zatanna in 413-415, 419, 421.

REPRINT FEATURES

Animal Man in 412, 414, 415, 420, 421. Aqualad in 494. Aquaman in 491-493, 495-499, 501-503. Black Canary in 491, 492. Capt. Marvel in 493-495, 497-499, 501, 502. Enchantress in 417, 419. Guardian/Newsboy Legion in 503. Hawkman in 413. Jimmy Olsen/Legion in 500, 503. Johnny Thunder in 416. Legion of Super-Heroes in 403, 409-411, 491-497, 498 (Bouncing Boy origin), 499-503. Merry, Phantom Lady in 416. Phantom Stranger in 419. Plastic Man in 498, 499, 501-503. The Ray in 501. Robotman in 413. Sandman by Simon & Kirby in 491, 492, 495, 496, 499. Shining Knight in 417. Spectre in 491-499, 501, 502. Superboy in 317-338, 340-345, 356, 356. Superboy/Mon-El in 491. Supergirl in 390, 398, 416. Superman in 339, 420. Wonder Woman in 416. Zatanna in 493, 502, 503.

ADVENTURERS
Aircel/Adventure; 1 Aug 1986-10 1987

	$Good	$Fine	$N.Mint	£Good	£Fine	£N.Mint
0 ND origin issue (July 1988)	$0.60	$1.80	$3.00	£0.40	£1.20	£2.00
1 ND light blue cover	$1.20	$3.60	$6.00	£0.80	£2.40	£4.00
1 ND limited edition, skeleton cover	$2.00	$6.00	$10.00	£1.50	£4.50	£7.50
1 2nd printing, ND dark blue cover, 1st Elf-Warrior	$0.55	$1.65	$2.75	£0.35	£1.05	£1.75
2 ND	$0.45	$1.35	$2.25	£0.30	£0.90	£1.50
3 ND 1st Adventure Comics issue	$0.45	$1.35	$2.25	£0.30	£0.90	£1.50
4-10 ND	$0.40	$1.20	$2.00	£0.25	£0.75	£1.25
Title Value:	$8.05	$24.15	$40.25	£5.40	£16.20	£27.00

ADVENTURERS BOOK 2
Adventure; 1 1987-9 1989

	$Good	$Fine	$N.Mint	£Good	£Fine	£N.Mint
1 ND regular edition	$0.45	$1.35	$2.25	£0.30	£0.90	£1.50
1 ND limited edition	$0.55	$1.65	$2.75	£0.35	£1.05	£1.75
2-9 ND	$0.40	$1.20	$2.00	£0.25	£0.75	£1.25
Title Value:	$4.20	$12.60	$21.00	£2.65	£7.95	£13.25

ADVENTURERS BOOK 3
Adventure; 1 Oct 1989-6 1990

	$Good	$Fine	$N.Mint	£Good	£Fine	£N.Mint
1 ND regular edition	$0.45	$1.35	$2.25	£0.30	£0.90	£1.50
1 ND limited edition	$0.55	$1.65	$2.75	£0.35	£1.05	£1.75
2-6 ND	$0.40	$1.20	$2.00	£0.25	£0.75	£1.25
Title Value:	$3.00	$9.00	$15.00	£1.90	£5.70	£9.50
Trade Paperback (B&W)				£1.00	£3.00	£5.00
Adventurers Graphic Novel Three Pack (May1991) - The Chaos Gate/The Halls of Anubis/The Ways of the Worm)				£1.40	£4.20	£7.00

ADVENTURES IN THE MYSTWOOD
Blackthorne; 1 1986

	$Good	$Fine	$N.Mint	£Good	£Fine	£N.Mint
1 ND Williams art	$0.30	$0.90	$1.50	£0.20	£0.60	£1.00
Title Value:	$0.30	$0.90	$1.50	£0.20	£0.60	£1.00

	$Good	$Fine	$N.Mint	£Good	£Fine	£N.Mint
Trade Paperback (B&W)				£1.00	£3.00	£5.00

ADVENTURES INTO THE UNKNOWN
ACG; 1 Autumn 1948-174 Aug 1967

	$Good	$Fine	$N.Mint	£Good	£Fine	£N.Mint
1 ND adaptation of gothic novel Castle of Otranto; Fred Guardineer art featured	$160.00	$480.00	$800.00	£110.00	£330.00	£550.00
2 ND	$70.00	$210.00	$350.00	£50.00	£150.00	£250.00
3 ND	$75.00	$225.00	$375.00	£52.50	£155.00	£265.00
4-5 ND	$40.00	$120.00	$200.00	£27.00	£80.00	£135.00
6-10 ND	$35.00	$105.00	$175.00	£23.00	£67.50	£115.00
11-20 ND	$25.00	$75.00	$125.00	£17.00	£50.00	£85.00
21-30 ND	$20.00	$60.00	$100.00	£14.00	£42.00	£70.00
31-50 ND	$17.00	$50.00	$85.00	£12.00	£36.00	£60.00
51 ND scarce in the U.K. 3-D cover and story	$22.50	$67.50	$157.50	£15.00	£45.00	£105.00
52-58 ND scarce in the U.K. 3-D cover and story	$19.00	$57.50	$135.00	£12.50	£39.00	£90.00
59 ND scarce in the U.K. 3-D story	$12.50	$39.00	$90.00	£8.50	£26.00	£60.00
60 ND	$7.75	$23.50	$55.00	£5.50	£17.00	£40.00
61 ND	$6.25	$19.00	$45.00	£4.25	£12.50	£30.00
62-70 ND	$5.75	$17.50	$35.00	£4.15	£12.50	£25.00
71-80 ND	$4.15	$12.50	$25.00	£2.90	£8.75	£17.50
81-90 ND	$4.15	$12.50	$25.00	£2.50	£7.50	£15.00
91 ND Williamson art	$5.75	$17.50	$35.00	£3.75	£11.00	£22.50
92-95 ND	$4.15	$12.50	$25.00	£2.50	£7.50	£15.00
96 ND Williamson art	$5.75	$17.50	$35.00	£3.75	£11.00	£22.50
97-106 ND	$4.15	$12.50	$25.00	£2.50	£7.50	£15.00
107 ND Williamson art	$5.75	$17.50	$35.00	£3.75	£11.00	£22.50
108-110 ND	$4.15	$12.50	$25.00	£2.50	£7.50	£15.00
1st official distribution in the U.K.						
111-115	$4.15	$12.50	$25.00	£2.50	£7.50	£15.00
116 Williamson art	$5.75	$17.50	$35.00	£3.75	£11.00	£22.50
117	$4.15	$12.50	$25.00	£2.50	£7.50	£15.00
118 painted cover	$4.15	$12.50	$25.00	£2.50	£7.50	£15.00
119-127	$4.15	$12.50	$25.00	£2.50	£7.50	£15.00
128 Williamson reprint	$4.15	$12.50	$25.00	£2.50	£7.50	£15.00
129-150	$3.30	$10.00	$20.00	£2.05	£6.25	£12.50
151-153	$2.90	$8.75	$17.50	£1.80	£5.50	£11.00
154 1st appearance/origin Nemesis	$3.30	$10.00	$20.00	£2.05	£6.25	£12.50
155-160	$2.90	$8.75	$17.50	£1.80	£5.50	£11.00
161-167	$3.00	$9.00	$15.00	£2.00	£6.00	£10.00
168 Steve Ditko art	$4.00	$12.00	$25.00	£2.80	£8.25	£14.00
169-174	$3.00	$9.00	$15.00	£2.00	£6.00	£10.00
Title Value:	$1975.85	$5921.75	$10677.50	£1335.75	£3999.50	£7205.50

ADVENTURES INTO THE UNKNOWN (2ND SERIES)
A Plus Comics; 1 Oct 1990-5 1991

	$Good	$Fine	$N.Mint	£Good	£Fine	£N.Mint
1 ND 48pgs, Frank Frazetta cover; reprints of ACG series begin	$0.45	$1.35	$2.25	£0.30	£0.90	£1.50
2 ND 48pgs, Williamson, Steve Ditko, Mike Zeck art, Frank Frazetta cover	$0.45	$1.35	$2.25	£0.30	£0.90	£1.50
3 ND 48pgs, Williamson, Wood art	$0.45	$1.35	$2.25	£0.30	£0.90	£1.50
4-5 ND 48pgs	$0.45	$1.35	$2.25	£0.30	£0.90	£1.50
Title Value:	$2.25	$6.75	$11.25	£1.50	£4.50	£7.50

Note: bi-monthly

	$Good	$Fine	$N.Mint	£Good	£Fine	£N.Mint
Halloween Special (Nov 1991), 48pgs				£0.30	£0.90	£1.50

ADVENTURES OF BARON MUNCHAUSEN
Now Comics,MS; 1 Jul 1989-4 Oct 1989

	$Good	$Fine	$N.Mint	£Good	£Fine	£N.Mint
1-4 ND movie adaptation in colour	$0.40	$1.20	$2.00	£0.25	£0.75	£1.25
Title Value:	$1.60	$4.80	$8.00	£1.00	£3.00	£5.00

ADVENTURES OF BOB HOPE
(see Bob Hope)

ADVENTURES OF CAPT JACK
(see Captain Jack)

ADVENTURES OF CAPTAIN NEMO, THE
Rip Off Press,MS; 1 Jun 1992-3 Aug 1992

	$Good	$Fine	$N.Mint	£Good	£Fine	£N.Mint
1-3 ND	$0.45	$1.35	$2.25	£0.30	£0.90	£1.50
Title Value:	$1.35	$4.05	$6.75	£0.90	£2.70	£4.50

ADVENTURES OF CHUK, THE
White Wolf/Avatar; 1 Jul 1986-3 1987 (Avatar #3 Only)
(becomes Chuk the Barbaric with #3)

	$Good	$Fine	$N.Mint	£Good	£Fine	£N.Mint
1-2 ND	$0.25	$0.75	$1.25	£0.15	£0.45	£0.75
3 ND scarce in the U.K.	$0.30	$0.90	$1.50	£0.20	£0.60	£1.00
Title Value:	$0.80	$2.40	$4.00	£0.50	£1.50	£2.50

ADVENTURES OF CYCLOPS & PHOENIX, THE
Marvel Comics Group,MS; 1 May 1994-4 Aug 1994

	$Good	$Fine	$N.Mint	£Good	£Fine	£N.Mint
1 Scott Lobdell script begins	$0.90	$2.70	$4.50	£0.60	£1.80	£3.00
2	$0.80	$2.40	$4.00	£0.50	£1.50	£2.00
3-4	$0.70	$2.10	$3.50	£0.45	£1.35	£2.25
Title Value:	$3.10	$9.30	$15.50	£2.00	£6.00	£10.00

ADVENTURES OF JERRY LEWIS
(see Jerry Lewis)

VERY GENERAL PERCENTAGE CONVERSION CHART WHICH MAY BE USED TO CALCULATE LOW AND INBETWEEN GRADES:

ADVENTURES OF LUTHER ARKWRIGHT
(see British section and Luther Arkwright)

ADVENTURES OF MR.PYRIDINE
Fantagraphics,Magazine OS; nn Dec 1988

	$Good	$Fine	$N.Mint	£Good	£Fine	£N.Mint
nn ND Singh art	$0.45	$1.35	$2.25	£0.30	£0.90	£1.50
Title Value:	$0.45	$1.35	$2.25	£0.30	£0.90	£1.50

ADVENTURES OF SUPERMAN
(see Superman #424 onwards)

ADVENTURES OF THE OUTSIDERS
(see Batman and the Outsiders)

ADVENTURES ON THE PLANET OF THE APES
Marvel Comics Group, Film; 1 Oct 1975-11 Dec 1976

	$Good	$Fine	$N.Mint	£Good	£Fine	£N.Mint
1 ND Jim Starlin cover	$0.45	$1.35	$2.25	£0.30	£0.90	£1.50
2-11 ND	$0.40	$1.20	$2.00	£0.25	£0.75	£1.25
Title Value:	$4.45	$13.35	$22.25	£2.80	£8.40	£14.00

AESOP'S FABLES
Fantagraphics; 1 Feb 1991-3 1991

	$Good	$Fine	$N.Mint	£Good	£Fine	£N.Mint
1-3 ND	$0.45	$1.35	$2.25	£0.30	£0.90	£1.50
Title Value:	$1.35	$4.05	$6.75	£0.90	£2.70	£4.50

AFTER DARK
Millennium,OS; nn Mar 1995

	$Good	$Fine	$N.Mint	£Good	£Fine	£N.Mint
nn ND horror anthology; black and white	$0.60	$1.80	$3.00	£0.40	£1.20	£2.00
Title Value:	$0.60	$1.80	$3.00	£0.40	£1.20	£2.00

AGAINST BLACKSHARD: 3-D
Sirius; 1 Aug 1986

	$Good	$Fine	$N.Mint	£Good	£Fine	£N.Mint
1 ND Scott Hampton inks	$0.45	$1.35	$2.25	£0.30	£0.90	£1.50
Title Value:	$0.45	$1.35	$2.25	£0.30	£0.90	£1.50

AGE OF REPTILES
Dark Horse,MS; 1 Nov 1993-4 Feb 1994

	$Good	$Fine	$N.Mint	£Good	£Fine	£N.Mint
1-4 ND Ricardo Delgado script and art	$0.45	$1.35	$2.25	£0.30	£0.90	£1.50
Title Value:	$1.80	$5.40	$9.00	£1.20	£3.60	£6.00

AGENT LIBERTY SPECIAL
DC Comics,OS; 1 Jan 1992
(see Superman [2nd Series] #60)

	$Good	$Fine	$N.Mint	£Good	£Fine	£N.Mint
1 48pgs	$0.40	$1.20	$2.00	£0.25	£0.75	£1.25
Title Value:	$0.40	$1.20	$2.00	£0.25	£0.75	£1.25

AGENT UNKNOWN
Renegade; 1 Oct 1987-3 Feb 1988

	$Good	$Fine	$N.Mint	£Good	£Fine	£N.Mint
1-3 ND Dell Barras art	$0.40	$1.20	$2.00	£0.25	£0.75	£1.25
Title Value:	$1.20	$3.60	$6.00	£0.75	£2.25	£3.75

AGENTS OF LAW
Dark Horse; 1 Mar 1995-present

	$Good	$Fine	$N.Mint	£Good	£Fine	£N.Mint
1-6 ND Keith Giffen co-script; spin off from Comics Greatest World	$0.45	$1.35	$2.25	£0.30	£0.90	£1.50
Title Value:	$2.70	$8.10	$13.50	£1.80	£5.40	£9.00

AIDS AWARENESS
Chaos City Comics,OS; 1 Dec 1993

	$Good	$Fine	$N.Mint	£Good	£Fine	£N.Mint
1 ND features art by Dave Gibbons, Liam Sharp, Bryan Hitch, John Higgins, Kev O'Neill with Simon Bisley painted cover; black and white, printed on heavy stock paper	$0.75	$2.25	$3.75	£0.50	£1.50	£2.50
1 ND Limited Edition	$1.50	$4.50	$7.50	£1.00	£3.00	£5.00
Title Value:	$2.25	$6.75	$11.25	£1.50	£4.50	£7.50

AIR RAIDERS
Marvel Comics Group, Toy; 1 Jan 1988-5 Mar 1988

	$Good	$Fine	$N.Mint	£Good	£Fine	£N.Mint
1-5	$0.15	$0.45	$0.75	£0.10	£0.30	£0.50
Title Value:	$0.75	$2.25	$3.75	£0.50	£1.50	£2.50

AIRBOY
Eclipse; 1 Jul 1986-50 Oct 1989
(see Airfighters, Airmaidens, Target: Airboy)

	$Good	$Fine	$N.Mint	£Good	£Fine	£N.Mint
1 20pgs, bi-weekly, 50¢ cover		$1.80	$3.00	£0.40	£1.20	£2.00
2	$0.40	$1.20	$2.00	£0.25	£0.75	£1.25
3 The Heap begins (looks very much like Marvel's Man-Thing)	$0.40	$1.20	$2.00	£0.25	£0.75	£1.25
4	$0.40	$1.20	$2.00	£0.25	£0.75	£1.25
5 rare in the U.K., Dave Stevens cover, re-intro Valkyrie	$0.75	$2.25	$3.75	£0.50	£1.50	£2.50
6	$0.40	$1.20	$2.00	£0.25	£0.75	£1.25
7 Gulacy cover	$0.40	$1.20	$2.00	£0.25	£0.75	£1.25
8	$0.40	$1.20	$2.00	£0.25	£0.75	£1.25
9 Skywolf begins	$0.40	$1.20	$2.00	£0.25	£0.75	£1.25
10	$0.40	$1.20	$2.00	£0.25	£0.75	£1.25
11 origin Airboy retold	$0.40	$1.20	$2.00	£0.25	£0.75	£1.25
12 Dave Dorman cover	$0.40	$1.20	$2.00	£0.25	£0.75	£1.25
13-16	$0.40	$1.20	$2.00	£0.25	£0.75	£1.25
17 Steacy painted cover	$0.40	$1.20	$2.00	£0.25	£0.75	£1.25
18-23	$0.40	$1.20	$2.00	£0.25	£0.75	£1.25
24 The Heap returns	$0.40	$1.20	$2.00	£0.25	£0.75	£1.25
25-27	$0.40	$1.20	$2.00	£0.25	£0.75	£1.25
28 Mr. Monster vs. The Heap back-up story	$0.40	$1.20	$2.00	£0.25	£0.75	£1.25
29-32	$0.40	$1.20	$2.00	£0.25	£0.75	£1.25
33 painted Steacy cover	$0.40	$1.20	$2.00	£0.25	£0.75	£1.25
34 1st monthly issue	$0.40	$1.20	$2.00	£0.25	£0.75	£1.25
35-45	$0.40	$1.20	$2.00	£0.25	£0.75	£1.25
46-49 Airboy Diary story	$0.40	$1.20	$2.00	£0.25	£0.75	£1.25
50 48pgs, DS squarebound, Joe Kubert cover, Andy and Adam Kubert art	$0.80	$2.40	$4.00	£0.50	£1.50	£2.50
Title Value:	$20.95	$62.85	$104.75	£13.15	£39.45	£65.75

Note: all Non-Distributed on the news-stands in the U.K.

AIRBOY AND MR.MONSTER SPECIAL
Eclipse,OS; 1 Aug 1987

	$Good	$Fine	$N.Mint	£Good	£Fine	£N.Mint
1 ND Michael T. Gilbert script/art	$0.45	$1.35	$2.25	£0.30	£0.90	£1.50
Title Value:	$0.45	$1.35	$2.25	£0.30	£0.90	£1.50

AIRBOY MEETS PROWLER
Eclipse,OS; 1 Dec 1987

	$Good	$Fine	$N.Mint	£Good	£Fine	£N.Mint
1 ND	$0.45	$1.35	$2.25	£0.30	£0.90	£1.50
Title Value:	$0.45	$1.35	$2.25	£0.30	£0.90	£1.50

AIRBOY VERSUS THE AIR MAIDENS
Eclipse,OS; 1 Jul 1988

	$Good	$Fine	$N.Mint	£Good	£Fine	£N.Mint
1 ND	$0.45	$1.35	$2.25	£0.30	£0.90	£1.50
Title Value:	$0.45	$1.35	$2.25	£0.30	£0.90	£1.50

AIRFIGHTERS CLASSICS
Eclipse; 1 Nov 1987-6 May 1989

	$Good	$Fine	$N.Mint	£Good	£Fine	£N.Mint
1 ND 64pgs, squarebound, classic contraversial Japanese fighter pilot cover reprinted, black and white	$0.90	$2.70	$4.50	£0.60	£1.80	£3.00
2-6 ND 64pgs, squarebound, Golden Age Airboy reprints, black and white	$0.80	$2.40	$4.00	£0.50	£1.50	£2.50
Title Value:	$4.90	$14.70	$24.50	£3.10	£9.30	£15.50

Note: all bookshelf format. Issue #1 reprints Airfighters #2 originally published by Hillman Periodicals from Nov 1942 on. Issues #2-6 reprints original issues #3-7.

AIRFIGHTERS MEET SGT.STRIKE
Eclipse,OS; 1 Jan 1988

	$Good	$Fine	$N.Mint	£Good	£Fine	£N.Mint
1 ND Tom Lyle cover and art (colour), card stock covers	$0.45	$1.35	$2.25	£0.30	£0.90	£1.50
Title Value:	$0.45	$1.35	$2.25	£0.30	£0.90	£1.50

AIRMAIDENS SPECIAL
Eclipse,OS; 1 Aug 1987

	$Good	$Fine	$N.Mint	£Good	£Fine	£N.Mint
1 ND Airboy tie-in, Larry Elmore cover and art; colour	$0.45	$1.35	$2.25	£0.30	£0.90	£1.50
Title Value:	$0.45	$1.35	$2.25	£0.30	£0.90	£1.50

AIRMAN
Malibu,OS; 1 Mar 1993

	$Good	$Fine	$N.Mint	£Good	£Fine	£N.Mint
1 ND Protectors spin-off	$0.40	$1.20	$2.00	£0.25	£0.75	£1.25
Title Value:	$0.40	$1.20	$2.00	£0.25	£0.75	£1.25

AIRTIGHT GARAGE, THE
Marvel Comics Group/Epic,MS; 1 Jul 1993-4 Oct 1993

	$Good	$Fine	$N.Mint	£Good	£Fine	£N.Mint
1 ND reprint of Moebius Graphic Novel #3 begins	$0.45	$1.35	$2.25	£0.30	£0.90	£1.50
2-4 ND	$0.45	$1.35	$2.25	£0.30	£0.90	£1.50
Title Value:	$1.80	$5.40	$9.00	£1.20	£3.60	£6.00

AIRWAVES
Caliber Press; 1 Apr 1991-6 1991

	$Good	$Fine	$N.Mint	£Good	£Fine	£N.Mint
1-6 ND	$0.45	$1.35	$2.25	£0.30	£0.90	£1.50
Title Value:	$2.70	$8.10	$13.50	£1.80	£5.40	£9.00

AKIRA
Marvel Comics Group/Epic; 1 Nov 1988-33 1992; 34 Oct 1995-38 Feb 1996

	$Good	$Fine	$N.Mint	£Good	£Fine	£N.Mint
1 ND scarce in the U.K.	$2.40	$7.00	$12.00	£1.60	£4.80	£8.00
1 2nd printing ND	$0.90	$2.70	$4.50	£0.60	£1.80	£3.00
2 ND	$1.80	$5.25	$9.00	£1.20	£3.60	£6.00
2 2nd printing ND	$0.80	$2.40	$4.00	£0.50	£1.50	£2.50
3 ND very scarce in the U.K.	$2.40	$7.00	$12.00	£1.60	£4.80	£8.00
4 ND scarce in the U.K.	$2.10	$6.25	$10.50	£1.40	£4.20	£7.00
5 ND scarce in the U.K.	$2.00	$6.00	$10.00	£1.30	£3.90	£6.50
6-10 ND	$1.50	$4.50	$7.50	£1.00	£3.00	£5.00
11-15 ND	$1.20	$3.60	$6.00	£0.80	£2.40	£4.00
16-24 ND	$1.00	$3.00	$5.00	£0.70	£2.10	£3.50
25 ND scarce in the U.K.	$2.00	$6.00	$10.00	£1.30	£3.90	£6.50
26-30 ND	$0.90	$2.70	$4.50	£0.60	£1.80	£3.00
31-33 ND	$0.80	$2.40	$4.00	£0.50	£1.50	£2.50
34-35 ND	$1.20	$3.60	$6.00	£0.80	£2.40	£4.00
36-38 ND	$1.40	$4.20	$7.00	£0.90	£2.70	£4.50
Title Value:	$50.40	$150.60	$253.00	£33.60	£100.80	£168.00

Note: all 64pgs, Bookshelf Format. Japanese post-holocaust story, translation by Mary Jo Duffy. Mature Readers. Note also: last five issues very delayed in frequency.

	£Good	£Fine	£N.Mint
Trade paperback 1 (May 1991), reprints issues #1-3	£2.25	£6.75	£11.25
Trade paperback 2 (Aug 1991), reprints issues #4-6	£2.00	£6.00	£10.00
Trade paperback 3 (Jan 1992), reprints issues #7-9	£2.00	£6.00	£10.00
Trade paperback 4 (May 1992), reprints issues #10-12	£2.00	£6.00	£10.00
Trade paperback 5 (Jul 1992), reprints issues #13-15	£2.00	£6.00	£10.00
Trade paperback 6 (Sep 1992), reprints issues #16-18	£2.00	£6.00	£10.00
Trade paperback 7 (Feb 1993), reprints issues #19-21	£2.00	£6.00	£10.00
Trade paperback 8 (May 1993), reprints issues #22-24	£2.00	£6.00	£10.00

MINT = 100% / NEAR MINT (inc. +/-) = 90-99% / VERY FINE (inc. +/-) = 75-89% / FINE (inc. +/-) = 55-74%
VERY GOOD (inc. +/-) = 35-54% / GOOD (inc. +/-) = 15-34% / FAIR = 5-14% / POOR = 1-4%

193

	$Good	$Fine	$N.Mint	£Good	£Fine	£N.Mint

Trade paperback 9 (Aug 1993), reprints issues #25-27

| | | | | £2.00 | £6.00 | £10.00 |

Trade paperback 10 (Nov 1993), reprints issues #28-30

| | | | | £2.00 | £6.00 | £10.00 |

ALADDIN
Marvel Comics Group; 1 Oct 1994-12 Sep 1995
1-12 ND new new adventures

| | $0.30 | $0.90 | $1.50 | £0.20 | £0.60 | £1.00 |
| Title Value: | $3.60 | $10.80 | $18.00 | £2.40 | £7.20 | £12.00 |

Aladdin Volume 1 (Jun 1995)
Trade paperback reprints issues #1-4

| | | | | £1.30 | £3.90 | £6.50 |

ALARMING ADVENTURES
Harvey; 1 Oct 1962-3 Feb 1963
1 rare in the U.K., Crandall/Williamson art; distributed in the U.K.

| | $8.25 | $25.00 | $50.00 | £5.00 | £15.00 | £30.00 |

2-3 rare in the U.K, Crandall/Williamson art; distributed in the U.K.

| | $6.50 | $19.50 | $40.00 | £4.00 | £12.00 | £25.00 |
| Title Value: | $21.25 | $64.00 | $130.00 | £13.00 | £39.00 | £80.00 |

ALBEDO
Thoughts and Images; 0 Apr 1985-15 1989
0 1st printing, blue cover

| | $3.00 | $9.00 | $15.00 | £2.00 | £6.00 | £10.00 |

0 2nd printing, blue cover, "Second printing" on cover and price removed

| | $1.50 | $4.50 | $7.50 | £1.00 | £3.00 | £5.00 |

0 3rd printing, blue cover; "Third printing" on cover and new address in indicia

| | $0.60 | $1.80 | $3.00 | £0.40 | £1.20 | £2.00 |

0 4th printing

| | $0.45 | $1.35 | $2.25 | £0.30 | £0.90 | £1.50 |

1 dark red cover, 1st appearance Usagi Yojimbo

| | $2.00 | $6.00 | $10.00 | £1.50 | £4.50 | £7.50 |

1 bright red cover variation

	$2.00	$6.00	$10.00	£1.50	£4.50	£7.50
2	$1.50	$4.50	$7.50	£1.00	£3.00	£5.00
3	$0.90	$2.70	$4.50	£0.60	£1.80	£3.00
4-8	$0.60	$1.80	$3.00	£0.40	£1.20	£2.00
9-15	$0.40	$1.20	$2.00	£0.25	£0.75	£1.25
Title Value:	$17.75	$53.25	$88.75	£12.05	£36.15	£60.25

Note: all Non-Distributed on the news-stands in the U.K.

ALBEDO COLOR SPECIAL
Antarctic Press,OS; 1 Sep 1993
1 ND Steve Gallacci's first story for Albedo re-done in colour

| | $0.60 | $1.80 | $3.00 | £0.40 | £1.20 | £2.00 |
| Title Value: | $0.60 | $1.80 | $3.00 | £0.40 | £1.20 | £2.00 |

ALBEDO VOLUME 2
Antarctic Press; 1 Aug 1991-10 1993

1 ND	$0.55	$1.65	$2.75	£0.35	£1.05	£1.75
1 2nd printing ND	$0.45	$1.35	$2.25	£0.30	£0.90	£1.50
2-10 ND	$0.45	$1.35	$2.25	£0.30	£0.90	£1.50
Title Value:	$5.05	$15.15	$25.25	£3.35	£10.05	£16.75

ALBEDO VOLUME 3
Antarctic Press; 1 Feb 1994-3 Apr 1994
1-3 ND Steve Gallacci script and art

| | $0.60 | $1.80 | $3.00 | £0.40 | £1.20 | £2.00 |
| Title Value: | $1.80 | $5.40 | $9.00 | £1.20 | £3.60 | £6.00 |

ALEX
Fantagraphics; 1 Mar 1994-2 1994
1-2 ND Mark Kalesniko script and art; black and white

| | $0.45 | $1.35 | $2.25 | £0.30 | £0.90 | £1.50 |
| Title Value: | $0.90 | $2.70 | $4.50 | £0.60 | £1.80 | £3.00 |

ALF
Marvel Comics Group, TV; 1 Mar 1988-50 Feb 1992

1 ND	$0.30	$0.90	$1.50	£0.20	£0.60	£1.00
1 2nd printing ND	$0.20	$0.60	$1.00	£0.15	£0.45	£0.75
2-10 ND	$0.20	$0.60	$1.00	£0.15	£0.45	£0.75
11-28 ND	$0.15	$0.45	$0.75	£0.10	£0.35	£0.60

29 ND mock 3-D cover

	$0.15	$0.45	$0.75	£0.10	£0.35	£0.60
30-49 ND	$0.15	$0.45	$0.75	£0.10	£0.35	£0.60
50 DS	$0.20	$0.60	$1.00	£0.15	£0.45	£0.75
Title Value:	$8.35	$25.05	$43.00	£5.75	£19.20	£32.65

ALF ANNUAL
Marvel Comics Group, TV; 1 1988-3 1990

| **1** ND | $0.30 | $0.90 | $1.50 | £0.25 | £0.75 | £1.25 |
| **2** ND | $0.25 | $0.75 | $1.25 | £0.20 | £0.60 | £1.00 |

3 ND New Age Melmutant Abstract Turtles appear

| | $0.25 | $0.75 | $1.25 | £0.20 | £0.60 | £1.00 |
| Title Value: | $0.80 | $2.40 | $4.00 | £0.65 | £1.95 | £3.25 |

ALF HOLIDAY SPECIAL
Marvel Comics Group,OS; 1 Jul 1988
1 ND 64pgs, squarebound, Wolverine appears

| | $0.30 | $0.90 | $1.50 | £0.25 | £0.75 | £1.25 |
| Title Value: | $0.30 | $0.90 | $1.50 | £0.25 | £0.75 | £1.25 |

ALF SPECIAL EDITION
Marvel Comics Group,OS; 1 Aug 1990
1 reprints Alf #1-#3, photo cover from #1

| | $0.50 | $1.50 | $2.50 | £0.35 | £1.05 | £1.75 |
| Title Value: | $0.50 | $1.50 | $2.50 | £0.35 | £1.05 | £1.75 |

Note: Bookshelf Format

ALF SPRING SPECIAL
Marvel Comics Group,OS; 1 Feb 1989
1 ND 64pgs, squarebound

| | $0.40 | $1.20 | $2.00 | £0.25 | £0.75 | £1.25 |
| Title Value: | $0.40 | $1.20 | $2.00 | £0.25 | £0.75 | £1.25 |

ALFRED HITCHCOCK'S PSYCHO
Innovation,MS; 1 Nov 1991-3 Aug 1992

| **1-3** ND | $0.45 | $1.35 | $2.25 | £0.30 | £0.90 | £1.50 |
| Title Value: | $1.35 | $4.05 | $6.75 | £0.90 | £2.70 | £4.50 |

ALI BABA: SCOURGE OF THE DESERT
Caliber Press,OS; 1 Jan 1993
1 ND cover layouts by Dave Sim, finishes by Dale Keown

| | $0.60 | $1.80 | $3.00 | £0.40 | £1.20 | £2.00 |

1 ND signed, limited edition; metallic logo, 3,000 copies

| | $0.90 | $2.70 | $4.50 | £0.60 | £1.80 | £3.00 |
| Title Value: | $1.50 | $4.50 | $7.50 | £1.00 | £3.00 | £5.00 |

ALI-BABA: THETA'S REVENGE
Caliber Press,OS; 1 Sep 1993

| **1** ND | $0.60 | $1.80 | $3.00 | £0.40 | £1.20 | £2.00 |
| Title Value: | $0.60 | $1.80 | $3.00 | £0.40 | £1.20 | £2.00 |

ALIAS: STORMFRONT
Now Comics; 1,2 1990

| **1-2** ND Jeff Starling art | $0.45 | $1.35 | $2.25 | £0.30 | £0.90 | £1.50 |
| Title Value: | $0.90 | $2.70 | $4.50 | £0.60 | £1.80 | £3.00 |

ALICE COOPER: LAST TEMPTATION OF ALICE
Marvel Comics Group,MS; 1 Aug 1994-3 Nov 1994
1-3 ND Neil Gaiman script, Michael Zulli art, Dave McKean covers

| | $0.90 | $2.70 | $4.50 | £0.60 | £1.80 | £3.00 |
| Title Value: | $2.70 | $8.10 | $13.50 | £1.80 | £5.40 | £9.00 |

Alice Cooper: The Complete Last Temptation (May 1995)
Trade paperback reprints mini-series with Dave McKean cover

| | | | | £2.00 | £6.00 | £10.00 |

ALIEN
Avon Books,OS; nn Sep 1979
nn ND scarce in the U.K. 100pgs, softcover; Dan O'Bannon screenplay illustrated with several hundred movie stills

| | $22.50 | $67.50 | $112.50 | £15.00 | £45.00 | £75.00 |
| Title Value: | $22.50 | $67.50 | $112.50 | £15.00 | £45.00 | £75.00 |

ALIEN 3 MOVIE
Dark Horse,MS; 1 Aug 1992-3 Sep 1992
1-3 ND adaptation of film, Arthur Suydam covers, bi-weekly

| | $0.45 | $1.35 | $2.25 | £0.30 | £0.90 | £1.50 |
| Title Value: | $1.35 | $4.05 | $6.75 | £0.90 | £2.70 | £4.50 |

Alien 3 Movie Special - U.K. Edition (Feb 1993)
magazine, 44pgs, behind-the-scenes material

| | | | | £0.35 | £1.05 | £1.75 |

ALIEN ENCOUNTERS
Eclipse; 1 Jun 1985-14 Aug 1987

| **1** ND | $0.55 | $1.65 | $2.75 | £0.35 | £1.05 | £1.75 |
| **2-7** ND | $0.45 | $1.35 | $2.25 | £0.30 | £0.90 | £1.50 |

8 ND Marilyn Monroe cover

| | $0.45 | $1.35 | $2.25 | £0.30 | £0.90 | £1.50 |
| **9-13** ND | $0.45 | $1.35 | $2.25 | £0.30 | £0.90 | £1.50 |

14 ND John Ridgway art, John Bolton cover

| | $0.45 | $1.35 | $2.25 | £0.30 | £0.90 | £1.50 |
| Title Value: | $6.40 | $19.20 | $32.00 | £4.25 | £12.75 | £21.25 |

ALIEN FIRE
Kitchen Sink; 1 Jan 1987-3 Jul 1987

| **1-3** ND | $0.45 | $1.35 | $2.25 | £0.30 | £0.90 | £1.50 |
| Title Value: | $1.35 | $4.05 | $6.75 | £0.90 | £2.70 | £4.50 |

Alien Fire: Pass in Thunder (May 1995)
64pgs, new novella plus reprint of two-part story from
Dark Horse Presents; black and white

| | | | | £0.90 | £2.70 | £4.50 |

ALIEN FIRE: PASS IN THUNDER
Kitchen Sink,OS; 1 Aug 1993
1 ND reprints Alien Fire stories from Dark Horse Presents with extra art pages

| | $0.80 | $2.40 | $4.00 | £0.50 | £1.50 | £2.50 |
| Title Value: | $0.80 | $2.40 | $4.00 | £0.50 | £1.50 | £2.50 |

Note: originally announced as a mini-series

ALIEN LEGION
Marvel Comics Group/Epic; 1 Apr 1984-20 Sep 1987
(see Marvel Graphic Novel)

| **1** ND DS | $0.70 | $2.10 | $3.50 | £0.45 | £1.35 | £2.25 |
| **2-5** ND | $0.55 | $1.65 | $2.75 | £0.35 | £1.05 | £1.75 |

6-8 ND Portacio inks

	$0.55	$1.65	$2.75	£0.35	£1.05	£1.75
9-20 ND	$0.45	$1.35	$2.25	£0.30	£0.90	£1.50
Title Value:	$9.95	$29.85	$49.75	£6.50	£19.50	£32.50

Note: all high quality paper.
Alien Legion: Slaughter-World (Nov 1991)
Trade paperback reprints #1,7-11

| | | | | £1.10 | £3.30 | £5.50 |

ALIEN LEGION (2ND SERIES)
Marvel Comics Group/Epic; 1 Aug 1987-18 Aug 1990

1 ND	$0.45	$1.35	$2.25	£0.30	£0.90	£1.50
2-18 ND	$0.40	$1.20	$2.00	£0.25	£0.75	£1.25
Title Value:	$7.25	$21.75	$36.25	£4.55	£13.65	£22.75

Note: Mature Readers.

ALIEN LEGION: BINARY DEEP
Marvel Comics Group/Epic,OS; 1 Nov 1993
1 48pgs, Chuck Dixon and Quique Alcatena; bound-in trading card

| | $0.60 | $1.80 | $3.00 | £0.40 | £1.20 | £2.00 |
| Title Value: | $0.60 | $1.80 | $3.00 | £0.40 | £1.20 | £2.00 |

ALIEN LEGION: ON THE EDGE
Marvel Comics Group/Epic,MS; 1 Jan 1991-3 Mar 1991

| **1-3** ND 48pgs | $0.75 | $2.25 | $3.75 | £0.50 | £1.50 | £2.50 |
| Title Value: | $2.25 | $6.75 | $11.25 | £1.50 | £4.50 | £7.50 |

Note: Bookshelf Format

ALIEN LEGION: ONE PLANET AT A TIME
Marvel Comics Group/Epic,MS; 1 Jul 1993-3 Sep 1993

| **1-3** ND | $0.90 | $2.70 | $4.50 | £0.60 | £1.80 | £3.00 |
| Title Value: | $2.70 | $8.10 | $13.50 | £1.80 | £5.40 | £9.00 |

	$Good	$Fine	$N.Mint	£Good	£Fine	£N.Mint
ALIEN LEGION: TENANTS OF HELL						
Marvel Comics Group,Epic,MS; 1 Sep 1991-2 Oct 1991						
1 ND continues on from On The Edge story						
	$0.90	$2.70	$4.50	£0.60	£1.80	£3.00
2 ND	$0.90	$2.70	$4.50	£0.60	£1.80	£3.00
Title Value:	$1.80	$5.40	$9.00	£1.20	£3.60	£6.00
ALIEN NATION						
DC Comics,OS,Film; 1 Dec 1988						
1 58pgs, squarebound						
	$0.30	$0.90	$1.50	£0.20	£0.60	£1.00
Title Value:	$0.30	$0.90	$1.50	£0.20	£0.60	£1.00
ALIEN NATION: A BREED APART						
Adventure,MS; 1 1990-4 Apr 1991						
1-4 ND	$0.45	$1.35	$2.25	£0.30	£0.90	£1.50
Title Value:	$1.80	$5.40	$9.00	£1.20	£3.60	£6.00
ALIEN NATION: PUBLIC ENEMY						
Adventure,MS; 1 Feb 1992-4 May 1992						
1-4 ND	$0.45	$1.35	$2.25	£0.30	£0.90	£1.50
Title Value:	$1.80	$5.40	$9.00	£1.20	£3.60	£6.00
ALIEN NATION: THE FIRSTCOMERS						
Adventure,MS; 1 Jul 1991-4 Oct 1991						
1-4 ND	$0.45	$1.35	$2.25	£0.30	£0.90	£1.50
Title Value:	$1.80	$5.40	$9.00	£1.20	£3.60	£6.00
ALIEN NATION: THE LOST EPISODE						
Adventure,OS; 1 Aug 1992						
1 ND 48pgs, ties up plot-lines left when TV series was cancelled, photo cover						
	$0.75	$2.25	$3.75	£0.50	£1.50	£2.50
Title Value:	$0.75	$2.25	$3.75	£0.50	£1.50	£2.50
ALIEN NATION: THE SKIN TRADE						
Adventure,MS; 1 May 1991-4 Aug 1991						
1-4 ND	$0.45	$1.35	$2.25	£0.30	£0.90	£1.50
Title Value:	$1.80	$5.40	$9.00	£1.20	£3.60	£6.00
ALIEN NATION: THE SPARTANS						
Adventure,MS; 1 Sep 1990-4 Dec 1990						
1 ND cover available in 4 different colours						
	$0.55	$1.65	$2.75	£0.35	£1.05	£1.75
1 ND Limited Edition (Sep 1990) - 5,000 copies exclusive to Diamond Distributors with gold embossed logo on card-stock cover: limited number on top left of cover						
	$1.50	$4.50	$7.50	£1.00	£3.00	£5.00
2nd printing ND	$0.45	$1.35	$2.25	£0.30	£0.90	£1.50
2-4 ND	$0.45	$1.35	$2.25	£0.30	£0.90	£1.50
Title Value:	$3.85	$11.55	$19.25	£2.55	£7.65	£12.75
Special Edition (of #1), runs in conjunction with regular series with additional art and embossed logo, 40pgs				£0.60	£1.80	£3.00
Trade Paperback (Sep 1991), reprints mini-series				£1.00	£3.00	£5.00
ALIEN WORLDS						
Pacific/Eclipse; 1 Dec 1982-9 Jan 1985						
(see Three Dimensional Alien Worlds)						
1 Al Williamson, Tim Conrad and Val Mayerik art featured						
	$0.80	$2.40	$4.00	£0.50	£1.50	£2.50
2 Aurora by Dave Stevens; Bruce Jones, Ken Steacy cover						
	$0.60	$1.80	$3.00	£0.40	£1.20	£2.00
3 Scott Hampton, Tom Yeates, Ken Steacy art; Bill Stout cover						
	$0.60	$1.80	$3.00	£0.40	£1.20	£2.00
4 Dave Stevens, Jeff Jones, Ken Steacy, Bo Hampton art; Stevens cover						
	$0.60	$1.80	$3.00	£0.40	£1.20	£2.00
5 John Bolton, Ken Steacy, Adolpho Buylla, Tom Yeates art; Bolton cover						
	$0.60	$1.80	$3.00	£0.40	£1.20	£2.00
6 Brunner/Mignola, Roy Krenkel, Arthur Suydam art; Brunner cover						
	$0.60	$1.80	$3.00	£0.40	£1.20	£2.00
7 Richard Corben, Brent Anderson, Gray Morrow, George Perez art; Corben cover						

	$Good	$Fine	$N.Mint	£Good	£Fine	£N.Mint
	$0.60	$1.80	$3.00	£0.40	£1.20	£2.00
8 Al Williamson, Ken Steacy, Paul Rivoche art						
	$0.60	$1.80	$3.00	£0.40	£1.20	£2.00
9 Bo Hampton, Frank Brunner art; John Bolton cover						
	$0.60	$1.80	$3.00	£0.40	£1.20	£2.00
Title Value:	$5.60	$16.80	$28.00	£3.70	£11.10	£18.50
Note: all Non-Distributed on the news-stands in the U.K.						
Note also: publication delays between issues #7-9.						
ALIEN WORLDS (2ND SERIES)						
Blackthorne; 1 1986						
nn ND Book 1: Williamson, Conrad, Jones, Perez, Bo Hampton, Yeates, Brent Anderson, Barry Smith, John Bolton reprints. Hardcover, scarce in the U.K.						
	$3.00	$9.00	$15.00	£2.00	£6.00	£10.00
nn ND softcover	$1.50	$4.50	$7.50	£1.00	£3.00	£5.00
Title Value:	$4.50	$13.50	$22.50	£3.00	£9.00	£15.00
ALIEN WORLDS GRAPHIC NOVEL						
Eclipse; nn May 1988						
(Eclipse Graphic Novel #22)						
nn ND Bruce Jones script, Reese, Shanower, Yeates, Wray art						
	$0.90	$2.70	$4.50	£0.60	£1.80	£3.00
Title Value:	$0.90	$2.70	$4.50	£0.60	£1.80	£3.00
Note: Bookshelf Format						
ALIENS						
Dark Horse,MS Film; 1 May 1988-6 1989						
(see Dark Horse Presents #24)						
1 Mark Nelson art begins						
	$6.00	$18.00	$30.00	£3.50	£10.50	£17.50
1 2nd printing, new art inside cover						
	$1.50	$4.50	$7.50	£1.00	£3.00	£5.00
1 3rd printing	$0.90	$2.70	$4.50	£0.60	£1.80	£3.00
1 4th printing	$0.80	$2.40	$4.00	£0.50	£1.50	£2.50
1 5th printing	$0.60	$1.80	$3.00	£0.40	£1.20	£2.00
2	$3.50	$10.50	$17.50	£2.00	£6.00	£10.00
2 2nd printing	$0.90	$2.70	$4.50	£0.60	£1.80	£3.00
2 3rd printing	$0.60	$1.80	$3.00	£0.40	£1.20	£2.00
2 4th printing	$0.45	$1.35	$2.25	£0.30	£0.90	£1.50
3	$1.80	$5.25	$9.00	£1.20	£3.60	£6.00
3 2nd printing	$0.60	$1.80	$3.00	£0.40	£1.20	£2.00
3 3rd printing	$0.45	$1.35	$2.25	£0.30	£0.90	£1.50
4	$1.50	$4.50	$7.50	£1.00	£3.00	£5.00
4 2nd printing	$0.60	$1.80	$3.00	£0.40	£1.20	£2.00
4 3rd printing	$0.45	$1.35	$2.25	£0.30	£0.90	£1.50
5 scarce in the U.K.	$2.00	$6.00	$10.00	£1.30	£3.90	£6.50
5 2nd printing	$0.60	$1.80	$3.00	£0.40	£1.20	£2.00
5 3rd printing	$0.45	$1.35	$2.25	£0.30	£0.90	£1.50
6	$0.90	$2.70	$4.50	£0.60	£1.80	£3.00
Title Value:	$24.60	$73.65	$123.00	£15.50	£46.50	£77.50
Note: all Non-Distributed on the news-stands in the U.K.						
Book 1, Trade paperback, reprints #1-6 plus story from Dark Horse Presents #24				£1.50	£4.50	£7.50
(2nd print - Oct 1991)				£1.40	£4.20	£7.00
Book 1, Hardcover (Apr 1990), reprints #1-6				£3.50	£10.50	£17.50
Signed and Numbered Edition, Hardcover (1,000 copies)				£6.00	£18.00	£30.00
ALIENS II						
Dark Horse,MS Film; 1 Aug 1989-4 May 1990						
1 colour art begins	$1.50	$4.50	$7.50	£1.00	£3.00	£5.00
1 2nd printing	$0.70	$2.10	$3.50	£0.50	£1.50	£2.50
2	$1.00	$3.00	$5.00	£0.60	£1.80	£3.00
2 2nd printing	$0.55	$1.65	$2.75	£0.35	£1.05	£1.75
3	$0.90	$2.70	$4.50	£0.60	£1.80	£3.00
3 2nd printing	$0.55	$1.65	$2.75	£0.35	£1.05	£1.75

Alien Encounters #10

All American Comics #19

All Flash #2

	$Good	$Fine	$N.Mint	£Good	£Fine	£N.Mint
4	$0.80	$2.40	$4.00	£0.50	£1.50	£2.50
Title Value:	$6.00	$18.00	$30.00	£3.90	£11.70	£19.50

Note: all Non-Distributed on the news-stands in the U.K.

Aliens II Collection, Trade paperback (Oct 1990),
reprints the above series (3 printings) £1.60 £4.80 £8.00

Signed, Limited Edition Hardcover (2,500 copies)
signed and numbered, reprints #1-4 £6.00 £18.00 £30.00

ALIENS VS. PREDATOR
Dark Horse,MS; 0 Jun 1990-4 Dec 1990

0 ND (Jul 1990), collects Dark Horse Presents #34-#36, new Mignola cover

	$Good	$Fine	$N.Mint	£Good	£Fine	£N.Mint
	$1.50	$4.50	$7.50	£1.00	£3.00	£5.00

1 ND story continues from Dark Horse Presents #34-#36 in colour, has similar art on front/back covers

	$1.20	$3.60	$6.00	£0.80	£2.40	£4.00

1 2nd printing, ND has "Give Me Liberty" ad on back cover

	$Good	$Fine	$N.Mint	£Good	£Fine	£N.Mint
	$0.45	$1.35	$2.25	£0.30	£0.90	£1.50
2 ND	$0.80	$2.40	$4.00	£0.50	£1.50	£2.50

3 ND extra pages of story/art

	$0.80	$2.40	$4.00	£0.50	£1.50	£2.50
4 ND	$0.80	$2.40	$4.00	£0.50	£1.50	£2.50
Title Value:	$5.55	$16.65	$27.75	£3.60	£10.80	£18.00

Note: bi-monthly

Aliens Vs. Predator Collection (Feb 1992)
reprints Aliens Vs. Predator mini-series plus prequel stories
from Dark Horse Presents #34-#36, all colour £2.60 £7.80 £13.00
(2nd printing - Feb 1993, 3rd print - Aug 1994) £2.50 £7.50 £12.50

Aliens Vs. Predator Hardcover Edition (Feb 1993)
custom hardcover binding & slipcase; 1,000 copies £10.00 £30.00 £50.00

ALIENS VS. PREDATOR: DUEL
Dark Horse,MS; 1 Mar 1995-2 Apr 1995

1-2 ND Javier Saltares and Jimmy Palmiotti art

	$Good	$Fine	$N.Mint	£Good	£Fine	£N.Mint
	$0.45	$1.35	$2.25	£0.30	£0.90	£1.50
Title Value:	$0.90	$2.70	$4.50	£0.60	£1.80	£3.00

ALIENS VS. PREDATOR: THE DEADLIEST OF THE SPECIES
Dark Horse,MS; 1 Jul 1993-12 Jul 1995

1 ND Chris Claremont script, Guice and Beatty art begins; painted covers by John Bolton

	$Good	$Fine	$N.Mint	£Good	£Fine	£N.Mint
	$0.45	$1.35	$2.25	£0.30	£0.90	£1.50

1 ND Limited Edition (Jul 1993) - silver foil embossed cover

	$1.80	$5.25	$9.00	£1.20	£3.60	£6.00
2-12 ND	$0.45	$1.35	$2.25	£0.30	£0.90	£1.50
Title Value:	$7.20	$21.45	$36.00	£4.80	£14.40	£24.00

ALIENS VS. PREDATOR: WAR
Dark Horse,OS; 1 Apr 1995

1 ND collects story from Dark Horse Insider #1-14 with additional art, cover by Richard Corben

	$Good	$Fine	$N.Mint	£Good	£Fine	£N.Mint
	$0.45	$1.35	$2.25	£0.30	£0.90	£1.50
Title Value:	$0.45	$1.35	$2.25	£0.30	£0.90	£1.50

ALIENS VS. PREDATOR: WAR (LIMITED SERIES)
Dark Horse,MS; 1 May 1995-4 Aug 1995

1-4 ND Richard Corben covers

	$Good	$Fine	$N.Mint	£Good	£Fine	£N.Mint
	$0.45	$1.35	$2.25	£0.30	£0.90	£1.50
Title Value:	$1.80	$5.40	$9.00	£1.20	£3.60	£6.00

ALIENS, THE (CAPTAIN JOHNER AND..)
(see Captain Johner And The Aliens)

ALIENS: BERSERKER
Dark Horse,MS; 1 Jan 1995-4 Apr 1995

1-4 ND John Wagner script

	$Good	$Fine	$N.Mint	£Good	£Fine	£N.Mint
	$0.45	$1.35	$2.25	£0.30	£0.90	£1.50
Title Value:	$1.80	$5.40	$9.00	£1.20	£3.60	£6.00

ALIENS: COLONIAL MARINES
Dark Horse,MS; 1 Jan 1993-10 Jun 1994

1 ND painted covers by Robert Mentor begin

	$Good	$Fine	$N.Mint	£Good	£Fine	£N.Mint
	$0.45	$1.35	$2.25	£0.30	£0.90	£1.50
2-10 ND	$0.45	$1.35	$2.25	£0.30	£0.90	£1.50
Title Value:	$4.50	$13.50	$22.50	£3.00	£9.00	£15.00

ALIENS: EARTH ANGEL
Dark Horse,OS; 1 Aug 1994

1 ND collects together the John Byrne strip from Previews magazine, new John Byrne cover

	$Good	$Fine	$N.Mint	£Good	£Fine	£N.Mint
	$0.60	$1.80	$3.00	£0.40	£1.20	£2.00
Title Value:	$0.60	$1.80	$3.00	£0.40	£1.20	£2.00

Aliens: Earth Angel Deluxe Hardcover Edition (Aug 1994)
24pg story plus 8pg interview with John Byrne;
1,000 copies randomly signed £2.50 £7.50 £12.50

ALIENS: EARTH WAR
Dark Horse,MS; 1 Jun 1990-4 Oct 1990

1 ND Sam Kieth art begins and John Bolton painted covers begin

	$Good	$Fine	$N.Mint	£Good	£Fine	£N.Mint
	$1.00	$3.00	$5.00	£0.70	£2.10	£3.50

1 2nd printing, ND has "Give Me Liberty" ad on back cover

	$0.45	$1.35	$2.25	£0.30	£0.90	£1.50
2 ND	$0.80	$2.40	$4.00	£0.50	£1.50	£2.50
3 ND	$0.70	$2.10	$3.50	£0.45	£1.35	£2.25

4 ND extra pages of story/art

	$0.70	$2.10	$3.50	£0.45	£1.35	£2.25
Title Value:	$3.65	$10.95	$18.25	£2.40	£7.20	£12.00

Note: bi-monthly, colour interior art

Earth War Collection (Sep 1991),
reprints mini-series, cover painting by John Bolton £1.60 £4.80 £8.00

Earth War Collection - Limited Edition (Feb 1992),
new dust-jacket illustration by John Bolton,
signed by Sam Kieth (2,000 copies) £8.00 £24.00 £40.00

ALIENS: GENOCIDE
Dark Horse,MS; 1 Jan 1992-4 Apr 1992

1 ND Arthur Suydam covers begin

	$Good	$Fine	$N.Mint	£Good	£Fine	£N.Mint
	$0.45	$1.35	$2.25	£0.30	£0.90	£1.50

	$Good	$Fine	$N.Mint	£Good	£Fine	£N.Mint
2-3 ND	$0.45	$1.35	$2.25	£0.30	£0.90	£1.50

4 ND mini-poster of cover without text included

	$0.45	$1.35	$2.25	£0.30	£0.90	£1.50
Title Value:	$1.80	$5.40	$9.00	£1.20	£3.60	£6.00

Aliens: Genocide Softcover Collection (Jan 1993)
112pgs, reprints issues #1-4 £1.70 £5.10 £8.50

ALIENS: HIVE
Dark Horse,MS; 1 Apr 1992-4 Jul 1992

1-4 ND Kelley Jones art

	$Good	$Fine	$N.Mint	£Good	£Fine	£N.Mint
	$0.45	$1.35	$2.25	£0.30	£0.90	£1.50
Title Value:	$1.80	$5.40	$9.00	£1.20	£3.60	£6.00

Aliens: Hive Softcover Collection (Apr 1993)
reprints issues #1-4, painted cover by Dave Dorman £1.75 £5.25 £8.75

Aliens: Hive Trade Paperback (Aug 1994)
as above with new painted cover by Dave Dorman £1.75 £5.25 £8.75

ALIENS: LABYRINTH
Dark Horse,MS; 1 Sep 1993-4 Jan 1994

1-4 ND Jim Woodring & Kilian Plunkett

	$Good	$Fine	$N.Mint	£Good	£Fine	£N.Mint
	$0.45	$1.35	$2.25	£0.30	£0.90	£1.50
Title Value:	$1.80	$5.40	$9.00	£1.20	£3.60	£6.00

Aliens: Labyrinth (Jun 1995)
Trade paperback reprints mini-series with new Kilian Plunkett cover £2.40 £7.20 £12.00

ALIENS: MONDO PEST
Dark Horse,OS; 1 Mar 1995

1 ND reprints stories from Dark Horse Comics #22-24 plus sketches

	$Good	$Fine	$N.Mint	£Good	£Fine	£N.Mint
	$0.60	$1.80	$3.00	£0.40	£1.20	£2.00
Title Value:	$0.60	$1.80	$3.00	£0.40	£1.20	£2.00

ALIENS: MUSIC OF THE SPEARS
Dark Horse,MS; 1 Jan 1994-4 Apr 1994

1-4 ND Williamson, Hamilton and Bradstreet

	$Good	$Fine	$N.Mint	£Good	£Fine	£N.Mint
	$0.45	$1.35	$2.25	£0.30	£0.90	£1.50
Title Value:	$1.80	$5.40	$9.00	£1.20	£3.60	£6.00

ALIENS: NEWT'S TALE
Dark Horse,MS; 1 Jul 1992-2 Aug 1992

1-2 ND John Bolton covers

	$Good	$Fine	$N.Mint	£Good	£Fine	£N.Mint
	$0.90	$2.70	$4.50	£0.60	£1.80	£3.00
Title Value:	$1.80	$5.40	$9.00	£1.20	£3.60	£6.00

ALIENS: ROGUE
Dark Horse,MS; 1 Apr 1993-4 Aug 1993

	$Good	$Fine	$N.Mint	£Good	£Fine	£N.Mint
1-4 ND	$0.45	$1.35	$2.25	£0.30	£0.90	£1.50
Title Value:	$1.80	$5.40	$9.00	£1.20	£3.60	£6.00

Aliens: Rogue (Aug 1994)
Trade paperback reprints mini-series, painted cover by Nelson £2.00 £6.00 £10.00

ALIENS: SACRIFICE
Dark Horse,OS; 1 May 1993

1 ND 48pgs, squarebound, collects material originally published in U.K. Aliens title; Peter Milligan script,
Paul Johnson art

	$Good	$Fine	$N.Mint	£Good	£Fine	£N.Mint
	$1.00	$3.00	$5.00	£0.65	£1.95	£3.25
Title Value:	$1.00	$3.00	$5.00	£0.65	£1.95	£3.25

ALIENS: SALVATION
Dark Horse,OS; 1 Nov 1993

1 ND 48pgs, Dave Gibbons script, Mignola and Nowlan art

	$Good	$Fine	$N.Mint	£Good	£Fine	£N.Mint
	$1.00	$3.00	$5.00	£0.65	£1.95	£3.25
Title Value:	$1.00	$3.00	$5.00	£0.65	£1.95	£3.25

ALIENS: STRONGHOLD
Dark Horse,MS; 1 May 1994-4 Aug 1994

	$Good	$Fine	$N.Mint	£Good	£Fine	£N.Mint
1-4 ND	$0.45	$1.35	$2.25	£0.30	£0.90	£1.50
Title Value:	$1.80	$5.40	$9.00	£1.20	£3.60	£6.00

ALIENS: THE ILLUSTRATED STORY
Heavy Metal; nn 1979

nn ND 56pgs, scarce; Archie Goodwin script, Walt Simonson art

	$Good	$Fine	$N.Mint	£Good	£Fine	£N.Mint
	$5.25	$15.50	$26.25	£3.50	£10.50	£17.50

nn U.K. Edition, published by Futura (1979)

	$3.75	$11.00	$18.75	£2.50	£7.50	£12.50
Title Value:	$9.00	$26.50	$45.00	£6.00	£18.00	£30.00

ALIENS: TRIBES HARDCOVER GRAPHIC NOVEL
Dark Horse,OS; nn Jan 1992

1 ND Steve Bissette script, Dave Dorman art

	$Good	$Fine	$N.Mint	£Good	£Fine	£N.Mint
	$4.50	$13.50	$22.50	£3.00	£9.00	£15.00
Title Value:	$4.50	$13.50	$22.50	£3.00	£9.00	£15.00

Aliens: Tribes Softcover Graphic Novel (Apr 1993)
softcover version of the above, Dave Dorman cover £1.50 £4.50 £7.50

ALL STAR ARCHIVES
DC Comics; 1 Jul 1992-2 1993

1 ND 272pgs, reprints All Star Comics #3-#6 featuring the first cases of the Justice Society of America

	$Good	$Fine	$N.Mint	£Good	£Fine	£N.Mint
	$10.00	$30.00	$50.00	£6.50	£19.50	£32.50

2 ND 256pgs, reprints All Star Comics #7-#10

	$9.00	$27.00	$45.00	£6.00	£18.00	£30.00
Title Value:	$19.00	$57.00	$95.00	£12.50	£37.50	£62.50

ALL STAR COMICS
National Periodical Publications; 1 Summer 1940-57 Feb/Mar 1951

1 The Flash, Hourman, Hawkman, Spectre, Sandman begin

	$Good	$Fine	$N.Mint	£Good	£Fine	£N.Mint
	$1075.00	$3250.00	$9750.00	£800.00	£2400.00	£7250.00

2 Green Lantern feature begins

	$530.00	$1575.00	$4250.00	£355.00	£1050.00	£2850.00

3 scarce in the U.K. origin and 1st appearance Justice Society of America (see Famous First Edition F-7);
historically important as the 1st major super-team

	$2500.00	$7500.00	$30000.00	£1825.00	£5500.00	£22000.00

[Prices may vary widely on this comic]

4	$570.00	$1700.00	$4000.00	£390.00	£1175.00	£2750.00

5 1st appearance Hawkgirl, DC's first costumed super-heroine (see All-American Comics #20)

	$530.00	$1600.00	$3750.00	£355.00	£1050.00	£2500.00

	$Good	$Fine	$N.Mint	£Good	£Fine	£N.Mint

6 Johnny Thunder joins Justice Society of America
| | $320.00 | $960.00 | $2250.00 | £210.00 | £640.00 | £1500.00 |

7 Superman, Batman cameo appearance
| | $385.00 | $1150.00 | $2700.00 | £255.00 | £770.00 | £1800.00 |

8 origin and 1st appearance Wonder Woman (8pg origin added to comic)
| | $1500.00 | $4500.00 | $15000.00 | £1000.00 | £3000.00 | £10000.00 |

9-10
| | $320.00 | $960.00 | $2250.00 | £210.00 | £640.00 | £1500.00 |

11-14
| | $260.00 | $790.00 | $1850.00 | £175.00 | £520.00 | £1225.00 |

15 1st appearance and origin Brain Wave
| | $260.00 | $790.00 | $1850.00 | £175.00 | £520.00 | £1225.00 |

16-20
| | $210.00 | $640.00 | $1500.00 | £140.00 | £425.00 | £1000.00 |

21
| | $155.00 | $470.00 | $1100.00 | £100.00 | £310.00 | £725.00 |

22 classic flag cover
| | $155.00 | $470.00 | $1100.00 | £100.00 | £310.00 | £725.00 |

23 1st appearance and origin Psycho Pirate
| | $155.00 | $470.00 | $1100.00 | £100.00 | £310.00 | £725.00 |

24-25
| | $155.00 | $470.00 | $1100.00 | £100.00 | £310.00 | £725.00 |

26 robot cover
| | $155.00 | $470.00 | $1100.00 | £95.00 | £285.00 | £675.00 |

27-30
| | $155.00 | $470.00 | $1100.00 | £95.00 | £285.00 | £675.00 |

31-32
| | $140.00 | $425.00 | $1000.00 | £92.50 | £275.00 | £650.00 |

33 Solomon Grundy appears
| | $275.00 | $820.00 | $2200.00 | £180.00 | £550.00 | £1475.00 |

34-35
| | $140.00 | $425.00 | $1000.00 | £92.50 | £275.00 | £650.00 |

36 Superman and Batman appear, 1st time they appear together in the same story
(pre their adventures in World's Finest Comics from #71 onwards)
| | $275.00 | $820.00 | $2200.00 | £180.00 | £550.00 | £1475.00 |

37 origin Injustice Society
| | $155.00 | $470.00 | $1100.00 | £100.00 | £300.00 | £700.00 |

38 Black Canary appears; classic Alex Toth cover
| | $200.00 | $600.00 | $1400.00 | £125.00 | £385.00 | £900.00 |

39-40
| | $110.00 | $330.00 | $775.00 | £70.00 | £210.00 | £500.00 |

41 Black Canary joins Justice Society of America
| | $110.00 | $330.00 | $775.00 | £70.00 | £210.00 | £500.00 |

42 new costumes for Hawkman and Atom, cover concept used for Justice League of America #6
| | $110.00 | $330.00 | $775.00 | £70.00 | £210.00 | £500.00 |

43 cover concept used for Brave and the Bold #29
| | $110.00 | $330.00 | $775.00 | £70.00 | £210.00 | £500.00 |

44-49
| | $110.00 | $330.00 | $775.00 | £70.00 | £210.00 | £500.00 |

50 part Frank Frazetta art
| | $125.00 | $375.00 | $875.00 | £80.00 | £245.00 | £575.00 |

51-55
| | $100.00 | $300.00 | $700.00 | £62.50 | £190.00 | £450.00 |

56 scarce in the U.K.
| | $100.00 | $300.00 | $700.00 | £70.00 | £210.00 | £500.00 |

57 very scarce in the U.K. part Kubert art
| | $125.00 | $385.00 | $900.00 | £92.50 | £275.00 | £650.00 |

Title Value: $15475.00 $46605.00 $129350.00 £10440.00 £31440.00 £88400.00

Note: none of these comics were officially distributed into the U.K. but some **may** have come over during the War Years with American G.I.'s that were stationed here or through American relatives of U.K. residents.
Note also: most issues of this title are scarce in the U.K., in common with most Golden Age comics.

ALL STAR COMICS (2ND SERIES)
DC Comics; 58 Jan/Feb 1976-74 Sep/Oct 1978
(numbering continues from Golden Age All Star Comics)
58 Flash, Hawkman, Dr.Mid-Nite, Robin, Green Lantern, Dr.Fate, Wildcat, Star-Spangled Kid
(Justice Society of America characters); 1st appearance Power Girl, Wood art
| | $0.85 | $2.55 | $4.25 | £0.55 | £1.65 | £2.75 |

59 ND Wood art
| | $0.70 | $2.10 | $3.50 | £0.45 | £1.35 | £2.25 |

60 Wood art
| | $0.45 | $1.35 | $2.25 | £0.30 | £0.90 | £1.50 |

61 ND Wood art
| | $0.60 | $1.80 | $3.00 | £0.40 | £1.20 | £2.00 |

62 scarce in the U.K.
| | $0.55 | $1.65 | $2.75 | £0.35 | £1.05 | £1.75 |

63 Wood art
| | $0.45 | $1.35 | $2.25 | £0.30 | £0.90 | £1.50 |

64 scarce in the U.K.
| | $0.55 | $1.65 | $2.75 | £0.35 | £1.05 | £1.75 |

65 ND Wood art
| | $0.60 | $1.80 | $3.00 | £0.40 | £1.20 | £2.00 |

66 scarce in the U.K.
| | $0.45 | $1.35 | $2.25 | £0.30 | £0.90 | £1.50 |

67-69 Wood art
| | $0.40 | $1.20 | $2.00 | £0.25 | £0.75 | £1.25 |

70 scarce in the U.K.
| | $0.45 | $1.35 | $2.25 | £0.30 | £0.90 | £1.50 |

71-73 Wood art
| | $0.40 | $1.20 | $2.00 | £0.25 | £0.75 | £1.25 |

74 scarce in the U.K. 44pgs
| | $0.80 | $2.40 | $4.00 | £0.50 | £1.50 | £2.50 |

Title Value: $8.85 $26.55 $44.25 £5.70 £17.10 £28.50

FEATURES
Justice Society of America and Super Squad in all. (See DC Special 29 & Adventure Comics #461-466)

ALL-AMERICAN COMICS
National Periodical Publications; 1 Apr 1939-102 Oct 1948
(becomes All American Western #103-#126 then All American Men of War #127 onwards)
1 anthology of "funnies" such as Scribbly and Mutt & Jeff begin plus adventure strips like Hop Harrigan
| | $530.00 | $1575.00 | $4250.00 | £355.00 | £1050.00 | £2850.00 |

2
| | $175.00 | $520.00 | $1225.00 | £125.00 | £385.00 | £900.00 |

3
| | $120.00 | $360.00 | $850.00 | £85.00 | £255.00 | £600.00 |

4 rare in the U.K.
| | $120.00 | $360.00 | $850.00 | £92.50 | £275.00 | £650.00 |

5
| | $120.00 | $360.00 | $850.00 | £85.00 | £255.00 | £600.00 |

6
| | $110.00 | $330.00 | $775.00 | £75.00 | £225.00 | £525.00 |

7 very scarce in the U.K.
| | $110.00 | $330.00 | $775.00 | £80.00 | £245.00 | £575.00 |

8 Gary Concord the Ultra-Man begins
| | $130.00 | $390.00 | $1050.00 | £87.50 | £260.00 | £700.00 |

9
| | $110.00 | $330.00 | $775.00 | £75.00 | £225.00 | £525.00 |

10 Christmas cover
| | $110.00 | $330.00 | $775.00 | £75.00 | £225.00 | £525.00 |

11 very scarce in the U.K.
| | $95.00 | $285.00 | $675.00 | £70.00 | £210.00 | £500.00 |

12-15
| | $95.00 | $285.00 | $675.00 | £62.50 | £190.00 | £450.00 |

16 very rare in the U.K. origin and 1st appearance Golden Age Green Lantern; estimated 40 extant copies
in any condition; created/drawn by Martin Nodell, inspired by Aladdin's Lamp
| | $5000.00 | $15000.00 | $60000.00 | £3300.00 | £10000.00 | £40000.00 |
[Rare in high grade - Very Fine+ or better]
[Prices may vary widely on this comic]

17 rare in the U.K., 2nd appearance Green Lantern
| | $1400.00 | $4200.00 | $11250.00 | £930.00 | £2800.00 | £7500.00 |
[Very scarce in high grade - Very Fine+ or better]

18 3rd appearance Green Lantern
| | $920.00 | $2750.00 | $7400.00 | £620.00 | £1875.00 | £5000.00 |

19 origin and 1st appearance Golden Age Atom, last Ultra Man
| | $1400.00 | $4200.00 | $11250.00 | £930.00 | £2800.00 | £7500.00 |

20 scarce in the U.K. 1st appearance Golden Age Red Tornado (Ma Hunkle), DC's first costumed heroine
(see All Star Comics #5), part origin Green Lantern
| | $410.00 | $1225.00 | $2900.00 | £285.00 | £850.00 | £2000.00 |

21-23
| | $220.00 | $660.00 | $1550.00 | £145.00 | £435.00 | £1025.00 |

24 origin Sargon the Sorcerer and Dr. Mid-Nite in illustrated text
| | $285.00 | $850.00 | $1995.00 | £185.00 | £560.00 | £1325.00 |

25 origin and 1st appearance Dr. Mid-Nite
| | $800.00 | $2400.00 | $7250.00 | £520.00 | £1575.00 | £4750.00 |

26 origin and 1st story appearance Sargon the Sorcerer
| | $340.00 | $1025.00 | $2400.00 | £225.00 | £680.00 | £1600.00 |

27 1st appearance Doiby Dickles as Green Lantern's comic partner
| | $390.00 | $1175.00 | $2750.00 | £260.00 | £780.00 | £1825.00 |

28-30
| | $135.00 | $405.00 | $950.00 | £87.50 | £265.00 | £625.00 |

31-40
| | $110.00 | $330.00 | $775.00 | £75.00 | £225.00 | £525.00 |

41-46
| | $92.50 | $275.00 | $650.00 | £60.00 | £180.00 | £425.00 |

47 non-Green Lantern cover (Hop Harrigan)
| | $92.50 | $275.00 | $650.00 | £60.00 | £180.00 | £425.00 |

48-50
| | $92.50 | $275.00 | $650.00 | £60.00 | £180.00 | £425.00 |

51
| | $77.50 | $235.00 | $550.00 | £50.00 | £150.00 | £350.00 |

52 intro The Silhouette
| | $77.50 | $235.00 | $550.00 | £50.00 | £150.00 | £350.00 |

53-60
| | $77.50 | $235.00 | $550.00 | £50.00 | £150.00 | £350.00 |

61 origin and 1st appearance Solomon Grundy
| | $350.00 | $1050.00 | $2800.00 | £230.00 | £690.00 | £1850.00 |

62-69
| | $65.00 | $200.00 | $470.00 | £45.00 | £135.00 | £315.00 |

70 Kubert art
| | $65.00 | $200.00 | $470.00 | £45.00 | £135.00 | £315.00 |

71-76
| | $60.00 | $180.00 | $425.00 | £41.00 | £120.00 | £285.00 |

77 non-Green Lantern cover (Hop Harrigan)
| | $60.00 | $180.00 | $425.00 | £41.00 | £120.00 | £285.00 |

78
| | $60.00 | $180.00 | $425.00 | £41.00 | £120.00 | £285.00 |

79 non-Green Lantern cover (Mutt & Jeff)
| | $60.00 | $180.00 | $425.00 | £41.00 | £120.00 | £285.00 |

80-82
| | $60.00 | $180.00 | $425.00 | £41.00 | £120.00 | £285.00 |

83 non-Green Lantern cover (Mutt & Jeff)
| | $60.00 | $180.00 | $425.00 | £41.00 | £120.00 | £285.00 |

| | $60.00 | $180.00 | $425.00 | £41.00 | £120.00 | £285.00 |

89 origin and 1st appearance of The Harlequin
| | $70.00 | $210.00 | $500.00 | £46.00 | £135.00 | £325.00 |

90 origin and 1st appearance The Icicle
| | $70.00 | $210.00 | $500.00 | £46.00 | £135.00 | £325.00 |

91-95
| | $60.00 | $180.00 | $425.00 | £41.00 | £120.00 | £285.00 |

96 Alex Toth cover and art featured
| | $60.00 | $180.00 | $425.00 | £41.00 | £120.00 | £285.00 |

97 Alex Toth cover
| | $60.00 | $180.00 | $425.00 | £41.00 | £120.00 | £285.00 |

98 Alex Toth cover and art featured
| | $60.00 | $180.00 | $425.00 | £41.00 | £120.00 | £285.00 |

99 Alex Toth cover and art featured, last Green Lantern cover
| | $60.00 | $180.00 | $425.00 | £41.00 | £120.00 | £285.00 |

100 scarce in the U.K. 1st appearance Johnny Thunder (Western character) by Alex Toth, Toth cover
| | $110.00 | $330.00 | $775.00 | £77.50 | £235.00 | £550.00 |

101 scarce in the U.K. Alex Toth cover and art
| | $95.00 | $285.00 | $675.00 | £67.50 | £200.00 | £475.00 |

102 very scarce in the U.K. Alex Toth cover and art
| | $120.00 | $360.00 | $850.00 | £92.50 | £275.00 | £650.00 |

Title Value: $19940.00 $59835.00 $171800.00 £13329.00 £40065.00 £114905.00

Note: though not officially distributed in the U.K., some copies **may** have come over through American G.I's or U.S. relatives of U.K. citizens. **Note also:** most issues of this title are at least scarce in the U.K.

ALL-AMERICAN MEN OF WAR
National Periodical Publications; 1 (#128) Oct/Nov 1952-117 Oct 1966
(see All American Western)
1 Krigstein art; numbered #128 on cover which is a continuation of All American Western title
| | $55.00 | $170.00 | $400.00 | £39.00 | £115.00 | £275.00 |

2-3 no number on cover, Krigstein art
| | $46.00 | $135.00 | $325.00 | £32.00 | £95.00 | £225.00 |

4 no number on cover
| | $46.00 | $135.00 | $325.00 | £32.00 | £95.00 | £225.00 |

5
| | $46.00 | $135.00 | $325.00 | £32.00 | £95.00 | £225.00 |

6-10
| | $29.00 | $85.00 | $200.00 | £20.00 | £60.00 | £140.00 |

11-18
| | $25.00 | $75.00 | $175.00 | £16.00 | £49.00 | £115.00 |

19-28
| | $17.50 | $52.50 | $125.00 | £12.00 | £36.00 | £85.00 |

29-30 Wood art
| | $18.50 | $55.00 | $130.00 | £13.50 | £41.00 | £95.00 |

31
| | $13.50 | $41.00 | $95.00 | £9.25 | £28.00 | £65.00 |

32 Wood art
| | $18.50 | $55.00 | $130.00 | £12.00 | £36.00 | £85.00 |

33-40
| | $13.50 | $41.00 | $95.00 | £9.25 | £28.00 | £65.00 |

41-50
| | $10.50 | $32.00 | $75.00 | £7.00 | £21.00 | £50.00 |

51-66
| | $8.50 | $26.00 | $60.00 | £5.50 | £17.00 | £40.00 |

	$Good	$Fine	$N.Mint	£Good	£Fine	£N.Mint
67 1st appearance Gunner & Sarge						
	$21.00	$62.50	$150.00	£11.00	£34.00	£80.00
68-70	$8.50	$26.00	$60.00	£5.50	£17.00	£40.00
71-74	$5.50	$17.00	$40.00	£3.90	£11.50	£27.50
75 scarce in the U.K.						
	$5.50	$17.00	$40.00	£4.25	£12.50	£30.00
1st official distribution in the U.K.						
76-80 scarce in the U.K.						
	$6.50	$20.00	$40.00	£5.00	£15.00	£30.00
81 scarce in the U.K.						
	$5.00	$15.00	$30.00	£3.75	£11.00	£22.50
82 scarce in the U.K. 1st appearance Johnny Cloud						
	$9.50	$29.00	$57.50	£4.15	£12.50	£25.00
83-85 scarce in the U.K.						
	$5.00	$15.00	$30.00	£3.75	£11.00	£22.50
86-100	$4.15	$12.50	$25.00	£2.90	£8.75	£17.50
101-113	$3.30	$10.00	$20.00	£2.05	£6.25	£12.50
114-117 ND	$3.30	$10.00	$20.00	£2.25	£6.75	£13.50
Title Value:	$1431.35	$4302.00	$9927.50	£965.90	£2913.50	£6729.00

NEW FEATURES
Balloon Buster in 112-114, 116. Johnny Cloud in 82-111, 115, 117.

ALL-AMERICAN WESTERN

National Periodical Publications; 103 Nov 1948-127 Aug/Sep 1952
(formerly All-American Comics #1-#102; becomes All American Men of War #127 onwards)

	$Good	$Fine	$N.Mint	£Good	£Fine	£N.Mint
103 Johnny Thunder by Alex Toth continues from All-American Comics						
	$45.00	$135.00	$315.00	£30.00	£90.00	£210.00
104 Kubert art featured						
	$30.00	$90.00	$210.00	£20.00	£60.00	£140.00
105 Kubert art featured						
	$25.00	$75.00	$175.00	£16.00	£49.00	£115.00
106	$17.50	$52.50	$125.00	£12.00	£36.00	£85.00
107 Kubert art featured						
	$25.00	$75.00	$175.00	£16.00	£49.00	£115.00
108-109	$17.50	$52.50	$125.00	£12.00	£36.00	£85.00
110 rare in the U.K.						
	$17.50	$52.50	$125.00	£12.00	£36.00	£85.00
111 rare in the U.K., Kubert art						
	$20.00	$60.00	$140.00	£13.50	£41.00	£95.00
112 rare in the U.K.						
	$17.50	$52.50	$125.00	£12.00	£36.00	£85.00
113 rare in the U.K., 1st appearance Swift Deer						
	$23.50	$70.00	$165.00	£15.50	£47.00	£110.00
114-116 rare in the U.K., Kubert art						
	$20.50	$60.00	$145.00	£13.50	£41.00	£95.00
117 rare in the U.K., origin Super-Chief						
	$15.50	$47.00	$110.00	£10.50	£32.00	£75.00
118-119 rare in the U.K.						
	$15.50	$47.00	$110.00	£10.50	£32.00	£75.00
120	$15.50	$47.00	$110.00	£10.50	£32.00	£75.00
121 Kubert art	$15.50	$47.00	$110.00	£10.50	£32.00	£75.00
122-126	$15.50	$47.00	$110.00	£10.50	£32.00	£75.00
127 cover title changes to "All American Men of War"						
	$77.50	$235.00	$550.00	£52.50	£160.00	£375.00
Title Value:	$550.00	$1652.50	$3890.00	£369.00	£1119.00	£2620.00

Note: all Non-Distributed on the news-stands in the U.K.

ALL-FLASH

National Periodical Publications; 1 Summer 1941-32 Dec/Jan 1947/1948

	$Good	$Fine	$N.Mint	£Good	£Fine	£N.Mint
1 origin of the Golden Age Flash retold						
	$1075.00	$3250.00	$9750.00	£720.00	£2150.00	£6500.00
[Scarce in high grade - Very Fine+ or better]						
2	$255.00	$770.00	$1800.00	£170.00	£510.00	£1200.00
3-4	$150.00	$450.00	$1050.00	£100.00	£300.00	£700.00
5	$105.00	$320.00	$750.00	£70.00	£210.00	£500.00
6-10	$92.50	$275.00	$650.00	£60.00	£180.00	£425.00
11-13	$75.00	$225.00	$525.00	£50.00	£150.00	£350.00
14 Golden Age Green Lantern appears						
	$92.50	$275.00	$650.00	£60.00	£180.00	£425.00
15	$75.00	$225.00	$525.00	£50.00	£150.00	£350.00
16-20	$67.50	$200.00	$475.00	£50.00	£150.00	£360.00
21-30	$60.00	$180.00	$425.00	£39.00	£115.00	£275.00
31	$55.00	$170.00	$400.00	£38.00	£110.00	£265.00
32 very scarce in the U.K. origin and 1st appearance The Fiddler						
	$80.00	$245.00	$575.00	£55.00	£165.00	£385.00
Title Value:	$3662.50	$11005.00	$28000.00	£2453.00	£7325.00	£18750.00

Note: most of these issues are at least scarce in the U.K.

ALL-NEW COLLECTOR'S EDITION

Tabloid; C-53 Jan 1978 - C-56, C-58, C-60, C-62 1979
(see Famous First Edition, Limited Collector's Edition)
(for other numbers see Famous First Edition, Limited Collector's Edition)

	£Good	£Fine	£N.Mint
C-53 ND 76pgs, Rudolph the Red-Nosed Reindeer	£0.40	£1.20	£2.00
C-54 ND 76pgs, Superman vs Wonder Woman	£0.60	£1.80	£3.00
C-55 ND 76pgs, Superboy & the Legion of Super-Heroes	£1.00	£3.00	£5.00
C-56 ND 76pgs, Superman vs Muhammad Ali;			
Neal Adams art, wraparound cover	£0.80	£2.40	£4.00
C-58 ND 76pgs, Superman vs Shazam	£0.60	£1.80	£3.00
C-60 ND Rudolph	£0.40	£1.20	£2.00
C-62 68pgs, Superman: the Movie	£0.40	£1.20	£2.00

Note: owing to their size, original mail packaging and display, truly near mint copies are very scarce

ALL-OUT WAR

DC Comics; 1 Sep/Oct 1979-6 Jul/Aug 1980

	$Good	$Fine	$N.Mint	£Good	£Fine	£N.Mint
1 ND 68pgs	$0.45	$1.35	$2.25	£0.30	£0.90	£1.50
2-6 ND 68pgs	$0.40	$1.20	$2.00	£0.25	£0.75	£1.25
Title Value:	$2.45	$7.35	$12.25	£1.55	£4.65	£7.75

FEATURES
Viking Commando in all, plus various war stories.

ALL-STAR INDEX, THE

ICG/Eclipse; 1 Feb 1987

	$Good	$Fine	$N.Mint	£Good	£Fine	£N.Mint
1 ND scarce in the U.K. information and colour cover repros All Star Comics #1-4 and DC Special #29 plus detailed character indexes						
	$0.80	$2.40	$4.00	£0.50	£1.50	£2.50
Title Value:	$0.80	$2.40	$4.00	£0.50	£1.50	£2.50

ALL-STAR SQUADRON

DC Comics; 1 Sep 1981-67 Mar 1987
(see Justice League of America #193)

	$Good	$Fine	$N.Mint	£Good	£Fine	£N.Mint
1 original Dr.Mid-Nite, Atom, Plastic Man Hawkman, Johnny Quick, Liberty Belle, Shining Knight begin; origin Robotman retold						
	$0.40	$1.20	$2.00	£0.25	£0.75	£1.25
2	$0.30	$0.90	$1.50	£0.20	£0.60	£1.00
3 Solomon Grundy appears						
	$0.25	$0.75	$1.25	£0.15	£0.45	£0.75
4 Justice Society of America appears						
	$0.25	$0.75	$1.25	£0.15	£0.45	£0.75
5 1st new Firebrand						
	$0.25	$0.75	$1.25	£0.15	£0.45	£0.75
6-11	$0.25	$0.75	$1.25	£0.15	£0.45	£0.75
12 Golden Age Hawkman origin retold						
	$0.25	$0.75	$1.25	£0.15	£0.45	£0.75
13-14	$0.25	$0.75	$1.25	£0.15	£0.45	£0.75
15 Masters of the Universe insert, Justice League of America/Justice Society of America appear						
	$0.25	$0.75	$1.25	£0.15	£0.45	£0.75
16-20	$0.25	$0.75	$1.25	£0.15	£0.45	£0.75
21-22	$0.15	$0.45	$0.75	£0.10	£0.35	£0.60
23 origin Amazing-Man						
	$0.15	$0.45	$0.75	£0.10	£0.35	£0.60
24 Golden Age Batman and Robin appear						
	$0.25	$0.75	$1.25	£0.15	£0.45	£0.75
25 1st appearance Infinity Inc.						
	$0.45	$1.35	$2.25	£0.30	£0.90	£1.50
26 origin Infinity Inc., Golden Age Batman and Robin appear, ties in with Annual #2						
	$0.40	$1.20	$2.00	£0.25	£0.75	£1.25
27-28 Justice Society of America appears						
	$0.15	$0.45	$0.75	£0.10	£0.35	£0.60
29 Seven Soldiers of Victory appear						
	$0.15	$0.45	$0.75	£0.10	£0.35	£0.60
30 Justice Society of America appears						
	$0.15	$0.45	$0.75	£0.10	£0.35	£0.60
31 Freedom Fighters (Earth-X) origin begins, Golden Age Batman appears						
	$0.15	$0.45	$0.75	£0.10	£0.35	£0.60
32-34 Freedom Fighters appear						
	$0.15	$0.45	$0.75	£0.10	£0.35	£0.60
35 Freedom Fighters origin concludes, death of Red Bee, Batman appears (1 panel)						
	$0.15	$0.45	$0.75	£0.10	£0.35	£0.60
36-37 Shazam appears						
	$0.15	$0.45	$0.75	£0.10	£0.35	£0.60
38-40	$0.15	$0.45	$0.75	£0.10	£0.35	£0.60
41 origin Starman	$0.15	$0.45	$0.75	£0.10	£0.35	£0.60
42-46	$0.15	$0.45	$0.75	£0.10	£0.35	£0.60
47 origin Dr.Fate, early Todd McFarlane pencils						
	$0.60	$1.80	$3.00	£0.40	£1.20	£2.00
48 Shining Knight and Blackhawk appear						
	$0.15	$0.45	$0.75	£0.10	£0.35	£0.60
49 Dr. Occult returns (after nearly 50 years!)						
	$0.15	$0.45	$0.75	£0.10	£0.35	£0.60
50 DS, Crisis X-over						
	$0.30	$0.90	$1.50	£0.20	£0.60	£1.00
51 Crisis X-over	$0.25	$0.75	$1.25	£0.15	£0.45	£0.75
52 Crisis X-over, Shazam appears						
	$0.25	$0.75	$1.25	£0.15	£0.45	£0.75
53-55 Crisis X-over						
	$0.25	$0.75	$1.25	£0.15	£0.45	£0.75
56 Crisis X-over, Seven Soldiers of Victory appear						
	$0.25	$0.75	$1.25	£0.15	£0.45	£0.75
57 Atom, Starman and Wonder Woman spotlighted						
	$0.15	$0.45	$0.75	£0.10	£0.35	£0.60
58-59	$0.15	$0.45	$0.75	£0.10	£0.35	£0.60
60 unofficial Crisis X-over, Justice Society of America appear						
	$0.15	$0.45	$0.75	£0.10	£0.35	£0.60
61 origin Liberty Belle						
	$0.15	$0.45	$0.75	£0.10	£0.35	£0.60
62 origin Shining Knight						
	$0.15	$0.45	$0.75	£0.10	£0.35	£0.60
63 origin Robotman						
	$0.15	$0.45	$0.75	£0.10	£0.35	£0.60
64 Wayne Boring (Golden and Silver Age Superman artist) pencils						
	$0.15	$0.45	$0.75	£0.10	£0.35	£0.60
65 origin Johnny Quick						
	$0.15	$0.45	$0.75	£0.10	£0.35	£0.60
66 origin Tarantula						
	$0.15	$0.45	$0.75	£0.10	£0.35	£0.60
67 Justice Society of America's 1st case						
	$0.15	$0.45	$0.75	£0.10	£0.35	£0.60
Title Value:	$14.10	$42.30	$70.50	£8.95	£28.65	£48.35

Note: JSA appears in 15, 19, 27, 28, 30, 36, 37, 51, 60, 67. Seven Soldiers of Victory appear in 29, 56.

	$Good	$Fine	$N.Mint	£Good	£Fine	£N.Mint

ARTISTS

Jerry Ordway inks in 1-14. Pencils in 23-26. Art in 19-22. Ordway covers 19-26, 29-31, 33-39, 41, 60. Joe Kubert covers 2,7-18.

ALL-STAR SQUADRON ANNUAL

DC Comics; 1 Nov 1982-3 Sep 1984

1 Golden Age Atom, Guardian, Wildcat origins retold

	$0.30	$0.90	$1.50	£0.20	£0.60	£1.00

2 Infinity Inc. X-over, Jerry Ordway cover and art

	$0.30	$0.90	$1.50	£0.20	£0.60	£1.00

3 Batman and Justice Society of America appear

	$0.40	$1.20	$2.00	£0.25	£0.75	£1.25
Title Value:	$1.00	$3.00	$5.00	£0.65	£1.95	£3.25

ALL-STAR WESTERN

National Periodical Publications; 58 Apr/May 1951-119 Jun/Jul 1961

(formerly All Star Comics #1-57)

58 Strong Bow Indian Warrior and Trigger Twins begin

	$42.00	$125.00	$295.00	£28.00	£82.50	£195.00
59	$21.00	$62.50	$150.00	£14.00	£43.00	£100.00

60 Infantino cover

	$21.00	$62.50	$150.00	£14.00	£43.00	£100.00
61-64 Toth art	$16.00	$49.00	$115.00	£10.50	£32.00	£75.00

65 Infantino cover

	$16.00	$49.00	$115.00	£10.50	£32.00	£75.00
66	$16.00	$49.00	$115.00	£10.50	£32.00	£75.00

67 Johnny Thunder by Gil Kane

	$20.00	$60.00	$140.00	£12.50	£39.00	£90.00
68-81	$8.50	$26.00	$60.00	£5.50	£17.00	£40.00
82-98	$7.75	$23.50	$55.00	£5.25	£16.00	£37.50
99 Frazetta art	$8.50	$26.00	$60.00	£5.50	£17.00	£40.00
100	$8.50	$26.00	$60.00	£5.50	£17.00	£40.00
101-107	$5.50	$17.00	$40.00	£3.90	£11.50	£27.50

108 origin Johnny Thunder

	$13.50	$41.00	$95.00	£9.25	£28.00	£65.00
109	$5.50	$17.00	$40.00	£3.90	£11.50	£27.50

1st official distribution in the U.K.

110-116 rare in the U.K.

	$6.50	$20.00	$40.00	£5.00	£15.00	£30.00

117 rare in the U.K.

	$10.00	$30.00	$60.00	£6.50	£20.00	£40.00

118-119 rare in the U.K.

	$6.50	$20.00	$40.00	£5.00	£15.00	£30.00
Title Value:	$593.75	$1806.50	$4155.00	£400.70	£1218.50	£2807.50

ALL-STAR WESTERN (2ND SERIES)

DC Comics; 1 Aug/Sep 1970-11 Apr/May 1972

1 reprints (Pow Wow Smith)

	$0.60	$1.80	$3.00	£0.40	£1.20	£2.00

2 scarce in the U.K. 1st Diablo, 1st Outlaw, Williamson inks

	$0.70	$2.10	$3.50	£0.45	£1.35	£2.25
3 origin El Diablo	$0.60	$1.80	$3.00	£0.40	£1.20	£2.00
4-6	$0.40	$1.20	$2.00	£0.25	£0.75	£1.25
7-8 52pgs	$0.45	$1.35	$2.25	£0.30	£0.90	£1.50

9 52pgs, Frazetta reprint

	$0.60	$1.80	$3.00	£0.40	£1.20	£2.00

10 52pgs, 1st appearance Jonah Hex

	$12.50	$39.00	$90.00	£7.00	£21.00	£50.00

11 52pgs, 2nd appearance Jonah Hex

	$5.00	$15.00	$35.00	£3.00	£9.00	£21.00
Title Value:	$22.10	$67.80	$148.00	£13.00	£39.00	£86.00

FEATURES

Billy the Kid in 6-8. El Diablo in 2-5,7,10,11. Jonah Hex in 10,11. Outlaw in 2-8.

REPRINT FEATURES

Bat Lash in 9-11. Buffalo Bill in 7-9. Davy Crockett in 7,8. Pow-Wow Smith in 1,8,9,11.

ALLIANCE, THE

Image; 1 Aug 1995-present

1 ND Jim Valentino script/art

	$0.50	$1.50	$2.50	£0.30	£0.90	£1.50
1 ND variant cover	$0.50	$1.50	$2.50	£0.30	£0.90	£1.50

2 ND Jim Valentino script/art

	$0.50	$1.50	$2.50	£0.30	£0.90	£1.50
2 ND variant cover	$0.50	$1.50	$2.50	£0.30	£0.90	£1.50

3 ND Jim Valentino script/art

	$0.50	$1.50	$2.50	£0.30	£0.90	£1.50
3 ND variant cover	$0.50	$1.50	$2.50	£0.30	£0.90	£1.50

4 ND Jim Valentino script/art

	$0.50	$1.50	$2.50	£0.30	£0.90	£1.50
4 ND variant cover	$0.50	$1.50	$2.50	£0.30	£0.90	£1.50
Title Value:	$4.00	$12.00	$20.00	£2.40	£7.20	£12.00

ALLIES, THE

Image; 1 Oct 1995-present

1 ND Diehard, Glory, Roman, Superpatriot and Battlestone begin; Len Wein script, Fabian Ribiero art

	$0.50	$1.50	$2.50	£0.30	£0.90	£1.50
2-3 ND	$0.50	$1.50	$2.50	£0.30	£0.90	£1.50
Title Value:	$1.50	$4.50	$7.50	£0.90	£2.70	£4.50

ALMURIC GRAPHIC NOVEL

Dark Horse,OS; nn Aug 1991

nn ND reprints from Marvel's Epic Illustrated; Roy Thomas script, Tim Conrad art

	$1.95	$5.75	$9.75	£1.30	£3.90	£6.50
Title Value:	$1.95	$5.75	$9.75	£1.30	£3.90	£6.50

ALONE IN THE SHADE SPECIAL

Alchemy Studios; 1 1990

1 ND black and white

	$0.25	$0.75	$1.25	£0.15	£0.45	£0.75
Title Value:	$0.25	$0.75	$1.25	£0.15	£0.45	£0.75

ALPHA FLIGHT

Marvel Comics Group; 1 Aug 1983-130 Mar 1994

(see X-Men #120, X-Men vs Alpha Flight)

1 ND 52pgs, John Byrne art begins

	$1.00	$3.00	$5.00	£0.70	£2.10	£3.50

2 origin Marrina and Alpha Flight, John Byrne art

	$0.60	$1.80	$3.00	£0.40	£1.20	£2.00

3 origin Marrina and Alpha Flight continued, Sub-Mariner and Sue Richards guest-star, John Byrne art

	$0.60	$1.80	$3.00	£0.40	£1.20	£2.00

4-5 John Byrne art

	$0.60	$1.80	$3.00	£0.40	£1.20	£2.00

6 Dr. Strange guest-stars, John Byrne art

	$0.60	$1.80	$3.00	£0.40	£1.20	£2.00

7-8 John Byrne art

	$0.60	$1.80	$3.00	£0.40	£1.20	£2.00

9 origin Sasquatch, Wolverine guest-stars, John Byrne art

	$0.80	$2.40	$4.00	£0.50	£1.50	£2.50
10 John Byrne art	$0.60	$1.80	$3.00	£0.40	£1.20	£2.00

11 LD in the U.K., origin Sasquatch concluded, John Byrne art

	$0.80	$2.40	$4.00	£0.50	£1.50	£2.50

12 DS Guardian dies, John Byrne art

	$0.90	$2.70	$4.50	£0.60	£1.80	£3.00

13 Wolverine appears, John Byrne art

	$0.90	$2.70	$4.50	£0.60	£1.80	£3.00

14 Sub-Mariner appears, John Byrne art

	$0.45	$1.35	$2.25	£0.30	£0.90	£1.50

15 LD in the U.K. Sub-Mariner vs. Marrina, John Byrne art

	$0.60	$1.80	$3.00	£0.40	£1.20	£2.00

All Out War #2

Alpha Flight #13

Amazing Adventures (2nd) #2

MINT = 100% / NEAR MINT (inc. +/-) = 90–99% / VERY FINE (inc. +/-) = 75–89% / FINE (inc. +/-) = 55–74%
VERY GOOD (inc. +/-) = 35–54% / GOOD (inc. +/-) = 15–34% / FAIR = 5–14% / POOR = 1–4%

199

Issue / Description	$Good	$Fine	$N.Mint	£Good	£Fine	£N.Mint
16 Sub-Mariner appears, Wolverine appears (1pg), John Byrne art	$0.80	$2.40	$4.00	£0.50	£1.50	£2.50
17 Wolverine and X-Men appear, John Byrne art	$0.90	$2.70	$4.50	£0.60	£1.80	£3.00
18-22 John Byrne art	$0.40	$1.20	$2.00	£0.25	£0.75	£1.25
23 LD in the U.K. Sasquatch battles Sasquatch, John Byrne art	$0.60	$1.80	$3.00	£0.40	£1.20	£2.00
24 DS John Byrne art	$0.45	$1.35	$2.25	£0.30	£0.90	£1.50
25-27 John Byrne art	$0.40	$1.20	$2.00	£0.25	£0.75	£1.25
28 Secret Wars II X-over, Hulk appears, John Byrne art (last)	$0.45	$1.35	$2.25	£0.30	£0.90	£1.50
29 LD in the U.K. Alpha Flight vs. Hulk	$0.55	$1.65	$2.75	£0.35	£1.05	£1.75
30-31 LD in the U.K.	$0.40	$1.20	$2.00	£0.25	£0.75	£1.25
32 LD in the U.K. 1st appearance new Vindicator	$0.40	$1.20	$2.00	£0.25	£0.75	£1.25
33 LD in the U.K. Wolverine/X-Men appear	$0.90	$2.70	$4.50	£0.60	£1.80	£3.00
34 Wolverine/X-Men appear; 1st full appearance Lady Deathstroke, part origin Wolverine's claws and adamantium skeleton	$0.70	$2.10	$3.50	£0.50	£1.50	£2.50
35 Wolverine appears	$0.40	$1.20	$2.00	£0.25	£0.75	£1.25
36 Avengers and Dr. Strange appear	$0.30	$0.90	$1.50	£0.20	£0.60	£1.00
37	$0.30	$0.90	$1.50	£0.20	£0.60	£1.00
38 Sub-Mariner appears	$0.30	$0.90	$1.50	£0.20	£0.60	£1.00
39 Whilce Portacio inks, Sub-Mariner and Avengers appear	$0.30	$0.90	$1.50	£0.20	£0.60	£1.00
40-41	$0.30	$0.90	$1.50	£0.20	£0.60	£1.00
42 Whilce Portacio inks	$0.30	$0.90	$1.50	£0.20	£0.60	£1.00
43 Sentinels appear	$0.30	$0.90	$1.50	£0.20	£0.60	£1.00
44-46	$0.30	$0.90	$1.50	£0.20	£0.60	£1.00
47-49 LD in the U.K.	$0.40	$1.20	$2.00	£0.25	£0.75	£1.25
50 DS Whilce Portacio co-artist	$0.45	$1.35	$2.25	£0.30	£0.90	£1.50
51 Jim Lee art (his 1st art on a mutant comic), Whilce Portacio inks	$1.00	$3.00	$5.00	£0.70	£2.10	£3.50
52 ND scarce in the U.K. Wolverine appears	$0.80	$2.40	$4.00	£0.50	£1.50	£2.50
53 ND scarce in the U.K. Jim Lee art, Wolverine appears	$1.40	$4.20	$7.00	£0.90	£2.70	£4.50
54 ND Portacio inks	$0.40	$1.20	$2.00	£0.25	£0.75	£1.25
55-57 ND Jim Lee art	$0.45	$1.35	$2.25	£0.30	£0.90	£1.50
58-60 Jim Lee art	$0.40	$1.20	$2.00	£0.25	£0.75	£1.25
61 ND Jim Lee art; paper stock changes to a more glossy format	$0.45	$1.35	$2.25	£0.30	£0.90	£1.50
62 ND Jim Lee art	$0.45	$1.35	$2.25	£0.30	£0.90	£1.50
63 ND	$0.40	$1.20	$2.00	£0.25	£0.75	£1.25
64 ND Jim Lee art	$0.45	$1.35	$2.25	£0.30	£0.90	£1.50
65-73 ND	$0.40	$1.20	$2.00	£0.25	£0.75	£1.25
74 ND Spiderman appears: Wolverine in last panel	$0.40	$1.20	$2.00	£0.25	£0.75	£1.25
75 ND 48pgs, Wolverine appears	$0.45	$1.35	$2.25	£0.30	£0.90	£1.50
76-78 ND	$0.40	$1.20	$2.00	£0.25	£0.75	£1.25
79-80 ND Acts of Vengeance tie-in	$0.40	$1.20	$2.00	£0.25	£0.75	£1.25
81-82 ND Quest for Northstar	$0.40	$1.20	$2.00	£0.25	£0.75	£1.25
83-86 ND	$0.40	$1.20	$2.00	£0.25	£0.75	£1.25
87-90 ND Building Blocks story; new direction for title, Wolverine appears	$0.40	$1.20	$2.00	£0.25	£0.75	£1.25
91-92 ND Fantastic Four appear	$0.40	$1.20	$2.00	£0.25	£0.75	£1.25
93-94 ND	$0.40	$1.20	$2.00	£0.25	£0.75	£1.25
95 ND line-up changes	$0.40	$1.20	$2.00	£0.25	£0.75	£1.25
96 ND Michael Golden cover	$0.40	$1.20	$2.00	£0.25	£0.75	£1.25
97-99 ND The Final Option story	$0.40	$1.20	$2.00	£0.25	£0.75	£1.25
100 ND DS The Final Option concludes, Avengers and Galactus appear	$0.60	$1.80	$3.00	£0.40	£1.20	£2.00
101 ND Dr. Strange and Avengers appear	$0.40	$1.20	$2.00	£0.25	£0.75	£1.25
102-103 ND	$0.40	$1.20	$2.00	£0.25	£0.75	£1.25
104 ND new costumes	$0.40	$1.20	$2.00	£0.25	£0.75	£1.25
105 ND	$0.40	$1.20	$2.00	£0.25	£0.75	£1.25
106 ND Northstar declares his homosexuality (1st in comics? - see Flash [2nd Series] #53)	$0.75	$2.25	$3.75	£0.50	£1.50	£2.50

Issue / Description	$Good	$Fine	$N.Mint	£Good	£Fine	£N.Mint
106 2nd printing ND	$0.40	$1.20	$2.00	£0.25	£0.75	£1.25
107 ND X-Factor appear	$0.40	$1.20	$2.00	£0.25	£0.75	£1.25
108-109 ND	$0.40	$1.20	$2.00	£0.25	£0.75	£1.25
110 ND Infinity War X-over	$0.40	$1.20	$2.00	£0.25	£0.75	£1.25
111-112 ND Infinity War X-over	$0.30	$0.90	$1.50	£0.20	£0.60	£1.00
113 ND Infinity War aftermath	$0.30	$0.90	$1.50	£0.20	£0.60	£1.00
114 ND	$0.30	$0.90	$1.50	£0.20	£0.60	£1.00
115 ND intro Wyre	$0.30	$0.90	$1.50	£0.20	£0.60	£1.00
116-119 ND	$0.30	$0.90	$1.50	£0.20	£0.60	£1.00
120 ND pre-bagged 10th anniversary issue; 11"x17" poster	$0.45	$1.35	$2.25	£0.30	£0.90	£1.50
121 ND Spiderman guest-stars, Wolverine cameo	$0.30	$0.90	$1.50	£0.20	£0.60	£1.00
122-126 ND Infinity Crusade X-over	$0.30	$0.90	$1.50	£0.20	£0.60	£1.00
127 ND Infinity Crusade epilogue	$0.30	$0.90	$1.50	£0.20	£0.60	£1.00
128-129 ND	$0.30	$0.90	$1.50	£0.20	£0.60	£1.00
130 ND 48pgs, leads into Northstar mini-series	$0.40	$1.20	$2.00	£0.25	£0.75	£1.25
Title Value:	$58.90	$176.70	$294.50	£38.10	£114.30	£190.50

ALPHA FLIGHT ANNUAL
Marvel Comics Group; 1 Sep 1986-2 Dec 1987

Issue / Description	$Good	$Fine	$N.Mint	£Good	£Fine	£N.Mint
1 ND	$0.45	$1.35	$2.25	£0.30	£0.90	£1.50
2 ND	$0.40	$1.20	$2.00	£0.25	£0.75	£1.25
Title Value:	$0.85	$2.55	$4.25	£0.55	£1.65	£2.75

ALPHA FLIGHT SPECIAL
Marvel Comics Group,MS; 1 Jul 1991-4 Oct 1991

Issue / Description	$Good	$Fine	$N.Mint	£Good	£Fine	£N.Mint
1-4 ND	$0.45	$1.35	$2.25	£0.30	£0.90	£1.50
Title Value:	$1.80	$5.40	$9.00	£1.20	£3.60	£6.00

Note: reprints Alpha Flight #97-100, one per issue with altered logo, as a market-tester to establish viability of returning title to news-stand distribution

ALPHA FLIGHT SPECIAL (2ND SERIES)
Marvel Comics Group,OS; 1 Jun 1992

Issue / Description	$Good	$Fine	$N.Mint	£Good	£Fine	£N.Mint
1 ND 48pgs, origin Alpha Flight	$0.45	$1.35	$2.25	£0.30	£0.90	£1.50
Title Value:	$0.45	$1.35	$2.25	£0.30	£0.90	£1.50

ALPHA ILLUSTRATED
Alpha Productions; 1 1991

Issue / Description	$Good	$Fine	$N.Mint	£Good	£Fine	£N.Mint
1 ND 48pgs, black and white anthology	$0.60	$1.80	$3.00	£0.40	£1.20	£2.00
Title Value:	$0.60	$1.80	$3.00	£0.40	£1.20	£2.00

ALPHA WAVE
Darkline Comics; 1 1987

Issue / Description	$Good	$Fine	$N.Mint	£Good	£Fine	£N.Mint
1 ND colour	$0.40	$1.20	$2.00	£0.25	£0.75	£1.25
Title Value:	$0.40	$1.20	$2.00	£0.25	£0.75	£1.25

ALTER EGO
First,MS; 1 May 1986-4 Nov 1986

Issue / Description	$Good	$Fine	$N.Mint	£Good	£Fine	£N.Mint
1-4 ND Roy Thomas script, Ron Harris art; colour	$0.40	$1.20	$2.00	£0.25	£0.75	£1.25
Title Value:	$1.60	$4.80	$8.00	£1.00	£3.00	£5.00

AMAZING ADULT FANTASY
Marvel Comics Group; 7 Dec 1961-14 Jul 1962
(formerly Amazing Adventures, becomes Amazing Fantasy)

Issue / Description	$Good	$Fine	$N.Mint	£Good	£Fine	£N.Mint
7	$82.50	$250.00	$500.00	£50.00	£150.00	£300.00
8 last 10¢ issue	$65.00	$200.00	$400.00	£42.00	£125.00	£250.00
9-13	$46.00	$135.00	$275.00	£42.00	£125.00	£250.00
14 "The Boy Who Could Fly" - the first mutant story in the Marvel Universe?	$46.00	$135.00	$275.00	£42.00	£125.00	£250.00
Title Value:	$423.50	$1260.00	$2550.00	£344.00	£1025.00	£2050.00

Note: all have Ditko art throughout. Ditko covers #7-13

AMAZING ADVENTURES
Marvel Comics Group; 1 Jun 1961-6 Nov 1961
(becomes Amazing Adult Fantasy)

Issue / Description	$Good	$Fine	$N.Mint	£Good	£Fine	£N.Mint
1 origin Dr. Droom (1st Marvel Age Super-Hero; see Weird Wonder Tales #19	$140.00	$425.00	$1000.00	£92.50	£275.00	£650.00
2 Dr. Droom	$62.50	$190.00	$450.00	£39.00	£115.00	£275.00
3-4 Dr. Droom	$52.50	$160.00	$375.00	£32.00	£95.00	£225.00
5 no Dr. Droom	$52.50	$160.00	$375.00	£29.00	£85.00	£200.00
6 Dr. Droom	$52.50	$160.00	$375.00	£32.00	£95.00	£225.00
Title Value:	$412.50	$1255.00	$2950.00	£256.50	£760.00	£1800.00

Note: Ditko, Kirby art 1-6. Kirby covers 1-6.

AMAZING ADVENTURES (2ND SERIES)
Marvel Comics Group; 1 Aug 1970-39 Aug 1976

Issue / Description	$Good	$Fine	$N.Mint	£Good	£Fine	£N.Mint
1 ND Inhumans/Black Widow begin	$2.50	$7.50	$15.00	£1.25	£3.75	£7.50
2 ND Fantastic Four appear in Inhumans story	$1.50	$4.50	$7.50	£1.00	£3.00	£5.00
3	$1.05	$3.15	$5.25	£0.70	£2.10	£3.50
4	$0.90	$2.70	$4.50	£0.60	£1.80	£3.00
5 Neal Adams art	$2.00	$6.00	$10.00	£1.30	£3.90	£6.50
6-7 Neal Adams art	$1.80	$5.25	$9.00	£1.20	£3.60	£6.00
8 last Black Widow; Avengers appear in Inhumans story; Thor vs. Black Bolt, Neal Adams art	$1.80	$5.25	$9.00	£1.20	£3.60	£6.00
9 very scarce in the U.K. Magneto vs. Inhumans	$1.80	$5.25	$9.00	£1.20	£3.60	£6.00

	$Good	$Fine	$N.Mint	£Good	£Fine	£N.Mint
10 scarce in the U.K. X-over Avengers #95, Magneto vs. Inhumans	$1.50	$4.50	$7.50	£1.00	£3.00	£5.00
11 scarce in the U.K. Beast series begins, X-Men appear	$5.00	$15.00	$30.00	£1.25	£3.75	£7.50
12 scarce in the U.K.	$1.50	$4.50	$7.50	£1.00	£3.00	£5.00
13 scarce in the U.K. Brotherhood of Evil Mutants appear	$1.40	$4.20	$7.00	£0.90	£2.70	£4.50
14 scarce in the U.K. Iron Man appears	$1.20	$3.60	$6.00	£0.80	£2.40	£4.00
15 scarce in the U.K. Angel appears	$1.40	$4.20	$7.00	£0.90	£2.70	£4.50
16 scarce in the U.K. Beast battles Juggernaut; Spiderman and Avengers appear on cover only	$1.40	$4.20	$7.00	£0.90	£2.70	£4.50
17 scarce in the U.K. cover and 2pgs Jim Starlin art, rest edited reprint of X-Men #49, #53; origin Beast, X-Men and Magneto appear	$1.40	$4.20	$7.00	£0.90	£2.70	£4.50
18 1st War of the Worlds/Killraven, Neal Adams and Howard Chaykin art	$1.20	$5.25	$9.00	£1.20	£3.60	£6.00
19 Chaykin art	$0.85	$2.55	$4.25	£0.55	£1.65	£2.75
20	$0.70	$2.10	$3.50	£0.45	£1.35	£2.25
21-22	$0.60	$1.80	$3.00	£0.40	£1.20	£2.00
23-25 ND	$0.60	$1.80	$3.00	£0.60	£1.80	£3.00
26-34	$0.45	$1.35	$2.25	£0.30	£0.90	£1.50
35 Giffen art (his first in comics?)	$0.45	$1.35	$2.25	£0.30	£0.90	£1.50
36-37	$0.45	$1.35	$2.25	£0.30	£0.90	£1.50
38 Man-Thing, Iron Man, Dr. Strange cameos, Gerald Ford appears, Giffen art	$0.45	$1.35	$2.25	£0.30	£0.90	£1.50
39 Giffen inks	$0.45	$1.35	$2.25	£0.30	£0.90	£1.50
Title Value:	$42.60	$127.05	$220.50	£26.30	£78.90	£134.00

Note: issues 11-17 very often have ink-staining along one or more edges.

ARTISTS

Kirby in 1-4. Ploog in 12. P.Craig Russell in 33, 39. Adams covers 6-8

FEATURES

Inhumans in 1-10. Black Widow in 1-8. Beast in 11-17 (17 part reprint). War of the Worlds (Killraven) in 18-28; Killraven 29-39.

AMAZING ADVENTURES (3RD SERIES)
Marvel Comics Group; 1 Dec 1979-14 Jan 1981

	$Good	$Fine	$N.Mint	£Good	£Fine	£N.Mint
1 ND reprints first half of X-Men #1	$1.05	$3.15	$5.25	£0.70	£2.10	£3.50
2 ND reprints second half of X-Men #1	$0.80	$2.40	$4.00	£0.50	£1.50	£2.50
3-4 ND reprints X-Men #2	$0.60	$1.80	$3.00	£0.40	£1.20	£2.00
5-6 ND reprints X-Men #3	$0.60	$1.80	$3.00	£0.40	£1.20	£2.00
7-8 ND reprints X-Men #4	$0.60	$1.80	$3.00	£0.40	£1.20	£2.00
9 ND reprints X-Men #5, Steranko back-up reprint	$0.60	$1.80	$3.00	£0.40	£1.20	£2.00
10 ND reprints X-Men #5	$0.60	$1.80	$3.00	£0.40	£1.20	£2.00
11-12 ND reprints X-Men #6	$0.60	$1.80	$3.00	£0.40	£1.20	£2.00
13 ND reprints X-Men #7	$0.60	$1.80	$3.00	£0.40	£1.20	£2.00
14 ND reprints X-Men #8	$0.60	$1.80	$3.00	£0.40	£1.20	£2.00
Title Value:	$9.05	$27.15	$45.25	£6.00	£18.00	£30.00

Note: issues 1-12 have reprinted back-up features. Selected issues re-draw the original X-Men covers from 1-8. These are noted as follows in brackets: 1(1), 4(2), 5(3), 7(4), 10(5), 12(6), 13(7), 14(8).

AMAZING ADVENTURES (4TH SERIES)
Marvel Comics Group,OS; 1 Jul 1988

	$Good	$Fine	$N.Mint	£Good	£Fine	£N.Mint
1 ND 64pgs, squarebound, art by Mayerik, Golden and Ridgway	$0.80	$2.40	$4.00	£0.50	£1.50	£2.50
Title Value:	$0.80	$2.40	$4.00	£0.50	£1.50	£2.50

AMAZING COMICS PREMIERES
Amazing Publishing; 1 1987-5 Aug 1987

	$Good	$Fine	$N.Mint	£Good	£Fine	£N.Mint
1 ND Ninja Bots; black and white begins	$0.40	$1.20	$2.00	£0.25	£0.75	£1.25
2 ND Untouchabots	$0.30	$0.90	$1.50	£0.20	£0.60	£1.00
3 ND Shadowalker and the Ghost Chasers	$0.30	$0.90	$1.50	£0.20	£0.60	£1.00
4 ND The Great American Murder Bar; 10pgs Sam Kieth art, Sam Kieth cover	$0.40	$1.20	$2.00	£0.25	£0.75	£1.25
5 ND Friends; 5pgs Ron Lim art, Ron Lim cover; 1st Legends of the Stargrazers	$0.40	$1.20	$2.00	£0.25	£0.75	£1.25
Title Value:	$1.80	$5.40	$9.00	£1.15	£3.45	£5.75

AMAZING CYNICALMAN
Eclipse,OS; 1 Jun 1987

	$Good	$Fine	$N.Mint	£Good	£Fine	£N.Mint
1 ND Matt Feazell art	$0.30	$0.90	$1.50	£0.20	£0.60	£1.00
Title Value:	$0.30	$0.90	$1.50	£0.20	£0.60	£1.00

AMAZING FANTASY
Marvel Comics Group; 15 Aug 1962; 16 Dec 1995-18 Mar 1996
(formerly Amazing Adult Fantasy)

	$Good	$Fine	$N.Mint	£Good	£Fine	£N.Mint
15 origin and 1st appearance of Spiderman by Stan Lee and Steve Ditko, Jack Kirby/Steve Ditko cover (alternative cover version can be found in Spiderman index no.1)	$1650.00	$5000.00	$25000.00	£930.00	£2800.00	£14000.00

[Prices may vary widely on this comic]

[Very scarce in high grade - Very Fine+ or better]

	$Good	$Fine	$N.Mint	£Good	£Fine	£N.Mint
15 ND Marvel Milestone Edition (Mar 1992), reprints original issue with ads, silver border around cover	$0.60	$1.80	$3.00	£0.40	£1.20	£2.00
16 ND Kurt Busiek script, Paul Lee painted art; Spiderman's adventures days after his origin; UV coated cover	$0.80	$2.40	$4.00	£0.50	£1.50	£2.50
17-18 ND Kurt Busiek script, Paul Lee painted art; UV coated cover	$0.80	$2.40	$4.00	£0.50	£1.50	£2.50
Title Value:	$1653.00	$5009.00	$25015.00	£931.90	£2805.70	£14009.50

AMAZING HIGH ADVENTURE
Marvel Comics Group; 1 Aug 1984-5 Dec 1986

	$Good	$Fine	$N.Mint	£Good	£Fine	£N.Mint
1 ND Severin art	$0.55	$1.65	$2.75	£0.35	£1.05	£1.75
2 ND Paul Smith art, Williamson inks	$0.55	$1.65	$2.75	£0.35	£1.05	£1.75
3 ND Mike Mignola art	$0.45	$1.35	$2.25	£0.30	£0.90	£1.50
4 ND John Bolton art	$0.45	$1.35	$2.25	£0.30	£0.90	£1.50
5 ND scarce in the U.K. Bissette and Ridgway art, Bolton cover	$0.45	$1.35	$2.25	£0.30	£0.90	£1.50
Title Value:	$2.45	$7.35	$12.25	£1.60	£4.80	£8.00

Note: all Baxter paper.

AMAZING SCARLET SPIDER
Marvel Comics Group; 1 Nov 1995-2 Jan 1996

	$Good	$Fine	$N.Mint	£Good	£Fine	£N.Mint
1 ND J.M. DeMatteis script, Mark Bagley and Larry Mahlstedt art, coontinued in Scarlet Spider #1; metallic ink cover	$0.40	$1.20	$2.00	£0.25	£0.75	£1.25
2 ND continued in Scarlet Spider #2	$0.40	$1.20	$2.00	£0.25	£0.75	£1.25
Title Value:	$0.80	$2.40	$4.00	£0.50	£1.50	£2.50

AMAZING SPIDERMAN COLLECTION
Marvel Comics Group,MS; 1 May 1995-4 Aug 1995

	$Good	$Fine	$N.Mint	£Good	£Fine	£N.Mint
1-4 ND reprints the set of Fleer Spiderman '93 trading cards	$0.60	$1.80	$3.00	£0.40	£1.20	£2.00
Title Value:	$2.40	$7.20	$12.00	£1.60	£4.80	£8.00

AMAZING SPIDERMAN, THE
Marvel Comics Group; 1 Mar 1963-406 Oct 1995; 407 Jan 1996-present
(see Amazing Fantasy, Deadly Foes of.., Marvel Fanfare, Marvel Graphic Novel, Marvel Special Edition, Marvel Tales, Marvel Team Up, Marvel Treasury Edition, Official Index to.., Sensational Spiderman, Spectacular Spiderman, Spiderman Digest, Spiderman vs. Wolverine, Spidey Super Stories, Superman vs. Spiderman, Web of Spiderman)

	$Good	$Fine	$N.Mint	£Good	£Fine	£N.Mint
1 retells origin, Fantastic Four appear, intro J. Jonah Jameson, The Chameleon, Steve Ditko art begins (ends #38); Jack Kirby cover	$1350.00	$4050.00	$19000.00	£710.00	£2125.00	£10000.00

[Prices may vary widely on this comic]

	$Good	$Fine	$N.Mint	£Good	£Fine	£N.Mint
1 ND very scarce in the U.K. reprint (1966)	$17.50	$52.50	$125.00	£10.00	£30.00	£70.00
1 ND very rare in the U.K reprint with Golden Record to form complete sealed package	$39.00	$115.00	$275.00	£21.00	£62.50	£150.00
1 ND Marvel Milestone Edition (Dec 1992), reprints original issue with ads	$0.50	$1.50	$2.50	£0.30	£0.90	£1.50
2 1st appearance Vulture, 1st appearance The Tinkerer	$315.00	$950.00	$2850.00	£175.00	£530.00	£1600.00
3 1st appearance Dr. Octopus, Human Torch cameo	$215.00	$650.00	$1750.00	£125.00	£375.00	£1000.00
3 ND Marvel Milestone Edition (Mar 1995) - metallic ink cover	$0.60	$1.80	$3.00	£0.40	£1.20	£2.00
4 less common in the U.K. 1st appearance Betty Brant and Liz Allen, origin and 1st appearance The Sandman	$175.00	$520.00	$1400.00	£100.00	£300.00	£800.00
5 Dr. Doom appears (1st encounter with Spiderman)	$165.00	$500.00	$1350.00	£92.50	£280.00	£750.00
6 1st appearance The Lizard	$140.00	$430.00	$1150.00	£80.00	£240.00	£650.00
7 2nd appearance The Vulture	$100.00	$300.00	$800.00	£52.50	£155.00	£425.00
8 scarce in the U.K. (Jan 1964), Fantastic Four X-over (in back-up story)	$100.00	$300.00	$800.00	£60.00	£185.00	£495.00
9 origin and 1st appearance Electro	$105.00	$315.00	$850.00	£60.00	£185.00	£495.00
10 1st appearance Big Man and the Enforcers	$100.00	$300.00	$800.00	£52.50	£155.00	£425.00
11 2nd appearance Dr. Octopus	$67.50	$200.00	$475.00	£41.00	£120.00	£285.00
12 3rd appearance Dr. Octopus; Spiderman unmasked by Dr. Octopus	$67.50	$200.00	$475.00	£41.00	£120.00	£285.00
13 1st appearance Mysterio	$77.50	$235.00	$550.00	£46.00	£135.00	£325.00
14 1st appearance of the original Green Goblin (Norman Osborn), Hulk appears	$155.00	$465.00	$1400.00	£87.50	£265.00	£800.00
15 origin and 1st appearance Kraven the Hunter, 1st mention Mary Jane Watson though unseen	$60.00	$180.00	$425.00	£38.00	£110.00	£265.00
16 Daredevil vs. Spiderman (see Daredevil #16/17), 4th ever appearance of Daredevil (in original costume)	$45.00	$135.00	$325.00	£28.00	£82.50	£195.00
17 less common in the U.K. 2nd appearance Green Goblin	$70.00	$210.00	$495.00	£45.00	£135.00	£315.00
18 rare in the U.K., Fantastic Four appear, 1st appearance Ned Leeds (later Hobgoblin), Green Goblin cameo (3 panels thus 3rd appearance) and Kraven cameo (2 panels thus 2nd appearance)	$46.00	$135.00	$325.00	£32.00	£95.00	£225.00
19 rare in the U.K., Human Torch appears, 1st appearance Scorpion (not in costume)	$41.00	$120.00	$285.00	£31.00	£90.00	£215.00
20 very scarce in the U.K., scarce in the U.S. (Jan 1965), origin and 1st appearance The Scorpion	$46.00	$135.00	$325.00	£31.00	£90.00	£215.00
21 2nd appearance The Beetle (see Strange Tales #123)						

#	Description	$Good	$Fine	$N.Mint	£Good	£Fine	£N.Mint
22	1st appearance Princess Python	$32.00	$95.00	$225.00	£17.50	£52.50	£125.00
23	4th appearance Green Goblin	$32.00	$95.00	$225.00	£17.50	£52.50	£125.00
24	2nd appearance Mysterio, Sandman and Vulture cameos	$44.00	$130.00	$310.00	£26.00	£75.00	£180.00
25	1st Mary Jane Watson? cameo only, face unseen..., 1st appearance Spider-Slayer	$27.00	$80.00	$190.00	£15.50	£47.00	£110.00
26	1st appearance Crimemaster, 5th appearance Green Goblin	$34.00	$100.00	$225.00	£17.50	£52.50	£125.00
27	Green Goblin cover and story	$32.00	$95.00	$225.00	£18.50	£55.00	£130.00
28	origin and 1st appearance Molten Man; Peter Parker graduates [Very scarce in high grade - Very Fine+ or better]	$30.00 / $46.00	$90.00 / $135.00	$210.00 / $325.00	£15.50 / £25.00	£47.00 / £75.00	£110.00 / £175.00
29	scarce in the U.K. 2nd appearance Scorpion	$21.00	$62.50	$150.00	£13.50	£41.00	£95.00
30	1st appearance The Cat (not to be confused with Tigra who was previously called The Cat)	$21.00	$62.50	$150.00	£12.50	£39.00	£90.00
31	less common in the U.K. 1st Harry Osborn (later 2nd Green Goblin), 1st appearance Gwen Stacy and Professor Warren; last Silver Age issue indicia-dated Dec 1965	$19.00	$57.50	$135.00	£12.00	£36.00	£85.00
32	(Jan 1966)	$19.00	$57.50	$135.00	£10.50	£32.00	£75.00
33	classic interior sequence considered by many as among Steve Ditko's finest work on Spiderman	$19.00	$57.50	$135.00	£10.50	£32.00	£75.00
34	3rd appearance Kraven	$19.00	$57.50	$135.00	£10.50	£32.00	£75.00
35	2nd appearance Molten Man	$19.00	$57.50	$135.00	£10.50	£32.00	£75.00
36	1st appearance The Looter	$19.00	$57.50	$135.00	£10.50	£32.00	£75.00
37	Norman Osborn character introduced: not yet known that he's Green Goblin	$19.00	$57.50	$135.00	£10.50	£32.00	£75.00
38	last Steve Ditko art, 2nd Mary Jane Watson? (cameo), face unseen and...	$19.00	$57.50	$135.00	£10.50	£32.00	£75.00
39	Green Goblin appears and reveals he's Norman Osborn, 1st John Romita Snr. art, classic cover	$27.00	$80.00	$190.00	£15.50	£47.00	£110.00
40	Green Goblin appears, origin told for 1st time	$36.00	$105.00	$285.00	£20.00	£60.00	£160.00
41	less common in the U.K. 1st appearance The Rhino	$19.00	$57.50	$135.00	£10.50	£32.00	£75.00
42	scarce in the U.K. 3rd Mary Jane Watson? (cameo), face fully shown in one panel (last)	$17.50	$52.50	$125.00	£10.00	£30.00	£70.00
43	scarce in the U.K. 1st full appearance Mary Jane Watson, 2nd appearance Rhino	$12.50	$39.00	$90.00	£7.75	£23.50	£55.00
44	less common in the U.K. (Jan 1967), 2nd appearance Lizard	$12.50	$39.00	$90.00	£7.00	£21.00	£50.00
45	3rd appearance Lizard	$12.50	$39.00	$90.00	£6.00	£18.00	£42.50
46	1st appearance The Shocker	$12.50	$39.00	$90.00	£6.00	£18.00	£42.50
47	Kraven appears	$12.50	$39.00	$90.00	£6.00	£18.00	£42.50
48-49	Vulture appears	$12.50	$39.00	$90.00	£6.00	£18.00	£42.50
50	scarce in the U.K. 1st appearance Kingpin, origin retold, classic cover	$50.00	$155.00	$365.00	£29.00	£85.00	£200.00
51	2nd appearance Kingpin	$19.00	$57.50	$135.00	£9.25	£28.00	£65.00
52	1st appearance Joe Robertson	$11.50	$35.00	$70.00	£5.75	£17.50	£35.00
53-55	Dr. Octopus appears	$11.50	$35.00	$70.00	£5.75	£17.50	£35.00
56	(Jan 1968), 1st appearance Captain George Stacy (Gwen Stacy's father), Dr. Octopus appears	$11.50	$35.00	$70.00	£5.75	£17.50	£35.00
57-58	Ka-Zar appears	$11.50	$35.00	$70.00	£5.75	£17.50	£35.00
59-60		$11.50	$35.00	$70.00	£5.75	£17.50	£35.00
61-62		$8.25	$25.00	$50.00	£4.55	£13.50	£27.50
63	Green Goblin cameo	$8.25	$25.00	$50.00	£4.55	£13.50	£27.50
64-67		$8.25	$25.00	$50.00	£4.55	£13.50	£27.50
68	(Jan 1969), Kingpin appears	$8.25	$25.00	$50.00	£4.55	£13.50	£27.50
69-70	Kingpin appears	$8.25	$25.00	$50.00	£4.55	£13.50	£27.50
71		$8.25	$25.00	$50.00	£4.15	£12.50	£25.00
72	2nd appearance Shocker	$8.25	$25.00	$50.00	£4.15	£12.50	£25.00
73		$8.25	$25.00	$50.00	£4.15	£12.50	£25.00
74	last 12¢ issue	$8.25	$25.00	$50.00	£4.15	£12.50	£25.00
75-76		$7.00	$21.00	$42.00	£3.30	£10.00	£20.00
77	Human Torch appears	$7.00	$21.00	$42.00	£3.30	£10.00	£20.00
78	1st appearance The Prowler	$7.00	$21.00	$42.00	£4.15	£12.50	£25.00
79		$7.00	$21.00	$42.00	£3.30	£10.00	£20.00
80	(Jan 1970)	$7.00	$21.00	$42.00	£3.30	£10.00	£20.00
81	1st appearance Kangaroo	$7.00	$21.00	$42.00	£3.30	£10.00	£20.00
82		$7.00	$21.00	$42.00	£3.30	£10.00	£20.00
83	1st appearance Schemer	$7.00	$21.00	$42.00	£3.30	£10.00	£20.00
84-85		$7.00	$21.00	$42.00	£3.30	£10.00	£20.00
86	Black Widow appears	$7.00	$21.00	$42.00	£2.90	£8.75	£17.50
87		$7.00	$21.00	$42.00	£2.90	£8.75	£17.50
88-89	Dr. Octopus appears	$7.00	$21.00	$42.00	£2.90	£8.75	£17.50
90	less common in the U.K. Captain Stacy dies, Dr. Octopus appears	$8.00	$24.00	$48.00	£3.75	£11.00	£22.50
91		$7.00	$21.00	$42.00	£2.90	£8.75	£17.50
92	(Jan 1971), Iceman appears	$7.00	$21.00	$42.00	£2.90	£8.75	£17.50
93		$7.00	$21.00	$42.00	£2.90	£8.75	£17.50
94	scarce in the U.K. origin retold	$10.50	$33.00	$65.00	£5.00	£15.00	£30.00
95	scarce in the U.K.	$7.00	$21.00	$42.00	£4.15	£12.50	£25.00
96-98	scarce in the U.K. non Code-approved drugs story, Green Goblin appears	$13.00	$40.00	$80.00	£5.00	£15.00	£30.00
99		$7.00	$21.00	$42.00	£2.90	£8.75	£17.50
100	scarce in the U.K. anniversary issue and retrospective (Dr. Octopus, Green Goblin and Kingpin in dream sequence), Spiderman with six arms	$25.00	$75.00	$175.00	£13.50	£41.00	£95.00
101	scarce in the U.K. 1st appearance Morbius the Living Vampire, Lizard appears; last 15 cents issue	$25.00	$75.00	$175.00	£12.50	£39.00	£90.00
101	ND reprint (Sep 1992) - silver metallic ink cover; released to tie in with Morbius #1 (same cover date month)	$0.40	$1.20	$2.00	£0.25	£0.75	£1.25
102	scarce in the U.K. 52pgs, origin and 2nd appearance Morbius (spelt incorrectly on cover as "Moribus"), Lizard appears	$17.00	$50.00	$120.00	£10.50	£32.00	£75.00
103	scarce in the U.K. Ka-Zar and Kraven appear; Gil Kane cover	$4.15	$12.50	$25.00	£2.90	£8.75	£17.50
104	scarce in the U.K. (Jan 1972), Ka-Zar and Kraven appear; Gil Kane cover	$4.15	$12.50	$25.00	£2.90	£8.75	£17.50
105-108	scarce in the U.K.	$4.15	$12.50	$25.00	£2.90	£8.75	£17.50
109	scarce in the U.K. Dr. Strange appears	$4.15	$12.50	$25.00	£2.90	£8.75	£17.50
110	scarce in the U.K. 1st appearance The Gibbon	$4.15	$12.50	$25.00	£2.90	£8.75	£17.50
111	scarce in the U.K.	$4.15	$12.50	$25.00	£2.50	£7.50	£15.00
112	scarce in the U.K. Dr. Octopus appears	$4.15	$12.50	$25.00	£2.50	£7.50	£15.00
113	scarce in the U.K. 1st appearance Hammerhead, Dr. Octopus appears; part Starlin art	$4.15	$12.50	$25.00	£2.50	£7.50	£15.00
114	scarce in the U.K. Dr. Octopus appears; part Starlin art	$4.15	$12.50	$25.00	£2.50	£7.50	£15.00
115	Dr. Octopus appears	$4.15	$12.50	$25.00	£2.05	£6.25	£12.50
116	(Jan 1973)	$4.15	$12.50	$25.00	£2.05	£6.25	£12.50
117-118	scarce in the U.K.	$4.15	$12.50	$25.00	£2.50	£7.50	£15.00
119-120	scarce in the U.K. Spiderman vs. Hulk	$6.50	$20.00	$40.00	£3.30	£10.00	£20.00
121	ND Gwen Stacy dies (murdered by The Green Goblin)(Note: this was the first issue of this title to be officially Non Distributed in the U.K.)	$17.50	$52.50	$125.00	£10.50	£32.00	£75.00
122	ND Green Goblin (Norman Osborn) dies	$20.00	$60.00	$140.00	£12.00	£36.00	£85.00
123	ND Luke Cage appears	$4.15	$12.50	$25.00	£2.50	£7.50	£15.00
124	ND 1st appearance Man-Wolf (J. Jonah Jameson's son)	$4.15	$12.50	$25.00	£2.90	£8.75	£17.50
125	ND 2nd appearance Man-Wolf	$4.15	$12.50	$25.00	£2.05	£6.25	£12.50
126	ND	$4.15	$12.50	$25.00	£2.05	£6.25	£12.50
127	ND Vulture returns	$4.15	$12.50	$25.00	£2.05	£6.25	£12.50
128	ND (Jan 1974), Vulture returns	$4.15	$12.50	$25.00	£2.05	£6.25	£12.50
129	ND 1st appearance Punisher, 1st appearance The Jackal	$42.00	$125.00	$295.00	£26.00	£77.50	£185.00
130-131	ND Dr. Octopus appears	$2.90	$8.75	$17.50	£1.65	£5.00	£10.00
132-133	ND	$2.90	$8.75	$17.50	£1.65	£5.00	£10.00
134	ND scarce in the U.K. Punisher cameo, 1st appearance Tarantula	$4.15	$12.50	$25.00	£3.00	£9.00	£18.00
135	ND 2nd full appearance Punisher	$11.50	$35.00	$70.00	£6.50	£20.00	£40.00
136	ND 1st appearance Green Goblin II (Harry Osborn)	$7.50	$22.50	$45.00	£3.00	£9.00	£18.00
137	ND Green Goblin II appears (full story and cover)	$7.50	$22.50	$45.00	£2.00	£6.00	£12.00
138-139	ND	$2.50	$7.50	$15.00	£1.30	£4.00	£8.00
140	ND (Jan 1975)	$2.50	$7.50	$15.00	£1.30	£4.00	£8.00
141	ND Morbius and Green Goblin cameos in dream sequence; 1st appearance Mysterio II	$2.90	$8.75	$17.50	£1.30	£4.00	£8.00
142	ND Gwen Stacy clone cameo	$4.15	$12.50	$25.00	£2.05	£6.25	£12.50

# / Description	$Good	$Fine	$N.Mint	£Good	£Fine	£N.Mint
143 ND Gwen Stacy clone cameo; 1st appearance Cyclone	$4.15	$12.50	$25.00	£2.05	£6.25	£12.50
144 ND 1st full appearance Gwen Stacy clone	$4.15	$12.50	$25.00	£2.05	£6.25	£12.50
145-146 ND Gwen Stacy clone	$3.30	$10.00	$20.00	£1.65	£5.00	£10.00
147 ND Spiderman learns of Gwen Stacy clone	$3.30	$10.00	$20.00	£1.65	£5.00	£10.00
148 ND The Jackal revealed as Professor Warren	$5.00	$15.00	$30.00	£2.50	£7.50	£15.00
149 ND 1st appearance Spiderman clone, origin Jackal	$11.00	$34.00		£7.75	£23.50	£55.00
149 ND Marvel Milestone Edition (Nov 1994) - silver border cover	$0.60	$1.80	$3.00	£0.40	£1.20	£2.00
150 ND Spiderman clone appears	$8.25	$25.00	$50.00	£5.75	£17.50	£35.00
150 ND Marvel Milestone Edition (1995) - silver border cover	$0.60	$1.80	$3.00	£0.40	£1.20	£2.00
151 ND Spiderman clone appears	$5.75	$17.50	$35.00	£3.75	£11.00	£22.50
152 ND (Jan 1976)	$2.50	$7.50	$15.00	£1.30	£4.00	£8.00
153-154 ND	$2.50	$7.50	$15.00	£1.30	£4.00	£8.00
155-156 ND	$2.50	$7.50	$15.00	£1.15	£3.50	£7.00
157-159 ND Dr. Octopus appears	$2.50	$7.50	$15.00	£1.15	£3.50	£7.00
160 ND	$2.50	$7.50	$15.00	£1.15	£3.50	£7.00
161 ND Nightcrawler appears, Punisher, Wolverine, Colossus cameos; Jigsaw appears though hidden	$2.90	$8.75	$17.50	£1.25	£3.75	£7.50
162 ND Punisher, Nightcrawler appear, 1st full appearance Jigsaw	$3.30	$10.00	$20.00	£1.65	£5.00	£10.00
163 ND	$1.50	$4.50	$9.00	£0.80	£2.50	£5.00
164 ND (Jan 1977)	$1.50	$4.50	$9.00	£0.80	£2.50	£5.00
165-166 ND	$1.50	$4.50	$9.00	£0.80	£2.50	£5.00
167 ND 1st appearance Barton Hamilton (later Green Goblin III in #176)	$1.50	$4.50	$9.00	£0.80	£2.50	£5.00
168-170 ND	$1.50	$4.50	$9.00	£0.80	£2.50	£5.00
171 ND Nova appears, X-over Nova #12	$1.50	$4.50	$9.00	£0.80	£2.50	£5.00
172-173 ND	$1.50	$4.50	$9.00	£0.80	£2.50	£5.00
174-175 ND Punisher appears	$3.30	$10.00	$20.00	£1.65	£5.00	£10.00
176 ND (Jan 1978), 1st appearance Green Goblin III (Barton Hamilton)	$3.00	$9.00	$18.00	£1.05	£3.25	£6.50
177-179 ND Green Goblin III appears	$3.00	$9.00	$18.00	£1.05	£3.25	£6.50
180 ND Green Goblin II & III appear	$3.00	$9.00	$18.00	£1.05	£3.25	£6.50
181 ND origin retold	$1.50	$4.50	$9.00	£0.80	£2.50	£5.00
182-184 ND	$1.50	$4.50	$9.00	£0.80	£2.50	£5.00
185 ND Peter Parker's graduation (1st graduation in #28!)	$1.50	$4.50	$9.00	£0.80	£2.50	£5.00
186 ND	$1.50	$4.50	$9.00	£0.80	£2.50	£5.00
187 ND Jim Starlin art, Captain America appears	$1.50	$4.50	$9.00	£0.80	£2.50	£5.00
188 ND (Jan 1979)	$1.50	$4.50	$9.00	£0.80	£2.50	£5.00
189-190 ND Man-Wolf appears, John Byrne art	$1.50	$4.50	$9.00	£0.80	£2.50	£5.00
191-193 ND	$1.30	$4.00	$8.00	£0.65	£2.00	£4.00
194 ND 1st appearance Black Cat	$3.00	$9.00	$18.00	£1.25	£3.75	£7.50
195-199 ND	$1.30	$4.00	$8.00	£0.65	£2.00	£4.00
200 ND (Jan 1980), DS, origin retold, return of burglar that killed Peter Parker's uncle in Amazing Fantasy #15	$5.25	$16.00	$32.00	£1.65	£5.00	£10.00
201-202 ND Punisher appears	$3.30	$10.00	$20.00	£1.65	£5.00	£10.00
203 ND 2nd appearance Dazzler	$1.30	$4.00	$8.00	£0.65	£2.00	£4.00
204-205 ND Black Cat appears	$1.30	$4.00	$8.00	£0.65	£2.00	£4.00
206 ND John Byrne art	$1.30	$4.00	$8.00	£0.65	£2.00	£4.00
207-208 ND	$1.30	$4.00	$8.00	£0.65	£2.00	£4.00
209 ND 1st appearance Calypso	$2.00	$6.00	$12.00	£0.80	£2.50	£5.00
210 ND	$1.30	$4.00	$8.00	£0.65	£2.00	£4.00
211 ND Sub-Mariner appears	$1.30	$4.00	$8.00	£0.65	£2.00	£4.00
212 ND (Jan 1981), 1st appearance Hydroman	$1.30	$4.00	$8.00	£0.65	£2.00	£4.00
213 ND	$1.30	$4.00	$8.00	£0.65	£2.00	£4.00
214 ND Sub-Mariner appears	$1.30	$4.00	$8.00	£0.65	£2.00	£4.00
215 Sub-Mariner X-over/origin	$1.30	$4.00	$8.00	£0.55	£1.75	£3.50
216-218 ND	$1.30	$4.00	$8.00	£0.55	£1.75	£3.50
219 Frank Miller cover	$1.30	$4.00	$8.00	£0.55	£1.75	£3.50
220 Moon Knight appears	$1.30	$4.00	$8.00	£0.55	£1.75	£3.50
221-223 ND	$1.30	$4.00	$8.00	£0.50	£1.50	£3.00
224 (Jan 1982)	$1.30	$4.00	$8.00	£0.50	£1.50	£3.00

# / Description	$Good	$Fine	$N.Mint	£Good	£Fine	£N.Mint
225 Foolkiller appears	$1.30	$4.00	$8.00	£0.50	£1.50	£3.00
226-227 Black Cat appears	$1.30	$4.00	$8.00	£0.50	£1.50	£3.00
228 LD in the U.K.	$1.30	$4.00	$8.00	£0.50	£1.60	£3.25
229-231 LD in the U.K. Juggernaut appears	$1.30	$4.00	$8.00	£0.50	£1.60	£3.25
232-233 LD in the U.K.	$1.30	$4.00	$8.00	£0.50	£1.60	£3.25
234 LD in the U.K. free insert - Marvel Guide to Collecting Comics	$1.30	$4.00	$8.00	£0.50	£1.60	£3.25
234 as above but without insert	$1.00	$3.00	$5.00	£0.50	£1.50	£2.50
235 LD in the U.K. Walt Simonson cover	$1.30	$4.00	$8.00	£0.50	£1.50	£3.00
236 LD in the U.K. (Jan 1983)	$1.30	$4.00	$8.00	£0.50	£1.50	£3.00
237 LD in the U.K.	$1.30	$4.00	$8.00	£0.50	£1.50	£3.00
238 LD in the U.K. 1st appearance Hobgoblin (Ned Leeds), issue includes free stick-on skin tattoos	$14.00	$43.00	$85.00	£5.00	£15.00	£30.00
238 as above but without tattoos	$5.00	$15.00	$30.00	£3.30	£10.00	£20.00
239 LD in the U.K. 2nd appearance Hobgoblin	$7.50	$22.50	$45.00	£2.50	£7.50	£15.00
240-242 LD in the U.K.	$1.30	$4.00	$8.00	£0.40	£1.25	£2.50
243 LD in the U.K. return of Mary Jane Watson	$1.30	$4.00	$8.00	£0.40	£1.25	£2.50
244 LD in the U.K. Hobgoblin appears (cameo)	$2.00	$6.00	$12.00	£0.55	£1.75	£3.50
245 LD in the U.K. "Hobgoblin" (Lefty Donovan) vs. Spiderman	$2.50	$7.50	$15.00	£0.65	£2.00	£4.00
246 LD in the U.K. Avengers and Fantastic Four cameos	$1.30	$4.00	$8.00	£0.40	£1.25	£2.50
247 LD in the U.K.	$1.30	$4.00	$8.00	£0.40	£1.25	£2.50
248 LD in the U.K. (Jan 1984)	$1.30	$4.00	$8.00	£0.40	£1.25	£2.50
249-251 LD in the U.K. Hobgoblin vs. Spiderman	$2.50	$7.50	$15.00	£0.75	£2.25	£4.50
252 LD in the U.K. 1st appearance (alien) black costume which later transforms into Venom (see Secret Wars I and Marvel Team Up #141)	$6.25	$18.50	$37.50	£1.50	£4.50	£9.00
253 LD in the U.K. 1st appearance Rose	$1.65	$5.00	$10.00	£0.55	£1.75	£3.50
254 LD in the U.K. Jack O'Lantern appears	$1.15	$3.50	$7.00	£0.40	£1.25	£2.50
255 LD in the U.K. 1st appearance Black Fox; Red Ghost appears	$1.15	$3.50	$7.00	£0.40	£1.25	£2.50
256 LD in the U.K. 1st appearance Puma	$1.00	$3.00	$6.00	£0.50	£1.50	£3.00
257 LD in the U.K. Hobgoblin cameo; Hobgoblin costume discovered to be alive	$2.00	$6.00	$12.00	£0.55	£1.75	£3.50
258 LD in the U.K. Hobgoblin cameo, Fantastic Four appear	$2.00	$6.00	$12.00	£0.55	£1.75	£3.50
259 LD in the U.K. Hobgoblin appears, old costume returns alternating with black costume, Fantastic Four appear; origin of Mary Jane Watson told	$4.15	$12.50	$25.00	£0.80	£2.50	£5.00
260 (Jan 1985), Hobgoblin appears	$2.00	$6.00	$12.00	£0.65	£2.00	£4.00
261 Hobgoblin appears	$2.00	$6.00	$12.00	£0.65	£2.00	£4.00
262 photo cover	$1.65	$5.00	$10.00	£0.40	£1.25	£2.50
263-264	$1.00	$3.00	$6.00	£0.30	£1.00	£2.00
265 1st appearance Silver Sable	$1.65	$5.00	$10.00	£0.65	£2.00	£4.00
265 2nd printing, ND (Jun 1992) - metallic ink cover	$0.40	$1.20	$2.00	£0.25	£0.75	£1.25
266 Peter David's 1st published script for Marvel though the script for Spectacular Spiderman #103 was commissioned earlier	$0.80	$2.50	$5.00	£0.30	£1.00	£2.00
267 Human Torch appears	$0.80	$2.50	$5.00	£0.30	£1.00	£2.00
268 Secret Wars X-over, John Byrne cover	$0.80	$2.50	$5.00	£0.30	£1.00	£2.00
269 LD in the U.K. Firelord appears	$0.80	$2.50	$5.00	£0.35	£1.10	£2.25
270 LD in the U.K. Avengers appear	$0.80	$2.50	$5.00	£0.35	£1.10	£2.25
271	$0.80	$2.50	$5.00	£0.30	£1.00	£2.00
272 (Jan 1986)	$0.80	$2.50	$5.00	£0.30	£1.00	£2.00
273 LD in the U.K. Secret Wars X-over; alien black costume appears	$0.80	$2.50	$5.00	£0.35	£1.10	£2.25
274 Secret Wars X-over, Zarathos (The Spirit of Vengeance) appears	$0.80	$2.50	$5.00	£0.30	£1.00	£2.00
275 LD in the U.K. DS, Hobgoblin appears, Spiderman origin reprinted (Steve Ditko art)	$2.50	$7.50	$15.00	£0.65	£2.00	£4.00
276 LD in the U.K. Hobgoblin appears	$2.00	$6.00	$12.00	£0.50	£1.50	£3.00
277 Daredevil, Kingpin appear, Charles Vess art	$0.80	$2.50	$5.00	£0.30	£1.00	£2.00
278 Hobgoblin appears on last page	$0.80	$2.50	$5.00	£0.30	£1.00	£2.00

VERY GENERAL PERCENTAGE CONVERSION CHART WHICH MAY BE USED TO CALCULATE LOW AND INBETWEEN GRADES:

Issue / Description	$Good	$Fine	$N.Mint	£Good	£Fine	£N.Mint
279 Silver Sable vs. Jack O' Lantern	$0.80	$2.50	$5.00	£0.30	£1.00	£2.00
280 Silver Sable appears	$0.80	$2.50	$5.00	£0.30	£1.00	£2.00
281 Hobgoblin vs. Jack O'Lantern, Silver Sable appears	$2.00	$6.00	$12.00	£0.50	£1.50	£3.00
282 LD in the U.K. X-Factor appear	$0.80	$2.50	$5.00	£0.40	£1.25	£2.50
283 LD in the U.K. Hobgoblin appears	$1.65	$5.00	$10.00	£0.40	£1.25	£2.50
284 (Jan 1987), Punisher cameo, Hobgoblin appears, Daredevil appears, Gang War story begins	$1.65	$5.00	$10.00	£0.55	£1.75	£3.50
285 Punisher, Hobgoblin appear, Zeck art	$2.00	$6.00	$12.00	£0.80	£2.50	£5.00
286 Hobgoblin cameo	$1.15	$3.50	$7.00	£0.40	£1.25	£2.50
287 Spiderman vs. Daredevil, Hobgoblin cameo, Falcon appears; 1st Erik Larsen art on Spiderman	$1.00	$3.00	$6.00	£0.50	£1.50	£3.00
288 LD in the U.K. Gang War ends, Hobgoblin appears, Punisher appears (2 panels), Black Cat and Daredevil appear	$1.65	$5.00	$10.00	£0.50	£1.50	£3.00
289 DS, Hobgoblin's identity revealed, X-over with Web of Spiderman #30, death of Ned Leeds (original Hobgoblin), Philip Macendale (Jack O'Lantern) becomes Hobgoblin II, Wolverine cameo	$4.15	$12.50	$25.00	£1.15	£3.50	£7.00
290 LD in the U.K. Peter Parker proposes marriage to Mary J. Watson	$0.80	$2.50	$5.00	£0.30	£1.00	£2.00
291-292 LD in the U.K.	$0.80	$2.50	$5.00	£0.30	£1.00	£2.00
293-294 Kraven Saga, Zeck art	$1.30	$4.00	$8.00	£0.55	£1.75	£3.50
295 LD in the U.K. Sienkiewicz cover	$1.00	$3.00	$6.00	£0.30	£1.00	£2.00
296 LD in the U.K. (Jan 1988)	$1.00	$3.00	$6.00	£0.30	£1.00	£2.00
297 LD in the U.K.	$1.00	$3.00	$6.00	£0.30	£1.00	£2.00
298 LD in the U.K. 1st Todd McFarlane art, 1st Venom without costume (cameo)	$6.50	$20.00	$40.00	£2.50	£7.50	£15.00
299 LD in the U.K. Todd McFarlane art, 1st appearance Venom (cameo)	$4.55	$13.50	$27.50	£1.65	£5.00	£10.00
300 LD in the U.K. DS, Todd McFarlane art, Spiderman fully returns to old costume, 1st full appearance Venom, Thing appears; 25th anniversary issue	$12.50	$38.00	$75.00	£3.30	£10.00	£20.00
301-302 LD in the U.K. Todd McFarlane art, Silver Sable appears	$2.50	$7.50	$15.00	£1.00	£3.00	£6.00
303 LD in the U.K. Todd McFarlane art, Silver Sable and Sandman appear	$2.50	$7.50	$15.00	£1.00	£3.00	£6.00
304-305 Todd McFarlane art; bi-weekly	$2.00	$6.00	$12.00	£0.65	£2.00	£4.00
306 Todd McFarlane art, Black Cat appears; bi-weekly - cover based on Action Comics #1	$2.00	$6.00	$12.00	£0.65	£2.00	£4.00
307 Todd McFarlane art, origin Chameleon retold; bi-weekly	$2.00	$6.00	$12.00	£0.65	£2.00	£4.00
308-309 Todd McFarlane art; bi-weekly	$2.00	$6.00	$12.00	£0.65	£2.00	£4.00
310 Todd McFarlane art	$2.00	$6.00	$12.00	£0.65	£2.00	£4.00
311 (Jan 1989), Todd McFarlane art, Mysterio appears, Inferno tie-in	$2.00	$6.00	$12.00	£0.65	£2.00	£4.00
312 LD in the U.K. Todd McFarlane art, Hobgoblin II vs. Green Goblin II, Inferno tie-in	$4.15	$12.50	$25.00	£1.00	£3.00	£6.00
313 Todd McFarlane art, Lizard appears, Inferno tie-in	$2.00	$6.00	$12.00	£0.65	£2.00	£4.00
314 Todd McFarlane art	$2.00	$6.00	$12.00	£0.65	£2.00	£4.00
315-316 Todd McFarlane art, Venom appears	$3.30	$10.00	$20.00	£0.80	£2.50	£5.00
317 Todd McFarlane art, Thing appears, Venom appears	$3.30	$10.00	$20.00	£0.80	£2.50	£5.00
318 Todd McFarlane art	$1.30	$4.00	$8.00	£0.55	£1.75	£3.50
319 Todd McFarlane art; bi-weekly	$1.30	$4.00	$8.00	£0.55	£1.75	£3.50
320-321 Silver Sable appears, Todd McFarlane art; bi-weekly	$1.30	$4.00	$8.00	£0.55	£1.75	£3.50
322 Silver Sable appears, Sabretooth appears (unidentified), Todd McFarlane art; bi-weekly	$1.30	$4.00	$8.00	£0.55	£1.75	£3.50
323 Silver Sable appears, Todd McFarlane art	$1.30	$4.00	$8.00	£0.55	£1.75	£3.50
324 LD in the U.K. Sabretooth appears; Silver Sable appears, Erik Larsen art, Todd McFarlane cover, Acts of Vengeance tie-in	$2.50	$7.50	$15.00	£0.80	£2.50	£5.00
325 Silver Sable appears, Todd McFarlane art	$1.30	$4.00	$8.00	£0.55	£1.75	£3.50
326 Acts of Vengeance tie-in	$0.75	$2.25	$4.50	£0.25	£0.75	£1.50
327 Acts of Vengeance tie-in, Erik Larsen art, Magneto appears, Cosmic Spiderman (see Spectacular Spiderman #158)	$0.75	$2.25	$4.50	£0.25	£0.75	£1.50
328 LD in the U.K. (Jan 1990), Acts of Vengeance tie-in, last Todd McFarlane art, Hulk vs. Cosmic Spiderman (temporarily stronger than Hulk)	$2.00	$6.00	$12.00	£0.65	£2.00	£4.00
329 Erik Larsen art run begins, Acts of Vengeance tie-in, Cosmic Spiderman	$0.75	$2.25	$4.50	£0.25	£0.75	£1.50
330 Punisher appears (continued in Punisher War Journal #14), Larsen art	$0.75	$2.25	$4.50	£0.25	£0.75	£1.50
331 Punisher appears (continued in Punisher War Journal #15), Larsen art	$0.75	$2.25	$4.50	£0.25	£0.75	£1.50
332-333 Venom appears, Larsen art	$2.00	$6.00	$12.00	£0.25	£0.85	£1.75
334-336 Sinister Six, Larsen art	$0.50	$1.50	$3.00	£0.20	£0.60	£1.25
337 Sinister Six, Hobgoblin appears, Larsen art	$0.50	$1.50	$3.00	£0.20	£0.60	£1.25
338 Sinister Six, Larsen art; Hobgoblin appears	$0.50	$1.50	$3.00	£0.20	£0.60	£1.25
339 Sinister Six, Larsen art	$0.50	$1.50	$3.00	£0.20	£0.60	£1.25
340-342 Larsen art	$0.50	$1.50	$3.00	£0.20	£0.60	£1.25
343 (Jan 1991), Larsen art, 1st appearance Cardiac (cameo)	$0.50	$1.50	$3.00	£0.20	£0.60	£1.25
344 LD in the U.K. 1st full appearance Cardiac, 1st appearance (cameo) Cletus Kasady (later Carnage), Larsen art	$1.00	$3.00	$6.00	£0.30	£1.00	£2.00
345 LD in the U.K. Venom appears, 1st full appearance Cletus Kasady, Larsen art	$2.50	$7.50	$15.00	£0.80	£2.50	£5.00
346 ND scarce in the U.K. Venom appears, Larsen art	$1.65	$5.00	$10.00	£0.55	£1.75	£3.50
347 ND Venom appears, Larsen art	$1.65	$5.00	$10.00	£0.40	£1.25	£2.50
348 ND The Avengers guest-star, Larsen art	$0.50	$1.50	$3.00	£0.20	£0.60	£1.25
349 ND Black Fox appears, Larsen art	$0.50	$1.50	$3.00	£0.20	£0.60	£1.25
350 ND DS Black Fox appears, last Larsen art, origin retold; pin-up gallery included	$0.55	$1.75	$3.50	£0.30	£1.00	£2.00
351 ND Mark Bagley art begins, Nova appears	$0.50	$1.50	$2.50	£0.25	£0.75	£1.25
352 ND New Warriors appear, Mark Bagley art	$0.50	$1.50	$2.50	£0.25	£0.75	£1.25
353 ND Round Robin part 1, Darkhawk, Punisher appear, Mark Bagley art, bi-weekly issue	$0.50	$1.50	$2.50	£0.25	£0.75	£1.25
354 ND Round Robin story, Darkhawk, Punisher, Nova appear, Mark Bagley art, bi-weekly issue	$0.50	$1.50	$2.50	£0.25	£0.75	£1.25
355 ND Round Robin story, Darkhawk, Puisher, Nova, Moon Knight appear, Mark Bagley art, bi-weekly issue	$0.50	$1.50	$2.50	£0.25	£0.75	£1.25
356 ND Round Robin story, Daredevil, Punisher, Moon Knight, Nova appear, Mark Bagley art, bi-weekly issue	$0.50	$1.50	$2.50	£0.25	£0.75	£1.25
357 ND (Jan 1992), Round Robin story, Punisher, Darkhawk, Moon Knight appear, Mark Bagley art, bi-weekly issue	$0.50	$1.50	$2.50	£0.25	£0.75	£1.25
358 ND Round Robin story concludes, Punisher, Darkhawk, Moon Knight, Nova, Night Thrasher appear, Mark Bagley art, gatefold cover, bi-weekly issue	$0.50	$1.50	$2.50	£0.25	£0.75	£1.25
359 ND $1.25 cover begins, Cardiac appears, Carnage cameo	$0.70	$2.10	$3.50	£0.30	£0.90	£1.50
360 ND fuller appearance of Carnage, Cardiac appears	$2.00	$6.00	$10.00	£0.40	£1.20	£2.00
361 ND 1st full appearance of Carnage	$4.40	$13.00	$22.00	£1.20	£3.60	£6.00
361 2nd printing, ND silver ink cover	$0.40	$1.20	$2.00	£0.25	£0.75	£1.25
362 ND Carnage, Venom and Human Torch appear	$2.00	$6.00	$10.00	£0.70	£2.10	£3.50
362 2nd printing, ND silver ink cover	$0.30	$0.90	$1.50	£0.20	£0.60	£1.00
363 ND Spiderman and Venom vs. Carnage, Mr. Fantastic and Human Torch appear	$2.00	$6.00	$10.00	£0.70	£2.10	£3.50
364 ND	$0.40	$1.20	$2.00	£0.25	£0.75	£1.25
365 ND 80pgs, 30th anniversary issue, origin retold, silver hologram cover, previews Spider 2099 (1st appearance), poster by John Romita Jnr, contributions from Stan Lee and Steve Ditko	$1.20	$3.60	$6.00	£0.60	£1.80	£3.00
365 2nd printing, ND gold hologram cover	$0.80	$2.40	$4.00	£0.50	£1.50	£2.50
366-367 ND Red Skull appears	$0.30	$0.90	$1.50	£0.20	£0.60	£1.00
368-370 ND Invasion of the Spider Slayers, bi-weekly	$0.30	$0.90	$1.50	£0.20	£0.60	£1.00
371 ND Invasion of the Spider Slayers, bi-weekly	$0.30	$0.90	$1.50	£0.15	£0.45	£0.75
372 ND (Jan 1993), Invasion of the Spider Slayers, bi-weekly	$0.30	$0.90	$1.50	£0.15	£0.45	£0.75
373 ND Invasion of the Spider Slayers, bi-weekly; Venom back-up story	$0.30	$0.90	$1.50	£0.15	£0.45	£0.75
374 ND Venom appears	$0.30	$0.90	$1.50	£0.15	£0.45	£0.75
375 ND 64pgs, 30th anniversary issue, holo-grafix metallic ink cover, Spiderman vs. Venom	$1.20	$3.60	$6.00	£0.50	£1.50	£2.50
376-377 ND Cardiac appears	$0.30	$0.90	$1.50	£0.15	£0.45	£0.75
378 ND Maximum Carnage part 3, continued in Spiderman #35	$0.30	$0.90	$1.50	£0.15	£0.45	£0.75
379 ND Maximum Carnage part 7, continued in Spiderman #36	$0.30	$0.90	$1.50	£0.15	£0.45	£0.75

MINT = 100% / NEAR MINT (inc. +/-) = 90–99% / VERY FINE (inc. +/-) = 75–89% / FINE (inc. +/-) = 55–74%
VERY GOOD (inc. +/-) = 35–54% / GOOD (inc. +/-) = 15–34% / FAIR = 5–14% / POOR = 1–4%

205

	$Good	$Fine	$N.Mint	£Good	£Fine	£N.Mint
Left column						

380 ND Maximum Carnage part 11 continued in Spiderman #37

| | $0.30 | $0.90 | $1.50 | £0.15 | £0.45 | £0.75 |

381-382 ND Hulk guest-stars, Doc Samson appears

| | $0.30 | $0.90 | $1.50 | £0.15 | £0.45 | £0.75 |

383-384 ND

| | $0.30 | $0.90 | $1.50 | £0.15 | £0.45 | £0.75 |

385 ND (Jan 1994) $0.30 $0.90 $1.50 £0.15 £0.45 £0.75

386 ND Lifetheft story

| | $0.30 | $0.90 | $1.50 | £0.15 | £0.45 | £0.75 |

387 ND Lifetheft story, reveals his identity to parents

| | $0.30 | $0.90 | $1.50 | £0.15 | £0.45 | £0.75 |

388 ND 64pgs, Collector's Edition with red foil cover; Lifetheft story; the true fate of Spiderman's parents revealed

| | $0.45 | $1.35 | $2.25 | £0.40 | £1.20 | £2.00 |

388 Newstand edition, ND 64pgs, without cover enhancement; Lifetheft story; the true fate of Spiderman's parents revealed

| | $0.45 | $1.35 | $2.25 | £0.30 | £0.90 | £1.50 |

389 ND Pursuit part 4 (conclusion); Spiderman vs. Chameleon; with free Spiderman's Amazing Powers card sheet

| | $0.30 | $0.90 | $1.50 | £0.15 | £0.45 | £0.75 |

390 ND Shriek and Carrion appear

| | $0.30 | $0.90 | $1.50 | £0.15 | £0.45 | £0.75 |

390 ND Collector's Edition, pre-bagged with 16pg preview and animation cel from Spiderman TV series; metallic ink cover

| | $0.60 | $1.80 | $3.00 | £0.40 | £1.20 | £2.00 |

391 ND

| | $0.30 | $0.90 | $1.50 | £0.15 | £0.45 | £0.75 |

392 ND cover based on issue #50 (a classic!)

| | $0.30 | $0.90 | $1.50 | £0.15 | £0.45 | £0.75 |

393 ND

| | $0.30 | $0.90 | $1.50 | £0.15 | £0.45 | £0.75 |

394 ND Power and Responsibility part 2

| | $0.30 | $0.90 | $1.50 | £0.15 | £0.45 | £0.75 |

394 ND 48pgs, Power and Responsibility part 2, foil stamped cover; incorporates 16pg flip-book with second foil stamped cover; continued in Spiderman #51

| | $0.80 | $2.40 | $4.00 | £0.40 | £1.20 | £2.00 |

395 ND Puma appears

| | $0.30 | $0.90 | $1.50 | £0.20 | £0.60 | £1.00 |

396 ND Spiderman and Daredevil vs. The Vulture and The Owl (see Spectacular Spiderman #219)

| | $0.30 | $0.90 | $1.50 | £0.20 | £0.60 | £1.00 |

397 ND (Jan 1995), Web of Death part 1, continued in Spectacular Spiderman #220; Dr. Octopus appears

| | $0.45 | $1.35 | $2.25 | £0.30 | £0.90 | £1.50 |

398 ND Web of Death part 3, continued in Spectacular Spiderman #221; Dr. Octopus appears

| | $0.30 | $0.90 | $1.50 | £0.20 | £0.60 | £1.00 |

399 ND The Jackal appears

| | $0.30 | $0.90 | $1.50 | £0.20 | £0.60 | £1.00 |

400 ND 64pgs, the death of Aunt May

| | $0.60 | $1.80 | $3.00 | £0.40 | £1.20 | £2.00 |

400 ND 64pgs, Enhanced Edition - die-cut multi-level debossed cover

| | $1.20 | $3.60 | $6.00 | £0.60 | £1.80 | £3.00 |

400 ND white cover variant Edition

| | $3.50 | $10.50 | $17.50 | £2.50 | £7.50 | £12.50 |

401 ND The Mark of Kaine part 2, continued in Spiderman #58

| | $0.30 | $0.90 | $1.50 | £0.20 | £0.60 | £1.00 |

402 ND continued in Spiderman #59

| | $0.30 | $0.90 | $1.50 | £0.20 | £0.60 | £1.00 |

403 ND The Trial of Peter Parker part 2, continued in Spiderman #60; Carnage appears

| | $0.30 | $0.90 | $1.50 | £0.20 | £0.60 | £1.00 |

404 ND Maximum Clonage part 3, continued in Spiderman #61; Spiderman vs. The Scarlet Spider

| | $0.30 | $0.90 | $1.50 | £0.20 | £0.60 | £1.00 |

405 ND Exiled part 2, continued in Spiderman #62

| | $0.30 | $0.90 | $1.50 | £0.20 | £0.60 | £1.00 |

406 ND The Great Responsibility part 1, continued in Spiderman #63; 1st new Dr. Octopus; Angel Medina guest art

| | $0.30 | $0.90 | $1.50 | £0.20 | £0.60 | £1.00 |

407 ND The Return of Spiderman part 2, Spiderman vs. Sandman, Human Torch appears; continued Spiderman #64

| | $0.30 | $0.90 | $1.50 | £0.20 | £0.60 | £1.00 |

408 ND Media Blizzard part 2, continued in Spiderman #65

| | $0.30 | $0.90 | $1.50 | £0.20 | £0.60 | £1.00 |

409 ND The Return of Kaine part 3, continued in Spiderman #66

| | $0.30 | $0.90 | $1.50 | £0.20 | £0.60 | £1.00 |

Title Value: $5409.10 $16261.45 $48698.75 £2932.45 £8807.80 £26400.00

Sensational Spiderman (1988)
Trade paperback reprints Annual #14, #15 (Miller art) plus issue #8 back-up featuring Human Torch (Ditko art) — £0.80 £2.40 £4.00

Spiderman Hardcover (Jun 1989), reprints 6 part Kraven Saga, Mike Zeck art — £2.40 £7.20 £12.00

Alien Costume
Trade paperback reprints issues #252-259 — £1.60 £4.80 £8.00
(2nd printing - Aug 1990) — £1.50 £4.50 £7.50
(3rd printing - Dec 1992) — £1.50 £4.50 £7.50

Nothing Can Stop The Juggernaut (Sep 1989)
Trade paperback [Headlined: The Sensational Spiderman]
reprints issues #229,#230 — £0.50 £1.50 £2.50
(2nd printing - Oct 1990) — £0.45 £1.35 £2.25

Spiderman vs. Venom
Trade paperback
reprints issues #298 & #299 as 1 pagers plus #300, #315-317 — £1.00 £3.00 £5.00

Spiderman: Kraven's Last Hunt (Sep 1990)
Trade paperback reprints Kraven Saga, Mike Zeck art — £1.00 £3.00 £5.00
(2nd printing - Dec 1992) — £0.80 £2.40 £4.00

The Death of Jean DeWolff
Trade paperback, 96pgs, reprints 4 part story — £1.00 £3.00 £5.00

Spiderman's Wedding (Nov 1991)
Trade paperback

reprints lead-up to wedding plus syndicated newspaper material — £1.50 £4.50 £7.50

Spiderman: Assassination Plot
Trade paperback (Jul 1992) reprints Amazing Spiderman #320-325 — £2.00 £6.00 £10.00
(2nd print - Jun 1993) — £1.90 £5.70 £9.50

Spiderman: The Cosmic Adventures
Trade paperback (Mar 1993)
196pgs, reprints Spectacular Spiderman #158-#160, Web of Spiderman #59-#61, Amazing Spiderman #327-#329, Ron Lim cover — £2.50 £7.50 £12.50

Spiderman: Venom Returns (May 1993)
Trade paperback
reprints Amazing Spiderman #331-333, #344-347 — £1.60 £4.80 £8.00

Spiderman: Origin of Hobgoblin (Jul 1993)
Trade paperback
reprints Amazing Spiderman #238, 239, 244, 245, 249-251 — £1.80 £5.40 £9.00

Spiderman: Carnage (Aug 1993)
Trade paperback
reprints Amazing Spiderman #361-363 — £0.90 £2.70 £4.50

The Complete Frank Miller Spiderman (Jun 1994)
Hardback with embossed dust-wrapper,
reprints Annual #14,15 plus Marvel Team Up #100, Annual #4 and Spectacular Spiderman #27 and 28 — £4.00 £12.00 £20.00

Spiderman: Round Robin (Jul 1994)
Trade paperback, reprints — £2.00 £6.00 £10.00

Spiderman: Maximum Carnage (Oct 1994)
Trade paperback
336pgs, reprints Maximum Carnage storyline — £3.30 £9.90 £16.50

Spiderman: Return of the Sinister Six (Nov 1994)
Trade paperback reprints Spiderman #334-339 — £2.00 £6.00 £10.00

Very Best of Spiderman (Dec 1994)
Trade paperback 176pgs, classic reprints — £2.00 £6.00 £10.00

Spiderman: Revenge of the Sinister Six (Jan 1995)
reprints Spiderman #18-23 with Erik Larsen art — £2.00 £6.00 £10.00

Spiderman: Invasion of the Spider-Slayers (Apr 1995)
Trade paperback 144pgs, reprints issues #368-373 — £2.00 £6.00 £10.00

Spiderman: Carnage (Apr 1995)
80pgs Bookshelf Edition, reprints issues #361-363 — £0.90 £2.70 £4.50

Spiderman: Clone Genesis (Aug 1995)
Trade paperback
reprints the Clone Saga from Spiderman #141-151 — £2.30 £6.90 £11.50

Spiderman vs. Dr. Doom (Sep 1995)
reprints Amazing Spiderman #349/350 with new cover — £0.90 £2.70 £4.50

Spiderman vs. Green Goblin (Oct 1995)
Trade paperback reprints classic encounters — £2.00 £6.00 £10.00

Spiderman Premiere (Nov 1995)
boxed set of Web of Spiderman #117, Spiderman #51, Amazing Spiderman #394, Spectacular Spiderman #217 that make up the "Power and Responsibility" story — £1.50 £4.50 £7.50

AMAZING SPIDERMAN, THE ANNUAL

Marvel Comics Group; 1 1964-9 1973; 10 Jun 1976-present

1 scarce in the U.K. 72pgs, origin retold, 1st appearance Sinister Six; Steve Ditko art

| | $62.50 | $187.50 | $500.00 | £35.00 | £105.00 | £280.00 |

[Scarce in high grade - Very Fine+ or better]

2 72pgs, Dr. Strange appears; reprints from issues #1,#2 and #5; Steve Ditko art

| | $36.00 | $105.00 | $250.00 | £17.50 | £52.50 | £125.00 |

3 72pgs, Avengers vs. Hulk

| | $13.50 | $41.00 | $81.00 | £7.00 | £21.00 | £42.00 |

4 72pgs, Spiderman vs. Human Torch (new 40pg story)

| | $12.50 | $38.00 | $75.00 | £6.00 | £18.00 | £36.00 |

5 72pgs, Peter Parker's parents appear, Red Skull appears (see 30th anniversay issues of Spiderman), Fantastic Four appear

| | $13.50 | $41.00 | $81.00 | £7.00 | £21.00 | £42.00 |

6 68pgs, Sinister Six appear (story reprinted from Annual #1)

| | $6.00 | $18.00 | $36.00 | £3.00 | £9.00 | £18.00 |

7 68pgs, reprints Spiderman #1, #6 (Lizard)

| | $5.00 | $15.00 | $30.00 | £2.50 | £7.50 | £15.00 |

8 ND scarce in the U.K. 68pgs

| | $5.00 | $15.00 | $30.00 | £2.50 | £7.50 | £15.00 |

9 ND very scarce in the U.K. 52pgs, reprints edited version of story from Spectacular Spiderman Magazine #2 with Green Goblin (hard to find without inking stains around edges)

| | $5.00 | $15.00 | $30.00 | £3.50 | £10.50 | £21.00 |

10 ND scarce in the U.K. 52pgs

| | $2.00 | $6.00 | $12.00 | £1.25 | £3.75 | £7.50 |

11 ND 52pgs, John Romita Jnr. art (very early - 1st?)

| | $1.80 | $5.25 | $9.00 | £1.00 | £3.00 | £5.00 |

12 ND 52pgs, John Byrne cover

| | $1.80 | $5.25 | $9.00 | £0.80 | £2.40 | £4.00 |

13 ND 52pgs, John Byrne art

| | $1.80 | $5.25 | $9.00 | £1.00 | £3.00 | £5.00 |

14 ND 52pgs, Frank Miller art (Ditkoesque Dr. Strange)

| | $1.80 | $5.25 | $9.00 | £1.00 | £3.00 | £5.00 |

15 ND 52pgs, Frank Miller art, Dr. Octopus/Punisher appear

| | $4.00 | $12.00 | $20.00 | £1.50 | £4.50 | £7.50 |

16 ND 52pgs, 1st appearance new Captain Marvel (female)

| | $1.60 | $4.80 | $8.00 | £0.60 | £1.80 | £3.00 |

17-19 ND $1.60 $4.80 $8.00 £0.50 £1.50 £2.50

20 scarce in the U.K. 1st appearance Iron Man of 2020

| | $1.60 | $4.80 | $8.00 | £0.60 | £1.80 | £3.00 |

21 ND Peter Parker, Mary Jane wed, costume cover

| | $1.80 | $5.25 | $9.00 | £0.60 | £1.80 | £3.00 |

21 ND Peter Parker, Mary Jane wed, plain clothes cover

TRADE PAPERBACKS, GRAPHIC NOVELS AND OTHER COLLECTIONS ARE PRICED IN POUNDS STERLING ONLY. CONVERT AT 1.5 FOR DOLLARS.

	$Good	$Fine	$N.Mint	£Good	£Fine	£N.Mint
	$1.80	$5.25	$9.00	£0.60	£1.80	£3.00
22 ND 64pgs, squarebound, Evolutionary War, Ron Lim art on back-up	$1.60	$4.80	$8.00	£0.40	£1.20	£2.00
23 ND squarebound, Atlantis Attacks part 4, She-Hulk appears, Rob Liefeld art	$1.60	$4.80	$8.00	£0.50	£1.50	£2.50
24 ND squarebound, Spiderman's Totally Tiny Adventure part 1, continues in Spectacular Spiderman Annual #10, Sandman back-up by Zeck	$1.00	$3.00	$5.00	£0.35	£1.05	£1.75
25 ND The Vibranium Vendetta part 1, continued in Spectacular Spiderman Annual #11; 1st solo Venom story	$2.40	$7.00	$12.00	£0.80	£2.40	£4.00
26 ND The Hero Killers part 1, New Warriors and Venom appear, continued in Spectacular Spiderman Annual #12	$1.60	$4.80	$8.00	£0.35	£1.05	£1.75
27 ND pre-bagged with trading card; Tom Lyle art	$0.60	$1.80	$3.00	£0.40	£1.20	£2.00
28 ND Spiderman vs. Carnage	$0.60	$1.80	$3.00	£0.40	£1.20	£2.00
Title Value:	$193.20	$577.00	$1286.00	£97.65	£292.95	£663.50

Note: #3-8 titled "Special". #9 titled "King Size". #1-3 have back-up reprints. #6-8, 12 are all reprint.

Note also that Annual 1 & 2 occasionally turn up with blank back and inside covers (see Fantastic Four Annuals #1-3, Sgt. Fury Annual #1, Strange Tales Annual #2). These were originally subscription copies sent over to this country as left-overs. They are very scarce and with their white back covers they show soiling and wear that much more easily. They are very rare in near mint condition.

AMAZING WORLD OF DC COMICS, THE
DC Comics; 1 Jul/Aug 1974-17 Apr 1978

	$Good	$Fine	$N.Mint	£Good	£Fine	£N.Mint
1 ND 48pgs, Joe Kubert interview, unpublished Jack Kirby story	$1.50	$4.50	$7.50	£1.00	£3.00	£5.00
2 ND 48pgs, Fifties issue	$1.40	$4.20	$7.00	£0.90	£2.70	£4.50
3 ND 48pgs, Julius Schwartz issue, unpublished Golden Age Green Lantern story	$1.40	$4.20	$7.00	£0.90	£2.70	£4.50
4 ND 48pgs, Batman issue, Jerry Robinson interview	$1.80	$5.25	$9.00	£1.20	£3.60	£6.00
5 ND 48pgs, Sheldon Mayer/Golden Age issue	$1.20	$3.60	$6.00	£0.80	£2.40	£4.00
6 ND 48pgs	$1.20	$3.60	$6.00	£0.80	£2.40	£4.00
7 ND 48pgs, Superman issue, Mort Weisinger/Curt Swan interviews	$1.50	$4.50	$7.50	£1.00	£3.00	£5.00
8 ND 48pgs, Carmine Infantino issue	$1.20	$3.60	$6.00	£0.80	£2.40	£4.00
9 ND 48pgs, Legion of Super-Heroes issue, Legion check-list	$1.80	$5.25	$9.00	£1.20	£3.60	£6.00
10 ND 48pgs, feature on Showcase title	$1.20	$3.60	$6.00	£0.80	£2.40	£4.00
11 ND 48pgs, Super-Villain issue	$1.20	$3.60	$6.00	£0.80	£2.40	£4.00
12 ND 48pgs, Sci-Fi issue, Mike Grell feature	$1.20	$3.60	$6.00	£0.80	£2.40	£4.00
13 ND 48pgs, Humour issue, Wonder Woman feature	$1.20	$3.60	$6.00	£0.80	£2.40	£4.00
14 ND 48pgs, Justice League of America issue	$1.80	$5.25	$9.00	£1.20	£3.60	£6.00
15 ND 48pgs, Wonder Woman issue	$1.20	$3.60	$6.00	£0.80	£2.40	£4.00
16 ND 48pgs, Golden Age issue, Silver Age comics feature	$1.50	$4.50	$7.50	£1.00	£3.00	£5.00
17 ND 48pgs, Shazam issue	$1.20	$3.60	$6.00	£0.80	£2.40	£4.00
Title Value:	$23.50	$70.05	$117.50	£15.60	£46.80	£78.00

Note: magazine format professional "fanzine" published by DC Comics. Each issue carries check-list/covers of DC comics to be published that month.

AMAZON WARRIORS
AC Comics,OS; 1 1989

	$Good	$Fine	$N.Mint	£Good	£Fine	£N.Mint
1 ND black and white	$0.45	$1.35	$2.25	£0.30	£0.90	£1.50
Title Value:	$0.45	$1.35	$2.25	£0.30	£0.90	£1.50

AMAZON, THE
Comico,MS; 1 Mar 1989-3 May 1989

	$Good	$Fine	$N.Mint	£Good	£Fine	£N.Mint
1-3 ND Tim Sale art, colour	$0.40	$1.20	$2.00	£0.25	£0.75	£1.25
Title Value:	$1.20	$3.60	$6.00	£0.75	£2.25	£3.75

AMBUSH BUG
DC Comics,MS; 1 Jun 1985-4 Sep 1985

	$Good	$Fine	$N.Mint	£Good	£Fine	£N.Mint
1-4 Keith Giffen art	$0.25	$0.75	$1.25	£0.15	£0.45	£0.75
Title Value:	$1.00	$3.00	$5.00	£0.60	£1.80	£3.00

AMBUSH BUG NOTHING SPECIAL
DC Comics,OS; 1 Sep 1992

	$Good	$Fine	$N.Mint	£Good	£Fine	£N.Mint
1 64pgs, Lobo, Death, Sandman, Aquaman appear	$0.45	$1.35	$2.25	£0.30	£0.90	£1.50
Title Value:	$0.45	$1.35	$2.25	£0.30	£0.90	£1.50

AMBUSH BUG STOCKING STUFFER
DC Comics,OS; nn Feb 1986

	$Good	$Fine	$N.Mint	£Good	£Fine	£N.Mint
nn 48pgs, Giffen art; Joker cameo	$0.25	$0.75	$1.25	£0.15	£0.45	£0.75
Title Value:	$0.25	$0.75	$1.25	£0.15	£0.45	£0.75

AMBUSH BUG, SON OF
DC Comics,MS; 1 Jul 1986-2 Dec 1986

	$Good	$Fine	$N.Mint	£Good	£Fine	£N.Mint
1-6 Giffen art	$0.15	$0.45	$0.75	£0.10	£0.35	£0.60
Title Value:	$0.90	$2.70	$4.50	£0.60	£2.10	£3.60

AMERICA VERSUS THE JUSTICE SOCIETY
DC Comics,MS; 1 Jan 1985-4 Apr 1985

	$Good	$Fine	$N.Mint	£Good	£Fine	£N.Mint
1-4 ND 48pgs	$0.45	$1.35	$2.25	£0.30	£0.90	£1.50
Title Value:	$1.80	$5.40	$9.00	£1.20	£3.60	£6.00

AMERICA'S BEST TV COMICS
ABC; nn 1967

	$Good	$Fine	$N.Mint	£Good	£Fine	£N.Mint
nn ND scarce in the U.K. 64pgs, squarebound; promotion for cartoon show, reprints F.F. #19, Spiderman #51	$12.00	$36.00	$60.00	£8.00	£24.00	£40.00
Title Value:	$12.00	$36.00	$60.00	£8.00	£24.00	£40.00

AMERICAN FLAGG!
First; 1 Oct 1983-50 Mar 1988

	$Good	$Fine	$N.Mint	£Good	£Fine	£N.Mint
1 ND Chaykin story/art begins, ends #26	$1.20	$3.60	$6.00	£0.80	£2.40	£4.00
2-3 ND	$0.75	$2.25	$3.75	£0.50	£1.50	£2.50
4-5 ND	$0.60	$1.80	$3.00	£0.40	£1.20	£2.00
6-10 ND	$0.45	$1.35	$2.25	£0.30	£0.90	£1.50
11-18 ND	$0.40	$1.20	$2.00	£0.25	£0.75	£1.25
19 ND scarce in the U.K.	$1.40	$4.20	$7.00	£0.90	£2.70	£4.50
20 ND	$0.40	$1.20	$2.00	£0.25	£0.75	£1.25
21 ND Alan Moore back-up	$0.55	$1.65	$2.75	£0.35	£1.05	£1.75
22 ND scarce in the U.K. Moore back-up	$0.80	$2.40	$4.00	£0.50	£1.50	£2.50
23-25 ND Moore back-up	$0.55	$1.65	$2.75	£0.35	£1.05	£1.75
26 ND Moore back-up, last Chaykin art	$0.55	$1.65	$2.75	£0.35	£1.05	£1.75
27 ND Alan Moore script, Don Lomax art	$0.55	$1.65	$2.75	£0.35	£1.05	£1.75
28-30 ND Staton art	$0.40	$1.20	$2.00	£0.25	£0.75	£1.25

Amazing Spiderman #161

Amazing Spiderman Annual #9

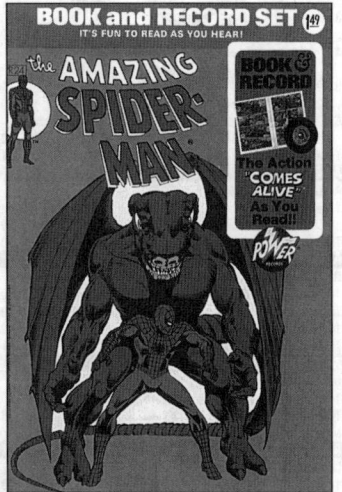

Amazing Spiderman Book and Record Set PR - 24

	$Good	$Fine	$N.Mint	£Good	£Fine	£N.Mint

31-45 ND Badger art
| | $0.40 | $1.20 | $2.00 | £0.25 | £0.75 | £1.25 |

46 ND retrospective/apology issue
| | $0.45 | $1.35 | $2.25 | £0.30 | £0.90 | £1.50 |

47-49 ND Paul Smith art
| | $0.45 | $1.35 | $2.25 | £0.30 | £0.90 | £1.50 |

50 ND Chaykin art | $0.45 | $1.35 | $2.25 | £0.30 | £0.90 | £1.50 |

Title Value: | $24.70 | $74.10 | $123.50 | £15.85 | £47.55 | £79.25 |

Hard Times: Trade paperback,
reprints #1-3, plus new material
| | | | | £1.50 | £4.50 | £7.50 |

Southern Comfort: Trade paperback,
reprints #4-6, plus new material
| | | | | £1.50 | £4.50 | £7.50 |

AMERICAN FLAGG! (2ND SERIES)
First,MS; 1 May 1988-12 Apr 1989
1 ND Chaykin story/breakdowns/part art begins
| | $0.45 | $1.35 | $2.25 | £0.30 | £0.90 | £1.50 |

2-12 ND | $0.35 | $1.05 | $1.75 | £0.25 | £0.75 | £1.25 |

Title Value: | $4.30 | $12.90 | $21.50 | £3.05 | £9.15 | £15.25 |

AMERICAN FLAGG! SPECIAL
First,OS; 1 Nov 1986
1 ND 1st Time 2 | $0.55 | $1.65 | $2.75 | £0.35 | £1.05 | £1.75 |

Title Value: | $0.55 | $1.65 | $2.75 | £0.35 | £1.05 | £1.75 |

AMERICAN FREAK: A TALE OF THE UN-MEN
DC Comics/Vertigo,MS; 1 Feb 1994-5 Jun 1994
1-5 Dave Louapre script, Vince Locke art
| | $0.40 | $1.20 | $2.00 | £0.25 | £0.75 | £1.25 |

Title Value: | $2.00 | $6.00 | $10.00 | £1.25 | £3.75 | £6.25 |

AMERICAN SPLENDOUR SPECIAL: A STEP OUT OF THE NEST
Dark Horse,OS; 1 Aug 1994
1 ND Harvey Pekar script; comic sized version of American Splendour book
| | $0.60 | $1.80 | $3.00 | £0.40 | £1.20 | £2.00 |

Title Value: | $0.60 | $1.80 | $3.00 | £0.40 | £1.20 | £2.00 |

AMERICAN SPLENDOUR: WINDFALL
Dark Horse,MS; 1 Sep 1995-2 Oct 1995
1-2 ND 40pgs, Harvey Pekar script; black and white
| | $0.80 | $2.40 | $4.00 | £0.50 | £1.50 | £2.50 |

Title Value: | $1.60 | $4.80 | $8.00 | £1.00 | £3.00 | £5.00 |

AMERICAN, THE
Dark Horse; 1 Aug 1987-8 1989
1 ND scarce in the U.K. Mark Veheiden script/Chris Warner art begins
| | $1.50 | $4.50 | $7.50 | £1.00 | £3.00 | £5.00 |

2 ND scarce in the U.K.
| | $1.40 | $4.20 | $7.00 | £0.90 | £2.70 | £4.50 |

3 ND | $0.40 | $1.20 | $2.00 | £0.40 | £1.20 | £2.00 |

4-5 ND | $0.35 | $1.05 | $1.75 | £0.30 | £0.90 | £1.50 |

6-8 ND | $0.35 | $1.05 | $1.75 | £0.25 | £0.75 | £1.25 |

Title Value: | $5.05 | $15.15 | $25.25 | £3.65 | £10.95 | £18.25 |

Book 1, reprints #1-4 | | | | £0.80 | £2.40 | £4.00 |

Special (Jul 1990), story continues from issue 8, colour | | | | £0.30 | £0.90 | £1.50 |

AMERICAN: LOST IN AMERICA, THE
Dark Horse,MS; 1 Jul 1992-4 Dec 1992
1 ND Dave Dorman cover
| | $0.45 | $1.35 | $2.25 | £0.30 | £0.90 | £1.50 |

2-3 ND | $0.45 | $1.35 | $2.25 | £0.30 | £0.90 | £1.50 |

4 ND Mike Mignola cover
| | $0.45 | $1.35 | $2.25 | £0.30 | £0.90 | £1.50 |

Title Value: | $1.80 | $5.40 | $9.00 | £1.20 | £3.60 | £6.00 |

AMERICOMICS
AC Comics; 1 Apr 1983-6 Mar 1984
1 ND intro The Shade, Captain Freedom; Perez cover
| | $0.40 | $1.20 | $2.00 | £0.25 | £0.75 | £1.25 |

2 ND intro Messenger (Ordway art - 13pgs) Shade appears; Ordway cover
| | $0.40 | $1.20 | $2.00 | £0.25 | £0.75 | £1.25 |

3 ND Blue Beetle returns; Shade appears
| | $0.40 | $1.20 | $2.00 | £0.25 | £0.75 | £1.25 |

4 ND 1st colour issue, origin Shade, Dragonfly; Ordway cover
| | $0.40 | $1.20 | $2.00 | £0.25 | £0.75 | £1.25 |

5 ND intro Commando D, Captain Freedom appears
| | $0.40 | $1.20 | $2.00 | £0.25 | £0.75 | £1.25 |

6 ND origin Scarlet Scorpion; Steve Lightle and Jerry Ordway cover
| | $0.40 | $1.20 | $2.00 | £0.25 | £0.75 | £1.25 |

Title Value: | $2.40 | $7.20 | $12.00 | £1.50 | £4.50 | £7.50 |

AMERICOMICS SPECIAL
AC Comics; 1 Aug 1983
1 ND Blue Beetle, Question, Nightshade, Captain Atom (Sentinels of Justice)
| | $0.40 | $1.20 | $2.00 | £0.25 | £0.75 | £1.25 |

Title Value: | $0.40 | $1.20 | $2.00 | £0.25 | £0.75 | £1.25 |

AMETHYST
DC Comics; 1 Jan 1985-16 Aug 1986
1-12 | $0.15 | $0.45 | $0.75 | £0.10 | £0.35 | £0.60 |

13 Crisis X-over | $0.25 | $0.75 | $1.25 | £0.15 | £0.45 | £0.75 |

14-16 | $0.15 | $0.45 | $0.75 | £0.10 | £0.35 | £0.60 |

Title Value: | $2.50 | $7.50 | $12.50 | £1.65 | £5.70 | £9.75 |

AMETHYST (LIMITED SERIES)
DC Comics,MS; 1 Nov 1987-4 Feb 1988
1-4 | $0.15 | $0.45 | $0.75 | £0.10 | £0.35 | £0.60 |

Title Value: | $0.60 | $1.80 | $3.00 | £0.40 | £1.40 | £2.40 |

Note: New Format

AMETHYST ANNUAL
DC Comics; 1 Sep 1984
1 48pgs | $0.25 | $0.75 | $1.25 | £0.15 | £0.45 | £0.75 |

Title Value: | $0.25 | $0.75 | $1.25 | £0.15 | £0.45 | £0.75 |

AMETHYST SPECIAL
DC Comics,OS; nn Sep 1986
nn Giffen plot | $0.25 | $0.75 | $1.25 | £0.15 | £0.45 | £0.75 |

Title Value: | $0.25 | $0.75 | $1.25 | £0.15 | £0.45 | £0.75 |

AMETHYST, PRINCESS OF GEMWORLD
DC Comics,MS; 1 May 1983-12 May 1984
1 60¢ cover | $0.15 | $0.45 | $0.75 | £0.10 | £0.35 | £0.60 |

1 ND very scarce in the U.K., 35¢ cover, (distributed to certain U.S. states only)
| | $0.45 | $1.35 | $2.25 | £0.30 | £0.90 | £1.50 |

2 | $0.15 | $0.45 | $0.75 | £0.10 | £0.35 | £0.60 |

2 ND scarce in the U.K., 35¢ cover, (distributed to certain U.S. states only)
| | $0.60 | $1.80 | $3.00 | £0.40 | £1.20 | £2.00 |

3-4 | $0.15 | $0.45 | $0.75 | £0.10 | £0.35 | £0.60 |

5-12 George Perez co-over artist
| | $0.15 | $0.45 | $0.75 | £0.10 | £0.35 | £0.60 |

Title Value: | $2.85 | $8.55 | $14.25 | £1.90 | £6.30 | £10.70 |

AMUSING STORIES
Renegade; 1 Mar 1986-3 1986
1-3 ND | $0.30 | $0.90 | $1.50 | £0.20 | £0.60 | £1.00 |

Title Value: | $0.90 | $2.70 | $4.50 | £0.60 | £1.80 | £3.00 |

AMY PAPUDA
Northstar,MS; 1 1990-4 1991
1-4 ND Michael Pearlstein script/art, black and white
| | $0.45 | $1.35 | $2.25 | £0.30 | £0.90 | £1.50 |

Title Value: | $1.80 | $5.40 | $9.00 | £1.20 | £3.60 | £6.00 |

Amy Papuda Collection (May 1993)
collects mini-series plus Amy Papuda Returns | | | | £1.20 | £3.60 | £6.00 |

AMY PAPUDA, THE RETURN OF
Northstar,OS; 1 Dec 1992
1 ND | $0.45 | $1.35 | $2.25 | £0.30 | £0.90 | £1.50 |

Title Value: | $0.45 | $1.35 | $2.25 | £0.30 | £0.90 | £1.50 |

AN AMERICAN TAIL II
Marvel Comics Group,MS; 1 Jan 1992-3 Feb 1992
1-3 ND adaptation of Don Bluth animated film, bi-weekly
| | $0.25 | $0.75 | $1.25 | £0.15 | £0.45 | £0.75 |

Title Value: | $0.75 | $2.25 | $3.75 | £0.45 | £1.35 | £2.25 |

ANDREW VACHSS' UNDERGROUND
Dark Horse,MS; 1 Nov 1993-4 Feb 1994
1-4 ND 48pgs, anthology
| | $0.75 | $2.25 | $3.75 | £0.50 | £1.50 | £2.50 |

Title Value: | $3.00 | $9.00 | $15.00 | £2.00 | £6.00 | £10.00 |

ANDROMEDA
Andromeda; 1 1976; Andromeda/Silver Snail; 1 1977-7 1979
1-6 ND colour cover
| | $0.55 | $1.65 | $2.75 | £0.35 | £1.05 | £1.75 |

7 ND scarce in the U.K. colour cover
| | $0.60 | $1.80 | $3.00 | £0.40 | £1.20 | £2.00 |

Title Value: | $3.90 | $11.70 | $19.50 | £2.50 | £7.50 | £12.50 |

ANGEL AND THE APE
National Periodical Publications; 1 Nov/Dec 1968-7 Nov/Dec 1969
(see Showcase #77)
(becomes Meet Angel with issue #7)
1 | $3.75 | $11.00 | $22.50 | £2.50 | £7.50 | £15.00 |

2 Wood inks | $2.50 | $7.50 | $12.50 | £1.40 | £4.20 | £7.00 |

3 scarce in the U.K. Wood inks
| | $2.50 | $7.50 | $12.50 | £1.50 | £4.50 | £7.50 |

4-6 rare in the U.K. Wood inks
| | $2.50 | $7.50 | $12.50 | £1.50 | £4.50 | £7.50 |

7 ND title becomes "Meet Angel", Wood art
| | $1.40 | $4.20 | $7.00 | £0.90 | £2.70 | £4.50 |

Title Value: | $17.65 | $52.70 | $92.00 | £10.80 | £32.40 | £56.50 |

ANGEL AND THE APE (2ND SERIES)
DC Comics,MS; 1 Mar 1990-4 Jun 1991
1 | $0.15 | $0.45 | $0.75 | £0.10 | | £0.50 |

2 Guy Gardner, Dumb Bunny appear
| | $0.15 | $0.45 | $0.75 | £0.10 | £0.30 | £0.50 |

3-4 Inferior Five appear
| | $0.15 | $0.45 | $0.75 | £0.10 | £0.30 | £0.50 |

Title Value: | $0.60 | $1.80 | $3.00 | £0.40 | £1.20 | £2.00 |

ANGEL LOVE
DC Comics,MS; 1 Aug 1986-8 Mar 1987
1-8 Barbara Slate script/art
| | $0.15 | $0.45 | $0.75 | £0.10 | £0.35 | £0.60 |

Title Value: | $1.20 | $3.60 | $6.00 | £0.80 | £2.80 | £4.80 |

ANGEL LOVE SPECIAL
DC Comics,OS; 1 Apr 1987
1 48pgs, Barbara Slate script/art
| | $0.15 | $0.45 | $0.75 | £0.10 | £0.35 | £0.60 |

Title Value: | $0.15 | $0.45 | $0.75 | £0.10 | £0.35 | £0.60 |

ANGEL OF DEATH
Innovation,MS; 1 Jan 1991-4 Apr 1991
1-4 ND black and white
| | $0.45 | $1.35 | $2.25 | £0.30 | £0.90 | £1.50 |

Title Value: | $1.80 | $5.40 | $9.00 | £1.20 | £3.60 | £6.00 |

ANGELA
Image,MS; 1 Dec 1994-3 Feb 1995
nn ND Pennington cover art, Angela in pirate's costume alone on cover
| | $3.00 | $9.00 | $15.00 | £2.40 | £7.00 | £12.00 |

nn ND Pennington cover art, Angela and Spawn featured on cover, issued with box of Ultra-Pro mylar sleeves, contains story originaly presented in issue above
| | $3.00 | $9.00 | $15.00 | £2.40 | £7.00 | £12.00 |

1 ND Neil Gaiman script, Greg Capullo art, Spawn app.

	$Good	$Fine	$N.Mint	£Good	£Fine	£N.Mint
	$1.50	$4.50	$7.50	£1.20	£3.60	£6.00
2 ND Neil Gaiman script, Greg Capullo art; Spawn appears						
	$1.20	$3.60	$6.00	£1.00	£3.00	£5.00
3 ND Neil Gaiman script, Greg Capullo art; Spawn appears						
	$1.20	$3.60	$6.00	£0.80	£2.40	£4.00
Title Value:	$9.90	$29.70	$49.50	£7.80	£23.00	£39.00

Angela (Nov 1995)

	$Good	$Fine	$N.Mint	£Good	£Fine	£N.Mint
Trade paperback reprints mini-series, new cover by Greg Capullo				£1.30	£3.90	£6.50

ANGRY SHADOWS
Innovation; 1 1989

	$Good	$Fine	$N.Mint	£Good	£Fine	£N.Mint
1 ND 48pgs, squarebound, black and white horror anthology, John Bolton cover						
	$0.90	$2.70	$4.50	£0.60	£1.80	£3.00
Title Value:	$0.90	$2.70	$4.50	£0.60	£1.80	£3.00

ANIMA
DC Comics; 0 Oct 1994; 1 Mar 1994-present

	$Good	$Fine	$N.Mint	£Good	£Fine	£N.Mint
0 (Oct 1994) Zero Hour X-over, origin revealed						
	$0.40	$1.20	$2.00	£0.25	£0.75	£1.25
1 spin-off from Bloodbath storyline from 1993 DC annuals						
	$0.30	$0.90	$1.50	£0.20	£0.60	£1.00
2-6	$0.30	$0.90	$1.50	£0.20	£0.60	£1.00
7 Zero Hour X-over						
	$0.30	$0.90	$1.50	£0.20	£0.60	£1.00
8-9	$0.30	$0.90	$1.50	£0.20	£0.60	£1.00
10 Superboy appears						
	$0.30	$0.90	$1.50	£0.20	£0.60	£1.00
11	$0.30	$0.90	$1.50	£0.20	£0.60	£1.00
12-13 Hawkman appears						
	$0.30	$0.90	$1.50	£0.20	£0.60	£1.00
14	$0.30	$0.90	$1.50	£0.20	£0.60	£1.00
Title Value:	$4.60	$13.80	$23.00	£3.05	£9.15	£15.25

ANIMAL CONFIDENTIAL
Dark Horse, OS; 1 Jul 1994

	$Good	$Fine	$N.Mint	£Good	£Fine	£N.Mint
1 ND anthology of parody pulp animal stories						
	$0.45	$1.35	$2.25	£0.30	£0.90	£1.50
Title Value:	$0.45	$1.35	$2.25	£0.30	£0.90	£1.50

ANIMAL MAN
DC Comics/Vertigo; 1 Sep 1988-89 Nov 1995

	$Good	$Fine	$N.Mint	£Good	£Fine	£N.Mint
1 Grant Morrison scripts, Bolland covers begin						
	$2.00	$6.00	$10.00	£1.50	£4.50	£7.50
2	$1.50	$4.50	$7.50	£1.00	£3.00	£5.00
3-4	$1.10	$3.30	$5.50	£0.70	£2.10	£3.50
5 "Wile E.Coyote" story						
	$1.10	$3.30	$5.50	£0.70	£2.10	£3.50
6 Invasion X-over	$0.90	$2.70	$4.50	£0.60	£1.80	£3.00
7-8	$0.90	$2.70	$4.50	£0.60	£1.80	£3.00
9 new Mirror Master appears						
	$0.90	$2.70	$4.50	£0.60	£1.80	£3.00
10	$0.90	$2.70	$4.50	£0.60	£1.80	£3.00
11 co-stars The Vixen						
	$0.70	$2.10	$3.50	£0.50	£1.50	£2.50
12-15	$0.70	$2.10	$3.50	£0.50	£1.50	£2.50
16 Justice League Europe appears						
	$0.60	$1.80	$3.00	£0.40	£1.20	£2.00
17-20	$0.60	$1.80	$3.00	£0.40	£1.20	£2.00
21-23	$0.45	$1.35	$2.25	£0.30	£0.90	£1.50
24 Arkham Asylum featured						
	$0.45	$1.35	$2.25	£0.30	£0.90	£1.50
25-26	$0.35	$1.05	$1.75	£0.25	£0.75	£1.25
27 Pete Milligan scripts begin						
	$0.35	$1.05	$1.75	£0.25	£0.75	£1.25
28-32	$0.35	$1.05	$1.75	£0.25	£0.75	£1.25
33 Tom Veitch scripts and Steve Dillon art begins						
	$0.35	$1.05	$1.75	£0.25	£0.75	£1.25
34-39	$0.35	$1.05	$1.75	£0.25	£0.75	£1.25
40 War of the Gods X-over						
	$0.35	$1.05	$1.75	£0.25	£0.75	£1.25
41-43	$0.35	$1.05	$1.75	£0.25	£0.75	£1.25
44 The Vixen appears						
	$0.35	$1.05	$1.75	£0.25	£0.75	£1.25
45-46	$0.35	$1.05	$1.75	£0.25	£0.75	£1.25
47 B'wana Beast appears						
	$0.35	$1.05	$1.75	£0.25	£0.75	£1.25
48-49	$0.35	$1.05	$1.75	£0.25	£0.75	£1.25
50 48pgs, last Tom Veitch script						
	$0.60	$1.80	$3.00	£0.40	£1.20	£2.00
51 Jamie Delano scripts begin, new direction for title						
	$0.35	$1.05	$1.75	£0.25	£0.75	£1.25
52-56	$0.35	$1.05	$1.75	£0.25	£0.75	£1.25
57 Recreation part 1, 1st issue under "Vertigo" banner						
	$0.35	$1.05	$1.75	£0.25	£0.75	£1.25
58-59 John Higgins art						
	$0.35	$1.05	$1.75	£0.25	£0.75	£1.25
60 John Higgins art, $1.95 cover price begin						
	$0.35	$1.05	$1.75	£0.25	£0.75	£1.25
61-66	$0.35	$1.05	$1.75	£0.25	£0.75	£1.25
67 ties in with Animal Man Annual #1						
	$0.35	$1.05	$1.75	£0.25	£0.75	£1.25
68-78	$0.35	$1.05	$1.75	£0.25	£0.75	£1.25
79 last Jamie Delano script						
	$0.35	$1.05	$1.75	£0.25	£0.75	£1.25
80-82	$0.35	$1.05	$1.75	£0.25	£0.75	£1.25
83-89	$0.45	$1.35	$2.25	£0.30	£0.90	£1.50

	$Good	$Fine	$N.Mint	£Good	£Fine	£N.Mint
Title Value:	$43.30	$129.90	$216.50	£30.05	£90.15	£150.25

Note: New Format

Trade paperback (Sep 1991), reprints issues #1-9 with covers; intro by Grant Morrison, new painted cover by Brian Bolland

	$Good	$Fine	$N.Mint	£Good	£Fine	£N.Mint
				£2.40	£7.20	£12.00

ANIMAL MAN ANNUAL
DC Comics/Vertigo; 1 Dec 1993

	$Good	$Fine	$N.Mint	£Good	£Fine	£N.Mint
1 The Children's Crusade part 3, continued in Swamp Thing Annual #7; Brian Bolland cover						
	$0.75	$2.25	$3.75	£0.50	£1.50	£2.50
Title Value:	$0.75	$2.25	$3.75	£0.50	£1.50	£2.50

ANIMAL MYSTIC
CFD Productions; 1 1993-4 1995

	$Good	$Fine	$N.Mint	£Good	£Fine	£N.Mint
1 ND	$7.00	$21.00	$35.00	£5.00	£15.00	£25.00
1 2nd printing ND	$1.40	$4.20	$7.00	£1.00	£3.00	£5.00
1 Variant Edition, ND signed & numbered; contains 8 new pages plus pin-ups						
	$17.00	$51.00	$85.00	£8.00	£24.00	£40.00
2 ND 1st app. Klor						
	$6.00	$18.00	$30.00	£4.00	£12.00	£20.00
2 2nd printing, ND 1st appearance Klor						
	$1.00	$3.00	$5.00	£0.60	£1.80	£3.00
3 ND	$1.50	$4.50	$7.50	£1.50	£4.50	£7.50
4 ND DS, contains poster insert						
	$1.00	$3.00	$5.00	£1.00	£3.00	£5.00
Title Value:	$34.90	$104.70	$174.50	£21.10	£63.30	£105.50

ANIMANIACS
DC Comics; 1 May 1995-present

	$Good	$Fine	$N.Mint	£Good	£Fine	£N.Mint
1-11 based on cartoon show						
	$0.30	$0.90	$1.50	£0.20	£0.60	£1.00
Title Value:	$3.30	$9.90	$16.50	£2.20	£6.60	£11.00

ANIMANIACS: A CHRISTMAS SPECIAL
DC Comics, OS; 1 Jan 1995

	$Good	$Fine	$N.Mint	£Good	£Fine	£N.Mint
1	$0.30	$0.90	$1.50	£0.20	£0.60	£1.00
Title Value:	$0.30	$0.90	$1.50	£0.20	£0.60	£1.00

ANIMAX
Marvel Comics Group/Star, Toy; 1 Dec 1986-4 Jun 1987

	$Good	$Fine	$N.Mint	£Good	£Fine	£N.Mint
1-4	$0.15	$0.45	$0.75	£0.10	£0.30	£0.50
Title Value:	$0.60	$1.80	$3.00	£0.40	£1.20	£2.00

ANNEX
Marvel Comics Group, MS; 1 Aug 1994-4 Nov 1994

	$Good	$Fine	$N.Mint	£Good	£Fine	£N.Mint
1-4 spin-off from Amazing Spiderman Annual #27						
	$0.30	$0.90	$1.50	£0.20	£0.60	£1.00
Title Value:	$1.20	$3.60	$6.00	£0.80	£2.40	£4.00

ANNIE
Marvel Comics Group, MS Film; 1 Oct 1982-2 Nov 1982

	$Good	$Fine	$N.Mint	£Good	£Fine	£N.Mint
1-2 ND	$0.15	$0.45	$0.75	£0.10	£0.30	£0.50
Title Value:	$0.30	$0.90	$1.50	£0.20	£0.60	£1.00

ANNIE (2ND SERIES)
Marvel Comics Group, Tabloid OS; 1 Oct 1982

	$Good	$Fine	$N.Mint	£Good	£Fine	£N.Mint
1 ND reprints mini-series						
	$0.30	$0.90	$1.50	£0.20	£0.60	£1.00
Title Value:	$0.30	$0.90	$1.50	£0.20	£0.60	£1.00

ANT BOY
Steeldragon Press; 1 1987-2 1987

	$Good	$Fine	$N.Mint	£Good	£Fine	£N.Mint
1 ND Matt Feazell story and art						
	$0.35	$1.05	$1.75	£0.25	£0.75	£1.25
1 2nd printing ND	$0.30	$0.90	$1.50	£0.20	£0.60	£1.00
2 ND	$0.35	$1.05	$1.75	£0.25	£0.75	£1.25
Title Value:	$1.00	$3.00	$5.00	£0.70	£2.10	£3.50

ANTHRO
National Periodical Publications; 1 Jul/Aug 1968-6 Jul/Aug 1969
(see Showcase #74)

	$Good	$Fine	$N.Mint	£Good	£Fine	£N.Mint
1	$5.75	$17.50	$35.00	£4.15	£12.50	£25.00
2	$4.00	$12.00	$20.00	£2.50	£7.50	£12.50
3-5	$4.00	$12.00	$20.00	£2.00	£6.00	£10.00
6 Wood cover/inks						
	$4.00	$12.00	$20.00	£2.50	£7.50	£12.50
Title Value:	$25.75	$77.50	$135.00	£15.15	£45.50	£80.00

ANTI-HITLER COMICS
New England Comics; 1 Aug 1992

	$Good	$Fine	$N.Mint	£Good	£Fine	£N.Mint
1 ND reprints Golden Age stories						
	$0.45	$1.35	$2.25	£0.30	£0.90	£1.50
Title Value:	$0.45	$1.35	$2.25	£0.30	£0.90	£1.50

ANTIQUITIES WAR ON THE WORLD OF MAGIC: THE GATHERING
Acclaim Comics/Armada, MS; 1 Nov 1995-4 Feb 1996

	$Good	$Fine	$N.Mint	£Good	£Fine	£N.Mint
1 ND George Pratt painted cover						
	$0.50	$1.50	$2.50	£0.30	£0.90	£1.50
2-4 ND	$0.50	$1.50	$2.50	£0.30	£0.90	£1.50
Title Value:	$2.00	$6.00	$10.00	£1.20	£3.60	£6.00

ANXIETY TIMES
Eclipse; 1 Aug 1992

	$Good	$Fine	$N.Mint	£Good	£Fine	£N.Mint
1 ND 48pgs, anthology of tales featuring work by Gilbert Hernandez, Don McGregor, Gene Colan						
	$0.90	$2.70	$4.50	£0.60	£1.80	£3.00
Title Value:	$0.90	$2.70	$4.50	£0.60	£1.80	£3.00

ANYTHING GOES
Fantagraphics, MS; 1 Oct 1986-6 Oct 1987

	$Good	$Fine	$N.Mint	£Good	£Fine	£N.Mint
1 Flaming Carrot in colour by Burden (4pgs); Gilbert Hernandez (4pgs), Gil Kane (4pgs), Toth (1pg), Gil Kane cover						
	$0.60	$1.80	$3.00	£0.80	£2.40	£4.00
2 very scarce in the U.K. "Pictopia" by Alan Moore, Fujitaki, Spiegelman, J.Hernandez (4pgs), Simpson, Kirby pin-ups (4), Frank Miller cover						
	$0.40	$1.20	$2.00	£0.60	£1.80	£3.00
3 Cerebus text story by Sim (3pgs), Spiegelman, Clowes, Cruise art, Neal Adams Cerebus cover						

	$Good	$Fine	$N.Mint	£Good	£Fine	£N.Mint
	$0.40	$1.20	$2.00	£0.40	£1.20	£2.00

4 Gilbert Hernandez art on Heart Break Soup, Popeye by Segar, Orphan Annie by Gray, Journey by Messner-Loebs, Peter Bagge story, Perez cover

	$Good	$Fine	$N.Mint	£Good	£Fine	£N.Mint
	$0.40	$1.20	$2.00	£0.40	£1.20	£2.00

5 Turtles cover and story by Eastman & Laird, Journey by Messner-Loebs, Crumb, Sutton, Lomax art, Orphan Annie reprints by Gray

	$Good	$Fine	$N.Mint	£Good	£Fine	£N.Mint
	$0.40	$1.20	$2.00	£0.60	£1.80	£3.00

6 Keif Llama by Howarth, Eddie Campbell, Phill Elliott, Mark Martin, Sutton art, Stan Sakai cover

	$Good	$Fine	$N.Mint	£Good	£Fine	£N.Mint
	$0.40	$1.20	$2.00	£0.40	£1.20	£2.00
Title Value:	$2.60	$7.80	$13.00	£3.20	£9.60	£16.00

Note: all Non-Distributed on the news-stands in the U.K.

APACHE DICK
Eternity,MS; 1 Feb 1990-4 May 1990

	$Good	$Fine	$N.Mint	£Good	£Fine	£N.Mint
1-4 ND black and white	$0.35	$1.05	$1.75	£0.25	£0.75	£1.25
Title Value:	$1.40	$4.20	$7.00	£1.00	£3.00	£5.00
Graphic Novel (1991), reprints #1-4				£1.30	£3.90	£6.50

APE CITY
Adventure,MS; 1 Aug 1990-4 Nov 1990

	$Good	$Fine	$N.Mint	£Good	£Fine	£N.Mint
1 ND	$0.45	$1.35	$2.25	£0.30	£0.90	£1.50
2-4 ND	$0.35	$1.05	$1.75	£0.25	£0.75	£1.25
Title Value:	$1.50	$4.50	$7.50	£1.05	£3.15	£5.25

Note: based on Planet of the Apes

APE NATION
Adventure,MS; 1 Feb 1991-4 Jun 1991

	$Good	$Fine	$N.Mint	£Good	£Fine	£N.Mint
1 ND	$0.50	$1.50	$2.50	£0.35	£1.05	£1.75

1 ND Limited Edition (Feb 1991) - 8,000 copies exclusive to Diamond Distributors with silver embossed logo and card-stock cover: limited number in top right of cover

	$Good	$Fine	$N.Mint	£Good	£Fine	£N.Mint
	$1.50	$4.50	$7.50	£1.00	£3.00	£5.00
2-4 ND	$0.45	$1.35	$2.25	£0.30	£0.90	£1.50
Title Value:	$3.35	$10.05	$16.75	£2.25	£6.75	£11.25
Special Edition (8,000 copies)				£1.00	£3.00	£5.00
Special Edition (5,000 copies), foil embossed cover by Peter Hsu				£0.80	£2.40	£4.00

APE WORLD
Comax Productions; 1 Aug 1991

	$Good	$Fine	$N.Mint	£Good	£Fine	£N.Mint
1 ND Butch Burcham script/art	$0.45	$1.35	$2.25	£0.30	£0.90	£1.50

1 ND as above, 1500 copies signed and numbered

	$Good	$Fine	$N.Mint	£Good	£Fine	£N.Mint
	$0.60	$1.80	$3.00	£0.40	£1.20	£2.00
Title Value:	$1.05	$3.15	$5.25	£0.70	£2.10	£3.50

APOCALYPSE STRIKE FILES, THE
Marvel Comics Group,OS; 1 Apr 1995

1 ND additional information tied into "The Age of Apocalypse" storyline (see X-Planations title header)

	$Good	$Fine	$N.Mint	£Good	£Fine	£N.Mint
	$0.45	$1.35	$2.25	£0.30	£0.90	£1.50
Title Value:	$0.45	$1.35	$2.25	£0.30	£0.90	£1.50

APPARITION: ABANDONED, THE
Caliber Press,OS; 1 Apr 1995

1 ND 48pgs, spin-off from the Negative Burn anthology; black and white

	$Good	$Fine	$N.Mint	£Good	£Fine	£N.Mint
	$0.80	$2.40	$4.00	£0.50	£1.50	£2.50
Title Value:	$0.80	$2.40	$4.00	£0.50	£1.50	£2.50

APPLESEED
Eclipse; 1 Sep 1988-5 Jan 1989

1 ND scarce in the U.K. serialisation of Japanese Graphic Novel begins

	$Good	$Fine	$N.Mint	£Good	£Fine	£N.Mint
	$3.00	$9.00	$15.00	£2.00	£6.00	£10.00
2 ND	$1.00	$3.00	$5.00	£1.00	£3.00	£5.00
3 ND	$0.80	$2.40	$4.00	£0.80	£2.40	£4.00
4-5 ND	$0.60	$1.80	$3.00	£0.60	£1.80	£3.00
Title Value:	$6.00	$18.00	$30.00	£5.00	£15.00	£25.00
Trade paperback: The Promethean Challenge reprints #1-5				£1.50	£4.50	£7.50
2nd print (Nov 1991)				£1.40	£4.20	£7.00

APPLESEED BOOK 2
Eclipse,MS; 1 Feb 1989-5 Jun 1989

	$Good	$Fine	$N.Mint	£Good	£Fine	£N.Mint
1 ND Art Adams cover	$0.60	$1.80	$3.00	£0.60	£1.80	£3.00
2-5 ND Art Adams cover	$0.60	$1.80	$3.00	£0.50	£1.50	£2.50
Title Value:	$3.00	$9.00	$15.00	£2.60	£7.80	£13.00
Trade paperback: Prometheus Unbound, reprints #1-5				£1.50	£4.50	£7.50
Hardcover (Apr 1991)				£5.00	£15.00	£25.00
Limited Edition Hardcover, 300 signed by Masamune Shirow (May 1991)				£10.00	£30.00	£50.00

APPLESEED BOOK 3
Eclipse,MS; 1-5 1991

	$Good	$Fine	$N.Mint	£Good	£Fine	£N.Mint
1-5 ND	$0.60	$1.80	$3.00	£0.50	£1.50	£2.50
Title Value:	$3.00	$9.00	$15.00	£2.50	£7.50	£12.50
Trade paperback: The Scales of Prometheus (Aug 1991), reprints #1-5				£1.70	£5.10	£8.50
Hardcover (Aug 1991)				£5.00	£15.00	£25.00
Deluxe Hardcover (Aug 1991)				£7.00	£21.00	£35.00
Limited Edition Hardcover (Aug 1995)				£11.00	£33.00	£55.00

APPLESEED BOOK 4
Eclipse,MS; 1 Feb 1991-2 Mar 1991

	$Good	$Fine	$N.Mint	£Good	£Fine	£N.Mint
1-2 ND 64pgs	$0.60	$1.80	$3.00	£0.40	£1.20	£2.00
Title Value:	$1.20	$3.60	$6.00	£0.80	£2.40	£4.00
Appleseed Book 4 Collection (Mar 1993) reprints mini-series, now published by Dark Horse Comics				£1.60	£4.80	£8.00

APPLESEED DATABOOK
Dark Horse,MS; 1 Mar 1994-2 Apr 1994

	$Good	$Fine	$N.Mint	£Good	£Fine	£N.Mint
1-2 ND 48pgs	$0.60	$1.80	$3.00	£0.40	£1.20	£2.00
Title Value:	$1.20	$3.60	$6.00	£0.80	£2.40	£4.00

Appleseed Databook (Aug 1995) Trade paperback collects issues #1,2

	$Good	$Fine	$N.Mint	£Good	£Fine	£N.Mint
with wraparound cover by Masamune Shirow				£1.70	£5.10	£8.50

AQUAMAN
National Periodical Publications/DC Comics; 1 Jan/Feb 1962-56 Mar/Apr 1971; 57 Aug/Sep 1977-63 Aug/Sep 1978

(see Action, Adventure, Aquaman Special, Brave and the Bold, DC Comics Presents, DC Comics Presents, DC Special, Detective, Five-Star Super-Hero Spectacular, Secret Origins, Showcase, Super DC Giant, Super-Team Family, World's Finest)

	$Good	$Fine	$N.Mint	£Good	£Fine	£N.Mint
1 1st appearance Quisp	$57.50	$170.00	$575.00	£30.00	£90.00	£300.00
2	$27.00	$80.00	$245.00	£11.00	£33.00	£100.00
3	$17.50	$52.50	$140.00	£8.75	£26.00	£70.00
4-5	$15.50	$47.00	$125.00	£7.50	£22.50	£60.00
6-8	$10.00	$30.00	$80.00	£5.00	£15.00	£40.00
9 Sea Devils appear	$10.00	$30.00	$80.00	£5.00	£15.00	£40.00
10	$10.00	$30.00	$80.00	£5.00	£15.00	£40.00
11 1st appearance Mera	$8.00	$24.00	$65.00	£3.75	£11.00	£30.00
12-17	$8.00	$24.00	$65.00	£3.10	£9.25	£25.00
18 Aquaman & Mera wed, Justice League of America cameo	$8.00	$24.00	$65.00	£3.10	£9.25	£25.00
19-20	$8.00	$24.00	$65.00	£3.10	£9.25	£25.00
21-22	$7.75	$23.50	$55.00	£2.50	£7.50	£17.50
23 birth of Aquababy	$7.75	$23.50	$55.00	£2.50	£7.50	£17.50
24-28	$7.75	$23.50	$55.00	£2.50	£7.50	£17.50
29 1st appearance Ocean Master	$7.75	$23.50	$55.00	£2.85	£8.50	£20.00
30 Batman appears	$7.75	$23.50	$55.00	£2.50	£7.50	£17.50
31-32	$7.75	$23.50	$55.00	£2.10	£6.25	£15.00
33 1st appearance Aquagirl (later killed in Crisis); see Adventure Comics #266	$10.00	$30.00	$70.00	£2.85	£8.50	£20.00
34	$7.75	$23.50	$55.00	£2.10	£6.25	£15.00
35 1st appearance Black Manta	$7.75	$23.50	$55.00	£2.10	£6.25	£15.00
36-40	$7.75	$23.50	$55.00	£1.75	£5.25	£12.50
41-49	$4.25	$12.50	$30.00	£1.05	£3.20	£7.50
50 Neal Adams art on Deadman	$5.50	$17.00	$40.00	£1.75	£5.25	£12.50
51 scarce in the U.K. Neal Adams art on Deadman	$5.50	$17.00	$40.00	£2.10	£6.25	£15.00
52 Neal Adams art on Deadman	$5.50	$17.00	$40.00	£1.75	£5.25	£12.50
53-55	$2.10	$6.25	$15.00	£0.55	£1.70	£4.00
56 series cancelled; continues as back-up in Adventure #434-437, #441-452 before returning to continue numbering	$2.10	$6.25	$15.00	£0.55	£1.70	£4.00
57 Aquababy dies	$1.00	$3.00	$6.00	£0.40	£1.25	£2.50
58 origin retold	$1.00	$3.00	$6.00	£0.40	£1.25	£2.50
59-60	$1.00	$3.00	$6.00	£0.40	£1.25	£2.50
61 Batman and Green Lantern appear	$1.00	$3.00	$6.00	£0.40	£1.25	£2.50
62-63	$1.00	$3.00	$6.00	£0.25	£0.85	£1.75
Title Value:	$490.40	$1472.50	$3867.00	£186.50	£559.30	£1504.50

FEATURES
Aquaman solo in 26,41,42,47,50-52,54,56. Aquaman/Aqualad in 1-25, 27-40,43-46,48,49,53,56. Aquagirl in 56. Deadman (linked to Aquaman) in 50-52. Mera in 58-60.

AQUAMAN (1ST LIMITED SERIES)
DC Comics,MS; 1 Feb 1986-4 May 1986

	$Good	$Fine	$N.Mint	£Good	£Fine	£N.Mint
1 scarce in the U.K. Neal Pozner script, Craig Hamilton art, new costume	$0.80	$2.40	$4.00	£0.40	£1.20	£2.00
2-4 Neal Pozner script, Craig Hamilton art	$0.50	$1.50	$2.50	£0.20	£0.60	£1.00
Title Value:	$2.30	$6.90	$11.50	£1.00	£3.00	£5.00

AQUAMAN (2ND LIMITED SERIES)
DC Comics,MS; 1 Jun 1989-5 Oct 1989

	$Good	$Fine	$N.Mint	£Good	£Fine	£N.Mint
1-5	$0.25	$0.75	$1.25	£0.15	£0.45	£0.75
Title Value:	$1.25	$3.75	$6.25	£0.75	£2.25	£3.75

AQUAMAN (2ND SERIES)
DC Comics; 1 Dec 1991-13 Dec 1992

	$Good	$Fine	$N.Mint	£Good	£Fine	£N.Mint
1 Martian Manhunter, Blue Beetle appear	$0.30	$0.90	$1.50	£0.20	£0.60	£1.00
2-4	$0.25	$0.75	$1.25	£0.15	£0.45	£0.75
5 New Titans and Martian Manhunter appear	$0.25	$0.75	$1.25	£0.15	£0.45	£0.75
6	$0.25	$0.75	$1.25	£0.15	£0.45	£0.75
7 Justice League appear	$0.25	$0.75	$1.25	£0.15	£0.45	£0.75
8 Batman guest-stars	$0.25	$0.75	$1.25	£0.15	£0.45	£0.75
9-10 Eco-Wars story, Sea Devils appear	$0.25	$0.75	$1.25	£0.15	£0.45	£0.75
11 dinosaur cover	$0.25	$0.75	$1.25	£0.15	£0.45	£0.75
12-13	$0.25	$0.75	$1.25	£0.15	£0.45	£0.75
Title Value:	$3.30	$9.90	$16.50	£2.00	£6.00	£10.00
Aquaman Multi-Pack 1 (Dec 1992), ND pre-bagged with header card containing issues 1-3 (#1 is 2nd print) with four stickers				£0.35	£1.05	£1.75

Aquaman Multi-Pack 2 (Dec 1992),

	$Good	$Fine	$N.Mint	£Good	£Fine	£N.Mint
ND pre-bagged with header card containing issues 4-6 with same four illustrated stickers				£0.35	£1.05	£1.75

AQUAMAN (3RD SERIES)
DC Comics; 0 Oct 1994; 1 Aug 1994-present

	$Good	$Fine	$N.Mint	£Good	£Fine	£N.Mint
0 (Oct 1994) Zero Hour, new facts about origin						
	$0.50	$1.50	$2.50	£0.30	£0.90	£1.50
1 Peter David script begins						
	$0.60	$1.80	$3.00	£0.40	£1.20	£2.00
2 Aquaman loses hand						
	$0.60	$1.80	$3.00	£0.30	£0.90	£1.50
3 Aquaman vs. Superboy, new costume; Aqualad and Dolphin appear						
	$0.40	$1.20	$2.00	£0.30	£0.90	£1.50
4 Aquaman vs. Lobo						
	$0.40	$1.20	$2.00	£0.30	£0.90	£1.50
5 new costume	$0.40	$1.20	$2.00	£0.30	£0.90	£1.50
6 Aquaman finds a new son						
	$0.35	$1.05	$1.75	£0.25	£0.75	£1.25
7	$0.35	$1.05	$1.75	£0.25	£0.75	£1.25
8 Aqualad meets Aquaman's wizard father, Atlan						
	$0.35	$1.05	$1.75	£0.25	£0.75	£1.25
9	$0.35	$1.05	$1.75	£0.25	£0.75	£1.25
10 Green Lantern guest-stars						
	$0.35	$1.05	$1.75	£0.25	£0.75	£1.25
11	$0.35	$1.05	$1.75	£0.25	£0.75	£1.25
12 Dolphin vs. Mera						
	$0.35	$1.05	$1.75	£0.25	£0.75	£1.25
13	$0.35	$1.05	$1.75	£0.25	£0.75	£1.25
14 Underworld Unleashed tie-in						
	$0.35	$1.05	$1.75	£0.25	£0.75	£1.25
15 Walt Simonson cover						
	$0.35	$1.05	$1.75	£0.25	£0.75	£1.25
16-17 Justice League guest-stars						
	$0.35	$1.05	$1.75	£0.25	£0.75	£1.25
18 origin retold Dolphin						
	$0.35	$1.05	$1.75	£0.25	£0.75	£1.25
Title Value:	$7.45	$22.35	$37.25	£5.15	£15.45	£25.75

AQUAMAN (3RD SERIES) ANNUAL
DC Comics; 1 Jul 1995-present

	$Good	$Fine	$N.Mint	£Good	£Fine	£N.Mint
1 56pgs, Year One, Superman and Wonder Woman guest-star						
	$0.80	$2.40	$4.00	£0.50	£1.50	£2.50
Title Value:	$0.80	$2.40	$4.00	£0.50	£1.50	£2.50

AQUAMAN SPECIAL
DC Comics,OS; 1 1988

	$Good	$Fine	$N.Mint	£Good	£Fine	£N.Mint
1 George Freeman art						
	$0.30	$0.90	$1.50	£0.20	£0.60	£1.00
Title Value:	$0.30	$0.90	$1.50	£0.20	£0.60	£1.00

AQUAMAN SPECIAL, LEGEND OF
DC Comics,OS; 1 Jun 1989

	$Good	$Fine	$N.Mint	£Good	£Fine	£N.Mint
1 48pgs, Keith Giffen layouts						
	$0.40	$1.20	$2.00	£0.25	£0.75	£1.25
Title Value:	$0.40	$1.20	$2.00	£0.25	£0.75	£1.25

AQUAMAN: TIME & TIDE
DC Comics,MS; 1 Dec 1993-4 Mar 1994

	$Good	$Fine	$N.Mint	£Good	£Fine	£N.Mint
1 Peter David script begins, Aquaman: Year One-type story; The Flash (Barry Allen) appears						
	$0.50	$1.50	$2.50	£0.30	£0.90	£1.50
2-3 Aquaman's origin continues						
	$0.40	$1.20	$2.00	£0.25	£0.75	£1.25
4 Ocean Master's origin; appearances by Mera, Aqualad, Tula and Aquababy						
	$0.40	$1.20	$2.00	£0.25	£0.75	£1.25
Title Value:	$1.70	$5.10	$8.50	£1.05	£3.15	£5.25
Aquaman: Time & Tide (Mar 1996)						

	$Good	$Fine	$N.Mint	£Good	£Fine	£N.Mint
Trade paperback reprints mini-series, new cover by Kirk Jarvinen	£1.30	£3.90	£6.50			

ARAK, SON OF THUNDER
DC Comics; 1 Sep 1981-50 Nov 1985
(see Warlord #48)

	$Good	$Fine	$N.Mint	£Good	£Fine	£N.Mint
1 origin Arak, 1st appearance Angelica						
	$0.15	$0.45	$0.75	£0.10	£0.35	£0.60
2	$0.15	$0.45	$0.75	£0.10	£0.35	£0.60
3 intro Valda	$0.15	$0.45	$0.75	£0.10	£0.35	£0.60
4-7	$0.15	$0.45	$0.75	£0.10	£0.35	£0.60
8-11 Viking Prince						
	$0.15	$0.45	$0.75	£0.10	£0.35	£0.60
12-23	$0.15	$0.45	$0.75	£0.10	£0.35	£0.60
24 DS	$0.25	$0.75	$1.25	£0.15	£0.45	£0.75
25-49	$0.15	$0.45	$0.75	£0.10	£0.35	£0.60
50 DS	$0.25	$0.75	$1.25	£0.15	£0.45	£0.75
Title Value:	$7.70	$23.10	$38.50	£5.10	£17.70	£30.30

ARAK, SON OF THUNDER ANNUAL
DC Comics; 1 Oct 1984

	$Good	$Fine	$N.Mint	£Good	£Fine	£N.Mint
1 48pgs	$0.25	$0.75	$1.25	£0.15	£0.45	£0.75
Title Value:	$0.25	$0.75	$1.25	£0.15	£0.45	£0.75

ARCANA ANNUAL
DC Comics,OS; 1 Feb 1994

	$Good	$Fine	$N.Mint	£Good	£Fine	£N.Mint
1 ND 64pgs Children's Crusade part 6, concluded in Children's Crusade #2						
	$0.85	$2.55	$4.25	£0.55	£1.65	£2.75
Title Value:	$0.85	$2.55	$4.25	£0.55	£1.65	£2.75

ARCANE COMIX
Arcane/Eclipse; 1 Dec 1987-5 1990

	$Good	$Fine	$N.Mint	£Good	£Fine	£N.Mint
1 128pgs, "Bad Moon"						
	$0.70	$2.10	$3.50	£0.50	£1.50	£2.50
2 224pgs, "Fly In My Eye", part Clive Barker text Bissette, Talbot, Howarth, McKeever, SMS, Bolton art						
	$1.00	$3.00	$5.00	£1.00	£3.00	£5.00
3 "Saturday Mourning"						
	$1.00	$3.00	$5.00	£1.00	£3.00	£5.00
4 "Daughters of Fly in My Eye"						
	$1.00	$3.00	$5.00	£1.00	£3.00	£5.00
5 128pgs, "Fly In My Eye Exposed", Clive Barker cover						
	$1.20	$3.60	$6.00	£1.20	£3.60	£6.00
Title Value:	$4.90	$14.70	$24.50	£4.70	£14.10	£23.50
Note: all Non-Distributed on the news-stands in the U.K.						

ARCHANGEL
Marvel Comics Group,OS; 1 Feb 1996

	$Good	$Fine	$N.Mint	£Good	£Fine	£N.Mint
1 ND Peter Milligan script, Steve Lightle art						
	$0.50	$1.50	$2.50	£0.30	£0.90	£1.50
Title Value:	$0.50	$1.50	$2.50	£0.30	£0.90	£1.50

ARCHER & ARMSTRONG
Valiant; 0 Jul 1992- 26 Sep 1994

	$Good	$Fine	$N.Mint	£Good	£Fine	£N.Mint
0 Barry Windsor-Smith art begins, 1st appearance Archer & Armstrong						
	$0.70	$2.10	$3.50	£0.40	£1.20	£2.00
0 gold embossed cover						
	$3.00	$9.00	$15.00	£2.00	£6.00	£10.00
1 Unity: Chapter 3, Eternal Warrior appears						
	$0.60	$1.80	$3.00	£0.40	£1.20	£2.00
2 Unity: Chapter 11, 2nd appearance Turok, Walt Simonson cover						
	$0.50	$1.50	$2.50	£0.30	£0.90	£1.50
3-7	$0.45	$1.35	$2.25	£0.25	£0.75	£1.25
8 48pgs, Archer & Armstrong and Eternal Warrior as The Three Musketeers, 1st appearance of Ivar						
(note: single issue shared with Eternal Warrior #8)						
	$0.70	$2.10	$3.50	£0.40	£1.20	£2.00
9	$0.45	$1.35	$2.25	£0.25	£0.75	£1.25
10 Solar guest-stars, Ivar appears						
	$0.45	$1.35	$2.25	£0.20	£0.60	£1.00

Aquaman (1st) #3

Aquaman (3rd) #1

Astonishing Tales #1

MINT = 100% / NEAR MINT (inc. +/-) = 90–99% / VERY FINE (inc. +/-) = 75–89% / FINE (inc. +/-) = 55–74%
VERY GOOD (inc. +/-) = 35–54% / GOOD (inc. +/-) = 15–34% / FAIR = 5–14% / POOR = 1–4%

	$Good	$Fine	$N.Mint	£Good	£Fine	£N.Mint
11-12	$0.45	$1.35	$2.25	£0.20	£0.60	£1.00
13-14 Mike Baron script						
	$0.45	$1.35	$2.25	£0.20	£0.60	£1.00
15-20	$0.45	$1.35	$2.25	£0.20	£0.60	£1.00
21 with free Upper Deck card bound-in at centre-fold						
	$0.45	$1.35	$2.25	£0.20	£0.60	£1.00
22-24	$0.45	$1.35	$2.25	£0.20	£0.60	£1.00
25 continued in Eternal Warrior #25						
	$0.45	$1.35	$2.25	£0.20	£0.60	£1.00
26 Chaos Effect tie-in; shared issue with Eternal Warrior #26 (see #8 for similar idea)						
	$0.45	$1.35	$2.25	£0.25	£0.75	£1.25
Title Value:	$15.85	$47.55	$79.25	£8.45	£25.35	£42.25

Note: all Non-Distributed at the news-stands in the U.K.

ARCHIE'S JOKE BOOK MAGAZINE
Archie Comics; 1 1953-3 Summer 1954; 15 Autumn 1954-288 Dec 1982

	$Good	$Fine	$N.Mint	£Good	£Fine	£N.Mint
1 very scarce in the U.K.						
	$67.50	$200.00	$475.00	£47.00	£140.00	£330.00
2 scarce in the U.K.						
	$39.00	$115.00	$275.00	£26.00	£77.50	£185.00
3 scarce in the U.K.						
	$26.00	$77.50	$185.00	£17.50	£52.50	£125.00
[Note: no issues #4-14]						
15-17 Katy Keene appears						
	$18.50	$55.00	$130.00	£12.50	£38.00	£87.50
18-20	$18.50	$55.00	$130.00	£12.50	£38.00	£87.50
21-30	$13.00	$40.00	$80.00	£8.75	£26.00	£52.50
31-40	$8.25	$25.00	$50.00	£5.25	£16.00	£32.50
41 scarce in the U.K. Neal Adams 1st professional comic book art (Jul 1959), 1 page - hard to tell which one!						
	$20.50	$62.50	$125.00	£13.50	£41.00	£82.50
42-43	$8.25	$25.00	$50.00	£5.25	£16.00	£32.50
44 Neal Adams art (3rd ever?)						
	$10.50	$33.00	$65.00	£7.75	£23.50	£47.50
45-47 Neal Adams art (1/2pgs)						
	$10.00	$30.00	$60.00	£6.50	£20.00	£40.00
48 Neal Adams art (4pgs)						
	$10.50	$33.00	$65.00	£7.75	£23.50	£47.50
49-50	$3.30	$10.00	$20.00	£2.25	£6.75	£13.50
51-60	$3.15	$9.50	$19.00	£2.05	£6.25	£12.50
61-80	$1.80	$5.50	$11.00	£1.20	£3.60	£7.25
81-100	$0.80	$2.50	$5.00	£0.50	£1.60	£3.25
101-150	$0.40	$1.25	$2.50	£0.25	£0.85	£1.75
151-200	$0.35	$1.05	$1.75	£0.25	£0.75	£1.25
201-280	$0.25	$0.75	$1.25	£0.15	£0.45	£0.75
281-288	$0.30	$0.90	$1.50	£0.20	£0.60	£1.00
Title Value:	$694.00	$2098.20	$4417.00	£462.10	£1398.80	£2957.50

Note: most issues after Nov 1959 distributed on the news-stands in the U.K. but became more irregular in the late 1970s/early '80s.

ARCHIE'S MADHOUSE
Archie Comics; 1 Sep 1959-66 Feb 1969

	$Good	$Fine	$N.Mint	£Good	£Fine	£N.Mint
1 scarce in the U.K.						
	$31.00	$92.50	$185.00	£20.50	£62.50	£125.00
2 scarce in the U.K.						
	$15.00	$45.00	$90.00	£10.00	£30.00	£60.00
3-4 scarce in the U.K.						
	$9.50	$29.00	$57.50	£6.25	£19.00	£38.00
1st official distribution in the U.K.						
5 scarce in the U.K. Archie mask at centre-fold (often missing!)						
	$9.50	$29.00	$57.50	£6.25	£19.00	£38.00
6-10	$6.50	$20.00	$40.00	£4.55	£13.50	£27.50
11-17	$4.55	$13.50	$27.50	£3.30	£10.00	£20.00
18-21	$1.65	$5.00	$10.00	£1.25	£3.75	£7.50
22 scarce in the U.K. 1st appearance Sabrina						
	$9.00	$28.00	$55.00	£6.25	£18.50	£37.50
23-30	$1.65	$5.00	$10.00	£1.25	£3.75	£7.50
31-40	$0.80	$2.50	$5.00	£0.50	£1.60	£3.25
41-66	$0.35	$1.05	$1.75	£0.25	£0.75	£1.25
Title Value:	$184.75	$559.30	$1110.50	£127.85	£386.00	£769.00

ARCHIE'S SUPER HERO COMICS DIGEST MAGAZINE
Archie Comics, Digest; 2 Aug 1979

(previously Archie's Super-Hero Special)

	$Good	$Fine	$N.Mint	£Good	£Fine	£N.Mint
2 148pgs, previously unpublished Neal Adams Black Hood story; limited distribution in the U.K.						
	$0.90	$2.70	$4.50	£0.60	£1.80	£3.00
Title Value:	$0.90	$2.70	$4.50	£0.60	£1.80	£3.00

ARCHIE'S SUPER-HERO SPECIAL
Archie Comics, Digest; 1 1978

(becomes Archie's Super Hero Comic Digest Magazine)

	$Good	$Fine	$N.Mint	£Good	£Fine	£N.Mint
1 148pgs, Joe Simon and Jack Kirby art; all reprints: Fly, Black Hood, Web, Jaguar appear; limited distribution in the U.K.						
	$0.55	$1.65	$2.75	£0.35	£1.05	£1.75
Title Value:	$0.55	$1.65	$2.75	£0.35	£1.05	£1.75

ARCHIE'S SUPERTEENS
Archie Comics; 1 Aug 1994-2 1994

	$Good	$Fine	$N.Mint	£Good	£Fine	£N.Mint
1 ND 48pgs, Archie returns as Pureheart the Powerful, Jughead as Captain Hero, Betty as Superteen and Reggie as Evilheart; Elliot S! Maggin script, Joe Staton art						
	$0.40	$1.20	$2.00	£0.25	£0.75	£1.25
2 ND	$0.40	$1.20	$2.00	£0.25	£0.75	£1.25
Title Value:	$0.80	$2.40	$4.00	£0.50	£1.50	£2.50

AREA 88
Eclipse/Viz; 1 1987-42 May 1989

	$Good	$Fine	$N.Mint	£Good	£Fine	£N.Mint
1 Kaoru Shintani script/art (translated Japanese reprint) begins; black and white						
	$0.45	$1.35	$2.25	£0.30	£0.90	£1.50
1 2nd printing	$0.40	$1.20	$2.00	£0.25	£0.75	£1.25

	$Good	$Fine	$N.Mint	£Good	£Fine	£N.Mint
2	$0.35	$1.05	$1.75	£0.25	£0.75	£1.25
2 2nd printing	$0.30	$0.90	$1.50	£0.20	£0.60	£1.00
3	$0.35	$1.05	$1.75	£0.25	£0.75	£1.25
4-36	$0.30	$0.90	$1.50	£0.20	£0.60	£1.00
37 1st Viz Comics issue, photo-cover						
	$0.40	$1.20	$2.00	£0.25	£0.75	£1.25
38-42	$0.30	$0.90	$1.50	£0.20	£0.60	£1.00
Title Value:	$13.65	$40.95	$68.25	£9.10	£27.30	£45.50

Note: all Non-Distributed on the news-stands in the U.K.

				£Good	£Fine	£N.Mint
Graphic Novel 1 (Apr 1991), 200pgs, reprints				£1.40	£4.20	£7.00
Graphic Novel 2 (Jun 1991), 200pgs, reprints				£1.40	£4.20	£7.00

ARGONAUTS
Eternity; 1 1991-5 1992?

	$Good	$Fine	$N.Mint	£Good	£Fine	£N.Mint
1-5 ND	$0.25	$0.75	$1.25	£0.15	£0.45	£0.75
Title Value:	$1.25	$3.75	$6.25	£0.75	£2.25	£3.75

ARGONAUTS: SYSTEM CRASH, THE
Alpha Productions,MS; 1 Jan 1994-present ?

	$Good	$Fine	$N.Mint	£Good	£Fine	£N.Mint
1 ND	$0.45	$1.35	$2.25	£0.30	£0.90	£1.50
Title Value:	$0.45	$1.35	$2.25	£0.30	£0.90	£1.50

Note: solicited and advertised, but probably never came out

ARGOSY, THE
Caliber Press,OS; 1 Dec 1991

	$Good	$Fine	$N.Mint	£Good	£Fine	£N.Mint
1 ND reprints from Dark Horse Presents						
	$0.45	$1.35	$2.25	£0.30	£0.90	£1.50
Title Value:	$0.45	$1.35	$2.25	£0.30	£0.90	£1.50

ARGUS
DC Comics,MS; 1 Apr 1995-6 Oct 1995

	$Good	$Fine	$N.Mint	£Good	£Fine	£N.Mint
1-6 spin-off from The Flash series						
	$0.35	$1.05	$1.75	£0.20	£0.60	£1.00
Title Value:	$2.10	$6.30	$10.50	£1.20	£3.60	£6.00

ARIANE AND BLUEBEARD
Eclipse,OS; nn 1989

	$Good	$Fine	$N.Mint	£Good	£Fine	£N.Mint
nn ND squarebound, P. Craig Russell cover and art						
	$0.40	$1.20	$2.00	£0.25	£0.75	£1.25
Title Value:	$0.40	$1.20	$2.00	£0.25	£0.75	£1.25

Note: based on opera by Maeterlinck

ARIK KHAN
Silver Snail; 1 1977-3 1979

	$Good	$Fine	$N.Mint	£Good	£Fine	£N.Mint
1-3 ND	$0.30	$0.90	$1.50	£0.20	£0.60	£1.00
Title Value:	$0.90	$2.70	$4.50	£0.60	£1.80	£3.00

ARIK KHAN (2ND SERIES)
A Plus Comics; 1 Jul 1991-3 1991

	$Good	$Fine	$N.Mint	£Good	£Fine	£N.Mint
1-3 ND 48pgs	$0.45	$1.35	$2.25	£0.30	£0.90	£1.50
Title Value:	$1.35	$4.05	$6.75	£0.90	£2.70	£4.50

ARION, LORD OF ATLANTIS
DC Comics; 1 Nov 1982-35 Sep 1985

	$Good	$Fine	$N.Mint	£Good	£Fine	£N.Mint
1-35	$0.15	$0.45	$0.60	£0.10	£0.35	£0.60
Title Value:	$5.25	$15.75	$26.25	£3.50	£12.25	£21.00

ARION, LORD OF ATLANTIS SPECIAL
DC Comics; 1 1985

	$Good	$Fine	$N.Mint	£Good	£Fine	£N.Mint
1	$0.25	$0.75	$1.25	£0.15	£0.45	£0.75
Title Value:	$0.25	$0.75	$1.25	£0.15	£0.45	£0.75

ARION, THE IMMORTAL
DC Comics,MS; 1 Jul 1992-6 Dec 1992

	$Good	$Fine	$N.Mint	£Good	£Fine	£N.Mint
1-5	$0.25	$0.75	$1.25	£0.15	£0.45	£0.75
6 Power Girl guest stars						
	$0.25	$0.75	$1.25	£0.15	£0.45	£0.75
Title Value:	$1.50	$4.50	$7.50	£0.90	£2.70	£4.50

ARISTOCRATIC X-TRATERRESTRIAL TIME-TRAVELLING THIEVES
Fictioneer; 1 Aug 1986; 1 Feb 1987-12 1988

(becomes X-Thieves)

	$Good	$Fine	$N.Mint	£Good	£Fine	£N.Mint
1 ND one shot issue; black and white						
	$0.35	$1.05	$1.75	£0.25	£0.75	£1.25
1 ND regular series begins; black and white						
	$0.35	$1.05	$1.75	£0.25	£0.75	£1.25
1 2nd printing, ND as above						
	$0.30	$0.90	$1.50	£0.20	£0.60	£1.00
2-12 ND	$0.30	$0.90	$1.50	£0.20	£0.60	£1.00
Title Value:	$4.30	$12.90	$21.50	£2.90	£8.70	£14.50

ARMAGEDDON 2001
Cross-over series running throughout the DC summer 1991 annuals and tied into a limited series of the same name. The order of the story is as follows:
1) Armageddon 2001 1
2) Superman Annual 3
3) Batman Annual 15
4) Justice League America Annual 5
5) Hawk and Dove Annual 2
6) Hawkworld Annual 2
7) Flash Annual 4
8) Action Comics Annual 3
9) Legion '91 Annual 2
10) New Titans Annual 7
11) Adventures of Superman Annual 3
12) Detective Comics Annual 4
13) Justice League Europe Annual 2
14) Armageddon 2001 2

ARMAGEDDON 2001 (LIMITED SERIES)
DC Comics,MS; 1 May 1991-2 Oct 1991

	$Good	$Fine	$N.Mint	£Good	£Fine	£N.Mint
1 64pgs, multi cross-over series, most major DC characters appear, 1st appearance Waverider						
	$0.50	$1.50	$2.50	£0.30	£0.90	£1.50
1 2nd printing, "II" in box on cover						
	$0.40	$1.20	$2.00	£0.25	£0.75	£1.25

	$Good	$Fine	$N.Mint	£Good	£Fine	£N.Mint
1 3rd printing	$0.40	$1.20	$2.00	£0.25	£0.75	£1.25
2 64pgs	$0.40	$1.20	$2.00	£0.25	£0.75	£1.25
Title Value:	$1.70	$5.10	$8.50	£1.05	£3.15	£5.25

ARMAGEDDON: INFERNO
DC Comics,MS; 1 Apr 1992-4 Jul 1992

	$Good	$Fine	$N.Mint	£Good	£Fine	£N.Mint
1 Batman, Creeper, Spectre appear	$0.15	$0.45	$0.75	£0.10	£0.35	£0.60
2 Superman, Flash, Lobo, Wonder Woman, Hawkman appear	$0.15	$0.45	$0.75	£0.10	£0.35	£0.60
3-4 Justice Society of America appears	$0.15	$0.45	$0.75	£0.10	£0.35	£0.60
Title Value:	$0.60	$1.80	$3.00	£0.40	£1.40	£2.40

ARMAGEDDON: THE ALIEN AGENDA
DC Comics,MS; 1 Nov 1991-4 Feb 1992

	$Good	$Fine	$N.Mint	£Good	£Fine	£N.Mint
1 sequel to Armageddon: 2001, Jerry Ordway art	$0.15	$0.45	$0.75	£0.10	£0.35	£0.60
2 Nasser art	$0.15	$0.45	$0.75	£0.10	£0.35	£0.60
3 Weiss art	$0.15	$0.45	$0.75	£0.10	£0.35	£0.60
4 George Perez art	$0.15	$0.45	$0.75	£0.10	£0.35	£0.60
Title Value:	$0.60	$1.80	$3.00	£0.40	£1.40	£2.40

ARMED & DANGEROUS
Acclaim Comics/Armada,MS; 1 Apr 1996-present

	$Good	$Fine	$N.Mint	£Good	£Fine	£N.Mint
1 ND Bob Hall script and art; black and white	$0.40	$1.20	$2.00	£0.25	£0.75	£1.25
Title Value:	$0.40	$1.20	$2.00	£0.25	£0.75	£1.25

ARMOR
Continuity; 1 Sep 1985; 1 1987-14 1991

	$Good	$Fine	$N.Mint	£Good	£Fine	£N.Mint
1 Neal Adams, Grindberg, Murray art; silver logo on Neal Adams cover; indicia reads "Revengers featuring Armor and Silver Streak"	$0.45	$1.35	$2.25	£0.30	£0.90	£1.50
1 Neal Adams, Grindberg, Murray art; red logo on Neal Adams cover	$0.35	$1.05	$1.75	£0.25	£0.75	£1.25
2 Neal Adams cover; intro The Silver Streak	$0.35	$1.05	$1.75	£0.25	£0.75	£1.25
3-5 Neal Adams cover	$0.35	$1.05	$1.75	£0.25	£0.75	£1.25
6-10 Neal Adams cover	$0.30	$0.90	$1.50	£0.20	£0.60	£1.00
11-12 Son of Sacraman story	$0.30	$0.90	$1.50	£0.20	£0.60	£1.00
13 Son of Sacraman story, Neal Adams cover	$0.30	$0.90	$1.50	£0.20	£0.60	£1.00
14 Son of Sacraman story	$0.30	$0.90	$1.50	£0.20	£0.60	£1.00
Title Value:	$4.90	$14.70	$24.50	£3.35	£10.05	£16.75

Note: irregularly published and Non-Distributed on the news-stands in the U.K.

ARMOR (2ND SERIES)
Continuity; 1 Apr 1993-6 1994

	$Good	$Fine	$N.Mint	£Good	£Fine	£N.Mint
1 Deathwatch 2000 part 3; pre-bagged with 2 trading cards, Mike Golden silver embossed cover	$0.35	$1.05	$1.75	£0.25	£0.75	£1.25
2 Deathwatch 2000 part 9; pre-bagged with trading card	$0.35	$1.05	$1.75	£0.25	£0.75	£1.25
3 Deathwatch 2000 part 15; pre-bagged with trading card; Tyvek indestructible cover	$0.35	$1.05	$1.75	£0.25	£0.75	£1.25
4 Rise of Magic X-over, embossed parchment cover	$0.35	$1.05	$1.75	£0.25	£0.75	£1.25
5-6 Rise of Magic X-over, Michael Golden parchment cover	$0.35	$1.05	$1.75	£0.25	£0.75	£1.25
Title Value:	$2.10	$6.30	$10.50	£1.50	£4.50	£7.50

Note: all Non-Distributed on the news-stands in the U.K.

ARMORINES
Valiant; 1 Jul 1994-12 Jun 1995

	$Good	$Fine	$N.Mint	£Good	£Fine	£N.Mint
1	$0.40	$1.20	$2.00	£0.25	£0.75	£1.25
1 Valiant Validated Signature Series Edition (Jun 1994), signed by at least one creator; 5,300 copies with certificate and Mylar sleeve	$1.50	$4.50	$7.50	£1.00	£3.00	£5.00
2-4	$0.40	$1.20	$2.00	£0.20	£0.60	£1.00
5 Chaos Effect tie-in	$0.40	$1.20	$2.00	£0.20	£0.60	£1.00
6-12	$0.40	$1.20	$2.00	£0.20	£0.60	£1.00
Title Value:	$6.30	$18.90	$31.50	£3.45	£10.35	£17.25

Nore: all Non-Distributed on the news-stands in the U.K.

ARMORINES YEARBOOK
Valiant; 1 Jun 1995

	$Good	$Fine	$N.Mint	£Good	£Fine	£N.Mint
1 ND intro Linhoff	$0.40	$1.20	$2.00	£0.25	£0.75	£1.25
Title Value:	$0.40	$1.20	$2.00	£0.25	£0.75	£1.25

ARMY AT WAR
DC Comics; 1 Oct/Nov 1978
(see also Our Army at War)

	$Good	$Fine	$N.Mint	£Good	£Fine	£N.Mint
1 ND 44pgs, Kubert cover	$0.40	$1.20	$2.00	£0.25	£0.75	£1.25
Title Value:	$0.40	$1.20	$2.00	£0.25	£0.75	£1.25

ARMY ATTACK (1ST SERIES)
Charlton; 1 Jul 1964-4 Feb 1965

	$Good	$Fine	$N.Mint	£Good	£Fine	£N.Mint
1 distributed in the U.K.	$2.90	$8.75	$17.50	£1.65	£5.00	£10.00
2-4 distributed in the U.K.	$1.65	$5.00	$10.00	£1.05	£3.25	£6.50
Title Value:	$7.85	$23.75	$47.50	£4.80	£14.75	£29.50

ARMY ATTACK (2ND SERIES)
Charlton; 38 Jul 1965-47 Feb 1967
(formerly US Air Force Comics #1-37)

	$Good	$Fine	$N.Mint	£Good	£Fine	£N.Mint
38-40 distributed in the U.K.	$1.65	$5.00	$10.00	£1.00	£3.00	£6.00
41-47 distributed in the U.K.	$2.00	$6.00	$10.00	£1.00	£3.00	£5.00
Title Value:	$18.95	$57.00	$100.00	£10.00	£30.00	£53.00

ARMY SURPLUS COMICS
(see Cutey Bunny)

ARMY WAR HEROES
Charlton; 1 Dec 1963-38 Jun 1970

	$Good	$Fine	$N.Mint	£Good	£Fine	£N.Mint
1 distributed in the U.K.	$3.00	$9.00	$18.00	£2.00	£6.00	£12.00
2-10 distributed in the U.K.	$1.50	$4.50	$9.00	£1.00	£3.00	£6.00
11-20 distributed in the U.K.	$1.50	$4.50	$7.50	£1.00	£3.00	£5.00
21 distributed in the U.K.	$1.40	$4.20	$7.00	£0.90	£2.70	£4.50
22 1st appearance Iron Corporal; distributed in the U.K.	$1.40	$4.20	$7.00	£0.90	£2.70	£4.50
23-30 distributed in the U.K.	$1.40	$4.20	$7.00	£0.90	£2.70	£4.50
31-38 distributed in the U.K.	$1.20	$3.60	$6.00	£0.80	£2.40	£4.00
Title Value:	$55.10	$165.30	$292.00	£36.40	£109.20	£193.00

ARRGH!
Marvel Comics Group; 1 Dec 1974-5 Sep 1975

	$Good	$Fine	$N.Mint	£Good	£Fine	£N.Mint
1-2 ND scarce in the U.K.	$0.80	$2.40	$4.00	£0.50	£1.50	£2.50
3-5 ND scarce in the U.K.	$0.45	$1.35	$2.25	£0.30	£0.90	£1.50
Title Value:	$2.95	$8.85	$14.75	£1.90	£5.70	£9.50

Note: all satire material.

ARROW, THE
Malibu,OS; 1 Oct 1992

	$Good	$Fine	$N.Mint	£Good	£Fine	£N.Mint
1 ND Protectors spin-off, Protectors guest star; Lee Moder pencils, colour	$0.30	$0.90	$1.50	£0.20	£0.60	£1.00
Title Value:	$0.30	$0.90	$1.50	£0.20	£0.60	£1.00

ART OF ERIK LARSEN
Image,OS; nn Feb 1995

	$Good	$Fine	$N.Mint	£Good	£Fine	£N.Mint
1 ND 48pgs, information and artwork and even helpful hints!	$0.90	$2.70	$4.50	£0.60	£1.80	£3.00
Title Value:	$0.90	$2.70	$4.50	£0.60	£1.80	£3.00

ART OF HOMAGE STUDIOS, THE
Image,OS; 1 Dec 1993

	$Good	$Fine	$N.Mint	£Good	£Fine	£N.Mint
1 ND 48pgs, squarebound; pin-ups, art and sketches by Lee, Silvestri, Williams and Portacio amongst others	$0.90	$2.70	$4.50	£0.60	£1.80	£3.00
Title Value:	$0.90	$2.70	$4.50	£0.60	£1.80	£3.00

ASH
Event Comics; 1 Nov 1994-present

	$Good	$Fine	$N.Mint	£Good	£Fine	£N.Mint
1 ND Joe Quesada and Jimmy Palmiotti story and art; pin-up by Barry Smith	$3.00	$9.00	$15.00	£2.00	£6.00	£10.00
1 ND Connoisseur's Kit (May 1995) - signed and numbered #1 with certificate and lithograph, all pre-bagged	$5.00	$15.00	$25.00	£3.00	£9.00	£15.00
2 ND Joe Quesada and Jimmy Palmiotti story and art; pin-up by Mike Mignola	$2.40	$7.00	$12.00	£1.60	£4.80	£8.00
3 ND Joe Quesada and Jimmy Palmiotti story and art	$0.80	$2.40	$4.00	£0.80	£2.40	£4.00
4 ND Joe Quesada and Jimmy Palmiotti story and art	$0.50	$1.50	$2.50	£0.35	£1.05	£1.75
4 Gold Fahrenheit Edition, ND scarce in the U.K. limited to 2,500 copies	$5.50	$16.50	$27.50	£4.00	£12.00	£20.00
4 Red Fahrenheit Edition, ND scarce in the U.K. limited to 1,500 copies	$8.00	$24.00	$40.00	£6.00	£18.00	£30.00
4 White Fahrenheit Edition, ND scarce in the U.K. limited to 500 copies	$14.00	$42.00	$70.00	£10.00	£30.00	£50.00
5 ND Joe Quesada and Jimmy Palmiotti story and art	$0.50	$1.50	$2.50	£0.35	£1.05	£1.75
5 ND variant cover by The Brothers Hildebrandt	$0.60	$1.80	$3.00	£0.40	£1.20	£2.00
6 ND Joe Quesada and Jimmy Palmiotti story and art	$0.50	$1.50	$2.50	£0.30	£0.90	£1.50
6 ND variant cover by Mark Texeira	$0.50	$1.50	$2.50	£0.30	£0.90	£1.50
Title Value:	$41.30	$123.70	$206.50	£29.10	£87.30	£145.50

ASHES
Caliber Press,MS; 1 Sep 1990-6 May 1991

	$Good	$Fine	$N.Mint	£Good	£Fine	£N.Mint
1-6 ND 48pgs, horror anthology by John Bergin	$0.45	$1.35	$2.25	£0.30	£0.90	£1.50
Title Value:	$2.70	$8.10	$13.50	£1.80	£5.40	£9.00

Note: issue 4 has #3 in indicia.

ASSASSIN
TSR; 1 1990-4 1991

	$Good	$Fine	$N.Mint	£Good	£Fine	£N.Mint
1-4 distributed in the U.K.	$0.40	$1.20	$2.00	£0.25	£0.75	£1.25
Title Value:	$1.60	$4.80	$8.00	£1.00	£3.00	£5.00

ASSASSIN FORCE
Greater Mercury Comics; 1 Feb 1992-2 Mar 1992

	$Good	$Fine	$N.Mint	£Good	£Fine	£N.Mint
1 regular team story begins with seven different cover versions/origin story extras; Maxwell Faraday cover and origin story	$0.35	$1.05	$1.75	£0.25	£0.75	£1.25
1 Sting/Ray cover and origin story	$0.35	$1.05	$1.75	£0.25	£0.75	£1.25

	$Good	$Fine	$N.Mint	£Good	£Fine	£N.Mint
1 Crimson Cougar cover and origin story						
	$0.35	$1.05	$1.75	£0.25	£0.75	£1.25
1 Grips cover and origin story						
	$0.35	$1.05	$1.75	£0.25	£0.75	£1.25
1 Death Hawk cover and origin story						
	$0.35	$1.05	$1.75	£0.25	£0.75	£1.25
1 Death Lord cover and origin story						
	$0.35	$1.05	$1.75	£0.25	£0.75	£1.25
1 Vengeance cover and origin story						
	$0.35	$1.05	$1.75	£0.25	£0.75	£1.25
2	$0.35	$1.05	$1.75	£0.25	£0.75	£1.25
Title Value:	$2.80	$8.40	$14.00	£2.00	£6.00	£10.00

Note: cover colours for variants are: Dark Blue, Green, Grey, Light Blue, Orange, Red and Yellow. All Non-Distributed on the news-stands in the U.K.

ASSASSINETTE
Pocket Change Comics; 1 1995-present

	$Good	$Fine	$N.Mint	£Good	£Fine	£N.Mint
1-8 ND Bob Dixon script, Ed Ball art; black and white						
	$0.45	$1.35	$2.25	£0.30	£0.90	£1.50
Title Value:	$3.60	$10.80	$18.00	£2.40	£7.20	£12.00

ASSASSINETTE: HARDCORE
Pocket Change Comics,MS; 1 Jun 1995-2 Aug 1995

	$Good	$Fine	$N.Mint	£Good	£Fine	£N.Mint
1-2 ND Bob Dixon script, Scott Shriver art; black and white						
	$0.45	$1.35	$2.25	£0.30	£0.90	£1.50
Title Value:	$0.90	$2.70	$4.50	£0.60	£1.80	£3.00

ASSASSINS INC.
Silverline Comics; 1-4 1987

	$Good	$Fine	$N.Mint	£Good	£Fine	£N.Mint
1-4 ND Rich Buckler inks						
	$0.25	$0.75	$1.25	£0.15	£0.45	£0.75
Title Value:	$1.00	$3.00	$5.00	£0.60	£1.80	£3.00

ASTER
Entity Comics; 0 May 1995; 1 Oct 1994-4 Feb 1995

	$Good	$Fine	$N.Mint	£Good	£Fine	£N.Mint
0 ND origin told, George Perez cover						
	$0.70	$2.10	$3.50	£0.40	£1.20	£2.00
1 ND foil-stamped cover by Jae lee						
	$0.80	$2.40	$4.00	£0.50	£1.50	£2.50
1 ND Signed Limited Edition (May 1995) - in protective case with certificate; 500 copies						
	$4.50	$13.50	$22.50	£2.50	£7.50	£12.50
1 ND Ashcan Signed and Numbered (May 1995) - in protective case with certificate; 500 copies						
	$3.00	$9.00	$15.00	£2.00	£6.00	£10.00
1 2nd printing, ND (Mar 1995)						
	$0.60	$1.80	$3.00	£0.40	£1.20	£2.00
2-3 ND foil-stamped cover by Joe Quesada						
	$0.60	$1.80	$3.00	£0.40	£1.20	£2.00
3 ND variant cover $1.00	$3.00	$5.00	£0.50	£1.50	£2.50
4 ND foil-stamped cover by Joe Quesada						
	$0.60	$1.80	$3.00	£0.40	£1.20	£2.00
Title Value:	$12.40	$37.20	$62.00	£7.50	£22.50	£37.50

Aster (May 1995)
Trade paperback reprints issues #1-4 with pin-ups
by Jae Lee, Joe Quesada and others

				£1.70	£5.10	£8.50

ASTER: THE LAST CELESTIAL KNIGHT
Entity Comics; 1 Jul 1995-2 1995

	$Good	$Fine	$N.Mint	£Good	£Fine	£N.Mint
1 ND Narcisco and Ronaldo Roxas script and art; chromium covers						
	$0.80	$2.40	$4.00	£0.50	£1.50	£2.50
2 ND	$0.80	$2.40	$4.00	£0.50	£1.50	£2.50
Title Value:	$1.60	$4.80	$8.00	£1.00	£3.00	£5.00

ASTONISHING TALES
Marvel Comics Group; 1 Aug 1970-36 Jul 1976
(see Ka-Zar, X-Men #10)

	$Good	$Fine	$N.Mint	£Good	£Fine	£N.Mint
1 ND Ka-Zar and Dr. Doom in separate stories begin (Ka-Zar vs. Kraven, part Jack Kirby art, Wood inks						
	$3.75	$11.00	$22.50	£2.50	£7.50	£15.00
2 Ka-Zar vs. Kraven, Jack Kirby art, Wood inks						
	$1.80	$5.25	$9.00	£1.20	£3.60	£6.00
3-4 part Barry Smith art						
	$2.50	$7.50	$12.50	£1.20	£3.60	£6.00
5 Dr. Doom vs. Red Skull, part Barry Smith art						
	$2.50	$7.50	$12.50	£1.20	£3.60	£6.00
6 Black Panther appears, part Barry Smith art						
	$2.50	$7.50	$12.50	£1.20	£3.60	£6.00
7 Black Panther appears						
	$1.50	$4.50	$7.50	£0.70	£2.10	£3.50
8 ND 48pgs, squarebound, last Dr. Doom story and cover credit						
	$1.50	$4.50	$7.50	£1.00	£3.00	£5.00
9 Gill Kane cover, features Lorna the Jungle Girl reprint (1950s)						
	$0.70	$2.10	$3.50	£0.45	£1.35	£2.25
10 Gill Kane cover, part Barry Smith art, features Lorna the Jungle Girl reprint (1950s)						
	$1.20	$3.60	$6.00	£0.80	£2.40	£4.00
11 Gill Kane cover, origin Ka-Zar and Zabu						
	$0.90	$2.70	$4.50	£0.60	£1.80	£3.00
12 origin Man-Thing retold, Neal Adams art						
	$1.50	$4.50	$7.50	£1.00	£3.00	£5.00
13 Man-Thing vs. Ka-Zar						
	$0.70	$2.10	$3.50	£0.45	£1.35	£2.25
14-15 Gil Kane cover						
	$0.45	$1.35	$2.25	£0.30	£0.90	£1.50
16	$0.45	$1.35	$2.25	£0.30	£0.90	£1.50
17 Nick Fury appears						
	$0.45	$1.35	$2.25	£0.30	£0.90	£1.50
18 Nick Fury appears, X-over Spiderman #104, Gil Kane cover						
	$0.45	$1.35	$2.25	£0.30	£0.90	£1.50
19-20 Nick Fury appears						
	$0.45	$1.35	$2.25	£0.30	£0.90	£1.50

	$Good	$Fine	$N.Mint	£Good	£Fine	£N.Mint
21 1st appearance It! the Colossus, Steve Ditko back-up reprint						
	$0.45	$1.35	$2.25	£0.30	£0.90	£1.50
22-23	$0.45	$1.35	$2.25	£0.30	£0.90	£1.50
24 ND It! vs. Fin Fang Foom						
	$0.45	$1.35	$2.25	£0.30	£0.90	£1.50
25 1st appearance Deathlok, George Perez' 1st professional artwork (last two pages only - see Creatures on the Loose #33)						
	$5.75	$17.50	$35.00	£3.50	£10.50	£20.00
26 2nd appearance Deathlok						
	$2.50	$7.50	$12.50	£1.50	£4.50	£7.50
27 LD in the U.K. Deathlok						
	$2.50	$7.50	$12.50	£1.50	£4.50	£7.50
28 Deathlok	$2.00	$6.00	$10.00	£1.20	£3.60	£6.00
29 Guardians of the Galaxy: 1st appearance reprinted from Marvel Super-Heroes #18, no Deathlok						
	$2.05	$6.25	$12.50	£1.25	£3.75	£7.50
30 Deathlok	$1.50	$4.50	$7.50	£1.00	£3.00	£5.00
31 Deathlok, Wrightson cover						
	$1.50	$4.50	$7.50	£1.00	£3.00	£5.00
32-36 Deathlok	$1.50	$4.50	$7.50	£1.00	£3.00	£5.00
Title Value:	$53.80	$161.35	$282.25	£33.00	£98.75	£172.50

ARTISTS
Wood art 1-4.
FEATURES
Ka-Zar in 1-20. Dr.Doom in 1-8. Man Thing in 12, 13. It! in 21-24. Deathlok in 25-28, 30-36.
REPRINT FEATURES
The Watcher in 31.

ASTRO BOY
Gold Key,OS TV; 1 Aug 1965

	$Good	$Fine	$N.Mint	£Good	£Fine	£N.Mint
1 very scarce in the U.K. thought to be distributed in the U.K.						
	$45.00	$135.00	$270.00	£30.00	£90.00	£180.00
Title Value:	$45.00	$135.00	$270.00	£30.00	£90.00	£180.00

ASTRO BOY, THE ORIGINAL
Now Comics, TV; 1 Sep 1987-20 1989

	$Good	$Fine	$N.Mint	£Good	£Fine	£N.Mint
1 ND Ken Steacy cover/art begins						
	$0.60	$1.80	$3.00	£0.40	£1.20	£2.00
2-3 ND	$0.45	$1.35	$2.25	£0.30	£0.90	£1.50
4-20 ND	$0.35	$1.05	$1.75	£0.25	£0.75	£1.25
Title Value:	$7.45	$22.35	$37.25	£5.25	£15.75	£26.25

ASTRO CITY
Image; 1 Aug 1995-present

	$Good	$Fine	$N.Mint	£Good	£Fine	£N.Mint
1 ND Kurt Busiek script, Brent Anderson art; Alex Ross cover and poster at centrefold						
	$0.45	$1.35	$2.25	£0.30	£0.90	£1.50
2-5 ND	$0.45	$1.35	$2.25	£0.30	£0.90	£1.50
Title Value:	$2.25	$6.75	$11.25	£1.50	£4.50	£7.50

ASTROBOYS WAVE WARRIORS
Herbie Fletcher Productions; 1 1987

	$Good	$Fine	$N.Mint	£Good	£Fine	£N.Mint
1 ND colour	$0.15	$0.45	$0.75	£0.10	£0.35	£0.60
Title Value:	$0.15	$0.45	$0.75	£0.10	£0.35	£0.60

ASYLUM
New Comics Group; 1 Jun 1989-4 1990

	$Good	$Fine	$N.Mint	£Good	£Fine	£N.Mint
1 ND Wrightson cover, Alex Nino/Jon B. Bright art						
	$0.30	$0.90	$1.50	£0.20	£0.60	£1.00
2-4 ND	$0.30	$0.90	$1.50	£0.20	£0.60	£1.00
Title Value:	$1.20	$3.60	$6.00	£0.80	£2.40	£4.00

ASYLUM
Millennium; 1 Sep 1993-6 1994

	$Good	$Fine	$N.Mint	£Good	£Fine	£N.Mint
1-2 ND	$0.45	$1.35	$2.25	£0.25	£0.75	£1.25
3 ND 48pgs	$0.45	$1.35	$2.25	£0.50	£1.50	£2.50
4-6 ND	$0.45	$1.35	$2.25	£0.25	£0.75	£1.25
Title Value:	$2.70	$8.10	$13.50	£1.75	£5.25	£8.75

The Best of Asylum Volume 1 (Jun 1994)
John Bolton, Neil Gaiman, P. Craig Russell work featured

				£1.00	£3.00	£5.00

The Best of Asylum Volume 2 (Jul 1994)
John Bolton work featured

				£1.00	£3.00	£5.00

ASYLUM
Maximum Comic Press; 1 Dec 1995-present

	$Good	$Fine	$N.Mint	£Good	£Fine	£N.Mint
1 ND Rob Liefeld, Stephen Platt, Arthur Adams creative team begins						
	$0.60	$1.80	$3.00	£0.40	£1.20	£2.00
Title Value:	$0.60	$1.80	$3.00	£0.40	£1.20	£2.00

ASYLUM: THE BEGINNING
Millennium; 1 Jan 1995

	$Good	$Fine	$N.Mint	£Good	£Fine	£N.Mint
1 ND contributors include Nancy Collins, Jim Higgins and John Bergin						
	$0.60	$1.80	$3.00	£0.40	£1.20	£2.00
Title Value:	$0.60	$1.80	$3.00	£0.40	£1.20	£2.00

ATARI FORCE
DC Comics; 1 Jan 1984-20 May 1985
(see Teen Titans #27)

	$Good	$Fine	$N.Mint	£Good	£Fine	£N.Mint
1 1st appearance Dart, Tempest, Babe, Packrat, Morphea; Garcia Lopez art						
	$0.15	$0.45	$0.75	£0.10	£0.35	£0.60
2-12 Garcia Lopez art						
	$0.15	$0.45	$0.75	£0.10	£0.35	£0.60
13 Keith Giffen back-up story						
	$0.15	$0.45	$0.75	£0.10	£0.35	£0.60
14-20	$0.15	$0.45	$0.75	£0.10	£0.35	£0.60
Title Value:	$3.00	$9.00	$15.00	£2.00	£7.00	£12.00

ATARI FORCE SPECIAL
DC Comics; 1 Apr 1986

	$Good	$Fine	$N.Mint	£Good	£Fine	£N.Mint
1 ND Rogers art	$0.25	$0.75	$1.25	£0.15	£0.45	£0.75
Title Value:	$0.25	$0.75	$1.25	£0.15	£0.45	£0.75

ATLANTIS CHRONICLES
DC Comics,MS; 1 Mar 1990-7 Sep 1990
1-7 Peter David script

	$Good	$Fine	$N.Mint	£Good	£Fine	£N.Mint
	$0.45	$1.35	$2.25	£0.30	£0.90	£1.50
Title Value:	$3.15	$9.45	$15.75	£2.10	£6.30	£10.50

Note: all 48pgs, Deluxe Format

ATLAS
Dark Horse,MS; 1 Feb 1994-4 Aug 1994

	$Good	$Fine	$N.Mint	£Good	£Fine	£N.Mint
1-4 ND Bruce Zick script and art	$0.45	$1.35	$2.25	£0.30	£0.90	£1.50
Title Value:	$1.80	$5.40	$9.00	£1.20	£3.60	£6.00

ATOM ANT
Gold Key,OS TV; 1 Jan 1966

	$Good	$Fine	$N.Mint	£Good	£Fine	£N.Mint
1 very scarce in the U.K.	$33.00	$100.00	$200.00	£20.50	£62.50	£125.00
Title Value:	$33.00	$100.00	$200.00	£20.50	£62.50	£125.00

ATOM SPECIAL, SWORD OF THE
DC Comics; 1 Jul 1984-3 Jun 1988

	$Good	$Fine	$N.Mint	£Good	£Fine	£N.Mint
1-2 48pgs, Gil Kane cover and art	$0.25	$0.75	$1.25	£0.15	£0.45	£0.75
3 48pgs	$0.25	$0.75	$1.25	£0.15	£0.45	£0.75
Title Value:	$0.75	$2.25	$3.75	£0.45	£1.35	£2.25

ATOM SPECIAL, THE
DC Comics; 1 May 1993; 2 Jan 1995

	$Good	$Fine	$N.Mint	£Good	£Fine	£N.Mint
1 64pgs, squarebound, Steve Dillon art	$0.45	$1.35	$2.25	£0.30	£0.90	£1.50
2 64pgs, Atom re-discovers himself and his powers	$0.60	$1.80	$3.00	£0.40	£1.20	£2.00
Title Value:	$1.05	$3.15	$5.25	£0.70	£2.10	£3.50

ATOM THE CAT
A Plus Comics; 1 Aug 1991

	$Good	$Fine	$N.Mint	£Good	£Fine	£N.Mint
1 ND	$0.35	$1.05	$1.75	£0.25	£0.75	£1.25
Title Value:	$0.35	$1.05	$1.75	£0.25	£0.75	£1.25

ATOM, POWER OF THE
DC Comics; 1 Aug 1988-18 Nov 1989

	$Good	$Fine	$N.Mint	£Good	£Fine	£N.Mint
1	$0.25	$0.75	$1.25	£0.15	£0.45	£0.75
2-5	$0.15	$0.45	$0.75	£0.10	£0.35	£0.60
6 John Byrne pencils	$0.25	$0.75	$1.25	£0.15	£0.45	£0.75
7-8 Invasion X-over	$0.15	$0.45	$0.75	£0.10	£0.35	£0.60
9 Justice League International appear	$0.15	$0.45	$0.75	£0.10	£0.35	£0.60
10-18	$0.15	$0.45	$0.75	£0.10	£0.35	£0.60
Title Value:	$2.90	$8.70	$14.50	£1.90	£6.50	£11.10

ATOM, SWORD OF THE
DC Comics,MS; 1 Sep 1983-4 Dec 1983

	$Good	$Fine	$N.Mint	£Good	£Fine	£N.Mint
1-4 Gil Kane art	$0.15	$0.45	$0.75	£0.10	£0.35	£0.60
Title Value:	$0.60	$1.80	$3.00	£0.40	£1.40	£2.40

ATOM, THE
National Periodical Publications; 1 Jun/Jul 1962-45 Oct/Nov 1969

(see Action,Brave and the Bold,DC Comics Presents,Detective,Five-Star Super-Hero Spectacular,Power of the Atom,Showcase,Super-Team Family,World's Finest) (title becomes Atom and Hawkman with issue #39)

	$Good	$Fine	$N.Mint	£Good	£Fine	£N.Mint
1 1st appearance Jason Woodrue (Plant Master)	$92.50	$280.00	$750.00	£55.00	£165.00	£450.00
2	$38.00	$110.00	$300.00	£21.50	£65.00	£175.00
3 1st Time Pool story, origin and 1st appearance Chronos	$25.00	$75.00	$200.00	£12.50	£38.00	£100.00
4-5	$16.50	$50.00	$135.00	£8.75	£26.00	£70.00
6	$14.00	$43.00	$115.00	£7.50	£22.50	£60.00
7 1st Atom and Hawkman team-up (pre Hawkman #1)	$28.00	$82.50	$250.00	£12.50	£38.00	£115.00
8 Dr. Light, Justice League of America X-over	$14.00	$43.00	$115.00	£7.50	£22.50	£60.00
9-10	$14.00	$43.00	$115.00	£6.25	£18.50	£50.00
11-15	$10.00	$30.00	$80.00	£3.75	£11.00	£30.00
16-18	$8.00	$24.00	$65.00	£2.80	£8.25	£22.50
19 2nd appearance Zatanna (see Hawkman #4)	$8.00	$24.00	$65.00	£3.10	£9.25	£25.00
20	$8.00	$24.00	$65.00	£2.80	£8.25	£22.50
21-25	$6.25	$19.00	$45.00	£2.50	£7.50	£17.50
26-28	$6.25	$19.00	$45.00	£2.10	£6.25	£15.00
29 1st solo Silver Age appearance Golden Age Atom	$15.50	$47.00	$125.00	£5.50	£16.50	£45.00
30	$6.25	$19.00	$45.00	£2.10	£6.25	£15.00
31 Hawkman X-over	$6.25	$19.00	$45.00	£1.40	£4.25	£10.00
32-35	$6.25	$19.00	$45.00	£1.40	£4.25	£10.00
36 Golden Age Atom appears	$6.75	$20.50	$55.00	£2.15	£6.50	£17.50
37 1st appearance Major Mynah	$6.25	$19.00	$45.00	£1.40	£4.25	£10.00
38	$6.25	$19.00	$45.00	£1.40	£4.25	£10.00
39 title becomes Atom and Hawkman	$5.75	$17.50	$35.00	£1.65	£5.00	£10.00
40	$5.75	$17.50	$35.00	£1.65	£5.00	£10.00
41-42	$5.75	$17.50	$35.00	£1.40	£4.25	£8.50
43 1st appearance Gentleman Ghost	$5.75	$17.50	$35.00	£1.50	£4.50	£9.00
44 origin retold	$5.75	$17.50	$35.00	£1.50	£4.50	£9.00
45	$5.75	$17.50	$35.00	£1.40	£4.25	£8.50
Title Value:	$525.00	$1583.50	$4100.00	£228.40	£684.25	£1808.50

FEATURES
Atom solo, Hawkman solo in 40,41,43,44. Atom and Hawkman in 39,42,45.

ATOMIC AGE
Marvel Comics Group/Epic,MS; 1 Jan 1991-4 Apr 1991

	$Good	$Fine	$N.Mint	£Good	£Fine	£N.Mint
1-4 ND 48pgs	$0.80	$2.40	$4.00	£0.50	£1.50	£2.50
Title Value:	$3.20	$9.60	$16.00	£2.00	£6.00	£10.00

Note: Bookshelf Format

ATOMIC BUNNY
Charlton; 12 Aug 1958-19 Dec 1959

(previously Atomic Rabbit)

	$Good	$Fine	$N.Mint	£Good	£Fine	£N.Mint
12 distributed in the U.K.	$10.00	$30.00	$60.00	£6.50	£20.00	£40.00
13-19 distributed in the U.K.	$5.75	$17.50	$35.00	£3.75	£11.00	£22.50
Title Value:	$50.25	$152.50	$305.00	£32.75	£97.00	£197.50

ATOMIC CLONES
Comico; 1 1990-5 1991

	$Good	$Fine	$N.Mint	£Good	£Fine	£N.Mint
1-5 ND	$0.45	$1.35	$2.25	£0.30	£0.90	£1.50
Title Value:	$2.25	$6.75	$11.25	£1.50	£4.50	£7.50

ATOMIC MAN COMICS
Blackthorne; 1 Dec 1986-3 1987

	$Good	$Fine	$N.Mint	£Good	£Fine	£N.Mint
1-3 ND Bonivert art	$0.30	$0.90	$1.50	£0.20	£0.60	£1.00
Title Value:	$0.90	$2.70	$4.50	£0.60	£1.80	£3.00

ATOMIC MOUSE
A Plus Comics; 1 Feb 1991-2 1991

	$Good	$Fine	$N.Mint	£Good	£Fine	£N.Mint
1-2 ND reprints from 1950s/60s	$0.45	$1.35	$2.25	£0.30	£0.90	£1.50
Title Value:	$0.90	$2.70	$4.50	£0.60	£1.80	£3.00

ATOMIC RABBIT
Charlton; 1 Aug 1955-11 Mar 1958

(becomes Atomic Bunny)

1 scarce in the U.K. 1st appearance Atomic Rabbit

The Atom #2

Avengelyne Swimsuit Edition

Avengers #183

	$Good	$Fine	$N.Mint	£Good	£Fine	£N.Mint
	$18.50	$55.00	$112.50	£12.50	£38.00	£75.00
2-3 scarce in the U.K.						
	$7.50	$22.50	$45.00	£5.00	£15.00	£30.00
4-10	$5.75	$17.50	$35.00	£3.75	£11.00	£22.50
11 scarce in the U.K. giant						
	$7.50	$22.50	$45.00	£5.00	£15.00	£30.00
Title Value:	**$81.25**	**$245.00**	**$482.50**	**£53.75**	**£160.00**	**£322.50**

Note: the last two issue have been recorded with distribution stamps ie. distributed in the U.K. All the other issues were probably Non-Distributed.

ATTACK
Charlton; 1 Sep 1971-48 Oct 1984

	$Good	$Fine	$N.Mint	£Good	£Fine	£N.Mint
1 distributed in the U.K.						
	$0.45	$1.35	$2.25	£0.30	£0.90	£1.50
2-10 distributed in the U.K.						
	$0.35	$1.05	$1.75	£0.25	£0.75	£1.25
11-47 distributed in the U.K.						
	$0.30	$0.90	$1.50	£0.20	£0.60	£1.00
48 reprint; limited distributed in the U.K.						
	$0.30	$0.90	$1.50	£0.20	£0.60	£1.00
Title Value:	**$15.00**	**$45.00**	**$75.00**	**£10.15**	**£30.45**	**£50.75**

ATTACK OF THE MUTANT MONSTERS
A Plus Comics; 1 May 1991-2 1991

	$Good	$Fine	$N.Mint	£Good	£Fine	£N.Mint
1 ND 48pgs, Steve Ditko monster reprints						
	$0.45	$1.35	$2.25	£0.30	£0.90	£1.50
2 ND 48pgs, Reptisaurus reprints						
	$0.45	$1.35	$2.25	£0.30	£0.90	£1.50
Title Value:	**$0.90**	**$2.70**	**$4.50**	**£0.60**	**£1.80**	**£3.00**

AUTUMN
Caliber Press; 1 Oct 1995

	$Good	$Fine	$N.Mint	£Good	£Fine	£N.Mint
1 ND black and white						
	$0.60	$1.80	$3.00	£0.40	£1.20	£2.00
Title Value:	**$0.60**	**$1.80**	**$3.00**	**£0.40**	**£1.20**	**£2.00**

AVALON
Comico,MS; 1 Nov 1993-2 1994

	$Good	$Fine	$N.Mint	£Good	£Fine	£N.Mint
1 ND	$0.35	$1.05	$1.75	£0.25	£0.75	£1.25
1 ND Deluxe Edition, emerald foil logo						
	$0.60	$1.80	$3.00	£0.40	£1.20	£2.00
2 ND	$0.35	$1.05	$1.75	£0.25	£0.75	£1.25
2 ND Deluxe Edition, ruby foil logo						
	$0.60	$1.80	$3.00	£0.40	£1.20	£2.00
Title Value:	**$1.90**	**$5.70**	**$9.50**	**£1.30**	**£3.90**	**£6.50**

AVANT GUARD
Day One Comics; 1 Mar 1994

	$Good	$Fine	$N.Mint	£Good	£Fine	£N.Mint
1 ND Stephen Conley script and art; black and white						
	$0.45	$1.35	$2.25	£0.30	£0.90	£1.50
Title Value:	**$0.45**	**$1.35**	**$2.25**	**£0.30**	**£0.90**	**£1.50**

AVATAR COMICS
DC Comics,MS; 1 Dec 1990-3 Apr 1991

	$Good	$Fine	$N.Mint	£Good	£Fine	£N.Mint
1-3 96pgs	$0.60	$1.80	$3.00	£0.40	£1.20	£2.00
Title Value:	**$1.80**	**$5.40**	**$9.00**	**£1.20**	**£3.60**	**£6.00**

Note: based on TSR role-playing games. Issued every six weeks

Note also that these issues are prone to crinkly spines owing to the production process

AVENGELYNE
Maximum Comic Press; 1 May 1995-3 Aug 1995

	$Good	$Fine	$N.Mint	£Good	£Fine	£N.Mint
0 Ashcan Edition, 8.5" x 5.5" Blue card cover, featuring the same cover as Avengelyne #1						
	$3.00	$9.00	$15.00	£2.00	£6.00	£10.00
1 Gold Edition ND	$5.00	$15.00	$25.00	£3.00	£9.00	£15.00
1 Newstand Edition, ND Cathy Christian photo cover						
	$1.00	$3.00	$5.00	£1.00	£3.00	£5.00
1 Version A, ND Direct Marker Edition with wraparound chromium cover, Cathy Christian photo insert standing with spear						
	$1.40	$4.20	$7.00	£1.00	£3.00	£5.00
1 Version B, ND Direct Marker Edition with wraparound chromium cover, Cathy Christian photo insert standing with sword						
	$1.40	$4.20	$7.00	£1.00	£3.00	£5.00
1 Version C, ND Direct Marker Edition with wraparound chromium cover, Cathy Christian photo insert kneeling with sword						
	$1.40	$4.20	$7.00	£1.00	£3.00	£5.00
1 Version D, ND Direct Market Edition with wraparound chromium cover, Cathy Christian photo insert folded arms						
	$1.40	$4.20	$7.00	£1.00	£3.00	£5.00
2 ND pre-bagged with trading card						
	$0.80	$2.40	$4.00	£0.70	£2.10	£3.50
3 ND	$0.70	$2.10	$3.50	£0.50	£1.50	£2.50
3 ND Variant cover, Arthur Adams cover art						
	$2.00	$6.00	$10.00	£1.50	£4.50	£7.50
Title Value:	**$18.10**	**$54.30**	**$90.50**	**£12.70**	**£38.10**	**£63.50**

AVENGELYNE SWIMSUIT EDITION
Maximum Comic Press,OS; 1 Aug 1995

	$Good	$Fine	$N.Mint	£Good	£Fine	£N.Mint
1 ND photographs of Cathy Christian (sigh!) and pin-ups by Rob Liefeld, Mike Deodato, Dan Fraga and others; four cover variations available						
	$0.60	$1.80	$3.00	£0.40	£1.20	£2.00
Title Value:	**$0.60**	**$1.80**	**$3.00**	**£0.40**	**£1.20**	**£2.00**

AVENGELYNE/GLORY
Image,OS; 1 Sep 1995

	$Good	$Fine	$N.Mint	£Good	£Fine	£N.Mint
1 ND Rob Liefeld art, Robert Napton script; wraparound chromium cover						
	$0.80	$2.40	$4.00	£0.60	£1.80	£3.00
1 Variant cover, ND Glory on the left hand side of the cover back to back with Avengelyne						
	$1.00	$3.00	$5.00	£0.80	£2.40	£4.00
Title Value:	**$1.80**	**$5.40**	**$9.00**	**£1.40**	**£4.20**	**£7.00**

AVENGELYNE: POWER
Maximum Comic Press; 1 Oct 1995-present

	$Good	$Fine	$N.Mint	£Good	£Fine	£N.Mint
1 ND Rob Liefeld, Robert Napton script, John Stinsman art						
	$0.50	$1.50	$2.50	£0.30	£0.90	£1.50
2 ND	$0.50	$1.50	$2.50	£0.30	£0.90	£1.50
2 ND photo cover variant of Cathy Christian						
	$0.50	$1.50	$2.50	£0.30	£0.90	£1.50
3 ND	$0.50	$1.50	$2.50	£0.30	£0.90	£1.50
3 ND photo cover variant - holding sword aloft						
	$0.50	$1.50	$2.50	£0.30	£0.90	£1.50
3 ND photo cover variant - mini-crossbow						
	$0.50	$1.50	$2.50	£0.30	£0.90	£1.50
Title Value:	**$3.00**	**$9.00**	**$15.00**	**£1.80**	**£5.40**	**£9.00**

AVENGER, THE
I.W. Comics; 9 1964

	$Good	$Fine	$N.Mint	£Good	£Fine	£N.Mint
9 scarce distributed in the U.K. 50s reprints						
	$2.90	$8.75	$17.50	£1.65	£5.00	£10.00
Title Value:	**$2.90**	**$8.75**	**$17.50**	**£1.65**	**£5.00**	**£10.00**

AVENGERS
Marvel Comics Group; 1 Sep 1963-present

	$Good	$Fine	$N.Mint	£Good	£Fine	£N.Mint
1 origin and 1st appearance The Avengers (Thor, Iron Man, Ant-Man, Hulk, Wasp), Loki appears						
	$280.00	$840.00	$2250.00	£180.00	£540.00	£1450.00
1 ND Marvel Milestone Edition (Sep 1993), reprints issue #1						
	$0.60	$1.80	$3.00	£0.40	£1.20	£2.00
2 1st appearance Avengers Mansion and Space Phantom; Hulk leaves temporarily						
	$85.00	$255.00	$600.00	£55.00	£165.00	£395.00
3 scarce in the U.K. Sub-Mariner appears (teams with the Hulk against the Avengers); Spiderman appears; X-Men appear (joint 3rd appearance along with Tales of Suspense #49 and X-Men #3, all cover-dated Jan. 1964)						
	$55.00	$170.00	$400.00	£41.00	£120.00	£285.00
				[Scarce in high grade - Very Fine+ or better]		
4 Captain America first revived (his 1st Silver Age appearance), joins Avengers; storyline continues in Fantastic Four #26; 1st Silver Age appearance Baron Zemo I						
	$175.00	$520.00	$1400.00	£75.00	£225.00	£600.00
4 ND scarce in the U.K reprint (1966)						
	$14.00	$43.00	$100.00	£8.50	£26.00	£60.00
4 ND very rare in the U.K reprint (1966) with Golden Record to form complete sealed package						
	$28.00	$82.50	$195.00	£17.50	£52.50	£125.00
4 ND Marvel Milestone Edition (Mar 1995), metallic ink cover						
	$0.60	$1.80	$3.00	£0.40	£1.20	£2.00
5 less common in the U.K. Hulk leaves team for good						
	$32.00	$95.00	$225.00	£21.00	£62.50	£150.00
6 less common in the U.K. 1st appearance Baron Zemo teamed with The Masters of Evil						
	$26.00	$77.50	$185.00	£17.50	£52.50	£125.00
7	$25.00	$75.00	$175.00	£16.00	£49.00	£115.00
8 1st appearance Kang the Conqueror						
	$25.00	$75.00	$175.00	£16.00	£49.00	£115.00
9 very rare in the U.K. 1st appearance Wonder Man (dies - see #131)						
	$26.00	$77.50	$185.00	£17.50	£52.50	£150.00
10 scarce in the U.K. 1st appearance Immortus, 3rd Crime Circus, Hercules appears						
	$22.50	$67.50	$160.00	£15.50	£47.00	£110.00
11 scarce in the U.K. Spiderman appears (origin briefly retold)						
	$25.00	$75.00	$175.00	£16.00	£49.00	£115.00
12 Avengers vs. The Mole Man						
	$15.00	$45.00	$105.00	£10.00	£30.00	£70.00
13 Avengers vs. Count Nefaria						
	$15.00	$45.00	$105.00	£10.00	£30.00	£70.00
14	$15.00	$45.00	$105.00	£10.00	£30.00	£70.00
15 Baron Zemo dies	$15.00	$45.00	$105.00	£10.00	£30.00	£70.00
16 1st main line-up change: Hawkeye, Scarlet Witch, Quicksilver, Captain America (Thor, Giant Man, Wasp and Iron Man leave)						
	$17.00	$50.00	$120.00	£11.00	£34.00	£80.00
16 ND Marvel Milestone Edition (Oct 1993), reprints issue #16						
	$0.60	$1.80	$3.00	£0.40	£1.20	£2.00
17-18	$10.50	$32.00	$75.00	£7.00	£21.00	£50.00
19 1st appearance Swordsman, origin Hawkeye						
	$10.50	$32.00	$75.00	£7.00	£21.00	£50.00
20 Wood inks	$7.75	$23.50	$55.00	£5.00	£15.00	£35.00
21 Wood inks, 1st appearance original Powerman						
	$7.75	$23.50	$55.00	£5.00	£15.00	£35.00
22 Wood inks	$7.75	$23.50	$55.00	£5.00	£15.00	£35.00
23 last Silver Age issue, indicia-dated December 1965						
	$5.50	$17.00	$40.00	£4.00	£12.00	£28.00
24	$5.50	$17.00	$40.00	£4.00	£12.00	£28.00
25 Dr. Doom vs. Avengers, Fantastic Four appear						
	$5.50	$17.00	$40.00	£4.00	£12.00	£28.00
26-27	$5.50	$17.00	$40.00	£4.00	£12.00	£28.00
28 Giant-Man becomes Goliath						
	$5.50	$17.00	$40.00	£4.00	£12.00	£28.00
29-30	$5.50	$17.00	$40.00	£4.00	£12.00	£28.00
31-32	$4.00	$12.00	$28.00	£2.50	£7.50	£17.50
33-34 scarce in the U.K.						
	$4.00	$12.00	$28.00	£2.70	£8.00	£19.00
35 Goliath's power altered (height set)						
	$4.00	$12.00	$28.00	£2.50	£7.50	£17.50
36-37	$4.00	$12.00	$28.00	£2.50	£7.50	£17.50
38 Hercules joins	$4.00	$12.00	$28.00	£2.50	£7.50	£17.50
39	$4.00	$12.00	$28.00	£2.50	£7.50	£17.50
40 Sub-Mariner appears						
	$4.00	$12.00	$28.00	£2.50	£7.50	£17.50
41-42	$2.85	$8.50	$20.00	£1.70	£5.00	£12.00
43 1st appearance Red Guardian						
	$2.85	$8.50	$20.00	£1.70	£5.00	£12.00

VERY GENERAL PERCENTAGE CONVERSION CHART WHICH MAY BE USED TO CALCULATE LOW AND INBETWEEN GRADES:

	$Good	$Fine	$N.Mint	£Good	£Fine	£N.Mint
44-46	$2.85	$8.50	$20.00	£1.70	£5.00	£12.00
47 Magneto appears	$3.55	$10.50	$25.00	£2.10	£6.25	£15.00
48 1st appearance new Black Knight, Magneto appears	$3.55	$10.50	$25.00	£2.50	£7.50	£17.50
49 Magneto appears	$2.85	$8.50	$20.00	£2.10	£6.25	£15.00
50	$2.85	$8.50	$20.00	£1.70	£5.00	£12.00
51 Thor and Iron Man appear, Goliath's powers restored (variable height)	$3.30	$10.00	$20.00	£2.00	£6.00	£12.00
52	$3.30	$10.00	$20.00	£2.00	£6.00	£12.00
53 less common in the U.K. Avengers vs. original X-Men; story continues from X-Men #45	$5.00	$15.00	$30.00	£3.30	£10.00	£20.00
54 1st appearance of new Masters of Evil	$3.30	$10.00	$20.00	£2.00	£6.00	£12.00
55	$3.30	$10.00	$20.00	£2.00	£6.00	£12.00
56	$3.30	$10.00	$20.00	£1.80	£5.50	£11.00
57 1st appearance The Vision	$11.50	$35.00	$70.00	£5.75	£17.50	£35.00
58 rare in the U.K., origin The Vision	$7.50	$22.50	$45.00	£4.15	£12.50	£25.00
59 scarce in the U.K. 1st appearance Yellowjacket	$3.30	$10.00	$20.00	£2.30	£7.00	£14.00
60 scarce in the U.K. Yellowjacket and Wasp's wedding	$3.30	$10.00	$20.00	£2.30	£7.00	£14.00
61 scarce in the U.K. Dr. Strange appears	$3.30	$10.00	$20.00	£2.00	£6.00	£12.00
62 scarce in the U.K.	$3.30	$10.00	$20.00	£2.00	£6.00	£12.00
63 1st appearance new Goliath (Hawkeye)	$3.30	$10.00	$20.00	£1.80	£5.50	£11.00
64-65	$3.30	$10.00	$20.00	£1.80	£5.50	£11.00
66-67 Barry Smith art	$3.30	$10.00	$20.00	£2.30	£7.00	£14.00
68	$2.50	$7.50	$15.00	£1.65	£5.00	£10.00
69 1st Justice League of America inspired Squadron Sinister (later Squadron Supreme), 1st appearance Nighthawk	$2.50	$7.50	$15.00	£1.80	£5.50	£11.00
70 scarce in the U.K.	$2.50	$7.50	$15.00	£2.00	£6.00	£12.00
71 scarce in the U.K. 1st modern teaming of Golden Age Captain America, Human Torch & Sub-Mariner (later The Invaders), Black Knight appears	$3.65	$11.00	$22.00	£2.30	£7.00	£14.00
72-79	$2.30	$7.00	$14.00	£1.50	£4.50	£9.00
80 1st appearance Red Wolf and Lobo (not to be confused with DC's Lobo!)	$2.30	$7.00	$14.00	£1.50	£4.50	£9.00
81	$2.30	$7.00	$14.00	£1.50	£4.50	£9.00
82 Daredevil appears	$2.30	$7.00	$14.00	£1.50	£4.50	£9.00
83 scarce in the U.K. 1st appearance Valkyrie (Enchantress disguised), intro The Liberators	$2.30	$7.00	$14.00	£1.55	£4.75	£9.50
84 scarce in the U.K.	$2.30	$7.00	$14.00	£1.55	£4.75	£9.50
85-86	$2.30	$7.00	$14.00	£1.50	£4.50	£9.00
87 Black Panther's origin retold	$4.50	$13.50	$27.00	£2.50	£7.50	£15.00
88 Hulk and Professor X appear; story continues in Hulk #140	$2.30	$7.00	$14.00	£1.55	£4.75	£9.50
89 scarce in the U.K. Captain Marvel appears	$2.30	$7.00	$14.00	£1.65	£5.00	£10.00
90 scarce in the U.K.	$2.30	$7.00	$14.00	£1.65	£5.00	£10.00
91 scarce in the U.K. Captain Marvel appears	$2.30	$7.00	$14.00	£1.65	£5.00	£10.00
92 scarce in the U.K. Neal Adams cover	$2.30	$7.00	$14.00	£1.65	£5.00	£10.00
93 52pgs, scarce in the U.K., Neal Adams art, Kree-Skrull War begins, Fantastic Four appear	$8.25	$25.00	$50.00	£5.75	£17.50	£35.00
94 very scarce in the U.K. Neal Adams art	$5.00	$15.00	$30.00	£4.15	£12.50	£25.00
95-96 scarce in the U.K. Neal Adams art	$5.00	$15.00	$30.00	£3.65	£11.00	£22.00
97 scarce in the U.K. Gil Kane cover, Golden Age Captain America, Blazing Skull, Sub-Mariner, Human Torch, Patriot, Fin, Angel, Vision cameos, Kree/Skrull War ends	$3.00	$9.00	$18.00	£2.15	£6.50	£13.00
98 scarce in the U.K. Barry Smith art, Goliath reverts back to Hawkeye	$4.65	$14.00	$28.00	£2.80	£8.50	£17.00
99 scarce in the U.K. Barry Smith art	$4.65	$14.00	$28.00	£2.80	£8.50	£17.00
100 very scarce in the U.K. Barry Smith art; features everyone who had been an Avenger up to that point	$14.00	$43.00	$85.00	£6.25	£18.50	£37.50
101-106 scarce in the U.K.	$2.00	$6.00	$10.00	£1.60	£4.80	£8.00
107 scarce in the U.K. Jim Starlin art	$2.00	$6.00	$12.00	£1.70	£5.00	£8.50
108-109	$2.00	$6.00	$10.00	£1.40	£4.20	£7.00
110 original X-Men and Magneto appear, ties into Daredevil #99	$4.00	$12.00	$20.00	£2.00	£6.00	£10.00
111 original X-Men and Magneto appear, Daredevil and Black Widow guest-star; ties into Hulk #172 and Daredevil #100	$4.00	$12.00	$20.00	£2.00	£6.00	£10.00
112 1st appearance Mantis						

	$Good	$Fine	$N.Mint	£Good	£Fine	£N.Mint
	$3.00	$9.00	$15.00	£1.80	£5.25	£9.00
113-114	$1.60	$4.80	$8.00	£1.30	£3.90	£6.50
115 story continues in Defenders #8	$2.00	$6.00	$10.00	£1.50	£4.50	£7.50
116 Silver Surfer appears (vs. Vision), ties into Defenders #9	$2.00	$6.00	$10.00	£1.50	£4.50	£7.50
117 Silver Surfer and Sub-Mariner appear, ties into Defenders #10	$2.00	$6.00	$10.00	£1.50	£4.50	£7.50
118 Silver Surfer and original Defenders appear, cameos of many Marvel heroes	$2.00	$6.00	$10.00	£1.50	£4.50	£7.50
119-120	$1.60	$4.80	$8.00	£1.30	£3.90	£6.50
121-122 ND	$1.60	$4.80	$8.00	£1.40	£4.20	£7.00
123 ND origin Mantis	$1.60	$4.80	$8.00	£1.40	£4.20	£7.00
124 ND	$1.60	$4.80	$8.00	£1.40	£4.20	£7.00
125 ND Thanos cover and cameo	$2.40	$7.00	$12.00	£1.60	£4.80	£8.00
126 ND	$1.60	$4.80	$8.00	£1.30	£3.90	£6.50
127 ND Fantastic Four and the Inhumans appear	$1.60	$4.80	$8.00	£1.30	£3.90	£6.50
128 ND Fantastic Four appear	$1.60	$4.80	$8.00	£1.30	£3.90	£6.50
129-130 ND	$1.60	$4.80	$8.00	£1.30	£3.90	£6.50
131 ND scarce in the U.K. 2nd appearance Wonderman (raised from the dead); Legion of the Dead appear (inc. Frankenstein and original Human Torch)	$1.60	$4.80	$8.00	£1.70	£5.00	£8.50
132 ND 3rd appearance Wonderman, Legion of the Dead appear (inc. Frankenstein and original Human Torch)	$1.40	$4.20	$7.00	£1.30	£3.90	£6.50
133 ND	$1.40	$4.20	$7.00	£1.10	£3.30	£5.50
134-135 ND scarce in the U.K. "true" origin Vision	$1.60	$4.80	$8.00	£1.20	£3.60	£6.00
136 ND all reprint (Amazing Adventures #12 featuring Beast vs. Iron Man)	$1.40	$4.20	$7.00	£1.10	£3.30	£5.50
137 ND Beast joins	$1.40	$4.20	$7.00	£1.10	£3.30	£5.50
138-140 ND	$1.40	$4.20	$7.00	£1.10	£3.30	£5.50
141-143 ND	$1.20	$3.60	$6.00	£1.00	£3.00	£5.00
144 ND 1st appearance Hellcat (formerly The Cat)	$1.40	$4.20	$7.00	£1.20	£3.60	£6.00
145-147 ND	$1.20	$3.60	$6.00	£1.00	£3.00	£5.00
148 ND Squadron Supreme appears	$1.20	$3.60	$6.00	£1.00	£3.00	£5.00
149 ND	$1.20	$3.60	$6.00	£1.00	£3.00	£5.00
150 ND anniversary special; new line-up debated in re-cap of Avengers history: Yellowjacket, Scarlet Witch, Wasp, Captain America, Beast, Vision, Iron Man; part Perez and Kirby art	$1.20	$3.60	$6.00	£1.00	£3.00	£5.00
151 ND George Perez art, Jack Kirby cover, new line-up takes effect, Wonderman returns	$1.00	$3.00	$5.00	£0.90	£2.70	£4.50
152 ND Jack Kirby cover, Wonderman appears	$1.00	$3.00	$5.00	£0.90	£2.70	£4.50
153 Jack Kirby cover	$1.00	$3.00	$5.00	£0.70	£2.10	£3.50
154-155 George Perez art, Jack Kirby cover	$1.00	$3.00	$5.00	£0.70	£2.10	£3.50
156-158 Jack Kirby cover	$1.00	$3.00	$5.00	£0.70	£2.10	£3.50
159	$1.00	$3.00	$5.00	£0.70	£2.10	£3.50
160 George Perez art	$1.00	$3.00	$5.00	£0.70	£2.10	£3.50
161-162 George Perez art	$1.00	$3.00	$5.00	£0.60	£1.80	£3.00
163 Iceman with The Champions appear (no Ghost Rider however)	$1.00	$3.00	$5.00	£0.60	£1.80	£3.00
164-166 John Byrne art	$1.20	$3.60	$6.00	£0.70	£2.10	£3.50
167-168 LD in the U.K. George Perez art, Guardians of the Galaxy appear	$1.00	$3.00	$5.00	£0.80	£2.40	£4.00
169	$0.80	$2.40	$4.00	£0.50	£1.50	£2.50
170 George Perez art	$0.80	$2.40	$4.00	£0.50	£1.50	£2.50
171 scarce in the U.K. George Perez art	$0.80	$2.40	$4.00	£0.55	£1.65	£2.75
172 scarce in the U.K.	$0.80	$2.40	$4.00	£0.55	£1.65	£2.75
173 scarce in the U.K. Korvac Saga begins, Guardians of the Galaxy appear	$0.80	$2.40	$4.00	£0.55	£1.65	£2.75
174-176 scarce in the U.K. Korvac Saga, Guardians of the Galaxy appear	$0.80	$2.40	$4.00	£0.55	£1.65	£2.75
177 scarce in the U.K. Korvac Saga epilogue, Guardians of the Galaxy appear	$0.80	$2.40	$4.00	£0.55	£1.65	£2.75
178-180	$0.80	$2.40	$4.00	£0.50	£1.50	£2.50
181 John Byrne art, new line-up: Captain America, Scarlet Witch, Beast, Vision, Iron Man, Wasp, Falcon; Guardians of the Galaxy appear	$0.60	$1.80	$3.00	£0.60	£1.80	£3.00
182 John Byrne art	$0.60	$1.80	$3.00	£0.40	£1.20	£2.00
183 ND scarce in the U.K. John Byrne art, Ms. Marvel appears	$1.20	$3.60	$6.00	£1.20	£3.60	£6.00
184 John Byrne art, Ms. Marvel joins team	$0.60	$1.80	$3.00	£0.40	£1.20	£2.00
185 John Byrne art, origin Quicksilver and Scarlet Witch	$0.60	$1.80	$3.00	£0.40	£1.20	£2.00

MINT = 100% / NEAR MINT (inc. +/-) = 90–99% / VERY FINE (inc. +/-) = 75–89% / FINE (inc. +/-) = 55–74% / VERY GOOD (inc. +/-) = 35–54% / GOOD (inc. +/-) = 15–34% / FAIR = 5–14% / POOR = 1–4%

217

	$Good	$Fine	$N.Mint	£Good	£Fine	£N.Mint
186-187 LD in the U.K. John Byrne art	$1.20	$3.60	$6.00	£0.60	£1.80	£3.00
188 John Byrne art, Inhumans appear, ties into Avengers Annual #9	$0.60	$1.80	$3.00	£0.40	£1.20	£2.00
189 John Byrne art	$0.60	$1.80	$3.00	£0.40	£1.20	£2.00
190 John Byrne art, Daredevil appears	$0.60	$1.80	$3.00	£0.40	£1.20	£2.00
191 John Byrne art	$0.50	$1.50	$2.50	£0.30	£0.90	£1.50
192	$0.50	$1.50	$2.50	£0.30	£0.90	£1.50
193 Frank Miller cover	$0.50	$1.50	$2.50	£0.30	£0.90	£1.50
194-196 George Perez art	$0.50	$1.50	$2.50	£0.30	£0.90	£1.50
197 George Perez art	$0.50	$1.50	$2.50	£0.30	£0.90	£1.50
198-199 George Perez art	$0.50	$1.50	$2.50	£0.30	£0.90	£1.50
200 ND DS George Perez art, anniversary issue	$0.60	$1.80	$3.00	£0.70	£2.10	£3.50
201-202 George Perez art	$0.50	$1.50	$2.50	£0.30	£0.90	£1.50
203	$0.50	$1.50	$2.50	£0.30	£0.90	£1.50
204-205 ND	$0.50	$1.50	$2.50	£0.40	£1.20	£2.00
206 Human Torch appears	$0.50	$1.50	$2.50	£0.30	£0.90	£1.50
207-210	$0.50	$1.50	$2.50	£0.30	£0.90	£1.50
211 new line-up: Captain America, Wasp, Tigra, Iron Man, Thor, Yellowjacket; Angel/Iceman (with Champions), Moonknight cameos	$0.50	$1.50	$2.50	£0.30	£0.90	£1.50
212-213	$0.50	$1.50	$2.50	£0.30	£0.90	£1.50
214 Ghost Rider and Angel appear	$0.50	$1.50	$2.50	£0.30	£0.90	£1.50
215-216 Silver Surfer appears	$0.60	$1.80	$3.00	£0.40	£1.20	£2.00
217-218	$0.50	$1.50	$2.50	£0.25	£0.75	£1.25
219-220 Drax the Destroyer appears	$0.50	$1.50	$2.50	£0.25	£0.75	£1.25
221 Frank Miller cover, She-Hulk joins, Hawkeye returns, Spiderman appears	$0.50	$1.50	$2.50	£0.25	£0.75	£1.25
222-224	$0.50	$1.50	$2.50	£0.25	£0.75	£1.25
225 very LD Black Knight returns	$0.50	$1.50	$2.50	£0.40	£1.20	£2.00
226 LD in the U.K.	$0.60	$1.80	$3.00	£0.45	£1.35	£2.25
227 LD in the U.K. new (female) Captain Marvel joins, Ant-Man/Giant-Man/Goliath/Yellowjacket, Wasp origins retold	$0.60	$1.80	$3.00	£0.45	£1.35	£2.25
228-230 LD in the U.K.	$0.60	$1.80	$3.00	£0.40	£1.20	£2.00
231 LD in the U.K. Nick Fury appears	$0.60	$1.80	$3.00	£0.40	£1.20	£2.00
232 LD in the U.K. Starfox joins	$0.60	$1.80	$3.00	£0.40	£1.20	£2.00
233 LD in the U.K. John Byrne art, Fantastic Four appear	$0.60	$1.80	$3.00	£0.40	£1.20	£2.00
234 LD in the U.K. origin Quicksilver and Scarlet Witch, X-Men and Dr. Strange appear; continues from Fantastic Four #256	$0.60	$1.80	$3.00	£0.35	£1.05	£1.75
235 LD in the U.K.	$0.60	$1.80	$3.00	£0.35	£1.05	£1.75
236 LD in the U.K. Spiderman appears	$0.60	$1.80	$3.00	£0.35	£1.05	£1.75
237 very LD Spiderman appears	$0.50	$1.50	$2.50	£0.40	£1.20	£2.00
238 LD in the U.K.	$0.60	$1.80	$3.00	£0.35	£1.05	£1.75
239 LD in the U.K. David Letterman parody	$0.60	$1.80	$3.00	£0.35	£1.05	£1.75
240 LD in the U.K. return of Spiderwoman, Dr. Strange appears	$0.60	$1.80	$3.00	£0.35	£1.05	£1.75
241-245 LD in the U.K.	$0.60	$1.80	$3.00	£0.30	£0.90	£1.50
246-249 LD in the U.K. Eternals appear	$0.60	$1.80	$3.00	£0.30	£0.90	£1.50
250 DS, Avengers West Coast X-over	$0.70	$2.10	$3.50	£0.40	£1.20	£2.00
251 Paladin appears	$0.50	$1.50	$2.50	£0.25	£0.75	£1.25
252-255	$0.50	$1.50	$2.50	£0.25	£0.75	£1.25
256-257 Ka-Zar appears	$0.50	$1.50	$2.50	£0.25	£0.75	£1.25
258 Spiderman appears (in black costume), Ka-Zar appears	$0.50	$1.50	$2.50	£0.25	£0.75	£1.25
259	$0.50	$1.50	$2.50	£0.25	£0.75	£1.25
260 LD in the U.K. Secret Wars II X-over, Fantastic Four appear	$0.60	$1.80	$3.00	£0.35	£1.05	£1.75
261 Secret Wars II X-over	$0.50	$1.50	$2.50	£0.25	£0.75	£1.25
262 Hercules battles Sub-Mariner	$0.50	$1.50	$2.50	£0.25	£0.75	£1.25
263 LD in the U.K. 1st X-Factor story (see Fantastic Four #286 for continuation); Jean Grey cocoon found	$1.50	$4.50	$7.50	£0.70	£2.10	£3.50
264 1st appearance Yellowjacket II	$0.50	$1.50	$2.50	£0.25	£0.75	£1.25
265 Secret Wars II X-over	$0.50	$1.50	$2.50	£0.25	£0.75	£1.25
266 Secret Wars II X-over (epilogue), Silver Surfer appears	$0.50	$1.50	$2.50	£0.25	£0.75	£1.25
267 Hulk, Storm and Colossus appear	$0.50	$1.50	$2.50	£0.25	£0.75	£1.25
268 John Byrne cover	$0.50	$1.50	$2.50	£0.25	£0.75	£1.25
269-270	$0.50	$1.50	$2.50	£0.25	£0.75	£1.25
271 Paladin appears	$0.50	$1.50	$2.50	£0.20	£0.60	£1.00
272 Alpha Flight appears	$0.50	$1.50	$2.50	£0.20	£0.60	£1.00
273 LD in the U.K.	$0.60	$1.80	$3.00	£0.25	£0.75	£1.25
274-286	$0.50	$1.50	$2.50	£0.20	£0.60	£1.00
287 Machine Man appears	$0.50	$1.50	$2.50	£0.20	£0.60	£1.00
288-290	$0.50	$1.50	$2.50	£0.20	£0.60	£1.00
291-297 Simonson script	$0.50	$1.50	$2.50	£0.20	£0.60	£1.00
298 Inferno X-over, Simonson script	$0.50	$1.50	$2.50	£0.20	£0.60	£1.00
299 Inferno X-over, Simonson script, Mr. Fantastic appears	$0.50	$1.50	$2.50	£0.20	£0.60	£1.00
300 LD in the U.K. 64pgs, Walt Simonson art in back up story, Inferno, new line-up: Thor, Invisible Woman, The Captain, Mr. Fantastic, Gilgamesh: Simonson script , squarebound (many copies, 25%? with crinkled spines)	$0.80	$2.40	$4.00	£0.40	£1.20	£2.00
301 Nova appears	$0.40	$1.20	$2.00	£0.20	£0.60	£1.00
302 very LD re-intro Quasar, Nova appears	$0.50	$1.50	$2.50	£0.50	£1.50	£2.50
303 Fantastic Four, Quasar, Firelord, West Coast Avengers and Nova appear	$0.40	$1.20	$2.00	£0.20	£0.60	£1.00
304	$0.40	$1.20	$2.00	£0.20	£0.60	£1.00
305 everybody who was an Avenger appears, John Byrne scripts begin (ends #317)	$0.40	$1.20	$2.00	£0.20	£0.60	£1.00
306-310	$0.40	$1.20	$2.00	£0.20	£0.60	£1.00
311 LD in the U.K. Acts of Vengeance tie-in	$0.60	$1.80	$3.00	£0.30	£0.90	£1.50
312 LD in the U.K. Acts of Vengeance tie-in	$0.60	$1.80	$3.00	£0.40	£1.20	£2.00
313 Acts of Vengeance tie-in	$0.40	$1.20	$2.00	£0.20	£0.60	£1.00
314-318 Spiderman considers joining storyline	$0.40	$1.20	$2.00	£0.15	£0.45	£0.75
319-324 The Crossing Line story	$0.40	$1.20	$2.00	£0.15	£0.45	£0.75
325 intro the Skull, Byrne cover	$0.40	$1.20	$2.00	£0.15	£0.45	£0.75
326 new line up, 1st appearance Rage	$1.00	$3.00	$5.00	£0.30	£0.90	£1.50
327 story based on Avengers #1, Rage appears	$0.40	$1.20	$2.00	£0.15	£0.45	£0.75
328 origin Rage	$0.80	$2.40	$4.00	£0.30	£0.90	£1.50
329	$0.40	$1.20	$2.00	£0.15	£0.45	£0.75
330 line up change	$0.40	$1.20	$2.00	£0.15	£0.45	£0.75
331-333	$0.40	$1.20	$2.00	£0.15	£0.45	£0.75
334-339 bi-weekly issue, Collection Obsession story	$0.40	$1.20	$2.00	£0.15	£0.45	£0.75
340-342 New Warriors guest star	$0.40	$1.20	$2.00	£0.15	£0.45	£0.75
343	$0.30	$0.90	$1.50	£0.15	£0.45	£0.75
344 $1.25 cover begins	$0.30	$0.90	$1.50	£0.15	£0.45	£0.75
345 Galactic Storm part 5	$0.30	$0.90	$1.50	£0.15	£0.45	£0.75
346 Galactic Storm part 12	$0.30	$0.90	$1.50	£0.15	£0.45	£0.75
347 DS Galactic Storm part 19 (conclusion)	$0.40	$1.20	$2.00	£0.25	£0.75	£1.25
348	$0.30	$0.90	$1.50	£0.15	£0.45	£0.75
349 Rage appears	$0.30	$0.90	$1.50	£0.15	£0.45	£0.75
350 64pgs, Cyclops and Professor X appear, reprints of past Avengers covers, gatefold cover	$0.50	$1.50	$2.50	£0.30	£0.90	£1.50
351-353 bi-weekly	$0.30	$0.90	$1.50	£0.15	£0.45	£0.75
354-355	$0.30	$0.90	$1.50	£0.15	£0.45	£0.75
356 Black Panther appears	$0.30	$0.90	$1.50	£0.15	£0.45	£0.75
357-359	$0.30	$0.90	$1.50	£0.15	£0.45	£0.75
360 30th anniversary issue, embossed all-bronze foil cover	$1.00	$3.00	$5.00	£0.40	£1.20	£2.00
361-362	$0.30	$0.90	$1.50	£0.20	£0.60	£1.00
363 48pgs, embossed all-silver foil cover 30th anniversary celebration issue	$0.60	$1.80	$3.00	£0.40	£1.20	£2.00
364 Giant-Man returns to the Avengers	$0.30	$0.90	$1.50	£0.20	£0.60	£1.00
365	$0.30	$0.90	$1.50	£0.20	£0.60	£1.00
366 64pgs, squarebound, embossed all-gold foil cover 30th anniversary actual issue (by date)	$0.80	$2.40	$4.00	£0.50	£1.50	£2.50
367	$0.30	$0.90	$1.50	£0.20	£0.60	£1.00

	$Good	$Fine	$N.Mint	£Good	£Fine	£N.Mint
368 Bloodties part 1, continued in X-Men #26	$0.30	$0.90	$1.50	£0.30	£0.90	£1.50
369 48pgs, platinum foil embossed cover, Bloodties part 5 (conclusion)	$0.60	$1.80	$3.00	£0.40	£1.20	£2.00
370-373	$0.30	$0.90	$1.50	£0.20	£0.60	£1.00
374 with free Spiderman vs. Venom card sheet	$0.30	$0.90	$1.50	£0.20	£0.60	£1.00
375 48pgs, Thunderstrike returns	$0.40	$1.20	$2.00	£0.25	£0.75	£1.25
375 48pgs, Thunderstrike returns; bound-in poster	$0.45	$1.35	$2.25	£0.30	£0.90	£1.50
376 Black Panther appears	$0.30	$0.90	$1.50	£0.20	£0.60	£1.00
377	$0.30	$0.90	$1.50	£0.20	£0.60	£1.00
378 Magneto and High Evolutionary appear	$0.30	$0.90	$1.50	£0.20	£0.60	£1.00
379-384	$0.30	$0.90	$1.50	£0.20	£0.60	£1.00
385 ties into Captain America #438	$0.30	$0.90	$1.50	£0.20	£0.60	£1.00
386 ties into Captain America #439	$0.30	$0.90	$1.50	£0.20	£0.60	£1.00
387 Taking AIM part 2, continued in Captain America #441	$0.30	$0.90	$1.50	£0.20	£0.60	£1.00
388 Taking AIM part 4 (conclusion)	$0.30	$0.90	$1.50	£0.20	£0.60	£1.00
389	$0.30	$0.90	$1.50	£0.20	£0.60	£1.00
390 Avengers: The Crossing prelude and lead into Avengers/Ultraforce team-up, Mike Deodato art	$0.30	$0.90	$1.50	£0.20	£0.60	£1.00
391-394 Avengers: The Crossing tie-in, Mike Deodato art	$0.30	$0.90	$1.50	£0.20	£0.60	£1.00
395 Avengers: Timeslide	$0.30	$0.90	$1.50	£0.20	£0.60	£1.00
396 The First Sign part 4 (conclusion from Iron Man #326)	$0.30	$0.90	$1.50	£0.20	£0.60	£1.00
Title Value:	$1467.20	$4408.55	$10170.25	£920.75	£2764.25	£6351.25

Greatest Battles of the Avengers (Oct 1993)

	$Good	$Fine	$N.Mint	£Good	£Fine	£N.Mint
Trade paperback reprints issues #54,55, 79,160 plus Annuals #7,10			$2.00		£6.00	£10.00

Avengers Anniversary Cover Set (Jan 1994)

	$Good	$Fine	$N.Mint	£Good	£Fine	£N.Mint
collects the four foil cover issues Avengers #360, 363, 366 and 369			$2.70		£8.10	£13.50

Avengers: Yesterday Quest (Oct 1994)

	$Good	$Fine	$N.Mint	£Good	£Fine	£N.Mint
Trade paperback reprints issues #181,182 and #185-187			£0.90		£2.70	£4.50

ARTISTS
Paul Neary art in 292-329. Paul Neary covers 293, 294, 298-307, 309-312, 315, 319. John Byrne covers 239, 247-254, 290, 308, 313. Mike Zeck covers 224, 258, 259, 261-270, 272, 273, 275, 276, 278-289, 321, 323-326, 332,334,337.

AVENGERS ANNIVERSARY MAGAZINE
Marvel Comics Group,OS; 1 Nov 1993

	$Good	$Fine	$N.Mint	£Good	£Fine	£N.Mint
1 ND 48pgs, features and articles on The Avengers; 8.5" x 11"	$0.90	$2.70	$4.50	£0.60	£1.80	£3.00
Title Value:	$0.90	$2.70	$4.50	£0.60	£1.80	£3.00

AVENGERS ANNUAL, THE
Marvel Comics Group; 1 Sep 1967-5 1972; 6 1976-present

	$Good	$Fine	$N.Mint	£Good	£Fine	£N.Mint
1 68pgs, all new 40pg story; original Avengers team-up with current team of the time, Sub-Mariner and Nick Fury appear	$7.75	$23.50	$55.00	£5.00	£15.00	£35.00
2 68pgs, all new story; original Avengers vs. new Avengers, Dr. Strange cameo	$3.85	$11.50	$27.00	£2.10	£6.25	£15.00
3 scarce in the U.K. 68pgs, reprints #4 (1st Silver Age Captain America) plus three new stories by Jack Kirby	$3.85	$11.50	$27.00	£2.55	£7.50	£18.00
4 scarce in the U.K. 68pgs, reprints issues #5,6	$2.00	$6.00	$12.00	£1.50	£4.50	£9.00
5 ND very scarce in the U.K. 52pgs, (often ink-stained), Spiderman appears (reprint of #11)	$2.00	$6.00	$12.00	£1.50	£4.50	£9.00
6 ND 52pgs, George Perez art	$1.50	$4.50	$7.50	£0.90	£2.70	£4.50
7 ND 52pgs, Jim Starlin cover & art, Captain Marvel and Thanos appear, death of Warlock; story continues in Marvel Two-In-One Annual #2	$5.00	$15.00	$25.00	£2.60	£7.75	£13.00
8 ND scarce in the U.K. 52pgs, Dr. Strange with Ms. Marvel and Thundra appear, George Perez art	$1.20	$3.60	$6.00	£0.90	£2.70	£4.50
9 ND scarce in the U.K. 52pgs	$1.20	$3.60	$6.00	£0.90	£2.70	£4.50
10 ND 52pgs, Golden art, 1st appearance Rogue, 1st appearance Madelyn Prior (see X-Men #168), Spiderman appears, X-Men cameo	$5.00	$15.00	$25.00	£1.50	£4.50	£7.50
11 ND 52pgs, Silver Surfer appears; Avengers vs. Defenders	$0.80	$2.40	$4.00	£0.60	£1.80	£3.00
12 ND 52pgs, Guice art, Inhumans appear	$0.80	$2.40	$4.00	£0.40	£1.20	£2.00
13 ND Hulk appears, Ditko pencils, John Byrne inks	$0.80	$2.40	$4.00	£0.40	£1.20	£2.00
14 ND Fantastic Four appears, John Byrne and Kyle Baker art	$0.80	$2.40	$4.00	£0.40	£1.20	£2.00
15 ND Freedom Force, Ditko and Janson art; ties into West Coast Avengers Annual #1	$0.80	$2.40	$4.00	£0.40	£1.20	£2.00
16 ND Avengers vs. Legion of the Dead inc. Captain Marvel and Drax, Silver Surfer and Green Goblin appear, Marshall Rogers art	$0.80	$2.40	$4.00	£0.50	£1.50	£2.50
17 ND 64pgs, Evolutionary War	$0.60	$1.80	$3.00	£0.40	£1.20	£2.00
18 ND Atlantis Attacks part 8	$0.60	$1.80	$3.00	£0.35	£1.05	£1.75
19 ND Terminus Factor part 5 (see Captain America/Thor/Iron Man/West Coast Avengers Annuals)	$0.60	$1.80	$3.00	£0.30	£0.90	£1.50
20 ND Subterranean Odyssey part 1 (continued in Hulk Annual #17)	$0.60	$1.80	$3.00	£0.30	£0.90	£1.50
21 ND 64pgs, Citizen Kang part 4 (conclusion), Fantastic Four appear	$0.50	$1.50	$2.50	£0.30	£0.90	£1.50
22 ND 64pgs, pre-bagged with trading card introducing Bloodwraith	$0.60	$1.80	$3.00	£0.40	£1.20	£2.00
23 ND 64pgs, Hercules appears	$0.60	$1.80	$3.00	£0.40	£1.20	£2.00
Title Value:	$42.25	$126.90	$247.00	£24.60	£73.55	£145.75

Note: 1, 2 have back-up reprints; 3-5 all reprint. 1-6 called King Size Special.

AVENGERS DOUBLE FEATURE
Marvel Comics Group,MS; 1 Oct 1994-4 Jan 1995

	$Good	$Fine	$N.Mint	£Good	£Fine	£N.Mint
1 ND 48pgs, flip-book format; features Avengers #379 plus Giant Man #1; George Perez 1st script for Marvel	$0.45	$1.35	$2.25	£0.30	£0.90	£1.50
2 ND 48pgs, flip-book format; Avengers #380 plus Giant Man back-up story	$0.45	$1.35	$2.25	£0.30	£0.90	£1.50
3 ND 48pgs, flip-book format; Avengers #381 plus Giant Man back-up story	$0.45	$1.35	$2.25	£0.30	£0.90	£1.50
4 ND 48pgs, flip-book format; Avengers #382 plus Giant Man back-up story	$0.45	$1.35	$2.25	£0.30	£0.90	£1.50
Title Value:	$1.80	$5.40	$9.00	£1.20	£3.60	£6.00

AVENGERS GIANT SIZE
Marvel Comics Group; 1 Aug 1974-5 Dec 1975

	$Good	$Fine	$N.Mint	£Good	£Fine	£N.Mint
1 ND scarce in the U.K. 68pgs, All Winner's Squad appear; Rich Buckler's Kirbyesque art	$2.25	$6.75	$11.25	£1.50	£4.50	£7.50
2 ND scarce in the U.K. 68pgs, Kang and Rama-Tut appear	$2.00	$6.00	$10.00	£1.35	£4.05	£6.75
3 ND rare in the U.K. 68pgs						

Avengers Giant Size #3

Avenging World #1

Barbi Twins Adventures #1

	$Good	$Fine	$N.Mint	£Good	£Fine	£N.Mint
	$2.40	$7.00	$12.00	£1.60	£4.80	£8.00

4 ND rare in the U.K. 68pgs, wedding of Scarlet Witch and Vision

	$Good	$Fine	$N.Mint	£Good	£Fine	£N.Mint
	$2.40	$7.00	$12.00	£1.60	£4.80	£8.00

5 ND 68pgs, all reprint (Avengers King Size Special #1)

	$Good	$Fine	$N.Mint	£Good	£Fine	£N.Mint
	$1.40	$4.20	$7.00	£1.00	£3.00	£5.00
Title Value:	$10.45	$30.95	$52.25	£7.05	£21.15	£35.25

AVENGERS LOG
Marvel Comics Group,OS; 1 Feb 1994

1 ND 48pgs, reference index from Avengers #1 to present; George Perez cover

	$Good	$Fine	$N.Mint	£Good	£Fine	£N.Mint
	$0.40	$1.20	$2.00	£0.25	£0.75	£1.25
Title Value:	$0.40	$1.20	$2.00	£0.25	£0.75	£1.25

AVENGERS STRIKE FILE
Marvel Comics Group,OS; 1 Jan 1994

1 ND Avengers pin-ups plus operation: Galactic Storm re-told

	$Good	$Fine	$N.Mint	£Good	£Fine	£N.Mint
	$0.30	$0.90	$1.50	£0.20	£0.60	£1.00
Title Value:	$0.30	$0.90	$1.50	£0.20	£0.60	£1.00

AVENGERS UNPLUGGED
Marvel Comics Group; 1 Oct 1995-present

1 ND new stories begin, cover priced at 99 cents

	$Good	$Fine	$N.Mint	£Good	£Fine	£N.Mint
	$0.20	$0.60	$1.00	£0.10	£0.35	£0.65
2-3 ND	$0.20	$0.60	$1.00	£0.10	£0.35	£0.65
Title Value:	$0.60	$1.80	$3.00	£0.30	£1.05	£1.95

Note: originally announced as Avengers Unleashed

AVENGERS, OFFICIAL INDEX TO
Marvel Comics Group,MS; 1 Oct 1994-6 Mar 1995

1 ND information and cover repros of issues #1-62

	$Good	$Fine	$N.Mint	£Good	£Fine	£N.Mint
	$0.40	$1.20	$2.00	£0.25	£0.75	£1.25

2 ND information and cover repros of issues #63-121

	$Good	$Fine	$N.Mint	£Good	£Fine	£N.Mint
	$0.40	$1.20	$2.00	£0.25	£0.75	£1.25

3 ND information and cover repros of issues #122-180

	$Good	$Fine	$N.Mint	£Good	£Fine	£N.Mint
	$0.40	$1.20	$2.00	£0.25	£0.75	£1.25

4 ND information and cover repros of issues #181-240

	$Good	$Fine	$N.Mint	£Good	£Fine	£N.Mint
	$0.40	$1.20	$2.00	£0.25	£0.75	£1.25

5 ND information and cover repros of issues #241-299

	$Good	$Fine	$N.Mint	£Good	£Fine	£N.Mint
	$0.40	$1.20	$2.00	£0.25	£0.75	£1.25

6 ND information and cover repros of issues #300-360

	$Good	$Fine	$N.Mint	£Good	£Fine	£N.Mint
	$0.40	$1.20	$2.00	£0.25	£0.75	£1.25
Title Value:	$2.40	$7.20	$12.00	£1.50	£4.50	£7.50

AVENGERS, THE
Gold Key, TV; 1 Nov 1968

1 rare in the U.K. features Steed and Mrs. Peel from the TV series, photo cover

	$Good	$Fine	$N.Mint	£Good	£Fine	£N.Mint
	$33.00	$100.00	$200.00	£20.50	£62.50	£125.00
Title Value:	$33.00	$100.00	$200.00	£20.50	£62.50	£125.00

AVENGERS, THE OFFICIAL MARVEL INDEX TO
Marvel Comics Group,MS; 1 Jun 1987-7 Aug 1988

1 ND 48pgs, squarebound; information and colour cover reproductions Avengers #1-#23

	$Good	$Fine	$N.Mint	£Good	£Fine	£N.Mint
	$0.50	$1.50	$2.50	£0.35	£1.05	£1.75

2 ND 48pgs, squarebound; information and colour cover reproductions Avengers #24-#45, Annual #1, cover and splash page by Mark Texeira

	$Good	$Fine	$N.Mint	£Good	£Fine	£N.Mint
	$0.50	$1.50	$2.50	£0.35	£1.05	£1.75

3 ND 48pgs, squarebound; information and colour cover reproductions Avengers #46-#66, Annual #2, Marvel Super-Heroes #17

	$Good	$Fine	$N.Mint	£Good	£Fine	£N.Mint
	$0.50	$1.50	$2.50	£0.35	£1.05	£1.75

4 ND 48pgs, squarebound; information and colour cover reproductions Avengers #67-#87, Annual #3-#5, Ka-Zar (1st Series) #1

	$Good	$Fine	$N.Mint	£Good	£Fine	£N.Mint
	$0.50	$1.50	$2.50	£0.35	£1.05	£1.75

5 ND 48pgs, squarebound; information and colour cover reproductions Avengers #88-#108 Annual #3-#5, Avengers Special Edition #1,#2

	$Good	$Fine	$N.Mint	£Good	£Fine	£N.Mint
	$0.50	$1.50	$2.50	£0.35	£1.05	£1.75

6 ND 48pgs, squarebound; information and colour cover reproductions Avengers #109-#126, Avengers Giant Size #1, Defenders #8-#11, Jim Valentino cover and splash page pencils

	$Good	$Fine	$N.Mint	£Good	£Fine	£N.Mint
	$0.50	$1.50	$2.50	£0.35	£1.05	£1.75

7 ND 48pgs, squarebound; information and colour cover reproductions Avengers #127-#145, Avengers Giant Size #2-#5

	$Good	$Fine	$N.Mint	£Good	£Fine	£N.Mint
	$0.50	$1.50	$2.50	£0.35	£1.05	£1.75
Title Value:	$3.50	$10.50	$17.50	£2.45	£7.35	£12.25

Note: Volume 5 in Official Marvel Index Series of 5.

AVENGERS/ULTRAFORCE
Marvel Comics Group/Malibu Ultraverse,OS; 1 Oct 1995

(see Ultraforce/Avengers)

1 ND 48pgs, Loki vs. the Avengers and Ultraforce; Glenn Herdling and Angel Medina art, wraparound cover by George Perez with silver foil logo

	$Good	$Fine	$N.Mint	£Good	£Fine	£N.Mint
	$0.80	$2.40	$4.00	£0.50	£1.50	£2.50
Title Value:	$0.80	$2.40	$4.00	£0.50	£1.50	£2.50

AVENGERS: THE CROSSING
Marvel Comics Group,OS; nn Sep 1995

nn ND Mike Deodato art, chromium cover; tie-in with Avengers #390

	$Good	$Fine	$N.Mint	£Good	£Fine	£N.Mint
	$1.00	$3.00	$5.00	£0.65	£1.95	£3.25
Title Value:	$1.00	$3.00	$5.00	£0.65	£1.95	£3.25

AVENGERS: THE TERMINATRIX OBJECTIVE
Marvel Comics Group,MS; 1 Sep 1993-4 Dec 1993

1 ND sequel to "Citizen Kang" begins; holo-grafix starfield foil pattern cover.

	$Good	$Fine	$N.Mint	£Good	£Fine	£N.Mint
	$0.35	$1.05	$1.75	£0.25	£0.75	£1.25
2-4 ND	$0.25	$0.75	$1.25	£0.15	£0.45	£0.75
Title Value:	$1.10	$3.30	$5.50	£0.70	£2.10	£3.50

AVENGERS: TIMESLIDE
Marvel Comics Group,OS; 1 Feb 1995

1 ND 48pgs, metallic chrome cover, continued in Force Works #20

	$Good	$Fine	$N.Mint	£Good	£Fine	£N.Mint
	$1.00	$3.00	$5.00	£0.65	£1.95	£3.25
Title Value:	$1.00	$3.00	$5.00	£0.65	£1.95	£3.25

AVENGING WORLD
Bruce Hershenson,OS; 1 1973

1 ND 32pgs, black and white; Steve Ditko art and cover; the second in an intended series of quarterly magazines, Mr. A #1 being the first

	$Good	$Fine	$N.Mint	£Good	£Fine	£N.Mint
	$0.90	$2.70	$4.50	£0.60	£1.80	£3.00
Title Value:	$0.90	$2.70	$4.50	£0.60	£1.80	£3.00

AVENUE X
Innovation,MS; 1 Oct 1992

1 ND black and white

	$Good	$Fine	$N.Mint	£Good	£Fine	£N.Mint
	$0.45	$1.35	$2.25	£0.30	£0.90	£1.50
Title Value:	$0.45	$1.35	$2.25	£0.30	£0.90	£1.50

Note: cancelled mini-series

AXA
First American (Eclipse); 1 1983-9 1988

1-8 ND complete newspaper strip reprints

	$Good	$Fine	$N.Mint	£Good	£Fine	£N.Mint
	$1.00	$3.00	$5.00	£0.70	£2.10	£3.50

9 ND includes unfinished strip "The Betrayal"

	$Good	$Fine	$N.Mint	£Good	£Fine	£N.Mint
	$1.20	$3.60	$6.00	£0.80	£2.40	£4.00
Title Value:	$9.20	$27.60	$46.00	£6.40	£19.20	£32.00

AXA (2ND SERIES)
Eclipse; 1 Apr 1987-2 Jun 1987

1-2 ND new Romero art

	$Good	$Fine	$N.Mint	£Good	£Fine	£N.Mint
	$0.45	$1.35	$2.25	£0.30	£0.90	£1.50
Title Value:	$0.90	$2.70	$4.50	£0.60	£1.80	£3.00

AXED FILES, THE
Entity Comics,OS; 1 Aug 1995

1 ND parody of X-Files; black and white

	$Good	$Fine	$N.Mint	£Good	£Fine	£N.Mint
	$0.50	$1.50	$2.50	£0.30	£0.90	£1.50
Title Value:	$0.50	$1.50	$2.50	£0.30	£0.90	£1.50

AXEL PRESSBUTTON
Eclipse/Quality; 1 Nov 1984-6 Sep 1985

(see Laser Eraser)

1 Steve Dillon art, Brian Bolland cover; 4pgs Bolland art in Zirk back-up story

	$Good	$Fine	$N.Mint	£Good	£Fine	£N.Mint
	$0.40	$1.20	$2.00	£0.25	£0.75	£1.25

2 Steve Dillon art, Alan Moore script and Garry Leach art on "Cold War, Cold Warrior", 2pg Gibbons back-up (classic time-loop tale), Dave Gibbons cover

	$Good	$Fine	$N.Mint	£Good	£Fine	£N.Mint
	$0.40	$1.20	$2.00	£0.25	£0.75	£1.25

3 Steve Dillon art, John Ridgway and Cam Kennedy back-ups, Alan Davis cover

	$Good	$Fine	$N.Mint	£Good	£Fine	£N.Mint
	$0.40	$1.20	$2.00	£0.25	£0.75	£1.25

4 Steve Dillon art, Garry Leach and Cam Kennedy back-ups, Austin painted cover

	$Good	$Fine	$N.Mint	£Good	£Fine	£N.Mint
	$0.40	$1.20	$2.00	£0.25	£0.75	£1.25

5 Alan Davis cover and art, Hunt Emerson back-up

	$Good	$Fine	$N.Mint	£Good	£Fine	£N.Mint
	$0.40	$1.20	$2.00	£0.25	£0.75	£1.25

6 Steve Dillon art throughout, Austin painted cover

	$Good	$Fine	$N.Mint	£Good	£Fine	£N.Mint
	$0.40	$1.20	$2.00	£0.25	£0.75	£1.25
Title Value:	$2.40	$7.20	$12.00	£1.50	£4.50	£7.50

Note: made up entirely from Warrior Magazine reprints. Some limited distribution on the news-stands in the U.K. of issues #2-6

AXIS ALPHA
Axis Comics; nn Feb 1994

nn ND 30pgs, 1st appearances of Dethgrip, Beasties, W, Shelter plus a prequel to Tribe #1; Larry Stroman cover and art featured

	$Good	$Fine	$N.Mint	£Good	£Fine	£N.Mint
	$0.40	$1.20	$2.00	£0.25	£0.75	£1.25
Title Value:	$0.40	$1.20	$2.00	£0.25	£0.75	£1.25

AXIS BETA
Axis Comics; 1 Apr 1994

1 ND continuation of Axis Alpha; 1st appearances Quantum 5, Marcus Arena, Power, Night Avenger

	$Good	$Fine	$N.Mint	£Good	£Fine	£N.Mint
	$0.40	$1.20	$2.00	£0.25	£0.75	£1.25
Title Value:	$0.40	$1.20	$2.00	£0.25	£0.75	£1.25

AXIS SOURCE BOOK
Axis Comics,OS; 1 Jun 1994

1 ND information about all Axis characters

	$Good	$Fine	$N.Mint	£Good	£Fine	£N.Mint
	$0.40	$1.20	$2.00	£0.25	£0.75	£1.25
Title Value:	$0.40	$1.20	$2.00	£0.25	£0.75	£1.25

AZ
Comico; 1 Feb 1983-2 1984

(see Primer)

	$Good	$Fine	$N.Mint	£Good	£Fine	£N.Mint
1 ND	$0.60	$1.80	$3.00	£0.40	£1.20	£2.00
2 ND	$0.45	$1.35	$2.25	£0.30	£0.90	£1.50
Title Value:	$1.05	$3.15	$5.25	£0.70	£2.10	£3.50

AZRAEL
DC Comics; 1 Feb 1995-present

1 Denny O'Neil script and Barry Kitson pencils begin

	$Good	$Fine	$N.Mint	£Good	£Fine	£N.Mint
	$1.00	$3.00	$5.00	£0.40	£1.20	£2.00
2-3	$0.60	$1.80	$3.00	£0.30	£0.90	£1.50
4	$0.40	$1.20	$2.00	£0.25	£0.75	£1.25

5 upgraded coated paper stock (Miraweb Format) begins

	$Good	$Fine	$N.Mint	£Good	£Fine	£N.Mint
	$0.40	$1.20	$2.00	£0.25	£0.75	£1.25

6 Ra's Al Ghul appears

	$Good	$Fine	$N.Mint	£Good	£Fine	£N.Mint
	$0.40	$1.20	$2.00	£0.25	£0.75	£1.25
7-9	$0.40	$1.20	$2.00	£0.25	£0.75	£1.25

10 Underworld Unleashed tie-in; Batman, Robin and Lady Shiva appear

	$Good	$Fine	$N.Mint	£Good	£Fine	£N.Mint
	$0.40	$1.20	$2.00	£0.25	£0.75	£1.25

11 Batman guest-stars

	$Good	$Fine	$N.Mint	£Good	£Fine	£N.Mint
	$0.40	$1.20	$2.00	£0.25	£0.75	£1.25
12	$0.40	$1.20	$2.00	£0.25	£0.75	£1.25

13 Demon Time story

	$Good	$Fine	$N.Mint	£Good	£Fine	£N.Mint
	$0.40	$1.20	$2.00	£0.25	£0.75	£1.25

14 Demon Time story, bi-monthly

	$Good	$Fine	$N.Mint	£Good	£Fine	£N.Mint
	$0.40	$1.20	$2.00	£0.25	£0.75	£1.25

15 Contagion part 5, continued in Batman #529

	$Good	$Fine	$N.Mint	£Good	£Fine	£N.Mint
	$0.40	$1.20	$2.00	£0.25	£0.75	£1.25
Title Value:	$7.00	$21.00	$35.00	£4.00	£12.00	£20.00

	$Good	$Fine	$N.Mint	£Good	£Fine	£N.Mint

AZRAEL ANNUAL

DC Comics; 1 Oct 1995-present

1 56pgs, Year One, Denny O'Neil script, Barry Kitson art

	$Good	$Fine	$N.Mint	£Good	£Fine	£N.Mint
	$0.60	$1.80	$3.00	£0.40	£1.20	£2.00
Title Value:	$0.60	$1.80	$3.00	£0.40	£1.20	£2.00

AZTEC ACE

Eclipse; 1 Mar 1984-15 Sep 1985

	$Good	$Fine	$N.Mint	£Good	£Fine	£N.Mint
1 ND 52pgs	$0.50	$1.50	$2.50	£0.35	£1.05	£1.75
2-3 ND scarce in the U.K.						
	$0.45	$1.35	$2.25	£0.30	£0.90	£1.50
4-15 ND	$0.40	$1.20	$2.00	£0.25	£0.75	£1.25
Title Value:	$6.20	$18.60	$31.00	£3.95	£11.85	£19.75

AZTEC ACE (2ND SERIES)

Eclipse; 1 Jul 1992-2 Jul 1992?

1 ND Doug Moench script begins

	$Good	$Fine	$N.Mint	£Good	£Fine	£N.Mint
	$0.45	$1.35	$2.25	£0.30	£0.90	£1.50
2 ND	$0.45	$1.35	$2.25	£0.30	£0.90	£1.50
Title Value:	$0.90	$2.70	$4.50	£0.60	£1.80	£3.00

B

B.E.A.S.T.I.E.S.

Axis Comics; 1 Apr 1994

1 ND Javier Saltares script and art

	$Good	$Fine	$N.Mint	£Good	£Fine	£N.Mint
	$0.40	$1.20	$2.00	£0.25	£0.75	£1.25
Title Value:	$0.40	$1.20	$2.00	£0.25	£0.75	£1.25

Note: Issues #2-4 were advertised and solicited but never came out.

BABE

Dark Horse/Legend,MS; 1 Jul 1994-4 Oct 1994

1-4 ND John Byrne script, art and covers

	$Good	$Fine	$N.Mint	£Good	£Fine	£N.Mint
	$0.45	$1.35	$2.25	£0.30	£0.90	£1.50
Title Value:	$1.80	$5.40	$9.00	£1.20	£3.60	£6.00

BABE 2

Dark Horse,MS; 1 Feb 1995-2 Mar 1995

1-2 ND John Byrne script and art

	$Good	$Fine	$N.Mint	£Good	£Fine	£N.Mint
	$0.45	$1.35	$2.25	£0.30	£0.90	£1.50
Title Value:	$0.90	$2.70	$4.50	£0.60	£1.80	£3.00

BABY HUEY, THE BABY GIANT

Harvey; 1 Sep 1956-103 1991?

	$Good	$Fine	$N.Mint	£Good	£Fine	£N.Mint
1	$40.00	$120.00	$240.00	£25.00	£75.00	£150.00
2	$19.00	$57.50	$115.00	£12.50	£38.00	£75.00
3	$11.50	$35.00	$70.00	£7.50	£22.50	£45.00
4-5	$8.25	$25.00	$50.00	£5.25	£16.00	£32.50
6-10	$4.15	$12.50	$25.00	£2.65	£8.00	£16.00
11-20	$2.90	$8.75	$17.50	£1.80	£5.50	£11.00
21-40	$2.15	$6.50	$13.00	£1.50	£4.50	£9.00
41-60	$1.80	$5.25	$9.00	£1.20	£3.60	£6.00
61-79	$1.40	$4.20	$7.00	£0.90	£2.70	£4.50
80-95 giant	$1.80	$5.25	$9.00	£1.20	£3.60	£6.00
96-97 giant	$1.50	$4.50	$7.50	£1.00	£3.00	£5.00
98-99	$0.60	$1.80	$3.00	£0.40	£1.20	£2.00
100-103	$0.30	$0.90	$1.50	£0.20	£0.60	£1.00
Title Value:	$276.55	$827.50	$1569.00	£180.65	£544.20	£1024.50

Note: while no official distribution date in known, it is thought that most issues after about 1958/59 were distributed in the U.K.

BABYLON 5

DC Comics, TV; 1 Jan 1995-11 Dec 1995

1 Mike Kaluta painted cover

	$Good	$Fine	$N.Mint	£Good	£Fine	£N.Mint
	$0.80	$2.40	$4.00	£0.80	£2.40	£4.00
2	$0.80	$2.40	$4.00	£0.80	£2.40	£4.00
3	$0.60	$1.80	$3.00	£0.60	£1.80	£3.00
4	$0.40	$1.20	$2.00	£0.40	£1.20	£2.00
5 upgraded paper format begins						
	$0.40	$1.20	$2.00	£0.40	£1.20	£2.00
6-8	$0.45	$1.35	$2.25	£0.30	£0.90	£1.50
9-10 David Gerrold script						
	$0.50	$1.50	$2.50	£0.30	£0.90	£1.50
11	$0.50	$1.50	$2.50	£0.30	£0.90	£1.50
Title Value:	$5.85	$17.55	$29.75	£4.80	£14.40	£24.00

BABYLON CRUSH

Boneyard Press,MS; 1 May 1995-present ?

1-3 ND Hart Fisher script, Thomas Derenick and Joseph Eiden art; black and white

	$Good	$Fine	$N.Mint	£Good	£Fine	£N.Mint
	$0.60	$1.80	$3.00	£0.40	£1.20	£2.00
Title Value:	$1.80	$5.40	$9.00	£1.20	£3.60	£6.00

BACCHUS COLOR SPECIAL

Dark Horse,OS; 1 Apr 1995

1 ND Eddy Campbell and Terry Kristiansen

	$Good	$Fine	$N.Mint	£Good	£Fine	£N.Mint
	$0.60	$1.80	$3.00	£0.40	£1.20	£2.00
Title Value:	$0.60	$1.80	$3.00	£0.40	£1.20	£2.00

BACK DOWN THE LINE HARDCOVER

Eclipse,OS; 1 Sep 1991

1 ND 48pgs, John Bolton early stories

	$Good	$Fine	$N.Mint	£Good	£Fine	£N.Mint
	$5.00	$15.00	$25.00	£3.50	£10.50	£17.50
Title Value:	$5.00	$15.00	$25.00	£3.50	£10.50	£17.50

BACKLASH

Image; 1 Oct 1994-present

1 ND Ty Templeton art

	$Good	$Fine	$N.Mint	£Good	£Fine	£N.Mint
	$0.50	$1.50	$2.50	£0.30	£0.90	£1.50
2-5 ND	$0.50	$1.50	$2.50	£0.30	£0.90	£1.50
6 ND WetWorks guest-star						
	$0.50	$1.50	$2.50	£0.30	£0.90	£1.50

	$Good	$Fine	$N.Mint	£Good	£Fine	£N.Mint
7 ND	$0.50	$1.50	$2.50	£0.30	£0.90	£1.50

8 ND Wildstorm Rising part 8, continued in Stormwatch #22; with two foil-bagged painted trading cards. Cover by Barry Windsor-Smith.

	$Good	$Fine	$N.Mint	£Good	£Fine	£N.Mint
	$0.50	$1.50	$2.50	£0.30	£0.90	£1.50
8 Newsstand edition, ND without trading cards						
	$0.40	$1.20	$2.00	£0.25	£0.75	£1.25
9 ND	$0.50	$1.50	$2.50	£0.30	£0.90	£1.50
10 ND 1st appearance Crimson						
	$0.50	$1.50	$2.50	£0.30	£0.90	£1.50
11 ND	$0.50	$1.50	$2.50	£0.30	£0.90	£1.50
12 ND $2.95 cover						
	$0.60	$1.80	$3.00	£0.40	£1.20	£2.00
13 ND	$0.45	$1.35	$2.25	£0.30	£0.90	£1.50
14 ND Deathblow appears						
	$0.50	$1.50	$2.50	£0.30	£0.90	£1.50
15 ND	$0.50	$1.50	$2.50	£0.30	£0.90	£1.50
Title Value:	$7.95	$23.85	$39.75	£4.85	£14.55	£24.25

BAD GIRLS OF BLACKOUT

Blackout Comics; 0 Apr 1995

0 ND Extreme Violet, Lady Vampre, Ms. Cyanide and Ice appear; Outbreed 999 also appears

	$Good	$Fine	$N.Mint	£Good	£Fine	£N.Mint
	$0.80	$2.40	$4.00	£0.50	£1.50	£2.50
Title Value:	$0.80	$2.40	$4.00	£0.50	£1.50	£2.50

BAD GIRLS OF BLACKOUT: HARI KARI, LADY VAMPRE & VIOLET ANNUAL

Blackout Comics; 1 Oct 1995

1 ND Guy Dorian art

	$Good	$Fine	$N.Mint	£Good	£Fine	£N.Mint
	$0.70	$2.10	$3.50	£0.50	£1.50	£2.50
Title Value:	$0.70	$2.10	$3.50	£0.50	£1.50	£2.50

BAD GIRLS OF BLACKOUT: VIOLET, LADY VAMPRE, MS. CYANIDE & ICE

Blackout Comics,OS; 1 Jun 1995

1 ND Dell Barras and Jake Jacobsen art

	$Good	$Fine	$N.Mint	£Good	£Fine	£N.Mint
	$0.60	$1.80	$3.00	£0.40	£1.20	£2.00
Title Value:	$0.60	$1.80	$3.00	£0.40	£1.20	£2.00

BAD NEWS

Fantagraphics; 1 1988-3 Oct 1988

1-3 ND 48pgs, oversized

	$Good	$Fine	$N.Mint	£Good	£Fine	£N.Mint
	$0.60	$1.80	$3.00	£0.40	£1.20	£2.00
Title Value:	$1.80	$5.40	$9.00	£1.20	£3.60	£6.00

BADAXE

Adventure,MS; 1 Oct 1989-3 Dec 1989

1-3 ND black and white

	$Good	$Fine	$N.Mint	£Good	£Fine	£N.Mint
	$0.45	$1.35	$2.25	£0.30	£0.90	£1.50
Title Value:	$1.35	$4.05	$6.75	£0.90	£2.70	£4.50

BADE BIKER & ORSON

Mirage Studios; 1 Sep 1986-5 1987

	$Good	$Fine	$N.Mint	£Good	£Fine	£N.Mint
1-5 ND	$0.30	$0.90	$1.50	£0.20	£0.60	£1.00
Title Value:	$1.50	$4.50	$7.50	£1.00	£3.00	£5.00
Collection, reprints #1-4 plus 14 new pages				£1.30	£3.90	£6.50

BADGER

Capital/First; 1 Oct 1983-70 Feb 1991

(see Coyote #14 [Marvel])

	$Good	$Fine	$N.Mint	£Good	£Fine	£N.Mint
1 Jeff Butler art	$1.20	$3.60	$6.00	£0.80	£2.40	£4.00
2-4 Butler art	$0.80	$2.40	$4.00	£0.60	£1.80	£3.00
5 1st First issue, Bill Reinhold art						
	$0.80	$2.40	$4.00	£0.60	£1.80	£3.00
6-10	$0.70	$2.10	$3.50	£0.50	£1.50	£2.50
11-16	$0.55	$1.65	$2.75	£0.35	£1.05	£1.75
17 Butler art	$0.55	$1.65	$2.75	£0.35	£1.05	£1.75
18-20	$0.55	$1.65	$2.75	£0.35	£1.05	£1.75
21-22	$0.45	$1.35	$2.25	£0.30	£0.90	£1.50
23 Beckam art	$0.45	$1.35	$2.25	£0.30	£0.90	£1.50
24-39	$0.45	$1.35	$2.25	£0.30	£0.90	£1.50
40 Ron Lim art	$0.45	$1.35	$2.25	£0.35	£1.05	£1.75
41-49 Ron Lim art	$0.45	$1.35	$2.25	£0.30	£0.90	£1.50
50 48pgs, prestige issue with die-cut cover, Jeff Butler and Mark E. Nelson art, Ron Lim art						
	$0.70	$2.10	$3.50	£0.50	£1.50	£2.50
51 Ron Lim art	$0.45	$1.35	$2.25	£0.30	£0.90	£1.50
52-54 Tim Vigil art						
	$0.45	$1.35	$2.25	£0.30	£0.90	£1.50
55-67	$0.35	$1.05	$1.75	£0.25	£0.75	£1.25
68 George Freeman guest pencils						
	$0.35	$1.05	$1.75	£0.25	£0.75	£1.25
69-70	$0.35	$1.05	$1.75	£0.25	£0.75	£1.25
Title Value:	$34.55	$103.65	$172.75	£23.65	£70.95	£118.25

Note: all Non-Distributed on the news-stands in the U.K.

BADGER GOES BERSERK

First,MS; 1 Sep 1989-4 Dec 1989

1 script by Mike Baron, variety of artist pgs/panels throughout the 4 issues inc. John Beatty,John Butler Paul Chadwick, Denys Cowan,Steve Epting,J.Geldhof,Flint Henry,Malcolm Jones III,Mark Nelson,Mitch

	$Good	$Fine	$N.Mint	£Good	£Fine	£N.Mint
	$0.45	$1.35	$2.25	£0.30	£0.90	£1.50
2-4 script by Mike Baron, variety of artist pgs/panels throughout the 4 issues inc. John Beatty,John Butler,Paul Chad-wick,Denys Cowan,Steve Epting,J.Geldhof,Flint Henry,Malcolm Jones III,Mark Nelson,Mitch						
	$0.45	$1.35	$2.25	£0.30	£0.90	£1.50
Title Value:	$1.80	$5.40	$9.00	£1.20	£3.60	£6.00

Note: all Non-Distributed on the news-stands in the U.K.

BADGER: BEDLAM

First,OS; 1 Mar 1991

1 ND 48pgs, squarebound, Baron and Butler

	$Good	$Fine	$N.Mint	£Good	£Fine	£N.Mint
	$1.00	$3.00	$5.00	£0.65	£1.95	£3.25
Title Value:	$1.00	$3.00	$5.00	£0.65	£1.95	£3.25

BADGER: SHATTERED MIRROR

Dark Horse,MS; 1 Jul 1994-4 Oct 1994

1-4 ND Mike Baron script, Jill Thompson art

	$Good	$Fine	$N.Mint	£Good	£Fine	£N.Mint
	$0.45	$1.35	$2.25	£0.30	£0.90	£1.50
Title Value:	$1.80	$5.40	$9.00	£1.20	£3.60	£6.00

BADGER: ZEN POP FUNNY ANIMAL VERSION
Dark Horse,MS; 1 Jul 1994-2 Aug 1994
1-2 ND Mike Baron script, Steve Butler and Val Mayerik art

	$Good	$Fine	$N.Mint	£Good	£Fine	£N.Mint
	$0.45	$1.35	$2.25	£0.30	£0.90	£1.50
Title Value:	$0.90	$2.70	$4.50	£0.60	£1.80	£3.00

BADLANDS
Vortex,OS; 1 1990
1 black and white

	$Good	$Fine	$N.Mint	£Good	£Fine	£N.Mint
	$0.50	$1.50	$2.50	£0.30	£0.90	£1.50
Title Value:	$0.50	$1.50	$2.50	£0.30	£0.90	£1.50

BADLANDS (2ND SERIES)
Dark Horse; 1 Sep 1991-6 Feb 1992
1-6 ND Kennedy assassination story

	$Good	$Fine	$N.Mint	£Good	£Fine	£N.Mint
	$0.45	$1.35	$2.25	£0.30	£0.90	£1.50
Title Value:	$2.70	$8.10	$13.50	£1.80	£5.40	£9.00

Note: Vortex series suddenly cancelled and rights picked up by Dark Horse
Badlands Softcover Collection (May 1993)
reprints mini-series, intro by Frank Miller £1.65 £4.95 £8.25

BADROCK AND COMPANY
Image,MS; 1 Sep 1994-6 Feb 1995
1-5 ND Keith Giffen script, Todd Nauck art

	$Good	$Fine	$N.Mint	£Good	£Fine	£N.Mint
	$0.45	$1.35	$2.25	£0.30	£0.90	£1.50

6 ND Keith Giffen script, Todd Nauck art; Shadowhawk guest-stars

	$Good	$Fine	$N.Mint	£Good	£Fine	£N.Mint
	$0.45	$1.35	$2.25	£0.30	£0.90	£1.50
Title Value:	$2.70	$8.10	$13.50	£1.80	£5.40	£9.00

BADROCK ANNUAL
Image; 1 Sep 1995-present
1 ND Tom and Mary Bierbaum script, Todd Nauck art

	$Good	$Fine	$N.Mint	£Good	£Fine	£N.Mint
	$0.60	$1.80	$3.00	£0.40	£1.20	£2.00
Title Value:	$0.60	$1.80	$3.00	£0.40	£1.20	£2.00

BADROCK!
Image; 1 Mar 1995-present
1 ND Rob Liefeld script, Eric Stephenson art; Cover A variant inked by Todd McFarlane

	$Good	$Fine	$N.Mint	£Good	£Fine	£N.Mint
	$0.40	$1.20	$2.00	£0.25	£0.75	£1.25

1 ND Rob Liefeld script, Eric Stephenson art; Cover B variant inked by Stephen Platt

	$Good	$Fine	$N.Mint	£Good	£Fine	£N.Mint
	$0.40	$1.20	$2.00	£0.25	£0.75	£1.25

1 ND Rob Liefeld script, Eric Stephenson art; Cover C variant inked by Dan Fraga

	$Good	$Fine	$N.Mint	£Good	£Fine	£N.Mint
	$0.40	$1.20	$2.00	£0.25	£0.75	£1.25

2 ND guest-starring Savage Dragon

	$Good	$Fine	$N.Mint	£Good	£Fine	£N.Mint
	$0.40	$1.20	$2.00	£0.25	£0.75	£1.25

3 ND guest-starring Savage Dragon; Badrock vs. The Overlord

	$Good	$Fine	$N.Mint	£Good	£Fine	£N.Mint
	$0.40	$1.20	$2.00	£0.25	£0.75	£1.25
Title Value:	$2.00	$6.00	$10.00	£1.25	£3.75	£6.25

BAKER STREET
Caliber Press; 1 1989-10 1992

	$Good	$Fine	$N.Mint	£Good	£Fine	£N.Mint
1 ND	$0.60	$1.80	$3.00	£0.40	£1.20	£2.00
2-5 ND	$0.45	$1.35	$2.25	£0.30	£0.90	£1.50
6-10 ND	$0.40	$1.20	$2.00	£0.25	£0.75	£1.25
Title Value:	$4.40	$13.20	$22.00	£2.85	£8.55	£14.25

Honour Among Punks (Aug 1990)
Trade paperback reprints #1-5 (softcover) £1.70 £5.10 £8.50
Hardcover (500 copies), signed by Gary Reed and Guy Davis £4.00 £12.00 £20.00

BAKER STREET GRAPHITTI
Caliber Press,OS; 1 Nov 1991
1 ND includes reprints from Caliber Presents

	$Good	$Fine	$N.Mint	£Good	£Fine	£N.Mint
	$0.55	$1.65	$2.75	£0.35	£1.05	£1.75
Title Value:	$0.55	$1.65	$2.75	£0.35	£1.05	£1.75

BALANCE OF POWER
Mu Press,MS; 1 May 1990-6 Mar 1991
1-6 ND ND Paula Shoudy script, Mike Raabe art; black and white

	$Good	$Fine	$N.Mint	£Good	£Fine	£N.Mint
	$0.30	$0.90	$1.50	£0.20	£0.60	£1.00
Title Value:	$1.80	$5.40	$9.00	£1.20	£3.60	£6.00

BALDER THE BRAVE
Marvel Comics Group,MS; 1 Nov 1985-4 Feb 1986
1-4 ND Simonson script, Sal Buscema art

	$Good	$Fine	$N.Mint	£Good	£Fine	£N.Mint
	$0.25	$0.75	$1.25	£0.15	£0.45	£0.75
Title Value:	$1.00	$3.00	$5.00	£0.60	£1.80	£3.00

BALLISTIC
Image; 1 Sep 1995-present
1 ND Brian Haberlin script, Michael Turner art; Wetworks appear

	$Good	$Fine	$N.Mint	£Good	£Fine	£N.Mint
	$0.60	$1.80	$3.00	£0.35	£1.05	£1.75

2 ND Wetworks appear

	$Good	$Fine	$N.Mint	£Good	£Fine	£N.Mint
	$0.50	$1.50	$2.50	£0.30	£0.90	£1.50

3 ND

	$Good	$Fine	$N.Mint	£Good	£Fine	£N.Mint
	$0.50	$1.50	$2.50	£0.30	£0.90	£1.50
Title Value:	$1.60	$4.80	$8.00	£0.95	£2.85	£4.75

BALLISTIC IMAGERY
Image,OS; 1 Nov 1995
1 ND antholohy series begins; Hell Cop, Heavy Space and True Tales of Cyberforce

	$Good	$Fine	$N.Mint	£Good	£Fine	£N.Mint
	$0.50	$1.50	$2.50	£0.30	£0.90	£1.50
Title Value:	$0.50	$1.50	$2.50	£0.30	£0.90	£1.50

BAOH
Viz Communications,MS; 1 Feb 1990-8 Sep 1990
1 ND 48pgs, squarebound, Japanese reprint material in black and white, art by Hirohiko Araki

	$Good	$Fine	$N.Mint	£Good	£Fine	£N.Mint
	$0.60	$1.80	$3.00	£0.40	£1.20	£2.00

2-8 ND 48pgs, squarebound, Japanese reprint material in black and white, art by Hirohiko Araki

	$Good	$Fine	$N.Mint	£Good	£Fine	£N.Mint
	$0.55	$1.65	$2.75	£0.35	£1.05	£1.75
Title Value:	$4.45	$13.35	$22.25	£2.85	£8.55	£14.25

Baoh Graphic Novel Vol. 1 (May 1995) reprints mini-series £2.00 £6.00 £10.00
Baoh Graphic Novel Vol. 2 (Jul 1995) reprints mini-series £2.00 £6.00 £10.00

BAR SINISTER
Valiant/Windjammer,MS; 1 Jun 1995-4 Sep 1995
1 ND Mike Grell script and cover, storyline continued from Shaman's Tears #4

	$Good	$Fine	$N.Mint	£Good	£Fine	£N.Mint
	$0.45	$1.35	$2.25	£0.30	£0.90	£1.50

2-4 ND Mike Grell script and cover

	$Good	$Fine	$N.Mint	£Good	£Fine	£N.Mint
	$0.45	$1.35	$2.25	£0.30	£0.90	£1.50
Title Value:	$1.80	$5.40	$9.00	£1.20	£3.60	£6.00

BARABBAS
Slave Labor; 1 Aug 1986-4 May 1987
1-4 ND black and white

	$Good	$Fine	$N.Mint	£Good	£Fine	£N.Mint
	$0.25	$0.75	$1.25	£0.15	£0.45	£0.75
Title Value:	$1.00	$3.00	$5.00	£0.60	£1.80	£3.00

BARB WIRE
Dark Horse; 1 Apr 1994-9 Feb 1995
1 ND Arcudi, Moder and Parks creative team begins; spin-off from Comics Greatest World series

	$Good	$Fine	$N.Mint	£Good	£Fine	£N.Mint
	$0.90	$2.70	$4.50	£0.50	£1.50	£2.50
2-3 ND	$0.60	$1.80	$3.00	£0.40	£1.20	£2.00
4-9 ND	$0.45	$1.35	$2.25	£0.30	£0.90	£1.50
Title Value:	$4.80	$14.40	$24.00	£3.10	£9.30	£15.50

BARBARIANS
Atlas; 1 Jun 1975
(see Ironjaw)
1 Ironjaw and Andrax appear; distributed in the U.K.

	$Good	$Fine	$N.Mint	£Good	£Fine	£N.Mint
	$0.30	$0.90	$1.50	£0.20	£0.60	£1.00
Title Value:	$0.30	$0.90	$1.50	£0.20	£0.60	£1.00

BARBARIC TALES
Pyramid Comics; 1 1986
1 ND black and white

	$Good	$Fine	$N.Mint	£Good	£Fine	£N.Mint
	$0.30	$1.00	$1.70	£0.20	£0.60	£1.00
Title Value:	$0.30	$1.00	$1.70	£0.20	£0.60	£1.00

BARBI TWINS ADVENTURES, THE
Topps,OS; 1 Mar 1995
1 ND the stunning adventures of Shane and Sia Barbi

	$Good	$Fine	$N.Mint	£Good	£Fine	£N.Mint
	$0.45	$1.35	$2.25	£0.30	£0.90	£1.50
Title Value:	$0.45	$1.35	$2.25	£0.30	£0.90	£1.50

BARBIE
Marvel Comics Group; 1 Jan 1991-present
1 ND pre-bagged with free "credit card"

	$Good	$Fine	$N.Mint	£Good	£Fine	£N.Mint
	$0.20	$0.60	$1.00	£0.15	£0.45	£0.75
2-39 ND	$0.15	$0.45	$0.75	£0.10	£0.35	£0.60

40 ND Trina Robbins and Mary Wilshire

	$Good	$Fine	$N.Mint	£Good	£Fine	£N.Mint
	$0.15	$0.45	$0.75	£0.10	£0.35	£0.60

41 ND Trina Robbins

	$Good	$Fine	$N.Mint	£Good	£Fine	£N.Mint
	$0.15	$0.45	$0.75	£0.10	£0.35	£0.60
42-49 ND	$0.15	$0.45	$0.75	£0.10	£0.35	£0.60
50 ND 48pgs	$0.35	$1.05	$1.75	£0.25	£0.75	£1.25
51-60 ND	$0.20	$0.60	$1.00	£0.15	£0.45	£0.75
61-63 ND	$0.30	$0.90	$1.50	£0.20	£0.60	£1.00
Title Value:	$10.65	$31.95	$53.25	£7.30	£24.30	£41.30

Barbie Trade paperback (Jul 1992), reprints most popular stories from the first year of Barbie and Barbie Fashion £1.00 £3.00 £5.00

BARBIE FASHION
Marvel Comics Group; 1 Jan 1991-55 Jul 1995
1 ND pre-bagged with Barbie door-hanger

	$Good	$Fine	$N.Mint	£Good	£Fine	£N.Mint
	$0.20	$0.60	$1.00	£0.15	£0.45	£0.75
2-49 ND	$0.15	$0.45	$0.75	£0.10	£0.35	£0.60
50 ND 48pgs	$0.25	$0.75	$1.25	£0.15	£0.45	£0.75
51-55 ND	$0.15	$0.45	$0.75	£0.10	£0.35	£0.60
Title Value:	$8.40	$25.20	$42.00	£5.60	£19.45	£33.30

BAREFOOTZ - THE COMIC BOOK STORIES
Renegade; 1 Mar 1986
1 ND Howard Cruse art; reprints

	$Good	$Fine	$N.Mint	£Good	£Fine	£N.Mint
	$0.30	$0.90	$1.50	£0.20	£0.60	£1.00
Title Value:	$0.30	$0.90	$1.50	£0.20	£0.60	£1.00

BARON WEIRWULF'S HAUNTED LIBRARY
(see Haunted)

BART SIMPSON'S TREEHOUSE OF HORROR
Bongo Comics,OS; 1 Oct 1995

	$Good	$Fine	$N.Mint	£Good	£Fine	£N.Mint
1 ND 48pgs	$0.60	$1.80	$3.00	£0.40	£1.20	£2.00
Title Value:	$0.60	$1.80	$3.00	£0.40	£1.20	£2.00

BARTMAN
Bongo Comics; 1 Dec 1993-3 Feb 1994; 4 May 1995-present
1 ND silver foil cover, pull-out poster

	$Good	$Fine	$N.Mint	£Good	£Fine	£N.Mint
	$0.70	$2.10	$3.50	£0.50	£1.50	£2.50

1 Newstand edition, without poster insert

	$Good	$Fine	$N.Mint	£Good	£Fine	£N.Mint
	$0.50	$1.50	$2.50	£0.40	£1.20	£2.00
2-6 ND	$0.45	$1.35	$2.25	£0.30	£0.90	£1.50
Title Value:	$3.45	$10.35	$17.25	£2.40	£7.20	£12.00

BASIL WOLVERTON'S FANTASTIC FABLES
Dark Horse; 1 Oct 1993-2 Dec 1993

	$Good	$Fine	$N.Mint	£Good	£Fine	£N.Mint
1-2 ND	$0.45	$1.35	$2.25	£0.30	£0.90	£1.50
Title Value:	$0.90	$2.70	$4.50	£0.60	£1.80	£3.00

BASIL WOLVERTON'S GATEWAY TO HORROR
Dark Horse; 1 Jun 1988
1 ND Bissette cover, black and white sci-fi and horror reprints

	$Good	$Fine	$N.Mint	£Good	£Fine	£N.Mint
	$0.45	$1.35	$2.25	£0.30	£0.90	£1.50
Title Value:	$0.45	$1.35	$2.25	£0.30	£0.90	£1.50

BASIL WOLVERTON'S PLANET OF TERROR
Dark Horse; 1 Oct 1987
1 ND Alan Moore cover

	$Good	$Fine	$N.Mint	£Good	£Fine	£N.Mint
	$0.45	$1.35	$2.25	£0.30	£0.90	£1.50
Title Value:	$0.45	$1.35	$2.25	£0.30	£0.90	£1.50

VERY GENERAL PERCENTAGE CONVERSION CHART WHICH MAY BE USED TO CALCULATE LOW AND INBETWEEN GRADES:

BASIL WOLVERTON'S SPACE FUNNIES
Robert Brosch/Archival Photography; 1 Nov 1990- 2 1991

	$Good	$Fine	$N.Mint	£Good	£Fine	£N.Mint
1 ND reprints Spacehawk/Space Patrol in colour from 1940s "Target Comics"	$0.90	$2.70	$4.50	£0.60	£1.80	£3.00
2 ND	$0.90	$2.70	$4.50	£0.60	£1.80	£3.00
Title Value:	$1.80	$5.40	$9.00	£1.20	£3.60	£6.00

BAT LASH
National Periodical Publications; 1 Oct/Nov 1968-7 Oct/Nov 1969
(see Jonah Hex, Jonah Hex Spectacular, Showcase #76, Weird Western Tales)

	$Good	$Fine	$N.Mint	£Good	£Fine	£N.Mint
1 2nd appearance of Bat Lash (see showcase #76)	$2.50	$7.50	$15.00	£1.65	£5.00	£10.00
2-7	$2.00	$6.00	$10.00	£1.00	£3.00	£5.00
Title Value:	$14.50	$43.50	$75.00	£7.65	£23.00	£40.00

BAT MASTERSON
Dell; (Four Color #1013) 1 Oct 1959-9 Nov 1961/Jan 1962

	$Good	$Fine	$N.Mint	£Good	£Fine	£N.Mint
1 Four Color #1013; Gene Barry photo covers begin	$14.00	$43.00	$85.00	£9.00	£28.00	£55.00
2-3	$7.50	$22.50	$45.00	£5.00	£15.00	£30.00
4-9	$6.50	$20.00	$40.00	£4.15	£12.50	£25.00
Title Value:	$68.00	$208.00	$415.00	£43.90	£133.00	£265.00

Note: all Limited Distribution on the news-stands in the U.K.

BAT, THE
Apple Comics,OS; 1 1990

	$Good	$Fine	$N.Mint	£Good	£Fine	£N.Mint
1 ND	$0.60	$1.80	$3.00	£0.40	£1.20	£2.00
Title Value:	$0.60	$1.80	$3.00	£0.40	£1.20	£2.00

Note: based on 1930s pulp hero, a direct antecedent of Batman

BAT, THE (2ND SERIES)
Adventure,OS; 1 Aug 1992

	$Good	$Fine	$N.Mint	£Good	£Fine	£N.Mint
1 ND adaptation of Mary Roberts Rinehart 1926 play that influenced the creation of Batman	$0.45	$1.35	$2.25	£0.30	£0.90	£1.50
Title Value:	$0.45	$1.35	$2.25	£0.30	£0.90	£1.50

BATGIRL SPECIAL
DC Comics,OS; 1 Mar 1988

	$Good	$Fine	$N.Mint	£Good	£Fine	£N.Mint
1 48pgs, Barry Kitson art	$1.00	$3.00	$5.00	£0.60	£1.80	£3.00
Title Value:	$1.00	$3.00	$5.00	£0.60	£1.80	£3.00

BATMAN
National Periodical Publications/DC Comics; 0 Oct 1994; 1 Spring 1940-present
(see Arkham Asylum, Batman: The Cult, Batman Family, Batman: The Son of the Demon, Batman 3D, Best of DC, Brave and the Bold, The Dark Knight Returns, DC Special, Detective, Dynamic Classics, Eighty Page Giant, Famous First Edition, Gotham by Gaslight, Greatest Batman Stories Ever Told, The Killing Joke, Legends of the Dark Knight, Limited Collector's Edition, One Hundred Page Super-Spectacular, Batman and the Outsiders, Saga of Ra's Al Ghul, Shadow of the Batman, Untold Legend of the Batman)

	$Good	$Fine	$N.Mint	£Good	£Fine	£N.Mint
0 (Oct 1994) Zero Hour X-over, origin retold; continued in Batman: Shadow of the Bat #31	$0.20	$0.60	$1.00	£0.15	£0.45	£0.75

1 (Spring 1940), 1st appearance The Joker and The Cat (later Catwoman), 2 page origin from Detective Comics #33 reprinted; around 300 copies extant in any condition

	$Good	$Fine	$N.Mint	£Good	£Fine	£N.Mint
	$4150.00	$12500.00	$50000.00	£3000.00	£9000.00	£36000.00

[Prices may vary widely on this comic]

2 less common/scarce in the U.S, scarce/very scarce in the U.K.; 2nd appearance of The Joker and Catwoman (though she is out of costume)

	$Good	$Fine	$N.Mint	£Good	£Fine	£N.Mint
	$1175.00	$3550.00	$9500.00	£780.00	£2325.00	£6250.00

3 scarce in the U.S, very scarce in the U.K. 1st appearance Catwoman in costume (and her 3rd ever appearance. 1st ever villainess in costume?)

	$Good	$Fine	$N.Mint	£Good	£Fine	£N.Mint
	$830.00	$2500.00	$6700.00	£530.00	£1575.00	£4250.00

4 5th ever appearance of The Joker (see Detective Comics #45)

	$Good	$Fine	$N.Mint	£Good	£Fine	£N.Mint
	$650.00	$1950.00	$5000.00	£435.00	£1300.00	£3500.00

5 (Spring 1941), 1st appearance of the Batmobile classic with bat-head front

	$Good	$Fine	$N.Mint	£Good	£Fine	£N.Mint
	$465.00	$1400.00	$3750.00	£315.00	£950.00	£2550.00
6-7	$365.00	$1100.00	$2950.00	£250.00	£750.00	£2000.00

8 (Dec/Jan 1942), classic infinity cover effect

	$Good	$Fine	$N.Mint	£Good	£Fine	£N.Mint
	$335.00	$1000.00	$2700.00	£175.00	£520.00	£1400.00

9 classic cover that was repeated in reverse on Batman #16

	$Good	$Fine	$N.Mint	£Good	£Fine	£N.Mint
	$335.00	$1000.00	$2700.00	£175.00	£520.00	£1400.00

10 Catwoman appears

	$Good	$Fine	$N.Mint	£Good	£Fine	£N.Mint
	$335.00	$1000.00	$2700.00	£175.00	£520.00	£1400.00

11 classic Joker cover with playing card background; Penguin appears for 1st time in title

	$Good	$Fine	$N.Mint	£Good	£Fine	£N.Mint
	$520.00	$1575.00	$5250.00	£350.00	£1050.00	£3500.00
12	$250.00	$750.00	$2000.00	£165.00	£500.00	£1350.00

13 Superman's co-creator Jerry Siegel appears in one of the Batman stories

	$Good	$Fine	$N.Mint	£Good	£Fine	£N.Mint
	$280.00	$840.00	$2250.00	£185.00	£560.00	£1500.00

14 (Dec/Jan 1943), 1st Penguin cover and story in title

	$Good	$Fine	$N.Mint	£Good	£Fine	£N.Mint
	$255.00	$760.00	$2050.00	£170.00	£510.00	£1375.00

15 Catwoman appears

	$Good	$Fine	$N.Mint	£Good	£Fine	£N.Mint
	$250.00	$750.00	$2000.00	£165.00	£500.00	£1350.00

16 1st appearance Alfred the Butler (fat rather than skinny as later Alfred came to be)

	$Good	$Fine	$N.Mint	£Good	£Fine	£N.Mint
	$500.00	$1500.00	$4500.00	£330.00	£1000.00	£3000.00

17 classic patriotic cover; Batman and Robin on American Eagle (see Superman #14); Penguin appears

	$Good	$Fine	$N.Mint	£Good	£Fine	£N.Mint
	$155.00	$475.00	$1275.00	£105.00	£315.00	£850.00

18 Hirohito, Mussolini and Hitler on cover

	$Good	$Fine	$N.Mint	£Good	£Fine	£N.Mint
	$155.00	$475.00	$1275.00	£105.00	£315.00	£850.00
19	$155.00	$475.00	$1275.00	£105.00	£315.00	£850.00

20 (Dec/Jan 1944), classic Batmobile cover

	$Good	$Fine	$N.Mint	£Good	£Fine	£N.Mint
	$155.00	$475.00	$1275.00	£105.00	£315.00	£850.00

21 Penguin appears; Alfred becomes skinny (for no apparent reason! Lousy editing?)

	$Good	$Fine	$N.Mint	£Good	£Fine	£N.Mint
	$130.00	$390.00	$1050.00	£87.50	£260.00	£700.00

22 Alfred begins solo story series (much like Lois Lane in Superman); Catwoman appears

	$Good	$Fine	$N.Mint	£Good	£Fine	£N.Mint
	$130.00	$390.00	$1050.00	£87.50	£260.00	£700.00

23 classic Joker cover and story

	$Good	$Fine	$N.Mint	£Good	£Fine	£N.Mint
	$180.00	$540.00	$1450.00	£115.00	£355.00	£950.00

[Very scarce in high grade - Very Fine+ or better]

24 1st Batman and Robin sent back through time by Professor Carter Nichols (the first of about 30 occasions)

	$Good	$Fine	$N.Mint	£Good	£Fine	£N.Mint
	$130.00	$390.00	$1050.00	£87.50	£260.00	£700.00

25 Joker and Penguin team (reprinted in Wanted #2); 1st DC "super-villain team-up" (see Fantastic Four #6)

	$Good	$Fine	$N.Mint	£Good	£Fine	£N.Mint
	$180.00	$550.00	$1475.00	£125.00	£375.00	£1000.00

26 (Dec/Jan 1945)

	$Good	$Fine	$N.Mint	£Good	£Fine	£N.Mint
	$125.00	$375.00	$1000.00	£82.50	£250.00	£675.00

27 classic Christmas cover; Penguin appears

	$Good	$Fine	$N.Mint	£Good	£Fine	£N.Mint
	$150.00	$450.00	$1200.00	£100.00	£300.00	£800.00
28-30	$125.00	$375.00	$1000.00	£82.50	£250.00	£675.00

[Note: most of these Golden Age issues are at least scarce in the U.K.]

31 infinity cover effect (see Batman #8)

	$Good	$Fine	$N.Mint	£Good	£Fine	£N.Mint
	$92.50	$280.00	$750.00	£62.50	£185.00	£500.00

32 (Dec/Jan 1946), origin of Robin recapped

	$Good	$Fine	$N.Mint	£Good	£Fine	£N.Mint
	$92.50	$280.00	$750.00	£62.50	£185.00	£500.00

33 Christmas cover

	$Good	$Fine	$N.Mint	£Good	£Fine	£N.Mint
	$105.00	$315.00	$850.00	£70.00	£215.00	£575.00
34	$92.50	$280.00	$750.00	£62.50	£185.00	£500.00

35 Catwoman appears

	$Good	$Fine	$N.Mint	£Good	£Fine	£N.Mint
	$92.50	$280.00	$750.00	£62.50	£185.00	£500.00

36 Penguin appears

	$Good	$Fine	$N.Mint	£Good	£Fine	£N.Mint
	$92.50	$280.00	$750.00	£62.50	£185.00	£500.00

37 Joker cover and story

	$Good	$Fine	$N.Mint	£Good	£Fine	£N.Mint
	$110.00	$335.00	$900.00	£75.00	£225.00	£600.00

38 (Dec/Jan 1947), Penguin cover and story

	$Good	$Fine	$N.Mint	£Good	£Fine	£N.Mint
	$100.00	$300.00	$800.00	£65.00	£200.00	£535.00

39 Catwoman story

	$Good	$Fine	$N.Mint	£Good	£Fine	£N.Mint
	$100.00	$300.00	$800.00	£65.00	£200.00	£535.00

40 Joker cover and story

	$Good	$Fine	$N.Mint	£Good	£Fine	£N.Mint
	$115.00	$345.00	$925.00	£77.50	£230.00	£625.00

41 "Batman, Interplanetary Policeman" - 1st sci-fi Batman story (a theme which was to become dominant in the 1950s); Penguin appears

Batman #2

Batman #6

Batman #14

MINT = 100% / NEAR MINT (inc. +/-) = 90–99% / VERY FINE (inc. +/-) = 75–89% / FINE (inc. +/-) = 55–74%
VERY GOOD (inc. +/-) = 35–54% / GOOD (inc. +/-) = 15–34% / FAIR = 5–14% / POOR = 1–4%

223

Issue / Description	$Good	$Fine	$N.Mint	£Good	£Fine	£N.Mint
	$75.00	$225.00	$600.00	£50.00	£150.00	£400.00
42 2nd Catwoman cover (1st in Batman title - see Detective Comics #122), Catwoman story	$87.50	$260.00	$700.00	£57.50	£175.00	£475.00
43 Penguin cover and story	$87.50	$260.00	$700.00	£57.50	£175.00	£475.00
44 (Dec/Jan 1948), Joker cover and story	$115.00	$345.00	$925.00	£77.50	£230.00	£625.00
45 1st appearance Vicki Vale, Christmas cover	$80.00	$240.00	$650.00	£55.00	£165.00	£450.00
46	$75.00	$225.00	$600.00	£50.00	£150.00	£400.00
47 classic origin of Batman, more detailed than Detective Comics #33	$280.00	$840.00	$2250.00	£185.00	£560.00	£1500.00
48 1000 Secrets of the Batcave	$87.50	$260.00	$700.00	£57.50	£175.00	£475.00
49 1st appearance The Mad Hatter (see Detective Comics #230), 2nd appearance Vicki Vale, Joker cover and story	$110.00	$335.00	$900.00	£75.00	£225.00	£600.00
50 (Dec/Jan 1949), Two Face returns	$75.00	$225.00	$600.00	£50.00	£150.00	£400.00
51	$65.00	$195.00	$525.00	£44.00	£130.00	£350.00
52 Joker cover and story	$80.00	$240.00	$650.00	£52.50	£155.00	£425.00
53 Joker appears	$70.00	$215.00	$575.00	£48.00	£140.00	£385.00
54	$65.00	$195.00	$525.00	£44.00	£130.00	£350.00
55 Joker cover and story	$80.00	$240.00	$650.00	£52.50	£155.00	£425.00
56 (Dec/Jan 1950)	$65.00	$195.00	$525.00	£44.00	£130.00	£350.00
57 calendar for 1950 at centrefold (often missing!)	$65.00	$195.00	$525.00	£44.00	£130.00	£350.00
58 Penguin cover and story	$70.00	$210.00	$560.00	£47.00	£140.00	£375.00
59 classic "Batman in the Future" story and cover; 1st appearance Deadshot (not to be confused with later DC hero)	$67.50	$205.00	$550.00	£47.00	£140.00	£375.00
60 Joker appears	$67.50	$205.00	$550.00	£47.00	£140.00	£375.00
61 origin Bat-Plane II	$67.50	$205.00	$550.00	£47.00	£140.00	£375.00
62 (Dec/Jan 1951), origin Catwoman, Catwoman cover and story	$90.00	$270.00	$725.00	£60.00	£180.00	£485.00
63 origin and 1st appearance Killer Moth; Joker appears	$55.00	$165.00	$450.00	£38.00	£110.00	£300.00
64	$52.50	$155.00	$425.00	£35.00	£105.00	£280.00
65 Catwoman cover and story	$55.00	$165.00	$450.00	£38.00	£110.00	£300.00
66 Joker cover and story	$65.00	$195.00	$525.00	£44.00	£130.00	£350.00
67	$52.50	$155.00	$425.00	£35.00	£105.00	£280.00
68 (Dec/Jan 1952), Two Face story	$52.50	$155.00	$425.00	£36.00	£105.00	£285.00
69 Catwoman cover and story	$55.00	$165.00	$450.00	£38.00	£110.00	£300.00
70-71	$52.50	$155.00	$425.00	£35.00	£105.00	£280.00
72 last 52pg issue	$52.50	$155.00	$425.00	£35.00	£105.00	£280.00
73 Joker cover and story	$65.00	$195.00	$525.00	£44.00	£130.00	£350.00
74 (Dec/Jan 1953), Joker story	$55.00	$165.00	$450.00	£38.00	£110.00	£300.00
75-77	$52.50	$155.00	$425.00	£35.00	£105.00	£280.00
78 Roh Kar, The Manhunter From Mars character/story (pre J'onn J'onzz in Detective #225)	$65.00	$195.00	$525.00	£44.00	£130.00	£350.00
79 Vicki Vale appears	$52.50	$155.00	$425.00	£35.00	£105.00	£280.00
80 (Dec/Jan 1954), Joker appears	$55.00	$165.00	$450.00	£38.00	£110.00	£300.00
81 Two Face cover and story	$52.50	$155.00	$425.00	£35.00	£105.00	£280.00
82 flying Batman (see Detective Comics #153)	$50.00	$150.00	$400.00	£34.00	£100.00	£270.00
83	$48.00	$140.00	$385.00	£33.00	£97.50	£260.00
84 Catwoman cover and story	$55.00	$165.00	$450.00	£38.00	£110.00	£300.00
85	$49.00	$145.00	$395.00	£33.00	£97.50	£260.00
86 1st Bat-Submarine	$50.00	$150.00	$410.00	£33.00	£97.50	£265.00
87-88	$49.00	$145.00	$395.00	£33.00	£97.50	£260.00
89 (Feb 1955), 1st Aunt Agatha (later became Aunt Harriet for the 1960s Batman TV series)	$49.00	$145.00	$395.00	£33.00	£97.50	£260.00
90 scarce in the U.K. 1st Code-approved issue	$41.00	$120.00	$325.00	£28.00	£82.50	£225.00
91 very scarce in the U.K.	$41.00	$120.00	$325.00	£29.00	£85.00	£230.00
92 very scarce in the U.K. 1st Bat-Hound	$52.50	$155.00	$425.00	£38.00	£110.00	£300.00
93-96 very scarce in the U.K.	$41.00	$120.00	$325.00	£28.00	£82.50	£225.00
97 very scarce in the U.K. (Feb 1956), return of Bat-Hound (2nd appearance)	$41.00	$120.00	$325.00	£28.00	£82.50	£225.00
98 very scarce in the U.K.	$41.00	$120.00	$325.00	£28.00	£82.50	£225.00
99 very scarce in the U.K. Penguin story, on cover as statuette						
	$41.00	$120.00	$325.00	£28.00	£82.50	£225.00
100 scarce in the U.K. cover features reproductions of six early issues (#1, #23, #25, #47, #48, #61)	$160.00	$480.00	$1600.00	£110.00	£330.00	£1100.00
[Very scarce in high grade - Very Fine+ or better]						
101-104	$46.00	$135.00	$325.00	£31.00	£92.50	£220.00
105 (Feb 1957), 2nd appearance Batwoman and 1st Batwoman in Batman title (see Detective Comics #233)	$52.50	$160.00	$380.00	£37.00	£110.00	£260.00
106-109	$46.00	$135.00	$325.00	£31.00	£92.50	£220.00
110 1st appearance of The Joker in Silver Age	$50.00	$150.00	$350.00	£34.00	£100.00	£235.00
111-112	$32.00	$95.00	$225.00	£21.00	£62.50	£150.00
113 (Feb 1958), 1st science-fiction type story of Batman-on-strange-worlds, the theme to dominate for the next 6 years	$32.00	$95.00	$225.00	£21.00	£62.50	£150.00
114-120	$32.00	$95.00	$225.00	£21.00	£62.50	£150.00
121 (Feb 1959)	$23.50	$70.00	$165.00	£15.50	£47.00	£110.00
122 marriage of Batman and Batwoman story	$23.50	$70.00	$165.00	£15.50	£47.00	£110.00
123 Joker story	$26.00	$75.00	$180.00	£17.00	£50.00	£120.00
124-125	$23.50	$70.00	$165.00	£15.50	£47.00	£110.00
126 Batwoman/Batman/Robin team-up	$26.00	$75.00	$180.00	£17.00	£50.00	£120.00
127 Joker story, Superman cameo, "Thor" appears (note Marvel character); copies known with distribution (pence) stamp	$23.50	$70.00	$165.00	£15.50	£47.00	£110.00
1st official distribution in the U.K.						
128	$23.50	$70.00	$165.00	£14.00	£43.00	£100.00
129 (Feb 1960), origin Robin retold	$29.00	$85.00	$200.00	£15.50	£47.00	£110.00
130	$23.50	$70.00	$165.00	£14.00	£43.00	£100.00
131 1st Batman and Robin II; 1st imaginary Batman story?	$19.00	$57.50	$135.00	£10.50	£32.00	£75.00
132	$17.00	$50.00	$120.00	£10.00	£30.00	£70.00
133 3rd appearance Bat-Mite	$17.00	$50.00	$120.00	£10.50	£32.00	£75.00
134	$17.00	$50.00	$120.00	£10.00	£30.00	£70.00
135 scarce in the U.K.	$17.00	$50.00	$120.00	£10.50	£32.00	£75.00
136 Joker cover and story	$22.50	$67.50	$160.00	£13.50	£41.00	£95.00
137 scarce in the U.K. (Feb 1961)	$17.00	$50.00	$120.00	£10.50	£32.00	£75.00
138	$17.00	$50.00	$120.00	£10.00	£30.00	£70.00
139 1st appearance original Batgirl	$17.00	$50.00	$120.00	£10.50	£32.00	£75.00
140 Joker story, Superman cameo	$17.00	$50.00	$120.00	£10.50	£32.00	£75.00
141-142	$17.00	$50.00	$120.00	£10.00	£30.00	£70.00
143 last 10 cents issue	$17.00	$50.00	$120.00	£10.00	£30.00	£70.00
144 Joker story, Bat-Mite meets original Batgirl	$17.00	$50.00	$120.00	£10.00	£30.00	£70.00
145 (Feb 1962), Joker cover and story ("Son of the Joker" - only appearance?)	$19.00	$57.50	$135.00	£10.50	£32.00	£75.00
146 Bat-Mite appears	$14.00	$43.00	$100.00	£7.00	£21.00	£50.00
147	$14.00	$43.00	$100.00	£7.00	£21.00	£50.00
148 Joker cover and story	$14.00	$43.00	$101.25	£9.50	£29.00	£67.50
149-150	$14.00	$43.00	$100.00	£7.00	£21.00	£50.00
151-152	$10.50	$32.00	$75.00	£5.00	£15.00	£35.00
153 (Feb 1963), 1st 3-part full length story (features Batwoman and original Batgirl)	$10.50	$32.00	$75.00	£5.00	£15.00	£35.00
154	$10.50	$32.00	$75.00	£5.00	£15.00	£35.00
155 1st Silver Age appearance of The Penguin (last seen in issue #99)	$36.00	$105.00	$285.00	£18.50	£55.00	£150.00
156-158	$10.50	$32.00	$75.00	£4.25	£12.50	£30.00
159 Joker cover and story, original Bat-Girl appears; back-up story featuring Bruce Wayne Jnr.	$12.00	$36.00	$85.00	£6.25	£19.00	£45.00
160-161	$10.50	$32.00	$75.00	£4.25	£12.50	£30.00
162 (Feb 1964)	$10.50	$32.00	$75.00	£4.25	£12.50	£30.00
163 Joker cover and story; last appearance original Bat-girl	$12.00	$36.00	$85.00	£6.25	£19.00	£45.00
164 new-look Batman, new Batmobile (see Detective Comics #327)	$10.50	$32.00	$75.00	£5.00	£15.00	£35.00
165	$10.00	$30.00	$70.00	£3.85	£11.50	£27.00
166-168	$10.00	$30.00	$70.00	£3.55	£10.50	£25.00
169 (Feb 1965), Penguin cover and story	$15.50	$47.00	$110.00	£4.25	£12.50	£30.00
170	$10.00	$30.00	$70.00	£3.55	£10.50	£25.00
171 1st Silver Age appearance of The Riddler (1st since Dec. 1948 in Detective Comics #142 making this his 3rd ever appearance)	$50.00	$150.00	$400.00	£25.00	£75.00	£200.00
172-175	$7.00	$21.00	$50.00	£3.20	£9.50	£22.50
176 scarce in the U.K. 80pgs, Giant G-17, Joker cover and story, Catwoman story; last Silver Age issue (indicadated Dec 1965)	$8.50	$26.00	$60.00	£4.25	£12.50	£30.00
177	$7.00	$21.00	$50.00	£2.85	£8.50	£20.00
178 (Feb 1966)	$7.00	$21.00	$50.00	£2.85	£8.50	£20.00
179 rare in the U.K., scarce in the U.S. (see note below), 2nd appearance Silver Age Riddler	$15.50	$47.00	$110.00	£11.00	£34.00	£80.00
180 rare in the U.K., scarce in the U.S. (see note below)						

TRADE PAPERBACKS, GRAPHIC NOVELS AND OTHER COLLECTIONS ARE PRICED IN POUNDS STERLING ONLY. CONVERT AT 1.5 FOR DOLLARS.

FORBIDDEN PLANET

THE MIGHTIEST HEROES OF ANY UNIVERSE

Issue / Description	$Good	$Fine	$N.Mint	£Good	£Fine	£N.Mint
	$7.00	$21.00	$50.00	£8.50	£26.00	£60.00
181 1st appearance Poison Ivy, centre-spread pin-up poster of Batman and Robin (often missing!)	$8.50	$26.00	$60.00	£3.90	£11.50	£27.50
182 80pgs, Giant G-24, Joker cover and story	$8.50	$26.00	$60.00	£3.90	£11.50	£27.50
183 2nd appearance Poison Ivy	$7.00	$21.00	$50.00	£2.85	£8.50	£20.00
184	$7.00	$21.00	$50.00	£2.50	£7.50	£17.50
185 80pgs, Giant G-27, all Robin reprints including the classic "Robin Dies At Dawn"	$7.00	$21.00	$50.00	£3.20	£9.50	£22.50
186 Joker cover and story	$6.25	$19.00	$45.00	£2.85	£8.50	£20.00
187 80pgs, (Jan 1967), Giant G-30, Joker cover and story	$8.50	$26.00	$60.00	£3.55	£10.50	£25.00
188	$4.25	$12.50	$30.00	£2.10	£6.25	£15.00
189 1st appearance Silver Age Scarecrow	$10.00	$30.00	$70.00	£2.85	£8.50	£20.00
190 Penguin cover and story	$5.50	$17.00	$40.00	£2.10	£6.25	£15.00
191-192	$4.25	$12.50	$30.00	£1.75	£5.25	£12.50
193 80pgs, Giant G-37, reprints "bizarre action roles" including "The Flying Batman"	$6.25	$19.00	$45.00	£2.85	£8.50	£20.00
194-196	$4.25	$12.50	$30.00	£1.40	£4.25	£10.00
197 1st Silver Age appearance of Catwoman in Batman title (see Lois Lane #70); 4th overall	$10.00	$30.00	$70.00	£3.90	£11.50	£27.50
198 80pgs, (Feb 1968), Giant G-43, reprints origin from Batman #47 (1948), Joker cover and story, Penguin and Catwoman reprints and cover appearances	$11.00	$34.00	$80.00	£4.60	£13.50	£32.50
199	$4.25	$12.50	$30.00	£1.40	£4.25	£10.00
200 retells origin, Joker on cover by Neal Adams	$22.50	$67.50	$160.00	£10.50	£32.00	£75.00
201 Joker and Catwoman cameos	$4.50	$13.50	$27.00	£2.05	£6.25	£12.50
202	$3.00	$9.00	$18.00	£1.30	£4.00	£8.00
203 80pgs, Giant G-49, "Secrets of the Bat-Cave", Neal Adams cover	$5.75	$17.50	$35.00	£2.90	£8.75	£17.50
204-207	$3.00	$9.00	$18.00	£1.30	£4.00	£8.00
208 80pgs, (Feb 1969), Giant G-55; new origin Batman by Gil Kane (see note below)	$5.75	$17.50	$35.00	£3.30	£10.00	£20.00
209-210	$3.00	$9.00	$18.00	£1.30	£4.00	£8.00
211	$3.00	$9.00	$18.00	£1.25	£3.75	£7.50
212 last 12 cents issue	$3.00	$9.00	$18.00	£1.25	£3.75	£7.50
213 68pgs, Giant G-61, origin Alfred (from Batman #16), Robin (from Detective #38), Joker (from Detective #168), Clayface II (Detective #298)	$7.00	$21.00	$50.00	£3.55	£10.50	£25.00
214-216	$3.00	$9.00	$18.00	£1.25	£3.75	£7.50
217 Robin leaves, Bat-Cave closed down, Neal Adams cover	$3.00	$9.00	$18.00	£1.25	£3.75	£7.50
218 68pgs, (Feb 1970), Giant G-67; reprints 1944 syndicated newspaper story, Neal Adams cover	$5.75	$17.50	$35.00	£2.90	£8.75	£17.50
219 Neal Adams art; solo Batman without Robin begins in title (temporary)	$5.00	$15.00	$30.00	£2.50	£7.50	£15.00
220 Neal Adams cover	$2.50	$7.50	$15.00	£1.25	£3.75	£7.50
221	$2.50	$7.50	$15.00	£1.05	£3.25	£6.50
222 scarce in the U.K. "Beatles" cover and story, Robin appears	$5.00	$15.00	$30.00	£2.50	£7.50	£15.00
223 68pgs, Giant G-73, Neal Adams cover	$4.15	$12.50	$25.00	£2.05	£6.25	£12.50
224-225 Neal Adams covers	$2.50	$7.50	$15.00	£1.05	£3.25	£6.50
226-227	$2.50	$7.50	$15.00	£0.90	£2.75	£5.50
228 68pgs, (Feb 1971), Giant G-79	$4.15	$12.50	$25.00	£1.65	£5.00	£10.00
229	$2.50	$7.50	$15.00	£0.90	£2.75	£5.50
230 Neal Adams cover	$2.50	$7.50	$15.00	£0.90	£2.75	£5.50
231	$2.50	$7.50	$15.00	£0.90	£2.75	£5.50
232 Neal Adams art, 1st appearance Ra's Al Ghul, Robin appears	$10.00	$30.00	$60.00	£4.15	£12.50	£25.00
233 68pgs, Giant G-85	$4.15	$12.50	$25.00	£1.50	£4.50	£9.00
234 52pgs, Neal Adams art, 1st modern appearance (not Silver Age!) Two Face	$14.00	$43.00	$100.00	£5.00	£15.00	£35.00
235-236 52pgs	$2.00	$6.00	$12.00	£1.00	£3.00	£6.00
237 52pgs, Neal Adams art, back-up reprint of Detective Comics #37, Robin appears	$5.75	$17.50	$35.00	£2.50	£7.50	£15.00
238 scarce in the U.K. 100pgs, (Jan 1972), DC-100pg Super Spectacular #8; reprints My Greatest Adventure #80 (1st Doom Patrol), Neal Adams cover	$2.50	$7.50	$15.00	£1.65	£5.00	£10.00
239 52pgs	$2.00	$6.00	$12.00	£1.00	£3.00	£6.00
240 scarce in the U.K. 52pgs, Neal Adams cover	$2.00	$6.00	$12.00	£1.05	£3.25	£6.50
241-242 scarce in the U.K. 52pgs	$2.00	$6.00	$12.00	£1.05	£3.25	£6.50
243 Neal Adams art, classic Ra's Al Ghul story, Robin appears	$3.30	$10.00	$20.00	£2.05	£6.25	£12.50
244-245 Neal Adams art, classic Ra's Al Ghul story	$3.30	$10.00	$20.00	£2.05	£6.25	£12.50
246 scarce in the U.K. Robin appears	$2.00	$6.00	$12.00	£1.15	£3.50	£7.00
247 (Feb 1973), Robin appears	$2.00	$6.00	$12.00	£1.00	£3.00	£6.00
248-249	$2.00	$6.00	$12.00	£0.90	£2.75	£5.50
250	$2.00	$6.00	$12.00	£1.00	£3.00	£6.00
251 Neal Adams art, classic Joker rendition, first appearance in title since issue #201	$6.50	$20.00	$40.00	£3.75	£11.00	£22.50
252	$2.00	$6.00	$12.00	£0.80	£2.50	£5.00
253 Batman/Shadow team-up	$2.00	$6.00	$12.00	£1.00	£3.00	£6.00
254 100pgs, (Feb 1974)	$2.50	$7.50	$15.00	£1.30	£4.00	£8.00
255 100pgs, Neal Adams art	$4.15	$12.50	$25.00	£2.05	£6.25	£12.50
256 100pgs	$2.50	$7.50	$15.00	£1.30	£4.00	£8.00
257 100pgs, Joker reprint	$2.50	$7.50	$15.00	£1.30	£4.00	£8.00
258-259 100pgs	$2.50	$7.50	$15.00	£1.30	£4.00	£8.00
260 100pgs, (Feb 1975), Joker cover and new story, Catwoman and Penguin reprints	$5.75	$17.50	$35.00	£2.05	£6.25	£12.50
261 100pgs	$2.50	$7.50	$15.00	£1.25	£3.75	£7.50
262 scarce in the U.K. 68pgs	$1.25	$3.75	$7.50	£1.00	£3.00	£6.00
263-264	$1.25	$3.75	$7.50	£0.65	£2.00	£4.00
265 Wrightson part-inks	$1.25	$3.75	$7.50	£0.75	£2.25	£4.50
266	$1.25	$3.75	$7.50	£0.65	£2.00	£4.00
267 scarce in the U.K.	$1.25	$3.75	$7.50	£0.75	£2.25	£4.50
268	$1.25	$3.75	$7.50	£0.65	£2.00	£4.00
269-270 scarce in the U.K.	$1.25	$3.75	$7.50	£0.75	£2.25	£4.50
271 (Jan 1976)	$1.25	$3.75	$7.50	£0.65	£2.00	£4.00
272-276	$1.25	$3.75	$7.50	£0.65	£2.00	£4.00
277-282 scarce in the U.K.	$1.25	$3.75	$7.50	£0.75	£2.25	£4.50
283 scarce in the U.K. (Jan 1977)	$1.25	$3.75	$7.50	£0.75	£2.25	£4.50
284 scarce in the U.K.	$1.25	$3.75	$7.50	£0.75	£2.25	£4.50
285 ND scarce in the U.K.	$1.25	$3.75	$7.50	£1.00	£3.00	£6.00
286 scarce in the U.K. Joker cover and story	$1.65	$5.00	$10.00	£0.75	£2.25	£4.50
287-290 scarce in the U.K. Grell art	$1.15	$3.50	$7.00	£0.75	£2.25	£4.50
291 Joker and Catwoman appear	$1.65	$5.00	$10.00	£0.75	£2.25	£4.50
292	$1.15	$3.50	$7.00	£0.65	£2.00	£4.00
293 Lex Luthor and Superman appear	$1.15	$3.50	$7.00	£0.65	£2.00	£4.00
294 Joker cover and story	$1.65	$5.00	$10.00	£0.75	£2.25	£4.50
295 scarce in the U.K. (Jan 1978), Michael Golden art	$1.15	$3.50	$7.00	£0.65	£2.00	£4.00
296-299	$1.15	$3.50	$7.00	£0.65	£2.00	£4.00
300 48pgs	$1.65	$5.00	$10.00	£1.00	£3.00	£6.00
301-302	$1.60	$4.80	$8.00	£0.70	£2.10	£3.50
303 ND 44pgs, Golden art	$1.60	$4.80	$8.00	£1.30	£3.90	£6.50
304-305 ND 44pgs	$1.60	$4.80	$8.00	£1.00	£3.00	£5.00
306	$1.60	$4.80	$8.00	£0.70	£2.10	£3.50
307 (Jan 1979)	$1.60	$4.80	$8.00	£0.70	£2.10	£3.50
308-310	$1.60	$4.80	$8.00	£0.70	£2.10	£3.50
311 Batgirl guest stars	$1.60	$4.80	$8.00	£0.70	£2.10	£3.50
312-317	$1.60	$4.80	$8.00	£0.70	£2.10	£3.50
318 1st appearance Firebug	$1.60	$4.80	$8.00	£0.70	£2.10	£3.50
319 (Jan 1980)	$1.60	$4.80	$8.00	£0.70	£2.10	£3.50
320	$1.60	$4.80	$8.00	£0.70	£2.10	£3.50
321 Joker cover and story, Walt Simonson art	$2.00	$6.00	$10.00	£1.10	£3.30	£5.50
322	$1.60	$4.80	$8.00	£0.70	£2.10	£3.50
323-324 Catwoman appears	$1.60	$4.80	$8.00	£0.80	£2.40	£4.00
325-326	$1.60	$4.80	$8.00	£0.70	£2.10	£3.50
327 Arkham Asylum	$1.60	$4.80	$8.00	£0.70	£2.10	£3.50
328-330	$1.60	$4.80	$8.00	£0.70	£2.10	£3.50
331 (Jan 1981)	$1.60	$4.80	$8.00	£0.70	£2.10	£3.50
332-335 Catwoman story	$1.60	$4.80	$8.00	£0.80	£2.40	£4.00
336-338	$1.60	$4.80	$8.00	£0.70	£2.10	£3.50
339 scarce in the U.K. Vicki Vale returns	$1.60	$4.80	$8.00	£0.80	£2.40	£4.00
340 Gene Colan art	$1.60	$4.80	$8.00	£0.70	£2.10	£3.50
341-342	$1.60	$4.80	$8.00	£0.70	£2.10	£3.50
343 (Jan 1982)	$1.60	$4.80	$8.00	£0.70	£2.10	£3.50
344-352	$1.60	$4.80	$8.00	£0.70	£2.10	£3.50
353 Joker cover/story, free 16pg insert "Masters of the Universe"	$2.00	$6.00	$10.00	£1.10	£3.30	£5.50

	$Good	$Fine	$N.Mint	£Good	£Fine	£N.Mint
354	$1.40	$4.20	$7.00	£0.70	£2.10	£3.50
355 (Jan 1983), Catwoman appears	$1.40	$4.20	$7.00	£0.70	£2.25	£3.75
356	$1.40	$4.20	$7.00	£0.70	£2.10	£3.50
357 1st appearance Jason Todd (later the new Robin); see Detective #524 (2nd appearance)	$1.50	$4.50	$7.50	£0.90	£2.70	£4.50
358	$1.40	$4.20	$7.00	£0.70	£2.10	£3.50
359 Joker cover and story	$2.00	$6.00	$10.00	£0.90	£2.70	£4.50
360	$1.40	$4.20	$7.00	£0.70	£2.10	£3.50
361 Man Bat appears	$1.40	$4.20	$7.00	£0.70	£2.10	£3.50
362 Riddler appears	$1.40	$4.20	$7.00	£0.70	£2.10	£3.50
363-365	$1.40	$4.20	$7.00	£0.60	£1.80	£3.00
366 1st new Robin in costume, Joker cover and story	$4.00	$12.00	$20.00	£2.50	£7.50	£12.50
367 (Jan 1984)	$1.40	$4.20	$7.00	£0.60	£1.80	£3.00
368 1st official introduction of Jason Todd as new Robin (see Detective #535)	$2.00	$6.00	$10.00	£1.60	£4.80	£8.00
369-373	$1.40	$4.20	$7.00	£0.60	£1.80	£3.00
374 Penguin appears	$0.80	$2.40	$4.00	£0.60	£1.80	£3.00
375-378	$0.80	$2.40	$4.00	£0.60	£1.80	£3.00
379 (Jan 1985)	$0.80	$2.40	$4.00	£0.60	£1.80	£3.00
380-381	$0.80	$2.40	$4.00	£0.60	£1.80	£3.00
382 Catwoman appears and "dies"	$0.80	$2.40	$4.00	£0.70	£2.10	£3.50
383-387	$0.80	$2.40	$4.00	£0.60	£1.80	£3.00
388 Mirror Master and Captain Boomerang appear	$0.80	$2.40	$4.00	£0.60	£1.80	£3.00
389-390	$0.80	$2.40	$4.00	£0.60	£1.80	£3.00
391 (Jan 1986)	$0.80	$2.40	$4.00	£0.60	£1.80	£3.00
392	$0.80	$2.40	$4.00	£0.60	£1.80	£3.00
393-394 Gulacy art	$0.80	$2.40	$4.00	£0.60	£1.80	£3.00
395-399	$0.80	$2.40	$4.00	£0.60	£1.80	£3.00
400 64pgs, "Dark Knight" special, intro by Stephen King, Bolland, Sienkiewicz, Art Adams, George Perez art, 1pg John Byrne	$4.00	$12.00	$20.00	£2.50	£7.50	£12.50
401 Legends X-over (1st), John Byrne cover	$0.70	$2.10	$3.50	£0.50	£1.50	£2.50
402 Jim Starlin art, 1st Batman's "long ears", very popular look in the 1990s	$0.70	$2.10	$3.50	£0.50	£1.50	£2.50
403 (Jan 1987)	$0.70	$2.10	$3.50	£0.50	£1.50	£2.50
404 Batman Year One by Frank Miller begins; 1st appearance new style Catwoman (as Selina Kyle only)	$2.60	$7.75	$13.00	£1.20	£3.60	£6.00
405 Batman Year One	$1.10	$3.30	$5.50	£0.75	£2.25	£3.75
406 Batman Year One, 1st appearance new style Catwoman in costume	$1.30	$3.90	$6.50	£0.90	£2.70	£4.50
407 Batman Year One	$1.10	$3.30	$5.50	£0.70	£2.10	£3.50
408 new origin Jason Todd (Robin II) begins	$0.90	$2.70	$4.50	£0.60	£1.80	£3.00
409-410 new origin Jason Todd (Robin II) continued	$0.90	$2.70	$4.50	£0.50	£1.50	£2.50
411-413	$0.50	$1.50	$2.50	£0.35	£1.05	£1.75
414 Jim Starlin script	$0.50	$1.50	$2.50	£0.35	£1.05	£1.75
415 (Jan 1988), Jim Starlin script, Millennium X-over	$0.50	$1.50	$2.50	£0.35	£1.05	£1.75
416 Jim Starlin script	$0.50	$1.50	$2.50	£0.35	£1.05	£1.75
417 Ten Nights of the Beast, Jim Starlin script, Mike Zeck cover	$1.80	$5.25	$9.00	£1.20	£3.60	£6.00
418 Ten Nights of the Beast, Jim Starlin script, Mike Zeck cover	$1.80	$5.25	$9.00	£0.80	£2.40	£4.00
419-420 Ten Nights of the Beast, Jim Starlin script, Mike Zeck cover	$1.80	$5.25	$9.00	£0.75	£2.25	£3.75
421-422 Jim Starlin script	$0.50	$1.50	$2.50	£0.30	£0.90	£1.50
423 Jim Starlin script, Todd McFarlane cover	$0.50	$1.50	$2.50	£0.30	£0.90	£1.50
423 2nd printing	$0.25	$0.75	$1.25	£0.15	£0.45	£0.75
423 3rd printing	$0.15	$0.45	$0.75	£0.10	£0.35	£0.60
424 Jim Starlin script	$0.50	$1.50	$2.50	£0.30	£0.90	£1.50
424 2nd printing	$0.25	$0.75	$1.25	£0.15	£0.45	£0.75
425 Jim Starlin script	$0.50	$1.50	$2.50	£0.30	£0.90	£1.50
426 A Death in the Family begins	$1.60	$4.80	$8.00	£1.10	£3.30	£5.50
427 DS, regular edition	$1.40	$4.20	$7.00	£1.00	£3.00	£5.00
427 DS (phone number inside cover)	$1.40	$4.20	$7.00	£1.00	£3.00	£5.00
428 (Jan 1989), death of Robin II (Jason Todd)	$1.40	$4.20	$7.00	£1.00	£3.00	£5.00
429 Death in the Family ends, Superman appears, Joker cover	$1.00	$3.00	$5.00	£0.55	£1.65	£2.75
430-432	$0.40	$1.20	$2.00	£0.25	£0.75	£1.25
433-435 Many Deaths of Batman, John Byrne script	$0.40	$1.20	$2.00	£0.25	£0.75	£1.25
436 Year 3 part 1, blue DC logo; 1st appearance Timothy Drake	$0.80	$2.40	$4.00	£0.45	£1.35	£2.25
436 2nd printing, green DC logo	$0.25	$0.75	$1.25	£0.15	£0.45	£0.75
437-438 Year 3 parts 2,3	$0.40	$1.20	$2.00	£0.25	£0.75	£1.25
439 Year 3 part 4, George Perez cover	$0.40	$1.20	$2.00	£0.25	£0.75	£1.25
440 A Lonely Place of Dying, X-over with New Teen Titans #60, #61; George Perez cover	$0.40	$1.20	$2.00	£0.25	£0.75	£1.25
441 A Lonely Place of Dying continues, George Perez cover	$0.40	$1.20	$2.00	£0.25	£0.75	£1.25
442 last part A Lonely Place of Dying, 1st appearance Tim Drake in new Robin costume (see #457); George Perez cover	$0.80	$2.40	$4.00	£0.30	£0.90	£1.50
443 (Jan 1990), free 16pg insert	$0.30	$0.90	$1.50	£0.20	£0.60	£1.00
444	$0.30	$0.90	$1.50	£0.20	£0.60	£1.00
445-447 Bolland covers	$0.30	$0.90	$1.50	£0.20	£0.60	£1.00
448-449 bi-weekly X-over with Detective #615, Penguin appears	$0.30	$0.90	$1.50	£0.20	£0.60	£1.00
450-451 bi-weekly X-over with Detective #617, The Joker appears	$0.30	$0.90	$1.50	£0.20	£0.60	£1.00
452-454 Riddler story by Pete Milligan	$0.30	$0.90	$1.50	£0.20	£0.60	£1.00
455-456 Identity Crisis story; Scarecrow appears	$0.30	$0.90	$1.50	£0.20	£0.60	£1.00

Batman #108

Batman #171

Batman #208

	$Good	$Fine	$N.Mint	£Good	£Fine	£N.Mint

457 Identity Crisis part 3; Tim Drake becomes the new Robin (III), Scarecrow appears
(Note: the direct sales edition has "000" instead of "457" in indicia at the bottom of the 1st page)
$1.40 / $4.20 / $7.00 / £0.60 / £1.80 / £3.00

457 2nd printing, (Jan 1991)
$0.15 / $0.45 / $0.75 / £0.10 / £0.35 / £0.60

458-459 Sarah Essen (from Batman: Year One) appears
$0.30 / $0.90 / $1.50 / £0.20 / £0.60 / £1.00

460-461 Sister in Arms story, Catwoman appears
$0.30 / $0.90 / $1.50 / £0.20 / £0.60 / £1.00

462-463 $0.30 / $0.90 / $1.50 / £0.20 / £0.60 / £1.00

464-466 bi-weekly $0.30 / $0.90 / $1.50 / £0.20 / £0.60 / £1.00

467-469 The Shadow Box, sequel to Robin mini-series, Louise Simonson script, bi-weekly
$0.30 / $0.90 / $1.50 / £0.20 / £0.60 / £1.00

470 War of the Gods X-over
$0.30 / $0.90 / $1.50 / £0.20 / £0.60 / £1.00

471 $0.25 / $0.75 / $1.25 / £0.15 / £0.45 / £0.75

472 The Idiot Root part 1, X-over with Detective #639
$0.25 / $0.75 / $1.25 / £0.15 / £0.45 / £0.75

473 (Jan 1992), The Idiot Root part 3, X-over with Detective #440
$0.25 / $0.75 / $1.25 / £0.15 / £0.45 / £0.75

474 Destroyer part 1, continued in Legends of the Dark Knight #27
$0.25 / $0.75 / $1.25 / £0.15 / £0.45 / £0.75

475 X-over with Detective Comics #642
$0.25 / $0.75 / $1.25 / £0.15 / £0.45 / £0.75

476 Batman "reveals" identity to Vicki Vale
$0.25 / $0.75 / $1.25 / £0.15 / £0.45 / £0.75

477 A Gotham Tale story, bi-weekly issue, photo cover, $1.25 cover begins
$0.25 / $0.75 / $1.25 / £0.15 / £0.45 / £0.75

478 A Gotham Tale story, bi-weekly issue, photo cover
$0.25 / $0.75 / $1.25 / £0.15 / £0.45 / £0.75

479-480 bi-weekly
$0.25 / $0.75 / $1.25 / £0.15 / £0.45 / £0.75

481-482 Messenger of Zeus story, bi-weekly
$0.25 / $0.75 / $1.25 / £0.15 / £0.45 / £0.75

483 The Ballad of Crash story
$0.25 / $0.75 / $1.25 / £0.15 / £0.45 / £0.75

484 $0.25 / $0.75 / $1.25 / £0.15 / £0.45 / £0.75

485 Mike Golden cover
$0.25 / $0.75 / $1.25 / £0.15 / £0.45 / £0.75

486-487 $0.25 / $0.75 / $1.25 / £0.15 / £0.45 / £0.75

488 (Jan 1993), continued from Batman: Sword of Azrael #4, Travis Charest cover
$2.00 / $6.00 / $10.00 / £0.80 / £2.40 / £4.00

489 Azrael dons Batman costume for 1st time; Travis Charest cover
$1.60 / $4.80 / $8.00 / £0.70 / £2.10 / £3.50

490 Bane and Azrael appear; Riddler appears, Travis Charest cover
$1.40 / $4.20 / $7.00 / £0.60 / £1.80 / £3.00

491 Joker cover and story; Azrael and Bane appear, Knightfall prequel
$1.00 / $3.00 / $5.00 / £0.50 / £1.50 / £2.50

492 Knightfall part 1, bi-weekly; continued in Detective Comics #659
$1.20 / $3.60 / $6.00 / £0.55 / £1.65 / £2.75

492 2nd printing $0.30 / $0.90 / $1.50 / £0.20 / £0.60 / £1.00

492 ND Platinum Edition - made available by DC at the Capital City Distribution Sales Conference; enlarged "492" no date no price and platinum coloured logo background
$2.40 / $7.00 / $12.00 / £1.40 / £4.20 / £7.00

493 Knightfall part 3, bi-weekly; continued in Detective Comics #660
$0.80 / $2.40 / $4.00 / £0.40 / £1.20 / £2.00

494 Knightfall part 5, bi-weekly; continued in Detective Comics #661; Joker appears
$0.60 / $1.80 / $3.00 / £0.30 / £0.90 / £1.50

495 Knightfall part 7, bi-weekly; continued in Detective Comics #662; Bane and Joker cameos
$0.60 / $1.80 / $3.00 / £0.30 / £0.90 / £1.50

496 Knightfall part 9, bi-weekly; continued in Detective Comics #663; Joker and Bane appear
$0.60 / $1.80 / $3.00 / £0.25 / £0.75 / £1.25

497 Knightfall part 11, bi-weekly; continued in Detective Comics #664; protective outer half cover, Batman vs. Bane - "the breaking of Batman"
$1.20 / $3.60 / $6.00 / £0.55 / £1.65 / £2.75

497 2nd printing, no outer cover
$0.30 / $0.90 / $1.50 / £0.20 / £0.60 / £1.00

497 Newstand edition, as 1st printing but without outer cover
$0.40 / $1.20 / $2.00 / £0.20 / £0.60 / £1.00

498 Knightfall part 15; continued in Detective Comics #665; Bane and Catwoman appear
$0.40 / $1.20 / $2.00 / £0.25 / £0.75 / £1.25

499 Knightfall part 17; continued in Detective Comics #666; Kelley Jones cover; Bane appears
$0.40 / $1.20 / $2.00 / £0.25 / £0.75 / £1.25

500 64pgs, Knightfall part 19; Azrael takes over as Batman with new costume, cover by Kelley Jones
$0.50 / $1.50 / $2.50 / £0.30 / £0.90 / £1.50

500 ND Collector's Edition - 64pgs, die-cut outer cover with foil enhancement by Joe Quesada
$0.80 / $2.40 / $4.00 / £0.50 / £1.50 / £2.50

501 Knightquest: The Crusade part 3, continued in Batman: Shadow of the Bat #20, Kelley Jones cover
$0.30 / $0.90 / $1.50 / £0.20 / £0.60 / £1.00

502 Knightquest: The Crusade part 6, continued in Detective Comics #669; Kelley Jones cover
$0.30 / $0.90 / $1.50 / £0.20 / £0.60 / £1.00

503 (Jan 1994), Knightquest: The Crusade story, Kelley Jones cover; continued in Catwoman #6
$0.30 / $0.90 / $1.50 / £0.20 / £0.60 / £1.00

504 Knightquest: The Crusade story, Kelley Jones cover; continued in Catwoman #7
$0.30 / $0.90 / $1.50 / £0.20 / £0.60 / £1.00

505 Knightquest: The Crusade story, Kelley Jones cover; continued in Batman: Shadow of the Bat #26
$0.30 / $0.90 / $1.50 / £0.20 / £0.60 / £1.00

506-507 Knightquest: The Crusade story, Ballistic appears; Kelley Jones cover
$0.30 / $0.90 / $1.50 / £0.20 / £0.60 / £1.00

508 Knightquest: The Crusade story conclusion; continued in Batman: Shadow of the Bat #28, Kelley Jones cover $0.30 / $0.90 / $1.50 / £0.20 / £0.60 / £1.00

509 48pgs, Knightsend part 1, continued in Batman: Shadow of the Bat #29

$0.30 / $0.90 / $1.50 / £0.20 / £0.60 / £1.00

510 Knightsend part 7, continued in Batman: Shadow of the Bat #30; Kelley Jones cover
$0.30 / $0.90 / $1.50 / £0.20 / £0.60 / £1.00

511 Zero Hour X-over
$0.30 / $0.90 / $1.50 / £0.20 / £0.60 / £1.00

512 Dick Grayson as Batman vs. Killer Croc
$0.30 / $0.90 / $1.50 / £0.20 / £0.60 / £1.00

513 Dick Grayson as Batman vs. Two-Face
$0.30 / $0.90 / $1.50 / £0.20 / £0.60 / £1.00

514 (Jan 1995) $0.30 / $0.90 / $1.50 / £0.20 / £0.60 / £1.00

515 The Troika part 1, continued in Batman: Shadow of the Bat #35
$0.30 / $0.90 / $1.50 / £0.20 / £0.60 / £1.00

515 ND Collector's Edition, embossed black cover
$0.45 / $1.35 / $2.25 / £0.30 / £0.90 / £1.50

516-518 $0.30 / $0.90 / $1.50 / £0.20 / £0.60 / £1.00

519 upgraded coated paper stock (Miraweb Format) begins
$0.40 / $1.20 / $2.00 / £0.25 / £0.75 / £1.25

520-521 $0.40 / $1.20 / $2.00 / £0.25 / £0.75 / £1.25

522 Swamp Thing appears
$0.40 / $1.20 / $2.00 / £0.25 / £0.75 / £1.25

523-524 $0.40 / $1.20 / $2.00 / £0.25 / £0.75 / £1.25

525 Underworld Unleashed tie-in, Mr. Freeze appears
$0.40 / $1.20 / $2.00 / £0.25 / £0.75 / £1.25

526 (Jan 1996) $0.40 / $1.20 / $2.00 / £0.25 / £0.75 / £1.25

527 Two-Face appears
$0.40 / $1.20 / $2.00 / £0.25 / £0.75 / £1.25

528 Two-Face appears
$0.40 / $1.20 / $2.00 / £0.25 / £0.75 / £1.25

529 Contagion Part 6
$0.40 / $1.20 / $2.00 / £0.25 / £0.75 / £1.25

Title Value: $20389.70 / $61232.50 / $179928.50 / £13495.85 / £40404.05 / £120058.70

Note: Joker covers - 100, 200. Joker covers and stories - 136, 145, 148, 159, 163, 176, 181, 182, 183, 184, 185, 186, 187, 193, 198, 251, 266, 286, 291, 294, 321, 353, 359, 366, 429, 450, 451. Joker stories - 110, 123, 127, 140, 144, 152, 201.

FEATURES

Atom (previously unpublished GA story) in 238. Batman/Commissioner Gordon in 328, 331. Bruce Wayne in 304. Catwoman solo in 332. Robin solo in 227, 229-231, 234-236, 239-242, 244, 245, 248-250, 252, 254, 337-339, 341-343. Tales of Gotham City in 334. Unsolved Cases of the Batman in 303, 305, 306.

REPRINT FEATURES

Batman/Robin in 176, 182, 185, 187, 193, 198, 203, 208, 213, 218, 223, 228, 233-242, 254-262. Alfred in 255, 257, 260. Doom Patrol, Plastic Man, Sargon the Sorcerer, Aquaman, Legion in 238.

Challenge of the Man-Bat (May 1989)
Trade Paperback black and white reprints of Detective Comics issues #395, #397, #400, #402 Neal Adams art / £1.00 / £3.00 / £5.00

Vow from the Grave (1989)
Trade Paperback
Titan Edition. B&W reprints of classic Neal Adams art / £1.00 / £3.00 / £5.00

The Demon Awakes (1989)
Trade Paperback
Titan Edition. B&W Neal Adams reprints / £1.00 / £3.00 / £5.00

The Joker's Revenge (1990)
Trade Paperback
Titan Edition. B&W Neal Adams reprints. Great foreword! / £1.00 / £3.00 / £5.00

The Frightened City (1990)
Trade Paperback
Titan Edition. B&W Neal Adams reprints. Even greater foreword! / £1.00 / £3.00 / £5.00

Red Water, Crimson Death (1990)
Trade Paperback Titan Edition.
B&W Neal Adams reprints. The best foreword of them all! / £1.00 / £3.00 / £5.00

Batman: A Death in the Family (1988)
Trade paperback, 144pgs, reprints #425-428 / £1.00 / £3.00 / £5.00
(Note: 5 prints available - story title colour in red/purple/ green/ yellow/orange; 2nd-5th prints at 80% of above)

Batman: Year One (1988)
Hardback, with dustjacket
ND, reprints #404-407 with corrections / £2.00 / £6.00 / £10.00

Batman: Year One (1988)
Softback, as above, Titan (UK)/DC Edition / £1.00 / £3.00 / £5.00
2nd/3rd prints DC Edition (1988) / £0.90 / £2.70 / £4.50

Batman: Year Two (Jan 1990)
Trade paperback reprints Detective #575-578,
104pgs McFarlane/Davis/Neary art / £1.00 / £3.00 / £5.00

Batman: A Lonely Place of Dying (Sep 1990)
Trade paperback, reprints Batman #440-442,
New Titans #60, #61, new cover by Perez / £0.50 / £1.50 / £2.50

Batman: Tales of the Demon (Sep 1991)
Trade paperback, reprints Ra's Al Ghul mini-series,
Detective #485, #489, #490, DC Special Series #15 / £2.50 / £7.50 / £12.50

The Many Deaths of Batman (Apr 1992)
Trade paperback, reprints Batman #433-435 by John Byrne.
John Byrne cover / £0.50 / £1.50 / £2.50

Batman: Blind Justice (Apr 1992)
Trade paperback, reprints Detective Comics
#598-600, new intro by Sam Hamm / £0.90 / £2.70 / £4.50

Batman: Night Cries (Apr 1993)
Trade paperback, Scott Hampton art and painted cover / £1.60 / £4.80 / £8.00

Multi-Pack (1990), three issues from #397-399 or
#414-416, pre-bagged with illustrated header card, ND / £0.30 / £0.90 / £1.50

Batman: Sword of Azrael (Aug 1993)
Trade paperback reprints four issue mini-series,
new cover by Joe Quesada and Kevin Nowlan / £1.30 / £3.90 / £6.50

Batman: Venom (Oct 1993)

VERY GENERAL PERCENTAGE CONVERSION CHART WHICH MAY BE USED TO CALCULATE LOW AND INBETWEEN GRADES:

	$Good	$Fine	$N.Mint	£Good	£Fine	£N.Mint

Trade paperback reprints Batman: Legends of the Dark Knight #16-20, new embossed painted cover by Russell Braun — £1.30 £3.90 £6.50

Batman: Knightfall Vol 1 (Mar 1994)
Tarde paperback reprints Batman #491-497, Detective #659-663; Kelley Jones cover — £1.70 £5.10 £8.50

Batman: Knightfall Vol 2 (Mar 1994)
Trade paperback reprints Batman #498,500,Detective #664-666, Showcase '93 #7&8, Batman: Shadow of the Bat #16-18 — £1.70 £5.10 £8.50

Batman: Ten Nights of the Beast (Aug 1994)
Trade paperback reprints issues #417-420, new painted cover by Mike Zeck — £0.80 £2.40 £4.00

Knightsend (Jun 1995)
Trade paperback reprints Batman #509/510, Batman: Shadow of the Bat #29/30, Detective Comics #676/677, Batman: Legends of the Dark Knight #62/63, Catwoman #12, Robin #8 and 17pgs of Robin #9 — £2.00 £6.00 £10.00

Batman: Featuring The Riddler & Two-Face (Aug 1995)
Trade paperback 192pgs, classic collection of reprints from Golden Age to present — £1.70 £5.10 £8.50

Note: The front cover of #208 often bears ink marks, the result of inferior printing inks detaching from the back covers when the copies were originally stacked. Superman #207 and New Teen Titans 4 often suffer the same defacement. Perfect mint copies are scarce. **Note also:** A large percentage of the print-runs of #179 and #180 were distributed to American cinemas to promote the Batman film, and many were destroyed resulting in today's rarity.

BATMAN 3-D
National Periodical Publications,Magazine; nn 1953, nn 1966
nn ND rare in the U.K., Batman and Tommy Tomorrow reprints — $105.00 $315.00 $735.00 £70.00 £210.00 £490.00
nn scarce in the U.K. reprints the above — $39.00 $115.00 $275.00 £26.00 £77.50 £185.00
Title Value: $144.00 $430.00 $1010.00 £96.00 £287.50 £675.00
Note: if 3-D glasses are detached deduct 15%, if missing deduct 25%

BATMAN 3-D GRAPHIC ALBUM
DC Comics,OS; nn Dec 1990
nn ND 80pgs, John Byrne art, Penguin, Joker, Two Face, Riddler appear plus 3-D pin-ups featuring work by Art Adams, Dave Gibbons. Reprint from 1953 3-D comic included. With glasses — $1.50 $4.50 $7.50 £1.00 £3.00 £5.00
Title Value: $1.50 $4.50 $7.50 £1.00 £3.00 £5.00

BATMAN ADVENTURES
DC Comics; 1 Nov 1992-36 Oct 1995
1 based on US animated series, Ty Templeton art begins, bi-weekly — $1.00 $3.00 $5.00 £0.60 £1.80 £3.00
2 — $0.40 $1.20 $2.00 £0.25 £0.75 £1.25
3 Joker story and cover — $0.40 $1.20 $2.00 £0.25 £0.75 £1.25
4-5 — $0.40 $1.20 $2.00 £0.25 £0.75 £1.25
6 — $0.30 $0.90 $1.50 £0.20 £0.60 £1.00
7 pre-bagged with Batman vs. Man-Bat trading card — $1.20 $3.60 $6.00 £0.50 £1.50 £2.50
8-10 — $0.30 $0.90 $1.50 £0.20 £0.60 £1.00
11-17 — $0.25 $0.75 $1.25 £0.15 £0.45 £0.75
18 Batgirl appears — $0.25 $0.75 $1.25 £0.15 £0.45 £0.75
19-21 — $0.25 $0.75 $1.25 £0.15 £0.45 £0.75
22 Two Face appears — $0.25 $0.75 $1.25 £0.15 £0.45 £0.75
23-24 — $0.25 $0.75 $1.25 £0.15 £0.45 £0.75
25 48pgs, Superman guest-stars — $0.45 $1.35 $2.25 £0.30 £0.90 £1.50
26 Robin and Batgirl team-up — $0.25 $0.75 $1.25 £0.15 £0.45 £0.80
27-28 — $0.25 $0.75 $1.25 £0.15 £0.45 £0.80
29 Talia returns — $0.25 $0.75 $1.25 £0.15 £0.45 £0.80
30 — $0.25 $0.75 $1.25 £0.15 £0.45 £0.80
31 Alan Grant script — $0.25 $0.75 $1.25 £0.15 £0.45 £0.80
32-33 — $0.35 $1.05 $1.75 £0.20 £0.60 £1.00
34-36 Catwoman appears — $0.35 $1.05 $1.75 £0.20 £0.60 £1.00
Title Value: $12.20 $36.60 $61.00 £7.20 £21.60 £36.30

Batman: The Collected Adventures (Jan 1994)
Trade paperback reprints #1-6 with new wraparound cover — £0.80 £2.50 £4.00

Batman: The Collected Adventures (Jul 1994)
Trade paperback reprints #7-12 with new painted cover — £0.80 £2.50 £4.00

BATMAN ADVENTURES ANNUAL, THE
DC Comics; 1 Nov 1994-2 1995
1 64pgs, Joker appears; Matt Wagner art featured — $0.80 $2.40 $4.00 £0.50 £1.50 £2.50
2 56pgs, Batman vs. Demon; Ra's Al Ghul appears — $0.80 $2.40 $4.00 £0.50 £1.50 £2.50
Title Value: $1.60 $4.80 $8.00 £1.00 £3.00 £5.00

BATMAN ADVENTURES HOLIDAY SPECIAL, THE
DC Comics; 1 Feb 1995
1 ND 48pgs Bruce Timm cover and art — $0.60 $1.80 $3.00 £0.40 £1.20 £2.00
Title Value: $0.60 $1.80 $3.00 £0.40 £1.20 £2.00

BATMAN ADVENTURES, THE - MAD LOVE
DC Comics,OS; 1 Feb 1994; 1 Sep 1995
1 64pgs, squarebound, origin of Harley Quinn — $0.80 $2.40 $4.00 £0.50 £1.50 £2.50
1 ND 64pgs, Prestige Format with new painted cover by Bruce Timm — $1.00 $3.00 $5.00 £0.65 £1.95 £3.25

Title Value: $1.80 $5.40 $9.00 £1.15 £3.45 £5.75

BATMAN AND OTHER DC CLASSICS
DC Comics,OS; nn Jan 1990
nn ND giveaway advertising material from DC Trade paperbacks; reprints the origin of Batman from Batman #47 (1948) — $0.30 $0.90 $1.50 £0.20 £0.60 £1.00
Title Value: $0.30 $0.90 $1.50 £0.20 £0.60 £1.00

BATMAN AND ROBIN ADVENTURES, THE
DC Comics; 1 Nov 1995-present
1 based on US animated series, Two-Face appears — $0.40 $1.20 $2.00 £0.25 £0.75 £1.25
2 Two-Face appears — $0.40 $1.20 $2.00 £0.25 £0.75 £1.25
3 Riddler appears — $0.35 $1.05 $1.75 £0.25 £0.75 £1.25
4 Penguin appears — $0.35 $1.05 $1.75 £0.25 £0.75 £1.25
5 The Joker appears — $0.35 $1.05 $1.75 £0.25 £0.75 £1.25
Title Value: $1.85 $5.55 $9.25 £1.25 £3.75 £6.25

BATMAN AND THE OUTSIDERS
DC Comics; 1 Aug 1983-46 Jun 1987
(see Outsiders) (becomes Adventures of the Outsiders with issue #33)
1 scarce in the U.K. Batman, Black Lightning, Katana, Halo, Geo-Force, Metamorpho begin — $0.40 $1.20 $2.00 £0.70 £2.10 £3.50
2 scarce in the U.K. — $0.30 $0.90 $1.50 £0.40 £1.20 £2.00
3-4 — $0.30 $0.90 $1.50 £0.30 £0.90 £1.50
5 New Teen Titans X-over, Mando (higher quality) paper begins — $0.30 $0.90 $1.50 £0.30 £0.90 £1.50
6-10 — $0.25 $0.75 $1.25 £0.20 £0.60 £1.00
11 — $0.20 $0.60 $1.00 £0.15 £0.45 £0.75
12 origin Katana — $0.20 $0.60 $1.00 £0.15 £0.45 £0.75
13-21 — $0.20 $0.60 $1.00 £0.15 £0.45 £0.75
22-32 Alan Davis art — $0.25 $0.75 $1.25 £0.20 £0.60 £1.00
33 Alan Davis art, title becomes Adventures of the Outsiders — $0.25 $0.75 $1.25 £0.20 £0.60 £1.00
34-36 Alan Davis and Paul Neary art — $0.25 $0.75 $1.25 £0.20 £0.60 £1.00
37-38 — $0.20 $0.60 $1.00 £0.15 £0.45 £0.75
39 reprints from The Outsiders #1 onwards begin — $0.20 $0.60 $1.00 £0.15 £0.45 £0.75
40-46 — $0.20 $0.60 $1.00 £0.15 £0.45 £0.75
Title Value: $10.80 $32.40 $54.00 £9.15 £27.45 £45.75

BATMAN AND THE OUTSIDERS ANNUAL
DC Comics; 1 Sep 1984-2 Sep 1985
1 Frank Miller/Jim Aparo cover — $0.30 $0.90 $1.50 £0.20 £0.60 £1.00
2 Metamorpho and Sapphire Stagg wed — $0.30 $0.90 $1.50 £0.20 £0.60 £1.00
Title Value: $0.60 $1.80 $3.00 £0.40 £1.20 £2.00

BATMAN ANNUAL
National Periodical Publications/DC Comics; 1 Sep/Oct 1961-7 Jul 1964; 8 Oct 1982-present
1 80pgs, classic reprints featuring re-telling of origin plus origin of The Bat-Cave from Detective #205 — $55.00 $165.00 $500.00 £35.00 £105.00 £315.00
[Scarce in high grade - Very Fine+ or better]
2 80pgs, classic reprints including 1st Bat-Marine from Batman #86, The Super Batman from #113; Batman calendar and back cover pin-up — $26.00 $75.00 $230.00 £13.50 £42.00 £125.00
3 80pgs, Joker cover/story, includes 1st Mad Hatter from Detective #230, 1st Mirror Man from Detective #213 and Two Face from Batman #68 — $26.00 $77.50 $235.00 £13.50 £42.00 £125.00
4 80pgs, reprints include 1st Bat-Woman from Detective #233 and The First Batman from Detective #235 — $12.50 $38.00 $115.00 £7.00 £21.50 £65.00
5 80pgs, "Strange Lives" reprints including Batman #110, #118, #119 and World's Finest #109; covers of Batman #1 and Detective #27 on the back — $12.50 $38.00 $115.00 £7.00 £21.50 £65.00
6 scarce in the U.K. 80pgs, reprints include Batman #91, #94 and Detective #255 — $10.50 $32.00 $95.00 £5.50 £16.50 £50.00
7 80pgs, reprints include 1st Bat-Mite from Detective #267 and 1st original Bat-Girl from Batman #139 — $10.50 $32.00 $95.00 £4.70 £14.00 £42.50
8 — $0.90 $2.70 $4.50 £0.60 £1.80 £3.00
9 Nino/Paul Smith art, painted cover, high quality paper — $0.70 $2.10 $3.50 £0.60 £1.80 £3.00
10 — $0.70 $2.10 $3.50 £0.60 £1.80 £3.00
11 Alan Moore story, John Byrne cover — $1.00 $3.00 $5.00 £0.80 £2.40 £4.00
12 Mike Baron story — $0.70 $2.10 $3.50 £0.50 £1.50 £2.50
13 LD in the U.K. 64pgs, squarebound, George Pratt pencils, Gray Morrow inks — $0.90 $2.70 $4.50 £0.60 £1.80 £3.00
14 follows on from Year One, Harvey Dent appears with origin Two-Face retold; Neal Adams cover — $0.80 $2.40 $4.00 £0.50 £1.50 £2.50
15 64pgs, Armageddon: 2001 tie-in, Joker/Catwoman/Anarky appear — $0.80 $2.40 $4.00 £0.50 £1.50 £2.50
15 2nd printing, Feb 1992 — $0.40 $1.20 $2.00 £0.25 £0.75 £1.25
16 64pgs, Eclipso: The Darkness Within tie-in, Joker cover and story, Sam Kieth cover — $0.50 $1.50 $2.50 £0.30 £0.90 £1.50
17 64pgs, Bloodlines part 8, 1st appearance Decimator, continued in Justice League International Annual #4 — $0.50 $1.50 $2.50 £0.30 £0.90 £1.50

MINT = 100% / NEAR MINT (inc. +/-) = 90-99% / VERY FINE (inc. +/-) = 75-89% / FINE (inc. +/-) = 55-74%
VERY GOOD (inc. +/-) = 35-54% / GOOD (inc. +/-) = 15-34% / FAIR = 5-14% / POOR = 1-4%

229

	$Good	$Fine	$N.Mint	£Good	£Fine	£N.Mint

18 64pgs, Elseworlds story by Doug Moench

| | $0.50 | $1.50 | $2.50 | £0.30 | £0.90 | £1.50 |

19 56pgs, Year One, Batman vs. Scarecrow and origins told of both

| | $0.80 | $2.40 | $4.00 | £0.50 | £1.50 | £2.50 |
| **Title Value:** | $162.20 | $485.10 | $1431.00 | £92.55 | £281.55 | £819.25 |

Note: Many 80pg Giants and Annuals from the early '60s, and in particular Batman Annual #1-7, have crinkled covers at the spine, (particularly #2) caused by uneven drying of the glue. Perfectly flat (and therefore Near Mint or Mint) copies are rare.

BATMAN ARCHIVES

DC Comics; nn Oct 1990; nn Jul 1991; nn 1992
(see Superman Archives)
nn ND 306pgs, Hardcover; reprints Detective Comics #27-50 by Bob Kane and Jerry Robinson plus covers and ads

| | $7.50 | $22.50 | $37.50 | £5.00 | £15.00 | £25.00 |

nn ND 288pgs, Hardcover; reprints Detective Comics #51-70 by Bob Kane and Jerry Robinson plus covers and ads

| | $7.50 | $22.50 | $37.50 | £5.00 | £15.00 | £25.00 |

nn ND 224pgs, Hardcover; reprints Detective Comics #71-86 by Bob Kane and Jerry Robinson plus covers and ads

| | $7.50 | $22.50 | $37.50 | £5.00 | £15.00 | £25.00 |
| **Title Value:** | $22.50 | $67.50 | $112.50 | £15.00 | £45.00 | £75.00 |

BATMAN BOOK AND RECORD SET

Power Records; PR-27, PR-30 1974
27 scarce in the U.K. features The Joker in a 20pg booklet with 45 rpm record

| | $2.25 | $6.75 | $11.25 | | £4.50 | £7.50 |

30 scarce in the U.K. features Man-Bat in a 20pg booklet with 45 rpm record

| | $1.80 | $5.25 | $9.00 | £1.20 | £3.60 | £6.00 |
| **Title Value:** | $4.05 | $12.00 | $20.25 | £2.70 | £8.10 | £13.50 |

BATMAN CHRONICLES, THE

DC Comics; 1 Summer 1995-present
1 ND 48pgs, three stories each issue; Huntress and Anarky appear, work by Alan Grant, Doug Moench and Bill Sienkiewicz (art and cover inks) feature

| | $0.60 | $1.80 | $3.00 | £0.40 | £1.20 | £2.00 |

2 ND 48pgs, continued from Batman: Shadow of the Bat #42

| | $0.60 | $1.80 | $3.00 | £0.40 | £1.20 | £2.00 |

3 ND The Riddler and Killer Croc appear; Brian Bolland cover

| | $0.60 | $1.80 | $3.00 | £0.40 | £1.20 | £2.00 |
| **Title Value:** | $1.80 | $5.40 | $9.00 | £1.20 | £3.60 | £6.00 |

Note: quarterly frequency and rotating creative teams

BATMAN COLLECTION, THE

DC Comics; OS; nn Jul 1992; Vol 2 Aug 1992
nn Special Slipcase Set featuring Trade paperbacks Batman: The Dark Knight Returns, Batman: Year One, Batman: Arkham Asylum and Catwoman: Her Sister's Keeper; all latest printings as of date

| | $6.00 | $18.00 | $30.00 | £4.00 | £12.00 | £20.00 |

2 (Volume 2), Special Slipcase Set featuring Trade paperbacks The Greatest Batman Stories Ever Told, Batman: The Cult and Batman: Gotham By Gaslight

| | $5.00 | $15.00 | $25.00 | £3.50 | £10.50 | £17.50 |
| **Title Value:** | $11.00 | $33.00 | $55.00 | £7.50 | £22.50 | £37.50 |

BATMAN FAMILY

DC Comics; 1 Sep/Oct 1975-20 Oct/Nov 1978
(see Detective #481-483)
1 scarce in the U.K. 68pgs, Neal Adams reprint

| | $2.00 | $6.00 | $10.00 | £1.50 | £4.50 | £7.50 |

2-4 68pgs

| | $1.00 | $3.00 | $5.00 | £1.20 | £3.60 | £6.00 |

5-6 ND 52pgs

| | $1.00 | $3.00 | $5.00 | £1.30 | £3.90 | £6.50 |

7 scarce in the U.K. 52pgs

| | $0.80 | $2.40 | $4.00 | £1.10 | £3.30 | £5.50 |

8 scarce in the U.K. 52pgs, Catwoman cover

| | $0.80 | $2.40 | $4.00 | £1.10 | £3.30 | £5.50 |

9 52pgs, 1st appearance Penguin's, Riddler's and Scarecrow's daughters

| | $1.00 | $3.00 | $5.00 | £1.00 | £3.00 | £5.00 |

10 52pgs

| | $0.80 | $2.40 | $4.00 | £0.80 | £2.40 | £4.00 |

11 scarce in the U.K. 52pgs, Rogers art; 1st Commissioner Gordon and Alfred team-up

| | $1.00 | $3.00 | $5.00 | £1.10 | £3.30 | £5.50 |

12-13 scarce in the U.K. 52pgs, Rogers art

| | $1.00 | $3.00 | $5.00 | £1.10 | £3.30 | £5.50 |

14 scarce in the U.K. 52pgs

| | $0.80 | $2.40 | $4.00 | £1.00 | £3.00 | £5.00 |

15 scarce in the U.K. 52pgs, Golden art

| | $0.80 | $2.40 | $4.00 | £1.00 | £3.00 | £5.00 |

16 52pgs, Golden art

| | $0.80 | $2.40 | $4.00 | £0.80 | £2.40 | £4.00 |

17 scarce in the U.K. 80pgs, Demon appears, Huntress arrives on Earth 1 from Earth 2, Golden art on Man-Bat

| | $1.00 | $3.00 | $5.00 | £1.20 | £3.60 | £6.00 |

18 scarce in the U.K. 80pgs, Huntress, Staton and Golden art

| | $0.80 | $2.40 | $4.00 | £1.00 | £3.00 | £5.00 |

19-20 ND scarce in the U.K. 80pgs, Huntress, Staton and Golden art

| | $0.80 | $2.40 | $4.00 | £1.20 | £3.60 | £6.00 |
| **Title Value:** | $19.20 | $57.60 | $96.50 | £22.40 | £67.20 | £112.00 |

BATMAN FOREVER MOVIE ADAPTATION

DC Comics; Film; 1 Aug 1995
1 ND 64pgs, Prestige Edition, Denny O'Neil script, Michael Dutkiewicz art, painted cover by John Hanley

| | $1.00 | $3.00 | $5.00 | £0.70 | £2.10 | £3.50 |

1 64pgs, Standard Edition, as above with alternate cover by Michael Dutkiewicz

| | $0.70 | $2.10 | $3.50 | £0.50 | £1.50 | £2.50 |
| **Title Value:** | $1.70 | $5.10 | $8.50 | £1.20 | £3.60 | £6.00 |

BATMAN GALLERY, THE

DC Comics; OS; 1 Sep 1992
1 ND collection of poster and promotional material by Frank Miller, McKean, Bolton, Todd McFarlane, Mazzucchelli, Mike Zeck etc; Joe Quesada cover

| | $0.45 | $1.35 | $2.25 | £0.30 | £0.90 | £1.50 |
| **Title Value:** | $0.45 | $1.35 | $2.25 | £0.30 | £0.90 | £1.50 |

BATMAN PIZZA HUT GIVEAWAY

DC Comics/Pizza Hut; nn 1977
(see Superman, Wonder Woman)
nn ND scarce in the U.K. Batman #122 and #123 reprinted in their entirety only different ads and Pizza Hut banner on cover. Cover colour differs from original on #123

| | $0.60 | $1.80 | $3.00 | £1.00 | £3.00 | £5.00 |
| **Title Value:** | $0.60 | $1.80 | $3.00 | £1.00 | £3.00 | £5.00 |

BATMAN RETURNS MOVIE ADAPTATION

DC Comics; 1 Aug 1992
1 ND 64pgs, Prestige Edition adaptation of Batman film sequel

| | $1.00 | $3.00 | $5.00 | £0.70 | £2.10 | £3.50 |

1 Newsstand edition 64pgs

| | $0.60 | $1.80 | $3.00 | £0.40 | £1.20 | £2.00 |
| **Title Value:** | $1.60 | $4.80 | $8.00 | £1.10 | £3.30 | £5.50 |

BATMAN SPECIAL

DC Comics; OS; 1 Jun 1984
1 48pgs, Mike Golden art

| | $1.05 | $3.15 | $5.25 | £0.70 | £2.10 | £3.50 |
| **Title Value:** | $1.05 | $3.15 | $5.25 | £0.70 | £2.10 | £3.50 |

BATMAN SPECTACULAR

DC Comics; 15 Summer 1978
(DC Special Series #15)
15 ND scarce in the U.K. 68pgs, Rogers, Nasser, Golden art

| | $1.00 | $3.00 | $5.00 | £1.20 | £3.60 | £6.00 |
| **Title Value:** | $1.00 | $3.00 | $5.00 | £1.20 | £3.60 | £6.00 |

BATMAN VS THE INCREDIBLE HULK

DC/Marvel Co-production, Tabloid; nn Autumn 1981
(DC Special Series #27)
nn ND 68pgs, Garcia Lopez art; Joker appears

| | $1.20 | $3.60 | $6.00 | £0.80 | £2.40 | £4.00 |
| **Title Value:** | $1.20 | $3.60 | $6.00 | £0.80 | £2.40 | £4.00 |

BATMAN VS. PREDATOR

DC Comics/Dark Horse, MS; 1 Jan 1992-3 Mar 1992
1 script by Dave Gibbons, art by Andy and Adam Kubert, cover by Chris Warner

| | $0.45 | $1.35 | $2.25 | £0.30 | £0.90 | £1.50 |

1 ND as above but painted cover by Arthur Suydam and uncut sheet of eight trading cards

| | $1.05 | $3.15 | $5.25 | £0.70 | £2.10 | £3.50 |

2 script by Dave Gibbons, art by Andy and Adam Kubert, cover by Chris Warner

| | $0.40 | $1.20 | $2.00 | £0.25 | £0.75 | £1.25 |

2 ND as above but painted cover by Arthur Suydam and 16 pin-up pages

| | $1.05 | $3.15 | $5.25 | £0.70 | £2.10 | £3.50 |

3 script by Dave Gibbons, art by Andy and Adam Kubert, cover by Chris Warner

| | $0.40 | $1.20 | $2.00 | £0.25 | £0.75 | £1.25 |

3 ND as above but painted cover by Arthur Suydam and eight trading cards

| | $0.90 | $2.70 | $4.50 | £0.60 | £1.80 | £3.00 |
| **Title Value:** | $4.25 | $12.75 | $21.25 | £2.80 | £8.40 | £14.00 |

Trade paperback (Feb 1993)
128pgs, reprints mini-series with new introduction and new wraparound cover by Dave Gibbons

| | | | | £0.75 | £2.25 | £3.75 |

BATMAN VS. PREDATOR II: BLOODMATCH

DC Comics/Dark Horse, MS; 1 Dec 1994-4 Mar 1995
1-4 ND Doug Moench script, Paul Gulacy and Terry Austin art

| | $0.45 | $1.35 | $2.25 | £0.30 | £0.90 | £1.50 |
| **Title Value:** | $1.80 | $5.40 | $9.00 | £1.20 | £3.60 | £6.00 |

Batman Vs. Predator II: Bloodmatch (Dec 1995)
Trade paperback reprints mini-series with new Simon Bisley cover £0.90 £2.70 £4.50

BATMAN, SHADOW OF THE

DC Comics, MS; 1 Dec 1985-5 Apr 1986
1 very scarce in the U.K. Rogers reprints

| | $1.00 | $3.00 | $5.00 | £1.40 | £4.20 | £7.00 |

2-5 very scarce in the U.K. Rogers reprints

| | $0.80 | $2.40 | $4.00 | £1.20 | £3.60 | £6.00 |
| **Title Value:** | $4.20 | $12.60 | $21.00 | £6.20 | £18.60 | £31.00 |

Note: reprints classic Detective #471-478 by Englehart/Rogers/Austin. New cover art on each issue.

BATMAN/DRACULA: RED RAIN GRAPHIC NOVEL

DC Comics; OS; nn Jan 1992
nn ND scarce in the U.K. 96pgs, Doug Moench script and Kelley Jones art

| | $6.75 | $20.00 | $33.75 | £4.50 | £13.50 | £22.50 |
| **Title Value:** | $6.75 | $20.00 | $33.75 | £4.50 | £13.50 | £22.50 |

Trade paperback (Jul 1992),
softcover version of the above, new cover by Kelley Jones £1.25 £3.75 £6.25

BATMAN/GREEN ARROW: THE POISON TOMORROW

DC Comics; OS; 1 Nov 1992
1 ND 64pgs, Poison Ivy and Black Canary appear

| | $1.00 | $3.00 | $5.00 | £0.70 | £2.10 | £3.50 |
| **Title Value:** | $1.00 | $3.00 | $5.00 | £0.70 | £2.10 | £3.50 |

BATMAN/GRENDEL

DC Comics, MS; 1,2 Aug 1993
1 ND 48pgs, squarebound, Matt Wagner script and art; sub-titled "Devil's Riddle", bi-weekly

| | $1.05 | $3.15 | $5.25 | £0.70 | £2.10 | £3.50 |

2 ND 48pgs, squarebound, Matt Wagner script and art; sub-titled "Devil's Masque", bi-weekly

| | $1.05 | $3.15 | $5.25 | £0.70 | £2.10 | £3.50 |
| **Title Value:** | $2.10 | $6.30 | $10.50 | £1.40 | £4.20 | £7.00 |

BATMAN/HOUDINI: THE DEVIL'S WORKSHOP

DC Comics; OS; 1 Oct 1993
1 ND 64pgs, squarebound, Howard Chaykin and John Francis Moore script, Mark Chiarello art

| | $1.00 | $3.00 | $5.00 | £0.70 | £2.10 | £3.50 |
| **Title Value:** | $1.00 | $3.00 | $5.00 | £0.70 | £2.10 | £3.50 |

BATMAN/JUDGE DREDD: JUDGEMENT ON GOTHAM

DC Comics, OS; 1 Dec 1991
(see British section)
1 ND 64pgs, story by Alan Grant and John Wagner, art by Simon Bisley, Judge Anderson and

	$Good	$Fine	$N.Mint	£Good	£Fine	£N.Mint
The Scarecrow appear						
	$1.20	$3.60	$6.00	£0.80	£2.40	£4.00
1 2nd printing, ND Aug 1992						
	$1.00	$3.00	$5.00	£0.65	£1.95	£3.25
Title Value:	$2.20	$6.60	$11.00	£1.45	£4.35	£7.25

BATMAN/JUDGE DREDD: THE ULTIMATE RIDDLE
DC Comics,OS; 1 Sep 1995

	$Good	$Fine	$N.Mint	£Good	£Fine	£N.Mint
1 ND 48pgs, Alan Grant script, Carl Critchlow and Dermot Power cover; Critchlow painted cover						
	$1.00	$3.00	$5.00	£0.65	£1.95	£3.25
Title Value:	$1.00	$3.00	$5.00	£0.65	£1.95	£3.25

BATMAN/JUDGE DREDD: VENDETTA IN GOTHAM
DC Comics,OS; 1 Dec 1993

	$Good	$Fine	$N.Mint	£Good	£Fine	£N.Mint
1 ND 48pgs, squarebound; Alan Grant/John Wagner script, Cam Kennedy art, Mike Mignola cover						
	$1.00	$3.00	$5.00	£0.70	£2.10	£3.50
Title Value:	$1.00	$3.00	$5.00	£0.70	£2.10	£3.50

BATMAN/PUNISHER: LAKE OF FIRE
DC Comics,OS; 1 Aug 1994

	$Good	$Fine	$N.Mint	£Good	£Fine	£N.Mint
1 ND 48pgs, squarebound, Barry Kitson cover and art						
	$0.60	$1.80	$3.00	£0.40	£1.20	£2.00
Title Value:	$0.60	$1.80	$3.00	£0.40	£1.20	£2.00

BATMAN/SPAWN: WAR DEVIL
DC Comics,OS; 1 May 1994

	$Good	$Fine	$N.Mint	£Good	£Fine	£N.Mint
1 ND 48pgs, Doug Moench, Chuck Dixon and Alan Grant script, Klaus Janson art						
	$1.00	$3.00	$5.00	£0.65	£1.95	£3.25
Title Value:	$1.00	$3.00	$5.00	£0.65	£1.95	£3.25

BATMAN: ARKHAM ASYLUM
DC Comics; nn Nov 1989

	$Good	$Fine	$N.Mint	£Good	£Fine	£N.Mint
nn ND DC Hardcover; Grant Morrison script, Dave McKean painted art and cover						
	$4.50	$13.50	$22.50	£3.00	£9.00	£15.00
nn ND Titan Hardcover; Grant Morrison script, Dave McKean painted art and cover						
	$4.00	$12.00	$20.00	£2.50	£7.50	£12.50
Title Value:	$8.50	$25.50	$42.50	£5.50	£16.50	£27.50

Note: there were some production problems on the DC copy which resulted in defective bindings causing loose pages.
Softcover (May 1990) new painted cover by Dave McKean £1.80 £5.40 £9.00

BATMAN: BIRTH OF THE DEMON
DC Comics; nn Jan 1993

	$Good	$Fine	$N.Mint	£Good	£Fine	£N.Mint
nn ND Hardcover 112pgs, origin of Ra'S Al Ghul; Denny O'Neill script, Norm Breyfogle art						
	$4.50	$13.50	$22.50	£3.00	£9.00	£15.00
Title Value:	$4.50	$13.50	$22.50	£3.00	£9.00	£15.00
Softcover (Sep 1993), as above				£1.60	£4.80	£8.00

BATMAN: BLOODSTORM
DC Comics,OS; nn Jan 1995

	$Good	$Fine	$N.Mint	£Good	£Fine	£N.Mint
1 ND 96pgs, hardcover; Doug Moench script, Kelley Jones and John Beatty art						
	$4.50	$13.50	$22.50	£3.00	£9.00	£15.00
Title Value:	$4.50	$13.50	$22.50	£3.00	£9.00	£15.00

Batman: Bloodstorm (Jul 1995)
Softcover version of the above with cover by Kelley Jones £1.70 £5.10 £8.50

BATMAN: BRIDE OF THE DEMON
DC Comics,OS; nn Jan 1991

	$Good	$Fine	$N.Mint	£Good	£Fine	£N.Mint
nn ND 96pgs, Hardcover sequel to Son of the Demon; Barr and Grindberg						
	$4.00	$12.00	$20.00	£2.50	£7.50	£12.50
Title Value:	$4.00	$12.00	$20.00	£2.50	£7.50	£12.50

BATMAN: BROTHERHOOD OF THE BAT
DC Comics,OS; nn Nov 1995

	$Good	$Fine	$N.Mint	£Good	£Fine	£N.Mint
1 ND Doug Moench script with a variety of Batman artists in a story centred around different costume designs						
	$1.00	$3.00	$5.00	£0.65	£1.95	£3.25
Title Value:	$1.00	$3.00	$5.00	£0.65	£1.95	£3.25

BATMAN: CASTLE OF THE BAT
DC Comics,OS; 1 Dec 1994

1 ND 64pgs, Bo Hampton art

	$Good	$Fine	$N.Mint	£Good	£Fine	£N.Mint
	$1.00	$3.00	$5.00	£0.70	£2.10	£3.50
Title Value:	$1.00	$3.00	$5.00	£0.70	£2.10	£3.50

BATMAN: CATWOMAN DEFIANT
DC Comics,OS; 1 Jul 1992

	$Good	$Fine	$N.Mint	£Good	£Fine	£N.Mint
1 ND 48pgs, foil finish logo, cover painted by Brian Stelfreeze which inter-locks with cover of Batman: Penguin Triumphant						
	$1.00	$3.00	$5.00	£0.65	£1.95	£3.25
Title Value:	$1.00	$3.00	$5.00	£0.65	£1.95	£3.25

BATMAN: DARK ALLEGIANCES
DC Comics/Elseworlds,OS; 1 Feb 1996

	$Good	$Fine	$N.Mint	£Good	£Fine	£N.Mint
1 ND 64pgs, Howard Chaykin script and art						
	$1.20	$3.60	$6.00	£0.80	£2.40	£4.00
Title Value:	$1.20	$3.60	$6.00	£0.80	£2.40	£4.00

BATMAN: DARK JOKER - THE WILD
DC Comics,OS; 1 Dec 1993; 1 Sep 1994

	$Good	$Fine	$N.Mint	£Good	£Fine	£N.Mint
1 96pgs, hardcover with holographic foil enhanced dust-jacket						
	$5.00	$15.00	$25.00	£3.50	£10.50	£17.50
1 96pgs, softcover (Sep 1994)						
	$2.00	$6.00	$10.00	£1.30	£3.90	£6.50
Title Value:	$7.00	$21.00	$35.00	£4.80	£14.40	£24.00

BATMAN: DARK KNIGHT ARCHIVES
DC Comics; 1 Jul 1992; 2 Apr 1995

	$Good	$Fine	$N.Mint	£Good	£Fine	£N.Mint
1 reprints Batman #1-4 featuring the first appearances of The Joker and Catwoman						
	$7.50	$22.50	$37.50	£5.00	£15.00	£25.00
2 reprints Batman #5-8						
	$12.00	$36.00	$60.00	£8.00	£24.00	£40.00
Title Value:	$19.50	$58.50	$97.50	£13.00	£39.00	£65.00

BATMAN: DARK KNIGHT GALLERY
DC Comics,OS; 1 Jan 1996

	$Good	$Fine	$N.Mint	£Good	£Fine	£N.Mint
1 ND pin-ups by Klaus Jansen, Bill Sienkiewicz, Barry Kitson and others						
	$0.70	$2.10	$3.50	£0.50	£1.50	£2.50
Title Value:	$0.70	$2.10	$3.50	£0.50	£1.50	£2.50

BATMAN: DIGITAL JUSTICE
DC Comics; nn 1990

	$Good	$Fine	$N.Mint	£Good	£Fine	£N.Mint
nn ND Hardcover 110pgs; computer-generated art by Pepe Moreno						
	$4.00	$12.00	$20.00	£2.00	£6.00	£10.00
Title Value:	$4.00	$12.00	$20.00	£2.00	£6.00	£10.00

BATMAN: FULL CIRCLE
DC Comics,OS; 1 Jul 1991

	$Good	$Fine	$N.Mint	£Good	£Fine	£N.Mint
1 ND 64pgs, Alan Davis art						
	$1.00	$3.00	$5.00	£0.70	£2.10	£3.50
Title Value:	$1.00	$3.00	$5.00	£0.70	£2.10	£3.50

BATMAN: GHOSTS - A LEGEND OF THE DARK KNIGHT HALLOWEEN SPECIAL
DC Comics,OS; 1 Dec 1995

	$Good	$Fine	$N.Mint	£Good	£Fine	£N.Mint
1 ND 48pgs, Jeph Loeb script, Tim Sale art						
	$1.00	$3.00	$5.00	£0.65	£1.95	£3.25
Title Value:	$1.00	$3.00	$5.00	£0.65	£1.95	£3.25

BATMAN: GOTHAM BY GASLIGHT
DC Comics,OS; 1 Jan 1990

	$Good	$Fine	$N.Mint	£Good	£Fine	£N.Mint
1 ND Mike Mignola, P.Craig Russell art; Batman meets Jack the Ripper in non-continuity story in "Elseworlds" series	$0.90	$2.70	$4.50	£0.60	£1.80	£3.00
1 Titan edition	$0.80	$2.40	$4.00	£0.50	£1.50	£2.50
Title Value:	$1.70	$5.10	$8.50	£1.10	£3.30	£5.50

BATMAN: GOTHAM NIGHTS
DC Comics,MS; 1 Mar 1992-4 Jun 1992

	$Good	$Fine	$N.Mint	£Good	£Fine	£N.Mint
1-4 Anton Furst's designs from Batman film used throughout	$0.25	$0.75	$1.25	£0.15	£0.45	£0.75
Title Value:	$1.00	$3.00	$5.00	£0.60	£1.80	£3.00

BATMAN: GOTHAM NIGHTS II
DC Comics,MS; 1 Mar 1995-4 Jun 1995

	$Good	$Fine	$N.Mint	£Good	£Fine	£N.Mint
1-4	$0.40	$1.20	$2.00	£0.25	£0.75	£1.25

Batman Chronicles #3

Batman: Mitefall

Batman: The Last Angel

	$Good	$Fine	$N.Mint	£Good	£Fine	£N.Mint
Title Value:	$1.60	$4.80	$8.00	£1.00	£3.00	£5.00

BATMAN: GREATEST STORIES EVER TOLD

DC Comics; nn May 1990; nn Aug 1990; Vol 2 Jul 1992

	$Good	$Fine	$N.Mint	£Good	£Fine	£N.Mint
nn ND Hardcover; classic reprints including Batman #1, #47, #156 and Detective Comics #31, #32, #211 and #500	$6.00	$18.00	$30.00	£4.00	£12.00	£20.00
nn ND Softcover; classic reprints including Batman #1 (1st Catwoman) and Detective Comics #58 (1st Penguin)	$3.00	$9.00	$15.00	£2.00	£6.00	£10.00
Title Value:	$9.00	$27.00	$45.00	£6.00	£18.00	£30.00
Vol 1 Trade Paperback (Softcover)				£2.00	£6.00	£10.00

BATMAN: IN DARKEST KNIGHT

DC Comics,OS; 1 Feb 1994

	$Good	$Fine	$N.Mint	£Good	£Fine	£N.Mint
1 ND 48pgs, squarebound, Mike Barr script and Jerry Bingham art, embossed logo	$1.00	$3.00	$5.00	£0.65	£1.95	£3.25
Title Value:	$1.00	$3.00	$5.00	£0.65	£1.95	£3.25

BATMAN: JAZZ

DC Comics, MS; 1 Apr 1995-3 Jun 1995

	$Good	$Fine	$N.Mint	£Good	£Fine	£N.Mint
1-3 Gerard Jones script, Mark Badger art	$1.35	$2.25	£0.30	£0.90	£1.50
Title Value:	$1.35	$4.05	$6.75	£0.90	£2.70	£4.50

BATMAN: KELLOG'S AND POPTARTS GIVEAWAYS

Kellogs/National Periodical Publications; nn 1966

	$Good	$Fine	$N.Mint	£Good	£Fine	£N.Mint
nn ND rare in the U.K., 6 different small size comics (3" x 5.5")	$5.00	$15.00	$25.00	£4.00	£12.00	£20.00
Title Value:	$5.00	$15.00	$25.00	£4.00	£12.00	£20.00

Titles are as follows:
The Case of Batman II, The Catwoman's Catnapping Caper, The Joker's Happy Victims, The Mad Hatter's Hat Crimes, The Man in the Iron Mask, The Penguin's Fowl Play

BATMAN: KNIGHT GALLERY

DC Comics,OS; 1 Oct 1995

	$Good	$Fine	$N.Mint	£Good	£Fine	£N.Mint
1 ND designs for Batman costume by Neal Adams, Norm Breyfogle, Jim Aparo, George Perez and others	$0.80	$2.40	$4.00	£0.50	£1.50	£2.50
Title Value:	$0.80	$2.40	$4.00	£0.50	£1.50	£2.50

BATMAN: KNIGHTFALL

Multi-part storyline that leads to the breaking of Batman by the villain Bane and the introduction of the new Batman of Jean Paul Valley, formerly known as Azrael. The parts are as follows:
Part 1 - Batman #492; **Part 2** - Detective Comics #659; **Part 3** - Batman #493; **Part 4** - Detective Comics #660; **Part 5** - Batman #494; **Part 6** - Detective Comics #661; **Part 7** - Batman #495; **Part 8** - Detective Comics #662; **Part 9** - Batman #496; **Part 10** - Detective Comics #663; **Part 11** - Batman #497; **Part 12** - Detective Comics #664; **Part 13** - Showcase '93 #7; **Part 14** - Showcase '93 #8; **Part 15** - Batman #498; **Part 16** - Detective Comics #665; **Part 17** - Batman #499; **Part 18** - Detective Comics #666; **Part 19** - Batman #500

BATMAN: LEGENDS OF THE DARK KNIGHT

DC Comics; 0 Oct 1994; 1 Nov 1989-present

	$Good	$Fine	$N.Mint	£Good	£Fine	£N.Mint
0 (Oct 1994) Zero Hour X-over, exploring the psyche of Batman	$0.40	$1.20	$2.00	£0.25	£0.75	£1.25
1 LD in the U.K. George Pratt cover, available in four different colour variations (see note below)	$1.40	$4.20	$7.00	£0.90	£2.70	£4.50
2 George Pratt cover	$0.60	$1.80	$3.00	£0.40	£1.20	£2.00
3-4 George Pratt covers	$0.50	$1.50	$2.50	£0.30	£0.90	£1.50
5 George Pratt cover	$0.50	$1.50	$2.50	£0.30	£0.90	£1.50
6 Grant Morrison story "Gothic" begins	$0.50	$1.50	$2.50	£0.40	£1.20	£2.00
7-10 Gothic	$0.50	$1.50	$2.50	£0.30	£0.90	£1.50
11-15 Prey by Moench, art by Gulacy/Austin	$0.50	$1.50	$2.50	£0.30	£0.90	£1.50
16 LD in the U.K. Venom by O'Neil, art by Von Eeden/Garcia Lopez	$0.90	$2.70	$4.50	£0.60	£1.80	£3.00
17 LD in the U.K. Venom by O'Neil, art by Von Eeden/Garcia Lopez	$0.60	$1.80	$3.00	£0.40	£1.20	£2.00
18-20 Venom by O'Neil, art by Von Eeden/Garcia Lopez	$0.50	$1.50	$2.50	£0.30	£0.90	£1.50
21-23 Faith	$0.40	$1.20	$2.00	£0.25	£0.75	£1.25
24-26 Flyer by Howard Chaykin and Gil Kane	$0.40	$1.20	$2.00	£0.25	£0.75	£1.25
27 Destroyer part 2, continued in Detective Comics #641	$0.40	$1.20	$2.00	£0.25	£0.75	£1.25
28 Faces part 1, Matt Wagner script and art begins	$0.40	$1.20	$2.00	£0.25	£0.75	£1.25
29-30 Faces	$0.40	$1.20	$2.00	£0.25	£0.75	£1.25
31 Brent Anderson art, bi-weekly	$0.40	$1.20	$2.00	£0.25	£0.75	£1.25
32-34 Blades, bi-weekly	$0.40	$1.20	$2.00	£0.25	£0.75	£1.25
35 Destiny story, Viking Prince appears, Bo Hampton cover/art, bi-weekly	$0.40	$1.20	$2.00	£0.25	£0.75	£1.25
36 Destiny story, Viking Prince appears, Bo Hampton cover/art	$0.40	$1.20	$2.00	£0.25	£0.75	£1.25
37	$0.40	$1.20	$2.00	£0.25	£0.75	£1.25
38 Bat-Mite returns	$0.40	$1.20	$2.00	£0.25	£0.75	£1.25
39-40 Mask story, Bryan Talbot script and art	$0.40	$1.20	$2.00	£0.25	£0.75	£1.25
41 previews Scarlett series	$0.40	$1.20	$2.00	£0.25	£0.75	£1.25
42-43 Hothouse story, Poison Ivy appears	$0.40	$1.20	$2.00	£0.25	£0.75	£1.25
44-45	$0.40	$1.20	$2.00	£0.25	£0.75	£1.25
46 Russ Heath art	$0.40	$1.20	$2.00	£0.25	£0.75	£1.25

	$Good	$Fine	$N.Mint	£Good	£Fine	£N.Mint
47 Catwoman vs. Catman, Russ Heath art	$0.40	$1.20	$2.00	£0.25	£0.75	£1.25
48-49 Russ Heath art, bi-weekly	$0.40	$1.20	$2.00	£0.25	£0.75	£1.25
50 64pgs, the 1st case of Batman vs. The Joker, holo-grafix foil cover, pin-up gallery	$0.80	$2.40	$4.00	£0.50	£1.50	£2.50
51	$0.40	$1.20	$2.00	£0.25	£0.75	£1.25
52-53 Tao by Alan Grant and Arthur Ranson	$0.40	$1.20	$2.00	£0.25	£0.75	£1.25
54 Mike Mignola art	$0.40	$1.20	$2.00	£0.25	£0.75	£1.25
55-57 Mike McMahon art	$0.40	$1.20	$2.00	£0.25	£0.75	£1.25
58 John Higgins cover and art	$0.40	$1.20	$2.00	£0.25	£0.75	£1.25
59-60 Quarry story	$0.40	$1.20	$2.00	£0.25	£0.75	£1.25
61 Quarry story, continued in Robin #7	$0.40	$1.20	$2.00	£0.25	£0.75	£1.25
62 Knightsend part 4, continued in Robin #8; Mignola cover	$0.40	$1.20	$2.00	£0.25	£0.75	£1.25
63 Knightsend part 10 (conclusion), continued in Robin #9	$0.40	$1.20	$2.00	£0.25	£0.75	£1.25
64 Jamie Delano and Chris Bachalo one-off story	$0.40	$1.20	$2.00	£0.25	£0.75	£1.25
65-68 Joker appears	$0.40	$1.20	$2.00	£0.25	£0.75	£1.25
69-70 Mike Zeck art	$0.40	$1.20	$2.00	£0.25	£0.75	£1.25
71-73 Werewolf story, John Watkiss painted cover	$0.40	$1.20	$2.00	£0.25	£0.75	£1.25
74-75 Ted McKeever cover and art	$0.40	$1.20	$2.00	£0.25	£0.75	£1.25
76-78 Scott Hampton script and art	$0.40	$1.20	$2.00	£0.25	£0.75	£1.25
79 Mark Millar script, Steve Yeowell and Dick Giordano art	$0.40	$1.20	$2.00	£0.25	£0.75	£1.25
80-81	$0.40	$1.20	$2.00	£0.25	£0.75	£1.25
Title Value:	$36.70	$110.10	$183.50	£22.95	£68.85	£114.75

Note: series designed to contain 5 issue stories by a variety of artists and writers, harder-hitting but no Mature Readers label. Four different protective covers produced for #1: blue/orange/yellow/pink. The blue cover seems to be the most popular.

Batman: Gothic (Jul 1992)
Trade paperback, reprints issues #6-10, new cover by Klaus Janson

	£Good	£Fine	£N.Mint
	£1.40	£4.20	£7.00

Batman: Prey (Dec 1992)
Trade paperback, reprints issues #11-15, new cover by Paul Gulacy

	£Good	£Fine	£N.Mint
	£1.50	£4.50	£7.50

Batman: Shaman (Feb 1993)
Trade paperback, reprints issues #1-5, new painted cover by George Pratt

	£Good	£Fine	£N.Mint
	£1.50	£4.50	£7.50

Batman: The Collected Legends of the Dark Knight (Apr 1994)
Trade paperback, reprints issues #32-34, #38 and #42,43

	£Good	£Fine	£N.Mint
	£1.70	£5.10	£8.50

Batman: Faces (Aug 1995)
Trade paperback
reprints issues #28-30, Matt Wagner painted cover

	£Good	£Fine	£N.Mint
	£1.30	£3.90	£6.50

BATMAN: LEGENDS OF THE DARK KNIGHT ANNUAL

DC Comics; 1 Dec 1991-present

	$Good	$Fine	$N.Mint	£Good	£Fine	£N.Mint
1 64pgs, Joker, Two Face, Penguin appear, Mignola cover	$0.80	$2.40	$4.00	£0.50	£1.50	£2.50
2 64pgs	$0.80	$2.40	$4.00	£0.50	£1.50	£2.50
3 64pgs, Bloodlines (Wave Two) part 21, 1st appearance Cardinal Sin and Samaritan, continued in Team Titans Annual #1	$0.70	$2.10	$3.50	£0.45	£1.35	£2.25
4 64pgs, Elseworlds	$0.70	$2.10	$3.50	£0.45	£1.35	£2.25
5 64pgs, Year One, origin of Man-Bat featured	$0.80	$2.40	$4.00	£0.50	£1.50	£2.50
Title Value:	$3.80	$11.40	$19.00	£2.40	£7.20	£12.00

BATMAN: LEGENDS OF THE DARK KNIGHT HALLOWEEN SPECIAL

DC Comics,OS; 1 Dec 1993

	$Good	$Fine	$N.Mint	£Good	£Fine	£N.Mint
1 ND 48pgs, squarebound; Tim Sale art, embossed cover	$1.20	$3.60	$6.00	£0.80	£2.40	£4.00
Title Value:	$1.20	$3.60	$6.00	£0.80	£2.40	£4.00

BATMAN: MADNESS

DC Comics,OS; 1 Nov 1994

	$Good	$Fine	$N.Mint	£Good	£Fine	£N.Mint
1 ND 48pgs, Jeph Loeb and Tim Sale; follow up Halloween Special	$0.90	$2.70	$4.50	£0.60	£1.80	£3.00
Title Value:	$0.90	$2.70	$4.50	£0.60	£1.80	£3.00

BATMAN: MAN-BAT

DC Comics,MS; 1 Oct 1995-3 Dec 1995

	$Good	$Fine	$N.Mint	£Good	£Fine	£N.Mint
1-3 ND 48pgs, Jamie Delano script, John Bolton painted art	$1.00	$3.00	$5.00	£1.95	£1.95	£3.25
Title Value:	$3.00	$9.00	$15.00	£1.95	£5.85	£9.75

BATMAN: MASK OF THE PHANTASM

DC Comics,OS; 1 Feb 1994

	$Good	$Fine	$N.Mint	£Good	£Fine	£N.Mint
1 64pgs, squarebound; adaptation of the Twentieth Century Fox Batman animated film	$1.00	$3.00	$5.00	£0.65	£1.95	£3.25
Title Value:	$1.00	$3.00	$5.00	£0.65	£1.95	£3.25

BATMAN: MASTER OF THE FUTURE

DC Comics,OS; 1 Jan 1992

	$Good	$Fine	$N.Mint	£Good	£Fine	£N.Mint
1 ND 48pgs, part of "Elseworlds Series" imaginary stories						
	$1.00	$3.00	$5.00	£0.70	£2.10	£3.50
Title Value:	$1.00	$3.00	$5.00	£0.70	£2.10	£3.50

BATMAN: MITEFALL
DC Comics,OS; 1 Mar 1995

	$Good	$Fine	$N.Mint	£Good	£Fine	£N.Mint
1 ND 48pgs, Alan Grant script, Kev O'Neill art						
	$1.00	$3.00	$5.00	£0.65	£1.95	£3.25
Title Value:	$1.00	$3.00	$5.00	£0.65	£1.95	£3.25

BATMAN: MOVIE ADAPTATION
DC Comics; nn Aug 1989

	$Good	$Fine	$N.Mint	£Good	£Fine	£N.Mint
nn ND Standard Format; Denny O'Neill script, Jerry Ordway art						
	$0.50	$1.50	$2.50	£0.35	£1.05	£1.75
nn ND Prestige Format; Denny O'Neill script, Jerry Ordway art						
	$0.75	$2.25	$3.75	£0.50	£1.50	£2.50
Title Value:	$1.25	$3.75	$6.25	£0.85	£2.55	£4.25

BATMAN: PENGUIN TRIUMPHANT
DC Comics,OS; 1 Jul 1992

	$Good	$Fine	$N.Mint	£Good	£Fine	£N.Mint
1 ND 48pgs, foil finish logo, cover painted by Brian Stelfreeze which interlocks with cover of Batman: Catwoman Defiant						
	$1.00	$3.00	$5.00	£0.65	£1.95	£3.25
Title Value:	$1.00	$3.00	$5.00	£0.65	£1.95	£3.25

BATMAN: RIDDLER - THE RIDDLE FACTORY
DC Comics,OS; nn Aug 1995

	$Good	$Fine	$N.Mint	£Good	£Fine	£N.Mint
nn ND 48pgs, Matt Wagner script, Dave Taylor art, painted cover by Brian Stelfreeze						
	$1.00	$3.00	$5.00	£0.65	£1.95	£3.25
Title Value:	$1.00	$3.00	$5.00	£0.65	£1.95	£3.25

BATMAN: RUN RIDDLER RUN
DC Comics,MS; 1 Jun 1992-3 Aug 1992

	$Good	$Fine	$N.Mint	£Good	£Fine	£N.Mint
1 ND 48pgs, Batman vs. Riddler by Gerard Jones and Mark Badger begins						
	$1.00	$3.00	$5.00	£0.65	£1.95	£3.25
2-3 ND 48pgs	$1.00	$3.00	$5.00	£0.65	£1.95	£3.25
Title Value:	$3.00	$9.00	$15.00	£1.95	£5.85	£9.75

BATMAN: SCAR OF THE BAT
DC Comics,OS; 1 Mar 1996

	$Good	$Fine	$N.Mint	£Good	£Fine	£N.Mint
1 ND Max Allan Collins script, Eduardo Barreto art						
	$1.00	$3.00	$5.00	£0.65	£1.95	£3.25
Title Value:	$1.00	$3.00	$5.00	£0.65	£1.95	£3.25

BATMAN: SEDUCTION OF THE GUN
DC Comics,OS; 1 Feb 1993

	$Good	$Fine	$N.Mint	£Good	£Fine	£N.Mint
1 ND 64pgs, deals with gun-control issue						
	$0.45	$1.35	$2.25	£0.30	£0.90	£1.50
Title Value:	$0.45	$1.35	$2.25	£0.30	£0.90	£1.50

BATMAN: SHADOW OF THE BAT
DC Comics; 0 Oct 1994; 1 Jul 1992-present

	$Good	$Fine	$N.Mint	£Good	£Fine	£N.Mint
0 (Oct 1994) Zero Hour X-over, origin retold; continued from Batman #0						
	$0.40	$1.20	$2.00	£0.25	£0.75	£1.25
1 Alan Grant script begins, painted covers by Brian Stelfreeze begin, bi-weekly						
	$0.40	$1.20	$2.00	£0.25	£0.75	£1.25
1 ND Collector's Edition, pre-bagged, features a pull-out poster, a pop-up and blueprint plans of Arham Asylum and a book-mark						
	$0.80	$2.40	$4.00	£0.50	£1.50	£2.50
2 bi-weekly	$0.30	$0.90	$1.50	£0.20	£0.60	£1.00
3-4 Nightwing appears, bi-weekly						
	$0.30	$0.90	$1.50	£0.20	£0.60	£1.00
5 Black Spider appears						
	$0.30	$0.90	$1.50	£0.20	£0.60	£1.00
6 Catwoman appears						
	$0.30	$0.90	$1.50	£0.20	£0.60	£1.00
7 The Misfits story begins, intro Chancer						
	$0.30	$0.90	$1.50	£0.20	£0.60	£1.00
8 The Misfits story, Brian Stelfreeze cover; $1.75 cover begins						
	$0.30	$0.90	$1.50	£0.20	£0.60	£1.00
9 The Misfits story, Brian Stelfreeze cover						
	$0.30	$0.90	$1.50	£0.20	£0.60	£1.00
10-13 Brian Stelfreeze cover						
	$0.30	$0.90	$1.50	£0.20	£0.60	£1.00
14-15 Gotham Freaks story						
	$0.30	$0.90	$1.50	£0.20	£0.60	£1.00
16-18 The God of Fear, Brian Stelfreeze cover, bi-weekly						
	$0.30	$0.90	$1.50	£0.20	£0.60	£1.00
19 Knightquest: The Crusade part 2, continued in Batman #501; Brian Stelfreeze cover						
	$0.30	$0.90	$1.50	£0.20	£0.60	£1.00
20 Knightquest: The Crusade part 4, continued in Detective Comics #668; Brian Stelfreeze cover						
	$0.30	$0.90	$1.50	£0.20	£0.60	£1.00
21-24 Knightquest: The Crusade, Brian Stelfreeze cover						
	$0.30	$0.90	$1.50	£0.20	£0.60	£1.00
25 Knightquest: The Crusade, Brian Stelfreeze cover; Joe Public appears						
	$0.30	$0.90	$1.50	£0.20	£0.60	£1.00
26-27 Knightquest: The Crusade, Brian Stelfreeze cover						
	$0.30	$0.90	$1.50	£0.20	£0.60	£1.00
28 Knightquest: The Crusade, Brian Stelfreeze cover; continued in Detective Comics #675						
	$0.30	$0.90	$1.50	£0.20	£0.60	£1.00
29 48pgs, Knightsend part 2, continued in Detective Comics #676						
	$0.45	$1.35	$2.25	£0.30	£0.90	£1.50
30 Knightsend part 8, continued in Detective Comics #677						
	$0.40	$1.20	$2.00	£0.25	£0.75	£1.25
31 Zero Hour X-over						
	$0.40	$1.20	$2.00	£0.25	£0.75	£1.25
32-33 Two Face appears						
	$0.40	$1.20	$2.00	£0.25	£0.75	£1.25
34	$0.40	$1.20	$2.00	£0.25	£0.75	£1.25
35 The Troika part 2, continued in Detective Comics #682						
	$0.40	$1.20	$2.00	£0.25	£0.75	£1.25
35 ND Collector's Edition, embossed black cover						
	$0.60	$1.80	$3.00	£0.40	£1.20	£2.00
36 Black Canary appears						
	$0.40	$1.20	$2.00	£0.25	£0.75	£1.25
37	$0.40	$1.20	$2.00	£0.25	£0.75	£1.25
38 The Joker appears						
	$0.40	$1.20	$2.00	£0.25	£0.75	£1.25
39 upgraded coated paper stock (Miraweb Format) begins						
	$0.40	$1.20	$2.00	£0.25	£0.75	£1.25
40-41	$0.40	$1.20	$2.00	£0.25	£0.75	£1.25
42 continued in Batman Chronicles #2						
	$0.40	$1.20	$2.00	£0.25	£0.75	£1.25
43 The Secret of the Universe part 1, continued in Catwoman #26; painted cover by Brian Stelfreeze						
	$0.40	$1.20	$2.00	£0.25	£0.75	£1.25
44 The Secret of the Universe part 3, continued from Catwoman #26; painted cover by Brian Stelfreeze						
	$0.40	$1.20	$2.00	£0.25	£0.75	£1.25
45-47	$0.40	$1.20	$2.00	£0.25	£0.75	£1.25
48 Contagion part 1, continued in Detective Comics #695						
	$0.40	$1.20	$2.00	£0.25	£0.75	£1.25
Title Value:	$18.35	$55.05	$91.75	£11.85	£35.55	£59.25
Batman: The Last Arkham (Jan 1996)						
Trade paperback reprints issues #1-4, new Brian Stelfreeze cover				£1.70	£5.10	£8.50

BATMAN: SHADOW OF THE BAT ANNUAL
DC Comics; 1 Jul 1993-present

	$Good	$Fine	$N.Mint	£Good	£Fine	£N.Mint
1 64pgs, Bloodlines part 3, 1st appearance Joe Public, continued in Flash Annual #6						
	$0.70	$2.10	$3.50	£0.45	£1.35	£2.25
2 64pgs, Elseworlds story; Alan Grant script						
	$0.70	$2.10	$3.50	£0.45	£1.35	£2.25
3 56pgs, Year One; Poison Ivy appears, painted cover by Brian Stelfreeze						
	$0.80	$2.40	$4.00	£0.50	£1.50	£2.50
Title Value:	$2.20	$6.60	$11.00	£1.40	£4.20	£7.00

BATMAN: SON OF THE DEMON
DC Comics,OS; nn Sep 1987
(see Batman: Bride of the Demon)

	$Good	$Fine	$N.Mint	£Good	£Fine	£N.Mint
nn scarce in the U.K. 80pgs, Hardcover with dust-jacket						
	$8.00	$24.00	$40.00	£5.00	£15.00	£25.00
nn 80pgs, Softcover; new cover art						
	$2.40	$7.00	$12.00	£1.50	£4.50	£7.50
Title Value:	$10.40	$31.00	$52.00	£6.50	£19.50	£32.50

Note: 1700 hardback copies were signed by writer and artist. These would be valued at approximately 30% more than the hardback price above

BATMAN: SWORD OF AZRAEL
DC Comics,MS; 1 Oct 1992-4 Jan 1993

	$Good	$Fine	$N.Mint	£Good	£Fine	£N.Mint
1 Joe Quesada cover and art begins, wraparound three-part gatefold cover						
	$3.00	$9.00	$15.00	£1.00	£3.00	£5.00
2-3	$1.60	$4.80	$8.00	£0.90	£2.70	£4.50
4 continued in Batman #488						
	$1.50	$4.50	$7.50	£0.80	£2.40	£4.00
Title Value:	$7.70	$23.10	$38.50	£3.60	£10.80	£18.00

BATMAN: THE ANIMATED MOVIE
DC Comics,OS; 1 Feb 1994

	$Good	$Fine	$N.Mint	£Good	£Fine	£N.Mint
1 64pgs, squarebound, adaptation of animated film "The Mask of the Phantasm"						
	$0.60	$1.80	$3.00	£0.40	£1.20	£2.00
1 64pgs, squarebound, adaptation of animated film "The Mask of the Phantasm", painted cover						
	$1.00	$3.00	$5.00	£0.65	£1.95	£3.25
Title Value:	$1.60	$4.80	$8.00	£1.05	£3.15	£5.25

BATMAN: THE BLUE, THE GREY AND THE BAT
DC Comics,OS; 1 Jan 1993

	$Good	$Fine	$N.Mint	£Good	£Fine	£N.Mint
1 ND 64pgs, "Elseworlds" story set during the American Civil War, parchment-style covers						
	$1.00	$3.00	$5.00	£0.70	£2.10	£3.50
Title Value:	$1.00	$3.00	$5.00	£0.70	£2.10	£3.50

BATMAN: THE CULT
DC Comics,MS; 1 Sep 1988-4 Dec 1988

	$Good	$Fine	$N.Mint	£Good	£Fine	£N.Mint
1 ND 2nd DC embossed cover; Jim Starlin script, Bernie Wrightson art begins						
	$1.50	$4.50	$7.50	£1.00	£3.00	£5.00
2 ND scarce in the U.K.						
	$1.20	$3.60	$6.00	£1.00	£3.00	£5.00
3 ND	$1.20	$3.60	$6.00	£0.80	£2.40	£4.00
4 ND some pages bound out of sequence						
	$1.20	$3.60	$6.00	£0.80	£2.40	£4.00
Title Value:	$5.10	$15.30	$25.50	£3.60	£10.80	£18.00

Note: 48pgs, Dark Knight format, UV (glossy) coated.
Trade paperback (Mar 1991),
new cover painting by Berni Wrightson £1.40 £4.20 £7.00

BATMAN: THE DAILIES
DC Comics; 1 Jan 1991-3 1991
(see Batman: The Sunday Classics)

	$Good	$Fine	$N.Mint	£Good	£Fine	£N.Mint
1 reprints daily newspaper strips from 25/10/43 to 28/10/44 plus features						
	$1.80	$5.25	$9.00	£1.20	£3.60	£6.00
2 reprints daily newspaper strips from 30/10/44 to 24/11/45 plus features						
	$1.80	$5.25	$9.00	£1.20	£3.60	£6.00
3 reprints daily newpaper strips from 26/11/45 to 2/11/46 plus features						
	$1.80	$5.25	$9.00	£1.20	£3.60	£6.00
Title Value:	$5.40	$15.75	$27.00	£3.60	£10.80	£18.00
Limited Hardcover Edition (Feb 1992),						
all three volumes collected into a slipcase				£7.50	£22.50	£37.50

Batman: The Dailies 1943-1946 Hardcover Signed & Numbered (Feb 1995)
signed by the five surviving Batman creators £20.00 £60.00 £100.00

BATMAN: THE DARK KNIGHT RETURNS
DC Comics,MS; 1 Mar 1986-4 1986

	$Good	$Fine	$N.Mint	£Good	£Fine	£N.Mint
1 ND Frank Miller story/art begins	$3.50	$10.50	$17.50	£2.80	£8.25	£14.00
1 2nd printing ND	$0.80	$2.40	$4.00	£0.80	£2.40	£4.00
1 3rd printing ND	$0.60	$1.80	$3.00	£0.60	£1.80	£3.00
2 ND Carrie Kelly (female) becomes new Robin	$2.00	$6.00	$10.00	£1.40	£4.20	£7.00
2 2nd printing, ND (see note below)	$0.60	$1.80	$3.00	£0.60	£1.80	£3.00
2 3rd printing ND	$0.50	$1.50	$2.50	£0.50	£1.50	£2.50
3 ND death of The Joker	$1.20	$3.60	$6.00	£1.00	£3.00	£5.00
3 2nd printing ND	$0.50	$1.50	$2.50	£0.50	£1.50	£2.50
4 ND Alfred dies	$1.00	$3.00	$5.00	£0.80	£2.40	£4.00
Title Value:	$10.70	$32.10	$53.50	£9.00	£26.85	£45.00
Hardcover (1986), with dustjacket, signed & numbered (4,000 copies)				£30.00	£90.00	£150.00
Hardcover (1986), with dustjacket, Trade edition ND				£6.00	£18.00	£30.00
Trade paperback, Warner Books edition ND, scarce, reprints #1-4 with corrections				£1.80	£5.40	£9.00
Trade paperback, as above, DC edition ND				£1.75	£5.25	£8.75
Trade paperback, as above, Titan (UK) edition, Alan Moore intro (7 printings available)				£1.60	£4.80	£8.00

Note: due to a printer's error, the indicia of issue 2 has no mention of first and second prints; however, they can be identified as follows: Issue 2 (1st print) has a slight grey "ghosting" around the ears of the bat-shadow on the inside front cover; this had been corrected for the second print, which is noticeably crisper. The 3rd print of issue 2 is clearly marked as such.

BATMAN: THE HOLY TERROR
DC Comics,OS; 1 Oct 1991

	$Good	$Fine	$N.Mint	£Good	£Fine	£N.Mint
1 48pgs, 1st "Elseworlds Series" where major characters have alternative adventures	$1.00	$3.00	$5.00	£0.70	£2.10	£3.50
Title Value:	$1.00	$3.00	$5.00	£0.70	£2.10	£3.50

BATMAN: THE KILLING JOKE
DC Comics,OS; nn 1988

	$Good	$Fine	$N.Mint	£Good	£Fine	£N.Mint
nn ND Alan Moore script, Brian Bolland art begins; 1st DC embossed logo; 1st print (green logo)	$2.00	$6.00	$10.00	£1.20	£3.60	£6.00
nn 2nd printing, ND (green logo)	$1.00	$3.00	$5.00	£0.80	£2.40	£4.00
nn 3rd printing ND	$0.90	$2.70	$4.50	£0.60	£1.80	£3.00
nn 4th printing ND	$0.80	$2.40	$4.00	£0.60	£1.80	£3.00
nn 5th printing, ND (blue logo)	$0.60	$1.80	$3.00	£0.50	£1.50	£2.50
nn 6th printing ND (pink logo)	$0.60	$1.80	$3.00	£0.50	£1.50	£2.50
nn 7th printing ND (light green logo)	$0.60	$1.80	$3.00	£0.50	£1.50	£2.50
nn 8th printing, ND (silver logo)	$0.60	$1.80	$3.00	£0.50	£1.50	£2.50
nn Titan (U.K.) Edition; 1st print (green embossed logo)	$0.60	$1.80	$3.00	£0.45	£1.35	£2.25
nn Titan (U.K.) Edition; 2nd print (pink logo)	$0.60	$1.80	$3.00	£0.45	£1.35	£2.25
Title Value:	$8.30	$24.90	$41.50	£6.10	£18.30	£30.50

Note: 48pgs Prestige Format, UV (glossy) coated cover.

BATMAN: THE LAST ANGEL
DC Comics,OS; 1 Nov 1994

	$Good	$Fine	$N.Mint	£Good	£Fine	£N.Mint
1 ND 96pgs, squarebound, Catwoman and The Joker appear; Eric Lustbader script; Lee Moder and Scott Hanna art	$2.55	$7.50	$12.75	£1.70	£5.00	£8.50
Title Value:	$2.55	$7.50	$12.75	£1.70	£5.00	£8.50

BATMAN: THE SUNDAY CLASSICS
DC Comics; nn 1994
(see Batman: The Dailies)

	$Good	$Fine	$N.Mint	£Good	£Fine	£N.Mint
nn ND 208pgs, reprints Sunday paper strips from 1943-1946	$5.00	$15.00	$25.00	£3.50	£10.50	£17.50
Title Value:	$5.00	$15.00	$25.00	£3.50	£10.50	£17.50
Batman: The Sunday Classics 1943-1946 Hardcover Signed & Numbered (Feb 1995), 208pgs, signed and numbered by the five surviving Batman creators				£20.00	£60.00	£100.00

BATMAN: THE ULTIMATE EVIL
DC Comics,MS; 1 Dec 1995-2 Jan 1996

	$Good	$Fine	$N.Mint	£Good	£Fine	£N.Mint
1-2 ND 48pgs, adaptation of Andrew Vachss' novel; Denys Cowan and Prentis Rollins art	$1.20	$3.60	$6.00	£0.80	£2.40	£4.00
Title Value:	$2.40	$7.20	$12.00	£1.60	£4.80	£8.00

BATMAN: TWO-FACE - CRIME AND PUNISHMENT
DC Comics,OS; nn Aug 1995

	$Good	$Fine	$N.Mint	£Good	£Fine	£N.Mint
nn ND 48pgs, J.M. DeMatteis script, Scott McDaniel art painted cover by Brian Stelfreeze	$1.00	$3.00	$5.00	£0.65	£1.95	£3.25
Title Value:	$1.00	$3.00	$5.00	£0.65	£1.95	£3.25

BATMAN: TWO-FACE STRIKES TWICE
DC Comics,MS; 1 Dec 1993-2 Jan 1994

	$Good	$Fine	$N.Mint	£Good	£Fine	£N.Mint
1-2 ND 48pgs, flip-book format with Golden Age story with cover by Dick Sprang and Modern Age story with cover by Daerrick Gross	$1.00	$3.00	$5.00	£0.65	£1.95	£3.25
Title Value:	$2.00	$6.00	$10.00	£1.30	£3.90	£6.50

BATMAN: UNTOLD LEGEND OF THE
DC Comics,MS; 1 Jul 1980-3 Sep 1980

	$Good	$Fine	$N.Mint	£Good	£Fine	£N.Mint
1 John Byrne art	$1.00	$3.00	$5.00	£0.80	£2.40	£4.00
2 scarce in the U.K.	$0.80	$2.40	$4.00	£0.70	£2.10	£3.50
3	$0.70	$2.10	$3.50	£0.60	£1.80	£3.00
Title Value:	$2.50	$7.50	$12.50	£2.10	£6.30	£10.50

MPI Audio Edition (1980), same issues with stiffer card covers, featuring Golden and Silver Age Batman covers inside. Each issue came with a 30 minute audio cassette of that part of the story. Smaller than standard comic size. ND

	$Good	$Fine	$N.Mint	£Good	£Fine	£N.Mint
				£1.00	£3.00	£5.00

BATMAN: VENGEANCE OF BANE
DC Comics,OS; 1 Jan 1993

	$Good	$Fine	$N.Mint	£Good	£Fine	£N.Mint
1 64pgs, 1st appearance of Bane; ties in with "Venom" story from Batman: Legends of the Dark Knight	$3.50	$10.50	$17.50	£2.40	£7.00	£12.00
Title Value:	$3.50	$10.50	$17.50	£2.40	£7.00	£12.00

BATMAN: VENGEANCE OF BANE II - THE REDEMPTION
DC Comics,OS; 1 Oct 1995

	$Good	$Fine	$N.Mint	£Good	£Fine	£N.Mint
1 ND Graham Nolan and Eduardo Barreto art	$0.80	$2.40	$4.00	£0.50	£1.50	£2.50
Title Value:	$0.80	$2.40	$4.00	£0.50	£1.50	£2.50

BATPAC SPECIAL
National Periodical Publications; B-6 Jun 1966

	$Good	$Fine	$N.Mint	£Good	£Fine	£N.Mint
6 rare in the U.K. Batman #181, JLA #45, Metal Men #20, World's Finest #158 in sealed plastic bag attached to illustrated header card; priced 47¢	$15.00	$45.00	$75.00	£10.00	£30.00	£50.00
Title Value:	$15.00	$45.00	$75.00	£10.00	£30.00	£50.00

Note: not distributed on U.K. news-stands

BATS, CATS AND CADILLACS
Now Comics; 1 1990-6 1991

	$Good	$Fine	$N.Mint	£Good	£Fine	£N.Mint
1-6 ND	$0.30	$0.90	$1.50	£0.20	£0.60	£1.00
Title Value:	$1.80	$5.40	$9.00	£1.20	£3.60	£6.00

BATS, CATS AND CADILLACS ANNUAL
Innovation; 1 May 1991

	$Good	$Fine	$N.Mint	£Good	£Fine	£N.Mint
1 ND 48pgs	$0.60	$1.80	$3.00	£0.40	£1.20	£2.00
Title Value:	$0.60	$1.80	$3.00	£0.40	£1.20	£2.00

BATTLE
Atlas/Marvel Comics Group; 63 Nov 1959-70 Jun 1960
(Atlas Comics company title 1-62)

	$Good	$Fine	$N.Mint	£Good	£Fine	£N.Mint
63 ND scarce in the U.K. Steve Ditko art	$3.75	$11.00	$22.50	£2.50	£7.50	£15.00
64 ND scarce in the U.K. Jack Kirby art	$3.75	$11.00	$22.50	£2.50	£7.50	£15.00
65-66 ND scarce in the U.K. Jack Kirby art	$4.50	$13.50	$27.00	£3.00	£9.00	£18.00
67 ND scarce in the U.K. part Jack Kirby art	$3.75	$11.00	$22.50	£2.50	£7.50	£15.00
68 ND scarce in the U.K. part Jack Kirby and Steve Ditko art	$3.75	$11.00	$22.50	£2.50	£7.50	£15.00
69 ND scarce in the U.K. Jack Kirby art	$4.50	$13.50	$27.00	£3.00	£9.00	£18.00
70 rare in the U.K., Jack Kirby and Steve Ditko art	$5.25	$16.00	$32.00	£4.55	£13.50	£27.50
Title Value:	$33.75	$100.50	$203.00	£23.55	£70.50	£141.50

Note: all Ditko, Kirby art throughout.

BATTLE ANGEL ALITA
Viz Communications,MS; 1 Sep 1992-9 May 1993

	$Good	$Fine	$N.Mint	£Good	£Fine	£N.Mint
1-9 ND Yukito Kishiro; black and white	$0.55	$1.65	$2.75	£0.35	£1.05	£1.75
Title Value:	$4.95	$14.85	$24.75	£3.15	£9.45	£15.75
Battle Angel Alita Vol 1 (1994) 208pgs, reprints of series begin; black and white				£2.00	£6.00	£10.00
Battle Angel Alita Vol 2: Tears of an Angel (Oct 1994) 208pgs, reprints of series continue; black and white				£2.00	£6.00	£10.00

BATTLE ANGEL ALITA BOOK 2
Viz Communications,MS; 1 Jun 1993-7 Dec 1993

	$Good	$Fine	$N.Mint	£Good	£Fine	£N.Mint
1-7 ND Yukito Kishiro; black and white	$0.55	$1.65	$2.75	£0.35	£1.05	£1.75
Title Value:	$3.85	$11.55	$19.25	£2.45	£7.35	£12.25

BATTLE ANGEL ALITA BOOK 3
Viz Communications,MS; 1 Jan 1994-13 Jan 1995

	$Good	$Fine	$N.Mint	£Good	£Fine	£N.Mint
1-13 ND Yukito Kishiro; black and white	$0.55	$1.65	$2.75	£0.35	£1.05	£1.75
Title Value:	$7.15	$21.45	$35.75	£4.55	£13.65	£22.75

BATTLE ANGEL ALITA PART 4
Viz Communications,MS; 1 Dec 1994-7 Jun 1995

	$Good	$Fine	$N.Mint	£Good	£Fine	£N.Mint
1-7 ND Yukito Kishiro; black and white	$0.55	$1.65	$2.75	£0.35	£1.05	£1.75
Title Value:	$3.85	$11.55	$19.25	£2.45	£7.35	£12.25
Battle Angel Alita: Angel of Victory (Aug 1995) Trade paperback reprints mini-series				£2.10	£6.30	£10.50

BATTLE ANGEL ALITA PART 5
Viz Communications,MS; 1 Jul 1995-7 Jan 1996

	$Good	$Fine	$N.Mint	£Good	£Fine	£N.Mint
1-7 ND Yukito Kishiro script and art; black and white	$0.55	$1.65	$2.75	£0.35	£1.05	£1.75
Title Value:	$3.85	$11.55	$19.25	£2.45	£7.35	£12.25

BATTLE ANGEL ALITA: KILLING ANGEL
Viz Communications,OS; nn Jun 1995

	$Good	$Fine	$N.Mint	£Good	£Fine	£N.Mint
nn ND 184pgs, Yukito Kishiro script and art; 5" x 7"	$3.00	$9.00	$15.00	£2.00	£6.00	£10.00
Title Value:	$3.00	$9.00	$15.00	£2.00	£6.00	£10.00

BATTLE ARMOR
Eternity; 1 1988-4 1988

	$Good	$Fine	$N.Mint	£Good	£Fine	£N.Mint
1-4 ND game tie-in	$0.40	$1.20	$2.00	£0.25	£0.75	£1.25
Title Value:	$1.60	$4.80	$8.00	£1.00	£3.00	£5.00

BATTLE CLASSICS
DC Comics; 1 Sep/Oct 1978

	$Good	$Fine	$N.Mint	£Good	£Fine	£N.Mint
1 ND 44pgs	$0.40	$1.20	$2.00	£0.25	£0.75	£1.25
Title Value:	$0.40	$1.20	$2.00	£0.25	£0.75	£1.25

Note: was intended as an on-going series (see Dynamic Classics) Johnny Cloud/Sgt. Rock story

	$Good	$Fine	$N.Mint	£Good	£Fine	£N.Mint

REPRINT FEATURES

Johnny Cloud/Sgt. Rock story

BATTLE FOR A THREE-DIMENSIONAL WORLD

3-D Cosmic, OS; 1 1982

1 ND Ray Zone script, Jack Kirby art plus photos; back cover features 1st full-colour 3-D in comics; with 3-D glasses (25% less if without glasses)

	$0.60	$1.80	$3.00	£0.40	£1.20	£2.00
Title Value:	$0.60	$1.80	$3.00	£0.40	£1.20	£2.00

Note: 1st 1980s 3-D comic.

BATTLE GROUP PEIPER

Tome Press; 1 1991

1 ND black and white

	$0.30	$0.90	$1.50	£0.15	£0.45	£0.75
Title Value:	$0.30	$0.90	$1.50	£0.15	£0.45	£0.75

BATTLE OF THE PLANETS

Gold Key/Whitman, TV; 1 Jun 1979-10 Dec 1980

1 scarce in the U.K.

	$0.60	$1.80	$3.00	£0.40	£1.20	£2.00
2-5	$0.40	$1.20	$2.00	£0.25	£0.75	£1.25
6-10	$0.30	$0.90	$1.50	£0.20	£0.60	£1.00
Title Value:	$3.70	$11.10	$18.50	£2.40	£7.20	£12.00

Note: there was Limited Distribution of this title on U.K. new-stands

BATTLE STORIES

Super Comics; 10-12, 15-18 1963-1964

10-12 1950s war reprints begin

	$0.35	$1.10	$2.25	£0.25	£0.75	£1.50

15-18 1950s war reprints

	$0.30	$1.00	$2.00	£0.20	£0.60	£1.25
Title Value:	$2.25	$7.30	$14.75	£1.55	£4.65	£9.50

BATTLE TO THE DEATH

Eternity; 1 Sep 1987-2 Nov 1987

1-2 ND black and white

	$0.30	$0.90	$1.50	£0.15	£0.45	£0.75
	$0.60	$1.80	$3.00	£0.30	£0.90	£1.50
Title Value:	$0.60	$1.80	$3.00	£0.30	£0.90	£1.50

BATTLEFORCE

Blackthorne; 1 Oct 1988-2 1988

1-2 ND

	$0.40	$1.20	$2.00	£0.20	£0.60	£1.00
Title Value:	$0.80	$2.40	$4.00	£0.40	£1.20	£2.00

BATTLESTAR GALACTICA

Marvel Comics Group, TV; 1 Mar 1979-23 Jan 1981

(see also Marvel Super Special #8)

1 ND	$0.30	$0.90	$1.50	£0.20	£0.60	£1.00
2	$0.25	$0.75	$1.25	£0.15	£0.45	£0.75
3 ND	$0.20	$0.60	$1.00	£0.20	£0.60	£1.00

4-5 ND Walt Simonson art

	$0.20	$0.60	$1.00	£0.20	£0.60	£1.00
6-8 ND	$0.20	$0.60	$1.00	£0.15	£0.45	£0.75
9	$0.20	$0.60	$1.00	£0.10	£0.35	£0.60
10 ND Barreto art	$0.20	$0.60	$1.00	£0.15	£0.45	£0.75

11-13 ND Walt Simonson art

	$0.20	$0.60	$1.00	£0.15	£0.45	£0.75
14 ND	$0.20	$0.60	$1.00	£0.15	£0.45	£0.75

15-18 ND Walt Simonson art

	$0.20	$0.60	$1.00	£0.15	£0.45	£0.75

19 Walt Simonson art

	$0.20	$0.60	$1.00	£0.10	£0.35	£0.60

20 ND Walt Simonson art

	$0.20	$0.60	$1.00	£0.15	£0.45	£0.75

21 ND Brent Anderson art

	$0.20	$0.60	$1.00	£0.15	£0.45	£0.75

22 ND Walt Simonson cover

	$0.20	$0.60	$1.00	£0.15	£0.45	£0.75

23 ND Walt Simonson cover and art

	$0.20	$0.60	$1.00	£0.15	£0.45	£0.75
Title Value:	$4.75	$14.25	$23.75	£3.55	£10.75	£17.95

BATTLESTAR GALACTICA: THE ENEMY WITHIN

Maximum Comic Press; 1 Nov 1995-3 Jan 1996

1 ND Rob Liefeld story, Robert Knapton script, Hector Gomez and Rene Micheletti art

	$0.50	$1.50	$2.50	£0.30	£0.90	£1.50
2-3 ND	$0.45	$1.35	$2.25	£0.30	£0.90	£1.50
Title Value:	$1.40	$4.20	$7.00	£0.90	£2.70	£4.50

BATTLESTONE

Image, MS; 1 Nov 1994-2 Dec 1994

1-2 ND Youngblood spin-off

	$0.45	$1.35	$2.25	£0.30	£0.90	£1.50
Title Value:	$0.90	$2.70	$4.50	£0.60	£1.80	£3.00

BATTLETECH

Blackthorne; 1 Aug 1987-12 1988

1 ND	$0.40	$1.20	$2.00	£0.25	£0.75	£1.25
1 ND 3-D issue	$0.45	$1.35	$2.25	£0.30	£0.90	£1.50
2 ND	$0.40	$1.20	$2.00	£0.25	£0.75	£1.25

2 ND 3-D issue

	$0.45	$1.35	$2.25	£0.30	£0.90	£1.50
3-12 ND	$0.40	$1.20	$2.00	£0.25	£0.75	£1.25
Title Value:	$5.70	$17.10	$28.50	£3.60	£10.80	£18.00
Annual 1				£0.50	£1.50	£2.50

Note: first six issues in black and white

BATTLETECH: FALL OUT

Malibu; 0 Feb 1995; 1 Dec 1994-4 Mar 1995

0 ND three stories plus guide to Battletech universe

	$0.45	$1.35	$2.25	£0.30	£0.90	£1.50

1 ND based on video game

	$0.45	$1.35	$2.25	£0.30	£0.90	£1.50

1 ND Hologram Cover Edition (Dec 1994)

	$0.80	$2.40	$4.00	£0.60	£1.80	£3.00

1 ND Foil Logo Edition (Dec 1994)

	$0.80	$2.40	$4.00	£0.60	£1.80	£3.00

2-4 ND based on video game

	$0.45	$1.35	$2.25	£0.30	£0.90	£1.50
Title Value:	$3.85	$11.55	$19.25	£2.70	£8.10	£13.50

BATTRON

New England Comics; 1 Oct 1992-3 1993

1-3 ND	$0.45	$1.35	$2.25	£0.30	£0.90	£1.50
Title Value:	$1.35	$4.05	$6.75	£0.90	£2.70	£4.50

BEACH PARTY

Eternity, OS; 1 Aug 1989

1 ND Dale Keown cover

	$0.45	$1.35	$2.25	£0.30	£0.90	£1.50
Title Value:	$0.45	$1.35	$2.25	£0.30	£0.90	£1.50

BEAST WARRIORS OF SHAOLIN

Pied Piper Comics; 1 Jul 1987-5 1988

1-5 ND Glen Johnson art

	$0.20	$0.60	$1.00	£0.15	£0.45	£0.75
Title Value:	$1.00	$3.00	$5.00	£0.75	£2.25	£3.75

BEATLES LIFE STORY, THE

Dell; 1 Sep/Nov 1964

1 very scarce in the U.K., scarce in the U.S. Giant; colour pin-ups and photos

	$57.50	$175.00	$525.00	£39.00	£115.00	£350.00
Title Value:	$57.50	$175.00	$525.00	£39.00	£115.00	£350.00

BEAUTIFUL STORIES FOR UGLY CHILDREN

DC Comics/Piranha Press; 1 1989-30 1994

1-10 ND 40pgs	$0.40	$1.20	$2.00	£0.30	£0.90	£1.50

Battlestar Galactica #1

Best of DC Digest #3

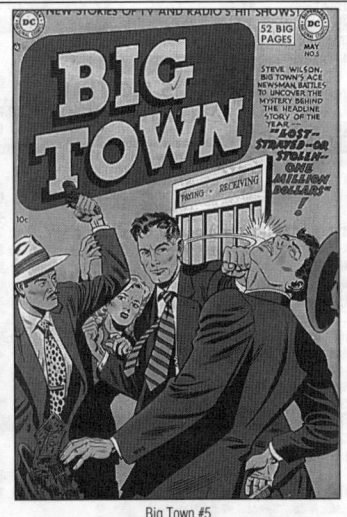

Big Town #5

MINT = 100% / NEAR MINT (inc. +/-) = 90–99% / VERY FINE (inc. +/-) = 75–89% / FINE (inc. +/-) = 55–74% / VERY GOOD (inc. +/-) = 35–54% / GOOD (inc. +/-) = 15–34% / FAIR = 5–14% / POOR = 1–4%

235

	$Good	$Fine	$N.Mint	£Good	£Fine	£N.Mint
11-18 ND 40pgs	$0.35	$1.05	$1.75	£0.25	£0.75	£1.25
19 ND 112pgs, quarterly format begins	$1.00	$3.00	$5.00	£0.70	£2.10	£3.50
20 ND 112pgs, What If This Were Heaven, Wouldn't That Be Hell?	$1.50	$4.50	$7.50	£1.00	£3.00	£5.00
21 ND Dances With Cows	$0.35	$1.05	$1.75	£0.25	£0.75	£1.25
22 ND Prince: Alter Ego, promo for Prince album Diamonds and Pearls	$0.35	$1.05	$1.75	£0.25	£0.75	£1.25
23 ND Tiny Writhing Slimy Thing	$0.35	$1.05	$1.75	£0.25	£0.75	£1.25
24 ND I Am Paul's Dog	$0.35	$1.05	$1.75	£0.25	£0.75	£1.25
25 ND A Legion of Ogs	$0.35	$1.05	$1.75	£0.25	£0.75	£1.25
26 ND Dead, Like Me	$0.35	$1.05	$1.75	£0.25	£0.75	£1.25
27 ND The No-Wax Killing Floor	$0.35	$1.05	$1.75	£0.25	£0.75	£1.25
28 ND The Guilty Orphan	$0.35	$1.05	$1.75	£0.25	£0.75	£1.25
29 ND Gravity Sucks	$0.35	$1.05	$1.75	£0.25	£0.75	£1.25
30 ND The Dream is Dead	$0.35	$1.05	$1.75	£0.25	£0.75	£1.25
Title Value:	$12.80	$38.40	$64.00	£9.20	£27.60	£46.00

Note: 1-18 all black and white art by Dave Louapre and Dan Sweetman

BEAUTY & THE BEAST
Disney,MS; 1 Sep 1992-2 Oct 1992

	$Good	$Fine	$N.Mint	£Good	£Fine	£N.Mint
1-2 ND prequel to animated feature film	$0.30	$0.90	$1.50	£0.20	£0.60	£1.00
Title Value:	$0.60	$1.80	$3.00	£0.40	£1.20	£2.00

BEAUTY AND THE BEAST
First; 1 May 1989-3 1990

	$Good	$Fine	$N.Mint	£Good	£Fine	£N.Mint
1 ND 48pgs, squarebound, script/art by Wendy Pini, based on TV series (blue and red cover logos available)	$1.00	$3.00	$5.00	£0.70	£2.10	£3.50
2 ND 48pgs, squarebound, script/art by Wendy Pini	$1.00	$3.00	$5.00	£0.70	£2.10	£3.50
3 ND 56pgs, Barb Rausch art	$1.00	$3.00	$5.00	£0.70	£2.10	£3.50
Title Value:	$3.00	$9.00	$15.00	£2.10	£6.30	£10.50

Note: embossed covers on all

BEAUTY AND THE BEAST
Marvel Comics Group; 1 Sep 1994-13 Sep 1995

	$Good	$Fine	$N.Mint	£Good	£Fine	£N.Mint
1-13 ND new adventures	$0.30	$0.90	$1.50	£0.20	£0.60	£1.00
Title Value:	$3.90	$11.70	$19.50	£2.60	£7.80	£13.00
Beauty & The Beast (May 1995)						
Trade paperback reprints first four issues				£1.30	£3.90	£6.50

BEAUTY AND THE BEAST
Innovation; 1 Mar 1993-9 1993

	$Good	$Fine	$N.Mint	£Good	£Fine	£N.Mint
1 ND	$0.45	$1.35	$2.25	£0.30	£0.90	£1.50
1 ND special edition - pre-bagged with poster	$0.80	$2.40	$4.00	£0.50	£1.50	£2.50
2-9 ND	$0.45	$1.35	$2.25	£0.30	£0.90	£1.50
Title Value:	$4.85	$14.55	$24.25	£3.20	£9.60	£16.00

BEAUTY AND THE BEAST MOVIE ADAPTATION
Disney,OS; 1 Dec 1991

	$Good	$Fine	$N.Mint	£Good	£Fine	£N.Mint
1 ND Prestige Format version	$1.00	$3.00	$5.00	£0.65	£1.95	£3.25
1 Newstand edition ND	$0.45	$1.35	$2.25	£0.30	£0.90	£1.50
Title Value:	$1.45	$4.35	$7.25	£0.95	£2.85	£4.75

BEAUTY AND THE BEAST, THE
Marvel Comics Group,MS; 1 Jan 1985-4 Apr 1985

	$Good	$Fine	$N.Mint	£Good	£Fine	£N.Mint
1 ND Dazzler/Beast appear, Dr. Doom cameo, Bill Sienkiewicz cover	$0.45	$1.35	$2.25	£0.30	£0.90	£1.50
2-4 ND Dazzler/Beast appear, Dr. Doom cameo, Bill Sienkiewicz cover	$0.40	$1.20	$2.00	£0.25	£0.75	£1.25
Title Value:	$1.65	$4.95	$8.25	£1.05	£3.15	£5.25

BEAVIS & BUTT-HEAD
Marvel Comics Group; 1 Mar 1994-present

	$Good	$Fine	$N.Mint	£Good	£Fine	£N.Mint
1 ND Mike Lackey and Rick Parker creative team begin	$0.90	$2.70	$4.50	£0.60	£1.80	£3.00
2 ND	$0.60	$1.80	$3.00	£0.40	£1.20	£2.00
3 ND	$0.45	$1.35	$2.25	£0.30	£0.90	£1.50
4-25 ND	$0.40	$1.20	$2.00	£0.25	£0.75	£1.25
Title Value:	$10.75	$32.25	$53.75	£6.80	£20.40	£34.00
Beavis & Butt-Head Greatest Hits (Aug 1994)						
Trade paperback ND, reprints issues #1-4, 96pgs				£1.70	£5.10	£8.50
Beavis & Butt-Head: Trashcan Edition (Jan 1995)						
Trade paperback ND, reprints issues #5-8, 96pgs				£1.70	£5.10	£8.50
Beavis & Butt-Head: Holidazed and Confused (Jun 1995)						
Trade paperback ND, collection of holiday stories				£1.70	£5.10	£8.50
Beavis & Butt-Head: Wanted (Jan 1996)						
Trade paperback ND reprints issues #9,13,15,16				£1.70	£5.10	£8.50

BECK & CAUL
Caliber Press; 1 1994-6 1995?

	$Good	$Fine	$N.Mint	£Good	£Fine	£N.Mint
1-6 ND black and white	$0.50	$1.50	$2.50	£0.35	£1.05	£1.75
Title Value:	$3.00	$9.00	$15.00	£2.10	£6.30	£10.50

Beck & Caul Special (Aug 1994)

	$Good	$Fine	$N.Mint	£Good	£Fine	£N.Mint
reprints issues #1 & 2 plus short story from U.N. Files #1				£0.65	£1.95	£3.25

BECK AND CAUL ANNUAL
Caliber Press; 1 May 1995-present?

	$Good	$Fine	$N.Mint	£Good	£Fine	£N.Mint
1 ND 48pgs, black and white	$0.80	$2.40	$4.00	£0.50	£1.50	£2.50
Title Value:	$0.80	$2.40	$4.00	£0.50	£1.50	£2.50

BEDLAM
Eclipse,MS; 1 Sep 1985-2 Oct 1985

	$Good	$Fine	$N.Mint	£Good	£Fine	£N.Mint
1-2 ND Bisette/Veitch reprints	$0.45	$1.35	$2.25	£0.30	£0.90	£1.50
Title Value:	$0.90	$2.70	$4.50	£0.60	£1.80	£3.00

BEETLE BAILEY
King Comics; 54 Aug 1966-65 Dec 1967; Charlton; 67 Feb 1969-119 Nov 1976; Gold Key; 120 Apr 1978-132 Apr 1980

	$Good	$Fine	$N.Mint	£Good	£Fine	£N.Mint
54	$0.60	$1.80	$3.00	£0.40	£1.20	£2.00
55-75	$0.45	$1.35	$2.25	£0.30	£0.90	£1.50
76-120	$0.40	$1.20	$2.00	£0.25	£0.75	£1.25
121-132	$0.30	$0.90	$1.50	£0.20	£0.60	£1.00
Title Value:	$31.65	$94.95	$158.25	£20.35	£61.05	£101.75

BENEATH THE PLANET OF THE APES
Gold Key, Film; 30044-012 Dec 1970

	$Good	$Fine	$N.Mint	£Good	£Fine	£N.Mint
30044-012 rare in the UK, with pull-out poster (value less if poster missing)	$6.50	$19.50	$40.00	£5.00	£15.00	£30.00
Title value:	$6.50	$19.50	$40.00	£5.00	£15.00	£30.00

BENEATH THE PLANET OF THE APES GRAPHIC ALBUM
Adventure,OS; 1 Apr 1991

	$Good	$Fine	$N.Mint	£Good	£Fine	£N.Mint
1 ND 164pgs, reprints 1970s Marvel series plus unseen photos from film	$1.50	$4.50	$7.50	£1.00	£3.00	£5.00
Title Value:	$1.50	$4.50	$7.50	£1.00	£3.00	£5.00

BEOWULF
DC Comics; 1 Apr/May 1975-6 Feb/Mar 1976

	$Good	$Fine	$N.Mint	£Good	£Fine	£N.Mint
1-3	$0.15	$0.45	$0.75	£0.10	£0.35	£0.60
4 scarce in the U.K.	$0.15	$0.45	$0.75	£0.20	£0.60	£1.00
5	$0.15	$0.45	$0.75	£0.10	£0.35	£0.60
6 scarce in the U.K.	$0.15	$0.45	$0.75	£0.20	£0.60	£1.00
Title Value:	$0.90	$2.70	$4.50	£0.80	£2.60	£4.40

BEOWULF
First; nn 1976

	$Good	$Fine	$N.Mint	£Good	£Fine	£N.Mint
nn ND Graphic Novel (the first one the company produced); Jerry Bingham art	$1.20	$3.60	$6.00	£0.80	£2.40	£4.00
Title Value:	$1.20	$3.60	$6.00	£0.80	£2.40	£4.00

BERNI WRIGHTSON. MASTER OF THE MACABRE
Pacific/Eclipse; 1 Jul 1983-5 Nov 1984

	$Good	$Fine	$N.Mint	£Good	£Fine	£N.Mint
1 ND classic Edgar Allan Poe adaptation of The Black Cat, reprint; all Berni Wrightson covers	$0.40	$1.20	$2.00	£0.30	£0.90	£1.50
2-4 ND all reprint	$0.40	$1.20	$2.00	£0.30	£0.90	£1.50
5 ND Eclipse issue, reprints	$0.40	$1.20	$2.00	£0.30	£0.90	£1.50
Title Value:	$2.00	$6.00	$10.00	£1.50	£4.50	£7.50

BERSERKERS
Image,MS; 1 Aug 1995-4 Nov 1995

	$Good	$Fine	$N.Mint	£Good	£Fine	£N.Mint
1 ND Beau Smith script, Dan Fraga art	$0.50	$1.50	$2.50	£0.30	£0.90	£1.50
1 Variant Edition, ND Joe Quesada/Jimmy Palmiotti cover art	$0.80	$2.40	$4.00	£0.50	£1.50	£2.50
2-4 ND Beau Smith script, Dan Fraga art	$0.50	$1.50	$2.50	£0.30	£0.90	£1.50
Title Value:	$2.80	$8.40	$14.00	£1.70	£5.10	£8.50

BERZERKER
Gauntlet Comics,MS; 1 Feb 1993-6 1994

	$Good	$Fine	$N.Mint	£Good	£Fine	£N.Mint
1-6 ND Angel Medina art, black and white	$0.40	$1.20	$2.00	£0.30	£0.90	£1.50
Title Value:	$2.40	$7.20	$12.00	£1.80	£5.40	£9.00

BEST OF DC, THE
DC Comics,Digest; 1 Sep/Oct 1979-71 Dec 1985

	$Good	$Fine	$N.Mint	£Good	£Fine	£N.Mint
1 ND Superman	$0.60	$1.80	$3.00	£0.40	£1.20	£2.00
2 ND Batman, celebrates 40th anniversary with reprints including Batman #7 and #251 (Neal Adams)	$0.60	$1.80	$3.00	£0.40	£1.20	£2.00
3 ND Super Friends, Garcia Lopez painted cover	$0.45		$2.25	£0.30	£0.90	£1.50
4 ND Rudolph the Red Nosed Reindeer	$0.40	$1.20	$2.00	£0.25	£0.75	£1.25
5 ND 132pgs, Year's Best Comic Stories 1979	$0.45	$1.35	$2.25	£0.30	£0.90	£1.50
6 ND Superman, mostly 1960s reprints	$0.40	$1.20	$2.00	£0.25	£0.75	£1.25
7 ND Superboy, mostly 1960s reprints	$0.40	$1.20	$2.00	£0.25	£0.75	£1.25
8 ND Superman	$0.40	$1.20	$2.00	£0.25	£0.75	£1.25
9 ND Batman	$0.40	$1.20	$2.00	£0.25	£0.75	£1.25
10 ND Secret Origins of Super-Villains	$0.40	$1.20	$2.00	£0.25	£0.75	£1.25
11 ND 132pgs, Year's Best Comic Stories 1980	$0.45	$1.35	$2.25	£0.30	£0.90	£1.50
12 ND Superman	$0.40	$1.20	$2.00	£0.25	£0.75	£1.25
13 ND DC Comics Presents (Superman team up)	$0.40	$1.20	$2.00	£0.25	£0.75	£1.25

14 ND Batman's Villains, Marshall Rogers reprint and Neal Adams reprint from Batman #234 (1st modern age Two Face)

	$Good	$Fine	$N.Mint	£Good	£Fine	£N.Mint
	$0.45	$1.35	$2.25	£0.30	£0.90	£1.50
15 ND Superboy, mostly 1960s reprints						
	$0.40	$1.20	$2.00	£0.25	£0.75	£1.25
16 ND Superman, anniversary reprints inc. origin of Superman from Superman #53						
	$0.45	$1.35	$2.25	£0.30	£0.90	£1.50
17 ND Supergirl	$0.40	$1.20	$2.00	£0.25	£0.75	£1.25
18 ND New Teen Titans, new story which was later reprinted in Tales of the Teen Titans #59						
	$0.60	$1.80	$3.00	£0.40	£1.20	£2.00
19 ND Superman, reprints classic Superman Red and Superman Blue						
	$0.40	$1.20	$2.00	£0.25	£0.75	£1.25
20 ND World's Finest Comics (Superman and Batman)						
	$0.40	$1.20	$2.00	£0.25	£0.75	£1.25
21 ND Justice Society of America, featuring Golden Age reprint						
	$0.45	$1.35	$2.25	£0.30	£0.90	£1.50
22 ND Christmas with the Super-Heroes, features unpublished Sandman story by Jack Kirby (18pgs)						
	$0.60	$1.80	$3.00	£0.40	£1.20	£2.00
23 ND 148pgs, Year's Best Comic Stories 1981						
	$0.45	$1.35	$2.25	£0.30	£0.90	£1.50
24 ND Legion of Super-Heroes, new story featured						
	$0.60	$1.80	$3.00	£0.40	£1.20	£2.00
25 ND Superman, featuring kid pals						
	$0.40	$1.20	$2.00	£0.25	£0.75	£1.25
26 ND Brave and the Bold (Batman team up plus Robin Hood, Suicide Squad, Viking Prince, Silent Knight and Cave Carson)						
	$0.40	$1.20	$2.00	£0.25	£0.75	£1.25
27 ND Superman vs. Luthor						
	$0.40	$1.20	$2.00	£0.25	£0.75	£1.25
28 ND Binky's Summer Fun						
	$0.30	$0.90	$1.50	£0.20	£0.60	£1.00
29 ND Sugar and Spike						
	$0.40	$1.20	$2.00	£0.25	£0.75	£1.25
30 ND Detective Comics						
	$0.45	$1.35	$2.25	£0.30	£0.90	£1.50
31 ND Justice League of America, special initiation issue						
	$0.30	$0.90	$1.50	£0.20	£0.60	£1.00
32 ND Superman	$0.40	$1.20	$2.00	£0.25	£0.75	£1.25
33 ND Legion of Super-Heroes						
	$0.45	$1.35	$2.25	£0.30	£0.90	£1.50
34 ND Metal Men, reprints Showcase #37-40; has #497 on cover (intended for Adveture Comics?)						
	$0.45	$1.35	$2.25	£0.30	£0.90	£1.50
35 ND 148pgs, Year's Best Comic Stories 1982						
	$0.45	$1.35	$2.25	£0.30	£0.90	£1.50
36 ND Superman vs. Kryptonite						
	$0.40	$1.20	$2.00	£0.25	£0.75	£1.25
37 ND Funny Stuff	$0.25	$0.75	$1.25	£0.15	£0.45	£0.75
38 ND Superman: The Supernatural, features some 40s and 50s reprints						
	$0.40	$1.20	$2.00	£0.25	£0.75	£1.25
39 ND Binky and His Buddies						
	$0.30	$0.90	$1.50	£0.20	£0.60	£1.00
40 ND Superman: The Fabulous World of Krypton						
	$0.40	$1.20	$2.00	£0.25	£0.75	£1.25
41 ND Sugar and Spike						
	$0.30	$0.90	$1.50	£0.20	£0.60	£1.00
42 ND Superman vs. Aliens, 1950s/1960s classic reprints						
	$0.30	$0.90	$1.50	£0.20	£0.60	£1.00
43 ND Funny Stuff						
	$0.30	$0.90	$1.50	£0.20	£0.60	£1.00
44 ND Legion of Super-Heroes (reprints Adventure Comics #319-323)						
	$0.45	$1.35	$2.25	£0.30	£0.90	£1.50
45 ND Binky and His Buddies						
	$0.25	$0.75	$1.25	£0.15	£0.45	£0.75
46 ND Jimmy Olsen, reprints Jimmy Olsen #1 and #2						
	$0.40	$1.20	$2.00	£0.25	£0.75	£1.25
47 ND Sugar and Spike						
	$0.40	$1.20	$2.00	£0.25	£0.75	£1.25
48 ND Superman Team Up Action						
	$0.40	$1.20	$2.00	£0.25	£0.75	£1.25
49 ND Funny Stuff	$0.25	$0.75	$1.25	£0.15	£0.45	£0.75
50 ND Year's Best Superman Stories						
	$0.45	$1.35	$2.25	£0.30	£0.90	£1.50
51 ND Batman Family, Neal Adams, Marshall Rogers reprints						
	$0.60	$1.80	$3.00	£0.40	£1.20	£2.00
52 ND 148pgs, Year's Best Comic Stories 1983						
	$0.45	$1.35	$2.25	£0.30	£0.90	£1.50
53 ND Binky and His Buddies						
	$0.25	$0.75	$1.25	£0.15	£0.45	£0.75
54 ND Superman Battles Weird Villains						
	$0.40	$1.20	$2.00	£0.25	£0.75	£1.25
55 ND Funny Stuff						
	$0.25	$0.75	$1.25	£0.15	£0.45	£0.75
56 ND Superman vs. More Aliens						
	$0.30	$0.90	$1.50	£0.20	£0.60	£1.00
57 ND	$0.30	$0.90	$1.50	£0.20	£0.60	£1.00
58 ND Super Jrs. Holiday Special						
	$0.30	$0.90	$1.50	£0.20	£0.60	£1.00
59 ND Superman Sagas						
	$0.40	$1.20	$2.00	£0.25	£0.75	£1.25
60 ND Plop!	$0.40	$1.20	$2.00	£0.25	£0.75	£1.25
61 ND 148pgs, Year's Best Comic Stories 1984 inc. Swamp Thing #21 (Alan Moore)						
	$0.45	$1.35	$2.25	£0.30	£0.90	£1.50
62 ND Year's Best Batman Stories						
	$0.45	$1.35	$2.25	£0.30	£0.90	£1.50
63 ND Plop!	$0.40	$1.20	$2.00	£0.25	£0.75	£1.25
64 ND Legion of Super-Heroes (reprints Adventure Comics #330-334)						
	$0.30	$0.90	$1.50	£0.20	£0.60	£1.00
65 ND Sugar and Spike						
	$0.30	$0.90	$1.50	£0.20	£0.60	£1.00
66 ND Superman Team Up Action						
	$0.30	$0.90	$1.50	£0.20	£0.60	£1.00
67 ND Legion of Super-Heroes						
	$0.45	$1.35	$2.25	£0.30	£0.90	£1.50
68 ND Sugar and Spike Halloween Special						
	$0.30	$0.90	$1.50	£0.20	£0.60	£1.00
69 ND Year's Best Team Stories						
	$0.40	$1.20	$2.00	£0.25	£0.75	£1.25
70 ND Binky's Buddies						
	$0.25	$0.75	$1.25	£0.15	£0.45	£0.75
71 ND 148pgs, Year's Best Comic Stories 1985 inc. Swamp Thing #34						
	$0.45	$1.35	$2.25	£0.30	£0.90	£1.50
Title Value:	$28.30	$84.90	$141.50	£18.30	£54.90	£91.50

Note: unless otherwise stated, issues are 100pgs.

ARTISTS

Adams reprints in 2,14,16,18,25,26. Rogers reprints in 14. Kirby in 22 (previously unpublished Sandman 7). Perez in 24.

FEATURES

Batman in 10. Legion of Super-Heroes in 24 (with 16pgs of new costumes). Teen Titans in 18. Sandman in 22. One page origins of various villains in 14.

REPRINT FEATURES

(other than featured character) Aquaman in 10. Batman in 5,11,22,23. Batman/Deadman in 26. Captain Marvel/Crimson Avenger in 23. Captain Marvel Jnr. in 22. Cave Carson, Robin Hood, Silent Knight, Suicide Squad, Viking Prince/Sgt. Rock in 5. Flash in 10. Green Arrow, Green Lantern in 10. Green Lantern Corps, New Teen Titans in 23. Hawkman in 10. Jimmy Olsen in 6,16. Jonah Hex in 5,11,23. JLA in 3. Legion in 11. Lois Lane in 6,19. Robin in 22. Sgt. Rock in 11,23. Starman/Black Canary in 21. Superman in 5,10,11,13,23. Superman/Aquaman in 13. Superman/Batgirl, Superman/Batman, Superman/Green Arrow, Superman/ Lantern, Superman/Supergirl in 13. Superman/Batman in 19,20. Superman/Deadman in 11. Superman/Dr. Fate in 20. Teen Titans in 3,18,22.

BEST OF MARVEL 1994

Marvel Comics Group,OS; nn Dec 1994

nn ND 240pgs, Trade paperback. Ten reprints from 1994 featuring X-Men, X-Factor, Spiderman, Thunderstrike and others

	$Good	$Fine	$N.Mint	£Good	£Fine	£N.Mint
	$2.55	$7.50	$12.75	£1.70	£5.00	£8.50
Title Value:	$2.55	$7.50	$12.75	£1.70	£5.00	£8.50

BEST OF MARVEL 1995

Marvel Comics Group,OS; nn Jan 1996

nn ND 224pgs, Trade paperback. Reprints iclude Generation X #5,6, Amazing Spiderman #400, Spiderman #57, Spectacular Spiderman #223, Hulk #345 among others

	$Good	$Fine	$N.Mint	£Good	£Fine	£N.Mint
	$4.00	$12.00	$20.00	£2.70	£8.00	£13.50
Title Value:	$4.00	$12.00	$20.00	£2.70	£8.00	£13.50

BEST OF SORCERY, THE

Millennium,MS; 1 Dec 1992

1 ND 48pgs, reprints begin from Red Circle's Sorcery and Madhouse featuring work by Chaykin, Williamson, Morrow and Toth; new John Bolton cover

	$Good	$Fine	$N.Mint	£Good	£Fine	£N.Mint
	$0.40	$1.20	$2.00	£0.30	£0.90	£1.50
Title Value:	$0.40	$1.20	$2.00	£0.30	£0.90	£1.50

BEST OF THE BRAVE AND THE BOLD

DC Comics,MS; 1 Oct 1988-6 Mar 1989

1-6 ND Neal Adams reprints

	$Good	$Fine	$N.Mint	£Good	£Fine	£N.Mint
	$0.40	$1.20	$2.00	£0.30	£0.90	£1.50
Title Value:	$2.40	$7.20	$12.00	£1.80	£5.40	£9.00

REPRINT FEATURES

Batman/Aquaman (from Brave & Bold 82) in 3; Batman/Creeper (from Brave & Bold 80) in 4; Batman/Flash (from B&B 81) in 2; Batman/Green Arrow (from Brave & Bold 85) in 1; Batman/House of Mystery (from B&B 93) in 5; Batman/Teen Titans (from B&B 83) in 6. Golden Gladiator in 3-5. Robin Hood in 2-6. Silent Knight (from B&B 1) in 1. Viking Prince in 1-6.

BETTY BEING BAD

Eros Comix,OS; 1 Feb 1991

1 ND rare in the U.K., rare photos of 1950s pin-up Betty Page

	$Good	$Fine	$N.Mint	£Good	£Fine	£N.Mint
	$0.80	$2.40	$4.00	£0.50	£1.50	£2.50
Title Value:	$0.80	$2.40	$4.00	£0.50	£1.50	£2.50

BETTY BOOP IN 3-D

Blackthorne; (3-D Series #11) Nov 1986

1 ND 1934 reprints by Bud Counihan; with bound-in 3-D glasses (25% less if without glasses)

	$Good	$Fine	$N.Mint	£Good	£Fine	£N.Mint
	$0.45	$1.35	$2.25	£0.30	£0.90	£1.50
Title Value:	$0.45	$1.35	$2.25	£0.30	£0.90	£1.50

Note: see also Little Nemo in Slumberland as this is also numbered Blackthorne 3-D Series #11 in the indicia

BETTY BOOP'S BIG BREAK

First,OS; 1 Oct 1990

1 ND 48pgs, squarebound

	$Good	$Fine	$N.Mint	£Good	£Fine	£N.Mint
	$1.00	$3.00	$5.00	£0.70	£2.10	£3.50
Title Value:	$1.00	$3.00	$5.00	£0.70	£2.10	£3.50

BETTY PAGE 3-D COMICS

The 3-D Zone,OS; 1 Apr 1991

1 ND with glasses (25% less if without glasses); oversize issue (8"x10")

	$Good	$Fine	$N.Mint	£Good	£Fine	£N.Mint
	$0.80	$2.40	$4.00	£0.50	£1.50	£2.50
Title Value:	$0.80	$2.40	$4.00	£0.50	£1.50	£2.50

BETTY PAGE 3-D PICTURE BOOK, THE

The 3-D Zone,OS; 1 1989

1 ND scarce in the U.K. topless photos of Betty Page, with bound-in 3-D glasses (25% less if without glasses); intro by Dave Stevens

	$Good	$Fine	$N.Mint	£Good	£Fine	£N.Mint
	$1.20	$3.60	$6.00	£0.80	£2.40	£4.00
Title Value:	$1.20	$3.60	$6.00	£0.80	£2.40	£4.00

BETTY PAGE CAPTURED JUNGLE GIRL 3-D

The 3-D Zone,OS; 1 1990

	$Good	$Fine	$N.Mint	£Good	£Fine	£N.Mint

1 ND scarce in the U.K. bondage pin-ups of Betty Page, with bound-in (excuse pun) 3-D glasses (25% less if without glasses)

| | $0.90 | $2.70 | $4.50 | £0.60 | £1.80 | £3.00 |
| Title Value: | $0.90 | $2.70 | $4.50 | £0.60 | £1.80 | £3.00 |

BEWARE THE CREEPER
(see Creeper)

BEWARE!
Marvel Comics Group; 1 Mar 1973-8 May 1974
(becomes Tomb of Darkness)

1 ND scarce in the U.K. horror reprints from the 1950s/early 1960s begin

| | $0.90 | $2.70 | $4.50 | £0.60 | £1.80 | £3.00 |

2-3 ND scarce in the U.K.

| | $0.80 | $2.40 | $4.00 | £0.50 | £1.50 | £2.50 |

4 ND scarce in the U.K. Gil Kane cover

| | $0.70 | $2.10 | $3.50 | £0.45 | £1.35 | £2.25 |

5-8 ND scarce in the U.K.

| | $0.70 | $2.10 | $3.50 | £0.45 | £1.35 | £2.25 |
| Title Value: | $6.00 | $18.00 | $30.00 | £3.85 | £11.55 | £19.25 |

BEYOND THE GRAVE
Charlton; 1 Jul 1975-6 Jun 1976; 7 Jan 1983-17 Oct 1984

1 distributed in the U.K.

| | $0.35 | $1.05 | $1.75 | £0.25 | £0.75 | £1.25 |

2-5 distributed in the U.K.

| | $0.30 | $0.90 | $1.50 | £0.20 | £0.60 | £1.00 |

6-17 distributed in the U.K.

| | $0.25 | $0.75 | $1.25 | £0.15 | £0.45 | £0.75 |
| Title Value: | $4.55 | $13.65 | $22.75 | £2.85 | £8.55 | £14.25 |

BIFF THUNDERSAUR
Innovation,OS; 1 1991

1 ND black and white

| | $0.40 | $1.20 | $2.00 | £0.25 | £0.75 | £1.25 |
| Title Value: | $0.40 | $1.20 | $2.00 | £0.25 | £0.75 | £1.25 |

BIG BANG COMICS
Caliber Press; 0 Sep 1994; 1 Spring 1994-present?

0 ND 16pgs, information and timeline on Big Bang characters

| | $0.20 | $0.60 | $1.00 | £0.15 | £0.45 | £0.75 |

1 ND 64pgs, Sheldon Moldoff cover; 1940s period feel

| | $0.60 | $1.80 | $3.00 | £0.40 | £1.20 | £2.00 |

2 ND Curt Swan and Murphy Anderson cover

| | $0.45 | $1.35 | $2.25 | £0.30 | £0.90 | £1.50 |

3 ND Silver Age issue

| | $0.40 | $1.20 | $2.00 | £0.25 | £0.75 | £1.25 |

4 ND The Free Agents appear

| | $0.40 | $1.20 | $2.00 | £0.25 | £0.75 | £1.25 |
| Title Value: | $2.05 | $6.15 | $10.25 | £1.35 | £4.05 | £6.75 |

Note: Golden Age homage/parody

BIG BLACK KISS
Vortex,MS; 1 Sep 1989-3 Nov 1989

1 ND reprints of Black Kiss begin

| | $0.80 | $2.40 | $4.00 | £0.50 | £1.50 | £2.50 |

2-3 ND reprints of Black Kiss begin

| | $0.70 | $2.10 | $3.50 | £0.45 | £1.35 | £2.25 |
| Title Value: | $2.20 | $6.60 | $11.00 | £1.40 | £4.20 | £7.00 |

BIG BOOK OF CONSPIRACIES, THE
DC Comics/Paradox Press,OS; nn Aug 1995

nn ND 224pgs, Doug Moench script with art by Rick Geary, Kev O'Neill, Brett Ewins, Bryan Talbot and others

| | $2.50 | $7.50 | $12.50 | £1.50 | £4.50 | £7.50 |
| Title Value: | $2.50 | $7.50 | $12.50 | £1.50 | £4.50 | £7.50 |

BIG BOOK OF DEATH, THE
DC Comics/Paradox Press,OS; nn Jun 1995

nn ND 224pgs, squarebound, everything you wanted to know about death; black and white

| | $2.50 | $7.50 | $12.50 | £1.50 | £4.50 | £7.50 |
| Title Value: | $2.50 | $7.50 | $12.50 | £1.50 | £4.50 | £7.50 |

BIG BOOK OF URBAN LEGENDS, THE
DC Comics/Paradox Press; nn Jan 1995

nn ND 224pgs, contributions from Art Adams, Terry Austin, Mike Mignola among others

| | $2.50 | $7.50 | $12.50 | £1.50 | £4.50 | £7.50 |
| Title Value: | $2.50 | $7.50 | $12.50 | £1.50 | £4.50 | £7.50 |

BIG BOOK OF WEIRDOS, THE
DC Comics/Paradox Press,OS; nn Mar 1995

nn ND 224pgs, contributors include Joe Staton and Mike Zeck; black and white

| | $2.50 | $7.50 | $12.50 | £1.50 | £4.50 | £7.50 |
| Title Value: | $2.50 | $7.50 | $12.50 | £1.50 | £4.50 | £7.50 |

BIG GUY & RUSTY THE BOY ROBOT, THE
Dark Horse,MS; 1 Jul 1995-2 Aug 1995

1 ND Frank Miller script, Geoff Darrow art, cover by Darrow, Olivia and Lynn Varley; 9" x 12.5" format

| | $1.00 | $3.00 | $5.00 | £0.65 | £1.95 | £3.25 |

2 ND Frank Miller script, Geoff Darrow art, cover by Geoff Darrow and Lynn Varley; 9" x 12.5" format

| | $1.00 | $3.00 | $5.00 | £0.65 | £1.95 | £3.25 |
| Title Value: | $2.00 | $6.00 | $10.00 | £1.30 | £3.90 | £6.50 |

BIG NUMBERS
(see British section)

BIG PRIZE, THE
Eternity; 1 May 1988-2 Sep 1988

| **1-2** ND | $0.40 | $1.20 | $2.00 | £0.25 | £0.75 | £1.25 |
| Title Value: | $0.80 | $2.40 | $4.00 | £0.50 | £1.50 | £2.50 |

BIG TOWN
National Periodical Publications; 1 Jan 1951-50 Mar/Apr 1958

1 scarce in the U.K.

| | $50.00 | $150.00 | $350.00 | £34.00 | £100.00 | £235.00 |

2 scarce in the U.K.

	$Good	$Fine	$N.Mint	£Good	£Fine	£N.Mint
	$24.00	$72.50	$170.00	£16.00	£49.00	£115.00

3-5 scarce in the U.K.

| | $16.00 | $49.00 | $115.00 | £10.50 | £32.00 | £75.00 |

6-10 scarce in the U.K.

	$14.00	$43.00	$100.00	£9.25	£28.00	£65.00
11-20	$9.25	$28.00	$65.00	£6.00	£18.00	£42.50
21-30	$6.25	$19.00	$45.00	£4.25	£12.50	£30.00
31-50	$4.60	$13.50	$32.50	£3.20	£9.50	£22.50
Title Value:	$439.00	$1324.50	$3115.00	£294.25	£880.00	£2075.00

BIKER MICE FROM MARS
Marvel Comics Group, TV; 1 Nov 1993-6 Apr 1994

1 adaptation of animated TV film

	$0.30	$0.90	$1.50	£0.20	£0.60	£1.00
2-6	$0.30	$0.90	$1.50	£0.20	£0.60	£1.00
Title Value:	$1.80	$5.40	$9.00	£1.20	£3.60	£6.00

BILL & TED II MOVIE ADAPTATION
Marvel Comics Group,OS; 1 Sep 1991

1 adaptation of film, news-stand edition

| | $0.45 | $1.35 | $2.25 | £0.30 | £0.90 | £1.50 |

1 ND adaptation of film, bookshelf format, direct sales edition

| | $0.90 | $2.70 | $4.50 | £0.60 | £1.80 | £3.00 |
| Title Value: | $1.35 | $4.05 | $6.75 | £0.90 | £2.70 | £4.50 |

BILL & TED'S EXCELLENT COMIC BOOK
Marvel Comics Group; 1 Dec 1991-12 Nov 1992

| **1** based on film | $0.20 | $0.60 | $1.00 | £0.10 | £0.35 | £0.60 |
| **2** | $0.20 | $0.60 | $1.00 | £0.10 | £0.35 | £0.60 |

3 $1.25 cover begins

	$0.20	$0.60	$1.00	£0.10	£0.35	£0.60
4-12	$0.20	$0.60	$1.00	£0.10	£0.35	£0.60
Title Value:	$2.40	$7.20	$12.00	£1.20	£4.20	£7.20

BILL BLACK'S FUN COMICS
Paragon/AC Comics; 1 Dec 1982-4 Mar 1983

1 ND oversize, intro Captain Paragon

| | $0.35 | $1.05 | $1.75 | £0.25 | £0.75 | £1.25 |

2 ND oversize, Commando D

| | $0.35 | $1.05 | $1.75 | £0.25 | £0.75 | £1.25 |

3 ND oversize, Captain Paragon, Nightveil

| | $0.35 | $1.05 | $1.75 | £0.25 | £0.75 | £1.25 |

4 ND 1st Colour, 1st Americomics issue, Phantom Lady becomes Nightfall

| | $0.35 | $1.05 | $1.75 | £0.25 | £0.75 | £1.25 |
| Title Value: | $1.40 | $4.20 | $7.00 | £1.00 | £3.00 | £5.00 |

BILLI 99
Dark Horse,MS; 1 Nov 1991-4 Feb 1992

| **1-4** ND 48pgs | $0.60 | $1.80 | $3.00 | £0.40 | £1.20 | £2.00 |
| Title Value: | $2.40 | $7.20 | $12.00 | £1.60 | £4.80 | £8.00 |

BILL THE GALACTIC HERO
Topps,MS; 1 Jul 1994-3 Sep 1994

1-3 48pgs, adaptation of Harry Harrison characters

| | $1.00 | $3.00 | $5.00 | £0.65 | £1.95 | £3.25 |
| Title Value: | $3.00 | $9.00 | $15.00 | £1.95 | £5.85 | £9.75 |

BILLY NGUYEN
Caliber Press,MS; 1 Feb 1991-2 May 1991

| **1-2** ND | $0.45 | $1.35 | $2.25 | £0.30 | £0.90 | £1.50 |
| Title Value: | $0.90 | $2.70 | $4.50 | £0.60 | £1.80 | £3.00 |

Compilation Novel, reprints early adventures published by Attitude Zone Comics — £6.75

BILLY THE KID
Charlton; 9 Nov 1957-153 Mar 1983
(#1-8 called The Masked Raider)

9	$8.25	$25.00	$50.00	£5.75	£17.50	£35.00
10	$5.00	$15.00	$30.00	£3.30	£10.00	£20.00
11 origin	$5.25	$16.00	$32.50	£3.65	£11.00	£22.00
12	$5.00	$15.00	$30.00	£3.30	£10.00	£20.00
13 Williamson art	$5.75	$17.50	$35.00	£4.00	£12.00	£24.00
14	$5.00	$15.00	$30.00	£3.30	£10.00	£20.00

15-16 part Williamson art

	$5.75	$17.50	$35.00	£4.00	£12.00	£24.00
17-19	$5.00	$15.00	$30.00	£3.30	£10.00	£20.00
20-26	$5.75	$17.50	$35.00	£4.00	£12.00	£24.00
27-30	$3.30	$10.00	$20.00	£2.30	£7.00	£14.00
31-40	$2.50	$7.50	$15.00	£1.65	£5.00	£10.00
41-60	$1.65	$5.00	$10.00	£1.15	£3.50	£7.00
61-80	$1.00	$3.00	$5.00	£0.65	£1.95	£3.25
81-99	$0.60	$1.80	$3.00	£0.40	£1.20	£2.00
100	$0.90	$2.70	$4.50	£0.60	£1.80	£3.00
101-125	$0.45	$1.35	$2.25	£0.30	£0.90	£1.50
126-153	$0.40	$1.20	$2.00	£0.25	£0.75	£1.25
Title Value:	$226.95	$685.25	$1316.50	£153.60	£463.60	£891.50

BINKY
National Periodical Publications; 61 Jun/Jul 1968-81 Oct/Nov 1971; OS; 82 1977
(see Super DC Giant, Showcase) (previous issues ND)

61-71 titled Leave It To Binky

| | $1.90 | $5.50 | $9.50 | £1.20 | £3.60 | £6.00 |

72-81 title becomes Binky

	$0.90	$2.70	$4.50	£0.60	£1.80	£3.00
82	$0.45	$1.35	$2.25	£0.30	£0.90	£1.50
Title Value:	$30.35	$88.85	$151.75	£19.50	£58.50	£97.50

BINKY'S BUDDIES
National Periodical Publications; 1 Jan/Feb 1969-12 Nov/Dec 1970

1	$0.80	$2.40	$4.00	£0.50	£1.50	£2.50
2-12	$0.40	$1.20	$2.00	£0.25	£0.75	£1.25
Title Value:	$5.20	$15.60	$26.00	£3.25	£9.75	£16.25

	$Good	$Fine	$N.Mint	£Good	£Fine	£N.Mint
BIO-BOOSTER ARMOR GUYVER						
Viz Communications,MS; 1 Dec 1993-12 Nov 1994						
1-12 ND Yoshiki Takaya; black and white						
	$0.45	$1.35	$2.25	£0.30	£0.90	£1.50
Title Value:	$5.40	$16.20	$27.00	£3.60	£10.80	£18.00
Bio-Booster Armor Guyver Graphic Novel (Apr 1995)						
collects issues #1-6 retelling origin				£2.00	£6.00	£10.00
BIO-BOOSTER ARMOR GUYVER PART 2						
Viz Communications,MS; 1 Oct 1994-6 Mar 1995						
1-6 ND Yoshiki Takaya; black and white						
	$0.45	$1.35	$2.25	£0.30	£0.90	£1.50
Title Value:	$2.70	$8.10	$13.50	£1.80	£5.40	£9.00
Bio-Booster Armor Guyver: Revenge of Chronos (Jun 1995)						
Trade paperback reprints issues #1-6				£2.10	£6.30	£10.50
BIO-BOOSTER ARMOR GUYVER PART 3						
Viz Communications,MS; 1 Apr 1995-7 Oct 1995						
1-7 ND Yoshiki Takaya script and art; black and white						
	$0.45	$1.35	$2.25	£0.30	£0.90	£1.50
Title Value:	$3.15	$9.45	$15.75	£2.10	£6.30	£10.50
BIONEERS						
Mirage/Next Comics; 1 Aug 1994-3 1994						
1-2 ND A.C. Farley script and art						
	$0.45	$1.35	$2.25	£0.30	£0.90	£1.50
3 ND A.C. Farley script and art; with two bound-in trading cards						
	$0.45	$1.35	$2.25	£0.30	£0.90	£1.50
Title Value:	$1.35	$4.05	$6.75	£0.90	£2.70	£4.50
BIONIC WOMAN, THE ALL NEW						
Charlton, TV; 1 Oct 1977-5 Jun 1978						
1 distributed in the U.K.						
	$0.60	$1.80	$3.00	£0.40	£1.20	£2.00
2-5 distributed in the U.K.						
	$0.55	$1.65	$2.75	£0.35	£1.05	£1.75
Title Value:	$2.80	$8.40	$14.00	£1.80	£5.40	£9.00
BIRDLAND						
Eros Comix,MS; 1 Oct 1990-3 Apr 1991						
1 ND scarce in the U.K. features Bang Bang and Inez from Love and Rockets, Gilbert Hernandez art; adult material						
	$1.50	$4.50	$7.50	£0.90	£2.70	£4.50
2-3 ND scarce in the U.K. features Bang Bang and Inez from Love and Rockets, Gilbert Hernandez art; adult material						
	$0.90	$2.70	$4.50	£0.60	£1.80	£3.00
Title Value:	$3.30	$9.90	$16.50	£2.10	£6.30	£10.50
BIRTH RITE						
(see British Section)						
BISHOP						
Marvel Comics Group,MS; 1 Dec 1994-4 Mar 1995						
1-4 foil stamped cover						
	$0.60	$1.80	$3.00	£0.40	£1.20	£2.00
Title Value:	$2.40	$7.20	$12.00	£1.60	£4.80	£8.00
Bishop Mini Masterpiece (Nov 1995)						
boxed set of issues #1-4, ND				£1.50	£4.50	£7.50
Bishop: Mountjoy Crisis (Mar 1996)						
Trade paperback ND collects mini-series				£1.70	£5.10	£8.50
BIZARRE 3-D ZONE						
Blackthorne; (3-D Series #5) 1 Jul 1986						
1 ND Spain, Strand, Pound, Stout, Scott Shaw, Sekowsky, Robert Williams art, with 3-D glasses						
(25% less without glasses)						
	$0.45	$1.35	$2.25	£0.30	£0.90	£1.50
Title Value:	$0.45	$1.35	$2.25	£0.30	£0.90	£1.50
BIZARRE ADVENTURES						
Marvel Comics Group,Magazine; 25 Mar 1981-34 Feb 1983						
(formerly Marvel Preview)						
25 ND Lethal Ladies; Rogers/Gulacy/Golden art						
	$0.40	$1.20	$2.00	£0.50	£1.50	£2.50
26 ND Kull; Bolton art						
	$0.40	$1.20	$2.00	£0.50	£1.50	£2.50
27 ND X-Men; Phoenix, Iceman, Nightcrawler; John Buscema art on Phoenix story, George Perez art on Iceman story, Dave Cockrum art on Nightcrawler story						
	$0.60	$1.80	$3.00	£0.70	£2.10	£3.50
28 ND Unlikely Heroes; Miller's Elektra, Neal Adams, Golden art						
	$0.60	$1.80	$3.00	£0.70	£2.10	£3.50
29 ND Horror; 1st appearance Greenberg the Vampire, Walt Simonson art						
	$0.40	$1.20	$2.00	£0.50	£1.50	£2.50
30 ND Paradox						
	$0.40	$1.20	$2.00	£0.30	£0.90	£1.50
31 ND Violence issue; Frank Miller, John Byrne art						
	$0.40	$1.20	$2.00	£0.30	£0.90	£1.50
32 ND scarce in the U.K. Gods (inc. Thor); Bolton art						
	$0.60	$1.80	$3.00	£0.40	£1.20	£2.00
33 ND Horror stories						
	$0.40	$1.20	$2.00	£0.30	£0.90	£1.50
34 ND Son of Santa; Howard the Duck by Paul Smith						
	$0.40	$1.20	$2.00	£0.30	£0.90	£1.50
Title Value:	$4.60	$13.80	$23.00	£4.50	£13.50	£22.50
Note: #34 in comic and magazine format.						
BLACK AND WHITE						
Image,MS; 1 Oct 1994-3 Dec 1994						
1-3 ND Art Thibert art						
	$0.40	$1.20	$2.00	£0.25	£0.75	£1.25
Title Value:	$1.20	$3.60	$6.00	£0.75	£2.25	£3.75
BLACK AXE						
Marvel UK; 1 Apr 1993-10 Jan 1994						
1 Simon Jowett script, Death's Head II appears, cover pencils by John Romita Jnr.						
	$0.30	$0.90	$1.50	£0.20	£0.60	£1.00
2-3 Death's Head II appears						
	$0.30	$0.90	$1.50	£0.20	£0.60	£1.00
4 Liam Sharp cover						
	$0.30	$0.90	$1.50	£0.20	£0.60	£1.00
5 1st appearance Afrikaa, Black Panther appears						
	$0.30	$0.90	$1.50	£0.20	£0.60	£1.00
6-7 Black Panther appears						
	$0.30	$0.90	$1.50	£0.20	£0.60	£1.00
8 Liam Sharp cover						
	$0.30	$0.90	$1.50	£0.20	£0.60	£1.00
9-10						
	$0.30	$0.90	$1.50	£0.20	£0.60	£1.00
Title Value:	$3.00	$9.00	$15.00	£2.00	£6.00	£10.00
BLACK CANARY						
DC Comics,MS; 1 Nov 1991-4 Feb 1992						
1-4 Trevor Von Eeden art						
	$0.30	$0.90	$1.50	£0.20	£0.60	£1.00
Title Value:	$1.20	$3.60	$6.00	£0.80	£2.40	£4.00
BLACK CANARY (2ND SERIES)						
DC Comics; 1 Jan 1993-12 Dec 1993						
1-5	$0.25	$0.75	$1.25	£0.15	£0.45	£0.75
6 leads into Green Arrow #75						
	$0.25	$0.75	$1.25	£0.15	£0.45	£0.75
7-10	$0.25	$0.75	$1.25	£0.15	£0.45	£0.75
11 Nightwing and Huntress appear						
	$0.25	$0.75	$1.25	£0.15	£0.45	£0.75
12	$0.25	$0.75	$1.25	£0.15	£0.45	£0.75
Title Value:	$3.00	$9.00	$15.00	£1.80	£5.40	£9.00
BLACK CANARY/ORACLE: BIRDS OF PREY						
DC Comics,OS; 1 Jan 1996						

Black Axe #1

Black Panther #9

Blackhawk #172

1 ND 48pgs, Chuck Dixon script, Gary Frank and John Dell art

	$Good	$Fine	$N.Mint	£Good	£Fine	£N.Mint
	$0.80	$2.40	$4.00	£0.50	£1.50	£2.50
Title Value:	$0.80	$2.40	$4.00	£0.50	£1.50	£2.50

BLACK CAT
Harvey; 63 Oct 1962-65 Apr 1963
63-65 scarce in the U.K. giant size, all reprint; distributed in the U.K.

	$Good	$Fine	$N.Mint	£Good	£Fine	£N.Mint
	$9.25	$28.00	$65.00	£5.50	£17.00	£40.00
Title Value:	$27.75	$84.00	$195.00	£16.50	£51.00	£120.00

BLACK CAT, ALFRED HARVEY'S
Lorne Harvey Publications/Recollections,MS; 1 Aug 1995-2 Oct 1995
1 ND 52pgs, new costume and new origin by Mark Evanier and Murphy Anderson plus Lee Elias reprint; cover by the Brothers Hildebrandt

	$Good	$Fine	$N.Mint	£Good	£Fine	£N.Mint
	$0.70	$2.10	$3.50	£0.50	£1.50	£2.50

2 ND origin continues plus the origin of Ms. Fortune

	$Good	$Fine	$N.Mint	£Good	£Fine	£N.Mint
	$0.70	$2.10	$3.50	£0.50	£1.50	£2.50
Title Value:	$1.40	$4.20	$7.00	£1.00	£3.00	£5.00

BLACK CAT, FELICIA HARDY
Marvel Comics Group,MS; 1 Jul 1994-4 Oct 1994
1-2 Spiderman appears

	$Good	$Fine	$N.Mint	£Good	£Fine	£N.Mint
	$0.25	$0.75	$1.25	£0.15	£0.45	£0.75

3-4 Spiderman and Cardiac appear

	$Good	$Fine	$N.Mint	£Good	£Fine	£N.Mint
	$0.25	$0.75	$1.25	£0.15	£0.45	£0.75
Title Value:	$1.00	$3.00	$5.00	£0.60	£1.80	£3.00

BLACK CAT, THE ORIGINAL
Recollections; 1 Sep 1988-2 1988; Lorne-Harvey; 3 1990-11 1992
1 ND Lee Elias/Joe Kubert reprints begin

	$Good	$Fine	$N.Mint	£Good	£Fine	£N.Mint
	$0.30	$0.90	$1.50	£0.20	£0.60	£1.00

2-11 ND

	$Good	$Fine	$N.Mint	£Good	£Fine	£N.Mint
	$0.30	$0.90	$1.50	£0.20	£0.60	£1.00
Title Value:	$3.30	$9.90	$16.50	£2.20	£6.60	£11.00

BLACK COMMANDO: DARK DYNAMO
AC Comics; 1 Jan 1993
1 ND Thunder Agents tie-in; flash-back sequence by Wally Wood

	$Good	$Fine	$N.Mint	£Good	£Fine	£N.Mint
	$0.35	$1.05	$1.75	£0.25	£0.75	£1.25
Title Value:	$0.35	$1.05	$1.75	£0.25	£0.75	£1.25

BLACK CONDOR, THE
DC Comics; 1 Jun 1992-12 May 1993

	$Good	$Fine	$N.Mint	£Good	£Fine	£N.Mint
1-8	$0.25	$0.75	$1.25	£0.15	£0.45	£0.75

9-10 The Ray appears

	$Good	$Fine	$N.Mint	£Good	£Fine	£N.Mint
	$0.25	$0.75	$1.25	£0.15	£0.45	£0.75

11 origin

	$Good	$Fine	$N.Mint	£Good	£Fine	£N.Mint
	$0.25	$0.75	$1.25	£0.15	£0.45	£0.75

12 Batman appears

	$Good	$Fine	$N.Mint	£Good	£Fine	£N.Mint
	$0.25	$0.75	$1.25	£0.15	£0.45	£0.75
Title Value:	$3.00	$9.00	$15.00	£1.80	£5.40	£9.00

BLACK CROSS SPECIAL
Dark Horse,OS; 1 Jan 1988
1 ND Dark Horse Presents reprints

	$Good	$Fine	$N.Mint	£Good	£Fine	£N.Mint
	$0.90	$2.70	$4.50	£0.60	£1.80	£3.00
Title Value:	$0.90	$2.70	$4.50	£0.60	£1.80	£3.00

BLACK DIAMOND
Americomics, Film; 1 May 1983-5 Apr 1984
(see Colt Special)
1 ND Sybil Danning photos/features

	$Good	$Fine	$N.Mint	£Good	£Fine	£N.Mint
	$0.35	$1.05	$1.75	£0.25	£0.75	£1.25

2-4 ND Colt backups, Gulacy covers

	$Good	$Fine	$N.Mint	£Good	£Fine	£N.Mint
	$0.35	$1.05	$1.75	£0.25	£0.75	£1.25

5 ND Colt backup, Gulacy cover, Sybil Danning/"V" feature

	$Good	$Fine	$N.Mint	£Good	£Fine	£N.Mint
	$0.35	$1.05	$1.75	£0.25	£0.75	£1.25
Title Value:	$1.75	$5.25	$8.75	£1.25	£3.75	£6.25

BLACK DOMINION
Anubis Press; 1 Jul 1993
1 ND black and white

	$Good	$Fine	$N.Mint	£Good	£Fine	£N.Mint
	$0.35	$1.05	$1.75	£0.25	£0.75	£1.25
Title Value:	$0.35	$1.05	$1.75	£0.25	£0.75	£1.25

BLACK DRAGON, THE
Marvel Comics Group/Epic,MS; 1 May 1985-6 Oct 1985
1 ND scarce in the U.K. Claremont scripts, Bolton art begins

	$Good	$Fine	$N.Mint	£Good	£Fine	£N.Mint
	$0.60	$1.80	$3.00	£0.50	£1.50	£2.50
2-6 ND Bolton art	$0.30	$0.90	$1.50	£0.30	£0.90	£1.50
Title Value:	$2.10	$6.30	$10.50	£2.00	£6.00	£10.00

The Black Dragon (Sep 1994)
Trade paperback reprints mini-series
with new painted cover by John Bolton £2.00 £6.00 £10.00
Note: this edition published by Dark Horse Comics

BLACK ENCHANTRESS
Heroic Publishing; 1 Jan 1995-2 1995
1 ND origin told

	$Good	$Fine	$N.Mint	£Good	£Fine	£N.Mint
	$0.40	$1.20	$2.00	£0.25	£0.75	£1.25
2 ND	$0.40	$1.20	$2.00	£0.25	£0.75	£1.25
Title Value:	$0.80	$2.40	$4.00	£0.50	£1.50	£2.50

BLACK FLAG
Image; 1 Jun 1994
1 ND black and white

	$Good	$Fine	$N.Mint	£Good	£Fine	£N.Mint
	$0.40	$1.20	$2.00	£0.25	£0.75	£1.25
Title Value:	$0.40	$1.20	$2.00	£0.25	£0.75	£1.25

BLACK FLAG (2ND SERIES)
Maximum Comic Press; 0 Jul 1995; 1 Jan 1995-present
0 ND Dan Fraga script and part art

	$Good	$Fine	$N.Mint	£Good	£Fine	£N.Mint
	$0.45	$1.35	$2.25	£0.30	£0.90	£1.50

1 ND Dan Fraga script, Eric Stephenson art; gatefold cover

	$Good	$Fine	$N.Mint	£Good	£Fine	£N.Mint
	$0.45	$1.35	$2.25	£0.30	£0.90	£1.50
2 ND	$0.45	$1.35	$2.25	£0.30	£0.90	£1.50

2 Variant Edition, ND Black Flag solo on cover; Stephen Platt/Dan Fraga cover art

	$Good	$Fine	$N.Mint	£Good	£Fine	£N.Mint
	$0.60	$1.80	$3.00	£0.40	£1.20	£2.00
3-4 ND	$0.45	$1.35	$2.25	£0.30	£0.90	£1.50

4 Variant Edition, ND same as regular issue but with white background

	$Good	$Fine	$N.Mint	£Good	£Fine	£N.Mint
	$0.45	$1.35	$2.25	£0.30	£0.90	£1.50
5-6 ND	$0.45	$1.35	$2.25	£0.30	£0.90	£1.50
Title Value:	$4.20	$12.60	$21.00	£2.80	£8.40	£14.00

BLACK FLAG PREVIEW EDITION
Image,OS; 1 Jun 1994
1 ND previews series, black and white; 100,000 copies

	$Good	$Fine	$N.Mint	£Good	£Fine	£N.Mint
	$0.40	$1.20	$2.00	£0.25	£0.75	£1.25
Title Value:	$0.40	$1.20	$2.00	£0.25	£0.75	£1.25

BLACK FURY
Charlton; 1 May 1955-57 Mar/Apr 1966

	$Good	$Fine	$N.Mint	£Good	£Fine	£N.Mint
1	$5.25	$16.00	$32.00	£3.30	£10.00	£20.00
2	$2.50	$7.50	$15.00	£1.65	£5.00	£10.00
3-5	$1.50	$4.50	$9.00	£1.00	£3.00	£6.00
6-15	$1.15	$3.50	$7.00	£0.75	£2.25	£4.50

16-18 Steve Ditko art

	$Good	$Fine	$N.Mint	£Good	£Fine	£N.Mint
	$5.00	$15.00	$30.00	£3.30	£10.00	£20.00
19-20	$1.15	$3.50	$7.00	£0.75	£2.25	£4.50
21-30	$0.80	$2.50	$5.00	£0.55	£1.75	£3.50
31-57	$0.55	$1.75	$3.50	£0.40	£1.25	£2.50
Title Value:	$63.90	$196.25	$392.50	£43.15	£132.25	£264.50

Note: Limited Distribution in the U.K. after 1959.

BLACK GOLIATH
Marvel Comics Group; 1 Feb 1976-5 Nov 1976
(see Powerman #24)

	$Good	$Fine	$N.Mint	£Good	£Fine	£N.Mint
1	$0.45	$1.35	$2.25	£0.30	£0.90	£1.50
2-3	$0.30	$0.90	$1.50	£0.20	£0.60	£1.00

4 Black Goliath vs. Stiltman, Jack Kirby cover

	$Good	$Fine	$N.Mint	£Good	£Fine	£N.Mint
	$0.30	$0.90	$1.50	£0.20	£0.60	£1.00
5	$0.30	$0.90	$1.50	£0.20	£0.60	£1.00
Title Value:	$1.65	$4.95	$8.25	£1.10	£3.30	£5.50

Note: #2-5 Claremont script

BLACK HOLE
Kitchen Sink,OS; 1 Mar 1995
1 ND Charles Burns script and art

	$Good	$Fine	$N.Mint	£Good	£Fine	£N.Mint
	$0.80	$2.40	$4.00	£0.50	£1.50	£2.50
Title Value:	$0.80	$2.40	$4.00	£0.50	£1.50	£2.50

BLACK HOLE, THE
Whitman, Film; 1 Mar 1980-3 Jul 1980
1-2 adaptation of Walt Disney film, photo cover

	$Good	$Fine	$N.Mint	£Good	£Fine	£N.Mint
	$0.30	$0.90	$1.50	£0.20	£0.60	£1.00

3 titled "Beyond The Black Hole"; new adventures, photo cover

	$Good	$Fine	$N.Mint	£Good	£Fine	£N.Mint
	$0.30	$0.90	$1.50	£0.20	£0.60	£1.00
Title Value:	$0.90	$2.70	$4.50	£0.60	£1.80	£3.00

Note: Limited Distribution in the U.K.

BLACK HOOD
Red Circle; 1 Jan 1983-3 Oct 1983
1 ND Gray Morrow and Doug Wildey art, Alex Toth cover

	$Good	$Fine	$N.Mint	£Good	£Fine	£N.Mint
	$0.30	$0.90	$1.50	£0.20	£0.60	£1.00

2 ND Alex Toth art on The Fox back-up, Alex Toth cover

	$Good	$Fine	$N.Mint	£Good	£Fine	£N.Mint
	$0.30	$0.90	$1.50	£0.20	£0.60	£1.00

3 ND Gray Morrow art on The Fox back-up, Alex Toth cover

	$Good	$Fine	$N.Mint	£Good	£Fine	£N.Mint
	$0.30	$0.90	$1.50	£0.20	£0.60	£1.00
Title Value:	$0.90	$2.70	$4.50	£0.60	£1.80	£3.00

BLACK HOOD
DC Comics/Impact; 1 Dec 1991-12 Dec 1992

	$Good	$Fine	$N.Mint	£Good	£Fine	£N.Mint
1-12	$0.15	$0.45	$0.75	£0.10	£0.35	£0.60
Title Value:	$1.80	$5.40	$9.00	£1.20	£4.20	£7.20

BLACK HOOD ANNUAL
DC Comics/Impact; 1 Jun 1992
1 64pgs, Earthquest part 6 (see other Impact annuals), includes trading card

	$Good	$Fine	$N.Mint	£Good	£Fine	£N.Mint
	$0.30	$0.90	$1.50	£0.20	£0.60	£1.00
Title Value:	$0.30	$0.90	$1.50	£0.20	£0.60	£1.00

BLACK KISS
Vortex,MS; 1 Jun 1988-12 Jul 1989
(see Big Black Kiss)
1 Chaykin story/art begins, 2-colour cover

	$Good	$Fine	$N.Mint	£Good	£Fine	£N.Mint
	$1.20	$3.60	$6.00	£0.80	£2.40	£4.00
1 2nd printing	$0.60	$1.80	$3.00	£0.40	£1.20	£2.00
1 3rd printing	$0.45	$1.35	$2.25	£0.30	£0.90	£1.50
2	$0.90	$2.70	$4.50	£0.60	£1.80	£3.00
2 2nd printing	$0.60	$1.80	$3.00	£0.40	£1.20	£2.00
3	$0.75	$2.25	$3.75	£0.50	£1.50	£2.50
3 2nd printing	$0.40	$1.20	$2.00	£0.25	£0.75	£1.25
4	$0.65	$1.95	$3.25	£0.45	£1.35	£2.25
4 2nd printing	$0.40	$1.20	$2.00	£0.25	£0.75	£1.25

5 1st full-colour cover

	$Good	$Fine	$N.Mint	£Good	£Fine	£N.Mint
	$0.60	$1.80	$3.00	£0.40	£1.20	£2.00
6-12	$0.60	$1.80	$3.00	£0.40	£1.20	£2.00
Title Value:	$10.75	$32.25	$53.75	£7.15	£21.45	£35.75

Note: all Non-Distributed on the news-stands in the U.K. All pre-bagged. At the time, there were fears about the plastic being low grade/acidic so most were torn off (and also to enjoy the content!). Intact pre-bagged issues are very scarce

Thick Black Kiss (Sep 1993)
138pgs, softcover; collects 12 part series £1.20 £3.60 £6.00

BLACK KNIGHT
Marvel Comics Group,MS; 1 Jun 1990-4 Sep 1990
(see Avengers, Avengers Spotlight)

	$Good	$Fine	$N.Mint	£Good	£Fine	£N.Mint
1 ND	$0.30	$0.90	$1.50	£0.20	£0.60	£1.00

2 ND Captain Britain appears

VERY GENERAL PERCENTAGE CONVERSION CHART WHICH MAY BE USED TO CALCULATE LOW AND INBETWEEN GRADES:

	$Good	$Fine	$N.Mint	£Good	£Fine	£N.Mint
	$0.30	$0.90	$1.50	£0.20	£0.60	£1.00
3-4 ND Dr. Strange appears						
	$0.30	$0.90	$1.50	£0.20	£0.60	£1.00
Title Value:	$1.20	$3.60	$6.00	£0.80	£2.40	£4.00

BLACK KNIGHT
Super Comics; 11 1963
11 scarce, distributed in the U.K. All reprints

	$Good	$Fine	$N.Mint	£Good	£Fine	£N.Mint
	$2.90	$8.75	$17.50	£2.05	£6.25	£12.50
Title Value:	$2.90	$8.75	$17.50	£2.05	£6.25	£12.50

BLACK LIGHTNING
DC Comics; 1 Apr 1977-11 Sep/Oct 1978
(see DC Comics Presents, Detective, World's Finest)

	$Good	$Fine	$N.Mint	£Good	£Fine	£N.Mint
1 scarce in the U.K. Von Eeden art						
	$0.55	$1.65	$2.75	£0.35	£1.05	£1.75
2-3 Von Eeden art	$0.40	$1.20	$2.00	£0.25	£0.75	£1.25
4-5 Von Eeden art, Superman appears						
	$0.40	$1.20	$2.00	£0.25	£0.75	£1.25
6-10 Von Eeden art						
	$0.30	$0.90	$1.50	£0.20	£0.60	£1.00
11 44pgs, The Ray appears						
	$0.40	$1.20	$2.00	£0.25	£0.75	£1.25
Title Value:	$4.05	$12.15	$20.25	£2.60	£7.80	£13.00

BLACK LIGHTNING (2ND SERIES)
DC Comics; 1 Feb 1995-13 Feb 1996

	$Good	$Fine	$N.Mint	£Good	£Fine	£N.Mint
1 Tony Isabella script begins						
	$0.40	$1.20	$2.00	£0.25	£0.75	£1.25
2-4	$0.40	$1.20	$2.00	£0.25	£0.75	£1.25
5	$0.45	$1.35	$2.25	£0.30	£0.90	£1.50
6-8 Gangbuster guest-stars						
	$0.45	$1.35	$2.25	£0.30	£0.90	£1.50
9-11	$0.45	$1.35	$2.25	£0.30	£0.90	£1.50
12-13 Batman appears						
	$0.45	$1.35	$2.25	£0.30	£0.90	£1.50
Title Value:	$5.65	$16.95	$28.25	£3.70	£11.10	£18.50

BLACK MAGIC
Crestwood Publishing; Vol 7 #3 Jul/Aug 1960-Vol 8 #5 Nov/Dec 1961
(previous issues ND)

	$Good	$Fine	$N.Mint	£Good	£Fine	£N.Mint
Vol 7/ 3-6 distributed in the U.K.						
	$5.00	$15.00	$30.00	£3.30	£10.00	£20.00
Vol 8/ 1 distributed in the U.K.						
	$5.00	$15.00	$30.00	£3.30	£10.00	£20.00
Vol 8/ 2 Steve Ditko art; distributed in the U.K.						
	$5.25	$16.00	$32.00	£3.75	£11.00	£22.50
Vol 8/ 3-5 distributed in the U.K.						
	$4.55	$13.50	$27.50	£3.30	£10.00	£20.00
Title Value:	$43.90	$131.50	$264.50	£30.15	£91.00	£182.50

BLACK MAGIC
DC Comics; 1 Oct/Nov 1973-9 Apr/May 1975

	$Good	$Fine	$N.Mint	£Good	£Fine	£N.Mint
1 Simon & Jack Kirby pre-code horror reprints begin						
	$0.40	$1.20	$2.00	£0.25	£0.75	£1.25
2-9	$0.30	$0.90	$1.50	£0.20	£0.60	£1.00
Title Value:	$2.80	$8.40	$14.00	£1.85	£5.55	£9.25

BLACK MASK
DC Comics,MS; 1 Nov 1993-3 Jan 1994

	$Good	$Fine	$N.Mint	£Good	£Fine	£N.Mint
1-3 ND 48pgs, squarebound, Brian Augustyn and Jim Baikie						
	$0.75	$2.25	$3.75	£0.50	£1.50	£2.50
Title Value:	$2.25	$6.75	$11.25	£1.50	£4.50	£7.50

BLACK MIST: ANGUISH OF THE MIST GRAPHIC NOVEL
Caliber Press,OS; nn Apr 1995

	$Good	$Fine	$N.Mint	£Good	£Fine	£N.Mint
nn ND Negative Burn anthology spin-off						
	$2.50	$7.50	$12.50	£1.50	£4.50	£7.50
Title Value:	$2.50	$7.50	$12.50	£1.50	£4.50	£7.50

BLACK ORCHID
DC Comics,MS; 1 Nov 1988-3 Jan 1989
(see Adventure #428)

	$Good	$Fine	$N.Mint	£Good	£Fine	£N.Mint
1 ND Neil Gaiman script, Dave McKean painted art begins						
	$1.00	$3.00	$5.00	£0.60	£1.80	£3.00
2 ND Arkham Asylum						
	$1.00	$3.00	$5.00	£0.60	£1.80	£3.00
3 ND	$1.00	$3.00	$5.00	£0.60	£1.80	£3.00
Title Value:	$3.00	$9.00	$15.00	£1.80	£5.40	£9.00

Note: 48pg Dark Knight format, UV glossy coated, squarebound
Trade paperback (Aug 1991), 160pgs reprints mini-series
with new Dave McKean cover $2.50 £7.50 £12.50

BLACK ORCHID (2ND SERIES)
DC Comics/Vertigo; 1 Sep 1993-22 Jun 1995

	$Good	$Fine	$N.Mint	£Good	£Fine	£N.Mint
1 Dave McKean painted covers begin						
	$0.40	$1.20	$2.00	£0.25	£0.75	£1.25
1 Platinum edition ND						
	$3.00	$9.00	$15.00	£2.00	£6.00	£10.00
2-16	$0.40	$1.20	$2.00	£0.25	£0.75	£1.25
17-22 Twisted Season story						
	$0.40	$1.20	$2.00	£0.25	£0.75	£1.25
Title Value:	$11.80	$35.40	$59.00	£7.50	£22.50	£37.50

BLACK ORCHID ANNUAL
DC Comics; 1 Dec 1993

	$Good	$Fine	$N.Mint	£Good	£Fine	£N.Mint
1 ND 64pgs, Children's Crusade part 2, continued in Animal Man Annual #1						
	$0.80	$2.40	$4.00	£0.50	£1.50	£2.50
Title Value:	$0.80	$2.40	$4.00	£0.50	£1.50	£2.50

BLACK PANTHER, THE
Marvel Comics Group; 1 Jan 1977-15 May 1979
(see also Jungle Action)

	$Good	$Fine	$N.Mint	£Good	£Fine	£N.Mint
1 1st appearance King Solomon's frog (!), Jack Kirby art						
	$0.90	$2.70	$4.50	£0.50	£1.50	£2.50
2-3 ND Jack Kirby art						
	$0.70	$2.10	$3.50	£0.45	£1.35	£2.25
4-6 ND Jack Kirby art						
	$0.60	$1.80	$3.00	£0.40	£1.20	£2.00
7-12 Jack Kirby art						
	$0.45	$1.35	$2.25	£0.30	£0.90	£1.50
13 Bingham/Day art						
	$0.30	$0.90	$1.50	£0.20	£0.60	£1.00
14 Bingham/Day art, Avengers appear						
	$0.30	$0.90	$1.50	£0.20	£0.60	£1.00
15 scarce in the U.K. Bingham/Day art, Avengers appear						
	$0.30	$0.90	$1.50	£0.25	£0.75	£1.25
Title Value:	$7.70	$23.10	$38.50	£5.05	£15.15	£25.25

BLACK PANTHER, THE (LIMITED SERIES)
Marvel Comics Group,MS; 1 Jul 1988-4 Oct 1988

	$Good	$Fine	$N.Mint	£Good	£Fine	£N.Mint
1-4 ND Cowan art	$0.30	$0.90	$1.50	£0.20	£0.60	£1.00
Title Value:	$1.20	$3.60	$6.00	£0.80	£2.40	£4.00

BLACK PANTHER: PANTHER'S PREY
Marvel Comics Group,MS; 1 May 1991-4 Aug 1991

	$Good	$Fine	$N.Mint	£Good	£Fine	£N.Mint
1-4 ND 48pgs	$0.70	$2.10	$3.50	£0.45	£1.35	£2.25
Title Value:	$2.80	$8.40	$14.00	£1.80	£5.40	£9.00

Note: Bookshelf Format. Originally solicited for Oct 1990 but series delayed

BLACK PHANTOM
AC Comics; 1 1989-3 1990

	$Good	$Fine	$N.Mint	£Good	£Fine	£N.Mint
1-3 ND new colour stories by Bill Black plus black and white reprints featuring Black Phantom and Red Mask						
	$0.45	$1.35	$2.25	£0.30	£0.90	£1.50
Title Value:	$1.35	$4.05	$6.75	£0.90	£2.70	£4.50

BLACK RIDER
Atlas Comics; 8 Mar 1950-27 Mar 1955
(Western Winners #1-7)

	$Good	$Fine	$N.Mint	£Good	£Fine	£N.Mint
8 scarce in the U.K.						
	$30.00	$90.00	$240.00	£20.00	£60.00	£160.00
9 48pgs	$17.50	$52.50	$125.00	£11.00	£34.00	£80.00
10 48pgs, origin retold						
	$19.00	$57.50	$135.00	£12.50	£39.00	£90.00
11-14 48pgs	$12.00	$36.00	$85.00	£7.75	£23.50	£55.00
15-18	$10.00	$30.00	$70.00	£6.25	£19.00	£45.00
19-20 Two Gun Kid story						
	$10.00	$30.00	$70.00	£6.25	£19.00	£45.00
21-22	$9.25	$28.00	$65.00	£6.00	£18.00	£42.50
23 Two Gun Kid story						
	$9.25	$28.00	$65.00	£6.00	£18.00	£42.50
24-25	$9.25	$28.00	$65.00	£6.00	£18.00	£42.50
26-27 Kid Colt story						
	$9.25	$28.00	$65.00	£6.00	£18.00	£42.50
Title Value:	$239.25	$720.00	$1715.00	£154.00	£467.00	£1117.50

Note: all Non-Distributed on the news-stands in the U.K.

BLACK SCORPION
Special Studio; 1 Apr 1991

	$Good	$Fine	$N.Mint	£Good	£Fine	£N.Mint
1 ND black and white	$0.45	$1.35	$2.25	£0.30	£0.90	£1.50
Title Value:	$0.45	$1.35	$2.25	£0.30	£0.90	£1.50

BLACK SEPTEMBER: INFINITY
Marvel Comics Group,OS; nn Nov 1995

	$Good	$Fine	$N.Mint	£Good	£Fine	£N.Mint
nn ND Dan Danko and Roland Mann script, Steve Butler and M.C. Wyman art; follow on from Ultraforce/Avengers and how the Marvel Universe and Malibu Ultraverse will merge						
	$0.60	$1.80	$3.00	£0.40	£1.20	£2.00
Title Value:	$0.60	$1.80	$3.00	£0.40	£1.20	£2.00

BLACK TERROR
Eclipse,MS; 1 Oct 1989-3 1990

	$Good	$Fine	$N.Mint	£Good	£Fine	£N.Mint
1-3 ND	$0.80	$2.40	$4.00	£0.50	£1.50	£2.50
Title Value:	$2.40	$7.20	$12.00	£1.50	£4.50	£7.50

Note: 48pgs, squarebound, painted art by Daniel Brereton
Graphic Album Softcover (Dec 1991),
reprints 3 issue mini-series £1.90 £5.70 £9.50
Graphic Album Hardcover Deluxe (Dec 1991)
reprints mini-series, signed and numbered £5.00 £15.00 £25.00

BLACK THUNDER
Breeze Comics; 1 1991

	$Good	$Fine	$N.Mint	£Good	£Fine	£N.Mint
1 ND black and white	$0.30	$0.90	$1.50	£0.20	£0.60	£1.00
Title Value:	$0.30	$0.90	$1.50	£0.20	£0.60	£1.00

BLACK ZEPPELIN, GENE DAY'S
Renegade; 1 Apr 1985-5 1986

	$Good	$Fine	$N.Mint	£Good	£Fine	£N.Mint
1 ND scarce in the U.K. Gene/Dan Day art						
	$0.45	$1.35	$2.25	£0.30	£0.90	£1.50
2-5 ND Gene/Dan Day art						
	$0.30	$0.90	$1.50	£0.20	£0.60	£1.00
Title Value:	$1.65	$4.95	$8.25	£1.10	£3.30	£5.50

BLACK-BOW
Artline Studios; 1 Mar 1991

	$Good	$Fine	$N.Mint	£Good	£Fine	£N.Mint
1 ND black and white						
	$0.30	$0.90	$1.50	£0.20	£0.60	£1.00
Title Value:	$0.30	$0.90	$1.50	£0.20	£0.60	£1.00

BLACKBALL COMICS
Blackball Comics; 1 Mar 1994-present ?

	$Good	$Fine	$N.Mint	£Good	£Fine	£N.Mint
1-2 ND 48pgs, Kev O'Neill and Keith Giffen art						
	$0.35	$1.05	$1.75	£0.25	£0.75	£1.25
3 ND 48pgs, Kev O'Neill and Keith Giffen art; Mr. Monster vs. Trencher by Keith Giffen and Michael T. Gilbert						
	$0.35	$1.05	$1.75	£0.25	£0.75	£1.25

MINT = 100% / NEAR MINT (inc. +/-) = 90–99% / VERY FINE (inc. +/-) = 75–89% / FINE (inc. +/-) = 55–74%
VERY GOOD (inc. +/-) = 35–54% / GOOD (inc. +/-) = 15–34% / FAIR = 5–14% / POOR = 1–4%

241

	$Good	$Fine	$N.Mint	£Good	£Fine	£N.Mint

4 ND 48pgs, Kev O'Neill and Keith Giffen art; Mr. Monster vs. Trencher by Keith Giffen and Michael T. Gilbert; cover by Simon Bisley

| | $0.35 | $1.05 | $1.75 | £0.25 | £0.75 | £1.25 |
| Title Value: | $1.40 | $4.20 | $7.00 | £1.00 | £3.00 | £5.00 |

Note: it is unclear whether #4 came out

BLACKBALL COMICS SPECIAL
Blackball Comics,OS; 1 Aug 1994

1 ND Mark Wheatley, Bill Wray and Keith Giffen work featured

| | $0.45 | $1.35 | $2.25 | £0.30 | £0.90 | £1.50 |
| Title Value: | $0.45 | $1.35 | $2.25 | £0.30 | £0.90 | £1.50 |

BLACKHAWK
National Periodical Publications/DC Comics; 108 Jan 1957-243 Oct/Nov 1968; 244 Jan/Feb 1976-250 Jan/Feb 1977; 251 Oct 1982-273 Nov 1984
(see also Brave and the Bold #167)
(previously published as Uncle Sam #1-8. #9-107 published by Quality Comics)

108 1st DC issue

| | $47.00 | $140.00 | $375.00 | £31.00 | £92.50 | £250.00 |
| 109-117 | $17.50 | $52.50 | $125.00 | £10.50 | £32.00 | £75.00 |

118 Frazetta reprint

	$18.50	$55.00	$130.00	£11.00	£34.00	£80.00
119-130	$10.50	$32.00	$75.00	£7.00	£21.00	£50.00
131-132	$7.75	$23.50	$55.00	£6.25	£19.00	£45.00

133 1st appearance Lady Blackhawk

| | $7.75 | $23.50 | $55.00 | £6.25 | £19.00 | £45.00 |

1st official distribution in the U.K.

| 134-138 | $7.75 | $23.50 | $55.00 | £5.25 | £16.00 | £37.50 |

139 Lady Blackhawk returns

	$7.75	$23.50	$55.00	£5.25	£16.00	£37.50
140	$7.75	$23.50	$55.00	£5.25	£16.00	£37.50
141-142	$6.25	$19.00	$45.00	£4.25	£12.50	£30.00

143 dinosaur cover

| | $6.25 | $19.00 | $45.00 | £4.25 | £12.50 | £30.00 |
| 144-150 | $6.25 | $19.00 | $45.00 | £4.25 | £12.50 | £30.00 |

151 Lady Blackhawk with super powers (like a Supergirl-in-uniform!)

	$6.25	$19.00	$45.00	£4.25	£12.50	£30.00
152-163	$6.25	$19.00	$45.00	£4.25	£12.50	£30.00
164 origin retold	$6.25	$19.00	$45.00	£4.25	£12.50	£30.00
165	$6.25	$19.00	$45.00	£4.25	£12.50	£30.00

166 last 10 cents issue

	$6.25	$19.00	$45.00	£4.25	£12.50	£30.00
167-180	$2.50	$7.50	$17.50	£1.75	£5.25	£12.50
181-196	$1.75	$5.25	$12.50	£1.10	£3.40	£8.00

197 "new look" begins with new uniforms and change of direction for title

| | $1.75 | $5.25 | $12.50 | £1.10 | £3.40 | £8.00 |

198 origins of these "new" Blackhawks retold

| | $1.75 | $5.25 | $12.50 | £1.10 | £3.40 | £8.00 |
| 199 | $1.75 | $5.25 | $12.50 | £1.10 | £3.40 | £8.00 |

200 scarce in the U.K.

| | $1.75 | $5.25 | $12.50 | £1.20 | £3.60 | £8.50 |
| 201-202 | $1.40 | $4.25 | $10.00 | £0.70 | £2.10 | £5.00 |

203 origin Chop-Chop

	$1.40	$4.25	$10.00	£0.70	£2.10	£5.00
204-210	$1.40	$4.25	$10.00	£0.70	£2.10	£5.00
211-227	$1.00	$3.00	$6.00	£0.55	£1.75	£3.50

228 Superman, Batman, Green Lantern, Flash cameos

| | $1.00 | $3.00 | $6.00 | £0.55 | £1.75 | £3.50 |
| 229 | $1.00 | $3.00 | $6.00 | £0.55 | £1.75 | £3.50 |

230 Blackhawks become super-heroes; The Leaper, The Golden Centurion, Dr. Hands, The Listener, M'Sieu Machine, The Weapons Master

| | $1.00 | $3.00 | $6.00 | £0.55 | £1.75 | £3.50 |
| 231-241 | $0.80 | $2.50 | $5.00 | £0.50 | £1.50 | £3.00 |

242 original costumes return

	$0.80	$2.50	$5.00	£0.50	£1.50	£3.00
243	$0.80	$2.50	$5.00	£0.50	£1.50	£3.00
244-249	$0.45	$1.35	$2.25	£0.30	£0.90	£1.50

250 Chuck dies

	$0.45	$1.35	$2.25	£0.30	£0.90	£1.50
251 origin retold	$0.30	$0.90	$1.50	£0.20	£0.60	£1.00
252-256	$0.30	$0.90	$1.50	£0.20	£0.60	£1.00

257 Chaykin cover

| | $0.30 | $0.90 | $1.50 | £0.20 | £0.60 | £1.00 |

258 Blackhawk Island destroyed, Chaykin "Iwo Jima" cover

| | $0.30 | $0.90 | $1.50 | £0.20 | £0.60 | £1.00 |

259-260 Chaykin cover

| | $0.30 | $0.90 | $1.50 | £0.20 | £0.60 | £1.00 |
| 261 | $0.30 | $0.90 | $1.50 | £0.20 | £0.60 | £1.00 |

262 Chaykin cover

	$0.30	$0.90	$1.50	£0.20	£0.60	£1.00
263-273	$0.30	$0.90	$1.50	£0.20	£0.60	£1.00
Title Value:	$713.45	$2155.65	$5080.25	£464.30	£1397.80	£3310.50

BLACKHAWK (2ND SERIES)
DC Comics; 1 Apr 1989-16 Aug 1990

1-6	$0.25	$0.75	$1.25	£0.15	£0.45	£0.75
7 DS	$0.30	$0.90	$1.50	£0.20	£0.60	£1.00
8-16	$0.25	$0.75	$1.25	£0.15	£0.45	£0.75
Title Value:	$4.05	$12.15	$20.25	£2.45	£7.35	£12.25

Note: Mature Readers, New Format

BLACKHAWK (LIMITED SERIES)
DC Comics,MS; 1 Mar 1988-3 May 1988

1-3 ND 48pgs, Chaykin art

| | $0.60 | $1.80 | $3.00 | £0.40 | £1.20 | £2.00 |
| Title Value: | $1.80 | $5.40 | $9.00 | £1.20 | £3.60 | £6.00 |

Note: Prestige Format

BLACKHAWK ANNUAL
DC Comics; 1 Jun 1989

| 1 | $0.40 | $1.20 | $2.00 | £0.30 | £0.90 | £1.50 |
| Title Value: | $0.40 | $1.20 | $2.00 | £0.30 | £0.90 | £1.50 |

Note: Mature Readers, New Format

BLACKHAWK SPECIAL
DC Comics,OS; 1 Dec 1992

| 1 64pgs | $0.60 | $1.80 | $3.00 | £0.40 | £1.20 | £2.00 |
| Title Value: | $0.60 | $1.80 | $3.00 | £0.40 | £1.20 | £2.00 |

BLACKMASK
Eastern; 1 1988-6 1990

1-6 ND 48pgs, original Korean art

| | $0.30 | $0.90 | $1.50 | £0.20 | £0.60 | £1.00 |
| Title Value: | $1.80 | $5.40 | $9.00 | £1.20 | £3.60 | £6.00 |

BLACKMOON
US Comics; 1 1985-2 1986

1-2 ND black and white

| | $0.15 | $0.45 | $0.75 | £0.10 | £0.35 | £0.60 |
| Title Value: | $0.30 | $0.90 | $1.50 | £0.20 | £0.70 | £1.20 |

BLACKTHORNE 3-IN-1
Blackthorne; 1 Dec 1986-2 Feb 1987

1-2 ND Axis & Pandor, Starlight Squad, Merlinrealm

| | $0.30 | $0.90 | $1.50 | £0.20 | £0.60 | £1.00 |
| Title Value: | $0.60 | $1.80 | $3.00 | £0.40 | £1.20 | £2.00 |

BLACKWATCH
Heroic Comics; 1 Sep 1993

1 ND Daerick Gross script/art begins

| | $0.60 | $1.80 | $3.00 | £0.40 | £1.20 | £2.00 |
| Title Value: | $0.60 | $1.80 | $3.00 | £0.40 | £1.20 | £2.00 |

BLACKWULF
Marvel Comics Group; 1 Jun 1994-10 Mar 1995

1 Angel Medina pencils begin, foil embossed cover

| | $0.30 | $0.90 | $1.50 | £0.20 | £0.60 | £1.00 |
| 2-3 | $0.30 | $0.90 | $1.50 | £0.20 | £0.60 | £1.00 |

4 Giant Man guest-stars

| | $0.30 | $0.90 | $1.50 | £0.20 | £0.60 | £1.00 |
| 5-8 | $0.30 | $0.90 | $1.50 | £0.20 | £0.60 | £1.00 |

9 Daredevil guest-stars

	$0.30	$0.90	$1.50	£0.20	£0.60	£1.00
10	$0.30	$0.90	$1.50	£0.20	£0.60	£1.00
Title Value:	$3.00	$9.00	$15.00	£2.00	£6.00	£10.00

BLADE OF SHURIKEN
Eternity; 1 1987-8 1988

| 1-8 ND | $0.35 | $1.05 | $1.75 | £0.25 | £0.75 | £1.25 |
| Title Value: | $2.80 | $8.40 | $14.00 | £2.00 | £6.00 | £10.00 |

BLADE: THE VAMPIRE HUNTER
Marvel Comics Group; 1 Jul 1994-11 May 1995

1 foil stamped cover

| | $0.50 | $1.50 | $2.50 | £0.30 | £0.90 | £1.50 |

2-3 Blade vs. Dracula

| | $0.40 | $1.20 | $2.00 | £0.25 | £0.75 | £1.25 |
| 4-9 | $0.40 | $1.20 | $2.00 | £0.25 | £0.75 | £1.25 |

10-11 Dracula appears

| | $0.40 | $1.20 | $2.00 | £0.25 | £0.75 | £1.25 |
| Title Value: | $4.50 | $13.50 | $22.50 | £2.80 | £8.40 | £14.00 |

BLADERUNNER
Marvel Comics Group,MS Film; 1 Oct 1982-2 Nov 1982

1-2 ND Al Williamson art

| | $0.25 | $0.75 | $1.25 | £0.15 | £0.45 | £0.75 |
| Title Value: | $0.50 | $1.50 | $2.50 | £0.30 | £0.90 | £1.50 |

Note: movie adaptation, reprinted from Marvel Super Special 22, Williamson art.

BLANCHE GOES TO HOLLYWOOD
Dark Horse,OS; 1 Oct 1993

1 ND Rick Geary script and art

| | $0.35 | $1.05 | $1.75 | £0.25 | £0.75 | £1.25 |
| Title Value: | $0.35 | $1.05 | $1.75 | £0.25 | £0.75 | £1.25 |

BLANDMAN
Eclipse,OS; 1 Jul 1992

1 ND parody of Sandman, black and white

| | $0.45 | $1.35 | $2.25 | £0.30 | £0.90 | £1.50 |
| Title Value: | $0.45 | $1.35 | $2.25 | £0.30 | £0.90 | £1.50 |

BLAST-OFF
Harvey; 1 Oct 1965
(Three Rocketeers)

1 ND rare in the U.K. Jack Kirby, Williamson, Crandall art

| | $3.75 | $11.00 | $22.50 | £2.50 | £7.50 | £15.00 |
| Title Value: | $3.75 | $11.00 | $22.50 | £2.50 | £7.50 | £15.00 |

BLASTERS SPECIAL
DC Comics,OS; 1 May 1989

| 1 48pgs | $0.25 | $0.75 | $1.25 | £0.15 | £0.45 | £0.75 |
| Title Value: | $0.25 | $0.75 | $1.25 | £0.15 | £0.45 | £0.75 |

Note: Invasion spin-off

BLAZE
Marvel Comics Group,MS; 1 Dec 1993-4 Mar 1994

1 John Blaze (the former Ghost Rider) stars

	$0.40	$1.20	$2.00	£0.25	£0.75	£1.25
2-4	$0.40	$1.20	$2.00	£0.25	£0.75	£1.25
Title Value:	$1.60	$4.80	$8.00	£1.00	£3.00	£5.00

BLAZE (2ND SERIES)
Marvel Comics Group; 1 Aug 1994-12 Jul 1995

1 foil stamped cover

| | $0.60 | $1.80 | $3.00 | £0.30 | £0.90 | £1.50 |

	$Good	$Fine	$N.Mint	£Good	£Fine	£N.Mint
2	$0.40	$1.20	$2.00	£0.25	£0.75	£1.25
3 X-Force appear	$0.40	$1.20	$2.00	£0.25	£0.75	£1.25
4	$0.40	$1.20	$2.00	£0.25	£0.75	£1.25
5-6 Warpath of X-Force appears						
	$0.40	$1.20	$2.00	£0.25	£0.75	£1.25
7-10	$0.40	$1.20	$2.00	£0.25	£0.75	£1.25
11 Punisher appears						
	$0.40	$1.20	$2.00	£0.25	£0.75	£1.25
12	$0.40	$1.20	$2.00	£0.25	£0.75	£1.25
Title Value:	$5.00	$15.00	$25.00	£3.05	£9.15	£15.25

BLAZING BATTLE TALES (FEATURING SGT. HAWK)
Atlas; 1 Jul 1975
1 Frank Thorne cover; distributed in the U.K.

	$Good	$Fine	$N.Mint	£Good	£Fine	£N.Mint
	$0.20	$0.60	$1.00	£0.10	£0.35	£0.60
Title Value:	$0.20	$0.60	$1.00	£0.10	£0.35	£0.60

BLAZING COMBAT
Warren,Magazine; 1 Oct 1965-4 Jul 1966
1 scarce, distributed in the U.K.

	$Good	$Fine	$N.Mint	£Good	£Fine	£N.Mint
	$12.50	$38.00	$75.00	£8.25	£25.00	£50.00
2 distributed in the U.K.						
	$4.50	$13.50	$22.50	£3.00	£9.00	£15.00
3-4 not distributed in the U.K.						
	$4.00	$12.00	$20.00	£2.50	£7.50	£12.50
Title Value:	$25.00	$75.50	$137.50	£16.25	£49.00	£90.00

Note: all have Crandall, Wood, Williamson art; Frazetta covers.

BLAZING COMBAT WW I & II
Apple Comics,MS; 1 Oct 1993-2 Nov 1993
1-2 ND Wally Wood and Alex Toth reprints

	$Good	$Fine	$N.Mint	£Good	£Fine	£N.Mint
	$0.80	$2.40	$4.00	£0.50	£1.50	£2.50
Title Value:	$1.60	$4.80	$8.00	£1.00	£3.00	£5.00

BLIP AND THE C.C.A.D.S.
Amazing Comics; 1 1987

	$Good	$Fine	$N.Mint	£Good	£Fine	£N.Mint
1 ND	$0.25	$0.75	$1.25	£0.10	£0.35	£0.60
Title Value:	$0.25	$0.75	$1.25	£0.10	£0.35	£0.60

BLITZ
Night Wynd,MS; 1 May 1992-4 Aug 1992
1-4 ND Barry Blair script and art; black and white

	$Good	$Fine	$N.Mint	£Good	£Fine	£N.Mint
	$0.45	$1.35	$2.25	£0.30	£0.90	£1.50
Title Value:	$1.80	$5.40	$9.00	£1.20	£3.60	£6.00

BLITZKRIEG
DC Comics; 1 Jan/Feb 1976-5 Sep/Oct 1976

	$Good	$Fine	$N.Mint	£Good	£Fine	£N.Mint
1-5	$0.25	$0.75	$1.25	£0.15	£0.45	£0.75
Title Value:	$1.25	$3.75	$6.25	£0.75	£2.25	£3.75

FEATURES
WWII stories as seen through the enemy's eyes.

BLONDIE, CHIC YOUNG'S
King Comics; 164 Aug 1966-175 Dec 1967; Charlton; 177 Feb 1969-222 Nov 1976

	$Good	$Fine	$N.Mint	£Good	£Fine	£N.Mint
164-167	$2.00	$6.00	$10.00	£1.30	£3.90	£6.50
168-175	$1.00	$3.00	$5.00	£0.65	£1.95	£3.25
177-200	$0.80	$2.40	$4.00	£0.50	£1.50	£2.50
201-222	$0.60	$1.80	$3.00	£0.40	£1.20	£2.00
Title Value:	$48.40	$145.20	$242.00	£31.20	£93.60	£156.00

Note: all Limited Distribution in the U.K.

BLOOD & ROSES ADVENTURES
Knight Press; 1 Apr 1995-4 1995
1 ND Bob Hickey script, picks up storyline from Sky Comics series; black and white

	$Good	$Fine	$N.Mint	£Good	£Fine	£N.Mint
	$0.60	$1.80	$3.00	£0.40	£1.20	£2.00
2 ND black and white						
	$0.60	$1.80	$3.00	£0.40	£1.20	£2.00
3-4 ND	$0.60	$1.80	$3.00	£0.40	£1.20	£2.00
Title Value:	$2.40	$7.20	$12.00	£1.60	£4.80	£8.00

BLOOD & ROSES: SEARCH FOR THE TIME STONE
Sky Comics; 0 Jul 1994; 1 Feb 1994; 2 Nov 1994
0 ND Leif Jones script and art

	$Good	$Fine	$N.Mint	£Good	£Fine	£N.Mint
	$0.40	$1.20	$2.00	£0.25	£0.75	£1.25

1 ND Bob Hickey script, Gene Gonzales art; painted cover by Daerick Gross

	$Good	$Fine	$N.Mint	£Good	£Fine	£N.Mint
	$0.40	$1.20	$2.00	£0.25	£0.75	£1.25
2 ND	$0.40	$1.20	$2.00	£0.25	£0.75	£1.25
Title Value:	$1.20	$3.60	$6.00	£0.75	£2.25	£3.75
Blood & Roses (Feb 1995)						
Trade paperback reprints mini-series plus new pin-ups				£1.70	£5.10	£8.50

Note: Trade paperback published by Knight Press

BLOOD & SHADOWS
DC Comics/Vertigo,MS; 1 Mar 1996-present
1 ND 48pgs, Joe R. Lansdale script, Mark Nelson art

	$Good	$Fine	$N.Mint	£Good	£Fine	£N.Mint
	$1.20	$3.60	$6.00	£0.80	£2.40	£4.00
Title Value:	$1.20	$3.60	$6.00	£0.80	£2.40	£4.00

BLOOD 'N GUTS
Aircel,MS; 1 Nov 1990-3 Jan 1991
1-3 ND Barry Blair script and art; black and white

	$Good	$Fine	$N.Mint	£Good	£Fine	£N.Mint
	$0.40	$1.20	$2.00	£0.25	£0.75	£1.25
Title Value:	$1.20	$3.60	$6.00	£0.75	£2.25	£3.75

BLOOD FEAST
Eternity,OS; 1 Feb 1991
1 ND film adaptation, graphic photo cover

	$Good	$Fine	$N.Mint	£Good	£Fine	£N.Mint
	$0.40	$1.20	$2.00	£0.25	£0.75	£1.25
Title Value:	$0.40	$1.20	$2.00	£0.25	£0.75	£1.25

BLOOD GOTHIC
Fantaco,MS; 1 Feb 1995-2 Mar 1995
1-2 ND Dave Stephenson script and art; black and white

	$Good	$Fine	$N.Mint	£Good	£Fine	£N.Mint
	$0.80	$2.40	$4.00	£0.55	£1.65	£2.75
Title Value:	$1.60	$4.80	$8.00	£1.10	£3.30	£5.50

BLOOD IS THE HARVEST
Eclipse/FX Comix,MS; 1 Jul 1992-4 Oct 1992
1 ND based on film; bound-in FX scratchcard; black and white begins

	$Good	$Fine	$N.Mint	£Good	£Fine	£N.Mint
	$0.35	$1.05	$1.75	£0.25	£0.75	£1.25
2-4 ND based on film						
	$0.35	$1.05	$1.75	£0.25	£0.75	£1.25
Title Value:	$1.40	$4.20	$7.00	£1.00	£3.00	£5.00

BLOOD JUNKIES ON CAPITOL HILL
Eternity,MS; 1 Aug 1992-2 Nov 1992
1-2 ND black and white

	$Good	$Fine	$N.Mint	£Good	£Fine	£N.Mint
	$0.30	$0.90	$1.50	£0.20	£0.60	£1.00
Title Value:	$0.60	$1.80	$3.00	£0.40	£1.20	£2.00

BLOOD LINES
Aircel/Vortex; 1 Jun 1987-7 Mar 1988

	$Good	$Fine	$N.Mint	£Good	£Fine	£N.Mint
1-2 ND	$0.35	$1.05	$1.75	£0.25	£0.75	£1.25
3 ND 1st Vortex issue						
	$0.35	$1.05	$1.75	£0.25	£0.75	£1.25
4-7 ND	$0.35	$1.05	$1.75	£0.25	£0.75	£1.25
Title Value:	$2.45	$7.35	$12.25	£1.75	£5.25	£8.75

BLOOD OF DRACULA
Apple Comics; 1 Nov 1987-18 1990?

	$Good	$Fine	$N.Mint	£Good	£Fine	£N.Mint
1-14 ND	$0.30	$0.90	$1.50	£0.20	£0.60	£1.00
15 ND flexidisc	$0.30	$0.90	$1.50	£0.20	£0.60	£1.00
16-18 ND	$0.30	$0.90	$1.50	£0.20	£0.60	£1.00
Title Value:	$5.40	$16.20	$27.00	£3.60	£10.80	£18.00

BLOOD OF THE APES, THE
Adventure,MS; 1 Jan 1992-4 Apr 1992

	$Good	$Fine	$N.Mint	£Good	£Fine	£N.Mint
1-4 ND	$0.35	$1.05	$1.75	£0.25	£0.75	£1.25
Title Value:	$1.40	$4.20	$7.00	£1.00	£3.00	£5.00

Blood Sword #1

Blue Beetle (Charlton) #1

Blue Beetle (DC) #1

BLOOD OF THE INNOCENT
Warp,MS; 1-4 Jul 1986

	$Good	$Fine	$N.Mint	£Good	£Fine	£N.Mint
1-4 ND	$0.35	$1.05	$1.75	£0.25	£0.75	£1.25
Title Value:	$1.40	$4.20	$7.00	£1.00	£3.00	£5.00

BLOOD PACK
DC Comics,MS; 1 Mar 1995-4 Jun 1995

	$Good	$Fine	$N.Mint	£Good	£Fine	£N.Mint
1 Sparx, Geist, Nightblade, Razorsharp and Loria begin as a team	$0.30	$0.90	$1.50	£0.20	£0.60	£1.00
2 Superboy guest-stars	$0.30	$0.90	$1.50	£0.20	£0.60	£1.00
3-4	$0.30	$0.90	$1.50	£0.20	£0.60	£1.00
Title Value:	$1.20	$3.60	$6.00	£0.80	£2.40	£4.00

BLOOD POOL
Image,MS; 1 Aug 1995-4 Nov 1995

	$Good	$Fine	$N.Mint	£Good	£Fine	£N.Mint
1-4 ND Jo Duffy script, Pat Lee art	$0.50	$1.50	$2.50	£0.30	£0.90	£1.50
Title Value:	$2.00	$6.00	$10.00	£1.20	£3.60	£6.00

BLOOD SWORD
Jademan; 1 Aug 1988-56 Mar 1993

	$Good	$Fine	$N.Mint	£Good	£Fine	£N.Mint
1 ND	$0.40	$1.20	$2.00	£0.50	£1.50	£2.50
2-3 ND	$0.30	$0.90	$1.50	£0.40	£1.20	£2.00
4-10 ND	$0.30	$0.90	$1.50	£0.30	£0.90	£1.50
11-20 ND	$0.30	$0.90	$1.50	£0.25	£0.75	£1.25
21-40 ND	$0.30	$0.90	$1.50	£0.20	£0.60	£1.00
41-56 ND	$0.25	$0.75	$1.25	£0.15	£0.45	£0.75
Title Value:	$16.10	$48.30	$80.50	£12.30	£36.90	£61.50
Collectors Album 1,2 scarce in the U.K.				£1.20	£3.60	£6.00

BLOOD SWORD DYNASTY
Jademan; 1 1989-43 Mar 1993

	$Good	$Fine	$N.Mint	£Good	£Fine	£N.Mint
1 ND	$0.50	$1.50	$2.50	£0.50	£1.50	£2.50
2-5 ND	$0.30	$0.90	$1.50	£0.40	£1.20	£2.00
6-10 ND	$0.30	$0.90	$1.50	£0.30	£0.90	£1.50
11-20 ND	$0.30	$0.90	$1.50	£0.25	£0.75	£1.25
21-30 ND	$0.30	$0.90	$1.50	£0.20	£0.60	£1.00
31-43 ND	$0.25	$0.75	$1.25	£0.15	£0.45	£0.75
Title Value:	$12.45	$37.35	$62.25	£10.05	£30.15	£50.25

Note: 36pgs, Japanese material

BLOOD SYNDICATE
DC Comics/Milestone; 1 Apr 1993-35 Feb 1996

	$Good	$Fine	$N.Mint	£Good	£Fine	£N.Mint
1	$0.40	$1.20	$2.00	£0.25	£0.75	£1.25
1 ND Direct Market Edition - pre-bagged with poster, profile, trading card and jig-saw puzzle pieces	$0.60	$1.80	$3.00	£0.40	£1.20	£2.00
2-9	$0.30	$0.90	$1.50	£0.20	£0.60	£1.00
10 48pgs, spot varnished cover by Walt Simonson	$0.45	$1.35	$2.25	£0.30	£0.90	£1.50
11-14	$0.30	$0.90	$1.50	£0.20	£0.60	£1.00
15 John Byrne cover	$0.30	$0.90	$1.50	£0.20	£0.60	£1.00
16 Worlds Collide X-over, continued in Worlds Collide #1	$0.30	$0.90	$1.50	£0.20	£0.60	£1.00
17 Worlds Collide X-over, continued in Static #14	$0.30	$0.90	$1.50	£0.20	£0.60	£1.00
18-24	$0.30	$0.90	$1.50	£0.20	£0.60	£1.00
25 48pgs	$0.45	$1.35	$2.25	£0.30	£0.90	£1.50
26-28	$0.40	$1.20	$2.00	£0.25	£0.75	£1.25
29 special 99 cents issue	$0.20	$0.60	$1.00	£0.10	£0.35	£0.60
30-31	$0.40	$1.20	$2.00	£0.25	£0.75	£1.25
32 cover by Howard Chaykin	$0.40	$1.20	$2.00	£0.25	£0.75	£1.25
33 special price of 99 cents	$0.20	$0.60	$1.00	£0.10	£0.35	£0.60
34	$0.45	$1.35	$2.25	£0.30	£0.90	£1.50
35	$0.70	$2.10	$3.50	£0.50	£1.50	£2.50
Title Value:	$12.45	$37.35	$62.25	£8.15	£24.55	£40.95

BLOOD WING
Eternity; 1 Jan 1988-5 1988

	$Good	$Fine	$N.Mint	£Good	£Fine	£N.Mint
1-5 ND	$0.40	$1.20	$2.00	£0.25	£0.75	£1.25
Title Value:	$2.00	$6.00	$10.00	£1.25	£3.75	£6.25

BLOOD: A TALE
Marvel Comics Group/Epic,MS; 1 Feb 1988-4 May 1988

	$Good	$Fine	$N.Mint	£Good	£Fine	£N.Mint
1 ND scarce in the U.K. Kent Williams art	$1.05	$3.15	$5.25	£0.70	£2.10	£3.50
2-4 ND Williams art	$0.60	$1.80	$3.00	£0.40	£1.20	£2.00
Title Value:	$2.85	$8.55	$14.25	£1.90	£5.70	£9.50

Note: Bookshelf Format, Mature Readers;

	$Good	$Fine	$N.Mint	£Good	£Fine	£N.Mint
Trade paperback (1989). Reprints #1-4				£1.80	£5.40	£9.00
(2nd print Dec 1990)				£1.75	£5.25	£8.75

BLOODBATH
DC Comics,MS; 1 Early Dec 1993-2 Late Dec 1993

	$Good	$Fine	$N.Mint	£Good	£Fine	£N.Mint
1-2 64pgs, conclusion to the Bloodlines story, Superman appears	$0.45	$1.35	$2.25	£0.30	£0.90	£1.50
Title Value:	$0.90	$2.70	$4.50	£0.60	£1.80	£3.00

BLOODBROTHERS
Eternity; 1 Oct 1988-4 Jan 1989

	$Good	$Fine	$N.Mint	£Good	£Fine	£N.Mint
1-4 ND	$0.40	$1.20	$2.00	£0.25	£0.75	£1.25
Title Value:	$1.60	$4.80	$8.00	£1.00	£3.00	£5.00

BLOODCHILDE
Millennium; 0 Oct 1995; 1 1995-5 1995

	$Good	$Fine	$N.Mint	£Good	£Fine	£N.Mint
0 ND origin told, Faye Perozich script, Daerick Gross art	$0.60	$1.80	$3.00	£0.40	£1.20	£2.00
1-5 ND Faye Perozich script from a Neil Gaiman story	$0.60	$1.80	$3.00	£0.40	£1.20	£2.00
Title Value:	$3.60	$10.80	$18.00	£2.40	£7.20	£12.00

BLOODFIRE
Lightning Comics; 0 Jun 1994; 1 Aug 1993-12 1994

	$Good	$Fine	$N.Mint	£Good	£Fine	£N.Mint
0 ND (Jun 1994) origin Brian Reace	$0.60	$1.80	$3.00	£0.40	£1.20	£2.00
1 ND foil-stamped cover	$0.80	$2.40	$4.00	£0.55	£1.65	£2.75
1 ND Signed Edition (Oct 1994), pre-bagged with certificate; 1,000 copies	$2.50	$7.50	$12.50	£1.50	£4.50	£7.50
1 Platinum edition ND	$2.50	$7.50	$12.50	£1.50	£4.50	£7.50
2 ND origin Bloodfire	$0.60	$1.80	$3.00	£0.40	£1.20	£2.00
3 ND 1st appearances of Dreadwolf, Perg and Judgement Day	$0.60	$1.80	$3.00	£0.40	£1.20	£2.00
3 ND Signed & Numbered Edition (Feb 1995) - pre-bagged, limited to 4,000 copies	$1.50	$4.50	$7.50	£1.00	£3.00	£5.00
4 ND	$0.60	$1.80	$3.00	£0.40	£1.20	£2.00
5 ND pre-bagged with trading card	$0.60	$1.80	$3.00	£0.40	£1.20	£2.00
6-12 ND	$0.60	$1.80	$3.00	£0.40	£1.20	£2.00
Title Value:	$14.50	$43.50	$72.50	£9.35	£28.05	£46.75

BLOODFIRE/HELLINA
Lightning Comics; 1 Aug 1995

	$Good	$Fine	$N.Mint	£Good	£Fine	£N.Mint
1 ND	$0.60	$1.80	$3.00	£0.40	£1.20	£2.00
1 Nude Edition, ND Mike Deodato cover art, polybagged	$2.00	$6.00	$10.00	£1.20	£3.60	£6.00
1 Variant cover, ND Trent Kaniuga cover art	$1.00	$3.00	$5.00	£0.60	£1.80	£3.00
Title Value:	$3.60	$10.80	$18.00	£2.20	£6.60	£11.00

BLOODLINES
The cross over story for the 1993 DC Annuals that introduces one new super-hero in each or as DC put it "introducing new blood into the DC Universe". The parts of the story are as follows:
Part 1 - Lobo Annual #1; Part 2 - Superman: The Man of Steel Annual #2; Part 3 - Batman: Shadow of the Bat Annual #1; Part 4 - Flash Annual #6 Part 5 - New Titans Annual #9; Part 6 - Superman (2nd) Annual #5 Part 7 - Green Lantern Annual #2; Part 8 - Batman Annual #17; Part 9 - Justice League International Annual #5; Part 10 - Robin Annual #2; Part 11 - Action Comics Annual #5; Part 12 - Legion of Super-Heroes Annual #4 Part 13 - Green Arrow Annual #6; Part 14 - Detective Comics Annual #6 Part 15 - Justice League America Annual #7; Part 16 - Superman (1st) Annual #5; Part 17 - Hawkman Annual #1; Part 18 - Deathstroke the Terminator Annual #2; Part 19 - Eclipso Annual #1; Part 20 - Demon Annual #2; Part 21 - Batman: Legends of the Dark Knight Annual #3; Part 22 - Team Titans Annual #1; Part 23 - Legion '93 Annual #4. Concluded in Bloodbath #1, #2

BLOODLINES: A TALE FROM THE HEART OF AFRICA
Marvel Comics Group/Epic,OS; 1 Oct 1992

	$Good	$Fine	$N.Mint	£Good	£Fine	£N.Mint
1 ND 48pgs, sequel to Temporary Natives, Brian Stelfreeze cover	$1.05	$3.15	$5.25	£0.70	£2.10	£3.50
Title Value:	$1.05	$3.15	$5.25	£0.70	£2.10	£3.50

BLOODLUST
Slave Labor,MS; 1 Dec 1990-2 1991

	$Good	$Fine	$N.Mint	£Good	£Fine	£N.Mint
1-2 ND black and white	$0.30	$0.90	$1.50	£0.20	£0.60	£1.00
Title Value:	$0.60	$1.80	$3.00	£0.40	£1.20	£2.00

BLOODRUSH
Marvel Comics Group,OS; 1 Dec 1993

	$Good	$Fine	$N.Mint	£Good	£Fine	£N.Mint
1 contains four-card uncut sheet	$0.35	$1.05	$1.75	£0.25	£0.75	£1.25
Title Value:	$0.35	$1.05	$1.75	£0.25	£0.75	£1.25

BLOODSCENT
Comico,OS; 1 Oct 1988

	$Good	$Fine	$N.Mint	£Good	£Fine	£N.Mint
1 ND Gene Colan art (colour)	$0.35	$1.05	$1.75	£0.25	£0.75	£1.25
Title Value:	$0.35	$1.05	$1.75	£0.25	£0.75	£1.25

BLOODSEED
Marvel UK/Frontier,MS; 1 Sep 1993-3 Nov 1993

	$Good	$Fine	$N.Mint	£Good	£Fine	£N.Mint
1 Paul Neary script, Liam Sharp art begins; gold-ink enhanced background on cover	$0.35	$1.05	$1.75	£0.25	£0.75	£1.25
2-3 gold ink enhanced cover	$0.35	$1.05	$1.75	£0.25	£0.75	£1.25
Title Value:	$1.05	$3.15	$5.25	£0.75	£2.25	£3.75

BLOODSHOT
Valiant/Acclaim Comics; 1 Jan 1993-present

	$Good	$Fine	$N.Mint	£Good	£Fine	£N.Mint
0 (Mar 1994) - Chromium wrap around cover; Kevin Van Hook art with Dick Giordano inks	$0.45	$1.35	$2.25	£0.30	£0.90	£1.50
0 Valiant Validated Signature Series Edition (Jun 1994), signed by Kevin Van Horn and Dick Giordano; 5,300 copies with certificate and Mylar sleeve	$1.80	$5.25	$9.00	£1.00	£3.00	£5.00
1 Barry Smith cover, fold-out poster, chromium metallic cover	$0.60	$1.80	$3.00	£0.35	£1.05	£1.75
2-3	$0.40	$1.20	$2.00	£0.25	£0.75	£1.25
4 Eternal Warrior cameo	$0.40	$1.20	$2.00	£0.25	£0.75	£1.25
5 Rai Guest-stars	$0.40	$1.20	$2.00	£0.25	£0.75	£1.25
6 1st appearance of Ninjak (cameo)	$0.50	$1.50	$2.50	£0.35	£1.05	£1.75
7 1st full appearance of Ninjak	$0.45	$1.35	$2.25	£0.30	£0.90	£1.50
8 The Coming of the Darque Age story; prelude to Secret Weapons #1	$0.40	$1.20	$2.00	£0.25	£0.75	£1.25
9-10	$0.40	$1.20	$2.00	£0.25	£0.75	£1.25
11 Empirical Dynasty part 2, continued from Secret Weapons #3						

	$Good	$Fine	$N.Mint	£Good	£Fine	£N.Mint
	$0.40	$1.20	$2.00	£0.25	£0.75	£1.25
12-19	$0.40	$1.20	$2.00	£0.25	£0.75	£1.25
20 Chaos Effect tie-in						
21-23	$0.40	$1.20	$2.00	£0.25	£0.75	£1.25
24 Geomancer appears						
	$0.40	$1.20	$2.00	£0.25	£0.75	£1.25
25-26	$0.40	$1.20	$2.00	£0.25	£0.75	£1.25
27-28 Bloodshot Rampage story						
	$0.40	$1.20	$2.00	£0.25	£0.75	£1.25
29 Bloodshot Rampage story; Ninjak appears						
	$0.40	$1.20	$2.00	£0.25	£0.75	£1.25
30 1st Acclaim Comics issue; Norm Breyfogle art begins; bi-weekly						
	$0.40	$1.20	$2.00	£0.25	£0.75	£1.25
31-39 bi-weekly	$0.40	$1.20	$2.00	£0.25	£0.75	£1.25
40 Jackson Guice art; bi-weekly						
	$0.40	$1.20	$2.00	£0.25	£0.75	£1.25
41 Paul Gulacy art; bi-weekly						
	$0.45	$1.35	$2.25	£0.30	£0.90	£1.50
42-45 bi-weekly	$0.45	$1.35	$2.25	£0.30	£0.90	£1.50
Title Value:	$20.85	$62.40	$104.25	£13.05	£39.15	£65.25

Note: all Non-Distributed at the news-stands in the U.K.

BLOODSHOT YEARBOOK

Valiant; 1 Jul 1994; 2 Apr 1995

	$Good	$Fine	$N.Mint	£Good	£Fine	£N.Mint
1 ND Kevin van Hook script, Michael Bair art						
	$0.50	$1.50	$2.50	£0.35	£1.05	£1.75
2 ND Mike Grell script, Tommy Lee Edwards art						
	$0.50	$1.50	$2.50	£0.35	£1.05	£1.75
Title Value:	$1.00	$3.00	$5.00	£0.70	£2.10	£3.50

BLOODSHOT: LAST STAND

Valiant/Acclaim Comics, OS; 1 Nov 1995

	$Good	$Fine	$N.Mint	£Good	£Fine	£N.Mint
1 ND 48pgs, Mike Zeck art						
	$1.20	$3.60	$6.00	£0.80	£2.40	£4.00
Title Value:	$1.20	$3.60	$6.00	£0.80	£2.40	£4.00

BLOODSTRIKE

Image; 1 Apr 1993-present

	$Good	$Fine	$N.Mint	£Good	£Fine	£N.Mint
1 Rob Liefeld plot/layouts, Dan Fraga pencils and Danny Miki inks begin						
	$0.60	$1.80	$3.00	£0.40	£1.20	£2.00
2-6	$0.45	$1.35	$2.25	£0.30	£0.90	£1.50
7	$0.40	$1.20	$2.00	£0.25	£0.75	£1.25
8 Chapel joins the team						
	$0.40	$1.20	$2.00	£0.25	£0.75	£1.25
9	$0.40	$1.20	$2.00	£0.25	£0.75	£1.25
10 Extreme Prejudice part 7, with coupon						
	$0.40	$1.20	$2.00	£0.25	£0.75	£1.25
11 Savage Dragon appears						
	$0.40	$1.20	$2.00	£0.25	£0.75	£1.25
12 team disbands temporarily						
	$0.40	$1.20	$2.00	£0.25	£0.75	£1.25
13-14	$0.45	$1.35	$2.25	£0.30	£0.90	£1.50
15 War Games storyline, X-over with Prophet #8						
	$0.45	$1.35	$2.25	£0.30	£0.90	£1.50
16 War Games storyline, Prophet appears						
	$0.45	$1.35	$2.25	£0.30	£0.90	£1.50
17	$0.45	$1.35	$2.25	£0.30	£0.90	£1.50
18 Extreme Sacrifice part 2, continued in Brigade #16; pre-bagged with trading card						
	$0.45	$1.35	$2.25	£0.30	£0.90	£1.50
19	$0.45	$1.35	$2.25	£0.30	£0.90	£1.50
20 Lily and Bailout join team						
	$0.45	$1.35	$2.25	£0.30	£0.90	£1.50
21-24	$0.45	$1.35	$2.25	£0.30	£0.90	£1.50
25 cover-dated May 1994; issued in between issues #10 and 11 as part of "Images of Tomorrow", showing what the 25th issues of titles will look'read like						
	$0.45	$1.35	$2.25	£0.30	£0.90	£1.50
Title Value:	$11.10	$33.30	$55.50	£7.30	£21.90	£36.50

Note: all Non-Distributed on the news-stands in the U.K.

Blood Brothers (Aug 1994)

Trade paperback reprints the Extreme prejudice storyline including early issues of Bloodstrike

				£1.70	£5.10	£8.50

BLOODSTRIKE: ASSASSIN

Image; 0 Oct 1995; 1 Jun 1995-present

	$Good	$Fine	$N.Mint	£Good	£Fine	£N.Mint
0 ND Robert Napton script, Karl Altstaetter art						
	$0.45	$1.35	$2.50	£0.30	£0.90	£1.50
1 ND Robert Napton script, Karl Alstaetter art begins						
	$0.45	$1.35	$2.25	£0.30	£0.90	£1.50
2-4 ND	$0.45	$1.35	$2.25	£0.30	£0.90	£1.50
Title Value:	$2.30	$6.90	$11.75	£1.50	£4.50	£7.50

BLOODTHIRST: THE NIGHTFALL CONSPIRACY

Alpha Productions, MS; 1 Jul 1994-2 Aug 1994

	$Good	$Fine	$N.Mint	£Good	£Fine	£N.Mint
1-2 ND black and white						
	$0.45	$1.35	$2.25	£0.30	£0.90	£1.50
Title Value:	$0.90	$2.70	$4.50	£0.60	£1.80	£3.00

BLOODWULF

Image, MS; 1 Feb 1995-4 May 1995

	$Good	$Fine	$N.Mint	£Good	£Fine	£N.Mint
1-4 ND Andy Mangels script, Daerick Gross art						
	$0.45	$1.35	$2.25	£0.30	£0.90	£1.50
Title Value:	$1.80	$5.40	$9.00	£1.20	£3.60	£6.00

BLOODWULF SPECIAL

Image, OS; 1 Aug 1995

	$Good	$Fine	$N.Mint	£Good	£Fine	£N.Mint
1 ND	$0.50	$1.50	$2.50	£0.30	£0.90	£1.50
Title Value:	$0.50	$1.50	$2.50	£0.30	£0.90	£1.50

BLUE BEETLE

DC Comics; 1 Jun 1986-24 May 1988

	$Good	$Fine	$N.Mint	£Good	£Fine	£N.Mint
1 origin retold	$0.30	$0.90	$1.50	£0.20	£0.60	£1.00
2-4	$0.20	$0.60	$1.00	£0.15	£0.45	£0.75
5-7 The Question X-over						
	$0.20	$0.60	$1.00	£0.15	£0.45	£0.75
8	$0.20	$0.60	$1.00	£0.15	£0.45	£0.75
9-10 Legends X-over						
	$0.20	$0.60	$1.00	£0.15	£0.45	£0.75
11-13 Titans X-over						
	$0.15	$0.45	$0.75	£0.10	£0.35	£0.60
14-17	$0.15	$0.45	$0.75	£0.10	£0.35	£0.60
18 original Blue Beetle appears						
	$0.15	$0.45	$0.75	£0.10	£0.35	£0.60
19	$0.15	$0.45	$0.75	£0.10	£0.35	£0.60
20-21 Millennium X-over						
	$0.15	$0.45	$0.75	£0.10	£0.35	£0.60
22-24	$0.15	$0.45	$0.75	£0.10	£0.35	£0.60
Title Value:	$4.20	$12.60	$21.00	£2.95	£9.55	£16.15

BLUE BEETLE (2ND SERIES)

Charlton; 1 Jun 1964-5 Mar/Apr 1965; V3 50 Jul 1965-54 Feb/Mar 1966; 1Jun 1967-5 Oct 1968

(previously Unusual Tales #1-49, becomes Ghostly Tales #55-169) (all distributed in the U.K.)

	$Good	$Fine	$N.Mint	£Good	£Fine	£N.Mint
v2 1 origin retold; 1st Silver Age appearance Blue Beetle			$5.00	$15.00	$30.00	
v2 2-5			$3.00	$9.00	$18.00	
v3 50-54			$2.50	$7.50	$15.00	
1 Question begins; Steve Ditko art			$6.00	$18.00	$40.00	
2 origin Blue Beetle (Ted Kord); Steve Ditko art			$2.50	$7.50	$15.00	
3-5 Steve Ditko art			$1.75	$5.25	$10.50	

BLUE DEVIL

DC Comics; 1 Jun 1984-31 Dec 1986

	$Good	$Fine	$N.Mint	£Good	£Fine	£N.Mint
1-2	$0.20	$0.60	$1.00	£0.15	£0.45	£0.75
3 Blue Devil vs. Metallo; Superman appears						
	$0.20	$0.60	$1.00	£0.15	£0.45	£0.75
4 origin Nebiros	$0.20	$0.60	$1.00	£0.15	£0.45	£0.75
5	$0.20	$0.60	$1.00	£0.15	£0.45	£0.75
6 Flash Force 2000 insert						
	$0.20	$0.60	$1.00	£0.15	£0.45	£0.75
7 Gil Kane art	$0.20	$0.60	$1.00	£0.15	£0.45	£0.75
8-9 Blue Devil vs. The Trickster						
10	$0.20	$0.60	$1.00	£0.15	£0.45	£0.75
11-12	$0.15	$0.45	$0.75	£0.10	£0.35	£0.60
13 Green Lantern and Zatanna appear						
	$0.15	$0.45	$0.75	£0.10	£0.35	£0.60
14 Detective #38 cover parody (Kid Devil instead of Robin bursting through the hoop)						
	$0.15	$0.45	$0.75	£0.10	£0.35	£0.60
15-16	$0.15	$0.45	$0.75	£0.10	£0.35	£0.60
17-18 Crisis X-over						
	$0.15	$0.45	$0.75	£0.10	£0.35	£0.60
19 Robin appears	$0.15	$0.45	$0.75	£0.10	£0.35	£0.60
20-22	$0.15	$0.45	$0.75	£0.10	£0.35	£0.60
23 Blue Devil vs. Firestorm						
	$0.15	$0.45	$0.75	£0.10	£0.35	£0.60
24-29	$0.15	$0.45	$0.75	£0.10	£0.35	£0.60
30 DS Flash's Rogue's Gallery appear						
	$0.20	$0.60	$1.00	£0.15	£0.45	£0.75
31 DS	$0.20	$0.60	$1.00	£0.15	£0.45	£0.75
Title Value:	$5.25	$15.75	$26.25	£3.70	£12.05	£20.40

BLUE DEVIL ANNUAL

DC Comics; 1 Nov 1985

	$Good	$Fine	$N.Mint	£Good	£Fine	£N.Mint
1 Black Orchid, Creeper, Demon, Man-Bat, Madame Xanadu, Phantom Stranger appear, Bollandesque pin-up re-done from Superman #400						
	$0.20	$0.60	$1.00	£0.15	£0.45	£0.75
Title Value:	$0.20	$0.60	$1.00	£0.15	£0.45	£0.75

BLUE LILY, THE

Dark Horse, MS; 1 Mar 1993-4 Jun 1993

	$Good	$Fine	$N.Mint	£Good	£Fine	£N.Mint
1-4 ND 48pgs, Angus McKie script and art						
	$0.60	$1.80	$3.00	£0.40	£1.20	£2.00
Title Value:	$2.40	$7.20	$12.00	£1.60	£4.80	£8.00

BLUE RIBBON COMICS

Red Circle (Archie); 1 Oct 1983-14 Dec 1985

	$Good	$Fine	$N.Mint	£Good	£Fine	£N.Mint
1 reprints Adventures of the Fly #1 by Kirby						
	$0.20	$0.60	$1.00	£0.15	£0.45	£0.75
2 Mr. Justice by Trevor von Eeden and Alex Nino						
	$0.15	$0.45	$0.75	£0.10	£0.35	£0.60
3 Steel Sterling	$0.15	$0.45	$0.75	£0.10	£0.35	£0.60
4 Fly by Von Eeden/Buckler						
	$0.15	$0.45	$0.75	£0.10	£0.35	£0.60
5 Shield (reprints, including origin by Joe Simon & Jack Kirby from Double Life of Private Strong), new Jack Kirby/Buckler cover						
	$0.15	$0.45	$0.75	£0.10	£0.35	£0.60
6-7 The Fox	$0.15	$0.45	$0.75	£0.10	£0.35	£0.60
8 Black Hood by Morrow, Williamson, Neal Adams reprint						
	$0.15	$0.45	$0.75	£0.10	£0.35	£0.60
9 Agents of Atlantis, Adamsesque art						
	$0.15	$0.45	$0.75	£0.10	£0.35	£0.60
10 The Fly (50s reprints)						
	$0.15	$0.45	$0.75	£0.10	£0.35	£0.60
11	$0.15	$0.45	$0.75	£0.10	£0.35	£0.60
12 ThunderAgents						
	$0.15	$0.45	$0.75	£0.10	£0.35	£0.60

13 Thunderbunny

	$Good	$Fine	$N.Mint	£Good	£Fine	£N.Mint
	$0.15	$0.45	$0.75	£0.10	£0.35	£0.60

14 Web and Jaguar

	$Good	$Fine	$N.Mint	£Good	£Fine	£N.Mint
	$0.15	$0.45	$0.75	£0.10	£0.35	£0.60
Title Value:	$2.15	$6.45	$10.75	£1.45	£5.00	£8.55

Note: all Non-Distributed on the news-stands in the U.K.

BLUEBERRY
Marvel Comics Group/Epic Graphic Novel; 1 1989-8 1992
(see Moebius)

	$Good	$Fine	$N.Mint	£Good	£Fine	£N.Mint
1 ND 96pgs, Chihuahua Pearl, Charlier script; Moebius art begins						
	$1.80	$5.25	$9.00	£1.20	£3.60	£6.00
2 ND 120pgs, Ballad for a Coffin Graphic Novel						
	$1.80	$5.25	$9.00	£1.20	£3.60	£6.00
3 ND 96pgs, Angel Face						
	$1.80	$5.25	$9.00	£1.20	£3.60	£6.00
4 ND 96pgs, The Ghost Tribe						
	$1.80	$5.25	$9.00	£1.20	£3.60	£6.00
5 ND 96pgs, End of the Trail						
	$1.50	$4.50	$7.50	£1.00	£3.00	£5.00
6 ND 48pgs, The Iron Horse						
	$1.50	$4.50	$7.50	£1.00	£3.00	£5.00
7 ND 48pgs, Steel Finger						
	$1.50	$4.50	$7.50	£1.00	£3.00	£5.00
8 ND 48pgs, General Golden Mane						
	$2.50	$7.50	$12.50	£1.50	£4.50	£7.50
Title Value:	$14.20	$42.00	$71.00	£9.30	£27.90	£46.50

Note: script by J.M. Lofficier, art by Moebius. Titan Editions of 1,2 available

BOB HOPE, THE ADVENTURES OF
National Periodical Publications; 1 Feb/Mar 1950-109 Feb/Mar 1968

	$Good	$Fine	$N.Mint	£Good	£Fine	£N.Mint
1	$125.00	$385.00	$900.00	£85.00	£255.00	£600.00
2	$62.50	$190.00	$450.00	£43.00	£125.00	£300.00
3-4	$40.00	$120.00	$280.00	£26.00	£77.50	£185.00
5-10	$32.00	$95.00	$225.00	£21.00	£62.50	£150.00
11-20	$18.50	$55.00	$130.00	£12.00	£36.00	£85.00
21-30	$12.50	$39.00	$90.00	£8.50	£26.00	£60.00
31-40	$10.00	$30.00	$70.00	£6.75	£20.00	£47.50
41-48	$9.25	$28.00	$65.00	£6.25	£19.00	£45.00
1st official distribution in the U.K.						
49-50	$9.00	$28.00	$55.00	£5.75	£17.50	£35.00
51-60	$5.75	$17.50	$35.00	£4.15	£12.50	£25.00
61-70	$5.25	$16.00	$32.50	£3.75	£11.00	£22.50
71-93	$3.30	$10.00	$20.00	£2.30	£7.00	£14.00
94 Aquaman appears						
	$3.30	$10.00	$20.00	£2.30	£7.00	£14.00
95-96	$3.30	$10.00	$20.00	£2.30	£7.00	£14.00
97 Batman and Robin X-over, Joker's Health Club story						
	$4.55	$13.50	$27.50	£2.90	£8.75	£17.50
98-100	$3.30	$10.00	$20.00	£2.30	£7.00	£14.00
101-105	$3.00	$9.00	$18.00	£2.00	£6.00	£12.00
106-109 scarce in the U.K. Neal Adams art						
	$5.25	$16.00	$32.50	£3.30	£10.00	£20.00
Title Value:	$1207.75	$3652.50	$8292.50	£811.80	£2433.75	£5563.50

Note: early issues at least scarce in the U.K.

BOB MARLEY: TALE OF THE TUFF GONG BOOK
Marvel Comics Group,MS; 1 Oct 1994-3 Dec 1994

	$Good	$Fine	$N.Mint	£Good	£Fine	£N.Mint
1-3 ND 48pgs, Gene Colan art						
	$1.00	$3.00	$5.00	£0.70	£2.10	£3.50
Title Value:	$3.00	$9.00	$15.00	£2.10	£6.30	£10.50

BOB, THE GALACTIC BUM
DC Comics,MS; 1 Feb 1995-4 Jun 1995

	$Good	$Fine	$N.Mint	£Good	£Fine	£N.Mint
1-4 Alan Grant and John Wagner script, Carlos Ezquerra art						
	$0.40	$1.20	$2.00	£0.25	£0.75	£1.25
Title Value:	$1.60	$4.80	$8.00	£1.00	£3.00	£5.00

BODY COUNT
Aircel,MS; 1 Dec 1989-4 Apr 1990

	$Good	$Fine	$N.Mint	£Good	£Fine	£N.Mint
1-4 ND Barry Blair script/lay-outs, Dave Cooper finishes						
	$0.45	$1.35	$2.25	£0.30	£0.90	£1.50
Title Value:	$1.80	$5.40	$9.00	£1.20	£3.60	£6.00

BODY COUNT
Marvel UK,OS; 1 Oct 1993

	$Good	$Fine	$N.Mint	£Good	£Fine	£N.Mint
1 ND Marvel UK arist and writer information and listings; originally given away for free						
	$0.30	$0.90	$1.50	£0.20	£0.60	£1.00
Title Value:	$0.30	$0.90	$1.50	£0.20	£0.60	£1.00

BODY GUARD
Aircel,MS; 1 Nov 1990-3 Jan 1991

	$Good	$Fine	$N.Mint	£Good	£Fine	£N.Mint
1-3 ND reprints from Australian Penthouse						
	$0.45	$1.35	$2.25	£0.30	£0.90	£1.50
Title Value:	$1.35	$4.05	$6.75	£0.90	£2.70	£4.50

BOLD ADVENTURE
Pacific; 1 Nov 1983-3 Jun 1984

	$Good	$Fine	$N.Mint	£Good	£Fine	£N.Mint
1 ND Time Force begins						
	$0.15	$0.45	$0.75	£0.10	£0.35	£0.60
2 ND Alex Nino art	$0.15	$0.45	$0.75	£0.10	£0.35	£0.60
3 ND Mike Kaluta cover						
	$0.15	$0.45	$0.75	£0.10	£0.35	£0.60
Title Value:	$0.45	$1.35	$2.25	£0.30	£1.05	£1.80

BOLT & STARFORCE SIX
AC Comics; 1 Mar 1984
(see Starforce Six Special)

	$Good	$Fine	$N.Mint	£Good	£Fine	£N.Mint
1 ND	$0.30	$0.90	$1.50	£0.20	£0.60	£1.00
Title Value:	$0.30	$0.90	$1.50	£0.20	£0.60	£1.00

BOLT SPECIAL
AC Comics; 1 1984

	$Good	$Fine	$N.Mint	£Good	£Fine	£N.Mint
1 ND 52pgs, black and white						
	$0.30	$0.90	$1.50	£0.20	£0.60	£1.00
Title Value:	$0.30	$0.90	$1.50	£0.20	£0.60	£1.00

BOMARC
Night Wynd,MS; 1 Sep 1992-5 Jan 1993

	$Good	$Fine	$N.Mint	£Good	£Fine	£N.Mint
1-5 ND Ken Branch script/art						
	$0.35	$1.05	$1.75	£0.25	£0.75	£1.25
Title Value:	$1.75	$5.25	$8.75	£1.25	£3.75	£6.25

BOMBA, THE JUNGLE BOY
National Periodical Publications, TV; 1 Sep/Oct 1967-7 Sep/Oct 1968

	$Good	$Fine	$N.Mint	£Good	£Fine	£N.Mint
1 1st appearance Bomba; Infantino/Anderson cover						
	$2.90	$8.75	$17.50	£2.05	£6.25	£12.50
2-7	$1.30	$4.00	$8.00	£1.00	£3.00	£6.00
Title Value:	$10.70	$32.75	$65.50	£8.05	£24.25	£48.50

BOMBAST
Topps,OS; 1 Apr 1993

	$Good	$Fine	$N.Mint	£Good	£Fine	£N.Mint
1 ND pre-bagged with coupon #3 for Secret City Saga #0 plus Bombast chrome trading card; Savage Dragon appears; Jack Kirby cover						
	$0.30	$0.90	$1.50	£0.20	£0.60	£1.00
1 ND without coupon/card						
	$0.20	$0.60	$1.00	£0.15	£0.45	£0.75
Title Value:	$0.50	$1.50	$2.50	£0.35	£1.05	£1.75

BONE
Cartoon Books/Image Comics; 1 1992-present

	$Good	$Fine	$N.Mint	£Good	£Fine	£N.Mint
1 Jeff Smith script/art begins; black and white						
	$40.00	$120.00	$200.00	£25.00	£75.00	£125.00
1 2nd printing	$5.00	$15.00	$25.00	£3.00	£9.00	£15.00
1 3rd printing	$1.50	$4.50	$7.50	£1.00	£3.00	£5.00
1 4th printing	$0.90	$2.70	$4.50	£0.60	£1.80	£3.00
1 5th printing	$0.60	$1.80	$3.00	£0.40	£1.20	£2.00
1 6th printing	$0.60	$1.80	$3.00	£0.40	£1.20	£2.00
2	$25.00	$75.00	$125.00	£15.00	£45.00	£75.00
2 2nd printing	$0.90	$2.70	$4.50	£0.60	£1.80	£3.00
2 3rd printing	$0.55	$1.65	$2.75	£0.35	£1.05	£1.75
3	$18.00	$52.50	$90.00	£11.00	£33.00	£55.00
3 2nd printing	$0.90	$2.70	$4.50	£0.60	£1.80	£3.00
3 3rd printing	$0.60	$1.80	$3.00	£0.40	£1.20	£2.00
3 4th printing	$0.55	$1.65	$2.75	£0.35	£1.05	£1.75
4	$10.00	$30.00	$50.00	£6.00	£18.00	£30.00
5	$9.00	$27.00	$45.00	£5.00	£15.00	£25.00
6	$6.00	$18.00	$30.00	£4.00	£12.00	£20.00
7	$5.00	$15.00	$25.00	£3.00	£9.00	£15.00
8	$4.00	$12.00	$20.00	£2.50	£7.50	£12.50
9-10	$2.40	$7.00	$12.00	£1.20	£3.60	£6.00
11-13	$0.80	$2.40	$4.00	£0.50	£1.50	£2.50
13 1/2, Wizard send-away promotion						
	$2.00	$6.00	$10.00	£1.20	£3.60	£6.00
13 1/2 Gold edition	$3.00	$9.00	$15.00	£2.00	£6.00	£10.00
14-20	$0.60	$1.80	$3.00	£0.40	£1.20	£2.00
21 1st Image Comics issue						
	$0.60	$1.80	$3.00	£0.40	£1.20	£2.00
22	$0.60	$1.80	$3.00	£0.40	£1.20	£2.00
Title Value:	$146.70	$438.20	$733.50	£89.90	£269.70	£449.50

Note: all Non-Distributed on the news-stands in the U.K.

	£Good	£Fine	£N.Mint
The Complete Bone Adventures (Aug 1993) reprints issues #1-6, foreword by Will Eisner	£1.75	£5.25	£8.25
Holiday Special (1993), 16pgs, larger size format; free with Hero Illustrated	£0.25	£0.75	£1.25
The Complete Bone Adventures Vol. 2 (Jul 1994) reprints issues #7-12, foreword by Neil Gaiman	£1.70	£5.10	£8.50
Bone Volume One Hardcover: Out From Boneville (Jul 1995) reprints issues #1-6 with dust-jacket	£3.00	£9.00	£15.00
The Complete Bone Adventures Vol. 3 (Aug 1995) reprints issues #13-18, foreword by Frank Miller	£1.70	£5.10	£8.50

BONE (2ND SERIES)
Image; 1 Nov 1995-present

	$Good	$Fine	$N.Mint	£Good	£Fine	£N.Mint
1 ND reprint of #1 celebrating Image Comics taking over the title						
	$0.60	$1.80	$3.00	£0.40	£1.20	£2.00
2 ND reprints issue #2 of original series						
	$0.60	$1.80	$3.00	£0.40	£1.20	£2.00
Title Value:	$1.20	$3.60	$6.00	£0.80	£2.40	£4.00

BONE SAW
Tundra,OS; 1 1992

	$Good	$Fine	$N.Mint	£Good	£Fine	£N.Mint
1 ND horror anthology featuring John Bergin art, black and white and colour						
	$3.00	$9.00	$15.00	£2.00	£6.00	£10.00
Title Value:	$3.00	$9.00	$15.00	£2.00	£6.00	£10.00

BONE SOURCEBOOK
Image,OS; 1 Sep 1995

	$Good	$Fine	$N.Mint	£Good	£Fine	£N.Mint
1 ND black and white giveaway to celebrate Bone joining Image						
	$0.20	$0.60	$1.00	£0.10	£0.35	£0.65
Title Value:	$0.20	$0.60	$1.00	£0.10	£0.35	£0.65

BONES
Malibu; 1 Aug 1987-4 Nov 1987

	$Good	$Fine	$N.Mint	£Good	£Fine	£N.Mint
1-4 ND	$0.20	$0.60	$1.00	£0.15	£0.45	£0.75
Title Value:	$0.80	$2.40	$4.00	£0.60	£1.80	£3.00

BOOF
Image; 1 Jul 1994-6 Dec 1994

	$Good	$Fine	$N.Mint	£Good	£Fine	£N.Mint
1-6 ND John Cleary art						
	$0.30	$0.90	$1.50	£0.20	£0.60	£1.00
Title Value:	$1.80	$5.40	$9.00	£1.20	£3.60	£6.00

BOOF AND THE BRUISE CREW
Image; 1 Jul 1994-6 Dec 1994

	$Good	$Fine	$N.Mint	£Good	£Fine	£N.Mint
1-6 ND Tim Harkins art	$0.30	$0.90	$1.50	£0.20	£0.60	£1.00
Title Value:	$1.80	$5.40	$9.00	£1.20	£3.60	£6.00

BOOK OF NIGHT, CHARLES VESS'
Dark Horse; 1 Jul 1987-3 Oct 1987

	$Good	$Fine	$N.Mint	£Good	£Fine	£N.Mint
1-3 ND Charles Vess art	$0.45	$1.35	$2.25	£0.30	£0.90	£1.50
Title Value:	$1.35	$4.05	$6.75	£0.90	£2.70	£4.50
Book of Night Softcover (Nov 1991), reprints mini-series				£1.40	£4.20	£7.00
Book of Night Hardcover (Nov 1991), slipcase with foil stamping, signed and numbered (500 copies)				£7.00	£21.00	£35.00

BOOK OF THE DEAD
Marvel Comics Group, MS; 1 Dec 1993-4 Mar 1994

	$Good	$Fine	$N.Mint	£Good	£Fine	£N.Mint
1 ND 48pgs, Man-Thing and Frankenstein reprints begin	$0.30	$0.90	$1.50	£0.20	£0.60	£1.00
2 ND 48pgs, Adventure Into Fear #10 reprinted (1st Man-Thing)	$0.30	$0.90	$1.50	£0.20	£0.60	£1.00
3-4 ND 48pgs	$0.30	$0.90	$1.50	£0.20	£0.60	£1.00
Title Value:	$1.20	$3.60	$6.00	£0.80	£2.40	£4.00

BOOKS OF MAGIC
DC Comics, MS; 1 Dec 1990-4 Apr 1991

	$Good	$Fine	$N.Mint	£Good	£Fine	£N.Mint
1 ND Phantom Stranger/Arion/Zatara/Sargon/John Constantine/Spectre/Dr. Fate/Deadman/Zatanna/Mister E appear in this series	$1.80	$5.25	$9.00	£0.80	£2.40	£4.00
2 ND	$1.40	$4.20	$7.00	£0.70	£2.10	£3.50
3 ND scarce in the U.K. Sandman appears	$1.40	$4.20	$7.00	£0.80	£2.40	£4.00
4 ND Death appears	$1.80	$5.25	$9.00	£0.80	£2.40	£4.00
Title Value:	$6.40	$18.90	$32.00	£3.10	£9.30	£15.50

Note: painted art by John Bolton, Charles Vess, Scott Hampton and Paul Johnson in #1-4 respectively; script by Neil Gaiman in all. Prestige Format
Trade paperback (Mar 1993)

	$Good	$Fine	$N.Mint	£Good	£Fine	£N.Mint
200pgs, reprints mini-series, foil-enhanced cover and new introduction by Roger Zelazny				£2.50	£7.50	£12.50

BOOKS OF MAGIC, THE
DC Comics/Vertigo; 1 May 1994-present

	$Good	$Fine	$N.Mint	£Good	£Fine	£N.Mint
1 John Reiber script, Gary Amaro art; painted cover by Charles Vess	$1.00	$3.00	$5.00	£0.40	£1.20	£2.00
2	$0.60	$1.80	$3.00	£0.30	£0.90	£1.50
3-12	$0.40	$1.20	$2.00	£0.25	£0.75	£1.25
13 upgraded paper format begins	$0.45	$1.35	$2.25	£0.30	£0.90	£1.50
14-22	$0.45	$1.35	$2.25	£0.30	£0.90	£1.50
Title Value:	$10.10	$30.30	$51.00	£6.20	£18.60	£31.00

The Books of Magic: Bindings (Mar 1995)

	$Good	$Fine	$N.Mint	£Good	£Fine	£N.Mint
Trade paperback reprints issues #1-4				£1.70	£5.10	£8.50

BOOSTER GOLD
DC Comics; 1 Feb 1986-25 Feb 1988
(see Adventures of Superman, Justice League)

	$Good	$Fine	$N.Mint	£Good	£Fine	£N.Mint
1 Superman appears	$0.20	$0.60	$1.00	£0.15	£0.45	£0.75
2-5	$0.15	$0.45	$0.75	£0.10	£0.35	£0.60
6 origin	$0.15	$0.45	$0.75	£0.10	£0.35	£0.60
7	$0.15	$0.45	$0.75	£0.10	£0.35	£0.60
8 Legion of Super-Heroes appear	$0.15	$0.45	$0.75	£0.10	£0.35	£0.60
9-21	$0.15	$0.45	$0.75	£0.10	£0.35	£0.60
22 Justice League International appear	$0.15	$0.45	$0.75	£0.10	£0.35	£0.60
23	$0.15	$0.45	$0.75	£0.10	£0.35	£0.60
24-25 Millennium X-over	$0.15	$0.45	$0.75	£0.10	£0.35	£0.60
Title Value:	$3.80	$11.40	$19.00	£2.55	£8.85	£15.15

BORDER WORLDS
Kitchen Sink; 1 Jul 1986-7 Aug 1987

	$Good	$Fine	$N.Mint	£Good	£Fine	£N.Mint
1-6 ND Don Simpson story/art	$0.35	$1.05	$1.75	£0.25	£0.75	£1.25
7 ND Don Simpson story/art; with printing error	$0.35	$1.05	$1.75	£0.25	£0.75	£1.25
7 ND Don Simpson story/art; 2nd print "Corrected Edition" on cover	$0.35	$1.05	$1.75	£0.25	£0.75	£1.25
Title Value:	$2.80	$8.40	$14.00	£2.00	£6.00	£10.00

BORDER WORLDS: MAROONED
Kitchen Sink, OS; 1 1990

	$Good	$Fine	$N.Mint	£Good	£Fine	£N.Mint
1 ND Don Simpson script/art	$0.35	$1.05	$1.75	£0.25	£0.75	£1.25
Title Value:	$0.35	$1.05	$1.75	£0.25	£0.75	£1.25

BORDERGUARD
Eternity; 1 Nov 1987-2 Mar 1988

	$Good	$Fine	$N.Mint	£Good	£Fine	£N.Mint
1-2 ND	$0.20	$0.60	$1.00	£0.15	£0.45	£0.75
Title Value:	$0.40	$1.20	$2.00	£0.30	£0.90	£1.50

BORIS ADVENTURE MAGAZINE
Nicotat; 1 Aug 1988

	$Good	$Fine	$N.Mint	£Good	£Fine	£N.Mint
1 ND Rocketeer parody cover	$0.45	$1.35	$2.25	£0.30	£0.90	£1.50
Title Value:	$0.45	$1.35	$2.25	£0.30	£0.90	£1.50

BORIS KARLOFF TALES OF MYSTERY
Gold Key; 3 Apr 1963-97 Feb 1980
(previously Boris Karloff Thriller)

	$Good	$Fine	$N.Mint	£Good	£Fine	£N.Mint
3-8	$3.30	$10.00	$20.00	£2.30	£7.00	£14.00
9 Wally Wood art	$4.15	$12.50	$25.00	£2.80	£8.50	£17.00
10	$3.30	$10.00	$20.00	£2.30	£7.00	£14.00
11 Williamson art	$4.15	$12.50	$25.00	£2.80	£8.50	£17.00
12	$3.00	$9.00	$18.00	£2.00	£6.00	£12.00
13-14	$2.50	$7.50	$15.00	£1.65	£5.00	£10.00
15 Crandall, Evans art	$2.50	$7.50	$15.00	£1.65	£5.00	£10.00
16-20	$2.50	$7.50	$15.00	£1.65	£5.00	£10.00
21 Jeff Jones art	$3.00	$9.00	$18.00	£2.00	£6.00	£12.00
22	$2.00	$6.00	$10.00	£1.30	£3.90	£6.50
23 reprint	$2.00	$6.00	$10.00	£1.30	£3.90	£6.50
24-30	$2.00	$6.00	$10.00	£1.30	£3.90	£6.50
31-50	$1.40	$4.20	$7.00	£0.90	£2.70	£4.50
51-69	$1.00	$3.00	$5.00	£0.65	£1.95	£3.25
70-97	$0.50	$1.50	$2.50	£0.35	£1.05	£1.75
Title Value:	$136.40	$410.00	$741.00	£90.75	£273.55	£495.25

Note: all Limited Distribution on the news-stands in the U.K.

BORIS KARLOFF THRILLER
Gold Key; 1 Oct 1962-2 Jan 1963
(becomes Boris Karloff Tales of Mystery)

	$Good	$Fine	$N.Mint	£Good	£Fine	£N.Mint
1 scarce, very limited distributed in the U.K. 80pgs	$7.50	$22.50	$45.00	£5.00	£15.00	£30.00
2 scarce, very limited distributed in the U.K. 80pgs	$5.25	$15.50	$31.50	£3.50	£10.50	£21.00
Title Value:	$12.75	$38.00	$76.50	£8.50	£25.50	£51.00

BORIS THE BEAR
Nicotat/Dark Horse; 1 1986-24 1989; 25 1990-37 1993?

	$Good	$Fine	$N.Mint	£Good	£Fine	£N.Mint
1	$0.60	$1.80	$3.00	£0.40	£1.20	£2.00

Book of the Dead #2

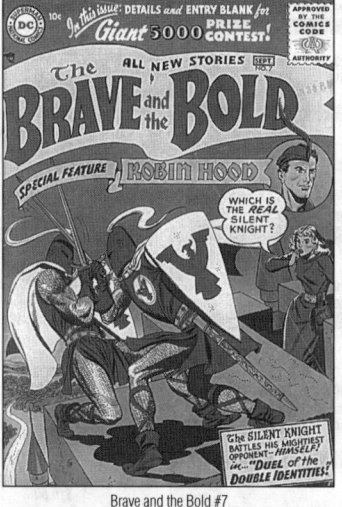

Brave and the Bold #7

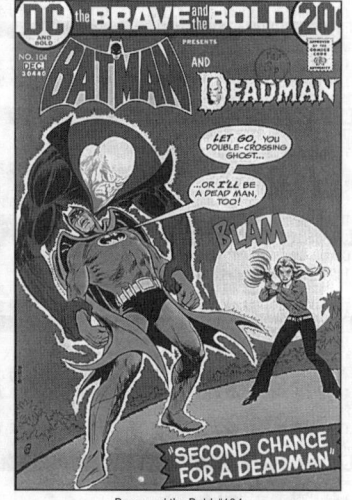

Brave and the Bold #104

MINT = 100% / NEAR MINT (inc. +/-) = 90–99% / VERY FINE (inc. +/-) = 75–89% / FINE (inc. +/-) = 55–74% / VERY GOOD (inc. +/-) = 35–54% / GOOD (inc. +/-) = 15–34% / FAIR = 5–14% / POOR = 1–4%

247

	$Good	$Fine	$N.Mint	£Good	£Fine	£N.Mint
1 2nd printing	$0.45	$1.35	$2.25	£0.30	£0.90	£1.50
2 scarce in the U.K.	$0.45	$1.35	$2.25	£0.30	£0.90	£1.50
3 Secret Wars parody	$0.45	$1.35	$2.25	£0.30	£0.90	£1.50
4 origin, "Man of Steel" parody, 2 covers exist	$0.45	$1.35	$2.25	£0.30	£0.90	£1.50
5 Swamp Thing parody	$0.45	$1.35	$2.25	£0.30	£0.90	£1.50
6 Batman parody (Bat-Bear)	$0.35	$1.05	$1.75	£0.25	£0.75	£1.25
7 Elfquest parody	$0.35	$1.05	$1.75	£0.25	£0.75	£1.25
8 DS	$0.35	$1.05	$1.75	£0.25	£0.75	£1.25
9-12	$0.35	$1.05	$1.75	£0.25	£0.75	£1.25
13 1st Nicotat issue, Punisher parody	$0.35	$1.05	$1.75	£0.25	£0.75	£1.25
14-24	$0.35	$1.05	$1.75	£0.25	£0.75	£1.25
25 Southern Squadron appears	$0.30	$0.90	$1.50	£0.20	£0.60	£1.00
26-33	$0.30	$0.90	$1.50	£0.20	£0.60	£1.00
34-37 The Return of Blackbear	$0.30	$0.90	$1.50	£0.20	£0.60	£1.00
Title Value:	$13.40	$40.20	$67.00	£9.25	£27.75	£46.25

Note: all Non-Distributed on the news-stands in the U.K.

BORIS THE BEAR INSTANT COLOR CLASSICS
Dark Horse; 1 Jul 1987-7 1988

	$Good	$Fine	$N.Mint	£Good	£Fine	£N.Mint
1-7 ND reprints from Boris the Bear, in colour	$0.35	$1.05	$1.75	£0.25	£0.75	£1.25
Title Value:	$2.45	$7.35	$12.25	£1.75	£5.25	£8.75

BORN TO BE WILD
Eclipse,OS; 1 Dec 1991

1 ND 72pgs, features work by Neil Gaiman, Grant Morrison, Moebius, Starlin, David Lloyd, Todd McFarlane and others for animal charities

	$Good	$Fine	$N.Mint	£Good	£Fine	£N.Mint
	$1.50	$4.50	$7.50	£1.00	£3.00	£5.00
Title Value:	$1.50	$4.50	$7.50	£1.00	£3.00	£5.00

BORN TO KILL
Aircel; 1 May 1991-2 1991

	$Good	$Fine	$N.Mint	£Good	£Fine	£N.Mint
1-2 ND black and white	$0.35	$1.05	$1.75	£0.25	£0.75	£1.25
Title Value:	$0.70	$2.10	$3.50	£0.50	£1.50	£2.50

BOSTON BOMBERS, THE
Caliber Press,MS; 1 Nov 1990-6 Sep 1991

	$Good	$Fine	$N.Mint	£Good	£Fine	£N.Mint
1-6 ND	$0.35	$1.05	$1.75	£0.25	£0.75	£1.25
Title Value:	$2.10	$6.30	$10.50	£1.50	£4.50	£7.50

BOUNTY
Caliber Press; 1 Aug 1991-3 Oct 1991

	$Good	$Fine	$N.Mint	£Good	£Fine	£N.Mint
1-3 ND	$0.35	$1.05	$1.75	£0.25	£0.75	£1.25
Title Value:	$1.05	$3.15	$5.25	£0.75	£2.25	£3.75

BOY AND HIS BOT
Now Comics; 1 Jan 1987

	$Good	$Fine	$N.Mint	£Good	£Fine	£N.Mint
1 ND	$0.35	$1.05	$1.75	£0.25	£0.75	£1.25
Title Value:	$0.35	$1.05	$1.75	£0.25	£0.75	£1.25

BOY COMMANDOS
DC Comics; 1 Sep/Oct 1973-2 Nov/Dec 1973

	$Good	$Fine	$N.Mint	£Good	£Fine	£N.Mint
1 Golden Age Joe Simon & Jack Kirby reprints from Boy Commandoes #1 and Detective Comics #66	$0.60	$1.80	$3.00	£0.40	£1.20	£2.00
2 Golden Age Joe Simon & Jack Kirby reprints	$0.55	$1.65	$2.75	£0.35	£1.05	£1.75
Title Value:	$1.15	$3.45	$5.75	£0.75	£2.25	£3.75

BOZO THE CLOWN IN 3-D
Blackthorne; (3-D Series #24) 1 Autumn 1987

	$Good	$Fine	$N.Mint	£Good	£Fine	£N.Mint
1 ND with bound-in 3-D glasses (25% less if without glasses)	$0.40	$1.20	$2.00	£0.25	£0.75	£1.25
Title Value:	$0.40	$1.20	$2.00	£0.25	£0.75	£1.25

BOZZ CHRONICLES, THE
Marvel Comics Group/Epic; 1 Dec 1985-6 May 1986

	$Good	$Fine	$N.Mint	£Good	£Fine	£N.Mint
1-6 ND	$0.35	$1.05	$1.75	£0.25	£0.75	£1.25
Title Value:	$2.10	$6.30	$10.50	£1.50	£4.50	£7.50

Note: all high-quality paper.

BRAIN BOY
Dell; 1 Apr/Jun 1962-6 Sep/Nov 1963

	$Good	$Fine	$N.Mint	£Good	£Fine	£N.Mint
1 scarce, distributed in the U.K.	$14.00	$43.00	$100.00	£9.25	£28.00	£65.00
2-6 distributed in the U.K.	$7.75	$23.50	$55.00	£5.25	£16.00	£37.50
Title Value:	$52.75	$160.50	$375.00	£35.50	£108.00	£252.50

BRAM STOKER'S BURIAL OF THE RATS
Cosmic Comics; 1 Apr 1995-3 1995

	$Good	$Fine	$N.Mint	£Good	£Fine	£N.Mint
1-3 ND Jerry Prosser script, Val Mayerik art; based on film	$0.45	$1.35	$2.25	£0.30	£0.90	£1.50
Title Value:	$1.35	$4.05	$6.75	£0.90	£2.70	£4.50

BRATPACK
Tundra Publishing,MS; 1 Aug 1990-5 1991

	$Good	$Fine	$N.Mint	£Good	£Fine	£N.Mint
1 ND Rick Veitch story/art	$0.60	$1.80	$3.00	£0.40	£1.20	£2.00
1 2nd printing ND	$0.45	$1.35	$2.25	£0.30	£0.90	£1.50
2-5 ND	$0.50	$1.50	$2.50	£0.35	£1.05	£1.75
Title Value:	$3.05	$9.15	$15.25	£2.10	£6.30	£10.50

Note: bi-monthly.

BRATS BIZARRE
Marvel Comics Group/Epic,MS; 1 May 1994-4 Aug 1994

1-4 ND Pat Mills and Tony Skinner script

	$Good	$Fine	$N.Mint	£Good	£Fine	£N.Mint
	$0.35	$1.05	$1.75	£0.25	£0.75	£1.25
Title Value:	$1.40	$4.20	$7.00	£1.00	£3.00	£5.00

BRAVE AND THE BOLD SPECIAL, THE
DC Comics; 8 1978
(DC Special Series #8)

	$Good	$Fine	$N.Mint	£Good	£Fine	£N.Mint
8 ND 52pgs, features Batman and Sgt. Rock, Deadman and Sherlock Holmes	$0.90	$2.70	$4.50	£0.60	£1.80	£3.00
Title Value:	$0.90	$2.70	$4.50	£0.60	£1.80	£3.00

BRAVE AND THE BOLD, THE
National Periodical Publications/DC Comics; 1 Aug/Sep 1955-200 Jul 1983
(see Best of the Brave and the Bold, Super DC Giant 16)

	$Good	$Fine	$N.Mint	£Good	£Fine	£N.Mint
1 Viking Prince by Kubert, Golden Gladiator and Silent Knight all begin	$250.00	$750.00	$2250.00	£165.00	£500.00	£1500.00
2	$100.00	$300.00	$900.00	£65.00	£200.00	£600.00
3-4	$60.00	$180.00	$550.00	£42.00	£125.00	£375.00
5 Robin Hood begins	$60.00	$180.00	$550.00	£42.00	£125.00	£375.00
6 no Viking Prince	$46.00	$135.00	$365.00	£31.00	£90.00	£245.00
7-10	$46.00	$135.00	$365.00	£31.00	£90.00	£245.00
11-21	$34.00	$100.00	$275.00	£23.00	£67.50	£185.00
22 last Silent Knight	$34.00	$100.00	$275.00	£23.00	£67.50	£185.00
23 origin Viking Prince by Kubert; 1st small logo	$43.00	$125.00	$340.00	£28.00	£82.50	£225.00
24	$34.00	$100.00	$275.00	£23.00	£67.50	£185.00
25 rare in the U.K., 1st appearance Suicide Squad	$39.00	$115.00	$310.00	£27.00	£80.00	£215.00

1st official distribution in the U.K.

	$Good	$Fine	$N.Mint	£Good	£Fine	£N.Mint
26 very scarce in the U.K. Suicide Squad	$33.00	$97.50	$265.00	£21.50	£65.00	£175.00
27 scarce in the U.K. Suicide Squad	$33.00	$97.50	$265.00	£20.50	£60.00	£165.00
28 1st appearance Justice League of America, origin and 1st appearance Snapper Carr	$430.00	$1275.00	$4750.00	£305.00	£920.00	£3400.00

[Scarce in high grade - Very Fine+ or better]

	$Good	$Fine	$N.Mint	£Good	£Fine	£N.Mint
28 ND Silver Age Classic reprint (Mar 1992)	$0.25	$0.75	$1.25	£0.15	£0.50	£0.85
29 2nd appearance Justice League of America	$210.00	$630.00	$2100.00	£125.00	£375.00	£1250.00
30 scarce in the U.K., 3rd appearance Justice League of America, 1st appearance Amazo	$170.00	$510.00	$1700.00	£125.00	£375.00	£1250.00

[Scarce in high grade - Very Fine+ or better]

	$Good	$Fine	$N.Mint	£Good	£Fine	£N.Mint
31 1st appearance Cave Carson	$31.00	$92.50	$250.00	£20.50	£60.00	£165.00
32 rare in the U.K., 2nd appearance Cave Carson	$21.50	$65.00	$175.00	£15.00	£45.00	£120.00
33 3rd appearance Cave Carson	$21.50	$65.00	$175.00	£13.50	£41.00	£110.00
34 origin and 1st appearance Silver Age Hawkman by Kubert; classic cover	$175.00	$520.00	$1750.00	£120.00	£360.00	£1200.00

[Scarce in high grade - Very Fine+ or better]

	$Good	$Fine	$N.Mint	£Good	£Fine	£N.Mint
35 2nd appearance Silver Age Hawkman by Kubert	$62.50	$185.00	$500.00	£43.00	£125.00	£340.00
36 3rd appearance Silver Age Hawkman by Kubert	$50.00	$155.00	$415.00	£34.00	£100.00	£275.00
37 Suicide Squad	$31.00	$92.50	$250.00	£20.50	£60.00	£165.00
38-39 Suicide Squad	$25.00	$75.00	$200.00	£16.50	£50.00	£135.00
40-41 Cave Carson	$16.50	$50.00	$135.00	£11.00	£34.00	£90.00
42 Hawkman by Kubert	$36.00	$105.00	$285.00	£23.50	£70.00	£190.00
43 Hawkman origin retold by Kubert	$38.00	$115.00	$345.00	£26.00	£75.00	£230.00
44 Hawkman by Kubert, painted cover	$30.00	$90.00	$240.00	£20.00	£60.00	£160.00
45-49 Strange Sports	$8.50	$26.00	$60.00	£5.00	£15.00	£35.00
50 1st team-up issue, Green Arrow and Manhunter from Mars	$17.50	$52.50	$160.00	£10.50	£32.00	£95.00
51 Aquaman and Hawkman (pre-dates Hawkman #1)	$24.00	$72.50	$220.00	£8.75	£27.00	£80.00
52 scarce in the U.K. Sgt. Rock & 3 Battle Aces; Kubert art	$12.50	$38.00	$100.00	£7.50	£22.50	£60.00
53 Atom and Flash, art by Alex Toth	$8.50	$26.00	$60.00	£5.00	£15.00	£35.00
54 Kid Flash, Robin and Aqualad; 1st "Teen Titans"	$35.00	$105.00	$245.00	£21.00	£62.50	£150.00
55 Metal Men and Atom	$5.50	$17.00	$40.00	£3.55	£10.50	£25.00
56 Flash and Manhunter from Mars	$5.50	$17.00	$40.00	£3.55	£10.50	£25.00
57 1st appearance Metamorpho	$19.00	$57.50	$135.00	£9.25	£28.00	£65.00
58 2nd appearance Metamorpho	$9.25	$28.00	$65.00	£5.00	£15.00	£35.00
59 Batman team-ups begin; Green Lantern	$12.50	$39.00	$90.00	£7.00	£21.00	£50.00
60 Teen Titans (first time title used: see Showcase #59)	$10.50	$32.00	$75.00	£7.00	£21.00	£50.00

#	Description	$Good	$Fine	$N.Mint	£Good	£Fine	£N.Mint
61	Starman and Black Canary, 1pg text origins of both	$16.50	$50.00	$100.00	£5.00	£15.00	£30.00
62	Starman and Black Canary; 1st Silver Age Wildcat	$16.50	$50.00	$100.00	£5.00	£15.00	£30.00
63	Supergirl and Wonder Woman; last Silver Age issue cover-dated January but indicia-dated December 1965/January 1966	$4.15	$12.50	$25.00	£2.50	£7.50	£15.00
64	2nd Batman team-up, with and versus Eclipso	$9.00	$28.00	$55.00	£5.75	£17.50	£35.00
65	Flash and Doom Patrol	$2.50	$7.50	$15.00	£1.65	£5.00	£10.00
66	Metamorpho and Metal Men	$2.50	$7.50	$15.00	£1.65	£5.00	£10.00
67	Batman and Flash by Infantino	$5.75	$17.50	$35.00	£3.75	£11.00	£22.50
68	Batman (as Bat-Hulk) and Metamorpho; Joker, Riddler and Penguin appear	$9.50	$29.00	$57.50	£5.00	£15.00	£30.00
69	Batman and Green Lantern	$4.15	$12.50	$25.00	£2.50	£7.50	£15.00
70	Batman and Hawkman	$4.15	$12.50	$25.00	£2.50	£7.50	£15.00
71	Batman and Green Arrow	$4.15	$12.50	$25.00	£2.05	£6.25	£12.50
72	Flash and Spectre	$4.15	$12.50	$25.00	£1.65	£5.00	£10.00
73	Aquaman and Atom	$4.15	$12.50	$25.00	£1.65	£5.00	£10.00
74	Batman and Metal Men; regular Batman team-ups begin (end #200)	$3.65	$11.00	$22.00	£2.05	£6.25	£12.50
75	Spectre	$4.15	$12.50	$25.00	£1.65	£5.00	£10.00
76	Plastic Man	$3.65	$11.00	$22.00	£1.65	£5.00	£10.00
77	Atom	$3.65	$11.00	$22.00	£1.65	£5.00	£10.00
78	Wonder Woman, Batgirl	$3.65	$11.00	$22.00	£1.65	£5.00	£10.00
79	Neal Adams art, Deadman; the first issue of a classic run	$5.75	$17.50	$35.00	£3.30	£10.00	£20.00
80	Neal Adams art, Creeper appears	$5.00	$15.00	$30.00	£2.30	£7.00	£14.00
81	Neal Adams art, Flash appears	$5.00	$15.00	$30.00	£2.30	£7.00	£14.00
82	Neal Adams art, Aquaman appears	$5.00	$15.00	$30.00	£2.30	£7.00	£14.00
83	Neal Adams art, Teen Titans appears	$6.50	$20.00	$40.00	£3.30	£10.00	£20.00
84	Neal Adams art, Sgt. Rock appears	$5.00	$15.00	$30.00	£2.30	£7.00	£14.00
85	Neal Adams art, Green Arrow appears (1st "new look" Green Arrow with new costume and goatee beard)	$5.00	$15.00	$30.00	£2.30	£7.00	£14.00
86	Neal Adams art, Deadman appears	$5.00	$15.00	$30.00	£2.30	£7.00	£14.00
87	Wonder Woman	$3.30	$10.00	$20.00	£1.65	£5.00	£10.00
88	Wildcat	$3.30	$10.00	$20.00	£1.65	£5.00	£10.00
89	Phantom Stranger	$3.30	$10.00	$20.00	£1.65	£5.00	£10.00
90	Adam Strange	$3.30	$10.00	$20.00	£1.65	£5.00	£10.00
91	Black Canary	$3.30	$10.00	$20.00	£1.65	£5.00	£10.00
92	Bat Squad	$3.30	$10.00	$20.00	£1.65	£5.00	£10.00
93	Neal Adams art, House of Mystery	$4.55	$13.50	$27.50	£2.50	£7.50	£15.00
94	Teen Titans	$2.00	$6.00	$12.00	£1.15	£3.50	£7.00
95	Plastic Man	$1.80	$5.50	$11.00	£1.00	£3.00	£6.00
96	Sgt. Rock	$1.80	$5.50	$11.00	£1.00	£3.00	£6.00
97	52pgs, Wildcat; Deadman origin	$1.80	$5.50	$11.00	£1.00	£3.00	£6.00
98	52pgs, Phantom Stranger	$1.80	$5.50	$11.00	£1.00	£3.00	£6.00
99	52pgs, Flash	$1.80	$5.50	$11.00	£1.00	£3.00	£6.00
100	52pgs, Neal Adams art on Deadman reprints, Green Lantern, Green Arrow, Black Canary and Robin appear	$4.15	$12.50	$25.00	£1.65	£5.00	£10.00
101	52pgs, Metamorpho	$0.80	$2.50	$5.00	£0.50	£1.60	£3.25
102	Neal Adams art, Teen Titans appear	$1.30	$4.00	$8.00	£0.80	£2.50	£5.00
103	Metal Men	$0.80	$2.50	$5.00	£0.50	£1.60	£3.25
104	Deadman	$0.80	$2.50	$5.00	£0.50	£1.60	£3.25
105	Wonder Woman	$0.80	$2.50	$5.00	£0.50	£1.60	£3.25
106	Green Arrow	$0.80	$2.50	$5.00	£0.50	£1.60	£3.25
107	Black Canary	$0.80	$2.50	$5.00	£0.50	£1.60	£3.25
108	Sgt. Rock	$0.80	$2.50	$5.00	£0.50	£1.60	£3.25
109	Demon	$0.80	$2.50	$5.00	£0.50	£1.60	£3.25
110	Wildcat	$0.80	$2.50	$5.00	£0.50	£1.60	£3.25
111	The Joker	$0.80	$2.50	$5.00	£1.15	£3.50	£7.00
112	100pgs, Mister Miracle; reprints Brave and the Bold #15, #51, #58	$1.30	$4.00	$8.00	£0.80	£2.50	£5.00
113	100pgs, Metal Men; reprints Brave and the Bold #34 (1st Silver Age Hawkman)	$1.30	$4.00	$8.00		£2.50	£5.00
114	100pgs, Aquaman; reprints Brave and the Bold #50	$1.30	$4.00	$8.00	£0.80	£2.50	£5.00
115	100pgs, Atom; reprints Showcase #55	$1.30	$4.00	$8.00	£0.80	£2.50	£5.00
116	100pgs, Spectre; reprints Brave and the Bold #2, #78, Teen Titans #16	$1.30	$4.00	$8.00	£0.80	£2.50	£5.00
117	100pgs, Sgt.Rock; reprints Brave and the Bold #24, Secret Six #1	$1.30	$4.00	$8.00	£0.80	£2.50	£5.00
118	Wildcat and The Joker	$1.80	$5.50	$11.00	£1.15	£3.50	£7.00
119	Man-Bat	$0.55	$1.75	$3.50	£0.35	£1.10	£2.25
120	scarce in the U.K. 68pgs, Kamandi The Last Boy On Earth	$0.55	$1.75	$3.50	£0.55	£1.75	£3.50
121	scarce in the U.K. Metal Men	$0.55	$1.75	$3.50	£0.50	£1.50	£3.00
122	scarce in the U.K. Swamp Thing	$0.55	$1.75	$3.50	£0.50	£1.50	£3.00
123	Plastic Man and Metamorpho	$0.55	$1.75	$3.50	£0.35	£1.10	£2.25
124	Sgt. Rock	$0.55	$1.75	$3.50	£0.35	£1.10	£2.25
125	scarce in the U.K. Flash	$0.55	$1.75	$3.50	£0.40	£1.25	£2.50
126	scarce in the U.K. Aquaman	$0.55	$1.75	$3.50	£0.40	£1.25	£2.50
127	Wildcat	$0.55	$1.75	$3.50	£0.35	£1.10	£2.25
128	scarce in the U.K. Mister Miracle	$0.55	$1.75	$3.50	£0.40	£1.25	£2.50
129	ND Green Arrow, Joker and Two Face appear	$1.80	$5.50	$11.00	£1.15	£3.50	£7.00
130	Two-Face, Joker, Green Arrow and Atom	$1.80	$5.50	$11.00	£1.00	£3.00	£6.00
131	scarce in the U.K. Wonder Woman; Catwoman appears	$0.55	$1.75	$3.50	£0.40	£1.25	£2.50
132	scarce in the U.K. Richard Dragon Kung Fu Fighter	$0.55	$1.75	$3.50	£0.40	£1.25	£2.50
133	scarce in the U.K. Deadman	$0.55	$1.75	$3.50	£0.40	£1.25	£2.50
134	Green Lantern	$0.50	$1.50	$3.00	£0.30	£1.00	£2.00
135	Metal Men	$0.50	$1.50	$3.00	£0.30	£1.00	£2.00
136	Green Arrow and Metal Men	$0.50	$1.50	$3.00	£0.30	£1.00	£2.00
137	Demon	$0.50	$1.50	$3.00	£0.30	£1.00	£2.00
138	Mister Miracle	$0.50	$1.50	$3.00	£0.30	£1.00	£2.00
139	scarce in the U.K. Hawkman	$0.50	$1.50	$3.00	£0.35	£1.10	£2.25
140	Wonder Woman	$0.50	$1.50	$3.00	£0.30	£1.00	£2.00
141	Black Canary; Joker appears	$1.65	$5.00	$10.00	£0.80	£2.50	£5.00
142	Aquaman	$0.50	$1.50	$3.00	£0.25	£0.75	£1.50
143	scarce in the U.K. 44pgs, Creeper	$0.50	$1.50	$3.00	£0.30	£1.00	£2.00
144	scarce in the U.K. 44pgs, Green Arrow	$0.50	$1.50	$3.00	£0.30	£1.00	£2.00
145	Phantom Stranger	$0.50	$1.50	$3.00	£0.25	£0.75	£1.50
146	Unknown Soldier	$0.50	$1.50	$3.00	£0.25	£0.75	£1.50
147	Supergirl	$0.50	$1.50	$3.00	£0.25	£0.75	£1.50
148	Plastic Man	$0.50	$1.50	$3.00	£0.25	£0.75	£1.50
149	Teen Titans	$0.50	$1.50	$3.00	£0.25	£0.75	£1.50
150	Superman	$0.50	$1.50	$3.00	£0.25	£0.75	£1.50
151	Flash	$0.40	$1.25	$2.50	£0.25	£0.75	£1.50
152	Atom	$0.40	$1.25	$2.50	£0.25	£0.75	£1.50
153	Red Tornado	$0.40	$1.25	$2.50	£0.25	£0.75	£1.50
154	Metamorpho	$0.40	$1.25	$2.50	£0.25	£0.75	£1.50
155	Green Lantern	$0.40	$1.25	$2.50	£0.25	£0.75	£1.50
156	Dr. Fate	$0.40	$1.25	$2.50	£0.25	£0.75	£1.50
157	Kamandi	$0.40	$1.25	$2.50	£0.25	£0.75	£1.50
158	Wonder Woman	$0.40	$1.25	$2.50	£0.25	£0.75	£1.50
159	R'as Al Ghul	$0.40	$1.25	$2.50	£0.25	£0.75	£1.50
160	Supergirl	$0.40	$1.25	$2.50	£0.25	£0.75	£1.50
161	Adam Strange	$0.40	$1.25	$2.50	£0.25	£0.75	£1.50
162	Sgt. Rock	$0.40	$1.25	$2.50	£0.25	£0.75	£1.50
163	Black Lightning	$0.40	$1.25	$2.50	£0.25	£0.75	£1.50
164	Hawkman	$0.40	$1.25	$2.50	£0.25	£0.75	£1.50
165	Man-Bat	$0.40	$1.25	$2.50	£0.25	£0.75	£1.50
166	Black Canary; Penguin appears	$0.40	$1.25	$2.50	£0.25	£0.75	£1.50
167	Blackhawk	$0.40	$1.25	$2.50	£0.25	£0.75	£1.50
168	Green Arrow	$0.40	$1.25	$2.50	£0.25	£0.75	£1.50
169	Zatanna	$0.40	$1.25	$2.50	£0.25	£0.75	£1.50
170	Nemesis	$0.40	$1.25	$2.50	£0.25	£0.75	£1.50
171	Scalphunter	$0.30	$1.00	$2.00	£0.20	£0.60	£1.25
172	Firestorm	$0.30	$1.00	$2.00	£0.20	£0.60	£1.25
173	Guardians of the Universe	$0.30	$1.00	$2.00	£0.20	£0.60	£1.25
174	Green Lantern	$0.30	$1.00	$2.00	£0.20	£0.60	£1.25
175	Lois Lane	$0.30	$1.00	$2.00	£0.20	£0.60	£1.25
176	Swamp Thing, Kaluta cover						

	$Good	$Fine	$N.Mint	£Good	£Fine	£N.Mint
	$0.30	$1.00	$2.00	£0.20	£0.60	£1.25
177 Elongated Man	$0.30	$1.00	$2.00	£0.20	£0.60	£1.25
178 Creeper	$0.30	$1.00	$2.00	£0.20	£0.60	£1.25
179 Legion of Super-Heroes						
	$0.30	$1.00	$2.00	£0.20	£0.60	£1.25
180 The Spectre	$0.30	$1.00	$2.00	£0.20	£0.60	£1.25
181 Hawk and the Dove						
	$0.30	$1.00	$2.00	£0.20	£0.60	£1.25
182 Earth-2 Robin	$0.30	$1.00	$2.00	£0.20	£0.60	£1.25
183 Riddler	$0.30	$1.00	$2.00	£0.20	£0.60	£1.25
184 Huntress	$0.30	$1.00	$2.00	£0.20	£0.60	£1.25
185 Green Arrow	$0.30	$1.00	$2.00	£0.20	£0.60	£1.25
186 Hawkman	$0.30	$1.00	$2.00	£0.20	£0.60	£1.25
187 Metal Men	$0.30	$1.00	$2.00	£0.20	£0.60	£1.25
188-189 Rose and the Thorn						
	$0.30	$1.00	$2.00	£0.20	£0.60	£1.25
190 Adam Strange	$0.30	$1.00	$2.00	£0.20	£0.60	£1.25
191 LD in the U.K. Joker						
	$0.80	$2.40	$4.00	£0.50	£1.50	£2.50
192 Superboy	$0.30	$1.00	$2.00	£0.20	£0.60	£1.25
193 Nemesis	$0.30	$1.00	$2.00	£0.20	£0.60	£1.25
194 Flash	$0.30	$1.00	$2.00	£0.20	£0.60	£1.25
195 "I" Vampire	$0.30	$1.00	$2.00	£0.20	£0.60	£1.25
196 Ragman	$0.30	$1.00	$2.00	£0.20	£0.60	£1.25
197 Catwoman, Staton art; Earth-2 Batman marries Catwoman						
	$0.40	$1.25	$2.50	£0.25	£0.75	£1.50
198 Karate Kid	$0.30	$1.00	$2.00	£0.20	£0.60	£1.25
199 Spectre	$0.30	$1.00	$2.00	£0.20	£0.60	£1.25
200 68pgs, Earth-1 and Earth-2 Batman team, Gibbons art; 1st appearance Batman & the Outsiders (preview)						
	$1.15	$3.50	$7.00	£0.75	£2.25	£4.50
Title Value:	$3188.40	$9516.65	$28017.25	£2093.25	£6250.60	£18560.10

Note: Joker covers and stories-68, 111, 118, 129, 130, 141, 191.
Note also that Neal Adams finished the artwork for issue 102 when Jim Aparo fell ill.

BRAVE AND THE BOLD, THE (2ND SERIES)
DC Comics,MS; 1 Dec 1991-6 Jun 1992

	$Good	$Fine	$N.Mint	£Good	£Fine	£N.Mint
1 Green Arrow, Black Canary, Butcher and The Question feature, Mike Grell covers begin						
	$0.30	$0.90	$1.50	£0.20	£0.60	£1.00
2-6	$0.30	$0.90	$1.50	£0.20	£0.60	£1.00
Title Value:	$1.80	$5.40	$9.00	£1.20	£3.60	£6.00

BRAVESTARR IN 3-D
Blackthorne; (3-D Series #27,#40); 1 Autumn 1987-2 Apr 1988

	$Good	$Fine	$N.Mint	£Good	£Fine	£N.Mint
1-2 ND with bound-in 3-D glasses (25% less if without glasses)						
	$0.40	$1.20	$2.00	£0.25	£0.75	£1.25
Title Value:	$0.80	$2.40	$4.00	£0.50	£1.50	£2.50

BRAVURA
Hero Illustrated; ½ Feb 1994

	$Good	$Fine	$N.Mint	£Good	£Fine	£N.Mint
½ ND 16pgs, presented free with Hero Illustrated #9; previews Bravura titles						
	$0.25	$0.75	$1.25	£0.15	£0.50	£0.85
Title Value:	$0.25	$0.75	$1.25	£0.15	£0.50	£0.85

BREAK THE CHAIN
Marvel Comics Group; 1 Aug 1994

	$Good	$Fine	$N.Mint	£Good	£Fine	£N.Mint
1 ND pre-bagged with audio cassette						
	$1.00	$3.00	$5.00	£0.65	£1.95	£3.25
Title Value:	$1.00	$3.00	$5.00	£0.65	£1.95	£3.25

BREAK-THRU
Malibu Ultraverse; 1 Dec 1993-2 Jan 1994

	$Good	$Fine	$N.Mint	£Good	£Fine	£N.Mint
1 ND George Perez art and cover; continued directly from Exiles #4						
	$0.35	$1.05	$1.75	£0.25	£0.75	£1.25
2 ND George Perez art and cover						
	$0.35	$1.05	$1.75	£0.25	£0.75	£1.25
Title Value:	$0.70	$2.10	$3.50	£0.50	£1.50	£2.50

BREATHTAKER
DC Comics,MS; 1 Sep 1990-4 Dec 1990

	$Good	$Fine	$N.Mint	£Good	£Fine	£N.Mint
1-4 ND 48pgs	$0.60	$1.80	$3.00	£0.40	£1.20	£2.00
Title Value:	$2.40	$7.20	$12.00	£1.60	£4.80	£8.00

Note: Prestige Format, Mature Readers
Breathtaker (Jun 1994) Trade paperback
reprints mini-series, new introduction by Neil Gaiman £2.00 £6.00 £10.00

BREED
Malibu Bravura,MS; 1 Jan 1994-6 Jun 1994

	$Good	$Fine	$N.Mint	£Good	£Fine	£N.Mint
1 ND Jim Starlin script and art begins						
	$0.60	$1.80	$3.00	£0.40	£1.20	£2.00
1 Newstand edition, ND pre-bagged but with alternative cover						
	$0.60	$1.80	$3.00	£0.40	£1.20	£2.00
2-6 ND	$0.45	$1.35	$2.25	£0.30	£0.90	£1.50
Title Value:	$3.45	$10.35	$17.25	£2.30	£6.90	£11.50

Breed Collection Softcover (Sep 1994) Trade paperback
reprints mini-series, digitally re-mastered. Bagged £1.70 £5.10 £8.50
Breed Collection Softcover Limited Signed Edition (Sep 1994)
as above, signed by Jim Starlin. 500 copies £4.00 £12.00 £20.00

BREED II: THE BOOK OF REVELATIONS
Malibu Bravura,MS; 1 Nov 1994-6 Apr 1995

	$Good	$Fine	$N.Mint	£Good	£Fine	£N.Mint
1 ND 40pgs, Jim Starlin script and art						
	$0.50	$1.50	$2.50	£0.35	£1.05	£1.75
1 ND Gold Foil Edition (Mar 1995)						
	$1.80	$5.25	$9.00	£1.20	£3.60	£6.00
2-6 ND 40pgs, Jim Starlin script and art						
	$0.45	$1.35	$2.25	£0.30	£0.90	£1.50
Title Value:	$4.55	$13.50	$22.75	£3.05	£9.15	£15.25

BRENDA STARR, REPORTER
Charlton; 13 Jun 1955-15 Oct 1955

	$Good	$Fine	$N.Mint	£Good	£Fine	£N.Mint
13-15 scarce, not distributed in the U.K.						
	$30.00	$90.00	$180.00	£20.00	£60.00	£120.00
Title Value:	$90.00	$270.00	$540.00	£60.00	£180.00	£360.00

BRENDA STARR, REPORTER (2ND SERIES)
Blackthorne; 1 Apr 1986

	$Good	$Fine	$N.Mint	£Good	£Fine	£N.Mint
1 ND 72pgs, squarebound						
	$0.45	$1.35	$2.25	£0.30	£0.90	£1.50
Title Value:	$0.45	$1.35	$2.25	£0.30	£0.90	£1.50

BRIAN BOLLAND'S BLACK BOOK
Eclipse/Quality,OS; 1 Jul 1985

	$Good	$Fine	$N.Mint	£Good	£Fine	£N.Mint
1 ND reprints left-over inventory from House of Hammer magazine (packaged by then Quality editor Dez Skinn)						
	$0.60	$1.80	$3.00	£0.40	£1.20	£2.00
Title Value:	$0.60	$1.80	$3.00	£0.40	£1.20	£2.00

BRIGADE
Image,MS; 1 Aug 1992-4 Apr 1993

	$Good	$Fine	$N.Mint	£Good	£Fine	£N.Mint
1 Rob Liefeld script and cover art, includes two trading cards						
	$0.80	$2.40	$4.00	£0.50	£1.50	£2.50
1 gold embossed cover						
	$1.80	$5.25	$9.00	£1.20	£3.60	£6.00
1 gold embossed cover, signed by Rob Liefeld						
	$3.00	$9.00	$15.00	£2.00	£6.00	£10.00
2 contains Image #0 coupon 4						
	$0.60	$1.80	$3.00	£0.40	£1.20	£2.00
2 without coupon	$0.45	$1.35	$2.25	£0.30	£0.90	£1.50
3 with 2 trading cards						
	$0.45	$1.35	$2.25	£0.30	£0.90	£1.50
4	$0.45	$1.35	$2.25	£0.30	£0.90	£1.50
Title Value:	$7.55	$22.50	$37.75	£5.00	£15.00	£25.00

Note: all Non-Distributed on the news-stands in the U.K.

BRIGADE (2ND SERIES)
Image; 0 Sep 1993; 1 May 1993-present

	$Good	$Fine	$N.Mint	£Good	£Fine	£N.Mint
0 (Sep 1993) Jeff Matsuda and Norm Rapmund art						
	$0.40	$1.20	$2.00	£0.25	£0.75	£1.25
1 Rob Liefeld script, Marat Mychaels and Norm Rapmund art begin; gatefold cover						
	$0.50	$1.50	$2.50	£0.30	£0.90	£1.50
2 silver foil embossed cover						
	$0.50	$1.50	$2.50	£0.30	£0.90	£1.50
3	$0.40	$1.20	$2.00	£0.25	£0.75	£1.25
4 new facts about Seahawk's and Coldsnap's origins						
	$0.40	$1.20	$2.00	£0.25	£0.75	£1.25
5-7	$0.40	$1.20	$2.00	£0.25	£0.75	£1.25
8 Extreme Prejudice part 2						
	$0.40	$1.20	$2.00	£0.25	£0.75	£1.25
9 Extreme Prejudice part 6, with coupon						
	$0.40	$1.20	$2.00	£0.25	£0.75	£1.25
10 Extreme Prejudice Aftermath						
	$0.40	$1.20	$2.00	£0.25	£0.75	£1.25
11 Brigade vs. Wildc.a.t.s.						
	$0.40	$1.20	$2.00	£0.25	£0.75	£1.25
12-13	$0.40	$1.20	$2.00	£0.25	£0.75	£1.25
14-15 ties into issue #25						
	$0.40	$1.20	$2.00	£0.25	£0.75	£1.25
16 Extreme Sacrifice part 3, continued in Newmen #10; pre-bagged with trading card						
	$0.40	$1.20	$2.00	£0.25	£0.75	£1.25
17-19	$0.40	$1.20	$2.00	£0.25	£0.75	£1.25
20 Alien Cult Saga concludes						
	$0.40	$1.20	$2.00	£0.25	£0.75	£1.25
20 Variant cover, Joe Quesada/Jimmy Palmiotti cover art						
	$0.80	$2.40	$4.00	£0.50	£1.50	£2.50
21	$0.40	$1.20	$2.00	£0.25	£0.75	£1.25
22 Supreme Apocalypse part 4, continued in Supreme #30						
	$0.40	$1.20	$2.00	£0.25	£0.75	£1.25
23-24	$0.40	$1.20	$2.00	£0.25	£0.75	£1.25
25 cover-dated May 1994, issued between issues #9 and 10 as part of "Images of Tomorrow" previewing what the 25th issue will read/look like						
	$0.40	$1.20	$2.00	£0.25	£0.75	£1.25
26	$0.40	$1.20	$2.00	£0.25	£0.75	£1.25
27 Extreme Babewatch						
	$0.50	$1.50	$2.50	£0.30	£0.90	£1.50
Title Value:	$12.30	$36.90	$61.50	£7.65	£22.95	£38.25

Note: all Non-Distributed on the news-stands in the U.K.

BRIGADE SOURCEBOOK
Image; 1 Aug 1994

	$Good	$Fine	$N.Mint	£Good	£Fine	£N.Mint
1 ND information and statistics about Brigade characters						
	$0.45	$1.35	$2.25	£0.30	£0.90	£1.50
Title Value:	$0.45	$1.35	$2.25	£0.30	£0.90	£1.50

BRINKE OF ETERNITY
Chaos Comics,MS; 1 Apr 1994-3 Jun 1994

	$Good	$Fine	$N.Mint	£Good	£Fine	£N.Mint
1-3 ND scream queen Brinke Stevens appears, (yummy)						
	$0.55	$1.65	$2.75	£0.35	£1.05	£1.75
Title Value:	$1.65	$4.95	$8.25	£1.05	£3.15	£5.25

BRONX
Eternity,MS; 1 Sep 1991-3 Nov 1991

	$Good	$Fine	$N.Mint	£Good	£Fine	£N.Mint
1-3 ND	$0.45	$1.35	$2.25	£0.30	£0.90	£1.50
Title Value:	$1.35	$4.05	$6.75	£0.90	£2.70	£4.50

BROOKLYN DREAMS
DC Comics/Paradox Press,MS; 1 Jan 1995-4 Apr 1995

	$Good	$Fine	$N.Mint	£Good	£Fine	£N.Mint
1-4 ND 96pgs, black and white; unusual 5" x 8" size						
	$0.90	$2.70	$4.50	£0.60	£1.80	£3.00
Title Value:	$3.60	$10.80	$18.00	£2.40	£7.20	£12.00

BROTHER BILLY, THE PAIN FROM THE PLAINS
Marvel Comics Group,Magazine OS; 1 1979

1 ND Jimmy Carter satire

	$Good	$Fine	$N.Mint	£Good	£Fine	£N.Mint
1 ND Jimmy Carter satire	$0.45	$1.35	$2.25	£0.30	£0.90	£1.50
Title Value:	$0.45	$1.35	$2.25	£0.30	£0.90	£1.50

BROTHER POWER, THE GEEK
(see Geek)

BROTHERS OF THE SPEAR
Gold Key; 1 Jun 1972-17 Feb 1976; Whitman; 18 May 1982

	$Good	$Fine	$N.Mint	£Good	£Fine	£N.Mint
1 scarce in the U.K. Dan-El and Natongo stories continue from Tarzan back-up; Jesse Santos art begins (ends #12)	$3.00	$9.00	$15.00	£2.00	£6.00	£10.00
2 painted covers begin	$1.80	$5.25	$9.00	£1.20	£3.60	£6.00
3	$1.05	$3.15	$5.25	£0.70	£2.10	£3.50
4-10	$0.90	$2.70	$4.50	£0.60	£1.80	£3.00
11	$0.60	$1.80	$3.00	£0.40	£1.20	£2.00
12 line drawn cover, reprints #1	$0.60	$1.80	$3.00	£0.40	£1.20	£2.00
13 Dan Spiegle art begins (ends #17)	$0.60	$1.80	$3.00	£0.40	£1.20	£2.00
14-16	$0.60	$1.80	$3.00	£0.40	£1.20	£2.00
17 last painted cover	$0.60	$1.80	$3.00	£0.40	£1.20	£2.00
18 scarce in the U.K. reprints #2, line-drawn cover	$0.80	$2.40	$4.00	£0.50	£1.50	£2.50
Title Value:	$17.15	$51.30	$85.75	£11.40	£34.20	£57.00

Note: all Limited Distribution on the news-stands in the U.K.

BRUCE JONES' OUTER EDGE
Innovation,OS; 1 Nov 1992

	$Good	$Fine	$N.Mint	£Good	£Fine	£N.Mint
1 ND four sci-fi stories	$0.45	$1.35	$2.25	£0.30	£0.90	£1.50
Title Value:	$0.45	$1.35	$2.25	£0.30	£0.90	£1.50

BRUCE JONES' RAZOR EDGE
Innovation,OS; 1 Dec 1992

	$Good	$Fine	$N.Mint	£Good	£Fine	£N.Mint
1 ND four horror stories	$0.45	$1.35	$2.25	£0.30	£0.90	£1.50
Title Value:	$0.45	$1.35	$2.25	£0.30	£0.90	£1.50

BRUCE LEE
Malibu,MS; 1 Jul 1994-6 Dec 1994

	$Good	$Fine	$N.Mint	£Good	£Fine	£N.Mint
1-6 Mike Baron script and Val Mayerik art	$0.45	$1.35	$2.25	£0.30	£0.90	£1.50
Title Value:	$2.70	$8.10	$13.50	£1.80	£5.40	£9.00

Note: all Non-Distributed on the newsstands in the U.K.

BRUTE & BABE MONUMENT SET
Ominous Press; 1 Jul 1994-2 1994?

	$Good	$Fine	$N.Mint	£Good	£Fine	£N.Mint
1 ND Bart Sears script, Andy Smith art; 16pg unstapled comic forming a single splash page included in a clear plastic slipcase	$0.80	$2.40	$4.00	£0.50	£1.50	£2.50
2 ND Bart Sears script, Andy Smith art; 16pg unstapled comic forming a single splash page included in a clear plastic slipcase	$1.00	$3.00	$5.00	£0.65	£1.95	£3.25
Title Value:	$1.80	$5.40	$9.00	£1.15	£3.45	£5.75

BRUTE & BABE: CHAKALL, SHE-SLAVE FROM BEYOND
Ominous Press,MS; 1 Dec 1994

	$Good	$Fine	$N.Mint	£Good	£Fine	£N.Mint
1 ND Bart Sears script	$0.40	$1.20	$2.00	£0.25	£0.75	£1.25
Title Value:	$0.40	$1.20	$2.00	£0.25	£0.75	£1.25

BRUTE & BABE: INFINITY
Ominous Press,OS; nn Oct 1994

	$Good	$Fine	$N.Mint	£Good	£Fine	£N.Mint
nn ND Bart Sears script, Andy Smith art	$0.40	$1.20	$2.00	£0.25	£0.75	£1.25
Title Value:	$0.40	$1.20	$2.00	£0.25	£0.75	£1.25

BRUTE & BABE: MAEL'S RAGE
Ominous Press,OS; 1 Aug 1994

	$Good	$Fine	$N.Mint	£Good	£Fine	£N.Mint
1 ND story continued from Monument Set 1	$0.40	$1.20	$2.00	£0.25	£0.75	£1.25
Title Value:	$0.40	$1.20	$2.00	£0.25	£0.75	£1.25

BRUTE & BABE: OMEN
Ominous Press,OS; nn Sep 1994

	$Good	$Fine	$N.Mint	£Good	£Fine	£N.Mint
nn ND Bart Sears script, Mark Pennington art	$0.40	$1.20	$2.00	£0.25	£0.75	£1.25
Title Value:	$0.40	$1.20	$2.00	£0.25	£0.75	£1.25

BRUTE FORCE
Marvel Comics Group,MS; 1 Aug 1990-4 Nov 1990

	$Good	$Fine	$N.Mint	£Good	£Fine	£N.Mint
1-4	$0.15	$0.45	$0.75	£0.10	£0.30	£0.50
Title Value:	$0.60	$1.80	$3.00	£0.40	£1.20	£2.00

Note: eco-theme comic

BRUTE, THE
Atlas; 1 Feb 1975-3 Jun 1975

	$Good	$Fine	$N.Mint	£Good	£Fine	£N.Mint
1-2 Mike Sekowsky art; distributed in the U.K.	$0.25	$0.75	$1.25	£0.15	£0.45	£0.75
3 distributed in the U.K.	$0.15	$0.50	$0.90	£0.10	£0.35	£0.60
Title Value:	$0.65	$2.00	$3.40	£0.40	£1.25	£2.10

BUBBLEGUM CRISIS: GRAND MAL
Dark Horse,MS; 1 Mar 1994-4 Jun 1994

	$Good	$Fine	$N.Mint	£Good	£Fine	£N.Mint
1-4 ND Adam Warren script and art	$0.45	$1.35	$2.25	£0.30	£0.90	£1.50
	$1.80	$5.40	$9.00	£1.20	£3.60	£6.00
Bubblegum Crisis: Grand Mal (Aug 1995)						
Trade paperback collects issues #1-4				£2.00	£6.00	£10.00

BUCCANEER
I.W. Comics; 1,8 1963; 12 1964

	$Good	$Fine	$N.Mint	£Good	£Fine	£N.Mint
1 Captain Daring, Black Roger, Eric Falcon reprints, Crandall art; distributed in the U.K.	$1.85	$5.50	$11.25	£1.25	£3.75	£7.50
Title Value:	$1.85	$5.50	$11.25	£1.25	£3.75	£7.50

BUCK ROGERS
Gold Key/Whitman; 1 Oct 1964; 2 Aug 1979-6 Feb 1980; Whitman; 7 Aug 1980-16 1982

	$Good	$Fine	$N.Mint	£Good	£Fine	£N.Mint
1 rare in the U.K.	$5.25	$15.50	$31.50	£3.50	£10.50	£21.00
2-4 film adaptation; Frank Bolle and Al McWilliams art; painted cover	$0.60	$1.80	$3.00	£0.40	£1.20	£2.00
5 new stories begin, Al McWilliams art and painted covers begin	$0.40	$1.20	$2.00	£0.25	£0.75	£1.25
6	$0.40	$1.20	$2.00	£0.25	£0.75	£1.25
7 1st Whitman issue	$0.40	$1.20	$2.00	£0.25	£0.75	£1.25
8-10	$0.40	$1.20	$2.00	£0.25	£0.75	£1.25
11 J.M. DeMatteis script	$0.30	$0.90	$1.50	£0.20	£0.60	£1.00
12 Mike Roy art begins	$0.30	$0.90	$1.50	£0.20	£0.60	£1.00
13 last painted cover	$0.30	$0.90	$1.50	£0.20	£0.60	£1.00
14 line-drawn covers begin	$0.30	$0.90	$1.50	£0.20	£0.60	£1.00
15-16	$0.30	$0.90	$1.50	£0.20	£0.60	£1.00
Title Value:	$11.25	$33.50	$61.50	£7.40	£22.20	£40.50

Note: issues #2-16 had Limited Distribution in the U.K.

BUCK ROGERS (2ND SERIES)
TSR; 1 1990-12 1991?

	$Good	$Fine	$N.Mint	£Good	£Fine	£N.Mint
1-12 ND	$0.55	$1.65	$2.75	£0.35	£1.05	£1.75
Title Value:	$6.60	$19.80	$33.00	£4.20	£12.60	£21.00

Brothers of the Spear #2

Buck Rogers #2

Cage #1

	$Good	$Fine	$N.Mint	£Good	£Fine	£N.Mint

BUCKAROO BANZAI
Marvel Comics Group,MS Film; 1 Dec 1984-2 Feb 1985
1-2 Mark Texeira cover and pencil art

| | $0.15 | $0.45 | $0.75 | £0.10 | £0.30 | £0.50 |
| Title Value: | $0.30 | $0.90 | $1.50 | £0.20 | £0.60 | £1.00 |

Note: reprints Marvel Super Special #33

BUCKY O'HARE (1ST SERIES)
Continuity; 1 1988
1 ND reprints series from Echoes of Future Past #1-6

| | $0.80 | $2.40 | $4.00 | £0.50 | £1.50 | £2.50 |
| Title Value: | $0.80 | $2.40 | $4.00 | £0.50 | £1.50 | £2.50 |

Deluxe Hardcover Edition (1988), 52pgs, reprints the above

| | | | | £5.00 | £15.00 | £25.00 |

BUCKY O'HARE (2ND SERIES)
Continuity; 1 Jan 1991-6 1992
1-5 ND

	$0.40	$1.20	$2.00	£0.25	£0.75	£1.25
6 ND $2.50 cover	$0.45	$1.35	$2.25	£0.30	£0.90	£1.50
Title Value:	$2.45	$7.35	$12.25	£1.55	£4.65	£7.75

BUCKY O'HARE (3RD SERIES)
Continuity; 1 Aug 1993
1 ND 48pgs, Neal Adams cover with green flock on figure of Bucky

| | $0.70 | $2.10 | $3.50 | £0.45 | £1.35 | £2.25 |
| Title Value: | $0.70 | $2.10 | $3.50 | £0.45 | £1.35 | £2.25 |

BUG
Planet X Productions,OS; 1 1986
1 ND Tony Basilicato script/art; black and white

| | $0.30 | $0.90 | $1.50 | £0.20 | £0.60 | £1.00 |
| Title Value: | $0.30 | $0.90 | $1.50 | £0.20 | £0.60 | £1.00 |

BUGS BUNNY
DC Comics,MS; 1 Jun 1990-3 Sep 1990
1-3 ND scarce in the U.K.

| | $0.15 | $0.45 | $0.75 | £0.10 | £0.35 | £0.60 |
| Title Value: | $0.45 | $1.35 | $2.25 | £0.30 | £1.05 | £1.80 |

Multi-pack (Dec 1990), ND pre-bagged set of #1-3
with illustrated header card

| | | | | £0.30 | £0.90 | £1.50 |

BULLET CROW, FOWL OF FORTUNE
Eclipse,MS; 1 Feb 1987-2 Apr 1987
1-2 ND

| | $0.25 | $0.75 | $1.25 | £0.15 | £0.45 | £0.75 |
| Title Value: | $0.50 | $1.50 | $2.50 | £0.30 | £0.90 | £1.50 |

Note: based on role-playing game

BULLWINKLE AND ROCKY
Marvel Comics Group/Star; 1 Jun 1988-9 Mar 1989
1-9 scarce in the U.K., Dave Manak scripts

| | $0.15 | $0.45 | $0.75 | £0.10 | £0.30 | £0.50 |
| Title Value: | $1.35 | $4.05 | $6.75 | £0.90 | £2.70 | £4.50 |

Trade paperback (Mar 1992), selected reprints from issues #1-9

| | | | | £0.65 | £1.95 | £3.25 |

BULLWINKLE AND ROCKY IN 3-D
Blackthorne; (3-D Series #18) 1 Mar 1987
1 ND with bound-in 3-D glasses (25% less if without glasses)

| | $0.40 | $1.20 | $2.00 | £0.25 | £0.75 | £1.25 |
| Title Value: | $0.40 | $1.20 | $2.00 | £0.25 | £0.75 | £1.25 |

BULLWINKLE FOR PRESIDENT IN 3-D
Blackthorne; (3-D Series #50) 1 Autumn 1988
1 ND with bound-in 3-D glasses (25% less if without glasses)

| | $0.40 | $1.20 | $2.00 | £0.25 | £0.75 | £1.25 |
| Title Value: | $0.40 | $1.20 | $2.00 | £0.25 | £0.75 | £1.25 |

BULWARK
Millennium; 1 Jul 1995
1 ND Brian Main script and art; black and white

| | $0.60 | $1.80 | $3.00 | £0.40 | £1.20 | £2.00 |
| Title Value: | $0.60 | $1.80 | $3.00 | £0.40 | £1.20 | £2.00 |

BURIED TERROR
New England Comics; 1 Jan 1995-2 1995
1-2 ND horror reprints; black and white

| | $0.55 | $1.65 | $2.75 | £0.35 | £1.05 | £1.75 |
| Title Value: | $1.10 | $3.30 | $5.50 | £0.70 | £2.10 | £3.50 |

BURIED TREASURE
Caliber Press; 1 Apr 1990-5 Dec 1990
(previously published by Pure Imagination)
1 ND Joe Simon/Jack Kirby, Williamson, Toth, Kubert

| | $0.35 | $1.05 | $1.75 | £0.25 | £0.75 | £1.25 |

2 ND Jack Kirby, Kubert, Wally Wood

| | $0.35 | $1.05 | $1.75 | £0.25 | £0.75 | £1.25 |

3 ND Wally Wood, Frank Frazetta

| | $0.35 | $1.05 | $1.75 | £0.25 | £0.75 | £1.25 |

4 ND all Frazetta issue

| | $0.35 | $1.05 | $1.75 | £0.25 | £0.75 | £1.25 |

5 ND Joe Simon/Jack Kirby, Toth, Jack Cole, Jerry Robinson

| | $0.35 | $1.05 | $1.75 | £0.25 | £0.75 | £1.25 |
| Title Value: | $1.75 | $5.25 | $8.75 | £1.25 | £3.75 | £6.25 |

Note: all reprint featuring classic art-work of the 1940s/1950s

BUSHIDO
Eternity; 1 1988-6 1989
1-6 ND

| | $0.40 | $1.20 | $2.00 | £0.25 | £0.75 | £1.25 |
| Title Value: | $2.40 | $7.20 | $12.00 | £1.50 | £4.50 | £7.50 |

BUSHIDO BLADE OF ZATOICHI WALRUS
Solson Publications; 1,2 1986
1-2 ND

| | $0.40 | $1.20 | $2.00 | £0.25 | £0.75 | £1.25 |
| Title Value: | $0.80 | $2.40 | $4.00 | £0.50 | £1.50 | £2.50 |

BUTCHER, THE
DC Comics,MS; 1 May 1990-5 Sep 1990

	$0.25	$0.75	$1.25	£0.15	£0.45	£0.75
1-5	$0.25	$0.75	$1.25	£0.15	£0.45	£0.75
Title Value:	$1.25	$3.75	$6.25	£0.75	£2.25	£3.75

Note: Mature Readers, New Format

C

CABINET OF DR. CALIGARI, THE
Monster Comics,MS; 1 Jun 1992-3 Oct 1992
1-3 ND 24pgs, painted art

| | $0.40 | $1.20 | $2.00 | £0.25 | £0.75 | £1.25 |
| Title Value: | $1.20 | $3.60 | $6.00 | £0.75 | £2.25 | £3.75 |

CABLE
Marvel Comics Group,MS; 1 Oct 1992-2 Nov 1992
1 ND Cable vs. Stryfe, John Romita Jnr. art begins

| | $0.60 | $1.80 | $3.00 | £0.35 | £1.05 | £1.75 |

2 ND sequel to X-Cutioner's Song (see X-Force #18)

| | $0.50 | $1.50 | $2.50 | £0.30 | £0.90 | £1.50 |
| Title Value: | $1.10 | $3.30 | $5.50 | £0.65 | £1.95 | £3.25 |

Cable Trade paperback (Sep 1992)
176pgs, reprints New Mutants #87-94

| | | | | £2.20 | £6.60 | £11.00 |

(2nd print - Apr 1993)

| | | | | £2.00 | £6.00 | £10.00 |

CABLE & X-FORCE '95
Marvel Comics Group,OS; nn Dec 1995
nn ND 48pgs, Mark Waid and Jeph Loeb script, Matt Ryan art; Impossible Man appears

| | $0.80 | $2.40 | $4.00 | £0.50 | £1.50 | £2.50 |
| Title Value: | $0.80 | $2.40 | $4.00 | £0.50 | £1.50 | £2.50 |

CABLE (2ND SERIES)
Marvel Comics Group; 1 May 1993-20 Feb 1995; 21 Jul 1995-present
(becomes X-Man)
1 Art Thibert art begins

| | $1.00 | $3.00 | $5.00 | £0.50 | £1.50 | £2.50 |

1 ND Signed Limited Edition (Jun 1993) - signed by Art Thibert; 3,000 copies

	$2.50	$7.50	$12.50	£1.50	£4.50	£7.50
2-5	$0.45	$1.35	$2.25	£0.30	£0.90	£1.50
6-7	$0.40	$1.20	$2.00	£0.25	£0.75	£1.25

8 Cyclops, Jean Grey and Professor X appear

| | $0.40 | $1.20 | $2.00 | £0.25 | £0.75 | £1.25 |

9

| | $0.40 | $1.20 | $2.00 | £0.25 | £0.75 | £1.25 |

10 Nightcrawler and Kitty Pryde appear

| | $0.40 | $1.20 | $2.00 | £0.25 | £0.75 | £1.25 |

11 with free Spiderman and his Deadly Foes card sheet

| | $0.40 | $1.20 | $2.00 | £0.25 | £0.75 | £1.25 |
| 12-15 | $0.40 | $1.20 | $2.00 | £0.25 | £0.75 | £1.25 |

16 ND Direct Market edition, foil stamped cover; ties into the formation of Generation X

| | $1.20 | $2.40 | $4.00 | £0.80 | £2.40 | £4.00 |

16 Newstand edition, ties into the formation of Generation X

| | $0.60 | $1.80 | $3.00 | £0.40 | £1.20 | £2.00 |
| 17 | $0.30 | $0.90 | $1.50 | £0.20 | £0.60 | £1.00 |

17 ND Deluxe Edition - printed on glossy stock paper

| | $0.40 | $1.20 | $2.00 | £0.25 | £0.75 | £1.25 |
| 18 | $0.30 | $0.90 | $1.50 | £0.20 | £0.60 | £1.00 |

18 ND Deluxe Edition - printed on glossy stock paper

| | $0.40 | $1.20 | $2.00 | £0.25 | £0.75 | £1.25 |
| 19 | $0.30 | $0.90 | $1.50 | £0.20 | £0.60 | £1.00 |

19 ND Deluxe Edition - printed on glossy stock paper

| | $0.40 | $1.20 | $2.00 | £0.25 | £0.75 | £1.25 |
| 20 | $0.30 | $0.90 | $1.50 | £0.20 | £0.60 | £1.00 |

20 ND Deluxe Edition - printed on glossy stock paper plus bound-in Fleer trading card; see X-Man #1

| | $0.40 | $1.20 | $2.00 | £0.25 | £0.75 | £1.25 |

21 continued from X-Men: Prime; Jeph Loeb script, Ian Churchill art

| | $0.40 | $1.20 | $2.00 | £0.25 | £0.75 | £1.25 |
| 22-24 | $0.40 | $1.20 | $2.00 | £0.25 | £0.75 | £1.25 |

25 48pgs, prismatic foil cover

	$0.80	$2.40	$4.00	£0.50	£1.50	£2.50
26-29	$0.40	$1.20	$2.00	£0.25	£0.75	£1.25
Title Value:	$17.90	$53.70	$89.50	£11.20	£33.60	£56.00

CADILLACS AND DINOSAURS
Marvel Comics Group/Epic,MS; 1 Nov 1990-6 Apr 1991
1 ND reprints of Mark Schultz's Xenozoic Tales begins

	$0.45	$1.35	$2.25	£0.30	£0.90	£1.50
2-6 ND	$0.40	$1.20	$2.00	£0.25	£0.75	£1.25
Title Value:	$2.45	$7.35	$12.25	£1.55	£4.65	£7.75

Note: all new covers by Mark Schultz

CADILLACS AND DINOSAURS (2ND SERIES)
Topps,MS; 1 Feb 1994-3 Apr 1994
1 ND Roy Thomas script and Dick Giordano art begin

| | $0.45 | $1.35 | $2.25 | £0.30 | £0.90 | £1.50 |

1 ND Collector's Edition, foil embossed logo on card-stock cover

	$0.60	$1.80	$3.00	£0.40	£1.20	£2.00
2-3 ND	$0.45	$1.35	$2.25	£0.30	£0.90	£1.50
Title Value:	$1.95	$5.85	$9.75	£1.30	£3.90	£6.50

CADILLACS AND DINOSAURS: MAN-EATER
Topps,MS; 1 Jun 1994-3 Aug 1994
1 ND Roy Thomas script, Claude St. Aubin art

| | $0.45 | $1.35 | $2.25 | £0.30 | £0.90 | £1.50 |

1 ND Collector's Edition with Sam Kieth cover

| | $0.45 | $1.35 | $2.25 | £0.30 | £0.90 | £1.50 |

2 ND Roy Thomas script, Claude St. Aubin art

| | $0.45 | $1.35 | $2.25 | £0.30 | £0.90 | £1.50 |

2 ND Collector's Edition with Sam Kieth cover

| | $0.45 | $1.35 | $2.25 | £0.30 | £0.90 | £1.50 |

VERY GENERAL PERCENTAGE CONVERSION CHART WHICH MAY BE USED TO CALCULATE LOW AND INBETWEEN GRADES:

	$Good	$Fine	$N.Mint	£Good	£Fine	£N.Mint

3 ND Roy Thomas script, Claude St. Aubin art

	$0.45	$1.35	$2.25	£0.30	£0.90	£1.50

3 ND Collector's Edition with Sam Kieth cover

	$0.45	$1.35	$2.25	£0.30	£0.90	£1.50
Title Value:	$2.70	$8.10	$13.50	£1.80	£5.40	£9.00

CADILLACS AND DINOSAURS: THE WILD ONES
Topps,MS; 1 Sep 1994-3 Nov 1994

1-3 ND Roy Thomas script, Esteban Maroto art

	$0.45	$1.35	$2.25	£0.30	£0.90	£1.50
Title Value:	$1.35	$4.05	$6.75	£0.90	£2.70	£4.50

CAGE
Marvel Comics Group; 1 Apr 1992-20 Nov 1993
(see Luke Cage Hero for Hire, Powerman and Iron Fist, Punisher #60)

1 ND originally advertised as having an acetate cover overlay which never appeared owing to production problems

	$0.25	$0.75	$1.25	£0.20	£0.60	£1.00

2 ND

	$0.25	$0.75	$1.25	£0.15	£0.45	£0.75

3-4 ND Punisher guest stars

	$0.25	$0.75	$1.25	£0.15	£0.45	£0.75

5-8 ND

	$0.25	$0.75	$1.25	£0.15	£0.45	£0.75

9-10 ND Cage vs. Rhino; Hulk appears

	$0.25	$0.75	$1.25	£0.15	£0.45	£0.75

11 ND

	$0.25	$0.75	$1.25	£0.15	£0.45	£0.75

12 ND DS Cage (Powerman) vs. Iron Fist

	$0.25	$0.75	$1.25	£0.20	£0.60	£1.00

13-14 ND

	$0.25	$0.75	$1.25	£0.15	£0.45	£0.75

15 ND Silver Sable appears; X-over with Silver Sable #13

	$0.25	$0.75	$1.25	£0.15	£0.45	£0.75

16 ND Silver Sable appears; X-over with Silver Sable #14

	$0.25	$0.75	$1.25	£0.15	£0.45	£0.75

17 Infinity Crusade tie-in

	$0.25	$0.75	$1.25	£0.15	£0.45	£0.75

18-19 The Dark story

	$0.25	$0.75	$1.25	£0.15	£0.45	£0.75

20 Fantastic Four appear

	$0.25	$0.75	$1.25	£0.15	£0.45	£0.75
Title Value:	$5.00	$15.00	$25.00	£3.10	£9.30	£15.50

CAGES
Tundra Publishing,Magazine MS; 1 Feb 1991-8 1992?

1 ND 48pgs, Dave McKean black and white art

	$1.60	$4.80	$8.00	£0.60	£1.80	£3.00

2-8 ND 48pgs, Dave McKean black and white art

	$1.20	$3.60	$6.00	£0.50	£1.50	£2.50
Title Value:	$10.00	$30.00	$38.00	£4.10	£12.30	£20.50

Note: bi-monthly

CAIN
Harris Comics; 1 Jul 1993-4 1993

1-4 ND	$0.50	$1.50	$2.50	£0.35	£1.05	£1.75
Title Value:	$2.00	$6.00	$10.00	£1.40	£4.20	£7.00

CALIBER CHRISTMAS, A
Caliber Press,OS; 1 Dec 1989

1 64pgs, squarebound; new anthology featuring Aniverse, Baker Street, Crow, Deadworld, Frost, Fugitive, Gideon's, The Realm, Street Shadows; black and white

	$0.90	$2.70	$4.50	£0.60	£1.80	£3.00
Title Value:	$0.90	$2.70	$4.50	£0.60	£1.80	£3.00

CALIBER PRESENTS
Caliber Press; 1 Jun 1989-24 1992

1 1st appearance The Crow

	$20.00	$60.00	$100.00	£10.00	£30.00	£50.00

2 Deadworld cover and story (see realm #4)

	$0.90	$2.70	$4.50	£0.50	£1.50	£2.50
3-5	$0.45	$1.35	$2.25	£0.30	£0.90	£1.50

6-7 Tim Vigil art featured

	$0.45	$1.35	$2.25	£0.30	£0.90	£1.50

8 Deadworld cover and story (see Realm #4)

	$0.45	$1.35	$2.25	£0.30	£0.90	£1.50

9 Baker Street cover and story

	$0.45	$1.35	$2.25	£0.30	£0.90	£1.50

10 Realm cover and story

	$0.45	$1.35	$2.25	£0.30	£0.90	£1.50
11-14	$0.45	$1.35	$2.00	£0.25	£0.75	£1.25

15 64pgs, previews final issue of The Crow

	$4.00	$12.00	$20.00	£1.50	£4.50	£7.50
16 64pgs	$0.45	$1.35	$2.25	£0.30	£0.90	£1.50

17 64pgs, new Deadworld story

	$0.45	$1.35	$2.25	£0.30	£0.90	£1.50
18-24 64pgs	$0.45	$1.35	$2.25	£0.30	£0.90	£1.50
Title Value:	$34.15	$102.45	$170.75	£18.10	£54.30	£90.50

Note: anthology series. 1-14 are all 48pgs and Non-Distributed on the news-stands in the U.K.

CALIBER SPOTLIGHT SPECIAL
Caliber Press; OS; 1 May 1995

1 ND 64pgs, new stories featuring Kabuki, Oz and Kilroy

	$0.60	$1.80	$3.00	£0.40	£1.20	£2.00
Title Value:	$0.60	$1.80	$3.00	£0.40	£1.20	£2.00

CALIBRATIONS
Caliber Press,OS; 1 1992

1 ND 48pgs, Baker Street, Airwaves, Fringe, Deadworld included; originally announced as "Caliber Summer Special"; black and white

	$0.80	$2.40	$4.00	£0.50	£1.50	£2.50
Title Value:	$0.80	$2.40	$4.00	£0.50	£1.50	£2.50

CALIFORNIA GIRLS
Eclipse; 1 Jun 1987-8 May 1988

1-8 ND Trina Robbins script and art

	$0.35	$1.05	$1.75	£0.25	£0.75	£1.25
Title Value:	$2.80	$8.40	$14.00	£2.00	£6.00	£10.00

CALIFORNIA RAISINS IN 3-D, THE
Blackthorne; (3-D Series #31,#44,#46,#63); 1 Dec 1987-4 1988

1 ND inside front and back covers are printed upside-down on most copies with the indicia for Blackthorne 3-D Series #32 (not #31); all with 3-D glasses (25% less if without glasses)

	$0.35	$1.05	$1.75	£0.25	£0.75	£1.25
2-4 ND	$0.35	$1.05	$1.75	£0.25	£0.75	£1.25
Title Value:	$1.40	$4.20	$7.00	£1.00	£3.00	£5.00

CALIGARI 2050
Monster Comics,MS; 1 Jul 1992

1 ND	$0.35	$1.05	$1.75	£0.25	£0.75	£1.25
Title Value:	$0.35	$1.05	$1.75	£0.25	£0.75	£1.25

Note: announced as a mini-series and then cancelled after one issue

CAMELOT 3000
DC Comics,MS; 1 Dec 1982-12 Apr 1985

1 ND Brian Bolland art begins

	$0.50	$1.50	$2.50	£0.40	£1.20	£2.00
2-3 ND	$0.50	$1.50	$2.50	£0.35	£1.05	£1.75
4 ND	$0.50	$1.50	$2.50	£0.30	£0.90	£1.50

5 ND 1st appearance Knights of New Camelot

	$0.50	$1.50	$2.50	£0.30	£0.90	£1.50
6-11 ND	$0.50	$1.50	$2.50	£0.30	£0.90	£1.50

12 ND scarce in the U.K.

	$0.80	$2.40	$4.00	£0.50	£1.50	£2.50
Title Value:	$6.30	$18.90	$31.50	£4.00	£12.00	£20.00

Note: a long delay between issues #11 and 12 owing to production problems and art delivery

Trade paperback (Titan UK Edition/DC Edition)				£1.40	£4.20	£7.00

CAMELOT ETERNAL
Caliber Press; 1 1990-8 1991

1-8 ND	$0.35	$1.05	$1.75	£0.25	£0.75	£1.25
Title Value:	$2.80	$8.40	$14.00	£2.00	£6.00	£10.00

CAMP CANDY
Marvel Comics Group, Film; 1 May 1990-7 Nov 1990

1-7 ND	$0.15	$0.45	$0.75	£0.10	£0.35	£0.60
	$1.05	$3.15	$5.25	£0.70	£2.45	£4.20

Note: based on cartoon TV series

CANNON
Heroes Inc; 1 1969-4 1971

1 ND scarce in the U.K. Steve Ditko, Wally Wood art reprints begin

	$4.50	$13.50	$22.50	£3.00	£9.00	£15.00

2-4 ND scarce in the U.K.

	$3.60	$10.50	$18.00	£2.40	£7.00	£12.00
Title Value:	$15.30	$45.00	$76.50	£10.20	£30.00	£51.00

CANNON (2ND SERIES)
Eros Comix,MS; 1 Feb 1991-8 Sep 1991

1-8 ND reprints from newspaper strips by Wally Wood

	$0.45	$1.35	$2.25	£0.30	£0.90	£1.50
Title Value:	$3.60	$10.80	$18.00	£2.40	£7.20	£12.00

Note: contains nudity and sexual situations

CAP'N QUICK & A FOOZLE
Eclipse; 1 Jul 1984-3 Aug 1985
(see Eclipse Magazine)

1-2 ND Rogers art

	$0.30	$0.90	$1.50	£0.20	£0.60	£1.00

3 ND titled "Foozle", Rogers art

	$0.30	$0.90	$1.50	£0.20	£0.60	£1.00
Title Value:	$0.90	$2.70	$4.50	£0.60	£1.80	£3.00

CAPTAIN 3-D
Harvey,OS; 1 Dec 1953

1 ND scarce in the U.K. features Jack Kirby and Steve Ditko artwork, with bound-in 3-D glasses (25% less without glasses); this is thought to be Steve Ditko's 2nd ever work in comics

	$10.00	$30.00	$60.00	£7.00	£21.00	£42.00
Title Value:	$10.00	$30.00	$60.00	£7.00	£21.00	£42.00

CAPTAIN ACTION
National Periodical Publications; 1 Oct/Nov 1968-5 Jun/Jul 1969

1 origin, Wally Wood inks; Superman appears on the cover

	$8.25	$25.00	$50.00	£5.25	£16.00	£32.50

2-3 Wally Wood inks

	$5.00	$15.00	$30.00	£3.30	£10.00	£20.00
4	$4.15	$12.50	$25.00	£2.65	£8.00	£16.00

5 Wally Wood inks

	$5.00	$15.00	$30.00	£3.30	£10.00	£20.00
Title Value:	$27.40	$82.50	$165.00	£17.80	£54.00	£108.50

Captain Action and Action Boy (1967), Ideal Toy Giveaway, ND rare in the U.K.				£5.00	£15.00	£25.00

CAPTAIN AMERICA
Marvel Comics Group; 100 Apr 1968-present
(see also Avengers #4, The Invaders, Marvel Double Feature, Marvel Fanfare, Marvel Super Action, Marvel Super Heroes, Marvel Team Up, Marvel Treasury, Edition) (formerly Tales of Suspense up to #99)

100 Jack Kirby art, flashbacks of revival with Avengers, Black Panther appears

	$46.00	$135.00	$325.00	£29.00	£85.00	£200.00

101 scarce in the U.K. Jack Kirby art

	$12.00	$36.00	$85.00	£7.00	£21.00	£50.00

102 very scarce in the U.K. Jack Kirby art

	$6.25	$19.00	$45.00	£4.60	£13.50	£32.50

103-105 Jack Kirby art

	$6.25	$19.00	$45.00	£4.25	£12.50	£30.00

106-108 Jack Kirby art

	$6.00	$18.00	$42.50	£4.00	£12.00	£28.00

109 (Jan 1969), origin retold, Jack Kirby art

MINT = 100% / NEAR MINT (inc. +/-) = 90-99% / VERY FINE (inc. +/-) = 75-89% / FINE (inc. +/-) = 55-74%
VERY GOOD (inc. +/-) = 35-54% / GOOD (inc. +/-) = 15-34% / FAIR = 5-14% / POOR = 1-4%

253

Issue / Description	$Good	$Fine	$N.Mint	£Good	£Fine	£N.Mint
(continued)	$10.00	$30.00	$70.00	£5.00	£15.00	£35.00
110 Captain America battles Hulk, Jim Steranko art	$9.25	$28.00	$65.00	£5.00	£15.00	£35.00
111 classic cover, Jim Steranko art	$9.25	$28.00	$65.00	£5.00	£15.00	£35.00
112 less common in the U.K. Iron Man recounts Captain America's origin and life story, Jack Kirby art	$4.25	$12.50	$30.00	£2.55	£7.50	£18.00
113 ND scarce in the U.K. Steranko art, classic cover	$9.25	$28.00	$65.00	£5.50	£17.00	£40.00
114 scarce in the U.K. Avengers and Nick Fury appear	$3.40	$10.00	$24.00	£2.00	£6.00	£14.00
115 ND Cosmic Cube appears	$3.40	$10.00	$24.00	£2.10	£6.25	£15.00
116 ND Avengers appear	$3.40	$10.00	$24.00	£2.10	£6.25	£15.00
117 very scarce in the U.K. 1st appearance Falcon	$5.00	$15.00	$35.00	£4.25	£12.50	£30.00
118-120	$4.00	$12.00	$24.00	£2.00	£6.00	£12.00
121 (Jan 1970), retells origin	$2.00	$6.00	$12.00	£1.15	£3.50	£7.00
122-126	$2.00	$6.00	$12.00	£1.15	£3.50	£7.00
127 Nick Fury appears	$2.00	$6.00	$12.00	£1.15	£3.50	£7.00
128	$2.00	$6.00	$12.00	£1.15	£3.50	£7.00
129 Red Skull appears	$2.00	$6.00	$12.00	£1.15	£3.50	£7.00
130 Hulk appears	$2.00	$6.00	$12.00	£1.15	£3.50	£7.00
131 Bucky re-appears	$2.00	$6.00	$12.00	£1.00	£3.00	£6.00
132 scarce in the U.K.	$2.00	$6.00	$12.00	£1.15	£3.50	£7.00
133 scarce in the U.K. (Jan 1971), origin Modok	$2.00	$6.00	$12.00	£1.15	£3.50	£7.00
134 scarce in the U.K. Falcon shares title on cover	$2.00	$6.00	$12.00	£1.15	£3.50	£7.00
135-136 scarce in the U.K.	$2.00	$6.00	$12.00	£1.15	£3.50	£7.00
137-138 scarce in the U.K. Spiderman appears	$2.00	$6.00	$12.00	£1.25	£3.75	£7.50
139 scarce in the U.K.	$2.00	$6.00	$12.00	£1.15	£3.50	£7.00
140-142 ND	$2.00	$6.00	$12.00	£1.00	£3.00	£6.00
143 ND 52pgs	$1.30	$4.00	$8.00	£1.15	£3.25	£6.50
144 ND Gray Morrow back-up	$1.30	$4.00	$8.00	£1.00	£3.00	£6.00
145 ND (Jan 1972)	$1.30	$4.00	$8.00	£1.00	£3.00	£6.00
146-150 ND	$1.30	$4.00	$8.00	£1.00	£3.00	£6.00
151-152 ND	$1.50	$4.50	$7.50	£1.00	£3.00	£5.00
153 ND 1st appearance (cameo) Jack Monroe (later Nomad II)	$1.60	$4.80	$8.00	£1.20	£3.60	£6.00
154 ND 1st full appearance Jack Monroe, Avengers appear	$1.60	$4.80	$8.00	£1.20	£3.60	£6.00
155 ND "secret origin" Captain America, origin Jack Monroe	$1.50	$4.50	$7.50	£1.00	£3.00	£5.00
156 ND Captain America vs. Captain America	$1.50	$4.50	$7.50	£1.00	£3.00	£5.00
157 ND (Jan 1973)	$1.50	$4.50	$7.50	£1.00	£3.00	£5.00
158 ND Captain America gains super-strength (temporarily)	$1.50	$4.50	$7.50	£1.00	£3.00	£5.00
159 1st display of super-strength	$1.50	$4.50	$7.50	£0.70	£2.10	£3.50
160 scarce in the U.K. 1st appearance Solarr	$1.50	$4.50	$7.50	£0.80	£2.40	£4.00
161-163	$1.50	$4.50	$7.50	£0.70	£2.10	£3.50
164 Jim Starlin colours	$1.50	$4.50	$7.50	£0.70	£2.10	£3.50
165-167	$1.50	$4.50	$7.50	£0.60	£1.80	£3.00
168 1st appearance Baron Zemo II	$1.50	$4.50	$7.50	£0.60	£1.80	£3.00
169 (Jan 1974), Black Panther appears (and meets Falcon for 1st time)	$1.50	$4.50	$7.50	£0.60	£1.80	£3.00
170 Black Panther appears	$1.50	$4.50	$7.50	£0.60	£1.80	£3.00
171 Black Panther and Iron Man appear; new Falcon costume, Falcon "flies"	$1.50	$4.50	$7.50	£0.60	£1.80	£3.00
172-175 ND old X-Men appear	$2.80	$8.25	$14.00	£1.30	£3.90	£6.50
176 history of Captain America retold; Thor, Iron Man and Vision appear	$1.50	$4.50	$7.50	£0.60	£1.80	£3.00
177 Beast appears	$1.50	$4.50	$7.50	£0.60	£1.80	£3.00
178	$1.50	$4.50	$7.50	£0.60	£1.80	£3.00
179 Hawkeye appears	$1.50	$4.50	$7.50	£0.60	£1.80	£3.00
180 1st appearance Steve Rogers as Nomad I, Hawkeye appears	$2.00	$6.00	$10.00	£0.70	£2.10	£3.50
181 (Jan 1975), Nomad appears, origin new Captain America, Sub-Mariner appears	$1.50	$4.50	$7.50	£0.60	£1.80	£3.00
182 Nomad appears	$1.00	$3.00	$5.00	£0.40	£1.20	£2.00
183 death of new Captain America, Nomad (Steve Rogers) returns to being Captain America, Beast cameo	$1.50	$4.50	$7.50	£0.60	£1.80	£3.00
184-185	$1.00	$3.00	$5.00	£0.40	£1.20	£2.00
186 origin Falcon	$1.00	$3.00	$5.00	£0.40	£1.20	£2.00
187-190	$1.00	$3.00	$5.00	£0.40	£1.20	£2.00
191 Ghost Rider appears (2pgs)	$0.80	$2.40	$4.00	£0.35	£1.05	£1.75
192	$0.80	$2.40	$4.00	£0.35	£1.05	£1.75
193 (Jan 1976), Jack Kirby art, his return to drawing Captain America	$0.80	$2.40	$4.00	£0.35	£1.05	£1.75
194-200 Jack Kirby art	$0.80	$2.40	$4.00	£0.35	£1.05	£1.75
201-204 Jack Kirby art	$0.60	$1.80	$3.00	£0.30	£0.90	£1.50
205 (Jan 1977), Jack Kirby art	$0.60	$1.80	$3.00	£0.30	£0.90	£1.50
206-210 Jack Kirby art	$0.60	$1.80	$3.00	£0.30	£0.90	£1.50
211-214 Jack Kirby art	$0.60	$1.80	$3.00	£0.25	£0.75	£1.25
215 origin retold, Invaders and original Avengers appear	$0.60	$1.80	$3.00	£0.25	£0.75	£1.25
216 reprints Strange Tales #114 (1st appearance of Captain America since Golden Age, actually The Acrobat disguised), Captain America battles Human Torch	$0.60	$1.80	$3.00	£0.25	£0.75	£1.25
217 (Jan 1978), Iron Man appears	$0.60	$1.80	$3.00	£0.25	£0.75	£1.25
218 origin retold; secret history of Steve Rogers begins (ends #225)	$0.60	$1.80	$3.00	£0.25	£0.75	£1.25
219	$0.60	$1.80	$3.00	£0.25	£0.75	£1.25
220 Falcon back-up story	$0.60	$1.80	$3.00	£0.25	£0.75	£1.25
221 Rick Jones back-up story	$0.60	$1.80	$3.00	£0.25	£0.75	£1.25
222-223	$0.60	$1.80	$3.00	£0.25	£0.75	£1.25
224 1st Mike Zeck art on Captain America	$0.60	$1.80	$3.00	£0.25	£0.75	£1.25
225-228	$0.60	$1.80	$3.00	£0.25	£0.75	£1.25
229 (Jan 1979), Quasar appears	$0.60	$1.80	$3.00	£0.25	£0.75	£1.25
230 Quasar and Hulk appear	$0.60	$1.80	$3.00	£0.25	£0.75	£1.25
231 Hulk appears	$0.60	$1.80	$3.00	£0.25	£0.75	£1.25
232-233	$0.60	$1.80	$3.00	£0.25	£0.75	£1.25
234-236 Daredevil appears	$0.60	$1.80	$3.00	£0.25	£0.75	£1.25
237-240	$0.60	$1.80	$3.00	£0.25	£0.75	£1.25
241 (Jan 1980), Punisher appears, Frank Miller cover	$4.15	$12.50	$25.00	£2.30	£7.00	£14.00
242	$0.60	$1.80	$3.00	£0.25	£0.75	£1.25
243 George Perez cover	$0.60	$1.80	$3.00	£0.25	£0.75	£1.25
244-245 Frank Miller cover	$0.60	$1.80	$3.00	£0.25	£0.75	£1.25
246 George Perez cover	$0.60	$1.80	$3.00	£0.25	£0.75	£1.25
247-252 John Byrne art	$0.70	$2.10	$3.50	£0.40	£1.20	£2.00
253 (Jan 1981), John Byrne art	$0.70	$2.10	$3.50	£0.40	£1.20	£2.00
254 ND John Byrne art	$0.70	$2.10	$3.50	£0.50	£1.50	£2.50
255 ND John Byrne art, anniversary issue	$0.70	$2.10	$3.50	£0.60	£1.80	£3.00
256	$0.40	$1.20	$2.00	£0.25	£0.75	£1.25
257 Hulk appears	$0.40	$1.20	$2.00	£0.25	£0.75	£1.25
258-259 Mike Zeck art	$0.40	$1.20	$2.00	£0.25	£0.75	£1.25
260	$0.40	$1.20	$2.00	£0.25	£0.75	£1.25
261-263 Mike Zeck art	$0.40	$1.20	$2.00	£0.25	£0.75	£1.25
264 Mike Zeck art; X-Men appear in dream sequence	$0.40	$1.20	$2.00	£0.25	£0.75	£1.25
265 (Jan 1982), Spiderman appears, Mike Zeck art	$0.40	$1.20	$2.00	£0.25	£0.75	£1.25
266 Spiderman appears, Mike Zeck art	$0.40	$1.20	$2.00	£0.25	£0.75	£1.25
267 1st appearance Everyman, Mike Zeck art	$0.40	$1.20	$2.00	£0.25	£0.75	£1.25
268 Mike Zeck art; ties into Defenders #104, #106	$0.40	$1.20	$2.00	£0.25	£0.75	£1.25
269 Mike Zeck art, 1st appearance Team America	$0.40	$1.20	$2.00	£0.25	£0.75	£1.25
270 Mike Zeck art	$0.40	$1.20	$2.00	£0.25	£0.75	£1.25
271	$0.40	$1.20	$2.00	£0.25	£0.75	£1.25
272-276 Mike Zeck art	$0.40	$1.20	$2.00	£0.25	£0.75	£1.25
277 (Jan 1983), Mike Zeck art	$0.40	$1.20	$2.00	£0.25	£0.75	£1.25
278 Mike Zeck art	$0.40	$1.20	$2.00	£0.25	£0.75	£1.25
279 LD in the U.K. Mike Zeck art, Iron Man appears	$0.40	$1.20	$2.00	£0.30	£0.90	£1.50
280 LD in the U.K. Mike Zeck art						

	$Good	$Fine	$N.Mint	£Good	£Fine	£N.Mint
	$0.40	$1.20	$2.00	£0.30	£0.90	£1.50
281 LD in the U.K. Mike Zeck art, Spiderwoman and Bucky appear	$0.40	$1.20	$2.00	£0.30	£0.90	£1.50
282 LD in the U.K. 1st appearance Nomad II (Jack Monroe), Spiderwoman appears, Mike Zeck art	$2.40	$7.00	$12.00	£0.80	£2.40	£4.00
282 2nd printing, ND (1992) - silver ink cover	$0.40	$1.20	$2.00	£0.25	£0.75	£1.25
283 LD in the U.K. 2nd appearance Nomad II, Mike Zeck art	$0.80	$2.40	$4.00	£0.35	£1.05	£1.75
284 Nomad appears	$0.40	$1.20	$2.00	£0.25	£0.75	£1.25
285	$0.40	$1.20	$2.00	£0.25	£0.75	£1.25
286 LD in the U.K. Deathlok appears, Zeck art	$0.60	$1.80	$3.00	£0.60	£1.80	£3.00
287-288 LD in the U.K. Deathlok appears, Zeck art	$0.60	$1.80	$3.00	£0.50	£1.50	£2.50
289 (Jan 1984), Deathlok cameo, Mike Zeck art	$0.40	$1.20	$2.00	£0.25	£0.75	£1.25
290-291 LD in the U.K. John Byrne cover, Nomad appears	$0.40	$1.20	$2.00	£0.30	£0.90	£1.50
292-296 Nomad appears	$0.40	$1.20	$2.00	£0.25	£0.75	£1.25
297 LD in the U.K.	$0.40	$1.20	$2.00	£0.30	£0.90	£1.50
298 LD in the U.K. origin Red Skull retold	$0.40	$1.20	$2.00	£0.35	£1.05	£1.75
299 LD in the U.K.	$0.40	$1.20	$2.00	£0.30	£0.90	£1.50
300 LD in the U.K. Captain America vs. The Red Skull	$0.60	$1.80	$3.00	£0.40	£1.20	£2.00
301 LD in the U.K. (Jan 1985), Avengers and Nomad appear	$0.40	$1.20	$2.00	£0.30	£0.90	£1.50
302-304 LD in the U.K.	$0.40	$1.20	$2.00	£0.25	£0.75	£1.25
305 LD in the U.K. Captain Britain appears	$0.40	$1.20	$2.00	£0.25	£0.75	£1.25
306 LD in the U.K. Captain Britain by Paul Neary	$0.40	$1.20	$2.00	£0.40	£1.20	£2.00
307 Captain Britain by Paul Neary, Nomad appears	$0.40	$1.20	$2.00	£0.30	£0.90	£1.50
308 Secret Wars X-over	$0.40	$1.20	$2.00	£0.25	£0.75	£1.25
309 Nomad appears	$0.40	$1.20	$2.00	£0.25	£0.75	£1.25
310-311	$0.40	$1.20	$2.00	£0.20	£0.60	£1.00
312 LD in the U.K.	$0.40	$1.20	$2.00	£0.25	£0.75	£1.25
313 LD in the U.K. (Jan 1986)	$0.40	$1.20	$2.00	£0.25	£0.75	£1.25
314-320 LD in the U.K.	$0.40	$1.20	$2.00	£0.25	£0.75	£1.25
321-322	$0.40	$1.20	$2.00	£0.20	£0.60	£1.00
323 1st appearance new Super Patriot	$1.00	$3.00	$5.00	£0.30	£0.90	£1.50
324	$0.40	$1.20	$2.00	£0.20	£0.60	£1.00
325 (Jan 1987), Nomad appears	$0.40	$1.20	$2.00	£0.20	£0.60	£1.00
326	$0.40	$1.20	$2.00	£0.20	£0.60	£1.00
327 LD in the U.K.	$0.60	$1.80	$3.00	£0.25	£0.75	£1.25
328 LD in the U.K. origin and 1st appearance D Man	$0.60	$1.80	$3.00	£0.30	£0.90	£1.50
329-331 LD in the U.K.	$0.40	$1.20	$2.00	£0.25	£0.75	£1.25
332 LD in the U.K. Captain America resigns						
	$2.00	$6.00	$10.00	£0.80	£2.40	£4.00
333 very LD new Super Patriot becomes new Captain America	$1.20	$3.60	$6.00	£0.80	£2.40	£4.00
334 1st appearance new Bucky	$1.00	$3.00	$5.00	£0.40	£1.20	£2.00
335 LD in the U.K.	$1.00	$3.00	$5.00	£0.40	£1.20	£2.00
336	$1.00	$3.00	$5.00	£0.35	£1.05	£1.75
337 LD in the U.K. (Jan 1988), cover based on classic Avengers #4, return of Steve Rogers	$1.00	$3.00	$5.00	£0.50	£1.50	£2.50
338 LD in the U.K.	$1.00	$3.00	$5.00	£0.40	£1.20	£2.00
339 Fall of Mutants, ties into Iron Man #238	$1.00	$3.00	$5.00	£0.30	£0.90	£1.50
340	$1.00	$3.00	$5.00	£0.30	£0.90	£1.50
341 LD in the U.K. Captain America battles Iron Man	$0.40	$1.20	$2.00	£0.35	£1.05	£1.75
342-343	$0.30	$0.90	$1.50	£0.25	£0.75	£1.25
344 DS	$0.50	$1.50	$2.50	£0.30	£0.90	£1.50
345	$0.30	$0.90	$1.50	£0.25	£0.75	£1.25
346 Freedom Force	$0.30	$0.90	$1.50	£0.25	£0.75	£1.25
347-348	$0.30	$0.90	$1.50	£0.25	£0.75	£1.25
349 (Jan 1989)	$0.30	$0.90	$1.50	£0.25	£0.75	£1.25
350 LD in the U.K. 64pgs, squarebound, origin Red Skull, John Byrne art (most copies have spine crinkling); return of Steve Rogers to original Captain America	$0.80	$2.40	$4.00	£0.40	£1.20	£2.00
351-356	$0.30	$0.90	$1.50	£0.20	£0.60	£1.00
357 LD in the U.K. Captain America and Diamondback in separate stories, Bloodstone story begins, bi-weekly	$0.30	$0.90	$1.50	£0.25	£0.75	£1.25
358-359 Bloodstone story, bi-weekly issue	$0.30	$0.90	$1.50	£0.20	£0.60	£1.00
360-362 Bloodstone story, bi-weekly issue	$0.30	$0.90	$1.50	£0.15	£0.45	£0.75
363 Bloodstone story concludes	$0.30	$0.90	$1.50	£0.15	£0.45	£0.75
364	$0.30	$0.90	$1.50	£0.15	£0.45	£0.75
365 Acts of Vengeance tie-in, Captain America battles Sub-Mariner	$0.30	$0.90	$1.50	£0.15	£0.45	£0.75
366 (Jan 1990), Acts of Vengeance tie-in, 1st Ron Lim art on Captain America	$0.30	$0.90	$1.50	£0.15	£0.45	£0.75
367 Acts of Vengeance tie-in, Magneto appears, no Lim art	$0.30	$0.90	$1.50	£0.15	£0.45	£0.75
368-371 Ron Lim art	$0.30	$0.90	$1.50	£0.15	£0.45	£0.75
372-377 Streets of Poison story, bi-weekly issue, Ron Lim art	$0.30	$0.90	$1.50	£0.15	£0.45	£0.75
378 Ron Lim art	$0.30	$0.90	$1.50	£0.15	£0.45	£0.75
379 Quasar appears, Ron Lim art	$0.30	$0.90	$1.50	£0.15	£0.45	£0.75
380 Ron Lim art	$0.30	$0.90	$1.50	£0.15	£0.45	£0.75
381 (Jan 1991), Ron Lim art	$0.30	$0.90	$1.50	£0.15	£0.45	£0.75
382 Ron Lim art	$0.30	$0.90	$1.50	£0.15	£0.45	£0.75
383 LD in the U.K. 64pgs, 50th anniversary issue, Ron Lim art, Jim Lee cover	$1.00	$3.00	$5.00	£0.40	£1.20	£2.00
384 Ron Lim art	$0.30	$0.90	$1.50	£0.15	£0.45	£0.75
385-386 West Coast Avengers appear, Ron Lim art	$0.30	$0.90	$1.50	£0.15	£0.45	£0.75
387-392 Superia Stratagem story, bi-weekly issue	$0.30	$0.90	$1.50	£0.15	£0.45	£0.75

Captain America #175

Captain America Annual #4

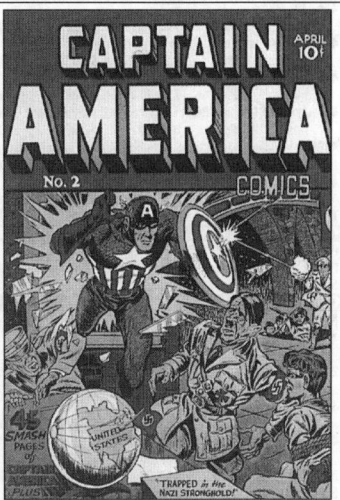

Captain America Comics #2

	$Good	$Fine	$N.Mint	£Good	£Fine	£N.Mint
393	$0.30	$0.90	$1.50	£0.15	£0.45	£0.75
394-395 Heart of the Viper story, Red Skull appears	$0.30	$0.90	$1.50	£0.15	£0.45	£0.75
396 (Jan 1992), Heart of the Viper story, Red Skull appears	$0.30	$0.90	$1.50	£0.15	£0.45	£0.75
397 Heart of the Viper story, Red Skull appears, $1.25 cover	$0.30	$0.90	$1.50	£0.15	£0.45	£0.75
398 Galactic Storm part 1	$0.30	$0.90	$1.50	£0.15	£0.45	£0.75
399 Galactic Storm part 8	$0.30	$0.90	$1.50	£0.15	£0.45	£0.75
400 I.D in the U.K. 96pgs, Galactic Storm part 15, reprints Avengers #4, gatefold cover	$0.60	$1.80	$3.00	£0.40	£1.20	£2.00
401 Galactic Storm: Aftermath	$0.25	$0.75	$1.25	£0.15	£0.45	£0.75
402-406 The Man & The Wolf story, Wolverine appears, bi-weekly	$0.25	$0.75	$1.25	£0.15	£0.45	£0.75
407 The Man & The Wolf (conclusion), Captain America vs. Cable, Wolverine appears, bi-weekly	$0.25	$0.75	$1.25	£0.15	£0.45	£0.75
408 Falcon, Red Skull appear	$0.25	$0.75	$1.25	£0.15	£0.45	£0.75
409	$0.25	$0.75	$1.25	£0.15	£0.45	£0.75
410 Falcon appears	$0.25	$0.75	$1.25	£0.15	£0.45	£0.75
411 (Jan 1993), Falcon becomes Captain America's partner again	$0.25	$0.75	$1.25	£0.15	£0.45	£0.75
412-413 Master of Kung Fu appears	$0.25	$0.75	$1.25	£0.15	£0.45	£0.75
414-417 Ka-Zar and Black Panther appear	$0.25	$0.75	$1.25	£0.15	£0.45	£0.75
418 Daredevil appears	$0.25	$0.75	$1.25	£0.15	£0.45	£0.75
419 Silver Sable appers	$0.25	$0.75	$1.25	£0.15	£0.45	£0.75
420	$0.25	$0.75	$1.25	£0.15	£0.45	£0.75
420 ND pre-bagged with Dirt Magazine and sticker	$0.60	$1.80	$3.00	£0.40	£1.20	£2.00
421	$0.25	$0.75	$1.25	£0.15	£0.45	£0.75
422 (Jan 1994)	$0.25	$0.75	$1.25	£0.15	£0.45	£0.75
423-424	$0.25	$0.75	$1.25	£0.15	£0.45	£0.75
425 48pgs, Fighting Chance story begins (ends #436)	$0.40	$1.20	$2.00	£0.25	£0.75	£1.25
425 ND Collector's Edition, multi-level foil embossed cover	$0.60	$1.80	$3.00	£0.40	£1.20	£2.00
426	$0.25	$0.75	$1.25	£0.15	£0.45	£0.75
427 with free Spiderman vs. Venom card sheet	$0.25	$0.75	$1.25	£0.15	£0.45	£0.75
428-430	$0.25	$0.75	$1.25	£0.15	£0.45	£0.75
431-434	$0.30	$0.90	$1.50	£0.20	£0.60	£1.00
435 (Jan 1995)	$0.30	$0.90	$1.50	£0.20	£0.60	£1.00
436 Fighting Chance part 12 (conclusion)	$0.30	$0.90	$1.50	£0.20	£0.60	£1.00
437 Iron Man and Giant Man appear	$0.30	$0.90	$1.50	£0.20	£0.60	£1.00
438 Captain America dons a new exo-skeleton armour, Iron Man and Nick Fury appear	$0.30	$0.90	$1.50	£0.20	£0.60	£1.00
439	$0.30	$0.90	$1.50	£0.20	£0.60	£1.00
440 Taking AIM part 1, continued in Avengers #387	$0.30	$0.90	$1.50	£0.20	£0.60	£1.00
441 Taking AIM part 3, continued in Avengers #388	$0.30	$0.90	$1.50	£0.20	£0.60	£1.00
442-443	$0.30	$0.90	$1.50	£0.20	£0.60	£1.00
444 Mark Waid scripts begin	$0.80	$2.40	$4.00	£0.50	£1.50	£2.50
445 Operation Rebirth story, Red Skull and the Cosmic Cube appear	$0.60	$1.80	$3.00	£0.40	£1.20	£2.00
446 Operation Rebirth story, Red Skull and the Cosmic Cube appear	$0.45	$1.35	$2.25	£0.30	£0.90	£1.50
447 (Jan 1996), Operation Rebirth story, Red Skull and the Cosmic Cube appear	$0.30	$0.90	$1.50	£0.25	£0.75	£1.25
448 48pgs, Operation Rebirth concludes, Red Skull and Cosmic Cube appear; metallic fifth ink cover	$0.55	$1.75	$2.95	£0.40	£1.20	£2.00
449 The First Sign part 1; Captain America, Thor and Iron Man return to the Avengers; continued in Thor #496	$0.30	$0.90	$1.50	£0.20	£0.60	£1.00
Title Value:	**$412.70**	**$1236.15**	**$2456.45**	**£235.80**	**£705.35**	**£1421.50**

CAPTAIN AMERICA AND THE FALCON BOOK AND RECORD SET
Power Records; PR-12 1974

	$Good	$Fine	$N.Mint	£Good	£Fine	£N.Mint
PR-12 scarce, 20pg booklet with 45 rpm record				£1.00	£3.00	£5.00

Note: the item would be valued 50% less without record

CAPTAIN AMERICA ANNUAL
Marvel Comics Group; 1 Jan 1971-7 1983; 8 Sep 1986-present

	$Good	$Fine	$N.Mint	£Good	£Fine	£N.Mint
1 68pgs, all reprint, origin retold	$2.50	$7.50	$15.00	£1.65	£5.00	£10.00
2 ND scarce in the U.K. 68pgs, all reprint	$2.00	$6.00	$12.00	£1.30	£4.00	£8.00
3 ND 52pgs, Jack Kirby art	$0.55	$1.75	$3.50	£0.55	£1.75	£3.50
4 ND very scarce in the U.K. 52pgs, Captain America vs. Magneto, Jack Kirby cover and art	$0.80	$2.50	$5.00	£1.00	£3.00	£6.00
5 ND 52pgs	$0.50	$1.50	$3.00	£0.30	£1.00	£2.00
6 ND 52pgs, Invaders appear	$0.60	$1.80	$3.00	£0.40	£1.20	£2.00
7 ND 52pgs, Cosmic Cube story	$0.60	$1.80	$3.00	£0.40	£1.20	£2.00
8 ND Wolverine appears, Mike Zeck art	$5.00	$15.00	$25.00	£2.00	£6.00	£10.00
9 ND The Terminus Factor part 1, Nomad appears, continues in Iron Man Annual #11	$1.00	$3.00	$5.00	£0.30	£0.90	£1.50
10 ND Von Strucker Gambit, story concludes from Daredevil Annual #7/Punisher Annual #4	$0.50	$1.50	$2.50	£0.30	£0.90	£1.50
11 ND Citizen Kang part 1, Gilgamesh appears, continued in Thor Annual #17	$0.50	$1.50	$2.50	£0.30	£0.90	£1.50
12 ND 64pgs, pre-bagged with trading card introducing The Battling Bantam	$0.50	$1.50	$2.50	£0.40	£1.20	£2.00
13 ND 64pgs, Captain America vs. Red Skull	$0.60	$1.80	$3.00	£0.40	£1.20	£2.00
Title Value:	**$15.65**	**$47.15**	**$85.00**	**£9.30**	**£28.25**	**£52.00**

Note: King Size Special #1-2, Annual 3 on.

CAPTAIN AMERICA ASHCAN
Marvel Comics Group; nn Mar 1995

	$Good	$Fine	$N.Mint	£Good	£Fine	£N.Mint
1 ND 16pgs, previews the latest storylines and changes for Captain America	$0.15	$0.45	$0.75	£0.10	£0.30	£0.50
	$0.15	$0.45	$0.75	£0.10	£0.30	£0.50

CAPTAIN AMERICA COLLECTORS' PREVIEW
Marvel Comics Group,OS; 1 Mar 1995

	$Good	$Fine	$N.Mint	£Good	£Fine	£N.Mint
1 ND 48pgs, previews storylines plus articles and features	$0.40	$1.20	$2.00	£0.25	£0.75	£1.25
Title Value:	**$0.40**	**$1.20**	**$2.00**	**£0.25**	**£0.75**	**£1.25**

CAPTAIN AMERICA COMICS
Timely/Atlas/Marvel; 1 Mar 1941-75 Feb 1950; 76 May 1954-78 Sep 1954

	$Good	$Fine	$N.Mint	£Good	£Fine	£N.Mint
1 origin and 1st appearance Captain America and Bucky by Joe Simon and Jack Kirby; 68pgs begin	$5000.00	$15000.00	$50000.00	£3500.00	£10500.00	£35000.00
1 ND 48pgs, Marvel Milestone Edition (Mar 1995) - metallic ink cover	$0.80	$2.40	$4.00	£0.50	£1.50	£2.50
2	$1050.00	$3150.00	$8500.00	£710.00	£2125.00	£5700.00
3 1st ever text work by Stan Lee and his first job as Assistant Editor	$810.00	$2425.00	$6500.00	£530.00	£1600.00	£4300.00
4	$530.00	$1600.00	$4300.00	£355.00	£1050.00	£2850.00
5	$475.00	$1425.00	$3800.00	£325.00	£970.00	£2600.00
6	$410.00	$1225.00	$3300.00	£275.00	£820.00	£2200.00
7 Red Skull appears	$450.00	$1350.00	$3600.00	£300.00	£900.00	£2400.00
8-9	$340.00	$1025.00	$2750.00	£230.00	£690.00	£1850.00
10 (Jan 1942), last issue by Simon and Kirby	$340.00	$1025.00	$2750.00	£230.00	£690.00	£1850.00
11	$290.00	$880.00	$2350.00	£190.00	£580.00	£1550.00
12-15	$265.00	$800.00	$2150.00	£180.00	£540.00	£1450.00
16 classic Captain America vs. Red Skull, Red Skull on cover	$310.00	$930.00	$2500.00	£205.00	£620.00	£1675.00
17	$235.00	$710.00	$1900.00	£155.00	£475.00	£1275.00
18	$185.00	$560.00	$1500.00	£125.00	£375.00	£1000.00
19 Human Torch back-up begins	$185.00	$560.00	$1500.00	£125.00	£375.00	£1000.00
20 Sub-Mariner appears	$185.00	$560.00	$1500.00	£125.00	£375.00	£1000.00
21	$175.00	$520.00	$1400.00	£115.00	£355.00	£950.00
22 (Jan 1943)	$175.00	$520.00	$1400.00	£115.00	£355.00	£950.00
22 very rare in the U.K., rare in the U.S. 128pgs, same cover as #22 but with contents of Marvel Mystery #33 and Captain America #18; Canadian issue	$1600.00	$4800.00	$16000.00	£850.00	£2550.00	£8500.00
23-25	$175.00	$520.00	$1400.00	£115.00	£355.00	£950.00
26	$155.00	$465.00	$1250.00	£100.00	£305.00	£825.00
27 last 68pg issue	$155.00	$465.00	$1250.00	£100.00	£305.00	£825.00
28-30	$155.00	$465.00	$1250.00	£100.00	£305.00	£825.00
31-33	$130.00	$390.00	$1050.00	£87.50	£260.00	£700.00
34 (Jan 1944)	$130.00	$390.00	$1050.00	£87.50	£260.00	£700.00
35	$130.00	$390.00	$1050.00	£87.50	£260.00	£700.00
36 Hitler on cover - the classic confrontation	$200.00	$600.00	$1600.00	£135.00	£410.00	£1100.00
37 Red Skull appears	$150.00	$450.00	$1200.00	£100.00	£300.00	£800.00
38-40	$130.00	$390.00	$1050.00	£87.50	£260.00	£700.00
41-43	$125.00	$375.00	$1000.00	£82.50	£250.00	£675.00
44 (Jan 1945)	$125.00	$375.00	$1000.00	£82.50	£250.00	£675.00
45-50	$125.00	$375.00	$1000.00	£82.50	£250.00	£675.00
51	$105.00	$315.00	$850.00	£67.50	£205.00	£550.00
52 (Jan 1946)	$105.00	$315.00	$850.00	£67.50	£205.00	£550.00
53-58	$105.00	$315.00	$850.00	£67.50	£205.00	£550.00
59 origin retold	$215.00	$650.00	$1750.00	£150.00	£450.00	£1200.00
60 (Jan 1947)	$105.00	$315.00	$850.00	£67.50	£205.00	£550.00
61 Red Skull cover and story	$155.00	$475.00	$1275.00	£105.00	£315.00	£850.00
62-64	$100.00	$300.00	$800.00	£62.50	£185.00	£500.00
65 (Jan 1948)	$100.00	$300.00	$800.00	£62.50	£185.00	£500.00
66 scarce in the U.K. Golden Girl appears, origin Golden Girl	$130.00	$390.00	$1050.00	£87.50	£260.00	£700.00
67 Golden Girl appears	$115.00	$355.00	$950.00	£77.50	£230.00	£625.00
68 Sub-Mariner appears	$115.00	$355.00	$950.00	£77.50	£230.00	£625.00
69 Human Torch appears	$115.00	$355.00	$950.00	£77.50	£230.00	£625.00
70 Sub-Mariner appears						

	$Good	$Fine	$N.Mint	£Good	£Fine	£N.Mint
	$115.00	$355.00	$950.00	£77.50	£230.00	£625.00
71	$100.00	$300.00	$800.00	£62.50	£185.00	£500.00
72 (Jan 1949)	$100.00	$300.00	$800.00	£62.50	£185.00	£500.00
73	$100.00	$300.00	$800.00	£62.50	£185.00	£500.00

74 very scarce in the U.K. titled "Captain America's Weird Tales", classic Red Skull cover

	$260.00	$780.00	$2100.00	£175.00	£520.00	£1400.00

75 very scarce in the U.K. (Feb 1950), titled "Captain America's Weird Tales"

	$115.00	$355.00	$950.00	£77.50	£230.00	£625.00

76 scarce in the U.K. (May 1954), Human Torch and Toro appear, classic cover headline begins: "Captain America...Commie Smasher!"

	$67.50	$200.00	$540.00	£47.00	£140.00	£375.00

77-78 scarce in the U.K. Human Torch and Toro appear

	$67.50	$200.00	$540.00	£47.00	£140.00	£375.00
Title Value:	$21268.30	$63902.40	$184349.00	£14106.50	£42391.50	£122377.50

Note: though not officially distributed on the news-stands in the U.K. copies are thought to have come over with American G.I.'s or through US relatives of UK citizens. A copy of #50 has been recorded with a 9 (old) pence stamp on the cover. **Note also**: most issues of this title are at least scarce in the U.K.

CAPTAIN AMERICA GIANT SIZE
Marvel Comics Group; 1 Dec 1975
1 ND scarce in the U.K. 68pgs, all reprint

	$Good	$Fine	$N.Mint	£Good	£Fine	£N.Mint
	$1.80	$5.25	$9.00	£1.20	£3.60	£6.00
Title Value:	$1.80	$5.25	$9.00	£1.20	£3.60	£6.00

CAPTAIN AMERICA GOES TO WAR AGAINST DRUGS
Marvel Comics Group; nn Dec 1990
nn ND script by Peter David highlighting drugs problem among kids; promotional giveaway

	$0.30	$0.90	$1.50	£0.20	£0.60	£1.00
Title Value:	$0.30	$0.90	$1.50	£0.20	£0.60	£1.00

CAPTAIN AMERICA MOVIE ADAPTATION
Marvel Comics Group,OS; 1 May 1992
1 ND 48pgs, Stan Lee script; printed on special coated stock paper

	$0.45	$1.35	$2.25	£0.30	£0.90	£1.50
Title Value:	$0.45	$1.35	$2.25	£0.30	£0.90	£1.50

Note: originally scheduled for 1991 release but held over and re-formatted as the film was not distributed and went straight to video.

CAPTAIN AMERICA SPECIAL EDITION
Marvel Comics Group; 1 Feb 1984-2 Mar 1984
1 ND reprints Captain America #110, #111

	$0.55	$1.65	$2.75	£0.35	£1.05	£1.75

2 ND reprints Captain America #113

	$0.55	$1.65	$2.75	£0.35	£1.05	£1.75
Title Value:	$1.10	$3.30	$5.50	£0.70	£2.10	£3.50

Note: all Jim Steranko reprints on Baxter paper.

CAPTAIN AMERICA, THE ADVENTURES OF
Marvel Comics Group,MS; 1 Sep 1991-4 Dec 1991
1 ND Year One origin type story, Kevin Maguire art with Terry Austin inks on all; full embossed cover figure and title

	$1.05	$3.15	$5.25	£0.70	£2.10	£3.50

2 ND meeting with Bucky, Kevin Maguire art

	$1.00	$3.00	$5.00	£0.65	£1.95	£3.25

3 ND Kevin Maguire art

	$1.00	$3.00	$5.00	£0.65	£1.95	£3.25

4 ND Steve Carr/Kevin West art

	$1.00	$3.00	$5.00	£0.65	£1.95	£3.25
Title Value:	$4.05	$12.15	$20.25	£2.65	£7.95	£13.25

CAPTAIN AMERICA: DRUG WARS
Marvel Comics Group,OS; nn Apr 1994
nn ND New Warriors guest-star

	$0.40	$1.20	$2.00	£0.25	£0.75	£1.25
Title Value:	$0.40	$1.20	$2.00	£0.25	£0.75	£1.25

CAPTAIN AMERICA: THE CLASSIC YEARS
Marvel Comics Group; nn Dec 1990
Hardcover
ND Two volume set reprinting original 1940s Simon and Kirby issues #1-10 in slipcase

				£7.20	£21.60	£36.00

CAPTAIN AMERICA: THE MEDUSA EFFECT
Marvel Comics Group,OS; 1 Mar 1994
1 ND 64pgs, Golden Age Captain America and Bucky vs. Baron Zemo

	$0.60	$1.80	$3.00	£0.40	£1.20	£2.00
Title Value:	$0.60	$1.80	$3.00	£0.40	£1.20	£2.00

CAPTAIN ATOM
Charlton; 78 Dec 1965-89 Dec 1967
(previously Strange Suspense Stories)
78 ND Steve Ditko art

	$8.50	$26.00	$60.00	£5.50	£17.00	£40.00

79 ND Steve Ditko art

	$6.50	$20.00	$40.00	£5.00	£15.00	£30.00

80-82 Steve Ditko art; distributed in the U.K.

	$6.50	$20.00	$40.00	£4.15	£12.50	£25.00

83-87 Blue Beetle appears, Steve Ditko art; distributed in the U.K.

	$5.75	$17.50	$35.00	£3.75	£11.00	£22.50

88-89 Nightshade appears, Steve Ditko art; distributed in the U.K.

	$5.75	$17.50	$35.00	£3.75	£11.00	£22.50
Title Value:	$74.75	$228.50	$465.00	£49.20	£146.50	£302.50

Note: stories intended for issue #90 appeared in Charlton Bullseye #1,2

CAPTAIN ATOM (2ND SERIES)
DC Comics; 1 Mar 1987-57 Sep 1991
1 44pgs, origin, 1st DC appearance, new costume; Pat Broderick art begins (ends #27)

	$0.40	$1.20	$2.00	£0.25	£0.75	£1.25
2-4	$0.25	$0.75	$1.25	£0.15	£0.45	£0.75

5 Captain Atom vs. Firestorm

	$0.25	$0.75	$1.25	£0.15	£0.45	£0.75
6-10	$0.25	$0.75	$1.25	£0.15	£0.45	£0.75

11 Millennium X-over

	$0.25	$0.75	$1.25	£0.15	£0.45	£0.75
12-13	$0.25	$0.75	$1.25	£0.15	£0.45	£0.75

14 Nightshade guest-stars

	$0.25	$0.75	$1.25	£0.15	£0.45	£0.75

15 Captain Atom vs. Major Force

	$0.25	$0.75	$1.25	£0.15	£0.45	£0.75

16 Justice League X-over

	$0.25	$0.75	$1.25	£0.15	£0.45	£0.75

17 Swamp Thing appears

	$0.25	$0.75	$1.25	£0.15	£0.45	£0.75
18-19	$0.25	$0.75	$1.25	£0.15	£0.45	£0.75

20 Blue Beetle appears

	$0.25	$0.75	$1.25	£0.15	£0.45	£0.75
21-23	$0.15	$0.45	$0.75	£0.10	£0.35	£0.60

24-25 Invasion X-over

	$0.15	$0.45	$0.75	£0.10	£0.35	£0.60

26-28 Captain Atom File story; Blue Beetle, Mister Miracle, Booster Gold appear - leads into "true" origin

	$0.15	$0.45	$0.75	£0.10	£0.35	£0.60
29	$0.15	$0.45	$0.75	£0.10	£0.35	£0.60

30 Janus Directive tie-in, Captain Atom vs. Black Manta

	$0.15	$0.45	$0.75	£0.10	£0.35	£0.60
31-32	$0.15	$0.45	$0.75	£0.10	£0.35	£0.60

33 Batman appears; cover in style of classic 60s Batman/Robin pin-up

	$0.15	$0.45	$0.75	£0.10	£0.35	£0.60
34-41	$0.15	$0.45	$0.75	£0.10	£0.35	£0.60
42 Death appears	$0.30	$0.90	$1.50	£0.20	£0.60	£1.00
43-45	$0.15	$0.45	$0.75	£0.10	£0.35	£0.60

46-47 Superman guest-stars

	$0.15	$0.45	$0.75	£0.10	£0.35	£0.60

48 Red Tornado appears

	$0.15	$0.45	$0.75	£0.10	£0.35	£0.60
49	$0.15	$0.45	$0.75	£0.10	£0.35	£0.60
50 48pgs	$0.20	$0.60	$1.00	£0.15	£0.45	£0.75
51-52	$0.15	$0.45	$0.75	£0.10	£0.35	£0.60

53 Aquaman appears

	$0.15	$0.45	$0.75	£0.10	£0.35	£0.60
54-57	$0.15	$0.45	$0.75	£0.10	£0.35	£0.60
Title Value:	$10.90	$32.70	$54.50	£6.95	£22.60	£38.25

Note: previously a Charlton Comics character

CAPTAIN ATOM ANNUAL
DC Comics; 1 1987-2 1988

	$0.30	$0.90	$1.50	£0.20	£0.60	£1.00
1-2 48pgs	$0.30	$0.90	$1.50	£0.20	£0.60	£1.00
Title Value:	$0.60	$1.80	$3.00	£0.40	£1.20	£2.00

CAPTAIN BRITAIN
Marvel UK; nn Nov 1988
(see Excalibur)
Trade Paperback
196pgs, reprints British issues of Captain Britain #1-14, Mighty World of Marvel #14-16 Alan Davis art

				£1.25	£3.75	£6.25
(2nd print, 1990)				£1.00	£3.00	£5.00
(3rd print. Oct 1991)				£1.85	£5.55	£9.25

CAPTAIN CANUCK
Comely/CKR; 1 Jul 1975-4 Jul 1977; 4 Jul/Aug 1979-14 Mar/Apr 1981
1 1st appearance Captain Canuck

	$0.60	$1.80	$3.00	£0.40	£1.20	£2.00
2-3	$0.45	$1.35	$2.25	£0.30	£0.90	£1.50

4 1st printing, rare in the U.K. signed and numbered, with certificate

	$2.50	$7.50	$12.50	£1.00	£3.00	£5.00

4 2nd printing, extremely rare; 15 copies, orange card cover, none known in the UK at time of going to press

	$5.00	$15.00	$25.00	£2.00	£6.00	£10.00
4 3rd printing	$0.30	$0.90	$1.50	£0.20	£0.60	£1.00
5 origin	$0.30	$0.90	$1.50	£0.20	£0.60	£1.00
6-14	$0.25	$0.75	$1.25	£0.15	£0.45	£0.75
Title Value:	$11.85	$35.55	$59.25	£5.75	£17.25	£28.75

Note: all Non-Distributed on the news-stands in the U.K.

CAPTAIN CANUK FIRST SUMMER SPECIAL
CKR; 1 Jul/Sep 1980
1 ND 64pgs, Gene Day, Dave Sim pin-ups & biographies

	$0.60	$1.80	$3.00	£0.40	£1.20	£2.00
Title Value:	$0.60	$1.80	$3.00	£0.40	£1.20	£2.00

CAPTAIN CARROT AND HIS AMAZING ZOO CREW
DC Comics; 1 Mar 1982-20 Nov 1983
(see New Teen Titans #16, OZ-Wonderland War)
1 Superman appears

	$0.15	$0.45	$0.75	£0.10	£0.35	£0.60
2-11	$0.15	$0.45	$0.75	£0.10	£0.35	£0.60

12 Art Adams pin-up (his first published comic work)

	$0.15	$0.45	$0.75	£0.10	£0.35	£0.60
13-19	$0.15	$0.45	$0.75	£0.10	£0.35	£0.60

20 Changeling appears

	$0.15	$0.45	$0.75	£0.10	£0.35	£0.60
Title Value:	$3.00	$9.00	$15.00	£2.00	£7.00	£12.00

CAPTAIN CONFEDERACY
Steeldragon Press; 1 1986-12 1987
1 ND Ant Boy back-up by Matt Feazell; black and white

	$0.35	$1.05	$1.75	£0.25	£0.75	£1.25

2-12 ND Ant Boy back-up by Matt Feazell; black and white

	$0.30	$0.90	$1.50	£0.20	£0.60	£1.00
Title Value:	$3.65	$10.95	$18.25	£2.45	£7.35	£12.25

CAPTAIN CONFEDERACY SPECIAL
Steeldragon Press; 1 1986-3 1987

	$Good	$Fine	$N.Mint	£Good	£Fine	£N.Mint
1 ND	$0.40	$1.20	$2.00	£0.25	£0.75	£1.25

	$Good	$Fine	$N.Mint	£Good	£Fine	£N.Mint
2-3 ND	$0.30	$0.90	$1.50	£0.20	£0.60	£1.00
Title Value:	$1.00	$3.00	$5.00	£0.65	£1.95	£3.25

CAPTAIN CONFERACY
Marvel Comics Group/Epic,MS; 1 Nov 1991-4 Feb 1992

	$Good	$Fine	$N.Mint	£Good	£Fine	£N.Mint
1 ND computer-generated colours begin	$0.35	$1.05	$1.75	£0.25	£0.75	£1.25
2-4 ND	$0.35	$1.05	$1.75	£0.25	£0.75	£1.25
Title Value:	$1.40	$4.20	$7.00	£1.00	£3.00	£5.00

CAPTAIN EO 3-D
Eclipse, Film; (3-D Special 18) 1 Jul 1987

	$Good	$Fine	$N.Mint	£Good	£Fine	£N.Mint
1 ND adapts Michael Jackson film, Tom Yeates art, painted cover; glasses included (25% less without glasses)	$0.60	$1.80	$3.00	£0.40	£1.20	£2.00
1 ND souvenir edition, treasury size	$1.20	$3.60	$6.00	£0.80	£2.40	£4.00
Title Value:	$1.80	$5.40	$9.00	£1.20	£3.60	£6.00

CAPTAIN GALLANT
Charlton, TV; 1 1955; 2 Jan 1956-4 Sep 1956

	$Good	$Fine	$N.Mint	£Good	£Fine	£N.Mint
1 ND Buster Crabbe photo feature; Don Heck art	$7.75	$23.50	$55.00	£5.00	£15.00	£35.00
2-4 ND	$6.75	$20.00	$47.50	£3.90	£11.50	£27.50
Title Value:	$28.00	$83.50	$197.50	£16.70	£49.50	£117.50

CAPTAIN GLORY
Topps,OS; 1 Apr 1993

	$Good	$Fine	$N.Mint	£Good	£Fine	£N.Mint
1 ND pre-bagged with coupon #2 for Secret City Saga #0 with chrome trading card; Steve Ditko art and Jack Kirby cover	$0.30	$0.90	$1.50	£0.20	£0.60	£1.00
1 ND without coupon/card	$0.20	$0.60	$1.00	£0.15	£0.45	£0.75
Title Value:	$0.50	$1.50	$2.50	£0.35	£1.05	£1.75

CAPTAIN HARLOCK
Eternity; 1 Oct 1989-13 Oct 1990

	$Good	$Fine	$N.Mint	£Good	£Fine	£N.Mint
1-13 ND	$0.35	$1.05	$1.75	£0.25	£0.75	£1.25
Title Value:	$4.55	$13.65	$22.75	£3.25	£9.75	£16.25

CAPTAIN HARLOCK CHRISTMAS SPECIAL
Eternity,OS; 1 Feb 1992

	$Good	$Fine	$N.Mint	£Good	£Fine	£N.Mint
1 ND	$0.45	$1.35	$2.25	£0.30	£0.90	£1.50
Title Value:	$0.45	$1.35	$2.25	£0.30	£0.90	£1.50

CAPTAIN HARLOCK: DEATHSHADOW RISING
Eternity,MS; 1 Jul 1991-6 Dec 1991

	$Good	$Fine	$N.Mint	£Good	£Fine	£N.Mint
1-6 ND	$0.35	$1.05	$1.75	£0.25	£0.75	£1.25
Title Value:	$2.10	$6.30	$10.50	£1.50	£4.50	£7.50

CAPTAIN HARLOCK: FALL OF THE EMPIRE
Eternity,MS; 1 Oct 1992-4 Dec 1992

	$Good	$Fine	$N.Mint	£Good	£Fine	£N.Mint
1-4 ND	$0.35	$1.05	$1.75	£0.25	£0.75	£1.25
Title Value:	$1.40	$4.20	$7.00	£1.00	£3.00	£5.00

CAPTAIN HARLOCK: THE MACHINE PEOPLE
Eternity; 1 Jul 1993-4 Oct 1993

	$Good	$Fine	$N.Mint	£Good	£Fine	£N.Mint
1-4 ND	$0.35	$1.05	$1.75	£0.25	£0.75	£1.25
Title Value:	$1.40	$4.20	$7.00	£1.00	£3.00	£5.00

CAPTAIN JACK, THE ADVENTURES OF
Fantagraphics; 1 Jun 1986-12 1987

	$Good	$Fine	$N.Mint	£Good	£Fine	£N.Mint
1-12 ND DS, black and white	$0.35	$1.05	$1.75	£0.25	£0.75	£1.25
Title Value:	$4.20	$12.60	$21.00	£3.00	£9.00	£15.00

CAPTAIN JOHNER AND THE ALIENS
Gold Key/Whitman; 1 Sep/Dec 1967; Whitman; 2 May 1982

	$Good	$Fine	$N.Mint	£Good	£Fine	£N.Mint
1 scarce in the U.K. reprints back-up from Magnus Robot Fighter #1,3,4,6-10 by Russ Manning; distributed in the U.K.	$3.00	$9.00	$15.00	£2.00	£6.00	£10.00
2 reprints Magnus Robot Fighter #1 by Russ Manning; Limited Distribution in the U.K.	$1.00	$3.00	$5.00	£1.00	£3.00	£5.00
Title Value:	$4.00	$12.00	$20.00	£3.00	£9.00	£15.00

Note: reprints from Magnus, Robot Fighter with Russ Manning art

CAPTAIN JOHNER AND THE ALIENS, THE ORIGINAL
Valiant/Western Publishing; 1 Apr 1995-2 May 1995

	$Good	$Fine	$N.Mint	£Good	£Fine	£N.Mint
1-2 ND reprints from original back-up stories in Gold Key's Magnus Robot Fighter	$0.60	$1.80	$3.00	£0.40	£1.20	£2.00
Title Value:	$1.20	$3.60	$6.00	£0.80	£2.40	£4.00

CAPTAIN JUSTICE
Marvel Comics Group,MS TV; 1 Mar 1988-2 Apr 1988

	$Good	$Fine	$N.Mint	£Good	£Fine	£N.Mint
1-2	$0.15	$0.45	$0.75	£0.10	£0.30	£0.50
Title Value:	$0.30	$0.90	$1.50	£0.20	£0.60	£1.00

CAPTAIN MARVEL
(see Adventure, DC Comics Presents, Justice League of America, Shazam!, World's Finest)

CAPTAIN MARVEL
Marvel Comics Group; 1 May 1968-19 Dec 1969; 20 Jun 1970-21 Aug 1970; 22 Sep 1972-62 May 1979
(see Marvel Graphic Novel, Marvel Spotlight, Marvel Super Heroes #12)

	$Good	$Fine	$N.Mint	£Good	£Fine	£N.Mint
1	$20.00	$60.00	$100.00	£13.00	£39.00	£65.00
2 Captain Marvel battles Super Skrull	$6.50	$19.50	$32.50	£4.50	£13.50	£22.50
3 Super Skrull appears	$4.50	$13.50	$22.50	£3.00	£9.00	£15.00
4 Captain Marvel battles Sub-Mariner	$4.50	$13.50	$22.50	£3.00	£9.00	£15.00
5	$4.50	$13.50	$22.50	£3.00	£9.00	£15.00
6-10	$2.80	$8.25	$14.00	£1.60	£4.80	£8.00
11-13	$1.60	$4.80	$8.00	£1.10	£3.30	£5.50
14 Iron Man appears	$1.60	$4.80	$8.00	£1.10	£3.30	£5.50
15-16	$1.60	$4.80	$8.00	£1.10	£3.30	£5.50
17 new costume; Captain America, Bucky appear	$1.60	$4.80	$8.00	£1.10	£3.30	£5.50
18-19	$1.60	$4.80	$8.00	£1.10	£3.30	£5.50
20 LD in the U.K.	$1.80	$5.25	$9.00	£1.20	£3.60	£6.00
21 Captain Marvel vs. Hulk; Gil Kane art	$1.60	$4.80	$8.00	£1.10	£3.30	£5.50
22 ND scarce in the U.K. Wayne Boring art, Gil Kane cover	$1.80	$5.25	$9.00	£1.20	£3.60	£6.00
23-24 ND scarce in the U.K. Wayne Boring art	$1.80	$5.25	$9.00	£1.20	£3.60	£6.00
25 scarce in the U.K. 1st Jim Starlin cover and art, Thanos cameo, battles many old foes inc. Hulk and Sub-Mariner	$4.50	$13.50	$22.50	£3.00	£9.00	£15.00
26 scarce in the U.K. Jim Starlin art, Captain Marvel battles Thing; 2nd full appearance of Thanos, 1st Thanos cover	$6.00	$18.00	$30.00	£3.50	£10.50	£17.50
27 Jim Starlin art, Captain Marvel battles Super Skrull, 3rd appearance of Thanos, 1st Eros & Mentor	$4.50	$13.50	$22.50	£3.00	£9.00	£15.00
28 Jim Starlin art, part script. Avengers appear. Thanos battles Drax the Destroyer, Thanos on cover	$3.00	$9.00	$15.00	£2.00	£6.00	£10.00
29 Jim Starlin art/script, Captain Marvel gets Cosmic Powers	$2.00	$6.00	$10.00	£1.40	£4.20	£7.00
30 Jim Starlin art, Thanos in 4 panels, Captain Marvel's 1st use of Cosmic Power, Avengers appear	$2.00	$6.00	$10.00	£1.40	£4.20	£7.00
31 ND classic Jim Starlin art and Thanos War. Drax and Avengers appear	$2.25	$6.75	$11.25	£1.50	£4.50	£7.50
32 ND classic Jim Starlin art, Thanos War. Drax and Avengers appear	$2.25	$6.75	$11.25	£1.50	£4.50	£7.50
33 ND scarce in the U.K. 1st origin Thanos, Captain Marvel vs. Thanos, Jim Starlin art	$4.50	$13.50	$22.50	£3.00	£9.00	£15.00
34 last full Jim Starlin art, Avengers appear	$1.20	$3.60	$6.00	£0.80	£2.40	£4.00
35	$0.40	$1.20	$2.00	£0.25	£0.75	£1.25
36 Starlin art (3pgs), reprints 1st Captain Marvel story from Marvel Super-Heroes #12	$0.80	$2.40	$4.00	£0.50	£1.50	£2.50
37-38	$0.40	$1.20	$2.00	£0.25	£0.75	£1.25
39 origin the Watcher retold	$0.40	$1.20	$2.00	£0.25	£0.75	£1.25
40	$0.40	$1.20	$2.00	£0.25	£0.75	£1.25
41 Wrightson part inks, P. Craig Russell part inks	$0.40	$1.20	$2.00	£0.25	£0.75	£1.25
42 Drax the Destroyer appears	$0.40	$1.20	$2.00	£0.25	£0.75	£1.25
43 Wrightson part inks, Captain Marvel battles Drax	$0.40	$1.20	$2.00	£0.25	£0.75	£1.25
44 Drax appears	$0.40	$1.20	$2.00	£0.25	£0.75	£1.25
45-46	$0.40	$1.20	$2.00	£0.25	£0.75	£1.25
47 Human Torch appears	$0.40	$1.20	$2.00	£0.25	£0.75	£1.25
48	$0.40	$1.20	$2.00	£0.25	£0.75	£1.25
49 ND part Jim Starlin art	$0.40	$1.20	$2.00	£0.30	£0.90	£1.50
50 ND Captain Marvel and the Avengers battles the Super Adaptoid	$0.40	$1.20	$2.00	£0.30	£0.90	£1.50
51 ND Avengers appear	$0.40	$1.20	$2.00	£0.30	£0.90	£1.50
52 ND	$0.40	$1.20	$2.00	£0.30	£0.90	£1.50
53 Inhumans appear	$0.40	$1.20	$2.00	£0.25	£0.75	£1.25
54 Wonder Man appears	$0.40	$1.20	$2.00	£0.25	£0.75	£1.25
55-56 Broderick art	$0.40	$1.20	$2.00	£0.25	£0.75	£1.25
57 Captain Marvel battles Thor, Thanos appearance in flashback	$0.70	$2.10	$3.50	£0.30	£0.90	£1.50
58 Broderick art, Drax returns	$0.40	$1.20	$2.00	£0.25	£0.75	£1.25
59-62 Broderick art, Drax appears	$0.40	$1.20	$2.00	£0.25	£0.75	£1.25
Title Value:	$121.30	$362.55	$605.50	£78.90	£236.70	£394.50

Trade Paperback (Dec 1990), reprints Iron Man #55, Marvel Feature #12, Captain Marvel #25-34, Avengers Annual #7

	$Good	$Fine	$N.Mint	£Good	£Fine	£N.Mint
Marvel Two-in-One Annual #2				£1.40	£4.20	£7.00

CAPTAIN MARVEL
MF; 1 Jun 1966-4 Nov 1966
(becomes Captain Marvel Presents the Terrible 5)

	$Good	$Fine	$N.Mint	£Good	£Fine	£N.Mint
1 giant, origin told; limited distribution in the U.K.	$3.50	$10.50	$17.50	£2.50	£7.50	£12.50
2 LD in the U.K. giant	$1.80	$5.25	$9.00	£1.20	£3.60	£6.00
3 giant (titled ...Fights The Bat); limited distribution in the U.K.	$2.00	$6.00	$10.00	£1.40	£4.20	£7.00
4 LD in the U.K. giant	$1.80	$5.25	$9.00	£1.20	£3.60	£6.00
Title Value:	$9.10	$27.00	$45.50	£6.30	£18.90	£31.50

CAPTAIN MARVEL (2ND SERIES)
Marvel Comics Group; 1 Dec 1995-present

	$Good	$Fine	$N.Mint	£Good	£Fine	£N.Mint
1 ND Fabian Nicieza script, Ed Benes art on the son of Mar-vell; foil-stamped cover	$0.60	$1.80	$3.00	£0.40	£1.20	£2.00
2-4 ND	$0.40	$1.20	$2.00	£0.25	£0.75	£1.25
Title Value:	$1.80	$5.40	$9.00	£1.15	£3.45	£5.75

CAPTAIN MARVEL ADVENTURES

Fawcett; nn Spring 1941-150 Nov 1953
(see Whiz Comics)

	$Good	$Fine	$N.Mint	£Good	£Fine	£N.Mint
nn (#1), scarce, Jack Kirby cover and art						
	$2250.00	$6700.00	$22500.00	£1650.00	£4950.00	£16500.00
2 Jack Kirby cover and art						
	$330.00	$990.00	$2650.00	£215.00	£650.00	£1750.00
3 Jack Kirby cover and art						
	$215.00	$650.00	$1750.00	£140.00	£430.00	£1150.00
4 Jack Kirby cover and art						
	$130.00	$390.00	$1050.00	£92.50	£280.00	£750.00
5	$105.00	$315.00	$850.00	£67.50	£205.00	£550.00
6	$75.00	$225.00	$600.00	£50.00	£150.00	£400.00
7-10	$77.50	$230.00	$625.00	£52.50	£155.00	£425.00
11-15	$67.50	$205.00	$550.00	£46.00	£135.00	£370.00
16	$65.00	$195.00	$525.00	£44.00	£130.00	£350.00
17 painted cover - "Captain Marvel Smacks the Axis"						
	$65.00	$195.00	$525.00	£44.00	£130.00	£350.00
18 1st appearance Mary Marvel, painted cover						
	$95.00	$290.00	$775.00	£65.00	£195.00	£525.00
19 Christmas cover						
	$65.00	$195.00	$525.00	£44.00	£130.00	£350.00
20	$65.00	$195.00	$525.00	£44.00	£130.00	£350.00
21	$52.50	$155.00	$425.00	£34.00	£100.00	£275.00
22 1st appearance Mr. Mind						
	$70.00	$210.00	$560.00	£48.00	£140.00	£380.00
23-25	$52.50	$155.00	$425.00	£34.00	£100.00	£275.00
26 patriotic flag cover						
	$46.00	$135.00	$320.00	£30.00	£90.00	£210.00
27-30	$46.00	$135.00	$320.00	£30.00	£90.00	£210.00
31-35	$39.00	$115.00	$275.00	£26.00	£77.50	£185.00
36-40	$35.00	$105.00	$245.00	£25.00	£75.00	£175.00
41	$28.00	$82.50	$195.00	£18.50	£55.00	£130.00
42 Christmas cover						
	$28.00	$82.50	$195.00	£18.50	£55.00	£130.00
43-45	$28.00	$82.50	$195.00	£18.50	£55.00	£130.00
46-50	$25.00	$75.00	$175.00	£17.50	£52.50	£122.50
51-53	$22.00	$65.00	$155.00	£14.00	£43.00	£100.00
54 68pgs	$25.00	$75.00	$175.00	£17.50	£52.50	£125.00
55-60	$22.00	$65.00	$155.00	£14.00	£43.00	£100.00
61 The Cult of the Curse story begins (ends #66)						
	$27.00	$80.00	$190.00	£19.00	£57.50	£135.00
62-65	$20.00	$60.00	$140.00	£13.50	£41.00	£95.00
66 famous Atomic War story						
	$20.00	$60.00	$140.00	£13.50	£41.00	£95.00
67-71	$20.00	$60.00	$140.00	£13.50	£41.00	£95.00
72 "Flash" cover (running in mid-air with speed-lines behind him)						
	$20.00	$60.00	$140.00	£13.50	£41.00	£95.00
73-77	$20.00	$60.00	$140.00	£13.50	£41.00	£95.00
78 1st appearance Mr. Atom (robot), origin Mr. Tawney						
	$22.00	$65.00	$155.00	£14.00	£43.00	£100.00
79	$20.00	$60.00	$140.00	£13.50	£41.00	£95.00
80 origin Captain Marvel re-told						
	$39.00	$115.00	$275.00	£26.00	£77.50	£185.00
81-90	$17.50	$52.50	$125.00	£12.00	£36.00	£85.00
91-99	$15.50	$47.00	$110.00	£10.00	£31.00	£72.50
100 origin re-told						
	$32.00	$95.00	$225.00	£21.00	£62.50	£150.00
101-120	$15.00	$45.00	$105.00	£10.00	£30.00	£70.00
121 origin re-told						
	$22.00	$65.00	$155.00	£15.00	£45.00	£105.00
122-137	$15.00	$45.00	$105.00	£10.00	£30.00	£70.00
138 flying saucer paranoia story						
	$15.00	$45.00	$105.00	£10.00	£30.00	£70.00
139-148	$15.00	$45.00	$105.00	£10.00	£30.00	£70.00
149 scarce in the U.K.						
	$17.50	$52.50	$125.00	£12.00	£36.00	£85.00
150 scarce in the U.S, very scarce in the U.K.						
	$22.50	$67.50	$157.50	£15.00	£45.00	£105.00
Title Value:	$7017.00	$20960.50	$58242.50	£4840.00	£14517.00	£40465.00

Note: though not officially distributed on the news-stands in the U.K. many copies were sent over in bundles as ballast on ships. There have been hundreds of instances of copies with British pence stamps on the cover. **Note also**: most of these issues, particularly before #100, are at least scarce in the U.K.

CAPTAIN MARVEL GIANT SIZE

Marvel Comics Group; 1 Dec 1975

	$Good	$Fine	$N.Mint	£Good	£Fine	£N.Mint
1 ND scarce in the U.K. 68pgs, all reprint from Captain Marvel #19, #20 and #21 (Captain Marvel vs. Hulk), all Gil Kane art						
	$1.80	$5.25	$9.00	£1.20	£3.60	£6.00
Title Value:	$1.80	$5.25	$9.00	£1.20	£3.60	£6.00

CAPTAIN MARVEL PRESENTS THE TERRIBLE 5

MF; 1 Aug 1966; 5 Sep 1967
(previously Captain Marvel)

	$Good	$Fine	$N.Mint	£Good	£Fine	£N.Mint
1 giant, distributed in the U.K.						
	$3.00	$9.00	$15.00	£2.00	£6.00	£10.00
5 giant, distributed in the U.K.						
	$1.80	$5.25	$9.00	£1.20	£3.60	£6.00
Title Value:	$4.80	$14.25	$24.00	£3.20	£9.60	£16.00

CAPTAIN MARVEL SPECIAL

Marvel Comics Group, OS; 1 Nov 1989

	$Good	$Fine	$N.Mint	£Good	£Fine	£N.Mint
1 ND 48pgs, new career and new powers for female version						
	$0.40	$1.20	$2.00	£0.25	£0.75	£1.25
Title Value:	$0.40	$1.20	$2.00	£0.25	£0.75	£1.25

CAPTAIN MARVEL, DEATH OF

Marvel Comics Group, OS; nn Oct 1994

	$Good	$Fine	$N.Mint	£Good	£Fine	£N.Mint
nn ND 64pgs, reprints the first Marvel Graphic Novel with new cover by Jim Starlin						
	$1.50	$4.50	$7.50	£1.00	£3.00	£5.00
Title Value:	$1.50	$4.50	$7.50	£1.00	£3.00	£5.00

CAPTAIN MARVEL, THE LIFE OF

Marvel Comics Group, MS; 1 Aug 1985-5 Dec 1985
(see Captain Marvel)

	$Good	$Fine	$N.Mint	£Good	£Fine	£N.Mint
1 ND Jim Starlin reprints from Captain Marvel begin, Baxter paper						
	$0.60	$1.80	$3.00	£0.40	£1.20	£2.00
2-5 ND	$0.60	$1.80	$3.00	£0.40	£1.20	£2.00
Title Value:	$3.00	$9.00	$15.00	£2.00	£6.00	£10.00
The Life of Captain Marvel (Dec 1995) Trade paperback						
224pgs, collects 5 issue mini-series				£2.00	£6.00	£10.00

CAPTAIN MARVEL: SPEAKING WITHOUT CONCERN

Marvel Comics Group, OS; nn Feb 1994

	$Good	$Fine	$N.Mint	£Good	£Fine	£N.Mint
nn ND 48pgs, female Captain Marvel story about racism						
	$0.40	$1.20	$2.00	£0.25	£0.75	£1.25
Title Value:	$0.40	$1.20	$2.00	£0.25	£0.75	£1.25

CAPTAIN NAUTICUS AND THE OCEAN FORCE

Entity Comics/National Maritime Center; 1 Oct 1994-3 1995?

	$Good	$Fine	$N.Mint	£Good	£Fine	£N.Mint
1-3 ND Bill Maus script and art						
	$0.60	$1.80	$3.00	£0.40	£1.20	£2.00
Title Value:	$1.80	$5.40	$9.00	£1.20	£3.60	£6.00

CAPTAIN PARAGON

AC Comics, MS; 1 Dec 1983-4 Jun 1984
(see Americomics, Bill Black's Fun Comics)

	$Good	$Fine	$N.Mint	£Good	£Fine	£N.Mint
1-4 ND	$0.30	$0.90	$1.50	£0.20	£0.60	£1.00
Title Value:	$1.20	$3.60	$6.00	£0.80	£2.40	£4.00

Captain Atom #79

Captain Marvel #22

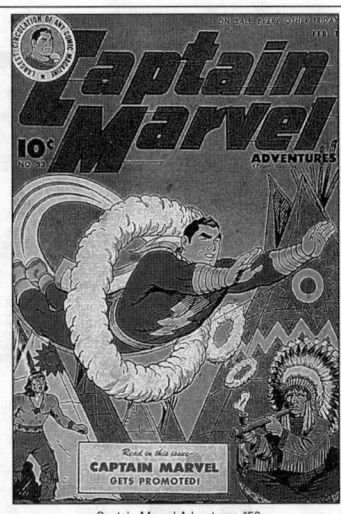

Captain Marvel Adventures #53

MINT = 100% / NEAR MINT (inc. +/-) = 90–99% / VERY FINE (inc. +/-) = 75–89% / FINE (inc. +/-) = 55–74%
VERY GOOD (inc. +/-) = 35–54% / GOOD (inc. +/-) = 15–34% / FAIR = 5–14% / POOR = 1–4%

259

CAPTAIN PARAGON & THE SENTINELS OF JUSTICE
AC Comics; 1 Apr 1985-6 1986
(becomes Sentinels of Justice)

	$Good	$Fine	$N.Mint	£Good	£Fine	£N.Mint
1-6 ND	$0.35	$1.05	$1.75	£0.25	£0.75	£1.25
Title Value:	$2.10	$6.30	$10.50	£1.50	£4.50	£7.50

CAPTAIN PLANET
Marvel Comics Group,MS; 1 Oct 1991-12 Oct 1992

	$Good	$Fine	$N.Mint	£Good	£Fine	£N.Mint
1 based on U.S. animated series	$0.15	$0.45	$0.75	£0.10	£0.35	£0.60
2-4	$0.15	$0.45	$0.75	£0.10	£0.35	£0.60
5 $1.25 cover begins	$0.15	$0.45	$0.75	£0.10	£0.35	£0.60
6-12	$0.15	$0.45	$0.75	£0.10	£0.35	£0.60
Title Value:	$5.40		$9.00		£4.20	£7.20

CAPTAIN POWER (AND THE SOLDIERS OF THE FUTURE)
Continuity; 1 Aug 1988-2 Jan 1989

	$Good	$Fine	$N.Mint	£Good	£Fine	£N.Mint
1-2 ND Neal Adams pencils, co-plot and cover	$0.35	$1.05	$1.75	£0.25	£0.75	£1.25
Title Value:	$0.70	$2.10	$3.50	£0.50	£1.50	£2.50

CAPTAIN SATAN
Millennium; 1 Jul 1994-2 1994

	$Good	$Fine	$N.Mint	£Good	£Fine	£N.Mint
1 ND Steven Seagle script, Sean Shaw art	$0.60	$1.80	$3.00	£0.40	£1.20	£2.00
1 ND Collector's Edition with Matt Wagner cover	$0.80	$2.40	$4.00	£0.50	£1.50	£2.50
2 ND	$0.60	$1.80	$3.00	£0.40	£1.20	£2.00
Title Value:	$2.00	$6.00		£1.30	£3.90	£6.50

CAPTAIN SAVAGE AND HIS LEATHERNECK RAIDERS
Marvel Comics Group; 1 Jan 1968-19 Mar 1970
(see Sgt. Fury #10)

	$Good	$Fine	$N.Mint	£Good	£Fine	£N.Mint
1 Sgt. Fury cameo	$2.20	$6.50	$11.00	£1.40	£4.20	£7.00
2-3	$1.20	$3.60	$6.00	£0.60	£1.80	£3.00
4 origin of Hydra	$1.20	$3.60	$6.00	£0.60	£1.80	£3.00
5-6	$1.20	$3.60	$6.00	£0.60	£1.80	£3.00
7 Ben Grimm appears	$1.20	$3.60	$6.00	£0.60	£1.80	£3.00
8 scarce in the U.K.	$1.20	$3.60	$6.00	£0.70	£2.10	£3.50
9-10	$1.20	$3.60	$6.00	£0.60	£1.80	£3.00
11 Sgt. Fury appears	$0.80	$2.40	$4.00	£0.50	£1.50	£2.50
12-14	$0.80	$2.40	$4.00	£0.50	£1.50	£2.50
15-18 ND	$0.80	$2.40	$4.00	£0.55	£1.65	£2.75
19	$0.80	$2.40	$4.00	£0.50	£1.50	£2.50
Title Value:	$20.20	$60.50	$101.00	£11.60	£34.80	£58.00

CAPTAIN STORM
National Periodical Publications; 1 May/Jun 1964-18 Mar/Apr 1967
(see Unknown Soldier)

	$Good	$Fine	$N.Mint	£Good	£Fine	£N.Mint
1	$3.30	$10.00	$20.00	£2.05	£6.25	£12.50
2	$1.80	$5.50	$11.00	£1.15	£3.50	£7.00
3 Kubert art	$1.80	$5.50	$11.00	£1.15	£3.50	£7.00
4-5	$1.80	$5.50	$11.00	£1.15	£3.50	£7.00
6 Kubert art	$1.80	$5.50	$11.00	£1.15	£3.50	£7.00
7-10	$1.80	$5.50	$11.00	£1.15	£3.50	£7.00
11	$1.65	$5.00	$10.00	£1.00	£3.00	£6.00
12 Kubert cover	$1.65	$5.00	$10.00	£1.00	£3.00	£6.00
13 Kubert art	$1.65	$5.00	$10.00	£1.00	£3.00	£6.00
14-17	$1.65	$5.00	$10.00	£1.00	£3.00	£6.00
18 scarce in the U.K.	$1.65	$5.00	$10.00	£1.15	£3.50	£7.00
Title Value:	$32.70	$99.50	$199.00	£20.55	£62.25	£124.50

CAPTAIN THUNDER
Hero; 1 Aug 1992-3 Mar 1993

	$Good	$Fine	$N.Mint	£Good	£Fine	£N.Mint
1-3 ND Roy and Dann Thomas script	$0.45	$1.35	$2.25	£0.30	£0.90	£1.50
Title Value:	$1.35	$4.05	$6.75	£0.90	£2.70	£4.50

CAPTAIN THUNDER & BLUE BOLT
Hero; 1 Sep 1987-12 1988

	$Good	$Fine	$N.Mint	£Good	£Fine	£N.Mint
1-12 ND	$0.40	$1.20	$2.00	£0.25	£0.75	£1.25
Title Value:	$4.80	$14.40	$24.00	£3.00	£9.00	£15.00
The Complete Captain Thunder (Mar 1993) reprints 12 issue mini-series				£3.00	£9.00	£15.00

CAPTAIN THUNDER (2ND SERIES)
Heroic Publishing; 1 Jan 1995

	$Good	$Fine	$N.Mint	£Good	£Fine	£N.Mint
1 ND original stories of Captain Thunder and Blue Bolt reprinted	$0.40	$1.20	$2.00	£0.25	£0.75	£1.25
Title Value:	$0.40	$1.20	$2.00	£0.25	£0.75	£1.25

CAPTAIN VENTURE AND THE LAND BENEATH THE SEA
Gold Key; 1 Oct 1968-2 Oct 1969

	$Good	$Fine	$N.Mint	£Good	£Fine	£N.Mint
1 Space Family Robinson reprint; limited distribution in the U.K.	$6.00	$18.00	$30.00	£4.00	£12.00	£20.00
2 LD in the U.K.	$5.25	$15.50	$26.25	£3.50	£10.50	£17.50
Title Value:	$11.25	$33.50	$56.25	£7.50	£22.50	£37.50

CAPTAIN VICTORY AND THE GALACTIC RANGERS
Pacific; 1 Nov 1981-13 Nov 1983

	$Good	$Fine	$N.Mint	£Good	£Fine	£N.Mint
1-2 ND Jack Kirby art	$0.25	$0.75	$1.25	£0.15	£0.45	£0.75
3 ND Ms. Mystic back-up, Neal Adams art	$0.30	$0.90	$1.50	£0.20	£0.60	£1.00
4-5 ND Jack Kirby art	$0.25	$0.75	$1.25	£0.15	£0.45	£0.75
6 ND Jack Kirby art, Missing Man by Steve Ditko	$0.30	$0.90	$1.50	£0.20	£0.60	£1.00
7-10 ND Jack Kirby art	$0.25	$0.75	$1.25	£0.15	£0.45	£0.75
11 ND origin, Jack Kirby, Conrad art	$0.25	$0.75	$1.25	£0.15	£0.45	£0.75
12-13 ND Jack Kirby art	$0.25	$0.75	$1.25	£0.15	£0.45	£0.75
Title Value:	$3.35	$10.05	$16.75	£2.05	£6.15	£10.25

CAPTAIN VICTORY SPECIAL
Pacific; 1 Oct 1983

	$Good	$Fine	$N.Mint	£Good	£Fine	£N.Mint
1 ND Jack Kirby cover and art	$0.25	$0.75	$1.25	£0.15	£0.45	£0.75
Title Value:	$0.25	$0.75	$1.25	£0.15	£0.45	£0.75

CAR WARRIORS
Marvel Comics Group,Epic,MS; 1 Jun 1991-4 Sep 1991

	$Good	$Fine	$N.Mint	£Good	£Fine	£N.Mint
1-4 ND	$0.40	$1.20	$2.00	£0.25	£0.75	£1.25
Title Value:	$1.60	$4.80	$8.00	£1.00	£3.00	£5.00

CARAVAN KIDD
Dark Horse; 1 Jul 1992-10 Apr 1993

	$Good	$Fine	$N.Mint	£Good	£Fine	£N.Mint
1 ND Johji Manabe script/art begins	$0.60	$1.80	$3.00	£0.40	£1.20	£2.00
2 ND	$0.55	$1.65	$2.75	£0.35	£1.05	£1.75
3-9 ND	$0.45	$1.35	$2.25	£0.30	£0.90	£1.50
Title Value:	$4.30	$12.90	$21.50	£2.85	£8.55	£14.25

CARAVAN KIDD HOLIDAY SPECIAL
Dark Horse,OS; 1 Nov 1993

	$Good	$Fine	$N.Mint	£Good	£Fine	£N.Mint
1 ND Johji Manabe script and art, black and white	$0.45	$1.35	$2.25	£0.30	£0.90	£1.50
Title Value:	$0.45	$1.35	$2.25	£0.30	£0.90	£1.50

CARAVAN KIDD PART 2
Dark Horse,MS; 1 May 1993-10 Apr 1994

	$Good	$Fine	$N.Mint	£Good	£Fine	£N.Mint
1-10 ND black and white	$0.45	$1.35	$2.25	£0.30	£0.90	£1.50
Title Value:	$4.50	$13.50	$22.50	£3.00	£9.00	£15.00

CARAVAN KIDD PART 3
Dark Horse,MS; 1 May 1994-8 Dec 1994

	$Good	$Fine	$N.Mint	£Good	£Fine	£N.Mint
1-6 ND black and white	$0.45	$1.35	$2.25	£0.30	£0.90	£1.50
7 ND 48pgs, black and white	$0.60	$1.80	$3.00	£0.40	£1.20	£2.00
8 ND black and white	$0.45	$1.35	$2.25	£0.30	£0.90	£1.50
Title Value:	$3.75	$11.25	$18.75	£2.50	£7.50	£12.50

CARAVAN KIDD VALENTINE'S DAY SPECIAL
Dark Horse,OS; 1 Feb 1994

	$Good	$Fine	$N.Mint	£Good	£Fine	£N.Mint
1 ND Johji Manabe script and art, black and white	$0.45	$1.35	$2.25	£0.30	£0.90	£1.50
Title Value:	$0.45	$1.35	$2.25	£0.30	£0.90	£1.50

CARE BEARS
Marvel Comics Group/Star, TV; 1 Nov 1985-20 Jan 1990

	$Good	$Fine	$N.Mint	£Good	£Fine	£N.Mint
1-20 scarce in the U.K.	$0.15	$0.45	$0.75	£0.10	£0.30	£0.50
Title Value:	$3.00	$9.00	$15.00	£2.00	£6.00	£10.00

CARNAGE
Eternity; 1,2 1987

	$Good	$Fine	$N.Mint	£Good	£Fine	£N.Mint
1 ND	$0.40	$1.20	$2.00	£0.25	£0.75	£1.25
Title Value:	$0.40	$1.20	$2.00	£0.25	£0.75	£1.25

CARNAGE: MINDBOMB
Marvel Comics Group,OS; 1 Feb 1996

	$Good	$Fine	$N.Mint	£Good	£Fine	£N.Mint
1 ND Warren Ellis script, Kyle Hotz art; foil stamped cover	$0.60	$1.80	$3.00	£0.40	£1.20	£2.00
Title Value:	$0.60	$1.80	$3.00	£0.40	£1.20	£2.00

CARNIVAL OF SOULS
Malibu,OS; 1 Sep 1991

	$Good	$Fine	$N.Mint	£Good	£Fine	£N.Mint
1 ND 48pgs, squarebound, black and white horror anthology	$0.90	$2.70	$4.50	£0.60	£1.80	£3.00
Title Value:	$0.90	$2.70	$4.50	£0.60	£1.80	£3.00

CASES OF SHERLOCK HOLMES
Renegade/Northstar; 1 May 1986-24 1990?

	$Good	$Fine	$N.Mint	£Good	£Fine	£N.Mint
1 ND Dan Day art begins	$0.40	$1.20	$2.00	£0.25	£0.75	£1.25
2-24 ND	$0.40	$1.20	$2.00	£0.25	£0.75	£1.25
Title Value:	$9.60	$28.80	$48.00	£6.00	£18.00	£30.00
Vol I Collection Trade paperback, reprints issues #1-5				£1.00	£3.00	£5.00
Vol II Collection Trade paperback, reprints issues #6-9				£1.00	£3.00	£5.00

Note: all adaptations of Sir Arthur Conan Doyle stories

CASEY JONES & RAPHAEL
Mirage Studios; 1 Oct 1994-5 1995

	$Good	$Fine	$N.Mint	£Good	£Fine	£N.Mint
1-5 ND Kevin Eastman script, Simon Bisley art	$0.55	$1.65	$2.75	£0.35	£1.05	£1.75
Title Value:	$2.75	$8.25	$13.75	£1.75	£5.25	£8.75

CASPER, THE FRIENDLY GHOST
Harvey; 1 Aug 1958-224 Oct 1982; 225 Oct 1986-253 1989

	$Good	$Fine	$N.Mint	£Good	£Fine	£N.Mint
1 scarce in the U.K.	$18.50	$55.00	$112.50	£12.50	£38.00	£75.00
2 scarce in the U.K.	$9.25	$28.00	$56.25	£6.25	£18.50	£37.50
3-5 scarce in the U.K.	$5.50	$16.50	$33.75	£3.75	£11.00	£22.50
6-10	$4.50	$13.50	$27.00	£3.00	£9.00	£18.00
11-20	$3.00	$9.00	$18.00	£2.00	£6.00	£12.00
21-30	$1.85	$5.50	$11.25	£1.25	£3.75	£7.50
31-40	$1.50	$4.50	$9.00	£1.00	£3.00	£6.00

	$Good	$Fine	$N.Mint	£Good	£Fine	£N.Mint
41-50	$1.05	$3.15	$6.30	£0.70	£2.10	£4.20
51-100	$0.75	$2.25	$4.50	£0.50	£1.50	£3.00
101-125	$0.80	$2.40	$4.00	£0.50	£1.50	£2.50
126-150	$0.60	$1.80	$3.00	£0.40	£1.20	£2.00
151-159	$0.45	$1.35	$2.25	£0.30	£0.90	£1.50
160-163 giants	$0.80	$2.40	$4.00	£0.50	£1.50	£2.50
164-175	$0.45	$1.35	$2.25	£0.30	£0.90	£1.50
176-200	$0.40	$1.20	$2.00	£0.25	£0.75	£1.25
201-210	$0.30	$0.90	$1.50	£0.20	£0.60	£1.00
211-224	$0.25	$0.75	$1.25	£0.15	£0.45	£0.75
225-253	$0.15	$0.50	$0.90	£0.10	£0.30	£0.60
Title Value:	$246.75	$740.95	$1422.35	£163.55	£491.60	£940.15

Note: most issues distributed on the news-stands in the U.K. though more irregularly after #225

CAT AND MOUSE
Aircel; 1 Mar 1990-18 Nov 1991
1 ND 48pgs, squarebound; black and white begins

	$Good	$Fine	$N.Mint	£Good	£Fine	£N.Mint
	$0.40	$1.20	$2.00	£0.25	£0.75	£1.25
2-18 ND	$0.40	$1.20	$2.00	£0.25	£0.75	£1.25
Title Value:	$7.20	$21.60	$36.00	£4.50	£13.50	£22.50
Collection 1, reprints #1-4				£1.00	£3.00	£5.00
Hardcover, reprints early issues				£2.50	£7.50	£12.50
Collection 2, reprints #5-8				£1.00	£3.00	£5.00

Tooth and Nail Trade paperback (Jan 1993)
reprints issues #9-12 — £0.75 / £2.25 / £3.75

CAT CLAW
Eternity; 1 Sep 1990-9 May 1991
1 ND black and white begins

	$Good	$Fine	$N.Mint	£Good	£Fine	£N.Mint
	$0.45	$1.35	$2.25	£0.30	£0.90	£1.50
1 2nd printing ND	$0.45	$1.35	$2.25	£0.30	£0.90	£1.50
2 ND	$0.45	$1.35	$2.25	£0.30	£0.90	£1.50
3 ND pre-bagged (25% less if non-bagged)	$0.60	$1.80	$3.00	£0.40	£1.20	£2.00
4-5 ND	$0.45	$1.35	$2.25	£0.30	£0.90	£1.50
6-9 ND	$0.40	$1.20	$2.00	£0.25	£0.75	£1.25
Title Value:	$4.45	$13.35	$22.25	£2.90	£8.70	£14.50
Graphic Album (Aug 1991)				£1.00	£3.00	£5.00

CAT TALES
Eternity,OS; 1 May 1989
1 ND Felix the Cat in 3-D

	$Good	$Fine	$N.Mint	£Good	£Fine	£N.Mint
	$0.45	$1.35	$2.25	£0.30	£0.90	£1.50
Title Value:	$0.45	$1.35	$2.25	£0.30	£0.90	£1.50

CAT, BEWARE! THE CLAWS OF THE
Marvel Comics Group; 1 Nov 1972-4 Jun 1973
1 ND origin and 1st appearance The Cat (later becomes Tigra), Severin/Wood art

	$Good	$Fine	$N.Mint	£Good	£Fine	£N.Mint
	$2.80	$8.25	$14.00	£1.60	£4.80	£8.00
2 ND Severin inks, The Owl appears	$1.50	$4.50	$7.50	£1.00	£3.00	£5.00
3 ND Bill Everett inks	$1.50	$4.50	$7.50	£1.00	£3.00	£5.00
4 ND Jim Starlin art, part reprint from X-Men #57, Weiss inks	$1.50	$4.50	$7.50	£1.00	£3.00	£5.00
Title Value:	$7.30	$21.75	$36.50	£4.60	£13.80	£23.00

CATALYST: AGENTS OF CHANGE
Dark Horse/Comics Greatest World; 1 Feb 1994-7 Sep 1994
1-7 ND spin-off from Comics' Greatest World series

	$Good	$Fine	$N.Mint	£Good	£Fine	£N.Mint
	$0.40	$1.20	$2.00	£0.25	£0.75	£1.25
Title Value:	$2.80	$8.40	$14.00	£1.75	£5.25	£8.75

CATFIGHT
Lightning Comics/Insomnia Press; 1 Jun 1995
1 ND Hellina appears

	$Good	$Fine	$N.Mint	£Good	£Fine	£N.Mint
	$0.55	$1.65	$2.75	£0.35	£1.05	£1.75
1 ND Gold Edition (Jun 1995)	$0.80	$2.40	$4.00	£0.50	£1.50	£2.50
1 ND Signed Edition (May 1995) - pre-bagged in mylar, signed by Steven Zyskowski; 1,500 copies	$1.00	$3.00	$5.00	£0.65	£1.95	£3.25
Title Value:	$2.35	$7.05	$11.75	£1.50	£4.50	£7.50

CATFIGHT: DREAM WARRIOR
Lightning Comics; 1 Jun 1995
1 ND Steven Zyskowski script; black and white

	$Good	$Fine	$N.Mint	£Good	£Fine	£N.Mint
	$0.60	$1.80	$3.00	£0.35	£1.05	£1.75
1 ND variant cover, 25% of the print run	$0.90	$2.70	$4.50	£0.60	£1.80	£3.00
Title Value:	$1.50	$4.50	$7.50	£0.95	£2.85	£4.75

CATMAN ASHCAN EDITION
AC Comics; nn Apr 1995
nn ND black and white, cover by L.B. Cole; 2,000 copies

	$Good	$Fine	$N.Mint	£Good	£Fine	£N.Mint
	$1.05	$3.15	$5.25	£0.70	£2.10	£3.50
Title Value:	$1.05	$3.15	$5.25	£0.70	£2.10	£3.50

CATSEYE AGENCY
Rip Off Press; 1 Jul 1992

	$Good	$Fine	$N.Mint	£Good	£Fine	£N.Mint
1 ND	$0.45	$1.35	$2.25	£0.30	£0.90	£1.50
Title Value:	$0.45	$1.35	$2.25	£0.30	£0.90	£1.50

CATWOMAN
DC Comics,MS; 1 Mar 1989-4 June 1989
(see Batman, Detective, Lois Lane)

	$Good	$Fine	$N.Mint	£Good	£Fine	£N.Mint
1-2	$1.60	$4.80	$8.00	£0.80	£2.40	£4.00
3-4 Batman appears	$0.80	$2.40	$4.00	£0.50	£1.50	£2.50
Title Value:	$4.80	$14.40	$22.00	£2.60	£7.80	£13.00

Note: alternative perspective to Batman Year One (#404-407)
Trade paperback (Jul 1991), reprints mini-series
with new cover painting by Brian Stelfreeze — £1.10 / £3.30 / £5.50

CATWOMAN (2ND SERIES)
DC Comics; 0 Oct 1994; 1 Aug 1993-present
0 (Oct 1994) Zero Hour X-over, origin retold

	$Good	$Fine	$N.Mint	£Good	£Fine	£N.Mint
			$2.00	£0.25	£0.75	£1.25
1 spot-varnished black embossed cover; spin-off from the "Knightfall" story in Batman	$1.05	$3.15	$5.25	£0.70	£2.10	£3.50
2	$0.60	$1.80	$3.00	£0.40	£1.20	£2.00
3	$0.55	$1.65	$2.75	£0.35	£1.05	£1.75
4-5	$0.35	$1.05	$1.75	£0.25	£0.75	£1.25
6 Knightquest: The Crusade, continued from Batman #503	$0.40	$1.20	$2.00	£0.25	£0.75	£1.25
7 Knightquest: The Crusade, continued from Batman #505	$0.35	$1.05	$1.75	£0.25	£0.75	£1.25
8-10	$0.35	$1.05	$1.75	£0.25	£0.75	£1.25
11	$0.30	$0.90	$1.50	£0.20	£0.60	£1.00
12 Knightsend part 6, continued in Batman #510	$0.30	$0.90	$1.50	£0.20	£0.60	£1.00
13 Knightsend: Aftermath part 2 (of 2)	$0.30	$0.90	$1.50	£0.20	£0.60	£1.00
14 Zero Hour X-over	$0.30	$0.90	$1.50	£0.20	£0.60	£1.00
15 new direction for title	$0.30	$0.90	$1.50	£0.20	£0.60	£1.00
16-20	$0.30	$0.90	$1.50	£0.20	£0.60	£1.00
21-24	$0.40	$1.20	$2.00	£0.25	£0.75	£1.25
25 48pgs	$0.60	$1.80	$3.00	£0.40	£1.20	£2.00
26 The Secret of the Universe, continued in Batman: Shadow of the Bat #44	$0.40	$1.20	$2.00	£0.25	£0.75	£1.25
27 Underworld Unleashed tie-in, Gorilla Grodd appears	$0.40	$1.20	$2.00	£0.25	£0.75	£1.25
28	$0.40	$1.20	$2.00	£0.25	£0.75	£1.25
29 Penguin appears	$0.40	$1.20	$2.00	£0.25	£0.75	£1.25
30 bi-monthly	$0.40	$1.20	$2.00	£0.25	£0.75	£1.25
31 Contagion part 4, continued in Azrael #15	$0.40	$1.20	$2.00	£0.25	£0.75	£1.25
Title Value:	$12.70	$38.10	$63.50	£8.35	£25.05	£41.75

CATWOMAN ANNUAL
DC Comics; 1 May 1994-present
1 64pgs, Elseworlds story

	$Good	$Fine	$N.Mint	£Good	£Fine	£N.Mint
	$0.60	$1.80	$3.00	£0.40	£1.20	£2.00
2 56pgs, Year One, origin retold	$0.80	$2.40	$4.00	£0.50	£1.50	£2.50
Title Value:	$1.40	$4.20	$7.00	£0.90	£2.70	£4.50

CAULDRON
Real Comics; 1 Oct 1995
1 ND Steve Brown script and art

	$Good	$Fine	$N.Mint	£Good	£Fine	£N.Mint
	$0.60	$1.80	$3.00	£0.40	£1.20	£2.00
1 ND variant cover by Glenn Fabry (20% of print run)	$0.60	$1.80	$3.00	£0.40	£1.20	£2.00
Title Value:	$1.20	$3.60	$6.00	£0.80	£2.40	£4.00

CAVEWOMAN
Basement Comics; 1 1994-5 1994?
1 ND Budd Root script and art begins; black and white

	$Good	$Fine	$N.Mint	£Good	£Fine	£N.Mint
	$0.60	$1.80	$3.00	£0.40	£1.20	£2.00
1 ND 2nd printing, (Mar 1995)	$0.60	$1.80	$3.00	£0.40	£1.20	£2.00
2-5 ND black and white	$0.60	$1.80	$3.00	£0.40	£1.20	£2.00
Title Value:	$3.60	$10.80	$18.00	£2.40	£7.20	£12.00

CECIL KUNKLE
Renegade; 1 May 1986

	$Good	$Fine	$N.Mint	£Good	£Fine	£N.Mint
1 ND	$0.30	$0.90	$1.50	£0.20	£0.60	£1.00
Title Value:	$0.30	$0.90	$1.50	£0.20	£0.60	£1.00

CECIL KUNKLE (2ND SERIES)
Darkline/Renegade; 1 1987-2 1988

	$Good	$Fine	$N.Mint	£Good	£Fine	£N.Mint
1-2 ND	$0.30	$0.90	$1.50	£0.20	£0.60	£1.00
Title Value:	$0.60	$1.80	$3.00	£0.40	£1.20	£2.00

CECIL KUNKLE CHRISTMAS SPECIAL
Renegade; 1 1988

	$Good	$Fine	$N.Mint	£Good	£Fine	£N.Mint
1 ND	$0.40	$1.20	$2.00	£0.25	£0.75	£1.25
Title Value:	$0.40	$1.20	$2.00	£0.25	£0.75	£1.25

CELESTIAL MECHANICS
Innovation; 1 Nov 1990

	$Good	$Fine	$N.Mint	£Good	£Fine	£N.Mint
1 ND	$0.40	$1.20	$2.00	£0.25	£0.75	£1.25
Title Value:	$0.40	$1.20	$2.00	£0.25	£0.75	£1.25

CENOTAPH: CYBER-GODDESS
Northstar; 1 Jan 1995
1 ND Tony Akins script and art; black and white

	$Good	$Fine	$N.Mint	£Good	£Fine	£N.Mint
	$0.80	$2.40	$4.00	£0.50	£1.50	£2.50
1 ND Signed & Numbered Edition, pre-bagged with gold foil cover; 2,500 copies	$2.00	$6.00	$10.00	£1.30	£3.90	£6.50
Title Value:	$2.80	$8.40	$14.00	£1.80	£5.40	£9.00

CENTRIFUGAL BUMBLE-PUPPY
Fantagraphics,Magazine; 1 Sep 1987-8 1988

	$Good	$Fine	$N.Mint	£Good	£Fine	£N.Mint
1-8 ND	$0.45	$1.35	$2.25	£0.30	£0.90	£1.50
Title Value:	$3.60	$10.80	$18.00	£2.40	£7.20	£12.00

CENTURIONS
DC Comics,MS Toy; 1 Jun 1987-4 Sep 1987
1-4 scarce in the U.K.

	$Good	$Fine	$N.Mint	£Good	£Fine	£N.Mint
	$0.15	$0.45	$0.75	£0.10	£0.30	£0.50
Title Value:	$0.60	$1.80	$3.00	£0.40	£1.20	£2.00

	$Good	$Fine	$N.Mint	£Good	£Fine	£N.Mint
CENTURY: DISTANT SONS						
Marvel Comics Group, OS; 1 Feb 1996						
1 ND 48pgs, Dan Abnett/Andy Lanning script, Jim Calafiore and Peter Palmiotti art; wraparound fifth ink cover						
	$0.60	$1.80	$3.00	£0.40	£1.20	£2.00
Title Value:	$0.60	$1.80	$3.00	£0.40	£1.20	£2.00
CEREBUS BI-WEEKLY						
Aardvark-Vanaheim; 1 Dec 1988-25 May 1989						
1 ND reprints Cerebus the Aardvark #1						
	$0.45	$1.35	$2.25	£0.30	£0.90	£1.50
2 ND reprints issue #2						
	$0.35	$1.05	$1.75	£0.25	£0.75	£1.25
3-25 ND	$0.35	$1.05	$1.75	£0.25	£0.75	£1.25
Title Value:	$8.85	$26.55	$44.25	£6.30	£18.90	£31.50
Note: there was an un-numbered issue published after #25 which reprinted the two stories set in continuity in Swords of Cerebus #4. It would be valued at approximately £1.50 ($2.25) at the time of going to press						
CEREBUS HIGH SOCIETY						
Aardvark-Vanaheim; 1 Jun 1989-25 Jun 1991						
(continues from Cerebus Bi-Weekly)						
1 ND reprints Cerebus #26						
	$0.45	$1.35	$2.25	£0.30	£0.90	£1.50
2 ND reprints Cerebus #27						
	$0.35	$1.05	$1.75	£0.25	£0.75	£1.25
3-24 ND	$0.35	$1.05	$1.75	£0.25	£0.75	£1.25
25 ND reprints issue #50						
	$0.35	$1.05	$1.75	£0.25	£0.75	£1.25
Title Value:	$8.85	$26.55	$44.25	£6.30	£18.90	£31.50
Trade Paperback (Apr 1991), reprints #26-50				£3.00	£9.00	£15.00
CEREBUS JAM						
Aardvark-Vanaheim; 1 Apr 1985						
1 ND Eisner, Anderson, Scott/Bo Hampton, Austin art, Sienkiewicz cover						
	$1.00	$3.00	$5.00	£0.70	£2.10	£3.50
Title Value:	$1.00	$3.00	$5.00	£0.70	£2.10	£3.50
CEREBUS THE AARDVARK						
Aardvark-Vanaheim; 1 Dec 1977-present						
(see A-V in 3-D, Cerebus Jam)						
0 1st printing, (Jun 1993) pre-bagged with gold ink logo and Cerebus hologram trading card; Mothers and Daughters storyline from #151-200 reprinted						
	$1.50	$4.50	$7.50	£1.00	£3.00	£5.00
0 2nd printing, (Jun 1993) - Mothers and Daughters storyline from #151-200 reprinted						
	$0.60	$1.80	$3.00	£0.40	£1.20	£2.00
1	$31.00	$92.50	$185.00	£20.00	£60.00	£120.00
1 counterfeit, see note below						
	$0.00	$0.00	$0.00	£0.00	£0.00	£0.00
2	$10.00	$30.00	$50.00	£7.00	£21.00	£35.00
3 1st Red Sophia						
	$7.00	$21.00	$35.00	£5.00	£15.00	£25.00
4 1st Elric of Melvinbone						
	$6.00	$18.00	$30.00	£4.50	£13.50	£22.50
5-6	$6.00	$18.00	$30.00	£4.00	£12.00	£20.00
7-10	$4.50	$13.50	$22.50	£3.00	£9.00	£15.00
11 origin Captain Cockroach						
	$5.25	$15.50	$26.25	£3.50	£10.50	£17.50
12	$3.75	$11.00	$18.75	£2.50	£7.50	£12.50
13-15	$2.25	$6.75	$11.25	£1.50	£4.50	£7.50
16-20	$1.80	$5.25	$9.00	£1.20	£3.60	£6.00
21 scarce in the U.K.						
	$6.50	$19.50	$32.50	£4.40	£13.00	£22.00
22 scarce in the U.K. Captain Cockroach and Bunky						
	$2.40	$7.00	$12.00	£1.60	£4.80	£8.00
23-24	$1.40	$4.20	$7.00	£0.90	£2.70	£4.50
25	$1.20	$3.60	$6.00	£0.80	£2.40	£4.00
26 High Society begins						
	$1.20	$3.60	$6.00	£0.80	£2.40	£4.00
27-30	$1.20	$3.60	$6.00	£0.80	£2.40	£4.00
31 Moonroach origin						
	$1.80	$5.25	$9.00	£1.20	£3.60	£6.00
32-40	$0.90	$2.70	$4.50	£0.60	£1.80	£3.00
41-50	$0.80	$2.40	$4.00	£0.50	£1.50	£2.50
51 Interlude						
	$1.50	$4.50	$7.50	£1.00	£3.00	£5.00
52 Church & State I begins						
	$0.90	$2.70	$4.50	£0.60	£1.80	£3.00
53 Wolveroach cameo (1st appearance)						
	$1.50	$4.50	$7.50	£1.00	£3.00	£5.00
54 1st Wolveroach full story						
	$1.50	$4.50	$7.50	£1.00	£3.00	£5.00
55-56 Wolveroach						
	$1.20	$3.60	$6.00	£0.80	£2.40	£4.00
57-60	$0.80	$2.40	$4.00	£0.50	£1.50	£2.50
61-62 Flaming Carrot back-up						
	$1.05	$3.15	$5.25	£0.70	£2.10	£3.50
63-73	$0.80	$2.40	$4.00	£0.50	£1.50	£2.50
74 scarce in the U.K.						
	$1.50	$4.50	$7.50	£1.00	£3.00	£5.00
75-80	$0.60	$1.80	$3.00	£0.40	£1.20	£2.00
81 Church & State II begins						
	$0.80	$2.40	$4.00	£0.50	£1.50	£2.50
82-84	$0.60	$1.80	$3.00	£0.40	£1.20	£2.00
85-99	$0.45	$1.35	$2.25	£0.30	£0.90	£1.50
100	$0.60	$1.80	$3.00	£0.40	£1.20	£2.00
101-103	$0.45	$1.35	$2.25	£0.30	£0.90	£1.50

	$Good	$Fine	$N.Mint	£Good	£Fine	£N.Mint
104 Flaming Carrot appears						
	$1.50	$4.50	$7.50	£1.00	£3.00	£5.00
105 scarce in the U.K.						
	$0.90	$2.70	$4.50	£0.60	£1.80	£3.00
106-111	$0.45	$1.35	$2.25	£0.30	£0.90	£1.50
112-113 double issue, interlude						
	$0.70	$2.10	$3.50	£0.45	£1.35	£2.25
114 Jaka's story begins						
	$0.60	$1.80	$3.00	£0.40	£1.20	£2.00
115-136	$0.45	$1.35	$2.25	£0.30	£0.90	£1.50
137-138 Jaka's Story Epilogues						
	$0.45	$1.35	$2.25	£0.30	£0.90	£1.50
139 Melmoth Zero						
	$0.45	$1.35	$2.25	£0.30	£0.90	£1.50
140 Melmoth story begins (ends #149)						
	$0.45	$1.35	$2.25	£0.30	£0.90	£1.50
141-149	$0.45	$1.35	$2.25	£0.30	£0.90	£1.50
150 Melmoth storyline epilogue						
	$0.45	$1.35	$2.25	£0.30	£0.90	£1.50
151 Mothers & Daughters story begins						
	$0.80	$2.40	$4.00	£0.50	£1.50	£2.50
151 2nd printing, (Jun 1992)						
	$0.45	$1.35	$2.25	£0.30	£0.90	£1.50
151 3rd printing	$0.45	$1.35	$2.25	£0.30	£0.90	£1.50
152	$0.55	$1.65	$2.75	£0.35	£1.05	£1.75
152 2nd printing, (Jul 1992)						
	$0.45	$1.35	$2.25	£0.30	£0.90	£1.50
153	$0.45	$1.35	$2.25	£0.30	£0.90	£1.50
153 2nd printing, (Aug 1992)						
	$0.45	$1.35	$2.25	£0.30	£0.90	£1.50
154-162	$0.45	$1.35	$2.25	£0.30	£0.90	£1.50
163 Mothers & Daughters Book 2 - Women story begins						
	$0.60	$1.80	$3.00	£0.40	£1.20	£2.00
163 2nd printing, (Aug 1993)						
	$0.45	$1.35	$2.25	£0.30	£0.90	£1.50
164	$0.55	$1.65	$2.75	£0.35	£1.05	£1.75
164 2nd printing, (Aug 1993)						
	$0.45	$1.35	$2.25	£0.30	£0.90	£1.50
165 Dave McKean parody cover						
	$0.55	$1.65	$2.75	£0.35	£1.05	£1.75
165 2nd printing, (Aug 1993)						
	$0.45	$1.35	$2.25	£0.30	£0.90	£1.50
166-173	$0.45	$1.35	$2.25	£0.30	£0.90	£1.50
174 Mothers & Daughters Book Two: Women conclusion						
	$0.45	$1.35	$2.25	£0.30	£0.90	£1.50
175 Mothers & Daughters Book Three begins						
	$0.45	$1.35	$2.25	£0.30	£0.90	£1.50
176-185	$0.45	$1.35	$2.25	£0.30	£0.90	£1.50
186 Mothers & Daughters Book Three concludes						
	$0.45	$1.35	$2.25	£0.30	£0.90	£1.50
187-200	$0.45	$1.35	$2.25	£0.30	£0.90	£1.50
Title Value:	$235.70	$705.00	$1208.50	£156.65	£469.75	£803.25

Note: all Non-Distributed on the news-stands in the U.K.

Trade Paperback collections:

	£Good	£Fine	£N.Mint
Cerebus Book One, reprints #1-25	£3.50	£10.50	£17.50
(2nd printing - 1991)	£3.00	£9.00	£15.00
Cerebus Book Two: High Society, reprints #26-50	£3.50	£10.50	£17.50
Cerebus Book Three: Church & State 1, reprints #52-80	£4.00	£12.00	£20.00
Cerebus Book Four: Church & State II, reprints #81-111:			
1st print, Limited Edition, 435 copies, signed	£10.00	£30.00	£50.00
2nd print	£4.00	£12.00	£20.00
Swords of Cerebus:			
Vol 1, reprints #1-4 plus new story	£1.25	£3.75	£6.25
Vol 1 2nd/3rd/4th print	£1.00	£3.00	£5.00
Vol 2, reprints #5-8 plus new story	£1.00	£3.00	£5.00
Vol 2 2nd/3rd print	£0.90	£2.70	£4.50
Vol 3 (1st,2nd) reprints #9-12 plus new story	£1.00	£3.00	£5.00
Vol 4 (1st,2nd) reprints #13-16 plus 2 new stories	£1.00	£3.00	£5.00
Vol 5 (1st,2nd) reprints #17-20 plus new story	£1.00	£3.00	£5.00
Vol 6 reprints #21-25 plus new story; contains supplement insert	£1.00	£3.00	£5.00
Cerebus Book Five: Jaka's Story Trade paperback (Nov 1992)			
reprints issues #114-136	£3.00	£9.00	£15.00
Cerebus Book Six: Melmoth Trade paperback (Feb 1993)			
reprints issues #139-150	£2.00	£6.00	£10.00
Cerebus Book Seven: Mothers & Daughters Vol. I - Flight			
Trade paperback (Jun 1993) reprints issues #151-200. 1st prints			
signed and numbered by Dave Sim and Gerhard	£3.00	£9.00	£15.00
2nd prints, unsigned	£2.40	£7.20	£12.00
Cerebus Book Eight: Mothers & Daughters Vol. II - Women (May 1994)			
Trade paperback reprints issues #163-174. 1st prints			
signed and numbered by Dave Sim and Gerhard	£3.25	£9.75	£16.25
2nd prints, unsigned	£2.40	£7.20	£12.00
Cerebus Book Nine: Mothers & Daughters Vol. III - Reads (Apr 1995)			
Trade paperback reprints issues #175-186. 1st prints signed			
and numbered by Dave Sim and Gerhard	£3.25	£9.75	£16.25
2nd prints, unsigned (Apr 1995)	£2.40	£7.20	£12.00
Cerebus World Tour Book '95 (Feb 1995)			
reprints back-up and supplementary stories from			
Swords of Cerebus	£0.40	£1.20	£2.00

Note: counterfeit copies of #1 exist. The inside covers of the counterfeit copies have a glossy black finish, whereas the genuine copies have a matt black inside cover and the black background on the counterfeit front cover appears flecked with white. **The Guide does not give a value and thereby promote forgery.**

262

SOME INDEPENDENT COMICS MAY NOT HAVE APPEARED ALTHOUGH THEY WERE ADVERTISED AND SOLICITED.

	$Good	$Fine	$N.Mint	£Good	£Fine	£N.Mint

CEREBUS: CHURCH AND STATE
Aardvark-Vanaheim; 1 Apr 1991-30 Jun 1992
(continues from Cerebus High Society)

	$Good	$Fine	$N.Mint	£Good	£Fine	£N.Mint
1 reprints Cerebus #51, bi-weekly begins						
	$0.35	$1.05	$1.75	£0.25	£0.75	£1.25
2 reprints Cerebus #52 etc						
	$0.35	$1.05	$1.75	£0.25	£0.75	£1.25
3-30	$0.35	$1.05	$1.75	£0.25	£0.75	£1.25
Title Value:	$10.50	$31.50	$52.50	£7.50	£22.50	£37.50

CHAIN GANG WAR
DC Comics; 1 Jul 1993-12 Jun 1994

	$Good	$Fine	$N.Mint	£Good	£Fine	£N.Mint
1 Alan Grant and John Wagner script begins						
	$0.35	$1.05	$1.75	£0.25	£0.75	£1.25
1 ND Platinum Edition - silver embossed logo and chain design on left of cover						
	$1.20	$3.60	$6.00	£0.80	£2.40	£4.00
2-6	$0.35	$1.05	$1.75	£0.25	£0.75	£1.25
7 Gary Erskine guest art						
	$0.35	$1.05	$1.75	£0.25	£0.75	£1.25
8-9	$0.35	$1.05	$1.75	£0.25	£0.75	£1.25
10 Deathstroke the Terminator appears						
	$0.35	$1.05	$1.75	£0.25	£0.75	£1.25
11 Batman appears						
	$0.35	$1.05	$1.75	£0.25	£0.75	£1.25
12	$0.35	$1.05	$1.75	£0.25	£0.75	£1.25
Title Value:	$5.40	$16.20	$27.00	£3.80	£11.40	£19.00

CHAINGANG
Northstar; 1 Apr 1990-2 1990

	$Good	$Fine	$N.Mint	£Good	£Fine	£N.Mint
1 ND scarce in the U.K. "Night City" back-ups by Mark Nelson begin						
	$2.25	$6.75	$11.25	£1.50	£4.50	£7.50
2 ND scarce in the U.K. part Tim Vigil, part Mark Nelson art						
	$1.50	$4.50	$7.50	£1.00	£3.00	£5.00
Title Value:	$3.75	$11.25	$18.75	£2.50	£7.50	£12.50

CHAINGANG, REX MILLER'S
Northstar; 1 May 1992

	$Good	$Fine	$N.Mint	£Good	£Fine	£N.Mint
1 ND	$0.45	$1.35	$2.25	£0.30	£0.90	£1.50
Title Value:	$0.45	$1.35	$2.25	£0.30	£0.90	£1.50

CHAINS OF CHAOS
Harris Comics,MS; 1 Nov 1994-3 Jan 1995

	$Good	$Fine	$N.Mint	£Good	£Fine	£N.Mint
1 ND Vampirella appears						
	$0.60	$1.80	$3.00	£0.50	£1.50	£2.50
2-3 ND Vampirella appears						
	$0.60	$1.80	$3.00	£0.40	£1.20	£2.00
Title Value:	$1.80	$5.40	$9.00	£1.30	£3.90	£6.50

CHALLENGERS OF THE UNKNOWN
DC Comics; 1 Apr/May 1958-77 Dec/Jan 1970/71; 78 Feb 1973-80 Jun/Jul 1973; 81 Jun/Jul 1977-87 Jun/Jul 1978
(see Secret Origins, Showcase, Super DC Giant, Super-Team Family)

	$Good	$Fine	$N.Mint	£Good	£Fine	£N.Mint
1 Jack Kirby/Stein art						
	$190.00	$570.00	$1900.00	£125.00	£375.00	£1250.00
2 Jack Kirby/Stein art						
	$87.50	$260.00	$700.00	£57.50	£175.00	£475.00
3 Jack Kirby/Stein art						
	$70.00	$215.00	$575.00	£48.00	£140.00	£385.00
4-8 Jack Kirby/Wood art						
	$57.50	$175.00	$470.00	£40.00	£120.00	£320.00
9-10	$29.00	$87.50	$235.00	£20.00	£60.00	£160.00
1st official distribution in the U.K.						
11-13	$25.00	$75.00	$175.00	£17.00	£50.00	£120.00
14 origin Multi-Man						
	$25.00	$75.00	$175.00	£17.00	£50.00	£120.00
15	$25.00	$75.00	$175.00	£17.00	£50.00	£120.00

	$Good	$Fine	$N.Mint	£Good	£Fine	£N.Mint
16-17	$20.00	$60.00	$140.00	£13.50	£41.00	£95.00
18 intro Cosmo, Challengers' space-pet						
	$20.00	$60.00	$140.00	£13.50	£41.00	£95.00
19-20	$20.00	$60.00	$140.00	£13.50	£41.00	£95.00
21	$20.00	$60.00	$140.00	£12.00	£36.00	£85.00
22 last 10 cents issue						
	$20.00	$60.00	$140.00	£12.00	£36.00	£85.00
23-30	$10.50	$32.00	$75.00	£7.75	£23.50	£55.00
31 origin retold	$12.00	$36.00	$85.00	£8.00	£24.50	£57.50
32-40	$5.25	$16.00	$37.50	£3.55	£10.50	£25.00
41-42	$2.70	$8.00	$19.00	£1.75	£5.25	£12.50
43 new look begins						
	$2.70	$8.00	$19.00	£1.75	£5.25	£12.50
44-45	$2.70	$8.00	$19.00	£1.75	£5.25	£12.50
46 last Silver Age issue indicia dated November 1965						
	$2.70	$8.00	$19.00	£1.75	£5.25	£12.50
47	$3.15	$9.50	$19.00	£1.90	£5.75	£11.50
48 Doom Patrol appears						
	$3.15	$9.50	$19.00	£1.90	£5.75	£11.50
49 intro Challenger Corps						
	$3.15	$9.50	$19.00	£1.90	£5.75	£11.50
50	$3.15	$9.50	$19.00	£1.90	£5.75	£11.50
51 Sea Devils X-over						
	$3.15	$9.50	$19.00	£1.90	£5.75	£11.50
52-54	$3.15	$9.50	$19.00	£1.90	£5.75	£11.50
55 Red Ryan dies	$3.15	$9.50	$19.00	£1.90	£5.75	£11.50
56-59	$3.15	$9.50	$19.00	£1.90	£5.75	£11.50
60 Red Ryan returns						
	$3.15	$9.50	$19.00	£1.90	£5.75	£11.50
61-62	$1.15	$3.50	$7.00	£0.65	£2.00	£4.00
63 scarce in the U.K.						
	$1.15	$3.50	$7.00	£0.75	£2.35	£4.75
64 Jack Kirby art, origin retold (reprints #1); Joe Kubert cover						
	$1.15	$3.50	$7.00	£0.65	£2.00	£4.00
65 Jack Kirby art, origin retold (reprints #1)						
	$1.15	$3.50	$7.00	£0.65	£2.00	£4.00
66 Joe Kubert cover						
	$1.15	$3.50	$7.00	£0.65	£2.00	£4.00
67 Neal Adams cover						
	$1.15	$3.50	$7.00	£0.65	£2.00	£4.00
68	$1.15	$3.50	$7.00	£0.65	£2.00	£4.00
69 intro Corinna Stark						
	$1.15	$3.50	$7.00	£0.65	£2.00	£4.00
70 new costumes, Neal Adams cover						
	$1.15	$3.50	$7.00	£0.65	£2.00	£4.00
71	$1.15	$3.50	$7.00	£0.55	£1.75	£3.50
72 Neal Adams cover						
	$1.15	$3.50	$7.00	£0.55	£1.75	£3.50
73	$1.15	$3.50	$7.00	£0.55	£1.75	£3.50
74 Deadman by George Tuska and Neal Adams, also 1pg Wrightson art, Neal Adams cover						
	$2.65	$8.00	$16.00	£1.30	£4.00	£8.00
75 reprints Showcase #7						
	$1.40	$4.20	$7.00	£0.60	£1.80	£3.00
76 reprints stories from issues #2 and #3; Joe Kubert cover						
	$1.40	$4.20	$7.00	£0.60	£1.80	£3.00
77 reprints Showcase #12						
	$1.40	$4.20	$7.00	£0.60	£1.80	£3.00
78 scarce in the U.K. reprints stories from issues #6 and #7						
	$1.00	$3.00	$5.00	£0.45	£1.35	£2.25
79 scarce in the U.K. reprints stories from issues #1 and #2; Joe Kubert cover						
	$1.00	$3.00	$5.00	£0.45	£1.35	£2.25

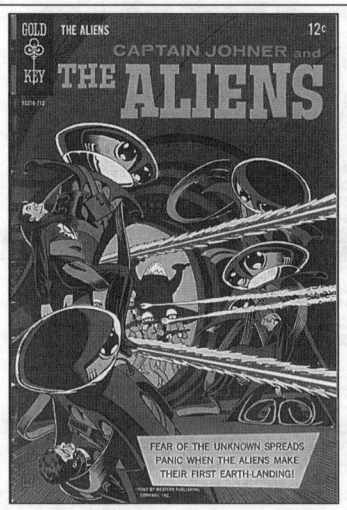

Captain Johner and the Aliens #1

Cerebus the Aardvark #7

Challengers of the Unknown #80

	$Good	$Fine	$N.Mint	£Good	£Fine	£N.Mint
80 scarce in the U.K. reprints Showcase #11	$1.00	$3.00	$5.00	£0.45	£1.35	£2.25
81 scarce in the U.K. Nasser art, Neal Adams cover inks	$1.00	$3.00	$5.00	£0.45	£1.35	£2.25
82 Swamp Thing X-over, Nasser art	$1.00	$3.00	$5.00	£0.40	£1.20	£2.00
83 Swamp Thing X-over	$1.00	$3.00	$5.00	£0.40	£1.20	£2.00
84-85 Swamp Thing and Deadman X-over	$1.00	$3.00	$5.00	£0.40	£1.20	£2.00
86 Swamp Thing and Deadman X-over, Keith Giffen art	$1.00	$3.00	$5.00	£0.40	£1.20	£2.00
87 Swamp Thing and Deadman X-over	$1.00	$3.00	$5.00	£0.40	£1.20	£2.00
Title Value:	$1193.35	$3603.10	$9430.50	£801.60	£2403.60	£6322.75

CHALLENGERS OF THE UNKNOWN (2ND SERIES)
DC Comics,MS; 1 Mar 1991-8 Oct 1991

	$Good	$Fine	$N.Mint	£Good	£Fine	£N.Mint
1 Brian Bolland cover	$0.30	$0.90	$1.50	£0.20	£0.60	£1.00
2-6	$0.30	$0.90	$1.50	£0.20	£0.60	£1.00
7 Art Adams cover	$0.30	$0.90	$1.50	£0.20	£0.60	£1.00
8	$0.30	$0.90	$1.50	£0.20	£0.60	£1.00
Title Value:	$2.40	$7.20	$12.00	£1.60	£4.80	£8.00

CHAMBER OF CHILLS
Marvel Comics Group; 1 Nov 1972-25 Nov 1976

	$Good	$Fine	$N.Mint	£Good	£Fine	£N.Mint
1 ND P. Craig Russell/Russ Heath art	$1.00	$3.00	$5.00	£0.60	£1.80	£3.00
2-4 ND Brunner art	$0.80	$2.40	$4.00	£0.50	£1.50	£2.50
5 ND	$0.60	$1.80	$3.00	£0.40	£1.20	£2.00
6-18 ND	$0.45	$1.35	$2.25	£0.30	£0.90	£1.50
19-20	$0.45	$1.35	$2.25	£0.25	£0.75	£1.25
21 ND	$0.45	$1.35	$2.25	£0.30	£0.90	£1.50
22	$0.45	$1.35	$2.25	£0.25	£0.75	£1.25
23-24 ND	$0.45	$1.35	$2.25	£0.30	£0.90	£1.50
25	$0.45	$1.35	$2.25	£0.25	£0.75	£1.25
Title Value:	$13.00	$39.00	$65.00	£8.30	£24.90	£41.50

FEATURES
Brak the Barbarian in 2, 3. 8 is all 1950s horror reprints.

CHAMBER OF DARKNESS
Marvel Comics Group; 1 Oct 1969-8 Dec 1970
(becomes Monsters on the Prowl)

	$Good	$Fine	$N.Mint	£Good	£Fine	£N.Mint
1 Buscema art	$4.60	$13.50	$32.50	£3.10	£9.25	£22.00
2 Neal Adams co-script	$2.80	$8.25	$14.00	£1.50	£4.50	£7.50
3 ND Barry Smith art (7pgs)	$2.80	$8.25	$14.00	£1.60	£4.80	£8.00
4 ND Barry Smith art on Conan "try out", reprinted in Conan #16	$5.00	$15.00	$35.00	£2.85	£8.50	£20.00
5 ND Jack Kirby script and art (6pgs)	$1.20	$3.60	$6.00	£0.60	£1.80	£3.00
6 Steve Ditko reprint	$1.20	$3.60	$6.00	£0.50	£1.50	£2.50
7 Wrightson art (1st Marvel work), self-cameo on first and last page	$2.00	$6.00	$10.00	£1.20	£3.60	£6.00
8 Wrightson cover, Bill Everett inks	$1.00	$3.00	$5.00	£0.50	£1.50	£2.50
Title Value:	$20.60	$61.20	$122.50	£11.85	£35.45	£71.50

ARTISTS
Kirby in 4, 5.
FEATURES
All issues have new fantasy/horror stories, except reprints in 6 (one story), 7 (two stories), 8 (three stories)

CHAMBER OF DARKNESS SPECIAL
Marvel Comics Group; 1 Jan 1972

	$Good	$Fine	$N.Mint	£Good	£Fine	£N.Mint
1 ND scarce in the U.K. 52pgs, all reprints	$0.80	$2.40	$4.00	£0.50	£1.50	£2.50
Title Value:	$0.80	$2.40	$4.00	£0.50	£1.50	£2.50

CHAMPION SPORTS
DC Comics; 1 Oct/Nov 1973-3 Feb/Mar 1974

	$Good	$Fine	$N.Mint	£Good	£Fine	£N.Mint
1-3	$0.25	$0.75	$1.25	£0.15	£0.45	£0.75
Title Value:	$0.75	$2.25	$3.75	£0.45	£1.35	£2.25

CHAMPIONS
Eclipse, Game; 1 Jun 1986-6 Feb 1987

	$Good	$Fine	$N.Mint	£Good	£Fine	£N.Mint
1 ND Carol Lay art, colour; based on role playing game and includes character stats	$0.30	$0.90	$1.50	£0.20	£0.60	£1.00
2-6 ND Chris Marrinan art, with stats	$0.30	$0.90	$1.50	£0.20	£0.60	£1.00
Title Value:	$1.80	$5.40	$9.00	£1.20	£3.60	£6.00

CHAMPIONS (2ND SERIES)
Hero, Game; 1 Sep 1987-15 1990

	$Good	$Fine	$N.Mint	£Good	£Fine	£N.Mint
1-2 ND	$0.35	$1.05	$1.75	£0.25	£0.75	£1.25
3 ND Flare vs. Champions	$0.35	$1.05	$1.75	£0.25	£0.75	£1.25
4 ND intro Icicle	$0.35	$1.05	$1.75	£0.25	£0.75	£1.25
5-7 ND	$0.35	$1.05	$1.75	£0.25	£0.75	£1.25
8 ND origin Foxbat	$0.35	$1.05	$1.75	£0.25	£0.75	£1.25
9-15 ND	$0.35	$1.05	$1.75	£0.25	£0.75	£1.25
Title Value:	$5.25	$15.75	$26.25	£3.75	£11.25	£18.75

CHAMPIONS ADVENTURES
Heroic Publishing; 1 Feb 1994-3 1994

	$Good	$Fine	$N.Mint	£Good	£Fine	£N.Mint
1-3 ND 44pgs	$0.60	$1.80	$3.00	£0.40	£1.20	£2.00
Title Value:	$1.80	$5.40	$9.00	£1.20	£3.60	£6.00

CHAMPIONS ANNUAL
Hero; 1 1988-2 1989

	$Good	$Fine	$N.Mint	£Good	£Fine	£N.Mint
1-2 ND	$0.60	$1.80	$3.00	£0.40	£1.20	£2.00
Title Value:	$1.20	$3.60	$6.00	£0.80	£2.40	£4.00

CHAMPIONS CLASSICS
Hero; 1 Jan 1992-5 May 1992

	$Good	$Fine	$N.Mint	£Good	£Fine	£N.Mint
1 ND 20pgs, new and reprint material begins, George Perez cover	$0.25	$0.75	$1.25	£0.15	£0.45	£0.75
2-5 ND 20pgs	$0.25	$0.75	$1.25	£0.15	£0.45	£0.75
Title Value:	$1.25	$3.75	$6.25	£0.75	£2.25	£3.75

CHAMPIONS, THE
Marvel Comics Group; 1 Oct 1975-17 Jan 1978

	$Good	$Fine	$N.Mint	£Good	£Fine	£N.Mint
1 Angel, Black Widow, Ghost Rider, Ice Man, Hercules begin (Note: as with many of these mid '70s Marvels, the British pence version has "Marvel All-Colour Comics" at the top)	$2.50	$7.50	$12.50	£1.20	£3.60	£6.00
2	$1.40	$4.20	$7.00	£0.70	£2.10	£3.50
3-10	$1.40	$4.20	$7.00	£0.60	£1.80	£3.00
11-12 Black Goliath appears, Byrne art	$1.40	$4.20	$7.00	£0.70	£2.10	£3.50
13 ND Black Goliath appears, Byrne art	$1.40	$4.20	$7.00	£0.80	£2.40	£4.00
14-15 ND Byrne art	$1.40	$4.20	$7.00	£0.80	£2.40	£4.00
16 ND Magneto and Beast appear	$1.40	$4.20	$7.00	£0.80	£2.40	£4.00
17 ND very scarce in the U.K. Hulk appears, Byrne inks	$2.25	$6.75	$11.25	£1.50	£4.50	£7.50
Title Value:	$25.75	$77.25	$128.75	£12.80	£38.40	£64.00

Note: Ghost Rider on cover of 1-4,7,8,10,14,16,17.

CHAOS BIBLE
Chaos Comics,OS; nn Oct 1995

	$Good	$Fine	$N.Mint	£Good	£Fine	£N.Mint
nn, ND , 40pgs	$0.70	$2.10	$3.50	£0.50	£1.50	£2.50
Title Value:	$0.70	$2.10	$3.50	£0.50	£1.50	£2.50

CHAOS EFFECT EPILOGUE
Valiant,MS; 1,2 Jan 1995

	$Good	$Fine	$N.Mint	£Good	£Fine	£N.Mint
1-2 ND Kevin van Hook script, Louis Small Jnr. art	$0.30	$0.90	$1.50	£0.20	£0.60	£1.00
Title Value:	$0.60	$1.80	$3.00	£0.40	£1.20	£2.00

CHAOS EFFECT, THE
Valiant,MS; 1,2 Oct 1994

	$Good	$Fine	$N.Mint	£Good	£Fine	£N.Mint
1 ND 16pgs, The Chaos Effect - Alpha. Promotional giveaway featuring a preview of The Visitor with free trading card checklist	$0.30	$0.90	$1.50	£0.20	£0.60	£1.00
2 ND The Chaos Effect - Omega. Conclusion to the 18 part cross-over story. Timewalker preview	$0.30	$0.90	$1.50	£0.20	£0.60	£1.00
Title Value:	$0.60	$1.80	$3.00	£0.40	£1.20	£2.00

CHAOS QUARTERLY
Chaos Comics; 1 Sep 1995-present

	$Good	$Fine	$N.Mint	£Good	£Fine	£N.Mint
1 ND 48pgs, Lady Death by Pulido and Hughes plus Purgatori, Bedlam and Cremator stories; cover by Julie Bell	$1.00	$3.00	$5.00	£0.65	£1.95	£3.25
1 Limited Edition, ND limited to 7,500 copies	$3.00	$9.00	$15.00	£2.00	£6.00	£10.00
Title Value:	$4.00	$12.00	$20.00	£2.65	£7.95	£13.25

CHAPEL
Image,MS; 1 Feb 1995-2 Mar 1995

	$Good	$Fine	$N.Mint	£Good	£Fine	£N.Mint
1 ND Tom Tenney art	$0.45	$1.35	$2.25	£0.30	£0.90	£1.50
1 Variant Edition ND	$1.00	$3.00	$5.00	£0.60	£1.80	£3.00
2 ND Tom Tenney art	$0.45	$1.35	$2.25	£0.30	£0.90	£1.50
Title Value:	$1.90	$5.70	$9.50	£1.20	£3.60	£6.00

CHAPEL (2ND SERIES)
Image; 1 Aug 1995-present

	$Good	$Fine	$N.Mint	£Good	£Fine	£N.Mint
1 ND Brian Witten script, Calvin Irving art	$0.45	$1.35	$2.25	£0.30	£0.90	£1.50
1 Variant cover, ND Joe Quesada/Jimmy Palmiotti cover art	$0.80	$2.40	$4.00	£0.50	£1.50	£2.50
2-3 ND Brian Witten script, Calvin Irving art	$0.45	$1.35	$2.25	£0.30	£0.90	£1.50
4 ND Extreme Babewatch; Brian Witten script, Calvin Irving art	$0.45	$1.35	$2.25	£0.30	£0.90	£1.50
5 ND Hell on Earth part 1, Spawn appears	$0.50	$1.50	$2.50	£0.30	£0.90	£1.50
Title Value:	$3.10	$9.30	$15.50	£2.00	£6.00	£10.00

CHARLEMAGNE
Defiant; 0 Feb 1994; 1 Mar 1994-8 Oct 1994

	$Good	$Fine	$N.Mint	£Good	£Fine	£N.Mint
0 ND (Feb 1994) - presented free with Hero Illustrated #9	$0.30	$0.90	$1.50	£0.20	£0.60	£1.00
1 ND 48pgs, Jim Shooter plot; Adam Pollina and Mike Witherby art	$0.30	$0.90	$1.50	£0.20	£0.60	£1.00
2-5 ND	$0.30	$0.90	$1.50	£0.20	£0.60	£1.00
6 ND Schism X-over; continued in War Dancer #7	$0.30	$0.90	$1.50	£0.20	£0.60	£1.00
7-8 ND	$0.30	$0.90	$1.50	£0.20	£0.60	£1.00
Title Value:	$2.70	$8.10	$13.50	£1.80	£5.40	£9.00

CHARLIE CHAN, THE NEW ADVENTURES OF
National Periodical Publications; 1 May/Jun 1958-6 Mar/Apr 1959

	$Good	$Fine	$N.Mint	£Good	£Fine	£N.Mint
1 rare in the U.K.	$55.00	$165.00	$385.00	£36.00	£105.00	£250.00
2 very scarce in the U.K.	$39.00	$115.00	$275.00	£25.00	£75.00	£175.00
3-6 very scarce in the U.K.						

	$Good	$Fine	$N.Mint	£Good	£Fine	£N.Mint
	$32.00	$95.00	$225.00	£21.00	£62.50	£150.00
Title Value:	$222.00	$660.00	$1560.00	£145.00	£430.00	£1025.00

CHARLTON BULLSEYE, THE
Charlton,Magazine; 1 1975-5 1976

Description	$Good	$Fine	$N.Mint	£Good	£Fine	£N.Mint
1 scarce in the U.K. newszine devoted to Charlton material; Captain Atom by John Byrne and Steve Ditko; all black and white with card cover	$2.40	$7.00	$12.00	£1.20	£3.60	£6.00
2 scarce in the U.K. Captain Atom by John Byrne and Steve Ditko; black and white with colour cover by Joe Staton	$2.20	$6.50	$11.00	£1.00	£3.00	£5.00
3 Kung-Fu issue	$1.60	$4.80	$8.00	£0.80	£2.40	£4.00
4 Doomsday + 1 by John Byrne	$2.00	$6.00	$10.00	£1.00	£3.00	£5.00
5 Doomsday + 1 by John Byrne, The Question by Alex Toth; Toth front cover and Neal Adams back cover art	$2.20	$6.50	$11.00	£1.00	£3.00	£5.00
Title Value:	$10.40	$30.80	$52.00	£5.00	£15.00	£25.00

Note: all Non-Distributed on the news-stands in the U.K.

CHARLTON BULLSEYE, THE (2ND SERIES)
Charlton; 1 Jun 1981-10 Dec 1982

Description	$Good	$Fine	$N.Mint	£Good	£Fine	£N.Mint
1 Blue Beetle and The Question team-up	$0.60	$1.80	$3.00	£0.40	£1.20	£2.00
2 Cap'n Catnip, 1st Neil the Horse	$0.45	$1.35	$2.25	£0.30	£0.90	£1.50
3 science fiction stories	$0.30	$0.90	$1.50	£0.20	£0.60	£1.00
4 The Vanguards	$0.30	$0.90	$1.50	£0.20	£0.60	£1.00
5 Warhound	$0.30	$0.90	$1.50	£0.20	£0.60	£1.00
6 Thunderbunny	$0.30	$0.90	$1.50	£0.20	£0.60	£1.00
7 Captain Atom	$0.45	$1.35	$2.25	£0.30	£0.90	£1.50
8 mystery stories	$0.30	$0.90	$1.50	£0.20	£0.60	£1.00
9 Bludd the Ultimate Barbarian	$0.30	$0.90	$1.50	£0.20	£0.60	£1.00
10 Thunderbunny	$0.30	$0.90	$1.50	£0.20	£0.60	£1.00
Title Value:	$3.60	$10.80	$18.00	£2.40	£7.20	£12.00

Note: all Limited Distribution on the new-stands in the U.K.

CHARLTON CLASSICS
Charlton; 1 Apr 1980-9 Aug 1981

Description	$Good	$Fine	$N.Mint	£Good	£Fine	£N.Mint
1-9 reprints; distributed in the U.K.	$0.30	$0.90	$1.50	£0.20	£0.60	£1.00
Title Value:	$2.70	$8.10	$13.50	£1.80	£5.40	£9.00

CHARLTON PREMIERE
Charlton; 1 Sep 1967-4 May 1968

Description	$Good	$Fine	$N.Mint	£Good	£Fine	£N.Mint
1 Trio,1st appearance the Tyro Team, Shape & Spookman in separate stories	$0.60	$1.80	$3.00	£0.35	£1.05	£1.75
2 Children of Doom	$0.60	$1.80	$3.00	£0.35	£1.05	£1.75
3 scarce in the U.K., Sinistro Boy Fiend	$0.60	$1.80	$3.00	£0.40	£1.20	£2.00
4 scarce in the U.K., Unlikely Tales	$0.60	$1.80	$3.00	£0.40	£1.20	£2.00
Title Value:	$2.40	$7.20	$12.00	£1.50	£4.50	£7.50

CHASER PLATOON
Aircel,MS; 1 Feb 1991-6 Jul 1991

Description	$Good	$Fine	$N.Mint	£Good	£Fine	£N.Mint
1-6 ND black and white	$0.35	$1.05	$1.75	£0.25	£0.75	£1.25
Title Value:	$2.10	$6.30	$10.50	£1.50	£4.50	£7.50

CHECKMATE
DC Comics; 1 Apr 1988-33 Dec 1990
(see Action #598)

Description	$Good	$Fine	$N.Mint	£Good	£Fine	£N.Mint
1	$0.25	$0.75	$1.25	£0.15	£0.45	£0.75
2 Gil Kane cover	$0.25	$0.75	$1.25	£0.15	£0.45	£0.75
3 part Rob Liefeld cover	$0.25	$0.75	$1.25	£0.15	£0.45	£0.75
4 Gil Kane cover	$0.25	$0.75	$1.25	£0.15	£0.45	£0.75
5	$0.25	$0.75	$1.25	£0.15	£0.45	£0.75
6 Gil Kane cover	$0.25	$0.75	$1.25	£0.15	£0.45	£0.75
7 Art Thibert cover	$0.25	$0.75	$1.25	£0.15	£0.45	£0.75
8 Gil Kane cover	$0.25	$0.75	$1.25	£0.15	£0.45	£0.75
9 Art Thibert cover	$0.25	$0.75	$1.25	£0.15	£0.45	£0.75
10 Gil Kane cover	$0.25	$0.75	$1.25	£0.15	£0.45	£0.75
11 Invasion X-over, Gil Kane cover	$0.25	$0.75	$1.25	£0.15	£0.45	£0.75
12 Invasion X-over, Art Thibert cover	$0.25	$0.75	$1.25	£0.15	£0.45	£0.75
13-14	$0.25	$0.75	$1.25	£0.15	£0.45	£0.75
15 The Janus Directive, X-over Suicide Squad #27	$0.25	$0.75	$1.25	£0.15	£0.45	£0.75
16 The Janus Directive, X-over Suicide Squad #28, Gil Kane cover	$0.25	$0.75	$1.25	£0.15	£0.45	£0.75
17-18 Janus Directive tie-in, Gil Kane cover	$0.25	$0.75	$1.25	£0.15	£0.45	£0.75
19-33	$0.25	$0.75	$1.25	£0.15	£0.45	£0.75
Title Value:	$8.00	$24.00	$40.00	£4.80	£14.40	£24.00

CHEQUE MATE, THE
Fantagraphics,OS; 1 May 1992

Description	$Good	$Fine	$N.Mint	£Good	£Fine	£N.Mint
1 ND reprints early and rare work of Eddie Campbell	$0.70	$2.10	$3.50	£0.45	£1.35	£2.25
Title Value:	$0.70	$2.10	$3.50	£0.45	£1.35	£2.25

CHEVAL NOIR
Dark Horse; 1 Feb 1989-50 Jan 1994

Description	$Good	$Fine	$N.Mint	£Good	£Fine	£N.Mint
1 Loan Sloane by Phillipe Druillet, Fever in Urbicand by Schusten, Fred and Bob by Cailleteau and Vatine, Adele and the Beast by Tardi, Angel Fusion by Hiroyuki Kato, Rork by Andreas. Dave Stevens cover	$1.05	$3.15	$5.25	£0.70	£2.10	£3.50
2 Lone Sloane/Fever/Adele continue plus Oscar Hellion by John Bolton, The Auction by Cossu and Jamsin Poison by Leo Duranon	$0.90	$2.70	$4.50	£0.60	£1.80	£3.00
3 Lone Sloane/Fever/Adele continue plus Dark Horse by Brian Bolland, The Eyeball Kid by Eddie Campbell/Ed Hillyer, Geoff- The Man by Geoff Darrow God is Love by Bolland. Rick Geary illustrations pg 1,3	$0.80	$2.40	$4.00	£0.50	£1.50	£2.50
4 Lone Sloane/Fever/Adele plus The Promise by John Bolton/Steve Moore, painted cover John Bolton	$0.80	$2.40	$4.00	£0.50	£1.50	£2.50
5 Lone Sloane/Fever plus Eddie Campbell, Geary, Bolland, The Demon of the Eiffel Tower by Tardi, cover by Moebius	$0.80	$2.40	$4.00	£0.50	£1.50	£2.50
6 Sunstroke by Kaluta, Tardi, Bolland, Geary	$0.80	$2.40	$4.00	£0.50	£1.50	£2.50
7 Cailleteau/Vatine, Bolland, Geary, Eddie Campbell, Jacques Tardi, cover by Dave Stevens	$0.80	$2.40	$4.00	£0.50	£1.50	£2.50
8 80pgs, Demon of Eiffel Tower by Tardi, Fun by Brian Bolland, Cailleteau/Vatine/Druillet art featured	$0.90	$2.70	$4.50	£0.60	£1.80	£3.00
9 80pgs, The Tower by Schuiten and Peeters plus Bolland, Druillet, Eddie Campbell, Rick Geary, a fold-out Geof Darrow poster. Cover by Moebius	$0.90	$2.70	$4.50	£0.60	£1.80	£3.00
10 Jacques Tardi's "The Roach Killer" begins plus Druillet, Cailleteau and Vatine and article on the art of H.R. Giger	$0.80	$2.40	$4.00	£0.50	£1.50	£2.50
11 80pgs, features art by Jacques Tardi, Druillet, Rick Geary, Geof Darrow	$0.90	$2.70	$4.50	£0.60	£1.80	£3.00
12 80pgs, Jacques Tardi, Druillet, cover by Mignola	$0.80	$2.40	$4.00	£0.50	£1.50	£2.50
13 80pgs, Tardi, Bolland, Geary, cover by Paul Chadwick	$0.90	$2.70	$4.50	£0.60	£1.80	£3.00
14 72pgs, Tardi, Bolland, Darrow, Geary	$0.80	$2.40	$4.00	£0.50	£1.50	£2.50
15 80pgs, Jacques Tardi's Mad Scientist begins plus Bolland. Cailleteau and Vatine, Geary	$0.90	$2.70	$4.50	£0.60	£1.80	£3.00
16 64pgs, Tardi, Bolland, Darrow, Geary	$0.80	$2.40	$4.00	£0.50	£1.50	£2.50
17 80pgs, Eddie Campbell, Tardi, Bolland, Darrow, Geary	$0.90	$2.70	$4.50	£0.60	£1.80	£3.00
18 64pgs, Eddie Campbell, Tardi, Bolland, Darrow, Geary	$0.80	$2.40	$4.00	£0.50	£1.50	£2.50
19 64pgs, Tardi's "The Mummies On Parade" begins, Bolland, Darrow, Geary	$0.80	$2.40	$4.00	£0.50	£1.50	£2.50
20 80pgs, Angriest Dog in the World by David Lynch begins, John Bolton cover	$0.90	$2.70	$4.50	£0.60	£1.80	£3.00
21 64pgs, Chris Warner cover	$1.05	$3.15	$5.25	£0.70	£2.10	£3.50
22 64pgs, The Great Power of the Chninkel concludes	$0.90	$2.70	$4.50	£0.60	£1.80	£3.00
23 64pgs, The Forever War Book Three concludes	$0.80	$2.40	$4.00	£0.50	£1.50	£2.50
24 64pgs, Izo the Man Cleaver by Masahi Tanaka begins, Adieu Brindavoine by Tardi begins, Arthur Suydam cover	$1.05	$3.15	$5.25	£0.70	£2.10	£3.50
25 64pgs, Matt Wagner cover painting	$0.80	$2.40	$4.00	£0.50	£1.50	£2.50
26 64pgs, The Man From Ciguri by Moebius begins, cover painting by Moebius	$0.80	$2.40	$4.00	£0.50	£1.50	£2.50
27 32pgs, cover painting by Kelley Jones	$0.60	$1.80	$3.00	£0.40	£1.20	£2.00
28 32pgs, The Flower and The Rifle by Tardi begins	$0.60	$1.80	$3.00	£0.40	£1.20	£2.00
29-30 32pgs	$0.60	$1.80	$3.00	£0.40	£1.20	£2.00
31 32pgs, cover painting by Steve Pugh	$0.60	$1.80	$3.00	£0.40	£1.20	£2.00
32 32pgs, Sabotage by Daniel Torres begins, cover painting by Dave Gibbons	$0.60	$1.80	$3.00	£0.40	£1.20	£2.00
33-35 32pgs	$0.60	$1.80	$3.00	£0.40	£1.20	£2.00
36 32pgs, painted cover by Tom Sutton	$0.60	$1.80	$3.00	£0.40	£1.20	£2.00
37 32pgs, painted cover by Olivier Vatine	$0.60	$1.80	$3.00	£0.40	£1.20	£2.00
38-39 32pgs	$0.60	$1.80	$3.00	£0.40	£1.20	£2.00
40 32pgs, Dave Mazzucchelli painted cover	$0.60	$1.80	$3.00	£0.40	£1.20	£2.00
41-45 32pgs	$0.60	$1.80	$3.00	£0.40	£1.20	£2.00
46 32pgs, Moebius cover	$0.60	$1.80	$3.00	£0.40	£1.20	£2.00
47-48 32pgs	$0.60	$1.80	$3.00	£0.40	£1.20	£2.00
49 32pgs, John Bolton painted cover	$0.60	$1.80	$3.00	£0.40	£1.20	£2.00
50 48pgs	$0.80	$2.40	$4.00	£0.50	£1.50	£2.50
Title Value:	$37.05	$111.15	$185.25	£24.20	£72.60	£121.00

Note: all Non-Distributed on the news-stands in the U.K.
Note: owing to bad printing, many copies of issue #1 were returned

CHEYENNE
Dell; (Four Color #734) 1 Oct 1956-25 Dec 1961/Jan 1962

Description	$Good	$Fine	$N.Mint	£Good	£Fine	£N.Mint
1 (Four Color #734) photo cover Clint Walker	$20.00	$60.00	$140.00	£13.00	£40.00	£92.50
2 (Four Color #772) photo cover Clint Walker	$10.50	$31.50	$63.00	£7.00	£21.00	£42.00
3 (Four Color #803) photo cover Clint Walker	$10.00	$30.00	$60.00	£6.50	£19.50	£40.00

MINT = 100% / NEAR MINT (inc. +/-) = 90-99% / VERY FINE (inc. +/-) = 75-89% / FINE (inc. +/-) = 55-74%
VERY GOOD (inc. +/-) = 35-54% / GOOD (inc. +/-) = 15-34% / FAIR = 5-14% / POOR = 1-4%

265

	$Good	$Fine	$N.Mint	£Good	£Fine	£N.Mint

4-9 Clint Walker photo cover

| | $6.50 | $19.50 | $40.00 | £4.00 | £12.00 | £25.00 |

10

| | $6.50 | $19.50 | $40.00 | £4.00 | £12.00 | £25.00 |

11-12

| | $5.25 | $16.00 | $32.50 | £2.90 | £8.75 | £17.50 |

13 Clint Walker photo covers return (ends #25)

| | $5.25 | $16.00 | $32.50 | £2.90 | £8.75 | £17.50 |

14-25

| | $5.25 | $16.00 | $32.50 | £2.90 | £8.75 | £17.50 |

| Title Value: | $164.75 | $498.00 | $1070.50 | £98.00 | £295.75 | £612.00 |

Note: limited distribution in the U.K. after 1959

CHEYENNE KID
Charlton; 8 Jul 1957-99 Nov 1973
(Wild Frontier #1-7)

| **8** scarce in the U.K. | $5.75 | $17.50 | $35.00 | £3.75 | £11.00 | £22.50 |
| **9** | $3.30 | $10.00 | $20.00 | £2.05 | £6.25 | £12.50 |

10 Williamson art, Steve Ditko cover

| | $7.75 | $23.50 | $47.50 | £5.25 | £16.00 | £32.00 |

11-12 Williamson art

| | $7.75 | $23.50 | $47.50 | £5.25 | £16.00 | £32.00 |

13-14 part Williamson art

| | $5.25 | $16.00 | $32.00 | £3.30 | £10.00 | £20.00 |

15-17

| | $3.30 | $10.00 | $20.00 | £2.05 | £6.25 | £12.50 |

18 part Williamson art

	$3.30	$10.00	$20.00	£2.05	£6.25	£12.50
19	$3.30	$10.00	$20.00	£2.05	£6.25	£12.50
20-22	$3.65	$11.00	$22.00	£2.15	£6.50	£13.00
23	$1.65	$5.00	$10.00	£1.15	£3.50	£7.00
24-25	$3.65	$11.00	$22.00	£2.15	£6.50	£13.00
26	$2.50	$7.50	$15.00	£1.65	£5.00	£10.00
27-29	$1.65	$5.00	$10.00	£1.15	£3.50	£7.00
30	$2.50	$7.50	$15.00	£1.65	£5.00	£10.00
31-40	$1.00	$3.00	$6.00	£0.65	£2.00	£4.00
41-60	$0.80	$2.50	$5.00	£0.50	£1.60	£3.25
61-80	$0.80	$2.40	$4.00	£0.50	£1.50	£2.50
81-99	$0.60	$1.80	$3.00	£0.40	£1.20	£2.00
Title Value:	$142.55	$432.20	$838.50	£91.15	£277.80	£539.50

Note: most issues distributed in the U.K. after 1959

CHEYENNE KID (2ND SERIES)
A Plus Comics; 1 Jan 1992
1 ND reprints from original series

| | $0.45 | $1.35 | $2.25 | £0.30 | £0.90 | £1.50 |
| Title Value: | $0.45 | $1.35 | $2.25 | £0.30 | £0.90 | £1.50 |

CHIAROSCURO: THE PRIVATE LIVES OF LEONARDO DA VINCI
DC Comics/Vertigo,MS; 1 Jul 1995-present
1-9 ND Dave Rawson script, Chas Truog art

| | $0.60 | $1.80 | $3.00 | £0.40 | £1.20 | £2.00 |
| Title Value: | $5.40 | $16.20 | $27.00 | £3.60 | £10.80 | £18.00 |

CHILD'S PLAY 2
Innovation,MS Film; 1 Nov 1991-3 Jan 1991
1-3 ND film adaptation; colour

| | $0.55 | $1.65 | $2.75 | £0.35 | £1.05 | £1.75 |
| Title Value: | $1.65 | $4.95 | $8.25 | £1.05 | £3.15 | £5.25 |

Trade Paperback (1991)
68pgs, squarebound, film adaptation in full

| | | | | £0.90 | £2.70 | £4.50 |

CHILD'S PLAY 3
Innovation, Film; 1 Oct 1991-3 Nov 1991
1-3 ND film adaptation

| | $0.45 | $1.35 | $2.25 | £0.30 | £0.90 | £1.50 |
| Title Value: | $1.35 | $4.05 | $6.75 | £0.90 | £2.70 | £4.50 |

Graphic Novel (Jan 1992), reprints mini-series

| | | | | £0.90 | £2.70 | £4.50 |

CHILD'S PLAY: THE SERIES
Innovation; 1 May 1991-5 Jan 1992
1-5 ND

| | $0.40 | $1.20 | $2.00 | £0.25 | £0.75 | £1.25 |
| Title Value: | $2.00 | $6.00 | $10.00 | £1.25 | £3.75 | £6.25 |

CHILDREN OF FIRE
Fantagor; 1-3 1988
1 ND scarce in the U.K. Corben art begins

| | $0.80 | $2.40 | $4.00 | £0.50 | £1.50 | £2.50 |

2 ND scarce in the U.K. includes redrawn reprint from Promethian Enterprises #3

| | $0.80 | $2.40 | $4.00 | £0.50 | £1.50 | £2.50 |

3 ND scarce in the U.K. includes reprint from Fantagor #3

| | $0.80 | $2.40 | $4.00 | £0.50 | £1.50 | £2.50 |
| Title Value: | $2.40 | $7.20 | $12.00 | £1.50 | £4.50 | £7.50 |

Note: last series in "Corben-color".

CHILDREN OF THE NIGHT
Night Wynd,MS; 1 Sep 1992-4 Dec 1992
1-4 ND Barry Blair and Jimmy Palmiotti script/art; black and white

| | $0.45 | $1.35 | $2.25 | £0.30 | £0.90 | £1.50 |
| Title Value: | $1.80 | $5.40 | $9.00 | £1.20 | £3.60 | £6.00 |

CHILDREN OF THE VOYAGER
Marvel UK/Frontier,MS; 1 Sep 1993-4 Dec 1993
1 Nick Abadzis and Paul Johnson begin; embossed, glow-in-the-dark cover

	$0.40	$1.20	$2.00	£0.25	£0.75	£1.25
2-4	$0.40	$1.20	$2.00	£0.25	£0.75	£1.25
Title Value:	$1.60	$4.80	$8.00	£1.00	£3.00	£5.00

CHILDREN'S CRUSADE, THE
DC Comics/Vertigo,MS; 1 Dec 1993-2 Jan 1994
1 64pgs, Neil Gaiman and Chris Bachalo

| | $0.75 | $2.25 | $3.75 | £0.50 | £1.50 | £2.50 |

2 64pgs, Neil Gaiman; painted cover by John Totleben

| | $0.75 | $2.25 | $3.75 | £0.50 | £1.50 | £2.50 |
| Title Value: | $1.50 | $4.50 | $7.50 | £1.00 | £3.00 | £5.00 |

CHILI
Marvel Comics Group; 1 May 1969-17 Sep 1970; 18 Aug 1972-26 Dec 1973
1 ND scarce in the U.K.

| | $3.60 | $10.50 | $18.00 | £2.40 | £7.00 | £12.00 |

2 ND scarce in the U.K.

| | $1.80 | $5.25 | $9.00 | £1.20 | £3.60 | £6.00 |

3-5 ND scarce in the U.K.

	$1.20	$3.60	$6.00	£0.80	£2.40	£4.00
6-10 ND	$1.05	$3.15	$5.25	£0.70	£2.10	£3.50
11-18 ND	$0.80	$2.40	$4.00	£0.50	£1.50	£2.50
19-26 ND	$0.45	$1.35	$2.25	£0.30	£0.90	£1.50
Title Value:	$24.25	$72.30	$121.25	£15.90	£47.50	£79.50

CHILI ANNUAL
Marvel Comics Group; 1 Dec 1971
1 ND very scarce in the U.K.

| | $1.50 | $4.50 | $7.50 | £1.00 | £3.00 | £5.00 |
| Title Value: | $1.50 | $4.50 | $7.50 | £1.00 | £3.00 | £5.00 |

CHILLER
Marvel Comics Group/Epic,MS; 1 Nov 1993-2 Dec 1993
1-2 ND James Hudnall and John Ridgway

| | $1.50 | $4.50 | $7.50 | £1.00 | £3.00 | £5.00 |
| Title Value: | $3.00 | $9.00 | $15.00 | £2.00 | £6.00 | £10.00 |

CHILLERS GIANT SIZE
Marvel Comics Group; 1 Jun 1974
(becomes Dracula Giant Size)
1 ND 52pgs, 1st appearance Lilith (daughter of Dracula); Gene Colan art

| | $1.50 | $4.50 | $7.50 | £1.00 | £3.00 | £5.00 |
| Title Value: | $1.50 | $4.50 | $7.50 | £1.00 | £3.00 | £5.00 |

CHILLERS GIANT SIZE (2ND SERIES)
Marvel Comics Group; 1 Feb 1975-3 Aug 1975
1 ND scarce in the U.K. 68pgs, Dave Gibbons art featured

| | $1.20 | $3.60 | $6.00 | £0.80 | £2.40 | £4.00 |

2 ND 68pgs, all reprint, Wrightson/Smith reprint

| | $0.90 | $2.70 | $4.50 | £0.60 | £1.80 | £3.00 |

3 ND 68pgs, all reprint, Wrightson/Smith reprint

| | $0.80 | $2.40 | $4.00 | £0.50 | £1.50 | £2.50 |
| Title Value: | $2.90 | $8.70 | $14.50 | £1.90 | £5.70 | £9.50 |

CHILLING ADVENTURES IN SORCERY
Red Circle; 1 Sep 1972-5 Feb 1974
(becomes Red Circle Sorcery)
1 Sabrina appears; distributed in the U.K.

| | $0.30 | $0.90 | $1.50 | £0.20 | £0.60 | £1.00 |

2 Sabrina appears; distributed in the U.K.

| | $0.25 | $0.75 | $1.25 | £0.15 | £0.45 | £0.75 |

3-5 Gray Morrow art; distributed in the U.K.

| | $0.25 | $0.75 | $1.25 | £0.15 | £0.45 | £0.75 |
| Title Value: | $1.30 | $3.90 | $6.50 | £0.80 | £2.40 | £4.00 |

CHINA SEA
Night Wynd,MS; 1 Dec 1991-4 Mar 1992
1-4 ND Barry Blair script and art; black and white

| | $0.45 | $1.35 | $2.25 | £0.30 | £0.90 | £1.50 |
| Title Value: | $1.80 | $5.40 | $9.00 | £1.20 | £3.60 | £6.00 |

CHIP 'N DALE RESCUE RANGERS
Disney; 1 May 1990-20 Dec 1991
1-20 ND

| | $0.30 | $0.90 | $1.50 | £0.20 | £0.60 | £1.00 |
| Title Value: | $6.00 | $18.00 | $30.00 | £4.00 | £12.00 | £20.00 |

CHIPS & VANILLA
Kitchen Sink,OS; 1 Jun 1988
1 ND Doug Potter script and art

| | $0.40 | $1.20 | $2.00 | £0.25 | £0.75 | £1.25 |
| Title Value: | $0.40 | $1.20 | $2.00 | £0.25 | £0.75 | £1.25 |

CHOLLY AND FLYTRAP, NEW ADVENTURES OF
Marvel Comics Group/Epic,MS; 1 Dec 1990-3 Feb 1991
1-3 ND characters from Epic Illustrated, Arthur Suydam script/art

| | $0.75 | $2.25 | $3.75 | £0.50 | £1.50 | £2.50 |
| Title Value: | $2.25 | $6.75 | $11.25 | £1.50 | £4.50 | £7.50 |

CHOSEN
Click! Comics; 1 Jul 1995-2 1995
1-2 ND

| | $0.50 | $1.50 | $2.50 | £0.30 | £0.90 | £1.50 |
| Title Value: | $1.00 | $3.00 | $5.00 | £0.60 | £1.80 | £3.00 |

CHRISTMAS WITH SUPERSWINE
Fantagraphics,OS; 1 Feb 1989
1 ND Gary Fields art; black and white

| | $0.40 | $1.20 | $2.00 | £0.25 | £0.75 | £1.25 |
| Title Value: | $0.40 | $1.20 | $2.00 | £0.25 | £0.75 | £1.25 |

CHRISTMAS WITH THE SUPER-HEROES
DC Comics; 1 Dec 1988; 2 Dec 1989
1 ND reprints Frank Miller Batman, John Byrne cover

| | $0.55 | $1.65 | $2.75 | £0.35 | £1.05 | £1.75 |

2 ND squarebound, features Batman fable-story by Gibbons, art on Superman by Chadwick

| | $0.55 | $1.65 | $2.75 | £0.35 | £1.05 | £1.75 |
| Title Value: | $1.10 | $3.30 | $5.50 | £0.70 | £2.10 | £3.50 |

CHROMA-TICK SPECIAL EDITION, THE
New England Press; 1 Apr 1992-11 1993
1 ND 40pgs, reprints begin of Tick series in colour; with 4 bound-in trading cards at centrefold

| | $0.70 | $2.10 | $3.50 | £0.45 | £1.35 | £2.25 |

2 ND 40pgs, with 4 bound-in trading cards at centrefold

| | $0.70 | $2.10 | $3.50 | £0.45 | £1.35 | £2.25 |

3 ND

| | $0.70 | $2.10 | $3.50 | £0.45 | £1.35 | £2.25 |

4 ND issue available with 3 different outer covers predicting the outcome of the 1992 Presidential Election

| | $0.70 | $2.10 | $3.50 | £0.45 | £1.35 | £2.25 |

5 ND

| | $0.70 | $2.10 | $3.50 | £0.45 | £1.35 | £2.25 |

	$Good	$Fine	$N.Mint	£Good	£Fine	£N.Mint
6 ND bound-in trading card						
	$0.70	$2.10	$3.50	£0.45	£1.35	£2.25
7-11 ND	$0.70	$2.10	$3.50	£0.45	£1.35	£2.25
Title Value:	$7.70	$23.10	$38.50	£4.95	£14.85	£24.75

CHROME
Hot; 1 Oct 1986-3 Mar 1987

	$Good	$Fine	$N.Mint	£Good	£Fine	£N.Mint
1 ND Peter Gillis script, Kelly Jones art begins						
	$0.35	$1.05	$1.75	£0.25	£0.75	£1.25
2 ND (1 on indicia)	$0.35	$1.05	$1.75	£0.25	£0.75	£1.25
3 ND	$0.35	$1.05	$1.75	£0.25	£0.75	£1.25
Title Value:	$1.05	$3.15	$5.25	£0.75	£2.25	£3.75

CHROMIUM MAN, THE
Triumphant Comics; 0 Apr 1994; 1 Jan 1993-15 1994

	$Good	$Fine	$N.Mint	£Good	£Fine	£N.Mint
0 (Apr 1994)	$0.30	$0.90	$1.50	£0.20	£0.60	£1.00
0 Signed Edition (Aug 1994), pre-bagged with backing board						
	$0.60	$1.80	$3.00	£0.40	£1.20	£2.00
0 Blue Logo Edition (Oct 1994) - pre-bagged with backing board; 2,000 copies						
	$0.70	$2.10	$3.50	£0.50	£1.50	£2.50
1 Ash Can Edition	$0.30	$0.90	$1.50	£0.20	£0.60	£1.00
2	$0.30	$0.90	$1.50	£0.20	£0.60	£1.00
2 Limited Edition - signed by creators with mini-poster photo-print; pre-bagged with backing board						
	$0.60	$1.80	$3.00	£0.40	£1.20	£2.00
3	$0.30	$0.90	$1.50	£0.20	£0.60	£1.00
4 Unleashed X-over						
	$0.30	$0.90	$1.50	£0.20	£0.60	£1.00
5-10	$0.30	$0.90	$1.50	£0.20	£0.60	£1.00
11 dual issue with Prince Vandal #8 (Note: there is only one comic between the two titles)						
	$0.30	$0.90	$1.50	£0.20	£0.60	£1.00
11 Signed Edition (Oct 1994) - pre-bagged with mini-poster photo-print and backing board						
	$0.60	$1.80	$3.00	£0.40	£1.20	£2.00
12 dual issue with Prince Vandal #9 (Note: there is only one comic between the two titles)						
	$0.30	$0.90	$1.50	£0.20	£0.60	£1.00
13-15	$0.30	$0.90	$1.50	£0.20	£0.60	£1.00
Title Value:	$7.30	$21.90	$36.50	£4.90	£14.70	£24.50

Note: all Non-Distributed on the news-stands in the U.K.

CHROMIUM MAN: VIOLENT PAST
Triumphant Comics,MS; 1,2 Jan 1994

	$Good	$Fine	$N.Mint	£Good	£Fine	£N.Mint
1 ND	$0.45	$1.35	$2.25	£0.30	£0.90	£1.50
1 ND Signed Edition with mini-poster photo-print; pre-bagged with backing board						
	$0.70	$2.10	$3.50	£0.50	£1.50	£2.50
2 ND	$0.45	$1.35	$2.25	£0.30	£0.90	£1.50
2 ND Signed Edition with mini-poster photo-print; pre-bagged with backing board						
	$0.70	$2.10	$3.50	£0.50	£1.50	£2.50
Title Value:	$2.30	$6.90	$11.50	£1.60	£4.80	£8.00

CHRONIC IDIOCY
Caliber Press,MS; 1 Nov 1991-3 Jan 1992

	$Good	$Fine	$N.Mint	£Good	£Fine	£N.Mint
1-3 ND	$0.45	$1.35	$2.25	£0.30	£0.90	£1.50
Title Value:	$1.35	$4.05	$6.75	£0.90	£2.70	£4.50

CHRONICLES OF CORUM
First; 1 Jan 1987-12 Nov 1988
(see Corum)

	$Good	$Fine	$N.Mint	£Good	£Fine	£N.Mint
1 ND Knight of the Swords begins, Mignola covers and art begins						
	$0.40	$1.20	$2.00	£0.25	£0.75	£1.25
2-4 ND	$0.40	$1.20	$2.00	£0.25	£0.75	£1.25
5 ND Queen of the Swords begins						
	$0.40	$1.20	$2.00	£0.25	£0.75	£1.25
6 ND last Mignola cover and art						
	$0.40	$1.20	$2.00	£0.25	£0.75	£1.25
7-8 ND Jackson Guice and Kelly Jones cover and art						
	$0.40	$1.20	$2.00	£0.25	£0.75	£1.25
9 ND King of the Swords begins, Ken Hooper and Kelly Jones cover and art						

	$Good	$Fine	$N.Mint	£Good	£Fine	£N.Mint
	$0.40	$1.20	$2.00	£0.25	£0.75	£1.25
10 ND Ken Hooper and Kelly Jones cover and art						
	$0.40	$1.20	$2.00	£0.25	£0.75	£1.25
11 ND Ken Hooper and Kelly Jones art, Mignola cover						
	$0.40	$1.20	$2.00	£0.25	£0.75	£1.25
12 ND Jill Thompson and Kelly Jones art, Mignola cover						
	$0.40	$1.20	$2.00	£0.25	£0.75	£1.25
Title Value:	$4.80	$14.40	$24.00	£3.00	£9.00	£15.00

CHRONICLES OF PANDA KHAN
Apple/Abacus Press; 1 Feb 1987-2 Jul 1987
(becomes Panda Khan)

	$Good	$Fine	$N.Mint	£Good	£Fine	£N.Mint
1-2 ND	$0.40	$1.20	$2.00	£0.25	£0.75	£1.25
Title Value:	$0.80	$2.40		£0.50	£1.50	£2.50

CHRONICLES OF PANDA KHAN BOOK 2
Abacus Press; 1 1990-4 1991?

	$Good	$Fine	$N.Mint	£Good	£Fine	£N.Mint
1-4 ND titled Panda Khan						
	$0.40	$1.20	$2.00	£0.25	£0.75	£1.25
Title Value:	$1.60	$4.80	$8.00	£1.00	£3.00	£5.00
Special (Aug 1990), 48pgs; ties up plot lines; Bryan Talbot art featured				£0.35	£1.05	£1.75

CHUCK NORRIS
Marvel Comics Group/Star; 1 Jan 1987-5 Sep 1987

	$Good	$Fine	$N.Mint	£Good	£Fine	£N.Mint
1-5 ND	$0.15	$0.45	$0.75	£0.10	£0.35	£0.60
Title Value:	$0.75	$2.25	$3.75	£0.50	£1.75	£3.00

CINDER AND ASHE
DC Comics,MS; 1 May 1988-4 Aug 1988

	$Good	$Fine	$N.Mint	£Good	£Fine	£N.Mint
1-4 ND Jose Garcia Lopez art						
	$0.45	$1.35	$2.25	£0.30	£0.90	£1.50
Title Value:	$1.80	$5.40	$9.00	£1.20	£3.60	£6.00

CITY KNIGHTS
Acclaim Comics/Windjammer,MS; 1 Jun 1995-3 Aug 1995

	$Good	$Fine	$N.Mint	£Good	£Fine	£N.Mint
1-3 ND Jeff Gomez script, Val Mayerik art						
	$0.45	$1.35	$2.25	£0.30	£0.90	£1.50
Title Value:	$1.35	$4.05	$6.75	£0.90	£2.70	£4.50

CITYSCAPE
NC Venture; 1 Jun 1990-2 1990

	$Good	$Fine	$N.Mint	£Good	£Fine	£N.Mint
1 ND card-stock cover; black and white						
	$0.40	$1.20	$2.00	£0.25	£0.75	£1.25
2 ND black and white						
	$0.40	$1.20	$2.00	£0.25	£0.75	£1.25
Title Value:	$0.80	$2.40	$4.00	£0.50	£1.50	£2.50

CIVIL WAR TALES
ACG,MS; 1 Jul 1995-3 Sep 1995

	$Good	$Fine	$N.Mint	£Good	£Fine	£N.Mint
1-3 ND features story and art by Sam Glanzman						
	$0.50	$1.50	$2.50	£0.30	£0.90	£1.50
Title Value:	$1.50	$4.50	$7.50	£0.90	£2.70	£4.50

CIVIL WAR, THE
Eclipse; 1,2 Jun 1993

	$Good	$Fine	$N.Mint	£Good	£Fine	£N.Mint
1 ND 96pgs, Richard Rockwell and Fred Fredericks painted art, Earl Norem painted cover						
	$2.40	$7.00	$12.00	£1.50	£4.50	£7.50
2 96pgs, Angelo Torres and George Woodbridge painted art, Earl Norem painted cover						
	$2.40	$7.00	$12.00	£1.50	£4.50	£7.50
Title Value:	$4.80	$14.00	$24.00	£3.00	£9.00	£15.00

CLANDESTINE
Marvel Comics Group; 1 Oct 1994-12 Sep 1995

	$Good	$Fine	$N.Mint	£Good	£Fine	£N.Mint
1 Alan Davis script and art, inks by Mark Farmer; foil stamped cover						
	$0.60	$1.80	$3.00	£0.40	£1.20	£2.00
2-5	$0.45	$1.35	$2.25	£0.30	£0.90	£1.50
6-7 Spiderman guest-stars						
	$0.45	$1.35	$2.25	£0.30	£0.90	£1.50
8 Dr. Strange and The Invaders guest-star; last Alan Davis art						

Charlton Premiere #1

Cheval Noir #1

Chili #1

Issue	$Good	$Fine	$N.Mint	£Good	£Fine	£N.Mint
	$0.45	$1.35	$2.25	£0.30	£0.90	£1.50
9	$0.45	$1.35	$2.25	£0.30	£0.90	£1.50
10 Britanic appears	$0.45	$1.35	$2.25	£0.30	£0.90	£1.50
11-12	$0.45	$1.35	$2.25	£0.30	£0.90	£1.50
Title Value:	$5.55	$16.65	$27.75	£3.70	£11.10	£18.50

Note: issues 13-14 were advertised and solicited, but never appeared

CLANDESTINE PREVIEW
Marvel Comics Group,OS; nn Oct 1994

nn ND previews Clandestine series and spotlights Alan Davis' work for Marvel

Issue	$Good	$Fine	$N.Mint	£Good	£Fine	£N.Mint
	$0.30	$0.90	$1.50	£0.20	£0.60	£1.00
Title Value:	$0.30	$0.90	$1.50	£0.20	£0.60	£1.00

CLASH
DC Comics,MS; 1 Nov 1991-3 Jan 1992

1-3 ND Tom Veitch script, Adam Kubert art

Issue	$Good	$Fine	$N.Mint	£Good	£Fine	£N.Mint
	$0.90	$2.70	$4.50	£0.60	£1.80	£3.00
Title Value:	$2.70	$8.10	$13.50	£1.80	£5.40	£9.00

CLASSIC GIRLS
Eternity; 1 Feb 1991-4 May 1991

1 ND reprints Trouble With Girls #1 etc. New Paul Gulacy cover

Issue	$Good	$Fine	$N.Mint	£Good	£Fine	£N.Mint
1	$0.40	$1.20	$2.00	£0.25	£0.75	£1.25
2-4 ND	$0.40	$1.20	$2.00	£0.25	£0.75	£1.25
Title Value:	$1.60	$4.80	$8.00	£1.00	£3.00	£5.00

CLASSIC STAR WARS
Dark Horse; 1 Sep 1992-20 May 1994

1 ND reprints of 1980s US newspaper strip begins by Goodwin and Williamson; new Williamson covers

Issue	$Good	$Fine	$N.Mint	£Good	£Fine	£N.Mint
1	$0.45	$1.35	$2.25	£0.30	£0.90	£1.50
2-19 ND	$0.45	$1.35	$2.25	£0.30	£0.90	£1.50
20 ND 48pgs	$0.80	$2.40	$4.00	£0.50	£1.50	£2.50
Title Value:	$9.35	$28.05	$46.75	£6.20	£18.60	£31.00

Classic Star Wars Volume 1 (1995)

Issue	£Good	£Fine	£N.Mint
Trade paperback reprints issues #1-7, new Al Williamson cover	£2.20	£6.60	£11.00

Classic Star Wars Volume 2 (Jun 1995)

Issue	£Good	£Fine	£N.Mint
Trade paperback reprints issues #8-14, new Al Williamson cover	£2.20	£6.60	£11.00

Classic Star Wars: Star Wars Trilogy Boxed Set (Oct 1995)

Issue	£Good	£Fine	£N.Mint
collects the three Star Wars films adaptations in slip-case	£4.00	£12.00	£20.00

CLASSIC STAR WARS: A NEW HOPE
Dark Horse,MS; 1 Jun 1994-2 Jul 1994

1-2 ND reprints film adaptation from the first issues of Star Wars, newly recoloured, covers by Adam Hughes

Issue	$Good	$Fine	$N.Mint	£Good	£Fine	£N.Mint
	$0.80	$2.40	$4.00	£0.50	£1.50	£2.50
Title Value:	$1.60	$4.80	$8.00	£1.00	£3.00	£5.00

Classic Star Wars: A New Hope (Oct 1995)

Issue	£Good	£Fine	£N.Mint
Trade paperback collects mini-series	£1.30	£3.90	£6.50

CLASSIC STAR WARS: RETURN OF THE JEDI
Dark Horse,MS; 1 Oct 1994-2 Nov 1994

1-2 ND film adaptation reprinted from Marvel's comic series; pre-bagged with trading acrd

Issue	$Good	$Fine	$N.Mint	£Good	£Fine	£N.Mint
	$0.80	$2.40	$4.00	£0.50	£1.50	£2.50
Title Value:	$1.60	$4.80	$8.00	£1.00	£3.00	£5.00

Classic Star Wars: Return of the Jedi (Oct 1995)

Issue	£Good	£Fine	£N.Mint
Trade paperback collects mini-series	£1.30	£3.90	£6.50

CLASSIC STAR WARS: THE EARLY ADVENTURES
Dark Horse,MS; 1 Aug 1994-9 Apr 1995

1-9 ND Russ Manning strip reformatted and coloured

Issue	$Good	$Fine	$N.Mint	£Good	£Fine	£N.Mint
	$0.45	$1.35	$2.25	£0.30	£0.90	£1.50
Title Value:	$4.05	$12.15	$20.25	£2.70	£8.10	£13.50

CLASSIC STAR WARS: THE EMPIRE STRIKES BACK
Dark Horse,MS; 1 Aug 1994-2 Sep 1994

1-2 ND reprints film adaptation from Marvel Star Wars comic with new Al Williamson covers

Issue	$Good	$Fine	$N.Mint	£Good	£Fine	£N.Mint
	$0.80	$2.40	$4.00	£0.50	£1.50	£2.50
Title Value:	$1.60	$4.80	$8.00	£1.00	£3.00	£5.00

Classic Star Wars: The Empire Strikes Back (Oct 1995)

Issue	£Good	£Fine	£N.Mint
Trade paperback collects mini-series	£1.30	£3.90	£6.50

CLASSIC STAR WARS: THE VANDELHEIM MISSION
Dark Horse,OS; 1 Mar 1995

1 ND reprinted from newspaper strip by Archie Goodwin and Al Williamson

Issue	$Good	$Fine	$N.Mint	£Good	£Fine	£N.Mint
	$0.45	$1.35	$2.25	£0.30	£0.90	£1.50
Title Value:	$0.45	$1.35	$2.25	£0.30	£0.90	£1.50

CLASSIC X-MEN
Marvel Comics Group; 1 Sep 1986-110 Sep 1995

Issue	$Good	$Fine	$N.Mint	£Good	£Fine	£N.Mint
1 LD in the U.K. reprints Giant Size #1, additional back up material with John Bolton art begins	$1.50	$4.50	$7.50	£1.00	£3.00	£5.00
2 LD in the U.K. reprints X-Men #94, John Bolton art	$0.85	$2.55	$4.25	£0.55	£1.65	£2.75
3 LD in the U.K. reprints X-Men #95, John Bolton art	$0.80	$2.40	$4.00	£0.50	£1.50	£2.50
4 ND John Bolton art	$0.70	$2.10	$3.50	£0.45	£1.35	£2.25
5-9 LD in the U.K. John Bolton art	$0.60	$1.80	$3.00	£0.40	£1.20	£2.00
10 ND Wolverine stalked by Sabretooth, John Bolton art	$0.75	$2.25	$3.75	£0.50	£1.50	£2.50
11 ND John Bolton art	$0.55	$1.65	$2.75	£0.35	£1.05	£1.75
12 ND more facts about Magneto's origin	$0.55	$1.65	$2.75	£0.35	£1.05	£1.75
13-15 ND John Bolton art	$0.55	$1.65	$2.75	£0.35	£1.05	£1.75
16 ND John Bolton art	$0.45	$1.35	$2.25	£0.30	£0.90	£1.50
17 ND Wolverine cover, John Bolton art	$0.45	$1.35	$2.25	£0.30	£0.90	£1.50
18 ND John Bolton art	$0.45	$1.35	$2.25	£0.30	£0.90	£1.50
19 ND John Bolton art; Magneto's Vengeance story	$0.60	$1.80	$3.00	£0.40	£1.20	£2.00
20 ND John Bolton art	$0.45	$1.35	$2.25	£0.30	£0.90	£1.50
21-25 John Bolton art	$0.40	$1.20	$2.00	£0.25	£0.75	£1.25
26 Wolverine cover, John Bolton art; reprints X-Men #120	$0.40	$1.20	$2.00	£0.25	£0.75	£1.25
27 ND reprints #121, John Bolton art	$0.40	$1.20	$2.00	£0.25	£0.75	£1.25
28 ND John Bolton art	$0.40	$1.20	$2.00	£0.25	£0.75	£1.25
29 ND no John Bolton art in back up material	$0.40	$1.20	$2.00	£0.25	£0.75	£1.25
30-35 ND John Bolton art	$0.40	$1.20	$2.00	£0.25	£0.75	£1.25
36-38 ND	$0.40	$1.20	$2.00	£0.25	£0.75	£1.25
39 ND Jim Lee art in back up; 2nd Jim Lee work on X-Men (see X-Men #248)	$0.60	$1.80	$3.00	£0.40	£1.20	£2.00
40-42 ND	$0.40	$1.20	$2.00	£0.25	£0.75	£1.25
43 ND DS reprints X-Men #137 Death of Phoenix	$0.40	$1.20	$2.00	£0.25	£0.75	£1.25
44 ND reprints X-Men #138, new Rogue story by Nocenti and Barta (last new material in title)	$0.40	$1.20	$2.00	£0.25	£0.75	£1.25
45 ND	$0.40	$1.20	$2.00	£0.25	£0.75	£1.25
46 ND title becomes "X-Men Classic"	$0.40	$1.20	$2.00	£0.25	£0.75	£1.25
47 ND last Byrne reprint	$0.40	$1.20	$2.00	£0.25	£0.75	£1.25
48-50 ND	$0.40	$1.20	$2.00	£0.25	£0.75	£1.25
51-53 ND	$0.30	$0.90	$1.50	£0.20	£0.60	£1.00
54 ND DS	$0.30	$0.90	$1.50	£0.20	£0.60	£1.00
55-60 ND	$0.30	$0.90	$1.50	£0.20	£0.60	£1.00
61-65 ND	$0.25	$0.75	$1.25	£0.15	£0.45	£0.75
66 ND Mike Mignola cover	$0.25	$0.75	$1.25	£0.15	£0.45	£0.75
67 ND	$0.25	$0.75	$1.25	£0.15	£0.45	£0.75
68-69 ND Mike Mignola cover	$0.25	$0.75	$1.25	£0.15	£0.45	£0.75
70 ND DS, reprints X-Men #166, Mike Mignola cover	$0.25	$0.75	$1.25	£0.15	£0.45	£0.75
71-89 ND	$0.25	$0.75	$1.25	£0.15	£0.45	£0.75
90 ND 48pgs, Bart Sears cover	$0.30	$0.90	$1.50	£0.20	£0.60	£1.00
91-92 ND Bart Sears cover	$0.25	$0.75	$1.25	£0.15	£0.45	£0.75
93-100 ND	$0.25	$0.75	$1.25	£0.15	£0.45	£0.75
101-103 ND	$0.30	$0.90	$1.50	£0.20	£0.60	£1.00
104 ND 48pgs, reprints X-Men #200	$0.40	$1.20	$2.00	£0.25	£0.75	£1.25
105-108 ND	$0.30	$0.90	$1.50	£0.20	£0.60	£1.00
109 ND reprints X-Men #205 with new Jae Lee cover	$0.30	$0.90	$1.50	£0.20	£0.60	£1.00
110 ND reprints X-Men 206	$0.30	$0.90	$1.50	£0.20	£0.60	£1.00
Title Value:	$41.10	$123.30	$205.50	£26.10	£78.30	£130.50

Note: chronologically reprints new X-Men stories with new back-up material by Claremont, Nocenti & Bolton (Bolton not in issues #29, #36-39)

CLASSICS ILLUSTRATED
Berkley/First Publishing; 1 Feb 1990-27 Jun 1991

Issue	$Good	$Fine	$N.Mint	£Good	£Fine	£N.Mint
1 The Raven and Other Poems, Graham Wilson art	$0.80	$2.40	$4.00	£0.50	£1.50	£2.50
2 Great Expectations, Rick Geary art	$0.80	$2.40	$4.00	£0.50	£1.50	£2.50
3 Through The Looking Glass, Kyle Baker art	$0.80	$2.40	$4.00	£0.50	£1.50	£2.50
4 Moby Dick, Bill Sienkiewicz art	$0.90	$2.70	$4.50	£0.60	£1.80	£3.00
5 Hamlet, Tom Mandrake art	$0.80	$2.40	$4.00	£0.50	£1.50	£2.50
6 The Scarlet Letter, layouts by P. Craig Russell	$0.80	$2.40	$4.00	£0.50	£1.50	£2.50
7 The Count of Monte Cristo, Dan Spiegle art	$0.80	$2.40	$4.00	£0.50	£1.50	£2.50
8 Dr. Jekyll and Mr. Hyde, John K. Snyder III art	$0.80	$2.40	$4.00	£0.50	£1.50	£2.50
9 The Adventures of Tom Sawyer, Michael Ploog art	$0.80	$2.40	$4.00	£0.50	£1.50	£2.50
10 The Call of the Wild, Ricardo Villagran art	$0.80	$2.40	$4.00	£0.50	£1.50	£2.50
11 Rip Van Winkle, Jeffrey Busch art	$0.80	$2.40	$4.00	£0.50	£1.50	£2.50
12 The Island of Dr. Moreau, Eric Vincent art	$0.80	$2.40	$4.00	£0.50	£1.50	£2.50
13 Wuthering Heights, Rick Geary art	$0.80	$2.40	$4.00	£0.50	£1.50	£2.50
14 Fall of the House of Usher, P. Craig Russell art	$0.80	$2.40	$4.00	£0.50	£1.50	£2.50
15 The Gift of the Magi	$0.80	$2.40	$4.00	£0.50	£1.50	£2.50

	$Good	$Fine	$N.Mint	£Good	£Fine	£N.Mint

16 A Christmas Carol, Joe Staton art
| | $0.80 | $2.40 | $4.00 | £0.50 | £1.50 | £2.50 |

17 Treasure Island, Pat Boyette art
| | $0.80 | $2.40 | $4.00 | £0.50 | £1.50 | £2.50 |

18 Devil's Dictionary, Graham Wilson art
| | $0.80 | $2.40 | $4.00 | £0.50 | £1.50 | £2.50 |

19 Secret Agent, John K. Snyder III art
| | $0.80 | $2.40 | $4.00 | £0.50 | £1.50 | £2.50 |

20 Invisible Man, Rick Geary art
| | $0.80 | $2.40 | $4.00 | £0.50 | £1.50 | £2.50 |

21 Cyrano de Bergerac
| | $0.80 | $2.40 | $4.00 | £0.50 | £1.50 | £2.50 |

22 The Jungle Books
| | $0.80 | $2.40 | $4.00 | £0.50 | £1.50 | £2.50 |

23 Robinson Crusoe, Pat Boyette art
| | $0.80 | $2.40 | $4.00 | £0.50 | £1.50 | £2.50 |

24 Rime of the Ancient Mariner, Dean Motter art
| | $0.80 | $2.40 | $4.00 | £0.50 | £1.50 | £2.50 |

25 Ivanhoe
| | $0.80 | $2.40 | $4.00 | £0.50 | £1.50 | £2.50 |

26 Aesop's Fables
| | $0.80 | $2.40 | $4.00 | £0.50 | £1.50 | £2.50 |

27 The Jungle
| | $0.80 | $2.40 | $4.00 | £0.50 | £1.50 | £2.50 |

| Title Value: | $21.70 | $65.10 | $108.50 | £13.60 | £40.80 | £68.00 |

Note: all Non-Distributed on the news-stands in the U.K. Note: all 48pgs, squarebound
Note also: issues #28-35 were advertised but never appeared owing to the collapse of the project. The intended titles were: #28 Kidnapped; #29 Around the World in 80 Days; #30 The Red Badge of Courage; #31 20,000 Leagues Under the Sea; #32 Candide; #33 Hunchback of Notre Dame; #34 Last of the Mohicans; #35 The Sea Wolf. #31 and #34 were taken over by Dark Horse Comics to become Dark Horse Classics (see entry).

CLAW THE UNCONQUERED
DC Comics; 1 May/Jun 1975-9 Sep/Oct 1976; 10 Apr/May 1978-12 Aug/Sep 1978
(see Warlord)
| 1 | $0.30 | $0.90 | $1.50 | £0.20 | £0.60 | £1.00 |
| 2-9 | $0.25 | $0.75 | $1.25 | £0.15 | £0.45 | £0.75 |
10-12 Kubert cover
| | $0.25 | $0.75 | $1.25 | £0.15 | £0.45 | £0.75 |
| Title Value: | $3.05 | $9.15 | $15.25 | £1.85 | £5.55 | £9.25 |

CLINT
Eclipse; 1 Sep 1986-2 Jan 1987
(see Adolescent Radioactive Black Belt Hamsters)
1 ND Dark Knight parody - "Clint, The Hamster Triumphant"; Mike Drigenberg inks
| | $0.40 | $1.20 | $2.00 | £0.25 | £0.75 | £1.25 |
2 ND Apocalypse Now parody; Mike Drigenberg inks
| | $0.40 | $1.20 | $2.00 | £0.25 | £0.75 | £1.25 |
| Title Value: | $0.80 | $2.40 | $4.00 | £0.50 | £1.50 | £2.50 |

CLIVE BARKER'S TAPPING THE VEIN
Eclipse; 1 May 1990-5 1991
1 ND Scott Hampton, P. Craig Russell art, John Bolton cover
| | $1.50 | $4.50 | $7.50 | £1.00 | £3.00 | £5.00 |
1 2nd printing ND | $1.20 | $3.60 | $6.00 | £0.80 | £2.40 | £4.00 |
2 ND Klaus Janson, John Bolton art, Scott Hampton cover
| | $1.20 | $3.60 | $6.00 | £0.80 | £2.40 | £4.00 |
2 2nd printing ND | $1.10 | $3.30 | $5.50 | £0.75 | £2.25 | £3.75 |
3 ND Denys Cowan, Bo Hampton art, Dave McKean cover
| | $1.20 | $3.60 | $6.00 | £0.80 | £2.40 | £4.00 |
3 2nd printing ND | $1.10 | $3.30 | $5.50 | £0.75 | £2.25 | £3.75 |
4 ND Jim Pearson/Alan Okamato, Stan Woch art, die-cut outer cover
| | $1.20 | $3.60 | $6.00 | £0.80 | £2.40 | £4.00 |
4 2nd printing ND | $1.10 | $3.30 | $5.50 | £0.75 | £2.25 | £3.75 |
5 ND Tim Conrad art featured
| | $1.20 | $3.60 | $6.00 | £0.80 | £2.40 | £4.00 |
| Title Value: | $10.80 | $32.40 | $54.00 | £7.25 | £21.75 | £36.25 |

Note: adapts Books of Blood stories, all 64pgs, painted art.
Titan versions (cover dated Sep-Oct 1990) of #1-4 available at cover price.
Folio Edition 1 (May 1991), reprints #1,2
with foil-embossed painted cover by Simon Bisley
| Softcover | | | | £1.85 | £5.55 | £9.25 |
| Hardcover | | | | £4.50 | £13.50 | £22.50 |

CLOAK AND DAGGER
Marvel Comics Group; 1 Jul 1985-11 Jan 1987
(see also Marvel Fanfare, Marvel Graphic Novel, Strange Tales 2nd Series)
| 1 ND | $0.45 | $1.35 | $2.25 | £0.30 | £0.90 | £1.50 |
| 2 ND | $0.40 | $1.20 | $2.00 | £0.25 | £0.75 | £1.25 |
3 ND Spiderman appears
| | $0.40 | $1.20 | $2.00 | £0.25 | £0.75 | £1.25 |
4 ND Secret Wars II X-over
| | $0.40 | $1.20 | $2.00 | £0.25 | £0.75 | £1.25 |
| 5-7 ND | $0.40 | $1.20 | $2.00 | £0.25 | £0.75 | £1.25 |
8 ND Mike Mignola art
| | $0.40 | $1.20 | $2.00 | £0.25 | £0.75 | £1.25 |
9 ND Art Adams art
| | $0.40 | $1.20 | $2.00 | £0.25 | £0.75 | £1.25 |
| 10 ND | $0.40 | $1.20 | $2.00 | £0.25 | £0.75 | £1.25 |
11 ND DS Larry Stroman art
| | $0.45 | $1.35 | $2.25 | £0.30 | £0.90 | £1.50 |
| Title Value: | $4.50 | $13.50 | $22.50 | £2.85 | £8.55 | £14.25 |

CLOAK AND DAGGER (LIMITED SERIES)
Marvel Comics Group,MS; 1 Oct 1983-4 Jan 1984
| 1-3 ND | $0.40 | $1.20 | $2.00 | £0.25 | £0.75 | £1.25 |
4 ND scarce in the U.K.
| | $0.45 | $1.35 | $2.25 | £0.30 | £0.90 | £1.50 |

| Title Value: | $1.65 | $4.95 | $8.25 | £1.05 | £3.15 | £5.25 |

CLOAK AND DAGGER, THE MUTANT MISADVENTURES OF
Marvel Comics Group; 1 Nov 1988-19 Aug 1991
1 ND X-Factor appear
| | $0.40 | $1.20 | $2.00 | £0.25 | £0.75 | £1.25 |
| 2-3 ND | $0.40 | $1.20 | $2.00 | £0.25 | £0.75 | £1.25 |
4 ND New Mutants appear, Inferno X-over
| | $0.40 | $1.20 | $2.00 | £0.25 | £0.75 | £1.25 |
| 5-7 ND | $0.40 | $1.20 | $2.00 | £0.25 | £0.75 | £1.25 |
8 ND Acts of Vengeance tie-in
| | $0.40 | $1.20 | $2.00 | £0.25 | £0.75 | £1.25 |
9 ND DS Acts of Vengeance tie-in, Avengers appear
| | $0.40 | $1.20 | $2.00 | £0.25 | £0.75 | £1.25 |
| 10-11 ND | $0.40 | $1.20 | $2.00 | £0.25 | £0.75 | £1.25 |
12-13 ND Dr. Doom appears
14 ND new direction; Steve Gerber scripts begin
| | $0.40 | $1.20 | $2.00 | £0.25 | £0.75 | £1.25 |
| 15 ND | $0.40 | $1.20 | $2.00 | £0.25 | £0.75 | £1.25 |
16 ND Spiderman appears
| | $0.40 | $1.20 | $2.00 | £0.25 | £0.75 | £1.25 |
17-18 ND Ghost Rider/Spiderman appear
| | $0.40 | $1.20 | $2.00 | £0.25 | £0.75 | £1.25 |
19 ND "true" origin
| | $0.40 | $1.20 | $2.00 | £0.25 | £0.75 | £1.25 |
| Title Value: | $7.60 | $22.80 | $38.00 | £4.75 | £14.25 | £23.75 |
Note: bi-monthly

CLONEZONE SPECIAL
Dark Horse; 1 1989
1 ND Mike Baron script
| | $0.30 | $0.90 | $1.50 | £0.20 | £0.60 | £1.00 |
| Title Value: | $0.30 | $0.90 | $1.50 | £0.20 | £0.60 | £1.00 |

COBALT 60
Tundra; 1 1992
1 ND 48pgs, Mark Bode carries on the unfinished work of Vaughn Bode after his death in 1975
| | $0.90 | $2.70 | $4.50 | £0.60 | £1.80 | £3.00 |
| Title Value: | $0.90 | $2.70 | $4.50 | £0.60 | £1.80 | £3.00 |

COBALT BLUE
Power Comics; 1 Jan 1977
1 ND black and white
| | $0.30 | $0.90 | $1.50 | £0.20 | £0.60 | £1.00 |
| Title Value: | $0.30 | $0.90 | $1.50 | £0.20 | £0.60 | £1.00 |

COBALT BLUE (2ND SERIES)
Innovation; 1 Sep 1989-2 Oct 1989
1-2 ND Mike Gustovich script/art
| | $0.40 | $1.20 | $2.00 | £0.25 | £0.75 | £1.25 |
| Title Value: | $0.80 | $2.40 | $4.00 | £0.50 | £1.50 | £2.50 |

COBRA
Viz Communications,MS; 1 Apr 1990-12 Mar 1991
| 1-12 ND | $0.60 | $1.80 | $3.00 | £0.40 | £1.20 | £2.00 |
| Title Value: | $7.20 | $21.60 | $36.00 | £4.80 | £14.40 | £24.00 |

CODA
Coda Publishing; 1 Aug 1986-4 Mar 1987
| 1-4 ND | $0.30 | $0.90 | $1.50 | £0.20 | £0.60 | £1.00 |
| Title Value: | $1.20 | $3.60 | $6.00 | £0.80 | £2.40 | £4.00 |

CODENAME SPITFIRE
Marvel Comics Group/New Universe; 10 Jul 1987-12 Oct 1987
(formerly Spitfire and the Troubleshooters)
| 10-12 | $0.15 | $0.45 | $0.75 | £0.10 | £0.30 | £0.50 |
| Title Value: | $0.45 | $1.35 | $2.25 | £0.30 | £0.90 | £1.50 |

CODENAME: DANGER
Lodestone; 1 Aug 1985-4 1986
| 1-4 ND colour | $0.30 | $0.90 | $1.50 | £0.20 | £0.60 | £1.00 |
| Title Value: | $1.20 | $3.60 | $6.00 | £0.80 | £2.40 | £4.00 |

CODENAME: FIREARM
Malibu Ultraverse/Marvel Comics Group,MS; 0 Aug 1995-5 Oct 1995
0 ND 40pgs, Marv Wolfman and David Quinn script, Gabriel Gecko art, covers bt George Perez; bi-weekly
| | $0.60 | $1.80 | $3.00 | £0.40 | £1.20 | £2.00 |
1-5 ND 40pgs, Marv Wolfman and David Quinn script, Gabriel Gecko art, covers bt George Perez; bi-weekly
| | $0.45 | $1.35 | $2.25 | £0.30 | £0.90 | £1.50 |
| Title Value: | $2.85 | $8.55 | $14.25 | £1.90 | £5.70 | £9.50 |

CODENAME: STRYKEFORCE
Image; 0 May 1995; 1 Jan 1994-present
0 (May 1995) origin told
| | $0.45 | $1.35 | $2.25 | £0.30 | £0.90 | £1.50 |
1 Marc Silvestri script, Brandon Peterson art begins
| | $0.40 | $1.20 | $2.00 | £0.25 | £0.75 | £1.25 |
| 2-3 | $0.40 | $1.20 | $2.00 | £0.25 | £0.75 | £1.25 |
4-5 Stormwatch guest-stars
6 Stormwatch guest-stars, Kill Razor dies
	$0.40	$1.20	$2.00	£0.25	£0.75	£1.25
7-12	$0.40	$1.20	$2.00	£0.25	£0.75	£1.25
13-14	$0.45	$1.35	$2.25	£0.30	£0.90	£1.50
Title Value:	$6.15	$18.45	$30.75	£3.90	£11.70	£19.50
Note: all Non-Distributed on the news-stands in the U.K.
Codename: Strykeforce (Mar 1995)
Trade paperback reprints issues #1-4, cover by Brandon Peterson | £1.30 | £3.90 | £6.50 |

COFFIN BLOOD
Monster Comics; 1 Jul 1992
1 ND 48pgs, horror anthology
| | $0.55 | $1.65 | $2.75 | £0.35 | £1.05 | £1.75 |
| Title Value: | $0.55 | $1.65 | $2.75 | £0.35 | £1.05 | £1.75 |

	$Good	$Fine	$N.Mint	£Good	£Fine	£N.Mint

COLD BLOODED
Northstar; 1 May 1993-5 1994

	$Good	$Fine	$N.Mint	£Good	£Fine	£N.Mint
1 32pgs, centre-fold poster by Kelley Jones						
	$0.60	$1.80	$3.00	£0.40	£1.20	£2.00
1 48pgs, centre-fold poster by Jim O'Barr and embossed cover by Kelley Jones; Kyle Hotz black and white art						
	$0.90	$2.70	$4.50	£0.60	£1.80	£3.00
2 32pgs	$0.60	$1.80	$3.00	£0.40	£1.20	£2.00
2 silver foil embossed						
	$0.90	$2.70	$4.50	£0.60	£1.80	£3.00
3 32pgs	$0.60	$1.80	$3.00	£0.40	£1.20	£2.00
3 silver foil embossed						
	$0.90	$2.70	$4.50	£0.60	£1.80	£3.00
4 32pgs	$0.60	$1.80	$3.00	£0.40	£1.20	£2.00
4 silver foil embossed						
	$0.90	$2.70	$4.50	£0.60	£1.80	£3.00
5 32pgs	$0.60	$1.80	$3.00	£0.40	£1.20	£2.00
5 silver foil embossed						
	$0.90	$2.70	$4.50	£0.60	£1.80	£3.00
Title Value:	$7.50	$22.50	$37.50	£5.00	£15.00	£25.00

Note: all Non-Distributed on the news-stands in the U.K.
Cold-Blooded (Mar 1995)

Trade paperback reprints issues #1-5				£1.30	£3.90	£6.50

COLD-BLOODED CHAMELEON COMMANDOS
Blackthorne; 1 Jun 1986-6 1987

	$Good	$Fine	$N.Mint	£Good	£Fine	£N.Mint
1-6 ND	$0.30	$0.90	$1.50	£0.20	£0.60	£1.00
Title Value:	$1.80	$5.40	$9.00	£1.20	£3.60	£6.00

COLD-BLOODED: THE SLAYER
Northstar; 1 Feb 1995

	$Good	$Fine	$N.Mint	£Good	£Fine	£N.Mint
1 ND 40pgs, Vincent Proce art; black and white						
	$0.60	$1.80	$3.00	£0.40	£1.20	£2.00
1 ND Gold Signed & Numbered Edition (Feb 1995) - pre-bagged with gold foil cover; 2,500 copies						
	$1.00	$3.00	$5.00	£0.70	£2.10	£3.50
Title Value:	$1.60	$4.80	$8.00	£1.10	£3.30	£5.50

COLORS IN BLACK
Dark Horse; 1 Mar 1995-4 Jun 1995

	$Good	$Fine	$N.Mint	£Good	£Fine	£N.Mint
1-4 ND anthology in association with Spike Lee						
	$0.60	$1.80	$3.00	£0.40	£1.20	£2.00
Title Value:	$2.40	$7.20	$12.00	£1.60	£4.80	£8.00

COLOSSUS: GOD'S COUNTRY
Marvel Comics Group,OS; 1 Oct 1994

	$Good	$Fine	$N.Mint	£Good	£Fine	£N.Mint
1 ND 64pgs, squarebound, Ann Nocenti script, P. Craig Russell art						
	$1.20	$3.60	$6.00	£0.80	£2.40	£4.00
Title Value:	$1.20	$3.60	$6.00	£0.80	£2.40	£4.00

COLOUR OF MAGIC
Innovation,MS; 1 Feb 1991-4 Sep 1991

	$Good	$Fine	$N.Mint	£Good	£Fine	£N.Mint
1-4 ND adaptation of Terry Pratchett's "Discworld"						
	$0.45	$1.35	$2.25	£0.30	£0.90	£1.50
Title Value:	$1.80	$5.40	$9.00	£1.20	£3.60	£6.00

COLT SPECIAL
AC Comics; 1 1985
(see Black Diamond)

	$Good	$Fine	$N.Mint	£Good	£Fine	£N.Mint
1 ND scarce in the U.K. .52pgs						
	$0.45	$1.35	$2.25	£0.30	£0.90	£1.50
Title Value:	$0.45	$1.35	$2.25	£0.30	£0.90	£1.50

COLUMBUS
Dark Horse,OS; 1 Oct 1992

	$Good	$Fine	$N.Mint	£Good	£Fine	£N.Mint
1 ND	$0.45	$1.35	$2.25	£0.30	£0.90	£1.50
Title Value:	$0.45	$1.35	$2.25	£0.30	£0.90	£1.50

COMBAT
Image,MS; 1 Jan 1996-present

	$Good	$Fine	$N.Mint	£Good	£Fine	£N.Mint
1 ND	$0.50	$1.50	$2.50	£0.30	£0.90	£1.50
Title Value:	$0.50	$1.50	$2.50	£0.30	£0.90	£1.50

COMBAT KELLY AND THE DEADLY DOZEN
Marvel Comics Group; 1 Jun 1972-9 Oct 1973

	$Good	$Fine	$N.Mint	£Good	£Fine	£N.Mint
1 ND 1st appearance Combat Kelly						
	$0.40	$1.20	$2.00	£0.25	£0.75	£1.25
2-9 ND	$0.40	$1.20	$2.00	£0.25	£0.75	£1.25
Title Value:	$3.60	$10.80	$18.00	£2.25	£6.75	£11.25

FEATURES
All new war stories; all characters killed off in the last issue

COMET
DC Comics/Impact; 1 Jul 1991-18 Dec 1992

	$Good	$Fine	$N.Mint	£Good	£Fine	£N.Mint
1-9	$0.15	$0.45	$0.75	£0.10	£0.35	£0.60
10 continued from The Fly #8						
	$0.15	$0.45	$0.75	£0.10	£0.35	£0.60
11 previews Crusaders #1 (see Jaguar #9), includes trading cards						
	$0.15	$0.45	$0.75	£0.10	£0.35	£0.60
12-18	$0.15	$0.45	$0.75	£0.10	£0.35	£0.60
Title Value:	$2.70	$8.10	$13.50	£1.80	£6.30	£10.80

COMET ANNUAL, THE
DC Comics/Impact; 1 Jun 1992

	$Good	$Fine	$N.Mint	£Good	£Fine	£N.Mint
1 64pgs, ties into Crusaders #1 (see Jaguar #9), includes trading cards						
	$0.30	$0.90	$1.50	£0.20	£0.60	£1.00
Title Value:	$0.30	$0.90	$1.50	£0.20	£0.60	£1.00

COMET MAN, THE
Marvel Comics Group,MS; 1 Feb 1987-6 Jul 1987

	$Good	$Fine	$N.Mint	£Good	£Fine	£N.Mint
1-2 ND	$0.30	$0.90	$1.50	£0.20	£0.60	£1.00
3 ND Hulk appears	$0.30	$0.90	$1.50	£0.20	£0.60	£1.00
4-5 ND Fantastic Four appear						
	$0.30	$0.90	$1.50	£0.20	£0.60	£1.00
6 ND	$0.30	$0.90	$1.50	£0.20	£0.60	£1.00
Title Value:	$1.80	$5.40	$9.00	£1.20	£3.60	£6.00

Note: Sienkiewicz covers on all. Created and written by Billy Mumy/Miguel Ferrer

COMET, THE
Red Circle (Archie); 1 Oct 1983-2 Dec 1983
(un-finished 6 issue series)

	$Good	$Fine	$N.Mint	£Good	£Fine	£N.Mint
1-2 Carmine Infantino pencils, Alex Nino inks; limited distriburion in the U.K.						
	$0.40	$1.20	$2.00	£0.25	£0.75	£1.25
Title Value:	$0.80	$2.40	$4.00	£0.50	£1.50	£2.50

COMIC CAVALCADE
National Periodical Publications; 1 Winter 1942-63 Jun/Jul 1954

	$Good	$Fine	$N.Mint	£Good	£Fine	£N.Mint
1 scarce in the U.K. The Flash, Wonder Woman, Green Lantern (cover features) and Wildcat and Black Pirate features begin						
	$750.00	$2250.00	$6750.00	£500.00	£1500.00	£4500.00
2 Mutt & Jeff begin (replacing Black Pirate)						
	$210.00	$640.00	$1500.00	£155.00	£470.00	£1100.00
3 Hop Harrigan and Sargon the Sorcerer begin						
	$160.00	$490.00	$1150.00	£110.00	£330.00	£775.00
4	$125.00	$385.00	$900.00	£85.00	£255.00	£600.00
5 Christmas cover						
	$125.00	$385.00	$900.00	£85.00	£255.00	£600.00
6-10	$100.00	$310.00	$725.00	£67.50	£205.00	£485.00
11-12	$85.00	$255.00	$600.00	£55.00	£170.00	£400.00
13 Solomon Grundy appears; Christmas cover						
	$140.00	$425.00	$1000.00	£95.00	£285.00	£675.00
14-18	$85.00	$255.00	$600.00	£55.00	£170.00	£400.00
19 Christmas cover						
	$85.00	$255.00	$600.00	£55.00	£170.00	£400.00
20	$85.00	$255.00	$600.00	£55.00	£170.00	£400.00
21	$82.50	$245.00	$580.00	£55.00	£165.00	£385.00
22 scarce in the U.K.						
	$82.50	$245.00	$580.00	£55.00	£170.00	£400.00
23	$82.50	$245.00	$580.00	£55.00	£165.00	£385.00
24 Solomon Grundy battles Green Lantern						
	$100.00	$310.00	$725.00	£67.50	£205.00	£485.00
25 scarce in the U.K.						
	$82.50	$245.00	$580.00	£55.00	£165.00	£385.00
26-28	$62.50	$190.00	$450.00	£43.00	£125.00	£300.00
29 Flash, Wonder Woman and Green Lantern features end; an indication of the decline of the super-hero genre after the War						
	$75.00	$225.00	$525.00	£50.00	£150.00	£350.00
30 1st appearance The Fox & The Crow; title becomes "Funny Animal" orientated						
	$44.00	$130.00	$310.00	£29.00	£87.50	£205.00
31-35	$21.00	$62.50	$150.00	£14.00	£43.00	£100.00
36-49	$14.00	$43.00	$100.00	£10.00	£30.00	£70.00
50-62 scarce in the U.K.						
	$18.50	$55.00	$130.00	£12.50	£38.00	£87.50
63 rare in the U.K.	$32.00	$95.00	$225.00	£21.00	£62.50	£150.00
Title Value:	$4085.00	$12359.50	$30520.00	£2751.50	£8324.00	£20537.50

Note: in common with all Golden Age comics, these were not officially distributed on the news-stands in the U.K. but some issues may have found their way over as ballast on ships or through serving personnel/relatives during the war. **Note also:** most of these issues are at least scarce in the U.K.

COMICO BLACK BOOK
Comico; 1 1987

	$Good	$Fine	$N.Mint	£Good	£Fine	£N.Mint
1 ND 5th anniversary retrospective						
	$0.40	$1.20	$2.00	£0.25	£0.75	£1.25
Title Value:	$0.40	$1.20	$2.00	£0.25	£0.75	£1.25

COMICO CHRISTMAS SPECIAL
Comico; 1 1988

	$Good	$Fine	$N.Mint	£Good	£Fine	£N.Mint
1 ND 40pgs, Mireault, Willingham/Warner, Steve Rude/Williamson art, Dave Stevens cover						
	$0.55	$1.65	$2.75	£0.35	£1.05	£1.75
Title Value:	$0.55	$1.65	$2.75	£0.35	£1.05	£1.75

COMICO COLLECTION
Comico; nn Oct 1987
(see Grendel: Devil's Vagary)

	$Good	$Fine	$N.Mint	£Good	£Fine	£N.Mint
nn rare, Slipcase containing poster, 10 Comico back issues (contents vary) and all-new 16pg 2-colour comic (Grendel - Devil's Vagary)				£15.00	£45.00	£75.00

Note: originally available shrink-wrapped. The item would be valued at approximately 10% more if un-opened. Non-Distributed on the news-stands in the U.K.

COMICO ILLUSTRATED
Comico; 1 Jul 1992

	$Good	$Fine	$N.Mint	£Good	£Fine	£N.Mint
1 ND anthology, black and white						
	$0.40	$1.20	$2.00	£0.25	£0.75	£1.25
Title Value:	$0.40	$1.20	$2.00	£0.25	£0.75	£1.25

COMICO PRIMER
(see Primer)

COMICS' GREATEST WORLD
Dark Horse,MS; 1 Jun 1993-16 Oct 1993

	$Good	$Fine	$N.Mint	£Good	£Fine	£N.Mint
1 (Arcadia Week 1) X (see Dark Horse Comics #8); Chris Warner pencils, Frank Miller cover						
	$0.40	$1.20	$2.00	£0.25	£0.75	£1.25
1 X Silver Edition - all silver cover, available only through Diamond Distributors						
	$2.00	$6.00	$10.00	£1.00	£3.00	£5.00
1 Press Proof Edition - approx. 1,500 copies, black and white						
	$2.40	$7.00	$12.00	£1.30	£3.90	£6.50
2 (Arcadia Week 2) Pit Bulls						
	$0.30	$0.90	$1.50	£0.20	£0.60	£1.00
3 (Arcadia Week 3) Ghost; Adam Hughes pencils, Dave Dorman cover						
	$0.30	$0.90	$1.50	£0.20	£0.60	£1.00
4 (Arcadia Week 4) Monster						
	$0.30	$0.90	$1.50	£0.20	£0.60	£1.00
4 Arcadia Week 1-4 limited collected edition; silver foil logo						
	$2.00	$6.00	$10.00	£1.00	£3.00	£5.00
5 (Golden City Week 1) Rebel; Jerry Ordway cover						
	$0.30	$0.90	$1.50	£0.20	£0.60	£1.00

VERY GENERAL PERCENTAGE CONVERSION CHART WHICH MAY BE USED TO CALCULATE LOW AND INBETWEEN GRADES:

	$Good	$Fine	$N.Mint	£Good	£Fine	£N.Mint
5 Rebel Gold Edition - all gold cover, available only through Diamond Distributors						
	$2.00	$6.00	$10.00	£1.00	£3.00	£5.00
6 (Golden City Week 2) Mecha						
	$0.30	$0.90	$1.50	£0.20	£0.60	£1.00
7 (Golden City Week 3) Titan; Walt Simonson cover						
	$0.30	$0.90	$1.50	£0.20	£0.60	£1.00
8 (Golden City Week 4) Catalyst: Agents of Change; George Perez cover						
	$0.30	$0.90	$1.50	£0.20	£0.60	£1.00
8 Golden City Week 1-4 limited collected edition; gold foil logo						
	$2.00	$6.00	$10.00	£1.00	£3.00	£5.00
9 (Steel Harbor Week 1) Barb Wire; Paul Gulacy pencils and cover						
	$0.60	$1.80	$3.00	£0.40	£1.20	£2.00
9 Barb Wire Silver Edition - all silver cover, available only through Diamond Distributors						
	$2.50	$7.50	$12.50	£1.30	£3.90	£6.50
10 (Steel Harbor Week 2) The Machine; Mike Mignola cover						
	$0.30	$0.90	$1.50	£0.20	£0.60	£1.00
11 (Steel Harbor Week 3) Wolf Gang						
	$0.30	$0.90	$1.50	£0.20	£0.60	£1.00
12 (Steel Harbor Week 4) Motorhead						
	$0.30	$0.90	$1.50	£0.20	£0.60	£1.00
12 Steel Harbor Week 1-4 limited collected edition; red foil logo						
	$2.00	$6.00	$10.00	£1.00	£3.00	£5.00
13 (The Vortex Week 1) Division 13						
	$0.30	$0.90	$1.50	£0.20	£0.60	£1.00
13 Division 13 Gold Edition - all gold cover, available only through Diamond Distributors						
	$2.00	$6.00	$10.00	£1.00	£3.00	£5.00
14 (The Vortex Week 2) Hero Zero; Eric Shanower art						
	$0.30	$0.90	$1.50	£0.20	£0.60	£1.00
15 (The Vortex Week 3) King Tiger						
	$0.30	$0.90	$1.50	£0.20	£0.60	£1.00
16 (The Vortex Week 4) Vortex; Bob McLeod art						
	$0.30	$0.90	$1.50	£0.20	£0.60	£1.00
16 The Vortex Week 1-4 limited collected edition; blue foil logo						
	$2.00	$6.00	$10.00	£1.00	£3.00	£5.00
Title Value:	$24.10	$72.10	$120.50	£13.05	£39.15	£65.25

Note: a continuing story, each issue 16pgs with card-stock glossy covers
Note: all Non-Distributed on the news-stands in the U.K.

COMICS' GREATEST WORLD: WILL TO POWER
Dark Horse,MS; 1 Jun 1994-12 Aug 1994

	$Good	$Fine	$N.Mint	£Good	£Fine	£N.Mint
1-12 ND Jerry Prosser script, Mike Manley art, bart Sears covers; weekly issues						
	$0.25	$0.75	$1.25	£0.15	£0.50	£0.85
Title Value:	$3.00	$9.00	$15.00	£1.80	£6.00	£10.20

COMIX BOOK
Marvel Comics Group,Magazine; 1 Oct 1974-3 Mar 1975

	$Good	$Fine	$N.Mint	£Good	£Fine	£N.Mint
1 ND Wolverton art (1pg)						
	$1.05	$3.15	$5.25	£0.70	£2.10	£3.50
2-3 ND scarce in the U.K.						
	$0.80	$2.40	$4.00	£0.50	£1.50	£2.50
Title Value:	$2.65	$7.95	$13.25	£1.70	£5.10	£8.50

Note: Marvel's experimental underground-style comic; issues 4, 5 published by Krupp Comics Works in 1976. Stan Lee had invited Denis Kitchen to produce an underground comic that would not tarnish Marvel's clean-cut image. A short-lived but vital project.

COMIX INTERNATIONAL
Warren; 1 Jul 1974-5 Spring 1977

	$Good	$Fine	$N.Mint	£Good	£Fine	£N.Mint
1 ND rare in the U.K.						
	$3.60	$10.50	$18.00	£2.40	£7.00	£12.00
2 ND	$2.40	$7.00	$12.00	£1.60	£4.80	£8.00
3-5 ND	$1.20	$3.60	$6.00	£0.80	£2.40	£4.00
Title Value:	$9.60	$28.30	$48.00	£6.40	£19.00	£32.00

COMIX ZONE
Marvel Comics Group; 1 Jan 1996-present

	$Good	$Fine	$N.Mint	£Good	£Fine	£N.Mint
1-3 ND based on Sega video game						
	$0.50	$1.50	$2.50	£0.30	£0.90	£1.50
Title Value:	$1.50	$4.50	$7.50	£0.90	£2.70	£4.50

COMMAND REVIEW
Thoughts and Images; 1 Jul 1986-3 1987

	$Good	$Fine	$N.Mint	£Good	£Fine	£N.Mint
1 ND reprints Albedo #1-4						
	$0.60	$1.80	$3.00	£0.40	£1.20	£2.00
2 ND reprints Albedo #5-8						
	$0.60	$1.80	$3.00	£0.40	£1.20	£2.00
3 ND reprints Albedo #9-12						
	$0.60	$1.80	$3.00	£0.40	£1.20	£2.00
Title Value:	$1.80	$5.40	$9.00	£1.20	£3.60	£6.00

COMMAND REVIEW (2ND SERIES)
Antarctic Press; 4 Jan 1994

	$Good	$Fine	$N.Mint	£Good	£Fine	£N.Mint
4 ND collects Albedo #14 and Albedo Vol. 2 #1 & 2; UV-coated cover						
	$0.90	$2.70	$4.50	£0.60	£1.80	£3.00
Title Value:	$0.90	$2.70	$4.50	£0.60	£1.80	£3.00

COMPANY X
Triumphant Comics; 1 Jun 1994-5 1994

	$Good	$Fine	$N.Mint	£Good	£Fine	£N.Mint
1-2 ND John Riley script, Bill Knapp art						
	$0.45	$1.35	$2.25	£0.30	£0.90	£1.50
3 ND dual issue with Doctor Chaos #10 (Note: there is only one issue between the two titles)						
	$0.45	$1.35	$2.25	£0.30	£0.90	£1.50
4 ND dual issue with Doctor Chaos #11 (Note: there is only one issue between the two titles)						
	$0.45	$1.35	$2.25	£0.30	£0.90	£1.50
5 ND	$0.45	$1.35	$2.25	£0.30	£0.90	£1.50
Title Value:	$2.25	$6.75	$11.25	£1.50	£4.50	£7.50

CONAN
Marvel Comics Group; 1 Aug 1995-present

	$Good	$Fine	$N.Mint	£Good	£Fine	£N.Mint
1 ND Larry Hama script, Barry Crain art begins						
	$0.60	$1.80	$3.00	£0.40	£1.20	£2.00
2-3 ND	$0.60	$1.80	$3.00	£0.40	£1.20	£2.00
4 ND Conan/Rune Prologue						
	$0.60	$1.80	$3.00	£0.40	£1.20	£2.00
5-7 ND	$0.60	$1.80	$3.00	£0.40	£1.20	£2.00
8 ND Godkiller story						
	$0.60	$1.80	$3.00	£0.40	£1.20	£2.00
Title Value:	$4.80	$14.40	$24.00	£3.20	£9.60	£16.00

CONAN CLASSIC
Marvel Comics Group; 1 Jun 1994-11 Apr 1995

	$Good	$Fine	$N.Mint	£Good	£Fine	£N.Mint
1 reprints begin from Conan the Barbarian #1						
	$0.30	$0.90	$1.50	£0.20	£0.60	£1.00
2-11	$0.30	$0.90	$1.50	£0.20	£0.60	£1.00
Title Value:	$3.30	$9.90	$16.50	£2.20	£6.60	£11.00

CONAN SAGA
Marvel Comics Group,Magazine; 1 Apr 1987-98 May 1995

	$Good	$Fine	$N.Mint	£Good	£Fine	£N.Mint
1 ND reprints Conan the Barbarian #1 by Smith						
	$0.60	$1.80	$3.00	£0.40	£1.20	£2.00
2-30 ND	$0.45	$1.35	$2.25	£0.30	£0.90	£1.50
31 ND Neal Adams reprint						
	$0.45	$1.35	$2.25	£0.30	£0.90	£1.50
32-36 ND	$0.45	$1.35	$2.25	£0.30	£0.90	£1.50
37-41 ND The Amra Saga						
	$0.45	$1.35	$2.25	£0.30	£0.90	£1.50
42-49 ND	$0.45	$1.35	$2.25	£0.30	£0.90	£1.50
50 ND reprints "Queen of the Black Coast" from Conan #57/58						
	$0.45	$1.35	$2.25	£0.30	£0.90	£1.50
51-52 ND "The Ballad of Belit" reprinted						
	$0.45	$1.35	$2.25	£0.30	£0.90	£1.50
53-74 ND	$0.45	$1.35	$2.25	£0.30	£0.90	£1.50

75 ND pre-bagged with Conan Handbook Comic

Cold Blooded #1

Comet #5

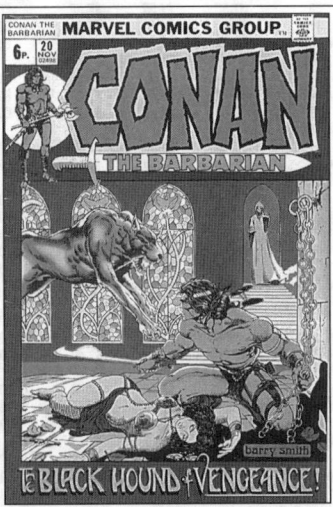
Conan the Barbarian #20

MINT = 100% / NEAR MINT (inc. +/-) = 90-99% / VERY FINE (inc. +/-) = 75-89% / FINE (inc. +/-) = 55-74%
VERY GOOD (inc. +/-) = 35-54% / GOOD (inc. +/-) = 15-34% / FAIR = 5-14% / POOR = 1-4%
271

	$Good	$Fine	$N.Mint	£Good	£Fine	£N.Mint
	$0.80	$2.40	$4.00	£0.50	£1.50	£2.50
76-98 ND	$0.45	$1.35	$2.25	£0.30	£0.90	£1.50
Title Value:	$44.60	$133.80	$223.00	£29.70	£89.10	£148.50

CONAN SPECIAL EDITION
Marvel Comics Group,OS; 1 1983

	$Good	$Fine	$N.Mint	£Good	£Fine	£N.Mint
1 ND reprints "Red Nails" by Barry Smith, in colour	$1.50	$4.50	$7.50	£1.00	£3.00	£5.00
Title Value:	$1.50	$4.50	$7.50	£1.00	£3.00	£5.00

Note: high-quality paper.

CONAN THE ADVENTURER
Marvel Comics Group; 1 Jun 1994-14 Jul 1995

	$Good	$Fine	$N.Mint	£Good	£Fine	£N.Mint
1 Roy Thomas script and Rafael Kayanan art begins; the adventures of the young Conan	$0.60	$1.80	$3.00	£0.40	£1.20	£2.00
2-14	$0.30	$0.90	$1.50	£0.20	£0.60	£1.00
Title Value:	$4.50	$13.50	$22.50	£3.00	£9.00	£15.00

CONAN THE BARBARIAN
Marvel Comics Group; 1 Oct 1970-275 Dec 1993

(see Chamber of Darkness #4, Conan Saga, Conan the Barbarian, Conan the King, Conan Universe, King Conan, Marvel Treasury Edition, Marvel Graphic Novel, Red Sonja, Savage Sword of Conan, Savage Tales)

	$Good	$Fine	$N.Mint	£Good	£Fine	£N.Mint
1 LD scarce in the U.K. origin and 1st appearance Conan by Barry Smith, King Kull appears in flashback (1st cameo appearance – see Creatures on the Loose #10)	$35.00	$105.00	$245.00	£20.00	£60.00	£140.00
2 ND	$17.00	$50.00	$102.00	£10.00	£30.00	£60.00
3 LD/scarce in the U.S. only	$17.00	$50.00	$102.00	£10.00	£30.00	£60.00
4	$10.00	$31.00	$62.50	£5.00	£15.00	£30.00
5	$10.00	$31.00	$62.50	£4.50	£13.50	£27.00
6	$7.00	$21.00	$42.00	£3.50	£10.50	£21.00
7 ND	$7.00	$21.00	$42.00	£4.00	£12.00	£24.00
8 ND scarce in the U.K.	$7.00	$21.00	$42.00	£4.50	£13.50	£27.00
9 ND	$7.00	$21.00	$42.00	£4.00	£12.00	£24.00
10 ND 52pgs, 4th appearance Kull (in back-up story)	$9.00	$28.00	$55.00	£4.50	£13.50	£27.00
11 scarce in the U.K. 52pgs, (most copies ink-stained in some way)	$9.00	$28.00	$55.00	£4.00	£12.00	£24.00
12 scarce in the U.K. part Gil Kane art	$5.00	$15.00	$30.00	£2.50	£7.50	£15.00
13 scarce in the U.K.	$5.00	$15.00	$30.00	£2.50	£7.50	£15.00
14 scarce in the U.K. 1st appearance Elric	$7.50	$22.50	$45.00	£4.00	£12.00	£24.00
15 scarce in the U.K. 2nd appearance Elric	$7.50	$22.50	$45.00	£3.75	£11.00	£22.50
16 scarce in the U.K. reprints Savage Tales #1 in colour	$4.50	$13.50	$27.00	£3.00	£9.00	£18.00
17-18 part Gil Kane art	$2.00	$6.00	$12.00	£2.00	£6.00	£12.00
19-20	$4.50	$13.50	$27.00	£1.75	£5.25	£10.50
21 scarce in the U.K. (award winner)	$5.00	$15.00	$25.00	£1.80	£5.25	£9.00
22 reprints issue #1	$5.00	$15.00	$25.00	£1.60	£4.80	£8.00
23 1st appearance Red Sonja	$7.00	$21.00	$35.00	£3.50	£10.50	£17.50
24 last Smith art, 2nd appearance Red Sonja (in a full story)	$6.00	$18.00	$30.00	£2.50	£7.50	£12.50
25 1st John Buscema art	$2.50	$7.50	$12.50	£1.50	£4.50	£7.50
26 2nd John Buscema art	$1.50	$4.50	$7.50	£1.00	£3.00	£5.00
27-30	$1.50	$4.50	$7.50	£0.70	£2.10	£3.50
31-35	$1.00	$3.00	$5.00	£0.60	£1.80	£3.00
36 ND	$1.00	$3.00	$5.00	£0.80	£2.40	£4.00
37 ND Neal Adams art	$1.50	$4.50	$7.50	£1.00	£3.00	£5.00
38-40 ND	$1.00	$3.00	$5.00	£0.80	£2.40	£4.00
41-43	$0.60	$1.80	$3.00	£0.40	£1.20	£2.00
44-45 Neal Adams inks	$0.60	$1.80	$3.00	£0.45	£1.35	£2.25
46-48	$0.60	$1.80	$3.00	£0.35	£1.05	£1.75
49 Neal Adams inks	$0.60	$1.80	$3.00	£0.40	£1.20	£2.00
50	$0.60	$1.80	$3.00	£0.35	£1.05	£1.75
51-53	$0.60	$1.80	$3.00	£0.30	£0.90	£1.50
54-56 ND	$0.60	$1.80	$3.00	£0.40	£1.20	£2.00
57	$0.60	$1.80	$3.00	£0.30	£0.90	£1.50
58 2nd appearance Belit (see Giant Size Conan #1); Note: this is her first appearance chronologically in the Conan universe	$1.00	$3.00	$5.00	£0.35	£1.05	£1.75
59 origin Belit	$0.60	$1.80	$3.00	£0.30	£0.90	£1.50
60-63	$0.60	$1.80	$3.00	£0.25	£0.75	£1.25
64 Jim Starlin art on reprint from Savage Sword of Conan	$0.60	$1.80	$3.00	£0.30	£0.90	£1.50
65-81	$0.40	$1.20	$2.00	£0.25	£0.75	£1.25
82-99 ND	$0.40	$1.20	$2.00	£0.30	£0.90	£1.50
100 52pgs, death of Belit	$1.00	$3.00	$5.00	£0.40	£1.20	£2.00
101-114 ND	$0.40	$1.20	$2.00	£0.25	£0.75	£1.25
115 ND 52pgs	$0.60	$1.80	$3.00	£0.30	£0.90	£1.50
116 ND Neal Adams inks						
117-120 ND	$0.40	$1.20	$2.00	£0.25	£0.75	£1.25
121-138	$0.40	$1.20	$2.00	£0.20	£0.60	£1.00
139-149 LD in the U.K.	$0.40	$1.20	$2.00	£0.25	£0.75	£1.25
150-162	$0.40	$1.20	$2.00	£0.20	£0.60	£1.00
163 Charles Vess inks	$0.40	$1.20	$2.00	£0.20	£0.60	£1.00
164-193	$0.40	$1.20	$2.00	£0.20	£0.60	£1.00
194 ND scarce in the U.K.	$0.40	$1.20	$2.00	£0.30	£0.90	£1.50
195-199 ND	$0.40	$1.20	$2.00	£0.25	£0.75	£1.25
200 ND 48pgs	$0.60	$1.80	$3.00	£0.40	£1.20	£2.00
201-215 ND	$0.40	$1.20	$2.00	£0.20	£0.60	£1.00
216 ND scarce in the U.K.	$0.40	$1.20	$2.00	£0.25	£0.75	£1.25
217-227 ND	$0.40	$1.20	$2.00	£0.20	£0.60	£1.00
228-231	$0.40	$1.20	$2.00	£0.15	£0.45	£0.75
232 Ron Lim art begins, new direction that explores Conan, "Conan Year 1"	$0.40	$1.20	$2.00	£0.15	£0.45	£0.75
233-236 Ron Lim art	$0.40	$1.20	$2.00	£0.15	£0.45	£0.75
237-249	$0.40	$1.20	$2.00	£0.15	£0.45	£0.75
250 DS	$0.60	$1.80	$3.00	£0.25	£0.75	£1.25
251-252	$0.40	$1.20	$2.00	£0.15	£0.45	£0.75
253 $1.25 cover begins	$0.40	$1.20	$2.00	£0.15	£0.45	£0.75
254-274	$0.40	$1.20	$2.00	£0.15	£0.45	£0.75
275 64pgs	$0.60	$1.80	$3.00	£0.25	£0.75	£1.25
Title Value:	$321.60	$966.80	$1902.50	£172.45	£516.95	£979.50

Note: 64, 78, 87 are reprint.

ARTISTS
Barry Smith in 1-16, 19-24. Ploog in 57. Wood back-up reprint in 47. Gil Kane in 17, 18, 127-134.

CONAN THE BARBARIAN ANNUAL
Marvel Comics Group; 1 Sep 1973; 2 Jun 1976-5 Dec 1979; 6 Nov 1981-12 1987

	$Good	$Fine	$N.Mint	£Good	£Fine	£N.Mint
1 ND 52pgs, all Barry Smith reprints (issues #2 and #4)	$1.40	$4.20	$7.00	£1.00	£3.00	£5.00
2 ND 52pgs	$0.80	$2.40	$4.00	£0.50	£1.50	£2.50
3 ND 52pgs, Neal Adams inks	$0.60	$1.80	$3.00	£0.50	£1.50	£2.50
4-5 ND 52pgs	$0.40	$1.20	$2.00	£0.40	£1.20	£2.00
6 ND 52pgs	$0.40	$1.20	$2.00	£0.30	£0.90	£1.50
7-12 ND 52pgs	$0.30	$0.90	$1.50	£0.20	£0.60	£1.00
Title Value:	$5.80	$17.40	$29.00	£4.30	£12.90	£21.50

CONAN THE BARBARIAN BOOK AND RECORD SET
Power Records; PR-31 1974

	$Good	$Fine	$N.Mint	£Good	£Fine	£N.Mint
PR-31 scarce, 20pg booklet with 45 rpm record				£0.80	£2.40	£4.00

Note: item would be valued 50% less without record

CONAN THE BARBARIAN GIANT SIZE
Marvel Comics Group; 1 Sep 1974-5 1975

	$Good	$Fine	$N.Mint	£Good	£Fine	£N.Mint
1 ND 68pgs, 1st appearance Belit (see Conan #58); this is her first appearance in Marvel publication terms though the story is set years after her death	$1.50	$4.50	$7.50	£1.00	£3.00	£5.00
2 ND 68pgs	$1.20	$3.60	$6.00	£0.80	£2.40	£4.00
3 ND 68pgs	$1.00	$3.00	$5.00	£0.70	£2.10	£3.50
4 ND 68pgs	$0.90	$2.70	$4.50	£0.60	£1.80	£3.00
5 ND 68pgs, Jack Kirby cover	$0.90	$2.70	$4.50	£0.60	£1.80	£3.00
Title Value:	$5.50	$16.50	$27.50	£3.70	£11.10	£18.50

CONAN THE BARBARIAN MOVIE SPECIAL
Marvel Comics Group,MS; 1 Oct 1982-2 Nov 1982

	$Good	$Fine	$N.Mint	£Good	£Fine	£N.Mint
1-2 ND	$0.30	$0.90	$1.50	£0.20	£0.60	£1.00
Title Value:	$0.60	$1.80	$3.00	£0.40	£1.20	£2.00

Note: adapts film

CONAN THE DESTROYER MOVIE SPECIAL
Marvel Comics Group,MS; 1 Jan 1985-2 Mar 1985

	$Good	$Fine	$N.Mint	£Good	£Fine	£N.Mint
1-2 ND	$0.30	$0.90	$1.50	£0.20	£0.60	£1.00
Title Value:	$0.60	$1.80	$3.00	£0.40	£1.20	£2.00

Note: adapts film, reprint from Marvel Super Special

CONAN THE KING
(see King Conan)

CONAN THE SAVAGE
Marvel Comics Group,Magazine; 1 Aug 1995-present

	$Good	$Fine	$N.Mint	£Good	£Fine	£N.Mint
1 ND Simon Bisley cover; black and white	$0.60	$1.80	$3.00	£0.40	£1.20	£2.00
2-3 ND black and white	$0.60	$1.80	$3.00	£0.40	£1.20	£2.00
4 ND Conan/Rune tie-in, set years after the Conan/Rune first encounter; black and white	$0.60	$1.80	$3.00	£0.40	£1.20	£2.00
5 ND Mike Baron script, Val Mayerik art; black and white	$0.60	$1.80	$3.00	£0.40	£1.20	£2.00
6 ND cover by Brothers Hildebrandt; black and white	$0.60	$1.80	$3.00	£0.40	£1.20	£2.00
7-8 ND black and white	$0.60	$1.80	$3.00	£0.40	£1.20	£2.00
Title Value:	$4.80	$14.40	$24.00	£3.20	£9.60	£16.00

CONAN UNIVERSE
Marvel Comics Group,OS; 1 1990

	$Good	$Fine	$N.Mint	£Good	£Fine	£N.Mint
1 ND guide to characters in Conan series; Kaluta wraparound cover	$0.45	$1.35	$2.25	£0.30	£0.90	£1.50
Title Value:	$0.45	$1.35	$2.25	£0.30	£0.90	£1.50

	$Good	$Fine	$N.Mint	£Good	£Fine	£N.Mint

CONAN, SAVAGE SWORD OF
Marvel Comics Group,Magazine; 1 Aug 1974-235 Jul 1995
1 part Neal Adams art, Barry Smith reprint, origin Blackmark by Gil Kane, Red Sonja (3rd appearance)

	$Good	$Fine	$N.Mint	£Good	£Fine	£N.Mint
1	$12.00	$36.00	$85.00	£5.50	£17.00	£40.00
2 Neal Adams inks, Chaykin art						
	$6.25	$18.50	$37.50	£3.30	£10.00	£20.00
3 Barry Smith art	$3.75	$11.00	$22.50	£2.50	£7.50	£15.00
4 Neal Adams/Gil Kane art, Corben reprints						
	$2.90	$8.75	$17.50	£1.80	£5.50	£11.00
5 Jim Starlin art	$2.05	$6.25	$12.50	£1.30	£4.00	£8.00
6 Nino art						
	$2.00	$6.00	$12.00	£1.05	£3.25	£6.50
7-10	$2.00	$6.00	$12.00	£1.05	£3.25	£6.50
11-13	$2.00	$6.00	$10.00	£1.00	£3.00	£5.00
14 Neal Adams art	$2.40	$7.00	$12.00	£1.20	£3.60	£6.00
15	$2.00	$6.00	$10.00	£0.90	£2.70	£4.50
16 Barry Smith/Tim Conrad art						
	$2.00	$6.00	$10.00	£0.90	£2.70	£4.50
17 Tim Conrad art	$2.00	$6.00	$10.00	£0.90	£2.70	£4.50
18-21	$2.00	$6.00	$10.00	£0.90	£2.70	£4.50
22-29	$1.80	$5.25	$9.00	£0.70	£2.10	£3.50
30 ND Brunner art	$1.80	$5.25	$9.00	£0.70	£2.10	£3.50
31-40 ND	$1.60	$4.80	$8.00	£0.60	£1.80	£3.00
41-59 ND	$1.40	$4.20	$7.00	£0.50	£1.50	£2.50
60 ND Neal Adams story-boards for film						
	$1.20	$3.60	$6.00	£0.50	£1.50	£2.50
61-80 ND	$1.20	$3.60	$6.00	£0.50	£1.50	£2.50
81-82 ND	$1.00	$3.00	$5.00	£0.40	£1.20	£2.00
83 ND reprints Red Sonja by Neal Adams from issue 1						
	$1.00	$3.00	$5.00	£0.40	£1.20	£2.00
84-100 ND	$1.00	$3.00	$5.00	£0.40	£1.20	£2.00
101-177 ND	$0.80	$2.40	$4.00	£0.30	£0.90	£1.50
178 ND 54pgs, story featuring dinosaurs						
	$0.45	$1.35	$2.25	£0.30	£0.90	£1.50
179-189 ND	$0.45	$1.35	$2.25	£0.30	£0.90	£1.50
190 ND Skull on the Seas part 1, classic creative team of Thomas, Buscema and DeZuniga reunited						
	$0.45	$1.35	$2.25	£0.30	£0.90	£1.50
191 ND Skull on the Seas						
	$0.45	$1.35	$2.25	£0.30	£0.90	£1.50
192-193 ND Skull on the Seas						
	$0.45	$1.35	$2.25	£0.30	£0.90	£1.50
194-195 ND	$0.45	$1.35	$2.25	£0.30	£0.90	£1.50
196 ND Valeria appears						
	$0.45	$1.35	$2.25	£0.30	£0.90	£1.50
197-201 ND	$0.45	$1.35	$2.25	£0.30	£0.90	£1.50
202-205 ND The City of Magicians story						
	$0.45	$1.35	$2.25	£0.30	£0.90	£1.50
206 ND	$0.45	$1.35	$2.25	£0.30	£0.90	£1.50
207-210 ND Conan and the Spider God						
	$0.45	$1.35	$2.25	£0.30	£0.90	£1.50
211-221 ND	$0.45	$1.35	$2.25	£0.30	£0.90	£1.50
222 ND features John Buscema's pencilled version of Conan the Barbarian #1						
	$0.45	$1.35	$2.25	£0.30	£0.90	£1.50
223-224 ND	$0.45	$1.35	$2.25	£0.30	£0.90	£1.50
225 ND John Buscema art						
	$0.45	$1.35	$2.25	£0.30	£0.90	£1.50
226 ND	$0.45	$1.35	$2.25	£0.30	£0.90	£1.50
227 ND John Buscema art						
	$0.45	$1.35	$2.25	£0.30	£0.90	£1.50
228 ND	$0.45	$1.35	$2.25	£0.30	£0.90	£1.50
229-233 ND Red Sonja and King Kull appear						
	$0.45	$1.35	$2.25	£0.30	£0.90	£1.50
234-235 ND	$0.45	$1.35	$2.25	£0.30	£0.90	£1.50
Title Value:	$251.05	$751.25	$1218.25	£110.95	£334.15	£583.00

CONAN, SAVAGE SWORD OF ANNUAL
Marvel Comics Group; 1 1975
1 ND 88pgs, squarebound, all reprint featuring Barry Smith art

	$Good	$Fine	$N.Mint	£Good	£Fine	£N.Mint
1	$1.50	$4.50	$7.50	£1.00	£3.00	£5.00
Title Value:	$1.50	$4.50	$7.50	£1.00	£3.00	£5.00

CONAN/RUNE
Marvel Comics Group/Malibu Ultraverse,OS; 1 Nov 1995
1 ND Barry Windsor-Smith cover, script and art

	$Good	$Fine	$N.Mint	£Good	£Fine	£N.Mint
1	$0.60	$1.80	$3.00	£0.40	£1.20	£2.00
Title Value:	$0.60	$1.80	$3.00	£0.40	£1.20	£2.00

CONCRETE
Dark Horse; 1 Mar 1987-10 1989
(see Dark Horse Presents)
1 ND Paul Chadwick story/art begins; black and white

	$Good	$Fine	$N.Mint	£Good	£Fine	£N.Mint
1	$3.00	$9.00	$15.00	£2.00	£6.00	£10.00
1 2nd printing ND	$0.80	$2.40	$4.00	£0.50	£1.50	£2.50
2 ND scarce in the U.K.						
	$1.80	$5.25	$9.00	£1.20	£3.60	£6.00
3 ND origin	$1.40	$4.20	$7.00	£0.90	£2.70	£4.50
4-5 ND	$1.05	$3.15	$5.25	£0.70	£2.10	£3.50
6-10 ND	$0.90	$2.70	$4.50	£0.60	£1.80	£3.00
Title Value:	$13.60	$40.65	$68.00	£9.00	£27.00	£45.00
Colour Special 1 (new story and reprint of first 2 adventures from Dark Horse Presents, all colour)				£0.70	£2.10	£3.50
Concrete: Land and Sea (1989), reprints #1,2 with new material				£0.70	£2.10	£3.50
Concrete: A New Life (1989), reprints #3,4				£0.55	£1.65	£2.75
Concrete: Earth Day Special, features a						

(right column top — Concrete continued)
	$Good	$Fine	$N.Mint	£Good	£Fine	£N.Mint
wordless S/F tale by Moebius, 4pg Charles Vess story				£0.60	£1.80	£3.00
Concrete: Odd Jobs (Jul 1990), reprints and new material, 48pgs squarebound				£0.50	£1.50	£2.50
Concrete: Complete Short Stories, reprints Dark Horse Presents material				£1.80	£5.40	£9.00
(2nd printing - Apr 1993)				£1.75	£5.25	£8.75
Hardcover (May 1991 - 2000 copies)				£5.00	£15.00	£25.00
The Complete Concrete (Aug 1994)						
Trade paperback 320pgs, reprints all 10 issues, black and white				£3.40	£10.20	£17.00

CONCRETE: ELECTICA
Dark Horse,MS; 1 Apr 1993-2 May 1993
1-2 Paul Chadwick script/art

	$Good	$Fine	$N.Mint	£Good	£Fine	£N.Mint
1-2	$0.60	$1.80	$3.00	£0.40	£1.20	£2.00
Title Value:	$1.20	$3.60	$6.00	£0.80	£2.40	£4.00

CONCRETE: FRAGILE CREATURE
Dark Horse,MS; 1 Jun 1991-4 Jun 1992
1-4 ND Paul and Elizabeth Chadwick

	$Good	$Fine	$N.Mint	£Good	£Fine	£N.Mint
1-4	$0.40	$1.20	$2.00	£0.25	£0.75	£1.25
Title Value:	$1.60	$4.80	$8.00	£1.00	£3.00	£5.00

Note: issues printed on "environmentally-friendly" recycled paper
Concrete: Fragile Creature (Jul 1994)
Trade paperback reprints mini-series plus essay by Paul Chadwick £2.00 £6.00 £10.00

CONCRETE: KILLER SMILE
Dark Horse/Legend,MS; 1 Jul 1994-4 Oct 1994
1-4 ND Paul Chadwick script, art and painted covers

	$Good	$Fine	$N.Mint	£Good	£Fine	£N.Mint
1-4	$0.60	$1.80	$3.00	£0.40	£1.20	£2.00
Title Value:	$2.40	$7.20	$12.00	£1.60	£4.80	£8.00

Concrete: Killer Smile (Sep 1995)
Trade paperback reprints mini-series with new Paul Chadwick cover £2.30 £6.90 £11.50

CONDOM-MAN
Aaaahh!! Comics; 1 Jun 1994; 2 Jul 1995-present
1 ND 20pgs, signed by the creator (Chris Swafford); black and white

	$Good	$Fine	$N.Mint	£Good	£Fine	£N.Mint
1	$0.70	$2.10	$3.50	£0.50	£1.50	£2.50
2-5 ND 24pgs, black and white						
	$0.70	$2.10	$3.50	£0.50	£1.50	£2.50
Title Value:	$3.50	$10.50	$17.50	£2.50	£7.50	£12.50

CONDORMAN
Whitman; 1 Oct 1981-3 Jan 1982
1-2 scarce in the U.K. adaptation of Walt Disney film with Michael Crawford; photo cover

	$Good	$Fine	$N.Mint	£Good	£Fine	£N.Mint
1-2	$0.45	$1.35	$2.25	£0.40	£1.20	£2.00
3 new story; photo cover						
	$0.45	$1.35	$2.25	£0.30	£0.90	£1.50
Title Value:	$1.35	$4.05	$6.75	£1.10	£3.30	£5.50

Note: limited distribution on the news-stands in the U.K.

CONEHEADS
Marvel Comics Group,MS; 1 Jun 1994-4 Sep 1994
1-4 ND based on cult film and "Saturday Night Live" TV sketch

	$Good	$Fine	$N.Mint	£Good	£Fine	£N.Mint
1-4	$0.30	$0.90	$1.50	£0.20	£0.60	£1.00
Title Value:	$1.20	$3.60	$6.00	£0.80	£2.40	£4.00

CONFESSIONS OF THE LOVELORN
ACG; 109 Nov 1959-114 Jun/Jul 1960
(previous issues ND)
109-114 distributed in the U.K.

	$Good	$Fine	$N.Mint	£Good	£Fine	£N.Mint
109-114	$1.50	$4.50	$9.00	£1.00	£3.00	£6.00
Title Value:	$9.00	$27.00	$54.00	£6.00	£18.00	£36.00

CONGO BILL
National Periodical Publications; 1 Aug/Sep 1954-7 Aug/Sep 1955
1 very rare in the U.K.

	$Good	$Fine	$N.Mint	£Good	£Fine	£N.Mint
1	$70.00	$210.00	$500.00	£45.00	£135.00	£315.00
2 very rare in the U.K.						
	$60.00	$180.00	$425.00	£39.00	£115.00	£275.00
3-7 very rare in the U.K.						
	$52.50	$160.00	$375.00	£34.00	£100.00	£240.00
Title Value:	$392.50	$1190.00	$2850.00	£254.00	£750.00	£1790.00

CONGORILLA
DC Comics,MS; 1 Nov 1992-4 Feb 1993
1 Brian Bolland cover

	$Good	$Fine	$N.Mint	£Good	£Fine	£N.Mint
1	$0.25	$0.75	$1.25	£0.15	£0.45	£0.75
2-4	$0.25	$0.75	$1.25	£0.15	£0.45	£0.75
Title Value:	$1.00	$3.00	$5.00	£0.60	£1.80	£3.00

CONQUEROR OF THE BARREN EARTH
DC Comics,MS; 1 Feb 1985-4 May 1985
(see Warlord)
1-4 Ron Randall art

	$Good	$Fine	$N.Mint	£Good	£Fine	£N.Mint
1-4	$0.15	$0.45	$0.75	£0.10	£0.35	£0.60
Title Value:	$0.60	$1.80	$3.00	£0.40	£1.40	£2.40

CONSTRUCT
Mirage Studios,MS; 1 Mar 1995-6 Aug 1995
1-6 ND Paul Jenkins script, Leo Duranona art

	$Good	$Fine	$N.Mint	£Good	£Fine	£N.Mint
1-6	$0.55	$1.65	$2.75	£0.35	£1.05	£1.75
Title Value:	$3.30	$9.90	$16.50	£2.10	£6.30	£10.50

CONTEMPORARY BIO-GRAPHICS
Revolutionary Comics; 1 Dec 1991
1 ND Stan Lee

	$Good	$Fine	$N.Mint	£Good	£Fine	£N.Mint
1	$0.45	$1.35	$2.25	£0.30	£0.90	£1.50
Title Value:	$0.45	$1.35	$2.25	£0.30	£0.90	£1.50

CONTINUUM
Continuum Comics; 1 Oct 1988
1 ND 1st appearance The Dark and 1st appearance of Dawn in ad for Cry For Dawn #1; 4pgs Linsner script/art (1st?)

	$Good	$Fine	$N.Mint	£Good	£Fine	£N.Mint
1	$12.00	$36.00	$60.00	£6.00	£18.00	£30.00
Title Value:	$12.00	$36.00	$60.00	£6.00	£18.00	£30.00

	$Good	$Fine	$N.Mint	£Good	£Fine	£N.Mint

CONTRACTORS
Eclipse; 1 Jun 1987
1 ND Ken Macklin script and art; black and white

	$Good	$Fine	$N.Mint	£Good	£Fine	£N.Mint
	$0.45	$1.35	$2.25	£0.30	£0.90	£1.50
Title Value:	$0.45	$1.35	$2.25	£0.30	£0.90	£1.50

CONVOCATIONS - A MAGIC: THE GATHERING GALLERY
Acclaim Comics/Armada,OS; 1 Jan 1996
1 ND pin-ups by Charles Vess, Mike Kaluta, Alex Maleev and others

	$Good	$Fine	$N.Mint	£Good	£Fine	£N.Mint
	$0.50	$1.50	$2.50	£0.30	£0.90	£1.50
Title Value:	$0.50	$1.50	$2.50	£0.30	£0.90	£1.50

COOL WORLD
DC Comics,MS; 1 May 1992-4 Jul 1992
1-2 ND based on animated film, bi-weekly

	$Good	$Fine	$N.Mint	£Good	£Fine	£N.Mint
	$0.25	$0.75	$1.25	£0.15	£0.45	£0.75

3-4 ND based on animated film

	$Good	$Fine	$N.Mint	£Good	£Fine	£N.Mint
	$0.25	$0.75	$1.25	£0.15	£0.45	£0.75
Title Value:	$1.00	$3.00	$5.00	£0.60	£1.80	£3.00

COOL WORLD MOVIE ADAPTATION
DC Comics,OS; 1 Aug 1992
1 ND 64pgs, adapts animated film

	$Good	$Fine	$N.Mint	£Good	£Fine	£N.Mint
	$0.45	$1.35	$2.25	£0.30	£0.90	£1.50
Title Value:	$0.45	$1.35	$2.25	£0.30	£0.90	£1.50

COPS
DC Comics,MS Toy; 1 Aug 1988-15 Oct 1989

	$Good	$Fine	$N.Mint	£Good	£Fine	£N.Mint
1 DS LD	$0.15	$0.45	$0.75	£0.10	£0.30	£0.50
2-15 ND	$0.15	$0.45	$0.75	£0.10	£0.30	£0.50
Title Value:	$2.25	$6.75	$11.25	£1.50	£4.50	£7.50

COPS: THE JOB
Marvel Comics Group,MS; 1 Jun 1992-4 Sep 1992
1-4 Michael Golden covers

	$Good	$Fine	$N.Mint	£Good	£Fine	£N.Mint
	$0.15	$0.45	$0.75	£0.10	£0.35	£0.60
Title Value:	$0.60	$1.80	$3.00	£0.40	£1.40	£2.40

CORBEN SPECIAL
Pacific,OS; 1 May 1984
1 ND House of Usher, Richard Corben art

	$Good	$Fine	$N.Mint	£Good	£Fine	£N.Mint
	$0.45	$1.35	$2.25	£0.30	£0.90	£1.50
Title Value:	$0.45	$1.35	$2.25	£0.30	£0.90	£1.50

CORBO
Sword in Stone; 1 Feb 1987
1 ND Mike Kaluta cover

	$Good	$Fine	$N.Mint	£Good	£Fine	£N.Mint
	$0.25	$0.75	$1.25	£0.15	£0.45	£0.75
Title Value:	$0.25	$0.75	$1.25	£0.15	£0.45	£0.75

CORMAC MAC ART
Dark Horse,MS; 1 Mar 1990-4 Jun 1990

	$Good	$Fine	$N.Mint	£Good	£Fine	£N.Mint
1-3 ND	$0.40	$1.20	$2.00	£0.25	£0.75	£1.25

4 ND John Bolton cover

	$Good	$Fine	$N.Mint	£Good	£Fine	£N.Mint
	$0.40	$1.20	$2.00	£0.25	£0.75	£1.25
Title Value:	$1.60	$4.80	$8.00	£1.00	£3.00	£5.00

CORUM: THE BULL AND THE SPEAR
First,MS; 1 Jan 1989-4 Jul 1989
(see Chronicles of Corum)
1-4 ND Jill Thompson art begins; Mike Mignola cover

	$Good	$Fine	$N.Mint	£Good	£Fine	£N.Mint
	$0.40	$1.20	$2.00	£0.25	£0.75	£1.25
Title Value:	$1.60	$4.80	$8.00	£1.00	£3.00	£5.00

COSMIC BOOK
Ace; 1 1987
1 ND 40pgs, Alex Toth, Wally Wood art

	$Good	$Fine	$N.Mint	£Good	£Fine	£N.Mint
	$0.30	$0.90	$1.50	£0.20	£0.60	£1.00
Title Value:	$0.30	$0.90	$1.50	£0.20	£0.60	£1.00

COSMIC BOY
DC Comics,MS; 1 Dec 1986-4 Mar 1987
(see Adventure Comics, Legion of Super-Heroes)
1-4 Legends tie-in, Giffen art

	$Good	$Fine	$N.Mint	£Good	£Fine	£N.Mint
	$0.25	$0.75	$1.25	£0.15	£0.45	£0.75
Title Value:	$1.00	$3.00	$5.00	£0.60	£1.80	£3.00

COSMIC HEROES
Eternity; 1 Oct 1988-11 Dec 1989
1 ND 48pgs, squarebound begins; 1930s Buck Rogers reprints by Phil Nowlan/Dick Calkins; all black and white

	$Good	$Fine	$N.Mint	£Good	£Fine	£N.Mint
	$0.40	$1.20	$2.00	£0.25	£0.75	£1.25

2-6 ND Buck Rogers

	$Good	$Fine	$N.Mint	£Good	£Fine	£N.Mint
	$0.40	$1.20	$2.00	£0.25	£0.75	£1.25
7-11 ND	$0.40	$1.20	$2.00	£0.25	£0.75	£1.25
Title Value:	$4.40	$13.20	$22.00	£2.75	£8.25	£13.75

COSMIC ODYSSEY
DC Comics,MS; 1 Dec 1988-4 Mar 1989
1 ND 48pgs, features New Gods, Superman, Batman, Starfire, Martian Manhunter, Green Lantern (John Stewart)

	$Good	$Fine	$N.Mint	£Good	£Fine	£N.Mint
	$0.80	$2.40	$4.00	£0.55	£1.65	£2.75
2-4 ND 48pgs	$0.80	$2.40	$4.00	£0.55	£1.65	£2.75
Title Value:	$3.20	$9.60	$16.00	£2.20	£6.60	£11.00

Note: all Prestige Format, squarebound
Trade paperback (Aug 1992),
reprints issues #1-4, painted cover by Mike Mignola £2.50 £7.50 £12.50

COSMIC POWERS
Marvel Comics Group,MS; 1 Mar 1994-6 Aug 1994
1 ND 48pgs, Thanos appears; Ron Lim art

	$Good	$Fine	$N.Mint	£Good	£Fine	£N.Mint
	$0.45	$1.35	$2.25	£0.30	£0.90	£1.50

2 ND 48pgs, Thanos and Terrax appear; Moore art

	$Good	$Fine	$N.Mint	£Good	£Fine	£N.Mint
	$0.45	$1.35	$2.25	£0.30	£0.90	£1.50

3 ND 48pgs, Thanos and Terrax with Jack of Hearts and Ganymede; Ron Lim cover

	$Good	$Fine	$N.Mint	£Good	£Fine	£N.Mint
	$0.45	$1.35	$2.25	£0.30	£0.90	£1.50

4 ND 48pgs, Legacy appears

	$Good	$Fine	$N.Mint	£Good	£Fine	£N.Mint
	$0.45	$1.35	$2.25	£0.30	£0.90	£1.50

5 ND 48pgs, Thanos appears

	$Good	$Fine	$N.Mint	£Good	£Fine	£N.Mint
	$0.45	$1.35	$2.25	£0.30	£0.90	£1.50

6 ND 48pgs, Thanos, Galactus and Terrax appear

	$Good	$Fine	$N.Mint	£Good	£Fine	£N.Mint
	$0.45	$1.35	$2.25	£0.30	£0.90	£1.50
Title Value:	$2.70	$8.10	$13.50	£1.80	£5.40	£9.00

COSMIC POWERS UNLIMITED
Marvel Comics Group; 1 May 1995-present
1 ND 64pgs, Silver Surfer vs. Thanos, Death and Captain Marvel back-up

	$Good	$Fine	$N.Mint	£Good	£Fine	£N.Mint
	$0.80	$2.40	$4.00	£0.50	£1.50	£2.50

2 ND 64pgs, Silver Surfer vs. Cosmic Enclave, Jack of Hearts back-up

	$Good	$Fine	$N.Mint	£Good	£Fine	£N.Mint
	$0.80	$2.40	$4.00	£0.50	£1.50	£2.50

3 ND 64pgs, Silver Surfer and Jack of Hearts

	$Good	$Fine	$N.Mint	£Good	£Fine	£N.Mint
	$0.80	$2.40	$4.00	£0.50	£1.50	£2.50

4 ND continued from Star Masters #3

	$Good	$Fine	$N.Mint	£Good	£Fine	£N.Mint
	$0.80	$2.40	$4.00	£0.50	£1.50	£2.50
Title Value:	$3.20	$9.60	$16.00	£2.00	£6.00	£10.00

Note: quarterly frequency

COTTON CANDY AUTOPSY, A
DC Comics/Piranha Press; nn 1991
nn ND Trade paperback, reprints Beautiful Stories for Ugly Children #1,13 plus new Sweetman/Louapre story

	$Good	$Fine	$N.Mint	£Good	£Fine	£N.Mint
	$2.40	$7.00	$12.00	£1.60	£4.80	£8.00
Title Value:	$2.40	$7.00	$12.00	£1.60	£4.80	£8.00

COUGAR, THE
Atlas; 1 Apr 1975-2 Jun 1975
1-2 Frank Springer art; distributed in the U.K.

	$Good	$Fine	$N.Mint	£Good	£Fine	£N.Mint
	$0.25	$0.75	$1.25	£0.15	£0.45	£0.75
Title Value:	$0.50	$1.50	$2.50	£0.30	£0.90	£1.50

COUNT DUCKULA
Marvel Comics Group; 1 Feb 1989-15 Jan 1991

	$Good	$Fine	$N.Mint	£Good	£Fine	£N.Mint
1-15 ND	$0.15	$0.45	$0.75	£0.10	£0.35	£0.60
Title Value:	$2.25	$6.75	$11.25	£1.50	£5.25	£9.00

COUTOO
Dark Horse,OS; 1 Apr 1994
1 ND French strip collected from reprints in Cheval Noir

	$Good	$Fine	$N.Mint	£Good	£Fine	£N.Mint
	$0.70	$2.10	$3.50	£0.45	£1.35	£2.25
Title Value:	$0.70	$2.10	$3.50	£0.45	£1.35	£2.25

COWABUNGA COMICS
Mirage Studios,OS; nn Mar 1991
nn ND 16pgs, features pin-ups and unpublished art of the Turtles by Eastman and Laird and others; card stock covers and painted cover

	$Good	$Fine	$N.Mint	£Good	£Fine	£N.Mint
	$0.45	$1.35	$2.25	£0.30	£0.90	£1.50
Title Value:	$0.45	$1.35	$2.25	£0.30	£0.90	£1.50

COYOTE
Marvel Comics Group/Epic; 1 Jun 1983-16 Mar 1986
1 ND origin

	$Good	$Fine	$N.Mint	£Good	£Fine	£N.Mint
	$0.30	$0.90	$1.50	£0.20	£0.60	£1.00

2 ND origin concludes

	$Good	$Fine	$N.Mint	£Good	£Fine	£N.Mint
	$0.30	$0.90	$1.50	£0.20	£0.60	£1.00
3-10 ND	$0.30	$0.90	$1.50	£0.20	£0.60	£1.00

11 ND McFarlane art back up (Slash) - his first professional work

	$Good	$Fine	$N.Mint	£Good	£Fine	£N.Mint
	$0.45	$1.35	$2.25	£0.30	£0.90	£1.50

12-13 ND McFarlane art back up

	$Good	$Fine	$N.Mint	£Good	£Fine	£N.Mint
	$0.45	$1.35	$2.25	£0.30	£0.90	£1.50

14 ND Badger X-over, McFarlane art back up

	$Good	$Fine	$N.Mint	£Good	£Fine	£N.Mint
	$0.45	$1.35	$2.25	£0.30	£0.90	£1.50
15-16 ND	$0.30	$0.90	$1.50	£0.20	£0.60	£1.00
Title Value:	$5.40	$16.20	$27.00	£3.60	£10.80	£18.00

Note: all Baxter paper.

CRASH RYAN
Marvel Comics Group/Epic,MS; 1 Oct 1984-4 Jan 1985

	$Good	$Fine	$N.Mint	£Good	£Fine	£N.Mint
1-4 ND	$0.25	$0.75	$1.25	£0.15	£0.45	£0.75
Title Value:	$1.00	$3.00	$5.00	£0.60	£1.80	£3.00

Note: all the above on Baxter paper

CRAZY
Marvel Comics Group; 1 Feb 1973-3 Jun 1973
1 ND features X-Men, Avengers, Spiderman parodies

	$Good	$Fine	$N.Mint	£Good	£Fine	£N.Mint
	$0.30	$0.90	$1.50	£0.40	£1.20	£2.00

2 ND Fantastic Four and Spiderman romance issue parodies

	$Good	$Fine	$N.Mint	£Good	£Fine	£N.Mint
	$0.30	$0.90	$1.50	£0.40	£1.20	£2.00

3 ND Fantastic Four and Superman origin parodies

	$Good	$Fine	$N.Mint	£Good	£Fine	£N.Mint
	$0.30	$0.90	$1.50	£0.40	£1.20	£2.00
Title Value:	$0.90	$2.70	$4.50	£1.20	£3.60	£6.00

Note: all reprints from Not Brand Echh.
ARTISTS
Eisner in 9-16. Ploog in 1, 4, 7.

CRAZY (2ND SERIES)
Marvel Comics Group,Magazine; 1 Oct 1973-94 Mar 1983

	$Good	$Fine	$N.Mint	£Good	£Fine	£N.Mint
1 ND	$0.50	$1.50	$2.50	£0.40	£1.20	£2.00

2 ND Neal Adams art

	$Good	$Fine	$N.Mint	£Good	£Fine	£N.Mint
	$0.50	$1.50	$2.50	£0.40	£1.20	£2.00
3-10 ND	$0.40	$1.20	$2.00	£0.25	£0.75	£1.25

11-21 ND scarce in the U.K.

	$Good	$Fine	$N.Mint	£Good	£Fine	£N.Mint
	$0.55	$1.65	$2.75	£0.35	£1.05	£1.75
22-81 ND	$0.40	$1.20	$2.00	£0.25	£0.75	£1.25
82 ND Rogers art	$0.55	$1.65	$2.75	£0.35	£1.05	£1.75
83-87 ND	$0.40	$1.20	$2.00	£0.25	£0.75	£1.25

88 ND contains re-lettered version of Death of Phoenix from Uncanny X-Men #137, Byrne art

	$Good	$Fine	$N.Mint	£Good	£Fine	£N.Mint
	$0.40	$1.20	$2.00	£0.25	£0.75	£1.25
89-94 ND	$0.40	$1.20	$2.00	£0.25	£0.75	£1.25
Title Value:	$39.60	$118.80	$198.00	£25.00	£75.00	£125.00

CRAZY SUMMER SPECIAL
Marvel Comics Group,Magazine; 1 Summer 1975

	$Good	$Fine	$N.Mint	£Good	£Fine	£N.Mint
1 ND 100pgs, Neal Adams reprint	$0.60	$1.80	$3.00	£0.40	£1.20	£2.00
Title Value:	$0.60	$1.80	$3.00	£0.40	£1.20	£2.00

CRAZYMAN
Continuity; 1 Nov 1991-2 1992

	$Good	$Fine	$N.Mint	£Good	£Fine	£N.Mint
1 ND	$0.40	$1.20	$2.00	£0.25	£0.75	£1.25
2 ND Neal Adams pencils and Brian Bolland inks on cover	$0.40	$1.20	$2.00	£0.25	£0.75	£1.25
Title Value:	$0.80	$2.40	$4.00	£0.50	£1.50	£2.50

CRAZYMAN (2ND SERIES)
Continuity; 1 May 1993-7 1994

	$Good	$Fine	$N.Mint	£Good	£Fine	£N.Mint
1-3 ND	$0.35	$1.05	$1.75	£0.25	£0.75	£1.25
4 ND parchment embossed cover	$0.35	$1.05	$1.75	£0.25	£0.75	£1.25
5-7 ND	$0.35	$1.05	$1.75	£0.25	£0.75	£1.25
Title Value:	$2.45	$7.35	$12.25	£1.75	£5.25	£8.75

CREATURES GIANT SIZE
Marvel Comics Group; 1 Jul 1974
(becomes Werewolf Giant Size)

	$Good	$Fine	$N.Mint	£Good	£Fine	£N.Mint
1 ND 52pgs, Werewolf, Tigra appear; secret origin of Tigra	$1.50	$4.50	$7.50	£1.00	£3.00	£5.00
Title Value:	$1.50	$4.50	$7.50	£1.00	£3.00	£5.00

CREATURES OF THE ID
Caliber Press,OS; 1 1990

	$Good	$Fine	$N.Mint	£Good	£Fine	£N.Mint
1 ND features Bernie Mireault art; black and white	$0.40	$1.20	$2.00	£0.25	£0.75	£1.25
Title Value:	$0.40	$1.20	$2.00	£0.25	£0.75	£1.25

CREATURES ON THE LOOSE
Marvel Comics Group; 10 Mar 1971-37 Sep 1975
(formerly Tower of Shadows)

	$Good	$Fine	$N.Mint	£Good	£Fine	£N.Mint
10 scarce in the U.K. 1st appearance King Kull, Wrightson art	$4.50	$13.50	$27.00	£2.50	£7.50	£15.00
11	$0.55	$1.65	$2.75	£0.35	£1.05	£1.75
12 ND Wrightson cover	$0.55	$1.65	$2.75	£0.35	£1.05	£1.75
13-15 ND	$0.55	$1.65	$2.75	£0.35	£1.05	£1.75
16 ND 1st appearance Gullivar Jones, Warrior of Mars, Gil Kane art	$0.80	$2.40	$4.00	£0.50	£1.50	£2.50
17-19 ND Gullivar Jones	$0.45	$1.35	$2.25	£0.30	£0.90	£1.50
20 ND Gullivar Jones, Gray Morrow art	$0.45	$1.35	$2.25	£0.30	£0.90	£1.50
21 ND Gullivar Jones, Gray Morrow art	$0.40	$1.20	$2.00	£0.25	£0.75	£1.25
22 ND 1st appearance Thongor (Conanesque character), Steranko cover	$0.40	$1.20	$2.00	£0.25	£0.75	£1.25
23-29 ND Thongor appears	$0.40	$1.20	$2.00	£0.25	£0.75	£1.25
30 ND 1st of Man-Wolf series	$0.45	$1.35	$2.25	£0.30	£0.90	£1.50
31 LD in the U.K. Man-Wolf	$0.45	$1.35	$2.25	£0.30	£0.90	£1.50
32 Man-Wolf	$0.40	$1.20	$2.00	£0.25	£0.75	£1.25
33 George Perez' 1st full professional artwork in comics (see Astonishing Tales #25), Man-Wolf	$0.45	$1.35	$2.25	£0.30	£0.90	£1.50
34-37 Man-Wolf, George Perez art	$0.40	$1.20	$2.00	£0.25	£0.75	£1.25
Title Value:	$16.80	$50.40	$88.50	£10.35	£31.05	£54.25

ARTISTS
Morrow in 20, 21. Perez in 33-37. Steranko covers 20-22.

FEATURES
King Kull in 10. 50s/60s fantasy reprints in 10-15. Gullivar Jones in 16-21. Thongor in 22-29. Man-Wolf in 30-37.

CREED
Hall of Heroes; 1 Dec 1994-2 Jan 1995

	$Good	$Fine	$N.Mint	£Good	£Fine	£N.Mint
1 ND scarce in the U.K, scarce in the U.S. 7000 print run	$7.00	$21.00	$35.00	£8.00	£24.00	£40.00
2 ND scarce in the U.K, scarce in the U.S. 3500 print run	$7.00	$21.00	$35.00	£8.00	£24.00	£40.00
Title Value:	$14.00	$42.00	$70.00	£16.00	£48.00	£80.00

CREED (2ND SERIES)
Lightning Comics; 1 Jul 1995

	$Good	$Fine	$N.Mint	£Good	£Fine	£N.Mint
1 ND 48pgs, Trent Kaniuga script; reprints 2 issue Hall of Heroes comics, black and white	$1.50	$4.50	$7.50	£1.50	£4.50	£7.50
1 Gold Edition, ND 48pgs, Trent Kaniuga script	$5.00	$15.00	$25.00	£3.00	£9.00	£15.00
Title Value:	$6.50	$19.50	$32.50	£4.50	£13.50	£22.50

CREED (3RD SERIES)
Lightning Comics; 1 Sep 1995-present

	$Good	$Fine	$N.Mint	£Good	£Fine	£N.Mint
1 ND Trent Kaniuga script, Steven Zyskowski art	$0.80	$2.40	$4.00	£0.70	£2.10	£3.50
1 ND variant cover edition; Creed swinging from a branch	$1.50	$4.50	$7.50	£1.00	£3.00	£5.00
1 ND Commemorative Edition (Sep 1995) - pre-bagged with signed certificate, metallic ink cover: limited to 3000 copies	$2.40	$7.20	$12.00	£2.00	£6.00	£10.00
1 ND Variant cover, Signed, Numbered Edition (Oct 1995) - pre-bagged with certificate; 1,500 copies	$2.40	$7.20	$12.00	£2.00	£6.00	£10.00
Title Value:	$7.10	$21.30	$35.50	£5.70	£17.10	£28.50

CREEPER, BEWARE THE
National Periodical Publications; 1 May/Jun 1968-6 Mar/Apr 1969
(see Brave and the Bold, First Issue Special, Showcase #73, Super-Team Family, World's Finest)

	$Good	$Fine	$N.Mint	£Good	£Fine	£N.Mint
1 Steve Ditko art	$8.50	$26.00	$60.00	£5.00	£15.00	£35.00
2-5 Steve Ditko art	$5.00	$15.00	$30.00	£2.80	£8.50	£17.00
6 part Steve Ditko art	$5.00	$15.00	$30.00	£2.80	£8.50	£17.00
Title Value:	$33.50	$101.00	$210.00	£19.00	£57.50	£120.00

CREEPSVILLE
Go-Go Comics,OS; 1 1991

	$Good	$Fine	$N.Mint	£Good	£Fine	£N.Mint
1 ND black and white humour anthology, bound-in set of 6 trading cards	$0.60	$1.80	$3.00	£0.40	£1.20	£2.00
Title Value:	$0.60	$1.80	$3.00	£0.40	£1.20	£2.00

CREEPY
Warren; 1 no date (1964)-146 1985

	$Good	$Fine	$N.Mint	£Good	£Fine	£N.Mint
1 distributed in the U.K.	$12.00	$36.00	$85.00	£5.50	£17.00	£40.00
2 distributed in the U.K.	$7.50	$22.50	$45.00	£3.30	£10.00	£20.00
3 distributed in the U.K.	$5.00	$15.00	$30.00	£2.50	£7.50	£15.00
4-8 distributed in the U.K.	$3.30	$10.00	$20.00	£1.50	£4.50	£9.00
9 Wrightson's first published work (one panel), distributed	$3.30	$10.00	$20.00	£1.65	£5.00	£10.00
10-13 distributed in the U.K.	$2.50	$7.50	$15.00	£1.25	£3.75	£7.50
14 distributed in the U.K.	$4.15	$12.50	$25.00	£1.50	£4.50	£9.00
15-50 distributed in the U.K.	$1.65	$5.00	$10.00	£0.80	£2.50	£5.00

Concrete #1

Crazy #1

Creatures on the Loose #16

	$Good	$Fine	$N.Mint	£Good	£Fine	£N.Mint
51-61	$1.00	$3.00	$6.00	£0.65	£2.00	£4.00
62-63 Wrightson art						
	$1.00	$3.00	$6.00	£0.65	£2.00	£4.00
64-70	$1.00	$3.00	$6.00	£0.65	£2.00	£4.00
71-100 distributed in the U.K.						
	$1.00	$3.00	$5.00	£0.60	£1.80	£3.00
101-112	$1.00	$3.00	$5.00	£0.50	£1.50	£2.50
113 Bernie Wrightson art						
	$1.50	$4.50	$7.50	£0.60	£1.80	£3.00
114-146	$1.00	$3.00	$5.00	£0.50	£1.50	£2.50
Title Value:	$214.35	$645.50	$1165.00	£109.85	£334.80	£634.50

CREEPY (2ND SERIES)
Harris Publications/Dark Horse,MS; 1 May 1992-4 Aug 1992
1-4 ND 48pgs, squarebound, all new anthology begins, Peter David scripts featured

	$0.80	$2.40	$4.00	£0.50	£1.50	£2.50
Title Value:	$3.20	$9.60	$16.00	£2.00	£6.00	£10.00

CREEPY ANNUAL
Warren; 1 1968-4 1971
1968 reprints; distributed in the U.K.

	$1.65	$5.00	$10.00	£1.00	£3.00	£6.00

1969-1971 Neal Adams reprints; distributed in the U.K.

	$1.65	$5.00	$10.00	£1.00	£3.00	£6.00
Title Value:	$6.60	$20.00	$40.00	£4.00	£12.00	£24.00

CREEPY FEARBOOK
Harris Comics,OS; 1 Feb 1993
1 ND 44pgs, Dan Brereton "Vampirella" cover; Peter David and Art Adams work featured

	$0.80	$2.40	$4.00	£0.50	£1.50	£2.50
Title Value:	$0.80	$2.40	$4.00	£0.50	£1.50	£2.50

CREEPY THINGS
Charlton; 1 Jul 1975-6 Jun 1976
1 distributed in the U.K. painted cover

	$0.30	$0.90	$1.50	£0.20	£0.60	£1.00

2 distributed in the U.K.

	$0.30	$0.90	$1.50	£0.20	£0.60	£1.00

3 Steve Ditko art; distributed in the U.K.

	$0.30	$0.90	$1.50	£0.20	£0.60	£1.00

4 distributed in the U.K.

	$0.30	$0.90	$1.50	£0.20	£0.60	£1.00

5 Steve Ditko art; distributed in the U.K.

	$0.30	$0.90	$1.50	£0.20	£0.60	£1.00

6 distributed in the U.K.

	$0.30	$0.90	$1.50	£0.20	£0.60	£1.00
Title Value:	$1.80	$5.40	$9.00	£1.20	£3.60	£6.00

CREEPY TRADE PAPERBACK
Dark Horse,OS; 1 Oct 1991
1 ND 112pgs, features reprints by Frazetta, Toth, Adams, Crandall, Williamson, Steve Ditko and others

	$2.10	$6.25	$10.50	£1.40	£4.20	£7.00
Title Value:	$2.10	$6.25	$10.50	£1.40	£4.20	£7.00

CRIME CLASSICS
Eternity; 1 Sep 1988-13 1989
1-13 ND Shadow newspaper strip reprints

	$0.40	$1.20	$2.00	£0.25	£0.75	£1.25
Title Value:	$5.20	$15.60	$26.00	£3.25	£9.75	£16.25

CRIME SUSPENSTORIES
E.C. Comics; 1 Oct/Nov 1950-27 Mar 1955
1 Wally Wood art (Note: copies of #1 exist with Vault of Horror #15 on inside front cover, blacked out and with #1 printed over it)

	$92.50	$275.00	$650.00	£62.50	£190.00	£450.00

2 Jack Kamen art

	$50.00	$150.00	$350.00	£36.00	£105.00	£250.00

3 Wally Wood art, Johnny Craig cover and art

	$37.00	$110.00	$260.00	£25.00	£75.00	£175.00

4 Ingels art

	$37.00	$110.00	$260.00	£25.00	£75.00	£175.00

5 Jack Kamen art

	$37.00	$110.00	$260.00	£25.00	£75.00	£175.00

6 Jack Davis art

	$29.00	$85.00	$200.00	£19.00	£57.50	£135.00
7-10	$29.00	$85.00	$200.00	£19.00	£57.50	£135.00
11-12	$21.00	$62.50	$150.00	£14.00	£43.00	£100.00

13 Al Williamson art

	$24.00	$72.50	$170.00	£16.00	£49.00	£115.00
14-15	$21.00	$62.50	$150.00	£14.00	£43.00	£100.00

16 Al Williamson, Johnny Craig cover and art

	$24.00	$72.50	$170.00	£16.00	£49.00	£115.00

17 Frazetta and Williamson art, Johnny Craig cover and art

	$26.00	$77.50	$185.00	£17.50	£52.50	£125.00

18 Johnny Craig cover and art

	$19.00	$57.50	$135.00	£12.50	£39.00	£90.00

19 Johnny Craig art

	$19.00	$57.50	$135.00	£12.50	£39.00	£90.00

20 Johnny Craig cover and art; famous "hanging noose" cover

	$24.00	$72.50	$170.00	£16.00	£49.00	£115.00

21 Crandall, Johnny Craig cover and art

	$13.50	$41.00	$95.00	£9.50	£29.00	£67.50

22 Johnny Craig cover

	$13.50	$41.00	$95.00	£9.50	£29.00	£67.50

23 Jack Kamen art

	$13.50	$41.00	$95.00	£9.50	£29.00	£67.50
24 Krigstein art	$13.50	$41.00	$95.00	£9.50	£29.00	£67.50

25-27 Jack Kamen cover and art

	$13.50	$41.00	$95.00	£9.50	£29.00	£67.50
Title Value:	$713.00	$2127.00	$5010.00	£481.50	£1460.00	£3422.50

Note: all Non-Distributed on the news-stands in the U.K.

CRIME SUSPENSTORIES (2ND SERIES)
Russ Cochran/EC Comics; 1 Nov 1992-present
1 ND reprints begin from original 1950s EC series with exact cover and interior reproduction

	$0.30	$0.90	$1.50	£0.20	£0.60	£1.00
2-13 ND	$0.30	$0.90	$1.50	£0.20	£0.60	£1.00
Title Value:	$3.90	$11.70	$19.50	£2.60	£7.80	£13.00

Crime Suspenstories Annual #1 (Oct 1994)
reprints issues #1-5 with covers

				£1.20	£3.60	£6.00

CRIMEBUSTER
AC Comics; 0 Apr 1995
0 ND 40pgs, flip-book format with issue #1 of Crimebuster Classics included; spin-off from Fem Force; black and white

	$0.60	$1.80	$3.00	£0.40	£1.20	£2.00
Title Value:	$0.60	$1.80	$3.00	£0.40	£1.20	£2.00

CRIMSON AVENGER, THE
DC Comics,MS; 1 Jun 1988-4 Sep 1988
(see Secret Origins)

1 Greg Brooks art	$0.15	$0.45	$0.75	£0.10	£0.35	£0.60
2 Greg Brookes art	$0.15	$0.45	$0.75	£0.10	£0.35	£0.60

3-4 Greg Brooks art

	$0.15	$0.45	$0.75	£0.10	£0.35	£0.60
Title Value:	$0.60	$1.80	$3.00	£0.40	£1.40	£2.40

CRIMSON COUGAR
Greater Mercury Comics; 1 Dec 1990
1 ND black and white

	$0.40	$1.20	$2.00	£0.25	£0.75	£1.25
Title Value:	$0.40	$1.20	$2.00	£0.25	£0.75	£1.25

CRISIS ON INFINITE EARTHS

Cross-over series that re-shaped the continuity problems of the DC Universe that had accrued over four decades. The number of different planet Earths each with their own heroes started with the story in Flash #123 that saw the Silver Age Flash (Barry Allen) meet his Golden Age Flash counter-part (Jay Garrick). Thereafter, the Golden Age heroes were said to exist on Earth II. Further complications followed introducing other groups of heroes and complicated plot-lines. This series resolved to combine all the various Earths into one and a number of heroes died as a result. It was seen at the time as a great clearing-out process by DC and represents a water-shed in their history. The core mini-series had (appropriately) an almost infinite number of cross-overs listed below in alphabetical rather than chronological order.

1) All Star Squadron 50
2) All Star Squadron 51
3) All Star Squadron 52
4) All Star Squadron 53
5) All Star Squadron 54
6) All Star Squadron 55
7) All Star Squadron 56
8) All Star Squadron 60 - Unofficial X-over
9) Amethyst (1986 series) 13
10) Blue Devil 17
11) Blue Devil 18
12) DC Comics Presents 78
13) DC Comics Presents 86
14) DC Comics Presents 87
15) DC Comics Presents 88
16) DC Comics Presents 94 - post Crisis epilogue
17) DC Comics Presents 95 - unofficial X-over
18) Detective Comics 558 - unofficial X-over
19) Fury of Firestorm 41
20) Fury of Firestorm 42
21) Green Lantern 194
22) Green Lantern 195
23) Green Lantern 196 - unofficial X-over
24) Green Lantern 198
25) Infinity Inc. 18
26) Infinity Inc. 19
27) Infinity Inc. 20
28) Infinity Inc. 21
29) Infinity Inc. 22
30) Infinity Inc. 23
31) Infinity Inc. 24
32) Infinity Inc. 25 - unofficial X-over
33) Infinity Inc. Annual 1
34) Justice League of America 244
35) Justice League of America 245
36) Justice League of America Annual 3
37) Legion of Super-Heroes (2nd Series) 16 - unofficial X-over
38) Legion of Super-Heroes 18
39) Losers Special 1 - Crisis first appears
40) New Teen Titans (2nd Series) 13
41) New Teen Titans (2nd Series) 14
42) Omega Men 31
43) Omega Men 33 - unofficial X-over
44) Superman 413 - unofficial X-over
45) Superman 414
46) Superman 415
47) Swamp Thing (2nd Series) 44 - unofficial X-over
48) Swamp Thing (2nd series) 46
49) Wonder Woman 327
50) Wonder Woman 328
51) Wonder Woman 329
Note: an unofficial cross-over means that the Crisis storyline is referred to in the comic but it is not emblazoned as such on the cover.

CRISIS ON INFINITE EARTHS (LIMITED SERIES)
DC Comics,MS; 1 Apr 1985-12 Mar 1986
1 LD in the U.K. George Perez art

	$Good	$Fine	$N.Mint	£Good	£Fine	£N.Mint
	$1.50	$4.50	$7.50	£1.00	£3.00	£5.00
2 LD in the U.K. George Perez art; Joker appers	$1.20	$3.60	$6.00	£0.80	£2.40	£4.00
3 George Perez art; death of Kid Psycho and Nighthawk (Western)	$0.50	$1.50	$2.50	£0.40	£1.20	£2.00
4 George Perez art; death of The Monitor, 1st appearance new Dr. Light	$0.50	$1.50	$2.50	£0.40	£1.20	£2.00
5 George Perez art; 1st appearance Anti-Monitor	$0.50	$1.50	$2.50	£0.40	£1.20	£2.00
6 George Perez art; 1st appearance the new Wildcat	$0.50	$1.50	$2.50	£0.40	£1.20	£2.00
7 DS LD George Perez art; death of Supergirl	$0.90	$2.70	$4.50	£0.60	£1.80	£3.00
8 George Perez art; death of Flash (Barry Allen)	$0.70	$2.10	$3.50	£0.50	£1.50	£2.50
9 George Perez art; death of Earth 2 Luthor; Joker appears	$0.50	$1.50	$2.50	£0.40	£1.20	£2.00
10 George Perez art; The Molder cameo (the only other appearance Flash #253, actually Elongated Man disguised)	$0.50	$1.50	$2.50	£0.40	£1.20	£2.00
11 George Perez art	$0.50	$1.50	$2.50	£0.40	£1.20	£2.00
12 DS LD George Perez art; Dove, Kole, Lori Lemaris, Sunburst, Golden Age Robin, Golden Age Huntress die, 1st appearance new Flash (Wally West)	$0.70	$2.10	$3.50	£0.50	£1.50	£2.50
Title Value:	$8.50	$25.50	$42.50	£6.20	£18.60	£31.00

CRISIS ON INFINITE EARTHS - THE EARTH INDEX

Over the years, DC had built up a very complex set of universes and thus very complex continuity problems which was the main reason for having their "clearout". Prior to the events of the mini-series, the known Earths of the DC Universe are as follows:

Earth 1 - where the DC super-heroes and characters from the Silver Age onwards are based. All stories unless otherwise stated from cover date September 1956 (ie. Showcase #4) take place on Earth 1

Earth 2 - where the DC super-heroes and characters from the Golden Age to just before the beginning of the Silver Age are based. All stories from cover date June 1938 (ie. Action Comics #1) to about 1955/56 take place on Earth 2.

Earth 3 - very similar in make-up to Earth 1 but the only super-powered beings are in The Crime Syndicate of America (Ultraman, Super-Woman, Johnny Quick, Owl Man and Power Ring). Alexander Luthor is the only (short-lived) super-hero and his son, Alex Luthor, escaped to Earth 1.

Earth 4 - inhabited by the Charlton Comics characters. These are Captain Atom, Blue Beetle, Nightshade, Thunderbolt, Son of Vulcan, Peacemaker and The Question.

Earth 5 - to my knowledge, an Earth 5 has never been mentioned.

Earth 6 - inhabited by a super-powered family comprising Lord Volt, Lady Quark and their daughter Princess Fern.

Earth S - inhabited by the Shazam family of characters. These are principally Captain Marvel, Mary Marvel, Captain Marvel Junior.

Earth X - a world where the Second World War lasted 40 years and becomes the home of The Freedom Fighters (The Ray, Black Condor, Phantom Lady, Uncle Sam, Human Bomb and Doll Man - all Golden Age heroes.

Earth Quality - a world that also has Freedom Fighter counter-parts plus Kid Eternity, The Spirit, Lady Luck and Mr. Mystic.

Earth B - a world created by DC editorial staff to allow for the many inconsistencies in Brave and the Bold and World's Finest stories. It is named after "The 3 B's": editor Murray Bolintoff and writers Bob Haney and E. Nelson Bridwell. The mini-series DC Challenge takes place here.

Earth C - inhabited by DC's "funny animals" such as Captain Carrot and co.

Earth C Minus - a world discovered by Captain Carrot in his civillian identity of cartoonist Rodney Rabbit where living versions of the cartoon characters he created announced they were from.

Earth Prime - the "real" world where super-heroes only exist as comic book characters.

CRITICAL ERROR
Dark Horse,OS; 1 Oct 1992

	$Good	$Fine	$N.Mint	£Good	£Fine	£N.Mint
1 ND early John Byrne black and white story in full colour	$0.45	$1.35	$2.25	£0.30	£0.90	£1.50
Title Value:	$0.45	$1.35	$2.25	£0.30	£0.90	£1.50

CRITICAL MASS
Marvel Comics Group/Epic,MS; 1 Jan 1989-7 Jul 1990

	$Good	$Fine	$N.Mint	£Good	£Fine	£N.Mint
1 ND Janson/Sienkiewicz/Kev O'Neill/Gray Morrow art	$0.90	$2.70	$4.50	£0.60	£1.80	£3.00
2 ND Kev O'Neill/Kyle Baker/Mark Texiera art featured	$0.85	$2.55	$4.25	£0.55	£1.65	£2.75
3 ND Ron Randall/Gray Morrow/John Ridgway/Denys Cowan/Kent Williams art	$0.85	$2.55	$4.25	£0.55	£1.65	£2.75
4 ND features John Ridgway, Jim Lee art	$0.90	$2.70	$4.50	£0.60	£1.80	£3.00
5 ND features John Ridgway art	$0.85	$2.55	$4.25	£0.55	£1.65	£2.75
6 ND features Gray Morrow art	$0.85	$2.55	$4.25	£0.55	£1.65	£2.75
7 ND 80pgs, The Shadowline Saga concludes	$0.90	$2.70	$4.50	£0.60	£1.80	£3.00
Title Value:	$6.10	$18.30	$30.50	£4.00	£12.00	£20.00

Note: issues #1-6 are squarebound 64 pgs
FEATURES
Dr. Zero in 1, 2 Powerline in 1, 3 St. George in 2, 3

CRITTERS
Fantagraphics; 1 Jun 1986-50 Mar 1990

	$Good	$Fine	$N.Mint	£Good	£Fine	£N.Mint
1 giant, Usagi Yojimbo and Cutey Bunny appear; black and white	$0.60	$1.80	$3.00	£0.60	£1.80	£3.00
1 2nd printing, (Sep 1991)	$0.45	$1.35	$2.25	£0.30	£0.90	£1.50
2	$0.40	$1.20	$2.00	£0.35	£1.05	£1.75
3 Usagi Yojimbo appears	$0.40	$1.20	$2.00	£0.35	£1.05	£1.75
4-9	$0.40	$1.20	$2.00	£0.35	£1.05	£1.75
10 Usagi Yojimbo appears	$0.40	$1.20	$2.00	£0.35	£1.05	£1.75
11 68pgs, Christmas Special, Usagi Yojimbo appears	$0.40	$1.20	$2.00	£0.30	£0.90	£1.50
12-13	$0.40	$1.20	$2.00	£0.30	£0.90	£1.50
14 Usagi Yojimbo appears	$0.40	$1.20	$2.00	£0.30	£0.90	£1.50
15-21	$0.40	$1.20	$2.00	£0.30	£0.90	£1.50
22 Watchmen parody; two different covers rumoured to exist	$0.40	$1.20	$2.00	£0.30	£0.90	£1.50
23 64pgs, flexi-disc included, Alan Moore's Sinister Ducks story (text- 2pgs), 1pg Sam Kieth art, (without disc = 25% less)	$0.70	$2.10	$3.50	£0.50	£1.50	£2.50
24-30	$0.40	$1.20	$2.00	£0.30	£0.90	£1.50
31-37	$0.35	$1.05	$1.75	£0.25	£0.75	£1.25
38 48pgs, Usagi Yojimbo appears	$0.35	$1.05	$1.75	£0.25	£0.75	£1.25
39-49	$0.35	$1.05	$1.75	£0.25	£0.75	£1.25
50 80pgs, Neil the Horse, Sam and Max, Usagi Yojimbo among others	$0.70	$2.10	$3.50	£0.50	£1.50	£2.50
Title Value:	$20.30	$60.90	$101.50	£15.50	£46.50	£77.50

Note: all Non-Distributed on the news-stands in the U.K.

CRITTERS SPECIAL
Fantagraphics; 1 1988

	$Good	$Fine	$N.Mint	£Good	£Fine	£N.Mint
1 ND Nilson Groundthumper reprints by Stan Sakai	$0.45	$1.35	$2.25	£0.30	£0.90	£1.50
Title Value:	$0.45	$1.35	$2.25	£0.30	£0.90	£1.50

CROMWELL STONE
Dark Horse,OS; 1 Apr 1992

	$Good	$Fine	$N.Mint	£Good	£Fine	£N.Mint
1 ND	$0.70	$2.10	$3.50	£0.45	£1.35	£2.25
Title Value:	$0.70	$2.10	$3.50	£0.45	£1.35	£2.25

CRONA
Dagger Enterprises; 1 Aug 1994-2 1994

	$Good	$Fine	$N.Mint	£Good	£Fine	£N.Mint
1 ND Bart Sears cover	$0.45	$1.35	$2.25	£0.30	£0.90	£1.50
2 ND	$0.45	$1.35	$2.25	£0.30	£0.90	£1.50
3 ND	$0.90	$2.70	$4.50	£0.60	£1.80	£3.00

CROSS
Dark Horse,MS; 0 Oct 1995-present

	$Good	$Fine	$N.Mint	£Good	£Fine	£N.Mint
0-2 ND Andrew Vachss script, Geoff Darrow covers	$0.50	$1.50	$2.50	£0.30	£0.90	£1.50
Title Value:	$1.50	$4.50	$8.50	£0.90	£2.70	£4.50

CROSSFIRE
Eclipse; 1 May 1984-26 Feb 1988

	$Good	$Fine	$N.Mint	£Good	£Fine	£N.Mint
1 ND Mark Evanier script and Dan Spiegle art begin; colour issues begin	$0.40	$1.20	$2.00	£0.25	£0.75	£1.25
2-16 ND	$0.40	$1.20	$2.00	£0.25	£0.75	£1.25
17 ND last colour issue	$0.40	$1.20	$2.00	£0.25	£0.75	£1.25
18-26 ND	$0.40	$1.20	$2.00	£0.25	£0.75	£1.25
Title Value:	$10.40	$31.20	$52.00	£6.50	£19.50	£32.50

CROSSFIRE & RAINBOW
Eclipse,MS; 1 Jun 1986-4 Sep 1986

	$Good	$Fine	$N.Mint	£Good	£Fine	£N.Mint
1 ND Jerry Ordway cover	$0.30	$0.90	$1.50	£0.20	£0.60	£1.00
2-3 ND	$0.30	$0.90	$1.50	£0.20	£0.60	£1.00
4 ND Dave Stevens cover	$0.30	$0.90	$1.50	£0.20	£0.60	£1.00
Title Value:	$1.20	$3.60	$6.00	£0.80	£2.40	£4.00

CROSSOVER CLASSICS: THE MARVEL/DC COLLECTION
Marvel Comics Group/DC Comics,OS; 1 Jan 1992

	$Good	$Fine	$N.Mint	£Good	£Fine	£N.Mint
1 ND 320pgs, reprints Superman vs. Spiderman (1976), Batman vs. Hulk (1981) and Teen Titans vs. The X-Men (1982)	$3.75	$11.00	$18.75	£2.50	£7.50	£12.50
1 2nd printing,ND (Apr 1993)	$3.35	$10.00	$16.88	£2.25	£6.75	£11.25
Title Value:	$7.10	$21.00	$35.63	£4.75	£14.25	£23.75

CROSSROADS
First,MS; 1 Jul 1988-5 Nov 1988

	$Good	$Fine	$N.Mint	£Good	£Fine	£N.Mint
1 ND Whisper/Sable by S. Grant/C. Martin	$0.80	$2.40	$4.00	£0.50	£1.50	£2.50
1 2nd printing ND	$0.55	$1.65	$2.75	£0.35	£1.05	£1.75
2 ND Sable/Badger by Baron/Medina/Whigham	$0.70	$2.10	$3.50	£0.45	£1.35	£2.25
3 ND Badger/Luther Ironheart by Salick/Staton	$0.70	$2.10	$3.50	£0.45	£1.35	£2.25
4 ND Grimjack/Judah Maccabee by Salick/McManus	$0.70	$2.10	$3.50	£0.45	£1.35	£2.25
5 ND Grimjack/Dreadstar/Nexus by Baron/McDonnell	$0.70	$2.10	$3.50	£0.45	£1.35	£2.25
Title Value:	$4.15	$12.45	$20.75	£2.65	£7.95	£13.25

Note: all Bookshelf Format; Steve Rude painted covers on all

CROW OF THE BEAR CLAW
Blackthorne; 1 Sep 1986-6 Jul 1987

	$Good	$Fine	$N.Mint	£Good	£Fine	£N.Mint
1-6 ND	$0.40	$1.20	$2.00	£0.25	£0.75	£1.25
Title Value:	$2.40	$7.20	$12.00	£1.50	£4.50	£7.50

CROW, THE
Caliber Press,MS; 1 Feb 1989-4 Dec 1990

	$Good	$Fine	$N.Mint	£Good	£Fine	£N.Mint
1 ND	$10.50	$33.00	$65.00	£5.75	£17.50	£35.00
1 2nd printing, ND (Oct 1989)	$1.50	$4.50	$7.50	£1.00	£3.00	£5.00
1 3rd printing ND	$0.90	$2.70	$4.50	£0.60	£1.80	£3.00
2 ND	$6.00	$18.00	$30.00	£4.00	£12.00	£20.00

MINT = 100% / NEAR MINT (inc. +/-) = 90-99% / VERY FINE (inc. +/-) = 75-89% / FINE (inc. +/-) = 55-74%
VERY GOOD (inc. +/-) = 35-54% / GOOD (inc. +/-) = 15-34% / FAIR = 5-14% / POOR = 1-4%

277

	$Good	$Fine	$N.Mint	£Good	£Fine	£N.Mint

2 2nd printing, ND (Dec 1989)
| | $0.70 | $2.10 | $3.50 | £0.50 | £1.50 | £2.50 |

2 3rd printing ND
| | $0.45 | $1.35 | $2.25 | £0.30 | £0.90 | £1.50 |

3 ND limited print run
| | $5.50 | $16.50 | $27.50 | £3.00 | £9.00 | £15.00 |

3 2nd printing, ND (Jun 1990)
| | $0.70 | $2.10 | $3.50 | £0.50 | £1.50 | £2.50 |

4 ND
| | $5.50 | $16.50 | $27.50 | £3.00 | £9.00 | £15.00 |
| Title Value: | $31.75 | $96.75 | $171.25 | £18.65 | £56.20 | £99.50 |

CROW, THE (2ND SERIES)
Tundra; 1-3 1992
1 ND 64pgs, reprints Crow #1,2 with new covers
| | $2.00 | $6.00 | $10.00 | £1.20 | £3.60 | £6.00 |
2-3 ND
| | $2.00 | $6.00 | $10.00 | £1.20 | £3.60 | £6.00 |
| Title Value: | $6.00 | $18.00 | $30.00 | £3.60 | £10.80 | £18.00 |

CRUCIBLE
DC Comics/Impact,MS; 1 Feb 1993-6 Jul 1993
1 ND Shield, Black Hood and The Comet appear, special cover price of 99 cents; Joe Quesada art featured
| | $0.15 | $0.45 | $0.75 | £0.10 | £0.35 | £0.60 |
2-6 ND Joe Quesada art featured
| | $0.15 | $0.45 | $0.75 | £0.10 | £0.35 | £0.60 |
| Title Value: | $0.90 | $2.70 | $4.50 | £0.60 | £2.10 | £3.60 |

CRUSADERS
Guild Publications,Magazine; 1 Aug 1982
(becomes Southern Knights)
1 ND very scarce in the U.K. black and white
| | $3.75 | $11.00 | $18.75 | £2.50 | £7.50 | £12.50 |
| Title Value: | $3.75 | $11.00 | $18.75 | £2.50 | £7.50 | £12.50 |

CRUSADERS, THE
DC Comics/Impact; 1 May 1992-8 Dec 1992
1 The Fly, Jaguar, Fireball, Comet and The Web begin as team, includes trading cards
| | $0.15 | $0.45 | $0.75 | £0.10 | £0.35 | £0.60 |
2-8 ND
| | $0.15 | $0.45 | $0.75 | £0.10 | £0.35 | £0.60 |
| Title Value: | $1.20 | $3.60 | $6.00 | £0.80 | £2.80 | £4.80 |

CRUSH, THE
Image,MS; 1 Mar 1996-present
1 ND Mike Baron script, N. Steven Harris and Reggie Jones art
| | $0.45 | $1.35 | $2.25 | £0.30 | £0.90 | £1.50 |
| Title Value: | $0.45 | $1.35 | $2.25 | £0.30 | £0.90 | £1.50 |

CRY FOR DAWN
Cry For Dawn; 1 Spring 1989-10 1992
1 scarce in the U.K. Joseph Michael Linsner art, black and white begins
| | $31.00 | $92.50 | $185.00 | £12.50 | £38.00 | £75.00 |
| | [Prices may vary widely on this comic] | | | | | |

1 2nd printing, (1989/1990)
| | $19.00 | $55.00 | $95.00 | £7.00 | £21.00 | £35.00 |
1 3rd printing
| | $12.00 | $36.00 | $60.00 | £4.00 | £12.00 | £20.00 |
2 Joseph Michael Linsner art & interior (8pgs)
| | $20.00 | $60.00 | $120.00 | £9.00 | £28.00 | £55.00 |
2 2nd printing
| | $7.00 | $21.00 | $35.00 | £2.50 | £7.50 | £12.50 |
3
| | $11.50 | $35.00 | $70.00 | £5.75 | £17.50 | £35.00 |
4-5
| | $7.50 | $22.50 | $45.00 | £4.15 | £12.50 | £25.00 |
5 2nd printing, (Aug 1993)
| | $1.50 | $4.50 | $7.50 | £0.70 | £2.10 | £3.50 |
6
| | $9.00 | $27.00 | $45.00 | £4.00 | £12.00 | £20.00 |
6 2nd printing, (Jan 1994)
| | $1.50 | $4.50 | $7.50 | £0.70 | £2.10 | £3.50 |
7
| | $5.00 | $15.00 | $25.00 | £2.50 | £7.50 | £12.50 |
7 2nd printing, (Jan 1994)
| | $1.50 | $4.50 | $7.50 | £0.70 | £2.10 | £3.50 |
8
| | $5.00 | $15.00 | $25.00 | £2.50 | £7.50 | £12.50 |
8 2nd printing, (Jan 1994)
| | $1.50 | $4.50 | $7.50 | £0.70 | £2.10 | £3.50 |
9 Joseph Michael Linsner art & interior (20pgs)
| | $5.00 | $15.00 | $25.00 | £2.50 | £7.50 | £12.50 |
10
| | $5.00 | $15.00 | $25.00 | £2.50 | £7.50 | £12.50 |
| Title Value: | $150.50 | $449.50 | $830.00 | £65.85 | £199.40 | £366.50 |
Note: all Non-Distributed on the news-stands in the U.K.

CRYING FREEMAN
Viz Communications; 1 1989-8 Jul 1990
1 ND DS
| | $0.80 | $2.40 | $4.00 | £0.50 | £1.50 | £2.50 |
2-8 ND
| | $0.80 | $2.40 | $4.00 | £0.50 | £1.50 | £2.50 |
| Title Value: | $6.40 | $19.20 | $32.00 | £4.00 | £12.00 | £20.00 |
Crying Freeman: Portrait of a Killer
Part 1, reprints issues #1-4
| | | | | £2.00 | £6.00 | £10.00 |
Part 2, reprints #5-8
| | | | | £2.00 | £6.00 | £10.00 |
Crying Freeman Perfect Collection: Portarint of a Killer
(Aug 1995) 456pgs, collects volumes 1 and 2
| | | | | 2.70 | 8.10 | 13.50 |
Note: Manga series by Ikegami (Mai) and Koike (Lone Wolf); contains violence and nudity

CRYING FREEMAN (2ND SERIES)
Viz Communications; 1 Oct 1990-9 1991
1-9 ND
| | $0.80 | $2.40 | $4.00 | £0.50 | £1.50 | £2.50 |
| Title Value: | $7.20 | $21.60 | $36.00 | £4.50 | £13.50 | £22.50 |

CRYING FREEMAN (3RD SERIES)
Viz Communications,MS; 1 Jul 1991-10 Apr 1992
1-10 ND 40pgs
| | $0.90 | $2.70 | $4.50 | £0.60 | £1.80 | £3.00 |
| Title Value: | $9.00 | $27.00 | $45.00 | £6.00 | £18.00 | £30.00 |
Crying Freeman: A Taste of Revenge Part 1 (Jan 1993)
184pgs, reprints #1-5
| | | | | £2.00 | £6.00 | £10.00 |
Crying Freeman: A Taste of Revenge Part 2 (Mar 1993)
184pgs, reprints #6-10
| | | | | £2.00 | £6.00 | £10.00 |
Crying Freeman: A Taste of Revenge Perfect Collection

(Sep 1995) collects part 1 and part 2
| | | | | £2.70 | £8.10 | £13.50 |

CRYING FREEMAN (4TH SERIES)
Viz Communications,MS; 1 May 1992-8 Jan 1993
1-8 ND 40pgs
| | $0.90 | $2.70 | $4.50 | £0.60 | £1.80 | £3.00 |
| Title Value: | $7.20 | $21.60 | $36.00 | £4.80 | £14.40 | £24.00 |

CRYING FREEMAN (5TH SERIES)
Viz Communications,MS; 1 Feb 1993-11 Dec 1993
1-11 ND Rumiko Takahashi; black and white
| | $0.55 | $1.65 | $2.75 | £0.35 | £1.05 | £1.75 |
| Title Value: | $6.05 | $18.15 | $30.25 | £3.85 | £11.55 | £19.25 |
Crying Freeman: Journey to Freedom (Sep 1994)
168pgs, reprints first half of series
| | | | | £2.00 | £6.00 | £10.00 |
Crying Freeman: Journey to Fredom (Nov 1994)
168pgs, reprints second half of series
| | | | | £2.00 | £6.00 | £10.00 |

CRYPT
Image,MS; 1 Aug 1995-2 Sep 1995
1-2 ND Robert Napton script, John Fang art
| | $0.50 | $1.50 | $2.50 | £0.30 | £0.90 | £1.50 |
| Title Value: | $1.00 | $3.00 | $5.00 | £0.60 | £1.80 | £3.00 |

CRYPT OF SHADOWS
Marvel Comics Group; 1 Jan 1973-21 Nov 1975
1 ND horror reprints begin
| | $0.80 | $2.40 | $4.00 | £0.50 | £1.50 | £2.50 |
2-3 ND
| | $0.60 | $1.80 | $3.00 | £0.40 | £1.20 | £2.00 |
4-5 ND
| | $0.45 | $1.35 | $2.25 | £0.30 | £0.90 | £1.50 |
6-20 ND
| | $0.40 | $1.20 | $2.00 | £0.25 | £0.75 | £1.25 |
21
| | $0.30 | $0.90 | $1.50 | £0.20 | £0.60 | £1.00 |
| Title Value: | $9.20 | $27.60 | $46.00 | £5.85 | £17.55 | £29.25 |

CRYSTAR CRYSTAL WARRIOR, SAGA OF
Marvel Comics Group; 1 May 1983-11 Jan/Feb 1985
1-2 ND
| | $0.25 | $0.75 | $1.25 | £0.15 | £0.45 | £0.75 |
3 ND Doctor Strange appears, Golden cover
| | $0.25 | $0.75 | $1.25 | £0.15 | £0.45 | £0.75 |
4-5 ND Golden cover
| | $0.25 | $0.75 | $1.25 | £0.15 | £0.45 | £0.75 |
6 ND Nightcrawler appears, Golden cover
| | $0.25 | $0.75 | $1.25 | £0.15 | £0.45 | £0.75 |
7-8 ND Golden cover
| | $0.25 | $0.75 | $1.25 | £0.15 | £0.45 | £0.75 |
9-10 ND
| | $0.25 | $0.75 | $1.25 | £0.15 | £0.45 | £0.75 |
11 DS, Alpha Flight X-over
| | $0.25 | $0.75 | $1.25 | £0.15 | £0.45 | £0.75 |
| Title Value: | $2.75 | $8.25 | $13.75 | £1.65 | £4.95 | £8.25 |
Note: only issues 1-7 have full title on cover. Painted covers on issues 1,4-7,9-11.

CUD COMICS
Fantagraphics; 1 Aug 1992-8 Dec 1994
1 ND Terry LaBan script and art; black and white begins
| | $0.60 | $1.80 | $3.00 | £0.40 | £1.20 | £2.00 |
2-8 ND Terry LaBan script and art
| | $0.60 | $1.80 | $3.00 | £0.40 | £1.20 | £2.00 |
| Title Value: | $4.80 | $14.40 | $24.00 | £3.20 | £9.60 | £16.00 |

CUD COMICS (2ND SERIES)
Dark Horse; 1 Nov 1995-present
1 ND Terry LaBan script and art; black and white
| | $0.60 | $1.80 | $3.00 | £0.40 | £1.20 | £2.00 |
| Title Value: | $0.60 | $1.80 | $3.00 | £0.40 | £1.20 | £2.00 |

CUDA
Rebel Studios; 1 Jun 1995
1 ND 16pgs, Tim Vigil and Adam McDaniel; black and white
| | $0.40 | $1.20 | $2.00 | £0.25 | £0.75 | £1.25 |
| Title Value: | $0.40 | $1.20 | $2.00 | £0.25 | £0.75 | £1.25 |

CURSE OF THE MOLEMEN
Kitchen Sink,OS; 1 Oct 1991
1 ND reprints Charles Burns' story from Raw in colour
| | $1.00 | $3.00 | $5.00 | £0.65 | £1.95 | £3.25 |
| Title Value: | $1.00 | $3.00 | $5.00 | £0.65 | £1.95 | £3.25 |

CURSE OF THE WEIRD
Marvel Comics Group,MS; 1 Dec 1993-4 Mar 1994
1 pre super-hero reprints by Steve Ditko, Basil Wolverton and Bill Everett; Ditko cover
| | $0.25 | $0.75 | $1.25 | £0.15 | £0.45 | £0.75 |
2 Steve Ditko cover
| | $0.25 | $0.75 | $1.25 | £0.15 | £0.45 | £0.75 |
3 Wolverton, Heath and Kubert reprints
| | $0.25 | $0.75 | $1.25 | £0.15 | £0.45 | £0.75 |
4 Bill Everett reprint plus Steve Ditko's 1st work for Marvel
| | $0.25 | $0.75 | $1.25 | £0.15 | £0.45 | £0.75 |
| Title Value: | $1.00 | $3.00 | $5.00 | £0.60 | £1.80 | £3.00 |

CUTEY BUNNY, ARMY SURPLUS COMICS FEATURING
Army Surplus/Eclipse; 1 1982-7 1986
1-4 ND
| | $0.45 | $1.35 | $2.25 | £0.30 | £0.90 | £1.50 |
5 ND X-Men parody
| | $0.45 | $1.35 | $2.25 | £0.30 | £0.90 | £1.50 |
6-7 ND
| | $0.45 | $1.35 | $2.25 | £0.30 | £0.90 | £1.50 |
| Title Value: | $3.15 | $9.45 | $15.75 | £2.10 | £6.30 | £10.50 |

CUTTING EDGE
Marvel Comics Group,OS; 1 Dec 1995
1 ND 48pgs, Ghosts of the Future tie-in, Hulk appears
| | $0.60 | $1.80 | $3.00 | £0.40 | £1.20 | £2.00 |
| Title Value: | $0.60 | $1.80 | $3.00 | £0.40 | £1.20 | £2.00 |

CYBER 7
Eclipse; 1 Mar 1989-7 Sep 1989
1-7 ND script and art by Shuto Itahishi; black and white

	$Good	$Fine	$N.Mint	£Good	£Fine	£N.Mint
	$0.40	$1.20	$2.00	£0.25	£0.75	£1.25
Title Value:	$2.80	$8.40	$14.00	£1.75	£5.25	£8.75

CYBER 7 BOOK TWO
Eclipse; 1 Oct 1989-10 Jul 1990

	$Good	$Fine	$N.Mint	£Good	£Fine	£N.Mint
1-10 ND script and art by Shuto Itahishi; black and white	$0.35	$1.05	$1.75	£0.25	£0.75	£1.25
Title Value:	$3.50	$10.50	$17.50	£2.50	£7.50	£12.50

CYBER CITY: PART ONE
CPM Comics,MS; 1,2 Sep 1995

	$Good	$Fine	$N.Mint	£Good	£Fine	£N.Mint
1-2 ND 24pgs, Tim Eldred script with Studio Go!	$0.60	$1.80	$3.00	£0.40	£1.20	£2.00
Title Value:	$1.20	$3.60	$6.00	£0.80	£2.40	£4.00

CYBER CITY: PART TWO
CPM Comics,MS; 1 Oct 1995-2 Nov 1995

	$Good	$Fine	$N.Mint	£Good	£Fine	£N.Mint
1-2 ND 24pgs, Tim Eldred script and Go! Studios art	$0.60	$1.80	$3.00	£0.40	£1.20	£2.00
Title Value:	$1.20	$3.60	$6.00	£0.80	£2.40	£4.00

CYBERFORCE
Image; 0 Sep 1993; Malibu/Image; 1 Oct 1992-4 Jul 1993

	$Good	$Fine	$N.Mint	£Good	£Fine	£N.Mint
0 (Sep 1993) Walt Simonson script and art	$0.45	$1.35	$2.25	£0.30	£0.90	£1.50
1 Marc Silvestri script/art begins; contains Image #0 coupon 3	$1.20	$3.60	$6.00	£0.80	£2.40	£4.00
1 without coupon	$0.80	$2.40	$4.00	£0.50	£1.50	£2.50
1 Ash Can, 8.5" x 5.5" yellow card cover, black and white interior, limited to 5,500 copies (numbered in silver bottom right of cover, each signed in silver ink on cover by Marc Silvestri)	$2.50	$7.50	$12.50	£1.50	£4.50	£7.50
2	$0.60	$1.80	$3.00	£0.40	£1.20	£2.00
2 Ash Can, 8.5" x 5.5" yellow card cover, black and white interior, limited to 5,000 copies (numbered in silver bottom right of cover, each signed in silver ink on cover by Marc Silvestri	$2.50	$7.50	$12.50	£1.50	£4.50	£7.50
3 Badrock of Youngblood appears	$0.60	$1.80	$3.00	£0.40	£1.20	£2.00
4 silver embossed logo	$0.60	$1.80	$3.00	£0.40	£1.20	£2.00
Title Value:	$9.25	$27.75	$46.25	£5.80	£17.40	£29.00

Note; all Non-Distributed on the news-stands in the U.K.
Cyberforce: The Tin Men of War (Dec 1993)

	$Good	$Fine	$N.Mint	£Good	£Fine	£N.Mint
Trade paperback reprints issues #1-4 plus pin-ups; holografix foil embossed				£2.00	£6.00	£10.00

CYBERFORCE (2ND SERIES)
Image; 1 Nov 1993-present

	$Good	$Fine	$N.Mint	£Good	£Fine	£N.Mint
1 Marc Silvestri plot and pencils begin	$0.45	$1.35	$2.25	£0.30	£0.90	£1.50
1 Gold edition	$2.50	$7.50	$12.50	£1.50	£4.50	£7.50
2	$0.40	$1.20	$2.00	£0.25	£0.75	£1.25
2 Silver edition	$2.50	$7.50	$12.50	£1.50	£4.50	£7.50
3	$0.40	$1.20	$2.00	£0.25	£0.75	£1.25
3 Gold edition	$2.50	$7.50	$12.50	£1.50	£4.50	£7.50
4-7	$0.40	$1.20	$2.00	£0.25	£0.75	£1.25
8 Image X Month tie-in	$0.40	$1.20	$2.00	£0.25	£0.75	£1.25
9 Chris Claremont script begins; cover painting by Joe Chiodo	$0.40	$1.20	$2.00	£0.25	£0.75	£1.25
10-12	$0.40	$1.20	$2.00	£0.25	£0.75	£1.25
13-15	$0.45	$1.35	$2.25	£0.30	£0.90	£1.50
16 Ripclaw origin	$0.45	$1.35	$2.25	£0.30	£0.90	£1.50
17-18	$0.45	$1.35	$2.25	£0.30	£0.90	£1.50
Title Value:	$15.05	$45.15	$75.25	£9.35	£28.05	£46.75

CYBERFORCE ANNUAL
Image; 1 Feb 1995-present

	$Good	$Fine	$N.Mint	£Good	£Fine	£N.Mint
1 ND Velocity falls into a coma	$0.50	$1.50	$2.50	£0.30	£0.90	£1.50
Title Value:	$0.50	$1.50	$2.50	£0.30	£0.90	£1.50

CYBERFORCE ORIGINS
Image; 1 Jan 1995-present

	$Good	$Fine	$N.Mint	£Good	£Fine	£N.Mint
1 ND origin Cyblade	$0.50	$1.50	$2.50	£0.30	£0.90	£1.50
2 ND origin Stryker	$0.50	$1.50	$2.50	£0.30	£0.90	£1.50
3 ND origin Impact; Marc Silvestri script, Randy Queen art	$0.50	$1.50	$2.50	£0.30	£0.90	£1.50
4 ND	$0.50	$1.50	$2.50	£0.30	£0.90	£1.50
5 ND origin Misery by Brandon Peterson	$0.50	$1.50	$2.50	£0.30	£0.90	£1.50
Title Value:	$2.50	$7.50	$12.50	£1.50	£4.50	£7.50

CYBERFORCE UNIVERSE SOURCEBOOK
Image; 1 Aug 1994-present

	$Good	$Fine	$N.Mint	£Good	£Fine	£N.Mint
2 ND information and statistics on Cyberforce characters	$0.45	$1.35	$2.25	£0.30	£0.90	£1.50
3 ND	$0.45	$1.35	$2.25	£0.30	£0.90	£1.50
Title Value:	$0.90	$2.70	$4.50	£0.60	£1.80	£3.00

CYBERFORCE/CODENAME STRYEFORCE - OPPOSING FORCES
Image; 1 Sep 1995-2 Oct 1995

	$Good	$Fine	$N.Mint	£Good	£Fine	£N.Mint
1 ND Marc Silvestri and Steve Gerber script	$0.50	$1.50	$2.50	£0.30	£0.90	£1.50
2 ND	$0.50	$1.50	$2.50	£0.30	£0.90	£1.50
Title Value:	$1.00	$3.00	$5.00	£0.60	£1.80	£3.00

CYBERHOOD
Entity Comics; 0 Oct 1995

	$Good	$Fine	$N.Mint	£Good	£Fine	£N.Mint
0 ND Bill Maus script and art	$0.50	$1.50	$2.50	£0.30	£0.90	£1.50
0 ND Interactive Videogame Edition (Oct 1995), pre-bagged with floppy disk	$1.40	$4.20	$7.00	£0.95	£2.85	£4.75
Title Value:	$1.90	$5.70	$9.50	£1.25	£3.75	£6.25

CYBERNARY
Image,MS; 1 Nov 1995-present

	$Good	$Fine	$N.Mint	£Good	£Fine	£N.Mint
1 ND Steve Gerber script, Jeff Rebner and Richard Friend art	$0.50	$1.50	$2.50	£0.30	£0.90	£1.50
2 ND	$0.50	$1.50	$2.50	£0.30	£0.90	£1.50
Title Value:	$1.00	$3.00	$5.00	£0.60	£1.80	£3.00

CYBERPUNK
Innovative Corp; 1 Sep 1989-2 1989

	$Good	$Fine	$N.Mint	£Good	£Fine	£N.Mint
1-2 ND	$0.40	$1.20	$2.00	£0.25	£0.75	£1.25
Title Value:	$0.80	$2.40	$4.00	£0.50	£1.50	£2.50
Graphic Novel 1, reprints issues #1,2, squarebound with new material (1990)				£0.80	£2.40	£4.00

CYBERPUNK (2ND SERIES)
Innovation; 1 Nov 1990-2 Dec 1990

	$Good	$Fine	$N.Mint	£Good	£Fine	£N.Mint
1-2 ND painted art by Doug Talalla	$0.45	$1.35	$2.25	£0.30	£0.90	£1.50
Title Value:	$0.90	$2.70	$4.50	£0.60	£1.80	£3.00
Graphic Novel 2, reprints issues #1,2				£0.80	£2.40	£4.00

CYBERPUNK: THE SERAPHIM FILES
Innovation,MS; 1 Sep 1990-2 Nov 1990

	$Good	$Fine	$N.Mint	£Good	£Fine	£N.Mint
1-2 ND	$0.45	$1.35	$2.25	£0.30	£0.90	£1.50
Title Value:	$0.90	$2.70	$4.50	£0.60	£1.80	£3.00

CYBERPUNK: THE SERAPHIM PROJECT GRAPHIC NOVEL
Innovation; nn 1991
nn ND reprints 1st Seraphim story plus mini-series, painted cover by Doug Talalla (no number on cover)

Crisis on Infinite Earths #12

Cry For Dawn #1 (2nd print)

Cyberforce Origins #1

	$Good	$Fine	$N.Mint	£Good	£Fine	£N.Mint
	$1.40	$4.20	$7.00	£0.90	£2.70	£4.50
Title Value:	$1.40	$4.20	$7.00	£0.90	£2.70	£4.50

CYBERRAD
Continuity; 1 Mar 1991-7 Dec 1991

	$Good	$Fine	$N.Mint	£Good	£Fine	£N.Mint
1 Neal Adams lay-outs; 1st appearance Cyberrad	$0.35	$1.05	$1.75	£0.25	£0.75	£1.25
2-4 Neal Adams lay-outs	$0.35	$1.05	$1.75	£0.25	£0.75	£1.25
5 Neal Adams lay-outs; glow-in-the-dark cover	$0.35	$1.05	$1.75	£0.25	£0.75	£1.25
6 Neal Adams lay-outs; pull-out poster	$0.35	$1.05	$1.75	£0.25	£0.75	£1.25
7 Neal Adams lay-outs; "see-thru" cel overlay cover	$0.35	$1.05	$1.75	£0.25	£0.75	£1.25
Title Value:	$2.45	$7.35	$12.25	£1.75	£5.25	£8.75

Note: all Non-Distributed on the news-stands in the U.K.

CYBERRAD (2ND SERIES)
Continuity; 1 Nov 1992-2 Aug 1993

	$Good	$Fine	$N.Mint	£Good	£Fine	£N.Mint
1 die-cut hologram cover, Neal Adams layouts and sketches	$0.35	$1.05	$1.75	£0.30	£0.90	£1.50
1 Limited Edition - silver foil logo	$1.50	$4.50	$7.50	£1.00	£3.00	£5.00
1 Newstand edition, (no holgram, no sketches)	$0.35	$1.05	$1.75	£0.25	£0.75	£1.25
2 Neal Adams layouts; acetate cel overlay cover	$0.35	$1.05	$1.75	£0.30	£0.90	£1.50
Title Value:	$2.55	$7.65	$12.75	£1.85	£5.55	£9.25

Note: all Non-Distributed on the news-stands in the U.K.

CYBERRAD (3RD SERIES)
Continuity; 1 Apr 1993-2 1993

	$Good	$Fine	$N.Mint	£Good	£Fine	£N.Mint
1 Deathwatch 2000 part 7, pre-bagged with 2 trading cards, Neal Adams cover	$0.35	$1.05	$1.75	£0.25	£0.75	£1.25
1 un-bagged/without cards	$0.30	$0.90	$1.50	£0.20	£0.60	£1.00
2 Deathwatch 2000, pre-bagged with trading cards	$0.35	$1.05	$1.75	£0.25	£0.75	£1.25
2 un-bagged/without cards	$0.30	$0.90	$1.50	£0.20	£0.60	£1.00
Title Value:	$1.30	$3.90	$6.50	£0.90	£2.70	£4.50

Note: all Non-Distributed on the news-stands in the U.K.

CYBERSPACE 3000
Marvel UK; 1 Jul 1993-7 Jan 1994

	$Good	$Fine	$N.Mint	£Good	£Fine	£N.Mint
1 Galactus appears, glow-in-the-dark cover by Liam Sharp	$0.30	$0.90	$1.50	£0.20	£0.60	£1.00
2 Galactus appears	$0.30	$0.90	$1.50	£0.20	£0.60	£1.00
3-5 Galactus and Silver Surfer appear	$0.30	$0.90	$1.50	£0.20	£0.60	£1.00
6 Warlock appears; gold ink enhanced cover	$0.30	$0.90	$1.50	£0.20	£0.60	£1.00
7	$0.30	$0.90	$1.50	£0.20	£0.60	£1.00
Title Value:	$2.10	$6.30	$10.50	£1.40	£4.20	£7.00

CYBERSUIT ARKADYNE
Janus Publications; 1 Mar 1992-6 Aug 1992

	$Good	$Fine	$N.Mint	£Good	£Fine	£N.Mint
1-6 ND black and white	$0.30	$0.90	$1.50	£0.20	£0.60	£1.00
Title Value:	$1.80	$5.40	$9.00	£1.20	£3.60	£6.00

CYBLADE/SHI SPECIAL - THE BATTLE FOR INDEPENDENTS
Image,OS; 1 Sep 1995

	$Good	$Fine	$N.Mint	£Good	£Fine	£N.Mint
1 ND Co-wriiten and co-pencilled by Marc Silvestri and William Tucci; cover by Marc Silvestri	$0.60	$1.80	$3.00	£0.40	£1.20	£2.00
1 Preview Edition, ND Marc Silvestri cover art, distributed at the San Diego comic convention; marked "Special Preview Teaser" along top of comic	$3.00	$9.00	$15.00	£2.00	£6.00	£10.00
1 Variant Edition, ND Tucci cover art, Cyblade & Shi faces shown only	$1.00	$3.00	$5.00	£0.60	£1.80	£3.00
Title Value:	$4.60	$13.80	$23.00	£3.00	£9.00	£15.00

Cyblade/Shi Limited Edition Boxed Set A (Dec 1995)
collects all 4 variants in slipcase plus new fifth
cover edition; signed by Marc Silvestri and William Tucci £8.00 £24.00 £40.00

Cyblade/Shi Limited Edition Boxed Set B (Dec 1995)
collects all 4 variants in slipcase plus new fifth
cover edition; signed by Marc Silvestri £6.50 £19.50 £32.50

Cyblade/Shi Limited Edition Boxed Set C (Dec 1995)
collects all 4 variants in slipcase plus new fifth cover edition £4.50 £13.50 £22.50

CYBRID
Maximum Comic Press; 1 Jul 1995-present

	$Good	$Fine	$N.Mint	£Good	£Fine	£N.Mint
1 ND Rob Liefeld plot and cover, Sam Liu and Danny Miki art	$0.60	$1.80	$3.00	£0.40	£1.20	£2.00
Title Value:	$0.60	$1.80	$3.00	£0.40	£1.20	£2.00

CYCLOPS: RETRIBUTION
Marvel Comics Group,OS; 1 Jan 1995

	$Good	$Fine	$N.Mint	£Good	£Fine	£N.Mint
1 ND 64pgs, reprints from Marvel Comics Presents with Ron Lim art	$1.00	$3.00	$5.00	£0.70	£2.10	£3.50
Title Value:	$1.00	$3.00	$5.00	£0.70	£2.10	£3.50

CYCOPS
Comics Interview,MS; 1-3 Summer 1988

	$Good	$Fine	$N.Mint	£Good	£Fine	£N.Mint
1-3 ND	$0.40	$1.20	$2.00	£0.25	£0.75	£1.25
Title Value:	$1.20	$3.60	$6.00	£0.75	£2.25	£3.75
Trade Paperback, reprints #1-3				£1.20	£3.60	£6.00

CYNDER
Immortelle Studios,MS; 1 Apr 1995-present

	$Good	$Fine	$N.Mint	£Good	£Fine	£N.Mint
1 ND David and Michael Hernandez script and art, Cynder centrefold by Rob Liefeld; black and white	$0.45	$1.35	$2.25	£0.30	£0.90	£1.50
2-3 ND David and Michael Hernandez script and art; centrefold by William Tucci; black and white	$0.45	$1.35	$2.25	£0.30	£0.90	£1.50
Title Value:	$1.35	$4.05	$6.75	£0.90	£2.70	£4.50

D

DADAVILLE
Caliber Press,OS; 1 Nov 1991

	$Good	$Fine	$N.Mint	£Good	£Fine	£N.Mint
1 ND	$0.35	$1.05	$1.75	£0.25	£0.75	£1.25
Title Value:	$0.35	$1.05	$1.75	£0.25	£0.75	£1.25

DAEMON MASK
Amazing Comics; 1 1987

	$Good	$Fine	$N.Mint	£Good	£Fine	£N.Mint
1 ND black and white	$0.30	$0.90	$1.50	£0.20	£0.60	£1.00
Title Value:	$0.30	$0.90	$1.50	£0.20	£0.60	£1.00

DAEMON'S BLOOD
Greater Mercury Comics; 1 Dec 1990-3 1991

	$Good	$Fine	$N.Mint	£Good	£Fine	£N.Mint
1-3 ND black and white	$0.25	$0.75	$1.25	£0.15	£0.45	£0.75
Title Value:	$0.75	$2.25	$3.75	£0.45	£1.35	£2.25

DAGAR THE INVINCIBLE
Gold Key; 1 Oct 1972-18 Dec 1976; Whitman; 19 Apr 1982

	$Good	$Fine	$N.Mint	£Good	£Fine	£N.Mint
1 scarce in the U.K. origin and 1st appearance Dagar; painted covers begin (sub-titled Tales of Sword and Sorcery)	$2.50	$7.50	$12.50	£1.60	£4.80	£8.00
2 16pg Kenner catalogue insert	$1.50	$4.50	$7.50	£0.80	£2.40	£4.00
3 vampire issue	$1.20	$3.60	$6.00	£0.70	£2.10	£3.50
4-5	$1.20	$3.60	$6.00	£0.70	£2.10	£3.50
6 16pg Kenner catalogue insert	$0.80	$2.40	$4.00	£0.50	£1.50	£2.50
7 slight logo change (this issue only)	$0.80	$2.40	$4.00	£0.50	£1.50	£2.50
8-12	$0.80	$2.40	$4.00	£0.50	£1.50	£2.50
13	$0.60	$1.80	$3.00	£0.40	£1.20	£2.00
14 origin briefly retold (Dagar witnessing his own origin as intangible)	$0.60	$1.80	$3.00	£0.40	£1.20	£2.00
15	$0.60	$1.80	$3.00	£0.40	£1.20	£2.00
16-17	$0.45	$1.35	$2.25	£0.30	£0.90	£1.50
18 last painted cover	$0.45	$1.35	$2.25	£0.30	£0.90	£1.50
19 scarce in the U.K. line-drawn cover	$0.60	$1.80	$3.00	£0.40	£1.20	£2.00
Title Value:	$16.95	$50.85	$84.75	£10.50	£31.50	£52.50

Note: some issues distributed in the news-stands in the U.K.

DAI KAMIKAZE!
Now Comics; 1 Jun 1987-12 Aug 1988

	$Good	$Fine	$N.Mint	£Good	£Fine	£N.Mint
1 ND 1st appearance Speed Racer; says July 1987 in indicia	$0.30	$0.90	$1.50	£0.20	£0.60	£1.00
1 2nd printing ND	$0.25	$0.75	$1.25	£0.15	£0.45	£0.75
2-12 ND	$0.30	$0.90	$1.50	£0.20	£0.60	£1.00
Title Value:	$3.85	$11.55	$19.25	£2.55	£7.65	£12.75

DAIKAZU VS. GUGURON
Ground Zero Comics,MS; 1 Sep 1991-3 Dec 1991

	$Good	$Fine	$N.Mint	£Good	£Fine	£N.Mint
1-3 ND	$0.30	$0.90	$1.50	£0.20	£0.60	£1.00
Title Value:	$0.90	$2.70	$4.50	£0.60	£1.80	£3.00

DAILY PLANET INVASION EDITION
DC Comics,Tabloid OS; nn Nov 1988

	$Good	$Fine	$N.Mint	£Good	£Fine	£N.Mint
1 ND 16pgs, Invasion tie-in, newspaper articles and reports format	$0.30	$0.90	$1.50	£0.20	£0.60	£1.00
Title Value:	$0.30	$0.90	$1.50	£0.20	£0.60	£1.00

DAKOTA NORTH
Marvel Comics Group; 1 Oct 1986-5 Feb 1987

	$Good	$Fine	$N.Mint	£Good	£Fine	£N.Mint
1-5 ND	$0.15	$0.45	$0.75	£0.10	£0.35	£0.60
Title Value:	$0.75	$2.25	$3.75	£0.50	£1.75	£3.00

DALGODA
Fantagraphics; 1 Aug 1984-8 Feb 1986

	$Good	$Fine	$N.Mint	£Good	£Fine	£N.Mint
1 ND DS Fujitaki art, Kevin Nowlan back-up	$0.45	$1.35	$2.25	£0.30	£0.90	£1.50
2-6 ND Fujitaki art, Kevin Nowlan back-up	$0.45	$1.35	$2.25	£0.30	£0.90	£1.50
7 ND Fujitaki art, Journey back-up story by Loebs	$0.45	$1.35	$2.25	£0.30	£0.90	£1.50
8 ND Fujitaki art, Bojeffries back-up story by Moore and Parkhouse	$0.45	$1.35	$2.25	£0.30	£0.90	£1.50
Title Value:	$3.60	$10.80	$18.00	£2.40	£7.20	£12.00

DALGODA: FLESH AND BONES
Fantagraphics,MS; 1-4 1986

	$Good	$Fine	$N.Mint	£Good	£Fine	£N.Mint
1-4 ND Dalgoda by Fujitaki, Bojefries by Alan Moore and Steve Parkhouse	$0.35	$1.05	$1.75	£0.25	£0.75	£1.25
Title Value:	$1.40	$4.20	$7.00	£1.00	£3.00	£5.00

DAMAGE
DC Comics; 0 Oct 1994; 1 Apr 1994-20 Jan 1996

	$Good	$Fine	$N.Mint	£Good	£Fine	£N.Mint
0 (Oct 1994) Zero Hour X-over, origins revealed	$0.35	$1.05	$1.75	£0.25	£0.75	£1.25
1 Bill Marimon and Tom McWeeny art	$0.30	$0.90	$1.50	£0.20	£0.60	£1.00
2-4	$0.30	$0.90	$1.50	£0.20	£0.60	£1.00
5 New Titans appear						

	$Good	$Fine	$N.Mint	£Good	£Fine	£N.Mint
	$0.30	$0.90	$1.50	£0.20	£0.60	£1.00
6 X-over New Titans #114						
	$0.30	$0.90	$1.50	£0.20	£0.60	£1.00
7-8	$0.30	$0.90	$1.50	£0.20	£0.60	£1.00
9 Damage vs. Dr. Polaris						
	$0.30	$0.90	$1.50	£0.20	£0.60	£1.00
10-11	$0.30	$0.90	$1.50	£0.20	£0.60	£1.00
12 photo cover	$0.30	$0.90	$1.50	£0.20	£0.60	£1.00
13 New Titans appear						
	$0.35	$1.05	$1.75	£0.25	£0.75	£1.25
14 The Ray appears; X-over with Justice League Task Force #25						
	$0.35	$1.05	$1.75	£0.25	£0.75	£1.25
15	$0.35	$1.05	$1.75	£0.25	£0.75	£1.25
16 The Siege of Zi Charam part 4, continued in New Titans #125; Green Lantern appears						
	$0.35	$1.05	$1.75	£0.25	£0.75	£1.25
17	$0.35	$1.05	$1.75	£0.25	£0.75	£1.25
18 Underworld Unleashed tie-in						
	$0.35	$1.05	$1.75	£0.25	£0.75	£1.25
19 Underworld Unleashed tie-in						
	$0.45	$1.35	$2.25	£0.30	£0.90	£1.50
20	$0.35	$1.05	$1.75	£0.25	£0.75	£1.25
Title Value:	**$6.85**	**$20.55**	**$34.25**	**£4.70**	**£14.10**	**£23.50**

DAMAGE CONTROL
Marvel Comics Group,MS; 1 May 1989-4 Aug 1989

	$Good	$Fine	$N.Mint	£Good	£Fine	£N.Mint
1 ND Spiderman appears						
	$0.25	$0.75	$1.25	£0.15	£0.45	£0.75
2 ND Dr. Doom appears						
	$0.25	$0.75	$1.25	£0.15	£0.45	£0.75
3 ND Iron Man appears						
	$0.25	$0.75	$1.25	£0.15	£0.45	£0.75
4 ND X-Men appear, Wolverine on cover; Inferno tie-in						
	$0.25	$0.75	$1.25	£0.15	£0.45	£0.75
Title Value:	**$1.00**	**$3.00**	**$5.00**	**£0.60**	**£1.80**	**£3.00**
Trade paperback (Jun 1991), reprints above				£0.55	£1.65	£2.75

DAMAGE CONTROL II
Marvel Comics Group,MS; 1 Dec 1989-4 Feb 1990

	$Good	$Fine	$N.Mint	£Good	£Fine	£N.Mint
1 ND Acts of Vengeance tie-in, features Captain America, Falcon and Thor						
	$0.25	$0.75	$1.25	£0.15	£0.45	£0.75
2 ND Acts of Vengeance, Punisher and Dr. Doom appear						
	$0.25	$0.75	$1.25	£0.15	£0.45	£0.75
3 ND Acts of Vengeance tie-in, She-Hulk and original Avengers appear						
	$0.25	$0.75	$1.25	£0.15	£0.45	£0.75
4 ND Acts of Vengeance tie-in, Shield, Captain America, Thor and Punisher appear						
	$0.25	$0.75	$1.25	£0.15	£0.45	£0.75
Title Value:	**$1.00**	**$3.00**	**$5.00**	**£0.60**	**£1.80**	**£3.00**

DAMAGE CONTROL III
Marvel Comics Group,MS; 1 Jun 1991-4 Sep 1991

	$Good	$Fine	$N.Mint	£Good	£Fine	£N.Mint
1 ND Spiderman appears						
	$0.25	$0.75	$1.25	£0.15	£0.45	£0.75
2 ND Hulk, New Warriors appear						
	$0.25	$0.75	$1.25	£0.15	£0.45	£0.75
3 ND West Coast Avengers, Wonder Man, Silver Surfer appear						
	$0.25	$0.75	$1.25	£0.15	£0.45	£0.75
4 ND Silver Surfer appears plus most other Marvel characters						
	$0.25	$0.75	$1.25	£0.15	£0.45	£0.75
Title Value:	**$1.00**	**$3.00**	**$5.00**	**£0.60**	**£1.80**	**£3.00**

DAN TURNER: HOMICIDE HUNCH
Eternity,OS; 1 Sep 1991

	$Good	$Fine	$N.Mint	£Good	£Fine	£N.Mint
1 ND	$0.30	$0.90	$1.50	£0.20	£0.60	£1.00
Title Value:	**$0.30**	**$0.90**	**$1.50**	**£0.20**	**£0.60**	**£1.00**

DAN TURNER: THE STAR CHAMBER
Eternity,OS; 1 Nov 1991

	$Good	$Fine	$N.Mint	£Good	£Fine	£N.Mint
1 ND	$0.30	$0.90	$1.50	£0.20	£0.60	£1.00
Title Value:	**$0.30**	**$0.90**	**$1.50**	**£0.20**	**£0.60**	**£1.00**

DANCES WITH DEMONS
Marvel UK/Frontier; 1 Sep 1993-4 Dec 1993

	$Good	$Fine	$N.Mint	£Good	£Fine	£N.Mint
1 Simon Jowett & Charlie Adlard; foil embossed cover						
	$0.30	$0.90	$1.50	£0.20	£0.60	£1.00
2-4	$0.30	$0.90	$1.50	£0.20	£0.60	£1.00
Title Value:	**$1.20**	**$3.60**	**$6.00**	**£0.80**	**£2.40**	**£4.00**

DANGER COMIX
Danger Graphix; 1 Nov 1990

	$Good	$Fine	$N.Mint	£Good	£Fine	£N.Mint
1 ND black and white						
	$0.30	$0.90	$1.50	£0.20	£0.60	£1.00
Title Value:	**$0.30**	**$0.90**	**$1.50**	**£0.20**	**£0.60**	**£1.00**

DANGER IS OUR BUSINESS
I.W. Comics; 9 1964

	$Good	$Fine	$N.Mint	£Good	£Fine	£N.Mint
9 Williams and Frazetta reprints; distributed in the U.K.						
	$9.00	$28.00	$55.00	£5.75	£17.50	£35.00
Title Value:	**$9.00**	**$28.00**	**$55.00**	**£5.75**	**£17.50**	**£35.00**

DANGER MAN
Dell,TV; 1231 Sep/Nov 1961

	$Good	$Fine	$N.Mint	£Good	£Fine	£N.Mint
1231 scarce, distributed in the U.K.						
	$11.00	$34.00	$67.50	£7.50	£22.50	£45.00
Title Value:	**$11.00**	**$34.00**	**$67.50**	**£7.50**	**£22.50**	**£45.00**

DANGER TRAIL
National Periodical Publications; 1 Jul/Aug 1950-5 Mar/Apr 1951

	$Good	$Fine	$N.Mint	£Good	£Fine	£N.Mint
1 very scarce in the U.K. King Faraday begins, Alex Toth art						
	$87.50	$260.00	$700.00	£57.50	£175.00	£475.00
2 very scarce in the U.K. Alex Toth art						
	$70.00	$210.00	$500.00	£50.00	£150.00	£350.00
3 very rare in the U.K. Alex Toth art; a leading US dealer/historian believes there to be no more than						
10 extant copies						
	$105.00	$320.00	$750.00	£70.00	£210.00	£500.00
4 scarce in the U.K. Alex Toth art						
	$62.50	$190.00	$450.00	£43.00	£125.00	£300.00
5 scarce in the U.K. Johnny Peril, logo change; Alex Toth art						
	$62.50	$190.00	$450.00	£43.00	£125.00	£300.00
Title Value:	**$387.50**	**$1170.00**	**$2850.00**	**£263.50**	**£785.00**	**£1925.00**

DANGER TRAIL (2ND SERIES)
DC Comics; 1 Apr 1993-4 Jul 1993

	$Good	$Fine	$N.Mint	£Good	£Fine	£N.Mint
1 King Faraday begins, Infantino pencils begin; Paul Gulacy covers begin						
	$0.25	$0.75	$1.25	£0.15	£0.50	£0.85
2-4 Kobra appears						
	$0.25	$0.75	$1.25	£0.15	£0.50	£0.85
Title Value:	**$1.00**	**$3.00**	**$5.00**	**£0.60**	**£2.00**	**£3.40**

DANGER UNLIMITED
Dark Horse/Legend,MS; 1 Feb 1994-4 May 1994

	$Good	$Fine	$N.Mint	£Good	£Fine	£N.Mint
1-4 ND John Byrne script and art						
	$0.40	$1.20	$2.00	£0.25	£0.75	£1.25
Title Value:	**$1.60**	**$4.80**	**$8.00**	**£1.00**	**£3.00**	**£5.00**
Danger Unlimited (Mar 1995) Trade paperback						
collects mini-series plus story from San Diego Comicon						
Comics #2 plus a new last page and new cover by John Byrne				£2.00	£6.00	£10.00
Danger Unlimited Limited Edition Hardcover (Jul 1995)						
foil-stamped cover with dust-jacket; 1,000 copies				£8.00	£24.00	£40.00

DANGEROUS TIMES
Evolution Comics; 1 Jan 1991-4 1991

	$Good	$Fine	$N.Mint	£Good	£Fine	£N.Mint
1 ND Mike Kaluta art						
	$0.30	$0.90	$1.50	£0.20	£0.60	£1.00
1 2nd printing ND	$0.25	$0.75	$1.25	£0.15	£0.45	£0.75
2 ND Murphy Anderson cover						
	$0.30	$0.90	$1.50	£0.20	£0.60	£1.00
2 2nd printing ND	$0.25	$0.75	$1.25	£0.15	£0.45	£0.75
3 ND Marshall Rogers cover						
	$0.30	$0.90	$1.50	£0.20	£0.60	£1.00
3 2nd printing ND	$0.25	$0.75	$1.25	£0.15	£0.45	£0.75
4 ND George Perez cover						
	$0.30	$0.90	$1.50	£0.20	£0.60	£1.00
Title Value:	**$1.95**	**$5.85**	**$9.75**	**£1.25**	**£3.75**	**£6.25**

DANSE
Blackthorne; 1 1987

	$Good	$Fine	$N.Mint	£Good	£Fine	£N.Mint
1 ND	$0.30	$0.90	$1.50	£0.20	£0.60	£1.00
Title Value:	**$0.30**	**$0.90**	**$1.50**	**£0.20**	**£0.60**	**£1.00**

DARE
Monster Comics,MS; 1 Dec 1991-4 Aug 1992

	$Good	$Fine	$N.Mint	£Good	£Fine	£N.Mint
1-4 ND reprints of Dan Dare by Grant Morrison and Rian Hughes from Revolver magazine in U.K.						
	$0.30	$0.90	$1.50	£0.20	£0.60	£1.00
Title Value:	**$1.20**	**$3.60**	**$6.00**	**£0.80**	**£2.40**	**£4.00**

DAREDEVIL
Marvel Comics Group; 1 Apr 1964-present
(see Marvel Adventure, Fantastic Four, Marvel Graphic Novel, Marvel Team Up, Marvel Two-in-One, Spiderman) (...and the Black Widow #92-107)

	$Good	$Fine	$N.Mint	£Good	£Fine	£N.Mint
1 origin and 1st appearance Daredevil, Bill Everett cover and art						
	$185.00	$550.00	$1850.00	£140.00	£420.00	£1400.00
[Scarce in high grade - Very Fine+ or better]						
2 scarce in the U.K. Thing appears, Fantastic Four cameo, 2nd appearance Electro (see Amazing Spiderman #9)						
	$65.00	$195.00	$525.00	£44.00	£130.00	£350.00
[Very scarce in high grade - Very Fine+ or better]						
3 scarce in the U.K. origin and 1st appearance The Owl						
	$39.00	$115.00	$315.00	£25.00	£75.00	£200.00
4 rare in the U.K., 1st appearance The Purple Man						
	$38.00	$110.00	$300.00	£24.00	£72.50	£195.00
5 Wood art	$25.00	$75.00	$200.00	£15.50	£47.00	£125.00
6 (Feb 1965), Wood art						
	$18.00	$52.50	$145.00	£11.00	£34.00	£90.00
7 new red costume, Sub-Mariner battles Daredevil						
	$25.00	$75.00	$200.00	£15.50	£47.00	£125.00
[Scarce in high grade - Very Fine+ or better]						
8 Wood art, origin and 1st appearance Stiltman						
	$18.00	$52.50	$145.00	£11.00	£34.00	£90.00
9-10 Wood art	$18.00	$52.50	$145.00	£11.00	£34.00	£90.00
11 Wood inks; last Silver Age issue indicia-dated December 1965						
	$10.50	$32.00	$85.00	£6.25	£18.50	£50.00
12 (Jan 1966), John Romita Snr's 1st 1960s work at Marvel, Ka-Zar appears						
	$10.50	$32.00	$85.00	£6.25	£18.50	£50.00
13 Jack Kirby art, part Ka-Zar origin						
	$10.50	$32.00	$85.00	£6.25	£18.50	£50.00
14 Ka-Zar appears						
	$10.50	$32.00	$85.00	£6.25	£18.50	£50.00
15	$10.50	$32.00	$85.00	£6.25	£18.50	£50.00
16 scarce in the U.K. Spiderman X-over; John Romita Snr's 1st art on Spiderman (pre Amazing Spiderman #39)						
	$11.50	$36.00	$95.00	£7.50	£22.50	£60.00
17 Spiderman X-over						
	$11.00	$34.00	$90.00	£6.75	£20.50	£55.00
18 origin and 1st appearance The Gladiator (not to be confused with the Shiar Imperial Guard of the same name)						
	$6.75	$20.50	$55.00	£4.35	£13.00	£35.00
19-20	$6.75	$20.50	$55.00	£4.35	£13.00	£35.00
21-23 scarce in the U.K.						
	$5.00	$15.00	$35.00	£2.85	£8.50	£20.00
24 (Jan 1967)	$5.00	$15.00	$35.00	£2.85	£8.50	£20.00
25-26	$5.00	$15.00	$35.00	£2.85	£8.50	£20.00
27 Spiderman appears						

Issue / Description	$Good	$Fine	$N.Mint	£Good	£Fine	£N.Mint
	$6.00	$18.00	$42.50	£3.55	£10.50	£25.00
28-29	$5.00	$15.00	$35.00	£2.85	£8.50	£20.00
30 Thor appears	$5.00	$15.00	$35.00	£2.85	£8.50	£20.00
31-34	$3.70	$11.00	$26.00	£2.50	£7.50	£17.50
35 scarce in the U.K.	$3.70	$11.00	$26.00	£2.85	£8.50	£20.00
36 (Jan 1968), Fantastic Four appear	$3.70	$11.00	$26.00	£2.50	£7.50	£17.50
37 Dr. Doom appears, Galactus appears (1 panel); Doom rides Surfer's board! Cool.	$3.70	$11.00	$26.00	£2.50	£7.50	£17.50
38 Dr. Doom appears, X-over with Fantastic Four #73	$3.70	$11.00	$26.00	£2.50	£7.50	£17.50
39 1st appearance Exterminator (later becomes Deathstalker)	$3.70	$11.00	$26.00	£2.50	£7.50	£17.50
40	$3.70	$11.00	$26.00	£2.50	£7.50	£17.50
41 death of Mike Murdock (Daredevil's "brother")	$3.30	$10.00	$20.00	£2.00	£6.00	£12.00
42 1st appearance The Jester (note DC's The Joker!)	$3.30	$10.00	$20.00	£2.00	£6.00	£12.00
43 Captain America vs Daredevil; Jack Kirby cover	$3.30	$10.00	$20.00	£2.00	£6.00	£12.00
44 scarce in the U.K.	$3.30	$10.00	$20.00	£2.15	£6.50	£13.00
45 scarce in the U.K. photo cover	$3.30	$10.00	$20.00	£2.15	£6.50	£13.00
46 scarce in the U.K.	$3.30	$10.00	$20.00	£2.15	£6.50	£13.00
47	$3.30	$10.00	$20.00	£2.00	£6.00	£12.00
48 (Jan 1969)	$3.30	$10.00	$20.00	£2.00	£6.00	£12.00
49	$3.30	$10.00	$20.00	£2.00	£6.00	£12.00
50-51 Barry Smith art	$4.15	$12.50	$25.00	£2.50	£7.50	£15.00
52 Barry Smith art, Black Panther appears	$4.15	$12.50	$25.00	£2.50	£7.50	£15.00
53 origin retold, classic cover	$4.15	$12.50	$25.00	£2.50	£7.50	£15.00
54 scarce in the U.K. Spiderman appears	$2.05	$6.25	$12.50	£1.65	£5.00	£10.00
55	$2.00	$6.00	$12.00	£1.15	£3.50	£7.00
56 1st appearance Death's Head (not to be confused with Marvel U.K. character)	$2.00	$6.00	$12.00	£1.15	£3.50	£7.00
57 Daredevil reveals I.D. to Karen Page	$2.00	$6.00	$12.00	£1.15	£3.50	£7.00
58-59	$2.00	$6.00	$12.00	£1.15	£3.50	£7.00
60 (Jan 1970)	$2.00	$6.00	$12.00	£1.15	£3.50	£7.00
61	$1.65	$5.00	$10.00	£1.00	£3.00	£6.00
62 1st appearance Nighthawk	$1.65	$5.00	$10.00	£1.00	£3.00	£6.00
63-68	$1.65	$5.00	$10.00	£1.00	£3.00	£6.00
69 Black Panther appears	$1.65	$5.00	$10.00	£1.00	£3.00	£6.00
70-71	$1.65	$5.00	$10.00	£1.00	£3.00	£6.00
72 scarce in the U.K. (Jan 1971)	$1.65	$5.00	$10.00	£1.05	£3.25	£6.50
73 Iron Man appears	$1.65	$5.00	$10.00	£1.00	£3.00	£6.00
74-76	$1.65	$5.00	$10.00	£1.00	£3.00	£6.00
77 scarce in the U.K. Sub-Mariner and Spiderman appear	$1.65	$5.00	$10.00	£1.05	£3.25	£6.50
78-80 scarce in the U.K.	$1.65	$5.00	$10.00	£1.05	£3.25	£6.50
81 52pgs, scarce in the U.K., 1st Black Widow in title	$2.00	$6.00	$12.00	£1.15	£3.50	£7.00
82 very scarce in the U.K.	$2.00	$6.00	$12.00	£1.15	£3.50	£7.00
83 scarce in the U.K. (Jan 1972), Smith layouts	$1.65	$5.00	$10.00	£1.05	£3.25	£6.50
84-89 scarce in the U.K.	$1.65	$5.00	$10.00	£1.00	£3.00	£6.00
90-91 scarce in the U.K.	$1.50	$4.50	$9.00	£0.90	£2.75	£5.50
92 scarce in the U.K. Black Widow shares title (till #124)	$1.50	$4.50	$9.00	£0.90	£2.75	£5.50
93-94 scarce in the U.K.	$1.50	$4.50	$9.00	£0.90	£2.75	£5.50
95 scarce in the U.K. (Jan 1973)	$1.50	$4.50	$9.00	£0.90	£2.75	£5.50
96-98	$1.50	$4.50	$9.00	£0.75	£2.25	£4.50
99 Hawkeye appears	$1.50	$4.50	$9.00	£0.75	£2.25	£4.50
100 scarce in the U.K. origin retold	$4.15	$12.50	$25.00	£2.00	£6.00	£12.00
101-102	$1.50	$4.50	$7.50	£0.80	£2.40	£4.00
103 Spiderman appears	$1.50	$4.50	$7.50	£0.90	£2.70	£4.50
104 Kraven appears	$1.50	$4.50	$7.50	£0.80	£2.40	£4.00
105 Jim Starlin art (5pgs), origin of Moondragon; Thanos cameo	$2.40	$7.00	$12.00	£1.20	£3.60	£6.00
106 Moondragon appears	$1.50	$4.50	$7.50	£0.80	£2.40	£4.00
107 (Jan 1974), Jim Starlin cover, Captain Marvel and Moondragon appear, Thanos cameo;						
last Black Widow co-title on cover though she still appears inside until issue #124	$2.00	$6.00	$10.00	£0.80	£2.40	£4.00
108 Gulacy inks	$1.50	$4.50	$7.50	£0.75	£2.25	£3.75
109 ND	$1.50	$4.50	$7.50	£1.00	£3.00	£5.00
110 ND Thing cameo (X-over with Marvel Two-in-One #3)	$1.50	$4.50	$7.50	£1.00	£3.00	£5.00
111 ND	$1.50	$4.50	$7.50	£1.00	£3.00	£5.00
112	$1.50	$4.50	$7.50	£0.60	£1.80	£3.00
113 1st appearance Deathstalker (cameo)	$1.50	$4.50	$7.50	£0.60	£1.80	£3.00
114 1st full appearance Deathstalker, Man-Thing appears	$2.00	$6.00	$10.00	£0.80	£2.40	£4.00
115-116	$1.50	$4.50	$7.50	£0.60	£1.80	£3.00
117 (Jan 1975)	$1.50	$4.50	$7.50	£0.60	£1.80	£3.00
118-119	$1.50	$4.50	$7.50	£0.60	£1.80	£3.00
120 1st appearance El Jaguar	$1.50	$4.50	$7.50	£0.60	£1.80	£3.00
121	$1.00	$3.00	$5.00	£0.50	£1.50	£2.50
122 last Black Widow joint character illustration on cover	$1.00	$3.00	$5.00	£0.50	£1.50	£2.50
123	$1.00	$3.00	$5.00	£0.50	£1.50	£2.50
124 1st appearance Copperhead, last Black Widow co-title appearance	$1.00	$3.00	$5.00	£0.50	£1.50	£2.50
125-128	$1.00	$3.00	$5.00	£0.50	£1.50	£2.50
129 (Jan 1976)	$1.00	$3.00	$5.00	£0.50	£1.50	£2.50
130	$1.00	$3.00	$5.00	£0.50	£1.50	£2.50
131 scarce in the U.K. 2nd appearance/origin Bullseye, (see Nick Fury, Agent of Shield #15)	$4.50	$13.50	$22.50	£2.00	£6.00	£10.00
132 3rd appearance Bullseye	$1.50	$4.50	$7.50	£1.00	£3.00	£5.00
133 Uri Geller appears	$1.00	$3.00	$5.00	£0.45	£1.35	£2.25
134-137	$1.00	$3.00	$5.00	£0.45	£1.35	£2.25
138 Ghost Rider appears (X-over with Ghost Rider #20), Death's Head appears, Byrne art	$1.65	$5.00	$10.00	£1.00	£3.00	£6.00
139-140 LD in the U.K.	$1.00	$3.00	$5.00	£0.50	£1.50	£2.50
141 LD in the U.K. (Jan 1977)	$1.00	$3.00	$5.00	£0.50	£1.50	£2.50
142 LD in the U.K. Nova cameo (2 panels)	$1.00	$3.00	$5.00	£0.50	£1.50	£2.50
143-147 LD in the U.K.	$1.00	$3.00	$5.00	£0.50	£1.50	£2.50
148 LD in the U.K. (30 and 35 cent issues exist)	$0.90	$2.70	$4.50	£0.50	£1.50	£2.50
149 LD in the U.K.	$1.00	$3.00	$5.00	£0.50	£1.50	£2.50
150 ND scarce in the U.K. (Jan 1978), 1st appearance Paladin	$1.00	$3.00	$5.00	£1.00	£3.00	£5.00
151 Daredevil reveals I.D. to Heather Glenn	$1.00	$3.00	$5.00	£0.40	£1.20	£2.00
152 2nd appearance Paladin	$1.00	$3.00	$5.00	£0.40	£1.20	£2.00
153-154	$1.00	$3.00	$5.00	£0.40	£1.20	£2.00
155 LD in the U.K. Avengers, Hercules and Black Widow appear	$1.00	$3.00	$5.00	£0.50	£1.50	£2.50
156 LD in the U.K. (Jan 1979), Avengers appear	$1.00	$3.00	$5.00	£0.50	£1.50	£2.50
157 LD in the U.K. Avengers appear	$1.00	$3.00	$5.00	£0.50	£1.50	£2.50
158 Frank Miller art begins, origin and death of Deathstalker	$5.75	$17.50	$35.00	£3.30	£10.00	£20.00
159 Frank Miller art	$3.30	$10.00	$20.00	£2.05	£6.25	£12.50
160 Frank Miller art	$1.65	$5.00	$10.00	£1.65	£5.00	£10.00
161 ND rare in the U.K., Frank Miller art	$1.65	$5.00	$10.00	£2.50	£7.50	£15.00
162 ND (Jan 1980), Steve Ditko art	$0.65	$2.00	$4.00	£0.50	£1.50	£3.00
163 Hulk battles Daredevil, Frank Miller art	$1.65	$5.00	$10.00	£1.25	£3.75	£7.50
164 origin retold, Avengers appear, Frank Miller art	$1.65	$5.00	$10.00	£1.15	£3.50	£7.00
165-167 Frank Miller art	$1.25	$3.75	$7.50	£1.00	£3.00	£6.00
168 (Jan 1981), 1st appearance Elektra, Frank Miller art	$5.00	$15.00	$30.00	£2.50	£7.50	£15.00
169 ND Elektra appears, Frank Miller art	$1.65	$5.00	$10.00	£2.05	£6.25	£12.50
170-172 LD in the U.K. Frank Miller art	$1.50	$4.50	$7.50	£0.90	£2.70	£4.50
173	$1.00	$3.00	$5.00	£0.60	£1.80	£3.00
174-177 Elektra appears, Frank Miller art	$1.00	$3.00	$5.00	£0.70	£2.10	£3.50
178 (Jan 1982), Elektra appears, Powerman and Iron Fist appear, Frank Miller art	$0.80	$2.40	$4.00	£0.70	£2.10	£3.50
179-180 Elektra appears, Frank Miller art	$0.80	$2.40	$4.00	£0.70	£2.10	£3.50
181 DS, death of Elektra, Punisher and Bullseye appear, Frank Miller art	$1.80	$5.25	$9.00	£1.00	£3.00	£5.00
182 Punisher cameo, Frank Miller art	$2.00	$6.00	$10.00	£0.90	£2.70	£4.50

Issue / Notes	$Good	$Fine	$N.Mint	£Good	£Fine	£N.Mint
183-184 Punisher cameo, Frank Miller art	$2.00	$6.00	$10.00	£1.00	£3.00	£5.00
185-186 Frank Miller credited as the story-teller only	$0.60	$1.80	$3.00	£0.50	£1.50	£2.50
187 new Black Widow appears, Frank Miller story-teller only, Elektra's ressurrection begins	$0.60	$1.80	$3.00	£0.50	£1.50	£2.50
188-189 Frank Miller credited as the story-teller only	$0.60	$1.80	$3.00	£0.50	£1.50	£2.50
190 (Jan 1983), DS, Elektra saga ends, partial origin Elektra	$0.60	$1.80	$3.00	£0.60	£1.80	£3.00
191 last Frank Miller Daredevil	$0.60	$1.80	$3.00	£0.40	£1.20	£2.00
192-195	$0.50	$1.50	$2.50	£0.30	£0.90	£1.50
196 Wolverine appears	$3.00	$9.00	$15.00	£1.00	£3.00	£5.00
197-199	$0.50	$1.50	$2.50	£0.30	£0.90	£1.50
200 Bullseye appears, John Byrne cover	$0.50	$1.50	$2.50	£0.40	£1.20	£2.00
201	$0.50	$1.50	$2.50	£0.30	£0.90	£1.50
202 (Jan 1984)	$0.50	$1.50	$2.50	£0.30	£0.90	£1.50
203-205	$0.50	$1.50	$2.50	£0.30	£0.90	£1.50
206 1st Mazzuchelli art	$0.50	$1.50	$2.50	£0.30	£0.90	£1.50
207	$0.50	$1.50	$2.50	£0.30	£0.90	£1.50
208 Harlan Ellison script	$0.50	$1.50	$2.50	£0.30	£0.90	£1.50
209-213	$0.50	$1.50	$2.50	£0.30	£0.90	£1.50
214 (Jan 1985)	$0.40	$1.20	$2.00	£0.30	£0.90	£1.50
215-216	$0.40	$1.20	$2.00	£0.30	£0.90	£1.50
217 Barry Windsor-Smith cover	$0.40	$1.20	$2.00	£0.30	£0.90	£1.50
218 LD in the U.K.	$0.40	$1.20	$2.00	£0.40	£1.20	£2.00
219 Frank Miller story	$0.40	$1.20	$2.00	£0.40	£1.20	£2.00
220-222 LD in the U.K.	$0.40	$1.20	$2.00	£0.35	£1.05	£1.75
223 LD in the U.K. Secret Wars X-over	$0.40	$1.20	$2.00	£0.35	£1.05	£1.75
224-225 LD in the U.K.	$0.40	$1.20	$2.00	£0.35	£1.05	£1.75
226 LD in the U.K. (Jan 1986), Frank Miller plot	$0.60	$1.80	$3.00	£0.80	£2.40	£4.00
227 LD in the U.K. Frank Miller story only	$1.20	$3.60	$6.00	£1.00	£3.00	£5.00
228 Frank Miller	$0.50	$1.50	$2.50	£0.50	£1.50	£2.50
229 very LD Frank Miller	$0.50	$1.50	$2.50	£0.60	£1.80	£3.00
230-233 Frank Miller	$0.50	$1.50	$2.50	£0.50	£1.50	£2.50
234-235 Steve Ditko art	$0.40	$1.20	$2.00	£0.25	£0.75	£1.25
236 Barry Smith art, Nocenti scripts begin	$0.40	$1.20	$2.00	£0.30	£0.90	£1.50
237	$0.40	$1.20	$2.00	£0.30	£0.75	£1.25
238 LD in the U.K. (Jan 1987), Mutant Massacre, Sabretooth X-over, Art Adams art	$1.50	$4.50	$7.50	£0.80	£2.40	£4.00
239-240	$0.40	$1.20	$2.00	£0.25	£0.75	£1.25
241 Todd McFarlane art, Mike Zeck cover	$0.60	$1.80	$3.00	£0.40	£1.20	£2.00
242-246	$0.40	$1.20	$2.00	£0.25	£0.75	£1.25
247 Keith Giffen art	$0.40	$1.20	$2.00	£0.25	£0.75	£1.25
248-249 LD in the U.K. Wolverine appears, Williamson inks	$1.50	$4.50	$7.50	£0.80	£2.40	£4.00
250 LD in the U.K. (Jan 1988)	$0.40	$1.20	$2.00	£0.40	£1.20	£2.00
251 LD in the U.K.	$0.40	$1.20	$2.00	£0.40	£1.20	£2.00
252 LD in the U.K. DS, Fall of the Mutants	$0.60	$1.80	$3.00	£0.70	£2.10	£3.50
253 LD in the U.K.	$0.40	$1.20	$2.00	£0.40	£1.20	£2.00
254 LD in the U.K. origin and 1st appearance Typhoid Mary	$2.40	$7.00	$12.00	£1.30	£3.90	£6.50
255 2nd appearance of Typhoid Mary	$1.00	$3.00	$5.00	£0.60	£1.80	£3.00
256 3rd appearance of Typhoid Mary	$0.80	$2.40	$4.00	£0.40	£1.20	£2.00
257 X-over with Punisher #10	$2.00	$6.00	$10.00	£1.50	£4.50	£7.50
258 Ron Lim art	$0.40	$1.20	$2.00	£0.35	£1.05	£1.75
259 LD in the U.K. Typhoid Mary appears	$0.80	$2.40	$4.00	£0.40	£1.20	£2.00
260 DS Typhoid Mary, Kingpin appear	$0.30	$0.90	$1.50	£0.15	£0.45	£0.75
261 LD in the U.K. Human Torch/Typhoid Mary	$0.40	$1.20	$2.00	£0.30	£0.90	£1.50
262 (Jan 1989), Inferno tie-in	$0.30	$0.90	$1.50	£0.15	£0.45	£0.75
263 Inferno tie-in	$0.30	$0.90	$1.50	£0.15	£0.45	£0.75
264	$0.30	$0.90	$1.50	£0.15	£0.45	£0.75
265 Inferno tie-in	$0.30	$0.90	$1.50	£0.15	£0.45	£0.75
266-268	$0.30	$0.90	$1.50	£0.15	£0.45	£0.75
269 LD in the U.K. Blob/Pyro battle Daredevil	$0.40	$1.20	$2.00	£0.30	£0.90	£1.50
270 Spiderman co-stars, 1st appearance Black Heart	$0.30	$0.90	$1.50	£0.15	£0.45	£0.75
271	$0.30	$0.90	$1.50	£0.15	£0.45	£0.75
272 Inhumans appear, 1st appearance Shotgun	$0.30	$0.90	$1.50	£0.15	£0.45	£0.75
273-274 Inhumans appear	$0.30	$0.90	$1.50	£0.15	£0.45	£0.75
275 Acts of Vengeance tie-in	$0.30	$0.90	$1.50	£0.15	£0.45	£0.75
276 (Jan 1990), Acts of Vengeance tie-in	$0.30	$0.90	$1.50	£0.15	£0.45	£0.75
277-280	$0.30	$0.90	$1.50	£0.15	£0.45	£0.75
281 Silver Surfer appears (cameo)	$0.30	$0.90	$1.50	£0.15	£0.45	£0.75
282 Silver Surfer appears	$0.30	$0.90	$1.50	£0.15	£0.45	£0.75
283 Captain America appears	$0.30	$0.90	$1.50	£0.15	£0.45	£0.75
284-286	$0.30	$0.90	$1.50	£0.15	£0.45	£0.75
287 Bullseye as Daredevil	$0.30	$0.90	$1.50	£0.15	£0.45	£0.75
288 (Jan 1991), Bullseye as Daredevil	$0.30	$0.90	$1.50	£0.15	£0.45	£0.75
289 Bullseye as Daredevil	$0.30	$0.90	$1.50	£0.15	£0.45	£0.75
290	$0.30	$0.90	$1.50	£0.15	£0.45	£0.75
291 last Nocenti script	$0.30	$0.90	$1.50	£0.15	£0.45	£0.75

Dagar the Invincible #2

Daredevil #8

Daredevil #131

MINT = 100% / NEAR MINT (inc. +/-) = 90-99% / VERY FINE (inc. +/-) = 75-89% / FINE (inc. +/-) = 55-74%
VERY GOOD (inc. +/-) = 35-54% / GOOD (inc. +/-) = 15-34% / FAIR = 5-14% / POOR = 1-4%

283

	$Good	$Fine	$N.Mint	£Good	£Fine	£N.Mint
292-293 Punisher guest-stars	$0.30	$0.90	$1.50	£0.15	£0.45	£0.75
294	$0.30	$0.90	$1.50	£0.15	£0.45	£0.75
295 Ghost Rider guest-stars	$0.30	$0.90	$1.50	£0.15	£0.45	£0.75
296	$0.30	$0.90	$1.50	£0.15	£0.45	£0.75
297 Last Rites (Fall of the Kingpin) part 1, Typhoid Mary appears	$0.30	$0.90	$1.50	£0.15	£0.45	£0.75
298 Last Rites part 2, Nick Fury guest stars	$0.30	$0.90	$1.50	£0.15	£0.45	£0.75
299 Last Rites part 3	$0.30	$0.90	$1.50	£0.15	£0.45	£0.75
300 (Jan 1992), DS Last Rites part 4; "red spot varnish" cover was solicited but it only came out as vaguely fluorescent	$0.80	$2.40	$4.00	£0.30	£0.90	£1.50
301 $1.25 cover begins	$0.30	$0.90	$1.50	£0.15	£0.45	£0.75
302-304	$0.30	$0.90	$1.50	£0.15	£0.45	£0.75
305-306 Spiderman appears	$0.30	$0.90	$1.50	£0.15	£0.45	£0.75
307 Dead Man's Hand part 1, Punisher and Nomad appear, continues in Nomad #4	$0.30	$0.90	$1.50	£0.15	£0.45	£0.75
308 Dead Man's Hand part 4, Punisher and Tombstone appear	$0.30	$0.90	$1.50	£0.15	£0.45	£0.75
309 Dead Man's Hand part 7, Punisher and Nomad appear	$0.30	$0.90	$1.50	£0.15	£0.45	£0.75
310-311 Calypso appears	$0.30	$0.90	$1.50	£0.15	£0.45	£0.75
312 (Jan 1993)	$0.30	$0.90	$1.50	£0.15	£0.45	£0.75
313-314	$0.30	$0.90	$1.50	£0.15	£0.45	£0.75
315 1st appearance Shock	$0.30	$0.90	$1.50	£0.15	£0.45	£0.75
316 ties into Daredevil #304	$0.30	$0.90	$1.50	£0.15	£0.45	£0.75
317-318	$0.30	$0.90	$1.50	£0.15	£0.45	£0.75
319 ND Fall From Grace prologue, Silver Sable appears	$2.00	$6.00	$10.00	£1.50	£4.50	£7.50
319 2nd printing, ND (Jan 1994), cover colours reversed	$0.25	$0.75	$1.25	£0.15	£0.45	£0.80
320 ND Fall From Grace story, Silver Sable appears	$1.80	$5.25	$9.00	£1.40	£4.20	£7.00
321 ND Fall From Grace story; glow in the dark cover	$1.20	$3.60	$6.00	£0.70	£2.10	£3.50
321 ND Fall From Grace story; no glow in the dark cover	$0.60	$1.80	$3.00	£0.35	£1.05	£1.75
322 ND Fall From Grace story	$0.80	$2.40	$4.00	£0.50	£1.50	£2.50
323 ND Fall From Grace story, painted cover	$0.50	$1.50	$2.50	£0.35	£1.05	£1.75
324 ND (Jan 1994), Fall From Grace story, Morbius and Elektra appear	$0.50	$1.50	$2.50	£0.35	£1.05	£1.75
325 ND 48pgs, Fall From Grace story, Morbius and Elekta appear; bound-in poster at centre-fold	$0.50	$1.50	$2.50	£0.35	£1.05	£1.75
326 ND Tree of Knowledge story begins (ends #330)	$0.30	$0.90	$1.50	£0.20	£0.60	£1.00
327	$0.30	$0.90	$1.50	£0.20	£0.60	£1.00
328 with free Spiderman's Amazing Powers card sheet	$0.30	$0.90	$1.50	£0.20	£0.60	£1.00
329-330 Gambit guest-stars	$0.30	$0.90	$1.50	£0.20	£0.60	£1.00
331 Captain America appears	$0.30	$0.90	$1.50	£0.20	£0.60	£1.00
332 Captain America and Gambit appear	$0.30	$0.90	$1.50	£0.20	£0.60	£1.00
333-335	$0.30	$0.90	$1.50	£0.20	£0.60	£1.00
336 (Jan 1995)	$0.30	$0.90	$1.50	£0.20	£0.60	£1.00
337 Blackwulf and Kingpin appear	$0.30	$0.90	$1.50	£0.20	£0.60	£1.00
338-339	$0.30	$0.90	$1.50	£0.20	£0.60	£1.00
340-342 Kingpin appears	$0.30	$0.90	$1.50	£0.20	£0.60	£1.00
343	$0.30	$0.90	$1.50	£0.20	£0.60	£1.00
344 Over The Edge tie-in, J.M. DeMatteis script and Ron Wagner art begin	$0.40	$1.20	$2.00	£0.25	£0.75	£1.25
345-347	$0.40	$1.20	$2.00	£0.25	£0.75	£1.25
348 (Jan 1996)	$0.40	$1.20	$2.00	£0.25	£0.75	£1.25
349	$0.40	$1.20	$2.00	£0.25	£0.75	£1.25
350 48pgs	$0.60	$1.80	$3.00	£0.40	£1.20	£2.00
350 48pgs, fifth ink aqueous coated cover	$0.70	$2.10	$3.50	£0.50	£1.50	£2.50
Title Value:	$962.20	$2876.95	$7166.75	£619.60	£1862.40	£4701.80

Note: Al Williamson inks #248-267

Daredevil and Punisher: Child's Play

	£Good	£Fine	£N.Mint
Trade paperback, reprints #182-184	£1.10	£3.30	£5.50
(2nd print - May 1991)	£1.00	£3.00	£5.00

Daredevil: Born Again

	£Good	£Fine	£N.Mint
Trade paperback, reprints #226-229	£1.25	£3.75	£6.25
(2nd print. Nov 1989)	£1.20	£3.60	£6.00

Daredevil: Love and War

	£Good	£Fine	£N.Mint
Trade paperback, reprints #230-233	£1.25	£3.75	£6.25
(2nd print. Dec 1989)	£1.20	£3.60	£6.00

Daredevil: Marked For Death

	£Good	£Fine	£N.Mint
Trade paperback (May 1990) reprints #159-161,163,164	£1.40	£4.20	£7.00

Daredevil: Gang War

	£Good	£Fine	£N.Mint
Trade paperback (May 1992) reprints #169-172, 180	£1.40	£4.20	£7.00

Daredevil: Fall of the Kingpin (Apr 1993)

	£Good	£Fine	£N.Mint
Trade paperback, reprints #297-#300	£1.65	£4.95	£8.25

Daredevil: Fall From Grace (Nov 1994)
Trade paperback

	£Good	£Fine	£N.Mint
reprints issues #319-325 plus 12 new pages	£2.60	£7.80	£13.00

Marvel Limited: Daredevil, Man Without Fear

	£Good	£Fine	£N.Mint
Trade paperback 192pgs, reprints mini-series	£2.60	£7.80	£13.00

Daredevil: Man Without Fear (Dec 1994)

	£Good	£Fine	£N.Mint
160pgs, reprints mini-series in softcover format	£2.00	£6.00	£10.00

Daredevil Megahit (Nov 1995)

	£Good	£Fine	£N.Mint
ND boxed set of Daredevil: Man Without Fear mini-series, with limited quantities	£2.00	£6.00	£10.00

Daredevil Mini-Masterpiece (Nov 1995)

	£Good	£Fine	£N.Mint
ND boxed set of Daredevil #319-325 (#319 2nd print), with limited quantities	£1.40	£4.20	£7.00

DAREDEVIL ANNUAL
Marvel Comics Group; 1 Sep 1967; 2 Feb 1971-3 Jan 1972; 4 Oct 1976; 4 Sep 1989-present

	$Good	$Fine	$N.Mint	£Good	£Fine	£N.Mint
1 68pgs, all new stories; Daredevil vs. The Emissaries of Evil	$5.25	$16.00	$32.00	£3.30	£10.00	£20.00
2 ND scarce in the U.K. 52pgs, reprints issues #10, #11	$2.15	$6.50	$13.00	£1.15	£3.50	£7.00
3 ND very scarce in the U.K. 52pgs, reprints Daredevil #16, #17 featuring Spiderman	$2.15	$6.50	$13.00	£1.30	£4.00	£8.00
4 ND 52pgs, all new, Black Panther and Sub-Mariner appear	$1.00	$3.00	$5.00	£0.60	£1.80	£3.00
4 52pgs, squarebound, Atlantis Attacks tie-in, Jim Lee and Whilce Portacio; accidentally mis-numbered by Marvel	$0.60	$1.80	$3.00	£0.40	£1.20	£2.00
6 ND 64pgs, Lifeform part 2, continues in Hulk Annual #16	$0.45	$1.35	$2.25	£0.30	£0.90	£1.50
7 ND story continues in Punisher Annual #4	$0.45	$1.35	$2.25	£0.30	£0.90	£1.50
8 ND The System Bytes part 2, Deathlok appears, continued in Wonderman Annual #1	$0.45	$1.35	$2.25	£0.30	£0.90	£1.50
9 ND 64pgs, pre-bagged with trading card introducing Devourer	$0.60	$1.80	$3.00	£0.40	£1.20	£2.00
10 ND 64pgs, Master of Kung Fu and Black Widow appear	$0.60	$1.80	$3.00	£0.40	£1.20	£2.00
Title Value:	$13.70	$41.45	$78.75	£8.45	£25.60	£48.50

Note: Marvel mistakenly issued a 2nd Annual 4, not realising they had already done so in 1976. There is no Annual 5.

DAREDEVIL GIANT SIZE
Marvel Comics Group; 1 1975

	$Good	$Fine	$N.Mint	£Good	£Fine	£N.Mint
1 ND very scarce in the U.K. 68pgs, reprints Daredevil King Size Annual #1	$2.00	$6.00	$10.00	£1.30	£3.90	£6.50
Title Value:	$2.00	$6.00	$10.00	£1.30	£3.90	£6.50

DAREDEVIL: MAN WITHOUT FEAR
Marvel Comics Group,MS; 1 Oct 1993-5 Feb 1994

	$Good	$Fine	$N.Mint	£Good	£Fine	£N.Mint
1 ND Frank Miller script, John Romita Jnr. pencils begin; red foil embossed card-stock cover	$1.00	$3.00	$5.00	£0.60	£1.80	£3.00
2 ND scarce in the U.K. Matt Murdock's first meeting with Elektra; foil etched cover	$1.00	$3.00	$5.00	£0.60	£1.80	£3.00
3 ND Daredevil's origin explored in more detail	$1.00	$3.00	$5.00	£0.50	£1.50	£2.50
4-5 ND red foil embossed cover	$1.00	$3.00	$5.00	£0.50	£1.50	£2.50
Title Value:	$5.00	$15.00	$25.00	£2.70	£8.10	£13.50

DARERAT/TADPOLE
Mighty Pumpkin; nn Feb 1987
(see Gnatrat, Happy Birthdat Gnatrat)

	$Good	$Fine	$N.Mint	£Good	£Fine	£N.Mint
nn ND scarce in the U.K. Daredevil/Elektra/Frank Miller parody by Mark Martin	$0.60	$1.80	$3.00	£0.40	£1.20	£2.00
Title Value:	$0.60	$1.80	$3.00	£0.40	£1.20	£2.00

DARING ADVENTURES
I.W. Super; 9-12,15-18 1963-1964

	$Good	$Fine	$N.Mint	£Good	£Fine	£N.Mint
9 scarce in the U.K. all reprint	$5.00	$15.00	$30.00	£3.30	£10.00	£20.00
10-11 scarce in the U.K. all reprint	$2.50	$7.50	$15.00	£1.65	£5.00	£10.00
12 scarce in the U.K. Phantom Lady reprints	$14.00	$43.00	$85.00	£9.00	£28.00	£55.00
15 scarce in the U.K. Hooded Menace reprint	$8.25	$25.00	$50.00	£5.00	£15.00	£30.00
16-18 scarce in the U.K. all reprint	$2.50	$7.50	$15.00	£1.65	£5.00	£10.00
Title Value:	$39.75	$120.50	$240.00	£25.55	£78.00	£155.00

DARING NEW ADVENTURES OF SUPERGIRL
(see Supergirl)

DARK ASSASSIN
Greater Mercury Comics; 1 Aug 1989-6 1992?

	$Good	$Fine	$N.Mint	£Good	£Fine	£N.Mint
1 ND Kris Silver script, Richard Carter art; black and white	$0.30	$0.90	$1.50	£0.20	£0.60	£1.00
2-6 ND black and white	$0.30	$0.90	$1.50	£0.20	£0.60	£1.00
Title Value:	$1.80	$5.40	$9.00	£1.20	£3.60	£6.00

DARK CRYSTAL, THE
Marvel Comics Group,MS Film; 1 Apr 1983-2 May 1983

	$Good	$Fine	$N.Mint	£Good	£Fine	£N.Mint
1-2 ND adapts film	$0.15	$0.45	$0.75	£0.10	£0.35	£0.60

	$Good	$Fine	$N.Mint	£Good	£Fine	£N.Mint

DARK DESTINY
Alpha Productions; 1 Oct 1994

	$Good	$Fine	$N.Mint	£Good	£Fine	£N.Mint
1 ND black and white; Paul Pelletier cover	$0.80	$2.40	$4.00	£0.50	£1.50	£2.50
Title Value:	$0.80	$2.40	$4.00	£0.50	£1.50	£2.50

DARK DOMINION
Defiant; 1 Oct 1993-13 Oct 1994

	$Good	$Fine	$N.Mint	£Good	£Fine	£N.Mint
1 ND Len Wein script begins	$0.30	$0.90	$1.50	£0.20	£0.60	£1.00
2-10 ND	$0.30	$0.90	$1.50	£0.20	£0.60	£1.00
11 ND Schism X-over	$0.30	$0.90	$1.50	£0.20	£0.60	£1.00
12-13 ND	$0.30	$0.90	$1.50	£0.20	£0.60	£1.00
Title Value:	$3.90	$11.70	$19.50	£2.60	£7.80	£13.00

Dark Dominion #0 Special Edition (Aug 1994)
Trade paperback

	$Good	$Fine	$N.Mint	£Good	£Fine	£N.Mint
new Joe James art, Jim Shooter's original script; 10,000 copies				$2.70	£8.10	£13.50

DARK FANTASY
Apple Comics; 1 May 1992

	$Good	$Fine	$N.Mint	£Good	£Fine	£N.Mint
1 ND Kevin Schnaper script/art; horror/fantasy anthology (3 stories); black and white	$0.35	$1.05	$1.75	£0.25	£0.75	£1.25
Title Value:	$0.35	$1.05	$1.75	£0.25	£0.75	£1.25

DARK GUARD
Marvel UK; 1 Oct 1993-3 Dec 1993

	$Good	$Fine	$N.Mint	£Good	£Fine	£N.Mint
1 Dan Abnett script and Carlos Pacheco art begin; features Death's Head II, Motormouth, Killpower and Dark Angel; card stock cover with silver foil logo	$0.35	$1.05	$1.75	£0.25	£0.75	£1.25
2-3	$0.30	$0.90	$1.50	£0.20	£0.60	£1.00
Title Value:	$0.95	$2.85	$4.75	£0.65	£1.95	£3.25

DARK HORSE CLASSICS
Dark Horse; 1 Jul 1992-2 1992

	$Good	$Fine	$N.Mint	£Good	£Fine	£N.Mint
1 ND 48pgs, Last of the Mohicans	$0.80	$2.40	$4.00	£0.50	£1.50	£2.50
2 ND 48pgs, 20,000 Leagues Under The Sea	$0.80	$2.40	$4.00	£0.50	£1.50	£2.50
Title Value:	$1.60	$4.80	$8.00	£1.00	£3.00	£5.00

DARK HORSE COMICS
Dark Horse; 1 Aug 1992-25 Sep 1994

	$Good	$Fine	$N.Mint	£Good	£Fine	£N.Mint
1 anthology of new stories featuring Predator, Robocop plus Renegade by Claremont and Time Cop by Verheiden, double gatefold cover by Dave Dorman	$0.45	$1.35	$2.25	£0.30	£0.90	£1.50
2	$0.45	$1.35	$2.25	£0.30	£0.90	£1.50
3 Aliens: Horror Show by Sarah Byam and David Roach begins, David Roach cover	$0.45	$1.35	$2.25	£0.30	£0.90	£1.50
4-5	$0.45	$1.35	$2.25	£0.30	£0.90	£1.50
6 Robocop by Steven Grant and Bruce Patterson begins	$0.45	$1.35	$2.25	£0.30	£0.90	£1.50
7 Star Wars: Tales of the Jedi by Tom Veitch begins (1st)	$0.80	$2.40	$4.00	£0.50	£1.50	£2.50
8 Star Wars, RoboCop: Invasions, James Bond 1st appearance X	$0.80	$2.40	$4.00	£0.50	£1.50	£2.50
9 Star Wars, RoboCop: Invasions, James Bond, X	$0.45	$1.35	$2.25	£0.30	£0.90	£1.50
10 Predator, Godzilla, James Bond, X	$0.45	$1.35	$2.25	£0.30	£0.90	£1.50
11 Predator, Godzilla, James Bond, Aliens: Taste; Art Adams cover	$0.45	$1.35	$2.25	£0.30	£0.90	£1.50
12 Aliens/Predator special	$0.45	$1.35	$2.25	£0.30	£0.90	£1.50
13 Aliens, Predator, Thing from Another World	$0.45	$1.35	$2.25	£0.30	£0.90	£1.50
14 The Mark	$0.45	$1.35	$2.25	£0.30	£0.90	£1.50
15 The Mark, Aliens: Cargo	$0.45	$1.35	$2.25	£0.30	£0.90	£1.50
16 Predator: The Hunted City	$0.45	$1.35	$2.25	£0.30	£0.90	£1.50
17-18 Aliens, Star Wars: Droids, Predator	$0.45	$1.35	$2.25	£0.30	£0.90	£1.50
19-20 Predator	$0.45	$1.35	$2.25	£0.30	£0.90	£1.50
21 Mecha, Predator	$0.45	$1.35	$2.25	£0.30	£0.90	£1.50
22 Aliens, Mecha	$0.45	$1.35	$2.25	£0.30	£0.90	£1.50
23 Aliens, The Machine	$0.45	$1.35	$2.25	£0.30	£0.90	£1.50
24 Aliens, The Machine	$0.45	$1.35	$2.25	£0.30	£0.90	£1.50
25 James Bond by Doug Moench and Russ Heath, Aliens vs. Predator; Russ Heath cover	$0.45	$1.35	$2.25	£0.30	£0.90	£1.50
Title Value:	$11.95	$35.85	$59.75	£7.90	£23.70	£39.50

Note: all Non-Distributed on the news-stands in the U.K.

DARK HORSE DOWNUNDER
Dark Horse; 1 May 1994-3 Jul 1994

	$Good	$Fine	$N.Mint	£Good	£Fine	£N.Mint
1 ND features Eddie Campbell script and art; anthology, black and white	$0.45	$1.35	$2.25	£0.30	£0.90	£1.50
2-3 ND features by Australian creative teams continue	$0.45	$1.35	$2.25	£0.30	£0.90	£1.50
Title Value:	$1.35	$4.05	$6.75	£0.90	£2.70	£4.50

DARK HORSE FUTURES
Dark Horse; 1989-1994

	$Good	$Fine	$N.Mint	£Good	£Fine	£N.Mint
1989-1990 ND promotional giveaway	$0.30	$0.90	$1.50	£0.20	£0.60	£1.00
1991 ND promotional giveaway featuring an Aliens mini-poster by Dave Dorman	$0.30	$0.90	$1.50	£0.20	£0.60	£1.00
1992-1994 ND promotional giveaway	$0.30	$0.90	$1.50	£0.20	£0.60	£1.00
Title Value:	$1.80	$5.40	$9.00	£1.20	£3.60	£6.00

DARK HORSE INSIDER
Dark Horse; 1 Dec 1991-present

	$Good	$Fine	$N.Mint	£Good	£Fine	£N.Mint
1 ND promotional material begins plus Aliens vs. Predator story (ends #14)	$0.15	$0.45	$0.75	£0.10	£0.30	£0.50
2-48 ND	$0.15	$0.45	$0.75	£0.10	£0.30	£0.50
Title Value:	$7.20	$21.60	$36.00	£4.80	£14.40	£24.00

DARK HORSE PRESENTS
Dark Horse; 1 Jul 1986-present

	$Good	$Fine	$N.Mint	£Good	£Fine	£N.Mint
1 1st appearance Concrete by Chadwick, Black Cross	$2.40	$7.00	$12.00	£1.20	£3.60	£6.00
1 reprint of #1 (Oct 1992) - silver border around cover	$0.40	$1.20	$2.00	£0.25	£0.75	£1.25
1 2nd printing	$0.80	$2.40	$4.00	£0.50	£1.50	£2.50
2 Concrete	$1.40	$4.20	$7.00	£0.80	£2.40	£4.00
3 Concrete, Boris the Bear	$1.20	$3.60	$6.00	£0.80	£2.40	£4.00
4 1st Trekker, Concrete	$1.00	$3.00	$5.00	£0.60	£1.80	£3.00
5 Concrete, Gulacy cover	$1.00	$3.00	$5.00	£0.60	£1.80	£3.00
6 Concrete	$0.60	$1.80	$3.00	£0.40	£1.20	£2.00
7	$0.60	$1.80	$3.00	£0.40	£1.20	£2.00
8 Concrete	$0.60	$1.80	$3.00	£0.40	£1.20	£2.00
9	$0.60	$1.80	$3.00	£0.40	£1.20	£2.00
10 Concrete	$0.80	$2.40	$4.00	£0.50	£1.50	£2.50
11	$0.40	$1.20	$2.00	£0.30	£0.90	£1.50
12 Concrete	$0.40	$1.20	$2.00	£0.30	£0.90	£1.50
13	$0.40	$1.20	$2.00	£0.30	£0.90	£1.50
14 Mr. Monster	$0.40	$1.20	$2.00	£0.30	£0.90	£1.50
15 no number on cover	$0.40	$1.20	$2.00	£0.30	£0.90	£1.50
16 Concrete	$0.40	$1.20	$2.00	£0.30	£0.90	£1.50
17 full length Roachmill story	$0.40	$1.20	$2.00	£0.30	£0.90	£1.50
18-19	$0.40	$1.20	$2.00	£0.30	£0.90	£1.50
20 64pgs, (Annual), Concrete, Flaming Carrot; many were produced with crinkled spines owing to the way the glue dried	$0.60	$1.80	$3.00	£0.40	£1.20	£2.50
21-22 Trekker	$0.40	$1.20	$2.00	£0.30	£0.90	£1.50
23	$0.40	$1.20	$2.00	£0.30	£0.90	£1.50
24 1st appearance Aliens; Mark A. Nelson plot/art, Mark Verheiden text	$3.00	$9.00	$15.00	£2.00	£6.00	£10.00
25-27	$0.45	$1.35	$2.25	£0.30	£0.90	£1.50
28 DS, Concrete, Roachmill	$0.70	$2.10	$3.50	£0.50	£1.50	£2.50
29-31	$0.40	$1.20	$2.00	£0.30	£0.90	£1.50
32 64pgs, (Annual), Concrete, American	$0.90	$2.70	$4.50	£0.60	£1.80	£3.00
33 40pgs	$0.40	$1.20	$2.00	£0.30	£0.90	£1.50
34 scarce in the U.K. Aliens story that builds to Aliens vs. Predator	$1.20	$3.60	$6.00	£0.80	£2.40	£4.00
35 scarce in the U.K. Predator story that builds to Aliens vs. Predator	$1.20	$3.60	$6.00	£0.80	£2.40	£4.00
36 Aliens vs. Predator (1st - predates Aliens vs. Predator mini-series), painted cover with black surround	$1.80	$5.25	$9.00	£1.20	£3.60	£6.00
36 Aliens vs. Predator (1st - predates Aliens vs. Predator mini-series), line-drawn cover with blue and mauve background	$1.80	$5.25	$9.00	£1.20	£3.60	£6.00
37-39	$0.40	$1.20	$2.00	£0.30	£0.90	£1.50
40 48pgs, Trekker, Bacchus	$0.60	$1.80	$3.00	£0.40	£1.20	£2.00
41	$0.40	$1.20	$2.00	£0.30	£0.90	£1.50
42-43 Aliens	$0.60	$1.80	$3.00	£0.40	£1.20	£2.00
44 Crash Ryan returns	$0.40	$1.20	$2.00	£0.30	£0.90	£1.50
45	$0.40	$1.20	$2.00	£0.30	£0.90	£1.50
46 Predator	$0.40	$1.20	$2.00	£0.30	£0.90	£1.50
47-49	$0.40	$1.20	$2.00	£0.30	£0.90	£1.50
50 George Perez art featured	$0.60	$1.80	$3.00	£0.40	£1.20	£2.00
51 Sin City by Frank Miller continues from 5th Anniversary Special (1st appearance in title)	$0.60	$1.80	$3.00	£0.40	£1.20	£2.00
52 Eddie Campbell cover	$0.40	$1.20	$2.00	£0.30	£0.90	£1.50
53 Frank Miller cover	$0.40	$1.20	$2.00	£0.30	£0.90	£1.50
54 previews John Byrne's Next Men (1st appearance)	$1.50	$4.50	$7.50	£1.00	£3.00	£5.00
55 previews John Byrne's Next Men, Frank Miller cover	$1.20	$3.60	$6.00	£0.80	£2.40	£4.00
56 64pgs, Next Men, Sin City continues, cover based on DC's famous Superman Annual #7	$0.90	$2.70	$4.50	£0.60	£1.80	£3.00
57 48pgs, Next Men concludes, cover by John Byrne and Frank Miller based on Marvel's Daredevil #1	$0.90	$2.70	$4.50	£0.60	£1.80	£3.00
58	$0.40	$1.20	$2.00	£0.30	£0.90	£1.50
59-60 20pgs Sin City by Frank Miller, cover by Frank Miller and Lynn Varley	$0.40	$1.20	$2.00	£0.30	£0.90	£1.50

	$Good	$Fine	$N.Mint	£Good	£Fine	£N.Mint

61 Sin City by Frank Miller, cover by Frank Miller and Lynn Varley
| | $0.40 | $1.20 | $2.00 | £0.30 | £0.90 | £1.50 |

62 full length Sin City conclusion by Frank Miller, cover by Frank Miller and Lynn Varley
| | $0.40 | $1.20 | $2.00 | £0.30 | £0.90 | £1.50 |

63 Moebius story and cover
| | $0.40 | $1.20 | $2.00 | £0.30 | £0.90 | £1.50 |

64 Matt Wagner story and cover
| | $0.40 | $1.20 | $2.00 | £0.30 | £0.90 | £1.50 |

65 inter-active do-it-yourself-story
| | $0.40 | $1.20 | $2.00 | £0.30 | £0.90 | £1.50 |

66 Concrete by Chadwick returns
| | $0.40 | $1.20 | $2.00 | £0.30 | £0.90 | £1.50 |

67 64pgs, squarebound, Predator mini-series begins that previews Predator: Race War
| | $0.60 | $1.80 | $3.00 | £0.40 | £1.20 | £2.00 |

68-69 Predator: Race War continues
| | $0.40 | $1.20 | $2.00 | £0.30 | £0.90 | £1.50 |

70 Madwoman of the Sacred Heart begins by Moebius, Moebius cover
| | $0.40 | $1.20 | $2.00 | £0.30 | £0.90 | £1.50 |

71 Madwoman of the Sacred Heart
| | $0.40 | $1.20 | $2.00 | £0.30 | £0.90 | £1.50 |

72-74 Madwoman of the Sacred Heart, Eudaemon

75-76 Madwoman of the Sacred Heart
| | $0.40 | $1.20 | $2.00 | £0.30 | £0.90 | £1.50 |

77 Hermes vs. The Eyeball Kid by Eddie Campbell begins
| | $0.40 | $1.20 | $2.00 | £0.30 | £0.90 | £1.50 |

78 painted cover by Charles Vess
| | $0.40 | $1.20 | $2.00 | £0.30 | £0.90 | £1.50 |

79 The Shadow Empires
| | $0.40 | $1.20 | $2.00 | £0.30 | £0.90 | £1.50 |

80 The Shadow Empires, Monkeyman and O'Brien by Arthur Adams; Arthur Adams cover
| | $0.40 | $1.20 | $2.00 | £0.30 | £0.90 | £1.50 |

81 The Shadow Empires, Buoy 77 by F. Solano Lopez
| | $0.40 | $1.20 | $2.00 | £0.30 | £0.90 | £1.50 |

82 Eddie Campbell cover
| | $0.40 | $1.20 | $2.00 | £0.30 | £0.90 | £1.50 |

83 David Lloyd cover (and featured art)
| | $0.40 | $1.20 | $2.00 | £0.30 | £0.90 | £1.50 |

84 Solano Lopez and Eddie Campbell stories conclude, Bryan Talbot art featured
| | $0.40 | $1.20 | $2.00 | £0.30 | £0.90 | £1.50 |

85-86
| | $0.40 | $1.20 | $2.00 | £0.30 | £0.90 | £1.50 |

87 features Paul Chadwick and Rick Geary work
| | $0.40 | $1.20 | $2.00 | £0.30 | £0.90 | £1.50 |

88-91 Hellboy by Mike Mignola
| | $0.40 | $1.20 | $2.00 | £0.30 | £0.90 | £1.50 |

92 Shannon Wheeler's Too Much Coffee Man, Rick Geary strip
| | $0.40 | $1.20 | $2.00 | £0.30 | £0.90 | £1.50 |

93 Shannon Wheeler's Too Much Coffee Man
| | $0.40 | $1.20 | $2.00 | £0.30 | £0.90 | £1.50 |

94-95 Shannon Wheeler's Too Much Coffee Man, Eddie Campbell's Eyeball Kid
| | $0.40 | $1.20 | $2.00 | £0.30 | £0.90 | £1.50 |

96-98 Eyeball Kid
| | $0.40 | $1.20 | $2.00 | £0.30 | £0.90 | £1.50 |

99 Eyeball Kid, also features work by Harvey Pekar and Jamie Delano
| | $0.40 | $1.20 | $2.00 | £0.30 | £0.90 | £1.50 |

100 Frank Miller and Lynn Varley dinosaur cover, Dave Stevens back cover; 1st in a weekly mini-series of 5 issues
| | $0.45 | $1.35 | $2.25 | £0.30 | £0.90 | £1.50 |

100 Issue #2; Hell boy cover by Bernie Wrightson, Hellboy's origin by Mike Mignola, Alec by Eddie Campbell
| | $0.45 | $1.35 | $2.25 | £0.30 | £0.90 | £1.50 |

100 Issue #3; Concrete cover by Paul Chadwick and Lynn Varley, features Concrete
| | $0.45 | $1.35 | $2.25 | £0.30 | £0.90 | £1.50 |

100 Issue #4; Dave Gibbons cover and story featuring Martha Washington, Black Cross by Chris Warner, Bird Dog by Ed Brubaker
| | $0.45 | $1.35 | $2.25 | £0.30 | £0.90 | £1.50 |

100 Issue #5; Mike Allred wraparound cover and features work by Jeff Smith, Evan Dorkin and Art Adams
| | $0.45 | $1.35 | $2.25 | £0.30 | £0.90 | £1.50 |

101 Aliens by Ron Marz and Bernie Wrightson, work by Paul Pope and Harvey Pekar, painted back cover by John Bolton
| | $0.45 | $1.35 | $2.25 | £0.30 | £0.90 | £1.50 |

102 Aliens by Ron Marz and Bernie Wrightson, work by Paul Pope and Harvey Pekar; cover by Bernie Wrightson
| | $0.45 | $1.35 | $2.25 | £0.30 | £0.90 | £1.50 |

103 work by Paul Pope and Stan Shaw; cover by Stan Shaw
| | $0.45 | $1.35 | $2.25 | £0.30 | £0.90 | £1.50 |

104
| | $0.60 | $1.80 | $3.00 | £0.40 | £1.20 | £2.00 |

| Title Value: | $63.85 | $191.05 | $318.75 | £44.25 | £132.75 | £221.25 |

Note: all Non-Distributed on the news-stands in the U.K.
Note: Concrete stories in 1-6,8,10,12,14,16,18,20,22,28,32.

Sin City Softcover Collection (Jan 1993)
| 208pgs, reprints from Dark Horse Presents on re-cycled paper | | | $2.00 | £6.00 | £10.00 |
| 2nd printing (Mar 1993), 3rd printing (1994) | | | $1.80 | £5.40 | £9.00 |

DARK HORSE PRESENTS FIFTH ANNIVERSARY SPECIAL

Dark Horse, OS; 1 Oct 1991
1 ND 112pgs, features work by Miller, Gibbons, Bisley, Chadwick, Wagner, Janson; 1st chapter Frank Miller's "Sin City"
| | $1.80 | $5.25 | $9.00 | £1.20 | £3.60 | £6.00 |
| Title Value: | $1.80 | $5.25 | $9.00 | £1.20 | £3.60 | £6.00 |

DARK HORSE PRESENTS, BEST OF

Dark Horse; 1 1989-3 1991
1 ND 128pgs, reprints selected stories from Dark Horse Presents #1-20; Concrete by Chadwick, Mr. Monster by Gilbert plus Rick Geary, Geoff Darrow, Rich Rice and others
| | $1.50 | $4.50 | $7.50 | £1.00 | £3.00 | £5.00 |

2 ND 112pgs, reprints selected stories from Dark Horse Presents #21-30 featuring Paul Chadwick, Rick Geary
| | $1.50 | $4.50 | $7.50 | £1.00 | £3.00 | £5.00 |

3 ND 144pgs, reprints selected stories from Dark Horse Presents #31-50 featuring Matt Wagner, Eddie Campbell, Rick Geary
| | $2.25 | $6.75 | $11.25 | £1.50 | £4.50 | £7.50 |
| Title Value: | $5.25 | $15.75 | $26.25 | £3.50 | £10.50 | £17.50 |

DARK HORSE PRESENTS: ALIENS

Dark Horse, OS; 1 May 1992
1 ND reprints black and white Aliens stories from Dark Horse Presents #24, #42, #43, 5th Anniversary Special and #56. New cover by Simon Bisley
| | $0.90 | $2.70 | $4.50 | £0.60 | £1.80 | £3.00 |

1 ND Platinum Edition, contents as above
| | $1.50 | $4.50 | $7.50 | £0.80 | £2.40 | £4.00 |
| Title Value: | $2.40 | $7.20 | $12.00 | £1.40 | £4.20 | £7.00 |

DARK MANSION OF FORBIDDEN LOVE, THE

DC Comics; 1 Sep/Oct 1971-4 Mar/Apr 1972
(becomes Forbidden Tales of the Dark Mansion)
1 52pgs
| | $3.00 | $9.00 | $15.00 | £0.60 | £1.80 | £3.00 |

2-4 ND 52pgs
| | $2.00 | $6.00 | $10.00 | £0.40 | £1.20 | £2.00 |
| Title Value: | $9.00 | $27.00 | $45.00 | £1.80 | £5.40 | £9.00 |

FEATURES
Gothic romance, mystery stories

DARK PASSION

Hero, MS; 1 Dec 1992-2 1993
1-2 ND
| | $0.40 | $1.20 | $2.00 | £0.30 | £0.90 | £1.50 |
| Title Value: | $0.80 | $2.40 | $4.00 | £0.60 | £1.80 | £3.00 |

DARK SHADOWS

Gold Key; 1 Mar 1969-35 Feb 1976
1 with poster; painted and photo covers begin (to #30)
| | $31.00 | $92.50 | $185.00 | £20.50 | £62.50 | £125.00 |

1 without poster
| | $11.00 | $34.00 | $67.50 | £7.50 | £22.50 | £45.00 |

2
| | $10.50 | $33.00 | $65.00 | £7.50 | £22.50 | £45.00 |

3 with poster
| | $15.00 | $45.00 | $90.00 | £10.00 | £30.00 | £60.00 |

3 without poster
| | $7.50 | $22.50 | $45.00 | £5.00 | £15.00 | £30.00 |

4-6
| | $11.50 | $35.00 | $57.50 | £7.00 | £21.00 | £35.00 |

7 last photo cover
| | $11.50 | $35.00 | $57.50 | £7.00 | £21.00 | £35.00 |

8-10
| | $9.00 | $27.00 | $45.00 | £6.00 | £18.00 | £30.00 |

11-20
| | $7.00 | $21.00 | $35.00 | £4.50 | £13.50 | £22.50 |

21-29
| | $5.00 | $15.00 | $25.00 | £3.00 | £9.00 | £15.00 |

30 last painted cover
| | $5.00 | $15.00 | $25.00 | £3.00 | £9.00 | £15.00 |

31 line drawn covers begin (to #35)
| | $5.00 | $15.00 | $25.00 | £3.00 | £9.00 | £15.00 |

32-35
| | $5.00 | $15.00 | $25.00 | £3.00 | £9.00 | £15.00 |
| Title Value: | $293.00 | $883.00 | $1542.50 | £186.50 | £560.50 | £985.00 |

Note: most issues distributed on the news-stands in the U.K.
Dark Shadows: Old Friends (Sep 1993) Trade paperback reprints series with 16pgs of designs and paintings
| | | | | £1.30 | £3.90 | £6.50 |

DARK SHADOWS BOOK 1

Innovation; 1 May 1992-4 Feb 1993
1-4 ND based on US TV series
| | $0.45 | $1.35 | $2.25 | £0.30 | £0.90 | £1.50 |
| Title Value: | $1.80 | $5.40 | $9.00 | £1.20 | £3.60 | £6.00 |

DARK SHADOWS BOOK 2

Innovation; 1 Apr 1993-4 Aug 1993
1-4 ND Maggie Thompson script
| | $0.45 | $1.35 | $2.25 | £0.30 — | £0.90 | £1.50 |
| Title Value: | $1.80 | $5.40 | $9.00 | £1.20 | £3.60 | £6.00 |

DARK SHADOWS BOOK 3

Innovation, MS; 1 Nov 1993-4 Feb 1994
1-4 ND Felipe Echevarria painted art
| | $0.45 | $1.35 | $2.25 | £0.30 | £0.90 | £1.50 |
| Title Value: | $1.80 | $5.40 | $9.00 | £1.20 | £3.60 | £6.00 |

DARK STAR

Rebel Studios; 1 Aug 1991
1 ND Kirbyesque art and Japanese animation
| | $0.45 | $1.35 | $2.25 | £0.30 | £0.90 | £1.50 |
| Title Value: | $0.45 | $1.35 | $2.25 | £0.30 | £0.90 | £1.50 |

DARK WOLF

Malibu; 1 Jul 1987-4 Oct 1987
1-4 ND Butch Burcham art; black and white
| | $0.40 | $1.20 | $2.00 | £0.25 | £0.75 | £1.25 |
| Title Value: | $1.60 | $4.80 | $8.00 | £1.00 | £3.00 | £5.00 |

DARK WOLF (2ND SERIES)

Eternity; 1 Feb 1988-4 May 1988
1-4 ND Butch Burcham art; black and white
| | $0.40 | $1.20 | $2.00 | £0.25 | £0.75 | £1.25 |
| Title Value: | $1.60 | $4.80 | $8.00 | £1.00 | £3.00 | £5.00 |

The Dark Wolf Collection (1988) reprints issues #1-4, new Butch Burcham cover and intro by Archie Goodwin
| | | | | £1.00 | £3.00 | £5.00 |

DARK WOLF (3RD SERIES)

Comax Productions; 1 1991
1 ND Butch Burcham script/art, black and white; Halloween special
| | $0.30 | $0.90 | $1.50 | £0.20 | £0.60 | £1.00 |
| Title Value: | $0.30 | $0.90 | $1.50 | £0.20 | £0.60 | £1.00 |

DARK WORLD #1: VAMPIRES

Millennium, OS; 1 Dec 1994
1 ND Jae Lee, Colleen Doran, Daerick Gross art featured
| | $0.60 | $1.80 | $3.00 | £0.40 | £1.20 | £2.00 |
| Title Value: | $0.60 | $1.80 | $3.00 | £0.40 | £1.20 | £2.00 |

	$Good	$Fine	$N.Mint	£Good	£Fine	£N.Mint
DARK, THE						
Continuum Comics; 1 Sep 1991-4 1992						
1 ND quarterly frequency begins, Larry Stroman part pencils, black and white						
	$0.45	$1.35	$2.25	£0.30	£0.90	£1.50
2-4 ND	$0.40	$1.20	$2.00	£0.25	£0.75	£1.25
Title Value:	$1.65	$4.95	$8.25	£1.05	£3.15	£5.25
DARK, THE (2ND SERIES)						
Continuum Comics; 1 Jun 1993-7 1994						
1 ND part George Perez art and cover; foil enhanced card stock cover						
	$0.40	$1.20	$2.00	£0.25	£0.75	£1.25
1 ND red non-foil cover						
	$0.40	$1.20	$2.00	£0.25	£0.75	£1.25
1 2nd printing, ND blue foil enhanced cover						
	$0.40	$1.20	$2.00	£0.25	£0.75	£1.25
2 ND part George Perez art and cover; foil enhanced card stock cover						
	$0.40	$1.20	$2.00	£0.25	£0.75	£1.25
2 2nd printing, (Mar 1994), new foil enhanced cover						
	$0.40	$1.20	$2.00	£0.25	£0.75	£1.25
3-5 ND part George Perez art and cover; foil enhanced card stock cover						
	$0.40	$1.20	$2.00	£0.25	£0.75	£1.25
6-7 ND part Perez art; foil enhanced card stock cover						
	$0.40	$1.20	$2.00	£0.25	£0.75	£1.25
Title Value:	$4.00	$12.00	$20.00	£2.50	£7.50	£12.50
DARK, THE (3RD SERIES)						
August House; 1 Jan 1995-present						
1 ND 40pgs, foil enhanced cardstock cover, part art George Perez; bound-in Foodang character card by Bart Sears						
	$0.45	$1.35	$2.25	£0.30	£0.90	£1.50
1 ND Signed Limited Edition (Jun 1995) - foil cover; 1,000 copies with certificate						
	$0.45	$1.35	$2.25	£0.30	£0.90	£1.50
2 ND foil-enhanced cover by Mike Zeck						
	$0.45	$1.35	$2.25	£0.30	£0.90	£1.50
3 ND foil-enhanced cover by Todd Lidstone and Mike Hoff						
	$0.45	$1.35	$2.25	£0.30	£0.90	£1.50
4 ND painted cover by John Rheaume						
	$0.45	$1.35	$2.25	£0.30	£0.90	£1.50
5 ND	$0.45	$1.35	$2.25	£0.30	£0.90	£1.50
Title Value:	$2.70	$8.10	$13.50	£1.80	£5.40	£9.00

Note: the contents of issue #1 were originally published in part as The Dark #7 by Continuum Comics. New pages have been added throughout the story

	$Good	$Fine	$N.Mint	£Good	£Fine	£N.Mint
DARKER IMAGE						
Image; 1 Mar 1993						
1 ND 24pgs, anthology of try-out characters; Bloodwulf by Liefeld, The Maxx by Sam Kieth and Deathblow by Jim Lee; pre-bagged with The Maxx trading card						
	$0.50	$1.50	$2.50	£0.30	£0.90	£1.50
1 ND Premium Edition - pre-bagged with gold embossed logo						
	$3.00	$9.00	$15.00	£2.00	£6.00	£10.00
1 ND Platinum Edition, embossed silver logo; available for every 100 copies of regular issue ordered						
	$4.50	$13.50	$22.50	£3.00	£9.00	£15.00
Title Value:	$8.00	$24.00	$40.00	£5.30	£15.90	£26.50

Note: originally solicited as a mini-series but cancelled after one issue.

	$Good	$Fine	$N.Mint	£Good	£Fine	£N.Mint
DARKEWOOD						
Aircel,MS; 1-5 1988						
1-5 ND	$0.30	$0.90	$1.50	£0.20	£0.60	£1.00
Title Value:	$1.50	$4.50	$7.50	£1.00	£3.00	£5.00
DARKHAWK						
Marvel Comics Group; 1 Mar 1991-50 Apr 1995						
1 ND origin and 1st appearance Darkhawk						
	$0.60	$1.80	$3.00	£0.30	£0.90	£1.50
2-3 ND Spiderman and Hobgoblin appear						
	$0.60	$1.80	$3.00	£0.25	£0.75	£1.25

	$Good	$Fine	$N.Mint	£Good	£Fine	£N.Mint
4-5 ND	$0.40	$1.20	$2.00	£0.20	£0.60	£1.00
6 ND Captain America/Daredevil appear						
	$0.40	$1.20	$2.00	£0.20	£0.60	£1.00
7-8 ND	$0.40	$1.20	$2.00	£0.20	£0.60	£1.00
9 ND Punisher appears						
	$0.40	$1.20	$2.00	£0.20	£0.60	£1.00
10 ND	$0.40	$1.20	$2.00	£0.20	£0.60	£1.00
11 ND	$0.30	$0.90	$1.50	£0.15	£0.45	£0.75
12 ND Tombstone appears						
	$0.30	$0.90	$1.50	£0.15	£0.45	£0.75
13-14 ND Darkhawk vs. Venom						
	$0.30	$0.90	$1.50	£0.15	£0.45	£0.75
15-18 ND	$0.30	$0.90	$1.50	£0.15	£0.45	£0.75
19 ND Spiderman appears						
	$0.30	$0.90	$1.50	£0.15	£0.45	£0.75
20 ND Darkhawk vs. Brotherhood of Evil Mutants, Spiderman, Sleepwalker appear; continued in Sleepwalker #17						
	$0.30	$0.90	$1.50	£0.15	£0.45	£0.75
21 ND Return To Forever story begins that reveals Darkhawk's true origin						
	$0.30	$0.90	$1.50	£0.15	£0.45	£0.75
22 Ghost Rider guest-stars						
	$0.30	$0.90	$1.50	£0.15	£0.45	£0.75
23-24 ND	$0.30	$0.90	$1.50	£0.15	£0.45	£0.75
25 DS anniversary issue, holo-grafix foil cover, double-gatefold poster of covers #21-24						
	$0.40	$1.20	$2.00	£0.20	£0.75	£1.25
26 New Warriors appear						
	$0.25	$0.75	$1.25	£0.15	£0.45	£0.75
27	$0.25	$0.75	$1.25	£0.15	£0.45	£0.75
28-29 New Warriors appear						
	$0.25	$0.75	$1.25	£0.15	£0.45	£0.75
30 Infinity Crusade tie-in						
	$0.25	$0.75	$1.25	£0.15	£0.45	£0.75
31 Infinity Crusade tie-in, X-Men appear						
	$0.25	$0.75	$1.25	£0.15	£0.45	£0.75
32-34 ND	$0.25	$0.75	$1.25	£0.15	£0.45	£0.75
35-37 Venom guest-stars						
	$0.25	$0.75	$1.25	£0.15	£0.45	£0.75
38 Amulet Quest story begins; new costume and new powers						
	$0.25	$0.75	$1.25	£0.15	£0.45	£0.75
39 with free Spiderman vs. Venom card sheet						
	$0.25	$0.75	$1.25	£0.15	£0.45	£0.75
40-41	$0.25	$0.75	$1.25	£0.15	£0.45	£0.75
42 Darkhawk reveals identity to parents						
	$0.25	$0.75	$1.25	£0.15	£0.45	£0.75
43-46 ND	$0.25	$0.75	$1.25	£0.15	£0.45	£0.75
47 ties into Spiderman: Friends & Enemies #1						
	$0.25	$0.75	$1.25	£0.15	£0.45	£0.75
48-49 ND	$0.25	$0.75	$1.25	£0.15	£0.45	£0.75
50 48pgs, metallic ink cover						
	$0.30	$0.90	$1.50	£0.20	£0.60	£1.00
Title Value:	$15.50	$46.50	$77.50	£8.35	£25.05	£41.75
DARKHAWK ANNUAL						
Marvel Comics Group; 1 Jul 1992-3 1994						
1 ND Assault On Armor City part 1, Iron Man appears, continued in West Coast Avengers Annual #7						
	$0.40	$1.20	$2.00	£0.25	£0.75	£1.25
2 ND 64pgs, pre-bagged with trading card introducing Dreamkiller						
	$0.40	$1.20	$2.00	£0.25	£0.75	£1.25
3 ND 64pgs	$0.40	$1.20	$2.00	£0.25	£0.75	£1.25
Title Value:	$1.20	$3.60	$6.00	£0.75	£2.25	£3.75
DARKHOLD						
Marvel Comics Group; 1 Oct 1992-16 Jan 1994						

Dark Horse Comics #8

Dark Horse Presents #5

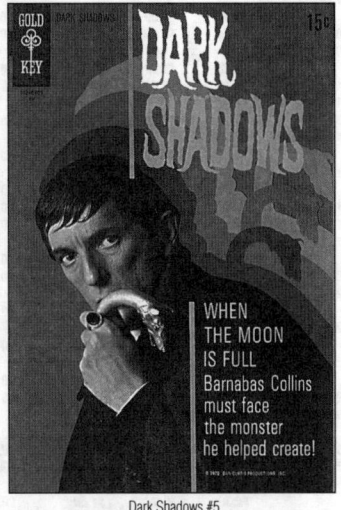

Dark Shadows #5

	$Good	$Fine	$N.Mint	£Good	£Fine	£N.Mint
1 ND DS Rise of the Midnight Sons part 4, pre-bagged with poster by Andy and Adam Kubert	$0.45	$1.35	$2.25	£0.30	£0.90	£1.50
2 ND	$0.40	$1.20	$2.00	£0.25	£0.75	£1.25
3 ND Scarlet Witch cameo; Modred the Mystic returns	$0.40	$1.20	$2.00	£0.25	£0.75	£1.25
4 ND Sabretooth appears	$0.40	$1.20	$2.00	£0.25	£0.75	£1.25
5 ND Ghost Rider and Punisher appear	$0.40	$1.20	$2.00	£0.25	£0.75	£1.25
6 ND Modred the Mystic vs. Dr. Strange	$0.40	$1.20	$2.00	£0.25	£0.75	£1.25
7-10 ND	$0.40	$1.20	$2.00	£0.25	£0.75	£1.25
11 ND Midnight Massacre part 3, gold-ink black parchment outer cover	$0.30	$0.90	$1.50	£0.20	£0.60	£1.00
12-14 ND	$0.30	$0.90	$1.50	£0.20	£0.60	£1.00
15 ND Siege of Darkness part 4; Ghost Rider appears	$0.30	$0.90	$1.50	£0.20	£0.60	£1.00
16 ND Siege of Darkness part 12; spot varnish cover	$0.30	$0.90	$1.50	£0.20	£0.60	£1.00
Title Value:	$5.85	$17.55	$29.25	£3.75	£11.25	£18.75

DARKLON THE MYSTIC
Pacific; 1 Nov 1983

	$Good	$Fine	$N.Mint	£Good	£Fine	£N.Mint
1 ND DS, Jim Starlin art, reprint	$0.40	$1.20	$2.00	£0.25	£0.75	£1.25
Title Value:	$0.40	$1.20	$2.00	£0.25	£0.75	£1.25

DARKMAN
Marvel Comics Group,MS; 1 Apr 1993-6 Sep 1993

	$Good	$Fine	$N.Mint	£Good	£Fine	£N.Mint
1 48pgs, card-stock covers begin	$0.45	$1.35	$2.25	£0.30	£0.90	£1.50
2-6	$0.45	$1.35	$2.25	£0.30	£0.90	£1.50
Title Value:	$2.70	$8.10	$13.50	£1.80	£5.40	£9.00

DARKMAN MOVIE MAGAZINE
Marvel Comics Group,OS; 1 Sep 1990

	$Good	$Fine	$N.Mint	£Good	£Fine	£N.Mint
1 ND 64pgs, black and white adaptation of film	$0.40	$1.20	$2.00	£0.25	£0.75	£1.25
Title Value:	$0.40	$1.20	$2.00	£0.25	£0.75	£1.25

DARKMAN MOVIE MAGAZINE COMIC
Marvel Comics Group,MS; 1 Oct 1990-3 Dec 1990

	$Good	$Fine	$N.Mint	£Good	£Fine	£N.Mint
1-3 ND comics version of the above	$0.15	$0.45	$0.75	£0.10	£0.35	£0.60
Title Value:	$0.45	$1.35	$2.25	£0.30	£1.05	£1.80

DARKSEID VS. GALACTUS: THE HUNGER
DC Comics/Marvel Comics Group,OS; 1 Oct 1995

	$Good	$Fine	$N.Mint	£Good	£Fine	£N.Mint
1 ND John Byrne script and art, Darkseid, Galactus and Silver Surfer appear	$1.00	$3.00	$5.00	£0.65	£1.95	£3.25
Title Value:	$1.00	$3.00	$5.00	£0.65	£1.95	£3.25

DARKSTAR II
Rebel Studios; 1 Aug 1993-2 1993

	$Good	$Fine	$N.Mint	£Good	£Fine	£N.Mint
1-2 ND	$0.45	$1.35	$2.25	£0.30	£0.90	£1.50
Title Value:	$0.90	$2.70	$4.50	£0.60	£1.80	£3.00

DARKSTARS, THE
DC Comics; 0 Oct 1994; 1 Oct 1992-38 Jan 1996

	$Good	$Fine	$N.Mint	£Good	£Fine	£N.Mint
0 (Oct 1994) Zero Hour X-over, history of Darkstars revealed	$0.40	$1.20	$2.00	£0.25	£0.75	£1.25
1 Larry Stroman art begins, Travis Charest cover	$0.40	$1.20	$2.00	£0.25	£0.75	£1.25
2-3 Travis Charest cover	$0.30	$0.90	$1.50	£0.20	£0.60	£1.00
4 1st Travis Charest art on Darkstars	$0.40	$1.20	$2.00	£0.25	£0.75	£1.25
5-6 Hawkman and Hawkwoman appear, Travis Charest art	$0.30	$0.90	$1.50	£0.20	£0.60	£1.00
7 Travis Charest art	$0.30	$0.90	$1.50	£0.20	£0.60	£1.00
8	$0.30	$0.90	$1.50	£0.20	£0.60	£1.00
9 Travis Charest art	$0.30	$0.90	$1.50	£0.20	£0.60	£1.00
10	$0.30	$0.90	$1.50	£0.20	£0.60	£1.00
11 Trinity part 4, Travis Charest art	$0.30	$0.90	$1.50	£0.20	£0.60	£1.00
12 X-over with DC Universe: Trinity #2	$0.30	$0.90	$1.50	£0.20	£0.60	£1.00
13 Travis Charest cover	$0.30	$0.90	$1.50	£0.20	£0.60	£1.00
14-17	$0.30	$0.90	$1.50	£0.20	£0.60	£1.00
18 Flash appears	$0.30	$0.90	$1.50	£0.20	£0.60	£1.00
19 Flash appears; Alan Davis and Mark Farmer cover	$0.30	$0.90	$1.50	£0.20	£0.60	£1.00
20 Flash appears	$0.30	$0.90	$1.50	£0.20	£0.60	£1.00
21-23 prelude to Zero Hour	$0.30	$0.90	$1.50	£0.20	£0.60	£1.00
24 Zero Hour X-over	$0.30	$0.90	$1.50	£0.20	£0.60	£1.00
25 John Stewart takes command of The Darkstars	$0.30	$0.90	$1.50	£0.20	£0.60	£1.00
26-29	$0.30	$0.90	$1.50	£0.20	£0.60	£1.00
30 Green Lantern appears	$0.30	$0.90	$1.50	£0.20	£0.60	£1.00
31	$0.30	$0.90	$1.50	£0.20	£0.60	£1.00
32 The Crimelord/Syndicate War part 3, continued in New Titans #122; Supergirl, New Titans and Deathstroke guest-star	$0.30	$0.90	$1.50	£0.20	£0.60	£1.00
33	$0.30	$0.90	$1.50	£0.20	£0.60	£1.00
34 The Siege of Zi Charam part 3, continued in Damage #16	$0.30	$0.90	$1.50	£0.20	£0.60	£1.00
35-36 Flash guest-stars	$0.30	$0.90	$1.50	£0.20	£0.60	£1.00
37 story continued from Guy Gardner #35	$0.30	$0.90	$1.50	£0.20	£0.60	£1.00
38	$0.30	$0.90	$1.50	£0.20	£0.60	£1.00
Title Value:	$12.00	$36.00	$60.00	£7.95	£23.85	£39.75

DARKWING DUCK
Disney,MS; 1 Oct 1991-4 Jan 1992

	$Good	$Fine	$N.Mint	£Good	£Fine	£N.Mint
1-4 ND	$0.30	$0.90	$1.50	£0.20	£0.60	£1.00
Title Value:	$1.20	$3.60	$6.00	£0.80	£2.40	£4.00

DATE WITH DEBBI
National Periodical Publications; 1 Jan/Feb 1969-17 Sep/Oct 1971; 18 Oct/Nov 1972

	$Good	$Fine	$N.Mint	£Good	£Fine	£N.Mint
1 scarce in the U.K.	$1.85	$5.50	$11.25	£1.25	£3.75	£7.50
2	$1.50	$4.50	$7.50	£1.00	£3.00	£5.00
3-5	$1.20	$3.60	$6.00	£0.80	£2.40	£4.00
6-18	$0.90	$2.70	$4.50	£0.60	£1.80	£3.00
Title Value:	$18.65	$55.90	$95.25	£12.45	£37.35	£63.50

DATE WITH JUDY, A
National Periodical Publications; 67 Oct/Nov 1959-79 Oct/Nov 1960
(previous issues ND)

	$Good	$Fine	$N.Mint	£Good	£Fine	£N.Mint
67-70	$2.90	$8.75	$17.50	£2.05	£6.25	£12.50
71-79	$2.65	$8.00	$16.00	£1.65	£5.00	£10.00
Title Value:	$35.45	$107.00	$214.00	£23.05	£70.00	£140.00

DAUGHTERS OF TIME
The Three-D Zone,OS; 1 Nov 1991

	$Good	$Fine	$N.Mint	£Good	£Fine	£N.Mint
1 ND Steve Ditko, Kurt Schaffenberger cover, with glasses	$0.60	$1.80	$3.00	£0.40	£1.20	£2.00
Title Value:	$0.60	$1.80	$3.00	£0.40	£1.20	£2.00

DAWN
Sirius Entertainment,MS; 1 Jul 1995-present

	$Good	$Fine	$N.Mint	£Good	£Fine	£N.Mint
1 ND Joseph Michael Linsner art and script	$1.20	$3.60	$6.00	£0.80	£2.40	£4.00
1 "Black Light" edition ND	$5.00	$15.00	$25.00	£3.00	£9.00	£15.00
1 "Look Sharp" edition ND	$7.00	$21.00	$35.00	£5.00	£15.00	£25.00
1 "White Trash" edition ND	$7.00	$21.00	$35.00	£4.00	£12.00	£20.00
2 ND	$0.90	$2.70	$4.50	£0.60	£1.80	£3.00
3 ND	$0.60	$1.80	$3.00	£0.40	£1.20	£2.00
Title Value:	$21.70	$65.10	$108.50	£13.80	£41.40	£69.00

DAYS OF DARKNESS
Apple Comics,MS; 1 Mar 1992-4 Sep 1992

	$Good	$Fine	$N.Mint	£Good	£Fine	£N.Mint
1-4 ND chronicle of events leading to Pearl Harbour	$0.55	$1.65	$2.75	£0.35	£1.05	£1.75
Title Value:	$2.20	$6.60	$11.00	£1.40	£4.20	£7.00

DAZZLER, THE
Marvel Comics Group; 1 Mar 1981-42 Mar 1986
(see Marvel Graphic Novel, X-Men #130)

	$Good	$Fine	$N.Mint	£Good	£Fine	£N.Mint
1 ND X-Men, Spiderman and Avengers appear	$0.55	$1.65	$2.75	£0.35	£1.05	£1.75
2 X-Men, Spiderman and Fantastic Four appear	$0.40	$1.20	$2.00	£0.25	£0.75	£1.25
3-4 Dr. Doom and Fantastic Four appear	$0.30	$0.90	$1.50	£0.20	£0.60	£1.00
5 intro Blue Shield	$0.30	$0.90	$1.50	£0.20	£0.60	£1.00
6-7 Hulk appears	$0.30	$0.90	$1.50	£0.20	£0.60	£1.00
8	$0.30	$0.90	$1.50	£0.20	£0.60	£1.00
9 Quasar appears, Sienkiewicz cover	$0.30	$0.90	$1.50	£0.20	£0.60	£1.00
10 Galactus appears	$0.30	$0.90	$1.50	£0.20	£0.60	£1.00
11 Galactus appears	$0.25	$0.75	$1.25	£0.15	£0.45	£0.75
12-13	$0.25	$0.75	$1.25	£0.15	£0.45	£0.75
14 She-Hulk appears	$0.25	$0.75	$1.25	£0.15	£0.45	£0.75
15 Spiderwoman appears, Sienkiewicz cover	$0.25	$0.75	$1.25	£0.15	£0.45	£0.75
16 Sienkiewicz cover	$0.25	$0.75	$1.25	£0.15	£0.45	£0.75
17 Angel appears	$0.25	$0.75	$1.25	£0.15	£0.45	£0.75
18 Fantastic Four appear, Angel cameo, Sienkiewicz cover	$0.25	$0.75	$1.25	£0.15	£0.45	£0.75
19 Black Bolt appears, Fantastic Four and Angel cameos	$0.25	$0.75	$1.25	£0.15	£0.45	£0.75
20 Angel cameo	$0.25	$0.75	$1.25	£0.15	£0.45	£0.75
21 DS, photo cover, Angel, Avengers, Fantastic Four and Spiderman cameos	$0.25	$0.75	$1.25	£0.15	£0.45	£0.75
22 LD in the U.K. Rogue and Angel appear, Angel appears	$0.45	$1.35	$2.25	£0.30	£0.90	£1.50
23 Rogue and Angel appear, Luke Cage and Iron Fist appear	$0.25	$0.75	$1.25	£0.15	£0.45	£0.75
24 Powerman and Iron Fist appear, Rogue and Angel appear	$0.25	$0.75	$1.25	£0.15	£0.45	£0.75
25	$0.25	$0.75	$1.25	£0.15	£0.45	£0.75
26 LD in the U.K.	$0.30	$0.90	$1.50	£0.20	£0.60	£1.00
27 LD in the U.K. Sienkiewicz run of covers begin, Angel appears	$0.30	$0.90	$1.50	£0.20	£0.60	£1.00

VERY GENERAL PERCENTAGE CONVERSION CHART WHICH MAY BE USED TO CALCULATE LOW AND INBETWEEN GRADES:

	$Good	$Fine	$N.Mint	£Good	£Fine	£N.Mint
28 LD in the U.K. Rogue appears	$0.30	$0.90	$1.50	£0.20	£0.60	£1.00
29-31	$0.25	$0.75	$1.25	£0.15	£0.45	£0.75
32 Inhumans appear	$0.25	$0.75	$1.25	£0.15	£0.45	£0.75
33-34	$0.25	$0.75	$1.25	£0.15	£0.45	£0.75
35 last Sienkiewicz cover	$0.25	$0.75	$1.25	£0.15	£0.45	£0.75
36 Byrne cover	$0.25	$0.75	$1.25	£0.15	£0.45	£0.75
37	$0.25	$0.75	$1.25	£0.15	£0.45	£0.75
38 very scarce in the U.K. X-Men appear, Paul Chadwick art	$1.00	$3.00	$5.00	£0.70	£2.10	£3.50
39 ND Chadwick art	$0.25	$0.75	$1.25	£0.20	£0.60	£1.00
40 ND Secret Wars II, Chadwick art	$0.25	$0.75	$1.25	£0.20	£0.60	£1.00
41 ND Chadwick art	$0.25	$0.75	$1.25	£0.20	£0.60	£1.00
42 ND scarce in the U.K. Beast appears, Chadwick art	$0.45	$1.35	$2.25	£0.30	£0.90	£1.50
Title Value:	**$12.65**	**$37.95**	**$63.25**	**£8.15**	**£24.45**	**£40.75**

DC 100-PAGE SUPER SPECTACULAR
DC Comics; 4 1971-13 Jun 1972; 14 Feb 1973-22 Nov 1973
(No issues #1-3. Becomes 100-Page Super Spectacular #14-22)

	$Good	$Fine	$N.Mint	£Good	£Fine	£N.Mint
4 Weird Mystery Tales; Wrightson art (1pg) and cover	$1.05	$3.15	$5.25	£0.70	£2.10	£3.50
5 ND very scarce in the U.K. Love Stories	$1.40	$4.20	$7.00	£0.90	£2.70	£4.50
6 World's Greatest Super-Heroes, reprints Justice League of America #21 (1st Justice Society of America appearance in Silver Age); Neal Adams cover	$1.50	$4.50	$7.50	£1.00	£3.00	£5.00
14 Batman; reprints classic two-part Batman vs. The Mad Monk story from Detective Comics #31 and #32 and Atom's origin from Showcase #34	$1.80	$5.25	$9.00	£1.20	£3.60	£6.00
15 Superboy; reprints Detective Comics #65 the 2nd Boy Commandoes by Joe Simon and Jack Kirby	$1.05	$3.15	$5.25	£0.70	£2.10	£3.50
16 Sgt. Rock; features Haunted Tank, Johnny Cloud, Mlle. Marie reprints	$0.80	$2.40	$4.00	£0.50	£1.50	£2.50
17 Justice League of America; reprints Golden Age Sandman from Adventure Comics #66	$1.20	$3.60	$6.00	£0.80	£2.40	£4.00
18 Superman; reprints classic "Superman Red and Superman Blue" from Superman #166	$1.05	$3.15	$5.25	£0.70	£2.10	£3.50
19 ND Tarzan; Russ Manning newspaper strip reprints	$1.05	$3.15	$5.25	£0.70	£2.10	£3.50
20 Batman; reprints 1st appearance of Two-Face from Detective Comics #66 and #68	$1.80	$5.25	$9.00	£1.20	£3.60	£6.00
21 Superboy; reprints 1st appearance Teen Titans from Brave and the Bold #54	$1.05	$3.15	$5.25	£0.70	£2.10	£3.50
22 Flash; Golden Age Flash reprint from All Flash #13	$0.90	$2.70	$4.50	£0.60	£1.80	£3.00
Title Value:	**$14.65**	**$43.65**	**$73.25**	**£9.70**	**£29.10**	**£48.50**

Note: Numbers 7 to 13 are listed under the individual titles in which they appeared: 7 (Superman #245), 8 (Batman #238), 9 (Our Army at War #242), 10 (Adventure Comics #416), 11 (Flash #214), 12 (Superboy #185), 13 (Superman #252).

ARTISTS

Neal Adams wraparound cover on 6. Part Wrightson art in 4. Wood inks in 5.

FEATURES

Spectre, Johnny Quick, Vigilante, Wildcat, Hawkman, JLA, JSA in 6. Johnny Peril, Phantom Stranger in 4.

REPRINT FEATURES

Aquaman, Dial H for Hero in 15. Atom in 14. Batman in 14, 20. Black Canary in 20. Blackhawk in 14, 20. Boy Commandoes, Hawk and Dove in 15. Captain Storm in 16. Captain Triumph, Hourman, Superman, TNT and Dan the Dynamite in 18. Dollman, Wildcat, Wonder Woman in 14. Dr. Mid-Nite in 20. Elongated Man in 22. Flash, GA Flash, Johnny Quick in 22. Flash, Kid Flash, Robin, Aqualad in 21. Gunner & Sarge, Haunted Tank, Johnny Cloud, Mlle. Marie, Sgt. Rock in 16. JLA, Spectre, Johnny Quick, Vigilante, Wildcat, Hawkman in 6. JLA/JSA in 17. Kid Eternity/LSH in 21. Mystery stories, including Phantom Stranger in 4. Sandman in 15,17. Spectre, Starman in 20.Superboy in 15, 21. Tarzan (Russ Manning newspaper reprints) in 19. Wildcat in 20.

DC CHALLENGE
DC Comics,MS; 1 Nov 1985-12 Oct 1986

	$Good	$Fine	$N.Mint	£Good	£Fine	£N.Mint
1-4 ND	$0.15	$0.45	$0.75	£0.10	£0.35	£0.60
5 ND features Dave Gibbons art	$0.15	$0.45	$0.75	£0.10	£0.35	£0.60
6 ND	$0.15	$0.45	$0.75	£0.10	£0.35	£0.60
7-8 ND Joker appears	$0.15	$0.45	$0.75	£0.10	£0.35	£0.60
9-11 ND	$0.15	$0.45	$0.75	£0.10	£0.35	£0.60
12 ND DS Darkseid appears	$0.15	$0.45	$0.75	£0.10	£0.35	£0.60
Title Value:	**$1.80**	**$5.40**	**$9.00**	**£1.20**	**£4.20**	**£7.20**

Note: all 32pgs; round-robin series, wherein different creative teams continue the previous issue's storyline.

FEATURES/ARTISTS

(Note: main characters only) 1 Superman, Batman, Wonder Woman by Evanier / Colan / Bob Smith; 2 Superman, Batman, Jonah Hex by Wein / Patton / DeCarlo; 3 Viking Prince, Hawkman, Aquaman by Moench / Infantino / Bob Smith; 4 Superman, Zatanna, Detective Chimp by Levitz / Kane / Janson; 5 Dr.Fate, Captain Marvel, Adam Strange by Mike Barr / Dave Gibbons / Farmer; 6 Silent Knight, Batman, Adam Strange by Maggin / Jurgens / Malstedt; 7 Blackhawk, Plastic Man, Deadman, Batman, Joker by Kupperberg / Staton / Mitchell; 8 Batman, Joker, Blackhawk, New Gods by Conway / Hoberg / Giordano; 9 Superman, New Teen Titans, Guardians of Oa, Wonder Woman, Batman, Adam Strange by Roy Thomas / Don Heck; 10 Superman, Deadman, Hawkman, Vigilante, A.Strange by Miskin / Swan / Austin; 11 Dr. Fate, Superman, Batman by Wolfman / Bates / Giffen / Hunt; 12 Superman, Batman, Deadman, Dr. Fate & others by various.

DC COMIC COLLECTION
DC Comics; 1 Jul 1989-2 1989

	$Good	$Fine	$N.Mint	£Good	£Fine	£N.Mint
1 very LD bound collection of selected DC comics - some inc. Batman #417 Ten Nights of the Beast part 1	$1.20	$3.60	$6.00	£0.80	£2.40	£4.00
2 very LD bound collection of selected DC comics	$0.80	$2.40	$4.00	£0.50	£1.50	£2.50
Title Value:	**$2.00**	**$6.00**	**$10.00**	**£1.30**	**£3.90**	**£6.50**

DC COMICS PRESENTS
DC Comics; 1 Jul/Aug 1978-97 Sep 1986
(see Best of DC 13)

[Note: Superman appears in every issue, teamed with the character(s) listed.]

	$Good	$Fine	$N.Mint	£Good	£Fine	£N.Mint
1 Flash	$0.35	$1.05	$1.75	£0.25	£0.75	£1.25
2 ND Flash	$0.30	$0.90	$1.50	£0.30	£0.90	£1.50
3 ND 44pgs, Adam Strange	$0.30	$0.90	$1.50	£0.30	£0.90	£1.50
4 Metal Men	$0.25	$0.75	$1.25	£0.15	£0.45	£0.75
5 Aquaman	$0.25	$0.75	$1.25	£0.15	£0.45	£0.75
6 Green Lantern	$0.25	$0.75	$1.25	£0.15	£0.45	£0.75
7 Red Tornado	$0.25	$0.75	$1.25	£0.15	£0.45	£0.75
8 Swamp Thing	$0.25	$0.75	$1.25	£0.15	£0.45	£0.75
9 Wonder Woman	$0.25	$0.75	$1.25	£0.15	£0.45	£0.75
10 Sgt. Rock	$0.25	$0.75	$1.25	£0.15	£0.45	£0.75
11 Hawkman	$0.25	$0.75	$1.25	£0.15	£0.45	£0.75
12 Mister Miracle	$0.25	$0.75	$1.25	£0.15	£0.45	£0.75
13 Legion of Super-Heroes	$0.25	$0.75	$1.25	£0.15	£0.45	£0.75
14 Superboy	$0.25	$0.75	$1.25	£0.15	£0.45	£0.75
15 Atom	$0.25	$0.75	$1.25	£0.15	£0.45	£0.75
16 Black Lightning	$0.25	$0.75	$1.25	£0.15	£0.45	£0.75
17 Firestorm	$0.25	$0.75	$1.25	£0.15	£0.45	£0.75
18 Zatanna	$0.25	$0.75	$1.25	£0.15	£0.45	£0.75
19 Batgirl	$0.25	$0.75	$1.25	£0.15	£0.45	£0.75
20 Green Arrow	$0.25	$0.75	$1.25	£0.15	£0.45	£0.75
21 Elongated Man	$0.25	$0.75	$1.25	£0.15	£0.45	£0.75
22 Captain Comet	$0.25	$0.75	$1.25	£0.15	£0.45	£0.75
23 Dr. Fate	$0.25	$0.75	$1.25	£0.15	£0.45	£0.75
24 Deadman	$0.25	$0.75	$1.25	£0.15	£0.45	£0.75
25 Phantom Stranger	$0.25	$0.75	$1.25	£0.15	£0.45	£0.75
26 52pgs, Green Lantern; 1st appearance New Teen Titans in insert; Jim Starlin art, George Perez art	$1.20	$3.60	$6.00	£0.80	£2.40	£4.00
27 Jim Starlin art, Manhunter from Mars	$0.25	$0.75	$1.25	£0.15	£0.45	£0.80
28 Jim Starlin art, Supergirl	$0.25	$0.75	$1.25	£0.15	£0.45	£0.80
29 Jim Starlin art, Spectre	$0.25	$0.75	$1.25	£0.15	£0.45	£0.80
30 Black Canary	$0.25	$0.75	$1.25	£0.15	£0.45	£0.75
31 Robin	$0.25	$0.75	$1.25	£0.15	£0.45	£0.75
32 Wonder Woman	$0.25	$0.75	$1.25	£0.15	£0.45	£0.75
33 Shazam	$0.25	$0.75	$1.25	£0.15	£0.45	£0.75
34 Shazam Family	$0.25	$0.75	$1.25	£0.15	£0.45	£0.75
35 Man-Bat	$0.25	$0.75	$1.25	£0.15	£0.45	£0.75
36 Jim Starlin art, Starman	$0.25	$0.75	$1.25	£0.15	£0.45	£0.80
37 Jim Starlin art, Hawkgirl	$0.25	$0.75	$1.25	£0.15	£0.45	£0.80
38 George Perez cover, Flash	$0.25	$0.75	$1.25	£0.15	£0.45	£0.75
39 Plastic Man	$0.25	$0.75	$1.25	£0.15	£0.45	£0.75
40 Metamorpho	$0.25	$0.75	$1.25	£0.15	£0.45	£0.75
41 52pgs, The Joker; Wonder Woman insert, 1st new costume	$0.60	$1.80	$3.00	£0.40	£1.20	£2.00
42 Unknown Soldier	$0.25	$0.75	$1.25	£0.15	£0.45	£0.75
43 Legion of Super-Heroes	$0.25	$0.75	$1.25	£0.15	£0.45	£0.75
44 Dial H For Hero	$0.25	$0.75	$1.25	£0.15	£0.45	£0.75
45 Firestorm	$0.25	$0.75	$1.25	£0.15	£0.45	£0.75
46 The Global Guardians	$0.25	$0.75	$1.25	£0.15	£0.45	£0.75
47 Masters of the Universe	$0.25	$0.75	$1.25	£0.15	£0.45	£0.75
48 Aquaman	$0.25	$0.75	$1.25	£0.15	£0.45	£0.75
49 Shazam	$0.25	$0.75	$1.25	£0.15	£0.45	£0.75
50 Clark Kent; 2pg pin-up of 65 previous co-stars	$0.25	$0.75	$1.25	£0.15	£0.45	£0.75
51 Atom; 16pg Masters of the Universe insert	$0.25	$0.75	$1.25	£0.15	£0.45	£0.75
52 New Doom Patrol; 1st appearance Ambush Bug, cameos of Judge Dredd, Cerebus, Skywise from Elfquest, Giffen art	$0.60	$1.80	$3.00	£0.40	£1.20	£2.00
53 The House of Mystery, 16pg Atari Force insert	$0.25	$0.75	$1.25	£0.15	£0.45	£0.75
54 Green Arrow	$0.25	$0.75	$1.25	£0.15	£0.45	£0.75
55 Airwave; Superboy and original Airwave cameo	$0.25	$0.75	$1.25	£0.15	£0.45	£0.75
56 Power Girl	$0.25	$0.75	$1.25	£0.15	£0.45	£0.75
57 The Atomic Knights	$0.25	$0.75	$1.25	£0.15	£0.45	£0.75

MINT = 100% / NEAR MINT (inc. +/-) = 90–99% / VERY FINE (inc. +/-) = 75–89% / FINE (inc. +/-) = 55–74%
VERY GOOD (inc. +/-) = 35–54% / GOOD (inc. +/-) = 15–34% / FAIR = 5–14% / POOR = 1–4%

289

	$Good	$Fine	$N.Mint	£Good	£Fine	£N.Mint
58 Robin, Elongated Man	$0.25	$0.75	$1.25	£0.15	£0.45	£0.75
59 Legion of Substitute-Heroes, Ambush Bug appears, Giffen art	$0.25	$0.75	$1.25	£0.15	£0.45	£0.80
60 Guardians of the Universe	$0.25	$0.75	$1.25	£0.15	£0.45	£0.75
61 George Perez art, Omac	$0.25	$0.75	$1.25	£0.15	£0.45	£0.80
62 Freedom Fighters	$0.15	$0.50	$0.90	£0.10	£0.35	£0.60
63 Amethyst	$0.15	$0.50	$0.90	£0.10	£0.35	£0.60
64 Kamandi	$0.15	$0.50	$0.90	£0.10	£0.35	£0.60
65 Gray Morrow art, Madame Xanadu	$0.25	$0.75	$1.25	£0.15	£0.45	£0.80
66 Joe Kubert art, Demon	$0.15	$0.50	$0.90	£0.10	£0.35	£0.60
67 Curt Swan and Murphy Anderson art, Santa Claus	$0.15	$0.50	$0.90	£0.10	£0.35	£0.60
68 The Vixen	$0.15	$0.50	$0.90	£0.10	£0.35	£0.60
69 Blackhawk	$0.15	$0.50	$0.90	£0.10	£0.35	£0.60
70 Metal Men	$0.15	$0.50	$0.90	£0.10	£0.35	£0.60
71 Bizarro	$0.15	$0.50	$0.90	£0.10	£0.35	£0.60
72 Phantom Stranger; Joker appears	$0.25	$0.75	$1.25	£0.15	£0.45	£0.75
73 Flash, Infantino art	$0.15	$0.50	$0.90	£0.10	£0.35	£0.60
74 Hawkman	$0.15	$0.50	$0.90	£0.10	£0.35	£0.60
75 Arion	$0.15	$0.50	$0.90	£0.10	£0.35	£0.60
76 Wonder Woman	$0.15	$0.50	$0.90	£0.10	£0.35	£0.60
77 The Forgotten Heroes; Dolphin, Animal Man, Congo Bill, Rick Flagg, Rip Hunter, Cave Carson	$0.45	$1.35	$2.25	£0.30	£0.90	£1.50
78 The Forgotten Villains; Ultivac, Atom Master, Krakow, Mr. Poseidon, Enchantress, Faceless Hunter; Space Cabby, Animal Man appear, unofficial Crisis X-over	$0.40	$1.20	$2.00	£0.25	£0.75	£1.25
79 Clark Kent	$0.15	$0.50	$0.90	£0.10	£0.35	£0.60
80 Legion of Super-Heroes	$0.25	$0.75	$1.25	£0.15	£0.45	£0.75
81 Giffen art, Ambush Bug	$0.25	$0.75	$1.25	£0.15	£0.45	£0.75
82 Garcia Lopez art, Adam Strange	$0.15	$0.50	$0.90	£0.10	£0.35	£0.60
83 Batman and the Outsiders	$0.30	$0.90	$1.50	£0.20	£0.60	£1.00
84 Jack Kirby and Toth art, Challengers of the Unknown	$0.25	$0.75	$1.25	£0.15	£0.45	£0.75
85 Swamp Thing, Alan Moore story	$0.40	$1.20	$2.00	£0.25	£0.75	£1.25
86 Supergirl; Crisis X-over	$0.25	$0.75	$1.25	£0.15	£0.45	£0.75
87 Superboy; Crisis X-over, Superman's existence explored	$0.25	$0.75	$1.25	£0.15	£0.45	£0.75
88 Giffen art, Creeper; Crisis X-over	$0.25	$0.75	$1.25	£0.15	£0.45	£0.75
89 Omega Men	$0.15	$0.50	$0.90	£0.10	£0.35	£0.60
90 Firestorm and Captain Atom	$0.15	$0.50	$0.90	£0.10	£0.35	£0.60
91 Captain Comet	$0.15	$0.50	$0.90	£0.10	£0.35	£0.60
92 Vigilante	$0.15	$0.50	$0.90	£0.10	£0.35	£0.60
93 The Elastic Four (Elongated Man, Plastic Man, Elastic Lad, Malleable Man)	$0.15	$0.50	$0.90	£0.10	£0.35	£0.60
94 George Perez cover, Harbinger, Lady Quark, Pariah; post-Crisis issue	$0.25	$0.75	$1.25	£0.15	£0.45	£0.75
95 Hawkman, unofficial Crisis X-over	$0.15	$0.50	$0.90	£0.10	£0.35	£0.60
96 Blue Devil	$0.15	$0.50	$0.90	£0.10	£0.35	£0.60
97 DS, Phantom Zone Villains: Jax-Ur, Dr. Xadu, Faora, General Zod	$0.30	$0.90	$1.50	£0.20	£0.60	£1.00
Title Value:	$24.50	$74.60	$125.80	£15.45	£47.45	£79.85

FEATURES

As above, plus: Air Wave in 40. Earth-2 Atom in 305. Congorilla in 27. Crimson Avenger in 38. Dr.Mid-Nite in 29. Hourman in 25. Johnny Thunder in 28. Mark Merlin, Prince Ra-Man in 32. Rex the Wonder Dog in 35. Richard Dragon in 39. Rip Hunter in 37. Robotman in 31. Sandman in 42. Sargon the Sorcerer in 26. Star Hawkins in 33.

DC COMICS PRESENTS ANNUAL
DC Comics; 1 Sep 1982-4 Oct 1985

	$Good	$Fine	$N.Mint	£Good	£Fine	£N.Mint
1 ND scarce in the U.K. 52pgs, co-stars Golden Age Superman	$0.40	$1.20	$2.00	£0.25	£0.75	£1.25
2 52pgs, Pollard art, 1st appearance Superwoman	$0.30	$0.90	$1.50	£0.20	£0.60	£1.00
3 52pgs, Gill Kane art, co-stars Shazam; intro Captain Thunder	$0.30	$0.90	$1.50	£0.20	£0.60	£1.00
4 52pgs, Barreto art, co-stars Superwoman	$0.30	$0.90	$1.50	£0.20	£0.60	£1.00
Title Value:	$1.30	$3.90	$6.50	£0.85	£2.55	£4.25

DC FOCUS
DC Comics,OS; 1 Summer 1987

	$Good	$Fine	$N.Mint	£Good	£Fine	£N.Mint
1 ND Giveaway checklist and features promotional comic	$0.15	$0.45	$0.75	£0.10	£0.30	£0.50
Title Value:	$0.15	$0.45	$0.75	£0.10	£0.30	£0.50

DC GRAPHIC NOVEL
DC Comics; 1 Nov 1983-7 1986

	$Good	$Fine	$N.Mint	£Good	£Fine	£N.Mint
1 ND Garcia Lopez art, Star Raiders	$1.20	$3.60	$6.00	£0.80	£2.40	£4.00
2 ND Warlords (not from Warlord series)	$1.05	$3.15	$5.25	£0.70	£2.10	£3.50
3 ND The Medusa Chain	$1.05	$3.15	$5.25	£0.70	£2.10	£3.50
4 ND very scarce in the U.K. Jack Kirby art, The Hunger Dogs	$2.25	$6.75	$11.25	£1.50	£4.50	£7.50
5 ND Me and Joe Priest	$1.20	$3.60	$6.00	£0.80	£2.40	£4.00
6 ND Kevin O'Neill art, Metalzoic (later serialized in British comic 2000AD)	$1.50	$4.50	$7.50	£1.00	£3.00	£5.00
7 ND Alex Nino art, Space Clusters	$1.05	$3.15	$5.25	£0.70	£2.10	£3.50
Title Value:	$9.30	$27.90	$46.50	£6.20	£18.60	£31.00

Note: all are 68pgs.

DC SAMPLER
DC Comics; 1 Apr 1984-3 Oct 1984
(see DC Spotlight)

	$Good	$Fine	$N.Mint	£Good	£Fine	£N.Mint
1-3 ND 32pgs	$0.15	$0.45	$0.75	£0.10	£0.30	£0.50
Title Value:	$0.45	$1.35	$2.25	£0.30	£0.90	£1.50

Note: contains news, features on current DC titles. No. 3 has "published monthly" in indicia but it was never to be.

DC SCIENCE FICTION GRAPHIC NOVEL
DC Comics; 1 1985-7 1987

	$Good	$Fine	$N.Mint	£Good	£Fine	£N.Mint
1 ND Keith Giffen art, Hell on Earth by Robert Bloch	$1.00	$3.00	$5.00	£0.65	£1.95	£3.25
2 ND Nightwings by Robert Silverberg	$1.00	$3.00	$5.00	£0.65	£1.95	£3.25
3 ND Frost and Fire by Ray Bradbury	$1.00	$3.00	$5.00	£0.65	£1.95	£3.25
4 ND Merchants of Venus by Frederik Pohl	$1.00	$3.00	$5.00	£0.65	£1.95	£3.25
5 ND Rogers art, Demon with a Glass Hand by Harlan Ellison	$1.20	$3.60	$6.00	£0.80	£2.40	£4.00
6 ND The Magic Goes Away by Larry Niven	$1.00	$3.00	$5.00	£0.65	£1.95	£3.25
7 ND Sandkings by George R.R. Martin	$1.00	$3.00	$5.00	£0.65	£1.95	£3.25
Title Value:	$7.20	$21.60	$36.00	£4.70	£14.10	£23.50

Note: adaptations of popular sci-fi books

DC SNEAK PREVIEWS
DC Comics; 1 1991

	$Good	$Fine	$N.Mint	£Good	£Fine	£N.Mint
1 ND 16pgs, promotional giveaway featuring Justice Society of America and Green Lantern: Emerald Dawn II	$0.25	$0.75	$1.25	£0.15	£0.45	£0.75
Title Value:	$0.25	$0.75	$1.25	£0.15	£0.45	£0.75

DC SPECIAL
National Periodical Publications/DC Comics; 1 Oct/Dec 1968-15 Nov/Dec 1971; 16 Spring 1975-29 Aug/Sep 1977

	$Good	$Fine	$N.Mint	£Good	£Fine	£N.Mint
1 68pgs, all Carmine Infantino art	$2.25	$6.75	$11.25	£1.50	£4.50	£7.50
2 scarce in the U.K. 68pgs, Teen Favourites (Binky)	$1.20	$3.60	$6.00	£0.80	£2.40	£4.00
3 very scarce in the U.K. 68pgs, all-Heroines issue; features an un-published Golden Age Wonder Woman story and reprints Green Lantern #16 (1st modern Star Sapphire)	$1.80	$5.25	$9.00	£1.20	£3.60	£6.00
4 68pgs, Mystery Tales	$0.80	$2.40	$4.00	£0.50	£1.50	£2.50
5 68pgs, all Kubert issue (cover and art)	$0.90	$2.70	$4.50	£0.60	£1.80	£3.00
6 68pgs, Wild Frontier	$0.80	$2.40	$4.00	£0.50	£1.50	£2.50
7 68pgs, Strange Sports	$0.80	$2.40	$4.00	£0.50	£1.50	£2.50
8 68pgs, Wanted: The World's Most Dangerous Villains, Joker story/featured on cover	$1.05	$3.15	$5.25	£0.70	£2.10	£3.50
9 68pgs, Strange Sports	$0.80	$2.40	$4.00	£0.50	£1.50	£2.50
10 68pgs, Stop! In the Name of the Law	$0.60	$1.80	$3.00	£0.40	£1.20	£2.00
11 68pgs, The Monsters are Here	$0.60	$1.80	$3.00	£0.40	£1.20	£2.00
12 68pgs, Viking Prince, Kubert reprints	$0.90	$2.70	$4.50	£0.60	£1.80	£3.00
13 68pgs, Strange Sports	$0.60	$1.80	$3.00	£0.40	£1.20	£2.00
14 52pgs, Wanted: The World's Most Dangerous Villains	$0.80	$2.40	$4.00	£0.50	£1.50	£2.50
15 52pgs, Plastic Man, all Jack Cole reprints, including origin from Police Comics #1	$1.05	$3.15	$5.25	£0.70	£2.10	£3.50
16 Super-Heroes vs. Super-Gorillas (see Super-Heroes Battle Super Gorillas)	$0.40	$1.20	$2.00	£0.25	£0.75	£1.25
17 Green Lantern	$0.45	$1.35	$2.25	£0.30	£0.90	£1.50
18 Earth Shaking Disasters	$0.40	$1.20	$2.00	£0.25	£0.75	£1.25
19 ND War Against the Giants	$0.45	$1.35	$2.25	£0.30	£0.90	£1.50
20 Green Lantern	$0.45	$1.35	$2.25	£0.30	£0.90	£1.50
21 ND Super-Heroes War against the Monsters	$0.60	$1.80	$3.00	£0.40	£1.20	£2.00
22-25 Three Musketeers & Robin Hood	$0.40	$1.20	$2.00	£0.25	£0.75	£1.25

	$Good	$Fine	$N.Mint	£Good	£Fine	£N.Mint

26 scarce in the U.K. Kubert cover and all art, Enemy Ace

	$1.00	$3.00	$5.00	£0.65	£1.95	£3.25

27 scarce in the U.K. Dinosaurs at Large, all new Captain Comet/Tommy Tomorrow appear; Justice League of America cameo

	$1.00	$3.00	$5.00	£0.65	£1.95	£3.25

28 scarce in the U.K. Earth Shattering Disasters, all new Batman/Aquaman/Legion stories

	$1.00	$3.00	$5.00	£1.00	£3.00	£5.00

29 scarce in the U.K. Untold Origin of the Justice Society of America, Neal Adams cover

	$1.00	$3.00	$5.00	£1.00	£3.00	£5.00
Title Value:	$23.30	$69.75	$116.50	£15.90	£47.70	£79.50

Note: issues 1-13, 16-21 are 68pgs; 14, 15, 22-29 are 52pgs.

FEATURES

All issues are reprint apart from the following new features: Aquaman/Batman in 28. Black Canary in 3 (previously unpublished GA story). Captain Comet in 27. Justice Society of America in 29. Legion of Super-Heroes in 28. Three Musketeers in 22-25.

REPRINT FEATURES

Adam Strange in 1. Batman in 1, 14, 16. Buffalo Bill, Davy Crockett, Daniel Boone, Kit Carson, Pow-Wow Smith, Tomahawk in 6. Captain Marvel in 18. Detective Chimp in 1. Enemy Ace in 26. Flash in 1, 8, 14, 16. Golden Gladiator, Silent Knight in 12. Green Lantern in 3, 8, 14, 16. Hawkman in 5, 8. Marvel Family in 21. Plastic Man in 15. Robin Hood in 12, 22-25. Sgt.Rock in 5. Strange Sports in 1, 7, 9, 13. Supergirl in 3. Superman in 14, 16, 18, 19, 21. Superman/Batman in 8. Viking Prince in 5, 12, 24, 25. War That Time Forgot in 21. Wonder Woman in 3, 16, 19.

DC SPECIAL BLUE RIBBON DIGEST

DC Comics, Digest; 1 Mar/Apr 1980-24 Aug 1982

1 Legion of Super-Heroes

	$0.50	$1.50	$2.50	£0.50	£1.50	£2.50

2 Flash

	$1.50	$2.50		£0.50	£1.50	£2.50

3 Justice Society of America

4 Green Lantern

	$0.50	$1.50	$2.50	£0.50	£1.50	£2.50

5 Secret Origins of Super-Heroes

	$0.50	$1.50	$2.50	£0.50	£1.50	£2.50

6 Ghosts

	$0.50	$1.50	$2.50	£0.50	£1.50	£2.50

7 Sgt.Rock's Prize Battle Tales

8 Legion of Super-Heroes

	$0.50	$1.50	$2.50	£0.50	£1.50	£2.50

9 Secret Origins of Super-Heroes

	$0.50	$1.50	$2.50	£0.50	£1.50	£2.50

10 Warlord

	$0.50	$1.50	$2.50	£0.50	£1.50	£2.50

11 Justice League of America

12 Haunted Tank

	$0.50	$1.50	$2.50	£0.50	£1.50	£2.50

13 Strange Sports Stories

14 UFO Invaders

	$0.50	$1.50	$2.50	£0.50	£1.50	£2.50

15 Secret Origins of Super-Villains

16 Green Lantern, all Neal Adams reprints

	$0.50	$1.50	$2.50	£0.50	£1.50	£2.50

17 Ghosts

	$0.50	$1.50	$2.50	£0.50	£1.50	£2.50

18 Sgt. Rock

	$0.50	$1.50	$2.50	£0.50	£1.50	£2.50

19 Doom Patrol

	$0.50	$1.50	$2.50	£0.50	£1.50	£2.50

20 Dark Mansion of Forbidden Love

	$0.50	$1.50	$2.50	£0.50	£1.50	£2.50

21 Our Army at War

	$0.50	$1.50	$2.50	£0.50	£1.50	£2.50

22 Secret Origins of Super-Heroes

	$0.50	$1.50	$2.50	£0.50	£1.50	£2.50

23 Green Arrow

	$0.50	$1.50	$2.50	£0.50	£1.50	£2.50

24 House of Mystery

	$0.50	$1.50	$2.50	£0.50	£1.50	£2.50
Title Value:	$12.00	$36.00	$60.00	£12.00	£36.00	£60.00

DC SPECIAL SERIES

DC Comics; 1 1977-27 Fall 1981

Note: All Non-Distributed on the news-stands in the U.K. See listings under individual titles, as follows:

1 Five Star Super-Hero Spectacular
2, **14**, **17**, **20** Original Swamp Thing Saga
3 Sgt. Rock Special
4 Unexpected Special
5 Superman Spectacular
6 Secret Society of Super-Villains Special
7 Ghosts Special
8 Brave and the Bold Special
9 Wonder Woman Spectacular
10 Secret Origins of Super-Heroes Special
11 Flash Spectacular
12 Secrets of Haunted House Special
13 Sgt. Rock Spectacular
15 Batman Spectacular
16 Jonah Hex Spectacular
18 Sgt. Rock's Prize Battle Tales
19 Secret Origins of Super-Heroes
21 Super-Star Holiday Special
22 G.I.Combat
23 World's Finest Comics Digest
24 The Flash Digest
25 Superman II, The Adventure Continues
26 Superman and His Incredible Fortress of Solitude
27 Batman vs. The Incredible Hulk

Note: Numbers **18**, **19**, **23**, **24** are digest size; numbers **25**, **26**, **27** are tabloid size.

DC SPOTLIGHT

DC Comics, OS; 1 1985

(50th anniversary special giveaway)

1 ND 32pgs, Garcia Lopez cover

	$0.15	$0.45	$0.75	£0.10	£0.30	£0.50
Title Value:	$0.15	$0.45	$0.75	£0.10	£0.30	£0.50

Note: contains features on the year's DC projects, including Crisis on Infinite Earths; 1st published appearance of the Watchmen (1 panel).

DC SUPER-STARS

DC Comics; 1 Mar 1976-18 Jan/Feb 1978

1 Teen Titans

	$0.60	$1.80	$3.00	£0.40	£1.20	£2.00

2 scarce in the U.K. Super Stars of Space

	$0.60	$1.80	$3.00	£0.40	£1.20	£2.00

3 ND scarce in the U.K. Legion of Super-Heroes

	$1.50	$4.50	$7.50	£1.00	£3.00	£5.00

4 Super Stars of Space

	$0.30	$0.90	$1.50	£0.20	£0.60	£1.00

5 Flash

	$0.40	$1.20	$2.00	£0.25	£0.75	£1.25

6 scarce in the U.K. Super Stars of Space

	$0.55	$1.65	$2.75	£0.35	£1.05	£1.75

7 Aquaman

	$0.40	$1.20	$2.00	£0.25	£0.75	£1.25

8 Super Stars of Space, reprints 1st Space Ranger from Showcase #15

	$0.30	$0.90	$1.50	£0.20	£0.60	£1.00

9 Man Behind the Gun

	$0.30	$0.90	$1.50	£0.20	£0.60	£1.00

10 scarce in the U.K. Strange Sports Stories featuring Superman, Batman, Luthor and Joker in new lead story

	$0.60	$1.80	$3.00	£0.40	£1.20	£2.00

11 Magic

	$0.30	$0.90	$1.50	£0.20	£0.60	£1.00

12 scarce in the U.K. Superboy

	$0.45	$1.35	$2.25	£0.30	£0.90	£1.50

Dazzler #38

DC Special #8

DC Superstars #3

	$Good	$Fine	$N.Mint	£Good	£Fine	£N.Mint

13 scarce in the U.K. Sergio Aragones art

| | $0.45 | $1.35 | $2.25 | £0.30 | £0.90 | £1.50 |

14 scarce in the U.K. Secret Origins of Super-Villains, new origins of Gorilla Grodd, Two Face, Dr. Light

| | $0.60 | $1.80 | $3.00 | £0.40 | £1.20 | £2.00 |

15 scarce in the U.K. Sgt. Rock, Unknown Soldier

| | $0.45 | $1.35 | $2.25 | £0.30 | £0.90 | £1.50 |

16 ND 1st appearance Star Hunters

| | $0.60 | $1.80 | $3.00 | £0.40 | £1.20 | £2.00 |

17 ND Secret Origins of Super-Heroes, 1st appearance Huntress, origins Legion/Green Arrow retold

| | $1.80 | $5.25 | $9.00 | £1.20 | £3.60 | £6.00 |

18 Deadman, Phantom Stranger

| | $0.40 | $1.20 | $2.00 | £0.25 | £0.75 | £1.25 |
| Title Value: | $10.60 | $31.65 | $53.00 | £7.00 | £21.00 | £35.00 |

Note: 1, 2 are 68pgs; 3-18 are 52pgs.

FEATURES

Deadman/Phantom Stranger in 18. Dr.Light, Super-Gorilla Grodd/Green Lantern, Two-Face in 14. GA Flash story re-done in 5. Green Arrow, Huntress, Legion in 17. Sergio Aragones cartoons in 13. Sgt.Rock/Unknown Soldier in 15. Star Hunters in 16. Superboy in 12. Super Heroes vs Super-Villains in 10.

REPRINT FEATURES

Adam Strange in 2, 4, 6, 8. Aqualad, Aquaman in 7. Atomic Knights, Knights of the Galaxy in 2. Captain Comet in 4, 6. Flash in 5, 11; Kid Flash in 5. Green Lantern in 10. Legion in 3. Nighthawk in 9. Space Cabby, Tommy Tomorrow in 6. Space Ranger in 4, 8. Star Rovers in 8. Teen Titans in 1. Zatanna in 11.

DC UNIVERSE: TRINITY

DC Comics,MS; 1 Aug 1993-2 Sep 1993

1-2 ND 48pgs, squarebound, holo-grafix foil cover; Legion '93, Green Lantern Corps and Darkstars begin; features art by Kitson and Charest

| | $0.45 | $1.35 | $2.25 | £0.30 | £0.90 | £1.50 |
| Title Value: | $0.90 | $2.70 | $4.50 | £0.60 | £1.80 | £3.00 |

DC VERSUS MARVEL

DC Comics/Marvel Comics Group,MS; 1 Jan 1996-present

1 ND Ron Marz script begins, Dan Jurgens/ Claudio Castellini pencils, Josef Rubenstein/Paul Neary inks; most DC and Marvel major characters appear; card-stock cover

| | $1.00 | $3.00 | $5.00 | £0.70 | £2.10 | £3.50 |

1 ND 2nd print

| | $0.80 | $2.40 | $4.00 | £0.50 | £1.50 | £2.50 |
| Title Value: | $1.80 | $5.40 | $9.00 | £1.20 | £3.60 | £6.00 |

DEAD CLOWN

Malibu; 1 Oct 1993-2 1993

1-2 ND Chris Ulm script, Joel Thomas pencils

| | $0.30 | $0.90 | $1.50 | £0.20 | £0.60 | £1.00 |
| Title Value: | $0.60 | $1.80 | $3.00 | £0.40 | £1.20 | £2.00 |

DEAD CREW

Fathom Press,OS; 1 Jun 1992

1 ND black and white

| | $0.35 | $1.05 | $1.75 | £0.25 | £0.75 | £1.25 |
| Title Value: | $0.35 | $1.05 | $1.75 | £0.25 | £0.75 | £1.25 |

DEAD HEAT, THE

All American Comics; 1 1990

1 ND

| | $0.30 | $0.90 | $1.50 | £0.20 | £0.60 | £1.00 |
| Title Value: | $0.30 | $0.90 | $1.50 | £0.20 | £0.60 | £1.00 |

DEAD IN THE WEST

Dark Horse,MS; 1 Oct 1993-2 Jan 1994

1-2 ND 48pgs, painted cover by Tim Truman

| | $0.80 | $2.40 | $4.00 | £0.50 | £1.50 | £2.50 |
| Title Value: | $1.60 | $4.80 | $8.00 | £1.00 | £3.00 | £5.00 |

DEAD OF NIGHT

Marvel Comics Group; 1 Dec 1973-11 Sep 1975

1-3 ND

| | $0.40 | $1.20 | $2.00 | £0.25 | £0.75 | £1.25 |

4 ND Werewolf issue

| | $0.40 | $1.20 | $2.00 | £0.25 | £0.75 | £1.25 |

5 ND

| | $0.40 | $1.20 | $2.00 | £0.25 | £0.75 | £1.25 |

6 ND Jack the Ripper appears

| | $0.40 | $1.20 | $2.00 | £0.25 | £0.75 | £1.25 |

7-9 ND

| | $0.40 | $1.20 | $2.00 | £0.25 | £0.75 | £1.25 |

10 Kirby/Ditko reprints

| | $0.40 | $1.20 | $2.00 | £0.25 | £0.75 | £1.25 |

11 ND 1st appearance Scarecrow (note DC villain of the same name)

| | $0.40 | $1.20 | $2.00 | £0.25 | £0.75 | £1.25 |
| Title Value: | $4.40 | $13.20 | $22.00 | £2.75 | £8.25 | £13.75 |

DEAD WALKERS

Aircel,MS; 1 Jan 1991-4 Apr 1991

1-4 ND black and white

| | $0.40 | $1.20 | $2.00 | £0.25 | £0.75 | £1.25 |
| Title Value: | $1.60 | $4.80 | $8.00 | £1.00 | £3.00 | £5.00 |

DEADBEATS

Claypool Comics; 1 Jun 1993-present

1-13 ND black and white

| | $0.45 | $1.35 | $2.25 | £0.30 | £0.90 | £1.50 |

14 ND

| | $0.45 | $1.35 | $2.25 | £0.30 | £0.90 | £1.50 |
| Title Value: | $6.30 | $18.90 | $31.50 | £4.20 | £12.60 | £21.00 |

DEADFACE

(see British section)

DEADFACE: DOING THE ISLANDS WITH BACCHUS

Dark Horse,MS; 1 Jul 1991-3 Sep 1991

1-3 ND 48pgs, Eddie Campbell script and art

| | $0.55 | $1.65 | $2.75 | £0.35 | £1.05 | £1.75 |
| Title Value: | $1.65 | $4.95 | $8.25 | £1.05 | £3.15 | £5.25 |

DEADFACE: EARTH, AIR, FIRE & WATER

Dark Horse,MS; 1 Aug 1992-4 Dec 1992

1-4 ND Eddie Campbell script and art

| | $0.45 | $1.35 | $2.25 | £0.30 | £0.90 | £1.50 |
| Title Value: | $1.80 | $5.40 | $9.00 | £1.20 | £3.60 | £6.00 |

DEADLINE U.S.A.

Dark Horse; 1 Nov 1991-3 Jan 1992

1-3 ND 96pgs, features work from British Deadline magazine

| | $1.60 | $4.80 | $8.00 | £1.05 | £3.15 | £5.25 |
| Title Value: | $4.80 | $14.40 | $24.00 | £3.15 | £9.45 | £15.75 |

DEADLINE USA (2ND SERIES)

Dark Horse; 1 Jun 1992-8 1993

1 ND 48pgs, reprints from UK's Deadline magazine plus new US material

| | $0.80 | $2.40 | $4.00 | £0.50 | £1.50 | £2.50 |

2-8 ND 48pgs

| | $0.80 | $2.40 | $4.00 | £0.50 | £1.50 | £2.50 |
| Title Value: | $6.40 | $19.20 | $32.00 | £4.00 | £12.00 | £20.00 |

DEADLY DUO

Image; 1 Nov 1994-4 Feb 1995

1 ND Erik Larsen script, spoofing superheroes

| | $0.45 | $1.35 | $2.25 | £0.30 | £0.90 | £1.50 |

2 ND Pitt guest-stars

| | $0.45 | $1.35 | $2.25 | £0.30 | £0.90 | £1.50 |

3 ND Roman from Brigade appears

| | $0.45 | $1.35 | $2.25 | £0.30 | £0.90 | £1.50 |

4 ND Savage Dragon appears

| | $0.45 | $1.35 | $2.25 | £0.30 | £0.90 | £1.50 |
| Title Value: | $1.80 | $5.40 | $9.00 | £1.20 | £3.60 | £6.00 |

DEADLY DUO II

Image; 1 Jun 1995-present

1 ND Erik Larsen script, John Cleary art; Spawn appears

| | $0.45 | $1.35 | $2.25 | £0.30 | £0.90 | £1.50 |

2 ND Freak Force appear

| | $0.45 | $1.35 | $2.25 | £0.30 | £0.90 | £1.50 |

3 ND

| | $0.45 | $1.35 | $2.25 | £0.30 | £0.90 | £1.50 |

4 ND Riptide appears

| | $0.45 | $1.35 | $2.25 | £0.30 | £0.90 | £1.50 |
| Title Value: | $1.80 | $5.40 | $9.00 | £1.20 | £3.60 | £6.00 |

DEADLY HANDS OF KUNG-FU

Marvel Comics Group,Magazine; 1 Apr 1974-33 Feb 1977

1 ND origin Shang-Chi, Jim Starlin art

| | $0.80 | $2.40 | $4.00 | £0.50 | £1.50 | £2.50 |

2 ND Jim Starlin reprint

| | $0.55 | $1.65 | $2.75 | £0.35 | £1.05 | £1.75 |

3 ND Gulacy art

| | $0.55 | $1.65 | $2.75 | £0.35 | £1.05 | £1.75 |

4 ND Bruce Lee cover, 8 page biography on Bruce Lee

| | $0.55 | $1.65 | $2.75 | £0.35 | £1.05 | £1.75 |

5 ND

| | $0.55 | $1.65 | $2.75 | £0.35 | £1.05 | £1.75 |

6-7 George Perez art

| | $0.70 | $2.10 | $3.50 | £0.45 | £1.35 | £2.25 |

8 scarce, George Perez art

| | $0.80 | $2.40 | $4.00 | £0.50 | £1.50 | £2.50 |

9-11 ND

| | $0.55 | $1.65 | $2.75 | £0.35 | £1.05 | £1.75 |

12 James Bond feature, George Perez art

| | $0.60 | $1.80 | $3.00 | £0.40 | £1.20 | £2.00 |

13-14 ND

| | $0.45 | $1.35 | $2.25 | £0.30 | £0.90 | £1.50 |

15 Annual 1 (Summer 1975), Englehart script, Jim Starlin/Gulacy art, Man Thing appears

| | $0.55 | $1.65 | $2.75 | £0.35 | £1.05 | £1.75 |

16-17 ND

| | $0.45 | $1.35 | $2.25 | £0.30 | £0.90 | £1.50 |

18 Broderick/Austin art

| | $0.45 | $1.35 | $2.25 | £0.30 | £0.90 | £1.50 |

19 George Perez art, Jim Starlin pin-up

| | $0.60 | $1.80 | $3.00 | £0.40 | £1.20 | £2.00 |

20 origin White Tiger, George Perez art

| | $0.60 | $1.80 | $3.00 | £0.40 | £1.20 | £2.00 |

21 George Perez art

| | $0.55 | $1.65 | $2.75 | £0.35 | £1.05 | £1.75 |

22

| | $0.45 | $1.35 | $2.25 | £0.30 | £0.90 | £1.50 |

23 Jack of Hearts appears, Gil Kane art

| | $0.45 | $1.35 | $2.25 | £0.30 | £0.90 | £1.50 |

24 Keith Giffen art

| | $0.45 | $1.35 | $2.25 | £0.30 | £0.90 | £1.50 |

25 Broderick art

| | $0.45 | $1.35 | $2.25 | £0.30 | £0.90 | £1.50 |

26-27

| | $0.40 | $1.20 | $2.00 | £0.25 | £0.75 | £1.25 |

28 full length Bruce Lee life story, Joe Staton art

| | $0.40 | $1.20 | $2.00 | £0.25 | £0.75 | £1.25 |

29 origin Jack of Hearts

| | $0.40 | $1.20 | $2.00 | £0.25 | £0.75 | £1.25 |

30 Jack of Hearts appears, George Perez art

| | $0.55 | $1.65 | $2.75 | £0.35 | £1.05 | £1.75 |

31 Jack of Hearts appears, Staton art

| | $0.40 | $1.20 | $2.00 | £0.25 | £0.75 | £1.25 |

32-33 scarce, Marshall Rogers art

| | $0.80 | $2.40 | $4.00 | £0.50 | £1.50 | £2.50 |
| Title Value: | $17.95 | $53.85 | $89.75 | £11.55 | £34.65 | £57.75 |

Special Album Edition (Summer 1974)

(sub-titled Deadliest Hands of Kung-Fu)

Neal Adams art, very scarce

| | | | | £0.75 | £2.25 | £3.75 |

Note: Neal Adams painted covers on 1, 2-4, 11, 12, 14, 17. Some others feature covers by Earl Norem.

DEADMAN

DC Comics,MS; 1 May 1985-7 Nov 1985

1 ND Carmine Infantino, Neal Adams reprints

| | $0.45 | $1.35 | $2.25 | £0.30 | £0.90 | £1.50 |

2-7 ND Neal Adams reprints

| | $0.45 | $1.35 | $2.25 | £0.30 | £0.90 | £1.50 |
| Title Value: | $3.15 | $9.45 | $15.75 | £2.10 | £6.30 | £10.50 |

Note: reprints Strange Adventures #206-216, Brave & Bold #79.

DEADMAN (LIMITED SERIES)

DC Comics,MS; 1 Mar 1986-4 Jun 1986

	$Good	$Fine	$N.Mint	£Good	£Fine	£N.Mint
1 LD in the U.K. Garcia Lopez art begins	$0.30	$0.90	$1.50	£0.20	£0.60	£1.00
2-3	$0.25	$0.75	$1.25	£0.15	£0.45	£0.75
4 John Byrne cover	$0.25	$0.75	$1.25	£0.15	£0.45	£0.75
Title Value:	$1.05	$3.15	$5.25	£0.65	£1.95	£3.25

DEADMAN: EXORCISM
DC Comics,MS; 1 Dec 1992-2 Jan 1993

	$Good	$Fine	$N.Mint	£Good	£Fine	£N.Mint
1-2 ND 48pgs, Mike Baron script, Kelly Jones art	$0.90	$2.70	$4.50	£0.60	£1.80	£3.00
Title Value:	$1.80	$5.40	$9.00	£1.20	£3.60	£6.00
Deadman: Lost Souls (May 1995)						
Trade paperback reprints Love & Death and						
Exorcism mini-series				£2.70	£8.10	£13.50

DEADMAN: LOVE AFTER DEATH
DC Comics,MS; 1 Dec 1989-2 Jan 1990

	$Good	$Fine	$N.Mint	£Good	£Fine	£N.Mint
1-2 ND 48pgs, Mike Baron story, Kelly Jones art, squarebound	$0.85	$2.55	$4.25	£0.55	£1.65	£2.75
Title Value:	$1.70	$5.10	$8.50	£1.10	£3.30	£5.50

DEADPOOL
Marvel Comics Group,MS; 1 Aug 1993-4 Nov 1993

	$Good	$Fine	$N.Mint	£Good	£Fine	£N.Mint
1 ND embossed Deadpool figure and recessed logo with metallic ink on cover	$0.50	$1.50	$2.50	£0.35	£1.05	£1.75
2-4 ND	$0.45	$1.35	$2.25	£0.30	£0.90	£1.50
Title Value:	$1.85	$5.55	$9.25	£1.25	£3.75	£6.25

DEADPOOL (2ND SERIES)
Marvel Comics Group,MS; 1 Aug 1994-4 Nov 1994

	$Good	$Fine	$N.Mint	£Good	£Fine	£N.Mint
1 ND	$1.00	$3.00	$5.00	£0.60	£1.80	£3.00
2 ND	$0.60	$1.80	$3.00	£0.40	£1.20	£2.00
3-4 ND	$0.45	$1.35	$2.25	£0.30	£0.90	£1.50
Title Value:	$2.50	$7.50	$12.50	£1.60	£4.80	£8.00
X-Men Premiere (Dec 1995)						
ND boxed set collecting issues #1-4				£1.10	£3.30	£5.50

DEADSHOT
DC Comics,MS; 1 Nov 1988-4 Feb 1989
(see Suicide Squad)

	$Good	$Fine	$N.Mint	£Good	£Fine	£N.Mint
1 Batman appears	$0.20	$0.60	$1.00	£0.15	£0.45	£0.75
2-4	$0.20	$0.60	$1.00	£0.15	£0.45	£0.75
Title Value:	$0.80	$2.40	$4.00	£0.60	£1.80	£3.00

DEADTALES: A BODY
Caliber Press,OS; 1 Dec 1991

	$Good	$Fine	$N.Mint	£Good	£Fine	£N.Mint
1 ND reprints from Deadworld #10-13	$0.55	$1.65	$2.75	£0.35	£1.05	£1.75
Title Value:	$0.55	$1.65	$2.75	£0.35	£1.05	£1.75

DEADTIME STORIES
Now Comics,OS; 1 Nov 1987

	$Good	$Fine	$N.Mint	£Good	£Fine	£N.Mint
1 ND Bissette, Breyfogle art, Mike Mignola, Jim Starlin, Art Adams, Gulacy, Walt Simonson, Jones illustrations	$0.45	$1.35	$2.25	£0.30	£0.90	£1.50
Title Value:	$0.45	$1.35	$2.25	£0.30	£0.90	£1.50

DEADWORLD
Arrow; 1 Nov 1987-26 Nov 1992 (Caliber 11 on)

	$Good	$Fine	$N.Mint	£Good	£Fine	£N.Mint
1 ND	$0.90	$2.70	$4.50	£0.60	£1.80	£3.00
2 ND very scarce in the U.K.	$1.20	$3.60	$6.00	£0.80	£2.40	£4.00
3 ND scarce in the U.K.	$0.80	$2.40	$4.00	£0.50	£1.50	£2.50
4-5 ND scarce in the U.K	$0.60	$1.80	$3.00	£0.40	£1.20	£2.00
6-10 ND	$0.55	$1.65	$2.75	£0.35	£1.05	£1.75
11-25 ND	$0.45	$1.35	$2.25	£0.30	£0.90	£1.50
26 ND $3.50 cover	$0.60	$1.80	$3.00	£0.40	£1.20	£2.00
Title Value:	$14.20	$42.60	$71.00	£9.35	£28.05	£46.75

Note: issues #5-24 are published with 2 cover versions, "graphic" or "tame"; prices are the same for either.

Trade paperback: Deadworld Book 1
reprints issues #1-7 — £1.50 £4.50 £7.50

Trade paperback: Deadworld Book 2
reprints issues #8-16 — £1.50 £4.50 £7.50

DEADWORLD (2ND SERIES)
Caliber Press; 1 May 1993-present

	$Good	$Fine	$N.Mint	£Good	£Fine	£N.Mint
1 ND black and white begins	$0.60	$1.80	$3.00	£0.40	£1.20	£2.00
1 ND Limited Edition - red foil enhanced cover	$1.20	$3.60	$6.00	£0.80	£2.40	£4.00
2 ND	$0.60	$1.80	$3.00	£0.40	£1.20	£2.00
2 ND Limited Edition - signed, pre-bagged with poster	$1.20	$3.60	$6.00	£0.80	£2.40	£4.00
3-4 ND	$0.60	$1.80	$3.00	£0.40	£1.20	£2.00
5 ND die-cut cover $0.60	$1.80	$3.00	£0.40	£1.20	£2.00	
5 ND Collector's Set - pre-bagged with a copy of issue #1 and trading card	$1.20	$3.60	$6.00	£0.80	£2.40	£4.00
6-9 ND	$0.60	$1.80	$3.00	£0.40	£1.20	£2.00
10-15 ND Death Call story	$0.60	$1.80	$3.00	£0.40	£1.20	£2.00
Title Value:	$12.60	$37.80	$63.00	£8.40	£25.20	£42.00

DEADWORLD ARCHIVES
Caliber Press; 1 Jan 1993-4 Apr 1993

	$Good	$Fine	$N.Mint	£Good	£Fine	£N.Mint
1 ND reprints from Deadworld series begin; solid black cover with red droplets	$0.45	$1.35	$2.25	£0.30	£0.90	£1.50

	$Good	$Fine	$N.Mint	£Good	£Fine	£N.Mint
2-4 ND	$0.45	$1.35	$2.25	£0.30	£0.90	£1.50
Title Value:	$1.80	$5.40	$9.00	£1.20	£3.60	£6.00

DEADWORLD: BITS AND PIECES
Caliber Press,OS; 1 Oct 1991

	$Good	$Fine	$N.Mint	£Good	£Fine	£N.Mint
1 ND reprints from Caliber Presents #2 and #8 being the first Deadworld story	$0.55	$1.65	$2.75	£0.35	£1.05	£1.75
Title Value:	$0.55	$1.65	$2.75	£0.35	£1.05	£1.75

DEADWORLD: TO KILL A KING
Caliber Press,MS; 1 1992-3 Aug 1993

	$Good	$Fine	$N.Mint	£Good	£Fine	£N.Mint
1 ND	$0.60	$1.80	$3.00	£0.40	£1.20	£2.00
1 ND Limited Edition	$1.20	$3.60	$6.00	£0.80	£2.40	£4.00
2 ND	$0.60	$1.80	$3.00	£0.40	£1.20	£2.00
2 ND Limited Edition	$1.20	$3.60	$6.00	£0.80	£2.40	£4.00
3 ND	$0.55	$1.65	$2.75	£0.35	£1.05	£1.75
Title Value:	$4.15	$12.45	$20.75	£2.75	£8.25	£13.75

DEATH DEALER
Verotik; 1 Jul 1995

	$Good	$Fine	$N.Mint	£Good	£Fine	£N.Mint
1 ND 48pgs, squarebound; Glenn Danzig script, Simon Bisley art, cover by Frank Frazetta	$1.20	$3.60	$6.00	£1.00	£3.00	£5.00
Title Value:	$1.20	$3.60	$6.00	£1.00	£3.00	£5.00

DEATH DUTY
Marvel UK; 1 Dec 1993

	$Good	$Fine	$N.Mint	£Good	£Fine	£N.Mint
1 ND contains four-card uncut sheet	$0.45	$1.35	$2.25	£0.30	£0.90	£1.50
Title Value:	$0.45	$1.35	$2.25	£0.30	£0.90	£1.50

DEATH GALLERY
DC Comics,OS; 1 Jan 1994

	$Good	$Fine	$N.Mint	£Good	£Fine	£N.Mint
1 ND pin-ups of Death by Arthur Adams, Brian Bolland, Dave Gibbons plus Kaluta, McKean, Quesada, Talbot, Vess and lots of others	$0.60	$1.80	$3.00	£0.40	£1.20	£2.00
Title Value:	$0.60	$1.80	$3.00	£0.40	£1.20	£2.00

DEATH HAWK
Adventure; 1 May 1988-3 Nov 1988

	$Good	$Fine	$N.Mint	£Good	£Fine	£N.Mint
1 ND Hughes art	$0.40	$1.20	$2.00	£0.25	£0.75	£1.25
2-3 ND	$0.40	$1.20	$2.00	£0.25	£0.75	£1.25
Title Value:	$1.20	$3.60	$6.00	£0.75	£2.25	£3.75

DEATH HUNT
Eternity; 1,2 1987

	$Good	$Fine	$N.Mint	£Good	£Fine	£N.Mint
1-2 ND	$0.40	$1.20	$2.00	£0.25	£0.75	£1.25
Title Value:	$0.80	$2.40	$4.00	£0.50	£1.50	£2.50

DEATH III
Marvel UK,MS; 1 Sep 1993-4 Dec 1993

	$Good	$Fine	$N.Mint	£Good	£Fine	£N.Mint
1 foil embossed cover	$0.45	$1.35	$2.25	£0.30	£0.90	£1.50
2 Death's Head II appears with Ghost Rider, Kingpin, Thing, Dr. Octopus and Iron Man	$0.40	$1.20	$2.00	£0.25	£0.75	£1.25
3 Death's Head II appears with Hulk, Storm, Cable and Thing	$0.40	$1.20	$2.00	£0.25	£0.75	£1.25
4 Death's Head II appears	$0.40	$1.20	$2.00	£0.25	£0.75	£1.25
Title Value:	$1.65	$4.95	$8.25	£1.05	£3.15	£5.25

DEATH METAL VS. GENETIX
Marvel UK,MS; 1 Dec 1993-4 Mar 1994

	$Good	$Fine	$N.Mint	£Good	£Fine	£N.Mint
1 pre-bagged with 2 trading cards	$0.45	$1.35	$2.25	£0.30	£0.90	£1.50
2-4	$0.40	$1.20	$2.00	£0.25	£0.75	£1.25
Title Value:	$1.65	$4.95	$8.25	£1.05	£3.15	£5.25

DEATH RACE 2020
Cosmic Comics; 1 Apr 1995-present

	$Good	$Fine	$N.Mint	£Good	£Fine	£N.Mint
1-3 ND Pat Mills script, Tony Skinner and Kev O'Neill art; based on Roger Corman's film Deathrace 2000; bi-monthly	$0.45	$1.35	$2.25	£0.30	£0.90	£1.50
4 ND Pat Mills script, Kev O'Neill and Tony Skinner art; based on Roger Corman's film Death Race 2000	$0.45	$1.35	$2.25	£0.30	£0.90	£1.50
5-8 ND Pat Mills and Tony Skinner script	$0.45	$1.35	$2.25	£0.30	£0.90	£1.50
Title Value:	$3.60	$10.80	$18.00	£2.40	£7.20	£12.00

DEATH RATTLE
Kitchen Sink; 1 Oct 1985-18 Sep 1988
(previous series Underground-type comic)

	$Good	$Fine	$N.Mint	£Good	£Fine	£N.Mint
1 ND Richard Corben cover, colour begins	$0.45	$1.35	$2.25	£0.30	£0.90	£1.50
2-4 ND	$0.45	$1.35	$2.25	£0.30	£0.90	£1.50
5 ND last colour issue	$0.45	$1.35	$2.25	£0.30	£0.90	£1.50
6-7 ND	$0.45	$1.35	$2.25	£0.30	£0.90	£1.50
8 ND Xenozoic Tales preview	$0.45	$1.35	$2.25	£0.30	£0.90	£1.50
9 ND	$0.45	$1.35	$2.25	£0.30	£0.90	£1.50
10 ND Charles Burns cover	$0.45	$1.35	$2.25	£0.30	£0.90	£1.50
11 ND photo cover	$0.45	$1.35	$2.25	£0.30	£0.90	£1.50
12-17 ND	$0.45	$1.35	$2.25	£0.30	£0.90	£1.50
18 ND 44pgs, Frank Miller cover	$0.55	$1.65	$2.75	£0.35	£1.05	£1.75
Title Value:	$8.20	$24.60	$41.00	£5.45	£16.35	£27.25

DEATH RATTLE (2ND SERIES)
Kitchen Sink; 1 Oct 1995-present

1 ND Mark Schultz cover and lead story

	$Good	$Fine	$N.Mint	£Good	£Fine	£N.Mint
	$0.60	$1.80	$3.00	£0.40	£1.20	£2.00
Title Value:	$0.60	$1.80	$3.00	£0.40	£1.20	£2.00

DEATH TALKS ABOUT LIFE
DC Comics;OS; nn 1993
nn ND 8pgs, promotional giveaway with Death talking about AIDS; Neil Gaiman script, Dave McKean art

	$Good	$Fine	$N.Mint	£Good	£Fine	£N.Mint
	$0.15	$0.45	$0.75	£0.10	£0.30	£0.50
Title Value:	$0.15	$0.45	$0.75	£0.10	£0.30	£0.50

DEATH'S HEAD
Crystal; 1 Dec 1987-2 Feb 1988
1-2 ND black and white (note: no relation to Marvel character!)

	$Good	$Fine	$N.Mint	£Good	£Fine	£N.Mint
	$0.40	$1.20	$2.00	£0.25	£0.75	£1.25
Title Value:	$0.80	$2.40	$4.00	£0.50	£1.50	£2.50

DEATH'S HEAD
Marvel Comics Group; 1 Mar 1989-10 Dec 1989
(see Marvel Graphic Novel)

	$Good	$Fine	$N.Mint	£Good	£Fine	£N.Mint
1	$1.50	$4.50	$7.50	£1.00	£3.00	£5.00
2	$0.90	$2.70	$4.50	£0.60	£1.80	£3.00
3-5	$0.80	$2.40	$4.00	£0.50	£1.50	£2.50
6-7	$0.60	$1.80	$3.00	£0.40	£1.20	£2.00
8 Dr. Who appears						
	$0.60	$1.80	$3.00	£0.40	£1.20	£2.00
9 Simonson cover						
	$0.60	$1.80	$3.00	£0.40	£1.20	£2.00
10 less common in the U.K.						
	$0.60	$1.80	$3.00	£0.50	£1.50	£2.50
Title Value:	$7.80	$23.40	$39.00	£5.20	£15.60	£26.00
Trade paperback (1991), reprints				£1.25	£3.75	£6.25

DEATH'S HEAD II
Marvel Comics Group,MS; 1 Mar 1992-4 Jun 1992

	$Good	$Fine	$N.Mint	£Good	£Fine	£N.Mint
1 Dan Abnett script begins, Liam Sharp art; origin Death's Head II						
	$0.70	$2.10	$3.50	£0.50	£1.50	£2.50
1 2nd printing, silver ink cover						
	$0.45	$1.35	$2.25	£0.30	£0.90	£1.50
2 Fantastic Four appear						
	$0.60	$1.80	$3.00	£0.40	£1.20	£2.00
2 2nd printing, silver ink cover						
	$0.40	$1.20	$2.00	£0.25	£0.75	£1.25
3 less common in the U.K. 1st appearance Tuck, origin Charnel						
	$0.60	$1.80	$3.00	£0.50	£1.50	£2.50
4 alternate future Spiderman, Punisher, Daredevil, She-Hulk and Wolverine appear						
	$0.60	$1.80	$3.00	£0.40	£1.20	£2.00
Title Value:	$3.35	$10.05	$16.75	£2.35	£7.05	£11.75

Treat Pedigree Collection (1992)
ND Issues #1-4 (all 1st prints) sealed in plastic display case;

	£Good	£Fine	£N.Mint
50,000 units with gold seal on outside	£2.50	£7.50	£12.50

DEATH'S HEAD II (2ND SERIES)
Marvel UK; 1 Dec 1992-16 Mar 1994

	$Good	$Fine	$N.Mint	£Good	£Fine	£N.Mint
1 X-Men appear, Liam Sharp art begins						
	$0.45	$1.35	$2.25	£0.30	£0.90	£1.50
2 Lotus FX story begins (ends #4); Wolverine appears						
	$0.40	$1.20	$2.00	£0.25	£0.75	£1.25
3 1st appearance Raptor						
	$0.40	$1.20	$2.00	£0.25	£0.75	£1.25
4 X-Men appear						
	$0.40	$1.20	$2.00	£0.25	£0.75	£1.25
5 MyS-TECH Wars X-over, Warheads appear, Dell Barras art						
	$0.40	$1.20	$2.00	£0.25	£0.75	£1.25
6 $1.95 cover begins; Simon Coleby art begins						
	$0.40	$1.20	$2.00	£0.25	£0.75	£1.25
7 Liam Sharp cover only						
	$0.40	$1.20	$2.00	£0.25	£0.75	£1.25
8 Liam-Sharp cover only; Anthony Williams art						
	$0.40	$1.20	$2.00	£0.25	£0.75	£1.25
9	$0.40	$1.20	$2.00	£0.25	£0.75	£1.25
10 The Origin of Death's Head II; Dougie Braithewaite art						
	$0.40	$1.20	$2.00	£0.25	£0.75	£1.25
11-13	$0.40	$1.20	$2.00	£0.25	£0.75	£1.25
14 metallic blue foil cover with flip-side 8pg Death's Head Gold #0 prologue; Sal Larocca art						
	$0.70	$2.10	$3.50	£0.45	£1.35	£2.25
15-16	$0.40	$1.20	$2.00	£0.25	£0.75	£1.25
Title Value:	$6.75	$20.25	$33.75	£4.25	£12.75	£21.25

Note: #5 not reprinted in Overkill
Death's Head II Gold #0 (Jan 1994)

	£Good	£Fine	£N.Mint
Liam Sharp story and pencils	£0.45	£1.35	£2.25

DEATH'S HEAD II/DIE CUT
Marvel UK,MS; 1 Aug 1993-2 Sep 1993

	$Good	$Fine	$N.Mint	£Good	£Fine	£N.Mint
1 foil embossed logo on cover						
	$0.45	$1.35	$2.25	£0.30	£0.90	£1.50
2 Liam Sharp cover						
	$0.40	$1.20	$2.00	£0.25	£0.75	£1.25
Title Value:	$0.85	$2.55	$4.25	£0.55	£1.65	£2.75

DEATH'S HEAD II/KILLPOWER: BATTLETIDE
Marvel UK,MS; 1 Dec 1992-4 Mar 1993

	$Good	$Fine	$N.Mint	£Good	£Fine	£N.Mint
1 Wolverine, Captain America and Hulk appear						
	$0.45	$1.35	$2.25	£0.30	£0.90	£1.50
2 Wolverine, Dark Angel, Hercules appear						
	$0.40	$1.20	$2.00	£0.25	£0.75	£1.25
3 Wolverine, Hercules, Psylocke, Dark Angel appear						
	$0.40	$1.20	$2.00	£0.25	£0.75	£1.25
4 Wolverine, Psylocke, Dark Angel appear						
	$0.40	$1.20	$2.00	£0.25	£0.75	£1.25
Title Value:	$1.65	$4.95	$8.25	£1.05	£3.15	£5.25

DEATH'S HEAD II/KILLPOWER: BATTLETIDE II
Marvel UK,MS; 1 Aug 1993-4 Nov 1993

	$Good	$Fine	$N.Mint	£Good	£Fine	£N.Mint
1-4 Hulk appears	$0.40	$1.20	$2.00	£0.25	£0.75	£1.25
Title Value:	$1.60	$4.80	$8.00	£1.00	£3.00	£5.00

DEATH'S HEAD, THE INCOMPLETE
Marvel UK,MS; 1 Jan 1993-12 Dec 1993

	$Good	$Fine	$N.Mint	£Good	£Fine	£N.Mint
1 DS reprints begin from original Marvel UK series Dr. Who Monthly with new linking art, die-cut cover						
	$0.45	$1.35	$2.25	£0.30	£0.90	£1.50
2-4	$0.40	$1.20	$2.00	£0.25	£0.75	£1.25
5 Dr. Who appears						
	$0.40	$1.20	$2.00	£0.25	£0.75	£1.25
6-11	$0.40	$1.20	$2.00	£0.25	£0.75	£1.25
12 48pgs	$0.45	$1.35	$2.25	£0.30	£0.90	£1.50
Title Value:	$4.90	$14.70	$24.50	£3.10	£9.30	£15.50

Note: contains new linking material by Dan Abnett and Simon Coleby

DEATH: THE HIGH COST OF LIVING
DC Comics/Vertigo,MS; 1 Mar 1993-3 May 1993
(see Sandman [2nd Series])

	$Good	$Fine	$N.Mint	£Good	£Fine	£N.Mint
1 features Sandman's sister Death, scripts by Neil Gaiman, pencils by Chris Bachalo, inks by Mark Buckingham, covers by Dave McKean						
	$0.45	$1.35	$2.25	£0.30	£0.90	£1.50
1 Gold Edition ND (Jun 1993) - 7,500 copies, signed by Chris Bachalo with certificate of authenticity						
	$3.00	$9.00	$15.00	£2.00	£6.00	£10.00
1 Platinum Edition ND						
	$4.00	$12.00	$20.00	£3.00	£9.00	£15.00
2 less common in the U.K.						
	$0.45	$1.35	$2.25	£0.50	£1.50	£2.50
3	$0.45	$1.35	$2.25	£0.30	£0.90	£1.50
Title Value:	$8.35	$25.05	$41.75	£6.10	£18.30	£30.50

Death: The High Cost Of Living (Jan 1994)

	£Good	£Fine	£N.Mint
Hardcover Edition with dust-jacket	£2.70	£8.10	£13.50

DEATHBLOW
Image; 1 May 1993-present

	$Good	$Fine	$N.Mint	£Good	£Fine	£N.Mint
1 Jim Lee and Brandon Choi story begins with Jim Lee art plus Cybernary back-up featuring Steve Gerber script and Nick Manabat art						
	$0.60	$1.80	$3.00	£0.40	£1.20	£2.00
2 detachable Deathblow poster included						
	$0.45	$1.35	$2.25	£0.30	£0.90	£1.50
3	$0.45	$1.35	$2.25	£0.30	£0.90	£1.50
4 Tim Sale art	$0.45	$1.35	$2.25	£0.30	£0.90	£1.50
5 Tim Sale art	$0.45	$1.35	$2.25	£1.20	£3.60	£6.00
5 Variant cover, ND cover forms larger picture when combined with variant covers of Gen 13 #5, Kindred #3, Stormwatch #10, Team 7 #1, Union #0, Wetworks #2, WildC.A.T.S #11						
	$2.00	$6.00	$10.00	£2.00	£6.00	£10.00
6-13 Tim Sale art	$0.45	$1.35	$2.25	£0.30	£0.90	£1.50
14 Johnny Savoy from WetWorks appears, Tim Sale art						
	$0.45	$1.35	$2.25	£0.30	£0.90	£1.50
15 Tim Sale art	$0.45	$1.35	$2.25	£0.30	£0.90	£1.50
16 Wildstorm Rising part 6, continued in Wetworks #8; with two foil-bagged painted trading cards. Cover by Barry Windor-Smith						
	$0.45	$1.35	$2.25	£0.30	£0.90	£1.50
16 Newstand edition, without trading cards						
	$0.40	$1.20	$2.00	£0.25	£0.75	£1.25
17-20	$0.45	$1.35	$2.25	£0.30	£0.90	£1.50
21 Brothers in Arms part 2, guest starring Gen 13						
	$0.45	$1.35	$2.25	£0.30	£0.90	£1.50
22 Brothers in Arms part 3, guest starring Dane from Wetworks						
	$0.45	$1.35	$2.25	£0.30	£0.90	£1.50
23 Brothers in Arms part 4, guest starring Backlash						
	$0.50	$1.50	$2.50	£0.30	£0.90	£1.50
Title Value:	$12.95	$38.85	$64.75	£10.15	£30.45	£50.75

Note: all Non-Distributed on the news-stands in the U.K.
Deathblow (Sep 1995)

	£Good	£Fine	£N.Mint
Trade paperback reprints The Black Angel Saga	£2.70	£8.10	£13.50

DEATHLOK
Marvel Comics Group; 1 Jul 1991-34 Apr 1994
(see Astonishing Tales)

	$Good	$Fine	$N.Mint	£Good	£Fine	£N.Mint
1 ND story continues from mini-series						
	$0.60	$1.80	$3.00	£0.30	£0.90	£1.50
2 ND The Cybernet Saga part 1, Dr. Doom appears						
	$0.35	$1.05	$1.75	£0.25	£0.75	£1.25
3 ND The Cybernet Saga, Deathlok vs. Dr. Doom						
	$0.35	$1.05	$1.75	£0.25	£0.75	£1.25
4 ND The Cybernet Saga, X-Men, Fantastic Four, Vision appear						
	$0.35	$1.05	$1.75	£0.25	£0.75	£1.25
5 ND The Cybernet Saga, X-Men, Fantastic Four appear						
	$0.35	$1.05	$1.75	£0.25	£0.75	£1.25
6 ND Deathlok vs. Punisher						
	$0.35	$1.05	$1.75	£0.25	£0.75	£1.25
6 ND Punisher appears, signed by artist Denys Cowan (5,000 copies)						
	$1.20	$3.60	$6.00	£0.80	£2.40	£4.00
7 ND Punisher appears						
	$0.35	$1.05	$1.75	£0.25	£0.75	£1.25
8 ND	$0.35	$1.05	$1.75	£0.25	£0.75	£1.25
9-10 ND Ghost Rider appears						
	$0.35	$1.05	$1.75	£0.25	£0.75	£1.25
11 ND	$0.30	$0.90	$1.50	£0.20	£0.60	£1.00
12 ND Biohazard Agenda part 1, Nick Fury appears						
	$0.30	$0.90	$1.50	£0.20	£0.60	£1.00
13-15 ND Biohazard Agenda						
	$0.30	$0.90	$1.50	£0.20	£0.60	£1.00
16 ND Infinity War X-over						

	$Good	$Fine	$N.Mint	£Good	£Fine	£N.Mint
17 ND Cyberwar story begins	$0.30	$0.90	$1.50	£0.20	£0.60	£1.00
18-19 ND Cyberwar story, Silver Sable appears	$0.30	$0.90	$1.50	£0.20	£0.60	£1.00
20 ND Cyberwar story	$0.30	$0.90	$1.50	£0.20	£0.60	£1.00
21 ND Cyberwar story, Nick Fury appears	$0.30	$0.90	$1.50	£0.20	£0.60	£1.00
22-24 ND Black Panther appears	$0.30	$0.90	$1.50	£0.20	£0.60	£1.00
25 ND 48pgs, Black Panther appears, holo-grafix foil cover	$0.45	$1.35	$2.25	£0.30	£0.90	£1.50
26 ND Hobgoblin appears; new direction for title	$0.25	$0.75	$1.25	£0.15	£0.45	£0.75
27 ND	$0.25	$0.75	$1.25	£0.15	£0.45	£0.75
28-29 ND Infinity Crusade X-over	$0.25	$0.75	$1.25	£0.15	£0.45	£0.75
30 ND the original Deathlok returns	$0.25	$0.75	$1.25	£0.15	£0.45	£0.75
31-34 ND	$0.25	$0.75	$1.25	£0.15	£0.45	£0.75
Title Value:	$11.85	$35.55	$59.25	£7.80	£23.40	£39.00

Note: Bookshelf Format

DEATHLOK (LIMITED SERIES)
Marvel Comics Group,MS; 1 Jul 1990-4 Oct 1990

	$Good	$Fine	$N.Mint	£Good	£Fine	£N.Mint
1 ND 48pgs, squarebound card cover format begins	$1.05	$3.15	$5.25	£0.70	£2.10	£3.50
2 ND 48pgs	$1.05	$3.15	$5.25	£0.70	£2.10	£3.50
3-4 ND 48pgs, Nick Fury appears	$1.05	$3.15	$5.25	£0.70	£2.10	£3.50
Title Value:	$4.20	$12.60	$21.00	£2.80	£8.40	£14.00

DEATHLOK ANNUAL
Marvel Comics Group; 1 Aug 1992-2 1993

	$Good	$Fine	$N.Mint	£Good	£Fine	£N.Mint
1 ND Timestream story	$0.45	$1.35	$2.25	£0.30	£0.90	£1.50
2 ND 64pgs, pre-bagged with trading card, 1st appearance The Tracer	$0.45	$1.35	$2.25	£0.30	£0.90	£1.50
Title Value:	$0.90	$2.70	$4.50	£0.60	£1.80	£3.00

DEATHLOK SPECIAL
Marvel Comics Group,MS; 1 May 1991-4 Jun 1991

	$Good	$Fine	$N.Mint	£Good	£Fine	£N.Mint
1-4 ND 48pgs, reprints mini-series, issued bi-weekly	$0.40	$1.20	$2.00	£0.25	£0.75	£1.25
Title Value:	$1.60	$4.80	$8.00	£1.00	£3.00	£5.00

DEATHMARK
Lightning Comics; 1 Dec 1994

	$Good	$Fine	$N.Mint	£Good	£Fine	£N.Mint
1 ND Steven Zyskowski script	$0.55	$1.65	$2.75	£0.35	£1.05	£1.75
Title Value:	$0.55	$1.65	$2.75	£0.35	£1.05	£1.75

DEATHMATE
Valiant/Image,MS; 1 Sep 1993-6 Feb 1994

	$Good	$Fine	$N.Mint	£Good	£Fine	£N.Mint
1 PROLOGUE: Solar meets Void, card stock cover by Jim Lee and Bob Layton; silver border	$0.60	$1.80	$3.00	£0.40	£1.20	£2.00
1 PROLOGUE: Gold Edition	$1.50	$4.50	$7.50	£1.00	£3.00	£5.00
1 PROLOGUE: Pink Edition, available with Ultra-Pro comic sleeves, one per box	$1.00	$3.00	$5.00	£0.70	£2.10	£3.50
2 BLUE: 48pgs squarebound; includes Chapter 1 (Magnus/Battlestone), Chapter 2 (Livewire/Stronghold/Striker/Impact), Chapter 3 (Harbinger/Brigade), Chapter 4 (Solar/Supreme)	$0.80	$2.40	$4.00	£0.50	£1.50	£2.50
2 BLUE: Gold Edition	$2.00	$6.00	$10.00	£1.00	£3.00	£5.00

	$Good	$Fine	$N.Mint	£Good	£Fine	£N.Mint
3 YELLOW: 48pgs squarebound; includes Chapter 1 (Ivar/Armstrong), Chapter 2 (H.A.R.D.C.A.T.S.), Chapter 3 (Ninjak/Zealot), Chapter 4 (Shadowman/Grifter)	$0.80	$2.40	$4.00	£0.50	£1.50	£2.50
3 YELLOW: Gold Edition	$2.00	$6.00	$10.00	£1.00	£3.00	£5.00
4 BLACK: 48pgs squarebound; Wildc.a.t.s/Hard Corps; 1st app. Gen 13	$1.50	$4.50	$7.50	£0.70	£2.10	£3.50
4 BLACK: Gold Edition	$2.40	$7.00	$12.00	£1.20	£3.60	£6.00
5 RED: 48pgs squarebound; Youngblood/Eternal Warrior	$0.80	$2.40	$4.00	£0.60	£1.80	£3.00
5 RED: Gold Edition	$2.00	$6.00	$10.00	£1.00	£3.00	£5.00
6 EPILOGUE: Silver foil cover; Solar, Supreme, Master D'Arque, Dr. Eclipse	$0.60	$1.80	$3.00	£0.40	£1.20	£2.00
6 EPILOGUE: Gold Edition	$1.50	$4.50	$7.50	£1.00	£3.00	£5.00
Title Value:	$17.50	$52.30	$87.50	£10.00	£30.00	£50.00

Note: all Non-Distributed on the news-stands in the U.K.

DEATHSTROKE THE TERMINATOR
DC Comics; 1 Aug 1991-present

	$Good	$Fine	$N.Mint	£Good	£Fine	£N.Mint
0 (Oct 1994) Zero Hour X-over; title changes here to Deathstroke the Hunted (effective in title as of #41)	$0.40	$1.20	$2.00	£0.25	£0.75	£1.25
1 Mike Zeck covers begin	$0.80	$2.40	$4.00	£0.50	£1.50	£2.50
1 2nd printing, (1992) - gold ink cover	$0.30	$0.90	$1.50	£0.20	£0.60	£1.00
2	$0.60	$1.80	$3.00	£0.40	£1.20	£2.00
3	$0.55	$1.65	$2.75	£0.35	£1.05	£1.75
4	$0.45	$1.35	$2.25	£0.30	£0.90	£1.50
5	$0.40	$1.20	$2.00	£0.25	£0.75	£1.25
6 Batman appears (cameo)	$0.40	$1.20	$2.00	£0.25	£0.75	£1.25
7 Batman appears	$0.40	$1.20	$2.00	£0.25	£0.75	£1.25
8	$0.40	$1.20	$2.00	£0.25	£0.75	£1.25
9 Batman appears	$0.40	$1.20	$2.00	£0.25	£0.75	£1.25
10 Guns and Roses part 1, 1st appearance new Vigilante (female)	$0.40	$1.20	$2.00	£0.25	£0.75	£1.25
11 Guns and Roses part 2	$0.30	$0.90	$1.50	£0.20	£0.60	£1.00
12	$0.30	$0.90	$1.50	£0.20	£0.60	£1.00
13 Superman, Aquaman, Green Lantern, Flash appear, continued from Superman #68	$0.30	$0.90	$1.50	£0.20	£0.60	£1.00
14 Total Chaos part 1, continued in New Titans #90	$0.30	$0.90	$1.50	£0.20	£0.60	£1.00
15 Total Chaos part 4, continued in New Titans #91	$0.30	$0.90	$1.50	£0.20	£0.60	£1.00
16 Total Chaos part 7, continued in New Titans #92	$0.30	$0.90	$1.50	£0.20	£0.60	£1.00
17 Titans Sell-Out part 2, new costume	$0.30	$0.90	$1.50	£0.20	£0.60	£1.00
18	$0.30	$0.90	$1.50	£0.20	£0.60	£1.00
19 new Speedy appears, nuclear explosion cover	$0.30	$0.90	$1.50	£0.20	£0.60	£1.00
20-21	$0.30	$0.90	$1.50	£0.20	£0.60	£1.00
22-25 bi-weekly	$0.30	$0.90	$1.50	£0.20	£0.60	£1.00
26	$0.30	$0.90	$1.50	£0.20	£0.60	£1.00
27 Deathstroke's World Tour part 1 (of 8)	$0.30	$0.90	$1.50	£0.20	£0.60	£1.00
28	$0.30	$0.90	$1.50	£0.20	£0.60	£1.00

Deadworld #1

Death's Head #1

Defenders #5

MINT = 100% / NEAR MINT (inc. +/-) = 90–99% / VERY FINE (inc. +/-) = 75–89% / FINE (inc. +/-) = 55–74%
VERY GOOD (inc. +/-) = 35–54% / GOOD (inc. +/-) = 15–34% / FAIR = 5–14% / POOR = 1–4%

295

	$Good	$Fine	$N.Mint	£Good	£Fine	£N.Mint
29 continued in Deathstroke Annual #2						
	$0.30	$0.90	$1.50	£0.20	£0.60	£1.00
30-32	$0.30	$0.90	$1.50	£0.20	£0.60	£1.00
33 Vigilante guest-stars						
	$0.30	$0.90	$1.50	£0.20	£0.60	£1.00
34 change of direction for title, promising a new and grittier Deathstroke..						
	$0.30	$0.90	$1.50	£0.20	£0.60	£1.00
35-40	$0.30	$0.90	$1.50	£0.20	£0.60	£1.00
41 title changes to Deathstroke the Hunted (see issue #0)						
	$0.30	$0.90	$1.50	£0.20	£0.60	£1.00
42 Guy Gardner appears						
	$0.30	$0.90	$1.50	£0.20	£0.60	£1.00
43 Deathstroke vs. Hawkman						
	$0.30	$0.90	$1.50	£0.20	£0.60	£1.00
44	$0.30	$0.90	$1.50	£0.20	£0.60	£1.00
45 The New Titans guest-star						
	$0.30	$0.90	$1.50	£0.20	£0.60	£1.00
46 the title now becomes simply "Deathstroke"						
	$0.40	$1.20	$2.00	£0.25	£0.75	£1.25
47 1st appearance the new Vigilante (female)						
	$0.40	$1.20	$2.00	£0.25	£0.75	£1.25
48 The Crimelord/Syndicate War, New Titans guest-star; continued in New Titans #122						
	$0.40	$1.20	$2.00	£0.25	£0.75	£1.25
49 The Crimelord/Syndicate War, New Titans guest-star; continued from Darkstars #32						
	$0.40	$1.20	$2.00	£0.25	£0.75	£1.25
50 48pgs, guest-starring New Titans, Outsiders, Hawkman, Steel and Deadshot; continued in Deathstroke Annual #4						
	$0.80	$2.40	$4.00	£0.50	£1.50	£2.50
51-52 Deathstroke of the future vs. Hawkman						
	$0.45	$1.35	$2.25	£0.30	£0.90	£1.50
53-57	$0.45	$1.35	$2.25	£0.30	£0.90	£1.50
Title Value:	$21.55	$64.65	$107.75	£14.10	£42.30	£70.50

Note: spin-off from New Teen Titans
Deathstroke The Terminator: Full Cycle (1993)
Trade paperback
reprints New Titans #70, Deathstroke #1-5; new
cover and cover gallery by Mike Zeck | | | | £1.60 | £4.80 | £8.00

DEATHSTROKE THE TERMINATOR ANNUAL

DC Comics; 1 Sep 1992-present

	$Good	$Fine	$N.Mint	£Good	£Fine	£N.Mint
1 64pgs, Eclipso: The Darkness Within tie-in, Nightwing appears						
	$0.60	$1.80	$3.00	£0.40	£1.20	£2.00
2 64pgs, Bloodlines (Wave Two) part 18, 1st appearance Gunfire, continued in Eclipso Annual #1						
	$0.60	$1.80	$3.00	£0.40	£1.20	£2.00
3 64pgs, Elseworlds						
	$0.60	$1.80	$3.00	£0.40	£1.20	£2.00
4 56pgs, Year One, continued from Deathstroke #50						
	$0.80	$2.40	$4.00	£0.50	£1.50	£2.50
Title Value:	$2.60	$7.80	$13.00	£1.70	£5.10	£8.50

DEATHWATCH 2000

Continuity Comics re-launch (yet again!) with a 20 part series. Parts 1 & 2 were only available as send-away items and part 3 as the first distributed to the normal outlets.
The parts (to date) are as follows:
Part 1 - Megalith (3rd Series) #0
Part 2 - Hybrids (2nd Series) #0
Part 3 - Armor (2nd Series) #1
Part 4 - Hybrids (2nd Series) #1
Part 5 - Megalith (3rd Series) #1
Part 6 - Urth 4 (2nd Series) #1
Part 7 - Cyberrad (3rd Series) #1
Part 8 - Ms. Mystic (3rd Series) #1

DEATHWISH

DC Comics/Milestone,MS; 1 Dec 1994-4 Mar 1995

	$Good	$Fine	$N.Mint	£Good	£Fine	£N.Mint
1-4 ND	$0.45	$1.35	$2.25	£0.30	£0.90	£1.50
Title Value:	$1.80	$5.40	$9.00	£1.20	£3.60	£6.00

DEATHWORLD

Adventure,MS; 1 Nov 1990-4 Feb 1991

	$Good	$Fine	$N.Mint	£Good	£Fine	£N.Mint
1-4 ND John Holland script based on Harry Harrison novel, Marcello Campos art; black and white						
	$0.40	$1.20	$2.00	£0.25	£0.75	£1.25
Title Value:	$1.60	$4.80	$8.00	£1.00	£3.00	£5.00

DEATHWORLD BOOK 2

Adventure,MS; 1 Apr 1991-4 Jul 1991

	$Good	$Fine	$N.Mint	£Good	£Fine	£N.Mint
1-4 ND	$0.40	$1.20	$2.00	£0.25	£0.75	£1.25
Title Value:	$1.60	$4.80	$8.00	£1.00	£3.00	£5.00

DEATHWORLD BOOK 3

Adventure,MS; 1 Sep 1991-4 Dec 1991

	$Good	$Fine	$N.Mint	£Good	£Fine	£N.Mint
1-4 ND	$0.40	$1.20	$2.00	£0.25	£0.75	£1.25
Title Value:	$1.60	$4.80	$8.00	£1.00	£3.00	£5.00

DEBBI'S DATES

National Periodical Publications; 1 Apr/May 1969-11 Dec/Jan 1970/71

	$Good	$Fine	$N.Mint	£Good	£Fine	£N.Mint
1	$1.50	$4.50	$7.50	£1.00	£3.00	£5.00
2-3	$0.90	$2.70	$4.50	£0.60	£1.80	£3.00
4 Neal Adams text illustration						
	$1.50	$4.50	$7.50	£1.00	£3.00	£5.00
5-11	$0.90	$2.70	$4.50	£0.60	£1.80	£3.00
Title Value:	$11.10	$33.30	$55.50	£7.40	£22.20	£37.00

DEEP DIMENSION OF HORROR

AC Comics; 1 Sep 1994

	$Good	$Fine	$N.Mint	£Good	£Fine	£N.Mint
1 ND horror anthology, Bill Black cover; black and white						
	$0.60	$1.80	$3.00	£0.40	£1.20	£2.00
Title Value:	$0.60	$1.80	$3.00	£0.40	£1.20	£2.00

DEEP, THE

Marvel Comics Group,OS Film; 1 Nov 1977

	$Good	$Fine	$N.Mint	£Good	£Fine	£N.Mint
1 ND 52pgs, adapts film						
	$0.45	$1.35	$2.25	£0.30	£0.90	£1.50
Title Value:	$0.45	$1.35	$2.25	£0.30	£0.90	£1.50

DEFENDERS

Marvel Comics Group; 1 Aug 1972-152 Feb 1986
(see Marvel Feature,Marvel Treasury Edition, Sub-Mariner #34,35)

	$Good	$Fine	$N.Mint	£Good	£Fine	£N.Mint
1 ND Hulk, Dr Strange, Sub-Mariner begin						
	$10.00	$30.00	$70.00	£6.25	£19.00	£45.00
2 ND Silver Surfer appears						
	$5.75	$17.50	$35.00	£3.30	£10.00	£20.00
3 ND Silver Surfer appears						
	$4.15	$12.50	$25.00	£2.50	£7.50	£15.00
4-5	$4.15	$12.50	$25.00	£2.05	£6.25	£12.50
6 Silver Surfer appears						
	$2.90	$8.75	$17.50	£1.80	£5.50	£11.00
7 Silver Surfer and Hawkeye appear						
	$2.90	$8.75	$17.50	£1.80	£5.50	£11.00
8 ND Surfer appears, story continues from Avengers #115						
	$2.90	$8.75	$17.50	£2.05	£6.25	£12.50
9 Iron Man appears, Silver Surfer appears (6 panels)						
	$2.90	$8.75	$17.50	£1.80	£5.50	£11.00
10 ND scarce in the U.K. Avengers, Silver Surfer appear, Thor vs Hulk						
	$8.25	$24.50	$41.25	£5.50	£16.50	£27.50
11 Silver Surfer and Avengers appear						
	$1.65	$5.00	$10.00	£0.90	£2.75	£5.50
12	$1.65	$5.00	$10.00	£0.90	£2.75	£5.50
13 ND	$1.65	$5.00	$10.00	£1.00	£3.00	£6.00
14 ND Sub-Mariner leaves, Nighthawk joins						
	$1.65	$5.00	$10.00	£1.00	£3.00	£6.00
15-16 Professor X, Magneto and The Brotherhood of Evil Mutants appear						
	$2.00	$6.00	$12.00	£1.15	£3.50	£7.00
17 Luke Cage appears						
	$1.25	$3.75	$7.50	£0.65	£2.00	£4.00
18-19	$1.25	$3.75	$7.50	£0.65	£2.00	£4.00
20 The Thing appears						
	$1.25	$3.75	$7.50	£0.65	£2.00	£4.00
21-23	$1.00	$3.00	$6.00	£0.50	£1.50	£3.00
24 Son of Satan, Yellowjacket and Daredevil appear						
	$1.00	$3.00	$6.00	£0.50	£1.50	£3.00
25 Powerman, Son of Satan, Yellowjacket and Daredevil appear						
	$1.00	$3.00	$6.00	£0.50	£1.50	£3.00
26 Guardians of the Galaxy appear						
	$1.30	$4.00	$8.00	£0.65	£2.00	£4.00
27 Guardians of the Galaxy appear; Starhawk cameo						
	$1.30	$4.00	$8.00	£0.65	£2.00	£4.00
28 1st full appearance Starhawk, Guardians of the Galaxy appear						
	$1.30	$4.00	$8.00	£0.65	£2.00	£4.00
29 Guardians of the Galaxy appear						
	$1.30	$4.00	$8.00	£0.65	£2.00	£4.00
30-35	$0.65	$2.00	$4.00	£0.40	£1.25	£2.50
36	$0.70	$2.10	$3.50	£0.45	£1.35	£2.25
37 Luke Cage appears						
	$0.70	$2.10	$3.50	£0.45	£1.35	£2.25
38-40	$0.70	$2.10	$3.50	£0.45	£1.35	£2.25
41	$0.60	$1.80	$3.00	£0.40	£1.20	£2.00
42 1st Giffen art on title (ends #54)						
	$0.60	$1.80	$3.00	£0.40	£1.20	£2.00
43-46	$0.60	$1.80	$3.00	£0.40	£1.20	£2.00
47 Moon Knight, Wonderman appear						
	$0.60	$1.80	$3.00	£0.40	£1.20	£2.00
48-50 Moon Knight appears						
	$0.60	$1.80	$3.00	£0.40	£1.20	£2.00
51 Moon Knight appears, George Perez cover						
	$0.55	$1.65	$2.75	£0.35	£1.05	£1.75
52 Giffen art	$0.55	$1.65	$2.75	£0.35	£1.05	£1.75
53 Golden art and part Giffen art; Red Guardian re-born						
	$0.55	$1.65	$2.75	£0.35	£1.05	£1.75
54 Golden art, some Giffen art, George Perez cover						
	$0.55	$1.65	$2.75	£0.35	£1.05	£1.75
55 ND origin Red Guardian						
	$0.55	$1.65	$2.75	£0.35	£1.05	£1.75
56 ND	$0.55	$1.65	$2.75	£0.35	£1.05	£1.75
57 ND Ms. Marvel appears						
	$0.55	$1.65	$2.75	£0.35	£1.05	£1.75
58 ND 1st appearance Devil-Slayer (John Buscema's "Demon-Slayer" taken from Atlas to Marvel)						
	$0.55	$1.65	$2.75	£0.35	£1.05	£1.75
59-60 ND	$0.55	$1.65	$2.75	£0.35	£1.05	£1.75
61 ND Spiderman appears						
	$0.45	$1.35	$2.25	£0.30	£0.90	£1.50
62 ND Havok, Polaris appear (Angel on cover but not inside), Nova, Black Goliath, Hercules and Paladin appear						
	$0.45	$1.35	$2.25	£0.30	£0.90	£1.50
63 ND Havok, Polaris, Nova, Paladin, Black Goliath, Iron Man and Hercules appear						
	$0.45	$1.35	$2.25	£0.30	£0.90	£1.50
64 ND Nova, Hercules, Captain Marvel, Paladin, Black Goliath, Jack of Hearts, Havok and Iron Fist appear						
	$0.45	$1.35	$2.25	£0.30	£0.90	£1.50
65-70 ND	$0.45	$1.35	$2.25	£0.30	£0.90	£1.50
71-72	$0.40	$1.20	$2.00	£0.25	£0.75	£1.25
73 Foolkiller appearance (1 panel)						
	$0.40	$1.20	$2.00	£0.25	£0.75	£1.25
74 Foolkiller appears						
	$0.40	$1.20	$2.00	£0.25	£0.75	£1.25

	$Good	$Fine	$N.Mint	£Good	£Fine	£N.Mint
75 Foolkiller appears, Omega the Unknown appears, resolving plot-lines from his own title						
	$0.40	$1.20	$2.00	£0.25	£0.75	£1.25
76 Omega the Unknown						
	$0.40	$1.20	$2.00	£0.25	£0.75	£1.25
77 origin Omega the Unknown						
	$0.40	$1.20	$2.00	£0.25	£0.75	£1.25
78 the return of the original Defenders						
	$0.40	$1.20	$2.00	£0.25	£0.75	£1.25
79-88						
	$0.40	$1.20	$2.00	£0.25	£0.75	£1.25
89-91 Daredevil appears						
	$0.40	$1.20	$2.00	£0.25	£0.75	£1.25
92 ND Son of Satan returns						
	$0.40	$1.20	$2.00	£0.30	£0.90	£1.50
93 ND Son of Satan appears						
	$0.40	$1.20	$2.00	£0.30	£0.90	£1.50
94 Son of Satan appears						
	$0.40	$1.20	$2.00	£0.25	£0.75	£1.25
95 Dracula and Son of Satan appear						
	$0.40	$1.20	$2.00	£0.25	£0.75	£1.25
96 Ghost Rider and Son of Satan appear						
	$0.40	$1.20	$2.00	£0.25	£0.75	£1.25
97 Son of Satan and Man-Thing appear						
	$0.40	$1.20	$2.00	£0.25	£0.75	£1.25
98 Son of Satan appears						
	$0.40	$1.20	$2.00	£0.25	£0.75	£1.25
99 Silver Sufer, Hulk, Sub-Mariner and Son of Satan appear						
	$0.40	$1.20	$2.00	£0.25	£0.75	£1.25
100 52pgs, Silver Surfer, Hulk and Sub-Mariner and Son of Satan appear						
	$0.45	$1.35	$2.25	£0.30	£0.90	£1.50
101 Silver Surfer appears; Son of Satan appears (cameo)						
	$0.30	$0.90	$1.50	£0.20	£0.60	£1.00
102-104						
	$0.30	$0.90	$1.50	£0.20	£0.60	£1.00
105 Son of Satan appears, Beast and Mr. Fantastic appear						
	$0.30	$0.90	$1.50	£0.20	£0.60	£1.00
106 death of Nighthawk; Son of Satan, Beast, Daredevil and Captain America appear						
	$0.30	$0.90	$1.50	£0.20	£0.60	£1.00
107 Silver Surfer, Son of Satan, Beast, Daredevil and Captain America appear						
	$0.30	$0.90	$1.50	£0.20	£0.60	£1.00
108-109 Son of Satan, Beast and Spiderman appear						
	$0.30	$0.90	$1.50	£0.20	£0.60	£1.00
110-111						
	$0.30	$0.90	$1.50	£0.20	£0.60	£1.00
112 Silver Surfer, Squadron Supreme appear						
	$0.30	$0.90	$1.50	£0.20	£0.60	£1.00
113 Silver Surfer, Squadron Supreme and Son of Satan appear						
	$0.30	$0.90	$1.50	£0.20	£0.60	£1.00
114 Silver Surfer, Squadron Supreme appear						
	$0.30	$0.90	$1.50	£0.20	£0.60	£1.00
115-116 Son of Satan appears						
	$0.30	$0.90	$1.50	£0.20	£0.60	£1.00
117						
	$0.30	$0.90	$1.50	£0.20	£0.60	£1.00
118 Son of Satan appears						
	$0.30	$0.90	$1.50	£0.20	£0.60	£1.00
119						
	$0.30	$0.90	$1.50	£0.20	£0.60	£1.00
120-121 Son of Satan appears						
	$0.30	$0.90	$1.50	£0.20	£0.60	£1.00
122 Son of Satan appears, Silver Surfer guest-stars						
	$0.30	$0.90	$1.50	£0.20	£0.60	£1.00
123-124 Silver Surfer appears						
	$0.30	$0.90	$1.50	£0.20	£0.60	£1.00
125 DS 1st new Defenders; Hell Cat and Son of Satan wed, Silver Surfer appears						
	$0.60	$1.80	$3.00	£0.40	£1.20	£2.00
126-127 Mike Zeck cover						
	$0.25	$0.75	$1.25	£0.15	£0.45	£0.75
128						
	$0.25	$0.75	$1.25	£0.15	£0.45	£0.75
129 New Mutants appear						
	$0.25	$0.75	$1.25	£0.15	£0.45	£0.75
130 Mike Zeck art						
	$0.25	$0.75	$1.25	£0.15	£0.45	£0.75
131 Sienkiewicz cover						
	$0.25	$0.75	$1.25	£0.15	£0.45	£0.75
132-134						
	$0.25	$0.75	$1.25	£0.15	£0.45	£0.75
135-136 Sienkiewicz cover						
	$0.25	$0.75	$1.25	£0.15	£0.45	£0.75
137-149						
	$0.25	$0.75	$1.25	£0.15	£0.45	£0.75
150 DS Captain America appears						
	$0.45	$1.35	$2.25	£0.30	£0.90	£1.50
151						
	$0.25	$0.75	$1.25	£0.15	£0.45	£0.75
152 DS scarce, Secret Wars tie-in, X-over with X-Factor						
	$0.50	$1.50	$2.50	£0.35	£1.05	£1.75
Title Value:	$124.30	$374.15	$704.00	£75.30	£227.75	£427.00

Note: title "New Defenders" #125-152

DEFENDERS ANNUAL
Marvel Comics Group; 1 Nov 1976

	$Good	$Fine	$N.Mint	£Good	£Fine	£N.Mint
1 ND 52pgs, Luke Cage appears						
	$0.90	$2.70	$4.50	£0.60	£1.80	£3.00
Title Value:	$0.90	$2.70	$4.50	£0.60	£1.80	£3.00

DEFENDERS GIANT SIZE
Marvel Comics Group; 1 Jul 1974-5 Jul 1975

	$Good	$Fine	$N.Mint	£Good	£Fine	£N.Mint
1 ND 68pgs, Everett Sub-Mariner, Kirby Hulk, Kirby Surfer reprints, 9pgs new Starlin art						
	$2.00	$6.00	$10.00	£1.30	£3.90	£6.50
2 ND 68pgs, Son of Satan appears						
	$1.80	$5.25	$9.00	£1.20	£3.60	£6.00
3 ND scarce in the U.K. 68pgs, Daredevil appears, Starlin lay-outs, Silver Surfer appears						
	$1.50	$4.50	$7.50	£1.00	£3.00	£5.00
4 ND 68pgs, Squadron Supreme appears						
	$1.50	$4.50	$7.50	£1.00	£3.00	£5.00
5 ND 68pgs, Guardians of the Galaxy appear						
	$1.80	$5.25	$9.00	£1.20	£3.60	£6.00
Title Value:	$8.60	$25.50	$43.00	£5.70	£17.10	£28.50

DEFENDERS OF DYNATRON CITY
Marvel Comics Group,MS Game; 1 Feb 1992-6 Jul 1992

	$Good	$Fine	$N.Mint	£Good	£Fine	£N.Mint
1-6	$0.15	$0.45	$0.75	£0.10	£0.35	£0.60
Title Value:	$0.90	$2.70	$4.50	£0.60	£2.10	£3.60

DEFENDERS OF THE EARTH
Marvel Comics Group/Star, TV; 1 Jan 1987-5 Sep 1987

	$Good	$Fine	$N.Mint	£Good	£Fine	£N.Mint
1-5 ND	$0.15	$0.45	$0.75	£0.10	£0.35	£0.60
Title Value:	$0.75	$2.25	$3.75	£0.50	£1.75	£3.00

DEFENSELESS DEAD, THE
Adventure,MS; 1 Feb 1991-3 Apr 1991

	$Good	$Fine	$N.Mint	£Good	£Fine	£N.Mint
1-3 ND adaptation of Larry Niven novel; black and white						
	$0.35	$1.05	$1.75	£0.25	£0.75	£1.25
Title Value:	$1.05	$3.15	$5.25	£0.75	£2.25	£3.75

DEFIANT ANNIVERSARY TRADE PAPERBACK
Defiant,OS; nn Sep 1994

	$Good	$Fine	$N.Mint	£Good	£Fine	£N.Mint
nn ND 96pgs, reprints Dark Dominion, Charlemagne, Plasm, Glory and Grimmax #0 issues						
	$0.75	$2.25	$3.75	£0.50	£1.50	£2.50
Title Value:	$0.75	$2.25	$3.75	£0.50	£1.50	£2.50

DEFIANT GENESIS
Defiant,OS; 1 Oct 1993

	$Good	$Fine	$N.Mint	£Good	£Fine	£N.Mint
1 ND 16pgs	$0.30	$0.90	$1.50	£0.15	£0.45	£0.75
1 ND (Feb 1994) 16pgs, published version with updated text; re-titled The Origin of the Defiant Universe						
	$0.25	$0.75	$1.25	£0.15	£0.45	£0.75
Title Value:	$0.55	$1.65	$2.75	£0.30	£0.90	£1.50

DELIRIUM
Metro Comics; 1,2 1987

	$Good	$Fine	$N.Mint	£Good	£Fine	£N.Mint
1 ND	$0.35	$1.05	$1.75	£0.25	£0.75	£1.25
2 ND Keith Giffen art						
	$0.35	$1.05	$1.75	£0.25	£0.75	£1.25
Title Value:	$0.70	$2.10	$3.50	£0.50	£1.50	£2.50

DEMOLITION MAN
DC Comics,MS; 1 Nov 1993-4 Feb 1994

	$Good	$Fine	$N.Mint	£Good	£Fine	£N.Mint
1-4 based on Sylvester Stallone film						
	$0.25	$0.75	$1.25	£0.15	£0.45	£0.75
Title Value:	$1.00	$3.00	$5.00	£0.60	£1.80	£3.00

DEMON BLADE
New Comics Group; 1 1989

	$Good	$Fine	$N.Mint	£Good	£Fine	£N.Mint
1 ND Alex Nino art; black and white						
	$0.30	$0.90	$1.50	£0.20	£0.60	£1.00
Title Value:	$0.30	$0.90	$1.50	£0.20	£0.60	£1.00

DEMON DREAMS
Pacific,MS; 1 Feb 1984-2 May 1984

	$Good	$Fine	$N.Mint	£Good	£Fine	£N.Mint
1-2 ND Arthur Suydam reprints; colour						
	$0.35	$1.05	$1.75	£0.25	£0.75	£1.25
Title Value:	$0.70	$2.10	$3.50	£0.50	£1.50	£2.50

DEMON DREAMS OF DOCTOR DREW
AC Comics; 1 Oct 1994

	$Good	$Fine	$N.Mint	£Good	£Fine	£N.Mint
1 ND Jerry Grandenetti reprints (in Will Eisner-esque style)						
	$0.35	$1.05	$1.75	£0.25	£0.75	£1.25
Title Value:	$0.35	$1.05	$1.75	£0.25	£0.75	£1.25

DEMON HUNTER
Atlas; 1 Sep 1975

	$Good	$Fine	$N.Mint	£Good	£Fine	£N.Mint
1 Rich Buckler art; distributed in the U.K.						
	$0.25	$0.75	$1.25	£0.15	£0.45	£0.75
Title Value:	$0.25	$0.75	$1.25	£0.15	£0.45	£0.75

DEMON HUNTER (2ND SERIES)
Aircel; 1 Mar 1989-4 1989

	$Good	$Fine	$N.Mint	£Good	£Fine	£N.Mint
1-4 ND	$0.30	$0.90	$1.50	£0.20	£0.60	£1.00
Title Value:	$1.20	$3.60	$6.00	£0.80	£2.40	£4.00

DEMON WARRIOR, THE
Eastern; 1 Aug 1987-14 1988

	$Good	$Fine	$N.Mint	£Good	£Fine	£N.Mint
1 ND Jae hak Lee script and art (1st professional work by Jae Lee?); black and white						
	$0.30	$0.90	$1.50	£0.20	£0.60	£1.00
2 ND black and white; some copies have indicia information for #1 on the inside						
	$0.30	$0.90	$1.50	£0.20	£0.60	£1.00
3-14 ND black and white						
	$0.30	$0.90	$1.50	£0.20	£0.60	£1.00
Title Value:	$4.20	$12.60	$21.00	£2.80	£8.40	£14.00

DEMON'S TAILS
Adventure,MS; 1 Mar 1993-4 Jun 1993

	$Good	$Fine	$N.Mint	£Good	£Fine	£N.Mint
1-4 ND	$0.30	$0.90	$1.50	£0.20	£0.60	£1.00
Title Value:	$1.20	$3.60	$6.00	£0.80	£2.40	£4.00

DEMON, THE
National Periodical Publications; 1 Aug/Sep 1972-16 Jan 1974
(see Brave and the Bold, Detective #482-485))

	$Good	$Fine	$N.Mint	£Good	£Fine	£N.Mint
1 ND origin and 1st appearance The Demon by Jack Kirby						
	$4.55	$13.50	$32.00	£2.85	£8.50	£20.00
2 scarce in the U.K.						
	$3.00	$9.00	$18.00	£1.65	£5.00	£10.00
3 scarce in the U.K.						
	$3.00	$9.00	$18.00	£1.30	£4.00	£8.00
4-5	$3.00	$9.00	$18.00	£1.15	£3.50	£7.00
6-7	$2.50	$7.50	$15.00	£0.65	£2.00	£4.00
8 scarce in the U.K.						
	$2.50	$7.50	$15.00	£0.75	£2.25	£4.50

	$Good	$Fine	$N.Mint	£Good	£Fine	£N.Mint
9-10	$2.50	$7.50	$15.00	£0.65	£2.00	£4.00
11-14	$2.00	$6.00	$12.00	£0.55	£1.75	£3.50
15 some words missing from front cover word balloon						
	$2.00	$6.00	$12.00	£0.55	£1.75	£3.50
16	$2.00	$6.00	$12.00	£0.55	£1.75	£3.50
Title Value:	$41.05	$123.00	$251.00	£14.75	£45.25	£93.50

Note: Jack Kirby art in all.

DEMON, THE (2ND SERIES)
DC Comics; 0 Oct 1994; 1 Jul 1990-58 May 1995

	$Good	$Fine	$N.Mint	£Good	£Fine	£N.Mint
0 (Oct 1994) Zero Hour X-over, origin retold						
	$0.40	$1.20	$2.00	£0.25	£0.75	£1.25
1	$0.60	$1.80	$3.00	£0.40	£1.20	£2.00
2	$0.45	$1.35	$2.25	£0.30	£0.90	£1.50
3 Batman appears	$0.45	$1.35	$2.25	£0.30	£0.90	£1.50
4-5	$0.45	$1.35	$2.25	£0.30	£0.90	£1.50
6-7	$0.40	$1.20	$2.00	£0.25	£0.75	£1.25
8 Batman/Arkham Asylum appear						
	$0.40	$1.20	$2.00	£0.25	£0.75	£1.25
9-10	$0.40	$1.20	$2.00	£0.25	£0.75	£1.25
11 Lobo appears, Apokalypse Now story						
	$0.40	$1.20	$2.00	£0.25	£0.75	£1.25
12 Demon vs. Lobo, Apokalypse Now story						
	$0.40	$1.20	$2.00	£0.25	£0.75	£1.25
13-15 Lobo appears, Apokalypse Now story						
	$0.40	$1.20	$2.00	£0.25	£0.75	£1.25
16	$0.40	$1.20	$2.00	£0.25	£0.75	£1.25
17 War of the Gods X-over						
	$0.40	$1.20	$2.00	£0.25	£0.75	£1.25
18	$0.40	$1.20	$2.00	£0.25	£0.75	£1.25
19 40pgs, secret origin The Demon, Demon and Lobo mini-poster						
	$0.40	$1.20	$2.00	£0.25	£0.75	£1.25
20	$0.40	$1.20	$2.00	£0.25	£0.75	£1.25
21 Lobo appears	$0.40	$1.20	$2.00	£0.25	£0.75	£1.25
22 Matt Wagner script/art						
	$0.40	$1.20	$2.00	£0.25	£0.75	£1.25
23 Return of the Howler part 1, Robin appears						
	$0.40	$1.20	$2.00	£0.25	£0.75	£1.25
24 Return of the Howler part 2, Batman and Robin appear						
	$0.40	$1.20	$2.00	£0.25	£0.75	£1.25
25	$0.40	$1.20	$2.00	£0.25	£0.75	£1.25
26 Political Asylum story						
	$0.40	$1.20	$2.00	£0.25	£0.75	£1.25
27 Political Asylum story, Superman appears						
	$0.40	$1.20	$2.00	£0.25	£0.75	£1.25
28-29 Political Asylum story, Superman vs. Demon						
	$0.40	$1.20	$2.00	£0.25	£0.75	£1.25
30	$0.40	$1.20	$2.00	£0.25	£0.75	£1.25
31 Lobo appears	$0.40	$1.20	$2.00	£0.25	£0.75	£1.25
32 Lobo and Wonder Woman appear						
	$0.40	$1.20	$2.00	£0.25	£0.75	£1.25
33 Lobo appears	$0.40	$1.20	$2.00	£0.25	£0.75	£1.25
34-37 The Eternity Quest, Lobo appears						
	$0.40	$1.20	$2.00	£0.25	£0.75	£1.25
38 Lobo appears	$0.40	$1.20	$2.00	£0.25	£0.75	£1.25
39	$0.40	$1.20	$2.00	£0.25	£0.75	£1.25
40 Garth Ennis and John McCrea creative team begins						
	$0.40	$1.20	$2.00	£0.25	£0.75	£1.25
41 guest-written and drawn by Kevin Altieri of the Fox Batman animated TV series						
	$0.40	$1.20	$2.00	£0.25	£0.75	£1.25
42 Ennis and McCrea return						
	$0.40	$1.20	$2.00	£0.25	£0.75	£1.25
43-45 Hitman appears						
	$0.40	$1.20	$2.00	£0.25	£0.75	£1.25
46-48 Haunted Tank appears						
	$0.40	$1.20	$2.00	£0.25	£0.75	£1.25
49	$0.40	$1.20	$2.00	£0.25	£0.75	£1.25
50 48pgs	$0.55	$1.65	$2.75	£0.35	£1.05	£1.75
51-58	$0.40	$1.20	$2.00	£0.25	£0.75	£1.25
Title Value:	$24.15	$72.45	$120.75	£15.20	£45.60	£76.00

Note: New Format, script by Alan Grant.

DEMON, THE (2ND SERIES) ANNUAL
DC Comics; 1 Aug 1992-2 1993

	$Good	$Fine	$N.Mint	£Good	£Fine	£N.Mint
1 64pgs, Eclipso: The Darkness Within tie-in						
	$0.55	$1.65	$2.75	£0.35	£1.05	£1.75
2 64pgs, Bloodlines (Wave Two) part 20, 1st appearance Hitman, continued in Batman: Legends of the Dark Knight Annual #3						
	$0.55	$1.65	$2.75	£0.35	£1.05	£1.75
Title Value:	$1.10	$3.30	$5.50	£0.70	£2.10	£3.50

DEMON, THE (LIMITED SERIES)
DC Comics,MS; 1 Jan 1987-4 Apr 1987

	$Good	$Fine	$N.Mint	£Good	£Fine	£N.Mint
1	$0.30	$0.90	$1.50	£0.20	£0.60	£1.00
2 "4 of 4" on cover						
	$0.30	$0.90	$1.50	£0.20	£0.60	£1.00
3-4	$0.30	$0.90	$1.50	£0.20	£0.60	£1.00
Title Value:	$1.20	$3.60	$6.00	£0.80	£2.40	£4.00

Note: Matt Wagner script/art in all.

DEMONIC TOYS
Eternity,MS; 1 Jun 1992-4 May 1992

	$Good	$Fine	$N.Mint	£Good	£Fine	£N.Mint
1-4 ND	$0.35	$1.05	$1.75	£0.25	£0.75	£1.25
Title Value:	$1.40	$4.20	$7.00	£1.00	£3.00	£5.00

DEMONIQUE
London Night Studios,MS; 1 Nov 1994-4 Apr 1995

	$Good	$Fine	$N.Mint	£Good	£Fine	£N.Mint
1-4 ND Skye Owens script and art; black and white						
	$0.45	$1.35	$2.25	£0.30	£0.90	£1.50
Title Value:	$1.80	$5.40	$9.00	£1.20	£3.60	£6.00

DEN
Fantagor; 1 1988-10 1989

	$Good	$Fine	$N.Mint	£Good	£Fine	£N.Mint
1-10 ND Richard Corben story and art						
	$0.60	$1.80	$3.00	£0.40	£1.20	£2.00
Title Value:	$6.00	$18.00	$30.00	£4.00	£12.00	£20.00
Den 1: Neverwhere (Sep 1991), selected reprints, 112pgs softcover				£1.90	£5.70	£9.50

DENIZENS OF DEEP CITY
Kitchen Sink; 1 Dec 1988-9 May 1990

	$Good	$Fine	$N.Mint	£Good	£Fine	£N.Mint
1-9 ND Doug Potter script and art, black and white; bi-monthly frequency						
	$0.60	$1.80	$3.00	£0.40	£1.20	£2.00
Title Value:	$5.40	$16.20	$27.00	£3.60	£10.80	£18.00

DENNIS THE MENACE
Marvel Comics Group; 1 Nov 1981-13 Nov 1982

	$Good	$Fine	$N.Mint	£Good	£Fine	£N.Mint
1-13 ND	$0.15	$0.45	$0.75	£0.10	£0.35	£0.60
Title Value:	$1.95	$5.85	$9.75	£1.30	£4.55	£7.80

DESCENDING ANGELS
Millennium; 1 Apr 1995-2 1995

	$Good	$Fine	$N.Mint	£Good	£Fine	£N.Mint
1 ND black and white						
	$0.60	$1.80	$3.00	£0.40	£1.20	£2.00
2 ND Houses of the Holy story						
	$0.60	$1.80	$3.00	£0.40	£1.20	£2.00
Title Value:	$1.20	$3.60	$6.00	£0.80	£2.40	£4.00

DESERT PEACH, THE
Mu Press; 1 Nov 1989-14 1991

	$Good	$Fine	$N.Mint	£Good	£Fine	£N.Mint
1-14 ND black and white						
	$0.30	$0.90	$1.50	£0.20	£0.60	£1.00
Title Value:	$4.20	$12.60	$21.00	£2.80	£8.40	£14.00

DESERT STORM JOURNAL
Apple Comics; 1 Jul 1991-7 1992

	$Good	$Fine	$N.Mint	£Good	£Fine	£N.Mint
1-7 ND Don Lomax script and art						
	$0.30	$0.90	$1.50	£0.20	£0.60	£1.00
Title Value:	$2.10	$6.30	$10.50	£1.40	£4.20	£7.00

DESERT STREAMS
DC Comics/Piranha Press,OS; 1 1989

	$Good	$Fine	$N.Mint	£Good	£Fine	£N.Mint
1 ND 104pgs, half-size trade paperback format (8" x 5"), Alison Marek script/art						
	$0.90	$2.70	$4.50	£0.60	£1.80	£3.00
Title Value:	$0.90	$2.70	$4.50	£0.60	£1.80	£3.00

DESTROY!
Eclipse,Tabloid; nn 1986

	$Good	$Fine	$N.Mint	£Good	£Fine	£N.Mint
nn ND Scott McLeod script and art						
	$1.50	$4.50	$7.50	£1.00	£3.00	£5.00
Title Value:	$1.50	$4.50	$7.50	£1.00	£3.00	£5.00

DESTROY! IN THREE-D
Eclipse; (3-D Special 17) 1 Mar 1987

	$Good	$Fine	$N.Mint	£Good	£Fine	£N.Mint
1 ND Scott McLeod script/art 3-D version; glasses included (less 25% without)						
	$0.45	$1.35	$2.25	£0.30	£0.90	£1.50
Title Value:,	$0.45	$1.35	$2.25	£0.30	£0.90	£1.50

DESTROYER DUCK
Eclipse; 1 Feb 1982-7 1984

	$Good	$Fine	$N.Mint	£Good	£Fine	£N.Mint
1 ND Jack Kirby art, 1st appearance of Groo in back-up story						
	$0.80	$2.40	$4.00		£1.20	£3.60	£6.00
2-3 ND Jack Kirby art	$0.45	$1.35	$2.25	£0.30	£0.90	£1.50
4-6 ND	$0.45	$1.35	$2.25	£0.30	£0.90	£1.50
7 ND Frank Miller cover						
	$0.45	$1.35	$2.25	£0.30	£0.90	£1.50
Title Value:	$3.50	$10.50	$17.50	£3.00	£9.00	£15.00

DESTROYER, THE
Marvel Comics Group,Magazine; 1 Dec 1989-10 Jun 1990

	$Good	$Fine	$N.Mint	£Good	£Fine	£N.Mint
1-5 ND	$0.30	$0.90	$1.50	£0.20	£0.60	£1.00
6 ND Infantino art	$0.30	$0.90	$1.50	£0.20	£0.60	£1.00
7-10 ND	$0.30	$0.90	$1.50	£0.20	£0.60	£1.00
Title Value:	$3.00	$9.00	$15.00	£2.00	£6.00	£10.00
Trade Paperback (Dec 1991), reprints selected stories in colour for first time				£1.10	£3.30	£5.50

DESTROYER, THE (2ND SERIES)
Marvel Comics Group,OS; 1 Mar 1991

	$Good	$Fine	$N.Mint	£Good	£Fine	£N.Mint
1 ND Lee Weeks art and painted cover						
	$0.30	$0.90	$1.50	£0.20	£0.60	£1.00
Title Value:	$0.30	$0.90	$1.50	£0.20	£0.60	£1.00

DESTROYER, THE
Valiant; 0 Apr 1995

	$Good	$Fine	$N.Mint	£Good	£Fine	£N.Mint
0 ND spin-off from Solar, Man of the Atom; Mike Manley art						
	$0.45	$1.35	$2.25	£0.30	£0.90	£1.50
Title Value:	$0.45	$1.35	$2.25	£0.30	£0.90	£1.50

DESTROYER: TERROR, THE
Marvel Comics Group,MS; 1 Dec 1991-4 Mar 1992

	$Good	$Fine	$N.Mint	£Good	£Fine	£N.Mint
1	$0.30	$0.90	$1.50	£0.20	£0.60	£1.00
2-4 Simonson cover						
	$0.30	$0.90	$1.50	£0.20	£0.60	£1.00
Title Value:	$1.20	$3.60	$6.00	£0.80	£2.40	£4.00

DESTRUCTOR, THE
Atlas; 1 Feb 1975-4 Aug 1975

	$Good	$Fine	$N.Mint	£Good	£Fine	£N.Mint
1-2 Steve Ditko, Wally Wood art; distributed in the U.K.						
	$0.25	$0.75	$1.25	£0.15	£0.45	£0.75
3 Steve Ditko art; distributed in the U.K.						
	$0.25	$0.75	$1.25	£0.15	£0.45	£0.75
4 Steve Ditko, Al Milgrom art; distributed in the U.K.						

	$Good	$Fine	$N.Mint	£Good	£Fine	£N.Mint
	$0.25	$0.75	$1.25	£0.15	£0.45	£0.75
Title Value:	$1.00	$3.00	$5.00	£0.60	£1.80	£3.00

DETECTIVE COMICS

National Periodical Publications/DC Comics; 0 Oct 1994; 1 Mar 1937-present
(see Batman, Best of DC, Famous First Edition C-28)

0 (Oct 1994) Zero Hour X-over, origin retold

	$0.40	$1.20	$2.00	£0.25	£0.75	£1.25

1 very rare in the U.K., rare in the U.S. about 30 or less extant copies, classic "Chinaman" cover by Vincent Sullivan; historically important as the first successful anthology of detectives & policemen

	$7500.00	$22500.00	$75000.00	£5000.00	£15000.00	£50000.00

[Extremely Rare in high grade - Very Fine or better]
[Prices may vary widely on this comic]

2 rare in the U.S., very rare in the U.K. fewer than 30 extant copies

	$1775.00	$5300.00	$16000.00	£940.00	£2800.00	£8500.00

3 rare in the U.S., very rare in the U.K. fewer than 20 extant copies

	$1250.00	$3750.00	$11250.00	£830.00	£2500.00	£7500.00

4-5 very scarce in the U.S. rare in the U.K.

	$620.00	$1875.00	$5000.00	£415.00	£1250.00	£3350.00

6-7 scarce in the U.S. very scarce in the U.K.

	$465.00	$1400.00	$3750.00	£310.00	£930.00	£2500.00

8 scarce in the U.S, very scarce in the U.K. classic Mister Chang cover

	$590.00	$1775.00	$4750.00	£405.00	£1200.00	£3250.00

9-10 scarce in the U.K.

	$435.00	$1300.00	$3500.00	£280.00	£840.00	£2250.00

[please note that the above are approximate values only, as copies very rarely come onto the UK market.]
[Note also that the first three issues have been given theoretical values for Near Mint]

11-14 scarce in the U.S., very scarce in the U.K.

	$340.00	$1025.00	$2750.00	£230.00	£690.00	£1850.00

15 1pg advertisement for Action Comics #1

	$340.00	$1025.00	$2750.00	£230.00	£690.00	£1850.00

16-17

	$340.00	$1025.00	$2750.00	£230.00	£690.00	£1850.00

18 scarce in the U.S., very scarce in the U.K. classic Fu Manchu cover

	$465.00	$1400.00	$3750.00	£310.00	£930.00	£2500.00

19

	$340.00	$1025.00	$2750.00	£230.00	£690.00	£1850.00

20 scarce in the U.S., very scarce in the U.K. 1st appearance The Crimson Avenger

	$530.00	$1575.00	$4250.00	£355.00	£1050.00	£2850.00

21

	$325.00	$970.00	$2275.00	£210.00	£640.00	£1500.00

22 only Crimson Avenger cover

	$390.00	$1175.00	$2750.00	£260.00	£790.00	£1850.00

23

	$325.00	$970.00	$2275.00	£210.00	£640.00	£1500.00

24 very scarce in the U.S. rare in the U.K.

	$325.00	$970.00	$2275.00	£225.00	£680.00	£1600.00

25

	$325.00	$970.00	$2275.00	£210.00	£640.00	£1500.00

26 advertises "The Bat-Man" coming next issue

	$340.00	$1025.00	$2400.00	£225.00	£680.00	£1600.00

27 1st appearance of The Bat-Man, 1st Commissioner Gordon, scarcer than Action Comics #1 at about 65 extant copies and arguably as important in publishing history

	$11600.00	$35000.00	$140000.00	£7900.00	£23700.00	£95000.00

[Prices may vary widely on this comic]

27 ND rare in the U.K., 14pgs (paper cover) Oreo Cookies Giveaway - reprints lead stories from Detective #27 (1st Batman), #38 (1st Robin) plus Batman #1 (1st Joker)

	$4.50	$13.50	$22.50	£3.00	£9.00	£15.00

28 2nd appearance of Batman, non Batman cover

	$1625.00	$4850.00	$13000.00	£1075.00	£3250.00	£8750.00

29 3rd appearance of Batman, Dr. Death story, (2nd ever Batman cover)

	$2200.00	$6600.00	$20000.00	£1575.00	£4750.00	£14250.00

30 Dr. Death story part 2

	$620.00	$1875.00	$5000.00	£435.00	£1300.00	£3500.00

31 1st appearance Julie Madison (Batman's first girlfriend), 1st use of Bat-Gyro and Batarang,

the classic Batman cover

	$2000.00	$6000.00	$20000.00	£1400.00	£4200.00	£14000.00

32 very scarce in the U.K. and U.S. classic opening page

	$620.00	$1875.00	$5000.00	£435.00	£1300.00	£3500.00

33 1st details of the origin of Batman (there was no origin in #27); Batman-wearing-gun-holster cover

	$2650.00	$7900.00	$26500.00	£1750.00	£5200.00	£17500.00

34 Crimson Avenger cover?

	$500.00	$1500.00	$4000.00	£340.00	£1025.00	£2750.00

35 regular Batman covers begin; long "bat-ears" and classic hypodermic needle cover

	$810.00	$2425.00	$6500.00	£530.00	£1575.00	£4250.00

36 scarce in both US and UK origin and 1st appearance Hugo Strange

	$560.00	$1675.00	$4500.00	£375.00	£1125.00	£3000.00

37

	$530.00	$1600.00	$4300.00	£355.00	£1050.00	£2850.00

38 origin and 1st appearance Robin the Boy Wonder

	$2500.00	$7500.00	$25000.00	£1750.00	£5200.00	£17500.00

39

	$560.00	$1675.00	$4500.00	£375.00	£1125.00	£3000.00

40 origin and 1st appearance Clayface I (Basil Karlo), 1st Joker cover (face re-coloured clay-brown to denote Clayface, probably last minute, as Joker story originally intended here was used in Batman #1)

	$600.00	$1800.00	$5400.00	£425.00	£1275.00	£3850.00

41 1st solo Robin story

	$280.00	$840.00	$2250.00	£200.00	£600.00	£1600.00

42-44

	$185.00	$560.00	$1500.00	£120.00	£365.00	£975.00

45 1st Joker story in Detective Comics

	$280.00	$840.00	$2250.00	£185.00	£560.00	£1500.00

46-47

	$180.00	$550.00	$1475.00	£120.00	£365.00	£975.00

48 1st mention of Batmobile (see Batman #5), 1st mention of Gotham City

	$190.00	$580.00	$1550.00	£130.00	£390.00	£1050.00

49-50

	$180.00	$550.00	$1475.00	£120.00	£365.00	£975.00

51

	$115.00	$355.00	$950.00	£77.50	£230.00	£625.00

52 opium den cover

	$115.00	$355.00	$950.00	£77.50	£230.00	£625.00

53-57

	$115.00	$355.00	$950.00	£77.50	£230.00	£625.00

58 1st appearance The Penguin

	$275.00	$830.00	$2500.00	£190.00	£580.00	£1750.00

59 2nd appearance The Penguin

	$150.00	$450.00	$1200.00	£100.00	£300.00	£800.00

60 1st appearance Air Wave

	$135.00	$410.00	$1100.00	£90.00	£270.00	£725.00

61

	$115.00	$355.00	$950.00	£77.50	£230.00	£625.00

62 Joker cover and story by Jerry Robinson

	$175.00	$520.00	$1400.00	£80.00	£240.00	£650.00

63

	$115.00	$355.00	$950.00	£77.50	£230.00	£625.00

64 origin and 1st appearance Boy Commandos by Joe Simon and Jack Kirby

	$305.00	$910.00	$2750.00	£205.00	£610.00	£1850.00

65 classic Boy Commandos cover by Simon and Kirby

	$265.00	$800.00	$2150.00	£175.00	£520.00	£1400.00

66 origin and 1st appearance Two Face

	$235.00	$710.00	$2150.00	£155.00	£465.00	£1400.00

67 1st Penguin cover

	$155.00	$465.00	$1250.00	£105.00	£315.00	£850.00

68 Two Face cover and story (continued from #66)

	$130.00	$390.00	$1050.00	£95.00	£290.00	£775.00

69 Joker cover and story, classic Joker holding Colt .45's by Jerry Robinson

	$130.00	$390.00	$1050.00	£95.00	£290.00	£775.00

70 classic montage cover by Jerry Robinson

	$95.00	$290.00	$775.00	£65.00	£195.00	£525.00

71 Joker cover and story; classic "calendar" cover by Jerry Robinson

	$110.00	$335.00	$900.00	£75.00	£225.00	£600.00

72

	$87.50	$260.00	$700.00	£57.50	£175.00	£475.00

73 Scarecrow cover and story

Demon Warrior #1

Detective Comics #4

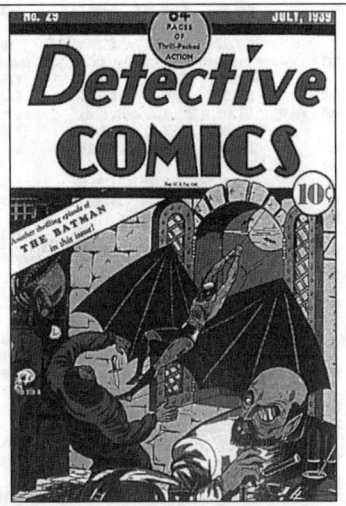

Detective Comics #29

Issue	$Good	$Fine	$N.Mint	£Good	£Fine	£N.Mint
	$87.50	$260.00	$700.00	£57.50	£175.00	£475.00
74 1st appearance Tweedledum and Tweedledee	$87.50	$260.00	$700.00	£57.50	£175.00	£475.00
75	$87.50	$260.00	$700.00	£57.50	£175.00	£475.00
76 Joe Simon and Jack Kirby art, Joker cover and story	$140.00	$430.00	$1150.00	£95.00	£290.00	£775.00
77-79	$95.00	$290.00	$775.00	£65.00	£195.00	£525.00
80 Two Face appears	$105.00	$315.00	$850.00	£67.50	£205.00	£550.00
81 1st appearance The Cavalier	$82.50	$250.00	$675.00	£55.00	£165.00	£450.00
82	$77.50	$230.00	$625.00	£52.50	£155.00	£425.00
83 1st appearance of the more familiar "skinny" Alfred (see cover Batman #22 for 1st cover appearance in this style)	$82.50	$250.00	$675.00	£55.00	£165.00	£450.00
84	$77.50	$230.00	$625.00	£52.50	£155.00	£425.00
85 Joker cover and story	$100.00	$305.00	$825.00	£67.50	£205.00	£550.00
86-90	$75.00	$225.00	$600.00	£50.00	£150.00	£400.00
91 Joker cover and story	$92.50	$280.00	$750.00	£62.50	£185.00	£500.00
92-95	$65.00	$195.00	$525.00	£44.00	£130.00	£350.00
96 Alfred's surname known to be "Beagle" which became "Pennyworth" in later years	$65.00	$195.00	$525.00	£44.00	£130.00	£350.00
97-98	$65.00	$195.00	$525.00	£44.00	£130.00	£350.00
99 Penguin cover	$100.00	$300.00	$800.00	£67.50	£205.00	£550.00
100	$105.00	$315.00	$850.00	£70.00	£215.00	£575.00
[Note: issues before #100 generally scarce in the U.K.]						
101	$75.00	$225.00	$525.00	£50.00	£150.00	£350.00
102 Joker cover and story	$100.00	$300.00	$700.00	£67.50	£200.00	£475.00
103-107	$75.00	$225.00	$525.00	£50.00	£150.00	£350.00
108 1st appearance of the Bat-Plane, classic bat-symbol and bat-plane cover	$75.00	$225.00	$525.00	£50.00	£150.00	£350.00
109 Joker cover and story	$95.00	$285.00	$675.00	£62.50	£190.00	£450.00
110-113	$70.00	$210.00	$500.00	£48.00	£140.00	£335.00
114 Joker cover and story, 1st smaller cover logo	$95.00	$285.00	$675.00	£62.50	£190.00	£450.00
115-117	$70.00	$210.00	$500.00	£48.00	£140.00	£335.00
118 Joker cover and story	$95.00	$285.00	$665.00	£62.50	£190.00	£450.00
119	$70.00	$210.00	$500.00	£48.00	£140.00	£335.00
120 Penguin cover (predominantly white and prone to foxing and/or dust shadows)	$120.00	$360.00	$850.00	£80.00	£245.00	£575.00
121	$70.00	$210.00	$500.00	£48.00	£140.00	£335.00
122 1st Catwoman cover in Detective title	$125.00	$375.00	$875.00	£82.50	£250.00	£585.00
123	$70.00	$210.00	$500.00	£48.00	£140.00	£335.00
124 Joker cover and story	$92.50	$275.00	$650.00	£60.00	£180.00	£425.00
125	$70.00	$210.00	$500.00	£48.00	£140.00	£335.00
126 Penguin cover	$95.00	$285.00	$675.00	£62.50	£190.00	£450.00
127	$70.00	$210.00	$500.00	£48.00	£140.00	£335.00
128 Joker cover and story	$92.50	$275.00	$650.00	£60.00	£180.00	£425.00
129-130	$70.00	$210.00	$500.00	£48.00	£140.00	£335.00
131-134	$62.50	$190.00	$450.00	£43.00	£125.00	£300.00
135 Batman meets Frankenstein	$62.50	$190.00	$450.00	£43.00	£125.00	£300.00
136	$62.50	$190.00	$450.00	£43.00	£125.00	£300.00
137 Joker cover and story	$75.00	$225.00	$525.00	£50.00	£150.00	£350.00
138 origin Robotman (though the 1st appeared in Star Spangled Comics #7)	$110.00	$340.00	$800.00	£75.00	£225.00	£525.00
139	$62.50	$190.00	$450.00	£43.00	£125.00	£300.00
140 scarce in both US and UK 1st appearance The Riddler, Riddler cover	$375.00	$1125.00	$3000.00	£260.00	£780.00	£2100.00
141	$62.50	$190.00	$450.00	£43.00	£125.00	£300.00
142 2nd Riddler, Riddler cover	$110.00	$330.00	$775.00	£75.00	£225.00	£525.00
143-146	$62.50	$190.00	$450.00	£43.00	£125.00	£300.00
147 1st appearance Tiger Shark (note Marvel villain!)	$62.50	$190.00	$450.00	£43.00	£125.00	£300.00
148	$62.50	$190.00	$450.00	£43.00	£125.00	£300.00
149 Joker cover and story	$75.00	$225.00	$525.00	£50.00	£150.00	£350.00
150	$62.50	$190.00	$450.00	£43.00	£125.00	£300.00
151 origin and 1st appearance Pow-Wow Smith	$70.00	$210.00	$500.00	£46.00	£135.00	£325.00
152	$60.00	$180.00	$425.00	£41.00	£120.00	£285.00
153 1st appearance Roy Raymond, TV Detective; also The Flying Batman (see Batman #82)	$67.50	$200.00	$475.00	£46.00	£135.00	£325.00
154-155	$60.00	$180.00	$425.00	£41.00	£120.00	£285.00
156 new Batmobile with bubble canopy and bat-wing fin on top	$85.00	$255.00	$600.00	£55.00	£170.00	£400.00
157	$60.00	$180.00	$425.00	£41.00	£120.00	£285.00
158 Joker face on cover	$60.00	$180.00	$425.00	£41.00	£120.00	£285.00
159-167	$60.00	$180.00	$425.00	£41.00	£120.00	£285.00
168 scarce in the U.S., very scarce in the U.K. 1st origin The Joker ("The Man in the Red Hood") since his first appearance in Batman #1 in 1940, classic cover	$300.00	$900.00	$2400.00	£215.00	£650.00	£1750.00
[Very rare in high grade - Very Fine+ or better]						
169-170 scarce in both US and UK	$60.00	$180.00	$425.00	£41.00	£120.00	£285.00
171 Penguin cover	$92.50	$275.00	$650.00	£60.00	£180.00	£425.00
172-175	$55.00	$170.00	$400.00	£39.00	£115.00	£275.00
176 last 52pg issue	$55.00	$170.00	$400.00	£39.00	£115.00	£275.00
177-179	$50.00	$150.00	$350.00	£35.00	£105.00	£245.00
180 Joker cover and story	$52.50	$160.00	$375.00	£40.00	£120.00	£280.00
181-185	$50.00	$150.00	$350.00	£35.00	£105.00	£245.00
186 The Flying Batcave (see Detective #317)	$50.00	$150.00	$350.00	£35.00	£105.00	£245.00
187 Two Face appears	$55.00	$165.00	$385.00	£38.00	£110.00	£262.50
188-189	$50.00	$150.00	$350.00	£35.00	£105.00	£245.00
190 origin retold	$70.00	$210.00	$500.00	£46.00	£135.00	£325.00
191-192	$50.00	$150.00	$350.00	£35.00	£105.00	£245.00
193 Joker cover and story	$55.00	$165.00	$385.00	£40.00	£120.00	£280.00
194-199	$50.00	$150.00	$350.00	£35.00	£105.00	£245.00
200 scarce in the U.K.	$65.00	$195.00	$460.00	£43.00	£125.00	£300.00
201-202	$46.00	$135.00	$325.00	£31.00	£92.50	£220.00
203 Catwoman cover	$50.00	$150.00	$350.00	£34.00	£100.00	£235.00
204	$46.00	$135.00	$325.00	£31.00	£92.50	£220.00
205 origin Batcave	$62.50	$190.00	$450.00	£43.00	£125.00	£300.00
206-210	$46.00	$135.00	$325.00	£31.00	£92.50	£220.00
211 Catwoman cover	$48.00	$140.00	$335.00	£32.00	£95.00	£225.00
212	$46.00	$135.00	$325.00	£31.00	£92.50	£220.00
213 origin and 1st appearance Mirror Man (note the later Flash villain Mirror Master)	$62.50	$190.00	$450.00	£43.00	£125.00	£300.00
214-220	$43.00	$125.00	$300.00	£29.00	£85.00	£200.00
221-224	$39.00	$115.00	$275.00	£26.00	£77.50	£185.00
225 origin and 1st appearance John Jones the Martian Manhunter, the first recognised new Silver Age super-hero (The Flash, though more important, was a revival)	$375.00	$1125.00	$4500.00	£250.00	£750.00	£3000.00
225 ND Silver Age Classic reprint (Mar 1992)	$0.25	$0.75	$1.25	£0.15	£0.45	£0.80
226 2nd appearance Martian Manhunter, origin continued	$125.00	$375.00	$1000.00	£82.50	£250.00	£670.00
227 3rd appearance Martian Manhunter	$60.00	$180.00	$420.00	£40.00	£120.00	£280.00
228-229	$60.00	$180.00	$420.00	£40.00	£120.00	£280.00
230 1st appearance Silver Age Mad Hatter (see Batman #49)	$62.50	$190.00	$450.00	£43.00	£125.00	£300.00
231 origin Martian Manhunter retold in brief	$39.00	$115.00	$275.00	£26.00	£77.50	£185.00
232	$39.00	$115.00	$275.00	£26.00	£77.50	£185.00
233 origin and 1st appearance Batwoman	$130.00	$390.00	$1050.00	£87.50	£260.00	£700.00
234	$39.00	$115.00	$275.00	£26.00	£77.50	£185.00
235 scarce in the U.K. origin partly retold; Bruce Wayne's father Thomas wears a bat-costume to a fancy dress party and prevents a robbery; influences Bruce on choice of name/costume	$55.00	$165.00	$450.00	£39.00	£115.00	£315.00
236 Martian Manhunter contacts Mars	$43.00	$125.00	$300.00	£29.00	£85.00	£200.00
237-238	$34.00	$100.00	$240.00	£22.50	£67.50	£160.00
239 scarce in the U.K. painted (grey-tone) cover	$37.00	$110.00	$260.00	£25.00	£75.00	£175.00
240	$34.00	$100.00	$240.00	£22.50	£67.50	£160.00
241-250	$32.00	$95.00	$225.00	£21.00	£62.50	£150.00
251-254	$29.00	$85.00	$200.00	£19.00	£57.50	£135.00
255 "Dinasaur" mis-spelling on cover	$29.00	$85.00	$200.00	£19.00	£57.50	£135.00
256-260	$29.00	$85.00	$200.00	£19.00	£57.50	£135.00
261-264	$22.50	$67.50	$160.00	£15.50	£47.00	£110.00
265 Batman's origin retold	$33.00	$97.50	$230.00	£22.50	£67.50	£160.00
266	$22.50	$67.50	$160.00	£15.50	£47.00	£110.00
267 origin and 1st appearance Bat-Mite	$30.00	$90.00	$210.00	£20.00	£60.00	£140.00
268-270	$22.50	$67.50	$160.00	£15.50	£47.00	£110.00
271 Martian Manhunter origin retold	$22.50	$67.50	$160.00	£15.50	£47.00	£110.00
272	$17.50	$52.50	$125.00	£11.00	£34.00	£80.00
1st official distribution in the U.K.						
273 Jonn Jonzz reveals identity	$19.00	$57.50	$135.00	£12.00	£36.00	£85.00
274-275	$17.50	$52.50	$125.00	£10.50	£32.00	£75.00
276 2nd appearance Bat-Mite	$17.50	$52.50	$125.00	£10.50	£32.00	£75.00
277-280	$17.50	$52.50	$125.00	£10.50	£32.00	£75.00
281-286	$14.00	$43.00	$100.00	£7.75	£23.50	£55.00
287 origin Martian Manhunter retold						

VERY GENERAL PERCENTAGE CONVERSION CHART WHICH MAY BE USED TO CALCULATE LOW AND INBETWEEN GRADES:

Issue / Description	$Good	$Fine	$N.Mint	£Good	£Fine	£N.Mint
	$14.00	$43.00	$100.00	£7.75	£23.50	£55.00
288-290	$14.00	$43.00	$100.00	£7.75	£23.50	£55.00
291-296	$12.50	$39.00	$90.00	£7.00	£21.00	£50.00
297 last 10 cents issue	$12.50	$39.00	$90.00	£7.00	£21.00	£50.00
298 1st appearance Clayface II (Matt Hagen)	$23.50	$70.00	$190.00	£14.00	£43.00	£115.00
299	$10.50	$32.00	$75.00	£6.00	£18.00	£42.50
300	$12.00	$36.00	$85.00	£6.25	£19.00	£45.00
301 Martian Manhunter returns to Mars	$10.00	$30.00	$70.00	£5.00	£15.00	£35.00
302-309	$7.75	$23.50	$55.00	£4.00	£12.00	£28.00
310 scarce in the U.K.	$7.75	$23.50	$55.00	£4.25	£12.50	£30.00
311-316	$7.75	$23.50	$55.00	£4.00	£12.00	£28.00
317 flying Batcave	$7.75	$23.50	$55.00	£4.00	£12.00	£28.00
318-320	$7.75	$23.50	$55.00	£4.00	£12.00	£28.00
321	$7.75	$23.50	$55.00	£3.40	£10.00	£24.00
322 1st original Batgirl in title	$7.75	$23.50	$55.00	£3.40	£10.00	£24.00
323-326	$7.75	$23.50	$55.00	£3.40	£10.00	£24.00
327 new look Batman costume, 1st official Silver Age Batman (according to DC - debateable however); 1st Elongated Man series	$13.50	$41.00	$95.00	£6.25	£19.00	£45.00
327 ND Silver Age Classic reprint (Mar 1992)	$0.25	$0.75	$1.25	£0.15	£0.45	£0.80
328 Alfred "dies" (later returns as The Outsider in #340)	$11.00	$34.00	$80.00	£5.50	£17.00	£40.00
329-330	$7.75	$23.50	$55.00	£3.40	£10.00	£24.00
331	$5.50	$17.00	$40.00	£2.50	£7.50	£17.50
332 Joker cover and story	$7.00	$21.00	$50.00	£3.20	£9.50	£22.50
333-339	$5.50	$17.00	$40.00	£2.50	£7.50	£17.50
340 The Outsider appears	$5.50	$17.00	$40.00	£2.50	£7.50	£17.50
341 Joker cover and story	$6.25	$19.00	$45.00	£3.00	£9.00	£21.00
342	$5.50	$17.00	$40.00	£2.50	£7.50	£17.50
343 Elongated Man appears	$5.50	$17.00	$40.00	£2.50	£7.50	£17.50
344	$5.50	$17.00	$40.00	£2.50	£7.50	£17.50
345 1st appearance Block Buster	$6.25	$19.00	$45.00	£2.85	£8.50	£20.00
346 last Silver Age issue indicia dated December 1965	$5.50	$17.00	$40.00	£2.50	£7.50	£17.50
347 Earth II Batman appears, Justice League of America cameo	$5.50	$17.00	$40.00	£2.50	£7.50	£17.50
348-349 Kubert cover	$5.50	$17.00	$40.00	£2.50	£7.50	£17.50
350	$5.50	$17.00	$40.00	£2.50	£7.50	£17.50
351	$6.50	$20.00	$40.00	£2.50	£7.50	£15.00
352 pin-up poster at centre-fold (often missing!)	$6.50	$20.00	$40.00	£2.50	£7.50	£15.00
353 Batman vs. Weather Wizard, Flash appears on cover	$6.50	$20.00	$40.00	£2.50	£7.50	£15.00
354-355	$6.50	$20.00	$40.00	£2.50	£7.50	£15.00
356 Alfred returns from his period as The Outsider	$6.50	$20.00	$40.00	£2.50	£7.50	£15.00
357	$6.50	$20.00	$40.00	£2.50	£7.50	£15.00
358 1st appearance Spellbinder	$6.50	$20.00	$40.00	£2.90	£8.75	£17.50
359 origin and 1st appearance new Batgirl (prompted by TV Show)	$9.25	$28.00	$65.00	£4.25	£12.50	£30.00
360-364	$6.50	$20.00	$40.00	£2.50	£7.50	£15.00
365 Joker cover and story	$7.50	$22.50	$45.00	£3.00	£9.00	£18.00
366-368	$6.50	$20.00	$40.00	£2.50	£7.50	£15.00
369 Neal Adams art on Elongated Man back-up, Catwoman appears (cameo) - 3rd Silver Age appearance?	$10.00	$30.00	$60.00	£5.00	£15.00	£30.00
370	$6.50	$20.00	$40.00	£2.50	£7.50	£15.00
371 new Batmobile modelled on TV show version	$6.50	$20.00	$40.00	£2.50	£7.50	£15.00
372-376	$5.00	$15.00	$30.00	£2.05	£6.25	£12.50
377 Riddler appers	$5.00	$15.00	$30.00	£2.05	£6.25	£12.50
378	$5.00	$15.00	$30.00	£2.05	£6.25	£12.50
379-380 scarce in the U.K.	$5.00	$15.00	$30.00	£2.50	£7.50	£15.00
381-384	$5.00	$15.00	$30.00	£2.05	£6.25	£12.50
385 Neal Adams cover	$5.00	$15.00	$30.00	£2.05	£6.25	£12.50
386	$5.00	$15.00	$30.00	£2.05	£6.25	£12.50
387 scarce in the U.K. 30th anniversary; reprints 1st Batman story in Detective #27 (May 1939), Joker and Penguin on cover	$10.00	$30.00	$60.00	£4.55	£13.50	£27.50
388 Joker cover and story; last 12 cents issue	$6.50	$20.00	$40.00	£2.50	£7.50	£15.00
389-390	$5.00	$15.00	$30.00	£1.65	£5.00	£10.00
391 Neal Adams cover	$3.30	$10.00	$20.00	£1.30	£4.00	£8.00
392-394	$3.30	$10.00	$20.00	£1.30	£4.00	£8.00
395 Neal Adams art	$3.30	$10.00	$20.00	£2.25	£6.75	£13.50
396	$3.30	$10.00	$20.00	£1.30	£4.00	£8.00
397 Neal Adams art	$3.30	$10.00	$20.00	£2.25	£6.75	£13.50
398	$2.50	$7.50	$15.00	£1.25	£3.75	£7.50
399 Neal Adams cover	$2.50	$7.50	$15.00	£1.25	£3.75	£7.50
400 Neal Adams art; 1st appearance Man-Bat	$10.00	$30.00	$60.00	£4.55	£13.50	£27.50
401	$2.00	$6.00	$12.00	£1.25	£3.75	£7.50
402 Neal Adams art	$2.90	$8.75	$17.50	£2.25	£6.75	£13.50
403 Neal Adams cover	$2.00	$6.00	$12.00	£1.25	£3.75	£7.50
404 Neal Adams art	$2.90	$8.75	$17.50	£2.25	£6.75	£13.50
405-406	$2.00	$6.00	$12.00	£1.25	£3.75	£7.50
407-408 Neal Adams art	$2.90	$8.75	$17.50	£2.05	£6.25	£12.50
409	$2.00	$6.00	$12.00	£1.25	£3.75	£7.50
410 Neal Adams art	$2.90	$8.75	$17.50	£2.05	£6.25	£12.50
411-413 Neal Adams covers	$2.40	$7.00	$12.00	£1.20	£3.60	£6.00
414-417 scarce in the U.K. 52pgs	$2.40	$7.00	$12.00	£1.50	£4.50	£7.50
418 scarce in the U.K. 52pgs, Creeper appears	$2.40	$7.00	$12.00	£1.50	£4.50	£7.50
419-420 scarce in the U.K. 52pgs	$2.40	$7.00	$12.00	£1.50	£4.50	£7.50
421-424 scarce in the U.K. 52pgs	$2.00	$6.00	$10.00	£1.40	£4.20	£7.00
425-427	$2.00	$6.00	$10.00	£1.20	£3.60	£6.00
428 ND	$2.00	$6.00	$10.00	£1.50	£4.50	£7.50
429-433	$2.00	$6.00	$10.00	£1.00	£3.00	£5.00
434-436 scarce in the U.K.	$2.00	$6.00	$10.00	£1.20	£3.60	£6.00
437 scarce in the U.K. 1st modern Manhunter, Walt Simonson art (ends 443)	$2.40	$7.00	$12.00	£1.70	£5.00	£8.50
438 100pgs	$4.40	$13.00	$22.00	£1.60	£4.80	£8.00
439 100pgs, origin briefly retold, Adamsesque art by Vin and Sal Amendola	$4.40	$13.00	$22.00	£1.80	£5.25	£9.00
440 100pgs	$4.40	$13.00	$22.00	£1.60	£4.80	£8.00
441 100pgs, Chaykin art on Batman	$4.40	$13.00	$22.00	£1.60	£4.80	£8.00
442 100pgs, Toth art on Batman	$4.40	$13.00	$22.00	£1.60	£4.80	£8.00
443 100pgs, death of Manhunter; origin Creeper retold	$4.40	$13.00	$22.00	£1.80	£5.25	£9.00
444-445 100pgs	$4.40	$13.00	$22.00	£1.50	£4.50	£7.50
446	$1.60	$4.80	$8.00	£0.80	£2.40	£4.00
447 Creeper appears	$1.60	$4.80	$8.00	£0.80	£2.40	£4.00
448	$1.60	$4.80	$8.00	£0.80	£2.40	£4.00
449 scarce in the U.K.	$1.60	$4.80	$8.00	£0.90	£2.70	£4.50
450 scarce in the U.K. Walt Simonson art	$1.60	$4.80	$8.00	£1.00	£3.00	£5.00
451-454 scarce in the U.K.	$1.60	$4.80	$8.00	£0.90	£2.70	£4.50
455-456	$1.60	$4.80	$8.00	£0.80	£2.40	£4.00
457 origin updated	$1.60	$4.80	$8.00	£0.90	£2.70	£4.50
458	$1.60	$4.80	$8.00	£0.80	£2.40	£4.00
459 Batman and Catwoman vs. Green Arrow and Black Canary, Bolland cover	$1.60	$4.80	$8.00	£0.90	£2.70	£4.50
460	$1.60	$4.80	$8.00	£0.80	£2.40	£4.00
461 ND	$1.20	$3.60	$6.00	£1.00	£3.00	£5.00
462 scarce in the U.K.	$1.20	$3.60	$6.00	£0.80	£2.40	£4.00
463 ND	$1.20	$3.60	$6.00	£1.00	£3.00	£5.00
464-465 scarce in the U.K.	$1.20	$3.60	$6.00	£0.90	£2.70	£4.50
466 ND Rogers art on Green Arrow	$3.00	$9.00	$15.00	£1.40	£4.20	£7.00
467 scarce in the U.K. Rogers art on Hawkman	$3.00	$9.00	$15.00	£1.20	£3.60	£6.00
468 scarce in the U.K. Rogers art on Batman	$3.00	$9.00	$15.00	£1.60	£4.80	£8.00
469-470 scarce in the U.K. Walt Simonson art	$1.20	$3.60	$6.00	£0.90	£2.70	£4.50
471 scarce in the U.K. Rogers art on Batman	$3.00	$9.00	$15.00	£1.60	£4.80	£8.00
472 very scarce/rare in the U.K. Rogers art on Batman, classic cover	$3.00	$9.00	$15.00	£3.00	£9.00	£15.00
473-474 scarce in the U.K. Rogers art on Batman	$3.00	$9.00	$15.00	£1.60	£4.80	£8.00
475 classic Rogers art on Batman and Joker	$5.00	$15.00	$25.00	£2.50	£7.50	£12.50
476 Rogers art on Batman and Joker	$5.00	$15.00	$25.00	£2.00	£6.00	£10.00

MINT = 100% / NEAR MINT (inc. +/-) = 90-99% / VERY FINE (inc. +/-) = 75-89% / FINE (inc. +/-) = 55-74%
VERY GOOD (inc. +/-) = 35-54% / GOOD (inc. +/-) = 15-34% / FAIR = 5-14% / POOR = 1-4%

301

Description	$Good	$Fine	$N.Mint	£Good	£Fine	£N.Mint
477 3pgs Rogers art; Neal Adams reprint	$3.60	$10.50	$18.00	£1.40	£4.20	£7.00
478 Rogers art on Batman, 1st appearance Clayface III	$3.00	$9.00	$15.00	£1.60	£4.80	£8.00
479 ND 44pgs, Rogers art on Batman	$3.00	$9.00	$15.00	£1.60	£4.80	£8.00
480 ND 44pgs	$1.20	$3.60	$6.00	£1.30	£3.90	£6.50
481 ND 68pgs, Jim Starlin, Rogers art	$2.40	$7.00	$12.00	£1.50	£4.50	£7.50
482 ND 68pgs, Jim Starlin, Rogers and Golden art	$1.60	$4.80	$8.00	£1.50	£4.50	£7.50
483 ND 68pgs, 40th anniversary issue; origin retold	$2.00	$6.00	$10.00	£1.00	£3.00	£5.00
484-490 ND 68pgs	$1.00	$3.00	$5.00	£0.80	£2.40	£4.00
491-495 ND 68pgs	$1.10	$3.35	$5.62	£0.75	£2.25	£3.75
496-499	$0.90	$2.70	$4.50	£0.60	£1.80	£3.00
500 ND 80pgs, Deadman X-over	$2.40	$7.00	$12.00	£1.20	£3.60	£6.00
501-503	$0.85	$2.55	$4.25	£0.55	£1.65	£2.75
504 Joker cover and story	$1.05	$3.15	$5.25	£0.70	£2.10	£3.50
505-511	$0.85	$2.55	$4.25	£0.55	£1.65	£2.75
512 45th anniversary issue	$0.85	$2.55	$4.25	£0.55	£1.65	£2.75
513-523	$0.85	$2.55	$4.25	£0.55	£1.65	£2.75
524 2nd appearance Jason Todd (cameo; see Batman #357)	$1.05	$3.15	$5.25	£0.70	£2.10	£3.50
525 3rd appearance Jason Todd	$0.90	$2.70	$4.50	£0.60	£1.80	£3.00
526 68pgs, Batman's 500th appearance in title, Joker cover and story	$3.00	$9.00	$15.00	£1.20	£3.60	£6.00
527-531	$0.80	$2.40	$4.00	£0.50	£1.50	£2.50
532 Joker appears	$1.00	$3.00	$5.00	£0.70	£2.10	£3.50
533-534	$0.80	$2.40	$4.00	£0.50	£1.50	£2.50
535 intro new Robin (Jason Todd; see Batman #368)	$1.00	$3.00	$5.00	£0.70	£2.10	£3.50
536-550	$0.80	$2.40	$4.00	£0.50	£1.50	£2.50
551-553	$0.70	$2.10	$3.50	£0.45	£1.35	£2.25
554 1st appearance new Black Canary	$0.80	$2.40	$4.00	£0.50	£1.50	£2.50
555-557	$0.70	$2.10	$3.50	£0.45	£1.35	£2.25
558 unofficial Crisis X-over	$0.70	$2.10	$3.50	£0.45	£1.35	£2.25
559 LD in the U.K. Catwoman appears	$0.90	$2.70	$4.50	£0.60	£1.80	£3.00
560 LD in the U.K.	$0.85	$2.55	$4.25	£0.55	£1.65	£2.75
561-566	$0.70	$2.10	$3.50	£0.45	£1.35	£2.25
567 Harlan Ellison story	$0.70	$2.10	$3.50	£0.45	£1.35	£2.25
568 Legends X-over, Janson art	$0.70	$2.10	$3.50	£0.45	£1.35	£2.25
569-570 Alan Davis/Paul Neary Joker rendition	$1.10	$3.30	$5.50	£0.70	£2.10	£3.50
571 Alan Davis/Paul Neary art	$1.05	$3.15	$5.25	£0.70	£2.10	£3.50
572 DS, 50th anniversary, Sherlock Holmes appears, Alan Davis art	$1.20	$3.60	$6.00	£0.80	£2.40	£4.00
573-574 Alan Davis/Paul Neary art	$1.05	$3.15	$5.25	£0.70	£2.10	£3.50
575 LD in the U.K. Davis/Neary art, Batman Year Two	$2.00	$6.00	$10.00	£1.30	£3.90	£6.50
576-578 Todd McFarlane art, Year Two	$1.80	$5.25	$9.00	£0.90	£2.70	£4.50
579 Breyfogle art	$0.55	$1.65	$2.75	£0.35	£1.05	£1.75
580-581 Jim Baikie art	$0.55	$1.65	$2.75	£0.35	£1.05	£1.75
582 Breyfogle art, Millennium X-over	$0.55	$1.65	$2.75	£0.35	£1.05	£1.75
583 Breyfogle art, Alan Grant/John Wagner scripts begin	$0.55	$1.65	$2.75	£0.35	£1.05	£1.75
584-585	$0.55	$1.65	$2.75	£0.35	£1.05	£1.75
586-594	$0.45	$1.35	$2.25	£0.30	£0.90	£1.50
595 Invasion X-over	$0.45	$1.35	$2.25	£0.30	£0.90	£1.50
596-597	$0.45	$1.35	$2.25	£0.30	£0.90	£1.50
598 LD in the U.K. giant squarebound, Part I Blind Justice, script by Sam Hamm (writer of Batman film), art by Cowans	$1.50	$4.50	$7.50	£1.00	£3.00	£5.00
599 Part II Blind Justice, script by Sam Hamm	$0.80		$4.00	£0.50	£1.50	£2.50
600 LD in the U.K. 80pgs, squarebound, Sam Hamm script Part III Blind Justice	$0.90	$2.70	$4.50	£0.60	£1.80	£3.00
601	$0.40	$1.20	$2.00	£0.25	£0.75	£1.25
602-603 The Demon appears	$0.40	$1.20	$2.00	£0.25	£0.75	£1.25
604 Mud Pack story continues from Secret Origins 44; bi-weekly issue; mini-poster with painted art by Norm Breyfogle	$0.40	$1.20	$2.00	£0.25	£0.75	£1.25
605-606 Mud Pack story continues; bi-weekly issue	$0.40	$1.20	$2.00	£0.25	£0.75	£1.25
607 Mud Pack story continues; bi-weekly issue; mini-poster with painted art by Norm Breyfogle	$0.40	$1.20	$2.00	£0.25	£0.75	£1.25
608-609	$0.40	$1.20	$2.00	£0.25	£0.75	£1.25
610-614	$0.30	$0.90	$1.50	£0.20	£0.60	£1.00
615 X-over with Batman 448/449	$0.30	$0.90	$1.50	£0.20	£0.60	£1.00
616-617 bi-weekly issue	$0.30	$0.90	$1.50	£0.20	£0.60	£1.00
618 bi-weekly issue, Joker cameo (1 panel)	$0.30	$0.90	$1.50	£0.20	£0.60	£1.00
619 bi-weekly issue	$0.30	$0.90	$1.50	£0.20	£0.60	£1.00
620	$0.30	$0.90	$1.50	£0.20	£0.60	£1.00
621	$0.25	$0.75	$1.25	£0.15	£0.45	£0.75
622-624 The Demon Within story, covers by DickSprang, Mike McKone/Flint Henry art	$0.25	$0.75	$1.25	£0.15	£0.45	£0.75
625	$0.25	$0.75	$1.25	£0.15	£0.45	£0.75
626 Sarah Essen from Year: One appears	$0.25	$0.75	$1.25	£0.15	£0.45	£0.75
627 80pgs, 600th appearance of Batman in title, first story from Detective #27 reprinted, and re-worked by a variety of artists/writers, cover painting by Breyfogle based on Detective #27	$0.60	$1.80	$3.00	£0.40	£1.20	£2.00
628-630	$0.25	$0.75	$1.25	£0.15	£0.45	£0.75
631-634 bi-weekly issues	$0.25	$0.75	$1.25	£0.15	£0.45	£0.75
635-636 bi-weekly issues, Arkham Asylum story by Louise Simonson	$0.25	$0.75	$1.25	£0.15	£0.45	£0.75
637-638	$0.25	$0.75	$1.25	£0.15	£0.45	£0.75
639 The Idiot Root part 2, continues in Batman #473	$0.25	$0.75	$1.25	£0.15	£0.45	£0.75
640 The Idiot Root part 4 (conclusion)	$0.25	$0.75	$1.25	£0.15	£0.45	£0.75
641 Destroyer part 3 (conclusion)	$0.25	$0.75	$1.25	£0.15	£0.45	£0.75
642 X-over with Batman #476, Batman reveals identity to Vicki Vale	$0.25	$0.75	$1.25	£0.15	£0.45	£0.75
643	$0.25	$0.75	$1.25	£0.15	£0.45	£0.75
644-646 Electric City story	$0.25	$0.75	$1.25	£0.15	£0.45	£0.75
647-649 Return of the Cluemaster, bi-weekly	$0.25	$0.75	$1.25	£0.15	£0.45	£0.75
650-651 bi-weekly	$0.25	$0.75	$1.25	£0.15	£0.45	£0.75
652 Graham Nolan art, Travis Charest cover; prelude to Robin III mini-series, Huntress appears (origin retold), bi-weekly,	$0.25	$0.75	$1.25	£0.15	£0.45	£0.75
653 Travis Charest cover, Huntress appears	$0.25	$0.75	$1.25	£0.15	£0.45	£0.75
654-657 Sam Kieth cover	$0.25	$0.75	$1.25	£0.15	£0.45	£0.75
658 bi-weekly, Sam Kieth cover, Knightfall prequel	$0.30	$0.90	$1.50	£0.20	£0.60	£1.00
659 Knightfall part 2, continued in Batman #493; bi-weekly, Sam Kieth cover	$0.90	$2.70	$4.50	£0.50	£1.50	£2.50
660 Knightfall part 4, continued in Batman #494; bi-weekly, Sam Kieth cover featuring Bane	$0.90	$2.70	$4.50	£0.40	£1.20	£2.00
661 Knightfall part 6, continued in Batman #495; bi-weekly; Joker and Riddler cameos	$0.80	$2.40	$4.00	£0.30	£0.90	£1.50
662 Knightfall part 8, continued in Batman #496; bi-weekly; Riddler appears	$0.60	$1.80	$3.00	£0.25	£0.75	£1.25
663 Knightfall part 10, continued in Batman #497; bi-weekly	$0.60	$1.80	$3.00	£0.25	£0.75	£1.25
664 Knightfall part 12, continued in Showcase '93 #7; bi-weekly; Bane and Joker appear	$0.60	$1.80	$3.00	£0.25	£0.75	£1.25
665 Knightfall part 16, continued in Batman: Shadow of the Bat #16; bi-weekly	$0.40	$1.20	$2.00	£0.25	£0.75	£1.25
666 Knightfall part 18, continued in Batman #500	$0.40	$1.20	$2.00	£0.25	£0.75	£1.25
667 Knightquest: The Crusade part 1, continued in Batman: Shadow of the Bat #19; Kelley Jones cover	$0.40	$1.20	$2.00	£0.25	£0.75	£1.25
668 Knightquest: The Crusade part 5, continued in Batman #502; Kelley Jones cover; leads into Robin #1	$0.25	$0.75	$1.25	£0.15	£0.45	£0.75
669 Knightquest: The Crusade part 7, Kelley Jones cover	$0.25	$0.75	$1.25	£0.15	£0.45	£0.75
670 Knightquest: The Crusade story, Kelley Jones cover	$0.25	$0.75	$1.25	£0.15	£0.45	£0.75
671 Knightquest: The Crusade story, Kelley Jones cover; Joker appears (in a pony-tail - excellent)	$0.25	$0.75	$1.25	£0.15	£0.45	£0.75
672-673 Knightquest: The Crusade story, Kelley Jones cover; Joker appears	$0.25	$0.75	$1.25	£0.15	£0.45	£0.75
674 Knightquest: The Crusade story, Kelley Jones cover	$0.25	$0.75	$1.25	£0.15	£0.45	£0.75
675 Knightquest: The Crusade story the conclusion, continued in Robin #7; Kelley Jones cover	$0.25	$0.75	$1.25	£0.15	£0.45	£0.75
675 ND Collector's Edition, embossed blue and gold foil cover	$0.60	$1.80	$3.00	£0.40	£1.20	£2.00
676 48pgs, Knightsend part 3, continued in Batman: Legends of the Dark Knight #62	$0.45	$1.35	$2.25	£0.30	£0.90	£1.50
677 Knightsend part 9, continued in Batman: Legends of the Dark Knight #63						

	$Good	$Fine	$N.Mint	£Good	£Fine	£N.Mint
	$0.30	$0.90	$1.50	£0.20	£0.60	£1.00
678 Zero Hour X-over						
	$0.30	$0.90	$1.50	£0.20	£0.60	£1.00
679	$0.30	$0.90	$1.50	£0.20	£0.60	£1.00
680 Dick Grayson as Batman vs. Two Face						
	$0.30	$0.90	$1.50	£0.20	£0.60	£1.00
681	$0.30	$0.90	$1.50	£0.20	£0.60	£1.00
682 The Troika part 3, concluded in Robin #14						
	$0.30	$0.90	$1.50	£0.20	£0.60	£1.00
682 ND Collector's Edition, embossed black cover						
	$0.45	$1.35	$2.25	£0.30	£0.90	£1.50
683-684 The Penguin appears						
	$0.30	$0.90	$1.50	£0.20	£0.60	£1.00
685	$0.30	$0.90	$1.50	£0.20	£0.60	£1.00
686 Batman vs. King Snake and Lynx; upgraded coated paper stock (Miraweb Format) begins						
	$0.40	$1.20	$2.00	£0.25	£0.75	£1.25
687-690	$0.40	$1.20	$2.00	£0.25	£0.75	£1.25
691 Underworld Unleashed tie-in; death of Spellbinder and intro new Spellbinder						
	$0.40	$1.20	$2.00	£0.25	£0.75	£1.25
692 Underworld Unleashed tie-in, Spellbinder appears						
	$0.40	$1.20	$2.00	£0.25	£0.75	£1.25
693-694 Poison Ivy appears						
	$0.40	$1.20	$2.00	£0.25	£0.75	£1.25
695 Contagion part 2, continued in Robin #27						
	$0.40	$1.20	$2.00	£0.25	£0.75	£1.25
Title Value: $66724.65	$200552.70	$607762.73		£44662.10	£133760.60	£407046.60

Note: Joker cover: 387 Joker cover and stories: 332, 341, 365, 388, 475, 476, 504, 526, 532, 566, 569, 570

ARTISTS
Ditko in 483-485, 487. Golden in 482. Rogers in 466-468, 471-479, 481.

FEATURES
Alfred in 486, 489. Atom in 432, 463, 489. Aquaman in 293-300. Batgirl in 384, 385, 388, 389, 392, 393, 396, 397, 404-424, 481-488, 490-499, 501, 502, 505, 506, 508-510, 512-517. Batman in 27-date; Unsolved Cases of the Batman in 484. Batman/Deadman in 500. Black Canary in 464. Black Lightning in 490, 491, 494, 495. Bat-Mite in 482. Demon in 482-485. Dr. Phosphorus in 469. Elongated Man in 327-383, 426, 430, 436, 444, 449, 453, 456, 457, 462, 465, 488, 500. Green Arrow in 466. Hawkman in 428, 434, 446, 452, 454, 455, 467, 479, 480, 500. Human Target in 483, 484, 486, 493. Jason Bard in 425, 427, 429, 431, 433, 435. Man-Bat in 458, 459, 481, 485, 492. Manhunter in 437-442; Manhunter/Batman in 443. Martian Manhunter in 273-326. Odd Man in 487. Robin solo in 386, 390, 391, 394, 398, 399, 402, 403, 445, 447, 450, 451, 481-488, 490-495; Robin/Batgirl in 400, 401, 489. Roy Raymond in 273-292, 487. Slam Bradley in 500. Tales of Gotham City in 488-495, 504, 507 (featuring Red Tornado in 493). Tim Trench, Private Detective in 460, 461.

REPRINT FEATURES
Alfred in 417, 421. Atom in 438, 439. Batman in 387, 438, 440-443. Black Canary, Guardian in 442. Doll Man, Manhunter in 440. Dr.Fate in 439, 442. Dr.Mid-Nite in 445. Elongated Man in 439, 442, 444, 445. Green Lantern in 438; GA Green Lantern in 440, 443. Hawkman in 438-440, 442. Ibis, The Spider, Eclipso, Kid Eternity in 439, 444. Plastic Man in 441. Rex the Wonder Dog in 416. Robin in 438, 440, 442-444. Roy Raymond in 419, 444, 445. Sierra Smith in 418, 444. Spectre, Creeper (origin) in 443. Star Hawkins in 444, 445.

DETECTIVE COMICS ANNUAL
DC Comics; 1 Aug 1988-present

	$Good	$Fine	$N.Mint	£Good	£Fine	£N.Mint
1 48pgs, Janson art, ties in with Green Arrow Annual #1, Question Annual #1						
	$1.05	$3.15	$5.25	£0.70	£2.10	£3.50
2 64pgs, squarebound, Bolland cover						
	$0.55	$1.65	$2.75	£0.35	£1.05	£1.75
3 64pgs, Archie Goodwin script						
	$0.45	$1.35	$2.25	£0.30	£0.90	£1.50
4 64pgs, Armageddon: 2001 tie-in						
	$0.80	$2.40	$4.00	£0.50	£1.50	£2.50
5 64pgs, Sam Kieth cover art,Eclipso: The Darkness Within tie-in						
	$0.45	$1.35	$2.25	£0.30	£0.90	£1.50

	$Good	$Fine	$N.Mint	£Good	£Fine	£N.Mint
6 64pgs, Bloodlines (Wave Two) part 14, 1st appearance Geist, continued in Justice League America Annual #7						
	$0.45	$1.35	$2.25	£0.30	£0.90	£1.50
7 64pgs, Elseworlds story; Chuck Dixon script, Alcatena art; "Joker" appears						
	$0.55	$1.65	$2.75	£0.35	£1.05	£1.75
8 64pgs, Year One, origin of the Riddler retold						
	$0.80	$2.40	$4.00	£0.50	£1.50	£2.50
Title Value:	$5.10	$15.30	$25.50	£3.30	£9.90	£16.50

DETECTIVES INC.
Eclipse,MS; 1,2 Apr 1985

	$Good	$Fine	$N.Mint	£Good	£Fine	£N.Mint
1-2 ND reprints graphic novel in colour						
	$0.45	$1.35	$2.25	£0.30	£0.90	£1.50
Title Value:	$0.90	$2.70	$4.50	£0.60	£1.80	£3.00

DETECTIVES INC: A TERROR OF DREAMS
Eclipse,MS; 1 Oct 1987-3 Dec 1987

	$Good	$Fine	$N.Mint	£Good	£Fine	£N.Mint
1-3 ND Gene Colan art, printed in sepia and black						
	$0.40	$1.20	$2.00	£0.25	£0.75	£1.25
Title Value:	$1.20	$3.60	$6.00	£0.75	£2.25	£3.75

DETECTIVES, THE
Alpha Productions,OS; 1 Apr 1993

	$Good	$Fine	$N.Mint	£Good	£Fine	£N.Mint
1 ND 48pgs, squarebound, new anthology featuring Maze Agency and Mike Mauser among others; Adam Hughes cover						
	$0.60	$1.80	$3.00	£0.40	£1.20	£2.00
1 ND Gold Edition (Sep 1993); signed by one or more of the creators (inc. Mike Barr, Paul Petellier, Cuti, Staton, Beatty); gold foil logo						
	$1.20	$3.60	$6.00	£0.80	£2.40	£4.00
Title Value:	$1.80	$5.40	$9.00	£1.20	£3.60	£6.00

DETHGRIP
Immortal Comics; 1 Sep 1994-4 1995

	$Good	$Fine	$N.Mint	£Good	£Fine	£N.Mint
1-2 ND Beau Smith script, Jim Callahan and Tim Dzon art						
	$0.40	$1.20	$2.00	£0.25	£0.75	£1.25
3-4 ND	$0.40	$1.20	$2.00	£0.25	£0.75	£1.25
Title Value:	$1.60	$4.80	$8.00	£1.00	£3.00	£5.00

Note: originally solicited by Axis Comics for Mar 1994 cover date

DETONATOR
Chaos Comics,MS; 1 Dec 1994-2 Jan 1995

	$Good	$Fine	$N.Mint	£Good	£Fine	£N.Mint
1-2 ND Brian Pulido script, Steven Hughes art						
	$0.60	$1.80	$3.00	£0.40	£1.20	£2.00
Title Value:	$1.20	$3.60	$6.00	£0.80	£2.40	£4.00

DEVIL CHEF
Dark Horse,OS; nn Jul 1994

	$Good	$Fine	$N.Mint	£Good	£Fine	£N.Mint
1 ND Jack Pollock script/art; black and white						
	$0.45	$1.35	$2.25	£0.30	£0.90	£1.50
Title Value:	$0.45	$1.35	$2.25	£0.30	£0.90	£1.50

DEVIL DINOSAUR
Marvel Comics Group; 1 Apr 1978-9 Dec 1978

	$Good	$Fine	$N.Mint	£Good	£Fine	£N.Mint
1-9 ND Jack Kirby art						
	$0.40	$1.20	$2.00	£0.25	£0.75	£1.25
Title Value:	$3.60	$10.80	$18.00	£2.25	£6.75	£11.25

DEVILINA
Atlas Seaboard,Magazine OS; 1 1975

	$Good	$Fine	$N.Mint	£Good	£Fine	£N.Mint
1 distributed in the U.K.						
	$0.80	$2.40	$4.00	£0.50	£1.50	£2.50
Title Value:	$0.80	$2.40	$4.00	£0.50	£1.50	£2.50

DEVILMAN
Verotik; 1 Jun 1995-present

	$Good	$Fine	$N.Mint	£Good	£Fine	£N.Mint
1 ND Go Nagai script and art begins						
	$0.70	$2.10	$3.50	£0.50	£1.50	£2.50
2-5 ND	$0.60	$1.80	$3.00	£0.40	£1.20	£2.00
Title Value:	$3.10	$9.30	$15.50	£2.10	£6.30	£10.50

Detective Comics #226

Detective Comics #339

Devil Dinosaur #2

DICK TRACY
Harvey; 141 Aug 1960-145 Apr 1961

	$Good	$Fine	$N.Mint	£Good	£Fine	£N.Mint
141-142 rare in the U.K., giant	$7.50	$22.50	$45.00	£5.00	£15.00	£30.00
143 very scarce in the U.K. giant	$6.75	$20.00	$40.50	£4.50	£13.50	£27.00
144-145 rare in the U.K., giant	$7.50	$22.50	$45.00	£5.00	£15.00	£30.00
Title Value:	$36.75	$110.00	$220.50	£24.50	£73.50	£147.00

Note: all reprints, Prestige Format and all distributed on the news-stands in the U.K.

DICK TRACY ALBUM, THE ORIGINAL
Gladstone; 1 Sep 1990-6 1991

	$Good	$Fine	$N.Mint	£Good	£Fine	£N.Mint
1 ND 48pgs, Mumbles appears	$1.00	$3.00	$5.00	£0.65	£1.95	£3.25
2 ND 48pgs, origin of two-way wrist radio	$1.00	$3.00	$5.00	£0.65	£1.95	£3.25
3-6 ND 48pgs	$1.00	$3.00	$5.00	£0.65	£1.95	£3.25
Title Value:	$6.00	$18.00	$30.00	£3.90	£11.70	£19.50

Note: bi-monthly

DICK TRACY IN 3-D
Blackthorne; (3-D Series #8) 1 Jul 1986

	$Good	$Fine	$N.Mint	£Good	£Fine	£N.Mint
1 ND reprints by Chester Gould; with bound-1n 3-D glasses (25% less if without)	$0.55	$1.65	$2.75	£0.35	£1.05	£1.75
Title Value:	$0.55	$1.65	$2.75	£0.35	£1.05	£1.75

DICK TRACY MAGAZINE
Gladstone; 1 Aug 1991-2 1991

	$Good	$Fine	$N.Mint	£Good	£Fine	£N.Mint
1-2 ND 48pgs	$0.80	$2.40	$4.00	£0.50	£1.50	£2.50
Title Value:	$1.60	$4.80	$8.00	£1.00	£3.00	£5.00

DICK TRACY MONTHLY/WEEKLY
Blackthorne; 1 Jun 1986-108 1992

	$Good	$Fine	$N.Mint	£Good	£Fine	£N.Mint
1 ND 72pgs, squarebound begins (ends #25)	$0.45	$1.35	$2.25	£0.30	£0.90	£1.50
2-25 ND	$0.45	$1.35	$2.25	£0.30	£0.90	£1.50
26 ND becomes Dick Tracy Weekly	$0.40	$1.20	$2.00	£0.25	£0.75	£1.25
27-96 ND	$0.40	$1.20	$2.00	£0.25	£0.75	£1.25
97 ND Moon Maid appears	$0.40	$1.20	$2.00	£0.25	£0.75	£1.25
98-99 ND	$0.40	$1.20	$2.00	£0.25	£0.75	£1.25
100 ND DS	$0.45	$1.35	$2.25	£0.30	£0.90	£1.50
101-108 ND	$0.40	$1.20	$2.00	£0.25	£0.75	£1.25
Title Value:	$44.50	$133.50	$222.50	£28.30	£84.90	£141.50
Special 1 (Jan 1988)				£0.45	£1.35	£2.25
Special 2,3				£0.40	£1.20	£2.00

DICK TRACY MOVIE ADAPTATION
Disney,OS; Film; nn Oct 1990

	$Good	$Fine	$N.Mint	£Good	£Fine	£N.Mint
nn ND 64pgs, regular edition of Prestige Format series (Big City Blues #3)	$0.55	$1.65	$2.75	£0.35	£1.05	£1.75
Title Value:	$0.55	$1.65	$2.75	£0.35	£1.05	£1.75

DICK TRACY, THE ORIGINAL
Gladstone; 1 Jul 1990-5 1991

	$Good	$Fine	$N.Mint	£Good	£Fine	£N.Mint
1 ND 64pgs, Dick Tracy vs. Mrs. Prune-Face	$0.40	$1.20	$2.00	£0.25	£0.75	£1.25
2 ND 64pgs, "Influence" story	$0.40	$1.20	$2.00	£0.25	£0.75	£1.25
3 ND 64pgs, "The Extortioner" story	$0.40	$1.20	$2.00	£0.25	£0.75	£1.25
4-5 ND 64pgs	$0.40	$1.20	$2.00	£0.25	£0.75	£1.25
Title Value:	$2.00	$6.00	$10.00	£1.25	£3.75	£6.25

Note: bi-monthly

DICK TRACY: BIG CITY BLUES
Disney,MS; 1 Apr 1990-3 Jun 1990

	$Good	$Fine	$N.Mint	£Good	£Fine	£N.Mint
1 ND 48pgs, Kyle Baker art begins	$0.70	$2.10	$3.50	£0.50	£1.50	£2.50
2 ND 64pgs, Tracy vs. The Underworld	$1.00	$3.00	$5.00	£0.70	£2.10	£3.50
3 ND 64pgs, Len Wein/Kyle Baker adaptation of Warren Beatty film (never legally imported into the U.K. though a very few issues found their way through)	$1.00	$3.00	$5.00	£0.70	£2.10	£3.50
Title Value:	$2.70	$8.10	$13.50	£1.90	£5.70	£9.50

True Hearts and Tommy Guns (Oct 1990)
Trade paperback reprints the above
(never legally imported into the U.K. though a few issues found their way through) £1.50 £4.50 £7.50

Note: issue #3 and Trade paperback only legally available as Fleetway reprints

DICK TRACY: THE UNPRINTED STORIES
Blackthorne; 1 Sep 1987-4 1988

	$Good	$Fine	$N.Mint	£Good	£Fine	£N.Mint
1-3 ND	$0.60	$1.80	$3.00	£0.40	£1.20	£2.00
4 ND Flat-Top Junior appears	$0.60	$1.80	$3.00	£0.40	£1.20	£2.00
Title Value:	$2.40	$7.20	$12.00	£1.60	£4.80	£8.00

DIE-CUT
Marvel UK; 1 Nov 1993-2 1993

	$Good	$Fine	$N.Mint	£Good	£Fine	£N.Mint
1 Beast appears; die-cut cover	$0.40	$1.20	$2.00	£0.25	£0.75	£1.25
2 X-Beast appears	$0.40	$1.20	$2.00	£0.25	£0.75	£1.25
Title Value:	$0.80	$2.40	$4.00	£0.50	£1.50	£2.50

DIE-CUT VS. G-FORCE
Marvel UK,MS; 1 Nov 1993-2 Dec 1993

	$Good	$Fine	$N.Mint	£Good	£Fine	£N.Mint
1 Liam Sharp cover	$0.35	$1.05	$1.75	£0.25	£0.75	£1.25
2 gold foil enhanced cover	$0.35	$1.05	$1.75	£0.25	£0.75	£1.25
Title Value:	$0.70	$2.10	$3.50	£0.50	£1.50	£2.50

DIGITEK
Marvel UK,MS; 1 Dec 1992-4 Mar 1993
(see Overkill in British section)

	$Good	$Fine	$N.Mint	£Good	£Fine	£N.Mint
1 origin Digitek, Dermot Power art	$0.30	$0.90	$1.50	£0.20	£0.60	£1.00
2-3 Deathlok appears	$0.30	$0.90	$1.50	£0.20	£0.60	£1.00
4	$0.30	$0.90	$1.50	£0.20	£0.60	£1.00
Title Value:	$1.20	$3.60	$6.00	£0.80	£2.40	£4.00

DILLINGER
Rip Off Press,OS; 1 1991

	$Good	$Fine	$N.Mint	£Good	£Fine	£N.Mint
1 ND black and white	$0.45	$1.35	$2.25	£0.30	£0.90	£1.50
Title Value:	$0.45	$1.35	$2.25	£0.30	£0.90	£1.50

DINO ISLAND
Mirage Studios,MS; 1 Feb 1993-2 Mar 1993

	$Good	$Fine	$N.Mint	£Good	£Fine	£N.Mint
1-2 ND	$0.45	$1.35	$2.25	£0.30	£0.90	£1.50
Title Value:	$0.90	$2.70	$4.50	£0.60	£1.80	£3.00

DINO RIDERS
Marvel Comics Group, Toy; 1 Feb 1989-5 Jun 1989

	$Good	$Fine	$N.Mint	£Good	£Fine	£N.Mint
1-5 ND	$0.15	$0.45	$0.75	£0.10	£0.30	£0.50
Title Value:	$0.75	$2.25	$3.75	£0.50	£1.50	£2.50

DINO, THE ALL-NEW FLINTSTONES STARRING
Charlton; 1 Aug 1973-20 Jan 1977

	$Good	$Fine	$N.Mint	£Good	£Fine	£N.Mint
1 distributed in the U.K.	$0.90	$2.70	$4.50	£0.60	£1.80	£3.00
2 distributed in the U.K.	$0.60	$1.80	$3.00	£0.40	£1.20	£2.00
3 distributed in the U.K.	$0.45	$1.35	$2.25	£0.30	£0.90	£1.50
4-20 distributed in the U.K.	$0.40	$1.20	$2.00	£0.25	£0.75	£1.25
Title Value:	$8.75	$26.25	$43.75	£5.55	£16.65	£27.75

DINOSAUR BOP
Monster Comics,MS; 1 Aug 1991-4 Dec 1991

	$Good	$Fine	$N.Mint	£Good	£Fine	£N.Mint
1-4 ND Jim Arnon's Kirbyesque art	$0.40	$1.20	$2.00	£0.25	£0.75	£1.25
Title Value:	$1.60	$4.80	$8.00	£1.00	£3.00	£5.00

DINOSAUR REX
Upshot Graphics/Fantagraphics,MS; 1-3 1987

	$Good	$Fine	$N.Mint	£Good	£Fine	£N.Mint
1 ND colour; Henry Mayo art; Dennis Fujitaki art on The Dragons of Summer back-up	$0.40	$1.20	$2.00	£0.25	£0.75	£1.25
2-3 ND black and white	$0.40	$1.20	$2.00	£0.25	£0.75	£1.25
Title Value:	$1.20	$3.60	$6.00	£0.75	£2.25	£3.75

DINOSAURS ATTACK!
Eclipse,MS; 1 Feb 1992-3 Apr 1992

	$Good	$Fine	$N.Mint	£Good	£Fine	£N.Mint
1-3 ND 48pgs, based on series of gum cards	$0.70	$2.10	$3.50	£0.45	£1.35	£2.25
Title Value:	$2.10	$6.30	$10.50	£1.35	£4.05	£6.75

DINOSAURS FOR HIRE
Eternity; 1 Mar 1988-9 1989

	$Good	$Fine	$N.Mint	£Good	£Fine	£N.Mint
1 ND	$0.35	$1.05	$1.75	£0.25	£0.75	£1.25
1 2nd printing ND	$0.35	$1.05	$1.75	£0.25	£0.75	£1.25
2-9 ND	$0.35	$1.05	$1.75	£0.25	£0.75	£1.25
Title Value:	$3.50	$10.50	$17.50	£2.50	£7.50	£12.50
Fall Classic				£0.30	£0.90	£1.50
Guns 'N Lizards				£0.70	£2.10	£3.50
Dinosaurs For Hire 3-D				£0.35	£1.05	£1.75

DINOSAURS FOR HIRE (2ND SERIES)
Malibu; 1 Feb 1993-13 Feb 1994

	$Good	$Fine	$N.Mint	£Good	£Fine	£N.Mint
1 ND	$0.30	$0.90	$1.50	£0.20	£0.60	£1.00
1 ND Ash Can, 16pgs, black and white interior, normal comic size (unusually), signed on cover by Tom Mason; banner stating "Distributed exclusively by Great Eastern Conventions January 22-24 1993"	$1.20	$3.60	$6.00	£0.80	£2.40	£4.00
2-5 ND	$0.30	$0.90	$1.50	£0.20	£0.60	£1.00
6 ND Jurassic Park parody	$0.30	$0.90	$1.50	£0.20	£0.60	£1.00
7 ND	$0.30	$0.90	$1.50	£0.20	£0.60	£1.00
8 ND Genesis Tie-In; pre-bagged with free Sky-Cap (some bags have two)	$0.30	$0.90	$1.50	£0.20	£0.60	£1.00
9-13 ND Genesis Tie-In	$0.30	$0.90	$1.50	£0.20	£0.60	£1.00
Title Value:	$5.10	$15.30	$25.50	£3.40	£10.20	£17.00

DINOSAURS: A CELEBRATION
Marvel Comics Group/Epic,MS; 1-4 Dec 1992

	$Good	$Fine	$N.Mint	£Good	£Fine	£N.Mint
1 ND 48pgs, Terrible Claws and Tyrants, Kevin Walker cover	$0.60	$1.80	$3.00	£0.40	£1.20	£2.00
2 ND 48pgs, Egg Stealers and Earth Shakers, John Bolton cover	$0.60	$1.80	$3.00	£0.40	£1.20	£2.00
3 ND 48pgs, Boneheads and Duckbills, Garry Leach cover	$0.60	$1.80	$3.00	£0.40	£1.20	£2.00
4 ND 48pgs, Horns and Heavy Armour, Richard Dolan cover	$0.60	$1.80	$3.00	£0.40	£1.20	£2.00
Title Value:	$2.40	$7.20	$12.00	£1.60	£4.80	£8.00

DIRTY PAIR
Eclipse,MS; 1 Dec 1988-4 Mar 1989

	$Good	$Fine	$N.Mint	£Good	£Fine	£N.Mint
1-4 ND	$0.80	$2.40	$4.00	£0.50	£1.50	£2.50
Title Value:	$3.20	$9.60	$16.00	£2.00	£6.00	£10.00

Dirty Pair: Bio-Hazards (1990)

	$Good	$Fine	$N.Mint	£Good	£Fine	£N.Mint
reprints mini-series				£1.10	£3.30	£5.50
2nd print (Nov 1991)				£1.00	£3.00	£5.00

DIRTY PAIR ANIME COMICS
Viz Communications,MS; 1 Sep 1994-5 Jan 1995

	$Good	$Fine	$N.Mint	£Good	£Fine	£N.Mint
1-5 ND 48pgs, adapted from scripts and cels from the animated series; colour	$1.00	$3.00	$5.00	£0.65	£1.95	£3.25
Title Value:	$5.00	$15.00	$25.00	£3.25	£9.75	£16.25

DIRTY PAIR II
Eclipse,MS; 1 Oct 1989-4 Jan 1990

	$Good	$Fine	$N.Mint	£Good	£Fine	£N.Mint
1-4 ND	$0.55	$1.65	$2.75	£0.35	£1.05	£1.75
Title Value:	$2.20	$6.60	$11.00	£1.40	£4.20	£7.00
Dirty Pair II: Dangerous						
Acquaintances (Sep 1991), reprints mini-series, softcover				£1.40	£4.20	£7.00
Hardcover (Oct 1991)				£4.00	£12.00	£20.00
Signed, numbered hardcover				£5.00	£15.00	£25.00

DIRTY PAIR III: A PLAGUE OF ANGELS
Eclipse,MS; 1 Jul 1990-5 Sep 1991

	$Good	$Fine	$N.Mint	£Good	£Fine	£N.Mint
1-5 ND	$0.40	$1.20	$2.00	£0.25	£0.75	£1.25
Title Value:	$2.00	$6.00	$10.00	£1.25	£3.75	£6.25
The Dirty Pair Book Three: A Plague of Angels (1994)						
Trade paperback reprints mini-series; black and white				£1.70	£5.10	£8.50

Note: this edition published by Dark Horse Comics

DIRTY PAIR: FATAL BUT NOT SERIOUS
Dark Horse,MS; 1 Jul 1995-1 Nov 1995

	$Good	$Fine	$N.Mint	£Good	£Fine	£N.Mint
1-2 ND Adam Warren script and art	$0.60	$1.80	$3.00	£0.40	£1.20	£2.00
3-4 ND	$0.60	$1.80	$3.00	£0.40	£1.20	£2.00
Title Value:	$2.40	$7.20	$12.00	£1.60	£4.80	£8.00

DIRTY PAIR: SIM HELL
Dark Horse,MS; 1 May 1993-4 Aug 1993

	$Good	$Fine	$N.Mint	£Good	£Fine	£N.Mint
1-4 ND Adam Warren script/art	$0.45	$1.35	$2.25	£0.30	£0.90	£1.50
Title Value:	$1.80	$5.40	$9.00	£1.20	£3.60	£6.00
The Dirty Pair: Sim Hell (Nov 1994)						
Trade paperback reprints mini-series, painted cover by Adam Warren				£1.70	£5.10	£8.50

DIRTY PICTURES
Aircel; 1 Apr 1991

	$Good	$Fine	$N.Mint	£Good	£Fine	£N.Mint
1 ND black and white illustrations from "spicy" 1930s pulp fiction	$0.40	$1.20	$2.00	£0.25	£0.75	£1.25
Title Value:	$0.40	$1.20	$2.00	£0.25	£0.75	£1.25

DIRTY PLOTTE
Drawn and Quarterly; 1 1990-present

	$Good	$Fine	$N.Mint	£Good	£Fine	£N.Mint
1 ND Julie Doucet script and art begins; black and white	$0.90	$2.70	$4.50	£0.60	£1.80	£3.00
2 ND	$0.70	$2.10	$3.50	£0.50	£1.50	£2.50
3-4 ND	$0.60	$1.80	$3.00	£0.40	£1.20	£2.00
4 2nd printing, ND (Jan 1995)	$0.45	$1.35	$2.25	£0.30	£0.90	£1.50
5-9 ND	$0.60	$1.80	$3.00	£0.40	£1.20	£2.00
Title Value:	$6.25	$18.75	$31.25	£4.20	£12.60	£21.00

DISHMAN, THE MUNDANE ADVENTURES OF
McLeod; 1 Aug 1985-3 Aug 1986; Eclipse; 1 Sep 1988

	$Good	$Fine	$N.Mint	£Good	£Fine	£N.Mint
1 ND mini-comic (500 copies)	$0.30	$0.90	$1.50	£0.20	£0.60	£1.00
1 2nd printing ND	$0.15	$0.45	$0.75	£0.10	£0.35	£0.60
1 3rd printing ND	$0.15	$0.45	$0.75	£0.10	£0.30	£0.50
2 ND mini-comic (1000 copies)	$0.30	$0.90	$1.50	£0.20	£0.60	£1.00
2 2nd printing ND	$0.15	$0.45	$0.75	£0.10	£0.30	£0.50
3 ND full size comic, reprints #1,2	$0.30	$0.90	$1.50	£0.20	£0.60	£1.00
Title Value:	$1.35	$4.05	$6.75	£0.90	£2.75	£4.60

DISNEY AFTERNOON
Marvel Comics Group; 1 Nov 1994-10 Sep 1995

	$Good	$Fine	$N.Mint	£Good	£Fine	£N.Mint
1-10 ND	$0.30	$0.90	$1.50	£0.20	£0.60	£1.00
Title Value:	$3.00	$9.00	$15.00	£2.00	£6.00	£10.00

DISNEY COMIC ALBUM
Gladstone/Disney; 1 Jul 1990-8 1991

	$Good	$Fine	$N.Mint	£Good	£Fine	£N.Mint
1 ND Donald Duck/Gyro Gearloose	$0.30	$0.90	$1.50	£0.20	£0.60	£1.00
2 ND Uncle Scrooge	$0.30	$0.90	$1.50	£0.20	£0.60	£1.00
3 ND 64pgs, Donald Duck	$0.75	$2.25	$3.75	£0.50	£1.50	£2.50
4 ND 64pgs, Mickey Mouse/Phantom Blot	$0.75	$2.25	$3.75	£0.50	£1.50	£2.50
5 ND 64pgs, Chip 'N Dale, all new stories	$0.75	$2.25	$3.75	£0.50	£1.50	£2.50
6 ND 64pgs, Uncle Scrooge	$0.75	$2.25	$3.75	£0.50	£1.50	£2.50
7 ND 64pgs, Donald Duck	$0.75	$2.25	$3.75	£0.50	£1.50	£2.50
8 ND 64pgs, Super-Goof	$0.75	$2.25	$3.75	£0.50	£1.50	£2.50
Title Value:	$5.10	$15.30	$25.50	£3.40	£10.20	£17.00
Special (Oct 1990): Super Goof Adventures, all reprint, 64pgs				£0.90	£2.70	£4.50

Note: Carl Barks/Floyd Gottfredson reprints packaged by Gladstone for Disney, bi-weekly

DISNEY COMIC HITS
Marvel Comics Group; 1 Oct 1995-present

	$Good	$Fine	$N.Mint	£Good	£Fine	£N.Mint
1 ND Aladdin	$0.30	$0.90	$1.50	£0.20	£0.60	
2 ND Lion King: Stories from the Prideland						

	$Good	$Fine	$N.Mint	£Good	£Fine	£N.Mint
	$0.30	$0.90	$1.50	£0.20	£0.60	£1.00
3 ND Pocahontas	$0.30	$0.90	$1.50	£0.20	£0.60	£1.00
4 ND 48pgs, Disney's Toy Story movie adaptation	$0.30	$0.90	$1.50	£0.20	£0.60	£1.00
5 ND Pocahontas	$0.45	$1.35	$2.25	£0.30	£0.90	£1.50
6 ND Toy Story	$0.45	$1.35	$2.25	£0.30	£0.90	£1.50
Title Value:	$2.10	$6.30	$10.50	£1.40	£4.20	£7.00

Note: originally announced as Disney Presents

DISNEY COMICS FIRST ISSUE COLLECTORS EDITION
Disney,OS; nn 1991

	$Good	$Fine	$N.Mint	£Good	£Fine	£N.Mint
nn ND scarce in the U.K. set of six of the all-new Disney comics boxed with certificate	$7.50	$22.50	$37.50	£5.00	£15.00	£25.00
Title Value:	$7.50	$22.50	$37.50	£5.00	£15.00	£25.00

DISNEY COMICS IN 3-D
Disney,OS; 1 May 1992

	$Good	$Fine	$N.Mint	£Good	£Fine	£N.Mint
1 ND 48pgs, Barks, van Horn and Rosa art, with 3-D glasses (25% less without glasses)	$0.45	$1.35	$2.25	£0.30	£0.90	£1.50
Title Value:	$0.45	$1.35	$2.25	£0.30	£0.90	£1.50

DISNEY HOLIDAY PARADE
Disney; 1 Jan 1991-2 1991

	$Good	$Fine	$N.Mint	£Good	£Fine	£N.Mint
1 ND 64pgs	$0.45	$1.35	$2.25	£0.30	£0.90	£1.50
2 ND 64pgs, Christmas stories	$0.45	$1.35	$2.25	£0.30	£0.90	£1.50
Title Value:	$0.90	$2.70	$4.50	£0.60	£1.80	£3.00

DISNEY'S POCAHONTAS MOVIE ADAPTATION
Marvel Comics Group,OS; 1 Aug 1995

	$Good	$Fine	$N.Mint	£Good	£Fine	£N.Mint
1 ND 48pgs, adaptation of Disney film, Dan Spiegle art	$1.00	$3.00	$5.00	£0.65	£1.95	£3.25
Title Value:	$1.00	$3.00	$5.00	£0.65	£1.95	£3.25

DISNEY'S TOY STORE
Marvel Comics Group,OS; 1 Jan 1996

	$Good	$Fine	$N.Mint	£Good	£Fine	£N.Mint
1 ND adaptation of Disney film	$1.00	$3.00	$5.00	£0.65	£1.95	£3.25
Title Value:	$1.00	$3.00	$5.00	£0.65	£1.95	£3.25

DISNEYLAND BIRTHDAY PARTY
Gladstone; 1 1985

	$Good	$Fine	$N.Mint	£Good	£Fine	£N.Mint
1 ND 20pgs Carl Barks art	$1.05	$3.15	$5.25	£0.70	£2.10	£3.50
Title Value:	$1.05	$3.15	$5.25	£0.70	£2.10	£3.50

DISTANT SOIL, A
Warp Graphics,Magazine; 1 Dec 1983-10 1985

	$Good	$Fine	$N.Mint	£Good	£Fine	£N.Mint
1 ND Panda Khan appears	$0.45	$1.35	$2.25	£0.30	£0.90	£1.50
2-10 ND	$0.45	$1.35	$2.25	£0.30	£0.90	£1.50
Title Value:	$4.50	$13.50	$22.50	£3.00	£9.00	£15.00
Graphic Novel 1				£0.75	£2.25	£3.75
Graphic Album 2: Knights of the Angel				£1.50	£4.50	£7.50

Note: In October 1994, Aria Press offered the remaining copies of this Graphic Album that they had obtained from the publisher The Donning Company at $12.95

DISTANT SOIL, A (2ND SERIES)
Aria Press; 1 Aug 1991-present?

	$Good	$Fine	$N.Mint	£Good	£Fine	£N.Mint
1 ND Colleen Doran script/art begins; black and white reprints	$0.40	$1.20	$2.00	£0.25	£0.75	£1.25
1 2nd printing, ND (Sep 1991)	$0.30	$0.90	$1.50	£0.20	£0.60	£1.00
1 3rd printing ND	$0.30	$0.90	$1.50	£0.20	£0.60	£1.00
1 4th printing, ND (Sep 1995)	$0.30	$0.90	$1.50	£0.20	£0.60	£1.00
2 ND	$0.40	$1.20	$2.00	£0.25	£0.75	£1.25
2 2nd printing ND	$0.30	$0.90	$1.50	£0.20	£0.60	£1.00
3 ND	$0.40	$1.20	$2.00	£0.25	£0.75	£1.25
3 2nd printing, ND (Jan 1994)	$0.30	$0.90	$1.50	£0.20	£0.60	£1.00
4 ND	$0.40	$1.20	$2.00	£0.25	£0.75	£1.25
4 2nd printing, ND (Apr 1995)	$0.30	$0.90	$1.50	£0.20	£0.60	£1.00
5-11 ND	$0.40	$1.20	$2.00	£0.25	£0.75	£1.25
12 ND all new material begins	$0.40	$1.20	$2.00	£0.25	£0.75	£1.25
Title Value:	$6.60	$19.80	$33.00	£4.20	£12.60	£21.00
A Distant Soil Starter Pack (Jan 1994) set of the first three issues plus limited edition print				£0.80	£2.40	£4.00
Dexluxe Edition (Jan 1994), as above with another signed print and signed certificate				£3.00	£9.00	£15.00
A Distant Soil: Immigrant's Song Deluxe Graphic Novel (Oct 1995)reprints issues #1,2, pre-bagged with colour print and certificate				£2.00	£6.00	£10.00
A Distant Soil: Knights of the Angel Deluxe Graphic Novel (Dec 1994)reprints issues #3-11, pre-bagged with colour print and certificate				£2.70	£8.10	£13.50

DITKO'S WORLD
Renegade; 1 May 1986-3 Jul 1986
(see Frisky Frolics Annual, Murder, Revolver)

	$Good	$Fine	$N.Mint	£Good	£Fine	£N.Mint
1-3 ND	$0.40	$1.20	$2.00	£0.25	£0.75	£1.25
Title Value:	$1.20	$3.60	$6.00	£0.75	£2.25	£3.75

DIVA'S
Caliber Press; 1 Feb 1992-2 Mar 1992

	$Good	$Fine	$N.Mint	£Good	£Fine	£N.Mint
1-2 ND	$0.45	$1.35	$2.25	£0.30	£0.90	£1.50
Title Value:	$0.90	$2.70	$4.50	£0.60	£1.80	£3.00

DIVISION 13
Dark Horse/Comics Greatest World,MS; 1 Aug 1994-4 Nov 1994
1 ND spin-off from Comics' Greatest World series; Art Adams cover

	$Good	$Fine	$N.Mint	£Good	£Fine	£N.Mint
	$0.45	$1.35	$2.25	£0.30	£0.90	£1.50
2-4 ND	$0.45	$1.35	$2.25	£0.30	£0.90	£1.50
Title Value:	$1.80	$5.40	$9.00	£1.20	£3.60	£6.00

DJANGO & ANGEL
Caliber Press; 1 Jun 1990-5 1990
1 ND Donne Avenell script and Florenci Clave art; black and white

	$Good	$Fine	$N.Mint	£Good	£Fine	£N.Mint
	$0.30	$0.90	$1.50	£0.20	£0.60	£1.00
2-5 ND	$0.30	$0.90	$1.50	£0.20	£0.60	£1.00
Title Value:	$1.50	$4.50	$7.50	£1.00	£3.00	£5.00

DNAGENTS
Eclipse; 1 Mar 1983-24 Jul 1985

	$Good	$Fine	$N.Mint	£Good	£Fine	£N.Mint
1-17 ND	$0.30	$0.90	$1.50	£0.20	£0.60	£1.00
18 ND infinity cover						
	$0.30	$0.90	$1.50	£0.20	£0.60	£1.00
19-23 ND	$0.30	$0.90	$1.50	£0.20	£0.60	£1.00
24 ND guest art by Dan Spiegle, Dave Stevens cover; story continues in Crossfire #14						
	$0.30	$0.90	$1.50	£0.20	£0.60	£1.00
Title Value:	$7.20	$21.60	$36.00	£4.80	£14.40	£24.00

DNAGENTS, THE NEW
Eclipse; 1 Oct 1985-17 Mar 1987
1 ND Mark Evanier script begins, colour

	$Good	$Fine	$N.Mint	£Good	£Fine	£N.Mint
	$0.30	$0.90	$1.50	£0.20	£0.60	£1.00
2-8 ND	$0.30	$0.90	$1.50	£0.20	£0.60	£1.00
9 ND 1st appearance New Wave team (preview)						
	$0.30	$0.90	$1.50	£0.20	£0.60	£1.00
10 ND Airboy preview, continues in Airboy #1; Jerry Ordway cover						
	$0.30	$0.90	$1.50	£0.20	£0.60	£1.00
11 ND Summer Fun issue						
	$0.30	$0.90	$1.50	£0.20	£0.60	£1.00
12 ND	$0.30	$0.90	$1.50	£0.20	£0.60	£1.00
13-15 ND Erik Larsen cover and art						
	$0.45	$1.35	$2.25	£0.30	£0.90	£1.50
16 ND Erik Larsen art, Erik Larsen and Jerry Ordway cover						
	$0.45	$1.35	$2.25	£0.30	£0.90	£1.50
17 ND Erik Larsen cover and art						
	$0.45	$1.35	$2.25	£0.30	£0.90	£1.50
Title Value:	$5.85	$17.55	$29.25	£3.90	£11.70	£19.50

DOC SAMSON
Marvel Comics Group,MS; 1 Jan 1996-4 Apr 1996
1-2 ND She-Hulk appears, Ken Lashley art

	$Good	$Fine	$N.Mint	£Good	£Fine	£N.Mint
	$0.40	$1.20	$2.00	£0.25	£0.75	£1.25
3 ND Punisher appears, Ken Lashley art						
	$0.40	$1.20	$2.00	£0.25	£0.75	£1.25
4 ND Ken Lashley art						
	$0.40	$1.20	$2.00	£0.25	£0.75	£1.25
Title Value:	$1.60	$4.80	$8.00	£1.00	£3.00	£5.00

DOC SAVAGE
DC Comics; 1 Nov 1988-24 Sep 1990

	$Good	$Fine	$N.Mint	£Good	£Fine	£N.Mint
1-16 ND	$0.25	$0.75	$1.25	£0.15	£0.45	£0.75
17-18 ND X-over with Shadow Strikes #5, 6						
	$0.25	$0.75	$1.25	£0.15	£0.45	£0.75
19-24 ND	$0.25	$0.75	$1.25	£0.15	£0.45	£0.75
Title Value:	$6.00	$18.00	$30.00	£3.60	£10.80	£18.00

Note: Deluxe Format, Baxter paper.

DOC SAVAGE
Gold Key; 1 Nov 1966
1 very scarce in the U.K. though distributed on the news-stands

	$Good	$Fine	$N.Mint	£Good	£Fine	£N.Mint
	$10.00	$30.00	$60.00	£6.50	£20.00	£40.00
Title Value:	$10.00	$30.00	$60.00	£6.50	£20.00	£40.00

DOC SAVAGE
Marvel Comics Group; 1 Nov 1972-8 Jan 1974
(see DC series)

	$Good	$Fine	$N.Mint	£Good	£Fine	£N.Mint
1 ND	$0.80	$2.40	$4.00	£0.50	£1.50	£2.50
2-3 ND Steranko covers						
	$0.60	$1.80	$3.00	£0.40	£1.20	£2.00
4-8 ND	$0.45	$1.35	$2.25	£0.30	£0.90	£1.50
Title Value:	$4.25	$12.75	$21.25	£2.80	£8.40	£14.00

Note: Pulp novels adapted as follows: **1, 2** The Man of Bronze; **3, 4** Death in Silver; **5, 6** The Monsters; **7, 8** Brand of the Werewolf. Tom Palmer inks throughout.

DOC SAVAGE (LIMITED SERIES)
DC Comics,MS; 1 Jul 1987-4 Oct 1987
1-4 Adam & Andy Kubert art

	$Good	$Fine	$N.Mint	£Good	£Fine	£N.Mint
	$0.30	$0.90	$1.50	£0.20	£0.60	£1.00
Title Value:	$1.20	$3.60	$6.00	£0.80	£2.40	£4.00

DOC SAVAGE (MAGAZINE SERIES)
Marvel Comics Group,Magazine; 1 Aug 1975-8 Apr 1977
1 ND Doug Moench scripts and Tony DeZuniga art begins, painted covers by Ken Barr; cover from film poster

	$Good	$Fine	$N.Mint	£Good	£Fine	£N.Mint
	$0.45	$1.35	$2.25	£0.30	£0.90	£1.50
2 interview with Ron Ely and Doc Savage movie						
	$0.40	$1.20	$2.00	£0.25	£0.75	£1.25
3-8	$0.40	$1.20	$2.00	£0.25	£0.75	£1.25
Title Value:	$3.25	$9.75	$16.25	£2.05	£6.15	£10.25

DOC SAVAGE ANNUAL
DC Comics; 1 Jun 1989

	$Good	$Fine	$N.Mint	£Good	£Fine	£N.Mint
1 ND 48pgs	$0.60	$1.80	$3.00	£0.40	£1.20	£2.00
Title Value:	$0.60	$1.80	$3.00	£0.40	£1.20	£2.00

DOC SAVAGE GIANT SIZE
Marvel Comics Group; 1 1975
1 68pgs, reprints issues #1, #2

	$Good	$Fine	$N.Mint	£Good	£Fine	£N.Mint
	$1.05	$3.15	$5.25	£0.70	£2.10	£3.50
Title Value:	$1.05	$3.15	$5.25	£0.70	£2.10	£3.50

DOC SAVAGE: CURSE OF THE FIRE GOD
Dark Horse,MS; 1 Sep 1995-4 Dec 1995
1-4 ND Steve Vance script, Pat Broderick art

	$Good	$Fine	$N.Mint	£Good	£Fine	£N.Mint
	$0.60	$1.80	$3.00	£0.40	£1.20	£2.00
Title Value:	$2.40	$7.20	$12.00	£1.60	£4.80	£8.00

DOC SAVAGE: DOOM DYNASTY
Millennium,MS; 1 May 1992-2 Jun 1992
1-2 ND Brian Stelfreeze cover

	$Good	$Fine	$N.Mint	£Good	£Fine	£N.Mint
	$0.45	$1.35	$2.25	£0.30	£0.90	£1.50
Title Value:	$0.90	$2.70	$4.50	£0.60	£1.80	£3.00

DOC SAVAGE: MAN OF BRONZE
Millennium,MS; 1 Dec 1991-4 Mar 1992
1 ND Brian Stelfreeze cover

	$Good	$Fine	$N.Mint	£Good	£Fine	£N.Mint
	$0.45	$1.35	$2.25	£0.30	£0.90	£1.50
2-4 ND	$0.45	$1.35	$2.25	£0.30	£0.90	£1.50
Title Value:	$1.80	$5.40	$9.00	£1.20	£3.60	£6.00

DOC SAVAGE: REPEL
Millennium,MS; 1 Dec 1992-2 Jan 1993

	$Good	$Fine	$N.Mint	£Good	£Fine	£N.Mint
1-2 ND	$0.45	$1.35	$2.25	£0.30	£0.90	£1.50
Title Value:	$0.90	$2.70	$4.50	£0.60	£1.80	£3.00

DOC SAVAGE: THE DEVIL'S THOUGHTS
Millennium,MS; 1 Aug 1992-3 Oct 1992

	$Good	$Fine	$N.Mint	£Good	£Fine	£N.Mint
1-3 ND	$0.45	$1.35	$2.25	£0.30	£0.90	£1.50
Title Value:	$1.35	$4.05	$6.75	£0.90	£2.70	£4.50

DOC SAVAGE: THE MANUAL OF BRONZE
Millennium,OS; 1 Aug 1992
1 ND features art by Tim Truman and Adam Hughes, cover by Brian Stelfreeze

	$Good	$Fine	$N.Mint	£Good	£Fine	£N.Mint
	$0.45	$1.35	$2.25	£0.30	£0.90	£1.50
	$0.45	$1.35	$2.25	£0.30	£0.90	£1.50

DOCTOR CHAOS
Triumphant Comics; 0 Jun 1994; 1 Nov 1993-12 Oct 1994
0 origin of Doctor Chaos

	$Good	$Fine	$N.Mint	£Good	£Fine	£N.Mint
	$0.30	$0.90	$1.50	£0.20	£0.60	£1.00
0 Signed Edition (Oct 1994) - pre-bagged with mini-poster photo-print and backing board						
	$0.90	$2.70	$4.50	£0.60	£1.80	£3.00
1 serially numbered at top of cover; Unleashed X-over						
	$0.30	$0.90	$1.50	£0.20	£0.60	£1.00
2-3	$0.30	$0.90	$1.50	£0.20	£0.60	£1.00
3 Signed Edition with mini-poster photo-print; pre-bagged with backing board						
	$0.90	$2.70	$4.50	£0.60	£1.80	£3.00
4	$0.30	$0.90	$1.50	£0.20	£0.60	£1.00
4 Limited Edition - signed by Adam Post and Eric Shefferman with Doctor Chaos mini-print. 18,000 print run						
	$0.90	$2.70	$4.50	£0.60	£1.80	£3.00
5-9	$0.30	$0.90	$1.50	£0.20	£0.60	£1.00
10 dual issue with Company X #3 (Note: there is only one issue between the two titles)						
	$0.30	$0.90	$1.50	£0.20	£0.60	£1.00
11 dual issue with Company X #4 (Note: there is only one issue between the two titles)						
	$0.30	$0.90	$1.50	£0.20	£0.60	£1.00
12	$0.30	$0.90	$1.50	£0.20	£0.60	£1.00
Title Value:	$6.60	$19.80	$33.00	£4.40	£13.20	£22.00

Note: All Non-Distributed on news-stands in the U.K.

DOCTOR FATE
DC Comics; 1 Winter 1988-41 Jun 1992
1 "Return Of Dr.Fate" on cover

	$Good	$Fine	$N.Mint	£Good	£Fine	£N.Mint
	$0.25	$0.75	$1.25	£0.15	£0.45	£0.75
2-14	$0.25	$0.75	$1.25	£0.15	£0.45	£0.75
15 Justice League International appears						
	$0.25	$0.75	$1.25	£0.15	£0.45	£0.75
16-18	$0.25	$0.75	$1.25	£0.15	£0.45	£0.75
19-20 guest stars Phantom Stranger						
	$0.25	$0.75	$1.25	£0.15	£0.45	£0.75
21-24	$0.25	$0.75	$1.25	£0.15	£0.45	£0.75
25 1st appearance new Dr. Fate (female); new direction/creative team						
	$0.25	$0.75	$1.25	£0.15	£0.45	£0.75
26-31	$0.25	$0.75	$1.25	£0.15	£0.45	£0.75
32-33 War of the Gods tie-in						
	$0.25	$0.75	$1.25	£0.15	£0.45	£0.75
34-39	$0.25	$0.75	$1.25	£0.15	£0.45	£0.75
40 Wonder Woman appears						
	$0.25	$0.75	$1.25	£0.15	£0.45	£0.75
41	$0.25	$0.75	$1.25	£0.15	£0.45	£0.75
Title Value:	$10.25	$30.75	$51.25	£6.15	£18.45	£30.75

Note: New Format

DOCTOR FATE (LIMITED SERIES)
DC Comics,MS; 1 Jul 1987-4 Oct 1987

	$Good	$Fine	$N.Mint	£Good	£Fine	£N.Mint
1-4 Keith Giffen art	$0.40	$1.20	$2.00	£0.25	£0.75	£1.25
Title Value:	$1.60	$4.80	$8.00	£1.00	£3.00	£5.00

DOCTOR FATE ANNUAL
DC Comics; 1 Sep 1989-present

	$Good	$Fine	$N.Mint	£Good	£Fine	£N.Mint
1 ND	$0.45	$1.35	$2.25	£0.30	£0.90	£1.50
Title Value:	$0.45	$1.35	$2.25	£0.30	£0.90	£1.50

DOCTOR FATE, THE IMMORTAL
DC Comics,MS; 1 Jan 1985-3 Mar 1985
1 Walt Simonson reprint from First Issue Special #9 plus Golden Age reprint, also included Dr. Fate by Staton

	$Good	$Fine	$N.Mint	£Good	£Fine	£N.Mint
	$0.30	$0.90	$1.50	£0.20	£0.60	£1.00
2 Giffen part reprint						
	$0.30	$0.90	$1.50	£0.20	£0.60	£1.00
3 reprints	$0.30	$0.90	$1.50	£0.20	£0.60	£1.00
Title Value:	$0.90	$2.70	$4.50	£0.60	£1.80	£3.00

Note: issues 2 and 3 reprint back-up stories from Flash #306-#313

DOCTOR GIGGLES
Dark Horse,MS; 1,2 Dec 1992

	$Good	$Fine	$N.Mint	£Good	£Fine	£N.Mint
1-2 ND adaptation of horror film	$0.45	$1.35	$2.25	£0.30	£0.90	£1.50
Title Value:	$0.90	$2.70	$4.50	£0.60	£1.80	£3.00

DOCTOR GORPON
Eternity,MS; 1 Aug 1991-3 Oct 1991

	$Good	$Fine	$N.Mint	£Good	£Fine	£N.Mint
1-3 ND	$0.45	$1.35	$2.25	£0.30	£0.90	£1.50
Title Value:	$1.35	$4.05	$6.75	£0.90	£2.70	£4.50

DOCTOR MIRAGE, THE SECOND LIFE OF
Valiant; 1 Nov 1993-19 Jun 1995

	$Good	$Fine	$N.Mint	£Good	£Fine	£N.Mint
1 Master D'Arque appears; Bernard Chang art begins	$0.30	$0.90	$1.50	£0.20	£0.60	£1.00
2-3 Master D'Arque appears	$0.30	$0.90	$1.50	£0.20	£0.60	£1.00
4-6	$0.30	$0.90	$1.50	£0.20	£0.60	£1.00
7 with free Upper Deck trading card	$0.30	$0.90	$1.50	£0.20	£0.60	£1.00
8-10	$0.30	$0.90	$1.50	£0.20	£0.60	£1.00
11 Chaos Effect tie-in	$0.30	$0.90	$1.50	£0.20	£0.60	£1.00
12-19	$0.30	$0.90	$1.50	£0.20	£0.60	£1.00
Title Value:	$6.75	$17.10	$28.50	£3.80	£11.40	£19.00

Note: all Non-Distributed at the news-stands in the U.K.

DOCTOR OCCULT (VERTIGO VISIONS)
DC Comics/Vertigo,OS; 1 Jul 1994

	$Good	$Fine	$N.Mint	£Good	£Fine	£N.Mint
1 ND 64pgs	$0.80	$2.40	$4.00	£0.50	£1.50	£2.50
Title Value:	$0.80	$2.40	$4.00	£0.50	£1.50	£2.50

DOCTOR SOLAR MAN OF THE ATOM, THE ORIGINAL
Valiant/Western Publishing; 1 Apr 1995-3 Jun 1995

	$Good	$Fine	$N.Mint	£Good	£Fine	£N.Mint
1 ND reprints from the Gold Key series begin; Paul Smith cover	$0.45	$1.35	$2.25	£0.30	£0.90	£1.50
2-3 ND reprints from the Gold Key series begin; Dave Ross cover	$0.45	$1.35	$2.25	£0.30	£0.90	£1.50
Title Value:	$1.35	$4.05	$6.75	£0.90	£2.70	£4.50

DOCTOR SOLAR, MAN OF THE ATOM
Gold Key; 1 Oct 1962-27 Apr 1969; Whitman; 28 Apr 1981-31 1982

	$Good	$Fine	$N.Mint	£Good	£Fine	£N.Mint
1 distributed in the U.K.	$43.00	$125.00	$300.00	£29.00	£85.00	£200.00
2 distributed in the U.K.	$16.50	$50.00	$100.00	£10.50	£33.00	£65.00
3-5 distributed in the U.K.	$10.50	$33.00	$65.00	£7.50	£22.50	£45.00
6-10 distributed in the U.K.	$7.00	$21.00	$42.50	£4.15	£12.50	£25.00
11-14 distributed in the U.K.	$5.75	$17.50	$35.00	£3.30	£10.00	£20.00
15 distributed in the U.K.	$7.00	$21.00	$42.50	£4.55	£13.50	£27.50
16-20 distributed in the U.K.	$7.00	$21.00	$35.00	£4.00	£12.00	£20.00
21-27 distributed in the U.K.	$3.75	$11.00	$22.50	£2.50	£7.50	£15.00
28 scarce in the U.K. line drawn covers and new logo begins; Solar by Roger McKenzie and Frank Bolle begins	$2.40	$7.00	$12.00	£1.20	£3.60	£6.00
29 scarce in the U.K. Magnus Robot Fighter back-up and his origin re-told	$2.40	$7.00	$12.00	£1.20	£3.60	£6.00
30 scarce in the U.K. Magnus Robot Fighter back-up	$2.40	$7.00	$12.00	£1.20	£3.60	£6.00
31 very scarce in the U.K. Magnus Robot Fighter back-up	$2.40	$7.00	$12.00	£1.40	£4.20	£7.00
Title Value:	$226.85	$680.00	$1373.00	£143.00	£429.00	£862.50

Note: painted covers #1-27 and also back cover pin-ups without cover logo

DOCTOR STRANGE (1ST SERIES)
Marvel Comics Group; 169 Jun 1968-183 Nov 1969
(formerly Strange Tales)
(see Marvel Fanfare, Marvel Graphic Novel, Marvel Premiere, Marvel Treasury Edition, Strange Tales 2nd Series)

	$Good	$Fine	$N.Mint	£Good	£Fine	£N.Mint
169 origin retold	$20.00	$60.00	$140.00	£11.00	£34.00	£80.00
170-175	$10.00	$30.00	$60.00	£4.15	£12.50	£25.00
176	$6.25	$18.50	$37.50	£3.30	£10.00	£20.00
177 new costume	$6.25	$18.50	$37.50	£3.30	£10.00	£20.00
178	$6.25	$18.50	$37.50	£3.30	£10.00	£20.00
179 very LD all reprint from Spiderman Annual #2, Ditko art	$6.25	$18.50	$37.50	£3.65	£11.00	£22.00
180 scarce in the U.K. part photo cover	$6.25	$18.50	$37.50	£3.65	£11.00	£22.00
181 ND	$6.25	$18.50	$37.50	£3.65	£11.00	£22.00
182 scarce in the U.K. Dr. Strange vs. Juggernaut	$6.25	$18.50	$37.50	£3.30	£10.00	£20.00
183 scarce in the U.K.	$6.25	$18.50	$37.50	£3.30	£10.00	£20.00
Title Value:	$130.00	$388.00	$730.00	£63.35	£192.00	£396.00

DOCTOR STRANGE (2ND SERIES)
Marvel Comics Group; 1 Jun 1974-81 Feb 1987

	$Good	$Fine	$N.Mint	£Good	£Fine	£N.Mint
1 ND scarce in the U.K. Brunner art	$4.50	$13.50	$22.50	£3.00	£9.00	£15.00
2 ND Defenders appear, Brunner art	$2.50	$7.50	$15.00	£1.65	£5.00	£10.00
3 ND 2pgs Brunner art, rest reprint	$1.65	$5.00	$10.00	£1.05	£3.25	£6.50
4-5 Brunner art	$1.30	$4.00	$8.00	£0.80	£2.50	£5.00
6-10	$1.20	$3.60	$6.00	£0.80	£2.40	£4.00
11-12	$0.90	$2.70	$4.50	£0.60	£1.80	£3.00
13 Gene Colan art	$0.90	$2.70	$4.50	£0.60	£1.80	£3.00
14 Dracula appears	$1.05	$3.15	$5.25	£0.70	£2.10	£3.50
15-16	$0.80	$2.40	$4.00	£0.50	£1.50	£2.50
17 Gene Colan art	$0.80	$2.40	$4.00	£0.50	£1.50	£2.50
18-20	$0.80	$2.40	$4.00	£0.50	£1.50	£2.50
21 reprints origin from Strange Tales #169	$0.60	$1.80	$3.00	£0.40	£1.20	£2.00
22 ND scarce in the U.K. Brunner cover	$0.80	$2.40	$4.00	£0.50	£1.50	£2.50
23-24 ND Jim Starlin art	$0.60	$1.80	$3.00	£0.50	£1.50	£2.50
25 ND	$0.60	$1.80	$3.00	£0.50	£1.50	£2.50
26 Jim Starlin art	$0.55	$1.65	$2.75	£0.35	£1.05	£1.75
27-30	$0.55	$1.65	$2.75	£0.35	£1.05	£1.75
31-45	$0.45	$1.35	$2.25	£0.30	£0.90	£1.50
46 LD in the U.K. Golden art	$0.40	$1.20	$2.00	£0.25	£0.75	£1.25
47 LD in the U.K.	$0.40	$1.20	$2.00	£0.25	£0.75	£1.25
48-50 LD in the U.K. Rogers art	$0.45	$1.35	$2.25	£0.30	£0.90	£1.50
51-53 ND Rogers art	$0.40	$1.20	$2.00	£0.25	£0.75	£1.25
54 LD in the U.K. Paul Smith art	$0.45	$1.35	$2.25	£0.30	£0.90	£1.50
55 LD in the U.K. Golden art	$0.40	$1.20	$2.00	£0.25	£0.75	£1.25

Destroyer Duck #1

Doc Savage Giant Size #1

Doctor Solar #29

MINT = 100% / NEAR MINT (inc. +/-) = 90–99% / VERY FINE (inc. +/-) = 75–89% / FINE (inc. +/-) = 55–74%
VERY GOOD (inc. +/-) = 35–54% / GOOD (inc. +/-) = 15–34% / FAIR = 5–14% / POOR = 1–4%

307

	$Good	$Fine	$N.Mint	£Good	£Fine	£N.Mint
56 LD in the U.K. origin retold, Paul Smith art	$0.45	$1.35	$2.25	£0.30	£0.90	£1.50
57-61 LD in the U.K.	$0.40	$1.20	$2.00	£0.25	£0.75	£1.25
62 LD in the U.K. Dracula appears, death of all vampires	$0.60	$1.80	$3.00	£0.40	£1.20	£2.00
63-64 LD in the U.K.	$0.40	$1.20	$2.00	£0.25	£0.75	£1.25
65-66 LD in the U.K. Paul Smith art	$0.45	$1.35	$2.25	£0.30	£0.90	£1.50
67 LD in the U.K.	$0.40	$1.20	$2.00	£0.25	£0.75	£1.25
68-73 LD in the U.K. Paul Smith art	$0.45	$1.35	$2.25	£0.30	£0.90	£1.50
74 LD in the U.K. Secret Wars X-over	$0.45	$1.35	$2.25	£0.30	£0.90	£1.50
75-77 ND	$0.45	$1.35	$2.25	£0.30	£0.90	£1.50
78 ND scarce in the U.K. Cloak and Dagger appear	$0.90	$2.70	$4.50	£0.60	£1.80	£3.00
79-80 ND	$0.45	$1.35	$2.25	£0.30	£0.90	£1.50
81 ND scarce in the U.K.	$0.80	$2.40	$4.00	£0.50	£1.50	£2.50
Title Value:	$54.95	$165.10	$282.00	£36.15	£108.80	£185.75

DOCTOR STRANGE (3RD SERIES)
Marvel Comics Group; 1 Oct 1988-present

	$Good	$Fine	$N.Mint	£Good	£Fine	£N.Mint
1 ND	$0.80	$2.40	$4.00	£0.40	£1.20	£2.00
2-3 ND	$0.45	$1.35	$2.25	£0.30	£0.90	£1.50
4-5 ND New Defenders appear	$0.45	$1.35	$2.25	£0.30	£0.90	£1.50
6 ND 1st appearance Dread (Mephisto's daughter)	$0.40	$1.20	$2.00	£0.25	£0.75	£1.25
7-8 ND	$0.40	$1.20	$2.00	£0.25	£0.75	£1.25
9 ND scarce in the U.K. History of Vampires begins	$0.40	$1.20	$2.00	£0.25	£0.75	£1.25
10 ND Morbius returns (cover and story)	$0.40	$1.20	$2.00	£0.25	£0.75	£1.25
11-13 ND Acts of Vengeance tie-in	$0.60	$1.80	$3.00	£0.30	£0.75	£1.25
14 ND Vampiric Verses story; Morbius appears	$0.40	$1.20	$2.00	£0.25	£0.75	£1.25
15 ND Vampiric Verses story; Morbius appears	$0.60	$1.80	$3.00	£0.30	£0.90	£1.50
16-18 ND Vampiric Verses story; Morbius appears	$0.40	$1.20	$2.00	£0.25	£0.75	£1.25
19 ND	$0.40	$1.20	$2.00	£0.25	£0.75	£1.25
20 ND Morbius appears, Gene Colan art	$0.40	$1.20	$2.00	£0.25	£0.75	£1.25
21-24 ND The Dark Wars	$0.40	$1.20	$2.00	£0.25	£0.75	£1.25
25 ND Ron Lim art	$0.40	$1.20	$2.00	£0.25	£0.75	£1.25
26-27 ND Werewolf By Night appears	$0.40	$1.20	$2.00	£0.25	£0.75	£1.25
28 ND Ghost Rider appears, X-over from Ghost Rider #12	$0.45	$1.35	$2.25	£0.30	£0.90	£1.50
29-30 ND	$0.40	$1.20	$2.00	£0.25	£0.75	£1.25
31 ND Infinity Gauntlet tie-in, Silver Surfer appears	$0.30	$0.90	$1.50	£0.20	£0.60	£1.00
32-34 ND Infinity Gauntlet tie-in	$0.30	$0.90	$1.50	£0.20	£0.60	£1.00
35 ND Infinity Gauntlet tie-in, guest stars Hulk, Thor, Dr. Doom, Firelord, Drax vs. Thanos	$0.30	$0.90	$1.50	£0.20	£0.60	£1.00
36 ND Infinity Gauntlet tie-in, Warlock appears	$0.30	$0.90	$1.50	£0.20	£0.60	£1.00
37 ND	$0.30	$0.90	$1.50	£0.20	£0.60	£1.00
38-40 ND The Fear Lords Epic	$0.30	$0.90	$1.50	£0.20	£0.60	£1.00
41 ND Wolverine appears	$0.30	$0.90	$1.50	£0.20	£0.60	£1.00
42 ND Infinity War X-over (1st), Galactus appears	$0.30	$0.90	$1.50	£0.20	£0.60	£1.00
43-45 ND Infinity War X-over, Galactus appears	$0.30	$0.90	$1.50	£0.20	£0.60	£1.00
46 ND Infinity War X-over, Scarlet Witch appears	$0.30	$0.90	$1.50	£0.20	£0.60	£1.00
47 ND Infinity War X-over	$0.30	$0.90	$1.50	£0.20	£0.60	£1.00
48-49 ND Infinity War X-over	$0.30	$0.90	$1.50	£0.20	£0.60	£1.00
50 ND Hulk, Ghost Rider and Silver Surfer appear (leads in to Secret Defenders #1), holo-grafix cover	$0.60	$1.80	$3.00	£0.40	£1.20	£2.00
51 ND	$0.30	$0.90	$1.50	£0.20	£0.60	£1.00
52 ND X-over with Morbius #9	$0.30	$0.90	$1.50	£0.20	£0.60	£1.00
53 ND new direction for title	$0.30	$0.90	$1.50	£0.20	£0.60	£1.00
54-56 ND Infinity Crusade X-over	$0.30	$0.90	$1.50	£0.20	£0.60	£1.00
57-59 ND	$0.30	$0.90	$1.50	£0.20	£0.60	£1.00
60 ND Siege of Darkness part 7; neon ink/spot varnish cover	$0.45	$1.35	$2.25	£0.30	£0.90	£1.50
61 ND Siege of Darkness part 15; neon ink/spot varnish cover	$0.45	$1.35	$2.25	£0.30	£0.90	£1.50
62-63 ND Morbius appears	$0.30	$0.90	$1.50	£0.20	£0.60	£1.00
64 ND Mark Buckingham cover	$0.30	$0.90	$1.50	£0.20	£0.60	£1.00
65 ND Mark Buckingham cover; with free Spiderman vs. Venom card sheet	$0.30	$0.90	$1.50	£0.20	£0.60	£1.00
66 ND continued in Dr. Strange Annual #4	$0.30	$0.90	$1.50	£0.20	£0.60	£1.00
67 ND Clea returns	$0.30	$0.90	$1.50	£0.20	£0.60	£1.00
68 ND	$0.30	$0.90	$1.50	£0.20	£0.60	£1.00
69 ND Polaris appears	$0.30	$0.90	$1.50	£0.20	£0.60	£1.00
70-71 ND Hulk guest-stars	$0.30	$0.90	$1.50	£0.20	£0.60	£1.00
72-74 ND Last Rites story, metallic ink cover	$0.40	$1.20	$2.00	£0.25	£0.75	£1.25
75 ND 48pgs, Last Rites (conclusion)	$0.45	$1.35	$2.25	£0.30	£0.90	£1.50
75 ND Enhanced Cover Edition - prismatic-foil stamped cover	$0.80	$2.40	$4.00	£0.50	£1.50	£2.50
76 ND new look/new costume begins	$0.40	$1.20	$2.00	£0.25	£0.75	£1.25
77-79 ND	$0.40	$1.20	$2.00	£0.25	£0.75	£1.25
80 ND Warren Ellis script, Mark Buckingham and Kev Sutherland art begin	$0.40	$1.20	$2.00	£0.25	£0.75	£1.25
81 ND Over The Edge tie-in, Punisher, Ghost Rider and Nick Fury appear	$0.40	$1.20	$2.00	£0.25	£0.75	£1.25
82-83 ND	$0.40	$1.20	$2.00	£0.25	£0.75	£1.25
84 ND J.M. DeMatteis scripts with Mark Buckingham and Kev Sutherland art begins	$0.40	$1.20	$2.00	£0.25	£0.75	£1.25
85-87 ND	$0.40	$1.20	$2.00	£0.25	£0.75	£1.25
Title Value:	$33.60	$100.80	$166.00	£21.10	£63.30	£105.50

Note: issue #50 has been recorded with a normal non-holo grafix cover and a recorded sale of £10.00: an unknown and obviously very limited quantity slipped through the full production process.

DOCTOR STRANGE ANNUAL
Marvel Comics Group; 1 1976; 2 Jun 1992-present

	$Good	$Fine	$N.Mint	£Good	£Fine	£N.Mint
1 ND 52pgs, P. Craig Russell art	$0.90	$2.70	$4.50	£0.60	£1.80	£3.00
2 ND Return of the Defenders part 4 (conclusion)	$0.45	$1.35	$2.25	£0.30	£0.90	£1.50
3 ND 64pgs, pre-bagged with trading card introducing Killiam	$0.45	$1.35	$2.25	£0.30	£0.90	£1.50
4 ND 64pgs, Mark Buckingham cover	$0.45	$1.35	$2.25	£0.30	£0.90	£1.50
Title Value:	$2.25	$6.75	$11.25	£1.50	£4.50	£7.50

DOCTOR STRANGE ASHCAN
Marvel Comics Group, OS; nn Apr 1995

	$Good	$Fine	$N.Mint	£Good	£Fine	£N.Mint
1 ND 16pgs, black and white; previews changes and new costume in the current issue of the 3rd series	$0.15	$0.45	$0.75	£0.10	£0.30	£0.50
Title Value:	$0.15	$0.45	$0.75	£0.10	£0.30	£0.50

DOCTOR STRANGE CLASSICS
Marvel Comics Group; 1 Mar 1984-4 Jun 1984

	$Good	$Fine	$N.Mint	£Good	£Fine	£N.Mint
1-4 ND Steve Ditko reprint	$0.40	$1.20	$2.00	£0.25	£0.75	£1.25
Title Value:	$1.60	$4.80	$8.00	£1.00	£3.00	£5.00

DOCTOR STRANGE GIANT SIZE
Marvel Comics Group; 1 Nov 1975

	$Good	$Fine	$N.Mint	£Good	£Fine	£N.Mint
1 ND scarce in the U.K. 68pgs, all reprint	$1.50	$4.50	$7.50	£1.00	£3.00	£5.00
Title Value:	$1.50	$4.50	$7.50	£1.00	£3.00	£5.00

DOCTOR STRANGE SPECIAL EDITION
Marvel Comics Group; 1 Feb 1983

	$Good	$Fine	$N.Mint	£Good	£Fine	£N.Mint
1 ND features Silver Dagger, reprints Dr. Strange #1, #2, #4, #5 & Strange Tales #127, Wrightson cover	$0.60	$1.80	$3.00	£0.40	£1.20	£2.00
Title Value:	$0.60	$1.80	$3.00	£0.40	£1.20	£2.00

Note: high-quality paper.

DOCTOR STRANGE/GHOST RIDER SPECIAL
Marvel Comics Group, OS; 1 Apr 1991

	$Good	$Fine	$N.Mint	£Good	£Fine	£N.Mint
1 ND market-tester reprint of Doctor Strange #28 with new logo	$0.45	$1.35	$2.25	£0.30	£0.90	£1.50
Title Value:	$0.45	$1.35	$2.25	£0.30	£0.90	£1.50

DOCTOR WHO
Marvel Comics Group; 1 Oct 1984-23 Aug 1986
(see also Marvel Premiere #57-60)

	$Good	$Fine	$N.Mint	£Good	£Fine	£N.Mint
1 ND Dave Gibbons art begins (reprints)	$0.30	$0.90	$1.50	£0.20	£0.60	£1.00
2-8 ND	$0.30	$0.90	$1.50	£0.20	£0.60	£1.00
9 ND scarce in the U.K.	$0.45	$1.35	$2.25	£0.30	£0.90	£1.50
10-23 ND	$0.30	$0.90	$1.50	£0.20	£0.60	£1.00
Title Value:	$7.05	$21.15	$35.25	£4.70	£14.10	£23.50

Note: all reprints from British Doctor Who Magazine, Dave Gibbons art.

DOCTOR ZERO
Marvel Comics Group/Epic; 1 Apr 1988-8 Jun 1989

	$Good	$Fine	$N.Mint	£Good	£Fine	£N.Mint
1-3 ND Cowan/Sienkiewicz art	$0.30	$0.90	$1.50	£0.20	£0.60	£1.00
4 ND	$0.30	$0.90	$1.50	£0.20	£0.60	£1.00
5 ND DS, Brett Ewins/Steve Dillon art	$0.30	$0.90	$1.50	£0.20	£0.60	£1.00
6-8 ND	$0.30	$0.90	$1.50	£0.20	£0.60	£1.00
Title Value:	$2.40	$7.20	$12.00	£1.60	£4.80	£8.00

	$Good	$Fine	$N.Mint	£Good	£Fine	£N.Mint

DODEKAIN

Antarctic Press,MS; 1 Nov 1994-8 Jun 1995

1-8 ND Masajuki Fujiwara script and art; black and white

| | $0.45 | $1.35 | $2.25 | £0.30 | £0.90 | £1.50 |
| Title Value: | $3.60 | $10.80 | $18.00 | £2.40 | £7.20 | £12.00 |

DOG

Rebel Studios; 1 Aug 1991

1 ND Joe Vigil script/art

| | $0.45 | $1.35 | $2.25 | £0.30 | £0.90 | £1.50 |
| Title Value: | $0.45 | $1.35 | $2.25 | £0.30 | £0.90 | £1.50 |

DOG BOY

Fantagraphics; 1 Mar 1987-10 1988

1-10 ND Steve Lafler script/art; black and white

| | $1.20 | | $2.00 | £0.25 | £0.75 | £1.25 |
| Title Value: | $4.00 | $12.00 | $20.00 | £2.50 | £7.50 | £12.50 |

DOGS OF WAR

Defiant; 1 Apr 1994-8 Nov 1994

1-4 ND | $0.30 | $0.90 | $1.50 | £0.20 | £0.60 | £1.00 |

5 ND Schism X-over

	$0.30	$0.90	$1.50	£0.20	£0.60	£1.00
6-8 ND	$0.30	$0.90	$1.50	£0.20	£0.60	£1.00
Title Value:	$2.40	$7.20	$12.00	£1.60	£4.80	£8.00

DOLL

Rip Off Press; 1 1989-8 1991?

1 ND Guy Colwell script/art begins; black and white

	$0.90	$2.70	$4.50	£0.60	£1.80	£3.00
1 2nd printing ND	$0.45	$1.35	$2.25	£0.30	£0.90	£1.50
2 ND	$0.60	$1.80	$3.00	£0.40	£1.20	£2.00
2 2nd printing ND	$0.45	$1.35	$2.25	£0.30	£0.90	£1.50
3-8 ND	$0.45	$1.35	$2.25	£0.30	£0.90	£1.50
Title Value:	$5.10	$15.30	$25.50	£3.40	£10.20	£17.00
Trade Paperback, reprints #1-3				£1.20	£3.60	£6.00

DOLL MAN

I.W. Super; 11,15,17 1963-1964

11-17 scarce in the U.K. reprint; distributed in the U.K.

| | $3.30 | $10.00 | $20.00 | £2.00 | £6.00 | £12.00 |
| Title Value: | $9.90 | $30.00 | $60.00 | £6.00 | £18.00 | £36.00 |

DOLLMAN

Eternity,MS; 1 Nov 1991-4 Feb 1991

1 ND based on US film (not released in UK); great covers!

	$0.45	$1.35	$2.25	£0.30	£0.90	£1.50
2-4 ND	$0.45	$1.35	$2.25	£0.30	£0.90	£1.50
Title Value:	$1.80	$5.40	$9.00	£1.20	£3.60	£6.00

DOMINION

Eclipse,MS; 1 Dec 1989-6 Jul 1990

1-6 ND | $0.30 | $0.90 | $1.50 | £0.20 | £0.60 | £1.00 |

| Title Value: | $1.80 | $5.40 | $9.00 | £1.20 | £3.60 | £6.00 |

DOMINION SPECIAL

Dark Horse,OS; 1 Mar 1994

1 ND black and white

| | $0.45 | $1.35 | $2.25 | £0.30 | £0.90 | £1.50 |
| Title Value: | $0.45 | $1.35 | $2.25 | £0.30 | £0.90 | £1.50 |

DOMINIQUE

Caliber Press; 1 Jul 1994

1 ND spin-off character from Dark Horse Presents

| | $0.60 | $1.80 | $3.00 | £0.40 | £1.20 | £2.00 |
| Title Value: | $0.60 | $1.80 | $3.00 | £0.40 | £1.20 | £2.00 |

DOMINIQUE: KILLZONE

Caliber Press; 1 Apr 1995

1 ND Negative Burn anthology spin-off; black and white

| | $0.60 | $1.80 | $3.00 | £0.40 | £1.20 | £2.00 |
| Title Value: | $0.60 | $1.80 | $3.00 | £0.40 | £1.20 | £2.00 |

DOMINO CHANCE

Chance Ent.; 1 May/Jun 1982-9 May 1985

1 ND | $0.35 | $1.05 | $1.75 | £0.25 | £0.75 | £1.25 |

1 ND reprint (May 1985)

| | $0.30 | $0.90 | $1.50 | £0.20 | £0.60 | £1.00 |
| 2-6 ND | $0.30 | $0.90 | $1.50 | £0.20 | £0.60 | £1.00 |

7 ND 1st appearance Gizmo

| | $0.30 | $0.90 | $1.50 | £0.20 | £0.60 | £1.00 |

8 ND 1st full Gizmo story

	$0.30	$0.90	$1.50	£0.20	£0.60	£1.00
9 ND	$0.30	$0.90	$1.50	£0.20	£0.60	£1.00
Title Value:	$3.05	$9.15	$15.25	£2.05	£6.15	£10.25

DOMINO CHANCE: ROACH EXTRAORDINAIRE

Amazing Comics; 1-3 1987

1-3 ND | $0.40 | $1.20 | $2.00 | £0.25 | £0.75 | £1.25 |

| Title Value: | $1.20 | $3.60 | $6.00 | £0.75 | £2.25 | £3.75 |

DOMU: A CHILD'S DREAMS

Dark Horse,MS; 1 Mar 1995-3 May 1995

1-3 ND Katsuhiro Otomo script and art

| | $1.20 | $3.60 | $6.00 | £0.80 | £2.40 | £4.00 |
| Title Value: | $3.60 | $10.80 | $18.00 | £2.40 | £7.20 | £12.00 |

DON SIMPSON'S BIZARRE HEROES

Fiasco Comics; 0 Dec 1994; 1 Jul 1994-present

0 ND (Dec 1994) | $0.60 | $1.80 | $3.00 | £0.40 | £1.20 | £2.00 |

1 ND features Megaton Man; black and white begins

| | $0.60 | $1.80 | $3.00 | £0.40 | £1.20 | £2.00 |
| 2-6 ND | $0.60 | $1.80 | $3.00 | £0.40 | £1.20 | £2.00 |

7 ND page count now down from 32 to 24 pages but printed on heavier stock paper

| | | | | £0.40 | £1.20 | £2.00 |
| 8 ND | $0.60 | $1.80 | $3.00 | £0.40 | £1.20 | £2.00 |

---

9 ND Yarn Man returns

| | $0.60 | $1.80 | $3.00 | £0.40 | £1.20 | £2.00 |
| 10 ND | $0.60 | $1.80 | $3.00 | £0.40 | £1.20 | £2.00 |

11 ND The Search for Megaton Man story

	$0.60	$1.80	$3.00	£0.40	£1.20	£2.00
12-14 ND	$0.60	$1.80	$3.00	£0.40	£1.20	£2.00
Title Value:	$9.00	$27.00	$45.00	£6.00	£18.00	£30.00

Bizarre Heroes: The Apocalypse Affiliation (May 1995)

Trade paperback reprints issues #1-4 with Larry Marder intro | | | | £1.70 | £5.10 | £8.50 |

DONALD AND MICKEY

Gladstone/Disney; 1 Aug 1992-present

1-30 ND | $0.30 | $0.90 | $1.50 | £0.20 | £0.60 | £1.00 |

| Title Value: | $9.00 | $27.00 | $45.00 | £6.00 | £18.00 | £30.00 |

DONALD DUCK

Gladstone; 246 Oct 1986-279 1989; Gladstone/Disney; 280 Aug 1993-present

(see Donald Duck Adventures, Christmas Parade, Gladstone Album Series, Walt Disney's Comics)

(previously published by Whitman)

246 scarce in the U.K. 1st Gladstone issue, 75¢

| | $0.40 | $1.20 | $2.00 | £0.60 | £1.80 | £3.00 |

247 scarce in the U.K.

| | $0.40 | $1.20 | $2.00 | £0.30 | £0.90 | £1.50 |
| 248-249 | $0.40 | $1.20 | $2.00 | £0.25 | £0.75 | £1.25 |

250 64pgs, reprints 1st Carl Barks Donald Duck

| | $0.70 | $2.10 | $3.50 | £0.50 | £1.50 | £2.50 |

251 reprints 1945 Firestone giveaway

	$0.40	$1.20	$2.00	£0.25	£0.75	£1.25
252 1st 95¢ issue	$0.40	$1.20	$2.00	£0.25	£0.75	£1.25
253	$0.40	$1.20	$2.00	£0.25	£0.75	£1.25

254 scarce in the U.K. reprints Old California

| | $0.40 | $1.20 | $2.00 | £0.25 | £0.75 | £1.25 |
| 255-256 | $0.40 | $1.20 | $2.00 | £0.25 | £0.75 | £1.25 |

257 52pgs, Summer Special

| | $0.45 | $1.35 | $2.25 | £0.30 | £0.90 | £1.50 |
| 258-263 | $0.40 | $1.20 | $2.00 | £0.25 | £0.75 | £1.25 |

264 feature on various Donald Duck artists

	$0.40	$1.20	$2.00	£0.25	£0.75	£1.25
265	$0.40	$1.20	$2.00	£0.25	£0.75	£1.25
266-277	$0.30	$0.90	$1.50	£0.20	£0.60	£1.00

278 68pgs | $0.40 | $1.20 | $2.00 | £0.25 | £0.75 | £1.25 |

| 279 | $0.30 | $0.90 | $1.50 | £0.20 | £0.60 | £1.00 |

280 Carl Barks and Al Taliaferro reprints

| | $0.30 | $0.90 | $1.50 | £0.20 | £0.60 | £1.00 |
| 281-285 | $0.30 | $0.90 | $1.50 | £0.20 | £0.60 | £1.00 |

286 64pgs, 60th anniversary tribute

| | $0.60 | $1.80 | $3.00 | £0.40 | £1.20 | £2.00 |
| 287-291 | $0.30 | $0.90 | $1.50 | £0.20 | £0.60 | £1.00 |

292 $1.95 cover begins

	$0.40	$1.20	$2.00	£0.25	£0.75	£1.25
293-294 ND	$0.40	$1.20	$2.00	£0.25	£0.75	£1.25
Title Value:	$17.75	$53.25	$88.75	£11.90	£35.70	£59.50

Note: all Non-Distributed on the news-stands in the U.K.

DONALD DUCK ADVENTURES

Gladstone; 1 Nov 1987-20 Apr 1990; 21 Aug 1993-present

1-7 ND | $0.35 | $1.05 | $1.75 | £0.25 | £0.75 | £1.25 |

8 ND Crocodile Collector by Don Rosa

| | $0.35 | $1.05 | $1.75 | £0.25 | £0.75 | £1.25 |
| 9 ND | $0.35 | $1.05 | $1.75 | £0.25 | £0.75 | £1.25 |

10 ND classic Barks cover

| | $0.35 | $1.05 | $1.75 | £0.25 | £0.75 | £1.25 |
| 11 ND | $0.25 | $0.75 | $1.25 | £0.15 | £0.45 | £0.75 |

12 ND DS Don Rosa story/art, Barks poster

| | | $1.20 | $2.00 | £0.25 | £0.75 | £1.25 |
| 13-20 ND | $0.30 | $0.90 | $1.50 | £0.20 | £0.60 | £1.00 |

21 ND Carl Barks reprint; title now re-published by Gladstone

| | $0.30 | $0.90 | $1.50 | £0.20 | £0.60 | £1.00 |

22-29 ND Carl Barks reprint

| | $0.30 | $0.90 | $1.50 | £0.20 | £0.60 | £1.00 |

30 ND 64pgs, Carl Barks reprint

	$0.60	$1.80	$3.00	£0.40	£1.20	£2.00
31-32 ND	$0.30	$0.90	$1.50	£0.20	£0.60	£1.00
33-35 ND 64pgs	$0.60	$1.80	$3.00	£0.40	£1.20	£2.00
Title Value:	$12.25	$36.75	$61.25	£8.30	£24.90	£41.50

Note: Barks art in all

DONALD DUCK ADVENTURES (2ND SERIES)

Disney; 1 Jun 1990-38 Jun 1993

1 ND Don Rosa cover/art

| | $0.30 | $0.90 | $1.50 | £0.20 | £0.60 | £1.00 |

2 ND William van Horn begins, Carl Barks reprint

| | $0.30 | $0.90 | $1.50 | £0.20 | £0.60 | £1.00 |

3 ND Carl Barks reprint

| | $0.30 | $0.90 | $1.50 | £0.20 | £0.60 | £1.00 |
| 4-20 ND | $0.30 | $0.90 | $1.50 | £0.20 | £0.60 | £1.00 |

21 ND Barks reprints

| | $0.30 | $0.90 | $1.50 | £0.20 | £0.60 | £1.00 |
| 22 ND | $0.30 | $0.90 | $1.50 | £0.20 | £0.60 | £1.00 |

23 ND Barks reprints

| | $0.30 | $0.90 | $1.50 | £0.20 | £0.60 | £1.00 |
| 24-25 ND | $0.30 | $0.90 | $1.50 | £0.20 | £0.60 | £1.00 |

26 ND reprints "Race to the South Seas" from a 1948 giveaway by Carl Barks

| | $0.30 | $0.90 | $1.50 | £0.20 | £0.60 | £1.00 |

27-29 ND Carl Barks reprints

| | $0.30 | $0.90 | $1.50 | £0.20 | £0.60 | £1.00 |

	$Good	$Fine	$N.Mint	£Good	£Fine	£N.Mint
30-38 ND	$0.30	$0.90	$1.50	£0.20	£0.60	£1.00
Title Value:	$11.40	$34.20	$57.00	£7.60	£22.80	£38.00

DONALD DUCK AND MICKEY MOUSE
Gladstone/Disney; 1 Jun 1995-present?

	$Good	$Fine	$N.Mint	£Good	£Fine	£N.Mint
1 ND new material plus Carl Barks reprints begin	$0.30	$0.90	$1.50	£0.20	£0.60	£1.00
2-3 ND	$0.30	$0.90	$1.50	£0.20	£0.60	£1.00
Title Value:	$0.90	$2.70	$4.50	£0.60	£1.80	£3.00

DONALD DUCK DIGEST
Gladstone; 1 Oct 1986-5 1987

	$Good	$Fine	$N.Mint	£Good	£Fine	£N.Mint
1-5 ND	$0.30	$0.90	$1.50	£0.20	£0.60	£1.00
Title Value:	$1.50	$4.50	$7.50	£1.00	£3.00	£5.00

DONATELLO
Mirage Studios; 1 Aug 1985
(see Teenage Mutant Ninja Turtles)

	$Good	$Fine	$N.Mint	£Good	£Fine	£N.Mint
1 ND Jack Kirby tribute, Stan Sakai pin-up	$1.20	$3.60	$6.00	£0.80	£2.40	£4.00
Title Value:	$1.20	$3.60	$6.00	£0.80	£2.40	£4.00

DOOM 2099
Marvel Comics Group; 1 Jan 1993-present

	$Good	$Fine	$N.Mint	£Good	£Fine	£N.Mint
1 ND metallic foil (silver) stamped cover; Dr. Doom arrives in the year 2099	$0.30	$0.90	$1.50	£0.20	£0.60	£1.00
2-5 ND	$0.25	$0.75	$1.25	£0.15	£0.45	£0.75
6 ND virtual reality Hulk appears	$0.25	$0.75	$1.25	£0.15	£0.45	£0.75
7 ND	$0.25	$0.75	$1.25	£0.15	£0.45	£0.75
8 ND Ravage 2099 cameo	$0.25	$0.75	$1.25	£0.15	£0.45	£0.75
9 ND	$0.25	$0.75	$1.25	£0.15	£0.45	£0.75
10-12 ND covers fit together	$0.25	$0.75	$1.25	£0.15	£0.45	£0.75
13 ND	$0.25	$0.75	$1.25	£0.15	£0.45	£0.75
14 ND Dr. Doom vs. Loki	$0.25	$0.75	$1.25	£0.15	£0.45	£0.75
15-16 ND	$0.25	$0.75	$1.25	£0.15	£0.45	£0.75
17 ND with free Spiderman and his Deadly Foes card sheet	$0.25	$0.75	$1.25	£0.15	£0.45	£0.75
18-24 ND	$0.25	$0.75	$1.25	£0.15	£0.45	£0.75
25 ND new armour	$0.45	$1.35	$2.25	£0.30	£0.90	£1.50
25 ND foil-stamped multi-level embossed cover	$0.60	$1.80	$3.00	£0.40	£1.20	£2.00
26-28 ND	$0.30	$0.90	$1.50	£0.20	£0.60	£1.00
29 ND Doom invades America; upgraded paper stock begins	$0.40	$1.20	$2.00	£0.25	£0.75	£1.25
29 ND Doom invades America; clear chromium cover and upgraded paper	$0.80	$2.40	$4.00	£0.50	£1.50	£2.50
30-31 ND	$0.40	$1.20	$2.00	£0.25	£0.75	£1.25
32-35 ND One Nation Under Doom	$0.40	$1.20	$2.00	£0.25	£0.75	£1.25
36 ND continued from 2099 Apocalypse, guest-starring X-Men 2099; continued in X-Men 2099 #27	$0.40	$1.20	$2.00	£0.25	£0.75	£1.25
37 ND guest-starring X-Men 2099; continued in X-Men 2099 #28 and 2099 Genesis	$0.40	$1.20	$2.00	£0.25	£0.75	£1.25
38 ND continued in X-Men 2099 #29	$0.40	$1.20	$2.00	£0.25	£0.75	£1.25
39 ND X-Nation tie-in, continued in X-Men 2099 #30	$0.40	$1.20	$2.00	£0.25	£0.75	£1.25
Title Value:	$13.20	$39.60	$66.00	£8.20	£24.60	£41.00

DOOM FORCE SPECIAL
DC Comics,OS; 1 Jul 1992

	$Good	$Fine	$N.Mint	£Good	£Fine	£N.Mint
1 64pgs, Grant Morrison script, parody of Marvel Comics themes and styles	$0.35	$1.05	$1.75	£0.25	£0.75	£1.25
Title Value:	$0.35	$1.05	$1.75	£0.25	£0.75	£1.25

DOOM PATROL
National Periodical Publications; 86 Mar 1964-121 Sep/Oct 1968; 122 Feb 1973-124 Jun/Jul 1973
(see Brave and the Bold, DC Special Blue Ribbon Digest 19, Showcase #94-96)
(previously My Greatest Adventure)

	$Good	$Fine	$N.Mint	£Good	£Fine	£N.Mint
86 scarce in the U.K. 1pg origin	$12.00	$37.00	$110.00	£7.75	£23.00	£70.00
87	$10.00	$30.00	$80.00	£6.25	£18.50	£50.00
88 origin the Chief	$10.50	$32.00	$85.00	£6.75	£20.50	£55.00
89-90	$10.00	$30.00	$80.00	£6.25	£18.50	£50.00
91 1st appearance Mento	$9.25	$28.00	$75.00	£6.75	£20.50	£55.00
92-98	$9.25	$28.00	$75.00	£5.50	£16.50	£45.00
99 1st appearance Beast Boy later becomes Changeling in New Teen Titans	$9.25	$28.00	$75.00	£5.50	£16.50	£45.00
100 origin Beast Boy; last Silver Age issue cover-dated December 1965	$10.00	$30.00	$80.00	£6.25	£18.50	£50.00
101	$5.00	$15.00	$40.00	£3.40	£10.00	£27.50
102 Challengers of the Unknown X-over	$5.00	$15.00	$40.00	£3.40	£10.00	£27.50
103-105	$5.00	$15.00	$40.00	£3.40	£10.00	£27.50
106 origin Negative Man	$5.00	$15.00	$40.00	£3.40	£10.00	£27.50
107-110	$5.00	$15.00	$40.00	£3.40	£10.00	£27.50
111-120	$3.75	$11.00	$30.00	£2.50	£7.50	£20.00
121 very scarce in the U.K. Doom Patrol dies	$10.00	$30.00	$80.00	£6.25	£18.50	£50.00
122 scarce in the U.K. reprint	$0.80	$2.50	$5.00	£0.65	£2.00	£4.00
123 scarce in the U.K. reprint; Negative Man appears on cover without face bandages	$0.80	$2.50	$5.00	£0.65	£2.00	£4.00
124 scarce in the U.K. reprint	$0.80	$2.50	$5.00	£0.65	£2.00	£4.00
Title Value:	$245.65	$738.50	$1985.00	£157.45	£469.50	£1277.00

FEATURES
Beast Boy in 112-115. Elasti-Girl in 89. Private World of Negative Man in 106, 107, 109, 111. Robotman in 87, 100, 101, 105.

DOOM PATROL (2ND SERIES)
DC Comics; 1 Oct 1987-87 Feb 1995

	$Good	$Fine	$N.Mint	£Good	£Fine	£N.Mint
1-5	$0.30	$0.90	$1.50	£0.20	£0.60	£1.00
6-8 Erik Larsen art	$0.30	$0.90	$1.50	£0.20	£0.60	£1.00
9 Eric Larsen art, extra 16pg Doom Patrol story insert	$0.30	$0.90	$1.50	£0.20	£0.60	£1.00
10-15 Erik Larsen art	$0.30	$0.90	$1.50	£0.20	£0.60	£1.00
16	$0.30	$0.90	$1.50	£0.20	£0.60	£1.00
17 Invasion X-over, Aquaman, Aqualad, Sea Devils appear	$0.30	$0.90	$1.50	£0.20	£0.60	£1.00
18 Invasion X-over	$0.30	$0.90	$1.50	£0.20	£0.60	£1.00
19 1st Grant Morrison story; Crawling From The Wreckage part 1 (ends #22)	$1.80	$5.25	$9.00	£1.20	£3.60	£6.00
20	$1.20	$3.60	$6.00	£0.80	£2.40	£4.00
21-25	$0.90	$2.70	$4.50	£0.60	£1.80	£3.00
26-28	$0.80	$2.40		£0.50	£1.50	£2.50
29 Simon Bisley covers begin, Superman and Justice League of America appear	$0.80	$2.40	$4.00	£0.50	£1.50	£2.50
30	$0.80	$2.40	$4.00	£0.50	£1.50	£2.50
31-35	$0.60	$1.80	$3.00	£0.40	£1.20	£2.00
36-38	$0.45	$1.35	$2.25	£0.30	£0.90	£1.50
39 preview of new series World Without End	$0.45	$1.35	$2.25	£0.30	£0.90	£1.50
40	$0.45	$1.35	$2.25	£0.30	£0.90	£1.50
41-44	$0.40	$1.20	$2.00	£0.25	£0.75	£1.25
45 Brendan McCarthy art	$0.40	$1.20	$2.00	£0.25	£0.75	£1.25
46	$0.40	$1.20	$2.00	£0.25	£0.75	£1.25
47 $1.75 covers begin	$0.40	$1.20	$2.00	£0.25	£0.75	£1.25
48-49	$0.40	$1.20	$2.00	£0.25	£0.75	£1.25
50 DS pin-ups by Bisley, Bolland and others	$0.45	$1.35	$2.25	£0.30	£0.90	£1.50
51-52	$0.40	$1.20	$2.00	£0.25	£0.75	£1.25
53 Phantom Stranger, Hellblazer, Mister E appear	$0.40	$1.20	$2.00	£0.25	£0.75	£1.25
54 photo cover	$0.40	$1.20	$2.00	£0.25	£0.75	£1.25
55-56	$0.40	$1.20	$2.00	£0.25	£0.75	£1.25
57 48pgs, true history of the Doom Patrol	$0.45	$1.35	$2.25	£0.30	£0.90	£1.50
58-62	$0.40	$1.20	$2.00	£0.25	£0.75	£1.25
63 last Grant Morrison script, last Simon Bisley cover	$0.40	$1.20	$2.00	£0.25	£0.75	£1.25
64 1st issue scripted by Rachel Pollack, Brian Bolland covers begin, 1st issue under "Vertigo" banner	$0.40	$1.20	$2.00	£0.25	£0.75	£1.25
65	$0.40	$1.20	$2.00	£0.25	£0.75	£1.25
66 $1.95 cover begins	$0.40	$1.20	$2.00	£0.25	£0.75	£1.25
67 30th anniversary appearance of The Doom Patrol	$0.40	$1.20	$2.00	£0.25	£0.75	£1.25
68	$0.40	$1.20	$2.00	£0.25	£0.75	£1.25
69 John Higgins art	$0.40	$1.20	$2.00	£0.25	£0.75	£1.25
70-74	$0.40	$1.20	$2.00	£0.25	£0.75	£1.25
75-76 The Teiresias Wars story	$0.40	$1.20	$2.00	£0.25	£0.75	£1.25
77-78 The Teiresias Wars story; cover by Brian Bolland	$0.40	$1.20	$2.00	£0.25	£0.75	£1.25
79-87	$0.40	$1.20	$2.00	£0.25	£0.75	£1.25
Title Value:	$41.05	$123.00	$205.25	£26.45	£79.35	£132.25

Note: Direct sale from issue 19 as New Format. For Mature Readers from #37.
Doom Patrol: Crawling From The Wreckage (Aug 1992)
Trade paperback, reprints issues 19-25, painted cover by Simon Bisley £2.50 — £7.50 — £12.50

DOOM PATROL AND SUICIDE SQUAD SPECIAL
DC Comics,OS; 1 1988

	$Good	$Fine	$N.Mint	£Good	£Fine	£N.Mint
1 48pgs, Erik Larsen art	$0.40	$1.20	$2.00	£0.25	£0.75	£1.25
Title Value:	$0.40	$1.20	$2.00	£0.25	£0.75	£1.25

DOOM PATROL ANNUAL
DC Comics; 1 Nov 1988-2 1989

	$Good	$Fine	$N.Mint	£Good	£Fine	£N.Mint
1 48pgs	$0.40	$1.20	$2.00	£0.25	£0.75	£1.25
2 48pgs, The Children's Crusade part 5	$0.45	$1.35	$2.25	£0.30	£0.90	£1.50
Title Value:	$0.85	$2.55	$4.25	£0.55	£1.65	£2.75

DOOM'S IV
Image; 1 Jul 1994-4 Oct 1994

	$Good	$Fine	$N.Mint	£Good	£Fine	£N.Mint
1/2 ND Marc Pacella cover art, produced in conjunction with Wizard Comics; issued in a Wizard protective Mylar with certificate of authenticity	$1.50	$4.50	$7.50	£1.00	£3.00	£5.00
1 ND Rob Liefeld script, Mark Pacella art begin	$0.45	$1.35	$2.25	£0.30	£0.90	£1.50

	$Good	$Fine	$N.Mint	£Good	£Fine	£N.Mint

1 ND variant cover; part of four interlocking covers by Rob Liefield, limited to 25% of the print run
| | $1.00 | $3.00 | $5.00 | £0.50 | £1.50 | £2.50 |
2 ND
| | $0.45 | $1.35 | $2.25 | £0.30 | £0.90 | £1.50 |
2 ND variant cover; part of four interlocking covers by Rob Liefield, limited to 25% of the print run
| | $1.00 | $3.00 | $5.00 | £0.50 | £1.50 | £2.50 |
3-4 ND
| | $0.45 | $1.35 | $2.25 | £0.30 | £0.90 | £1.50 |
Title Value:
| | $5.30 | $15.90 | $26.50 | £3.20 | £9.60 | £16.00 |

DOOM'S IV SOURCEBOOK
Image; 1 Nov 1994
1 ND information and statistics about the characters
| | $0.45 | $1.35 | $2.25 | £0.30 | £0.90 | £1.50 |
Title Value:
| | $0.45 | $1.35 | $2.25 | £0.30 | £0.90 | £1.50 |

DOOMSDAY ANNUAL
DC Comics; 1 Dec 1996
1 ND 56pgs, Year One; four stories including origin before meeting Superman; Darkseid and the Green Lantern Corps appear
| | $0.80 | $2.40 | $4.00 | £0.50 | £1.50 | £2.50 |
Title Value:
| | $0.80 | $2.40 | $4.00 | £0.50 | £1.50 | £2.50 |

DOOMSDAY PLUS ONE
Charlton; 1 Jul 1975-6 May 1976; 7 Jun 1978-12 May 1979
1 John Byrne art; distributed in the U.K.
| | $1.20 | $3.60 | $6.00 | £1.00 | £3.00 | £5.00 |
2 John Byrne art; distributed in the U.K.
| | $1.00 | $3.00 | $5.00 | £0.80 | £2.40 | £4.00 |
3 John Byrne art; distributed in the U.K.
| | $1.20 | $3.60 | $6.00 | £1.00 | £3.00 | £5.00 |
4 John Byrne art; distributed in the U.K.
| | $1.00 | $3.00 | $5.00 | £0.80 | £2.40 | £4.00 |
5 John Byrne, Steve Ditko art; distributed in the U.K.
| | $1.00 | $3.00 | $5.00 | £0.80 | £2.40 | £4.00 |
6 John Byrne art; distributed in the U.K.
| | $1.05 | $3.15 | $5.25 | £0.70 | £2.10 | £3.50 |
7 reprints #1,2,4-6; distributed in the U.K.
| | $0.60 | $1.80 | $3.00 | £0.40 | £1.20 | £2.00 |
8-12 reprints #1,2,4-6; distributed in the U.K.
| | $0.45 | $1.35 | $2.25 | £0.30 | £0.90 | £1.50 |
Title Value:
| | $9.30 | $27.90 | $46.50 | £7.00 | £21.00 | £35.00 |

DOOMSDAY SQUAD
Fantagraphics; 1 Aug 1986-7 Jun 1987
1 ND John Byrne reprints from Doomsday + 1 begin, Dalgoda back-up, new Byrne cover
| | $0.45 | $1.35 | $2.25 | £0.30 | £0.90 | £1.50 |
2 ND Lloyd Llewellyn back-up, new John Byrne cover
| | $0.45 | $1.35 | $2.25 | £0.30 | £0.90 | £1.50 |
3 ND Usagi Yojimbo back-up, Gil Kane cover
| | $0.45 | $1.35 | $2.25 | £0.30 | £0.90 | £1.50 |
4 ND Miracle Squad back-up, new Neal Adams cover
| | $0.45 | $1.35 | $2.25 | £0.30 | £0.90 | £1.50 |
5 ND Captain Jack back-up, Gil Kane cover
| | $0.45 | $1.35 | $2.25 | £0.30 | £0.90 | £1.50 |
6 ND Keif Llama back-up, Gil Kane cover
| | $0.45 | $1.35 | $2.25 | £0.30 | £0.90 | £1.50 |
7 ND scarce in the U.K.
| | $0.60 | $1.80 | $3.00 | £0.40 | £1.20 | £2.00 |
Title Value:
| | $3.30 | $9.90 | $16.50 | £2.20 | £6.60 | £11.00 |
Note: all Non-Distributed on the news-stands in the U.K.

DOORWAY TO NIGHTMARE
DC Comics; 1 Jan/Feb 1978-5 Sep/Oct 1978
(see Books of Magic, Madame Xanadu, the Unexpected)
| 1-5 | $0.40 | $1.20 | $2.00 | £0.25 | £0.75 | £1.25 |
Title Value:
| | $2.00 | $6.00 | $10.00 | £1.25 | £3.75 | £6.25 |

FEATURES
Madame Xanadu in all issues.

DOUBLE DARE ADVENTURES
Harvey; 1 Dec 1966-2 Mar 1967
1 rare in the U.K. giant, Jack Kirby art featured, distributed in the U.K.
| | $6.50 | $20.00 | $40.00 | £4.15 | £12.50 | £25.00 |
2 scarce in the U.K. Williamson/Crandall reprint; distributed in the U.K.
| | $6.00 | $18.00 | $30.00 | £3.50 | £10.50 | £17.50 |
Title Value:
| | $12.50 | $38.00 | $70.00 | £7.65 | £23.00 | £42.50 |

DOUBLE DRAGON
Marvel Comics Group,MS; 1 Jul 1991-6 Dec 1991
| 1-6 ND | $0.15 | $0.45 | $0.75 | £0.10 | £0.35 | £0.60 |
Title Value:
| | $0.90 | $2.70 | $4.50 | £0.60 | £2.10 | £3.60 |
Note: based on Nintendo video game

DOUBLE EDGE
Night Wynd,MS; 1 Mar 1994-4 Jun 1994
1-4 ND Dwayne J. Ferguson script and art; black and white
| | $0.35 | $1.05 | $1.75 | £0.25 | £0.75 | £1.25 |
Title Value:
| | $1.40 | $4.20 | $7.00 | £1.00 | £3.00 | £5.00 |

DOUBLE EDGE: ALPHA
Marvel Comics Group,OS; 1 Sep 1995
1 ND 48pgs, Over The Edge story arc begins as The Punisher must kill Nick Fury; Larry Hama script, Kerry Gammill and Tom Palmer art; concluded in Double Edge: Omega
| | $1.00 | $3.00 | $5.00 | £0.65 | £1.95 | £3.25 |
Title Value:
| | $1.00 | $3.00 | $5.00 | £0.65 | £1.95 | £3.25 |

DOUBLE EDGE: OMEGA
Marvel Comics Group,OS; 1 Oct 1995
1 ND 48pgs, Over The Edge tie-in; Daredevil, Doc Samson, Ghost Rider, Nick Fury and Punisher appear; chromium cover by Joe Quesada and Jimmy Palmiotti; Nick Fury dies at the Punisher's hand
| | $1.00 | $3.00 | $5.00 | £0.65 | £1.95 | £3.25 |
Title Value:
| | $1.00 | $3.00 | $5.00 | £0.65 | £1.95 | £3.25 |

DOUBLE IMPACT
High Impact Studios; 1 Mar 1995-present
nn San Diego Collectors Edition, ND polybagged with a silver front outer cover; produced and distributed at the San Diego comic convention, limited to 5,000 copies
| | $8.00 | $24.00 | $40.00 | £5.00 | £15.00 | £25.00 |
1 ND Ricky Carralero art and script; chromium wraparound cover
| | $1.00 | $3.00 | $5.00 | £0.70 | £2.10 | £3.50 |
2 ND Ricky Carralero script and art; colour with 8 page black & white gallery pin-ups
| | $0.80 | $2.40 | $4.00 | £0.60 | £1.80 | £3.00 |
2 Nude Edition, ND limited to 5,000 copies
| | $5.00 | $15.00 | $25.00 | £3.00 | £9.00 | £15.00 |
3 ND Ricky Carralero script and art; black and white
| | $0.80 | $2.40 | $4.00 | £0.60 | £1.80 | £3.00 |
3 Variant cover ND
| | $1.60 | $4.80 | $8.00 | £1.00 | £3.00 | £5.00 |
4-5 ND
| | $0.60 | $1.80 | $3.00 | £0.40 | £1.20 | £2.00 |
5 Variant cover, ND white nude cover with gatefold back cover; limited to 600 copies - available to retailers for every 50 copies of the regular issue ordered
| | $7.00 | $21.00 | $35.00 | £4.00 | £12.00 | £20.00 |
Title Value:
| | $25.40 | $76.20 | $127.00 | £15.70 | £47.10 | £78.50 |

DOUBLE LIFE OF PRIVATE STRONG, THE
Archie; 1 Jun 1959-2 Aug 1959
1 rare in the U.K. origin The Shield, 1st appearance The Fly (Archie's 1st Silver Age super-hero), Joe Simon and Jack Kirby art; distributed in the U.K.
| | $62.50 | $190.00 | $450.00 | £43.00 | £125.00 | £300.00 |
2 scarce in the U.K. Fly appears, Joe Simon and Jack Kirby art; distributed in the U.K.
| | $43.00 | $125.00 | $300.00 | £29.00 | £85.00 | £200.00 |
Title Value:
| | $105.50 | $315.00 | $750.00 | £72.00 | £210.00 | £500.00 |

DP 7
Marvel Comics Group/New Universe; 1 Nov 1986-32 Jun 1989
| 1-29 ND | $0.15 | $0.45 | $0.75 | £0.10 | £0.35 | £0.60 |

Dollman #3

Doom's IV #2 (variant)

Dracula the Impaler #1

	$Good	$Fine	$N.Mint	£Good	£Fine	£N.Mint
30 ND intro Capt Manhattan						
	$0.15	$0.45	$0.75	£0.10	£0.35	£0.60
31-32 ND	$0.15	$0.45	$0.75	£0.10	£0.35	£0.60
Title Value:	$4.80	$14.40	$24.00	£3.20	£11.20	£19.20

DP 7 ANNUAL
Marvel Comics Group/New Universe; 1 Nov 1987

	$Good	$Fine	$N.Mint	£Good	£Fine	£N.Mint
1 ND intro The Witness						
	$0.25	$0.75	$1.25	£0.15	£0.45	£0.75
Title Value:	$0.25	$0.75	$1.25	£0.15	£0.45	£0.75

DR. BOOGIE
Media Arts Publishing; 1 1987

	$Good	$Fine	$N.Mint	£Good	£Fine	£N.Mint
1 ND cover inks by Nicola Cuti						
	$0.40	$1.20	$2.00	£0.25	£0.75	£1.25
Title Value:	$0.40	$1.20	$2.00	£0.25	£0.75	£1.25

DR. FU MANCHU
I.W. Comics; 1 1964

	$Good	$Fine	$N.Mint	£Good	£Fine	£N.Mint
1 rare in the U.K., Wally Wood art, all reprint; distributed in the U.K.						
	$9.00	$28.00	$55.00	£5.75	£17.50	£35.00
Title Value:	$9.00	$28.00	$55.00	£5.75	£17.50	£35.00

DR. GRAVES, ADVENTURES OF
A Plus Comics; 1 May 1991-2 1991

	$Good	$Fine	$N.Mint	£Good	£Fine	£N.Mint
1 ND 48pgs, Charlton Comics character revived						
	$0.40	$1.20	$2.00	£0.25	£0.75	£1.25
2 ND 48pgs	$0.40	$1.20	$2.00	£0.25	£0.75	£1.25
Title Value:	$0.80	$2.40	$4.00	£0.50	£1.50	£2.50

DR. GRAVES, THE MANY GHOSTS OF
Charlton; 1 May 1967-65 Apr 1978; 66 Jun 1981-75 Jan 1986

	$Good	$Fine	$N.Mint	£Good	£Fine	£N.Mint
1 scarce in the U.K.	$2.40	$7.00	$12.00	£1.20	£3.60	£6.00
2 scarce in the U.K.	$1.20	$3.60	$6.00	£0.60	£1.80	£3.00
3 scarce in the U.K.	$1.00	$3.00	$5.00	£0.40	£1.20	£2.00
4-50	$0.80	$2.40	$4.00	£0.30	£0.90	£1.50
51-65	$0.40	$1.20	$2.00	£0.25	£0.75	£1.25
66 reprints begin	$0.30	$0.90	$1.50	£0.20	£0.60	£1.00
67-75	$0.30	$0.90	$1.50	£0.20	£0.60	£1.00
Title Value:	$51.20	$153.40	$193.50	£22.05	£66.15	£110.25
Note: most issues distributed on the news-stands in the U.K.

DR. SPEKTOR, THE OCCULT FILES OF
Gold Key; 1 Apr 1973-24 Feb 1977; Whitman: 25 May 1982

	$Good	$Fine	$N.Mint	£Good	£Fine	£N.Mint
1 scarce in the U.K. 1st appearance Dr. Adam Spektor and Lakota; painted covers begin						
	$2.00	$6.00	$10.00	£1.20	£3.60	£6.00
2	$1.20	$3.60	$6.00	£0.70	£2.10	£3.50
3	$0.90	$2.70	$4.50	£0.60	£1.80	£3.00
4	$0.80	$2.40	$4.00	£0.50	£1.50	£2.50
5 16pg Kenner Catalogue insert						
	$0.85	$2.55	$4.25	£0.55	£1.65	£2.75
6-10	$0.60	$1.80	$3.00	£0.40	£1.20	£2.00
11 Dr. Spektor becomes a werewolf; 16pg Kenner Catalogue insert						
	$0.80	$2.40	$4.00	£0.50	£1.50	£2.00
12 Werewolf vs. Frankenstein						
	$0.60	$1.80	$3.00	£0.40	£1.20	£2.00
13	$0.45	$1.35	$2.25	£0.30	£0.90	£1.50
14 Dr. Solar Man of the Atom appears						
	$1.50	$4.50	$7.50	£1.00	£3.00	£5.00
15-24	$0.45	$1.35	$2.25	£0.30	£0.90	£1.50
25 scarce in the U.K. reprint; line drawn cover						
	$0.60	$1.80	$3.00	£0.40	£1.20	£2.00
Title Value:	$17.20	$51.60	$86.00	£11.15	£33.45	£55.75
Note: most issues distributed in the news-stands in the U.K.

DR. STRANGE VS. DRACULA
Marvel Comics Group, OS; 1 Mar 1994

	$Good	$Fine	$N.Mint	£Good	£Fine	£N.Mint
1 ND 48pgs, reprints Tomb of Dracula #44 and Dr. Strange (2nd Series) #14; Kyle Baker cover						
	$0.40	$1.20	$2.00	£0.25	£0.75	£1.25
Title Value:	$0.40	$1.20	$2.00	£0.25	£0.75	£1.25

DR. WEIRD
Caliber Press; 1 Oct 1994

	$Good	$Fine	$N.Mint	£Good	£Fine	£N.Mint
1 ND Frank Brunner cover; black and white						
	$0.45	$1.35	$2.25	£0.30	£0.90	£1.50
Title Value:	$0.45	$1.35	$2.25	£0.30	£0.90	£1.50

DR. WEIRD SPECIAL
Caliber Press, OS; 1 Feb 1994

	$Good	$Fine	$N.Mint	£Good	£Fine	£N.Mint
1 ND 64pgs, reprints Jim Starlin material						
	$0.90	$2.70	$4.50	£0.60	£1.80	£3.00
Title Value:	$0.90	$2.70	$4.50	£0.60	£1.80	£3.00

DR. WHO AND THE DALEKS
Dell, Film; 12-190-612 Dec 1966

	$Good	$Fine	$N.Mint	£Good	£Fine	£N.Mint
12 rare, distributed in the U.K. adapts film						
	$17.50	$52.50	$105.00	£10.50	£33.00	£65.00
Title Value:	$17.50	$52.50	$105.00	£10.50	£33.00	£65.00
Note: published as part of Dell's Movie Classics series

DRACULA
Dell; 12-231-212 1962; 2 Nov 1966-4 Mar 1967; 6 Jul 1972

	$Good	$Fine	$N.Mint	£Good	£Fine	£N.Mint
1 rare in the U.K. (Movie Classics #1) adapts film						
	$6.00	$18.00	$35.00	£2.50	£7.50	£15.00
2 origin of Dracula-as-super hero						
	$2.50	$7.50	$15.0	£1.50	£4.50	£7.50
3-4 scarce in the U.K.						
	$1.50	$4.50	$10.00	£0.80	£2.40	£4.00
6 scarce in the U.K. reprints #2						
	$1.25	$3.75	$7.50	£0.80	£2.40	£4.00
7-8 reprints #3,4	$0.80	$2.40	$5.00	£0.60	£1.80	£3.00
Title Value:	$14.35	$43.05	$87.50	£7.60	£22.80	£40.50
Note: all distributed on the news-stands in the U.K.

DRACULA (2ND SERIES)
Eternity, MS; 1 Dec 1989-4 May 1990

	$Good	$Fine	$N.Mint	£Good	£Fine	£N.Mint
1 ND black and white begins						
	$0.40	$1.20	$2.00	£0.25	£0.75	£1.25
1 2nd printing ND	$0.40	$1.20	$2.00	£0.25	£0.75	£1.25
2-4 ND	$0.40	$1.20	$2.00	£0.25	£0.75	£1.25
Title Value:	$2.00	$6.00	$10.00	£1.25	£3.75	£6.25

DRACULA (3RD SERIES)
Topps, MS; 1 Dec 1992-4 Mar 1993

	$Good	$Fine	$N.Mint	£Good	£Fine	£N.Mint
1 ND pre-bagged, adaptation of Francis Ford Coppola film, with four trading cards, Mike Mignola cover and art						
	$0.60	$1.80	$3.00	£0.40	£1.20	£2.00
1 ND Premium Edition, red-embossed logo						
	$3.00	$9.00	$15.00	£2.00	£6.00	£10.00
1 2nd printing, ND (printed on poly-bag)						
	$0.45	$1.35	$2.25	£0.30	£0.90	£1.50
2-4 ND pre-bagged, adaptation of Francis Ford Coppola film, with four trading cards, Mike Mignola cover and art						
	$0.45	$1.35	$2.25	£0.30	£0.90	£1.50
Title Value:	$5.40	$16.20	$27.00	£3.60	£10.80	£18.00

DRACULA BOOK AND RECORD SET
Power Records; PR-15 1974

	$Good	$Fine	$N.Mint	£Good	£Fine	£N.Mint
PR-15, scarce, 20pg booklet with 45 rpm record				£1.25	£3.75	£5.00
Note: the item would be valued at 50% less without record

DRACULA CHRONICLES
Topps, MS; 1 Apr 1995-3 Jun 1995

	$Good	$Fine	$N.Mint	£Good	£Fine	£N.Mint
1-3 ND Roy Thomas script, Esteban Maroto art						
	$0.40	$1.20	$2.00	£0.25	£0.75	£1.25
Title Value:	$1.20	$3.60	$6.00	£0.75	£2.25	£3.75

DRACULA GIANT SIZE
Marvel Comics Group; 2 Sep 1974-5 Jun 1975
(formerly Chillers Giant Size)

	$Good	$Fine	$N.Mint	£Good	£Fine	£N.Mint
2 ND 68pgs	$1.65	$4.95	$8.25	£1.10	£3.30	£5.50
3-4 ND 68pgs	$1.50	$4.50	$7.50	£1.00	£3.00	£5.00
5 ND 68pgs, 1st John Byrne art at Marvel						
	$1.80	$5.25	$9.00	£1.20	£3.60	£6.00
Title Value:	$6.45	$19.20	$32.25	£4.30	£12.90	£21.50

DRACULA IN HELL
Apple Comics, MS; 1 Jul 1991

	$Good	$Fine	$N.Mint	£Good	£Fine	£N.Mint
1 ND Tim Vigil cover						
	$0.40	$1.20	$2.00	£0.25	£0.75	£1.25
Title Value:	$0.40	$1.20	$2.00	£0.25	£0.75	£1.25
Note: cancelled mini-series

DRACULA LIVES ANNUAL
Marvel Comics Group, Magazine; 1 Summer 1975

	$Good	$Fine	$N.Mint	£Good	£Fine	£N.Mint
1 ND	$0.90	$2.70	$4.50	£0.60	£1.80	£3.00
Title Value:	$0.90	$2.70	$4.50	£0.60	£1.80	£3.00
Note: all reprint, includes Adams art.

DRACULA LIVES!
Marvel Comics Group, Magazine; 1 1973-13 Jul 1975

	$Good	$Fine	$N.Mint	£Good	£Fine	£N.Mint
1 ND	$1.20	$3.60	$6.00	£0.80	£2.40	£4.00
2 ND scarce in the U.K. Neal Adams art, origin of Dracula						
	$2.25	$6.75	$11.25	£1.50	£4.50	£7.50
3 ND Neal Adams inks						
	$1.00	$3.00	$5.00	£0.60	£1.80	£3.00
4 scarce in the U.K. $0.50	$1.50	$2.50	£0.50	£1.50	£2.50	
5-8	$0.45	$1.35	$2.25	£0.30	£0.90	£1.50
9-13 ND	$0.45	$1.35	$2.25	£0.40	£1.20	£2.00
Title Value:	$9.00	$27.00	$45.00	£6.60	£19.80	£33.00

DRACULA THE IMPALER
Comax Productions; 1 1991

	$Good	$Fine	$N.Mint	£Good	£Fine	£N.Mint
1 ND Butch Burcham script/art, black and white						
	$0.30	$0.90	$1.50	£0.20	£0.60	£1.00
Title Value:	$0.30	$0.90	$1.50	£0.20	£0.60	£1.00

DRACULA VERSUS ZORRO
Topps, MS; 1 Oct 1993-2 Nov 1993

	$Good	$Fine	$N.Mint	£Good	£Fine	£N.Mint
1 ND black cover with red foil logo and red metallic ink						
	$0.45	$1.35	$2.25	£0.30	£0.90	£1.50
2 ND pre-bagged with Zorro #0 included						
	$0.45	$1.35	$2.25	£0.30	£0.90	£1.50
Title Value:	$0.90	$2.70	$4.50	£0.60	£1.80	£3.00
Dracula vs. Zorro (Apr 1994) Trade paperback reprints mini-series with new wraparound cover by Tom Yeates				£0.80	£2.40	£4.00

DRACULA, BIG BAD BLOOD OF
Apple Comics, MS; 1 Oct 1991-2 Nov 1991

	$Good	$Fine	$N.Mint	£Good	£Fine	£N.Mint
1-2 ND	$0.35	$1.05	$1.75	£0.25	£0.75	£1.25
Title Value:	$0.70	$2.10	$3.50	£0.50	£1.50	£2.50

DRACULA, REQUIEM FOR
Marvel Comics Group, OS; 1 Feb 1993

	$Good	$Fine	$N.Mint	£Good	£Fine	£N.Mint
1 ND reprints Tomb of Dracula #69-#70						
	$0.35	$1.05	$1.75	£0.25	£0.75	£1.25
Title Value:	$0.35	$1.05	$1.75	£0.25	£0.75	£1.25

DRACULA, THE COLLECTOR'S
Millennium, MS; 1 Dec 1993-2 Jan 1994

	$Good	$Fine	$N.Mint	£Good	£Fine	£N.Mint
1-2 ND 48pgs, anthology featuring John Bolton among others						
	$0.60	$1.80	$3.00	£0.40	£1.20	£2.00
Title Value:	$1.20	$3.60	$6.00	£0.80	£2.40	£4.00

DRACULA, THE GHOSTS OF
Eternity, MS; 1 Sep 1991-5 Jan 1992

	$Good	$Fine	$N.Mint	£Good	£Fine	£N.Mint
1-5 ND	$0.35	$1.05	$1.75	£0.25	£0.75	£1.25
Title Value:	$1.75	$5.25	$8.75	£1.25	£3.75	£6.25

VERY GENERAL PERCENTAGE CONVERSION CHART WHICH MAY BE USED TO CALCULATE LOW AND INBETWEEN GRADES:

DRACULA, THE SAVAGE RETURN OF
Marvel Comics Group,OS; 1 Jan 1993

	$Good	$Fine	$N.Mint	£Good	£Fine	£N.Mint
1 ND 48pgs, reprints Tomb of Dracula #1,#2	$0.35	$1.05	$1.75	£0.25	£0.75	£1.25
Title Value:	$0.35	$1.05	$1.75	£0.25	£0.75	£1.25

DRACULA, THE WEDDING OF
Marvel Comics Group,OS; 1 Jan 1993

	$Good	$Fine	$N.Mint	£Good	£Fine	£N.Mint
1 ND 48pgs, reprints Tomb of Dracula #30, #45-#46	$0.40	$1.20	$2.00	£0.25	£0.75	£1.25
Title Value:	$0.40	$1.20	$2.00	£0.25	£0.75	£1.25

DRACULA: RETURN OF THE IMPALER
Slave Labor; 1 Sep 1993-3 1993; 4 Oct 1994-present

	$Good	$Fine	$N.Mint	£Good	£Fine	£N.Mint
1-4 ND b/w	$0.35	$1.05	$1.75	£0.25	£0.75	£1.25
Title Value:	$1.40	$4.20	$7.00	£1.00	£3.00	£5.00

DRACULA: THE SUICIDE CLUB
Adventure,MS; 1 Oct 1991-4 Jan 1993

	$Good	$Fine	$N.Mint	£Good	£Fine	£N.Mint
1-4 ND	$0.35	$1.05	$1.75	£0.25	£0.75	£1.25
Title Value:	$1.40	$4.20	$7.00	£1.00	£3.00	£5.00

DRACULA: VLAD THE IMPALER
Topps,MS; 1 Feb 1993-3 Apr 1993

	$Good	$Fine	$N.Mint	£Good	£Fine	£N.Mint
1 ND pre-bagged with 3 trading cards, Roy Thomas script, Esteban Marato art	$1.80	$5.25	$9.00	£1.20	£3.60	£6.00
1 ND Red foil embossed logo premium edition	$2.50	$7.50	$15.00	£1.25	£3.75	£7.50
2-3 ND pre-bagged with 3 trading cards, Roy Thomas script, Esteban Marato art	$0.45	$1.35	$2.25	£0.30	£0.90	£1.50
Title Value:	$5.20	$15.45	$28.50	£3.05	£9.15	£16.50

DRAFT, THE
New Universe,OS; 1 Jun 1988
(see also The Pitt, The War)

	$Good	$Fine	$N.Mint	£Good	£Fine	£N.Mint
1 ND part Kyle Baker art, Klaus Jansen inks	$0.80	$2.40	$4.00	£0.50	£1.50	£2.50
Title Value:	$0.80	$2.40	$4.00	£0.50	£1.50	£2.50

DRAG-STRIP HOTRODDERS
Charlton; 1 Summer 1963; 2 Jan 1965-16 Jul 1967

	$Good	$Fine	$N.Mint	£Good	£Fine	£N.Mint
1 scarce, distributed in the U.K.	$4.15	$12.50	$25.00	£2.50	£7.50	£15.00
2 distributed in the U.K.	$2.50	$7.50	$15.00	£1.65	£5.00	£10.00
3-5 distributed in the U.K.	$2.05	$6.25	$12.50	£1.25	£3.75	£7.50
6-10 distributed in the U.K.	$1.80	$5.50	$11.00	£0.80	£2.50	£5.00
11-16 distributed in the U.K.	$1.65	$5.00	$10.00	£0.65	£2.00	£4.00
Title Value:	$31.70	$96.25	$192.50	£15.80	£48.25	£96.50

DRAGON
Comics Interview,MS; 1-3 1988

	$Good	$Fine	$N.Mint	£Good	£Fine	£N.Mint
1-3 ND	$0.40	$1.20	$2.00	£0.25	£0.75	£1.25
Title Value:	$1.20	$3.60	$6.00	£0.75	£2.25	£3.75

DRAGON LINES
Marvel Comics Group/Epic,MS; 1 May 1993-4 Aug 1993

	$Good	$Fine	$N.Mint	£Good	£Fine	£N.Mint
1 ND Ron Lim pencils begin; embossed cover	$0.35	$1.05	$1.75	£0.25	£0.75	£1.25
2-4 ND	$0.35	$1.05	$1.75	£0.25	£0.75	£1.25
Title Value:	$1.40	$4.20	$7.00	£1.00	£3.00	£5.00

DRAGON LINES: WAY OF THE WARRIOR
Marvel Comics Group/Epic,MS; 1 Nov 1993-2 Dec 1993

	$Good	$Fine	$N.Mint	£Good	£Fine	£N.Mint
1-2 ND Ron Lim pencils; bound-in trading card	$0.35	$1.05	$1.75	£0.25	£0.75	£1.25
Title Value:	$0.70	$2.10	$3.50	£0.50	£1.50	£2.50

DRAGON STRIKE
Marvel Comics Group,OS, Game; 1 Feb 1994

	$Good	$Fine	$N.Mint	£Good	£Fine	£N.Mint
1 ND adaptation of TSR game	$0.25	$0.75	$1.25	£0.15	£0.45	£0.75
Title Value:	$0.25	$0.75	$1.25	£0.15	£0.45	£0.75

DRAGON'S CLAWS
Marvel Comics Group; 1 Oct 1988-10 Jul 1989
(see Transformers in British section)

	$Good	$Fine	$N.Mint	£Good	£Fine	£N.Mint
1 Simon Furman script, Geoff Senior art	$0.30	$0.90	$1.50	£0.20	£0.60	£1.00
2	$0.30	$0.90	$1.50	£0.20	£0.60	£1.00
3 1st cameo appearance Death's Head in mainstream Marvel Universe (on back cover one page strip)	$0.60	$1.80	$3.00	£0.40	£1.20	£2.00
4 Death's Head on back page advertisement announcing appearance next issue	$0.30	$0.90	$1.50	£0.20	£0.60	£1.00
5 1st full appearance of Death's Head in mainstream Marvel Universe (see Transformers #113 in UK section)	$1.00	$3.00	$5.00	£0.70	£2.10	£3.50
6-10	$0.30	$0.90	$1.50	£0.20	£0.60	£1.00
Title Value:	$4.00	$12.00	$20.00	£2.70	£8.10	£13.50

DRAGON'S STAR
Caliber Press,MS; 1 Sep 1993-2 1993

	$Good	$Fine	$N.Mint	£Good	£Fine	£N.Mint
1-2 ND b/w	$0.45	$1.35	$2.25	£0.30	£0.90	£1.50
Title Value:	$0.90	$2.70	$4.50	£0.60	£1.80	£3.00

DRAGON: BLOOD & GUTS
Image,MS; 1 Mar 1995-3 May 1995

	$Good	$Fine	$N.Mint	£Good	£Fine	£N.Mint
1-3 ND Jason Pearson and Karl Story script and art	$0.45	$1.35	$2.25	£0.30	£0.90	£1.50
Title Value:	$1.35	$4.05	$6.75	£0.90	£2.70	£4.50
Dragon: Blood & Guts (Nov 1995) Trade paperback collects mini-series, new cover by Jason Pearson				£1.10	£3.30	£5.50

DRAGONFIRE
Night Wynd,MS; 1 Feb 1992-4 May 1992

	$Good	$Fine	$N.Mint	£Good	£Fine	£N.Mint
1-4 ND Barry Blair script and art; black and white	$0.35	$1.05	$1.75	£0.25	£0.75	£1.25
Title Value:	$1.40	$4.20	$7.00	£1.00	£3.00	£5.00

DRAGONFIRE (2ND SERIES)
Night Wynd,MS; 1 Jun 1992-4 Sep 1992

	$Good	$Fine	$N.Mint	£Good	£Fine	£N.Mint
1-4 ND Barry Blair script and art; black and white	$0.35	$1.05	$1.75	£0.25	£0.75	£1.25
Title Value:	$1.40	$4.20	$7.00	£1.00	£3.00	£5.00

DRAGONFIRE: THE CLASSIFIED FILES
Night Wynd,MS; 1 Jul 1992-4 Oct 1992

	$Good	$Fine	$N.Mint	£Good	£Fine	£N.Mint
1-4 ND Barry Blair script and art; black and white	$0.35	$1.05	$1.75	£0.25	£0.75	£1.25
Title Value:	$1.40	$4.20	$7.00	£1.00	£3.00	£5.00

DRAGONFIRE: THE EARLY YEARS
Night Wynd,MS; 1 Apr 1993-8 Nov 1993

	$Good	$Fine	$N.Mint	£Good	£Fine	£N.Mint
1-8 ND Barry Blair and Dale Keown script and art; black and white	$0.35	$1.05	$1.75	£0.25	£0.75	£1.25
Title Value:	$2.80	$8.40	$14.00	£2.00	£6.00	£10.00

DRAGONFIRE: THE SAMURAI SWORD
Night Wynd,MS; 1 Oct 1993-2 1993

	$Good	$Fine	$N.Mint	£Good	£Fine	£N.Mint
1-2 ND Barry Blair script and art; black and white	$0.35	$1.05	$1.75	£0.25	£0.75	£1.25
Title Value:	$0.70	$2.10	$3.50	£0.50	£1.50	£2.50

DRAGONFIRE: UFO WARS
Night Wynd,MS; 1 Nov 1992-4 Mar 1993

	$Good	$Fine	$N.Mint	£Good	£Fine	£N.Mint
1-4 ND Barry Blair script and art; black and white	$0.35	$1.05	$1.75	£0.25	£0.75	£1.25
Title Value:	$1.40	$4.20	$7.00	£1.00	£3.00	£5.00

DRAGONFLIGHT
Eclipse,MS; 1 Feb 1991-3 Aug 1991

	$Good	$Fine	$N.Mint	£Good	£Fine	£N.Mint
1-3 ND 48pgs, adaptation Anne McCaffrey's book by Brynne Stephans, art by Lela Dowling & Cynthia Martin	$0.70	$2.10	$3.50	£0.50	£1.50	£2.50
Title Value:	$2.10	$6.30	$10.50	£1.50	£4.50	£7.50
Dragonflight Collection (Feb 1993)						
Softcover, reprints mini-series				£1.85	£5.55	£9.25
Hardcover, reprints mini-series				£4.20	£12.60	£21.00

DRAGONFLY
AC Comics; 1 1986-8 1987
(see Americomics, Fem Force)

	$Good	$Fine	$N.Mint	£Good	£Fine	£N.Mint
1-8 ND	$0.40	$1.20	$2.00	£0.25	£0.75	£1.25
Title Value:	$3.20	$9.60	$16.00	£2.00	£6.00	£10.00
Cycle of Fire Trade paperback, reworked reprint of issues #1,2 plus new art				£1.20	£3.60	£6.00

DRAGONFORCE
Aircel; 1 1988-13 1989

	$Good	$Fine	$N.Mint	£Good	£Fine	£N.Mint
1-13 ND	$0.40	$1.20	$2.00	£0.25	£0.75	£1.25
Title Value:	$5.20	$15.60	$26.00	£3.25	£9.75	£16.25

DRAGONLANCE COMICS
DC Comics, Game; 1 Dec 1988-34 Sep 1991

	$Good	$Fine	$N.Mint	£Good	£Fine	£N.Mint
1 based on the DragonLance books by Weis and Hickman	$0.50	$1.50	$2.50	£0.50	£1.50	£2.50
2-10	$0.45	$1.35	$2.25	£0.30	£0.90	£1.50
11-21	$0.30	$0.90	$1.50	£0.20	£0.60	£1.00
22-25 Taladas story	$0.30	$0.90	$1.50	£0.20	£0.60	£1.00
26-29	$0.30	$0.90	$1.50	£0.20	£0.60	£1.00
30-32 Dwarf War, covers by Mike Kaluta	$0.30	$0.90	$1.50	£0.20	£0.60	£1.00
33-34	$0.30	$0.90	$1.50	£0.20	£0.60	£1.00
Title Value:	$11.75	$35.25	$58.75	£8.00	£24.00	£40.00

DRAGONLANCE COMICS ANNUAL
DC Comics, Game; 1 Dec 1990

	$Good	$Fine	$N.Mint	£Good	£Fine	£N.Mint
1 64pgs, painted cover	$0.45	$1.35	$2.25	£0.30	£0.90	£1.50
Title Value:	$0.45	$1.35	$2.25	£0.30	£0.90	£1.50

DRAGONLANCE GRAPHIC NOVEL
TSR; 1,2 1988; 3 1989
(see DC's Dragonlance)

	$Good	$Fine	$N.Mint	£Good	£Fine	£N.Mint
1-2 ND Tom Yeates art	$2.00	$6.00	$10.00	£1.20	£3.60	£6.00
3 ND	$2.00	$6.00	$10.00	£1.20	£3.60	£6.00
Title Value:	$6.00	$18.00	$30.00	£3.60	£10.80	£18.00

DRAGONLANCE SAGA GRAPHIC NOVEL
DC Comics; 4 Apr 1990; 5 Apr 1991

	$Good	$Fine	$N.Mint	£Good	£Fine	£N.Mint
4-5 ND 80pgs	$2.00	$6.00	$10.00	£1.20	£3.60	£6.00
Title Value:	$4.00	$12.00	$20.00	£2.40	£7.20	£12.00

Note: first three volumes published by TSR Games

DRAGONRING
Aircel; 1-6 1986

	$Good	$Fine	$N.Mint	£Good	£Fine	£N.Mint
1-6 ND b/w	$0.40	$1.20	$2.00	£0.25	£0.75	£1.25
Title Value:	$2.40	$7.20	$12.00	£1.50	£4.50	£7.50

DRAGONRING (2ND SERIES)
Aircel; 1 Dec 1987-15 1988

	$Good	$Fine	$N.Mint	£Good	£Fine	£N.Mint
1-15 ND colour	$0.40	$1.20	$2.00	£0.25	£0.75	£1.25
Title Value:	$6.00	$18.00	$30.00	£3.75	£11.25	£18.75

DRAGONS IN THE MOON
Aircel,MS; 1 Aug 1990-4 Nov 1990

	$Good	$Fine	$N.Mint	£Good	£Fine	£N.Mint
1-4 ND	$0.45	$1.35	$2.25	£0.30	£0.90	£1.50
Title Value:	$1.80	$5.40	$9.00	£1.20	£3.60	£6.00

DRAGONSLAYER
Marvel Comics Group,MS Film; 1 Oct 1981-2 Nov 1981

MINT = 100% / NEAR MINT (inc. +/-) = 90-99% / VERY FINE (inc. +/-) = 75-89% / FINE (inc. +/-) = 55-74%
VERY GOOD (inc. +/-) = 35-54% / GOOD (inc. +/-) = 15-34% / FAIR = 5-14% / POOR = 1-4%

313

	$Good	$Fine	$N.Mint	£Good	£Fine	£N.Mint
1-2 ND	$0.15	$0.45	$0.75	£0.10	£0.35	£0.60
Title Value:	$0.30	$0.90	$1.50	£0.20	£0.70	£1.20

Note: reprints Marvel Super Special #20.

DRAMA
Sirius, OS; 1 1994

	$Good	$Fine	$N.Mint	£Good	£Fine	£N.Mint
1 ND Joe Linsner art $3.00		$9.00	$15.00	£1.60	£4.80	£8.00
1 ND signed and numbered edition						
	$6.00	$18.00	$30.00	£4.00	£12.00	£20.00
Title Value:	$8.00	$27.00	$45.00	£5.60	£16.80	£28.00

DREADLANDS
Marvel Comics Group,MS; 1 Jan 1992-4 Apr 1992

	$Good	$Fine	$N.Mint	£Good	£Fine	£N.Mint
1-4 ND 48pgs	$0.80	$2.40	$4.00	£0.50	£1.50	£2.50
Title Value:	$3.20	$9.60	$16.00	£2.00	£6.00	£10.00

DREADSTAR
Marvel Comics Group/Epic; 1 Nov 1982-26 Aug 1986
(see Marvel Graphic Novel) (published by First Comics #27 on)

	$Good	$Fine	$N.Mint	£Good	£Fine	£N.Mint
1 ND Jim Starlin story/art begins						
	$0.60	$1.80	$3.00	£0.40	£1.20	£2.00
2-5 ND	$0.45	$1.35	$2.25	£0.30	£0.90	£1.50
6-7 ND Wrightson art						
	$0.55	$1.65	$2.75	£0.35	£1.05	£1.75
8-15 ND	$0.45	$1.35	$2.25	£0.30	£0.90	£1.50
16 ND scarce in the U.K.						
	$0.55	$1.65	$2.75	£0.35	£1.05	£1.75
17-26 ND	$0.45	$1.35	$2.25	£0.30	£0.90	£1.50
Title Value:	$12.15	$36.45	$60.75	£8.05	£24.15	£40.25

DREADSTAR
First; 27 Sep 1986-64 Jan 1991
(previously published by Marvel)

	$Good	$Fine	$N.Mint	£Good	£Fine	£N.Mint
27-30 ND	$0.45	$1.35	$2.25	£0.30	£0.90	£1.50
31-49 ND	$0.40	$1.20	$2.00	£0.25	£0.75	£1.25
50 ND squarebound						
	$0.60	$1.80	$3.00	£0.40	£1.20	£2.00
51-64 ND	$0.40	$1.20	$2.00	£0.25	£0.75	£1.25
Title Value:	$15.60	$46.80	$78.00	£9.85	£29.55	£49.25

DREADSTAR AND CO.
Marvel Comics Group/Epic; 1 Jul 1985-6 Dec 1985

	$Good	$Fine	$N.Mint	£Good	£Fine	£N.Mint
1-6 ND reprints from Dreadstar series						
	$0.25	$0.75	$1.25	£0.15	£0.45	£0.75
Title Value:	$1.50	$4.50	$7.50	£0.90	£2.70	£4.50

DREADSTAR ANNUAL
Marvel Comics Group/Epic; 1 Dec 1983

	$Good	$Fine	$N.Mint	£Good	£Fine	£N.Mint
1 ND reprints "The Price" (see Eclipse Graphic Album series)						
	$0.60	$1.80	$3.00	£0.40	£1.20	£2.00
Title Value:	$0.60	$1.80	$3.00	£0.40	£1.20	£2.00

DREADSTAR, JIM STARLIN'S
Malibu Bravura,MS; 1 Apr 1994-6 Oct 1994

	$Good	$Fine	$N.Mint	£Good	£Fine	£N.Mint
1-6 ND Peter David script, Ernie Colon art						
	$0.45	$1.35	$2.25	£0.30	£0.90	£1.50
Title Value:	$2.70	$8.10	$13.50	£1.80	£5.40	£9.00

DREADWOLF
Lightning Comics; 1 Aug 1994-present

	$Good	$Fine	$N.Mint	£Good	£Fine	£N.Mint
1 ND	$0.80	$2.40	$4.00	£0.50	£1.50	£2.50
1 ND Ashcan Edition, black and white; 4,000 copies						
	$1.50	$4.50	$7.50	£0.80	£2.40	£4.00
1 ND Signed (by Joseph Zyskowski) Ashcan Edition, black and white; 1,000 copies						
	$1.60	$4.80	$8.00	£1.00	£3.00	£5.00
1 ND Signed & Numbered Edition (Feb 1995) - new metallic ink cover, pre-bagged and limited to 1,000 copies						
	$1.50	$4.50	$7.50	£0.80	£2.40	£4.00
1 Platinum edition ND						
	$1.05	$3.15	$5.25	£0.70	£2.10	£3.50
Title Value:	$6.45	$19.35	$32.25	£3.80	£11.40	£19.00

DREADWOLF, CURSE OF THE
Lightning Comics; 1 Sep 1994

	$Good	$Fine	$N.Mint	£Good	£Fine	£N.Mint
1 ND origin Dreadwolf; black and white						
	$0.55	$1.65	$2.75	£0.35	£1.05	£1.75
Title Value:	$0.55	$1.65	$2.75	£0.35	£1.05	£1.75

DREADWOLF, VENGEANCE OF
Lightning Comics; 1 Feb 1995

	$Good	$Fine	$N.Mint	£Good	£Fine	£N.Mint
1 ND b/w	$0.55	$1.65	$2.75	£0.35	£1.05	£1.75
Title Value:	$0.55	$1.65	$2.75	£0.35	£1.05	£1.75

DREAMER
Kitchen Sink; nn 1986

	$Good	$Fine	$N.Mint	£Good	£Fine	£N.Mint
nn ND Hardback, Will Eisner script and art, semi-auto biographical						
	$3.60	$10.50	$18.00	£2.40	£7.00	£12.00
Title Value:	$3.60	$10.50	$18.00	£2.40	£7.00	£12.00
Softback Edition				£0.90	£2.70	£4.50

DREAMERY, THE
Eclipse; 1 Dec 1986-14 Feb 1989

	$Good	$Fine	$N.Mint	£Good	£Fine	£N.Mint
1 ND Leila Dowling art begins						
	$0.40	$1.20	$2.00	£0.25	£0.75	£1.25
2-14 ND	$0.40	$1.20	$2.00	£0.25	£0.75	£1.25
Title Value:	$5.60	$16.80	$28.00	£3.50	£10.50	£17.50

Note: Alice in Wonderland #2-7. All Non-Distributed on the news-stands in the U.K.

DROIDS
Marvel Comics Group/Star, TV; 1 Apr 1986-8 Jun 1987

	$Good	$Fine	$N.Mint	£Good	£Fine	£N.Mint
1 ND R2-D2 and C-3PO from Star Wars begin						
	$0.15	$0.45	$0.75	£0.10	£0.35	£0.60
2-8 ND	$0.15	$0.45	$0.75	£0.10	£0.35	£0.60
Title Value:	$1.20	$3.60	$6.00	£0.80	£2.80	£4.80

DRONE
Dagger Enterprises; 1 Aug 1994-2 1994

	$Good	$Fine	$N.Mint	£Good	£Fine	£N.Mint
1-2 ND	$0.45	$1.35	$2.25	£0.30	£0.90	£1.50
Title Value:	$0.90	$2.70	$4.50	£0.60	£1.80	£3.00

DROOPY, TEX AVERY'S
Dark Horse,MS; 1 Oct 1995-3 Dec 1995

	$Good	$Fine	$N.Mint	£Good	£Fine	£N.Mint
1-3 ND Bill Morrison painted covers						
	$0.50	$1.50	$2.50	£0.30	£0.90	£1.50
Title Value:	$1.50	$4.50	$7.50	£0.90	£2.70	£4.50

DRUID
Marvel Comics Group; 1 May 1995-4 Aug 1995

	$Good	$Fine	$N.Mint	£Good	£Fine	£N.Mint
1 Warren Ellis script, Leonardo Manco art; card-stock cover						
	$0.40	$1.20	$2.00	£0.25	£0.75	£1.25
2-3	$0.40	$1.20	$2.00	£0.25	£0.75	£1.25
4 Daiman Hellstrom appears						
	$0.40	$1.20	$2.00	£0.25	£0.75	£1.25
Title Value:	$1.60	$4.80	$8.00	£1.00	£3.00	£5.00

DRUNKEN FIST
Jademan; 1 Aug 1988-56 Mar 1993

	$Good	$Fine	$N.Mint	£Good	£Fine	£N.Mint
1 ND	$0.70	$2.10	$3.50	£0.50	£1.50	£2.50
2-5 ND	$0.60	$1.80	$3.00	£0.40	£1.20	£2.00
6-10 ND	$0.45	$1.35	$2.25	£0.30	£0.90	£1.50
11-20 ND	$0.35	$1.05	$1.75	£0.25	£0.75	£1.25
21-30 ND	$0.30	$0.90	$1.50	£0.20	£0.60	£1.00
31-56 ND	$0.25	$0.75	$1.25	£0.15	£0.45	£0.75
Title Value:	$18.35	$55.05	$91.75	£12.00	£36.00	£60.00

Note: all Non-Distributed on the news-stands in the U.K.

DUCK TALES
Gladstone, TV; 1 Oct 1988-13 May 1989

	$Good	$Fine	$N.Mint	£Good	£Fine	£N.Mint
1-2 48pgs, features TV characters, Barks Uncle Scrooge back-up						
	$0.30	$0.90	$1.50	£0.20	£0.60	£1.00
3 36pgs	$0.30	$0.90	$1.50	£0.20	£0.60	£1.00
4 36pgs, no back-ups						
	$0.30	$0.90	$1.50	£0.20	£0.60	£1.00
5-13	$0.30	$0.90	$1.50	£0.20	£0.60	£1.00
Title Value:	$3.90	$11.70	$19.50	£2.60	£7.80	£13.00

Note: banned from distribution in the U.K.
Movie Adaptation Graphic Novel (Oct 1990)

	$Good	$Fine	$N.Mint	£Good	£Fine	£N.Mint
64pgs, Prestige Format				£0.90	£2.70	£4.50

DUCK TALES (2ND SERIES)
Disney; 1 Jun 1990-19 Nov 1991

	$Good	$Fine	$N.Mint	£Good	£Fine	£N.Mint
1-19 ND	$0.30	$0.90	$1.50	£0.20	£0.60	£1.00
Title Value:	$5.70	$17.10	$28.50	£3.80	£11.40	£19.00

DUCKMAN
Topps; 1 Nov 1994-5 Mar 1995?

	$Good	$Fine	$N.Mint	£Good	£Fine	£N.Mint
1 ND based on US animated show, with poster and 3-D cover enhancement						
	$0.45	$1.35	$2.25	£0.30	£0.90	£1.50
2-5 ND	$0.45	$1.35	$2.25	£0.30	£0.90	£1.50
Title Value:	$2.10	$6.75	$11.25	£1.50	£4.50	£7.50

Note: issues #6-8 were advertised and solicited, but never appeared?

DUCKMAN: THE MOB FROG SAGA
Topps,MS; 1 Nov 1994-3 Jan 1995

	$Good	$Fine	$N.Mint	£Good	£Fine	£N.Mint
1-3 ND based on US animated show						
	$0.45	$1.35	$2.25	£0.30	£0.90	£1.50
Title Value:	$1.35	$4.05	$6.75	£0.90	£2.70	£4.50

DUNE
Marvel Comics Group,MS Film; 1 Apr 1985-3 Jun 1985

	$Good	$Fine	$N.Mint	£Good	£Fine	£N.Mint
1-3 ND Sienkiewicz art; reprints Marvel Super Special #3						
	$0.45	$1.35	$2.25	£0.30	£0.90	£1.50
Title Value:	$1.35	$4.05	$6.75	£0.90	£2.70	£4.50

DUNGEONEERS
Silver Wolf; 1 Sep 1986-4 Dec 1986

	$Good	$Fine	$N.Mint	£Good	£Fine	£N.Mint
1-4 ND black and white						
	$0.30	$0.90	$1.50	£0.20	£0.60	£1.00
Title Value:	$1.20	$3.60	$6.00	£0.80	£2.40	£4.00

DYNAMIC CLASSICS
DC Comics; 1 Sep/Oct 1978

	$Good	$Fine	$N.Mint	£Good	£Fine	£N.Mint
1 ND scarce in the U.K. 44pgs, Neal Adams Batman and Walt Simonson Manhunter reprints, origin						
	$1.20	$3.60	$6.00	£0.80	£2.40	£4.00
Title Value:	$1.20	$3.60	$6.00	£0.80	£2.40	£4.00

Note: intended as on-going series (see Battle Classics)

DYNAMO
Tower Comics; 1 Aug 1966-4 Jun 1967

	$Good	$Fine	$N.Mint	£Good	£Fine	£N.Mint
1 rare in the U.K., giant, Wally Wood and Steve Ditko art						
	$7.50	$22.50	$37.50	£5.00	£15.00	£25.00
2-4 giants, Wood art						
	$5.00	$15.00	$25.00	£3.20	£9.50	£16.00
Title Value:	$22.50	$67.50	$112.50	£14.60	£43.50	£73.00

Note: all were distributed on the news-stands in the U.K.

DYNAMO JOE
First; 1 May 1986-15 Jan 1988
(see Mars #10-12, First Adventures #1-5, Grimjack #30)

	$Good	$Fine	$N.Mint	£Good	£Fine	£N.Mint
1-15 ND	$0.30	$0.90	$1.50	£0.20	£0.60	£1.00
Title Value:	$4.50	$13.50	$22.50	£3.00	£9.00	£15.00

Note: issues 1-3 marked as 3 issue mini-series

DYNAMO JOE SPECIAL
First,OS; 1 Jan 1987

	$Good	$Fine	$N.Mint	£Good	£Fine	£N.Mint
1 ND reprints Mars #10-12 plus new pages						
	$0.40	$1.20	$2.00	£0.25	£0.75	£1.25
Title Value:	$0.40	$1.20	$2.00	£0.25	£0.75	£1.25

DYNOMUTT
Marvel Comics Group, TV; 1 Nov 1977-6 Sep 1978

	$Good	$Fine	$N.Mint	£Good	£Fine	£N.Mint
1-6 ND	$0.15	$0.45	$0.75	£0.10	£0.35	£0.60
Title Value:	$0.90	$2.70	$4.50	£0.60	£2.10	£3.60

TRADE PAPERBACKS, GRAPHIC NOVELS AND OTHER COLLECTIONS ARE PRICED IN POUNDS STERLING ONLY. CONVERT AT 1.5 FOR DOLLARS.

E

	$Good	$Fine	$N.Mint	£Good	£Fine	£N.Mint

E-MAN
Charlton; 1 Oct 1973-10 Sep 1975
1 Joe Staton art

	$2.00	$6.00	$10.00	£1.20	£3.60	£6.00
2-3 Joe Staton, Steve Ditko art						
	$1.20	$3.60	$6.00	£0.80	£2.40	£4.00
4-5 Joe Staton, Steve Ditko art						
	$0.90	$2.70	$4.50	£0.60	£1.80	£3.00
6-7 Joe Staton, John Byrne art						
	$1.20	$3.60	$6.00	£0.80	£2.40	£4.00
8 Joe Staton	$0.80	$2.40	$4.00	£0.50	£1.50	£2.50
9-10 Joe Staton, John Byrne art						
	$1.20	$3.60	$6.00	£0.80	£2.40	£4.00
Title Value:	$11.80	$35.40	$59.00	£7.70	£23.10	£38.50

Note: all distributed on the news-stands in the U.K.

E-MAN (2ND SERIES)
First; 1 Apr 1983-25 Aug 1985
1 Joe Staton art begins, 1pg John Byrne art

	$0.30	$0.90	$1.50	£0.20	£0.60	£1.00
2 Joe Staton art, X-Men parody						
	$0.30	$0.90	$1.50	£0.20	£0.60	£1.00
3 Joe Staton art, X-Men parody (cover of X-Men #101)						
	$0.30	$0.90	$1.50	£0.20	£0.60	£1.00
4-10 Joe Staton art						
	$0.30	$0.90	$1.50	£0.20	£0.60	£1.00
11-25 Joe Staton art						
	$0.25	$0.75	$1.25	£0.15	£0.45	£0.75
Title Value:	$6.75	$20.25	$33.75	£4.25	£12.75	£21.25

Note: all Non-Distributed on the news-standsin the U.K.

E-MAN (3RD SERIES)
Comico,OS; 1 Sep 1989
1 ND colour, no ads, high quality paper

	$0.60	$1.80	$3.00	£0.40	£1.20	£2.00
Title Value:	$0.60	$1.80	$3.00	£0.40	£1.20	£2.00

E-MAN (4TH SERIES)
Comico,MS; 1 Jan 1990-3 Mar 1990
1-3 ND Staton cover/art, colour

	$1.35	$4.05	$6.75	£0.90	£2.70	£4.50
E-Man Limited Edition (May 1993)						
issues #1-3 pre-bagged with orange paper wrapper, ND				£0.70	£2.10	£3.50

E-MAN (5TH SERIES)
Alpha Productions; 1 Oct 1993-3 Jan 1994
1 ND Nicola Cuti script and Joe Staton art begins

	$0.45	$1.35	$2.25	£0.30	£0.90	£1.50
1 ND Special Limited Edition Ash Can Preview - 16pgs, limited to 3,000 copies						
	$1.00	$3.00	$5.00	£0.70	£2.10	£3.50
2 ND	$0.45	$1.35	$2.25	£0.30	£0.90	£1.50
2 ND pre-bagged with poster						
	$0.60	$1.80	$3.00	£0.40	£1.20	£2.00
3 ND	$0.45	$1.35	$2.25	£0.30	£0.90	£1.50
3 ND pre-bagged with poster						
	$0.60	$1.80	$3.00	£0.40	£1.20	£2.00
Title Value:	$3.55	$10.65	$17.75	£2.40	£7.20	£12.00

E-MAN RETURNS
Alpha Productions,OS; 1 Mar 1994
1 ND Nicola Cuti script, Joe Staton art; black and white

	$0.45	$1.35	$2.25	£0.30	£0.90	£1.50
Title Value:	$0.45	$1.35	$2.25	£0.30	£0.90	£1.50

E-MAN, THE ORIGINAL
First,MS; 1 Oct 1985-7 Apr 1986
1 ND reprints Charlton series, Michael Mauser back-ups begin

	$0.30	$0.90	$1.50	£0.20	£0.60	£1.00
2-7 ND	$0.30	$0.90	$1.50	£0.20	£0.60	£1.00
Title Value:	$2.10	$6.30	$10.50	£1.40	£4.20	£7.00

E-MAN: FUTURE TENSE
Alpha Productions; 1 Mar 1995
1 ND Nicola Cuti script, Joe Staton art; E-Man visits the time of The Morlocks who feature in H.G. Wells "The Time Machine"

	$0.55	$1.65	$2.75	£0.35	£1.05	£1.75
Title Value:	$0.55	$1.65	$2.75	£0.35	£1.05	£1.75

EAGLE
Crystal/Apple (#17 on); 1 Sep 1986-26 1991
1-11 ND

	$0.30	$0.90	$1.50	£0.20	£0.60	£1.00
12 ND DS, origin issue						
	$0.30	$0.90	$1.50	£0.20	£0.60	£1.00
13-26 ND	$0.30	$0.90	$1.50	£0.20	£0.60	£1.00
Title Value:	$7.80	$23.40	$39.00	£5.20	£15.60	£26.00

EAGLE: THE DARK MIRROR SAGA
Comic Zone; 1 Apr 1992-4 1992
1-4 ND black and white

	$0.30	$0.90	$1.50	£0.20	£0.60	£1.00
Title Value:	$1.20	$3.60	$6.00	£0.80	£2.40	£4.00

EARTH 4
Continuity; 1 Apr 1993-4 1994
1 ND Deathwatch 2000 part 6, embossed cover, pre-bagged with trading card

	$0.30	$0.90	$1.50	£0.20	£0.60	£1.00
2 ND Deathwatch 2000, pre-bagged with trading card						
	$0.30	$0.90	$1.50	£0.20	£0.60	£1.00
3 ND	$0.30	$0.90	$1.50	£0.20	£0.60	£1.00
4 ND Crossbreeds story						
	$0.30	$0.90	$1.50	£0.20	£0.60	£1.00
Title Value:	$1.20	$3.60	$6.00	£0.80	£2.40	£4.00

EARTHWORM JIM
Marvel Comics Group,MS; 1 Dec 1995-3 Feb 1996
1-3 ND based on video game and cartoon

	$0.45	$1.35	$2.25	£0.30	£0.90	£1.50
Title Value:	$1.35	$4.05	$6.75	£0.90	£2.70	£4.50

EASTER STORY, THE
Marvel Comics Group,OS; 1 Jan 1994
1 ND Louise Simonson script about The Ressurrection of Christ

	$0.45	$1.35	$2.25	£0.30	£0.90	£1.50
Title Value:	$0.45	$1.35	$2.25	£0.30	£0.90	£1.50

EB'NN THE RAVEN
Crowquill/Now; 1 Oct 1985-10 1987
1-9 ND

	$0.30	$0.90	$1.50	£0.20	£0.60	£1.00
10 ND colour	$0.30	$0.90	$1.50	£0.20	£0.60	£1.00
Title Value:	$3.00	$9.00	$15.00	£2.00	£6.00	£10.00

E.C. CLASSIC REPRINTS
East Coast; 1 1973-12 1976
1 scarce in the U.K. Crypt of Terror #1

	$1.20	$3.60	$6.00	£1.00	£3.00	£5.00
2 Weird Science #15						
	$1.00	$3.00	$5.00	£0.60	£1.80	£3.00
3 Shock-Suspenstories #12						
	$1.00	$3.00	$5.00	£0.60	£1.80	£3.00
4 Haunt of Fear #12						
	$1.00	$3.00	$5.00	£0.60	£1.80	£3.00
5 Weird Fantasy #13						
	$1.00	$3.00	$5.00	£0.60	£1.80	£3.00

Dragon's Claws #1

Dragstrip Hotrodders #5

E-Man Limited Edtion

	$Good	$Fine	$N.Mint	£Good	£Fine	£N.Mint
6 Crime-Suspenstories #25	$1.00	$3.00	$5.00	£0.60	£1.80	£3.00
7 scarce in the U.K. Vault of Horror #26	$1.00	$3.00	$5.00	£0.70	£2.10	£3.50
8 Shock-Suspenstories #6	$1.00	$3.00	$5.00	£0.60	£1.80	£3.00
9 Two-Fisted Tales #34	$1.00	$3.00	$5.00	£0.60	£1.80	£3.00
10 Haunt of Fear #23	$1.00	$3.00	$5.00	£0.60	£1.80	£3.00
11 scarce in the U.K. Weird Science #12	$1.00	$3.00	$5.00	£0.70	£2.10	£3.50
12 Shock-Suspenstories #2	$1.00	$3.00	$5.00	£0.60	£1.80	£3.00
Title Value:	$12.20	$36.60	$61.00	£7.80	£23.40	£39.00

Note: all Non-Distributed on the news-stands in the U.K.

E.C. CLASSICS
Russ Cochran; 1 Aug 1985-12 1988

	$Good	$Fine	$N.Mint	£Good	£Fine	£N.Mint
1 ND 56pgs, large format 8" x 11" reprints of classic EC Comics begins; Tales from the Crypt reprints, Jack Davis cover	$1.00	$3.00	$5.00	£0.70	£2.10	£3.50
2 ND Weird Science	$1.00	$3.00	$5.00	£0.70	£2.10	£3.50
3 ND Two Fisted Tales, Kurtzman cover	$1.00	$3.00	$5.00	£0.70	£2.10	£3.50
4 ND Shock Suspenstories, Wally Wood cover	$1.00	$3.00	$5.00	£0.70	£2.10	£3.50
5 ND Weird Fantasy, Feldstein cover	$1.00	$3.00	$5.00	£0.70	£2.10	£3.50
6 ND The Vault of Horror	$1.00	$3.00	$5.00	£0.70	£2.10	£3.50
7 ND Weird Science-Fantasy, Wally Wood cover	$1.00	$3.00	$5.00	£0.70	£2.10	£3.50
8 ND Crime Suspenstories	$1.00	$3.00	$5.00	£0.70	£2.10	£3.50
9 ND The Haunt of Fear	$1.00	$3.00	$5.00	£0.70	£2.10	£3.50
10 ND Panic	$1.00	$3.00	$5.00	£0.70	£2.10	£3.50
11 ND Tales From The Crypt	$1.00	$3.00	$5.00	£0.70	£2.10	£3.50
12 ND Weird Science, Wally Wood cover	$1.00	$3.00	$5.00	£0.70	£2.10	£3.50
Title Value:	$12.00	$36.00	$60.00	£8.40	£25.20	£42.00

ECHO OF FUTURE PAST
Continuity; 1 May 1984-9 Jan 1986

	$Good	$Fine	$N.Mint	£Good	£Fine	£N.Mint
1 48pgs, anthology begins; features Bucky O'Hare by Golden, Frankenstein by Adams, Mudwogs by Suydam	$0.50	$1.50	$2.50	£0.35	£1.05	£1.75
2 48pgs, Arthur Suydam, Neal Adams and Michael Golden art; Arthur Suydam cover	$0.50	$1.50	$2.50	£0.35	£1.05	£1.75
3 48pgs, Arthur Suydam, Neal Adams and Michael Golden art; Michael Golden cover	$0.50	$1.50	$2.50	£0.35	£1.05	£1.75
4 48pgs, Arthur Suydam, Neal Adams and Michael Golden art; Arthur Suydam cover	$0.50	$1.50	$2.50	£0.35	£1.05	£1.75
5 Arthur Suydam, Neal Adams and Michael Golden art featured; part Neal Adams cover	$0.50	$1.50	$2.50	£0.35	£1.05	£1.75
6 48pgs, Michael Golden, Neal Adams and Alex Toth art featured; Michael Golden cover	$0.50	$1.50	$2.50	£0.35	£1.05	£1.75
7 48pgs, part Neal Adams art, Alex Toth art; cover by Neal and Cory Adams	$0.50	$1.50	$2.50	£0.35	£1.05	£1.75
8 48pgs, part Neal Adams art featured	$0.50	$1.50	$2.50	£0.35	£1.05	£1.75
9 48pgs, Neal Adams part art and part cover art	$0.50	$1.50	$2.50	£0.35	£1.05	£1.75
Title Value:	$4.50	$13.50	$22.50	£3.15	£9.45	£15.75

Note: all Non-Distributed on the news-stands in the U.K.

ECLIPSE GRAPHIC ALBUM SERIES
Eclipse; 1 Oct 1978-31 1990

	$Good	$Fine	$N.Mint	£Good	£Fine	£N.Mint
1 Sabre (Oct 1978) by Don McGregor, Paul Gulacy art	$1.50	$4.50	$7.50	£1.00	£3.00	£5.00
1 2nd printing, (Jan 1979)	$1.20	$3.60	$6.00	£0.80	£2.40	£4.00
1 3rd printing	$1.05	$3.15	$5.25	£0.70	£2.10	£3.50
2 Night Music (Nov 1979) by P. Craig Russell	$0.90	$2.70	$4.50	£0.60	£1.80	£3.00
3 Detectives Inc: A Remembrance of Threatening Green (May 1980) by Marshall Rogers	$1.40	$4.20	$7.00	£0.90	£2.70	£4.50
4 Stewart the Rat (1980), Gene Colan art	$1.20	$3.60	$6.00	£0.80	£2.40	£4.00
5 The Price (Oct 1981) by Jim Starlin, features Dreadstar	$2.25	$6.75	$11.25	£1.50	£4.50	£7.50
6 I Am Coyote (Nov 1984), Marshall Rogers art	$1.20	$3.60	$6.00	£1.00	£3.00	£5.00
7 The Rocketeer (Sep 1985), Dave Stevens art	$1.80	$5.25	$9.00	£1.20	£3.60	£6.00
7 2nd printing	$1.40	$4.20	$7.00	£0.90	£2.70	£4.50
7 Signed, Limited Hardcover Edition, scarce	$9.00	$27.00	$45.00	£6.00	£18.00	£30.00
8 Zorro in Old California (1986)	$1.20	$3.60	$6.00	£0.80	£2.40	£4.00
9 Sacred and the Profane (1986), Ken Steacy art	$2.85	$8.50	$14.25	£1.90	£5.50	£9.50
9 Hardcover Edition	$4.50	$13.50	$22.50	£3.00	£9.00	£15.00
10 Somerset Holmes	$2.85	$8.50	$14.25	£1.90	£5.50	£9.50
10 Hardcover Edition	$4.50	$13.50	$22.50	£3.00	£9.00	£15.00
11 Floyd Farland, Citizen of the Future (1987)	$0.80	$2.40	$4.00	£0.40	£1.20	£2.00
12 Silverheels (1987)	$1.50	$4.50	$7.50	£1.00	£3.00	£5.00
12 Hardcover Edition	$3.00	$9.00	$15.00	£2.00	£6.00	£10.00
12 Signed, Limited Hardcover Edition	$4.50	$13.50	$22.50	£3.00	£9.00	£15.00
13 The Sisterhood of Steel (1987)	$1.80	$5.25	$9.00	£1.20	£3.60	£6.00
14 Samurai, Son of Death (1987)	$0.90	$2.70	$4.50	£0.60	£1.80	£3.00
14 2nd printing	$0.80	$2.40	$4.00	£0.50	£1.50	£2.50
15 Twisted Tales (Nov 1987), Dave Stevens cover	$0.80	$2.40	$4.00	£0.50	£1.50	£2.50
16 Airfighter Classics #1	$0.90	$2.70	$4.50	£0.60	£1.80	£3.00
17 Valkyrie, Prisoner of the Past (1988), reprints #1-3	$1.65	$4.95	$8.25	£1.10	£3.30	£5.50
18 Airfighter Classics #2	$0.90	$2.70	$4.50	£0.60	£1.80	£3.00
19 Scout: The Four Monsters (1988), reprints Scout #1-7	$3.00	$9.00	$15.00	£2.00	£6.00	£10.00
20 Airfighter Classics #3	$0.90	$2.70	$4.50	£0.60	£1.80	£3.00
21 XYR - role playing adventure with a number of possible endings, 48pgs squarebound, black and white	$0.80	$2.40	$4.00	£0.50	£1.50	£2.50
22 Alien Worlds #1 (May 1988), Bruce Jones script; Yeates, Reese, Shanover, Wray art	$1.00	$3.00	$5.00	£0.60	£1.80	£3.00
23 Airfighter Classics #4	$0.90	$2.70	$4.50	£0.60	£1.80	£3.00
24 Heartbreak	$0.90	$2.70	$4.50	£0.60	£1.80	£3.00
25 Zorro Volume #1 by Alex Toth	$1.80	$5.25	$9.00	£1.20	£3.60	£6.00
26 Zorro Volume #2 by Alex Toth	$1.80	$5.25	$9.00	£1.20	£3.60	£6.00
27 Fast Fiction	$1.05	$3.15	$5.25	£0.70	£2.10	£3.50
28 Miracleman Book 1: A Dream of Flying	$1.80	$5.25	$9.00	£1.20	£3.60	£6.00
29 Real Love: The Best of Simon and Kirby Romance Comics (Oct 1988)	$2.25	$6.75	$11.25	£1.50	£4.50	£7.50
30 Brought To Light (1988); Alan Moore script, Bill Sienkiewicz art	$1.80	$5.25	$9.00	£1.20	£3.60	£6.00
30 Limited Hardcover Edition	$5.25	$15.50	$26.25	£3.50	£10.50	£17.50
31 Pigeons From Hell (Nov 1988) by Robert E. Howard	$1.40	$4.20	$7.00	£0.90	£2.70	£4.50
31 Signed, Limited Hardcover Edition	$5.25	$15.50	$26.25	£3.50	£10.50	£17.50
Title Value:	$86.25	$257.25	$431.25	£57.30	£171.50	£286.50

Note: all Non-Distributed on the news-standsin the U.K.

ECLIPSE MONTHLY
Eclipse; 1 Aug 1983-10 Jul 1984

	$Good	$Fine	$N.Mint	£Good	£Fine	£N.Mint
1-10 ND	$0.30	$0.90	$1.50	£0.20	£0.60	£1.00
Title Value:	$3.00	$9.00	$15.00	£2.00	£6.00	£10.00

ECLIPSO
DC Comics; 1 Nov 1992-18 Apr 1994
(see House of Secrets #61)

	$Good	$Fine	$N.Mint	£Good	£Fine	£N.Mint
1 Eclipso: The Darkness Within spin-off	$0.25	$0.75	$1.25	£0.15	£0.45	£0.75
2	$0.25	$0.75	$1.25	£0.15	£0.45	£0.75
3-6 Cave Carson and Creeper appear	$0.25	$0.75	$1.25	£0.15	£0.45	£0.75
7 Ted McKeever art	$0.25	$0.75	$1.25	£0.15	£0.45	£0.75
8 Ted McKeever art, Sherlock Holmes appears	$0.25	$0.75	$1.25	£0.15	£0.45	£0.75
9 Johnny Peril appears	$0.25	$0.75	$1.25	£0.15	£0.45	£0.75
10 Darkseid appears	$0.25	$0.75	$1.25	£0.15	£0.45	£0.75
11-12 Creeper, Peacemaker, Mark Shaw: Manhunter, the new Wildcat, Dr. Midnight, Commander Steel and Major Victory appear	$0.25	$0.75	$1.25	£0.15	£0.45	£0.75
13 deaths of Creeper, Peacemaker, Mark Shaw: Manhunter, the new Wildcat, Dr. Midnight, Commander Steel and Major Victory	$0.25	$0.75	$1.25	£0.15	£0.45	£0.75
14-15	$0.25	$0.75	$1.25	£0.15	£0.45	£0.75
16 Green Lantern, Guy Gardner, Hourman, Jade, Obsidian, Green Arrow and Mister Miracle appear	$0.25	$0.75	$1.25	£0.15	£0.45	£0.75
17 Martian Manhunter, Wonder Woman, Flash, Bloodwynd, Booster Gold appear	$0.25	$0.75	$1.25	£0.15	£0.45	£0.75
18 Spectre vs. Eclipso, Justice League appear	$0.25	$0.75	$1.25	£0.15	£0.45	£0.75
Title Value:	$4.50	$13.50	$22.50	£2.70	£8.10	£13.50

ECLIPSO - THE DARKNESS WITHIN CROSSOVERS
Cross-over event for DC summer '92 annuals. A minor villain from the House of Secrets title, he is

transformed into an evil god of vengeance and plans to rule the Earth through his puppet soldiers - the heroes that defend the Earth. The story begins in Eclipso: The Darkness Within #1 and ends in number two with the annuals in between. The order is as follows:

Eclipso: The Darkness Within #1 Superman: The Man of Steel Annual #1 Green Lantern Annual #1 Detective Comics Annual #5 Superman Annual #4 Justice League America Annual #6 The Demon Annual #1 Green Arrow Annual #5 Flash Annual #5 Action Comics Annual #4 Hawkworld Annual #3 Robin Annual #1 Deathstroke, The Terminator Annual #1 New Titans Annual #8 Legion '92 Annual #3 Justice League Europe Annual #3 Wonder Woman Annual #3 Batman Annual #16 Adventures of Superman Annual #4 Eclipso: The Darkness Within #2

ECLIPSO ANNUAL
DC Comics; 1 Oct 1993
1 64pgs, Bloodlines (Wave Two) part 19, 1st appearance Prism, continued in Demon Annual #2

	$Good	$Fine	$N.Mint	£Good	£Fine	£N.Mint
	$0.30	$0.90	$1.50	£0.20	£0.60	£1.00
Title Value:	$0.30	$0.90	$1.50	£0.20	£0.60	£1.00

ECLIPSO: THE DARKNESS WITHIN
DC Comics; 1 Jul 1992-2 Dec 1992
1 ND 64pgs, The Darkness Within begins; Superman, Valor and Creeper appear, lead into summer '92 DC annual cross-overs, 3-D plastic purple diamond on cover. Direct Sales edition to comic shops

	$Good	$Fine	$N.Mint	£Good	£Fine	£N.Mint
	$0.45	$1.35	$2.25	£0.30	£0.90	£1.50

1 Newstand edition, without 3-D plastic diamond

	$0.35	$1.05	$1.75	£0.25	£0.75	£1.25

2 64pgs, The Darkness Within concludes, Hawkman, Aquaman, Blue Devil, Black Canary, Challengers and Suicide Squad appear

	$0.35	$1.05	$1.75	£0.25	£0.75	£1.25
Title Value:	$1.15	$3.45	$5.75	£0.80	£2.40	£4.00

ECTOKID
Marvel Comics Group/Razorline; 1 Sep 1993-9 May 1994
1 ND prismatic foil cover

	$0.30	$0.90	$1.50	£0.20	£0.60	£1.00
2-9 ND	$0.30	$0.90	$1.50	£0.20	£0.60	£1.00
Title Value:	$2.70	$8.10	$13.50	£1.80	£5.40	£9.00

ECTOKID UNLEASHED
Marvel Comics Group/Razorline, OS; 1 Oct 1994
1 ND 48pgs

	$0.45	$1.35	$2.25	£0.30	£0.90	£1.50
Title Value:	$0.45	$1.35	$2.25	£0.30	£0.90	£1.50

EDDIE CAMPBELL'S ALEC IN: THE DANCE OF LIFEY DEATH
Dark Horse, OS; 1 Jan 1994
1 ND 48pgs, black and white

	$0.80	$2.40	$4.00	£0.50	£1.50	£2.50
Title Value:	$0.80	$2.40	$4.00	£0.50	£1.50	£2.50

EDDIE CAMPBELL'S BACCHUS
Eddie Campbell Comics; 1 May 1995-present
1 ND reprints early adventures from Deadface with new art revisions plus new material

	$0.60	$1.80	$3.00	£0.40	£1.20	£2.00
2-6 ND	$0.60	$1.80	$3.00	£0.40	£1.20	£2.00
Title Value:	$3.60	$10.80	$18.00	£2.40	£7.20	£12.00

EDDY CURRENT
Mad Dog Graphics; 1 Jul 1987-12 Dec 1988
(see Splat! #3)
1 ND scarce in the U.K.

	$1.50	$4.50	$7.50	£1.20	£3.60	£6.00
2 ND	$1.20	$3.60	$6.00	£0.80	£2.40	£4.00

3 ND scarce in the U.K.

	$1.20	$3.60	$6.00	£1.00	£3.00	£5.00
4-5 ND	$1.00	$3.00	$5.00	£0.70	£2.10	£3.50
6-10 ND	$0.80	$2.40	$4.00	£0.50	£1.50	£2.50
11-12 ND	$0.60	$1.80	$3.00	£0.40	£1.20	£2.00
Title Value:	$11.10	$33.30	$55.50	£7.70	£23.10	£38.50

Hardcover Collection (Sep 1991), 360pgs with new cover

				£3.70	£11.10	£18.50

EDGE
Malibu Bravura, MS; 1 Jul 1994-4 Nov 1994
1-4 ND Gil Kane art

	$0.45	$1.35	$2.25	£0.30	£0.90	£1.50
Title Value:	$1.80	$5.40	$9.00	£1.20	£3.60	£6.00

Note; all Non-Distributed on the news-stands in the U.K.

EDGE OF CHAOS
Pacific; 1 Jul 1983-3 Dec 1983
1 ND origin issue, Gray Morrow art; colour begins

	$0.20	$0.60	$1.00	£0.15	£0.45	£0.75
2-3 ND Gray Morrrow art						
	$0.20	$0.60	$1.00	£0.15	£0.45	£0.75
Title Value:	$0.60	$1.80	$3.00	£0.45	£1.35	£2.25

EERIE
Avon Periodicals; 1 Jan 1947; 1 May 1951-17 Aug 1954
1 scarce in the U.K. widely acknowledged to be the first horror anthology comic

	$115.00	$355.00	$950.00	£77.50	£230.00	£625.00

1 scarce in the U.K. reprints original issue #1, classic "ghoul" cover

	$46.00	$135.00	$325.00	£32.00	£95.00	£225.00

2 classic Wally Wood bondage cover, Wood art

	$52.50	$160.00	$375.00	£36.00	£105.00	£250.00

3 Wally Wood cover and art, Joe Jubert art

	$52.50	$160.00	$375.00	£36.00	£105.00	£250.00

4-5 Wally Wood cover

	$43.00	$125.00	$300.00	£29.00	£85.00	£200.00
6	$18.50	$55.00	$130.00	£12.50	£39.00	£90.00

7 Wally Wood vampire cover, Kubert art

	$30.00	$90.00	$210.00	£20.00	£60.00	£140.00
8	$18.50	$55.00	$130.00	£12.50	£39.00	£90.00

9 Kubert art

	$21.00	$62.50	$150.00	£14.00	£43.00	£100.00
10	$17.00	$50.00	$120.00	£11.00	£34.00	£80.00
11	$15.50	$47.00	$110.00	£10.50	£32.00	£75.00

---

12 Dracula cover; Dracula story adaptation

	$Good	$Fine	$N.Mint	£Good	£Fine	£N.Mint
	$21.00	$62.50	$150.00	£14.00	£43.00	£100.00
13-14	$15.50	$47.00	$110.00	£10.50	£32.00	£75.00

15 reprints part issue #1 with different cover

	$12.00	$36.00	$85.00	£8.50	£26.00	£60.00

16 Wally Wood reprint; Mummy cover

	$13.50	$41.00	$95.00	£9.25	£28.00	£65.00

17 Wally Wood reprint

	$17.50	$52.50	$125.00	£12.00	£36.00	£85.00
Title Value:	$567.50	$1705.50	$4150.00	£384.75	£1149.00	£2785.00

Note; all Non-Distributed on the news-stands in the U.K.

EERIE (MAGAZINE)
Warren, Magazine; 1 Sep 1965; 2 Mar 1966-139 Feb 1983
1 very rare, distributed in the U.K.

	$39.00	$115.00	$275.00	£25.00	£75.00	£175.00

1 2nd printing, scarce in the U.K. distinguishable by its un-trimmed and therefore un-even edges

	$16.50	$50.00	$100.00	£10.50	£33.00	£65.00

2 distributed in the U.K.

	$8.25	$25.00	$50.00	£5.00	£15.00	£30.00

3 distributed in the U.K.

	$5.75	$17.50	$35.00	£3.30	£10.00	£20.00

4-5 distributed in the U.K.

	$4.15	$12.50	$25.00	£2.05	£6.25	£12.50

6-8 distributed in the U.K.

	$4.15	$12.50	$25.00	£1.65	£5.00	£10.00

9 scarce, distributed in the U.K. Neal Adams art

	$4.15	$12.50	$25.00	£2.05	£6.25	£12.50

10 distributed in the U.K.

	$4.15	$12.50	$25.00	£1.65	£5.00	£10.00

11 distributed in the U.K.

	$2.50	$7.50	$15.00	£1.15	£3.50	£7.00

12-14 distributed in the U.K.

	$2.50	$7.50	$15.00	£1.00	£3.00	£6.00

15 scarce, distributed in the U.K.

	$2.50	$7.50	$15.00	£1.15	£3.50	£7.00

16 distributed in the U.K.

	$2.50	$7.50	$15.00	£1.00	£3.00	£6.00

17-18 scarce, distributed in the U.K.

	$2.50	$7.50	$15.00	£1.15	£3.50	£7.00

19-20 distributed in the U.K.

	$2.50	$7.50	$15.00	£1.00	£3.00	£6.00

21-29 distributed in the U.K.

	$2.50	$7.50	$15.00	£0.80	£2.50	£5.00

30-33 distributed in the U.K.

	$2.00	$6.00	$10.00	£0.80	£2.40	£4.00

34 distributed in the U.K.

	$2.00	$6.00	$10.00	£0.70	£2.10	£3.50

35-37 distributed in the U.K.

	$2.00	$6.00	$10.00	£0.80	£2.40	£4.00

38 distributed in the U.K.

	$2.00	$6.00	$10.00	£0.70	£2.10	£3.50

39-40 distributed in the U.K.

	$2.00	$6.00	$10.00	£0.80	£2.40	£4.00
41-53	$1.60	$4.80	$8.00	£0.70	£2.10	£3.50

54-55 Eisner Spirit

	$2.00	$6.00	$10.00	£0.80	£2.40	£4.00
56-57	$1.60	$4.80	$8.00	£0.70	£2.10	£3.50
58 Wrightson art	$2.00	$6.00	$10.00	£0.80	£2.40	£4.00
59	$1.60	$4.80	$8.00	£0.70	£2.10	£3.50
60 Wrightson art	$2.00	$6.00	$10.00	£0.80	£2.40	£4.00
61	$1.60	$4.80	$8.00	£0.70	£2.10	£3.50
62 Wrightson art	$1.60	$4.80	$8.00	£0.60	£1.80	£3.00
63-64	$1.60	$4.80	$8.00	£0.70	£2.10	£3.50
65	$1.60	$4.80	$8.00	£0.60	£1.80	£3.00

66-68 distributed in the U.K.

	$1.60	$4.80	$8.00	£0.40	£1.20	£2.00

69 distributed in the U.K. Paul Neary art (Hunter story)

	$1.60	$4.80	$8.00	£0.40	£1.20	£2.00

70 distributed in the U.K.

	$1.60	$4.80	$8.00	£0.40	£1.20	£2.00

71 Paul Neary art featured

	$1.60	$4.80	$8.00	£0.40	£1.20	£2.00
72-80	$1.60	$4.80	$8.00	£0.40	£1.20	£2.00
81-139	$1.00	$3.00	$5.00	£0.30	£0.90	£1.50
Title Value:	$292.65	$877.30	$1633.00	£124.35	£376.25	£726.50

Eerie's Greatest Hits (Dec 1994)
Softcover collection of classic stories, black and white; Kelley Jones cover. Published by Harris Comics

				£1.70	£5.10	£8.50

EERIE ANNUAL
Warren, Magazine; 1-3 1970-1972
1 distributed in the U.K. reprints

	$3.00	$9.00	$15.00	£1.40	£4.20	£7.00

2 scarce in the U.K. reprints

	$3.00	$9.00	$15.00	£1.60	£4.80	£8.00

3 scarce in the U.K. reprints

	$2.40	$7.00	$12.00	£1.50	£4.50	£7.50
Title Value:	$8.40	$25.00	$42.00	£4.50	£13.50	£22.50

EERIE TALES
I.W. Super; 10,11,12,15,18 1963-1964
10-12 distributed in the U.K.

	$2.00	$6.00	$12.00	£1.15	£3.50	£7.00

15 distributed in the U.K.

	$4.55	$13.50	$27.50	£2.65	£8.00	£16.00

18 distributed in the U.K.

	$2.00	$6.00	$12.00	£1.15	£3.50	£7.00

	$Good	$Fine	$N.Mint	£Good	£Fine	£N.Mint
Title Value:	$12.55	$37.50	$75.50	£7.25	£22.00	£44.00

EGYPT
DC Comics/Vertigo,MS; 1 Aug 1995-7 Feb 1996

	$Good	$Fine	$N.Mint	£Good	£Fine	£N.Mint
1-7 ND Peter Milligan script, Glyn Dillon art	$0.50	$1.50	$2.50	£0.30	£0.90	£1.50
Title Value:	$3.50	$10.50	$17.50	£2.10	£6.30	£10.50

EIGHTBALL
Fantagraphics; 1 Jul 1990-present

	$Good	$Fine	$N.Mint	£Good	£Fine	£N.Mint
1 Dan Clowes story/art, Lloyd Llewellyn featured	$1.80	$5.25	$9.00	£1.20	£3.60	£6.00
1 2nd printing	$0.55	$1.65	$2.75	£0.35	£1.05	£1.75
1 3rd printing	$0.45	$1.35	$2.25	£0.30	£0.90	£1.50
1 4th printing	$0.40	$1.20	$2.00	£0.25	£0.75	£1.25
1 5th printing, (May 1993)	$0.40	$1.20	$2.00	£0.25	£0.75	£1.25
1 6th printing, (Aug 1994)	$0.60	$1.80	$3.00	£0.40	£1.20	£2.00
2	$1.20	$3.60	$6.00	£0.80	£2.40	£4.00
2 2nd printing	$0.55	$1.65	$2.75	£0.35	£1.05	£1.75
2 3rd/4th printing	$0.45	$1.35	$2.25	£0.30	£0.90	£1.50
3	$0.90	$2.70	$4.50	£0.60	£1.80	£3.00
3 2nd printing, (Nov 1991)	$0.45	$1.35	$2.25	£0.30	£0.90	£1.50
3 3rd/4th printing	$0.45	$1.35	$2.25	£0.30	£0.90	£1.50
4	$0.80	$2.40	$4.00	£0.50	£1.50	£2.50
4 2nd/3rd/4th printing	$0.45	$1.35	$2.25	£0.30	£0.90	£1.50
5	$0.80	$2.40	$4.00	£0.50	£1.50	£2.50
5 2nd printing, (Aug 1992)	$0.45	$1.35	$2.25	£0.30	£0.90	£1.50
6	$0.55	$1.65	$2.75	£0.35	£1.05	£1.75
6 2nd printing, (Sep 1992)	$0.45	$1.35	$2.25	£0.30	£0.90	£1.50
7	$0.45	$1.35	$2.25	£0.30	£0.90	£1.50
7 2nd printing, (Sep 1993)	$0.45	$1.35	$2.25	£0.30	£0.90	£1.50
8-9	$0.45	$1.35	$2.25	£0.30	£0.90	£1.50
10 conclusion "Like A Velvet Glove Cast In Iron"	$0.45	$1.35	$2.25	£0.30	£0.90	£1.50
11 $2.95 cover	$0.60	$1.80	$3.00	£0.40	£1.20	£2.00
12 $2.75 cover	$0.55	$1.65	$2.75	£0.35	£1.05	£1.75
13 $2.95 cover	$0.60	$1.80	$3.00	£0.40	£1.20	£2.00
13 (Nov 1994) An "improved" edition as the original issue #13 had colour and printing problems; heavier paper stock cover	$0.60	$1.80	$3.00	£0.40	£1.20	£2.00
14 $2.75 cover	$0.55	$1.65	$2.75	£0.35	£1.05	£1.75
15 $2.95 cover	$0.60	$1.80	$3.00	£0.40	£1.20	£2.00
16 $3.95 cover	$0.80	$2.40	$4.00	£0.50	£1.50	£2.50
Title Value:	$20.05	$60.00	$100.25	£13.15	£39.45	£65.75

Note: all Non-Distributed on the news-stands in the U.K.

EIGHTY PAGE GIANT MAGAZINE
National Periodical Publications/DC Comics; 1 Aug 1964-15 Oct 1965; 16 Nov 1965-89 Jul 1971

(#57-89 are actually 68pgs)

	$Good	$Fine	$N.Mint	£Good	£Fine	£N.Mint
1 Superman (not to be confused with Superman Annual 11); originally announced as Superman Annual #9	$31.00	$92.50	$375.00	£20.50	£62.50	£250.00
2 Jimmy Olsen	$18.50	$55.00	$225.00	£12.50	£38.00	£150.00
3 Lois Lane	$17.50	$52.50	$175.00	£11.50	£35.00	£115.00
4 The Flash, reprints Showcase #13 (cover story), #14 (cover story), Flash #105 (cover story), Flash #110 (cover story)	$17.50	$52.50	$175.00	£11.50	£35.00	£115.00
5 Batman, Silver anniversary issue; classic reprints	$16.00	$48.00	$160.00	£9.00	£27.00	£90.00
6 Superman, reprints including 1st Bizarro Lois Lane from Action Comics #255	$13.50	$41.00	$135.00	£9.00	£27.00	£90.00
7 rare in the U.K. Sgt. Rock's Prize Battle Tales	$13.50	$41.00	$135.00	£10.00	£30.00	£100.00
8 Secret Origins, reprints Justice League of America #9, Aquaman (Adventure #260), Robin origin re-told, Atom origin from Showcase #34, Superman #146	$33.00	$97.50	$325.00	£21.00	£62.50	£210.00
9 The Flash, reprints Flash #123	$13.50	$41.00	$135.00	£8.50	£26.00	£85.00
10 Superboy, reprints Adventure #271 (origin Luthor)	$13.50	$41.00	$135.00	£8.50	£26.00	£85.00
11 Superman, reprints Superboy #86 (4th Legion)	$13.50	$41.00	$135.00	£8.50	£26.00	£85.00
12 Batman	$13.50	$41.00	$135.00	£8.50	£26.00	£85.00
13 Jimmy Olsen	$13.50	$41.00	$135.00	£8.50	£26.00	£85.00
14 less common in the U.K. Lois Lane, reprints Superman #127 (1st Lori Lemaris)	$13.50	$41.00	$135.00	£9.00	£27.00	£90.00
15 Superman and Batman (World's Finest), Joker cover and story	$13.50	$41.00	$135.00	£9.00	£27.00	£90.00
Title Value:	$255.00	$767.00	$2650.00	£165.50	£501.00	£1725.00

Note: Many 80pg Giants and Annuals from the early '60s have crinkled covers at the spine, caused by uneven drying of the glue. Perfectly flat (and therefore Mint) copies are very scarce. Numbers 16-93 are included in the numbering of other titles, as follows:

16 Nov 1965-89 Oct/Nov 1971

#16: JLA 39. #17: Batman 176. #18: Superman 183. #19: Our Army at War 164. #20: Action 334. #21: Flash 160. #22: Superboy 129. #23: Superman 187. #24: Batman 182. #25: Jimmy Olsen 95. #26: Lois Lane 68. #27: Batman 185. #28: World's Finest 161. #29: JLA 48. #30: Batman 187. #31: Superman 193. #32: Our Army at War 177. #33: Action 347. #34: Flash 169. #35: Superboy 138. #36: Superman 198. #37: Batman 193. #38: Jimmy Olsen 104. #39: Lois Lane 77. #40: World's Finest 170. #41: JLA 58. #42: Superman 202. #43: Batman 198. #44: Our Army at War 190. #45: Action 360. #46: Flash 178. #47: Superboy 147. #48: Superman 207. #49: Batman 203. #50: Jimmy Olsen 113. #51: Lois Lane 86. #52: World's Finest 179. #53: JLA 67. #54: Superman 212. #55: Batman 208. #56: Our Army at War 203. #57: Action 373. #58: Flash 187. #59: Superboy 156. #60: Superman 217. #61: Batman 213. #62: Jimmy Olsen 122. #63: Lois Lane 95. #64 World's Finest 188. #65: JLA 76. #66: Superman 222. #67: Batman 218. #68: Our Army at War 216. #69: Adventure 390. #70: Flash 196. #71: Superboy 165. #72: Superman 227. #73: Batman 223. #74: Jimmy Olsen 131. #75: Lois Lane 104. #76: World's Finest 197. #77: JLA 85. #78: Superman 232. #79: Batman 228. #80: Our Army at War 229. #81: Adventure 403. #82: Flash 205. #83: Superboy 174. #84: Superman 239. #85: Batman 233. #86: Jimmy Olsen 140. #87: Lois Lane 113. #88: World's Finest 206. #89: JLA 93.

EL DIABLO
DC Comics; 1 Aug 1989-16 Dec 1990

	$Good	$Fine	$N.Mint	£Good	£Fine	£N.Mint
1-12 ND 48pgs	$0.25	$0.75	$1.25	£0.15	£0.45	£0.75
13-15 The River story	$0.25	$0.75	$1.25	£0.15	£0.45	£0.75
16	$0.25	$0.75	$1.25	£0.15	£0.45	£0.75
Title Value:	$4.00	$12.00	$20.00	£2.40	£7.20	£12.00

Note: New Format

EL SALVADOR: A HOUSE DIVIDED
Eclipse,OS; 1 1989

	$Good	$Fine	$N.Mint	£Good	£Fine	£N.Mint
1 ND Bill Tulp script/art; black and white	$0.30	$0.90	$1.50	£0.20	£0.60	£1.00
Title Value:	$0.30	$0.90	$1.50	£0.20	£0.60	£1.00

ELECTRIC BALLET
Caliber Press,MS; 1 Feb 1992-3 Apr 1993

	$Good	$Fine	$N.Mint	£Good	£Fine	£N.Mint
1-3 ND	$0.40	$1.20	$2.00	£0.25	£0.75	£1.25
Title Value:	$1.20	$3.60	$6.00	£0.75	£2.25	£3.75

ELECTRIC UNDERTOW
Marvel Comics Group,MS; 1 Dec 1989-5 Apr 1990

	$Good	$Fine	$N.Mint	£Good	£Fine	£N.Mint
1-5 ND 48pgs, squarebound, Mark Bagley pencils	$0.70	$2.10	$3.50	£0.40	£1.20	£2.00
Title Value:	$3.50	$10.50	$17.50	£2.40	£6.00	£10.00

Note: spin-off from Strikeforce: Morituri

ELECTRIC WARRIOR
DC Comics; 1 May 1986-18 Oct 1987

	$Good	$Fine	$N.Mint	£Good	£Fine	£N.Mint
1-18 ND Jim Baikie art	$0.25	$0.75	$1.25	£0.15	£0.45	£0.75
Title Value:	$4.50	$13.50	$22.50	£2.70	£8.10	£13.50

Note: Baxter paper.

ELEKTRA SAGA, THE
Marvel Comics Group/Epic,MS; 1 Feb 1984-4 Jun 1984

	$Good	$Fine	$N.Mint	£Good	£Fine	£N.Mint
1 ND	$1.00	$3.00	$5.00	£0.80	£2.40	£4.00
2-3 ND	$0.90	$2.70	$4.50	£0.70	£2.10	£3.50
4 ND	$1.20	$3.60	$6.00	£0.80	£2.40	£4.00
Title Value:	$4.00	$12.00	$20.00	£2.40	£7.20	£15.00
Note: edited reprints of Daredevil 168-190 with new covers, Miller story/art.						
Trade paperback (Nov 1989) Reprints of above				£2.00	£6.00	£10.00

ELEKTRA: ASSASSIN
Marvel Comics Group/Epic,MS; 1 Aug 1986-8 Mar 1987

	$Good	$Fine	$N.Mint	£Good	£Fine	£N.Mint
1 ND	$0.80	$2.40	$4.00	£0.50	£1.50	£2.50
2-8 ND	$0.60	$1.80	$3.00	£0.40	£1.20	£2.00
Title Value:	$5.00	$15.00	$25.00	£3.30	£9.90	£16.50
Trade Paperback, reprints #1-8				£1.25	£3.75	£6.25
Hardcover (2000 copies, signed and numbered. Jul 1989)				£5.00	£15.00	£25.00

Note: Miller story, Sienkiewicz art. Mature Readers.

ELEKTRA: ROOT OF EVIL
Marvel Comics Group,MS; 1 Mar 1995-4 Jun 1995

	$Good	$Fine	$N.Mint	£Good	£Fine	£N.Mint
1-4 foil stamped cover	$0.60	$1.80	$3.00	£0.40	£1.20	£2.00
Title Value:	$2.40	$7.20	$12.00	£1.60	£4.80	£8.00

ELEMENTALS
Comico; 1 Jun 1984-29 Sep 1988

(see Justice Machine)

	$Good	$Fine	$N.Mint	£Good	£Fine	£N.Mint
1 ND scarce in the U.K. 1st Comico flat-colour comic	$1.00	$3.00	$5.00	£1.00	£3.00	£5.00
2 ND	$0.60	$1.80	$3.00	£0.60	£1.80	£3.00
3 ND	$0.50	$1.50	$2.50	£0.40	£1.20	£2.00
4 ND	$0.40	$1.20	$2.00	£0.30	£0.90	£1.50
5-10 ND	$0.40	$1.20	$2.00	£0.25	£0.75	£1.25
11-29 ND	$0.30	$0.90	$1.50	£0.20	£0.60	£1.00
Title Value:	$10.60	$31.80	$53.00	£7.60	£22.80	£38.00
The Natural Order						
Trade paperback, reprints #1-5 plus story from Justice Machine Annual #1				£1.80	£5.40	£9.00
The Natural Order A (Dec 1992)						
as above with certificate and 11x17 print by Kelley Jones				£1.80	£5.40	£9.00
The Natural Order B (Dec 1992)						
as above plus reirnt of Monolith #1 and Vortex #1 and certificate. 2,000 copies				£2.00	£6.00	£10.00
Trade paperback (Sep 1991), reprints #6-10 with new cover by Bill Willingham				£2.00	£6.00	£10.00

ELEMENTALS OBLIVION WAR SPECIAL
Comico,MS; 1 Jul 1992-2 Aug 1992

	$Good	$Fine	$N.Mint	£Good	£Fine	£N.Mint
1 ND pin-ups, glow in the dark cover by Walt Simonson	$0.50	$1.50	$2.50	£0.30	£0.90	£1.50
1 ND Deluxe Format - silver embossed cover, 3,000 copies	$0.90	$2.70	$4.50	£0.60	£1.80	£3.00
2 ND includes two trading cards, cover by Walt Simonson	$0.50	$1.50	$2.50	£0.30	£0.90	£1.50
Title Value:	$1.90	$5.70	$9.50	£1.20	£3.60	£6.00

ELEMENTALS SEXY LINGERIE SPECIAL
Comico,OS; 1 Jan 1993

	$Good	$Fine	$N.Mint	£Good	£Fine	£N.Mint
1 ND includes giant pull-out poster						
	$1.00	$3.00	$5.00	£0.60	£1.80	£3.00
Title Value:	$1.00	$3.00	$5.00	£0.60	£1.80	£3.00
ELEMENTALS SPECIAL						
Comico; 1 Mar 1986; 2 Jan 1989						
1 ND	$0.30	$0.90	$1.50	£0.25	£0.75	£1.25
1 2nd printing, ND (Sep 1991)						
	$0.30	$0.90	$1.50	£0.20	£0.60	£1.00
2 ND	$0.30	$0.90	$1.50	£0.25	£0.75	£1.25
Title Value:	$0.90	$2.70	$4.50	£0.70	£2.10	£3.50
ELEMENTALS VOLUME 2						
Comico; 1 Mar 1989-32 1993						
1 ND Mike Leeke and Mike Chen art begins						
	$0.45	$1.35	$2.25	£0.30	£0.90	£1.50
2-15 ND	$0.40	$1.20	$2.00	£0.25	£0.75	£1.25
16 ND 1st appearance Strike Force America						
	$0.50	$1.50	$2.50	£0.30	£0.90	£1.50
17-24 ND	$0.30	$0.90	$1.50	£0.20	£0.60	£1.00
25 ND wraparound Kelley Jones cover						
	$0.40	$1.20	$2.00	£0.25	£0.75	£1.25
25 2nd printing, ND (May 1993)						
	$0.30	$0.90	$1.50	£0.20	£0.60	£1.00
26 ND origin of Strike Force America begins						
	$0.30	$0.90	$1.50	£0.20	£0.60	£1.00
27 ND	$0.30	$0.90	$1.50	£0.20	£0.60	£1.00
28 ND prism-embossed wraparound cover						
	$0.30	$0.90	$1.50	£0.20	£0.60	£1.00
29 ND	$0.30	$0.90	$1.50	£0.20	£0.60	£1.00
29 ND with giant poster by Walt Simonson						
	$0.80	$2.40	$4.00	£0.50	£1.50	£2.50
30 ND Oblivion War conclusion						
	$0.30	$0.90	$1.50	£0.20	£0.60	£1.00
30 ND 48pgs, Oblivion War conclusion, 16pg pin-up gallery; foil enhanced logo						
	$0.80	$2.40	$4.00	£0.50	£1.50	£2.50
31 ND sub-titled Birth of a Nation #0; new direction for title						
	$0.30	$0.90	$1.50	£0.20	£0.60	£1.00
32 ND	$0.30	$0.90	$1.50	£0.20	£0.60	£1.00
Title Value:	$13.35	$40.05	$66.75	£8.55	£25.65	£42.75
ELEMENTALS VOLUME 3						
Comico; 1 Aug 1995-present						
1 ND pre-bagged with trading card						
	$0.50	$1.50	$2.50	£0.30	£0.90	£1.50
2-4 ND	$0.50	$1.50	$2.50	£0.30	£0.90	£1.50
Title Value:	$2.00	$6.00	$10.00	£1.20	£3.60	£6.00
ELEMENTALS: GHOST OF A CHANCE GRAPHIC NOVEL						
Comico; OS; nn Jul 1995						
0 ND 48pgs, Alex Ross cover						
	$1.20	$3.60	$6.00	£0.80	£2.40	£4.00
Title Value:	$1.20	$3.60	$6.00	£0.80	£2.40	£4.00
ELEMENTALS: SEX, LIES, SANS VIDEOTAPE SPECIAL						
Comico,OS; 1 Oct 1991						
1 ND	$0.50	$1.50	$2.50	£0.30	£0.90	£1.50
Title Value:	$0.50	$1.50	$2.50	£0.30	£0.90	£1.50
ELEMENTALS: THE STRIKE FORCE LEGACY						
Comico,OS; 1 Jul 1993						
1 ND 64pgs	$0.60	$1.80	$3.00	£0.40	£1.20	£2.00
Title Value:	$0.60	$1.80	$3.00	£0.40	£1.20	£2.00
ELEVEN OR ONE						
Sirius, OS; 1 Apr 1995						
1 ND Joseph Michael Linsner cover & art, reprints Angry Christ Comic in colour						
	$1.00	$3.00	$5.00	£0.70	£2.10	£3.50
Title Value:	$1.00	$3.00	$5.00	£0.70	£2.10	£3.50
ELF TREK						
Dimension Graphics; 1 Jul 1986-2 Aug 1986						
1-2 ND parody of Star Trek, X-Men and Elflord, black and white						
	$0.25	$0.75	$1.25	£0.15	£0.45	£0.75
Title Value:	$0.50	$1.50	$2.50	£0.30	£0.90	£1.50
ELF-THING						
Eclipse,OS; 1 Mar 1987						
1 ND Elfquest/Swamp Thing/Hulk parody; black and white						
	$0.40	$1.20	$2.00	£0.25	£0.75	£1.25
Title Value:	$0.40	$1.20	$2.00	£0.25	£0.75	£1.25
ELF-WARRIOR						
Adventure/Quadrant; 1 1987-4 1988						
1-4 ND Peter Hsu art						
	$0.35	$1.05	$1.75	£0.25	£0.75	£1.25
Title Value:	$1.40	$4.20	$7.00	£1.00	£3.00	£5.00
ELFHEIM						
Night Wynd,MS; 1 Dec 1991-4 Mar 1992						
1-4 ND Barry Blair script and art; black and white						
	$0.35	$1.05	$1.75	£0.25	£0.75	£1.25
Title Value:	$1.40	$4.20	$7.00	£1.00	£3.00	£5.00
ELFHEIM (2ND SERIES)						
Night Wynd,MS; 1 Apr 1992-4 Jul 1992						
1-4 ND Barry Blair script and art; black and white						
	$0.35	$1.05	$1.75	£0.25	£0.75	£1.25
Title Value:	$1.40	$4.20	$7.00	£1.00	£3.00	£5.00
ELFHEIM (3RD SERIES)						
Night Wynd,MS; 1 Aug 1992-4 Nov 1992						
1-4 ND Barry Blair script and art; black and white						
	$0.35	$1.05	$1.75	£0.25	£0.75	£1.25
Title Value:	$1.40	$4.20	$7.00	£1.00	£3.00	£5.00
ELFHEIM (4TH SERIES)						
Night Wynd,MS; 1 Dec 1992-4 Apr 1993						
1-4 ND Barry Blair script and art; black and white						
	$0.35	$1.05	$1.75	£0.25	£0.75	£1.25
Title Value:	$1.40	$4.20	$7.00	£1.00	£3.00	£5.00
ELFHEIM: DRAGON'S DREAMS						
Night Wynd,MS; 1 Jul 1993-4 Aug 1993						
1-4 ND Barry Blair script and art; black and white						
	$0.35	$1.05	$1.75	£0.25	£0.75	£1.25
Title Value:	$1.40	$4.20	$7.00	£1.00	£3.00	£5.00
ELFHEIM: DRAGON'S EYE						
Night Wynd,MS; 1 Sep 1993-4 Feb 1994						
1-4 ND Barry Blair script and art; black and white						
	$0.35	$1.05	$1.75	£0.25	£0.75	£1.25
Title Value:	$1.40	$4.20	$7.00	£1.00	£3.00	£5.00
ELFHEIM: SHADE WARS						
Night Wynd,MS; 1 Jan 1994-4 Apr 1994						
1-4 ND Barry Blair script and art; black and white						
	$0.35	$1.05	$1.75	£0.25	£0.75	£1.25
Title Value:	$1.40	$4.20	$7.00	£1.00	£3.00	£5.00
ELFHEIM: TIME OF THE WOLF						
Night Wynd,MS; 1 Oct 1993-3 Dec 1993						
1-3 ND Barry Blair script and art						
	$0.35	$1.05	$1.75	£0.25	£0.75	£1.25
Title Value:	$1.05	$3.15	$5.25	£0.75	£2.25	£3.75
ELFLORD (1ST SERIES)						
Aircel; 1 1986-6 1986						
1 ND Barry Blair pencils begin; black and white						
	$0.40	$1.20	$2.00	£0.60	£1.80	£3.00
1 2nd printing ND	$0.35	$1.05	$1.75	£0.25	£0.75	£1.25

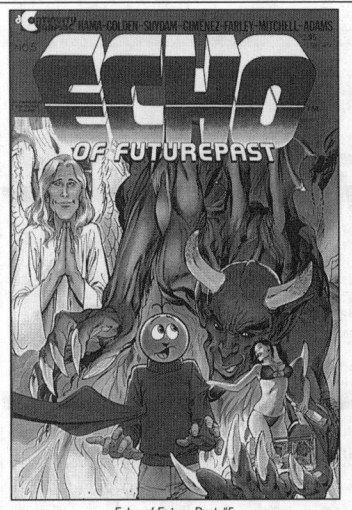

Echo of Future Past #5

Eclipse Monthly #1

Eighty Page Giant #7

MINT = 100% / NEAR MINT (inc. +/-) = 90–99% / VERY FINE (inc. +/-) = 75–89% / FINE (inc. +/-) = 55–74%
VERY GOOD (inc. +/-) = 35–54% / GOOD (inc. +/-) = 15–34% / FAIR = 5–14% / POOR = 1–4%

319

	$Good	$Fine	$N.Mint	£Good	£Fine	£N.Mint
2 ND	$0.30	$0.90	$1.50	£0.40	£1.20	£2.00
2 2nd printing ND	$0.35	$1.05	$1.75	£0.25	£0.75	£1.25
3-6 ND	$0.40	$1.20	$2.00	£0.30	£0.90	£1.50
Title Value:	$3.00	$9.00	$15.25	£2.70	£8.10	£13.50

ELFLORD (2ND SERIES)
Aircel; 1 1987-30 1989

	$Good	$Fine	$N.Mint	£Good	£Fine	£N.Mint
1-10 ND colour	$0.40	$1.20	$2.00	£0.30	£0.90	£1.50
11-20 ND colour	$0.35	$1.05	$1.75	£0.25	£0.75	£1.25
21 ND DS colour	$0.40	$1.20	$2.00	£0.30	£0.90	£1.50
22 ND last colour issue, new characters						
	$0.30	$0.90	$1.50	£0.20	£0.60	£1.00
23-30 ND	$0.30	$0.90	$1.50	£0.20	£0.60	£1.00
Title Value:	$10.60	$31.80	$53.00	£7.60	£22.80	£38.00

ELFLORD CHRONICLES
Aircel,MS; 1 Sep 1990-8 1991

	$Good	$Fine	$N.Mint	£Good	£Fine	£N.Mint
1 ND 40pgs, reprints begin, Barry Blair art begins						
	$0.35	$1.05	$1.75	£0.25	£0.75	£1.25
2-8 ND	$0.35	$1.05	$1.75	£0.25	£0.75	£1.25
Title Value:	$2.80	$8.40	$14.00	£2.00	£6.00	£10.00

ELFLORD: DRAGON'S EYE
Night Wynd,MS; 1 Aug 1993-4 Nov 1993

	$Good	$Fine	$N.Mint	£Good	£Fine	£N.Mint
1-4 ND Barry Blair script and art						
	$0.35	$1.05	$1.75	£0.25	£0.75	£1.25
Title Value:	$1.40	$4.20	$7.00	£1.00	£3.00	£5.00

ELFLORD: SHADOW SPELL
Night Wynd,MS; 1 Oct 1993-4 Mar 1994

	$Good	$Fine	$N.Mint	£Good	£Fine	£N.Mint
1-4 ND Barry Blair script and art; black and white						
	$0.35	$1.05	$1.75	£0.25	£0.75	£1.25
Title Value:	$1.40	$4.20	$7.00	£1.00	£3.00	£5.00

ELFLORD: SUMMER'S MAGIC
Night Wynd,MS; 1 Apr 1993-4 Jul 1993

	$Good	$Fine	$N.Mint	£Good	£Fine	£N.Mint
1-4 ND Barry Blair script and art						
	$0.35	$1.05	$1.75	£0.25	£0.75	£1.25
Title Value:	$1.40	$4.20	$7.00	£1.00	£3.00	£5.00

ELFLORD: THE RETURN OF THE KING
Night Wynd,MS; 1 Nov 1992-4 Mar 1993

	$Good	$Fine	$N.Mint	£Good	£Fine	£N.Mint
1-4 ND Barry Blair script and art						
	$0.35	$1.05	$1.75	£0.25	£0.75	£1.25
Title Value:	$1.40	$4.20	$7.00	£1.00	£3.00	£5.00

ELFLORE
Night Wynd,MS; 1 Apr 1992-4 Jul 1992

	$Good	$Fine	$N.Mint	£Good	£Fine	£N.Mint
1-4 ND Barry Blair script and art						
	$0.30	$0.90	$1.50	£0.20	£0.60	£1.00
Title Value:	$1.20	$3.60	$6.00	£0.80	£2.40	£4.00

ELFLORE (2ND SERIES)
Night Wynd,MS; 1 Aug 1992-4 Nov 1992

	$Good	$Fine	$N.Mint	£Good	£Fine	£N.Mint
1-4 ND Barry Blair script and art						
	$0.30	$0.90	$1.50	£0.20	£0.60	£1.00
Title Value:	$1.20	$3.60	$6.00	£0.80	£2.40	£4.00

ELFLORE (3RD SERIES)
Night Wynd,MS; 1 Dec 1992-4 Apr 1993

	$Good	$Fine	$N.Mint	£Good	£Fine	£N.Mint
1-4 ND Barry Blair script and art						
	$0.30	$0.90	$1.50	£0.20	£0.60	£1.00
Title Value:	$1.20	$3.60	$6.00	£0.80	£2.40	£4.00

ELFLORE: FIRE MOUNTAIN
Night Wynd,MS; 1 Jan 1994-4 Apr 1994

	$Good	$Fine	$N.Mint	£Good	£Fine	£N.Mint
1-4 ND Barry Blair script and art; black and white						
	$0.35	$1.05	$1.75	£0.25	£0.75	£1.25
Title Value:	$1.40	$4.20	$7.00	£1.00	£3.00	£5.00

ELFLORE: HIGH SEAS
Night Wynd,MS; 1 Jul 1993-4 Oct 1993

	$Good	$Fine	$N.Mint	£Good	£Fine	£N.Mint
1-4 ND Barry Blair script and art						
	$0.35	$1.05	$1.75	£0.25	£0.75	£1.25
Title Value:	$1.40	$4.20	$7.00	£1.00	£3.00	£5.00

ELFLORE: LAND OF DREAMS
Night Wynd,MS; 1 Sep 1993-3 Nov 1993

	$Good	$Fine	$N.Mint	£Good	£Fine	£N.Mint
1-3 ND Barry Blair script and art						
	$0.35	$1.05	$1.75	£0.25	£0.75	£1.25
Title Value:	$1.05	$3.15	$5.25	£0.75	£2.25	£3.75

ELFQUEST
Marvel Comics Group/Epic; 1 Aug 1985-32 Mar 1988

	$Good	$Fine	$N.Mint	£Good	£Fine	£N.Mint
1 ND	$0.60	$1.80	$3.00	£0.40	£1.20	£2.00
2-4	$0.40	$1.20	$2.00	£0.25	£0.75	£1.25
5 ND scarce in the U.K.						
	$0.40	$1.20	$2.00	£0.30	£0.90	£1.50
6	$0.30	$0.90	$1.50	£0.20	£0.60	£1.00
7 ND scarce in the U.K.						
	$0.30	$0.90	$1.50	£0.25	£0.75	£1.25
8-9	$0.30	$0.90	$1.50	£0.20	£0.60	£1.00
10-21	$0.25	$0.75	$1.25	£0.15	£0.45	£0.75
22-32 ND	$0.25	$0.75	$1.25	£0.20	£0.60	£1.00
Title Value:	$9.15	$27.45	$45.75	£6.30	£18.90	£31.50

ELFQUEST
Warp,Magazine; 1 Apr 1979; 2 Aug 1978-21 Feb 1985
(see other Elfquest titles,Fantasy Quarterly)

	$Good	$Fine	$N.Mint	£Good	£Fine	£N.Mint
1 Elfquest story from Fantasy Quarterly #1 reprinted; Wendy Pini story and art						
	$7.50	$22.50	$37.50	£4.00	£12.00	£20.00
1 2nd printing	$3.00	$9.00	$15.00	£1.00	£3.00	£5.00
1 3rd/4th printing, (slightly different cover on 4th print)						
	$0.80	$2.40	$4.00	£0.50	£1.50	£2.50
2	$5.00	$15.00	$25.00	£2.50	£7.50	£12.50
2 2nd/3rd/4th printings						
	$0.45	$1.35	$2.25	£0.30	£0.90	£1.50
3	$5.00	$15.00	$25.00	£2.00	£6.00	£10.00
3 2nd/3rd/4th printings						
	$0.45	$1.35	$2.25	£0.30	£0.90	£1.50
4	$4.00	$12.00	$20.00	£1.50	£4.50	£7.50
4 2nd/3rd/4th printings						
	$0.45	$1.35	$2.25	£0.30	£0.90	£1.50
5	$4.00	$12.00	$20.00	£1.50	£4.50	£7.50
5 2nd/3rd/4th printings						
	$0.45	$1.35	$2.25	£0.30	£0.90	£1.50
6	$2.00	$6.00	$10.00	£1.00	£3.00	£5.00
6 2nd/3rd printings	$0.40	$1.20	$2.00	£0.25	£0.75	£1.25
7	$2.00	$6.00	$10.00	£1.00	£3.00	£5.00
7 2nd/3rd printings	$0.40	$1.20	$2.00	£0.25	£0.75	£1.25
8	$2.00	$6.00	$10.00	£1.00	£3.00	£5.00
8 2nd/3rd printings	$0.40	$1.20	$2.00	£0.25	£0.75	£1.25
9	$2.00	$6.00	$10.00	£1.00	£3.00	£5.00
9 2nd/3rd printings	$0.40	$1.20	$2.00	£0.25	£0.75	£1.25
10-20	$1.20	$3.60	$6.00	£0.80	£2.40	£4.00
21 sketches and background information						
	$1.20	$3.60	$6.00	£0.80	£2.40	£4.00
Title Value:	$55.10	$165.30	$275.50	£28.80	£86.40	£144.00

Note: all Non-Distributed on the news-stands in the U.K.

Note also: the reason that issue #1 is dated later than #2 is that the creators, Richard and Wendy Pini, formed Warp Graphics after their original publisher went into receivership and continued the Fantasy Quarterly story as Elfquest #2. Issue #1, reprinting the first story, came out eight months later, around the time that issue #4 was released.

	£Good	£Fine	£N.Mint
Elfquest Book One: Fire and Flight, reprints #1-8 with additional art from the Marvel Epic Comics title	£2.00	£6.00	£10.00
Hardcover Edition (Jul 1993)	£3.00	£9.00	£15.00
Signed, Limited Edition #1-8 in slipcase	£25.00	£75.00	£125.00
Elfquest Book Two, reprints #9-16 plus new art	£2.00	£6.00	£10.00
Elfquest Book Three: Captives of Blue Mountain, reprints #17-24 with additional art	£2.00	£6.00	£10.00
Hardcover Edition (1994)	£3.00	£9.00	£15.00
Elfquest Book Four: Quest's End	£2.00	£6.00	£10.00
Elfquest Book Five: The Siege at Blue Mountain	£2.00	£6.00	£10.00
Elfquest Book Six: The Secret of Two-Edge	£2.00	£6.00	£10.00
Elfquest Book Seven: The Cry From Beyond	£2.00	£6.00	£10.00
Elfquest Book Eight: Kings of the Broken Wheel	£2.00	£6.00	£10.00

ELFQUEST GATHERUM
Warp; 1,2 1985

	$Good	$Fine	$N.Mint	£Good	£Fine	£N.Mint
1-2 ND 146pgs, new art	$3.00	$9.00	$15.00	£1.60	£4.80	£8.00
Title Value:	$6.00	$18.00	$30.00	£3.20	£9.60	£16.00
The Big Elfquest Gatherum (Nov 1994) selection from the two volumes plus new material. Hardcover				£2.70	£8.10	£13.50

ELFQUEST: BLOOD OF TEN CHIEFS
Warp Graphics; 1 Sep 1993-20 Sep 1995

	$Good	$Fine	$N.Mint	£Good	£Fine	£N.Mint
1 ND Richard Pini and Janine Johnson	$0.40	$1.20	$2.00	£0.25	£0.75	£1.25
2-20 ND	$0.40	$1.20	$2.00	£0.25	£0.75	£1.25
Title Value:	$8.00	$24.00	$40.00	£5.00	£15.00	£25.00

ELFQUEST: JINK
Warp Graphics; 1 Nov 1994-present

	$Good	$Fine	$N.Mint	£Good	£Fine	£N.Mint
1-5 ND John Ostrander script	$0.45	$1.35	$2.25	£0.30	£0.90	£1.50
6-9 ND	$0.45	$1.35	$2.25	£0.30	£0.90	£1.50
Title Value:	$4.05	$12.15	$20.25	£2.70	£8.10	£13.50

ELFQUEST: KAHVI
Warp Graphics,MS; 1 Oct 1995-present

	$Good	$Fine	$N.Mint	£Good	£Fine	£N.Mint
1-2 ND black and white	$0.45	$1.35	$2.25	£0.30	£0.90	£1.50
Title Value:	$0.90	$2.70	$4.50	£0.60	£1.80	£3.00

ELFQUEST: KINGS OF THE BROKEN WHEEL
Warp; 1 Aug 1990-9 Dec 1991

	$Good	$Fine	$N.Mint	£Good	£Fine	£N.Mint
1 ND	$0.50	$1.50	$2.50	£0.30	£0.90	£1.50
1 2nd printing ND	$0.40	$1.20	$2.00	£0.25	£0.75	£1.25
2-8 ND	$0.40	$1.20	$2.00	£0.25	£0.75	£1.25
9 ND conclusion of first story	$0.40	$1.20	$2.00	£0.25	£0.75	£1.25
Title Value:	$4.10	$12.30	$20.50	£2.55	£7.65	£12.75

Note: bi-monthly, carries on from Siege at Blue Mountain

ELFQUEST: NEW BLOOD
Warp Graphics,MS; 1 Oct 1992-present

	$Good	$Fine	$N.Mint	£Good	£Fine	£N.Mint
1 ND 64pgs	$0.50	$1.50	$2.50	£0.30	£0.90	£1.50
2-26 ND	$0.40	$1.20	$2.00	£0.25	£0.75	£1.25
27 ND $2.50 cover begins	$0.50	$1.50	$2.50	£0.30	£0.90	£1.50
28-33 ND	$0.50	$1.50	$2.50	£0.30	£0.90	£1.50
Title Value:	$14.00	$42.00	$70.00	£8.65	£25.95	£43.25
Elfquest: New Blood 1993 Summer Special (Sep 1993) 64pgs, new stories				£1.20	£3.60	£6.00
Elfquest: New Blood Collection (1994) Hard cover edition, collects first five issues				£2.40	£7.20	£12.00

ELFQUEST: SHARDS
Warp Graphics; 1 Aug 1994-present

	$Good	$Fine	$N.Mint	£Good	£Fine	£N.Mint
1 ND continues from Elfquest: The Hidden Years	$0.45	$1.35	$2.25	£0.30	£0.90	£1.50
2-9 ND	$0.45	$1.35	$2.25	£0.30	£0.90	£1.50
10 ND X-over Elfquest: The Hidden Years #23	$0.45	$1.35	$2.25	£0.30	£0.90	£1.50

	$Good	$Fine	$N.Mint	£Good	£Fine	£N.Mint
11-12 ND	$0.45	$1.35	$2.25	£0.30	£0.90	£1.50
Title Value:	$5.40	$16.20	$27.00	£3.60	£10.80	£18.00

ELFQUEST: SIEGE AT BLUE MOUNTAIN
Apple Comics,MS; 1 Mar 1987-8 Dec 1988

	$Good	$Fine	$N.Mint	£Good	£Fine	£N.Mint
1 ND Staton/Pini art begins, black and white	$1.00	$3.00	$5.00	£0.60	£1.80	£3.00
1 2nd printing ND	$0.45	$1.35	$2.25	£0.30	£0.90	£1.50
2 ND	$0.60	$1.80	$3.00	£0.30	£0.90	£1.50
2 2nd printing ND	$0.40	$1.20	$2.00	£0.25	£0.75	£1.25
3-5 ND	$0.45	$1.35	$2.25	£0.30	£0.90	£1.50
6-8 ND	$0.40	$1.20	$2.00	£0.25	£0.75	£1.25
Title Value:	$5.00	$15.00	$25.00	£3.10	£9.30	£15.50

ELFQUEST: THE HIDDEN YEARS
Warp Graphics; 1 Jul 1992-present

	$Good	$Fine	$N.Mint	£Good	£Fine	£N.Mint
1 ND Richard and Wendy Pini	$0.40	$1.20	$2.00	£0.25	£0.75	£1.25
2-9 ND	$0.40	$1.20	$2.00	£0.25	£0.75	£1.25
9 ND 48pgs, sub-titled "½" Wendy Pini and John Byrne	$0.60	$1.80	$3.00	£0.40	£1.20	£2.00
10-14 ND	$0.45	$1.35	$2.25	£0.30	£0.90	£1.50
15 ND 48pgs	$0.80	$2.40	$4.00	£0.50	£1.50	£2.50
16-25 ND	$0.45	$1.35	$2.25	£0.30	£0.90	£1.50
Title Value:	$11.75	$35.25	$58.75	£7.65	£22.95	£38.25
Elfquest: The Hidden Years Hardcover (1993) collects issues #1-5				£2.40	£7.20	£12.00
Elfquest: Hidden Years - Rogue's Challenge Hardcover (Feb 1994) collects issues #6-9 and #9 and a half				£2.70	£8.10	£13.50

ELFQUEST: THE REBELS
Warp Graphics; 1 Nov 1994-present

	$Good	$Fine	$N.Mint	£Good	£Fine	£N.Mint
1-10 ND	$0.45	$1.35	$2.25	£0.30	£0.90	£1.50
Title Value:	$4.50	$13.50	$22.75	£3.00	£9.00	£15.00

ELFQUEST: TWO SPEAR
Warp Graphics,MS; 1 Oct 1995-present

	$Good	$Fine	$N.Mint	£Good	£Fine	£N.Mint
1-2 ND Barry Blair art; black and white	$0.45	$1.35	$2.25	£0.30	£0.90	£1.50
Title Value:	$0.90	$2.70	$4.50	£0.60	£1.80	£3.00

ELFQUEST: WAVEDANCERS
Warp Graphics,MS; 1 Apr 1994-present

	$Good	$Fine	$N.Mint	£Good	£Fine	£N.Mint
1-6 ND	$0.40	$1.20	$2.00	£0.25	£0.75	£1.25
Title Value:	$2.40	$7.20	$12.00	£1.50	£4.50	£7.50

ELIMINATOR
Eternity,MS; 1 Jan 1992-3 Mar 1992

	$Good	$Fine	$N.Mint	£Good	£Fine	£N.Mint
1-3 ND	$0.35	$1.05	$1.75	£0.25	£0.75	£1.25
Title Value:	$1.05	$3.15	$5.25	£0.75	£2.25	£3.75

ELIMINATOR
Malibu Ultraverse; 0 Apr 1995; 1 May 1995-3 Jul 1995

	$Good	$Fine	$N.Mint	£Good	£Fine	£N.Mint
0 ND 40pgs, Godwheel spin-off, Mike Zeck cover and art	$0.40	$1.20	$2.00	£0.25	£0.75	£1.25
1 ND Mike Zeck cover and art; The Search for the Missing Infinity Gem story begins	$0.40	$1.20	$2.00	£0.25	£0.75	£1.25
1 ND Black Cover Limited Edition (May 1995) - solid black cover, limited to 5,000 copies	$0.60	$1.80	$3.00	£0.40	£1.20	£2.00
2-3 ND The Search for the Missing Infinity Gem, Mike Zeck cover	$0.40	$1.20	$2.00	£0.25	£0.75	£1.25
Title Value:	$2.20	$6.60	$11.00	£1.40	£4.20	£7.00

Note: no connection to 1st series called Eliminator by Eternity Comics

ELIMINATOR SPECIAL
Eternity,OS; 1 Oct 1991

	$Good	$Fine	$N.Mint	£Good	£Fine	£N.Mint
1 ND	$0.50	$1.50	$2.50	£0.30	£0.90	£1.50
Title Value:	$0.50	$1.50	$2.50	£0.30	£0.90	£1.50

ELITE PRESENTS
Elite Comics; 1 Jan 1987

	$Good	$Fine	$N.Mint	£Good	£Fine	£N.Mint
1 ND Night Wolf by Butch Burcham, colour	$0.30	$0.90	$1.50	£0.20	£0.60	£1.00
Title Value:	$0.30	$0.90	$1.50	£0.20	£0.60	£1.00

ELITE WARRIORS
Alchemy Studios,MS; 1 Sep 1991-2 1992

	$Good	$Fine	$N.Mint	£Good	£Fine	£N.Mint
1-2 ND	$0.30	$0.90	$1.50	£0.20	£0.60	£1.00
Title Value:	$0.60	$1.80	$3.00	£0.40	£1.20	£2.00

ELONGATED MAN
DC Comics,MS; 1 Dec 1991-4 Apr 1992
(see Flash [1st Series] #110)

	$Good	$Fine	$N.Mint	£Good	£Fine	£N.Mint
1	$0.15	$0.45	$0.75	£0.10	£0.35	£0.60
2-3 Flash appears	$0.15	$0.45	$0.75	£0.10	£0.35	£0.60
4	$0.15	$0.45	$0.75	£0.10	£0.35	£0.60
Title Value:	$0.60	$1.80	$3.00	£0.40	£1.40	£2.40

ELRIC OF MELNIBONE
Pacific; 1 Apr 1983-6 Apr 1984

	$Good	$Fine	$N.Mint	£Good	£Fine	£N.Mint
1 ND P. Craig Russell art begins	$0.40	$1.20	$2.00	£0.30	£0.90	£1.50
2-6 ND	$0.40	$1.20	$2.00	£0.30	£0.90	£1.50
Title Value:	$2.40	$7.20	$12.00	£1.80	£5.40	£9.00
Trade Paperback (First Publishing), reprints #1-6				£2.20	£6.60	£11.00

ELRIC: SAILOR ON THE SEAS OF FATE
First,MS; 1 Jun 1985-7 Jun 1986

	$Good	$Fine	$N.Mint	£Good	£Fine	£N.Mint
1 ND scarce in the U.K. Michael T. Gilbert art begins	$0.40	$1.20	$2.00	£0.40	£1.20	£2.00
2 ND scarce in the U.K.	$0.40	$1.20	$2.00	£0.35	£1.05	£1.75
3-7 ND	$0.40	$1.20	$2.00	£0.30	£0.90	£1.50
Title Value:	$2.80	$8.40	$14.00	£2.25	£6.75	£11.25
Trade Paperback, reprints #1-7				£2.20	£6.60	£11.00

ELRIC: THE BANE OF THE BLACK SWORD
First,MS; 1 Aug 1988-6 Jun 1989

	$Good	$Fine	$N.Mint	£Good	£Fine	£N.Mint
1-6 ND Mark Pacella art	$0.35	$1.05	$1.75	£0.25	£0.75	£1.25
Title Value:	$2.10	$6.30	$10.50	£1.50	£4.50	£7.50

ELRIC: THE VANISHING TOWER
First,MS; 1 Aug 1987-6 Jun 1990

	$Good	$Fine	$N.Mint	£Good	£Fine	£N.Mint
1-6 ND Jan Duursema art	$0.35	$1.05	$1.75	£0.25	£0.75	£1.25
Title Value:	$2.10	$6.30	$10.50	£1.50	£4.50	£7.50

ELRIC: WEIRD OF THE WHITE WOLF
First,MS; 1 Oct 1986-5 Jun 1987

	$Good	$Fine	$N.Mint	£Good	£Fine	£N.Mint
1-5 ND Michael T. Gilbert art	$0.35	$1.05	$1.75	£0.25	£0.75	£1.25
Title Value:	$1.75	$5.25	$8.75	£1.25	£3.75	£6.25

ELSEWHERE PRINCE
Marvel Comics Group/Epic,MS; 1 May 1990-6 Oct 1990

	$Good	$Fine	$N.Mint	£Good	£Fine	£N.Mint
1-6 ND Moebius/Lofficier/Shanower art/script	$0.35	$1.05	$1.75	£0.25	£0.75	£1.25
Title Value:	$2.10	$6.30	$10.50	£1.50	£4.50	£7.50

ELVEN
Malibu Ultraverse,MS; 0 Oct 1994; 1 Feb 1995-4 May 1995

	$Good	$Fine	$N.Mint	£Good	£Fine	£N.Mint
0 ND 48pgs, reprints Ultraverse Premiere material with new Norm Breyfogle sketches	$0.50	$1.50	$2.50	£0.30	£0.90	£1.50
1 ND Prime appears	$0.40	$1.20	$2.00	£0.25	£0.75	£1.25
1 ND Limited Foil Cover Edition (Feb 1995) - green foil logo	$0.50	$1.50	$2.50	£0.50	£1.50	£2.50
2-4 ND	$0.40	$1.20	$2.00	£0.25	£0.75	£1.25
Title Value:	$2.60	$7.80	$13.00	£1.80	£5.40	£9.00

ELVIRA'S HOUSE OF MYSTERY
DC Comics; 1 Jan 1986-11 Dec 1986
(see House of Mystery)

	$Good	$Fine	$N.Mint	£Good	£Fine	£N.Mint
1 64pgs, Bolland cover, photo back cover	$0.30	$0.90	$1.50	£0.20	£0.60	£1.00
2-5	$0.25	$0.75	$1.25	£0.15	£0.45	£0.75
6 entire issue reads sideways	$0.25	$0.75	$1.25	£0.15	£0.45	£0.75
7 sci-fi issue	$0.25	$0.75	$1.25	£0.15	£0.45	£0.75
8	$0.25	$0.75	$1.25	£0.15	£0.45	£0.75
9 photo cover	$0.25	$0.75	$1.25	£0.15	£0.45	£0.75
10-11	$0.25	$0.75	$1.25	£0.15	£0.45	£0.75
12 DS, Halloween issue	$0.30	$0.90	$1.50	£0.20	£0.60	£1.00
Title Value:	$3.10	$9.30	$15.50	£1.90	£5.70	£9.50

ELVIRA'S HOUSE OF MYSTERY SPECIAL
DC Comics; 1 Jan 1986

	$Good	$Fine	$N.Mint	£Good	£Fine	£N.Mint
1 48pgs	$0.30	$0.90	$1.50	£0.20	£0.60	£1.00
Title Value:	$0.30	$0.90	$1.50	£0.20	£0.60	£1.00

Note: cover labelled "Haunted Holidays".

ELVIRA, MISTRESS OF THE DARK
Claypool Comics; 1 May 1993-present

	$Good	$Fine	$N.Mint	£Good	£Fine	£N.Mint
1 ND photo cover	$0.35	$1.05	$1.75	£0.25	£0.75	£1.25
2-15 ND	$0.35	$1.05	$1.75	£0.25	£0.75	£1.25
16-30 ND	$0.45	$1.35	$2.25	£0.30	£0.90	£1.50
Title Value:	$12.00	$36.00	$60.00	£8.25	£24.75	£41.25

EMERALDAS
Eternity,MS; 1 Jan 1991-4 Apr 1991

	$Good	$Fine	$N.Mint	£Good	£Fine	£N.Mint
1-4 ND	$0.30	$0.90	$1.50	£0.20	£0.60	£1.00
Title Value:	$1.20	$3.60	$6.00	£0.80	£2.40	£4.00

EMERGENCY
Charlton,Magazine; 1 Jun 1976-4 Jan 1977

	$Good	$Fine	$N.Mint	£Good	£Fine	£N.Mint
1 Neal Adams art	$0.60	$1.80	$3.00	£0.80	£2.40	£4.00
2 Neal Adams art	$0.40	$1.20	$2.00	£0.50	£1.50	£2.50
3-4	$0.40	$1.20	$2.00	£0.50	£1.50	£2.50
Title Value:	$1.80	$5.40	$9.00	£2.30	£6.90	£11.50

Note: from TV series Limited Distribution on the news-stands in the U.K.

EMERGENCY (2ND SERIES)
Charlton, TV; 1 Jun 1976-4 Dec 1976

	$Good	$Fine	$N.Mint	£Good	£Fine	£N.Mint
1 ND John Byrne art	$1.00	$3.00	$5.00	£0.70	£2.10	£3.50
2-4 distributed in the U.K.	$0.50	$1.50	$2.50	£0.30	£0.90	£1.50
Title Value:	$2.50	$7.50	$12.50	£1.60	£4.80	£8.00

EMPIRE
Eternity; 1 Mar 1988-4 1988

	$Good	$Fine	$N.Mint	£Good	£Fine	£N.Mint
1-4 ND	$0.35	$1.05	$1.75	£0.25	£0.75	£1.25
Title Value:	$1.40	$4.20	$7.00	£1.00	£3.00	£5.00

EMPIRE LANES
Northern Lights; 1 Dec 1986-4 Aug 1987

	$Good	$Fine	$N.Mint	£Good	£Fine	£N.Mint
1-4 ND black and white	$0.35	$1.05	$1.75	£0.25	£0.75	£1.25
Title Value:	$1.40	$4.20	$7.00	£1.00	£3.00	£5.00
Collected (Dec 1989)				£0.40	£1.20	£2.00

EMPIRE LANES (2ND SERIES)
Comico; 1 Dec 1989

	$Good	$Fine	$N.Mint	£Good	£Fine	£N.Mint
1 ND 48pgs, squarebound	$0.45	$1.35	$2.25	£0.30	£0.90	£1.50
Title Value:	$0.45	$1.35	$2.25	£0.30	£0.90	£1.50

	$Good	$Fine	$N.Mint	£Good	£Fine	£N.Mint

EMPIRE LANES (ONE SHOT)
Comice,OS; 1 May 1990
1 ND 48pgs, squarebound

| | $0.45 | $1.35 | $2.25 | £0.30 | £0.90 | £1.50 |
| Title Value: | $0.45 | $1.35 | $2.25 | £0.30 | £0.90 | £1.50 |

ENCHANTER
Eclipse; 1 Apr 1987-3 Aug 1987
(cancelled 12 issue series)

| 1-3 ND | $0.35 | $1.05 | $1.75 | £0.25 | £0.75 | £1.25 |
| Title Value: | $1.05 | $3.15 | $5.25 | £0.75 | £2.25 | £3.75 |

ENDLESS GALLERY, THE
DC Comics,OS; 1 May 1995
1 ND pin-ups of Sandman characters by a variety of artists including Capullo, Chaykin and Al Davison

| | $0.80 | $2.40 | $4.00 | £0.50 | £1.50 | £2.50 |
| Title Value: | $0.80 | $2.40 | $4.00 | £0.50 | £1.50 | £2.50 |

ENEMY
Dark Horse,MS; 1 May 1994-5 Sep 1994
1-5 ND Mike Zeck covers

| | $0.45 | $1.35 | $2.25 | £0.30 | £0.90 | £1.50 |
| Title Value: | $2.25 | $6.75 | $11.25 | £1.50 | £4.50 | £7.50 |

ENEMY ACE SPECIAL
DC Comics,OS; 1 1990
(see Star Spangled War Stories #138)
1 LD in the U.K. reprints Our Army At War #151, #153 (1st and 2nd appearances), Joe Kubert cover

| | $0.35 | $1.05 | $1.75 | £0.25 | £0.75 | £1.25 |
| Title Value: | $0.35 | $1.05 | $1.75 | £0.25 | £0.75 | £1.25 |

ENEMY ACE: WAR IDYLL
DC Comics; nn Jan 1991
Hardcover Graphic Novel
nn Jan 1991 128pgs, George Pratt painted art

| | | | | £2.40 | £7.20 | £12.00 |

Softcover Graphic Novel
nn Jul 1991 128pgs, George Pratt painted art

| | | | | £1.80 | £5.40 | £9.00 |

Signed, Limited Edition (Nov 1991),
16 pages of new text/illustrations limited to 2,000 copies

| | | | | £9.50 | £28.50 | £47.50 |

ENIGMA
DC Comics/Vertigo,MS; 1 Mar 1993-8 Oct 1993
1-8 Peter Milligan script, Duncan Fegredo art and painted covers

| | $0.45 | $1.35 | $2.25 | £0.30 | £0.90 | £1.50 |
| Title Value: | $3.60 | $10.80 | $18.00 | £2.40 | £7.20 | £12.00 |

Enigma (Sep 1995) Trade paperback
reprints mini-series with new Duncan Fegredo cover

| | | | | £2.70 | £8.10 | £13.50 |

ENTERPRISE LOGS
Golden Press; 1-4 1976
1 ND very scarce in the U.K. 233pgs, compilation of Gold Key Star Trek issues #1-8 plus Kirk's psychofile, starship portrait and Scotty's diary

| | $8.00 | $24.00 | $40.00 | £5.50 | £16.50 | £27.50 |

2 ND scarce in the U.K. 224pgs, compilation of Gold Key Star Trek issues #9-17

| | $5.00 | $15.00 | $25.00 | £3.50 | £10.50 | £17.50 |

3 ND scarce in the U.K. 224pgs, compilation of Gold Key Star Trek issues #18-26 plus Spock's psychofile

| | $5.00 | $15.00 | $25.00 | £3.50 | £10.50 | £17.50 |

4 ND scarce in the U.K. 224pgs, compilation of Gold Key Star Trek issues #27,28,30,31,32,34,36 and 38 plus Enterprise history

| | $5.00 | $15.00 | $25.00 | £3.50 | £10.50 | £17.50 |
| Title Value: | $23.00 | $69.00 | $115.00 | £16.00 | £48.00 | £80.00 |

EO
Rebel Studios,MS; 1 Jun 1992-2 1992
1 ND Tim Vigil art, oversized format, wraparound cover

| | $2.00 | $6.00 | $10.00 | £1.20 | £3.60 | £6.00 |

1 ND Premiere Limited Edition (Aug 1992) – cardstock cover, signed by Tim Vigil, 2,000 copies

| | $9.00 | $27.00 | $45.00 | £5.00 | £15.00 | £25.00 |

1 2nd printing, ND (Aug 1994)

| | $0.60 | $1.80 | $3.00 | £0.40 | £1.20 | £2.00 |

2 ND Tim Vigil art

| | $1.20 | $3.60 | $6.00 | £0.80 | £2.40 | £4.00 |
| Title Value: | $12.80 | $38.40 | $64.00 | £7.40 | £22.20 | £37.00 |

EPIC
Marvel Comics Group,MS; 1 Jun 1992-4 Sep 1992
1 ND 48pgs, squarebound, anthology (Nightbreed/Stalkers/Wild Cards/Sleeze Brothers begin), Dave McKean cover

| | $0.90 | $2.70 | $4.50 | £0.60 | £1.80 | £3.00 |

2 ND 48pgs, squarebound, anthology, Dave Dorman cover

| | $0.90 | $2.70 | $4.50 | £0.60 | £1.80 | £3.00 |

3-4 ND 48pgs, squarebound, anthology, Dougie Braithwaite cover

| | $0.90 | $2.70 | $4.50 | £0.60 | £1.80 | £3.00 |
| Title Value: | $3.60 | $10.80 | $18.00 | £2.40 | £7.20 | £12.00 |

EPIC ILLUSTRATED
Marvel Comics Group,Magazine; 1 Spring 1980-34 Feb 1986
1 ND Silver Surfer story, Buscema art, cover by Frazetta; the Silver Surfer drawn with a belly button!

| | $2.40 | | | £1.00 | £3.00 | £5.00 |

2 ND Chaykin, Veitch and Bissette art, Corben cover

| | $0.60 | $1.80 | $3.00 | £0.50 | £1.50 | £2.50 |

3 ND Elric, Russell and Golden art, Gulacy cover and art

| | $0.60 | $1.80 | $3.00 | £0.50 | £1.50 | £2.50 |

4 ND Elric, Russell art

| | $0.60 | $1.80 | $3.00 | £0.50 | £1.50 | £2.50 |

5 ND Veitch art

| | $0.60 | $1.80 | $3.00 | £0.50 | £1.50 | £2.50 |

6 ND Bissette and Veitch art, Neal Adams cover

| | $0.60 | $1.80 | $3.00 | £0.50 | £1.50 | £2.50 |

7 ND Neal Adams and John Bolton art, Barry Smith interview and cover

| | $0.60 | $1.80 | $3.00 | £0.60 | £1.80 | £3.00 |

8 ND Suydam and Vess art, Chaykin cover

| | $0.60 | $1.80 | $3.00 | £0.50 | £1.50 | £2.50 |

9 ND

| | $0.60 | $1.80 | $3.00 | £0.50 | £1.50 | £2.50 |

10 ND Bolton cover and art

| | $0.60 | $1.80 | $3.00 | £0.50 | £1.50 | £2.50 |

11 ND scarce in the U.K. Bolton art, Brunner cover

| | $0.50 | $1.50 | $2.50 | £0.60 | £1.80 | £3.00 |

12 ND Wolverton Spacehawk reprint edited and re-coloured, Wolverton article, Bolton art

| | $0.50 | $1.50 | $2.50 | £0.50 | £1.50 | £2.50 |

13 ND

| | $0.50 | $1.50 | $2.50 | £0.50 | £1.50 | £2.50 |

14 ND Elric by Russell, Revenge of the Jedi preview, P. Craig Russell cover

| | $0.50 | $1.50 | $2.50 | £0.50 | £1.50 | £2.50 |

15 ND scarce in the U.K. Bolton and Corben art, Boris Vallejo cover and interview, tie-in with Dreadstar #1, Dreadstar by Jim Starlin

| | $0.50 | $1.50 | $2.50 | £0.70 | £2.10 | £3.50 |

16 ND Barry Smith cover/art, Dave Sim art

| | $0.50 | $1.50 | $2.50 | £0.60 | £1.80 | £3.00 |

17 ND Scott Hampton art, Walt Simonson art

| | $0.50 | $1.50 | $2.50 | £0.50 | £1.50 | £2.50 |

18 ND John Bolton cover and art

| | $0.50 | $1.50 | $2.50 | £0.50 | £1.50 | £2.50 |

19 ND Bode, Muth, Smith and Jones art, Steranko cover

| | $0.50 | $1.50 | $2.50 | £0.50 | £1.50 | £2.50 |

20 ND Muth, Williams and Pratt art

| | $0.50 | $1.50 | $2.50 | £0.50 | £1.50 | £2.50 |

21 ND Muth art

| | $0.50 | $1.50 | $2.50 | £0.40 | £1.20 | £2.00 |

22 ND Sienkiewicz art, John Bolton cover

| | $0.50 | $1.50 | $2.50 | £0.40 | £1.20 | £2.00 |

23 ND Bode art, John Bolton cover

| | $0.50 | $1.50 | $2.50 | £0.40 | £1.20 | £2.00 |

24-25 ND

| | $0.50 | $1.50 | $2.50 | £0.40 | £1.20 | £2.00 |

26 ND "The Last Galactus story" by John Byrne begins, ends #34; Dave Sim Cerebus story, Sienkiewicz cover

| | $0.50 | $1.50 | $2.50 | £0.80 | £2.40 | £4.00 |

27 ND Galactus by John Byrne, Groo by Aragones, Bode art

| | $0.50 | $1.50 | $2.50 | £0.60 | £1.80 | £3.00 |

28 ND Cerebus by Sim, Galactus by John Byrne

| | $0.50 | $1.50 | $2.50 | £0.60 | £1.80 | £3.00 |

29 ND scarce in the U.K. Galactus by John Byrne

| | $0.50 | $1.50 | $2.50 | £0.80 | £2.40 | £4.00 |

30 ND Cerebus by Sim, Galactus by John Byrne

| | $0.50 | $1.50 | $2.50 | £0.60 | £1.80 | £3.00 |

31 ND Galactus by John Byrne, John Bolton cover

| | $0.50 | $1.50 | $2.50 | £0.60 | £1.80 | £3.00 |

32 ND Cerebus by Sim, Galactus by John Byrne

| | $0.50 | $1.50 | $2.50 | £0.60 | £1.80 | £3.00 |

33 ND scarce in the U.K. Galactus by John Byrne, Kent Williams art, Totleben cover

| | $0.50 | $1.50 | $2.50 | £0.80 | £2.40 | £4.00 |

34 ND very scarce in the U.K. Alan Moore script, Wrightson, Barry Smith, Sienkiewicz art, Suydam cover

| | $0.50 | $1.50 | $2.50 | £1.20 | £3.60 | £6.00 |
| Title Value: | $18.20 | $54.60 | $91.00 | £19.60 | £58.80 | £98.00 |

ARTISTS
Bissette in 2,6. Bolton in 7, 10-12, 15, 24, 25, 31. Conrad in 7-9. Potts in 1, 13. P. Craig Russell in 2, 9, 33. Starlin in 1-9, 14. Steacy in 4, 6. Suydam in 1, 8, 10, 13, 14, 34. Veitch in 2, 4-6, 8, 28, 29, 34. Vess in 5, 8-10, 16, 21, 22, 24, 27. Wrightson in 22, 25.

FEATURES
Abraxas by Veitch in 10-17. Almuric by Tim Conrad in 2-5. Elric stories (by P. Craig Russell) in 3, 4, 14. Generation Zero by Pepe Moreno in 17-24. Last Galactus story in 26-34 (all by Byrne). Last of the Dragons by Carl Potts in 15-20. Marada the She-Wolf by Bolton in 10-12, 22, 23. Sacred and Profane by Ken Steacy in 20-25. Weirdworld in 9.

EPIC LITE
Marvel Comics Group,OS; 1 Sep 1991
1 ND anthology of humour stories

| | $0.90 | $2.70 | $4.50 | £0.50 | £1.50 | £2.50 |
| Title Value: | $0.90 | $2.70 | $4.50 | £0.50 | £1.50 | £2.50 |

EPICURUS THE SAGE
DC Comics/Piranha Press; 1 1990; 2 Aug 1991
1 ND

| | $2.00 | $6.00 | $10.00 | £1.30 | £3.90 | £6.50 |

1 2nd printing ND

| | $1.80 | $5.25 | $9.00 | £1.20 | £3.60 | £6.00 |

2 ND 48pgs

| | $1.60 | $4.80 | $8.00 | £1.00 | £3.00 | £5.00 |
| Title Value: | $5.40 | $16.05 | $27.00 | £3.50 | £10.50 | £17.50 |

EPSILON WAVE, THE
Independent Comics Group; 1 Oct 1985-2 Dec 1985
1-2 ND colour

| | $0.25 | $0.75 | $1.25 | £0.15 | £0.45 | £0.75 |
| Title Value: | $0.50 | $1.50 | $2.50 | £0.30 | £0.90 | £1.50 |

EQUINOX CHRONICLES
Innovation,MS; 1 Spring 1991-2 Summer 1991
1-2 ND black and white

| | $0.35 | $1.05 | $1.75 | £0.25 | £0.75 | £1.25 |
| Title Value: | $0.70 | $2.10 | $3.50 | £0.50 | £1.50 | £2.50 |

EQUINOX CHRONICLES SPECIAL EDITION
Gauntlet Comics/Caliber Press; 1 Aug 1993; 2 1993
1 ND 64pgs, Blind Faith; reprints previous series

| | $0.50 | $1.50 | $2.50 | £0.30 | £0.90 | £1.50 |

2 ND 64pgs, Circumstantial Saviours; reprints previous series

| | $0.50 | $1.50 | $2.50 | £0.30 | £0.90 | £1.50 |
| Title Value: | $1.00 | $3.00 | $5.00 | £0.60 | £1.80 | £3.00 |

ERADICATORS (2ND SERIES)
Greater Mercury Comics; 1 Jul 1990-6 Dec 1990
1-6 ND black and white

| | $0.25 | $0.75 | $1.25 | £0.15 | £0.45 | £0.75 |
| Title Value: | $1.50 | $4.50 | $7.50 | £0.90 | £2.70 | £4.50 |

ERADICATORS, THE
Silverwolf/Greater Mercury; 1-8 1986?
1 ND Ron Lim 1st pro work in comics

	$Good	$Fine	$N.Mint	£Good	£Fine	£N.Mint
	$0.50	$1.50	$2.50	£0.30	£0.90	£1.50
1 2nd printing ND	$0.40	$1.20	$2.00	£0.25	£0.75	£1.25
2 ND	$0.40	$1.20	$2.00	£0.25	£0.75	£1.25
3 ND Tim Vigil art	$0.40	$1.20	$2.00	£0.25	£0.75	£1.25
4-8 ND	$0.30	$0.90	$1.50	£0.20	£0.60	£1.00
Title Value:	$3.20	$9.60	$16.00	£2.05	£6.15	£10.25

EREWHON
Tome Press,OS; 1 1992

	$Good	$Fine	$N.Mint	£Good	£Fine	£N.Mint
1 ND based on book by Samuel Butler, black and white	$0.60	$1.80	$3.00	£0.40	£1.20	£2.00
Title Value:	$0.60	$1.80	$3.00	£0.40	£1.20	£2.00

EROTIC WORLDS OF FRANK THORNE, THE
Eros Comix,MS; 1 Oct 1990-6 1991

	$Good	$Fine	$N.Mint	£Good	£Fine	£N.Mint
1-6 ND black and white	$0.50	$1.50	$2.50	£0.30	£0.90	£1.50
Title Value:	$3.00	$9.00	$15.00	£1.80	£5.40	£9.00

ERT! NOT AVAILABLE COMICS 1987-1994 GRAPHIC NOVEL
Caliber Press,OS; nn Jul 1995

	$Good	$Fine	$N.Mint	£Good	£Fine	£N.Mint
nn ND 112pgs, collected strips by Matts Feazell; black and white	$2.50	$7.50	$13.00	£1.70	£5.10	£8.50
Title Value:	$2.50	$7.50	$13.00	£1.70	£5.10	£8.50

ESCAPE FROM THE PLANET OF THE APES GRAPHIC NOVEL
Adventure,OS; 1 Jul 1991

	$Good	$Fine	$N.Mint	£Good	£Fine	£N.Mint
1 ND reprints original material from Marvel Comics published in the 1970s	$1.50	$4.50	$7.50	£1.00	£3.00	£5.00
Title Value:	$1.50	$4.50	$7.50	£1.00	£3.00	£5.00

ESCAPE TO THE STARS
Solson Publications/Visionary; 1 1987-7 1988

	$Good	$Fine	$N.Mint	£Good	£Fine	£N.Mint
1-7 ND Rich Buckler art	$0.25	$0.75	$1.25	£0.15	£0.45	£0.75
Title Value:	$1.75	$5.25	$8.75	£1.05	£3.15	£5.25

ESCAPE TO THE STARS (2ND SERIES)
Visionary; 1,2 1988

	$Good	$Fine	$N.Mint	£Good	£Fine	£N.Mint
1-2 ND	$0.15	$0.45	$0.75	£0.10	£0.35	£0.60
Title Value:	$0.30	$0.90	$1.50	£0.20	£0.70	£1.20

ESCAPE VELOCITY
Escape Velocity Press; 1 1986

	$Good	$Fine	$N.Mint	£Good	£Fine	£N.Mint
1 ND black and white	$0.25	$0.75	$1.25	£0.15	£0.45	£0.75
Title Value:	$0.25	$0.75	$1.25	£0.15	£0.45	£0.75

ESPERS
Eclipse; 1 Jul 1986-5 Apr 1987
(see Interface)

	$Good	$Fine	$N.Mint	£Good	£Fine	£N.Mint
1-4 ND David Lloyd art	$0.35	$1.05	$1.75	£0.25	£0.75	£1.25
5 ND John Burns art	$0.35	$1.05	$1.75	£0.25	£0.75	£1.25
Title Value:	$1.75	$5.25	$8.75	£1.25	£3.75	£6.25

Note: pre-figures Marvel series Interface

	£Good	£Fine	£N.Mint
Espers (Oct 1990) Trade paperback 128pgs, reprints mini-series	£1.10	£3.30	£5.50

ETC
DC Comics/Piranha Press,MS; 1 1989-5 1989

	$Good	$Fine	$N.Mint	£Good	£Fine	£N.Mint
1-5 ND 48pgs, squarebound; Tim Conrad script, Michael Davis painted art	$0.80	$2.40	$4.00	£0.50	£1.50	£2.50
Title Value:	$4.00	$12.00	$20.00	£2.50	£7.50	£12.50

ETERNAL WARRIOR YEARBOOK
Valiant; 1 Dec 1993; 2 Mar 1995

	$Good	$Fine	$N.Mint	£Good	£Fine	£N.Mint
1 ND 48pgs, painted art	$0.70	$2.10	$3.50	£0.40	£1.20	£2.00
2 ND 48pgs	$0.70	$2.10	$3.50	£0.40	£1.20	£2.00
Title Value:	$1.40	$4.20	$7.00	£0.80	£2.40	£4.00

ETERNAL WARRIOR, THE
Valiant/Acclaim Comics; 1 Aug 1992-present

	$Good	$Fine	$N.Mint	£Good	£Fine	£N.Mint
1 Unity: Chapter 2	$0.70	$2.10	$3.50	£0.40	£1.20	£2.00
1 gold embossed cover (foil)	$2.40	$7.00	$12.00	£1.50	£4.50	£7.50
1 gold cover (flat)	$3.00	$9.00	$15.00	£2.00	£6.00	£10.00
2 Unity: Chapter 10, Archer and Sting appear, Walt Simonson cover	$0.50	$1.50	$2.50	£0.30	£0.90	£1.50
3	$0.50	$1.50	$2.50	£0.30	£0.90	£1.50
4 joint 1st appearance Bloodshot cameo (see Rai #0)	$0.80	$2.40	$4.00	£0.50	£1.20	£2.00
5 1st full appearance Bloodshot	$0.60	$1.80	$3.00	£0.40	£1.20	£2.00
6 Barry Windsor-Smith scripts begin	$0.45	$1.35	$2.25	£0.30	£0.90	£1.50
7	$0.45	$1.35	$2.25	£0.30	£0.90	£1.50
8 48pgs, special dual-issue with Archer & Armstrong #8 (note: there is only one single issue, not two different ones therefore cross-refer to Archer & Armstrong); 1st Ivar	$0.70	$2.10	$3.50	£0.40	£1.20	£2.00
9-10 The Book of the Geomancer story	$0.45	$1.35	$2.25	£0.30	£0.90	£1.50
11-15	$0.40	$1.20	$2.00	£0.25	£0.75	£1.25
16 Empirical Dynasty Prologue, continued in Secret Weapons #3	$0.40	$1.20	$2.00	£0.25	£0.75	£1.25
17 Master D'Arque appears	$0.40	$1.20	$2.00	£0.25	£0.75	£1.25
18 Dr. Mirage cameo	$0.40	$1.20	$2.00	£0.25	£0.75	£1.25
19 Dr. Mirage appears	$0.40	$1.20	$2.00	£0.25	£0.75	£1.25
20-23	$0.40	$1.20	$2.00	£0.25	£0.75	£1.25
24 features The Immortal Enemy	$0.40	$1.20	$2.00	£0.25	£0.75	£1.25
25 continued from Archer & Armstrong #25	$0.40	$1.20	$2.00	£0.25	£0.75	£1.25
26 Chaos Effect X-over; flip side Archer & Armstrong #26	$0.40	$1.20	$2.00	£0.25	£0.75	£1.25
27-34	$0.40	$1.20	$2.00	£0.25	£0.75	£1.25
35 1st Acclaim Comics issue; Paul Gulacy cover, shipped in a cover wrapper to obscure the graphic cover image; bi-weekly	$0.40	$1.20	$2.00	£0.25	£0.75	£1.25
36 Paul Gulacy cover and art; bi-weekly	$0.40	$1.20	$2.00	£0.25	£0.75	£1.25
37-42 bi-weekly	$0.40	$1.20	$2.00	£0.25	£0.75	£1.25
43-44 Jackson Guice art; bi-weekly	$0.40	$1.20	$2.00	£0.25	£0.75	£1.25
45 bi-weekly	$0.40	$1.20	$2.00	£0.25	£0.75	£1.25
46 bi-weekly	$0.45	$1.35	$2.25	£0.30	£0.90	£1.50
47-50 Jackson Guice art; bi-weekly	$0.45	$1.35	$2.25	£0.30	£0.90	£1.50
Title Value:	$27.25	$81.55	$136.25	£17.15	£51.45	£85.75

Note: all Non-Distributed on the news-stands in the U.K.

ETERNAL WARRIOR: THE WINGS OF JUSTICE
Valiant/Acclaim Comics,OS; 1 Oct 1995

	$Good	$Fine	$N.Mint	£Good	£Fine	£N.Mint
1 ND Geomancer appears	$0.50	$1.50	$2.50	£0.30	£0.90	£1.50
Title Value:	$0.50	$1.50	$2.50	£0.30	£0.90	£1.50

ETERNALS ANNUAL, THE
Marvel Comics Group; 1 Oct 1977

	$Good	$Fine	$N.Mint	£Good	£Fine	£N.Mint
1 ND 52pgs, Jack Kirby art	$0.50	$1.50	$2.50	£0.30	£0.90	£1.50

Eleven or One #1

Elfquest (Epic) #1

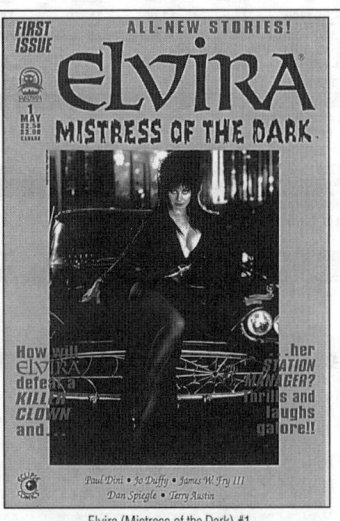

Elvira (Mistress of the Dark) #1

	$Good	$Fine	$N.Mint	£Good	£Fine	£N.Mint
Title Value:	$0.50	$1.50	$2.50	£0.30	£0.90	£1.50

ETERNALS GIANT SIZE SPECTACULAR
Marvel Comics Group,OS; 1 Nov 1991

	$Good	$Fine	$N.Mint	£Good	£Fine	£N.Mint
1 ND 64pgs, squarebound, many copies have crinkled spines; "The Herod Factor" story	$0.50	$1.50	$2.50	£0.25	£0.75	£1.25
Title Value:	$0.50	$1.50	$2.50	£0.25	£0.75	£1.25

ETERNALS, THE
Marvel Comics Group; 1 Jul 1976-19 Jan 1978

	$Good	$Fine	$N.Mint	£Good	£Fine	£N.Mint
1 origin	$0.80	$2.40	$4.00	£0.50	£1.50	£2.50
2 1st appearance The Celestials	$0.55	$1.65	$2.75	£0.35	£1.05	£1.75
3-13	$0.45	$1.35	$2.25	£0.30	£0.90	£1.50
14-15 Eternals vs. Hulk (cosmic-powered)	$0.45	$1.35	$2.25	£0.30	£0.90	£1.50
16-18	$0.45	$1.35	$2.25	£0.30	£0.90	£1.50
19 ND scarce in the U.K.	$0.45	$1.35	$2.25	£0.40	£1.20	£2.00
Title Value:	$9.00	$27.00	$45.00	£6.05	£18.15	£30.25

Note: all Jack Kirby art.

ETERNALS, THE (LIMITED SERIES)
Marvel Comics Group,MS; 1 Oct 1985-12 Sep 1986

	$Good	$Fine	$N.Mint	£Good	£Fine	£N.Mint
1 ND DS	$0.40	$1.20	$2.00	£0.30	£0.90	£1.50
2-8 ND	$0.30	$0.90	$1.50	£0.20	£0.60	£1.00
9-11 ND Walt Simonson script	$0.30	$0.90	$1.50	£0.20	£0.60	£1.00
12 DS ND Walt Simonson script, West Coast Avengers appear	$0.40	$1.20	$2.00	£0.30	£0.90	£1.50
Title Value:	$3.80	$11.40	$19.00	£2.60	£7.80	£13.00

ETERNITY SMITH
Renegade; 1 Sep 1986-5 May 1987

	$Good	$Fine	$N.Mint	£Good	£Fine	£N.Mint
1-5 ND Rick Hoberg art, colour	$0.30	$0.90	$1.50	£0.20	£0.60	£1.00
Title Value:	$1.50	$4.50	$7.50	£1.00	£3.00	£5.00

ETERNITY SMITH (2ND SERIES)
Hero; 1 Sep 1987-10 Jun 1988

	$Good	$Fine	$N.Mint	£Good	£Fine	£N.Mint
1-10 ND colour	$0.30	$0.90	$1.50	£0.20	£0.60	£1.00
Title Value:	$3.00	$9.00	$15.00	£2.00	£6.00	£10.00
Book 1				£0.90	£2.70	£4.50

ETERNITY SMITH (3RD SERIES)
Heroic Publishing; 1 Dec 1994

	$Good	$Fine	$N.Mint	£Good	£Fine	£N.Mint
1 ND reprints of second series	$0.30	$0.90	$1.50	£0.20	£0.60	£1.00
Title Value:	$0.30	$0.90	$1.50	£0.20	£0.60	£1.00

ETERNITY TRIPLE ACTION
Eternity; 1 May 1993-6 1993

	$Good	$Fine	$N.Mint	£Good	£Fine	£N.Mint
1-6 ND anthology title featuring three stories	$0.35	$1.05	$1.75	£0.25	£0.75	£1.25
Title Value:	$2.10	$6.30	$10.50	£1.50	£4.50	£7.50

EUDAEMON, THE
Dark Horse; 1 Aug 1993-3 Nov 1993

	$Good	$Fine	$N.Mint	£Good	£Fine	£N.Mint
1-3 ND script and art by Nelson	$0.45	$1.35	$2.25	£0.30	£0.90	£1.50
Title Value:	$1.35	$4.05	$6.75	£0.90	£2.70	£4.50

EUREKA!
Eureka; 1 Apr 1988

	$Good	$Fine	$N.Mint	£Good	£Fine	£N.Mint
1 ND Australian material	$0.30	$0.90	$1.50	£0.20	£0.60	£1.00
Title Value:	$0.30	$0.90	$1.50	£0.20	£0.60	£1.00

EVANGELINE
Comico; 1 Mar 1984-2 Jun 1984
(see Primer)

	$Good	$Fine	$N.Mint	£Good	£Fine	£N.Mint
1-2 ND	$0.50	$1.50	$2.50	£0.30	£0.90	£1.50
Title Value:	$1.00	$3.00	$5.00	£0.60	£1.80	£3.00

EVANGELINE (2ND SERIES)
First; 1 May 1987-12 Mar 1989

	$Good	$Fine	$N.Mint	£Good	£Fine	£N.Mint
1-12 ND	$0.35	$1.05	$1.75	£0.25	£0.75	£1.25
Title Value:	$4.20	$12.60	$21.00	£3.00	£9.00	£15.00

EVANGELINE SPECIAL
Lodestone; 1 1986

	$Good	$Fine	$N.Mint	£Good	£Fine	£N.Mint
1 ND reprints Comico series in colour	$0.50	$1.50	$2.50	£0.30	£0.90	£1.50
Title Value:	$0.50	$1.50	$2.50	£0.30	£0.90	£1.50

EVERYMAN, THE
Marvel Comics Group,OS; 1 Jan 1992

	$Good	$Fine	$N.Mint	£Good	£Fine	£N.Mint
1 ND Bernie Mireault art	$0.80	$2.40	$4.00	£0.50	£1.50	£2.50
Title Value:	$0.80	$2.40	$4.00	£0.50	£1.50	£2.50

EVIL DEAD: ARMY OF DARKNESS
Dark Horse,MS; 1 Jul 1992-3 Sep 1992

	$Good	$Fine	$N.Mint	£Good	£Fine	£N.Mint
1-3 ND adaptation of film, John Bolton cover and art	$0.50	$1.50	$2.50	£0.35	£1.05	£1.75
Title Value:	$1.50	$4.50	$7.50	£1.05	£3.15	£5.25

EVIL ERNIE
Eternity/Adventure,MS; 0 Dec 1993; 1 Dec 1991-5 Apr 1992

	$Good	$Fine	$N.Mint	£Good	£Fine	£N.Mint
0 ND Mark McKenna art	$1.50	$4.50	$7.50	£1.00	£3.00	£5.00
0 Platinum Edition, ND Mark McKenna art; Platinum colour cover	$10.00	$30.00	$50.00	£6.00	£18.00	£30.00

1 ND scarce in the U.K. Brian Pulido script, Steven Hughes art begin; 1st appearance Lady Death; approximately 12,000 print run

	$Good	$Fine	$N.Mint	£Good	£Fine	£N.Mint
	$30.00	$90.00	$150.00	£12.00	£36.00	£60.00

1 ND scarce in the U.K. special limited edition reprint (Aug 1992) - new 8pg story plus sketches

	$Good	$Fine	$N.Mint	£Good	£Fine	£N.Mint
	$12.00	$36.00	$60.00	£6.00	£18.00	£30.00

2 ND scarce in the U.K. Lady Death appears, 1st Lady Death cover; approximately 7,000 print run

	$Good	$Fine	$N.Mint	£Good	£Fine	£N.Mint
	$23.00	$67.50	$115.00	£10.00	£30.00	£50.00

3 ND scarce in the U.K. Lady Death appears; approximate;y 7,000 print run

	$Good	$Fine	$N.Mint	£Good	£Fine	£N.Mint
	$15.00	$45.00	$75.00	£7.00	£21.00	£35.00

4-5 ND scarce in the U.K. Lady Death appears; approximately 8,000 print run

	$Good	$Fine	$N.Mint	£Good	£Fine	£N.Mint
	$13.00	$39.00	$65.00	£5.00	£15.00	£25.00
Title Value:	$117.50	$351.00	$587.50	£52.00	£156.00	£260.00

Evil Ernie's Graphic Novel (Nov 1992)

	£Good	£Fine	£N.Mint
reprints issues #1-5, new cover by Steven Hughes	£1.40	£4.20	£7.00

Youth Gone Wild: Evil Ernie Trade Paperback (Nov 1994)

	£Good	£Fine	£N.Mint
reprints issues #1-5 plus sketches from issue #1	£1.30	£3.90	£6.50

EVIL ERNIE VS. THE SUPER HEROES
Chaos Comics,OS; 1 Aug 1995

	$Good	$Fine	$N.Mint	£Good	£Fine	£N.Mint
1 ND Brian Pullido script, Justiniano and Jimmy Palmiotti art	$0.80	$2.40	$4.00	£0.60	£1.80	£3.00
1 Limited Edition, red foil cover with green Evil Ernie logo, limited to 10,000 copies [Aug 1995	$8.00	$24.00	$40.00	£5.00	£15.00	£25.00
Title Value:	$8.80	$26.40	$44.00	£5.60	£16.80	£28.00

EVIL ERNIE/LADY DEATH
Chaos Comics; 1 1995

	$Good	$Fine	$N.Mint	£Good	£Fine	£N.Mint
1 Ashcan Edition, ND Orange card stock cover; 8.5" x 5.5"	$5.00	$15.00	$25.00	£3.00	£9.00	£15.00
Title Value:	$5.00	$15.00	$25.00	£3.00	£9.00	£15.00

EVIL ERNIE: REVENGE
Chaos Comics; 1 Oct 1994-4 Jan 1995

	$Good	$Fine	$N.Mint	£Good	£Fine	£N.Mint
1 ND Brian Pulido script, Steven Hughes art; Lady Death centre-fold	$1.60	$4.80	$8.00	£1.00	£3.00	£5.00
1 ND Glow in the dark edition - limited to 10,000 copies	$6.00	$18.00	$30.00	£3.50	£10.50	£17.50
1 Commemerative Edition, ND produced in conjunction with Comic Cavalcade	$5.00	$15.00	$25.00	£3.00	£9.00	£15.00
2 ND Brian Pulido script, Steven Hughes art; Lady Death centre-fold	$1.00	$3.00	$5.00	£0.70	£2.10	£3.50
3-4 ND Brian Pulido script, Steven Hughes art; Lady Death centre-fold	$0.80	$2.40	$4.00	£0.50	£1.50	£2.50
Title Value:	$15.20	$45.60	$76.00	£9.20	£27.60	£46.00

Evil Ernie: The Revenge (Oct 1995)

	£Good	£Fine	£N.Mint
Trade paperback reprints issues #1-4	£1.70	£5.10	£8.50

EVIL ERNIE: STRAIGHT TO HELL
Chaos Comics,MS; 1 Oct 1995-present

	$Good	$Fine	$N.Mint	£Good	£Fine	£N.Mint
1 ND Brian Pulido script, Justiniano art; coffin-shaped cover by Steven Hughes	$0.60	$1.80	$3.00	£0.40	£1.20	£2.00
2 ND Brian Pulido script, Justiniano art; cover by Steven Hughes	$0.60	$1.80	$3.00	£0.40	£1.20	£2.00
Title Value:	$1.20	$3.60	$6.00	£0.80	£2.40	£4.00

EVIL ERNIE: STRAIGHT TO HELL ASHCAN
Chaos Comics,OS; nn Sep 1995

	$Good	$Fine	$N.Mint	£Good	£Fine	£N.Mint
nn ND 24pgs, black and white	$0.30	$0.90	$1.50	£0.20	£0.60	£1.00
Title Value:	$0.30	$0.90	$1.50	£0.20	£0.60	£1.00

EVIL ERNIE: THE RESSURECTION
Chaos Comics,MS; 1 Jul 1993-4 Oct 1993

	$Good	$Fine	$N.Mint	£Good	£Fine	£N.Mint
1 ND Joe Quesada cover	$3.00	$9.00	$15.00	£1.50	£4.50	£7.50
1 ND Ashcan Edition, ND Yellow card stock cover	$8.00	$24.00	$40.00	£4.00	£12.00	£20.00
1 ND Gold Edition, ND Gold embossed logo	$6.00	$18.00	$30.00	£3.50	£10.50	£17.50
2 ND Chris Bachalo cover	$2.40	$7.00	$12.00	£1.00	£3.00	£5.00
3 ND poster insert by George Perez, Tom Morgan cover	$2.40	$7.00	$12.00	£1.00	£3.00	£5.00
4 ND 40pgs	$2.00	$6.00	$10.00	£0.80	£2.40	£4.00
Title Value:	$23.80	$71.00	$119.00	£11.80	£35.40	£59.00

Evil Ernie: The Ressurection (Dec 1994)

	£Good	£Fine	£N.Mint
Trade paperback reprints mini-series plus pin-ups by Jim Balent, George Perez and others	£2.00	£6.00	£10.00

EVIL ERNIE: YOUTH GONE WILD DIRECTOR'S CUT
Chaos Comics,OS; 1 Sep 1995

	$Good	$Fine	$N.Mint	£Good	£Fine	£N.Mint
1 ND 40pgs, limited to 15,000 copies; black and white interior	$1.00	$3.00	$5.00	£0.70	£2.10	£3.50
Title Value:	$1.00	$3.00	$5.00	£0.70	£2.10	£3.50

EWOKS
Marvel Comics Group/Star, TV; 1 Jun 1985-15 Sep 1987

	$Good	$Fine	$N.Mint	£Good	£Fine	£N.Mint
1-9	$0.15	$0.45	$0.75	£0.10	£0.30	£0.50
10 Williamson art	$0.15	$0.45	$0.75	£0.10	£0.30	£0.50
11-13	$0.15	$0.45	$0.75	£0.10	£0.30	£0.50
14 DS	$0.15	$0.45	$0.75	£0.10	£0.30	£0.50
15	$0.15	$0.45	$0.75	£0.10	£0.30	£0.50
Title Value:	$2.25	$6.75	$11.25	£1.50	£4.50	£7.50

EX-MUTANTS
Amazing/Eternity; 1 Aug 1986-15 1991
(see New Humans)

	$Good	$Fine	$N.Mint	£Good	£Fine	£N.Mint
1 Ron Lim art and cover	$0.60	$1.80	$3.00	£0.40	£1.20	£2.00
1 2nd printing	$0.40	$1.20	$2.00	£0.25	£0.75	£1.25
2 1st Eternity issue, Ron Lim cover	$0.40	$1.20	$2.00	£0.30	£0.90	£1.50
3 Ron Lim cover	$0.40	$1.20	$2.00	£0.30	£0.90	£1.50
4-15 scarce in the U.K.	$0.40	$1.20	$2.00	£0.30	£0.90	£1.50

	$Good	$Fine	$N.Mint	£Good	£Fine	£N.Mint
Title Value:	**$6.60**	**$19.80**	**$33.00**	**£4.85**	**£14.55**	**£24.25**
Note: all Non-Distributed on the news-stands in the U.K.						
Annual 1 (Apr 1988)				£0.30	£0.90	£1.50
Trade Paperback 1, reprints #1-3 with new material				£1.00	£3.00	£5.00
(2nd/3rd prints also)						
Trade paperback 2, all reprint				£1.00	£3.00	£5.00

EX-MUTANTS (2ND SERIES)
Malibu; 1 Nov 1992-18 Apr 1994

	$Good	$Fine	$N.Mint	£Good	£Fine	£N.Mint
1 ND Paul Pelletier cover and pencils begin, colour						
	$0.40	$1.20	$2.00	£0.25	£0.75	£1.25
1 ND silver foil-graphix cover edition - available to retailers who ordered 50 copies of #1						
	$1.00	$3.00	$5.00	£0.70	£2.10	£3.50
2-10 ND	$0.40	$1.20	$2.00	£0.25	£0.75	£1.25
11 ND Genesis Tie-In; pre-bagged with free Sky-Cap						
	$0.40	$1.20	$2.00	£0.25	£0.75	£1.25
12-16 ND Genesis Tie-In						
	$0.40	$1.20	$2.00	£0.25	£0.75	£1.25
17-18 ND	$0.40	$1.20	$2.00	£0.25	£0.75	£1.25
Title Value:	**$8.20**	**$24.60**	**$41.00**	**£5.20**	**£15.60**	**£26.00**

EX-MUTANTS MICRO SERIES
Pied Piper Comics,OS; 1 1987

	$Good	$Fine	$N.Mint	£Good	£Fine	£N.Mint
1 ND features Erin	$0.40	$1.20	$2.00	£0.25	£0.75	£1.25
Title Value:	**$0.40**	**$1.20**	**$2.00**	**£0.25**	**£0.75**	**£1.25**

EX-MUTANTS PIN-UP BOOK
Eternity; 1 1988

	$Good	$Fine	$N.Mint	£Good	£Fine	£N.Mint
1 ND	$0.40	$1.20	$2.00	£0.25	£0.75	£1.25
Title Value:	**$0.40**	**$1.20**	**$2.00**	**£0.25**	**£0.75**	**£1.25**

EX-MUTANTS SPECIAL EDITION
Amazing/Eternity; 1,2 1987

	$Good	$Fine	$N.Mint	£Good	£Fine	£N.Mint
1 ND	$0.40	$1.20	$2.00	£0.25	£0.75	£1.25
2 ND Winter Special						
	$0.40	$1.20	$2.00	£0.25	£0.75	£1.25
Title Value:	**$0.80**	**$2.40**	**$4.00**	**£0.50**	**£1.50**	**£2.50**

EX-MUTANTS: THE SHATTERED EARTH CHRONICLES
Eternity; 1 Apr 1988-15 1989

	$Good	$Fine	$N.Mint	£Good	£Fine	£N.Mint
1-15 ND	$0.40	$1.20	$2.00	£0.25	£0.75	£1.25
Title Value:	**$6.00**	**$18.00**	**$30.00**	**£3.75**	**£11.25**	**£18.75**

EXCALIBUR
Marvel Comics Group; 1 Oct 1988-86 Feb 1995; 87 Jul 1995-present
(see Excalibur Special Edition, Marvel Graphic Novel) (becomes X-Calibre)

	$Good	$Fine	$N.Mint	£Good	£Fine	£N.Mint
1 ND Alan Davis art						
	$1.50	$4.50	$7.50	£1.00	£3.00	£5.00
2-3 ND Alan Davis art						
	$1.00	$3.00	$5.00	£0.70	£2.10	£3.50
4-5 ND Alan Davis art						
	$0.80	$2.40	$4.00	£0.60	£1.80	£3.00
6-7 ND Inferno X-over, Alan Davis art						
	$0.70	$2.10	$3.50	£0.50	£1.50	£2.50
8 ND Ron Lim art	$0.70	$2.10	$3.50	£0.50	£1.50	£2.50
9 ND Alan Davis art						
	$0.70	$2.10	$3.50	£0.50	£1.50	£2.50
10 ND Rogers art	$0.70	$2.10	$3.50	£0.50	£1.50	£2.50
11 ND Rogers art	$0.60	$1.80	$3.00	£0.40	£1.20	£2.00
12-15 ND Alan Davis art						
	$0.60	$1.80	$3.00	£0.40	£1.20	£2.00
16-17 ND Alan Davis art						
	$0.50	$1.50	$2.50	£0.30	£0.90	£1.50
18-19 LD in the U.K.						
	$0.50	$1.50	$2.50	£0.30	£0.90	£1.50
20 LD in the U.K. Ron Lim art						
	$0.50	$1.50	$2.50	£0.30	£0.90	£1.50
21 LD in the U.K.	$0.50	$1.50	$2.50	£0.30	£0.90	£1.50
22 LD in the U.K. Cable appears						
	$0.50	$1.50	$2.50	£0.30	£0.90	£1.50
23 LD in the U.K. Alan Davis art						
	$0.50	$1.50	$2.50	£0.30	£0.90	£1.50
24 LD in the U.K. bi-weekly issue, Alan Davis art						
	$0.50	$1.50	$2.50	£0.30	£0.90	£1.50
25 LD in the U.K. bi-weekly issue, Galactus and Phoenix appear						
	$0.50	$1.50	$2.50	£0.30	£0.90	£1.50
26 LD in the U.K. Ron Lim art, bi-weekly issue						
	$0.40	$1.20	$2.00	£0.25	£0.75	£1.25
27 LD in the U.K. ties in with "Days of Future Past" story and other X-Men events, Barry Windsor-Smith and Bill Sienkiewicz art, bi-weekly issue						
	$0.60	$1.80	$3.00	£0.40	£1.20	£2.00
28 LD in the U.K. bi-weekly issue						
	$0.40	$1.20	$2.00	£0.25	£0.75	£1.25
29 LD in the U.K. last bi-weekly issue						
	$0.40	$1.20	$2.00	£0.25	£0.75	£1.25
30 LD in the U.K.	$0.40	$1.20	$2.00	£0.25	£0.75	£1.25
31 LD in the U.K. X-Men appear						
	$0.45	$1.35	$2.25	£0.30	£0.90	£1.50
32-34 LD in the U.K.						
	$0.40	$1.20	$2.00	£0.25	£0.75	£1.25
35 LD in the U.K. 1st appearance D'Spayre						
	$0.40	$1.20	$2.00	£0.25	£0.75	£1.25
36 LD in the U.K.	$0.40	$1.20	$2.00	£0.25	£0.75	£1.25
37-38 LD in the U.K. Promethium Exchange story, Avengers West Coast guest-star; covers 37-39 form one poster						
	$0.40	$1.20	$2.00	£0.25	£0.75	£1.25
39 LD in the U.K. Promethium Exchange story, Avengers West Coast guest-star; covers 37-39 form one poster, Spiderman appears						
	$0.40	$1.20	$2.00	£0.25	£0.75	£1.25
40 LD in the U.K.	$0.40	$1.20	$2.00	£0.25	£0.75	£1.25
41 LD in the U.K. Mutant Genesis tie-in, Wolverine and Cable appear						
	$0.60	$1.80	$3.00	£0.40	£1.20	£2.00
42 LD in the U.K. Alan Davis art begins, Captain Britain appears, Mutant Genesis tie-in, bi-weekly issue						
	$0.60	$1.80	$3.00	£0.40	£1.20	£2.00
43-45 LD in the U.K. Captain Britain appears, Alan Davis art, bi-weekly issue						
	$0.40	$1.20	$2.00	£0.25	£0.75	£1.25
46 LD in the U.K. bi-weekly issue, Alan Davis art						
	$0.40	$1.20	$2.00	£0.25	£0.75	£1.25
47 LD in the U.K. 1st appearance Cerise, Alan Davis art						
	$0.40	$1.20	$2.00	£0.25	£0.75	£1.25
48-49 LD in the U.K. Alan Davis art						
	$0.40	$1.20	$2.00	£0.25	£0.75	£1.25
50 ND 64pgs, Alan Davis art						
	$0.60	$1.80	$3.00	£0.40	£1.20	£2.00
51 LD in the U.K. Dougie Braithwaite art, new logo						
	$0.40	$1.20	$2.00	£0.25	£0.75	£1.25
52 LD in the U.K. Dougie Braithwaite art						
	$0.40	$1.20	$2.00	£0.25	£0.75	£1.25
53 LD in the U.K.	$0.40	$1.20	$2.00	£0.25	£0.75	£1.25
54-55 LD in the U.K. Alan Davis script/art						
	$0.40	$1.20	$2.00	£0.25	£0.75	£1.25
56 LD in the U.K. Alan Davis script/art, Psylocke appears, bi-weekly						
	$0.40	$1.20	$2.00	£0.25	£0.75	£1.25
57 LD in the U.K. Alan Davis script/art, X-Men appear, bi-weekly						
	$0.40	$1.20	$2.00	£0.25	£0.75	£1.25
58 LD in the U.K. X-Men appear, bi-weekly						
	$0.40	$1.20	$2.00	£0.25	£0.75	£1.25
59 LD in the U.K. bi-weekly, Captain America, Black Panther and Iron Man appear						
	$0.40	$1.20	$2.00	£0.25	£0.75	£1.25
60 LD in the U.K. Alan Davis script/art, Galactus appears						
	$0.40	$1.20	$2.00	£0.25	£0.75	£1.25
61 LD in the U.K. Phoenix returns						
	$0.40	$1.20	$2.00	£0.25	£0.75	£1.25
62-66 LD in the U.K.						
	$0.40	$1.20	$2.00	£0.25	£0.75	£1.25
67 LD in the U.K. last Alan Davis						
	$0.40	$1.20	$2.00	£0.25	£0.75	£1.25
68 LD in the U.K. Scott Lobdell scripts begin; new direction for title, Steve Buccellato art						
	$0.40	$1.20	$2.00	£0.25	£0.75	£1.25
69-70 LD in the U.K.						
	$0.40	$1.20	$2.00	£0.25	£0.75	£1.25
71 LD in the U.K. 48pgs, holo-gram cover; X-Men appear						
	$0.80	$2.40	$4.00	£0.50	£1.50	£2.50
72-74 LD in the U.K.						
	$0.40	$1.20	$2.00	£0.25	£0.75	£1.25
75 LD in the U.K. 48pgs						
	$0.45	$1.35	$2.25	£0.30	£0.90	£1.50
75 ND 48pgs, holo-grafix foil cover						
	$0.70	$2.10	$3.50	£0.45	£1.35	£2.25
76 LD in the U.K. continued tie-in fron X-Men Unlimited #4						
	$0.40	$1.20	$2.00	£0.25	£0.75	£1.25
77 LD in the U.K. Captain Britain guest-stars; with free Spiderman vs. Venom card sheet						
	$0.40	$1.20	$2.00	£0.25	£0.75	£1.25
78 LD in the U.K. Wolverine and Kitty Pryde appear						
	$0.40	$1.20	$2.00	£0.25	£0.75	£1.25
79-81	$0.40	$1.20	$2.00	£0.25	£0.75	£1.25
82 ND 48pgs	$0.45	$1.35	$2.25	£0.30	£0.90	£1.50
82 ND 48pgs, foil stamped cover						
	$0.80	$2.40	$4.00	£0.50	£1.50	£2.50
83 ND	$0.30	$0.90	$1.50	£0.20	£0.60	£1.00
83 ND Deluxe Edition - printed on glossy stock paper						
	$0.40	$1.20	$2.00	£0.25	£0.75	£1.25
84 ND	$0.30	$0.90	$1.50	£0.20	£0.60	£1.00
84 ND Deluxe Edition - printed on glossy stock paper						
	$0.40	$1.20	$2.00	£0.25	£0.75	£1.25
85 ND	$0.30	$0.90	$1.50	£0.20	£0.60	£1.00
85 ND Deluxe Edition - printed on glossy stock paper						
	$0.40	$1.20	$2.00	£0.25	£0.75	£1.25
86 ND	$0.30	$0.90	$1.50	£0.20	£0.60	£1.00
86 ND Deluxe Edition - printed on glossy stock paper plus bound-in Fleer trading card; see X-Calibre #1						
	$0.40	$1.20	$2.00	£0.25	£0.75	£1.25
87 ND continued from X-Men: Prime, leading into X-Men #42; Warren Ellis script, Ken Lashley art						
	$0.40	$1.20	$2.00	£0.25	£0.75	£1.25
88-89 ND	$0.40	$1.20	$2.00	£0.25	£0.75	£1.25
90 ND 48pgs, leads into Starjammers #1						
	$0.60	$1.80	$3.00	£0.40	£1.20	£2.00
91-93 ND	$0.40	$1.20	$2.00	£0.25	£0.75	£1.25
94 ND Karma and Psylocke appear						
	$0.40	$1.20	$2.00	£0.25	£0.75	£1.25
95 ND continued from X-Man #12						
	$0.40	$1.20	$2.00	£0.25	£0.75	£1.25
Title Value:	**$48.85**	**$146.55**	**$244.25**	**£31.50**	**£94.50**	**£157.50**

EXCALIBUR ANNUAL
Marvel Comics Group; 1 Sep 1993-present

	$Good	$Fine	$N.Mint	£Good	£Fine	£N.Mint
1 ND 64pgs, pre-bagged with trading card introducing Khaos						
	$0.60	$1.80	$3.00	£0.40	£1.20	£2.00
Title Value:	**$0.60**	**$1.80**	**$3.00**	**£0.40**	**£1.20**	**£2.00**

EXCALIBUR SPECIAL
Marvel Comics Group,OS; 1 Jul 1991

1 ND 48pgs, Meggan possessed story

MINT = 100% / NEAR MINT (inc. +/-) = 90–99% / VERY FINE (inc. +/-) = 75–89% / FINE (inc. +/-) = 55–74%
VERY GOOD (inc. +/-) = 35–54% / GOOD (inc. +/-) = 15–34% / FAIR = 5–14% / POOR = 1–4%

325

	$Good	$Fine	$N.Mint	£Good	£Fine	£N.Mint
	$0.60	$1.80	$3.00	£0.40	£1.20	£2.00
Title Value:	$0.60	$1.80	$3.00	£0.40	£1.20	£2.00

EXCALIBUR SPECIAL EDITION (1ST SERIES)
Marvel Comics Group; nn Apr 1988; nn Mar 1990
nn - ND **The Sword is Drawn**, 1st appearance "British" X-Men
by Chris Claremont, Alan Davis and Paul Neary

				£1.25	£3.75	£6.25
(2nd print - Oct 1989)				£1.00	£3.00	£5.00
(3rd print - Dec 1989)				£0.80	£2.40	£4.00
nn - ND DS **Mojo Mayhem** Art Adams art, X-Babies appear				£0.75	£2.25	£3.75

EXCALIBUR: AIR APPARENT
Marvel Comics Group, OS; 1 Dec 1991
1 ND 48pgs, squarebound, Ron Lim, Eric Larsen art featured

	$1.00	$3.00	$5.00	£0.65	£1.95	£3.25
Title Value:	$1.00	$3.00	$5.00	£0.65	£1.95	£3.25

EXCALIBUR: WILD, WILD LIFE
Marvel Comics Group, OS; 1 Apr 1995
1 ND 64pgs, reprints storyline from Marvel Comics Presents

	$1.20	$3.60	$6.00	£0.80	£2.40	£4.00
Title Value:	$1.20	$3.60	$6.00	£0.80	£2.40	£4.00

EXCALIBUR: XX CROSSING SPECIAL
Marvel Comics Group, OS; 1 Jul 1992
1 ND 48pgs, ties into Uncanny X-Men #1, featured art includes Ron Lim and Jackson Guice, Sam Kieth cover

	$0.45	$1.35	$2.25	£0.30	£0.90	£1.50
Title Value:	$0.45	$1.35	$2.25	£0.30	£0.90	£1.50

EXILES
Alpha Productions, MS; 1 May 1991-5 Sep 1991

1-5 ND	$0.35	$1.05	$1.75	£0.25	£0.75	£1.25
Title Value:	$1.75	$5.25	$8.75	£1.25	£3.75	£6.25

EXILES
Malibu Ultraverse; 1 Aug 1993-4 Nov 1993
1 ND Steve Gerber script begins

	$0.50	$1.50	$2.50	£0.30	£0.90	£1.50
2 ND	$0.40	$1.20	$2.00	£0.25	£0.75	£1.25
3 ND 40pgs, Rune insert						
	$0.50	$1.50	$2.50	£0.30	£0.90	£1.50
4 ND leads directly into Break Thru #1						
	$0.40	$1.20	$2.00	£0.25	£0.75	£1.25
Title Value:	$1.80	$5.40	$9.00	£1.10	£3.30	£5.50

EXILES, THE ALL NEW
Marvel Comics Group; 1 Dec 1995-present
1 ND Terry Kavanagh script, Ken Lashley art; cover by Jeff Matsuda and Steve Moncuse

	$0.30	$0.90	$1.50	£0.20	£0.60	£1.00
1 ND variant cover, computer painted cover by Chuck Maiden						
	$1.00	$3.00	$5.00	£0.70	£2.10	£3.50
1 ND E.T.M. Variant, exclusively produced by E.T.M.; Juggernaut & Shuriken on cover						
	$1.00	$3.00	$5.00	£0.70	£2.10	£3.50
2 ND flip-book format with Phoenix Ressurrection chapter						
	$0.30	$0.90	$1.50	£0.20	£0.60	£1.00
3 ND	$0.30	$0.90	$1.50	£0.20	£0.60	£1.00
4 ND Ultraforce guest-stars						
	$0.30	$0.90	$1.50	£0.20	£0.60	£1.00
Title Value:	$3.20	$9.60	$16.00	£2.20	£6.60	£11.00

EXILES: INFINITY, THE ALL NEW
Marvel Comics Group, OS; nn Nov 1995
nn ND Black September tie-in; introduces The Juggernaut leading a new team

	$0.50	$1.50	$2.50	£0.40	£1.20	£2.00
nn ND Signed Limited Edition (Dec 1995); 2,000 copies with certificate						
	$2.50	$7.50	$12.50	£1.50	£4.50	£7.50
nn ND Variant cover; 1 copy recieved for every 5 of regular ordered						
	$0.80	$2.40	$4.00	£0.50	£1.50	£2.50
Title Value:	$3.80	$11.40	$19.00	£2.40	£7.20	£12.00

EXOSQUAD
Topps, MS; 0 Jan 1994-3 Apr 1994
0 ND 16pgs, Len Wein script, Joe Staton art; card-stock cover

	$0.30	$0.90	$1.50	£0.20	£0.60	£1.00
1 ND origin told	$0.30	$0.90	$1.50	£0.20	£0.60	£1.00
2 ND	$0.30	$0.90	$1.50	£0.20	£0.60	£1.00
3 ND Michael Golden cover						
	$0.30	$0.90	$1.50	£0.20	£0.60	£1.00
Title Value:	$1.20	$3.60	$6.00	£0.80	£2.40	£4.00

EXOSQUAD THE SERIES
Topps; 1 Jan 1995
1 ND based on animated US show; Joe Staton art, Michael Golden cover

	$0.30	$0.90	$1.50	£0.20	£0.60	£1.00
Title Value:	$0.30	$0.90	$1.50	£0.20	£0.60	£1.00

EXQUISITE CORPSE
Dark Horse, OS; 1 Jul 1990
1 ND black and white, pre-bagged (25% less if un-bagged)

	$0.50	$1.50	$2.50	£0.30	£0.90	£1.50
Title Value:	$0.50	$1.50	$2.50	£0.30	£0.90	£1.50

Note: red/yellow/green variants available (logo and Dark Horse emblem on cover) and the issues may be read in any order.

EXTINCT
New England Comics; 1 Feb 1992-2 1992
1-2 ND 64pgs, 1940s and 1950s bizarre reprints

	$0.70	$2.10	$3.50	£0.40	£1.20	£2.00
Title Value:	$1.40	$4.20	$7.00	£0.80	£2.40	£4.00

EXTREME 3000 PRELUDE
Image, OS; nn Aug 1995
nn ND Rob Liefeld part script and part art

	$0.50	$1.50	$2.50	£0.30	£0.90	£1.50
Title Value:	$0.50	$1.50	$2.50	£0.30	£0.90	£1.50

EXTREME JUSTICE
DC Comics; 0 Jan 1995-present
0 Zero Hour spin-off. New team formed featuring Captain Atom, Maxima, Blue Beetle, Booster Gold and Amazing Man

	$0.40	$1.20	$2.00	£0.25	£0.75	£1.25
1-3	$0.35	$1.05	$1.75	£0.25	£0.75	£1.25
4 Firestorm the Nuclear Man returns						
	$0.35	$1.05	$1.75	£0.25	£0.75	£1.25
5 Firestorm, Captain Atom and Justice League appear						
	$0.35	$1.05	$1.75	£0.25	£0.75	£1.25
6 Captain Atom and Booster Gold appear						
	$0.35	$1.05	$1.75	£0.25	£0.75	£1.25
7-8 Captain Atom, Justice League and Monarch appear						
	$0.35	$1.05	$1.75	£0.25	£0.75	£1.25
9 Firestorm appears						
	$0.35	$1.05	$1.75	£0.25	£0.75	£1.25
10-11 Underworld Unleashed tie-in, Star Sapphire appears						
	$0.35	$1.05	$1.75	£0.25	£0.75	£1.25
12-14	$0.35	$1.05	$1.75	£0.25	£0.75	£1.25
Title Value:	$5.30	$15.90	$26.50	£3.75	£11.25	£18.75

EXTREME SACRIFICE
1994
Cross-over storyline from Image Comics scripted by Rob Liefeld and forcing changes in the Image Comics universe. The issues are as follows:
Prelude - Extreme Sacrifice Prelude
Part 0 - Youngblood Strikefile #11
Part 1 - Supreme #23
Part 2 - Bloodstrike #18
Part 3 - Brigade #16
Part 4 - Newmen #10
Part 5 - Team Youngblood #17
Part 6 - Prophet #10
Epilogue - Extreme Sacrifice Epilogue

EXTREME SACRIFICE EPILOGUE
Image, OS; 1 Jan 1995
1 ND Extreme Prejudice/Sacrifice storyline concludes, Stephen Platt art featured; pre-bagged with trading card

	$0.45	$1.35	$2.25	£0.30	£0.90	£1.50
Title Value:	$0.45	$1.35	$2.25	£0.30	£0.90	£1.50

EXTREME SACRIFICE PRELUDE
Image, OS; 1 Jan 1995
1 ND sequel to Extreme Prejudice X-over story, Stephen Platt art featured; pre-bagged with trading card

	$0.45	$1.35	$2.25	£0.30	£0.90	£1.50
Title Value:	$0.45	$1.35	$2.25	£0.30	£0.90	£1.50

EXTREME SACRIFICE TRADE PAPERBACK
Image, OS; nn Jul 1995
nn ND reprints Hearts #0-8 of Extreme Sacrifice storyline

	$3.40	$10.20	$17.00	£2.30	£6.90	£11.50
Title Value:	$3.40	$10.20	$17.00	£2.30	£6.90	£11.50

EXTREME STUDIOS TOUR BOOK
Extreme Studios, OS; 1 1993
1 ND biogs, pictures and pin-ups of Rob Liefeld, Brian Murray, Marat Mychaels, Dan Fraga, Danny Miki and others; gold/black embossed logo on black cover - 5,000 copies

	$2.80	$8.25	$14.00	£1.60	£4.80	£8.00
1 ND Gold Edition - as above but with gold logo embossed on gold cover - 1,000 copies						
	$3.50	$10.50	$17.50	£2.50	£7.50	£12.50
Title Value:	$6.30	$18.75	$31.50	£4.10	£12.30	£20.50

EXTREME SUPER CHRISTMAS SPECIAL
Image, OS; 1 Dec 1994
1 ND stories featuring Youngblood, Prophet and Team Youngblood by Liefeld, Platt and Matsuda

	$0.60	$1.80	$3.00	£0.40	£1.20	£2.00
Title Value:	$0.60	$1.80	$3.00	£0.40	£1.20	£2.00

EXTREMES OF VIOLET
Blackout Comics, MS; 0 Dec 1994; 1 Feb 1995-present?
0 ND wraparound cover

	$0.60	$1.80	$3.00	£0.40	£1.20	£2.00
0 ND Commemorative Edition (Jun 1995) - signed by Dell Barras and Bruce Schoengood in silver ink, large gold sticker on front cover; with certificate, 5000 print run						
	$3.00	$9.00	$15.00	£2.00	£6.00	£10.00
1-2 ND	$0.60	$1.80	$3.00	£0.40	£1.20	£2.00
Title Value:	$4.80	$14.40	$24.00	£3.20	£9.60	£16.00

Note: originally solicited as Extreme Violet

EXTREMIST, THE
DC Comics/Vertigo, MS; 1 Sep 1993-4 Dec 1993
1 Peter Milligan script, Ted McKeever art begins

	$0.40	$1.20	$2.00	£0.25	£0.75	£1.25
1 Platinum edition ND						
	$3.00	$9.00	$15.00	£1.50	£4.50	£7.50
2-4	$0.40	$1.20	$2.00	£0.25	£0.75	£1.25
Title Value:	$4.60	$13.80	$23.00	£2.50	£7.50	£12.50

EYEBALL KID
Dark Horse, MS; 1 Apr 1992-3 Jun 1992
1-3 ND reprints Eyeball Kid stories by Eddie Campbell and Ed Hillyer previously published by Harrier

	$0.45	$1.35	$2.25	£0.30	£0.90	£1.50
Title Value:	$1.35	$4.05	$6.75	£0.90	£2.70	£4.50

F

F-III BANDIT
Antarctic Press, MS; 1 Jan 1995-present
1-8 ND Ippongi Bang script and art; black and white

	$0.60	$1.80	$3.00	£0.40	£1.20	£2.00

	$Good	$Fine	$N.Mint	£Good	£Fine	£N.Mint
Title Value:	$4.80	$14.40	$24.00	£3.20	£9.60	£16.00

FACE
DC Comics/Vertigo,OS; 1 Jan 1995

	$Good	$Fine	$N.Mint	£Good	£Fine	£N.Mint
1 ND 64pgs, Peter Milligan script and Duncan Fegredo art						
	$0.90	$2.70	$4.50	£0.60	£1.80	£3.00
Title Value:	$0.90	$2.70	$4.50	£0.60	£1.80	£3.00

FACE, WHAT IS THE
Ace; 1 Dec 1986-3 Aug 1987

	$Good	$Fine	$N.Mint	£Good	£Fine	£N.Mint
1-3 ND Steve Ditko art						
	$0.40	$1.20	$2.00	£0.25	£0.75	£1.25
Title Value:	$1.20	$3.60	$6.00	£0.75	£2.25	£3.75

FACTOR X
Marvel Comics Group; 1 Mar 1995-4 Jun 1995

	$Good	$Fine	$N.Mint	£Good	£Fine	£N.Mint
1 ND J.F. Moore script, Epting and Milgrom art						
	$1.00	$3.00	$5.00	£0.60	£1.80	£3.00
2-3 ND J.F. Moore script, Epting and Milgrom art						
	$0.60	$1.80	$3.00	£0.30	£0.90	£1.50
4 ND J.F. Moore script, Epting and Milgrom art; continued in X-Men: Omega						
	$0.60	$1.80	$3.00	£0.30	£0.90	£1.50
Title Value:	$2.80	$8.40	$14.00	£1.50	£4.50	£7.50

Note: this title temporarily replaced X-Factor during the Age of Apocalypse storyline

The Ultimate Factor X (Jul 1995)
96pgs, Bookshelf Edition collects issues #1-4

	$Good	$Fine	$N.Mint	£Good	£Fine	£N.Mint
with etched gold cover				£1.20	£3.60	£6.00

FAFHRD & THE GREY MOUSER
Marvel Comics Group/Epic,MS; 1 Dec 1990-4 Mar 1991

	$Good	$Fine	$N.Mint	£Good	£Fine	£N.Mint
1-4 48pgs, Howard Chaykin script, Mike Mignola/Williamson art						
	$0.80	$2.40	$4.00	£0.50	£1.50	£2.50
Title Value:	$3.20	$9.60	$16.00	£2.00	£6.00	£10.00

Note: Bookshelf Format

FAILED UNIVERSE
Blackthorne,OS; 1 Dec 1986

	$Good	$Fine	$N.Mint	£Good	£Fine	£N.Mint
1 ND New Universe parody (see Marvel Comics); black and white						
	$0.40	$1.20	$2.00	£0.25	£0.75	£1.25
Title Value:	$0.40	$1.20	$2.00	£0.25	£0.75	£1.25

FALCON
Marvel Comics Group,MS; 1 Nov 1983-4 Feb 1984

	$Good	$Fine	$N.Mint	£Good	£Fine	£N.Mint
1 ND Paul Smith cover/part art						
	$0.30	$0.90	$1.50	£0.20	£0.60	£1.00
2 ND Paul Smith cover, Sentinels appear						
	$0.30	$0.90	$1.50	£0.20	£0.60	£1.00
3-4 ND						
	$0.30	$0.90	$1.50	£0.20	£0.60	£1.00
Title Value:	$1.20	$3.60	$6.00	£0.80	£2.40	£4.00

FALLEN ANGELS
Marvel Comics Group,MS; 1 Apr 1987-8 Nov 1987

	$Good	$Fine	$N.Mint	£Good	£Fine	£N.Mint
1 ND scarce in the U.K.						
	$0.40	$1.20	$2.00	£0.30	£0.90	£1.50
2-8 ND						
	$0.40	$1.20	$2.00	£0.25	£0.75	£1.25
Title Value:	$3.20	$9.60	$16.00	£2.05	£6.15	£10.25

Note: mainly stars New Mutants members.

FALLEN EMPIRES
Acclaim Comics/Armada,MS; 1 Oct 1995-2 Nov 1995

	$Good	$Fine	$N.Mint	£Good	£Fine	£N.Mint
1-2 ND Alexander Maleev art						
	$0.50	$1.50	$2.50	£0.30	£0.90	£1.50
Title Value:	$1.00	$3.00	$5.00	£0.60	£1.80	£3.00

Note: based on fantasy game Magic: The Gathering by Wizards of the Coast

Fallen Empires - A Magic: The Gathering (Oct 1995)
Trade paperback

	$Good	$Fine	$N.Mint	£Good	£Fine	£N.Mint
reprints issues #1,2, shrink-wrapped with booster pack				£0.65	£1.95	£3.25

FALLING IN LOVE
National Periodical Publications; 1 Sep/Oct 1955-143 Oct/Nov 1973

	$Good	$Fine	$N.Mint	£Good	£Fine	£N.Mint
1 very scarce in the U.K.						
	$33.00	$100.00	$200.00	£22.50	£67.50	£135.00
2 very scarce in the U.K.						
	$16.50	$50.00	$100.00	£11.50	£35.00	£70.00
3-5 scarce in the U.K.						
	$9.00	$28.00	$55.00	£5.75	£17.50	£35.00
6-10 scarce in the U.K.						
	$8.25	$25.00	$50.00	£5.00	£15.00	£30.00
11-20 scarce in the U.K.						
	$6.50	$20.00	$40.00	£4.15	£12.50	£25.00
21-30 scarce in the U.K.						
	$5.00	$15.00	$30.00	£3.30	£10.00	£20.00
1st official distribution in the U.K.						
31-40 scarce in the U.K.						
	$5.50	$16.50	$27.50	£3.50	£10.50	£17.50
41-46 scarce in the U.K.						
	$5.00	$15.00	$25.00	£3.00	£9.00	£15.00
47 scarce in the U.K. last 10 cents issue						
	$5.00	$15.00	$25.00	£3.00	£9.00	£15.00
48-50 scarce in the U.K.						
	$2.40	$7.00	$12.00	£1.60	£4.80	£8.00
51-70	$2.00	$6.00	$10.00	£1.40	£4.20	£7.00
71-100	$2.00	$6.00	$10.00	£1.20	£3.60	£6.00
101-107	$1.20	$3.60	$6.00	£0.80	£2.40	£4.00
108 Wood art	$2.00	$6.00	$10.00	£1.20	£3.60	£6.00
109-110	$1.20	$3.60	$6.00	£0.80	£2.40	£4.00
111-143	$1.20	$3.60	$6.00	£0.60	£1.80	£3.00
Title Value:	$482.35	$1457.20	$2663.00	£303.75	£914.00	£1675.00

FALLS THE GOTHAM RAIN
Comico,MS; 1 Feb 1992-2 Oct 1992

	$Good	$Fine	$N.Mint	£Good	£Fine	£N.Mint
1-2 ND 48pgs, duo-tone black and white art; reprints graphic novel						
	$0.45	$1.35	$2.25	£0.30	£0.90	£1.50
Title Value:	$0.90	$2.70	$4.50	£0.60	£1.80	£3.00

FAMILY MAN
DC Comics/Paradox Press,MS; 1 Apr 1995-3 Jul 1995

	$Good	$Fine	$N.Mint	£Good	£Fine	£N.Mint
1-3 ND 96pgs, black and white						
	$0.90	$2.70	$4.50	£0.60	£1.80	£3.00
Title Value:	$2.70	$8.10	$13.50	£1.80	£5.40	£9.00

FAMOUS FIRST EDITION
DC Comics,Tabloid; C-26 1974-F8 Aug/Sep 1975; C-61 Sep 1978

(see Limited Collector's Edition and
All New Collector's Edition)

	£Good	£Fine	£N.Mint
C-26 ND Action Comics #1	£2.50	£7.50	£12.50
C-28 Detective Comics #27	£5.00	£15.00	£25.00
C-30 ND Sensation Comics #1	£1.75	£5.25	£8.75
F-4 ND Whiz Comics #2 (1); cover not identical to original	£1.50	£4.50	£7.50
F-5 ND Batman #1 (indica misprinted F-6 on inside	£4.00	£12.00	£20.00
F-6 ND Wonder Woman #1	£1.50	£4.50	£7.50
F-7 ND All Star Comics #3	£1.50	£4.50	£7.50
F-8 ND Flash Comics #1	£1.50	£4.50	£7.50
C-61 Superman #1	£0.60	£1.80	£3.00

Note: F-6, F-7, F-8 are 68pgs; all other issues are 72pgs. All issues are exact, but larger reprints of the originals with new, thicker outer covers. Hard-bound editions (with dust-jackets) of C-26, C-28, C-30, F-4, F-6 are known. Some F-5 (Batman No.1) copies have no paper cover on inside. Owing to their size and consequent problems with mailing and display, perfectly flat, uncreased and unfolded near mint and mint copies are very scarce.

FAMOUS MONSTERS OF FILMLAND
Warren; 1 1962-160 1980

	$Good	$Fine	$N.Mint	£Good	£Fine	£N.Mint
1 scarce in the U.K.						
	$105.00	$325.00	$650.00	£65.00	£200.00	£400.00
2	$25.00	$75.00	$150.00	£16.50	£50.00	£100.00

Evil Ernie #1

Ex-Mutants #1

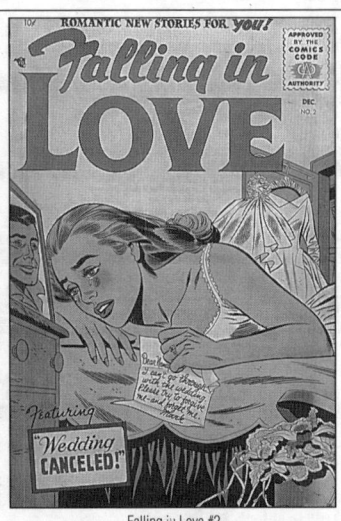

Falling in Love #2

	$Good	$Fine	$N.Mint	£Good	£Fine	£N.Mint
3-5	$15.00	$45.00	$90.00	£10.00	£30.00	£60.00
6-10	$11.50	$35.00	$70.00	£7.50	£22.50	£45.00
11-20	$9.00	$28.00	$55.00	£5.00	£15.00	£30.00
21-30	$6.50	$20.00	$40.00	£4.15	£12.50	£25.00
31	$4.15	$12.50	$25.00	£2.50	£7.50	£15.00
32 scarce in the U.K. Munsters	$4.15	$12.50	$25.00	£4.15	£12.50	£25.00
33-35	$4.15	$12.50	$25.00	£2.50	£7.50	£15.00
36-50	$3.00	$9.00	$15.00	£2.00	£6.00	£10.00
51-55	$2.40	$7.00	$12.00	£1.50	£4.50	£7.50
56 very rare in the U.K. Frankenstein cover	$3.00	$9.00	$15.00	£5.00	£15.00	£25.00
57-80	$2.40	$7.00	$12.00	£1.50	£4.50	£7.50
81-88	$2.00	$6.00	$10.00	£1.20	£3.60	£6.00
89 rare in the U.K., Werewolf cover	$2.00	$6.00	$10.00	£1.80	£5.25	£9.00
90-94	$1.50	$4.50	$7.50	£1.00	£3.00	£5.00
95 very rare in the U.K. Dracula	$2.00	$6.00	$10.00	£3.00	£9.00	£15.00
96-113	$1.00	$3.00	$5.00	£0.90	£2.70	£4.50
114 100pgs, special edition on Japanese monsters	$1.50	$4.50	$7.50	£1.00	£3.00	£5.00
115-139	$0.70	$2.10	$3.50	£0.70	£2.10	£3.50
140 scarce in the U.K. Frankenstein cover	$0.70	$2.10	$3.50	£0.80	£2.40	£4.00
141 scarce in the U.K. Close Encounters issue	$0.70	$2.10	$3.50	£0.80	£2.40	£4.00
142 scarce in the U.K. Star Wars issue	$0.70	$2.10	$3.50	£0.80	£2.40	£4.00
143-157	$0.60	$1.80	$3.00	£0.60	£1.80	£3.00
158 1980 Annual Giant Size	$0.70	$2.10	$3.50	£0.70	£2.10	£3.50
159-160	$0.60	$1.80	$3.00	£0.60	£1.80	£3.00
Title Value:	$603.35	$1832.00	$3470.50	£400.55	£1207.55	£2269.50

Note: most issues distributed on the news-stands in the U.K.

FAMOUS MONSTERS OF FILMLAND YEARBOOK
Warren; 1 1963-9 1971

	$Good	$Fine	$N.Mint	£Good	£Fine	£N.Mint
1 1963	$8.25	$25.00	$50.00	£5.75	£17.50	£35.00
2 1964	$5.75	$17.50	$35.00	£4.15	£12.50	£25.00
3 1965	$5.00	$15.00	$30.00	£3.30	£10.00	£20.00
4 1966	$4.50	$13.50	$22.50	£3.00	£9.00	£15.00
5 scarce in the U.K. 1967	$4.50	$13.50	$22.50	£3.00	£9.00	£15.00
6-8 1968-1971	$3.50	$10.50	$17.50	£2.40	£7.00	£12.00
9 1969-1971	$3.50	$10.50	$17.50	£2.40	£7.00	£12.00
Title Value:	$42.00	$126.50	$230.00	£28.80	£86.00	£158.00

Note: most issues distributed on the news-stands in the U.K.

FANG
Sirius Entertainment,MS; 1 Feb 1995-3 Jun 1995

	$Good	$Fine	$N.Mint	£Good	£Fine	£N.Mint
1-3 ND Kevin J. Taylor script and art	$0.60	$1.80	$3.00	£0.40	£1.20	£2.00
Title Value:	$1.80	$5.40	$9.00	£1.20	£3.60	£6.00

FANGORIA
O'Quinn Studios/Starlog Group; 1 1979-present

	$Good	$Fine	$N.Mint	£Good	£Fine	£N.Mint
1	$3.00	$9.00	$15.00	£2.00	£6.00	£10.00
2	$2.40	$7.00	$12.00	£1.50	£4.50	£7.50
3-5	$1.80	$5.25	$9.00	£1.20	£3.60	£6.00
6-10	$1.50	$4.50	$7.50	£1.00	£3.00	£5.00
11-19	$1.40	$4.20	$7.00	£0.90	£2.70	£4.50
20-39	$1.20	$3.60	$6.00	£0.80	£2.40	£4.00
40-55	$0.90	$2.70	$4.50	£0.60	£1.80	£3.00
56-130	$0.80	$2.40	$4.00	£0.50	£1.50	£2.50
131-145	$1.00	$3.00	$5.00	£0.65	£1.95	£3.25
146-149	$1.20	$3.60	$6.00	£0.80	£2.40	£4.00
Title Value:	$149.10	$446.65	$745.50	£96.25	£288.75	£481.25

Note: not distributed on the news-stands in the U.K.

FANGORIA HORROR SPECIAL/SPECTACULAR
O'Quinn Studios/Starlog Group; 1 1985-present

	$Good	$Fine	$N.Mint	£Good	£Fine	£N.Mint
1-10	$0.90	$2.70	$4.50	£0.60	£1.80	£3.00
Title Value:	$9.00	$27.00	$45.00	£6.00	£18.00	£30.00

Note: distrbuted on the news-stands in the U.K.

FANGS OF THE WIDOW
London Night Studios; 1 1995-present

	$Good	$Fine	$N.Mint	£Good	£Fine	£N.Mint
1-4 ND black and white	$0.60	$1.80	$3.00	£0.40	£1.20	£2.00
Title Value:	$2.40	$7.20	$12.00	£1.60	£4.80	£8.00

FANTASCI
Warp/Apple; 1 Jun 1986-9 Sep 1988

	$Good	$Fine	$N.Mint	£Good	£Fine	£N.Mint
1-9 ND	$0.40	$1.20	$2.00	£0.25	£0.75	£1.25
Title Value:	$3.60	$10.80	$18.00	£2.25	£6.75	£11.25

FANTASTC ADVENTURES (2ND SERIES)
Ace; 1 1987

	$Good	$Fine	$N.Mint	£Good	£Fine	£N.Mint
1 ND Golden Age reprints	$0.40	$1.20	$2.00	£0.25	£0.75	£1.25
Title Value:	$0.40	$1.20	$2.00	£0.25	£0.75	£1.25

FANTASTIC ADVENTURES
I.W. Super; 9,10-12,15,16-18 1963-1964

	$Good	$Fine	$N.Mint	£Good	£Fine	£N.Mint
9-10 reprints	$2.05	$6.25	$12.50	£1.30	£4.00	£8.00
11 reprints, Wally Wood art	$3.65	$11.00	$22.00	£2.30	£7.00	£14.00
12 reprints	$2.05	$6.25	$12.50	£1.30	£4.00	£8.00
15 reprints "The Gorilla" from Spook #23	$2.05	$6.25	$12.50	£1.30	£4.00	£8.00
16 reprints	$2.05	$6.25	$12.50	£1.30	£4.00	£8.00
17 reprints, Matt Baker art	$3.30	$10.00	$20.00	£2.05	£6.25	£12.50
18 reprints	$2.05	$6.25	$12.50	£1.30	£4.00	£8.00
Title Value:	$19.25	$58.50	$117.00	£12.15	£37.25	£74.50

Note: all distributed in the U.K.

FANTASTIC FABLES
Silverwolf Comics; 1 Feb 1987-2 1987

	$Good	$Fine	$N.Mint	£Good	£Fine	£N.Mint
1-2 ND features Tim Vigil art	$0.40	$1.20	$2.00	£0.25	£0.75	£1.25
Title Value:	$0.80	$2.40	$4.00	£0.50	£1.50	£2.50

FANTASTIC FORCE
Marvel Comics Group; 1 Oct 1994-present

	$Good	$Fine	$N.Mint	£Good	£Fine	£N.Mint
1 Psi-Lord, Vibraxis, Huntara and Gigantus begin; Black Panther appears; foil stamped cover	$0.45	$1.35	$2.25	£0.30	£0.90	£1.50
2-3	$0.35	$1.05	$1.75	£0.25	£0.75	£1.25
4 Captain America appears	$0.35	$1.05	$1.75	£0.25	£0.75	£1.25
5-6	$0.35	$1.05	$1.75	£0.25	£0.75	£1.25
7 ties into Fantastic Four #400	$0.35	$1.05	$1.75	£0.25	£0.75	£1.25
8-9 Atlantis Rising tie-in	$0.35	$1.05	$1.75	£0.25	£0.75	£1.25
10	$0.35	$1.05	$1.75	£0.25	£0.75	£1.25
11-12 Black Panther appears	$0.35	$1.05	$1.75	£0.25	£0.75	£1.25
13 Black Panther appears and She-Hulk joins the Fantastic Force	$0.35	$1.05	$1.75	£0.25	£0.75	£1.25
14-17	$0.35	$1.05	$1.75	£0.25	£0.75	£1.25
Title Value:	$6.05	$18.15	$30.25	£4.30	£12.90	£21.50

FANTASTIC FOUR
Marvel Comics Group; 1 Nov 1961-present
(see also Marvel Collector's Item Classics, Marvel's Greatest Comics, Marvel Treasury Edition, Marvel Triple Action, Official Marvel Index to.., What If?)

	$Good	$Fine	$N.Mint	£Good	£Fine	£N.Mint
1 origin/1st appearance Fantastic Four (Mr. Fantastic, Invisible Girl, Human Torch, The Thing), 1st appearance Mole Man; generally regarded as the comic that started "The Marvel Age of Comics"	$1500.00	$4500.00	$18000.00	£750.00	£2250.00	£9000.00
[Prices may vary widely on this comic]						
1 ND very scarce in the U.K. reprint (1966)	$26.00	$77.50	$185.00	£17.00	£50.00	£120.00
1 ND very rare in the U.K reprint with Golden Record to form complete sealed package	$39.00	$115.00	$270.00	£25.00	£75.00	£175.00
1 ND Marvel Milestone Edition (Nov 1991), reprints original issue with ads, silver border around cover	$0.60	$1.80	$3.00	£0.40	£1.20	£2.00
1 ND Marvel Milestone Edition (Nov 1994), reprints original issue with ads, metallic ink cover	$0.60	$1.80	$3.00	£0.40	£1.20	£2.00
2 (Jan 1962), 1st appearance The Skrulls	$360.00	$1075.00	$3250.00	£215.00	£650.00	£1950.00
3 1st appearance costumes, 1st Baxter Building and Fantasti-Car	$230.00	$700.00	$2100.00	£135.00	£415.00	£1250.00
4 Sub-Mariner returns (1st Silver Age appearance)	$285.00	$860.00	$2600.00	£165.00	£500.00	£1500.00
[Scarce in high grade - Very Fine+ or better]						
5 origin and 1st appearance Dr. Doom	$300.00	$900.00	$2700.00	£175.00	£530.00	£1600.00
5 ND Marvel Milestone Edition (Jan 1993) - silver border around cover	$0.60	$1.80	$3.00	£0.40	£1.20	£2.00
6 2nd appearance Dr. Doom, 2nd Silver Age Sub-Mariner appearance, 1st villain "Marvel Age" team-up; plans for Baxter Building shown	$185.00	$560.00	$1500.00	£100.00	£300.00	£800.00
7 very scarce in the U.K. (previously listed as Rare but more copies are turning up)	$82.50	$250.00	$675.00	£62.50	£185.00	£500.00
[Very scarce in high grade - Very Fine+ or better]						
8 scarce in the U.K. 1st appearance Puppet Master, 1st appearance Alicia Masters	$92.50	$275.00	$650.00	£55.00	£170.00	£400.00
9 3rd Silver Age Sub-Mariner appearance	$92.50	$275.00	$650.00	£55.00	£170.00	£400.00
10 (Jan 1963), 3rd appearance Dr. Doom	$92.50	$275.00	$650.00	£55.00	£170.00	£400.00
11 scarce in the U.K. origin and 1st appearance Impossible Man	$75.00	$225.00	$525.00	£50.00	£150.00	£350.00
12 Hulk appears (1st appearance in another title), 1st confrontation Hulk/Thing (1st ever Marvel X-over along with Amazing Spiderman #1)	$115.00	$345.00	$925.00	£57.50	£175.00	£475.00
13 1st appearance Red Ghost, 1st appearance The Watcher	$55.00	$165.00	$385.00	£34.00	£100.00	£240.00
14 less common in the U.K. Sub-Mariner appears; Steve Ditko cover?	$39.00	$115.00	$275.00	£24.00	£72.50	£170.00
15 scarce in the U.K. 1st appearance The Mad Thinker and Awesome Android	$41.00	$120.00	$290.00	£28.00	£82.50	£195.00
16 scarce in the U.K. Ant-Man and Dr. Doom appear	$39.00	$115.00	$275.00	£28.00	£82.50	£195.00
17 less common in the U.K. Ant-Man cameo	$39.00	$115.00	$275.00	£26.00	£77.50	£185.00
18 1st appearance Super Skrull	$39.00	$115.00	$275.00	£25.00	£75.00	£175.00
19 1st appearance Rama Tut	$39.00	$115.00	$275.00	£25.00	£75.00	£175.00
20 origin and 1st appearance Molecule Man	$44.00	$130.00	$310.00	£27.00	£80.00	£190.00
21 1st appearance Hate Monger, Nick Fury (CIA, pre-Shield), appears						

	$Good	$Fine	$N.Mint	£Good	£Fine	£N.Mint
	$29.00	$85.00	$200.00	£17.50	£52.50	£125.00

22 (Jan 1964), Mole Man appears
| $18.50 | $55.00 | $130.00 | £12.00 | £36.00 | £85.00 |

23 Dr. Doom appears
| $18.50 | $55.00 | $130.00 | £12.00 | £36.00 | £85.00 |

24 1st appearance The Infant ("Terrible")
| $18.50 | $55.00 | $130.00 | £12.00 | £36.00 | £85.00 |

25 classic Thing vs Hulk fight; the first of many! Avengers cameos including Captain America - technically his 2nd Silver Age appearance
| $50.00 | $150.00 | $360.00 | £35.00 | £105.00 | £245.00 |

26 Thing vs Hulk, Avengers X-over (1st) - story ties into Avengers #4
| $50.00 | $150.00 | $350.00 | £34.00 | £100.00 | £235.00 |

27 Sub-Mariner, Dr. Strange X-over (1st)
| $18.50 | $55.00 | $130.00 | £12.00 | £36.00 | £85.00 |

28 less common in the U.K. X-Men X-over (1st in title)
| $29.00 | $85.00 | $200.00 | £17.50 | £52.50 | £125.00 |

29 The Watcher appears
| $17.50 | $52.50 | $125.00 | £11.00 | £34.00 | £80.00 |

30 1st appearance Diablo
| $17.50 | $52.50 | $125.00 | £11.00 | £34.00 | £80.00 |

31 Avengers cameo; 1st appearance Dr. Franklin Storm, Mole Man appears
| $12.00 | $36.00 | $85.00 | £7.75 | £23.50 | £55.00 |

32 rare in the U.K., death of Franklin Storm (Sue & Johnny's father), Super Skrull appears
| $12.00 | $36.00 | $85.00 | £9.25 | £28.00 | £65.00 |

33 rare in the U.K., Sub-Mariner origin, photo-collage cover, 1st appearance Attuma
| $12.00 | $36.00 | $85.00 | £9.25 | £28.00 | £65.00 |

34 scarce in the U.K. (Jan 1965), 1st appearance Gideon
| $12.00 | $36.00 | $85.00 | £8.50 | £26.00 | £60.00 |

35 1st appearance Dragon Man, Reed and Sue engaged (later married in Annual #3)
| $12.00 | $36.00 | $85.00 | £7.75 | £23.50 | £55.00 |

36 1st appearance Frightful Four (Medusa, Paste-Pot Pete, Wizard, Sandman) (Note: this is the first appearance of Medusa)
| $12.00 | $36.00 | $85.00 | £7.75 | £23.50 | £55.00 |

37 Skrulls appear
| $12.00 | $36.00 | $85.00 | £7.75 | £23.50 | £55.00 |

38 Paste-Pot Pete becomes The Trapster, Frightful Four return
| $12.00 | $36.00 | $85.00 | £7.75 | £23.50 | £55.00 |

39 Daredevil X-over (a classic - D.D. battles Dr. Doom with powerless F.F.), classic cover
| $12.00 | $36.00 | $85.00 | £8.00 | £24.50 | £57.50 |

40 Daredevil X-over (a classic - D.D. battles Dr. Doom with powerless F.F.)
| $12.00 | $36.00 | $85.00 | £8.00 | £24.50 | £57.50 |

41-43 Frightful Four appear; Thing leaves F.F. temporarily
| $8.50 | $26.00 | $60.00 | £5.50 | £17.00 | £40.00 |

44 1st appearance Gorgon, Madame Medusa from Frightful Four appears
| $8.50 | $26.00 | $60.00 | £5.50 | £17.00 | £40.00 |

45 1st appearance Inhumans (Madame Medusa plus Crystal, Karnak, Black Bolt [cameo], Triton, Lockjaw); last Silver Age issue indicia-dated December 1965
| $8.50 | $26.00 | $60.00 | £5.50 | £17.00 | £40.00 |

46 (Jan 1966), 1st full appearance Black Bolt, 1st appearance The Seeker
| $8.50 | $26.00 | $60.00 | £5.50 | £17.00 | £40.00 |

47 1st appearance Maximus and The Great Refuge
| $8.50 | $26.00 | $60.00 | £5.50 | £17.00 | £40.00 |

48 1st appearance Silver Surfer (origin in Silver Surfer #1), 1st appearance Galactus (with part origin only)
| $90.00 | $275.00 | $825.00 | £50.00 | £150.00 | £450.00 |

49 2nd appearance Silver Surfer and Galactus
| $26.00 | $77.50 | $210.00 | £15.50 | £47.00 | £125.00 |

50 1st appearance Wyatt Wingfoot, 3rd Silver Surfer (vs. Galactus), classic cover
| $25.00 | $75.00 | $225.00 | £16.50 | £50.00 | £150.00 |

51 scarce in the U.K.
| $6.25 | $19.00 | $45.00 | £4.25 | £12.50 | £30.00 |

52 1st appearance Black Panther (in a cape!), Inhumans cameo
| $11.00 | $34.00 | $80.00 | £7.00 | £21.00 | £50.00 |

53 origin and 2nd appearance Black Panther
| $9.25 | $28.00 | $65.00 | £5.25 | £16.00 | £37.50 |

54 Black Panther and Inhumans guest-star
| $6.25 | $19.00 | $45.00 | £4.25 | £12.50 | £30.00 |

55 Silver Surfer battles The Thing
| $9.25 | $28.00 | $65.00 | £5.25 | £16.00 | £37.50 |

56 very scarce in the U.K. and U.S. (note: a slightly thinner paper was used on the cover resulting in many copies with spine splits)
| $7.75 | $23.50 | $55.00 | £5.25 | £16.00 | £37.50 |

57 very scarce in the U.K. Silver Surfer and Dr. Doom appear
| $7.75 | $23.50 | $55.00 | £5.25 | £16.00 | £37.50 |

58 (Jan 1967), Dr. Doom appear
| $7.75 | $23.50 | $55.00 | £4.60 | £13.50 | £32.50 |

59 Silver Surfer and Dr. Doom appear; Inhumans appear. Dr. Doom acquires Silver Surfer's board and powers
| $7.75 | $23.50 | $55.00 | £4.60 | £13.50 | £32.50 |

60 Silver Surfer and Dr. Doom appear
| $7.75 | $23.50 | $55.00 | £4.60 | £13.50 | £32.50 |

61 Silver Surfer and Dr. Doom appear
| $5.50 | $17.00 | $40.00 | £3.90 | £11.50 | £27.50 |

62 1st appearance Blastaar
| $5.50 | $17.00 | $40.00 | £3.90 | £11.50 | £27.50 |

63-65
| $5.50 | $17.00 | $40.00 | £3.90 | £11.50 | £27.50 |

66 1st appearance Warlock (as "Him"), still in "cocoon", partial origin told
| $12.00 | $36.00 | $85.00 | £6.25 | £19.00 | £45.00 |

67 2nd appearance "Him", emerges from "cocoon" (two panels only on last page - see Thor #165 for 1st full appearance)
| $14.00 | $43.00 | $100.00 | £7.00 | £21.00 | £50.00 |

68-69
| $5.25 | $16.00 | $37.50 | £2.85 | £8.50 | £20.00 |

70 (Jan 1968)
| $5.25 | $16.00 | $37.50 | £2.85 | £8.50 | £20.00 |

71
| $4.60 | $13.50 | $32.50 | £2.55 | £7.50 | £18.00 |

	$Good	$Fine	$N.Mint	£Good	£Fine	£N.Mint

72 less common in the U.K. Silver Surfer appears; classic cover
| $5.00 | $15.00 | $35.00 | £3.00 | £9.00 | £21.00 |

73 Thor, Spider-Man appear; X-over with Daredevil #38
| $4.60 | $13.50 | $32.50 | £2.55 | £7.50 | £18.00 |

74 Silver Surfer, Galactus appears, 1st different quality paper and covers (less glossy)
| $5.00 | $15.00 | $35.00 | £2.85 | £8.50 | £20.00 |

75 Silver Surfer, Galactus appear
| $5.00 | $15.00 | $35.00 | £2.85 | £8.50 | £20.00 |

76-77 Silver Surfer appears
| $5.00 | $15.00 | $35.00 | £2.85 | £8.50 | £20.00 |

78-80
| $4.60 | $13.50 | $32.50 | £2.55 | £7.50 | £18.00 |

81 Crystal joins F.F
| $3.55 | $10.50 | $25.00 | £2.00 | £6.00 | £14.00 |

82 (Jan 1969)
| $3.55 | $10.50 | $25.00 | £2.00 | £6.00 | £14.00 |

83
| $3.55 | $10.50 | $25.00 | £2.00 | £6.00 | £14.00 |

84-87 Dr.Doom story inspired by "The Prisoner" TV series
| $3.55 | $10.50 | $25.00 | £2.00 | £6.00 | £14.00 |

88 scarce in the U.K.
| $3.55 | $10.50 | $25.00 | £2.10 | £6.25 | £15.00 |

89-93
| $2.10 | $6.25 | $15.00 | £1.10 | £3.40 | £8.00 |

94 (Jan 1970), 1st appearance Agatha Harkness
| $2.10 | $6.25 | $15.00 | £1.10 | £3.40 | £8.00 |

95-97
| $2.10 | $6.25 | $15.00 | £1.10 | £3.40 | £8.00 |

98 Apollo mission story
| $2.10 | $6.25 | $15.00 | £1.10 | £3.40 | £8.00 |

99
| $2.10 | $6.25 | $15.00 | £1.10 | £3.40 | £8.00 |

100 very scarce in the U.K. guest-stars nearly every FF foe up to that point (as androids) under the control of the Puppet Master
| $10.00 | $30.00 | $70.00 | £5.50 | £17.00 | £40.00 |

101
| $2.05 | $6.25 | $12.50 | £1.15 | £3.50 | £7.00 |

102 Magneto X-over, Sub-Mariner appears; last Jack Kirby issue
| $2.05 | $6.25 | $12.50 | £1.15 | £3.50 | £7.00 |

103 Magneto X-over, Thing vs. Sub-Mariner
| $2.05 | $6.25 | $12.50 | £1.15 | £3.50 | £7.00 |

104 Magneto X-over
| $2.50 | $7.50 | $15.00 | £1.30 | £4.00 | £8.00 |

105
| $2.05 | $6.25 | $12.50 | £1.15 | £3.50 | £7.00 |

106 (Jan 1971)
| $2.05 | $6.25 | $12.50 | £1.15 | £3.50 | £7.00 |

107
| $2.05 | $6.25 | $12.50 | £1.15 | £3.50 | £7.00 |

108 part Jack Kirby art
| $2.05 | $6.25 | $12.50 | £1.15 | £3.50 | £7.00 |

109
| $2.05 | $6.25 | $12.50 | £1.15 | £3.50 | £7.00 |

110 (some copies have green misprinting on cover areas that are normally blue and yellow)
| $2.05 | $6.25 | $12.50 | £1.15 | £3.50 | £7.00 |

111
| $2.05 | $6.25 | $12.50 | £1.15 | £3.50 | £7.00 |

112 very scarce in the U.K. Hulk vs The Thing
| $9.00 | $28.00 | $55.00 | £4.15 | £12.50 | £25.00 |

113-115 scarce in the U.K.
| $2.05 | $6.25 | $12.50 | £1.25 | £3.75 | £7.50 |

116 very scarce in the U.K. 52pgs, origin The Stranger, Dr. Doom appears
| $1.65 | $5.00 | $10.00 | £1.30 | £4.00 | £8.00 |

117 scarce in the U.K.
| $1.65 | $5.00 | $10.00 | £1.15 | £3.50 | £7.00 |

118 scarce in the U.K. (Jan 1972)
| $1.65 | $5.00 | $10.00 | £1.15 | £3.50 | £7.00 |

119-120 scarce in the U.K.
| $1.65 | $5.00 | $10.00 | £1.15 | £3.50 | £7.00 |

121 very scarce in the U.K. Silver Surfer and Galactus appear, 1st appearance Gabriel (2nd herald of Galactus)
| $2.30 | $7.00 | $14.00 | £1.30 | £4.00 | £8.00 |

122-123 very scarce in the U.K. Silver Surfer and Galactus appear
| $2.30 | $7.00 | $14.00 | £1.30 | £4.00 | £8.00 |

124-125 scarce in the U.K.
| $1.50 | $4.50 | $9.00 | £1.15 | £3.50 | £7.00 |

126 scarce in the U.K. origin re-done from issue #1
| $2.00 | $6.00 | $12.00 | £1.15 | £3.50 | £7.00 |

127 scarce in the U.K.
| $2.00 | $6.00 | $12.00 | £1.15 | £3.50 | £7.00 |

128 high-quality colour 4pg centre-fold insert Friends and Foes
| $1.50 | $4.50 | $9.00 | £1.00 | £3.00 | £6.00 |

128 as above, but without insert
| $1.35 | $4.10 | $8.25 | £0.90 | £2.75 | £5.50 |

129 1st appearance Thundra
| $1.50 | $4.50 | $9.00 | £1.00 | £3.00 | £6.00 |

130 (Jan 1973), Jim Steranko cover
| $1.50 | $4.50 | $9.00 | £1.00 | £3.00 | £6.00 |

131 Inhumans appear, Steranko cover
| $1.30 | $4.00 | $8.00 | £0.75 | £2.25 | £4.50 |

132 Jim Steranko cover
| $1.30 | $4.00 | $8.00 | £0.75 | £2.25 | £4.50 |

133 Thing vs. Thundra
| $1.30 | $4.00 | $8.00 | £0.75 | £2.25 | £4.50 |

134-140
| $1.30 | $4.00 | $8.00 | £0.75 | £2.25 | £4.50 |

141
| $1.30 | $4.00 | $8.00 | £0.60 | £1.85 | £3.75 |

142 (Jan 1974)
| $1.30 | $4.00 | $8.00 | £0.60 | £1.85 | £3.75 |

143
| $1.30 | $4.00 | $8.00 | £0.60 | £1.85 | £3.75 |

144 ND scarce in the U.K.
| $2.00 | $6.00 | $12.00 | £1.25 | £3.75 | £7.50 |

145-146 ND
| $1.30 | $4.00 | $8.00 | £0.75 | £2.25 | £4.50 |

147 ND Thing vs. Sub-Mariner
| $1.30 | $4.00 | $8.00 | £0.75 | £2.25 | £4.50 |

148 ND
| $1.30 | $4.00 | $8.00 | £0.75 | £2.25 | £4.50 |

149 Sub-Mariner appears

Column headers (both columns): $Good | $Fine | $N.Mint | £Good | £Fine | £N.Mint

$Good	$Fine	$N.Mint	£Good	£Fine	£N.Mint
$1.30	$4.00	$8.00	£0.65	£2.00	£4.00

150 Crystal, Quicksilver wed, continues from Avengers #127

$1.30	$4.00	$8.00	£0.75	£2.25	£4.50

151-153

$1.50	$4.50	$7.50	£0.70	£2.10	£3.50

154 (Jan 1975), edited reprint of Strange Tales #127 with 7 new pages

$1.50	$4.50	$7.50	£0.70	£2.10	£3.50

155 Silver Surfer vs. Thing, cover based on #55

$1.60	$4.80	$8.00	£0.80	£2.40	£4.00

156-157 Silver Surfer/Dr. Doom

$1.60	$4.80	$8.00	£0.80	£2.40	£4.00

158

$1.50	$4.50	$7.50	£0.70	£2.10	£3.50

159 Inhumans appear

$1.50	$4.50	$7.50	£0.70	£2.10	£3.50

160

$1.50	$4.50	$7.50	£0.70	£2.10	£3.50

161

$1.00	$3.00	$5.00	£0.50	£1.50	£2.50

162 Thing vs. Thing

$1.00	$3.00	$5.00	£0.50	£1.50	£2.50

163

$1.00	$3.00	$5.00	£0.50	£1.50	£2.50

164 1st George Perez art on F.F., Marvel Boy returns as Crusader

$1.20	$3.60	$6.00	£0.60	£1.80	£3.00

165 George Perez art

$1.00	$3.00	$5.00	£0.50	£1.50	£2.50

166 (Jan 1976), George Perez art, Thing vs. Hulk

$1.00	$3.00	$5.00	£0.50	£1.50	£2.50

167 George Perez art

$1.00	$3.00	$5.00	£0.50	£1.50	£2.50

168-169 Luke Cage appears

$1.00	$3.00	$5.00	£0.50	£1.50	£2.50

170 Thing vs. Luke Cage

$1.00	$3.00	$5.00	£0.50	£1.50	£2.50

171 George Perez art

$0.80	$2.40	$4.00	£0.50	£1.50	£2.50

172 George Perez art, Galactus appears

$1.00	$3.00	$5.00	£0.60	£1.80	£3.00

173-174 Galactus appears

$1.00	$3.00	$5.00	£0.60	£1.80	£3.00

175 High Evolutionary vs. Galactus

$1.20	$3.60	$6.00	£0.60	£1.80	£3.00

176 ND Impossible Man, Marvel Bullpen appear, George Perez art

$0.80	$2.40	$4.00	£0.60	£1.80	£3.00

177 George Perez art

$0.80	$2.40	$4.00	£0.40	£1.20	£2.00

178 (Jan 1977), George Perez art

$0.80	$2.40	$4.00	£0.40	£1.20	£2.00

179

$0.80	$2.40	$4.00	£0.30	£0.90	£1.50

180 reprints issue #101

$0.80	$2.40	$4.00	£0.30	£0.90	£1.50

181-183

$0.80	$2.40	$4.00	£0.30	£0.90	£1.50

184-188 George Perez art

$0.80	$2.40	$4.00	£0.30	£0.90	£1.50

189 reprints part F.F. Annual #4 Human Torch vs. original Human Torch

$0.80	$2.40	$4.00	£0.30	£0.90	£1.50

190 LD in the U.K. (Jan 1978), history of F.F. retold; Silver Surfer and Galactus appear

$0.80	$2.40	$4.00	£0.50	£1.50	£2.50

191-192 George Perez art

$0.80	$2.40	$4.00	£0.30	£0.90	£1.50

193-199 ND

$0.80	$2.40	$4.00	£0.40	£1.20	£2.00

200 ND 52pgs, 17th anniversary, Mr. Fantastic vs. Dr. Doom

$1.50	$4.50	$7.50	£0.70	£2.10	£3.50

201 ND

$0.60	$1.80	$3.00	£0.40	£1.20	£2.00

202 ND (Jan 1979), Iron Man appears

$Good	$Fine	$N.Mint	£Good	£Fine	£N.Mint
$0.60	$1.80	$3.00	£0.40	£1.20	£2.00
$0.60	$1.80	$3.00	£0.40	£1.20	£2.00

203 ND

$0.60	$1.80	$3.00	£0.40	£1.20	£2.00

204 ND storyline introduces the new Champions (ends #209)

$0.60	$1.80	$3.00	£0.40	£1.20	£2.00

205-206 ND

$0.60	$1.80	$3.00	£0.40	£1.20	£2.00

207 ND Spider-Man vs Torch

$0.60	$1.80	$3.00	£0.40	£1.20	£2.00

208 ND

$0.60	$1.80	$3.00	£0.40	£1.20	£2.00

209 ND 1st appearance Herbie (robot), John Byrne art

$1.20	$3.60	$6.00	£0.60	£1.80	£3.00

210-211 ND Galactus appears, John Byrne art

$1.20	$3.60	$6.00	£0.50	£1.50	£2.50

212 Galactus appears, John Byrne art

$0.60	$1.80	$3.00	£0.40	£1.20	£2.00

213 ND John Byrne art

$0.60	$1.80	$3.00	£0.50	£1.50	£2.50

214 ND (Jan 1980), John Byrne art

$0.60	$1.80	$3.00	£0.50	£1.50	£2.50

215-216 ND John Byrne art

$0.60	$1.80	$3.00	£0.50	£1.50	£2.50

217 ND Dazzler appears, John Byrne art

$0.60	$1.80	$3.00	£0.50	£1.50	£2.50

218 ND Spider-Man appears, John Byrne art; continues from Spectacular Spiderman #42

$1.00	$3.00	$5.00	£0.50	£1.50	£2.50

219 ND Sub-Mariner appears, Sienkiewicz art

$0.60	$1.80	$3.00	£0.50	£1.50	£2.50

220 ND John Byrne art

$0.60	$1.80	$3.00	£0.50	£1.50	£2.50

221 ND John Byrne art

$0.60	$1.80	$3.00	£0.40	£1.20	£2.00

222-224 ND Sienkiewicz art

$0.60	$1.80	$3.00	£0.40	£1.20	£2.00

225 ND Sienkiewicz art, Thor appears

$0.60	$1.80	$3.00	£0.40	£1.20	£2.00

226 ND (Jan 1981), Shogun Warriors storyline completed, Sienkiewicz art

$0.60	$1.80	$3.00	£0.40	£1.20	£2.00

227-228 ND Sienkiewicz art

$0.60	$1.80	$3.00	£0.40	£1.20	£2.00

229 Sienkiewicz art

$0.60	$1.80	$3.00	£0.30	£0.90	£1.50

230 Sienkiewicz art, Avengers appear

$0.60	$1.80	$3.00	£0.30	£0.90	£1.50

231 Sienkiewicz art (cover character not Magneto as has been erroneously printed in other guides!)

$0.60	$1.80	$3.00	£0.30	£0.90	£1.50

232 John Byrne art begins (ends #293), credited as "Bjorn Heyn", start of new "old" direction, Dr. Strange cameo

$1.20	$3.60	$6.00	£0.40	£1.20	£2.00

233-234 John Byrne art

$0.80	$2.40	$4.00	£0.30	£0.90	£1.50

235 scarce in the U.K. John Byrne art

$0.80	$2.40	$4.00	£0.40	£1.20	£2.00

236 68pgs, Jack Kirby/John Byrne art, 20th anniversary, F.F. #5 re-done

$0.80	$2.40	$4.00	£0.30	£0.90	£1.50

237 John Byrne art

$0.80	$2.40	$4.00	£0.25	£0.75	£1.25

238 (Jan 1982), John Byrne art

$0.80	$2.40	$4.00	£0.25	£0.75	£1.25

239 scarce in the U.K. John Byrne art

$0.80	$2.40	$4.00	£0.30	£0.90	£1.50

240 scarce in the U.K. Crystal gives birth, Great Refuge moved to Moon, John Byrne art

$0.80	$2.40	$4.00	£0.30	£0.90	£1.50

Fantastic Adventures #15

Fantastic Four #149

Fantastic Giants #24

MINT = 100% / NEAR MINT (inc. +/-) = 90–99% / VERY FINE (inc. +/-) = 75–89% / FINE (inc. +/-) = 55–74% / VERY GOOD (inc. +/-) = 35–54% / GOOD (inc. +/-) = 15–34% / FAIR = 5–14% / POOR = 1–4%

331

# / Description	$Good	$Fine	$N.Mint	£Good	£Fine	£N.Mint
241 scarce in the U.K. Black Panther appears, John Byrne art	$0.80	$2.40	$4.00	£0.30	£0.90	£1.50
242 John Byrne art, Thor, Spiderman, Iron Man and Daredevil appear	$0.80	$2.40	$4.00	£0.25	£0.75	£1.25
243 scarce in the U.K. Avengers and Spiderman battle Galactus, Daredevil and Dr. Strange appear, John Byrne art	$0.80	$2.40	$4.00	£0.40	£1.20	£2.00
244 John Byrne art, Galactus appears; Frankie Raye becomes new Nova (later Galactus' herald)	$1.20	$3.60	$6.00	£0.25	£0.75	£1.25
245-248 John Byrne art	$0.80	$2.40	$4.00	£0.25	£0.75	£1.25
249 Gladiator battles F.F., X-Men appear, John Byrne art	$0.80	$2.40	$4.00	£0.30	£0.90	£1.50
250 52pgs, (Jan 1983), Spiderman and Avengers battle New X-Men, Captain America and Spiderman (disguised Skrulls referred to as "X-Factor"), John Byrne art	$0.80	$2.40	$4.00	£0.40	£1.20	£2.00
251 John Byrne art	$0.80	$2.40	$4.00	£0.25	£0.75	£1.25
252 sideways issue, John Byrne art (Note: an unknown number came with free Skin Tattoos - see Amazing Spiderman #238)	$0.80	$2.40	$4.00	£0.25	£0.75	£1.25
253-255 John Byrne art	$0.80	$2.40	$4.00	£0.25	£0.75	£1.25
256 continues in Thing #2, Avengers #234, John Byrne art	$0.80	$2.40	$4.00	£0.25	£0.75	£1.25
257-258 John Byrne art	$0.80	$2.40	$4.00	£0.25	£0.75	£1.25
259 Silver Surfer last page, John Byrne art	$0.80	$2.40	$4.00	£0.30	£0.90	£1.50
260 Silver Surfer, Alpha Flight X-over, Sub-Mariner appears, John Byrne art	$0.80	$2.40	$4.00	£0.40	£1.20	£2.00
261 Silver Surfer and Sub-Mariner appear, John Byrne art	$0.60	$1.80	$3.00	£0.40	£1.20	£2.00
262 (Jan 1984), new origin Galactus, John Byrne art	$0.60	$1.80	$3.00	£0.50	£1.50	£2.50
263 John Byrne art	$0.60	$1.80	$3.00	£0.25	£0.75	£1.25
264 John Byrne art, cover based on F.F. #1	$0.60	$1.80	$3.00	£0.25	£0.75	£1.25
265 John Byrne art, She-Hulk joins (temporarily), Avengers appear	$0.60	$1.80	$3.00	£0.25	£0.75	£1.25
266-272 John Byrne art	$0.60	$1.80	$3.00	£0.25	£0.75	£1.25
273 1st appearance Nathaniel Richards, John Byrne art	$0.80	$2.40	$4.00	£0.25	£0.75	£1.25
274 (Jan 1985), John Byrne art, Thing re-joins (continued from Thing #19)	$0.60	$1.80	$3.00	£0.25	£0.75	£1.25
275 John Byrne art, She-Hulk appears	$0.60	$1.80	$3.00	£0.25	£0.75	£1.25
276-277 Dr. Strange appears, John Byrne art	$0.60	$1.80	$3.00	£0.25	£0.75	£1.25
278 origin Dr. Doom retold, John Byrne art	$0.60	$1.80	$3.00	£0.25	£0.75	£1.25
279-280 John Byrne art	$0.60	$1.80	$3.00	£0.25	£0.75	£1.25
281 John Byrne art, Daredevil appears	$0.60	$1.80	$3.00	£0.25	£0.75	£1.25
282 LD in the U.K. Secret Wars II X-over, Power Pack appear, John Byrne art	$0.60	$1.80	$3.00	£0.30	£0.90	£1.50
283-284 John Byrne art	$0.60	$1.80	$3.00	£0.25	£0.75	£1.25
285 LD in the U.K. Secret Wars II X-over, John Byrne art	$0.60	$1.80	$3.00	£0.30	£0.90	£1.50
286 LD in the U.K. (Jan 1986), 2nd X-Factor tie-in (story continued in X-Factor #1), X-Men and Avengers appear, John Byrne art (see Avengers #263)	$1.20	$3.60	$6.00	£0.60	£1.80	£3.00
287 LD in the U.K. John Byrne art	$0.40	$1.20	$2.00	£0.30	£0.90	£1.50
288 LD in the U.K. Secret Wars II X-over, John Byrne art	$0.40	$1.20	$2.00	£0.30	£0.90	£1.50
289-290 Nick Fury appears, John Byrne art	$0.40	$1.20	$2.00	£0.25	£0.75	£1.25
291-292 Nick Fury appears, John Byrne art	$0.40	$1.20	$2.00	£0.20	£0.60	£1.00
293 last John Byrne art	$0.40	$1.20	$2.00	£0.20	£0.60	£1.00
294-295	$0.40	$1.20	$2.00	£0.20	£0.60	£1.00
296 DS, Thing re-joins, Barry Smith art	$0.60	$1.80	$3.00	£0.30	£0.90	£1.50
297	$0.40	$1.20	$2.00	£0.20	£0.60	£1.00
298 (Jan 1987)	$0.40	$1.20	$2.00	£0.20	£0.60	£1.00
299	$0.40	$1.20	$2.00	£0.20	£0.60	£1.00
300 Johnny Storm and Alicia Masters marry	$0.30	$0.90	$1.50	£0.20	£0.60	£1.00
301-304	$0.40	$1.20	$2.00	£0.20	£0.60	£1.00
305 Thing vs. Human Torch	$0.40	$1.20	$2.00	£0.20	£0.60	£1.00
306 line-up change: Mr. Fantastic and Invisible Woman leave	$0.40	$1.20	$2.00	£0.20	£0.60	£1.00
307 LD in the U.K. Ms. Marvel appears and joins to make (yet another) new team	$0.40	$1.20	$2.00	£0.25	£0.75	£1.25
308-309 LD in the U.K.	$0.40	$1.20	$2.00	£0.25	£0.75	£1.25
310 LD in the U.K. (Jan 1988), 1st new shape Thing appears, 1st new Ms. Marvel	$0.40	$1.20	$2.00	£0.25	£0.75	£1.25
311 LD in the U.K. Black Panther appears	$0.40	$1.20	$2.00	£0.25	£0.75	£1.25
312 LD in the U.K. Fall of the Mutants, Black Panther and X-Factor appear	$0.40	$1.20	$2.00	£0.30	£0.90	£1.50
313-314 LD in the U.K.	$0.40	$1.20	$2.00	£0.25	£0.75	£1.25
315 LD in the U.K. Morbius appears	$0.40	$1.20	$2.00	£0.25	£0.75	£1.25
316 LD in the U.K. Ka-Zar appears	$0.40	$1.20	$2.00	£0.25	£0.75	£1.25
317-318 LD in the U.K.	$0.40	$1.20	$2.00	£0.25	£0.75	£1.25
319 LD in the U.K. DS, Dr. Doom vs. The Beyonder	$0.40	$1.20	$2.00	£0.30	£0.90	£1.50
320 LD in the U.K. Thing vs. Grey Hulk	$0.40	$1.20	$2.00	£0.40	£1.20	£2.00
321 She-Hulk vs. She-Thing, Ron Lim art (1st on F.F.)	$0.40	$1.20	$2.00	£0.20	£0.60	£1.00
322 (Jan 1989), Inferno tie-in	$0.40	$1.20	$2.00	£0.20	£0.60	£1.00
323 Inferno tie-in	$0.40	$1.20	$2.00	£0.20	£0.60	£1.00
324-325 Inferno tie-in, Silver Surfer appears	$0.40	$1.20	$2.00	£0.20	£0.60	£1.00
326	$0.40	$1.20	$2.00	£0.20	£0.60	£1.00
327 LD in the U.K. Mr. Fantastic and Invisible Woman return	$0.40	$1.20	$2.00	£0.25	£0.75	£1.25
328-333 LD in the U.K.	$0.40	$1.20	$2.00	£0.25	£0.75	£1.25
334 Acts of Vengeance tie-in, Walt Simonson art	$0.40	$1.20	$2.00	£0.20	£0.60	£1.00
335 Acts of Vengeance tie-in, Walt Simonson story	$0.40	$1.20	$2.00	£0.20	£0.60	£1.00
336 (Jan 1990), Acts of Vengeance tie-in, Ron Lim art, Walt Simonson story	$0.40	$1.20	$2.00	£0.20	£0.60	£1.00
337 Walt Simonson story/art begins, Thor appears	$0.40	$1.20	$2.00	£0.20	£0.60	£1.00
338 Thor and Death's Head appear	$0.40	$1.20	$2.00	£0.20	£0.60	£1.00
339 Thor battles Gladiator	$0.40	$1.20	$2.00	£0.20	£0.60	£1.00
340-341 Thor and Iron Man appear	$0.40	$1.20	$2.00	£0.20	£0.60	£1.00
342-343 LD in the U.K.	$0.40	$1.20	$2.00	£0.25	£0.75	£1.25
344 ND scarce in the U.K.	$0.40	$1.20	$2.00	£0.30	£0.90	£1.50
345-346 ND	$0.40	$1.20	$2.00	£0.25	£0.75	£1.25
347 ND Ghost Rider, Wolverine, Spiderman appear, Art Adams cover/art	$1.20	$3.60	$6.00	£0.60	£1.80	£3.00
347 ND Ghost Rider, Wolverine, Spiderman appear, Art Adams cover/art (2nd print - gold cover)	$0.40	$1.20	$2.00	£0.40	£1.20	£2.00
348 ND (Jan 1991), Ghost Rider, Wolverine, Spiderman appear, Art Adams cover/art	$1.00	$3.00	$5.00	£0.50	£1.50	£2.50
348 ND Ghost Rider, Wolverine, Spiderman appear, Art Adams cover/art (2nd print - gold cover)	$0.40	$1.20	$2.00	£0.25	£0.75	£1.25
349 ND Ghost Rider, Wolverine, Spiderman appear (plus Punisher in a few panels), Art Adams art	$1.00	$3.00	$5.00	£0.30	£0.90	£1.50
350 ND DS The Thing returns, Walt Simonson story/art	$0.50	$1.50	$2.50	£0.35	£1.05	£1.75
351-352 LD in the U.K.	$0.40	$1.20	$2.00	£0.20	£0.60	£1.00
353 LD in the U.K. The Avengers guest-star	$0.40	$1.20	$2.00	£0.20	£0.60	£1.00
354 LD in the U.K. last Walt Simonson issue	$0.40	$1.20	$2.00	£0.20	£0.60	£1.00
355 LD in the U.K.	$0.40	$1.20	$2.00	£0.20	£0.60	£1.00
356 ND New Warriors appear, new direction for title	$0.40	$1.20	$2.00	£0.25	£0.75	£1.25
357 ND	$0.40	$1.20	$2.00	£0.25	£0.75	£1.25
358 ND 80pgs, 30th anniversary issue, die-cut card cover, John Byrne pin-up	$0.50	$1.50	$2.50	£0.40	£1.20	£2.00
359 LD in the U.K.	$0.40	$1.20	$2.00	£0.20	£0.60	£1.00
360 LD in the U.K. (Jan 1992)	$0.40	$1.20	$2.00	£0.20	£0.60	£1.00
361 LD in the U.K. $1.25 cover	$0.30	$0.90	$1.50	£0.20	£0.60	£1.00
362-363 LD in the U.K. Spiderman appears	$0.30	$0.90	$1.50	£0.20	£0.60	£1.00
364 LD in the U.K.	$0.30	$0.90	$1.50	£0.20	£0.60	£1.00
365 LD in the U.K. Alpha Flight appear	$0.30	$0.90	$1.50	£0.20	£0.60	£1.00
366-367 Infinity War X-over	$0.30	$0.90	$1.50	£0.20	£0.60	£1.00
368 Infinity War X-over, Hulk appears	$0.30	$0.90	$1.50	£0.20	£0.60	£1.00
369 Infinity War X-over, Thanos appears	$0.40	$1.20	$2.00	£0.20	£0.60	£1.00
370 Infinity War X-over						

	$Good	$Fine	$N.Mint	£Good	£Fine	£N.Mint
	$0.30	$0.90	$1.50	£0.20	£0.60	£1.00
371 embossed all-white cover showing Torch going super-nova (white-hot)						
	$0.70	$2.10	$3.50	£0.30	£0.90	£1.50
371 2nd printing, ND all-red embossed cover						
	$0.40	$1.20	$2.00	£0.30	£0.90	£1.50
372 (Jan 1993), Ms. Marvel and Silver Sable appear						
	$0.30	$0.90	$1.50	£0.20	£0.60	£1.00
373 Silver Sable appears						
	$0.30	$0.90	$1.50	£0.20	£0.60	£1.00
374 Spiderman, Ghost Rider, Hulk and Wolverine (the Secret Defenders) vs. Fantastic Four; Dr. Strange and Silver Sable appear						
	$0.30	$0.90	$1.50	£0.20	£0.60	£1.00
375 LD in the U.K. DS anniversary issue, Ms. Marvel appears, holo-grafix foil cover						
	$0.60	$1.80	$3.00	£0.40	£1.20	£2.00
376 ND pre-bagged with copy of "Dirt" magazine and audio cassette						
	$0.30	$0.90	$1.50	£0.25	£0.75	£1.25
377 lead into Fantastic Four Annual #26						
	$0.30	$0.90	$1.50	£0.20	£0.60	£1.00
378 Spiderman, Daredevil, Silver Surfer appear						
	$0.30	$0.90	$1.50	£0.20	£0.60	£1.00
379-380	$0.30	$0.90	$1.50	£0.20	£0.60	£1.00
381 Reed Richards and Dr. Doom "die"						
	$0.50	$1.50	$2.50	£0.30	£0.90	£1.50
382-383	$0.30	$0.90	$1.50	£0.15	£0.45	£0.75
384 (Jan 1994), Ant-Man "joins" the Fantastic Four						
	$0.30	$0.90	$1.50	£0.15	£0.45	£0.75
385-386 Starblast X-over						
	$0.30	$0.90	$1.50	£0.15	£0.45	£0.75
387 Nobody Gets Out Alive part 1						
	$0.30	$0.90	$1.50	£0.20	£0.60	£1.00
387 LD in the U.K. Collector's Edition, die-cut prismatic foil cover						
	$0.60	$1.80	$3.00	£0.40	£1.20	£2.00
388-389 Nobody Gets Out Alive story						
	$0.30	$0.90	$1.50	£0.15	£0.45	£0.75
390 Nobody Gets Out Alive story; Black Panther and Silver Surfer appear; cover based on issue #48						
	$0.30	$0.90	$1.50	£0.15	£0.45	£0.75
391 Nobody Gets Out Alive story; Black Panther begins to assemble Fantastic Force						
	$0.30	$0.90	$1.50	£0.15	£0.45	£0.75
392 Nobody Gets Out Alive story conclusion; 1st appearance Fantastic Force						
	$0.30	$0.90	$1.50	£0.15	£0.45	£0.75
393-394	$0.30	$0.90	$1.50	£0.15	£0.45	£0.75
394 ND pre-bagged with acetate print from Marvel Action Hour animated TV series						
	$0.60	$1.80	$3.00	£0.40	£1.20	£2.00
395 Thing vs. Wolverine						
	$0.30	$0.90	$1.50	£0.20	£0.60	£1.00
396 (Jan 1995)	$0.30	$0.90	$1.50	£0.20	£0.60	£1.00
397-398	$0.30	$0.90	$1.50	£0.20	£0.60	£1.00
398 ND Enhanced Edition - prismatic foil-enhanced cover						
	$0.60	$1.80	$3.00	£0.30	£0.90	£1.50
399	$0.30	$0.90	$1.50	£0.20	£0.60	£1.00
399 ND Enhanced Edition - prismatic foil-enhanced cover						
	$0.60	$1.80	$3.00	£0.30	£0.90	£1.50
400 LD in the U.K. 64pgs, prismatic foil-stamped cover, 10pg preview of Atlantis Rising						
	$0.80	$2.40	$4.00	£0.50	£1.50	£2.50
401 Atlantis Rising						
	$0.30	$0.90	$1.50	£0.20	£0.60	£1.00
402 Atlantis Rising; Namor vs. Black Bolt						
	$0.30	$0.90	$1.50	£0.20	£0.60	£1.00
403	$0.30	$0.90	$1.50	£0.20	£0.60	£1.00
404 Namor the Sub-Mariner appears; bi-weekly						
	$0.30	$0.90	$1.50	£0.20	£0.60	£1.00
405 Namor the Sub-Mariner joins the Fantastic Four; bi-weekly						
	$0.30	$0.90	$1.50	£0.20	£0.60	£1.00
406 The return of Dr. Doom...						
	$0.30	$0.90	$1.50	£0.20	£0.60	£1.00
407 The return of Reed Richards...						
	$0.30	$0.90	$1.50	£0.20	£0.60	£1.00
408 (Jan 1996)	$0.30	$0.90	$1.50	£0.20	£0.60	£1.00
409-410	$0.30	$0.90	$1.50	£0.20	£0.60	£1.00
Title Value:	**$4916.65**	**$14753.50**	**$44694.75**	**£2802.45**	**£8449.10**	**£25098.25**

Note: #154, #180, #189 are all reprint.

The Trial of Galactus
Trade paperback (Oct 1989) reprints edited version
of issues #244-262, John Byrne art £1.25 £3.75 £6.25
2nd print (Nov 1994) new John Byrne cover
Bookshelf Edition (Mar 1992), reprints issues #347-349 £0.75 £2.25 £3.75
Fantastic Four: Nobody Gets Out Alive (Feb 1995)
Trade paperback 144pgs,
reprints issues #387-392 plus new material £2.00 £6.00 £10.00
Greatest Villains of the Fantastic Four (Jun 1995)
Trade paperback 144pgs, classic reprints featuring Dr. Doom et al. £2.00 £6.00 £10.00

ARTISTS
Kirby art in 1-102, 108, 236. Perez art 164-172, 176-178, 184-188, 191, 192. Steranko covers on 130-132. Perez covers on 191, 192, 194-198, 208.

FANTASTIC FOUR 2099
Marvel Comics Group; 1 Jan 1996-present

	$Good	$Fine	$N.Mint	£Good	£Fine	£N.Mint
1 ND Karl Kesel script, Rick Leonardi and Al Williamson art; chromium cover						
	$0.80	$2.40	$4.00	£0.50	£1.50	£2.50
2-3 ND	$0.35	$1.15	$1.95	£0.25	£0.75	£1.25
Title Value:	**$1.50**	**$4.70**	**$7.90**	**£1.00**	**£3.00**	**£5.00**

FANTASTIC FOUR ANNUAL
Marvel Comics Group; 1 1963-9 1971; 10 1973; 11 1976-present

	$Good	$Fine	$N.Mint	£Good	£Fine	£N.Mint
1 origin Fantastic Four retold, reprints 1st part FF #1 and 2nd part Spiderman #1; Sub-Mariner appears (alternative cover in F.F. Index 2), Kirby cover and art						
	$67.50	$205.00	$550.00	£44.00	£130.00	£350.00
[Scarce in high grade - Very Fine+ or better]						
2 origin Dr. Doom retold from FF #5 plus new Dr. Doom story; Jack Kirby cover and art						
	$50.00	$150.00	$350.00	£29.00	£85.00	£200.00
3 Reed Richards & Sue Storm wed; X-Men, Avengers, Daredevil and The Watcher appear, Stan Lee & Jack Kirby cameo, reprints part FF #6, #11, Kirby cover and art						
	$21.00	$62.50	$150.00	£12.50	£39.00	£90.00
4 origin and 1st Silver Age appearance of Golden Age Human Torch, reprints part FF #25, #26, Jack Kirby cover and art						
	$14.00	$43.00	$85.00	£8.25	£25.00	£50.00
5 intro Psycho Man, Silver Surfer appears (1st solo story); Jack Kirby cover and art, Giacoia inks (not Sinnott as credited)						
	$12.50	$39.00	$90.00	£7.75	£23.50	£55.00
6 1st appearance Annihilus, Franklin Richards is born, Jack Kirby cover and art						
	$7.75	$23.50	$47.50	£4.55	£13.50	£27.50
7 reprints part FF #1 (Mole Man), Annual #2 (origin Dr. Doom), Jack Kirby cover and art						
	$4.15	$12.50	$25.00	£2.05	£6.25	£12.50
8 reprints part Annual #1 (Sub-Mariner story), Jack Kirby art						
	$2.05	$6.25	$12.50	£1.25	£3.75	£7.50
9 ND scarce in the U.K. reprints part Annual #3, Jack Kirby cover and art						
	$2.00	$6.00	$12.00	£1.75	£5.25	£10.50
10 ND scarce in the U.K. reprints part Annual #3, #4, Jack Kirby art						
	$2.00	$6.00	$12.00	£1.40	£4.20	£8.40
11 ND Invaders appear, continues in Marvel Two-In-One Annual #1, Jack Kirby cover						
	$1.20	$3.60	$6.00	£0.70	£2.10	£3.50
12-13 ND	$1.20	$3.60	$6.00	£0.50	£1.50	£2.50
14 ND George Perez art						
	$1.20	$3.60	$6.00	£0.55	£1.65	£2.75
15 ND George Perez art						
	$0.80	$2.40	$4.00	£0.50	£1.50	£2.50
16 ND Steve Ditko art						
	$0.80	$2.40	$4.00	£0.40	£1.20	£2.00
17 ND John Byrne art						
	$0.80	$2.40	$4.00	£0.40	£1.20	£2.00
18 ND John Byrne art; ties into X-Men #137, Wolverine appears						
	$0.80	$2.40	$4.00	£0.50	£1.50	£2.50
19 ND John Byrne art, Avengers appear						
	$0.80	$2.40	$4.00	£0.50	£1.50	£2.50
20 ND scarce in the U.K.						
	$0.80	$2.40	$4.00	£0.50	£1.50	£2.50
21 ND Evolutionary War, squarebound						
	$0.80	$2.40	$4.00	£0.40	£1.20	£2.00
22 ND part 14 (conclusion) Atlantis Attacks						
	$0.50	$1.50	$2.50	£0.30	£0.90	£1.50
23 ND Days of Future Present story (see X-Factor/ New Mutants/X-Men Annuals)						
	$0.50	$1.50	$2.50	£0.30	£0.90	£1.50
24 ND story continued in Thor Annual #16						
	$0.50	$1.50	$2.50	£0.30	£0.90	£1.50
25 ND 64pgs, Citizen Kang part 3, Black Widow, Falcon, Sersi, Hercules, Crystal and Black Knight appear, continued in Avengers Annual #21						
	$0.50	$1.50	$2.50	£0.30	£0.90	£1.50
26 ND 64pgs, pre-bagged with trading card introducing Black Marvel						
	$0.60	$1.80	$3.00	£0.40	£1.20	£2.00
27 ND 64pgs	$0.60	$1.80	$3.00	£0.40	£1.20	£2.00
Title Value:	**$196.55**	**$594.55**	**$1402.00**	**£119.85**	**£357.50**	**£848.15**

Note: 4-7 called Specials on cover. 7-10 are all reprint. 1-10 are 72pgs, 11-16 are 52pgs. 21 and 22 are 64pgs. Note also: Annuals 1-3 occasionally turn up with blank back and inside front and back covers (see also Spiderman Annual #1, 2, Sgt. Fury Annual #1, Strange Tales Annual #2). These were subscription copies sent over to this country as left-overs and are very scarce. With their white back covers which show soiling and wear that much more easily, they are very rare in mint condition.

FANTASTIC FOUR ASHCAN EDITION
Marvel Comics Group, OS; nn Jun 1995

	$Good	$Fine	$N.Mint	£Good	£Fine	£N.Mint
nn ND 16pgs, retells origin; black and white						
	$0.15	$0.45	$0.75	£0.10	£0.30	£0.50
Title Value:	**$0.15**	**$0.45**	**$0.75**	**£0.10**	**£0.30**	**£0.50**

FANTASTIC FOUR BOOK AND RECORD SET
Power Records; PR-13 1974
PR-13, scarce, 20pg booklet based on origin in issue #1
with 45 rpm record £1.20 £3.60 £6.00
Note: the item would retail for about 50% without record

FANTASTIC FOUR COLLECTOR'S PREVIEW
Marvel Comics Group, OS; 1 May 1995

	$Good	$Fine	$N.Mint	£Good	£Fine	£N.Mint
1 ND information, articles and interviews on the Fantastic Four; Alan Davis cover						
	$0.45	$1.35	$2.25	£0.30	£0.90	£1.50
Title Value:	**$0.45**	**$1.35**	**$2.25**	**£0.30**	**£0.90**	**£1.50**

FANTASTIC FOUR GIANT SIZE
Marvel Comics Group; 2 Aug 1974-6 Aug 1975
(formerly Super-Stars Giant Size)

	$Good	$Fine	$N.Mint	£Good	£Fine	£N.Mint
2 ND 68pgs	$2.40	$7.00	$12.00	£1.40	£4.20	£7.00
3 ND 68pgs	$2.00	$6.00	$10.00	£1.20	£3.60	£6.00
4 ND 68pgs, Professor X appears, 1st appearance Madrox the Multiplying Man						
	$2.00	$6.00	$10.00	£1.20	£3.60	£6.00
5-6 ND 68pgs	$1.60	$4.80	$8.00	£1.00	£3.00	£5.00
Title Value:	**$9.60**	**$28.60**	**$48.00**	**£5.80**	**£17.40**	**£29.00**

Note: #2-4 have back-up reprints; #5, #6 are all reprint.

FANTASTIC FOUR ROAST
Marvel Comics Group, OS; 1 May 1982
1 ND celebrates 20th anniversary, John Byrne, Hembeck, Frank Miller, Rogers, Buscema, Golden,

	$Good	$Fine	$N.Mint	£Good	£Fine	£N.Mint

Anderson, Sienkiewicz art

| | $0.45 | $1.35 | $2.25 | £0.30 | £0.90 | £1.50 |
| Title Value: | $0.45 | $1.35 | $2.25 | £0.30 | £0.90 | £1.50 |

FANTASTIC FOUR SPECIAL EDITION
Marvel Comics Group,OS; 1 May 1984
1 ND reprints F.F. Annual #1, John Byrne cover and few pages art

| | $0.60 | $1.80 | $3.00 | £0.40 | £1.20 | £2.00 |
| Title Value: | $0.60 | $1.80 | $3.00 | £0.40 | £1.20 | £2.00 |

FANTASTIC FOUR UNLIMITED
Marvel Comics Group; 1 Mar 1993-present
1 ND 64pgs, Black Panther appears

| | $0.80 | $2.40 | $4.00 | £0.50 | £1.50 | £2.50 |

2 ND 64pgs, Black Panther appears, Joe Quesada cover

| | $0.80 | $2.40 | $4.00 | £0.50 | £1.50 | £2.50 |

3 ND 64pgs

| | $0.80 | $2.40 | $4.00 | £0.50 | £1.50 | £2.50 |

4 ND 64pgs, Thing vs. Hulk

| | $0.80 | $2.40 | $4.00 | £0.50 | £1.50 | £2.50 |

5 ND 64pgs, Fantastic Four vs. The Frightful Four

| | $0.80 | $2.40 | $4.00 | £0.50 | £1.50 | £2.50 |

6 ND 64pgs, Fantastic Four vs. Namor the Sub-Mariner

| | $0.80 | $2.40 | $4.00 | £0.50 | £1.50 | £2.50 |

7 ND 64pgs, classic pre-super hero monsters appear

| | $0.80 | $2.40 | $4.00 | £0.50 | £1.50 | £2.50 |

8 ND 64pgs, Dr. Doom appears

| | $0.80 | $2.40 | $4.00 | £0.50 | £1.50 | £2.50 |

9 ND 64pgs, Thor guest-stars

| | $0.80 | $2.40 | $4.00 | £0.50 | £1.50 | £2.50 |

10 ND 64pgs, The Eternals appear

| | $0.80 | $2.40 | $4.00 | £0.50 | £1.50 | £2.50 |

11 ND 64pgs, The Inhumans mutate and Namor the Sub-Mariner appears

| | $0.80 | $2.40 | $4.00 | £0.50 | £1.50 | £2.50 |

12 ND 64pgs, Fantastic Four vs. Hyperstorm

| | $0.80 | $2.40 | $4.00 | £0.50 | £1.50 | £2.50 |

13 ND 64pgs

| | $0.80 | $2.40 | $4.00 | £0.50 | £1.50 | £2.50 |
| Title Value: | $10.40 | $31.20 | $52.00 | £6.50 | £19.50 | £32.50 |

Note: quarterly frequency

FANTASTIC FOUR UNPLUGGED
Marvel Comics Group; 1 Sep 1995-present
1 ND The Thing stars in his own bi-monthly series; cover priced at a special 99 cents

| | $0.20 | $0.60 | $1.00 | £0.10 | £0.35 | £0.65 |

2 ND

| | $0.20 | $0.60 | $1.00 | £0.10 | £0.35 | £0.65 |

3 ND ties into Fantastic Four #408

| | $0.20 | $0.60 | $1.00 | £0.10 | £0.35 | £0.65 |

4 ND

| | $0.20 | $0.60 | $1.00 | £0.10 | £0.35 | £0.65 |
| Title Value: | $0.80 | $2.40 | $4.00 | £0.40 | £1.40 | £2.60 |

Note: originally announced as Marvel: Fantastic Four

FANTASTIC FOUR VS THE X-MEN
Marvel Comics Group,MS; 1 Feb 1987-4 May 1987
1 ND Jon Bogdanove art begins

| | $0.45 | $1.35 | $2.25 | £0.30 | £0.90 | £1.50 |

2-4 ND

| | $0.45 | $1.35 | $2.25 | £0.30 | £0.90 | £1.50 |
| Title Value: | $1.80 | $5.40 | $9.00 | £1.20 | £3.60 | £6.00 |

Note: Jon Bogdanove art/Claremont script
Fantastic Four vs. The X-Men (Nov 1994) reprints mini-series £2.00 £6.00 £10.00

FANTASTIC FOUR, THE OFFICIAL MARVEL INDEX TO
Marvel Comics Group; 1 Dec 1985-12 Jan 1987
1 ND information and colour cover reproductions Fantastic Four #1-#15, new John Byrne cover; alternative original cover to F.F. #3 on back cover

| | $0.60 | $1.80 | $3.00 | £0.40 | £1.20 | £2.00 |

2 ND information and colour cover reproductions Fantastic Four #16-#30, Annual #1, Sienkiewicz cover; alternative original cover to F.F. Annual #1 on back cover

| | $0.60 | $1.80 | $3.00 | £0.40 | £1.20 | £2.00 |

3 ND information and colour cover reproductions Fantastic Four #31-#45, Annual #2,#3

| | $0.60 | $1.80 | $3.00 | £0.40 | £1.20 | £2.00 |

4 ND information and colour cover reproductions Fantastic Four #46-#65, Annual #4

| | $0.60 | $1.80 | $3.00 | £0.40 | £1.20 | £2.00 |

5 ND information and colour cover reproductions Fantastic Four #66-#84, Annual #5,#6

| | $0.60 | $1.80 | $3.00 | £0.40 | £1.20 | £2.00 |

6 ND information and colour cover reproductions Fantastic Four #85-#106, Annual #7,#8

| | $0.60 | $1.80 | $3.00 | £0.40 | £1.20 | £2.00 |

7 ND information and colour cover reproductions Fantastic Four #107-#125, Annual #9

| | $0.60 | $1.80 | $3.00 | £0.40 | £1.20 | £2.00 |

8 ND information and colour cover reproductions Fantastic Four #126-#141, Annual #10 and Giant Size Super Stars #1

| | $0.60 | $1.80 | $3.00 | £0.40 | £1.20 | £2.00 |

9 ND information and colour cover reproductions Fantastic Four #142-#160, Annual #10 and Giant Size #2,#3

| | $0.60 | $1.80 | $3.00 | £0.40 | £1.20 | £2.00 |

10 ND information and colour cover reproductions Fantastic Four #161-#176, Annual #11 and Giant Size #4-#6

| | $0.60 | $1.80 | $3.00 | £0.40 | £1.20 | £2.00 |

11 ND information and colour cover reproductions Fantastic Four #177-#198

| | $0.60 | $1.80 | $3.00 | £0.40 | £1.20 | £2.00 |

12 ND information and colour cover reproductions Fantastic Four #199-#214, Annual #12,#13

| | $0.60 | $1.80 | $3.00 | £0.40 | £1.20 | £2.00 |
| Title Value: | $7.20 | $21.60 | $36.00 | £4.80 | £14.40 | £24.00 |

Note: Volume 2 in Official Marvel Index Series of 5.

FANTASTIC FOUR/FORCE ASHCAN
Marvel Comics Group,OS; nn Oct 1994
nn ND 16pgs, reviews origin of FF and Fantastic Force

| | $0.25 | $0.75 | $1.25 | £0.15 | £0.45 | £0.75 |
| Title Value: | $0.25 | $0.75 | $1.25 | £0.15 | £0.45 | £0.75 |

FANTASTIC FOUR: ATLANTIS RISING
Marvel Comics Group,MS; 1 Jun 1995-2 Jul 1995

1-2 ND 48pgs, M.C. Wyman art, The Inhumans appear; acetate outer cover

| | $0.80 | $2.40 | $4.00 | £0.50 | £1.50 | £2.50 |
| Title Value: | $1.60 | $4.80 | $8.00 | £1.00 | £3.00 | £5.00 |

FANTASTIC GIANTS
Charlton; 24 Sep 1966
(previously Konga)
24 giant, new and reprint Steve Ditko art; Konga and Gorgo featured; distributed in the U.K.

| | $7.50 | $22.50 | $45.00 | £5.00 | £15.00 | £30.00 |
| Title Value: | $7.50 | $22.50 | $45.00 | £5.00 | £15.00 | £30.00 |

FANTASTIC TALES
I.W. Enterprises; 1 1958
1 reprints Avon Periodicals "City of the Living Dead"; distributed in the U.K.

| | $3.00 | $9.00 | $18.00 | £2.00 | £6.00 | £12.00 |
| Title Value: | $3.00 | $9.00 | $18.00 | £2.00 | £6.00 | £12.00 |

FANTASTIC VOYAGE
Gold Key; 1 Aug 1969-2 Dec 1969
1 based on TV cartoon rather than Raquel Welch film; distributed in the U.K.

| | $3.75 | $11.00 | $22.50 | £2.50 | £7.50 | £15.00 |

2 based on TV cartoon rather than Raquel Welch film; distributed in the U.K.

| | $3.30 | $10.00 | $20.00 | £2.30 | £7.00 | £14.00 |
| Title Value: | $7.05 | $21.00 | $42.50 | £4.80 | £14.50 | £29.00 |

FANTASY FEATURES
AC Comics; 1,2 1987
1-2 ND

| | $0.40 | $1.20 | $2.00 | £0.25 | £0.75 | £1.25 |
| Title Value: | $0.80 | $2.40 | $4.00 | £0.50 | £1.50 | £2.50 |

FANTASY MASTERPIECES
Marvel Comics Group; 1 Feb 1966-11 Oct 1967
(becomes Marvel Super-Heroes)
1 scarce in the U.K. 60s horror reprints featuring art by Steve Ditko (Amazing Fantasy #10) and Jack Kirby (Journey into Mystery #60)

| | $6.25 | $18.50 | $37.50 | £3.30 | £10.00 | £20.00 |

2 early 60s reprints including 1st appearance Fin Fang Foom from Strange Tales #89

| | $3.30 | $10.00 | $20.00 | £1.65 | £5.00 | £10.00 |

3 72pgs, Captain America 1940s reprints begin

| | $3.30 | $10.00 | $20.00 | £1.30 | £4.00 | £8.00 |

4-5 72pgs, Captain America reprints

| | $3.30 | $10.00 | $20.00 | £1.30 | £4.00 | £8.00 |

6 72pgs, Captain America reprints

| | $3.30 | $10.00 | $20.00 | £1.15 | £3.50 | £7.00 |

7 72pgs, begin Golden Age Sub-Mariner/Torch reprints

| | $4.00 | $12.00 | $20.00 | £1.40 | £4.20 | £7.00 |

8 72pgs, Golden Age Torch vs Sub-Mariner reprint from Marvel Mystery #9

| | $4.00 | $12.00 | $20.00 | £1.40 | £4.20 | £7.00 |

9 72pgs, reprints Golden Age Human Torch origin from Marvel Comics #1

| | $4.40 | $13.00 | $22.00 | £1.60 | £4.80 | £8.00 |

10 72pgs, All Winners Squad reprint

| | $4.00 | $12.00 | $20.00 | £1.20 | £3.60 | £6.00 |

11 72pgs, reprints origins Toro and Black Knight

| | $4.00 | $12.00 | $20.00 | £1.20 | £3.60 | £6.00 |
| Title Value: | $43.15 | $129.50 | $239.50 | £16.80 | £50.90 | £95.00 |

FANTASY MASTERPIECES (2ND SERIES)
Marvel Comics Group; 1 Dec 1979-14 Jan 1981
1 ND 52pgs, squarebound, reprints Silver Surfer #1

| | $1.50 | $4.50 | $7.50 | £1.00 | £3.00 | £5.00 |

2 ND 52pgs, squarebound, reprints Silver Surfer #2

| | $0.90 | $2.70 | $4.50 | £0.60 | £1.80 | £3.00 |

3 ND 52pgs, squarebound, reprints Silver Surfer #3

| | $0.90 | $2.70 | $4.50 | £0.60 | £1.80 | £3.00 |

4 ND 52pgs, squarebound, reprints Silver Surfer #4

| | $1.05 | $3.15 | $5.25 | £0.70 | £2.10 | £3.50 |

5 ND 52pgs, squarebound, reprints Silver Surfer #5

| | $0.90 | $2.70 | $4.50 | £0.60 | £1.80 | £3.00 |

6 ND 52pgs, squarebound, reprints Silver Surfer #6

| | $0.80 | $2.40 | $4.00 | £0.50 | £1.50 | £2.50 |

7 ND 52pgs, squarebound, reprints Silver Surfer #7

| | $0.80 | $2.40 | $4.00 | £0.50 | £1.50 | £2.50 |

8 ND 52pgs, squarebound, reprints Silver Surfer #8 and Warlock from Strange Tales #178

| | $0.90 | $2.70 | $4.50 | £0.60 | £1.80 | £3.00 |

9 ND 52pgs, squarebound, reprints Silver Surfer #9 and Warlock from Strange Tales #179

| | $0.80 | $2.40 | $4.00 | £0.50 | £1.50 | £2.50 |

10 ND 52pgs, squarebound, reprints Silver Surfer #10 and Warlock from Strange Tales #180

| | $0.80 | $2.40 | $4.00 | £0.50 | £1.50 | £2.50 |

11 ND 52pgs, squarebound, reprints Silver Surfer #11 and Warlock from Strange Tales #181

| | $0.80 | $2.40 | $4.00 | £0.40 | £1.20 | £2.00 |

12 ND 52pgs, reprints Silver Surfer #12 and Warlock #9

| | $0.80 | $2.40 | $4.00 | £0.40 | £1.20 | £2.00 |

13 ND 52pgs, reprints Silver Surfer #13 and Warlock #10

| | $0.80 | $2.40 | $4.00 | £0.50 | £1.50 | £2.50 |

14 ND 52pgs, reprints Silver Surfer #14 and Warlock #11 (plus cover repro)

| | $0.60 | $1.80 | $3.00 | £0.40 | £1.20 | £2.00 |
| Title Value: | $11.95 | $35.85 | $59.75 | £7.30 | £23.40 | £39.00 |

Note: all reprint from original Silver Surfer series. Warlock in 8-14 (Starlin art).

FANTASY QUARTERLY
IPS; 1 Spring 1978
1 ND 1st appearance Elfquest, Wendy Pini story/art

| | $7.00 | $21.00 | $35.00 | £5.00 | £15.00 | £25.00 |
| Title Value: | $7.00 | $21.00 | $35.00 | £5.00 | £15.00 | £25.00 |

FAREWELL TO WEAPONS DIRT BAG SPECIAL
Marvel Comics Group,OS; 1 Jun 1992
1 ND pre-bagged, Farewell To Arms comic by Katsuhiro Otomo, "Dirt" magazine, pop music cassette

| | $0.70 | $2.10 | $3.50 | £0.40 | £1.20 | £2.00 |
| Title Value: | $0.70 | $2.10 | $3.50 | £0.40 | £1.20 | £2.00 |

	$Good	$Fine	$N.Mint	£Good	£Fine	£N.Mint

FASHION IN ACTION SUMMER SPECIAL
Eclipse,OS; 1 Aug 1986

	$Good	$Fine	$N.Mint	£Good	£Fine	£N.Mint
1 ND John K. Snyder III art, Scout spin-off; colour	$0.45	$1.35	$2.25	£0.30	£0.90	£1.50
Title Value:	$0.45	$1.35	$2.25	£0.30	£0.90	£1.50

FASHION IN ACTION WINTER SPECIAL
Eclipse,OS; 1 Feb 1987

	$Good	$Fine	$N.Mint	£Good	£Fine	£N.Mint
1 ND John K. Snyder III art, Scout spin-off; colour	$0.45	$1.35	$2.25	£0.30	£0.90	£1.50
Title Value:	$0.45	$1.35	$2.25	£0.30	£0.90	£1.50

FAST FORWARD
DC Comics/Piranha Press,MS; 1 Dec 1992-2 1993

	$Good	$Fine	$N.Mint	£Good	£Fine	£N.Mint
1 ND 64pgs, Phobias; anthology featuring Grant Morrison story	$0.90	$2.70	$4.50	£0.60	£1.80	£3.00
2 ND 64pgs, anthology	$0.90	$2.70	$4.50	£0.60	£1.80	£3.00
Title Value:	$1.80	$5.40	$9.00	£1.20	£3.60	£6.00

FAT NINJA
Silverwolf Comics; 1 Aug 1986-8 1987

	$Good	$Fine	$N.Mint	£Good	£Fine	£N.Mint
1-8 ND black and white	$0.25	$0.75	$1.25	£0.15	£0.45	£0.75
Title Value:	$2.00	$6.00	$10.00	£1.20	£3.60	£6.00

FATE
DC Comics; 0 Oct 1994; 1 Nov 1994-present

	$Good	$Fine	$N.Mint	£Good	£Fine	£N.Mint
0 (Oct 1994) Zero Hour X-over, origin	$0.40	$1.20	$2.00	£0.25	£0.75	£1.25
1-4	$0.40	$1.20	$2.00	£0.25	£0.75	£1.25
5 Phantom Stranger and Dr. Occult appear	$0.40	$1.20	$2.00	£0.25	£0.75	£1.25
6-7	$0.40	$1.20	$2.00	£0.25	£0.75	£1.25
8-9	$0.45	$1.35	$2.25	£0.30	£0.90	£1.50
10 Zatanna guest-stars	$0.45	$1.35	$2.25	£0.30	£0.90	£1.50
11-12	$0.45	$1.35	$2.25	£0.30	£0.90	£1.50
13 Underworld Unleashed tie-in	$0.45	$1.35	$2.25	£0.30	£0.90	£1.50
14 Underworld Unleashed tie-in with Sentinel, Deadman and Zatanna	$0.45	$1.35	$2.25	£0.30	£0.90	£1.50
15-17	$0.45	$1.35	$2.25	£0.30	£0.90	£1.50
Title Value:	$7.70	$23.10	$38.50	£5.00	£15.00	£25.00

FATHER & SON
Kitchen Sink,MS; 1 Sep 1995-present

	$Good	$Fine	$N.Mint	£Good	£Fine	£N.Mint
1 ND Jeff Nicholson script and art; black and white	$0.55	$1.65	$2.75	£0.35	£1.05	£1.75
2-3 ND	$0.55	$1.65	$2.75	£0.35	£1.05	£1.75
Title Value:	$1.65	$4.95	$8.25	£1.05	£3.15	£5.25

FATHOM
Comico,MS; 1 May 1987-3 Jul 1987

	$Good	$Fine	$N.Mint	£Good	£Fine	£N.Mint
1-3 ND Elementals spin-off	$0.40	$1.20	$2.00	£0.25	£0.75	£1.25
Title Value:	$1.20	$3.60	$6.00	£0.75	£2.25	£3.75
Trade Paperback (Sep 1991), reprints mini-series plus new story, new cover by Bill Willingham				£1.50	£4.50	£7.50

FATHOM (2ND SERIES)
Comico,MS; 1 Nov 1992-3 Jun 1993

	$Good	$Fine	$N.Mint	£Good	£Fine	£N.Mint
1-3 ND colour	$0.40	$1.20	$2.00	£0.25	£0.75	£1.25
Title Value:	$1.20	$3.60	$6.00	£0.75	£2.25	£3.75

FATMAN THE HUMAN FLYING SAUCER
Lightning Comics/Milson Publishing; 1 Apr 1967-3 Aug/Sep 1967

	$Good	$Fine	$N.Mint	£Good	£Fine	£N.Mint
1 origin, script begins by Otto Binder, art begins by C.C. Beck	$8.00	$24.00	$40.00	£5.00	£15.00	£25.00
2	$5.50	$16.50	$27.50	£3.50	£10.50	£17.50
3 very scarce in the U.K., scarce in the U.S.	$9.00	$27.00	$45.00	£6.00	£18.00	£30.00
Title Value:	$22.50	$67.50	$112.50	£14.50	£43.50	£72.50

Note: irregular distribution in the U.K.

FATMAN THE HUMAN FLYING SAUCER (2ND SERIES)
A Plus Comics,MS; 1 Jan 1992-3 1992

	$Good	$Fine	$N.Mint	£Good	£Fine	£N.Mint
1 ND reprints from original series begin, C.C. Beck covers begin	$0.40	$1.20	$2.00	£0.25	£0.75	£1.25
2-3 ND	$0.40	$1.20	$2.00	£0.25	£0.75	£1.25
Title Value:	$1.20	$3.60	$6.00	£0.75	£2.25	£3.75

FAUNA REBELLION, THE
Fantagraphics,MS; 1 Mar 1990-3 May 1990

	$Good	$Fine	$N.Mint	£Good	£Fine	£N.Mint
1-3 ND ecology theme comic	$0.40	$1.20	$2.00	£0.25	£0.75	£1.25
Title Value:	$1.20	$3.60	$6.00	£0.75	£2.25	£3.75

FAUST
Northstar/Rebel Studios,MS; 1 1989-10 1995

	$Good	$Fine	$N.Mint	£Good	£Fine	£N.Mint
1 ND David Quinn and Tim Vigil art begins	$5.50	$16.50	$27.50	£3.00	£9.00	£15.00
1 2nd printing ND	$1.50	$4.50	$7.50	£1.00	£3.00	£5.00
1 3rd printing ND	$0.80	$2.40	$4.00	£0.50	£1.50	£2.50
1 4th printing ND	$0.40	$1.20	$2.00	£0.25	£0.75	£1.25
1 5th printing, ND (Aug 1994)	$0.45	$1.35	$2.25	£0.30	£0.90	£1.50
2 ND	$4.00	$12.00	$20.00	£2.00	£6.00	£10.00
2 2nd printing, ND	$0.90	$2.70	$4.50	£0.60	£1.80	£3.00
2 3rd printing ND	$0.60	$1.80	$3.00	£0.40	£1.20	£2.00
2 4th printing ND	$0.45	$1.35	$2.25	£0.30	£0.90	£1.50
3 ND	$3.00	$9.00	$15.00	£1.50	£4.50	£7.50
3 2nd printing ND	$0.80	$2.40	$4.00	£0.50	£1.50	£2.50
3 3rd printing ND	$0.45	$1.35	$2.25	£0.30	£0.90	£1.50
4 ND	$1.00	$3.00	$5.00	£1.00	£3.00	£5.00
4 2nd printing ND	$0.60	$1.80	$3.00	£0.40	£1.20	£2.00
4 3rd printing ND	$0.45	$1.35	$2.25	£0.30	£0.90	£1.50
5 ND	$0.80	$2.40	$4.00	£0.80	£2.40	£4.00
5 2nd printing ND	$0.45	$1.35	$2.25	£0.30	£0.90	£1.50
6 ND	$0.70	$2.10	$3.50	£0.60	£1.80	£3.00
7 ND scarce in the U.K. 1st Rebel Studios issue	$0.70	$2.10	$3.50	£0.60	£1.80	£3.00
7 2nd printing, ND (May 1993)	$0.45	$1.35	$2.25	£0.30	£0.90	£1.50
8 ND scarce in the U.K.	$0.70	$2.10	$3.50	£0.50	£1.50	£2.50
8 2nd printing, ND (Jun 1993)	$0.45	$1.35	$2.25	£0.30	£0.90	£1.50
9 ND scarce in the U.K.	$0.70	$2.10	$3.50	£0.50	£1.50	£2.50
9 2nd printing, ND (Sep 1993)	$0.45	$1.35	$2.25	£0.30	£0.90	£1.50
9 3rd printing ND	$0.45	$1.35	$2.25	£0.30	£0.90	£1.50
10 ND scarce in the U.K.	$0.70	$2.10	$3.50	£0.50	£1.50	£2.50
Title Value:	$27.45	$82.35	$137.25	£17.35	£52.05	£86.75

FAUST (2ND SERIES)
Rebel Studios,MS; 1 Aug 1992-6 Apr 1993

	$Good	$Fine	$N.Mint	£Good	£Fine	£N.Mint
1 reprints begin of original series with new covers, corrected art and editorial supplements	$0.60	$1.80	$3.00	£0.40	£1.20	£2.00
1 2nd printing	$0.45	$1.35	$2.25	£0.30	£0.90	£1.50
2	$0.45	$1.35	$2.25	£0.30	£0.90	£1.50
2 2nd printing, (Aug 1993)						

Fantasy Masterpieces (1st) #2

Fantasy Masterpieces (2nd) #2

Faust #1

	$Good	$Fine	$N.Mint	£Good	£Fine	£N.Mint
	$0.45	$1.35	$2.25	£0.30	£0.90	£1.50
3	$0.45	$1.35	$2.25	£0.30	£0.90	£1.50
3 2nd printing	$0.45	$1.35	$2.25	£0.30	£0.90	£1.50
4	$0.45	$1.35	$2.25	£0.30	£0.90	£1.50
4 2nd printing, (Oct 1993)	$0.45	$1.35	$2.25	£0.30	£0.90	£1.50
5	$0.45	$1.35	$2.25	£0.30	£0.90	£1.50
5 2nd printing, (Oct 1993)	$0.45	$1.35	$2.25	£0.30	£0.90	£1.50
6	$0.45	$1.35	$2.25	£0.30	£0.90	£1.50
6 2nd printing, (Nov 1993)	$0.45	$1.35	$2.25	£0.30	£0.90	£1.50
Title Value:	$5.55	$16.65	$27.75	£3.70	£11.10	£18.50

Note: all Non-Distributed on the news-stands in the U.K.

FAZE ONE FAZERS
AC Comics; 1 1986-4 1986

	$Good	$Fine	$N.Mint	£Good	£Fine	£N.Mint
1-4 ND	$0.40	$1.20	$2.00	£0.25	£0.75	£1.25
Title Value:	$1.60	$4.80	$8.00	£1.00	£3.00	£5.00

FAZERS
Dagger Enterprises; 1 Aug 1994

	$Good	$Fine	$N.Mint	£Good	£Fine	£N.Mint
0 ND Vic Bridges script and art	$0.40	$1.20	$2.00	£0.25	£0.75	£1.25
Title Value:	$0.40	$1.20	$2.00	£0.25	£0.75	£1.25

FEAR BOOK
Eclipse,OS; 1 Apr 1986

	$Good	$Fine	$N.Mint	£Good	£Fine	£N.Mint
1 ND Bissette/Veitch art	$0.40	$1.20	$2.00	£0.25	£0.75	£1.25
Title Value:	$0.40	$1.20	$2.00	£0.25	£0.75	£1.25

FEAR, ADVENTURE INTO
Marvel Comics Group; 1 Nov 1970-31 Dec 1975

	$Good	$Fine	$N.Mint	£Good	£Fine	£N.Mint
1 scarce in the U.K. 64pgs, titled "Fear"	$2.00	$6.00	$10.00	£1.50	£4.50	£7.50
2-4 scarce in the U.K. 64pgs	$1.20	$3.60	$6.00	£0.80	£2.40	£4.00
5-9 ND 48pgs	$0.70	$2.10	$3.50	£0.50	£1.50	£2.50
10 ND 1st of Man-Thing series, title becomes "Adventure into Fear", Howard Chaykin and Gray Morrow art	$1.60	$4.80	$8.00	£1.00	£3.00	£5.00
11 ND Neal Adams cover	$0.80	$2.40	$4.00	£0.60	£1.80	£3.00
12 ND Jim Starlin art	$0.80	$2.40	$4.00	£0.70	£2.10	£3.50
13 ND	$0.80	$2.40	$4.00	£0.60	£1.80	£3.00
14 ND Val Mayerik art	$0.80	$2.40	$4.00	£0.60	£1.80	£3.00
15-16 ND Val Mayerik art, Brunner cover	$0.80	$2.40	$4.00	£0.60	£1.80	£3.00
17 ND Man-Thing vs. Wundarr, Val Mayerik art, Brunner cover	$0.80	$2.40	$4.00	£0.60	£1.80	£3.00
18 ND Val Mayerik art, Brunner cover	$0.80	$2.40	$4.00	£0.60	£1.80	£3.00
19 ND 1st appearance of Howard the Duck (few panels only), Val Mayerik art, Brunner cover	$2.00	$6.00	$10.00	£1.20	£3.60	£6.00
20 ND Gulacy art, Morbius the Living Vampire series begins, very "Steranko-esque" art; X-Men and Spiderman appear in "flash-back"	$4.00	$12.00	$20.00	£2.40	£7.00	£12.00
21 ND	$2.00	$6.00	$10.00	£1.00	£3.00	£5.00
22 ND	$1.80	$5.25	$9.00	£0.80	£2.40	£4.00
23 P. Craig Russell art	$1.60	$4.80	$8.00	£0.70	£2.10	£3.50
24 Morbius vs. Blade, P. Craig Russell art	$1.60	$4.80	$8.00	£0.70	£2.10	£3.50
25	$1.40	$4.20	$7.00	£0.60	£1.80	£3.00
26-31	$1.40	$4.20	$7.00	£0.50	£1.50	£2.50
Title Value:	$39.90	$119.55	$199.50	£22.70	£67.90	£113.50

Note: Steve Gerber stories 21-24

FEATURES

Early 1960s horror/fantasy reprints in 1-9. Other reprints in 11-14,20-26. Man-Thing in 10-19. Morbius in 20-31.

FEM FANTASTIQUE
AC Comics; 1 Aug 1988

	$Good	$Fine	$N.Mint	£Good	£Fine	£N.Mint
1 ND	$0.40	$1.20	$2.00	£0.25	£0.75	£1.25
Title Value:	$0.40	$1.20	$2.00	£0.25	£0.75	£1.25

FEM FORCE
AC Comics; 1 Apr 1985-present

	$Good	$Fine	$N.Mint	£Good	£Fine	£N.Mint
1 ND DS rare in the U.K.	$1.00	$3.00	$5.00	£0.70	£2.10	£3.50
2 ND	$0.60	$1.80	$3.00	£0.40	£1.20	£2.00
3-5 ND	$0.55	$1.65	$2.75	£0.35	£1.05	£1.75
6-24 ND	$0.45	$1.35	$2.25	£0.30	£0.90	£1.50
25 ND 1st appearance new Ms. Victory	$0.45	$1.35	$2.25	£0.30	£0.90	£1.50
26-27 ND The Devil Below story	$0.45	$1.35	$2.25	£0.30	£0.90	£1.50
28-36 ND	$0.45	$1.35	$2.25	£0.30	£0.90	£1.50
37 ND The Bulleteer and Golden Age She-Cat appear	$0.45	$1.35	$2.25	£0.30	£0.90	£1.50
38 ND Blue Bulleteer vs. Lady Luger	$0.45	$1.35	$2.25	£0.30	£0.90	£1.50
39-43 ND	$0.45	$1.35	$2.25	£0.30	£0.90	£1.50
44 ND Catman and Kitten preview	$0.45	$1.35	$2.25	£0.30	£0.90	£1.50
45 ND	$0.45	$1.35	$2.25	£0.30	£0.90	£1.50

	$Good	$Fine	$N.Mint	£Good	£Fine	£N.Mint
46-49 ND	$0.55	$1.65	$2.75	£0.35	£1.05	£1.75
50 ND with flexi-disc and wraparound cover	$0.60	$1.80	$3.00	£0.40	£1.20	£2.00
51 ND photo cover	$0.55	$1.65	$2.75	£0.35	£1.05	£1.75
52 ND story continues in Good Girl Art Quarterly #9	$0.55	$1.65	$2.75	£0.35	£1.05	£1.75
53-56 ND	$0.55	$1.65	$2.75	£0.35	£1.05	£1.75
57 ND 1st full colour issue, with trading card	$0.60	$1.80	$3.00	£0.40	£1.20	£2.00
58-63 ND	$0.55	$1.65	$2.75	£0.35	£1.05	£1.75
63 ND pre-bagged with Rayda trading card	$0.70	$2.10	$3.50	£0.45	£1.35	£2.25
64-67 ND	$0.55	$1.65	$2.75	£0.35	£1.05	£1.75
67 ND pre-bagged with Brad Gorby print	$0.70	$2.10	$3.50	£0.45	£1.35	£2.25
68 ND	$0.55	$1.65	$2.75	£0.35	£1.05	£1.75
68 ND pre-bagged with print of Jillian Fontaine	$0.90	$2.70	$4.50	£0.60	£1.80	£3.00
69 ND $2.95 cover begins	$0.60	$1.80	$3.00	£0.40	£1.20	£2.00
69 ND pre-bagged with Pog	$0.80	$2.40	$4.00	£0.50	£1.50	£2.50
70-72 ND	$0.60	$1.80	$3.00	£0.40	£1.20	£2.00
72 ND pre-bagged with Sentinels of Justice mini-comic	$0.80	$2.40	$4.00	£0.50	£1.50	£2.50
73 ND	$0.60	$1.80	$3.00	£0.40	£1.20	£2.00
73 ND pre-bagged with Sentinels of Justice mini-comic	$0.60	$1.80	$3.00	£0.40	£1.20	£2.00
74 ND	$0.60	$1.80	$3.00	£0.40	£1.20	£2.00
74 ND pre-bagged with signed art print of Fear Force by Mark Heike	$1.00	$3.00	$5.00	£0.65	£1.95	£3.25
75 ND	$0.60	$1.80	$3.00	£0.40	£1.20	£2.00
75 ND prebagged with signed mini-poster art print of the wraparound cover by Brad Gorby	$1.00	$3.00	$5.00	£0.65	£1.95	£3.25
76 ND	$0.60	$1.80	$3.00	£0.40	£1.20	£2.00
76 ND pre-bagged with Captain Wings #1 mini-comic	$0.60	$1.80	$3.00	£0.40	£1.20	£2.00
77-78 ND	$0.60	$1.80	$3.00	£0.40	£1.20	£2.00
78 ND pre-bagged with Sentinels of Justice mini-comic	$1.00	$3.00	$5.00	£0.65	£1.95	£3.25
79 ND	$0.60	$1.80	$3.00	£0.40	£1.20	£2.00
79 ND pre-bagged with Volume 1 of the Fem Force Index	$1.20	$3.60	$6.00	£0.80	£2.40	£4.00
80 ND	$0.60	$1.80	$3.00	£0.40	£1.20	£2.00
80 ND pre-bagged with Volume 2 of the Fem Force Index	$1.20	$3.60	$6.00	£0.80	£2.40	£4.00
81 ND	$0.60	$1.80	$3.00	£0.40	£1.20	£2.00
81 ND pre-bagged with art supplement for Vols. 1 & 2 of the Fem Force Index	$1.20	$3.60	$6.00	£0.80	£2.40	£4.00
82 ND	$0.60	$1.80	$3.00	£0.40	£1.20	£2.00
82 ND pre-bagged with Volume 3 of the Fem Force Index	$1.20	$3.60	$6.00	£0.80	£2.40	£4.00
83 ND	$0.60	$1.80	$3.00	£0.40	£1.20	£2.00
83 ND pre-bagged with Ms. Victory print by Jackson Guice	$0.80	$2.40	$4.00	£0.50	£1.50	£2.50
84 ND	$0.60	$1.80	$3.00	£0.40	£1.20	£2.00
84 ND pre-bagged with Volume 4 of the Fem Force Index	$0.80	$2.40	$4.00	£0.50	£1.50	£2.50
85 ND	$0.60	$1.80	$3.00	£0.40	£1.20	£2.00
85 ND pre-bagged with trading card	$1.00	$3.00	$5.00	£0.65	£1.95	£3.25
86 ND	$0.60	$1.80	$3.00	£0.40	£1.20	£2.00
86 ND pre-bagged with part 5 of the AC Index	$1.20	$3.60	$6.00	£0.80	£2.40	£4.00
87 ND 10th anniversary edition	$0.80	$2.40	$4.00	£0.50	£1.50	£2.50
87 ND pre-bagged with special illustrated plate	$2.00	$6.00	$10.00	£1.30	£3.90	£6.50
88 ND pre-bagged with special illustrated plate	$2.00	$6.00	$10.00	£1.30	£3.90	£6.50
Title Value:	$66.30	$198.90	$331.50	£43.50	£130.50	£217.50

Femforce: The Capricorn Chronicles (Feb 1994)

	£Good	£Fine	£N.Mint
Trade paperback reprints issues #55-57, signed by ceators and limited to 1,000 copies	£3.20	£9.60	£16.00
Sisters in Sin Graphic Novel (Apr 1995) Brad Gorby art	£1.70	£5.10	£8.50
Signed Edition (Apr 1995)	£2.00	£6.00	£10.00

FEM FORCE FRIGHTBOOK
AC Comics,OS; 1 Dec 1992

	$Good	$Fine	$N.Mint	£Good	£Fine	£N.Mint
1 ND Halloween stories	$0.45	$1.35	$2.25	£0.30	£0.90	£1.50
Title Value:	$0.45	$1.35	$2.25	£0.30	£0.90	£1.50

FEM FORCE IN THE HOUSE OF HORROR
AC Comics; 1 1989

	$Good	$Fine	$N.Mint	£Good	£Fine	£N.Mint
1 ND 36pgs	$0.45	$1.35	$2.25	£0.30	£0.90	£1.50
Title Value:	$0.45	$1.35	$2.25	£0.30	£0.90	£1.50

FEM FORCE PIN-UP PORTFOLIO
AC Comics; 1 1987-present

	$Good	$Fine	$N.Mint	£Good	£Fine	£N.Mint
1 ND various artists inc. Art Adams	$0.45	$1.35	$2.25	£0.30	£0.90	£1.50
2-4 ND	$0.45	$1.35	$2.25	£0.30	£0.90	£1.50

5 ND Jerry Ordway cover with Brian Stelfreeze and Jackson Guice art featured

	$Good	$Fine	$N.Mint	£Good	£Fine	£N.Mint
	$0.45	$1.35	$2.25	£0.30	£0.90	£1.50
Title Value:	$2.25	$6.75	$11.25	£1.50	£4.50	£7.50

FEM FORCE SPECIAL
AC Comics; 1 1987

	$Good	$Fine	$N.Mint	£Good	£Fine	£N.Mint
1 ND 52pgs, 1st Miss Victory	$0.40	$1.20	$2.00	£0.25	£0.75	£1.25
Title Value:	$0.40	$1.20	$2.00	£0.25	£0.75	£1.25

FEM FORCE UP CLOSE
AC Comics; 1 Jun 1992-present

	$Good	$Fine	$N.Mint	£Good	£Fine	£N.Mint
1 ND black and white begins	$0.60	$1.80	$3.00	£0.40	£1.20	£2.00
2 ND	$0.60	$1.80	$3.00	£0.40	£1.20	£2.00
3 ND Dragonfly	$0.60	$1.80	$3.00	£0.40	£1.20	£2.00
4 ND Ms. Victory; pre-bagged with bumper sticker	$0.80	$2.40	$4.00	£0.50	£1.50	£2.50
4 ND Collector's Edition, She-Cat; pre-bagged with She-Cat trading card	$0.80	$2.40	$4.00	£0.50	£1.50	£2.50
5 ND Blue Bulleteer	$0.60	$1.80	$3.00	£0.40	£1.20	£2.00
5 ND Collector's Edition - pre-bagged with sticker	$0.80	$2.40	$4.00	£0.50	£1.50	£2.50
6-11 ND	$0.60	$1.80	$3.00	£0.40	£1.20	£2.00
Title Value:	$8.40	$25.20	$42.00	£5.50	£16.50	£27.50

FEM FORCE, THE UNTOLD ORIGIN OF
AC Comics,OS; 1 1992

	$Good	$Fine	$N.Mint	£Good	£Fine	£N.Mint
1 ND 64pgs, also reprints cover of Fem Force #1	$0.90	$2.70	$4.50	£0.60	£1.80	£3.00
Title Value:	$0.90	$2.70	$4.50	£0.60	£1.80	£3.00

FEM FORCE: NIGHT OF THE DEMON SPECIAL
AC Comics; 1 Dec 1990

	$Good	$Fine	$N.Mint	£Good	£Fine	£N.Mint
1 ND 36pgs	$0.45	$1.35	$2.25	£0.30	£0.90	£1.50
Title Value:	$0.45	$1.35	$2.25	£0.30	£0.90	£1.50

FEM FORCE: OUT OF THE ASYLUM SPECIAL
AC Comics; 1 1987

	$Good	$Fine	$N.Mint	£Good	£Fine	£N.Mint
1 ND 52pgs	$0.45	$1.35	$2.25	£0.30	£0.90	£1.50
Title Value:	$0.45	$1.35	$2.25	£0.30	£0.90	£1.50

FEMFORCE BAD GIRL BACKLASH
AC Comics,OS; 1 Nov 1995

	$Good	$Fine	$N.Mint	£Good	£Fine	£N.Mint
1 ND pin-ups with framing sequence by all-girl creative team	$1.00	$3.00	$5.00	£0.65	£1.95	£3.25
1 Signed Edition (Nov 1995) - signed by creators, pre-bagged	$1.40	$4.20	$7.00	£0.90	£2.70	£4.50
Title Value:	$2.40	$7.20	$12.00	£1.55	£4.65	£7.75

FEMFORCE TIMELINES
AC Comics,OS; nn Sep 1995

	$Good	$Fine	$N.Mint	£Good	£Fine	£N.Mint
nn ND 10th anniversary illustration of the birth and development of Fem Force; Compact Format	$0.60	$1.80	$3.00	£0.40	£1.20	£2.00
Title Value:	$0.60	$1.80	$3.00	£0.40	£1.20	£2.00

FERRET
Malibu,OS; 1 Sep 1992

	$Good	$Fine	$N.Mint	£Good	£Fine	£N.Mint
1 ND Thomas Derenick art	$0.40	$1.20	$2.00	£0.25	£0.75	£1.25
Title Value:	$0.40	$1.20	$2.00	£0.25	£0.75	£1.25

FERRET (2ND SERIES)
Malibu; 1 May 1993-10 Feb 1994

	$Good	$Fine	$N.Mint	£Good	£Fine	£N.Mint
1 entire die-cut comic following the outline of Ferret's head	$0.40	$1.20	$2.00	£0.25	£0.75	£1.25
2	$0.30	$0.90	$1.50	£0.20	£0.60	£1.00
2 Direct Sales Edition with pull-out poster	$0.35	$1.05	$1.75	£0.25	£0.75	£1.25
3	$0.30	$0.90	$1.50	£0.20	£0.60	£1.00
3 Direct Sales Edition with pull-out poster	$0.35	$1.05	$1.75	£0.25	£0.75	£1.25
4	$0.30	$0.90	$1.50	£0.20	£0.60	£1.00
5 Genesis Tie-In; pre-bagged with free Sky-Cap	$0.30	$0.90	$1.50	£0.20	£0.60	£1.00
6-10 Genesis Tie-In	$0.30	$0.90	$1.50	£0.20	£0.60	£1.00
Title Value:	$3.80	$11.40	$19.00	£2.55	£7.65	£12.75

Note: all Non-Distributed on the news-stands in the U.K.

FEUD
Marvel Comics Group/Epic,MS; 1 Jul 1993-4 Oct 1993

	$Good	$Fine	$N.Mint	£Good	£Fine	£N.Mint
1 ND Mike Baron script begins, embossed cover with metallic ink	$0.40	$1.20	$2.00	£0.25	£0.75	£1.25
2-4 ND	$0.40	$1.20	$2.00	£0.25	£0.75	£1.25
Title Value:	$1.60	$4.80	$8.00	£1.00	£3.00	£5.00

FIFTIES TERROR
Eternity; 1 Oct 1988-6 Apr 1989

	$Good	$Fine	$N.Mint	£Good	£Fine	£N.Mint
1-6 ND pre-Code horror reprints	$0.40	$1.20	$2.00	£0.25	£0.75	£1.25
Title Value:	$2.40	$7.20	$12.00	£1.50	£4.50	£7.50

FIFTY WHO MADE DC GREAT
DC Comics; nn 1985

	$Good	$Fine	$N.Mint	£Good	£Fine	£N.Mint
nn ND 56pgs, high quality paper; text and illustrations of 50 people and products that contributed to DC's 50 year history; released as part of the company's 50th anniversary	$0.90	$2.70	$4.50	£0.60	£1.80	£3.00
Title Value:	$0.90	$2.70	$4.50	£0.60	£1.80	£3.00

FIGHT-MAN ONE SHOT
Marvel Comics Group,OS; 1 Jun 1993

	$Good	$Fine	$N.Mint	£Good	£Fine	£N.Mint
1 ND Evan Dorkin script and art	$0.40	$1.20	$2.00	£0.25	£0.75	£1.25
Title Value:	$0.40	$1.20	$2.00	£0.25	£0.75	£1.25

FIGHTIN' AIR FORCE
Charlton; 3 Feb 1956-53 Feb/Mar 1966

	$Good	$Fine	$N.Mint	£Good	£Fine	£N.Mint
3 scarce in the U.K.	$4.55	$13.50	$27.50	£2.90	£8.75	£17.50
4-5 scarce in the U.K.	$2.50	$7.50	$15.00	£1.65	£5.00	£10.00
6-10	$2.50	$7.50	$15.00	£1.25	£3.75	£7.50
11 64pgs	$3.30	$10.00	$20.00	£1.65	£5.00	£10.00
12 scarce in the U.K. 100pgs, squarebound; 25 cents cover. There are copies known with pence stamps (as indeed for issues #13-21)	$4.15	$12.50	$25.00	£2.00	£6.00	£12.00
13-21	$2.05	$6.25	$12.50	£1.00	£3.00	£6.00
1st official distribution in the U.K.						
22-30	$2.05	$6.25	$12.50	£0.90	£2.75	£5.50
31-49	$1.50	$4.50	$9.00	£0.80	£2.50	£5.00
50 1st appearance American Eagle	$1.50	$4.50	$9.00	£0.80	£2.50	£5.00
51-53	$1.25	$3.75	$7.50	£0.80	£2.50	£5.00
Title Value:	$100.15	$302.25	$605.00	£51.60	£157.75	£315.50

Note: It is unclear what issues #1&2 were formerly known as.

FIGHTIN' ARMY
Charlton; 16 Jan 1956-127 Dec 1976; 128 Sep 1977-172 Nov 1984

	$Good	$Fine	$N.Mint	£Good	£Fine	£N.Mint
16 scarce in the U.K.	$4.55	$13.50	$27.50	£2.90	£8.75	£17.50
17-19	$2.50	$7.50	$15.00	£1.65	£5.00	£10.00
20 Steve Ditko art	$4.15	$12.50	$25.00	£2.50	£7.50	£15.00
21-23	$2.50	$7.50	$15.00	£1.30	£4.00	£8.00
24 giant	$2.90	$8.75	$17.50	£1.65	£5.00	£10.00
25-30	$2.50	$7.50	$15.00	£1.30	£4.00	£8.00
31-34	$2.05	$6.25	$12.50	£1.00	£3.00	£6.00
1st official distribution in the U.K.						
35-50	$2.05	$6.25	$12.50	£1.00	£3.00	£6.00
51-60	$1.65	$5.00	$10.00	£0.80	£2.50	£5.00
61-70	$1.25	$3.75	$7.50	£0.65	£2.00	£4.00
71-80	$1.20	$3.60	$6.00	£0.70	£2.10	£3.50
81-100	$0.90	$2.70	$4.50	£0.60	£1.80	£3.00
101-120	$0.60	$1.80	$3.00	£0.50	£1.50	£2.50
121-140	$0.50	$1.50	$2.50	£0.40	£1.20	£2.00
141-160	$0.50	$1.50	$2.50	£0.30	£0.90	£1.50
161-172	$0.50	$1.50	$2.50	£0.20	£0.60	£1.00
Title Value:	$179.60	$541.25	$1015.00	£103.60	£313.45	£581.50

Note: issues #1-15 were called Soldier and Marine

FIGHTIN' FIVE, THE
Charlton; 28 Jul 1964-41 Jan 1967; 42 Oct 1981-49 Dec 1982
(formerly Space War #1-27)

	$Good	$Fine	$N.Mint	£Good	£Fine	£N.Mint
28 scarce in the U.K.	$4.15	$12.50	$25.00	£2.50	£7.50	£15.00
29-30	$2.50	$7.50	$15.00	£1.65	£5.00	£10.00
31-39	$2.05	$6.25	$12.50	£1.30	£4.00	£8.00
40 Peacemaker appears	$4.15	$12.50	$25.00	£2.05	£6.25	£12.50
41	$2.05	$6.25	$12.50	£1.30	£4.00	£8.00
42 reprints begin	$0.40	$1.20	$2.00	£0.25	£0.75	£1.25
43-49	$0.40	$1.20	$2.00	£0.25	£0.75	£1.25
Title Value:	$37.00	$112.10	$221.00	£22.85	£69.75	£137.50

Note: all distributed on the news-stands in the U.K.

FIGHTIN' MARINES
Charlton; 14 May 1955-132 Nov 1976; 133 Oct 1977-176 Sep 1984

	$Good	$Fine	$N.Mint	£Good	£Fine	£N.Mint
14 scarce in the U.K.	$11.50	$35.00	$70.00	£8.25	£25.00	£50.00
15	$4.15	$12.50	$25.00	£2.50	£7.50	£15.00
16	$2.50	$7.50	$15.00	£1.65	£5.00	£10.00
17 Canteen Kate by Matt Baker	$8.25	$25.00	$50.00	£5.00	£15.00	£30.00
18-20	$2.50	$7.50	$15.00	£1.65	£5.00	£10.00
21-24	$2.30	$7.00	$14.00	£1.30	£4.00	£8.00
25 giant	$4.15	$12.50	$25.00	£2.50	£7.50	£15.00
26 scarce in the U.K. giant	$5.75	$17.50	$35.00	£3.30	£10.00	£20.00
27-30	$2.00	$6.00	$12.00	£1.25	£3.75	£7.50
31-44	$1.65	$5.00	$10.00	£1.05	£3.25	£6.50
1st official distribution in the U.K.						
45-50	$1.65	$5.00	$10.00	£1.05	£3.25	£6.50
51-80	$1.00	$3.00	$6.00	£0.55	£1.75	£3.50
81	$1.00	$3.00	$5.00	£0.60	£1.80	£3.00
82 giant	$1.60	$4.80	$8.00	£1.00	£3.00	£5.00
83-100	$1.00	$3.00	$5.00	£0.60	£1.80	£3.00
101-125	$0.60	$1.80	$3.00	£0.40	£1.20	£2.00
126-140	$0.30	$0.90	$1.50	£0.20	£0.60	£1.00
141-176	$0.25	$0.75	$1.25	£0.15	£0.45	£0.75
Title Value:	$173.10	$521.80	$994.50	£106.65	£325.90	£621.00

Note: previous issues published by St John (Approved Comics)

FIGHTIN' NAVY
Charlton; 74 Jan 1956-125 Apr/May 1966; 126 Aug 1983-133 Oct 1984

	$Good	$Fine	$N.Mint	£Good	£Fine	£N.Mint
74 scarce in the U.K.	$4.55	$13.50	$27.50	£2.90	£8.75	£17.50
75-80	$2.50	$7.50	$15.00	£1.65	£5.00	£10.00
81	$1.65	$5.00	$10.00	£1.25	£3.75	£7.50
82 Sam Glanzman art	$1.65	$5.00	$10.00	£1.25	£3.75	£7.50

83 100pgs, squarebound; some copies known with pence stamps (as well as issues #84-87)

MINT = 100% / NEAR MINT (inc. +/-) = 90–99% / VERY FINE (inc. +/-) = 75–89% / FINE (inc. +/-) = 55–74%
VERY GOOD (inc. +/-) = 35–54% / GOOD (inc. +/-) = 15–34% / FAIR = 5–14% / POOR = 1–4%

337

	$Good	$Fine	$N.Mint	£Good	£Fine	£N.Mint
	$2.00	$6.00	$12.00	£1.40	£4.25	£8.50
84-87	$1.15	$3.50	$7.00	£0.75	£2.25	£4.50
1st official distribution in the U.K.						
88-100	$1.05	$3.25	$6.50	£0.65	£2.00	£4.00
101-110	$0.75	$2.25	$4.50	£0.50	£1.50	£3.00
111-125	$0.80	$2.40	$4.00	£0.50	£1.50	£2.50
126-133	$0.45	$1.35	$2.25	£0.30	£0.90	£1.50
Title Value:	$66.20	$200.05	$385.00	£43.05	£130.20	£250.50

Note: issues #1-73 Don Winslow of the Navy

FIGHTING AMERICAN

Harvey; 1 Oct 1966

1 giant; Joe Simon and Jack Kirby reprints, 1pg Neal Adams art; distributed in the U.K.

	$Good	$Fine	$N.Mint	£Good	£Fine	£N.Mint
	$3.30	$10.00	$20.00	£2.05	£6.25	£12.50
Title Value:	$3.30	$10.00	$20.00	£2.05	£6.25	£12.50

FIGHTING AMERICAN

Marvel Comics Group; nn Mar 1990

nn Hardcover collection of all 7 issues of original Simon/Kirby Cold War comic of satire and super-heroics. Re-coloured. £2.00 £6.00 £10.00

FIGHTING AMERICAN

DC Comics,MS; 1 Feb 1994-6 Jul 1994

1 based on the 1950s creation by Joe Simon and Jack Kirby

	$Good	$Fine	$N.Mint	£Good	£Fine	£N.Mint
	$0.25	$0.75	$1.25	£0.15	£0.45	£0.75
2-6	$0.25	$0.75	$1.25	£0.15	£0.45	£0.75
Title Value:	$1.50	$4.50	$7.50	£0.90	£2.70	£4.50

FINAL CYCLE

Dragon's Teeth,MS; 1 Jul 1987-4 Oct 1987

1-3 ND Cirocco/Amaro art

	$Good	$Fine	$N.Mint	£Good	£Fine	£N.Mint
	$0.40	$1.20	$2.00	£0.25	£0.75	£1.25
4 ND Amaro art	$0.40	$1.20	$2.00	£0.25	£0.75	£1.25
Title Value:	$1.60	$4.80	$8.00	£1.00	£3.00	£5.00

FINAL FANTASY

Disney/Hollywood Comics,MS; 1 Jan 1992-2 1992

1-2 ND Mike Mignola cover, based on game

	$Good	$Fine	$N.Mint	£Good	£Fine	£N.Mint
	$0.30	$0.90	$1.50	£0.20	£0.60	£1.00
Title Value:	$0.60	$1.80	$3.00	£0.40	£1.20	£2.00

FIRE TRIPPER

Viz Comics; 1 1989

1 ND 64pgs, squarebound, black and white; script/art by Rumiko Takahashi

	$Good	$Fine	$N.Mint	£Good	£Fine	£N.Mint
	$0.60	$1.80	$3.00	£0.40	£1.20	£2.00
Title Value:	$0.60	$1.80	$3.00	£0.40	£1.20	£2.00

FIREARM

Malibu Ultraverse; 1 Sep 1993-18 Feb 1995

(see Codename: Firearm)

1 ND Cully Hamner art begins

	$Good	$Fine	$N.Mint	£Good	£Fine	£N.Mint
	$0.50	$1.50	$2.50	£0.30	£0.90	£1.50
2 ND 40pgs, Rune insert						
	$0.50	$1.50	$2.50	£0.30	£0.90	£1.50
3-4 ND	$0.35	$1.05	$1.75	£0.20	£0.60	£1.00
5 ND origins month tie-in						
	$0.35	$1.05	$1.75	£0.20	£0.60	£1.00
6-10 ND	$0.35	$1.05	$1.75	£0.20	£0.60	£1.00
11 ND flip-book format with Ultraverse Premiere #5						
	$0.50	$1.50	$2.50	£0.30	£0.90	£1.50
12-14 ND	$0.35	$1.05	$1.75	£0.20	£0.60	£1.00
15 ND tie-in with Freex #15 and Night Man #14						
	$0.35	$1.05	$1.75	£0.20	£0.60	£1.00
16 ND Howard Chaykin cover						
	$0.35	$1.05	$1.75	£0.20	£0.60	£1.00
17 ND	$0.35	$1.05	$1.75	£0.20	£0.60	£1.00
18 ND Prime, Nightman and Strangers all appear						
	$0.35	$1.05	$1.75	£0.20	£0.60	£1.00
Title Value:	$6.75	$20.25	$33.75	£3.90	£11.70	£19.50

FIREBALL XL5

(see Steve Zodiac)

FIREBRAND

DC Comics; 1 Feb 1996-present

1 ND Brian Augustyn script and Sal Velluto art begin

	$Good	$Fine	$N.Mint	£Good	£Fine	£N.Mint
	$0.35	$1.05	$1.75	£0.25	£0.75	£1.25
2 ND	$0.35	$1.05	$1.75	£0.25	£0.75	£1.25
Title Value:	$0.70	$2.10	$3.50	£0.50	£1.50	£2.50

FIREHAIR

I.W. Comics; 8 early 1960s

8 scarce, distributed in the U.K. all reprints

	$Good	$Fine	$N.Mint	£Good	£Fine	£N.Mint
	$2.50	$7.50	$15.00	£1.65	£5.00	£10.00
Title Value:	$2.50	$7.50	$15.00	£1.65	£5.00	£10.00

FIRESTAR

Marvel Comics Group,MS; 1 Mar 1988-4 Jun 1988

1 ND X-Men and New Mutants appear

	$Good	$Fine	$N.Mint	£Good	£Fine	£N.Mint
	$0.40	$1.20	$2.00	£0.25	£0.75	£1.25
2 ND	$0.40	$1.20	$2.00	£0.25	£0.75	£1.25
3 ND Wolverine appears						
	$0.40	$1.20	$2.00	£0.25	£0.75	£1.25
4 ND	$0.40	$1.20	$2.00	£0.25	£0.75	£1.25
Title Value:	$1.60	$4.80	$8.00	£1.00	£3.00	£5.00

FIRESTORM

DC Comics; 1 Mar 1978-5 Oct/Nov 1978

(see also Brave & the Bold, Captain Atom, DC Presents, Flash)

1 origin, 1st appearance Firestorm

	$Good	$Fine	$N.Mint	£Good	£Fine	£N.Mint
	$0.60	$1.80	$3.00	£0.40	£1.20	£2.00
2 origin Multiplex	$0.45	$1.35	$2.25	£0.30	£0.90	£1.50
3 origin Killer Frost						
	$0.45	$1.35	$2.25	£0.30	£0.90	£1.50
4 1st appearance Hyena (Summer Day)						
	$0.45	$1.35	$2.25	£0.30	£0.90	£1.50
5 ND 44pgs	$0.45	$1.35	$2.25	£0.35	£1.05	£1.75
Title Value:	$2.40	$7.20	$12.00	£1.65	£4.95	£8.25

FIRESTORM THE NUCLEAR MAN ANNUAL, THE FURY OF

DC Comics; 1 Nov 1983-5 Oct 1987

(becomes simply Firestorm The Nuclear Man Annual issue #4 onwards)

	$Good	$Fine	$N.Mint	£Good	£Fine	£N.Mint
1-5 48pgs	$0.30	$0.90	$1.50	£0.20	£0.60	£1.00
Title Value:	$1.50	$4.50	$7.50	£1.00	£3.00	£5.00

FIRESTORM THE NUCLEAR MAN, THE FURY OF

DC Comics; 1 Jun 1982-100 Aug 1990

(becomes Firestorm the Nuclear Man with issue 50)

1 intro Black Bison, origin briefly retold

	$Good	$Fine	$N.Mint	£Good	£Fine	£N.Mint
	$0.40	$1.20	$2.00	£0.20	£0.60	£1.25
2-5	$0.30	$0.90	$1.50	£0.20	£0.60	£1.00
6-16	$0.25	$0.75	$1.25	£0.15	£0.45	£0.75
17 1st appearance Firehawk						
	$0.30	$0.90	$1.50	£0.15	£0.45	£0.75
18-21	$0.25	$0.75	$1.25	£0.15	£0.45	£0.75
22 origin told	$0.25	$0.75	$1.25	£0.15	£0.45	£0.75
23	$0.25	$0.75	$1.25	£0.15	£0.45	£0.75
24 1st appearance Blue Devil						
	$0.30	$0.90	$1.50	£0.20	£0.60	£1.00
25-40	$0.25	$0.75	$1.25	£0.15	£0.45	£0.75
41-42 Crisis X-over						
	$0.30	$0.90	$1.50	£0.15	£0.45	£0.75
43-47	$0.25	$0.75	$1.25	£0.15	£0.45	£0.75
48 intro Moonbow						
	$0.25	$0.75	$1.25	£0.15	£0.45	£0.75
49	$0.25	$0.75	$1.25	£0.15	£0.45	£0.75
50 48pgs	$0.30	$0.90	$1.50	£0.20	£0.60	£1.00
51-52	$0.25	$0.75	$1.25	£0.15	£0.45	£0.75
53 origin, 1st appearance Silver Shade						
	$0.25	$0.75	$1.25	£0.15	£0.45	£0.75
54	$0.25	$0.75	$1.25	£0.15	£0.45	£0.75
55-56 Legends X-over						
	$0.25	$0.75	$1.25	£0.15	£0.45	£0.75
57-60	$0.25	$0.75	$1.25	£0.15	£0.45	£0.75
61 regular cover	$0.25	$0.75	$1.25	£0.15	£0.45	£0.75
61 ND test-cover, very rare in the U.K., rare in the US. (see note below)						
	$6.00	$18.00	$30.00	£7.00	£21.00	£35.00
62	$0.25	$0.75	$1.25	£0.15	£0.45	£0.75
63 Captain Atom X-over						
	$0.25	$0.75	$1.25	£0.15	£0.45	£0.75
64 Suicide Squad, Justice League X-over						
	$0.25	$0.75	$1.25	£0.15	£0.45	£0.75
65 Firestorm merges with Mikhail						
	$0.25	$0.75	$1.25	£0.15	£0.45	£0.75
66 Green Lantern X-over						
	$0.25	$0.75	$1.25	£0.15	£0.45	£0.75
67 Millennium X-over; Green Lantern Corps, Justice League of America, Batman and the Outsiders cameo						
	$0.25	$0.75	$1.25	£0.15	£0.45	£0.75
68 Millennium X-over, Justice League of America cameo, Captain Atom, Green Lantern, Driq, Harbinger appear						
	$0.25	$0.75	$1.25	£0.15	£0.45	£0.75
69-79	$0.25	$0.75	$1.25	£0.15	£0.45	£0.75
80-81 Invasion X-over						
	$0.25	$0.75	$1.25	£0.15	£0.45	£0.75
82-84	$0.25	$0.75	$1.25	£0.15	£0.45	£0.75
85 new costume, new identity						
	$0.25	$0.75	$1.25	£0.15	£0.45	£0.75
86 Janus Directive X-over						
	$0.25	$0.75	$1.25	£0.15	£0.45	£0.75
87-89	$0.25	$0.75	$1.25	£0.15	£0.45	£0.75
90 intro Naiad; Swamp Thing, Red Tornado appear - begin 4 part story						
				£0.15	£0.45	£0.75
91 Swamp Thing appears						
	$0.25	$0.75	$1.25	£0.15	£0.45	£0.75
92-93 Elemental war story continues, Red Tornado appears						
	$0.25	$0.75	$1.25	£0.15	£0.45	£0.75
94-99	$0.25	$0.75	$1.25	£0.15	£0.45	£0.75
100 giant issue with creators Gerry Conway and Al Milgrom presenting a new sequence of early adventures						
	$0.35	$1.05	$1.75	£0.20	£0.60	£1.00
Title Value:	$31.70	$95.10	$158.50	£22.45	£67.35	£112.25

Note: in a distribution experiment #61 was issued with alternative test-cover in some US states, very rare. It has a white cover as opposed to pink with a circular Superman logo in the top left hand corner (see Justice League International 3). Note also that the title became simply "Firestorm" in issues 55-58 and from 83 onwards.

FIRETEAM

Aircel,MS; 1 Dec 1990-6 May 1991

1-6 ND Don Lomax script and art

	$Good	$Fine	$N.Mint	£Good	£Fine	£N.Mint
	$0.40	$1.20	$2.00	£0.25	£0.75	£1.25
Title Value:	$2.40	$7.20	$12.00	£1.50	£4.50	£7.50

FIRST ADVENTURES

First; 1 Dec 1985-5 Apr 1986

1-5 ND Blaze Barlow, Whisper, Dynamo Joe

	$Good	$Fine	$N.Mint	£Good	£Fine	£N.Mint
	$0.30	$0.90	$1.50	£0.20	£0.60	£1.00
Title Value:	$1.50	$4.50	$7.50	£1.00	£3.00	£5.00

FIRST FOLIO

Pacific; 1 Mar 1984

1 ND Joe Kubert Art School graduates; Ron Randall, Adam and Andy Kubert

	$Good	$Fine	$N.Mint	£Good	£Fine	£N.Mint
	$0.30	$0.90	$1.50	£0.20	£0.60	£1.00
Title Value:	$0.30	$0.90	$1.50	£0.20	£0.60	£1.00

FIRST ISSUE SPECIAL
DC Comics; 1 Apr 1975-13 Apr 1976

	$Good	$Fine	$N.Mint	£Good	£Fine	£N.Mint
1 Atlas, Jack Kirby cover and art	$0.50	$1.50	$2.50	£0.30	£0.90	£1.50
2 Green Team, Joe Simon and Jerry Grandenetti art	$0.40	$1.20	$2.00	£0.25	£0.75	£1.25
3 Metamorpho	$0.40	$1.20	$2.00	£0.25	£0.75	£1.25
4 Lady Cop, mentions venereal disease	$0.40	$1.20	$2.00	£0.25	£0.75	£1.25
5 Jack Kirby cover and art, Manhunter	$0.40	$1.20	$2.00	£0.25	£0.75	£1.25
6 Jack Kirby cover and art, Dingbats	$0.40	$1.20	$2.00	£0.25	£0.75	£1.25
7 Steve Ditko cover and art, Creeper	$0.40	$1.20	$2.00	£0.25	£0.75	£1.25
8 Warlord by Grell, origin and 1st appearance; story continues in Warlord #1	$1.00	$3.00	$5.00	£1.00	£3.00	£5.00
9 Walt Simonson art, Kubert cover, Dr. Fate	$0.40	$1.20	$2.00	£0.25	£0.75	£1.25
10 scarce in the U.K. Outsiders	$0.30	$0.90	$1.50	£0.20	£0.60	£1.00
11 scarce in the U.K. Codename: Assassin	$0.30	$0.90	$1.50	£0.20	£0.60	£1.00
12 scarce in the U.K. Starman (a 70s version; see Adventure Comics #467)	$0.30	$0.90	$1.50	£0.20	£0.60	£1.00
13 scarce in the U.K. New Gods	$0.40	$1.20	$2.00	£0.25	£0.75	£1.25
Title Value:	$5.60	$16.80	$28.00	£3.90	£11.70	£19.50

FIRST KISS
Charlton; 1 Dec 1957-40 Jan 1965

	$Good	$Fine	$N.Mint	£Good	£Fine	£N.Mint
1 scarce in the U.K.	$3.30	$10.00	$20.00	£2.30	£7.00	£14.00
2-5	$2.00	$6.00	$12.00	£1.15	£3.50	£7.00
6-10	$1.65	$5.00	$10.00	£1.00	£3.00	£6.00
1st official distribution in the U.K.						
11-40	$0.75	$2.25	$4.50	£0.50	£1.50	£3.00
Title Value:	$42.05	$126.50	$253.00	£26.90	£81.00	£162.00

Note: issues distributed in the U.K. around 1958 onwards. It is possible that the title was distributed from issue #1 as an experiment.

FIRST SIX PACK
First; 1 Jul 1987-2 Nov 1987

	$Good	$Fine	$N.Mint	£Good	£Fine	£N.Mint
1 ND 50 cents; American Flagg, Badger, Dynamo Joe, Grim Jack, Jon Sable, Nexus previews in black and white; card stock covers, painted cover by Dave Dorman	$0.25	$0.75	$1.25	£0.15	£0.45	£0.75
2 ND 50 cents; American Flagg, Dreadstar, Jon Sable, Psychoblast, Shatter, Whisper previews in black and white; heavy stock paper cover	$0.25	$0.75	$1.25	£0.15	£0.45	£0.75
Title Value:	$0.50	$1.50	$2.50	£0.30	£0.90	£1.50

FISH POLICE (1ST SERIES)
Fishwrap; 1 Dec 1985-11 Nov 1987

	$Good	$Fine	$N.Mint	£Good	£Fine	£N.Mint
1 ND Steve Moncuse story/art begins, black and white	$0.40	$1.20	$2.00	£0.30	£0.90	£1.50
1 ND 2nd printing, (May 1986)	$0.35	$1.05	$1.75	£0.25	£0.75	£1.25
1 ND 3rd printing	$0.30	$0.90	$1.50	£0.20	£0.60	£1.00
2 ND	$0.35	$1.05	$1.75	£0.25	£0.75	£1.25
2 ND 2nd printing	$0.30	$0.90	$1.50	£0.20	£0.60	£1.00
3-11 ND	$0.35	$1.05	$1.75	£0.25	£0.75	£1.25
Title Value:	$4.85	$14.55	$24.25	£3.45	£10.35	£17.25

Hairballs Graphic Novel (Comico)
reprints #1-4 in colour, some new art, Harlan Ellison intro — £1.00 £3.00 £5.00

	$Good	$Fine	$N.Mint	£Good	£Fine	£N.Mint
Fish Police Bargain Prepack (Jun 1991), issues #18-20 pre-bagged				£0.60	£1.80	£3.00

FISH POLICE (2ND SERIES)
Comico; 0 Apr 1991; 5 Apr 1988-17 May 1989; Apple; 18 Aug 1989-26 Oct/Nov 1990

	$Good	$Fine	$N.Mint	£Good	£Fine	£N.Mint
0 ND previously unseen pilot issue from 1985, Art Adams cover (Apr 1991)	$0.35	$1.05	$1.75	£0.25	£0.75	£1.25
5 ND reprints from Fishwrap series begin; issues #1-5 in colour for the first time	$0.35	$1.05	$1.75	£0.25	£0.75	£1.25
6-10 ND	$0.35	$1.05	$1.75	£0.25	£0.75	£1.25
11 ND	$0.30	$0.90	$1.50	£0.20	£0.60	£1.00
12 ND new material begins, colour	$0.30	$0.90	$1.50	£0.20	£0.60	£1.00
13-17 ND	$0.30	$0.90	$1.50	£0.20	£0.60	£1.00
18 ND 1st Apple issue; reverts to black and white	$0.30	$0.90	$1.50	£0.20	£0.60	£1.00
19-22 ND	$0.30	$0.90	$1.50	£0.20	£0.60	£1.00
23 ND proposed issue #1 lay-outs shown for 1st time	$0.30	$0.90	$1.50	£0.20	£0.60	£1.00
24 ND	$0.30	$0.90	$1.50	£0.20	£0.60	£1.00
25-26 ND bi-weekly	$0.30	$0.90	$1.50	£0.20	£0.60	£1.00
Title Value:	$7.25	$21.75	$36.25	£4.95	£14.85	£24.75

FISH POLICE (3RD SERIES)
Marvel Comics Group,MS; 1 Oct 1992-6 Mar 1993

	$Good	$Fine	$N.Mint	£Good	£Fine	£N.Mint
1 ND reprints original series from Fishwrap in colour	$0.25	$0.75	$1.25	£0.15	£0.45	£0.75
2-6 ND	$0.25	$0.75	$1.25	£0.15	£0.45	£0.75
Title Value:	$1.50	$4.50	$7.50	£0.90	£2.70	£4.50

FISH POLICE SPECIAL
Comico; 1 Jul 1987

	$Good	$Fine	$N.Mint	£Good	£Fine	£N.Mint
1 ND story precedes issue #1	$0.40	$1.20	$2.00	£0.30	£0.90	£1.50
Title Value:	$0.40	$1.20	$2.00	£0.30	£0.90	£1.50

FISH SHTICKS
Apple Comics; 1 Sep 1991-5 1992

	$Good	$Fine	$N.Mint	£Good	£Fine	£N.Mint
1 ND return of the Fish Police begins	$0.30	$0.90	$1.50	£0.20	£0.60	£1.00
2-5 ND	$0.30	$0.90	$1.50	£0.20	£0.60	£1.00
Title Value:	$1.50	$4.50	$7.50	£1.00	£3.00	£5.00

FIST OF GOD
Eternity,MS; 1 May 1988-4 1988

	$Good	$Fine	$N.Mint	£Good	£Fine	£N.Mint
1-4 ND	$0.40	$1.20	$2.00	£0.25	£0.75	£1.25
Title Value:	$1.60	$4.80	$8.00	£1.00	£3.00	£5.00

FIST OF THE NORTH STAR
Viz Communications,MS; 1 1989-8 1989

	$Good	$Fine	$N.Mint	£Good	£Fine	£N.Mint
1-8 ND 52pgs, black and white	$0.55	$1.65	$2.75	£0.35	£1.05	£1.75
Title Value:	$4.40	$13.20	$22.00	£2.80	£8.40	£14.00

Fist of the Northstar Graphic Novel (Apr 1995)
collects 8 part mini-series — £2.70 £8.10 £13.50

FIST OF THE NORTH STAR PART 2
Viz Communications,MS; 1 Nov 1995-present

	$Good	$Fine	$N.Mint	£Good	£Fine	£N.Mint
1-5 ND black and white	$0.55	$1.65	$2.75	£0.35	£1.05	£1.75
Title Value:	$2.75	$8.25	$13.75	£1.75	£5.25	£8.75

FIVE-STAR SUPER-HERO SPECTACULAR
DC Comics,OS; nn Sep 1977
(see DC Special Series)

	$Good	$Fine	$N.Mint	£Good	£Fine	£N.Mint
nn ND 80pgs, Batman, Aquaman, Green Lantern, Flash, Atom and Kobra appear; Mike Nasser and Mike Golden art	$1.50	$4.50	$7.50	£1.00	£3.00	£5.00

Fear #6

Femforce #85

First Issue Special #1

	$Good	$Fine	$N.Mint	£Good	£Fine	£N.Mint
Title Value:	$1.50	$4.50	$7.50	£1.00	£3.00	£5.00

FLAMING CARROT (1ST SERIES)
Killan Barracks,Magazine; 1 Summer/Autumn 1981

	$Good	$Fine	$N.Mint	£Good	£Fine	£N.Mint
1 ND	$10.00	$30.00	$60.00	£7.50	£22.50	£45.00
Title Value:	$10.00	$30.00	$60.00	£7.50	£22.50	£45.00

FLAMING CARROT (2ND SERIES)
Aardvark/Renegade/Dark Horse; 1 Mar 1984-present?
(see Visions)

	$Good	$Fine	$N.Mint	£Good	£Fine	£N.Mint
1 ND Bob Burden script and art; black and white						
	$7.00	$21.00	$35.00	£4.00	£12.00	£20.00
2 ND Bob Burden script and art; black and white						
	$3.50	$10.50	$17.50	£2.50	£7.50	£12.50
3 ND Bob Burden script and art; black and white						
	$2.50	$7.50	$12.50	£1.50	£4.50	£7.50
4-6 ND Bob Burden script and art; black and white						
	$1.50	$4.50	$7.50	£1.00	£3.00	£5.00
7 1st Renegade issue						
	$1.00	$3.00	$5.00	£0.70	£2.10	£3.50
8-10	$1.00	$3.00	$5.00	£0.70	£2.10	£3.50
11-12	$0.90	$2.70	$4.50	£0.60	£1.80	£3.00
13-15	$0.60	$1.80	$3.00	£0.40	£1.20	£2.00
16-17	$0.45	$1.35	$2.25	£0.30	£0.90	£1.50
18 1st Dark Horse issue						
	$0.45	$1.35	$2.25	£0.30	£0.90	£1.50
19-20	$0.45	$1.35	$2.25	£0.30	£0.90	£1.50
21-23	$0.40	$1.20	$2.00	£0.25	£0.75	£1.25
24 giant						
	$0.55	$1.65	$2.75	£0.35	£1.05	£1.75
25-26	$0.40	$1.20	$2.00	£0.25	£0.75	£1.25
27 Todd McFarlane cover						
	$0.40	$1.20	$2.00	£0.25	£0.75	£1.25
28	$0.40	$1.20	$2.00	£0.25	£0.75	£1.25
29 $2.50 cover begins						
	$0.45	$1.35	$2.25	£0.30	£0.90	£1.50
30-31	$0.45	$1.35	$2.25	£0.30	£0.90	£1.50
Title Value:	$32.05	$96.15	$160.25	£20.70	£62.10	£103.50

Note: 25% of the print run of issue 15 appeared as "ash can" copies. There is no price on the cover, the ground on the cover is brown (not grey/green) and there is a contents banner at the top of the cover. While this is obviously scarcer than the regular edition, the Price Guide cannot offer a precise different value at this time though a figure of £7.50 has been suggested in questionnaires.

FLARE
Hero; 1 Nov 1985-4 1986
(see Champions)

	$Good	$Fine	$N.Mint	£Good	£Fine	£N.Mint
1-4 ND	$0.40	$1.20	$2.00	£0.25	£0.75	£1.25
Title Value:	$1.60	$4.80	$8.00	£1.00	£3.00	£5.00

FLARE (2ND SERIES)
Hero; 1 Nov 1990-17 1993

	$Good	$Fine	$N.Mint	£Good	£Fine	£N.Mint
1-10 ND	$0.60	$1.80	$3.00	£0.40	£1.20	£2.00
11 ND	$0.55	$1.65	$2.75	£0.35	£1.05	£1.75
12-13 ND 44pgs	$0.70	$2.10	$3.50	£0.45	£1.35	£2.25
14 ND pre-bagged with trading card						
	$0.70	$2.10	$3.50	£0.45	£1.35	£2.25
15-17 ND 44pgs	$0.60	$1.80	$3.00	£0.40	£1.20	£2.00
Title Value:	$10.45	$31.35	$52.25	£6.90	£20.70	£34.50

FLARE ADVENTURES
Hero; 1 Jan 1992-5 May 1992

	$Good	$Fine	$N.Mint	£Good	£Fine	£N.Mint
1-5 ND 20pgs, new and reprint material						
	$0.15	$0.45	$0.75	£0.10	£0.35	£0.60
Title Value:	$0.75	$2.25	$3.75	£0.50	£1.75	£3.00

FLARE ADVENTURES (2ND SERIES)
Heroic Publishing; 1 Apr 1994

	$Good	$Fine	$N.Mint	£Good	£Fine	£N.Mint
1 ND ties into Champion Adventures #2						
	$0.60	$1.80	$3.00	£0.40	£1.20	£2.00
Title Value:	$0.60	$1.80	$3.00	£0.40	£1.20	£2.00

FLARE ADVENTURES/CHAMPION CLASSICS
Hero,MS; 1 Jun 1992-17 1993

	$Good	$Fine	$N.Mint	£Good	£Fine	£N.Mint
1 ND flip-book format combination of the two previously individual titles begins						
	$0.50	$1.50	$2.50	£0.30	£0.90	£1.50
2-7 ND	$0.50	$1.50	$2.50	£0.30	£0.90	£1.50
8-12 ND $3.95 cover						
	$0.60	$1.80	$3.00	£0.40	£1.20	£2.00
13 ND $2.95 cover; title becomes "Champions Classics"						
	$0.60	$1.80	$3.00	£0.40	£1.20	£2.00
14-17 ND	$0.60	$1.80	$3.00	£0.40	£1.20	£2.00
Title Value:	$9.50	$28.50	$47.50	£6.10	£18.30	£30.50

FLARE FIRST EDITION
Innovation; 1 Jun 1991-13 1992

	$Good	$Fine	$N.Mint	£Good	£Fine	£N.Mint
1 ND 96pgs, squarebound, reprints Hero's Flare #1, Mark Beachum cover						
	$0.90	$2.70	$4.50	£0.60	£1.80	£3.00
2-13 ND	$0.60	$1.80	$3.00	£0.40	£1.20	£2.00
Title Value:	$8.10	$24.30	$40.50	£5.40	£16.20	£27.00

Flare First Edition Presents: Eternity Smith (Nov 1991)
3 original comics bound together with new cover, 6,000 print run £0.50 £1.50 £2.50

FLARE VS. THE TIGRESS
Hero,MS; 1 Aug 1992-2 Sep 1992

	$Good	$Fine	$N.Mint	£Good	£Fine	£N.Mint
1-2 ND	$0.60	$1.80	$3.00	£0.40	£1.20	£2.00
Title Value:	$1.20	$3.60	$6.00	£0.80	£2.40	£4.00

Flare vs. Tigress Trade paperback (Jan 1993)
reprints mini-series £1.85 £5.55 £9.25

FLASH (1ST SERIES)
National Periodical Publications/DC Comics; 105 Feb/Mar 1959-350 Oct 1985
(numbering continues from Flash Comics [Golden Age])

(see Adventure, Brave and the Bold, DC Comics Presents, DC Special Blue Ribbon Digest, DC Super-Stars, Eighty Page Giant Magazine, Famous First Edition, Five-Star Super-Hero Spectacular, Limited Collector's Edition, One Hundred Page Super Spectacular, Secret Origins, Super-Heroes Battle Super-Gorillas, Super-Team Family, World's Finest)

	$Good	$Fine	$N.Mint	£Good	£Fine	£N.Mint
105 origin Flash retold, 1st appearance Mirror Master						
	$500.00	$1500.00	$5000.00	£290.00	£870.00	£2900.00
[Very scarce in high grade - Very Fine+ or better]						
106 origin and 1st appearance Gorilla Grodd and Pied Piper						
	$130.00	$400.00	$1200.00	£77.50	£230.00	£700.00
107-108 Gorilla Grodd appears						
	$67.50	$205.00	$550.00	£44.00	£130.00	£350.00
1st official distribution in the U.K.						
109 2nd appearance The Mirror Master						
	$57.50	$175.00	$415.00	£38.00	£110.00	£265.00
110 origin and 1st appearance Kid Flash (later new Flash), 1st appearance Weather Wizard						
	$125.00	$380.00	$1150.00	£70.00	£215.00	£650.00
111 scarce in the U.K. 2nd appearance Kid Flash; Cloud Creatures appear						
	$41.00	$120.00	$285.00	£26.00	£77.50	£185.00
112 very scarce in the U.K. 1st appearance Elongated Man						
	$49.00	$145.00	$390.00	£31.00	£92.50	£250.00
113 origin and 1st appearance Trickster						
	$41.00	$120.00	$285.00	£26.00	£75.00	£180.00
114 Captain Cold appears and origin re-told (see Showcase #8)						
	$32.00	$95.00	$225.00	£20.00	£60.00	£140.00
115-116	$26.00	$77.50	$185.00	£16.00	£49.00	£115.00
117 origin and 1st appearance Captain Boomerang						
	$36.00	$105.00	$250.00	£21.00	£62.50	£150.00
118-120	$26.00	$77.50	$185.00	£16.00	£49.00	£115.00
121	$19.00	$57.50	$135.00	£10.50	£32.00	£75.00
122 origin and 1st appearance The Top						
	$19.00	$57.50	$135.00	£12.00	£36.00	£85.00
123 1st Earth 1/Earth 2 story, re-intro Golden Age Flash, classic story and cover; historically important to the shaping of the Silver Age DC Universe						
	$90.00	$275.00	$825.00	£55.00	£165.00	£500.00
124 last 10 cents issue						
	$17.50	$52.50	$125.00	£11.00	£34.00	£80.00
125-127	$15.00	$45.00	$105.00	£9.25	£28.00	£65.00
128 origin Abra-Kadabra						
	$15.00	$45.00	$105.00	£9.25	£28.00	£65.00
129 Golden Age Flash on cover, Justice Society of America cameo (first since 1950s)						
	$34.00	$100.00	$270.00	£18.50	£55.00	£150.00
130	$15.00	$45.00	$105.00	£8.50	£26.00	£60.00
131 Green Lantern co-stars						
	$15.00	$45.00	$105.00	£8.50	£26.00	£60.00
132-133	$15.00	$45.00	$105.00	£8.50	£26.00	£60.00
134 Elongated Man and Flash team, versus Captain Cold						
	$15.00	$45.00	$105.00	£8.50	£26.00	£60.00
135 Kid Flash appears, his costume is altered						
	$15.00	$45.00	$105.00	£8.50	£26.00	£60.00
136 1st appearance Dexter Miles, curator of the Flash Museum						
	$15.00	$45.00	$105.00	£8.50	£26.00	£60.00
137 Golden Age Flash on cover, Justice Society of America cameo and decision to re-form, 1st Silver Age appearance Vandal Savage, 1st full appearance Golden Age Green Lantern						
	$47.00	$140.00	$375.00	£16.50	£50.00	£135.00
138 Elongated Man and Flash team, versus Pied Piper						
	$15.00	$45.00	$105.00	£8.50	£26.00	£60.00
139 origin and 1st appearance Professor Zoom/Reverse Flash						
	$17.50	$52.50	$125.00	£10.50	£32.00	£75.00
140 1st appearance Heat Wave, Captain Cold appears						
	$15.00	$45.00	$105.00	£8.50	£26.00	£60.00
141 "Paul Gamby" appears, based on American-born/U.K. resident radio broadcaster/author Paul Gambaccini						
	$10.00	$30.00	$70.00	£5.25	£16.00	£37.50
142	$10.00	$30.00	$70.00	£5.25	£16.00	£37.50
143 co-stars Green Lantern						
	$10.50	$32.00	$75.00	£5.50	£17.00	£40.00
144-146	$10.00	$30.00	$70.00	£5.25	£16.00	£37.50
147 Reverse Flash appears, cover based on #123						
	$10.00	$30.00	$70.00	£5.25	£16.00	£37.50
148	$10.00	$30.00	$70.00	£5.25	£16.00	£37.50
149 Kid Flash co-stars						
	$10.00	$30.00	$70.00	£5.25	£16.00	£37.50
150	$10.00	$30.00	$70.00	£5.25	£16.00	£37.50
151 Golden Age Flash versus The Shade						
	$14.00	$43.00	$100.00	£5.00	£15.00	£35.00
152-154	$7.75	$23.50	$55.00	£3.55	£10.50	£25.00
155 1st Flash's Rogues Gallery (Pied Piper, Mirror Master, Captain Cold, The Top, Heatwave, Boomerang), Gorilla Grodd appears						
	$8.50	$26.00	$60.00	£3.55	£10.50	£25.00
156	$7.75	$23.50	$55.00	£3.55	£10.50	£25.00
157 last Silver Age issue, indicia dated December 1965						
	$7.75	$23.50	$55.00	£3.55	£10.50	£25.00
158-159	$7.75	$23.50	$55.00	£3.55	£10.50	£25.00
160 80pgs, scarce in the U.K., Giant G-21, reprints #107, Golden Age Flash reprint (Note: black cover makes this scarce in high grade)						
	$9.25	$28.00	$65.00	£4.25	£12.50	£30.00
161-164	$7.50	$22.50	$45.00	£3.30	£10.00	£20.00
165 Barry Allen marries Iris West						
	$7.50	$22.50	$45.00	£3.30	£10.00	£20.00
166	$7.50	$22.50	$45.00	£3.30	£10.00	£20.00
167 "true" origin The Flash (lightning bolt no accident..?)						
	$7.50	$22.50	$45.00	£3.30	£10.00	£20.00
168 Green Lantern guest-stars						

	$Good	$Fine	$N.Mint	£Good	£Fine	£N.Mint

	$Good	$Fine	$N.Mint	£Good	£Fine	£N.Mint
	$7.50	$22.50	$45.00	£3.75	£11.00	£22.50
169 80pgs, scarce in the U.K., Giant G-34, reprints #129						
	$10.50	$33.00	$65.00	£4.15	£12.50	£25.00
170 Golden Age Flash appears						
	$7.50	$22.50	$45.00	£3.30	£10.00	£20.00
171-172	$6.50	$20.00	$40.00	£2.50	£7.50	£15.00
173 Golden Age Flash/Kid Flash appear						
	$6.50	$20.00	$40.00	£2.50	£7.50	£15.00
174 Infantino art ends, Rogues Gallery return (see Secret Origins #41)						
	$6.50	$20.00	$40.00	£2.50	£7.50	£15.00
175 scarce in the U.K. 2nd Superman/Flash race, Justice League of America cameo						
(see Superman #199, World's Finest #198/199)						
	$15.00	$45.00	$105.00	£6.25	£19.00	£45.00
176-177	$6.50	$20.00	$40.00	£2.05	£6.25	£12.50
178 80pgs, Giant G-46						
	$8.25	$25.00	$50.00	£3.30	£10.00	£20.00
179-180	$6.50	$20.00	$40.00	£2.05	£6.25	£12.50
181-186	$4.15	$12.50	$25.00	£1.25	£3.75	£7.50
187 68pgs, Giant G-58						
	$6.50	$20.00	$40.00	£2.50	£7.50	£15.00
188-190	$4.15	$12.50	$25.00	£1.25	£3.75	£7.50
191-193	$4.15	$12.50	$25.00	£1.00	£3.00	£6.00
194-195 Neal Adams cover						
	$4.15	$12.50	$25.00	£1.00	£3.00	£6.00
196 Giant G-70, reprints #108						
	$6.50	$20.00	$40.00	£2.05	£6.25	£12.50
197-199	$4.15	$12.50	$25.00	£1.00	£3.00	£6.00
200 scarce in the U.K.						
	$4.15	$12.50	$25.00	£1.25	£3.75	£7.50
201-202	$2.50	$7.50	$12.50	£0.70	£2.10	£3.50
203 Superman cameo						
	$2.50	$7.50	$12.50	£0.70	£2.10	£3.50
204	$2.50	$7.50	$12.50	£0.70	£2.10	£3.50
205 68pgs, Giant G-82						
	$4.15	$12.50	$25.00	£1.50	£4.50	£9.00
206-207	$2.50	$7.50	$12.50	£0.70	£2.10	£3.50
208-210 52pgs	$2.50	$7.50	$12.50	£0.75	£2.25	£3.75
211 52pgs, Golden Age Flash origin from issue #104, last of original run						
	$2.50	$7.50	$12.50	£0.80	£2.40	£4.00
212 52pgs	$2.50	$7.50	$12.50	£0.75	£2.25	£3.75
213 52pgs, reprints #137						
	$2.50	$7.50	$12.50	£0.75	£2.25	£3.75
214 100pgs, DC-100pg Super Spectacular #11; origin Metal Men from Showcase #37,						
1st Golden Age Flash published story						
	$4.00	$12.00	$20.00	£1.50	£4.50	£7.50
215 52pgs, reprints 2nd Showcase #4 story "The Man Who Broke The Time Barrier"						
	$2.50	$7.50	$12.50	£1.00	£3.00	£5.00
216 52pgs	$1.10	$3.35	$5.62	£0.75	£2.25	£3.75
217-219 Neal Adams art on Green Lantern/Arrow back-up						
	$3.00	$9.00	$15.00	£1.60	£4.80	£8.00
220-221 Green Lantern appears						
	$1.50	$4.50	$7.50	£0.60	£1.80	£3.00
222	$1.50	$4.50	$7.50	£0.60	£1.80	£3.00
223 Neal Adams inks on Green Lantern back-up, Green Lantern teams with Flash (up to #228)						
	$1.50	$4.50	$7.50	£0.70	£2.10	£3.50
224 scarce in the U.K.						
	$1.50	$4.50	$7.50	£0.70	£2.10	£3.50
225	$1.50	$4.50	$7.50	£0.60	£1.80	£3.00
226 Neal Adams art						
	$2.40	$7.00	$12.00	£1.20	£3.60	£6.00
227	$1.50	$4.50	$7.50	£0.60	£1.80	£3.00
228 Cary Bates (scripter) appears						
	$1.50	$4.50	$7.50	£0.60	£1.80	£3.00
229 100pgs, Golden Age Flash appears						
	$1.65	$5.00	$10.00	£1.25	£3.75	£7.50
230-231 Green Lantern appears						
	$1.50	$4.50	$7.50	£0.60	£1.80	£3.00
232 100pgs	$1.65	$5.00	$10.00	£1.15	£3.50	£7.00
233-234 Green Lantern appears						
	$1.20	$3.60	$6.00	£0.50	£1.50	£2.50
235	$0.80	$2.40	$4.00	£0.50	£1.50	£2.50
236 ND	$0.80	$2.40	$4.00	£0.60	£1.80	£3.00
237-238 Green Lantern appears						
	$0.80	$2.40	$4.00	£0.50	£1.50	£2.50
239	$0.80	$2.40	$4.00	£0.50	£1.50	£2.50
240 Green Lantern appears						
	$0.80	$2.40	$4.00	£0.50	£1.50	£2.50
241-242 Green Lantern appears						
	$0.60	$1.80	$3.00	£0.40	£1.20	£2.00
243 LD in the U.K. death of The Top, Green Lantern appears						
	$0.80	$2.40	$4.00	£0.50	£1.50	£2.50
244 LD in the U.K.	$0.60	$1.80	$3.00	£0.45	£1.35	£2.25
245-246 LD in the U.K. Green Lantern appears						
	$0.60	$1.80	$3.00	£0.45	£1.35	£2.25
247-249 LD in the U.K.						
	$0.60	$1.80	$3.00	£0.45	£1.35	£2.25
250 LD in the U.K. 1st appearance Golden Glider						
	$0.60	$1.80	$3.00	£0.40	£1.20	£2.00
251-264	$0.60	$1.80	$3.00	£0.35	£1.05	£1.75
265 ND 44pgs	$0.60	$1.80	$3.00	£0.50	£1.50	£2.50
266 ND 44pgs, Kid Flash solo back-up						
	$0.60	$1.80	$3.00	£0.50	£1.50	£2.50

	$Good	$Fine	$N.Mint	£Good	£Fine	£N.Mint
267 ND 44pgs, origin of the Flash costume retold						
	$0.60	$1.80	$3.00	£0.50	£1.50	£2.50
268 features Flash Comics #26 as part of plot						
	$0.60	$1.80	$3.00	£0.30	£0.90	£1.50
269-274	$0.60	$1.80	$3.00	£0.30	£0.90	£1.50
275 Green Lantern cameo, Iris Allen dies						
	$0.60	$1.80	$3.00	£0.30	£0.90	£1.50
276-281	$0.60	$1.80	$3.00	£0.30	£0.90	£1.50
282 Green Lantern X-over						
	$0.60	$1.80	$3.00	£0.30	£0.90	£1.50
283-288	$0.60	$1.80	$3.00	£0.30	£0.90	£1.50
289 Firestorm back-up begins (8pgs) featuring 1st DC art by George Perez						
	$1.20	$3.60	$6.00	£0.50	£1.50	£2.50
290 George Perez art						
	$0.60	$1.80	$3.00	£0.35	£1.05	£1.75
291 George Perez art; Flash vs. The Sabertooth (not Marvel character!)						
	$0.60	$1.80	$3.00	£0.30	£0.90	£1.50
292 George Perez art						
	$0.60	$1.80	$3.00	£0.30	£0.90	£1.50
293 George Perez art; Flash and Firestorm team-up						
	$0.60	$1.80	$3.00	£0.30	£0.90	£1.50
294-295 Jim Starlin art						
	$0.50	$1.50	$2.50	£0.25	£0.75	£1.25
296 Jim Starlin, Infantino art, Flash vs. Elongated Man						
	$0.50	$1.50	$2.50	£0.25	£0.75	£1.25
297-299 Infantino, Cowan art						
	$0.50	$1.50	$2.50	£0.25	£0.75	£1.25
300 ND 52pgs, (no ads), 25th anniversary, Infantino art on Flash's life story						
	$1.00	$3.00	$5.00	£0.70	£2.10	£3.50
301-302 Infantino, Cowan art						
	$0.50	$1.50	$2.50	£0.20	£0.60	£1.00
303-304 Infantino art						
	$0.50	$1.50	$2.50	£0.20	£0.60	£1.00
305 Golden Age Flash X-over, Dr. Fate appears						
	$0.50	$1.50	$2.50	£0.20	£0.60	£1.00
306-308 Dr.Fate back-up by Giffen						
	$0.50	$1.50	$2.50	£0.25	£0.75	£1.25
309 Dr.Fate back-up by Giffen, origin The Flash retold						
	$0.50	$1.50	$2.50	£0.25	£0.75	£1.25
310-311 Dr.Fate back-up by Giffen						
	$0.50	$1.50	$2.50	£0.25	£0.75	£1.25
312 Infantino art, Giffen layouts on Dr. Fate						
	$0.50	$1.50	$2.50	£0.25	£0.75	£1.25
313 Dr.Fate back-up by Giffen						
	$0.50	$1.50	$2.50	£0.25	£0.75	£1.25
314-317	$0.40	$1.20	$2.00	£0.20	£0.60	£1.00
318-319 Gibbons art on Creeper back-up						
	$0.40	$1.20	$2.00	£0.20	£0.60	£1.00
320-323 Creeper back-up stories						
	$0.40	$1.20	$2.00	£0.20	£0.60	£1.00
324 scarce in the U.K. Reverse Flash dies						
	$0.40	$1.20	$2.00	£0.35	£1.05	£1.75
325 Kid Flash back-up						
	$0.40	$1.20	$2.00	£0.20	£0.60	£1.00
326-339	$0.40	$1.20	$2.00	£0.20	£0.60	£1.00
340 Flash on Trial begins						
	$0.40	$1.20	$2.00	£0.25	£0.75	£1.25
341-343 Flash on Trial						
	$0.40	$1.20	$2.00	£0.25	£0.75	£1.25
344 Flash on Trial, origin Kid Flash retold						
	$0.40	$1.20	$2.00	£0.25	£0.75	£1.25
345-347 Flash on Trial						
	$0.40	$1.20	$2.00	£0.25	£0.75	£1.25
348-349	$0.40	$1.20	$2.00	£0.20	£0.60	£1.00
350 very LD DS	$1.20	$3.60	$6.00	£0.80	£2.40	£4.00
Title Value:	$2280.30	$6863.55	$18064.62	£1257.30	£3777.20	£10098.50

Note: #340-347 are The Flash on Trial

FEATURES

Dr.Fate in 306-312. Elongated Man solo in 206, 208, 210, 212. Firestorm in 289-292, 294-299, 301-304. Firestorm/Flash in 293. Green Lantern in 220, 221, 223-228, 230, 231, 233, 234, 237, 238, 240-243, 245, 246. Green Lantern/Green Arrow in 217-219. GA Flash in 201. Kid Flash solo in 111, 112, 114, 116, 118, 112, 127, 130, 133, 138, 144, 202, 204, 207, 209, 211, 216, 265, 266.

REPRINT FEATURES

Flash in 160, 169, 178, 187, 196, 205, 208-215, 229, 232. Flash/Green Lantern, Flash/GA Flash in 178. Green Lantern in 229, 232. GA Flash in 160, 205,14, 216, 216, 232. Johnny Quick in 160, 205, 214, 229, 232. Kid Flash in 160, 205, 214, 229, 232. Metal Men in 214. Quicksilver in 214.

FLASH (1ST SERIES) ANNUAL

National Periodical Publications; 1 Nov/Dec 1963

	$Good	$Fine	$N.Mint	£Good	£Fine	£N.Mint
1 84pgs, reprints #106 (Gorilla Grodd), origins Elongated Man (#112), Kid Flash (#110) retold,						
Showcase #13 (Mr. Element), also 1st Golden Age Star Sapphire from Flash Comics						
	$41.00	$120.00	$325.00	£28.00	£82.50	£225.00

Note: copies often suffer from crinkled spines owing to original production process

FLASH (2ND SERIES)

DC Comics; 0 Oct 1994; 1 Jun 1987-present

	$Good	$Fine	$N.Mint	£Good	£Fine	£N.Mint
0 (Oct 1994) Zero Hour X-over, origin retold						
	$0.45	$1.35	$2.25	£0.30	£0.90	£1.50
1 Wally West as new Flash (see Crisis on Infinite Earths #12)						
	$0.90	$2.70	$4.50	£0.60	£1.80	£3.00
2	$0.70	$2.10	$3.50	£0.45	£1.35	£2.25
3	$0.45	$1.35	$2.25	£0.30	£0.90	£1.50
4-5	$0.40	$1.20	$2.00	£0.25	£0.75	£1.25

	$Good	$Fine	$N.Mint	£Good	£Fine	£N.Mint
6-7	$0.30	$0.90	$1.50	£0.20	£0.60	£1.00
8-9 Millennium X-over	$0.30	$0.90	$1.50	£0.20	£0.60	£1.00
10-11	$0.30	$0.90	$1.50	£0.20	£0.60	£1.00
12 free 16pg Bonus Book (Dr.Light)	$0.30	$0.90	$1.50	£0.20	£0.60	£1.00
13-18	$0.30	$0.90	$1.50	£0.20	£0.60	£1.00
19 free 16pg Bonus Book (Blue Trinity)	$0.30	$0.90	$1.50	£0.20	£0.60	£1.00
20	$0.30	$0.90	$1.50	£0.20	£0.60	£1.00
21 Invasion X-over	$0.30	$0.90		£0.20	£0.60	£1.00
22 Invasion X-over, new Manhunter appears	$0.30	$0.90	$1.50	£0.20	£0.60	£1.00
23-27	$0.30	$0.90	$1.50	£0.20	£0.60	£1.00
28 Captain Cold appears	$0.30	$0.90	$1.50	£0.20	£0.60	£1.00
29 new Phantom Lady appears	$0.30	$0.90	$1.50	£0.20	£0.60	£1.00
30-32	$0.30	$0.90	$1.50	£0.20	£0.60	£1.00
33 Joker cover and story	$0.30	$0.90	$1.50	£0.20	£0.60	£1.00
34	$0.30	$0.90	$1.50	£0.20	£0.60	£1.00
35 Elongated Man, Manhunter appear	$0.30	$0.90	$1.50	£0.20	£0.60	£1.00
36-44	$0.30	$0.90	$1.50	£0.20	£0.60	£1.00
45 Gorilla Grodd appears	$0.30	$0.90	$1.50	£0.20	£0.60	£1.00
46-47 The Vixen co-stars	$0.30	$0.90	$1.50	£0.20	£0.60	£1.00
48-49	$0.30	$0.90	$1.50	£0.20	£0.60	£1.00
50 48pgs, Vandal Savage appears	$0.40	$1.20	$2.00	£0.25	£0.75	£1.25
51-52	$0.25	$0.75	$1.25	£0.20	£0.60	£1.00
53 Superman/Jimmy Olsen appear; Pied Piper declares his homosexuality (pre Northstar in Alpha Flight #106)	$0.25	$0.75	$1.25	£0.20	£0.60	£1.00
54-61	$0.25	$0.75	$1.25	£0.20	£0.60	£1.00
62 Flash - Year One: Born To Run part 1, Silver Age Flash (Barry Allen) appears, bi-weekly	$0.25	$0.75	$1.25	£0.20	£0.60	£1.00
63 Flash - Year One: Born To Run part 2, Silver Age Flash (Barry Allen) appears, bi-weekly	$0.25	$0.75	$1.25	£0.20	£0.60	£1.00
64 Flash - Year One: Born To Run part 3, Mirror Master appears, bi-weekly	$0.25	$0.75	$1.25	£0.20	£0.60	£1.00
65 Flash - Year One: Born To Run part 4, bi-weekly	$0.25	$0.75	$1.25	£0.20	£0.60	£1.00
66 Flash vs. Aquaman, $1.25 cover begins	$0.25	$0.75	$1.25	£0.20	£0.60	£1.00
67-68	$0.25	$0.75	$1.25	£0.20	£0.60	£1.00
69 Gorilla Warfare part 2, Flash vs. Hector Hammond, continued in Green Lantern [2nd Series] #31	$0.25	$0.75	$1.25	£0.20	£0.60	£1.00
70 Gorilla Warfare part 4 (conclusion)	$0.25	$0.75	$1.25	£0.20	£0.60	£1.00
71-72	$0.25	$0.75	$1.25	£0.20	£0.60	£1.00
73 Golden Age Flash (Jay Garrick) appears		$0.75	$1.25	£0.20	£0.60	£1.00
74 Barry Allen (Silver Age Flash) appears	$0.25	$0.75	$1.25	£0.20	£0.60	£1.00
75 Barry Allen (Silver Age Flash) returns	$0.25	$0.75	$1.25	£0.20	£0.60	£1.00
76-78	$0.25	$0.75	$1.25	£0.20	£0.60	£1.00
79 64pgs, Barry Allen vs. Wally West	$0.45	$1.35	$2.25	£0.30	£0.90	£1.50
80 covers begin Alan Davis and Mark Farmer	$0.25	$0.75	$1.25	£0.20	£0.60	£1.00
80 ND Collector's Edition, foil-enhanced cover	$0.45	$1.35	$2.25	£0.30	£0.90	£1.50
81 Nightwing and Starfire appear	$0.25	$0.75	$1.25	£0.20	£0.60	£1.00
82 Alan Davis and Mark Farmer cover	$0.25	$0.75	$1.25	£0.20	£0.60	£1.00
83	$0.25	$0.75	$1.25	£0.20	£0.60	£1.00
84 Barry Kitson pencils, Alan Davis and Mark Farmer cover	$0.25	$0.75	$1.25	£0.20	£0.60	£1.00
85 Alan Davis and Mark Farmer art	$0.25	$0.75	$1.25	£0.20	£0.60	£1.00
86 Argus appears; Alan Davis and Mark Farmer art	$0.25	$0.75	$1.25	£0.20	£0.60	£1.00
87-91 Alan Davis and Mark Farmer cover	$0.30	$0.90	$1.50	£0.20	£0.60	£1.00
92 1st appearance Impulse (cameo), Alan Davis and Mark Farmer cover	$1.60	$4.80	$8.00	£0.70	£2.10	£3.50
93 1st full appearance Impulse	$0.60	$1.80	$3.00	£0.40	£1.20	£2.00
94 Zero Hour X-over	$0.40	$1.20	$2.00	£0.25	£0.75	£1.25
95 Terminal Velocity part 1 (ends #100)	$0.40	$1.20	$2.00	£0.25	£0.75	£1.25
96-99	$0.40	$1.20	$2.00	£0.25	£0.75	£1.25
100 Terminal Velocity concludes; Flash has increased speed powers	$0.45	$1.35	$2.25	£0.30	£0.90	£1.50
100 ND Collector's Edition - holographic foil-enhanced cover	$0.80	$2.40	$4.00	£0.50	£1.50	£2.50
101-104	$0.40	$1.20	$2.00	£0.25	£0.75	£1.25
105 Ron Lim cover and art	$0.40	$1.20	$2.00	£0.25	£0.75	£1.25
106	$0.40	$1.20	$2.00	£0.25	£0.75	£1.25
107 Underworld Unleashed tie-in, Captain Marvel teams up with Flash	$0.40	$1.20	$2.00	£0.25	£0.75	£1.25
108	$0.40	$1.20	$2.00	£0.25	£0.75	£1.25
109 Dead Heat part 2, continued in Impulse #10	$0.40	$1.20	$2.00	£0.25	£0.75	£1.25
110 Dead Heat part 4, continued in Impulse #11	$0.35	$1.05	$1.75	£0.20	£0.60	£1.00
111 Dead Heat part 6 (conclusion), continued from Impulse #11	$0.35	$1.05	$1.75	£0.20	£0.60	£1.00
Title Value:	$38.20	$114.60	$191.00	£25.85	£77.55	£129.25
Flash Multi-Pack (Feb 1992), contains issues #44 (2nd printing), #51, #52 plus illustrated header card				£0.40	£1.20	£2.00
The Flash: Terminal Velocity (Nov 1995) Trade paperback reprints Flash #0 and #95-100 with new cover				£1.70	£5.10	£8.50

FLASH (2ND SERIES) ANNUAL
DC Comics; 1 Sep 1987-present

	$Good	$Fine	$N.Mint	£Good	£Fine	£N.Mint
1 48pgs, Mike Baron story, Jackson Guice art	$0.45	$1.35	$2.25	£0.30	£0.90	£1.50
2 48pgs	$0.35	$1.05	$1.75	£0.25	£0.75	£1.25
3 48pgs, squarebound, features all three Flashes	$0.35	$1.05	$1.75	£0.25	£0.75	£1.25
4 64pgs, Armageddon: 2001 tie-in	$0.35	$1.05	$1.75	£0.25	£0.75	£1.25
5 64pgs, Eclipso: The Darkness Within tie-in, Travis Charest art	$0.45	$1.35	$2.25	£0.30	£0.90	£1.50
6 64pgs, Bloodlines part 4, 1st appearance Argus, continued in New Titans Annual #9	$0.45	$1.35	$2.25	£0.30	£0.90	£1.50
7 64pgs, Elseworlds story	$0.55	$1.65	$2.75	£0.35	£1.05	£1.75
8 56pgs, Year One, Flash (Wally West's) first mission vs. Hal Jordan Green Lantern	$0.80	$2.40	$4.00	£0.50	£1.50	£2.50
Title Value:	$3.75	$11.25	$18.75	£2.50	£7.50	£12.50

FLASH COMICS
National Periodical Publications; 1 Jan 1940-104 Feb 1949

	$Good	$Fine	$N.Mint	£Good	£Fine	£N.Mint
1 origin and 1st appearance Golden Age Flash (Jay Garrick), origin and 1st appearance Golden Age Hawkman, probably no more than 100 extant copies in any condition	$4150.00	$12400.00	$41500.00	£2750.00	£8200.00	£27500.00
[Prices may vary widely on this comic]						
2	$570.00	$1725.00	$4600.00	£375.00	£1125.00	£3000.00
3	$465.00	$1400.00	$3750.00	£265.00	£800.00	£2150.00
4	$360.00	$1075.00	$2900.00	£250.00	£750.00	£2000.00
5	$335.00	$1000.00	$2700.00	£215.00	£650.00	£1750.00
6 2nd Flash cover	$410.00	$1225.00	$3300.00	£250.00	£750.00	£2000.00
7 2nd Golden Age Hawkman app. on cover	$310.00	$930.00	$2500.00	£205.00	£610.00	£1650.00
8-10	$215.00	$650.00	$1750.00	£150.00	£450.00	£1200.00
11-20	$155.00	$470.00	$1100.00	£105.00	£320.00	£750.00
21-23	$110.00	$340.00	$800.00	£80.00	£240.00	£560.00
24 Shiera Sanders becomes Golden Age Hawkgirl (see All Star Comics #5), Flash vs. The Spidermen From Mars	$175.00	$530.00	$1250.00	£125.00	£375.00	£875.00
25-27	$110.00	$340.00	$800.00	£80.00	£240.00	£560.00
28 Hollywood cover	$110.00	$340.00	$800.00	£80.00	£240.00	£560.00
29-30	$110.00	$340.00	$800.00	£80.00	£240.00	£560.00
31-40	$92.50	$275.00	$650.00	£62.50	£190.00	£450.00
41-50	$85.00	$255.00	$600.00	£60.00	£180.00	£425.00
51-60	$80.00	$240.00	$560.00	£55.00	£165.00	£385.00
61	$70.00	$210.00	$490.00	£50.00	£150.00	£350.00
62 Joe Kubert art on Hawkman	$100.00	$300.00	$700.00	£70.00	£210.00	£490.00
63-65 Joe Kubert art on Hawkman	$85.00	$255.00	$600.00	£60.00	£180.00	£425.00
66-85	$75.00	$225.00	$525.00	£50.00	£150.00	£350.00
86 1st appearance Black Canary (Golden Age)	$190.00	$570.00	$1525.00	£130.00	£390.00	£1050.00
87-88	$87.50	$265.00	$625.00	£60.00	£180.00	£425.00
89 Flash vs. The Thorn	$87.50	$265.00	$625.00	£60.00	£180.00	£425.00
90	$87.50	$265.00	$625.00	£60.00	£180.00	£425.00
91 scarce in the U.K.	$87.50	$265.00	$625.00	£62.50	£190.00	£450.00
92 scarce in the U.K. 1st solo Black Canary story, classic cover	$250.00	$750.00	$2000.00	£165.00	£500.00	£1350.00
93-99 scarce in the U.K.	$110.00	$330.00	$775.00	£75.00	£225.00	£525.00
100 very scarce in the U.K.	$300.00	$900.00	$2100.00	£220.00	£660.00	£1550.00
101 very scarce in the U.K. Flash time travel story	$250.00	$750.00	$1750.00	£175.00	£520.00	£1225.00
102-103 very scarce in the U.K.	$250.00	$750.00	$1750.00	£175.00	£520.00	£1225.00
104 rare in the U.K., origin Flash retold, classic cover	$570.00	$1725.00	$4600.00	£410.00	£1225.00	£3300.00

	$Good	$Fine	$N.Mint	£Good	£Fine	£N.Mint
Title Value:	$17727.50	$53300.00	$141565.00	£12007.50	£36040.00	£95530.00

Note: in common with all Golden Age comics, these were not distributed on the news-stands in the U.K. but some may have come over during the war or in the late 1940s as ballast on ships. Most issues however are generally scarce in the U.K.

FLASH DIGEST, THE
DC Comics, Digest; 24 Feb 1981
(DC Special Series 24)

	$Good	$Fine	$N.Mint	£Good	£Fine	£N.Mint
24 ND 68pgs, Flash, Golden Age Flash reprints						
	$0.70	$2.10	$3.50	£0.50	£1.50	£2.50
Title Value:	$0.70	$2.10	$3.50	£0.50	£1.50	£2.50

FLASH GORDON (1ST SERIES)
Gold Key; 1 Jun 1965

	$Good	$Fine	$N.Mint	£Good	£Fine	£N.Mint
1 rare in the U.K., all reprint; distributed in the U.K.						
	$3.75	$11.00	$22.50	£2.50	£7.50	£15.00
Title Value:	$3.75	$11.00	$22.50	£2.50	£7.50	£15.00

FLASH GORDON (2ND LIMITED SERIES)
Marvel Comics Group, MS; 1 Jun 1995-2 Jul 1995

	$Good	$Fine	$N.Mint	£Good	£Fine	£N.Mint
1-2 ND Mark Schultz script, Al Williamson art						
	$0.60	$1.80	$3.00	£0.40	£1.20	£2.00
Title Value:	$1.20	$3.60	$6.00	£0.80	£2.40	£4.00

FLASH GORDON (2ND SERIES)
King Comics; 1 Sep 1966-11 Dec 1967; Charlton; 12 Feb 1969-18 Jan 1970; Gold Key; 19 Nov 1978-27 Jul 1980; Whitman; 28 Aug 1980-37 Mar 1982

	$Good	$Fine	$N.Mint	£Good	£Fine	£N.Mint
1 scarce, distributed in the U.K. Williamson art; painted covers begin						
	$5.25	$16.00	$32.50	£3.30	£10.00	£20.00
2 scarce, distributed in the U.K.						
	$2.50	$7.50	$15.00	£1.65	£5.00	£10.00
3-5 scarce, distributed in the U.K. Williamson art						
	$2.50	$7.50	$15.00	£1.65	£5.00	£10.00
6 scarce, distributed in the U.K. Crandall art						
	$2.50	$7.50	$15.00	£1.65	£5.00	£10.00
7-10 distributed in the U.K.						
	$2.05	$6.25	$12.50	£1.30	£4.00	£8.00
11 distributed in the U.K., Crandall art						
	$2.80	$8.25	$14.00	£1.40	£4.20	£7.00
12 rare in the U.K., Crandall art						
	$3.20	$9.50	$16.00	£1.60	£4.80	£8.00
13 rare in the U.K., Jones art						
	$3.20	$9.50	$16.00	£1.60	£4.80	£8.00
14-17 rare in the U.K.						
	$1.50	$4.50	$7.50	£1.00	£3.00	£5.00
18 rare in the U.K., Kaluta art						
	$1.80	$5.25	$9.00	£1.20	£3.60	£6.00
19-25	$0.80	$2.40	$4.00	£0.50	£1.50	£2.50
26-30	$0.60	$1.80	$3.00	£0.40	£1.20	£2.00
31-33 adapts Flash Gordon film with soundtrack by Queen, Al Williamson art; photo montage cover						
	$0.80	$2.40	$4.00	£0.50	£1.50	£2.50
34	$0.60	$1.80	$3.00	£0.40	£1.20	£2.00
35-37 line drawn cover						
	$0.60	$1.80	$3.00	£0.40	£1.20	£2.00
Title Value:	$56.35	$169.20	$314.50	£35.15	£106.20	£194.00

FLASH GORDON (LIMITED SERIES)
DC Comics, MS; 1 Jun 1988-9 Feb 1989

	$Good	$Fine	$N.Mint	£Good	£Fine	£N.Mint
1-9	$0.25	$0.75	$1.25	£0.15	£0.45	£0.75
Title Value:	$2.25	$6.75	$11.25	£1.35	£4.05	£6.75

Note: New Format

FLASH SPECIAL
DC Comics, OS; 1 Jul 1990

	$Good	$Fine	$N.Mint	£Good	£Fine	£N.Mint
1 80pgs, features all three Flashes, cover by Kubert						
	$0.60	$1.80	$3.00	£0.40	£1.20	£2.00
Title Value:	$0.60	$1.80	$3.00	£0.40	£1.20	£2.00

Note: celebrates Flash's 50th anniversary

FLASH SPECTACULAR
DC Comics; 11 1978
(DC Special Series 11)

	$Good	$Fine	$N.Mint	£Good	£Fine	£N.Mint
11 ND 80pgs, Flash, Golden Age Flash, Johnny Quick, Kid Flash reprints						
	$0.90	$2.70	$4.50	£0.60	£1.80	£3.00
Title Value:	$0.90	$2.70	$4.50	£0.60	£1.80	£3.00

FLASH TV SPECIAL
DC Comics, OS; 1 Jul 1991

	$Good	$Fine	$N.Mint	£Good	£Fine	£N.Mint
1 ND 80pgs, based on pilot film of CBS TV series plus pin-up pages						
	$0.60	$1.80	$3.00	£0.40	£1.20	£2.00
Title Value:	$0.60	$1.80	$3.00	£0.40	£1.20	£2.00

FLAXEN
Golden Apple Comics/Dark Horse, OS; 1 Sep 1992

	$Good	$Fine	$N.Mint	£Good	£Fine	£N.Mint
1 ND based on life story of Playboy model Suzie Owens, cover painting by Steve Rude						
	$0.50	$1.50	$2.50	£0.30	£0.90	£1.50
Title Value:	$0.50	$1.50	$2.50	£0.30	£0.90	£1.50

FLAXEN: ALTER EGO
Caliber Press; 1 Mar 1995

	$Good	$Fine	$N.Mint	£Good	£Fine	£N.Mint
1 ND David Mack art and back cover by Adam Hughes						
	$0.60	$1.80	$3.00	£0.40	£1.20	£2.00
Title Value:	$0.60	$1.80	$3.00	£0.40	£1.20	£2.00

FLESH AND BONES
(see Dalgoda)

FLINT ARMBUSTER JNR. SPECIAL
Alchemy Studios, OS; 1 1990

	$Good	$Fine	$N.Mint	£Good	£Fine	£N.Mint
1 ND Scot Eaton script/art						
	$0.50	$1.50	$2.50	£0.30	£0.90	£1.50
Title Value:	$0.50	$1.50	$2.50	£0.30	£0.90	£1.50

FLINTSTONE KIDS, THE
Marvel Comics Group/Star, TV; 1 Aug 1987-12 Apr 1989

	$Good	$Fine	$N.Mint	£Good	£Fine	£N.Mint
1-12	$0.15	$0.45	$0.75	£0.10	£0.35	£0.60
Title Value:	$1.80	$5.40	$9.00	£1.20	£4.20	£7.20

FLINTSTONES AND PEBBLES, THE
Charlton; 1 Nov 1970-50 Feb 1977

	$Good	$Fine	$N.Mint	£Good	£Fine	£N.Mint
1	$7.50	$22.50	$37.50	£4.00	£12.00	£20.00
2	$4.00	$12.00	$20.00	£2.50	£7.50	£12.50
3-10	$2.50	$7.50	$12.50	£1.50	£4.50	£7.50
11-20	$2.00	$6.00	$10.00	£1.20	£3.60	£6.00
21-36	$1.50	$4.50	$7.50	£1.00	£3.00	£5.00
37 John Byrne's 1st professional work (4 text illustrations) (May 1975)						
	$2.50	$7.50	$12.50	£1.50	£4.50	£7.50
38-41	$1.50	$4.50	$7.50	£1.00	£3.00	£5.00
42 John Byrne art (2pgs)						
	$1.80	$5.25	$9.00	£1.20	£3.60	£6.00
43-50	$1.50	$4.50	$7.50	£1.00	£3.00	£5.00
Title Value:	$97.80	$293.25	$489.00	£61.00	£183.60	£306.00

Note: most issues distributed in the U.K.

FLINTSTONES IN 3-D, THE
Blackthorne; (3-D Series #19,#22,#36,#42); 1 Apr 1987-4 Feb 1988

	$Good	$Fine	$N.Mint	£Good	£Fine	£N.Mint
1 ND all with bound-in 3-D glasses (25% less if without glasses)						
	$0.45	$1.35	$2.25	£0.30	£0.90	£1.50
2 ND	$0.45	$1.35	$2.25	£0.30	£0.90	£1.50
3 ND scarce in the U.K.						
	$0.45	$1.35	$2.25	£0.40	£1.20	£2.00
4 ND	$0.45	$1.35	$2.25	£0.30	£0.90	£1.50
Title Value:	$1.80	$5.40	$9.00	£1.30	£3.90	£6.50

FLINTSTONES, THE
Dell/Gold Key; 2 Nov/Dec 1961-60 Sep 1970

	$Good	$Fine	$N.Mint	£Good	£Fine	£N.Mint
2	$11.00	$34.00	$67.50	£7.50	£22.50	£45.00
3-6	$7.50	$22.50	$45.00	£5.00	£15.00	£30.00

Flaming Carrot #1

Flash #218

Flash Gordon #31

MINT = 100% / NEAR MINT (inc. +/-) = 90–99% / VERY FINE (inc. +/-) = 75–89% / FINE (inc. +/-) = 55–74%
VERY GOOD (inc. +/-) = 35–54% / GOOD (inc. +/-) = 15–34% / FAIR = 5–14% / POOR = 1–4%

343

(FLINTSTONES continued)

	$Good	$Fine	$N.Mint	£Good	£Fine	£N.Mint
7 1st Gold Key issue	$7.50	$22.50	$45.00	£5.00	£15.00	£30.00
8-10	$6.00	$18.00	$36.00	£4.00	£12.00	£24.00
11 1st Pebbles	$10.00	$30.00	$60.00	£6.25	£18.50	£37.50
12-15	$4.50	$13.50	$27.00	£3.00	£9.00	£18.00
16 1st Bamm-Bamm	$6.00	$18.00	$36.00	£4.00	£12.00	£24.00
17-20	$4.50	$13.50	$27.00	£3.00	£9.00	£18.00
21-30	$4.50	$13.50	$22.50	£3.00	£9.00	£15.00
31-33	$3.75	$11.00	$18.75	£2.50	£7.50	£12.50
34 1st appearance The Great Gazoo	$3.75	$11.00	$18.75	£2.50	£7.50	£12.50
35-40	$3.75	$11.00	$18.75	£2.50	£7.50	£12.50
41-60	$3.00	$9.00	$15.00	£2.00	£6.00	£10.00
Title Value:	$261.00	$781.50	$1425.00	£173.75	£521.00	£947.50

Note: all distributed on the news-stands in the U.K. **Note also:** issue #1 in Dell Giant #48

FLINTSTONES, THE
Marvel Comics Group, TV; 1 Oct 1977-9 Feb 1979

	$Good	$Fine	$N.Mint	£Good	£Fine	£N.Mint
1-9 ND	$0.15	$0.45	$0.75	£0.10	£0.35	£0.60
Title Value:	$1.35	$4.05	$6.75	£0.90	£3.15	£5.40

Note: see also Yogi Bear.

FLIPPER
Gold Key, TV; 1 Apr 1966-3 November 1967

	$Good	$Fine	$N.Mint	£Good	£Fine	£N.Mint
1 distributed in the U.K.	$9.00	$27.00	$45.00	£5.00	£15.00	£25.00
2-3 distributed in the U.K.	$5.50	$16.50	$27.50	£3.00	£9.00	£15.00
Title Value:	$20.00	$60.00	$100.00	£11.00	£33.00	£55.00

FLIPPITY AND FLOP
National Periodical Publications; 1 Dec 1951/Jan 1952-46 Aug/Oct 1959; 47 Sep 1960

	$Good	$Fine	$N.Mint	£Good	£Fine	£N.Mint
1 very scarce in the U.K.	$21.00	$62.50	$150.00	£13.50	£41.00	£95.00
2 scarce in the U.K.	$12.00	$36.00	$85.00	£7.75	£23.50	£55.00
3-5 scarce in the U.K.	$9.25	$28.00	$65.00	£5.50	£17.00	£40.00
6-10	$7.00	$21.00	$50.00	£4.25	£12.50	£30.00
11-20	$6.00	$18.00	$42.50	£3.55	£10.50	£25.00
21-46	$5.25	$16.00	$32.50	£3.30	£10.00	£20.00
1st official distribution in the U.K.						
47	$5.25	$16.00	$32.50	£3.30	£10.00	£20.00
Title Value:	$297.50	$899.50	$1982.50	£183.60	£553.00	£1210.00

FLOATERS
Dark Horse,MS; 1 Sep 1993-5 Jan 1994

	$Good	$Fine	$N.Mint	£Good	£Fine	£N.Mint
1-5 ND script by Cinque Lee (Spike's brother)	$0.45	$1.35	$2.25	£0.30	£0.90	£1.50
Title Value:	$2.25	$6.75	$11.25	£1.50	£4.50	£7.50

FLOOD RELIEF
Malibu/American Red Cross,OS; 1 Jan 1994

1 ND special charity comic produced for American Flood Relief agencies; features Ultraverse characters and available only through the mail; no price on cover, 15,000 copies

	$Good	$Fine	$N.Mint	£Good	£Fine	£N.Mint
	$0.90	$2.70	$4.50	£0.50	£1.50	£2.50
Title Value:	$0.90	$2.70	$4.50	£0.50	£1.50	£2.50

FLOYD FARLAND, CITIZEN OF THE FUTURE
Eclipse; Graphic Novel; 11 1987

	$Good	$Fine	$N.Mint	£Good	£Fine	£N.Mint
11 ND Chris Ware story/art	$0.60	$1.80	$3.00	£0.40	£1.20	£2.00
Title Value:	$0.60	$1.80	$3.00	£0.40	£1.20	£2.00

FLY
DC Comics/Impact; 1 Aug 1991-17 Dec 1992

	$Good	$Fine	$N.Mint	£Good	£Fine	£N.Mint
1-7	$0.15	$0.45	$0.75	£0.10	£0.35	£0.60
8 X-over with The Comet #10	$0.15	$0.45	$0.75	£0.10	£0.35	£0.60
9-17	$0.15	$0.45	$0.75	£0.10	£0.35	£0.60
Title Value:	$2.55	$7.65	$12.75	£1.70	£5.95	£10.20

Note: Archie Comics character acquired by DC. Events fall outside DC Universe continuity

FLY ANNUAL
DC Comics/Impact; 1 Jun 1992

1 64pgs, Earthquest part 5, ties into Crusaders #1 (see other Impact annuals), trading cards included

	$Good	$Fine	$N.Mint	£Good	£Fine	£N.Mint
	$0.30	$0.90	$1.50	£0.20	£0.60	£1.00
Title Value:	$0.30	$0.90	$1.50	£0.20	£0.60	£1.00

FLY IN MY EYE
(see Arcane Comix)

FLY, ADVENTURES OF THE
Archie; 1 Aug 1959-30 Oct 1964
(becomes Flyman)

	$Good	$Fine	$N.Mint	£Good	£Fine	£N.Mint
1 scarce in the U.K. origin The Fly, Joe Simon and Jack Kirby art	$52.50	$155.00	$425.00	£34.00	£100.00	£275.00
2 rare in the U.K., Jack Kirby, Williamson art	$36.00	$105.00	$250.00	£21.00	£62.50	£150.00
3 rare in the U.K., origin retold	$29.00	$85.00	$200.00	£17.50	£52.50	£125.00
4 scarce in the U.K. Neal Adams art (1 panel), second ever published art ?	$14.00	$43.00	$100.00	£9.25	£28.00	£65.00
5 rare in the U.K.	$10.50	$33.00	$65.00	£7.50	£22.50	£45.00
6-10	$10.00	$31.00	$62.50	£6.50	£20.00	£40.00
11-13	$6.25	$18.50	$37.50	£4.15	£12.50	£25.00
14 1st appearance Flygirl	$9.00	$28.00	$55.00	£5.75	£17.50	£35.00
15	$6.25	$18.50	$37.50	£4.15	£12.50	£25.00
16-20	$5.75	$17.50	$35.00	£3.30	£10.00	£20.00
21-30	$4.15	$12.50	$25.00	£2.90	£8.75	£17.50

(FLY, ADVENTURES OF THE continued)

	$Good	$Fine	$N.Mint	£Good	£Fine	£N.Mint
Title Value:	$296.25	$890.50	$1982.50	£189.60	£570.50	£1270.00

Note: all distributed on the news-stands in the U.K.

FLY, THE
Archie (Red Circle); 1 May 1983-3 Oct 1984

	$Good	$Fine	$N.Mint	£Good	£Fine	£N.Mint
1 ND origin Shield, Mr. Justice appears	$0.30	$0.90	$1.50	£0.20	£0.60	£1.00
2 ND Flygirl appears, Steranko cover	$0.30	$0.90	$1.50	£0.20	£0.60	£1.00
3-4 ND Steve Ditko art	$0.30	$0.90	$1.50	£0.20	£0.60	£1.00
5-7 ND	$0.30	$0.90	$1.50	£0.20	£0.60	£1.00
8 ND Steve Ditko cover and art	$0.30	$0.90	$1.50	£0.20	£0.60	£1.00
9 ND	$0.30	$0.90	$1.50	£0.20	£0.60	£1.00
Title Value:	$2.70	$8.10	$13.50	£1.80	£5.40	£9.00

FLYMAN
Archie; 31 May 1965-39 Sep 1966
(previously Fly; becomes Mighty Comics Presents)

	$Good	$Fine	$N.Mint	£Good	£Fine	£N.Mint
31 distributed in the U.K.	$5.00	$15.00	$30.00	£3.30	£10.00	£20.00
32-33 distributed in the U.K.	$4.55	$13.50	$27.50	£2.90	£8.75	£17.50
34-39 distributed in the U.K.	$3.30	$10.00	$20.00	£2.05	£6.25	£12.50
Title Value:	$33.90	$102.00	$205.00	£21.40	£65.00	£130.00

FOODANG
Continuum Comics; 1 Jul 1994

	$Good	$Fine	$N.Mint	£Good	£Fine	£N.Mint
1 ND 40pgs, Michael Duggan script and art; black and white	$0.35	$1.05	$1.75	£0.25	£0.75	£1.25
Title Value:	$0.35	$1.05	$1.75	£0.25	£0.75	£1.25

FOODANG (2ND SERIES)
August House; 1 Jan 1995-present

	$Good	$Fine	$N.Mint	£Good	£Fine	£N.Mint
1 ND 40pgs, Michael Duggan script and art with bound-in The Dark character card by Bart Sears	$0.35	$1.05	$1.75	£0.25	£0.75	£1.25
1 ND Special Edition (Jun 1995) - foil cover; 1,000 copies with certificate	$0.40	$1.20	$2.00	£0.25	£0.75	£1.25
2 ND foil-enhanced cover by Ben Edlund	$0.35	$1.05	$1.75	£0.25	£0.75	£1.25
3 ND foil-enhanced cover by Michael Duggan and Mike Sagara	$0.35	$1.05	$1.75	£0.25	£0.75	£1.25
4 ND	$0.35	$1.05	$1.75	£0.25	£0.75	£1.25
Title Value:	$1.80	$5.40	$9.00	£1.25	£3.75	£6.25

Note: originally solicited by Continuum Comics six months earlier. The contents were exactly the same but published now in full colour

FOOLKILLER
Marvel Comics Group,MS; 1 Oct 1990-10 Jul 1991
(see Omega the Unknown)

	$Good	$Fine	$N.Mint	£Good	£Fine	£N.Mint
1-7 ND	$0.30	$0.90	$1.50	£0.20	£0.60	£1.00
8 ND Spiderman appears	$0.30	$0.90	$1.50	£0.20	£0.60	£1.00
9 ND	$0.30	$0.90	$1.50	£0.20	£0.60	£1.00
10 ND scarce	$0.30	$0.90	$1.50	£0.20	£0.60	£1.00
Title Value:	$3.00	$9.00	$15.00	£2.00	£6.00	£10.00

Note: Mature Readers

FOOM
Marvel Comics Group; 1 Feb 1973-22 Autumn 1978
(see Amazing World of DC Comics)

	$Good	$Fine	$N.Mint	£Good	£Fine	£N.Mint
1 ND scarce in the U.K. 30pgs, Fantastic Four index/article; puzzles, games, advance information on Marvel comics begin	$9.00	$27.00	$45.00	£6.00	£18.00	£30.00
1 as above with original packaging containing free gifts; Steranko poster, 6 Marvel mini-labels, FOOM members card	$15.00	$45.00	$75.00	£10.00	£30.00	£50.00
2 ND Hulk index/article, Steranko cover	$6.00	$18.00	$30.00	£4.00	£12.00	£20.00
3 ND Spiderman index/article	$3.75	$11.00	$18.75	£2.50	£7.50	£12.50
4 ND	$1.50	$4.50	$7.50	£1.00	£3.00	£5.00
5 ND The Thing featured in article	$1.85	$5.50	$9.38	£1.25	£3.75	£6.25
6 ND	$1.50	$4.50	$7.50	£1.00	£3.00	£5.00
7 ND The Avengers	$1.50	$4.50	$7.50	£1.00	£3.00	£5.00
8 ND Captain America	$1.50	$4.50	$7.50	£1.00	£3.00	£5.00
9 ND Silver Surfer issue	$2.55	$7.50	$12.75	£1.70	£5.00	£8.50
10 ND X-Men issue	$1.80	$5.25	$9.00	£1.20	£3.60	£6.00
11 ND features a returning-to-Marvel Jack Kirby, John Byrne cover and centrefold (wrongly credited as Jack Byrne!)	$1.10	$3.35	$5.62	£0.75	£2.25	£3.75
12 ND The Avengers	$1.50	$4.50	$7.50	£1.00	£3.00	£5.00
13 ND Daredevil	$1.50	$4.50	$7.50	£1.00	£3.00	£5.00
14 ND Conan	$1.10	$3.35	$5.62	£0.75	£2.25	£3.75
15 ND Howard the Duck	$1.10	$3.35	$5.62	£0.75	£2.25	£3.75
16 ND	$1.10	$3.35	$5.62	£0.75	£2.25	£3.75
17 ND Stan Lee interview/profile	$1.10	$3.35	$5.62	£0.75	£2.25	£3.75
18 ND John Romita interview/profile						

	$Good	$Fine	$N.Mint	£Good	£Fine	£N.Mint
	$1.05	$3.15	$5.25	£0.70	£2.10	£3.50
19 ND Defenders	$0.90	$2.70	$4.50	£0.60	£1.80	£3.00
20 ND Edgar Rice Burroughs/John Carter of Mars/Tarzan						
	$1.05	$3.15	$5.25	£0.70	£2.10	£3.50
21 Sci-Fi/Star Wars issue						
	$1.50	$4.50	$7.50	£1.00	£3.00	£5.00
22 ND Marvel Heroes on TV						
	$0.90	$2.70	$4.50	£0.60	£1.80	£3.00
Title Value:	$59.85	$179.20	$299.98	£40.00	£119.90	£200.00

FOOZLE
(see Cap'n Quick)

FOR LOVERS ONLY
Charlton; 60 Aug 1971-87 Nov 1976

	$Good	$Fine	$N.Mint	£Good	£Fine	£N.Mint
60-87	$0.25	$0.75	$1.25	£0.15	£0.45	£0.75
Title Value:	$7.00	$21.00	$35.00	£4.20	£12.60	£21.00

Note: sporadic distribution in the U.K.

FOR YOUR EYES ONLY
Marvel Comics Group, Film; 1,2 1981

	$Good	$Fine	$N.Mint	£Good	£Fine	£N.Mint
1-2 Chaykin art, adapts James Bond film						
	$0.30	$0.90	$1.50	£0.20	£0.60	£1.00
Title Value:	$0.60	$1.80	$3.00	£0.40	£1.20	£2.00

FORBIDDEN KINGDOM
Eastern; 1 1988-11 1989

	$Good	$Fine	$N.Mint	£Good	£Fine	£N.Mint
1-11 ND	$0.40	$1.20	$2.00	£0.25	£0.75	£1.25
Title Value:	$4.40	$13.20	$22.00	£2.75	£8.25	£13.75

FORBIDDEN PLANET
Innovation,MS; 1 May 1992-4 Oct 1992

	$Good	$Fine	$N.Mint	£Good	£Fine	£N.Mint
1-4 ND adaptation of film						
	$0.45	$1.35	$2.25	£0.30	£0.90	£1.50
Title Value:	$1.80	$5.40	$9.00	£1.20	£3.60	£6.00
Forbidden Planet: The Saga of the Krell (May 1993)						

collects mini-series plus information on film; intro by Leslie Nielsen £1.20 £3.60 £6.00

FORBIDDEN TALES OF DARK MANSION
DC Comics; 5 May/Jun 1972-15 Feb/Mar 1974
(previously Dark Mansion of Forbidden Love)

	$Good	$Fine	$N.Mint	£Good	£Fine	£N.Mint
5 ND 52pgs	$1.00	$3.00	$5.00	£0.50	£1.50	£2.50
6 ND Jack Kirby art						
	$1.00	$3.00	$5.00	£0.50	£1.50	£2.50
7-10 ND	$1.00	$3.00	$5.00	£0.50	£1.50	£2.50
11-15 ND	$0.80	$2.40	$4.00	£0.40	£1.20	£2.00
Title Value:	$10.00	$30.00	$50.00	£5.00	£15.00	£25.00

ARTISTS
Nino in 8, 12, 15. Wood inks in 13.

FORBIDDEN WORLDS (1ST SERIES)
ACG; 84 Nov/Dec 1959-145 Aug 1967
(previous issues ND)

	$Good	$Fine	$N.Mint	£Good	£Fine	£N.Mint
84-90	$5.75	$17.50	$35.00	£3.30	£10.00	£20.00
91-93	$4.15	$12.50	$25.00	£2.50	£7.50	£15.00
94 Herbie appears						
	$8.25	$25.00	$50.00	£3.30	£10.00	£20.00
95-100	$4.15	$12.50	$25.00	£2.50	£7.50	£15.00
101-109	$3.30	$10.00	$20.00	£2.05	£6.25	£12.50
110 Herbie appears						
	$5.00	$15.00	$30.00	£2.50	£7.50	£15.00
111-113	$3.30	$10.00	$20.00	£2.05	£6.25	£12.50
114 Herbie appears						
	$4.15	$12.50	$25.00	£2.50	£7.50	£15.00
115	$3.30	$10.00	$20.00	£2.05	£6.25	£12.50
116 Herbie appears						
	$4.15	$12.50	$25.00	£2.50	£7.50	£15.00
117-120	$3.30	$10.00	$20.00	£2.05	£6.25	£12.50
121-124	$3.30	$10.00	$20.00	£1.65	£5.00	£10.00
125 1st appearance Magicman						
	$4.15	$12.50	$25.00	£2.05	£6.25	£12.50
126-130	$4.00	$12.00	$20.00	£2.00	£6.00	£10.00
131-136	$3.00	$9.00	$15.00	£1.80	£5.25	£9.00
137-138 Steve Ditko art						
	$3.00	$9.00	$15.00	£1.80	£5.25	£9.00
139	$3.00	$9.00	$15.00	£1.80	£5.25	£9.00
140 Steve Ditko art						
	$3.00	$9.00	$15.00	£1.80	£5.25	£9.00
141-145	$2.40	$7.00	$12.00	£1.50	£4.50	£7.50
Title Value:	$234.60	$707.50	$1355.00	£135.40	£407.50	£782.50

Note: all distributed on the news-stands in the U.K.

FORBIDDEN WORLDS (2ND SERIES)
A Plus Comics; 1 Jul 1993-1 1991

	$Good	$Fine	$N.Mint	£Good	£Fine	£N.Mint
1 ND 48pgs, two news stories plus Steve Ditko reprint						
	$0.45	$1.35	$2.25	£0.30	£0.90	£1.50
2 ND 48pgs, reprints 1st Herbie story						
	$0.45	$1.35	$2.25	£0.30	£0.90	£1.50
3 ND 48pgs, Williamson, Steve Ditko reprints featured						
	$0.45	$1.35	$2.25	£0.30	£0.90	£1.50
Title Value:	$1.35	$4.05	$6.75	£0.90	£2.70	£4.50

FORCE OF BUDDHA'S PALM
Jademan; 1 Aug 1988-56 Mar 1993

	$Good	$Fine	$N.Mint	£Good	£Fine	£N.Mint
1 ND	$0.70	$2.10	$3.50	£0.50	£1.50	£2.50
2-5 ND	$0.60	$1.80	$3.00	£0.40	£1.20	£2.00
6-10 ND	$0.45	$1.35	$2.25	£0.30	£0.90	£1.50
11-20 ND	$0.35	$1.05	$1.75	£0.25	£0.75	£1.25
21-30 ND	$0.30	$0.90	$1.50	£0.20	£0.60	£1.00
31-56 ND	$0.25	$0.75	$1.25	£0.15	£0.45	£0.75
Title Value:	$18.35	$55.05	$91.75	£12.00	£36.00	£60.00

FORCE WORKS
Marvel Comics Group; 1 Jul 1993-present

	$Good	$Fine	$N.Mint	£Good	£Fine	£N.Mint
1 48pgs, Abnett & Lanning script, Tenney & Garcia art begins; Iron Man, Scarlet Witch, Spider-Woman, US Agent, Wonder Man and Century begin; pop-up cover						
	$0.80	$2.40	$4.00	£0.50	£1.50	£2.50
1 ND Ashcan Edition, 12pgs, black and white						
	$0.30	$0.90	$1.50	£0.20	£0.60	£1.00
2-5	$0.30	$0.90	$1.50	£0.20	£0.60	£1.00
5 ND pre-bagged with acetate print from Marvel Action Hour TV series; neon ink cover						
	$0.60	$1.80	$3.00	£0.40	£1.20	£2.00
6 Hands of the Mandarin part 1, continued in War Machine #9						
	$0.30	$0.90	$1.50	£0.20	£0.60	£1.00
7 Hands of the Mandarin part 4, continued in War Machine #10						
	$0.30	$0.90	$1.50	£0.20	£0.60	£1.00
8 Quicksilver, Captain America and Hank Pym appear						
	$0.30	$0.90	$1.50	£0.20	£0.60	£1.00
9-10	$0.30	$0.90	$1.50	£0.20	£0.60	£1.00
11 X-over with War Machine #14						
	$0.30	$0.90	$1.50	£0.20	£0.60	£1.00
12 48pgs, flip-book format, continued in War Machine #15 and Iron Man #317						
	$0.45	$1.35	$2.25	£0.30	£0.90	£1.50
13-14 The Avengers guest-star						
	$0.30	$0.90	$1.50	£0.20	£0.60	£1.00
15	$0.30	$0.90	$1.50	£0.20	£0.60	£1.00
16-17 Avengers: The Crossing tie-in						
	$0.30	$0.90	$1.50	£0.20	£0.60	£1.00
18 Avengers: The Crossing tie-in; Hawkeye, War Machine and the Avengers appear						
	$0.30	$0.90	$1.50	£0.20	£0.60	£1.00
19 Avengers: The Crossing tie-in; Hawkeye and the Avengers appear						
	$0.30	$0.90	$1.50	£0.20	£0.60	£1.00
20 Avengers: Timeslide tie-in						
	$0.30	$0.90	$1.50	£0.20	£0.60	£1.00
21	$0.30	$0.90	$1.50	£0.20	£0.60	£1.00
Title Value:	$7.85	$23.55	$39.25	£5.20	£15.60	£26.00

FORD FAIRLANE
DC Comics, MS, Film; 1 May 1990-4 Aug 1990

	$Good	$Fine	$N.Mint	£Good	£Fine	£N.Mint
1-4 based on 20th Century Fox film						
	$0.25	$0.75	$1.25	£0.15	£0.45	£0.75
Title Value:	$1.00	$3.00	$5.00	£0.60	£1.80	£3.00

Note: New Format

FOREVER PEOPLE
DC Comics; 1 Feb/Mar 1971-11 Oct/Nov 1972

	$Good	$Fine	$N.Mint	£Good	£Fine	£N.Mint
1 Jack Kirby art begins, 1st full appearance Darkseid (see Jimmy Olsen #134 and New Gods #1)						
	$8.25	$25.00	$50.00	£4.15	£12.50	£25.00
2	$7.00	$21.00	$35.00	£3.00	£9.00	£15.00
3	$6.50	$19.50	$32.50	£2.00	£6.00	£10.00
4-5 52pgs, Joe Simon & Jack Kirby back-up reprints						
	$6.50	$19.50	$32.50	£2.00	£6.00	£10.00
6-9 52pgs, Joe Simon & Jack Kirby back-up reprints						
	$3.50	$10.50	$17.50	£1.30	£3.90	£6.50
10 Deadman X-over						
	$3.50	$10.50	$17.50	£1.30	£3.90	£6.50
11	$3.50	$10.50	$17.50	£1.30	£3.90	£6.50
Title Value:	$55.75	$167.50	$287.50	£20.95	£62.90	£109.00

FOREVER PEOPLE (LIMITED SERIES)
DC Comics,MS; 1 Feb 1988-6 Jul 1988

	$Good	$Fine	$N.Mint	£Good	£Fine	£N.Mint
1-6	$0.25	$0.75	$1.25	£0.15	£0.45	£0.75
Title Value:	$1.50	$4.50	$7.50	£0.90	£2.70	£4.50

Note: Deluxe Format

FORGOTTEN REALMS
DC Comics; 1 Sep 1989-25 Sep 1991

	$Good	$Fine	$N.Mint	£Good	£Fine	£N.Mint
1	$0.60	$1.80	$3.00	£0.40	£1.20	£2.00
2-5	$0.45	$1.35	$2.25	£0.30	£0.90	£1.50
6-15	$0.40	$1.20	$2.00	£0.25	£0.75	£1.25
16-19 Mad Gods and Paladins story						
	$0.30	$0.90	$1.50	£0.20	£0.60	£1.00
20-25	$0.30	$0.90	$1.50	£0.20	£0.60	£1.00
Title Value:	$9.40	$28.20	$47.00	£6.10	£18.30	£30.50

Note: New Format

FORGOTTEN REALMS ANNUAL
DC Comics; 1 Jan 1991

	$Good	$Fine	$N.Mint	£Good	£Fine	£N.Mint
1 painted cover by Gil Kane						
	$0.50	$1.50	$2.50	£0.30	£0.90	£1.50
Title Value:	$0.50	$1.50	$2.50	£0.30	£0.90	£1.50

FOUR COLOR (SERIES I)
Dell; 1 Sep 1939-25 1942

	$Good	$Fine	$N.Mint	£Good	£Fine	£N.Mint
1 rare in the U.K., Dick Tracy by Chester Gould; probably no more than 120 copies in any grade in existence						
	$600.00	$1800.00	$6000.00	£400.00	£1200.00	£4000.00
2 rare in the U.K., Don Winslow of the Navy						
	$150.00	$450.00	$1050.00	£100.00	£300.00	£700.00
3 scarce in the U.K. Myra North - Special Nurse						
	$90.00	$270.00	$630.00	£60.00	£180.00	£420.00
4 rare in the U.K. Donald Duck, script and art by Al Taliaferro; classic cover						
	$850.00	$2550.00	$8500.00	£570.00	£1725.00	£5775.00
5 Smilin' Jack, Mosely art						
	$75.00	$225.00	$525.00	£50.00	£150.00	£350.00
6 scarce in the U.S, very scarce in the U.K. Dick Tracy by Chester Gould						
	$150.00	$450.00	$1050.00	£100.00	£300.00	£700.00
7 Gang Busters	$45.00	$135.00	$315.00	£30.00	£90.00	£210.00
8 scarce in the U.K. Dick Tracy by Chester Gould						
	$85.00	$255.00	$595.00	£60.00	£180.00	£420.00
9 Terry and the Pirates						

Columns: $Good | $Fine | $N.Mint | £Good | £Fine | £N.Mint

Title	$Good	$Fine	$N.Mint	£Good	£Fine	£N.Mint
	$75.00	$225.00	$525.00	£50.00	£150.00	£350.00
10 Smilin' Jack	$65.00	$195.00	$455.00	£45.00	£135.00	£315.00
11 Smitty	$45.00	$135.00	$315.00	£30.00	£90.00	£210.00
12 Little Orphan Annie; reprints from newspaper strips	$60.00	$180.00	$420.00	£40.00	£120.00	£280.00
13 Walt Disney's The Reluctant Dragon; plus Donald Duck and Goofy stories	$180.00	$540.00	$1260.00	£120.00	£360.00	£840.00
14 Moon Mullins	$40.00	$120.00	$280.00	£26.00	£77.50	£182.00
15 Tillie the Toiler	$40.00	$120.00	$280.00	£26.00	£77.50	£182.00
16 Mickey Mouse Outwits the Phantom Blot; uncommon in high grade	$1100.00	$3300.00	$9900.00	£770.00	£2300.00	£6930.00
17 Walt Disney's Dumbo the Flying Elephant; plus Donald Duck, Mickey Mouse and Pluto stories	$215.00	$640.00	$1505.00	£145.00	£435.00	£1015.00
18 Jiggs and Maggie	$50.00	$150.00	$350.00	£33.00	£97.50	£231.00
19 Barney Google and Snuffy Smith; the sub-title "Four Color Comic" now appears on the cover	$45.00	$135.00	$315.00	£30.00	£90.00	£210.00
20 Tiny Tim	$35.00	$105.00	$245.00	£23.00	£67.50	£161.00
21 Dick Tracy by Chester Gould	$70.00	$210.00	$490.00	£45.00	£135.00	£315.00
22 Don Winslow of the Navy	$36.00	$105.00	$252.00	£24.00	£70.00	£168.00
23 Gang Busters	$32.00	$95.00	$224.00	£21.00	£62.50	£147.00
24 Captain Easy	$55.00	$165.00	$385.00	£37.00	£110.00	£259.00
25 Popeye	$95.00	$285.00	$665.00	£65.00	£195.00	£455.00
Title Value:	$4283.00	$12840.00	$36531.00	£2900.00	£8697.50	£24825.00

Note: not distributed on the news-stands in the U.K. and generally at least scarce/very scarce in the U.K.

FOUR COLOR (SERIES II)
Dell; 1 1942-1354 Apr 1962

Title	$Good	$Fine	$N.Mint	£Good	£Fine	£N.Mint
1 Little Jo; newspaper strip reprints	$55.00	$165.00	$385.00	£36.00	£105.00	£255.00
2 Harold Teen; newspaper strip reprints	$30.00	$90.00	$210.00	£20.00	£60.00	£140.00
3 Alley Oop; newspaper strip reprints	$55.00	$165.00	$385.00	£36.00	£105.00	£255.00
4 Smilin' Jack; Mosely art	$55.00	$165.00	$385.00	£36.00	£105.00	£255.00
5 Raggedy Ann and Andy; Mosely art	$55.00	$165.00	$385.00	£36.00	£105.00	£255.00
6 Smitty; newspaper strip reprints	$25.00	$75.00	$175.00	£16.00	£49.00	£115.00
7 Smokey Stover; newspaper strip reprints	$40.00	$120.00	$280.00	£26.00	£77.50	£185.00
8 Tillie the Toiler; newspaper strip reprints	$25.00	$75.00	$175.00	£16.00	£49.00	£115.00
9 Donald Duck Finds Pirate Gold; classic art by Carl Barks and a great cover	$750.00	$2250.00	$7500.00	£550.00	£1650.00	£5500.00
10 Flash Gordon by Alex Raymond	$70.00	$210.00	$490.00	£46.00	£135.00	£325.00
11 Wash Tubbs; newspaper strip reprints	$35.00	$105.00	$245.00	£23.50	£70.00	£165.00
12 Walt Disney's Bambi	$70.00	$210.00	$490.00	£46.00	£135.00	£325.00
13 Mr. District Attorney (later a classic DC title); newspaper strip reprints	$32.00	$95.00	$224.00	£21.00	£62.50	£150.00
14 Smilin' Jack; Mosely art	$42.00	$125.00	$294.00	£28.00	£82.50	£195.00
15 Felix The Cat; Otto Messmer cover and art	$85.00	$255.00	$595.00	£55.00	£165.00	£395.00
16 Porky Pig in "The Secret of the Haunted House"	$95.00	$285.00	$665.00	£62.50	£190.00	£445.00
17 Popeye; Segar art	$75.00	$225.00	$525.00	£50.00	£150.00	£350.00
18 Little Orphan Annie's Junior Commandores - patriotic flag cover	$45.00	$135.00	$315.00	£30.00	£90.00	£210.00
19 Walt Disney's Thumper meets The Seven Dwarfs	$70.00	$210.00	$490.00	£46.00	£135.00	£325.00
20 Barney Baxter; newspaper strip reprints	$28.00	$82.50	$196.00	£18.50	£55.00	£130.00
21 Oswald the Rabbit; Chester Gould cover and art	$65.00	$195.00	$455.00	£44.00	£130.00	£305.00
22 Tillie the Toiler; newspaper reprints	$20.00	$60.00	$140.00	£13.00	£40.00	£92.50
23 Raggedy Ann and Andy	$42.00	$125.00	$295.00	£28.00	£82.50	£195.00
24 Gang Busters; Crane art	$32.00	$95.00	$224.00	£21.00	£62.50	£150.00
25 Andy Panda; from Walter Lantz cartoon	$70.00	$210.00	$490.00	£46.00	£135.00	£325.00
26 Popeye; Segar art	$75.00	$225.00	$525.00	£50.00	£150.00	£350.00
27 Walt Disney's Mickey Mouse and the Seven Coloured Terror	$110.00	$330.00	$770.00	£72.50	£215.00	£510.00
28 Wash Tubbs; newspaper reprints	$25.00	$75.00	$175.00	£16.00	£49.00	£115.00
29 Donald Duck and The Mummy's Ring; Carl Barks art	$650.00	$1950.00	$6500.00	£435.00	£1300.00	£4350.00
30 Bambi's Children	$75.00	$225.00	$525.00	£50.00	£150.00	£350.00
31 Moon Mullins; newspaper reprints	$22.00	$65.00	$154.00	£15.00	£45.00	£105.00
32 Smitty	$20.00	$60.00	$140.00	£13.00	£40.00	£92.50
33 Bug's Bunny as Public Nuisance No. 1	$75.00	$225.00	$525.00	£50.00	£150.00	£350.00
34 Dick Tracy; Chester Gould art	$55.00	$165.00	$385.00	£36.00	£105.00	£255.00
35 Smokey Stover; newspaper reprints	$20.00	$60.00	$140.00	£13.00	£40.00	£92.50
36 Smilin' Jack; Moseley art	$25.00	$75.00	$175.00	£16.00	£49.00	£115.00
37 Bringing Up Father; newspaper rreprints	$22.00	$65.00	$154.00	£15.00	£45.00	£105.00
38 Roy Rogers; photo cover (great shirt!); 1st ever Western comic	$140.00	$420.00	$980.00	£92.50	£275.00	£650.00
39 Oswald the Rabbit	$50.00	$150.00	$350.00	£34.00	£100.00	£235.00
40 Barney Google and Snuffy Smith; newspaper reprints	$25.00	$75.00	$175.00	£16.00	£49.00	£115.00
41 Mother Goose and Nursery Rhyme Comics; Walt Kelly art	$28.00	$82.50	$196.00	£18.50	£55.00	£130.00
42 Tiny Tim; newspaper reprints	$22.00	$65.00	$154.00	£15.00	£45.00	£105.00
43 Popeye; newspaper reprints; Segar art	$40.00	$120.00	$280.00	£26.00	£77.50	£185.00
44 Terry and the Pirates; newspaper reprints; Milton Caniff cover and art	$50.00	$150.00	$350.00	£34.00	£100.00	£235.00
45 Raggedy Ann	$32.00	$95.00	$224.00	£21.00	£62.50	£150.00
46 Felix the Cat and The Haunted Castle; Otto Messmer cover and art	$55.00	$165.00	$385.00	£36.00	£105.00	£255.00
47 Gene Autry in The Ghost Mine	$50.00	$150.00	$350.00	£34.00	£100.00	£235.00
48 Porkie Pig of the Mounties; Carl Barks art	$140.00	$420.00	$980.00	£92.50	£275.00	£650.00
49 Snow White and the Seven Dwarfs	$85.00	$255.00	$595.00	£55.00	£165.00	£395.00
50 Fairy Tale Parade; Walt Kelly art	$32.00	$95.00	$224.00	£21.00	£62.50	£150.00
51 Bugs Bunny Finds The Lost Tresure	$40.00	$120.00	$280.00	£26.00	£77.50	£185.00
52 Little Orphan Annie; strip reprints	$38.00	$110.00	$266.00	£25.00	£75.00	£175.00
53 Wash Tubbs; strip reprints	$20.00	$60.00	$140.00	£13.00	£40.00	£92.50
54 Andy Panda	$40.00	$120.00	$280.00	£26.00	£77.50	£185.00
55 Tillie the Toiler; strip reprints	$16.00	$48.00	$112.00	£10.50	£32.00	£75.00
56 Dick Tracy; Chester Gould cover and art	$40.00	$120.00	$280.00	£26.00	£77.50	£185.00
57 Gene Autry; scarce, "Riders of the Range"	$42.00	$125.00	$294.00	£28.00	£82.50	£195.00
58 Smilin' Jack; Mosely art	$37.00	$110.00	$259.00	£25.00	£75.00	£175.00
59 Mother Goose and Nuresy Rhyme Comics; Walt Kelly cover and art	$22.00	$65.00	$154.00	£15.00	£45.00	£105.00
60 Tiny Folks Funnies	$18.00	$52.50	$126.00	£12.00	£36.00	£85.00
61 Santa Claus Funnies; Walt Kelly cover and art	$27.00	$80.00	$189.00	£17.50	£52.50	£125.00
62 Donald Duck in Frozen Gold; Carl Barks cover and art	$230.00	$690.00	$1610.00	£150.00	£460.00	£1075.00
63 Roy Rogers; photo cover	$55.00	$165.00	$385.00	£36.00	£105.00	£255.00
64 Smokey Stover; strip reprints	$17.00	$50.00	$119.00	£11.00	£34.00	£80.00
65 Smitty; strip reprints	$17.00	$50.00	$119.00	£11.00	£34.00	£80.00
66 Gene Autry; Marsh art	$42.00	$125.00	$294.00	£28.00	£82.50	£195.00
67 Oswald the Rabbit	$20.00	$60.00	$140.00	£13.00	£40.00	£92.50
68 Mother Goose and Nursery Rhyme Comics; Walt Kelly cover and art	$20.00	$60.00	$140.00	£13.00	£40.00	£92.50
69 Fairy Tale Parade; Walt Kelly cover and art	$32.00	$95.00	$224.00	£21.00	£62.50	£150.00
70 Popeye and Wimpy; newspaper strip reprints	$32.00	$95.00	$224.00	£21.00	£62.50	£150.00
71 Walt Disney's Three Caballeros; Walt Kelly cover and art	$110.00	$330.00	$770.00	£72.50	£215.00	£510.00
72 Raggedy Ann	$30.00	$90.00	$210.00	£20.00	£60.00	£140.00
73 The Gumps	$15.00	$45.00	$105.00	£10.00	£30.00	£70.00
74 Marge's Little Lulu (1st appearance); J. Stanley cover and art	$125.00	$375.00	$875.00	£82.50	£245.00	£580.00
75 Gene Autrey and the Wildcat; Marsh art	$35.00	$105.00	$245.00	£23.50	£70.00	£165.00
76 Little Orphan Annie; strip reprints	$30.00	$90.00	$210.00	£20.00	£60.00	£140.00
77 Felix the Cat; Otto Messmer cover and art	$45.00	$135.00	$315.00	£30.00	£90.00	£210.00
78 Porky Pig and the Bandit Twins	$28.00	$82.50	$196.00	£18.50	£55.00	£130.00
79 Walt Disney's Mickey Mouse in The Riddle of the Red Hat; Carl Barks cover and art	$150.00	$450.00	$1050.00	£100.00	£300.00	£700.00

# / Description	$Good	$Fine	$N.Mint	£Good	£Fine	£N.Mint
80 Smilin' Jack; Mosley art	$20.00	$60.00	$140.00	£13.00	£40.00	£92.50
81 Moon Mullins; strip reprints	$15.00	$45.00	$105.00	£10.00	£30.00	£70.00
82 Lone Ranger; strip reprints	$45.00	$135.00	$315.00	£30.00	£90.00	£210.00
83 Gene Autrey in "Outlaw Trail" (most copies have #84 printed inside)	$35.00	$105.00	$245.00	£23.50	£70.00	£165.00
84 Flash Gordon; Alex Raymond newspaper srtip reprints	$45.00	$135.00	$315.00	£30.00	£90.00	£210.00
85 Andy Panda and The Mad Dog Mystery (most copies have #86 printed inside)	$18.00	$52.50	$126.00	£12.00	£36.00	£85.00
86 Roy Rogers; photo cover (most copies have #87 printed indside)	$40.00	$120.00	$280.00	£26.00	£77.50	£185.00
87 Fairy Tale Parade; Walt Kelly art	$35.00	$105.00	$245.00	£23.50	£70.00	£165.00
88 Bugs Bunny's Great Adventure (most copies have #83 printed inside)	$28.00	$82.50	$196.00	£18.50	£55.00	£130.00
89 Tillie the Toiler; strip reprints	$16.00	$48.00	$112.00	£10.50	£32.00	£75.00
90 Christmas with Mother Goose; Walt Kelly cover and art	$20.00	$60.00	$140.00	£13.00	£40.00	£92.50
91 Santa Claus Funnies; Walt Kelly cover and art	$22.00	$65.00	$154.00	£15.00	£45.00	£105.00
92 Waly Disney's The Wonderful Adventures of Pinocchio, Donald Duck appears; Walt Kelly cover and art	$95.00	$285.00	$665.00	£62.50	£190.00	£445.00
93 Gene Autrey in "The Bandit of Black Rock"; Marsh art	$30.00	$90.00	$210.00	£20.00	£60.00	£140.00
94 Winnie Winkle; strip reprints	$15.00	$45.00	$105.00	£10.00	£30.00	£70.00
95 Roy Rogers Comics; photo cover	$40.00	$120.00	$280.00	£26.00	£77.50	£185.00
96 Dick Tracy; Chester Gould cover and art	$30.00	$90.00	$210.00	£20.00	£60.00	£140.00
97 Marge's Little Lulu; J. Stanley cover and art	$57.50	$170.00	$406.00	£39.00	£115.00	£270.00
98 The Lone Ranger; strip reprints	$35.00	$105.00	$245.00	£23.50	£70.00	£165.00
99 Smitty; strip reprints	$15.00	$45.00	$105.00	£10.00	£30.00	£70.00
100 Gene Autrey Comics; photo cover; Marsh art	$30.00	$90.00	$210.00	£20.00	£60.00	£140.00
101 Terry and The Pirates; Milton Caniff cover and art	$30.00	$90.00	$210.00	£20.00	£60.00	£140.00
102 Oswald the Rabbit; Walt Kelly art (1pg)	$18.00	$52.50	$126.00	£12.00	£36.00	£85.00
103 Easter with Mother Goose; Walt Kelly cover and art	$25.00	$75.00	$175.00	£16.00	£49.00	£115.00
104 Fairy Tale Parade; Walt Kelly cover and art	$25.00	$75.00	$175.00	£16.00	£49.00	£115.00
105 Albert the Alligator and Pogo Possum (1st appearance); Walt Kelly cover and art	$90.00	$270.00	$630.00	£60.00	£180.00	£420.00
106 Tillie the Toiler; newspaper strip reprints	$15.00	$45.00	$105.00	£10.00	£30.00	£70.00
107 Little Orphan Annie; strip reprints	$25.00	$75.00	$175.00	£16.00	£49.00	£115.00
108 Donald Duck in "The Terror of the River"; Carl Barks art	$180.00	$540.00	$1260.00	£120.00	£360.00	£840.00
109 Roy Rogers Comics; photo cover	$30.00	$90.00	$210.00	£20.00	£60.00	£140.00
110 Marge's Little Lulu; Jack Stanley cover and art	$40.00	$120.00	$280.00	£26.00	£77.50	£185.00
111 Captain Easy; Crane art	$18.00	$52.50	$126.00	£12.00	£36.00	£85.00
112 Porky Pig's Adventure in Gopher Gulch	$18.00	$52.50	$126.00	£12.00	£36.00	£85.00
113 Popeye (has #114 on inside indicia)	$18.00	$52.50	$126.00	£12.00	£36.00	£85.00
114 Fairy Tale Parade; Walt Kelly cover and art	$25.00	$75.00	$175.00	£16.00	£49.00	£115.00
115 Marge's Little Lulu; Jack Stanley cover and art	$40.00	$120.00	$280.00	£26.00	£77.50	£185.00
116 Mickey Mouse and The House of Many Mysteries	$30.00	$90.00	$210.00	£20.00	£60.00	£140.00
117 Roy Rogers Comics; photo cover	$22.00	$65.00	$154.00	£15.00	£45.00	£105.00
118 The Lone Ranger; strip reprints	$32.00	$95.00	$224.00	£21.00	£62.50	£150.00
119 Felix the Cat; Otto Messmer cover and art	$40.00	$120.00	$280.00	£26.00	£77.50	£185.00
120 Marge's Little Lulu; Jack Stanley cover and art	$35.00	$105.00	$245.00	£23.50	£70.00	£165.00
121 Fairy Tale Parade	$15.00	$45.00	$105.00	£10.00	£30.00	£70.00
122 Henry (1st appearance - has #121 on inside indicia)	$15.00	$45.00	$105.00	£10.00	£30.00	£70.00
123 Bugs Bunny's Dangerous Venture	$18.00	$52.50	$126.00	£12.00	£36.00	£85.00
124 Roy Rogers Comics; photo cover	$22.00	$65.00	$154.00	£15.00	£45.00	£105.00
125 The Lone Ranger; strip reprints	$25.00	$75.00	$175.00	£16.00	£49.00	£115.00
126 Christmas with Mother Goose; Walt Kelly cover and art	$22.00	$65.00	$154.00	£15.00	£45.00	£105.00
127 Popeye	$18.00	$52.50	$126.00	£12.00	£36.00	£85.00
128 Santa Claus Funnies featuring "A Mouse in the House" by Walt Kelly	$18.00	$52.50	$126.00	£12.00	£36.00	£85.00
129 Walt Disney's Uncle Remus and His Tales of Brer Rabbit (1st appearance)	$45.00	$135.00	$315.00	£30.00	£90.00	£210.00
130 Andy Panda by Walter Lantz	$15.00	$45.00	$105.00	£10.00	£30.00	£70.00
131 Marge's Little Lulu; Jack Stanley cover and art	$35.00	$105.00	$245.00	£23.50	£70.00	£165.00
132 Tillie the Toiler; newspaper reprints	$13.00	$39.00	$91.00	£8.50	£26.00	£60.00
133 Dick Tracy; Chester Gould cover and art	$25.00	$75.00	$175.00	£16.00	£49.00	£115.00
134 Tarzan and the Devil Ogre; Marsh cover and art (has #136 inside)	$75.00	$225.00	$525.00	£50.00	£150.00	£350.00
135 Felix the Cat; Otto Messmer cover and art	$30.00	$90.00	$210.00	£20.00	£60.00	£140.00
136 The Lone Ranger; strip reprints	$25.00	$75.00	$175.00	£16.00	£49.00	£115.00
137 Roy Rogers Comics; photo cover	$22.00	$65.00	$154.00	£15.00	£45.00	£105.00
138 Smitty; strip reprints	$13.00	$39.00	$91.00	£8.50	£26.00	£60.00
139 Marge's Little Lulu; Jack Stanley cover and art	$32.00	$95.00	$224.00	£21.00	£62.50	£150.00
140 Easter with Mother Gosse; Walt Kelly cover and art	$18.00	$52.50	$126.00	£12.00	£36.00	£85.00
141 Mickey Mouse and the Submarine Pirates						

Forbidden Worlds #131

Four Color #9

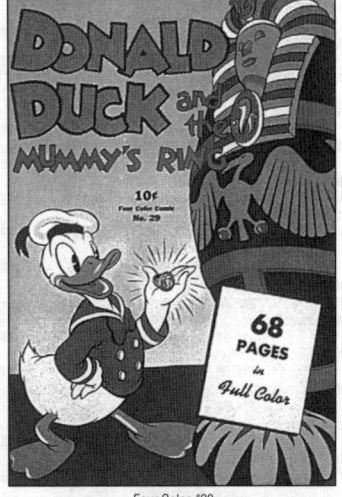

Four Color #29

# / Title	$Good	$Fine	$N.Mint	£Good	£Fine	£N.Mint
(continued from previous page)	$25.00	$75.00	$175.00	£16.00	£49.00	£115.00
142 Bugs Bunny and the Haunted Mountain	$18.00	$52.50	$126.00	£12.00	£36.00	£85.00
143 Oswald the Rabbit and the Prehistoric Egg	$13.00	$39.00	$91.00	£8.50	£26.00	£60.00
144 Roy Rogers Comics; photo cover	$22.00	$65.00	$154.00	£15.00	£45.00	£105.00
145 Popeye (has #134 on inside indicia)	$18.00	$52.50	$126.00	£12.00	£36.00	£85.00
146 Marge's Little Lulu; Jack Stanley cover and art	$32.00	$95.00	$224.00	£21.00	£62.50	£150.00
147 Donald Duck in Volcano Valley; Carl Barks cover and art	$110.00	$330.00	$770.00	£72.50	£215.00	£510.00
148 Albert the Alligator and Pogo Possum; Walt Kelly cover and art	$85.00	$255.00	$595.00	£55.00	£165.00	£395.00
149 Smilin' Jack; strip reprints	$15.00	$45.00	$105.00	£10.00	£30.00	£70.00
150 Tillie the Toiler; strip reprints	$12.00	$36.00	$84.00	£7.75	£23.50	£55.00
151 The Lone Ranger; strip reprints	$22.00	$65.00	$154.00	£15.00	£45.00	£105.00
152 Little Orphan Annie; strip reprints	$18.00	$52.50	$126.00	£12.00	£36.00	£85.00
153 Roy Rogers Comics; photo cover	$18.00	$52.50	$126.00	£12.00	£36.00	£85.00
154 Andy Panda by Walter Lantz	$12.00	$36.00	$84.00	£7.75	£23.50	£55.00
155 Henry	$12.00	$36.00	$84.00	£7.75	£23.50	£55.00
156 Porky Pig and The Phantom	$13.00	$39.00	$91.00	£8.50	£26.00	£60.00
157 Mickey Mouse and the Beanstalk	$30.00	$90.00	$210.00	£20.00	£60.00	£140.00
158 Marge's Little Lulu; Jack Stanley cover and art	$32.00	$95.00	$224.00	£21.00	£62.50	£150.00
159 Donald Duck and the Ghost of the Grotto; CArl Barks cover and art	$95.00	$285.00	$665.00	£62.50	£190.00	£445.00
160 Roy Rogers Comics; photo cover	$18.00	$52.50	$126.00	£12.00	£36.00	£85.00
161 Tarzan and the Fires of Tohr; Marsh cover and art	$60.00	$180.00	$420.00	£40.00	£120.00	£280.00
162 Felix the Cat; Otto Messmer cover and art	$22.00	$65.00	$154.00	£15.00	£45.00	£105.00
163 Dick Tracy; Chester Gould cover and art	$22.00	$65.00	$154.00	£15.00	£45.00	£105.00
164 Bugs Bunny Finds the Frozen Kingdom	$18.00	$52.50	$126.00	£12.00	£36.00	£85.00
165 Marge's Little Lulu; Jack Stanley cover and art	$32.00	$95.00	$224.00	£21.00	£62.50	£150.00
166 Roy Rogers Comics; photo cover	$18.00	$52.50	$126.00	£12.00	£36.00	£85.00
167 The Lone Ranger; strip reprints	$22.00	$65.00	$154.00	£15.00	£45.00	£105.00
168 Popeye	$18.00	$52.50	$126.00	£12.00	£36.00	£85.00
169 Woody Woodpecker (1st appearance) in The Manhunter From The North	$22.00	$65.00	$154.00	£15.00	£45.00	£105.00
170 Mickey Mouse on Spook's Island	$22.00	$65.00	$154.00	£15.00	£45.00	£105.00
171 Charlie McCarthy and the Twenty Thieves	$22.00	$65.00	$154.00	£15.00	£45.00	£105.00
172 Christmas with Mother Goose; Walt Kelly cover and art	$18.00	$52.50	$126.00	£12.00	£36.00	£85.00
173 Flash Gordon	$16.00	$48.00	$112.00	£10.50	£32.00	£75.00
174 Winnie Winkle; strip reprints	$11.00	$33.00	$77.00	£7.50	£22.50	£52.50
175 Santa Claus Funnies; Walt Kelly cover and art	$18.00	$52.50	$126.00	£12.00	£36.00	£85.00
176 Tillie the Toiler; strip reprints	$11.00	$33.00	$77.00	£7.50	£22.50	£52.50
177 Roy Rogers Comics; photo cover	$19.00	$55.00	$133.00	£12.50	£38.00	£87.50
178 Donald Duck in Christmas on Bear Mountain; Carl Barks cover and art	$115.00	$345.00	$805.00	£75.00	£230.00	£540.00
179 Uncle Wiggily; Walt Kelly cover	$18.00	$52.50	$126.00	£12.00	£36.00	£85.00
180 Ozark Ike; strip reprints	$11.00	$33.00	$77.00	£7.50	£22.50	£52.50
181 Walt Disney's Mickey Mouse in Jungle Magic	$22.00	$65.00	$154.00	£15.00	£45.00	£105.00
182 Porky Pig in Never-Never Land	$12.00	$36.00	$84.00	£7.75	£23.50	£55.00
183 Oswald the Rabbit by Walter Lantz (has #184 in inside indicia)	$11.00	$33.00	$77.00	£7.50	£22.50	£52.50
184 Tillie the Toiler; strip reprints (has #186 in inside indicia)	$12.00	$36.00	$84.00	£7.75	£23.50	£55.00
185 Easter with Mother Goose; Walt Kelly cover and art (has #187 in inside indicia)	$18.00	$52.50	$126.00	£12.00	£36.00	£85.00
186 Walt Disney's Bambi	$25.00	$75.00	$175.00	£16.00	£49.00	£115.00
187 Bugs Bunny and the Dreadful Dragon	$15.00	$45.00	$105.00	£10.00	£30.00	£70.00
188 Woody Woodpecker by Walter Lantz	$18.00	$52.50	$126.00	£12.00	£36.00	£85.00
189 Donald Duck in the Old Castle's Secret; Carl Barks cover and art	$95.00	$285.00	$665.00	£62.50	£190.00	£445.00
190 Flash Gordon	$15.00	$45.00	$105.00	£10.00	£30.00	£70.00
191 Porky Pig to the Rescue	$12.00	$36.00	$84.00	£7.75	£23.50	£55.00
192 The Brownies; Walt Kelly cover and art	$15.00	$45.00	$105.00	£10.00	£30.00	£70.00
193 M.G.M. Presents Tom and Jerry (1st comics appearance - has #192 in inside indicia)	$20.00	$60.00	$140.00	£13.00	£40.00	£92.50
194 Mickey Mouse in The World Under The Sea	$20.00	$60.00	$140.00	£13.00	£40.00	£92.50
195 Tiile the Toiler; strip reprints	$9.00	$27.00	$63.00	£6.00	£18.00	£42.00
196 Charlie McCarthy in The Haunted Hideout	$18.00	$52.50	$126.00	£12.00	£36.00	£85.00
197 Spirit of the Border by Zane Gey	$18.00	$52.50	$126.00	£12.00	£36.00	£85.00
198 Andy Panda	$11.00	$33.00	$77.00	£7.50	£22.50	£52.50
199 Donald Duck in Sheriff of Bullet Valley; Carl Barks cover and art (he appears himself on a wanted poster)	$92.50	$280.00	$655.00	£60.00	£185.00	£435.00
200 Bugs Bunny Super Sleuth	$15.00	$45.00	$105.00	£10.00	£30.00	£70.00
201 Christmas with Mother Goose; Walt Kelly cover and art	$15.00	$45.00	$105.00	£10.00	£30.00	£70.00
202 Woody Woodpecker	$11.00	$33.00	$77.00	£7.50	£22.50	£52.50
203 Donald Duck in The Golden Christmas Tree; Carl Barks cover and art	$75.00	$225.00	$525.00	£50.00	£150.00	£350.00
204 Flash Gordon	$15.00	$45.00	$105.00	£10.00	£30.00	£70.00
205 Santa Claus Funnies; Walt Kelly cover and art	$15.00	$45.00	$105.00	£10.00	£30.00	£70.00
206 Little Orphan Annie; strip reprints	$11.00	$33.00	$77.00	£7.50	£22.50	£52.50
207 King of The Royal Mounted	$22.00	$65.00	$154.00	£15.00	£45.00	£105.00
208 Brer Rabbit Does It Again	$13.00	$39.00	$91.00	£8.50	£26.00	£60.00
209 Harold Teen; strip reprints	$6.00	$18.00	$42.00	£4.00	£12.00	£28.00
210 Tippie and Cap Stubbs	$8.00	$24.00	$56.00	£5.25	£15.50	£37.00
211 Little Beaver	$9.00	$27.00	$63.00	£6.00	£18.00	£42.00
212 Dr. Bobbs	$6.00	$18.00	$42.00	£4.00	£12.00	£28.00
213 Tillie the Toiler; strip reprints	$7.00	$21.00	$49.00	£4.70	£14.00	£33.00
214 Mickey Mouse and His Sky Adventure	$18.00	$52.50	$126.00	£12.00	£36.00	£85.00
215 Sparkle Plenty; Chester Gould cover and art	$12.00	$36.00	$84.00	£7.75	£23.50	£55.00
216 Andy Panda and the Police Pup by Walter Lantz	$8.00	$24.00	$56.00	£5.25	£15.50	£37.00
217 Bugs Bunny in Court Jester	$15.00	$45.00	$105.00	£10.00	£30.00	£70.00
218 Three Little Pigs and the Wonderful Magic Lamp	$20.00	$60.00	$140.00	£13.00	£40.00	£92.50
219 Swee'pea	$11.00	$33.00	$77.00	£7.50	£22.50	£52.50
220 Easter with Mother Goose; Walt Kelly cover and art	$15.00	$45.00	$105.00	£10.00	£30.00	£70.00
221 Uncle Wiggily; part Walt Kelly cover	$12.00	$36.00	$84.00	£7.75	£23.50	£55.00
222 West of the Pecos by Zane Grey	$11.00	$33.00	$77.00	£7.50	£22.50	£52.50
223 Donald Duck in Lost in the Andes; Carl Barks cover and art	$85.00	$255.00	$595.00	£55.00	£165.00	£395.00
224 Little Iodine; Hatlo art	$12.00	$36.00	$84.00	£7.75	£23.50	£55.00
225 Oswald the Rabbit by Walter Lantz	$7.00	$21.00	$49.00	£4.70	£14.00	£33.00
226 Porky Pig and Spooky the Spook	$9.00	$27.00	$63.00	£6.00	£18.00	£42.00
227 Seven Dwarfs	$12.00	$36.00	$84.00	£7.75	£23.50	£55.00
228 The Mark of Zorro	$30.00	$90.00	$210.00	£18.50	£55.00	£130.00
229 Smokey Stover; strip reprints	$6.00	$18.00	$42.00	£4.00	£12.00	£28.00
230 Sunset Pass by Zane Grey	$9.00	$27.00	$63.00	£6.00	£18.00	£42.00
231 Mickey Mouse and the Rajah's Treasure	$18.00	$52.50	$126.00	£12.00	£36.00	£85.00
232 Woody Woodpecker by Walter Lantz	$9.00	$27.00	$63.00	£6.00	£18.00	£42.00
233 Bugs Bunny Sleepwalking Sleuth	$15.00	$45.00	$105.00	£10.00	£30.00	£70.00
234 Dumbo in Sky Voyage	$13.00	$39.00	$91.00	£8.50	£26.00	£60.00
235 Tiny Tim	$7.00	$21.00	$49.00	£4.70	£14.00	£33.00
236 Hertitage of the Desert by Zane Grey	$9.00	$27.00	$63.00	£6.00	£18.00	£42.00

VERY GENERAL PERCENTAGE CONVERSION CHART WHICH MAY BE USED TO CALCULATE LOW AND INBETWEEN GRADES:

#	Title	$Good	$Fine	$N.Mint	£Good	£Fine	£N.Mint
237	Tillie the Toiler; strip reprints	$7.00	$21.00	$49.00	£4.70	£14.00	£33.00
238	Donald Duck in Hoodoo Voodoo; Carl Barks cover and art	$75.00	$225.00	$525.00	£50.00	£150.00	£350.00
239	Adventure Bound	$7.00	$21.00	$49.00	£4.70	£14.00	£33.00
240	Andy Panda by Walter Lantz	$9.00	$27.00	$63.00	£6.00	£18.00	£42.00
241	Porky Pig, Mighty Hunter	$9.00	$27.00	$63.00	£6.00	£18.00	£42.00
242	Tippie and Cap Stubbs	$6.00	$18.00	$42.00	£4.00	£12.00	£28.00
243	Thumper Follows His Nose	$15.00	$45.00	$105.00	£10.00	£30.00	£70.00
244	The Brownies; Walt Kelly cover and art	$15.00	$45.00	$105.00	£10.00	£30.00	£70.00
245	Dick's Adventures in Dreamland; strip reprints	$7.00	$21.00	$49.00	£4.70	£14.00	£33.00
246	Thunder Mountain by Zane Grey	$6.00	$18.00	$42.00	£4.00	£12.00	£28.00
247	Flash Gordon	$15.00	$45.00	$105.00	£10.00	£30.00	£70.00
248	Mickey Mouse and the Black Sorceror	$18.00	$52.50	$126.00	£12.00	£36.00	£85.00
249	Woody Woodpecker in The Globetrotter	$9.00	$27.00	$63.00	£6.00	£18.00	£42.00
250	Bugs Bunny in Diamond Daze	$15.00	$45.00	$105.00	£10.00	£30.00	£70.00
251	Hubert at Camp Moonbeam	$6.00	$18.00	$42.00	£4.00	£12.00	£28.00
252	Pinocchio	$12.00	$36.00	$84.00	£7.75	£23.50	£55.00
253	Christmas with Mother Goose; Waly Kelly cover and art (has #254 on inside indicia)	$12.00	$36.00	$84.00	£7.75	£23.50	£55.00
254	Santa Claus Funnies; Walt Kelly cover and art plus Albert and Pogo story by Kelly (has #256 on inside indicia)	$18.00	$52.50	$126.00	£12.00	£36.00	£85.00
255	The Ranger by Zane Grey (has #256 on inside indicia)	$6.00	$18.00	$42.00	£4.00	£12.00	£28.00
256	Donald Duck in Luck of the North; Carl Barks cover and art (has #257 on inside indicia)	$50.00	$150.00	$350.00	£34.00	£100.00	£235.00
257	Little Iodine (has #258 on inside indicia)	$9.00	$27.00	$63.00	£6.00	£18.00	£42.00
258	Andy Panda and the Balloon Race by Walter Lantz	$9.00	$27.00	$63.00	£6.00	£18.00	£42.00
259	Santa and the Angel/Santa at the Zoo	$7.00	$21.00	$49.00	£4.70	£14.00	£33.00
260	Porky Pig Hero of the Wild West	$9.00	$27.00	$63.00	£6.00	£18.00	£42.00
261	Mickey Mouse and the Missing Key	$18.00	$52.50	$126.00	£12.00	£36.00	£85.00
262	Raggedy Ann and Andy	$7.00	$21.00	$49.00	£4.70	£14.00	£33.00
263	Donald Duck in The Land of the Totem Poles; Carl Barks cover and art	$50.00	$150.00	$350.00	£34.00	£100.00	£235.00
264	Woody Woodpecker in The Magic Lantern by Walter Lantz	$9.00	$27.00	$63.00	£6.00	£18.00	£42.00
265	King of the Royal Mounted by Zane Grey; strip reprints	$11.00	$33.00	$77.00	£7.50	£22.50	£52.50
266	Bugs Bunny on The Isle of Hercules	$11.00	$33.00	$77.00	£7.50	£22.50	£52.50
267	Little Beaver	$6.00	$18.00	$42.00	£4.00	£12.00	£28.00
268	Mickey Mouse's Surprise Visitor; Gottfredson art	$18.00	$52.50	$126.00	£12.00	£36.00	£85.00
269	Johnny Mack Brown	$25.00	$75.00	$175.00	£16.00	£49.00	£115.00
270	Drift Fence by Zane Grey	$6.00	$18.00	$42.00	£4.00	£12.00	£28.00
271	Porky Pig in Phantom of the Plains	$9.00	$27.00	$63.00	£6.00	£18.00	£42.00
272	Cinderella	$15.00	$45.00	$105.00	£10.00	£30.00	£70.00
273	Oswald the Rabbit	$7.00	$21.00	$49.00	£4.70	£14.00	£33.00
274	Bugs Bunny, Hare-Brained Reporter	$11.00	$33.00	$77.00	£7.50	£22.50	£52.50
275	Donald Duck in Ancient Persia; Carl Barks cover and art	$45.00	$135.00	$315.00	£30.00	£90.00	£210.00
276	Uncle Wiggily (has #277 on inside indicia)	$9.00	$27.00	$63.00	£6.00	£18.00	£42.00
277	Porky Pig in Desert Adventure	$9.00	$27.00	$63.00	£6.00	£18.00	£42.00
278	Bill Elliott Comics; photo cover	$15.00	$45.00	$105.00	£10.00	£30.00	£70.00
279	Mickey Mouse and Pluto Battle The Giant Ants (has #280 on inside indicia)	$15.00	$45.00	$105.00	£10.00	£30.00	£70.00
280	Andy Panda in The Isle of Mechanical Men by Walter Lantz	$9.00	$27.00	$63.00	£6.00	£18.00	£42.00
281	Bugs Bunny in The Great Circus Mystery	$11.00	$33.00	$77.00	£7.50	£22.50	£52.50
282	Donald Duck and The Pixilated Parrot; Carl Barks cover and story	$45.00	$135.00	$315.00	£30.00	£90.00	£210.00
283	King of the Royal Mounted	$11.00	$33.00	$77.00	£7.50	£22.50	£52.50
284	Porky Pig in The Kingdom of Nowhere	$9.00	$27.00	$63.00	£6.00	£18.00	£42.00
285	Bozo the Clown and his Minikin Circus	$18.00	$52.50	$126.00	£12.00	£36.00	£85.00
286	Mickey Mouse in The Uninvited Guest	$15.00	$45.00	$105.00	£10.00	£30.00	£70.00
287	Gene Autrey's Champion in The Ghost of Black Mountain	$15.00	$45.00	$105.00	£10.00	£30.00	£70.00
288	Woody Woodpecker in Klondike Gold by Walter Lantz	$9.00	$27.00	$63.00	£6.00	£18.00	£42.00
289	Bugs Bunny in Indian Trouble	$12.00	$36.00	$84.00	£7.75	£23.50	£55.00
290	The Chief	$6.00	$18.00	$42.00	£4.00	£12.00	£28.00
291	Donald Duck in The Magic Hourglass; Carl Barks cover and art	$45.00	$135.00	$315.00	£30.00	£90.00	£210.00
292	The Cisco Kid	$25.00	$75.00	$175.00	£16.00	£49.00	£115.00
293	The Brownies; Walt Kelly cover and art	$15.00	$45.00	$105.00	£10.00	£30.00	£70.00
294	Little Beaver	$6.00	$18.00	$42.00	£4.00	£12.00	£28.00
295	Porky Pig in President Porky	$9.00	$27.00	$63.00	£6.00	£18.00	£42.00
296	Mickey Mouse in Private Eye For Hire	$15.00	$45.00	$105.00	£10.00	£30.00	£70.00
297	Andy Panda in The Haunted Inn by Walter Lantz	$9.00	$27.00	$63.00	£6.00	£18.00	£42.00
298	Bugs Bunny in Sheik For A Day	$11.00	$33.00	$77.00	£7.50	£22.50	£52.50
299	Buck Jones and The iron Horse Trail	$18.00	$52.50	$126.00	£12.00	£36.00	£85.00
300	Donald Duck in Big Top Bedlam; Carl Barks cover and art	$45.00	$135.00	$315.00	£30.00	£90.00	£210.00
301	The Mysterious Rider by Zane Grey	$6.00	$18.00	$42.00	£4.00	£12.00	£28.00
302	Santa Claus Funnies	$5.00	$15.00	$35.00	£3.35	£10.00	£23.50
303	Porky Pig in The Land of the Monstrous Flies	$6.00	$18.00	$42.00	£4.00	£12.00	£28.00
304	Mickey Mouse in Tom-Tom Island	$9.00	$27.00	$63.00	£6.00	£18.00	£42.00
305	Woody Woodpecker	$6.00	$18.00	$42.00	£4.00	£12.00	£28.00
306	Raggedy Ann	$6.00	$18.00	$42.00	£4.00	£12.00	£28.00
307	Bugs Bunny in Lumberjack Rabbit	$9.00	$27.00	$63.00	£6.00	£18.00	£42.00
308	Donald Duck in Dangerous Disguise; Carl Bark cover and art	$40.00	$120.00	$280.00	£26.00	£77.50	£185.00
309	Betty Betz' Dollface and Her Gang	$6.00	$18.00	$42.00	£4.00	£12.00	£28.00
310	King of the Royal Mounted	$9.00	$27.00	$63.00	£6.00	£18.00	£42.00
311	Porky Pig in Midget Horses of Hidden Valley	$6.00	$18.00	$42.00	£4.00	£12.00	£28.00
312	Tonto	$18.00	$52.50	$126.00	£12.00	£36.00	£85.00
313	Mickey Mouse in The Mystery of the Double Cross Ranch	$9.00	$27.00	$63.00	£6.00	£18.00	£42.00
314	Ambush by Zane Grey (has #1 on inside indicia)	$6.00	$18.00	$42.00	£4.00	£12.00	£28.00
315	Oswald the Rabbit by Walter Lantz	$5.00	$15.00	$35.00	£3.35	£10.00	£23.50
316	Rex Allen; photo cover, Marsh art	$20.00	$60.00	$140.00	£13.00	£40.00	£92.50
317	Bugs Bunny in Hare Today Gone Tomorrow	$9.00	$27.00	$63.00	£6.00	£18.00	£42.00
318	Donald Duck in No Such Varmint; Carl Barks cover and art	$40.00	$120.00	$280.00	£26.00	£77.50	£185.00
319	Gene Autrey's Champion	$5.00	$15.00	$35.00	£3.35	£10.00	£23.50
320	Uncle Wiggily	$9.00	$27.00	$63.00	£6.00	£18.00	£42.00
321	Little Scouts	$4.00	$12.00	$28.00	£2.60	£7.75	£18.50
322	Porky Pig in Roaring Rockets	$6.00	$18.00	$42.00	£4.00	£12.00	£28.00
323	Susie Q. Smith	$6.00	$18.00	$42.00	£4.00	£12.00	£28.00
324	I Met A Handsome Cowboy	$9.00	$27.00	$63.00	£6.00	£18.00	£42.00
325	Mickey Mouse in The Haunted Castle	$11.00	$33.00	$77.00	£7.50	£22.50	£52.50
326	Andy Panda by Walter Lantz	$4.00	$12.00	$28.00	£2.60	£7.75	£18.50
327	Bugs Bunny and The Rajah's Treasure	$9.00	$27.00	$63.00	£6.00	£18.00	£42.00
328	Donald Duck in Old California; Carl Barks cover and art	$40.00	$120.00	$280.00	£26.00	£77.50	£185.00
329	Roy Roger's Trigger; photo cover	$15.00	$45.00	$105.00	£10.00	£30.00	£70.00
330	Porky Pig Meets The Bristled Bruiser	$6.00	$18.00	$42.00	£4.00	£12.00	£28.00
331	Alice in Wonderland	$20.00	$60.00	$140.00	£13.00	£40.00	£92.50
332	Little Beaver	$5.00	$15.00	$35.00	£3.35	£10.00	£23.50

MINT = 100% / NEAR MINT (inc. +/-) = 90–99% / VERY FINE (inc. +/-) = 75–89% / FINE (inc. +/-) = 55–74%
VERY GOOD (inc. +/-) = 35–54% / GOOD (inc. +/-) = 15–34% / FAIR = 5–14% / POOR = 1–4%

349

#	Title	$Good	$Fine	$N.Mint	£Good	£Fine	£N.Mint
333	Wilderness Trek by Zane Grey	$6.00	$18.00	$42.00	£4.00	£12.00	£28.00
334	Mickey Mouse and Yukon Gold	$9.00	$27.00	$63.00	£6.00	£18.00	£42.00
335	Francis the Famous Talking Mule	$11.00	$33.00	$77.00	£7.50	£22.50	£52.50
336	Woody Woodpecker by Walter Lantz	$5.00	$15.00	$35.00	£3.35	£10.00	£23.50
337	The Brownies; no Walt Kelly art	$5.00	$15.00	$35.00	£3.35	£10.00	£23.50
338	Bugs Bunny and the Rocking Horse Thieves	$9.00	$27.00	$63.00	£6.00	£18.00	£42.00
339	Donald Duck and The Magic Fountain; no Carl Barks art	$11.00	$33.00	$77.00	£7.50	£22.50	£52.50
340	King of the Royal Mounted	$9.00	$27.00	$63.00	£6.00	£18.00	£42.00
341	Unbirthday Party with Alice in Wonderland	$20.00	$60.00	$140.00	£13.00	£40.00	£92.50
342	Porky Pig in The Lucky Peppermint Mine	$5.00	$15.00	$35.00	£3.35	£10.00	£23.50
343	Mickey Mouse in The Ruby Eye of Homar-Guy-Am	$9.00	$27.00	$63.00	£6.00	£18.00	£42.00
344	Sergeant Preston from Challenge of the Yukon; based on TV show	$15.00	$45.00	$105.00	£10.00	£30.00	£70.00
345	Andy Panda in Scotland Yard by Walter Lantz	$5.00	$15.00	$35.00	£3.35	£10.00	£23.50
346	Hideout by Zane Grey (has #347 on inside indicia)	$6.00	$18.00	$42.00	£4.00	£12.00	£28.00
347	Bugs Bunny the Frigid Hare (has #349 on inside indicia)	$9.00	$27.00	$63.00	£6.00	£18.00	£42.00
348	Donald Duck in The Crocodile Collector; Carl Barks cover only	$25.00	$75.00	$175.00	£16.00	£49.00	£115.00
349	Uncle Wiggily	$9.00	$27.00	$63.00	£6.00	£18.00	£42.00
350	Woody Woodpecker by Walter Lantz	$5.00	$15.00	$35.00	£3.35	£10.00	£23.50
351	Porky Pig and The Grand Canyon Giant	$5.00	$15.00	$35.00	£3.35	£10.00	£23.50
352	Mickey Mouse in The Mystery of Painted Valley	$9.00	$27.00	$63.00	£6.00	£18.00	£42.00
353	Duck Album; Carl Barks cover only	$11.00	$33.00	$77.00	£7.50	£22.50	£52.50
354	Raggedy Ann and Andy	$6.00	$18.00	$42.00	£4.00	£12.00	£28.00
355	Bugs Bunny Hot Rod Hare	$9.00	$27.00	$63.00	£6.00	£18.00	£42.00
356	Donald Duck in Rags To Riches; Carl Barks cover only	$20.00	$60.00	$140.00	£13.00	£40.00	£92.50
357	Comeback by Zane Grey	$6.00	$18.00	$42.00	£4.00	£12.00	£28.00
358	Andy Panda by Walter Lantz	$5.00	$15.00	$35.00	£3.35	£10.00	£23.50
359	Frosty the Snowman	$9.00	$27.00	$63.00	£6.00	£18.00	£42.00
360	Porky Pig in Tree of Fortune	$5.00	$15.00	$35.00	£3.35	£10.00	£23.50
361	Santa Claus Funnies	$5.00	$15.00	$35.00	£3.35	£10.00	£23.50
362	Mickey Mouse and The Smuggled Diamonds	$9.00	$27.00	$63.00	£6.00	£18.00	£42.00
363	King of the Royal Mounted	$7.50	$23.00	$54.00	£5.00	£15.00	£36.00
364	Woody Woodpecker by Walter Lantz	$5.00	$15.00	$35.00	£3.35	£10.00	£23.50
365	The Brownies; no Walt Kelly art	$5.00	$15.00	$35.00	£3.35	£10.00	£23.50
366	Bugs Bunny in Uncle Buckskin Comes To Town	$9.00	$27.00	$63.00	£6.00	£18.00	£42.00
367	Donald Duck in A Christmas for Shacktown; Carl Barks cover and art	$40.00	$120.00	$280.00	£26.00	£77.50	£185.00
368	Bob Clampett's Beany and Cecil	$30.00	$90.00	$210.00	£20.00	£60.00	£140.00
369	The Lone Ranger's Famous Horse Hi-Yo Silver	$11.00	$33.00	$77.00	£7.50	£22.50	£52.50
370	Porky Pig in Trouble in the Big Trees	$5.00	$15.00	$35.00	£3.35	£10.00	£23.50
371	Mickey Mouse in The Inca Idol Case	$7.50	$23.00	$54.00	£5.00	£15.00	£36.00
372	Riders of the Purple Sage by Zane Grey	$5.00	$15.00	$35.00	£3.35	£10.00	£23.50
373	Sergeant Preston; based on TV show	$7.50	$23.00	$54.00	£5.00	£15.00	£36.00
374	Woody Woodpecker by Walter Lantz	$5.00	$15.00	$35.00	£3.35	£10.00	£23.50
375	John Carter of Mars; Jesse Marsh cover and art; origin John Carter	$30.00	$90.00	$210.00	£20.00	£60.00	£140.00
376	Bugs Bunny in The Magic Sneeze	$9.00	$27.00	$63.00	£6.00	£18.00	£42.00
377	Susie Q. Smith	$5.00	$15.00	$35.00	£3.35	£10.00	£23.50
378	Tom Corbett, Space Cadet (1st appearance in comics); based on TV show; Al McWilliams art	$20.00	$60.00	$140.00	£13.00	£40.00	£92.50
379	Donald Duck in Southern Hospitality; no Carl Barks art	$7.00	$21.00	$49.00	£4.70	£14.00	£33.00
380	Raggedy Ann and Andy (has #378 on inside indicia)	$6.00	$18.00	$42.00	£4.00	£12.00	£28.00
381	Marge's Tubby (1st appearance)	$20.00	$60.00	$140.00	£13.00	£40.00	£92.50
382	Snow White and the Seven Dwarfs	$20.00	$60.00	$140.00	£13.00	£40.00	£92.50
383	Andy Panda by Walter Lantz	$4.00	$12.00	$28.00	£2.60	£7.75	£18.50
384	King of the Royal Mounted (has #383 on inside indicia)	$7.00	$21.00	$49.00	£4.70	£14.00	£33.00
385	Porky Pig in The Isle of Missing Ships	$5.00	$15.00	$35.00	£3.35	£10.00	£23.50
386	Uncle Scrooge in Only a Poor Old Man (1st appearance); Carl Barks cover and art	$150.00	$450.00	$1050.00	£100.00	£300.00	£700.00
387	Mickey Mouse in High Tibet	$7.50	$23.00	$54.00	£5.00	£15.00	£36.00
388	Oswald the Rabbit by Walter Lantz	$5.00	$15.00	$35.00	£3.35	£10.00	£23.50
389	Andy Hardy Comics	$5.00	$15.00	$35.00	£3.35	£10.00	£23.50
390	Woody Woodpecker by Walter Lantz (has #389 on inside indicia)	$5.00	$15.00	$35.00	£3.35	£10.00	£23.50
391	Uncle Wiggily	$7.00	$21.00	$49.00	£4.70	£14.00	£33.00
392	Hi-Yo Silver	$6.00	$18.00	$42.00	£4.00	£12.00	£28.00
393	Bugs Bunny	$9.00	$27.00	$63.00	£6.00	£18.00	£42.00
394	Donald Duck in The Malaylaya; Carl Barks cover only	$20.00	$60.00	$140.00	£13.00	£40.00	£92.50
395	Forlorn River by Zane Grey	$6.00	$18.00	$42.00	£4.00	£12.00	£28.00
396	Tales of the Texas Rangers, photo cover; based on TV show	$15.00	$45.00	$105.00	£10.00	£30.00	£70.00
397	Sergeant Preston of the Yukon; based on TV show	$9.00	$27.00	$63.00	£6.00	£18.00	£42.00
398	The Brownies; no Walt Kelly art	$5.00	$15.00	$35.00	£3.35	£10.00	£23.50
399	Porky Pig in The Lost Gold Mine	$5.00	$15.00	$35.00	£3.35	£10.00	£23.50
400	Tom Corbett, Space Cadet; based on TV show; Al McWilliams art	$18.00	$52.50	$126.00	£12.00	£36.00	£85.00
401	Mickey Mouse and Goofy's Mechanical Wizard	$6.00	$18.00	$42.00	£4.00	£12.00	£28.00
402	Mary Jane and Sniffles	$11.00	$33.00	$77.00	£7.50	£22.50	£52.50
403	L'il Bad Wolf	$12.00	$36.00	$84.00	£7.75	£23.50	£55.00
404	The Range Rider; photo cover	$15.00	$45.00	$105.00	£10.00	£30.00	£70.00
405	Woody Woodpecker by Walter Lantz	$5.00	$15.00	$35.00	£3.35	£10.00	£23.50
406	Tweety and Sylvester	$9.00	$27.00	$63.00	£6.00	£18.00	£42.00
407	Bugs Bunny, Foreign Legion-Hare	$6.00	$18.00	$42.00	£4.00	£12.00	£28.00
408	Donald Duck and The Golden Helmet; Carl Barks cover and art	$35.00	$105.00	$245.00	£23.50	£70.00	£165.00
409	Andy Panda	$4.00	$12.00	$28.00	£2.60	£7.75	£18.50
410	Porky Pig in The Water Wizard	$5.00	$15.00	$35.00	£3.35	£10.00	£23.50
411	Mickey Mouse and The Old Sea Dog	$6.00	$18.00	$42.00	£4.00	£12.00	£28.00
412	Nevada by Zane Grey	$5.00	$15.00	$35.00	£3.35	£10.00	£23.50
413	Robin Hood; photo cover	$15.00	$45.00	$105.00	£10.00	£30.00	£70.00
414	Bob Clampett's Beany and Cecil	$22.00	$65.00	$154.00	£15.00	£45.00	£105.00
415	Rootie Kazootie	$12.00	$36.00	$84.00	£7.75	£23.50	£55.00
416	Woody Woodpecker by Walter Lantz	$5.00	$15.00	$35.00	£3.35	£10.00	£23.50
417	Double Trouble with Goober	$4.00	$12.00	$28.00	£2.60	£7.75	£18.50
418	Rusty Riley; A Boy, A Horse and A Dog; Godwin art	$5.00	$15.00	$35.00	£3.35	£10.00	£23.50
419	Sergeant Preston	$9.00	$27.00	$63.00	£6.00	£18.00	£42.00
420	Bugs Bunny in The Mysterious Buckaroo	$6.00	$18.00	$42.00	£4.00	£12.00	£28.00
421	Tom Corbett, Space Cadet; Al McWilliams art	$12.00	$36.00	$84.00	£7.75	£23.50	£55.00
422	Donald Duck and The Gilded Man; Carl Barks cover and art	$35.00	$105.00	$245.00	£23.50	£70.00	£165.00
423	Rhubarb, Owner of The Brooklyn Ball Club	$5.00	$15.00	$35.00	£3.35	£10.00	£23.50
424	Flash Gordon - Test Flight in Space	$9.00	$27.00	$63.00	£6.00	£18.00	£42.00
425	The Return of Zorro	$20.00	$60.00	$140.00	£13.00	£40.00	£92.50
426	Porky Pig in The Scallywag Leprechaun	$5.00	$15.00	$35.00	£3.35	£10.00	£23.50

TRADE PAPERBACKS, GRAPHIC NOVELS AND OTHER COLLECTIONS ARE PRICED IN POUNDS STERLING ONLY. CONVERT AT 1.5 FOR DOLLARS.

	$Good	$Fine	$N.Mint	£Good	£Fine	£N.Mint
427 Mickey Mouse and The Wonderful Whizzix	$5.00	$15.00	$35.00	£3.35	£10.00	£23.50
428 Uncle Wiggily	$5.00	$15.00	$35.00	£3.35	£10.00	£23.50
429 Pluto in Why Dogs Leave Home	$15.00	$45.00	$105.00	£10.00	£30.00	£70.00
430 Marge's Tubby, The Shadow of a Man-Eater	$9.00	$27.00	$63.00	£6.00	£18.00	£42.00
431 Woody Woodpecker by Walter Lantz	$4.00	$12.00	$28.00	£2.60	£7.75	£18.50
432 Bugs Bunny and The Rabbit Olympics	$6.00	$18.00	$42.00	£4.00	£12.00	£28.00
433 Wildfire by Zane Grey	$5.00	$15.00	$35.00	£3.35	£10.00	£23.50
434 Rin Tin Tin - In Dark Danger	$25.00	$75.00	$175.00	£16.00	£49.00	£115.00
435 Frosty the Snowman	$4.00	$12.00	$28.00	£2.60	£7.75	£18.50
436 The Brownies; no Walt Kelly art	$4.00	$12.00	$28.00	£2.60	£7.75	£18.50
437 John Carter of Mars; Marsh art	$20.00	$60.00	$140.00	£13.00	£40.00	£92.50
438 Annie Oakley	$18.00	$52.50	$126.00	£12.00	£36.00	£85.00
439 Little Hiawatha	$9.00	$27.00	$63.00	£6.00	£18.00	£42.00
440 Black Beauty	$4.00	$12.00	$28.00	£2.60	£7.75	£18.50
441 Fearless Fagan	$5.00	$15.00	$35.00	£3.35	£10.00	£23.50
442 Peter Pan	$9.00	$27.00	$63.00	£6.00	£18.00	£42.00
443 Ben Bowie and his Mountain Men	$9.00	$27.00	$63.00	£6.00	£18.00	£42.00
444 Marge's Tubby	$9.00	$27.00	$63.00	£6.00	£18.00	£42.00
445 Charlie McCarthy	$6.00	$18.00	$42.00	£4.00	£12.00	£28.00
446 Captain Hook and Peter Pan	$12.00	$36.00	$84.00	£7.75	£23.50	£55.00
447 Andy Hardy Comics	$3.00	$9.00	$21.00	£2.00	£6.00	£14.00
448 Bob Clampett's Beany and Cecil	$22.00	$65.00	$154.00	£15.00	£45.00	£105.00
449 Tapan's Burro by Zane Grey	$5.00	$15.00	$35.00	£3.35	£10.00	£23.50
450 Duck Album; Carl Barks cover	$7.50	$23.00	$54.00	£5.00	£15.00	£36.00
451 Rusty Riley; Godwin art	$5.00	$15.00	$35.00	£3.35	£10.00	£23.50
452 Raggedy Ann & Andy	$5.00	$15.00	$35.00	£3.35	£10.00	£23.50
453 Susie Q. Smith	$3.40	$10.00	$24.00	£2.25	£6.75	£16.00
454 Krazy Kat Comics; no George Herriman	$4.00	$12.00	$28.00	£2.60	£7.75	£18.50
455 Johnny Mack Brown Comics	$6.00	$18.00	$42.00	£4.00	£12.00	£28.00
456 Uncle Scrooge Back To The Klondike; Carl Barks cover and art	$75.00	$225.00	$525.00	£50.00	£150.00	£350.00
457 Daffy	$11.00	$33.00	$77.00	£7.50	£22.50	£52.50
458 Oswald the Rabbit	$3.40	$10.00	$24.00	£2.25	£6.75	£16.00
459 Rootie Kazootie	$9.00	$27.00	$63.00	£6.00	£18.00	£42.00
460 Buck Jones	$6.00	$18.00	$42.00	£4.00	£12.00	£28.00
461 Marge's Tubby; Stanley art	$9.00	$27.00	$63.00	£6.00	£18.00	£42.00
462 Little Scouts	$3.00	$9.00	$21.00	£2.00	£6.00	£14.00
463 Petunia	$4.00	$12.00	$28.00	£2.60	£7.75	£18.50
464 Bozo	$12.00	$36.00	$84.00	£7.75	£23.50	£55.00
465 Francis The Famous Talking Mule	$5.00	$15.00	$35.00	£3.35	£10.00	£23.50
466 Rhubarb, the Millionaire Cat	$3.40	$10.00	$24.00	£2.25	£6.75	£16.00
467 Desert Gold by Zane Grey	$5.00	$15.00	$35.00	£3.35	£10.00	£23.50
468 Goofy	$20.00	$60.00	$140.00	£13.00	£40.00	£92.50
469 Beetle Bailey; Walker art	$12.00	$36.00	$84.00	£7.75	£23.50	£55.00
470 Elmer Fudd	$3.00	$9.00	$21.00	£2.00	£6.00	£14.00
471 Double Trouble with Goober	$2.50	$7.50	$17.50	£1.60	£4.90	£11.50
472 Wild Bill Elliott	$6.00	$18.00	$42.00	£4.00	£12.00	£28.00
473 L'il Bad Wolf	$9.00	$27.00	$63.00	£6.00	£18.00	£42.00
474 Mary Jane and Sniffles	$9.00	$27.00	$63.00	£6.00	£18.00	£42.00
475 M.G.M's The Two Mouseketeers	$7.50	$23.00	$54.00	£5.00	£15.00	£36.00
476 Rin Tin Tin	$10.00	$30.00	$70.00	£6.50	£20.00	£47.00
477 Bob Clampett's Beany and Cecil	$20.00	$60.00	$140.00	£13.00	£40.00	£92.50
478 Charlie McCarthy	$6.00	$18.00	$42.00	£4.00	£12.00	£28.00
479 Queen of the West Dale Evans	$18.00	$52.50	$126.00	£12.00	£36.00	£85.00
480 Andy Hardy Comics	$3.00	$9.00	$21.00	£2.00	£6.00	£14.00
481 Annie Oakley and Tagg	$9.00	$27.00	$63.00	£6.00	£18.00	£42.00
482 The Brownies; no Walt Kelly	$3.40	$10.00	$24.00	£2.25	£6.75	£16.00
483 Little Beaver	$4.00	$12.00	$28.00	£2.60	£7.75	£18.50
484 River Feud by Zane Grey	$5.00	$15.00	$35.00	£3.35	£10.00	£23.50
485 The Little People by Walt Scott	$7.50	$23.00	$54.00	£5.00	£15.00	£36.00
486 Rusty Riley; Godwin art	$4.00	$12.00	$28.00	£2.60	£7.75	£18.50
487 Mowgli, the Jungle Book	$5.00	$15.00	$35.00	£3.35	£10.00	£23.50
488 John Carter of Mars; Marsh art	$20.00	$60.00	$140.00	£13.00	£40.00	£92.50
489 Tweety and Sylvester	$4.00	$12.00	$28.00	£2.60	£7.75	£18.50
490 Jungle Jim	$7.50	$23.00	$54.00	£5.00	£15.00	£36.00
491 Silvertip; Kinstler art	$10.00	$30.00	$70.00	£6.50	£20.00	£47.00
492 Duck Album	$7.50	$23.00	$54.00	£5.00	£15.00	£36.00
493 Johnny Mack Brown Comics	$7.00	$21.00	$49.00	£4.70	£14.00	£33.00

Four Color #147

Four Color #159

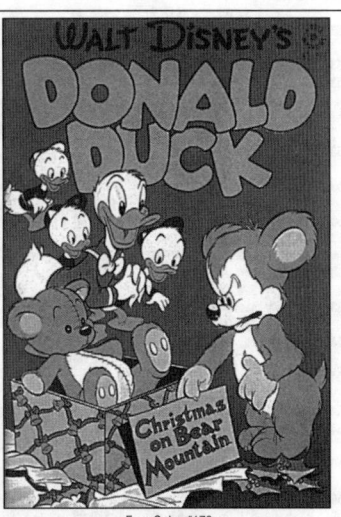

Four Color #178

#	Title	$Good	$Fine	$N.Mint	£Good	£Fine	£N.Mint
494	The Little King	$10.00	$30.00	$70.00	£6.50	£20.00	£47.00
495	Uncle Scrooge; Carl Barks cover and art	$55.00	$165.00	$385.00	£36.00	£105.00	£255.00
496	The Green Hornet	$35.00	$105.00	$245.00	£23.50	£70.00	£165.00
497	The Sword of Zorro	$18.00	$52.50	$126.00	£12.00	£36.00	£85.00
498	Bugs Bunny's Album	$5.00	$15.00	$35.00	£3.35	£10.00	£23.50
499	M.G.M's Spike and Tyke	$3.00	$9.00	$21.00	£2.00	£6.00	£14.00
500	Buck Jones	$6.00	$18.00	$42.00	£4.00	£12.00	£28.00
501	Francis The Talking Mule	$5.00	$15.00	$35.00	£3.35	£10.00	£23.50
502	Rootie Kazootie	$9.00	$27.00	$63.00	£6.00	£18.00	£42.00
503	Uncle Wiggily	$5.00	$15.00	$35.00	£3.35	£10.00	£23.50
504	Krazy Kat	$4.00	$12.00	$28.00	£2.60	£7.75	£18.50
505	The Sword and the Rose; photo cover of Disney film	$5.00	$15.00	$35.00	£3.35	£10.00	£23.50
506	The Little Scouts	$2.50	$7.50	$17.50	£1.60	£4.90	£11.50
507	Oswald the Rabbit	$3.00	$9.00	$21.00	£2.00	£6.00	£14.00
508	Bozo	$12.00	$36.00	$84.00	£7.75	£23.50	£55.00
509	Pluto	$7.50	$23.00	$54.00	£5.00	£15.00	£36.00
510	Son of Black Beauty (has #511 on inside indicia)	$3.40	$10.00	$24.00	£2.25	£6.75	£16.00
511	Outlaw Trail by Zane Grey; Kinstler art	$5.00	$15.00	$35.00	£3.35	£10.00	£23.50
512	Flash Gordon	$5.00	$15.00	$35.00	£3.35	£10.00	£23.50
513	Ben Bowie and his Mountain Men	$4.00	$12.00	$28.00	£2.60	£7.75	£18.50
514	Frosty the Snowman	$4.00	$12.00	$28.00	£2.60	£7.75	£18.50
515	Andy Hardy	$3.00	$9.00	$21.00	£2.00	£6.00	£14.00
516	Double Trouble with Goober	$3.00	$9.00	$21.00	£2.00	£6.00	£14.00
517	Chip 'n Dale	$11.00	$33.00	$77.00	£7.50	£22.50	£52.50
518	Rivets	$2.50	$7.50	$17.50	£1.60	£4.90	£11.50
519	Steve Canyon; no Milton Caniff art	$9.00	$27.00	$63.00	£6.00	£18.00	£42.00
520	Wild Bill Elliot; photo cover	$6.00	$18.00	$42.00	£4.00	£12.00	£28.00
521	Beetle Bailey	$5.00	$15.00	$35.00	£3.35	£10.00	£23.50
522	The Brownies (has #523 on inside indicia)	$3.40	$10.00	$24.00	£2.25	£6.75	£16.00
523	Rin Tin Tin; photo cover (has #524 on inside indicia)	$11.00	$33.00	$77.00	£7.50	£22.50	£52.50
524	Tweety and Sylvester	$4.00	$12.00	$28.00	£2.60	£7.75	£18.50
525	Santa Claus Funnies	$4.00	$12.00	$28.00	£2.60	£7.75	£18.50
526	Napoleon	$2.50	$7.50	$17.50	£1.60	£4.90	£11.50
527	Charlie McCarthy	$6.00	$18.00	$42.00	£4.00	£12.00	£28.00
528	Queen of the West Dale Evans; photo cover	$10.00	$30.00	$70.00	£6.50	£20.00	£47.00
529	Little Beaver	$4.00	$12.00	$28.00	£2.60	£7.75	£18.50
530	Bob Clampett's Beany and Cecil	$20.00	$60.00	$140.00	£13.00	£40.00	£92.50
531	Duck Album	$7.00	$21.00	$49.00	£4.70	£14.00	£33.00
532	The Rustlers by Zane Grey	$6.00	$18.00	$42.00	£4.00	£12.00	£28.00
533	Raggedy Ann and Andy	$6.00	$18.00	$42.00	£4.00	£12.00	£28.00
534	Western Marshall; Kinstler art	$6.00	$18.00	$42.00	£4.00	£12.00	£28.00
535	I Love Lucy; photo cover	$40.00	$120.00	$280.00	£26.00	£77.50	£185.00
536	Daffy Duck	$5.00	$15.00	$35.00	£3.35	£10.00	£23.50
537	Stormy the Thoroughbred and Pluto	$5.00	$15.00	$35.00	£3.35	£10.00	£23.50
538	The Mask of Zorro; Kinstler art	$20.00	$60.00	$140.00	£13.00	£40.00	£92.50
539	Ben and Me (has #540 on inside indicia)	$4.00	$12.00	$28.00	£2.60	£7.75	£18.50
540	The Knights of the Round Table; photo cover	$7.50	$23.00	$54.00	£5.00	£15.00	£36.00
541	Johnny MAck Brown	$7.00	$21.00	$49.00	£4.70	£14.00	£33.00
542	Super Circus	$7.00	$21.00	$49.00	£4.70	£14.00	£33.00
543	Uncle Wiggily	$7.00	$21.00	$49.00	£4.70	£14.00	£33.00
544	Rob Roy; Russ Manning art; photo cover	$10.00	$30.00	$70.00	£6.50	£20.00	£47.00
545	Pinocchio; part reprint Four Colour #92	$10.00	$30.00	$70.00	£6.50	£20.00	£47.00
546	Buck Jones	$6.00	$18.00	$42.00	£4.00	£12.00	£28.00
547	Francis The Talking Mule	$6.00	$18.00	$42.00	£4.00	£12.00	£28.00
548	Krazy Kat; no Herriman art	$4.00	$12.00	$28.00	£2.60	£7.75	£18.50
549	Oswald the Rabbit by Walter Lantz (has #548 on inside indicia)	$3.00	$9.00	$21.00	£2.00	£6.00	£14.00
550	The Little Scouts	$3.00	$9.00	$21.00	£2.00	£6.00	£14.00
551	Bozo	$12.00	$36.00	$84.00	£7.75	£23.50	£55.00
552	Beetle Bailey; Walker art	$5.00	$15.00	$35.00	£3.35	£10.00	£23.50
553	Susie Q. Smith	$4.00	$12.00	$28.00	£2.60	£7.75	£18.50
554	Rusty Riley; Godwin art, strip reprints	$4.00	$12.00	$28.00	£2.60	£7.75	£18.50
555	Range War by Zane Grey	$5.00	$15.00	$35.00	£3.35	£10.00	£23.50
556	Double Trouble with Goober	$3.00	$9.00	$21.00	£2.00	£6.00	£14.00
557	Ben Bowie and his Mountain Men (has #554 on inside indicia)	$5.00	$15.00	$35.00	£3.35	£10.00	£23.50
558	Elmer Fudd	$3.00	$9.00	$21.00	£2.00	£6.00	£14.00
559	I Love Lucy; photo cover	$30.00	$90.00	$210.00	£20.00	£60.00	£140.00
560	Duck Album	$7.50	$23.00	$54.00	£5.00	£15.00	£36.00
561	Mister Magoo	$11.00	$33.00	$77.00	£7.50	£22.50	£52.50
562	Goofy	$10.00	$30.00	$70.00	£6.50	£20.00	£47.00
563	Rhubarb the Millionaire Cat	$4.00	$12.00	$28.00	£2.60	£7.75	£18.50
564	L'il Bad Wolf	$7.50	$23.00	$54.00	£5.00	£15.00	£36.00
565	Jungle Jim	$4.00	$12.00	$28.00	£2.60	£7.75	£18.50
566	Son of Black Beauty	$4.00	$12.00	$28.00	£2.60	£7.75	£18.50
567	Prince Valiant; Bob Fuji art, photo cover from film	$10.00	$30.00	$70.00	£6.50	£20.00	£47.00
568	Gypsy Colt	$5.00	$15.00	$35.00	£3.35	£10.00	£23.50
569	Priscilla's Pop	$3.40	$10.00	$24.00	£2.25	£6.75	£16.00
570	Bob Clampett's Beany and Cecil	$22.00	$65.00	$154.00	£15.00	£45.00	£105.00
571	Charlie McCarthy	$6.00	$18.00	$42.00	£4.00	£12.00	£28.00
572	Silvertip; Kinstler art	$6.00	$18.00	$42.00	£4.00	£12.00	£28.00
573	Little People by Walt Scoot	$4.00	$12.00	$28.00	£2.60	£7.75	£18.50
574	The Hand of Zorro	$18.00	$52.50	$126.00	£12.00	£36.00	£85.00
575	Annie Oakley; photo cover	$9.00	$27.00	$63.00	£6.00	£18.00	£42.00
576	Angel	$3.00	$9.00	$21.00	£2.00	£6.00	£14.00
577	M.G.M's Spike and Tyke	$3.00	$9.00	$21.00	£2.00	£6.00	£14.00
578	Steve Canyon; no Milton Caniff art	$5.00	$15.00	$35.00	£3.35	£10.00	£23.50
579	Francis The Talking Mule	$5.00	$15.00	$35.00	£3.35	£10.00	£23.50
580	Luke Short and Six Gun Ranch	$5.00	$15.00	$35.00	£3.35	£10.00	£23.50
581	Chip 'n Dale	$5.00	$15.00	$35.00	£3.35	£10.00	£23.50
582	Mowgli, The Jungle Book	$4.00	$12.00	$28.00	£2.60	£7.75	£18.50
583	The Lost Wagon Train by Zane Grey	$5.00	$15.00	$35.00	£3.35	£10.00	£23.50
584	Johnny Mack Brown; photo cover	$7.00	$21.00	$49.00	£4.70	£14.00	£33.00
585	Bugs Bunny's Album	$5.00	$15.00	$35.00	£3.35	£10.00	£23.50
586	Duck Album	$6.00	$18.00	$42.00	£4.00	£12.00	£28.00
587	The Little Scouts	$3.00	$9.00	$21.00	£2.00	£6.00	£14.00
588	King Richard and the Crusades; Matt Baker art, photo cover	$12.00	$36.00	$84.00	£7.75	£23.50	£55.00
589	Buck Jones	$6.00	$18.00	$42.00	£4.00	£12.00	£28.00
590	Hansel and Gretel; photo collage cover	$6.00	$18.00	$42.00	£4.00	£12.00	£28.00
591	Western Marshall; Kinstler art	$6.00	$18.00	$42.00	£4.00	£12.00	£28.00
592	Super Circus	$6.00	$18.00	$42.00	£4.00	£12.00	£28.00
593	Oswald the Rabbit by Walter Lantz	$3.00	$9.00	$21.00	£2.00	£6.00	£14.00
594	Bozo	$12.00	$36.00	$84.00	£7.75	£23.50	£55.00
595	Pluto	$5.00	$15.00	$35.00	£3.35	£10.00	£23.50
596	Turok, Son of Stone (1st appearance); painted dinosaur cover	$85.00	$255.00	$595.00	£55.00	£165.00	£395.00
597	Little King	$7.50	$23.00	$54.00	£5.00	£15.00	£36.00
598	Captain Davy Jones	$3.40	$10.00	$24.00	£2.25	£6.75	£16.00
599	Ben Bowie and his Mountain Men						

SOME INDEPENDENT COMICS MAY NOT HAVE APPEARED ALTHOUGH THEY WERE ADVERTISED AND SOLICITED.

# / Title	$Good	$Fine	$N.Mint	£Good	£Fine	£N.Mint
600 Daisy Duck's Diary	$4.00	$12.00	$28.00	£2.60	£7.75	£18.50
601 Frosty the Snowman	$7.00	$21.00	$49.00	£4.70	£14.00	£33.00
602 Mister Magoo and Gerald McBoing-Boing	$4.00	$12.00	$28.00	£2.60	£7.75	£18.50
603 M.G.M's The Two Mouseketeers	$10.00	$30.00	$70.00	£6.50	£20.00	£47.00
604 Shadow on the Trail by Zane Grey	$5.00	$15.00	$35.00	£3.35	£10.00	£23.50
605 The Brownies; no Walt Kelly art	$5.00	$15.00	$35.00	£3.35	£10.00	£23.50
606 Sir Lancelot	$9.00	$27.00	$63.00	£6.00	£18.00	£42.00
607 Santa Claus Funnies	$4.00	$12.00	$28.00	£2.60	£7.75	£18.50
608 Silvertip in Valley of Vanishing Men; Kinstler art	$5.00	$15.00	$35.00	£3.35	£10.00	£23.50
609 The Littlest Outlaw (Disney); photo cover	$9.00	$27.00	$63.00	£6.00	£18.00	£42.00
610 Drum Beat; Alan Ladd photo cover	$12.00	$36.00	$84.00	£7.75	£23.50	£55.00
611 Duck Album	$7.50	$23.00	$54.00	£5.00	£15.00	£36.00
612 Little Beaver	$4.00	$12.00	$28.00	£2.60	£7.75	£18.50
613 Western Marshall; Kinstler art	$6.00	$18.00	$42.00	£4.00	£12.00	£28.00
614 20,000 Leagues Under the Sea (Disney); photo cover	$12.00	$36.00	$84.00	£7.75	£23.50	£55.00
615 Daffy Duck	$5.00	$15.00	$35.00	£3.35	£10.00	£23.50
616 To The Last Man by Zane Grey	$5.00	$15.00	$35.00	£3.35	£10.00	£23.50
617 The Quest of Zorro	$15.00	$45.00	$105.00	£10.00	£30.00	£70.00
618 Johnny Mack Brown; photo cover	$6.00	$18.00	$42.00	£4.00	£12.00	£28.00
619 Krazy Kat; no Herriman art	$5.00	$15.00	$35.00	£3.35	£10.00	£23.50
620 Mowgli Jungle Book	$5.00	$15.00	$35.00	£3.35	£10.00	£23.50
621 Francis The Talking Mule	$5.00	$15.00	$35.00	£3.35	£10.00	£23.50
622 Beetle Bailey	$5.00	$15.00	$35.00	£3.35	£10.00	£23.50
623 Oswald the Rabbit by Walter Lantz	$3.00	$9.00	$21.00	£2.00	£6.00	£14.00
624 Treasure Island (Disney); photo cover	$12.00	$36.00	$84.00	£7.75	£23.50	£55.00
625 Beaver Valley (Disney); photo cover	$9.00	$27.00	$63.00	£6.00	£18.00	£42.00
626 Ben Bowie and His Mountain Men	$5.00	$15.00	$35.00	£3.35	£10.00	£23.50
627 Goofy	$9.00	$27.00	$63.00	£6.00	£18.00	£42.00
628 Elmer Fudd	$3.00	$9.00	$21.00	£2.00	£6.00	£14.00
629 Lady and the Tramp	$7.00	$21.00	$49.00	£4.70	£14.00	£33.00
630 Priscilla's Pop	$3.40	$10.00	$24.00	£2.25	£6.75	£16.00
631 Davy Crockett, Indian Fighter; Fess Parker photo cover	$20.00	$60.00	$140.00	£13.00	£40.00	£92.50
632 Fighting Caravans by Zane Grey	$6.00	$18.00	$42.00	£4.00	£12.00	£28.00
633 Little People by Walt Scott	$6.00	$18.00	$42.00	£4.00	£12.00	£28.00
634 Walt Disney's Lady and the Tramp Album	$6.00	$18.00	$42.00	£4.00	£12.00	£28.00
635 Bob Clampett's Beany and Cecil	$20.00	$60.00	$140.00	£13.00	£40.00	£92.50
636 Chip 'n Dale	$3.00	$9.00	$21.00	£2.00	£6.00	£14.00
637 Silvertip; Kinstler art	$5.00	$15.00	$35.00	£3.35	£10.00	£23.50
638 M.G.M's Spike and Tyke	$3.00	$9.00	$21.00	£2.00	£6.00	£14.00
639 Davy Crockett at the Alamo; Fess Parker photo cover	$20.00	$60.00	$140.00	£13.00	£40.00	£92.50
640 Western Marshall; Kinstler art	$6.00	$18.00	$42.00	£4.00	£12.00	£28.00
641 Steve Canyon by Milton Caniff	$5.00	$15.00	$35.00	£3.35	£10.00	£23.50
642 M.G.M's The Two Mouseketeers	$4.00	$12.00	$28.00	£2.60	£7.75	£18.50
643 Wild Bill Elliot; photo cover	$5.00	$15.00	$35.00	£3.35	£10.00	£23.50
644 Sir Walter Raleigh (from the film "The Virgin Queen"); photo cover	$9.00	$27.00	$63.00	£6.00	£18.00	£42.00
645 Johnny Mack Brown; photo cover	$7.00	$21.00	$49.00	£4.70	£14.00	£33.00
646 Dottie Dripple and Taffy	$4.00	$12.00	$28.00	£2.60	£7.75	£18.50
647 Bugs Bunny Album	$6.00	$18.00	$42.00	£4.00	£12.00	£28.00
648 Tales of the Texas Rangers; photo cover	$7.00	$21.00	$49.00	£4.70	£14.00	£33.00
649 Duck Album	$6.00	$18.00	$42.00	£4.00	£12.00	£28.00
650 Prince Valiant by Bob Fuje	$6.00	$18.00	$42.00	£4.00	£12.00	£28.00
651 King Colt; Kinstler art	$5.00	$15.00	$35.00	£3.35	£10.00	£23.50
652 Buck Jones	$4.00	$12.00	$28.00	£2.60	£7.75	£18.50
653 Smokey Bear	$11.00	$33.00	$77.00	£7.50	£22.50	£52.50
654 Pluto	$5.00	$15.00	$35.00	£3.35	£10.00	£23.50
655 Francis The Talking Mule	$5.00	$15.00	$35.00	£3.35	£10.00	£23.50
656 Turok, Son of Stone (#2) - see #596	$50.00	$150.00	$350.00	£34.00	£100.00	£235.00
657 Ben Bowie and His Mountain Men	$5.00	$15.00	$35.00	£3.35	£10.00	£23.50
658 Goofy	$9.00	$27.00	$63.00	£6.00	£18.00	£42.00
659 Daisy Duck Diary	$6.00	$18.00	$42.00	£4.00	£12.00	£28.00
660 Little Beaver	$4.00	$12.00	$28.00	£2.60	£7.75	£18.50
661 Frosty the Snowman	$4.00	$12.00	$28.00	£2.60	£7.75	£18.50
662 Zoo Parade (TV)	$6.00	$18.00	$42.00	£4.00	£12.00	£28.00
663 Winky Dink (TV)	$9.00	$27.00	$63.00	£6.00	£18.00	£42.00
664 Davy Crockett in The Great Keelboat Race; Fess Parker photo cover	$20.00	$60.00	$140.00	£13.00	£40.00	£92.50
665 The African Lion (Disney)	$7.00	$21.00	$49.00	£4.70	£14.00	£33.00
666 Santa Claus Funnies	$4.00	$12.00	$28.00	£2.60	£7.75	£18.50
667 Silvertip and the Stolen Stallion; Kinstler art	$5.00	$15.00	$35.00	£3.35	£10.00	£23.50
668 Dumbo (1955)	$10.00	$30.00	$70.00	£6.50	£20.00	£47.00
668 668.2, Dumbo with different cover (1958)	$5.25	$15.50	$31.50	£3.50	£10.50	£21.00
669 Robin Hood; reprint of #413; photo cover	$6.00	$18.00	$42.00	£4.00	£12.00	£28.00
670 M.G.M's The Mouse Musketeers	$4.00	$12.00	$28.00	£2.60	£7.75	£18.50
671 Davy Crockett and the River Pirates; Fess Parker photo cover; Jesse Marsh art	$20.00	$60.00	$140.00	£13.00	£40.00	£92.50
672 Quentin Durward (Robert Taylor film); photo cover	$9.00	$27.00	$63.00	£6.00	£18.00	£42.00
673 Buffalo Bill Junior; photo cover	$9.00	$27.00	$63.00	£6.00	£18.00	£42.00
674 The Little Rascals (TV)	$9.00	$27.00	$63.00	£6.00	£18.00	£42.00
675 Steve Donovan, Western Marshal; Kinstler art; photo cover	$9.00	$27.00	$63.00	£6.00	£18.00	£42.00
676 Will-Yum!	$3.00	$9.00	$21.00	£2.00	£6.00	£14.00
677 The Little King	$7.00	$21.00	$49.00	£4.70	£14.00	£33.00
678 The Last Hunt; photo cover	$7.50	$23.00	$54.00	£5.00	£15.00	£36.00
679 Gunsmoke (TV)	$15.00	$45.00	$105.00	£10.00	£30.00	£70.00
680 Out Our Way with Worry Wart	$3.00	$9.00	$21.00	£2.00	£6.00	£14.00
681 Forever Darling with Lucille Ball	$13.00	$39.00	$91.00	£8.50	£26.00	£60.00
682 When Knighthood was in Flower; reprint of #505, photo cover	$9.00	$27.00	$63.00	£6.00	£18.00	£42.00
683 Hi and Lois	$3.00	$9.00	$21.00	£2.00	£6.00	£14.00
684 Helen of Troy; photo cover, John Buscema art	$15.00	$45.00	$105.00	£10.00	£30.00	£70.00
685 Johnny Mack Brown; photo cover	$7.50	$23.00	$54.00	£5.00	£15.00	£36.00
686 Duck Album	$7.50	$23.00	$54.00	£5.00	£15.00	£36.00
687 Indian Fighter; Kirk Douglas photo cover	$7.50	$23.00	$54.00	£5.00	£15.00	£36.00
688 Alexander the Great; photo cover, John Buscema art	$7.50	$23.00	$54.00	£5.00	£15.00	£36.00
689 Elmer Fudd	$3.00	$9.00	$21.00	£2.00	£6.00	£14.00
690 The Conqueror; John Wayne photo cover	$20.00	$60.00	$140.00	£13.00	£40.00	£92.50
691 Dottie Dripple and Taffy	$3.40	$10.00	$24.00	£2.25	£6.75	£16.00
692 Little People by Walt Scott	$3.40	$10.00	$24.00	£2.25	£6.75	£16.00
693 Song of the South; part reprint #129	$12.00	$36.00	$84.00	£7.75	£23.50	£55.00
694 Super Circus; photo cover	$6.00	$18.00	$42.00	£4.00	£12.00	£28.00
695 Little Beaver	$4.00	$12.00	$28.00	£2.60	£7.75	£18.50
696 Krazy Kat; no Herriman art	$4.00	$12.00	$28.00	£2.60	£7.75	£18.50
697 Oswald the Rabbit by Walter Lantz	$4.00	$12.00	$28.00	£2.60	£7.75	£18.50
698 Francis The Talking Mule	$5.00	$15.00	$35.00	£3.35	£10.00	£23.50
699 Prince Valiant by Bob Fuje						

#	Title	$Good	$Fine	$N.Mint	£Good	£Fine	£N.Mint
	(continued from previous page)	$6.00	$18.00	$42.00	£4.00	£12.00	£28.00
700	Water Birds & Olympic Elk (Disney); photo cover	$9.00	$27.00	$63.00	£6.00	£18.00	£42.00
701	Jiminy Cricket	$9.00	$27.00	$63.00	£6.00	£18.00	£42.00
702	Goofy Success Story	$9.00	$27.00	$63.00	£6.00	£18.00	£42.00
703	Scamp	$12.00	$36.00	$84.00	£7.75	£23.50	£55.00
704	Pricilla's Pop	$3.40	$10.00	$24.00	£2.25	£6.75	£16.00
705	Brave Eagle; photo cover	$7.00	$21.00	$49.00	£4.70	£14.00	£33.00
706	Bongo and Lumpjaw	$5.00	$15.00	$35.00	£3.35	£10.00	£23.50
707	Corky and White Shadow; photo cover	$9.00	$27.00	$63.00	£6.00	£18.00	£42.00
708	Smokey Bear	$5.00	$15.00	$35.00	£3.35	£10.00	£23.50
709	The Searchers; John Wayne photo cover	$35.00	$105.00	$245.00	£23.50	£70.00	£165.00
710	Francis The Talking Mule	$5.00	$15.00	$35.00	£3.35	£10.00	£23.50
711	The Two Mouseketeers	$3.00	$9.00	$21.00	£2.00	£6.00	£14.00
712	The Great Locomotive Chase; photo cover	$9.00	$27.00	$63.00	£6.00	£18.00	£42.00
713	The Animal World (Disney film)	$6.00	$18.00	$42.00	£4.00	£12.00	£28.00
714	Spin and Marty (Disney TV); photo cover	$15.00	$45.00	$105.00	£10.00	£30.00	£70.00
715	Timmy	$4.00	$12.00	$28.00	£2.60	£7.75	£18.50
716	Man In Space (Disney film)	$12.00	$36.00	$84.00	£7.75	£23.50	£55.00
717	Moby Dick; photo cover	$9.00	$27.00	$63.00	£6.00	£18.00	£42.00
718	Dottie Dripple and Daffy	$3.00	$9.00	$21.00	£2.00	£6.00	£14.00
719	Prince Valiant; Bob Fuje art	$7.00	$21.00	$49.00	£4.70	£14.00	£33.00
720	Gunsmoke; photo cover	$9.00	$27.00	$63.00	£6.00	£18.00	£42.00
721	Captain Kangaroo; photo cover	$18.00	$52.50	$126.00	£12.00	£36.00	£85.00
722	Johnny Mack Brown; photo cover	$7.50	$23.00	$54.00	£5.00	£15.00	£36.00
723	Santiago; Alan Ladd photo cover; Kinstler art	$15.00	$45.00	$105.00	£10.00	£30.00	£70.00
724	Bugs Bunny Album	$6.00	$18.00	$42.00	£4.00	£12.00	£28.00
725	Elmer Fudd	$3.00	$9.00	$21.00	£2.00	£6.00	£14.00
726	Duck Album	$6.00	$18.00	$42.00	£4.00	£12.00	£28.00
727	The Nature of Things; Jesse Marsh art	$9.00	$27.00	$63.00	£6.00	£18.00	£42.00
728	The Two Mouseketeers	$3.00	$9.00	$21.00	£2.00	£6.00	£14.00
729	Bob, Son of Battle	$3.40	$10.00	$24.00	£2.25	£6.75	£16.00
730	Smokey Stover	$3.40	$10.00	$24.00	£2.25	£6.75	£16.00
731	Silvertip; Kinstler art	$5.00	$15.00	$35.00	£3.35	£10.00	£23.50
732	The Challenge of Zorro	$18.00	$52.50	$126.00	£12.00	£36.00	£85.00
733	Buck Jones	$4.00	$12.00	$28.00	£2.60	£7.75	£18.50
734	Cheyenne; Clint Walker photo cover	$20.00	$60.00	$140.00	£13.00	£40.00	£92.50
735	Crusader Rabbit, scarce	$30.00	$90.00	$210.00	£20.00	£60.00	£140.00
736	Pluto	$6.00	$18.00	$42.00	£4.00	£12.00	£28.00
737	Steve Canyon; Milton Caniff art	$6.00	$18.00	$42.00	£4.00	£12.00	£28.00
738	Westward Ho The Wagons; Fess Parker photo cover	$13.00	$39.00	$91.00	£8.50	£26.00	£60.00
739	Bounty Guns; Drucker art	$5.00	$15.00	$35.00	£3.35	£10.00	£23.50
740	Chilly Willy by Walter Lantz	$5.00	$15.00	$35.00	£3.35	£10.00	£23.50
741	The Fastest Gun Alive; photo cover	$9.00	$27.00	$63.00	£6.00	£18.00	£42.00
742	Buffalo Bill Junior; photo cover	$5.00	$15.00	$35.00	£3.35	£10.00	£23.50
743	Daisy Duck's Diary	$6.00	$18.00	$42.00	£4.00	£12.00	£28.00
744	Little Beaver	$3.40	$10.00	$24.00	£2.25	£6.75	£16.00
745	Francis The Talking Mule	$5.00	$15.00	$35.00	£3.35	£10.00	£23.50
746	Dottie Dripple and Taffy	$3.00	$9.00	$21.00	£2.00	£6.00	£14.00
747	Goofy	$9.00	$27.00	$63.00	£6.00	£18.00	£42.00
748	Frosty the Snowman	$3.40	$10.00	$24.00	£2.25	£6.75	£16.00
749	Secrets of Life; photo cover	$7.50	$23.00	$54.00	£5.00	£15.00	£36.00
750	The Great Cat Family (Disney film)	$7.50	$23.00	$54.00	£5.00	£15.00	£36.00
751	Our Miss Brooks; photo cover	$9.00	$27.00	$63.00	£6.00	£18.00	£42.00
752	Mandrake the Magician	$11.00	$33.00	$77.00	£7.50	£22.50	£52.50
753	Walt Scott's The Little People	$4.00	$12.00	$28.00	£2.60	£7.75	£18.50
754	Smokey The Bear	$5.00	$15.00	$35.00	£3.35	£10.00	£23.50
755	The Littlest Snowman	$5.00	$15.00	$35.00	£3.35	£10.00	£23.50
756	Santa Claus Funnies	$4.00	$12.00	$28.00	£2.60	£7.75	£18.50
757	The Story of Jesse James; photo cover	$11.00	$33.00	$77.00	£7.50	£22.50	£52.50
758	Bear Country (Disney film)	$7.00	$21.00	$49.00	£4.70	£14.00	£33.00
759	Circus Boy; Mickey Dolenz photo cover	$13.00	$39.00	$91.00	£8.50	£26.00	£60.00
760	The Hardy Boys; photo cover	$15.00	$45.00	$105.00	£10.00	£30.00	£70.00
761	Howdy Doody	$11.00	$33.00	$77.00	£7.50	£22.50	£52.50
762	Sharkfighters; photo cover; John Buscema art	$15.00	$45.00	$105.00	£10.00	£30.00	£70.00
763	Grandma Duck's Farm Friends	$9.00	$27.00	$63.00	£6.00	£18.00	£42.00
764	The Two Mouseketeers	$3.00	$9.00	$21.00	£2.00	£6.00	£14.00
765	Will-Yum!	$3.00	$9.00	$21.00	£2.00	£6.00	£14.00
766	Buffalo Bill Junior; photo cover	$5.00	$15.00	$35.00	£3.35	£10.00	£23.50
767	Spin and Marty; photo cover	$10.00	$30.00	$70.00	£6.50	£20.00	£47.00
768	Steve Donovan; photo cover; Kinstler art	$7.00	$21.00	$49.00	£4.70	£14.00	£33.00
769	Gunsmoke	$7.00	$21.00	$49.00	£4.70	£14.00	£33.00
770	Brave Eagle; photo cover	$4.00	$12.00	$28.00	£2.60	£7.75	£18.50
771	Brand of Empire; Drucker art	$5.00	$15.00	$35.00	£3.35	£10.00	£23.50
772	Cheyenne; Clint Walker photo cover	$9.00	$27.00	$63.00	£6.00	£18.00	£42.00
773	The Brave One; photo cover	$6.00	$18.00	$42.00	£4.00	£12.00	£28.00
774	Hi and Lois	$3.00	$9.00	$21.00	£2.00	£6.00	£14.00
775	Sir Lancelot; photo cover; John Buscema art	$11.00	$33.00	$77.00	£7.50	£22.50	£52.50
776	Johnny Mack Brown; photo cover	$7.00	$21.00	$49.00	£4.70	£14.00	£33.00
777	Scamp	$7.50	$23.00	$54.00	£5.00	£15.00	£36.00
778	The Little Rascals	$4.00	$12.00	$28.00	£2.60	£7.75	£18.50
779	The Indian Fighter	$6.00	$18.00	$42.00	£4.00	£12.00	£28.00
780	scarce in the U.K. Captain Kangaroo	$18.00	$52.50	$126.00	£12.00	£36.00	£85.00
781	Fury; photo cover	$11.00	$33.00	$77.00	£7.50	£22.50	£52.50
782	Duck Album	$7.00	$21.00	$49.00	£4.70	£14.00	£33.00
783	Elmer Fudd	$3.00	$9.00	$21.00	£2.00	£6.00	£14.00
784	Around The World in Eighty Days; photo cover	$7.50	$23.00	$54.00	£5.00	£15.00	£36.00
785	Circus Boy; Mickey Dolenz photo cover	$12.00	$36.00	$84.00	£7.75	£23.50	£55.00
786	Cinderella - part reprint #272	$6.00	$18.00	$42.00	£4.00	£12.00	£28.00
787	Little Hiawatha	$6.00	$18.00	$42.00	£4.00	£12.00	£28.00
788	Prince Valiant; Bob Fuje art	$6.00	$18.00	$42.00	£4.00	£12.00	£28.00
789	Silvertip; Kinstler art	$5.00	$15.00	$35.00	£3.35	£10.00	£23.50
790	The Wings of Eagles; John Wayne photo cover; Alex Toth art	$20.00	$60.00	$140.00	£13.00	£40.00	£92.50
791	The 77th Bengal Lancers; photo cover	$9.00	$27.00	$63.00	£6.00	£18.00	£42.00
792	Oswald the Rabbit	$3.00	$9.00	$21.00	£2.00	£6.00	£14.00
793	Morty Meekle	$3.40	$10.00	$24.00	£2.25	£6.75	£16.00
794	The Count of Mont Cristo; John Buscema art	$11.00	$33.00	$77.00	£7.50	£22.50	£52.50
795	Jiminy Cricket	$7.00	$21.00	$49.00	£4.70	£14.00	£33.00
796	Madelein & Genevieve	$4.00	$12.00	$28.00	£2.60	£7.75	£18.50
797	Gunsmoke; photo cover	$7.50	$23.00	$54.00	£5.00	£15.00	£36.00
798	Buffalo Bill Junior; photo cover	$6.00	$18.00	$42.00	£4.00	£12.00	£28.00
799	Priscilla's Pop						

VERY GENERAL PERCENTAGE CONVERSION CHART WHICH MAY BE USED TO CALCULATE LOW AND INBETWEEN GRADES:

	$Good	$Fine	$N.Mint	£Good	£Fine	£N.Mint
	$3.40	$10.00	$24.00	£2.25	£6.75	£16.00
800 The Buccaneers; photo cover						
	$7.50	$23.00	$54.00	£5.00	£15.00	£36.00
801 Dottie Dripple and Taffy						
	$4.00	$12.00	$24.00	£2.65	£8.00	£16.00
802 Goofy						
	$10.00	$30.00	$60.00	£6.50	£20.00	£40.00
803 Cheyenne; Clint Walker photo cover						
	$10.00	$30.00	$60.00	£6.50	£20.00	£40.00
804 Steve Canyon; Milton Caniff art						
	$6.00	$18.00	$36.00	£4.00	£12.00	£24.00
805 Crusader Rabbit						
	$27.00	$80.00	$162.00	£18.00	£55.00	£110.00
806 Scamp						
	$9.00	$27.00	$54.00	£6.00	£18.00	£36.00
807 Savage Range; Drucker art						
	$6.00	$18.00	$36.00	£4.00	£12.00	£24.00
808 Spin and Marty; photo cover; less common						
	$12.00	$36.00	$72.00	£8.00	£24.00	£48.00
809 Walt Scott's The Little People						
	$4.00	$12.00	$24.00	£2.65	£8.00	£16.00
810 Francis The Talking Mule						
	$5.00	$15.00	$30.00	£3.30	£10.00	£20.00
811 Howdy Doody						
	$12.00	$36.00	$72.00	£8.00	£24.00	£48.00
812 The Big Land; Alan Ladd photo cover						
	$14.00	$42.00	$84.00	£9.00	£28.00	£55.00
813 Circus Boy; Mickey Dolenz photo cover						
	$14.00	$42.00	$84.00	£9.00	£28.00	£55.00
814 Covered Wagons, Ho! - Donald Duck and Mickey Mouse						
	$8.00	$24.00	$48.00	£5.25	£16.00	£32.00
815 Dragoon Wells Massacre; photo cover						
	$10.00	$30.00	$60.00	£6.50	£20.00	£40.00
816 Brave Eagle; photo cover						
	$5.00	$15.00	$30.00	£3.30	£10.00	£20.00
817 Little Beaver	$4.00	$12.00	$24.00	£2.65	£8.00	£16.00
818 Smokey the Bear						
	$6.00	$18.00	$36.00	£4.00	£12.00	£24.00
819 Mickey Mouse in Magicland						
	$5.00	$15.00	$30.00	£3.30	£10.00	£20.00
820 The Oklahoman; photo cover						
	$12.00	$36.00	$72.00	£8.00	£24.00	£48.00
821 Wringle Wrangle; Fess Parker photo cover; Jesse Marsh art						
	$12.00	$36.00	$72.00	£8.00	£24.00	£48.00
822 Paul Revere's Ride; scarce; Alex Toth art						
	$20.00	$60.00	$120.00	£13.00	£40.00	£80.00
823 Timmy	$4.00	$12.00	$24.00	£2.65	£8.00	£16.00
824 Pride and Passion; Cary Grant and Frank Sinatra photo cover						
	$12.00	$36.00	$72.00	£8.00	£24.00	£48.00
825 The Little Rascals						
	$5.00	$15.00	$30.00	£3.30	£10.00	£20.00
826 Spin and Marty and Annette; photo cover						
	$30.00	$90.00	$180.00	£20.00	£60.00	£120.00
827 Smokey Stover						
	$4.00	$12.00	$24.00	£2.65	£8.00	£16.00
828 Buffalo Bill Junior; photo cover						
	$6.00	$18.00	$36.00	£4.00	£12.00	£24.00
829 Tales of the Pony Express; painted cover						
	$6.00	$18.00	$36.00	£4.00	£12.00	£24.00
830 The Hardy Boys; photo cover						
	$14.00	$42.00	$84.00	£9.00	£28.00	£55.00
831 No Sleep Till Dawn - The Story of B52 Bombers						
	$8.00	$24.00	$48.00	£5.25	£16.00	£32.00
832 Lolly and Pepper						
	$4.00	$12.00	$24.00	£2.65	£8.00	£16.00
833 Scamp	$8.00	$24.00	$48.00	£5.25	£16.00	£32.00
834 Johnny Mack Brown; photo cover						
	$8.00	$24.00	$48.00	£5.25	£16.00	£32.00
835 Silvertip; Kinstler art						
	$5.00	$15.00	$30.00	£3.30	£10.00	£20.00
836 Man in Flight; Jesse Marsh art						
	$11.00	$33.00	$66.00	£7.25	£22.00	£44.00
837 All American Athlete Cotton Woods						
	$7.00	$21.00	$42.00	£4.65	£14.00	£28.00
838 Bugs Bunny's Life Story Album						
	$8.00	$24.00	$48.00	£5.25	£16.00	£32.00
839 Vigilantes	$11.00	$33.00	$66.00	£7.25	£22.00	£44.00
840 Duck Album	$8.00	$24.00	$48.00	£5.25	£16.00	£32.00
841 Elmer Fudd	$3.00	$9.00	$18.00	£2.00	£6.00	£12.00
842 The Nature of Things; Jesse Marsh art						
	$10.00	$30.00	$60.00	£6.50	£20.00	£40.00
843 The First Americans; Jesse Marsh art						
	$12.00	$36.00	$72.00	£8.00	£24.00	£48.00
844 Gunsmoke; photo cover						
	$8.00	$24.00	$48.00	£5.25	£16.00	£32.00
845 scarce in the U.K. The Land Unknown; Alex Toth art						
	$20.00	$60.00	$120.00	£13.00	£40.00	£80.00
846 Gun Glory; photo cover; Alex Toth art						
	$18.00	$52.50	$108.00	£12.00	£36.00	£72.50
847 Perri (Disney)						
	$10.00	$30.00	$60.00	£6.50	£20.00	£40.00
848 Marauder's Moon						
	$7.00	$21.00	$42.00	£4.65	£14.00	£28.00
849 Prince Valiant: Bob Fuje art						
	$7.00	$21.00	$42.00	£4.65	£14.00	£28.00
850 Buck Jones	$5.00	$15.00	$30.00	£3.30	£10.00	£20.00
851 The Story of Mankind; Vincent Price photo cover; Jesse Marsh art						
	$10.00	$30.00	$60.00	£6.50	£20.00	£40.00
852 Chilly Willy by Walter Lantz						
	$4.00	$12.00	$24.00	£2.65	£8.00	£16.00
853 Pluto	$6.00	$18.00	$36.00	£4.00	£12.00	£24.00
854 The Hunchback of Notre Dame; photo cover						
	$18.00	$52.50	$108.00	£12.00	£36.00	£72.50
855 Broken Arrow; photo cover						
	$7.00	$21.00	$42.00	£4.65	£14.00	£28.00
856 Buffalo Bill Junior; photo cover						
	$7.00	$21.00	$42.00	£4.65	£14.00	£28.00
857 The Goofy Adventure Story						
	$10.00	$30.00	$60.00	£6.50	£20.00	£40.00
858 Daisy Duck's Diary (#859 on inside indicia)						
	$5.00	$15.00	$30.00	£3.30	£10.00	£20.00
859 Topper and Neil						
	$5.00	$15.00	$30.00	£3.30	£10.00	£20.00
860 Wyatt Earp; photo cover; Russ Manning art						
	$18.00	$52.50	$108.00	£12.00	£36.00	£72.50
861 Frosty the Snowman						
	$4.00	$12.00	$24.00	£2.65	£8.00	£16.00
862 The Truth about Mother Goose						
	$10.00	$30.00	$60.00	£6.50	£20.00	£40.00
863 Francis The Talking Mule						
	$5.00	$15.00	$30.00	£3.30	£10.00	£20.00
864 The Littlest Snowman						
	$5.00	$15.00	$30.00	£3.30	£10.00	£20.00
865 Andy Burnett; photo cover						

Four Color #328

Four Color #339

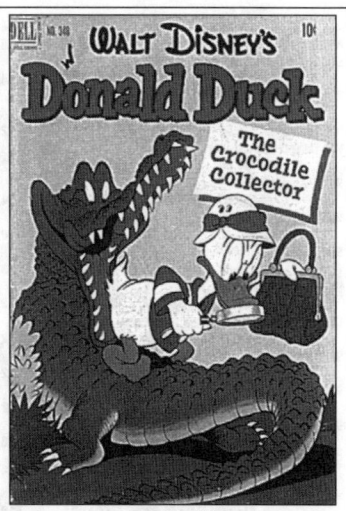

Four Color #348

MINT = 100% / NEAR MINT (inc. +/-) = 90–99% / VERY FINE (inc. +/-) = 75–89% / FINE (inc. +/-) = 55–74%
VERY GOOD (inc. +/-) = 35–54% / GOOD (inc. +/-) = 15–34% / FAIR = 5–14% / POOR = 1–4%

355

	$Good	$Fine	$N.Mint	£Good	£Fine	£N.Mint
	$18.00	$52.50	$108.00	£12.00	£36.00	£72.50
866 Mars and Beyond	$14.00	$42.00	$84.00	£9.00	£28.00	£55.00
867 Santa Claus Funnies	$4.00	$12.00	$24.00	£2.65	£8.00	£16.00
868 Walt Scott's The Little People	$4.00	$12.00	$24.00	£2.65	£8.00	£16.00
869 Old Yeller (Disney film); photo cover	$10.00	$30.00	$60.00	£6.50	£20.00	£40.00
870 Little Beaver	$4.00	$12.00	$24.00	£2.65	£8.00	£16.00
871 Curly Kayoe	$4.00	$12.00	$24.00	£2.65	£8.00	£16.00
872 Captain Kangaroo; photo cover	$20.00	$60.00	$120.00	£13.00	£40.00	£80.00
873 Grandma Duck's Farm Friends	$10.00	$30.00	$60.00	£6.50	£20.00	£40.00
874 Old Ironsides (Disney)	$10.00	$30.00	$60.00	£6.50	£20.00	£40.00
875 Trumpets West	$6.00	$18.00	$36.00	£4.00	£12.00	£24.00
876 Tales of Wells Fargo; photo cover	$14.00	$42.00	$84.00	£9.00	£28.00	£55.00
877 Frontier Doctor with Rex Allen; photo cover; Alex Toth art	$15.00	$45.00	$90.00	£10.00	£30.00	£60.00
878 Peanuts by Charles Schultz; scarce	$20.00	$60.00	$120.00	£13.00	£40.00	£80.00
879 Brave Eagle; photo cover	$4.00	$12.00	$24.00	£2.65	£8.00	£16.00
880 Steve Donovan; photo cover	$6.00	$18.00	$36.00	£4.00	£12.00	£24.00
881 Captain and the Kids	$5.00	$15.00	$30.00	£3.30	£10.00	£20.00
882 Zorro (Disney); Alex Toth art	$35.00	$105.00	$210.00	£23.00	£70.00	£140.00
883 The Little Rascals	$4.00	$12.00	$24.00	£2.65	£8.00	£16.00
884 Hawkeye and the Last of the Mohicans; photo cover	$10.00	$30.00	$60.00	£6.50	£20.00	£40.00
885 Fury; photo cover	$9.00	$27.00	$54.00	£6.00	£18.00	£36.00
886 Bongo and Lumpjaw	$4.00	$12.00	$24.00	£2.65	£8.00	£16.00
887 The Hardy Boys; photo cover	$15.00	$45.00	$90.00	£10.00	£30.00	£60.00
888 Elmer Fudd	$4.00	$12.00	$24.00	£2.65	£8.00	£16.00
889 Clint and Mac; photo cover; Alex Toth art	$20.00	$60.00	$120.00	£13.00	£40.00	£80.00
890 Wyatt Earp; photo cover; Russ Manning art	$11.00	$33.00	$66.00	£7.25	£22.00	£44.00
891 Light in the Forest; Fess Parker photo cover	$11.00	$33.00	$66.00	£7.25	£22.00	£44.00
892 Maverick; James Garner photo cover	$22.00	$65.00	$132.00	£14.50	£44.00	£87.50
893 Jim Bowie; photo cover	$7.00	$21.00	$42.00	£4.65	£14.00	£28.00
894 Oswald the Rabbit by Walter Lantz	$4.00	$12.00	$24.00	£2.65	£8.00	£16.00
895 Wagon Train; photo cover	$14.00	$42.00	$84.00	£9.00	£28.00	£55.00
896 The Adventures of Tinker Bell	$11.00	$33.00	$66.00	£7.25	£22.00	£44.00
897 Jiminy Cricket	$7.00	$21.00	$42.00	£4.65	£14.00	£28.00
898 Silvertip; Kinstler art	$7.00	$21.00	$42.00	£4.65	£14.00	£28.00
899 Goofy	$8.00	$24.00	$48.00	£5.25	£16.00	£32.00
900 Prince Valiant; Bob Fuje art	$7.00	$21.00	$42.00	£4.65	£14.00	£28.00
901 Little Hiawatha	$7.00	$21.00	$42.00	£4.65	£14.00	£28.00
902 Will-Yum!	$4.00	$12.00	$24.00	£2.65	£8.00	£16.00
903 Dottie Dripple and Taffy	$4.00	$12.00	$24.00	£2.65	£8.00	£16.00
904 The Indian Fighter	$6.00	$18.00	$36.00	£4.00	£12.00	£24.00
905 Annette; photo cover	$41.00	$120.00	$246.00	£28.00	£82.50	£165.00
906 Francis The Talking Mule	$5.00	$15.00	$30.00	£3.30	£10.00	£20.00
907 Sugarfoot; photo cover	$20.00	$60.00	$120.00	£13.00	£40.00	£80.00
908 Walt Scott's The Little People	$4.00	$12.00	$24.00	£2.65	£8.00	£16.00
909 Smitty and Herby	$4.00	$12.00	$24.00	£2.65	£8.00	£16.00
910 The Vikings; Kirk Douglas photo cover; John Buscema art	$14.00	$42.00	$84.00	£9.00	£28.00	£55.00
911 The Gray Ghost; photo cover; Russ Manning art	$10.00	$30.00	$60.00	£6.50	£20.00	£40.00
912 scarce in the U.K. Leave It To Beaver; photo cover	$27.00	$80.00	$160.00	£17.50	£52.50	£105.00
913 The Left-Handed Gun; Paul Newman photo cover	$15.00	$45.00	$90.00	£10.00	£30.00	£60.00
	$12.00	$36.00	$72.00	£8.00	£24.00	£48.00
914 No Time For Sergeants; photo cover; Alex Toth art	$12.00	$36.00	$72.00	£8.00	£24.00	£48.00
915 Casey Jones; photo cover	$8.00	$24.00	$48.00	£5.25	£16.00	£32.00
916 Red Ryder	$4.00	$12.00	$24.00	£2.65	£8.00	£16.00
917 Life of Riley; photo cover	$20.00	$60.00	$120.00	£13.00	£40.00	£80.00
918 Beep Beep, the Road Runner	$12.00	$36.00	$72.00	£8.00	£24.00	£48.00
919 Boots and Saddles; photo cover	$11.00	$33.00	$66.00	£7.25	£22.00	£44.00
920 Zorro; photo cover; Alex Toth art	$22.00	$65.00	$132.00	£14.50	£44.00	£87.50
921 Wyatt Earp; photo cover; Russ Manning art	$10.00	$30.00	$60.00	£6.50	£20.00	£40.00
922 Johnny Mack Brown; photo cover; Russ Manning art	$10.00	$30.00	$60.00	£6.50	£20.00	£40.00
923 Timmy	$4.00	$12.00	$24.00	£2.65	£8.00	£16.00
924 Colt .45; photo cover	$15.00	$45.00	$90.00	£10.00	£30.00	£60.00
925 Last of the Fast Guns; photo cover	$9.00	$27.00	$54.00	£6.00	£18.00	£36.00
926 Peter Pan; reprints #442	$7.00	$21.00	$42.00	£4.65	£14.00	£28.00
927 Top Gun; John Buscema art	$6.00	$18.00	$36.00	£4.00	£12.00	£24.00
928 Sea Hunt; Lloyd Bridges photo cover	$20.00	$60.00	$120.00	£13.00	£40.00	£80.00
929 Brave Eagle	$4.00	$12.00	$24.00	£2.65	£8.00	£16.00
930 Maverick; James Garner photo cover	$12.00	$36.00	$72.00	£8.00	£24.00	£48.00
931 Have Gun, Will Travel; photo cover	$18.00	$52.50	$108.00	£12.00	£36.00	£72.50
932 Smokey the Bear	$6.00	$18.00	$36.00	£4.00	£12.00	£24.00
933 Zorro; Alex Toth art	$22.00	$65.00	$132.00	£14.50	£44.00	£87.50
934 Restless Gun; photo cover	$18.00	$52.50	$108.00	£12.00	£36.00	£72.50
935 King of the Royal Mounted	$6.00	$18.00	$36.00	£4.00	£12.00	£24.00
936 The Little Rascals	$4.00	$12.00	$24.00	£2.65	£8.00	£16.00
937 Ruff and Reddy (Hanna-Barbera)	$20.00	$60.00	$120.00	£13.00	£40.00	£80.00
938 Elmer Fudd	$4.00	$12.00	$24.00	£2.65	£8.00	£16.00
939 Steve Canyon, no Caniff art	$6.00	$18.00	$36.00	£4.00	£12.00	£24.00
940 Lolly and Pepper	$4.00	$12.00	$24.00	£2.65	£8.00	£16.00
941 Pluto	$4.00	$12.00	$24.00	£2.65	£8.00	£16.00
942 Tales of the Pony Express	$6.00	$18.00	$36.00	£4.00	£12.00	£24.00
943 White Wilderness	$11.00	$33.00	$66.00	£7.25	£22.00	£44.00
944 The Seventh Voyage of Sinbad; John Buscema art	$20.00	$60.00	$120.00	£13.00	£40.00	£80.00
945 Maverick; James Garner photo cover	$12.00	$36.00	$72.00	£8.00	£24.00	£48.00
946 The Big Country; photo cover	$9.00	$27.00	$54.00	£6.00	£18.00	£36.00
947 Broken Arrow; photo cover	$7.00	$21.00	$42.00	£4.65	£14.00	£28.00
948 Daisy Duck's Diary	$6.00	$18.00	$36.00	£4.00	£12.00	£24.00
949 High Adventure - Lowell Thomas; photo cover; Alex Toth art	$7.00	$21.00	$42.00	£4.65	£14.00	£28.00
950 Frosty the Snowman	$4.00	$12.00	$24.00	£2.65	£8.00	£16.00
951 scarce in the U.K. The Lennon Sisters; photo cover; Alex Toth art	$24.00	$70.00	$144.00	£15.50	£48.00	£95.00
952 Goofy	$7.00	$21.00	$42.00	£4.65	£14.00	£28.00
953 Francis The Talking Mule	$5.00	$15.00	$30.00	£3.30	£10.00	£20.00
954 Man in Space (Disney)	$10.00	$30.00	$60.00	£6.50	£20.00	£40.00
955 Hi and Lois	$4.00	$12.00	$24.00	£2.65	£8.00	£16.00
956 scarce in the U.K. Ricky Nelson; photo cover	$35.00	$105.00	$210.00	£23.00	£70.00	£140.00
957 Buffalo Bee	$12.00	$36.00	$72.00	£8.00	£24.00	£48.00
958 Santa Claus Funnies	$4.00	$12.00	$24.00	£2.65	£8.00	£16.00
959 Christmas Stories; strip reprints	$5.00	$15.00	$30.00	£3.30	£10.00	£20.00
960 Zorro; Alex Toth art	$20.00	$60.00	$120.00	£13.00	£40.00	£80.00
961 Tales of the Texas Rangers; photo cover; Spiegle art	$7.00	$21.00	$42.00	£4.65	£14.00	£28.00
962 Maverick; James Garner photo cover	$12.00	$36.00	$72.00	£8.00	£24.00	£48.00
963 Johnny Mack Brown; photo cover						

	$Good	$Fine	$N.Mint	£Good	£Fine	£N.Mint
	$8.00	$24.00	$48.00	£5.25	£16.00	£32.00
964 The Hardy Boys; photo cover						
	$15.00	$45.00	$90.00	£10.00	£30.00	£60.00
965 Grandma Duck's Farm Friends						
	$7.00	$21.00	$42.00	£4.65	£14.00	£28.00
966 Tonka (Disney); photo cover						
	$14.00	$42.00	$84.00	£9.00	£28.00	£55.00
967 Chilly Willy by Walter Lantz						
	$4.00	$12.00	$24.00	£2.65	£8.00	£16.00
968 Tales of Wells Fargo; photo cover						
	$11.00	$33.00	$66.00	£7.25	£22.00	£44.00
969 Peanuts by Charles Schultz						
	$14.00	$42.00	$84.00	£9.00	£28.00	£55.00
970 Lawman; photo cover						
	$15.00	$45.00	$90.00	£10.00	£30.00	£60.00
971 Wagon Train; photo cover						
	$7.00	$21.00	$42.00	£4.65	£14.00	£28.00
972 Tom Thumb, scarce						
	$20.00	$60.00	$120.00	£13.00	£40.00	£80.00
973 Sleeping Beauty						
	$22.00	$65.00	$132.00	£14.50	£44.00	£87.50
974 The Little Rascals						
	$4.00	$12.00	$24.00	£2.65	£8.00	£16.00
975 Fury; photo cover						
	$9.00	$27.00	$54.00	£6.00	£18.00	£36.00
976 Zorro; photo cover; Alex Toth art						
	$20.00	$60.00	$120.00	£13.00	£40.00	£80.00
977 Elmer Fudd	$4.00	$12.00	$24.00	£2.65	£8.00	£16.00
978 Lolly and Pepper						
	$4.00	$12.00	$24.00	£2.65	£8.00	£16.00
979 Oswald the Rabbit by Walter Lantz						
	$4.00	$12.00	$24.00	£2.65	£8.00	£16.00
980 Maverick; James Garner photo cover						
	$12.00	$36.00	$72.00	£8.00	£24.00	£48.00
981 Ruff and Reddy (Hanna-Barbera)						
	$11.00	$33.00	$66.00	£7.25	£22.00	£44.00
982 The New Adventures of Tinker Bell						
	$10.00	$30.00	$60.00	£6.50	£20.00	£40.00
983 Have Gun, Will Travel; photo cover						
	$11.00	$33.00	$66.00	£7.25	£22.00	£44.00
984 Sleeping Beauty's Fairy Godmother						
	$18.00	$52.50	$108.00	£12.00	£36.00	£72.50
985 Shaggy Dog; photo cover						
	$8.00	$24.00	$48.00	£5.25	£16.00	£32.00
986 Restless Gun; photo cover						
	$10.00	$30.00	$60.00	£6.50	£20.00	£40.00
987 Goofy	$8.00	$24.00	$48.00	£5.25	£16.00	£32.00
988 Little Hiawatha						
	$9.00	$27.00	$54.00	£6.00	£18.00	£36.00
989 Jiminy Cricket						
	$8.00	$24.00	$48.00	£5.25	£16.00	£32.00
990 Huckleberry Hound; Yogi Bear appears						
	$20.00	$60.00	$120.00	£13.00	£40.00	£80.00
991 Francis The Talking Mule						
	$4.00	$12.00	$24.00	£2.65	£8.00	£16.00
992 Sugarfoot; photo cover; Alex Toth art						
	$18.00	$52.50	$108.00	£12.00	£36.00	£72.50
993 Jim Bowie; photo cover						
	$8.00	$24.00	$48.00	£5.25	£16.00	£32.00
994 Sea Hunt; Lloyd Bridges photo cover; Alex Toth art						
	$11.00	$33.00	$66.00	£7.25	£22.00	£44.00
995 Donald Duck Album						
	$8.00	$24.00	$48.00	£5.25	£16.00	£32.00
996 Nevada by Zane Grey						
	$5.00	$15.00	$30.00	£3.30	£10.00	£20.00
997 Tales of Texas John; photo cover						
	$11.00	$33.00	$66.00	£7.25	£22.00	£44.00
998 Ricky Nelson; photo cover						
	$30.00	$90.00	$180.00	£20.00	£60.00	£120.00
999 Leave It To Beaver; photo cover						
	$24.00	$70.00	$144.00	£15.50	£48.00	£95.00
1000 The Gray Ghost; photo cover						
	$10.00	$30.00	$60.00	£6.50	£20.00	£40.00
1001 High Adventure - Lowell Thomas; photo cover						
	$8.00	$24.00	$48.00	£5.25	£16.00	£32.00
1002 Buffalo Bee	$8.00	$24.00	$48.00	£5.25	£16.00	£32.00
1003 Zorro; photo cover; Alex Toth art						
	$20.00	$60.00	$120.00	£13.00	£40.00	£80.00
1004 Colt .45; photo cover						
	$11.00	$33.00	$66.00	£7.25	£22.00	£44.00
1005 Maverick; James Garner photo cover						
	$11.00	$33.00	$66.00	£7.25	£22.00	£44.00
1006 Hercules; John Buscema art						
	$14.00	$42.00	$84.00	£9.00	£28.00	£55.00
1007 John Paul Jones; Robert Stack photo cover						
	$7.00	$21.00	$42.00	£4.65	£14.00	£28.00
1008 Beep Beep, The Road Runner						
	$7.00	$21.00	$42.00	£4.65	£14.00	£28.00
1009 The Rifleman; Chuck Connors photo cover						
	$25.00	$75.00	$150.00	£16.50	£50.00	£100.00
1010 Grandma Duck's Farm Friends; Carl Barks art						
	$22.00	$65.00	$132.00	£14.50	£44.00	£87.50
1011 Buckskin; photo cover						
	$12.00	$36.00	$72.00	£8.00	£24.00	£48.00
1012 Last Train From Gun Hill; photo cover						
	$12.00	$36.00	$72.00	£8.00	£24.00	£48.00
1013 Bat Masterson; Gene Barry photo cover						
	$14.00	$43.00	$85.00	£9.00	£28.00	£55.00
1014 The Lennon Sisters; photo cover; Alex Toth art						
	$22.00	$65.00	$132.00	£14.50	£44.00	£87.50
1015 Peanuts by Charles Schultz						
	$14.00	$42.00	$84.00	£9.00	£28.00	£55.00
1016 Smokey the Bear Nature Stories						
	$5.00	$15.00	$30.00	£3.30	£10.00	£20.00
1017 Chilly Willy by Walter Lantz						
	$4.00	$12.00	$24.00	£2.65	£8.00	£16.00
1018 Rio Bravo; John Wayne and Dean Martin photo cover; Alex Toth art						
	$27.00	$80.00	$160.00	£17.50	£52.50	£105.00
1019 Wagon Train; photo cover						
	$7.00	$21.00	$42.00	£4.65	£14.00	£28.00
1020 Jungle Jim; McWilliams art						
	$4.00	$12.00	$24.00	£2.65	£8.00	£16.00
1021 Tales of Texas Rangers; photo cover						
	$6.00	$18.00	$36.00	£4.00	£12.00	£24.00
1022 Timmy	$4.00	$12.00	$24.00	£2.65	£8.00	£16.00
1023 Tales of Wells Fargo; photo cover						
	$11.00	$33.00	$66.00	£7.25	£22.00	£44.00
1024 Darby O'Gill and The Little People; Alex Toth art						
	$22.00	$65.00	$132.00	£14.50	£44.00	£87.50
1025 Vacation in Disneyland by Barl Barks						
	$30.00	$90.00	$180.00	£20.00	£60.00	£120.00
1026 Spin and Marty; photo cover						
	$10.00	$30.00	$60.00	£6.50	£20.00	£40.00
1027 The Texan; photo cover						
	$10.00	$30.00	$60.00	£6.50	£20.00	£40.00
1028 Rawhide; Clint Eastwood photo cover						
	$35.00	$105.00	$210.00	£23.00	£70.00	£140.00
1029 Boots and Saddles; photo cover						
	$7.00	$21.00	$42.00	£4.65	£14.00	£28.00
1030 The Little Rascals						
	$4.00	$12.00	$24.00	£2.65	£8.00	£16.00
1031 Fury; photo cover						
	$8.00	$24.00	$48.00	£5.25	£16.00	£32.00
1032 Elmer Fudd	$4.00	$12.00	$24.00	£2.65	£8.00	£16.00
1033 Steve Canyon; not Milton Caniff art; photo cover						
	$6.00	$18.00	$36.00	£4.00	£12.00	£24.00
1034 Nancy and Sluggo						
	$4.00	$12.00	$24.00	£2.65	£8.00	£16.00
1035 Lawman; photo cover; Alex Toth art						
	$8.00	$24.00	$48.00	£5.25	£16.00	£32.00
1036 The Big Circus; photo cover						
	$8.00	$24.00	$48.00	£5.25	£16.00	£32.00
1037 Zorro; Alex Toth art						
	$24.00	$70.00	$144.00	£15.50	£48.00	£95.00
1038 Ruff and Reddy (Hanna-Barbera)						
	$11.00	$33.00	$66.00	£7.25	£22.00	£44.00
1039 Pluto	$4.00	$12.00	$24.00	£2.65	£8.00	£16.00
1040 Quick Draw McGraw (Hanna-Barbera)						
	$15.00	$45.00	$90.00	£10.00	£30.00	£60.00
1041 Sea Hunt; Lloyd Bridges photo cover; Alex Toth art						
	$13.00	$39.00	$78.00	£8.75	£26.00	£52.50
1042 The Three Chipmunks						
	$5.00	$15.00	$30.00	£3.30	£10.00	£20.00
1043 scarce in the U.K. The Three Stooges; photo cover						
	$27.00	$80.00	$160.00	£17.50	£52.50	£105.00
1044 Have Gun, Will Travel; photo cover						
	$10.00	$30.00	$60.00	£6.50	£20.00	£40.00
1045 Restless Gun; photo cover						
	$11.00	$33.00	$66.00	£7.25	£22.00	£44.00
1046 Beep Beep, The Road Runner						
	$7.00	$21.00	$42.00	£4.65	£14.00	£28.00
1047 Gyro Gearloose						
	$27.00	$80.00	$160.00	£17.50	£52.50	£105.00
1048 The Horse Soldiers; John Wayne photo cover; Mike Sekowsky art						
	$27.00	$80.00	$160.00	£17.50	£52.50	£105.00
1049 Don't Give Up The Ship; Jerry Lewis photo cover						
	$9.00	$27.00	$54.00	£6.00	£18.00	£36.00
1050 Huckleberry Hound (Hanna-Barbera)						
	$10.00	$30.00	$60.00	£6.50	£20.00	£40.00
1051 Donald in Mathmagicland						
	$14.00	$42.00	$84.00	£9.00	£28.00	£55.00
1st official distribution in the U.K.						
1052 Ben Hur; Russ Manning art						
	$14.00	$42.00	$84.00	£9.00	£28.00	£55.00
1053 Goofy	$8.00	$24.00	$48.00	£5.25	£16.00	£32.00
1054 Huckleberry Hound						
	$9.00	$27.00	$54.00	£6.00	£18.00	£36.00
1055 Daisy Duck's Diary by Carl Barks						
	$15.00	$45.00	$90.00	£10.00	£30.00	£60.00
1056 Yellowstone Kelly; Clint Walker photo cover						
	$8.00	$24.00	$48.00	£5.25	£16.00	£32.00
1057 Mickey Mouse Album						
	$4.00	$12.00	$24.00	£2.65	£8.00	£16.00
1058 Colt .45; photo cover						

#	Title	$Good	$Fine	$N.Mint	£Good	£Fine	£N.Mint
	(continued from previous page)	$10.00	$30.00	$60.00	£6.50	£20.00	£40.00
1059	Sugarfoot; photo cover	$10.00	$30.00	$60.00	£6.50	£20.00	£40.00
1060	Journey To The Centre of the Earth; Pat Boone photo cover	$20.00	$60.00	$120.00	£13.00	£40.00	£80.00
1061	Buffalo Bee	$9.00	$27.00	$54.00	£6.00	£18.00	£36.00
1062	Christmas Stories; strip reprints	$4.00	$12.00	$24.00	£2.65	£8.00	£16.00
1063	Santa Claus Funnies	$4.00	$12.00	$24.00	£2.65	£8.00	£16.00
1064	Bugs Bunny's Merry Christmas	$6.00	$18.00	$36.00	£4.00	£12.00	£24.00
1065	Frosty the Snowman	$4.00	$12.00	$24.00	£2.65	£8.00	£16.00
1066	77 Sunset Strip; photo cover; Alex Toth art	$20.00	$60.00	$120.00	£13.00	£40.00	£80.00
1067	Yogi Bear (Hanna-Barbera)	$19.00	$55.00	$114.00	£12.50	£38.00	£75.00
1068	Francis The Talking Mule	$4.00	$12.00	$24.00	£2.65	£8.00	£16.00
1069	The FBI Story; James Stewart photo cover	$15.00	$45.00	$90.00	£10.00	£30.00	£60.00
1070	Solomon and Sheba; photo cover; Mike Sekowsky art	$12.00	$36.00	$72.00	£8.00	£24.00	£48.00
1071	The Real McCoys; photo cover; Alex Toth art	$15.00	$45.00	$90.00	£10.00	£30.00	£60.00
1072	Blythe	$7.00	$21.00	$42.00	£4.65	£14.00	£28.00
1073	Grandma Duck's Farm Friends by Carl Barks	$20.00	$60.00	$120.00	£13.00	£40.00	£80.00
1074	Chily Willy by Walter Lantz	$4.00	$12.00	$24.00	£2.65	£8.00	£16.00
1075	Tales of Wells Fargo; photo cover	$11.00	$33.00	$66.00	£7.25	£22.00	£44.00
1076	Johnny Yuma's Journal - The Rebel; photo cover; Mike Sekowsky art	$14.00	$42.00	$84.00	£9.00	£28.00	£55.00
1077	The Deputy; Henry Fonda photo cover; John Buscema art	$20.00	$60.00	$120.00	£13.00	£40.00	£80.00
1078	The Three Stooges; photo cover	$14.00	$42.00	$84.00	£9.00	£28.00	£55.00
1079	The Little Rascals	$4.00	$12.00	$24.00	£2.65	£8.00	£16.00
1080	Fury; photo cover	$9.00	$27.00	$54.00	£6.00	£18.00	£36.00
1081	Elmer Fudd	$4.00	$12.00	$24.00	£2.65	£8.00	£16.00
1082	Spin and Marty; photo cover	$10.00	$30.00	$60.00	£6.50	£20.00	£40.00
1083	Men into Space; photo cover	$10.00	$30.00	$60.00	£6.50	£20.00	£40.00
1084	Speedy Gonzales	$4.00	$12.00	$24.00	£2.65	£8.00	£16.00
1085	The Time Machine; Alex Toth art	$24.00	$70.00	$144.00	£15.50	£48.00	£95.00
1086	Lolly and Pepper	$4.00	$12.00	$24.00	£2.65	£8.00	£16.00
1087	Peter Gunn; photo cover	$12.00	$36.00	$72.00	£8.00	£24.00	£48.00
1088	A Dog of Flanders; photo cover	$7.00	$21.00	$42.00	£4.65	£14.00	£28.00
1089	Restless Gun; photo cover	$10.00	$30.00	$60.00	£6.50	£20.00	£40.00
1090	Francis The Talking Mule	$4.00	$12.00	$24.00	£2.65	£8.00	£16.00
1091	Jack's Diary	$8.00	$24.00	$48.00	£5.25	£16.00	£32.00
1092	Toby Tyler; photo cover	$10.00	$30.00	$60.00	£6.50	£20.00	£40.00
1093	MacKenzie's Raiders; photo cover	$9.00	$27.00	$54.00	£6.00	£18.00	£36.00
1094	Goofy	$7.00	$21.00	$42.00	£4.65	£14.00	£28.00
1095	Gyro Gearloose by Carl Barks	$16.00	$48.00	$96.00	£10.50	£33.00	£65.00
1096	The Texan; Rory Calhoun photo cover	$10.00	$30.00	$60.00	£6.50	£20.00	£40.00
1097	Rawhide; Clint Eastwood photo cover	$22.00	$65.00	$132.00	£14.50	£44.00	£87.50
1098	Sugarfoot; photo cover	$10.00	$30.00	$60.00	£6.50	£20.00	£40.00
1099	Donald Duck Album; Carl Barks cover only	$8.00	$24.00	$48.00	£5.25	£16.00	£32.00
1100	Annette's Life Story; photo cover	$27.00	$80.00	$160.00	£17.50	£52.50	£105.00
1101	Kidnapped; photo cover	$8.00	$24.00	$48.00	£5.25	£16.00	£32.00
1102	Wanted Dead or Alive; Steve McQueen photo cover	$19.00	$55.00	$114.00	£12.50	£38.00	£75.00
1103	Leave It To Beaver; photo cover	$22.00	$65.00	$132.00	£14.50	£44.00	£87.50
1104	Yogi Bear Goes to College (Hanna-Barbera)	$10.00	$30.00	$60.00	£6.50	£20.00	£40.00
1105	Gail Storm; photo cover; Alex Toth art	$20.00	$60.00	$120.00	£13.00	£40.00	£80.00
1106	77 Sunset Strip; photo cover; Alex Toth art	$12.00	$36.00	$72.00	£8.00	£24.00	£48.00
1107	Buckskin; photo cover	$10.00	$30.00	$60.00	£6.50	£20.00	£40.00
1108	The Troubleshooters; photo cover	$8.00	$24.00	$48.00	£5.25	£16.00	£32.00
1109	This Is Your Life Donald Duck; "origin" of Donald Duck	$25.00	$75.00	$150.00	£16.50	£50.00	£100.00
1110	Bonanza, scarce; photo cover	$45.00	$135.00	$270.00	£30.00	£90.00	£180.00
1111	Shotgun Slade; photo cover	$8.00	$24.00	$48.00	£5.25	£16.00	£32.00
1112	Pixie, Dixie and Mr. Jinks (Hanna-Barbera)	$8.00	$24.00	$48.00	£5.25	£16.00	£32.00
1113	Tales of Wells Fargo; photo cover	$10.00	$30.00	$60.00	£6.50	£20.00	£40.00
1114	The Adventures of Huckleberry Finn; photo cover	$7.00	$21.00	$42.00	£4.65	£14.00	£28.00
1115	Ricky Nelson; photo cover; not Russ Manning art	$22.00	$65.00	$132.00	£14.50	£44.00	£87.50
1116	Boots and Saddles; photo cover	$7.00	$21.00	$42.00	£4.65	£14.00	£28.00
1117	The Boy and the Pirates; photo cover	$8.00	$24.00	$48.00	£5.25	£16.00	£32.00
1118	The Sword and the Dragon; photo cover	$10.00	$30.00	$60.00	£6.50	£20.00	£40.00
1119	Smokey the Bear Nature Stories	$4.00	$12.00	$24.00	£2.65	£8.00	£16.00
1120	Dinosaurs! - painted cover	$10.00	$30.00	$60.00	£6.50	£20.00	£40.00
1121	Hercules Unchained; Reed Crandall art	$12.00	$36.00	$72.00	£8.00	£24.00	£48.00
1122	Chilly Willy by Walter Lantz	$4.00	$12.00	$24.00	£2.65	£8.00	£16.00
1123	Tombstone Territory; photo cover	$12.00	$36.00	$72.00	£8.00	£24.00	£48.00
1124	Whirlybirds; photo cover	$12.00	$36.00	$72.00	£8.00	£24.00	£48.00
1125	Laramie; photo cover; Russ Heath art	$12.00	$36.00	$72.00	£8.00	£24.00	£48.00
1126	Sundance; photo cover	$12.00	$36.00	$72.00	£8.00	£24.00	£48.00
1127	The Three Stooges; photo cover	$12.00	$36.00	$72.00	£8.00	£24.00	£48.00
1128	scarce in the U.K. Rocky and His Friends; photo cover	$37.00	$110.00	$222.00	£25.00	£75.00	£150.00
1129	Pollyana; photo cover	$14.00	$42.00	$84.00	£9.00	£28.00	£55.00
1130	The Deputy; Henry Fonda photo cover; John Buscema art	$12.00	$36.00	$72.00	£8.00	£24.00	£48.00
1131	Elmer Fudd	$3.00	$9.00	$18.00	£2.00	£6.00	£12.00
1132	less common in the U.K. Space Mouse by Walter Lantz	$6.00	$18.00	$36.00	£4.00	£12.00	£24.00
1133	Fury; photo cover	$8.00	$24.00	$48.00	£5.25	£16.00	£32.00
1134	The Real McCoys; photo cover; Alex Toth art	$15.00	$45.00	$90.00	£10.00	£30.00	£60.00
1135	The Mouseketeers	$3.00	$9.00	$18.00	£2.00	£6.00	£12.00
1136	Jungle Cat; photo cover	$10.00	$30.00	$60.00	£6.50	£20.00	£40.00
1137	The Little Rascals	$4.00	$12.00	$24.00	£2.65	£8.00	£16.00
1138	Johnny Yuma's Journal - The Rebel; photo cover	$12.00	$36.00	$72.00	£8.00	£24.00	£48.00
1139	Spartacus; Kirk Douglas photo cover; John Buscema art	$20.00	$60.00	$120.00	£13.00	£40.00	£80.00
1140	Donald Duck Album	$9.00	$27.00	$54.00	£6.00	£18.00	£36.00
1141	Huckleberry Hound	$9.00	$27.00	$54.00	£6.00	£18.00	£36.00
1142	Johnny Ringo; photo cover	$10.00	$30.00	$60.00	£6.50	£20.00	£40.00
1143	Pluto	$4.00	$12.00	$24.00	£2.65	£8.00	£16.00
1144	The Story of Ruth; photo cover	$15.00	$45.00	$90.00	£10.00	£30.00	£60.00
1145	The Lost World; photo cover; Gil Kane art	$16.00	$48.00	$96.00	£10.50	£33.00	£65.00
1146	Restless Gun; photo cover	$10.00	$30.00	$60.00	£6.50	£20.00	£40.00
1147	Sugarfoot; photo cover	$10.00	$30.00	$60.00	£6.50	£20.00	£40.00
1148	I Aim At The Stars; photo cover	$8.00	$24.00	$48.00	£5.25	£16.00	£32.00
1149	Goofy	$8.00	$24.00	$48.00	£5.25	£16.00	£32.00
1150	Daisy Duck's Diary by Carl Barks	$15.00	$45.00	$90.00	£10.00	£30.00	£60.00
1151	Mickey Mouse Album	$5.00	$15.00	$30.00	£3.30	£10.00	£20.00
1152	Rocky and His Friends	$30.00	$90.00	$180.00	£20.00	£60.00	£120.00
1153	Frosty the Snowman						

	$Good	$Fine	$N.Mint	£Good	£Fine	£N.Mint
	$4.00	$12.00	$24.00	£2.65	£8.00	£16.00
1154 Santa Claus Funnies						
	$5.00	$15.00	$30.00	£3.30	£10.00	£20.00
1155 North to Alaska; John Wayne photo cover						
	$20.00	$60.00	$120.00	£13.00	£40.00	£80.00
1156 Swiss Family Robinson; photo cover						
	$10.00	$30.00	$60.00	£6.50	£20.00	£40.00
1157 Master of the World						
	$7.00	$21.00	$42.00	£4.65	£14.00	£28.00
1158 The Three Worlds of Gulliver; photo cover						
	$7.00	$21.00	$42.00	£4.65	£14.00	£28.00
1159 77 Sunset Strip; photo cover; Alex Toth art						
	$12.00	$36.00	$72.00	£8.00	£24.00	£48.00
1160 Rawhide; Clint Eastwood photo cover						
	$20.00	$60.00	$120.00	£13.00	£40.00	£80.00
1161 Grandma Duck's Farm Friends by Carl Barks						
	$20.00	$60.00	$120.00	£13.00	£40.00	£80.00
1162 Yogi Bear Joins The Marines						
	$10.00	$30.00	$60.00	£6.50	£20.00	£40.00
1163 Daniel Boone; Jesse Marsh art						
	$9.00	$27.00	$54.00	£6.00	£18.00	£36.00
1164 Wanted Dead or Alive; Steve McQueen photo cover						
	$15.00	$45.00	$90.00	£10.00	£30.00	£60.00
1165 Ellery Queen, Detective						
	$16.00	$48.00	$96.00	£10.50	£33.00	£65.00
1166 Rocky and his Friends						
	$30.00	$90.00	$180.00	£20.00	£60.00	£120.00
1167 Tales of Wells Fargo; photo cover						
	$10.00	$30.00	$60.00	£6.50	£20.00	£40.00
1168 The Detectives; Robert Taylor photo cover						
	$12.00	$36.00	$72.00	£8.00	£24.00	£48.00
1169 The New Adventures of Sherlock Holmes						
	$22.00	$65.00	$132.00	£14.50	£44.00	£87.50
1170 The Three Stooges; photo cover						
	$14.00	$42.00	$84.00	£9.00	£28.00	£55.00
1171 Elmer Fudd	$4.00	$12.00	$24.00	£2.65	£8.00	£16.00
1172 Fury; photo cover						
	$8.00	$24.00	$48.00	£5.25	£16.00	£32.00
1173 The Twilight Zone; Crandall/Evans art						
	$25.00	$75.00	$150.00	£16.50	£50.00	£100.00
1174 The Little Rascals						
	$4.00	$12.00	$24.00	£2.65	£8.00	£16.00
1175 The Two Mouseketeers						
	$4.00	$12.00	$24.00	£2.65	£8.00	£16.00
1176 Dondi; photo cover						
	$7.00	$21.00	$42.00	£4.65	£14.00	£28.00
1177 Chilly Willy by Walter Lantz						
	$4.00	$12.00	$24.00	£2.65	£8.00	£16.00
1178 Ten Who Dared; painted cover						
	$10.00	$30.00	$60.00	£6.50	£20.00	£40.00
1179 Swamp Fox; Leslie Neilsen photo cover						
	$12.00	$36.00	$72.00	£8.00	£24.00	£48.00
1180 The Danny Thomas Show; Alex Toth art						
	$25.00	$75.00	$150.00	£16.50	£50.00	£100.00
1181 Texas John; photo cover						
	$10.00	$30.00	$60.00	£6.50	£20.00	£40.00
1182 Donald Duck Album						
	$6.00	$18.00	$36.00	£4.00	£12.00	£24.00
1183 101 Dalmatians						
	$12.00	$36.00	$72.00	£8.00	£24.00	£48.00
1184 Gyro Gearloose						

	$Good	$Fine	$N.Mint	£Good	£Fine	£N.Mint
	$15.00	$45.00	$90.00	£10.00	£30.00	£60.00
1185 Sweetie Pie	$5.00	$15.00	$30.00	£3.30	£10.00	£20.00
1186 Yak Yak	$11.00	$33.00	$66.00	£7.25	£22.00	£44.00
1187 The Three Stooges; photo cover						
	$14.00	$42.00	$84.00	£9.00	£28.00	£55.00
1188 Atlantis, The Lost Continent; photo cover						
	$14.00	$42.00	$84.00	£9.00	£28.00	£55.00
1189 Greyfriars Bobby; photo cover						
	$10.00	$30.00	$60.00	£6.50	£20.00	£40.00
1190 Donald and The Wheel by Carl Barks (cover only)						
	$8.00	$24.00	$48.00	£5.25	£16.00	£32.00
1191 Leave It To Beaver; photo cover						
	$22.00	$65.00	$132.00	£14.50	£44.00	£87.50
1192 Ricky Nelso; photo cover; Russ Manning art						
	$24.00	$70.00	$144.00	£15.50	£48.00	£95.00
1193 The Real McCoys; photo cover						
	$12.00	$36.00	$72.00	£8.00	£24.00	£48.00
1194 Pepe	$5.00	$15.00	$30.00	£3.30	£10.00	£20.00
1195 National Velvet; photo cover						
	$8.00	$24.00	$48.00	£5.25	£16.00	£32.00
1196 Pixie, Dixie and Mr. Jinks						
	$7.00	$21.00	$42.00	£4.65	£14.00	£28.00
1197 The Astronauts; photo cover						
	$8.00	$24.00	$48.00	£5.25	£16.00	£32.00
1198 Donald in Mathmagicland; reprints #1051						
	$8.00	$24.00	$48.00	£5.25	£16.00	£32.00
1199 The Absent Minded Professor; photo cover						
	$9.00	$27.00	$54.00	£6.00	£18.00	£36.00
1200 Hennesey; photo cover; Gil Kane art						
	$8.00	$24.00	$48.00	£5.25	£16.00	£32.00
1201 Goofy	$8.00	$24.00	$48.00	£5.25	£16.00	£32.00
1202 Rawhide; Clint Eastwood photo cover						
	$20.00	$60.00	$120.00	£13.00	£40.00	£80.00
1203 Pinocchio	$8.00	$24.00	$48.00	£5.25	£16.00	£32.00
1204 Scamp	$4.00	$12.00	$24.00	£2.65	£8.00	£16.00
1205 David and Goliath; photo cover						
	$9.00	$27.00	$54.00	£6.00	£18.00	£36.00
1206 Lolly and Pepper						
	$3.00	$9.00	$18.00	£2.00	£6.00	£12.00
1207 Johnny Yuma's Journal - The Rebel; photo cover; Mike Sekowsky art						
	$12.00	$36.00	$72.00	£8.00	£24.00	£48.00
1208 Rocky and his Friends						
	$30.00	$90.00	$180.00	£20.00	£60.00	£120.00
1209 Sugarfoot	$10.00	$30.00	$60.00	£6.50	£20.00	£40.00
1210 The Parent Trap						
	$15.00	$45.00	$90.00	£10.00	£30.00	£60.00
1211 77 Sunset Strip; photo cover; Russ Manning art						
	$12.00	$36.00	$72.00	£8.00	£24.00	£48.00
1212 Chilly Willy by Walter Lantz						
	$3.00	$9.00	$18.00	£2.00	£6.00	£12.00
1213 Mysterious Island; photo cover						
	$11.00	$33.00	$66.00	£7.25	£22.00	£44.00
1214 Smokey the Bear						
	$5.00	$15.00	$30.00	£3.30	£10.00	£20.00
1215 Tales of Wells Fargo; photo cover						
	$10.00	$30.00	$60.00	£6.50	£20.00	£40.00
1216 Whirlybirds; photo cover						
	$10.00	$30.00	$60.00	£6.50	£20.00	£40.00
1218 Fury; photo cover						
	$9.00	$27.00	$54.00	£6.00	£18.00	£36.00
1219 The Detectives; Robert Taylor and Adam West photo cover						

Four Color #1168

Four Color #1183

Four Color #1199

EXTREMELY HIGH GRADE COPIES MAY COMMAND MULTIPLES OF GUIDE ALTHOUGH THIS IS MORE PREVALENT IN THE US THAN IN THE UK

#	Title	$Good	$Fine	$N.Mint	£Good	£Fine	£N.Mint
		$11.00	$33.00	$66.00	£7.25	£22.00	£44.00
1220	Gunslinger; photo cover	$10.00	$30.00	$60.00	£6.50	£20.00	£40.00
1221	Bonanza; photo cover	$25.00	$75.00	$150.00	£16.50	£50.00	£100.00
1222	Elmer Fudd	$3.00	$9.00	$18.00	£2.00	£6.00	£12.00
1223	Laramie; photo cover; Gil Kane art	$8.00	$24.00	$48.00	£5.25	£16.00	£32.00
1224	The Little Rascals	$4.00	$12.00	$24.00	£2.65	£8.00	£16.00
1225	The Deputy; Henry Fonda photo cover	$12.00	$36.00	$72.00	£8.00	£24.00	£48.00
1226	Nikki, Wild Dog of the North; photo cover	$9.00	$27.00	$54.00	£6.00	£18.00	£36.00
1227	Morgan the Pirate; photo cover	$12.00	$36.00	$72.00	£8.00	£24.00	£48.00
1229	Thief of Bagdad; photo cover; George Evans art	$14.00	$42.00	$84.00	£9.00	£28.00	£55.00
1230	Voyage to the Bottom of the Sea; part photo cover	$11.00	$33.00	$66.00	£7.25	£22.00	£44.00
1231	Danger Man; Patrick McGoohan photo cover	$11.00	$34.00	$67.50	£7.50	£22.50	£45.00
1232	On the Double	$6.00	$18.00	$36.00	£4.00	£12.00	£24.00
1233	Tammy Tell Me True	$8.00	$24.00	$48.00	£5.25	£16.00	£32.00
1234	The Phantom Planet	$8.00	$24.00	$48.00	£5.25	£16.00	£32.00
1235	Mister Magoo	$6.00	$18.00	$36.00	£4.00	£12.00	£24.00
1236	King of Kings; photo cover	$10.00	$30.00	$60.00	£6.50	£20.00	£40.00
1237	The Untouchables; photo cover	$20.00	$60.00	$120.00	£13.00	£40.00	£80.00
1238	Deputy Dawg	$15.00	$45.00	$90.00	£10.00	£30.00	£60.00
1239	Donald Duck Album; Carl Barks cover	$10.00	$30.00	$60.00	£6.50	£20.00	£40.00
1240	The Detectives; Robert Taylor photo cover	$10.00	$30.00	$60.00	£6.50	£20.00	£40.00
1241	Sweetie Pie	$4.00	$12.00	$24.00	£2.65	£8.00	£16.00
1242	scarce in the U.K. King Leonard	$20.00	$60.00	$120.00	£13.00	£40.00	£80.00
1243	Ellery Queen, Detective	$10.00	$30.00	$60.00	£6.50	£20.00	£40.00
1244	Space Mouse by Walter Lantz	$6.00	$18.00	$36.00	£4.00	£12.00	£24.00
1245	The New Adventures of Sherlock Holmes	$22.00	$65.00	$132.00	£14.50	£44.00	£87.50
1246	Mickey Mouse Album	$5.00	$15.00	$30.00	£3.30	£10.00	£20.00
1247	Daisy Duck's Diary	$5.00	$15.00	$30.00	£3.30	£10.00	£20.00
1248	Pluto	$5.00	$15.00	$30.00	£3.30	£10.00	£20.00
1249	The Danny Thomas Show; photo cover; Russ Manning art	$22.00	$65.00	$132.00	£14.50	£44.00	£87.50
1250	The Four Horsemen of the Apocalypse; photo cover	$8.00	$24.00	$48.00	£5.25	£16.00	£32.00
1251	Everything's Ducky	$7.00	$21.00	$42.00	£4.65	£14.00	£28.00
1252	The Andy Griffith Show	$35.00	$105.00	$210.00	£23.00	£70.00	£140.00
1253	Space Man	$10.00	$30.00	$60.00	£6.50	£20.00	£40.00
1254	Diver Dan; photo cover	$8.00	$24.00	$48.00	£5.25	£16.00	£32.00
1255	The Wonders of Aladdin	$8.00	$24.00	$48.00	£5.25	£16.00	£32.00
1256	Kona, Monarch of Monster Isle; Sam Glanzman art	$8.00	$24.00	$48.00	£5.25	£16.00	£32.00
1257	Car 54, Where Are You?; photo cover	$10.00	$30.00	$60.00	£6.50	£20.00	£40.00
1258	The Frogmen; George Evans art	$11.00	$33.00	$66.00	£7.25	£22.00	£44.00
1259	El Cid; Charlton Heston photo cover	$8.00	$24.00	$48.00	£5.25	£16.00	£32.00
1260	The Horsemasters; photo cover	$15.00	$45.00	$90.00	£10.00	£30.00	£60.00
1261	Rawhide; Clint Eastwood photo cover	$20.00	$60.00	$120.00	£13.00	£40.00	£80.00
1262	Johnny Yuma's Journal - The Rebel; photo cover	$12.00	$36.00	$72.00	£8.00	£24.00	£48.00
1263	77 Sunset Strip; photo cover; Russ Manning art	$12.00	$36.00	$72.00	£8.00	£24.00	£48.00
1264	Pixie, Dixie and Mr. Jinks	$7.00	$21.00	$42.00	£4.65	£14.00	£28.00
1265	The Real McCoys; photo cover	$12.00	$36.00	$72.00	£8.00	£24.00	£48.00
1266	Spike and Tyke	$3.00	$9.00	$18.00	£2.00	£6.00	£12.00
1267	Gyro Gearloose, some Barks art	$10.00	$30.00	$60.00	£6.50	£20.00	£40.00
1268	Oswald the Rabbit by Walter Lantz	$3.00	$9.00	$18.00	£2.00	£6.00	£12.00
1269	Rawhide; Clint Eastwood photo cover	$20.00	$60.00	$120.00	£13.00	£40.00	£80.00
1270	Bullwinkle and Rocky	$25.00	$75.00	$150.00	£16.50	£50.00	£100.00
1271	Yogi Bear Birthday Party	$7.00	$21.00	$42.00	£4.65	£14.00	£28.00
1272	Frosty the Snowman	$4.00	$12.00	$24.00	£2.65	£8.00	£16.00
1273	Hans Brinker; photo cover	$10.00	$30.00	$60.00	£6.50	£20.00	£40.00
1274	Santa Claus Funnies	$4.00	$12.00	$24.00	£2.65	£8.00	£16.00
1275	Rocky and his Friends	$30.00	$90.00	$180.00	£20.00	£60.00	£120.00
1276	Dondi	$4.00	$12.00	$24.00	£2.65	£8.00	£16.00
1278	King Leonardo	$19.00	$55.00	$114.00	£12.50	£38.00	£75.00
1279	Grandma Duck's Farm Friends	$7.00	$21.00	$42.00	£4.65	£14.00	£28.00
1280	Hennesey; photo cover	$8.00	$24.00	$48.00	£5.25	£16.00	£32.00
1281	Chilly Willy by Walter Lantz	$3.50	$10.50	$21.00	£2.30	£7.00	£14.00
1282	Babes in Toyland; photo cover	$19.00	$55.00	$114.00	£12.50	£38.00	£75.00
1283	Bonanza; photo cover	$24.00	$70.00	$144.00	£15.50	£48.00	£95.00
1284	Laramie; photo cover; Russ Heath art	$8.00	$24.00	$48.00	£5.25	£16.00	£32.00
1285	Leave It To Beaver; photo cover	$22.00	$65.00	$132.00	£14.50	£44.00	£87.50
1286	The Untouchables; photo cover	$20.00	$60.00	$120.00	£13.00	£40.00	£80.00
1287	The Man From Wells Fargo; photo cover	$6.00	$18.00	$36.00	£4.00	£12.00	£24.00
1288	The Twilight Zone; Crandall/Evans art	$15.00	$45.00	$90.00	£10.00	£30.00	£60.00
1289	Ellery Queen, Detective	$10.00	$30.00	$60.00	£6.50	£20.00	£40.00
1290	The Two Mouseketeers	$3.00	$9.00	$18.00	£2.00	£6.00	£12.00
1291	77 Sunset Strip; photo cover; Russ Manning art	$12.00	$36.00	$72.00	£8.00	£24.00	£48.00
1293	Elmer Fudd	$3.00	$9.00	$18.00	£2.00	£6.00	£12.00
1294	Ripcord	$8.00	$24.00	$48.00	£5.25	£16.00	£32.00
1295	Mister Ed; photo cover	$19.00	$55.00	$114.00	£12.50	£38.00	£75.00
1296	Fury; photo cover	$8.00	$24.00	$48.00	£5.25	£16.00	£32.00
1297	The Little Rascals	$4.00	$12.00	$24.00	£2.65	£8.00	£16.00
1298	The Hathaways; photo cover	$7.00	$21.00	$42.00	£4.65	£14.00	£28.00
1299	Deputy Dawg	$15.00	$45.00	$90.00	£10.00	£30.00	£60.00
1300	The Comancheros; John Wayne photo cover	$24.00	$70.00	$144.00	£15.50	£48.00	£95.00
1301	Adventures in Paradise	$6.00	$18.00	$36.00	£4.00	£12.00	£24.00
1302	Johnny Jason, Teen Reporter	$3.00	$9.00	$18.00	£2.00	£6.00	£12.00
1303	Lad, A Dog; photo cover	$5.00	$15.00	$30.00	£3.30	£10.00	£20.00
1304	Nellie the Nurse	$12.00	$36.00	$72.00	£8.00	£24.00	£48.00
1305	Mister Magoo	$10.00	$30.00	$60.00	£6.50	£20.00	£40.00
1306	Target: The Corruptors; photo cover	$7.00	$21.00	$42.00	£4.65	£14.00	£28.00
1307	Margie	$5.00	$15.00	$30.00	£3.30	£10.00	£20.00
1308	Tales of the Wizard of Oz	$15.00	$45.00	$90.00	£10.00	£30.00	£60.00
1309	87th Precinct; photo cover	$12.00	$36.00	$72.00	£8.00	£24.00	£48.00
1310	Huckleberry Hound	$8.00	$24.00	$48.00	£5.25	£16.00	£32.00
1311	Rocky and his Friends	$30.00	$90.00	$180.00	£20.00	£60.00	£120.00
1312	National Velvet; photo cover	$5.00	$15.00	$30.00	£3.30	£10.00	£20.00
1313	Moon Pilot; photo cover	$11.00	$33.00	$66.00	£7.25	£22.00	£44.00
1328	The Underwater City; photo cover; George Evans art	$10.00	$30.00	$60.00	£6.50	£20.00	£40.00
1330	Brain Boy; Gil Kane art	$14.00	$43.00	$100.00	£9.25	£28.00	£65.00
1332	Bachelor Father	$11.00	$33.00	$66.00	£7.25	£22.00	£44.00
1333	Short Ribs	$7.00	$21.00	$42.00	£4.65	£14.00	£28.00
1335	Aggie Mack	$5.00	$15.00	$30.00	£3.30	£10.00	£20.00

VERY GENERAL PERCENTAGE CONVERSION CHART WHICH MAY BE USED TO CALCULATE LOW AND INBETWEEN GRADES:

	$Good	$Fine	$N.Mint	£Good	£Fine	£N.Mint
1336 On Stage	$6.00	$18.00	$36.00	£4.00	£12.00	£24.00
1337 Dr. Kildare; photo cover	$9.00	$27.00	$54.00	£6.00	£18.00	£36.00
1341 The Andy Griffith Show; photo cover	$35.00	$105.00	$210.00	£23.00	£70.00	£140.00
1348 Yak Yak; Jack Davis art	$10.00	$30.00	$60.00	£6.50	£20.00	£40.00
1349 Yogi Bear Visits the U.N.	$13.00	$39.00	$78.00	£8.75	£26.00	£52.50
1350 Commanche; reprints #466 with title change	$8.00	$24.00	$48.00	£5.25	£16.00	£32.00
1354 scarce in the U.K. Calvin and the Colonel	$11.00	$33.00	$66.00	£7.25	£22.00	£44.00
Title Value:	$20759.45	$62113.00	$143763.00	£13778.00	£41470.60	£96332.00

FOUR STAR BATTLE TALES
DC Comics; 1 Feb/Mar 1975-5 Nov/Dec 1975

	$Good	$Fine	$N.Mint	£Good	£Fine	£N.Mint
1-5 reprints	$0.25	$0.75	$1.25	£0.15	£0.45	£0.75
Title Value:	$1.25	$3.75	$6.25	£0.75	£2.25	£3.75

FOUR STAR SPECTACULAR
DC Comics; 1 Mar/Apr 1976-6 Jan/Feb 1977

	$Good	$Fine	$N.Mint	£Good	£Fine	£N.Mint
1 ND 68pgs	$0.40	$1.20	$2.00	£0.30	£0.90	£1.25
2-6 52pgs	$0.40	$1.20	$2.00	£0.25	£0.75	£1.25
Title Value:	$2.40	$7.20	$12.00	£1.55	£4.65	£7.75

FEATURES
Re-done GA Flash story in 1.
REPRINT FEATURES
Blackhawk in 6. Green Arrow, Vigilante in 5. Green Lantern, Supergirl/Superboy in 3. Hawkman in 1, 4. Kid Flash in 2. Superboy in 1, 2, 4-6. Wonder Woman in 1-6.

FOX AND THE CROW
National Periodical Publications; 62 Oct/Nov 1959-108 Feb/Mar 1968
(becomes Stanley and His Monster) (See also TV Screen Cartoons) (previous issues ND)

	$Good	$Fine	$N.Mint	£Good	£Fine	£N.Mint
62-80 scarce in the U.K.	$3.90	$11.50	$27.50	£2.55	£7.50	£18.00
81-94	$3.30	$10.00	$20.00	£2.05	£6.25	£12.50
95 origin and 1st appearance Stanley and His Monster	$3.75	$11.00	$22.50	£2.50	£7.50	£15.00
96-99	$2.25	$6.75	$13.50	£1.50	£4.50	£9.00
100	$3.00	$9.00	$18.00	£2.00	£6.00	£12.00
101-108	$2.25	$6.75	$13.50	£1.50	£4.50	£9.00
Title Value:	$154.05	$459.50	$1005.00	£99.65	£297.50	£652.00

FOXFIRE
Night Wynd,MS; 1 Apr 1992-3 Jun 1992

	$Good	$Fine	$N.Mint	£Good	£Fine	£N.Mint
1-3 ND Barry Blair script and art	$0.45	$1.35	$2.25	£0.30	£0.90	£1.50
Title Value:	$1.35	$4.05	$6.75	£0.90	£2.70	£4.50

FRAGGLE ROCK
Marvel Comics Group/Star; 1 Apr 1985-8 Sep 1986

	$Good	$Fine	$N.Mint	£Good	£Fine	£N.Mint
1-8	$0.15	$0.45	$0.75	£0.10	£0.30	£0.50
Title Value:	$1.20	$3.60	$6.00	£0.80	£2.40	£4.00

FRAGMENTS
Screaming Cat Productions; 1 1986

	$Good	$Fine	$N.Mint	£Good	£Fine	£N.Mint
1 ND Gregg Hinlicky script/art; black and white	$0.30	$0.90	$1.50	£0.20	£0.60	£1.00
Title Value:	$0.30	$0.90	$1.50	£0.20	£0.60	£1.00

FRANCIS, BROTHER OF THE UNIVERSE
Marvel Comics Group,OS; 1 1980

	$Good	$Fine	$N.Mint	£Good	£Fine	£N.Mint
1 ND scarce in the U.K. 52pgs, story of Francis Bernadone	$0.15	$0.45	$0.75	£0.10	£0.35	£0.60
Title Value:	$0.15	$0.45	$0.75	£0.10	£0.35	£0.60

FRANK
Nemesis,MS; 1 Mar 1994-4 Jun 1994

	$Good	$Fine	$N.Mint	£Good	£Fine	£N.Mint
1-4 ND D.G. Chichester script, Denys Cowan and Mike Manley art	$0.35	$1.05	$1.75	£0.25	£0.75	£1.25
Title Value:	$1.40	$4.20	$7.00	£1.00	£3.00	£5.00

FRANK FRAZETTA'S THUN'DA
(see Thun'da Tales)

FRANKENSTEIN
Dell; 12-283-305 Mar/May 1963; 1 Aug/Oct 1964; 2 Sep 1966-4 Mar 1967

	$Good	$Fine	$N.Mint	£Good	£Fine	£N.Mint
12-283-305 scarce in the U.K. adapts film	$6.00	$18.00	$35.00	£2.00	£6.00	£12.00
1 rare in the U.K.	$3.50	$10.50	$20.00	£1.30	£4.00	£8.00
2 scarce in the U.K. becomes super-hero title	$2.50	$7.50	$15.00	£1.00	£3.00	£5.00
3-4 scarce in the U.K.	$1.50	$4.50	$10.00	£0.70	£2.10	£3.50
Title Value:	$15.00	$45.00	$90.00	£5.70	£17.20	£32.00

Note: all distributed on the news-stands in the U.K.

FRANKENSTEIN (2ND SERIES)
Malibu,MS; 1-3 Dec 1994

	$Good	$Fine	$N.Mint	£Good	£Fine	£N.Mint
1 ND released to co-incide with Kenneth Branagh's film	$0.45	$1.35	$2.25	£0.30	£0.90	£1.50
1 ND Black Book Edition (Dec 1994) - black cover on thicker stock paper; 2,500 copies	$1.50	$4.50	$7.50	£1.00	£3.00	£5.00
2-3 ND released to co-incide with Kenneth Branagh's film	$0.45	$1.35	$2.25	£0.30	£0.90	£1.50
Title Value:	$2.85	$8.55	$14.25	£1.90	£5.70	£9.50

FRANKENSTEIN BOOK AND RECORD SET
Power Records; PR-14 1974

	$Good	$Fine	$N.Mint	£Good	£Fine	£N.Mint
PR-14 scarce, 20pg booklet with 45 rpm record, Neal Adams art featured				£1.25	£3.75	£6.25

Note: the item would be valued at 50% less without the record

FRANKENSTEIN OR THE MODERN PROMETHEUS
Caliber Press,OS; nn Oct 1994
nn ND 48pgs, Charles Yates art, Vince Locke painted cover

	$Good	$Fine	$N.Mint	£Good	£Fine	£N.Mint
	$0.60	$1.80	$3.00	£0.40	£1.20	£2.00
Title Value:	$0.60	$1.80	$3.00	£0.40	£1.20	£2.00

FRANKENSTEIN PAGES, THE LOST
Apple Comics,OS; 1 Jan 1992
1 ND 48pgs, Bernie Wrightson reprint from Marvel Comics with unpublished pages

	$Good	$Fine	$N.Mint	£Good	£Fine	£N.Mint
	$1.40	$4.20	$7.00	£0.90	£2.70	£4.50
Title Value:	$1.40	$4.20	$7.00	£0.90	£2.70	£4.50

FRANKENSTEIN, MARY SHELLEY'S
Topps,MS; 1 Oct 1994-4 Jan 1995
1 ND adaptation of Kenneth Branagh film, Timothy Bradstreet cover

	$Good	$Fine	$N.Mint	£Good	£Fine	£N.Mint
	$0.45	$1.35	$2.25	£0.30	£0.90	£1.50

1 ND Direct Market Edition (Oct 1994) - pre-bagged with trading card; John Bolton cover

	$Good	$Fine	$N.Mint	£Good	£Fine	£N.Mint
	$0.60	$1.80	$3.00	£0.40	£1.20	£2.00

2 ND adaptation of Kenneth Branagh film, Timothy Bradstreet cover

	$Good	$Fine	$N.Mint	£Good	£Fine	£N.Mint
	$0.45	$1.35	$2.25	£0.30	£0.90	£1.50

2 ND Direct Market Edition (Nov 1994) - pre-bagged with trading card; John Bolton cover

	$Good	$Fine	$N.Mint	£Good	£Fine	£N.Mint
	$0.60	$1.80	$3.00	£0.40	£1.20	£2.00

3 ND adaptation of Kenneth Branagh film, Timothy Bradstreet cover

	$Good	$Fine	$N.Mint	£Good	£Fine	£N.Mint
	$0.45	$1.35	$2.25	£0.30	£0.90	£1.50

3 ND Direct Market Edition (Dec 1994) - pre-bagged with trading card; John Bolton cover

	$Good	$Fine	$N.Mint	£Good	£Fine	£N.Mint
	$0.60	$1.80	$3.00	£0.40	£1.20	£2.00

4 ND adaptation of Kenneth Branagh film, Timothy Bradstreet cover

	$Good	$Fine	$N.Mint	£Good	£Fine	£N.Mint
	$0.45	$1.35	$2.25	£0.30	£0.90	£1.50

4 ND Direct market Edition (Jan 1995) - pre-bagged with trading card; John Bolton cover

	$Good	$Fine	$N.Mint	£Good	£Fine	£N.Mint
	$0.60	$1.80	$3.00	£0.40	£1.20	£2.00
Title Value:	$4.20	$12.60	$21.00	£2.80	£8.40	£14.00

Mary Shelley's Frankenstein Deluxe (Mar 1995)
Trade paperback reprints series with John Bolton covers
and new wraparound cover by Tim Bradstreet

	£Good	£Fine	£N.Mint
	£1.30	£3.90	£6.50

FRANKENSTEIN, THE MONSTER OF
Marvel Comics Group; 1 Jan 1973-18 Sep 1975
(see Marvel Illustrated Books)
1 ND Ploog art begins, ends #6

	$Good	$Fine	$N.Mint	£Good	£Fine	£N.Mint
	$3.60	$10.50	$18.00	£2.50	£7.50	£12.50
2 ND	$2.20	$6.50	$11.00	£1.50	£4.50	£7.50
3 ND	$1.50	$4.50	$7.50	£1.00	£3.00	£5.00
4-5 ND	$1.20	$3.60	$6.00	£0.80	£2.40	£4.00
6-7 ND	$0.90	$2.70	$4.50	£0.60	£1.80	£3.00
8-9 ND Dracula appears	$1.40	$4.20	$7.00	£0.90	£2.70	£4.50
10 ND	$0.90	$2.70	$4.50	£0.60	£1.80	£3.00
11 ND	$0.45	$1.35	$2.25	£0.50	£1.50	£2.50
12-18	$0.45	$1.35	$2.25	£0.30	£0.90	£1.50
Title Value:	$18.80	$56.00	$94.00	£12.80	£38.40	£64.00

FRANKENSTEIN/DRACULA WAR, THE
Topps,MS; 1 Feb 1995-3 Apr 1995

	$Good	$Fine	$N.Mint	£Good	£Fine	£N.Mint
1-3 ND Roy Thomas script, Mike Mignola cover	$0.45	$1.35	$2.25	£0.30	£0.90	£1.50
Title Value:	$1.35	$4.05	$6.75	£0.90	£2.70	£4.50

FREAK FORCE
Image; 1 Dec 1993-18 Jun 1995

	$Good	$Fine	$N.Mint	£Good	£Fine	£N.Mint
1 Erik Larsen script, Keith Giffen plot begins	$0.45	$1.35	$2.25	£0.30	£0.90	£1.50
2-3	$0.40	$1.20	$2.00	£0.25	£0.75	£1.25
4 features Vanguard	$0.40	$1.20	$2.00	£0.25	£0.75	£1.25
5	$0.40	$1.20	$2.00	£0.25	£0.75	£1.25
6 origin of Rapture	$0.40	$1.20	$2.00	£0.25	£0.75	£1.25
7	$0.40	$1.20	$2.00	£0.25	£0.75	£1.25
8 Vanguard appears	$0.45	$1.35	$2.25	£0.30	£0.90	£1.50
9 Cyberforce guest-stars	$0.40	$1.20	$2.00	£0.25	£0.75	£1.25
10 Savage Dragon guest-stars	$0.45	$1.35	$2.25	£0.30	£0.90	£1.50
11-18	$0.45	$1.35	$2.25	£0.30	£0.90	£1.50
Title Value:	$7.75	$23.25	$38.75	£5.05	£15.15	£25.25

Note: all Non-Distributed on the news-stands in the U.K.

FREAKS
Monster Comics,MS; 1 Jun 1992-3 1992

	$Good	$Fine	$N.Mint	£Good	£Fine	£N.Mint
1-3 ND Sam Kieth covers	$0.45	$1.35	$2.25	£0.30	£0.90	£1.50
Title Value:	$1.35	$4.05	$6.75	£0.90	£2.70	£4.50

FRED HEMBECK DESTROYS THE MARVEL UNIVERSE
Marvel Comics Group,OS; 1 Jul 1989
1 ND no advertisements

	$Good	$Fine	$N.Mint	£Good	£Fine	£N.Mint
	$0.30	$0.90	$1.50	£0.20	£0.60	£1.00
Title Value:	$0.30	$0.90	$1.50	£0.20	£0.60	£1.00

FRED HEMBECK SELLS THE MARVEL UNIVERSE
Marvel Comics Group,OS; 1 Oct 1990
1 ND reprints Marvel Age strips

	$Good	$Fine	$N.Mint	£Good	£Fine	£N.Mint
	$0.25	$0.75	$1.25	£0.15	£0.45	£0.75
Title Value:	$0.25	$0.75	$1.25	£0.15	£0.45	£0.75

FREDDY'S DEAD – THE FINAL NIGHTMARE
Innovation,MS; 1 Nov 1991-3 Jan 1992

	$Good	$Fine	$N.Mint	£Good	£Fine	£N.Mint
1-2 ND based on film	$0.45	$1.35	$2.25	£0.30	£0.90	£1.50

3 ND based on film; part 3-D issue (as the 6th film in the series is part 3-D or "Freddyvision");

MINT = 100% / NEAR MINT (inc. +/-) = 90–99% / VERY FINE (inc. +/-) = 75–89% / FINE (inc. +/-) = 55–74%
VERY GOOD (inc. +/-) = 35–54% / GOOD (inc. +/-) = 15–34% / FAIR = 5–14% / POOR = 1–4%

361

	$Good	$Fine	$N.Mint	£Good	£Fine	£N.Mint

no glasses were issued with the comic as they were issued when seeing the film

| | $0.45 | $1.35 | $2.25 | £0.30 | £0.90 | £1.50 |
| Title Value: | $1.35 | $4.05 | $6.75 | £0.90 | £2.70 | £4.50 |

Graphic Novel (Feb 1992),
reprints mini-series with cover by John Dismukes

| | | | | £0.90 | £2.70 | £4.50 |

FREEDOM AGENT
Gold Key; 1 Apr 1963
(see John Steele Secret Agent)
1 scarce, distributed in the U.K.

| | $2.05 | $6.25 | $12.50 | £1.25 | £3.75 | £7.50 |
| Title Value: | $2.05 | $6.25 | $12.50 | £1.25 | £3.75 | £7.50 |

FREEDOM FIGHTERS
DC Comics; 1 Mar/Apr 1976-15 Jul/Aug 1978
1 ND

| | $0.90 | $2.70 | $4.50 | £0.60 | £1.80 | £3.00 |

2-3 scarce in the U.K.

| | $0.40 | $1.20 | $2.00 | £0.40 | £1.20 | £2.00 |

4 scarce in the U.K. Wonder Woman appears

| | $0.30 | $0.90 | $1.50 | £0.30 | £0.90 | £1.50 |

5 Wonder Woman appears

| | $0.30 | $0.90 | $1.50 | £0.25 | £0.75 | £1.25 |

6

| | $0.30 | $0.90 | $1.50 | £0.25 | £0.75 | £1.25 |

7 Justice League of America appears

| | $0.30 | $0.90 | $1.50 | £0.25 | £0.75 | £1.25 |

8-9 scarce in the U.K.

| | $0.30 | $0.90 | $1.50 | £0.25 | £0.75 | £1.25 |

10 scarce in the U.K. origin Doll Man retold

| | $0.30 | $0.90 | $1.50 | £0.25 | £0.75 | £1.25 |

11 origin The Ray retold

| | $0.30 | $0.90 | $1.50 | £0.20 | £0.60 | £1.00 |

12-13

| | $0.30 | $0.90 | $1.50 | £0.20 | £0.60 | £1.00 |

14 Batwoman and Batgirl guest-star

| | $0.30 | $0.90 | $1.50 | £0.20 | £0.60 | £1.00 |

15

| | $0.30 | $0.90 | $1.50 | £0.20 | £0.60 | £1.00 |
| Title Value: | $5.30 | $15.90 | $26.50 | £4.20 | £12.60 | £21.00 |

FEATURES
Freedom Fighters (Black Condor, Uncle Sam, The Ray, Doll Man, Phantom Lady, Human Bomb) in all.

FREEJACK
Now Comics,MS; 1 Apr 1992-3 Jun 1992
1 ND based on film, bi-weekly

| | $0.40 | $1.20 | $2.00 | £0.25 | £0.75 | £1.25 |

1 ND direct market edition with free poster

| | $0.45 | $1.35 | $2.25 | £0.30 | £0.90 | £1.50 |

2 ND bi-weekly

| | $0.40 | $1.20 | $2.00 | £0.25 | £0.75 | £1.25 |

2 ND direct market edition with free poster

| | $0.45 | $1.35 | $2.25 | £0.30 | £0.90 | £1.50 |

3 ND bi-weekly

| | $0.40 | $1.20 | $2.00 | £0.25 | £0.75 | £1.25 |

3 ND direct market edition with free poster

| | $0.45 | $1.35 | $2.25 | £0.30 | £0.90 | £1.50 |
| Title Value: | $2.55 | $7.65 | $12.75 | £1.65 | £4.95 | £8.25 |

FREEX
Malibu Ultraverse; 1 Jul 1993-18 Dec 1994
1 pre-bagged with a trading card and large card coupon for Ultraverse #0

| | $0.50 | $1.50 | $2.50 | £0.30 | £0.90 | £1.50 |

1 without coupon/card

| | $0.45 | $1.35 | $2.25 | £0.25 | £0.75 | £1.25 |

1 Limited Edition - full hologram cover; 7,500 copies

| | $3.00 | $9.00 | $15.00 | £1.50 | £4.50 | £7.50 |

2-3

| | $0.50 | $1.50 | $2.50 | £0.30 | £0.90 | £1.50 |

4 40pgs, Rune insert

| | $0.50 | $1.50 | $2.50 | £0.30 | £0.90 | £1.50 |

5

| | $0.40 | $1.20 | $2.00 | £0.25 | £0.75 | £1.25 |

6 Break-Thru X-over

| | $0.40 | $1.20 | $2.00 | £0.25 | £0.75 | £1.25 |

7 Origins part 1: Pressure (ends #11)

| | $0.40 | $1.20 | $2.00 | £0.25 | £0.75 | £1.25 |

8-11

| | $0.40 | $1.20 | $2.00 | £0.25 | £0.75 | £1.25 |

12 Ultraforce tie-in

| | $0.40 | $1.20 | $2.00 | £0.25 | £0.75 | £1.25 |

13-14

| | $0.40 | $1.20 | $2.00 | £0.25 | £0.75 | £1.25 |

15 64pgs, flip-book format with Ultraverse Premiere #9

| | $0.70 | $2.10 | $3.50 | £0.30 | £0.90 | £1.50 |

16 prelude to Godwheel story

| | $0.40 | $1.20 | $2.00 | £0.25 | £0.75 | £1.25 |

17 Rune appears

| | $0.40 | $1.20 | $2.00 | £0.25 | £0.75 | £1.25 |

18

| | $0.40 | $1.20 | $2.00 | £0.25 | £0.75 | £1.25 |
| Title Value: | $11.35 | $34.05 | $56.75 | £6.50 | £19.50 | £32.50 |

Note: all Non-Distributed on the news-stands in the U.K.

FREEX, GIANT SIZE
Malibu Ultraverse; 1 Jul 1994
1 ND 40pgs

| | $0.40 | $1.20 | $2.00 | £0.25 | £0.75 | £1.25 |
| Title Value: | $0.40 | $1.20 | $2.00 | £0.25 | £0.75 | £1.25 |

FRENCH ICE
Renegade; 1 Jan 1987-13 Apr 1988
1-13 ND Carmen Cru translated reprints; black and white

| | | | | £0.25 | £0.75 | £1.25 |
| Title Value: | $5.20 | $15.60 | $26.00 | £3.25 | £9.75 | £16.25 |

FRIENDS
Renegade; 1 May 1987-3 Sep 1987
1-3 ND

| | $0.40 | $1.20 | $2.00 | £0.25 | £0.75 | £1.25 |
| Title Value: | $1.20 | $3.60 | $6.00 | £0.75 | £2.25 | £3.75 |

FRIGHT
Atlas; 1 Jun 1975

1 Son of Dracula by Frank Thorne; distributed in the U.K.

| | $0.40 | $1.20 | $2.00 | £0.25 | £0.75 | £1.25 |
| Title Value: | $0.40 | $1.20 | $2.00 | £0.25 | £0.75 | £1.25 |

FRIGHT (2ND SERIES)
Eternity; 1 Jul 1988-13 1989
1-13 ND

| | $0.40 | $1.20 | $2.00 | £0.25 | £0.75 | £1.25 |
| Title Value: | $5.20 | $15.60 | $26.00 | £3.25 | £9.75 | £16.25 |

FRIGHT NIGHT
Now Comics; 1 Oct 1988-22 Jul 1990
1-6 ND adapts film

| | $0.40 | $1.20 | $2.00 | £0.25 | £0.75 | £1.25 |

7-22 ND

| | $0.40 | $1.20 | $2.00 | £0.25 | £0.75 | £1.25 |
| Title Value: | $8.80 | $26.40 | $44.00 | £5.50 | £16.50 | £27.50 |

Fright Night Annual (1993)
includes centre-fold pin-up of all Fright Night covers

| | | | | | | £1.50 |

FRIGHT NIGHT 3-D HALLOWEEN SPECIAL
Now Comics,OS; 1 Dec 1992
1 ND pre-bagged with glasses (25% less without glasses)

| | $0.55 | $1.65 | $2.75 | £0.35 | £1.05 | £1.75 |
| Title Value: | $0.55 | $1.65 | $2.75 | £0.35 | £1.05 | £1.75 |

FRIGHT NIGHT 3-D SPECIAL
Now Comics,OS; 1 Jun 1992
1 ND with 3-D glasses (25% less without glasses)

| | $0.55 | $1.65 | $2.75 | £0.35 | £1.05 | £1.75 |
| Title Value: | $0.55 | $1.65 | $2.75 | £0.35 | £1.05 | £1.75 |

FRIGHT NIGHT 3-D SUMMER SPECIAL
Now Comics,OS; 1 Aug 1993
1 ND with 3-D glasses

| | $0.60 | $1.80 | $3.00 | £0.40 | £1.20 | £2.00 |
| Title Value: | $0.60 | $1.80 | $3.00 | £0.40 | £1.20 | £2.00 |

FRIGHT NIGHT 3-D WINTER SPECIAL
Now Comics,OS; 1 May 1993
1 ND pre-bagged with 3-D glasses (25% less without glasses)

| | $0.60 | $1.80 | $3.00 | £0.40 | £1.20 | £2.00 |
| Title Value: | $0.60 | $1.80 | $3.00 | £0.40 | £1.20 | £2.00 |

FRIGHT NIGHT II
Now Comics,OS; 1 1989
1 ND adapts film

| | $0.80 | $2.40 | $4.00 | £0.50 | £1.50 | £2.50 |
| Title Value: | $0.80 | $2.40 | $4.00 | £0.50 | £1.50 | £2.50 |

FRINGE
Caliber Press; 1 Feb 1990-8 1992
1-8 ND Paul Tobin script, Philip Hester art; black and white

| | $0.45 | $1.35 | $2.25 | £0.30 | £0.90 | £1.50 |
| Title Value: | $3.60 | $10.80 | $18.00 | £2.40 | £7.20 | £12.00 |

FRISKY FROLICS
Renegade; (Revolver 13) 1 Nov 1986
1 ND DS

| | $0.40 | $1.20 | $2.00 | £0.25 | £0.75 | £1.25 |
| Title Value: | $0.40 | $1.20 | $2.00 | £0.25 | £0.75 | £1.25 |

FROM BEYOND THE UNKNOWN
National Periodical Publications; 1 Oct/Nov 1969-25 Nov/Dec 1973
1 scarce in the U.K. reprints from Mystery in Space and Strange Adventures begin

| | $1.60 | $4.80 | $8.00 | £1.00 | £3.00 | £5.00 |

2-5 scarce in the U.K. all reprint

| | $1.00 | $3.00 | $5.00 | £0.60 | £1.80 | £3.00 |

6 scarce in the U.K. all reprint, Gil Kane art featured

| | $0.90 | $2.70 | $4.50 | £0.50 | £1.50 | £2.50 |

7 64pgs, new 12pg story by O'Neil/Anderson plus reprints, Kubert cover

| | $0.90 | $2.70 | $4.50 | £0.50 | £1.50 | £2.50 |

8 64pgs, new 12pg story by O'Neil/Anderson plus reprints

| | $0.90 | $2.70 | $4.50 | £0.50 | £1.50 | £2.50 |

9-10 64pgs, all reprint

| | $0.90 | $2.70 | $4.50 | £0.50 | £1.50 | £2.50 |

11 64pgs, all reprint

| | $0.60 | $1.80 | $3.00 | £0.40 | £1.20 | £2.00 |

12-14 48pgs, all reprint, Kubert cover

| | $0.60 | $1.80 | $3.00 | £0.40 | £1.20 | £2.00 |

15 scarce in the U.K. 48pgs, all reprint

| | $0.60 | $1.80 | $3.00 | £0.50 | £1.50 | £2.50 |

16-17 48pgs, all reprint

| | $0.60 | $1.80 | $3.00 | £0.40 | £1.20 | £2.00 |

18 all reprint

| | $0.40 | $1.20 | $2.00 | £0.25 | £0.75 | £1.25 |

19 all reprint, Kaluta cover

| | $0.50 | $1.50 | $2.50 | £0.30 | £0.90 | £1.50 |

20-21 all reprint, Kaluta cover

| | $0.50 | $1.50 | $2.50 | £0.30 | £0.90 | £1.50 |

22 all reprint, photo cover

| | $0.50 | $1.50 | $2.50 | £0.30 | £0.90 | £1.50 |

23-25 all reprint

| | $0.50 | $1.50 | $2.50 | £0.30 | £0.90 | £1.50 |
| Title Value: | $18.20 | $54.60 | $91.00 | £11.15 | £33.45 | £55.75 |

FEATURES
All science-fiction reprints except one new story each in 7, 8

FROM BEYONDE
Studio Insidio; 1 Feb 1991
1 ND 48pgs, black and white horror anthology

| | $0.60 | $1.80 | $3.00 | £0.40 | £1.20 | £2.00 |
| Title Value: | $0.60 | $1.80 | $3.00 | £0.40 | £1.20 | £2.00 |

FROM HELL
Tundra Publishing; 1 Apr 1991; 2 Aug 1993; 3 1993; Kitchen Sink; 4 Mar 1994-present
1 ND collects first 2 episodes of Alan Moore and Eddie Campbell "Jack the Ripper" story from Taboo

| | $1.05 | $3.15 | $5.25 | £0.70 | £2.10 | £3.50 |

1 2nd printing, ND (Jul 1992)

| | $0.90 | $2.70 | $4.50 | £0.60 | £1.80 | £3.00 |

1 3rd printing ND | $1.00 | $3.00 | $5.00 | £0.65 | £1.95 | £3.25 |

	$Good	$Fine	$N.Mint	£Good	£Fine	£N.Mint
2 ND	$1.00	$3.00	$5.00	£0.65	£1.95	£3.25
2 2nd printing, ND (Aug 1994) - new cover logo, updated appendix						
	$1.00	$3.00	$5.00	£0.65	£1.95	£3.25
3-8 ND	$1.00	$3.00	$5.00	£0.65	£1.95	£3.25
Title Value:	$10.95	$32.85	$54.75	£7.15	£21.45	£35.75

FROM THE DARK
Fantagor; 1 Apr 1991

	$Good	$Fine	$N.Mint	£Good	£Fine	£N.Mint
1 ND Richard Corben, Bruce Jones, black and white						
	$0.40	$1.20	$2.00	£0.25	£0.75	£1.25
Title Value:	$0.40	$1.20	$2.00	£0.25	£0.75	£1.25

FROM THE DARKNESS
Eternity,MS; 1 Oct 1990-4 Jan 1991

	$Good	$Fine	$N.Mint	£Good	£Fine	£N.Mint
1-4 ND black and white						
	$0.40	$1.20	$2.00	£0.25	£0.75	£1.25
Title Value:	$1.60	$4.80	$8.00	£1.00	£3.00	£5.00

FROM THE PIT
Fantagor; 1 Jul 1994-2 1994

	$Good	$Fine	$N.Mint	£Good	£Fine	£N.Mint
1-2 ND Richard Corben script and art						
	$1.00	$3.00	$5.00	£0.65	£1.95	£3.25
Title Value:	$2.00	$6.00	$10.00	£1.30	£3.90	£6.50

FROM THE VOID
Graphic Story Society; 1 1982

	$Good	$Fine	$N.Mint	£Good	£Fine	£N.Mint
1 ND	$0.30	$0.90	$1.50	£0.20	£0.60	£1.00
Title Value:	$0.30	$0.90	$1.50	£0.20	£0.60	£1.00

FRONTIER
Slave Labor; 1 Jul 1994

	$Good	$Fine	$N.Mint	£Good	£Fine	£N.Mint
1 ND Paul Duncan script, Steve Pugh art						
	$0.60	$1.80	$3.00	£0.40	£1.20	£2.00
Title Value:	$0.60	$1.80	$3.00	£0.40	£1.20	£2.00

FRONTIER FIGHTERS
National Periodical Publications; 1 Sep/Oct 1955-8 Nov/Dec 1956

	$Good	$Fine	$N.Mint	£Good	£Fine	£N.Mint
1 very rare in the U.K. Buffalo Bill and Davy Crockett by Joe Kubert begin						
	$44.00	$130.00	$350.00	£28.00	£82.50	£225.00
2 rare in the U.K.	$36.00	$105.00	$250.00	£21.00	£62.50	£150.00
3-8 rare in the U.K.						
	$32.00	$95.00	$225.00	£17.50	£52.50	£125.00
Title Value:	$272.00	$805.00	$1950.00	£154.00	£460.00	£1125.00

Note: all Non-Distributed on the news-stands in the U.K.

FRONTIER ROMANCES
I.W. Super; 9 1964

	$Good	$Fine	$N.Mint	£Good	£Fine	£N.Mint
9 reprints Avon Periodicals title; distributed in the U.K.						
	$1.50	$4.50	$9.00	£1.00	£3.00	£6.00
Title Value:	$1.50	$4.50	$9.00	£1.00	£3.00	£6.00

FRONTIER SCOUT DANIEL BOONE
Charlton; 10 Jan 1956-13 Aug 1956; 14 Mar 1965

	$Good	$Fine	$N.Mint	£Good	£Fine	£N.Mint
10 ND scarce in the U.K.						
	$6.00	$18.00	$36.00	£4.00	£12.00	£24.00
11-13 ND scarce in the U.K.						
	$3.75	$11.00	$22.50	£2.50	£7.50	£15.00
14 distributed in the U.K.						
	$1.85	$5.50	$11.25	£1.25	£3.75	£7.50
Title Value:	$19.10	$56.50	$114.75	£12.75	£38.25	£76.50

FRONTLINE COMBAT
E.C. Comics; 1 Jul/Aug 1951-15 Jan 1954

	$Good	$Fine	$N.Mint	£Good	£Fine	£N.Mint
1 Harvey Kurtzman cover and art						
	$60.00	$180.00	$425.00	£41.00	£120.00	£285.00
2 Harvey Kurtzman cover and art						
	$37.00	$110.00	$260.00	£25.00	£75.00	£175.00
3 Harvey Kurtzman cover						
	$26.00	$75.00	$180.00	£17.00	£50.00	£120.00
4 Harvey Kurtzman cover						
	$22.50	$67.50	$160.00	£15.00	£46.00	£108.00
5 Harvey Kurtzman cover						
	$20.00	$60.00	$140.00	£13.50	£41.00	£95.00
6 Harvey Kurtzman cover						
	$17.00	$50.00	$120.00	£11.00	£34.00	£80.00
7 Iwo Jima issue, Harvey Kurtzman cover						
	$17.00	$50.00	$120.00	£11.00	£34.00	£80.00
8 Harvey Kurtzman cover						
	$17.00	$50.00	$120.00	£11.00	£34.00	£80.00
9 Civil War issue, Harvey Kurtzman cover						
	$17.00	$50.00	$120.00	£11.00	£34.00	£80.00
10 Harvey Kurtzman cover						
	$17.00	$50.00	$120.00	£11.00	£34.00	£80.00
11	$12.50	$39.00	$90.00	£8.50	£26.00	£60.00
12 Air Force issue						
	$12.50	$39.00	$90.00	£8.50	£26.00	£60.00
13-15	$12.50	$39.00	$90.00	£8.50	£26.00	£60.00
Title Value:	$313.00	$937.50	$2215.00	£209.00	£632.00	£1483.00

Note: all Non-Distributed on the news-stands in the U.K.

FRONTLINE COMBAT (2ND SERIES)
E.C. Comics/Russ Cochran; 1 Jun 1995-present

	$Good	$Fine	$N.Mint	£Good	£Fine	£N.Mint
1 ND reprints begin from the original issue #1						
	$0.40	$1.20	$2.00	£0.25	£0.75	£1.25
2 ND	$0.35	$1.10	$1.88	£0.25	£0.75	£1.25
Title Value:	$0.75	$2.30	$3.88	£0.50	£1.50	£2.50

FROST
Caliber Press,OS; 1 1990

	$Good	$Fine	$N.Mint	£Good	£Fine	£N.Mint
1 ND	$0.30	$0.90	$1.50	£0.20	£0.60	£1.00
Title Value:	$0.30	$0.90	$1.50	£0.20	£0.60	£1.00
Frost Graphic Novel (1991), reprints issues #1,2 by Amazing Comics plus Caliber one-shot	$1.00	$3.00	£5.00			

FROST: THE DYING BREED
Caliber Press,MS; 1 Jun 1991-4 Feb 1992

	$Good	$Fine	$N.Mint	£Good	£Fine	£N.Mint
1-4 ND	$0.55	$1.65	$2.75	£0.35	£1.05	£1.75
Title Value:	$2.20	$6.60	$11.00	£1.40	£4.20	£7.00

FUGITIVE
Caliber Press,OS; 1 1989

	$Good	$Fine	$N.Mint	£Good	£Fine	£N.Mint
1 ND 48pgs, black and white						
	$0.45	$1.35	$2.25	£0.30	£0.90	£1.50
Title Value:	$0.45	$1.35	$2.25	£0.30	£0.90	£1.50

FUGITOID
Mirage Studios,Magazine; 1 Jan 1986

	$Good	$Fine	$N.Mint	£Good	£Fine	£N.Mint
1 ND ties in to Teenage Mutant Ninja Turtles #4-7, black and white						
	$1.20	$3.60	$6.00	£0.80	£2.40	£4.00
Title Value:	$1.20	$3.60	$6.00	£0.80	£2.40	£4.00

FULL THROTTLE
Aircel,MS; 1 Oct 1991-2 Nov 1991

	$Good	$Fine	$N.Mint	£Good	£Fine	£N.Mint
1-2 ND black and white						
	$0.45	$1.35	$2.25	£0.30	£0.90	£1.50
Title Value:	$0.90	$2.70	$4.50	£0.60	£1.80	£3.00

FUN AND GAMES MAGAZINE
Marvel Comics Group; 1 Sep 1979-8? Apr 1980

	$Good	$Fine	$N.Mint	£Good	£Fine	£N.Mint
1-8 ND	$0.30	$0.90	$1.50	£0.20	£0.60	£1.00
Title Value:	$2.40	$7.20	$12.00	£1.60	£4.80	£8.00

FUN COMICS
(see Bill Black's..)

FUNNY STUFF STOCKING STUFFER
DC Comics,OS; 1 Mar 1985

	$Good	$Fine	$N.Mint	£Good	£Fine	£N.Mint
1 48pgs, features most DC funny animals						
	$0.25	$0.75	$1.25	£0.15	£0.45	£0.75
Title Value:	$0.25	$0.75	$1.25	£0.15	£0.45	£0.75

Frank #2

Freex #1

Frontier Romances #9

FUNTASTIC WORLD OF HANNA-BARBERA, THE
Marvel Comics Group, Tabloid; 1 Dec 1977-3 Jun 1978

	$Good	$Fine	$N.Mint	£Good	£Fine	£N.Mint
1 ND scarce in the U.K. Flintstones' Christmas Party	$0.40	$1.20	$2.00	£0.25	£0.75	£1.25
2 ND scarce in the U.K. Yogi Bear's Easter Parade	$0.40	$1.20	$2.00	£0.25	£0.75	£1.25
3 ND scarce in the U.K. Laff-a-Lympics	$0.40	$1.20	$2.00	£0.25	£0.75	£1.25
Title Value:	$1.20	$3.60	$6.00	£0.75	£2.25	£3.75

FURRLOUGH
Antarctic Press; 1 Jan 1992-present

	$Good	$Fine	$N.Mint	£Good	£Fine	£N.Mint
1 ND 56pgs	$0.60	$1.80	$3.00	£0.40	£1.20	£2.00
2-20 ND 32pgs	$0.45	$1.35	$2.25	£0.30	£0.90	£1.50
21-22 ND 32pgs	$0.55	$1.65	$2.75	£0.35	£1.05	£1.75
23 ND 32pgs	$0.80	$2.40	$4.00	£0.50	£1.50	£2.50
24-34 ND 32pgs	$0.55	$1.65	$2.75	£0.35	£1.05	£1.75
35 ND 48pgs, 4th anniversary issue	$0.70	$2.10	$3.50	£0.50	£1.50	£2.50
Title Value:	$17.80	$53.40	$89.00	£11.65	£34.95	£58.25

Best of Furrlough Volume 1 (Jan 1995)
64pgs, collection of selected best tales, special gate-fold cover £0.50 £1.50 £2.50

FURY
Marvel Comics Group, OS; 1 May 1994

	$Good	$Fine	$N.Mint	£Good	£Fine	£N.Mint
1 ND 64pgs, Nick Fury and his origin re-told; Wolverine and Iron Man guest-star	$0.60	$1.80	$3.00	£0.40	£1.20	£2.00
Title Value:	$0.60	$1.80	$3.00	£0.40	£1.20	£2.00

FURY OF FIRESTORM THE NUCLEAR MAN
(see Firestorm the Nuclear Man)

FURY OF S.H.I.E.L.D.
Marvel Comics Group; 1 Apr 1995-4 Jul 1995

	$Good	$Fine	$N.Mint	£Good	£Fine	£N.Mint
1 foil-etched cover	$0.45	$1.35	$2.25	£0.30	£0.90	£1.50
2 Iron Man appears	$0.40	$1.20	$2.00	£0.25	£0.75	£1.25
3	$0.40	$1.20	$2.00	£0.25	£0.75	£1.25
4 bound-in decoder card	$0.45	$1.35	$2.25	£0.30	£0.90	£1.50
Title Value:	$1.70	$5.10	$8.50	£1.10	£3.30	£5.50

FUSION
Eclipse; 1 1987-17 1989

	$Good	$Fine	$N.Mint	£Good	£Fine	£N.Mint
1-17 ND	$0.40	$1.20	$2.00	£0.25	£0.75	£1.25
Title Value:	$6.80	$20.40	$34.00	£4.25	£12.75	£21.25

FUTURIANS
Lodestone; 1 Oct 1985-3 1986

	$Good	$Fine	$N.Mint	£Good	£Fine	£N.Mint
1-3 ND Dave Cockrum script and art	$0.40	$1.20	$2.00	£0.25	£0.75	£1.25
Title Value:	$1.20	$3.60	$6.00	£0.75	£2.25	£3.75

FUTURIANS (2ND SERIES)
Aardwolf Publications; 0 May 1995

	$Good	$Fine	$N.Mint	£Good	£Fine	£N.Mint
0 ND reprints from original series; 50,000 print run	$0.60	$1.80	$3.00	£0.40	£1.20	£2.00
0 ND Signed Edition (May 1995) - available to retailers for every 10 copies of issue #0 ordered	$0.60	$1.80	$3.00	£0.40	£1.20	£2.00
Title Value:	$1.20	$3.60	$6.00	£0.80	£2.40	£4.00

G

G-8 AND HIS BATTLE ACES
Gold Key; 1 Oct 1966

	$Good	$Fine	$N.Mint	£Good	£Fine	£N.Mint
1 scarce, distributed in the U.K.	$5.00	$15.00	$25.00	£3.00	£9.00	£15.00
Title Value:	$5.00	$15.00	$25.00	£3.00	£9.00	£15.00

G-8 AND HIS BATTLE ACES (2ND SERIES)
Blazing Comics; 1 1991

	$Good	$Fine	$N.Mint	£Good	£Fine	£N.Mint
1 ND Tim Truman cover and Sam Glanzman art, based on a 1940 story/characters; flip-book with The Spider's Web, all colour	$0.30	$0.90	$1.50	£0.20	£0.60	£1.00
Title Value:	$0.30	$0.90	$1.50	£0.20	£0.60	£1.00

G-8 AND HIS BATTLE ACES (3RD SERIES)
Millennium, MS; 1 Aug 1994-2 Sep 1994

	$Good	$Fine	$N.Mint	£Good	£Fine	£N.Mint
1-2 ND new stories	$0.60	$1.80	$3.00	£0.40	£1.20	£2.00
Title Value:	$1.20	$3.60	$6.00	£0.80	£2.40	£4.00

G-MEN
Caliber Press; 1 Oct 1991

	$Good	$Fine	$N.Mint	£Good	£Fine	£N.Mint
1 ND	$0.45	$1.35	$2.25	£0.30	£0.90	£1.50
Title Value:	$0.45	$1.35	$2.25	£0.30	£0.90	£1.50

G.I. COMBAT
National Periodical Publications; 44 Jan 1957-288 Mar 1987
(previous issues #1-43 published by Quality Comics)

	$Good	$Fine	$N.Mint	£Good	£Fine	£N.Mint
44 1st DC issue	$49.00	$145.00	$340.00	£32.00	£95.00	£225.00
45	$25.00	$75.00	$175.00	£17.50	£52.50	£125.00
46-50	$17.50	$52.50	$125.00	£10.50	£32.00	£75.00
51-60	$13.50	$41.00	$95.00	£7.00	£21.00	£50.00
61-66	$10.00	$30.00	$70.00	£5.50	£17.00	£40.00
67 1st appearance Tank Killer	$12.50	$39.00	$90.00	£6.75	£20.00	£47.50
1st official distribution in the U.K.						
68-77	$10.00	$30.00	$70.00	£5.50	£17.00	£40.00
78-80 scarce in the U.K.	$10.00	$30.00	$70.00	£6.00	£18.00	£42.50
81-82	$7.00	$21.00	$50.00	£4.25	£12.50	£30.00
83 scarce in the U.K. 1st appearances Big Al, Little Al, Charlie Cigar	$7.75	$23.50	$55.00	£5.00	£15.00	£35.00
84-85	$7.00	$21.00	$50.00	£4.25	£12.50	£30.00
86	$7.00	$21.00	$50.00	£3.55	£10.50	£25.00
87 scarce in the U.K. 1st appearance Haunted Tank (ends #246)	$23.50	$70.00	$190.00	£11.00	£34.00	£90.00
88-90 scarce in the U.K.	$7.00	$21.00	$50.00	£3.55	£10.50	£25.00
91-100 scarce in the U.K.	$5.00	$15.00	$35.00	£2.85	£8.50	£20.00
101-110	$5.00	$15.00	$30.00	£2.90	£8.75	£17.50
111-113	$4.15	$12.50	$25.00	£2.05	£6.25	£12.50
114 origin Haunted Tank	$9.25	$28.00	$65.00	£5.00	£15.00	£35.00
115-117	$4.15	$12.50	$25.00	£2.05	£6.25	£12.50
118-120 ND	$4.15	$12.50	$25.00	£2.50	£7.50	£15.00
121-135 ND	$4.15	$12.50	$25.00	£2.05	£6.25	£12.50
136 ND last 12 cents issue	$4.15	$12.50	$25.00	£2.05	£6.25	£12.50
137 ND	$4.15	$12.50	$25.00	£1.65	£5.00	£10.00
138 ND 1st appearance The Losers (Captain Storm/Gunner/Sarge/Johnny Cloud - see Losers Special)	$4.15	$12.50	$25.00	£1.65	£5.00	£10.00
139-140 ND	$4.15	$12.50	$25.00	£1.65	£5.00	£10.00
141-143 ND	$2.50	$7.50	$15.00	£1.25	£3.75	£7.50
144-146 ND 68pgs	$2.50	$7.50	$15.00	£1.65	£5.00	£10.00
147 scarce in the U.K. 68pgs	$2.50	$7.50	$15.00	£1.00	£3.00	£6.00
148-150 68pgs	$2.50	$7.50	$15.00	£0.80	£2.50	£5.00
151-152 52pgs	$2.00	$6.00	$10.00	£0.80	£2.40	£4.00
153 52pgs, Medal of Honour series by Maurer	$2.00	$6.00	$10.00	£0.80	£2.40	£4.00
154 52pgs	$2.00	$6.00	$10.00	£0.80	£2.40	£4.00
155-170	$2.00	$6.00	$10.00	£0.60	£1.80	£3.00
171-187	$1.00	$3.00	$5.00	£0.55	£1.65	£2.75
188 scarce in the U.K.	$1.00	$3.00	$5.00	£0.60	£1.80	£3.00
189-190	$1.00	$3.00	$5.00	£0.55	£1.65	£2.75
191-195 scarce in the U.K.	$1.00	$3.00	$5.00	£0.60	£1.80	£3.00
196-200	$1.00	$3.00	$5.00	£0.55	£1.65	£2.75
201 ND 80pgs	$0.80	$2.40	$4.00	£0.60	£1.80	£3.00
202 scarce in the U.K. 80pgs	$0.80	$2.40	$4.00	£0.55	£1.65	£2.75
203-210 ND 80pgs	$0.80	$2.40	$4.00	£0.60	£1.80	£3.00
211-223 ND 68pgs	$0.80	$2.40	$4.00	£0.55	£1.65	£2.75
224-231 ND 52pgs	$0.70	$2.10	$3.50	£0.45	£1.35	£2.25
232 ND 52pgs, origin Kana the Ninja	$0.70	$2.10	$3.50	£0.45	£1.35	£2.25
233 ND 52pgs	$0.70	$2.10	$3.50	£0.45	£1.35	£2.25
234-242 52pgs	$0.55	$1.65	$2.75	£0.35	£1.05	£1.75
243 ND 52pgs	$0.70	$2.10	$3.50	£0.45	£1.35	£2.25
244 ND 52pgs, death of Slim Stryker, 1st appearance Mercenaries	$0.80	$2.40	$4.00	£0.50	£1.50	£2.50
245 ND 52pgs	$0.70	$2.10	$3.50	£0.45	£1.35	£2.25
246 ND 72pgs, 30th anniversary issue	$0.80	$2.40	$4.00	£0.50	£1.50	£2.50
247-256	$0.30	$0.90	$1.50	£0.20	£0.60	£1.00
257 1st appearance Stuart's Raiders	$0.30	$0.90	$1.50	£0.20	£0.60	£1.00
258-259	$0.30	$0.90	$1.50	£0.20	£0.60	£1.00
260-263 64pgs	$0.55	$1.65	$2.75	£0.35	£1.05	£1.75
264 64pgs, 1st appearance Sgt.Bullet & the Bravos of Vietnam; origin Kana retold	$0.55	$1.65	$2.75	£0.35	£1.05	£1.75
265-273 64pgs	$0.55	$1.65	$2.75	£0.35	£1.05	£1.75
274 64pgs, 1st full physical appearance of The Monitor (see Crisis on Infinite Earths & New Teen Titans #21)	$0.85	$2.55	$4.25	£0.55	£1.65	£2.75
275-281 64pgs	$0.55	$1.65	$2.75	£0.35	£1.05	£1.75
282-288	$0.25	$0.75	$1.25	£0.15	£0.45	£0.75
Title Value:	$962.25	$2892.70	$6325.50	£529.55	£1600.15	£3547.50

G.I. COMBAT (SPECIAL)
DC Comics; nn Sep 1980
(DC Special Series 22)

	$Good	$Fine	$N.Mint	£Good	£Fine	£N.Mint
nn ND 68pgs, features Haunted Tank	$0.60	$1.80	$3.00	£0.40	£1.20	£2.00
Title Value:	$0.60	$1.80	$3.00	£0.40	£1.20	£2.00

G.I. JOE
Marvel Comics Group; 1 Jun 1982-155 Dec 1994

	$Good	$Fine	$N.Mint	£Good	£Fine	£N.Mint
1 ND Baxter paper	$1.20	$3.60	$6.00	£0.80	£2.40	£4.00
2 ND scarce in the U.K.	$1.00	$3.00	$5.00	£1.20	£3.60	£6.00
2 2nd printing, ND 75 cents cover	$0.55	$1.65	$2.75	£0.35	£1.05	£1.75
3-6 ND	$0.90	$2.70	$4.50	£0.60	£1.80	£3.00
6 2nd printing ND	$0.45	$1.35	$2.25	£0.30	£0.90	£1.50
7 ND	$0.80	$2.40	$4.00	£0.50	£1.50	£2.50

	$Good	$Fine	$N.Mint	£Good	£Fine	£N.Mint
7 2nd printing ND	$0.30	$0.90	$1.50	£0.20	£0.60	£1.00
8 ND	$0.80	$2.40	$4.00	£0.50	£1.50	£2.50
8 2nd printing ND	$0.45	$1.35	$2.25	£0.30	£0.90	£1.50
9-10 ND	$0.80	$2.40	$4.00	£0.50	£1.50	£2.50
10 2nd printing ND	$0.40	$1.20	$2.00	£0.25	£0.75	£1.25
11 ND	$0.80	$2.40	$4.00	£0.50	£1.50	£2.50
11 2nd printing ND	$0.40	$1.20	$2.00	£0.25	£0.75	£1.25
12 ND	$0.80	$2.40	$4.00	£0.50	£1.50	£2.50
12 2nd printing ND	$0.40	$1.20	$2.00	£0.25	£0.75	£1.25
13-14 ND	$0.80	$2.40	$4.00	£0.50	£1.50	£2.50
14 2nd printing ND	$0.30	$0.90	$1.50	£0.20	£0.60	£1.00
15-17 ND	$0.80	$2.40	$4.00	£0.50	£1.50	£2.50
17 2nd printing ND	$0.30	$0.90	$1.50	£0.20	£0.60	£1.00
18 ND	$0.80	$2.40	$4.00	£0.50	£1.50	£2.50
18 2nd printing ND	$0.30	$0.90	$1.50	£0.20	£0.60	£1.00
19 ND	$0.80	$2.40	$4.00	£0.50	£1.50	£2.50
19 2nd printing ND	$0.30	$0.90	$1.50	£0.20	£0.60	£1.00
20-21 ND	$0.80	$2.40	$4.00	£0.50	£1.50	£2.50
21 2nd printing ND	$0.30	$0.90	$1.50	£0.20	£0.60	£1.00
22-23 ND	$0.80	$2.40	$4.00	£0.50	£1.50	£2.50
23 2nd printing ND	$0.30	$0.90	$1.50	£0.20	£0.60	£1.00
24-25 ND	$0.80	$2.40	$4.00	£0.50	£1.50	£2.50
25 2nd printing ND	$0.30	$0.90	$1.50	£0.20	£0.60	£1.00
26 ND origin Snake Eyes	$0.80	$2.40	$4.00	£0.50	£1.50	£2.50
26 2nd printing ND	$0.30	$0.90	$1.50	£0.20	£0.60	£1.00
27 ND	$0.60	$1.80	$3.00	£0.40	£1.20	£2.00
27 2nd printing ND	$0.30	$0.90	$1.50	£0.20	£0.60	£1.00
28-35 ND	$0.60	$1.80	$3.00	£0.40	£1.20	£2.00
36 ND	$0.45	$1.35	$2.25	£0.30	£0.90	£1.50
36 2nd printing ND	$0.30	$0.90	$1.50	£0.20	£0.60	£1.00
37 ND	$0.45	$1.35	$2.25	£0.30	£0.90	£1.50
37 2nd printing ND	$0.30	$0.90	$1.50	£0.20	£0.60	£1.00
38-49 ND	$0.45	$1.35	$2.25	£0.30	£0.90	£1.50
50 ND DS, intro Special Missions	$0.60	$1.80	$3.00	£0.40	£1.20	£2.00
51 ND	$0.40	$1.20	$2.00	£0.25	£0.75	£1.25
51 2nd printing ND	$0.30	$0.90	$1.50	£0.20	£0.60	£1.00
52-59 ND	$0.40	$1.20	$2.00	£0.25	£0.75	£1.25
60 ND Todd McFarlane art	$0.60	$1.80	$3.00	£0.40	£1.20	£2.00
61-70 ND	$0.30	$0.90	$1.50	£0.20	£0.60	£1.00
71-84 ND	$0.25	$0.75	$1.25	£0.15	£0.45	£0.75
85 ND Ninja story with no dialogue	$0.25	$0.75	$1.25	£0.15	£0.45	£0.75
86-99 ND	$0.25	$0.75	$1.25	£0.15	£0.45	£0.75
100 ND 48pgs	$0.40	$1.20	$2.00	£0.25	£0.75	£1.25
101-107 ND	$0.25	$0.75	$1.25	£0.15	£0.45	£0.75
108 ND G.I. Joe Dossier feature begins	$0.25	$0.75	$1.25	£0.15	£0.45	£0.75
109-115 ND	$0.25	$0.75	$1.25	£0.15	£0.45	£0.75
116-118 ND Destro: Search and Destroy, pre-bagged with trading card	$0.30	$0.90	$1.50	£0.20	£0.60	£1.00
119 ND	$0.25	$0.75	$1.25	£0.15	£0.45	£0.75
120 ND Sam Kieth art on G.I. Joe Dossier feature	$0.25	$0.75	$1.25	£0.15	£0.45	£0.75
121-123 ND	$0.25	$0.75	$1.25	£0.15	£0.45	£0.75
124 ND three stories	$0.25	$0.75	$1.25	£0.15	£0.45	£0.75
125-126 ND two stories	$0.25	$0.75	$1.25	£0.15	£0.45	£0.75
127-134 ND	$0.25	$0.75	$1.25	£0.15	£0.45	£0.75
135-138 ND pre-bagged with G.I. Joe photographic trading card	$0.30	$0.90	$1.50	£0.20	£0.60	£1.00
139 ND Transformers Generation 2 back-up begins	$0.25	$0.75	$1.25	£0.15	£0.45	£0.75
140-141 ND	$0.25	$0.75	$1.25	£0.15	£0.45	£0.75
142 ND leads into Transformers: Generation 2 #1	$0.25	$0.75	$1.25	£0.15	£0.45	£0.75
143-149 ND	$0.25	$0.75	$1.25	£0.15	£0.45	£0.75
150 ND 48pgs	$0.30	$0.90	$1.50	£0.20	£0.60	£1.00
151-154 ND	$0.25	$0.75	$1.25	£0.15	£0.45	£0.75
155 ND	$0.30	$0.90	$1.50	£0.20	£0.60	£1.00
Title Value:	$69.70	$209.10	$348.50	£44.85	£134.55	£224.25

G.I. JOE (2ND SERIES)
Dark Horse,MS; 1 Dec 1995-present

	$Good	$Fine	$N.Mint	£Good	£Fine	£N.Mint
1 ND Frank Miller cover	$0.40	$1.20	$2.00	£0.25	£0.75	£1.25
Title Value:	$0.40	$1.20	$2.00	£0.25	£0.75	£1.25

G.I. JOE AND THE TRANSFORMERS
Marvel Comics Group,MS; 1 Jan 1987-4 Apr 1987

	$Good	$Fine	$N.Mint	£Good	£Fine	£N.Mint
1-4 ND	$0.25	$0.75	$1.25	£0.15	£0.45	£0.75
Title Value:	$0.25	$0.75	$1.25	£0.15	£0.45	£0.75
Bookshelf Edition (Apr 1993)						
96pgs, Higgins, Trimpe and Coletta, ND				£0.60	£1.80	£3.00

G.I. JOE COMICS MAGAZINE
Marvel Comics Group,Digest; 1 Dec 1986-13 1988

	$Good	$Fine	$N.Mint	£Good	£Fine	£N.Mint
1-13 ND	$0.25	$0.75	$1.25	£0.15	£0.45	£0.75
Title Value:	$3.25	$9.75	$16.25	£1.95	£5.85	£9.75

G.I. JOE EUROPEAN MISSIONS
Marvel Comics Group; 1 Oct 1988-15 Dec 1989

	$Good	$Fine	$N.Mint	£Good	£Fine	£N.Mint
1-15 ND	$0.25	$0.75	$1.25	£0.15	£0.45	£0.75

	$Good	$Fine	$N.Mint	£Good	£Fine	£N.Mint
Title Value:	$3.75	$11.25	$18.75	£2.25	£6.75	£11.25

G.I. JOE IN 3-D
Blackthorne; (3-D Series #20,#26,#35,#39,#52); 1 Jul 1987-5 1988

	$Good	$Fine	$N.Mint	£Good	£Fine	£N.Mint
1 ND all with bound-in 3-D glasses (25% less if without glasses)	$0.45	$1.35	$2.25	£0.30	£0.90	£1.50
2-5 ND	$0.45	$1.35	$2.25	£0.30	£0.90	£1.50
Title Value:	$2.25	$6.75	$11.25	£1.50	£4.50	£7.50

G.I. JOE ORDER OF BATTLE, THE
Marvel Comics Group,MS; 1 Dec 1986-4 Mar 1987

	$Good	$Fine	$N.Mint	£Good	£Fine	£N.Mint
1-4 ND	$0.40	$1.20	$2.00	£0.25	£0.75	£1.25
Title Value:	$1.60	$4.80	$8.00	£1.00	£3.00	£5.00

G.I. JOE SPECIAL MISSIONS
Marvel Comics Group; 1 Oct 1986-28 Dec 1989

	$Good	$Fine	$N.Mint	£Good	£Fine	£N.Mint
1-28 ND	$0.25	$0.75	$1.25	£0.15	£0.45	£0.75
Title Value:	$7.00	$21.00	$35.00	£4.20	£12.60	£21.00
Trade Paperback reprints issues #1-4				£0.75	£2.25	£3.75

G.I. JOE SPECIAL TREASURY EDITION
Marvel Comics Group; nn 1982

	$Good	$Fine	$N.Mint	£Good	£Fine	£N.Mint
nn ND reprints issue #1; extremely rare in the U.K.	$3.60	$10.50	$18.00	£2.40	£7.00	£12.00
Title Value:	$3.60	$10.50	$18.00	£2.40	£7.00	£12.00

G.I. JOE THREE-PACK
Marvel Comics Group; nn Oct 1990

	$Good	$Fine	$N.Mint	£Good	£Fine	£N.Mint
nn ND scarce in the U.K. 2nd printings of Issues #2, #26 and #27; pre-bagged	$0.60	$1.80	$3.00	£0.40	£1.20	£2.00
Title Value:	$0.60	$1.80	$3.00	£0.40	£1.20	£2.00

G.I. JOE YEARBOOK
Marvel Comics Group; 1 Mar 1985-4 Feb 1988

	$Good	$Fine	$N.Mint	£Good	£Fine	£N.Mint
1 ND 48pgs, reprints issue #1 with selected history of subsequent events plus feature on G.I. Joe animated series, painted cover by Michael Golden	$0.40	$1.20	$2.00	£0.25	£0.75	£1.25
2 ND 48pgs, Mike Golden cover and art	$0.40	$1.20	$2.00	£0.25	£0.75	£1.25
3-4 ND 48pgs	$0.40	$1.20	$2.00	£0.25	£0.75	£1.25
Title Value:	$1.60	$4.80	$8.00	£1.00	£3.00	£5.00

Note: many copies of #1 were mis-cut

G.I. JOE, TALES OF
Marvel Comics Group; 1 Jan 1988-15 1989

	$Good	$Fine	$N.Mint	£Good	£Fine	£N.Mint
1 ND DS, reprints from GI Joe begin	$0.25	$0.75	$1.25	£0.15	£0.45	£0.75
2-15 ND	$0.25	$0.75	$1.25	£0.15	£0.45	£0.75
Title Value:	$3.75	$11.25	$18.75	£2.25	£6.75	£11.25

G.I. WAR TALES
DC Comics; 1 Mar/Apr 1973-4 Oct/Nov 1973

	$Good	$Fine	$N.Mint	£Good	£Fine	£N.Mint
1 reprints begin	$0.45	$1.35	$2.25	£0.30	£0.90	£1.50
2 Neal Adams reprint	$0.60	$1.80	$3.00	£0.40	£1.20	£2.00
3-4	$0.30	$0.90	$1.50	£0.20	£0.60	£1.00
Title Value:	$1.65	$4.95	$8.25	£1.10	£3.30	£5.50

G.I.JOE IN 3-D ANNUAL
Blackthorne; (3-D Series #62) 1 1988

	$Good	$Fine	$N.Mint	£Good	£Fine	£N.Mint
1 ND	$0.55	$1.65	$2.75	£0.35	£1.05	£1.75
Title Value:	$0.55	$1.65	$2.75	£0.35	£1.05	£1.75

G.O.T.H.
Verotik,MS; 1 Nov 1995-present

	$Good	$Fine	$N.Mint	£Good	£Fine	£N.Mint
1 ND Glenn Danzig script, Liam Sharp art	$0.60	$1.80	$3.00	£0.40	£1.20	£2.00
Title Value:	$0.60	$1.80	$3.00	£0.40	£1.20	£2.00

G.R.I.P., THE
Eclipse; 1 Apr 1994-2 1994

	$Good	$Fine	$N.Mint	£Good	£Fine	£N.Mint
1-2 ND Brad Gorby art	$0.55	$1.65	$2.75	£0.35	£1.05	£1.75
Title Value:	$1.10	$3.30	$5.50	£0.70	£2.10	£3.50

GABRIEL
Caliber Press; 1 Jul 1995

	$Good	$Fine	$N.Mint	£Good	£Fine	£N.Mint
1 ND 48pgs, black and white	$0.80	$2.40	$4.00	£0.50	£1.50	£2.50
Title Value:	$0.80	$2.40	$4.00	£0.50	£1.50	£2.50

GAIJIN
Caliber Press,OS; 1 Feb 1991

	$Good	$Fine	$N.Mint	£Good	£Fine	£N.Mint
1 ND 64pgs, black and white	$0.60	$1.80	$3.00	£0.40	£1.20	£2.00
Title Value:	$0.60	$1.80	$3.00	£0.40	£1.20	£2.00

GALACTIC GUARDIANS
Marvel Comics Group,MS; 1 Jul 1994-4 Oct 1994

	$Good	$Fine	$N.Mint	£Good	£Fine	£N.Mint
1 Future History part 2, concluded in Guardians of the Galaxy Annual #4	$0.25	$0.75	$1.25	£0.15	£0.45	£0.75
2-4	$0.25	$0.75	$1.25	£0.15	£0.45	£0.75
Title Value:	$1.00	$3.00	$5.00	£0.60	£1.80	£3.00

GALACTIC PATROL
Eternity,MS; 1 Jul 1990-5 Nov 1990
(see Lensman)

	$Good	$Fine	$N.Mint	£Good	£Fine	£N.Mint
1-5 ND based on Lensman series	$0.40	$1.20	$2.00	£0.25	£0.75	£1.25
Title Value:	$2.00	$6.00	$10.00	£1.25	£3.75	£6.25

GALACTUS: THE ORIGIN
(see Super Villain Classics)

GALL FORCE: ETERNAL STORY
CPM Comics; 1 Mar 1995-4 1995?

	$Good	$Fine	$N.Mint	£Good	£Fine	£N.Mint
1-3 ND based on anime series	$0.60	$1.80	$3.00	£0.40	£1.20	£2.00
4 ND	$0.60	$1.80	$3.00	£0.40	£1.20	£2.00

	$Good	$Fine	$N.Mint	£Good	£Fine	£N.Mint
Title Value:	$2.40	$7.20	$12.00	£1.60	£4.80	£8.00

GAMBIT
Marvel Comics Group,MS; 1 Dec 1993-4 Mar 1994

	$Good	$Fine	$N.Mint	£Good	£Fine	£N.Mint
1 embossed gold foil stamped cover						
	$1.00	$3.00	$5.00	£0.70	£2.10	£3.50
1 Gold Edition ND	$5.00	$15.00	$25.00	£2.50	£7.50	£12.50
2 Rogue appears						
	$0.60	$1.80	$3.00	£0.30	£0.90	£1.50
3-4	$0.60	$1.80	$3.00	£0.30	£0.90	£1.50
Title Value:	$7.80	$23.40	$39.00	£4.10	£12.30	£20.50

Gambit (Sep 1995)

				£Good	£Fine	£N.Mint
Trade Paperback collects four issue series, new Lee Weeks cover				£1.70	£5.10	£8.50

GAMBIT & THE X-TERNALS
Marvel Comics Group; 1 Mar 1995-4 Jun 1995

	$Good	$Fine	$N.Mint	£Good	£Fine	£N.Mint
1 Fabian Nicieza script, Danial and Conrad art						
	$1.00	$3.00	$5.00	£0.60	£1.80	£3.00
2-3 Fabian Nicieza script, Danial and Conrad art						
	$0.60	$1.80	$3.00	£0.30	£0.90	£1.50
4 Fabian Nicieza script, Danial and Conrad art; continued in X-Men: Omega						
	$0.60	$1.80	$3.00	£0.30	£0.90	£1.50
Title Value:	$2.80	$8.40	$14.00	£1.50	£4.50	£7.50

Note: this title temporarily replaced X-Force in the Age of Apocalypse storyline

The Ultimate Gambit & The X-Ternals (Jul 1995)
96pgs, Bookshelf Edition collects issues #1-4

				£Good	£Fine	£N.Mint
with etched gold cover				£1.20	£3.60	£6.00

GAMMARAUDERS
DC Comics, Game; 1 Jan 1989-10 Dec 1989

	$Good	$Fine	$N.Mint	£Good	£Fine	£N.Mint
1-10 ND	$0.25	$0.75	$1.25	£0.15	£0.45	£0.75
Title Value:	$2.50	$7.50	$12.50	£1.50	£4.50	£7.50

GARGOYLE
Marvel Comics Group,MS; 1 Jun 1985-4 Sep 1985

	$Good	$Fine	$N.Mint	£Good	£Fine	£N.Mint
1-4 ND Badger art						
	$0.30	$0.90	$1.50	£0.20	£0.60	£1.00
Title Value:	$1.20	$3.60	$6.00	£0.80	£2.40	£4.00

GARGOYLES
Marvel Comics Group,MS TV; 1 Feb 1995-present

	$Good	$Fine	$N.Mint	£Good	£Fine	£N.Mint
1 ND based on US TV series; embossed UV-coated cover						
	$0.45	$1.35	$2.25	£0.30	£0.90	£1.50
2-7 ND	$0.30	$0.90	$1.50	£0.20	£0.60	£1.00
8-9 ND bi-weekly	$0.30	$0.90	$1.50	£0.20	£0.60	£1.00
10-14 ND	$0.30	$0.90	$1.50	£0.20	£0.60	£1.00
Title Value:	$4.35	$13.05	$21.75	£2.90	£8.70	£14.50

GASP!
ACG; 1 Mar 1967-4 Aug 1967

	$Good	$Fine	$N.Mint	£Good	£Fine	£N.Mint
1 distributed in the U.K.						
	$4.50	$13.50	$22.50	£3.00	£9.00	£15.00
2-4 distributed in the U.K.						
	$2.25	$6.75	$11.25	£1.50	£4.50	£7.50
Title Value:	$11.25	$33.75	$56.25	£7.50	£22.50	£37.50

GATES OF THE NIGHT, THE
Jademan,MS; 1 Oct 1990-6 Mar 1991

	$Good	$Fine	$N.Mint	£Good	£Fine	£N.Mint
1-6 ND 48pgs, squarebound						
	$0.70	$2.10	$3.50	£0.45	£1.35	£2.25
Title Value:	$4.20	$12.60	$21.00	£2.70	£8.10	£13.50

GEEK, BROTHER POWER, THE
National Periodical Publications; 1 Sep/Oct 1968-2 Nov/Dec 1968

	$Good	$Fine	$N.Mint	£Good	£Fine	£N.Mint
1 scarce in the U.K.						
	$3.75	$11.00	$22.50	£2.50	£7.50	£15.00
2 scarce in the U.K.						
	$3.00	$9.00	$15.00	£2.00	£6.00	£10.00
Title Value:	$6.75	$20.00	$37.50	£4.50	£13.50	£25.00

Note: unusually cult comic owing to its focus on Sixties "flower power" culture, bizarre title and short-lived run

GEEK, THE
DC Comics/Vertigo,OS; 1 Jun 1993

	$Good	$Fine	$N.Mint	£Good	£Fine	£N.Mint
1 ND 64pgs	$0.80	$2.40	$4.00	£0.50	£1.50	£2.50
Title Value:	$0.80	$2.40	$4.00	£0.50	£1.50	£2.50

GEHENNA
White Wolf,MS; 1 Aug 1991

	$Good	$Fine	$N.Mint	£Good	£Fine	£N.Mint
1 ND	$0.45	$1.35	$2.25	£0.30	£0.90	£1.50
Title Value:	$0.45	$1.35	$2.25	£0.30	£0.90	£1.50

Note: originally announced as a mini-series

GEN 13
Image,MS; 0 Aug 1994; 1 Feb 1994-5 Jul 1994

	$Good	$Fine	$N.Mint	£Good	£Fine	£N.Mint
½ ND produced in conjunction with Wizard Comics; issued in protective Mylar with certificate of authenticity						
	$5.00	$15.00	$25.00	£3.00	£9.00	£15.00
0 (Aug 1994) short stories focusing on individual characters						
	$1.20	$3.60	$6.00	£0.80	£2.40	£4.00
1 Jim Lee and Brandon Choi script, J. Scott Campbell and Alex Garner art begins; fold-out poster at centre-fold						
	$7.00	$21.00	$35.00	£4.00	£12.00	£20.00
1 2nd printing, (Jul 1994)						
	$0.45	$1.35	$2.25	£0.30	£0.90	£1.50
2	$7.00	$21.00	$35.00	£4.40	£13.00	£22.00
3	$6.00	$18.00	$30.00	£3.60	£10.50	£18.00
4	$4.40	$13.00	$22.00	£2.40	£7.00	£12.00
5	$3.00	$9.00	$15.00	£2.00	£6.00	£10.00
5 Variant cover, ND Whilce Portacio cover art; cover forms larger picture when combined with variant covers of Deathblow #5, Kindred #3, Stormwatch #10, Team 7 #1, Union #0, Wetworks #2, WildC.A.T.S. #11						
	$5.00	$15.00	$25.00	£2.40	£7.00	£12.00
Title Value:	$39.05	$116.95	$195.25	£22.90	£67.80	£114.50

Note: all Non-Distributed on the news-stands in the U.K.

Gen 13 (Dec 1994)

				£Good	£Fine	£N.Mint
Trade paperback collects 5 issue mini-series				£1.70	£5.10	£8.50

Gen 13 Hardcover Collection (Jun 1995)
reprints mini-series, case-bound limited edition

				£Good	£Fine	£N.Mint
signed and numbered; 1,000 copies				£5.20	£15.60	£26.00

GEN 13 (2ND SERIES)
Image; 1 Apr 1995-present

	$Good	$Fine	$N.Mint	£Good	£Fine	£N.Mint
1 Cover A - "Charge", ND Brandon Choi script, J. Scott Campbell art; Fairchild, Grunge, Freefall, Burnout and Rainmaker begin						
	$1.20	$3.60	$6.00	£0.80	£2.40	£4.00
1 Cover B - "Thumbs Up" ND						
	$1.20	$3.60	$6.00	£0.80	£2.40	£4.00
1 Cover C - "Lil Gen", ND Arthur Adams cover art						
	$3.60	$10.50	$18.00	£2.00	£6.00	£10.00
1 Cover D - "Barbari-Gen", ND Simon Bisley cover art						
	$3.60	$10.50	$18.00	£2.00	£6.00	£10.00
1 Cover E - "Friendley Neighborhood Grunge", ND John Cleary cover art						
	$3.00	$9.00	$15.00	£2.00	£6.00	£10.00
1 Cover F - "Gen13 Goes Madison Ave.", ND Michael Golden cover art						
	$3.60	$10.50	$18.00	£2.00	£6.00	£10.00
1 Cover G - "Lin-Gen-re", ND Michael Lopez cover art						
	$4.40	$13.00	$22.00	£3.00	£9.00	£15.00
1 Cover H - "Gen-et-Jackson", ND Jason Pearson cover art						
	$4.40	$13.00	$22.00	£3.00	£9.00	£15.00
1 Cover I - "That's the Way We Became Gen", ND J. Scott Campbell/Chuck Gibson cover art						
	$3.60	$10.50	$18.00	£2.00	£6.00	£10.00
1 Cover J - "All Dolled Up", ND J. Scott Campbell/Tom McWeeney cover art						
	$3.00	$9.00	$15.00	£2.00	£6.00	£10.00
1 Cover K - "Verti-Gen", ND Joe Dunn cover art						
	$3.00	$9.00	$15.00	£2.00	£6.00	£10.00
1 Cover L - "Picto-Fiction" ND						
	$3.00	$9.00	$15.00	£2.00	£6.00	£10.00
1 Cover M - "Do-It-Yourself-Cover" ND						
	$3.00	$9.00	$15.00	£2.00	£6.00	£10.00
2 ND Wildstorm Rising part 4, continued in Grifter #1; with two foil-bagged painted trading cards. Cover by Barry Windsor-Smith and extra cover by J. Scott Campbell						
	$0.60	$1.80	$3.00	£0.50	£1.50	£2.50
2 Newsstand edition, ND without trading cards						
	$0.40	$1.20	$2.00	£0.25	£0.75	£1.25
3 ND	$0.50	$1.50	$2.50	£0.40	£1.20	£2.00
4-6 ND	$0.45	$1.35	$2.25	£0.30	£0.90	£1.50
7 ND Jim Lee art	$0.50	$1.50	$2.50	£0.30	£0.90	£1.50
Title Value:	$43.95	$130.25	$219.75	£27.95	£83.85	£139.75

GEN 13 LIMITED EDITION COLLECTOR'S PACK
Image; nn Jun 1995

	$Good	$Fine	$N.Mint	£Good	£Fine	£N.Mint
nn Collector's Pack featuring all 13 variant editions plus chromium variant, signed by 1 creator (4 different)						
	$40.00	$120.00	$200.00	£25.00	£75.00	£125.00
Title Value:	$40.00	$120.00	$200.00	£25.00	£75.00	£125.00

GEN 13 RAVE
Image,OS; nn Mar 1995

	$Good	$Fine	$N.Mint	£Good	£Fine	£N.Mint
nn ND Creator interviews and sketch book showing creation of Gen 13						
	$1.50	$4.50	$7.50	£1.20	£3.60	£6.00
Title Value:	$1.50	$4.50	$7.50	£1.20	£3.60	£6.00

GEN 13/MAXX
Image,OS; 1 Dec 1995

	$Good	$Fine	$N.Mint	£Good	£Fine	£N.Mint
1 ND	$0.70	$2.10	$3.50	£0.45	£1.35	£2.25
Title Value:	$0.70	$2.10	$3.50	£0.45	£1.35	£2.25

GENE DAY'S BLACK ZEPPELIN
(see Black Zeppelin)

GENE DOGS
Marvel UK,MS; 1 Oct 1993-3 Dec 1993

	$Good	$Fine	$N.Mint	£Good	£Fine	£N.Mint
1 pre-bagged with trading cards and poster						
	$0.55	$1.65	$2.75	£0.35	£1.05	£1.75
2-3	$0.40	$1.20	$2.00	£0.25	£0.75	£1.25
Title Value:	$1.35	$4.05	$6.75	£0.85	£2.55	£4.25

GENERATION X
Marvel Comics Group; 1 Nov 1994-Feb 1995; 5 Jul 1995-present
(becomes The Mutants: Generation Next)

	$Good	$Fine	$N.Mint	£Good	£Fine	£N.Mint
½ ND San Diego comic convention give away						
	$1.50	$4.50	$7.50	£1.20	£3.60	£6.00
1 48pgs, chromium cover; Scott Lobdell, Chris Bachalo and Mark Buckingham creative team						
	$1.20	$3.60	$6.00	£1.00	£3.00	£5.00
2	$0.60	$1.80	$3.00	£0.60	£1.80	£3.00
3	$0.40	$1.20	$2.00	£0.25	£0.75	£1.25
3 Deluxe Edition - printed on glossy stock paper						
	$0.50	$1.50	$2.50	£0.30	£0.90	£1.50
4	$0.40	$1.20	$2.00	£0.25	£0.75	£1.25
4 Deluxe Edition: bound-in Fleer trading card; see Mutants: Generation Next #1						
	$0.50	$1.50	$2.50	£0.30	£0.90	£1.50
5 continued from X-Men: Prime; Scott Lobdell script, Chris Bachalo and Mark Buckingham art						
	$0.40	$1.20	$2.00	£0.25	£0.75	£1.25
6 Wolverine appears, continued in Wolverine #92						
	$0.40	$1.20	$2.00	£0.25	£0.75	£1.25
7-8	$0.40	$1.20	$2.00	£0.25	£0.75	£1.25
9 Tom Grummett guest pencil art						
	$0.40	$1.20	$2.00	£0.25	£0.75	£1.25
10 Banshee vs. Omega Red						
	$0.40	$1.20	$2.00	£0.25	£0.75	£1.25
11-13	$0.40	$1.20	$2.00	£0.25	£0.75	£1.25
Title Value:	$8.70	$26.10	$43.50	£6.15	£18.45	£30.75

GENERATION X '95
Marvel Comics Group,OS; nn Nov 1995

nn ND 64pgs, Scott Lobdell script, Ashley Wood art; Mondo joins team

VERY GENERAL PERCENTAGE CONVERSION CHART WHICH MAY BE USED TO CALCULATE LOW AND INBETWEEN GRADES:

	$Good	$Fine	$N.Mint	£Good	£Fine	£N.Mint
	$0.80	$2.40	$4.00	£0.50	£1.50	£2.50
Title Value:	$0.80	$2.40	$4.00	£0.50	£1.50	£2.50

Note: issued in place of planned Generation X Annual

GENERATION X ASHCAN
Marvel Comics Group,OS; nn Nov 1994

	$Good	$Fine	$N.Mint	£Good	£Fine	£N.Mint
nn ND 16pgs, previews Generation X						
	$0.30	$0.90	$1.50	£0.20	£0.60	£1.00
Title Value:	$0.30	$0.90	$1.50	£0.20	£0.60	£1.00

GENERATION X COLLECTOR'S PREVIEW
Marvel Comics Group,OS; 1 Oct 1994

	$Good	$Fine	$N.Mint	£Good	£Fine	£N.Mint
1 ND 48pgs, inside information on Generation X						
	$0.40	$1.20	$2.00	£0.50	£1.50	£2.50
Title Value:	$0.40	$1.20	$2.00	£0.50	£1.50	£2.50

GENERATION ZERO GRAPHIC NOVEL
DC Comics,OS; 1 Nov 1991

	$Good	$Fine	$N.Mint	£Good	£Fine	£N.Mint
1 ND 120pgs, reprints Pepe Moreno's Generation Zero, originally published in Marvel Comics' Epic Illustrated						
	$2.55	$7.50	$12.75	£1.70	£5.00	£8.50
Title Value:	$2.55	$7.50	$12.75	£1.70	£5.00	£8.50

GENERIC COMIC BOOK, THE
Marvel Comics Group,OS; 1 Apr 1984

	$Good	$Fine	$N.Mint	£Good	£Fine	£N.Mint
1 ND	$0.15	$0.45	$0.75	£0.10	£0.35	£0.60
Title Value:	$0.15	$0.45	$0.75	£0.10	£0.35	£0.60

GENESIS
Malibu,OS; 0 October 1993

	$Good	$Fine	$N.Mint	£Good	£Fine	£N.Mint
0 ND Widowmaker, Ex-Mutants, Dinosaurs for Hire and Protectors stories; all foil card-stock cover						
	$0.50	$1.50	$2.50	£0.30	£0.90	£1.50
Title Value:	$0.50	$1.50	$2.50	£0.30	£0.90	£1.50

GENETIX
Marvel UK,MS; 1 Oct 1993-6 Mar 1994

	$Good	$Fine	$N.Mint	£Good	£Fine	£N.Mint
1 pre-bagged with trading cards; Phil Gascoine art begins						
	$0.55	$1.65	$2.75	£0.35	£1.05	£1.75
2-3	$0.40	$1.20	$2.00	£0.25	£0.75	£1.25
4 Genetix vs. The Gene Dogs						
	$0.40	$1.20	$2.00	£0.25	£0.75	£1.25
5-6	$0.40	$1.20	$2.00	£0.25	£0.75	£1.25
Title Value:	$2.55	$7.65	$12.75	£1.60	£4.80	£8.00

GENOCYBER
Viz Communications,MS; 1 Jun 1993-6 Nov 1993

	$Good	$Fine	$N.Mint	£Good	£Fine	£N.Mint
1-6 ND	$0.55	$1.65	$2.75	£0.35	£1.05	£1.75
Title Value:	$3.30	$9.90	$16.50	£2.10	£6.30	£10.50

GENSAGA: ANCIENT WARRIOR
Entity Comics; 1 Aug 1995-present

	$Good	$Fine	$N.Mint	£Good	£Fine	£N.Mint
1 ND Raff Ienco script and art; Kabuki pin-up by David Mack						
	$0.50	$1.50	$2.50	£0.30	£0.90	£1.50
1 ND Videogame Edition (Aug 1995) - pre-bagged with floppy disk game Sango Fighter						
	$1.40	$4.20	$7.00	£0.90	£2.70	£4.50
2-3 ND	$0.50	$1.50	$2.50	£0.30	£0.90	£1.50
Title Value:	$2.90	$8.70	$14.50	£1.80	£5.40	£9.00

GEOMANCER
Valiant; 1 Nov 1994-8 Jun 1995

	$Good	$Fine	$N.Mint	£Good	£Fine	£N.Mint
1 story continued from Eternal Warrior #27						
	$0.40	$1.20	$2.00	£0.25	£0.75	£1.25
2 Eternal Warrior vs. Geomancer						
	$0.40	$1.20	$2.00	£0.20	£0.60	£1.00
3-8	$0.40	$1.20	$2.00	£0.20	£0.60	£1.00
Title Value:	$3.20	$9.60	$16.00	£1.65	£4.95	£8.25

Note: all Non-Distributed on the news-stands in the U.K.

GET LOST
NCG; 1 Oct 1987-3 1988

	$Good	$Fine	$N.Mint	£Good	£Fine	£N.Mint
1 ND classic Ross Andru/Esposito humour reprints begin						
	$0.40	$1.20	$2.00	£0.25	£0.75	£1.25

	$Good	$Fine	$N.Mint	£Good	£Fine	£N.Mint
2 ND	$0.40	$1.20	$2.00	£0.25	£0.75	£1.25
2 ND Gold Medal Edition, signed and numbered (1200 copies)						
	$1.05	$3.15	$5.25	£0.70	£2.10	£3.50
3 ND	$0.40	$1.20	$2.00	£0.25	£0.75	£1.25
Title Value:	$2.25	$6.75	$11.25	£1.45	£4.35	£7.25

GETALONG GANG, THE
Marvel Comics Group/Star, TV; 1 May 1985-6 1986

	$Good	$Fine	$N.Mint	£Good	£Fine	£N.Mint
1-6 ND features Saturday morning TV characters						
	$0.15	$0.45	$0.75	£0.10	£0.30	£0.50
Title Value:	$0.90	$2.70	$4.50	£0.60	£1.80	£3.00

GHOST
Dark Horse; 1 Apr 1995-present

	$Good	$Fine	$N.Mint	£Good	£Fine	£N.Mint
1 ND Eric Luke script, Adam Hughes and Mark Farmer art begins; spin-off from Comics' Greatest World						
	$1.20	$3.60	$6.00	£0.70	£2.10	£3.50
2 ND	$0.80	$2.40	$4.00	£0.50	£1.50	£2.50
3-4 ND	$0.45	$1.35	$2.25	£0.30	£0.90	£1.50
5 ND Predator X-over (see Motorhead #1, X #18 and Agents of Law #6)						
	$0.45	$1.35	$2.25	£0.30	£0.90	£1.50
6-9 ND	$0.45	$1.35	$2.25	£0.30	£0.90	£1.50
Title Value:	$5.15	$15.45	$26.00	£3.30	£9.90	£16.50

Ghost

	$Good	$Fine	$N.Mint	£Good	£Fine	£N.Mint
Trade paperback 96pgs, reprints Ghost appearances from Comics' Greatest World, X #8 and Ghost Special plus sketches				£1.20	£3.60	£6.00

GHOST IN THE SHELL, THE
Dark Horse,MS; 1 Feb 1995-8 Sep 1995

	$Good	$Fine	$N.Mint	£Good	£Fine	£N.Mint
1-8 ND Masamune Shirow script and art; colour and black and white						
	$0.80	$2.40	$4.00	£0.50	£1.50	£2.50
Title Value:	$6.40	$19.20	$32.00	£4.00	£12.00	£20.00

GHOST MANOR (1ST SERIES)
Charlton; 1 Jul 1968-19 Jul 1971
(becomes Ghostly Haunts #20 on)

	$Good	$Fine	$N.Mint	£Good	£Fine	£N.Mint
1 distributed in the U.K.						
	$1.50	$4.50	$7.50	£1.00	£3.00	£5.00
2-3 distributed in the U.K.						
	$0.90	$2.70	$4.50	£0.60	£1.80	£3.00
4-10 distributed in the U.K.						
	$0.80	$2.40	$4.00	£0.50	£1.50	£2.50
11-12 distributed in the U.K.						
	$0.60	$1.80	$3.00	£0.40	£1.20	£2.00
16 Steve Ditko art; distributed in the U.K.						
	$0.80	$2.40	$4.00	£0.50	£1.50	£2.50
17 distributed in the U.K.						
	$0.60	$1.80	$3.00	£0.40	£1.20	£2.00
18-19 Steve Ditko art; distributed in the U.K.						
	$0.80	$2.40	$4.00	£0.50	£1.50	£2.50
Title Value:	$13.10	$39.30	$65.50	£8.40	£25.20	£42.00

GHOST MANOR (2ND SERIES)
Charlton; 1 Oct 1971-32 Dec 1976; 33 Sep 1977-77 Nov 1984

	$Good	$Fine	$N.Mint	£Good	£Fine	£N.Mint
1 distributed in the U.K.						
	$1.50	$4.50	$7.50	£1.00	£3.00	£5.00
2-3 distributed in the U.K.						
	$0.90	$2.70	$4.50	£0.60	£1.80	£3.00
4-7 distributed in the U.K.						
	$0.80	$2.40	$4.00	£0.50	£1.50	£2.50
8 distributed in the U.K. Wally Wood art						
	$0.90	$2.70	$4.50	£0.60	£1.80	£3.00
9-10 distributed in the U.K.						
	$0.80	$2.40	$4.00	£0.50	£1.50	£2.50
11-20 distributed in the U.K.						
	$0.60	$1.80	$3.00	£0.40	£1.20	£2.00
21-56 distributed in the U.K.						

Gabriel #1

Galactus the Origin #1

Ghost Manor #1

MINT = 100% / NEAR MINT (inc. +/-) = 90-99% / VERY FINE (inc. +/-) = 75-89% / FINE (inc. +/-) = 55-74%
VERY GOOD (inc. +/-) = 35-54% / GOOD (inc. +/-) = 15-34% / FAIR = 5-14% / POOR = 1-4%

367

	$Good	$Fine	$N.Mint	£Good	£Fine	£N.Mint
	$0.45	$1.35	$2.25	£0.30	£0.90	£1.50
57 Steve Ditko art; distributed in the U.K.						
	$0.80	$2.40	$4.00	£0.50	£1.50	£2.50
58-60 distributed in the U.K.						
	$0.45	$1.35	$2.25	£0.30	£0.90	£1.50
61-77 distributed in the U.K.						
	$0.30	$0.90	$1.50	£0.20	£0.60	£1.00
Title Value:	$38.45	$115.35	$192.25	£25.40	£76.20	£127.00

GHOST RIDER

Marvel Comics Group; 1 Sep 1973-81 Jun 1983
(see Marvel Spotlight)

	$Good	$Fine	$N.Mint	£Good	£Fine	£N.Mint
1 Johnny Blaze as Ghost Rider begins; 1st appearance Daimon Hellstrom (cameo and face unseen)						
	$12.00	$36.00	$85.00	£5.50	£17.00	£40.00
2 2nd appearance Daimon Hellstrom (cameo - Son of Satan costume partially seen; face unseen); his appearance continues directly in Marvel Spotlight #12						
	$7.00	$21.00	$35.00	£3.00	£9.00	£15.00
3 new motorcycle, 2nd full appearance Son of Satan (see Marvel Spotlight #12/13)						
	$5.00	$15.00	$25.00	£2.50	£7.50	£12.50
4	$4.00	$12.00	$20.00	£1.60	£4.80	£8.00
5-6 ND	$4.00	$12.00	$20.00	£1.80	£5.25	£9.00
7	$3.00	$9.00	$15.00	£1.60	£4.80	£8.00
8 ND	$3.00	$9.00	$15.00	£1.80	£5.25	£9.00
9 Jesus Christ appears (called "friend")						
	$3.00	$9.00	$15.00	£1.50	£4.50	£7.50
10 Ploog art, reprints origin from Marvel Spotlight #5, Hulk appears						
	$3.00	$9.00	$15.00	£1.50	£4.50	£7.50
11 Ghost Rider vs. Hulk						
	$2.50	$7.50	$12.50	£1.00	£3.00	£5.00
12-16	$2.50	$7.50	$12.50	£1.00	£3.00	£5.00
17 team-up with Son of Satan						
	$2.50	$7.50	$12.50	£1.00	£3.00	£5.00
18 Spiderman, Thing, Hercules and Black Widow appear						
	$2.50	$7.50	$12.50	£1.00	£3.00	£5.00
19	$2.50	$7.50	$12.50	£1.00	£3.00	£5.00
20 ND John Byrne art, Death's Head appears, tie-in with Daredevil #138						
	$3.00	$9.00	$15.00	£1.20	£3.60	£6.00
21 ND Ghost Rider vs. The Gladiator, Gil Kane art						
	$1.50	$4.50	$7.50	£0.70	£2.10	£3.50
22 LD in the U.K.	$1.50	$4.50	$7.50	£0.60	£1.80	£3.00
23-25 ND	$1.50	$4.50	$7.50	£0.70	£2.10	£3.50
26 ND Ghost Rider vs. Dr. Druid						
	$1.50	$4.50	$7.50	£0.70	£2.10	£3.50
27 ND Hawkeye appears						
	$1.50	$4.50	$7.50	£0.70	£2.10	£3.50
28 ND	$1.50	$4.50	$7.50	£0.70	£2.10	£3.50
29-30 ND Ghost Rider vs. Dr. Strange						
	$1.50	$4.50	$7.50	£0.70	£2.10	£3.50
31 ND Dr. Strange appears						
	$1.20	$3.60	$6.00	£0.60	£1.80	£3.00
32-34 ND	$1.20	$3.60	$6.00	£0.60	£1.80	£3.00
35 ND Jim Starlin layouts						
	$1.20	$3.60	$6.00	£0.70	£2.10	£3.50
36-37	$1.20	$3.60	$6.00	£0.50	£1.50	£2.50
38	$1.20	$3.60	$6.00	£0.60	£1.80	£3.00
39-40	$1.20	$3.60	$6.00	£0.50	£1.50	£2.50
41-42	$1.00	$3.00	$5.00	£0.45	£1.35	£2.25
43 Infantino art, Ghost Rider vs. Johnny Blaze						
	$1.00	$3.00	$5.00	£0.45	£1.35	£2.25
44-49	$1.00	$3.00	$5.00	£0.45	£1.35	£2.25
50 ND 52pgs, Night Rider (original Ghost Rider) battles Ghost Rider						
	$1.20	$3.60	$6.00	£0.70	£2.10	£3.50
51 Infantino art	$0.80	$2.40	$4.00	£0.40	£1.20	£2.00
52	$0.80	$2.40	$4.00	£0.40	£1.20	£2.00
53-54 ND	$0.80	$2.40	$4.00	£0.45	£1.35	£2.25
55-57	$0.80	$2.40	$4.00	£0.40	£1.20	£2.00
58 Sienkiewicz cover						
	$0.80	$2.40	$4.00	£0.40	£1.20	£2.00
59-71	$0.80	$2.40	$4.00	£0.40	£1.20	£2.00
72-77 less common in the U.K.						
	$0.80	$2.40	$4.00	£0.50	£1.50	£2.50
78 LD in the U.K. Son of Satan, Dr. Strange and Dr. Druid cameos						
	$0.90	$2.70	$4.50	£0.60	£1.80	£3.00
79 ND	$0.80	$2.40	$4.00	£0.55	£1.65	£2.75
80 ND scarce in the U.K.						
	$1.20	$3.60	$6.00	£0.80	£2.40	£4.00
81 ND very scarce in the U.K						
	$1.50	$4.50	$7.50	£1.00	£3.00	£5.00
Title Value:	$136.70	$410.10	$709.50	£64.60	£193.85	£335.50

Note: part origin stories of Ghost Rider in #6 and #68.

GHOST RIDER & BLAZE: SPIRITS OF VENGEANCE

Marvel Comics Group; 1 Aug 1992-23 Jun 1994

	$Good	$Fine	$N.Mint	£Good	£Fine	£N.Mint
1 ND 48pgs, pre-bagged, fold-out poster, ties in with Rise of the Midnight Sons						
	$0.60	$1.80	$3.00	£0.30	£0.90	£1.50
2-4 ND Rise of the Midnight Sons tie-in						
	$0.40	$1.20	$2.00	£0.25	£0.75	£1.25
5 ND Spirits of Venom part 2, continued in Web of Spiderman #96						
	$0.40	$1.20	$2.00	£0.25	£0.75	£1.25
6 ND Spirits of Venom part 4 (conclusion), Spiderman and Venom appear						
	$0.40	$1.20	$2.00	£0.25	£0.75	£1.25
7-8 ND	$0.40	$1.20	$2.00	£0.25	£0.75	£1.25
9 ND Adam Kubert cover, 1st appearance of Vengeance						
	$0.50	$1.50	$2.50	£0.30	£0.90	£1.50
10 ND Vengeance appears						
	$0.40	$1.20	$2.00	£0.25	£0.75	£1.25
11 ND	$0.40	$0.90	$1.50	£0.20	£0.60	£1.00
12 ND glow-in-the-dark cover by Andy and Adam Kubert, new logo						
	$0.30	$0.90	$1.50	£0.20	£0.60	£1.00
13 ND Midnight Massacre part 5 (conclusion), gold-printed black parchment outer cover						
	$0.30	$0.90	$1.50	£0.20	£0.60	£1.00
14 ND X-over with Ghost Rider #42						
	$0.30	$0.90	$1.50	£0.20	£0.60	£1.00
15 ND X-over with Ghost Rider #43						
	$0.30	$0.90	$1.50	£0.20	£0.60	£1.00
16 ND Road to Vengeance: The Missing Link conclusion, neon ink cover						
	$0.30	$0.90	$1.50	£0.20	£0.60	£1.00
17 ND Siege of Darkness part 8, black cover with enhanced inks						
	$0.30	$0.90	$1.50	£0.20	£0.60	£1.00
18 ND Siege of Darkness conclusion; Ghost Rider dies						
	$0.30	$0.90	$1.50	£0.20	£0.60	£1.00
19-21 ND	$0.30	$0.90	$1.50	£0.20	£0.60	£1.00
22 ND with free Spiderman and his Deadly Foes card sheet						
	$0.30	$0.90	$1.50	£0.20	£0.60	£1.00
23 ND	$0.30	$0.90	$1.50	£0.20	£0.60	£1.00
Title Value:	$8.20	$24.60	$41.00	£5.20	£15.60	£26.00

Ghost Rider & Spiderman: Spirits of Venom (Jan 1994)
Trade paperback reprints Spirits of Vengeance #5 and Web of Spiderman #95, 96; new painted cover by Adam Kubert and Ken Steacy £1.30 £3.90 £6.50

GHOST RIDER (2ND SERIES)

Marvel Comics Group; 1 May 1990-present

	$Good	$Fine	$N.Mint	£Good	£Fine	£N.Mint
1 ND 48pgs, Kingpin appears, Texeira art begins						
	$1.50	$4.50	$7.50	£1.20	£3.60	£6.00
1 2nd printing ND	$0.60	$1.80	$3.00	£0.40	£1.20	£2.00
2-3 ND Kingpin appears						
	$1.30	$3.90	$6.50	£0.80	£2.40	£4.00
4 ND scarce in the U.K., scarce only in the U.S.						
	$1.30	$3.90	$6.50	£0.80	£2.40	£4.00
5 ND 1st Punisher/Ghost Rider team-up						
	$1.30	$3.90	$6.50	£0.80	£2.40	£4.00
5 2nd printing, Gold cover; this is the only gold edition available even though it's called 2nd print (ie. there's no 1st print Gold Edition)						
	$0.90	$2.70	$4.50	£0.60	£1.80	£3.00
6 ND Punisher co-stars						
	$0.80	$2.40	$4.00	£0.60	£1.80	£3.00
7-8 ND	$0.70	$2.10	$3.50	£0.40	£1.20	£2.00
9 ND X-Factor appear						
	$0.70	$2.10	$3.50	£0.40	£1.20	£2.00
10 ND	$0.70	$2.10	$3.50	£0.40	£1.20	£2.00
11 ND Dr. Strange appears						
	$0.50	$1.50	$2.50	£0.30	£0.90	£1.50
12 ND X-over with Dr. Strange #28						
	$0.50	$1.50	$2.50	£0.30	£0.90	£1.50
13-14 ND Ghost Rider vs. Johnny Blaze (original super-hero Ghost Rider)						
	$0.50	$1.50	$2.50	£0.30	£0.90	£1.50
15 ND Ghost Rider vs. Johnny Blaze (original super-hero Ghost Rider), glow-in-the-dark cover						
	$1.00	$3.00	$5.00	£0.50	£1.50	£2.50
15 2nd printing, ND different glow-in-the-dark cover						
	$0.60	$1.80	$3.00	£0.40	£1.20	£2.00
16 ND Johnny Blaze appears, Hobgoblin and Spiderman appear						
	$0.60	$1.80	$3.00	£0.30	£0.90	£1.50
17 ND Johnny Blaze appears, sequel to Spiderman #6,7 (Hobgoblin and Spiderman appear)						
	$0.60	$1.80	$3.00	£0.30	£0.90	£1.50
18-20 ND	$0.50	$1.50	$2.50	£0.30	£0.90	£1.50
21 ND Ron Wagner pencils, inks only by Texeira						
	$0.40	$1.20	$2.00	£0.25	£0.75	£1.25
22-23 ND	$0.40	$1.20	$2.00	£0.25	£0.75	£1.25
24 ND Johnny Blaze cameo						
	$0.40	$1.20	$2.00	£0.25	£0.75	£1.25
25 ND 48pgs, celebrates 20th anniversary, die-cut pop-up centre-spread						
	$0.55	$1.65	$2.75	£0.35	£1.05	£1.75
26 ND X-over with X-Men #9						
	$0.50	$1.50	$2.50	£0.30	£0.90	£1.50
27 ND X-Men guest-star, Jim Lee cover						
	$0.50	$1.50	$2.50	£0.30	£0.90	£1.50
28 ND Rise of the Midnight Sons part 1, pre-bagged with fold-out poster and gatefold centre-spread, Andy and Joe Kubert art						
	$0.50	$1.50	$2.50	£0.30	£0.90	£1.50
29 ND Wolverine and Beast appear, Rise of the Midnight Sons tie-in						
	$0.40	$1.20	$2.00	£0.25	£0.75	£1.25
30 ND more deatails of Ghost Rider's origin						
	$0.40	$1.20	$2.00	£0.25	£0.75	£1.25
31 ND pre-bagged, Rise of the Midnight Sons part 6 (conclusion), all characters in this storyline appear including Morbius and Dr. Strange						
	$0.55	$1.65	$2.75	£0.35	£1.05	£1.75
32 ND Dr. Strange guest-stars						
	$0.40	$1.20	$2.00	£0.25	£0.75	£1.25
33-36 ND	$0.40	$1.20	$2.00	£0.25	£0.75	£1.25
37 ND Archangel appears						
	$0.40	$1.20	$2.00	£0.25	£0.75	£1.25
38-39 ND	$0.40	$1.20	$2.00	£0.25	£0.75	£1.25
40 ND Midnight Massacre part 2, gold-ink black parchment outer cover						
	$0.40	$1.20	$2.00	£0.25	£0.75	£1.25
41 ND Road to Vengeance: The Missing Link begins, neon ink covers begin; continued in Ghost Rider & Blaze: Spirits of Vengeance #14						
	$0.40	$1.20	$2.00	£0.25	£0.75	£1.25

	$Good	$Fine	$N.Mint	£Good	£Fine	£N.Mint
42 ND Road to Vengeance: The Missing Link story; continued in Ghost Rider & Blaze: Spirits of Vengeance #15	$0.40	$1.20	$2.00	£0.25	£0.75	£1.25
43 ND Road to Vengeance: The Missing Link story; continued in Ghost Rider & Blaze: Spirits of Vengeance #16	$0.40	$1.20	$2.00	£0.25	£0.75	£1.25
44 ND Siege of Darkness part 2, neon ink/spot varnish cover	$0.40	$1.20	$2.00	£0.25	£0.75	£1.25
45 ND Siege of Darkness part 10, neon ink/spot varnish cover	$0.40	$1.20	$2.00	£0.25	£0.75	£1.25
46 ND Vengeance becomes new Ghost Rider	$0.40	$1.20	$2.00	£0.25	£0.75	£1.25
47-48 ND	$0.40	$1.20	$2.00	£0.25	£0.75	£1.25
49 ND with free Spiderman and his Deadly Foes card sheet	$0.40	$1.20	$2.00	£0.25	£0.75	£1.25
50 ND 48pgs, John Blaze appears	$0.45	$1.35	$2.25	£0.30	£0.90	£1.50
50 ND Collector's Edition, John Blaze appears; die-cut foil stamped cover	$0.60	$1.80	$3.00	£0.40	£1.20	£2.00
51-54 ND	$0.40	$1.20	$2.00	£0.25	£0.75	£1.25
55 ND Werewolf By Night appears	$0.40	$1.20	$2.00	£0.25	£0.75	£1.25
56 ND	$0.40	$1.20	$2.00	£0.25	£0.75	£1.25
57 ND Wolverine appears, X-over with Wolverine #89	$0.40	$1.20	$2.00	£0.25	£0.75	£1.25
58 ND Nick Fury appears	$0.40	$1.20	$2.00	£0.25	£0.75	£1.25
59 ND Hulk appears	$0.40	$1.20	$2.00	£0.25	£0.75	£1.25
60 ND	$0.40	$1.20	$2.00	£0.25	£0.75	£1.25
61 ND 48pgs, Daredevil, Nick Fury and Punisher appear	$0.45	$1.35	$2.25	£0.30	£0.90	£1.50
62-63 ND Nick Fury appears	$0.40	$1.20	$2.00	£0.25	£0.75	£1.25
64 ND Avengers and Nick Fury appear	$0.40	$1.20	$2.00	£0.25	£0.75	£1.25
65 ND Over The Edge tie-in, Punisher appears	$0.40	$1.20	$2.00	£0.25	£0.75	£1.25
66 ND Ghost Rider vs. Blackout	$0.40	$1.20	$2.00	£0.25	£0.75	£1.25
67 ND Gambit guest-stars	$0.40	$1.20	$2.00	£0.25	£0.75	£1.25
68 ND Gambit and Wolverine appear	$0.40	$1.20	$2.00	£0.25	£0.75	£1.25
69-71 ND	$0.40	$1.20	$2.00	£0.25	£0.75	£1.25
Title Value:	$39.80	$119.40	$199.00	£24.80	£74.40	£124.00

Ghost Rider: Ressurrected

	£Good	£Fine	£N.Mint
Trade paperback (Jan 1992) reprints issues #1-7	£1.60	£4.80	£8.00
(2nd printing - Dec 1992)	£1.50	£4.50	£7.50

Ghost Rider Poster Book (Jul 1992), magazine format with posters featuring the work of McFarlane, Lee, Texeira and Golden; sixteen of the posters are double-page spreads £0.65 £1.95 £3.25

Ghost Rider: Midnight Sons (Aug 1993) Trade paperback reprints Ghost Rider #28,31, Morbius #1, Nightstalkers #1, Darkhold #1 and Spirits of Vengeance #1; wraparound cover with embossed gold logo £2.75 £8.25 £13.75

GHOST RIDER (2ND SERIES) ANNUAL
Marvel Comics Group; 1 Sep 1993-present

	$Good	$Fine	$N.Mint	£Good	£Fine	£N.Mint
1 ND 64pgs, pre-bagged with trading card introducing Night Terror; Chris Bachalo and Mark Buckingham art	$0.50	$1.50	$2.50	£0.30	£0.90	£1.50
2 ND 64pgs, Warren Ellis script	$0.50	$1.50	$2.50	£0.30	£0.90	£1.50
Title Value:	$1.00	$3.00	$5.00	£0.60	£1.80	£3.00

GHOST RIDER 2099
Marvel Comics Group; 1 May 1994-present

	$Good	$Fine	$N.Mint	£Good	£Fine	£N.Mint
1 ND Chris Bachalo and Mark Buckingham art begins	$0.30	$0.90	$1.50	£0.20	£0.60	£1.00
1 ND Collector's Edition, prismatic foil enhanced cover; with free Spiderman's Amazing Powers card sheet	$0.45	$1.35	$2.25	£0.30	£0.90	£1.50
2-6 ND	$0.30	$0.90	$1.50	£0.20	£0.60	£1.00
7 ND Spiderman 2099 appears	$0.30	$0.90	$1.50	£0.20	£0.60	£1.00
8 ND	$0.30	$0.90	$1.50	£0.20	£0.60	£1.00
9 ND Mark Buckingham art	$0.30	$0.90	$1.50	£0.20	£0.60	£1.00
10 ND photographic cover	$0.30	$0.90	$1.50	£0.20	£0.60	£1.00
11 ND	$0.30	$0.90	$1.50	£0.20	£0.60	£1.00
12 ND computer-generated cover	$0.30	$0.90	$1.50	£0.20	£0.60	£1.00
13-15 ND	$0.40	$1.20	$2.00	£0.25	£0.75	£1.25
16 ND One Nation Under Doom	$0.40	$1.20	$2.00	£0.25	£0.75	£1.25
17-20 ND	$0.40	$1.20	$2.00	£0.25	£0.75	£1.25
21 ND ties-into 2099 Genesis	$0.40	$1.20	$2.00	£0.25	£0.75	£1.25
22 ND Ghost Rider 2099 vs. Vengeance 2099	$0.40	$1.20	$2.00	£0.25	£0.75	£1.25
23 ND	$0.40	$1.20	$2.00	£0.25	£0.75	£1.25
Title Value:	$8.45	$25.35	$42.25	£5.45	£16.35	£27.25

GHOST RIDER AND THE MIDNIGHT SONS MAGAZINE
Marvel Comics Group,Magazine OS; 1 Dec 1993

	$Good	$Fine	$N.Mint	£Good	£Fine	£N.Mint
1 ND 48pgs, George Pratt cover	$0.80	$2.40	$4.00	£0.50	£1.50	£2.50
Title Value:	$0.80	$2.40	$4.00	£0.50	£1.50	£2.50

GHOST RIDER RIDES AGAIN, THE ORIGINAL
Marvel Comics Group,MS; 1 Jul 1991-7 Jan 1992

	$Good	$Fine	$N.Mint	£Good	£Fine	£N.Mint
1 ND reprints from Ghost Rider (super-hero) 1st series begin with issues #68,#69	$0.30	$0.90	$1.50	£0.20	£0.60	£1.00
2 ND reprints issues #70,#71	$0.30	$0.90	$1.50	£0.20	£0.60	£1.00
3 ND reprints issues #72,#73	$0.30	$0.90	$1.50	£0.20	£0.60	£1.00
4 ND reprints issues #74,#75	$0.30	$0.90	$1.50	£0.20	£0.60	£1.00
5 ND reprints issues #76,#77	$0.30	$0.90	$1.50	£0.20	£0.60	£1.00
6 ND reprints issues #78,#79	$0.30	$0.90	$1.50	£0.20	£0.60	£1.00
7 ND reprints issues #80,#81	$0.30	$0.90	$1.50	£0.20	£0.60	£1.00
Title Value:	$2.10	$6.30	$10.50	£1.40	£4.20	£7.00

GHOST RIDER, THE
Marvel Comics Group; 1 Feb 1967-7 Nov 1967
(see Nightrider, Western Gunfighters)

	$Good	$Fine	$N.Mint	£Good	£Fine	£N.Mint
1 origin and 1st appearance Ghost Rider (Western), Kid Colt begins	$7.50	$22.50	$45.00	£3.30	£10.00	£20.00
2	$4.00	$12.00	$20.00	£2.50	£7.50	£12.50
3-7	$3.50	$10.50	$17.50	£2.00	£6.00	£10.00
Title Value:	$29.00	$87.00	$152.50	£15.80	£47.50	£82.50

Note: not to be confused with the later super-hero title. All the above were reprinted under the title "Night Rider".

GHOST RIDER, THE ORIGINAL
Marvel Comics Group; 1 Jul 1992-20 Feb 1994

	$Good	$Fine	$N.Mint	£Good	£Fine	£N.Mint
1 ND reprints Marvel Spotlight (1st Series) #5 featuring the 1st appearance of Ghost Rider; reprints from this series begin in order	$0.30	$0.90	$1.50	£0.20	£0.60	£1.00
2-7 ND	$0.30	$0.90	$1.50	£0.20	£0.60	£1.00
8 ND reprints begin from Ghost Rider (1st series) #1	$0.30	$0.90	$1.50	£0.20	£0.60	£1.00
9 ND reprints Ghost Rider (1st Series) #2	$0.30	$0.90	$1.50	£0.20	£0.60	£1.00
10 ND reprints Marvel Spotlight (1st Series) #12 with the first full appearance of Son of Satan	$0.30	$0.90	$1.50	£0.20	£0.60	£1.00
11 ND reprints Ghost Rider #3, Hellstorm appears	$0.30	$0.90	$1.50	£0.20	£0.60	£1.00
12-17 ND	$0.30	$0.90	$1.50	£0.20	£0.60	£1.00
18 ND reprints Ghost Rider #11, Hulk appears	$0.30	$0.90	$1.50	£0.20	£0.60	£1.00
19 ND	$0.30	$0.90	$1.50	£0.20	£0.60	£1.00
20 ND Mike Ploog cover	$0.30	$0.90	$1.50	£0.20	£0.60	£1.00
Title Value:	$6.00	$18.00	$30.00	£4.00	£12.00	£20.00

GHOST RIDER/CABLE SPECIAL
Marvel Comics Group,OS; 1 Sep 1992

	$Good	$Fine	$N.Mint	£Good	£Fine	£N.Mint
1 ND reprints Marvel Comics Presents #90-98, new covers on heavier card-stock	$0.80	$2.40	$4.00	£0.50	£1.50	£2.50
Title Value:	$0.80	$2.40	$4.00	£0.50	£1.50	£2.50

GHOST RIDER/WOLVERINE/PUNISHER: THE DARK DESIGN
Marvel Comics Group,OS; 1 Feb 1995

	$Good	$Fine	$N.Mint	£Good	£Fine	£N.Mint
1 ND 48pgs, sequel to Hearts of Darkness	$1.20	$3.60	$6.00	£0.80	£2.40	£4.00
Title Value:	$1.20	$3.60	$6.00	£0.80	£2.40	£4.00

GHOST RIDER: FEAR
Marvel Comics Group,OS; 1 Dec 1992

	$Good	$Fine	$N.Mint	£Good	£Fine	£N.Mint
1 ND 48pgs, team-up with Captain America, gatefold cover	$1.00	$3.00	$5.00	£0.70	£2.10	£3.50
Title Value:	$1.00	$3.00	$5.00	£0.70	£2.10	£3.50

GHOST RIDERS: CROSS ROADS
Marvel Comics Group,OS; nn Dec 1995

	$Good	$Fine	$N.Mint	£Good	£Fine	£N.Mint
nn ND 48pgs, features original Ghost Rider and Spirit of Vengeance; die-cut cover	$0.80	$2.40	$4.00	£0.50	£1.50	£2.50
Title Value:	$0.80	$2.40	$4.00	£0.50	£1.50	£2.50

GHOST SPECIAL
Dark Horse/Comics Greatest World,OS; 1 Jul 1994

	$Good	$Fine	$N.Mint	£Good	£Fine	£N.Mint
1 ND 48pgs, Adam Hughes cover	$0.80	$2.40	$4.00	£0.50	£1.50	£2.50
Title Value:	$0.80	$2.40	$4.00	£0.50	£1.50	£2.50

Ghost

	£Good	£Fine	£N.Mint
Trade paperback (Feb 1995) reprints early appearances from Comics' Greatest World with Adam Hughes cover	£1.20	£3.60	£6.00

GHOSTBUSTERS
First, TV; 1 Feb 1986-6 Aug 1987
(see Real Ghostbusters)

	$Good	$Fine	$N.Mint	£Good	£Fine	£N.Mint
1-6 ND based on animated TV show	$0.25	$0.75	$1.25	£0.15	£0.45	£0.75
Title Value:	$1.50	$4.50	$7.50	£0.90	£2.70	£4.50

GHOSTDANCING
DC Comics,MS; 1 Mar 1995-6 Sep 1995

	$Good	$Fine	$N.Mint	£Good	£Fine	£N.Mint
1-2 Jamie Delano script, Richard Case art	$0.40	$1.20	$2.00	£0.25	£0.75	£1.25
3 Jamie Delano script, Richard Case art; upgraded paper format begins	$0.40	$1.20	$2.00	£0.25	£0.75	£1.25
4-6 Jamie Delano script, Richard Case art	$0.40	$1.20	$2.00	£0.25	£0.75	£1.25

	$Good	$Fine	$N.Mint	£Good	£Fine	£N.Mint
Title Value:	$2.40	$7.20	$12.00	£1.50	£4.50	£7.50

GHOSTLY HAUNTS
Charlton; 20 Sep 1971-53 Dec 1976; 54 Sep 1977-58 Apr 1978
(formerly Ghost Manor #1-19)

	$Good	$Fine	$N.Mint	£Good	£Fine	£N.Mint
20-40 distributed in the U.K.						
	$0.60	$1.80	$3.00	£0.40	£1.20	£2.00
41-51 distributed in the U.K.						
	$0.45	$1.35	$2.25	£0.30	£0.90	£1.50
52 Pat Boyette cover; distributed in the U.K.						
	$0.45	$1.35	$2.25	£0.30	£0.90	£1.50
53-58 distributed in the U.K.						
	$0.45	$1.35	$2.25	£0.30	£0.90	£1.50
Title Value:	$20.70	$62.10	$103.50	£13.80	£41.40	£69.00

Note: most issues have Ditko art

GHOSTLY TALES
Charlton; 55 Apr/May 1966-124 Dec 1976; 125 Sep 1977-169 Oct 1984
(previously Unusual Tales #1-49; Blue Beetle 2nd Series #50-54)

	$Good	$Fine	$N.Mint	£Good	£Fine	£N.Mint
55 origin/1st appearance Dr. Graves						
	$1.50	$4.50	$7.50	£1.00	£3.00	£5.00
56-60 Dr. Graves appears						
	$0.90	$2.70	$4.50	£0.60	£1.80	£3.00
61-70 Dr. Graves appears						
	$0.80	$2.40	$4.00	£0.50	£1.50	£2.50
71-124	$0.60	$1.80	$3.00	£0.40	£1.20	£2.00
125-169	$0.45	$1.35	$2.25	£0.30	£0.90	£1.50
Title Value:	$66.65	$199.95	$333.25	£44.10	£132.30	£220.50

Note: most issues have Ditko art. All were distributed in the U.K.

GHOSTS
DC Comics; 1 Sep/Oct 1971-112 May 1982
(see DC Special Blue Ribbon Digest, Limited Collector's Edition)

	$Good	$Fine	$N.Mint	£Good	£Fine	£N.Mint
1 48pgs	$2.40	$7.00	$12.00	£1.30	£3.90	£6.50
2 48pgs, Wood art	$1.00	$3.00	$5.00	£0.60	£1.80	£3.00
3-5 48pgs	$0.70	$2.10	$3.50	£0.40	£1.20	£2.00
6-20	$0.50	$1.50	$2.50	£0.30	£0.90	£1.50
21-39	$0.40	$1.20	$2.00	£0.25	£0.75	£1.25
40 scarce in the U.K. 64pgs, squarebound						
	$0.45	$1.35	$2.25	£0.30	£0.90	£1.50
41-42	$0.30	$0.90	$1.50	£0.20	£0.60	£1.00
43 ND	$0.30	$0.90	$1.50	£0.25	£0.75	£1.25
44-46	$0.30	$0.90	$1.50	£0.20	£0.60	£1.00
47-49 scarce in the U.K.						
	$0.30	$0.90	$1.50	£0.25	£0.75	£1.25
50-60	$0.30	$0.90	$1.50	£0.20	£0.60	£1.00
61-67	$0.25	$0.75	$1.25	£0.15	£0.45	£0.75
68-70 ND 44pgs	$0.25	$0.75	$1.25	£0.20	£0.60	£1.00
71-87	$0.25	$0.75	$1.25	£0.15	£0.45	£0.75
88 Golden art						
	$0.25	$0.75	$1.25	£0.15	£0.45	£0.75
89-96	$0.25	$0.75	$1.25	£0.15	£0.45	£0.75
97-99 Dr. Geist by Mike Nasser, Dr. 13 Ghostbreaker vs. The Spectre back-up						
	$0.40	$1.20	$2.00	£0.20	£0.60	£1.00
100	$0.25	$0.75	$1.25	£0.15	£0.45	£0.75
101-103	$0.15	$0.45	$0.75	£0.10	£0.35	£0.60
104 Giffen art	$0.15	$0.45	$0.75	£0.10	£0.35	£0.60
105-112	$0.15	$0.45	$0.75	£0.10	£0.35	£0.60
Title Value:	$39.30	$117.70	$196.50	£24.35	£73.65	£122.95

ARTISTS
Ditko in 77, 111. Nino in 35, 37, 57. Wood in 2.
FEATURES
All-new mystery stories except some reprints in 1-5, 40. Dr.13 in 95, 96, 101, 102. Dr.13/Spectre in 97-99.

GHOSTS SPECIAL
DC Comics; nn 1977
nn ND 52pgs, Alex Nino art

	$Good	$Fine	$N.Mint	£Good	£Fine	£N.Mint
	$0.45	$1.35	$2.25	£0.30	£0.90	£1.50
Title Value:	$0.45	$1.35	$2.25	£0.30	£0.90	£1.50

GHOUL GALLERY
AC Comics; 1 Apr 1994-2 1994
1-2 ND black and white

	$Good	$Fine	$N.Mint	£Good	£Fine	£N.Mint
	$0.60	$1.80	$3.00	£0.40	£1.20	£2.00
Title Value:	$1.20	$3.60	$6.00	£0.80	£2.40	£4.00

GIANT-SIZE MINI COMICS
Eclipse; 1 Aug 1986-4 Feb 1987
1-4 ND Mini-comics reprints in black and white featuring Ronald Reagan

	$Good	$Fine	$N.Mint	£Good	£Fine	£N.Mint
	$0.30	$0.90	$1.50	£0.20	£0.60	£1.00
Title Value:	$1.20	$3.60	$6.00	£0.80	£2.40	£4.00

GIFT, THE
First,OS; 1 Jan 1991
1 ND 48pgs, features Badger, Nexus, Grimjack, Meta-4, Squalor, Zero Tolerance

	$Good	$Fine	$N.Mint	£Good	£Fine	£N.Mint
	$1.20	$3.60	$6.00	£0.80	£2.40	£4.00
Title Value:	$1.20	$3.60	$6.00	£0.80	£2.40	£4.00

GIL KANE'S SAVAGE
Fantagraphics,Magazine; 1 1987
1 ND reprints "His Name Is Savage", new cover

	$Good	$Fine	$N.Mint	£Good	£Fine	£N.Mint
	$0.55	$1.65	$2.75	£0.35	£1.05	£1.75
Title Value:	$0.55	$1.65	$2.75	£0.35	£1.05	£1.75

GILGAMESH II
DC Comics,MS; 1 April 1989-4 July 1989
1-4 ND squarebound, Jim Starlin script/art

	$Good	$Fine	$N.Mint	£Good	£Fine	£N.Mint
	$0.70	$2.10	$3.50	£0.45	£1.35	£2.25
Title Value:	$2.80	$8.40	$14.00	£1.80	£5.40	£9.00

Note: Mature Readers

GINGER FOX
Comico,MS; 1 Sep 1988-4 Dec 1988
(see World of Ginger Fox)
1-4 ND Pander Bros. art

	$Good	$Fine	$N.Mint	£Good	£Fine	£N.Mint
	$0.40	$1.20	$2.00	£0.25	£0.75	£1.25
Title Value:	$1.60	$4.80	$8.00	£1.00	£3.00	£5.00

GIRL FROM U.N.C.L.E., THE
Gold Key, TV; 1 Oct 1966-5 Oct 1967
(see Man From Uncle)

	$Good	$Fine	$N.Mint	£Good	£Fine	£N.Mint
1 scarce, distributed in the U.K.						
	$12.00	$36.00	$60.00	£7.00	£21.00	£35.00
2-5 scarce, distributed in the U.K.						
	$9.00	$27.00	$45.00	£6.00	£18.00	£30.00
Title Value:	$48.00	$144.00	$240.00	£31.00	£93.00	£155.00

GIRL'S LOVE STORIES
National Periodical Publications/DC Comics; 1 Aug/Sep 1949-180 Nov/Dec 1973

	$Good	$Fine	$N.Mint	£Good	£Fine	£N.Mint
1 very scarce in the U.K. photo cover						
	$45.00	$135.00	$315.00	£30.00	£90.00	£210.00
2 very scarce in the U.K. photo cover						
	$22.50	$67.50	$157.50	£15.00	£45.00	£105.00
3-9 scarce in the U.K. photo cover						
	$14.00	$43.00	$100.00	£9.25	£28.00	£65.00
10 scarce in the U.K.						
	$14.00	$43.00	$100.00	£9.25	£28.00	£65.00
11-20 scarce in the U.K.						
	$10.50	$32.00	$75.00	£6.25	£19.00	£45.00
21-30 scarce in the U.K.						
	$7.00	$21.00	$50.00	£4.25	£12.50	£30.00
31-50 scarce in the U.K.						
	$6.50	$20.00	$40.00	£4.15	£12.50	£25.00
51-65 scarce in the U.K.						
	$4.55	$13.50	$27.50	£2.50	£7.50	£15.00
1st official distribution in the U.K.						
66-82 scarce in the U.K.						
	$4.55	$13.50	$27.50	£2.05	£6.25	£12.50
83 scarce in the U.K. last 10 cents issue						
	$4.15	$12.50	$25.00	£2.05	£6.25	£12.50
84-90 scarce in the U.K.						
	$4.15	$12.50	$25.00	£2.05	£6.25	£12.50
91-99	$5.00	$15.00	$25.00	£2.20	£6.50	£11.00
100	$5.50	$16.50	$27.50	£2.50	£7.50	£12.50
101-110	$3.00	$9.00	$15.00	£1.50	£4.50	£7.50
111-130	$3.00	$9.00	$15.00	£1.20	£3.60	£6.00
131-150	$2.40	$7.00	$12.00	£1.00	£3.00	£5.00
151-160	$1.20	$3.60	$6.00	£0.80	£2.40	£4.00
161-170 48pgs	$1.20	$3.60	$6.00	£0.90	£2.70	£4.50
171-180	$1.00	$3.00	$5.00	£0.70	£2.10	£3.50
Title Value:	$885.80	$2672.00	$5485.00	£501.05	£1507.75	£3149.00

GIRL'S ROMANCES
National Periodical Publications/DC Comics; 1 Feb/Mar 1950-160 Oct 1971

	$Good	$Fine	$N.Mint	£Good	£Fine	£N.Mint
1 very scarce in the U.K. photo cover						
	$45.00	$135.00	$315.00	£30.00	£90.00	£210.00
2 very scarce in the U.K. photo cover						
	$22.50	$67.50	$157.50	£15.00	£45.00	£105.00
3-6 scarce in the U.K. photo cover						
	$14.00	$43.00	$100.00	£9.25	£28.00	£65.00
7-10 scarce in the U.K.						
	$12.50	$39.00	$90.00	£8.50	£26.00	£60.00
11-20 scarce in the U.K.						
	$10.00	$30.00	$70.00	£6.25	£19.00	£45.00
21-30 scarce in the U.K.						
	$5.50	$17.00	$40.00	£3.55	£10.50	£25.00
31-50 scarce in the U.K.						
	$5.75	$17.50	$35.00	£3.30	£10.00	£20.00
51-63 scarce in the U.K.						
	$3.75	$11.00	$22.50	£2.50	£7.50	£15.00
1st official distribution in the U.K.						
64-79 scarce in the U.K.						
	$3.00	$9.00	$18.00	£2.00	£6.00	£12.00
80 scarce in the U.K. last 10 cents issue						
	$3.00	$9.00	$18.00	£2.00	£6.00	£12.00
81-90	$3.00	$9.00	$18.00	£1.80	£5.50	£11.00
91-99	$3.60	$10.50	$18.00	£2.00	£6.00	£10.00
100	$4.00	$12.00	$20.00	£2.50	£7.50	£12.50
101-108	$3.00	$9.00	$15.00	£1.80	£5.25	£9.00
109 Beatles story and cover appearance						
	$8.25	$25.00	$50.00	£5.00	£15.00	£30.00
110	$3.00	$9.00	$15.00	£1.80	£5.25	£9.00
111-120	$2.50	$7.50	$12.50	£1.60	£4.80	£8.00
121-133	$2.00	$6.00	$10.00	£1.20	£3.60	£6.00
134 Neal Adams cover						
	$2.40	$7.00	$12.00	£1.40	£4.20	£7.00
135-140	$2.00	$6.00	$10.00	£1.20	£3.60	£6.00
141-158	$1.20	$3.60	$6.00	£0.80	£2.40	£4.00
159-160 scarce in the U.K. 48pgs						
	$1.20	$3.60	$6.00	£0.90	£2.70	£4.50
Title Value:	$734.30	$2217.00	$4625.00	£462.60	£1393.45	£2919.50

GIVE ME LIBERTY
Dark Horse,MS; 1 Aug 1990-4 Apr 1991
1 ND Frank Miller script, Dave Gibbons art

	$Good	$Fine	$N.Mint	£Good	£Fine	£N.Mint
	$1.05	$3.15	$5.25	£0.70	£2.10	£3.50
2-4 ND Frank Miller script, Dave Gibbons art						

	$Good	$Fine	$N.Mint	£Good	£Fine	£N.Mint
	$1.00	$3.00	$5.00	£0.65	£1.95	£3.25
Title Value:	$4.05	$12.15	$20.25	£2.65	£7.95	£13.25
Trade paperback (Sep 1991)						
(published by Penguin Books) reprints #1–4				£1.80	£5.40	£9.00
Hardcover				£3.00	£9.00	£15.00
Hardcover distributed by Titan with signed						
plate by Miller and Gibbons				£3.50	£10.50	£17.50
Trade paperback (Feb 1992) - published by						
Dark Horse), reprints #1–4				£2.00	£6.00	£10.00
(2nd print - Sep 1994) $19.95 cover				£2.50	£7.50	£12.50
Signed and Numbered Limited Edition Hardcover						
(Dec 1994) with slipcase, new sketched included				£15.00	£45.00	£75.00
Give Me Liberty Trade Paperback - Dell Edition (Jul 1995)						
reprints mini-series. Note: only distributed in the U.S. not U.K.			£2.00	£6.00	£10.00

GIZMO
Chance,OS; 1 May 1985
1 ND Turtles X-over

	$1.05	$3.15	$5.25	£0.70	£2.10	£3.50
Title Value:	$1.05	$3.15	$5.25	£0.70	£2.10	£3.50
Trade Paperback, reprints #1–6, plus new material			£1.70	£5.10	£8.50

GIZMO (2ND SERIES)
Mirage Studios; 1 Feb 1986-6 Jul 1987
1 ND black and white

	$0.45	$1.35	$2.25	£0.30	£0.90	£1.50
2-6 ND black and white						
	$0.40	$1.20	$2.00	£0.25	£0.75	£1.25
Title Value:	$2.45	$7.35	$12.25	£1.55	£4.65	£7.75

GIZMO AND THE FUGITOID
Mirage Studios,MS; 1 Jun 1989-2 Jul 1989

	$Good	$Fine	$N.Mint	£Good	£Fine	£N.Mint
1-2 ND	$0.40	$1.20	$2.00	£0.25	£0.75	£1.25
Title Value:	$0.80	$2.40	$4.00	£0.50	£1.50	£2.50

GLADSTONE COMIC ALBUM
Gladstone; 1 1987-28 1990
1 Uncle Scrooge: Mines of King Solomon, plus 2 shorts by Barks

	$1.50	$4.50	$7.50	£1.00	£3.00	£5.00
2 Donald Duck: Terror of the River, plus 2 shorts by Barks						
	$1.40	$4.20	$7.00	£0.90	£2.70	£4.50
3 Mickey Mouse: Lair of Wolf Barker, Mickey's Nephew by Gottfredson						
	$1.40	$4.20	$7.00	£0.90	£2.70	£4.50
4 Uncle Scrooge: Back to the Klondike (includes restored artwork), plus 2 shorts by Barks						
	$1.40	$4.20	$7.00	£0.90	£2.70	£4.50
5 Donald Duck: Sheriff of Bullet Valley plus 2 shorts by Barks						
	$1.40	$4.20	$7.00	£0.90	£2.70	£4.50
6 Uncle Scrooge: Land Beneath the Ground & Pipeline to Danger by Barks						
	$1.20	$3.60	$6.00	£0.80	£2.40	£4.00
7 The Brittle Mastery of Donald Duck (5 shorts by Barks)						
	$1.20	$3.60	$6.00	£0.80	£2.40	£4.00
8 Mickey Mouse: Hoppy the Kangaroo, Mount Fishflake Expedition by Gottfredson						
	$1.20	$3.60	$6.00	£0.80	£2.40	£4.00
9 Bambi: movie adaptation						
	$1.20	$3.60	$6.00	£0.80	£2.40	£4.00
10 Donald Duck: In Ancient Persia, plus 2 shorts by Barks						
	$1.20	$3.60	$6.00	£0.80	£2.40	£4.00
11 Uncle Scrooge: Hawaiian Hideaway, plus 2 shorts by Barks						
	$1.20	$3.60	$6.00	£0.80	£2.40	£4.00
12 Donald and Daisy: 5 stories by Barks						
	$1.20	$3.60	$6.00	£0.80	£2.40	£4.00
13 Donald Duck: The Golden Helmet, plus 2 shorts by Barks						
	$1.20	$3.60	$6.00	£0.80	£2.40	£4.00
14 Uncle Scrooge	$1.20	$3.60	$6.00	£0.80	£2.40	£4.00
15-16 Donald Duck						

	$Good	$Fine	$N.Mint	£Good	£Fine	£N.Mint
	$1.20	$3.60	$6.00	£0.80	£2.40	£4.00
17 Mickey Mouse	$1.20	$3.60	$6.00	£0.80	£2.40	£4.00
18 Junior Woodchucks						
	$1.20	$3.60	$6.00	£0.80	£2.40	£4.00
19-20 Uncle Scrooge						
	$1.20	$3.60	$6.00	£0.80	£2.40	£4.00
21 Duck Family	$1.20	$3.60	$6.00	£0.80	£2.40	£4.00
22 Mickey Mouse	$1.20	$3.60	$6.00	£0.80	£2.40	£4.00
23 Donald Duck/Halloween						
	$1.20	$3.60	$6.00	£0.80	£2.40	£4.00
24 Uncle Scrooge	$1.20	$3.60	$6.00	£0.80	£2.40	£4.00
25 Donald Duck, Christmas issue						
	$1.20	$3.60	$6.00	£0.80	£2.40	£4.00
26 Mickey and Donald						
	$1.10	$3.35	$5.62	£0.75	£2.25	£3.75
27 Donald Duck	$1.10	$3.35	$5.62	£0.75	£2.25	£3.75
28 Scrooge and Donald						
	$1.10	$3.35	$5.62	£0.75	£2.25	£3.75
Title Value:	$34.40	$103.35	$172.36	£22.85	£68.55	£114.25
Note: all Non-Distributed on the news-stands in the U.K.						
Special 1 (1989), reprints Donald Duck						
Finds Pirate Gold from Four Color #9			£1.20	£3.60	£6.00
Special 2 (1989), Uncle Scrooge and						
Donald Duck, reprints Uncle Scrooge #5			£1.10	£3.30	£5.50
Special 3 (1990), Mickey Mouse reprint			£1.10	£3.30	£5.50
Special 4 (1990), Uncle Scrooge reprints 104 pgs			£1.40	£4.20	£7.00
Special 5 (1990), Donald Duck reprints 104 pgs			£1.40	£4.20	£7.00
Special 6 (1990), Uncle Scrooge reprints 104 pgs			£1.50	£4.50	£7.50
Special 7 (1990), Mickey Mouse reprints 104 pgs			£1.60	£4.80	£8.00

GLORY
Image; 0 Feb 1996; 1 Mar 1995-present
0 ND (Feb 1996), origin of Glory

	$0.45	$1.35	$2.25	£0.30	£0.90	£1.50
1 ND Mike Deodato Jnr. art begins						
	$0.45	$1.35	$2.25	£0.30	£0.90	£1.50
1 ND variant cover						
	$0.45	$1.35	$2.25	£0.30	£0.90	£1.50
2-4 ND	$0.45	$1.35	$2.25	£0.30	£0.90	£1.50
4 Variant cover, ND Joe Quesada/Jimmy Palmiotti cover art						
	$0.80	$2.40	$4.00	£0.50	£1.50	£2.50
5 ND Supreme Apocalypse part 3, continued in Brigade #22						
	$0.45	$1.35	$2.25	£0.30	£0.90	£1.50
6-7 ND	$0.45	$1.35	$2.25	£0.30	£0.90	£1.50
8 ND Extreme Babewatch						
	$0.45	$1.35	$2.25	£0.30	£0.90	£1.50
Title Value:	$5.30	$15.90	$26.50	£3.50	£10.50	£17.50
Glory (Jul 1995) reprints issues #1–4						
with new cover by Mike Deodato			£1.30	£3.90	£6.50

GLORY/AVENGELYNE
Image,OS; 1 Oct 1995
1 ND Rob Liefeld art, Robert Napton script; wraparound chromium cover

	$0.80	$2.40	$4.00	£0.60	£1.80	£3.00
1 ND variant cover, Rob Liefeld art; Glory in foreground/Avengelyne in background						
	$1.00	$3.00	$5.00	£0.80	£2.40	£4.00
Title Value:	$1.80	$7.40	$9.00	£1.40	£4.20	£7.00

GLORY & FRIENDS BIKINI FEST
Image,OS; 1 Sep 1995
1 ND pin-ups by Mike Deodato, Rob Liefeld, Stephen Platt, Dan Fraga and others

	$0.50	$1.50	$2.50	£0.30	£0.90	£1.50
Title Value:	$0.50	$1.50	$2.50	£0.30	£0.90	£1.50

GI Joe (2nd print) #2

Girls' Love Stories #62

Gobbledygook #1

	$Good	$Fine	$N.Mint	£Good	£Fine	£N.Mint

GLORY & FRIENDS CHRISTMAS SPECIAL
Image,OS; 1 Dec 1995

	$Good	$Fine	$N.Mint	£Good	£Fine	£N.Mint
1 ND	$0.50	$1.50	$2.50	£0.30	£0.90	£1.50
Title Value:	$0.50	$1.50	$2.50	£0.30	£0.90	£1.50

GNAT RAT: THE DARK GNAT RETURNS
Prelude; 1 1986
(see also Happy Birthday Gnat Rat, Darerat)
1 ND Dark Knight parody, Mark Martin art

	$Good	$Fine	$N.Mint	£Good	£Fine	£N.Mint
	$0.45	$1.35	$2.25	£0.30	£0.90	£1.50
Title Value:	$0.45	$1.35	$2.25	£0.30	£0.90	£1.50

GO-MAN!
Caliber Press; 1 Nov 1989-4 Jun 1990
1-4 ND black and white

	$Good	$Fine	$N.Mint	£Good	£Fine	£N.Mint
	$0.45	$1.35	$2.25	£0.30	£0.90	£1.50
Title Value:	$1.80	$5.40	$9.00	£1.20	£3.60	£6.00

GOBBLEDYGOOK
Mirage Studios; 1,2 1984
1 ND very scarce in the U.K. 1st appearance of Teenage Mutant Ninja Turtles

	$Good	$Fine	$N.Mint	£Good	£Fine	£N.Mint
	$30.00	$90.00	$150.00	£20.00	£60.00	£100.00

2 ND very scarce in the U.K.

	$Good	$Fine	$N.Mint	£Good	£Fine	£N.Mint
	$22.50	$67.50	$112.50	£15.00	£45.00	£75.00
Title Value:	$52.50	$157.50	$262.50	£35.00	£105.00	£175.00

Note: 1st Mirage comic title.

GOBBLEDYGOOK (2ND SERIES)
Mirage Studios; OS; 1 Dec 1986
1 ND new 10pg Turtles story

	$Good	$Fine	$N.Mint	£Good	£Fine	£N.Mint
	$0.60	$1.80	$3.00	£0.40	£1.20	£2.00
Title Value:	$0.60	$1.80	$3.00	£0.40	£1.20	£2.00

GOBLIN, THE
Warren; 1 Jul 1982-4 Dec 1982
1-4 ND

	$Good	$Fine	$N.Mint	£Good	£Fine	£N.Mint
	$0.60	$1.80	$3.00	£0.40	£1.20	£2.00
Title Value:	$2.40	$7.20	$12.00	£1.60	£4.80	£8.00

GOD'S HAMMER
Caliber Press; 1 Mar 1990-3 May 1990
1-3 ND black and white

	$Good	$Fine	$N.Mint	£Good	£Fine	£N.Mint
	$0.30	$0.90	$1.50	£0.20	£0.60	£1.00
Title Value:	$0.90	$2.70	$4.50	£0.60	£1.80	£3.00

GODDESS
DC Comics,MS; 1 Jun 1995-8 Jan 1996
1 Garth Ennis script, Phil Winslade art

	$Good	$Fine	$N.Mint	£Good	£Fine	£N.Mint
	$0.90	$2.70	$4.50	£0.60	£1.80	£3.00

2 Garth Ennis script, Phil Winslade art

	$Good	$Fine	$N.Mint	£Good	£Fine	£N.Mint
	$0.70	$2.10	$3.50	£0.50	£1.50	£2.50

3-8 Garth Ennis script, Phil Winslade art

	$Good	$Fine	$N.Mint	£Good	£Fine	£N.Mint
	$0.60	$1.80	$3.00	£0.40	£1.20	£2.00
Title Value:	$5.20	$15.60	$26.00	£3.50	£10.50	£17.50

GODWHEEL
Malibu Ultraverse,MS; 0-3 Jan 1995
0-3 ND Lord Pumpkin, Rune, NecroMantra, Primevil appear, bi-weekly; Marvel's Thor appears; art by George Perez and Gary Frank amongst others

	$Good	$Fine	$N.Mint	£Good	£Fine	£N.Mint
	$0.45	$1.35	$2.25	£0.30	£0.90	£1.50
Title Value:	$1.80	$5.40	$9.00	£1.20	£3.60	£6.00

Godwheel: Wheel of Thunder (Apr 1995)
Trade paperback reprints mini-series featuring
Thor's debut as an Ultraverse character

				£1.30	£3.90	£6.50

GODZILLA
Marvel Comics Group; 1 Aug 1977-24 Jul 1979

	$Good	$Fine	$N.Mint	£Good	£Fine	£N.Mint
1 ND	$0.30	$0.90	$1.50	£0.20	£0.60	£1.00
2 ND	$0.25	$0.75	$1.25	£0.15	£0.45	£0.75
3 ND Champions X-over	$0.25	$0.75	$1.25	£0.15	£0.45	£0.75
4-9 ND	$0.25	$0.75	$1.25	£0.15	£0.45	£0.75
10 ND Champions X-over	$0.25	$0.75	$1.25	£0.15	£0.45	£0.75
11-20 ND	$0.25	$0.75	$1.25	£0.15	£0.45	£0.75
21-22 ND Fantastic Four appear	$0.25	$0.75	$1.25	£0.15	£0.45	£0.75
23 ND Fantastic Four and Avengers appear	$0.25	$0.75	$1.25	£0.15	£0.45	£0.75
24 ND Fantastic Four, Spiderman and Avengers appear	$0.25	$0.75	$1.25	£0.15	£0.45	£0.75
Title Value:	$6.05	$18.15	$30.25	£3.65	£10.95	£18.25

GODZILLA (LIMITED SERIES 1)
Dark Horse,MS; 1 May 1988-6 Jan 1989
1 ND Japanese art, American script, Mark Nelson covers begin

	$Good	$Fine	$N.Mint	£Good	£Fine	£N.Mint
	$0.45	$1.35	$2.25	£0.30	£0.90	£1.50

2-6 ND Japanese art, American script, Mark Nelson covers begin

	$Good	$Fine	$N.Mint	£Good	£Fine	£N.Mint
	$0.40	$1.20	$2.00	£0.25	£0.75	£1.25
Title Value:	$2.45	$7.35	$12.25	£1.55	£4.65	£7.75

Godzilla Collection (Aug 1990)
Trade paperback reprints mini-series

				£1.00	£3.00	£5.00

Godzilla (May 1995)
Trade paperback 2nd Edition of the above with filmography
and new painted cover by Bob Eggleton

				£2.40	£7.20	£12.00

GODZILLA (LIMITED SERIES 2)
Dark Horse,MS; 0 May 1995; 1 Jun 1995-present
0 ND combination of new art and reprints from Dark Horse Comics #10 and 11

	$Good	$Fine	$N.Mint	£Good	£Fine	£N.Mint
	$0.45	$1.35	$2.25	£0.30	£0.90	£1.50

1 ND Kevin Maguire script, Brandon McKinney and Keith Aiken art; Art Adams covers begin

	$Good	$Fine	$N.Mint	£Good	£Fine	£N.Mint
	$0.45	$1.35	$2.25	£0.30	£0.90	£1.50
2-7	$0.45	$1.35	$2.25	£0.30	£0.90	£1.50
Title Value:	$3.60	$10.80	$18.00	£2.40	£7.20	£12.00

GODZILLA COLOUR SPECIAL
Dark Horse,OS; 1 Summer 1992
1 ND 40pgs, Art Adams art

	$Good	$Fine	$N.Mint	£Good	£Fine	£N.Mint
	$0.90	$2.70	$4.50	£0.60	£1.80	£3.00
Title Value:	$0.90	$2.70	$4.50	£0.60	£1.80	£3.00

GODZILLA SPECIAL
Dark Horse,OS; 1 Aug 1987
1 ND Bissette, Randall, Salmons art, Chadwick, Geary, Giffen, Vess, Alan Moore pin-ups

	$Good	$Fine	$N.Mint	£Good	£Fine	£N.Mint
	$0.40	$1.20	$2.00	£0.25	£0.75	£1.25
Title Value:	$0.40	$1.20	$2.00	£0.25	£0.75	£1.25

GODZILLA VS. BARKLEY
Dark Horse,OS; 1 Dec 1993
1 ND Mike Baron script, Jeff Butler pencils

	$Good	$Fine	$N.Mint	£Good	£Fine	£N.Mint
	$0.60	$1.80	$3.00	£0.40	£1.20	£2.00
Title Value:	$0.60	$1.80	$3.00	£0.40	£1.20	£2.00

GODZILLA VS. HERO ZERO
Dark Horse,OS; 1 Jun 1995
1 ND Art Adams cover

	$Good	$Fine	$N.Mint	£Good	£Fine	£N.Mint
	$0.45	$1.35	$2.25	£0.30	£0.90	£1.50
Title Value:	$0.45	$1.35	$2.25	£0.30	£0.90	£1.50

GOJIN
Antarctic Press,MS; 1 Apr 1995-present
1-7 ND Kazuho Takizawa script, Yutaka Kondo art; black and white

	$Good	$Fine	$N.Mint	£Good	£Fine	£N.Mint
	$0.60	$1.80	$3.00	£0.40	£1.20	£2.00
Title Value:	$4.20	$12.60	$21.00	£2.80	£8.40	£14.00

GOKU
Antarctic Press; 1 Oct 1993-5 Feb 1994
1-5 ND Ippongi Bang script/art; black and white

	$Good	$Fine	$N.Mint	£Good	£Fine	£N.Mint
	$0.60	$1.80	$3.00	£0.40	£1.20	£2.00
Title Value:	$3.00	$9.00	$15.00	£2.00	£6.00	£10.00

GOLD DIGGER
Antarctic Press; 1 Jul 1993-present
1-26 ND Fred Perry script/art; black and white

	$Good	$Fine	$N.Mint	£Good	£Fine	£N.Mint
	$0.55	$1.65	$2.75	£0.35	£1.05	£1.75
Title Value:	$14.30	$42.90	$71.50	£9.10	£27.30	£45.50

Gold Digger Graphic Novel Volume 1 (Oct 1994)
collects four issue limited series with new sketches and artwork

				£1.30	£3.90	£6.50

Gold Digger Graphic Novel Volume 2 (Mar 1995)
collects first four issues of on-going series with new cover

				£1.30	£3.90	£6.50

Gold Digger Graphic Novel Volume 3 (Oct 1995)
collects issues #5-8

				£1.30	£3.90	£6.50

GOLD DIGGER ANNUAL
Antarctic Press; 1 Sep 1995-present
1 ND 48pgs, black and white

	$Good	$Fine	$N.Mint	£Good	£Fine	£N.Mint
	$0.80	$2.40	$4.00	£0.50	£1.50	£2.50
Title Value:	$0.80	$2.40	$4.00	£0.50	£1.50	£2.50

GOLD KEY CHAMPION
Gold Key; 1 Mar 1978-2 May 1978
1 scarce in the U.K. 48pgs, Space Family Robinson, painted cover

	$Good	$Fine	$N.Mint	£Good	£Fine	£N.Mint
	$0.60	$1.80	$3.00	£0.40	£1.20	£2.00

2 scarce in the U.K. 48pgs, Mighty Samson, painted cover

	$Good	$Fine	$N.Mint	£Good	£Fine	£N.Mint
	$0.60	$1.80	$3.00	£0.40	£1.20	£2.00
Title Value:	$1.20	$3.60	$6.00	£0.80	£2.40	£4.00

Note: thought not to be distributed in the U.K. but as yet unconfirmed. Both above issues are part reprint.

GOLD KEY SPOTLIGHT
Gold Key; 1 May 1976-11 Feb 1978
1 scarce in the U.K. Tom, Dick and Harriet

	$Good	$Fine	$N.Mint	£Good	£Fine	£N.Mint
	$0.60	$1.80	$3.00	£0.40	£1.20	£2.00

2 Wacky Adventures of Cracky

	$Good	$Fine	$N.Mint	£Good	£Fine	£N.Mint
	$0.40	$1.20	$2.00	£0.25	£0.75	£1.25

3 Wacky Witch

	$Good	$Fine	$N.Mint	£Good	£Fine	£N.Mint
	$0.40	$1.20	$2.00	£0.25	£0.75	£1.25

4 Tom, Dick and Harriet

	$Good	$Fine	$N.Mint	£Good	£Fine	£N.Mint
	$0.40	$1.20	$2.00	£0.25	£0.75	£1.25

5 Wacky Adventures of Cracky

	$Good	$Fine	$N.Mint	£Good	£Fine	£N.Mint
	$0.40	$1.20	$2.00	£0.25	£0.75	£1.25

6 Dagar the Invincible, painted cover

	$Good	$Fine	$N.Mint	£Good	£Fine	£N.Mint
	$0.60	$1.80	$3.00	£0.40	£1.20	£2.00

7 Wacky Witch and Greta Ghost

	$Good	$Fine	$N.Mint	£Good	£Fine	£N.Mint
	$0.40	$1.20	$2.00	£0.25	£0.75	£1.25

8 The Occult Files of Dr. Spektor, painted cover

	$Good	$Fine	$N.Mint	£Good	£Fine	£N.Mint
	$0.60	$1.80	$3.00	£0.40	£1.20	£2.00

9 Tragg and the Sky Gods, Dan Spiegle art, painted cover

	$Good	$Fine	$N.Mint	£Good	£Fine	£N.Mint
	$0.60	$1.80	$3.00	£0.40	£1.20	£2.00

10 O.G. Whiz

	$Good	$Fine	$N.Mint	£Good	£Fine	£N.Mint
	$0.30	$0.90	$1.50	£0.20	£0.60	£1.00

11 Tom, Dick and Harriet

	$Good	$Fine	$N.Mint	£Good	£Fine	£N.Mint
	$0.30	$0.90	$1.50	£0.20	£0.60	£1.00
Title Value:	$5.00	$15.00	$25.00	£3.25	£9.75	£16.25

Note: very irregular distribution in the U.K.

GOLDEN AGE GREATS
AC Comics; 1 Oct 1994-present
1 ND 76pgs, squarebound; reprints Catman and Kitten, Rocket-Man and Rocket-Girl, The Hood, Green Lama from over 45 years ago; black and white

	$Good	$Fine	$N.Mint	£Good	£Fine	£N.Mint
	$2.00	$6.00	$10.00	£1.30	£3.90	£6.50

2 ND 96pgs, Phantom Lady reprints with Matt Baker art; black and white

	$Good	$Fine	$N.Mint	£Good	£Fine	£N.Mint
	$2.00	$6.00	$10.00	£1.30	£3.90	£6.50

3 ND 80pgs, Lou Fine's The Flame, Will Eisner's Espionage: Black X; black and white

	$Good	$Fine	$N.Mint	£Good	£Fine	£N.Mint
	$2.00	$6.00	$10.00	£1.30	£3.90	£6.50

4 ND 96pgs, Bulletman, Mr. Scarlet, Ibis the Invincible, Minute Man

	$Good	$Fine	$N.Mint	£Good	£Fine	£N.Mint
	$2.00	$6.00	$10.00	£1.30	£3.90	£6.50

5 ND 84pgs, Iron Jaw vs. Crimebuster

	$Good	$Fine	$N.Mint	£Good	£Fine	£N.Mint
	$2.25	$6.75	$11.25	£1.50	£4.50	£7.50

6 ND Black Cat, Blonde Phantom, Lorna Queen of the Jungle

VERY GENERAL PERCENTAGE CONVERSION CHART WHICH MAY BE USED TO CALCULATE LOW AND INBETWEEN GRADES:

	$Good	$Fine	$N.Mint	£Good	£Fine	£N.Mint
	$2.00	$6.00	$10.00	£1.30	£3.90	£6.50
Title Value:	$12.25	$36.75	$61.25	£8.00	£24.00	£40.00

GOLDEN AGE, THE
DC Comics,MS; 1 Sep 1993-4 Dec 1993

	$Good	$Fine	$N.Mint	£Good	£Fine	£N.Mint
1-4 ND 48pgs, squarebound, James Robinson script, Paul Smith art; embossed logo	$1.00	$3.00	$5.00	£0.70	£2.10	£3.50
Title Value:	$4.00	$12.00	$20.00	£2.80	£8.40	£14.00
The Golden Age (Sep 1995)						
Trade paperback reprints mini-series with Howard Chaykin intro				£2.70	£8.10	£13.50

GOLDYN IN 3-D
Blackthorne; (3-D Series #4) 1 Jun 1986

	$Good	$Fine	$N.Mint	£Good	£Fine	£N.Mint
1 ND reprints	$0.45	$1.35	$2.25	£0.30	£0.90	£1.50
Title Value:	$0.45	$1.35	$2.25	£0.30	£0.90	£1.50

GOOD GIRL ART QUARTERLY
AC Comics; 1 1990-present

	$Good	$Fine	$N.Mint	£Good	£Fine	£N.Mint
1 ND new lead story plus classic "good girl art" reprints begin; black and white	$0.70	$2.10	$3.50	£0.45	£1.35	£2.25
2-8 ND	$0.55	$1.65	$2.75	£0.35	£1.05	£1.75
9 ND X-over with Femforce #52	$0.55	$1.65	$2.75	£0.35	£1.05	£1.75
10 ND $3.95 cover begins	$0.80	$2.40	$4.00	£0.50	£1.50	£2.50
11-16 ND	$0.80	$2.40	$4.00	£0.50	£1.50	£2.50
17 ND title becomes Good Girl Comics	$0.80	$2.40	$4.00	£0.50	£1.50	£2.50
18 ND	$0.80	$2.40	$4.00	£0.50	£1.50	£2.50
Title Value:	$12.30	$36.90	$61.50	£7.75	£23.25	£38.75

GOOD GIRLS
Fantagraphics; 1 Apr 1987-6 1987

	$Good	$Fine	$N.Mint	£Good	£Fine	£N.Mint
1 ND Carol Lay story and art	$0.55	$1.65	$2.75	£0.35	£1.05	£1.75
2 ND Carol Lay story and art	$0.45	$1.35	$2.25	£0.30	£0.90	£1.50
3-6 ND Carol Lay story and art	$0.40	$1.20	$2.00	£0.25	£0.75	£1.25
Title Value:	$2.60	$7.80	$13.00	£1.65	£4.95	£8.25

GOOD GUYS, THE
Defiant; 1 Nov 1993-12 Oct 1994

	$Good	$Fine	$N.Mint	£Good	£Fine	£N.Mint
1 ND part Jim Shooter script	$0.80	$2.40	$4.00	£0.50	£1.50	£2.50
1½ ND reprints the story originally serialized in Previews magazine	$0.45	$1.35	$2.25	£0.30	£0.90	£1.50
2-9 ND part Jim Shooter script	$0.70	$2.10	$3.50	£0.45	£1.35	£2.25
10 ND Schism X-over, part Jim Shooter script	$0.45	$1.35	$2.25	£0.30	£0.90	£1.50
11-12 ND	$0.45	$1.35	$2.25	£0.30	£0.90	£1.50
Title Value:	$8.20	$24.60	$41.00	£5.30	£15.90	£26.50

GOOFY ADVENTURES
Disney; 1 Jun 1990-17 Sep 1991

	$Good	$Fine	$N.Mint	£Good	£Fine	£N.Mint
1-5 ND new stories	$0.30	$0.90	$1.50	£0.20	£0.60	£1.00
6 ND new stories, reprints Super Goof #1 (1965)	$0.30	$0.90	$1.50	£0.20	£0.60	£1.00
7 ND part reprints	$0.30	$0.90	$1.50	£0.20	£0.60	£1.00
8-17 ND	$0.30	$0.90	$1.50	£0.20	£0.60	£1.00
Title Value:	$5.10	$15.30	$25.50	£3.40	£10.20	£17.00

Note: banned from distribution in UK

GORE SHRIEK
Fantaco; 1 Sep 1986-6 1990

	$Good	$Fine	$N.Mint	£Good	£Fine	£N.Mint
1-3 ND	$0.60	$1.80	$3.00	£0.40	£1.20	£2.00
4 ND Mars Attacks special	$0.80	$2.40	$4.00	£0.50	£1.50	£2.50
5-6 ND	$0.60	$1.80	$3.00	£0.40	£1.20	£2.00
6½ ND very rare in the U.K 16pgs, special issue featuring unused art and stories, available only direct from the publisher	$2.25	$6.75	$11.25	£1.50	£4.50	£7.50
Title Value:	$6.05	$18.15	$30.25	£4.00	£12.00	£20.00

GORE SHRIEK ANNUAL
Fantaco,OS; 1 Dec 1990

	$Good	$Fine	$N.Mint	£Good	£Fine	£N.Mint
1 ND 100pgs, black and white humour/horror anthology featuring Gurchain Singh art	$0.90	$2.70	$4.50	£0.60	£1.80	£3.00
Title Value:	$0.90	$2.70	$4.50	£0.60	£1.80	£3.00

GORE SHRIEK VOLUME TWO
Eternity; 1 1990-4 1991

	$Good	$Fine	$N.Mint	£Good	£Fine	£N.Mint
1 ND	$0.70	$2.10	$3.50	£0.45	£1.35	£2.25
1 ND all pin-up edition of an amalgamated issue 1 and 2 by Gurchain Singh, limited edition	$0.80	$2.40	$4.00	£0.50	£1.50	£2.50
2 ND	$0.60	$1.80	$3.00	£0.40	£1.20	£2.00
3-4 ND	$0.45	$1.35	$2.25	£0.30	£0.90	£1.50
Title Value:	$3.00	$9.00	$15.00	£1.95	£5.85	£9.75

GORE SHRIEK VOLUME TWO ANNUAL
Fantaco; 1 Jun 1995

	$Good	$Fine	$N.Mint	£Good	£Fine	£N.Mint
1 ND over 20 artists and writers feature; black and white	$1.00	$3.00	$5.00	£0.65	£1.95	£3.25
Title Value:	$1.00	$3.00	$5.00	£0.65	£1.95	£3.25

GORGO
Charlton; 1 May 1961-23 Sep 1965
(see Gorgo's Revenge,Return of...)

	$Good	$Fine	$N.Mint	£Good	£Fine	£N.Mint
1 very scarce in the U.K. Steve Ditko art	$31.00	$92.50	$185.00	£20.50	£62.50	£125.00
2-3 scarce in the U.K. Steve Ditko art						

	$Good	$Fine	$N.Mint	£Good	£Fine	£N.Mint
	$15.00	$45.00	$90.00	£9.00	£28.00	£55.00
4 Steve Ditko cover	$9.00	$28.00	$55.00	£5.75	£17.50	£35.00
5	$9.00	$28.00	$55.00	£5.75	£17.50	£35.00
6-10	$9.00	$28.00	$55.00	£5.00	£15.00	£30.00
11 Steve Ditko art	$7.50	$22.50	$45.00	£4.55	£13.50	£27.50
12	$3.75	$11.00	$22.50	£2.05	£6.25	£12.50
13-16 Steve Ditko art	$7.00	$21.00	$42.50	£4.15	£12.50	£25.00
17-23	$3.75	$11.00	$22.50	£2.05	£6.25	£12.50
Title Value:	$189.50	$573.00	$1145.00	£112.55	£342.00	£682.50

Note: all distributed in the U.K.

GORGO'S REVENGE
Charlton; nn 1962
(becomes Return of Gorgo)

	$Good	$Fine	$N.Mint	£Good	£Fine	£N.Mint
nn distributed in the U.K.	$4.50	$13.50	$22.50	£3.00	£9.00	£15.00
Title Value:	$4.50	$13.50	$22.50	£3.00	£9.00	£15.00

GRAFIK MUZIK
Caliber Press; 1 Nov 1990-6 1991

	$Good	$Fine	$N.Mint	£Good	£Fine	£N.Mint
1 ND 48pgs, colour; Michael Dalton Allred script and art	$0.70	$2.10	$3.50	£0.45	£1.35	£2.25
2 ND	$0.45	$1.35	$2.25	£0.30	£0.90	£1.50
3-6 ND	$0.40	$1.20	$2.00	£0.25	£0.75	£1.25
Title Value:	$2.75	$8.25	$13.75	£1.75	£5.25	£8.75

Note: formerly published by Slave Labor

GRAPHIC
Fantaco; 1 Sep 1990

	$Good	$Fine	$N.Mint	£Good	£Fine	£N.Mint
1 ND horror anthology	$0.70	$2.10	$3.50	£0.45	£1.35	£2.25
Title Value:	$0.70	$2.10	$3.50	£0.45	£1.35	£2.25

GRAPHIC FANTASY
Ajax; 1 1982
(see Megaton)
1 ND very rare in the U.K 1st draft appearance Savage Dragon (prior to Megaton #3 and #4). Self-published fanzine rather than a distributed comic

	$Good	$Fine	$N.Mint	£Good	£Fine	£N.Mint
	$15.00	$45.00	$75.00	£10.00	£30.00	£50.00
Title Value:	$15.00	$45.00	$75.00	£10.00	£30.00	£50.00

GRAPHIC STORY MONTHLY
Fantagraphics; 1 Feb 1990-12 1991

	$Good	$Fine	$N.Mint	£Good	£Fine	£N.Mint
1-4 ND Tardi, Ward Kimball, Paul Ollswang, Rick Geary work featured	$0.70	$2.10	$3.50	£0.45	£1.35	£2.25
5 ND Jacques Tardi's "Fog Over Tolbiac Bridge" concludes	$0.60	$1.80	$3.00	£0.40	£1.20	£2.00
6 ND Roger Langridge story	$0.60	$1.80	$3.00	£0.40	£1.20	£2.00
7 ND	$0.60	$1.80	$3.00	£0.40	£1.20	£2.00
8-9 ND 52pgs, Billie Holiday story by Carlos Sampayo and Jose Munoz	$0.80	$2.40	$4.00	£0.50	£1.50	£2.50
10 ND 48pgs, Billie Holiday plus Jacques Tardi's "Griffu"	$0.80	$2.40	$4.00	£0.50	£1.50	£2.50
11-12 ND	$0.60	$1.80	$3.00	£0.40	£1.20	£2.00
Title Value:	$8.20	$24.60	$41.00	£5.30	£15.90	£26.50

Note: black and white magazine format, 48pgs

GRAPHIQUE MUSIQUE
Slave Labor; 1 Dec 1989-3 May 1990

	$Good	$Fine	$N.Mint	£Good	£Fine	£N.Mint
1-3 ND 48pgs, black and white	$0.45	$1.35	$2.25	£0.30	£0.90	£1.50
Title Value:	$1.35	$4.05	$6.75	£0.90	£2.70	£4.50

GRATEFUL DEAD COMIX
Kitchen Sink,Magazine MS; 1 Jul 1991-6 1992

	$Good	$Fine	$N.Mint	£Good	£Fine	£N.Mint
1 ND Tim Truman art featured; 8" x 11"" format begins and great painted cover by Dean Armstrong	$1.20	$3.60	$6.00	£0.80	£2.40	£4.00
2-3 ND Tim Truman art featured	$1.05	$3.15	$5.25	£0.70	£2.10	£3.50
4 ND Tim Truman and Mary Fleener art featured, Gilbert Shelton cover	$1.05	$3.15	$5.25	£0.70	£2.10	£3.50
5 ND Tim Truman art featured, painted cover by Dean Armstrong	$1.05	$3.15	$5.25	£0.70	£2.10	£3.50
6 ND	$1.05	$3.15	$5.25	£0.70	£2.10	£3.50
Title Value:	$6.45	$19.35	$32.25	£4.30	£12.90	£21.50
Grateful Dead Limited Edition (Dec 1992)						
signed, hardcover, 500 copies				£20.00	£60.00	£100.00

GRATEFUL DEAD COMIX (2ND SERIES)
Kitchen Sink; 1 Jun 1993-2 1993

	$Good	$Fine	$N.Mint	£Good	£Fine	£N.Mint
1-2 ND Tim Truman art featured	$0.80	$2.40	$4.00	£0.50	£1.50	£2.50
Title Value:	$1.60	$4.80	$8.00	£1.00	£3.00	£5.00

GRAVE TALES
Bruce Hamilton Publishing,Magazine; 1 Oct 1991-3 1992

	$Good	$Fine	$N.Mint	£Good	£Fine	£N.Mint
1-3 ND Joe Staton, Gray Morrow, Pat Boyette art featured; black and white	$0.80	$2.40	$4.00	£0.50	£1.50	£2.50
Title Value:	$2.40	$7.20	$12.00	£1.50	£4.50	£7.50

GRAVESTONE
Malibu; 1 Jul 1993-7 Jan 1994

	$Good	$Fine	$N.Mint	£Good	£Fine	£N.Mint
1 Protectors spin-off	$0.40	$1.20	$2.00	£0.25	£0.75	£1.25
2	$0.40	$1.20	$2.00	£0.25	£0.75	£1.25
3 Genesis Tie-In; pre-bagged with free Sky-Cap	$0.40	$1.20	$2.00	£0.25	£0.75	£1.25
4 Genesis Tie-In	$0.40	$1.20	$2.00	£0.25	£0.75	£1.25
5 Genesis Tie-In, Frank Miller cover						

MINT = 100% / NEAR MINT (inc. +/-) = 90-99% / VERY FINE (inc. +/-) = 75-89% / FINE (inc. +/-) = 55-74%
VERY GOOD (inc. +/-) = 35-54% / GOOD (inc. +/-) = 15-34% / FAIR = 5-14% / POOR = 1-4%

373

	$Good	$Fine	$N.Mint	£Good	£Fine	£N.Mint
	$0.40	$1.20	$2.00	£0.25	£0.75	£1.25
6-7 Genesis Tie-In	$0.40	$1.20	$2.00	£0.25	£0.75	£1.25
Title Value:	$2.80	$8.40	$14.00	£1.75	£5.25	£8.75

Note: all Non-Distributed on the news-stands in the U.K.

GREAT ACTION COMICS
IW Comics; 1,8,9 1958-1960

	$Good	$Fine	$N.Mint	£Good	£Fine	£N.Mint
1 scarce in the U.K. reprints; distributed in the U.K.	$1.85	$5.50	$11.25	£1.25	£3.75	£7.50
8-9 rare in the U.K., Phantom Lady reprints; distributed in the U.K.	$9.25	$28.00	$56.25	£6.25	£18.50	£37.50
Title Value:	$20.35	$61.50	$123.75	£13.75	£40.75	£82.50

GREAT MOUSE DETECTIVE GRAPHIC NOVEL, THE
Disney,OS; 1 Apr 1991

	$Good	$Fine	$N.Mint	£Good	£Fine	£N.Mint
1 ND 48pgs, adaptation of film	$1.00	$3.00	$5.00	£0.65	£1.95	£3.25
Title Value:	$1.00	$3.00	$5.00	£0.65	£1.95	£3.25

GREAT WESTERN
I.W. Comics; 1,2,8,9 early 1960s

	$Good	$Fine	$N.Mint	£Good	£Fine	£N.Mint
1-2 distributed in the U.K. all reprints	$1.50	$4.50	$9.00	£1.00	£3.00	£6.00
8 all reprint featuring origin Ghost Rider; distributed in the U.K.	$1.85	$5.50	$11.25	£1.25	£3.75	£7.50
9 distributed in the U.K.	$1.50	$4.50	$9.00	£1.00	£3.00	£6.00
Title Value:	$6.35	$19.00	$38.25	£4.25	£12.75	£25.50

GREATER MERCURY COMICS ACTION
Greater Mercury Comics; 1 1989-5 1990

	$Good	$Fine	$N.Mint	£Good	£Fine	£N.Mint
1-5 ND	$0.40	$1.20	$2.00	£0.25	£0.75	£1.25
Title Value:	$2.00	$6.00	$10.00	£1.25	£3.75	£6.25

GREATEST 1950S STORIES EVER TOLD, THE
nn Dec 1990

	£Good	£Fine	£N.Mint
nn - 288pgs, Hardcover. Many stories never reprinted before	£2.75	£8.25	£13.75
Softcover	£2.00	£6.00	£10.00

GREATEST 1960S STORIES EVER TOLD
nn Mar 1992

	£Good	£Fine	£N.Mint
nn - two volume slip-case set featuring the major DC characters with art by Neal Adams, Gil Kane, Carmine Infantino, Alex Toth etc	£6.00	£18.00	£30.00

GREATEST FLASH STORIES EVER TOLD, THE
nn Feb 1991

	£Good	£Fine	£N.Mint
nn - 288pgs, Hardcover Reprints of classic Flash stories inc. Showcase #4	£2.75	£8.25	£13.75
Softcover (Jun 1992)	£1.80	£5.40	£9.00

GREATEST GOLDEN AGE STORIES EVER TOLD
nn Feb 1990

	£Good	£Fine	£N.Mint
nn - 288pgs, Hardcover. Reprints of classic Golden Age stories. Intro by Roy Thomas. New dust-jacket illustration by Jerry Ordway	£2.75	£8.25	£13.75

GREATEST TEAM-UP STORIES EVER TOLD, THE
nn Jan 1990

	£Good	£Fine	£N.Mint
nn - 288pgs, Hardcover. 15 classic reprints inc. Flash #123	£2.75	£8.25	£13.75
Softcover (Jul 1990)	£2.10	£6.30	£10.50

GREEN ARROW
DC Comics; 0 Oct 1994; 1 Feb 1988-present

	$Good	$Fine	$N.Mint	£Good	£Fine	£N.Mint
0 (Oct 1994) Zero Hour X-over, origin retold	$0.40	$1.20	$2.00	£0.25	£0.75	£1.25
1 Mike Grell script begins	$0.80	$2.40	$4.00	£0.50	£1.50	£2.50
2-5 scarce in the U.K.	$0.50	$1.50	$2.50	£0.30	£0.90	£1.50
6-15 scarce in the U.K.	$0.40	$1.20	$2.00	£0.25	£0.75	£1.25
16-20	$0.30	$0.90	$1.50	£0.20	£0.60	£1.00
21-24 bi-weekly issues	$0.30	$0.90	$1.50	£0.20	£0.60	£1.00
25-26	$0.30	$0.90	$1.50	£0.20	£0.60	£1.00
27-28 The Warlord appears	$0.30	$0.90	$1.50	£0.20	£0.60	£1.00
29-34	$0.30	$0.90	$1.50	£0.20	£0.60	£1.00
35-38 Black Arrow saga, bi-weekly issues	$0.30	$0.90	$1.50	£0.20	£0.60	£1.00
39-40	$0.30	$0.90	$1.50	£0.20	£0.60	£1.00
41-43	$0.25	$0.75	$1.25	£0.15	£0.45	£0.75
44-45 Rock and Runes story	$0.25	$0.75	$1.25	£0.15	£0.45	£0.75
46-49	$0.25	$0.75	$1.25	£0.15	£0.45	£0.75
50 DS	$0.50	$1.50	$2.50	£0.30	£0.90	£1.50
51-54	$0.25	$0.75	$1.25	£0.15	£0.45	£0.75
55 ties in with Green Arrow: The Longbow Hunters	$0.25	$0.75	$1.25	£0.15	£0.45	£0.75
56-58	$0.25	$0.75	$1.25	£0.15	£0.45	£0.75
59 Predator part 1	$0.25	$0.75	$1.25	£0.15	£0.45	£0.75
60 Predator part 2, bi-weekly	$0.25	$0.75	$1.25	£0.15	£0.45	£0.75
61-62 bi-weekly	$0.25	$0.75	$1.25	£0.15	£0.45	£0.75
63 The Hunt for the Red Dragon story begins, "Mature Readers" label dropped from cover, bi-weekly	$0.25	$0.75	$1.25	£0.15	£0.45	£0.75
64-67	$0.25	$0.75	$1.25	£0.15	£0.45	£0.75
68 $1.75 cover begins	$0.30	$0.90	$1.50	£0.20	£0.60	£1.00
69-74	$0.30	$0.90	$1.50	£0.20	£0.60	£1.00
75 48pgs, Speedy appears; Green Arrow and Black Canary split up	$0.45	$1.35	$2.25	£0.30	£0.90	£1.50

	$Good	$Fine	$N.Mint	£Good	£Fine	£N.Mint
76-84	$0.30	$0.90	$1.50	£0.20	£0.60	£1.00
85 Deathstroke the Terminator appears	$0.30	$0.90	$1.50	£0.20	£0.60	£1.00
86 Catwoman appears	$0.30	$0.90	$1.50	£0.20	£0.60	£1.00
87 $1.95 cover begins	$0.40	$1.20	$2.00	£0.25	£0.75	£1.25
88 Martian Manhunter and Blue Beetle appear	$0.40	$1.20	$2.00	£0.25	£0.75	£1.25
89	$0.40	$1.20	$2.00	£0.25	£0.75	£1.25
90 Zero Hour X-over	$0.40	$1.20	$2.00	£0.25	£0.75	£1.25
91-96	$0.40	$1.20	$2.00	£0.25	£0.75	£1.25
97 $2.25 cover begins	$0.45	$1.35	$2.25	£0.30	£0.90	£1.50
98-99	$0.45	$1.35	$2.25	£0.30	£0.90	£1.50
100 48pgs, holographic foil-stamped cover, Superman guest-stars	$0.80	$2.40	$4.00	£0.50	£1.50	£2.50
101 Superman and Black Canary guest-star	$0.45	$1.35	$2.25	£0.30	£0.90	£1.50
102-103 Underworld Unleashed tie-in	$0.45	$1.35	$2.25	£0.30	£0.90	£1.50
104 Green Lantern guest-stars	$0.45	$1.35	$2.25	£0.30	£0.90	£1.50
105 Robin guest-stars	$0.45	$1.35	$2.25	£0.30	£0.90	£1.50
106	$0.45	$1.35	$2.25	£0.30	£0.90	£1.50
Title Value:	$36.40	$109.20	$182.00	£23.25	£69.75	£116.25

Note: all are New Format, Baxter paper. Mature Readers label.

GREEN ARROW (LIMITED SERIES)
DC Comics,MS; 1 May 1983-4 Aug 1983

(see Action, Adventure, Brave & the Bold, DC Super-Stars #17, Flash, Green Arrow: The Longbow Hunters, Green Lantern, World's Finest)

	$Good	$Fine	$N.Mint	£Good	£Fine	£N.Mint
1 Von Eeden art begins, origin retold, Speedy cameo	$0.40	$1.20	$2.00	£0.25	£0.75	£1.25
2-4	$0.40	$1.20	$2.00	£0.25	£0.75	£1.25
Title Value:	$1.60	$4.80	$8.00	£1.00	£3.00	£5.00

GREEN ARROW ANNUAL
DC Comics; 1 1988-present

	$Good	$Fine	$N.Mint	£Good	£Fine	£N.Mint
1 48pgs, ties in with Detective Annual #1, Question Annual #1	$0.60	$1.80	$3.00	£0.40	£1.20	£2.00
2 concluded from Question Annual #2	$0.60	$1.80	$3.00	£0.40	£1.20	£2.00
3-4 64pgs	$0.60	$1.80	$3.00	£0.40	£1.20	£2.00
5 64pgs, Eclipso: The Darkness Within, Batman appears	$0.60	$1.80	$3.00	£0.40	£1.20	£2.00
6 64pgs, Bloodlines (Wave Two) part 13, 1st appearance The Hook, continued in Detective Comics Annual #6	$0.60	$1.80	$3.00	£0.40	£1.20	£2.00
7 56pgs, Year One story	$0.60	$1.80	$3.00	£0.50	£1.50	£2.50
Title Value:	$4.20	$12.60	$21.00	£2.90	£8.70	£14.50

GREEN ARROW: THE LONGBOW HUNTERS
DC Comics,MS; 1 Aug 1987-3 Oct 1987

	$Good	$Fine	$N.Mint	£Good	£Fine	£N.Mint
1 ND Mike Grell cover/art begins	$1.20	$3.60	$6.00	£0.80	£2.40	£4.00
1 2nd printing ND	$0.80	$2.40	$4.00	£0.50	£1.50	£2.50
2 ND scarce in the U.K.	$0.70	$2.10	$3.50	£0.50	£1.50	£2.50
2 2nd printing ND	$0.60	$1.80	$3.00	£0.40	£1.20	£2.00
3 ND	$0.70	$2.10	$3.50	£0.50	£1.50	£2.50
Title Value:	$4.00	$12.00	$20.00	£2.70	£8.10	£13.50

Note: all are Prestige format, squarebound. Mature Readers label.

	£Good	£Fine	£N.Mint
Trade paperback (Jun 1989), 160 pgs. Reprints three issue MS with covers. New wraparound painted cover by Mike Grell	£1.00	£3.00	£5.00

GREEN ARROW: THE WONDER YEAR
DC Comics,MS; 1 Feb 1993-4 May 1993

	$Good	$Fine	$N.Mint	£Good	£Fine	£N.Mint
1 Mike Grell and Gray Morrow story presenting Green Arrow: Year One	$0.30	$0.90	$1.50	£0.20	£0.60	£1.00
2 Green Arrow meets Brianna Stone	$0.30	$0.90	$1.50	£0.20	£0.60	£1.00
3-4	$0.30	$0.90	$1.50	£0.20	£0.60	£1.00
Title Value:	$1.20	$3.60	$6.00	£0.80	£2.40	£4.00

GREEN CANDLES
DC Comics/Paradox Press,MS; 1 Nov 1995-3 Jan 1996

	$Good	$Fine	$N.Mint	£Good	£Fine	£N.Mint
1-3 ND 96pgs, Tom DeHaven script, Robin Smith art; Compact Format	$1.20	$3.60	$6.00	£0.80	£2.40	£4.00
Title Value:	$3.60	$10.80	$18.00	£2.40	£7.20	£12.00

GREEN GOBLIN
Marvel Comics Group; 1 Oct 1995-present

	$Good	$Fine	$N.Mint	£Good	£Fine	£N.Mint
1 ND Tom DeFalco script, Scott McDaniel art; prismatic foil-stamped cover	$0.60	$1.80	$3.00	£0.40	£1.20	£2.00
2 ND Rhino appears	$0.40	$1.20	$2.00	£0.25	£0.75	£1.25
3 ND storyline tie-in from Amazing Scarlet Spider #2	$0.40	$1.20	$2.00	£0.25	£0.75	£1.25
4-5 ND Green Goblin vs. Hobgoblin	$0.40	$1.20	$2.00	£0.25	£0.75	£1.25
6 ND Green Goblin vs. Daredevil	$0.40	$1.20	$2.00	£0.25	£0.75	£1.25
Title Value:	$2.60	$7.80	$13.00	£1.65	£4.95	£8.25

GREEN HORNET
Gold Key, TV; 1 Feb 1967-3 Aug 1967

	$Good	$Fine	$N.Mint	£Good	£Fine	£N.Mint
1 scarce in the U.K. Bruce Lee cover; distributed in the U.K.	$21.00	$62.50	$150.00	£13.50	£41.00	£95.00
2-3 scarce in the U.K. Bruce Lee cover; distributed in the U.K.	$12.50	$39.00	$90.00	£8.50	£26.00	£60.00
Title Value:	$46.00	$140.50	$330.00	£30.50	£93.00	£215.00

GREEN HORNET 3-D SPECIAL
Now Comics,OS; 1 Oct 1993

	$Good	$Fine	$N.Mint	£Good	£Fine	£N.Mint
1 ND with 3-D glasses	$0.60	$1.80	$3.00	£0.40	£1.20	£2.00
Title Value:	$0.60	$1.80	$3.00	£0.40	£1.20	£2.00

GREEN HORNET ANNIVERSARY SPECIAL, TALES OF THE
Now Comics; 1 Sep 1992

	$Good	$Fine	$N.Mint	£Good	£Fine	£N.Mint
1 ND pre-bagged with hologram trading card, direct market editions of 3rd Series Tales begins, but cancelled	$0.45	$1.35	$2.25	£0.30	£0.90	£1.50
Title Value:	$0.45	$1.35	$2.25	£0.30	£0.90	£1.50

GREEN HORNET ANNIVERSARY SPECIAL, THE
Now Comics; 1 Aug 1992-3 1992

	$Good	$Fine	$N.Mint	£Good	£Fine	£N.Mint
1 Newstand edition of #12 (2nd Series), pre-bagged with badge, new cover	$0.45	$1.35	$2.25	£0.30	£0.90	£1.50
2-3 Newstand edition of #13/14 (2nd Series), new cover	$0.45	$1.35	$2.25	£0.30	£0.90	£1.50
Title Value:	$1.35	$4.05	$6.75	£0.90	£2.70	£4.50

GREEN HORNET ANNUAL
Now Comics; 1 Dec 1992-3 1994

	$Good	$Fine	$N.Mint	£Good	£Fine	£N.Mint
1-2 ND	$0.45	$1.35	$2.25	£0.30	£0.90	£1.50
3 ND metallic green cover	$0.60	$1.80	$3.00	£0.40	£1.20	£2.00
Title Value:	$1.50	$4.50	$7.50	£1.00	£3.00	£5.00

GREEN HORNET LEGACY SPECIAL, THE
Now Comics,OS; 1 May 1993

	$Good	$Fine	$N.Mint	£Good	£Fine	£N.Mint
1 ND origin of Green Hornet II, pin-up of Van Williams	$0.45	$1.35	$2.25	£0.30	£0.90	£1.50
Title Value:	$0.45	$1.35	$2.25	£0.30	£0.90	£1.50

GREEN HORNET SPECIAL MINI SERIES
Now Comics,MS; 1 Jul 1990-2 Aug 1990

	$Good	$Fine	$N.Mint	£Good	£Fine	£N.Mint
1-2 ND script by Van Williams, TV's Green Hornet	$0.40	$1.20	$2.00	£0.25	£0.75	£1.25
Title Value:	$0.80	$2.40	$4.00	£0.50	£1.50	£2.50

GREEN HORNET, STING OF THE
Now Comics; 1 Jun 1992-4 Sep 1992

	$Good	$Fine	$N.Mint	£Good	£Fine	£N.Mint
1 ND	$0.45	$1.35	$2.25	£0.30	£0.90	£1.50
1 ND Collector's Edition, pre-bagged with poster	$0.55	$1.65	$2.75	£0.35	£1.05	£1.75
2 ND	$0.45	$1.35	$2.25	£0.30	£0.90	£1.50
2 ND Collector's Edition, pre-bagged with poster	$0.55	$1.65	$2.75	£0.35	£1.05	£1.75
3 ND	$0.45	$1.35	$2.25	£0.30	£0.90	£1.50
3 ND Collector's Edition, pre-bagged with poster	$0.55	$1.65	$2.75	£0.35	£1.05	£1.75
4 ND	$0.45	$1.35	$2.25	£0.30	£0.90	£1.50
4 ND Collector's Edition, pre-bagged with poster	$0.55	$1.65	$2.75	£0.35	£1.05	£1.75
Title Value:	$4.00	$12.00	$20.00	£2.60	£7.80	£13.00

GREEN HORNET, TALES OF THE
Now Comics,MS; 1 Sep 1990-2 Oct 1990

	$Good	$Fine	$N.Mint	£Good	£Fine	£N.Mint
1-2 ND script by Van Williams (TV's Green Hornet); painted covers by Dell Barras	$0.40	$1.20	$2.00	£0.25	£0.75	£1.25
Title Value:	$0.80	$2.40	$4.00	£0.50	£1.50	£2.50

GREEN HORNET, TALES OF THE (2ND SERIES)
Now Comics; 1 Jan 1992-4 Apr 1992

1 ND Neal Adams cover

	$Good	$Fine	$N.Mint	£Good	£Fine	£N.Mint
	$0.40	$1.20	$2.00	£0.25	£0.75	£1.25
2-4 ND	$0.40	$1.20	$2.00	£0.25	£0.75	£1.25
Title Value:	$1.60	$4.80	$8.00	£1.00	£3.00	£5.00

GREEN HORNET, TALES OF THE (3RD SERIES)
Now Comics; 1 Sep 1992-3 Nov 1992

	$Good	$Fine	$N.Mint	£Good	£Fine	£N.Mint
1-3 ND	$0.45	$1.35	$2.25	£0.30	£0.90	£1.50
Title Value:	$1.35	$4.05	$6.75	£0.90	£2.70	£4.50

GREEN HORNET, THE
Now Comics; 1 Nov 1989-4 Apr 1991

	$Good	$Fine	$N.Mint	£Good	£Fine	£N.Mint
1 DS painted cover by Jim Steranko	$2.00	$6.00	$10.00	£2.00	£6.00	£10.00
1 2nd printing, new cover	$0.70	$2.10	$3.50	£0.45	£1.35	£2.25
2	$1.80	$5.25	$9.00	£1.20	£3.60	£6.00
3	$1.20	$3.60	$6.00	£0.80	£2.40	£4.00
4	$0.90	$2.70	$4.50	£0.60	£1.80	£3.00
5 death original (1930s) Green Hornet	$0.90	$2.70	$4.50	£0.60	£1.80	£3.00
6	$0.80	$2.40	$4.00	£0.50	£1.50	£2.50
7 new Kato	$0.80	$2.40	$4.00	£0.50	£1.50	£2.50
8-10	$0.60	$1.80	$3.00	£0.40	£1.20	£2.00
11-18	$0.45	$1.35	$2.25	£0.30	£0.90	£1.50
Title Value:	$14.50	$43.35	$72.50	£10.25	£30.75	£51.25

Note: all Non-Distributed on the news-stands in the U.K.
Note also: issue #1 depicts 1940s character, #2-4 depict 1960s television characters. Issues #15-18 were solicited and advertised, but may not have appeared.

	$Good	$Fine	$N.Mint	£Good	£Fine	£N.Mint
Trade Paperback (1991), reprints issues #1-7 plus new cover				£1.30	£3.90	£6.50

GREEN HORNET, THE (2ND SERIES)
Now Comics; 1 Sep 1991-39 Dec 1994 ?

	$Good	$Fine	$N.Mint	£Good	£Fine	£N.Mint
1 ND	$0.45	$1.35	$2.25	£0.30	£0.90	£1.50
2-7 ND	$0.40	$1.20	$2.00	£0.25	£0.75	£1.25
8 ND intro new Black Beauty car	$0.40	$1.20	$2.00	£0.25	£0.75	£1.25
9-11 ND	$0.40	$1.20	$2.00	£0.25	£0.75	£1.25
12 ND 3rd anniversary edition, pre-bagged with Green Hornet badge	$0.45	$1.35	$2.25	£0.30	£0.90	£1.50
13-15 ND	$0.40	$1.20	$2.00	£0.25	£0.75	£1.25
16 ND ties-in to Green Hornet #8	$0.40	$1.20	$2.00	£0.25	£0.75	£1.25
17-18 ND	$0.40	$1.20	$2.00	£0.25	£0.75	£1.25
19 ND pre-bagged with Green Hornet hologram card (2 different covers available)	$0.80	$2.40	$4.00	£0.50	£1.50	£2.50
20-27 ND	$0.40	$1.20	$2.00	£0.25	£0.75	£1.25
27 ND pre-bagged with trading card - 1993 Anniversary Special	$0.60	$1.80	$3.00	£0.40	£1.20	£2.00
28-30 ND	$0.40	$1.20	$2.00	£0.25	£0.75	£1.25
31 ND	$0.45	$1.35	$2.25	£0.30	£0.90	£1.50
32-39 ND	$0.40	$1.20	$2.00	£0.25	£0.75	£1.25
Title Value:	$16.85	$50.55	$84.25	£10.65	£31.95	£53.25

Note: issues #40-46 were solicited and advertised, but did not appear.

GREEN HORNET: DARK TOMORROW
Now Comics,MS; 1 Jun 1993-3 Aug 1993

	$Good	$Fine	$N.Mint	£Good	£Fine	£N.Mint
1-3 ND	$0.45	$1.35	$2.25	£0.30	£0.90	£1.50
Title Value:	$1.35	$4.05	$6.75	£0.90	£2.70	£4.50

GREEN HORNET: SOLITARY SENTINEL
Now Comics,MS; 1 Dec 1992-3 Feb 1993

	$Good	$Fine	$N.Mint	£Good	£Fine	£N.Mint
1-3 ND	$0.45	$1.35	$2.25	£0.30	£0.90	£1.50
Title Value:	$1.35	$4.05	$6.75	£0.90	£2.70	£4.50

GREEN LANTERN (1ST SERIES)
National Periodical Publications; 1 Sep 1941-38 May/Jun 1949
(see All American Comics, All Flash Quarterly, All Star Comics)

Gold Key Spotlight #9

Good Girls #1

Gore Shriek (2nd) #1

Issue / Description	$Good	$Fine	$N.Mint	£Good	£Fine	£N.Mint
1 scarce in the U.K. Green Lantern's origin retold; quarterly frequency begins (to #18)	$2100.00	$6300.00	$21000.00	£1400.00	£4200.00	£14000.00
[Scarce in high grade - Very Fine+ or better]						
2	$580.00	$1725.00	$4650.00	£375.00	£1125.00	£3000.00
3	$430.00	$1275.00	$3450.00	£280.00	£840.00	£2250.00
4 patriotic war cover	$310.00	$930.00	$2500.00	£205.00	£620.00	£1675.00
5 scarce in the U.K. patriotic war cover	$215.00	$650.00	$1750.00	£150.00	£450.00	£1200.00
6-9	$150.00	$450.00	$1200.00	£100.00	£300.00	£800.00
10 origin Vandal Savage - "The Man Who Wanted The World"	$150.00	$450.00	$1200.00	£100.00	£305.00	£825.00
11	$125.00	$375.00	$875.00	£85.00	£255.00	£595.00
12 scarce in the U.K. 1st appearance The Gambler	$125.00	$375.00	$875.00	£85.00	£260.00	£610.00
13-17	$125.00	$375.00	$875.00	£85.00	£255.00	£595.00
18 classic Christmas cover	$140.00	$425.00	$1000.00	£92.50	£275.00	£650.00
19-20	$125.00	$375.00	$875.00	£85.00	£255.00	£595.00
21-24	$115.00	$350.00	$825.00	£77.50	£235.00	£550.00
25 scarce in the U.K.	$115.00	$350.00	$825.00	£80.00	£245.00	£575.00
26	$115.00	$350.00	$825.00	£77.50	£235.00	£550.00
27 Green Lantern vs. The Sky Pirate	$125.00	$385.00	$900.00	£85.00	£255.00	£600.00
28 Green Lantern vs. The Sportsmaster	$115.00	$350.00	$825.00	£77.50	£235.00	£550.00
29 Green Lantern vs. The Harlequin	$115.00	$350.00	$825.00	£77.50	£235.00	£550.00
30 1st appearance Streak the Wonder Dog	$115.00	$350.00	$825.00	£77.50	£235.00	£550.00
31-35	$92.50	$275.00	$650.00	£62.50	£190.00	£450.00
36-38 very scarce in the U.K., scarce in the U.S.	$120.00	$360.00	$850.00	£87.50	£265.00	£625.00
Title Value:	**$7632.50**	**$22920.00**	**$62350.00**	**£5127.50**	**£15440.00**	**£41870.00**

Note: all Non-Distributed on the news-stands in the U.K. but some issues may have come over with personnel movement during the Second World War or as cheap ballast on ships after the war. Most issues of this title however are generally scarce in the U.K.

GREEN LANTERN (2ND SERIES)

National Periodical Publications/DC Comics; 1 Jul/Aug 1960-89 Apr/May 1972; 90 Aug/Sep 1976-224 May 1988

(see Action, Adventure, Brave & the Bold, DC Comics Presents, DC Special, Emerald Dawn I & II, Five-Star Super-Hero Spectacular, Flash, Green Lantern: Mosaic, Showcase, Secret Origins, Super-Team Family, Tales of the Green Lantern Corps, World's Finest) (becomes Green Lantern Corps with issue #201)

Issue / Description	$Good	$Fine	$N.Mint	£Good	£Fine	£N.Mint
1 origin retold, Gil Kane art begins	$295.00	$880.00	$2950.00	£195.00	£580.00	£1950.00
2 1st appearance Pieface	$87.50	$260.00	$700.00	£55.00	£165.00	£450.00
3	$52.50	$155.00	$425.00	£31.00	£92.50	£250.00
4	$44.00	$130.00	$350.00	£21.50	£65.00	£175.00
5 1st appearance Hector Hammond	$44.00	$130.00	$350.00	£21.50	£65.00	£175.00
6 less common in the U.K. 1st appearance Tomar-re (alien Green Lantern)	$38.00	$110.00	$300.00	£17.50	£52.50	£140.00
7 origin and 1st appearance Sinestro	$34.00	$100.00	$275.00	£17.50	£52.50	£140.00
8 painted grey-tone cover	$36.00	$105.00	$290.00	£18.50	£55.00	£150.00
9 last 10 cents issue	$31.00	$92.50	$250.00	£15.00	£45.00	£120.00
10 the secret of Green Lantern's oath is told	$31.00	$92.50	$250.00	£15.00	£45.00	£120.00
11-12	$25.00	$75.00	$175.00	£13.50	£41.00	£95.00
13 Flash guest stars	$29.00	$85.00	$200.00	£15.50	£47.00	£110.00
14-15	$22.00	$62.50	$150.00	£11.00	£34.00	£80.00
16 origin and 1st appearance Star Sapphire	$25.00	$75.00	$175.00	£12.50	£39.00	£90.00
17-19	$21.00	$62.50	$150.00	£9.25	£28.00	£65.00
20 Flash guest stars	$21.00	$62.50	$150.00	£9.25	£28.00	£65.00
21 origin Dr. Polaris	$17.50	$52.50	$125.00	£8.50	£26.00	£60.00
22	$17.50	$52.50	$125.00	£7.75	£23.50	£55.00
23 1st appearance Tattooed Man	$17.50	$52.50	$125.00	£8.50	£26.00	£60.00
24 origin Shark	$17.50	$52.50	$125.00	£8.50	£26.00	£60.00
25	$17.50	$52.50	$125.00	£7.75	£23.50	£55.00
26-28	$17.50	$52.50	$125.00	£6.25	£19.00	£45.00
29 Justice League of America cameo	$17.50	$52.50	$125.00	£8.50	£26.00	£60.00
30	$17.50	$52.50	$125.00	£6.25	£19.00	£45.00
31-37	$14.00	$43.00	$100.00	£5.00	£15.00	£35.00
38 Tomar-Re appears	$14.00	$43.00	$100.00	£5.00	£15.00	£35.00
39	$14.00	$43.00	$100.00	£5.00	£15.00	£35.00
40 1st appearance Crisis, origin of the Guardians, GA Green Lantern co-stars (1st full SA appearance in title. 2nd solo appearance in SA). (1st cameo in Flash 129, 1st full appearance in Flash #137)	$57.50	$175.00	$475.00	£18.50	£55.00	£150.00
41 Star Sapphire vs. Green Lantern; last Silver Age issue, indicia dated December 1965	$10.50	$32.00	$75.00	£4.25	£12.50	£30.00
42 3rd appearance Zatanna	$12.50	$38.00	$75.00	£4.15	£12.50	£25.00
43-44	$12.50	$38.00	$75.00	£4.15	£12.50	£25.00
45 Golden Age Green Lantern appears (2nd full Silver Age appearance in title)	$15.50	$47.00	$110.00	£5.25	£16.00	£37.50
46-49	$12.50	$38.00	$75.00	£4.15	£12.50	£25.00
50 scarce in the U.K.	$12.50	$38.00	$75.00	£5.00	£15.00	£30.00
51	$9.00	$28.00	$55.00	£3.30	£10.00	£20.00
52 Golden Age Green Lantern X-over	$9.00	$28.00	$55.00	£3.75	£11.00	£22.50
53-55	$9.00	$28.00	$55.00	£3.30	£10.00	£20.00
56-58	$9.00	$28.00	$55.00	£2.50	£7.50	£15.00
59 1st appearance Guy Gardner; in an imaginary story he becomes a Green Lantern (see #116)	$25.00	$75.00	$175.00	£11.00	£34.00	£80.00
60	$5.75	$17.50	$35.00	£1.65	£5.00	£10.00
61 Golden Age Green Lantern X-over	$6.50	$20.00	$40.00	£2.05	£6.25	£12.50
62	$5.75	$17.50	$35.00	£1.65	£5.00	£10.00
63 Neal Adams cover	$5.75	$17.50	$35.00	£1.65	£5.00	£10.00
64-65	$5.75	$17.50	$35.00	£1.65	£5.00	£10.00
66-68	$5.75	$17.50	$35.00	£1.25	£3.75	£7.50
69 last 12 cents issue	$5.75	$17.50	$35.00	£1.25	£3.75	£7.50
70-72	$3.30	$10.00	$20.00	£1.00	£3.00	£6.00
73 Star Sapphire appears	$3.30	$10.00	$20.00	£1.00	£3.00	£6.00
74 Star Sapphire and Sinestro appear	$3.30	$10.00	$20.00	£1.00	£3.00	£6.00
75 less common in the U.K.	$3.30	$10.00	$20.00	£1.05	£3.25	£6.50
76 rare in the U.K., 1st Green Arrow/Green Lantern, Neal Adams art, classic and award-winning issue, comic credited as starting the "Bronze Age" of comics' history	$20.00	$60.00	$140.00	£12.50	£39.00	£90.00
[Scarce in high grade - Very Fine+ or better]						
76 ND Silver Age Classic reprint (Mar 1992)	$0.25	$0.75	$1.25	£0.15	£0.45	£0.75
77 Neal Adams art	$8.25	$25.00	$50.00	£4.15	£12.50	£25.00
78-80 Neal Adams art	$5.75	$17.50	$35.00	£2.90	£8.75	£17.50
81-83 Neal Adams art	$5.00	$15.00	$30.00	£2.50	£7.50	£15.00
84 Neal Adams art; last 15 cents issue	$5.00	$15.00	$30.00	£2.50	£7.50	£15.00
85 48pgs, (says 52pgs on cover up to #89 as they count the covers in the U.S.), scarce in the U.K., Neal Adams art, drugs issues	$7.00	$21.00	$42.50	£2.90	£8.75	£17.50
86 48pgs, scarce in the U.K., Neal Adams art, drugs issues	$7.00	$21.00	$42.50	£2.90	£8.75	£17.50
87 48pgs, Neal Adams art, 2nd appearance Guy Gardner (cameo), 1st John Stewart Green Lantern	$4.15	$12.50	$25.00	£2.50	£7.50	£15.00
88 48pgs, Neal Adams art (1pg), reprint of Showcase #23 (2nd Silver Age Green Lantern), unpublished Golden Age Green Lantern story from unreleased #39	$2.00	$6.00	$12.00	£1.25	£3.75	£7.50
89 48pgs, story continues in Flash #217, Neal Adams art	$2.50	$7.50	$15.00	£1.50	£4.50	£9.00
90 scarce in the U.K.	$0.80	$2.40	$4.00	£0.70	£2.10	£3.50
91-96 scarce in the U.K.	$0.80	$2.40	$4.00	£0.50	£1.50	£2.50
97-98	$0.55	$1.65	$2.75	£0.35	£1.05	£1.75
99 ND	$0.55	$1.65	$2.75	£0.60	£1.80	£3.00
100 ND scarce in the U.K. 48pgs, 1st appearance Air Wave II	$1.20	$3.60	$6.00	£1.00	£3.00	£5.00
101-107	$0.60	$1.80	$3.00	£0.30	£0.90	£1.50
108 44pgs, scarce, Golden Age Green Lantern back-up	$0.60	$1.80	$3.00	£0.50	£1.50	£2.50
109-110 ND Golden Age Green Lantern back-up	$0.60	$1.80	$3.00	£0.50	£1.50	£2.50
111 Green Lantern and Golden Age Green Lantern team-up	$0.60	$1.80	$3.00	£0.30	£0.90	£1.50
112 Golden Age Green Lantern origin retold	$1.20	$3.60	$6.00	£0.30	£0.90	£1.50
113-115	$0.60	$1.80	$3.00	£0.25	£0.75	£1.25
116 3rd appearance Guy Gardner, 1st as a Green Lantern	$5.50	$16.50	$27.50	£1.00	£3.00	£5.00
117-121	$0.60	$1.80	$3.00	£0.25	£0.75	£1.25
122 last Green Lantern/Green Arrow cover title, Guy Gardner appears, Superman and Flash appear	$0.60	$1.80	$3.00	£0.25	£0.75	£1.25
123 Green Lantern goes solo, Superman cameo, Gil Kane cover, Guy Gardner appears	$1.20	$3.60	$6.00	£0.30	£0.90	£1.50
124-126	$0.40	$1.20	$2.00	£0.25	£0.75	£1.25
127 Bolland cover, his first published DC work	$0.40	$1.20	$2.00	£0.30	£0.90	£1.50
128 Cockrum art	$0.40	$1.20	$2.00	£0.25	£0.75	£1.25
129-130	$0.40	$1.20	$2.00	£0.25	£0.75	£1.25
131 Bolland cover (2nd DC work?)	$0.40	$1.20	$2.00	£0.25	£0.75	£1.25
132 Adam Strange back-up begins (ends #147)	$0.40	$1.20	$2.00	£0.25	£0.75	£1.25
133-135	$0.40	$1.20	$2.00	£0.25	£0.75	£1.25
136 Space Ranger and Eclipso appear; 1st appearance The Citadel						

	$Good	$Fine	$N.Mint	£Good	£Fine	£N.Mint
	$0.40	$1.20	$2.00	£0.25	£0.75	£1.25
137 Space Ranger appears	$0.40	$1.20	$2.00	£0.25	£0.75	£1.25
138 Green Lantern vs. Eclipso	$0.40	$1.20	$2.00	£0.25	£0.75	£1.25
139-140	$0.40	$1.20	$2.00	£0.25	£0.75	£1.25
141 1st appearance Omega Men	$0.60	$1.80	$3.00	£0.30	£0.90	£1.50
142 Omega Men appear	$0.40	$1.20	$2.00	£0.25	£0.75	£1.25
143-144 Omega Men appear	$0.40	$1.20	$2.00	£0.25	£0.60	£1.00
145-149	$0.40	$1.20	$2.00	£0.20	£0.60	£1.00
150 44pgs, anniversary issue	$0.60	$1.80	$3.00	£0.30	£0.90	£1.50
151-155	$0.40	$1.20	$2.00	£0.20	£0.60	£1.00
156 Gil Kane cover and art	$0.40	$1.20	$2.00	£0.20	£0.60	£1.00
157-159	$0.40	$1.20	$2.00	£0.20	£0.60	£1.00
160 Omega Men X-over	$0.40	$1.20	$2.00	£0.20	£0.60	£1.00
161 Dave Gibbons art, Omega Men X-over	$0.40	$1.20	$2.00	£0.20	£0.60	£1.00
162 Dave Gibbons art	$0.40	$1.20	$2.00	£0.20	£0.60	£1.00
163	$0.40	$1.20	$2.00	£0.20	£0.60	£1.00
164-167 Gibbons art	$0.40	$1.20	$2.00	£0.20	£0.60	£1.00
168-170	$0.40	$1.20	$2.00	£0.20	£0.60	£1.00
171-174 Gibbons art	$0.40	$1.20	$2.00	£0.20	£0.60	£1.00
175 Gibbons art; no number on cover	$0.40	$1.20	$2.00	£0.20	£0.60	£1.00
176 Gibbons art	$0.40	$1.20	$2.00	£0.20	£0.60	£1.00
177 Cockrum art	$0.40	$1.20	$2.00	£0.20	£0.60	£1.00
178-181 Gibbons art	$0.40	$1.20	$2.00	£0.20	£0.60	£1.00
182 John Stewart takes over as Green Lantern, Kevin O'Neill, Gibbons art	$0.40	$1.20	$2.00	£0.20	£0.60	£1.00
183 Gibbons art	$0.40	$1.20	$2.00	£0.20	£0.60	£1.00
184 John Stewart/Hal Jordan/Guy Gardner Green Lanterns appear	$0.40	$1.20	$2.00	£0.20	£0.60	£1.00
185 John Stewart origin as Green Lantern, Eclipso appears, Gibbons art	$0.40	$1.20	$2.00	£0.20	£0.60	£1.00
186 John Stewart vs. Eclipso	$0.40	$1.20	$2.00	£0.20	£0.60	£1.00
187 Marshall Rogers art	$0.40	$1.20	$2.00	£0.20	£0.60	£1.00
188 Moore script, Gibbons art	$0.40	$1.20	$2.00	£0.20	£0.60	£1.00
189-193	$0.40	$1.20	$2.00	£0.20	£0.60	£1.00
194 Crisis X-over	$1.00	$3.00	$5.00	£0.20	£0.60	£1.00
195 Crisis X-over, Guy Gardner becomes Green Lantern	$2.00	$6.00	$10.00	£0.50	£1.50	£2.50
196 unofficial Crisis X-over	$0.40	$1.20	$2.00	£0.20	£0.60	£1.00
197 Guy Gardner vs. John Stewart	$0.40	$1.20	$2.00	£0.20	£0.60	£1.00
198 DS, Crisis X-over, alien Green Lantern Tomar-Re dies	$0.40	$1.20	$2.00	£0.25	£0.75	£1.25
199 Hal Jordan returns as Green Lantern	$0.40	$1.20	$2.00	£0.20	£0.60	£1.00
200 DS, anniversary issue, various past Green Lantern friends and foes return in flashback	$0.60	$1.80	$3.00	£0.25	£0.75	£1.25
201 title becomes Green Lantern Corps (Jun 1986)	$0.25	$0.75	$1.25	£0.15	£0.45	£0.75
202-206	$0.25	$0.75	$1.25	£0.15	£0.45	£0.75
207 Legends X-over	$0.25	$0.75	$1.25	£0.15	£0.45	£0.75
208-213	$0.25	$0.75	$1.25	£0.15	£0.45	£0.75
214-216 Ian Gibson art	$0.25	$0.75	$1.25	£0.15	£0.45	£0.75
217-219	$0.25	$0.75	$1.25	£0.15	£0.45	£0.75
220-221 Millennium X-over	$0.25	$0.75	$1.25	£0.15	£0.45	£0.75
222	$0.25	$0.75	$1.25	£0.15	£0.45	£0.75
223 LD in the U.K.	$0.25	$0.75	$1.25	£0.20	£0.60	£1.00
224 LD in the U.K. 48pgs	$0.30	$0.90	$1.50	£0.20	£0.60	£1.00
Title Value:	**$1738.95**	**$5216.75**	**$13158.25**	**£840.90**	**£2530.45**	**£6571.25**

Note: content changed to Green Lantern Corps with issue #201.

Green Lantern/Green Arrow Collection 1 (Jun 1992)
Trade paperback, reprints issues #76-82, new intro by Denny O'Neill — £1.60 £4.80 £8.00

Green Lantern/Green Arrow Collection 2 (May 1993)
Trade paperback, reprints issues #84-87, #89 and Flash #217-219, new Neal Adams cover, intro by Dick Giordano — £1.60 £4.80 £8.00

ARTISTS
Wrightson inks in 84.

FEATURES
Adam Strange in 132-147. Earth's First Green Lantern in 149. Green Lantern/Green Arrow in 76-86, 99-99, 101-122. Green Arrow solo in 87. Green Arrow/ Black Canary in 100. GA Green Lantern in 108-110. Tales of the Green Lantern Corps in 130-132, 148, 151-172, 188.

REPRINT FEATURES
Green Lantern in 85, 87, 88. GA Green Lantern in 86, 88, 89.

GREEN LANTERN (3RD SERIES)
DC Comics; 0 Oct 1994; 1 Jun 1990-present

	$Good	$Fine	$N.Mint	£Good	£Fine	£N.Mint
0 (Oct 1994) Zero Hour X-over, Kyle Rayner vs. Hal Jordan	$0.40	$1.20	$2.00	£0.25	£0.75	£1.25
1 Batman appears	$0.60	$1.80	$3.00	£0.40	£1.20	£2.00
2	$0.40	$1.20	$2.00	£0.30	£0.90	£1.50
3-8	$0.40	$1.20	$2.00	£0.25	£0.75	£1.25
9-10 origin G'Nort story	$0.40	$1.20	$2.00	£0.25	£0.75	£1.25
11-12 origin G'Nort story	$0.30	$0.90	$1.50	£0.20	£0.60	£1.00
13 48pgs, three story issue	$0.40	$1.20	$2.00	£0.25	£0.75	£1.25
14-15 John Stewart/Guardians story	$0.30	$0.90	$1.50	£0.20	£0.60	£1.00
16-17 John Stewart/Guardians story	$0.25	$0.75	$1.25	£0.15	£0.45	£0.75
18	$0.25	$0.75	$1.25	£0.15	£0.45	£0.75
19 48pgs, 50th anniversary issue, Golden Age Green Lantern appears, part art by Martin Nodell who originally drew G.L. in the 1940s	$0.30	$0.90	$1.50	£0.20	£0.60	£1.00
19 ND Signed Edition by Martin Nodell (Jul 1992), 2,000 copies only - one copy was issued per retailer's account by their distributor	$3.00	$9.00	$15.00	£2.00	£6.00	£10.00
20-24	$0.25	$0.75	$1.25	£0.15	£0.45	£0.75
25 48pgs, leads into Green Lantern: Mosaic #1	$0.30	$0.90	$1.50	£0.20	£0.60	£1.00
26-28 Evil Star Rising story	$0.25	$0.75	$1.25	£0.15	£0.45	£0.75
29	$0.25	$0.75	$1.25	£0.15	£0.45	£0.75
30 Gorilla Warfare part 1, Gorilla Grodd, Detective Chimp and Rex the Wonder Dog appear, continued in Flash [2nd Series] #69	$0.25	$0.75	$1.25	£0.15	£0.45	£0.75
31 Gorilla Warfare part 2, continued in Flash #70	$0.25	$0.75	$1.25	£0.15	£0.45	£0.75
32-33 bi-weekly	$0.25	$0.75	$1.25	£0.15	£0.45	£0.75
34 1st appearance Entropy	$0.25	$0.75	$1.25	£0.15	£0.45	£0.75
35-37	$0.25	$0.75	$1.25	£0.15	£0.45	£0.75
38 Adam Strange appears	$0.25	$0.75	$1.25	£0.15	£0.45	£0.75
39 Adam Strange appears, bi-weekly	$0.25	$0.75	$1.25	£0.15	£0.45	£0.75
40 Darkstar appears, bi-weekly	$0.25	$0.75	$1.25	£0.15	£0.45	£0.75
41 DC's Predator, Deathstroke and Eclipso appear, bi-weekly	$0.25	$0.75	$1.25	£0.15	£0.45	£0.75
42 DC's Predator, Deathstroke appear, bi-weekly	$0.25	$0.75	$1.25	£0.15	£0.45	£0.75
43	$0.25	$0.75	$1.25	£0.15	£0.45	£0.75
44 Trinity part 2, continued in Legion '93 #57	$0.25	$0.75	$1.25	£0.15	£0.45	£0.75
45 Trinity part 5, continued in Legion '93 #58	$0.25	$0.75	$1.25	£0.15	£0.45	£0.75
46 Reign of the Supermen part 19, continued in Superman #82	$0.90	$2.70	$4.50	£0.50	£1.50	£2.50
46 2nd printing	$0.25	$0.75	$1.25	£0.15	£0.45	£0.75
47 Green Lantern and Green Arrow team returns	$0.25	$0.75	$1.25	£0.15	£0.45	£0.75
48 Emerald Twilight part 1	$0.60	$1.80	$3.00	£0.40	£1.20	£2.00
49 Emerald Twilight part 2	$0.50	$1.50	$2.50	£0.35	£1.05	£1.75
50 48pgs, Emerald Twilight part 3, Green Lantern vs. Sinestro; 1st appearance new Green Lantern (Kyle Rayner) with new costume/powers; death of Sinestro, death Killowog, end of Green Lantern Corps and Guardians of Oa; green glow-in-the-dark cover	$0.80	$2.40	$4.00	£0.90	£2.70	£4.50
51 cyborg Superman appears	$0.40	$1.20	$2.00	£0.25	£0.75	£1.25
52	$0.30	$0.90	$1.50	£0.20	£0.60	£1.00
53 Superman appears	$0.30	$0.90	$1.50	£0.20	£0.60	£1.00
54	$0.30	$0.90	$1.50	£0.20	£0.60	£1.00
55 Zero Hour X-over	$0.30	$0.90	$1.50	£0.20	£0.60	£1.00
56	$0.30	$0.90	$1.50	£0.20	£0.60	£1.00
57 continued in New Titans #116	$0.30	$0.90	$1.50	£0.20	£0.60	£1.00
58-59	$0.30	$0.90	$1.50	£0.20	£0.60	£1.00
60 Guy Gardner guest-stars	$0.30	$0.90	$1.50	£0.20	£0.60	£1.00
61-62	$0.30	$0.90	$1.50	£0.20	£0.60	£1.00
63-64 Parallax View: the resurrection of Hal Jordan (who "died" in Zero Hour); Superman, Flash, Aquaman, Green Arrow, Black Canary, Martian Manhunter appear	$0.40	$1.20	$2.00	£0.25	£0.75	£1.25
65 The Siege of Zi Charam, continued in Darkstars #34. Ron Lim cover and art	$0.40	$1.20	$2.00	£0.25	£0.75	£1.25
66-67 Flash guest-stars						

	$Good	$Fine	$N.Mint	£Good	£Fine	£N.Mint
68-69 Underworld Unleashed tie-in	$0.40	$1.20	$2.00	£0.25	£0.75	£1.25
70 Supergirl guest-stars	$0.40	$1.20	$2.00	£0.25	£0.75	£1.25
71	$0.40	$1.20	$2.00	£0.25	£0.75	£1.25
72 Green Lantern teams with Captain Marvel	$0.40	$1.20	$2.00	£0.25	£0.75	£1.25
Title Value:	$27.80	$83.40	$139.00	£18.00	£54.00	£90.00

Note: early issues of series spotlight Hal Jordan/Guy Gardner/John Stewart incarnations of Green Lantern.

Green Lantern: The Road Back (Jun 1992)

	$Good	$Fine	$N.Mint	£Good	£Fine	£N.Mint
Trade paperback, reprints issues #1-8, new cover painting by Brian Stelfreeze				£1.10	£3.30	£5.50

GREEN LANTERN ANNUAL
DC Comics; 1 Jul 1992-present

	$Good	$Fine	$N.Mint	£Good	£Fine	£N.Mint
1 64pgs, Eclipso: The Darkness Within tie-in	$0.45	$1.35	$2.25	£0.30	£0.90	£1.50
2 64pgs, Bloodlines part 7, 1st appearance Nightblade, continued in Batman Annual #17	$0.45	$1.35	$2.25	£0.30	£0.90	£1.50
3 64pgs, Elseworlds story, Adolf Hitler appears	$0.60	$1.80	$3.00	£0.35	£1.05	£1.75
4 64pgs, Year One	$0.80	$2.40	$4.00	£0.50	£1.50	£2.50
Title Value:	$2.30	$6.90	$11.50	£1.45	£4.35	£7.25

GREEN LANTERN ARCHIVES
DC Comics; 1 Jan 1993

	$Good	$Fine	$N.Mint	£Good	£Fine	£N.Mint
1 ND 224pgs, reprints Showcase #22-#24, Green Lantern #1-#5	$7.50	$22.50	$37.50	£5.00	£15.00	£25.00
Title Value:	$7.50	$22.50	$37.50	£5.00	£15.00	£25.00

GREEN LANTERN CORPS ANNUAL
DC Comics; 2 Dec 1986-3 Aug 1987
(previously Tales of the ...)

	$Good	$Fine	$N.Mint	£Good	£Fine	£N.Mint
2 Moore script, Kev O'Neill art, non-code approved	$0.40	$1.20	$2.00	£0.25	£0.75	£1.25
3 Moore scripts, John Byrne, Kevin Nowlan art	$0.40	$1.20	$2.00	£0.25	£0.75	£1.25
Title Value:	$0.80	$2.40	$4.00	£0.50	£1.50	£2.50

Note: issue 3 titled "Green Lantern Annual".

GREEN LANTERN CORPS ANNUAL, TALES OF THE
DC Comics; 1 Jan 1985
(becomes Green Lantern Corps Annual)

	$Good	$Fine	$N.Mint	£Good	£Fine	£N.Mint
1 48pgs, Gil Kane cover/art	$0.45	$1.35	$2.25	£0.30	£0.90	£1.50
Title Value:	$0.45	$1.35	$2.25	£0.30	£0.90	£1.50

GREEN LANTERN CORPS QUARTERLY
DC Comics; 1 Jun 1992-8 Mar 1994

	$Good	$Fine	$N.Mint	£Good	£Fine	£N.Mint
1-6 64pgs, Golden Age Green Lantern appears	$0.45	$1.35	$2.25	£0.30	£0.90	£1.50
7 64pgs, Golden Age Green Lantern appears; special Halloween issue focusing on fear	$0.45	$1.35	$2.25	£0.30	£0.90	£1.50
8 64pgs, Golden Age Green Lantern appears	$0.45	$1.35	$2.25	£0.30	£0.90	£1.50
Title Value:	$3.60	$10.80	$18.00	£2.40	£7.20	£12.00

GREEN LANTERN CORPS, TALES OF THE
DC Comics, MS; 1 May 1981-3 Jul 1981

	$Good	$Fine	$N.Mint	£Good	£Fine	£N.Mint
1-3 origin Green Lantern & the Guardians retold	$0.25	$0.75	$1.25	£0.15	£0.45	£0.75
Title Value:	$0.75	$2.25	$3.75	£0.45	£1.35	£2.25

GREEN LANTERN SPECIAL
DC Comics; 1 1988-2 1989

	$Good	$Fine	$N.Mint	£Good	£Fine	£N.Mint
1 48pgs	$0.25	$0.75	$1.25	£0.15	£0.45	£0.75
2 plotlines from Action Comics Weekly resolved	$0.25	$0.75	$1.25	£0.15	£0.45	£0.75
Title Value:	$0.50	$1.50	$2.50	£0.30	£0.90	£1.50

GREEN LANTERN/GREEN ARROW
DC Comics; 1 Oct 1983-7 Apr 1984

	$Good	$Fine	$N.Mint	£Good	£Fine	£N.Mint
1 52pgs, Neal Adams reprints begin	$0.45	$1.35	$2.25	£0.30	£0.90	£1.50
2-7 52pgs	$0.45	$1.35	$2.25	£0.30	£0.90	£1.50
Title Value:	$3.15	$9.45	$15.75	£2.10	£6.30	£10.50

GREEN LANTERN/SILVER SURFER
DC Comics/Marvel Comics Group, OS; 1 Jan 1996

	$Good	$Fine	$N.Mint	£Good	£Fine	£N.Mint
1 ND 48pgs, Ron Marz script, Darryl Banks and Terry Austin art	$1.00	$3.00	$5.00	£0.65	£1.95	£3.25
Title Value:	$1.00	$3.00	$5.00	£0.65	£1.95	£3.25

GREEN LANTERN: EMERALD DAWN
DC Comics, MS; 1 Dec 1989-6 May 1990

	$Good	$Fine	$N.Mint	£Good	£Fine	£N.Mint
1 origin retold	$0.70	$2.10	$3.50	£0.40	£1.20	£2.00
2-3	$0.50	$1.50	$2.50	£0.30	£0.90	£1.50
4-6	$0.40	$1.20	$2.00	£0.25	£0.75	£1.25
Title Value:	$2.90	$8.70	$14.50	£1.75	£5.25	£8.75
Trade Paperback (May 1991), reprints mini-series				£0.70	£2.10	£3.50

GREEN LANTERN: EMERALD DAWN II
DC Comics, MS; 1 Apr 1991-6 Sep 1991

	$Good	$Fine	$N.Mint	£Good	£Fine	£N.Mint
1-6	$0.40	$1.20	$2.00	£0.25	£0.75	£1.25
Title Value:	$2.40	$7.20	$12.00	£1.50	£4.50	£7.50

GREEN LANTERN: GANTHET'S TALE
DC Comics, OS; 1 Nov 1992

	$Good	$Fine	$N.Mint	£Good	£Fine	£N.Mint
1 64pgs, Larry Niven script, John Byrne art	$1.00	$3.00	$5.00	£0.70	£2.10	£3.50
Title Value:	$1.00	$3.00	$5.00	£0.70	£2.10	£3.50

GREEN LANTERN: MOSAIC
DC Comics; 1 Jun 1992-18 Nov 1993

	$Good	$Fine	$N.Mint	£Good	£Fine	£N.Mint
1 John Stewart (Green Lantern) begins	$0.25	$0.75	$1.25	£0.15	£0.45	£0.75
2	$0.25	$0.75	$1.25	£0.15	£0.45	£0.75
3 ties in with Eclipso: The Darkness Within and Guy Gardner: Reborn series	$0.25	$0.75	$1.25	£0.15	£0.45	£0.75
4-15	$0.25	$0.75	$1.25	£0.15	£0.45	£0.75
16 Flash, Power Girl and Martian Manhunter appear	$0.25	$0.75	$1.25	£0.15	£0.45	£0.75
17	$0.25	$0.75	$1.25	£0.15	£0.45	£0.75
18 Guy Gardner, Hal Jordan, Flash, Power Girl, Martian Manhunter appear with John Stewart	$0.25	$0.75	$1.25	£0.15	£0.45	£0.75
Title Value:	$4.50	$13.50	$22.50	£2.70	£8.10	£13.50

GREENHAVEN
Aircel; 1-3 1988

	$Good	$Fine	$N.Mint	£Good	£Fine	£N.Mint
1 ND Barry Blair script/art begins (colour)	$0.40	$1.20	$2.00	£0.25	£0.75	£1.25
2 ND	$0.40	$1.20	$2.00	£0.25	£0.75	£1.25
3 ND conclusion in Elflord #21 (2nd Series)	$0.40	$1.20	$2.00	£0.25	£0.75	£1.25
Title Value:	$1.20	$3.60	$6.00	£0.75	£2.25	£3.75

GREENLOCK
Aircel, OS; 1 Mar 1991

	$Good	$Fine	$N.Mint	£Good	£Fine	£N.Mint
1 ND Barry Blair script/art, black and white	$0.30	$0.90	$1.50	£0.20	£0.60	£1.00
Title Value:	$0.30	$0.90	$1.50	£0.20	£0.60	£1.00

GREGORY
DC Comics/Piranha Press, OS; 1 1989

	$Good	$Fine	$N.Mint	£Good	£Fine	£N.Mint
1 ND Marc Hempel script/art	$1.50	$4.50	$7.50	£1.00	£3.00	£5.00
1 2nd printing, ND (1990)	$1.40	$4.20	$7.00	£0.90	£2.70	£4.50
Title Value:	$2.90	$8.70	$14.50	£1.90	£5.70	£9.50

GREGORY II
DC Comics/Piranha Press, OS; 1993

	$Good	$Fine	$N.Mint	£Good	£Fine	£N.Mint
1 ND 64pgs, black and white	$0.90	$2.70	$4.50	£0.60	£1.80	£3.00
Title Value:	$0.90	$2.70	$4.50	£0.60	£1.80	£3.00

GREGORY III
DC Comics/Piranha Press, OS; 1 Jul 1993

	$Good	$Fine	$N.Mint	£Good	£Fine	£N.Mint
1 ND 48pgs Marc Hempel script/art	$1.00	$3.00	$5.00	£0.65	£1.95	£3.25
Title Value:	$1.00	$3.00	$5.00	£0.65	£1.95	£3.25

GREGORY IV: FAT BOY
DC Comics/Piranha Press, OS; 1 Dec 1993

	$Good	$Fine	$N.Mint	£Good	£Fine	£N.Mint
1 ND Marc Hempel script/art	$1.00	$3.00	$5.00	£0.65	£1.95	£3.25
Title Value:	$1.00	$3.00	$5.00	£0.65	£1.95	£3.25

GRENDEL
Comico; 1 Mar 1983-3 Feb 1984
(see Primer #2)

	$Good	$Fine	$N.Mint	£Good	£Fine	£N.Mint
1 ND very scarce in the U.K.	$15.00	$45.00	$75.00	£10.00	£30.00	£50.00
2 ND scarce in the U.K.	$12.00	$36.00	$60.00	£8.00	£24.00	£40.00
3 ND scarce in the U.K.	$10.00	$30.00	$50.00	£7.00	£21.00	£35.00
Title Value:	$37.00	$111.00	$185.00	£25.00	£75.00	£125.00

GRENDEL (2ND SERIES)
Comico; 1 Oct 1986-40 Feb 1990
(see Mage)

	$Good	$Fine	$N.Mint	£Good	£Fine	£N.Mint
1 Christine Spar becomes Grendel, Wagner scripts, Pander Bros. art begins	$1.80	$5.25	$9.00	£1.20	£3.60	£6.00
1 2nd printing	$0.80	$2.40	$4.00	£0.50	£1.50	£2.50
2	$1.20	$3.60	$6.00	£0.80	£2.40	£4.00
3	$1.05	$3.15	$5.25	£0.70	£2.10	£3.50
4	$0.90	$2.70	$4.50	£0.60	£1.80	£3.00
5-10	$0.80	$2.40	$4.00	£0.50	£1.50	£2.50
11	$0.60	$1.80	$3.00	£0.40	£1.20	£2.00
12 last Pander Bros.	$0.60	$1.80	$3.00	£0.40	£1.20	£2.00
13-15 Bernie Mireault art	$0.60	$1.80	$3.00	£0.40	£1.20	£2.00
16 painted Mage back-up by Wagner begins	$1.80	$5.25	$9.00	£1.20	£3.60	£6.00
17-19 Mage back-up	$0.90	$2.70	$4.50	£0.60	£1.80	£3.00
20 Wagner art	$0.45	$1.35	$2.25	£0.30	£0.90	£1.50
21-22 Hannibal King art	$0.45	$1.35	$2.25	£0.30	£0.90	£1.50
23 Tim Sale art	$0.45	$1.35	$2.25	£0.30	£0.90	£1.50
24-25 Snyder/J.Geldhof art	$0.45	$1.35	$2.25	£0.30	£0.90	£1.50
26-32	$0.40	$1.20	$2.00	£0.25	£0.75	£1.25
33 44pgs	$0.60	$1.80	$3.00	£0.40	£1.20	£2.00
34-39	$0.40	$1.20	$2.00	£0.25	£0.75	£1.25
40 giant, scarce; flip-book featuring Grendel Tales Preview Special	$1.05	$3.15	$5.25	£0.70	£2.10	£3.50
Title Value:	$27.60	$82.50	$138.00	£17.95	£53.85	£89.75

Note: all Non-Distributed on the news-stands in the U.K.

	$Good	$Fine	$N.Mint	£Good	£Fine	£N.Mint
Grendel: Devil's Legacy Trade paperback (1988), reprints #1-12				£2.00	£6.00	£10.00
Hardcover, Limited Edition				£3.00	£9.00	£15.00

	$Good	$Fine	$N.Mint	£Good	£Fine	£N.Mint

Grendel: Devil by the Deed,
pink cover; re-tells story of original Grendel from

	$Good	$Fine	$N.Mint	£Good	£Fine	£N.Mint
Christine Spar's point of view				£1.50	£4.50	£7.50
2nd print, blue cover				£1.00	£3.00	£5.00
Dark Horse Edition (Aug 1993), new cover by Matt Wagner				£0.50	£1.50	£2.50

GRENDEL CLASSICS
Dark Horse,MS; 1 Jul 1995-2 Aug 1995

	$Good	$Fine	$N.Mint	£Good	£Fine	£N.Mint
1 ND reprints issues 16 and 17 of original series with Matt Wagner art						
	$0.80	$2.40	$4.00	£0.50	£1.50	£2.50
2 ND reprints issues 18 and 19 from original series with Matt Wagner art						
	$0.80	$2.40	$4.00	£0.50	£1.50	£2.50
Title Value:	$1.60	$4.80	$8.00	£1.00	£3.00	£5.00

GRENDEL CYCLE
Dark Horse, OS; nn Oct 1995

	$Good	$Fine	$N.Mint	£Good	£Fine	£N.Mint
nn, ND , 64pgs	$1.20	$3.60	$6.00	£0.80	£2.40	£4.00
Title Value:	$1.20	$3.60	$6.00	£0.80	£2.40	£4.00

GRENDEL TALES: DEVIL IN OUR MIDST
Dark Horse,MS; 1 May 1994-5 Sep 1994

	$Good	$Fine	$N.Mint	£Good	£Fine	£N.Mint
1-5 ND Paul Grist art						
	$0.60	$1.80	$3.00	£0.40	£1.20	£2.00
Title Value:	$3.00	$9.00	$15.00	£2.00	£6.00	£10.00

GRENDEL TALES: DEVIL MAY CARE
Dark Horse,MS; 1 Dec 1995-present

	$Good	$Fine	$N.Mint	£Good	£Fine	£N.Mint
1 ND Terry LaBan script, Peter Doherty art						
	$0.60	$1.80	$3.00	£0.40	£1.20	£2.00
Title Value:	$0.60	$1.80	$3.00	£0.40	£1.20	£2.00

GRENDEL TALES: DEVIL'S CHOICES
Dark Horse,MS; 1 Mar 1995-4 Jun 1995

	$Good	$Fine	$N.Mint	£Good	£Fine	£N.Mint
1-4 ND Darko Macan script, Edvin Biukovic art with back-up feature by Matt Wagner						
	$0.60	$1.80	$3.00	£0.40	£1.20	£2.00
Title Value:	$2.40	$7.20	$12.00	£1.60	£4.80	£8.00

GRENDEL TALES: DEVILS & DEATHS
Dark Horse,MS; 1 Oct 1994-2 Nov 1994

	$Good	$Fine	$N.Mint	£Good	£Fine	£N.Mint
1-2 ND Matt Wagner painted back-up story amd painted cover						
	$0.60	$1.80	$3.00	£0.40	£1.20	£2.00
Title Value:	$1.20	$3.60	$6.00	£0.80	£2.40	£4.00

GRENDEL TALES: FOUR DEVILS, ONE HELL
Dark Horse,MS; 1 Aug 1993-6 Jan 1994

	$Good	$Fine	$N.Mint	£Good	£Fine	£N.Mint
1-6 ND Matt Wagner cover paintings and "creative direction"						
	$0.60	$1.80	$3.00	£0.40	£1.20	£2.00
Title Value:	$3.60	$10.80	$18.00	£2.40	£7.20	£12.00
Grendel Tales: Four Devils, One Hell (Nov 1994)						
Trade paperback reprints mini-series plus sketches				£2.40	£7.20	£12.00

GRENDEL TALES: HOMECOMING
Dark Horse,MS; 1 Dec 1994-3 Feb 1995

	$Good	$Fine	$N.Mint	£Good	£Fine	£N.Mint
1-3 ND Pat McEwon script and art, painted cover by Matt Wagner						
	$0.60	$1.80	$3.00	£0.40	£1.20	£2.00
Title Value:	$1.80	$5.40	$9.00	£1.20	£3.60	£6.00

GRENDEL TALES: THE DEVIL'S HAMMER
Dark Horse,MS; 1 Feb 1994-3 Apr 1994

	$Good	$Fine	$N.Mint	£Good	£Fine	£N.Mint
1-3 ND Bernie Mirault art						
	$0.55	$1.65	$2.75	£0.35	£1.05	£1.75
Title Value:	$1.65	$4.95	$8.25	£1.05	£3.15	£5.25

GRENDEL: DEVIL QUEST
Dark Horse, OS; 1 Nov 1995

	$Good	$Fine	$N.Mint	£Good	£Fine	£N.Mint
1 ND 56pgs, Matt Wagner script and art						
	$1.00	$3.00	$5.00	£0.65	£1.95	£3.25
Title Value:	$1.00	$3.00	$5.00	£0.65	£1.95	£3.25

GRENDEL: DEVIL'S VAGARY
Comico; nn 1987
(see Comico Collection)

	$Good	$Fine	$N.Mint	£Good	£Fine	£N.Mint
nn ND rare in the U.K., 16pgs, Wagner script, Motter art, printed in						
black & red, published as part of the Comico Collection				£4.00	£12.00	£20.00

GRENDEL: THE DEVIL INSIDE
Comics,OS; 1 Jun 1989

	$Good	$Fine	$N.Mint	£Good	£Fine	£N.Mint
1 ND 80pgs, squarebound						
	$2.40	$7.00	$12.00	£1.60	£4.80	£8.00
Title Value:	$2.40	$7.00	$12.00	£1.60	£4.80	£8.00

GRENDEL: WAR CHILD
Dark Horse,MS; 1 Aug 1992-10 Jun 1993

	$Good	$Fine	$N.Mint	£Good	£Fine	£N.Mint
1 ND Matt Wagner script and inks begin, Patrick McKeown pencils; picks up after events in Grendel #40, Simon Bisley painted covers begin						
	$0.90	$2.70	$4.50	£0.60	£1.80	£3.00
2 ND	$0.80	$2.40	$4.00	£0.50	£1.50	£2.50
3 ND	$0.60	$1.80	$3.00	£0.40	£1.20	£2.00
4-9 ND	$0.45	$1.35	$2.25	£0.30	£0.90	£1.50
10 ND 48pgs, $3.50 cover						
	$0.80	$2.40	$4.00	£0.50	£1.50	£2.50
Title Value:	$5.80	$17.40	$29.00	£3.80	£11.40	£19.00
Grendel: War Child Limited Edition Hardcover (Oct 1994)						
1,000 signed and numbered copies, reprinting mini-series				£14.00	£42.00	£70.00
Grendel: War Child (1995)						
Trade paperback reprints mini-series plus covers				£2.40	£7.20	£12.00
(2nd print - Sep 1995)				£2.30	£6.90	£11.50

GREY
Viz; 1 1988-9 1989

	$Good	$Fine	$N.Mint	£Good	£Fine	£N.Mint
1-9 ND 72pgs, black & white						
	$0.60	$1.80	$3.00	£0.40	£1.20	£2.00
Title Value:	$5.40	$16.20	$27.00	£3.60	£10.80	£18.00

GREYLORE
Sirius; 1 Dec 1985-5 Sep 1986

	$Good	$Fine	$N.Mint	£Good	£Fine	£N.Mint
1-5 ND	$0.40	$1.20	$2.00	£0.25	£0.75	£1.25
Title Value:	$2.00	$6.00	$10.00	£1.25	£3.75	£6.25

GRID, THE
Dark Horse; 1 Jul 1990-3 1990

	$Good	$Fine	$N.Mint	£Good	£Fine	£N.Mint
1 ND reprints Warlock 5 issues #1-5, new painted covers by Beauvais begin						
	$1.40	$4.20	$7.00	£0.90	£2.70	£4.50
2 ND reprints rest of Warlock 5 issues by Beauvais						
	$1.40	$4.20	$7.00	£0.90	£2.70	£4.50
3 ND new material	$1.40	$4.20	$7.00	£0.90	£2.70	£4.50
Title Value:	$4.20	$12.60	$21.00	£2.70	£8.10	£13.50

GRIFFIN
Slave Labor; 1 Jul 1988-3 1988

	$Good	$Fine	$N.Mint	£Good	£Fine	£N.Mint
1-3 ND	$0.40	$1.20	$2.00	£0.25	£0.75	£1.25
Title Value:	$1.20	$3.60	$6.00	£0.75	£2.25	£3.75

GRIFFIN, THE
DC Comics,MS; 1 Nov 1991-6 Apr 1992

	$Good	$Fine	$N.Mint	£Good	£Fine	£N.Mint
1-6 ND 48pgs, Matt Wagner cover						
	$0.80	$2.40	$4.00	£0.50	£1.50	£2.50
Title Value:	$4.80	$14.40	$24.00	£3.00	£9.00	£15.00

Note: originally published by Slave Labor Graphics but never completed

GRIFTER
Image; 1 May 1995-present

	$Good	$Fine	$N.Mint	£Good	£Fine	£N.Mint
1 ND Wildstorm Rising part 5, continued in Deathblow #16; with two foil-bagged painted trading cards. Cover by Barry Windsor-Smith, Keith Giffen co-plot and pencils						
	$0.45	$1.35	$2.25	£0.30	£0.90	£1.50
1 Newstand edition, ND without trading cards						
	$0.40	$1.20	$2.00	£0.25	£0.75	£1.25
2-8 ND	$0.45	$1.35	$2.25	£0.30	£0.90	£1.50
Title Value:	$4.00	$12.00	$20.50	£2.65	£7.95	£13.25

GRIFTER/BADROCK
Image,MS; 1 Oct 1995-3 Dec 1995

Green Lantern (1st) #4

Green Lantern (2nd) #80

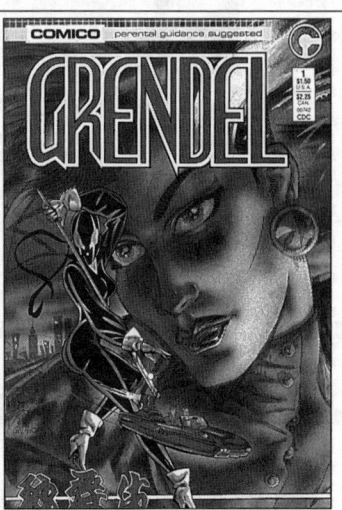

Grendel #1

MINT = 100% / NEAR MINT (inc. +/-) = 90-99% / VERY FINE (inc. +/-) = 75-89% / FINE (inc. +/-) = 55-74%
VERY GOOD (inc. +/-) = 35-54% / GOOD (inc. +/-) = 15-34% / FAIR = 5-14% / POOR = 1-4%

379

	$Good	$Fine	$N.Mint	£Good	£Fine	£N.Mint
1 ND Rob Liefeld script and art with Chap Yaep and Jonathan Sibal						
	$0.50	$1.50	$2.50	£0.30	£0.90	£1.50
2 ND	$0.50	$1.50	$2.50	£0.30	£0.90	£1.50
3 ND	$0.70	$2.10	$3.50	£0.45	£1.35	£2.25
Title Value:	$1.70	$5.10	$8.50	£1.05	£3.15	£5.25

GRIFTER: ONE-SHOT
Image,OS; 1 Jan 1995
1 ND 48pgs, squarebound, Steve Seagle script, Dan Norton pencils

	$1.00	$3.00	$5.00	£0.65	£1.95	£3.25
Title Value:	$1.00	$3.00	$5.00	£0.65	£1.95	£3.25

GRIM GHOST
Atlas; 1 Jan 1975-3 Jul 1975
1-3 distributed in the U.K.

	$0.25	$0.75	$1.25	£0.15	£0.45	£0.75
Title Value:	$0.75	$2.25	$3.75	£0.45	£1.35	£2.25

GRIMJACK
First; 1 Aug 1984-81 Jan 1991
(see Starslayer)

1 ND	$0.45	$1.35	$2.25	£0.30	£0.90	£1.50
2-21 ND	$0.40	$1.20	$2.00	£0.25	£0.75	£1.25
22 ND Brian Bolland backup (18pgs)						
	$0.60	$1.80	$3.00	£0.40	£1.20	£2.00
23-25 ND	$0.40	$1.20	$2.00	£0.25	£0.75	£1.25
26 ND 1st colour Teenage Mutant Ninja Turtles story						
	$0.50	$1.50	$2.50	£0.30	£0.90	£1.50
27-45 ND	$0.40	$1.20	$2.00	£0.25	£0.75	£1.25
46 ND Eddie Current in colour						
	$0.60	$1.80	$3.00	£0.40	£1.20	£2.00
47-50 ND	$0.40	$1.20	$2.00	£0.25	£0.75	£1.25
51-54 ND	$0.30	$0.90	$1.50	£0.20	£0.60	£1.00
55 ND 1st appearance new Grimjack						
	$0.45	$1.35	$2.25	£0.30	£0.90	£1.50
56-60 ND	$0.30	$0.90	$1.50	£0.20	£0.60	£1.00
61 ND no logo on cover						
	$0.30	$0.90	$1.50	£0.20	£0.60	£1.00
62-65 ND	$0.30	$0.90	$1.50	£0.20	£0.60	£1.00
66-67 ND Demon Wars						
	$0.30	$0.90	$1.50	£0.20	£0.60	£1.00
68-74 ND	$0.30	$0.90	$1.50	£0.20	£0.60	£1.00
75 ND 48pgs, squarebound, final confrontation with The Major, fold-out map of Cynosure						
	$1.05	$3.15	$5.25	£0.70	£2.10	£3.50
76-81 ND	$0.90	$2.70	$1.50	£0.20	£0.60	£1.00
Title Value:	$30.75	$92.25	$153.75	£19.70	£59.10	£98.50
Demon Knight Graphic Novel (1990)				£1.00	£3.00	£5.00

GRIMJACK CASEFILES
First; 1 Sep 1990-6 Feb 1991
1 ND reprints from "Starslayer" begin

	$0.40	$1.20	$2.00	£0.25	£0.75	£1.25
2 ND	$0.40	$1.20	$2.00	£0.25	£0.75	£1.25
3 ND reprints Grimjack #1						
	$0.40	$1.20	$2.00	£0.25	£0.75	£1.25
4 ND reprints Grimjack #2						
	$0.40	$1.20	$2.00	£0.25	£0.75	£1.25
5-6 ND	$0.40	$1.20	$2.00	£0.25	£0.75	£1.25
Title Value:	$2.40	$7.20	$12.00	£1.50	£4.50	£7.50

GRIMM TALES
Eclipse,OS; 1 Jul 1993

1 ND	$1.20	$3.60	$6.00	£0.80	£2.40	£4.00
Title Value:	$1.20	$3.60	$6.00	£0.80	£2.40	£4.00

GRIMM'S GHOST STORIES
Gold Key; 1 Jan 1972-54 Nov 1979; Whitman; 55 Mar 1980-60 19
1 scarce in the U.K. painted covers begin (unless otherwise noted)

	$0.90	$2.70	$4.50	£0.60	£1.80	£3.00
2-5	$0.60	$1.80	$3.00	£0.40	£1.20	£2.00
6-10	$0.45	$1.35	$2.25	£0.30	£0.90	£1.50
11-42	$0.40	$1.20	$2.00	£0.25	£0.75	£1.25
43 48pgs, photo cover						
	$0.45	$1.35	$2.25	£0.30	£0.90	£1.50
44 48pgs	$0.45	$1.35	$2.25	£0.30	£0.90	£1.50
45 photo cover	$0.40	$1.20	$2.00	£0.25	£0.75	£1.25
46-54	$0.40	$1.20	$2.00	£0.25	£0.75	£1.25
55 1st Whitman issue						
	$0.40	$1.20	$2.00	£0.25	£0.75	£1.25
56 last painted cover						
	$0.40	$1.20	$2.00	£0.25	£0.75	£1.25
57 line-drawn covers begin						
	$0.30	$0.90	$1.50	£0.20	£0.60	£1.00
58-60	$0.30	$0.90	$1.50	£0.20	£0.60	£1.00
Title Value:	$25.75	$75.75	$126.25	£16.10	£48.30	£80.50

Note: most issues distributed in the U.K. if irregularly

GRIMMAX, THE GREAT
Defiant,OS; 0 Aug 1994
0 ND 8pgs, free with Hero Illustrated; colour

	$0.15	$0.45	$0.75	£0.10	£0.30	£0.50
Title Value:	$0.15	$0.45	$0.75	£0.10	£0.30	£0.50

GRIPS
Silverwolf/Greater Mercury Comics; 1 Sep 1986-4 1987

1 ND Tim Vigil art	$3.00	$9.00	$15.00	£2.00	£6.00	£10.00
1 2nd printing, ND scarce in the U.K. (bootleg copy only)						
	$1.50	$4.50	$7.50	£1.00	£3.00	£5.00
2 ND Tim Vigil art	$2.25	$6.75	$11.25	£1.50	£4.50	£7.50
3 ND Tim Vigil art	$1.50	$4.50	$7.50	£1.00	£3.00	£5.00

	$Good	$Fine	$N.Mint	£Good	£Fine	£N.Mint
4 ND scarce in the U.K. Tim Vigil art						
	$1.80	$5.25	$9.00	£1.20	£3.60	£6.00
Title Value:	$10.05	$30.00	$50.25	£6.70	£20.10	£33.50

GRIPS (2ND SERIES)
Silverwolf/Greater Mercury Comics; 1 1989-12 1991
1 ND black and white

	$0.55	$1.65	$2.75	£0.35	£1.05	£1.75
1 ND Special Edition (May 1992) - no cover copy or logos, 2,500 copies						
	$2.25	$6.75	$11.25	£1.50	£4.50	£7.50
2-3 ND	$0.45	$1.35	$2.25	£0.30	£0.90	£1.50
4-6 ND	$0.40	$1.20	$2.00	£0.25	£0.75	£1.25
7-9 ND Web of the Spyder story						
	$0.40	$1.20	$2.00	£0.25	£0.75	£1.25
10-11 ND	$0.40	$1.20	$2.00	£0.25	£0.75	£1.25
12 ND Mistaken Identity story						
	$0.40	$1.20	$2.00	£0.25	£0.75	£1.25
Title Value:	$7.30	$21.90	$36.50	£4.70	£14.10	£23.50
Special Graphic Novel 1 (Nov 1990)						
128pgs squarebound, black and white				£1.20	£3.60	£6.00
Gold Edition Special Graphic Novel 1,						
limited print run, gold-trimmed cover				£2.00	£6.00	£10.00
2nd printing (Aug 1991)				£1.10	£3.30	£5.50

GRIPS ADVENTURES
Greater Mercury Comics; 1 May 1989-10 1990
1 ND DS featuring Legion X-II

	$0.45	$1.35	$2.25	£0.30	£0.90	£1.50
2-6 ND	$0.40	$1.20	$2.00	£0.25	£0.75	£1.25
7-8 ND One Man's Army story						
	$0.40	$1.20	$2.00	£0.25	£0.75	£1.25
9-10 ND Chasing Time story						
	$0.40	$1.20	$2.00	£0.25	£0.75	£1.25
Title Value:	$4.05	$12.15	$20.25	£2.55	£7.65	£12.75

GRIPS SPECIAL
Greater Mercury Comics,OS; 1 Apr 1992
1 ND anorexia nervosa story

	$0.45	$1.35	$2.25	£0.30	£0.90	£1.50
Title Value:	$0.45	$1.35	$2.25	£0.30	£0.90	£1.50

GRIPS VOLUME TWO
Greater Mercury Comics; 1 Aug 1989-12 1991

1 ND	$0.45	$1.35	$2.25		£0.90	£1.50
1 ND special printing, 2,500 copies, alternate cover						
	$0.90	$2.70	$4.50	£0.60	£1.80	£3.00
2-6 ND	$0.45	$1.35	$2.25	£0.30	£0.90	£1.50
7 ND	$0.40	$1.20	$2.00	£0.25	£0.75	£1.25
8-9 ND Web of the Spider story						
	$0.40	$1.20	$2.00	£0.25	£0.75	£1.25
10-11 ND River of Blood story						
	$0.40	$1.20	$2.00	£0.25	£0.75	£1.25
12 ND	$0.40	$1.20	$2.00	£0.25	£0.75	£1.25
Title Value:	$6.00	$18.00	$30.00	£3.90	£11.70	£19.50

GROO
Pacific; 1 Dec 1982-8 Mar 1984
(see Destroyer Duck #1, Groo [Marvel], Starslayer #5)

1 ND	$6.00	$18.00	$30.00	£4.00	£12.00	£20.00
2 ND	$3.50	$10.50	$17.50	£2.50	£7.50	£12.50
3 ND	$2.40	$7.00	$12.00	£1.60	£4.80	£8.00
4-6 ND scarce in the U.K.						
	$2.70	$8.00	$13.50	£1.80	£5.25	£9.00
7 ND very scarce in the U.K.						
	$2.70	$8.00	$13.50	£2.50	£7.50	£12.50
8 ND scarce in the U.K.						
	$2.70	$8.00	$13.50	£1.80	£5.25	£9.00
Title Value:	$25.40	$75.50	$127.00	£17.80	£52.80	£89.00

GROO (2ND SERIES)
Image; 1 Dec 1994-present
1 ND Sergio Aragones with Mark Evanier begins

	$0.40	$1.20	$2.00	£0.25	£0.75	£1.25
2-6 ND	$0.40	$1.20	$2.00	£0.25	£0.75	£1.25
7-12 ND	$0.45	$1.35	$2.25	£0.30	£0.90	£1.50
Title Value:	$5.10	$15.30	$25.50	£3.30	£9.90	£16.50

GROO CHRONICLES
Marvel Comics Group/Epic,MS; 1 Jul 1989-6 Feb 1990
1 ND squarebound, reprints of Pacific Groo/Eclipse Groo one-shot stories, re-coloured with new art by Aragones and new text by Evanier

	$0.80	$2.40	$4.00	£0.50	£1.50	£2.50
2 ND	$0.80	$2.40	$4.00	£0.50	£1.50	£2.50
3-6 ND	$0.60	$1.80	$3.00	£0.40	£1.20	£2.00
Title Value:	$4.00	$12.00	$20.00	£2.60	£7.80	£13.00
Hardback (by Graphitti), (1991), Signed.				£5.25	£15.75	£26.25

GROO SPECIAL
Eclipse,OS; 1 Oct 1984
1 ND scarce in the U.K.

	$7.00	$21.00	$35.00	£5.00	£15.00	£25.00
Title Value:	$7.00	$21.00	$35.00	£5.00	£15.00	£25.00

GROO THE WANDERER
Marvel Comics Group/Epic; 1 Mar 1985-120 Jan 1995
(see also Groo [Pacific], Groo Special [Eclipse], Destroyer Duck #1 [Eclipse], Starslayer #5 [First], Marvel Graphic Novel)
1 ND Sergio Aragones art begins

	$2.50	$7.50	$12.50	£2.50	£7.50	£12.50
2 ND	$1.20	$3.60	$6.00	£1.60	£4.80	£8.00
3 ND	$1.00	$3.00	$5.00	£1.40	£4.20	£7.00

TRADE PAPERBACKS, GRAPHIC NOVELS AND OTHER COLLECTIONS ARE PRICED IN POUNDS STERLING ONLY. CONVERT AT 1.5 FOR DOLLARS.

	$Good	$Fine	$N.Mint	£Good	£Fine	£N.Mint
4 ND	$1.00	$3.00	$5.00	£1.20	£3.60	£6.00
5-6 ND scarce in the U.K.	$1.00	$3.00	$5.00	£1.40	£4.20	£7.00
7 ND very scarce in the U.K.	$1.00	$3.00	$5.00	£1.50	£4.50	£7.50
8-10 ND	$1.00	$3.00	$5.00	£1.00	£3.00	£5.00
11-12 ND	$0.60	$1.80	$3.00	£0.80	£2.40	£4.00
13-26	$0.60	$1.80	$3.00	£0.40	£1.20	£2.00
27-30 ND	$0.60	$1.80	$3.00	£0.45	£1.35	£2.25
31-38 ND	$0.40	$1.20	$2.00	£0.35	£1.05	£1.75
39-45	$0.40	$1.20	$2.00	£0.25	£0.75	£1.25
46-49	$0.30	$0.90	$1.50	£0.20	£0.60	£1.00
50 LD in the U.K. DS	$0.30	$0.90	$1.50	£0.25	£0.75	£1.25
51-54	$0.30	$0.90	$1.50	£0.20	£0.60	£1.00
55 LD in the U.K.	$0.30	$0.90	$1.50	£0.25	£0.75	£1.25
56-79	$0.30	$0.90	$1.50	£0.20	£0.60	£1.00
80 Thaiis the Warrior Woman introduced	$0.30	$0.90	$1.50	£0.20	£0.60	£1.00
81-86	$0.30	$0.90	$1.50	£0.20	£0.60	£1.00
87 ND $2.25 covers begin	$0.40	$1.20	$2.00	£0.25	£0.75	£1.25
88-99 ND	$0.40	$1.20	$2.00	£0.25	£0.75	£1.25
100 ND DS	$0.60	$1.80	$3.00	£0.40	£1.20	£2.00
101-120 ND	$0.40	$1.20	$2.00	£0.25	£0.75	£1.25
Title Value:	$55.80	$167.40	$279.00	£44.50	£133.50	£222.50
The Groo Adventurer Trade paperback (1991), reprints issues #1-4				£1.00	£3.00	£5.00
The Groo Adventurer Trade paperback (Mar 1992), reprints issues #5-8				£1.10	£3.00	£5.00
The Groo Carnival Trade paperback (Apr 1992), reprints issues #9-12, new foreword by Evanier				£1.00	£3.00	£5.00
The Groo Adventurer Trade paperback (1992), reprints issues #13-16				£1.00	£3.00	£5.00
Groo: Expose Trade paperback (Apr 1993), reprints issues #17-20				£1.00	£3.00	£5.00
Groo: Festival Trade paperback (Oct 1993), reprints issues #21-24				£1.50	£4.50	£7.50
Groo: Garden Trade paperback (Apr 1994), reprints issues #25-28				£1.50	£4.50	£7.50

Note: Evanier/Aragones scripts, Aragones art in all.

GROOTLORE
Fantagraphics,MS; 1 Mar 1989-2 Apr 1989

	$Good	$Fine	$N.Mint	£Good	£Fine	£N.Mint
1-2 ND Peter Gullerud script and art, black and white	$0.30	$0.90	$1.50	£0.20	£0.60	£1.00
Title Value:	$0.60	$1.80	$3.00	£0.40	£1.20	£2.00

GROOVY
Marvel Comics Group; 1 Mar 1968-3 Jul 1968

	$Good	$Fine	$N.Mint	£Good	£Fine	£N.Mint
1 rare in the U.K.	$5.00	$15.00	$25.00	£3.00	£9.00	£15.00
2-3 rare in the U.K.	$4.00	$12.00	$20.00	£2.00	£6.00	£10.00
Title Value:	$13.00	$39.00	$65.00	£7.00	£21.00	£35.00

Note: no CCA code on any of the comics

GROUND POUND COMIX
Blackthorne; nn Jan 1987

	$Good	$Fine	$N.Mint	£Good	£Fine	£N.Mint
nn ND 52pgs, all John Byrne reprints	$0.55	$1.65	$2.75	£0.35	£1.05	£1.75
Title Value:	$0.55	$1.65	$2.75	£0.35	£1.05	£1.75

GROUND ZERO
Eternity,MS; 1 Nov 1991-4 Feb 1992

	$Good	$Fine	$N.Mint	£Good	£Fine	£N.Mint
1-4 ND	$0.45	$1.35	$2.25	£0.30	£0.90	£1.50
Title Value:	$1.80	$5.40	$9.00	£1.20	£3.60	£6.00

GROUP LARUE, THE
Innovation,MS; 1 Sep 1989-3 Nov 1989

	$Good	$Fine	$N.Mint	£Good	£Fine	£N.Mint
1-3 ND Mike Baron plot, colour	$0.30	$0.90	$1.50	£0.20	£0.60	£1.00
Title Value:	$0.90	$2.70	$4.50	£0.60	£1.80	£3.00

GRUNTS
Mirage Studios,OS; 1 Nov 1987
(see Teenage Mutant Ninja Turtles)

	$Good	$Fine	$N.Mint	£Good	£Fine	£N.Mint
1 ND Triceraton story	$0.90	$2.70	$4.50	£0.60	£1.80	£3.00
Title Value:	$0.90	$2.70	$4.50	£0.60	£1.80	£3.00

GUARDIANS OF METROPOLIS, THE
DC Comics,MS; 1 Nov 1994-4 Feb 1995

	$Good	$Fine	$N.Mint	£Good	£Fine	£N.Mint
1-4 The Guardian and The Newsboy Legion	$0.25	$0.75	$1.25	£0.15	£0.45	£0.75
Title Value:	$1.00	$3.00	$5.00	£0.60	£1.80	£3.00

GUARDIANS OF THE GALAXY
Marvel Comics Group; 1 Jul 1990-62 Jul 1995
(see Defenders, Marvel Team Up)

	$Good	$Fine	$N.Mint	£Good	£Fine	£N.Mint
1 ND Valentino art begins	$0.80	$2.40	$4.00	£0.80	£2.40	£4.00
2-3 ND	$0.50	$1.50	$2.50	£0.50	£1.50	£2.50
4-6 ND	$0.40	$1.20	$2.00	£0.40	£1.20	£2.00
7 ND George Perez inks (1st Marvel work for some years)	$0.40	$1.20	$2.00	£0.40	£1.20	£2.00
8 ND	$0.40	$1.20	$2.00	£0.40	£1.20	£2.00
9-10 ND World of Mutants	$0.40	$1.20	$2.00	£0.40	£1.20	£2.00
11-12 ND World of Mutants	$0.30	$0.90	$1.50	£0.30	£0.90	£1.50
13-14 Ghost Rider of the 31st Century appears	$0.30	$0.90	$1.50	£0.30	£0.90	£1.50
15	$0.30	$0.90	$1.50	£0.30	£0.90	£1.50
16 DS Martinex loses hand	$0.30	$0.90	$1.50	£0.20	£0.60	£1.00
17 new direction for title, 1st appearance Crazy Nate	$0.30	$0.90	$1.50	£0.20	£0.60	£1.00
18 Crazy Nate undergoes operation on eye - it is replaced with a bionic one; thought at one point to be the 1st origin of Cable but now disproved	$0.30	$0.90	$1.50	£0.20	£0.60	£1.00
19 1st appearance Talon, Crazy Nate shown with glowing eye (thought at one point to be proof that Nathan Summers is Cable and now not the case)	$0.30	$0.90	$1.50	£0.20	£0.60	£1.00
20	$0.30	$0.90	$1.50	£0.20	£0.60	£1.00
21 $1.25 cover begins	$0.30	$0.90	$1.50	£0.20	£0.60	£1.00
22 ND Starhawk returns	$0.30	$0.90	$1.50	£0.20	£0.60	£1.00
23 Starhawk appears, Mark Texeira art	$0.30	$0.90	$1.50	£0.20	£0.60	£1.00
24 LD in the U.K. Silver Surfer appears	$0.30	$0.90	$1.50	£0.25	£0.75	£1.25
25 LD in the U.K. 48pgs, Silver Surfer appears, foil-stamped cover ("prismatic")	$0.70	$2.10	$3.50	£0.40	£1.20	£2.00
25 2nd printing, non foil-cover	$0.45	$1.35	$2.25	£0.30	£0.90	£1.50
26 "secret" origin told	$0.25	$0.75	$1.25	£0.15	£0.45	£0.75
27-28 Infinity War X-over	$0.25	$0.75	$1.25	£0.15	£0.45	£0.75
29 Infinity War X-over, Dr. Octopus appears	$0.25	$0.75	$1.25	£0.15	£0.45	£0.75
30	$0.25	$0.75	$1.25	£0.15	£0.45	£0.75
31 Captain America appears	$0.25	$0.75	$1.25	£0.15	£0.45	£0.75
32-33 Dr. Strange appears	$0.25	$0.75	$1.25	£0.15	£0.45	£0.75
34-36	$0.25	$0.75	$1.25	£0.15	£0.45	£0.75
37 Dr. Doom appears	$0.25	$0.75	$1.25	£0.15	£0.45	£0.75
38 Inhumans appear	$0.25	$0.75	$1.25	£0.15	£0.45	£0.75
39 48pgs, Rancor vs. Dr. Doom (wearing Wolverine's exo-skeleton)	$0.50	$1.50	$2.50	£0.30	£0.90	£1.50
40-43 Thor of 31st Century appears	$0.25	$0.75	$1.25	£0.15	£0.45	£0.75
44-47	$0.25	$0.75	$1.25	£0.15	£0.45	£0.75
48 with free Spiderman and his Deadly Foes card sheet	$0.25	$0.75	$1.25	£0.15	£0.45	£0.75
49	$0.25	$0.75	$1.25	£0.15	£0.45	£0.75
50 ND Direct Market Edition - 48pgs, foil embossed cover; Future History part 1, continued in Galactic Guardians #1	$0.50	$1.50	$2.50	£0.30	£0.90	£1.50
50 Newsstand edition	$0.40	$1.20	$2.00	£0.25	£0.75	£1.25
51-53	$0.25	$0.75	$1.25	£0.15	£0.45	£0.75
54 Spiderman appears	$0.25	$0.75	$1.25	£0.15	£0.45	£0.75
55-59	$0.25	$0.75	$1.25	£0.15	£0.45	£0.75
60 30th Century Silver Surfer appears	$0.25	$0.75	$1.25	£0.15	£0.45	£0.75
61	$0.25	$0.75	$1.25	£0.15	£0.45	£0.75
62 48pgs	$0.45	$1.35	$2.25	£0.30	£0.90	£1.50
Title Value:	$20.30	$60.90	$101.50	£14.90	£44.70	£74.50

The Quest for the Shield (Apr 1992)

	$Good	$Fine	$N.Mint	£Good	£Fine	£N.Mint
Trade paperback, reprints issues #1-6, new cover by Jim Valentino				£1.40	£4.20	£7.00

GUARDIANS OF THE GALAXY ANNUAL
Marvel Comics Group; 1 Jul 1991-present

	$Good	$Fine	$N.Mint	£Good	£Fine	£N.Mint
1 ND The Korvac Quest, continued from Silver Surfer Annual #4	$0.45	$1.35	$2.25	£0.30	£0.90	£1.50
2 ND The System Bytes part 4 (of 4), Ghost Rider and Firelord appear, continued from Wonder Man Annual #1	$0.45	$1.35	$2.25	£0.30	£0.90	£1.50
3 ND 64pgs, pre-bagged with trading card introducing Cuchulain	$0.45	$1.35	$2.25	£0.30	£0.90	£1.50
4 ND 64pgs	$0.45	$1.35	$2.25	£0.30	£0.90	£1.50
Title Value:	$1.80	$5.40	$9.00	£1.20	£3.60	£6.00

GUMBY 3-D
Blackthorne; (3-D Series #10,#14,#17,#21,#28,#33,#38); 1 Oct 1986-7 Apr 1988

	$Good	$Fine	$N.Mint	£Good	£Fine	£N.Mint
1 ND all come with 3-D bound-in glasses (25% less if without glasses)	$0.55	$1.65	$2.75	£0.35	£1.05	£1.75
2-7 ND	$0.55	$1.65	$2.75	£0.35	£1.05	£1.75
Title Value:	$3.85	$11.55	$19.25	£2.45	£7.35	£12.25

GUMBY'S SUMMER FUN SPECIAL
Comico; 1 Jul 1987

	$Good	$Fine	$N.Mint	£Good	£Fine	£N.Mint
1 ND Bob Burden script, Art Adams art and cover	$0.80	$2.40	$4.00	£0.50	£1.50	£2.50
Title Value:	$0.80	$2.40	$4.00	£0.50	£1.50	£2.50

GUMBY'S WINTER FUN SPECIAL
Comico; 1 Dec 1988

	$Good	$Fine	$N.Mint	£Good	£Fine	£N.Mint
1 ND 40pgs, Steve Purcell script, Art Adams art	$0.70	$2.10	$3.50	£0.45	£1.35	£2.25
Title Value:	$0.70	$2.10	$3.50	£0.45	£1.35	£2.25

GUN FURY
Aircel; 1 Jan 1988-10 1988

	$Good	$Fine	$N.Mint	£Good	£Fine	£N.Mint
1 ND	$1.05	$3.15	$5.25	£0.70	£2.10	£3.50
2-3 ND	$0.70	$2.10	$3.50	£0.45	£1.35	£2.25
4-10 ND	$0.45	$1.35	$2.25	£0.30	£0.90	£1.50
Title Value:	$5.60	$16.80	$28.00	£3.70	£11.10	£18.50

GUN FURY RETURNS
Aircel,MS; 1 Aug 1990-4 Nov 1990

	$Good	$Fine	$N.Mint	£Good	£Fine	£N.Mint
1-4 ND	$0.40	$1.20	$2.00	£0.25	£0.75	£1.25
Title Value:	$1.60	$4.80	$8.00	£1.00	£3.00	£5.00

GUN RUNNER
Marvel UK,MS; 1 Oct 1993-3 Dec 1993

	$Good	$Fine	$N.Mint	£Good	£Fine	£N.Mint
1 pre-bagged with trading cards, Dan Abnett/Andy Lanning script begins; Terry Clarke art; Ghost Rider appears						
	$0.50	$1.60	$2.70	£0.35	£1.05	£1.80
2 Ghost Rider appears; Anthony Williams art						
	$0.40	$1.20	$2.00	£0.25	£0.75	£1.25
3 Anthony Williams art						
	$0.40	$1.20	$2.00	£0.25	£0.75	£1.25
Title Value:	$1.30	$4.00	$6.70	£0.85	£2.55	£4.30

Note: originally solicited as a six issue mini-series

GUNFIGHTERS, THE
Charlton; 51 Oct 1966-85 Jul 1984
(formerly Kid Montana #1-50)

	$Good	$Fine	$N.Mint	£Good	£Fine	£N.Mint
51-52 distributed in the U.K.						
	$0.90	$2.70	$4.50	£0.60	£1.80	£3.00
53-70 distributed in the U.K.						
	$0.80	$2.40	$4.00	£0.50	£1.50	£2.50
71-80 distributed in the U.K.						
	$0.60	$1.80	$3.00	£0.40	£1.20	£2.00
81-85 distributed in the U.K.						
	$0.45	$1.35	$2.25	£0.30	£0.90	£1.50
Title Value:	$24.45	$73.35	$122.25	£15.70	£47.10	£78.50

Note: Williamson reprints #53,54

GUNFIRE
DC Comics; 0 Oct 1994; 1 May 1994-13 Jun 1995

	$Good	$Fine	$N.Mint	£Good	£Fine	£N.Mint
0 (Oct 1994) Zero Hour X-over, origin retold						
	$0.40	$1.20	$2.00	£0.25	£0.75	£1.25
1 Len Wein script, Steve Irwin and Brian Garvey art						
	$0.40	$1.20	$2.00	£0.25	£0.75	£1.25
2-5	$0.30	$0.90	$1.50	£0.20	£0.60	£1.00
6 new costume	$0.30	$0.90	$1.50	£0.20	£0.60	£1.00
7-13	$0.30	$0.90	$1.50	£0.20	£0.60	£1.00
Title Value:	$4.40	$13.20	$22.00	£2.90	£8.70	£14.50

GUNHAWKS, THE
Marvel Comics Group; 1 Oct 1972-7 Oct 1973

	$Good	$Fine	$N.Mint	£Good	£Fine	£N.Mint
1 ND Reno Jones and Kid Cassidy begin; Gary Friedrich script and Sid Shores art begins						
	$0.80	$2.40	$4.00	£0.50	£1.50	£2.50
2 ND	$0.55	$1.65	$2.75	£0.35	£1.05	£1.75
3-5 ND	$0.45	$1.35	$2.25	£0.30	£0.90	£1.50
6 ND Kid Cassidy dies; Dick Ayers and Vince Coletta art						
	$0.45	$1.35	$2.25	£0.30	£0.90	£1.50
7 titled Reno Jones, Gunhawk; Gardner Fox script (he of classic Silver Age DC J.L.A. tales)						
	$0.40	$1.20	$2.00	£0.25	£0.75	£1.25
Title Value:	$3.55	$10.65	$17.75	£2.30	£6.90	£11.50

GUNHED
Viz,MS; 1 Jan 1991-3 May 1991

	$Good	$Fine	$N.Mint	£Good	£Fine	£N.Mint
1-3 ND 48pgs, 1st full colour series from Viz, measures 7" x 9", squarebound; story and art by Kia Asamiya						
	$1.05	$3.15	$5.25	£0.70	£2.10	£3.50
Title Value:	$3.15	$9.45	$15.75	£2.10	£6.30	£10.50
Graphic Novel (Dec 1991), collects mini-series				£1.90	£5.70	£9.50

GUNMASTER
Charlton; 84 Jul 1965-88 Mar/Apr 1966; 89 Oct 1967
(becomes Judomaster)

	$Good	$Fine	$N.Mint	£Good	£Fine	£N.Mint
84-86 distributed in the U.K.						
	$1.50	$4.50	$9.00	£1.00	£3.00	£6.00
87-89 distributed in the U.K.						
	$1.20	$3.60	$6.00	£0.80	£2.40	£4.00
Title Value:	$8.10	$24.30	$45.00	£5.40	£16.20	£30.00

GUNS OF SHAR-PEI
Caliber Press,MS; 1 Dec 1991-3 Mar 1992

	$Good	$Fine	$N.Mint	£Good	£Fine	£N.Mint
1-3 ND black and white						
	$0.55	$1.65	$2.75	£0.35	£1.05	£1.75
Title Value:	$1.65	$4.95	$8.25	£1.05	£3.15	£5.25

GUNSMITH CATS
Dark Horse; 1 Apr 1995-10 Jan 1996

	$Good	$Fine	$N.Mint	£Good	£Fine	£N.Mint
1-10 ND Kenichi Sonada script and art (translated by Dana Lewis and Toren Smith)						
	$0.60	$1.80	$3.00	£0.40	£1.20	£2.00
Title Value:	$6.00	$18.00	$30.00	£4.00	£12.00	£20.00

GUNSMOKE WESTERN
Atlas/Marvel Comics Group; 32 Dec 1955-77 Jul 1963 (Atlas #32-35)

	$Good	$Fine	$N.Mint	£Good	£Fine	£N.Mint
32 scarce in the U.K. Wyatt Earp and Kid Colt begin						
	$11.00	$34.00	$78.75	£7.50	£22.50	£52.50
33 scarce in the U.K. Williamson art						
	$7.50	$22.50	$52.50	£5.00	£15.00	£35.00
34 scarce in the U.K. Matt Baker art						
	$5.25	$15.50	$36.75	£3.50	£10.50	£24.50
35-36 scarce in the U.K. Williamson art						
	$7.50	$22.50	$52.50	£5.00	£15.00	£35.00
37-39 scarce in the U.K.						
	$6.00	$18.00	$36.00	£4.00	£12.00	£24.00
40 scarce in the U.K. Williamson art						
	$6.75	$20.00	$40.50	£4.50	£13.50	£27.00
41-49 scarce in the U.K.						
	$3.75	$11.00	$22.50	£2.50	£7.50	£15.00
50 scarce in the U.K. Reed Crandall art						
	$3.75	$11.00	$22.50	£2.50	£7.50	£15.00
51-55 scarce in the U.K.						
	$3.00	$9.00	$18.00	£2.00	£6.00	£12.00
56 scarce in the U.K. Matt Baker art						
	$3.75	$11.00	$22.50	£2.50	£7.50	£15.00
57 scarce in the U.K. 1st appearance Two Gun Kid by Stan Lee and Marie Severin						
	$4.50	$13.50	$27.00	£3.00	£9.00	£18.00
1st official distribution in the U.K.						
58 scarce in the U.K.						
	$3.00	$9.00	$18.00	£2.00	£6.00	£12.00
59-60 rare in the U.K.						
	$4.50	$13.50	$27.00	£3.00	£9.00	£18.00
61-64 rare in the U.K.						
	$3.75	$11.00	$22.50	£2.50	£7.50	£15.00
65-71	$2.25	$6.75	$13.50	£1.50	£4.50	£9.00
72 origin Kid Colt retold						
	$2.25	$6.75	$13.50	£1.50	£4.50	£9.00
73-77	$2.25	$6.75	$13.50	£1.50	£4.50	£9.00
Title Value:	$180.50	$538.25	$1123.50	£120.50	£361.50	£749.00

Note: issues after around 1958 distributed on the news-stands in the U.K. though irregularly before official distribution

ARTISTS
Kirby art in 59, 32, 36, 65-67, 69-71, 73, 77. Ditko art in 66.

FEATURES
Kid Colt in all issues (origin in 72); Two-Gun Kid in 59-63, 66; Wyatt Earp in 58.

GUTTER RAT
Gauntlet Comics,MS; 1 Jul 1993

	$Good	$Fine	$N.Mint	£Good	£Fine	£N.Mint
1 ND	$0.60	$1.80	$3.00	£0.40	£1.20	£2.00
Title Value:	$0.60	$1.80	$3.00	£0.40	£1.20	£2.00

Note: cancelled after 1 issue

GUY GARDNER
DC Comics; 0 Oct 1994; 1 Oct 1992-present
(see Green Lantern #59) (becomes Guy Gardner: Warrior with #17)

	$Good	$Fine	$N.Mint	£Good	£Fine	£N.Mint
0 (Oct 1994) Zero Hour X-over, Guy Gardner's new powers revealed						
	$0.40	$1.20	$2.00	£0.25	£0.75	£1.25
1-4	$0.30	$0.90	$1.50	£0.20	£0.60	£1.00
5-7 Hal Jordan guest stars						
	$0.30	$0.90	$1.50	£0.20	£0.60	£1.00
8 Lobo vs. Guy Gardner						
	$0.30	$0.90	$1.50	£0.20	£0.60	£1.00
9-10	$0.30	$0.90	$1.50	£0.20	£0.60	£1.00
11-13 Guy Gardner: Year One						
	$0.30	$0.90	$1.50	£0.20	£0.60	£1.00
14 Guy Gardner: Year One, X-over Justice League America #72						
	$0.30	$0.90	$1.50	£0.20	£0.60	£1.00
15-16	$0.30	$0.90	$1.50	£0.20	£0.60	£1.00
17 Guy Gardner renames himself Warrior (1st appearance)						
	$0.30	$0.90	$1.50	£0.20	£0.60	£1.00
18	$0.30	$0.90	$1.50	£0.20	£0.60	£1.00
19 Golden Age Green Lantern appears						
	$0.30	$0.90	$1.50	£0.20	£0.60	£1.00
20 Green Lantern, Golden Age Green Lantern, Martian Manhunter, The Ray, Wonder Woman, Darkstar and Captain Atom appear						
	$0.30	$0.90	$1.50	£0.20	£0.60	£1.00
21 Green Lantern vs. Warrior						
	$0.30	$0.90	$1.50	£0.20	£0.60	£1.00
22-23	$0.30	$0.90	$1.50	£0.20	£0.60	£1.00
24 Zero Hour X-over						
	$0.30	$0.90	$1.50	£0.20	£0.60	£1.00
25 48pgs, Adam Hughes art featured						
	$0.30	$0.90	$1.50	£0.20	£0.60	£1.00
26-27	$0.30	$0.90	$1.50	£0.20	£0.60	£1.00
28 story concluded in Green Lantern #60						
	$0.30	$0.90	$1.50	£0.20	£0.60	£1.00
29	$0.30	$0.90	$1.50	£0.20	£0.60	£1.00
29 ND Collector's Edition, barn-door style fold-out cover						
	$0.60	$1.80	$3.00	£0.40	£1.20	£2.00
30 story continued from Action Comics #709						
	$0.30	$0.90	$1.50	£0.20	£0.60	£1.00
31 Supergirl and Sentinel (the former Golden Age Green Lantern) guest-star						
	$0.35	$1.05	$1.75	£0.25	£0.75	£1.25
32 Way of the Warrior part 1, continued in Justice League America #101						
	$0.35	$1.05	$1.75	£0.25	£0.75	£1.25
33 Way of the Warrior part 4, continued in Justice League America #102						
	$0.35	$1.05	$1.75	£0.25	£0.75	£1.25
34 Way of the Warrior part 7 (conclusion)						
	$0.35	$1.05	$1.75	£0.25	£0.75	£1.25
35	$0.35	$1.05	$1.75	£0.25	£0.75	£1.25
36 Underworld Unleashed tie-in						
	$0.35	$1.05	$1.75	£0.25	£0.75	£1.25
37 Underworld Unleashed tie-in, continued in Darkstars #37						
	$0.35	$1.05	$1.75	£0.25	£0.75	£1.25
38-40	$0.35	$1.05	$1.75	£0.25	£0.75	£1.25
Title Value:	$13.50	$40.50	$67.50	£9.15	£27.45	£45.75

GUY GARDNER: REBORN
DC Comics,MS; 1 Jul 1992-3 Sep 1992

	$Good	$Fine	$N.Mint	£Good	£Fine	£N.Mint
1 ND 48pgs, aftermath of losing to the Hal Jordan Green Lantern in Green Lantern #25						
	$0.90	$2.70	$4.50	£0.60	£1.80	£3.00
2-3 ND 48pgs, Lobo appears						
	$0.90	$2.70	$4.50	£0.60	£1.80	£3.00
Title Value:	$2.70	$8.10	$13.50	£1.80	£5.40	£9.00

	$Good	$Fine	$N.Mint	£Good	£Fine	£N.Mint

GUY GARDNER: WARRIOR ANNUAL
DC Comics; 1 Jul 1995-present

	$Good	$Fine	$N.Mint	£Good	£Fine	£N.Mint
1 56pgs, Year One						
	$0.80	$2.40	$4.00	£0.50	£1.50	£2.50
Title Value:	$0.80	$2.40	$4.00	£0.50	£1.50	£2.50

H

H.A.R.D. CORPS, THE
Valiant; 1 Nov 1992-30 May 1995

	$Good	$Fine	$N.Mint	£Good	£Fine	£N.Mint
1 gatefold cover by Jim Lee						
	$0.50	$1.50	$2.50	£0.30	£0.90	£1.50
1 Gold Logo Edition						
	$1.50	$4.50	$7.50	£1.00	£3.00	£5.00
2-3	$0.50	$1.50	$2.50	£0.30	£0.90	£1.50
4	$0.40	$1.20	$2.00	£0.25	£0.75	£1.25
5 Bloodshot appears						
	$0.40	$1.20	$2.00	£0.25	£0.75	£1.25
5 Comic Defense System Pro-Skins Giveaway - red logo, no cover price						
	$0.80	$2.40	$4.00	£0.50	£1.50	£2.50
6	$0.40	$1.20	$2.00	£0.25	£0.75	£1.25
7 Hotshot joins						
	$0.40	$1.20	$2.00	£0.25	£0.75	£1.25
8-9	$0.40	$1.20	$2.00	£0.25	£0.75	£1.25
10 Turok, Dinosaur Hunter appears						
	$0.40	$1.20	$2.00	£0.25	£0.75	£1.25
11 Harbinger appear						
	$0.40	$1.20	$2.00	£0.25	£0.75	£1.25
12-16	$0.40	$1.20	$2.00	£0.25	£0.75	£1.25
17 H.A.R.D. Corps vs. Armorines						
	$0.40	$1.20	$2.00	£0.25	£0.75	£1.25
18-19	$0.40	$1.20	$2.00	£0.25	£0.75	£1.25
20 guest stars Harbinger; continued from Harbinger #31						
	$0.40	$1.20	$2.00	£0.25	£0.75	£1.25
21-22	$0.40	$1.20	$2.00	£0.25	£0.75	£1.25
23 Chaos Effect tie-in						
	$0.40	$1.20	$2.00	£0.25	£0.75	£1.25
24-30	$0.40	$1.20	$2.00	£0.25	£0.75	£1.25
Title Value:	$14.60	$43.80	$73.00	£9.15	£27.45	£45.75

note: all Non-Distributed on the news-stands in the U.K.

H.P. LOVECRAFT'S CTHULHU
Millennium; 1 Feb 1992-3 Apr 1992

	$Good	$Fine	$N.Mint	£Good	£Fine	£N.Mint
1-3 ND bound-in trading card						
	$0.45	$1.35	$2.25	£0.30	£0.90	£1.50
Title Value:	$1.35	$4.05	$6.75	£0.90	£2.70	£4.50

H.P. LOVECRAFT'S CTHULHU: FESTIVAL OF DEATH
Millennium,MS; 1 Sep 1993-3 May 1994

	$Good	$Fine	$N.Mint	£Good	£Fine	£N.Mint
1-3 ND Roy Thomas script						
	$0.45	$1.35	$2.25	£0.30	£0.90	£1.50
Title Value:	$1.35	$4.05	$6.75	£0.90	£2.70	£4.50

H.P. LOVECRAFT'S CTHULHU: THE FESTIVAL
Millennium,OS; nn Jun 1995

	$Good	$Fine	$N.Mint	£Good	£Fine	£N.Mint
nn ND 80pgs, David Mack script						
	$2.40	$7.00	$12.00	£1.60	£4.80	£8.00
Title Value:	$2.40	$7.00	$12.00	£1.60	£4.80	£8.00

H.P. LOVECRAFT'S CTHULHU: THE HOUNDS OF TINDALOS
Millennium,MS; 1 Jul 1992-2 Aug 1992

	$Good	$Fine	$N.Mint	£Good	£Fine	£N.Mint
1-2 ND	$0.45	$1.35	$2.25	£0.30	£0.90	£1.50
Title Value:	$0.90	$2.70	$4.50	£0.60	£1.80	£3.00

HACKER FILES, THE
DC Comics,MS; 1 Aug 1992-12 Jul 1993

	$Good	$Fine	$N.Mint	£Good	£Fine	£N.Mint
1 Mark Buckingham inks; computer-generated cover art begins						
	$0.25	$0.75	$1.25	£0.15	£0.45	£0.75
2-4 Mark Buckingham inks						
	$0.25	$0.75	$1.25	£0.15	£0.45	£0.75
5 1st appearance of Barbara Gordon as Oracle; Mark Buckingham inks						
	$0.25	$0.75	$1.25	£0.15	£0.45	£0.75
6 Barbara Gordon appears as Oracle, Green Lantern guest stars; Mark Buckingham inks						
	$0.25	$0.75	$1.25	£0.15	£0.45	£0.75
7-10 Mark Buckingham inks						
	$0.25	$0.75	$1.25	£0.15	£0.45	£0.75
11-12 Justice League appear; Mark Buckingham inks						
	$0.25	$0.75	$1.25	£0.15	£0.45	£0.75
Title Value:	$3.00	$9.00	$15.00	£1.80	£5.40	£9.00

HAGAR THE HORRIBLE
ACG,OS; 0 Jul 1995

	$Good	$Fine	$N.Mint	£Good	£Fine	£N.Mint
0 ND Frank Roberge script and art						
	$0.40	$1.20	$2.00	£0.25	£0.75	£1.25
Title Value:	$0.40	$1.20	$2.00	£0.25	£0.75	£1.25

HAIRY CROWS
Caliber Press; 1 Dec 1991

	$Good	$Fine	$N.Mint	£Good	£Fine	£N.Mint
1 ND horror anthology						
	$0.55	$1.65	$2.75	£0.35	£1.05	£1.75
Title Value:	$0.55	$1.65	$2.75	£0.35	£1.05	£1.75

HALLOWEEN HORROR
Eclipse; 1 Oct 1987
(Seduction of the Innocent #7)

	$Good	$Fine	$N.Mint	£Good	£Fine	£N.Mint
1 ND pre-Code horror reprints, colour						
	$0.30	$0.90	$1.50	£0.20	£0.60	£1.00
Title Value:	$0.30	$0.90	$1.50	£0.20	£0.60	£1.00

HALLOWEEN TERROR
Eternity,OS; 1 Sep 1990

	$Good	$Fine	$N.Mint	£Good	£Fine	£N.Mint
1 ND horror anthology, black and white						
	$0.40	$1.20	$2.00	£0.25	£0.75	£1.25
Title Value:	$0.40	$1.20	$2.00	£0.25	£0.75	£1.25

HAMMER HORROR
Marvel Comics Group,Magazine; 1 Apr 1995-5 1995?

	$Good	$Fine	$N.Mint	£Good	£Fine	£N.Mint
1 ND the history of Hammer films told in photo art						
	$1.05	$3.15	$5.25	£0.70	£2.10	£3.50
2-5 ND	$1.05	$3.15	$5.25	£0.70	£2.10	£3.50
Title Value:	$5.25	$15.75	$26.25	£3.50	£10.50	£17.50

HAMMER OF GOD
First,MS; 1 Feb 1990-4 May 1990

	$Good	$Fine	$N.Mint	£Good	£Fine	£N.Mint
1-3 ND	$0.40	$1.20	$2.00	£0.25	£0.75	£1.25
Title Value:	$1.20	$3.60	$6.00	£0.75	£2.25	£3.75

HAMMER OF GOD: BUTCH
Dark Horse,MS; 1 Apr 1994-3 Jun 1994

	$Good	$Fine	$N.Mint	£Good	£Fine	£N.Mint
1-3 ND Mike Baron script						
	$0.45	$1.35	$2.25	£0.30	£0.90	£1.50
Title Value:	$1.35	$4.05	$6.75	£0.90	£2.70	£4.50

HAMMER OF GOD: PENTATHLON
Dark Horse,OS; 1 Dec 1993

	$Good	$Fine	$N.Mint	£Good	£Fine	£N.Mint
1 ND	$0.45	$1.35	$2.25	£0.30	£0.90	£1.50
Title Value:	$0.45	$1.35	$2.25	£0.30	£0.90	£1.50

HAMMER OF GOD: SWORD OF JUSTICE
First,MS; 1 Feb 1991-2 Mar 1991

	$Good	$Fine	$N.Mint	£Good	£Fine	£N.Mint
1-2 ND 48pgs	$1.00	$3.00	$5.00	£0.65	£1.95	£3.25
Title Value:	$2.00	$6.00	$10.00	£1.30	£3.90	£6.50

HAMMERLOCKE
DC Comics,MS; 1 Sep 1992-9 May 1993

	$Good	$Fine	$N.Mint	£Good	£Fine	£N.Mint
1 48pgs	$0.30	$0.90	$1.50	£0.20	£0.60	£1.00
2-9	$0.25	$0.75	$1.25	£0.15	£0.45	£0.75

Grips (2nd) #7

Gunhawks #6

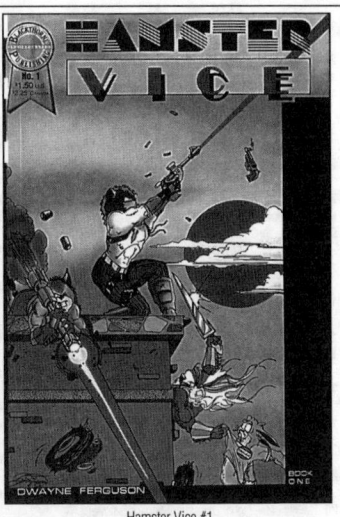

Hamster Vice #1

	$Good	$Fine	$N.Mint	£Good	£Fine	£N.Mint
Title Value:	$2.30	$6.90	$11.50	£1.40	£4.20	£7.00

HAMSTER VICE
Blackthorne; 1 Jun 1986-9 1987
1 ND Miami Vice parody begins; black and white

	$Good	$Fine	$N.Mint	£Good	£Fine	£N.Mint
	$0.40	$1.20	$2.00	£0.25	£0.75	£1.25
2-9 ND	$0.30	$0.90	$1.50	£0.20	£0.60	£1.00
Title Value:	$2.80	$8.40	$14.00	£1.85	£5.55	£9.25

HAMSTER VICE IN 3-D
Blackthorne; (3-D Series #12,15); 1 Nov 1986-2 Dec 1986
1-2 ND with bound-in 3-D glasses (25% less without glasses)

	$Good	$Fine	$N.Mint	£Good	£Fine	£N.Mint
	$0.55	$1.65	$2.75	£0.35	£1.05	£1.75
Title Value:	$1.10	$3.30	$5.50	£0.70	£2.10	£3.50

HAND OF FATE
Eclipse,MS; 1 Feb 1988-3 Apr 1988
1-2 ND colour

	$Good	$Fine	$N.Mint	£Good	£Fine	£N.Mint
	$0.40	$1.20	$2.00	£0.25	£0.75	£1.25
3 ND black & white	$0.40	$1.20	$2.00	£0.25	£0.75	£1.25
Title Value:	$1.20	$3.60	$6.00	£0.75	£2.25	£3.75

HANDBOOK TO THE MALIBU ULTRAVERSE
Marvel Comics Group,MS; 1 Mar 1996-2 Apr 1996
1-2 ND 48pgs, information and character biographies

	$Good	$Fine	$N.Mint	£Good	£Fine	£N.Mint
	$0.60	$1.80	$3.00	£0.40	£1.20	£2.00
Title Value:	$1.20	$3.60	$6.00	£0.80	£2.40	£4.00

HANDS OF THE DRAGON
Atlas; 1 Jun 1975
1 scarce though distributed in the U.K.

	$Good	$Fine	$N.Mint	£Good	£Fine	£N.Mint
	$0.25	$0.75	$1.25	£0.15	£0.45	£0.75
Title Value:	$0.25	$0.75	$1.25	£0.15	£0.45	£0.75

HANNA-BARBERA SPOTLIGHT
Marvel Comics Group; 1 Sep 1978-4 Mar 1979
1 ND Huckleberry Hound

	$Good	$Fine	$N.Mint	£Good	£Fine	£N.Mint
	$0.15	$0.45	$0.75	£0.10	£0.35	£0.60
2 ND Quick Draw McGraw						
	$0.15	$0.45	$0.75	£0.10	£0.35	£0.60
3 ND The Jetsons	$0.15	$0.45	$0.75	£0.10	£0.35	£0.60
4 ND Magilla Gorilla						
	$0.15	$0.45	$0.75	£0.10	£0.35	£0.60
Title Value:	$0.60	$1.80	$3.00	£0.40	£1.40	£2.40

HANNA-BARBERA SUPER TV HEROES
Gold Key; 1 Apr 1968-7 Oct 1969
1 Birdman, Herculoids, Mighty Mightor, Young Sampson begin

	$Good	$Fine	$N.Mint	£Good	£Fine	£N.Mint
	$18.00	$52.50	$90.00	£11.00	£33.00	£55.00
2	$13.00	$40.00	$80.00	£7.50	£22.50	£45.00
3 Space Ghost appears						
	$12.50	$38.00	$75.00	£7.50	£22.50	£45.00
4	$12.50	$38.00	$75.00	£7.50	£22.50	£45.00
5-7 Space Ghost appears						
	$12.50	$38.00	$75.00	£7.50	£22.50	£45.00
Title Value:	$93.50	$282.50	$545.00	£56.00	£168.00	£325.00

Note: issues patchily distributed on the news-stands in the U.K.

HAPPY BIRTHDAY GNATRAT
Prelude; 1 1986
(see Gnatrat, Darerat)
1 ND Batman #400 parody, Mark Martin art

	$Good	$Fine	$N.Mint	£Good	£Fine	£N.Mint
	$0.70	$2.10	$3.50	£0.45	£1.35	£2.25
Title Value:	$0.70	$2.10	$3.50	£0.45	£1.35	£2.25

HARBINGER
Valiant; 1 Jan 1992-41 Jun 1995
0 rare in the U.K. (red cover); available from Valiant in return for coupons #1-6; print run estimated at
approximately 5000 copies

	$Good	$Fine	$N.Mint	£Good	£Fine	£N.Mint
	$3.00	$9.00	$15.00	£2.00	£6.00	£10.00

0 (blue cover); available from Valiant, a separate item poly-bagged together with Harbinger trade paperback

	$1.00	$3.00	$5.00	£0.30	£0.90	£1.50

1 scarce in the U.K. (with coupon intact. Less approx. 30% without coupon for issues #1-6)

	$2.40	$7.00	$12.00	£1.60	£4.80	£8.00
2 with coupon	$1.40	$4.20	$7.00	£1.00	£3.00	£5.00
3 with coupon	$1.20	$3.60	$6.00	£0.80	£2.40	£4.00

4 scarce in the U.K. with coupon

	$1.40	$4.20	$7.00	£1.00	£3.00	£5.00

5 Sting vs. Solar, Man of the Atom; with coupon

	$1.20	$3.60	$6.00	£0.80	£2.40	£4.00

6 scarce in the U.K. Torque dies; with coupon

	$0.70	$2.10	$3.50	£0.50	£1.50	£2.50
7	$0.70	$2.10	$3.50	£0.50	£1.50	£2.50
8 Unity: Chapter 8	$0.70	$2.10	$3.50	£0.50	£1.50	£2.50

9 Unity: Chapter 9, Magnus Robot Fighter appears, Walt Simonson cover

	$0.70	$2.10	$3.50	£0.50	£1.50	£2.50

10 1st appearance H.A.R.D. Corps

	$0.70	$2.10	$3.50	£0.50	£1.50	£2.50

11 1st full appearance H.A.R.D. Corps

	$0.50	$1.50	$2.50	£0.30	£0.90	£1.50
12-13	$0.50	$1.50	$2.50	£0.30	£0.90	£1.50

14 1st appearance Stronghold (cameo)

	$0.50	$1.50	$2.50	£0.30	£0.90	£1.50

15 1st full appearance Stronghold and Livewire

	$0.50	$1.50	$2.50	£0.30	£0.90	£1.50
16-21	$0.40	$1.20	$2.00	£0.25	£0.75	£1.25

22 Archer & Armstrong guest-star

	$0.40	$1.20	$2.00	£0.25	£0.75	£1.25

23-24 Twilight of the Eighth Day story

	$0.40	$1.20	$2.00	£0.25	£0.75	£1.25

25 Twilight of the Eighth Day story; Sting loses powers

	$Good	$Fine	$N.Mint	£Good	£Fine	£N.Mint
	$0.50	$1.50	$2.50	£0.30	£0.90	£1.50

26 titled "The New Harbingers", Sean Chen pencils begin

	$0.40	$1.20	$2.00	£0.25	£0.75	£1.25
27-28	$0.40	$1.20	$2.00	£0.25	£0.75	£1.25

29 with free Valiant Upper Deck card bound-in at centre-fold

	$0.40	$1.20	$2.00	£0.25	£0.75	£1.25
30	$0.40	$1.20	$2.00	£0.25	£0.75	£1.25

31 guest stars H.A.R.D Corps; continued in H.A.R.D. Corps #20

	$0.40	$1.20	$2.00	£0.25	£0.75	£1.25

32 guest-stars Eternal Warrior

	$0.40	$1.20	$2.00	£0.25	£0.75	£1.25

33 Dr. Eclipse appears

	$0.40	$1.20	$2.00	£0.25	£0.75	£1.25

34 Chaos Effect tie-in

	$0.40	$1.20	$2.00	£0.25	£0.75	£1.25
35-41	$0.40	$1.20	$2.00	£0.25	£0.75	£1.25
Title Value:	$28.10	$84.10	$140.50	£18.05	£54.15	£90.25

Note: a special issue "0" was made available by sending coupons from the first 6 issues of the title.

Note also: all Non-Distributed on the news-stands in the U.K.

Harbinger Trade paperback (Jan 1993)
contains issue 0 and reprints issues #1-4

				£2.00	£6.00	£10.00

(2nd print - Jul 1993), no Harbinger #0 included

				£1.30	£3.90	£6.50

Harbinger Trade paperback (Feb 1993),
as above but with blue logo specially
produced by Diamond Distributors

				£5.00	£15.00	£25.00

Harbinger #2 (Jun 1995)
Trade paperback reprints issues #6,7,10,11

				£1.30	£3.90	£6.50

HARBINGER FILES: HARADA
Valiant; 1 Jun 1994; 2 Feb 1995
1 ND story continued directly after Solar Man of the Atom #3; features the origin of Harada

	$Good	$Fine	$N.Mint	£Good	£Fine	£N.Mint
	$0.40	$1.20	$2.00	£0.25	£0.75	£1.25

2 ND the debut of The Harbinger, Harada's secret weapon

	$0.40	$1.20	$2.00	£0.25	£0.75	£1.25
Title Value:	$0.80	$2.40	$4.00	£0.50	£1.50	£2.50

HARD BOILED
Dark Horse,MS; 1 Sep 1990-3 May 1992
1 ND Frank Miller script/Geoff Darrow art begins

	$Good	$Fine	$N.Mint	£Good	£Fine	£N.Mint
	$1.05	$3.15	$5.25	£0.70	£2.10	£3.50
2-3 ND larger format - $5.95 cover						
	$1.10	$3.35	$5.62	£0.75	£2.25	£3.75
Title Value:	$3.25	$9.85	$16.49	£2.20	£6.60	£11.00

Note: magazine format

Hard Boiled Softcover Collection (Apr 1993)
reprints mini-series with new cover

				£2.00	£6.00	£10.00

Signed and Numbered Limited Edition Hardcover
(Dec 1994) with slipcase and additional sketches

				£13.50	£40.50	£67.50

Hard Boiled Trade Paperback - Dell Edition (Jul 1995)
reprints mini-series with new cover by Geof Darrow.
Note: only distributed in the U.S. not U.K.

				£2.00	£6.00	£10.00

HARD LOOKS
Dark Horse; 1 Dec 1991-10 Sep 1993
1 ND anthology series begins, Dave Gibbons art featured

	$Good	$Fine	$N.Mint	£Good	£Fine	£N.Mint
	$0.45	$1.35	$2.25	£0.30	£0.90	£1.50

2 ND David Lloyd art featured

	$0.45	$1.35	$2.25	£0.30	£0.90	£1.50

3 ND George Pratt art featured

	$0.45	$1.35	$2.25	£0.30	£0.90	£1.50
4-6 ND	$0.45	$1.35	$2.25	£0.30	£0.90	£1.50
7-9 ND	$0.55	$1.65	$2.75	£0.35	£1.05	£1.75
10 ND 40pgs	$0.70	$2.10	$3.50	£0.45	£1.35	£2.25
Title Value:	$5.05	$15.15	$25.25	£3.30	£9.90	£16.50

Andrew Vachss' Hard Looks Book One (Jun 1995)
Trade paperback reprints plus four new stories

				£2.00	£6.00	£10.00

HARDCASE
Malibu Ultraverse; 1 Jun 1993-26 Aug 1995
1 Dave Gibbons cover, 1st appearance Hardcase; Ultraverse #0 card coupon

	$Good	$Fine	$N.Mint	£Good	£Fine	£N.Mint
	$0.70	$2.10	$3.50	£0.40	£1.20	£2.00

1 Limited Edition (Jun 1993) - full hologram cover; 7,500 copies (re-offered by Marvel in Sep 1995)

	$3.00	$9.00	$15.00	£1.50	£4.50	£7.50
2	$0.50	$1.50	$2.50	£0.40	£1.20	£2.00
3	$0.40	$1.20	$2.00	£0.30	£0.90	£1.50

4 gatefold cover, Hardcase/Strangers team up

	$0.40	$1.20	$2.00	£0.30	£0.90	£1.50

5 40pgs, Rune insert

	$0.40	$1.20	$2.00	£0.30	£0.90	£1.50
6	$0.50	$1.50	$2.50	£0.30	£0.90	£1.50

7 Break Thru X-over

	$0.40	$1.20	$2.00	£0.25	£0.75	£1.25

8 Solution guest-stars; Solitaire origin by George Perez

	$0.40	$1.20	$2.00	£0.25	£0.75	£1.25

9-10 The Origin of Choice

	$0.40	$1.20	$2.00	£0.25	£0.75	£1.25
11-15	$0.40	$1.20	$2.00	£0.25	£0.75	£1.25

16 64pgs, flip-book format with Ultraverse Premiere #7

	$0.50	$1.50	$2.50	£0.30	£0.90	£1.50
17-18	$0.40	$1.20	$2.00	£0.25	£0.75	£1.25

19 prelude to Godwheel story

	$0.40	$1.20	$2.00	£0.25	£0.75	£1.25
20-22	$0.40	$1.20	$2.00	£0.25	£0.75	£1.25

23 Marvel's Loki appears, making his Ultraverse debut. The Loki Connection continues in Mantra #22

	$0.40	$1.20	$2.00	£0.25	£0.75	£1.25
24	$0.40	$1.20	$2.00	£0.25	£0.75	£1.25

	$Good	$Fine	$N.Mint	£Good	£Fine	£N.Mint
25 1st issue under Marvel Comics solicitation						
	$0.40	$1.20	$2.00	£0.25	£0.75	£1.25
26 $2.95 cover, no ads						
	$0.50	$1.50	$2.50	£0.30	£0.90	£1.50
Title Value:	$14.10	$42.30	$70.50	£8.60	£25.80	£43.00

Note: all Non-Distributed on the news-stands in the U.K.

HARDCORE
Cry For Dawn; 1 Aug 1995-present?

	$Good	$Fine	$N.Mint	£Good	£Fine	£N.Mint
1 ND adult material; black and white						
	$0.55	$1.65	$2.75	£0.35	£1.05	£1.75
Title Value:	$0.55	$1.65	$2.75	£0.35	£1.05	£1.75

HARDKORR
Aircel,OS; 1 Jun 1991

	$Good	$Fine	$N.Mint	£Good	£Fine	£N.Mint
1 ND Barry Blair script/art, black and white						
	$0.45	$1.35	$2.25	£0.30	£0.90	£1.50
Title Value:	$0.45	$1.35	$2.25	£0.30	£0.90	£1.50

HARDWARE
DC Comics/Milestone; 1 Apr 1993-present

	$Good	$Fine	$N.Mint	£Good	£Fine	£N.Mint
1	$0.30	$0.90	$1.50	£0.20	£0.60	£1.00
1 ND Direct Market Edition - pre-bagged with poster, profile, trading card and jig-saw puzzle pieces						
	$0.50	$1.50	$2.50	£0.30	£0.90	£1.50
1 ND Platinum Edition - 6,000 copies available from Diamond Distributors						
	$1.00	$3.00	$5.00	£0.80	£2.40	£4.00
2-3 bi-weekly	$0.25	$0.75	$1.25	£0.15	£0.45	£0.75
4-10	$0.25	$0.75	$1.25	£0.15	£0.45	£0.75
11 Shadow War part 1, continued in Icon #9; spot-varnished cover by Walt Simonson						
	$0.30	$0.90	$1.50	£0.20	£0.60	£1.00
12-14	$0.30	$0.90	$1.50	£0.20	£0.60	£1.00
15 part Walt Simonson cover						
	$0.30	$0.90	$1.50	£0.20	£0.60	£1.00
16 John Byrne cover						
	$0.30	$0.90	$1.50	£0.20	£0.60	£1.00
16 ND Collector's Edition, 48pgs, "barn door" style gatefold cover by John Byrne						
	$0.80	$2.40	$4.00	£0.50	£1.50	£2.50
17 Worlds Collide X-over, continued in Superboy #6						
	$0.30	$0.90	$1.50	£0.20	£0.60	£1.00
18 Worlds Collide X-over, continued in Superman: The Man of Steel #36						
	$0.30	$0.90	$1.50	£0.20	£0.60	£1.00
19-24	$0.30	$0.90	$1.50	£0.20	£0.60	£1.00
25 48pgs, metallic ink cover						
	$0.55	$1.65	$2.75	£0.35	£1.05	£1.75
26-28	$0.30	$0.90	$1.50	£0.20	£0.60	£1.00
29 upgraded paper stock begins; cover priced at 99 cents						
	$0.20	$0.60	$1.00	£0.15	£0.45	£0.75
30-32	$0.45	$1.35	$2.25	£0.30	£0.90	£1.50
33 Howard Chaykin cover						
	$0.45	$1.35	$2.25	£0.30	£0.90	£1.50
34-37	$0.45	$1.35	$2.25	£0.30	£0.90	£1.50
Title Value:	$14.30	$42.90	$72.00	£9.45	£28.35	£47.25

HARI KARI
Blackout Comics; 0 Sep 1995; 1 Nov 1995-present

	$Good	$Fine	$N.Mint	£Good	£Fine	£N.Mint
0-1 ND Gilbert King script, Guy Dorian art						
	$0.60	$1.80	$3.00	£0.40	£1.20	£2.00
Title Value:	$1.20	$3.60	$6.00	£0.80	£2.40	£4.00

HARLAN ELLISON'S DREAM CORRIDOR
Dark Horse; 1 Mar 1995-present

	$Good	$Fine	$N.Mint	£Good	£Fine	£N.Mint
1-3 ND sci-fi anthology featuring Harlan Ellison, John Byrne and Eric Shanower						
	$0.60	$1.80	$3.00	£0.40	£1.20	£2.00
4-5 ND featuring Harlan Ellison, John Byrne and Eric Shanower, Peter David and Mike Deodato						
	$0.60	$1.80	$3.00	£0.40	£1.20	£2.00
6 ND Harlan Ellison and others						
	$0.60	$1.80	$3.00	£0.40	£1.20	£2.00
Title Value:	$3.60	$10.80	$18.00	£2.40	£7.20	£12.00

HARLAN ELLISON'S DREAM CORRIDOR SPECIAL
Dark Horse,OS; 1 Jan 1995

	$Good	$Fine	$N.Mint	£Good	£Fine	£N.Mint
1 ND 48pgs, sci-fi anthology						
	$1.00	$3.00	$5.00	£0.65	£1.95	£3.25
Title Value:	$1.00	$3.00	$5.00	£0.65	£1.95	£3.25

HAROLD HEDD
Kitchen Sink,MS; 1,2 1984

	$Good	$Fine	$N.Mint	£Good	£Fine	£N.Mint
1-2 ND reprints underground colour strip from the 1970s						
	$0.80	$2.40	$4.00	£0.50	£1.50	£2.50
Title Value:	$1.60	$4.80	$8.00	£1.00	£3.00	£5.00

HARRIERS
Entity Comics,MS; 1 Jun 1995-3 Aug 1995

	$Good	$Fine	$N.Mint	£Good	£Fine	£N.Mint
1 ND Aster/Harriers poster at centre-fold						
	$0.60	$1.80	$3.00	£0.40	£1.20	£2.00
2-3 ND	$0.60	$1.80	$3.00	£0.40	£1.20	£2.00
Title Value:	$1.80	$5.40	$9.00	£1.20	£3.60	£6.00

HARROWERS
Marvel Comics Group/Epic,MS; 1 Dec 1993-6 May 1994

	$Good	$Fine	$N.Mint	£Good	£Fine	£N.Mint
1-6 ND Clive Barker's Pinhead featured						
	$0.40	$1.20	$2.00	£0.25	£0.75	£1.25
Title Value:	$2.40	$7.20	$12.00	£1.50	£4.50	£7.50

HARSH REALM
Harris Publications,MS; 1 Feb 1994-6 Jul 1994

	$Good	$Fine	$N.Mint	£Good	£Fine	£N.Mint
1-6 ND John Ridgway inks						
	$0.60	$1.80	$3.00	£0.40	£1.20	£2.00
Title Value:	$3.60	$10.80	$18.00	£2.40	£7.20	£12.00

HARTE OF DARKNESS
Eternity,MS; 1 Oct 1991-4 Jan 1992

	$Good	$Fine	$N.Mint	£Good	£Fine	£N.Mint
1-4 ND	$0.45	$1.35	$2.25	£0.30	£0.90	£1.50

	$Good	$Fine	$N.Mint	£Good	£Fine	£N.Mint
Title Value:	$1.80	$5.40	$9.00	£1.20	£3.60	£6.00

HARVEY
Marvel Comics Group; 1 Oct 1970-6 Dec 1972

	$Good	$Fine	$N.Mint	£Good	£Fine	£N.Mint
1 ND scarce in the U.K. Stan Lee scripts begin						
	$0.60	$1.80	$3.00	£0.40	£1.20	£2.00
2-6 ND scarce in the U.K.						
	$0.45	$1.35	$2.25	£0.30	£0.90	£1.50
Title Value:	$2.85	$8.55	$14.25	£1.90	£5.70	£9.50

HARVEY KURTZMAN'S STRANGE ADVENTURES HARDCOVER
Marvel Comics Group/Epic,OS; 1 Jan 1991

	$Good	$Fine	$N.Mint	£Good	£Fine	£N.Mint
1 ND 80pgs, tribute to Kurtzman by a variety of leading artists including Gibbons/Aragones/ Moebius						
	$2.70	$8.00	$13.50	£1.80	£5.25	£9.00
Title Value:	$2.70	$8.00	$13.50	£1.80	£5.25	£9.00

HATE
Fantagraphics; 1 Jun 1990-present

	$Good	$Fine	$N.Mint	£Good	£Fine	£N.Mint
1 Peter Bagge script/art begins; black and white						
	$0.90	$2.70	$4.50	£0.60	£1.80	£3.00
1 2nd printing, (Jan 1992)						
	$0.55	$1.65	$2.75	£0.35	£1.05	£1.75
1 3rd/4th printing	$0.45	$1.35	$2.25	£0.30	£0.90	£1.50
2	$0.60	$1.80	$3.00	£0.40	£1.20	£2.00
2 2nd printing, (Feb 1992)						
	$0.55	$1.65	$2.75	£0.35	£1.05	£1.75
2 3rd/4th printing	$0.45	$1.35	$2.25	£0.30	£0.90	£1.50
3	$0.55	$1.65	$2.75	£0.35	£1.05	£1.75
3 2nd printing, (Mar 1992)						
	$0.45	$1.35	$2.25	£0.30	£0.90	£1.50
3 3rd printing	$0.40	$1.20	$2.00	£0.25	£0.75	£1.25
4	$0.45	$1.35	$2.25	£0.30	£0.90	£1.50
4 2nd printing, (Jun 1992)						
	$0.40	$1.20	$2.00	£0.25	£0.75	£1.25
4 3rd printing	$0.45	$1.20	$2.00	£0.25	£0.90	£1.25
5	$0.40	$1.20	$2.00	£0.25	£0.75	£1.25
5 2nd printing, (Aug 1992)						
	$0.40		$2.00	£0.25	£0.75	£1.25
6	$0.40	$1.20	$2.00	£0.25	£0.75	£1.25
6 2nd printing, (1994)						
	$0.45	$1.35	$2.25	£0.30	£0.90	£1.50
6 3rd printing	$0.45	$1.35	$2.25	£0.30	£0.90	£1.50
7	$0.40	$1.20	$2.00	£0.25	£0.75	£1.25
7 2nd printing, (Nov 1994)						
	$0.45	$1.35	$2.25	£0.30	£0.90	£1.50
8	$0.40	$1.20	$2.00	£0.25	£0.75	£1.25
8 2nd printing, (Jul 1993)						
	$0.40	$1.20	$2.00	£0.25	£0.75	£1.25
8 3rd printing	$0.45	$1.35	$2.25	£0.30	£0.90	£1.50
9	$0.40	$1.20	$2.00	£0.25	£0.75	£1.25
9 2nd printing, (Jan 1994)						
	$0.45	$1.35	$2.25	£0.30	£0.90	£1.50
10	$0.40	$1.20	$2.00	£0.25	£0.75	£1.25
11 $2.50 cover begins						
	$0.45	$1.35	$2.25	£0.30	£0.90	£1.50
11 2nd printing, (Jan 1995)						
	$0.45	$1.35	$2.25	£0.30	£0.90	£1.50
12	$0.45	$1.35	$2.25	£0.30	£0.90	£1.50
12 2nd printing, (Oct 1995)						
	$0.50	$1.50	$2.50	£0.30	£0.90	£1.50
13-14	$0.45	$1.35	$2.25	£0.30	£0.90	£1.50
15-16	$0.60	$1.80	$3.00	£0.40	£1.20	£2.00
17 full colour begins						
	$0.60	$1.80	$3.00	£0.40	£1.20	£2.00
18-20	$0.60	$1.80	$3.00	£0.40	£1.20	£2.00
Title Value:	$18.90	$56.70	$94.50	£12.35	£37.05	£61.75

Note: all Non-Distributed on the news-stands in the U.K.

Note: Buddy Bradley character continues from Neat Stuff; bi-monthly

HAUNT OF FEAR
E.C. Comics; 1 May/Jun 1950-28 Nov/Dec 1954

(formerly Fat & Slat #1-4, becomes Gunfighter #5-14)

	$Good	$Fine	$N.Mint	£Good	£Fine	£N.Mint
1 very scarce in the U.K., scarce in the U.S. has #15 on cover						
	$215.00	$650.00	$1750.00	£145.00	£440.00	£1175.00
2 scarce in the U.K. has #16 on cover						
	$100.00	$300.00	$700.00	£65.00	£200.00	£470.00
3 scarce in the U.K. has #17 on cover; origin Vault of Horror and Crypt of Terror						
	$105.00	$320.00	$750.00	£70.00	£210.00	£500.00
4	$75.00	$225.00	$525.00	£50.00	£150.00	£350.00
5 famous eye-injury panel						
	$55.00	$170.00	$400.00	£39.00	£115.00	£270.00
6-10	$39.00	$115.00	$275.00	£26.00	£77.50	£185.00
11-15	$29.00	$85.00	$200.00	£19.00	£57.50	£135.00
16 Ray Bradbury adaptation						
	$29.00	$85.00	$200.00	£19.00	£57.50	£135.00
17	$29.00	$85.00	$200.00	£19.00	£57.50	£135.00
18 Ray Bradbury adaptation						
	$29.00	$85.00	$200.00	£19.00	£57.50	£135.00
19 classic cover featuring bondage and beheading						
	$43.00	$125.00	$300.00	£29.00	£85.00	£200.00
20	$29.00	$85.00	$200.00	£19.00	£57.50	£135.00
21-27	$17.50	$52.50	$125.00	£12.00	£36.00	£85.00
28 scarce in both US and UK						
	$26.00	$75.00	$180.00	£17.00	£50.00	£120.00
Title Value:	$1197.50	$3572.50	$8655.00	£800.00	£2407.00	£5820.00

Note: all Non-Distributed on the news-stands in the U.K.

MINT = 100% / NEAR MINT (inc. +/-) = 90-99% / VERY FINE (inc. +/-) = 75-89% / FINE (inc. +/-) = 55-74%
VERY GOOD (inc. +/-) = 35-54% / GOOD (inc. +/-) = 15-34% / FAIR = 5-14% / POOR = 1-4%

385

	$Good	$Fine	$N.Mint	£Good	£Fine	£N.Mint

HAUNT OF FEAR (2ND SERIES)
Gladstone; 1 May 1991-2 1991

1 ND 64pgs, reprints Haunt of Fear #7 and Weird Science Fantasy #28

	$Good	$Fine	$N.Mint	£Good	£Fine	£N.Mint
	$0.40	$1.20	$2.00	£0.25	£0.75	£1.25

2 ND 64pgs, reprints Haunt of Fear #5 and Weird Science Fantasy #29

	$0.40	$1.20	$2.00	£0.25	£0.75	£1.25
Title Value:	$0.80	$2.40	$4.00	£0.50	£1.50	£2.50

Note: sub-titled "Tales from the Crypt presents". Note also: issue #3 was advertised but never appeared.

HAUNT OF FEAR (3RD SERIES)
Russ Cochran/EC Comics; 1 Aug 1991-5 May 1992

1 ND reprints Haunt of Fear #14 and Weird Fantasy #13

	$Good	$Fine	$N.Mint	£Good	£Fine	£N.Mint
	$0.60	$1.80	$3.00	£0.40	£1.20	£2.00

2 ND reprints Haunt of Fear #18, Weird Fantasy #14

	$0.40	$1.20	$2.00	£0.25	£0.75	£1.25

3 ND reprints Haunt of Fear #19, Weird Fantasy #18

	$0.40	$1.20	$2.00	£0.25	£0.75	£1.25

4 ND reprints Haunt of Fear #16, Weird Fantasy #15

	$0.40	$1.20	$2.00	£0.25	£0.75	£1.25

5 ND reprints Haunt of Fear #27, Weird Fantasy #22

	$0.40	$1.20	$2.00	£0.25	£0.75	£1.25
Title Value:	$2.20	$6.60	$11.00	£1.40	£4.20	£7.00

Note: issues #6,7 were advertised but never appeared.

HAUNT OF FEAR (4TH SERIES)
Russ Cochran/EC Comics; 1 Nov 1992-present

1 ND reprints begin from original 1950s EC series with exact cover and interior reproduction

	$Good	$Fine	$N.Mint	£Good	£Fine	£N.Mint
	$0.30	$0.90	$1.50	£0.20	£0.60	£1.00
2-7 ND	$0.30	$0.90	$1.50	£0.20	£0.60	£1.00
8-13 ND	$0.40	$1.20	$2.00	£0.25	£0.75	£1.25
Title Value:	$4.50	$13.50	$22.38	£2.90	£8.70	£14.50

Haunt of Fear Annual 1 (Oct 1994)

reprints issues #1-5 with covers

				£1.20	£3.60	£6.00

HAUNT OF HORROR
Marvel Comics Group, Digest; 1 Jun 1973-2 Aug 1973

	$Good	$Fine	$N.Mint	£Good	£Fine	£N.Mint
1-2 ND	$0.45	$1.35	$2.25	£0.30	£0.90	£1.50
Title Value:	$0.90	$2.70	$4.50	£0.60	£1.80	£3.00

HAUNT OF HORROR (2ND SERIES)
Marvel Comics Group, Magazine; 1 May 1974-5 Jan 1975

1 64pgs, Gabriel Devil-Hunter begins, Walt Simonson art featured

	$Good	$Fine	$N.Mint	£Good	£Fine	£N.Mint
	$0.90	$2.70	$4.50	£0.60	£1.80	£3.00

2 64pgs, Satana appears and in a text story, Gene Colan art featured; Earl Norem cover

	$0.80	$2.40	$4.00	£0.50	£1.50	£2.50
3 64pgs	$0.80	$2.40	$4.00	£0.50	£1.50	£2.50

4 64pgs, Satana appears; Satana text story with illustrations by Pat Broderick and The Crusty Bunkers - a collection of inkers including Neal Adams

	$0.80	$2.40	$4.00	£0.50	£1.50	£3.00

5 very scarce in the U.K. 64pgs, Satana appears, Dick Giordano cover

	$0.80	$2.40	$4.00	£0.80	£2.40	£4.00
Title Value:	$4.10	$12.30	$20.50	£3.00	£9.00	£15.00

Note: issue #6 was advertised but never appeared.

HAUNTED
Charlton; 1 Sep 1971-30 Nov 1976; 31 Sep 1977-75 Sep 1984
(becomes Baron Weirwulf's Haunted Library #20 on)

1 Steve Ditko art and cover

	$Good	$Fine	$N.Mint	£Good	£Fine	£N.Mint
	$1.80	$5.25	$9.00	£1.20	£3.60	£6.00

2-5 Steve Ditko art and cover

	$0.90	$2.70	$4.50	£0.60	£1.80	£3.00

6-8 Steve Ditko art and cover

	$0.60	$1.80	$3.00	£0.40	£1.20	£2.00
9-10	$0.45	$1.35	$2.25	£0.30	£0.90	£1.50

11 Steve Ditko art and cover

	$0.60	$1.80	$3.00	£0.40	£1.20	£2.00

12-13 Steve Ditko art

	$0.60	$1.80	$3.00	£0.40	£1.20	£2.00

14 Steve Ditko art and cover

	$0.60	$1.80	$3.00	£0.40	£1.20	£2.00
15 Steve Ditko art	$0.60	$1.80	$3.00	£0.40	£1.20	£2.00

16 Steve Ditko art and cover

	$0.60	$1.80	$3.00	£0.40	£1.20	£2.00
17	$0.45	$1.35	$2.25	£0.30	£0.90	£1.50
18 Steve Ditko art	$0.60	$1.80	$3.00	£0.40	£1.20	£2.00
19-20	$0.45	$1.35	$2.25	£0.30	£0.90	£1.50
21-22	$0.30	$0.90	$1.50	£0.20	£0.60	£1.00

23-24 Steve Ditko art

	$0.40	$1.20	$2.00	£0.25	£0.75	£1.25
25-27	$0.30	$0.90	$1.50	£0.20	£0.60	£1.00
28 Steve Ditko art	$0.40	$1.20	$2.00	£0.25	£0.75	£1.25
29	$0.30	$0.90	$1.50	£0.20	£0.60	£1.00

30 Steve Ditko art and cover

	$0.40	$1.20	$2.00	£0.25	£0.75	£1.25
31-40	$0.30	$0.90	$1.50	£0.20	£0.60	£1.00

41 Steve Ditko cover

	$0.30	$0.90	$1.50	£0.20	£0.60	£1.00
42-46	$0.30	$0.90	$1.50	£0.20	£0.60	£1.00

47 Steve Ditko cover

	$0.30	$0.90	$1.50	£0.20	£0.60	£1.00
48	$0.30	$0.90	$1.50	£0.20	£0.60	£1.00

49-50 Steve Ditko cover

	$0.30	$0.90	$1.50	£0.20	£0.60	£1.00

51 Steve Ditko cover, reprints issue #1

	$0.30	$0.90	$1.50	£0.20	£0.60	£1.00
52-56	$0.30	$0.90	$1.50	£0.20	£0.60	£1.00
57 Steve Ditko art	$0.40	$1.20	$2.00	£0.25	£0.75	£1.25
58-59	$0.30	$0.90	$1.50	£0.20	£0.60	£1.00
60 Steve Ditko art	$0.40	$1.20	$2.00	£0.25	£0.75	£1.25
61-75	$0.30	$0.90	$1.50	£0.20	£0.60	£1.00
Title Value:	$30.75	$92.10	$153.75	£20.40	£61.20	£102.00

Note: all Limited Distribution in the U.K.

HAUNTED LOVE
Charlton; 1 Apr 1973-11 Sep 1975

	$Good	$Fine	$N.Mint	£Good	£Fine	£N.Mint
1	$0.90	$2.70	$4.50	£0.60	£1.80	£3.00
2-3	$0.45	$1.35	$2.25	£0.30	£0.90	£1.50

4-5 Steve Ditko art

	$0.60	$1.80	$3.00	£0.40	£1.20	£2.00
6-11	$0.45	$1.35	$2.25	£0.30	£0.90	£1.50
Title Value:	$5.70	$17.10	$28.50	£3.80	£11.40	£19.00

Note: all Limited Distribution in the U.K.

HAVE GUN WILL TRAVEL
Dell; (Four Color #931) 1 Aug 1958-14 Sep 1962

1 (Four Color #931) photo cover

	$Good	$Fine	$N.Mint	£Good	£Fine	£N.Mint
	$18.00	$54.00	$108.00	£12.00	£36.00	£72.50

2 (Four Color #983) photo cover

	$11.00	$33.00	$66.00	£7.25	£22.00	£44.00

3 (Four Color #1044) photo cover

	$10.00	$30.00	$60.00	£6.50	£19.50	£40.00

4 all photo covers (ends #14)

	$6.00	$18.00	$36.00	£4.00	£12.00	£24.00
5-14	$6.00	$18.00	$36.00	£4.00	£12.00	£24.00
Title Value:	$105.00	$315.00	$630.00	£69.75	£209.50	£420.50

Note: all distributed on the news-stands in the U.K.

HAVOK AND WOLVERINE: MELTDOWN
Marvel Comics Group/Epic,MS; 1 Nov 1988-4 Jun 1989

	$Good	$Fine	$N.Mint	£Good	£Fine	£N.Mint
1 ND 48pgs	$1.00	$3.00	$5.00	£0.70	£2.10	£3.50
2-3 ND 48pgs	$0.80	$2.40	$4.00	£0.50	£1.50	£2.50

4 ND scarce in the U.K. 48pgs

	$0.80	$2.40	$4.00	£0.60	£1.80	£3.00
Title Value:	$3.40	$10.20	$17.00	£2.30	£6.90	£11.50

Note: Bookshelf Format. Walt/Louise Simonson script, Jon J. Muth/Kent Williams art

Trade Paperback (1991), reprints issues #1-4

				£1.60	£4.80	£8.00

HAWK AND DOVE ANNUAL
DC Comics; 1 Sep 1990-2 1991

1 ND Rob Liefeld cover

	$Good	$Fine	$N.Mint	£Good	£Fine	£N.Mint
	$0.45	$1.35	$2.25	£0.30	£0.90	£1.50

2 ND Armageddon: 2001 tie-in

	$0.45	$1.35	$2.25	£0.30	£0.90	£1.50
Title Value:	$0.90	$2.70	$4.50	£0.60	£1.80	£3.00

HAWK AND DOVE, THE
DC Comics,MS; 1 Oct 1988-5 Feb 1989

	$Good	$Fine	$N.Mint	£Good	£Fine	£N.Mint
1 Rob Liefeld art	$0.80	$2.40	$4.00	£0.60	£1.80	£3.00
2 Rob Liefeld art	$0.60	$1.80	$3.00	£0.50	£1.50	£2.50
3-5 Rob Liefeld art	$0.50	$1.50	$2.50	£0.40	£1.20	£2.00
Title Value:	$2.90	$8.70	$14.50	£2.30	£6.90	£11.50

Hawk and Dove Trade paperback (Dec 1993)

reprints 5 issue mini-series with unpublished costume designs

				£1.30	£3.90	£6.50

HAWK AND DOVE, THE (2ND SERIES)
DC Comics; 1 Jun 1989-28 Oct 1991

	$Good	$Fine	$N.Mint	£Good	£Fine	£N.Mint
1	$0.30	$0.90	$1.50	£0.20	£0.60	£1.00
2-10	$0.25	$0.75	$1.25	£0.15	£0.45	£0.75

11 New Titans guest-star

	$0.25	$0.75	$1.25	£0.15	£0.45	£0.75
12-17	$0.25	$0.75	$1.25	£0.15	£0.45	£0.75

18-19 Creeper appears

	$0.25	$0.75	$1.25	£0.15	£0.45	£0.75
20-24	$0.25	$0.75	$1.25	£0.15	£0.45	£0.75
25 48pgs	$0.30	$0.90	$1.50	£0.20	£0.60	£1.00
26-27	$0.25	$0.75	$1.25	£0.15	£0.45	£0.75
28 64pgs	$0.30	$0.90	$1.50	£0.20	£0.60	£1.00
Title Value:	$7.15	$21.45	$35.75	£4.35	£13.05	£21.75

HAWK AND THE DOVE, THE
National Periodical Publications; 1 Aug/Sep 1968-6 Jun/Jul 1969
(see Brave and the Bold, Showcase #75, Teen Titans)

	$Good	$Fine	$N.Mint	£Good	£Fine	£N.Mint
1 Steve Ditko art	$7.00	$21.00	$50.00	£4.25	£12.50	£30.00
2 Steve Ditko art	$6.25	$18.50	$37.50	£2.90	£8.75	£17.50
3 Gil Kane art	$6.25	$18.50	$37.50	£2.90	£8.75	£17.50
4 Gil Kane art	$6.25	$18.50	$37.50	£2.50	£7.50	£15.00

5 Gil Kane art, Teen Titans cameo

	$6.25	$18.50	$37.50	£2.50	£7.50	£15.00
6 Gil Kane art	$6.25	$18.50	$37.50	£2.50	£7.50	£15.00
Title Value:	$38.25	$113.50	$237.50	£17.55	£52.50	£110.00

Note: original Dove killed in Crisis on Infinite Earths.

HAWKEYE
Marvel Comics Group,MS; 1 Sep 1983-4 Dec 1983

1-2 ND scarce in the U.K.

	$Good	$Fine	$N.Mint	£Good	£Fine	£N.Mint
	$0.40	$1.20	$2.00	£0.40	£1.20	£2.00
3-4 ND	$0.30	$0.90	$1.50	£0.30	£0.90	£1.50
Title Value:	$1.40	$4.20	$6.50	£1.40	£4.20	£7.00

Trade Paperback, reprints #1-4

				£1.00	£3.00	£5.00
(2nd print. 1991)				£1.00	£3.00	£5.00

HAWKEYE (2ND SERIES)
Marvel Comics Group,MS; 1 Jan 1994-4 Apr 1994

	$Good	$Fine	$N.Mint	£Good	£Fine	£N.Mint
1-3	$0.40	$1.20	$2.00	£0.25	£0.75	£1.25
4 new costume	$0.40	$1.20	$2.00	£0.25	£0.75	£1.25
Title Value:	$1.60	$4.80	$8.00	£1.00	£3.00	£5.00

HAWKMAN
National Periodical Publications; 1 Apr/May 1964-27 Aug/Sep 1968

	$Good	$Fine	$N.Mint	£Good	£Fine	£N.Mint
(see Atom and Hawkman, Brave and the Bold, DC Presents, Detective Mystery in Space, Shadow War of the..., Showcase, World's Finest)						
1 Murphy Anderson art						
	$65.00	$195.00	$525.00	£34.00	£100.00	£275.00
2	$26.00	$77.50	$185.00	£12.50	£39.00	£90.00
3	$15.50	$47.00	$110.00	£7.75	£23.50	£55.00
4 1st appearance Zatanna						
	$19.00	$57.50	$135.00	£8.50	£26.00	£60.00
5	$15.50	$47.00	$110.00	£6.25	£19.00	£45.00
6-8	$12.00	$36.00	$85.00	£4.25	£12.50	£30.00
9 Atom X-over	$12.00	$36.00	$85.00	£4.25	£12.50	£30.00
10	$12.00	$36.00	$85.00	£4.25	£12.50	£30.00
11 last Silver Age issue, indicia dated Dec 1965/Jan 1966						
	$8.50	$26.00	$60.00	£3.55	£10.50	£25.00
12-15	$10.00	$30.00	$60.00	£3.75	£11.00	£22.50
16-17	$8.25	$25.00	$50.00	£3.30	£10.00	£20.00
18 Adam Strange appears						
	$8.25	$25.00	$50.00	£3.30	£10.00	£20.00
19-20	$8.25	$25.00	$50.00	£3.30	£10.00	£20.00
21-24	$7.50	$22.50	$45.00	£2.90	£8.75	£17.50
25 Golden Age Hawkman reprint						
	$7.50	$22.50	$45.00	£2.90	£8.75	£17.50
26-27	$7.50	$22.50	$45.00	£2.90	£8.75	£17.50
Title Value:	$343.25	$1032.50	$2355.00	£145.60	£435.75	£1012.50
Trade Paperback (Sep 1989)						
Reprints classic Gardner Fox/Joe Kubert stories including Brave and the Bold #34				£2.80	£8.40	£14.00

HAWKMAN (2ND SERIES)
DC Comics; 1 Aug 1986-17 Dec 1987

	$Good	$Fine	$N.Mint	£Good	£Fine	£N.Mint
1	$0.30	$0.90	$1.50	£0.20	£0.60	£1.00
2-9	$0.25	$0.75	$1.25	£0.15	£0.45	£0.75
10 John Byrne cover, Superman cameo						
	$0.25	$0.75	$1.25	£0.15	£0.45	£0.75
11-17	$0.25	$0.75	$1.25	£0.15	£0.45	£0.75
Title Value:	$4.30	$12.90	$21.50	£2.60	£7.80	£13.00

HAWKMAN (3RD SERIES)
DC Comics; 0 Oct 1994; 1 Sep 1993-present

	$Good	$Fine	$N.Mint	£Good	£Fine	£N.Mint
0 (Oct 1994) Zero Hour X-over, Hawkman discovers new powers						
	$0.40	$1.20	$2.00	£0.25	£0.75	£1.25
1 new powers and new costume, gold foil embossed cover						
	$0.45	$1.35	$2.25	£0.30	£0.90	£1.50
2-3	$0.40	$1.20	$2.00	£0.25	£0.75	£1.25
4 Justice League of America appear						
	$0.40	$1.20	$2.00	£0.25	£0.75	£1.25
5	$0.40	$1.20	$2.00	£0.25	£0.75	£1.25
6 The Eradicator appears						
	$0.40	$1.20	$2.00	£0.25	£0.75	£1.25
7-8 King of the Netherworld story						
	$0.40	$1.20	$2.00	£0.25	£0.75	£1.25
9 prelude to Zero Hour mini-series begins						
	$0.40	$1.20	$2.00	£0.25	£0.75	£1.25
10-12	$0.40	$1.20	$2.00	£0.25	£0.75	£1.25
13 Zero Hour X-over						
	$0.40	$1.20	$2.00	£0.25	£0.75	£1.25
14 Hawkman with new powers discovered during Zero Hour						
	$0.40	$1.20	$2.00	£0.25	£0.75	£1.25
15 Hawkman vs. Aquaman						
	$0.40	$1.20	$2.00	£0.25	£0.75	£1.25
16 Diana Prince appears						
	$0.40	$1.20	$2.00	£0.25	£0.75	£1.25
17-18	$0.40	$1.20	$2.00	£0.25	£0.75	£1.25

	$Good	$Fine	$N.Mint	£Good	£Fine	£N.Mint
19 Hawkwoman vs. Vigilante						
	$0.40	$1.20	$2.00	£0.25	£0.75	£1.25
20	$0.40	$1.20	$2.00	£0.25	£0.75	£1.25
21 Ron Lim cover and art						
	$0.45	$1.35	$2.25	£0.30	£0.90	£1.50
22 Way of the Warrior part 3, continued in Guy Gardner: Warrior #33. Cover by Ron Lim						
	$0.45	$1.35	$2.25	£0.30	£0.90	£1.50
23 Way of the Warrior part 3, continued in Guy Gardner: Warrior #34. Cover by Ron Lim						
	$0.45	$1.35	$2.25	£0.30	£0.90	£1.50
24 Ron Lim cover	$0.45	$1.35	$2.25	£0.30	£0.90	£1.50
25 Kent Williams painted cover						
	$0.45	$1.35	$2.25	£0.30	£0.90	£1.50
26 Underworld Unleashed tie-in, Scarecrow appears						
	$0.45	$1.35	$2.25	£0.30	£0.90	£1.50
27 Underworld Unleashed tie-in, Ron Lim cover						
	$0.45	$1.35	$2.25	£0.30	£0.90	£1.50
28 Hawkman vs. Doctor Polaris						
	$0.45	$1.35	$2.25	£0.30	£0.90	£1.50
29-30 Howard Chaykin cover						
	$0.45	$1.35	$2.25	£0.30	£0.90	£1.50
Title Value:	$12.95	$38.85	$64.75	£8.30	£24.90	£41.50

HAWKMAN ANNUAL
DC Comics; 1 Oct 1993-present

	$Good	$Fine	$N.Mint	£Good	£Fine	£N.Mint
1 64pgs, Bloodlines (Wave Two) part 17, 1st appearance Mongrel, continued in Deathstroke the Terminator Annual #2						
	$0.70	$2.10	$3.50	£0.50	£1.50	£2.50
2 56pgs, Year One	$0.80	$2.40	$4.00	£0.50	£1.50	£2.50
Title Value:	$1.50	$4.50	$7.50	£1.00	£3.00	£5.00

HAWKMAN SPECIAL
DC Comics; 1 Mar 1986

	$Good	$Fine	$N.Mint	£Good	£Fine	£N.Mint
1 48pgs	$0.30	$0.90	$1.50	£0.20	£0.60	£1.00
Title Value:	$0.30	$0.90	$1.50	£0.20	£0.60	£1.00

HAWKMAN, SHADOW WAR OF
DC Comics,MS; 1 May 1985-4 Aug 1985

	$Good	$Fine	$N.Mint	£Good	£Fine	£N.Mint
1-4	$0.25	$0.75	$1.25	£0.15	£0.45	£0.75
Title Value:	$1.00	$3.00	$5.00	£0.60	£1.80	£3.00

HAWKMOON: THE JEWEL IN THE SKULL
First,MS; 1 May 1986-4 Nov 1986

	$Good	$Fine	$N.Mint	£Good	£Fine	£N.Mint
1-4 ND	$0.45	$1.35	$2.25	£0.30	£0.90	£1.50
Title Value:	$1.80	$5.40	$9.00	£1.20	£3.60	£6.00
Trade Paperback (1988), reprints #1-4				£1.00	£3.00	£5.00

HAWKMOON: THE MAD GOD'S AMULET
First,MS; 1 Jan 1987-4 Jul 1987

	$Good	$Fine	$N.Mint	£Good	£Fine	£N.Mint
1-4 ND	$0.45	$1.35	$2.25	£0.30	£0.90	£1.50
Title Value:	$1.80	$5.40	$9.00	£1.20	£3.60	£6.00

HAWKMOON: THE RUNESTAFF
First,MS; 1 Jun 1988-4 Dec 1988

	$Good	$Fine	$N.Mint	£Good	£Fine	£N.Mint
1-4 ND	$0.45	$1.35	$2.25	£0.30	£0.90	£1.50
Title Value:	$1.80	$5.40	$9.00	£1.20	£3.60	£6.00

HAWKMOON: THE SWORD OF THE DAWN
First,MS; 1 Sep 1987-4 Feb 1988

	$Good	$Fine	$N.Mint	£Good	£Fine	£N.Mint
1-4 ND	$0.55	$1.65	$2.75	£0.35	£1.05	£1.75
Title Value:	$2.20	$6.60	$11.00	£1.40	£4.20	£7.00

HAWKWORLD
DC Comics; 1 Jun 1990-32 Mar 1993

	$Good	$Fine	$N.Mint	£Good	£Fine	£N.Mint
1 Graham Nolan art begins						
	$0.40	$1.20	$2.00	£0.25	£0.75	£1.25
2-10	$0.30	$0.90	$1.50	£0.20	£0.60	£1.00
11-14	$0.25	$0.75	$1.25	£0.15	£0.45	£0.75
15-16 War of the Gods tie-in						
	$0.25	$0.75	$1.25	£0.15	£0.45	£0.75

Hardware #1 Collector's Edition

Harvey #1

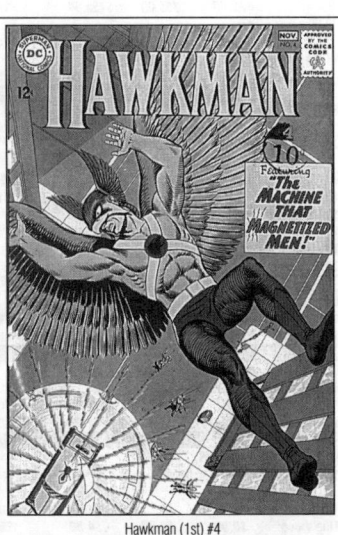

Hawkman (1st) #4

	$Good	$Fine	$N.Mint	£Good	£Fine	£N.Mint
17-20	$0.25	$0.75	$1.25	£0.15	£0.45	£0.75
21 Golden Age Hawkman guest-stars	$0.25	$0.75	$1.25	£0.15	£0.45	£0.75
22-24	$0.25	$0.75	$1.25	£0.15	£0.45	£0.75
25 new costumes	$0.25	$0.75	$1.25	£0.15	£0.45	£0.75
26	$0.25	$0.75	$1.25	£0.15	£0.45	£0.75
27-29 Flight's End story	$0.25	$0.75	$1.25	£0.15	£0.45	£0.75
30 Flight's End story, Tim Truman art begins	$0.25	$0.75	$1.25	£0.15	£0.45	£0.75
31-32 Flight's End story	$0.25	$0.75	$1.25	£0.15	£0.45	£0.75
Title Value:	$8.60	$25.80	$43.00	£5.35	£16.05	£26.75

Note: New Format
Trade Paperback (Oct 1991), reprints four issue series, wraparound cover by Tim Truman — £2.10 £6.30 £10.50

HAWKWORLD (LIMITED SERIES)
DC Comics,MS; 1 Jun 1989-3 Aug 1989

	$Good	$Fine	$N.Mint	£Good	£Fine	£N.Mint
1-3 ND	$1.00	$3.00	$5.00	£0.60	£1.80	£3.00
Title Value:	$3.00	$9.00	$15.00	£1.80	£5.40	£9.00

Note: Bookshelf Format, 48pgs. Tim Truman story/art. Mature Readers label.

HAWKWORLD ANNUAL
DC Comics; 1 Nov 1990-3 1992

	$Good	$Fine	$N.Mint	£Good	£Fine	£N.Mint
1 48pgs, Flash guest-stars	$0.45	$1.35	$2.25	£0.30	£0.90	£1.50
2 64pgs, Armageddon: 2001 tie-in	$0.45	$1.35	$2.25	£0.30	£0.90	£1.50
2 2nd printing, silver ink cover	$0.40	$1.20	$2.00	£0.25	£0.75	£1.25
3 64pgs, Eclipso: The Darkness Within tie-in	$0.45	$1.35	$2.25	£0.30	£0.90	£1.50
Title Value:	$1.75	$5.25	$8.75	£1.15	£3.45	£5.75

HAYWIRE
DC Comics; 1 Oct 1988-13 Sep 1989

	$Good	$Fine	$N.Mint	£Good	£Fine	£N.Mint
1-13	$0.15	$0.45	$0.75	£0.10	£0.35	£0.60
Title Value:	$1.95	$5.85	$9.75	£1.30	£4.55	£7.80

Note: high quality paper

HE-MAN, THE MOVIE
Marvel Comics Group/Star, Film; 1 Nov 1987

	$Good	$Fine	$N.Mint	£Good	£Fine	£N.Mint
1 scarce in the U.K. 48pgs, adapts film; George Tuska art	$0.25	$0.75	$1.25	£0.15	£0.45	£0.75
Title Value:	$0.25	$0.75	$1.25	£0.15	£0.45	£0.75

HEAP, THE
Skywald; 1 Sep 1971

	$Good	$Fine	$N.Mint	£Good	£Fine	£N.Mint
1 giant, scarce, part reprint; distributed in the U.K.	$1.00	$3.00	$5.00	£1.20	£3.60	£6.00
Title Value:	$1.00	$3.00	$5.00	£1.20	£3.60	£6.00

HEART OF DARKNESS
Hardline Studios; 1 1994

	$Good	$Fine	$N.Mint	£Good	£Fine	£N.Mint
1 ND Mike Miller co-script and pencils, Matthew Osborne inks	$0.60	$1.80	$3.00	£0.40	£1.20	£2.00
Title Value:	$0.60	$1.80	$3.00	£0.40	£1.20	£2.00

HEART OF THE BEAST GRAPHIC NOVEL
DC Comics; nn Jul 1994

	$Good	$Fine	$N.Mint	£Good	£Fine	£N.Mint
nn ND 96pgs, Hardcover; Dean Motter script, Sean Phillips art and cover	$4.00	$12.00	$20.00	£2.50	£7.50	£12.50
Title Value:	$4.00	$12.00	$20.00	£2.50	£7.50	£12.50

HEART THROBS
National Periodical Publications; 47 Apr/May 1959-146 Oct 1972
(previously published by Quality Comics; becomes Love Stories)

	$Good	$Fine	$N.Mint	£Good	£Fine	£N.Mint
47 scarce in the U.K. 1st DC issue	$22.00	$65.00	$155.00	£14.00	£43.00	£100.00
48-60 scarce in the U.K.	$10.00	$30.00	$60.00	£6.25	£18.50	£37.50
61 scarce in the U.K.	$6.50	$20.00	$40.00	£5.00	£15.00	£30.00
1st official distribution in the U.K.						
62-70 scarce in the U.K.	$6.50	$20.00	$40.00	£4.15	£12.50	£25.00
71-100 scarce in the U.K.	$5.00	$15.00	$30.00	£3.30	£10.00	£20.00
101 Beatles cover	$10.50	$33.00	$65.00	£5.00	£15.00	£30.00
102-119	$3.00	$9.00	$15.00	£1.50	£4.50	£7.50
120 Neal Adams cover	$3.00	$9.00	$15.00	£1.50	£4.50	£7.50
121-146	$1.50	$4.50	$7.50	£0.80	£2.40	£4.00
Title Value:	$473.50	$1426.00	$2780.00	£290.90	£873.90	£1719.00

HEARTBREAK COMICS
David Boswell; 1 Aug 1984

	$Good	$Fine	$N.Mint	£Good	£Fine	£N.Mint
1 ND	$0.90	$2.70	$4.50	£0.60	£1.80	£3.00
Title Value:	$0.90	$2.70	$4.50	£0.60	£1.80	£3.00

HEARTBREAK COMICS (2ND SERIES)
Eclipse; 1 May 1988

	$Good	$Fine	$N.Mint	£Good	£Fine	£N.Mint
1 ND magazine, Boswell art, Reid Flemming appears	$0.55	$1.65	$2.75	£0.35	£1.05	£1.75
Title Value:	$0.55	$1.65	$2.75	£0.35	£1.05	£1.75

HEARTS OF DARKNESS
Marvel Comics Group,OS; 1 Feb 1992

	$Good	$Fine	$N.Mint	£Good	£Fine	£N.Mint
1 ND 48pgs, Ghost Rider, Punisher, Wolverine appear, John Romita Jnr and Klaus Janson art, double gatefold cover	$0.90	$2.70	$4.50	£0.60	£1.80	£3.00
Title Value:	$0.90	$2.70	$4.50	£0.60	£1.80	£3.00

HEARTSTOPPER
Millennium,MS; 1 Dec 1994-4 Oct 1995

	$Good	$Fine	$N.Mint	£Good	£Fine	£N.Mint
1-2 ND Steve Roman script, Uriel Caton part art	$0.60	$1.80	$3.00	£0.40	£1.20	£2.00
3-4 ND Fauve and Alan Larsen art	$0.60	$1.80	$3.00	£0.40	£1.20	£2.00
Title Value:	$2.40	$7.20	$12.00	£1.60	£4.80	£8.00

HEAT: DEADWORLD CHRONICLES
Caliber Press; 1 Jul 1994

	$Good	$Fine	$N.Mint	£Good	£Fine	£N.Mint
1 ND black and white	$0.60	$1.80	$3.00	£0.40	£1.20	£2.00
Title Value:	$0.60	$1.80	$3.00	£0.40	£1.20	£2.00

HEATHCLIFF
Marvel Comics Group/Star; 1 Apr 1985-57 1991

	$Good	$Fine	$N.Mint	£Good	£Fine	£N.Mint
1-49	$0.15	$0.45	$0.75	£0.10	£0.30	£0.50
50 48pgs	$0.15	$0.50	$0.90	£0.10	£0.35	£0.60
51-57	$0.15	$0.45	$0.75	£0.10	£0.30	£0.50
Title Value:	$8.55	$25.70	$42.90	£5.70	£17.15	£28.60

HEAVY HITTERS ANNUAL
Marvel Comics Group/Epic,OS; 1 Nov 1993

	$Good	$Fine	$N.Mint	£Good	£Fine	£N.Mint
1 ND 64pgs, features Spyke, Lawdog, Trouble With Girls, Alien Legion and Feud; bound-in trading card	$0.80	$2.40	$4.00	£0.50	£1.50	£2.50
Title Value:	$0.80	$2.40	$4.00	£0.50	£1.50	£2.50

HEAVY METAL
Heavy Metal; 1 Apr 1977-present

	$Good	$Fine	$N.Mint	£Good	£Fine	£N.Mint
Apr 1977				£4.00	£12.00	£20.00
May 1977				£3.00	£9.00	£15.00
Jun 1977				£1.50	£4.50	£7.50
Jul 1977-Dec 1979				£1.00	£3.00	£5.00
Jan 1980-Dec 1982				£0.70	£2.10	£3.50
Jan 1983-Dec 1985 (#105, last monthly)				£0.50	£1.50	£2.50
Winter 1986 1st Quarterly, squarebound				£0.80	£2.40	£4.00
Spring 1986-Winter 1989				£0.70	£2.10	£3.50
Mar 1989 1st bi-monthly				£0.70	£2.10	£3.50
May 1989 onwards				£0.60	£1.80	£3.00
Son of Heavy Metal (all new)				£0.70	£2.10	£3.50
Bride of Heavy Metal (all new)				£0.70	£2.10	£3.50
Best of Heavy Metal, all reprint				£0.70	£2.10	£3.50
Best of Heavy Metal II, all reprint				£0.70	£2.10	£3.50
Even Heavier Metal, all new				£0.70	£2.10	£3.50

HECKLER, THE
DC Comics; 1 Sep 1992-7 Mar 1993

	$Good	$Fine	$N.Mint	£Good	£Fine	£N.Mint
1 Keith Giffin script/art begins	$0.30	$0.90	$1.50	£0.20	£0.60	£1.00
2-7	$0.25	$0.75	$1.25	£0.15	£0.45	£0.75
Title Value:	$1.80	$5.40	$9.00	£1.10	£3.30	£5.50

HELL'S ANGEL
Marvel UK; 1 Jul 1992-17 Dec 1993
(see Overkill in British section) (title becomes Dark Angel with #8)

	$Good	$Fine	$N.Mint	£Good	£Fine	£N.Mint
1 origin Hell's Angel, X-Men guest-star; Jaye and Senior script/art	$0.40	$1.20	$2.00	£0.25	£0.75	£1.25
2-3	$0.40	$1.20	$2.00	£0.25	£0.75	£1.25
4-5 X-Men appear	$0.40	$1.20	$2.00	£0.25	£0.75	£1.25
6 becomes Dark Angel, X-Men appear	$0.40	$1.20	$2.00	£0.25	£0.75	£1.25
7 Psylocke guest-stars	$0.40	$1.20	$2.00	£0.25	£0.75	£1.25
8 Psylocke guest-stars; title change to "Dark Angel" owing to copyright problems actioned by Hell's Angels in America	$0.40	$1.20	$2.00	£0.25	£0.75	£1.25
9 Punisher appears	$0.40	$1.20	$2.00	£0.25	£0.75	£1.25
10 MyS-TECH Wars X-over, X-Men and the Avengers appear	$0.40	$1.20	$2.00	£0.25	£0.75	£1.25
11-12 X-Men appear	$0.40	$1.20	$2.00	£0.25	£0.75	£1.25
13 X-Men and Death's Head II appear	$0.40	$1.20	$2.00	£0.25	£0.75	£1.25
14-16 Death's Head II appears	$0.40	$1.20	$2.00	£0.25	£0.75	£1.25
17	$0.40	$1.20	$2.00	£0.25	£0.75	£1.25
Title Value:	$6.80	$20.40	$34.00	£4.25	£12.75	£21.25

HELLBLAZER
DC Comics; 1 Jan 1988-present

	$Good	$Fine	$N.Mint	£Good	£Fine	£N.Mint
1 John Constantine begins, John Ridgway art and Jamie Delano scripts begin	$3.50	$10.50	$17.50	£2.00	£6.00	£10.00
2	$2.00	$6.00	$10.00	£1.20	£3.60	£6.00
3 LD in the U.K. "Yuppies from Hell", Maggie Thatcher election issue	$2.00	$6.00	$10.00	£1.60	£4.80	£8.00
4-5	$1.60	$4.80	$8.00	£1.00	£3.00	£5.00
6-8	$1.20	$3.60	$6.00	£0.80	£2.40	£4.00
9 LD in the U.K. X-over Swamp Thing #76	$1.20	$3.60	$6.00	£0.90	£2.70	£4.50
10 story continued from Swamp Thing #76	$1.20	$3.60	$6.00	£0.80	£2.40	£4.00
11 Newcastle story, "origin"	$1.00	$3.00	$5.00	£0.70	£2.10	£3.50
12-15	$1.00	$3.00	$5.00	£0.70	£2.10	£3.50
16-20	$0.90	$2.70	$4.50	£0.60	£1.80	£3.00
21-24	$0.80	$2.40	$4.00	£0.50	£1.50	£2.50
25 Grant Morrison script	$0.80	$2.40	$4.00	£0.50	£1.50	£2.50

	$Good	$Fine	$N.Mint	£Good	£Fine	£N.Mint
26 Grant Morrison script						
	$0.60	$1.80	$3.00	£0.40	£1.20	£2.00
27-30	$0.60	$1.80	$3.00	£0.40	£1.20	£2.00
31-32	$0.45	$1.35	$2.25	£0.30	£0.90	£1.50
33 Dean Motter pencils						
	$0.45	$1.35	$2.25	£0.30	£0.90	£1.50
34-35	$0.45	$1.35	$2.25	£0.30	£0.90	£1.50
36-39	$0.40	$1.20	$2.00	£0.25	£0.75	£1.25
40 48pgs, previews Kid Eternity series						
	$0.45	$1.35	$2.25	£0.30	£0.90	£1.50
41 Garth Ennis script/Will Simpson art begins, John Constantine learns he has cancer						
	$0.40	$1.20	$2.00	£0.25	£0.75	£1.25
42-45	$0.40	$1.20	$2.00	£0.25	£0.75	£1.25
46 cancer story conclusion						
	$0.40	$1.20	$2.00	£0.25	£0.75	£1.25
47-49 painted photo cover						
	$0.40	$1.20	$2.00	£0.25	£0.75	£1.25
50 48pgs, painted photo cover, pin-ups by Will Simpson						
	$0.60	$1.80	$3.00	£0.40	£1.20	£2.00
51	$0.40	$1.20	$2.00	£0.25	£0.75	£1.25
52 Royal Blood part 1, Glenn Fabry painted covers begin						
	$0.40	$1.20	$2.00	£0.25	£0.75	£1.25
53-55 Royal Blood story						
	$0.40	$1.20	$2.00	£0.25	£0.75	£1.25
56 David Lloyd art	$0.40	$1.20	$2.00	£0.25	£0.75	£1.25
57-58 Steve Dillon art						
	$0.40	$1.20	$2.00	£0.25	£0.75	£1.25
59 Guys & Dolls story, Garth Ennis script						
	$0.40	$1.20	$2.00	£0.25	£0.75	£1.25
60 Guys & Dolls story, Garth Ennis script; 1st appearance Genesis						
	$1.40	$4.20	$7.00	£0.70	£2.10	£3.50
61 Guys & Dolls story, Garth Ennis script; Genesis appears						
	$0.80	$2.40	$4.00	£0.50	£1.50	£2.50
62 Steve Dillon art, Garth Ennis script; Gaiman and McKean back-up AIDS story						
	$0.40	$1.20	$2.00	£0.25	£0.75	£1.25
63 Steve Dillon art and Garth Ennis scripts begin under "Vertigo", metallic ink logo. 1st issue under "Vertigo" line of comics; Swamp Thing cameo						
	$0.40	$1.20	$2.00	£0.25	£0.75	£1.25
64-65 Fear & Loathing story						
	$0.40	$1.20	$2.00	£0.25	£0.75	£1.25
66 Fear & Loathing story, $1.95 cover begins						
	$0.40	$1.20	$2.00	£0.25	£0.75	£1.25
67-71	$0.40	$1.20	$2.00	£0.25	£0.75	£1.25
72-74 Damnation's Flame story						
	$0.40	$1.20	$2.00	£0.25	£0.75	£1.25
75 48pgs, Damnation's Flame conclusion						
	$0.60	$1.80	$3.00	£0.40	£1.20	£2.00
76-77	$0.40	$1.20	$2.00	£0.25	£0.75	£1.25
78 Rake At The Gates Of Hell story (ends #83)						
	$0.40	$1.20	$2.00	£0.25	£0.75	£1.25
79-84	$0.40	$1.20	$2.00	£0.25	£0.75	£1.25
85-88 Sean Philips cover and art						
	$0.40	$1.20	$2.00	£0.25	£0.75	£1.25
89-91 Sean Philips cover and art						
	$0.45	$1.35	$2.25	£0.30	£0.90	£1.50
92-96 Critical Mass story, Sean Philips cover and art						
	$0.45	$1.35	$2.25	£0.30	£0.90	£1.50
97-99	$0.45	$1.35	$2.25	£0.30	£0.90	£1.50
Title Value:	$63.45	$190.35	$317.25	£41.00	£123.00	£205.00

Note: all are New Format, Mature Readers label. Issue 36 previews World Without End series.

ARTISTS

John Ridgway art in #1-9. Richard Piers Rayner/Mark Buckingham art in 10, 11.

	£Good	£Fine	£N.Mint
Trade paperback (Titan) 1	£1.40	£4.20	£7.00
Trade paperback (Titan) 2	£1.30	£3.90	£6.50
Trade paperback (Titan) 3	£1.30	£3.90	£6.50
Trade paperback (Titan) 4	£1.30	£3.90	£6.50
Hellblazer: Original Sins			
Trade paperback			
reprints issues #1-9, new cover by Dave McKean	£2.70	£8.10	£13.50
Hellblazer: Dangerous Habits (Mar 1994)			
Trade paperback			
reprints issues #41-46, new cover by Glenn Fabry	£2.00	£6.00	£10.00

HELLBLAZER ANNUAL
DC Comics; 1 Sep 1989-present

	$Good	$Fine	$N.Mint	£Good	£Fine	£N.Mint
1 ND Bryan Talbot art featured						
	$0.80	$2.40	$4.00	£0.50	£1.50	£2.50
Title Value:	$0.80	$2.40	$4.00	£0.50	£1.50	£2.50

HELLBLAZER SPECIAL
DC Comics; 1 Oct 1993-present

	$Good	$Fine	$N.Mint	£Good	£Fine	£N.Mint
1 64pgs, Garth Ennis and Steve Dillon						
	$0.80	$2.40	$4.00	£0.50	£1.50	£2.50
Title Value:	$0.80	$2.40	$4.00	£0.50	£1.50	£2.50

HELLBOY: SEED OF DESTRUCTION
Dark Horse/Legend,MS; 1 Mar 1994-4 Jun 1994

	$Good	$Fine	$N.Mint	£Good	£Fine	£N.Mint
1 ND scarce in the U.K. Mike Mignola script and cover, John Byrne art						
	$1.00	$3.00	$5.00	£0.60	£1.80	£3.00
2-4 ND Mike Mignola script and cover, John Byrne art						
	$0.60	$1.80	$3.00	£0.30	£0.90	£1.50
Title Value:	$2.80	$8.40	$14.00	£1.50	£4.50	£7.50

Hellboy: Seeds of Destruction (Oct 1995)
Trade paperback

	£Good	£Fine	£N.Mint
reprints mini-series plus new artwork by Mignola	£2.40	£7.20	£12.00
Signed, Limited Hardcover Edition (Feb 1995)			
foil-embossed slipcase. 1,000 copies	£13.50	£40.50	£67.50

HELLBOY: THE WOLVES OF ST. AUGUST
Dark Horse,OS; 1 Nov 1995

	$Good	$Fine	$N.Mint	£Good	£Fine	£N.Mint
1 ND 48pgs, Mike Mignola script and art						
	$1.00	$3.00	$5.00	£0.65	£1.95	£3.25
Title Value:	$1.00	$3.00	$5.00	£0.65	£1.95	£3.25

HELLHOUND
Marvel Comics Group/Epic,MS; 1 Dec 1993-4 Mar 1994

	$Good	$Fine	$N.Mint	£Good	£Fine	£N.Mint
1-4 ND John Miller and Floyd Hughes						
	$0.45	$1.35	$2.25	£0.30	£0.90	£1.50
Title Value:	$1.80	$5.40	$9.00	£1.20	£3.60	£6.00

HELLHOUNDS: PANZER COPS
Dark Horse; 1 Feb 1994-6 Jul 1994

	$Good	$Fine	$N.Mint	£Good	£Fine	£N.Mint
1-5 ND Mamoru Oshii and Kamui Fugiwara; black and white						
	$0.45	$1.35	$2.25	£0.30	£0.90	£1.50
6 ND 48pgs, Mamoru Oshii and Kamui Fugiwara; black and white						
	$0.60	$1.80	$3.00	£0.40	£1.20	£2.00
Title Value:	$2.85	$8.55	$14.25	£1.90	£5.70	£9.50

Note: title simply called Hellhounds for issues #1 and 2

HELLINA
Lightning Comics; 1 Sep 1994-present

	$Good	$Fine	$N.Mint	£Good	£Fine	£N.Mint
1 ND Steven Zyskowski script; black and white						
	$1.20	$3.60	$6.00	£0.60	£1.80	£3.00
1 ND Commemerative edition, Signed and Numbered, limited to 1500 copies						
	$3.00	$9.00	$15.00	£1.40	£4.20	£7.00
1 ND Signed Edition (May 1995) - pre-bagged in mylar, signed by Steven Zyskowski, 1,500 copies						
	$3.00	$9.00	$15.00	£1.40	£4.20	£7.00
1 2nd printing, ND (May 1995) - new cover and Hellina sketches						
	$0.55	$1.65	$2.75	£0.35	£1.05	£1.75
1 ND Signed Edition (May 1995) - pre-bagged in mylar, signed by Steven Zyskowski; 1,500 copies						
	$3.00	$9.00	$15.00	£1.40	£4.20	£7.00
Title Value:	$7.75	$23.25	$38.75	£3.75	£11.25	£18.75

Hellina (Feb 1995)
Trade paperback

	£Good	£Fine	£N.Mint
reprints stories from Perg #4-7, Hellina #1 and Fury of Hellina #1	£1.20	£3.60	£6.00

HELLINA, THE FURY OF
Lightning Comics,OS; 1 Jan 1995

	$Good	$Fine	$N.Mint	£Good	£Fine	£N.Mint
1 ND Steven Zyskowski script; black and white						
	$0.60	$1.80	$3.00	£0.40	£1.20	£2.00
1 ND Commemorative Edition (Jan 1995) - metallic silver ink cover, pre-bagged; 1,000 copies						
	$2.00	$6.00	$10.00	£1.30	£3.90	£6.50
1 ND Signed and Numbered Edition (Apr 1995) - signed and numbered by Steven Zyskowski, shipped in mylar bag						
	$2.00	$6.00	$10.00	£1.30	£3.90	£6.50
Title Value:	$4.60	$13.80	$23.00	£3.00	£9.00	£15.00

HELLINA/CATFIGHT
Lightning Comics,OS; 1 Oct 1995

	$Good	$Fine	$N.Mint	£Good	£Fine	£N.Mint
1 ND	$0.55	$1.65	$2.75	£0.35	£1.05	£1.75
1 ND Signed Edition (Oct 1995) - gold metallic ink cover						
	$1.20	$3.60	$6.00	£0.80	£2.40	£4.00
1 ND Nude Signed Edition (Oct 1995) - Paul Abrams/Gary Barnes cover, signed						
	$2.00	$6.00	$10.00	£1.30	£3.90	£6.50
1 ND Signed & Numbered Edition (Nov 1995) - 1,500 copies pre-bagged with certificate						
	$2.00	$6.00	$10.00	£1.30	£3.90	£6.50
1 ND Commemorative Edition; gold metallic ink cover, pre-bagged with certificate of authenticity; limited to 2500 copies						
	$2.50	$7.50	$12.50	£1.50	£4.50	£7.50
Title Value:	$8.25	$24.75	$41.25	£5.25	£15.75	£26.25

HELLINA: KISS OF DEATH
Lightning Comics; 1 Jul 1995

	$Good	$Fine	$N.Mint	£Good	£Fine	£N.Mint
1 ND Steven Zyskowski script, Paul Abrams and Gary Barnes art; black and white						
	$0.55	$1.65	$2.75	£0.35	£1.05	£1.75
1 ND 20% of the print run has this variant cover						
	$1.50	$4.50	$7.50	£0.60	£1.80	£3.00
1 ND Nude version - pre-bagged with numbered certificate						
	$3.00	$9.00	$15.00	£1.50	£4.50	£7.50
1 ND Signed and Numbered Edition (Aug 1995) - pre-bagged with certificate; 1,500 copies						
	$2.00	$6.00	$10.00	£1.30	£3.90	£6.50
Title Value:	$7.05	$21.15	$35.25	£3.75	£11.25	£18.75

HELLINA: TAKING BACK THE NIGHT
Lightning Comics; 1 Apr 1995

	$Good	$Fine	$N.Mint	£Good	£Fine	£N.Mint
1 ND Lawrence and Anderson art, Clarke Hawbaker cover						
	$0.55	$1.65	$2.75	£0.35	£1.05	£1.75
1 ND Nude Version; pre-bagged with certificate, Lawrence and Anderson art, Clarke Hawbaker cover						
	$2.00	$6.00	$10.00	£1.30	£3.90	£6.50
1 ND Signed Edition (Jun 1995) with certificate; 1,500 copies						
	$2.00	$6.00	$10.00	£1.30	£3.90	£6.50
Title Value:	$4.55	$13.65	$22.75	£2.95	£8.85	£14.75

HELLINA: WICKED WAYS
Lightning Comics,OS; 1 Nov 1995

	$Good	$Fine	$N.Mint	£Good	£Fine	£N.Mint
1 ND black and white						
	$0.55	$1.65	$2.75	£0.35	£1.05	£1.75
1 Nude Cover variant, ND signed by Joe Zyskowski						
	$2.00	$6.00	$10.00	£1.40	£4.20	£7.00
1 Signed Numbered Edition (Nov 1995), ND pre-bagged, pencilled and inked by Trent Kaniuga; black and white						
	$1.20	$3.60	$6.00	£0.80	£2.40	£4.00
Title Value:	$3.75	$11.25	$18.75	£2.55	£7.65	£12.75

HELLRAISER 1993 SPECIAL
Marvel Comics Group/Epic,OS; 1 Jan 1994

	$Good	$Fine	$N.Mint	£Good	£Fine	£N.Mint
1 ND 64pgs, anthology featuring work by Ann Nocenti and Scott Hampton; Scott Hampton painted cover						
	$1.50	$4.50	$7.50	£1.00	£3.00	£5.00

	$Good	$Fine	$N.Mint	£Good	£Fine	£N.Mint
Title Value:	$1.50	$4.50	$7.50	£1.00	£3.00	£5.00

HELLRAISER HOLIDAY SPECIAL
Marvel Comics Group/Epic,OS; 1 Jan 1993

	$Good	$Fine	$N.Mint	£Good	£Fine	£N.Mint
1 ND 48pgs, anthology of Clive Barker stories	$0.90	$2.70	$4.50	£0.60	£1.80	£3.00
Title Value:	$0.90	$2.70	$4.50	£0.60	£1.80	£3.00

HELLRAISER III: HELL ON EARTH BOOKSHELF EDITION
Marvel Comics Group/Epic; 1 Oct 1992

	$Good	$Fine	$N.Mint	£Good	£Fine	£N.Mint
1 ND 48pgs, adaptation of film	$0.90	$2.70	$4.50	£0.60	£1.80	£3.00
Title Value:	$0.90	$2.70	$4.50	£0.60	£1.80	£3.00

HELLRAISER III: HELL ON EARTH MAGAZINE EDITION
Marvel Comics Group/Epic; 1 Oct 1992

	$Good	$Fine	$N.Mint	£Good	£Fine	£N.Mint
1 ND 48pgs, adaptation of film	$0.50	$1.60	$2.70	£0.35	£1.05	£1.80
Title Value:	$0.50	$1.60	$2.70	£0.35	£1.05	£1.80

HELLRAISER SPRING SLAUGHTER: RAZING HELL
Marvel Comics Group/Epic,OS; 1 May 1994

	$Good	$Fine	$N.Mint	£Good	£Fine	£N.Mint
1 ND 48pgs, three stories	$1.40	$4.20	$7.00	£0.90	£2.70	£4.50
Title Value:	$1.40	$4.20	$7.00	£0.90	£2.70	£4.50

HELLRAISER SUMMER SPECIAL
Marvel Comics Group/Epic,OS; 1 Sep 1992

	$Good	$Fine	$N.Mint	£Good	£Fine	£N.Mint
1 ND	$1.10	$3.35	$5.62	£0.75	£2.25	£3.75
Title Value:	$1.10	$3.35	$5.62	£0.75	£2.25	£3.75

HELLRAISER, CLIVE BARKER'S
Marvel Comics Group/Epic; 1 Feb 1990-20 1993

	$Good	$Fine	$N.Mint	£Good	£Fine	£N.Mint
1 ND Bolton art	$1.50	$4.50	$7.50	£1.00	£3.00	£5.00
2 ND Simon Bisley cover	$1.20	$3.60	$6.00	£0.80	£2.40	£4.00
3 ND features John Ridgway art	$1.10	$3.35	$5.62	£0.75	£2.25	£3.75
4 ND	$1.10	$3.35	$5.62	£0.75	£2.25	£3.75
5 ND Ted McKeever cover	$1.05	$3.15	$5.25	£0.70	£2.10	£3.50
6 ND Billy Mumy/Miguel Ferrer scripts featured	$1.05	$3.15	$5.25	£0.70	£2.10	£3.50
7 ND John Bolton/Kyle Baker art featured	$1.05	$3.15	$5.25	£0.70	£2.10	£3.50
8 ND Texeira art featured	$1.00	$3.00	$5.00	£0.65	£1.95	£3.25
9 ND Scott Hampton art featured	$1.00	$3.00	$5.00	£0.65	£1.95	£3.25
10 ND 48pgs, foil embossed cover	$1.00	$3.00	$5.00	£0.65	£1.95	£3.25
11-13 ND 48pgs	$0.90	$2.70	$4.50	£0.60	£1.80	£3.00
14 ND 48pgs, $4.95 cover begins	$0.90	$2.70	$4.50	£0.60	£1.80	£3.00
15-20 ND 48pgs	$0.90	$2.70	$4.50	£0.60	£1.80	£3.00
Title Value:	$20.05	$60.25	$100.49	£13.35	£40.05	£66.75
Trade Paperback (Apr 1991), selected stories reprinted from issues #1-4, new John Bolton cover		$1.60		£4.80		£8.00

Note: Mature Readers only. Based on the Hellraiser and Hellbound films. Issues #1-9 64pgs. Issues #1-6 quarterly frequency. Bi-monthly from issue #7

HELLRAISER: BOOK OF THE DAMNED
Marvel Comics Group; 1 Oct 1991-4 1992

	$Good	$Fine	$N.Mint	£Good	£Fine	£N.Mint
1-4 ND 48pgs, journal format of photos, notes and press cuttings, foil embossed cover by Simon Bisley	$1.00	$3.00	$5.00	£0.65	£1.95	£3.25
Title Value:	$4.00	$12.00	$20.00	£2.60	£7.80	£13.00

HELLSHOCK
Image,MS; 1 Jul 1994-4 Oct 1994

	$Good	$Fine	$N.Mint	£Good	£Fine	£N.Mint
1 ND Jae Lee script and art	$0.45	$1.35	$2.25	£0.30	£0.90	£1.50
2-4 ND Jae Lee script and art	$0.40	$1.20	$2.00	£0.25	£0.75	£1.25
Title Value:	$1.65	$4.95	$8.25	£1.05	£3.15	£5.25

HELLSTORM
Marvel Comics Group; 1 Apr 1993-21 Dec 1994

	$Good	$Fine	$N.Mint	£Good	£Fine	£N.Mint
1 Daimon Hellstrom (Son of Satan) begins, parchment stock cover with thermographic (raised) red ink	$0.40	$1.20	$2.00	£0.25	£0.75	£1.25
2 Dr. Strange and Gargoyle appear	$0.40	$1.20	$2.00	£0.25	£0.75	£1.25
3	$0.40	$1.20	$2.00	£0.25	£0.75	£1.25
4 Ghost Rider appears	$0.40	$1.20	$2.00	£0.25	£0.75	£1.25
5	$0.40	$1.20	$2.00	£0.25	£0.75	£1.25
6 Mark Beachum guest pencils	$0.40	$1.20	$2.00	£0.25	£0.75	£1.25
7-13	$0.40	$1.20	$2.00	£0.25	£0.75	£1.25
14 with free Spiderman vs. Venom card sheet	$0.40	$1.20	$2.00	£0.25	£0.75	£1.25
15	$0.40	$1.20	$2.00	£0.25	£0.75	£1.25
16 Warren Ellis script begins, Brian Bolland cover	$0.40	$1.20	$2.00	£0.25	£0.75	£1.25
17 Satana returns	$0.40	$1.20	$2.00	£0.25	£0.75	£1.25
18-20	$0.40	$1.20	$2.00	£0.25	£0.75	£1.25
21 Duncan Fegredo cover	$0.40	$1.20	$2.00	£0.25	£0.75	£1.25
Title Value:	$8.40	$25.20	$42.00	£5.25	£15.75	£26.25

HEMBECK
Eclipse,Magazine; 1,2 1988?

	$Good	$Fine	$N.Mint	£Good	£Fine	£N.Mint
1-2 ND reprints	$0.30	$0.90	$1.50	£0.20	£0.60	£1.00

	$Good	$Fine	$N.Mint	£Good	£Fine	£N.Mint
Title Value:	$0.60	$1.80	$3.00	£0.40	£1.20	£2.00

HENRY V
Caliber/Tome Press,MS; 1-3 1991

	$Good	$Fine	$N.Mint	£Good	£Fine	£N.Mint
1-3 ND black and white	$0.40	$1.20	$2.00	£0.25	£0.75	£1.25
Title Value:	$1.20	$3.60	$6.00	£0.75	£2.25	£3.75

HEPCATS
Double Diamond Press; 1 1989-present

	$Good	$Fine	$N.Mint	£Good	£Fine	£N.Mint
1 Martin Wagner script and art begins; black and white	$0.90	$2.70	$4.50	£0.60	£1.80	£3.00
1 Special Edition (Nov 1991) - reprints issue 1, 2,000 signed and numbered copies	$0.60	$1.80	$3.00	£0.40	£1.20	£2.00
1 Special Edition 2nd printing (Aug 1994) - new cover, new back-up story	$0.40	$1.20	$2.00	£0.25	£0.75	£1.25
1 2nd printing	$0.45	$1.35	$2.25	£0.30	£0.90	£1.50
2	$0.70	$2.10	$3.50	£0.45	£1.35	£2.25
2 Special Edition (Aug 1994) - contains L'il Hepcats story from Usagi Yojimbo #87	$0.40	$1.20	$2.00	£0.25	£0.75	£1.25
2 2nd printing	$0.45	$1.35	$2.25	£0.30	£0.90	£1.50
2 3rd printing	$0.45	$1.35	$2.25	£0.30	£0.90	£1.50
3 Martin Wagner script/art	$0.55	$1.65	$2.75	£0.35	£1.05	£1.75
4-6 Martin Wagner script/art	$0.45	$1.35	$2.25	£0.30	£0.90	£1.50
6 2nd printing, (Apr 1993)	$0.40	$1.20	$2.00	£0.25	£0.75	£1.25
7 Martin Wagner script/art	$0.45	$1.35	$2.25	£0.30	£0.90	£1.50
7 2nd printing, (Jun 1993)	$0.45	$1.35	$2.25	£0.30	£0.90	£1.50
8-11 Martin Wagner script/art	$0.45	$1.35	$2.25	£0.30	£0.90	£1.50
12-13 40pgs, Martin Wagner script and art	$0.45	$1.35	$2.25	£0.30	£0.90	£1.50
14-15 40pgs, Martin Wagner script and art	$0.55	$1.65	$2.75	£0.35	£1.05	£1.75
Title Value:	$11.35	$34.05	$56.75	£7.45	£22.35	£37.25

Note: all Non-Distributed on the news-stands in the U.K.

	£Good	£Fine	£N.Mint
The First Hepcats Book (1991), reprints newspaper strips	£1.00	£3.00	£5.00
The Second Hepcats Book (1991), reprints newspaper strips	£1.00	£3.00	£5.00
The Collegiate Hepcats (1994) collects all early Hepcats strips from Martin Wagner's college days, signed	£1.30	£3.90	£6.50
Snowblind Part One (Mar 1995) Trade paperback reprints issues #3-10	£2.00	£6.00	£10.00

HEPCATS LITTERBOX, THE
Double Diamond Press,OS; nn Aug 1995

	$Good	$Fine	$N.Mint	£Good	£Fine	£N.Mint
nn ND sampler comic reprinting early excerpts and introducing characters	$0.50	$1.50	$2.50	£0.30	£0.90	£1.50
Title Value:	$0.50	$1.50	$2.50	£0.30	£0.90	£1.50

HERBIE
ACG; 1 Apr/May 1964-23 Feb 1967

	$Good	$Fine	$N.Mint	£Good	£Fine	£N.Mint
1	$20.50	$62.50	$125.00	£12.50	£38.00	£75.00
2-4	$12.50	$38.00	$75.00	£6.25	£18.50	£37.50
5 Beatles appear	$12.50	$38.00	$75.00	£7.50	£22.50	£45.00
6-7	$9.00	$27.00	$45.00	£6.00	£18.00	£30.00
8 origin	$12.00	$36.00	$60.00	£7.00	£21.00	£35.00
9-10	$9.00	$27.00	$45.00	£6.00	£18.00	£30.00
11-15	$6.00	$18.00	$30.00	£4.00	£12.00	£20.00
16-20	$5.25	$15.50	$26.25	£3.50	£10.50	£17.50
21-22	$4.50	$13.50	$22.50	£3.00	£9.00	£15.00
23 part reprint of 1st Herbie from Forbidden World's #73	$4.50	$13.50	$22.50	£3.00	£9.00	£15.00
Title Value:	$188.25	$566.50	$983.75	£116.25	£348.50	£620.00

Note: all distributed in the U.K.

HERBIE (2ND SERIES)
A Plus Comics; 1 Oct 1990-7 1991

	$Good	$Fine	$N.Mint	£Good	£Fine	£N.Mint
1 ND 48pgs, reprints of original series begin, Trina Robbins cover that parodies Batman and Spiderman; black and white	$0.40	$1.20	$2.00	£0.25	£0.75	£1.25
2-5 ND 48pgs, Rog 2000 by John Byrne reprint; black and white	$0.40	$1.20	$2.00	£0.25	£0.75	£1.25
6 ND 48pgs, Star Trek parody cover; black and white	$0.40	$1.20	$2.00	£0.25	£0.75	£1.25
7 ND 48pgs, black and white	$0.40	$1.20	$2.00	£0.25	£0.75	£1.25
Title Value:	$2.80	$8.40	$14.00	£1.75	£5.25	£8.75

HERBIE (3RD SERIES)
Dark Horse; 1 Sep 1992-7 Mar 1993

	$Good	$Fine	$N.Mint	£Good	£Fine	£N.Mint
1 ND Ogden Whitney art in colour begins; 8pgs John Byrne art, John Byrne cover	$0.45	$1.35	$2.25	£0.30	£0.90	£1.50
2 ND	$0.45	$1.35	$2.25	£0.30	£0.90	£1.50
3 ND Bob Burden cover	$0.45	$1.35	$2.25	£0.30	£0.90	£1.50
4 ND Art Adams cover	$0.45	$1.35	$2.25	£0.30	£0.90	£1.50
5-7 ND	$0.45	$1.35	$2.25	£0.30	£0.90	£1.50
Title Value:	$3.15	$9.45	$15.75	£2.10	£6.30	£10.50

Note: originally announced as a 12 issue series

HERCULES
Charlton; 1 Oct 1967-13 Sep 1969

1 distributed in the U.K.

	$Good	$Fine	$N.Mint	£Good	£Fine	£N.Mint
	$1.50	$4.50	$7.50	£1.00	£3.00	£5.00
2-8 distributed in the U.K.						
	$1.20	$3.60	$6.00	£0.80	£2.40	£4.00
9-13 distributed in the U.K.						
	$0.90	$2.70	$4.50	£0.60	£1.80	£3.00
Title Value:	$114.40	$43.20	$72.00	£9.60	£28.80	£48.00

HERCULES (2ND SERIES)
Charlton,Magazine; 8 Dec 1968
8 rare in the U.K., very rare in the U.S.

	$Good	$Fine	$N.Mint	£Good	£Fine	£N.Mint
	$4.00	$12.00	$20.00	£3.00	£9.00	£15.00
Title Value:	$4.00	$12.00	$20.00	£3.00	£9.00	£15.00

Note: magazine size. Reprint of #1 plus new story

HERCULES (3RD SERIES)
A Plus Comics; 1 Sep 1991-2 1991
1-2 ND reprints Charlton series with new dialogue

	$Good	$Fine	$N.Mint	£Good	£Fine	£N.Mint
	$0.45	$1.35	$2.25	£0.30	£0.90	£1.50
Title Value:	$0.90	$2.70	$4.50	£0.60	£1.80	£3.00

HERCULES UNBOUND
DC Comics; 1 Oct/Nov 1975-12 Aug/Sep 1977
1 Garcia Lopez art begins (ends #6), Wood inks begin

	$Good	$Fine	$N.Mint	£Good	£Fine	£N.Mint
	$0.25	$0.75	$1.25	£0.15	£0.45	£0.75
2-6	$0.25	$0.75	$1.25	£0.15	£0.45	£0.75
7-9 Walt Simonson art						
	$0.25	$0.75	$1.25	£0.15	£0.45	£0.75
10 Walt Simonson art, Atomic Knights X-over						
	$0.25	$0.75	$1.25	£0.15	£0.45	£0.75
11-12 Walt Simonson art						
	$0.25	$0.75	$1.25	£0.15	£0.45	£0.75
Title Value:	$3.00	$9.00	$15.00	£1.80	£5.40	£9.00

HERCULES, PRINCE OF POWER
Marvel Comics Group,MS; 1 Sep 1982-4 Dec 1982
(see Marvel Graphic Novel)
1-4 ND Bob Layton art

	$Good	$Fine	$N.Mint	£Good	£Fine	£N.Mint
	$0.25	$0.75	$1.25	£0.15	£0.45	£0.75
Title Value:	$1.00	$3.00	$5.00	£0.60	£1.80	£3.00
Trade Paperback, reprints #1-4.				£0.70	£2.10	£3.50

HERCULES, PRINCE OF POWER (2ND SERIES)
Marvel Comics Group,MS; 1 Mar 1984-4 Jun 1984
1-4 ND Bob Layton art

	$Good	$Fine	$N.Mint	£Good	£Fine	£N.Mint
	$0.25	$0.75	$1.25	£0.15	£0.45	£0.75
Title Value:	$1.00	$3.00	$5.00	£0.60	£1.80	£3.00

HERMES VS. THE EYEBALL KID
Dark Horse,MS; 1 Dec 1994-3 Feb 1995
1-3 ND Eddie Campbell script and art

	$Good	$Fine	$N.Mint	£Good	£Fine	£N.Mint
	$0.60	$1.80	$3.00	£0.40	£1.20	£2.00
Title Value:	$1.80	$5.40	$9.00	£1.20	£3.60	£6.00

HERO
Marvel Comics Group,MS; 1 May 1990-6 Oct 1990

	$Good	$Fine	$N.Mint	£Good	£Fine	£N.Mint
1-6 ND	$0.25	$0.75	$1.25	£0.15	£0.45	£0.75
Title Value:	$1.50	$4.50	$7.50	£0.90	£2.70	£4.50

Note: role-playing game tie-in

HERO ALLIANCE
Wonder,OS; 1 May 1987
1 ND story continues from Pied Piper Graphic Novel

	$Good	$Fine	$N.Mint	£Good	£Fine	£N.Mint
	$0.55	$1.65	$2.75	£0.35	£1.05	£1.75
Title Value:	$0.55	$1.65	$2.75	£0.35	£1.05	£1.75
Graphic Novel, Hardcover				£1.70	£5.10	£8.50
Annual 1 (Jul 1990), wraparound cover by Paul Smith				£0.30	£0.90	£1.50

HERO ALLIANCE (2ND SERIES)
Innovation; 1 Sep 1989-18 1991

	$Good	$Fine	$N.Mint	£Good	£Fine	£N.Mint
1 ND Ron Lim art	$0.45	$1.35	$2.25	£0.30	£0.90	£1.50
2-9 ND	$0.40	$1.20	$2.00	£0.25	£0.75	£1.25
10 ND ties in with Annual #1						
	$0.40	$1.20	$2.00	£0.25	£0.75	£1.25
11-18 ND	$0.40	$1.20	$2.00	£0.25	£0.75	£1.25
Title Value:	$7.25	$21.75	$36.25	£4.55	£13.65	£22.75

HERO ALLIANCE QUARTERLY
Innovation; 1 Jun 1991-4 1992

	$Good	$Fine	$N.Mint	£Good	£Fine	£N.Mint
1 ND	$0.45	$1.35	$2.25	£0.30	£0.90	£1.50
2-3 ND Brian Stelfreeze cover						
	$0.45	$1.35	$2.25	£0.30	£0.90	£1.50
4 ND	$0.45	$1.35	$2.25	£0.30	£0.90	£1.50
Title Value:	$1.80	$5.40	$9.00	£1.20	£3.60	£6.00

HERO ALLIANCE SPECIAL
Innovation,OS; 1 Sep 1992
1 ND prelude to re-vamped series

	$Good	$Fine	$N.Mint	£Good	£Fine	£N.Mint
	$0.45	$1.35	$2.25	£0.30	£0.90	£1.50
Title Value:	$0.45	$1.35	$2.25	£0.30	£0.90	£1.50

HERO ALLIANCE VS. JUSTICE MACHINE
Innovation; 1 Nov 1990
1 ND follows events after Annual #1

	$Good	$Fine	$N.Mint	£Good	£Fine	£N.Mint
	$0.80	$2.40	$4.00	£0.50	£1.50	£2.50
Title Value:	$0.80	$2.40	$4.00	£0.50	£1.50	£2.50

HERO ALLIANCE; END OF THE GOLDEN AGE
Innovation,MS; 1 Jul 1989-3 Aug 1989
1-3 ND Bart Sears/Ron Lim art, part reprint

	$Good	$Fine	$N.Mint	£Good	£Fine	£N.Mint
	$0.55	$1.65	$2.75	£0.35	£1.05	£1.75
Title Value:	$1.65	$4.95	$8.25	£1.05	£3.15	£5.25

Note: bi-weekly

HERO HOTLINE
DC Comics,MS; 1 May 1989-6 Oct 1989

	$Good	$Fine	$N.Mint	£Good	£Fine	£N.Mint
1-6	$0.15	$0.45	$0.75	£0.10	£0.35	£0.60
Title Value:	$0.90	$2.70	$4.50	£0.60	£2.10	£3.60

Note: high quality paper

HERO PREMIERE EDITION
Warrior Publications; 1 Jul 1993-11 1995

1 Premiere Edition #1 (issued with Hero Illustrated #1) - Star Trek: Deep Space Nine; all Ash Can 5.5" x 8.5" unless otherwise stated; blue cover, 8pgs

	$Good	$Fine	$N.Mint	£Good	£Fine	£N.Mint
	$0.60	$1.80	$3.00	£0.40	£1.20	£2.00

2 Premiere Edition #2 (issued with Hero Illustrated #1) - Batman/Grendel; red foil enhanced cover, 16pgs

	$0.60	$1.80	$3.00	£0.40	£1.20	£2.00

3 Premiere Edition #3 (issued with Hero Illustrated #2) - Aliens: Deadliest of the Species; all red foil cover, 5.5" x 8.5" Ash Can size, 16pgs with 8 in colour and 8 in black and white

	$0.60	$1.80	$3.00	£0.40	£1.20	£2.00

4 Premiere Edition #4 (issued with Hero Illustrated #2) - Madman Adventures; red foil enhanced cover, 16pgs

	$0.60	$1.80	$3.00	£0.40	£1.20	£2.00

5 Premiere Edition #5 (issued with Hero Illustrated #3) - Q Unit; 16pgs

	$0.60	$1.80	$3.00	£0.40	£1.20	£2.00

6 Premiere Edition #6 (issued with Hero Illustrated #3) - Horus, Lord of Light; 16pgs

	$0.60	$1.80	$3.00	£0.40	£1.20	£2.00

7 Premiere Edition #7 - 2099 Unlimited #1; gold foil cover, 16pgs, numbered with seal of authenticity; 10,000

	$0.80	$2.40	$4.00	£0.50	£1.50	£2.50

8 Premiere Edition #8 - Shadowhawk III #1

	$0.60	$1.80	$3.00	£0.40	£1.20	£2.00

9 Premiere Edition #9 - Aliens vs. Predator: deadliest of the Species gold/blue foil cover

	$0.60	$1.80	$3.00	£0.40	£1.20	£2.00

10 Premiere Edition #10 (issued with Hero Illustrated #6) - Pitt #3; red foil enhanced cover, 16pgs

	$0.45	$1.35	$2.25	£0.30	£0.90	£1.50

11 Premiere Edition #11 (issued with Hero Illustrated #7) - Wetworks; 16pgs

	$0.45	$1.35	$2.25	£0.30	£0.90	£1.50

11 Premiere Edition Holiday Special (issued with Hero Illustrated #7) - Bone; 7" x 10" normal comic size

	$0.60	$1.80	$3.00	£0.40	£1.20	£2.00

Heart Throbs #68

Hercules (1st) #1

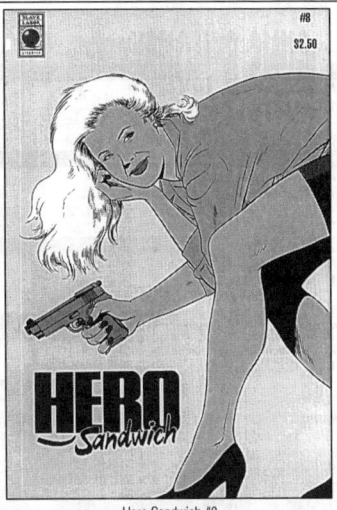

Hero Sandwich #8

MINT = 100% / NEAR MINT (inc. +/-) = 90-99% / VERY FINE (inc. +/-) = 75-89% / FINE (inc. +/-) = 55-74%
VERY GOOD (inc. +/-) = 35-54% / GOOD (inc. +/-) = 15-34% / FAIR = 5-14% / POOR = 1-4%

391

	$Good	$Fine	$N.Mint	£Good	£Fine	£N.Mint
Title Value:	$7.10	$21.30	$35.50	£4.70	£14.10	£23.50

Note: only available with Hero Magazine; not distributed in the U.K.

HERO SANDWICH
Slave Labor; 1 1988-9 1990

	$Good	$Fine	$N.Mint	£Good	£Fine	£N.Mint
1-7 ND	$0.45	$1.35	$2.25	£0.30	£0.90	£1.50
7 ND single issue amalgamation of issues #7 and #8 (Apr 1990)						
	$0.55	$1.65	$2.75	£0.35	£1.05	£1.75
8-9 ND	$0.45	$1.35	$2.25	£0.30	£0.90	£1.50
Title Value:	$4.60	$13.80	$23.00	£3.05	£9.15	£15.25

HERO ZERO
Dark Horse, OS; 0 Sep 1994

	$Good	$Fine	$N.Mint	£Good	£Fine	£N.Mint
0 ND spin-off from Comics' Greatest World series						
	$0.45	$1.35	$2.25	£0.30	£0.90	£1.50
Title Value:	$0.45	$1.35	$2.25	£0.30	£0.90	£1.50

HEROES AGAINST HUNGER
DC Comics, OS; nn 1986

(see Heroes For Hope)

	$Good	$Fine	$N.Mint	£Good	£Fine	£N.Mint
nn ND famine relief benefit book; Superman and Batman feature, Neal Adams cover and part art						
	$0.40	$1.20	$2.00	£0.25	£0.75	£1.25
Title Value:	$0.40	$1.20	$2.00	£0.25	£0.75	£1.25

HEROES FOR HOPE STARRING THE X-MEN
Marvel Comics Group, OS; nn Dec 1985

	$Good	$Fine	$N.Mint	£Good	£Fine	£N.Mint
nn ND 52pgs, proceeds donated to famine relief; Ellison, Morre and Stephen King scripts, Wrightson, Corben, Miller, Neal Adams and Bolton art						
	$0.80	$2.40	$4.00	£0.50	£1.50	£2.50
Title Value:	$0.80	$2.40	$4.00	£0.50	£1.50	£2.50

HERU, SON OF AUSAR
Afrocentric Comic Books; 1 Apr 1993-3 1993

	$Good	$Fine	$N.Mint	£Good	£Fine	£N.Mint
1 ND bound-in trading card by Erik Larsen						
	$0.40	$1.20	$2.00	£0.25	£0.75	£1.25
2-3 ND	$0.40	$1.20	$2.00	£0.25	£0.75	£1.25
Title Value:	$1.20	$3.60	$6.00	£0.75	£2.25	£3.75

HEX
DC Comics; 1 Sep 1985-18 Feb 1987

(see Jonah Hex, Jonah Hex Spectacular, Weird Western Tales)

	$Good	$Fine	$N.Mint	£Good	£Fine	£N.Mint
1 Mark Texeira art, new storyline, Hex in future						
	$0.40	$1.20	$2.00	£0.25	£0.75	£1.25
2-3 Mark Texira art						
	$0.30	$0.90	$1.50	£0.20	£0.60	£1.00
4 Mark Texeira cover						
	$0.25	$0.75	$1.25	£0.15	£0.45	£0.75
5 Mark Texeira cover and art						
	$0.25	$0.75	$1.25	£0.15	£0.45	£0.75
6 Mark Texeira cover and art, origin Stiletto						
	$0.25	$0.75	$1.25	£0.15	£0.45	£0.75
7 Mark Texeira cover and art						
	$0.25	$0.75	$1.25	£0.15	£0.45	£0.75
8	$0.25	$0.75	$1.25	£0.15	£0.45	£0.75
9 Mark Texeira cover and art						
	$0.25	$0.75	$1.25	£0.15	£0.45	£0.75
10	$0.25	$0.75	$1.25	£0.15	£0.45	£0.75
11-12 Mark Texeira cover and art, Batman appears						
	$0.30	$0.90	$1.50	£0.20	£0.60	£1.00
13-14 Mark Texeira cover and art						
	$0.25	$0.75	$1.25	£0.15	£0.45	£0.75
15 Giffen cover and art						
	$0.25	$0.75	$1.25	£0.15	£0.45	£0.75
16-18 Giffen art	$0.25	$0.75	$1.25	£0.15	£0.45	£0.75
Title Value:	$4.85	$14.55	$24.25	£3.00	£9.00	£15.00

HEXBREAKER
(see Badger)

HIDING PLACE, THE
DC Comics/Piranha Press; nn Aug 1990

	$Good	$Fine	$N.Mint	£Good	£Fine	£N.Mint
nn ND 104pgs, Trade paperback format, Steve Parkhouse art						
	$2.30	$6.75	$11.50	£1.50	£4.50	£7.50
Title Value:	$2.30	$6.75	$11.50	£1.50	£4.50	£7.50

HIGH SHINING BRASS
Apple Comics; 1 Aug 1990-4 Oct 1991

	$Good	$Fine	$N.Mint	£Good	£Fine	£N.Mint
1-4 ND story by Vietnam Veteran Don Lomax						
	$0.45	$1.35	$2.25	£0.30	£0.90	£1.50
Title Value:	$1.80	$5.40	$9.00	£1.20	£3.60	£6.00

HIGHBROW ENTERTAINMENT ASHCAN
Image, OS; nn Nov 1994

	$Good	$Fine	$N.Mint	£Good	£Fine	£N.Mint
nn ND information on Erik Larsen's projects for 1995/96						
	$0.30	$0.90	$1.50	£0.20	£0.60	£1.00
Title Value:	$0.30	$0.90	$1.50	£0.20	£0.60	£1.00

HIS NAME IS SAVAGE
Adventure House, Magazine; 1 Jun 1968

	$Good	$Fine	$N.Mint	£Good	£Fine	£N.Mint
1 ND Gil Kane art, black & white						
	$4.50	$13.50	$22.50	£3.00	£9.00	£15.00
Title Value:	$4.50	$13.50	$22.50	£3.00	£9.00	£15.00

HISTORY OF THE DC UNIVERSE
DC Comics, MS; 1 Sep 1986-2 Nov 1986

	$Good	$Fine	$N.Mint	£Good	£Fine	£N.Mint
1-2 ND 48pgs, George Perez art						
	$0.90	$2.70	$4.50	£0.60	£1.80	£3.00
Title Value:	$1.80	$5.40	$9.00	£1.20	£3.60	£6.00

Note: Dark Knight format, glossy paper (Silent Knight accidentally appears in 2 separate periods of history, and Tommy Tomorrow is miscoloured throughout as Rip Hunter.)

	£Good	£Fine	£N.Mint
Deluxe Hardback Edition with dustjacket and limited edition enamel pin	£4.20	£12.60	£21.00
Deluxe Hardback Edition with dustjacket, signed and numbered with limited edition gold-plated pin	£12.00	£36.00	£60.00

HITCH-HIKER'S GUIDE TO THE GALAXY, THE
DC Comics, MS; 1 Nov 1993-3 Jan 1994

(see Restaurant At The End Of The Universe)

	$Good	$Fine	$N.Mint	£Good	£Fine	£N.Mint
1-3 ND 48pgs, squarebound; John Carnell script, Steve Leialoha art						
	$1.00	$3.00	$5.00	£0.60	£1.80	£3.00
Title Value:	$3.00	$9.00	$15.00	£1.80	£5.40	£9.00

HITOMI II
Antarctic Press, MS; 1 Aug 1993-10 Sep 1995

	$Good	$Fine	$N.Mint	£Good	£Fine	£N.Mint
1 ND Dave Wilson script and art, black and white						
	$0.45	$1.35	$2.25	£0.30	£0.90	£1.50
2-6 ND black and white						
	$0.45	$1.35	$2.25	£0.30	£0.90	£1.50
7 ND title becomes "Hitomi: Geohammer"; black and white						
	$0.55	$1.65	$2.75	£0.35	£1.05	£1.75
8-9 ND black and white						
	$0.55	$1.65	$2.75	£0.35	£1.05	£1.75
10 ND 40pgs, black and white						
	$0.60	$1.80	$3.00	£0.40	£1.20	£2.00
Title Value:	$4.95	$14.85	$24.75	£3.25	£9.75	£16.25

HOBBIT, THE
Eclipse, MS; 1 Apr 1990-3 Jun 1990

	$Good	$Fine	$N.Mint	£Good	£Fine	£N.Mint
1 ND 48pgs, adaptation of Tolkien novel						
	$0.85	$2.55	$4.25	£0.55	£1.65	£2.75
1 2nd printing ND	$0.80	$2.40	$4.00	£0.50	£1.50	£2.50
2-3 ND 48pgs	$0.85	$2.55	$4.25	£0.55	£1.65	£2.75
Title Value:	$3.35	$10.05	$16.75	£2.15	£6.45	£10.75
Graphic Album (1991), softcover				£1.50	£4.50	£7.50
Graphic Album (1991), hardcover				£4.50	£13.50	£22.50

HOKUM & HEX
Marvel Comics Group/Razorline; 1 Sep 1993-9 May 1994

	$Good	$Fine	$N.Mint	£Good	£Fine	£N.Mint
1 ND prismatic foil cover						
	$0.45	$1.35	$2.25	£0.30	£0.90	£1.50
2-9 ND	$0.40	$1.20	$2.00	£0.25	£0.75	£1.25
Title Value:	$3.65	$10.95	$18.25	£2.30	£6.90	£11.50

HOLIDAY FOR SCREAMS
Malibu, OS; 1 Feb 1992

	$Good	$Fine	$N.Mint	£Good	£Fine	£N.Mint
1 ND 48pgs, squarebound, black and white horror anthology						
	$0.90	$2.70	$4.50	£0.60	£1.80	£3.00
Title Value:	$0.90	$2.70	$4.50	£0.60	£1.80	£3.00

HOLIDAY OUT
Renegade; 1 Mar 1987-4 Jun 1987

	$Good	$Fine	$N.Mint	£Good	£Fine	£N.Mint
1-4 ND	$0.40	$1.20	$2.00	£0.25	£0.75	£1.25
Title Value:	$1.60	$4.80	$8.00	£1.00	£3.00	£5.00

HOLLYWOOD DETECTIVES, THE
Eternity, OS; 1 Jul 1991

	$Good	$Fine	$N.Mint	£Good	£Fine	£N.Mint
1 ND Dan Turner, Queenie Smith feature						
	$0.80	$2.40	$4.00	£0.50	£1.50	£2.50
Title Value:	$0.80	$2.40	$4.00	£0.50	£1.50	£2.50

HOLLYWOOD SECRETS OF ROMANCE
I.W. Super; 9 1964

	$Good	$Fine	$N.Mint	£Good	£Fine	£N.Mint
9 reprints Quality Comics Title "Hollywood Secrets"; Reed Crandall art; distributed in the U.K.						
	$1.15	$3.50	$7.00	£0.75	£2.25	£4.50
Title Value:	$1.15	$3.50	$7.00	£0.75	£2.25	£4.50

HOLLYWOOD SUPERSTARS
Marvel Comics Group/Epic; 1 Dec 1990-5 Apr 1991

	$Good	$Fine	$N.Mint	£Good	£Fine	£N.Mint
1-5 ND 48pgs	$0.45	$1.35	$2.25	£0.30	£0.90	£1.50
Title Value:	$2.25	$6.75	$11.25	£1.50	£4.50	£7.50

HOLOCAUST
DC Comics/Milestone, MS; 1 Feb 1995-5 Jun 1995

	$Good	$Fine	$N.Mint	£Good	£Fine	£N.Mint
1-5	$0.30	$0.90	$1.50	£0.20	£0.60	£1.00
Title Value:	$1.50	$4.50	$7.50	£1.00	£3.00	£5.00

HOLY KNIGHT, THE
Pocket Change Comics; 1 1995-present

	$Good	$Fine	$N.Mint	£Good	£Fine	£N.Mint
1-8 ND 24pgs, Bob Dixon script, Xavier and Kaleb art; black and white						
	$0.50	$1.50	$2.50	£0.30	£0.90	£1.50
9 ND Bob Dixon script, Philip Xavier art; black and white						
	$0.50	$1.50	$2.50	£0.30	£0.90	£1.50
Title Value:	$4.50	$13.50	$22.50	£2.70	£8.10	£13.50

HOMER THE HAPPY GHOST
Marvel Comics Group; 1 Nov 1969-5 Jul 1970

	$Good	$Fine	$N.Mint	£Good	£Fine	£N.Mint
1 scarce in the U.K.						
	$0.90	$2.70	$4.50	£0.60	£1.80	£3.00
2-5 scarce in the U.K.						
	$0.80	$2.40	$4.00	£0.50	£1.50	£2.50
Title Value:	$4.10	$12.30	$20.50	£2.60	£7.80	£13.00

HOMICIDE
Dark Horse, OS; 1 Apr 1990

	$Good	$Fine	$N.Mint	£Good	£Fine	£N.Mint
1 ND	$0.40	$1.20	$2.00	£0.25	£0.75	£1.25
Title Value:	$0.40	$1.20	$2.00	£0.25	£0.75	£1.25

HONEYMOONERS
Lodestone, TV; 1 Oct 1986

	$Good	$Fine	$N.Mint	£Good	£Fine	£N.Mint
1 ND	$0.55	$1.65	$2.75	£0.35	£1.05	£1.75
Title Value:	$0.55	$1.65	$2.75	£0.35	£1.05	£1.75

HONEYMOONERS (2ND SERIES)
Triad, TV; 1 Sep 1987-13 1988

	$Good	$Fine	$N.Mint	£Good	£Fine	£N.Mint
1 ND	$0.60	$1.80	$3.00	£0.40	£1.20	£2.00
2-3 ND	$0.55	$1.65	$2.75	£0.35	£1.05	£1.75
4 ND squarebound	$0.60	$1.80	$3.00	£0.40	£1.20	£2.00
5-13 ND	$0.45	$1.35	$2.25	£0.30	£0.90	£1.50
Title Value:	$6.35	$19.05	$31.75	£4.20	£12.60	£21.00

HONEYMOONERS CHRISTMAS SPECIAL
Triad, TV; 1 1988

	$Good	$Fine	$N.Mint	£Good	£Fine	£N.Mint
1 ND	$0.80	$2.40	$4.00	£0.50	£1.50	£2.50
Title Value:	$0.80	$2.40	$4.00	£0.50	£1.50	£2.50

HONK!
Fantagraphics,Magazine; 1 1987-5 1988

	$Good	$Fine	$N.Mint	£Good	£Fine	£N.Mint
1-5 ND	$0.60	$1.80	$3.00	£0.40	£1.20	£2.00
Title Value:	$3.00	$9.00	$15.00	£2.00	£6.00	£10.00

HOODOO
The 3-D Zone,OS; 1 Nov 1988
1 ND Mary Fleener art

	$Good	$Fine	$N.Mint	£Good	£Fine	£N.Mint
	$0.45	$1.35	$2.25	£0.30	£0.90	£1.50
Title Value:	$0.45	$1.35	$2.25	£0.30	£0.90	£1.50

HOOK
Marvel Comics Group,MS; 1 Jan 1992-4 Feb 1992
1-4 adapted and inked by Charles Vess, bi-weekly

	$Good	$Fine	$N.Mint	£Good	£Fine	£N.Mint
	$0.15	$0.45	$0.75	£0.10	£0.35	£0.60
Title Value:	$0.60	$1.80	$3.00	£0.40	£1.40	£2.40

HOOK BOOKSHELF EDITION
Marvel Comics Group,OS; nn Jan 1992
nn ND 64pgs, adaptation of Steven Spielberg film

	$Good	$Fine	$N.Mint	£Good	£Fine	£N.Mint
	$1.10	$3.30	$5.50	£0.75	£2.25	£3.75
Title Value:	$1.10	$3.30	$5.50	£0.75	£2.25	£3.75

HOOK SUPER SPECIAL
Marvel Comics Group,Magazine OS Film; 1 Jan 1992
1 ND 80pgs, adaptation of Steven Spielberg film, John Ridgway and Charles Vess art

	$Good	$Fine	$N.Mint	£Good	£Fine	£N.Mint
	$0.70	$2.10	$3.50	£0.45	£1.35	£2.25
Title Value:	$0.70	$2.10	$3.50	£0.45	£1.35	£2.25

HOROBI
Viz; 1 Apr 1990-8 1991
1-7 ND 64pgs, squarebound, Japanes manga adapted by Len Wein

	$Good	$Fine	$N.Mint	£Good	£Fine	£N.Mint
	$0.70	$2.10	$3.50	£0.45	£1.35	£2.25

8 ND 72pgs, squarebound, Japanes manga adapted by Len Wein

	$Good	$Fine	$N.Mint	£Good	£Fine	£N.Mint
	$0.80	$2.40	$4.00	£0.50	£1.50	£2.50
Title Value:	$5.70	$17.10	$28.50	£3.65	£10.95	£18.25

HOROBI BOOK TWO
Viz; 1 1991-7 1991

	$Good	$Fine	$N.Mint	£Good	£Fine	£N.Mint
1 ND	$0.90	$2.70	$4.50	£0.60	£1.80	£3.00
2-7 ND	$0.85	$2.55	$4.25	£0.55	£1.65	£2.75
Title Value:	$6.00	$18.00	$30.00	£3.90	£11.70	£19.50

HORROR HOUSE
AC Comics; 1 Nov 1994
1 ND horror anthology with classic Wally Wood cover; black and white

	$Good	$Fine	$N.Mint	£Good	£Fine	£N.Mint
	$0.60	$1.80	$3.00	£0.40	£1.20	£2.00
Title Value:	$0.60	$1.80	$3.00	£0.40	£1.20	£2.00

HORROR IN THE DARK
Fantagor,MS; 1 Aug 1991-5 Dec 1991
1-5 ND Richard Corben art, black and white; painted covers

	$Good	$Fine	$N.Mint	£Good	£Fine	£N.Mint
	$0.40	$1.20	$2.00	£0.25	£0.75	£1.25
Title Value:	$2.00	$6.00	$10.00	£1.25	£3.75	£6.25

HORROR SHOW: TALES OF FEAR AND FANTASY
Caliber Press,OS; 1 Oct 1991
1 ND 64pgs, Richard Sala cover, black and white

	$Good	$Fine	$N.Mint	£Good	£Fine	£N.Mint
	$0.70	$2.10	$3.50	£0.45	£1.35	£2.25
Title Value:	$0.70	$2.10	$3.50	£0.45	£1.35	£2.25

HORRORIST, THE
DC Comics/Vertigo,MS; 1 Dec 1995-2 Jan 1996
1-2 ND 48pgs, John Constantine appears, Jamie Delano script, David Lloyd art

	$Good	$Fine	$N.Mint	£Good	£Fine	£N.Mint
	$1.20	$3.60	$6.00	£0.80	£2.40	£4.00
Title Value:	$2.40	$7.20	$12.00	£1.60	£4.80	£8.00

HORRORS OF THE HAUNTER
AC Comics; 1 Sep 1994
1 ND Bill Black cover; black and white

	$Good	$Fine	$N.Mint	£Good	£Fine	£N.Mint
	$0.60	$1.80	$3.00	£0.40	£1.20	£2.00
Title Value:	$0.60	$1.80	$3.00	£0.40	£1.20	£2.00

HORUS, SON OF OSIRIS
Acme Comics,Magazine MS; 1 Apr 1991-3 Jun 1991

	$Good	$Fine	$N.Mint	£Good	£Fine	£N.Mint
1 ND 64pgs	$0.55	$1.65	$2.75	£0.35	£1.05	£1.75

1 ND 64pgs, Deluxe Edition on high quality paper

	$Good	$Fine	$N.Mint	£Good	£Fine	£N.Mint
	$0.60	$1.80	$3.00	£0.40	£1.20	£2.00
2-3 ND 64pgs	$0.55	$1.65	$2.75	£0.35	£1.05	£1.75
Title Value:	$2.25	$6.75	$11.25	£1.45	£4.35	£7.25

HOSTILE TAKEOVER ASHCAN
Malibu Ultraverse,OS; nn Sep 1994
1 ND 16pgs, black and white; previews storyline starting in Night Man #12

	$Good	$Fine	$N.Mint	£Good	£Fine	£N.Mint
	$0.15	$0.45	$0.75	£0.10	£0.30	£0.50
Title Value:	$0.15	$0.45	$0.75	£0.10	£0.30	£0.50

HOT AND COLD HEROES
A Plus Comics; 1 Oct 1990-2 1991
1 ND 48pgs, John Byrne's "Rog 2000" reprinted plus other old and new heroes, Mike Zeck art featured; black and white

	$Good	$Fine	$N.Mint	£Good	£Fine	£N.Mint
	$0.40	$1.20	$2.00	£0.25	£0.75	£1.25

2 ND 48pgs, ACG reprints continue; black and white

	$Good	$Fine	$N.Mint	£Good	£Fine	£N.Mint
	$0.40	$1.20	$2.00	£0.25	£0.75	£1.25
Title Value:	$0.80	$2.40	$4.00	£0.50	£1.50	£2.50

HOT SHOTS: AVENGERS
Marvel Comics Group,OS; 1 Oct 1995
1 ND fully painted pin-ups by Sienkiewicz, Steacy, Zeck, Golden, Jusko and others; fold-out format

	$Good	$Fine	$N.Mint	£Good	£Fine	£N.Mint
	$0.60	$1.80	$3.00	£0.40	£1.20	£2.00
Title Value:	$0.60	$1.80	$3.00	£0.40	£1.20	£2.00

HOT SHOTS: SPIDERMAN
Marvel Comics Group,OS; 1 Jan 1996
1 ND pin-ups by Joe Jusko, Alex Ross, Charles Vess and others; fold-out format

	$Good	$Fine	$N.Mint	£Good	£Fine	£N.Mint
	$0.60	$1.80	$3.00	£0.40	£1.20	£2.00
Title Value:	$0.60	$1.80	$3.00	£0.40	£1.20	£2.00

HOT SHOTS: X-MEN
Marvel Comics Group; 1 Feb 1996
1 ND pin-ups by Alan Davis, Bill Sienkiewicz, Alex Ross and others; fold-out format

	$Good	$Fine	$N.Mint	£Good	£Fine	£N.Mint
	$0.60	$1.80	$3.00	£0.40	£1.20	£2.00
Title Value:	$0.60	$1.80	$3.00	£0.40	£1.20	£2.00

HOT STUF'
Quarruccio,Magazine; 1 1975-8 1983?

	$Good	$Fine	$N.Mint	£Good	£Fine	£N.Mint
1-2 ND 64pgs	$0.90	$2.70	$4.50	£0.60	£1.80	£3.00

3 ND 64pgs, Tim Kirk and Richard Corben art

	$Good	$Fine	$N.Mint	£Good	£Fine	£N.Mint
	$1.05	$3.15	$5.25	£0.70	£2.10	£3.50

4 ND 64pgs, Alex Toth and Gray Morrow art

	$Good	$Fine	$N.Mint	£Good	£Fine	£N.Mint
	$0.90	$2.70	$4.50	£0.60	£1.80	£3.00
5-7 ND 64pgs	$0.90	$2.70	$4.50	£0.60	£1.80	£3.00

8 ND 64pgs, Erik Larsen art, Neal Adams painted cover

	$Good	$Fine	$N.Mint	£Good	£Fine	£N.Mint
	$0.85	$2.55	$4.25	£0.55	£1.65	£2.75
Title Value:	$7.30	$21.90	$36.50	£4.85	£14.55	£24.25

HOT WHEELS
DC Comics, TV Toy; 1 Mar/Apr 1970-6 Jan/Feb 1971

	$Good	$Fine	$N.Mint	£Good	£Fine	£N.Mint
1	$9.00	$28.00	$55.00	£4.15	£12.50	£25.00
2 rare in the U.K.	$4.50	$13.50	$22.50	£2.50	£7.50	£12.50

3 Neal Adams cover

	$Good	$Fine	$N.Mint	£Good	£Fine	£N.Mint
	$6.50	$19.50	$32.50	£2.00	£6.00	£10.00
4 rare in the U.K.	$4.50	$13.50	$22.50	£2.50	£7.50	£12.50
5	$4.50	$13.50	$22.50	£2.00	£6.00	£10.00

6 scarce in the U.K. Neal Adams art and cover

	$Good	$Fine	$N.Mint	£Good	£Fine	£N.Mint
	$7.50	$22.50	$37.50	£3.00	£9.00	£15.00
Title Value:	$36.50	$110.50	$192.50	£16.15	£48.50	£85.00

HOTEL HARBOUR VIEW
Viz; nn Dec 1990
nn ND graphic album of Japanese manga material with a film noir look

	$Good	$Fine	$N.Mint	£Good	£Fine	£N.Mint
	$1.65	$4.95	$8.25	£1.10	£3.30	£5.50
Title Value:	$1.65	$4.95	$8.25	£1.10	£3.30	£5.50

HOTSPUR
Eclipse,MS; 1 Jun 1987-3 Oct 1987

	$Good	$Fine	$N.Mint	£Good	£Fine	£N.Mint
1-3 ND	$0.40	$1.20	$2.00	£0.25	£0.75	£1.25
Title Value:	$1.20	$3.60	$6.00	£0.75	£2.25	£3.75

HOUSE II - THE SECOND STORY
Marvel Comics Group, Film; 1 1987
1 ND DS adaptation of film

	$Good	$Fine	$N.Mint	£Good	£Fine	£N.Mint
	$0.40	$1.20	$2.00	£0.25	£0.75	£1.25
Title Value:	$0.40	$1.20	$2.00	£0.25	£0.75	£1.25

HOUSE OF FRIGHTENSTEIN
AC Comics; 1 Dec 1994
1 ND horror anthology; black and white

	$Good	$Fine	$N.Mint	£Good	£Fine	£N.Mint
	$0.60	$1.80	$3.00	£0.40	£1.20	£2.00
Title Value:	$0.60	$1.80	$3.00	£0.40	£1.20	£2.00

HOUSE OF MYSTERY
National Periodical Publications/DC Comics; 1 Dec/Jan 1951/52-321 Oct 1983
(see Brave and the Bold, Super DC Giant, Super-Star Holiday Special)
1 scarce in the U.K.

	$Good	$Fine	$N.Mint	£Good	£Fine	£N.Mint
	$165.00	$500.00	$1350.00	£110.00	£335.00	£900.00

2 scarce in the U.K.

	$Good	$Fine	$N.Mint	£Good	£Fine	£N.Mint
	$85.00	$255.00	$600.00	£55.00	£170.00	£400.00

3 scarce in the U.K.

	$Good	$Fine	$N.Mint	£Good	£Fine	£N.Mint
	$65.00	$195.00	$455.00	£44.00	£130.00	£305.00
4-5	$52.50	$160.00	$375.00	£36.00	£105.00	£250.00
6-10	$39.00	$115.00	$275.00	£26.00	£77.50	£185.00
11-15	$30.00	$90.00	$210.00	£20.00	£60.00	£140.00
16-25	$25.00	$75.00	$175.00	£16.00	£49.00	£115.00
26-35	$17.50	$52.50	$125.00	£11.50	£35.00	£82.50
36-49	$15.00	$45.00	$105.00	£10.00	£30.00	£70.00

50 features script of Orson Welles' War of the Worlds broadcast

	$Good	$Fine	$N.Mint	£Good	£Fine	£N.Mint
	$15.00	$45.00	$105.00	£10.00	£30.00	£70.00
51-60	$12.50	$39.00	$90.00	£8.50	£26.00	£60.00
61 Jack Kirby art	$12.00	$36.00	$85.00	£8.00	£24.50	£57.50
62	$8.50	$26.00	$60.00	£5.50	£17.00	£40.00
63 Jack Kirby art	$12.00	$36.00	$85.00	£8.00	£24.50	£57.50
64	$8.50	$26.00	$60.00	£5.50	£17.00	£40.00

65-66 Jack Kirby art

	$Good	$Fine	$N.Mint	£Good	£Fine	£N.Mint
	$12.00	$36.00	$85.00	£8.00	£24.50	£57.50
67-69	$8.50	$26.00	$60.00	£5.50	£17.00	£40.00
70 Jack Kirby art	$12.00	$36.00	$85.00	£8.00	£24.50	£57.50
71	$7.75	$23.50	$55.00	£5.25	£15.50	£37.00
72 Jack Kirby art	$12.00	$36.00	$85.00	£8.00	£24.50	£57.50
73-75	$7.75	$23.50	$55.00	£5.25	£15.50	£37.00
76 Jack Kirby art	$12.00	$36.00	$85.00	£8.00	£24.50	£57.50
77-83	$7.75	$23.50	$55.00	£5.25	£15.50	£37.00

84-85 Jack Kirby art

	$Good	$Fine	$N.Mint	£Good	£Fine	£N.Mint
	$11.00	$34.00	$80.00	£7.50	£22.50	£52.50
86-91	$7.75	$23.50	$55.00	£5.00	£15.00	£35.00

1st official distribution in the U.K.

	$Good	$Fine	$N.Mint	£Good	£Fine	£N.Mint
92-99	$7.75	$23.50	$55.00	£4.25	£12.50	£30.00
100	$10.50	$32.00	$75.00	£5.50	£17.00	£40.00
101-115	$8.25	$25.00	$50.00	£4.15	£12.50	£25.00

116 last 10 cents issue

	$Good	$Fine	$N.Mint	£Good	£Fine	£N.Mint
	$8.25	$25.00	$50.00	£4.15	£12.50	£25.00
117-119	$7.50	$22.50	$45.00	£3.30	£10.00	£20.00
120 Toth art	$8.25	$25.00	$50.00	£4.15	£12.50	£25.00
121-130	$7.50	$22.50	$45.00	£2.50	£7.50	£15.00
131-142	$6.50	$20.00	$40.00	£2.05	£6.25	£12.50

143 scarce in the U.K. Martian Manhunter series begins, ends #173; storyline continuation from Detective

	$Good	$Fine	$N.Mint	£Good	£Fine	£N.Mint			$Good	$Fine	$N.Mint	£Good	£Fine	£N.Mint
Comics #326									$1.00	$3.00	$5.00	£0.60	£1.80	£3.00
	$36.00	$105.00	$250.00	£21.00	£62.50	£150.00	260	44pgs, scarce	$1.00	$3.00	$5.00	£0.50	£1.50	£2.50
144	$20.50	$62.50	$125.00	£12.50	£38.00	£75.00	261-262 ND	44pgs	$1.00	$3.00	$5.00	£0.60	£1.80	£3.00
145	$15.00	$45.00	$90.00	£8.25	£25.00	£50.00	263-273		$1.00	$3.00	$5.00	£0.30	£0.90	£1.50
146-149	$15.00	$45.00	$90.00	£7.50	£22.50	£45.00	274	Rogers art	$1.00	$3.00	$5.00	£0.30	£0.90	£1.50
150-154	$14.00	$43.00	$85.00	£5.75	£17.50	£35.00	275		$1.00	$3.00	$5.00	£0.30	£0.90	£1.50
155 last Silver Age issue, indicia dated December 1965							276	Nasser art	$1.00	$3.00	$5.00	£0.30	£0.90	£1.50
	$14.00	$43.00	$85.00	£5.75	£17.50	£35.00	277-280		$1.00	$3.00	$5.00	£0.30	£0.90	£1.50
156 1st Dial H For Hero, ends #173							281		$1.00	$3.00	$5.00	£0.25	£0.75	£1.25
	$14.00	$43.00	$100.00	£7.00	£21.00	£50.00	282 68pgs, Jim Starlin art on insert							
157-159	$14.00	$43.00	$85.00	£5.00	£15.00	£30.00			$1.00	$3.00	$5.00	£0.30	£0.90	£1.50
160 Dial H for Hero as Plastic Man (see Plastic Man #1 for 1st Silver Age appearance)							283-300		$1.00	$3.00	$5.00	£0.20	£0.60	£1.00
	$21.50	$65.00	$130.00	£8.25	£25.00	£50.00	301-321		$0.80	$2.40	$4.00	£0.15	£0.45	£0.75
161-172	$10.50	$33.00	$65.00	£4.55	£13.50	£27.50	Title Value:	$2833.60	$8565.90	$19196.50	£1651.85	£4980.65	£11389.50
173 last Martian Manhunter							**ARTISTS**							
	$10.50	$33.00	$65.00	£4.55	£13.50	£27.50	Adams inks reprint in 224. Ditko art in 236, 247, 254, 258, 276. Kaluta art (2pgs) in 195. Kirby reprints in							
174 change to mystery format, new-style cover							194, 199, 225. Nino art in 204, 212, 213, 220, 224, 225, 245, 250, 252-256, 283. Wood art in 180, 183-							
	$4.15	$12.50	$25.00	£1.65	£5.00	£10.00	185, 189, 199, 251. Wrightson reprints in 224, 226, 228, 229.							
175-177	$4.15	$12.50	$25.00	£1.65	£5.00	£10.00	**FEATURES**							
178 scarce in the U.K. Neal Adams art							Dial H for Hero in 156-173. I...Vampire in 290, 291, 293, 295, 297, 299, 302-319. Martian Manhunter in							
	$5.00	$15.00	$30.00	£2.05	£6.25	£12.50	143-173. Remainder are mystery stories.							
179 scarce in the U.K. Neal Adams art, Wrightson art (1st pro work)							**REPRINT FEATURES**							
	$10.00	$30.00	$60.00	£4.15	£12.50	£25.00	Phantom Stranger in 225, 226. Spectre in 224, 225. Various Mystery stories in 174, 194-203, 224-229.							
180 Wrightson art; last 12 cents issue							**HOUSE OF SECRETS**							
	$3.75	$11.00	$22.50	£1.65	£5.00	£10.00	National Periodical Publications/DC Comics; 1 Nov/Dec 1956-80 Sep/Oct 1966; 81 Aug/Sep							
181 Wrightson art							1969-140 Feb/Mar 1976; 141 Aug/Sep 1976-154 Oct/Nov 1978							
	$3.75	$11.00	$22.50	£1.65	£5.00	£10.00	1 scarce in the U.K.							
182 Toth art	$3.30	$10.00	$20.00	£1.25	£3.75	£7.50			$125.00	$375.00	$1000.00	£82.50	£250.00	£675.00
183 Wrightson art	$3.75	$11.00	$22.50	£1.65	£5.00	£10.00	2		$55.00	$170.00	$400.00	£39.00	£115.00	£275.00
184	$2.50	$7.50	$15.00	£0.80	£2.50	£5.00	3 Jack Kirby cover/art							
185 Williamson/Kaluta art									$50.00	$150.00	$350.00	£34.00	£100.00	£240.00
	$2.50	$7.50	$15.00	£1.25	£3.75	£7.50	4 Jack Kirby art	$39.00	$115.00	$275.00	£26.00	£77.50	£185.00
186 Neal Adams, Wrightson art							5-7		$25.00	$75.00	$175.00	£17.00	£50.00	£120.00
	$2.50	$7.50	$15.00	£1.30	£4.00	£8.00	8 Jack Kirby art	$29.00	$85.00	$200.00	£19.00	£57.50	£135.00
187	$1.30	$4.00	$8.00	£0.65	£2.00	£4.00	9-11		$20.00	$60.00	$140.00	£13.50	£41.00	£95.00
188 Wrightson art	$2.50	$7.50	$15.00	£1.00	£3.00	£6.00	12 Jack Kirby cover/art							
189 scarce in the U.K. Wood inks									$22.50	$67.50	$160.00	£15.50	£47.00	£110.00
	$1.30	$4.00	$8.00	£0.80	£2.50	£5.00	13-15		$14.00	$43.00	$100.00	£10.00	£30.00	£70.00
190	$1.30	$4.00	$8.00	£0.65	£2.00	£4.00	16-20		$12.00	$36.00	$85.00	£8.50	£26.00	£60.00
191 Wrightson art	$2.50	$7.50	$15.00	£1.00	£3.00	£6.00	21-22		$11.00	$34.00	$80.00	£7.00	£21.00	£50.00
192-193	$1.30	$4.00	$8.00	£0.55	£1.75	£3.50	23 origin and 1st appearance Mark Merlin							
194 48pgs	$1.30	$4.00	$8.00	£0.65	£2.00	£4.00			$12.50	$39.00	$90.00	£8.50	£26.00	£60.00
195 48pgs, Wrightson art							**1st official distribution in the U.K.**							
	$2.50	$7.50	$15.00	£1.00	£3.00	£6.00	24-30		$11.00	$34.00	$80.00	£7.00	£21.00	£50.00
196-198 48pgs	$1.30	$4.00	$8.00	£0.65	£2.00	£4.00	31-40		$10.00	$30.00	$60.00	£5.75	£17.50	£35.00
199 48pgs, (says 52pgs on the covers of #199-203 as in US they count the covers)							41-47		$10.00	$30.00	$60.00	£5.00	£15.00	£30.00
	$1.65	$5.00	$10.00	£0.65	£2.00	£4.00	48 Toth art	$10.00	$30.00	$60.00	£5.75	£17.50	£35.00
200 scarce in the U.K. 48pgs, Kaluta art							49		$10.00	$30.00	$60.00	£5.00	£15.00	£30.00
	$1.30	$4.00	$8.00	£0.80	£2.50	£5.00	50 last 10 cents issue							
201 48pgs, features Wrightson art									$10.00	$30.00	$60.00	£5.00	£15.00	£30.00
	$1.40	$4.20	$7.00	£0.90	£2.70	£4.50	51-60		$9.00	$28.00	$55.00	£4.15	£12.50	£25.00
202-203 48pgs	$1.40	$4.20	$7.00	£0.70	£2.10	£3.50	61 1st appearance Eclipso							
204 Wrightson art	$1.60	$4.80	$8.00	£0.70	£2.10	£3.50			$25.00	$75.00	$150.00	£12.50	£38.00	£75.00
205	$1.00	$3.00	$5.00	£0.50	£1.50	£2.50	62 2nd appearance Eclipso							
206 Wrightson art	$1.00	$3.00	$5.00	£0.70	£2.10	£3.50			$14.00	$43.00	$85.00	£7.50	£22.50	£45.00
207 2pgs Jim Starlin art							63-65 Toth art	$11.50	$35.00	$70.00	£5.00	£15.00	£30.00
	$1.00	$3.00	$5.00	£0.70	£2.10	£3.50	66 Toth art, 1st Eclipso cover							
208-210	$1.00	$3.00	$5.00	£0.50	£1.50	£2.50			$15.00	$45.00	$90.00	£7.50	£22.50	£45.00
211-220	$1.00	$3.00	$5.00	£0.40	£1.20	£2.00	67 Toth art	$11.50	$35.00	$70.00	£5.00	£15.00	£30.00
221 Wrightson/Kaluta art							68-70		$9.00	$28.00	$55.00	£4.15	£12.50	£25.00
	$1.00	$3.00	$5.00	£0.70	£2.10	£3.50	71-74		$9.00	$28.00	$55.00	£3.75	£11.00	£22.50
222-223	$1.00	$3.00	$5.00	£0.40	£1.20	£2.00	75 last Silver Age issue, indicia dated Nov/Dec 1965							
224 100pgs	$1.60	$4.80	$8.00	£1.00	£3.00	£5.00			$9.00	$28.00	$55.00	£3.75	£11.00	£22.50
225-227 100pgs	$1.00	$3.00	$5.00	£0.80	£2.40	£4.00	76-79		$8.25	$25.00	$50.00	£3.30	£10.00	£20.00
228 100pgs, Neal Adams inks							80 last Eclipso	$8.25	$25.00	$50.00	£3.30	£10.00	£20.00
	$1.40	$4.20	$7.00	£1.00	£3.00	£5.00	81 1st mystery format, 1st appearance Abel							
229 100pgs	$1.00	$3.00	$5.00	£0.80	£2.40	£4.00			$1.80	$5.25	$9.00	£1.20	£3.60	£6.00
230-235	$1.00	$3.00	$5.00	£0.40	£1.20	£2.00	82 Neal Adams inks (cover)							
236 Neal Adams inks, part Ditko art; Wrightson cover									$1.60	$4.80	$8.00	£1.00	£3.00	£5.00
	$1.20	$3.60	$6.00	£0.60	£1.80	£3.00	83		$1.60	$4.80	$8.00	£0.80	£2.40	£4.00
237-240	$1.00	$3.00	$5.00	£0.40	£1.20	£2.00	84 Neal Adams cover							
241-242 scarce in the U.K.									$1.60	$4.80	$8.00	£0.80	£2.40	£4.00
	$1.00	$3.00	$5.00	£0.50	£1.50	£2.50	85 Neal Adams inks and cover							
243 ND	$1.00	$3.00	$5.00	£0.60	£1.80	£3.00			$1.60	$4.80	$8.00	£1.00	£3.00	£5.00
244 scarce in the U.K.							86 Neal Adams and cover							
	$1.00	$3.00	$5.00	£0.50	£1.50	£2.50			$1.60	$4.80	$8.00	£0.80	£2.40	£4.00
245 ND	$1.00	$3.00	$5.00	£0.60	£1.80	£3.00	87 Wrightson/Kaluta art, Neal Adams cover							
246-249 scarce in the U.K.									$1.60	$4.80	$8.00	£1.00	£3.00	£5.00
	$1.00	$3.00	$5.00	£0.50	£1.50	£2.50	88 Neal Adams cover							
250-251	$1.00	$3.00	$5.00	£0.60	£1.80	£3.00			$1.60	$4.80	$8.00	£0.80	£2.40	£4.00
252 80pgs, scarce; Neal Adams cover; pin-up poster of The House							89		$1.60	$4.80	$8.00	£0.80	£2.40	£4.00
	$1.00	$3.00	$5.00		£1.80	£3.00	90 Neal Adams inks, Buckler art (very early work)							
253 80pgs, scarce; Neal Adams cover									$1.60	$4.80	$8.00	£1.20	£3.60	£6.00
	$1.00	$3.00	$5.00		£1.80	£3.00	91		$1.60	$4.80	$8.00	£0.80	£2.40	£4.00
254 80pgs, scarce, Rogers art							92 scarce in the U.K. 1st appearance of Swamp Thing by Bernie Wrightson							
	$1.00	$3.00	$5.00	£0.60	£1.80	£3.00			$45.00	$135.00	$450.00	£25.00	£75.00	£250.00
255-256 ND 80pgs							[Scarce in high grade - Very Fine+ or better]							
	$1.00	$3.00	$5.00	£0.60	£1.80	£3.00	92 ND Silver Age Classic reprint (Mar 1992)							
257 ND 80pgs, Golden art									$0.25	$0.75	$1.25	£0.15	£0.45	£0.75
	$1.00	$3.00	$5.00	£0.60	£1.80	£3.00	93 48pgs	$1.00	$3.00	$5.00	£0.55	£1.65	£2.75
258 ND 80pgs	$1.00	$3.00	$5.00	£0.60	£1.80	£3.00	94 48pgs, Wrightson inks							
259 ND 80pgs, Golden art									$1.00	$3.00	$5.00	£0.70	£2.10	£3.50

	$Good	$Fine	$N.Mint	£Good	£Fine	£N.Mint
95 48pgs	$1.00	$3.00	$5.00	£0.55	£1.65	£2.75
96 48pgs, (says 52pgs on cover up to #98 as they count the covers in the U.S)						
	$1.00	$3.00	$5.00	£0.55	£1.65	£2.75
97 48pgs	$1.00	$3.00	$5.00	£0.55	£1.65	£2.75
98 48pgs, Kaluta art						
	$1.00	$3.00	$5.00	£0.55	£1.65	£2.75
99	$1.00	$3.00	$5.00	£0.40	£1.20	£2.00
100 scarce in the U.K. Bernie Wrightson cover						
	$1.00	$3.00	$5.00	£0.60	£1.80	£3.00
101 Kaluta cover	$0.55	$1.65	$2.75	£0.35	£1.05	£1.75
102	$0.55	$1.65	$2.75	£0.35	£1.05	£1.75
103 scarce in the U.K. Bernie Wrightson cover						
	$0.55	$1.65	$2.75	£0.50	£1.50	£2.50
104-105	$0.55	$1.65	$2.75	£0.35	£1.05	£1.75
106 Bernie Wrightson cover and 1pg art						
	$0.55	$1.65	$2.75	£0.35	£1.05	£1.75
107-110	$0.55	$1.65	$2.75	£0.35	£1.05	£1.75
111-120	$0.55	$1.65	$2.75	£0.30	£0.90	£1.50
121-134	$0.55	$1.65	$2.75	£0.25	£0.75	£1.25
135 Bernie Wrightson cover						
	$0.50	$1.50	$2.50	£0.25	£0.75	£1.25
136-139	$0.50	$1.50	$2.50	£0.25	£0.75	£1.25
140 origin Patchwork Man						
	$0.50	$1.50	$2.50	£0.30	£0.90	£1.50
141-147	$0.40	$1.20	$2.00	£0.15	£0.45	£0.75
148 Steve Ditko and Mike Golden art						
	$0.40	$1.20	$2.00	£0.15	£0.45	£0.75
149 Mike Golden art (1pg)						
	$0.40	$1.20	$2.00	£0.15	£0.45	£0.75
150	$0.40	$1.20	$2.00	£0.15	£0.45	£0.75
151 Mike Golden art						
	$0.40	$1.20	$2.00	£0.25	£0.75	£1.25
152-153	$0.30	$0.90	$1.50	£0.15	£0.45	£0.75
154 ND 44pgs	$0.40	$1.20	$2.00	£0.30	£0.90	£1.50
Title Value:	$1270.40	$3847.80	$8624.75	£750.30	£2254.55	£5156.75

ARTISTS
Ditko art in 139, 148. Nino art in 101, 103, 106, 109, 115, 117, 126, 128, 131, 147, 153. Wood art in 91, 96.

FEATURES
Eclipso in 61-80. Mark Merlin in 26-73 (origin in 58). Prince Ra-Man in 73-80. Swamp Thing in 92. Remainder are mystery stories.

REPRINT FEATURES
Various mystery stories in 93-98.

HOUSE OF YANG
Charlton; 1 Jul 1975-6 Jun 1976
(see Yang)

	$Good	$Fine	$N.Mint	£Good	£Fine	£N.Mint
1 distributed in the U.K. painted cover						
	$0.40	$1.20	$2.00	£0.25	£0.75	£1.25
2-6 distributed in the U.K.						
	$0.30	$0.90	$1.50	£0.20	£0.60	£1.00
Title Value:	$1.90	$5.70	$9.50	£1.25	£3.75	£6.25

HOW TO DRAW COMICS COMIC, THE
Solson Publications,OS; 1 1985

	$Good	$Fine	$N.Mint	£Good	£Fine	£N.Mint
1 ND John Byrne and John Romita guide to professional comic drawing; black and white sketches						
	$0.40	$1.20	$2.00	£0.25	£0.75	£1.25
Title Value:	$0.40	$1.20	$2.00	£0.25	£0.75	£1.25

HOWARD CHAYKIN'S AMERICAN FLAG
(see American Flagg!)

HOWARD THE DUCK
Marvel Comics Group; 1 Jan 1976-31 May 1979; 32 Jan 1986-33 Sep 1986
(see Fear 19, Giant Size Man-Thing 4, 5,She-Hulk)

	$Good	$Fine	$N.Mint	£Good	£Fine	£N.Mint
1 scarce in the U.K. Brunner art, Spiderman appears						
	$1.40	$4.20	$7.00	£0.70	£2.10	£3.50
2 scarce in the U.K. Brunner art, Jim Starlin "script lay-out"						
	$0.60	$1.80	$3.00	£0.40	£1.20	£2.00
3 classic "Master of Quack Fu" story						
	$0.40	$1.20	$2.00	£0.25	£0.75	£1.25
4-7	$0.40	$1.20	$2.00	£0.25	£0.75	£1.25
8 Dr. Strange cameo						
	$0.40	$1.20	$2.00	£0.25	£0.75	£1.25
9-10	$0.40	$1.20	$2.00	£0.25	£0.75	£1.25
11	$0.30	$0.90	$1.50	£0.20	£0.60	£1.00
12-13 Kiss appear						
	$0.55	$1.65	$2.75	£0.35	£1.05	£1.75
14-15 Son of Satan appears						
	$0.40	$1.20	$2.00	£0.25	£0.75	£1.25
16-21	$0.30	$0.90	$1.50	£0.20	£0.60	£1.00
22 Man-Thing appears, Mayerik art						
	$0.30	$0.90	$1.50	£0.20	£0.60	£1.00
23 Star Wars parody, Mayerik art						
	$0.30	$0.90	$1.50	£0.20	£0.60	£1.00
24-31	$0.30	$0.90	$1.50	£0.20	£0.60	£1.00
32 ND Paul Smith art						
	$0.30	$0.90	$1.50	£0.20	£0.60	£1.00
33 ND	$0.30	$0.90	$1.50	£0.20	£0.60	£1.00
Title Value:	$12.80	$38.40	$64.00	£8.10	£24.30	£40.50

Note: Colan art 4-20, 24-27, 29, 30. Infantino art 21, 28. Also 32, 33 are high quality paper.

HOWARD THE DUCK (2ND SERIES)
Marvel Comics Group,Magazine; 1 Oct 1979-9 Mar 1981

	$Good	$Fine	$N.Mint	£Good	£Fine	£N.Mint
1 ND Golden art	$0.90	$2.70	$4.50	£0.60	£1.80	£3.00
2-4 ND	$0.60	$1.80	$3.00	£0.40	£1.20	£2.00
5-6 ND Golden art	$0.60	$1.80	$3.00	£0.40	£1.20	£2.00
7 ND 1pg John Byrne art						
	$0.80	$2.40	$4.00	£0.50	£1.50	£2.50
8 ND Rogers art	$0.80	$2.40	$4.00	£0.50	£1.50	£2.50
9 ND	$0.60	$1.80	$3.00	£0.40	£1.20	£2.00
Title Value:	$6.10	$18.30	$30.50	£4.00	£12.00	£20.00

HOWARD THE DUCK ANNUAL
Marvel Comics Group; 1 Sep 1977

	$Good	$Fine	$N.Mint	£Good	£Fine	£N.Mint
1 scarce in the U.K. 52pgs, Val Mayerik art						
	$0.60	$1.80	$3.00	£0.40	£1.20	£2.00
Title Value:	$0.60	$1.80	$3.00	£0.40	£1.20	£2.00

HOWARD THE DUCK: THE MOVIE
Marvel Comics Group,MS Film; 1 Dec 1986-3 Feb 1987

	$Good	$Fine	$N.Mint	£Good	£Fine	£N.Mint
1-3 ND adapts film, Kyle Baker art						
	$0.25	$0.75	$1.25	£0.15	£0.45	£0.75
Title Value:	$0.75	$2.25	$3.75	£0.45	£1.35	£2.25

HOWL
Eternity; 1 Nov 1988-2 1989

	$Good	$Fine	$N.Mint	£Good	£Fine	£N.Mint
1-2 ND reprints	$0.45	$1.35	$2.25	£0.30	£0.90	£1.50
Title Value:	$0.90	$2.70	$4.50	£0.60	£1.80	£3.00

HUGO
Fantagraphics; 1 Nov 1984-3 1985

	$Good	$Fine	$N.Mint	£Good	£Fine	£N.Mint
1-3 ND	$0.40	$1.20	$2.00	£0.25	£0.75	£1.25
Title Value:	$1.20	$3.60	$6.00	£0.75	£2.25	£3.75

HULK 2099
Marvel Comics Group; 1 Dec 1994-10 Sep 1995

	$Good	$Fine	$N.Mint	£Good	£Fine	£N.Mint
1 ND foil stamped cover						
	$0.40	$1.20	$2.00	£0.25	£0.75	£1.25
2-4 ND	$0.30	$0.90	$1.50	£0.20	£0.60	£1.00
5 ND The Hulk of 2099 mutates						
	$0.30	$0.90	$1.50	£0.20	£0.60	£1.00
6 ND	$0.30	$0.90	$1.50	£0.20	£0.60	£1.00

House of Mystery #126

House of Secrets #70

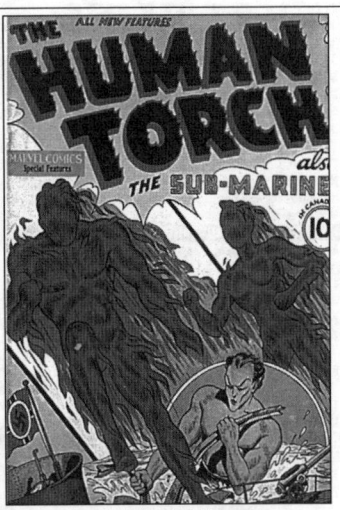

Human Torch #2

	$Good	$Fine	$N.Mint	£Good	£Fine	£N.Mint
7 ND upgraded paper stock begins	$0.30	$0.90	$1.50	£0.20	£0.60	£1.00
8 ND	$0.30	$0.90	$1.50	£0.20	£0.60	£1.00
9-10 ND One Nation Under Doom	$0.30	$0.90	$1.50	£0.20	£0.60	£1.00
Title Value:	$3.10	$9.30	$15.50	£2.05	£6.15	£10.25

HUMAN FLY
IW Super; 1,10 1963, 1964

	$Good	$Fine	$N.Mint	£Good	£Fine	£N.Mint
1 reprint; rare in the U.K. though distributed	$1.50	$4.50	$9.00	£1.00	£3.00	£6.00
10 reprint; scarce in the U.K. though distributed	$0.75	$2.25	$4.50	£0.50	£1.50	£3.00
Title Value:	$2.25	$6.75	$13.50	£1.50	£4.50	£9.00

HUMAN FLY
Marvel Comics Group; 1 Sep 1977-19 Mar 1979

	$Good	$Fine	$N.Mint	£Good	£Fine	£N.Mint
1 Spiderman appears	$0.15	$0.45	$0.75	£0.10	£0.35	£0.60
2 Ghost Rider appears	$0.15	$0.45	$0.75	£0.10	£0.35	£0.60
3-7	$0.15	$0.45	$0.75	£0.10	£0.35	£0.60
8 White Tiger appears	$0.15	$0.45	$0.75	£0.10	£0.35	£0.60
9 Daredevil and White Tiger appear	$0.15	$0.45	$0.75	£0.10	£0.35	£0.60
10-19	$0.15	$0.45	$0.75	£0.10	£0.35	£0.60
Title Value:	$2.85	$8.55	$14.25	£1.90	£6.65	£11.40

HUMAN GARGOYLES
Eternity; 1-4 1988

	$Good	$Fine	$N.Mint	£Good	£Fine	£N.Mint
1-4 ND	$0.40	$1.20	$2.00	£0.25	£0.75	£1.25
Title Value:	$1.60	$4.80	$8.00	£1.00	£3.00	£5.00

HUMAN TARGET SPECIAL, THE
DC Comics,OS; 1 Nov 1991

	$Good	$Fine	$N.Mint	£Good	£Fine	£N.Mint
1 48pgs, ties in with U.S. TV series	$0.30	$0.90	$1.50	£0.20	£0.60	£1.00
Title Value:	$0.30	$0.90	$1.50	£0.20	£0.60	£1.00

HUMAN TORCH (1ST SERIES)
Timely/Atlas; 2 Autumn 1940-15 Spring 1944; 16 Autumn 1944-35 Mar 1949; 36 Apr 1954-38 Aug 1954

(see Red Raven Comics for issue #1)

2 scarce in the U.K. origin and 1st appearance Toro, Sub-Mariner back-up story begins (co-title on cover until #6); no number on cover (actually issue #1), Bill Everett cover and art

	$Good	$Fine	$N.Mint	£Good	£Fine	£N.Mint
(issue 2)	$1675.00	$5000.00	$18500.00	£1125.00	£3400.00	£12500.00
3 Bill Everett art; no number on cover (actually issue #2)	$465.00	$1400.00	$3750.00	£310.00	£930.00	£2500.00
4 Alex Schomburg covers begin; no number on cover (actually issue #3)	$350.00	$1050.00	$2800.00	£235.00	£710.00	£1900.00
5 no number on cover (actually issue #4)	$260.00	$780.00	$2100.00	£175.00	£520.00	£1400.00
5 no number on cover (the "real" issue #5), Human Torch vs. Sub-Mariner	$415.00	$1250.00	$3350.00	£275.00	£820.00	£2200.00
6 1st number on cover	$155.00	$465.00	$1250.00	£100.00	£305.00	£825.00
7	$155.00	$465.00	$1250.00	£100.00	£305.00	£825.00
8 Human Torch vs. Sub-Mariner	$260.00	$780.00	$2100.00	£175.00	£520.00	£1400.00
9	$155.00	$465.00	$1250.00	£100.00	£305.00	£825.00
10 Human Torch vs. Sub-Mariner	$195.00	$590.00	$1575.00	£130.00	£390.00	£1050.00
11-15	$140.00	$425.00	$1000.00	£92.50	£275.00	£650.00
16-19	$105.00	$320.00	$750.00	£70.00	£210.00	£500.00
20 1st war theme cover	$105.00	$320.00	$750.00	£70.00	£210.00	£500.00
21-30	$95.00	$285.00	$675.00	£62.50	£190.00	£450.00
31-32	$80.00	$245.00	$575.00	£52.50	£160.00	£375.00
33	$85.00	$255.00	$600.00	£55.00	£170.00	£400.00
34	$77.50	$235.00	$550.00	£50.00	£150.00	£360.00
35	$82.50	$250.00	$585.00	£55.00	£165.00	£385.00
36-37 scarce in the U.K.	$77.50	$235.00	$550.00	£50.00	£150.00	£360.00
38 very scarce in the U.K.	$82.50	$250.00	$585.00	£52.50	£160.00	£375.00
Title Value:	$6902.50	$20770.00	$58005.00	£4580.00	£13795.00	£38665.00

Note: as with all Golden Age material, this title was not distributed on the news-stands in the U.K. but copies may have come over with personnel movements during the Second World War or as cheap ballast on ships. Most issues in this title however are generally scarce in the U.K.

HUMAN TORCH (2ND SERIES)
Marvel Comics Group; 1 Sep 1974-8 Nov 1975

(see Strange Tales)

	$Good	$Fine	$N.Mint	£Good	£Fine	£N.Mint
1 ND reprints from Strange Tales #101 onwards begin	$0.70	$2.10	$3.50	£0.45	£1.35	£2.25
2-6 ND	$0.55	$1.65	$2.75	£0.35	£1.05	£1.75
7 ND reprints, Strange Tales #107 (vs Sub-Mariner)	$0.55	$1.65	$2.75	£0.35	£1.05	£1.75
8 reprints Strange Tales #108 and Marvel Tales #16 (1948)	$0.45	$1.35	$2.25	£0.30	£0.90	£1.50
Title Value:	$4.45	$13.35	$22.25	£2.85	£8.55	£14.25

Note: Golden Age & 1960s reprints in all.

HUMAN TORCH, SAGA OF THE ORIGINAL
Marvel Comics Group,MS; 1 Apr 1990-4 Jul 1990

	$Good	$Fine	$N.Mint	£Good	£Fine	£N.Mint
1 ND	$0.30	$0.90	$1.50	£0.20	£0.60	£1.00
2 Captain America/Sub-Mariner appear	$0.30	$0.90	$1.50	£0.20	£0.60	£1.00
3 Invaders/All Winners Squad/Liberty Legion appear	$0.30	$0.90	$1.50	£0.20	£0.60	£1.00
4	$0.30	$0.90	$1.50	£0.20	£0.60	£1.00
Title Value:	$1.20	$3.60	$6.00	£0.80	£2.40	£4.00

HUMANTS
Legacy Comics; 1 1992

	$Good	$Fine	$N.Mint	£Good	£Fine	£N.Mint
1 ND 48pgs, black and white	$0.45	$1.35	$2.25	£0.30	£0.90	£1.50
Title Value:	$0.45	$1.35	$2.25	£0.30	£0.90	£1.50

HUNTER'S HEART
DC Comics/Paradox Press,MS; 1 Aug 1995-3 Oct 1995

	$Good	$Fine	$N.Mint	£Good	£Fine	£N.Mint
1 ND 96pgs, Randy DuBurke script and art; black and white	$1.00	$3.00	$5.00	£0.60	£1.80	£3.00
2-3 ND 96pgs, Randy DuBurke script and art; black and white	$0.60	$1.80	$3.00	£0.40	£1.20	£2.00
Title Value:	$2.20	$6.60	$11.00	£1.40	£4.20	£7.00

HUNTRESS, THE
DC Comics; 1 Mar 1989-19 Sep 1990

	$Good	$Fine	$N.Mint	£Good	£Fine	£N.Mint
1	$0.30	$0.90	$1.50	£0.20	£0.60	£1.00
2-16	$0.25	$0.75	$1.25	£0.15	£0.45	£0.75
17-19 Batman appears	$0.25	$0.75	$1.25	£0.15	£0.45	£0.75
Title Value:	$4.80	$14.40	$24.00	£2.90	£8.70	£14.50

Note: Mature Readers label.

HUNTRESS, THE (2ND SERIES)
DC Comics,MS; 1 Jun 1994-4 Sep 1994

	$Good	$Fine	$N.Mint	£Good	£Fine	£N.Mint
1-4 Chuck Dixon script, Michael Netzer art	$0.25	$0.75	$1.25	£0.15	£0.45	£0.75
Title Value:	$1.00	$3.00	$5.00	£0.60	£1.80	£3.00

HURRICANE GIRLS
Antarctic Press,MS; 1 Jul 1995-7 Jan 1996

	$Good	$Fine	$N.Mint	£Good	£Fine	£N.Mint
1-7 ND Hiroshi Yakumo script and art; black and white	$0.70	$2.10	$3.50	£0.50	£1.50	£2.50
Title Value:	$4.90	$14.70	$24.50	£3.50	£10.50	£17.50

HYBRIDS
Continuity; 1 Sep 1992

	$Good	$Fine	$N.Mint	£Good	£Fine	£N.Mint
1 ND Neal Adams cover	$0.45	$1.35	$2.25	£0.30	£0.90	£1.50
Title Value:	$0.45	$1.35	$2.25	£0.30	£0.90	£1.50

HYBRIDS (2ND SERIES)
Continuity; 0 Apr 1993; 1 Apr 1993-5 Dec 1993

0 Deathwatch 2000 part 2, silver foil embossed cover, part cover art by Neal Adams (originally came pre-bagged as an "incentive pack" with Megalith (3rd) #0)

	$Good	$Fine	$N.Mint	£Good	£Fine	£N.Mint
(0)	$1.50	$4.50	$7.50	£1.00	£3.00	£5.00
0 as above but un-bagged individual issue	$0.60	$1.80	$3.00	£0.40	£1.20	£2.00
0 red foil embossed cover, part cover art by Neal Adams	$4.50	$13.50	$22.50	£3.00	£9.00	£15.00
1 Deathwatch 2000 part 4, pre-bagged with 2 trading cards, die-cut cover, Neal Adams plot	$0.45	$1.35	$2.25	£0.30	£0.90	£1.50
2 Deathwatch 2000 part 13, pre-bagged with trading card	$0.45	$1.35	$2.25	£0.30	£0.90	£1.50
3 Deathwatch 2000, pre-bagged with trading card, Tyvek "indestructible" cover	$0.45	$1.35	$2.25	£0.30	£0.90	£1.50
4-5 guest-stars Valeria the She-Bat and the Werebreds	$0.45	$1.35	$2.25	£0.30	£0.90	£1.50
Title Value:	$8.85	$26.55	$44.25	£5.90	£17.70	£29.50

Note: all Non-Distributed on the news-stands in the U.K.

HYBRIDS (3RD SERIES)
Continuity; 1 Jan 1994

	$Good	$Fine	$N.Mint	£Good	£Fine	£N.Mint
1 ND Rise of Magic X-over; parchment embossed cover; part Neal Adams cover and inks	$0.45	$1.35	$2.25	£0.30	£0.90	£1.50
Title Value:	$0.45	$1.35	$2.25	£0.30	£0.90	£1.50

HYDE-25
Harris Comics; 0 May 1995-1 1995

	$Good	$Fine	$N.Mint	£Good	£Fine	£N.Mint
0 ND spin-off from Vampirella series, Flint Henry cover	$0.60	$1.80	$3.00	£0.40	£1.20	£2.00
1 ND	$0.60	$1.80	$3.00	£0.40	£1.20	£2.00
Title Value:	$1.20	$3.60	$6.00	£0.80	£2.40	£4.00

HYPERKIND
Marvel Comics Group/Razorline; 1 Sep 1993-9 May 1994

	$Good	$Fine	$N.Mint	£Good	£Fine	£N.Mint
1 ND prismatic foil cover	$0.45	$1.35	$2.25	£0.30	£0.90	£1.50
2-9 ND	$0.40	$1.20	$2.00	£0.25	£0.75	£1.25
Title Value:	$3.65	$10.95	$18.25	£2.30	£6.90	£11.50

HYPERKIND UNLEASHED
Marvel Comics Group/Razorline; 1 Sep 1994

	$Good	$Fine	$N.Mint	£Good	£Fine	£N.Mint
1 ND	$0.60	$1.80	$3.00	£0.40	£1.20	£2.00
Title Value:	$0.60	$1.80	$3.00	£0.40	£1.20	£2.00

I

I AM COYOTE
Eclipse; (Graphic Novel 6) Nov 1984

	$Good	$Fine	$N.Mint	£Good	£Fine	£N.Mint
nn ND	$1.80	$5.25	$9.00	£1.00	£3.00	£5.00
Title Value:	$1.80	$5.25	$9.00	£1.00	£3.00	£5.00

I AM LEGEND
Eclipse,MS; 1 Apr 1991-4 Oct 1991

	$Good	$Fine	$N.Mint	£Good	£Fine	£N.Mint
1-4 ND 64pgs, squarebound, black and white	$1.05	$3.15	$5.25	£0.70	£2.10	£3.50
Title Value:	$4.20	$12.60	$21.00	£2.80	£8.40	£14.00

	$Good	$Fine	$N.Mint	£Good	£Fine	£N.Mint

I BEFORE E
Fantagraphics,MS; 1 Aug 1991-2 Sep 1991

1 ND 48pgs, Sam Kieth cover and art; black and white

	$Good	$Fine	$N.Mint	£Good	£Fine	£N.Mint
	$0.90	$2.70	$4.50	£0.60	£1.80	£3.00

1 2nd printing, ND 48pgs, (May 1994)

| | $0.80 | $2.40 | $4.00 | £0.50 | £1.50 | £2.50 |

2 ND 48pgs, Sam Kieth cover and art; black and white

| | $0.80 | $2.40 | $4.00 | £0.50 | £1.50 | £2.50 |

2 2nd printing, ND 48pgs, (Jun 1994)

| | $0.80 | $2.40 | $4.00 | £0.50 | £1.50 | £2.50 |
| Title Value: | $3.30 | $9.90 | $16.50 | £2.10 | £6.30 | £10.50 |

I COME IN PEACE
Greater Mercury Comics,MS; 1 Oct 1991-2 Apr 1991

1-2 ND colour, film adaptation

	$Good	$Fine	$N.Mint	£Good	£Fine	£N.Mint
	$0.30	$0.90	$1.50	£0.20	£0.60	£1.00
Title Value:	$0.60	$1.80	$3.00	£0.40	£1.20	£2.00

I LOVE LUCY
Eternity,MS; 1 May 1990-6 Oct 1990

	$Good	$Fine	$N.Mint	£Good	£Fine	£N.Mint
1-6 ND	$0.55	$1.65	$2.75	£0.35	£1.05	£1.75
Title Value:	$3.30	$9.90	$16.50	£2.10	£6.30	£10.50

I LOVE LUCY BOOK TWO
Eternity,MS; 1-3 1991

	$Good	$Fine	$N.Mint	£Good	£Fine	£N.Mint
1-3 ND	$0.55	$1.65	$2.75	£0.35	£1.05	£1.75
Title Value:	$1.65	$4.95	$8.25	£1.05	£3.15	£5.25

I LOVE YOU
Charlton; 7 Sep 1955-121 Dec 1976; 122 Mar 1979-130 May 1980

7 scarce in the U.K. Jack Kirby cover

	$Good	$Fine	$N.Mint	£Good	£Fine	£N.Mint
	$7.50	$22.50	$45.00	£5.00	£15.00	£30.00

8-10 scarce in the U.K.

	$3.00	$9.00	$18.00	£2.00	£6.00	£12.00
11-15	$1.85	$5.50	$11.25	£1.25	£3.75	£7.50
16	$1.50	$4.50	$9.00	£1.00	£3.00	£6.00
17 giant	$1.85	$5.50	$11.25	£1.25	£3.75	£7.50
18-20	$1.50	$4.50	$9.00	£1.00	£3.00	£6.00
21-22	$1.15	$3.50	$7.00	£0.75	£2.25	£4.50

1st official distribution in the U.K.

	$Good	$Fine	$N.Mint	£Good	£Fine	£N.Mint
23-30	$1.15	$3.50	$7.00	£0.75	£2.25	£4.50
31-59	$0.75	$2.25	$4.50	£0.50	£1.50	£3.00

60 Elvis Presley appears

	$7.50	$22.50	$45.00	£5.00	£15.00	£30.00
61-65	$0.75	$2.25	$4.50	£0.50	£1.50	£3.00
66-80	$0.60	$1.80	$3.00	£0.40	£1.20	£2.00
81-100	$0.45	$1.35	$2.25	£0.30	£0.90	£1.50
101-130	$0.30	$0.90	$1.50	£0.20	£0.60	£1.00
Title Value:	$105.10	$315.50	$605.50	£70.00	£210.00	£402.00

Note: most issues distributed in the U.K. after 1958. Issues #1-6 called "In Love"

I WANT TO BE YOUR DOG
Eros Comix,MS; 1 Oct 1990-5 Mar 1991

1 ND Ho Che Anderson script and art; black and white, adult material

	$Good	$Fine	$N.Mint	£Good	£Fine	£N.Mint
	$0.45	$1.35	$2.25	£0.30	£0.90	£1.50

2-5 ND Ho Che Anderson script and art; black and white, adult material

| | $0.40 | $1.20 | $2.00 | £0.25 | £0.75 | £1.25 |
| Title Value: | $2.05 | $6.15 | $10.25 | £1.30 | £3.90 | £6.50 |

I.F.S. ZONE
KBH; 1 Sep 1987

1 ND black and white

	$Good	$Fine	$N.Mint	£Good	£Fine	£N.Mint
	$0.25	$0.75	$1.25	£0.15	£0.45	£0.75
Title Value:	$0.25	$0.75	$1.25	£0.15	£0.45	£0.75

ICARUS
Aircel; 1 1987-6 1988

	$Good	$Fine	$N.Mint	£Good	£Fine	£N.Mint
1-6 ND	$0.40	$1.20	$2.00	£0.25	£0.75	£1.25
Title Value:	$2.40	$7.20	$12.00	£1.50	£4.50	£7.50

ICE AGE - A MAGIC: THE GATHERING LIMITED SERIES
Acclaim Comics,MS; 1 Jul 1995-4 Oct 1995

1-4 ND Jeff Gomez script, Rafael Kayanan art; painted cover by Charles Vess

	$Good	$Fine	$N.Mint	£Good	£Fine	£N.Mint
	$0.45	$1.35	$2.25	£0.30	£0.90	£1.50
Title Value:	$1.80	$5.40	$9.00	£1.20	£3.60	£6.00

Note: based on fantasy game Magic: The Gathering by Wizards of the Coast

Ice Age on the World of Magic: The Gathering 1 (Sep 1995)

Trade paperback collects issues #1,2 £0.65 | £1.95 | £3.25

Ice Age on the World of Magic: The Gathering 2 (Sep 1995)

Trade paperback collects issues #3,4 £0.65 | £1.95 | £3.25

ICEMAN
Marvel Comics Group,MS; 1 Dec 1984-4 Jun 1985

	$Good	$Fine	$N.Mint	£Good	£Fine	£N.Mint
1-2 ND	$0.45	$1.35	$2.25	£0.30	£0.90	£1.50

3 ND original X-Men, Defenders and Champions appear

	$0.45	$1.35	$2.25	£0.30	£0.90	£1.50
4 ND	$0.45	$1.35	$2.25	£0.30	£0.90	£1.50
Title Value:	$1.80	$5.40	$9.00	£1.20	£3.60	£6.00

ICICLE
Hero,MS; 1 Jul 1992-7 Jan 1993

1 ND Flare and Lady Arcane appear

	$Good	$Fine	$N.Mint	£Good	£Fine	£N.Mint
	$0.55	$1.65	$2.75	£0.35	£1.05	£1.75
2-7 ND	$0.55	$1.65	$2.75	£0.35	£1.05	£1.75
Title Value:	$3.85	$11.55	$19.25	£2.45	£7.35	£12.25

ICON
DC Comics/Milestone; 1 May 1993-present

	$Good	$Fine	$N.Mint	£Good	£Fine	£N.Mint
1	$0.30	$0.90	$1.50	£0.20	£0.60	£1.00

1 ND Direct Market Edition, pre-bagged with poster, trading card and jigsaw puzzle pieces

| | $0.60 | $1.80 | $3.00 | £0.40 | £1.20 | £2.00 |
| 2-8 | $0.30 | $0.90 | $1.50 | £0.20 | £0.60 | £1.00 |

9 spot varnish ink cover by Walt Simonson, continued in Xombi #0

| | $0.30 | $0.90 | $1.50 | £0.20 | £0.60 | £1.00 |
| 10-13 | $0.30 | $0.90 | $1.50 | £0.20 | £0.60 | £1.00 |

14 John Byrne cover

| | $0.30 | $0.90 | $1.50 | £0.20 | £0.60 | £1.00 |

15 Worlds Collide X-over, continued in Steel #6

| | $0.30 | $0.90 | $1.50 | £0.20 | £0.60 | £1.00 |

16 Worlds Collide X-over, continued in Steel #7

	$0.30	$0.90	$1.50	£0.20	£0.60	£1.00
17-24	$0.30	$0.90	$1.50	£0.20	£0.60	£1.00
25 48pgs	$0.60	$1.80	$3.00	£0.40	£1.20	£2.00
26	$0.40	$1.20	$2.00	£0.25	£0.75	£1.25
27-30	$0.45	$1.35	$2.25	£0.30	£0.90	£1.50

31 Howard Chaykin cover; special price of 99 cents

	$0.20	$0.60	$0.75	£0.15	£0.45	£0.75
32-35	$0.45	$1.35	$2.25	£0.30	£0.90	£1.50
Title Value:	$12.60	$37.80	$63.50	£8.40	£25.20	£42.00

ICZER ONE, GOLDEN WARRIOR
Antarctic Press,MS; 1 Mar 1994-5 Aug 1994

1-5 ND black and white

	$Good	$Fine	$N.Mint	£Good	£Fine	£N.Mint
	$0.55	$1.65	$2.75	£0.35	£1.05	£1.75
Title Value:	$2.75	$8.25	$13.75	£1.75	£5.25	£8.75

IDOL
Marvel Comics Group,MS; 1 May 1992-3 Jul 1992

	$Good	$Fine	$N.Mint	£Good	£Fine	£N.Mint
1-3 ND 48pgs	$0.55	$1.65	$2.75	£0.35	£1.05	£1.75
Title Value:	$1.65	$4.95	$8.25	£1.05	£3.15	£5.25

IGRAT
Verotik,MS; 1 Nov 1995-present

1 ND Glenn Danzig script, Eric Canete art

	$Good	$Fine	$N.Mint	£Good	£Fine	£N.Mint
	$0.60	$1.80	$3.00	£0.40	£1.20	£2.00
Title Value:	$0.60	$1.80	$3.00	£0.40	£1.20	£2.00

IKE GARUDA, THE TRANSMUTATION OF
Marvel Comics Group/Epic,MS; 1 Sep 1991-2 Mar 1992

	$Good	$Fine	$N.Mint	£Good	£Fine	£N.Mint
1-2 ND	$0.80	$2.40	$4.00	£0.50	£1.50	£2.50
Title Value:	$1.60	$4.80	$8.00	£1.00	£3.00	£5.00

ILLEGAL ALIENS
Eclipse; 1 Sep 1992

1 ND famous film monsters featured

	$Good	$Fine	$N.Mint	£Good	£Fine	£N.Mint
	$0.45	$1.35	$2.25	£0.30	£0.90	£1.50
Title Value:	$0.45	$1.35	$2.25	£0.30	£0.90	£1.50

ILLUMINATOR
Marvel Comics Group,MS; 1 Jan 1993-3 Apr 1994

1-3 ND 48pgs, squarebound

	$Good	$Fine	$N.Mint	£Good	£Fine	£N.Mint
	$1.00	$3.00	$5.00	£0.65	£1.95	£3.25
Title Value:	$3.00	$9.00	$15.00	£1.95	£5.85	£9.75

Note: originally announced as "Crucible" but changed owing to a DC title of the same name appearing around the same time.

ILLUMINATUS!
Rip Off Press; 1,2 1990

1 ND re-done art from original issue #1 dated July 1987, Robert Shea art

	$Good	$Fine	$N.Mint	£Good	£Fine	£N.Mint
	$0.45	$1.35	$2.25	£0.30	£0.90	£1.50
2 ND	$0.45	$1.35	$2.25	£0.30	£0.90	£1.50
Title Value:	$0.90	$2.70	$4.50	£0.60	£1.80	£3.00

IMAGE COMICS ANNUAL INFORMATION CATALOGUE
Image,OS; 1994

1 ND details on titles, characters and artists up and coming for the year 1994

	$Good	$Fine	$N.Mint	£Good	£Fine	£N.Mint
	$0.45	$1.35	$2.25	£0.30	£0.90	£1.50
Title Value:	$0.45	$1.35	$2.25	£0.30	£0.90	£1.50

IMAGE COUPONS
Image; 1992/1993

The series of special Image Comics #0 coupons were bound-in with the following issues and all seven had to be sent away for the comic. The coupons are brightly coloured forms to be filled in and comics without the coupons are valued considerably lower:

Coupon 1 - Shadowhawk #1
Coupon 2 - Spawn #4
Coupon 3 - Cyberforce #1
Coupon 4 - Brigade #2
Coupon 5 - Wildc.a.t.s. #2
Coupon 6 - Savage Dragon #3
Coupon 7 - Youngblood #0

IMAGE PLUS
Image,OS; 1 May 1993

1 ND information on Image artists and writers; embossed logo on cover

	$Good	$Fine	$N.Mint	£Good	£Fine	£N.Mint
	$0.45	$1.35	$2.25	£0.30	£0.90	£1.50
Title Value:	$0.45	$1.35	$2.25	£0.30	£0.90	£1.50

IMAGE SWIMSUIT SPECIAL
Image,OS; 1 Apr 1993

1 ND pin-ups by Lee, Silvestri, Portacio and others; flip-cover by Lee and Silvestri

	$Good	$Fine	$N.Mint	£Good	£Fine	£N.Mint
	$0.40	$1.20	$2.00	£0.25	£0.75	£1.25
Title Value:	$0.40	$1.20	$2.00	£0.25	£0.75	£1.25

IMAGE ZERO
Image,OS; 0 Oct 1993

0 ND features art by Silvestri, Larsen, Lee, Valentino & includes 1st appearance of Troll by Liefeld

	$Good	$Fine	$N.Mint	£Good	£Fine	£N.Mint
	$2.00	$6.00	$10.00	£1.20	£3.60	£6.00
Title Value:	$2.00	$6.00	$10.00	£1.20	£3.60	£6.00

IMMORTAL DR FATE, THE
(see Doctor Fate)

IMMORTALIS
Marvel UK/Frontier,MS; 1 Sep 1993-4 Dec 1993

	$Good	$Fine	$N.Mint	£Good	£Fine	£N.Mint
1-4 Mark Buckingham art	$0.40	$1.20	$2.00	£0.25	£0.75	£1.25
Title Value:	$1.60	$4.80	$8.00	£1.00	£3.00	£5.00

MINT = 100% / NEAR MINT (inc. +/-) = 90–99% / VERY FINE (inc. +/-) = 75–89% / FINE (inc. +/-) = 55–74%
VERY GOOD (inc. +/-) = 35–54% / GOOD (inc. +/-) = 15–34% / FAIR = 5–14% / POOR = 1–4%

397

IMPACT COMICS WHO'S WHO

DC Comics/Impact,MS; 1 Sep 1991-2 Oct 1991; 3 May 1992

	$Good	$Fine	$N.Mint	£Good	£Fine	£N.Mint
1-2 ND 48pgs, loose-leaf format to fit in binder (issued separately)						
	$0.80	$2.40	$4.00	£0.50	£1.50	£2.50
3 ND 48pgs, loose-leaf format to fit in binder (issued separately), trading cards included						
	$0.80	$2.40	$4.00	£0.50	£1.50	£2.50
Title Value:	$2.40	$7.20	$12.00	£1.50	£4.50	£7.50

IMPACT COMICS WINTER SPECIAL

DC Comics/Impact,OS; 1 Jan 1992

	$Good	$Fine	$N.Mint	£Good	£Fine	£N.Mint
1 64pgs, features the Impact Line of heroes						
	$0.40	$1.20	$2.00	£0.25	£0.75	£1.25
Title Value:	$0.40	$1.20	$2.00	£0.25	£0.75	£1.25

IMPOSSIBLE MAN SUMMER VACATION SPECTACULAR

Marvel Comics Group; 1 Aug 1990; 2 Sep 1991

	$Good	$Fine	$N.Mint	£Good	£Fine	£N.Mint
1 ND 64pgs, Spiderman/Punisher appear, variety of artists/writers						
	$0.40	$1.20	$2.00	£0.25	£0.75	£1.25
2 ND Teenage Mutant Ninja Turtles parody cover by Golden						
	$0.40	$1.20	$2.00	£0.25	£0.75	£1.25
Title Value:	$0.80	$2.40	$4.00	£0.50	£1.50	£2.50

IMPULSE

DC Comics; 1 Apr 1995-present

(see Flash [2nd Series] #92,93)

	$Good	$Fine	$N.Mint	£Good	£Fine	£N.Mint
1 spin-off series from Flash (2nd Series) #100						
	$0.80	$2.40	$4.00	£0.50	£1.50	£2.50
2	$0.50	$1.50	$2.50	£0.30	£0.90	£1.50
3-7	$0.40	$1.20	$2.00	£0.25	£0.75	£1.25
8 Underworld Unleashed tie-in						
	$0.40	$1.20	$2.00	£0.25	£0.75	£1.25
9	$0.40	$1.20	$2.00	£0.25	£0.75	£1.25
10 Dead Heat part 3, continued in Flash #110						
	$0.40	$1.20	$2.00	£0.25	£0.75	£1.25
11 Dead Heat part 5, continued in Flash #111						
	$0.35	$1.05	$1.75	£0.25	£0.75	£1.25
12	$0.35	$1.05	$1.75	£0.25	£0.75	£1.25
Title Value:	$5.20	$15.60	$26.00	£3.30	£9.90	£16.50

IN HIS STEPS

Marvel Comics Group,OS; nn May 1994

	$Good	$Fine	$N.Mint	£Good	£Fine	£N.Mint
nn ND 96pgs, Trade paperback; neighbourhood and community programme story published in conjunction with Thomas Nelson Publishing						
	$2.00	$6.00	$10.00	£1.30	£3.90	£6.50
Title Value:	$2.00	$6.00	$10.00	£1.30	£3.90	£6.50

IN THE DAYS OF THE MOB

DC Comics/Hampshire Distribution,Magazine; 1 Fall 1971

	$Good	$Fine	$N.Mint	£Good	£Fine	£N.Mint
1 ND 48pgs, Jack Kirby art throughout, includes poster (John Dillinger), black and white						
	$3.00	$9.00	$15.00	£2.00	£6.00	£10.00
Title Value:	$3.00	$9.00	$15.00	£2.00	£6.00	£10.00

Note: a second issue was intended but never appeared. Some unpublished art by Kirby appears in The Amazing World of DC Comics #1

INCAL, THE

Marvel Comics Group/Epic; Graphic Novel; 1-3 1988

(see also Moebius)

	$Good	$Fine	$N.Mint	£Good	£Fine	£N.Mint
1 ND 96pgs	$1.65	$4.95	$8.25	£1.10	£3.30	£5.50
2 ND 120pgs	$1.80	$5.25	$9.00	£1.20	£3.60	£6.00
3 ND 96pgs	$1.65	$4.95	$8.25	£1.10	£3.30	£5.50
Title Value:	$5.10	$15.15	$25.50	£3.40	£10.20	£17.00

Note: all have Moebius art. Titan (UK) editions also exist.

INCREDIBLE HULK & WOLVERINE

Marvel Comics Group,OS; 1 Oct 1986

	$Good	$Fine	$N.Mint	£Good	£Fine	£N.Mint
1 ND reprints Hulk #180,#181 featuring the first appearance of Wolverine						
	$2.00	$6.00	$10.00	£1.40	£4.20	£7.00
1 2nd printing, (1991), squarebound, new cover art plus new pin-up inside back cover, titled "Wolverine Battles The Incredible Hulk"						
	$1.05	$3.15	$5.25	£0.70	£2.10	£3.50
Title Value:	$3.05	$9.15	$15.25	£2.10	£6.30	£10.50

INCREDIBLE HULK (1ST SERIES)

Marvel Comics Group; 1 May 1962-6 Mar 1963

(see Avengers, Marvel Fanfare, Marvel Team-Up, Marvel Treasury Edition, Rampaging Hulk)

	$Good	$Fine	$N.Mint	£Good	£Fine	£N.Mint
1 origin and 1st appearance of The Hulk (grey); Jack Kirby cover and art						
	$830.00	$2500.00	$10000.00	£500.00	£1500.00	£6000.00
[Very rare in high grade - Very Fine+ or better]						
1 ND Marvel Milestone Edition (May 1992), reprints original issue with ads						
	$0.50	$1.50	$3.00	£0.30	£0.90	£1.50
2 1st green Hulk; Jack Kirby and Steve Ditko cover and art						
	$300.00	$900.00	$3000.00	£140.00	£420.00	£1400.00
3 origin retold, 1st appearance Ringmaster; Jack Kirby cover and art						
	$185.00	$560.00	$1500.00	£100.00	£300.00	£800.00
4 origin re-told in brief; Jack Kirby cover and art						
	$165.00	$500.00	$1350.00	£87.50	£260.00	£700.00
5 scarce in the U.K. Jack Kirby cover and art						
	$165.00	$500.00	$1350.00	£92.50	£280.00	£750.00
6 less common in the U.K. 1st appearance Teen Brigade; all Steve Ditko cover and art						
	$235.00	$710.00	$1900.00	£110.00	£335.00	£900.00
Title Value:	$1880.50	$5671.50	$19102.50	£1030.30	£3095.90	£10551.50

Note: issue 1 has a dark blue cover which marks easily, particularly along the spine and edges and is therefore very rare in high grade. See also Fantastic Four #7.

ARTISTS
Kirby in 1-5, Ditko in 6.

INCREDIBLE HULK (2ND SERIES)

Marvel Comics Group; 102 Apr 1968-present

	$Good	$Fine	$N.Mint	£Good	£Fine	£N.Mint
102 origin retold; Warriors Three and Odin appear; Thor and Silver Surfer cameos						
	$26.00	$75.00	$180.00	£16.00	£49.00	£115.00
103 scarce in the U.K.						
	$11.50	$35.00	$70.00	£7.50	£22.50	£45.00
104 Rhino appears						
	$11.50	$35.00	$70.00	£6.25	£18.50	£37.50
105 1st appearance Missing Link						
	$9.00	$28.00	$55.00	£5.00	£15.00	£30.00
106-108	$9.00	$28.00	$55.00	£5.00	£15.00	£30.00
109-110 Ka-Zar appears						
	$6.50	$20.00	$40.00	£3.30	£10.00	£20.00
111 (Jan 1969)	$5.00	$15.00	$30.00	£2.50	£7.50	£15.00
112-115	$5.00	$15.00	$30.00	£2.50	£7.50	£15.00
116	$5.00	$15.00	$30.00	£2.05	£6.25	£12.50
117 last 12 cents issue						
	$5.00	$15.00	$30.00	£2.05	£6.25	£12.50
118 Hulk battles Sub-Mariner						
	$5.00	$15.00	$30.00	£2.05	£6.25	£12.50
119	$3.00	$9.00	$18.00	£1.50	£4.50	£9.00
120 Inhumans appear, classic cover by Herb Trimpe						
	$3.00	$9.00	$18.00	£1.50	£4.50	£9.00
121	$3.00	$9.00	$18.00	£1.50	£4.50	£9.00
122 Hulk battles The Thing (see Fantastic Four #25), Fantastic Four appear						
	$5.75	$17.50	$35.00	£2.00	£6.00	£12.00
123 (Jan 1970), Fantastic Four appear						
	$2.50	$7.50	$15.00	£1.15	£3.50	£7.00
124-125	$2.50	$7.50	$15.00	£1.15	£3.50	£7.00
126 Dr. Strange appears						
	$2.50	$7.50	$15.00	£1.15	£3.50	£7.00
127	$2.50	$7.50	$15.00	£1.15	£3.50	£7.00
128 Hulk battles Avengers						
	$2.50	$7.50	$15.00	£1.25	£3.75	£7.50
129-130	$2.50	$7.50	$15.00	£1.15	£3.50	£7.00
131 Iron Man vs. The Hulk						
	$1.65	$5.00	$10.00	£1.00	£3.00	£6.00
132-133	$1.65	$5.00	$10.00	£1.00	£3.00	£6.00
134 1st appearance Golem I (see Strange Tales #174)						
	$1.65	$5.00	$10.00	£1.00	£3.00	£6.00
135 (Jan 1971)	$1.65	$5.00	$10.00	£1.00	£3.00	£6.00
136-139	$1.65	$5.00	$10.00	£1.00	£3.00	£6.00
140 Harlan Ellison script, 1st appearance Jarella; story continues from Avengers #88						
	$1.65	$5.00	$10.00	£1.00	£3.00	£6.00
141 less common in the U.K. 1st appearance Doc Samson						
	$2.50	$7.50	$15.00	£2.05	£6.25	£12.50
142-143	$1.15	$3.50	$7.00	£0.75	£2.25	£4.50
144 Iron Man and Dr. Doom appear, classic cover						
	$1.15	$3.50	$7.00	£0.75	£2.25	£4.50
145 52pgs, origin retold						
	$1.65	$5.00	$10.00	£1.05	£3.25	£6.50
146	$1.15	$3.50	$7.00	£0.75	£2.25	£4.50
147 (Jan 1972)	$1.15	$3.50	$7.00	£0.75	£2.25	£4.50
148 Nick Fury appears						
	$1.15	$3.50	$7.00	£0.75	£2.25	£4.50
149 1st appearance The Inheritor						
	$1.15	$3.50	$7.00	£0.75	£2.25	£4.50
150 Lorna Dane, Havok appear						
	$1.15	$3.50	$7.00	£0.75	£2.25	£4.50
151	$1.15	$3.50	$7.00	£0.55	£1.75	£3.50
152 scarce in the U.K. Captain America, Daredevil, Fantastic Four, Nick Fury appear: Hulk on trial						
	$1.00	$3.00	$6.00	£1.00	£3.00	£6.00
153 ND very scarce in the U.K. Hulk on trial continued with above guests plus Spiderman and the Avengers						
	$1.00	$3.00	$6.00	£1.25	£3.75	£7.50
154 ND	$1.00	$3.00	$6.00	£0.75	£2.25	£4.50
155 ND scarce in the U.K.						
	$1.50	$4.50	$9.00	£1.00	£3.00	£6.00
156-157 ND	$1.00	$3.00	$6.00	£0.75	£2.25	£4.50
158 ND Counter Earth story, various cameo appearances including Warlock						
	$1.00	$3.00	$6.00	£0.80	£2.50	£5.00
159 ND (Jan 1973)	$1.00	$3.00	$6.00	£0.75	£2.25	£4.50
160 ND	$1.00	$3.00	$6.00	£0.75	£2.25	£4.50
161 Beast appears, death of Mimic						
	$0.80	$2.50	$5.00	£0.55	£1.75	£3.50
162 1st appearance Wendigo						
	$1.30	$4.00	$8.00	£0.80	£2.50	£5.00
163-165	$0.80	$2.50	$5.00	£0.55	£1.75	£3.50
166 1st appearance Zzzax, Hawkeye appears						
	$0.80	$2.50	$5.00	£0.55	£1.75	£3.50
167-170 ND	$0.80	$2.50	$5.00	£0.65	£2.00	£4.00
171 ND scarce in the U.K. (Jan 1974), Abomination/Rhino vs. Hulk						
	$1.25	$3.75	$7.50	£1.25	£3.75	£7.50
172 ND X-Men appear, ties in with Avengers #111						
	$1.25	$3.75	$7.50	£1.00	£3.00	£6.00
173-174 ND	$0.80	$2.50	$5.00	£0.55	£1.75	£3.50
175 ND Inhumans appear, Hulk vs. Black Bolt						
	$0.80	$2.50	$5.00	£0.55	£1.75	£3.50
176 ND Warlock X-over (cameo)						
	$0.80	$2.50	$5.00	£0.90	£2.75	£5.50
177 ND Warlock X-over; Warlock "dies" in last panel						
	$1.25	$3.75	$7.50	£1.00	£3.00	£6.00
178 ND Warlock X-over; rebirth of Warlock						
	$1.65	$5.00	$10.00	£1.15	£3.50	£7.00
179 ND	$0.80	$2.50	$5.00	£0.55	£1.75	£3.50
180 ND 1st appearance of Wolverine (one panel, last page)						
	$12.50	$38.00	$75.00	£8.25	£25.00	£50.00
181 ND 1st Wolverine story						

	$Good	$Fine	$N.Mint	£Good	£Fine	£N.Mint
	$50.00	$150.00	$350.00	£31.00	£92.50	£220.00
182 ND Wolverine cameo only						
	$9.00	$28.00	$55.00	£5.00	£15.00	£30.00
183 ND (Jan 1975)	$0.65	$2.00	$4.00	£0.50	£1.50	£3.00
184-189 ND	$0.65	$2.00	$4.00	£0.50	£1.50	£3.00
190 ND 1st appearance Glorian						
	$0.65	$2.00	$4.00	£0.50	£1.50	£3.00
191-194 ND	$0.55	$1.75	$3.50	£0.40	£1.25	£2.50
195 ND (Jan 1976)	$0.55	$1.75	$3.50	£0.40	£1.25	£2.50
196-197 ND	$0.55	$1.75	$3.50	£0.40	£1.25	£2.50
198-199 ND Man-Thing appears						
	$0.55	$1.75	$3.50	£0.40	£1.25	£2.50
200 ND anniversary issue, Silver Surfer appears in dream sequence						
	$4.15	$12.50	$25.00	£1.30	£4.00	£8.00
201-203 ND	$0.60	$1.80	$3.00	£0.40	£1.20	£2.00
204 ND origin retold						
	$0.60	$1.80	$3.00	£0.40	£1.20	£2.00
205-206 ND	$0.60	$1.80	$3.00	£0.40	£1.20	£2.00
207 ND (Jan 1977), Hulk battles Defenders						
	$0.60	$1.80	$3.00	£0.40	£1.20	£2.00
208-210 ND	$0.60	$1.80	$3.00	£0.40	£1.20	£2.00
211 ND	$0.60	$1.80	$3.00	£0.30	£0.90	£1.50
212 ND 1st appearance Constrictor						
	$0.60	$1.80	$3.00	£0.30	£0.90	£1.50
213 ND	$0.60	$1.80	$3.00	£0.30	£0.90	£1.50
214 ND Hulk battles Jack of Hearts						
	$0.60	$1.80	$3.00	£0.30	£0.90	£1.50
215-217 ND	$0.60	$1.80	$3.00	£0.30	£0.90	£1.50
218 ND 1st solo Doc Samson story						
	$0.60	$1.80	$3.00	£0.30	£0.90	£1.50
219 ND (Jan 1978)	$0.60	$1.80	$3.00	£0.30	£0.90	£1.50
220-221 ND	$0.60	$1.80	$3.00	£0.30	£0.90	£1.50
222 ND Jim Starlin layouts						
	$0.60	$1.80	$3.00	£0.30	£0.90	£1.50
223-226 ND	$0.60	$1.80	$3.00	£0.30	£0.90	£1.50
227 ND original Avengers appear						
	$0.60	$1.80	$3.00	£0.30	£0.90	£1.50
228 ND	$0.60	$1.80	$3.00	£0.30	£0.90	£1.50
229 ND Doc Samson appears						
	$0.60	$1.80	$3.00	£0.30	£0.90	£1.50
230 ND	$0.60	$1.80	$3.00	£0.30	£0.90	£1.50
231 ND (Jan 1979)	$0.60	$1.80	$3.00	£0.30	£0.90	£1.50
232 ND Captain America appears						
	$0.60	$1.80	$3.00	£0.30	£0.90	£1.50
233-234 ND	$0.60	$1.80	$3.00	£0.30	£0.90	£1.50
235-236 ND Machine Man appears						
	$0.60	$1.80	$3.00	£0.30	£0.90	£1.50
237-242 ND	$0.60	$1.80	$3.00	£0.30	£0.90	£1.50
243 ND (Jan 1980)	$0.60	$1.80	$3.00	£0.30	£0.90	£1.50
244 ND	$0.60	$1.80	$3.00	£0.30	£0.90	£1.50
245-246 ND Captain Marvel appears						
	$0.60	$1.80	$3.00	£0.30	£0.90	£1.50
247-248 ND	$0.60	$1.80	$3.00	£0.30	£0.90	£1.50
249 ND Steve Ditko art						
	$0.60	$1.80	$3.00	£0.30	£0.90	£1.50
250 ND 52pgs, Silver Surfer battles Hulk						
	$2.00	$6.00	$10.00	£1.00	£3.00	£5.00
251-252 ND	$0.60	$1.80	$3.00	£0.30	£0.90	£1.50
253 ND Doc Samson appears						
	$0.60	$1.80	$3.00	£0.30	£0.90	£1.50
254 ND	$0.60	$1.80	$3.00	£0.30	£0.90	£1.50

	$Good	$Fine	$N.Mint	£Good	£Fine	£N.Mint
255 ND (Jan 1981), Hulk vs. Thor						
	$0.60	$1.80	$3.00	£0.30	£0.90	£1.50
256-257 ND	$0.60	$1.80	$3.00	£0.30	£0.90	£1.50
258 Frank Miller cover						
	$0.60	$1.80	$3.00	£0.25	£0.75	£1.25
259-260	$0.60	$1.80	$3.00	£0.25	£0.75	£1.25
261 Frank Miller cover						
	$0.60	$1.80	$3.00	£0.25	£0.75	£1.25
262-263	$0.60	$1.80	$3.00	£0.25	£0.75	£1.25
264 Frank Miller cover						
	$0.60	$1.80	$3.00	£0.25	£0.75	£1.25
265-266	$0.60	$1.80	$3.00	£0.25	£0.75	£1.25
267 (Jan 1982)	$0.60	$1.80	$3.00	£0.25	£0.75	£1.25
268 Frank Miller cover						
	$0.60	$1.80	$3.00	£0.25	£0.75	£1.25
269-270	$0.60	$1.80	$3.00	£0.25	£0.75	£1.25
271 20th anniversary issue, 1st appearance Rocket Raccoon						
	$0.60	$1.80	$3.00	£0.25	£0.75	£1.25
272 Alpha Flight and Wendigo appear						
	$0.60	$1.80	$3.00	£0.25	£0.75	£1.25
273 Sasquatch and Wendigo appear						
	$0.60	$1.80	$3.00	£0.25	£0.75	£1.25
274-276	$0.60	$1.80	$3.00	£0.25	£0.75	£1.25
277 many Marvel heroes make cameo appearances						
	$0.60	$1.80	$3.00	£0.25	£0.75	£1.25
278 X-Men and Avengers cameos plus many other Marvel heroes						
	$0.60	$1.80	$3.00	£0.25	£0.75	£1.25
279 (Jan 1983), Alpha Flight, X-Men cameos and many other Marvel heroes						
	$0.60	$1.80	$3.00	£0.25	£0.75	£1.25
280	$0.60	$1.80	$3.00	£0.25	£0.75	£1.25
281 Avengers cameo						
	$0.60	$1.80	$3.00	£0.25	£0.75	£1.25
282-284 Avengers appear						
	$0.60	$1.80	$3.00	£0.25	£0.75	£1.25
285-290	$0.60	$1.80	$3.00	£0.25	£0.75	£1.25
291 (Jan 1984)	$0.60	$1.80	$3.00	£0.25	£0.75	£1.25
292	$0.60	$1.80	$3.00	£0.25	£0.75	£1.25
293 Fantastic Four appear						
	$0.60	$1.80	$3.00	£0.25	£0.75	£1.25
294	$0.60	$1.80	$3.00	£0.25	£0.75	£1.25
295 Sienkiewicz cover						
	$0.60	$1.80	$3.00	£0.25	£0.75	£1.25
296 Rom appears	$0.60	$1.80	$3.00	£0.25	£0.75	£1.25
297-298 Dr. Strange appears						
	$0.60	$1.80	$3.00	£0.25	£0.75	£1.25
299 LD in the U.K. Dr. Strange appears						
	$0.60	$1.80	$3.00	£0.30	£0.90	£1.50
300 LD in the U.K. DS, Spiderman, Thor, Avengers battle a rampaging Hulk, Dr. Strange, Daredevil and Luke Cage and Iron Fist appear						
	$1.05	$3.15	$5.25	£0.70	£2.10	£3.50
301 Dr. Strange appears, Sienkiewicz cover						
	$0.60	$1.80	$3.00	£0.25	£0.75	£1.25
302	$0.60	$1.80	$3.00	£0.25	£0.75	£1.25
303 (Jan 1985)	$0.60	$1.80	$3.00	£0.25	£0.75	£1.25
304	$0.60	$1.80	$3.00	£0.25	£0.75	£1.25
305 Dr. Strange and Avengers appear						
	$0.60	$1.80	$3.00	£0.25	£0.75	£1.25
306-311	$0.60	$1.80	$3.00	£0.25	£0.75	£1.25
312 LD in the U.K. Secret Wars X-over, origin retold						
	$0.60	$1.80	$3.00	£0.30	£0.90	£1.50
313 Alpha Flight	$0.60	$1.80	$3.00	£0.25	£0.75	£1.25

Incredible Hulk #141

Incredible Hulk #300

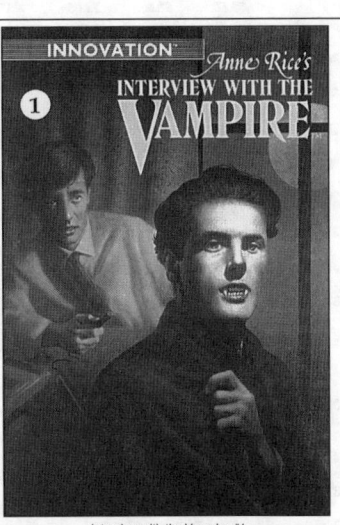

Interview with the Vampire #1

# / Description	$Good	$Fine	$N.Mint	£Good	£Fine	£N.Mint
314 LD in the U.K. John Byrne art begins	$1.20	$3.60	$6.00	£0.40	£1.20	£2.00
315 (Jan 1986), John Byrne art	$0.60	$1.80	$3.00	£0.30	£0.90	£1.50
316 Hulk battles West and East Coast Avengers, John Byrne art	$0.60	$1.80	$3.00	£0.30	£0.90	£1.50
317-319 John Byrne art	$0.60	$1.80	$3.00	£0.30	£0.90	£1.50
320 LD in the U.K.	$0.40	$1.20	$2.00	£0.30	£0.90	£1.50
321-323 LD in the U.K. Avengers vs Hulk	$0.40	$1.20	$2.00	£0.30	£0.90	£1.50
324 1st modern grey Hulk (since 1962!)	$2.00	$6.00	$10.00	£0.80	£2.40	£4.00
325 grey Hulk, 1st Steve Geiger art	$0.80	$2.40	$4.00	£0.60	£1.80	£3.00
326 grey Hulk vs. green Hulk, Geiger art	$1.20	$3.60	$6.00	£0.60	£1.80	£3.00
327 (Jan 1987), Geiger art	$0.80	$2.40	$4.00	£0.30	£0.90	£1.50
328 1st Peter David scripting, Geiger cover	$0.80	$2.40	$4.00	£0.60	£1.80	£3.00
329	$0.80	$2.40	$4.00	£0.40	£1.20	£2.00
330 Todd McFarlane art begins (ends #346)	$3.50	$10.50	$17.50	£1.40	£4.20	£7.00
331 LD in the U.K. grey Hulk series begins, 2nd Peter David script (to present except #360 and #389), Todd McFarlane art	$2.40	$7.00	$12.00	£1.20	£3.60	£6.00
332-334 Todd McFarlane art	$2.00	$6.00	$10.00	£0.80	£2.40	£4.00
335 Ridgway art	$0.60	$1.80	$3.00	£0.30	£0.90	£1.50
336-337 LD in the U.K. X-Factor X-over, Todd McFarlane art	$1.50	$4.50	$7.50	£1.20	£3.60	£6.00
338 Todd McFarlane art	$1.60	$4.80	$8.00	£0.80	£2.40	£4.00
339 (Jan 1988), Todd McFarlane art	$1.60	$4.80	$8.00	£0.80	£2.40	£4.00
340 LD in the U.K. Hulk vs. Wolverine, Todd McFarlane art	$6.00	$18.00	$30.00	£2.00	£6.00	£10.00
341-343 Todd McFarlane art	$1.20	$3.60	$6.00	£0.70	£2.10	£3.50
344 LD in the U.K. Todd McFarlane art	$1.20	$3.60	$6.00	£0.80	£2.40	£4.00
345 very LD DS, Todd McFarlane art	$1.60	$4.80	$8.00	£0.90	£2.70	£4.50
346 part Todd McFarlane art	$1.20	$3.60	$6.00	£0.50	£1.50	£2.50
347-348 Jeff Purves art	$0.60	$1.80	$3.00	£0.30	£0.90	£1.50
349 Jeff Purves art, Spiderman appears; ties into Web of Spiderman #46	$0.60	$1.80	$3.00	£0.30	£0.90	£1.50
350 LD in the U.K. Thing vs Hulk	$0.80	$2.40	$4.00	£0.50	£1.50	£2.50
351 (Jan 1989)	$0.60	$1.80	$3.00	£0.25	£0.75	£1.25
352-358	$0.60	$1.80	$3.00	£0.25	£0.75	£1.25
359 Hulk vs. "illusion" Wolverine, John Byrne cover	$1.00	$3.00	$5.00	£0.35	£1.05	£1.75
360	$0.60	$1.80	$3.00	£0.25	£0.75	£1.25
361 Iron Man battles Hulk	$0.60	$1.80	$3.00	£0.25	£0.75	£1.25
362	$0.60	$1.80	$3.00	£0.25	£0.75	£1.25
363 Acts of Vengeance tie-in	$0.60	$1.80	$3.00	£0.25	£0.75	£1.25
364 Walt Simonson cover, part 1 "Countdown"	$0.60	$1.80	$3.00	£0.25	£0.75	£1.25
365 (Jan 1990), Hulk battles Thing; Ms. Marvel appears, Walt Simonson cover	$0.60	$1.80	$3.00	£0.25	£0.75	£1.25
366 Walt Simonson cover	$0.60	$1.80	$3.00	£0.25	£0.75	£1.25
367 LD in the U.K. 1st Dale Keown art, part 4 (conclusion) "Countdown", Walt Simonson cover	$2.40	$7.00	$12.00	£1.20	£3.60	£6.00
368 Sam Keith art	$2.00	$6.00	$10.00	£0.60	£1.80	£3.00
369 2nd Dale Keown art, Hulk battles Freedom Force	$2.00	$6.00	$10.00	£0.70	£2.10	£3.50
370 Dale Keown art, Dr. Strange, Sub-Mariner appear (the original Defenders)	$2.00	$6.00	$10.00	£0.70	£2.10	£3.50
371 Dale Keown art, Dr. Strange, Sub-Mariner appear	$1.00	$3.00	$5.00	£0.60	£1.80	£3.00
372 Dale Keown art, green hulk re-emerges	$2.50	$7.50	$12.50	£0.80	£2.40	£4.00
373-375 Dale Keown art	$1.20	$3.60	$6.00	£0.60	£1.80	£3.00
376 Dale Keown art, green hulk vs grey hulk	$1.40	$4.20	$7.00	£0.80	£2.40	£4.00
377 LD in the U.K. (Jan 1991), grey/green Hulks merge to form 1st all-new Hulk, Dale Keown art, "flourescent" cover	$3.00	$9.00	$15.00	£1.00	£3.00	£5.00
377 ND grey/green Hulks merge, 2nd print - gold cover	$1.20	$3.60	$6.00	£0.60	£1.80	£3.00
377 ND reprints green cover (Nov 1994)	$0.40	$1.20	$2.00	£0.25	£0.75	£1.25
378 LD in the U.K. no Keown art	$0.60	$1.80	$3.00	£0.30	£0.90	£1.50
379 LD in the U.K. Dale Keown art	$1.20	$3.60	$6.00	£0.70	£2.10	£3.50
380 no Keown art, Doc Sampson appears	$0.60	$1.80	$3.00	£0.25	£0.75	£1.25
381-382 Dale Keown art	$0.60	$1.80	$3.00	£0.30	£0.90	£1.50
383-385 Infinity Gauntlet X-over, Dale Keown art	$0.60	$1.80	$3.00	£0.30	£0.90	£1.50
386-387 Dale Keown art	$0.60	$1.80	$3.00	£0.30	£0.90	£1.50
388 Dale Keown art, AIDS story	$0.60	$1.80	$3.00	£0.30	£0.90	£1.50
389 (Jan 1992), no Dale Keown art	$0.60	$1.80	$3.00	£0.25	£0.75	£1.25
390 X-Factor appear, $1.25 cover begins, Dale Keown art	$0.60	$1.80	$3.00	£0.25	£0.75	£1.25
391-392 X-Factor appear, Dale Keown art	$0.50	$1.50	$2.50	£0.20	£0.60	£1.00
393 64pgs, 30th anniversary issue, green foil back-ground, Dale Keown art plus Jim Starlin and Gil Kane	$0.80	$2.40	$4.00	£0.40	£1.20	£2.00
393 2nd printing, ND scarce in the U.K. grey cover	$0.80	$2.40	$4.00	£0.40	£1.20	£2.00
394 1st appearance Trauma, Andrew Wildman art	$0.40	$1.20	$2.00	£0.20	£0.60	£1.00
395 Punisher guest stars, Dale Keown art	$0.30	$0.90	$1.50	£0.20	£0.60	£1.00
396 Punisher and Dr. Octopus appear, Dale Keown art	$0.30	$0.90	$1.50	£0.20	£0.60	£1.00
397-398 Ghost of the Past story, Dale Keown art	$0.30	$0.90	$1.50	£0.20	£0.60	£1.00
399 Ghost of the Past story, Fantastic Four, Dr. Strange and Hank Pym appear; not Keown art	$0.30	$0.90	$1.50	£0.20	£0.60	£1.00
400 ND 64pgs, holo-grafix silver foil cover; reprints the Leader's 1st full appearance from Tales to Astonish #62; Flast Keown art	$0.60	$1.80	$3.00	£0.40	£1.20	£2.00
400 2nd printing, ND 64pgs, (May 1993), different back ground colour on cover	$0.45	$1.35	$2.25	£0.30	£0.90	£1.50
401 (Jan 1993)	$0.30	$0.90	$1.50	£0.20	£0.60	£1.00
402 Hulk vs. Juggernaut, Doc Samson returns	$0.30	$0.90	$1.50	£0.20	£0.60	£1.00
403 Red Skull and Avengers appear, Gary Frank pencils begin	$0.30	$0.90	$1.50	£0.20	£0.60	£1.00
404 Red Skull and Avengers appear	$0.30	$0.90	$1.50	£0.20	£0.60	£1.00
405-406	$0.30	$0.90	$1.50	£0.20	£0.60	£1.00
407 Ulysses origin in back-up story	$0.30	$0.90	$1.50	£0.20	£0.60	£1.00
408 Mad Man and Motormouth appear	$0.30	$0.90	$1.50	£0.20	£0.60	£1.00
409 Mad Man, Motormouth and Killpower appear	$0.30	$0.90	$1.50	£0.20	£0.60	£1.00
410 Nick Fury and SHIELD appear	$0.30	$0.90	$1.50	£0.20	£0.60	£1.00
411 Nick Fury and SHIELD appear	$0.30	$0.90	$1.50	£0.15	£0.45	£0.75
412	$0.30	$0.90	$1.50	£0.15	£0.45	£0.75
413 (Jan 1994), The Troyan War story	$0.30	$0.90	$1.50	£0.15	£0.45	£0.75
414 The Troyan War story	$0.30	$0.90	$1.50	£0.15	£0.45	£0.75
415 The Troyan War story, Silver Surfer appears	$0.30	$0.90	$1.50	£0.15	£0.45	£0.75
416 The Troyan War story; Future Imperfect storyline tie-in	$0.30	$0.90	$1.50	£0.15	£0.45	£0.75
417 with free Spiderman and his Deadly Foes card sheet	$0.30	$0.90	$1.50	£0.15	£0.45	£0.75
418 the wedding of Rick and Marlo	$0.30	$0.90	$1.50	£0.20	£0.60	£1.00
418 ND Collector's Edition, die-cut gate-fold wedding invitation cover	$0.60	$1.80	$3.00	£0.30	£0.90	£1.50
419	$0.30	$0.90	$1.50	£0.15	£0.45	£0.75
420 AIDS story	$0.30	$0.90	$1.50	£0.15	£0.45	£0.75
421 Thor appears	$0.30	$0.90	$1.50	£0.15	£0.45	£0.75
422-424	$0.30	$0.90	$1.50	£0.15	£0.45	£0.75
425 48pgs, (Jan 1995), new art team of Liam Sharpe and Robin Riggs	$0.45	$1.35	$2.25	£0.30	£0.90	£1.50
425 ND Deluxe Edition 48pgs, 2 channel holo-clear cover	$0.80	$2.40	$4.00	£0.50	£1.50	£2.50
426 the final fate of Betty Ross...	$0.30	$0.90	$1.50	£0.20	£0.60	£1.00
426 ND Deluxe Edition - superior paper stock and colouring	$0.40	$1.20	$2.00	£0.25	£0.75	£1.25
427 Man-Thing appears	$0.30	$0.90	$1.50	£0.20	£0.60	£1.00
427 ND Deluxe Edition - superior paper stock and colouring	$0.40	$1.20	$2.00	£0.25	£0.75	£1.25
428 Man-Thing appears	$0.30	$0.90	$1.50	£0.20	£0.60	£1.00
428 ND Deluxe Edition - superior paper stock and colouring	$0.40	$1.20	$2.00	£0.25	£0.75	£1.25
429-430	$0.40	$1.20	$2.00	£0.25	£0.75	£1.25

Issue / Description	$Good	$Fine	$N.Mint	£Good	£Fine	£N.Mint
431 The Abomination returns	$0.40	$1.20	$2.00	£0.25	£0.75	£1.25
432 Hulk vs. The Abomination	$0.40	$1.20	$2.00	£0.25	£0.75	£1.25
433 Over The Edge tie-in, Punisher appears	$0.40	$1.20	$2.00	£0.25	£0.75	£1.25
434 Over The Edge Epilogue; Wolverine, Forge and Banshee appear; funeral of Nick Fury (see Double Edge: Omega for death of Nick Fury)	$0.40	$1.20	$2.00	£0.25	£0.75	£1.25
435 48pgs, Rhino appears; features excerpts from Peter David's Hulk novel, previews new storyline and the new The Savage Hulk title	$0.45	$1.35	$2.25	£0.30	£0.90	£1.50
436 Ghosts of the Future part 1, continued in Cutting Edge #1	$0.40	$1.20	$2.00	£0.25	£0.75	£1.25
437 (Jan 1996), Ghosts of the Future part 2, the return of The Leader?	$0.40	$1.20	$2.00	£0.25	£0.75	£1.25
438-439 Ghosts of the Future story	$0.40	$1.20	$2.00	£0.25	£0.75	£1.25
Title Value:	$494.60	$1492.00	$2881.00	£271.60	£818.40	£1602.75

Incredible Hulk: Ground Zero (Aug 1991)
Trade paperback reprints issues #340-346, Todd McFarlane cover £1.70 £5.10 £8.50

INCREDIBLE HULK ANNUAL
Marvel Comics Group; 1 Oct 1968-2 Oct 1969; 3 Jan 1971-4 Jan 1972; 5 Oct 1976-present

Issue / Description	$Good	$Fine	$N.Mint	£Good	£Fine	£N.Mint
1 68pgs, Steranko cover, Hulk vs. The Inhumans	$11.50	$35.00	$70.00	£6.50	£20.00	£40.00
2 68pgs, origin reprinted (3pgs), reprints Hulk (1st Series) #3	$7.50	$22.50	$45.00	£2.90	£8.75	£17.50
3 68pgs	$1.65	$5.00	$10.00	£1.00	£3.00	£6.00
4 ND scarce in the U.K. 52pgs, all reprint	$1.50	$4.50	$9.00	£0.80	£2.50	£5.00
5 ND 52pgs	$1.00	$3.00	$6.00	£0.40	£1.25	£2.50
6 ND 52pgs, Dr. Strange appears, Warlock cameo	$0.80	$2.40	$4.00	£0.60	£1.80	£3.00
7 ND 52pgs, John Byrne art, Iceman, Angel appear; Sentinels ("Master Mould") storyline	$1.20	$3.60	$6.00	£0.80	£2.40	£4.00
8 ND 52pgs, Sasquatch appears	$0.80	$2.40	$4.00	£0.50	£1.50	£2.50
9 ND 52pgs	$0.60	$1.80	$3.00	£0.30	£0.90	£1.50
10 ND 52pgs, Bruce Banner as Captain Universe	$0.60	$1.80	$3.00	£0.30	£0.90	£1.50
11 ND 52pgs, Frank Miller's first Marvel art on a Doc Samson back-up story, (drawn before John Carter of Mars #18) but not first published	$0.80	$2.40	$4.00	£0.50	£1.50	£2.50
12-13 ND	$0.40	$1.20	$2.00	£0.25	£0.75	£1.25
14 ND John Byrne story	$0.40	$1.20	$2.00	£0.25	£0.75	£1.25
15 ND Mike Zeck cover	$0.40	$1.20	$2.00	£0.25	£0.75	£1.25
16 ND Lifeform part 3, continues in Silver Surfer Annual #3, Peter David and Alan Grant	$0.45	$1.35	$2.25	£0.30	£0.90	£1.50
17 ND Subterranean Odyssey part 2, continues in Namor Annual #1	$0.45	$1.35	$2.25	£0.30	£0.90	£1.50
18 ND Return of the Defenders part 1, Dr. Strange, Silver Surfer and Sub-Mariner appear, continued in Namor Annual #2, cover and art by Kevin Maguire, 1st story art (Thing vs. Hulk) by Travis Charest	$0.45	$1.35	$2.25	£0.30	£0.90	£1.50
19 ND 64pgs, pre-bagged with trading card introducing Lazarus	$0.60	$1.80	$3.00	£0.40	£1.20	£2.00
20 ND 64pgs, Peter David script; Hulk's history retold through the eyes of The Abomination	$0.60	$1.80	$3.00	£0.40	£1.20	£2.00
Title Value:	$32.10	$96.85	$184.75	£17.30	£52.60	£99.50

INCREDIBLE HULK ASHCAN
Marvel Comics Group; nn Jun 1994

Issue / Description	$Good	$Fine	$N.Mint	£Good	£Fine	£N.Mint
nn ND 16pgs, background information on the wedding of Rick Jones and Marlo	$0.30	$0.90	$1.50	£0.20	£0.60	£1.00
Title Value:	$0.30	$0.90	$1.50	£0.20	£0.60	£1.00

INCREDIBLE HULK BOOK AND RECORD SET
Power Records; PR-11 1974
PR-11 scarce, 20pg booklet with 45 rpm record £1.25 £3.75 £6.25
Note: the item would be valued at about 50% less without record

INCREDIBLE HULK GIANT SIZE
Marvel Comics Group; 1 1975

Issue / Description	$Good	$Fine	$N.Mint	£Good	£Fine	£N.Mint
1 ND scarce in the U.K. 68pgs, all reprint	$2.00	$6.00	$10.00	£1.30	£3.90	£6.50
Title Value:	$2.00	$6.00	$10.00	£1.30	£3.90	£6.50

INCREDIBLE HULK VS. QUASIMODO
Marvel Comics Group,OS; 1 Mar 1983

Issue / Description	$Good	$Fine	$N.Mint	£Good	£Fine	£N.Mint
1 ND scarce in the U.K. based on cartoon	$0.40	$1.20	$2.00	£0.25	£0.75	£1.25
Title Value:	$0.40	$1.20	$2.00	£0.25	£0.75	£1.25

INCREDIBLE HULK VS. VENOM
Marvel Comics Group,OS; 1 Aug 1994

Issue / Description	$Good	$Fine	$N.Mint	£Good	£Fine	£N.Mint
1 ND produced in association with the National Council for the Prevention of Child Abuse; Peter David script	$1.20	$3.60	$6.00	£1.40	£4.20	£7.00
Title Value:	$1.20	$3.60	$6.00	£1.40	£4.20	£7.00

INCREDIBLE HULK: FUTURE IMPERFECT
Marvel Comics Group,MS; 1 Feb 1993-2 Mar 1993

Issue / Description	$Good	$Fine	$N.Mint	£Good	£Fine	£N.Mint
1-2 ND 48pgs, squarebound, Peter David script, George Perez art; embossed cover	$1.20	$3.60	$6.00	£0.80	£2.40	£4.00
Title Value:	$2.40	$7.20	$12.00	£1.60	£4.80	£8.00

Incredible Hulk: Future Imperfect (Aug 1994)
Trade paperback reprints 2 issue mini-series £1.70 £5.10 £8.50
Marvel Limited: Incredible Hulk: Future Imperfect (Nov 1994)

Description	$Good	$Fine	$N.Mint	£Good	£Fine	£N.Mint
leather-bound hardcover, reprints 2 issue mini-series				£3.00	£5.00	£15.00

INCREDIBLE SCIENCE FICTION
E.C. Comics; 30 Jul/Aug 1955-33 Jan/Feb 1956
(formerly Weird Science Fantasy)

Issue / Description	$Good	$Fine	$N.Mint	£Good	£Fine	£N.Mint
30 Jack Davis cover	$30.00	$90.00	$240.00	£20.00	£60.00	£160.00
31 Jack Davis cover, Wood and Williamson art	$31.00	$92.50	$250.00	£20.00	£60.00	£160.00
32 Jack Davis cover, Williamson art	$31.00	$90.00	$245.00	£19.00	£57.50	£155.00
33 Weird Fantasy #18 reprinted, Wally Wood cover and art	$30.00	$90.00	$240.00	£18.50	£55.00	£150.00
Title Value:	$122.00	$362.50	$975.00	£77.50	£232.50	£625.00

Note: all Non-Distributed on the news-stands in the U.K.

INCREDIBLE SCIENCE FICTION (2ND SERIES)
Russ Cochran/EC Comics; 1 1993-11 1994

Issue / Description	$Good	$Fine	$N.Mint	£Good	£Fine	£N.Mint
1-11 ND	$0.30	$0.90	$1.50	£0.20	£0.60	£1.00
Title Value:	$3.30	$9.90	$16.50	£2.20	£6.60	£11.00

INDIANA JONES & THE IRON PHOENIX
Dark Horse,MS; 1 Dec 1994-4 Mar 1995

Issue / Description	$Good	$Fine	$N.Mint	£Good	£Fine	£N.Mint
1-4 ND Dave Dorman painted covers	$0.45	$1.35	$2.25	£0.30	£0.90	£1.50
Title Value:	$1.80	$5.40	$9.00	£1.20	£3.60	£6.00

INDIANA JONES AND THE SHRINE OF THE SEA DEVIL
Dark Horse,OS; 1 Sep 1994

Issue / Description	$Good	$Fine	$N.Mint	£Good	£Fine	£N.Mint
1 ND reprints serial from Dark Horse Comics #3-6	$0.45	$1.35	$2.25	£0.30	£0.90	£1.50
Title Value:	$0.45	$1.35	$2.25	£0.30	£0.90	£1.50

INDIANA JONES AND THE ARMS OF GOLD
Dark Horse; 1 Feb 1994-4 May 1994

Issue / Description	$Good	$Fine	$N.Mint	£Good	£Fine	£N.Mint
1-4 ND Lee Marrs script	$0.45	$1.35	$2.25	£0.30	£0.90	£1.50
Title Value:	$1.80	$5.40	$9.00	£1.20	£3.60	£6.00

INDIANA JONES AND THE FATE OF ATLANTIS
Dark Horse,MS; 1 May 1991-4 Nov 1991

Issue / Description	$Good	$Fine	$N.Mint	£Good	£Fine	£N.Mint
1 ND	$0.55	$1.65	$2.75	£0.35	£1.05	£1.75
1 2nd printing, ND (Dec 1991)	$0.45	$1.35	$2.25	£0.30	£0.90	£1.50
2-4 ND	$0.45	$1.35	$2.25	£0.30	£0.90	£1.50
Title Value:	$2.35	$7.05	$11.75	£1.55	£4.65	£7.75

INDIANA JONES AND THE GOLDEN FLEECE
Dark Horse,MS; 1 Jun 1994-2 Jul 1994

Issue / Description	$Good	$Fine	$N.Mint	£Good	£Fine	£N.Mint
1-2 ND	$0.45	$1.35	$2.25	£0.30	£0.90	£1.50
Title Value:	$0.90	$2.70	$4.50	£0.60	£1.80	£3.00

INDIANA JONES AND THE LAST CRUSADE
Marvel Comics Group,MS; 1 Oct 1989-3 Dec 1989
(see Further Adventures of...)

Issue / Description	$Good	$Fine	$N.Mint	£Good	£Fine	£N.Mint
1 ND	$0.30	$0.90	$1.50	£0.20	£0.60	£1.00
2 ND Todd McFarlane art	$0.40	$1.20	$2.00	£0.25	£0.75	£1.25
3 ND	$0.30	$0.90	$1.50	£0.20	£0.60	£1.00
Title Value:	$1.00	$3.00	$5.00	£0.65	£1.95	£3.25

Indiana Jones and the Last Crusade
80pg B&W magazine, David Michelinie and Bret Blevins £0.40 £1.20 £2.00

INDIANA JONES AND THE SARGASSO PIRATES
Dark Horse,MS; 1 Dec 1995-present

Issue / Description	$Good	$Fine	$N.Mint	£Good	£Fine	£N.Mint
1 ND painted cover by Alex Ross	$0.50	$1.50	$2.50	£0.30	£0.90	£1.50
Title Value:	$0.50	$1.50	$2.50	£0.30	£0.90	£1.50

INDIANA JONES AND THE SPEAR OF DESTINY
Dark Horse,MS; 1 Apr 1995-4 Aug 1995

Issue / Description	$Good	$Fine	$N.Mint	£Good	£Fine	£N.Mint
1-4 ND Elaine Lee script, Will Simpson and Dan Spiegle art	$0.45	$1.35	$2.25	£0.30	£0.90	£1.50
Title Value:	$1.80	$5.40	$9.00	£1.20	£3.60	£6.00

INDIANA JONES AND THE TEMPLE OF DOOM
Marvel Comics Group,MS; 1 Sep 1984-3 Nov 1984
(see Further Adventures of ...)

Issue / Description	$Good	$Fine	$N.Mint	£Good	£Fine	£N.Mint
1-3 ND reprints Marvel Super Special #30, Guice art	$0.30	$0.90	$1.50	£0.20	£0.60	£1.00
Title Value:	$0.90	$2.70	$4.50	£0.60	£1.80	£3.00

INDIANA JONES, FURTHER ADVENTURES OF
Marvel Comics Group; 1 Jan 1983-34 Mar 1986

Issue / Description	$Good	$Fine	$N.Mint	£Good	£Fine	£N.Mint
1 ND John Byrne script and layouts	$0.30	$0.90	$1.50	£0.20	£0.60	£1.00
2 ND John Byrne layouts	$0.25	$0.75	$1.25	£0.15	£0.45	£0.80
3 ND Gene Day art	$0.25	$0.75	$1.25	£0.15	£0.45	£0.80
4-5	$0.25	$0.75	$1.25	£0.15	£0.45	£0.75
6 Chaykin art	$0.25	$0.75	$1.25	£0.15	£0.45	£0.75
7-8	$0.25	$0.75	$1.25	£0.15	£0.45	£0.75
9-10 Chaykin cover	$0.25	$0.75	$1.25	£0.15	£0.45	£0.75
11-20	$0.25	$0.75	$1.25	£0.15	£0.45	£0.75
21 Steve Ditko art	$0.25	$0.75	$1.25	£0.15	£0.45	£0.75
22-24	$0.25	$0.75	$1.25	£0.15	£0.45	£0.75
25 Steve Ditko art	$0.25	$0.75	$1.25	£0.15	£0.45	£0.75
26 Steve Ditko art, Sienkiewicz cover	$0.25	$0.75	$1.25	£0.15	£0.45	£0.75
27-28 ND Steve Ditko art	$0.25	$0.75	$1.25	£0.15	£0.45	£0.75
29-31 ND	$0.25	$0.75	$1.25	£0.15	£0.45	£0.75
32-34 ND Steve Ditko art						

	$Good	$Fine	$N.Mint	£Good	£Fine	£N.Mint
	$0.25	$0.75	$1.25	£0.15	£0.45	£0.75
Title Value:	$8.55	$25.65	$42.75	£5.15	£15.45	£25.85

INDIANA JONES: THUNDER IN THE ORIENT
Dark Horse,MS; 1 Sep 1993-6 Feb 1994

	$Good	$Fine	$N.Mint	£Good	£Fine	£N.Mint
1-6 ND Dan Barry story and art; Dave Dorman cover	$0.45	$1.35	$2.25	£0.30	£0.90	£1.50
Title Value:	$2.70	$8.10	$13.50	£1.80	£5.40	£9.00

INDUSTRIAL GOTHIC
DC Comics/Vertigo,MS; 1 Dec 1995-5 Apr 1995

	$Good	$Fine	$N.Mint	£Good	£Fine	£N.Mint
1-5 ND 48pgs, Ted McKeever script and art	$0.50	$1.50	$2.50	£0.30	£0.90	£1.50
Title Value:	$2.50	$7.50	$12.50	£1.50	£4.50	£7.50

INFERIOR FIVE
National Periodical Publications; 1 Mar/Apr 1967-10 Sep/Oct 1968; 11 Aug/Sep 1972-12 Oct/Nov 1972
(see Showcase #62)

	$Good	$Fine	$N.Mint	£Good	£Fine	£N.Mint
1	$5.75	$17.50	$35.00	£3.75	£11.00	£22.50
2 Plastic Man X-over	$4.00	$12.00	$20.00	£2.50	£7.50	£12.50
3	$3.00	$9.00	$15.00	£2.00	£6.00	£10.00
4-6	$2.40	$7.00	$12.00	£1.40	£4.20	£7.00
7-9 ND	$2.40	$7.00	$12.00	£1.60	£4.80	£8.00
10 ND Superman appears; appearances by Spiderman and the Fantastic Four (unauthorised)	$2.40	$7.00	$12.00	£1.60	£4.80	£8.00
11 reprints Showcase #62 (1st appearance)	$2.40	$7.00	$12.00	£1.40	£4.20	£7.00
12 reprints Showcase #63 (2nd appearance)	$2.40	$7.00	$12.00	£1.40	£4.20	£7.00
Title Value:	$34.35	$101.50	$178.00	£21.65	£64.70	£112.00

INFERNO
Aircel,MS; 1 Oct 1990-4 Jan 1991

	$Good	$Fine	$N.Mint	£Good	£Fine	£N.Mint
1-4 ND horror anthology; pre-bagged	$0.40	$1.20	$2.00	£0.25	£0.75	£1.25
Title Value:	$1.60	$4.80	$8.00	£1.00	£3.00	£5.00

INFINITY CRUSADE, THE
Marvel Comics Group,MS; 1 Jun 1993-6 Nov 1993

	$Good	$Fine	$N.Mint	£Good	£Fine	£N.Mint
1 3rd part in the "Infinity trilogy", Jim Starlin script, Ron Lim art; Warlock, Silver Surfer and Thanos appear throughout	$0.60	$1.80	$3.00	£0.40	£1.20	£2.00
2-6	$0.45	$1.35	$2.25	£0.30	£0.90	£1.50
Title Value:	$2.85	$8.55	$14.25	£1.90	£5.70	£9.50

INFINITY GAUNTLET
Marvel Comics Group,MS; 1 Jul 1991-6 Dec 1991

	$Good	$Fine	$N.Mint	£Good	£Fine	£N.Mint
1 ND 1st part in the "Infinity trilogy", Jim Starlin script and George Perez art; Thanos appears	$1.00	$3.00	$5.00	£0.60	£1.80	£3.00
1 ND Gold Edition - 4,000 copies signed by George Perez in gold ink	$0.80	$2.40	$4.00	£0.50	£1.50	£2.50
1 ND Platinum Edition - 3,500 copies signed by George Perez in platinum ink	$2.00	$6.00	$10.00	£1.20	£3.60	£6.00
2 ND Thanos, Warlock ,Doctor Strange, Galactus appear	$0.80	$2.40	$4.00	£0.50	£1.50	£2.50
3 ND Thanos; Galactus, Celestials and The Watcher appear	$0.80	$2.40	$4.00	£0.50	£1.50	£2.50
4 ND Thanos, Annihilus appear	$0.60	$1.80	$3.00	£0.40	£1.20	£2.00
5 ND Thanos, Warlock appear	$0.60	$1.80	$3.00	£0.40	£1.20	£2.00
6 ND Thanos, Warlock, Silver Surfer, Dr. Strange appear	$0.60	$1.80	$3.00	£0.40	£1.20	£2.00
Title Value:	$7.20	$21.60	$36.00	£4.50	£13.50	£22.50

Note: other tie-ins include: Dr. Strange #31-33, Hulk #383-385, Quasar #26, Silver Surfer #51-55.

Infinity Gauntlet
Trade paperback reprints 6 issue mini-series

	£Good	£Fine	£N.Mint
	£3.00	£9.00	£15.00
(2nd print - Jun 1993)	£2.80	£8.40	£14.00

INFINITY INC.
DC Comics; 1 Mar 1984-53 Aug 1988

	$Good	$Fine	$N.Mint	£Good	£Fine	£N.Mint
1 ND Jerry Ordway cover and art begin (end #12).Fury, Jade, Brainwave Jnr, Huntress, Star Spangled Kid, Northwind, Nuklon, Power Girl, Obsidian, Silver Scarab begin	$0.40	$1.20	$2.00	£0.30	£0.90	£1.50
2 ND Dr.Mid-Nite Golden Age Flash, Wonderwoman, Dr. Fate, Hourman, Golden Age Green Lantern, Wildcat appear	$0.35	$1.05	$1.75	£0.25	£0.75	£1.25
3 ND	$0.35	$1.05	$1.75	£0.25	£0.75	£1.25
4-6 ND Justice Society of America appear	$0.35	$1.05	$1.75	£0.25	£0.75	£1.25
7 ND Golden Age Superman vs. Power Girl, Justice Society of America appear	$0.35	$1.05	$1.75	£0.25	£0.75	£1.25
8 ND	$0.35	$1.05	$1.75	£0.25	£0.75	£1.25
9 ND Justice Society of America cameo	$0.35	$1.05	$1.75	£0.25	£0.75	£1.25
10 ND Justice Society of America appear	$0.35	$1.05	$1.75	£0.25	£0.75	£1.25
11 ND origin Infinity Inc.	$0.35	$1.05	$1.75	£0.25	£0.75	£1.25
12 ND last Jerry Ordway cover and art	$0.35	$1.05	$1.75	£0.25	£0.75	£1.25
13 ND	$0.35	$1.05	$1.75	£0.25	£0.75	£1.25
14 ND Todd McFarlane art begins; his first professional mainstream art	$0.60	$1.80	$3.00	£0.40	£1.20	£2.00
15-17 ND Todd McFarlane art	$0.45	$1.35	$2.25	£0.30	£0.90	£1.50
18 ND Todd McFarlane art, Crisis X-over	$0.45	$1.35	$2.25	£0.30	£0.90	£1.50
19-20 ND scarce in the U.K. Todd McFarlane art, Crisis X-over; Justice Society of America and Infinity Inc. team-up	$0.45	$1.35	$2.25	£0.40	£1.20	£2.00
21 ND Todd McFarlane art, Crisis X-over, 1st appearance new Hourman and Dr.Midnight, Justice Society of America appear	$0.45	$1.35	$2.25	£0.30	£0.90	£1.50
22-24 ND Todd McFarlane art, Crisis X-over	$0.45	$1.35	$2.25	£0.30	£0.90	£1.50
25 ND Todd McFarlane art, unofficial Crisis X-over	$0.45	$1.35	$2.25	£0.30	£0.90	£1.50
26 ND Todd McFarlane art, 1st appearance new Wildcat (female)	$0.45	$1.35	$2.25	£0.30	£0.90	£1.50
27 ND Todd McFarlane art, Wonder Woman appears	$0.45	$1.35	$2.25	£0.30	£0.90	£1.50
28-29 ND Todd McFarlane art	$0.45	$1.35	$2.25	£0.30	£0.90	£1.50
30 ND Todd McFarlane art, Justice Society of America appear	$0.45	$1.35	$2.25	£0.30	£0.90	£1.50
31 ND Todd McFarlane art, Star Spangled Kid becomes Skyman	$0.40	$1.20	$2.00	£0.25	£0.75	£1.25
32 ND Todd McFarlane art, origin Northwind	$0.40	$1.20	$2.00	£0.25	£0.75	£1.25
33 ND Todd McFarlane art, origin Obsidian	$0.40	$1.20	$2.00	£0.25	£0.75	£1.25
34-36 ND Todd McFarlane art	$0.40	$1.20	$2.00	£0.25	£0.75	£1.25
37 ND last Todd McFarlane art	$0.40	$1.20	$2.00	£0.25	£0.75	£1.25
38-44 very LD	$0.40	$1.20	$2.00	£0.25	£0.75	£1.25
45 ND New Teen Titans guest-star	$0.40	$1.20	$2.00	£0.25	£0.75	£1.25
46 ND scarce in the U.K. Millennium X-over	$0.40	$1.20	$2.00	£0.30	£0.90	£1.50
47 ND Millennium X-over	$0.40	$1.20	$2.00	£0.25	£0.75	£1.25
48 ND origin Nuklon	$0.40	$1.20	$2.00	£0.25	£0.75	£1.25
49 ND 1970s Sandman appears; Lyta appears (story ties into her appearances in Sandman 2nd series)	$0.40	$1.20	$2.00	£0.25	£0.75	£1.25
50 ND DS 1970s Sandman and Lyta appear	$0.50	$1.50	$2.50	£0.30	£0.90	£1.50
51-53 ND.	$0.30	$0.90	$1.50	£0.20	£0.60	£1.00
Title Value:	$21.40	$64.20	$107.00	£14.40	£43.20	£72.00

Note: all 36 pgs, Baxter paper. Todd McFarlane art in #20, 23, 24, 33.
Note also: issue #38 is particularly scarce owing to a possible lost shipment.

INFINITY INC. ANNUAL
DC Comics; 1 Dec 1985-2 1986

	$Good	$Fine	$N.Mint	£Good	£Fine	£N.Mint
1 ND 48pgs, Crisis X-over	$0.40	$1.20	$2.00	£0.25	£0.75	£1.25
2 ND 48pgs	$0.40	$1.20	$2.00	£0.25	£0.75	£1.25
Title Value:	$0.80	$2.40	$4.00	£0.50	£1.50	£2.50

INFINITY INC. SPECIAL
DC Comics; 1 1987

	$Good	$Fine	$N.Mint	£Good	£Fine	£N.Mint
1 ND	$0.40	$1.20	$2.00	£0.25	£0.75	£1.25
Title Value:	$0.40	$1.20	$2.00	£0.25	£0.75	£1.25

INFINITY WAR, THE
Marvel Comics Group,MS; 1 Jun 1992-6 Nov 1992

	$Good	$Fine	$N.Mint	£Good	£Fine	£N.Mint
1 ND 48pgs, 2nd part of the "Infinity trilogy", Jim Starlin script, Ron Lim art, Thanos, Silver Surfer, Spiderman, Wolverine, Warlock and many other Marvel characters appear, gatefold cover by Ron Lim	$0.55	$1.65	$2.75	£0.35	£1.05	£1.75
2 ND 48pgs, Jim Starlin script, Ron Lim art, Thanos, Silver Surfer, Galactus, Spiderman appear, gatefold cover by Ron Lim	$0.45	$1.35	$2.25	£0.30	£0.90	£1.50
3-6 ND 48pgs, Jim Starlin script, Ron Lim art, Thanos, Silver Surfer, Galactus, Spiderman appear	$0.45	$1.35	$2.25	£0.30	£0.90	£1.50
Title Value:	$2.80	$8.40	$14.00	£1.85	£5.55	£9.25

INHUMANOIDS
Marvel Comics Group/Star, TV; 1 Jan 1987-4 Jul 1987

	$Good	$Fine	$N.Mint	£Good	£Fine	£N.Mint
1-4	$0.15	$0.45	$0.75	£0.10	£0.35	£0.60
Title Value:	$0.60	$1.80	$3.00	£0.40	£1.40	£2.40

Note: based on Hasbro toys

INHUMANS, THE
Marvel Comics Group; 1 Oct 1975-12 Aug 1977
(see Amazing Adventures, Marvel Graphic Novel)

	$Good	$Fine	$N.Mint	£Good	£Fine	£N.Mint
1 George Perez art	$1.20	$3.60	$6.00	£0.80	£2.40	£4.00
2 George Perez art	$0.90	$2.70	$4.50	£0.60	£1.80	£3.00
3 George Perez art, 1st Shatterstar (not to be confused with X-Force member of same name)	$0.80	$2.40	$4.00	£0.50	£1.50	£2.50
4 George Perez art	$0.60	$1.80	$3.00	£0.40	£1.20	£2.00
5-7 Gil Kane art	$0.60	$1.80	$3.00	£0.40	£1.20	£2.00
8 George Perez art	$0.60	$1.80	$3.00	£0.40	£1.20	£2.00
9 reprints Inhumans story from Amazing Adventures (2nd Series) 1,2	$0.60	$1.80	$3.00	£0.40	£1.20	£2.00
10-11 ND scarce in the U.K.	$0.60	$1.80	$3.00	£0.60	£1.80	£3.00
12 ND very scarce in the U.K. Inhumans vs. Hulk	$0.60	$1.80	$3.00	£0.70	£2.10	£3.50
Title Value:	$8.30	$24.90	$41.50	£6.20	£18.60	£31.00

INHUMANS, THE (2ND SERIES)
Marvel Comics Group,OS; 1 May 1995

1 ND 64pgs, Atlantis Rising tie-in (see Fantastic Four #401)

	$Good	$Fine	$N.Mint	£Good	£Fine	£N.Mint
	$0.80	$2.40	$4.00	£0.50	£1.50	£2.50
Title Value:	$0.80	$2.40	$4.00	£0.50	£1.50	£2.50

INHUMANS: THE UNTOLD SAGA
Marvel Comics Group,OS; 1 Apr 1990

	$Good	$Fine	$N.Mint	£Good	£Fine	£N.Mint
1 ND DS	$0.30	$0.90	$1.50	£0.20	£0.60	£1.00
Title Value:	$0.30	$0.90	$1.50	£0.20	£0.60	£1.00

INNOCENTS
Radical Comics; 1 Oct 1995
1 ND Simon Bisley cover

	$Good	$Fine	$N.Mint	£Good	£Fine	£N.Mint
	$0.50	$1.50	$2.50	£0.30	£0.90	£1.50
Title Value:	$0.50	$1.50	$2.50	£0.30	£0.90	£1.50

INNOVATION SOLICITATIONS
Innovation; 1 Mar 1989
1 ND previews forthcoming releases like Hero Alliance

	$Good	$Fine	$N.Mint	£Good	£Fine	£N.Mint
	$0.30	$0.90	$1.50	£0.10	£0.30	£0.50
Title Value:	$0.30	$0.90	$1.50	£0.10	£0.30	£0.50

INNOVATION SPECTACULAR
Innovation,OS; 1 1991
1 ND 100pgs, squarebound, Hero Alliance appear

	$Good	$Fine	$N.Mint	£Good	£Fine	£N.Mint
	$0.55	$1.65	$2.75	£0.35	£1.05	£1.75
Title Value:	$0.55	$1.65	$2.75	£0.35	£1.05	£1.75

INNOVATION'S SUMMER FUN SPECIAL
Innovation,OS; 1 Jul 1991

	$Good	$Fine	$N.Mint	£Good	£Fine	£N.Mint
1 ND	$0.70	$2.10	$3.50	£0.45	£1.35	£2.25
Title Value:	$0.70	$2.10	$3.50	£0.45	£1.35	£2.25

INSANE
Dark Horse; 1 Feb 1988-2 Sep 1988
1 ND X-Men, Godzilla, Munden's Bar parodies

	$Good	$Fine	$N.Mint	£Good	£Fine	£N.Mint
	$0.60	$1.80	$3.00	£0.40	£1.20	£2.00

2 ND Concrete, Lone Wolf & Cub parodies

	$Good	$Fine	$N.Mint	£Good	£Fine	£N.Mint
	$0.45	$1.35	$2.25	£0.30	£0.90	£1.50
Title Value:	$1.05	$3.15	$5.25	£0.70	£2.10	£3.50

INSIDE IMAGE
Image; 1 Mar 1993-present
1 ND promotional; details up and coming comics, poster at centrefold

	$Good	$Fine	$N.Mint	£Good	£Fine	£N.Mint
	$0.15	$0.45	$0.75	£0.10	£0.30	£0.50
2-30 ND	$0.15	$0.45	$0.75	£0.10	£0.30	£0.50
Title Value:	$4.50	$13.50	$22.50	£3.00	£9.00	£15.00

INSTANT PIANO
Dark Horse; 1 Aug 1994-present
1-4 ND cartoon anthology featuring Kyle Baker and Evan Dorkin amongst others

	$Good	$Fine	$N.Mint	£Good	£Fine	£N.Mint
	$0.80	$2.40	$4.00	£0.50	£1.50	£2.50
Title Value:	$3.20	$9.60	$16.00	£2.00	£6.00	£10.00

INTERACTIVE COMICS
Adventure; 1 Feb 1991
1 ND 56pgs, Dungeons and Dragons-game based

	$Good	$Fine	$N.Mint	£Good	£Fine	£N.Mint
	$0.90	$2.70	$4.50	£0.60	£1.80	£3.00
Title Value:	$0.90	$2.70	$4.50	£0.60	£1.80	£3.00

INTERFACE
Marvel Comics Group/Epic,MS; 1 Dec 1989-8 Feb 1991
1-6 ND Paul Johnson art

	$Good	$Fine	$N.Mint	£Good	£Fine	£N.Mint
	$0.30	$0.90	$1.50	£0.20	£0.60	£1.00
7-8 ND	$0.30	$0.90	$1.50	£0.20	£0.60	£1.00
Title Value:	$2.40	$7.20	$12.00	£1.60	£4.80	£8.00

INTERPLANETARY LIZARDS OF THE TEXAS PLAIN
Leadbelly Publications; 0 Jun 1994; 1 1992-7 Jul 1993

	$Good	$Fine	$N.Mint	£Good	£Fine	£N.Mint
0 ND (Jun 1994)	$0.45	$1.35	$2.25	£0.30	£0.90	£1.50
1-7 ND	$0.45	$1.35	$2.25	£0.30	£0.90	£1.50
Title Value:	$3.60	$10.80	$18.00	£2.40	£7.20	£12.00

INTERVIEW WITH THE VAMPIRE
Innovation,MS; 1 Sep 1991-11 1994

	$Good	$Fine	$N.Mint	£Good	£Fine	£N.Mint
1 ND John Bolton cover						
	$1.00	$3.00	$5.00	£0.70	£2.10	£3.50
2 ND John Bolton cover						
	$0.60	$1.80	$3.00	£0.40	£1.20	£2.00
3 ND	$0.60	$1.80	$3.00	£0.40	£1.20	£2.00
4-11 ND	$0.45	$1.35	$2.25	£0.30	£0.90	£1.50
Title Value:	$5.80	$17.40	$29.00	£3.90	£11.70	£19.50

Note: issue #12 was produced but held in storage when Innovation went bankrupt. Some issue have been reported in circulation.

INTIMATE CONFESSIONS
I.W. Comics; 9,10 1964
9 scarce in the U.K. classic "Duncan's Love Story"; distributed in the U.K.

	$Good	$Fine	$N.Mint	£Good	£Fine	£N.Mint
	$0.75	$2.25	$4.50	£0.50	£1.50	£3.00

10 scarce, distributed in the U.K.

	$Good	$Fine	$N.Mint	£Good	£Fine	£N.Mint
	$0.75	$2.25	$4.50	£0.50	£1.50	£3.00
Title Value:	$1.50	$4.50	$9.00	£1.00	£3.00	£6.00

INTRON DEPOT DELUXE
Dark Horse,OS; nn 1995
0 ND 148pgs, reprints the best of Masamune Shirow's work from 1981-1991

	$Good	$Fine	$N.Mint	£Good	£Fine	£N.Mint
	$8.00	$24.00	$40.00	£5.00	£15.50	£26.00
Title Value:	$8.00	$24.00	$40.00	£5.00	£15.50	£26.00

INTRUDER
TSR; 1-4 1990
1-4 ND based on role-playing game

	$Good	$Fine	$N.Mint	£Good	£Fine	£N.Mint
	$0.40	$1.20	$2.00	£0.25	£0.75	£1.25
Title Value:	$1.60	$4.80	$8.00	£1.00	£3.00	£5.00

INVADERS
Gold Key, TV; 1 Oct 1967-4 Oct 1968
1 distributed in the U.K.

	$Good	$Fine	$N.Mint	£Good	£Fine	£N.Mint
	$16.00	$48.00	$80.00	£9.00	£27.00	£45.00

2-4 distributed in the U.K.

	$Good	$Fine	$N.Mint	£Good	£Fine	£N.Mint
	$12.00	$36.00	$60.00	£7.00	£21.00	£35.00
Title Value:	$52.00	$156.00	$260.00	£30.00	£90.00	£150.00

INVADERS (LIMITED SERIES), THE
Marvel Comics Group,MS; 1 May 1993-4 Aug 1993
1 Roy Thomas script begins

	$Good	$Fine	$N.Mint	£Good	£Fine	£N.Mint
	$0.40	$1.20	$2.00	£0.25	£0.75	£1.25

2 the original Vision returns

	$Good	$Fine	$N.Mint	£Good	£Fine	£N.Mint
	$0.40	$1.20	$2.00	£0.25	£0.75	£1.25
3-4	$0.40	$1.20	$2.00	£0.25	£0.75	£1.25
Title Value:	$1.60	$4.80	$8.00	£1.00	£3.00	£5.00

INVADERS ANNUAL, THE
Marvel Comics Group; 1 Sep 1977
1 ND 52pgs, Avengers appear

	$Good	$Fine	$N.Mint	£Good	£Fine	£N.Mint
	$0.80	$2.40	$4.00	£0.50	£1.50	£2.50
Title Value:	$0.80	$2.40	$4.00	£0.50	£1.50	£2.50

INVADERS FROM HOME
DC Comics/Piranha Press,MS; 1 Aug 1990-6 Nov 1990
1-6 ND John Blair Moore

	$Good	$Fine	$N.Mint	£Good	£Fine	£N.Mint
	$0.50	$1.50	$2.50	£0.30	£0.90	£1.50
Title Value:	$3.00	$9.00	$15.00	£1.80	£5.40	£9.00

INVADERS FROM MARS GRAPHIC NOVEL
Eternity; 1 Jun 1991
1 ND adaptation of classic film

	$Good	$Fine	$N.Mint	£Good	£Fine	£N.Mint
	$1.50	$4.50	$7.50	£1.00	£3.00	£5.00
Title Value:	$1.50	$4.50	$7.50	£1.00	£3.00	£5.00

INVADERS FROM MARS II
Eternity,MS; 1 Aug 1991-3 Oct 1991

	$Good	$Fine	$N.Mint	£Good	£Fine	£N.Mint
1-3 ND	$0.40	$1.20	$2.00	£0.25	£0.75	£1.25
Title Value:	$1.20	$3.60	$6.00	£0.75	£2.25	£3.75

Invaders #2

Iron Man #70

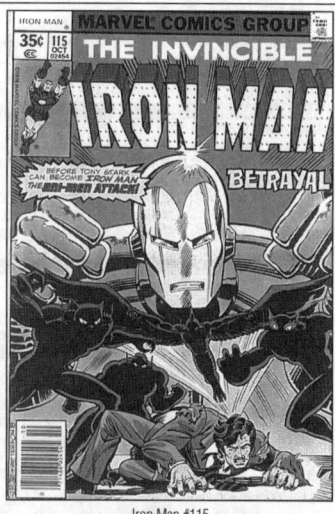

Iron Man #115

MINT = 100% / NEAR MINT (inc. +/-) = 90–99% / VERY FINE (inc. +/-) = 75–89% / FINE (inc. +/-) = 55–74%
VERY GOOD (inc. +/-) = 35–54% / GOOD (inc. +/-) = 15–34% / FAIR = 5–14% / POOR = 1–4%

INVADERS GIANT SIZE, THE
Marvel Comics Group; 1 Jun 1975

	$Good	$Fine	$N.Mint	£Good	£Fine	£N.Mint
1 ND 68pgs, 1st appearance The Invaders (see Avengers #71), Golden Age Sub-Mariner reprint	$1.50	$4.50	$7.50	£1.10	£3.30	£5.50
Title Value:	$1.50	$4.50	$7.50	£1.10	£3.30	£5.50

Note: pre-dates first issue of regular series

INVADERS, THE
Marvel Comics Group; 1 Aug 1975-41 Sep 1979

	$Good	$Fine	$N.Mint	£Good	£Fine	£N.Mint
1 ND Captain America, Sub-Mariner, Human Torch begin in World War II setting	$2.50	$7.50	$12.50	£1.20	£3.60	£6.00
2 ND untold origin of Toro	$1.40	$4.20	$7.00	£0.80	£2.40	£4.00
3-4	$1.20	$3.60	$6.00	£0.60	£1.80	£3.00
5 ties into Marvel Premiere #29	$1.20	$3.60	$6.00	£0.60	£1.80	£3.00
6 Liberty Legion appears, 25 & 30 cent issues exist, ties into Marvel Premiere #30	$1.20	$3.60	$6.00	£0.50	£1.50	£2.50
7	$1.20	$3.60	$6.00	£0.50	£1.50	£2.50
8 1st appearance Union Jack	$1.20	$3.60	$6.00	£0.50	£1.50	£2.50
9	$1.20	$3.60	$6.00	£0.50	£1.50	£2.50
10 Golden Age Captain America reprint	$1.20	$3.60	$6.00	£0.50	£1.50	£2.50
11-13	$0.80	$2.40	$4.00	£0.40	£1.20	£2.00
14 1st appearance Crusaders	$0.80	$2.40	$4.00	£0.40	£1.20	£2.00
15	$0.80	$2.40	$4.00	£0.40	£1.20	£2.00
16 Destroyer appears	$0.80	$2.40	$4.00	£0.40	£1.20	£2.00
17 intro Warrior Woman	$0.80	$2.40	$4.00	£0.40	£1.20	£2.00
18	$0.80	$2.40	$4.00	£0.40	£1.20	£2.00
19 Adolf Hitler appears	$0.80	$2.40	$4.00	£0.40	£1.20	£2.00
20 reprints the 1st ever appearance of Sub-Mariner from Motion Picture Funnies Weekly by Bill Everett (8pgs) with editiorial explanation	$0.80	$2.40	$4.00	£0.40	£1.20	£2.00
21 Golden Age Sub-Mariner reprint from Marvel Mystery #10	$0.80	$2.40	$4.00	£0.30	£0.90	£1.50
22 Golden Age Toro origin	$0.80	$2.40	$4.00	£0.30	£0.90	£1.50
23	$0.80	$2.40	$4.00	£0.30	£0.90	£1.50
24 reprints 1st Golden Age Human Torch and Sub-Mariner team-up from Marvel Mystery #17	$0.80	$2.40	$4.00	£0.30	£0.90	£1.50
25-30	$0.80	$2.40	$4.00	£0.30	£0.90	£1.50
31 Frankenstein appears	$0.80	$2.40	$4.00	£0.25	£0.75	£1.25
32-33 Thor, Adolf Hitler appear	$0.80	$2.40	$4.00	£0.25	£0.75	£1.25
34-37	$0.80	$2.40	$4.00	£0.25	£0.75	£1.25
38 1st appearance Lady Lotus	$0.80	$2.40	$4.00	£0.25	£0.75	£1.25
39-40	$0.80	$2.40	$4.00	£0.25	£0.75	£1.25
41 ND scarce in the U.K. 52pgs	$1.00	$3.00	$5.00	£0.40	£1.20	£2.00
Title Value:	$38.50	$115.50	$192.50	£16.20	£48.60	£81.00

INVASION '55
Apple Comics,MS; 1 Oct 1990-3 Dec 1990

	$Good	$Fine	$N.Mint	£Good	£Fine	£N.Mint
1-3 ND black and white	$0.45	$1.35	$2.25	£0.30	£0.90	£1.50
Title Value:	$1.35	$4.05	$6.75	£0.90	£2.70	£4.50

INVASION!
Cross-over series featuring most major DC heroes battling an invading alien force. The cross-over is listed below in alphabetical rather than chronological order.
Animal Man #6, Captain Atom #24,25, Checkmate #11,12, Detective Comics #595, Doom Patrol (2nd Series) #17,18, Firestorm #80,81, Flash #21,22, Justice League #22,23, Manhunter (2nd Series) #8,9, New Guardians #6, Spectre (2nd Series) #23, Starman #5,6, Superman #449, Superman (2nd Series) #26,27, Swamp Thing (2nd Series) #81, Wonder Woman (2nd Series) #25,26

INVASION! (LIMITED SERIES)
DC Comics,MS; 1 Oct 1988-3 Jan 1989

	$Good	$Fine	$N.Mint	£Good	£Fine	£N.Mint
1 LD in the U.K. Todd McFarlane art	$0.80	$2.40	$4.00	£0.50	£1.50	£2.50
2 ND Iwo Jima cover, part Todd McFarlane art	$0.80	$2.40	$4.00	£0.50	£1.50	£2.50
3 Bart Sears art	$0.60	$1.80	$3.00	£0.40	£1.20	£2.00
Title Value:	$2.20	$6.60	$11.00	£1.40	£4.20	£7.00

Note: all 80pgs squarebound; fourth DC cross over series (see Crisis, Legends, Millennium)

INVISIBLE PEOPLE
Kitchen Sink,MS; 1 Aug 1992-present?

	$Good	$Fine	$N.Mint	£Good	£Fine	£N.Mint
1 ND part 1: Sanctum, script and art by Will Eisner	$0.55	$1.65	$2.75	£0.35	£1.05	£1.75
Title Value:	$0.55	$1.65	$2.75	£0.35	£1.05	£1.75

INVISIBLES, THE
DC Comics/Vertigo; 1 Sep 1994-present

	$Good	$Fine	$N.Mint	£Good	£Fine	£N.Mint
1 48pgs, Grant Morrison script and Steve Yeowell art begin	$0.60	$1.80	$3.00	£0.40	£1.20	£2.00
2-4	$0.40	$1.20	$2.00	£0.25	£0.75	£1.25
5 Jill Thompson and Dennis Cramer art begins; there are four variant covers, all printed on plain brown paper with black ink graffiti slogans	$0.40	$1.20	$2.00	£0.25	£0.75	£1.25
6-8 painted cover by Sean Phillips	$0.40	$1.20	$2.00	£0.25	£0.75	£1.25
9-15 painted cover by Sean Phillips	$0.45	$1.35	$2.25	£0.30	£0.90	£1.50
16-18	$0.45	$1.35	$2.25	£0.30	£0.90	£1.50
Title Value:	$7.90	$23.70	$40.00	£5.15	£15.45	£25.75

IRON FIST
Marvel Comics Group; 1 Nov 1975-15 Sep 1977
(see Marvel Premiere, Powerman and Iron Fist)

	$Good	$Fine	$N.Mint	£Good	£Fine	£N.Mint
1 ND John Byrne art, Iron Man battles Iron Fist	$5.75	$17.50	$35.00	£3.30	£10.00	£20.00
2 ND scarce in the U.K. John Byrne art	$3.00	$9.00	$15.00	£2.00	£6.00	£10.00
3 John Byrne art	$2.40	$7.00	$12.00	£1.60	£4.80	£8.00
4-7 John Byrne art	$1.80	$5.25	$9.00	£1.20	£3.60	£6.00
8-10 ND John Byrne art	$1.80	$5.25	$9.00	£1.30	£3.90	£6.50
11 ND John Byrne art	$1.50	$4.50	$7.50	£1.10	£3.30	£5.50
12 ND John Byrne art, Captain America vs. Iron Fist	$1.50	$4.50	$7.50	£1.10	£3.30	£5.50
13 ND John Byrne art	$1.50	$4.50	$7.50	£1.10	£3.30	£5.50
14 ND John Byrne art, 1st appearance Sabretooth (see Powerman #66)	$23.00	$70.00	$140.00	£11.50	£35.00	£70.00
14 ND Marvel Milestone Edition (Jan 1992) - silver border around cover	$0.25	$0.75	$1.25	£0.15	£0.50	£0.85
15 ND John Byrne art, classic X-Men story, 30 cent cover	$4.15	$12.50	$25.00	£2.50	£7.50	£15.00
15 ND scarce in the U.K. John Byrne art, 35 cent cover	$4.80	$14.00	$24.00	£3.20	£9.50	£16.00
Title Value:	$60.45	$181.00	$337.75	£36.25	£109.30	£199.85

IRON JAW
Atlas; 1 Jan 1975-4 Jul 1975
(see Barbarians)

	$Good	$Fine	$N.Mint	£Good	£Fine	£N.Mint
1 Mike Sekowsky art, part Neal Adams cover; distributed in the U.K.	$0.25	$0.75	$1.25	£0.15	£0.45	£0.75
2-4 Pablo Marcos art; distributed in the U.K.	$0.25	$0.75	$1.25	£0.15	£0.45	£0.75
Title Value:	$1.00	$3.00	$5.00	£0.60	£1.80	£3.00

Note: Neal Adams cover on 2, origin in 4.

IRON MAN
Marvel Comics Group; 1 May 1968-present
(see Avengers, Marvel Double Feature, Marvel Fanfare, Marvel Graphic Novel, Marvel Team Up, Marvel Two-In-One, Tales of Suspense)

	$Good	$Fine	$N.Mint	£Good	£Fine	£N.Mint
1 origin retold; story continued from Iron Man and Sub-Mariner #1	$55.00	$170.00	$400.00	£32.00	£95.00	£225.00
2	$20.50	$62.50	$125.00	£12.50	£38.00	£75.00
3	$14.00	$43.00	$85.00	£9.00	£28.00	£55.00
4	$10.00	$30.00	$60.00	£6.25	£18.50	£37.50
5	$9.00	$28.00	$55.00	£5.75	£17.50	£35.00
6 The Crusher dies	$7.50	$22.50	$45.00	£4.55	£13.50	£27.50
7-8	$7.50	$22.50	$45.00	£4.55	£13.50	£27.50
9 Hulk appears (robot of the Mandarin)	$7.50	$22.50	$45.00	£4.55	£13.50	£27.50
10	$7.50	$22.50	$45.00	£4.55	£13.50	£27.50
11-15	$5.00	$15.00	$30.00	£3.00	£9.00	£18.00
16-17	$3.75	$11.00	$22.50	£2.30	£7.00	£14.00
18 Avengers appear	$3.75	$11.00	$22.50	£2.30	£7.00	£14.00
19-20	$3.75	$11.00	$22.50	£2.30	£7.00	£14.00
21	$3.30	$10.00	$20.00	£1.65	£5.00	£10.00
22 Janice Cord dies	$3.30	$10.00	$20.00	£1.65	£5.00	£10.00
23-24	$2.90	$8.75	$17.50	£1.65	£5.00	£10.00
25 Sub-Mariner battles Iron Man	$4.15	$12.50	$25.00	£2.50	£7.50	£15.00
26	$2.50	$7.50	$15.00	£1.65	£5.00	£10.00
27 1st appearance Fire Brand	$2.50	$7.50	$15.00	£1.65	£5.00	£10.00
28-30	$2.50	$7.50	$15.00	£1.65	£5.00	£10.00
31-34	$2.50	$7.50	$15.00	£1.30	£4.00	£8.00
35 Daredevil and Nick Fury appear	$2.50	$7.50	$15.00	£1.40	£4.25	£8.50
36-39	$2.50	$7.50	$15.00	£1.30	£4.00	£8.00
40-42 scarce in the U.K.	$2.50	$7.50	$15.00	£1.65	£5.00	£10.00
43 ND scarce in the U.K. 52pgs	$2.90	$8.75	$17.50	£2.25	£6.75	£13.50
44 ND Ant-Man story	$2.50	$7.50	$15.00	£1.65	£5.00	£10.00
45 ND	$2.50	$7.50	$15.00	£1.65	£5.00	£10.00
46 ND	$2.00	$6.00	$12.00	£1.30	£4.00	£8.00
47 origin retold, Barry Smith art	$2.90	$8.75	$17.50	£1.65	£5.00	£10.00
48-50 scarce in the U.K.	$2.00	$6.00	$12.00	£1.25	£3.75	£7.50
51-52 scarce in the U.K.	$2.00	$6.00	$10.00	£1.30	£3.90	£6.50
53 scarce in the U.K. part Jim Starlin art	$2.00	$6.00	$10.00	£1.30	£3.90	£6.50
54 scarce in the U.K. Sub-Mariner battles Iron Man, part Bill Everett art; 1st appearance Moondragon	$3.00	$9.00	$15.00	£1.60	£4.80	£8.00

#	Description	$Good	$Fine	$N.Mint	£Good	£Fine	£N.Mint
55	Jim Starlin art, origin and 1st appearance Drax the Destroyer, 1st appearance Thanos (cents copies seem to be scarce in the U.K.)	$10.00	$30.00	$50.00	£6.00	£18.00	£30.00
55 ND	Marvel Milestone Edition (Jan 1993) - silver border around cover	$0.50	$1.50	$2.50	£0.30	£0.90	£1.50
56	scarce in the U.K. Jim Starlin art	$4.00	$12.00	$20.00	£2.00	£6.00	£10.00
57-64		$2.00	$6.00	$10.00	£1.00	£3.00	£5.00
65	Thor appears (last panel)	$1.50	$4.50	$7.50	£1.00	£3.00	£5.00
66	Iron Man vs. Thor	$1.50	$4.50	$7.50	£0.90	£2.70	£4.50
67 ND		$1.50	$4.50	$7.50	£1.20	£3.60	£6.00
68 ND	Jim Starlin cover, origin retold	$2.00	$6.00	$10.00	£1.40	£4.20	£7.00
69		$1.50	$4.50	$7.50	£0.80	£2.40	£4.00
70 ND	scarce in the U.K.	$1.50	$4.50	$7.50	£1.40	£4.20	£7.00
71-75		$1.20	$3.60	$6.00	£0.60	£1.80	£3.00
76	reprints #9 (featuring Hulk)	$1.20	$3.60	$6.00	£0.70	£2.10	£3.50
77-79		$1.20	$3.60	$6.00	£0.60	£1.80	£3.00
80	Jack Kirby cover	$1.20	$3.60	$6.00	£0.60	£1.80	£3.00
81-82		$1.00	$3.00	$5.00	£0.50	£1.50	£2.50
83-84	Jack Kirby cover	$1.00	$3.00	$5.00	£0.50	£1.50	£2.50
85-87		$1.00	$3.00	$5.00	£0.50	£1.50	£2.50
88	Thanos appears in a flasback cameo	$1.00	$3.00	$5.00	£0.60	£1.80	£3.00
89	Daredevil appears	$1.00	$3.00	$5.00	£0.50	£1.50	£2.50
90	Avengers X-over, Jack Kirby cover	$1.00	$3.00	$5.00	£0.50	£1.50	£2.50
91-93		$1.00	$3.00	$5.00	£0.50	£1.50	£2.50
94-96	Jack Kirby cover	$1.00	$3.00	$5.00	£0.50	£1.50	£2.50
97		$1.00	$3.00	$5.00	£0.50	£1.50	£2.50
98	Iron Man vs. Sunfire	$1.00	$3.00	$5.00	£0.50	£1.50	£2.50
99		$1.00	$3.00	$5.00	£0.50	£1.50	£2.50
100	Jim Starlin cover	$1.60	$4.80	$8.00	£0.80	£2.40	£4.00
101	Frankenstein appears	$1.20	$3.60	$6.00	£0.50	£1.50	£2.50
102	1st appearance DreadKnight, George Perez cover	$1.20	$3.60	$6.00	£0.50	£1.50	£2.50
103-104	Jack of Hearts appears, George Perez cover	$1.20	$3.60	$6.00	£0.50	£1.50	£2.50
105	Jack of Hearts appears	$1.20	$3.60	$6.00	£0.50	£1.50	£2.50
106-109	Jack of Hearts appears	$1.20	$3.60	$6.00	£0.40	£1.20	£2.00
110	LD in the U.K. Jack of Hearts appears (his origin retold)	$1.20	$3.60	$6.00	£0.50	£1.50	£2.50
111	Jack of Hearts appears	$1.20	$3.60	$6.00	£0.40	£1.20	£2.00
112 ND	Jack of Hearts appears	$1.20	$3.60	$6.00	£0.50	£1.50	£2.50
113 ND		$1.20	$3.60	$6.00	£0.50	£1.50	£2.50
114 ND	Giffen art, Avengers X-over	$1.20	$3.60	$6.00	£0.50	£1.50	£2.50
115 ND	Avengers X-over, 1st John Romita Jnr. art	$1.20	$3.60	$6.00	£0.80	£2.40	£4.00
116 ND	2nd John Romita Jnr. art	$1.20	$3.60	$6.00	£0.60	£1.80	£3.00
117 ND	3rd John Romita Jnr. art	$1.20	$3.60	$6.00	£0.60	£1.80	£3.00
118 ND	John Byrne art	$1.50	$4.50	$7.50	£0.70	£2.10	£3.50
119 ND	John Byrne lay-outs	$1.00	$3.00	$5.00	£0.60	£1.80	£3.00
120 ND	Iron Man vs. Sub-Mariner	$1.00	$3.00	$5.00	£0.60	£1.80	£3.00
121 ND	Sub-Mariner appears	$0.60	$1.80	$3.00	£0.60	£1.80	£3.00
122	origin retold, Sub-Mariner appears	$0.60	$1.80	$3.00	£0.50	£1.50	£2.50
123-128	Tony Stark's alchohol struggle	$1.00	$3.00	$5.00	£0.45	£1.35	£2.25
129-130		$0.60	$1.80	$3.00	£0.30	£0.90	£1.50
131	Iron Man vs Hulk	$0.60	$1.80	$3.00	£0.30	£0.90	£1.50
132	LD in the U.K. Iron Man vs. Hulk	$0.60	$1.80	$3.00	£0.50	£1.50	£2.50
133	LD in the U.K. Hulk, Ant-Man appear	$0.60	$1.80	$3.00	£0.50	£1.50	£2.50
134-142		$0.60	$1.80	$3.00	£0.30	£0.90	£1.50
143 ND		$0.60	$1.80	$3.00	£0.40	£1.20	£2.00
144 ND	Tony Stark's 1st meeting with Jim Rhodes re-told	$0.60	$1.80	$3.00	£0.40	£1.20	£2.00
145		$0.60	$1.80	$3.00	£0.30	£0.90	£1.50
146 ND		$0.60	$1.80	$3.00	£0.40	£1.20	£2.00
147-149		$0.60	$1.80	$3.00	£0.30	£0.90	£1.50
150	48pgs, Iron Man vs. Dr. Doom		$3.00	$5.00	£0.40	£1.20	£2.00
151	Ant-Man appears	$0.60	$1.80	$3.00	£0.25	£0.75	£1.25
152	new armour, photo cover	$0.60	$1.80	$3.00	£0.25	£0.75	£1.25
153-158		$0.60	$1.80	$3.00	£0.25	£0.75	£1.25
159	Paul Smith art	$0.60	$1.80	$3.00	£0.30	£0.90	£1.50
160	Steve Ditko and Marie Severin art	$0.60	$1.80	$3.00	£0.25	£0.75	£1.25
161	Moon Knight appears	$0.60	$1.80	$3.00	£0.25	£0.75	£1.25
162-164		$0.60	$1.80	$3.00	£0.25	£0.75	£1.25
165-167	LD in the U.K.	$0.60	$1.80	$3.00	£0.30	£0.90	£1.50
168	LD in the U.K. Machine Man appears	$0.60	$1.80	$3.00	£0.30	£0.90	£1.50
169	LD in the U.K. Jim Rhodes replaces Tony Stark as Iron Man, Daredevil cameo	$2.40	$7.00	$12.00	£0.70	£2.10	£3.50
170	LD in the U.K. 2nd appearance new Iron Man	$1.20	$3.60	$6.00	£0.50	£1.50	£2.50
171	LD in the U.K.	$0.80	$2.40	$4.00	£0.30	£0.90	£1.50
172	LD in the U.K. Captain America appears	$0.60	$1.80	$3.00	£0.30	£0.90	£1.50
173-174	LD in the U.K.	$0.60	$1.80	$3.00	£0.30	£0.90	£1.50
175-188	LD in the U.K.	$0.60	$1.80	$3.00	£0.25	£0.75	£1.25
189	LD in the U.K.	$0.60	$1.80	$3.00	£0.30	£0.90	£1.50
190	LD in the U.K. Scarlet Witch appears	$0.60	$1.80	$3.00	£0.30	£0.90	£1.50
191	LD in the U.K. original Iron Man appears	$1.00	$3.00	$5.00	£0.30	£0.90	£1.50
192	LD in the U.K.	$0.60	$1.80	$3.00	£0.30	£0.90	£1.50
193-194	LD in the U.K. Hawkeye, Mockingbird X-over	$0.60	$1.80	$3.00	£0.30	£0.90	£1.50
195	LD in the U.K. Shaman appears	$0.60	$1.80	$3.00	£0.30	£0.90	£1.50
196	LD in the U.K.	$0.60	$1.80	$3.00	£0.30	£0.90	£1.50
197	Secret Wars X-over	$0.60	$1.80	$3.00	£0.25	£0.75	£1.25
198-199		$0.60	$1.80	$3.00	£0.25	£0.75	£1.25
200	LD in the U.K. DS Tony Stark returns as Iron Man in red/silver armour	$1.20	$3.60	$6.00	£0.40	£1.20	£2.00
201-207	LD in the U.K.	$0.60	$1.80	$3.00	£0.30	£0.90	£1.50
208-211		$0.60	$1.80	$3.00	£0.20	£0.60	£1.00
212	LD in the U.K. 1st appearance new Dominic Fortune (cameo)	$0.60	$1.80	$3.00	£0.25	£0.75	£1.25
213	1st full appearance new Dominic Fortune	$0.60	$1.80	$3.00	£0.20	£0.60	£1.00
214	Spiderwoman and Hawkeye appear	$0.60	$1.80	$3.00	£0.20	£0.60	£1.00
215	LD in the U.K.	$0.60	$1.80	$3.00	£0.25	£0.75	£1.25
216-222		$0.60	$1.80	$3.00	£0.20	£0.60	£1.00
223-224	build up to "Armour Wars"	$0.60	$1.80	$3.00	£0.35	£1.05	£1.75
225	LD in the U.K. DS, Armour Wars story begins, Ant-Man appears	$1.00	$3.00	$5.00	£0.60	£1.80	£3.00
226-230	Armour Wars	$0.60	$1.80	$3.00	£0.40	£1.20	£2.00
231	LD in the U.K. Armour Wars	$0.60	$1.80	$3.00	£0.45	£1.35	£2.25
232	very LD Barry Smith art	$0.60	$1.80	$3.00	£0.50	£1.50	£2.50
233	LD in the U.K. Ant-Man appears	$0.60	$1.80	$3.00	£0.25	£0.75	£1.25
234	Spiderman appears	$0.60	$1.80	$3.00	£0.25	£0.75	£1.25
235-242		$0.60	$1.80	$3.00	£0.20	£0.60	£1.00
243	Tony Stark shot, Barry Smith inks	$0.60	$1.80	$3.00	£0.25	£0.75	£1.25
244	DS new armour and origin Iron Man part retold	$1.00	$3.00	$5.00	£0.30	£0.90	£1.50
245-246		$0.40	$1.20	$2.00	£0.20	£0.60	£1.00
247	Hulk appears	$0.40	$1.20	$2.00	£0.20	£0.60	£1.00
248		$0.40	$1.20	$2.00	£0.20	£0.60	£1.00
249	Dr. Doom appears	$0.40	$1.20	$2.00	£0.20	£0.60	£1.00
250	48pgs, Dr. Doom appears, Acts of Vengeance tie-in	$0.60	$1.80	$3.00	£0.20	£0.60	£1.00
251-252	Acts of Vengeance tie-in	$0.30	$0.90	$1.50	£0.15	£0.45	£0.75
253-257		$0.30	$0.90	$1.50	£0.15	£0.45	£0.75
258-263	Armour Wars II, John Byrne script	$0.30	$0.90	$1.50	£0.15	£0.45	£0.75
264-266	Armour Wars II extra, John Byrne script	$0.30	$0.90	$1.50	£0.15	£0.45	£0.75
267	John Byrne script	$0.30	$0.90	$1.50	£0.15	£0.45	£0.75

	$Good	$Fine	$N.Mint	£Good	£Fine	£N.Mint
268 John Byrne script, more facts about origin	$0.30	$0.90	$1.50	£0.15	£0.45	£0.75
269 Black Widow appears, John Byrne script	$0.30	$0.90	$1.50	£0.15	£0.45	£0.75
270 John Byrne script	$0.30	$0.90	$1.50	£0.15	£0.45	£0.75
271 John Byrne script, Mandarin and Fin Fang Foom appear	$0.30	$0.90	$1.50	£0.15	£0.45	£0.75
272 John Byrne script, true origin Mandarin's rings	$0.30	$0.90	$1.50	£0.15	£0.45	£0.75
273 John Byrne script, Mandarin & Fin Fang Foom appear	$0.30	$0.90	$1.50	£0.15	£0.45	£0.75
274 John Byrne script	$0.30	$0.90	$1.50	£0.15	£0.45	£0.75
275 DS John Byrne script, Mandarin and Fin Fang Foom appear, back-up story and pin-up gallery	$0.30	$0.90	$1.50	£0.15	£0.45	£0.75
276 Black Widow appears	$0.30	$0.90	$1.50	£0.15	£0.45	£0.75
277 last John Byrne script, Black Widow appears, $1.25 cover begins	$0.30	$0.90	$1.50	£0.15	£0.45	£0.75
278 Galactic Storm part 6, Captain America appears	$0.30	$0.90	$1.50	£0.15	£0.45	£0.75
279 Galactic Storm part 13, guest stars Wonder Man, Hawkeye and the Avengers	$0.30	$0.90	$1.50	£0.15	£0.45	£0.75
280	$0.30	$0.90	$1.50	£0.15	£0.45	£0.75
281 1st appearance War Machine (cameo)	$0.30	$0.90	$1.50	£0.15	£0.45	£0.75
282 1st full appearance War Machine	$0.30	$0.90	$1.50	£0.15	£0.45	£0.75
283	$0.30	$0.90	$1.50	£0.15	£0.45	£0.75
284 Tony Stark cryogenically frozen	$0.30	$0.90	$1.50	£0.15	£0.45	£0.75
285-287	$0.30	$0.90	$1.50	£0.15	£0.45	£0.75
288 DS anniversary issue (Iron Man's 350th appearance)	$0.30	$0.90	$1.50	£0.15	£0.45	£0.75
289	$0.30	$0.90	$1.50	£0.15	£0.45	£0.75
290 Tony Stark returns as Iron Man, gold foil cover	$0.60	$1.80	$3.00	£0.40	£1.20	£2.00
291 Tony Stark vs. Jim Rhodes (War Machine)	$0.25	$0.75	$1.25	£0.25	£0.75	£1.25
292-293	$0.25	$0.75	$1.25	£0.20	£0.60	£1.00
294-295 Infinity Crusade X-over	$0.25	$0.75	$1.25	£0.20	£0.60	£1.00
296-299	$0.25	$0.75	$1.25	£0.20	£0.60	£1.00
300 LD in the U.K. 64pgs, new armour debuts, War Machine guest-stars; double embossed red and gold foil cover	$0.80	$2.40	$4.00	£0.50	£1.50	£2.50
300 64pgs, without foil cover	$0.45	$1.35	$2.25	£0.30	£0.90	£1.50
301-302	$0.30	$0.90	$1.50	£0.15	£0.45	£0.80
303 Venom appears	$0.30	$0.90	$1.50	£0.15	£0.45	£0.80
304 with free Spiderman and his Deadly Foes card sheet	$0.30	$0.90	$1.50	£0.15	£0.45	£0.80
305 Iron Man vs. Hulk	$0.30	$0.90	$1.50	£0.15	£0.45	£0.80
306-310	$0.30	$0.90	$1.50	£0.15	£0.45	£0.80
310 ND pre-bagged with acetate print from Marvel Action Hour TV series; neon ink cover; X-over War Machine #8	$0.60	$1.80	$3.00	£0.40	£1.20	£2.00
311 Hands of the Mandarin part 3, continued in Force Works #7	$0.30	$0.90	$1.50	£0.20	£0.60	£1.00
312 48pgs, Hands of the Mandarin part 6 (conclusion)	$0.45	$1.35	$2.25	£0.30	£0.90	£1.50
313-314	$0.30	$0.90	$1.50	£0.20	£0.60	£1.00
315-316 Black Widow guest-stars	$0.30	$0.90	$1.50	£0.20	£0.60	£1.00
317 48pgs, flip-book format, continued from War Machine #15	$0.45	$1.35	$2.25	£0.30	£0.90	£1.50
318	$0.30	$0.90	$1.50	£0.20	£0.60	£1.00
319 new Space Armour	$0.30	$0.90	$1.50	£0.20	£0.60	£1.00
320-321 Avengers: The Crossing tie-in; bi-weekly	$0.30	$0.90	$1.50	£0.20	£0.60	£1.00
322 Avengers: The Crossing tie-in	$0.30	$0.90	$1.50	£0.20	£0.60	£1.00
323-324 Iron Man vs. The Avengers	$0.30	$0.90	$1.50	£0.20	£0.60	£1.00
325 48pgs, Avengers: Timeslide tie-in; metallic fifth ink cover	$0.55	$1.75	$2.95	£0.40	£1.20	£2.00
326 The First Sign part 3, concludes in Avengers #396	$0.30	$0.90	$1.50	£0.20	£0.60	£1.00
Title Value:	**$482.05**	**$1453.25**	**$2742.95**	**£269.60**	**£810.75**	**£1549.50**

Note: two versions of Iron Man #232 exist; a version printed on the incorrect paper exists but is very hard to find. The Guide cannot give a value to this anomaly at this stage.

The Power of Iron Man

	£Good	£Fine	£N.Mint
Trade Paperback (1990), reprints Tony Stark's struggle with alcohol from issues #123-128	£1.10	£3.30	£5.50
(2nd printing - Apr 1991)	£1.00	£3.00	£5.00

Iron Man: Armor Wars (Jun 1990)

	£Good	£Fine	£N.Mint
Trade paperback 208pgs, reprints issues #225-232	£1.50	£4.50	£7.50

Iron Man: The Many Armours of Iron Man (Jan 1993)

	£Good	£Fine	£N.Mint
Trade paperback 208pgs, reprints stories showing the different types of armour over the years	£2.00	£6.00	£10.00

Iron Man vs. Dr. Doom (Feb 1995)

	£Good	£Fine	£N.Mint
Trade paperback 128pgs, reprints issues #149-150, #249-250	£1.70	£5.10	£8.50

IRON MAN 2020

Marvel Comics Group; OS; nn Aug 1994

	$Good	$Fine	$N.Mint	£Good	£Fine	£N.Mint
nn ND 64pgs, Walt Simonson and Bob Wiacek	$1.20	$3.60	$6.00	£0.80	£2.40	£4.00
Title Value:	**$1.20**	**$3.60**	**$6.00**	**£0.80**	**£2.40**	**£4.00**

IRON MAN AND SUB-MARINER

Marvel Comics Group, OS; 1 Apr 1968

	$Good	$Fine	$N.Mint	£Good	£Fine	£N.Mint
1 stories continue from Tales to Astonish #101, Tales of Suspense #99, continue in Iron Man #1 and Sub-Mariner #1	$24.00	$72.50	$170.00	£13.50	£41.00	£95.00
Title Value:	**$24.00**	**$72.50**	**$170.00**	**£13.50**	**£41.00**	**£95.00**

IRON MAN ANNUAL

Marvel Comics Group; 1 Aug 1970-2 Nov 1971; 3 Jun 1976-4 Aug 1977; 5 Dec 1982-present

	$Good	$Fine	$N.Mint	£Good	£Fine	£N.Mint
1 68pgs, all reprint inc. Iron Man vs. Sub-Mariner from Tales to Astonish #79,80,82	$4.15	$12.50	$25.00	£2.50	£7.50	£15.00
2 ND scarce in the U.K. 52pgs, reprints Tales of Suspense #81,92,91	$1.65	$5.00	$10.00	£1.25	£3.75	£7.50
3 ND 52pgs, Man-Thing appears	$1.20	$3.60	$6.00	£0.80	£2.40	£4.00
4 ND 52pgs, Champions (inc. Ghost Rider) appear	$1.00	$3.00	$5.00	£0.90	£2.70	£4.50
5 ND 52pgs, Black Panther appears	$0.60	$1.80	$3.00	£0.60	£1.80	£3.00
6 ND Eternals appear	$0.60	$1.80	$3.00	£0.50	£1.50	£2.50
7 ND West Coast Avengers X-over	$0.60	$1.80	$3.00	£0.50	£1.50	£2.50
8 ND X-Factor X-over	$0.60	$1.80	$3.00	£0.60	£1.80	£3.00
9 ND	$0.60	$1.80	$3.00	£0.30	£0.90	£1.50
10 ND Sub-Mariner appears, part 8 Atlantis Attacks	$0.45	$1.35	$2.25	£0.30	£0.90	£1.50
11 ND The Terminus Factor part 2, continues in Thor Annual #15, Machine Man appears	$0.45	$1.35	$2.25	£0.30	£0.90	£1.50
12 ND Subterranean Odyssey part 4, continues in Avengers West Coast Annual #6	$0.45	$1.35	$2.25	£0.30	£0.90	£1.50
13 ND Assault On Armor City part 3 (conclusion), Darkhawk appears	$0.45	$1.35	$2.25	£0.30	£0.90	£1.50
14 ND 64pgs, pre-bagged with trading card introducing Face Thief	$0.60	$1.80	$3.00	£0.40	£1.20	£2.00
15 ND 64pgs, The Controller appears	$0.60	$1.80	$3.00	£0.40	£1.20	£2.00
Title Value:	**$14.00**	**$42.10**	**$76.00**	**£9.95**	**£29.85**	**£53.50**

IRON MAN GIANT SIZE

Marvel Comics Group; 1 1975

	$Good	$Fine	$N.Mint	£Good	£Fine	£N.Mint
1 ND scarce in the U.K. 68pgs, all reprint from Tales of Suspense #49 (3rd X-Men), #57 (1st Hawkeye) and #58 (Iron Man vs. Captain America)	$2.00	$6.00	$10.00	£1.50	£4.50	£7.50
Title Value:	**$2.00**	**$6.00**	**$10.00**	**£1.50**	**£4.50**	**£7.50**

IRON MAN/FORCE WORKS COLLECTORS' PREVIEW

Marvel Comics Group, OS; 1 Nov 1994

	$Good	$Fine	$N.Mint	£Good	£Fine	£N.Mint
1 ND 48pgs, neon-ink wraparound cover	$0.40	$1.20	$2.00	£0.25	£0.75	£1.25
Title Value:	**$0.40**	**$1.20**	**$2.00**	**£0.25**	**£0.75**	**£1.25**

IRON MAN: AGE OF INNOCENCE

Marvel Comics Group, OS; 1 Feb 1996

	$Good	$Fine	$N.Mint	£Good	£Fine	£N.Mint
1 ND Avengers: Timeslide tie-in	$0.50	$1.50	$2.50	£0.30	£0.90	£1.50
Title Value:	**$0.50**	**$1.50**	**$2.50**	**£0.30**	**£0.90**	**£1.50**

IRON MANUAL

Marvel Comics Group, OS; 1 Mar 1993

	$Good	$Fine	$N.Mint	£Good	£Fine	£N.Mint
1 ND information on Iron Man technology, Bill Sienkiewicz painted cover	$0.30	$0.90	$1.50	£0.30	£0.90	£1.50
Title Value:	**$0.30**	**$0.90**	**$1.50**	**£0.30**	**£0.90**	**£1.50**

IRON MARSHAL

Jademan; 1 Jul 1990-33 Mar 1993
(see Jademan Special Issue)

	$Good	$Fine	$N.Mint	£Good	£Fine	£N.Mint
1-7 ND	$0.40	$1.20	$2.00	£0.25	£0.75	£1.25
8-33 ND	$0.30	$0.90	$1.50	£0.20	£0.60	£1.00
Title Value:	**$10.60**	**$31.80**	**$53.00**	**£6.95**	**£20.85**	**£34.75**

IRON SAGA'S ANTHOLOGY

Iron Saga Productions; 1 Jan 1987-2 Mar 1987

	$Good	$Fine	$N.Mint	£Good	£Fine	£N.Mint
1-2 ND black and white	$0.30	$0.90	$1.50	£0.20	£0.60	£1.00
Title Value:	**$0.60**	**$1.80**	**$3.00**	**£0.40**	**£1.20**	**£2.00**

IRONHAND OF ALMURIC

Dark Horse, MS; 1 Sep 1991-4 Feb 1992

	$Good	$Fine	$N.Mint	£Good	£Fine	£N.Mint
1-4 ND Roy Thomas script	$0.40	$1.20	$2.00	£0.25	£0.75	£1.25
Title Value:	**$1.60**	**$4.80**	**$8.00**	**£1.00**	**£3.00**	**£5.00**

IRONWOLF

DC Comics; nn 1986

	$Good	$Fine	$N.Mint	£Good	£Fine	£N.Mint
nn 48pgs, reprints Chaykin's Ironwolf series from Weird Worlds #8-10	$0.60	$1.80	$3.00	£0.40	£1.20	£2.00
Title Value:	**$0.60**	**$1.80**	**$3.00**	**£0.40**	**£1.20**	**£2.00**

IRONWOLF: FIRES OF THE REVOLUTION

DC Comics; nn 1992

nn ND Softcover Edition (May 1993); intro by Walt Simonson

	$Good	$Fine	$N.Mint	£Good	£Fine	£N.Mint
	$3.00	$9.00	$15.00	£2.00	£6.00	£10.00

nn ND Hardcover Edition, 104pgs; Howard Chaykin script, Mike Mignola andd Russell art

	$Good	$Fine	$N.Mint	£Good	£Fine	£N.Mint
	$6.00	$18.00	$30.00	£4.00	£12.00	£20.00
Title Value:	$9.00	$27.00	$45.00	£6.00	£18.00	£30.00

ISAAC ASIMOV'S I-BOTS
Tekno Comix; 1 Dec 1995-present
1 ND Steven Grant script, George Perez cover and art begin

	$Good	$Fine	$N.Mint	£Good	£Fine	£N.Mint
	$0.40	$1.20	$2.00	£0.25	£0.75	£1.25
2 ND	$0.40	$1.20	$2.00	£0.25	£0.75	£1.25
3 ND	$0.45	$1.35	$2.25	£0.30	£0.90	£1.50

4 ND pre-bagged with Tekno back-issue comic

	$Good	$Fine	$N.Mint	£Good	£Fine	£N.Mint
	$0.45	$1.35	$2.25	£0.30	£0.90	£1.50
Title Value:	$1.70	$5.10	$8.50	£1.10	£3.30	£5.50

ISIS, THE MIGHTY
DC Comics; 1 Oct/Nov 1976-8 Dec/Jan 1977/78
(see Shazam #25)
1 scarce in the U.K. Wood inks

	$Good	$Fine	$N.Mint	£Good	£Fine	£N.Mint
	$0.40	$1.20	$2.00	£0.25	£0.75	£1.25
2 Nasser art	$0.30	$0.90	$1.50	£0.20	£0.60	£1.00
3-6	$0.25	$0.75	$1.25	£0.15	£0.45	£0.75
7 origin Isis	$0.25	$0.75	$1.25	£0.15	£0.45	£0.75
8	$0.25	$0.75	$1.25	£0.15	£0.45	£0.75
Title Value:	$2.20	$6.60	$11.00	£1.35	£4.05	£6.75

ISLAND OF DR. MOREAU
Marvel Comics Group, Film; 1 Oct 1977
1 ND 52pgs, adapts film

	$Good	$Fine	$N.Mint	£Good	£Fine	£N.Mint
	$0.30	$0.90	$1.50	£0.20	£0.60	£1.00
Title Value:	$0.30	$0.90	$1.50	£0.20	£0.60	£1.00

IT! THE TERROR FROM BEYOND SPACE
Millennium,MS; 1 Nov 1992-4 Jul 1993
1 ND adaptation of classic 1950s sci-fi film, said to have inspired "Alien", begins; die-cut cover

	$Good	$Fine	$N.Mint	£Good	£Fine	£N.Mint
	$0.45	$1.35	$2.25	£0.30	£0.90	£1.50
2-4 ND	$0.45	$1.35	$2.25	£0.30	£0.90	£1.50
Title Value:	$1.80	$5.40	$9.00	£1.20	£3.60	£6.00

IT'S SCIENCE WITH DR. RADIUM
Slave Labor,OS; 1 Sep 1986
1 ND black and white; Samurai Penguin spin-off

	$Good	$Fine	$N.Mint	£Good	£Fine	£N.Mint
	$0.30	$0.90	$1.50	£0.20	£0.60	£1.00
Title Value:	$0.30	$0.90	$1.50	£0.20	£0.60	£1.00

ITCHY & SCRATCHY COMICS
Bongo Comics; 1 Jan 1994-present
1 ND Steve Vance script and Mike Milo art begin

	$Good	$Fine	$N.Mint	£Good	£Fine	£N.Mint
	$0.80	$2.40	$4.00	£0.50	£1.50	£2.50
2-3 ND	$0.45	$1.35	$2.25	£0.30	£0.90	£1.50
Title Value:	$1.70	$5.10	$8.50	£1.10	£3.30	£5.50

ITCHY & SCRATCHY'S HOLIDAY HIJINKS SPECIAL
Bongo Comics,OS; 1 Nov 1994

	$Good	$Fine	$N.Mint	£Good	£Fine	£N.Mint
1 ND	$0.45	$1.35	$2.25	£0.30	£0.90	£1.50
Title Value:	$0.45	$1.35	$2.25	£0.30	£0.90	£1.50

ITCHY PLANET
Fantagraphics; 1 Spring 1988-3 1989?
1 ND Nuclear issue; all black and white

	$Good	$Fine	$N.Mint	£Good	£Fine	£N.Mint
	$0.45	$1.35	$2.25	£0.30	£0.90	£1.50
2 ND Politics	$0.45	$1.35	$2.25	£0.30	£0.90	£1.50
3 ND Elections	$0.45	$1.35	$2.25	£0.30	£0.90	£1.50
Title Value:	$1.35	$4.05	$6.75	£0.90	£2.70	£4.50

J

J.N. WILLIAMSON'S MASQUES
Innovation; 1 Jul 1992
1 ND 48pgs, squarebound

	$Good	$Fine	$N.Mint	£Good	£Fine	£N.Mint
	$0.80	$2.40	$4.00	£0.50	£1.50	£2.50
Title Value:	$0.80	$2.40	$4.00	£0.50	£1.50	£2.50

JACK FROST
Amazing Comics; 1,2 1987

	$Good	$Fine	$N.Mint	£Good	£Fine	£N.Mint
1-2 ND	$0.40	$1.20	$2.00	£0.25	£0.75	£1.25
Title Value:	$0.80	$2.40	$4.00	£0.50	£1.50	£2.50

JACK KIRBY'S TEENAGENTS
Topps,MS; 1 Aug 1993-2 1993
1 pre-bagged with 3 trading cards (note: no Jack Kirby art)

	$Good	$Fine	$N.Mint	£Good	£Fine	£N.Mint
	$0.60	$1.80	$3.00	£0.40	£1.20	£2.00

2 pre-bagged with 2 trading cards (note: no Jack Kirby art)

	$Good	$Fine	$N.Mint	£Good	£Fine	£N.Mint
	$0.60	$1.80	$3.00	£0.40	£1.20	£2.00
Title Value:	$1.20	$3.60	$6.00	£0.80	£2.40	£4.00

JACK OF HEARTS
Marvel Comics Group,MS; 1 Jan 1984-4 Apr 1984
(see Deadly Hands of Kung Fu, Marvel Team Up)
1 ND S.H.I.E.L.D. appear, George Freeman art begins

	$Good	$Fine	$N.Mint	£Good	£Fine	£N.Mint
	$0.30	$0.90	$1.50	£0.20	£0.60	£1.00
2-3 ND	$0.30	$0.90	$1.50	£0.20	£0.60	£1.00

4 ND scarce in the U.K.

	$Good	$Fine	$N.Mint	£Good	£Fine	£N.Mint
	$0.30	$0.90	$1.50	£0.25	£0.75	£1.25
Title Value:	$1.20	$3.60	$6.00	£0.85	£2.55	£4.25

JACK THE RIPPER
Eternity,MS; 1 Dec 1989-3 Apr 1990
1-3 ND black and white

	$Good	$Fine	$N.Mint	£Good	£Fine	£N.Mint
	$0.55	$1.65	$2.75	£0.35	£1.05	£1.75
Title Value:	$1.65	$4.95	$8.25	£1.05	£3.15	£5.25
Graphic Album (Nov 1990), reprints #1-3				£1.00	£3.00	£5.00

JACKAROO
Eternity; 1 Mar 1990-3 May 1990
1-3 ND Gary Chaloner script/art; black and white

	$Good	$Fine	$N.Mint	£Good	£Fine	£N.Mint
	$0.30	$0.90	$1.50	£0.20	£0.60	£1.00
Title Value:	$0.90	$2.70	$4.50	£0.60	£1.80	£3.00

JADEMAN COLLECTION
Jademan; 1 Dec 1989-4 Mar 1990
1-4 64pgs, anthology title edited by Len Wein, colour art, plastic-coated covers; bound-in poster

	$Good	$Fine	$N.Mint	£Good	£Fine	£N.Mint
	$0.45	$1.35	$2.25	£0.30	£0.90	£1.50
Title Value:	$1.80	$5.40	$9.00	£1.20	£3.60	£6.00

JADEMAN KUNG-FU SPECIAL
Jademan; 1 1988
1 ND previews of Jademan titles

	$Good	$Fine	$N.Mint	£Good	£Fine	£N.Mint
	$0.30	$0.90	$1.50	£0.20	£0.60	£1.00
Title Value:	$0.30	$0.90	$1.50	£0.20	£0.60	£1.00

JADEMAN SPECIAL: GATES OF THE NIGHT
Jademan,MS; 1 Nov 1990-4 Feb 1991
1-4 68pgs, horror anthology

	$Good	$Fine	$N.Mint	£Good	£Fine	£N.Mint
	$0.80	$2.40	$4.00	£0.50	£1.50	£2.50
Title Value:	$3.20	$9.60	$16.00	£2.00	£6.00	£10.00

JAGUAR ANNUAL, THE
DC Comics/Impact; 1 Jun 1992
1 64pgs, ties into Crusaders #1 (see other Impact annuals), trading cards included

	$Good	$Fine	$N.Mint	£Good	£Fine	£N.Mint
	$0.30	$0.90	$1.50	£0.20	£0.60	£1.00
Title Value:	$0.30	$0.90	$1.50	£0.20	£0.60	£1.00

JAGUAR GOD
Verotik; 1 1995-present
0 ND (Aug 1995) Glenn Danzig script, Frank Teran art

	$Good	$Fine	$N.Mint	£Good	£Fine	£N.Mint
	$0.70	$2.10	$3.50	£0.50	£1.50	£2.50

1-3 ND Glenn Danzig script, Simon Bisley art

Island of Dr. Moreau #1

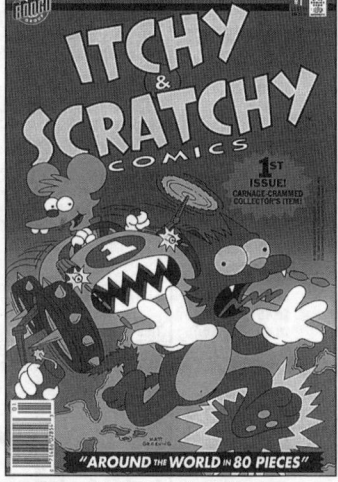

Itchy & Scratchy Comics #1

Jaguar (Archie) #1

	$Good	$Fine	$N.Mint	£Good	£Fine	£N.Mint

(continued)

	$Good	$Fine	$N.Mint	£Good	£Fine	£N.Mint
	$0.60	$1.80	$3.00	£0.40	£1.20	£2.00
4 ND new Frank Frazetta painted cover						
	$0.60	$1.80	$3.00	£0.40	£1.20	£2.00
Title Value:	$3.10	$9.30	$15.50	£2.10	£6.30	£10.50

JAGUAR STORIES
Comico; 1 Jul 1992-4 1992
1-4 Steve Seagle script in all

	$Good	$Fine	$N.Mint	£Good	£Fine	£N.Mint
	$0.40	$1.20	$2.00	£0.25	£0.75	£1.25
Title Value:	$1.60	$4.80	$8.00	£1.00	£3.00	£5.00

JAGUAR, ADVENTURES OF THE
Archie; 1 Sep 1961-15 Nov 1963
1 origin and 1st appearance The Jaguar; distributed in the U.K.

	$Good	$Fine	$N.Mint	£Good	£Fine	£N.Mint
	$18.50	$55.00	$112.50	£12.50	£38.00	£75.00
2-3 distributed in the U.K.						
	$9.25	$28.00	$56.25	£6.25	£18.50	£37.50
4-5 distributed in the U.K.						
	$6.00	$18.00	$36.00	£4.00	£12.00	£24.00
6-10 distributed in the U.K.						
	$4.50	$13.50	$27.00	£3.00	£9.00	£18.00
11-15 distributed in the U.K.						
	$3.75	$11.00	$22.50	£2.50	£7.50	£15.00
Title Value:	$90.25	$269.50	$544.50	£60.50	£181.50	£363.00

JAGUAR, THE
DC Comics/Impact; 1 Aug 1991-14 Oct 1992

	$Good	$Fine	$N.Mint	£Good	£Fine	£N.Mint
1-8	$0.15	$0.45	$0.75	£0.10	£0.35	£0.60
9 previews Crusaders #1 (see Web #9), trading cards included						
	$0.15	$0.45	$0.75	£0.10	£0.35	£0.60
10-14	$0.15	$0.45	$0.75	£0.10	£0.35	£0.60
Title Value:	$2.10	$6.30	$10.50	£1.40	£4.90	£8.40

Note: Archie character acquired (and revamped) by DC though events take place outside DC Universe continuity.

JAKE THRASH
Aircel,MS; 1 1988-3 1988
1-3 ND Barry Blair script, Dave Cooper art, black and white

	$Good	$Fine	$N.Mint	£Good	£Fine	£N.Mint
	$0.40	$1.20	$2.00	£0.25	£0.75	£1.25
Title Value:	$1.20	$3.60	$6.00	£0.75	£2.25	£3.75
Book One (1989)						
80pgs squarebound, reprints issues #1-3 (published by Malibu)				£0.50	£1.50	£2.50

JAM
Comico; 1 May 1988
1 ND Bernie Mireault art in colour; sub-titled "Super Cool Colour-Injected Turbo Adventure from Hell!"

	$Good	$Fine	$N.Mint	£Good	£Fine	£N.Mint
	$0.55	$1.65	$2.75	£0.35	£1.05	£1.75
Title Value:	$0.55	$1.65	$2.75	£0.35	£1.05	£1.75

JAM SPECIAL
Matrix Graphics; 1 Oct 1987-2 1988
1-2 ND 48pgs, Bernie Mireault script/art

	$Good	$Fine	$N.Mint	£Good	£Fine	£N.Mint
	$0.45	$1.35	$2.25	£0.30	£0.90	£1.50
Title Value:	$0.90	$2.70	$4.50	£0.60	£1.80	£3.00

JAM, THE
Slave Labor; 1 Nov 1989-4 May 1990; 5 May 1991; Dark Horse; 6-8 1994; Caliber Press; 9 Aug 1995-present
1-5 ND Bernie Mireault script/art, black and white

	$Good	$Fine	$N.Mint	£Good	£Fine	£N.Mint
	$0.40	$1.20	$2.00	£0.25	£0.75	£1.25
6-7 ND Bernie Mireault script/art, black and white; sub-titled Urban Adventure						
	$0.45	$1.35	$2.25	£0.30	£0.90	£1.50
8-9 ND Bernie Mireault script/art, black and white; sub-titled Urban Adventure						
	$0.60	$1.80	$3.00	£0.40	£1.20	£2.00
10 ND Bernie Mireault script/art; black and white						
	$0.60	$1.80	$3.00	£0.40	£1.20	£2.00
Title Value:	$4.70	$14.10	$23.50	£3.05	£9.15	£15.25

JAMES BOND 007: QUASIMODO GAMBIT
Dark Horse,MS; 1 Jan 1995-3 Mar 1995
1-3 ND Don McGregor script

	$Good	$Fine	$N.Mint	£Good	£Fine	£N.Mint
	$0.80	$2.40	$4.00	£0.50	£1.50	£2.50
Title Value:	$2.40	$7.20	$12.00	£1.50	£4.50	£7.50

JAMES BOND 007: SERPENT'S TOOTH
Dark Horse,MS; 1 Jul 1992-3 Dec 1992
1-3 ND 48pgs, Doug Moench script, Paul Gulacy art

	$Good	$Fine	$N.Mint	£Good	£Fine	£N.Mint
	$0.90	$2.70	$4.50	£0.60	£1.80	£3.00
Title Value:	$2.70	$8.10	$13.50	£1.80	£5.40	£9.00
James Bond 007: Serpent's Tooth (Dec 1994)						
Trade paperback reprints mini-series, Paul Gulacy painted cover				£2.00	£6.00	£10.00

JAMES BOND 007: SHATTERED HELIX
Dark Horse,MS; 1 May 1994-2 Jun 1994
1-2 ND David Lloyd cover and art

	$Good	$Fine	$N.Mint	£Good	£Fine	£N.Mint
	$0.45	$1.35	$2.25	£0.30	£0.90	£1.50
Title Value:	$0.90	$2.70	$4.50	£0.60	£1.80	£3.00

JAMES BOND JR.
Marvel Comics Group; 1 Feb 1992-12 Jan 1993
1 based on animated U.S. series, Dan Abnett script begin, bi-weekly

	$Good	$Fine	$N.Mint	£Good	£Fine	£N.Mint
	$0.25	$0.75	$1.25	£0.15	£0.45	£0.75
2 bi-weekly	$0.25	$0.75	$1.25	£0.15	£0.45	£0.75
3-12	$0.25	$0.75	$1.25	£0.15	£0.45	£0.75
Title Value:	$3.00	$9.00	$15.00	£1.80	£5.40	£9.00

JAMES BOND: A SILENT ARMAGEDDON
Dark Horse,MS; 1 Mar 1993-4 Oct 1993
1-4 ND Simon Jowett script and John Burns art

	$Good	$Fine	$N.Mint	£Good	£Fine	£N.Mint
	$0.60	$1.80	$3.00	£0.40	£1.20	£2.00
Title Value:	$2.40	$7.20	$12.00	£1.60	£4.80	£8.00

JAMES BOND: PERMISSION TO DIE
Acme/Eclipse Books; 1,2 1989
1-2 ND story/art by Mike Grell

	$Good	$Fine	$N.Mint	£Good	£Fine	£N.Mint
	$0.80	$2.40	$4.00	£0.50	£1.50	£2.50
Title Value:	$1.60	$4.80	$8.00	£1.00	£3.00	£5.00

JANUS DIRECTIVE, THE
(see in order) Checkmate #15, Suicide Squad #27, Checkmate #16, Suicide Squad #28, Checkmate #17, Manhunter #14, Firestorm #86, Suicide Squad #29, Checkmate #18, Suicide Squad #30, Captain Atom #30

JASON AND THE ARGONAUTS
Caliber/Tome Press; 1 Jul 1991-6 1991

	$Good	$Fine	$N.Mint	£Good	£Fine	£N.Mint
1-6 ND	$0.45	$1.35	$2.25	£0.30	£0.90	£1.50
Title Value:	$2.70	$8.10	$13.50	£1.80	£5.40	£9.00

JASON GOES TO HELL
Topps,MS; 1 Mar 1993-3 May 1993
1 ND pre-bagged with 3 trading cards, glow-in-the-dark cover

	$Good	$Fine	$N.Mint	£Good	£Fine	£N.Mint
	$0.80	$2.40	$4.00	£0.50	£1.50	£2.50
2-3 ND pre-bagged with 3 trading cards						
	$0.60	$1.80	$3.00	£0.40	£1.20	£2.00
Title Value:	$2.00	$6.00	$10.00	£1.30	£3.90	£6.50

JASON VS. LEATHERFACE
Topps,MS; 1 Oct 1995-present
1 ND Nancy Collins script, Jeff Butler and Steve Montano script

	$Good	$Fine	$N.Mint	£Good	£Fine	£N.Mint
	$0.60	$1.80	$3.00	£0.40	£1.20	£2.00
2 ND Nancy Collins script, Jeff Butler and Steve Montano script; Simon Bisley cover						
	$0.60	$1.80	$3.00	£0.40	£1.20	£2.00
Title Value:	$1.20	$3.60	$6.00	£0.80	£2.40	£4.00

JAVERTS
Firstlight Comixx,MS; 1 Aug 1994-5 Dec 1994
1 ND holo-foil enhanced cover by Bart Sears

	$Good	$Fine	$N.Mint	£Good	£Fine	£N.Mint
	$0.60	$1.80	$3.00	£0.40	£1.20	£2.00
1 ND Gold Edition, available to retailers with every 15 copies of #1						
	$1.50	$4.50	$7.50	£1.00	£3.00	£5.00
2-5 ND	$0.60	$1.80	$3.00	£0.40	£1.20	£2.00
Title Value:	$4.50	$13.50	$22.50	£3.00	£9.00	£15.00

JAZZ AGE CHRONICLES
Caliber Press; 1 May 1990-7 1991

	$Good	$Fine	$N.Mint	£Good	£Fine	£N.Mint
1-7 ND	$0.40	$1.20	$2.00	£0.25	£0.75	£1.25
Title Value:	$2.80	$8.40	$14.00	£1.75	£5.25	£8.75

JEMM, SON OF SATURN
DC Comics,MS; 1 Sep 1984-12 Aug 1985

	$Good	$Fine	$N.Mint	£Good	£Fine	£N.Mint
1-2	$0.15	$0.45	$0.75	£0.10	£0.35	£0.60
3 origin told	$0.15	$0.45	$0.75	£0.10	£0.35	£0.60
4 Superman appears						
	$0.15	$0.45	$0.75	£0.10	£0.35	£0.60
5-12	$0.15	$0.45	$0.75	£0.10	£0.35	£0.60
Title Value:	$1.80	$5.40	$9.00	£1.20	£4.20	£7.20

Note: Gene Colan art in all; series 1st intended to feature Martian Manhunter.

JEREMIAH: A FISTFUL OF SAND
Adventure,MS; 1,2 Aug 1991

	$Good	$Fine	$N.Mint	£Good	£Fine	£N.Mint
1-2 ND	$0.40	$1.20	$2.00	£0.25	£0.75	£1.25
Title Value:	$0.80	$2.40	$4.00	£0.50	£1.50	£2.50

JEREMIAH: BIRDS OF PREY
Adventure,MS; 1,2 Jan 1991

	$Good	$Fine	$N.Mint	£Good	£Fine	£N.Mint
1-2 ND	$0.40	$1.20	$2.00	£0.25	£0.75	£1.25
Title Value:	$0.80	$2.40	$4.00	£0.50	£1.50	£2.50

JEREMIAH: EYES LIKE BURNING COALS
Adventure,MS; 1,2 Oct 1991

	$Good	$Fine	$N.Mint	£Good	£Fine	£N.Mint
1-2 ND	$0.40	$1.20	$2.00	£0.25	£0.75	£1.25
Title Value:	$0.80	$2.40	$4.00	£0.50	£1.50	£2.50

JEREMIAH: THE HEIRS
Adventure,MS; 1,2 Sep 1991

	$Good	$Fine	$N.Mint	£Good	£Fine	£N.Mint
1-2 ND	$0.40	$1.20	$2.00	£0.25	£0.75	£1.25
Title Value:	$0.80	$2.40	$4.00	£0.50	£1.50	£2.50

JEREMIAH: THE HUNTERS
Adventure,MS; 1,2 Nov 1991

	$Good	$Fine	$N.Mint	£Good	£Fine	£N.Mint
1-2 ND	$0.45	$1.35	$2.25	£0.30	£0.90	£1.50
Title Value:	$0.90	$2.70	$4.50	£0.60	£1.80	£3.00

JERRY IGER'S FAMOUS FEATURES
Pacific,OS; 1 Jul 1984
1 ND Matt Baker Flamingo reprints; colour

	$Good	$Fine	$N.Mint	£Good	£Fine	£N.Mint
	$0.40	$1.20	$2.00	£0.25	£0.75	£1.25
Title Value:	$0.40	$1.20	$2.00	£0.25	£0.75	£1.25

JERRY IGER'S GOLDEN FEATURES
Blackthorne; 1 Feb 1986-6 Dec 1986
1 ND Flamingo by Matt Baker

	$Good	$Fine	$N.Mint	£Good	£Fine	£N.Mint
	$0.40	$1.20	$2.00	£0.25	£0.75	£1.25
2 ND Wonder Boy by Matt Baker						
	$0.40	$1.20	$2.00	£0.25	£0.75	£1.25
3 ND All-Girl issue	$0.40	$1.20	$2.00	£0.25	£0.75	£1.25
4 ND ZX-5 Spies in Action, Lou Fine, Jack Kirby art						
	$0.45	$1.35	$2.25	£0.30	£0.90	£1.50
5 ND All-Horror issue						
	$0.40	$1.20	$2.00	£0.25	£0.75	£1.25
6 ND All-Kids issue						
	$0.40	$1.20	$2.00	£0.25	£0.75	£1.25
Title Value:	$2.45	$7.35	$12.25	£1.55	£4.65	£7.75

JERRY LEWIS, THE ADVENTURES OF
National Periodical Publications; 41 Nov 1957-124 May/Jun 1971
(see Super DC Giant) (previous issues #1-40 titled Adventures of Dean Martin and Jerry Lewis, all ND)

	$Good	$Fine	$N.Mint	£Good	£Fine	£N.Mint
41-60	$7.00	$21.00	$42.50	£3.30	£10.00	£20.00
61-63	$5.25	$16.00	$32.50	£3.00	£9.00	£18.00
1st official distribution in the U.K.						
64-67	$5.25	$16.00	$32.50	£2.50	£7.50	£15.00
68 ND	$5.25	$16.00	$32.50	£3.00	£9.00	£18.00
69-73	$5.25	$16.00	$32.50	£2.50	£7.50	£15.00

	$Good	$Fine	$N.Mint	£Good	£Fine	£N.Mint
74 ND	$5.00	$15.00	$30.00	£3.00	£9.00	£18.00
75-80	$5.00	$15.00	$30.00	£2.50	£7.50	£15.00
81-91 ND	$3.75	$11.00	$22.50	£1.65	£5.00	£10.00
92 ND Superman cameo						
	$4.15	$12.50	$25.00	£2.05	£6.25	£12.50
93-96 ND	$2.90	$8.75	$17.50	£1.65	£5.00	£10.00
97 scarce in the U.K. Batman and Robin X-over, Joker cover and story						
	$5.00	$15.00	$30.00	£3.00	£9.00	£18.00
98-100 ND	$2.90	$8.75	$17.50	£1.65	£5.00	£10.00
101 ND Neal Adams art						
	$6.00	$18.00	$30.00	£3.00	£9.00	£15.00
102 ND scarce in the U.K. Neal Adams art, Beatles appear						
	$6.00	$18.00	$30.00	£4.00	£12.00	£20.00
103-104 ND Neal Adams art						
	$6.00	$18.00	$30.00	£3.00	£9.00	£15.00
105 ND Superman appears						
	$6.00	$18.00	$30.00	£3.00	£9.00	£15.00
106-111 ND	$1.60	$4.80	$8.00	£1.20	£3.60	£6.00
112 ND Flash appears						
	$4.00	$12.00	$20.00	£2.00	£6.00	£10.00
113-116 ND	$1.60	$4.80	$8.00	£1.20	£3.60	£6.00
117 ND Wonder Woman appears						
	$2.40	$7.00	$12.00	£2.00	£6.00	£10.00
118-124 ND	$1.20	$3.60	$6.00	£1.20	£3.60	£6.00
Title Value:	$374.75	$1124.95	$2199.00	£193.65	£583.95	£1127.50

JET POWER
IW Super; 1,2 1963
1-2 scarce, distributed in the U.K. all reprints

	$Good	$Fine	$N.Mint	£Good	£Fine	£N.Mint
	$3.00	$9.00	$18.00	£2.00	£6.00	£12.00
Title Value:	$6.00	$18.00	$36.00	£4.00	£12.00	£24.00

JETSONS, THE
Gold Key; 1 Jan 1963-36 Oct 1970

	$Good	$Fine	$N.Mint	£Good	£Fine	£N.Mint
1 scarce in the U.K.						
	$32.00	$95.00	$190.00	£20.50	£62.50	£125.00
2 scarce in the U.K.						
	$16.50	$50.00	$100.00	£10.50	£33.00	£65.00
3 scarce in the U.K.						
	$13.00	$40.00	$80.00	£9.00	£28.00	£55.00
4-5	$12.50	$38.00	$75.00	£8.25	£25.00	£50.00
6-10	$11.50	$35.00	$70.00	£7.50	£22.50	£45.00
11-20	$11.00	$33.00	$55.00	£6.00	£18.00	£30.00
21-30	$9.00	$27.00	$45.00	£5.00	£15.00	£25.00
31-36	$8.00	$24.00	$40.00	£4.50	£13.50	£22.50
Title Value:	$392.00	$1180.00	$2110.00	£231.00	£697.00	£1255.00

Note: all distributed on the news-stands in the U.K.

JETSONS, THE (2ND SERIES)
Charlton; 1 Nov 1970-20 Jan 1974

	$Good	$Fine	$N.Mint	£Good	£Fine	£N.Mint
1 scarce in the U.K.						
	$11.50	$35.00	$57.50	£7.00	£21.00	£35.00
2-3 scarce in the U.K.						
	$6.00	$18.00	$30.00	£3.00	£9.00	£15.00
4-5	$5.00	$15.00	$25.00	£2.00	£6.00	£10.00
6-10	$4.00	$12.00	$20.00	£1.50	£4.50	£7.50
11-20	$3.00	$9.00	$15.00	£1.00	£3.00	£5.00
Title Value:	$83.50	$251.00	$412.50	£34.50	£103.50	£172.50

Note: most issues distributed on the news-stands in the U.K.

JEZEBEL JADE
Comico,MS; 1 Oct 1988-3 Dec 1988
(see Jonny Quest)
1-3 ND Messner-Loebs script, Adam Kubert cover and art

	$Good	$Fine	$N.Mint	£Good	£Fine	£N.Mint
	$0.60	$1.80	$3.00	£0.40	£1.20	£2.00
Title Value:	$1.80	$5.40	$9.00	£1.20	£3.60	£6.00

JIGSAW
Harvey; 1 Sep 1966-2 Dec 1966

	$Good	$Fine	$N.Mint	£Good	£Fine	£N.Mint
1 Reed Crandall art; distributed in the U.K.						
	$1.25	$3.75	$7.50	£0.80	£2.50	£5.00
2 distributed in the U.K.						
	$0.75	$2.25	$4.50	£0.50	£1.50	£3.00
Title Value:	$2.00	$6.00	$12.00	£1.30	£4.00	£8.00

JIHAD
Marvel Comics Group,MS; 1 Dec 1991-2 Jan 1992
1 ND features The Cenobites from Clive Barker's Nightbreed, Paul Johnson painted cover and art

	$Good	$Fine	$N.Mint	£Good	£Fine	£N.Mint
	$0.90	$2.70	$4.50	£0.60	£1.80	£3.00
2 ND	$0.90	$2.70	$4.50	£0.60	£1.80	£3.00
Title Value:	$1.80	$5.40	$9.00	£1.20	£3.60	£6.00

JIHAD
White Wolf,MS; 1 Apr 1991

	$Good	$Fine	$N.Mint	£Good	£Fine	£N.Mint
1 ND (cancelled after 1 issue)						
	$0.45	$1.35	$2.25	£0.30	£0.90	£1.50
Title Value:	$0.45	$1.35	$2.25	£0.30	£0.90	£1.50

JIM
Fantagraphics,Magazine; 1 1988-3 1989?

	$Good	$Fine	$N.Mint	£Good	£Fine	£N.Mint
1 ND Jim Woodring story/art begins						
	$0.55	$1.65	$2.75	£0.35	£1.05	£1.75
2 ND scarce in the U.K.						
	$0.80	$2.40	$4.00	£0.50	£1.50	£2.50
3 ND	$0.45	$1.35	$2.25	£0.30	£0.90	£1.50
Title Value:	$1.80	$5.40	$9.00	£1.15	£3.45	£5.75

JIMBO
Bongo Comics; 1 Jun 1995

	$Good	$Fine	$N.Mint	£Good	£Fine	£N.Mint
1 ND Gary Panter art						
	$0.60	$1.80	$3.00	£0.40	£1.20	£2.00
Title Value:	$0.60	$1.80	$3.00	£0.40	£1.20	£2.00

JIMMY OLSEN, SUPERMAN'S PAL
National Periodical Publications/DC Comics; 1 Sep/Oct 1954-163 Feb/Mar 1974
(becomes Superman Family #164 on) (see also Superman, World's Finest)
1 rare in the U.K., less common/scarce in the U.S.

	$Good	$Fine	$N.Mint	£Good	£Fine	£N.Mint
	$350.00	$1050.00	$3500.00	$250.00	£750.00	£2500.00
[Very scarce in high grade - Very Fine+ or better]						
2 very scarce in the U.K.						
	$120.00	$360.00	$960.00	£82.50	£250.00	£675.00
3 very scarce in the U.K. (Jan/Feb 1955)						
	$75.00	$225.00	$600.00	£52.50	£155.00	£425.00
4-5 scarce in the U.K.						
	$50.00	$150.00	$400.00	£35.00	£105.00	£280.00
6-9	$35.00	$105.00	$280.00	£25.00	£75.00	£200.00
10 (Feb 1956)	$35.00	$105.00	$280.00	£25.00	£75.00	£200.00
11-17	$26.00	$75.00	$180.00	£17.00	£50.00	£120.00
18 (Feb 1957)	$26.00	$75.00	$180.00	£17.00	£50.00	£120.00
19-20	$26.00	$75.00	$180.00	£17.00	£50.00	£120.00
21-25	$17.00	$50.00	$120.00	£11.00	£34.00	£80.00
26 (Feb 1958)	$17.00	$50.00	$120.00	£11.00	£34.00	£80.00
27-28	$17.00	$50.00	$120.00	£11.00	£34.00	£80.00
29 Krypto appears						
	$17.00	$50.00	$120.00	£11.00	£34.00	£80.00
30	$17.00	$50.00	$120.00	£11.00	£34.00	£80.00
31 1st appearance Elastic Lad						
	$12.50	$39.00	$90.00	£8.50	£26.00	£60.00
32-33	$12.50	$39.00	$90.00	£8.50	£26.00	£60.00
34 (Feb 1959)	$12.50	$39.00	$90.00	£8.50	£26.00	£60.00
35	$12.50	$39.00	$90.00	£8.50	£26.00	£60.00
36 1st appearance Lucy Lane, sister of Lois Lane and long-time girl-friend of Jimmy						
	$12.50	$39.00	$90.00	£8.50	£26.00	£60.00
37-40	$12.50	$39.00	$90.00	£8.50	£26.00	£60.00
1st official distribution in the U.K.						
41	$10.50	$32.00	$75.00	£6.00	£18.00	£42.00
42 (Jan 1960)	$10.50	$32.00	$75.00	£6.00	£18.00	£42.00
43-47	$10.50	$32.00	$75.00	£6.00	£18.00	£42.00
48 1st Superman Emergency Squad						
	$10.50	$32.00	$75.00	£6.00	£18.00	£42.00
49 Congorilla appears						
	$10.50	$32.00	$75.00	£6.00	£18.00	£42.00
50 (Jan 1961), Bizarro and Supergirl appearances						
	$10.50	$32.00	$75.00	£6.00	£18.00	£42.00
51 Supergirl appears						
	$10.50	$33.00	$65.00	£4.15	£12.50	£25.00
52-55	$10.50	$33.00	$65.00	£4.15	£12.50	£25.00
56 last 10 cents issue						
	$10.50	$33.00	$65.00	£4.15	£12.50	£25.00
57 Supergirl appears						
	$5.75	$17.50	$35.00	£3.30	£10.00	£20.00
58 (Jan 1962)	$5.75	$17.50	$35.00	£3.30	£10.00	£20.00
59-60	$5.75	$17.50	$35.00	£3.30	£10.00	£20.00
61	$5.00	$15.00	$30.00	£1.65	£5.00	£10.00
62 Mon-El appearance						
	$5.00	$15.00	$30.00	£2.05	£6.25	£12.50
63 Legion of Super Villains appearance						
	$5.00	$15.00	$30.00	£2.05	£6.25	£12.50
64-65	$5.00	$15.00	$30.00	£1.65	£5.00	£10.00
66 (Jan 1963)	$5.00	$15.00	$30.00	£1.65	£5.00	£10.00
67-69	$5.00	$15.00	$30.00	£1.65	£5.00	£10.00
70 Element Lad X-over, 1st appearance Silver Kryponite (hoax)						
	$5.00	$15.00	$30.00	£1.65	£5.00	£10.00
71	$4.15	$12.50	$25.00	£1.25	£3.75	£7.50
72 Elastic Lad joins the Legion						
	$5.00	$15.00	$30.00	£1.65	£5.00	£10.00
73 Ultra Boy X-over						
	$4.15	$12.50	$25.00	£1.65	£5.00	£10.00
74 (Jan 1964)	$4.15	$12.50	$25.00	£1.25	£3.75	£7.50
75 Supergirl appears						
	$4.15	$12.50	$25.00	£1.25	£3.75	£7.50
76 Legion appears (Saturn Girl/Light Lass/Triplicate Girl)						
	$5.00	$15.00	$30.00	£1.65	£5.00	£10.00
77 Jimmy Olsen as Colossal Boy; Titano the Super-Ape appears						
	$4.15	$12.50	$25.00	£1.25	£3.75	£7.50
78 Aqualad appears						
	$4.15	$12.50	$25.00	£1.25	£3.75	£7.50
79 The Red Headed Beatle of 1,000 BC - cool!						
	$4.15	$12.50	$25.00	£1.25	£3.75	£7.50
80 Bizarro with Bizarro Lucy and Luthor appear						
	$4.15	$12.50	$25.00	£1.25	£3.75	£7.50
81	$3.30	$10.00	$20.00	£1.00	£3.00	£6.00
82 (Jan 1965)	$3.30	$10.00	$20.00	£1.00	£3.00	£6.00
83	$3.30	$10.00	$20.00	£1.00	£3.00	£6.00
84 Titano appears	$3.30	$10.00	$20.00	£1.00	£3.00	£6.00
85 Legion appear (3 panels)						
	$4.15	$12.50	$25.00	£1.15	£3.50	£7.00
86 Congorilla appears						
	$3.30	$10.00	$20.00	£1.00	£3.00	£6.00
87 Legion of Super Villains appear (inc. Brainiac and Luthor)						
	$4.15	$12.50	$25.00	£1.50	£4.50	£9.00
88 Star Boy appears (1 panel)						
	$4.15	$12.50	$25.00	£1.15	£3.50	£7.00

89 John F. Kennedy tribute; last Silver Age issue cover dated December 1965

MINT = 100% / NEAR MINT (inc. +/-) = 90–99% / VERY FINE (inc. +/-) = 75–89% / FINE (inc. +/-) = 55–74%
VERY GOOD (inc. +/-) = 35–54% / GOOD (inc. +/-) = 15–34% / FAIR = 5–14% / POOR = 1–4%

409

	$Good	$Fine	$N.Mint	£Good	£Fine	£N.Mint
	$3.30	$10.00	$20.00	£1.00	£3.00	£6.00
90 (Jan 1966)	$3.30	$10.00	$20.00	£0.80	£2.50	£5.00
91	$3.30	$10.00	$20.00	£0.80	£2.50	£5.00
92 Batman, Robin and Supergirl appear						
	$3.30	$10.00	$20.00	£1.00	£3.00	£6.00
93 Jimmy as Super-Batman						
	$3.30	$10.00	$20.00	£0.80	£2.50	£5.00
94 Supergirl cameo						
	$3.30	$10.00	$20.00	£0.80	£2.50	£5.00
95 80pgs, Giant G-25						
	$3.55	$10.50	$25.00	£1.75	£5.25	£12.50
96-98	$3.30	$10.00	$20.00	£0.80	£2.50	£5.00
99 (Jan 1967), Jimmy Olsen as Star Boy, Lightning Lad, Sun Boy						
	$3.30	$10.00	$20.00	£1.00	£3.00	£6.00
100 Legion cameo						
	$2.50	$7.50	$15.00	£1.00	£3.00	£6.00
101-103	$2.00	$6.00	$10.00	£0.70	£2.10	£3.50
104 80pgs, Giant G-38						
	$4.15	$12.50	$25.00	£2.05	£6.25	£12.50
105	$2.00	$6.00	$10.00	£0.70	£2.10	£3.50
106 Legion appears						
	$2.00	$6.00	$10.00	£0.80	£2.40	£4.00
107	$2.00	$6.00	$10.00	£0.70	£2.10	£3.50
108 (Jan 1968)	$2.00	$6.00	$10.00	£0.70	£2.10	£3.50
109 Neal Adams cover						
	$2.00	$6.00	$10.00	£0.70	£2.10	£3.50
110	$2.00	$6.00	$10.00	£0.70	£2.10	£3.50
111 Batman and Robin appear						
	$2.00	$6.00	$10.00	£0.60	£1.80	£3.00
112	$2.00	$6.00	$10.00	£0.60	£1.80	£3.00
113 80pgs, Giant G-50						
	$2.50	$7.50	$15.00	£1.50	£4.50	£9.00
114	$2.00	$6.00	$10.00	£0.60	£1.80	£3.00
115 Aquaman appears, Neal Adams cover						
	$2.00	$6.00	$10.00	£0.60	£1.80	£3.00
116 cover story reprints issue #10						
	$2.00	$6.00	$10.00	£0.60	£1.80	£3.00
117 (Jan 1969)	$2.00	$6.00	$10.00	£0.60	£1.80	£3.00
118-120	$2.00	$6.00	$10.00	£0.60	£1.80	£3.00
121	$2.00	$6.00	$10.00	£0.50	£1.50	£2.50
122 80pgs, Giant G-62						
	$2.50	$7.50	$15.00	£1.30	£4.00	£8.00
123-125	$2.00	$6.00	$10.00	£0.50	£1.50	£2.50
126 (Jan 1970)	$2.00	$6.00	$10.00	£0.50	£1.50	£2.50
127-130	$2.00	$6.00	$10.00	£0.50	£1.50	£2.50
131 80pgs, Giant G-74						
	$3.00	$9.00	$15.00	£1.60	£4.80	£8.00
132 scarce in the U.K.						
	$2.00	$6.00	$10.00	£0.70	£2.10	£3.50
133 1st of re-vamped series by Jack Kirby; Newsboy Legion appears						
	$3.30	$10.00	$20.00	£1.00	£3.00	£6.00
134 Jack Kirby art, 1st appearance Darkseid (cameo - 1 panel; see Forever People #1)						
	$5.00	$15.00	$20.00	£1.50	£4.50	£9.00
135 (Jan 1971), Jack Kirby art, 2nd appearance Darkseid (cameo)						
	$4.00	$12.00	$20.00	£1.40	£4.20	£7.00
136-139 Jack Kirby art						
	$1.00	$3.00	$5.00	£0.50	£1.50	£2.50
140 80pgs, Giant G-86						
	$2.50	$7.50	$15.00	£1.00	£3.00	£6.00
141 48pgs, (says 52pgs on cover to #150 as they count the covers in the U.S.), Jack Kirby art						
	$1.00	$3.00	$5.00	£0.50	£1.50	£2.50
142-144 48pgs, Jack Kirby art						
	$1.00	$3.00	$5.00	£0.50	£1.50	£2.50
145 48pgs, (Jan 1972), Jack Kirby art						
	$1.00	$3.00	$5.00	£0.50	£1.50	£2.50
146-148 48pgs, Jack Kirby art						
	$1.00	$3.00	$5.00	£0.50	£1.50	£2.50
149-150 48pgs, Golden Age Plastic Man reprints by Jack Cole						
	$0.60	$1.80	$3.00	£0.40	£1.20	£2.00
151-154	$1.00	$3.00	$5.00	£0.40	£1.20	£2.00
155 (Jan 1973)	$1.00	$3.00	$5.00	£0.40	£1.20	£2.00
156-161	$1.00	$3.00	$5.00	£0.40	£1.20	£2.00
162 (Jan 1974)	$1.00	$3.00	$5.00	£0.40	£1.20	£2.00
163	$1.00	$3.00	$5.00	£0.40	£1.20	£2.00
Title Value:	$1836.35	$5501.10	$13981.00	£1134.60	£3411.25	£8932.50

REPRINT FEATURES
Jimmy Olsen/Superman in 95, 104, 113, 122, 131, 140. Newsboy Legion by Simon & Kirby in 141-148.

JOE R. LANSDALE'S BY BIZARRE HANDS
Dark Horse; 1 Mar 1994-3 1994

	$Good	$Fine	$N.Mint	£Good	£Fine	£N.Mint
1-3 ND black and white						
	$0.45	$1.35	$2.25	£0.30	£0.90	£1.50
Title Value:	$1.35	$4.05	$6.75	£0.90	£2.70	£4.50

JOE SINN
Caliber Press,MS; 1 Aug 1993-3 1993

1-3 ND black and white						
	$0.55	$1.65	$2.75	£0.35	£1.05	£1.75
Title Value:	$1.65	$4.95	$8.25	£1.05	£3.15	£5.25

JOHN BOLTON HALLS OF HORROR
Eclipse,MS; 1,2 Jun 1985

1-2 ND reprints	$0.40	$1.20	$2.00	£0.25	£0.75	£1.25
Title Value:	$0.80	$2.40	$4.00	£0.50	£1.50	£2.50

JOHN BYRNE'S 2112 GRAPHIC NOVEL
Dark Horse,OS; 1 Nov 1991

	$Good	$Fine	$N.Mint	£Good	£Fine	£N.Mint
1 ND 64pgs, John Byrne script and art, ties in with Next Men, squarebound						
	$2.25	$6.75	$11.25	£1.50	£4.50	£7.50
1 2nd printing, ND (Nov 1993)						
	$2.00	$6.00	$10.00	£1.30	£3.90	£6.50
1 3rd printing ND	$2.00	$6.00	$10.00	£1.30	£3.90	£6.50
Title Value:	$6.25	$18.75	$31.25	£4.10	£12.30	£20.50
Hardcover Limited Edition (Nov 1991), one copy issued free to retailers with every 100 copies of the regular graphic novel ordered. Diamond Diamond Distributors and Dark Horse silver stamps on cover.				£15.00	£45.00	£75.00

JOHN CARTER OF MARS
Gold Key; 1 Apr 1964-3 Oct 1964

1 reprints; distributed in the U.K.						
	$3.75	$11.00	$22.50	£2.50	£7.50	£15.00
2-3 reprints; distributed in the U.K.						
	$3.00	$9.00	$18.00	£2.00	£6.00	£12.00
Title Value:	$9.75	$29.00	$58.50	£6.50	£19.50	£39.00

JOHN CARTER, WARLORD OF MARS
Marvel Comics Group; 1 Jun 1977-28 Oct 1979

1 ND origin, Gil Kane art begins						
	$0.30	$0.90	$1.50	£0.20	£0.60	£1.00
2-10 ND Gil Kane art						
	$0.25	$0.75	$1.25	£0.15	£0.45	£0.75
11 ND origin Dejah Thoris						
	$0.25	$0.75	$1.25	£0.15	£0.45	£0.75
12-14 ND	$0.25	$0.75	$1.25	£0.15	£0.45	£0.75
15 ND Walt Simonson art						
	$0.30	$0.90	$1.50	£0.20	£0.60	£1.00
16-17 ND	$0.25	$0.75	$1.25	£0.15	£0.45	£0.75
18 ND Frank Miller's first published work for Marvel (see Hulk Annual #11)						
	$0.60	$1.80	$3.00	£0.50	£1.50	£2.50
19-23 ND	$0.25	$0.75	$1.25	£0.15	£0.45	£0.75
24-28	$0.15	$0.45	$0.75	£0.10	£0.35	£0.60
Title Value:	$6.95	$20.85	$34.75	£4.40	£13.45	£22.50

JOHN CARTER, WARLORD OF MARS ANNUAL
Marvel Comics Group; 1 Oct 1977-3 Oct 1979

1-3 ND 52pgs	$0.30	$0.90	$1.50	£0.20	£0.60	£1.00
Title Value:	$0.90	$2.70	$4.50	£0.60	£1.80	£3.00

JOHN FORCE MAGIC AGENT
(see Magic Agent)

JOHN LAW, DETECTIVE
Eclipse; 1 Apr 1981

1 ND previously unpublished Eisner work in colour						
	$0.40	$1.20	$2.00	£0.25	£0.75	£1.25
Title Value:	$0.40	$1.20	$2.00	£0.25	£0.75	£1.25

JOHN PAIN SPECIAL
Blackball Comics; 1 Aug 1994

1 ND Kev O'Neill art, Mike Mignola pin-up						
	$0.60	$1.80	$3.00	£0.40	£1.20	£2.00
Title Value:	$0.60	$1.80	$3.00	£0.40	£1.20	£2.00

JOHN STEED AND EMMA PEEL
(see Avengers)

JOHN STEELE SECRET AGENT
Gold Key; 1 Dec 1964
(see Freedom Agent)

1 scarce, distributed in the U.K.						
	$11.00	$34.00	$67.50	£7.50	£22.50	£45.00
Title Value:	$11.00	$34.00	$67.50	£7.50	£22.50	£45.00

JOHNNY ATOMIC
Eternity,MS; 1 Oct 1991

1 ND (cancelled after 1 issue)						
	$1.00	$3.00	$5.00	£0.65	£1.95	£3.25
Title Value:	$1.00	$3.00	$5.00	£0.65	£1.95	£3.25

JOHNNY DEMON
Dark Horse,MS; 1 May 1994-3 Jul 1994

1-3 ND Steve Leialoha cover						
	$0.45	$1.35	$2.25	£0.30	£0.90	£1.50
Title Value:	$1.35	$4.05	$6.75	£0.90	£2.70	£4.50

JOHNNY DYNAMITE
Dark Horse,MS; 1 Sep 1994-4 Dec 1994

1-4 ND Max Allan Collins and Terry Beatty						
	$0.60	$1.80	$3.00	£0.40	£1.20	£2.00
Title Value:	$2.40	$7.20	$12.00	£1.60	£4.80	£8.00

JOHNNY NEMO MAGAZINE, THE
Eclipse; 1 Sep 1985-3 Feb 1986
(see Paradax, Strange Days)

1-3 ND sub-titled "Strange Days present", Milligan/Brett Ewins art, colour						
	$1.05	$3.15	$5.25	£0.70	£2.10	£3.50
Title Value:	$3.15	$9.45	$15.75	£2.10	£6.30	£10.50

Note: originally announced as a 6 issue mini-series.

JOHNNY THUNDER
DC Comics; 1 Feb/Mar 1973-3 Jul/Aug 1973
(see All-Star Western, DC Comics Presents 28)

1 scarce in the U.K. Alex Toth and Dan Barry art, Toth cover; reprints begin from All American Western						
	$0.50	$1.50	$2.50	£0.40	£1.20	£2.00
2-3	$0.50	$1.50	$2.50	£0.30	£0.90	£1.50
Title Value:	$1.50	$4.50	$7.50	£1.00	£3.00	£5.00

REPRINT FEATURES
Johnny Thunder, Nighthawk in 1-3. Trigger Twins in 2.

JOKER, THE
DC Comics; 1 May/Jun 1975-9 Sep/Oct 1976
(see Brave and the Bold, DC Comics Presents)

	$Good	$Fine	$N.Mint	£Good	£Fine	£N.Mint
1 Two Face appears	$3.00	$9.00	$15.00	£2.00	£6.00	£10.00
2	$1.80	$5.25	$9.00	£1.20	£3.60	£6.00
3 The Creeper appears	$1.50	$4.50	$7.50	£1.00	£3.00	£5.00
4 scarce in the U.K. Green Arrow appears	$1.40	$4.20	$7.00	£1.20	£3.60	£6.00
5 scarce in the U.K. Royal Flush Gang appears	$1.40	$4.20	$7.00	£1.20	£3.60	£6.00
6 scarce in the U.K. Sherlock Holmes appears	$1.40	$4.20	$7.00	£1.20	£3.60	£6.00
7 Lex Luthor appears	$1.20	$3.60	$6.00	£1.00	£3.00	£5.00
8 scarce in the U.K. Scarecrow appears	$1.20	$3.60	$6.00	£1.20	£3.60	£6.00
9 very scarce in the U.K. Catwoman appears	$1.20	$3.60	$6.00	£1.40	£4.20	£7.00
Title Value:	$14.10	$42.15	$70.50	£11.40	£34.20	£57.00

Note: Garcia Lopez art in #2-4

JOKER: DEVIL'S ADVOCATE, THE
DC Comics,OS; nn Jan 1996

	$Good	$Fine	$N.Mint	£Good	£Fine	£N.Mint
nn ND 96pgs, Hardcover graphic novel; Chuck Dixon script, Graham Nolan and Scott Hanna art	$5.00	$15.00	$25.00	£3.20	£9.50	£16.00
Title Value:	$5.00	$15.00	$25.00	£3.20	£9.50	£16.00

JOKER: GREATEST STORIES EVER TOLD.
DC Comics; nn 1989 Hardcover

	£Good	£Fine	£N.Mint
Classic reprints. Re-coloured.	£4.00	£12.00	£20.00
nn 1989 Trade paperback (Softcover)	£2.00	£6.00	£10.00
nn 1990 Expanded version with extra stories, leather bound cover	£5.00	£15.00	£25.00

JON SABLE, FREELANCE
First; 1 Jun 1983-56 Feb 1988
(see Mike Grell's Sable)

	$Good	$Fine	$N.Mint	£Good	£Fine	£N.Mint
1-10 ND	$0.40	$1.20	$2.00	£0.25	£0.75	£1.25
11-24 ND	$0.30	$0.90	$1.50	£0.20	£0.60	£1.00
25 ND 1st Shatter backup, ends #30	$0.40	$1.20	$2.00	£0.25	£0.75	£1.25
26-33 ND	$0.30	$0.90	$1.50	£0.20	£0.60	£1.00
34-56 ND Deluxe Format	$0.40	$1.20	$2.00	£0.25	£0.75	£1.25
Title Value:	$20.20	$60.60	$101.00	£12.90	£38.70	£64.50

Note: Mike Grell art in #1-43.

JONAH HEX
DC Comics; 1 Mar/Apr 1977-92 Aug 1985
(see All-Star Western, Weird Western Tales, Hex)

	$Good	$Fine	$N.Mint	£Good	£Fine	£N.Mint
1 scarce in the U.K.	$5.50	$17.00	$40.00	£4.25	£12.50	£30.00
2 scarce in the U.K.	$3.00	$9.00	$15.00	£2.00	£6.00	£10.00
3-5 scarce in the U.K.	$2.40	$7.00	$12.00	£1.50	£4.50	£7.50
6 scarce in the U.K.	$2.00	$6.00	$10.00	£1.00	£3.00	£5.00
7-8 scarce in the U.K. dis-figurement explained	$2.00	$6.00	$10.00	£1.00	£3.00	£5.00
9 scarce in the U.K. Wrightson cover	$2.00	$6.00	$10.00	£1.00	£3.00	£5.00
10	$2.00	$6.00	$10.00	£0.90	£2.70	£4.50
11	$1.20	$3.60	$6.00	£0.70	£2.10	£3.50
12 Jim Starlin cover	$1.20	$3.60	$6.00	£0.70	£2.10	£3.50
13-15	$1.20	$3.60	$6.00	£0.70	£2.10	£3.50
16-17 ND 44pgs	$1.20	$3.60	$6.00	£0.80	£2.40	£4.00
18-20 ND 44pgs	$1.20	$3.60	$6.00	£0.70	£2.10	£3.50
21-30 ND	$0.80	$2.40	$4.00	£0.50	£1.50	£2.50
31-32 ND origin retold	$0.80	$2.40	$4.00	£0.50	£1.50	£2.50
33-35 ND	$0.80	$2.40	$4.00	£0.50	£1.50	£2.50
36-44 ND	$0.80	$2.40	$4.00	£0.40	£1.20	£2.00
45 ND Jonah Hex weds	$0.80	$2.40	$4.00	£0.40	£1.20	£2.00
46-50 ND	$0.80	$2.40	$4.00	£0.40	£1.20	£2.00
51 ND Jonah Hex becomes a father	$0.60	$1.80	$3.00	£0.30	£0.90	£1.50
52-56 ND	$0.60	$1.80	$3.00	£0.30	£0.90	£1.50
57-89	$0.60	$1.80	$3.00	£0.30	£0.90	£1.50
90 Mark Texeira cover	$0.60	$1.80	$3.00	£0.30	£0.90	£1.50
91-92	$0.60	$1.80	$3.00	£0.30	£0.90	£1.50
Title Value:	$86.90	$260.60	$447.00	£48.95	£146.60	£253.50

FEATURES
Bat Lash in 49, 51, 52. El Diablo in 48, 56-60. Scalphunter in 40, 41, 45-47. Tejano in 53-55.

JONAH HEX AND OTHER WESTERN TALES
DC Comics, Digest; 1 Sep/Oct 1979-3 Jan/Feb 1980

	$Good	$Fine	$N.Mint	£Good	£Fine	£N.Mint
1-3 ND scarce in the U.K. 100pgs	$0.45	$1.35	$2.25	£0.30	£0.90	£1.50
Title Value:	$1.35	$4.05	$6.75	£0.90	£2.70	£4.50

ARTISTS
Adams reprints in 1, 2.
REPRINT FEATURES
Billy the Kid, El Diablo in 1, 2. Outlaw in 3. Jonah Hex, Scalphunter in 1-3.

JONAH HEX SPECTACULAR
DC Comics; nn Fall 1978
(DC Special Series #16)

	$Good	$Fine	$N.Mint	£Good	£Fine	£N.Mint
nn ND 68pgs, scarce in the U.K.; Jonah Hex dies, Scalphunter and Batlash appear	$1.20	$3.60	$6.00	£0.80	£2.40	£4.00
Title Value:	$1.20	$3.60	$6.00	£0.80	£2.40	£4.00

JONAH HEX: RIDERS OF THE WORM & SUCH
DC Comics,MS; 1 Mar 1995-5 Jul 1995

	$Good	$Fine	$N.Mint	£Good	£Fine	£N.Mint
1-5 ND Joe R. Lansdale script, Tim Truman and Sam Glanzman art	$0.60	$1.80	$3.00	£0.40	£1.20	£2.00
Title Value:	$3.00	$9.00	$15.00	£2.00	£6.00	£10.00

JONAH HEX: TWO-GUN MOJO
DC Comics/Vertigo,MS; 1 Aug 1993-5 Dec 1993

	$Good	$Fine	$N.Mint	£Good	£Fine	£N.Mint
1 ND Tim Truman art begins	$0.60	$1.80	$3.00	£0.40	£1.20	£2.00
1 Platinum edition ND	$4.50	$13.50	$22.50	£3.00	£9.00	£15.00
2-5 ND	$0.60	$1.80	$3.00	£0.40	£1.20	£2.00
Title Value:	$7.50	$22.50	$37.50	£5.00	£15.00	£25.00

Jonah Hex: Two-Gun Mojo (Oct 1994)

	£Good	£Fine	£N.Mint
Trade paperback reprints mini-series, new painted cover by Tim Truman	£1.70	£5.10	£8.50

JONNI THUNDER
DC Comics,MS; 1 Feb 1985-4 Aug 1985

	$Good	$Fine	$N.Mint	£Good	£Fine	£N.Mint
1-4	$0.15	$0.45	$0.75	£0.10	£0.35	£0.60
Title Value:	$0.60	$1.80	$3.00	£0.40	£1.40	£2.40

JONNY QUEST
Comico; 1 Jun 1986-31 Dec 1988

	$Good	$Fine	$N.Mint	£Good	£Fine	£N.Mint
1 ND Doug Wildey art	$0.60	$1.80	$3.00	£0.40	£1.20	£2.00

Jimmy Olsen #133

Journey into Mystery #117

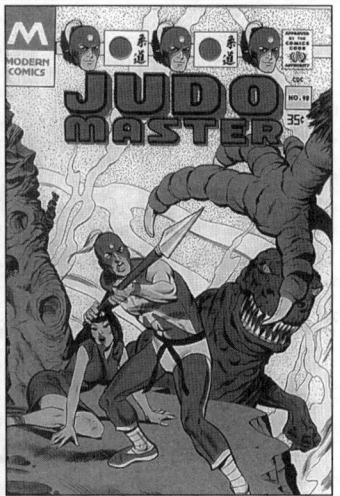

Judo Master #98

	$Good	$Fine	$N.Mint	£Good	£Fine	£N.Mint
2 ND Wendi Pini art, Pini/Rude cover	$0.45	$1.35	$2.25	£0.30	£0.90	£1.50
3 ND Dave Stevens cover	$0.45	$1.35	$2.25	£0.30	£0.90	£1.50
4 ND	$0.40	$1.20	$2.00	£0.25	£0.75	£1.25
5 ND Dave Stevens cover	$0.40	$1.20	$2.00	£0.25	£0.75	£1.25
6 ND Adam Kubert cover and art	$0.40	$1.20	$2.00	£0.25	£0.75	£1.25
7 ND Dan Spiegle art, Doug Wildey cover	$0.40	$1.20	$2.00	£0.25	£0.75	£1.25
8 ND Ken Steacy painted cover	$0.40	$1.20	$2.00	£0.25	£0.75	£1.25
9 ND Murphy Anderson art, Truman cover	$0.40	$1.20	$2.00	£0.25	£0.75	£1.25
10 ND	$0.40	$1.20	$2.00	£0.25	£0.75	£1.25
11 ND Bandit solo story, Staton art, Sienkiewicz cover	$0.40	$1.20	$2.00	£0.25	£0.75	£1.25
12 ND Dan Spiegle art	$0.40	$1.20	$2.00	£0.25	£0.75	£1.25
13 ND Carmine Infantino art	$0.40	$1.20	$2.00	£0.25	£0.75	£1.25
14-31 ND	$0.40	$1.20	$2.00	£0.25	£0.75	£1.25
Title Value:	$12.70	$38.10	$63.50	£8.00	£24.00	£40.00

JONNY QUEST CLASSICS
Comico; 1 May 1987-3 Jul 1987

	$Good	$Fine	$N.Mint	£Good	£Fine	£N.Mint
1-3 ND Doug Wildey cover and art	$0.45	$1.35	$2.25	£0.30	£0.90	£1.50
Title Value:	$1.35	$4.05	$6.75	£0.90	£2.70	£4.50

JONNY QUEST SPECIAL
Comico; 1 Sep 1988-2 Oct 1988

	$Good	$Fine	$N.Mint	£Good	£Fine	£N.Mint
1-2 ND	$0.40	$1.20	$2.00	£0.25	£0.75	£1.25
Title Value:	$0.80	$2.40	$4.00	£0.50	£1.50	£2.50

JONTAR RETURNS
Miller Publishing; 1-2 1990

	$Good	$Fine	$N.Mint	£Good	£Fine	£N.Mint
1-2 ND black and white	$0.15	$0.45	$0.75	£0.10	£0.30	£0.50
Title Value:	$0.30	$0.90	$1.50	£0.20	£0.60	£1.00

JOURNEY
Aardvark/Fantagraphics; 1 Mar 1983-27 July 1986

	$Good	$Fine	$N.Mint	£Good	£Fine	£N.Mint
1 ND scarce in the U.K.	$1.20	$3.60	$6.00	£0.80	£2.40	£4.00
2 ND	$0.80	$2.40	$4.00	£0.50	£1.50	£2.50
3-4 ND	$0.45	$1.35	$2.25	£0.30	£0.90	£1.50
5 ND scarce in the U.K.	$0.60	$1.80	$3.00	£0.40	£1.20	£2.00
6 ND scarce in the U.K.	$0.80	$2.40	$4.00	£0.50	£1.50	£2.50
7-13 ND	$0.45	$1.35	$2.25	£0.30	£0.90	£1.50
14 ND 44pgs	$0.55	$1.65	$2.75	£0.35	£1.05	£1.75
15-27 ND Fantagraphics issues	$0.45	$1.35	$2.25	£0.30	£0.90	£1.50
Title Value:	$13.85	$41.55	$69.25	£9.15	£27.45	£45.75

Journey Saga: Tall Tales
Trade paperback

	£Good	£Fine	£N.Mint
reprints #1-4 plus backups from Cerebus	£1.00	£3.00	£5.00
Book 2	£1.10	£3.30	£5.50

JOURNEY INTO MYSTERY
Atlas/Marvel Comics Group; 1 Jun 1952-125 Feb 1966
(becomes Thor)

	$Good	$Fine	$N.Mint	£Good	£Fine	£N.Mint
1 very scarce in the U.K.	$160.00	$490.00	$1800.00	£120.00	£365.00	£1350.00
2 very scarce in the U.K.	$77.50	$230.00	$625.00	£50.00	£150.00	£400.00
3-4 very scarce in the U.K.	$62.50	$185.00	$500.00	£43.00	£125.00	£340.00
5 very scarce in the U.K.	$44.00	$130.00	$350.00	£30.00	£90.00	£240.00
6-10 scarce in the U.K.	$41.00	$120.00	$325.00	£28.00	£82.50	£220.00
11-20	$33.00	$97.50	$260.00	£21.50	£65.00	£175.00
21 Kubert art	$33.00	$97.50	$260.00	£21.50	£65.00	£175.00
22 last pre-code issue	$33.00	$97.50	$260.00	£21.50	£65.00	£175.00
23-30	$20.50	$60.00	$165.00	£13.50	£41.00	£110.00
31-32	$20.00	$60.00	$160.00	£13.00	£39.00	£105.00
33 Ditko, Williamson art	$21.00	$62.50	$170.00	£14.00	£43.00	£115.00
34 Krigstein art	$20.00	$60.00	$160.00	£13.00	£39.00	£105.00
35-38	$20.00	$60.00	$160.00	£13.00	£39.00	£105.00
39 Wood art	$20.00	$60.00	$160.00	£13.00	£39.00	£105.00
40	$20.00	$60.00	$160.00	£13.00	£39.00	£105.00
41 Reed Crandall art	$16.50	$50.00	$135.00	£11.00	£34.00	£90.00
42-50	$16.50	$50.00	$135.00	£11.00	£34.00	£90.00
51 Jack Kirby, Wally Wood art	$16.50	$50.00	$135.00	£11.50	£36.00	£95.00
52-57	$15.00	$45.00	$120.00	£10.00	£30.00	£80.00
1st official distribution in the U.K.						
58 cover similar to Fantastic Four #1 (was F.F. #1 based on this?)	$15.00	$45.00	$120.00	£9.25	£28.00	£75.00
59-61	$15.00	$45.00	$120.00	£9.25	£28.00	£75.00

	$Good	$Fine	$N.Mint	£Good	£Fine	£N.Mint
62 1st appearance of Xemnu, called "The Hulk"	$22.50	$67.50	$180.00	£15.50	£47.00	£125.00
63-65	$15.00	$45.00	$120.00	£9.25	£28.00	£75.00
66 return of Xemnu, "The Hulk"	$19.00	$57.50	$155.00	£13.00	£39.00	£105.00
67-72	$14.00	$43.00	$115.00	£9.25	£28.00	£75.00
73 Spiderman prototype appears ? (unverified)	$21.00	$62.50	$170.00	£9.25	£28.00	£75.00
74	$14.00	$43.00	$115.00	£9.25	£28.00	£75.00
75 last 10 cents issue	$14.00	$43.00	$115.00	£9.25	£28.00	£75.00
76-77	$13.00	$39.00	$105.00	£8.75	£26.00	£70.00
78 Dr. Strange prototype (see Strange Tales #79 and Tales of Suspense #32)	$18.50	$55.00	$150.00	£10.00	£30.00	£80.00
79-82	$13.00	$39.00	$105.00	£8.75	£26.00	£70.00
83 origin and 1st appearance of Thor by Stan Lee and Jack Kirby	$500.00	$1500.00	$4500.00	£275.00	£830.00	£2500.00
[Scarce in high grade - Very Fine+ or better]						
83 ND very scarce in the U.K. reprint (1966)	$20.00	$60.00	$120.00	£13.00	£40.00	£80.00
83 ND very rare in the U.K reprint with Golden Record to form complete sealed package	$31.00	$92.50	$185.00	£20.50	£62.50	£125.00
84 scarce in the U.K. 2nd appearance Thor	$110.00	$335.00	$900.00	£75.00	£225.00	£600.00
[Scarce in high grade - Very Fine+ or better]						
85 1st appearance Loki, 1st appearance Heimdal, 1st appearance Odin (cameo)	$70.00	$215.00	$575.00	£44.00	£130.00	£350.00
86 1st full appearance Odin	$44.00	$130.00	$350.00	£27.00	£80.00	£215.00
87-88	$30.00	$90.00	$240.00	£18.50	£55.00	£150.00
89 reprints origin from #83	$30.00	$90.00	$240.00	£18.50	£55.00	£150.00
90 less common in the U.K. Ditko art	$18.00	$52.50	$145.00	£11.00	£34.00	£90.00
91 scarce in the U.K. Sinnott art	$15.00	$45.00	$120.00	£9.25	£28.00	£75.00
92 Sinnott art	$15.00	$45.00	$120.00	£8.75	£26.00	£70.00
93 Jack Kirby art	$18.00	$52.50	$145.00	£11.00	£34.00	£90.00
94-96 Sinnott art	$15.00	$45.00	$120.00	£8.75	£26.00	£70.00
97 Kirby art, "Tales of Asgard" begins, ends #125; 1st appearance Lava Man	$18.00	$52.50	$145.00	£10.50	£32.00	£85.00
98 1st appearance Human Cobra (later Cobra)	$15.00	$45.00	$120.00	£8.75	£26.00	£70.00
99 1st appearance Surtur, 1st appearance Mr.Hyde	$15.00	$45.00	$120.00	£8.75	£26.00	£70.00
100 less common in the U.K.	$15.00	$45.00	$120.00	£9.25	£28.00	£75.00
101 less common in the U.K. Avengers X-over	$12.00	$36.00	$85.00	£7.00	£21.00	£50.00
102 less common in the U.K. 1st appearance Sif	$12.00	$36.00	$85.00	£7.00	£21.00	£50.00
103 1st appearance Enchantress and Executioner	$12.00	$36.00	$85.00	£6.25	£19.00	£45.00
104	$12.00	$36.00	$85.00	£6.25	£19.00	£45.00
105-106 Jack Kirby art	$12.00	$36.00	$85.00	£6.00	£18.00	£42.50
107 1st appearance Grey Gargoyle	$12.00	$36.00	$85.00	£6.00	£18.00	£42.50
108 Jack Kirby art, Dr. Strange, Avengers appear	$12.00	$36.00	$85.00	£6.00	£18.00	£42.50
109 very rare in the U.K. Jack Kirby art, Magneto/Scarlet Witch/Quicksilver appear	$15.00	$45.00	$120.00	£11.00	£34.00	£90.00
[Scarce in high grade - Very Fine+ or better]						
110-111 scarce in the U.K.	$11.00	$34.00	$80.00	£6.00	£18.00	£42.50
112 very scarce in the U.K. Thor vs. Hulk, origin Loki	$18.50	$55.00	$150.00	£12.50	£38.00	£100.00
113 origin Loki	$10.50	$32.00	$75.00	£5.50	£17.00	£40.00
114	$10.50	$32.00	$75.00	£5.50	£17.00	£40.00
115 origin Loki retold, reveals more facts about origin	$12.50	$39.00	$90.00	£6.25	£19.00	£45.00
116-117	$10.00	$30.00	$70.00	£5.25	£16.00	£37.50
118 1st appearance Destroyer	$10.00	$30.00	$70.00	£5.25	£16.00	£37.50
119 1st appearance Hogun, Fandrall, Volstagg (Warriors Three)	$10.00	$30.00	$70.00	£5.25	£16.00	£37.50
120	$10.00	$30.00	$70.00	£5.25	£16.00	£37.50
121-122	$9.25	$28.00	$65.00	£4.60	£13.50	£32.50
123 last Silver Age issue cover dated December 1965	$9.25	$28.00	$65.00	£4.60	£13.50	£32.50
124 Hercules appears	$9.25	$28.00	$65.00	£4.60	£13.50	£32.50
125 Hercules appears, lead into Thor #126	$9.25	$28.00	$65.00	£5.00	£15.00	£35.00
Title Value:	$3340.25	$9997.00	$27460.00	£2109.90	£6352.00	£17482.50

ARTISTS
Kirby (Thor) art in 83-89, 93, 97, 101-125.

JOURNEY INTO MYSTERY (2ND SERIES)
Marvel Comics Group; 1 Oct 1972-19 Oct 1975

1 ND Gil Kane cover and art on Robert E. Howard adaptation, Jim Starlin art (6pgs)

	$Good	$Fine	$N.Mint	£Good	£Fine	£N.Mint
	$1.00	$3.00	$5.00	£0.60	£1.80	£3.00
2 ND Gil Kane art	$0.60	$1.80	$3.00	£0.40	£1.20	£2.00
3 ND Jim Starlin art						
	$0.60	$1.80	$3.00	£0.40	£1.20	£2.00
4 ND H.P.Lovecraft adaptation						
	$0.50	$1.50	$2.50	£0.30	£0.90	£1.50
5 ND last new material						
	$0.40	$1.20	$2.00	£0.25	£0.75	£1.25
6 ND horror/mystery reprints begin						
	$0.40	$1.20	$2.00	£0.25	£0.75	£1.25
7 ND	$0.40	$1.20	$2.00	£0.25	£0.75	£1.25
8-9	$0.40	$1.20	$2.00	£0.20	£0.60	£1.00
10-11 ND	$0.40	$1.20	$2.00	£0.25	£0.75	£1.25
12-18	$0.30	$0.90	$1.50	£0.20	£0.60	£1.00
19 ND scarce in the U.K.						
	$0.30	$0.90	$1.50	£0.30	£0.90	£1.50
Title Value:	$7.90	$23.70	$39.50	£5.05	£15.15	£25.25

JOURNEY INTO MYSTERY ANNUAL
Marvel Comics Group; 1 1965
(becomes Thor Annual)

	$Good	$Fine	$N.Mint	£Good	£Fine	£N.Mint
1 72pgs, 1st appearance Hercules, Jack Kirby art						
	$18.00	$52.50	$145.00	£10.50	£32.00	£85.00
[Scarce in high grade - Very Fine+ or better]						
Title Value:	$18.00	$52.50	$145.00	£10.50	£32.00	£85.00

JOURNEY: WARDRUMS
Fantagraphics; 1 May 1987; 2 Oct 1990; 3 Sep 1991

	$Good	$Fine	$N.Mint	£Good	£Fine	£N.Mint
1-3 ND printed in sepia						
	$0.40	$1.20	$2.00	£0.25	£0.75	£1.25
Title Value:	$1.20	$3.60	$6.00	£0.75	£2.25	£3.75

JUDGE DREDD
DC Comics; 1 Aug 1994-18 Jan 1996

	$Good	$Fine	$N.Mint	£Good	£Fine	£N.Mint
1 ND Andrew Hefler and Mike Oerning creative team						
	$0.40	$1.20	$2.00	£0.40	£1.20	£2.00
2-10 ND	$0.40	$1.20	$2.00	£0.25	£0.75	£1.25
11-18 ND	$0.45	$1.35	$2.25	£0.30	£0.90	£1.50
Title Value:	$7.60	$22.80	$38.00	£5.05	£15.15	£25.25

JUDGE DREDD
(see British section)

JUDGE DREDD: LEGENDS OF THE LAW
DC Comics; 1 Dec 1994-present

	$Good	$Fine	$N.Mint	£Good	£Fine	£N.Mint
1 ND Alan Grant and John Wagner script, Brent Anderson and Jimmy Palmiotti art. Painted cover by Dave Dorman						
	$0.40	$1.20	$2.00	£0.25	£0.75	£1.25
2-4 ND painted cover by Dave Dorman						
	$0.40	$1.20	$2.00	£0.25	£0.75	£1.25
5-6 ND painted cover by John Higgins						
	$0.40	$1.20	$2.00	£0.25	£0.75	£1.25
7 ND painted cover by John Higgins						
	$0.45	$1.35	$2.25	£0.30	£0.90	£1.50
8-10 ND John Byrne script						
	$0.45	$1.35	$2.25	£0.30	£0.90	£1.50
11-13 ND John Byrne cover						
	$0.45	$1.35	$2.25	£0.30	£0.90	£1.50
Title Value:	$5.55	$16.65	$27.75	£3.60	£10.80	£18.00

JUDGE DREDD: THE OFFICIAL MOVIE ADAPTATION
DC Comics, Film; nn Aug 1995

	$Good	$Fine	$N.Mint	£Good	£Fine	£N.Mint
nn ND 64pgs, Andrew Hefler script, Carlos Esquerra art						
	$1.20	$3.60	$6.00	£0.80	£2.40	£4.00
Title Value:	$1.20	$3.60	$6.00	£0.80	£2.40	£4.00

JUDGEMENT DAY
Lightning Comics; 1 Nov 1993-present

	$Good	$Fine	$N.Mint	£Good	£Fine	£N.Mint
1 ND gold prism cover						
	$0.90	$2.70	$4.50	£0.60	£1.80	£3.00
2 ND pre-bagged with trading card						
	$0.60	$1.80	$3.00	£0.40	£1.20	£2.00
2 ND signed and numbered edition						
	$1.80	$5.25	$9.00	£1.20	£3.60	£6.00
3-9 ND	$0.60	$1.80	$3.00	£0.40	£1.20	£2.00
10 ND 1st appearances Rook, Visage, Autobahn and Tracker						
	$0.60	$1.80	$3.00	£0.40	£1.20	£2.00
Title Value:	$8.10	$24.15	$40.50	£5.40	£16.20	£27.00

JUDO MASTER
Charlton; 89 May/Jun 1966-97 Oct 1967; Modern Comics; 98 Dec 1967
(see Special War Series) (previously Gunmaster)

	$Good	$Fine	$N.Mint	£Good	£Fine	£N.Mint
89 Judo Master vs. Mountain Storm; Frank McLaughlin art begins; distributed in the U.K.						
	$3.00	$9.00	$15.00	£2.00	£6.00	£10.00
90 distributed in the U.K.						
	$2.25	$6.75	$11.25	£1.50	£4.50	£7.50
91 Judo Master vs. The Cat, distributed in the U.K.; Sarge Steel back-up begins (ends #98)						
	$1.80	$5.25	$9.00	£1.20	£3.60	£6.00
92 The Smiling Skull appears; distributed in the U.K.						
	$1.80	$5.25	$9.00	£1.20	£3.60	£6.00
93 intro The Tiger who becomes Judo Master's partner; distributed in the U.K.						
	$1.80	$5.25	$9.00	£1.20	£3.60	£6.00
94 Mountain Storm appears; distributed in the U.K.						
	$1.80	$5.25	$9.00	£1.20	£3.60	£6.00
95-96 The Acrobat appears; distributed in the U.K.						
	$1.80	$5.25	$9.00	£1.20	£3.60	£6.00
97-98 distributed in the U.K.						
	$1.80	$5.25	$9.00	£1.20	£3.60	£6.00
Title Value:	$19.65	$57.75	$98.25	£13.10	£39.30	£65.50

JUGULAR
Blackout Comics; 0 Dec 1995-present

	$Good	$Fine	$N.Mint	£Good	£Fine	£N.Mint
0 ND Hari Kari appears, opening sequence by Mike Baron, Christopher Moeller						
	$0.60	$1.80	$3.00	£0.40	£1.20	£2.00
Title Value:	$0.60	$1.80	$3.00	£0.40	£1.20	£2.00

JUNGLE ACTION
Marvel Comics Group; 1 Oct 1972-24 Nov 1976
(see Black Panther)

	$Good	$Fine	$N.Mint	£Good	£Fine	£N.Mint
1 ND scarce in the U.K. 1950s reprints of minor classic jungle characters begins						
	$1.20	$3.60	$6.00	£0.50	£1.50	£2.50
2-4 ND	$0.60	$1.80	$3.00	£0.30	£0.90	£1.50
5 ND 1st of Black Panther series						
	$1.20	$3.60	$6.00	£0.60	£1.80	£3.00
6 ND	$0.80	$2.40	$4.00	£0.50	£1.50	£2.50
7 ND	$0.60	$1.80	$3.00	£0.40	£1.20	£2.00
8 ND origin retold	$0.60	$1.80	$3.00	£0.40	£1.20	£2.00
9-10 ND	$0.60	$1.80	$3.00	£0.40	£1.20	£2.00
11-13	$0.40	$1.20	$2.00	£0.25	£0.75	£1.25
14 terrific Gil Kane dinosaur cover						
	$0.40	$1.20	$2.00	£0.25	£0.75	£1.25
15-22	$0.40	$1.20	$2.00	£0.25	£0.75	£1.25
23 Daredevil appears						
	$0.40	$1.20	$2.00	£0.25	£0.75	£1.25
24 ND	$0.40	$1.20	$2.00	£0.25	£0.75	£1.25
Title Value:	$13.00	$39.00	$65.00	£7.60	£22.80	£38.00

JUNGLE ADVENTURES
I.W. Super; 10,12,15,17,18 1963-1964

	$Good	$Fine	$N.Mint	£Good	£Fine	£N.Mint
10-18 distributed in the U.K. all reprints						
	$2.25	$6.75	$13.50	£1.50	£4.50	£9.00
Title Value:	$11.25	$33.75	$67.50	£7.50	£22.50	£45.00

JUNGLE BOOK GRAPHIC ALBUM, THE
Disney,OS; nn Sep 1990

	$Good	$Fine	$N.Mint	£Good	£Fine	£N.Mint
nn ND 64pgs, adaptation of film						
	$1.05	$3.15	$5.25	£0.70	£2.10	£3.50
Title Value:	$1.05	$3.15	$5.25	£0.70	£2.10	£3.50
Comic Book Edition				£0.35	£1.05	£1.75

JUNGLE COMICS
Blackthorne; 1 May 1988-6 1988

	$Good	$Fine	$N.Mint	£Good	£Fine	£N.Mint
1 ND Bruce Jones scripts begin, Dave Stevens cover						
	$0.45	$1.35	$2.25	£0.30	£0.90	£1.50
2-6 ND	$0.40	$1.20	$2.00	£0.25	£0.75	£1.25
Title Value:	$2.45	$7.35	$12.25	£1.55	£4.65	£7.75

JUNGLE GIRLS
AC Comics; 1 1991-16 1993

	$Good	$Fine	$N.Mint	£Good	£Fine	£N.Mint
1 ND new material begins plus "jungle girl art" reprints such as Nyoka the Jungle Girl and Cave Girl by Bob Powell						
	$0.45	$1.35	$2.25	£0.30	£0.90	£1.50
2-16 ND	$0.45	$1.35	$2.25	£0.30	£0.90	£1.50
Title Value:	$7.20	$21.60	$36.00	£4.80	£14.40	£24.00

JUNGLE TALES OF TARZAN
Charlton; 1 Dec 1964-4 Jul 1965; 5 Sep 1965?

	$Good	$Fine	$N.Mint	£Good	£Fine	£N.Mint
1 rare, distributed in the U.K.						
	$3.75	$11.00	$22.50	£2.50	£7.50	£15.00
2-4 scarce, distributed in the U.K.						
	$3.00	$9.00	$18.00	£2.00	£6.00	£12.00
5 extremely rare (see note below)						
	$31.00	$92.50	$187.50	£20.50	£62.50	£125.00
Title Value:	$43.75	$130.50	$264.00	£29.00	£88.00	£176.00

Note: very few copies of issue #5 exist as virtually the entire print run was destroyed and it is therefore extremely rare in both the U.S. and U.K.

JUNGLE TWINS, THE (TONO AND KONO)
Gold Key; 1 Apr 1972-17 Nov 1975; Whitman; 18 May 1972

	$Good	$Fine	$N.Mint	£Good	£Fine	£N.Mint
1 scarce in the U.K. painted covers begin						
	$1.50	$4.50	$7.50	£1.00	£3.00	£5.00
2	$0.90	$2.70	$4.50	£0.60	£1.80	£3.00
3	$0.80	$2.40	$4.00	£0.50	£1.50	£2.50
4 16pg Fun Catalogue insert						
	$0.70	$2.10	$3.50	£0.45	£1.35	£2.25
5-11	$0.60	$1.80	$3.00	£0.40	£1.20	£2.00
12 dinosaur cover; 16pg Fun Catalogue insert						
	$0.70	$2.10	$3.50	£0.45	£1.35	£2.25
13 flying saucer cover						
	$0.60	$1.80	$3.00	£0.40	£1.20	£2.00
14-17	$0.60	$1.80	$3.00	£0.40	£1.20	£2.00
18 scarce in the U.K. reprint; line drawn cover						
	$0.45	$1.35	$2.25	£0.30	£0.90	£1.50
Title Value:	$12.25	$36.75	$61.25	£8.10	£24.30	£40.50

Note: irregularly distributed in the U.K.

JUNIOR CARROT PATROL
Dark Horse,OS; 1 May 1989

	$Good	$Fine	$N.Mint	£Good	£Fine	£N.Mint
1 ND Rick Geary art						
	$0.45	$1.35	$2.25	£0.30	£0.90	£1.50
Title Value:	$0.45	$1.35	$2.25	£0.30	£0.90	£1.50

JUNIOR WOODCHUCKS
Disney,MS; 1 Jun 1991-4 Sep 1991

	$Good	$Fine	$N.Mint	£Good	£Fine	£N.Mint
1-4 ND Carl Bark reprints plus new material						
	$0.25	$0.75	$1.25	£0.15	£0.45	£0.75
Title Value:	$1.00	$3.00	$5.00	£0.60	£1.80	£3.00

JUNKWAFFEL
Last Gasp; 1-4 1988

	$Good	$Fine	$N.Mint	£Good	£Fine	£N.Mint
1-4 ND Vaughn Bode script and art; black and white						
	$0.25	$0.75	$1.25	£0.15	£0.45	£0.75

	$Good	$Fine	$N.Mint	£Good	£Fine	£N.Mint
Title Value:	$1.00	$3.00	$5.00	£0.60	£1.80	£3.00

JURASSIC PARK
Topps,MS; 1 Jun 1993-4 Sep 1993
1 Gil Kane and George Perez art begins

	$0.45	$1.35	$2.25	£0.30	£0.90	£1.50

1 Collector's Edition - pre-bagged with 3 trading cards, Walt Simonson script with Gil Kane pencils and George Perez inks

	$0.80	$2.40	$4.00	£0.50	£1.50	£2.50

1 Gold Edition - gold prismatic cover

	$3.00	$9.00	$15.00	£1.50	£4.50	£7.50
2	$0.45	$1.35	$2.25	£0.30	£0.90	£1.50

2 Collector's Edition - pre-bagged with 3 trading cards, Walt Simonson script with Gil Kane pencils and George Perez inks

	$0.60	$1.80	$3.00	£0.40	£1.20	£2.00
3	$0.45	$1.35	$2.25	£0.30	£0.90	£1.50

3 Collector's Edition - pre-bagged with 3 trading cards, Walt Simonson script with Gil Kane pencils and George Perez inks

	$0.60	$1.80	$3.00	£0.40	£1.20	£2.00
4	$0.45	$1.35	$2.25	£0.30	£0.90	£1.50

4 Collector's Edition - pre-bagged with 3 trading cards, Walt Simonson script with Gil Kane pencils and George Perez inks

	$1.50	$4.50	$3.00	£1.00	£3.00	£2.00
Title Value:	$8.30	$24.90	$37.00	£5.00	£15.00	£22.00

Note: all Non-Distributed on the news-stands in the U.K.

JURASSIC PARK ADVENTURES
Topps; 1 Jul 1994-present
1-10 ND reprints Jurassic Park: Raptor titles

	$0.40	$1.20	$2.00	£0.25	£0.75	£1.25
Title Value:	$4.00	$12.00	$20.00	£2.50	£7.50	£12.50

JURASSIC PARK ANNUAL
Topps; 1 May 1995-present
1 ND two stories, Michael Golden cover

	$0.80	$2.40	$4.00	£0.50	£1.50	£2.50
Title Value:	$0.80	$2.40	$4.00	£0.50	£1.50	£2.50

JURASSIC PARK, RETURN TO
Topps; 1 Apr 1995-present
1 ND Steve Englehart script, Joe Staton and Rich Rankin art, Michael Golden cover - Direct Market Edition

	$0.45	$1.35	$2.25	£0.30	£0.90	£1.50

1 ND Steve Englehart script, Joe Staton and Rich Rankin art, Michael Golden cover - News-stand Edition

	$0.45	$1.35	$2.25	£0.30	£0.90	£1.50

2 ND Steve Englehart script, Joe Staton and Rich Rankin art, Michael Golden cover

	$0.45	$1.35	$2.25	£0.30	£0.90	£1.50

3-4 ND Steve Englehart script, Joe Staton and Rich Rankin art, Michael Golden cover; $2.95 cover

	$0.60	$1.80	$3.00	£0.40	£1.20	£2.00

5 ND Tom and Mary Bierbaum script, Armando Gil and Fred Carillo art; Michael Golden cover

	$0.60	$1.80	$3.00	£0.40	£1.20	£2.00
6-8 ND	$0.60	$1.80	$3.00	£0.40	£1.20	£2.00
Title Value:	$4.95	$14.85	$24.75	£3.30	£9.90	£16.50

JURASSIC PARK: RAPTOR
Topps,MS; 1 Nov 1993-2 Dec 1993
1 ND pre-bagged with trading cards plus Zorro #0; Michael Golden cover

	$0.45	$1.35	$2.25	£0.30	£0.90	£1.50

2 ND pre-bagged with trading cards; Michael Golden cover

	$0.45	$1.35	$2.25	£0.30	£0.90	£1.50
Title Value:	$0.90	$2.70	$4.50	£0.60	£1.80	£3.00

JURASSIC PARK: RAPTOR'S ATTACK
Topps,MS; 1 Mar 1994-4 Jun 1994
1-4 ND Steve Englehart script and Armando Gil art; covers by Michael Golden

	$0.45	$1.35	$2.25	£0.30	£0.90	£1.50
Title Value:	$1.80	$5.40	$9.00	£1.20	£3.60	£6.00

JURASSIC PARK: RAPTOR'S HIJACK
Topps,MS; 1 Jul 1994-4 Oct 1994
1-4 ND Steve Englehart script, Michael Golden cover

	$0.45	$1.35	$2.25	£0.30	£0.90	£1.50
Title Value:	$1.80	$5.40	$9.00	£1.20	£3.60	£6.00

JUST IMAGINE COMICS AND STORIES
Just Imagine; 1 1987-12 1987

1-12 ND	$0.25	$0.75	$1.25	£0.15	£0.45	£0.75
Title Value:	$3.00	$9.00	$15.00	£1.80	£5.40	£9.00

JUST IMAGINE COMICS AND STORIES SPECIAL
Just Imagine; 1 1987
1 ND features The Mildly Micro-Waved Pre-Pubescent Kung-Fu Gophers

	$0.30	$0.90	$1.50	£0.20	£0.60	£1.00
Title Value:	$0.30	$0.90	$1.50	£0.20	£0.60	£1.00

JUSTICE
Marvel Comics Group/New Universe; 1 Nov 1986-32 Jun 1989

1-3 ND	$0.25	$0.75	$1.25	£0.15	£0.45	£0.75

4-5 ND Salmons art

	$0.25	$0.75	$1.25	£0.15	£0.45	£0.75
6-8 ND	$0.25	$0.75	$1.25	£0.15	£0.45	£0.75

9-10 ND Giffen art

	$0.25	$0.75	$1.25	£0.15	£0.45	£0.75

11-14 ND Giffen art

	$0.15	$0.45	$0.75	£0.10	£0.35	£0.60

15 ND Peter David scripts begin (end 22), Nightmask X-over

	$0.15	$0.45	$0.75	£0.10	£0.35	£0.60
16-17 ND	$0.15	$0.45	$0.75	£0.10	£0.35	£0.60

18 ND The Pitt X-over

	$0.15	$0.45	$0.75	£0.10	£0.35	£0.60
19-28 ND	$0.15	$0.45	$0.75	£0.10	£0.35	£0.60

29 ND Psi-Force X-over

	$0.15	$0.45	$0.75	£0.10	£0.35	£0.60

	$Good	$Fine	$N.Mint	£Good	£Fine	£N.Mint
30-31 ND	$0.15	$0.45	$0.75	£0.10	£0.35	£0.60

32 ND unauthorised appearance of The Joker

	$0.60	$1.80	$3.00	£0.30	£0.90	£1.50
Title Value:	$6.25	$18.75	$31.25	£3.90	£12.75	£21.60

Note: Peter David scripts #19-31

JUSTICE INC.
DC Comics; 1 May/Jun 1975-4 Nov/Dec 1975
1 The Avenger begins

	$0.30	$0.90	$1.50	£0.20	£0.60	£1.00

2-4 ND Jack Kirby art

	$0.30	$0.90	$1.50	£0.20	£0.60	£1.00
Title Value:	$1.20	$3.60	$6.00	£0.80	£2.40	£4.00

JUSTICE INC. (2ND SERIES)
DC Comics,MS; 1 Aug 1989-2 Sep 1989
1-2 ND 48pgs, squarebound

	$0.70	$2.10	$3.50	£0.40	£1.20	£2.00
Title Value:	$1.40	$4.20	$7.00	£0.80	£2.40	£4.00

Note: Mature Readers label.

JUSTICE LEAGUE
DC Comics; 0 Oct 1994; 1 May 1987-present
(see Legends #6) (becomes Justice League International with issue #7) (reverts back to Justice League with issue #28)
0 (Oct 1994) Zero Hour X-over, the formation of a new Justice League

	$0.40	$1.20	$2.00	£0.25	£0.75	£1.25

1 LD in the U.K. new line-up: Batman, Blue Beetle, Captain Marvel, Black Canary, Green Lantern (Guy Gardner), Mister Miracle, Dr. Fate, Oberon, Martian Manhunter, Dr.Light; Giffen story, Maguire/Austin art begins

	$1.20	$3.60	$6.00	£0.80	£2.40	£4.00
2 LD in the U.K.	$0.80	$2.40	$4.00	£0.60	£1.80	£3.00
3 regular cover	$0.60	$1.80	$3.00	£0.50	£1.50	£2.50

3 ND test cover, very rare in the U.K. and rare in the U.S. (see note below)

	$12.00	$36.00	$60.00	£4.00	£12.00	£20.00

4 Booster Gold appears

	$0.60	$1.80	$3.00	£0.40	£1.20	£2.00

5 The Creeper appears, Batman vs Guy Gardner

	$0.60	$1.80	$3.00	£0.40	£1.20	£2.00

6 The Grey Man, Creeper appears

	$0.50	$1.50	$2.50	£0.30	£0.90	£1.50

7 48pgs, Maguire art; new direction, Captain Marvel leaves, Captain Atom/Rocket Red/Booster Gold join, Superman/President Reagan cameo

	$0.80	$2.40	$4.00	£0.50	£1.50	£2.50
8	$0.50	$1.50	$2.50	£0.30	£0.90	£1.50

9-10 Millennium X-over

	$0.50	$1.50	$2.50	£0.30	£0.90	£1.50
11-12	$0.40	$1.20	$2.00	£0.25	£0.75	£1.25

13 X-over with Suicide Squad #13

	$0.40	$1.20	$2.00	£0.25	£0.75	£1.25

14-15 no Maguire art

	$0.40	$1.20	$2.00	£0.25	£0.75	£1.25
16-17	$0.40	$1.20	$2.00	£0.25	£0.75	£1.25

18 Lobo vs. Guy Gardner

	$0.40	$1.20	$2.00	£0.25	£0.75	£1.25

19 Guy Gardner vs. Lobo

	$0.40	$1.20	$2.00	£0.25	£0.75	£1.25

20-21 no Maguire art, Lobo appears

	$0.40	$1.20	$2.00	£0.25	£0.75	£1.25

22-23 Invasion X-over

	$0.40	$1.20	$2.00	£0.25	£0.75	£1.25

24 DS new team intro to become Justice League Europe spin off

	$0.40	$1.20	$2.00	£0.25	£0.75	£1.25
25	$0.40	$1.20	$2.00	£0.25	£0.75	£1.25
26-30	$0.30	$0.90	$1.50	£0.20	£0.60	£1.00

31-32 Justice League Europe X-over

	$0.30	$0.90	$1.50	£0.20	£0.60	£1.00
33-36	$0.30	$0.90	$1.50	£0.20	£0.60	£1.00

37 X-over with Justice League Europe #13

	$0.30	$0.90	$1.50	£0.20	£0.60	£1.00
38-49	$0.30	$0.90	$1.50	£0.20	£0.60	£1.00

50 48pgs, conclusion General Glory story

	$0.45	$1.35	$2.25	£0.30	£0.90	£1.50
51	$0.25	$0.75	$1.25	£0.15	£0.45	£0.75

52 Blue Beetle vs. Guy Gardner, Batman guest-stars

	$0.25	$0.75	$1.25	£0.15	£0.45	£0.75
53	$0.25	$0.75	$1.25	£0.15	£0.45	£0.75

54 story continues in League Europe #30

	$0.25	$0.75	$1.25	£0.15	£0.45	£0.75

55 War of the Gods tie-in

	$0.25	$0.75	$1.25	£0.15	£0.45	£0.75

56 Breakdowns part 1, story continues in Justice League Europe #32

	$0.25	$0.75	$1.25	£0.15	£0.45	£0.75

57 story continues in Justice League Europe #33

	$0.25	$0.75	$1.25	£0.15	£0.45	£0.75

58 story continues in Justice League Europe #34

	$0.25	$0.75	$1.25	£0.15	£0.45	£0.75

59 story continues in Justice League Europe #35

	$0.25	$0.75	$1.25	£0.15	£0.45	£0.75

60 conclusion of Breakdowns story

	$0.25	$0.75	$1.25	£0.15	£0.45	£0.75

61 new direction for title, cover based on the classic Justice League of America #1

	$0.25	$0.75	$1.25	£0.15	£0.45	£0.75
62-68	$0.25	$0.75	$1.25	£0.15	£0.45	£0.75

69 LD in the U.K. Superman: Doomsday tie-in, story continued in Superman #74

	$Good	$Fine	$N.Mint	£Good	£Fine	£N.Mint
	$1.40	$4.20	$7.00	£0.60	£1.80	£3.00
69 2nd printing, II in box on cover	$0.25	$0.75	$1.25	£0.15	£0.45	£0.75
70 ties in with Superman #75; red card-stock part outer cover	$1.20	$3.60	$6.00	£0.40	£1.20	£2.00
70 2nd printing, II in box on cover	$0.25	$0.75	$1.25	£0.15	£0.45	£0.75
71	$0.25	$0.75	$1.25	£0.15	£0.45	£0.75
72 Justice League history re-told; Green Arrow, Black Canary and Atom return	$0.25	$0.75	$1.25	£0.15	£0.45	£0.75
73	$0.25	$0.75	$1.25	£0.15	£0.45	£0.75
74-75 original Justice League of America appear	$0.25	$0.75	$1.25	£0.15	£0.45	£0.75
76-78	$0.25	$0.75	$1.25	£0.15	£0.45	£0.75
79-80 bi-weekly	$0.25	$0.75	$1.25	£0.15	£0.45	£0.75
81	$0.25	$0.75	$1.25	£0.15	£0.45	£0.75
82 X-over Guy Gardner #14	$0.25	$0.75	$1.25	£0.15	£0.45	£0.75
83 X-over Guy Gardner #15	$0.25	$0.75	$1.25	£0.15	£0.45	£0.75
84-85	$0.25	$0.75	$1.25	£0.15	£0.45	£0.75
86-88 Cult of the Machine story	$0.25	$0.75	$1.25	£0.15	£0.45	£0.75
89 Judgement Day part 1, continued in Justice League Task Force #13	$0.25	$0.75	$1.25	£0.15	£0.45	£0.75
90 Judgement Day part 4, continued in Justice League Task Force #14	$0.25	$0.75	$1.25	£0.15	£0.45	£0.75
91 Aftershocks part 1, continued in Justice League Task Force #15	$0.30	$0.90	$1.50	£0.20	£0.60	£1.00
92 Zero Hour X-over	$0.30	$0.90	$1.50	£0.20	£0.60	£1.00
93-97	$0.30	$0.90	$1.50	£0.20	£0.60	£1.00
98 Blue Devil, Ice Maiden and the new Wonder Woman join the team	$0.30	$0.90	$1.50	£0.20	£0.60	£1.00
99	$0.30	$0.90	$1.50	£0.20	£0.60	£1.00
100 48pgs	$0.60	$1.80	$3.00	£0.40	£1.20	£2.00
100 48pgs, holographic foil-enhanced cover (different art to Standard Edition)	$0.80	$2.40	$4.00	£0.50	£1.50	£2.50
101 Way of the Warrior part 2, continued in Hawkman #22	$0.35	$1.05	$1.75	£0.25	£0.75	£1.25
102 Way of the Warrior part 5, continued in Hawkman #23	$0.35	$1.05	$1.75	£0.25	£0.75	£1.25
103-104	$0.35	$1.05	$1.75	£0.25	£0.75	£1.25
105-106 Underworld Unleashed tie-in	$0.35	$1.05	$1.75	£0.25	£0.75	£1.25
107-109	$0.35	$1.05	$1.75	£0.25	£0.75	£1.25
Title Value:	$52.50	$157.50	$262.50	£29.45	£88.35	£147.25

JUSTICE LEAGUE AMERICA
(see Justice League)

JUSTICE LEAGUE ANNUAL

DC Comics; 1 Sep 1987-present
(becomes Justice League International Annual with issue 2)
(becomes Justice League America Annual with issue 4)

	$Good	$Fine	$N.Mint	£Good	£Fine	£N.Mint
1 48pgs, Giffen, P. Craig Russell and other art	$0.45	$1.35	$2.25	£0.30	£0.90	£1.50
2 48pgs, Joker appears	$0.45	$1.35	$2.25	£0.40	£1.20	£2.00
3 48pgs	$0.45	$1.35	$2.25	£0.30	£0.90	£1.50
4 64pgs, squarebound, intro Justice League Antarctica	$0.45	$1.35	$2.25	£0.30	£0.90	£1.50
5 64pgs, Armageddon 2001 tie-in	$0.45	$1.35	$2.25	£0.30	£0.90	£1.50
5 2nd printing, silver ink cover (Feb 1992)	$0.40	$1.20	$2.00	£0.25	£0.75	£1.25
6 64pgs, Eclipso: The Darkness Within tie-in, Wonder Woman guest stars	$0.45	$1.35	$2.25	£0.30	£0.90	£1.50
7 64pgs, Bloodlines (Wave Two) part 15, 1st appearance Terrorsmith, continued in Adventures of Superman Annual #5	$0.45	$1.35	$2.25	£0.30	£0.90	£1.50
8 64pgs, Elseworlds	$0.55	$1.65	$2.75	£0.35	£1.05	£1.75
9 64pgs, Year One	$0.80	$2.40	$4.00	£0.50	£1.50	£2.50
Title Value:	$4.90	$14.70	$24.50	£3.30	£9.90	£16.50

JUSTICE LEAGUE EUROPE

DC Comics; 1 Apr 1989-68 Sep 1994
(title becomes "Justice League International with #51)

	$Good	$Fine	$N.Mint	£Good	£Fine	£N.Mint
1	$0.40	$1.20	$2.00	£0.30	£0.90	£1.50
2-5	$0.30	$0.90	$1.50	£0.25	£0.75	£1.25
6	$0.30	$0.90	$1.50	£0.20	£0.60	£1.00
7-8 Justice League America X-Over	$0.30	$0.90	$1.50	£0.20	£0.60	£1.00
9-10	$0.30	$0.90	$1.50	£0.20	£0.60	£1.00
11 Metamorpho appears	$0.25	$0.75	$1.25	£0.15	£0.45	£0.75
12 Metamorpho/Metal Men appear	$0.25	$0.75	$1.25	£0.15	£0.45	£0.75
13 X-over with Justice League America #37	$0.25	$0.75	$1.25	£0.15	£0.45	£0.75
14-20	$0.25	$0.75	$1.25	£0.15	£0.45	£0.75
21 line-up change	$0.25	$0.75	$1.25	£0.15	£0.45	£0.75
22-29	$0.25	$0.75	$1.25	£0.15	£0.45	£0.75
30 story continues in Justice League America #55	$0.25	$0.75	$1.25	£0.15	£0.45	£0.75
31 War of the Gods tie-in (unofficial)	$0.25	$0.75	$1.25	£0.15	£0.45	£0.75
32 new Doom Patrol cameo, story continued from Justice League America #56	$0.25	$0.75	$1.25	£0.15	£0.45	£0.75
33 story continued from Justice League America #57	$0.25	$0.75	$1.25	£0.15	£0.45	£0.75
34 story continued from Justice League America #58	$0.25	$0.75	$1.25	£0.15	£0.45	£0.75
35 story continued from Justice League America #59	$0.25	$0.75	$1.25	£0.15	£0.45	£0.75
36 Breakdowns epilogue, leads into Justice League Spectacular #1	$0.25	$0.75	$1.25	£0.15	£0.45	£0.75
37 Batman guest-stars, bi-weekly	$0.25	$0.75	$1.25	£0.15	£0.45	£0.75
38-40 bi-weekly	$0.25	$0.75	$1.25	£0.15	£0.45	£0.75
41 Wonder Woman and Metamorpho appear	$0.25	$0.75	$1.25	£0.15	£0.45	£0.75
42-44	$0.25	$0.75	$1.25	£0.15	£0.45	£0.75
45-49 Red Winter story	$0.25	$0.75	$1.25	£0.15	£0.45	£0.75
50 48pgs, Red Winter story conclusion	$0.30	$0.90	$1.50	£0.20	£0.60	£1.00
51 title becomes "Justice League International"	$0.25	$0.75	$1.25	£0.15	£0.45	£0.75
52-53	$0.25	$0.75	$1.25	£0.15	£0.45	£0.75
54-56 bi-weekly	$0.25	$0.75	$1.25	£0.15	£0.45	£0.75
57-60	$0.25	$0.75	$1.25	£0.15	£0.45	£0.75
61-64	$0.30	$0.90	$1.50	£0.20	£0.60	£1.00

Jungle Twins #4

Jurassic Park #1

Justice League of America #100

MINT = 100% / NEAR MINT (inc. +/-) = 90–99% / VERY FINE (inc. +/-) = 75–89% / FINE (inc. +/-) = 55–74%
VERY GOOD (inc. +/-) = 35–54% / GOOD (inc. +/-) = 15–34% / FAIR = 5–14% / POOR = 1–4%

415

	$Good	$Fine	$N.Mint	£Good	£Fine	£N.Mint
65 continued from Justice League Task Force #13, continued in Justice League America #90	$0.30	$0.90	$1.50	£0.20	£0.60	£1.00
66 concluded from Justice League Task Force #14	$0.30	$0.90	$1.50	£0.20	£0.60	£1.00
67 Aftershocks part 3 (of 3)	$0.30	$0.90	$1.50	£0.20	£0.60	£1.00
68 Zero Hour X-over	$0.30	$0.90	$1.50	£0.20	£0.60	£1.00
Title Value:	$18.05	$54.15	$90.25	£11.45	£34.35	£57.25

JUSTICE LEAGUE EUROPE ANNUAL

DC Comics; 1 Jun 1990-5 1994
(becomes Justice League International Annual with issue #4)

	$Good	$Fine	$N.Mint	£Good	£Fine	£N.Mint
1 48pgs, return of new Dr. Light	$0.45	$1.35	$2.25	£0.30	£0.90	£1.50
2 64pgs, Aramageddon: 2001 tie-in, Bat-Lash, Jonah Hex, Demon and Legion of Super-Heroes appear	$0.45	$1.35	$2.25	£0.30	£0.90	£1.50
3 64pgs, Eclipso: The Darkness Within tie-in, Power Girl "eclipsed"	$0.45	$1.35	$2.25	£0.30	£0.90	£1.50
4 64pgs, Bloodlines part 9, 1st appearance Lionheart, continued in Robin Annual #2	$0.45	$1.35	$2.25	£0.30	£0.90	£1.50
5 64pgs, Elseworlds story, Gerard Jones script and Kiki Chansamone art	$0.60	$1.80	$3.00	£0.40	£1.20	£2.00
Title Value:	$2.40	$7.20	$12.00	£1.60	£4.80	£8.00

JUSTICE LEAGUE INTERNATIONAL

(see Justice League #7-28, and Justice League Europe #51 onwards)

JUSTICE LEAGUE INTERNATIONAL SPECIAL

DC Comics; 1 Feb 1990-2 1991

	$Good	$Fine	$N.Mint	£Good	£Fine	£N.Mint
1 48pgs	$0.45	$1.35	$2.25	£0.30	£0.90	£1.50
2 48pgs, The Huntress appears	$0.45	$1.35	$2.25	£0.30	£0.90	£1.50
Title Value:	$0.90	$2.70	$4.50	£0.60	£1.80	£3.00

JUSTICE LEAGUE OF AMERICA

National Periodical Publications/DC Comics; 1 Oct/Nov 1960-261 Apr 1987

	$Good	$Fine	$N.Mint	£Good	£Fine	£N.Mint
1 scarce in the U.K. origin and 1st appearance Despero	$360.00	$1075.00	$3250.00	£270.00	£810.00	£2450.00
[Very scarce in high grade - Very Fine+ or better]						
2	$92.50	$280.00	$750.00	£62.50	£185.00	£500.00
3 origin and 1st appearance Kanjar Ro; see Mystery in Space #75	$75.00	$225.00	$600.00	£50.00	£150.00	£400.00
[Scarce in high grade - Very Fine or better]						
4 Green Arrow joins	$50.00	$150.00	$400.00	£34.00	£100.00	£270.00
5 origin and 1st appearance Dr. Destiny	$41.00	$120.00	$325.00	£26.00	£77.50	£210.00
6 origin Professor Amos Fortune	$33.00	$97.50	$265.00	£21.50	£65.00	£175.00
7-8	$33.00	$97.50	$265.00	£21.50	£65.00	£175.00
9 origin Justice League of America (origin untold in Brave and the Bold #28)	$46.00	$135.00	$415.00	£31.00	£90.00	£275.00
10 origin Felix Faust	$33.00	$97.50	$265.00	£21.50	£65.00	£175.00
11	$26.00	$75.00	$180.00	£15.50	£47.00	£110.00
12 origin and 1st appearance Dr. Light	$26.00	$75.00	$180.00	£15.50	£47.00	£110.00
13	$26.00	$75.00	$180.00	£15.50	£47.00	£110.00
14 Atom joins Justice League of America	$26.00	$75.00	$180.00	£15.50	£47.00	£110.00
15	$26.00	$75.00	$180.00	£15.50	£47.00	£110.00
16-20	$21.00	$62.50	$150.00	£11.50	£35.00	£82.50
21 1st re-appearance of Justice Society of America, 1st Silver Age Hourman and Dr. Fate, 1st appearance (as part of a team) Golden Age Green Lantern in Silver Age	$38.00	$110.00	$300.00	£20.50	£60.00	£165.00
22 Justice Society of America X-over, continues from #21, 2nd appearance (as part of a team) of Golden Age Green Lantern in Silver Age	$34.00	$100.00	$275.00	£17.50	£52.50	£140.00
23-28	$10.50	$32.00	$75.00	£5.50	£17.00	£40.00
29 2nd Justice Society of America X-over, 1st Silver Age appearance of Golden Age Starman	$15.50	$47.00	$110.00	£6.25	£19.00	£45.00
30 Justice Society of America X-over continues from #29	$13.50	$41.00	$95.00	£6.00	£18.00	£42.00
31 Hawkman joins	$10.00	$30.00	$70.00	£4.25	£12.50	£30.00
32 1st appearance Brainstorm	$7.75	$23.50	$55.00	£3.55	£10.50	£25.00
33	$7.75	$23.50	$55.00	£3.55	£10.50	£25.00
34 Joker cover and story	$8.50	$26.00	$60.00	£4.25	£12.50	£30.00
35-36	$7.75	$23.50	$55.00	£3.55	£10.50	£25.00
37 Justice Society of America X-over	$10.00	$30.00	$70.00	£4.25	£12.50	£30.00
38 Justice Society of America X-over, Mr. Terrific appears	$10.00	$30.00	$70.00	£4.25	£12.50	£30.00
39 80pgs, Giant G-16, reprints Brave and the Bold #28 (1st appearance Justice League of America) and #30 (3rd appearance)	$12.00	$36.00	$85.00	£5.00	£15.00	£35.00
40 3rd appearance Silver Age Penguin	$7.75	$23.50	$55.00	£3.20	£9.50	£22.50
41 last Silver Age issue, indicia dated December 1965	$7.75	$23.50	$55.00	£3.20	£9.50	£22.50
42-45	$5.00	$15.00	$35.00	£1.75	£5.25	£12.50
46 Justice Society of America X-over, 1st appearance Silver Age Sandman, 3rd Silver Age appearance Golden Age Spectre	$10.00	$30.00	$80.00	£3.75	£11.00	£30.00
47 Justice Society of America X-over	$5.50	$17.00	$40.00	£2.50	£7.50	£17.50
48 80pgs, Giant G-29, reprints #2,#3, Brave and the Bold #29 (2nd appearance J.L.A.)	$5.25	$16.00	$37.50	£2.85	£8.50	£20.00
49-50	$4.25	$12.50	$30.00	£1.75	£5.25	£12.50
51-54	$4.55	$13.50	$27.50	£1.65	£5.00	£10.00
55 1st Silver Age appearance of Golden Age Robin, Justice Society of America X-over	$7.00	$21.00	$50.00	£3.20	£9.50	£22.50
56 Justice Society of America X-over	$5.75	$17.50	$35.00	£1.65	£5.00	£10.00
57 United Nations story	$4.55	$13.50	$27.50	£1.25	£3.75	£7.50
58 80pgs, Giant G-41, reprints #1, #6, #8	$5.75	$17.50	$35.00	£2.05	£6.25	£12.50
59	$4.55	$13.50	$27.50	£1.65	£5.00	£10.00
60 Batgirl appears	$4.55	$13.50	$27.50	£1.65	£5.00	£10.00
61 all villain special	$3.65	$11.00	$22.00	£1.15	£3.50	£7.00
62	$3.65	$11.00	$22.00	£1.15	£3.50	£7.00
63 scarce in the U.K.	$3.65	$11.00	$22.00	£1.30	£4.00	£8.00
64 Justice Society of America X-over, origin and 1st appearance Red Tornado, Golden Age Black Canary, Dr. Fate, Flash, Starman and Hourman appear	$4.15	$12.50	$25.00	£1.30	£4.00	£8.00
65 Justice Society of America X-over	$3.65	$11.00	$22.00	£1.15	£3.50	£7.00
66 Neal Adams cover	$3.65	$11.00	$22.00	£1.15	£3.50	£7.00
67 80pgs, Giant G-53, reprints #4, #14, #31; Neal Adams cover	$4.55	$13.50	$27.50	£1.65	£5.00	£10.00
68-69	$3.65	$11.00	$22.00	£1.00	£3.00	£6.00
70 Neal Adams cover, The Creeper (early appearance) vs. Justice League of America	$3.65	$11.00	$22.00	£1.00	£3.00	£6.00
71	$2.80	$8.50	$17.00	£1.00	£3.00	£6.00
72 Joe Kubert cover	$2.80	$8.50	$17.00	£1.00	£3.00	£6.00
73 Justice Society of America X-over, Joe Kubert cover	$2.80	$8.50	$17.00	£1.00	£3.00	£6.00
74 Neal Adams cover, Justice Society of America X-over, Black Canary arrives on Earth 1 and is invited to stay	$1.65	$5.00	$10.00	£1.00	£3.00	£6.00
75 Black Canary replaces Wonder Woman	$1.65	$5.00	$10.00	£1.00	£3.00	£6.00
76 68pgs, Giant G-65, reprints #7, #12	$2.50	$7.50	$15.00	£1.30	£4.00	£8.00
77-78	$1.15	$3.50	$7.00	£0.75	£2.25	£4.50
79 Neal Adams cover	$1.15	$3.50	$7.00	£0.75	£2.25	£4.50
80	$1.15	$3.50	$7.00	£0.75	£2.25	£4.50
81 Neal Adams cover inks	$1.00	$3.00	$6.00	£0.65	£2.00	£4.00
82 Neal Adams cover, Justice Society of America X-over	$1.15	$3.50	$7.00	£0.75	£2.25	£4.50
83 Justice Society of America X-over	$1.15	$3.50	$7.00	£0.75	£2.25	£4.50
84	$1.00	$3.00	$6.00	£0.65	£2.00	£4.00
85 68pgs, Giant G-77, reprints #10, #11	$2.50	$7.50	$15.00	£1.00	£3.00	£6.00
86 very scarce in the U.K. Neal Adams cover	$1.00	$3.00	$6.00	£0.80	£2.50	£5.00
87 scarce in the U.K. Neal Adams cover	$1.00	$3.00	$6.00	£0.75	£2.25	£4.50
88 very scarce in the U.K. Neal Adams cover	$1.00	$3.00	$6.00	£0.80	£2.50	£5.00
89 scarce in the U.K. Neal Adams cover	$1.00	$3.00	$6.00	£0.75	£2.25	£4.50
90 ecology theme issue	$1.00	$3.00	$6.00	£0.65	£2.00	£4.00
91-92 52pgs, Neal Adams cover	$1.00	$3.00	$6.00	£0.80	£2.50	£5.00
93 68pgs, Giant G-89, reprints #13, #18	$2.50	$7.50	$15.00	£1.00	£3.00	£6.00
94 52pgs, 4pgs Neal Adams art, reprints origin Sandman, Starman (Adventure #40, #61)	$6.25	$18.50	$37.50	£2.05	£6.25	£12.50
95 52pgs, Neal Adams cover, reprints origin Dr.Fate (More Fun #57), Dr.Midnight (All American #25)	$2.30	$7.00	$14.00	£0.80	£2.50	£5.00
96 52pgs, Neal Adams cover, reprints origin Hourman (Adventure #48)	$2.30	$7.00	$14.00	£0.80	£2.50	£5.00
97 52pgs, Neal Adams cover, reprints #9 (origin Justice League of America)	$1.50	$4.50	$9.00	£0.75	£2.25	£4.50
98 52pgs, Neal Adams cover, Golden Age reprints	$1.50	$4.50	$9.00	£0.75	£2.25	£4.50
99 52pgs, Golden Age reprints	$1.50	$4.50	$9.00	£0.75	£2.25	£4.50
100 scarce in the U.K.	$1.30	$4.00	$8.00	£1.00	£3.00	£6.00
101 Justice Society of America X-over	$1.60	$4.80	$8.00	£0.80	£2.40	£4.00
102 Justice Society of America X-over, Red Tornado "dies"	$1.60	$4.80	$8.00	£0.80	£2.40	£4.00
103 Phantom Stranger joins	$1.00	$3.00	$5.00	£0.70	£2.10	£3.50

TRADE PAPERBACKS, GRAPHIC NOVELS AND OTHER COLLECTIONS ARE PRICED IN POUNDS STERLING ONLY. CONVERT AT 1.5 FOR DOLLARS.

	$Good	$Fine	$N.Mint	£Good	£Fine	£N.Mint
104	$1.00	$3.00	$5.00	£0.70	£2.10	£3.50
105 Elongated Man joins	$1.00	$3.00	$5.00	£0.70	£2.10	£3.50
106 new Red Tornado joins	$1.00	$3.00	$5.00	£0.70	£2.10	£3.50
107 Justice Society of America X-over, Freedom Fighters return - 1st appearance since Golden Age (Human Bomb, Phantom Lady, Doll Man, Uncle Sam, The Ray, Black Condor), 1st mention Earth X	$1.60	$4.80	$8.00	£0.80	£2.40	£4.00
108 Justice Society of America X-over, Freedom Fighters on cover	$1.60	$4.80	$8.00	£0.80	£2.40	£4.00
109 Hawkman resigns	$1.00	$3.00	$5.00	£0.70	£2.10	£3.50
110-113 100pgs	$1.20	$3.60	$6.00	£1.30	£3.90	£6.50
114 100pgs, reprints #22 (2nd part 1st Silver Age Justice Society of America)	$1.20	$3.60	$6.00	£1.30	£3.90	£6.50
115 100pgs	$1.20	$3.60	$6.00	£1.30	£3.90	£6.50
116 100pgs, 1st appearance Quizz, Joker appears	$1.20	$3.60	$6.00	£1.30	£3.90	£6.50
117 Hawkman rejoins	$0.80	$2.40	$4.00	£0.60	£1.80	£3.00
118-119	$0.80	$2.40	$4.00	£0.60	£1.80	£3.00
120-121 Adam Strange appears	$0.80	$2.40	$4.00	£0.60	£1.80	£3.00
122 scarce in the U.K.	$0.60	$1.80	$3.00	£0.70	£2.10	£3.50
123-124 scarce in the U.K. Justice Society of America X-over	$0.80	$2.40	$4.00	£0.80	£2.40	£4.00
125 scarce in the U.K. Two Face appears	$0.70	$2.10	$3.50	£0.70	£2.10	£3.50
126 scarce in the U.K.	$0.60	$1.80	$3.00	£0.60	£1.80	£3.00
127	$0.60	$1.80	$3.00	£0.50	£1.50	£2.50
128 Wonder Woman rejoins	$0.60	$1.80	$3.00	£0.50	£1.50	£2.50
129-131	$0.60	$1.80	$3.00	£0.50	£1.50	£2.50
132-134 scarce in the U.K.	$0.60	$1.80	$3.00	£0.60	£1.80	£3.00
135 ND Justice Society of America X-over	$0.80	$2.40	$4.00	£0.70	£2.10	£3.50
136 scarce in the U.K. Justice Society of America X-over, Joker appears	$0.80	$2.40	$4.00	£0.60	£1.80	£3.00
137 scarce in the U.K. classic Superman vs. Shazam	$0.60	$1.80	$3.00	£0.60	£1.80	£3.00
138 scarce in the U.K. Neal Adams cover, Adam Strange appears	$0.60	$1.80	$3.00	£0.60	£1.80	£3.00
139 scarce in the U.K. 52pgs, Neal Adams cover	$0.70	$2.10	$3.50	£0.70	£2.10	£3.50
140 scarce in the U.K. 52pgs	$0.70	$2.10	$3.50	£0.70	£2.10	£3.50
141 ND 52pgs	$0.70	$2.10	$3.50	£0.80	£2.40	£4.00
142 scarce in the U.K. 52pgs	$0.70	$2.10	$3.50	£0.70	£2.10	£3.50
143 very scarce in the U.K. 52pgs, Superman vs. Wonder Woman	$0.70	$2.10	$3.50	£0.90	£2.70	£4.50
144 scarce in the U.K. 52pgs, cameo appearances of 30 past DC characters from the Challengers of the Unknown and Congorilla to Plastic Man and Rex the Wonder Dog	$0.70	$2.10	$3.50	£0.70	£2.10	£3.50
145 ND scarce in the U.K. 52pgs	$0.70	$2.10	$3.50	£0.90	£2.70	£4.50
146-147 ND 52pgs	$0.70	$2.10	$3.50	£0.80	£2.40	£4.00
148 scarce in the U.K. 52pgs, Justice Society of America X-over, Legion of Super-Heroes appear	$0.70	$2.10	$3.50	£0.80	£2.40	£4.00
149 scarce in the U.K. 52pgs	$0.70	$2.10	$3.50	£0.70	£2.10	£3.50
150 ND very scarce in the U.K. 52pgs	$0.70	$2.10	$3.50	£1.20	£3.60	£6.00
151 scarce in the U.K. 52pgs	$0.60	$1.80	$3.00	£0.70	£2.10	£3.50
152-157 52pgs	$0.60	$1.80	$3.00	£0.40	£1.20	£2.00
158 scarce in the U.K. 44pgs	$0.60	$1.80	$3.00	£0.60	£1.80	£3.00
159 ND Jonah Hex, Enemy Ace, Viking Prince, Black Pirate, Miss Liberty, Justice Society of America appear	$0.50	$1.50	$2.50	£0.70	£2.10	£3.50
160 ND	$0.50	$1.50	$2.50	£0.60	£1.80	£3.00
161 Zatanna joins, new costume	$0.50	$1.50	$2.50	£0.35	£1.05	£1.75
162-170	$0.50	$1.50	$2.50	£0.35	£1.05	£1.75
171 Justice Society of America X-over	$0.50	$1.50	$2.50	£0.35	£1.05	£1.75
172 Justice Society off America X-over, Mr. Terrific dies	$0.50	$1.50	$2.50	£0.35	£1.05	£1.75
173 Black Lightning refuses to join	$0.50	$1.50	$2.50	£0.35	£1.05	£1.75
174-176	$0.50	$1.50	$2.50	£0.35	£1.05	£1.75
177 Martian Manhunter guest-stars, Despero appears	$0.50	$1.50	$2.50	£0.35	£1.05	£1.75
178 Jim Starlin cover, Martian Manhunter guest-stars, Despero appears	$0.50	$1.50	$2.50	£0.35	£1.05	£1.75
179 Jim Starlin cover, Firestorm joins	$0.50	$1.50	$2.50	£0.35	£1.05	£1.75
180 Jim Starlin cover	$0.50	$1.50	$2.50	£0.35	£1.05	£1.75
181	$0.50	$1.50	$2.50	£0.30	£0.90	£1.50
182 Green Arrow leaves, Elongated Man solo back-up	$0.50	$1.50	$2.50	£0.30	£0.90	£1.50
183 Jim Starlin cover, Justice Society of America X-over, Mr.Miracle, New Gods appear	$0.50	$1.50	$2.50	£0.35	£1.05	£1.75
184-185 George Perez art, Jim Starlin cover; Justice Society of America X-over	$0.50	$1.50	$2.50	£0.35	£1.05	£1.75
186 George Perez art	$0.50	$1.50	$2.50	£0.30	£0.90	£1.50
187-188	$0.50	$1.50	$2.50	£0.30	£0.90	£1.50
189-190 Bolland covers featuring Starro the Conqueror	$0.50	$1.50	$2.50	£0.30	£0.90	£1.50
191	$0.40	$1.20	$2.00	£0.25	£0.75	£1.25
192 George Perez art, true origin of Red Tornado begins (ends #193)	$0.40	$1.20	$2.00	£0.25	£0.75	£1.25
193 52pgs, George Perez art; 1st appearance All-Star Squadron (insert)	$0.50	$1.50	$2.50	£0.30	£0.90	£1.50
194 George Perez art	$0.40	$1.20	$2.00	£0.25	£0.75	£1.25
195-197 George Perez art, Justice Society of America X-over	$0.40	$1.20	$2.00	£0.25	£0.75	£1.25
198 Jonah Hex, Cinnamon, Bat Lash and Scalphunter appear	$0.40	$1.20	$2.00	£0.25	£0.75	£1.25
199 George Perez cover	$0.40	$1.20	$2.00	£0.25	£0.75	£1.25
200 76pgs, 1st Bolland Batman (5pgs), Aparo/Infantino/Gil Kane/Kubert/George Perez art, Green Arrow rejoins (virtually all copies have crinkled spines owing to the binding process)	$0.80	$2.40	$4.00	£0.80	£2.40	£4.00
201-205 George Perez cover	$0.40	$1.20	$2.00	£0.25	£0.75	£1.25
206	$0.40	$1.20	$2.00	£0.25	£0.75	£1.25
207 George Perez art; 20th annual Justice Society of America X-over, All Star Squadron appear	$0.40	$1.20	$2.00	£0.25	£0.75	£1.25
208 George Perez cover; 20th annual Justice Society of America X-over, All Star Squadron appear, Masters of the Universe insert	$0.40	$1.20	$2.00	£0.25	£0.75	£1.25
209 George Perez cover; 20th annual Justice Society of America X-over, All Star Squadron appear	$0.40	$1.20	$2.00	£0.25	£0.75	£1.25
210	$0.40	$1.20	$2.00	£0.25	£0.75	£1.25
211	$0.30	$0.90	$1.50	£0.20	£0.60	£1.00
212-215 George Perez cover	$0.30	$0.90	$1.50	£0.20	£0.60	£1.00
216	$0.30	$0.90	$1.50	£0.20	£0.60	£1.00
217 George Perez cover	$0.30	$0.90	$1.50	£0.20	£0.60	£1.00
217 ND rare in the U.K. SoMuchFun! Inc. issue (1983), same contents as above with same cover but the word "Classic" added to the logo	$0.80	$2.40	$4.00	£0.50	£1.50	£2.50
218	$0.30	$0.90	$1.50	£0.20	£0.60	£1.00
219-220 George Perez cover, Justice Society of America X-over	$0.30	$0.90	$1.50	£0.20	£0.60	£1.00
221-230	$0.30	$0.90	$1.50	£0.20	£0.60	£1.00
231-232 Justice Society of America X-over	$0.30	$0.90	$1.50	£0.20	£0.60	£1.00
233 Rebirth begins (ends #236); Vibe, Vixen, Steel and Gypsy introduced	$0.30	$0.90	$1.50	£0.20	£0.60	£1.00
234-242	$0.30	$0.90	$1.50	£0.20	£0.60	£1.00
243 Aquaman leaves	$0.30	$0.90	$1.50	£0.20	£0.60	£1.00
244-245 Crisis X-over, Justice Society of America and Infinity Inc. appear	$0.30	$0.90	$1.50	£0.20	£0.60	£1.00
246-249	$0.30	$0.90	$1.50	£0.20	£0.60	£1.00
250 DS anniversary issue, Batman re-joins	$0.40	$1.20	$2.00	£0.25	£0.75	£1.25
251-252	$0.30	$0.90	$1.50	£0.20	£0.60	£1.00
253 origin Despero retold	$0.30	$0.90	$1.50	£0.20	£0.60	£1.00
254-257	$0.30	$0.90	$1.50	£0.20	£0.60	£1.00
258 Legends X-over, death of Vibe	$0.30	$0.90	$1.50	£0.20	£0.60	£1.00
259-260 Legends X-over	$0.30	$0.90	$1.50	£0.20	£0.60	£1.00
261 LD in the U.K. Legends X-over	$0.60	$1.80	$3.00	£0.40	£1.20	£2.00
Title Value:	$1570.85	$4681.30	$12020.50	£966.80	£2900.80	£7539.50

REPRINT FEATURES

Atom in 99. Black Canary in 116. Flash in 92. Hourman in 91, 96. Johnny Peril in 116. JLA in 39, 48, 58, 67, 76, 85, 93, 97, 110-113, 115, 116. JLA/JSA in 114. Justice Society of America in 100, 113, 115. Knights of the Galaxy in 91. Sandman in 94, 99. Sargon in 98. Seven Soldiers of Victory in 111, 112. Starman in 94, 98, 116. Dr.Fate, Dr.Mid-Nite in 95. Wildcat in 96.

JUSTICE LEAGUE OF AMERICA ANNUAL
DC Comics; 1 Jul 1983-3 Nov 1985

	$Good	$Fine	$N.Mint	£Good	£Fine	£N.Mint
1 Dr. Destiny appears	$0.50	$1.50	$2.50	£0.30	£0.90	£1.50
2 intro new Justice League of America	$0.50	$1.50	$2.50	£0.30	£0.90	£1.50
3 Crisis X-over	$0.50	$1.50	$2.50	£0.30	£0.90	£1.50
Title Value:	$1.50	$4.50	$7.50	£0.90	£2.70	£4.50

JUSTICE LEAGUE OF AMERICA ARCHIVES
DC Comics; 1 Apr 1992-present

1 256pgs, hardcover reprint edition of Brave and the Bold #28-30, Justice League of America #1-6

	$Good	$Fine	$N.Mint	£Good	£Fine	£N.Mint
	$7.50	$22.50	$37.50	£5.00	£15.00	£25.00

2 256pgs, hardcover reprint edition of Justice League of America #7-14

	$7.50	$22.50	$37.50	£5.00	£15.00	£25.00

3 256pgs, hardcover reprint edition of Justice League of America #15-22

	$7.50	$22.50	$37.50	£5.00	£15.00	£25.00
Title Value:	$22.50	$67.50	$112.50	£15.00	£45.00	£75.00

JUSTICE LEAGUE QUARTERLY
DC Comics; 1 Winter 1990-17 Dec 1994

1 80pgs, Booster Gold plus Maxi-Man, Praxis, Gypsy, Echo, Vapor and Reverb

	$0.60	$1.80	$3.00	£0.40	£1.20	£2.00

2 80pgs, G'Nort appears

	$0.60	$1.80	$3.00	£0.40	£1.20	£2.00

3 80pgs, original Justice League of America appears

	$0.60	$1.80	$3.00	£0.40	£1.20	£2.00

4 80pgs, three complete stories

	$0.60	$1.80	$3.00	£0.40	£1.20	£2.00

5 80pgs

	$0.60	$1.80	$3.00	£0.40	£1.20	£2.00

6 80pgs, painted cover

	$0.60	$1.80	$3.00	£0.40	£1.20	£2.00

7-16 80pgs

	$0.60	$1.80	$3.00	£0.40	£1.20	£2.00

17 80pgs, special solo stories featuring Batman, Guy Gardner and others

	$0.60	$1.80	$3.00	£0.40	£1.20	£2.00
Title Value:	$10.20	$30.60	$51.00	£6.80	£20.40	£34.00

JUSTICE LEAGUE SPECTACULAR
DC Comics; 1 Apr 1992

1 48pgs, ties in with Justice League America #61 and Justice League Europe #37, two different covers available depicting new Justice League of America and Justice Legue International teams

	$0.40	$1.20	$2.00	£0.25	£0.75	£1.25
Title Value:	$0.40	$1.20	$2.00	£0.25	£0.75	£1.25

JUSTICE LEAGUE TASK FORCE
DC Comics; 0 Oct 1994; 1 Jun 1993-present

0 (Oct 1994) Zero Hour X-over, team re-formed

	$0.40	$1.20	$2.00	£0.25	£0.75	£1.25

1-4

	$0.30	$0.90	$1.50	£0.20	£0.60	£1.00

5 Knightquest: The Search part 1

	$0.40	$1.20	$2.00	£0.25	£0.75	£1.25

6 Knightquest: The Search part 3

	$0.30	$0.90	$1.50	£0.20	£0.60	£1.00

7-8 Peter David script

	$0.30	$0.90	$1.50	£0.20	£0.60	£1.00

9

	$0.30	$0.90	$1.50	£0.20	£0.60	£1.00

10-12 Purification story

	$0.30	$0.90	$1.50	£0.20	£0.60	£1.00

13 Judgement Day part 2, continued in Justice League America #65

	$0.30	$0.90	$1.50	£0.20	£0.60	£1.00

14 Judgement Day part 5, continued in Justice League America #66

	$0.30	$0.90	$1.50	£0.20	£0.60	£1.00

15 Aftershocks part 2, continued in Justice League #67

	$0.30	$0.90	$1.50	£0.20	£0.60	£1.00

16 Zero Hour X-over

	$0.30	$0.90	$1.50	£0.20	£0.60	£1.00

17-20 Vandal Savage appears

	$0.30	$0.90	$1.50	£0.20	£0.60	£1.00

21-23

	$0.30	$0.90	$1.50	£0.20	£0.60	£1.00

24

	$0.35	$1.05	$1.75	£0.25	£0.75	£1.25

25 Impulse and Damage guest-star

	$0.35	$1.05	$1.75	£0.25	£0.75	£1.25

26

	$0.35	$1.05	$1.75	£0.25	£0.75	£1.25

27-29 Despero appears

	$0.35	$1.05	$1.75	£0.25	£0.75	£1.25

30 Underworld Unleashed tie-in

	$0.35	$1.05	$1.75	£0.25	£0.75	£1.25

31-33

	$0.35	$1.05	$1.75	£0.25	£0.75	£1.25
Title Value:	$10.90	$32.70	$54.50	£7.40	£22.20	£37.00

JUSTICE MACHINE (1ST SERIES)
Noble/Texas; 1 Jun 1981-5 Nov 1983

1 ND magazine size

	$3.00	$9.00	$15.00	£2.00	£6.00	£10.00

2-3 ND magazine size

	$1.50	$4.50	$7.50	£1.00	£3.00	£5.00

4-5 ND DS slightly larger than regular comic size

	$0.90	$2.70	$4.50	£0.60	£1.80	£3.00
Title Value:	$7.80	$23.40	$39.00	£5.20	£15.60	£26.00

JUSTICE MACHINE (2ND SERIES)
Comico/Innovation; 1 Jan 1987-29 May 1989

1-18 ND

	$0.40	$1.20	$2.00	£0.25	£0.75	£1.25

19-25 ND The Earth/Georwell War

	$0.40	$1.20	$2.00	£0.25	£0.75	£1.25

26-29 ND

	$0.40	$1.20	$2.00	£0.25	£0.75	£1.25
Title Value:	$11.60	$34.80	$58.00	£7.25	£21.75	£36.25

Annual 1 (Jun 1989), last Comico issue

				£0.40	£1.20	£2.00

Summer Spectacular (1990),
1st Innovation issue, part Byrne cover

				£0.45	£1.35	£2.25

JUSTICE MACHINE (3RD SERIES)
Innovation; 1 Apr 1990-7 Apr 1991

1-4 ND

	$0.40	$1.20	$2.00	£0.25	£0.75	£1.25

5-7 ND The Demon Trilogy

	$0.40	$1.20	$2.00	£0.25	£0.75	£1.25
Title Value:	$2.80	$8.40	$14.00	£1.75	£5.25	£8.75

JUSTICE MACHINE ANNUAL
Texas,OS; 1 1984

1 ND 1st appearance Elementals, Willingham art, part Golden cover

	$3.00	$9.00	$15.00	£2.00	£6.00	£10.00
Title Value:	$3.00	$9.00	$15.00	£2.00	£6.00	£10.00

JUSTICE MACHINE FEATURING THE ELEMENTALS
Comico,MS; 1 May 1986-4 Aug 1986

1-4 ND

	$0.40	$1.20	$2.00	£0.25	£0.75	£1.25
Title Value:	$1.60	$4.80	$8.00	£1.00	£3.00	£5.00

JUSTICE MACHINE MINI-SERIES, THE NEW
Innovation,MS; 1 Nov 1989-3 Mar 1990

1-3 ND colour

	$0.40	$1.20	$2.00	£0.25	£0.75	£1.25
Title Value:	$1.20	$3.60	$6.00	£0.75	£2.25	£3.75

JUSTICE MACHINE: THE CHIMERA CONSPIRACY
Millennium,MS; 1 Nov 1992-3 Jan 1993

1-3 ND

	$0.45	$1.35	$2.25	£0.90	£0.90	£1.50
Title Value:	$1.35	$4.05	$6.75	£0.90	£2.70	£4.50

JUSTICE SOCIETY OF AMERICA (LIMITED SERIES)
DC Comics,MS; 1 Apr 1991-8 Nov 1991
(see Justice League of America #21)

1 Golden Age Flash (Jay Garrick) appears

	$0.25	$0.75	$1.25	£0.15	£0.45	£0.75

2 Golden Age Black Canary appears

	$0.25	$0.75	$1.25	£0.15	£0.45	£0.75

3 Golden Age Green Lantern appears

	$0.25	$0.75	$1.25	£0.15	£0.45	£0.75

4 Golden Age Hawkman appears

	$0.25	$0.75	$1.25	£0.15	£0.45	£0.75

5 Golden Age Hawkman and Flash appear

	$0.25	$0.75	$1.25	£0.15	£0.45	£0.75

6 Golden Age Black Canary and Green Lantern appear

	$0.25	$0.75	$1.25	£0.15	£0.45	£0.75

7 Justice Society re-united

	$0.25	$0.75	$1.25	£0.15	£0.45	£0.75

8 Justice Society vs. Vandal Savage

	$0.25	$0.75	$1.25	£0.15	£0.45	£0.75
Title Value:	$2.00	$6.00	$10.00	£1.20	£3.60	£6.00

JUSTICE SOCIETY OF AMERICA
DC Comics; 1 Aug 1992-10 May 1993
(see All Star Comics)

1-10

	$0.25	$0.75	$1.25	£0.15	£0.45	£0.75
Title Value:	$2.50	$7.50	$12.50	£1.50	£4.50	£7.50

JUSTICE: FOUR BALANCE
Marvel Comics Group,MS; 1 Sep 1994-4 Dec 1994

1-4 Thing, Yancy Street Gang, Night Thrasher and Firestar

	$0.30	$0.90	$1.50	£0.20	£0.60	£1.00
Title Value:	$1.20	$3.60	$6.00	£0.80	£2.40	£4.00

JUSTY
Viz,MS; 1 1988-9 1989

1-9 ND Japanese manga material

	$0.40	$1.20	$2.00	£0.25	£0.75	£1.25
Title Value:	$3.60	$10.80	$18.00	£2.25	£6.75	£11.25

K

KA-ZAR
Marvel Comics Group; 1 Aug 1970-3 Mar 1971
(see Savage Tales, X-Men #10)

1 68pgs, reprints X-Men #10 (1st Silver Age appearance), Daredevil #24; Hercules, Vision, Scarlet Witch, Quicksilver and Black Panther appear in new story

	$2.80	$8.25	$14.00	£1.60	£4.80	£8.00

2 68pgs, reprints origin Ka-Zar; new Angel back-up story; Daredevil appears

	$2.00	$6.00	$10.00	£1.20	£3.60	£6.00

3 68pgs, Daredevil appears (reprints issue 14); new Angel back-up continues in Marvel Tales #30

	$2.00	$6.00	$10.00	£1.20	£3.60	£6.00
Title Value:	$6.80	$20.25	$34.00	£4.00	£12.00	£20.00

KA-ZAR (2ND SERIES)
Marvel Comics Group; 1 Jan 1974-20 Feb 1977

1 ND	$0.60	$1.80	$3.00	£0.40	£1.20	£2.00
2 ND	$0.45	$1.35	$2.25	£0.30	£0.90	£1.50
3 ND	$0.40	$1.20	$2.00	£0.25	£0.75	£1.25

4 ND Brunner cover

	$0.30	$0.90	$1.50	£0.20	£0.60	£1.00
5-11	$0.30	$0.90	$1.50	£0.20	£0.60	£1.00
12 Russ Heath art	$0.30	$0.90	$1.50	£0.20	£0.60	£1.00
13-20	$0.30	$0.90	$1.50	£0.20	£0.60	£1.00
Title Value:	$6.55	$19.65	$32.75	£4.35	£13.05	£21.75

KA-ZAR THE SAVAGE
Marvel Comics Group; 1 Apr 1981-34 Oct 1984
(see Marvel Fanfare)

1 Brent Anderson art

	$0.30	$0.90	$1.50	£0.20	£0.60	£1.00

2-9 Brent Anderson art

	$0.25	$0.75	$1.25	£0.15	£0.45	£0.75

10 1st direct sale, Mando (heavier stock) paper begins, B. Anderson art

	$0.25	$0.75	$1.25	£0.15	£0.45	£0.75

11-12 Brent Anderson art

	$0.25	$0.75	$1.25	£0.15	£0.45	£0.75

13-20 ND

	$0.25	$0.75	$1.25	£0.15	£0.45	£0.75

21-26 Spiderman appears

	$0.25	$0.75	$1.25	£0.15	£0.45	£0.75

27-28 ND

	$0.25	$0.75	$1.25	£0.15	£0.45	£0.75

29 DS, Ka-Zar and Shanna wed

	$0.25	$0.75	$1.25	£0.15	£0.45	£0.75

	$Good	$Fine	$N.Mint	£Good	£Fine	£N.Mint
30	$0.25	$0.75	$1.25	£0.15	£0.45	£0.75
31-33 Paul Neary art						
	$0.25	$0.75	$1.25	£0.15	£0.45	£0.75
34 Neary art; Steranko-parody cover, many cancelled characters appear (cameo)						
	$0.30	$0.90	$1.50	£0.20	£0.60	£1.00
Title Value:	$8.60	$25.80	$43.00	£5.20	£15.60	£26.00

Note: Tales of Zabu in 11, 12, 14-18.

FEATURES

Tales of Zabu in 11, 12, 14-18.

KABUKI COLOUR GALLERY
Caliber Press,OS; nn Aug 1995

	$Good	$Fine	$N.Mint	£Good	£Fine	£N.Mint
nn ND painted pin-ups by David Mack, Tim Bradstreet, Colleen Doran and others						
	$0.60	$1.80	$3.00	£0.40	£1.20	£2.00
Title Value:	$0.60	$1.80	$3.00	£0.40	£1.20	£2.00

KABUKI: CIRCLE OF BLOOD
Caliber Press; 1 Jan 1995-6 Nov 1995

	$Good	$Fine	$N.Mint	£Good	£Fine	£N.Mint
1 ND 48pgs, David Mack script and art; black and white						
	$1.20	$3.60	$6.00	£0.70	£2.10	£3.50
1 ND 48pgs, red foil enhanced cover						
	$1.00	$3.00	$5.00	£0.80	£2.40	£4.00
2-6 ND 48pgs, David Mack script and art; black and white						
	$0.60	$1.80	$3.00	£0.40	£1.20	£2.00
Title Value:	$5.20	$15.60	$26.00	£3.50	£10.50	£17.50

KABUKI: DANCE OF DEATH
London Night Studios; 1 Jan 1995

	$Good	$Fine	$N.Mint	£Good	£Fine	£N.Mint
1 ND David Mack script and art; black and white						
	$0.60	$1.80	$3.00	£0.40	£1.20	£2.00
1 Commemerative Edition ND						
	$1.20	$3.60	$6.00	£0.70	£2.10	£3.50
Title Value:	$1.80	$5.40	$9.00	£1.10	£3.30	£5.50

KABUKI: FEAR THE REAPER
Caliber Press,OS; 1 Nov 1994

	$Good	$Fine	$N.Mint	£Good	£Fine	£N.Mint
1 ND 48pgs, spin-off from Shi, David Mack script and art; black and white						
	$0.80	$2.40	$4.00	£0.50	£1.50	£2.50
Title Value:	$0.80	$2.40	$4.00	£0.50	£1.50	£2.50
Kabuki Compilation Graphic Novel (Jul 1995) 80pgs, reprints Fear The Reaper and Dance of Death; black and white				£1.00	£3.00	£5.00

KAFKA
Renegade; 1 Apr 1987-6 Sep 1987

	$Good	$Fine	$N.Mint	£Good	£Fine	£N.Mint
1-6 ND	$0.40	$1.20	$2.00	£0.25	£0.75	£1.25
Title Value:	$2.40	$7.20	$12.00	£1.50	£4.50	£7.50

KAMANDI THE LAST BOY ON EARTH
DC Comics; 1 Oct/Nov 1972-59 Sep/Oct 1978

(see Brave and the Bold #120, #157)

	$Good	$Fine	$N.Mint	£Good	£Fine	£N.Mint
1 ND, origin and 1st appearance Kamandi, Jack Kirby art						
	$7.50	$22.50	$45.00	£2.50	£7.50	£15.00
2 Jack Kirby art	$5.50	$16.50	$27.50	£1.60	£4.80	£8.00
3 Jack Kirby art	$3.50	$10.50	$17.50	£1.00	£3.00	£5.00
4 intro Prince Tuftan of the Tigers, Jack Kirby art						
	$3.50	$10.50	$17.50	£1.00	£3.00	£5.00
5 Jack Kirby art	$3.50	$10.50	$17.50	£1.00	£3.00	£5.00
6-10 Jack Kirby art						
	$2.50	$7.50	$12.50	£0.60	£1.80	£3.00
11-17 Jack Kirby art						
	$1.40	$4.20	$7.00	£0.50	£1.50	£2.50
18 ND Jack Kirby art						
	$1.40	$4.20	$7.00	£0.60	£1.80	£3.00
19-20 Jack Kirby art						
	$1.40	$4.20	$7.00	£0.50	£1.50	£2.50
21-28 Jack Kirby art						
	$0.80	$2.40	$4.00	£0.40	£1.20	£2.00
29 Superman's costume appears, Jack Kirby art						
	$0.80	$2.40	$4.00	£0.50	£1.50	£2.50
30 Jack Kirby art	$0.80	$2.40	$4.00	£0.40	£1.20	£2.00
31 1st appearance Pyra, Jack Kirby art						
	$0.80	$2.40	$4.00	£0.30	£0.90	£1.50
32 scarce in the U.K. 68pgs, reprints issue #1, Jack Kirby art						
	$0.90	$2.70	$4.50	£0.60	£1.80	£3.00
33-39 Jack Kirby art						
	$0.80	$2.40	$4.00	£0.30	£0.90	£1.50
40 ND last Jack Kirby art						
	$0.80	$2.40	$4.00	£0.40	£1.20	£2.00
41-42	$0.60	$1.80	$3.00	£0.25	£0.75	£1.25
43 scarce in the U.K.						
	$0.60	$1.80	$3.00	£0.30	£0.90	£1.50
44 scarce in the U.K. Giffen art featured						
	$0.60	$1.80	$3.00	£0.30	£0.90	£1.50
45-46 scarce in the U.K. Giffen and Nasser art featured						
	$0.60	$1.80	$3.00	£0.30	£0.90	£1.50
47	$0.60	$1.80	$3.00	£0.25	£0.75	£1.25
48 scarce in the U.K.						
	$0.60	$1.80	$3.00	£0.30	£0.90	£1.50
49	$0.60	$1.80	$3.00	£0.25	£0.75	£1.25
50 Omac appears	$0.60	$1.80	$3.00	£0.30	£0.90	£1.50
51-57	$0.60	$1.80	$3.00	£0.25	£0.75	£1.25
58 Karate Kid appears						
	$0.60	$1.80	$3.00	£0.30	£0.90	£1.50
59 ND scarce in the U.K. 44pgs, Jim Starlin art on Omac						
	$0.70	$2.10	$3.50	£0.50	£1.50	£2.50
Title Value:	$77.60	$232.80	$395.50	£28.05	£84.15	£142.75

FEATURES

Omac in 59. Tales of the Great Disaster in 43-46.

KAMANDI: AT EARTH'S END
DC Comics,MS; 1 Jun 1993-6 Nov 1993

	$Good	$Fine	$N.Mint	£Good	£Fine	£N.Mint
1 Tom Veitch script begins						
	$0.40	$1.20	$2.00	£0.25	£0.75	£1.25
2-3	$0.40	$1.20	$2.00	£0.25	£0.75	£1.25
4-5 Superman appears						
	$0.40	$1.20	$2.00	£0.25	£0.75	£1.25
6	$0.40	$1.20	$2.00	£0.25	£0.75	£1.25
Title Va'ue:	$2.40	$7.20	$12.00	£1.50	£4.50	£7.50

KAMUI, LEGEND OF
Eclipse; 1 May 1987-38 Jul 1990

	$Good	$Fine	$N.Mint	£Good	£Fine	£N.Mint
1 ND Saripei Shirato script/art begins (translated Japanese reprint); black and white						
	$0.80	$2.40	$4.00	£0.50	£1.50	£2.50
1 2nd printing ND	$0.45	$1.35	$2.25	£0.30	£0.90	£1.50
2 ND	$0.45	$1.35	$2.25	£0.30	£0.90	£1.50
2 2nd printing ND	$0.30	$0.90	$1.50	£0.20	£0.60	£1.00
3 ND	$0.40	$1.20	$2.00	£0.25	£0.75	£1.25
3 2nd printing ND	$0.30	$0.90	$1.50	£0.20	£0.60	£1.00
4-10 ND	$0.30	$0.90	$1.50	£0.20	£0.60	£1.00
11-38 ND	$0.25	$0.80	$1.35	£0.15	£0.50	£0.90
Title Value:	$11.80	$36.80	$61.80	£7.35	£23.45	£40.95

KARATE KID
DC Comics; 1 Mar/Apr 1976-15 Jul/Aug 1978

(see Adventure, Legion of Super-Heroes, Superboy)

	$Good	$Fine	$N.Mint	£Good	£Fine	£N.Mint
1 scarce in the U.K. Legion of Super-Heroes appear						
	$0.60	$1.80	$3.00	£0.60	£1.80	£3.00
2-3 scarce in the U.K.						
	$0.40	$1.20	$2.00	£0.40	£1.20	£2.00
4-5	$0.30	$0.90	$1.50	£0.30	£0.90	£1.50
6 Legion of Super-Heroes appear						

Justice Machine Annual #1

Karate Kid #2

Kid Montana #43

	$Good	$Fine	$N.Mint	£Good	£Fine	£N.Mint
	$0.30	$0.90	$1.50	£0.25	£0.75	£1.25
7	$0.30	$0.90	$1.50	£0.25	£0.75	£1.25
8 scarce in the U.K.						
	$0.30	$0.90	$1.50	£0.30	£0.90	£1.50
9 Princess Projectra appears	$0.30	$0.90	$1.50	£0.25	£0.75	£1.25
10 Princess Projectra and Legion of Super-Heroes appear						
	$0.30	$0.90	$1.50	£0.25	£0.75	£1.25
11	$0.30	$0.90	$1.50	£0.20	£0.60	£1.00
12-13 Legion of Super-Heroes appear						
	$0.30	$0.90	$1.50	£0.20	£0.60	£1.00
14 Robin appears	$0.30	$0.90	$1.50	£0.20	£0.60	£1.00
15 X-over Kamandi #58						
	$0.30	$0.90	$1.50	£0.20	£0.60	£1.00
Title Value:	$5.00	$15.00	$25.00	£4.30	£12.90	£21.50

Note: Legion of Super-Heroes appear in #1,#2,#4,#6,#10,#12,#13.

KATMANDU

Antarctic Press; 1 Oct 1995-present

1-2 ND black and white

	$0.60	$1.80	$3.00	£0.40	£1.20	£2.00

3-6 ND black and white

	$0.55	$1.65	$2.75	£0.35	£1.05	£1.75
Title Value:	$3.40	$10.20	$17.00	£2.20	£6.60	£11.00

KATO THREE

Now Comics,MS; 1 Oct 1993-2 Nov 1993

1-2 ND Mike Baron script

	$0.45	$1.35	$2.25	£0.30	£0.90	£1.50
Title Value:	$0.90	$2.70	$4.50	£0.60	£1.80	£3.00

KATO OF THE GREEN HORNET

Now Comics,MS; 1 Nov 1991-4 Feb 1992

1-4 ND	$0.40	$1.20	$2.00	£0.25	£0.75	£1.25
Title Value:	$1.60	$4.80	$8.00	£1.00	£3.00	£5.00

KATO OF THE GREEN HORNET II

Now Comics; 1 Nov 1992-4 Feb 1993

1-4 ND	$0.45	$1.35	$2.25	£0.30	£0.90	£1.50
Title Value:	$1.80	$5.40	$9.00	£1.20	£3.60	£6.00

KATO: DRAGON'S IN EDEN GRAPHIC NOVEL

Now Comics,OS; nn Jul 1994

nn ND 48pgs, Mike Baron script, Bob Bilau art

	$1.00	$3.00	$5.00	£0.65	£1.95	£3.25
Title Value:	$1.00	$3.00	$5.00	£0.65	£1.95	£3.25

KATY KEENE SPECIAL

Red Circle (Archie); 1 Sep 1983

1 ND	$0.55	$1.65	$2.75	£0.35	£1.05	£1.75
Title Value:	$0.55	$1.65	$2.75	£0.35	£1.05	£1.75

KEGOR, MONSTER OF THE DEEP

A Plus Comics,MS; 1 Nov 1991

1 ND 48pgs, Steve Ditko art and cover

	$0.45	$1.35	$2.25	£0.30	£0.90	£1.50
Title Value:	$0.45	$1.35	$2.25	£0.30	£0.90	£1.50

KEIF LLAMA - XENO TECH

Fantagraphics; 1 1988-6 1988

(see Particle Dreams)

1-6 ND Matt Howarth script/art

	$0.40	$1.20	$2.00	£0.25	£0.75	£1.25
Title Value:	$2.40	$7.20	$12.00	£1.50	£4.50	£7.50

KELVIN MACE

Vortex; 1 1986; 2 1987

1 ND Schoenfeld art

	$0.80	$2.40	$4.00	£0.50	£1.50	£2.50

1 2nd printing, ND (stamped on 1st page)

	$0.40	$1.20	$2.00	£0.25	£0.75	£1.25
2 ND	$0.45	$1.35	$2.25	£0.30	£0.90	£1.50
Title Value:	$1.65	$4.95	$8.25	£1.05	£3.15	£5.25

KENDRA: LEGACY OF BLOOD

Perry Dog Press; 1 Feb/Mar 1987

1 ND black and white

	$0.25	$0.75	$1.25	£0.15	£0.45	£0.75
Title Value:	$0.25	$0.75	$1.25	£0.15	£0.45	£0.75

KI-GORR THE KILLER

AC Comics; 1 Feb 1995

1 ND Bill Black script, Brad Gorby cover; black and white

	$0.80	$2.40	$4.00	£0.50	£1.50	£2.50
Title Value:	$0.80	$2.40	$4.00	£0.50	£1.50	£2.50

KICKERS INC.

Marvel Comics Group/New Universe; 1 Nov 1986-12 Oct 1987

1-12 ND	$0.15	$0.45	$0.75	£0.10	£0.35	£0.60
Title Value:	$1.80	$5.40	$9.00	£1.20	£4.20	£7.20

KID 'N PLAY

Marvel Comics Group, TV; 1 Feb 1992-9 Oct 1993

1-9 ND	$0.15	$0.45	$0.75	£0.10	£0.35	£0.60
Title Value:	$1.35	$4.05	$6.75	£0.90	£3.15	£5.40

KID CANNIBAL

Eternity,MS; 1 Dec 1991-4 Mar 1992

1-4 ND	$0.45	$1.35	$2.25	£0.30	£0.90	£1.50
Title Value:	$1.80	$5.40	$9.00	£1.20	£3.60	£6.00

KID CODY, WESTERN ACTION STARRING

Atlas; 1 Feb 1975

1 Doug Wildey art; distributed in the U.K.

	$0.30	$0.90	$1.50	£0.20	£0.60	£1.00
Title Value:	$0.30	$0.90	$1.50	£0.20	£0.60	£1.00

KID COLT GIANT SIZE ANNUAL

Marvel Comics Group; 1 Jan 1975-3 Jul 1975

1-3 ND 68pgs, part reprint

	$0.70	$2.10	$3.50	£0.45	£1.35	£2.25
Title Value:	$2.10	$6.30	$10.50	£1.35	£4.05	£6.75

KID COLT OUTLAW

Atlas/Marvel Comics Group; 91 Jul 1960-139 Mar 1968; 140 Nov 1969-229 Apr 1979

(previous issues ND)

91	$1.65	$5.00	$10.12	£1.10	£3.35	£6.75
92-95 ND	$1.85	$5.50	$11.25	£1.25	£3.75	£7.50
96-99	$1.65	$5.00	$10.12	£1.10	£3.35	£6.75
100 scarce in the U.K.						
	$3.00	$9.00	$18.00	£2.00	£6.00	£12.00
101-104	$1.50	$4.50	$9.00	£1.00	£3.00	£6.00
105-108 very scarce in the U.K.						
	$1.85	$5.50	$11.25	£1.25	£3.75	£7.50
109	$1.50	$4.50	$9.00	£1.00	£3.00	£6.00
110 1st appearance Iron Mask						
	$1.50	$4.50	$9.00	£1.00	£3.00	£6.00
111-118	$1.50	$4.50	$9.00	£1.00	£3.00	£6.00
119-120 rare in the U.K.						
	$1.85	$5.50	$11.25	£1.25	£3.75	£7.50
121-129	$1.05	$3.15	$5.25	£0.70	£2.10	£3.50
130-132 64pgs, classic reprints						
	$1.40	$4.20	$7.00	£0.90	£2.70	£4.50
133-139	$0.90	$2.70	$4.50	£0.60	£1.80	£3.00
140-148 ND	$1.05	$3.15	$5.25	£0.70	£2.10	£3.50
149-154	$0.80	$2.40	$4.00	£0.50	£1.50	£2.50
155-156 ND scarce in the U.K.						
	$0.90	$2.70	$4.50	£0.60	£1.80	£3.00
157-169 ND	$0.80	$2.40	$4.00	£0.50	£1.50	£2.50
170 ND origin reprinted, Williamson art						
	$0.85	$2.55	$4.25	£0.55	£1.65	£2.75
171-199 ND	$0.60	$1.80	$3.00	£0.40	£1.20	£2.00
200 ND	$0.80	$2.40	$4.00	£0.50	£1.50	£2.50
201-229 ND	$0.40	$1.20	$2.00	£0.25	£0.75	£1.25
Title Value:	$127.80	$383.15	$692.35	£84.10	£252.55	£455.25

Note: issues 140, 142-200, 202-229 are all reprint. New Two Gun Kid story in 141, new Kid Colt story in 201.

KID ETERNITY

DC Comics,MS; 1 Apr 1991-3 Nov 1991

(see Secret Origins [1st Series] #4)

1-3 ND 48pgs, Grant Morrison script/Duncan Fegredo art and design by Rian Hughes

	$1.00	$3.00	$5.00	£0.70	£2.10	£3.50
Title Value:	$3.00	$9.00	$15.00	£2.10	£6.30	£10.50

Note: Prestige Format

KID ETERNITY (2ND SERIES)

DC Comics/Vertigo; 1 May 1993-16 Sep 1994

1 Sean Philips covers and art begins; under "Vertigo" banner

	$0.40	$1.35	$2.25	£0.30	£0.90	£1.50
2-6	$0.40	$1.20	$2.00	£0.25	£0.75	£1.25
7 Sean Schoffield guest art						
	$0.40	$1.20	$2.00	£0.25	£0.75	£1.25
8-12	$0.40	$1.20	$2.00	£0.25	£0.75	£1.25
13-16 A Date In Hell story						
	$0.40	$1.20	$2.00	£0.25	£0.75	£1.25
Title Value:	$6.45	$19.35	$32.25	£4.05	£12.15	£20.25

KID MONTANA

Charlton; 9 Nov 1957-50 Jan 1965

9 scarce in the U.K.	$5.25	$15.50	$31.50	£3.50	£10.50	£21.00
10 scarce in the U.K.						
	$3.00	$9.00	$18.00	£2.00	£6.00	£12.00
11-12	$1.85	$5.50	$11.25	£1.25	£3.75	£7.50
13 Williamson art	$2.25	$6.75	$13.50	£1.50	£4.50	£9.00
14-15	$1.85	$5.50	$11.25	£1.25	£3.75	£7.50
16-18	$1.50	$4.50	$9.00	£1.00	£3.00	£6.00
19-40 distributed in the U.K.						
	$1.15	$3.50	$7.00	£0.75	£2.25	£4.50
41-50 distributed in the U.K.						
	$0.75	$2.25	$4.50	£0.50	£1.50	£3.00
Title Value:	$55.20	$166.25	$334.00	£36.50	£109.50	£219.00

Note: reasonable distribution in the U.K. after 1959, issues #1-8 called "Davy Crockett, Frontier Fighter"

KIKU SAN

Aircel; 1 1988-6 1989

1-6 ND Barry Blair script and art

	$0.40	$1.20	$2.00	£0.25	£0.75	£1.25
Title Value:	$2.40	$7.20	$12.00	£1.50	£4.50	£7.50

KILG%RE

Renegade; 1 Nov 1987-5 1988

1-5 ND	$0.40	$1.20	$2.00	£0.25	£0.75	£1.25
Title Value:	$2.00	$6.00	$10.00	£1.25	£3.75	£6.25

KILL RAZOR SPECIAL

Image,OS; 1 Jun 1995

1 ND Codename: Strikeforce spin-off

	$0.45	$1.35	$2.25	£0.30	£0.90	£1.50
Title Value:	$0.45	$1.35	$2.25	£0.30	£0.90	£1.50

KILL YOUR BOYFRIEND

DC Comics/Vertigo,OS; 1 Jun 1995

1 ND 64pgs, Grant Morrison script and Phillip Bond art

	$0.90	$2.70	$4.50	£0.60	£1.80	£3.00
Title Value:	$0.90	$2.70	$4.50	£0.60	£1.80	£3.00

VERY GENERAL PERCENTAGE CONVERSION CHART WHICH MAY BE USED TO CALCULATE LOW AND INBETWEEN GRADES:

	$Good	$Fine	$N.Mint	£Good	£Fine	£N.Mint

KILLER SYNTHETIC TOADS
Artline Studios,OS; 1 Aug 1991

	$Good	$Fine	$N.Mint	£Good	£Fine	£N.Mint
1 ND	$0.40	$1.20	$2.00	£0.25	£0.75	£1.25
Title Value:	$0.40	$1.20	$2.00	£0.25	£0.75	£1.25

KILLER...TALES BY TIM TRUMAN
Eclipse,OS; 1 Mar 1985
1 ND Tim Truman cover and art

	$0.40	$1.20	$2.00	£0.25	£0.75	£1.25
Title Value:	$0.40	$1.20	$2.00	£0.25	£0.75	£1.25

KILLING STROKE, THE
Eternity,MS; 1 Jun 1991-4 Sep 1991
1 ND horror anthology featuring Mark Buckingham, D'Israeli, Shane Oakley, black and white;
   Intro by Jamie Delano

	$0.40	$1.20	$2.00	£0.25	£0.75	£1.25
2-4 ND	$0.40	$1.20	$2.00	£0.25	£0.75	£1.25
Title Value:	$1.60	$4.80	$8.00	£1.00	£3.00	£5.00

KILLPOWER: THE EARLY YEARS
Marvel UK,MS; 1 Aug 1993-4 Dec 1993
1 Codename: Genetix appear

	$0.55	$1.65	$2.75	£0.35	£1.05	£1.75
2-4 Codename: Genetix appear						
	$0.40	$1.20	$2.00	£0.25	£0.75	£1.25
Title Value:	$1.75	$5.25	$8.75	£1.10	£3.30	£5.50

KILROY IS HERE
Caliber Press; 1 Apr 1995-present?
1 ND Negative Burn spin-off; black and white

	$0.60	$1.80	$3.00	£0.40	£1.20	£2.00
1 ND Signed Edition (Sep 1995); black and white						
	$0.60	$1.80	$3.00	£0.40	£1.20	£2.00
2 ND Negative Burn spin-off; black and white						
	$0.60	$1.80	$3.00	£0.40	£1.20	£2.00
3-4 ND black and white						
	$0.60	$1.80	$3.00	£0.40	£1.20	£2.00
Title Value:	$3.00	$9.00	$15.00	£2.00	£6.00	£10.00

KIMURA
Night Wynd,MS; 1 Dec 1991-4 Mar 1992
1-4 ND Barry Blair script and art

	$0.45	$1.35	$2.25	£0.30	£0.90	£1.50
Title Value:	$1.80	$5.40	$9.00	£1.20	£3.60	£6.00

KINDRED, THE
Image; 1 Mar 1994-4 Jun 1994
1 ND Jim Lee and Brandon Choi script, Brett Booth art; bound-in scratch-off trading card

	$1.60	$4.80	$8.00	£1.00	£3.00	£5.00
2 ND Jim Lee and Brandon Choi script, Brett Booth art						
	$1.20	$3.60	$6.00	£0.80	£2.40	£4.00
3 ND Jim Lee and Brandon Choi script, Brett Booth art; 1st appearance Team 7						
	$1.00	$3.00	$5.00	£0.60	£1.80	£3.00
3 Variant cover, ND cover forms larger picture when combined with variant covers of Deathblow #5, Gen 13 #5, Stormwatch #10, Team 7 #1, Union #0, Wetworks #2, WildC.A.T.S. #11						
	$1.40	$4.20	$7.00	£1.00	£3.00	£5.00
4 ND Jim Lee and Brandon Choi script, Brett Booth art						
	$0.80	$2.40	$4.00	£0.50	£1.50	£2.50
Title Value:	$6.00	$18.00	$30.00	£3.90	£11.70	£19.50
Kindred (Feb 1995) Trade paperback reprints mini-series				£1.30	£3.90	£6.50

KING ARTHUR AND THE KNIGHTS OF JUSTICE
Marvel Comics Group,MS; 1 Dec 1993-3 Feb 1994
1 based on animated series; Michael Golden cover

	$0.25	$0.75	$1.25	£0.15	£0.45	£0.75
2 Michael Golden cover						
	$0.25	$0.75	$1.25	£0.15	£0.45	£0.75
3	$0.25	$0.75	$1.25	£0.15	£0.45	£0.75
Title Value:	$0.75	$2.25	$3.75	£0.45	£1.35	£2.25

KING CONAN
Marvel Comics Group; 1 Mar 1980-55 Nov 1989
1 ND 52pgs

	$0.55	$1.65	$2.75	£0.35	£1.05	£1.75
2-6 ND 52pgs	$0.45	$1.35	$2.25	£0.30	£0.90	£1.50
7 ND 52pgs, 1st Paul Smith art (2pgs)						
	$0.55	$1.65	$2.75	£0.35	£1.05	£1.75
8-19 ND 52pgs	$0.45	$1.35	$2.25	£0.30	£0.90	£1.50
20 ND 52pgs, title becomes Conan the King						
	$0.40	$1.20	$2.00	£0.25	£0.75	£1.25
21-30 ND 52pgs	$0.40	$1.20	$2.00	£0.25	£0.75	£1.25
31-55 ND 52pgs	$0.30	$0.90	$1.50	£0.20	£0.60	£1.00
Title Value:	$20.65	$61.95	$103.25	£13.55	£40.65	£67.75

KING KONG
Gold Key; 30036-809 Sep 1968
30036-809 no number on cover; distributed in the U.K. with painted cover

	$3.75	$11.00	$18.75	£2.50	£7.50	£12.50
Title Value:	$3.75	$11.00	$18.75	£2.50	£7.50	£12.50

KING KONG (2ND SERIES)
Monster Comics,MS; 1 Dec 1990-6 Mar 1992
1-3 ND adaptation of film; includes stills from 1933 version; Dave Stevens cover

	$0.40	$1.20	$2.00	£0.25	£0.75	£1.25
4-6 ND	$0.40	$1.20	$2.00	£0.25	£0.75	£1.25
Title Value:	$2.40	$7.20	$12.00	£1.50	£4.50	£7.50

KING OF THE DEAD
Fantaco; 1 1994-2 1994
1-2 ND Steve Niles script, Brian Clark art; black and white

	$0.40	$1.20	$2.00	£0.25	£0.75	£1.25
Title Value:	$0.80	$2.40	$4.00	£0.50	£1.50	£2.50

KINGDOM OF THE DWARFS
Comico,OS; 1 May 1991
1 ND 64pgs, squarebound; colour

	$0.90	$2.70	$4.50	£0.60	£1.80	£3.00
Title Value:	$0.90	$2.70	$4.50	£0.60	£1.80	£3.00

KINGS IN DISGUISE
Kitchen Sink,MS; 1 Mar 1988-6 Aug 1988

	$0.40	$1.20	$2.00	£0.25	£0.75	£1.25
1-6 ND	$0.40	$1.20	$2.00	£0.25	£0.75	£1.25
Title Value:	$2.40	$7.20	$12.00	£1.50	£4.50	£7.50
Kings in Disguise Collection (1990) softcover				£1.70	£5.10	£8.50
Signed and Numbered Hardcover				£2.75	£8.25	£13.75

KINGS OF THE NIGHT
Dark Horse,MS; 1 Aug 1990-2 Sep 1990
1-2 ND Roy and Dann Thomas script, painted covers by John Bolton

	$0.40	$1.20	$2.00	£0.25	£0.75	£1.25
Title Value:	$0.80	$2.40	$4.00	£0.50	£1.50	£2.50

KISS CLASSIC
Marvel Comics Group; nn Apr 1995
1 ND Trade paperback collecting Marvel Comics Super Special #1 and 5

	$2.00	$6.00	$10.00	£1.30	£3.90	£6.50
Title Value:	$2.00	$6.00	$10.00	£1.30	£3.90	£6.50

KISS OF DEATH
(see British section)

KISSYFUR
DC Comics,OS; 1 Sep 1989
1 ND scarce in the U.K.

	$0.25	$0.75	$1.25	£0.15	£0.45	£0.75
Title Value:	$0.25	$0.75	$1.25	£0.15	£0.45	£0.75
Note: based on TV cartoon						

KITTY PRYDE AND WOLVERINE
Marvel Comics Group,MS; 1 Nov 1984-6 Apr 1985
(see X-Men)

	$1.00	$3.00	$5.00	£0.80	£2.40	£4.00
1 ND	$1.00	$3.00	$5.00	£0.80	£2.40	£4.00
2-4 ND	$0.60	$1.80	$3.00	£0.60	£1.80	£3.00
5 ND scarce in the U.K.						
	$0.60	$1.80	$3.00	£0.80	£2.40	£4.00
6 ND very scarce in the U.K.						
	$0.60	$1.80	$3.00	£1.00	£3.00	£5.00
Title Value:	$4.00	$12.00	$20.00	£4.40	£13.20	£22.00

KITZ 'N' KATZ KOMICS
Phantasy/Eclipse; 1 1985-5 1986

	$0.30	$0.90	$1.50	£0.20	£0.60	£1.00
1-5 ND	$0.30	$0.90	$1.50	£0.20	£0.60	£1.00
Title Value:	$1.50	$4.50	$7.50	£1.00	£3.00	£5.00

KLOWN SHOCK
Northstar,MS; 1 Aug 1990-4 1991
1 ND 40pgs, horror material begins

	$0.55	$1.65	$2.75	£0.35	£1.05	£1.75
2-4 ND 32pgs	$0.45	$1.35	$2.25	£0.30	£0.90	£1.50
Title Value:	$1.90	$5.70	$9.50	£1.25	£3.75	£6.25

KLOWNSHOCK (2ND SERIES)
Northstar,MS; 1 Sep 1991-2 1991?

	$0.45	$1.35	$2.25	£0.30	£0.90	£1.50
1-2 ND	$0.45	$1.35	$2.25	£0.30	£0.90	£1.50
Title Value:	$0.90	$2.70	$4.50	£0.60	£1.80	£3.00

KLOWNSHOCK MADHOUSE
Northstar,OS; 1 Apr 1995
1 ND 48pgs, black and white

	$1.00	$3.00	$5.00	£0.65	£1.95	£3.25
Title Value:	$1.00	$3.00	$5.00	£0.65	£1.95	£3.25

KLOWNSHOCK: FREAK SHOW
Northstar,OS; 1 Feb 1994
1 ND 48pgs, foil-embossed cover logo; black and white

	$1.00	$3.00	$5.00	£0.65	£1.95	£3.25
Title Value:	$1.00	$3.00	$5.00	£0.65	£1.95	£3.25

KNIGHT WATCHMAN: GRAVEYARD SHIFT
Caliber Press,MS; 1 Sep 1994
1 ND black and white, cancelled mini-series?

	$0.60	$1.80	$3.00	£0.40	£1.20	£2.00
Title Value:	$0.60	$1.80	$3.00	£0.40	£1.20	£2.00

KNIGHTHAWK
Acclaim Comics/Windjammer,MS; 1 May 1995-6 Jul 1995
1-6 ND Neal Adams script and art with Peter Stone

	$0.45	$1.35	$2.25	£0.30	£0.90	£1.50
Title Value:	$2.70	$8.10	$13.50	£1.80	£5.40	£9.00
Note: originally solicited in early 1994 by Continuity Comics						

KNIGHTMARE
Antarctic Press; 1 Aug 1994-6 May 1995
1-6 ND black and white

	$0.55	$1.65	$2.75	£0.35	£1.05	£1.75
Title Value:	$3.30	$9.90	$16.50	£2.10	£6.30	£10.50

KNIGHTMARE (TALES)
Image; 0 Aug 1995; 1 Feb 1995-present
0 ND (Aug 1995), origin; wraparound chromium cover

	$0.80	$2.40	$4.00	£0.50	£1.50	£2.50
1-2 ND Marat Mychaels and Al Vey creative team						
	$0.45	$1.35	$2.25	£0.30	£0.90	£1.50
3 ND Marat Mychaels and Al Vey creative team; title becomes simply "Knightmare"						
	$0.45	$1.35	$2.25	£0.30	£0.90	£1.50
4 ND Marat Mychaels and Al Vey creative team						
	$0.45	$1.35	$2.25	£0.30	£0.90	£1.50
4 ND variant edition - Joe Quesada & Jimmy Palmiotti cover art						
	$0.80	$2.40	$4.00	£0.50	£1.50	£2.50
5 ND Rob Liefeld, Marat Mychaels and Al Vey						
	$0.45	$1.35	$2.25	£0.30	£0.90	£1.50
6 ND Savage Drgon appears						

MINT = 100% / NEAR MINT (inc. +/-) = 90–99% / VERY FINE (inc. +/-) = 75–89% / FINE (inc. +/-) = 55–74%
VERY GOOD (inc. +/-) = 35–54% / GOOD (inc. +/-) = 15–34% / FAIR = 5–14% / POOR = 1–4%

421

	$Good	$Fine	$N.Mint	£Good	£Fine	£N.Mint
	$0.45	$1.35	$2.25	£0.30	£0.90	£1.50
7 ND Extreme Babewatch tie-in						
	$0.50	$1.50	$2.50	£0.30	£0.90	£1.50
8 ND						
Title Value:	$4.95	$15.90	$26.50	£3.40	£10.20	£17.00

KNIGHTS OF PENDRAGON, THE
Marvel UK; 1 Jul 1990-18 Dec 1991

	$Good	$Fine	$N.Mint	£Good	£Fine	£N.Mint
1 Gary Erskine/Andy Lanning art begins; Captain Britain cameo						
	$0.40	$1.20	$2.00	£0.25	£0.75	£1.25
2-18						
	$0.30	$0.90	$1.50	£0.20	£0.60	£1.00
Title Value:	$5.50	$16.50	$27.50	£3.65	£10.95	£18.25

KNIGHTS OF PENDRAGON, THE (2ND SERIES)
Marvel UK; 1 Jul 1992-15 1993
(see Overkill in British section)

	$Good	$Fine	$N.Mint	£Good	£Fine	£N.Mint
1 Tomlinson and Abnett script, Gascoine and Buylla art; Iron Man co-stars						
	$0.30	$0.90	$1.50	£0.20	£0.60	£1.00
2 Black Knight appears						
	$0.30	$0.90	$1.50	£0.20	£0.60	£1.00
3-5						
	$0.30	$0.90	$1.50	£0.20	£0.60	£1.00
6-8 Spiderman guest-stars						
	$0.30	$0.90	$1.50	£0.20	£0.60	£1.00
9 Spiderman and the Warheads guest-star						
	$0.30	$0.90	$1.50	£0.20	£0.60	£1.00
10 origin Union Jack re-told, Baron Blood returns						
	$0.30	$0.90	$1.50	£0.20	£0.60	£1.00
11-12 MyS-TECH appear						
	$0.30	$0.90	$1.50	£0.20	£0.60	£1.00
13-15 Death's Head II appears						
	$0.30	$0.90	$1.50	£0.20	£0.60	£1.00
Title Value:	$4.50	$13.50	$22.50	£3.00	£9.00	£15.00

KNUCKLES THE MALEVOLENT NUN
Fantagraphics; 1 Aug 1991-2 1991

	$Good	$Fine	$N.Mint	£Good	£Fine	£N.Mint
1-2 ND black and white						
	$0.40	$1.20	$2.00	£0.25	£0.75	£1.25
Title Value:	$0.80	$2.40	$4.00	£0.50	£1.50	£2.50

KOBALT
DC Comics/Milestone; 1 Jun 1994-16 Aug 1995

	$Good	$Fine	$N.Mint	£Good	£Fine	£N.Mint
1-15						
	$0.30	$0.90	$1.50	£0.20	£0.60	£1.00
16 48pgs						
	$0.50	$1.50	$2.50	£0.30	£0.90	£1.50
Title Value:	$5.00	$15.00	$25.00	£3.30	£9.90	£16.50

KOBRA
DC Comics; 1 Feb/Mar 1976-7 Mar/Apr 1977
(see Five-Star Super-Hero Spectacular)

	$Good	$Fine	$N.Mint	£Good	£Fine	£N.Mint
1 Jack Kirby art with faces redrawn by Pablo Marcos - part of Kirby's resignation from DC Comics						
	$0.60	$1.80	$3.00	£0.40	£1.20	£2.00
2 scarce in the U.K.	$0.40	$1.20	$2.00	£0.30	£0.90	£1.50
3 Giffen art	$0.40	$1.20	$2.00	£0.30	£0.90	£1.50
4-5	$0.30	$0.90	$1.50	£0.20	£0.60	£1.00
6 Nasser art	$0.30	$0.90	$1.50	£0.20	£0.60	£1.00
7 scarce in the U.K. Nasser art						
	$0.30	$0.90	$1.50	£0.25	£0.75	£1.25
Title Value:	$2.60	$7.80	$13.00	£1.85	£5.55	£9.25

KOMAH
Anubis Press; 0 Oct 1994; 1 Dec 1994

	$Good	$Fine	$N.Mint	£Good	£Fine	£N.Mint
0 ND spin-off from Urban Decay; black and white, 5,000 copies						
	$0.55	$1.65	$2.75	£0.35	£1.05	£1.75
1 ND spin-off from Urban Decay; black and white						
	$0.55	$1.65	$2.75	£0.35	£1.05	£1.75
Title Value:	$1.10	$3.30	$5.50	£0.70	£2.10	£3.50

KONG THE UNTAMED
DC Comics; 1 Jun/Jul 1975-5 Feb/Mar 1976

	$Good	$Fine	$N.Mint	£Good	£Fine	£N.Mint
1 Wrightson cover	$0.30	$0.90	$1.50	£0.25	£0.75	£1.25
2 Wrightson cover	$0.30	$0.90	$1.50	£0.20	£0.60	£1.00
3-5	$0.25	$0.75	$1.25	£0.15	£0.45	£0.75
Title Value:	$1.35	$4.05	$6.75	£0.90	£2.70	£4.50

KONGA
Charlton; 1 1960; 2 Aug 1961-23 Nov 1965
(becomes Fantastic Giants)

	$Good	$Fine	$N.Mint	£Good	£Fine	£N.Mint
1 rare in the U.K.	$30.00	$90.00	$180.00	£20.00	£60.00	£120.00
2 scarce in the U.K.						
	$15.00	$45.00	$90.00	£10.00	£30.00	£60.00
3-5 scarce in the U.K. Steve Ditko art						
	$11.00	$34.00	$67.50	£7.50	£22.50	£45.00
6-10 scarce in the U.K. Steve Ditko art						
	$7.50	$22.50	$45.00	£5.00	£15.00	£30.00
11-15 scarce in the U.K. Steve Ditko art						
	$6.75	$20.00	$40.50	£4.50	£13.50	£27.00
16-23	$5.25	$15.50	$31.50	£3.50	£10.50	£21.00
Title Value:	$191.25	$573.50	$1152.00	£128.00	£384.00	£768.00

Note: all distributed in the U.K.

KONGA'S REVENGE
Charlton; 2 Summer 1963-3 Autumn 1963
(previously Return of Konga)

	$Good	$Fine	$N.Mint	£Good	£Fine	£N.Mint
1 reprints issue #3 (1968)						
	$3.00	$9.00	$18.00	£2.00	£6.00	£12.00
2-3 scarce in the U.K. Steve Ditko art						
	$5.25	$15.50	$31.50	£3.50	£10.50	£21.00
Title Value:	$13.50	$40.00	$81.00	£9.00	£27.00	£54.00

Note: all distributed in the U.K.

KONNY & CZU
Antarctic Press,MS; 1 Sep 1994-4 Mar 1995
1-4 ND Matt Howarth script and art; black and white

	$Good	$Fine	$N.Mint	£Good	£Fine	£N.Mint
	$0.55	$1.65	$2.75	£0.35	£1.05	£1.75
Title Value:	$2.20	$6.60	$11.00	£1.40	£4.20	£7.00

KOOL-AID MAN, ADVENTURES OF
DC Comics,OS; 1 1983

	$Good	$Fine	$N.Mint	£Good	£Fine	£N.Mint
1 ND 36pgs, promotional giveaway in U.S.						
	$0.15	$0.45	$0.75	£0.10	£0.35	£0.60
Title Value:	$0.15	$0.45	$0.75	£0.10	£0.35	£0.60

KORAK, SON OF TARZAN
Gold Key; 1 Jan 1964-45 Jan 1972
(published by DC issue #46 on)

	$Good	$Fine	$N.Mint	£Good	£Fine	£N.Mint
1 Russ Manning art						
	$7.50	$22.50	$45.00	£5.00	£15.00	£30.00
2-3 Russ Manning art						
	$3.00	$9.00	$18.00	£2.00	£6.00	£12.00
4-10 Russ Manning art						
	$2.25	$6.75	$13.50	£1.50	£4.50	£9.00
11 Russ Manning art						
	$1.85	$5.50	$11.25	£1.25	£3.75	£7.50
12-20	$1.85	$5.50	$11.25	£1.25	£3.75	£7.50
21-30	$1.50	$4.50	$7.50	£1.00	£3.00	£5.00
31-45	$1.20	$3.60	$6.00	£0.80	£2.40	£4.00
Title Value:	$80.75	$241.75	$453.00	£54.00	£162.00	£302.00

Note: all distributed in the U.K.

KORAK SON OF TARZAN
DC Comics; 46 May/Jun 1972-56 Feb/Mar 1974; 57 May/Jun 1975-59 Sep/Oct 1975
(previously published by Gold Key; becomes Tarzan Family)

	$Good	$Fine	$N.Mint	£Good	£Fine	£N.Mint
46 52pgs, Kaluta art						
	$0.80	$2.40	$4.00	£0.40	£1.20	£2.00
47-59 ND Kaluta art						
	$0.50	$1.50	$2.50	£0.30	£0.90	£1.50
Title Value:	$7.30	$21.90	$36.50	£4.30	£12.90	£21.50

ARTISTS
Kaluta art in 46-56. Manning reprint in 57-59.
FEATURES
Carson of Venus in 46-56. Pellucidar in 46.

KORG: 70,000 BC
Charlton; 1 May 1975-9 Nov 1976

	$Good	$Fine	$N.Mint	£Good	£Fine	£N.Mint
1 scarce in the U.K. based on TV show						
	$0.90	$2.70	$4.50	£0.60	£1.80	£3.00
2 John Byrne text illustration; Pat Boyette painted cover						
	$0.90	$2.70	$4.50	£0.60	£1.80	£3.00
3	$0.45	$1.35	$2.25	£0.30	£0.90	£1.50
4 Pat Boyette painted cover						
	$0.45	$1.35	$2.25	£0.30	£0.90	£1.50
5-9	$0.45	$1.35	$2.25	£0.30	£0.90	£1.50
Title Value:	$4.95	$14.85	$24.75	£3.30	£9.90	£16.50

Note: distributed irregularly in the U.K.

KREE/SKRULL WAR STARRING THE AVENGERS
Marvel Comics Group,MS; 1 Sep 1983-2 Oct 1983

	$Good	$Fine	$N.Mint	£Good	£Fine	£N.Mint
1 ND 68pgs, reprints classic Neal Adams Avengers #93, #94						
	$0.60	$1.80	$3.00	£0.40	£1.20	£2.00
2 ND 68pgs, reprints classic Neal Adams Avengers #95-97						
	$0.60	$1.80	$3.00	£0.40	£1.20	£2.00
Title Value:	$1.20	$3.60	$6.00	£0.80	£2.40	£4.00

KREY
Gauntlet Comics,MS; 1 Sep 1992-5 Aug 1993

	$Good	$Fine	$N.Mint	£Good	£Fine	£N.Mint
1-5 ND	$0.45	$1.35	$2.25	£0.30	£0.90	£1.50
Title Value:	$2.25	$6.75	$11.25	£1.50	£4.50	£7.50

KREY SPECIAL
Caliber Press,OS; 1 Sep 1993

	$Good	$Fine	$N.Mint	£Good	£Fine	£N.Mint
1 ND ties up plot from series; flip-book format						
	$0.70	$2.10	$3.50	£0.45	£1.35	£2.25
Title Value:	$0.70	$2.10	$3.50	£0.45	£1.35	£2.25

KRULL
Marvel Comics Group,MS; 1 Nov 1983-2 Dec 1983

	$Good	$Fine	$N.Mint	£Good	£Fine	£N.Mint
1-2 ND adapts film	$0.25	$0.75	$1.25	£0.15	£0.45	£0.75
Title Value:	$0.50	$1.50	$2.50	£0.30	£0.90	£1.50

KRUSTY COMICS
Bongo Comics,MS; 1 Jan 1995-3 Mar 1995

	$Good	$Fine	$N.Mint	£Good	£Fine	£N.Mint
1-3 ND Matt Groenig art						
	$0.45	$1.35	$2.25	£0.30	£0.90	£1.50
Title Value:	$1.35	$4.05	$6.75	£0.90	£2.70	£4.50

KRYPTON CHRONICLES
DC Comics,MS; 1 Sep 1981-3 Nov 1981
(see World of Krypton)

	$Good	$Fine	$N.Mint	£Good	£Fine	£N.Mint
1-3	$0.25	$0.75	$1.25	£0.15	£0.45	£0.75
Title Value:	$0.75	$2.25	$3.75	£0.45	£1.35	£2.25

KULL AND THE BARBARIANS
Marvel Comics Group,Magazine; 1 May 1975-3 Sep 1975

	$Good	$Fine	$N.Mint	£Good	£Fine	£N.Mint
1 scarce in the U.K. 2pgs Neal Adams art, reprints Kull the Conqueror #1						
	$1.50	$4.50	$7.50	£1.00	£3.00	£5.00
2 scarce in the U.K. Neal Adams inks, Gil Kane art, Red Sonja by Chaykin						
	$0.90	$2.70	$4.50	£0.60	£1.80	£3.00
3 Neal Adams inks, Solomon Kane appears, origin Red Sonja by Chaykin						
	$0.90	$2.70	$4.50	£0.60	£1.80	£3.00
Title Value:	$3.30	$9.90	$16.50	£2.20	£6.60	£11.00

KULL IN 3-D
Blackthorne; (3-D Series #51,#67); 1 Autumn 1988-2 Spring 1989

	$Good	$Fine	$N.Mint	£Good	£Fine	£N.Mint
1-2 ND with bound-in 3-D glasses (25% less if without glasses)						
	$0.45	$1.35	$2.25	£0.30	£0.90	£1.50
Title Value:	$0.90	$2.70	$4.50	£0.60	£1.80	£3.00

	$Good	$Fine	$N.Mint	£Good	£Fine	£N.Mint

KULL THE CONQUEROR

Marvel Comics Group; 1 Jun 1971-2 Sep 1971; 3 Jul 1972-15 Aug 1974; 16 Aug 1976-29 Oct 1978

(becomes Kull the Destroyer) (see Marvel Preview)

	$Good	$Fine	$N.Mint	£Good	£Fine	£N.Mint
1 origin and 2nd appearance Kull (see Creatures on the Loose #10), Wood inks						
	$1.50	$4.50	$7.50	£1.00	£3.00	£5.00
2 ND 3rd appearance Kull						
	$1.00	$3.00	$5.00	£0.70	£2.10	£3.50
3 ND	$1.00	$3.00	$5.00	£0.70	£2.10	£3.50
4-6 ND	$0.60	$1.80	$3.00	£0.40	£1.20	£2.00
7-10	$0.45	$1.35	$2.25	£0.30	£0.90	£1.50
11 Ploog art; titles becomes "Kull the Destroyer"						
	$0.60	$1.80	$3.00	£0.40	£1.20	£2.00
12-15 ND Ploog art						
	$0.40	$1.20	$2.00	£0.30	£0.90	£1.50
16-17 ND	$0.40	$1.20	$2.00	£0.25	£0.75	£1.25
18	$0.40	$1.20	$2.00	£0.20	£0.60	£1.00
19-29 ND	$0.40	$1.20	$2.00	£0.25	£0.75	£1.25
Title Value:	$14.90	$44.70	$74.50	£9.85	£29.55	£49.25

Note: Severin art 2-10

KULL THE CONQUEROR (2ND SERIES)

Marvel Comics Group; 1 Dec 1982-2 Mar 1983

	$Good	$Fine	$N.Mint	£Good	£Fine	£N.Mint
1 ND Buscema art	$0.45	$1.35	$2.25	£0.30	£0.90	£1.50
2 ND Bolton art	$0.45	$1.35	$2.25	£0.30	£0.90	£1.50
Title Value:	$0.90	$2.70	$4.50	£0.60	£1.80	£3.00

Note: 52pgs, Baxter paper.

KULL THE CONQUEROR (3RD SERIES)

Marvel Comics Group; 1 May 1983-10 Jun 1985

	$Good	$Fine	$N.Mint	£Good	£Fine	£N.Mint
1 ND	$0.40	$1.20	$2.00	£0.25	£0.75	£1.25
2 ND Sienkiewicz art						
	$0.30	$0.90	$1.50	£0.20	£0.60	£1.00
3 ND	$0.30	$0.90	$1.50	£0.20	£0.60	£1.00
4 ND Sienkiewicz/Bolton art						
	$0.30	$0.90	$1.50	£0.20	£0.60	£1.00
5-10 ND	$0.30	$0.90	$1.50	£0.20	£0.60	£1.00
Title Value:	$3.10	$9.30	$15.50	£2.05	£6.15	£10.25

KUNG FU FIGHTER

(see Richard Dragon, Kung Fu Fighter)

KUNG FU SPECIAL

Marvel Comics Group, Magazine; 1 1974

	$Good	$Fine	$N.Mint	£Good	£Fine	£N.Mint
1 ND 84pgs, features Iron Fist (part Neal Adams inks), Shang-Chi the Master of Kung-Fu, Sons of the Tiger						
	$0.80	$2.40	$4.00	£0.50	£1.50	£2.50
Title Value:	$0.80	$2.40	$4.00	£0.50	£1.50	£2.50

KYRA

Elsewhere Productions; 1 Winter 1985-5 Spring 1987

	$Good	$Fine	$N.Mint	£Good	£Fine	£N.Mint
1 ND black and white begins; this issue slightly larger size than normal						
	$0.30	$0.90	$1.50	£0.20	£0.60	£1.00
2-5 ND	$0.30	$0.90	$1.50	£0.20	£0.60	£1.00
Title Value:	$1.50	$4.50	$7.50	£1.00	£3.00	£5.00

L

L'IL GENIUS

Charlton; 1 1954-52 Jan 1965; 53 Oct 1965; 54 Oct 1985-55 Jan 1986

	$Good	$Fine	$N.Mint	£Good	£Fine	£N.Mint
1 scarce in the U.K.	$6.75	$20.00	$40.50	£4.50	£13.50	£27.00
2 scarce in the U.K.	$3.35	$10.00	$20.25	£2.25	£6.75	£13.50
3 scarce in the U.K.	$2.60	$7.75	$15.75	£1.75	£5.25	£10.50
4-10	$2.25	$6.75	$13.50	£1.50	£4.50	£9.00
11-15	$1.85	$5.50	$11.25	£1.25	£3.75	£7.50
16-17 68pgs	$2.25	$6.75	$13.50	£1.50	£4.50	£9.00

	$Good	$Fine	$N.Mint	£Good	£Fine	£N.Mint
18 scarce in the U.K. 100pgs						
	$3.75	$11.00	$22.50	£2.50	£7.50	£15.00
19-20	$1.85	$5.50	$11.25	£1.25	£3.75	£7.50
21-30	$1.50	$4.50	$9.00	£1.00	£3.00	£6.00
1st official distribution in the U.K.						
31-40	$0.90	$2.70	$5.40	£0.60	£1.80	£3.60
41-53	$0.60	$1.80	$3.60	£0.40	£1.20	£2.40
54-55 scarce in the U.K.						
	$0.30	$0.90	$1.50	£0.20	£0.60	£1.00
Title Value:	$82.05	$245.20	$493.05	£54.85	£164.55	£328.70

Note: distributed irregularly in the U.K. after 1958/59, prior to official distribution

L'IL GRUESOME

United Way Comics/Eclipse; 1 1988

	$Good	$Fine	$N.Mint	£Good	£Fine	£N.Mint
1 ND colour volunteer community youth comic						
	$0.15	$0.45	$0.75	£0.10	£0.30	£0.50
Title Value:	$0.15	$0.45	$0.75	£0.10	£0.30	£0.50

L'IL KIDS

Marvel Comics Group; 1 Aug 1970-2 Oct 1970; 3 Nov 1971-12 Jun 1973

	$Good	$Fine	$N.Mint	£Good	£Fine	£N.Mint
1 ND rare in the U.K.						
	$1.50	$4.50	$7.50	£1.00	£3.00	£5.00
2 ND rare in the U.K.						
	$0.85	$2.55	$4.25	£0.55	£1.65	£2.75
3-10 ND very scarce in the U.K.						
	$0.60	$1.80	$3.00	£0.40	£1.20	£2.00
11-12 ND very scarce in the U.K.						
	$0.55	$1.65	$2.75	£0.35	£1.05	£1.75
Title Value:	$8.25	$24.75	$41.25	£5.45	£16.35	£27.25

L'IL PALS

Marvel Comics Group; 1 Sep 1972-5 May 1973

	$Good	$Fine	$N.Mint	£Good	£Fine	£N.Mint
1 ND rare in the U.K.						
	$0.80	$2.40	$4.00	£0.50	£1.50	£2.50
2-5 ND rare in the U.K.						
	$0.55	$1.65	$2.75	£0.35	£1.05	£1.75
Title Value:	$3.00	$9.00	$15.00	£1.90	£5.70	£9.50

LA PACIFICA

DC Comics/Paradox,MS; 1 Jan 1995-3 Mar 1995

	$Good	$Fine	$N.Mint	£Good	£Fine	£N.Mint
1-3 ND 96pgs, black and white; digest size						
	$0.90	$2.70	$4.50	£0.60	£1.80	£3.00
Title Value:	$2.70	$8.10	$13.50	£1.80	£5.40	£9.00

LABYRINTH

Marvel Comics Group, Film; 1 Nov 1986-3 Jan 1987

	$Good	$Fine	$N.Mint	£Good	£Fine	£N.Mint
1-3 ND reprints Marvel Super Special #4						
	$0.25	$0.75	$1.25	£0.15	£0.45	£0.75
Title Value:	$0.75	$2.25	$3.75	£0.45	£1.35	£2.25

LADY ARCANE

Hero,MS; 1 Jul 1992-6 1993

	$Good	$Fine	$N.Mint	£Good	£Fine	£N.Mint
1 ND Flare appears	$0.55	$1.65	$2.75	£0.35	£1.05	£1.75
2-5 ND	$0.55	$1.65	$2.75	£0.35	£1.05	£1.75
6 ND 44pgs	$0.60	$1.80	$3.00	£0.40	£1.20	£2.00
Title Value:	$3.35	$10.05	$16.75	£2.15	£6.45	£10.75

LADY CRIME

AC Comics,OS; 1 Aug 1992

	$Good	$Fine	$N.Mint	£Good	£Fine	£N.Mint
1 ND	$0.55	$1.65	$2.75	£0.35	£1.05	£1.75
Title Value:	$0.55	$1.65	$2.75	£0.35	£1.05	£1.75

LADY DEATH

Chaos Comics,MS; 1 Mar 1994-3 May 1994

	$Good	$Fine	$N.Mint	£Good	£Fine	£N.Mint
½ ND produced in conjunction with Wizard Comics; issued in a Wizard protective Mylar with certificate of authenticity						
	$5.00	$15.00	$25.00	£2.50	£7.50	£12.50
½ Gold Edition, ND Gold embossed logo, produced in conjunction with Wizard Comics; issued in a Wizard protective Mylar with certificate of authenticity						

Korak #20

Krusty Comics #1

Lash Larue Western #72

	$Good	$Fine	$N.Mint	£Good	£Fine	£N.Mint
	$9.00	$27.00	$45.00	£3.50	£10.50	£17.50

½ Red Velvet Edition, ND Red velvet embossed logo, produced in conjunction with Wizard Comics; issued in a Wizard protective Mylar with certificate of authenticity

	$Good	$Fine	$N.Mint	£Good	£Fine	£N.Mint
	$10.00	$30.00	$50.00	£5.00	£15.00	£25.00

1 ND Steven Hughes art; chromium enhanced cover. Special guest appearance by Evil Ernie

| | $14.00 | $42.00 | $70.00 | £6.00 | £18.00 | £30.00 |

1 Commemorative Edition, ND Gold embossed logo, signed by creators on cover; limited to 5,000 copies

	$16.00	$48.00	$80.00	£8.00	£24.00	£40.00
2 ND	$7.00	$21.00	$35.00	£4.00	£12.00	£20.00
3 ND	$4.50	$13.50	$22.50	£3.00	£9.00	£15.00
Title Value:	$65.50	$196.50	$327.50	£32.00	£96.00	£160.00

Lady Death: The Reckoning (Jul 1994) Trade paperback
reprints mini-series with new cover by Steven Hughes £0.90 £2.70 £4.50
Lady Death Limited Edition Hardcover (Jul 1994)
reprints series, foil-stamped cover with
dust-jacket plus interviews and unpublished artwork £5.00 £15.00 £25.00
Lady Death: The Reckoning (Sep 1995)
Trade paperback reprints mini-series plus Lady Death ½
and Swimsuit Special £1.70 £5.10 £8.50

LADY DEATH II: BETWEEN HEAVEN & HELL
Chaos Comics,MS; 1 Feb 1995-4 Jun 1995
1 ND Brian Pulido script, Steven Hughes art; wraparound chromium cover

	$1.40	$4.20	$7.00	£0.90	£2.70	£4.50

1 ND Signed & Numbered Limited Edition (Mar 1995) - pre-bagged with certificate and mini-poster; 5,000 copies

| | $6.00 | $18.00 | $30.00 | £4.00 | £12.00 | £20.00 |

1 Black Velvet Edition ND

| | $8.00 | $24.00 | $40.00 | £4.00 | £12.00 | £20.00 |

1 Commemorative Edition, ND produced in conjuction with Comic Cavalcade, limited to 4,000 copies

| | $5.00 | $15.00 | $25.00 | £3.00 | £9.00 | £15.00 |

2-4 ND Brian Pulido script, Steven Hughes art

| | $1.00 | $3.00 | $5.00 | £0.50 | £1.50 | £2.50 |

4 Variant Edition, ND Lady Demon variant cover

| | $5.00 | $15.00 | $25.00 | £3.50 | £10.50 | £17.50 |
| Title Value: | $28.40 | $83.20 | $139.00 | £16.90 | £50.70 | £84.50 |

LADY DEATH IN LINGERIE
Chaos Comics,OS; 1 Aug 1995
1 ND Steven Hughes wraparound cover, pin-ups by Joe Quesada, Joe Linsner, David Mack, Tom Mandrake and others

	$0.60	$1.80	$3.00	£0.40	£1.20	£2.00

1 ND Leather Premium Edition (Aug 1995) - available to retailers with every 50 copies ordered of the regular edition

| | $10.00 | $30.00 | $50.00 | £7.00 | £21.00 | £35.00 |
| Title Value: | $10.60 | $31.80 | $53.00 | £7.40 | £22.20 | £37.00 |

LADY DEATH SWIMSUIT SPECIAL
Chaos Comics,OS; 1 May 1994
1 ND assorted eye-catching pin-ups...

	$0.90	$2.70	$4.50	£0.60	£1.80	£3.00

1 ND Signed & Numbered Edition (Sep 1994), pre-bagged with certificate

| | $4.50 | $13.50 | $22.50 | £3.00 | £9.00 | £15.00 |

1 Red Velvet Edition, ND limited to 10,000 copies [May 1994]

| | $9.00 | $27.00 | $45.00 | £5.00 | £15.00 | £25.00 |
| Title Value: | $14.40 | $43.20 | $72.00 | £8.60 | £25.80 | £43.00 |

LADY JUSTICE, NEIL GAIMAN'S
Tekno Comix; 1 May 1995-present
1 ND Neil Gaiman script, Bill Sienkiewicz cover and art

	$0.40	$1.20	$2.00	£0.25	£0.75	£1.25
2-4 ND	$0.40	$1.20	$2.00	£0.25	£0.75	£1.25
5 ND (non-Code approved issue)	$0.35	$1.10	$1.88	£0.25	£0.75	£1.25
6 ND (non-Code approved issue)	$0.45	$1.35	$2.25	£0.30	£0.90	£1.50
7 ND pre-bagged with Tekno back-issue comic	$0.45	$1.35	$2.25	£0.30	£0.90	£1.50
Title Value:	$2.85	$8.60	$14.14	£1.85	£5.55	£9.25

LADY RAWHIDE
Topps,MS; 1 Jul 1995-present
1 ND Don McGregor script, Mayhew & Palmiotti art begins

	$0.70	$2.10	$3.50	£0.50	£1.50	£2.50
2-3 ND	$0.60	$1.80	$3.00	£0.40	£1.20	£2.00
Title Value:	$1.90	$5.70	$9.50	£1.30	£3.90	£6.50

LADY RAWHIDE SPECIAL EDITION
Topps,OS; 1 Jun 1995
1 ND 64pgs, reprints stories from Zorro #2, #3 with new Adam Hughes cover

	$0.80	$2.40	$4.00	£0.50	£1.50	£2.50
Title Value:	$0.80	$2.40	$4.00	£0.50	£1.50	£2.50

LADY VAMPRE
Blackout Comics; 0 Mar 1995; 1 May 1995-present
0 ND Bob Berry script and art; black and white

	$0.55	$1.65	$2.75	£0.35	£1.05	£1.75

0 ND Commemorative Edition (Jul 1995) - signed by Bob Berry with new cover plus certificate; 5,000 copies

| | $2.00 | $6.00 | $10.00 | £1.20 | £3.60 | £6.00 |

1 ND Bruce Schoengood script, Gutierrez and Moussa art; black and white

| | $0.60 | $1.80 | $3.00 | £0.40 | £1.20 | £2.00 |
| Title Value: | $3.15 | $9.45 | $15.75 | £1.95 | £5.85 | £9.75 |

LADY VAMPRE, DEATH OF
Blackout Comics,OS; 1 Aug 1995
1 ND Mike Migola and Gene Colan flip-cover

	$0.60	$1.80	$3.00	£0.40	£1.20	£2.00
Title Value:	$0.60	$1.80	$3.00	£0.40	£1.20	£2.00

LAFF-A-LYMPICS, HANNA-BARBERA'S
Marvel Comics Group, TV; 1 Mar 1978-13 May 1979

(see Funtastic World of Hanna-Barbera)

	$Good	$Fine	$N.Mint	£Good	£Fine	£N.Mint
1-13 ND	$0.15	$0.45	$0.75	£0.10	£0.35	£0.60
Title Value:	$1.95	$5.85	$9.75	£1.30	£4.55	£7.80

LAFFIN' GAS
Blackthorne; 1 May 1987-12 Jun 1988
1 Adolescent Hamsters appear; parodies on every permutation of Mutant Turtles

	$0.30	$0.90	$1.50	£0.20	£0.60	£1.00
2 Dark Knight parody	$0.30	$0.90	$1.50	£0.20	£0.60	£1.00
3 He-Man parody	$0.30	$0.90	$1.50	£0.20	£0.60	£1.00
5 Boris Bear revenge issue	$0.30	$0.90	$1.50	£0.20	£0.60	£1.00
6 (Blackthorne 3-D Series 16)	$0.45	$1.35	$2.25	£0.30	£0.90	£1.50
7-12	$0.30	$0.90	$1.50	£0.20	£0.60	£1.00
Title Value:	$3.45	$10.35	$17.25	£2.30	£6.90	£11.50

Note: all Non-Distributed on the news-stands in the U.K.

LANCE BARNES: POST-NUKE DICK
Marvel Comics Group,MS; 1 Apr 1993-4 Jul 1993

	$Good	$Fine	$N.Mint	£Good	£Fine	£N.Mint
1-4 ND	$0.40	$1.20	$2.00	£0.25	£0.75	£1.25
Title Value:	$1.60	$4.80	$8.00	£1.00	£3.00	£5.00

LANCE CARRIGAN OF THE GALACTIC LEGION
Quest Publications; 1 Jul 1983

	$Good	$Fine	$N.Mint	£Good	£Fine	£N.Mint
1 ND	$0.25	$0.75	$1.25	£0.15	£0.45	£0.75
Title Value:	$0.25	$0.75	$1.25	£0.15	£0.45	£0.75

LAND OF THE GIANTS
Gold Key, TV; 1 Nov 1968-5 Sep 1969
1 distributed in the U.K. photo cover

	$10.00	$30.00	$50.00	£4.50	£13.50	£22.50

2 distributed in the U.K.

| | $6.00 | $18.00 | $30.00 | £3.00 | £9.00 | £15.00 |

3-5 distributed in the U.K.

| | $4.00 | $12.00 | $20.00 | £2.50 | £7.50 | £12.50 |
| Title Value: | $28.00 | $84.00 | $140.00 | £15.00 | £45.00 | £75.00 |

LARRY NIVEN'S A.R.M.
Adventure; 1 Sep 1990

	$Good	$Fine	$N.Mint	£Good	£Fine	£N.Mint
1 ND	$0.55	$1.65	$2.75	£0.35	£1.05	£1.75
Title Value:	$0.55	$1.65	$2.75	£0.35	£1.05	£1.75

Note: based on novella "Death By Ecstasy"

LARS OF MARS 3-D
Eclipse; (3-D Special 19) 1 Apr 1987
1 ND with bound-in 3-D glasses (25% less if without glasses), painted cover; reprints featuring Murphy Anderson pencils

	$0.55	$1.65	$2.75	£0.35	£1.05	£1.75

1 ND non-3-D issue (100 copies, signed)

| | $0.90 | $2.70 | $4.50 | £0.60 | £1.80 | £3.00 |
| Title Value: | $1.45 | $4.35 | $7.25 | £0.95 | £2.85 | £4.75 |

LASER ERASER & PRESSBUTTON
Eclipse; 1 Nov 1985-6 Jul 1986
(see Three-Dimensional...)
1 ND Steve Dillon art, Garry Leach cover

	$0.40	$1.20	$2.00	£0.25	£0.75	£1.25

2 ND David Lloyd art, Garry Leach cover

| | $0.40 | $1.20 | $2.00 | £0.25 | £0.75 | £1.25 |

3 ND Jerry Paris/Garry Leach art, Steve Dillon cover

| | $0.40 | $1.20 | $2.00 | £0.25 | £0.75 | £1.25 |

4-5 ND Mike Collins and Mark Farmer art

| | $0.40 | $1.20 | $2.00 | £0.25 | £0.75 | £1.25 |

6 ND Mike Collins and Mark Farmer art, Garry Leach cover

| | $0.40 | $1.20 | $2.00 | £0.25 | £0.75 | £1.25 |
| Title Value: | $2.40 | $7.20 | $12.00 | £1.50 | £4.50 | £7.50 |

LASH LARUE WESTERN
Charlton; 47 Mar/Apr 1954-84 Jun 1961
47 scarce in the U.K.

	$Good	$Fine	$N.Mint	£Good	£Fine	£N.Mint
	$11.50	$35.00	$81.00	£7.50	£23.00	£54.00
48	$9.00	$27.00	$63.00	£6.00	£18.00	£42.00
49-50	$7.50	$22.50	$52.50	£5.00	£15.00	£35.00
51-60	$6.00	$18.00	$36.00	£4.00	£12.00	£24.00
61-66	$4.50	$13.50	$27.00	£3.00	£9.00	£18.00
67-68 68pgs	$5.25	$15.50	$31.50	£3.50	£10.50	£21.00
69-70	$4.50	$13.50	$27.00	£3.00	£9.00	£18.00
71-73	$3.75	$11.00	$22.50	£2.50	£7.50	£15.00
1st official distribution in the U.K.						
74-83	$3.75	$11.00	$22.50	£2.50	£7.50	£15.00
84 scarce in the U.K.						
	$4.50	$13.50	$27.00	£3.00	£9.00	£18.00
Title Value:	$195.25	$582.50	$1207.50	£130.00	£390.50	£805.00

Note: some issues distributed in the U.K. after 1959/60, issues #1-46 published by Fawcett Comics

LASH LARUE WESTERN ANNUAL
AC Comics,OS; 1 Sep 1991
1 ND 40pgs, black and white cover and reprint art; $2.95 cover

	$0.50	$1.50	$2.50	£0.35	£1.05	£1.75
Title Value:	$0.50	$1.50	$2.50	£0.35	£1.05	£1.75

LAST ACTION HERO, THE
Topps,MS; 1 Jun 1993-3 Aug 1993
1-3 ND pre-bagged with 3 trading cards, film adaptation

	$0.60	$1.80	$3.00	£0.40	£1.20	£2.00
Title Value:	$1.80	$5.40	$9.00	£1.20	£3.60	£6.00

LAST AMERICAN, THE
Marvel Comics Group/Epic,MS; 1 Dec 1990-4 Mar 1991
1-4 ND script by John Wagner/Alan Grant, art by Steve McMahon

	$0.40	$1.20	$2.00	£0.25	£0.75	£1.25

	$Good	$Fine	$N.Mint	£Good	£Fine	£N.Mint

LEFT COLUMN

	$Good	$Fine	$N.Mint	£Good	£Fine	£N.Mint
Title Value:	$1.60	$4.80	$8.00	£1.00	£3.00	£5.00

LAST AVENGERS STORY, THE
Marvel Comics Group,MS; 1 Nov 1995-2 Dec 1995
1-2 ND 48pgs, Peter David script, Ariel Olivetti painted art; acetate outer cover

	$Good	$Fine	$N.Mint	£Good	£Fine	£N.Mint
	$1.20	$3.60	$6.00	£0.80	£2.40	£4.00
Title Value:	$2.40	$7.20	$12.00	£1.60	£4.80	£8.00

LAST DAYS OF THE JUSTICE SOCIETY SPECIAL
DC Comics,OS; 1986
1 LD in the U.K. 68pgs

	$Good	$Fine	$N.Mint	£Good	£Fine	£N.Mint
	$0.50	$1.50	$2.50	£0.30	£0.90	£1.50
Title Value:	$0.50	$1.50	$2.50	£0.30	£0.90	£1.50

LAST GENERATION
Black Tie; 1 Summer 1987-3 1988

	$Good	$Fine	$N.Mint	£Good	£Fine	£N.Mint
1 ND	$0.60	$1.80	$3.00	£0.40	£1.20	£2.00
2-3 ND	$0.55	$1.65	$2.75	£0.35	£1.05	£1.75
Title Value:	$1.70	$5.10	$8.50	£1.10	£3.30	£5.50

LAST OF THE VIKING HEROES
Genesis West; 1 Mar 1987-12 1991?
1 ND Michael Thibodeaux art begins; part Jack Kirby cover

	$Good	$Fine	$N.Mint	£Good	£Fine	£N.Mint
	$0.45	$1.35	$2.25	£0.30	£0.90	£1.50
1 ND Signed Edition (Dec 1992)						
	$0.45	$1.35	$2.25	£0.30	£0.90	£1.50
2-4 ND	$0.45	$1.35	$2.25	£0.30	£0.90	£1.50
5 ND (2 cover versions exist)						
	$0.45	$1.35	$2.25	£0.30	£0.90	£1.50
6-12 ND	$0.45	$1.35	$2.25	£0.30	£0.90	£1.50
Title Value:	$5.85	$17.55	$29.25	£3.90	£11.70	£19.50

Last of the Viking Heroes: Nidhogger Lives (Jun 1995)
Hardcover, reprints issues #4-12; limited to 100 gold engraved copies £6.50 | £19.50 | £32.50

LAST OF THE VIKING HEROES SUMMER SPECIAL
Genesis West; 1 Oct 1989-3 1991
1 ND Frank Frazetta cover

	$Good	$Fine	$N.Mint	£Good	£Fine	£N.Mint
	$0.60	$1.80	$3.00	£0.40	£1.20	£2.00
1 ND Signed Edition (Jan 1993)						
	$0.60	$1.80	$3.00	£0.40	£1.20	£2.00
2-3 ND	$0.60	$1.80	$3.00	£0.40	£1.20	£2.00
Title Value:	$2.40	$7.20	$12.00	£1.60	£4.80	£8.00

LAST ONE, THE
DC Comics/Vertigo,MS; 1 Jul 1993-6 Dec 1993
1-6 ND J.M. DeMatteis script

	$Good	$Fine	$N.Mint	£Good	£Fine	£N.Mint
	$0.45	$1.35	$2.25	£0.30	£0.90	£1.50
Title Value:	$2.70	$8.10	$13.50	£1.80	£5.40	£9.00

LAST STARFIGHTER, THE
Marvel Comics Group, Film; 1 Oct 1984-3 Dec 1984

	$Good	$Fine	$N.Mint	£Good	£Fine	£N.Mint
1-3 ND adapts film	$0.25	$0.75	$1.25	£0.15	£0.45	£0.75
Title Value:	$0.75	$2.25	$3.75	£0.45	£1.35	£2.25

LAUNCH
Elsewhere Productions; 1 1987

	$Good	$Fine	$N.Mint	£Good	£Fine	£N.Mint
1 ND	$0.40	$1.20	$2.00	£0.25	£0.75	£1.25
Title Value:	$0.40	$1.20	$2.00	£0.25	£0.75	£1.25

LAUNDRYLAND
Fantagraphics; 1 Oct 1990-4 Oct 1992

	$Good	$Fine	$N.Mint	£Good	£Fine	£N.Mint
1-4 ND black and white						
	$0.45	$1.35	$2.25	£0.30	£0.90	£1.50
Title Value:	$1.80	$5.40	$9.00	£1.20	£3.60	£6.00

LAUREL & HARDY IN 3-D
Blackthorne; (3-D Series #23,#34); 1 Autumn 1987-2 Dec 1987
1-2 ND with bound-in 3-D glasses (25% less if without glasses)

	$Good	$Fine	$N.Mint	£Good	£Fine	£N.Mint
	$0.45	$1.35	$2.25	£0.30	£0.90	£1.50
Title Value:	$0.90	$2.70	$4.50	£0.60	£1.80	£3.00

LAUREL AND HARDY
DC Comics,OS; 1 Jul/Aug 1972
1 ND very scarce in the U.K.

	$Good	$Fine	$N.Mint	£Good	£Fine	£N.Mint
	$0.80	$2.40	$4.00	£0.50	£1.50	£2.50
Title Value:	$0.80	$2.40	$4.00	£0.50	£1.50	£2.50

LAW & ORDER
Maximum Comic Press; 1 Aug 1995-present

	$Good	$Fine	$N.Mint	£Good	£Fine	£N.Mint
1-3 ND	$0.50	$1.50	$2.50	£0.30	£0.90	£1.50
Title Value:	$1.50	$4.50	$7.50	£0.90	£2.70	£4.50

LAWDOG
Marvel Comics Group/Epic; 1 May 1993-10 Feb 1994
1 ND embossed metallic ink cover

	$Good	$Fine	$N.Mint	£Good	£Fine	£N.Mint
	$0.45	$1.35	$2.25	£0.30	£0.90	£1.50
2-8 ND	$0.40	$1.20	$2.00	£0.25	£0.75	£1.25
9-10 ND bound-in trading card						
	$0.40	$1.20	$2.00	£0.25	£0.75	£1.25
Title Value:	$4.05	$12.15	$20.25	£2.55	£7.65	£12.75

LAWDOG VS. GRIMROD
Marvel Comics Group/Epic,OS; 1 Nov 1993
1 ND 48pgs, bound-in trading card

	$Good	$Fine	$N.Mint	£Good	£Fine	£N.Mint
	$0.70	$2.10	$3.50	£0.45	£1.35	£2.25
Title Value:	$0.70	$2.10	$3.50	£0.45	£1.35	£2.25

LAWNMOWER MAN GRAPHIC NOVEL, THE
Innovation, OS; 1 Jun 1992
1 ND 80pgs, based on film including scenes cut from final version

	$Good	$Fine	$N.Mint	£Good	£Fine	£N.Mint
	$1.40	$4.20	$7.00	£0.90	£2.70	£4.50
Title Value:	$1.40	$4.20	$7.00	£0.90	£2.70	£4.50

LAZARUS CHURCHYARD
Tundra,MS; 1 Aug 1992
1 ND reprints from British magazine "Blast!"

	$Good	$Fine	$N.Mint	£Good	£Fine	£N.Mint
	$0.80	$2.40	$4.00	£0.50	£1.50	£2.50
Title Value:	$0.80	$2.40	$4.00	£0.50	£1.50	£2.50

Note: announced as a mini-series but cancelled after one issue

LAZIEST SECRETARY IN THE WORLD, THE
DC Comics/Piranha Press; 1 Oct 1990
1 ND 80pgs, Jennifer Waters and Gil Ashley

	$Good	$Fine	$N.Mint	£Good	£Fine	£N.Mint
	$2.00	$6.00	$10.00	£1.30	£3.90	£6.50
Title Value:	$2.00	$6.00	$10.00	£1.30	£3.90	£6.50

LEADING COMICS
National Periodical Publications; 1 Winter 1941-77 Aug/Sep 1955
1 origin and 1st appearance The Seven Soldiers of Victory (Star Spangled Kid & Stripsey, Crimson Avenger, Green Arrow & Speedy, Vigilante, Shining Knight)

	$Good	$Fine	$N.Mint	£Good	£Fine	£N.Mint
	$330.00	$990.00	$2650.00	£225.00	£670.00	£1800.00
2	$125.00	$375.00	$875.00	£85.00	£255.00	£595.00
3	$110.00	$330.00	$775.00	£75.00	£225.00	£525.00
4-5	$80.00	$240.00	$560.00	£55.00	£165.00	£385.00
6-7	$70.00	$210.00	$490.00	£50.00	£150.00	£350.00
8 scarce in the U.K. classic hour-glass cover						
	$70.00	$210.00	$490.00	£50.00	£150.00	£350.00
9-10	$70.00	$210.00	$490.00	£50.00	£150.00	£350.00
11-14	$50.00	$150.00	$350.00	£35.00	£105.00	£245.00
15 contents change to all funny animal material such as King Oscar's Court						
	$25.00	$75.00	$175.00	£15.00	£45.00	£105.00
16-18	$10.50	$32.00	$75.00	£6.25	£19.00	£45.00
19 scarce in the U.K.						
	$10.50	$32.00	$75.00	£8.00	£24.00	£56.00
20-22	$10.50	$32.00	$75.00	£6.25	£19.00	£45.00
23 1st appearance of Peter Porkchops who becomes the main feature						
	$21.00	$62.50	$150.00	£15.00	£45.00	£105.00
24-30	$10.50	$32.00	$75.00	£6.25	£19.00	£45.00
31-32	$8.50	$26.00	$60.00	£5.00	£15.00	£35.00
33 scarce in the U.S, very scarce in the U.K.						
	$21.00	$62.50	$150.00	£14.00	£43.00	£100.00
34 title changes to "Leading Screen Comics" though contents are still funny animal						
	$8.50	$26.00	$60.00	£5.00	£15.00	£35.00
35-42	$8.50	$26.00	$60.00	£5.00	£15.00	£35.00
43-60	$7.00	$21.00	$50.00	£4.25	£12.50	£30.00
61-77	$7.00	$21.00	$50.00	£3.55	£10.50	£25.00
Title Value:	$1827.50	$5494.00	$13205.00	£1210.10	£3622.50	£8721.00

Note: all Non-Distributed on the news-stands in the U.K. but it is possible that copies found their way over through G.I.'s, Red Cross Parcels etc. Most issues in this title however are generally scarce in the U.K.

LEAF
NAB; 1-4 1990
1 ND black and white

	$Good	$Fine	$N.Mint	£Good	£Fine	£N.Mint
	$0.30	$0.90	$1.50	£0.20	£0.60	£1.00
1 ND black and white, Deluxe Edition						
	$0.80	$2.40	$4.00	£0.50	£1.50	£2.50
2-4 ND black and white						
	$0.30	$0.90	$1.50	£0.20	£0.60	£1.00
Title Value:	$2.00	$6.00	$10.00	£1.30	£3.90	£6.50

LEAGUE OF CHAMPIONS, THE
Hero; 1 Oct 1990-15 1992

	$Good	$Fine	$N.Mint	£Good	£Fine	£N.Mint
1-3 ND	$0.45	$1.35	$2.25	£0.30	£0.90	£1.50
4 ND $3.50 cover begins						
	$0.70	$2.10	$3.50	£0.45	£1.35	£2.25
5-6 ND	$0.70	$2.10	$3.50	£0.45	£1.35	£2.25
7-10 ND pre-bagged with trading card						
	$0.70	$2.10	$3.50	£0.45	£1.35	£2.25
11-12 ND 44pgs, $3.95 cover; pre-bagged with trading card						
	$0.80	$2.40	$4.00	£0.50	£1.50	£2.50
13-15 ND 44pgs	$0.60	$1.80	$3.00	£0.40	£1.20	£2.00
Title Value:	$9.65	$28.95	$48.25	£6.25	£18.75	£31.25

LEAGUE OF JUSTICE
DC Comics/Elseworlds,MS; 1 Nov 1995-2 Dec 1995
1-2 ND 48pgs, Elseworlds versions of the Justice League of America appear set in a medieval dimension

	$Good	$Fine	$N.Mint	£Good	£Fine	£N.Mint
	$1.20	$3.60	$6.00	£0.80	£2.40	£4.00
Title Value:	$2.40	$7.20	$12.00	£1.60	£4.80	£8.00

LEATHER AND LACE
Aircel; 1 Jul 1989-25 Nov 1991
1 Barry Blair script and art begins, black and white

	$Good	$Fine	$N.Mint	£Good	£Fine	£N.Mint
	$1.20	$3.60	$6.00	£0.80	£2.40	£4.00
1 2nd printing	$0.55	$1.65	$2.75	£0.35	£1.05	£1.75
2	$0.90	$2.70	$4.50	£0.60	£1.80	£3.00
2 2nd printing	$0.45	$1.35	$2.25	£0.30	£0.90	£1.50
3	$0.80	$2.40	$4.00	£0.50	£1.50	£2.50
3 2nd printing	$0.45	$1.35	$2.25	£0.30	£0.90	£1.50
4	$0.70	$2.10	$3.50	£0.45	£1.35	£2.25
4 2nd printing	$0.40	$1.20	$2.00	£0.25	£0.75	£1.25
5	$0.70	$2.10	$3.50	£0.45	£1.35	£2.25
5 2nd printing	$0.40	$1.20	$2.00	£0.25	£0.75	£1.25
6	$0.60	$1.80	$3.00	£0.40	£1.20	£2.00
6 2nd printing	$0.40	$1.20	$2.00	£0.25	£0.75	£1.25
7	$0.60	$1.80	$3.00	£0.40	£1.20	£2.00
7 2nd printing	$0.40	$1.20	$2.00	£0.25	£0.75	£1.25
8	$0.60	$1.80	$3.00	£0.40	£1.20	£2.00
8 2nd printing	$0.40	$1.20	$2.00	£0.25	£0.75	£1.25
9	$0.60	$1.80	$3.00	£0.40	£1.20	£2.00
9 2nd printing	$0.40	$1.20	$2.00	£0.25	£0.75	£1.25
10	$0.60	$1.80	$3.00	£0.40	£1.20	£2.00
10 2nd printing	$0.40	$1.20	$2.00	£0.25	£0.75	£1.25
11 1st banned issue in U.K.						
	$0.45	$1.35	$2.25	£0.30	£0.90	£1.50
12-21	$0.40	$1.20	$2.00	£0.25	£0.75	£1.25
22 $2.95 cover begins						

	$Good	$Fine	$N.Mint	£Good	£Fine	£N.Mint
	$0.55	$1.65	$2.75	£0.35	£1.05	£1.75
23-25	$0.55	$1.65	$2.75	£0.35	£1.05	£1.75
Title Value:	$18.20	$54.60	$91.00	£11.70	£35.10	£58.50

Note: all Non-Distributed on the news-stands in the U.K.

	$Good	$Fine	$N.Mint	£Good	£Fine	£N.Mint
Summer Special (Aug 1990)				£0.30	£0.90	£1.50

Search for Cindy Wilde Graphic Novel

	$Good	$Fine	$N.Mint	£Good	£Fine	£N.Mint
reprints issues #1-4, pre-bagged				£1.65	£4.95	£8.25

Holiday in Cambodia Graphic Album (Oct 1990)

	£Good	£Fine	£N.Mint
reprints #5-8 plus new 8pg story, pre-bagged	£1.65	£4.95	£8.25
Black Velvet Graphic Album (Jul 1991) reprints #9-12	£1.20	£3.60	£6.00

Note: adult content/nudity. Comics sealed in plastic bags. Opened bags would bring 50% of the above values. Artist on all, Barry Blair, also does a "tame" version of the same comics which sell for cover price. Back stocks from Aircel generally very good for both at the time.

LEATHER AND LACE II: BLOOD, SEX AND TEARS
Aircel,MS; 1 Dec 1991-4 Mar 1992

	$Good	$Fine	$N.Mint	£Good	£Fine	£N.Mint
1-4 ND	$0.55	$1.65	$2.75	£0.35	£1.05	£1.75
Title Value:	$2.20	$6.60	$11.00	£1.40	£4.20	£7.00

LEATHERFACE
Northstar; 1 Apr 1991-5 Jun 1992

1 ND based on Texas Chainsaw Massacre film, Dave Dorman cover

	$Good	$Fine	$N.Mint	£Good	£Fine	£N.Mint
	$0.60	$1.80	$3.00	£0.40	£1.20	£2.00
2-5 ND	$0.45	$1.35	$2.25	£0.30	£0.90	£1.50
Title Value:	$2.40	$7.20	$12.00	£1.60	£4.80	£8.00

LEATHERFACE (2ND SERIES)
Comico; 1-3 1991; Northstar; 4 1992-8 1993

	$Good	$Fine	$N.Mint	£Good	£Fine	£N.Mint
1 ND	$0.60	$1.80	$3.00	£0.40	£1.20	£2.00

1 2nd printing, ND (Apr 1992)

	$Good	$Fine	$N.Mint	£Good	£Fine	£N.Mint
	$0.45	$1.35	$2.25	£0.30	£0.90	£1.50
2-8 ND	$0.45	$1.35	$2.25	£0.30	£0.90	£1.50
Title Value:	$4.20	$12.60	$21.00	£2.80	£8.40	£14.00

LEATHERFACE SPECIAL
Northstar,OS; 1 May 1992

	$Good	$Fine	$N.Mint	£Good	£Fine	£N.Mint
1 ND	$0.55	$1.65	$2.75	£0.35	£1.05	£1.75
Title Value:	$0.55	$1.65	$2.75	£0.35	£1.05	£1.75

LEAVE IT TO BINKY
(see Binky)

LEGACY
Majestic Entertainment; 1 Oct 1993-6 1994

1 ND Tom Morgan and Stan Woch art begins; small glow in the dark image on cover

	$Good	$Fine	$N.Mint	£Good	£Fine	£N.Mint
	$0.55	$1.65	$2.75	£0.35	£1.05	£1.75
2-6 ND	$0.45	$1.35	$2.25	£0.30	£0.90	£1.50
Title Value:	$2.80	$8.40	$14.00	£1.85	£5.55	£9.25

LEGEND OF KAMUI
(see Kamui)

LEGEND OF MOTHER SARAH, THE
Dark Horse,MS; 1 Apr 1995-8 Nov 1995

1-8 ND Katsuhiro Otomo script and art (translated by Dana Lewis and Toren Smith)

	$Good	$Fine	$N.Mint	£Good	£Fine	£N.Mint
	$0.45	$1.35	$2.25	£0.30	£0.90	£1.50
Title Value:	$3.60	$10.80	$18.00	£2.40	£7.20	£12.00

LEGEND OF THE SHIELD
(see Shield...)

LEGEND OF WONDER WOMAN
(see Wonder Woman)

LEGENDS
Cross-over series that lead to the formation of the modern Suicide Squad and the new Justice League. The cross-overs are are listed outside the core mini-series of the same name in alphabetical rather than chronological order.

1) Batman #401,
2) Blue Beetle #9,
3) Blue Beetle #10,
4) Cosmic Boy #1,
5) Cosmic Boy #2,
6) Cosmic Boy #3,
7) Cosmic Boy #4,
8) Detective Comics #568,
9) Firestorm #55,
10) Firestorm #56,
11) Justice League of America #258,
12) Justice League of America #259,
13) Justice League of America #260,
14) Secret Origins (3rd Series) #10,
15) Shazam: The New Beginning #1,
16) Shazam: The New Beginning #2,
17) Shazam: The New Beginning #3,
18) Shazam: The New Beginning #4,
19) Superman, Adventures of #426,
20) Warlord #114,
21) Warlord #115

LEGENDS (LIMITED SERIES)
DC Comics,MS; 1 Nov 1986-6 Apr 1987

1 1st appearance new Captain Marvel

	$Good	$Fine	$N.Mint	£Good	£Fine	£N.Mint
	$0.40	$1.20	$2.00	£0.20	£0.60	£1.00
2	$0.40	$1.20	$2.00	£0.20	£0.60	£1.00

3 1st appearance new Suicide Squad (see Brave and the Bold #25 for original team)

	$Good	$Fine	$N.Mint	£Good	£Fine	£N.Mint
	$0.40	$1.20	$2.00	£0.20	£0.60	£1.00
4	$0.40	$1.20	$2.00	£0.20	£0.60	£1.00

5 new Justice League appear in last panel though un-named

	$Good	$Fine	$N.Mint	£Good	£Fine	£N.Mint
	$0.40	$1.20	$2.00	£0.20	£0.60	£1.00

6 1st appearance new Justice League

	$Good	$Fine	$N.Mint	£Good	£Fine	£N.Mint
	$0.50	$1.50	$2.50	£0.40	£1.20	£2.00
Title Value:	$2.50	$7.50	$12.50	£1.40	£4.20	£7.00

Note: Byrne cover/art in all. Multi cross-over title similar to Crisis on Infinite, Earths and Millennium. Last panel #5 features 1st assembly of new Justice League

	$Good	$Fine	$N.Mint	£Good	£Fine	£N.Mint
Legends (Jul 1993)						
Trade paperback reprints mini-series, new John Byrne cover				£1.85	£5.55	£9.25

LEGENDS OF THE STARGRAZERS
Innovation; 1 Jun 1989-5 1990

1-5 ND colour; "good girl in space" type story begins

	$Good	$Fine	$N.Mint	£Good	£Fine	£N.Mint
	$0.30	$0.90	$1.50	£0.20	£0.60	£1.00
Title Value:	$1.50	$4.50	$7.50	£1.00	£3.00	£5.00

LEGENDS OF THE WORLD'S FINEST
DC Comics,MS; 1 Feb 1994-3 Apr 1994

1-3 ND 48pgs, squarebound; Walt Simonson script, Daniel Brereton painted art

	$Good	$Fine	$N.Mint	£Good	£Fine	£N.Mint
	$1.00	$3.00	$5.00	£0.60	£1.80	£3.00
Title Value:	$3.00	$9.00	$15.00	£1.80	£5.40	£9.00

Legends of the World's Finest (Apr 1995) Trade paperback

	£Good	£Fine	£N.Mint
160pgs, reprints mini-series, new painted cover	£2.00	£6.00	£10.00

LEGION '89 (-'94)
DC Comics; 1 Feb 1989-70 Sep 1994

(Becomes Legion '90 with Jan 1990 issue, Legion '91 with Jan 1991 issue, Legion '92 with Jan 1992 issue, Legion '93 with Jan 1993 issue, Legion '94 with Jan 1994 issue)

1 Barry Kitson art begins, Keith Giffen/Alan Grant script begins

	$Good	$Fine	$N.Mint	£Good	£Fine	£N.Mint
	$0.50	$1.50	$2.50	£0.30	£0.90	£1.50
2	$0.40	$1.20	$2.00	£0.25	£0.75	£1.25

3 Lobo joins; appears in most issues hereafter

	$Good	$Fine	$N.Mint	£Good	£Fine	£N.Mint
	$0.50	$1.50	$2.50	£0.30	£0.90	£1.50
4-10	$0.40	$1.20	$2.00	£0.25	£0.75	£1.25

11 1st Legion '90 issue

	$Good	$Fine	$N.Mint	£Good	£Fine	£N.Mint
	$0.30	$0.90	$1.50	£0.20	£0.60	£1.00
12-22	$0.30	$0.90	$1.50	£0.20	£0.60	£1.00

23 48pgs, 1st Legion '91 issue

	$Good	$Fine	$N.Mint	£Good	£Fine	£N.Mint
	$0.40	$1.20	$2.00	£0.25	£0.75	£1.25
24-30	$0.30	$0.90	$1.50	£0.20	£0.60	£1.00

31 Captain Marvel appears

	$Good	$Fine	$N.Mint	£Good	£Fine	£N.Mint
	$0.30	$0.90	$1.50	£0.20	£0.60	£1.00
32-33	$0.30	$0.90	$1.50	£0.20	£0.60	£1.00

34 1st Legion '92 issue

	$Good	$Fine	$N.Mint	£Good	£Fine	£N.Mint
	$0.30	$0.90	$1.50	£0.20	£0.60	£1.00
35 Lobo "dies"	$0.30	$0.90	$1.50	£0.20	£0.60	£1.00
36-37	$0.30	$0.90	$1.50	£0.20	£0.60	£1.00

38 Lobo vs. Ice Man

	$Good	$Fine	$N.Mint	£Good	£Fine	£N.Mint
	$0.30	$0.90	$1.50	£0.20	£0.60	£1.00
39	$0.30	$0.90	$1.50	£0.20	£0.60	£1.00

40 Barry Kitson scripts begin

	$Good	$Fine	$N.Mint	£Good	£Fine	£N.Mint
	$0.30	$0.90	$1.50	£0.20	£0.60	£1.00
41-44 bi-weekly	$0.30	$0.90	$1.50	£0.20	£0.60	£1.00

45-47 Green Lantern (Hal Jordan) guest stars

	$Good	$Fine	$N.Mint	£Good	£Fine	£N.Mint
	$0.30	$0.90	$1.50	£0.20	£0.60	£1.00

48 $1.75 cover begins

	$Good	$Fine	$N.Mint	£Good	£Fine	£N.Mint
	$0.40	$1.20	$2.00	£0.25	£0.75	£1.25
49	$0.40	$1.20	$2.00	£0.25	£0.75	£1.25

50 64pgs, Lobo and Dox vs. Ig'nea

	$Good	$Fine	$N.Mint	£Good	£Fine	£N.Mint
	$0.60	$1.80	$3.00	£0.40	£1.20	£2.00
51-52	$0.40	$1.20	$2.00	£0.25	£0.75	£1.25
53-56 bi-weekly	$0.40	$1.20	$2.00	£0.25	£0.75	£1.25

57 Trinity part 3, continued in Darkstars #11

	$Good	$Fine	$N.Mint	£Good	£Fine	£N.Mint
	$0.40	$1.20	$2.00	£0.25	£0.75	£1.25

59 Trinity part 6, continued in Darkstars #12

	$Good	$Fine	$N.Mint	£Good	£Fine	£N.Mint
	$0.40	$1.20	$2.00	£0.25	£0.75	£1.25
60	$0.40	$1.20	$2.00	£0.25	£0.75	£1.25

61-62 Barry Kitson cover

	$Good	$Fine	$N.Mint	£Good	£Fine	£N.Mint
	$0.40	$1.20	$2.00	£0.25	£0.75	£1.25

63 Superman appears, Barry Kitson cover

	$Good	$Fine	$N.Mint	£Good	£Fine	£N.Mint
	$0.40	$1.20	$2.00	£0.25	£0.75	£1.25

64-68 Barry Kitson cover

	$Good	$Fine	$N.Mint	£Good	£Fine	£N.Mint
	$0.40	$1.20	$2.00	£0.25	£0.75	£1.25
69	$0.40	$1.20	$2.00	£0.25	£0.75	£1.25

70 48pgs, Zero Hour X-over, previews new team Rebels '94

	$Good	$Fine	$N.Mint	£Good	£Fine	£N.Mint
	$0.45	$1.35	$2.25	£0.30	£0.90	£1.50
Title Value:	$24.45	$73.35	$122.25	£15.75	£47.25	£78.75

Note: spin-off from Invasion mini-series New Format

LEGION '90 (-'94) ANNUAL
DC Comics; 1 Aug 1990-5 1994

1 48pgs, Superman guest-stars, Alan Grant script, continued from Adventures of Superman Annual 2

	$Good	$Fine	$N.Mint	£Good	£Fine	£N.Mint
	$0.50	$1.50	$2.50	£0.30	£0.90	£1.50

2 64pgs, Armageddon: 2001 tie-in

	$Good	$Fine	$N.Mint	£Good	£Fine	£N.Mint
	$0.50	$1.50	$2.50	£0.30	£0.90	£1.50

3 64pgs, Eclipso: The Darkness Within tie-in, Justice League appear

	$Good	$Fine	$N.Mint	£Good	£Fine	£N.Mint
	$0.50	$1.50	$2.50	£0.30	£0.90	£1.50

4 64pgs, Bloodlines (Wave Two) part 23, 1st appearance Pax, continued in Bloodbath Special #1

	$Good	$Fine	$N.Mint	£Good	£Fine	£N.Mint
	$0.50	$1.50	$2.50	£0.30	£0.90	£1.50

5 64pgs, Elseworlds story; Dick Sprang and Curt Swan art featured

	$Good	$Fine	$N.Mint	£Good	£Fine	£N.Mint
	$0.60	$1.80	$3.00	£0.40	£1.20	£2.00
Title Value:	$2.60	$7.80	$13.00	£1.60	£4.80	£8.00

LEGION ARCHIVES
DC Comics; 1 Dec 1991; 2 Dec 1992; 3 Oct 1993; 4 Oct 1994; 5 1995-present

1 ND 256pgs, reprints Legion appearances in chronological order from Adventure Comics #247-#305

	$Good	$Fine	$N.Mint	£Good	£Fine	£N.Mint
	$7.50	$22.50	$37.50	£5.00	£15.00	£25.00

2 ND 256pgs, reprints Legion appearances in chronological order from Adventure Comics #306-#317

	$Good	$Fine	$N.Mint	£Good	£Fine	£N.Mint
	$7.50	$22.50	$37.50	£5.00	£15.00	£25.00

3 ND 256pgs, reprints Legion appearances in chronological order from Adventure Comics #318-330

	$Good	$Fine	$N.Mint	£Good	£Fine	£N.Mint
	$7.50	$22.50	$37.50	£5.00	£15.00	£25.00

4 ND 224pgs, reprints Legion appearances in chronological order from Adventure Comics #329-339

	$Good	$Fine	$N.Mint	£Good	£Fine	£N.Mint
	$7.50	$22.50	$37.50	£5.00	£15.00	£25.00

	$Good	$Fine	$N.Mint	£Good	£Fine	£N.Mint
5 ND 224pgs, reprints Legion appearances in chronological order from Adventure Comics #340-349						
	$7.50	$22.50	$37.50	£5.00	£15.00	£25.00
Title Value:	$37.50	$112.50	$187.50	£25.00	£75.00	£125.00

LEGION OF MONSTERS
Marvel Comics Group, Magazine; 1 Sep 1975

	$Good	$Fine	$N.Mint	£Good	£Fine	£N.Mint
1 features Frankenstein, Dracula, Manphibian; limited distribution in the U.K.						
	$0.90	$2.70	$4.50	£0.60	£1.80	£3.00
Title Value:	$0.90	$2.70	$4.50	£0.60	£1.80	£3.00

LEGION OF NIGHT
Marvel Comics Group, MS; 1 Nov 1991-2 Dec 1991

	$Good	$Fine	$N.Mint	£Good	£Fine	£N.Mint
1-2 ND Steve Gerber script, Whilce Portacio art						
	$1.00	$3.00	$5.00	£0.60	£1.80	£3.00
Title Value:	$2.00	$6.00	$10.00	£1.20	£3.60	£6.00

LEGION OF STUPID HEROES
Blackthorne, OS; 1 Jan 1987

	$Good	$Fine	$N.Mint	£Good	£Fine	£N.Mint
1 ND Legion parody	$0.30	$0.90	$1.50	£0.20	£0.60	£1.00
Title Value:	$0.30	$0.90	$1.50	£0.20	£0.60	£1.00

LEGION OF SUBSTITUTE HEROES SPECIAL
DC Comics, OS; 1 Jul 1985

	$Good	$Fine	$N.Mint	£Good	£Fine	£N.Mint
1 Giffen cover, part art						
	$0.40	$1.20	$2.00	£0.25	£0.75	£1.25
Title Value:	$0.40	$1.20	$2.00	£0.25	£0.75	£1.25

LEGION OF SUPER-HEROES
(see Action Comics, Adventure Comics, All New Collector's Edition, Brave and the Bold, DC Comics Presents, DC Special, DC Special Blue Ribbon Digest, DC Super-Stars, Limited Collector's Edition, Secrets of the Legion of Super-Heroes, Secret Origins, Secret Origins of Super-Heroes, Superboy, Superboy and the Legion of Super-Heroes, Superman, Superman Annual, Super-Star Holiday Special)

Special Note: see Superboy #259-313 which was techically the third series of Legion adventures with the current one as the fourth. It was thought better to combine this third series as part of the Superboy run.

Special note: All appearances of the Legion prior to Adventure Comics #300 (Sep 1962, when they began their own regular series) are listed under the titles in which they occurred. For your information, here is a chronological list of all Legion appearances prior to Adventure #300:

1) Adventure Comics 247 (April 1958)
2) Adventure Comics 267 (December 1959)
3) Action Comics 267 (August 1960)
4) Superboy 86 (January 1961)
5) Adventure Comics 282 (March 1961)
6) Action Comics 276 (May 1961)
7) Superman 147 (August 1961)
8) Adventure Comics 289, statuettes in one panel only) (October 1961)
(Note: this is highly debateable as an actual appearance)
9) Adventure Comics 290 (November 1961)
10) Superman 149 (November 1961)
11) Superboy 93 (December 1961)
12) Superman Annual 4 (1961)
13) Action Comics 285 (February 1962)
14) Adventure Comics 293 (February 1962)
15) Action Comics 287 (April 1962)
16) Superman 152 (April 1962)
17) Action Comics 289 (June 1962)
18) Action Comics 290 (July 1962)
19) Superboy 98 (July 1962)
20) Superman 155 (August 1962)

Mon-El appearances prior to Adventure #300 are noted independently, as he was not a Legion member before that time. They are to be found in the following issues: Action Comics #284, 288; Jimmy Olsen #62; Lois Lane #33; Superboy #89 (1st appearance).

LEGION OF SUPER-HEROES (1ST SERIES)
DC Comics; 1 Feb 1973-4 Jul/Aug 1973

	$Good	$Fine	$N.Mint	£Good	£Fine	£N.Mint
1 scarce in the U.K. Legion and Tommy Tomorrow reprints begin from Adventure and Action Comics respectively						
	$1.50	$4.50	$7.50	£1.00	£3.00	£5.00
2-4 scarce in the U.K.						

	$Good	$Fine	$N.Mint	£Good	£Fine	£N.Mint
	$1.20	$3.60	$6.00	£0.80	£2.40	£4.00
Title Value:	$5.10	$15.30	$25.50	£3.40	£10.20	£17.00

LEGION OF SUPER-HEROES (2ND SERIES)
DC Comics; 1 Aug 1984-63 Aug 1989

	$Good	$Fine	$N.Mint	£Good	£Fine	£N.Mint
1 ND	$0.70	$2.10	$3.50	£0.50	£1.50	£2.50
2-3 ND scarce in the U.K.						
	$0.50	$1.50	$2.50	£0.30	£0.90	£1.50
4 ND Karate Kid dies						
	$0.40	$1.20	$2.00	£0.25	£0.75	£1.25
5 ND Nemesis Kid dies						
	$0.40	$1.20	$2.00	£0.25	£0.75	£1.25
6-11 ND	$0.40	$1.20	$2.00	£0.25	£0.75	£1.25
12 ND Cosmic Boy, Lighting Lad, Saturn Girl resign						
	$0.40	$1.20	$2.00	£0.25	£0.75	£1.25
13 ND	$0.40	$1.20	$2.00	£0.25	£0.75	£1.25
14 ND 1st appearance Tellus, Sensor Girl, Quislet						
	$0.40	$1.20	$2.00	£0.25	£0.75	£1.25
15 ND	$0.40	$1.20	$2.00	£0.25	£0.75	£1.25
16 ND Supergirl's death foreseen/remembered, X-over with Crisis #7						
	$0.40	$1.20	$2.00	£0.25	£0.75	£1.25
17 ND	$0.40	$1.20	$2.00	£0.25	£0.75	£1.25
18 ND Crisis X-over						
	$0.40	$1.20	$2.00	£0.25	£0.75	£1.25
19-22 ND	$0.40	$1.20	$2.00	£0.25	£0.75	£1.25
23 ND last Superboy in Legion						
	$0.40	$1.20	$2.00	£0.25	£0.75	£1.25
24 ND	$0.40	$1.20	$2.00	£0.25	£0.75	£1.25
25 ND Sensor Girl revealed as Princess Projectra						
	$0.40	$1.20	$2.00	£0.25	£0.75	£1.25
26-31 ND	$0.40	$1.20	$2.00	£0.25	£0.75	£1.25
32-35 ND "The Universo Proj"						
	$0.40	$1.20	$2.00	£0.25	£0.75	£1.25
36 ND	$0.40	$1.20	$2.00	£0.25	£0.75	£1.25
37 ND scarce in the U.K. Superboy returns (post-Crisis)						
	$2.00	$6.00	$10.00	£1.20	£3.60	£6.00
38 ND very scarce in the U.K. Superboy dies						
	$2.00	$6.00	$10.00	£2.00	£6.00	£10.00
39-41 ND	$0.40	$1.20	$2.00	£0.25	£0.75	£1.25
42 ND Millennium X-over, Laurel Kent revealed as a Manhunter						
	$0.40	$1.20	$2.00	£0.25	£0.75	£1.25
43 ND Millennium X-over						
	$0.40	$1.20	$2.00	£0.25	£0.75	£1.25
44 ND	$0.40	$1.20	$2.00	£0.25	£0.75	£1.25
45 ND 64pgs, 30th anniversary issue						
	$0.60	$1.80	$3.00	£0.40	£1.20	£2.00
46-49 ND	$0.40	$1.20	$2.00	£0.25	£0.75	£1.25
50 ND 48pgs	$0.50	$1.50	$2.50	£0.30	£0.90	£1.50
51-59 ND	$0.40	$1.20	$2.00	£0.25	£0.75	£1.25
60-63 ND Magic Wars story						
	$0.40	$1.20	$2.00	£0.25	£0.75	£1.25
Title Value:	$29.20	$87.60	$146.00	£19.00	£57.00	£95.00

Note: all Deluxe Format Baxter paper

LEGION OF SUPER-HEROES (3RD SERIES)
DC Comics; 0 Oct 1994; 1 Oct 1989-present

	$Good	$Fine	$N.Mint	£Good	£Fine	£N.Mint
0 (Oct 1994) Zero Hour X-over, origin retold						
	$0.40	$1.20	$2.00	£0.25	£0.75	£1.25
1 events take place 5 years after Magic Wars storyline						
	$0.50	$1.50	$2.50	£0.30	£0.90	£1.50
2-5	$0.40	$1.20	$2.00	£0.25	£0.75	£1.25
6 new Legionnaires						
	$0.40	$1.20	$2.00	£0.25	£0.75	£1.25

Laff-A-Lympics #1

Leading Comics #17

Legacy #1

MINT = 100% / NEAR MINT (inc. +/-) = 90–99% / VERY FINE (inc. +/-) = 75–89% / FINE (inc. +/-) = 55–74%
VERY GOOD (inc. +/-) = 35–54% / GOOD (inc. +/-) = 15–34% / FAIR = 5–14% / POOR = 1–4%

427

	$Good	$Fine	$N.Mint	£Good	£Fine	£N.Mint
7	$0.40	$1.20	$2.00	£0.25	£0.75	£1.25
8 origin re-worked	$0.40	$1.20	$2.00	£0.25	£0.75	£1.25
9-10	$0.40	$1.20	$2.00	£0.25	£0.75	£1.25
11 Matter-Eater Lad/Polar Boy appear	$0.40	$1.20	$2.00	£0.25	£0.75	£1.25
12 new costumes	$0.40	$1.20	$2.00	£0.25	£0.75	£1.25
13 Duo Damsel returns; gate-fold poster - compensate for comic being printed on Mando paper stock instead of its usual Standard stock	$0.40	$1.20	$2.00	£0.25	£0.75	£1.25
14 Matter-Eater Lad returns	$0.40	$1.20	$2.00	£0.25	£0.75	£1.25
15-18	$0.40	$1.20	$2.00	£0.25	£0.75	£1.25
19 continued from Adventures of Superman #478	$0.40	$1.20	$2.00	£0.25	£0.75	£1.25
20	$0.40	$1.20	$2.00	£0.25	£0.75	£1.25
21 The Quiet Darkness part 1, sequel to The Great Darkness Saga (Legion of Super-Heroes #290-294, Annual 2), Lobo and Darkseid appear	$0.30	$0.90	$1.50	£0.20	£0.60	£1.00
22 The Quiet Darkness part 2, Lobo and Darkseid appear	$0.30	$0.90	$1.50	£0.20	£0.60	£1.00
23 The Quiet Darkness part 3, Lobo vs. Timberwolf	$0.30	$0.90	$1.50	£0.20	£0.60	£1.00
24 The Quiet Darkness part 4 (conclusion), Lobo vs. Timberwolf	$0.30	$0.90	$1.50	£0.20	£0.60	£1.00
25 original Legion of Super-Heroes from Adventure Comics appear	$0.30	$0.90	$1.50	£0.20	£0.60	£1.00
26-27	$0.30	$0.90	$1.50	£0.20	£0.60	£1.00
28 origin Sun Boy retold	$0.30	$0.90	$1.50	£0.20	£0.60	£1.00
29 intro Monica Sade	$0.30	$0.90	$1.50	£0.20	£0.60	£1.00
30	$0.30	$0.90	$1.50	£0.20	£0.60	£1.00
31 guest pencils by Colleen Doran	$0.30	$0.90	$1.50	£0.20	£0.60	£1.00
32-34	$0.30	$0.90	$1.50	£0.20	£0.60	£1.00
35-37 bi-weekly	$0.30	$0.90	$1.50	£0.20	£0.60	£1.00
38 bi-weekly, full page illustrations with text story; Earth destroyed in nuclear explosion	$0.30	$0.90	$1.50	£0.20	£0.60	£1.00
39	$0.30	$0.90	$1.50	£0.20	£0.60	£1.00
40 Legionnaires preview	$0.30	$0.90	$1.50	£0.20	£0.60	£1.00
41 1st solo adventure of teen Legionnaires	$0.30	$0.90	$1.50	£0.20	£0.60	£1.00
42	$0.30	$0.90	$1.50	£0.20	£0.60	£1.00
43 Mordru Arises story, Martian Manhunter appears	$0.30	$0.90	$1.50	£0.20	£0.60	£1.00
44-48 Mordru Arises story	$0.30	$0.90	$1.50	£0.20	£0.60	£1.00
49	$0.30	$0.90	$1.50	£0.20	£0.60	£1.00
50 64pgs, features a wedding, a death, a re-birth and the return of a lost Legionnaire	$0.50	$1.50	$2.50	£0.30	£0.90	£1.50
51-53	$0.50	$1.50	$2.50	£0.30	£0.90	£1.50
54 new direction for title; die-cut, foil-stamped cover	$0.50	$1.50	$2.50	£0.30	£0.90	£1.50
55-58	$0.30	$0.90	$1.50	£0.20	£0.60	£1.00
59 leads into End of an Era storyline and Zero Hour mini-series	$0.30	$0.90	$1.50	£0.20	£0.60	£1.00
60 End of an Era part 3, continued in Legionnaires #18	$0.40	$1.20	$2.00	£0.25	£0.75	£1.25
61 End of an Era part 6 (conclusion); Zero Hour X-over	$0.40	$1.20	$2.00	£0.25	£0.75	£1.25
62 new members introduced	$0.40	$1.20	$2.00	£0.25	£0.75	£1.25
63-68	$0.40	$1.20	$2.00	£0.25	£0.75	£1.25
69	$0.45	$1.35	$2.25	£0.30	£0.90	£1.50
70-71 Alan Davis and Mark Farmer cover	$0.45	$1.35	$2.25	£0.30	£0.90	£1.50
72 Alan Davis and Mark Farmer cover; storyline continued from Legionnaires Annual #2	$0.45	$1.35	$2.25	£0.30	£0.90	£1.50
73 Alan Davis and Mark Farmer cover; storyline continued from Legionnaires #30	$0.45	$1.35	$2.25	£0.30	£0.90	£1.50
74 Future Tense part 2, continued in Legionnaires #31	$0.45	$1.35	$2.25	£0.30	£0.90	£1.50
75 Two Timer part 1, continued in Legionnaires #32	$0.45	$1.35	$2.25	£0.30	£0.90	£1.50
76-78 Alan Davis and Mark Farmer cover	$0.45	$1.35	$2.25	£0.30	£0.90	£1.50
Title Value:	**$28.70**	**$86.10**	**$143.50**	**£18.55**	**£55.65**	**£92.75**

Note: Deluxe Format, high quality paper

LEGION OF SUPER-HEROES ANNUAL (1ST SERIES)

DC Comics; 1 1982-5 Oct 1987
(becomes Tales of the Legion of Super-Heroes Annual with #4)

	$Good	$Fine	$N.Mint	£Good	£Fine	£N.Mint
1 ND 52pgs, scarce, Giffen cover/art, 1st appearance new Invisible Kid	$0.40	$1.20	$2.00	£0.40	£1.20	£2.00
2 52pgs, scarce, Giffen cover Karate Kid, Princess Projectra wed	$0.40	$1.20	$2.00	£0.30	£0.90	£1.50
3 52pgs	$0.30	$0.90	$1.50	£0.25	£0.75	£1.25
4-5 48pgs	$0.30	$0.90	$1.50	£0.20	£0.60	£1.00
Title Value:	**$1.70**		**$8.50**	**£1.35**	**£4.05**	**£6.75**

LEGION OF SUPER-HEROES ANNUAL (2ND SERIES)

DC Comics; 1 Oct 1985-4 1988

	$Good	$Fine	$N.Mint	£Good	£Fine	£N.Mint
1 ND	$0.45	$1.35	$2.25	£0.30	£0.90	£1.50
2 ND Dave Gibbons art	$0.45	$1.35	$2.25	£0.30	£0.90	£1.50
3 ND	$0.45	$1.35	$2.25	£0.30	£0.90	£1.50
4 ND Bolland cover, Gary Leach art (back-up)	$0.45	$1.35	$2.25	£0.30	£0.90	£1.50
Title Value:	**$1.80**	**$5.40**	**$9.00**	**£1.20**	**£3.60**	**£6.00**

Note: all 48pgs, Baxter paper

LEGION OF SUPER-HEROES ANNUAL (3RD SERIES)

DC Comics; 1 Aug 1990-present

	$Good	$Fine	$N.Mint	£Good	£Fine	£N.Mint
1-2 48pgs	$0.60	$1.80	$3.00	£0.40	£1.20	£2.00
3 64pgs, intro new-look Timber-Wolf	$0.70	$2.10	$3.50	£0.40	£1.20	£2.00
4 64pgs, Bloodlines (Wave Two) part 12, 1st appearance Jamm, continued in Green Arrow Annual #6	$0.70	$2.10	$3.50	£0.40	£1.20	£2.00
5 64pgs, Elseworlds story, features art by Colleen Doran and Ted McKeever	$0.70	$2.10	$3.50	£0.40	£1.20	£2.00
6 56pgs, Year One	$0.80	$2.40	$4.00	£0.50	£1.50	£2.50
Title Value:	**$4.10**	**$12.30**	**$21.00**	**£2.50**	**£7.50**	**£12.50**

Note: Deluxe Format

LEGION OF SUPER-HEROES SPECIAL

DC Comics,OS; 1 Apr 1985

	$Good	$Fine	$N.Mint	£Good	£Fine	£N.Mint
1 48pgs, Giffen art	$0.40	$1.20	$2.00	£0.25	£0.75	£1.25
Title Value:	**$0.40**	**$1.20**	**$2.00**	**£0.25**	**£0.75**	**£1.25**

LEGION X-1

Greater Mercury Comics; 1 1989-2 1989

	$Good	$Fine	$N.Mint	£Good	£Fine	£N.Mint
1 ND black and white	$0.45	$1.35	$2.25	£0.30	£0.90	£1.50
2 ND rare in the U.K. black and white	$1.50	$4.50	$7.50	£1.00	£3.00	£5.00
Title Value:	**$1.95**	**$5.85**	**$9.75**	**£1.30**	**£3.90**	**£6.50**

LEGION X-1 (2ND SERIES)

Greater Mercury Comics; 1 Aug 1989-6 Dec 1990

	$Good	$Fine	$N.Mint	£Good	£Fine	£N.Mint
1-6 ND black and white	$0.40	$1.20	$2.00	£0.25	£0.75	£1.25
Title Value:	**$2.40**	**$7.20**	**$12.00**	**£1.50**	**£4.50**	**£7.50**

LEGION X-2

Greater Mercury Comics; 1 Aug 1989-8 1991

	$Good	$Fine	$N.Mint	£Good	£Fine	£N.Mint
1-8 ND black and white	$0.40	$1.20	$2.00	£0.25	£0.75	£1.25
9-10 ND Split Decision story, black and white	$0.40	$1.20	$2.00	£0.25	£0.75	£1.25
Title Value:	**$4.00**	**$12.00**	**$20.00**	**£2.50**	**£7.50**	**£12.50**

LEGIONNAIRES

DC Comics; 0 Oct 1994; 1 Apr 1993-present

	$Good	$Fine	$N.Mint	£Good	£Fine	£N.Mint
0 (Oct 1994) Zero Hour X-over, origin retold	$0.40	$1.20	$2.00	£0.25	£0.75	£1.25
1 pre-bagged with trading card; spin-off from the destruction of Earth in Legion of Super-Heroes (3rd Series) #38; the covers of the first six issues make one giant montage	$0.30	$0.90	$1.50	£0.20	£0.60	£1.00
2-6	$0.25	$0.75	$1.25	£0.15	£0.45	£0.75
7 Adam Hughes pencils	$0.25	$0.75	$1.25	£0.15	£0.45	£0.75
8 Colleen Doran pencils	$0.25	$0.75	$1.25	£0.15	£0.45	£0.75
9	$0.25	$0.75	$1.25	£0.15	£0.45	£0.75
10 1st appearance new Kid Psycho	$0.25	$0.75	$1.25	£0.15	£0.45	£0.75
11 Kid Quantum joins	$0.30	$0.90	$1.50	£0.20	£0.60	£1.00
12-13	$0.30	$0.90	$1.50	£0.20	£0.60	£1.00
14-16 Adam Hughes cover	$0.30	$0.90	$1.50	£0.20	£0.60	£1.00
17 End of an Era part 1, continued in Valor #22; Adam Hughes cover	$0.30	$0.90	$1.50	£0.20	£0.60	£1.00
18 End of an Era part 4, continued in Valor #23; Adam Hughes cover	$0.30	$0.90	$1.50	£0.20	£0.60	£1.00
19-26	$0.30	$0.90	$1.50	£0.20	£0.60	£1.00
27 upgraded paper stock to Mando Format begins	$0.45	$1.35	$2.25	£0.30	£0.90	£1.50
28-29	$0.45	$1.35	$2.25	£0.30	£0.90	£1.50
30 continued from Legion of Super-Heroes #73	$0.45	$1.35	$2.25	£0.30	£0.90	£1.50
31 Future Tense part 3, continued from Legion of Super-Heroes #74	$0.45	$1.35	$2.25	£0.30	£0.90	£1.50
32 Underworld Unleashed tie-in, cover by Alan Davis and Mark Farmer	$0.45	$1.35	$2.25	£0.30	£0.90	£1.50
33-34 cover by Alan Davis and Mark Farmer	$0.45	$1.35	$2.25	£0.30	£0.90	£1.50
35	$0.45	$1.35	$2.25	£0.30	£0.90	£1.50
Title Value:	**$11.80**	**$35.40**	**$59.00**	**£7.70**	**£23.10**	**£38.50**

LEGIONNAIRES ANNUAL

DC Comics; 1 Jul 1994-present

	$Good	$Fine	$N.Mint	£Good	£Fine	£N.Mint
1 64pgs, Elseworlds story	$0.50	$1.50	$2.50	£0.30	£0.90	£1.50
2 56pgs, Year One	$0.80	$2.40	$4.00	£0.50	£1.50	£2.50
Title Value:	**$1.30**	**$3.90**	**$6.50**	**£0.80**	**£2.40**	**£4.00**

LEGIONNAIRES THREE

DC Comics,MS; 1 Jan 1986-4 May 1986

	$Good	$Fine	$N.Mint	£Good	£Fine	£N.Mint
1-4	$0.25	$0.75	$1.25	£0.15	£0.45	£0.75
Title Value:	**$1.00**	**$3.00**	**$5.00**	**£0.60**	**£1.80**	**£3.00**

LENSMAN

Eternity; 1 Apr 1990-6 Oct 1990

	$Good	$Fine	$N.Mint	£Good	£Fine	£N.Mint

(see Galactic Patrol)

(mini-series sub-titled The Secret of the Lens)

1 ND adaptation of animated Japanese feature begins based on E.E. "Doc" Smith's sci-fi series; black and white

| | $0.40 | $1.20 | $2.00 | £0.25 | £0.75 | £1.25 |

1 ND Collector's Edition (Feb 1990) - 56pgs, gold foil embossed logo, heavier stock paper covers, additional information and art

	$0.85	$2.55	$4.25	£0.55	£1.65	£2.75
2-6 ND	$0.40	$1.20	$2.00	£0.25	£0.75	£1.25
Title Value:	$3.25	$9.75	$16.25	£2.05	£6.15	£10.25
Birth of a Lensman Graphic Album (1991), reprints issues #1-3				£0.80	£2.40	£4.00
Secrets of the Lens Graphic Album, reprints issues #4-6				£0.80	£2.40	£4.00

LENSMAN: WAR OF THE GALAXIES
Eternity,MS; 1 Oct 1990-7 Apr 1991

| 1-7 ND | $0.40 | $1.20 | $2.00 | £0.25 | £0.75 | £1.25 |
| Title Value: | $2.80 | $8.40 | $14.00 | £1.75 | £5.25 | £8.75 |

LEONARDO
Mirage Studios,OS; 1 Dec 1986

1 ND Teenage Mutant Ninja Turtles tie-in

| | $1.20 | $3.60 | $6.00 | £0.80 | £2.40 | £4.00 |
| Title Value: | $1.20 | $3.60 | $6.00 | £0.80 | £2.40 | £4.00 |

LEOPARD
Millennium; 1 May 1995-2 1995

1 ND Dan and David Day script and art

| | $0.60 | $1.80 | $3.00 | £0.40 | £1.20 | £2.00 |

1 ND Signed Variant Edition (Jun 1995) - gold cover, signed by Dan and David Day

| | $0.80 | $2.40 | $4.00 | £0.50 | £1.50 | £2.50 |

2 ND Dan and David Day script and art

| | $0.60 | $1.80 | $3.00 | £0.40 | £1.20 | £2.00 |
| Title Value: | $2.00 | $6.00 | $10.00 | £1.30 | £3.90 | £6.50 |

LESTER GIRLS: THE LIZARD'S TRAIL
Eternity,MS; 1 Nov 1990-3 Jan 1991

1 ND Gerard Jones and Tim Hamilton, black and white; ties up plots from Trouble With Girls

	$0.45	$1.35	$2.25	£0.30	£0.90	£1.50
2-3 ND	$0.40	$1.20	$2.00	£0.25	£0.75	£1.25
Title Value:	$1.25	$3.75	$6.25	£0.80	£2.40	£4.00

LETHAL STRYKE
London Night Studios,MS; 0 Nov 1995; 1 Aug 1995-3 Nov 1995

| ¹/₂ ND | $1.00 | $3.00 | $5.00 | £0.80 | £2.40 | £4.00 |

0 ND Collector's Edition (Nov 1995) - gold foil cover

	$1.20	$3.60	$6.00	£0.80	£2.40	£4.00
1 ND	$1.00	$3.00	$5.00	£0.60	£1.80	£3.00
2-3 ND	$0.60	$1.80	$3.00	£0.40	£1.20	£2.00
Title Value:	$4.40	$13.20	$22.00	£3.00	£9.00	£15.00

LEX LUTHOR, THE UNAUTHORISED BIOGRAPHY OF
DC Comics,OS; 1 Jun 1989

1 ND 48pgs, squarebound

| | $0.60 | $1.80 | $3.00 | £0.40 | £1.20 | £2.00 |
| Title Value: | $0.60 | $1.80 | $3.00 | £0.40 | £1.20 | £2.00 |

LIBBY ELLIS
Malibu,MS; 1 Jul 1987-4 Dec 1988

| 1-4 ND | $0.40 | $1.20 | $2.00 | £0.25 | £0.75 | £1.25 |
| Title Value: | $1.60 | $4.80 | $8.00 | £1.00 | £3.00 | £5.00 |

LIBBY ELLIS (2ND SERIES)
Eternity,MS; 1 Jun 1988-4 Dec 1988

| 1-4 ND | $0.40 | $1.20 | $2.00 | £0.25 | £0.75 | £1.25 |
| Title Value: | $1.60 | $4.80 | $8.00 | £1.00 | £3.00 | £5.00 |

LIBERATOR
Malibu/Eternity; 1 Dec 1987-6 Dec 1988

1-6 ND Butch Burcham inks/covers

| | $0.40 | $1.20 | $2.00 | £0.25 | £0.75 | £1.25 |
| Title Value: | $2.40 | $7.20 | $12.00 | £1.50 | £4.50 | £7.50 |

LIBERTY PROJECT
Eclipse; 1 Jun 1987-8 May 1988

| 1-8 ND | $0.40 | $1.20 | $2.00 | £0.25 | £0.75 | £1.25 |
| Title Value: | $3.20 | $9.60 | $16.00 | £2.00 | £6.00 | £10.00 |

LIBRA
Eternity; 1 1987

| 1 ND | $0.30 | $0.90 | $1.50 | £0.20 | £0.60 | £1.00 |
| Title Value: | $0.30 | $0.90 | $1.50 | £0.20 | £0.60 | £1.00 |

LIEUTENANT BLUEBERRY
Marvel Comics Group/Epic Graphic Novel; 1 1991

(see Blueberry, Moebius)

1 ND Trail of the Sioux

| | $1.60 | $4.80 | $8.00 | £1.00 | £3.00 | £5.00 |
| Title Value: | $1.60 | $4.80 | $8.00 | £1.00 | £3.00 | £5.00 |

LIFE OF CHRIST: THE CHRISTMAS STORY
Marvel Comics Group,MS; 1 Feb 1993-2 Mar 1993

| 1-2 ND | $0.50 | $1.50 | $2.50 | £0.30 | £0.90 | £1.50 |
| Title Value: | $1.00 | $3.00 | $5.00 | £0.60 | £1.80 | £3.00 |

LIFE OF POPE JOHN PAUL II, THE
Marvel Comics Group,OS; 1 Jan 1983

| 1 ND 64pgs | $0.15 | $0.45 | $0.75 | £0.10 | £0.35 | £0.60 |
| Title Value: | $0.15 | $0.45 | $0.75 | £0.10 | £0.35 | £0.60 |

LIGHT AND DARKNESS WAR, THE
Marvel Comics Group/Epic,MS; 1 Oct 1988-6 Dec 1989

1 ND Cam Kennedy painted art begins

	$0.45	$1.35	$2.25	£0.30	£0.90	£1.50
2-6 ND	$0.45	$1.35	$2.25	£0.30	£0.90	£1.50
Title Value:	$2.70	$8.10	$13.50	£1.80	£5.40	£9.00

Note: Mature Readers

LIGHT FANTASTIC, THE
Innovation,MS; 1 Jun 1992-4 Sep 1992

1-4 ND adaptation of Terry Pratchett's 2nd Discworld novel; colour

| | $0.45 | $1.35 | $2.25 | £0.30 | £0.90 | £1.50 |
| Title Value: | $1.80 | $5.40 | $9.00 | £1.20 | £3.60 | £6.00 |

LIGHTNING COMICS PRESENTS
Lightning Comics,OS; 1 May 1994

1 ND War Party and Dreadwolf appear; red foil cover by Diamond Distributors

| | $0.80 | $2.40 | $4.00 | £0.50 | £1.50 | £2.50 |

1 ND War Party and Dreadwolf appear; black, yellow and blue cover by Capital Distribution

| | $0.80 | $2.40 | $4.00 | £0.50 | £1.50 | £2.50 |

1 ND War Party and Dreadwolf appear; red and yellow cover by Heroes World

| | $0.80 | $2.40 | $4.00 | £0.50 | £1.50 | £2.50 |

1 ND War Party and Dreadwolf appear; Platinum Edition

| | $0.80 | $2.40 | $4.00 | £0.50 | £1.50 | £2.50 |
| Title Value: | $3.20 | $9.60 | $16.00 | £2.00 | £6.00 | £10.00 |

LIMITED COLLECTOR'S EDITION
DC Comics,Tabloid; C-21 Summer 1973 - C-59 1978

(other numbers: see All New Collector's Edition, Famous First Edition)

C-21 Shazam				£0.60	£1.80	£3.00
C-22 ND, Tarzan				£0.75	£2.25	£3.75
C-23 House of Mystery				£0.50	£1.50	£2.50
C-24 ND, Rudolph the Red-Nosed Reindeer				£0.40	£1.20	£2.00
C-25 ND Batman, reprints art by Kane/Robinson/Sprang Infantino/Adams				£3.00	£9.00	£15.00
C-27 ND, Shazam				£0.75	£2.25	£3.75
C-29 ND, Tarzan				£0.75	£2.25	£3.75
C-31 ND, Superman, 4pgs Neal Adams art, reprints origin Superman 2001 from Superman #300				£1.00	£3.00	£5.00
C-32 ND, Ghosts				£0.50	£1.50	£2.50
C-33 ND, Rudolph				£0.35	£1.35	£1.75
C-34 ND, Christmas with the Super-Heroes reprints Miller Batman from Five Star Super-Hero Spectacular				£0.70	£2.10	£3.50
C-35 ND, Shazam				£0.70	£2.10	£3.50
C-36 ND, The Bible				£0.60	£1.80	£3.00
C-37 scarce, Batman, all villains, reprints Joker Penguin/Two Face/Scarecrow (origin)/Catwoman				£3.25	£9.75	£16.25
C-38 scarce, Superman, 2pgs Neal Adams art				£0.80	£2.40	£4.00
C-39 Secret Origins of Super-Villains, reprints Joker (origin from Detective #168)/Luthor Captain Cold/Dr. Sivana/Terra-Man				£0.80	£2.40	£4.00
C-40 ND scarce, Dick Tracy, newspaper reprints				£1.00	£3.00	£5.00
C-41 Super Friends				£0.30	£0.90	£1.50
C-42 ND, Rudolph				£0.35	£1.05	£1.75
C-43 ND, Christmas with the Super-Heroes, reprints Neal Adams Batman/Golden Age Superman, Wonder Woman, Simon and Kirby Sandman; Wrightson art on Mystery short				£0.60	£1.80	£3.00
C-44 ND scarce, Batman, reprints art by Infantino/Robinson/ Sprang/Adams				£3.00	£9.00	£15.00
C-45 ND, Secret Origins of Super-Villains Catwoman/Mirror Master Mr.Mxyzptlk/The Cheetah				£0.75	£2.25	£3.75
C-46 ND, Justice League of America				£0.75	£2.25	£3.75
C-47 ND, Superman Bicentennial; **Note:** interior features Tomahawk stories				£0.45	£1.35	£2.25
C-48 ND, Superman/Flash, 6pgs Neal Adams art				£1.50	£4.50	£7.50
C-49 ND, Superboy and the Legion of Super-Heroes				£0.90	£2.70	£4.50
C-50 ND, Rudolph				£0.30	£0.90	£1.50
C-51 ND, Batman, full length story reprint from Batman #232, 242, 243, 244; Neal Adams art featured				£3.00	£9.00	£15.00
C-52 ND, Best of DC, classic reprints, art by Adams (Batman), Toth (Firehair), Infantino (Flash)				£0.50	£1.50	£2.50
C-57 ND, Welcome Back Kotter				£0.30	£0.90	£1.50
C-59 ND scarce, Batman, classic reprints, Neal Adams ("A Vow from the Grave"), Berni Wrightson (from Swamp Thing #7)				£3.00	£9.00	£15.00

Note: all issues are reprint except some new stories in C-32, 33, 34. C36 is all new material. Issues 21-34, 51-59 are 84pgs, 35-41 are 68pgs, 42-50 are 60pgs. Owing to their size and consequent mail packaging or shop display, these items are rarely found in true MINT condition

ARTISTS

Adams reprints in C-23, 25, 39, 43, 44, 51, 52, 59. Kirby reprint in C-43. Wrightson reprints in C-23, 43, 59.

LION KING, THE
Marvel Comics Group,OS; 1 Jul 1994

1 ND 48pgs, adaptation of animated film

| | $0.45 | $1.35 | $2.25 | £0.30 | £0.90 | £1.50 |
| Title Value: | $0.45 | $1.35 | $2.25 | £0.30 | £0.90 | £1.50 |

LISA COMICS
Bongo Comics; 1 Apr 1995

1 ND Lisa Simpson stars; Matt Groenig art

| | $0.45 | $1.35 | $2.25 | £0.30 | £0.90 | £1.50 |
| Title Value: | $0.45 | $1.35 | $2.25 | £0.30 | £0.90 | £1.50 |

LITTLE DOT
Harvey; 1 Sep 1953-164 Apr 1976

1 1st appearance Little Dot and Richie Rich

	$92.50	$275.00	$650.00	£60.00	£180.00	£425.00
2	$36.00	$105.00	$250.00	£25.00	£75.00	£175.00
3	$23.50	$70.00	$165.00	£15.50	£47.00	£110.00
4-6	$17.00	$50.00	$120.00	£11.00	£34.00	£80.00
7-10	$12.00	$36.00	$85.00	£7.75	£23.50	£55.00
11-20	$10.50	$33.00	$65.00	£7.50	£22.50	£45.00
21-40	$5.75	$17.50	$35.00	£4.15	£12.50	£25.00
41-60	$2.90	$8.75	$17.50	£2.00	£6.00	£12.00
61-80	$2.00	$6.00	$10.00	£1.20	£3.60	£6.00
81-100	$1.20	$3.60	$6.00	£0.60	£1.80	£3.00
101-141	$0.60	$1.80	$3.00	£0.40	£1.20	£2.00
142-145 giant	$0.80	$2.40	$4.00	£0.50	£1.50	£2.50
146-164	$0.30	$0.90	$1.50	£0.20	£0.60	£1.00

	$Good	$Fine	$N.Mint	£Good	£Fine	£N.Mint
Title Value:	$626.50	$1891.50	$3952.50	£420.70	£1267.60	£2651.00

Note: most issues distributed in the U.K. after 1959

LITTLE DOT DOTLAND
Harvey; 1 Jul 1962-61 Dec 1973

	$Good	$Fine	$N.Mint	£Good	£Fine	£N.Mint
1	$7.50	$22.50	$45.00	£5.00	£15.00	£30.00
2-3	$3.75	$11.00	$22.50	£2.50	£7.50	£15.00
4-5	$3.00	$9.00	$18.00	£2.00	£6.00	£12.00
6-10	$1.85	$5.50	$11.25	£1.25	£3.75	£7.50
11-20	$1.50	$4.50	$9.00	£1.00	£3.00	£6.00
21-30	$0.90	$2.70	$4.50	£0.60	£1.80	£3.00
31-50	$0.60	$1.80	$3.00	£0.40	£1.20	£2.00
51-54 giant	$0.80	$2.40	$4.00	£0.50	£1.50	£2.50
55-61	$0.45	$1.35	$2.25	£0.30	£0.90	£1.50
Title Value:	$72.60	$217.05	$409.00	£48.35	£145.05	£272.00

Note: most issues distributed in the U.K.

LITTLE MERMAID COMIC EDITION, THE
Disney,OS; nn 1991
nn ND adaptation of film

	$Good	$Fine	$N.Mint	£Good	£Fine	£N.Mint
	$0.55	$1.65	$2.75	£0.35	£1.05	£1.75
Title Value:	$0.55	$1.65	$2.75	£0.35	£1.05	£1.75

LITTLE MERMAID GRAPHIC NOVEL, THE
Disney,OS; nn Nov 1990
nn ND 64pgs, adaptation of film

	$Good	$Fine	$N.Mint	£Good	£Fine	£N.Mint
	$1.00	$3.00	$5.00	£0.65	£1.95	£3.25
Title Value:	$1.00	$3.00	$5.00	£0.65	£1.95	£3.25

LITTLE MERMAID, THE
Disney; 1 Dec 1991-4 Apr 1992

	$Good	$Fine	$N.Mint	£Good	£Fine	£N.Mint
1-4 ND Peter David script	$0.30	$0.90	$1.50	£0.20	£0.60	£1.00
Title Value:	$1.20	$3.60	$6.00	£0.80	£2.40	£4.00

LITTLE MERMAID, THE
Marvel Comics Group; 1 Sep 1994-present

	$Good	$Fine	$N.Mint	£Good	£Fine	£N.Mint
1-13 ND new adventures; Trina Robbins script	$0.30	$0.90	$1.50	£0.20	£0.60	£1.00
Title Value:	$3.90	$11.70	$19.50	£2.60	£7.80	£13.00
The Little Mermaid (Apr 1995) Trade paperback reprints issues #1-4				£1.30	£3.90	£6.50

LITTLE NEMO IN SLUMBERLAND
Blackthorne; (3-D Series #11) Jan 1987
1 ND reprints by Windsor McCay; with bound-in 3-D glasses (25% less if without glasses)

	$Good	$Fine	$N.Mint	£Good	£Fine	£N.Mint
	$0.45	$1.35	$2.25	£0.30	£0.90	£1.50
Title Value:	$0.45	$1.35	$2.25	£0.30	£0.90	£1.50

Note: see also Betty Boop in 3-D as this is also numbered Blackthorne 3-D Series in the indicia

LITTLE NEMO IN SLUMBERLAND 3-D
Blackthorne; (3-D Series #13) 1 Jan 1987
nn ND indicia misprinted as #11

	$Good	$Fine	$N.Mint	£Good	£Fine	£N.Mint
	$0.55	$1.65	$2.75	£0.35	£1.05	£1.75
Title Value:	$0.55	$1.65	$2.75	£0.35	£1.05	£1.75

LITTLE NEMO IN THE PALACE OF ICE
Dover; nn 1976

	$Good	$Fine	$N.Mint	£Good	£Fine	£N.Mint
nn ND	$1.65	$4.95	$8.25	£1.10	£3.30	£5.50
Title Value:	$1.65	$4.95	$8.25	£1.10	£3.30	£5.50

LITTLE NINJAS IN WONDERLAND
Comax Productions; 1 1990
1 ND Butch Burcham script and art; adult material, black and white

	$Good	$Fine	$N.Mint	£Good	£Fine	£N.Mint
	$0.30	$0.90	$1.50	£0.20	£0.60	£1.00
Title Value:	$0.30	$0.90	$1.50	£0.20	£0.60	£1.00

LITTLE SHOP OF HORRORS
DC Comics,OS; 1 Feb 1987
1 ND 68pgs, adapts film, Gene Colan art

	$Good	$Fine	$N.Mint	£Good	£Fine	£N.Mint
	$0.30	$0.90	$1.50	£0.20	£0.60	£1.00
Title Value:	$0.30	$0.90	$1.50	£0.20	£0.60	£1.00

LIVINGSTONE MOUNTAIN
Adventure,MS; 1 Sep 1991-4 Dec 1991

	$Good	$Fine	$N.Mint	£Good	£Fine	£N.Mint
1-4 ND Steve Moncuse script/art	$0.40	$1.20	$2.00	£0.25	£0.75	£1.25
Title Value:	$1.60	$4.80	$8.00	£1.00	£3.00	£5.00

LIZARDS SUMMER FUN SPECIAL
Alchemy Studios,OS; 1 Sep 1991

	$Good	$Fine	$N.Mint	£Good	£Fine	£N.Mint
1 ND 36pgs	$0.45	$1.35	$2.25	£0.30	£0.90	£1.50
Title Value:	$0.45	$1.35	$2.25	£0.30	£0.90	£1.50

LLOYD LLEWELLYN
Fantagraphics,Magazine; 1 1986-6 1988

	$Good	$Fine	$N.Mint	£Good	£Fine	£N.Mint
1 ND Dan Clowes story/art begins	$1.80	$5.25	$9.00	£1.20	£3.60	£6.00
2 ND	$1.20	$3.60	$6.00	£0.80	£2.40	£4.00
3-6 ND	$0.90	$2.70	$4.50	£0.60	£1.80	£3.00
Title Value:	$6.60	$19.65	$33.00	£4.40	£13.20	£22.00
Collection (1990), reprints 13 stories				£1.10	£3.30	£5.50
The Many Worlds of Lloyd Llewellyn (May 1994) Hardcover collection of all stories published to date, 2,000 copies				£5.50	£16.50	£27.50

LLOYD LLEWELLYN SPECIAL
Fantagraphics; 1 Dec 1988
1 ND Dan Clowes story/art

	$Good	$Fine	$N.Mint	£Good	£Fine	£N.Mint
	$0.60	$1.80	$3.00	£0.40	£1.20	£2.00
1 2nd printing, ND (Dec 1992)	$0.55	$1.65	$2.75	£0.35	£1.05	£1.75
Title Value:	$1.15	$3.45	$5.75	£0.75	£2.25	£3.75

LOBO
DC Comics,MS; 1 Nov 1990-4 Feb 1991
(see Legion #89-94,Omega Men,Superman #41)
1 Keith Giffen/Alan Grant script, has cover splash with "only 99c", Simon Bisley art

---

	$Good	$Fine	$N.Mint	£Good	£Fine	£N.Mint
	$1.00	$3.00	$5.00	£0.60	£1.80	£3.00

1 2nd printing, has no cover splash?

	$Good	$Fine	$N.Mint	£Good	£Fine	£N.Mint
	$0.30	$0.90	$1.50	£0.20	£0.60	£1.00
2	$0.80	$2.40	$4.00	£0.50	£1.50	£2.50
3-4	$0.60	$1.80	$3.00	£0.40	£1.20	£2.00
Title Value:	$3.30	$9.90	$16.50	£2.10	£6.30	£10.50

Note: first issue sold at a special cut-price of 99 cents

	$Good	$Fine	$N.Mint	£Good	£Fine	£N.Mint
The Last Czarnian (Feb 1992) Trade paperback reprints issues #1-4 plus painted cover by Simon Bisley				£1.10	£3.30	£5.50
Lobo's Greatest Hits (Mar 1992) Trade paperback reprints early appearances from Omega Men, Justice League, Mister Miracle and Superman [2nd Series]				£1.60	£4.80	£8.00
Lobo Slipcase Package (Feb 1992), three trade paperbacks including The Wisdom of Lobo, pre-bagged in slipcase				£3.75	£11.25	£18.50

LOBO (2ND SERIES)
DC Comics; 0 Oct 1994; 1 Dec 1993-present

	$Good	$Fine	$N.Mint	£Good	£Fine	£N.Mint
0 (Oct 1994) Zero Hour X-over	$0.40	$1.20	$2.00	£0.25	£0.75	£1.25

1 Alan Grant script begins; foil embossed cover

	$Good	$Fine	$N.Mint	£Good	£Fine	£N.Mint
	$0.60	$1.80	$3.00	£0.40	£1.20	£2.00
2-15	$0.45	$1.20	$2.00	£0.25	£0.75	£1.25
16-20	$0.45	$1.35	$2.25	£0.30	£0.90	£1.50
21 Kev O'Neill art	$0.45	$1.35	$2.25	£0.30	£0.90	£1.50
22 Underworld Unleashed tie-in	$0.45	$1.35	$2.25	£0.30	£0.90	£1.50
23-25	$0.45	$1.35	$2.25	£0.30	£0.90	£1.50
Title Value:	$11.10	$33.30	$55.50	£7.15	£21.45	£35.75

LOBO ANNUAL
DC Comics; 1 Jul 1993-present
1 64pgs, Bloodlines part 1, continued in Superman: The Man of Steel Annual #2

	$Good	$Fine	$N.Mint	£Good	£Fine	£N.Mint
	$0.80	$2.40	$4.00	£0.50	£1.50	£2.50
2 64pgs, Elseworlds	$0.80	$2.40	$4.00	£0.50	£1.50	£2.50
3 56pgs, Year One	$0.80	$2.40	$4.00	£0.50	£1.50	£2.50
Title Value:	$2.40	$7.20	$12.00	£1.50	£4.50	£7.50

LOBO CONVENTION SPECIAL
DC Comics; 1 Sep 1993
1 Keith Giffen and Alan Grant script, Kev O'Neill art

	$Good	$Fine	$N.Mint	£Good	£Fine	£N.Mint
	$0.40	$1.20	$2.00	£0.25	£0.75	£1.25
Title Value:	$0.40	$1.20	$2.00	£0.25	£0.75	£1.25

LOBO PARAMILITARY CHRISTMAS SPECIAL
DC Comics,OS; 1 Jan 1992
1 48pgs, Keith Giffen, Alan Grant and Simon Bisley

	$Good	$Fine	$N.Mint	£Good	£Fine	£N.Mint
	$0.45	$1.35	$2.25	£0.30	£0.90	£1.50
Title Value:	$0.45	$1.35	$2.25	£0.30	£0.90	£1.50

LOBO'S BACK
DC Comics,MS; 1 May 1992-4 Sep 1992
1 Simon Bisley cover and art, Lobo "dies"

	$Good	$Fine	$N.Mint	£Good	£Fine	£N.Mint
	$0.45	$1.35	$2.25	£0.30	£0.90	£1.50
2 Simon Bisley cover and art, Lobo reincarnated as a woman	$0.40	$1.20	$2.00	£0.25	£0.75	£1.25
3 Simon Bisley art with Sam Kieth cover, Lobo reincarnated as a squirrel	$0.30	$0.90	$1.50	£0.20	£0.60	£1.00
4 Lobo reincarnated as Lobo again; (not Bisley art)	$0.30	$0.90	$1.50	£0.20	£0.60	£1.00
Title Value:	$1.45	$4.35	$7.25	£0.95	£2.85	£4.75
Lobo's Back Back (Sep 1993) Trade paperback 112pgs, reprints issues #1-4 with new die-cut cover				£1.30	£3.90	£6.50

LOBO'S BIG BABE SPRING BREAK SPECIAL
DC Comics,OS; 1 May 1995
1 Alan Grant script, Jim Balent art

	$Good	$Fine	$N.Mint	£Good	£Fine	£N.Mint
	$0.40	$1.20	$2.00	£0.25	£0.75	£1.25
Title Value:	$0.40	$1.20	$2.00	£0.25	£0.75	£1.25

LOBO/DEADMAN: THE BRAVE AND THE BALD
DC Comics,OS; 1 Feb 1995
1 Alan Grant script, Martin Edmond art

	$Good	$Fine	$N.Mint	£Good	£Fine	£N.Mint
	$0.80	$2.40	$4.00	£0.50	£1.50	£2.50
Title Value:	$0.80	$2.40	$4.00	£0.50	£1.50	£2.50

LOBO/JUDGE DREDD: PSYCHO BIKERS VS. MUTANTS FROM HELL
DC Comics,OS; 1 Jan 1996
1 ND 48pgs, Alan Grant script, Val Semeiks and John Dell art

	$Good	$Fine	$N.Mint	£Good	£Fine	£N.Mint
	$1.00	$3.00	$5.00	£0.65	£1.95	£3.25
Title Value:	$1.00	$3.00	$5.00	£0.65	£1.95	£3.25

LOBO: A CONTRACT ON GAWD
DC Comics,MS; 1 Apr 1994-4 Jul 1994

	$Good	$Fine	$N.Mint	£Good	£Fine	£N.Mint
1-4 Alan Grant script, Kieron Dwyer art	$0.30	$0.90	$1.50	£0.20	£0.60	£1.00
Title Value:	$1.20	$3.60	$6.00	£0.80	£2.40	£4.00

LOBO: BLAZING CHAIN OF LOVE
DC Comics,OS; 1 Sep 1992
1 Giffen, Grant and Cowan

	$Good	$Fine	$N.Mint	£Good	£Fine	£N.Mint
	$0.40	$1.20	$2.00	£0.25	£0.75	£1.25
Title Value:	$0.40	$1.20	$2.00	£0.25	£0.75	£1.25

LOBO: BOUNTY HUNTING FOR FUN & PROFIT
DC Comics,OS; 1 Apr 1995
1 ND 48pgs, Alan Grant script, Martin Edmond, Kev O'Neill among the artists

	$Good	$Fine	$N.Mint	£Good	£Fine	£N.Mint
	$1.00	$3.00	$5.00	£0.65	£1.95	£3.25
Title Value:	$1.00	$3.00	$5.00	£0.65	£1.95	£3.25

LOBO: I QUIT
DC Comics,OS; 1 Dec 1995
1 ND Alan Grant script, Carlos Esquerra art

	$Good	$Fine	$N.Mint	£Good	£Fine	£N.Mint
	$0.45	$1.35	$2.25	£0.30	£0.90	£1.50

	$Good	$Fine	$N.Mint	£Good	£Fine	£N.Mint
Title Value:	$0.45	$1.35	$2.25	£0.30	£0.90	£1.50

LOBO: IN THE CHAIR
DC Comics,OS; 1 Aug 1994

	$Good	$Fine	$N.Mint	£Good	£Fine	£N.Mint
1 Alan Grant and Martin Edmond						
	$0.40	$1.20	$2.00	£0.25	£0.75	£1.25
Title Value:	$0.40	$1.20	$2.00	£0.25	£0.75	£1.25

LOBO: INFANTICIDE
DC Comics,MS; 1 Oct 1992-4 Jan 1993

	$Good	$Fine	$N.Mint	£Good	£Fine	£N.Mint
1 Alan Grant script and Keith Giffen art						
	$0.40	$1.20	$2.00	£0.25	£0.75	£1.25
2-4 Alan Grant script and Keith Giffen art						
	$0.30	$0.90	$1.50	£0.20	£0.60	£1.00
Title Value:	$1.30	$3.90	$6.50	£0.85	£2.55	£4.25

LOBO: PORTRAITS OF A BASTICH
DC Comics,OS; nn Sep 1995
nn ND pin-ups by John Byrne, Carlos Esquerra, Kelley Jones, Barry Kitson, Mike Zeck and others; Simon Bisley cover

	$Good	$Fine	$N.Mint	£Good	£Fine	£N.Mint
	$0.80	$2.40	$4.00	£0.50	£1.50	£2.50
Title Value:	$0.80	$2.40	$4.00	£0.50	£1.50	£2.50

LOBO: PORTRAIT OF A VICTIM
DC Comics,OS; 1 May 1993

	$Good	$Fine	$N.Mint	£Good	£Fine	£N.Mint
1 Alan Grant script	$0.40	$1.20	$2.00	£0.25	£0.75	£1.25
Title Value:	$0.40	$1.20	$2.00	£0.25	£0.75	£1.25

LOBO: UNAMERICAN GLADIATORS
DC Comics,MS; 1 Jun 1993-4 Sep 1993

	$Good	$Fine	$N.Mint	£Good	£Fine	£N.Mint
1-4 Alan Grant and John Wagner script, Cam Kennedy art						
	$0.40	$1.20	$2.00	£0.25	£0.75	£1.25
Title Value:	$1.60	$4.80	$8.00	£1.00	£3.00	£5.00

LOBOCOP
DC Comics,OS; 1 Feb 1994

	$Good	$Fine	$N.Mint	£Good	£Fine	£N.Mint
1 Alan Grant script, Martin Emond art						
	$0.40	$1.20	$2.00	£0.25	£0.75	£1.25
Title Value:	$0.40	$1.20	$2.00	£0.25	£0.75	£1.25

LOCO VERSUS PULVERINE
Eclipse,OS; 1 Jul 1992

	$Good	$Fine	$N.Mint	£Good	£Fine	£N.Mint
1 ND parody of Lobo and Wolverine						
	$0.45	$1.35	$2.25	£0.30	£0.90	£1.50
Title Value:	$0.45	$1.35	$2.25	£0.30	£0.90	£1.50

LOGAN
Marvel Comics Group,OS; 1 Feb 1996

	$Good	$Fine	$N.Mint	£Good	£Fine	£N.Mint
1 ND 48pgs, Logan before he was Weapon X and Wolverine						
	$1.20	$3.60	$6.00	£0.80	£2.40	£4.00
Title Value:	$1.20	$3.60	$6.00	£0.80	£2.40	£4.00

LOGAN'S RUN
Adventure,MS; 1 Jun 1990-6 Apr 1991
(see Marvel Comics title)

	$Good	$Fine	$N.Mint	£Good	£Fine	£N.Mint
1 ND Barry Blair art begins; black and white						
	$0.40	$1.20	$2.00	£0.25	£0.75	£1.25
1 2nd printing ND	$0.40	$1.20	$2.00	£0.25	£0.75	£1.25
2-3 ND	$0.40	$1.20	$2.00	£0.25	£0.75	£1.25
4-6 ND title becomes Logan's Run						
	$0.40	$1.20	$2.00	£0.25	£0.75	£1.25
Title Value:	$2.80	$8.40	$14.00	£1.75	£5.25	£8.75

LOGAN'S RUN
Marvel Comics Group, Film; 1 Jan 1977-7 Jul 1977

	$Good	$Fine	$N.Mint	£Good	£Fine	£N.Mint
1 George Perez cover and art						
	$0.60	$1.80	$3.00	£0.40	£1.20	£2.00
2-5 George Perez cover and art						
	$0.45	$1.35	$2.25	£0.30	£0.90	£1.50
6 1st solo Thanos back-up story by Mike Zeck (very Starlinesque art)						
	$1.60	$4.80	$8.00	£0.70	£2.10	£3.50

	$Good	$Fine	$N.Mint	£Good	£Fine	£N.Mint
7	$0.45	$1.35	$2.25	£0.30	£0.90	£1.50
Title Value:	$4.45	$13.35	$22.25	£2.60	£7.80	£13.00

Note: 1-5 adapts film. 6,7 new material.

LOGAN'S WORLD
Adventure; 1 Jul 1991-6 Dec 1991

	$Good	$Fine	$N.Mint	£Good	£Fine	£N.Mint
1-6 ND	$0.40	$1.20	$2.00	£0.25	£0.75	£1.25
Title Value:	$2.40	$7.20	$12.00	£1.50	£4.50	£7.50

LOIS & CLARK: THE NEW ADVENTURES OF SUPERMAN
DC Comics; nn Jul 1994

	$Good	$Fine	$N.Mint	£Good	£Fine	£N.Mint
nn Trade paperback, 192pgs; reprints highlighting Lois and Clark stories; intro by John Byrne						
	$2.00	$6.00	$10.00	£1.35	£4.05	£6.75
Title Value:	$2.00	$6.00	$10.00	£1.35	£4.05	£6.75

LOIS LANE
DC Comics,MS; 1 Aug 1986-2 Sep 1986

	$Good	$Fine	$N.Mint	£Good	£Fine	£N.Mint
1-2 ND 52pgs, Gray Morrow art						
	$0.30	$0.90	$1.50	£0.20	£0.60	£1.00
Title Value:	$0.60	$1.80	$3.00	£0.40	£1.20	£2.00

LOIS LANE, SUPERMAN'S GIRLFRIEND
National Periodical Publications/DC Comics; 1 Mar/Apr 1958-137 Sep/Oct 1974
(see Brave and the Bold, 80-Page Giant, Lois Lane mini-series. Amalgamated with Superman Family after #137)

	$Good	$Fine	$N.Mint	£Good	£Fine	£N.Mint
1 very scarce in the U.K.						
	$225.00	$670.00	$2250.00	£165.00	£495.00	£1650.00
[Rare in high grade - Very Fine+ or better]						
2 very scarce in the U.K.						
	$95.00	$285.00	$760.00	£67.50	£205.00	£550.00
3 scarce in the U.K.						
	$62.50	$185.00	$500.00	£44.00	£130.00	£350.00
4-5	$48.00	$140.00	$380.00	£33.00	£97.50	£260.00
6 (Jan 1959)	$38.00	$110.00	$300.00	£25.00	£75.00	£200.00
7-8	$38.00	$110.00	$300.00	£25.00	£75.00	£200.00
9-10	$30.00	$90.00	$240.00	£18.50	£55.00	£150.00
11-12	$21.00	$62.50	$150.00	£12.50	£39.00	£90.00
13	$20.00	$60.00	$140.00	£11.00	£34.00	£80.00
1st official distribution in the U.K.						
14 (Jan 1960), Supergirl appears, Lois as Batgirl						
	$20.00	$60.00	$140.00	£12.00	£36.00	£85.00
15 3-part story (black cover - scarce in high grade)						
	$21.00	$62.50	$150.00	£12.00	£36.00	£85.00
16-20	$20.00	$60.00	$140.00	£9.25	£28.00	£65.00
21	$15.00	$45.00	$105.00	£6.25	£19.00	£45.00
22 (Jan 1961), Supergirl appears						
	$15.00	$45.00	$105.00	£6.25	£19.00	£45.00
23-25	$15.00	$45.00	$105.00	£6.25	£19.00	£45.00
26	$15.00	$45.00	$105.00	£5.00	£15.00	£35.00
27 Bizarro appears						
	$15.00	$45.00	$105.00	£5.00	£15.00	£35.00
28	$15.00	$45.00	$105.00	£5.00	£15.00	£35.00
29 Aquaman, Batman, Green Arrow cameo; last 10 cents issue (Note: white cover shows wear and dirt easily - scarce in high grade)						
	$15.00	$45.00	$105.00	£5.50	£17.00	£40.00
30 (Jan 1962)	$10.00	$30.00	$70.00	£3.55	£10.50	£25.00
31-32	$10.00	$30.00	$70.00	£3.55	£10.50	£25.00
33 Mon El cameo	$11.00	$34.00	$80.00	£3.90	£11.50	£27.50
34-35	$10.00	$30.00	$70.00	£3.55	£10.50	£25.00
36-37	$7.75	$23.50	$55.00	£3.20	£9.50	£22.50
38 (Jan 1963)	$7.75	$23.50	$55.00	£3.20	£9.50	£22.50
39 Supergirl cameo						
	$7.75	$23.50	$55.00	£3.20	£9.50	£22.50
40	$7.75	$23.50	$55.00	£3.20	£9.50	£22.50
41-45	$9.00	$28.00	$55.00	£2.90	£8.75	£17.50
46 (Jan 1964)	$9.00	$28.00	$55.00	£2.90	£8.75	£17.50

Logan's Run #7

Lois Lane #2

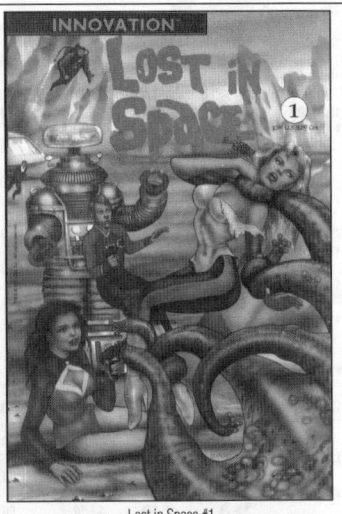

Lost in Space #1

	$Good	$Fine	$N.Mint	£Good	£Fine	£N.Mint
47 scarce in the U.K. Legion cameo						
	$9.00	$28.00	$55.00	£3.30	£10.00	£20.00
48-49	$9.00	$28.00	$55.00	£2.90	£8.75	£17.50
50 Phantom Girl, Shrinking Violet, Triplicate Girl appear						
	$8.25	$25.00	$50.00	£3.75	£11.00	£22.50
51 Supergirl appears						
	$6.50	$20.00	$40.00	£2.05	£6.25	£12.50
52-53	$6.50	$20.00	$40.00	£2.05	£6.25	£12.50
54 (Jan 1965), classic "The Monster That Loved Lois Lane"						
	$6.50	$20.00	$40.00	£2.05	£6.25	£12.50
55	$6.50	$20.00	$40.00	£2.05	£6.25	£12.50
56 Saturn Girl appears						
	$7.50	$22.50	$45.00	£2.05	£6.25	£12.50
57-58	$6.50	$20.00	$40.00	£2.05	£6.25	£12.50
59 Batman appears	$6.50	$20.00	$40.00	£2.05	£6.25	£12.50
60	$6.50	$20.00	$40.00	£2.05	£6.25	£12.50
61 Supergirl appears; last Silver Age issue, cover-dated Nov/Dec 1965						
	$6.50	$20.00	$40.00	£2.05	£6.25	£12.50
62 (Jan 1966)	$5.75	$17.50	$35.00	£1.50	£4.50	£9.00
63-67	$5.75	$17.50	$35.00	£1.50	£4.50	£9.00
68 less common in the U.K. 80pgs, Giant G-26						
	$7.00	$21.00	$50.00	£2.50	£7.50	£17.50
69	$5.75	$17.50	$35.00	£1.50	£4.50	£9.00
70 1st Silver Age appearance of Catwoman (pre-dates Batman #197 by more than a year)						
	$30.00	$90.00	$210.00	£12.50	£39.00	£90.00
71 (Jan 1967), 2nd Silver Age Catwoman; Batman/Robin cameo						
	$17.50	$52.50	$125.00	£7.75	£23.50	£55.00
72-73	$5.00	$15.00	$25.00	£1.50	£4.50	£7.50
74 1st appearance Bizarro Flash, Justice League of America appear						
	$7.00	$21.00	$35.00	£2.00	£6.00	£10.00
75	$5.00	$15.00	$25.00	£1.50	£4.50	£7.50
76	$5.00	$15.00	$25.00	£1.20	£3.60	£6.00
77 80pgs, Giant G-39, reprints cover story of #1						
	$5.00	$15.00	$30.00	£2.05	£6.25	£12.50
78	$5.00	$15.00	$25.00	£1.20	£3.60	£6.00
79 Neal Adams covers begin						
	$3.60	$10.50	$18.00	£1.20	£3.60	£6.00
80 (Jan 1968), Neal Adams cover						
	$2.50	$7.50	$12.50	£1.00	£3.00	£5.00
81-85 Neal Adams covers						
	$2.50	$7.50	$12.50	£0.80	£2.40	£4.00
86 Neal Adams cover, 80pg Giant G-51						
	$1.50	$4.50	$9.00	£1.50	£4.50	£9.00
87-88 Neal Adams covers						
	$2.50	$7.50	$12.50	£0.60	£1.80	£3.00
89 (Jan 1969), Neal Adams cover, Batman appears						
	$2.50	$7.50	$12.50	£0.70	£2.10	£3.50
90-92 Neal Adams cover						
	$2.50	$7.50	$12.50	£0.60	£1.80	£3.00
93 Neal Adams cover, Wonder Woman appears						
	$2.50	$7.50	$12.50	£0.70	£2.10	£3.50
94 Neal Adams cover						
	$2.50	$7.50	$12.50	£0.60	£1.80	£3.00
95 Neal Adams cover, 80pg Giant G-63						
	$4.15	$12.50	$25.00	£1.50	£4.50	£9.00
96-97	$1.20	$3.60	$6.00	£0.50	£1.50	£2.50
98 (Jan 1970)	$1.20	$3.60	$6.00	£0.50	£1.50	£2.50
99-100 Batman appears						
	$1.20	$3.60	$6.00	£0.60	£1.80	£3.00
101-103	$1.20	$3.60	$6.00	£0.50	£1.50	£2.50
104 scarce in the U.K. 80pgs, Giant G-75						
	$3.30	$10.00	$20.00	£1.50	£4.50	£9.00
105 1st appearance Rose and Thorn						
	$1.20	$3.60	$6.00	£0.50	£1.50	£2.50
106	$1.20	$3.60	$6.00	£0.40	£1.20	£2.00
107 (Jan 1971)	$1.20	$3.60	$6.00	£0.40	£1.20	£2.00
108 Neal Adams cover						
	$1.20	$3.60	$6.00	£0.40	£1.20	£2.00
109-110	$1.20	$3.60	$6.00	£0.40	£1.20	£2.00
111 Justice League of America appears						
	$1.00	$3.00	$5.00	£0.40	£1.20	£2.00
112 48pgs, (says 52pgs up to #123 as they count the covers in the U.S.)						
	$1.00	$3.00	$5.00	£0.50	£1.50	£2.50
113 80pgs, Giant G-87						
	$3.30	$10.00	$20.00	£1.25	£3.75	£7.50
114 48pgs	$1.00	$3.00	$5.00	£0.50	£1.50	£2.50
115 48pgs, Black Racer appears						
	$1.00	$3.00	$5.00	£0.50	£1.50	£2.50
116 48pgs, Darkseid cameo						
	$1.00	$3.00	$5.00	£0.50	£1.50	£2.50
117 48pgs	$1.00	$3.00	$5.00	£0.50	£1.50	£2.50
118 48pgs, (Jan 1972), Darkseid cameo, origin Morgan Edge						
	$1.00	$3.00	$5.00	£0.50	£1.50	£2.50
119 48pgs, Darkseid cameo						
	$1.00	$3.00	$5.00	£0.50	£1.50	£2.50
120-121 48pgs	$1.00	$3.00	$5.00	£0.50	£1.50	£2.50
122 48pgs, Thorn teams with Lois, solo Lois Lane story from Superman #30 reprinted						
	$1.00	$3.00	$5.00	£0.50	£1.50	£2.50
123 48pgs, reprints Golden Age Batman/Catwoman story from Batman #35						
	$0.90	$2.70	$4.50	£0.50	£1.50	£2.50
124 scarce in the U.K.						
	$0.70	$2.10	$3.50	£0.50	£1.50	£2.50

	$Good	$Fine	$N.Mint	£Good	£Fine	£N.Mint
125-127 less common in the U.K.						
	$0.70	$2.10	$3.50	£0.40	£1.20	£2.00
128 less common in the U.K. Justice League of America appear (principally Batman and Aquaman)						
	$0.70	$2.10	$3.50	£0.50	£1.50	£2.50
129 (Feb 1973)	$0.70	$2.10	$3.50	£0.30	£0.90	£1.50
130-131	$0.70	$2.10	$3.50	£0.30	£0.90	£1.50
132 Zatanna appears						
	$0.60	$1.80	$3.00	£0.30	£0.90	£1.50
133-135	$0.60	$1.80	$3.00	£0.30	£0.90	£1.50
136 (Jan 1974), Wonder Woman appears						
	$0.60	$1.80	$3.00	£0.35	£1.05	£1.75
137	$0.60	$1.80	$3.00	£0.30	£0.90	£1.50
Title Value:	$1472.50	$4406.70	$10996.00	£781.65	£2350.20	£6140.75

FEATURES

Melba in 132. Rose & the Thorn in 105-112, 115-121, 123-130. Zatanna in 132.

LOIS LANE ANNUAL, SUPERMAN'S GIRLFRIEND

National Periodical Publications, ; 1 Aug/Oct 1962-2 Aug/Oct 1963

	$Good	$Fine	$N.Mint	£Good	£Fine	£N.Mint
1 80pgs, reprints stories from Lois Lane #10, #11, Superman #131 and Adventure #261 among others						
	$19.00	$57.50	$175.00	£13.00	£40.00	£120.00
2 80pgs, reprints #14 and #16 among others						
	$11.00	$33.00	$100.00	£7.00	£21.50	£65.00
Title Value:	$30.00	$90.50	$275.00	£20.00	£61.50	£185.00

REPRINT FEATURES

Lois Lane/Superman in 1, 2.

LOMAX (POLICE ACTION FEATURING..)

Atlas; 1 Feb 1975

	$Good	$Fine	$N.Mint	£Good	£Fine	£N.Mint
1 Mike Sekowsky art; distributed in the U.K.						
	$0.25	$0.75	$1.25	£0.15	£0.45	£0.75
Title Value:	$0.25	$0.75	$1.25	£0.15	£0.45	£0.75

LONE RANGER AND TONTO, THE

Topps,MS; 1 Aug 1994-4 Nov 1994

	$Good	$Fine	$N.Mint	£Good	£Fine	£N.Mint
1-4 ND Joe R. Lansdale script, Tim Truman cover and art						
	$0.45	$1.35	$2.25	£0.30	£0.90	£1.50
Title Value:	$1.80	$5.40	$9.00	£1.20	£3.60	£6.00
The Lone Ranger and Tonto (Jan 1995) Trade paperback						
reprints mini-series with new wraparound cover by Tim Truman				£1.30	£3.90	£6.50

LONE WOLF & CUB

First; 1 May 1987-49 1991

	$Good	$Fine	$N.Mint	£Good	£Fine	£N.Mint
1 Frank Miller covers begin						
	$1.80	$5.25	$9.00	£1.20	£3.60	£6.00
1 2nd printing	$0.80	$2.40	$4.00	£0.50	£1.50	£2.50
1 3rd printing	$0.70	$2.10	$3.50	£0.45	£1.35	£2.25
2	$0.90	$2.70	$4.50	£0.60	£1.80	£3.00
2 2nd printing	$0.60	$1.80	$3.00	£0.40	£1.20	£2.00
3	$0.80	$2.40	$4.00	£0.50	£1.50	£2.50
3 2nd printing	$0.60	$1.80	$3.00	£0.40	£1.20	£2.00
4-5	$0.80	$2.40	$4.00	£0.50	£1.50	£2.50
6 origin issue	$0.85	$2.55	$4.25	£0.55	£1.65	£2.75
7-11	$0.80	$2.40	$4.00	£0.50	£1.50	£2.50
12 last Frank Miller cover						
	$0.80	$2.40	$4.00	£0.50	£1.50	£2.50
13-20 Bill Sienkiewicz covers						
	$0.80	$2.40	$4.00	£0.50	£1.50	£2.50
21-31	$0.80	$2.40	$4.00	£0.50	£1.50	£2.50
32 88pgs, Matt Wagner covers begin						
	$0.90	$2.70	$4.50	£0.60	£1.80	£3.00
33-36	$0.80	$2.40	$4.00	£0.50	£1.50	£2.50
37 Mike Ploog covers begin						
	$0.80	$2.40	$4.00	£0.50	£1.50	£2.50
38	$0.80	$2.40	$4.00	£0.50	£1.50	£2.50
39 120pgs	$1.20	$3.60	$6.00	£0.80	£2.40	£4.00
40	$0.80	$2.40	$4.00	£0.50	£1.50	£2.50
41 80pgs	$0.85	$2.55	$4.25	£0.55	£1.65	£2.75
42-48	$0.80	$2.40	$4.00	£0.50	£1.50	£2.50
49 Arthur Suydam cover						
	$0.80	$2.40	$4.00	£0.50	£1.50	£2.50
Title Value:	$43.60	$130.65	$218.00	£27.55	£82.65	£137.75

Note; all Non-Distributed on the news-stands in the U.K.
Deluxe Edition,

	$Good	$Fine	$N.Mint	£Good	£Fine	£N.Mint
reprints #1-7, colour section; Miller/Sienkiewicz cover				£2.40	£7.20	£12.00

LONG HOT SUMMER, THE

DC Comics/Milestone,MS; 1 Jul 1995-3 Sep 1995

	$Good	$Fine	$N.Mint	£Good	£Fine	£N.Mint
1 ND holographic foil-stamped cover; mini-series involving all the Milestone titles						
	$0.60	$1.80	$3.00	£0.40	£1.20	£2.00
2-3 ND	$0.60	$1.80	$3.00	£0.40	£1.20	£2.00
Title Value:	$1.80	$5.40	$9.00	£1.20	£3.60	£6.00

LONGSHOT

Marvel Comics Group,MS; 1 Sep 1985-6 Feb 1986

	$Good	$Fine	$N.Mint	£Good	£Fine	£N.Mint
1 ND 1st appearance Longshot, Art Adams pencils and Whilce Portacio inks in all						
	$2.00	$6.00	$10.00	£1.20	£3.60	£6.00
2 ND scarce in the U.K.						
	$1.60	$4.80	$8.00	£1.20	£3.60	£6.00
3 ND	$1.40	$4.20	$7.00	£0.90	£2.70	£4.50
4 ND Spiderman, She-Hulk appear						
	$1.40	$4.20	$7.00	£0.90	£2.70	£4.50
5 ND Dr. Strange appears						
	$1.40	$4.20	$7.00	£0.90	£2.70	£4.50
6 ND DS very scarce						
	$1.60	$4.80	$8.00	£1.20	£3.60	£6.00
Title Value:	$9.40	$28.20	$47.00	£6.30	£18.90	£31.50
Trade Paperback (1989) reprints issues #1-6				£2.50	£7.50	£12.50
2nd print (Dec 1992)				£2.25	£6.75	£11.25

	$Good	$Fine	$N.Mint	£Good	£Fine	£N.Mint
LOONEY TUNES						
DC Comics; 1 Apr 1994-present						
1 Bugs Bunny, Sylvester, Daffy Duck and others begin						
	$0.30	$0.90	$1.50	£0.20	£0.60	£1.00
2-19	$0.30	$0.90	$1.50	£0.20	£0.60	£1.00
20 title goes bi-monthly						
	$0.30	$0.90	$1.50	£0.20	£0.60	£1.00
21-22	$0.30	$0.90	$1.50	£0.20	£0.60	£1.00
Title Value:	$6.60	$19.80	$33.00	£4.40	£13.20	£22.00
LOONEY TUNES MAGAZINE						
DC Comics,Magazine; 1 Jan 1990-7 1990						
1-7 ND	$0.30	$0.90	$1.50	£0.20	£0.60	£1.00
Title Value:	$2.10	$6.30	$10.50	£1.40	£4.20	£7.00
Note: features Warner Bros cartoon characters like Bugs Bunny and Daffy Duck, other features and items, quarterly frequency.						
LOOSE CANNON						
DC Comics,MS; 1 Jun 1995-4 Sep 1995						
1 ND Jeph Loeb script and Adam Pollina art begins						
	$0.40	$1.20	$2.00	£0.25	£0.75	£1.25
2 ND The Eradicator appears						
	$0.40	$1.20	$2.00	£0.25	£0.75	£1.25
3-4 ND	$0.40	$1.20	$2.00	£0.25	£0.75	£1.25
Title Value:	$1.60	$4.80	$8.00	£1.00	£3.00	£5.00
LORD PUMPKIN						
Malibu,OS; 0 Oct 1994						
0 ND 40pgs, spin-off from Sludge #9						
	$0.45	$1.35	$2.25	£0.30	£0.90	£1.50
0 ND Signed Edition (Feb 1995) - signed with certificate; 2,000 copies						
	$2.50	$7.50	$12.50	£1.00	£3.00	£5.00
0 Newstand edition, ND (Feb 1995) - black etched cover						
	$0.45	$1.35	$2.25	£0.30	£0.90	£1.50
Title Value:	$3.40	$10.20	$17.00	£1.60	£4.80	£8.00
LORDS OF THE ULTRA REALM						
DC Comics,MS; 1 Jun 1986-6 Nov 1986						
1-6 ND scarce in the U.K.						
	$0.30	$0.90	$1.50	£0.20	£0.60	£1.00
Title Value:	$1.80	$5.40	$9.00	£1.20	£3.60	£6.00
LORDS OF THE ULTRA REALM SPECIAL						
DC Comics; 1 Dec 1987						
1 ND	$0.45	$1.35	$2.25	£0.30	£0.90	£1.50
Title Value:	$0.45	$1.35	$2.25	£0.30	£0.90	£1.50
LOSERS SPECIAL						
DC Comics,OS; 1 1985						
(see GI Combat #138, Our Fighting Forces #123)						
1 very LD 1st Crisis X-over comic, death of Capt. Storm, Gunner, Sarge & Johnny Cloud						
	$0.60	$1.80	$3.00	£0.40	£1.20	£2.00
Title Value:	$0.60	$1.80	$3.00	£0.40	£1.20	£2.00
LOST CONTINENT, THE						
Eclipse,MS; 1 Oct 1990-6 Mar 1991						
1-6 ND 64pgs, squarebound, Japanese material reprints of Akihiro Yamada work, black and white						
	$0.60	$1.80	$3.00	£0.40	£1.20	£2.00
Title Value:	$3.60	$10.80	$18.00	£2.40	£7.20	£12.00
LOST IN SPACE						
Gold Key, TV; 37 Oct 1973-54 Dec 1977; Whitman,TV; 55 Mar 1981-59 May 1982						
(previously Space Family Robinson)						
37 full cover title now reads "Space Family Robinson Lost in Space on Space Staion One"						
	$0.90	$2.70	$4.50	£0.60	£1.80	£3.00
38 16pg Kenner cartoon insert						
	$0.90	$2.70	$4.50	£0.60	£1.80	£3.00
39-41	$0.90	$2.70	$4.50	£0.60	£1.80	£3.00
42 16pg Kenner cartoon insert						
	$0.90	$2.70	$4.50	£0.60	£1.80	£3.00
43-54	$0.90	$2.70	$4.50	£0.60	£1.80	£3.00
55 all reprints begin	$0.60	$1.80	$3.00	£0.40	£1.20	£2.00
56 new logo begins	$0.60	$1.80	$3.00	£0.40	£1.20	£2.00
57-58	$0.60	$1.80	$3.00	£0.40	£1.20	£2.00
59 scarce in the U.K. line drawn cover						
	$0.80	$2.40	$4.00	£0.50	£1.50	£2.50
Title Value:	$19.40	$58.20	$97.00	£12.90	£38.70	£64.50
Note: most issue distributed in the U.K.						
LOST IN SPACE (2ND SERIES)						
Innovation,MS; 1 Aug 1991-18 Nov 1993						
1 co-written by Billy Mumy ("Will" in TV series)						
	$0.60	$1.80	$3.00	£0.40	£1.20	£2.00
1 special edition reprint (Mar 1992) - extra pages, recoloured						
	$0.55	$1.65	$2.75	£0.35	£1.05	£1.75
2	$0.55	$1.65	$2.75	£0.35	£1.05	£1.75
2 special edition reprint (Oct 1992) - extra pages, recoloured						
	$0.45	$1.35	$2.25	£0.30	£0.90	£1.50
3-6	$0.45	$1.35	$2.25	£0.30	£0.90	£1.50
7 co-plotted by Mark Goddard						
	$0.45	$1.35	$2.25	£0.30	£0.90	£1.50
8	$0.45	$1.35	$2.25	£0.30	£0.90	£1.50
9 co-written by Billy Mumy						
	$0.45	$1.35	$2.25	£0.30	£0.90	£1.50
10-12	$0.45	$1.35	$2.25	£0.30	£0.90	£1.50
13 Gold Collector's Edition (has #13 on cover), pre-bagged with poster and gold embossed logo						
	$3.00	$9.00	$15.00	£2.00	£6.00	£10.00
13 Gold foil card-stock cover						
	$0.50	$1.50	$2.50	£0.30	£0.90	£1.50
14-18 Voyage to the Bottom of the Soul story						
	$0.50	$1.50	$2.50	£0.30	£0.90	£1.50

	$Good	$Fine	$N.Mint	£Good	£Fine	£N.Mint
Title Value:	$12.65	$37.95	$63.25	£8.20	£24.60	£41.00
Note: all Non-Distributed on the news-stands in the U.K.						
Strangers Among Strangers Graphic Novel (Feb 1993)						
reprints issues #4-5 with new art, photo gallery and new cover painting					£0.75	£2.25	£3.75
LOST IN SPACE ANNUAL						
Innovation; 1 1992-2 1993						
1 ND Miguel Ferrer appears						
	$0.45	$1.35	$2.25	£0.30	£0.90	£1.50
2 ND script by Peter David and Billy Mumy						
	$0.45	$1.35	$2.25	£0.30	£0.90	£1.50
Title Value:	$0.90	$2.70	$4.50	£0.60	£1.80	£3.00
LOST IN SPACE: ARRIVAL						
Innovation; 1 Aug 1993-3 1993						
1 ND 44pgs - pre-bagged with trading card, gold foil-stamped cover						
	$0.60	$1.80	$3.00	£0.40	£1.20	£2.00
2-3 ND	$0.45	$1.35	$2.25	£0.30	£0.90	£1.50
Title Value:	$2.40	$7.20	$12.00	£1.60	£4.80	£8.00
LOST IN SPACE: PROJECT ROBINSON						
Innovation,MS; 1 Jan 1994						
1 ND	$0.45	$1.35	$2.25	£0.30	£0.90	£1.50
Title Value:	$0.45	$1.35	$2.25	£0.30	£0.90	£1.50
Note: Issue #2 was advertised & solicited but never came out.						
LOST PLANET						
Eclipse; 1 May 1987-5 Feb 1988; 6 Jan 1989						
1 ND Bo Hampton art, Scott Hampton art on back-up						
	$0.40	$1.20	$2.00	£0.25	£0.75	£1.25
2-3 ND Bo Hampton art						
	$0.40	$1.20	$2.00	£0.25	£0.75	£1.25
4 ND Bo Hampton art, Scott Hampton art on back-up						
	$0.40	$1.20	$2.00	£0.25	£0.75	£1.25
5-6 ND Bo Hampton art						
	$0.40	$1.20	$2.00	£0.25	£0.75	£1.25
Title Value:	$2.40	$7.20	$12.00	£1.50	£4.50	£7.50
LOST UNIVERSE, GENE RODDENBURY'S						
Tekno Comix; 0 Jul 1995; 1 Apr 1995-6 Nov 1995						
0 ND (Jul 1995), wraparound cover by Jae Lee						
	$0.45	$1.35	$2.25	£0.30	£0.90	£1.50
1 ND Lawrence Watts-Evans script, James Callahan and Aaron McClellan art; Bill Sienkiewicz painted cover						
	$0.40	$1.20	$2.00	£0.25	£0.75	£1.25
2-6 ND Bill Sienkiewicz painted cover						
	$0.40	$1.20	$2.00	£0.25	£0.75	£1.25
Title Value:	$2.85	$8.55	$14.25	£1.80	£5.40	£9.00
LOVE AND ROCKETS						
Hernandez Brothers/Fantagraphics; 1 Jul 1982-present						
(see Mechanics)						
1 black and white cover with no staples, $1.00 cover price, self-published, 800 copies						
	$13.00	$39.00	$65.00	£10.00	£30.00	£50.00
1 2nd printing, colour cover, 1st Fantagraphics issue						
	$8.00	$24.00	$40.00	£5.00	£15.00	£25.00
1 3rd printing	$0.90	$2.70	$4.50	£0.60	£1.80	£3.00
1 4th printing	$0.80	$2.40	$4.00	£0.50	£1.50	£2.50
2	$6.00	$18.00	$30.00	£4.00	£12.00	£20.00
2 2nd printing, (1990)						
	$0.80	$2.40	$4.00	£0.50	£1.50	£2.50
3	$4.00	$12.00	$20.00	£2.50	£7.50	£12.50
3 2nd printing, (1991)						
	$0.80	$2.40	$4.00	£0.50	£1.50	£2.50
4	$3.50	$10.50	$17.50	£2.50	£7.50	£12.50
4 2nd printing, (1991)						
	$0.80	$2.40	$4.00	£0.50	£1.50	£2.50
5	$3.00	$9.00	$15.00	£2.00	£6.00	£10.00
6	$1.50	$4.50	$7.50	£1.00	£3.00	£5.00
6 2nd printing	$0.60	$1.80	$3.00	£0.40	£1.20	£2.00
7	$1.50	$4.50	$7.50	£1.00	£3.00	£5.00
7 2nd printing	$0.60	$1.80	$3.00	£0.40	£1.20	£2.00
8	$1.50	$4.50	$7.50	£1.00	£3.00	£5.00
8 2nd printing, (Oct 1991)						
	$0.60	$1.80	$3.00	£0.40	£1.20	£2.00
9	$1.50	$4.50	$7.50	£1.00	£3.00	£5.00
9 2nd printing, (Nov 1991)						
	$0.60	$1.80	$3.00	£0.40	£1.20	£2.00
10	$1.50	$4.50	$7.50	£1.00	£3.00	£5.00
10 2nd printing, (Jan 1992)						
	$0.45	$1.35	$2.25	£0.30	£0.90	£1.50
11	$1.20	$3.60	$6.00	£0.80	£2.40	£4.00
11 2nd printing, (Feb 1992)						
	$0.45	$1.35	$2.25	£0.30	£0.90	£1.50
12	$1.20	$3.60	$6.00	£0.80	£2.40	£4.00
12 2nd printing, (Nov 1992)						
	$0.45	$1.35	$2.25	£0.30	£0.90	£1.50
13 Lloyd Llewellyn first ever story						
	$1.20	$3.60	$6.00	£0.80	£2.40	£4.00
13 2nd printing, (Dec 1992)						
	$0.45	$1.35	$2.25	£0.30	£0.90	£1.50
14	$1.20	$3.60	$6.00	£0.80	£2.40	£4.00
14 2nd printing, (Dec 1992)						
	$0.45	$1.35	$2.25	£0.30	£0.90	£1.50
15	$1.20	$3.60	$6.00	£0.80	£2.40	£4.00
15 2nd printing, (Nov 1993)						
	$0.45	$1.35	$2.25	£0.30	£0.90	£1.50

MINT = 100% / NEAR MINT (inc. +/-) = 90–99% / VERY FINE (inc. +/-) = 75–89% / FINE (inc. +/-) = 55–74%
VERY GOOD (inc. +/-) = 35–54% / GOOD (inc. +/-) = 15–34% / FAIR = 5–14% / POOR = 1–4%

433

	$Good	$Fine	$N.Mint	£Good	£Fine	£N.Mint
16	$1.00	$3.00	$5.00	£0.70	£2.10	£3.50
16 2nd printing, (Dec 1993)						
	$0.45	$1.35	$2.25	£0.30	£0.90	£1.50
17-20	$1.00	$3.00	$5.00	£0.70	£2.10	£3.50
21-25	$0.90	$2.70	$4.50	£0.60	£1.80	£3.00
26-28	$0.60	$1.80	$3.00	£0.40	£1.20	£2.00
28 2nd printing, (May 1995)						
	$0.60	$1.80	$3.00	£0.40	£1.20	£2.00
29	$0.60	$1.80	$3.00	£0.40	£1.20	£2.00
29 2nd printing, (May 1992)						
	$0.45	$1.35	$2.25	£0.30	£0.90	£1.50
30 bumper special						
	$0.80	$2.40	$4.00	£0.50	£1.50	£2.50
30 2nd printing, (Jun 1992)						
	$0.55	$1.65	$2.75	£0.35	£1.05	£1.75
31	$0.45	$1.35	$2.25	£0.30	£0.90	£1.50
31 2nd printing, (Jul 1992)						
	$0.45	$1.35	$2.25	£0.30	£0.90	£1.50
32-39	$0.45	$1.35	$2.25	£0.30	£0.90	£1.50
40 48pgs, Maggie returns						
	$0.70	$2.10	$3.50	£0.45	£1.35	£2.25
41-49	$0.60	$1.80	$3.00	£0.40	£1.20	£2.00
Title Value:	$85.55	$256.65	$427.75	£58.00	£174.00	£290.00

Note: all Non-Distributed on the news-stands in the U.K.

		£Good	£Fine	£N.Mint
Book 1: Music For Mechanics, hardcover reprints #1,2		£4.00	£12.00	£20.00
(2nd,3rd printings)		£2.50	£7.50	£12.50
(4th printing - Mar 1993)		£1.90	£5.70	£9.50
Book 1 softcover		£1.80	£5.40	£9.00
Book 2: Chelo's Burden, hardback, reprints #3,4		£3.60	£10.80	£18.00
Book 2 softcover		£1.80	£5.40	£9.00
Book 3: Las Mujeres Perdidas, hardcover, reprints #5-8		£3.60	£10.80	£18.00
Book 3 softcover		£1.70	£5.10	£8.50
Book 4: Tears from Heaven, hardcover, reprints #9-12		£3.60	£10.80	£18.00
Book 4 softback		£1.70	£5.10	£8.50
Book 4 Deluxe		£5.00	£15.00	£25.00
[Book 4: softcover, hardcover, deluxe all reprinted Sep 1991]				
Book 5: House of Raging Women, reprints #13-16, hardcover	£4.50	£13.50	£22.50
Book 5 softcover		£1.70	£5.10	£8.50
Book 5 2nd print (Jul 1995)		£2.20	£6.60	£11.00
Book 5 Deluxe		£5.00	£15.00	£25.00
Book 6: Duck Feet		£4.20	£12.60	£21.00
Book 6 softcover		£1.70	£5.10	£8.50
Book 6 2nd print (Aug 1995)		£2.20	£6.60	£11.00
Book 6 Deluxe		£5.00	£15.00	£25.00
Book 7: The Death of Speedy, hardcover		£4.00	£12.00	£20.00
Book 7 limited hardcover		£5.00	£15.00	£25.00
Book 7 softcover		£1.65	£4.95	£8.25
Book 8: Blood of Palomar, hardcover		£4.00	£12.00	£20.00
Book 8 limited hardcover		£5.00	£15.00	£25.00
Book 8 softcover		£1.65	£4.95	£8.25
Book 9: Flies on the Ceiling, softcover		£1.50	£4.50	£7.50
Book 9: hardcover		£4.20	£12.60	£21.00
Book 10 softcover		£1.50	£4.50	£7.50
Book 11: Wig Wam Bam softcover		£1.70	£5.10	£8.50
Book 11 Hardcover		£4.50	£13.50	£22.50
Book 11 Limited Hardcover		£5.00	£15.00	£25.00
Book 12 soft cover		£2.20	£6.60	£11.00
Book 12: Poison River Signed & Numbered hardcover		£5.00	£15.00	£25.00
Heartbreak Soup (Gilbert)		£1.50	£4.50	£7.50
The Reticent Heart (Gilbert)		£1.50	£4.50	£7.50
Short Stories (Jaimie)		£1.50	£4.50	£7.50
The Lost Women (Jaimie)		£1.50	£4.50	£7.50
Titan Books:				
Mechanics		£1.40	£4.20	£7.00
Love and Rockets		£1.30	£3.90	£6.50
Heartbreak Soup		£1.20	£3.60	£6.00
Duck Feet		£1.20	£3.60	£6.00
Human Diastrophism		£1.40	£4.20	£7.00
Ape Sex		£1.30	£3.90	£6.50

LOVE AND ROCKETS, TEN YEARS OF

Fantagraphics, OS; 1 Sep 1992

1 ND character indexes and background information plus new and old strips

	$Good	$Fine	$N.Mint	£Good	£Fine	£N.Mint
	$0.25	$0.75	$1.25	£0.15	£0.45	£0.75
Title Value:	$0.25	$0.75	$1.25	£0.15	£0.45	£0.75

LOVE STORIES

DC Comics; 147 Nov 1972-152 Oct/Nov 1973
(previously Heart Throbs)

	$Good	$Fine	$N.Mint	£Good	£Fine	£N.Mint
147-152 ND	$0.60	$1.80	$3.00	£0.40	£1.20	£2.00
Title Value:	$3.60	$10.80	$18.00	£2.40	£7.20	£12.00

LOVECRAFT

Adventure, MS; 1 Dec 1991-4 May 1992

1 ND The Lurking Fear

	$Good	$Fine	$N.Mint	£Good	£Fine	£N.Mint
	$0.55	$1.65	$2.75	£0.35	£1.05	£1.75

1 ND Limited Edition includes prose story, poster, embossed cover

	$1.10	$3.35	$5.62	£0.75	£2.25	£3.75

2 ND Beyond The Wall of Sleep

	$0.55	$1.65	$2.75	£0.35	£1.05	£1.75

3 ND The Tomb

	$0.55	$1.65	$2.75	£0.35	£1.05	£1.75

4 ND The Alchemist

	$0.55	$1.65	$2.75	£0.35	£1.05	£1.75
Title Value:	$3.30	$9.95	$16.62	£2.15	£6.45	£10.75

LOWLIFE

Caliber Press; 1 May 1991-3 1992; Aeon: 4 Oct 1994-6 1995

1 ND Ed Brubaker script and art, black and white; Chester Brown art featured

	$Good	$Fine	$N.Mint	£Good	£Fine	£N.Mint
	$0.45	$1.35	$2.25	£0.30	£0.90	£1.50

2 ND Beat Generation story

	$0.45	$1.35	$2.25	£0.30	£0.90	£1.50

3-6 ND

	$0.45	$1.35	$2.25	£0.30	£0.90	£1.50
Title Value:	$2.70	$8.10	$13.50	£1.80	£5.40	£9.00

Portable Lowlife (Dec 1994)

reprints issues #1 & 2 plus new 6pg story

				£0.65	£1.95	£3.25

LUCIFER'S HAMMER

Innovation, MS; 1 Nov 1993-4 1994

1 ND adaptation of Larry Niven and Jerry Pournelle novel begins

	$Good	$Fine	$N.Mint	£Good	£Fine	£N.Mint
	$0.45	$1.35	$2.25	£0.30	£0.90	£1.50

2-4 ND

	$0.45	$1.35	$2.25	£0.30	£0.90	£1.50
Title Value:	$1.80	$5.40	$9.00	£1.20	£3.60	£6.00

LUGER

Eclipse, MS; 1 Oct 1986-3 Feb 1987

1-3 ND Bo Hampton/Yeates art, colour

	$0.40	$1.20	$2.00	£0.25	£0.75	£1.25
Title Value:	$1.20	$3.60	$6.00	£0.75	£2.25	£3.75

LUKE CAGE, HERO FOR HIRE

Marvel Comics Group; 1 Jun 1972-16 Dec 1973
(becomes Powerman with #17, Powerman and Iron Fist with #50)

1 ND scarce in the U.K. origin and 1st appearance of Luke Cage

	$Good	$Fine	$N.Mint	£Good	£Fine	£N.Mint
	$6.50	$19.50	$32.50	£4.50	£13.50	£22.50

2 ND

	$2.40	$7.00	$12.00	£1.60	£4.80	£8.00

3 ND 1st appearance Mace

	$2.20	$6.50	$11.00	£1.50	£4.50	£7.50

4-5 ND

	$2.20	$6.50	$11.00	£1.50	£4.50	£7.50

6-7 ND

	$1.50	$4.50	$7.50	£1.00	£3.00	£5.00

8 ND Dr. Doom appears

	$1.50	$4.50	$7.50	£1.00	£3.00	£5.00

9 ND Luke Cage vs. Dr. Doom

	$1.50	$4.50	$7.50	£1.00	£3.00	£5.00

10 ND

	$1.50	$4.50	$7.50	£1.00	£3.00	£5.00

11 ND

	$1.40	$4.20	$7.00	£0.90	£2.70	£4.50

12 ND Spiderman cameo

	$1.40	$4.20	$7.00	£0.90	£2.70	£4.50

13 ND

	$1.40	$4.20	$7.00	£0.90	£2.70	£4.50

14 ND origin retold

$1.50	$4.50	$7.50	£1.00	£3.00	£5.00

15 ND includes Golden Age Sub-Mariner reprint by Everett

	$1.50	$4.50	$7.50	£1.00	£3.00	£5.00

16 ND origin Stiletto

	$1.40	$4.20	$7.00	£0.90	£2.70	£4.50
Title Value:	$31.60	$94.30	$158.00	£21.20	£63.60	£106.00

LUM

Viz; 1 1989-8 1990

1-8 ND Urusei Yatsura art

	$0.60	$1.80	$3.00	£0.40	£1.20	£2.00
Title Value:	$4.80	$14.40	$24.00	£3.20	£9.60	£16.00

Graphic Album 1, reprints				£1.65	£4.95	£8.25
Graphic Album 2, reprints				£1.65	£4.95	£8.25

Lum Urusei Yatsura Perfect Collection (Jul 1994)
400pgs, collects both the above in one volume;
softcover black and white

				£2.60	£7.80	£13.00

LUNATIK

Marvel Comics Group; 1 Dec 3 Feb 1996

1 ND Keith Giffen art begins

	$0.40	$1.20	$2.00	£0.25	£0.75	£1.25

2 ND Lunatik vs. The Avengers

	$0.40	$1.20	$2.00	£0.25	£0.75	£1.25

3 ND

	$0.40	$1.20	$2.00	£0.25	£0.75	£1.25
Title Value:	$1.20	$3.60	$6.00	£0.75	£2.25	£3.75

LUST OF THE NAZI WEASEL WOMEN

Fantagraphics; 1 Oct 1990-5 1991

1-5 ND Mitch Manzer script/art, black and white

	$0.40	$1.20	$2.00	£0.25	£0.75	£1.25
Title Value:	$2.00	$6.00	$10.00	£1.25	£3.75	£6.25

LUTHER ARKWRIGHT

Dark Horse, MS; 1 Mar 1990-9 Jan 1991
(see British section)

1 ND

	$0.45	$1.35	$2.25	£0.30	£0.90	£1.50

2-9 ND

	$0.40	$1.20	$2.00	£0.25	£0.75	£1.25
Title Value:	$3.65	$10.95	$18.25	£2.30	£6.90	£11.50

Note: reprints original series with new covers by Bryan Talbot; issued every 6 weeks

LUX AND ALBY

Dark Horse, MS; 1 Apr 1993-9 Dec 1993

1-9 ND Mark Millar script and Simon Fraser art

	$0.45	$1.35	$2.25	£0.30	£0.90	£1.50
Title Value:	$4.05	$12.15	$20.25	£2.70	£8.10	£13.50

LYCANTHROPE LEO

Viz, MS; 1 May 1994-7 Nov 1994

1-7 ND Kengo Kaji and Kenji Okamura; black and white

	$0.60	$1.80	$3.00	£0.40	£1.20	£2.00
Title Value:	$4.20	$12.60	$21.00	£2.80	£8.40	£14.00

LYNCH MOB

Chaos Comics, MS; 1 Jun 1994-4 Sep 1994

1-4 ND Brian Pulido script, Roman Morales art, cover by Greg Capullo

	$0.45	$1.35	$2.25	£0.30	£0.90	£1.50
Title Value:	$1.80	$5.40	$9.00	£1.20	£3.60	£6.00

TRADE PAPERBACKS, GRAPHIC NOVELS AND OTHER COLLECTIONS ARE PRICED IN POUNDS STERLING ONLY. CONVERT AT 1.5 FOR DOLLARS.

	$Good	$Fine	$N.Mint	£Good	£Fine	£N.Mint

M

M
Eclipse,MS; 1 Oct 1990-4 Aug 1992
1 ND Jon J. Muth script/art; bound-in flexi-disc

	$0.80	$2.40	$4.00	£0.50	£1.50	£2.50

2-4 ND Jon J. Muth script/art

	$0.80	$2.40	$4.00	£0.50	£1.50	£2.50
Title Value:	$3.20	$9.60	$16.00	£2.00	£6.00	£10.00

M.A.R.S. PATROL TOTAL WAR
Gold Key; 3 Sep 1966-10 Aug 1969
(previously Total War)
3 Wally Wood art, painted covers on all; distributed in the U.K.

	$5.75	$17.50	$35.00	£4.15	£12.50	£25.00

4-10 distributed in the U.K.

	$2.90	$8.75	$17.50	£2.00	£6.00	£12.00
Title Value:	$26.05	$78.75	$157.50	£18.15	£54.50	£109.00

Note: initials stand for Marine Attack Rescue Service - this is a war rather than sci-fi book

M.D. GEIST
CPM Comics,MS; 1 Jun 1995-3 Aug 1995
1-3 ND 24pgs, based on US animated video

	$0.60	$1.80	$3.00	£0.40	£1.20	£2.00
Title Value:	$1.80	$5.40	$9.00	£1.20	£3.60	£6.00

M.G.M'S MARVELOUS WIZARD OF OZ
Marvel/DC Co-Production; Tabloid,Film; 1 Nov 1975
1 ND 84pgs, adapts film

	$0.90	$2.70	$4.50	£0.60	£1.80	£3.00
Title Value:	$0.90	$2.70	$4.50	£0.60	£1.80	£3.00

M.I.C.R.A.
Comics Interview/Apple; 1 Nov 1986-8 1988
1-7 ND black and white

	$0.30	$0.90	$1.50	£0.20	£0.60	£1.00

8 ND 1st Apple issue, black and white

	$0.30	$0.90	$1.50	£0.20	£0.60	£1.00
Title Value:	$2.40	$7.20	$12.00	£1.60	£4.80	£8.00
Graphic Novel #1-3, reprints				£0.65	£1.95	£3.25

MACHINE MAN
Marvel Comics Group; 1 Apr 1978-9 Dec 1978; 10 Aug 1979-19 Feb 1981
(see 2001, A Space Odyssey)
1 ND Jack Kirby art

	$0.60	$1.80	$3.00	£0.30	£0.90	£1.50

2-9 ND Jack Kirby art

	$0.30	$0.90	$1.50	£0.20	£0.60	£1.00

10-13 Steve Ditko art

	$0.30	$0.90	$1.50	£0.20	£0.60	£1.00

14 Steve Ditko art, John Byrne cover

	$0.30	$0.90	$1.50	£0.20	£0.60	£1.00

15 Steve Ditko art, Fantastic Four appear

	$0.30	$0.90	$1.50	£0.20	£0.60	£1.00

16-17 Steve Ditko art

	$0.30	$0.90	$1.50	£0.20	£0.60	£1.00

18 Wendigo, Alpha Flight appear; ties in with X-Men #140, Steve Ditko art

	$0.80	$2.40	$4.00	£0.30	£0.90	£1.50

19 ND 1st appearance Jack O'Lantern (Philip Macendale – later Hobgoblin II), Steve Ditko art and Frank Miller cover

	$2.40	$7.00	$12.00	£0.40	£1.20	£2.00
Title Value:	$8.60	$25.60	$43.00	£4.20	£12.60	£21.00

ARTISTS
Ditko 10-19. Kirby 1-9.

MACHINE MAN (2ND SERIES)
Marvel Comics Group,MS; 1 Oct 1984-4 Jan 1985
1-2 ND Barry Windsor Smith inks

	$0.30	$0.90	$1.50	£0.25	£0.75	£1.25

3-4 ND Barry Windsor Smith art

	$0.30	$0.90	$1.50	£0.25	£0.75	£1.25
Title Value:	$1.20	$3.60	$6.00	£1.00	£3.00	£5.00
Trade Paperback, reprints #1-4, new cover by Barry Smith			£0.90	£2.70	£4.50	

MACHINE MAN 2020
Marvel Comics Group,MS; 1 Aug 1994-2 Sep 1994
1 48pgs, reprints mini-series issues #1,2

	$0.40	$1.20	$2.00	£0.25	£0.75	£1.25

2 48pgs, reprints mini-series issues #3,4

	$0.40	$1.20	$2.00	£0.25	£0.75	£1.25
Title Value:	$0.80	$2.40	$4.00	£0.50	£1.50	£2.50

MACHINE, THE
Dark Horse; 1 Nov 1994-4 Feb 1995
1-4 ND spin-off from Comics'Greatest World series

	$0.45	$1.35	$2.25	£0.30	£0.90	£1.50
Title Value:	$1.80	$5.40	$9.00	£1.20	£3.60	£6.00

MACKENZIE QUEEN
Matrix Graphics,MS; 1 Jun 1985-5 Apr 1986
1-5 ND Bernie Mireault art

	$0.40	$1.20	$2.00	£0.25	£0.75	£1.25
Title Value:	$2.00	$6.00	$10.00	£1.25	£3.75	£6.25

MACKENZIE QUEEN TRADE PAPERBACK
Caliber Press; nn 1991
nn ND reprints issues #1-5 originally published by Matrix Graphics

	$2.50	$7.50	$12.50	£1.50	£4.50	£7.50
Title Value:	$2.50	$7.50	$12.50	£1.50	£4.50	£7.50

MACROSS
Comico; 1 Dec 1984
(becomes Robotech: The Macross Saga)
1 ND colour, based on animated Japanese TV show

	$1.20	$3.60	$6.00	£0.60	£1.80	£3.00
Title Value:	$1.20	$3.60	$6.00	£0.60	£1.80	£3.00

MACROSS II
Viz,MS; 1 Nov 1993-10 1994
1-10 ND

	$0.50	$1.50	$2.50	£0.30	£0.90	£1.50
Title Value:	$5.00	$15.00	$25.00	£3.00	£9.00	£15.00

Macross II Graphic Novel (Jun 1994)

304pgs, collects mini-series; black and white				£2.20	£6.60	£11.00

MACROSS II: THE MICRON CONSPIRACY
Viz,MS; 1 Nov 1994-5 Mar 1995
1-5 ND James Hudnall and Schuloff Tam; black and white

	$0.50	$1.50	$2.50	£0.30	£0.90	£1.50
Title Value:	$2.50	$7.50	$12.50	£1.50	£4.50	£7.50

MAD
Extra-Large Comics; 1 Aug 1991
1 reprints issues #1-6 of original series

	$3.50	$10.50	$17.50	£2.50	£7.50	£12.50
Title Value:	$3.50	$10.50	$17.50	£2.50	£7.50	£12.50

Note: announced as an on-going series but cancelled after #1

MAD DOG
Marvel Comics Group,MS; 1 May 1993-6 Oct 1993
1-6 Evan Dorkin and Ty Templeton begin; based on US TV show

	$0.25	$0.75	$1.25	£0.15	£0.45	£0.75
Title Value:	$1.50	$4.50	$7.50	£0.90	£2.70	£4.50

MAD DOG MAGAZINE
Blackthorne; 1 Nov 1986-3 1987
1-3 ND

	$0.25	$0.75	$1.25	£0.15	£0.45	£0.75

M.A.R.S. Patrol #6

Magic Man #1

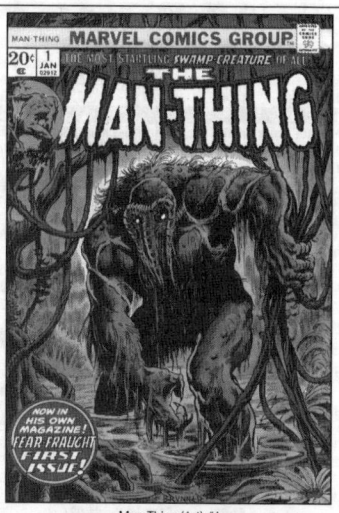

Man-Thing (1st) #1

	$Good	$Fine	$N.Mint	£Good	£Fine	£N.Mint
Title Value:	$0.75	$2.25	$3.75	£0.45	£1.35	£2.25

MAD DOGS
Comico,MS; 1 Apr 1992-3 Jun 1992

	$Good	$Fine	$N.Mint	£Good	£Fine	£N.Mint
1-3 ND	$0.40	$1.20	$2.00	£0.25	£0.75	£1.25
Title Value:	$1.20	$3.60	$6.00	£0.75	£2.25	£3.75

MAD MAGAZINE
E.C. Comics; 1 Oct/Nov 1952-present

	$Good	$Fine	$N.Mint	£Good	£Fine	£N.Mint
1 very scarce in the U.K. comic format begins; classic coverby Harvey Kurtzman; sub-titled "Tales Calculated to Drive You.."	$560.00	$1675.00	$4500.00	£375.00	£1125.00	£3000.00
2 scarce in the U.K. Jack Davis cover	$125.00	$385.00	$900.00	£80.00	£245.00	£575.00
3-4 Kurtzman cover	$77.50	$235.00	$550.00	£50.00	£150.00	£350.00
5 scarce in the U.K.	$120.00	$360.00	$850.00	£77.50	£235.00	£550.00
6-10 Kurtzman cover	$55.00	$170.00	$400.00	£39.00	£115.00	£275.00
11 classic Basil Wolverton cover and art	$46.00	$135.00	$325.00	£32.00	£95.00	£225.00
12	$46.00	$135.00	$325.00	£32.00	£95.00	£225.00
13 Kurtzman cover	$46.00	$135.00	$325.00	£32.00	£95.00	£225.00
14 Kurtzman Mona Lisa cover	$46.00	$135.00	$325.00	£32.00	£95.00	£225.00
15	$46.00	$135.00	$325.00	£32.00	£95.00	£225.00
16 Kurtzman cover	$36.00	$105.00	$250.00	£25.00	£75.00	£175.00
17	$36.00	$105.00	$250.00	£25.00	£75.00	£175.00
18 Kurtzman cover	$36.00	$105.00	$250.00	£25.00	£75.00	£175.00
19-20	$36.00	$105.00	$250.00	£25.00	£75.00	£175.00
21 famous Alfred E. Neuman character appears on cover in "small ad" (1st)	$36.00	$105.00	$250.00	£25.00	£75.00	£175.00
22 special Art issue	$36.00	$105.00	$250.00	£25.00	£75.00	£175.00
23	$36.00	$105.00	$250.00	£25.00	£75.00	£175.00
24 scarce in the U.K. 1st magazine format (July 1955); sub-titled The New Mad	$100.00	$310.00	$725.00	£67.50	£200.00	£475.00
25	$39.00	$115.00	$275.00	£26.00	£77.50	£185.00
26-29	$29.00	$85.00	$200.00	£19.00	£57.50	£135.00
30 1st classic Alfred E. Neuman cover	$41.00	$120.00	$290.00	£27.00	£80.00	£190.00
31-35	$20.00	$60.00	$140.00	£12.50	£39.00	£90.00
36-40	$13.00	$40.00	$80.00	£9.00	£28.00	£55.00
41-50	$10.00	$30.00	$60.00	£6.50	£20.00	£40.00
51-60	$9.00	$28.00	$55.00	£5.75	£17.50	£35.00
61-70	$6.50	$20.00	$40.00	£4.15	£12.50	£25.00
71-80	$5.75	$17.50	$35.00	£3.75	£11.00	£22.50
81-90	$5.00	$15.00	$30.00	£3.30	£10.00	£20.00
91-100	$4.15	$12.50	$25.00	£2.50	£7.50	£15.00
101-120	$3.30	$10.00	$20.00	£2.05	£6.25	£12.50
121-150	$2.50	$7.50	$15.00	£1.65	£5.00	£10.00
151-170	$2.40	$7.00	$12.00	£1.60	£4.80	£8.00
171-200	$1.80	$5.25	$9.00	£1.20	£3.60	£6.00
201-220	$1.20	$3.60	$6.00	£0.80	£2.40	£4.00
221-250	$1.00	$3.00	$5.00	£0.60	£1.80	£3.00
251-300	$0.70	$2.10	$3.50	£0.50	£1.50	£2.50
301-320	$0.45	$1.35	$2.25	£0.30	£0.90	£1.50
321-350	$0.40	$1.20	$2.00	£0.25	£0.75	£1.25
Title Value:	$2971.00	$8922.50	$20525.00	£1982.00	£5959.00	£13667.50

Note: see Mad Magazine in the British section

MADAME XANADU
DC Comics,OS; 1 Jul 1981

(see Doorway to Nightmare, Unexpected)

	$Good	$Fine	$N.Mint	£Good	£Fine	£N.Mint
1 32pgs, Bolland and Rogers art, Kaluta cover and art (2 pgs), includes poster, no ads	$0.40	$1.20	$2.00	£0.25	£0.75	£1.25
Title Value:	$0.40	$1.20	$2.00	£0.25	£0.75	£1.25

MADBALLS
Marvel Comics Group/Star; 1 Sep 1986-3 Nov 1986; 4 Jun 1987-10 Jun 1988

	$Good	$Fine	$N.Mint	£Good	£Fine	£N.Mint
1-10	$0.15	$0.45	$0.75	£0.10	£0.30	£0.50
Title Value:	$1.50	$4.50	$7.50	£1.00	£3.00	£5.00

MADHOUSE
Red Circle (Archie); 95 Sep 1974-97 Jan 1975; 98 Aug 1975-130 Oct 1982

	$Good	$Fine	$N.Mint	£Good	£Fine	£N.Mint
95-96 Gray Morrow cover and art	$0.70	$2.10	$3.50	£0.40	£1.20	£2.00
97 Williamson, Thorne, Morrow art	$0.30	$0.90	$1.50	£0.30	£0.90	£1.50
98-130	$0.30	$0.90	$1.50	£0.20	£0.60	£1.00
Title Value:	$11.60	$34.80	$58.00	£7.70	£23.10	£38.50

Note: all distributed in the U.K.

MADMAN
Tundra/Kitchen Sink; 1 May 1992-3 1992

	$Good	$Fine	$N.Mint	£Good	£Fine	£N.Mint
1 ND 48pgs, squarebound	$1.50	$4.50	$7.50	£1.00	£3.00	£5.00
1 2nd printing, ND (1993)	$0.80	$2.40	$4.00	£0.50	£1.50	£2.50
1 3rd printing ND	$0.80	$2.40	$4.00	£0.50	£1.50	£2.50
2 ND 48pgs, squarebound	$1.20	$3.60	$6.00	£0.80	£2.40	£4.00
3 ND 48pgs, squarebound	$1.00	$3.00	$5.00	£0.70	£2.10	£3.50
Title Value:	$5.30	$15.90	$26.50	£3.50	£10.50	£17.50

Madman Adventures Collection (Jan 1995) Trade paperback reprints mini-series with new cover by Mike Allred

	$Good	$Fine	$N.Mint	£Good	£Fine	£N.Mint
			$2.00		£6.00	£10.00

MADMAN COMICS
Dark Horse/Legend; 1 Apr 1994-present

	$Good	$Fine	$N.Mint	£Good	£Fine	£N.Mint
1 ND Mike Allred script and art; back cover by Frank Miller	$0.80	$2.40	$4.00	£0.40	£1.20	£2.00
2 ND	$0.60	$1.80	$3.00	£0.40	£1.20	£2.00
3 ND Alex Toth back cover	$0.60	$1.80	$3.00	£0.40	£1.20	£2.00
4 ND Dave Stevens back cover	$0.60	$1.80	$3.00	£0.40	£1.20	£2.00
5 ND	$0.60	$1.80	$3.00	£0.40	£1.20	£2.00
6 ND Frank Miller script; Bruce Timm back cover	$0.60	$1.80	$3.00	£0.40	£1.20	£2.00
7 ND Frank Miller script	$0.60	$1.80	$3.00	£0.40	£1.20	£2.00
8 ND Peter Bagge back cover	$0.60	$1.80	$3.00	£0.40	£1.20	£2.00
9 ND Paul Chadwick back cover	$0.60	$1.80	$3.00	£0.40	£1.20	£2.00
10 ND Alex Ross cover	$0.60	$1.80	$3.00	£0.40	£1.20	£2.00
Title Value:	$6.20	$18.60	$31.00	£4.00	£12.00	£20.00

MADRAVEN HALLOWEEN SPECIAL
Hamilton Comics; 1 Oct 1995

	$Good	$Fine	$N.Mint	£Good	£Fine	£N.Mint
1 ND features work by Nicola Cuti, Jan Duursema and Gray Morrow	$0.60	$1.80	$3.00	£0.40	£1.20	£2.00
Title Value:	$0.60	$1.80	$3.00	£0.40	£1.20	£2.00

MAELSTROM
Aircel; 1 1987-13 1988

	$Good	$Fine	$N.Mint	£Good	£Fine	£N.Mint
1-13 ND	$0.30	$0.90	$1.50	£0.20	£0.60	£1.00
Title Value:	$3.90	$11.70	$19.50	£2.60	£7.80	£13.00

MAGE
Comico; 1 Feb 1984-15 Dec 1986

	$Good	$Fine	$N.Mint	£Good	£Fine	£N.Mint
1 ND Comico's 1st colour comic, Matt Wagner script/art begins	$2.00	$6.00	$10.00	£2.00	£6.00	£10.00
2 ND	$1.50	$4.50	$7.50	£1.20	£3.60	£6.00
3-5 ND	$1.20	$3.60	$6.00	£1.00	£3.00	£5.00
6 ND 1st New Grendel (backup)	$3.60	$10.50	$18.00	£2.00	£6.00	£10.00
7-8 ND Grendel back up	$1.50	$4.50	$7.50	£1.20	£3.60	£6.00
9-10 ND Grendel back up	$1.20	$3.60	$6.00	£0.80	£2.40	£4.00
11-14 ND Grendel back up	$1.00	$3.00	$5.00	£0.70	£2.10	£3.50
15 ND DS	$1.20	$3.60	$6.00	£1.00	£3.00	£5.00
Title Value:	$21.30	$63.60	$106.50	£16.00	£48.00	£80.00

Grendel: The Devil Inside (Jun 1989)

	$Good	$Fine	$N.Mint	£Good	£Fine	£N.Mint
Trade paperback, reprints issues #6-15				£1.10	£3.30	£5.50
Mage: The Hero Discovered, reprints				£2.00	£6.00	£10.00
Signed and Numbered Edition, slipcase				£20.00	£60.00	£100.00
Mage II, reprints				£2.00	£6.00	£10.00
Signed and Numbered Edition, slipcase				£20.00	£60.00	£100.00
Mage III, reprints				£2.00	£6.00	£10.00
Signed and Numbered Edition, slipcase				£20.00	£60.00	£100.00

MAGGOTS
Gladstone/Hamilton Comics; 1 Sep 1991-4 1992

	$Good	$Fine	$N.Mint	£Good	£Fine	£N.Mint
1-4 ND 48pgs	$0.60	$1.80	$3.00	£0.40	£1.20	£2.00
Title Value:	$2.40	$7.20	$12.00	£1.60	£4.80	£8.00

MAGGOTS IN COLOUR
Hamilton Comics,OS; 1 Apr 1992

	$Good	$Fine	$N.Mint	£Good	£Fine	£N.Mint
1 ND reprints in colour	$0.25	$0.75	$1.25	£0.15	£0.45	£0.75
Title Value:	$0.25	$0.75	$1.25	£0.15	£0.45	£0.75

MAGIC AGENT, JOHN FORCE
ACG; 1 Jan/Feb 1961-3 May/Jun 1961

	$Good	$Fine	$N.Mint	£Good	£Fine	£N.Mint
1 distributed in the U.K.	$2.85	$8.50	$20.00	£2.00	£6.00	£14.00
2-3 distributed in the U.K.	$2.10	$6.25	$15.00	£1.40	£4.25	£10.00
Title Value:	$7.05	$21.00	$50.00	£4.80	£14.50	£34.00

MAGIC CARPET
Comix and Comix,Magazine; 1,2 1977

	$Good	$Fine	$N.Mint	£Good	£Fine	£N.Mint
1 ND Voltar appears	$0.40	$1.20	$2.00	£0.25	£0.75	£1.25
2 ND	$0.40	$1.20	$2.00	£0.25	£0.75	£1.25
Title Value:	$0.80	$2.40	$4.00	£0.50	£1.50	£2.50

MAGIC FLUTE, THE
Eclipse,MS; 1 Sep 1990-3 Nov 1990

	$Good	$Fine	$N.Mint	£Good	£Fine	£N.Mint
1-3 ND 64pgs, squarebound, P. Craig Russell art	$0.70	$2.10	$3.50	£0.50	£1.50	£2.50
Title Value:	$2.10	$6.30	$10.50	£1.50	£4.50	£7.50

MAGIC MAN
A Plus Comics; 1 1991

	$Good	$Fine	$N.Mint	£Good	£Fine	£N.Mint
1 ND 48pgs, Magic Man reprints from ACG comics; black and white	$0.40	$1.20	$2.00	£0.25	£0.75	£1.25
Title Value:	$0.40	$1.20	$2.00	£0.25	£0.75	£1.25

MAGIC: THE GATHERING – ARABIAN NIGHTS
Acclaim Comics/Armada,MS; 1 Dec 1995-present

	$Good	$Fine	$N.Mint	£Good	£Fine	£N.Mint
1-2 ND	$0.50	$1.50	$2.50	£0.30	£0.90	£1.50

	$Good	$Fine	$N.Mint	£Good	£Fine	£N.Mint
Title Value:	$1.00	$3.00	$5.00	£0.60	£1.80	£3.00

MAGIC: THE GATHERING – HOMELANDS
Acclaim Comics/Armada,OS; 1 Feb 1996

	$Good	$Fine	$N.Mint	£Good	£Fine	£N.Mint
1 ND 64pgs, pre-bagged with one of three Magic: The Gathering cards	$1.20	$3.60	$6.00	£0.80	£2.40	£4.00
Title Value:	$1.20	$3.60	$6.00	£0.80	£2.40	£4.00

MAGIC: THE GATHERING – LEGEND OF JEDIT OJANEN
Acclaim Comics/Armada,MS; 1 Mar 1996-2 Apr 1996

	$Good	$Fine	$N.Mint	£Good	£Fine	£N.Mint
1-2 ND	$0.50	$1.50	$2.50	£0.30	£0.90	£1.50
Title Value:	$1.00	$3.00	$5.00	£0.60	£1.80	£3.00

MAGIC: THE GATHERING – SHANDALAR
Acclaim Comics/Armada,MS; 1 Mar 1996-2 Apr 1996

	$Good	$Fine	$N.Mint	£Good	£Fine	£N.Mint
1-2 ND	$0.50	$1.50	$2.50	£0.30	£0.90	£1.50
Title Value:	$1.00	$3.00	$5.00	£0.60	£1.80	£3.00

MAGIC: THE GATHERING – THE SHADOW MAGE
Acclaim Comics/Armada,MS; 1 Jul 1995-4 Oct 1995

	$Good	$Fine	$N.Mint	£Good	£Fine	£N.Mint
1-4 ND Jeff Gomez script, Val Mayerik art and painted cover	$0.50	$1.50	$2.50	£0.30	£0.90	£1.50
Title Value:	$2.00	$6.00	$10.00	£1.20	£3.60	£6.00

Note: based on fantasy game Magic: The Gathering by Wizards of the Coast
Magic: The Gathering – Shadow Mage (Aug 1995)

				£Good	£Fine	£N.Mint
Trade paperback 48pgs, collects issues #1,2				£0.65	£1.95	£3.25

MAGIC: THE GATHERING – WAYFARER
Acclaim Comics/Armada,MS; 1 Nov 1995-5 Mar 1996

	$Good	$Fine	$N.Mint	£Good	£Fine	£N.Mint
1-2 ND Mike Kaluta painted covers	$0.50	$1.50	$2.50	£0.30	£0.90	£1.50
3-5 ND	$0.50	$1.50	$2.50	£0.30	£0.90	£1.50
Title Value:	$2.50	$7.50	$12.50	£1.50	£4.50	£7.50

MAGIC: THE GATHERING SPECIAL – NIGHTMARE
Acclaim Comics/Armada,OS; 1 Nov 1995

	$Good	$Fine	$N.Mint	£Good	£Fine	£N.Mint
1 ND Hilary Bader script	$0.50	$1.50	$2.50	£0.30	£0.90	£1.50
Title Value:	$0.50	$1.50	$2.50	£0.30	£0.90	£1.50

MAGIK: STORM AND ILLYANA
Marvel Comics Group,MS; 1 Dec 1983-4 Mar 1984

	$Good	$Fine	$N.Mint	£Good	£Fine	£N.Mint
1 ND Storm and Illyana (X-Men) begin	$0.60	$1.80	$3.00	£0.40	£1.20	£2.00
2 ND	$0.50	$1.50	$2.50	£0.40	£1.20	£2.00
3 ND scarce in the U.K.	$0.50	$1.50	$2.50	£0.50	£1.50	£2.50
4 ND rare in the U.K.	$0.50	$1.50	$2.50	£0.70	£2.10	£3.50
Title Value:	$2.10	$6.30	$10.50	£2.00	£6.00	£10.00

MAGNA-MAN: THE LAST SUPER-HERO
Comics Interview,MS; 1 Summer 1988-3 Spring 1989

	$Good	$Fine	$N.Mint	£Good	£Fine	£N.Mint
1-3 ND	$0.40	$1.20	$2.00	£0.25	£0.75	£1.25
Title Value:	$1.20	$3.60	$6.00	£0.75	£2.25	£3.75

MAGNETO
Marvel Comics Group,OS; 0 Aug 1993

	$Good	$Fine	$N.Mint	£Good	£Fine	£N.Mint
0 ND promotional issue from Marvel; reprints from Classic X-Men #12,#19 featuring John Bolton art, 3 new pages of art by Duursema/Panosian; foil embossed cover by Sienkiewicz	$1.00	$3.00	$5.00	£0.80	£2.40	£4.00
Title Value:	$1.00	$3.00	$5.00	£0.80	£2.40	£4.00

MAGNUS ROBOT FIGHTER
Gold Key; 1 Feb 1963-46 Jan 1977

	$Good	$Fine	$N.Mint	£Good	£Fine	£N.Mint
1 Magnus by Russ Manning, Aliens back-up begin	$42.00	$125.00	$250.00	£28.00	£82.50	£165.00
2-3 distributed in the U.K.	$21.50	$65.00	$130.00	£14.00	£43.00	£85.00
4-5 distributed in the U.K.	$15.00	$45.00	$90.00	£10.00	£30.00	£60.00
6-10 distributed in the U.K.	$12.50	$38.00	$75.00	£8.25	£25.00	£50.00
11-15 distributed in the U.K.	$8.25	$25.00	$50.00	£5.75	£17.50	£35.00
16-20 distributed in the U.K.	$7.50	$22.50	$45.00	£5.00	£15.00	£30.00
21 distributed in the U.K. last new Russ Manning art on Magnus	$6.50	$19.50	$32.50	£4.00	£12.00	£20.00
22 distributed in the U.K. reprints #1; 12 and 15 cents versions exist; last Manning art on Aliens back-up	$6.00	$18.00	$30.00	£3.60	£10.50	£18.00
23 distributed in the U.K. 12 and 15 cents versions exist	$6.00	$18.00	$30.00	£3.60	£10.50	£18.00
24-27 distributed in the U.K.	$6.50	$19.50	$32.50	£4.00	£12.00	£20.00
28 distributed in the U.K. last Aliens feature	$6.50	$19.50	$32.50	£4.00	£12.00	£20.00
29-32 distributed in the U.K. all reprints	$2.40	$7.00	$12.00	£1.60	£4.80	£8.00
33-46 ND all reprints	$2.40	$7.00	$12.00	£1.70	£5.00	£8.50
Title Value:	$350.45	$1051.50	$2011.00	£232.40	£698.20	£1337.00

Note: There was an 18-month gap in publication around issue #33-35.

MAGNUS ROBOT FIGHTER (2ND SERIES)
Valiant/Acclaim Comics; 0 1991; 1 May 1991-64 Jan 1996

	$Good	$Fine	$N.Mint	£Good	£Fine	£N.Mint
0 with trading card, ordered through mail	$3.50	$10.50	$17.50	£2.00	£6.00	£10.00
0 without trading card, sold through shops	$1.50	$4.50	$7.50	£1.40	£4.20	£7.00
1 (with coupon intact. Less 30% without coupon for #1-8)	$2.00	$6.00	$10.00	£1.40	£4.20	£7.00
2-4	$1.20	$3.60	$6.00	£0.80	£2.40	£4.00
5 scarce in the U.K. Rai back-up feature begins (1st appearance – flip side cover says Rai #1)	$1.20	$3.60	$6.00	£0.80	£2.40	£4.00
6-8 Rai back-up	$0.80	$2.40	$4.00	£0.50	£1.50	£2.50
9-11	$0.50	$1.50	$2.50	£0.30	£0.90	£1.50
12 1st anniversary special, 1st modern appearance of Turok	$2.00	$6.00	$10.00	£1.50	£4.50	£7.50
13-14 The Asylum Saga part 1, ties in with Magnus Robot Fighter (1st Series) #18	$0.40	$1.20	$2.00	£0.30	£0.90	£1.50
15 Unity: Chapter 4	$0.40	$1.20	$2.00	£0.30	£0.90	£1.50
16 Unity: Chapter 12, true origin of Magnus, Walt Simonson cover	$0.40	$1.20	$2.00	£0.30	£0.90	£1.50
17-19 Steve Ditko art featured	$0.40	$1.20	$2.00	£0.30	£0.90	£1.50
20	$0.40	$1.20	$2.00	£0.30	£0.90	£1.50
21 new direction for title; ties-in with the 1st Series Magnus Robot Fighter #17 and the destruction of the Earth	$0.40	$1.20	$2.00	£0.30	£0.90	£1.50
21 gold cover – 5,000 print run; gold logo and gold number/date box	$1.60	$4.80	$8.00	£1.20	£3.60	£6.00
22-23	$0.40	$1.20	$2.00	£0.25	£0.75	£1.25
24 leads into Rai and the Future Force #9	$0.40	$1.20	$2.00	£0.25	£0.75	£1.25
25 silver foil cover	$0.40	$1.20	$2.00	£0.30	£0.90	£1.50
25 Valiant Validated Signature Series Edition (Feb 1994), signed by John Ostrander and Bob Layton; 5,500 copies with certificate in Mylar sleeve	$1.50	$4.50	$7.50	£1.00	£3.00	£5.00
26-28	$0.40	$1.20	$2.00	£0.25	£0.75	£1.25
29 Eternal Warrior appears	$0.40	$1.20	$2.00	£0.25	£0.75	£1.25
30-32	$0.40	$1.20	$2.00	£0.25	£0.75	£1.25
33 Ivar the Timewalker appears	$0.40	$1.20	$2.00	£0.25	£0.75	£1.25
34-36	$0.40	$1.20	$2.00	£0.25	£0.75	£1.25
37 continued in Rai #22	$0.40	$1.20	$2.00	£0.25	£0.75	£1.25
38-40	$0.40	$1.20	$2.00	£0.25	£0.75	£1.25
41 Chaos Effect tie-in	$0.40	$1.20	$2.00	£0.25	£0.75	£1.25
42 ties-in with Rai #27	$0.40	$1.20	$2.00	£0.25	£0.75	£1.25
43-48	$0.40	$1.20	$2.00	£0.25	£0.75	£1.25
49 1st Acclaim Comics issue; bi-weekly	$0.40	$1.20	$2.00	£0.25	£0.75	£1.25
50 bi-weekly	$0.40	$1.20	$2.00	£0.25	£0.75	£1.25
51-54 Return of the Robots story; bi-weekly	$0.40	$1.20	$2.00	£0.25	£0.75	£1.25
55-64 bi-weekly	$0.40	$1.20	$2.00	£0.25	£0.75	£1.25
Title Value:	$41.60	$124.80	$208.00	£27.60	£82.80	£138.00

Note: all Non-Distributed on the news-stands in the U.K. Note: the first eight issues include 3 trading cards each. Note also that a special "0" issue was available, ordered from the publishers through the mail and obtained by sending coupons collected from the first 8 issues. This is with the special trading card. Otherwise a copy of issue #0 was given free to retailers with every 100 copies of Magnus #1 ordered. Note finally: There was also a #0 available on general sale in stores like Walmart at the time in America though how these differ, if at all, is unclear at this time.

				£Good	£Fine	£N.Mint
Steel Nation (Feb 1995) Trade paperback reprints issues #1-4				£1.30	£3.90	£6.50
Magnus Robot Fighter #2 Trade paperback reprints issues #5-8				£1.30	£3.90	£6.50

MAGNUS ROBOT FIGHTER YEARBOOK
Valiant; 1 Nov 1994

	$Good	$Fine	$N.Mint	£Good	£Fine	£N.Mint
1 ND Mike Baron script, Paul Smith art, Dave Dorman cover; story takes place between Magnus #1 and #2	$0.50	$1.50	$2.50	£0.30	£0.90	£1.50
Title Value:	$0.50	$1.50	$2.50	£0.30	£0.90	£1.50

MAGNUS ROBOT FIGHTER, THE ORIGINAL
Valiant/Western Publishing; 1 Apr 1995-3 Jun 1995

	$Good	$Fine	$N.Mint	£Good	£Fine	£N.Mint
1-3 ND reprints from the original Gold Key series begin featuring artwork by Russ Manning	$0.40	$1.20	$2.00	£0.25	£0.75	£1.25
Title Value:	$1.20	$3.60	$6.00	£0.75	£2.25	£3.75

MAGNUS ROBOT FIGHTER, THE VINTAGE
Valiant,MS; 1 May 1992-4 Aug 1992

	$Good	$Fine	$N.Mint	£Good	£Fine	£N.Mint
1 ND reprints from original Gold Key series begin; reprints issue #1	$0.40	$1.20	$2.00	£0.25	£0.75	£1.25
2 ND reprints issue #3	$0.40	$1.20	$2.00	£0.25	£0.75	£1.25
3 ND reprints issue #13	$0.40	$1.20	$2.00	£0.25	£0.75	£1.25
4 ND reprints issue #16	$0.40	$1.20	$2.00	£0.25	£0.75	£1.25
Title Value:	$1.60	$4.80	$8.00	£1.00	£3.00	£5.00

MAGNUS ROBOT FIGHTER/NEXUS
Valiant/Dark Horse,MS; 1 December 1993-2 Apr 1994

	$Good	$Fine	$N.Mint	£Good	£Fine	£N.Mint
1-2 ND Mike Baron script, Steve Rude art; card-stock cover; origin Magnus briefly re-told	$0.55	$1.65	$2.75	£0.35	£1.05	£1.75
Title Value:	$1.10	$3.30	$5.50	£0.70	£2.10	£3.50

MAI THE PSYCHIC GIRL
Eclipse; 1 May 1987-28 Jul 1988 (biweekly)

	$Good	$Fine	$N.Mint	£Good	£Fine	£N.Mint
1	$0.50	$1.50	$2.50	£0.30	£0.90	£1.50
1 2nd printing	$0.40	$1.20	$2.00	£0.25	£0.75	£1.25
2	$0.40	$1.20	$2.00	£0.25	£0.75	£1.25
2 2nd printing	$0.40	$1.20	$2.00	£0.25	£0.75	£1.25
3-5	$0.40	$1.20	$2.00	£0.25	£0.75	£1.25
6-28	$0.30	$0.90	$1.50	£0.20	£0.60	£1.00
Title Value:	$9.80	$29.40	$49.00	£6.40	£19.20	£32.00

	$Good	$Fine	$N.Mint	£Good	£Fine	£N.Mint

Note: all Non-Distributed on the news-stands in the U.K.

Mai the Psychic Girl Perfect Collection Vol 1 (Oct 1995)
368pgs, classic reprints in black and white — — — £2.70 £8.10 £13.50

MAISON IKKOKU
Viz Communications,MS; 1 Aug 1993-7 Feb 1994
1-7 ND Rumiko Takahashi; black and white

| | $0.60 | $1.80 | $3.00 | £0.40 | £1.20 | £2.00 |
| Title Value: | $4.20 | $12.60 | $21.00 | £2.80 | £8.40 | £14.00 |

MAISON IKKOKU GRAPHIC NOVEL
Viz Communications; nn Sep 1995
nn ND 264pgs, Romiko Takahashi script & art

| | $3.40 | $10.20 | $17.00 | £2.30 | £6.90 | £11.50 |
| Title Value: | $3.40 | $10.20 | $17.00 | £2.30 | £6.90 | £11.50 |

MAISON IKKOKU PART 2
Viz Communications,MS; 1 Mar 1994-6 Aug 1994
1-6 ND Rumiko Takahashi; black and white

| | $0.60 | $1.80 | $3.00 | £0.40 | £1.20 | £2.00 |
| Title Value: | $3.60 | $10.80 | $18.00 | £2.40 | £7.20 | £12.00 |

MAISON IKKOKU PART 3
Viz Communications,MS; 1 Jul 1994-6 Dec 1994
1-6 ND 48pgs, Rumiko Takahashi; black and white

| | $0.60 | $1.80 | $3.00 | £0.40 | £1.20 | £2.00 |
| Title Value: | $3.60 | $10.80 | $18.00 | £2.40 | £7.20 | £12.00 |

MAISON IKKOKU PART 4
Viz Communications,MS; 1 Dec 1994-10 Sep 1995
1-10 ND 40pgs, Rumiko Takahashi; black and white

| | $0.60 | $1.80 | $3.00 | £0.40 | £1.20 | £2.00 |
| Title Value: | $6.00 | $18.00 | $30.00 | £4.00 | £12.00 | £20.00 |

MAN CALLED A-X, THE
Malibu Bravura,MS; 0 Feb 1995; 1 Nov 1994-5 Mar 1995
0 ND Marv Wolfman script, Shawn McManus art; facts about origin revealed

| | $0.60 | $1.80 | $3.00 | £0.40 | £1.20 | £2.00 |

1 ND Marv Wolfman script, Shawn McManus art

| | $0.60 | $1.80 | $3.00 | £0.40 | £1.20 | £2.00 |

1 ND Gold Foil Edition (Mar 1995)

| | $2.00 | $6.00 | $10.00 | £1.00 | £3.00 | £5.00 |

2-5 ND Marv Wolfman script, Shawn McManus art

| | $0.50 | $1.50 | $2.50 | £0.30 | £0.90 | £1.50 |
| Title Value: | $5.20 | $15.60 | $26.00 | £3.00 | £9.00 | £15.00 |

The Man Called A-X Ashcan Edition (Feb 1995)
1,000 copies, signed by Marv Wolfman and Shawn McManus. ND £1.00 £3.00 £5.00

MAN CALLED LOCO, A
ACG,OS; nn Jul 1995
nn ND Western reprints with scripts by Denny O'Neil and art by Pete Morisi

| | $0.50 | $1.50 | $2.50 | £0.30 | £0.90 | £1.50 |
| Title Value: | $0.50 | $1.50 | $2.50 | £0.30 | £0.90 | £1.50 |

MAN FROG
Mad Dog Graphics; 1,2 1987

| 1-2 ND | $0.30 | $0.90 | $1.50 | £0.20 | £0.60 | £1.00 |
| Title Value: | $0.60 | $1.80 | $3.00 | £0.40 | £1.20 | £2.00 |

MAN FROM ATLANTIS
Marvel Comics Group,TV; 1 Feb 1978-7 Aug 1978
1 ND 80pgs, origin; based on TV series starring Patrick Duffy

	$0.30	$0.90	$1.50	£0.20	£0.60	£1.00
2-7 ND	$0.25	$0.75	$1.25	£0.15	£0.45	£0.75
Title Value:	$1.80	$5.40	$9.00	£1.10	£3.30	£5.50

MAN FROM PLANET X REPRINT COMIC, THE
Robert Brosch; 1 1990
1 ND reprints movie adaptation from 1951 with art by Kurt Schaffenberger, George Evans and Pete Costanza

| | $0.50 | $1.50 | $2.50 | £0.30 | £0.90 | £1.50 |
| Title Value: | $0.50 | $1.50 | $2.50 | £0.30 | £0.90 | £1.50 |

MAN FROM U.N.C.L.E., THE
Gold Key, TV; 1 Feb 1965-22 Apr 1969
1 scarce in the U.K. photo covers begin

| | $20.50 | $62.50 | $125.00 | £13.00 | £40.00 | £80.00 |

2 scarce in the U.K.

| | $11.50 | $35.00 | $70.00 | £7.50 | £22.50 | £45.00 |

3-5 scarce in the U.K.

| | $7.50 | $22.50 | $45.00 | £5.00 | £15.00 | £30.00 |

6-10 scarce in the U.K.

| | $6.50 | $20.00 | $40.00 | £4.55 | £13.50 | £27.50 |

11-15 scarce in the U.K.

| | $5.75 | $17.50 | $35.00 | £3.75 | £11.00 | £22.50 |

16-20 scarce in the U.K.

| | $5.00 | $15.00 | $30.00 | £3.30 | £10.00 | £20.00 |

21-22 scarce in the U.K. reprints

| | $4.55 | $13.50 | $27.50 | £2.90 | £8.75 | £17.50 |
| Title Value: | $149.85 | $454.50 | $910.00 | £99.30 | £297.50 | £600.00 |

Note: most issues distributed in the U.K.

MAN FROM U.N.C.L.E., THE (2ND SERIES)
Entertainment Publishing; 1 Feb 1987-11 1987
1 ND black and white begins

| | $0.40 | $1.20 | $2.00 | £0.25 | £0.75 | £1.25 |
| 2-4 ND | $0.40 | $1.20 | $2.00 | £0.25 | £0.75 | £1.25 |

5 ND scarce in the U.K. (owing to the fact that this was never imported into U.K. comic shops)

	$0.40	$1.20	$2.00	£0.50	£1.50	£2.50
6-11 ND	$0.30	$0.90	$1.50	£0.20	£0.60	£1.00
Title Value:	$3.80	$11.40	$19.00	£2.70	£8.10	£13.50

MAN FROM U.N.C.L.E.: THE BIRDS OF PREY AFFAIR
Millennium,MS; 1 Mar 1993-2 Apr 1993

| 1-2 ND | $0.50 | $1.50 | $2.50 | £0.30 | £0.90 | £1.50 |
| Title Value: | $1.00 | $3.00 | $5.00 | £0.60 | £1.80 | £3.00 |

The Man From U.N.C.L.E.: Birds of Prey Collection (Nov 1994)
reprints mini-series with new wraparound cover — — — £1.00 £3.00 £5.00

MAN FROM U.N.C.L.E.: THE END OF THE WORLD AFFAIR
Millennium,OS; 1 Apr 1994

| 1 ND photo cover | $0.50 | $1.50 | $2.50 | £0.30 | £0.90 | £1.50 |
| Title Value: | $0.50 | $1.50 | $2.50 | £0.30 | £0.90 | £1.50 |

MAN OF RUST
Blackthorne; 1A, 1B Nov 1986
1 ND (2 cover versions exist) parodies Man of Steel, Burchett art; cover 1A is chest emblem, cover 1B is rocket cover

| | $0.30 | $0.90 | $1.50 | £0.20 | £0.60 | £1.00 |
| Title Value: | $0.30 | $0.90 | $1.50 | £0.20 | £0.60 | £1.00 |

MAN OF WAR
Eclipse; 1 Aug 1987-3 Feb 1988
1-3 ND Bruce Jones script, Rick Burchett art

| | $0.40 | $1.20 | $2.00 | £0.25 | £0.75 | £1.25 |
| Title Value: | $1.20 | $3.60 | $6.00 | £0.75 | £2.25 | £3.75 |

MAN OF WAR (2ND SERIES)
Malibu; 1 Apr 1993-8 1993

| 1 ND | $0.30 | $0.90 | $1.50 | £0.20 | £0.60 | £1.00 |

1 ND Direct Market Edition – bound in poster and different cover

| | $0.40 | $1.20 | $2.00 | £0.25 | £0.75 | £1.25 |
| 2 ND | $0.30 | $0.90 | $1.50 | £0.20 | £0.60 | £1.00 |

2 ND Direct Market Edition – bound in poster and different cover

| | $0.40 | $1.20 | $2.00 | £0.25 | £0.75 | £1.25 |
| 3 ND | $0.30 | $0.90 | $1.50 | £0.20 | £0.60 | £1.00 |

3 ND Direct Market Edition – bound in poster and different cover

| | $0.40 | $1.20 | $2.00 | £0.25 | £0.75 | £1.25 |
| 4 ND | $0.30 | $0.90 | $1.50 | £0.20 | £0.60 | £1.00 |

4 ND Direct Market Edition – bound in poster and different cover

| | $0.40 | $1.20 | $2.00 | £0.25 | £0.75 | £1.25 |
| 5 ND | $0.30 | $0.90 | $1.50 | £0.20 | £0.60 | £1.00 |

5 ND Direct Market Edition – bound in poster and different cover

| | $0.40 | $1.20 | $2.00 | £0.25 | £0.75 | £1.25 |

6 ND Genesis Tie-In; pre-bagged with free Sky Cap

	$0.30	$0.90	$1.50	£0.20	£0.60	£1.00
7-8 ND	$0.30	$0.90	$1.50	£0.20	£0.60	£1.00
Title Value:	$4.40	$13.20	$22.00	£2.85	£8.55	£14.25

MAN-BAT
DC Comics; 1 Dec/Jan 1975/76-2 Feb/Mar 1976
(see Detective, Brave and the Bold, Batman Family)
1 Steve Ditko pencils, She Bat appears

| | $1.50 | $4.50 | $7.50 | £1.20 | £3.60 | £6.00 |

2 scarce in the U.K.

| | $1.20 | $3.60 | $6.00 | £1.00 | £3.00 | £5.00 |
| Title Value: | $2.70 | $8.10 | $13.50 | £2.20 | £6.60 | £11.00 |

MAN-BAT (2ND SERIES)
DC Comics,MS; 1 Feb 1996-present
1-2 ND Chuck Dixon script, Flint Henry and Eduardo Barreto art

| | $0.45 | $1.35 | $2.25 | £0.30 | £0.90 | £1.50 |
| Title Value: | $0.90 | $2.70 | $4.50 | £0.60 | £1.80 | £3.00 |

MAN-BAT (VERSUS BATMAN)
DC Comics,OS; 1 Dec 1984
1 ND 46pgs, reprints Neal Adams art from Detective Comics #400 and #402

| | $0.90 | $2.70 | $4.50 | £0.60 | £1.80 | £3.00 |
| Title Value: | $0.90 | $2.70 | $4.50 | £0.60 | £1.80 | £3.00 |

MAN-EATING COW
New England Comics; 1 Jun 1992-10 1993

| 1-10 ND | $0.50 | $1.50 | $2.50 | £0.30 | £0.90 | £1.50 |
| Title Value: | $5.00 | $15.00 | $25.00 | £3.00 | £9.00 | £15.00 |

MAN-THING
Marvel Comics Group; 1 Jan 1974-22 Oct 1975
(see Fear, Marvel Fanfare, Monsters Unleashed, Savage Tales)
1 ND 2nd Howard the Duck, continues from Fear #19

| | $3.00 | $9.00 | $15.00 | £2.00 | £6.00 | £10.00 |
| 2 ND | $1.50 | $4.50 | $7.50 | £1.00 | £3.00 | £5.00 |

3 ND 1st appearance original Foolkiller (see Omega The Unknown #8)

| | $1.50 | $4.50 | $7.50 | £1.00 | £3.00 | £5.00 |

4 ND origin and 2nd appearance (final) original Foolkiller

	$1.40	$4.20	$7.00	£0.90	£2.70	£4.50
5-7 ND Ploog art	$1.20	$3.60	$6.00	£0.80	£2.40	£4.00
8-11 Ploog art	$0.80	$2.40	$4.00	£0.50	£1.50	£2.50
12-15	$0.50	$1.50	$2.50	£0.30	£0.90	£1.50
16-19	$0.30	$0.90	$1.50	£0.20	£0.60	£1.00

20 Spiderman, Daredevil, Thing and Master of Kung Fu appear

| | $0.30 | $0.90 | $1.50 | £0.20 | £0.60 | £1.00 |
| 21 | $0.30 | $0.90 | $1.50 | £0.20 | £0.60 | £1.00 |

22 Howard the Duck cameo

| | $0.30 | $0.90 | $1.50 | £0.20 | £0.60 | £1.00 |
| Title Value: | $18.30 | $54.90 | $91.50 | £11.90 | £35.70 | £59.50 |

MAN-THING (2ND SERIES)
Marvel Comics Group; 1 Nov 1979-11 Jul 1981

| 1 | $0.30 | $0.90 | $1.50 | £0.20 | £0.60 | £1.00 |
| 2-3 ND | $0.25 | $0.75 | $1.25 | £0.15 | £0.45 | £0.75 |

4 ND ties into Dr. Strange (2nd Series) #41

| | $0.25 | $0.75 | $1.25 | £0.15 | £0.45 | £0.75 |
| 5 ND | $0.25 | $0.75 | $1.25 | £0.15 | £0.45 | £0.75 |

6 Michael Golden cover

	$0.25	$0.75	$1.25	£0.15	£0.45	£0.75
7-11 ND	$0.25	$0.75	$1.25	£0.15	£0.45	£0.75
Title Value:	$2.80	$8.40	$14.00	£1.70	£5.10	£8.50

MAN-THING GIANT SIZE

Marvel Comics Group; 1 Aug 1974-5 Aug 1975

	$Good	$Fine	$N.Mint	£Good	£Fine	£N.Mint
1 ND 64pgs, Ploog art; Steve Ditko and Jack Kirby pre-superhero reprints						
	$1.50	$4.50	$7.50	£1.00	£3.00	£5.00
2 ND 64pgs, Jack Kirby pre-superhero reprint						
	$1.20	$3.60	$6.00	£0.80	£2.40	£4.00
3 ND 64pgs, reprints Dr. Droom story from Amazing Adventures (1st Series) #6 and is re-named Dr. Druid (no relation to other Marvel character)						
	$1.00	$3.00	$5.00	£0.70	£2.10	£3.50
4 ND 64pgs, 2nd appearance Howard the Duck, Brunner art (see Fear #19)						
	$1.60	$4.80	$8.00	£1.20	£3.60	£6.00
5 ND 64pgs, 3rd appearance Howard the Duck, Brunner art						
	$1.40	$4.20	$7.00	£1.00	£3.00	£5.00
Title Value:	$6.70	$20.10	$33.50	£4.70	£14.10	£23.50

MANDRAKE

Marvel Comics Group,MS; 1 Apr 1995-3 Jun 1995

	$Good	$Fine	$N.Mint	£Good	£Fine	£N.Mint
1-3 ND Rob Ortaleza art painted art on glossy stock paper						
	$0.50	$1.50	$2.50	£0.30	£0.90	£1.50
Title Value:	$1.50	$4.50	$7.50	£0.90	£2.70	£4.50

MANDRAKE

Pioneer Comics,MS; 1 Dec 1989-3 Feb 1990

	$Good	$Fine	$N.Mint	£Good	£Fine	£N.Mint
1-3 ND never-before reprinted story						
	$1.20	$3.60	$6.00	£0.80	£2.40	£4.00
Title Value:	$3.60	$10.80	$18.00	£2.40	£7.20	£12.00

MANDRAKE THE MAGICIAN

King Comics; 1 Sep 1966-10 Nov 1967

	$Good	$Fine	$N.Mint	£Good	£Fine	£N.Mint
1 scarce in the U.K.	$5.00	$15.00	$30.00	£3.30	£10.00	£20.00
2-7 scarce in the U.K.						
	$2.90	$8.75	$17.50	£2.05	£6.25	£12.50
8 4pgs Jeff Jones art						
	$3.75	$11.00	$22.50	£2.50	£7.50	£15.00
9	$2.90	$8.75	$17.50	£2.05	£6.25	£12.50
10 Alex Raymond art						
	$3.75	$11.00	$22.50	£2.50	£7.50	£15.00
Title Value:	$32.80	$98.25	$197.50	£22.65	£68.75	£137.50

Note: all distributed on the news-stands in the U.K.

MANGA MONTHLY

Fathom Press; 0 Aug 1991

	$Good	$Fine	$N.Mint	£Good	£Fine	£N.Mint
0 ND 64pgs, Tim Tyler and Paris Cullins art						
	$0.50	$1.50	$2.50	£0.30	£0.90	£1.50
Title Value:	$0.50	$1.50	$2.50	£0.30	£0.90	£1.50

Note: series cancelled having been announced as ongoing

MANGA VIZION VOL. 1

Viz Communications; 1 Mar 1995-present

	$Good	$Fine	$N.Mint	£Good	£Fine	£N.Mint
1-7 ND 96pgs, anthology; black and white						
	$1.00	$3.00	$5.00	£0.60	£1.80	£3.00
Title Value:	$7.00	$21.00	$35.00	£4.20	£12.60	£21.00

MAGAZINE

Antarctic Press; 1 1985-5 Dec 1986

	$Good	$Fine	$N.Mint	£Good	£Fine	£N.Mint
1 ND scarce in the U.K. paper cover						
	$0.50	$1.50	$2.50	£0.30	£0.90	£1.50
1 2nd printing, ND glossy cover						
	$0.40	$1.20	$2.00	£0.25	£0.75	£1.25
2-5 ND	$0.30	$0.90	$1.50	£0.20	£0.60	£1.00
Title Value:	$2.10	$6.30	$10.50	£1.35	£4.05	£6.75

MAGAZINE VOLUME TWO

Antarctic Press; 1 Sep 1989-present

	$Good	$Fine	$N.Mint	£Good	£Fine	£N.Mint
1-9 ND	$0.40	$1.20	$2.00	£0.25	£0.75	£1.25
10-13 ND 40pgs	$0.45	$1.35	$2.25	£0.30	£0.90	£1.50
14-29 ND 40pgs	$0.55	$1.65	$2.75	£0.35	£1.05	£1.75
30-36 ND 32pgs	$0.60	$1.80	$3.00	£0.40	£1.20	£2.00
37 ND 48pgs, 10th anniversary issue; first time in full colour						
	$0.80	$2.40	$4.00	£0.50	£1.50	£2.50
38-39 ND 48pgs	$0.80	$2.40	$4.00	£0.50	£1.50	£2.50
40-41 ND 32pgs	$0.60	$1.80	$3.00	£0.40	£1.20	£2.00
Title Value:	$22.00	$66.00	$110.00	£14.15	£42.45	£70.75

MANGLE TANGLE TALES

Innovation; 1 1990

	$Good	$Fine	$N.Mint	£Good	£Fine	£N.Mint
1 ND funny animal material in colour, introduction by Harlan Ellison						
	$0.30	$0.90	$1.50	£0.20	£0.60	£1.00
Title Value:	$0.30	$0.90	$1.50	£0.20	£0.60	£1.00

MANHUNTER

DC Comics,OS; 1 May 1984

(see First Issue Special)

	$Good	$Fine	$N.Mint	£Good	£Fine	£N.Mint
1 ND 76pgs, Walt Simonson reprints from Detective Comics #437-443, Batman appears						
	$0.90	$2.70	$4.50	£0.60	£1.80	£3.00
Title Value:	$0.90	$2.70	$4.50	£0.60	£1.80	£3.00

Note: high quality paper.

MANHUNTER (2ND SERIES)

DC Comics; 1 Jul 1988-24 Apr 1990

(see First Issue Special #5, Millennium)

	$Good	$Fine	$N.Mint	£Good	£Fine	£N.Mint
1-3 part Sam Kieth art and cover						
	$0.25	$0.75	$1.25	£0.15	£0.45	£0.75
4-7	$0.25	$0.75	$1.25	£0.15	£0.45	£0.75
8-9 Invasion X-over, Flash appears						
	$0.25	$0.75	$1.25	£0.15	£0.45	£0.75
10	$0.25	$0.75	$1.25	£0.15	£0.45	£0.75
11-13	$0.15	$0.45	$0.75	£0.10	£0.35	£0.60
14 Kobra appears	$0.15	$0.45	$0.75	£0.10	£0.35	£0.60
15-16	$0.15	$0.45	$0.75	£0.10	£0.35	£0.60
17 Batman appears						
	$0.15	$0.45	$0.75	£0.10	£0.35	£0.60
18-23 Saints and Sinners story						
	$0.15	$0.45	$0.75	£0.10	£0.35	£0.60
24	$0.15	$0.45	$0.75	£0.10	£0.35	£0.60
Title Value:	$4.60	$13.80	$23.00	£2.90	£9.40	£15.90

MANHUNTER (3RD SERIES)

DC Comics; 0 Oct 1994; 1 Nov 1994-12 Nov 1995

	$Good	$Fine	$N.Mint	£Good	£Fine	£N.Mint
0 (Oct 1994) Zero Hour X-over, origin						
	$0.40	$1.20	$2.00	£0.25	£0.75	£1.25
1-6	$0.40	$1.20	$2.00	£0.25	£0.75	£1.25
7 Captain Atom appears						
	$0.40	$1.20	$2.00	£0.25	£0.75	£1.25
8-11	$0.40	$1.20	$2.00	£0.25	£0.75	£1.25
12 Underworld Unleashed tie-in						
	$0.40	$1.20	$2.00	£0.25	£0.75	£1.25
Title Value:	$5.20	$15.60	$26.00	£3.25	£9.75	£16.25

MANIMAL

Renegade,OS; 1 Jan 1986

	$Good	$Fine	$N.Mint	£Good	£Fine	£N.Mint
1 ND reprints from Hot Stuf; black and white, Ernie Colon art						
	$0.30	$0.90	$1.50	£0.20	£0.60	£1.00
Title Value:	$0.30	$0.90	$1.50	£0.20	£0.60	£1.00

MANOSAURS: THE ARMAGEDDON AGENDA

Entity Comics,MS; 1 Sep 1994-3 1994

	$Good	$Fine	$N.Mint	£Good	£Fine	£N.Mint
1-3 ND foil-stamped cover; black and white						
	$0.60	$1.80	$3.00	£0.40	£1.20	£2.00
Title Value:	$1.80	$5.40	$9.00	£1.20	£3.60	£6.00

MANTECH: ROBOT WARRIORS

Archie,MS; 1 Sep 1984-6 Jul 1985

	$Good	$Fine	$N.Mint	£Good	£Fine	£N.Mint
1-6 ND	$0.30	$0.90	$1.50	£0.20	£0.60	£1.00
Title Value:	$1.80	$5.40	$9.00	£1.20	£3.60	£6.00

Mandrake The Magician #7

Manimal #1

Mantra #8

MINT = 100% / NEAR MINT (inc. +/-) = 90–99% / VERY FINE (inc. +/-) = 75–89% / FINE (inc. +/-) = 55–74%
VERY GOOD (inc. +/-) = 35–54% / GOOD (inc. +/-) = 15–34% / FAIR = 5–14% / POOR = 1–4%

MANTRA
Malibu Ultraverse; 1 Jul 1993-24 Aug 1995

Item	$Good	$Fine	$N.Mint	£Good	£Fine	£N.Mint
1 pre-bagged with trading card plus large coupon for Ultraverse #0	$0.70	$2.10	$3.50	£0.50	£1.50	£2.50
1 without coupon/card	$0.50	$1.50	$2.50	£0.30	£0.90	£1.50
1 Limited Edition – full hologram cover; 7,500 copies	$3.00	$9.00	$15.00	£1.50	£4.50	£7.50
2	$0.50	$1.50	$2.50	£0.40	£1.20	£2.00
3	$0.50	$1.50	$2.50	£0.30	£0.90	£1.50
4 40pgs, Rune insert; Mantra's wedding	$0.50	$1.50	$2.50	£0.30	£0.90	£1.50
5	$0.50	$1.50	$2.50	£0.30	£0.90	£1.50
6	$0.40	$1.20	$2.00	£0.25	£0.75	£1.25
7 origin Prototype by Dan Jurgens and Terry Austin; Prime rescues Mantra	$0.40	$1.20	$2.00	£0.25	£0.75	£1.25
8 Warstrike appears	$0.40	$1.20	$2.00	£0.25	£0.75	£1.25
9	$0.40	$1.20	$2.00	£0.25	£0.75	£1.25
10 64pgs, flip-book format with Ultraverse Premiere #2	$0.50	$1.50	$2.50	£0.30	£0.90	£1.50
11	$0.40	$1.20	$2.00	£0.25	£0.75	£1.25
12 Strangers and Mantra team up	$0.40	$1.20	$2.00	£0.25	£0.75	£1.25
13-14	$0.40	$1.20	$2.00	£0.25	£0.75	£1.25
15-16 Prime appears	$0.40	$1.20	$2.00	£0.25	£0.75	£1.25
17 prelude to Godwheel story	$0.40	$1.20	$2.00	£0.25	£0.75	£1.25
18 Mantra becomes pregnant	$0.40	$1.20	$2.00	£0.25	£0.75	£1.25
19-21	$0.40	$1.20	$2.00	£0.25	£0.75	£1.25
22 The Loki Connection, Primevil appears; continued in Night Man #22	$0.40	$1.20	$2.00	£0.25	£0.75	£1.25
23 1st issue under Marvel Comics solicitation	$0.40	$1.20	$2.00	£0.25	£0.75	£1.25
24 Ghoul and Topaz appear	$0.40	$1.20	$2.00	£0.25	£0.75	£1.25
Title Value:	**$13.90**	**$41.70**	**$69.50**	**£8.40**	**£25.20**	**£42.00**

Note: all Non-Distributed on the news-stands in the U.K.

MANTRA (2ND SERIES)
Marvel Comics Group; 1 Dec 1995-present

Item	$Good	$Fine	$N.Mint	£Good	£Fine	£N.Mint
1 ND Mike Barr script, Dave Roberts and Jim Amash art	$0.30	$0.90	$1.50	£0.20	£0.60	£1.00
1 ND variant cover, computer painted cover by Chuck Maiden	$0.80	$2.40	$4.00	£0.50	£1.50	£2.50
2 ND flip-book format with Phoenix Ressurrection chapter	$0.30	$0.90	$1.50	£0.20	£0.60	£1.00
3-4 ND	$0.30	$0.90	$1.50	£0.20	£0.60	£1.00
Title Value:	**$2.00**	**$6.00**	**$10.00**	**£1.30**	**£3.90**	**£6.50**

MANTRA, GIANT SIZE
Malibu Ultraverse; 1 Jul 1994

Item	$Good	$Fine	$N.Mint	£Good	£Fine	£N.Mint
1 ND 40pgs	$0.45	$1.35	$2.25	£0.30	£0.90	£1.50
Title Value:	**$0.45**	**$1.35**	**$2.25**	**£0.30**	**£0.90**	**£1.50**

MANTRA: INFINITY
Marvel Comics Group,OS; nn Nov 1995

Item	$Good	$Fine	$N.Mint	£Good	£Fine	£N.Mint
nn ND Black September tie-in; introduces the new Mantra	$0.50	$1.50	$2.50	£0.30	£0.90	£1.50
Title Value:	**$0.50**	**$1.50**	**$2.50**	**£0.30**	**£0.90**	**£1.50**

MANTRA: SPEAR OF DESTINY
Malibu Ultraverse,MS; 1 Apr 1995-2 May 1995

Item	$Good	$Fine	$N.Mint	£Good	£Fine	£N.Mint
1-2 ND Joel Adams art	$0.45	$1.35	$2.25	£0.30	£0.90	£1.50
Title Value:	**$0.90**	**$2.70**	**$4.50**	**£0.60**	**£1.80**	**£3.00**

MANTUS FILES, THE
Eternity,MS; 1 Aug 1991-4 Nov 1991

Item	$Good	$Fine	$N.Mint	£Good	£Fine	£N.Mint
1-4 ND black and white	$0.40	$1.20	$2.00	£0.25	£0.75	£1.25
Title Value:	**$1.60**	**$4.80**	**$8.00**	**£1.00**	**£3.00**	**£5.00**

MANY LOVES OF DOBIE GILLIS
National Periodical Publications,TV; 1 May/Jun 1960-26 Oct 1964

Item	$Good	$Fine	$N.Mint	£Good	£Fine	£N.Mint
1 ND very scarce in the U.K.	$30.00	$90.00	$180.00	£20.00	£60.00	£120.00
2-5 ND scarce in the U.K.	$15.50	$48.00	$95.00	£10.50	£33.00	£65.00
6-10 ND	$11.50	$35.00	$70.00	£7.50	£22.50	£45.00
11-20 ND	$10.00	$30.00	$60.00	£6.50	£20.00	£40.00
21-26 ND	$9.00	$28.00	$55.00	£5.75	£17.50	£35.00
Title Value:	**$303.50**	**$925.00**	**$1840.00**	**£199.00**	**£609.50**	**£1215.00**

MARAUDER
Caliber Press,OS; 1 Apr 1993

Item	$Good	$Fine	$N.Mint	£Good	£Fine	£N.Mint
1 ND	$0.40	$1.20	$2.00	£0.25	£0.75	£1.25
Title Value:	**$0.40**	**$1.20**	**$2.00**	**£0.25**	**£0.75**	**£1.25**

MARCH HARE
Lodestone; 1 Aug 1986

Item	$Good	$Fine	$N.Mint	£Good	£Fine	£N.Mint
1 ND Keith Giffen art	$0.40	$1.20	$2.00	£0.25	£0.75	£1.25
Title Value:	**$0.40**	**$1.20**	**$2.00**	**£0.25**	**£0.75**	**£1.25**

MARCUS ARENA
Axis Comics; 1 Jun 1994-2 1994

Item	$Good	$Fine	$N.Mint	£Good	£Fine	£N.Mint
1-2 ND	$0.40	$1.20	$2.00	£0.25	£0.75	£1.25
Title Value:	**$0.80**	**$2.40**	**$4.00**	**£0.50**	**£1.50**	**£2.50**

MARINE WAR HEROES
Charlton; 1 Jan 1964-18 Mar 1967

Item	$Good	$Fine	$N.Mint	£Good	£Fine	£N.Mint
1 distributed in the U.K.	$2.50	$7.50	$15.00	£1.65	£5.00	£10.00
2-10 distributed in the U.K.	$1.25	$3.75	$7.50	£0.80	£2.50	£5.00
11-18 distributed in the U.K.	$1.20	$3.60	$6.00	£0.80	£2.40	£4.00
Title Value:	**$23.35**	**$70.05**	**$130.50**	**£15.25**	**£46.70**	**£87.00**

MARK HAZZARD: MERC
Marvel Comics Group/New Universe; 1 Nov 1986-12 Oct 1987

Item	$Good	$Fine	$N.Mint	£Good	£Fine	£N.Mint
1-2 ND Morrow art	$0.15	$0.45	$0.75	£0.10	£0.35	£0.60
3-4 ND Jack Fury art	$0.15	$0.45	$0.75	£0.10	£0.35	£0.60
5-6 ND Beechum art	$0.15	$0.45	$0.75	£0.10	£0.35	£0.60
7 ND Mayerick art	$0.15	$0.45	$0.75	£0.10	£0.35	£0.60
8-12 ND Morrow art	$0.15	$0.45	$0.75	£0.10	£0.35	£0.60
Title Value:	**$1.80**	**$5.40**	**$9.00**	**£1.20**	**£4.20**	**£7.20**

MARK HAZZARD: MERC ANNUAL
Marvel Comics Group/New Universe; 1 Nov 1987

Item	$Good	$Fine	$N.Mint	£Good	£Fine	£N.Mint
1 ND Mark Hazzard dies	$0.30	$0.90	$1.50	£0.20	£0.60	£1.00
Title Value:	**$0.30**	**$0.90**	**$1.50**	**£0.20**	**£0.60**	**£1.00**

MARK, THE
Dark Horse; 1 Sep 1987-6 Jan 1989

Item	$Good	$Fine	$N.Mint	£Good	£Fine	£N.Mint
1-6 ND	$0.50	$1.50	$2.50	£0.30	£0.90	£1.50
Title Value:	**$3.00**	**$9.00**	**$14.75**	**£1.80**	**£5.40**	**£9.00**

MARK, THE (2ND SERIES)
Dark Horse,MS; 1 Dec 1993-4 Mar 1994

Item	$Good	$Fine	$N.Mint	£Good	£Fine	£N.Mint
1-4 ND	$0.50	$1.50	$2.50	£0.30	£0.90	£1.50
Title Value:	**$2.00**	**$6.00**	**$10.00**	**£1.20**	**£3.60**	**£6.00**

MARK, THE (3RD SERIES)
Dark Horse,MS; 1 Sep 1995-4 Dec 1995

Item	$Good	$Fine	$N.Mint	£Good	£Fine	£N.Mint
1-4 ND Todd Johnson script, Larry Stroman art	$0.50	$1.50	$2.50	£0.30	£0.90	£1.50
Title Value:	**$2.00**	**$6.00**	**$10.00**	**£1.20**	**£3.60**	**£6.00**

MARKSMAN
Hero; 1 1987-5 Aug 1988

Item	$Good	$Fine	$N.Mint	£Good	£Fine	£N.Mint
1-5 ND spin-off from Champions	$0.30	$0.90	$1.50	£0.20	£0.60	£1.00
Title Value:	**$1.50**	**$4.50**	**$7.50**	**£1.00**	**£3.00**	**£5.00**

MARKSMAN ANNUAL
Hero; 1 1988

Item	$Good	$Fine	$N.Mint	£Good	£Fine	£N.Mint
1 ND 52pgs	$0.40	$1.20	$2.00	£0.25	£0.75	£1.25
Title Value:	**$0.40**	**$1.20**	**$2.00**	**£0.25**	**£0.75**	**£1.25**

MARRIED WITH CHILDREN
Now Comics; 1 Dec 1989-7 Jun 1990

Item	$Good	$Fine	$N.Mint	£Good	£Fine	£N.Mint
1 based on the US TV series	$1.20	$3.60	$6.00	£0.80	£2.40	£4.00
1 2nd printing	$0.50	$1.50	$2.50	£0.30	£0.90	£1.50
2 photo cover	$0.90	$2.70	$4.50	£0.60	£1.80	£3.00
2 2nd printing	$0.30	$0.90	$1.50	£0.20	£0.60	£1.00
3	$0.30	$0.90	$1.50	£0.20	£0.60	£1.00
3 2nd printing	$0.30	$0.90	$1.50	£0.20	£0.60	£1.00
4-7	$0.30	$0.90	$1.50	£0.30	£0.90	£1.50
Title Value:	**$4.70**	**$14.10**	**$23.50**	**£3.60**	**£10.80**	**£18.00**

Note: all Non-Distributed on the news-stands in the U.K.

Item	£Good	£Fine	£N.Mint
Married With Children Revisited Vol 1 (May 1991), 64pgs, reprints issues #1-3	£0.65	£1.95	£3.25

MARRIED WITH CHILDREN (2ND SERIES)
Now Comics; 1 Sep 1991-13 Mar 1992

Item	$Good	$Fine	$N.Mint	£Good	£Fine	£N.Mint
1 based on US TV series, focusing more on character of Kelly Bundy (photo cover)	$0.50	$1.50	$2.50	£0.30	£0.90	£1.50
2-13	$0.40	$1.20	$2.00	£0.25	£0.75	£1.25
Title Value:	**$5.30**	**$15.90**	**$26.50**	**£3.30**	**£9.90**	**£16.50**

Note: all Non-Distributed on the news-stands in the U.K.

MARRIED WITH CHILDREN 2099
Now Comics,MS; 1 Jun 1993-3 Aug 1993

Item	$Good	$Fine	$N.Mint	£Good	£Fine	£N.Mint
1-3 ND	$0.50	$1.50	$2.50	£0.30	£0.90	£1.50
Title Value:	**$1.50**	**$4.50**	**$7.50**	**£0.90**	**£2.70**	**£4.50**

MARRIED WITH CHILDREN 3-D SPECIAL
Now Comics; 1 Jun 1993

Item	$Good	$Fine	$N.Mint	£Good	£Fine	£N.Mint
1 ND with 3-D glasses (25% less without glasses)	$0.60	$1.80	$3.00	£0.40	£1.20	£2.00
Title Value:	**$0.60**	**$1.80**	**$3.00**	**£0.40**	**£1.20**	**£2.00**

MARRIED WITH CHILDREN FLASHBACK SPECIAL
Now Comics,MS; 1 Jun 1993-3 Mar 1993

Item	$Good	$Fine	$N.Mint	£Good	£Fine	£N.Mint
1-3 ND	$0.50	$1.50	$2.50	£0.30	£0.90	£1.50
Title Value:	**$1.50**	**$4.50**	**$7.50**	**£0.90**	**£2.70**	**£4.50**

MARRIED WITH CHILDREN: BUCK'S TALE
Now Comics,MS; 1 Apr 1993-3 Jun 1994

Item	$Good	$Fine	$N.Mint	£Good	£Fine	£N.Mint
1-3 ND	$0.50	$1.50	$2.50	£0.30	£0.90	£1.50
Title Value:	**$1.50**	**$4.50**	**$7.50**	**£0.90**	**£2.70**	**£4.50**

MARRIED WITH CHILDREN: KELLY BUNDY SPECIAL
Now Comics,MS; 1 Jul 1992-3 Sep 1993

Item	$Good	$Fine	$N.Mint	£Good	£Fine	£N.Mint
1-3 ND pre-bagged with poster	$0.50	$1.50	$2.50	£0.30	£0.90	£1.50
Title Value:	**$1.50**	**$4.50**	**$7.50**	**£0.90**	**£2.70**	**£4.50**

MARRIED WITH CHILDREN: KELLY GOES TO COLLEGE
Now Comics,MS; 1 Jun 1994-3 Aug 1994

	$Good	$Fine	$N.Mint	£Good	£Fine	£N.Mint
1-3 ND	$0.60	$1.80	$3.00	£0.40	£1.20	£2.00
Title Value:	$1.80	$5.40	$9.00	£1.20	£3.60	£6.00

MARRIED WITH CHILDREN: LOTTO FEVER!
Now Comics,MS; 1 Oct 1994-3 Dec 1994

	$Good	$Fine	$N.Mint	£Good	£Fine	£N.Mint
1-3 ND	$0.50	$1.50	$2.50	£0.25	£0.75	£1.25
Title Value:	$1.50	$4.50	$7.50	£0.75	£2.25	£3.75

MARRIED WITH CHILDREN: QUANTUM QUARTET
Now Comics,MS; 1 Oct 1993-2 Nov 1993; 3/4 Sep 1994

	$Good	$Fine	$N.Mint	£Good	£Fine	£N.Mint
1-2 ND	$0.50	$1.50	$2.50	£0.30	£0.90	£1.50

3 ND special flip-book format combining issues #3 and 4 that were originally solicited for Dec 1993/Jan 1994 cover date

	$Good	$Fine	$N.Mint	£Good	£Fine	£N.Mint
	$0.60	$1.80	$3.00	£0.40	£1.20	£2.00
Title Value:	$1.60	$4.80	$8.00	£1.00	£3.00	£5.00

MARRIED WITH CHILDREN: 2099 AND A HALF
Now Comics,MS; 1 Apr 1995-2 May 1995

1-2 ND sub-titled 'Turgid Ordeals of Retchh and Slobb"

	$Good	$Fine	$N.Mint	£Good	£Fine	£N.Mint
	$0.50	$1.50	$2.50	£0.30	£0.90	£1.50
Title Value:	$1.00	$3.00	$5.00	£0.60	£1.80	£3.00

MARRIED WITH CHILDREN: WE'RE DYSFUNCTIONAL
Now Comics,MS; 1 Jan 1995-3 Mar 1995

	$Good	$Fine	$N.Mint	£Good	£Fine	£N.Mint
1-3 ND	$0.50	$1.50	$2.50	£0.30	£0.90	£1.50
Title Value:	$1.50	$4.50	$7.50	£0.90	£2.70	£4.50

MARRIED WITH: OFF BROADWAY
Now Comics,OS; 1 Sep 1993

	$Good	$Fine	$N.Mint	£Good	£Fine	£N.Mint
1 ND	$0.50	$1.50	$2.50	£0.30	£0.90	£1.50
Title Value:	$0.50	$1.50	$2.50	£0.30	£0.90	£1.50

MARS
First; 1 Jan 1984-12 Mar 1985

	$Good	$Fine	$N.Mint	£Good	£Fine	£N.Mint
1-12 ND	$0.25	$0.75	$1.25	£0.10	£0.30	£0.50
Title Value:	$3.00	$9.00	$15.00	£1.20	£3.60	£6.00

MARS ATTACKS
Topps,MS; 1 May 1994-5 Sep 1994

1-4 ND Keith Giffen script, Charlie Adlard art

	$Good	$Fine	$N.Mint	£Good	£Fine	£N.Mint
	$0.50	$1.50	$2.50	£0.30	£0.90	£1.50

5 ND Keith Giffen script, Charlie Adlard art; bound-in tattoos

	$Good	$Fine	$N.Mint	£Good	£Fine	£N.Mint
	$0.50	$1.50	$2.50	£0.30	£0.90	£1.50
Title Value:	$2.50	$7.50	$12.50	£1.50	£4.50	£7.50

Mars Attacks (Dec 1994) Trade paperback collects mini-series with Simon Bisley front cover, John Bolton back cover — £1.70 / £5.10 / £8.50

MARS ATTACKS (2ND SERIES)
Topps; 1 Aug 1995-present

1 ND Keith Giffen part script, Charles Adlard art, Ken Steacy cover

	$Good	$Fine	$N.Mint	£Good	£Fine	£N.Mint
	$0.60	$1.80	$3.00	£0.40	£1.20	£2.00
2-4 ND	$0.60	$1.80	$3.00	£0.40	£1.20	£2.00
Title Value:	$2.40	$7.20	$12.00	£1.60	£4.80	£8.00

MARS ATTACKS MINI-COMICS
Pocket Comics; 1 Jul 1988-4 Oct 1988
(mini-comics, cancelled 54-part series)

	$Good	$Fine	$N.Mint	£Good	£Fine	£N.Mint
1-4 ND	$0.25	$0.75	$1.25	£0.15	£0.45	£0.75
Title Value:	$1.00	$3.00	$5.00	£0.60	£1.80	£3.00

MARS ON EARTH
DC Comics/Piranha Press,OS; 1 1992

	$Good	$Fine	$N.Mint	£Good	£Fine	£N.Mint
1 ND	$0.40	$1.20	$2.00	£0.25	£0.75	£1.25
Title Value:	$0.40	$1.20	$2.00	£0.25	£0.75	£1.25

MARSHAL BLUEBERRY GRAPHIC NOVEL
Marvel Comics Group,OS; 1 Dec 1991

1 ND features the last two Blueberry tales by Charlier and Moebius

	$Good	$Fine	$N.Mint	£Good	£Fine	£N.Mint
	$3.00	$9.00	$15.00	£2.00	£6.00	£10.00
Title Value:	$3.00	$9.00	$15.00	£2.00	£6.00	£10.00

MARSHAL LAW
Marvel Comics Group/Epic; 1 Dec 1987-6 May 1989
(see British section)

1 ND Pat Mills script, Kevin O'Neill painted art in all

	$Good	$Fine	$N.Mint	£Good	£Fine	£N.Mint
	$0.80	$2.40	$4.00	£0.70	£2.10	£3.50
2 ND	$0.60	$1.80	$3.00	£0.50	£1.50	£2.50
3-6 ND	$0.50	$1.50	$2.50	£0.40	£1.20	£2.00
Title Value:	$3.40	$10.20	$17.00	£2.80	£8.40	£14.00

Note: Mature Readers label

Crime and Punishment: Marshal Law Takes Manhattan (Jan 1990) Pat Mills and Kev O'Neill; Mature Readers label — £0.60 / £1.80 / £3.00

Trade Paperback (Aug 1990), reprints issues #1-6, new cover by Kev O'Neill — £1.60 / £4.80 / £8.00

MARSHAL LAW: CAPE FEAR
Dark Horse,MS; 1 Sep 1993-2 Oct 1993

	$Good	$Fine	$N.Mint	£Good	£Fine	£N.Mint
1-2 ND	$0.50	$1.50	$2.50	£0.30	£0.90	£1.50
Title Value:	$1.00	$3.00	$5.00	£0.60	£1.80	£3.00

MARSHAL LAW: SUPER BABYLON
Dark Horse,OS; 1 May 1992

	$Good	$Fine	$N.Mint	£Good	£Fine	£N.Mint
1 ND	$0.50	$1.50	$2.50	£0.30	£0.90	£1.50
Title Value:	$0.50	$1.50	$2.50	£0.30	£0.90	£1.50

MARTHA WASHINGTON GOES TO WAR
Dark Horse/Legend,MS; 1 May 1994-5 Sep 1994

1 ND Frank Miller script and Dave Gibbons art begin

	$Good	$Fine	$N.Mint	£Good	£Fine	£N.Mint
	$0.60	$1.80	$3.00	£0.40	£1.20	£2.00

1 ND Sky Blue Edition – produced in the UK by Chaos City Comics, signed by Dave Gibbons. 500 copies

	$Good	$Fine	$N.Mint	£Good	£Fine	£N.Mint
	$2.40	$7.00	$12.00	£1.60	£4.80	£8.00

1 ND Sunset Red Edition – produced in the UK by Chaos City Comics, signed by Dave Gibbons with 50% signed by Frank Miller. 100 copies

	$Good	$Fine	$N.Mint	£Good	£Fine	£N.Mint
	$4.50	$13.50	$22.50	£3.00	£9.00	£15.00
2-5	$0.60	$1.80	$3.00	£0.40	£1.20	£2.00
Title Value:	$9.90	$29.50	$49.50	£6.60	£19.80	£33.00

Note: all Non-Distributed on the news-stands in the U.K.

Martha Washington Goes to Washington (Oct 1995) Trade paperback collects issues #1-5 — £2.40 / £7.20 / £12.00

MARTHA WASHINGTON STRANDED IN SPACE
Dark Horse,OS; 1 Nov 1995

1 ND Frank Miller script, Dave Gibbons art

	$Good	$Fine	$N.Mint	£Good	£Fine	£N.Mint
	$0.60	$1.80	$3.00	£0.40	£1.20	£2.00
Title Value:	$0.60	$1.80	$3.00	£0.40	£1.20	£2.00

MARTHA WASHINGTON, HAPPY BIRTHDAY
Dark Horse/Legend,OS; 1 Feb 1995

1 ND Frank Miller script, Dave Gibbons art

	$Good	$Fine	$N.Mint	£Good	£Fine	£N.Mint
	$0.60	$1.80	$3.00	£0.40	£1.20	£2.00
Title Value:	$0.60	$1.80	$3.00	£0.40	£1.20	£2.00

MARTIAN MANHUNTER
DC Comics,MS; 1 May 1988-4 Aug 1988
(see Detective Comics, House of Mystery, Jemm Son of Saturn, Justice League, Justice League of America)

1 Mark Badger art begins, Batman appears

	$Good	$Fine	$N.Mint	£Good	£Fine	£N.Mint
	$0.25	$0.75	$1.25	£0.15	£0.45	£0.75

2 Batman appears

	$Good	$Fine	$N.Mint	£Good	£Fine	£N.Mint
	$0.25	$0.75	$1.25	£0.15	£0.45	£0.75
3-4	$0.25	$0.75	$1.25	£0.15	£0.45	£0.75
Title Value:	$1.00	$3.00	$5.00	£0.60	£1.80	£3.00

Note: all Deluxe Format.

MARTIAN MANHUNTER: AMERICAN SECRETS
DC Comics,MS; 1 Sep 1992-3 Nov 1992

	$Good	$Fine	$N.Mint	£Good	£Fine	£N.Mint
1-3 ND 48pgs, squarebound	$0.70	$2.10	$3.50	£0.50	£1.50	£2.50
Title Value:	$2.10	$6.30	$10.50	£1.50	£4.50	£7.50

MARVEL 1993 HOLIDAY SPECIAL
Marvel Comics Group,OS; 1 Jan 1994

1 ND 64pgs, features include Hulk by Peter David and Ron Lim, She-Hulk by John Byrne, Nick Fury by Howard Chaykin

	$Good	$Fine	$N.Mint	£Good	£Fine	£N.Mint
	$0.50	$1.50	$2.50	£0.30	£0.90	£1.50
Title Value:	$0.50	$1.50	$2.50	£0.30	£0.90	£1.50

MARVEL ACTION HOUR FEATURING FANTASTIC FOUR
Marvel Comics Group, TV; 1 Nov 1994-8 Jun 1995

1 ND based on US animated series

	$Good	$Fine	$N.Mint	£Good	£Fine	£N.Mint
	$0.30	$0.90	$1.50	£0.20	£0.60	£1.00

1 ND pre-bagged with acetate print from TV series

	$Good	$Fine	$N.Mint	£Good	£Fine	£N.Mint
	$0.60	$1.80	$3.00	£0.40	£1.20	£2.00

2-3 ND Puppet Master appears

	$Good	$Fine	$N.Mint	£Good	£Fine	£N.Mint
	$0.30	$0.90	$1.50	£0.20	£0.60	£1.00

4-5 ND Sub-Mariner appears

	$Good	$Fine	$N.Mint	£Good	£Fine	£N.Mint
	$0.30	$0.90	$1.50	£0.20	£0.60	£1.00

6 ND The Skrulls appear

	$Good	$Fine	$N.Mint	£Good	£Fine	£N.Mint
	$0.30	$0.90	$1.50	£0.20	£0.60	£1.00

7 ND Dr. Doom appears

	$Good	$Fine	$N.Mint	£Good	£Fine	£N.Mint
	$0.30	$0.90	$1.50	£0.20	£0.60	£1.00

8 ND The Skrulls appear

	$Good	$Fine	$N.Mint	£Good	£Fine	£N.Mint
	$0.30	$0.90	$1.50	£0.20	£0.60	£1.00
Title Value:	$3.00	$9.00	$15.00	£2.00	£6.00	£10.00

MARVEL ACTION HOUR FEATURING IRON MAN
Marvel Comics Group, TV; 1 Nov 1994-8 Jun 1995

1 ND based on US animated series

	$Good	$Fine	$N.Mint	£Good	£Fine	£N.Mint
	$0.30	$0.90	$1.50	£0.20	£0.60	£1.00

1 ND pre-bagged with acetate print from TV series

	$Good	$Fine	$N.Mint	£Good	£Fine	£N.Mint
	$0.60	$1.80	$3.00	£0.40	£1.20	£2.00

2 ND Iron Man vs. Mandarin

	$Good	$Fine	$N.Mint	£Good	£Fine	£N.Mint
	$0.30	$0.90	$1.50	£0.20	£0.60	£1.00

3 ND Hawkeye and Scarlet Witch appear

	$Good	$Fine	$N.Mint	£Good	£Fine	£N.Mint
	$0.30	$0.90	$1.50	£0.20	£0.60	£1.00

4 ND Force Works, Hawkeye and War Machine appear

	$Good	$Fine	$N.Mint	£Good	£Fine	£N.Mint
	$0.30	$0.90	$1.50	£0.20	£0.60	£1.00

5 ND origins of Iron man and Mandarin retold

	$Good	$Fine	$N.Mint	£Good	£Fine	£N.Mint
	$0.30	$0.90	$1.50	£0.20	£0.60	£1.00

6 ND Fin Fang Foom appears

	$Good	$Fine	$N.Mint	£Good	£Fine	£N.Mint
	$0.30	$0.90	$1.50	£0.20	£0.60	£1.00

7 ND origins of Iron Man and Mandarin retold

	$Good	$Fine	$N.Mint	£Good	£Fine	£N.Mint
	$0.30	$0.90	$1.50	£0.20	£0.60	£1.00

8 ND Mandarin and Modok appear

	$Good	$Fine	$N.Mint	£Good	£Fine	£N.Mint
	$0.30	$0.90	$1.50	£0.20	£0.60	£1.00
Title Value:	$3.00	$9.00	$15.00	£2.00	£6.00	£10.00

MARVEL ACTION UNIVERSE
Marvel Comics Group,OS TV; 1 Jan 1989

1 ND Spiderman, Iceman, Firestar appear

	$Good	$Fine	$N.Mint	£Good	£Fine	£N.Mint
	$0.25	$0.75	$1.25	£0.15	£0.45	£0.75
Title Value:	$0.25	$0.75	$1.25	£0.15	£0.45	£0.75

MARVEL ADVENTURE
Marvel Comics Group; 1 Dec 1975-6 Oct 1976

1 ND Daredevil reprints begin

	$Good	$Fine	$N.Mint	£Good	£Fine	£N.Mint
	$0.30	$0.90	$1.50	£0.30	£0.90	£1.50
2-5 ND	$0.30	$0.90	$1.50	£0.25	£0.75	£1.25

6 ND Spiderman appears (reprints Daredevil #27)

	$Good	$Fine	$N.Mint	£Good	£Fine	£N.Mint
	$0.30	$0.90	$1.50	£0.25	£0.75	£1.25
Title Value:	$1.80	$5.40	$9.00	£1.55	£4.65	£7.75

Note: reprints of Daredevil #22-27.

MARVEL AGE
Marvel Comics Group/Promotional; 1 Mar 1982-140 Aug 1994

	$Good	$Fine	$N.Mint	£Good	£Fine	£N.Mint
1 ND	$0.30	$0.90	$1.50	£0.20	£0.60	£1.00
2-13 ND	$0.25	$0.75	$1.25	£0.15	£0.45	£0.75

14 ND John Byrne cover art

	$Good	$Fine	$N.Mint	£Good	£Fine	£N.Mint
	$0.25	$0.75	$1.25	£0.15	£0.45	£0.75

	$Good	$Fine	$N.Mint	£Good	£Fine	£N.Mint
15-32 ND	$0.25	$0.75	$1.25	£0.15	£0.45	£0.75
33 ND Punisher (2pgs)	$0.25	$0.75	$1.25	£0.15	£0.45	£0.75
34-50 ND	$0.25	$0.75	$1.25	£0.15	£0.45	£0.75
51 ND Punisher	$0.25	$0.75	$1.25	£0.15	£0.45	£0.75
52 ND Silver Surfer issue	$0.25	$0.75	$1.25	£0.15	£0.45	£0.75
53-59 ND	$0.25	$0.75	$1.25	£0.15	£0.45	£0.75
60 ND Excalibur issue	$0.25	$0.75	$1.25	£0.15	£0.45	£0.75
61-66 ND	$0.25	$0.75	$1.25	£0.15	£0.45	£0.75
67 ND Punisher film preview	$0.25	$0.75	$1.25	£0.15	£0.45	£0.75
68 ND Havok and Wolverine	$0.25	$0.75	$1.25	£0.15	£0.45	£0.75
69-70 ND	$0.25	$0.75	$1.25	£0.15	£0.45	£0.75
71 ND Silver Surfer	$0.25	$0.75	$1.25	£0.15	£0.45	£0.75
72 ND Punisher film photo cover	$0.25	$0.75	$1.25	£0.15	£0.45	£0.75
73 ND	$0.25	$0.75	$1.25	£0.15	£0.45	£0.75
74 ND Moon Knight	$0.25	$0.75	$1.25	£0.15	£0.45	£0.75
75-87 ND	$0.25	$0.75	$1.25	£0.15	£0.45	£0.75
88 ND Guardians of the Galaxy	$0.25	$0.75	$1.25	£0.15	£0.45	£0.75
89-96 ND	$0.25	$0.75	$1.25	£0.15	£0.45	£0.75
97 ND Excalibur issue	$0.25	$0.75	$1.25	£0.15	£0.45	£0.75
98 ND	$0.25	$0.75	$1.25	£0.15	£0.45	£0.75
99 ND Infinity Gauntlet preview	$0.25	$0.75	$1.25	£0.15	£0.45	£0.75
100 ND Todd McFarlane/Jim Lee/Rob Liefeld interviews	$0.25	$0.75	$1.25	£0.15	£0.45	£0.75
101-103 ND	$0.25	$0.75	$1.25	£0.15	£0.45	£0.75
104 ND previews X-Men #1 by Claremont/Lee	$0.25	$0.75	$1.25	£0.15	£0.45	£0.75
105-109 ND	$0.25	$0.75	$1.25	£0.15	£0.45	£0.75
110 ND Luke Cage preview	$0.25	$0.75	$1.25	£0.15	£0.45	£0.75
111 ND	$0.25	$0.75	$1.25	£0.15	£0.45	£0.75
112 ND Captain America special	$0.25	$0.75	$1.25	£0.15	£0.45	£0.75
113 ND Punisher and Captain America	$0.25	$0.75	$1.25	£0.15	£0.45	£0.75
114 ND Spiderman's 30th anniversary	$0.25	$0.75	$1.25	£0.15	£0.45	£0.75
115 ND Cable mini-series feature	$0.25	$0.75	$1.25	£0.15	£0.45	£0.75
116 ND X-Men feature	$0.25	$0.75	$1.25	£0.15	£0.45	£0.75
117 ND 2099 preview, new 2099 strip begins	$0.25	$0.75	$1.25	£0.15	£0.45	£0.75
118 ND pre-bagged with Hulk Marvel Masterpiece trading card, George Perez cover	$0.40	$1.20	$1.25		£0.75	£1.25
119 ND	$0.25	$0.75	$1.25	£0.15	£0.45	£0.75
120 ND 10th anniversary issue	$0.25	$0.75	$1.25	£0.15	£0.45	£0.75
121 ND	$0.25	$0.75	$1.25	£0.15	£0.45	£0.75
122 ND $1.25 cover	$0.25	$0.75	$1.25	£0.15	£0.45	£0.75
123 ND Venom and Thunderstrike features	$0.25	$0.75	$1.25	£0.15	£0.45	£0.75
124 ND Infinity Crusade and Heavy Hitters features	$0.25	$0.75	$1.25	£0.15	£0.45	£0.75
125 ND flip-book covers	$0.25	$0.75	$1.25	£0.15	£0.45	£0.75
126 ND Marvel UK feature	$0.25	$0.75	$1.25	£0.15	£0.45	£0.75
127 ND Frank Miller cover	$0.25	$0.75	$1.25	£0.15	£0.45	£0.75
128 ND Wolverine cover	$0.25	$0.75	$1.25	£0.15	£0.45	£0.75
129 ND X-Men/Avengers poster part 1	$0.25	$0.75	$1.25	£0.15	£0.45	£0.75
130 ND X-Men/Avengers poster part 2	$0.25	$0.75	$1.25	£0.15	£0.45	£0.75
131 ND Joe, Andy and Adam Kubert cover	$0.25	$0.75	$1.25	£0.15	£0.45	£0.75
132 ND Alan Davis cover	$0.25	$0.75	$1.25	£0.15	£0.45	£0.75
133 ND X-Men cover by Andy Kubert	$0.25	$0.75	$1.25	£0.15	£0.45	£0.75
134 ND 3 card insert sheet celebrating the wedding of Scott Summers and Jean Grey	$0.30	$0.90	$1.50	£0.20	£0.60	£1.00
135 ND	$0.25	$0.75	$1.25	£0.15	£0.45	£0.75
136 ND Neil Gaiman on Alice Cooper; with free Spiderman vs. Venom card sheet	$0.25	$0.75	$1.25	£0.15	£0.45	£0.75
137 ND 48pgs, article on Spiderman animated TV series	$0.25	$0.75	$1.25	£0.15	£0.45	£0.75
138-140 ND	$0.25	$0.75	$1.25	£0.15	£0.45	£0.75
Title Value:	$35.25	$105.75	$176.25	£21.20	£63.60	£106.00

MARVEL AGE ANNUAL
Marvel Comics Group/Promotional; 1 1986-4 1993

	$Good	$Fine	$N.Mint	£Good	£Fine	£N.Mint
1 ND Sabretooth appears (1 panel only, outside Marvel continuity)	$0.25	$0.75	$1.25	£0.15	£0.45	£0.75
2 ND celebrates 25th Anniversary	$0.25	$0.75	$1.25	£0.15	£0.45	£0.75
3 ND Fred Hembeck issue	$0.25	$0.75	$1.25	£0.15	£0.45	£0.75
4 ND squarebound	$0.25	$0.75	$1.25	£0.15	£0.45	£0.75
Title Value:	$1.00	$3.00	$5.00	£0.60	£1.80	£3.00

MARVEL AGE PREVIEW SPECIAL
Marvel Comics Group/Promotional; 1 May 1990; 2 Mar 1992

	$Good	$Fine	$N.Mint	£Good	£Fine	£N.Mint
1 ND 48pgs, no ads, previewing future Marvel comics	$0.30	$0.90	$1.50	£0.20	£0.60	£1.00
2 ND 64pgs, squarebound, no ads, previewing future Marvel comics	$0.30	$0.90	$1.50	£0.20	£0.60	£1.00
Title Value:	$0.60	$1.80	$3.00	£0.40	£1.20	£2.00

MARVEL AND DC PRESENT
Marvel Comics Group/DC Comics,OS; 1 Nov 1982
(Marvel/DC Co-Production)

	$Good	$Fine	$N.Mint	£Good	£Fine	£N.Mint
1 ND 64pgs, Teen Titans, X-Men co-star, Deathstroke appears, Walt Simonson/Austin art	$2.00	$6.00	$10.00	£1.20	£3.60	£6.00
Title Value:	$2.00	$6.00	$10.00	£1.20	£3.60	£6.00

MARVEL CHILLERS
Marvel Comics Group; 1 Oct 1975-7 Oct 1976

	$Good	$Fine	$N.Mint	£Good	£Fine	£N.Mint
1 1st appearance Modred the Mystic, Gil Kane cover	$0.50	$1.50	$2.50	£0.30	£0.90	£1.50
2 Modred the Mystic	$0.40	$1.20	$2.00	£0.25	£0.75	£1.25
3 Tigra the Were-Woman begins (origin); ends #7	$0.40	$1.20	$2.00	£0.25	£0.75	£1.25
4 Tigra vs. Kraven	$0.40	$1.20	$2.00	£0.25	£0.75	£1.25
5 Red Wolf appears	$0.40	$1.20	$2.00	£0.25	£0.75	£1.25
6 ND scarce in the U.K. Red Wolf appears, John Byrne art	$0.40	$1.20	$2.00	£0.30	£0.90	£1.50
7 Tigra vs. Super-Skrull, Jack Kirby cover	$0.40	$1.20	$2.00	£0.25	£0.75	£1.25
Title Value:	$2.90	$8.70	$14.50	£1.85	£5.55	£9.25

MARVEL CLASSICS COMICS
Marvel Comics Group; 1 1976-36 Dec 1978

	$Good	$Fine	$N.Mint	£Good	£Fine	£N.Mint
1 Dr. Jekyll and Mr. Hyde	$0.60	$1.80	$3.00	£0.30	£0.90	£1.50
2 The Time Machine, Alex Nino art	$0.50	$1.50	$2.50	£0.25	£0.75	£1.25
3 The Hunchback of Notre Dame	$0.50	$1.50	$2.50	£0.25	£0.75	£1.25
4 20,000 Leagues Under The Sea	$0.50	$1.50	$2.50	£0.25	£0.75	£1.25
5 Black Beauty	$0.50	$1.50	$2.50	£0.25	£0.75	£1.25
6 Gulliver's Travels	$0.50	$1.50	$2.50	£0.25	£0.75	£1.25
7 Tom Sawyer	$0.50	$1.50	$2.50	£0.25	£0.75	£1.25
8 Moby Dick, Alex Nino art	$0.50	$1.50	$2.50	£0.25	£0.75	£1.25
9 Dracula	$0.50	$1.50	$2.50	£0.25	£0.75	£1.25
10 Red Badge of Courage	$0.50	$1.50	$2.50	£0.25	£0.75	£1.25
11 Mysterious Island	$0.50	$1.50	$2.50	£0.25	£0.75	£1.25
12 The Three Musketeers	$0.50	$1.50	$2.50	£0.25	£0.75	£1.25
13 The Last of the Mohicans	$0.50	$1.50	$2.50	£0.25	£0.75	£1.25
14 The War of the Worlds, Alex Nino art	$0.50	$1.50	$2.50	£0.25	£0.75	£1.25
15 Treasure Island	$0.50	$1.50	$2.50	£0.25	£0.75	£1.25
16 Ivanhoe	$0.50	$1.50	$2.50	£0.25	£0.75	£1.25
17 The Count of Monte Cristo	$0.50	$1.50	$2.50	£0.25	£0.75	£1.25
18 The Odyssey	$0.50	$1.50	$2.50	£0.25	£0.75	£1.25
19 Robinson Crusoe	$0.50	$1.50	$2.50	£0.25	£0.75	£1.25
20 Frankenstein	$0.50	$1.50	$2.50	£0.25	£0.75	£1.25
21 Master of the World	$0.50	$1.50	$2.50	£0.25	£0.75	£1.25
22 Food of the Gods	$0.50	$1.50	$2.50	£0.25	£0.75	£1.25
23 The Moonstone	$0.50	$1.50	$2.50	£0.25	£0.75	£1.25
24 She	$0.50	$1.50	$2.50	£0.25	£0.75	£1.25
25 The Invisible Man, Alex Nino art	$0.50	$1.50	$2.50	£0.25	£0.75	£1.25
26 The Iliad	$0.50	$1.50	$2.50	£0.25	£0.75	£1.25
27 Kidnapped	$0.50	$1.50	$2.50	£0.25	£0.75	£1.25
28 The Pit and the Pendulum, Michael Golden art	$0.50	$1.50	$2.50	£0.25	£0.75	£1.25
29 The Prisoner of Zenda	$0.50	$1.50	$2.50	£0.25	£0.75	£1.25
30 Arabian Nights	$0.50	$1.50	$2.50	£0.25	£0.75	£1.25
31 The First Men in the Moon	$0.50	$1.50	$2.50	£0.25	£0.75	£1.25

	$Good	$Fine	$N.Mint	£Good	£Fine	£N.Mint
32 White Fang	$0.50	$1.50	$2.50	£0.25	£0.75	£1.25
33 The Prince and the Pauper	$0.50	$1.50	$2.50	£0.25	£0.75	£1.25
34 Robin Hood	$0.50	$1.50	$2.50	£0.25	£0.75	£1.25
35 Alice in Wonderland	$0.50	$1.50	$2.50	£0.25	£0.75	£1.25
36 A Christmas Carol	$0.50	$1.50	$2.50	£0.25	£0.75	£1.25
Title Value:	$18.10	$54.30	$90.50	£9.05	£27.15	£45.25

Note: all 52pgs, no ads.

MARVEL COLLECTOR'S ITEM CLASSICS
Marvel Comics Group; 1 Feb 1965-22 Aug 1969
(becomes Marvel's Greatest Comics)

	$Good	$Fine	$N.Mint	£Good	£Fine	£N.Mint
1 68pgs, reprints from Fantastic Four (#2), Thor, Spiderman (#3), Antman (Tales To Astonish #36)	$8.00	$24.50	$57.50	£5.00	£15.00	£35.00
2 68pgs, reprints F.F. #3, Spiderman #4, Tales To Astonish #37	$5.75	$17.50	$35.00	£3.75	£11.00	£22.50
3 68pgs, reprints F.F. #4, Hulk #6, Tales of Suspense #40, Strange Tales #110	$5.00	$15.00	$30.00	£3.30	£10.00	£20.00
4 68pgs, reprints F.F. #7, Hulk #4 (1 story), Tales of Suspense #41, Strange Tales #111	$4.55	$13.50	$27.50	£2.50	£7.50	£15.00
5 68pgs, reprints F.F. #8, Hulk #4 (1 story), Tales of Suspense #42, Strange Tales #114	$3.30	$10.00	$20.00	£1.65	£5.00	£10.00
6 68pgs, reprints F.F. #9, Hulk #5, Tales of Suspense #43, Strange Tales #116	$3.30	$10.00	$20.00	£1.65	£5.00	£10.00
7 68pgs, reprints F.F. #13, Hulk #5, Tales of Suspense #44, Strange Tales #117	$3.30	$10.00	$20.00	£1.65	£5.00	£10.00
8 68pgs, reprints F.F. #10, Hulk #2, Tales of Suspense #45, Strange Tales #118	$3.30	$10.00	$20.00	£1.65	£5.00	£10.00
9 68pgs, reprints F.F. #14, Hulk #2, Tales of Suspense #46, Strange Tales #118	$3.30	$10.00	$20.00	£1.65	£5.00	£10.00
10 68pgs, reprints F.F. #15, Hulk #2, Tales of Suspense #47, Strange Tales #119	$3.30	$10.00	$20.00	£1.65	£5.00	£10.00
11 68pgs, reprints F.F. #16, Hulk #6, Tales of Suspense #48, Strange Tales #120; cover repros of early Marvels on cover end	$2.90	$8.75	$17.50	£1.25	£3.75	£7.50
12-22 68pgs	$2.90	$8.75	$17.50	£1.25	£3.75	£7.50
Title Value:	$77.90	$235.50	$480.00	£39.45	£118.50	£242.50

REPRINT FEATURES
Ant-Man in 1, 2, 22. Dr.Strange in 3-9, 11-22. Fantastic Four in 1-22. Hulk in 3-16. Iron Man in 3-22. Spiderman in 1, 2. Tales of Asgard in 1. Watcher in 3, 5, 10, 13, 21.

MARVEL COMICS
Timely/Atlas; 1 Oct/Nov 1939-92 Jun 1949

	$Good	$Fine	$N.Mint	£Good	£Fine	£N.Mint
1 origin and 1st distributed appearance Sub-Mariner, 1st appearance Human Torch, Ka-Zar and The Angel; most #1's have November cover with date blacked out, fewer have October. About 60 extant copies	$11200.00	$33700.00	$90000.00	£7500.00	£22500.00	£60000.00
[Prices may vary widely on this comic]						
2 origin retold of Human Torch (traditionally rarer than #1 – about 50 extant copies	$2000.00	$6000.00	$16000.00	£1375.00	£4100.00	£11000.00
3	$870.00	$2600.00	$7000.00	£560.00	£1675.00	£4500.00
4 1st appearance Electro	$680.00	$2050.00	$5500.00	£465.00	£1400.00	£3750.00
5 very scarce in the U.K.	$1500.00	$4500.00	$12000.00	£1000.00	£3000.00	£8000.00
6-7	$435.00	$1300.00	$3500.00	£280.00	£840.00	£2250.00
8 Human Torch vs. Sub Mariner, the first of their great battles	$530.00	$1575.00	$4250.00	£340.00	£1025.00	£2750.00
9 very scarce in the U.K. Human Torch vs. Sub-Mariner cover and story	$1550.00	$4650.00	$12500.00	£1050.00	£3150.00	£8500.00
10 Human Torch vs. Sub-Mariner	$350.00	$1050.00	$2800.00	£235.00	£710.00	£1900.00
11	$280.00	$840.00	$2250.00	£185.00	£560.00	£1500.00
12	$260.00	$780.00	$2100.00	£175.00	£520.00	£1400.00
13 1st appearance Golden Age The Vision by Joe Simon and Jack Kirby	$300.00	$900.00	$2400.00	£200.00	£600.00	£1600.00
14-16	$160.00	$485.00	$1300.00	£105.00	£315.00	£850.00
17 Human Torch and Sub-Mariner team up for 1st time cover and story	$185.00	$560.00	$1500.00	£125.00	£375.00	£1000.00
18-20	$155.00	$475.00	$1275.00	£105.00	£315.00	£850.00
21 1st appearance The Patriot	$150.00	$450.00	$1200.00	£100.00	£300.00	£800.00
22-30	$110.00	$335.00	$900.00	£75.00	£225.00	£600.00
31-40	$105.00	$315.00	$850.00	£70.00	£215.00	£575.00
41-48	$100.00	$300.00	$800.00	£67.50	£205.00	£550.00
49 origin Miss America	$130.00	$390.00	$1050.00	£87.50	£260.00	£700.00
50	$105.00	$315.00	$850.00	£70.00	£215.00	£575.00
51-60	$92.50	$280.00	$750.00	£62.50	£185.00	£500.00
61-62	$90.00	$270.00	$725.00	£57.50	£175.00	£475.00
63 Hitler on cover	$90.00	$270.00	$725.00	£57.50	£175.00	£475.00
64-65	$90.00	$270.00	$725.00	£57.50	£175.00	£475.00
66 last classic war cover	$90.00	$270.00	$725.00	£57.50	£175.00	£475.00
67-79	$80.00	$240.00	$650.00	£52.50	£155.00	£425.00
80 Captain America appears	$105.00	$315.00	$850.00	£70.00	£215.00	£575.00
81 Captain America appears	$82.50	$250.00	$675.00	£55.00	£165.00	£450.00
82 origin and 1st appearance Namora	$150.00	$450.00	$1200.00	£100.00	£300.00	£800.00
83	$80.00	$240.00	$650.00	£52.50	£155.00	£425.00
84 Captain America appears	$105.00	$315.00	$850.00	£70.00	£215.00	£575.00
85	$80.00	$240.00	$650.00	£52.50	£155.00	£425.00
86 Captain America appears	$92.50	$280.00	$750.00	£62.50	£185.00	£500.00
87 Captain America/Golden Girl team	$87.50	$260.00	$700.00	£57.50	£175.00	£475.00
88 Captain America appears	$92.50	$280.00	$750.00	£62.50	£185.00	£500.00
89 Captain America solo story	$92.50	$280.00	$750.00	£62.50	£185.00	£500.00
90 Captain America appears	$90.00	$270.00	$725.00	£57.50	£175.00	£475.00
91 scarce in the U.K. Captain America appears	$92.50	$280.00	$750.00	£62.50	£185.00	£500.00
92 very scarce in the U.K. Captain America appears, Human Torch "origin"	$175.00	$520.00	$1400.00	£115.00	£355.00	£950.00
Title Value:	$28575.00	$85925.00	$230125.00	£19105.00	£57340.00	£153650.00

Note: titled Marvel Mystery Comics from #2. Note also that these comics were not distributed on the news-stands in the U.K. like all Golden Age material but some copies have been noted with British pence stamps: these may have come over as ballast on ships during and after the war. However most issues of this title are at least scarce in the U.K.

MARVEL COMICS COLLECTION
Marvel Comics Group; 1-3 Jun 1992

	$Good	$Fine	$N.Mint	£Good	£Fine	£N.Mint
1-3 ND bound volumes of all the Marvel comics published for the month of June 1992 made available at the June Diamond Seminar; 600 sets made	$6.00	$18.00	$30.00	£4.00	£12.00	£20.00
Title Value:	$18.00	$54.00	$90.00	£12.00	£36.00	£60.00

MARVEL COMICS PRESENTS
Marvel Comics Group; 1 Sep 1988-175 Feb 1995

Marvel Classics Comic #9

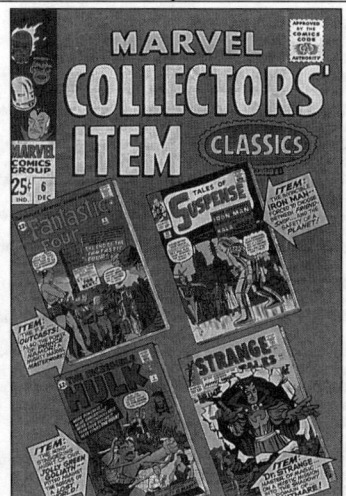

Marvel Collectors' Item Classics #6

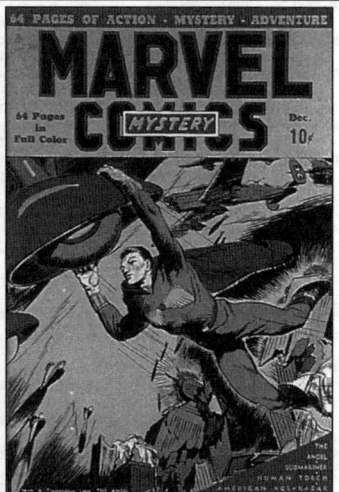

Marvel Mystery Comics #2

	$Good	$Fine	$N.Mint	£Good	£Fine	£N.Mint

1 ND Wolverine, Man-Thing, Master of Kung Fu, Silver Surfer
| | $1.50 | $4.50 | $7.50 | £0.70 | £2.10 | £3.50 |

2-5 ND Wolverine $0.80 | $2.40 | $4.00 | £0.40 | £1.20 | £2.00

6-10 ND Wolverine
| | $0.50 | $1.50 | $2.50 | £0.30 | £0.90 | £1.50 |

11-16 ND Colossus
| | $0.40 | $1.20 | $2.00 | £0.25 | £0.75 | £1.25 |

17 ND Cyclops $0.40 | $1.20 | $2.00 | £0.25 | £0.75 | £1.25

18 ND She-Hulk, Cyclops, Byrne art
| | $0.40 | $1.20 | $2.00 | £0.25 | £0.75 | £1.25 |

19-20 ND Cyclops $0.40 | $1.20 | $2.00 | £0.25 | £0.75 | £1.25

21-23 ND Cyclops $0.30 | $0.90 | $1.50 | £0.20 | £0.60 | £1.00

24 ND Cyclops, Havok
| | $0.30 | $0.90 | $1.50 | £0.20 | £0.60 | £1.00 |

25 ND Havok; 1st appearance Nth Man, The Ultimate Ninja
| | $0.30 | $0.90 | $1.50 | £0.20 | £0.60 | £1.00 |

26-28 ND Havok $0.30 | $0.90 | $1.50 | £0.20 | £0.60 | £1.00

29-30 ND Havok/Wolverine
| | $0.30 | $0.90 | $1.50 | £0.20 | £0.60 | £1.00 |

31 ND Havok, Excalibur, Erik Larsen art
| | $0.30 | $0.90 | $1.50 | £0.20 | £0.60 | £1.00 |

32 ND Excalibur, Erik Larsen art
| | $0.30 | $0.90 | $1.50 | £0.20 | £0.60 | £1.00 |

33 ND Excalibur, Erik Larsen art; Jim Lee art on Namor
| | $0.50 | $1.50 | $2.50 | £0.30 | £0.90 | £1.50 |

34-35 ND Excalibur
| | $0.30 | $0.90 | $1.50 | £0.20 | £0.60 | £1.00 |

36-37 LD in the U.K. Excalibur, Erik Larsen art
| | $0.30 | $0.90 | $1.50 | £0.20 | £0.60 | £1.00 |

38 LD in the U.K. Wolverine by Buscema, Excalibur by Larsen art
| | $0.50 | $1.50 | $2.50 | £0.30 | £0.90 | £1.50 |

39 LD in the U.K. Wolverine, Spiderman
| | $0.40 | $1.20 | $2.00 | £0.25 | £0.75 | £1.25 |

40-47 ND Wolverine
| | $0.40 | $1.20 | $2.00 | £0.25 | £0.75 | £1.25 |

48-49 LD in the U.K. Wolverine, Spiderman, Larsen art
| | $0.80 | $2.40 | $4.00 | £0.30 | £0.90 | £1.50 |

50 LD in the U.K. Wolverine, Spiderman, Silver Surfer appear, Larsen art
| | $0.80 | $2.40 | $4.00 | £0.30 | £0.90 | £1.50 |

51-53 Wolverine, Wild Child, Rob Liefeld art
| | $0.80 | $2.40 | $4.00 | £0.30 | £0.90 | £1.50 |

54-58 Wolverine, Hulk
| | $0.80 | $2.40 | $4.00 | £0.25 | £0.75 | £1.25 |

59 Wolverine, Hulk; Punisher appears
| | $0.80 | $2.40 | $4.00 | £0.25 | £0.75 | £1.25 |

60-61 Wolverine, Hulk
| | $0.80 | $2.40 | $4.00 | £0.25 | £0.75 | £1.25 |

62 Wolverine, Deathlok story
| | $0.80 | $2.40 | $4.00 | £0.25 | £0.75 | £1.25 |

63 Wolverine
| | $0.40 | $1.20 | $2.00 | £0.25 | £0.75 | £1.25 |

64-67 Wolverine/Ghost Rider, Texeira art
| | $0.40 | $1.20 | $2.00 | £0.30 | £0.90 | £1.50 |

68 ND Wolverine/Ghost Rider, Texeira art, bi-weekly
| | $0.40 | $1.20 | $2.00 | £0.30 | £0.90 | £1.50 |

69-71 Wolverine/Ghost Rider, bi-weekly
| | $0.40 | $1.20 | $2.00 | £0.30 | £0.90 | £1.50 |

72 LD in the U.K. Wolverine: Weapon X begins – Wolverine's origin, Barry Windsor-Smith art, bi-weekly issue
| | $1.50 | $4.50 | $7.50 | £0.75 | £2.25 | £3.75 |

73 Weapon X story, bi-weekly issue
| | $0.90 | $2.70 | $4.50 | £0.60 | £1.80 | £3.00 |

74 Weapon X story, bi-weekly issue
| | $0.80 | $2.40 | $4.00 | £0.50 | £1.50 | £2.50 |

75-83 Weapon X story, bi-weekly issue
| | $0.60 | $1.80 | $3.00 | £0.30 | £0.90 | £1.50 |

84 Weapon X story, wraparound cover by Barry Windsor-Smith, bi-weekly issue
| | $0.50 | $1.50 | $2.50 | £0.30 | £0.90 | £1.50 |

85 Wolverine by Peter David and Sam Kieth begins (1st Sam Kieth Wolverine), Liefeld art on X-Men back-up story, 1st Jae Lee art for Marvel, bi-weekly issue
| | $1.40 | $4.20 | $7.00 | £0.70 | £2.10 | £3.50 |

86-89 Wolverine by Peter David, Sam Kieth art, Jae Lee art, bi-weekly issue
| | $0.70 | $2.10 | $3.50 | £0.30 | £0.90 | £1.50 |

90 Wolverine by Peter David, Sam Kieth art, Jae Lee art, Ghost Rider and Cable begins, bi-weekly issue
| | $0.70 | $2.10 | $3.50 | £0.30 | £0.90 | £1.50 |

91-92 Wolverine by Peter David, Sam Kieth art, Jae Lee art, Ghost Rider and Cable, bi-weekly issue
| | $0.40 | $1.20 | $2.00 | £0.25 | £0.75 | £1.25 |

93-96 Wolverine by Tim Truman, Nova, Ghost Rider and Cable, bi-weekly issue
| | $0.40 | $1.20 | $2.00 | £0.25 | £0.75 | £1.25 |

97 Wolverine by Tim Truman, Ghost Rider and Cable, bi-weekly issue
| | $0.40 | $1.20 | $2.00 | £0.25 | £0.75 | £1.25 |

98 Wolverine by Tim Truman, Ghost Rider, bi-weekly issue
| | $0.40 | $1.20 | $2.00 | £0.25 | £0.75 | £1.25 |

99 Wolverine by Liefeld, Ghost Rider, Mary-Jane Parker, Captain America
| | $0.40 | $1.20 | $2.00 | £0.25 | £0.75 | £1.25 |

100 Ghost Rider, Dr. Doom, Wolverine and Nightmare in one full length story
| | $0.45 | $1.35 | $2.25 | £0.30 | £0.90 | £1.50 |

101-106 Ghost Rider and Dr. Strange, Wolverine and Nightcrawler, bi-weekly
| | $0.30 | $0.90 | $1.50 | £0.20 | £0.60 | £1.00 |

107 Wolverine and Nightcrawler, Ghost Rider and Werewolf, bi-weekly
| | $0.30 | $0.90 | $1.50 | £0.20 | £0.60 | £1.00 |

108 Infinity War X-over, Thanos appears, Wolverine and Nightcrawler, Ghost Rider and Werewolf, bi-weekly
| | $0.30 | $0.90 | $1.50 | £0.20 | £0.60 | £1.00 |

109-111 Infinity War X-over, Thanos appears, Wolverine and Typhoid Mary, Ghost Rider and Werewolf, bi-weekly
| | $0.30 | $0.90 | $1.50 | £0.20 | £0.60 | £1.00 |

112 Wolverine and Typhoid Mary, Ghost Rider and Werewolf, bi-weekly
| | $0.30 | $0.90 | $1.50 | £0.20 | £0.60 | £1.00 |

113 Wolverine and Typhoid Mary, Giant Man vs. Goliath, Werewolf By Night vs. Wendigo, Ghost Rider and Man-Thing, bi-weekly
| | $0.30 | $0.90 | $1.50 | £0.20 | £0.60 | £1.00 |

114-115 Wolverine and Typhoid Mary, Ghost Rider and Iron Fist, bi-weekly
| | $0.30 | $0.90 | $1.50 | £0.20 | £0.60 | £1.00 |

116 Wolverine and Typhoid Mary, Ghost Rider and Iron Fist, Iron Fist solo story, bi-weekly
| | $0.30 | $0.90 | $1.50 | £0.20 | £0.60 | £1.00 |

117 Wolverine and Venom by Sam Kieth, Ghost Rider and Iron Fist, Sam Kieth cover, bi-weekly; Ravage 2099 preview (1st appearance)
| | $0.50 | $1.50 | $2.50 | £0.30 | £0.90 | £1.50 |

118 Wolverine and Venom by Sam Kieth, Ghost Rider and Iron Fist, Sam Kieth cover, bi-weekly
| | $0.30 | $0.90 | $1.50 | £0.20 | £0.60 | £1.00 |

119 Wolverine and Venom by Sam Kieth, Ghost Rider and Cloak and Dagger, Sam Kieth cover, bi-weekly
| | $0.30 | $0.90 | $1.50 | £0.20 | £0.60 | £1.00 |

120 Wolverine and Venom by Sam Kieth, Ghost Rider and Cloak and Dagger, Spiderman solo story, Sam Kieth cover, bi-weekly
| | $0.30 | $0.90 | $1.50 | £0.20 | £0.60 | £1.00 |

121-122 Wolverine and Venom by Sam Kieth, Ghost Rider and Cloak and Dagger, Sam Kieth cover, bi-weekly
| | $0.30 | $0.90 | $1.50 | £0.20 | £0.60 | £1.00 |

123-124 Wolverine and Lynx, Ghost Rider and Typhoid Mary, Sam Kieth cover, bi-weekly
| | $0.30 | $0.90 | $1.50 | £0.20 | £0.60 | £1.00 |

125-130 Wolverine and Lynx, Ghost Rider and Typhoid Mary, Iron Fist, Sam Kieth cover, bi-weekly
| | $0.30 | $0.90 | $1.50 | £0.20 | £0.60 | £1.00 |

131 Wolverine and Cyber, Ghost Rider and Cage, Iron Fist, Shadowcat, bi-weekly
| | $0.30 | $0.90 | $1.50 | £0.20 | £0.60 | £1.00 |

132 Wolverine and Cyber, Ghost Rider and Cage, Iron Fist, Iron Man, bi-weekly
| | $0.30 | $0.90 | $1.50 | £0.20 | £0.60 | £1.00 |

133 Wolverine and Cyber, Ghost Rider and Cage, Iron Fist, Cloak & Dagger, bi-weekly
| | $0.30 | $0.90 | $1.50 | £0.20 | £0.60 | £1.00 |

134 Wolverine and Cyber, Ghost Rider and Cage, Iron Fist, Major Victory, bi-weekly
| | $0.30 | $0.90 | $1.50 | £0.20 | £0.60 | £1.00 |

135 Wolverine and Cyber, Ghost Rider and Cage, Iron Fist, Daredevil, bi-weekly
| | $0.30 | $0.90 | $1.50 | £0.20 | £0.60 | £1.00 |

136 Wolverine and Cyber, Ghost Rider and Cage, Iron Fist, Spiderman, bi-weekly
| | $0.30 | $0.90 | $1.50 | £0.20 | £0.60 | £1.00 |

137 Wolverine and Cyber, Ghost Rider and The Masters of Silence, Iron Fist, Ant-Man, bi-weekly
| | $0.30 | $0.90 | $1.50 | £0.20 | £0.60 | £1.00 |

138 Wolverine, Spellbound, Nightcrawler and Ghost Rider/Masters of Silence
| | $0.30 | $0.90 | $1.50 | £0.20 | £0.60 | £1.00 |

139 Wolverine, Spellbound, The Foreigner and Ghost Rider/Masters of Silence
| | $0.30 | $0.90 | $1.50 | £0.20 | £0.60 | £1.00 |

140 Wolverine, Spellbound, Captain Universe and Ghost Rider/Masters of Silence
| | $0.30 | $0.90 | $1.50 | £0.20 | £0.60 | £1.00 |

141 Wolverine, Spellbound, Iron Fist and Ghost Rider/Masters of Silence
| | $0.30 | $0.90 | $1.50 | £0.20 | £0.60 | £1.00 |

142 Wolverine, Spellbound, Mr. Fantastic and Ghost Rider/Masters of Silence
| | $0.30 | $0.90 | $1.50 | £0.20 | £0.60 | £1.00 |

143 Siege of Darkness part 3: Ghost Rider & Blaze, Werewolf, Scarlet Witch, Zarathos
| | $0.30 | $0.90 | $1.50 | £0.20 | £0.60 | £1.00 |

144 Siege of Darkness part 6: Ghost Rider & Blaze, Werewolf, Scarlet Witch, Morbius
| | $0.30 | $0.90 | $1.50 | £0.20 | £0.60 | £1.00 |

145 Siege of Darkness part 11: Ghost Rider & Blaze, Vengeance, Nightstalkers, Demonslayer, Morbius
| | $0.30 | $0.90 | $1.50 | £0.20 | £0.60 | £1.00 |

146 Siege of Darkness part 14: Ghost Rider, Nightstalkers, Dr. Strange, Darkhold
| | $0.30 | $0.90 | $1.50 | £0.20 | £0.60 | £1.00 |

147 Vengeance, American Eagle, Black Panther, Captain Universe
| | $0.30 | $0.90 | $1.50 | £0.20 | £0.60 | £1.00 |

148 Vengeance, American Eagle, Saints & Sinners, The Masters of Silence
| | $0.30 | $0.90 | $1.50 | £0.20 | £0.60 | £1.00 |

149 Wolverine vs. Typhoid Mary, Daredevil vs. Steel Shade
| | $0.30 | $0.90 | $1.50 | £0.20 | £0.60 | £1.00 |

150 The Four Marys story featuring Wolverine and Daredevil
| | $0.30 | $0.90 | $1.50 | £0.20 | £0.60 | £1.00 |

151-152 Vengeance, War Machine, Moon Knight, Wolverine
| | $0.30 | $0.90 | $1.50 | £0.20 | £0.60 | £1.00 |

153 Vengeance, War Machine, Moon Knight, Wolverine; with free Spiderman vs. Venom card sheet
| | $0.30 | $0.90 | $1.50 | £0.20 | £0.60 | £1.00 |

154 Vengeance, Namorita, War Machine, Wolverine
| | $0.30 | $0.90 | $1.50 | £0.20 | £0.60 | £1.00 |

155 Ghost Rider, Hawk (previously Hawkeye), Namorita, Nick Fury; with free Spiderman vs. Venom card sheet
| | $0.30 | $0.90 | $1.50 | £0.20 | £0.60 | £1.00 |

156 Vengeance, Hawkeye, New Warriors, Nick Fury
| | $0.30 | $0.90 | $1.50 | £0.20 | £0.60 | £1.00 |

157 Vengeance, Hawkeye, New Warriors, The Destroyer
| | $0.30 | $0.90 | $1.50 | £0.20 | £0.60 | £1.00 |

158 Vengeance, Master of Kung Fu, New Warriors, Clandestine by Alan Davis
| | $0.30 | $0.90 | $1.50 | £0.20 | £0.60 | £1.00 |

159 Vengeance, Hawkeye, New Warriors, Thing
| | $0.30 | $0.90 | $1.50 | £0.20 | £0.60 | £1.00 |

160-161 Vengeance, Hawkeye, New Warriors, Mace
| | $0.30 | $0.90 | $1.50 | £0.20 | £0.60 | £1.00 |

162-163 Vengeance, New Warriors, Mace, Tigra
| | $0.30 | $0.90 | $1.50 | £0.20 | £0.60 | £1.00 |

164 Vengeance, Speedball, Man-Thing, Tigra
| | $0.30 | $0.90 | $1.50 | £0.20 | £0.60 | £1.00 |

165 Vengeance, Rage, Man-Thing, Tigra
| | $0.30 | $0.90 | $1.50 | £0.20 | £0.60 | £1.00 |

166-167 Vengeance, Turbo, Man-Thing, Spiderwoman
| | $0.30 | $0.90 | $1.50 | £0.20 | £0.60 | £1.00 |

VERY GENERAL PERCENTAGE CONVERSION CHART WHICH MAY BE USED TO CALCULATE LOW AND INBETWEEN GRADES:

	$Good	$Fine	$N.Mint	£Good	£Fine	£N.Mint
168 Vengeance, Thing, Black Bolt, Spiderwoman	$0.30	$0.90	$1.50	£0.20	£0.60	£1.00
169 Vengeance, Mandarin, Century, It the Living Colossus	$0.30	$0.90	$1.50	£0.20	£0.60	£1.00
170 Vengeance, Mandarin, Force Works, Nick Fury	$0.30	$0.90	$1.50	£0.20	£0.60	£1.00
171 Vengeance, The Recorder, War Machine, Red Wolf	$0.30	$0.90	$1.50	£0.20	£0.60	£1.00
172 Vengeance, U.S Agent, Spiderwoman, Stingray	$0.30	$0.90	$1.50	£0.20	£0.60	£1.00
173 Vengeance, The Lunatics, Nick Fury, Sundragon	$0.30	$0.90	$1.50	£0.20	£0.60	£1.00
174 Vengeance, Lunatic/Silver Surfer, Nick Fury, Cage	$0.30	$0.90	$1.50	£0.20	£0.60	£1.00
175 Steel Raven, Lunatic/Silver Surfer, New Genix, Vengeance	$0.30	$0.90	$1.50	£0.20	£0.60	£1.00
Title Value:	$76.95	$230.85	$383.25	£43.75	£131.25	£218.75

Wolverine & Ghost Rider: Acts of Vengeance (Jan 1994)

	£Good	£Fine	£N.Mint
Trade paperback reprints Marvel Comics Presents #64-71	£0.90	£2.70	£4.50

Wolverine: Weapon X (Apr 1994)

	£Good	£Fine	£N.Mint
Trade paperback reprints Marvel Comics Presents #72-84	£1.70	£5.10	£8.50

FEATURES

American Eagle in 27. Ant-Man in 11,81. Aquarian in 46. Arabian Knight in 47. Beast in 85. Black Cat in 57. Black Knight in 72,73. Black Panther in 13-37. Black Widow and Silver Sable in 53. The Captain in 2. Captain America in 34, 47, 60, 80, 81. Clea in 20. Cloak in 9. Coldblood in 26- 35. Collective Man in 55. Colossus in 10-17. Comet Man in 50-53. Cyclops in 17-24. Daughters of the Dragon in 42,80. Daredevil in 5,49,81. Death's Head in 76 Devilslayer in 37,46-49. Dr. Strange in 19,20,44,61,79,80. El Aguila in 9. Excalibur in 31-38. Falcon in 23. Firestar in 82-85. Freedom Force in 41. Ghost Rider in 64-71. Gladiator in 49. Havok in 24-31. Hawkeye in 83. Hellcat in 36. Her in 35. Hercules in 12,39-41. Hulk in 6,26,38,45,52,54-61,75. Human Torch in 83. Iron Man in 83,43,51,58,78,82. Ka-Zar in 16. Leir in 30. Le Peregrine in 51. Longshot in 16. Machine Man in 10. Man-Thing in 1-12. Marvel Girl in 15. Master of Kung Fu in 1-8. Fantastic/Invisible Girl in 13. Namorita in 12. Nomad in 14. Nth Man in Overmind in 40. Paladin in 21. Poison in 60,61. Powerman in 82. Puma in 44. Punisher in 59. Quasar in 29. Red Wolf in 15. Rick Jones in 52. Scarlet Witch in 60, Shadowcat and Meggan in 78. Shamrock in 24. Shanna in 13,68-77. She-Hulk in 18. Shooting Star in 45. Sgt. Fury and Dracula in 77-79. Silver Surfer in 1,50. Sirya in 43. Slag in 11. Speedball in 14,56,85. Spiderman 39,48,50. Shroud in 54. Starfox in 22. Stingray in 53-56. Storm and Dr. Doo in 48. Sub-Mariner in 7,33,46,57-59,73,74. Sunfire in 32. Sunspot in 79. The Thing in 3,21. Thor in 4. Triton in 28. Union Jack in 42. Ursa Major in 25. Wasp in 48. Watcher in 17. Werewolf By Night in 54-59. Wheels of Wolfpack in 23. Willie Lumpkin in 18. Wolfsbane and Mirage in 22. Wolverine in 1-10,29,30,38-72. Wonderman in 38-45.

MARVEL DOUBLE FEATURE

Marvel Comics Group; 1 Dec 1973-21 Mar 1977

	$Good	$Fine	$N.Mint	£Good	£Fine	£N.Mint
1 ND Iron Man, Captain America reprints begin from Tales of Suspense #77 onwards	$1.00	$3.00	$5.00	£0.70	£2.10	£3.50
2 ND	$0.60	$1.80	$3.00	£0.40	£1.20	£2.00
3-5 ND	$0.50	$1.50	$2.50	£0.30	£0.90	£1.50
6-16 ND	$0.40	$1.20	$2.00	£0.25	£0.75	£1.25
17 ND reprints Iron Man and Sub-Mariner #1	$0.50	$1.50	$2.50	£0.30	£0.90	£1.50
18-19 ND reprints Iron Man #1	$0.50	$1.50	$2.50	£0.30	£0.90	£1.50
20-21 ND	$0.40	$1.20	$2.00	£0.25	£0.75	£1.25
Title Value:	$9.80	$29.40	$49.00	£6.15	£18.45	£30.75

MARVEL FANFARE

Marvel Comics Group; 1 Mar 1982-60 Dec 1991

	$Good	$Fine	$N.Mint	£Good	£Fine	£N.Mint
1 ND Spiderman/Angel team-up, Paul Smith/Golden art	$1.20	$3.60	$6.00	£0.80	£2.40	£4.00
2 ND Spiderman, Ka-Zar, Angel team, origin FF retold, Golden art	$1.40	$4.20	$7.00	£0.90	£2.70	£4.50
3 ND X-Men, Ka-Zar	$1.20	$3.60	$6.00	£0.80	£2.40	£4.00
4 ND Paul Smith's 1st work on X-Men, Iron Man/Deathlok by Golden	$1.20	$3.60	$6.00	£0.80	£2.40	£4.00
5 ND Dr. Strange by Rogers, Captain America	$0.40	$1.20	$2.00	£0.25	£0.75	£1.25
6 ND Spiderman/Scarlet Witch	$0.40	$1.20	$2.00	£0.25	£0.75	£1.25
7 ND Hulk/Daredevil	$0.40	$1.20	$2.00	£0.25	£0.75	£1.25
8 ND Dr. Strange, Wolf Boy by Sienkiewicz	$0.40	$1.20	$2.00	£0.25	£0.75	£1.25
9 ND Man-Thing by Morrow	$0.40	$1.20	$2.00	£0.25	£0.75	£1.25
10-13 ND Black Widow by George Perez	$0.40	$1.20	$2.00	£0.25	£0.75	£1.25
14 ND Vision and Scarlet Witch, Fantastic Four appear; Inhumans back-up story	$0.40	$1.20	$2.00	£0.25	£0.75	£1.25
15 ND The Thing by Barry Windsor Smith	$0.50	$1.50	$2.50	£0.30	£0.90	£1.50
16 ND Skywolf; Sub-Mariner back-up story	$0.40	$1.20	$2.00	£0.25	£0.75	£1.25
17 ND Skywolf; Hulk back-up story	$0.40	$1.20	$2.00	£0.25	£0.75	£1.25
18 ND Captain America, Frank Miller art	$0.50	$1.50	$2.50	£0.30	£0.90	£1.50
19 ND scarce in the U.K. Cloak & Dagger	$0.50	$1.50	$2.50	£0.30	£0.90	£1.50
20 ND Thing/Hulk, Jim Starlin art	$0.50	$1.50	$2.50	£0.30	£0.90	£1.50
21 ND Thing vs. Hulk, Jim Starlin art	$0.50	$1.50	$2.50	£0.30	£0.90	£1.50
22-23 ND Iron Man Vs Dr Octopus, Steacy art	$0.40	$1.20	$2.00	£0.25	£0.75	£1.25
24 ND Weirdworld, Wolverine, Nick Fury, Binary	$0.50	$1.50	$2.50	£0.30	£0.90	£1.50
25-26 ND Weirdworld, Ploog/Russell art	$0.50	$1.50	$2.50	£0.30	£0.90	£1.50
27 ND Daredevil, Spiderman	$0.50	$1.50	$2.50	£0.30	£0.90	£1.50
28 ND Alpha Flight, Steacy painted cover	$0.50	$1.50	$2.50	£0.30	£0.90	£1.50
29 ND Hulk, John Byrne cover and art	$0.50	$1.50	$2.50	£0.30	£0.90	£1.50
30 ND Moon Knight, Anderson art and painted cover	$0.50	$1.50	$2.50	£0.30	£0.90	£1.50
31-32 ND Captain America	$0.50	$1.50	$2.50	£0.30	£0.90	£1.50
33 ND X-Men	$0.80	$2.40	$4.00	£0.40	£1.20	£2.00
34-37 ND Warriors Three, Vess art	$0.50	$1.50	$2.50	£0.30	£0.90	£1.50
38 ND Rogue/Dazzler, Moon Knight by Sienkewicz	$0.50	$1.50	$2.50	£0.30	£0.90	£1.50
39 ND Hawkeye	$0.50	$1.50	$2.50	£0.30	£0.90	£1.50
40 ND Angel/Storm	$0.50	$1.50	$2.50	£0.30	£0.90	£1.50
41 ND Dr.Strange, Dave Gibbons art and painted cover	$0.50	$1.50	$2.50	£0.30	£0.90	£1.50
42 ND Spiderman	$0.50	$1.50	$2.50	£0.30	£0.90	£1.50
43 ND Submariner, Human Torch, Mignola and Craig Russell art	$0.50	$1.50	$2.50	£0.30	£0.90	£1.50
44 ND Iron Man, Dr Doom; Steacy painted cover	$0.50	$1.50	$2.50	£0.30	£0.90	£1.50
45 ND All pin-up issue. Art by Nowlan, A.Adams, Simonson, Vess, Mignola, Kaluta, Zeck, Ordway and others	$0.50	$1.50	$2.50	£0.30	£0.90	£1.50
46 ND Fantastic Four	$0.50	$1.50	$2.50	£0.30	£0.90	£1.50
47 ND Hulk/Spiderman, Michael Golden art	$0.50	$1.50	$2.50	£0.30	£0.90	£1.50
48 ND She-Hulk, Byrne art	$0.50	$1.50	$2.50	£0.30	£0.90	£1.50
49 ND Dr. Strange, Nick Fury	$0.50	$1.50	$2.50	£0.30	£0.90	£1.50
50 ND X-Factor, pin-up painted pages by Mark Badger	$0.60	$1.80	$3.00	£0.35	£1.05	£1.75
51 ND 48pgs, Silver Surfer, originally meant for first issue of new Surfer series	$0.60	$1.80	$3.00	£0.35	£1.05	£1.75
52-54 ND Black Knight, Mature Readers label	$0.40	$1.20	$2.00	£0.25	£0.75	£1.25
55 ND Power Pack	$0.40	$1.20	$2.00	£0.25	£0.75	£1.25
56 ND Shanna the She-Devil by Steve Gerber, Bret Blevins art begins	$0.40	$1.20	$2.00	£0.25	£0.75	£1.25
57 ND Shanna the She-Devil, new Captain Marvel. Norm Breyfogle art gallery	$0.40	$1.20	$2.00	£0.25	£0.75	£1.25
58 ND Shanna the She-Devil, Vision and Scarlet Witch. Michael Golden art gallery	$0.40	$1.20	$2.00	£0.25	£0.75	£1.25
59 ND Shanna the She-Devil	$0.40	$1.20	$2.00	£0.25	£0.75	£1.25
60 ND	$0.40	$1.20	$2.00	£0.25	£0.75	£1.25
Title Value:	$31.20	$93.60	$156.00	£19.15	£57.45	£95.75

Note: all ND, direct sale, slick paper.

MARVEL FEATURE

Marvel Comics Group; 1 Dec 1971-12 Nov 1973

	$Good	$Fine	$N.Mint	£Good	£Fine	£N.Mint
1 ND 48pgs, squarebound, origin, 1st appearance of The Defenders, 1950s Sub-Mariner reprint, Neal Adams cover	$10.50	$32.00	$75.00	£7.00	£21.00	£50.00
2 ND 48pgs, squarebound, 1950s Sub-Mariner reprint	$7.00	$21.00	$35.00	£4.50	£13.50	£22.50
3 ND Defenders	$6.00	$18.00	$30.00	£4.00	£12.00	£20.00
4 ND Ant-Man begins (1st appearance since 1960s), brief origin, guest stars Peter Parker, Spiderman appears	$3.00	$9.00	$15.00	£2.00	£6.00	£10.00
5-7 ND Ant-Man	$1.20	$3.60	$6.00	£0.80	£2.40	£4.00
8 ND reprints Tales to Astonish #44 (origin Wasp), 3pgs Starlin/Russell art framing sequence	$1.20	$3.60	$6.00	£0.80	£2.40	£4.00
9-10 ND Ant-Man	$1.20	$3.60	$6.00	£0.80	£2.40	£4.00
11 ND Thing/Hulk, Starlin art. 1st Thing team up (pre Marvel Two in One title)	$1.60	$4.80	$8.00	£1.20	£3.60	£6.00
12 ND Thing/Iron Man battle Thanos, Jim Starlin art	$2.40	$7.00	$12.00	£1.50	£4.50	£7.50
Title Value:	$37.70	$113.40		£25.00	£75.00	£140.00

MARVEL FEATURE (2ND SERIES)

Marvel Comics Group; 1 Nov 1975-7 Nov 1976

	$Good	$Fine	$N.Mint	£Good	£Fine	£N.Mint
1 ND Red Sonja begins (history retold), Neal Adams inks (reprint from Savage Sword of Conan)	$0.90	$2.70	$4.50	£0.60	£1.80	£3.00
2-6 Red Sonja	$0.50	$1.50	$2.50	£0.30	£0.90	£1.50
7 Conan appears	$0.50	$1.50	$2.50	£0.30	£0.90	£1.50
Title Value:	$3.90	$11.70	$19.50	£2.40	£7.20	£12.00

MARVEL FRONTIER COMICS UNLIMITED

Marvel UK,OS; 1 Jan 1994

	$Good	$Fine	$N.Mint	£Good	£Fine	£N.Mint
1 64pgs, Bloodseed, Children of the Voyager, Immortalis featured	$0.50	$1.50	$2.50	£0.30	£0.90	£1.50
Title Value:	$0.50	$1.50	$2.50	£0.30	£0.90	£1.50

MARVEL FUMETTI BOOK

Marvel Comics Group,OS; 1 Apr 1984

	$Good	$Fine	$N.Mint	£Good	£Fine	£N.Mint
1 ND photo-strips featuring the Marvel bullpen	$0.25	$0.75	$1.25	£0.15	£0.45	£0.75

MINT = 100% / NEAR MINT (inc. +/-) = 90–99% / VERY FINE (inc. +/-) = 75–89% / FINE (inc. +/-) = 55–74%
VERY GOOD (inc. +/-) = 35–54% / GOOD (inc. +/-) = 15–34% / FAIR = 5–14% / POOR = 1–4%

445

	$Good	$Fine	$N.Mint	£Good	£Fine	£N.Mint
Title Value:	**$0.25**	**$0.75**	**$1.25**	**£0.15**	**£0.45**	**£0.75**

MARVEL GRAPHIC NOVEL

Marvel Comics Group; 1 1982-1993

Title	$Good	$Fine	$N.Mint	£Good	£Fine	£N.Mint
1 DEATH OF CAPTAIN MARVEL						
Jim Starlin art				£3.00	£9.00	£15.00
2nd printing				£1.50	£4.50	£7.50
3rd-5th printings				£0.80	£2.40	£4.00
2 ELRIC: THE DREAMING CITY						
Roy Thomas, P.Craig Russell, scarce in th e U.K.				£1.00	£3.00	£5.00
3 DREADSTAR						
Jim Starlin art				£0.70	£2.10	£3.50
4 NEW MUTANTS						
Claremont & McLeod, origin told				£1.80	£5.40	£9.00
(2nd printing)				£1.00	£3.00	£5.00
(3rd printing. Nov 1990)				£0.80	£2.40	£4.00
5 X-MEN: GOD LOVES, MAN KILLS						
Claremont & Brent Anderson				£1.50	£4.50	£7.50
(2nd printing)				£1.00	£3.00	£5.00
(3rd printing)				£0.90	£2.70	£4.50
(4th printing. Nov 1990)				£0.80	£2.40	£4.00
6 STAR SLAMMERS						
Walt Simonson				£0.70	£2.10	£3.50
7 KILLRAVEN: WARRIOR OF THE WORLDS						
Don McGregor & P.Craig Russell				£0.80	£2.40	£4.00
8 SUPER BOXERS						
Ron Wilson, Byrne, Armando Gil				£0.55	£1.65	£3.75
9 THE FUTURIANS						
Dave Cockrum art				£1.00	£3.00	£5.00
10 HEARTBURST						
				£0.70	£2.10	£3.50
11 VOID INDIGO						
scarce in the U.K.,						
Note: will not be reprinted owing to sexual content/nudity				£1.00	£3.00	£5.00
12 DAZZLER: THE MOVIE						
Shooter, Springer/Coletta, scarce in the U.K.				£1.00	£3.00	£5.00
13 STARSTRUCK						
Mike Kaluta				£0.70	£2.10	£3.50
14 SWORDS OF THE SWASHBUCKLERS						
scarce in the U.K.				£0.80	£2.40	£4.00
15 THE RAVEN BANNER (Tales of Asgard)						
A.Zelenetz, Charles Vess				£0.70	£2.10	£3.50
16 THE ALADDIN EFFECT, Shooter, Michelinie						
LaRocque, Colletta				£0.70	£2.10	£3.50
17 REVENGE OF THE LIVING MONOLITH						
Michelinie, Silvestri, Isherwood				£0.70	£2.10	£3.50
nn SENSATIONAL SHE-HULK						
Byrne, DeMulder, Scotese				£1.10	£3.30	£5.50
(2nd printing – Sep 1991)				£1.00	£3.00	£5.00
nn CONAN: THE WITCH QUEEN OF ARCHERON						
Don Kraar, Gary Kwapisz, Art Nichols				£0.80	£2.40	£4.00
nn GREENBERG THE VAMPIRE						
DeMatteis & Badger				£1.00	£3.00	£5.00
nn MARADA THE SHE-WOLF						
Claremont & Bolton				£1.00	£3.00	£5.00
nn AMAZING SPIDERMAN: HOOKEY						
Sue Putney & Bernie Wrightson				£1.20	£3.60	£6.00
nn INTO SHAMBALLA (Dr.Strange)						
DeMatteis & Dan Green				£0.65	£1.95	£3.25
nn DAREDEVIL: LOVE AND WAR						
Miller script Sienkiewicz art				£1.00	£3.00	£5.00
nn DRACULA: A SYMPHONY IN MOONLIGHT AND NIGHTMARES						
Jon J. Muth				£0.70	£2.10	£3.50
(2nd printing)				£0.60	£1.80	£3.00
nn ALIEN LEGION						
Potts, Cirocco, Austin				£0.80	£2.40	£4.00
nn EMPEROR DOOM						
Michelinie & Bob Hall				£0.65	£1.95	£3.25
nn CONAN THE REAVER, Kraar,						
John & Marie Severin				£0.65	£1.95	£3.25
nn THING AND THE HULK: THE BIG CHANGE						
Starlin & Wrightson				£0.65	£1.95	£3.25
nn A SAILOR'S STORY						
Sam Glanzman				£0.65	£1.95	£3.25
nn WOLFPACK						
Hama, Wilson & Kyle Baker (1st appearance of Wolfpack)				£1.00	£3.00	£5.00
nn THE DEATH OF GROO						
(see Life of Groo further down) Aragones, Evanier				£0.65	£1.95	£3.25
nn THOR: I WHOM THE GODS WOULD DESTROY						
Shooter, Owsley, Ryan, Colletta				£0.65	£1.95	£3.25
nn CLOAK AND DAGGER: PREDATOR AND PREY						
Mantlo, Stroman, Williamson				£0.65	£1.95	£3.25
nn THE SHADOW: HITLER'S ASTROLOGER						
O'Neill, Kaluta, Heath (hardback, with dust-jacket)				£2.00	£6.00	£10.00
nn CRASH: IRON MAN						
Mike Saenz				£1.40	£4.20	£7.00
(2nd printing – 1991)				£1.20	£3.60	£6.00
nn WILLOW						
Duggy, Hall and Tanghal				£0.65	£1.95	£3.25
nn LAST OF THE DRAGONS						
Potts, O'Neill, Austin, Severin				£0.65	£1.95	£3.25
nn SILVER SURFER: JUDGEMENT DAY						
Stan Lee & Buscema (hardback, with dustjacket)				£2.00	£6.00	£10.00
nn SOMEPLACE STRANGE						
Nocenti, Bolton softback				£0.70	£2.10	£3.50
nn HERCULES: FULL CIRCLE						
Bob Layton				£0.65	£1.95	£3.25
nn THE INHUMANS						
Nocenti, Blevins, Williamson				£0.70	£2.10	£3.50
nn THE PUNISHER: ASSASSINS GUILD						
Duffy, Jorge Zaffino, Julie Michel				£1.20	£3.60	£6.00
nn PUNISHER HARDCOVER GRAPHIC NOVEL						
Steven Grant and Mike Zeck, all new material				£2.20	£6.60	£11.00
nn CONAN OF THE ISLES						
adapts Carter/ DeCamp novel				£0.80	£2.40	£4.00
nn ARENA Bruce Jones story and art				£0.65	£1.95	£3.25
nn WHO FRAMED ROGER RABBIT?						
Daan Jippes, Ferguson, Speigle. Marvel edition				£0.65	£1.95	£3.25
London Editions (U.K.), comic-sized, distributed				£0.20	£0.60	£1.00
nn AX						
Ernie Colon art				£0.65	£1.95	£3.25
nn DREAMWALKER						
(announced as DREAMWEAVER) Billy Mumy/Miguel Ferrer script				£0.65	£1.95	£3.25
nn KING KULL						
				£0.65	£1.95	£3.25
nn DR. DOOM/DR. STRANGE,						
Mignola and Badger art (Hardcover)				£2.20	£6.60	£11.00
nn NICK FURY/WOLVERINE						
(Hardcover) Chaykin art				£2.10	£6.30	£10.50
(2nd printing – 1991)				£2.00	£6.00	£10.00
nn A SAILOR'S STORY 2						
Sam Glanzman				£0.65	£1.95	£3.25
nn VOYAGER						
John Ridgway art, reprints Dr. Who Magazine #88, 89				£0.80	£2.40	£4.00
nn CONAN: THE SKULL OF SET						
				£0.70	£2.10	£3.50
nn THE SQUADRON SUPREME						
Williamson art				£0.90	£2.70	£4.50
nn ROGER RABBIT: THE RESSURRECTION OF DOOM				£0.70	£2.10	£3.50
nn SPIDERMAN: PARALLEL LIVES,						
Alex Saviuk art, Dr. Octopus appears				£0.80	£2.40	£4.00
nn PUNISHER: INTRUDER						
(Hardcover) Mike Baron/Bill Reinhold				£2.00	£6.00	£10.00
nn SOMEPLACE STRANGE						
(Limited) (1,200 copies) Hardback, signed and numbered;						
Ann Nocenti and John Bolton				£4.00	£12.00	£20.00
nn CLOAK AND DAGGER/POWER PACK						
Mantlo, Velluto and Farmer				£0.80	£2.40	£4.00
nn NEUROMANCER,						
adaptation of novel by William Gibson				£0.80	£2.40	£4.00
nn THE AGENT						
80pgs, John Ridgway art (Rick Mason as The Agent)				£0.80	£2.40	£4.00
nn RIO						
Doug Wildey script/art				£1.00	£3.00	£5.00
nn SILVER SURFER: THE ENSLAVERS						
(Hardcover)				£1.75	£5.25	£8.75
nn JHEREG						
adaptation of novel by Steven Brust				£0.90	£2.70	£4.50
nn CONAN: THE HORN OF AZOTH				£1.00	£3.00	£5.00
nn BLACK WIDOW: THE COLDEST WAR						
Daredevil/Avengers appear				£1.00	£3.00	£5.00
nn SILVER SURFER: JUDGEMENT DAY						
(Softcover) reprints Hardcover edition				£1.00	£3.00	£5.00
nn DR. DOOM/DR. STRANGE						
(Softcover) Mignola/Badger art				£1.00	£3.00	£5.00
nn KA-ZAR: GUNS OF THE SAVAGE LAND						
Dixon/Truman				£1.00	£3.00	£5.00
nn NICK FURY/WOLVERINE: THE SCORPIO CONNECTION						
Softcover reprint of Hardback Goodwin/Chaykin				£1.25	£3.75	£6.25
(2nd print – Nov 1990)				£1.20	£3.60	£6.00
nn ABSALOM DAAK – DALEK KILLER				£1.10	£3.30	£5.50
nn SPIDERMAN: SPIRITS OF THE EARTH						
(Hardcover), painted Vess art				£2.00	£6.00	£10.00
nn PUNISHER: KINGDOM GONE						
(Hardcover) C. Dixon and Zaffino				£2.00	£6.00	£10.00
nn DEATH'S HEAD: THE BODY IN QUESTION						
Walt Simonson cover, reprints Death's Head serial from Strip #13-20				£0.90	£2.70	£4.50
nn X-MEN: PRYDE OF THE X-MEN						
(see Trade paperbacks) based on cartoon				£1.00	£3.00	£5.00
nn PUNISHER: RETURN TO BIG NOTHING						
softcover of Hardback version				£1.20	£3.60	£6.00
nn EXCALIBUR: WEIRD WAR III				£0.90	£2.70	£4.50
nn ELEKTRA LIVES AGAIN						
(Hardcover) Frank Miller story/art				£3.00	£9.00	£15.00
(2nd print – 1991)				£2.90	£8.70	£14.50
nn HEARTS AND MINDS						
Doug Murray script, Russ Heath art				£1.00	£3.00	£5.00
nn SPIDERMAN: FEAR ITSELF						
Conway Andru and Esposito				£1.10	£3.30	£5.50
nn WOLVERINE: BLOODY CHOICES						
DeFalco and John Buscema, Nick Fury co-stars				£1.60	£4.80	£8.00
(2nd print – Sep 1993)				£1.50	£4.50	£7.50
nn AVENGERS – DEATHTRAP: THE VAULT						
Fingeroth, Lim and Emberlin				£1.20	£3.60	£6.00
nn NIGHTRAVEN : HOUSE OF CARDS						
Jamie Delano, David Lloyd				£1.85	£5.55	£9.25
nn CONAN THE ROGUE						
Roy Thomas, John Buscema				£1.10	£3.30	£5.50

	$Good	$Fine	$N.Mint	£Good	£Fine	£N.Mint

nn SILVER SURFER: HOMECOMING
Starlin and Reinhold — £1.60 / £4.80 / £8.00

nn WAR MAN
Dixon and Zanotto — £1.10 / £3.30 / £5.50

nn PUNISHER: BLOOD ON THE MOORS
(Hardcover) Alan Grant, John Wagner, Cam Kennedy — £2.10 / £6.30 / £10.50

nn BOY'S RANCH HARDCOVER
Jack Kirby and Joe Simon — £5.00 / £15.00 / £25.00

nn CONAN AND THE RAVAGERS OF TIME
Roy Thomas, Docherty & Alcala — £1.10 / £3.30 / £5.50

nn PUNISHER/BLACK WIDOW: SPINNING DOOMSDAY'S WEB
48pgs, Larry Stroman and Mark Farmer — £1.25 / £3.75 / £6.25

nn LIFE OF GROO
(May 1993 – originally solicited in 1991), Aragones and Evanier — £1.60 / £4.80 / £8.00

nn DAREDEVIL/BLACK WIDOW: ABATTOIR
(Sep 1993) Jim Starlin script, Joe Chiodo art — £2.00 / £6.00 / £10.00

Note: all of the above are Non Distributed on the news-stands in the U.K.

MARVEL GUIDE TO COLLECTING COMICS
Marvel Comics Group,OS; 1 1982
1 ND features on comic book collecting, first appeared in Spiderman #234, paper cover

	$Good	$Fine	$N.Mint	£Good	£Fine	£N.Mint
	$0.40	$1.20	$2.00	£0.25	£0.75	£1.25
Title Value:	$0.40	$1.20	$2.00	£0.25	£0.75	£1.25

MARVEL HOLIDAY SPECIAL
Marvel Comics Group; 1 Jan 1992; 2 Jan 1994; 3 Jan 1995
1 ND 64pgs, squarebound; X-Men, Captain America, Fantastic Four, Thor, Spiderman, Ghost Rider and others in Xmas season stories, cover by Art Adams (Note: many copies have crinkled spines)

	$Good	$Fine	$N.Mint	£Good	£Fine	£N.Mint
	$0.50	$1.50	$2.50	£0.30	£0.90	£1.50

2 ND 64pgs, Thanos and Wolverine appear in Christmas reprints

	$0.50	$1.50	$2.50	£0.30	£0.90	£1.50

3 ND 64pgs, X-Men, Thing, Beast and Iceman appear in Christmas reprints

	$0.50	$1.50	$2.50	£0.30	£0.90	£1.50
Title Value:	$1.50	$4.50	$7.50	£0.90	£2.70	£4.50

MARVEL ILLUSTRATED BOOKS
Marvel Comics Group; nn 1982
nn ND Frankenstein; 40 illustrations by Bernie Wrightson

	$Good	$Fine	$N.Mint	£Good	£Fine	£N.Mint
	$0.90	$2.70	$4.50	£0.60	£1.80	£3.00
Title Value:	$0.90	$2.70	$4.50	£0.60	£1.80	£3.00

MARVEL ILLUSTRATED SWIMSUIT SPECIAL
Marvel Comics Group,Magazine OS; 1 Mar 1991
nn ND magazine format; Lee, Guice, Nowlan, Perez and Zeck art featured

	$Good	$Fine	$N.Mint	£Good	£Fine	£N.Mint
	$0.80	$2.40	$4.00	£0.50	£1.50	£2.50

nn ND magazine format, (2nd print – Sep 1991)

	$0.80	$2.40	$4.00	£0.50	£1.50	£2.50
Title Value:	$1.60	$4.80	$8.00	£1.00	£3.00	£5.00

MARVEL MASTERPIECES COLLECTION, THE
Marvel Comics Group,MS; 1 May 1993-4 Aug 1993
1-4 ND Joe Jusko's Marvel Masterpieces trading cards reprinted in comic book format; each issue also has half a dozen new paintings

	$Good	$Fine	$N.Mint	£Good	£Fine	£N.Mint
	$0.60	$1.80	$3.00	£0.40	£1.20	£2.00
Title Value:	$2.40	$7.20	$12.00	£1.60	£4.80	£8.00

MARVEL MASTERPIECES COLLECTION 2, THE
Marvel Comics Group,MS; 1 Jul 1994-3 Sep 1994
1-3 ND reprints another collection of Marvel trading cards

	$Good	$Fine	$N.Mint	£Good	£Fine	£N.Mint
	$0.50	$1.50	$2.50	£0.30	£0.90	£1.50
Title Value:	$1.50	$4.50	$7.50	£0.90	£2.70	£4.50

MARVEL MASTERPIECES PREVIEW
Marvel Comics Group,OS; nn Dec 1995
nn ND previews Fleer's painted trading card set

	$Good	$Fine	$N.Mint	£Good	£Fine	£N.Mint
	$0.60	$1.80	$3.00	£0.40	£1.20	£2.00
Title Value:	$0.60	$1.80	$3.00	£0.40	£1.20	£2.00

MARVEL MASTERWORKS
Marvel Comics Group; 1 Nov 1987-present?

	$Good	$Fine	$N.Mint	£Good	£Fine	£N.Mint

1 less common in the U.K. Spiderman #1-#10, Amazing Fantasy #15 (1st printing)

	$9.00	$27.00	$45.00	£6.00	£18.00	£30.00

1 subsequent printings (3rd-7th)(7th print in Oct 1994)

	$6.00	$18.00	$30.00	£4.00	£12.00	£20.00

1 Spiderman #1-#10, Amazing Fantasy #15 softcover (May 1992)

	$2.50	$7.50	$12.50	£1.50	£4.50	£7.50

1 Spiderman #1-#10, Amazing Fantasy #15 softcover 2nd print (May 1993)

	$2.50	$7.50	$12.50	£1.50	£4.50	£7.50

1 2nd printing	$7.50	$22.50	$37.50	£5.00	£15.00	£25.00

2 Fantastic Four #1-#10

	$7.50	$22.50	$37.50	£5.00	£15.00	£25.00

3 X-Men #1-#10	$6.00	$18.00	$30.00	£4.00	£12.00	£20.00

3 X-Men #1-#10, 2nd print (Jun 1994)

	$6.00	$18.00	$30.00	£4.00	£12.00	£20.00

3 X-Men #1-#5 softcover (Apr 1993), new intro by Stan Lee

	$2.50	$7.50	$12.50	£1.50	£4.50	£7.50

4 Avengers #1-#10

	$6.00	$18.00	$30.00	£4.00	£12.00	£20.00

4 Avengers #1-5 softcover (Dec 1993)

	$2.50	$7.50	$12.50	£1.50	£4.50	£7.50

5 Spiderman #11-#20

	$6.00	$18.00	$30.00	£4.00	£12.00	£20.00

6 Fantastic Four #11-#20

	$6.00	$18.00	$30.00	£4.00	£12.00	£20.00

7 X-Men #11-#21	$6.00	$18.00	$30.00	£4.00	£12.00	£20.00

8 Incredible Hulk #1-#6

	$6.00	$18.00	$30.00	£4.00	£12.00	£20.00

9 Avengers #11-#20

	$6.00	$18.00	$30.00	£4.00	£12.00	£20.00

10 Spiderman #21-#30, Annual #1

	$6.00	$18.00	$30.00	£4.00	£12.00	£20.00

11 Giant Size X-Men #1, X-Men #94-#100

	$6.00	$18.00	$30.00	£4.00	£12.00	£20.00

11 Giant Size X-Men #1, X-Men #94-97 (Oct 1993); titled "X-Men: All New, All Different X-Men Masterworks Vol. 1"

	$2.50	$7.50	$12.50	£1.50	£4.50	£7.50

12 X-Men #101-#110	$6.00	$18.00	$30.00	£4.00	£12.00	£20.00

13 Fantastic Four #21-#30, Annual #1

	$6.00	$18.00	$30.00	£4.00	£12.00	£20.00

14 Tales of Suspense #59-#81

	$6.00	$18.00	$30.00	£4.00	£12.00	£20.00

15 Silver Surfer #1-#5

	$6.00	$18.00	$30.00	£4.00	£12.00	£20.00

16 Spiderman #31-#40, Annual #2

	$6.00	$18.00	$30.00	£4.00	£12.00	£20.00

17 Daredevil #1-#11

	$6.00	$18.00	$30.00	£4.00	£12.00	£20.00

18 Journey Into Mystery #83-#100

	$6.00	$18.00	$30.00	£4.00	£12.00	£20.00

19 Silver Surfer #6-#18

	$8.50	$26.00	$42.50	£5.50	£16.50	£27.50

20 Tales of Suspense #39-#50

	$6.00	$18.00	$30.00	£4.00	£12.00	£20.00

21 Fantastic Four #31-#40, Annual #2

	$6.00	$18.00	$30.00	£4.00	£12.00	£20.00

22 Spiderman #41-#50, Annual #3

	$6.00	$18.00	$30.00	£4.00	£12.00	£20.00

23 Strange Tales #110,#111,#114-141

Marvel Comics Presents #2

Marvel Feature (1st) #2

Marvel Guide to Collecting Comics

	$Good	$Fine	$N.Mint	£Good	£Fine	£N.Mint

	$Good	$Fine	$N.Mint	£Good	£Fine	£N.Mint
	$7.50	$22.50	$37.50	£5.00	£15.00	£25.00
24 Uncanny X-Men #111-120						
	$7.50	$22.50	$37.50	£5.00	£15.00	£25.00
25 Fantastic Four #41-50, Annual #3						
	$7.50	$22.50	$37.50	£5.00	£15.00	£25.00
26 Journey Into Mystery #101-110						
	$7.50	$22.50	$37.50	£5.00	£15.00	£25.00
27 Avengers #21-30						
	$7.50	$22.50	$37.50	£5.00	£15.00	£25.00
Title Value:	$208.50	$626.00	$1042.50	£138.00	£414.00	£690.00

MARVEL MINI BOOKS

Marvel Comics Group; nn 1966
(six different un-numbered issues)
Captain America, Spiderman, Hulk, Millie the Model, Thor, Sgt.Fury

				£Good	£Fine	£N.Mint
all Non-Distributed in the U.K.: each one				£0.50	£1.50	£3.00

Note: all 22mm x 16mm; smallest comics ever?

MARVEL MINI COMICS

Marvel Comics Group; nn Aug 1989
nn ND Spiderman, X-Men, Alf and Flinstone Kids comics available

	$Good	$Fine	$N.Mint	£Good	£Fine	£N.Mint
	$0.15	$0.45	$0.75	£0.10	£0.35	£0.60
Title Value:	$0.15	$0.45	$0.75	£0.10	£0.35	£0.60

Note: all intended for U.S. schools. Amazing Spiderman #1 is reprinted in the Spiderman comic as the 2nd story

MARVEL MOVIE PREMIERE

Marvel Comics Group,Magazine; 1 Sep 1975
1 ND scarce in the U.K. 68pgs, adapts Burroughs' Land That Time Forgot

	$Good	$Fine	$N.Mint	£Good	£Fine	£N.Mint
	$1.50	$4.50	$7.50	£1.20	£3.60	£6.00
Title Value:	$1.50	$4.50	$7.50	£1.20	£3.60	£6.00

MARVEL MOVIE SHOWCASE

Marvel Comics Group; 1 Nov 1982-2 Dec 1982
1 ND 68pgs, reprints Star Wars #1-3

	$Good	$Fine	$N.Mint	£Good	£Fine	£N.Mint
	$0.40	$1.20	$2.00	£0.25	£0.75	£1.25
2 ND 68pgs, reprints Star Wars #4-6						
	$0.40	$1.20	$2.00	£0.25	£0.75	£1.25
Title Value:	$0.80	$2.40	$4.00	£0.50	£1.50	£2.50

MARVEL MOVIE SPOTLIGHT

Marvel Comics Group; 1 Nov 1982
1 ND 68pgs, reprints Raiders of the Lost Ark

	$Good	$Fine	$N.Mint	£Good	£Fine	£N.Mint
	$0.40	$1.20	$2.00	£0.25	£0.75	£1.25
Title Value:	$0.40	$1.20	$2.00	£0.25	£0.75	£1.25

MARVEL MYSTERY #1 HARDCOVER

Marvel Comics Group; nn Dec 1990
nn ND reprints in full the first Marvel comic in the Golden Age with the Human Torch and Sub-Mariner;

	$Good	$Fine	$N.Mint	£Good	£Fine	£N.Mint
hardcover	$2.50	$7.50	$12.50	£1.50	£4.50	£7.50
Title Value:	$2.50	$7.50	$12.50	£1.50	£4.50	£7.50

MARVEL NO-PRIZE BOOK, THE

Marvel Comics Group,OS; 1 Jan 1983
1 ND Marvel's mistakes, Michael Golden Stan Lee/Dr.Doom cover

	$Good	$Fine	$N.Mint	£Good	£Fine	£N.Mint
	$0.30	$0.90	$1.50	£0.20	£0.60	£1.00
Title Value:	$0.30	$0.90	$1.50	£0.20	£0.60	£1.00

MARVEL PREMIERE

Marvel Comics Group; 1 Apr 1972-61 Aug 1981
1 ND origin Warlock, first appearance as a super-hero; Thor, Hulk and Fantastic Four cameos
(pre-dates Warlock #1)

	$Good	$Fine	$N.Mint	£Good	£Fine	£N.Mint
	$7.75	$23.50	$47.50	£5.00	£15.00	£30.00
2 ND Warlock, Gil Kane art, Jack Kirby reprint						
	$4.55	$13.50	$27.50	£2.90	£8.75	£17.50
3 ND Dr. Strange begins, Barry Smith art						
	$4.15	$12.50	$25.00	£2.50	£7.50	£15.00
4 ND Smith/Brunner art						
	$2.05	$6.25	$12.50	£1.25	£3.75	£7.50
5 ND	$1.50	$4.50	$9.00	£1.00	£3.00	£6.00
6 ND Brunner art	$1.25	$3.75	$7.50	£0.80	£2.50	£5.00
7 ND P. Craig Russell art						
	$1.25	$3.75	$7.50	£0.80	£2.50	£5.00
8 ND Jim Starlin/P. Craig Russell art						
	$1.25	$3.75	$7.50	£0.80	£2.50	£5.00
9 ND Brunner art	$1.25	$3.75	$7.50	£0.80	£2.50	£5.00
10 ND Brunner art, death of The Ancient One						
	$1.50	$4.50	$9.00	£1.00	£3.00	£6.00
11 ND reprints Dr. Strange origin by Steve Ditko						
	$0.80	$2.50	$5.00	£0.65	£2.00	£4.00
12-13 ND Brunner art						
	$0.80	$2.50	$5.00	£0.65	£2.00	£4.00
14 ND Frank Brunner, Neal Adams art						
	$0.80	$2.50	$5.00	£0.65	£2.00	£4.00
15 ND origin & 1st appearance of Iron Fist; Gil Kane art						
	$8.25	$25.00	$50.00	£5.75	£17.50	£35.00
16 ND 2nd appearance Iron Fist						
	$2.50	$7.50	$15.00	£1.65	£5.00	£10.00
17 ND	$2.05	$6.25	$12.50	£1.25	£3.75	£7.50
18-20 ND	$2.05	$6.25	$12.50	£1.00	£3.00	£6.00
21 ND scarce in the U.K.						
	$2.05	$6.25	$12.50	£1.05	£3.25	£6.50
22	$2.05	$6.25	$12.50	£0.80	£2.50	£5.00
23 ND scarce in the U.K.						
	$2.05	$6.25	$12.50	£1.00	£3.00	£6.00
24	$2.05	$6.25	$12.50	£0.80	£2.50	£5.00
25 ND 1st John Byrne art on Iron Fist						
	$2.90	$8.75	$17.50	£1.65	£5.00	£10.00
26 Hercules	$0.70	$2.10	$3.50	£0.30	£0.90	£1.50
27 Satana, Daughter of Satan						
	$0.70	$2.10	$3.50	£0.30	£0.90	£1.50

	$Good	$Fine	$N.Mint	£Good	£Fine	£N.Mint
28 Legion of Monsters – Ghost Rider, Werewolf, Man-Thing and Morbius (on cover also)						
	$2.50	$7.50	$12.50	£1.20	£3.60	£6.00
29 Liberty Legion, ties into Invaders #6						
	$0.40	$1.20	$2.00	£0.25	£0.75	£1.25
30 Liberty Legion	$0.40	$1.20	$2.00	£0.25	£0.75	£1.25
31 Woodgod, Giffen art						
	$0.40	$1.20	$2.00	£0.25	£0.75	£1.25
32 Monark Moonstalker, Chaykin art						
	$0.40	$1.20	$2.00	£0.25	£0.75	£1.25
33-34 Solomon Kane, Chaykin art						
	$0.40	$1.20	$2.00	£0.25	£0.75	£1.25
35 ND 1st appearance 3-D Man						
	$0.40	$1.20	$2.00	£0.25	£0.75	£1.25
36-37 ND 3-D Man						
	$0.40	$1.20	$2.00	£0.25	£0.75	£1.25
38 Weirdworld, Ploog art						
	$0.40	$1.20	$2.00	£0.25	£0.75	£1.25
39-40 The Torpedo						
	$0.40	$1.20	$2.00	£0.25	£0.75	£1.25
41 Seeker 3000	$0.40	$1.20	$2.00	£0.25	£0.75	£1.25
42 Tigra	$0.40	$1.20	$2.00	£0.25	£0.75	£1.25
43 Paladin	$0.40	$1.20	$2.00	£0.25	£0.75	£1.25
44 Jack of Hearts (1st solo story); some Giffen art						
	$0.40	$1.20	$2.00	£0.25	£0.75	£1.25
45-46 Man-Wolf, George Perez art						
	$0.40	$1.20	$2.00	£0.25	£0.75	£1.25
47 1st new Ant-Man, John Byrne art						
	$0.40	$1.20	$2.00	£0.25	£0.75	£1.25
48 Byrne art, Ant-Man						
	$0.40	$1.20	$2.00	£0.25	£0.75	£1.25
49 The Falcon; Captain America appears						
	$0.40	$1.20	$2.00	£0.25	£0.75	£1.25
50 Alice Cooper	$1.00	$3.00	$5.00	£0.70	£2.10	£3.50
51-53 Black Panther						
	$0.40	$1.20	$2.00	£0.25	£0.75	£1.25
54 Caleb Hammer, Chaykin art						
	$0.40	$1.20	$2.00	£0.25	£0.75	£1.25
55 Wonder Man	$0.40	$1.20	$2.00	£0.25	£0.75	£1.25
56 Dominic Fortune, Chaykin art						
	$0.40	$1.20	$2.00	£0.25	£0.75	£1.25
57 Dr. Who (1st U.S. appearance), Gibbons reprints begin, Simonson cover						
	$0.40	$1.50	$2.50	£0.30	£0.90	£1.50
58 ND Dr. Who	$0.40	$1.20	$2.00	£0.25	£0.75	£1.25
59 ND Dr. Who; Werewolf back-up story by Steven Grant						
	$0.40	$1.20	$2.00	£0.25	£0.75	£1.25
60 ND Dr. Who; Walt Simonson art on pin-ups						
	$0.40	$1.20	$2.00	£0.25	£0.75	£1.25
61 Starlord	$0.40	$1.20	$2.00	£0.25	£0.75	£1.25
Title Value:	$77.55	$234.40	$452.00	£46.95	£142.15	£273.75

FEATURES

Black Panther in 51-53. Caleb Hammer in 54. Dominic Fortune in 56. Falcon in 49. Jack of Hearts in 44.
Paladin in 43. Seeker 3000 in 41. 3-D Man in 35-37. Tigra in 42. Torpedo in 39, 40. Wonder Man in 55.

MARVEL PRESENTS

Marvel Comics Group; 1 Oct 1975-12 Aug 1977
1 1st appearance Bloodstone

	$Good	$Fine	$N.Mint	£Good	£Fine	£N.Mint
	$0.75	$2.25	$4.50	£0.50	£1.50	£3.00
2 Bloodstone origin						
	$0.50	$1.50	$3.00	£0.30	£1.00	£2.00
3 Guardians of the Galaxy begin, Steve Gerber scripts begin						
	$2.50	$7.50	$15.00	£1.25	£3.75	£7.50
4-7 Guardians of the Galaxy						
	$1.65	$5.00	$10.00	£0.80	£2.50	£5.00
8 Guardians of the Galaxy, Silver Surfer part reprint (issue 2, 1st series)						
	$2.50	$7.50	$15.00	£0.80	£2.50	£5.00
9 Guardians of the Galaxy						
	$1.65	$5.00	$10.00	£0.80	£2.50	£5.00
10 ND Guardians of the Galaxy, part Jim Starlin art						
	$1.65	$5.00	$10.00	£0.80	£2.50	£5.00
11-12 ND Guardians of the Galaxy						
	$1.65	$5.00	$10.00	£0.80	£2.50	£5.00
Title Value:	$19.45	$58.75	$117.50	£9.25	£28.75	£57.50

MARVEL PREVIEW

Marvel Comics Group,Magazine; 1 1975-24 Feb 1981
(becomes Bizarre Adventures)
1 scarce in the U.K. 82pgs, squarebound, Man Gods from Beyond the Stars; Doug Moench script,
Alex Nino art; Neal Adams art on cover; all black and white art from now on

	$Good	$Fine	$N.Mint	£Good	£Fine	£N.Mint
	$0.80	$2.40	$4.00		£1.50	£2.50
2 LD in the U.K. 82pgs, squarebound; origin The Punisher, 1st appearance Dominic Fortune (Chaykin art)						
	$15.50	$47.00	$110.00	£8.50	£26.00	£60.00
3 82pgs, squarebound, Blade the Vampire Slayer						
	$0.50	$1.50	$2.50	£0.30	£0.90	£1.50
4 74pgs, squarebound, 1st appearance Starlord, Steve Englehart script						
	$0.50	$1.50	$2.50	£0.30	£0.90	£1.50
5 Sherlock Holmes; adaptation of Hound of the Baskervilles by Doug Moench and Val Mayerik						
	$0.50	$1.50	$2.50	£0.30	£0.90	£1.50
6 Sherlock Holmes	$0.50	$1.50	$2.50	£0.30	£0.90	£1.50
7 Satana by Nasser and Sword in the Star by Giffen						
	$0.50	$1.50	$2.50	£0.30	£0.90	£1.50
8 Legion of Monsters (featuring Morbius and Blade), Colan/Ploog art; Sword in the Star by Giffen						
	$0.50	$1.50	$2.50	£0.60	£1.80	£3.00
9 Man-God by Roy Thomas and Tony DeZuniga; Earl Norem painted cover						
	$0.50	$1.50	$2.50	£0.30	£0.90	£1.50

	$Good	$Fine	$N.Mint	£Good	£Fine	£N.Mint

10 Thor, Jim Starlin art; Hercules back-up story
| | $0.50 | $1.50 | $2.50 | £0.30 | £0.90 | £1.50 |

11 Starlord; Chris Claremont script, John Byrne art
| | $0.50 | $1.50 | $2.50 | £0.30 | £0.90 | £1.50 |

12 Haunt of Horror featuring Dracula; Lilith story has 2pgs of George Perez art
| | $0.50 | $1.50 | $2.50 | £0.30 | £0.90 | £1.50 |

13 UFO Connection; Jim Starlin cover
| | $0.50 | $1.50 | $2.50 | £0.30 | £0.90 | £1.50 |

14 Starlord; Carmine Infantino art and Jim Starlin cover
| | $0.50 | $1.50 | $2.50 | £0.30 | £0.90 | £1.50 |

15 Starlord; Carmine Infantino art and Joe Jusko cover
| | $0.50 | $1.50 | $2.50 | £0.30 | £0.90 | £1.50 |

16 Masters of Terror featuring Hodiah Twist and Lilith
| | $0.50 | $1.50 | $2.50 | £0.30 | £0.90 | £1.50 |

17 Black Mark by Gil Kane
| | $0.50 | $1.50 | $2.50 | £0.30 | £0.90 | £1.50 |

18 ND Starlord
| | $0.50 | $1.50 | $2.50 | £0.30 | £0.90 | £1.50 |

19 ND Kull by Buscema/DeZuniga
| | $0.50 | $1.50 | $2.50 | £0.30 | £0.90 | £1.50 |

20 ND Bizarre Adventures featuring Dominic Fortune; Howard Chaykin cover and art
| | $0.50 | $1.50 | $2.50 | £0.30 | £0.90 | £1.50 |

21 ND Moon Knight, Sienkiewicz art; The Shroud back-up story by Steve Ditko
| | $1.00 | $3.00 | $5.00 | £0.70 | £2.10 | £3.50 |

22 ND Merlin by Doug Moench and John Buscema; Earl Norem painted cover
| | $0.50 | $1.50 | $2.50 | £0.30 | £0.90 | £1.50 |

23 ND Bizarre Adventures; Frank Miller art
| | $1.00 | $3.00 | $5.00 | £0.70 | £2.10 | £3.50 |

24 ND 1st appearance Paradox; Val Mayerik art, Paul Gulacy cover
| | $0.50 | $1.50 | $2.50 | £0.30 | £0.90 | £1.50 |

Title Value: $29.30 $88.40 $179.00 £16.70 £50.60 £101.00
ARTISTS
Adams art in 6 (1pg). Ditko in 21. Ploog in 8. Wrightson in 4 (1pg).

MARVEL PREVIEW 1993
Marvel Comics Group,Magazine OS; 1 Mar 1993

1 ND 48pgs, previews The Infinity Crusade and X-Men's 30th anniversary comics
| | $0.60 | $1.80 | $3.00 | £0.40 | £1.20 | £2.00 |

Title Value: $0.60 $1.80 $3.00 £0.40 £1.20 £2.00

MARVEL RIOT
Marvel Comics Group,OS; 1 Dec 1995

1 ND X-Men Age of Apocalypse spoof by Scott Lobdell, wraparound cover by Hilary Barta
| | $0.30 | $0.90 | $1.50 | £0.20 | £0.60 | £1.00 |

Title Value: $0.30 $0.90 $1.50 £0.20 £0.60 £1.00

MARVEL SAGA, THE
Marvel Comics Group; 1 Dec 1985-25 Dec 1987

1 ND new cameo origins of the major Marvel characters (5pgs); also part reprint Fantastic Four #1 and #2, Tales to Astonish #27 and reprint origin Guardian from Alpha Flight #12
| | $0.40 | $1.20 | $2.00 | £0.25 | £0.75 | £1.25 |

2 ND part reprints of Spiderman's origin from Amazing Fantasy #15, Hulk's origin from Hulk #1 and Sub-Mariner from Fantastic Four #4
| | $0.40 | $1.20 | $2.00 | £0.25 | £0.75 | £1.25 |

3 ND origin Dr. Doom re-told and history of Sub-Mariner from a variety of part reprints, conclusion origin Spiderman part reprinted from Amazing Fantasy #15
| | $0.40 | $1.20 | $2.00 | £0.25 | £0.75 | £1.25 |

4 ND origin and history of X-Men re-told from a variety of reprint sources, origin Thor part reprint Journey into Mystery #83, origin Ant-Man in costume from Tales to Astonish #35
| | $0.40 | $1.20 | $2.00 | £0.25 | £0.75 | £1.25 |

5 ND part reprints Fantastic Four #6,#7, Hulk #3, Strange Tales #101; origins Angel, Iceman and Loki from a variety of reprint sources
| | $0.40 | $1.20 | $2.00 | £0.25 | £0.75 | £1.25 |

6 ND origins of Iron Man, Odin, Asgard and the Puppet Master from a variety of reprint sources; origins Iceman and Cyclops reprinted from X-Men 44-46
| | $0.40 | $1.20 | $2.00 | £0.25 | £0.75 | £1.25 |

7 ND part reprint Spiderman #1, Iron Man's origin continued from Tales of Suspense #39; part reprints F.F. #9, Hulk #4, Strange Tales #103
| | $0.40 | $1.20 | $2.00 | £0.25 | £0.75 | £1.25 |

8 ND continued part reprint Spiderman #1, reprint F.F. 9-12, Hulk #6, Tales of Suspense #40; 3pgs new art by Bill Sienkiewicz Angel vs. Cyclops
| | $0.40 | $1.20 | $2.00 | £0.25 | £0.75 | £1.25 |

9 ND origin Vulture, Wasp, Watcher and Dr. Octopus from part reprints; 4pgs new art by Steve Geiger Angel vs. Cyclops
| | $0.40 | $1.20 | $2.00 | £0.25 | £0.75 | £1.25 |

10 ND origin Dr. Strange part reprint from Strange Tales #110, origins Jean Grey (Marvel Girl), Lizard, X-Men and Avengers from part reprints
| | $0.40 | $1.20 | $2.00 | £0.25 | £0.75 | £1.25 |

11 ND 1st appearance Magneto part reprint from X-Men #1, origin Molecule Man from F.F. #20
| | $0.30 | $0.90 | $1.50 | £0.20 | £0.60 | £1.00 |

12 ND history of Captain America reprinted from various including Avengers #4
| | $0.30 | $0.90 | $1.50 | £0.20 | £0.60 | £1.00 |

13 ND history and origins Daredevil and Elektra from various part reprints including Miller art
| | $0.30 | $0.90 | $1.50 | £0.20 | £0.60 | £1.00 |

14 ND origin and 1st appearance Green Goblin part reprinted from Spiderman #14 and #40, F.F. meet the X-Men from F.F. #28
| | $0.30 | $0.90 | $1.50 | £0.20 | £0.60 | £1.00 |

15 ND origins Hawkeye and Wonderman part reprinted
| | $0.30 | $0.90 | $1.50 | £0.20 | £0.60 | £1.00 |

16 ND X-Men vs. Avengers part reprint from X-Men #9
| | $0.30 | $0.90 | $1.50 | £0.20 | £0.60 | £1.00 |

17 ND origins Ka-Zar, The Leader and The Inhumans part reprint
| | $0.30 | $0.90 | $1.50 | £0.20 | £0.60 | £1.00 |

18 ND origin Nick Fury Agent of Shield part reprint, 1st cameo Mary Jane Watson
| | $0.30 | $0.90 | $1.50 | £0.20 | £0.60 | £1.00 |

19 ND 1st new Avengers line-up reprint
| | $0.30 | $0.90 | $1.50 | £0.20 | £0.60 | £1.00 |

20 ND part reprint F.F. #39,#40 (powerless FF vs. Dr. Doom)
| | $0.30 | $0.90 | $1.50 | £0.20 | £0.60 | £1.00 |

21 ND part reprint X-men vs. Juggernaut
| | $0.30 | $0.90 | $1.50 | £0.20 | £0.60 | £1.00 |

22 ND scarce in the U.K. history in reprint of Mary Jane Watson leading up to her marriage to Peter Parker (Spiderman)
| | $0.30 | $0.90 | $1.50 | £0.20 | £0.60 | £1.00 |

23 ND Reed Richards/Sue Storm wedding from F.F. Annual #3, Inhumans saga from F.F. #44-#47
| | $0.30 | $0.90 | $1.50 | £0.20 | £0.60 | £1.00 |

24 ND origin Galactus re-told in reprint history
| | $0.30 | $0.90 | $1.50 | £0.20 | £0.60 | £1.00 |

25 ND scarce in the U.K. origin Silver Surfer re-told in reprint history, Galactus appears
| | $0.40 | $1.20 | $2.00 | £0.25 | £0.75 | £1.25 |

Title Value: $8.70 $26.10 $43.50 £5.60 £16.80 £28.00
Note: reprints edited 1960s material in chronological order detailing origins and events in the Marvel Universe.

MARVEL SPECTACULAR
Marvel Comics Group; 1 Aug 1973-19 Nov 1975

1 ND scarce in the U.K. Jack Kirby Thor reprints begin (selected issues from Thor #128 on)
| | $0.60 | $1.80 | $3.00 | £0.40 | £1.20 | £2.00 |

2-5
| | $0.50 | $1.50 | $2.50 | £0.30 | £0.90 | £1.50 |

6-19
| | $0.40 | $1.20 | $2.00 | £0.25 | £0.75 | £1.25 |

Title Value: $8.20 $24.60 $41.00 £5.10 £15.30 £25.50

MARVEL SPOTLIGHT
Marvel Comics Group; 1 Nov 1971-33 Apr 1977

1 ND origin of Red Wolf (see Avengers #80), Wood inks, Neal Adams cover
| | $3.75 | $11.00 | $22.50 | £2.50 | £7.50 | £15.00 |

2 ND 52pgs, 1st origin and appearance of Werewolf by Night, Ploog art; Venus reprint
| | $7.00 | $21.00 | $42.50 | £4.55 | £13.50 | £27.50 |

3 ND 2nd appearance Werewolf, Ploog art
| | $2.50 | $7.50 | $15.00 | £1.65 | £5.00 | £10.00 |

4 ND 3rd appearance Werewolf, Ploog art
| | $2.05 | $6.25 | $12.50 | £1.25 | £3.75 | £7.50 |

5 ND scarce in the U.K. origin and 1st appearance Ghost Rider (super-hero)
| | $12.50 | $38.00 | $75.00 | £8.25 | £25.00 | £50.00 |

6 ND 2nd appearance Ghost Rider, Ploog art
| | $5.75 | $17.50 | $35.00 | £4.15 | £12.50 | £25.00 |

7 ND 3rd appearance Ghost Rider, Ploog art
| | $3.30 | $10.00 | $20.00 | £2.05 | £6.25 | £12.50 |

8-11 Ghost Rider
| | $2.05 | $6.25 | $12.50 | £1.30 | £4.00 | £8.00 |

12 origin and 1st full appearance Son of Satan (see Ghost Rider #2)
| | $2.05 | $6.25 | $12.50 | £1.25 | £3.75 | £7.50 |

13 3rd appearance Son of Satan (see Ghost Rider #3)
| | $0.80 | $2.50 | $5.00 | £0.65 | £2.00 | £4.00 |

14 ND 4th appearance Son of Satan
| | $0.80 | $2.50 | $5.00 | £0.65 | £2.00 | £4.00 |

15-21 ND
| | $0.80 | $2.50 | $5.00 | £0.65 | £2.00 | £4.00 |

22 ND Ghost Rider appears (cameo)
| | $0.80 | $2.50 | $5.00 | £0.65 | £2.00 | £4.00 |

23 ND
| | $0.80 | $2.50 | $5.00 | £0.65 | £2.00 | £4.00 |

24 ND last of Son of Satan series
| | $0.80 | $2.50 | $5.00 | £0.65 | £2.00 | £4.00 |

25 ND Sinbad
| | $0.50 | $1.50 | $3.00 | £0.30 | £1.00 | £2.00 |

26 Scarecrow
| | $0.50 | $1.50 | $3.00 | £0.30 | £1.00 | £2.00 |

27 Sub-Mariner
| | $0.50 | $1.50 | $3.00 | £0.30 | £1.00 | £2.00 |

28 Moon Knight (1st solo; see Werewolf by Night)
| | $1.65 | $5.00 | $10.00 | £0.80 | £2.50 | £5.00 |

29 Moon Knight (2nd solo; see Werewolf by Night), Kirby cover
| | $1.65 | $5.00 | $10.00 | £0.65 | £2.00 | £4.00 |

30 Warriors Three
| | $0.40 | $1.25 | $2.50 | £0.25 | £0.75 | £1.50 |

31 Nick Fury's longevity explained by Jim Starlin, Chaykin art
| | $0.40 | $1.25 | $2.50 | £0.25 | £0.75 | £1.50 |

32 ND origin (true origin) and 1st appearance of Spiderwoman, Nick Fury appears
| | $1.25 | $3.75 | $7.50 | £0.80 | £2.50 | £5.00 |

33 ND Deathlok, Devil-Slayer
| | $0.80 | $2.50 | $5.00 | £0.50 | £1.50 | £3.00 |

Title Value: $64.35 $195.75 $391.50 £42.80 £130.25 £261.00

MARVEL SPOTLIGHT (2ND SERIES)
Marvel Comics Group; 1 Jul 1979-11 Mar 1981

1 Captain Marvel, Drax the Destroyer, Broderick art
| | $0.40 | $1.20 | $2.00 | £0.25 | £0.75 | £1.25 |

2 Captain Marvel, Drax the Destroyer, Broderick art; Frank Miller cover
| | $0.30 | $0.90 | $1.50 | £0.20 | £0.60 | £1.00 |

3 Captain Marvel, Broderick art
| | $0.30 | $0.90 | $1.50 | £0.20 | £0.60 | £1.00 |

4 Captain Marvel
| | $0.30 | $0.90 | $1.50 | £0.20 | £0.60 | £1.00 |

5 Dragonlord, Frank Miller cover
| | $0.30 | $0.90 | $1.50 | £0.20 | £0.60 | £1.00 |

6 Starlord
| | $0.30 | $0.90 | $1.50 | £0.20 | £0.60 | £1.00 |

7 Starlord, Miller cover
| | $0.30 | $0.90 | $1.50 | £0.20 | £0.60 | £1.00 |

8 ND Captain Marvel, Frank Miller art
| | $0.80 | $2.40 | $4.00 | £0.50 | £1.50 | £2.50 |

9 Captain Universe (see Spectacular Spiderman #158)
| | $0.30 | $0.90 | $1.50 | £0.20 | £0.60 | £1.00 |

10-11 Captain Universe
| | $0.30 | $0.90 | $1.50 | £0.20 | £0.60 | £1.00 |

Title Value: $3.90 $11.70 $19.50 £2.55 £7.65 £12.75
Note: Spiderman's brief cosmic power derived from Captain Universe (see Spectacular Spiderman #158)
ARTISTS
Ditko in 4, 5, 9-11.

	$Good	$Fine	$N.Mint	£Good	£Fine	£N.Mint

MARVEL SPOTLIGHT ON CAPTAIN AMERICA
Marvel Comics Group,MS; 1-4 Mar 1995
1-4 ND 48pgs, classic reprints on glossy stock paper, weekly issues

	$0.60	$1.80	$3.00	£0.40	£1.20	£2.00
Title Value:	$2.40	$7.20	$12.00	£1.60	£4.80	£8.00

MARVEL SPOTLIGHT ON DOCTOR STRANGE
Marvel Comics Group,MS; 1-4 Apr 1995
1-4 ND 48pgs, classic reprints; weekly issues

	$0.60	$1.80	$3.00	£0.40	£1.20	£2.00
Title Value:	$2.40	$7.20	$12.00	£1.60	£4.80	£8.00

MARVEL SPOTLIGHT ON SILVER SURFER
Marvel Comics Group,MS; 1-4 May 1995
1-4 ND 48pgs, classic reprints; weekly issues

	$0.60	$1.80	$3.00	£0.40	£1.20	£2.00
Title Value:	$2.40	$7.20	$12.00	£1.60	£4.80	£8.00

MARVEL SPRING SPECIAL
Marvel Comics Group,Magazine OS; 1 1989
1 ND adaptation of Elvira The Movie

	$0.50	$1.50	$2.50	£0.30	£0.90	£1.50
Title Value:	$0.50	$1.50	$2.50	£0.30	£0.90	£1.50

MARVEL SUPER ACTION
Marvel Comics Group,Magazine OS; 1 May 1976
1 LD in the U.K. 72pgs, origin Dominic Fortune (Chaykin story/art) Punisher appears, 1st Weirdworld, Evans, Ploog art

	$8.50	$26.00	$60.00	£5.75	£17.25	£35.00
Title Value:	$8.50	$26.00	$60.00	£5.75	£17.25	£35.00

MARVEL SUPER ACTION (2ND SERIES)
Marvel Comics Group; 1 May 1977-37 Nov 1981
1 ND reprints Captain America #100

	$0.80	$2.40	$4.00	£0.50	£1.50	£2.50
2-3 ND	$0.50	$1.50	$2.50	£0.30	£0.90	£1.50

4 ND Marvel Boy (now Quasar) #1 reprinted

	$0.50	$1.50	$2.50	£0.30	£0.90	£1.50
5 ND	$0.50	$1.50	$2.50	£0.30	£0.90	£1.50
6-11 ND	$0.40	$1.20	$2.00	£0.25	£0.75	£1.25

12 reprints Captain America #110 (Steranko art)

	$0.40	$1.20	$2.00	£0.25	£0.75	£1.25

13 reprints Captain America #111 (Steranko art)

	$0.40	$1.20	$2.00	£0.25	£0.75	£1.25

14-37 ND Avengers reprints begin

	$0.30	$0.90	$1.50	£0.20	£0.60	£1.00
Title Value:	$13.20	$39.60	$66.00	£8.50	£25.50	£42.50

Note: early Captain America and Avengers reprints.
REPRINT FEATURES
Avengers in 14-38. Captain America in 1-13.

MARVEL SUPER SPECIAL
Marvel Comics Group,Magazine Film; 1 Sep 1977-41 Nov 1986
1 ND 66pgs, scarce in the U.K. Kiss; story (38pgs) by Steve Gerber, pencils by Alan Weiss, inks by John & Sal Buscema and Rick Buckler, The Avengers, Defenders, Dr. Doom and Mephisto appear; plus photos, features

	$10.00	$30.00	$60.00	£5.75	£17.50	£35.00

2 ND 66pgs, Savage Sword of Conan; John Buscema art, Earl Norem cover

	$0.50	$1.50	$2.50	£0.30	£0.90	£1.50

3 LD in the U.K. 48pgs, Close Encounters film adaptation; Walt Simonson and Klaus Janson art

	$0.50	$1.50	$2.50	£0.35	£1.05	£1.75

4 ND 66pgs, scarce in the U.K, the story of The Beatles; George Perez and Klaus Janson art; plus photos and features

	$2.50	$7.50	$15.00	£1.65	£5.00	£10.00

5 ND 54pgs, Kiss; story art by John Romita Jnr plus photos and features; bound-in poster at centre-fold (often missing!)

	$5.25	$16.00	$32.50	£3.30	£10.00	£20.00

6 ND 50pgs, Jaws II film adaptation; Gene Colan art

	$0.50	$1.50	$2.50	£0.30	£0.90	£1.50

7 ND extremely rare in the U.S. & the U.K., Sgt. Pepper's Lonely Heart's Club Band, only distributed in Japan (withdrawn from U.S. distribution)

	$14.00	$43.00	$100.00	£10.50	£32.00	£75.00

8 ND 50pgs, Battlestar Galactica; Ernie Colon art; plus photos and features

	$0.50	$1.50	$2.50	£0.30	£0.90	£1.50

9 LD in the U.K. 66pgs, Savage Sword of Conan; John Buscema art, Red Sonja back-up (15pgs) drawn by Howard Chaykin

	$0.50	$1.50	$2.50	£0.30	£0.90	£1.50

10 ND 66pgs, Starlord; Gene Colon art

	$0.50	$1.50	$2.50	£0.30	£0.90	£1.50

11 ND 56pgs, Warriors of the Shadow Realm Part I (Weirdworld); John Buscema and Rudy Nebres art

	$0.50	$1.50	$2.50	£0.30	£0.90	£1.50

12 ND 56pgs, Warriors of the Shadow Realm Part II (Weirdworld); John Buscema and Rudy Nebres art

	$0.50	$1.50	$2.50	£0.30	£0.90	£1.50

13 ND 56pgs, Warriors of the Shadow Realm Part III (Weirdworld); John Buscema and Rudy Nebres art; gatefold poster at centre-fold

	$0.50	$1.50	$2.50	£0.30	£0.90	£1.50

14 ND Meteor film adaptation (series now settled as adaptations of films — ends #41)

	$0.50	$1.50	$2.50	£0.40	£1.20	£2.00

15 ND 66pgs, Star Trek – The Motion Picture; Dave Cockrum and Klaus Janson art; plus photos and features

	$0.50	$1.50	$2.50	£0.40	£1.20	£2.00

16 ND 96pgs, The Empire Strikes Back; Al Williamson and Carlos Garzon art

	$0.50	$1.50	$2.50	£0.40	£1.20	£2.00

17 ND 66pgs, Xanadu; artists include Mike Nasser, Brent Anderson and Bill Sienkiewicz; plus photos and features

	$0.50	$1.50	$2.50	£0.30	£0.90	£1.50

18 ND 64pgs, Raiders of the Lost Ark; Walt Simonson script, John Buscema and Klaus Janson art

	$0.50	$1.50	$2.50	£0.30	£0.90	£1.50

19 LD in the U.K. 66pgs, For Your Eyes Only; Howard Chaykin and Vince Coletta art; plus photos and features

	$0.50	$1.50	$2.50	£0.30	£0.90	£1.50

20 ND 66pgs, Dragonslayer; Marie Severin and John Tartaglione art

	$0.50	$1.50	$2.50	£0.30	£0.90	£1.50

21 ND 66pgs, Conan the Movie

	$0.40	$1.20	$2.00	£0.25	£0.75	£1.25

22 ND 64pgs, Bladerunner; Al Williamson and Carlos Garzon art (Note: regular comic size, not magazine size); plus photos and features

	$0.40	$1.20	$2.00	£0.25	£0.75	£1.25

23 ND 64pgs, Annie; Win Mortimer and Vince Coletta art; plus photos and features

	$0.40	$1.20	$2.00	£0.25	£0.75	£1.25

24 ND 64pgs, The Dark Crystal; Bret Blevins and Vince Coletta art; plus photos and features

	$0.40	$1.20	$2.00	£0.25	£0.75	£1.25

25 ND 64pgs, Rock and Rule; specially adapted from the animated film plus photos and features

	$0.40	$1.20	$2.00	£0.25	£0.75	£1.25

26 ND 64pgs, Octopussy; Paul Neary art; plus photos and features

	$0.40	$1.20	$2.00	£0.25	£0.75	£1.25

27 ND 64pgs, Fire and Ice

	$0.40	$1.20	$2.00	£0.25	£0.75	£1.25

28 ND 64pgs, Krull; Bret Blevins and Vince Coletta art

	$0.40	$1.20	$2.00	£0.25	£0.75	£1.25

29 ND 64pgs, Greystoke – Tarzan of the Apes; Dan Spiegle art

	$0.40	$1.20	$2.00	£0.25	£0.75	£1.25

30 ND 64pgs, Indiana Jones and the Temple of Doom; Jackson Guice art featured

	$0.40	$1.20	$2.00	£0.25	£0.75	£1.25

31 ND 64pgs, The Last Starfighter; Bret Blevins and Tony Salmons art

	$0.40	$1.20	$2.00	£0.25	£0.75	£1.25

32 ND 64pgs, The Muppets Take Manhattan

	$0.40	$1.20	$2.00	£0.25	£0.75	£1.25

33 ND 64pgs, Buckeroo Banzai; Mark Texeira art

	$0.40	$1.20	$2.00	£0.25	£0.75	£1.25

34 ND 64pgs, Sheena; Gray Morrow art

	$0.40	$1.20	$2.00	£0.25	£0.75	£1.25

35 ND 64pgs, Conan the Destroyer; John Buscema art

	$0.40	$1.20	$2.00	£0.25	£0.75	£1.25

36 ND 64pgs, Dune; Sienkiewicz art

	$0.40	$1.20	$2.00	£0.25	£0.75	£1.25

37 ND 48pgs, 2010; Joe Barney, Larry Hama, Tom Palmer

	$0.40	$1.20	$2.00	£0.25	£0.75	£1.25

38 ND 48pgs, Red Sonja; Louise Simonson and Mary Wilshire

	$0.40	$1.20	$2.00	£0.25	£0.75	£1.25

39 ND 64pgs, Santa Claus: The Movie; Frank Springer art

	$0.40	$1.20	$2.00	£0.25	£0.75	£1.25

40 ND 64pgs, Labyrinth; John Buscema art

	$0.40	$1.20	$2.00	£0.25	£0.75	£1.25

41 ND 64pgs, Howard the Duck; Kyle Baker art

	$0.40	$1.20	$2.00	£0.25	£0.75	£1.25
Title Value:	$48.15	$145.70	$289.50	£31.60	£95.70	£192.00

Note: 11-13 each had a 25 copy special press run with gold seal and signed by artists (therefore rare) valued at about £30. Two different cover prices exist for #15 ($1.50 & $2.00). 22, 23 are normal comic size. #1-4 titled Marvel Comics Super Special.

MARVEL SUPER-HERO CONTEST OF CHAMPIONS
Marvel Comics Group,MS; 1 Jun 1982-3 Aug 1982
1 1st Marvel limited series; many Marvel heroes including X-Men appear

	$0.80	$2.40	$4.00	£0.60	£1.80	£3.00
2	$0.80	$2.40	$4.00	£0.60	£1.80	£3.00

3 ND scarce in the U.K.

	$0.80	$2.40	$4.00	£0.70	£2.10	£3.50
Title Value:	$2.40	$7.20	$12.00	£1.90	£5.70	£9.50

Note: most Marvel heroes appear.

MARVEL SUPER-HEROES
Marvel Comics Group; 12 Dec 1967-31 Nov 1971; 32 Sep 1972-106 Feb 1982
(previously Fantasy Masterpieces)
12 68pgs, issues begin; origin and 1st appearance Captain Marvel of the Kree

	$18.00	$55.00	$110.00	£12.50	£38.00	£75.00

13 2nd appearance Captain Marvel

	$9.00	$28.00	$55.00	£5.75	£17.50	£35.00

14 Spiderman features in a new full length story

	$17.50	$52.50	$105.00	£10.00	£30.00	£60.00

15 Medusa; Inhumans appear

	$2.50	$7.50	$15.00	£1.65	£5.00	£10.00

16 origin and 1st appearance Phantom Eagle

	$2.50	$7.50	$15.00	£1.65	£5.00	£10.00

17 origin Black Knight

	$2.50	$7.50	$15.00	£1.65	£5.00	£10.00

18 origin and 1st appearance Guardians of the Galaxy

	$10.00	$30.00	$60.00	£5.75	£17.50	£35.00

19 Ka-Zar, part Smith cover

	$2.05	$6.25	$12.50	£1.25	£3.75	£7.50

20 Dr. Doom

	$2.05	$6.25	$12.50	£1.25	£3.75	£7.50

21 X-Men #1 and #2 reprinted

	$0.80	$2.50	$5.00	£0.55	£1.75	£3.50

22 X-Men #3, Daredevil #2 reprinted

	$0.80	$2.50	$5.00	£0.55	£1.75	£3.50

23 new Watcher story, X-Men #4 reprinted (1st Brotherhood Evil Mutants/Scarlet Witch/Quicksilver), Daredevil #3

	$0.80	$2.50	$5.00	£0.55	£1.75	£3.50

24 X-Men #5 reprinted, Daredevil #4

	$0.80	$2.50	$5.00	£0.55	£1.75	£3.50

25 X-Men #6 reprinted, Daredevil #5

	$0.80	$2.50	$5.00	£0.55	£1.75	£3.50

26 X-Men #7 reprinted, Daredevil #6

	$0.80	$2.50	$5.00	£0.55	£1.75	£3.50

	$Good	$Fine	$N.Mint	£Good	£Fine	£N.Mint

27 X-Men #8 reprinted, Daredevil #7
$0.80 $2.50 $5.00 £0.55 £1.75 £3.50

28 Iron Man and Daredevil reprints takeover cover credit
$0.80 $2.50 $5.00 £0.55 £1.75 £3.50

29-30
$0.80 $2.50 $5.00 £0.55 £1.75 £3.50

31 ND last 68pg issue
$0.80 $2.50 $5.00 £0.55 £1.75 £3.50

32 ND reprints featuring Sub-Mariner and Hulk from Tales to Astonish take over cover credit (ends #55)
$0.40 $1.80 $3.00 £0.40 £1.20 £2.00

33-40 ND $0.60 $1.80 $3.00 £0.40 £1.20 £2.00

41-47 ND $0.50 $1.50 $2.50 £0.30 £0.90 £1.50

48 ND reprints Tales to Astonish #93 (Hulk vs. Silver Surfer)
$0.50 $1.50 $2.50 £0.30 £0.90 £1.50

49-50 ND $0.50 $1.50 $2.50 £0.30 £0.90 £1.50

51-55 ND $0.40 $1.20 $2.00 £0.25 £0.75 £1.25

56 ND reprints Hulk #102, origin retold
$0.40 $1.20 $2.00 £0.25 £0.75 £1.25

57-70 ND $0.40 $1.20 $2.00 £0.25 £0.75 £1.25

71-99 ND $0.30 $0.90 $1.50 £0.20 £0.60 £1.00

100 ND 52pgs $0.40 $1.20 $2.00 £0.25 £0.75 £1.25

101-106 ND $0.30 $0.90 $1.50 £0.20 £0.60 £1.00

Title Value: $104.20 $315.90 $601.50 £66.35 £201.30 £382.75

REPRINT FEATURES

All Winner's Squad in 17, 18. GA Black Knight in 12-16, 19. Black Marvel in 15. GA Captain America in 12 (by Romita), 13, 14, 15 (by Romita), 16, 20. Daredevil in 22-31. GA Destroyer in 12. Hulk in 21, 32-106. GA Human Torch in 12-14, 16, 17, 19, 20. Iron Man in 28-31. Marvel Boy in 19. Mercury in 14. Patriot in 16. GA Sub-Mariner in 12-20; Sub-Mariner in 21, 32-55. GA Vision in 13. X-Men in 21-27.

MARVEL SUPER-HEROES (2ND SERIES)

Marvel Comics Group; 1 May 1990-15 Dec 1993

1 80pgs, Moon Knight, Hercules, Black Panther, Hell Cat, Magik, Brother Voodoo, Speedball, features Ron Lim and Steve Ditko art among others
$0.50 $1.50 $2.50 £0.30 £0.90 £1.50

2 80pgs, Iron Man, Tigra, Falcon, Red Wolf, Rogue, Speedball, Daredevil, Steve Ditko art on Iron Man and Speedball
$0.50 $1.50 $2.50 £0.30 £0.90 £1.50

3 80pgs, Captain America, Captain Marvel, Wasp, Hulk, Blue Shield, Ditko/Rogers art featured
$0.50 $1.50 $2.50 £0.30 £0.90 £1.50

4 80pgs, Spiderman and Nick Fury, Daredevil, Speedball, Wonder Man, Spitfire, Black Knight. John Byrne cover
$0.50 $1.50 $2.50 £0.30 £0.90 £1.50

5 80pgs, Thor, Thing, Speedball, Doctor Strange
$0.50 $1.50 $2.50 £0.30 £0.90 £1.50

6 80pgs, X-Men, Power Pack, Speedball, Sabra
$0.50 $1.50 $2.50 £0.30 £0.90 £1.50

7 80pgs, X-Men, Cloak and Dagger by Peter David
$0.50 $1.50 $2.50 £0.30 £0.90 £1.50

8 80pgs, X-Men, Iron Man (Ditko art), Namor; Erik Larsen cover
$0.50 $1.50 $2.50 £0.30 £0.90 £1.50

9 80pgs, Avengers West Coast, Thor, Iron Man; Sam Kieth cover
$0.50 $1.50 $2.50 £0.30 £0.90 £1.50

10 80pgs, Sub-Mariner, Fantastic Four, Thor appear; story and cover to Ms. Marvel #24 appear (never published before – it had what would have been Sabretooth's 2nd appearance!)
$0.50 $1.50 $2.50 £0.30 £0.90 £1.50

11 80pgs, Ghost Rider, Giant Man plus the never before published Ms. Marvel #25 with Rogue appearance, Mark Texeira cover
$0.50 $1.50 $2.50 £0.30 £0.90 £1.50

12 80pgs, Dr. Strange, Falcon, Iron Man
$0.50 $1.50 $2.50 £0.30 £0.90 £1.50

13 80pgs, all-Iron Man issue to celebrate 30th anniversary
$0.50 $1.50 $2.50 £0.30 £0.90 £1.50

14 80pgs, Iron Man, Speedball, Dr. Strange
$0.50 $1.50 $2.50 £0.30 £0.90 £1.50

15 80pgs, Volstagg by Walt Simonson, Thor, Iron Man
$0.50 $1.50 $2.50 £0.30 £0.90 £1.50

Title Value: $7.50 $22.50 $37.50 £4.50 £13.50 £22.50

Note: quarterly frequency

MARVEL SUPER-HEROES (ONE SHOT)

Marvel Comics Group, OS; 1 Oct 1966

1 64pgs, reprints Daredevil #1 (origin), Avengers, Golden Age Sub-Mariner, Golden Age Human Torch reprint, 1st Marvel one-shot comic
$12.50 $38.00 $75.00 £8.25 £25.00 £50.00

Title Value: $12.50 $38.00 $75.00 £8.25 £25.00 £50.00

MARVEL SUPER-HEROES 1992 HOLIDAY SPECIAL

Marvel Comics Group, OS; 1 Jan 1993

1 ND 80pgs, stories featuring Hulk, Spiderman, Wolverine, Thanos, work by Sam Kieth, Jim Starlin and Golden
$0.50 $1.50 $2.50 £0.30 £0.90 £1.50

Title Value: $0.50 $1.50 $2.50 £0.30 £0.90 £1.50

MARVEL SUPER-HEROES MEGAZINE

Marvel Comics Group; 1 Oct 1994-6 1995

1 ND 96pgs, reprints FF #232, Daredevil #159, Iron Man #115 and Hulk #314
$0.50 $1.50 $2.50 £0.30 £0.90 £1.50

2 ND 96pgs, Human Torch, Daredevil and Hulk reprints; new Frank Miller cover
$0.50 $1.50 $2.50 £0.30 £0.90 £1.50

3 ND 96pgs, Fantastic Four, Daredevil and Iron Man reprints; Michael Golden cover
$0.50 $1.50 $2.50 £0.30 £0.90 £1.50

4 ND 96pgs, Fantastic Four, Daredevil and Iron Man reprints
$0.50 $1.50 $2.50 £0.30 £0.90 £1.50

5 ND 96pgs, all John Byrne issue with Fantastic Four, Thing and Hulk reprints; John Byrne cover
$0.50 $1.50 $2.50 £0.30 £0.90 £1.50

6 ND 96pgs, Fantastic Four, Daredevil, Iron Man and Hulk reprints
$0.50 $1.50 $2.50 £0.30 £0.90 £1.50

Title Value: $3.00 $9.00 $15.00 £1.80 £5.40 £9.00

MARVEL SUPER-HEROES SECRET WARS

Marvel Comics Group, MS; 1 May 1984-12 Apr 1985
(see Secret Wars II)

1 $0.90 $2.70 $4.50 £0.60 £1.80 £3.00

1 2nd printing $0.60 $1.80 $3.00 £0.40 £1.20 £2.00

1 3rd printing $0.50 $1.50 $2.50 £0.30 £0.90 £1.50

2-3 $0.60 $1.80 $3.00 £0.40 £1.20 £2.00

4-5 $0.50 $1.50 $2.50 £0.30 £0.90 £1.50

6 Wasp dies $0.50 $1.50 $2.50 £0.30 £0.90 £1.50

7 1st new Spiderwoman
$0.50 $1.50 $2.50 £0.30 £0.90 £1.50

8 origin Spiderman's black costume (see Spiderman #252, Spectacular Spiderman #90); costume later initiates origin of Venom
$3.50 $10.50 $17.50 £1.50 £4.50 £7.50

9-10 $0.50 $1.50 $2.50 £0.30 £0.90 £1.50

11 LD in the U.K. $0.50 $1.50 $2.50 £0.35 £1.05 £1.75

12 LD in the U.K. DS
$0.50 $1.50 $2.50 £0.40 £1.20 £2.00

Title Value: $10.70 $32.10 $53.50 £6.15 £18.45 £30.75

Secret Wars Trade paperback (Jun 1992), reprints issues #1-12, new cover by Mike Zeck £2.50 £7.50 £12.50

MARVEL SWIMSUIT SPECIAL 1992

Marvel Comics Group, OS; 1 Aug 1992

1 ND 48pgs $0.60 $1.80 $3.00 £0.40 £1.20 £2.00

Title Value: $0.60 $1.80 $3.00 £0.40 £1.20 £2.00

MARVEL SWIMSUIT SPECIAL 1993

Marvel Comics Group, Magazine OS; 1 Aug 1993

1 ND 48pgs, Adam Hughes and Kevin Maguire art featured
$0.60 $1.80 $3.00 £0.40 £1.20 £2.00

Title Value: $0.60 $1.80 $3.00 £0.40 £1.20 £2.00

Marvel Premiere #3

Marvel Spotlight (1st) #29

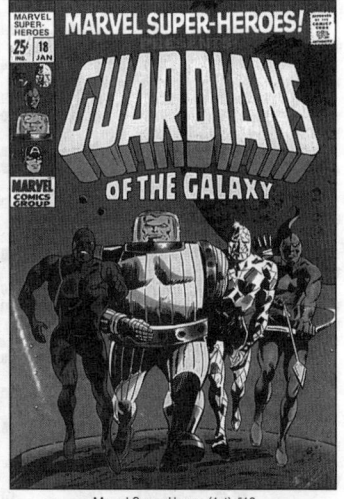

Marvel Super-Heroes (1st) #18

MINT = 100% / NEAR MINT (inc. +/-) = 90–99% / VERY FINE (inc. +/-) = 75–89% / FINE (inc. +/-) = 55–74%
VERY GOOD (inc. +/-) = 35–54% / GOOD (inc. +/-) = 15–34% / FAIR = 5–14% / POOR = 1–4%

451

	$Good	$Fine	$N.Mint	£Good	£Fine	£N.Mint

MARVEL SWIMSUIT SPECIAL 1994

Marvel Comics Group, Magazine OS; 1 Aug 1994

1 ND 48pgs, Adam Hughes cover

	$0.60	$1.80	$3.00	£0.40	£1.20	£2.00
Title Value:	$0.60	$1.80	$3.00	£0.40	£1.20	£2.00

MARVEL SWIMSUIT SPECIAL 1995

Marvel Comics Group, Magazine OS; 1 Oct 1995

1 ND 48pgs, Brian Stelfreeze, Gary Frank, Adam Hughes featured pin-ups, Gambit and Rogue cover by the Brothers Hildebrandt

	$0.60	$1.80	$3.00	£0.40	£1.20	£2.00
Title Value:	$0.60	$1.80	$3.00	£0.40	£1.20	£2.00

MARVEL TAILS, PETER PORKER SPECTACULAR SPIDERHAM

Marvel Comics Group, OS; 1 Nov 1983

1 ND

	$0.25	$0.75	$1.25	£0.15	£0.45	£0.75
Title Value:	$0.25	$0.75	$1.25	£0.15	£0.45	£0.75

MARVEL TALES

Marvel Comics Group; 3 Jul 1966-291 Nov 1994

(formerly Marvel Tales Annual)

3 64pgs, reprints Spiderman #6 (1st Lizard), Journey into Mystery #84 (2nd Thor), Strange Tales #101 (1st Human Torch series)

	$Good	$Fine	$N.Mint	£Good	£Fine	£N.Mint
	$6.25	$18.50	$37.50	£4.15	£12.50	£25.00
4-5	$2.90	$8.75	$17.50	£1.65	£5.00	£10.00
6 reprints Spiderman #9 (1st Electro)	$1.65	$5.00	$10.00	£1.00	£3.00	£6.00
7	$1.65	$5.00	$10.00	£1.00	£3.00	£6.00
8 reprints Spiderman #13 (1st Mysterio)	$1.65	$5.00	$10.00	£1.00	£3.00	£6.00
9 reprints Spiderman #14 (1st Green Goblin) plus cover	$2.05	$6.25	$12.50	£1.15	£3.50	£7.00
10 reprints Spiderman #15 (1st Kraven)	$1.65	$5.00	$10.00	£1.00	£3.00	£6.00
11-12 scarce in the U.K.	$1.25	$3.75	$7.50	£0.80	£2.50	£5.00
13 Marvel Boy reprint	$1.25	$3.75	$7.50	£0.80	£2.50	£5.00
14-15	$1.25	$3.75	$7.50	£0.80	£2.50	£5.00
16-20	$1.15	$3.50	$7.00	£0.75	£2.25	£4.50
21-29	$1.00	$3.00	$6.00	£0.65	£2.00	£4.00
30 new Angel story, continued from Ka-Zar #3 (1st series)	$1.00	$3.00	$6.00	£0.65	£2.00	£4.00
31	$1.00	$3.00	$6.00	£0.65	£2.00	£4.00
32 ND last 64pg issue	$1.00	$3.00	$6.00	£0.65	£2.00	£4.00
33 ND 48pgs	$0.90	$2.70	$4.50	£0.60	£1.80	£3.00
34-35 ND	$0.80	$2.40	$4.00	£0.50	£1.50	£2.50
36 ND reprints Spiderman #50 (1st Kingpin)	$0.80	$2.40	$4.00	£0.50	£1.50	£2.50
37-40 ND	$0.80	$2.40	$4.00	£0.50	£1.50	£2.50
41-60 ND	$0.60	$1.80	$3.00	£0.40	£1.20	£2.00
61-74 ND	$0.50	$1.50	$2.50	£0.30	£0.90	£1.50
75 ND reprints origin Spiderman	$0.60	$1.80	$3.00	£0.40	£1.20	£2.00
76 ND	$0.50	$1.50	$2.50	£0.30	£0.90	£1.50
77 ND reprints drug story (Spiderman #96)	$0.50	$1.50	$2.50	£0.30	£0.90	£1.50
78 ND reprints drug story (Spiderman #97)	$0.50	$1.50	$2.50	£0.30	£0.90	£1.50
79 ND reprints drug story (Spiderman #98)	$0.50	$1.50	$2.50	£0.30	£0.90	£1.50
80 ND	$0.50	$1.50	$2.50	£0.30	£0.90	£1.50
81 ND reprints newspaper strips as back-up	$0.30	$0.90	$1.50	£0.20	£0.60	£1.00
82-97	$0.30	$0.90	$1.50	£0.20	£0.60	£1.00
98 ND reprints death Gwen Stacy from Spiderman #121	$0.50	$1.50	$2.50	£0.30	£0.90	£1.50
99 ND reprints death Green Goblin from Spiderman #122	$0.50	$1.50	$2.50	£0.30	£0.90	£1.50
100 ND 52pgs, Nasser art on new Hawkeye/Two Gun Kid story	$0.50	$1.50	$2.50	£0.30	£0.90	£1.50
101-105	$0.30	$0.90	$1.50	£0.20	£0.60	£1.00
106 ND reprints 1st Punisher from Spiderman #129	$1.50	$4.50	$7.50	£0.80	£2.40	£4.00
107-110 ND	$0.30	$0.90	$1.50	£0.20	£0.60	£1.00
111 ND reprints Spiderman #134 (2nd appearance Punisher [cameo])	$0.50	$1.50	$2.50	£0.30	£0.90	£1.50
112 ND reprints Spiderman #135 (2nd full appearance Punisher)	$0.50	$1.50	$2.50	£0.30	£0.90	£1.50
113-122 ND	$0.30	$0.90	$1.50	£0.20	£0.60	£1.00
123 ND title becomes Marvel Tales Starring Spiderman						
124-136 ND	$0.30	$0.90	$1.50	£0.20	£0.60	£1.00
137 reprints 1st Spiderman from Amazing Fantasy #15 with unused original cover, reprints ist Dr. Strange from Strange Tales #110	$0.90	$2.70	$4.50	£0.60	£1.80	£3.00
138 reprints Spiderman #1	$0.70	$2.10	$3.50	£0.50	£1.50	£2.50
139 reprints Spiderman #2	$0.40	$1.20	$2.00	£0.25	£0.75	£1.25
140 reprints Spiderman #3	$0.40	$1.20	$2.00	£0.25	£0.75	£1.25
141 reprints Spiderman #4	$0.40	$1.20	$2.00	£0.25	£0.75	£1.25
142 reprints Spiderman #5	$0.40	$1.20	$2.00	£0.25	£0.75	£1.25
143 reprints Spiderman #6	$0.40	$1.20	$2.00	£0.25	£0.75	£1.25
144 reprints Spiderman #7	$0.40	$1.20	$2.00	£0.25	£0.75	£1.25
145 reprints Spiderman #8	$0.40	$1.20	$2.00	£0.25	£0.75	£1.25
146 reprints Spiderman #9	$0.40	$1.20	$2.00	£0.25	£0.75	£1.25
147 reprints Spiderman #10	$0.40	$1.20	$2.00	£0.25	£0.75	£1.25
148-149	$0.40	$0.90		£0.20	£0.60	£1.00
150 DS LD reprints Spiderman Annual #1 and #14	$0.50	$1.50	$2.50	£0.30	£0.90	£1.50
151	$0.30	$0.90	$1.50	£0.20	£0.60	£1.00
152 reprints Spiderman #14 (1st Green Goblin)	$0.30	$0.90	$1.50	£0.20	£0.60	£1.00
153-190	$0.30	$0.90	$1.50	£0.20	£0.60	£1.00
191 64pgs, reprints Spiderman #96-98	$0.30	$0.90	$1.50	£0.20	£0.60	£1.00
192 48pgs, reprints Spiderman #121, #122	$0.50	$1.50	$2.50	£0.30	£0.90	£1.50
193-197	$0.30	$0.90	$1.50	£0.20	£0.60	£1.00
198 new Spiderman/Thing story	$0.40	$1.20	$2.00	£0.25	£0.75	£1.25
199	$0.30	$0.90	$1.50	£0.20	£0.60	£1.00
200 DS Frank Miller reprint from Spiderman Annual #14	$0.40	$1.20	$2.00	£0.25	£0.75	£1.25
201-202 reprints Marvel Team Up #65,66	$0.25	$0.75	$1.25	£0.15	£0.45	£0.75
203-208	$0.25	$0.75	$1.25	£0.15	£0.45	£0.75
209 reprints 1st Punisher from Spiderman #129	$0.50	$1.50	$2.50	£0.30	£0.90	£1.50
210 reprints Spiderman #134, Punisher appears (1 panel)	$0.30	$0.90	$1.50	£0.20	£0.60	£1.00
211-212 Punisher appears	$0.30	$0.90	$1.50	£0.20	£0.60	£1.00
213 Punisher, Jack Kirby's Silver Surfer appear	$0.30	$0.90	$1.50	£0.20	£0.60	£1.00
214-215 Punisher/Nightcrawler	$0.30	$0.90	$1.50	£0.20	£0.60	£1.00
216-222 Punisher appears	$0.30	$0.90	$1.50	£0.20	£0.60	£1.00
223 Death Captain Stacy, Todd McFarlane covers begin	$0.25	$0.75	$1.25	£0.15	£0.45	£0.75
224-232	$0.25	$0.75	$1.25	£0.15	£0.45	£0.75
233 reprints X-Men #35	$0.25	$0.75	$1.25	£0.15	£0.45	£0.75
234 reprints Marvel Team Up #4 (X-Men and Morbius)	$0.25	$0.75	$1.25	£0.15	£0.45	£0.75
235-236	$0.25	$0.75	$1.25	£0.15	£0.45	£0.75
237-238 reprints Marvel Team Up #150 with the X-Men	$0.25	$0.75	$1.25	£0.15	£0.45	£0.75
239-240 Spiderman/Beast	$0.25	$0.75	$1.25	£0.15	£0.45	£0.75
241-242	$0.25	$0.75	$1.25	£0.15	£0.45	£0.75
243 reprints Marvel Team Up #117 with Wolverine	$0.25	$0.75	$1.25	£0.15	£0.45	£0.75
244 reprints Marvel Team Up #118 with Professor X	$0.25	$0.75	$1.25	£0.15	£0.45	£0.75
245-247	$0.25	$0.75	$1.25	£0.15	£0.45	£0.75
248 reprints Marvel Team Up Annual #6, new Rocket Racer back-up story	$0.25	$0.75	$1.25	£0.15	£0.45	£0.75
249	$0.25	$0.75	$1.25	£0.15	£0.45	£0.75
250 reprints Marvel Team Up #100	$0.25	$0.75	$1.25	£0.15	£0.45	£0.75
251 reprints Spiderman #100	$0.25	$0.75	$1.25	£0.15	£0.45	£0.75
252 reprints Spiderman #101	$0.25	$0.75	$1.25	£0.15	£0.45	£0.75
253 reprints Spiderman #102	$0.25	$0.75		£0.15	£0.45	£0.75
254 reprints Marvel Team Up #15 (Ghost Rider)	$0.25	$0.75	$1.25	£0.15	£0.45	£0.75
255 reprints Marvel Team Up #58 (Ghost Rider)	$0.25	$0.75	$1.25	£0.15	£0.45	£0.75
256-257	$0.25	$0.75	$1.25	£0.15	£0.45	£0.75
258 reprints Spiderman #238 (1st Hobgoblin)	$0.30	$0.90	$1.50	£0.20	£0.60	£1.00
259-261 reprints Spiderman #239, George Perez cover	$0.25	$0.75	$1.25	£0.15	£0.45	£0.75
262-263	$0.25	$0.75	$1.25	£0.15	£0.45	£0.75
264-265 reprints lead story from Spiderman Annual #5 with Peter Parker's parents to tie in with 30th anniversary plot-lines	$0.25	$0.75	$1.25	£0.15	£0.45	£0.75
266 reprints Spiderman #252 (1st Black Costume)	$0.25	$0.75	$1.25	£0.15	£0.45	£0.75
267-276	$0.25	$0.75	$1.25	£0.15	£0.45	£0.75
277 reprints 1st Silver Sable fron Amazing Spiderman #265	$0.25	$0.75	$1.25	£0.15	£0.45	£0.75
278-284 Ron Lim cover						

TRADE PAPERBACKS, GRAPHIC NOVELS AND OTHER COLLECTIONS ARE PRICED IN POUNDS STERLING ONLY. CONVERT AT 1.5 FOR DOLLARS.

	$Good	$Fine	$N.Mint	£Good	£Fine	£N.Mint
	$0.25	$0.75	$1.25	£0.15	£0.45	£0.75
285 Ron Lim cover, Wendigo back-up by Charles Vess						
	$0.25	$0.75	$1.25	£0.15	£0.45	£0.75
286 Tom Lyle cover						
	$0.25	$0.75	$1.25	£0.15	£0.45	£0.75
286 ND Collector's Edition, pre-bagged with 16pg preview and animation cel from the Spiderman animated TV series; metallic ink cover						
	$0.50	$1.50	$2.50	£0.30	£0.90	£1.50
287-291	$0.25	$0.75	$1.25	£0.15	£0.45	£0.75
Title Value:	**$138.20**	**$415.00**	**$737.00**	**£87.70**	**£264.40**	**£469.25**

Note: issue 3 occasionally turns up with blank back and inside covers. These were originally subscription copies sent as leftovers (see also Spiderman Annual #1,2, Fantastic Four Annual #1-3, Sgt. Fury Annual #1, Strange Tales Annual #2). With these white covers showing more easily signs of wear and soiling, near mint copies are extremely scarce both in the U.S. and U.K.

Note also: new Todd McFarlane covers begin from 223, new Spider-Ham back-up stories from 231.

REPRINT FEATURES
Ant-Man in 3-5. Dr.Strange in 28, 29, 31. Giant-Man in 13. Human Torch in 3-12, 14-27. Iron Man in 32. Marvel Boy in 13-16. Spiderman in 3-234. Thor in 3-27. Wasp in 6-12.

MARVEL TALES ANNUAL
Marvel Comics Group; 1 1964-2 1965

	$Good	$Fine	$N.Mint	£Good	£Fine	£N.Mint
1 scarce in the U.K. 68pgs, reprints first origins from first issues of Sgt. Fury, Spiderman, Hulk and Iron Man plus Giant-Man origin (Astonish #49)						
	$43.00	$130.00	$260.00	£22.50	£67.50	£135.00
2 68pgs, reprints origins of Avengers (Avengers #1), Dr. Strange (Strange Tales #110), X-Men (X-Men #1), and a Hulk story						
	$13.00	$40.00	$80.00	£10.00	£30.00	£60.00
Title Value:	**$56.00**	**$170.00**	**$340.00**	**£32.50**	**£97.50**	**£195.00**

MARVEL TEAM-UP
Marvel Comics Group; 1 Mar 1972-150 Feb 1985
(see Marvel Treasury Edition 18, Official Marvel Index to...)
[Spiderman teamed with each of the following]

	$Good	$Fine	$N.Mint	£Good	£Fine	£N.Mint
1 ND Human Torch						
	$11.00	$34.00	$80.00	£7.00	£21.00	£50.00
2 ND Human Torch	$5.25	$16.00	$32.50	£3.30	£10.00	£20.00
3 ND Spiderman and Human Torch vs. Morbius the Living Vampire (Morbius on cover)						
	$6.50	$20.00	$40.00	£3.75	£11.00	£22.50
4 ND X-Men, Morbius the Living Vampire appears, Gil Kane part art						
	$7.50	$22.50	$45.00	£5.00	£15.00	£30.00
5 ND Vision	$2.50	$7.50	$15.00	£1.65	£5.00	£10.00
6 ND The Thing	$2.50	$7.50	$15.00	£1.25	£3.75	£7.50
7 ND Thor	$2.50	$7.50	$15.00	£1.25	£3.75	£7.50
8 ND scarce in the U.K. The Cat						
	$2.50	$7.50	$15.00	£1.40	£4.25	£8.50
9 ND Iron Man	$2.50	$7.50	$15.00	£1.25	£3.75	£7.50
10 ND Human Torch						
	$2.50	$7.50	$15.00	£1.25	£3.75	£7.50
11 ND Inhumans	$1.65	$5.00	$10.00	£1.00	£3.00	£6.00
12 ND Werewolf by Night						
	$1.65	$5.00	$10.00	£1.25	£3.75	£7.50
13 ND Captain America						
	$1.65	$5.00	$10.00	£1.00	£3.00	£6.00
14 ND Sub-Mariner						
	$1.65	$5.00	$10.00	£1.00	£3.00	£6.00
15 ND Ghost Rider	$2.05	$6.25	$12.50	£1.25	£3.75	£7.50
16 ND Captain Marvel						
	$1.65	$5.00	$10.00	£1.00	£3.00	£6.00
17 ND Mr. Fantastic						
	$1.65	$5.00	$10.00	£1.00	£3.00	£6.00
18 ND Human Torch and Hulk, no Spiderman						
	$1.65	$5.00	$10.00	£1.00	£3.00	£6.00
19 ND Ka-Zar	$1.65	$5.00	$10.00	£1.00	£3.00	£6.00
20 ND Black Panther						
	$1.65	$5.00	$10.00	£1.00	£3.00	£6.00
21 ND Dr. Strange	$1.00	$3.00	$6.00	£0.80	£2.50	£5.00
22 ND Hawkeye	$1.00	$3.00	$6.00	£0.80	£2.50	£5.00
23 ND Human Torch and Iceman, no Spiderman						
	$1.00	$3.00	$6.00	£0.80	£2.50	£5.00
24 Brother Voodoo						
	$1.20	$3.60	$6.00	£0.70	£2.10	£3.50
25 Daredevil	$1.20	$3.60	$6.00	£0.70	£2.10	£3.50
26 Human Torch and Thor, no Spiderman						
	$1.20	$3.60	$6.00	£0.70	£2.10	£3.50
27 Hulk	$1.20	$3.60	$6.00	£0.70	£2.10	£3.50
28 Hercules	$1.20	$3.60	$6.00	£0.70	£2.10	£3.50
29 Human Torch and Iron Man, no Spiderman						
	$1.20	$3.60	$6.00	£0.70	£2.10	£3.50
30 Falcon	$1.20	$3.60	$6.00	£0.70	£2.10	£3.50
31 Iron Fist	$0.90	$2.70	$4.50	£0.60	£1.80	£3.00
32 Human Torch and Son of Satan, no Spiderman						
	$0.90	$2.70	$4.50	£0.60	£1.80	£3.00
33 Nighthawk	$0.90	$2.70	$4.50	£0.60	£1.80	£3.00
34 Valkyrie; Nighthawk appears						
	$0.90	$2.70	$4.50	£0.60	£1.80	£3.00
35 Dr. Strange	$0.90	$2.70	$4.50	£0.60	£1.80	£3.00
36 Frankenstein; Man-Wolf appears						
	$0.90	$2.70	$4.50	£0.60	£1.80	£3.00
37 Man-Wolf; Frankenstein appears						
	$0.90	$2.70	$4.50	£0.60	£1.80	£3.00
38 ND The Beast	$0.90	$2.70	$4.50	£0.90	£2.70	£4.50
39 Human Torch	$0.90	$2.70	$4.50	£0.60	£1.80	£3.00
40 Sons of the Tiger; Human Torch appears						
	$0.90	$2.70	$4.50	£0.60	£1.80	£3.00

	$Good	$Fine	$N.Mint	£Good	£Fine	£N.Mint
41 Scarlet Witch; Vision appears						
	$0.80	$2.40	$4.00	£0.50	£1.50	£2.50
42 Vision; Scarlet Witch appears						
	$0.80	$2.40	$4.00	£0.50	£1.50	£2.50
43 Dr. Doom; Vision and Scarlet Witch appear						
	$0.80	$2.40	$4.00	£0.50	£1.50	£2.50
44 Moondragon; Vision, Scarlet Witch and Iron Man appears						
	$0.80	$2.40	$4.00	£0.50	£1.50	£2.50
45 Killraven	$0.80	$2.40	$4.00	£0.50	£1.50	£2.50
46 Deathlok	$0.80	$2.40	$4.00	£0.50	£1.50	£2.50
47 The Thing	$0.80	$2.40	$4.00	£0.50	£1.50	£2.50
48-49 Iron Man	$0.80	$2.40	$4.00	£0.50	£1.50	£2.50
50 Dr. Strange	$0.80	$2.40	$4.00	£0.50	£1.50	£2.50
51 Iron Man; Dr. Strange appears						
	$0.70	$2.10	$3.50	£0.40	£1.20	£2.00
52 Captain America						
	$0.70	$2.10	$3.50	£0.40	£1.20	£2.00
53 Hulk, guest-stars New X-Men and Woodgod; John Byrne's 1st art on X-Men; story is linked to Marvel Team-Up Annual #1						
	$2.50	$7.50	$12.50	£1.50	£4.50	£7.50
54 Hulk, John Byrne art						
	$1.00	$3.00	$5.00	£0.70	£2.10	£3.50
55 Warlock, John Byrne art						
	$1.50	$4.50	$7.50	£1.00	£3.00	£5.00
56 Daredevil	$0.70	$2.10	$3.50	£0.40	£1.20	£2.00
57 Black Widow, John Byrne cover						
	$0.70	$2.10	$3.50	£0.40	£1.20	£2.00
58 Ghost Rider	$1.00	$3.00	$5.00	£0.70	£2.10	£3.50
59 Yellowjacket; Wasp appears, John Byrne cover and art						
	$1.00	$3.00	$5.00	£0.70	£2.10	£3.50
60 Wasp; Yellowjacket appears, John Byrne art						
	$1.00	$3.00	$5.00	£0.70	£2.10	£3.50
61 Human Torch, John Byrne art						
	$0.80	$2.40	$4.00	£0.50	£1.50	£2.50
62 Ms. Marvel, John Byrne art						
	$0.80	$2.40	$4.00	£0.50	£1.50	£2.50
63 Iron Fist, John Byrne art						
	$0.80	$2.40	$4.00	£0.50	£1.50	£2.50
64 Daughters of the Dragon, Iron Fist appears, John Byrne art						
	$0.80	$2.40	$4.00	£0.50	£1.50	£2.50
65 1st Captain Britain U.S. appearance, John Byrne art						
	$1.20	$3.60	$6.00	£1.00	£3.00	£5.00
66 Captain Britain, John Byrne art						
	$1.00	$3.00	$5.00	£0.80	£2.40	£4.00
67 Tigra, John Byrne art						
	$0.80	$2.40	$4.00	£0.50	£1.50	£2.50
68 Man-Thing, John Byrne art						
	$0.80	$2.40	$4.00	£0.50	£1.50	£2.50
69 Havok, John Byrne art						
	$0.80	$2.40	$4.00	£0.50	£1.50	£2.50
70 Thor/Havok, John Byrne art						
	$0.80	$2.40	$4.00	£0.50	£1.50	£2.50
71 Falcon; Captain America appears						
	$0.50	$1.50	$2.50	£0.30	£0.90	£1.50
72 Black Widow	$0.50	$1.50	$2.50	£0.30	£0.90	£1.50
73 Daredevil	$0.50	$1.50	$2.50	£0.30	£0.90	£1.50
74 The Not-Ready-For-Prime-Time Players						
	$0.50	$1.50	$2.50	£0.30	£0.90	£1.50
75 Powerman, John Byrne art						
	$0.50	$1.50	$2.50	£0.30	£0.90	£1.50
76-77 Dr. Strange, Ms. Marvel, part Chaykin art						
	$0.50	$1.50	$2.50	£0.30	£0.90	£1.50
78 Wonderman	$0.50	$1.50	$2.50	£0.30	£0.90	£1.50
79 Red Sonja, John Byrne cover and art						
	$0.50	$1.50	$2.50	£0.30	£0.90	£1.50
80 Dr. Strange	$0.50	$1.50	$2.50	£0.30	£0.90	£1.50
81 ND Satana	$0.50	$1.50	$2.50	£0.50	£1.50	£2.50
82 Black Widow	$0.40	$1.20	$2.00	£0.25	£0.75	£1.25
83 Nick Fury; Black Widow appears						
	$0.40	$1.20	$2.00	£0.25	£0.75	£1.25
84 Shang-Chi, Master of Kung Fu; Black Widow appears						
	$0.40	$1.20	$2.00	£0.25	£0.75	£1.25
85 Black Widow; Shang-Chi and Nick Fury appear						
	$0.40	$1.20	$2.00	£0.25	£0.75	£1.25
86 Guardians of the Galaxy						
	$0.60	$1.80	$3.00	£0.40	£1.20	£2.00
87 Black Panther	$0.40	$1.20	$2.00	£0.25	£0.75	£1.25
88 Invisible Girl	$0.40	$1.20	$2.00	£0.25	£0.75	£1.25
89 Nightcrawler, part Nasser art						
	$0.50	$1.50	$2.50	£0.30	£0.90	£1.50
90 The Beast	$0.40	$1.20	$2.00	£0.25	£0.75	£1.25
91 Ghost Rider	$0.50	$1.50	$2.50	£0.30	£0.90	£1.50
92 Hawkeye	$0.40	$1.20	$2.00	£0.25	£0.75	£1.25
93 Werewolf By Night						
	$0.40	$1.20	$2.00	£0.25	£0.75	£1.25
94 Shroud, Mike Zeck art						
	$0.40	$1.20	$2.00	£0.25	£0.75	£1.25
95 Mockingbird; Nick Fury appears, Frank Miller cover						
	$0.40	$1.20	$2.00	£0.25	£0.75	£1.25
96 Howard the Duck						
	$0.40	$1.20	$2.00	£0.25	£0.75	£1.25
97 Hulk and Spiderwoman, no Spiderman						

	$Good	$Fine	$N.Mint	£Good	£Fine	£N.Mint
	$0.40	$1.20	$2.00	£0.25	£0.75	£1.25
98 Black Widow	$0.40	$1.20	$2.00	£0.25	£0.75	£1.25
99 Machine Man, Frank Miller cover						
	$0.40	$1.20	$2.00	£0.25	£0.75	£1.25
100 ND 52pgs, Fantastic Four, Miller art; Storm, Havok, Black Panther appear, John Byrne art, 1st appearance and origin Karma						
	$1.50	$4.50	$7.50	£0.70	£2.10	£3.50
101 Nighthawk, Steve Ditko art						
	$0.30	$0.90	$1.50	£0.20	£0.60	£1.00
102 ND Doc Samson						
	$0.30	$0.90	$1.50	£0.25	£0.75	£1.25
103 ND Ant-Man	$0.30	$0.90	$1.50	£0.25	£0.75	£1.25
104 ND Hulk and Ka-Zar, no Spiderman						
	$0.30	$0.90	$1.50	£0.25	£0.75	£1.25
105 ND Hulk and Powerman and Iron Fist, no Spiderman						
	$0.30	$0.90	$1.50	£0.25	£0.75	£1.25
106 ND Captain America						
	$0.30	$0.90	$1.50	£0.25	£0.75	£1.25
107 ND She-Hulk	$0.30	$0.90	$1.50	£0.25	£0.75	£1.25
108 ND Paladin	$0.30	$0.90	$1.50	£0.25	£0.75	£1.25
109 ND Dazzler	$0.30	$0.90	$1.50	£0.25	£0.75	£1.25
110 ND Iron Man	$0.30	$0.90	$1.50	£0.25	£0.75	£1.25
111 ND Devilslayer; Defenders and Dr. Strange appear						
	$0.30	$0.90	$1.50	£0.25	£0.75	£1.25
112 Kull; Dr. Strange appears						
	$0.30	$0.90	$1.50	£0.20	£0.60	£1.00
113 Quasar	$0.30	$0.90	$1.50	£0.20	£0.60	£1.00
114 Falcon, Mike Zeck cover						
	$0.30	$0.90	$1.50	£0.20	£0.60	£1.00
115 Thor	$0.30	$0.90	$1.50	£0.20	£0.60	£1.00
116 Valkyrie; Thor appears						
	$0.30	$0.90	$1.50	£0.20	£0.60	£1.00
117 Wolverine	$2.50	$7.50	$12.50	£1.20	£3.60	£6.00
118 Professor X; Wolverine appears						
	$0.30	$2.40	$4.00	£0.50	£1.50	£2.50
119 Gargoyle	$0.30	$0.90	$1.50	£0.20	£0.60	£1.00
120 Dominic Fortune						
	$0.30	$0.90	$1.50	£0.20	£0.60	£1.00
121 Human Torch	$0.30	$0.90	$1.50	£0.20	£0.60	£1.00
122 Man-Thing	$0.30	$0.90	$1.50	£0.20	£0.60	£1.00
123 Daredevil	$0.30	$0.90	$1.50	£0.20	£0.60	£1.00
124 The Beast	$0.30	$0.90	$1.50	£0.20	£0.60	£1.00
125 Tigra	$0.30	$0.90	$1.50	£0.20	£0.60	£1.00
126 Spiderman and Hulk; Powerman and Son of Satan						
	$0.30	$0.90	$1.50	£0.20	£0.60	£1.00
127 The Watcher; Captain America appears						
	$0.30	$0.90	$1.50	£0.20	£0.60	£1.00
128 Captain America						
	$0.30	$0.90	$1.50	£0.20	£0.60	£1.00
129 Vision, John Byrne cover						
	$0.30	$0.90	$1.50		£0.60	£1.00
130 Scarlet Witch; The Vision appears						
	$0.30	$0.90	$1.50	£0.20	£0.60	£1.00
131 Frogman	$0.30	$0.90	$1.50	£0.20	£0.60	£1.00
132 Mr. Fantastic	$0.30	$0.90	$1.50	£0.20	£0.60	£1.00
133 Fantastic Four, John Byrne cover						
	$0.30	$0.90	$1.50	£0.20	£0.60	£1.00
134 Jack of Hearts; continued in Jack of Hearts mini-series						
	$0.30	$0.90	$1.50	£0.20	£0.60	£1.00
135 Kitty Pryde, X-Men cameo						
	$0.40	$1.20	$2.00	£0.25	£0.75	£1.25
136 Wonderman	$0.30	$0.90	$1.50	£0.20	£0.60	£1.00
137 Aunt May, Franklin Richards; Thing cameo						
	$0.30	$0.90	$1.50	£0.20	£0.60	£1.00
138 Sandman	$0.30	$0.90	$1.50	£0.20	£0.60	£1.00
139 Nick Fury	$0.30	$0.90	$1.50	£0.20	£0.60	£1.00
140 Black Widow	$0.30	$0.90	$1.50	£0.20	£0.60	£1.00
141 Daredevil, new Black Widow appears; ties for 1st appearance Spiderman black costume						
	$0.70	$2.10	$3.50	£0.40	£1.20	£2.00
142 Captain Marvel, Spiderman in black costume						
	$0.30	$0.90	$1.50	£0.20	£0.60	£1.00
143 Starfox, Spiderman in black costume						
	$0.30	$0.90	$1.50	£0.20	£0.60	£1.00
144 Moonknight, Spiderman in black costume						
	$0.30	$0.90	$1.50	£0.20	£0.60	£1.00
145 Iron Man, Spiderman in black costume						
	$0.30	$0.90	$1.50	£0.20	£0.60	£1.00
146 Nomad, Spiderman in black costume						
	$0.30	$0.90	$1.50	£0.20	£0.60	£1.00
147 Human Torch	$0.30	$0.90	$1.50	£0.20	£0.60	£1.00
148 LD in the U.K. Thor						
	$0.30	$0.90	$1.50	£0.25	£0.75	£1.25
149 Cannonball	$0.30	$0.90	$1.50	£0.25	£0.75	£1.25
150 LD in the U.K. DS, X-Men, Barry Smith cover						
	$1.00	$3.00	$5.00	£0.70	£2.10	£3.50
Title Value:	$143.45	$432.65	$799.50	£90.50	£271.75	£501.50

Note: Spiderman in black costume #141-146. Issue #74 had no number on the cover.

MARVEL TEAM-UP ANNUAL

Marvel Comics Group; 1 1976-7 Oct 1984

	$Good	$Fine	$N.Mint	£Good	£Fine	£N.Mint
1 ND 52pgs, Spiderman, X-Men; story linked to Marvel Team-Up #53						
	$2.50	$7.50	$15.00	£1.65	£5.00	£10.00
2 ND 52pgs, Spiderman, Hulk						

	$Good	$Fine	$N.Mint	£Good	£Fine	£N.Mint
	$0.60	$1.80	$3.00	£0.40	£1.20	£2.00
3 ND 52pgs, Hulk, Powerman, Iron Fist; Machine Man appears, Spiderman appears as cameo only; Frank Miller cover						
	$0.60	$1.80	$3.00	£0.40	£1.20	£2.00
4 ND 52pgs, Spiderman, Moonknight, Iron Fist, Daredevil, Powerman						
	$0.50	$1.50	$2.50	£0.30	£0.90	£1.50
5 ND 52pgs, Spiderman, Thing, Dr.Strange, Scarlet Witch, Quasar						
	$0.50	$1.50	$2.50	£0.30	£0.90	£1.50
6 ND 52pgs, Spiderman, New Mutants, Cloak and Dagger						
	$0.50	$1.50	$2.50	£0.30	£0.90	£1.50
7 ND 52pgs, Spiderman, Alpha Flight, John Byrne cover						
	$0.50	$1.50	$2.50	£0.30	£0.90	£1.50
Title Value:	$5.70	$17.10	$31.00	£3.65	£11.00	£20.00

MARVEL TEAM-UP, THE OFFICIAL MARVEL INDEX TO

Marvel Comics Group; 1 Jan 1986-6 Jul 1987

	$Good	$Fine	$N.Mint	£Good	£Fine	£N.Mint
1 ND scarce in the U.K. information and colour cover reproductions on Marvel Team-Up #1-#20						
	$0.50	$1.50	$2.50	£0.30	£0.90	£1.50
2 ND scarce in the U.K. information and colour cover reproductions on Marvel Team-Up #21-#42						
	$0.50	$1.50	$2.50	£0.30	£0.90	£1.50
3 ND scarce in the U.K. information and colour cover reproductions on Marvel Team-Up #43-#59, Annual #1; P. Craig Russell cover						
	$0.50	$1.50	$2.50	£0.30	£0.90	£1.50
4 ND scarce in the U.K. information and colour cover reproductions on Marvel Team-Up #60-#80						
	$0.50	$1.50	$2.50	£0.30	£0.90	£1.50
5 ND scarce in the U.K. information and colour cover reproductions on Marvel Team-Up #81-#98, Annual #2						
	$0.50	$1.50	$2.50	£0.30	£0.90	£1.50
6 ND scarce in the U.K. information and colour cover reproductions on Marvel Team-Up #99-#112, Annual #3,#4						
	$0.50	$1.50	$2.50	£0.30	£0.90	£1.50
Title Value:	$3.00	$9.00	$15.00	£1.80	£5.40	£9.00

MARVEL TREASURY EDITION

Marvel Comics Group, Tabloid; 1 1974-28 1981

	$Good	$Fine	$N.Mint	£Good	£Fine	£N.Mint
1 scarce in the U.K. Spiderman						
	$1.20	$3.60	$6.00	£0.80	£2.40	£4.00
2 Fantastic Four, issue #48 reprinted (origin Silver Surfer)						
	$1.00	$3.00	$5.00	£0.60	£1.80	£3.00
3 Thor	$1.00	$3.00	$5.00	£0.60	£1.80	£3.00
4 Conan, Smith reprints						
	$1.00	$3.00	$5.00	£0.60	£1.80	£3.00
5 Hulk, reprints origin						
	$1.00	$3.00	$5.00	£0.60	£1.80	£3.00
6 Dr. Strange	$0.80	$2.40	$4.00	£0.50	£1.50	£2.50
7 Avengers	$0.80	$2.40	$4.00	£0.50	£1.50	£2.50
8 Christmas Holiday Grab-Bag (Spiderman, Hulk, Nick Fury)						
	$0.80	$2.40	$4.00	£0.50	£1.50	£2.50
9 Super-Hero Team up						
	$0.80	$2.40	$4.00	£0.50	£1.50	£2.50
10 Thor	$0.80	$2.40	$4.00	£0.50	£1.50	£2.50
11 Fantastic Four	$0.80	$2.40	$4.00	£0.50	£1.50	£2.50
12 Howard the Duck, one new story plus Brunner reprints from Giant Size Man-Thing						
	$0.80	$2.40	$4.00	£0.50	£1.50	£2.50
13 Christmas Holiday Grab-Bag						
	$0.80	$2.40	$4.00	£0.50	£1.50	£2.50
14 less common in the U.K. Spiderman						
	$0.80	$2.40	$4.00	£0.50	£1.50	£2.50
15 Conan	$0.80	$2.40	$4.00	£0.50	£1.50	£2.50
16 Defenders, origin retold						
	$0.80	$2.40	$4.00	£0.50	£1.50	£2.50
17 Hulk	$0.80	$2.40	$4.00	£0.50	£1.50	£2.50
18 ND Spiderman, reprints 1st team-up with X-Men						
	$0.80	$2.40	$4.00	£0.50	£1.50	£2.50
19 ND Conan	$0.80	$2.40	$4.00	£0.60	£1.80	£3.00
20 ND Hulk	$0.80	$2.40	$4.00	£0.60	£1.80	£3.00
21 ND Fantastic Four						
	$0.80	$2.40	$4.00	£0.60	£1.80	£3.00
22 ND Spiderman	$0.80	$2.40	$4.00	£0.60	£1.80	£3.00
23 ND Conan	$0.80	$2.40	$4.00	£0.60	£1.80	£3.00
24 ND Hulk	$0.80	$2.40	$4.00	£0.60	£1.80	£3.00
25 ND Spiderman vs. Hulk						
	$0.80	$2.40	$4.00	£0.60	£1.80	£3.00
26 ND reprints Hulk #167-#170; new Wolverine and Hercules story (6pgs)						
	$1.20	$3.60	$6.00	£0.80	£2.40	£4.00
27 ND reprints Spiderman from Marvel Team Up #9-#11,#27, new Angel story (5pgs)						
	$1.00	$3.00	$5.00	£0.70	£2.10	£3.50
28 ND Superman and Spiderman, origins each retold						
	$1.00	$3.00	$5.00	£0.70	£2.10	£3.50
Title Value:	$24.40	$73.20	$122.00	£16.10	£48.30	£80.50

Note: owing to their large size and card covers, all are very scarce in true mint condition.

MARVEL TREASURY OF OZ

Marvel Comics Group, Tabloid; 1 1975

(see M.G.M.'s Marvelous...)

	$Good	$Fine	$N.Mint	£Good	£Fine	£N.Mint
1 ND The Marvelous Land of Oz, Buscema art						
	$0.90	$2.70	$4.50	£0.60	£1.80	£3.00
Title Value:	$0.90	$2.70	$4.50	£0.60	£1.80	£3.00

MARVEL TREASURY SPECIAL

Marvel Comics Group, Tabloid; 1974-1980

	£Good	£Fine	£N.Mint
1 ND 80pgs, Ditko Spiderman reprints, titled Marvel Special Edition	£0.60	£1.80	£3.00
1 2001 A Space Odyssey	£0.40	£1.20	£2.00
1 ND Land of Oz	£0.50	£1.50	£2.50
1 Captain America's Bicentennial Battles Kirby/Smith art	£0.45	£1.35	£2.25
1 Savage Fist of Kung Fu	£0.45	£1.35	£2.25
1 Giant Super-Hero Holiday Grab-Bag	£0.50	£1.50	£2.50
1 80pgs, reprints Star Wars #1-3	£0.35	£1.05	£1.75

	$Good	$Fine	$N.Mint	£Good	£Fine	£N.Mint
2 80pgs, reprints Star Wars #4-6				£0.30	£0.90	£1.50
2 ND Empire Strikes Back, reprints Star Wars #39-44				£0.50	£1.50	£2.50
3 ND reprints Star Wars #1-6				£0.60	£1.80	£3.00
3 Close Encounters, reprints Marvel Super Special #3				£0.35	£1.05	£1.75

MARVEL TRIPLE ACTION

Marvel Comics Group; 1 Feb 1972-24 Mar 1975; 25 Aug 1975-47 Apr 1979

	$Good	$Fine	$N.Mint	£Good	£Fine	£N.Mint
1 ND scarce in the U.K. 52pgs, Silver Surfer appears (reprints from Fantastic Four #57 onwards begin)						
	$1.00	$3.00	$5.00	£0.70	£2.10	£3.50
2-4 ND Silver Surfer appears						
	$0.60	$1.80	$3.00	£0.40	£1.20	£2.00
5 ND Avengers reprints begin (from #10 onwards omitting #11)						
	$0.60	$1.80	$3.00	£0.40	£1.20	£2.00
6-10 ND	$0.50	$1.50	$2.50	£0.30	£0.90	£1.50
11-19 ND	$0.40	$1.20	$2.00	£0.25	£0.75	£1.25
20-40 ND	$0.30	$0.90	$1.50	£0.20	£0.60	£1.00
41-44 ND	$0.25	$0.75	$1.25	£0.15	£0.45	£0.75
45 includes X-Men reprint						
	$0.25	$0.75	$1.25	£0.15	£0.45	£0.75
46-47 ND	$0.25	$0.75	$1.25	£0.15	£0.45	£0.75
Title Value:	$17.55	$52.65	$87.75	£11.30	£33.90	£56.50

Note: Fantastic Four reprints #1-4, Avengers reprints #5-46.

REPRINT FEATURES

Avengers in 5-47. Fantastic Four in 1-4. Silver Surfer in 1-3. X-Men in 45.

MARVEL TRIPLE ACTION GIANT SIZE

Marvel Comics Group; 1 May 1975-2 Jul 1975

	$Good	$Fine	$N.Mint	£Good	£Fine	£N.Mint
1 ND very scarce in the U.K. 64pgs, reprints Avengers #31, Daredevil #20, Strange Tales #122						
	$0.80	$2.40	$4.00	£0.80	£2.40	£4.00
2 ND very scarce in the U.K. 64pgs, reprints Avengers #32, Daredevil #21, Strange Tales #123						
	$0.70	$2.10	$3.50	£0.70	£2.10	£3.50
Title Value:	$1.50	$4.50	$7.50	£1.50	£4.50	£7.50

Note: Avengers reprints in 1, 2.

MARVEL TRY-OUT BOOK

Marvel Comics Group, OS; Oversize; nn 1986

	$Good	$Fine	$N.Mint	£Good	£Fine	£N.Mint
nn ND illustrations and exercises to complete						
	$3.50	$10.50	$17.50	£2.50	£7.50	£12.50
Title Value:	$3.50	$10.50	$17.50	£2.50	£7.50	£12.50

Note: the value of the item depends on the extent of completion inside. Untouched copies are very scarce in both the U.K. and U.S.

MARVEL TWO-IN-ONE

Marvel Comics Group; 1 Jan 1974-100 Jun 1983

[The Thing appears in every issue teamed with each of the following]

	$Good	$Fine	$N.Mint	£Good	£Fine	£N.Mint
1 ND Man-Thing	$5.00	$15.00	$30.00	£3.00	£10.00	£20.00
2 ND Sub-Mariner	$2.05	$6.25	$12.50	£1.25	£3.75	£7.50
3 ND Daredevil	$1.65	$5.00	$10.00	£1.05	£3.25	£6.50
4 ND Captain America						
	$1.65	$5.00	$10.00	£1.05	£3.25	£6.50
5 ND Guardians of the Galaxy; Captain America appears						
	$2.50	$7.50	$15.00	£1.25	£3.75	£7.50
6 ND Dr. Strange, Jim Starlin cover						
	$2.50	$7.50	$15.00	£1.05	£3.25	£6.50
7 ND Valkyrie	$1.30	$4.00	$8.00	£0.80	£2.50	£5.00
8 ND Ghost Rider	$2.05	$6.25	$12.50	£1.05	£3.25	£6.50
9 ND Thor	$1.30	$4.00	$8.00	£0.80	£2.50	£5.00
10 ND Black Widow						
	$1.30	$4.00	$8.00	£0.80	£2.50	£5.00
11 Golem	$0.80	$2.40	$4.00	£0.50	£1.50	£2.50
12 Iron Man	$0.80	$2.40	$4.00	£0.50	£1.50	£2.50
13 Powerman	$0.80	$2.40	$4.00	£0.50	£1.50	£2.50
14 Son of Satan	$0.80	$2.40	$4.00	£0.50	£1.50	£2.50
15 Morbius	$0.80	$2.40	$4.00	£0.50	£1.50	£2.50
16 Ka-Zar	$0.80	$2.40	$4.00	£0.50	£1.50	£2.50

	$Good	$Fine	$N.Mint	£Good	£Fine	£N.Mint
17 Spiderman; X-over Marvel Team Up #47						
	$0.80	$2.40	$4.00	£0.50	£1.50	£2.50
18 Scarecrow	$0.80	$2.40	$4.00	£0.50	£1.50	£2.50
19 Tigra	$0.80	$2.40	$4.00	£0.50	£1.50	£2.50
20 Liberty Legion, continues from Fantastic Four Annual #11						
	$0.80	$2.40	$4.00	£0.50	£1.50	£2.50
21 Doc Savage	$0.60	$1.80	$3.00	£0.40	£1.20	£2.00
22 Thor; Human Torch appears						
	$0.60	$1.80	$3.00	£0.40	£1.20	£2.00
23 Thor	$0.60	$1.80	$3.00	£0.40	£1.20	£2.00
24 Black Goliath	$0.60	$1.80	$3.00	£0.40	£1.20	£2.00
25 Iron Fist	$0.60	$1.80	$3.00	£0.40	£1.20	£2.00
26 Nick Fury; Deathlok appears on last page						
	$0.60	$1.80	$3.00	£0.40	£1.20	£2.00
27 Deathlok; Fantastic Four and Impossible Man appear						
	$1.00	$3.00	$5.00	£0.50	£1.50	£2.50
28 Sub-Mariner; Deathlok cameo (2pgs)						
	$0.60	$1.80	$3.00	£0.40	£1.20	£2.00
29 Master of Kung Fu; Spiderman appears on last page						
	$0.60	$1.80	$3.00	£0.40	£1.20	£2.00
30 Spiderwoman (2nd appearance)						
	$1.00	$3.00	$5.00	£0.50	£1.50	£2.50
31 Spiderwoman (3rd appearance)						
	$0.60	$1.80	$3.00	£0.30	£0.90	£1.50
32 Invisible Girl; Spiderwoman appears						
	$0.60	$1.80	$3.00	£0.30	£0.90	£1.50
33 Modred the Mystic; Spiderwoman appears						
	$0.60	$1.80	$3.00	£0.30	£0.90	£1.50
34 Nighthawk; Deathlok cameo						
	$0.60	$1.80	$3.00	£0.30	£0.90	£1.50
35 Skull the Slayer	$0.60	$1.80	$3.00	£0.30	£0.90	£1.50
36 Mr. Fantastic; Skull the Slayer appears						
	$0.60	$1.80	$3.00	£0.30	£0.90	£1.50
37 Matt Murdock (Daredevil)						
	$0.60	$1.80	$3.00	£0.30	£0.90	£1.50
38 Daredevil	$0.60	$1.80	$3.00	£0.30	£0.90	£1.50
39 Vision; Daredevil and Yellowjacket appear						
	$0.60	$1.80	$3.00	£0.30	£0.90	£1.50
40 Black Panther	$0.60	$1.80	$3.00	£0.30	£0.90	£1.50
41 Brother Voodoo; Black Panther appears						
	$0.50	$1.50	$2.50	£0.30	£0.90	£1.50
42 Captain America; Wundarr appears						
	$0.50	$1.50	$2.50	£0.30	£0.90	£1.50
43 Man-Thing and Captain America, Cosmic Cube featured, John Byrne art						
	$0.60	$1.80	$3.00	£0.40	£1.20	£2.00
44 Hercules	$0.50	$1.50	$2.50	£0.30	£0.90	£1.50
45 Captain Marvel	$0.50	$1.50	$2.50	£0.30	£0.90	£1.50
46 Hulk	$0.50	$1.50	$2.50	£0.30	£0.90	£1.50
47 The Yancy Street Gang						
	$0.50	$1.50	$2.50	£0.30	£0.90	£1.50
48 Jack of Hearts	$0.50	$1.50	$2.50	£0.30	£0.90	£1.50
49 Dr. Strange	$0.50	$1.50	$2.50	£0.30	£0.90	£1.50
50 Thing vs. Thing, John Byrne art						
	$0.60	$1.80	$3.00	£0.40	£1.20	£2.00
51 Frank Miller art, Beast, Ms.Marvel, Nick Fury, Wonderman						
	$0.80	$2.40	$4.00	£0.50	£1.50	£2.50
52 Moon Knight	$0.60	$1.80	$3.00	£0.40	£1.20	£2.00
53 Quasar, Deathlok on last page, John Byrne art; The Pegasus Project begins (ends #58)						
	$0.60	$1.80	$3.00	£0.40	£1.20	£2.00
54 Deathlok dies, John Byrne art						
	$2.00	$6.00	$10.00	£1.00	£3.00	£5.00

Marvel Super-Hero Secret Wars #1

Marvel Tales #6

Marvel Triple Action #2

#	Description	$Good	$Fine	$N.Mint	£Good	£Fine	£N.Mint
55	Giant-Man, John Byrne art	$0.60	$1.80	$3.00	£0.40	£1.20	£2.00
56	Thundra; Giant-Man appears, George Perez and Gene Day art	$0.40	$1.20	$2.00	£0.25	£0.75	£1.25
57	Wundarr; Giant-Man appears, George Perez art	$0.40	$1.20	$2.00	£0.25	£0.75	£1.25
58	Aquarian; Giant-Man appears, George Perez art	$0.40	$1.20	$2.00	£0.25	£0.75	£1.25
59	Human Torch	$0.40	$1.20	$2.00	£0.25	£0.75	£1.25
60	Impossible Man, George Perez art	$0.40	$1.20	$2.00	£0.25	£0.75	£1.25
61	Starhawk, George Perez art	$0.50	$1.50	$2.50	£0.30	£0.90	£1.50
62	Moondragon; Starhawk appears, George Perez art	$0.50	$1.50	$2.50	£0.30	£0.90	£1.50
63	Warlock (dead), Starhawk appears, George Perez art	$0.50	$1.50	$2.50	£0.30	£0.90	£1.50
64	Stingray; Wundarr and Fantastic Four appear, George Perez art	$0.40	$1.20	$2.00	£0.25	£0.75	£1.25
65	Triton; Stingray and Thundra appear, George Perez art	$0.40	$1.20	$2.00	£0.25	£0.75	£1.25
66	Scarlet Witch	$0.40	$1.20	$2.00	£0.25	£0.75	£1.25
67	Hyperion; Quasar and Thundra appear	$0.40	$1.20	$2.00	£0.25	£0.75	£1.25
68	Angel	$0.40	$1.20	$2.00	£0.25	£0.75	£1.25
69	Guardians of the Galaxy; Fantastic Four appear	$0.50	$1.50	$2.50	£0.30	£0.90	£1.50
70	The Yancy Street Gang	$0.40	$1.20	$2.00	£0.25	£0.75	£1.25
71	Mr. Fantastic; Triton, Inhumans, Fantastic Four and Stingray appear; 1st appearance Maelstrom	$0.30	$0.90	$1.50	£0.20	£0.60	£1.00
72	ND Inhumans	$0.30	$0.90	$1.50	£0.20	£0.60	£1.00
73	ND Quasar	$0.30	$0.90	$1.50	£0.20	£0.60	£1.00
74	Puppet Master	$0.30	$0.90	$1.50	£0.20	£0.60	£1.00
75	52pgs, Avengers, Beast appears	$0.30	$0.90	$1.50	£0.20	£0.60	£1.00
76	Iceman; Black Goliath appears	$0.30	$0.90	$1.50	£0.20	£0.60	£1.00
77	Man-Thing; Sgt. Fury appears in flash-back	$0.30	$0.90	$1.50	£0.20	£0.60	£1.00
78	Wonderman	$0.30	$0.90	$1.50	£0.20	£0.60	£1.00
79	Blue Diamond	$0.30	$0.90	$1.50	£0.20	£0.60	£1.00
80	Ghost Rider; Fantastic Four appear	$0.60	$1.80	$3.00	£0.40	£1.20	£2.00
81	Sub-Mariner; Black Goliath and Quasar appear	$0.30	$0.90	$1.50	£0.20	£0.60	£1.00
82	Captain America; Black Goliath and Fantastic Four appear	$0.30	$0.90	$1.50	£0.20	£0.60	£1.00
83	Sasquatch; Black Goliath and Fantastic Four appear	$0.40	$1.20	$2.00	£0.25	£0.75	£1.25
84	Alpha Flight; Black Goliath and Fantastic Four appear	$0.40	$1.20	$2.00	£0.25	£0.75	£1.25
85	Spiderwoman	$0.30	$0.90	$1.50	£0.20	£0.60	£1.00
86	Sandman	$0.30	$0.90	$1.50	£0.20	£0.60	£1.00
87	Ant-Man	$0.30	$0.90	$1.50	£0.20	£0.60	£1.0
88	She-Hulk	$0.30	$0.90	$1.50	£0.20	£0.60	£1.00
89	Human Torch	$0.30	$0.90	$1.50	£0.20	£0.60	£1.00
90	Machine Man	$0.30	$0.90	$1.50	£0.20	£0.60	£1.00
91	Sphinx; Dr. Strange appears	$0.30	$0.90	$1.50	£0.20	£0.60	£1.00
92	Jocasta; Machine Man appears	$0.30	$0.90	$1.50	£0.20	£0.60	£1.00
93	Machine Man (Jocasta dies)	$0.30	$0.90	$1.50	£0.20	£0.60	£1.00
94	Powerman/Iron Fist	$0.30	$0.90	$1.50	£0.20	£0.60	£1.00
95	The Living Mummy	$0.30	$0.90	$1.50	£0.20	£0.60	£1.00
96	The Sandman (and virtually all Marvel characters)	$0.30	$0.90	$1.50	£0.20	£0.60	£1.00
97	Iron Man	$0.30	$0.90	$1.50	£0.20	£0.60	£1.00
98	Video Wars	$0.30	$0.90	$1.50	£0.20	£0.60	£1.00
99	Rom	$0.30	$0.90	$1.50	£0.20	£0.60	£1.00
100	LD in the U.K. DS, Ben Grimm, John Byrne script	$0.60	$1.20	$2.00	£0.25	£0.75	£1.25
Title Value:		**$67.90**	**$204.30**	**$362.00**	**£40.80**	**£123.20**	**£218.00**

ARTISTS
Gene inks on 58, 60-70. Byrne covers on 56-58, 98, 99. Kirby covers 12, 19, 25, 27. Perez covers on 42, 51-52, 54-55, 61-66. Perez art: 56-58, 60, 64, 65, 75.

MARVEL TWO-IN-ONE ANNUAL
Marvel Comics Group; 1 1976-7 Oct 1982

#	Description	$Good	$Fine	$N.Mint	£Good	£Fine	£N.Mint
1	ND Thing, Liberty Legion, continued from Fantastic Four Annual #11 and continues in Marvel Two-in-One #20; Jack Kirby cover	$0.70	$2.10	$3.50	£0.50	£1.50	£2.50
2	ND scarce in the U.K. Jim Starlin art, Thing, Spiderman, Avengers, Warlock; Thanos dies, continues from Avengers Annual #7	$4.00	$12.00	$20.00	£2.50	£7.50	£12.50
3	ND scarce in the U.K. Thing/Nova	$0.50	$1.50	$2.50	£0.40	£1.20	£2.00
4	ND Thing, Black Bolt	$0.40	$1.20	$2.00	£0.25	£0.75	£1.25
5	ND Thing, Hulk	$0.40	$1.20	$2.00	£0.25	£0.75	£1.25
6	ND Thing, American Eagle; Ka-Zar appears, Gene Day inks	$0.40	$1.20	$2.00	£0.25	£0.75	£1.25
7	ND Thing, X-Men appear; cameos of many other heroes	$0.50	$1.50	$2.50	£0.30	£0.90	£1.50
Title Value:		**$6.90**	**$20.70**	**$34.50**	**£4.45**	**£13.35**	**£22.25**

MARVEL UNIVERSE – MASTER EDITION
Marvel Comics Group; 1 Dec 1990-36 Nov 1993

#	Description	$Good	$Fine	$N.Mint	£Good	£Fine	£N.Mint
1	ND 48pgs, loose-leaf spiral-bound format "who's who" of Marvel characters. Spiderman/Juggernaut featured	$0.80	$2.40	$4.00	£0.50	£1.50	£2.50
2	ND 48pgs, Captain America/Dr. Octopus featured	$0.80	$2.40	$4.00	£0.50	£1.50	£2.50
3	ND 48pgs, Ghost Rider/Elektra featured	$0.80	$2.40	$4.00	£0.50	£1.50	£2.50
4	ND 48pgs, Wolverine	$0.80	$2.40	$4.00	£0.50	£1.50	£2.50
5	ND 48pgs, Punisher/She-Hulk/Bullseye/ Nightcrawler featured	$0.80	$2.40	$4.00	£0.50	£1.50	£2.50
6	ND 48pgs, Hobgoblin	$0.80	$2.40	$4.00	£0.50	£1.50	£2.50
7	ND 48pgs, Daredevil/Callisto/Firestar/Nova/Black Knight featured	$0.80	$2.40	$4.00	£0.50	£1.50	£2.50
8	ND 48pgs, Hulk	$0.80	$2.40	$4.00	£0.50	£1.50	£2.50
9	ND 48pgs, Moon Knight/Scarlet Witch/Doc Samson featured	$0.80	$2.40	$4.00	£0.50	£1.50	£2.50
10	ND 48pgs, Captain Britain/Jigsaw/Wendigo/Odin featured	$0.80	$2.40	$4.00	£0.50	£1.50	£2.50
11	ND 48pgs, Storm, Madrox, Kid Nova featured	$0.80	$2.40	$4.00	£0.50	£1.50	£2.50
12	ND 48pgs, Silver Surfer, Black Cat, Loki featured	$0.80	$2.40	$4.00	£0.50	£1.50	£2.50
13	ND 48pgs, High Evolutionary, Werewolf, Shroud, Mysterio featured	$0.80	$2.40	$4.00	£0.50	£1.50	£2.50
14	ND 48pgs, Captain America, Avengers, Thor, Fin Fang Foom featured	$0.80	$2.40	$4.00	£0.50	£1.50	£2.50
15-17	ND 48pgs	$0.80	$2.40	$4.00	£0.50	£1.50	£2.50
18	ND 48pgs, Thing, She-Hulk	$0.80	$2.40	$4.00	£0.50	£1.50	£2.50
19	ND 48pgs	$0.80	$2.40	$4.00	£0.50	£1.50	£2.50
20	ND 48pgs, Dr. Doom, Archangel	$0.80	$2.40	$4.00	£0.50	£1.50	£2.50
21	ND 48pgs, Gambit, Watcher	$0.80	$2.40	$4.00	£0.50	£1.50	£2.50
22	ND 48pgs, Speedball, Nick Fury, Rogue, Silver Sable, Invisible Woman plus Venom feature	$0.80	$2.40	$4.00	£0.50	£1.50	£2.50
23	ND 48pgs, Deathlok, Batroc, Psylocke, Sunfire	$0.80	$2.40	$4.00	£0.50	£1.50	£2.50
24	ND 48pgs, Johnny Blaze, Human Torch, Iron Fist, Red Skull	$0.80	$2.40	$4.00	£0.50	£1.50	£2.50
25	ND 48pgs, Deadpool, Night Thrasher, Black Widow	$0.80	$2.40	$4.00	£0.50	£1.50	£2.50
26	ND 48pgs, Morbius, Stryfe, Mystique, Ikaris	$0.80	$2.40	$4.00	£0.50	£1.50	£2.50
27	ND 48pgs, Beta Ray Bill, Pip the Troll, Wonderman, Green Goblin	$0.80	$2.40	$4.00	£0.50	£1.50	£2.50
28	ND 48pgs, Dr. Strange, Blade, Scarecrow, Hellfire Club, Man-Beast, Starhawk, X-Men	$0.80	$2.40	$4.00	£0.50	£1.50	£2.50
29	ND 48pgs, Carnage, Dazzler, Puma, Sabretooth	$0.80	$2.40	$4.00	£0.50	£1.50	£2.50
30	ND 48pgs, Bishop, Dracula, Longshot, Magik, Rage	$0.80	$2.40	$4.00	£0.50	£1.50	£2.50
31	ND 48pgs, War Machine, Cardiac, Feral, Sleepwalker, Molecule Man, Vision, Destroyer and Killraven	$0.80	$2.40	$4.00	£0.50	£1.50	£2.50
32	ND 48pgs, Maverick, Captain Universe, the Kree, Lord Chaos, Mephisto	$0.80	$2.40	$4.00	£0.50	£1.50	£2.50
33	ND 48pgs, Warpath, Gideon, Avalanche, Bloodaxe, Crippler and Living Tribunal	$0.80	$2.40	$4.00	£0.50	£1.50	£2.50
34	ND 48pgs, Thunderstrike, Deathwatch, Caliban, Henry Pym, Turbo, Living Laser	$0.80	$2.40	$4.00	£0.50	£1.50	£2.50
35	ND 48pgs, Hellstrom, Omega Red, Lilith, Beyonder, Spiderman 2099	$0.80	$2.40	$4.00	£0.50	£1.50	£2.50
36	ND 48pgs, Morbius, Ravage 2099, Sunspot, Zarathos	$0.80	$2.40	$4.00	£0.50	£1.50	£2.50
Title Value:		**$28.80**	**$86.40**	**$144.00**	**£18.00**	**£54.00**	**£90.00**

Note: binder issued separately

MARVEL X-MEN COLLECTION
Marvel Comics Group,MS; 1 Jan 1994-3 Mar 1994

#	Description	$Good	$Fine	$N.Mint	£Good	£Fine	£N.Mint
1-3	ND 32pgs, reprints Jim Lee's set of 96 trading cards; gatefold back cover	$0.60	$1.80	$3.00	£0.40	£1.20	£2.00
Title Value:		**$1.80**	**$5.40**	**$9.00**	**£1.20**	**£3.60**	**£6.00**

MARVEL'S GREATEST COMICS
Marvel Comics Group; 23 Oct 1969-96 Jan 1981
(previously Marvel Collector's Item Classics)

#	Description	$Good	$Fine	$N.Mint	£Good	£Fine	£N.Mint
23-28	64pgs	$0.70	$2.10	$3.50	£0.50	£1.50	£2.50
29	64pgs, reprints Fantastic Four #12	$0.70	$2.10	$3.50	£0.50	£1.50	£2.50
30	64pgs	$0.70	$2.10	$3.50	£0.50	£1.50	£2.50
31	64pgs, reprints Fantastic Four #39, #40	$0.60	$1.80	$3.00	£0.40	£1.20	£2.00
32-34	64pgs	$0.60	$1.80	$3.00	£0.40	£1.20	£2.00
35	ND reprints 1st Silver Surfer (FF #48)	$0.90	$2.70	$4.50	£0.60	£1.80	£3.00
36	ND reprints 2nd Silver Surfer (FF #49)						

VERY GENERAL PERCENTAGE CONVERSION CHART WHICH MAY BE USED TO CALCULATE LOW AND INBETWEEN GRADES:

	$Good	$Fine	$N.Mint	£Good	£Fine	£N.Mint
	$0.70	$2.10	$3.50	£0.50	£1.50	£2.50
37 ND reprints 3rd Silver Surfer (FF #50)						
	$0.70	$2.10	$3.50	£0.50	£1.50	£2.50
38-40 ND	$0.60	$1.80	$3.00	£0.40	£1.20	£2.00
41 ND	$0.50	$1.50	$2.50	£0.30	£0.90	£1.50
42 ND reprints Fantastic Four #55						
	$0.50	$1.50	$2.50	£0.30	£0.90	£1.50
43-50 ND	$0.50	$1.50	$2.50	£0.30	£0.90	£1.50
51-96 ND	$0.40	$1.20	$2.00	£0.25	£0.75	£1.25
Title Value:	$35.50	$106.50	$177.50	£22.90	£68.70	£114.50

Note: Silver Surfer appears in #36,37,42

REPRINT FEATURES

Captain America 25-33. Dr.Strange 23-33. Fantastic Four in 23-96. Iron Man 23-33. Watcher in 23, 24.

MARVEL'S GREATEST SUPER-BATTLES
Marvel Comics Group; nn Aug 1994

nn ND 176pgs, softcover trade paperback, reprints include Uncanny X-Men #212/213, Amazing Spiderman #318/319 and Marvel Two in One Annual #7

	$Good	$Fine	$N.Mint	£Good	£Fine	£N.Mint
	$3.00	$9.00	$15.00	£2.00	£6.00	£10.00
Title Value:	$3.00	$9.00	$15.00	£2.00	£6.00	£10.00

MARVEL: 1989-95 THE YEAR IN REVIEW
Marvel Comics Group,Magazine; nn Jan 1990; nn Feb 1991; nn Feb 1992; nn Feb 1993; nn Feb 1994

nn ND 48pgs, based on Time Magazine format and style with articles and reviews; Todd McFarlane cover (1989)

	$0.60	$1.80	$3.00	£0.40	£1.20	£2.00

nn ND 48pgs, based on Time Magazine format and style with articles and reviews; Kevin Maguire cover (1990)

	$0.60	$1.80	$3.00	£0.40	£1.20	£2.00

nn ND 48pgs, based on Time Magazine format and style with articles and reviews (1991)

	$0.60	$1.80	$3.00	£0.40	£1.20	£2.00

nn ND 48pgs, comic-sized format rather than magazine with articles and reviews (1992)

	$0.60	$1.80	$3.00	£0.40	£1.20	£2.00

nn ND 48pgs, more satirical than in previous years; Sam Kieth cover

	$0.60	$1.80	$3.00	£0.40	£1.20	£2.00

nn ND 48pgs, back to factual review of the year with emphasis on art rather than text

	$0.60	$1.80	$3.00	£0.40	£1.20	£2.00
Title Value:	$3.60	$10.80	$18.00	£2.40	£7.20	£12.00

MARVEL: PORTRAIT OF THE UNIVERSE
Marvel Comics Group,MS; 1 Mar 1995-4 Jun 1995

1-4 ND Marvel history told in fully painted pin-ups; artists include Dave Gibbons, Brian Bolland, Simon Bisley and Mark Texeira

	$Good	$Fine	$N.Mint	£Good	£Fine	£N.Mint
	$0.60	$1.80	$3.00	£0.40	£1.20	£2.00
Title Value:	$2.40	$7.20	$12.00	£1.60	£4.80	£8.00

MARVELS
Marvel Comics Group,MS; 0 Aug 1994; 1 Jan 1994-4 Apr 1994

0 ND (Aug 1994) 8pg Human Torch origin story from Marvel Age plus sketches and designs

	$0.70	$2.10	$3.50	£0.50	£1.50	£2.50

1 ND 48pgs, acetate outer cover, Alex Ross painted art begins

	$1.50	$4.50	$7.50	£1.00	£3.00	£5.00

2 ND 48pgs, acetate outer cover, Alex Ross painted art

	$1.50	$4.50	$7.50	£1.00	£3.00	£5.00

3 ND 48pgs, acetate outer cover, Alex Ross painted art

	$1.20	$3.60	$6.00	£0.80	£2.40	£4.00

4 ND 48pgs, acetate outer cover, Alex Ross painted art

	$1.20	$3.60	$6.00	£0.70	£2.10	£3.50
Title Value:	$6.10	$18.30	$30.50	£4.00	£12.00	£20.00

Marvels Hardcover (Nov 1994) 216pgs, reprints mini-series with unpublished artwork and new Alex Ross painted cover — £4.50 £13.50 £22.50

Marvels (Jan 1995) Trade paperback 216pgs, reprints mini-series with new Alex Ross painted cover — £2.70 £8.10 £13.50

MASK (1ST SERIES)
DC Comics, Toy; 1 Feb 1987-9 Oct 1987

	$Good	$Fine	$N.Mint	£Good	£Fine	£N.Mint
1-9	$0.15	$0.45	$0.75	£0.10	£0.30	£0.50
Title Value:	$1.35	$4.05	$6.75	£0.90	£2.70	£4.50

MASK (LIMITED SERIES)
DC Comics,MS TV Toy; 1 Dec 1985-4 Mar 1986

	$Good	$Fine	$N.Mint	£Good	£Fine	£N.Mint
1-4	$0.15	$0.45	$0.75	£0.10	£0.30	£0.50
Title Value:	$0.60	$1.80	$3.00	£0.40	£1.20	£2.00

MASK IN SCHOOL SPIRITS HARDCOVER STORYBOOK
Dark Horse,OS; nn Aug 1995

nn ND 32pgs hardcover; Rick Geary scripts & art with Chris Chalenor

	$Good	$Fine	$N.Mint	£Good	£Fine	£N.Mint
	$2.30	$6.90	$11.00	£1.50	£4.50	£7.50
Title Value:	$2.30	$6.90	$11.00	£1.50	£4.50	£7.50

MASK RETURNS, THE
Dark Horse,MS; 1 Nov 1992-4 Feb 1993

1 ND with cut-out mask

	$Good	$Fine	$N.Mint	£Good	£Fine	£N.Mint
	$0.50	$1.50	$2.50	£0.30	£0.90	£1.50
2 ND	$0.50	$1.50	$2.50	£0.30	£0.90	£1.50
3 ND origin	$0.50	$1.50	$2.50	£0.30	£0.90	£1.50
4 ND	$0.50	$1.50	$2.50	£0.30	£0.90	£1.50
Title Value:	$2.00	$6.00	$10.00	£1.20	£3.60	£6.00

The Mask Returns (Jul 1994) Trade paperback reprints mini-series — £2.00 £6.00 £10.00

MASK SUMMER VACATION HARDCOVER, THE
Dark Horse,OS; nn Jun 1995

nn ND 32pgs, hardcover; Rick Geary script and art

	$Good	$Fine	$N.Mint	£Good	£Fine	£N.Mint
	$2.00	$6.00	$10.00	£1.20	£3.60	£6.00
Title Value:	$2.00	$6.00	$10.00	£1.20	£3.60	£6.00

MASK, THE
Dark Horse,MS; 0 Dec 1991; 1 Aug 1991-4 Nov 1991

0 ND reprints from Dark Horse Presents

	$Good	$Fine	$N.Mint	£Good	£Fine	£N.Mint
	$0.80	$2.40	$4.00	£0.50	£1.50	£2.50
1 ND	$1.20	$3.60	$6.00	£0.70	£2.10	£3.50
2 ND	$1.00	$3.00	$5.00	£0.60	£1.80	£3.00
3-4 ND	$0.80	$2.40	$4.00	£0.50	£1.50	£2.50
Title Value:	$4.60	$13.80	$23.00	£2.80	£8.40	£14.00

The Mask Softcover Collection (May 1993)

reprints mini-series plus new pages — £1.75 £5.25 £8.75

The Mask Limited Edition Collection (Jan 1995)

2 volume hardcover edition in slipcase reprinting both The Mask and The Mask Returns mini-series, 1,500 sets signed and numbered by John Arcudi and Doug Mahnke — £13.50 £40.50 £67.50

MASK, THE (2ND SERIES)
Dark Horse,MS; 1 Feb 1995-present

1 ND John Arcudi, Doug Mahnke and Keith Williams creative team

	$Good	$Fine	$N.Mint	£Good	£Fine	£N.Mint
	$0.60	$1.80	$3.00	£0.40	£1.20	£2.00

2-5 ND John Arcudi, Doug Mahnke and Keith Williams creative team

	$0.50	$1.50	$2.50	£0.30	£0.90	£1.50

6 ND The Hunt for Green October story (cover says first issue of four)

	$0.50	$1.50	$2.50	£0.30	£0.90	£1.50

7-9 ND The Hunt for Green October story

	$0.50	$1.50	$2.50	£0.30	£0.90	£1.50
Title Value:	$4.60	$13.80	$23.00	£2.80	£8.40	£14.00

MASK: THE MOVIE, THE
Dark Horse,MS Film; 1 Jul 1994-2 Aug 1994

1-2 ND adaptation of film starring Jim Carrey

	$Good	$Fine	$N.Mint	£Good	£Fine	£N.Mint
	$0.50	$1.50	$2.50	£0.30	£0.90	£1.50
Title Value:	$1.00	$3.00	$5.00	£0.60	£1.80	£3.00

MASKED MAN
Eclipse; 1 Jan 1985-11 Oct 1987

	$Good	$Fine	$N.Mint	£Good	£Fine	£N.Mint
1-11 ND	$0.30	$0.90	$1.50	£0.20	£0.60	£1.00
Title Value:	$3.30	$9.90	$16.50	£2.20	£6.60	£11.00

MASQUE OF THE RED DEATH
Dell, Movie; 12-490-410 Aug/Oct 1964

12-490-410 rare though distributed in the U.K., Vincent Price photo cover

	$Good	$Fine	$N.Mint	£Good	£Fine	£N.Mint
	$7.00	$21.00	$42.00	£6.00	£12.00	£24.00
Title Value:	$7.00	$21.00	$42.00	£6.00	£12.00	£24.00

Note: published under Dell series "Movie Classics"

MASTER OF KUNG FU
Marvel Comics Group; 17 Apr 1974-125 Jun 1983

(previously Special Marvel Edition)

17 ND Jim Starlin art, 1st appearance Black Jack Tarr

	$Good	$Fine	$N.Mint	£Good	£Fine	£N.Mint
	$2.90	$8.75	$17.50	£2.05	£6.25	£12.50

18 ND 1st Gulacy art

	$2.50	$7.50	$12.50	£1.50	£4.50	£7.50

19 ND Master of Kung Fu vs. Man-Thing, Gulacy art

	$2.00	$6.00	$10.00	£1.30	£3.90	£6.50
20 ND Gulacy art	$2.00	$6.00	$10.00	£1.30	£3.90	£6.50

21-22 ND Gulacy art

	$1.20	$3.60	$6.00	£0.80	£2.40	£4.00
23 ND	$1.00	$3.00	$5.00	£0.60	£1.80	£3.00

24 ND part Jim Starlin, part Walt Simonson art

	$1.00	$3.00	$5.00	£0.70	£2.10	£3.50
25 ND Gulacy art	$1.00	$3.00	$5.00	£0.60	£1.80	£3.00
26-28 ND Gulacy art	$1.00	$3.00	$5.00	£0.60	£1.80	£3.00

29-30 ND Gulacy art

	$1.00	$3.00	$5.00	£0.60	£1.80	£3.00
31 ND Gulacy art	$0.70	$2.10	$3.50	£0.50	£1.50	£2.50
32 ND	$0.70	$2.10	$3.50	£0.50	£1.50	£2.50

33-35 ND Gulacy art

	$0.70	$2.10	$3.50	£0.50	£1.50	£2.50
36-37	$0.60	$1.80	$3.00	£0.40	£1.20	£2.00
38-40 ND Gulacy art	$0.60	$1.80	$3.00	£0.40	£1.20	£2.00
41	$0.60	$1.80	$3.00	£0.30	£0.90	£1.50
42-50 ND Gulacy art	$0.60	$1.80	$3.00	£0.30	£0.90	£1.50
51-59	$0.60	$1.80	$3.00	£0.25	£0.75	£1.25

60 Dr. Doom appears

	$0.60	$1.80	$3.00	£0.25	£0.75	£1.25
61-70	$0.60	$1.80	$3.00	£0.25	£0.75	£1.25
71-89	$0.60	$1.80	$3.00	£0.20	£0.60	£1.00
90 Mike Zeck art	$0.60	$1.80	$3.00	£0.20	£0.60	£1.00
91-99	$0.60	$1.80	$3.00	£0.20	£0.60	£1.00
100 52pgs	$0.60	$1.80	$3.00	£0.30	£0.90	£1.50
101-117	$0.50	$1.50	$2.50	£0.20	£0.60	£1.00
118 DS	$0.50	$1.50	$2.50	£0.25	£0.75	£1.25
119-121	$0.50	$1.50	$2.50	£0.20	£0.60	£1.00
122-124 ND	$0.50	$1.50	$2.50	£0.25	£0.75	£1.25

125 ND scarce in the U.K. DS, Mike Mignola inks

	$0.50	$1.50	$2.50	£0.30	£0.90	£1.50
Title Value:	$74.80	$224.45	$377.00	£36.55	£109.75	£185.00

ARTISTS

Gene Day in 76, 77, 79-118.

MASTER OF KUNG FU ANNUAL
Marvel Comics Group; 1 1976

1 ND 52pgs, Iron Fist appears

	$Good	$Fine	$N.Mint	£Good	£Fine	£N.Mint
	$1.00	$3.00	$5.00	£0.60	£1.80	£3.00
Title Value:	$1.00	$3.00	$5.00	£0.60	£1.80	£3.00

MASTER OF KUNG FU GIANT SIZE
Marvel Comics Group; 1 Sep 1974-4 Jun 1975

1 ND 68pgs, Gulacy art

	$1.50	$4.50	$7.50	£1.00	£3.00	£5.00

2 ND 68pgs, Gulacy art

	$1.00	$3.00	$5.00	£0.80	£2.40	£4.00

3 ND 68pgs, Gulacy art

	$1.00	$3.00	$5.00	£0.70	£2.10	£3.50
4 ND 68pgs	$1.00	$3.00	$5.00	£0.60	£1.80	£3.00

MINT = 100% / NEAR MINT (inc. +/-) = 90–99% / VERY FINE (inc. +/-) = 75–89% / FINE (inc. +/-) = 55–74%
VERY GOOD (inc. +/-) = 35–54% / GOOD (inc. +/-) = 15–34% / FAIR = 5–14% / POOR = 1–4%

457

	$Good	$Fine	$N.Mint	£Good	£Fine	£N.Mint
Title Value:	$4.50	$13.50	$22.50	£3.10	£9.30	£15.50

MASTER OF KUNG FU: BLEEDING BLACK
Marvel Comics Group; nn Mar 1991

	$Good	$Fine	$N.Mint	£Good	£Fine	£N.Mint
nn ND 80pgs, Doug Moench script, David and Dan Day art	$0.50	$1.50	$2.50	£0.30	£0.90	£1.50
Title Value:	$0.50	$1.50	$2.50	£0.30	£0.90	£1.50

MASTER OF RAMPLING GATE, THE
Innovation,OS; 1 Jun 1991

	$Good	$Fine	$N.Mint	£Good	£Fine	£N.Mint
1 ND 76pgs, Colleen Doran art, adaptation of Anne Rice novel, painted cover by John Bolton	$1.20	$3.60	$6.00	£0.80	£2.40	£4.00
Title Value:	$1.20	$3.60	$6.00	£0.80	£2.40	£4.00

Anne Rice's Master of Rampling Gate Deluxe Edition (Aug1995)
64pgs, 150 copies sealed in archival bag with hand-embossed gold sticker

	$Good	$Fine	$N.Mint	£Good	£Fine	£N.Mint
				£3.00	£9.00	£15.00

MASTER, THE
New Comics Group; 1 1989-2 1989

	$Good	$Fine	$N.Mint	£Good	£Fine	£N.Mint
1-2 ND	$0.30	$0.90	$1.50	£0.20	£0.60	£1.00
Title Value:	$0.60	$1.80	$3.00	£0.40	£1.20	£2.00

MASTERS OF TERROR
Marvel Comics Group,Magazine; 1 Jul 1975-2 1975

	$Good	$Fine	$N.Mint	£Good	£Fine	£N.Mint
1 ND It!, all reprint, Neal Adams inks, Jim Starlin/Brunner/Smith art	$0.60	$1.80	$3.00	£0.40	£1.20	£2.00
2 ND Invisible Man, all reprint	$0.60	$1.80	$3.00	£0.40	£1.20	£2.00
Title Value:	$1.20	$3.60	$6.00	£0.80	£2.40	£4.00

MASTERS OF THE UNIVERSE
DC Comics,MS,TV,Toy; 1 Dec 1982-3 Feb 1983
(see Batman #353)

	$Good	$Fine	$N.Mint	£Good	£Fine	£N.Mint
1	$0.15	$0.45	$0.75	£0.10	£0.30	£0.50
2 origin He-Man	$0.15	$0.45	$0.75	£0.10	£0.30	£0.50
3	$0.15	$0.45	$0.75	£0.10	£0.30	£0.50
Title Value:	$0.45	$1.35	$2.25	£0.30	£0.90	£1.50

MASTERS OF THE UNIVERSE
Marvel Comics Group/Star,TV; 1 May 1986-13 May 1987

	$Good	$Fine	$N.Mint	£Good	£Fine	£N.Mint
1-12 ND	$0.15	$0.45	$0.75	£0.10	£0.30	£0.50
13 ND scarce in the U.K.	$0.15	$0.45	$0.75	£0.10	£0.35	£0.60
Title Value:	$1.95	$5.85	$9.75	£1.30	£3.95	£6.60

MASTERS OF THE UNIVERSE, THE MOTION PICTURE
Marvel Comics Group/Star,Film; 1 Nov 1987

	$Good	$Fine	$N.Mint	£Good	£Fine	£N.Mint
1 ND	$0.15	$0.45	$0.75	£0.10	£0.30	£0.50
Title Value:	$0.15	$0.45	$0.75	£0.10	£0.30	£0.50

MASTERWORKS SERIES OF GREAT COMIC BOOK ARTISTS
Seagate/DC Comics; 1 May 1983-3 Dec 1983

	$Good	$Fine	$N.Mint	£Good	£Fine	£N.Mint
1-2 ND Shining Knight reprints by Frank Frazetta	$0.40	$1.20	$2.00	£0.25	£0.75	£1.25
3 ND Berni Wrightson reprints	$0.40	$1.20	$2.00	£0.25	£0.75	£1.25
Title Value:	$1.20	$3.60	$6.00	£0.75	£2.25	£3.75

Note: the planned Neal Adams issue (#4) featuring his mystery, suspense and horror stories was advertised but never appeared. Shame.

MATT CHAMPION
Metro Comics,MS; 1-4 1987

	$Good	$Fine	$N.Mint	£Good	£Fine	£N.Mint
1-4 ND	$0.25	$0.75	$1.25	£0.15	£0.45	£0.75
Title Value:	$1.00	$3.00	$5.00	£0.60	£1.80	£3.00

MAVERICKS: THE NEW WAVE
Dagger Enterprises; 1 Jun 1994-4 Sep 1994

	$Good	$Fine	$N.Mint	£Good	£Fine	£N.Mint
1-4 ND Rich Buckler Snr. art	$0.40	$1.20	$2.00	£0.25	£0.75	£1.25
Title Value:	$1.60	$4.80	$8.00	£1.00	£3.00	£5.00

MAX THE MAGNIFICENT
Slave Labor,MS; 1 Jul 1987-3 Nov 1987

	$Good	$Fine	$N.Mint	£Good	£Fine	£N.Mint
1-3 ND Valentino art	$0.40	$1.20	$2.00	£0.25	£0.75	£1.25
Title Value:	$1.20	$3.60	$6.00	£0.75	£2.25	£3.75

MAXIMAGE
Image; 1 Dec 1995-present

	$Good	$Fine	$N.Mint	£Good	£Fine	£N.Mint
1,2 ND Rob Liefeld cover and story	$1.00	$3.00	$5.00	£0.60	£1.80	£3.00
Title Value:	$1.00	$3.00	$5.00	£0.60	£1.80	£3.00

MAXIMORTAL, THE
Kind Hell Press/Tundra; 1 Aug 1992-7 1993

	$Good	$Fine	$N.Mint	£Good	£Fine	£N.Mint
1 ND card-stock embossed cover	$0.60	$1.80	$3.00	£0.40	£1.20	£2.00
2 ND card-stock embossed cover	$0.50	$1.50	$2.50	£0.30	£0.90	£1.50
3-7 ND	$0.50	$1.50	$2.50	£0.30	£0.90	£1.50
Title Value:	$3.60	$10.80	$18.00	£2.20	£6.60	£11.00

MAXIMUM OVERLOAD
Dark Horse,Magazine; 1 Feb 1994-5 Jun 1994

	$Good	$Fine	$N.Mint	£Good	£Fine	£N.Mint
1 ND 64pgs, with free Lemmings stickers and promo poster	$0.80	$2.40	$4.00	£0.50	£1.50	£2.50
2-5 ND 64pgs	$0.80	$2.40	$4.00	£0.50	£1.50	£2.50
Title Value:	$4.00	$12.00	$20.00	£2.50	£7.50	£12.50

MAXIMUM PRESS PREVIEW
Maximum Comic Press,OS; 1 Mar 1995

	$Good	$Fine	$N.Mint	£Good	£Fine	£N.Mint
1 ND review of Maximum Press titles	$0.30	$0.90	$1.50	£0.20	£0.60	£1.00
Title Value:	$0.30	$0.90	$1.50	£0.20	£0.60	£1.00

MAXWELL MOUSE FOLLIES
Renegade; 1 Feb 1986-5 Oct 1986

	$Good	$Fine	$N.Mint	£Good	£Fine	£N.Mint
1-5 ND	$0.40	$1.20	$2.00	£0.25	£0.75	£1.25

	$Good	$Fine	$N.Mint	£Good	£Fine	£N.Mint
Title Value:	$2.00	$6.00	$10.00	£1.25	£3.75	£6.25

MAXX, THE
Image; 1 Mar 1993-present

	$Good	$Fine	$N.Mint	£Good	£Fine	£N.Mint
½ – available only with coupons sent from Wizard Price Guide magazinne	$2.00	$6.00	$10.00	£1.20	£3.60	£6.00
½ as above in black folder with gold logo; 1,100 copies available at Diamond Distributors seminar in June 1993 in Atlanta	$4.00	$12.00	$20.00	£2.50	£7.50	£12.50
1 Sam Kieth story and art begins	$1.00	$3.00	$5.00	£0.70	£2.10	£3.50
1 Glow in the dark edition	$4.00	$12.00	$20.00	£2.50	£7.50	£12.50
1 Blue Variant – misprint	$3.00	$9.00	$15.00	£2.00	£6.00	£10.00
1 Ash Can Edition – blue card cover, signed and numbered in gold pen on cover by Sam Kieth, 8.5" x 5.5"	$3.00	$9.00	$15.00	£2.00	£6.00	£10.00
2	$0.70	$2.10	$3.50	£0.50	£1.50	£2.50
2 Ash Can Edition – blue card cover, signed and numbered in gold pen on cover by Sam Kieth, 8.5" x 5.5"	$2.50	$7.50	$12.50	£1.50	£4.50	£7.50
3-5	$0.60	$1.80	$3.00	£0.40	£1.20	£2.00
6	$0.50	$1.50	$2.50	£0.30	£0.90	£1.50
7 Maxx vs. Pitt	$0.50	$1.50	$2.50	£0.30	£0.90	£1.50
8-10	$0.50	$1.50	$2.50	£0.30	£0.90	£1.50
11-20	$0.40	$1.20	$2.00	£0.25	£0.75	£1.25
21 Alan Moore guest script	$0.40	$1.20	$2.00	£0.25	£0.75	£1.25
Title Value:	$28.90	$86.70	$144.50	£18.35	£55.05	£91.75

Note: all Non-Distributed on the news-stands in the U.K.

Maxx (Mar 1995)

	$Good	$Fine	$N.Mint	£Good	£Fine	£N.Mint
Trade paperback reprints issues #1-5, new Sam Kieth cover				£1.70	£5.10	£8.50

MAYHEM
Dark Horse,MS; 1 May 1989-4 Sep 1989

	$Good	$Fine	$N.Mint	£Good	£Fine	£N.Mint
1 ND 48pgs, Mask appears	$2.50	$7.50	$12.50	£1.50	£4.50	£7.50
2-3 ND 48pgs, Mask appears	$2.00	$6.00	$10.00	£1.20	£3.60	£6.00
4 ND 48pgs, Mask appears	$2.00	$6.00	$10.00	£1.00	£3.00	£5.00
Title Value:	$8.50	$25.50	$42.50	£4.90	£14.70	£24.50

MAZE AGENCY
Comico/Innovation; 1 Dec 1988-23 1993 (Innovation #8 On)

	$Good	$Fine	$N.Mint	£Good	£Fine	£N.Mint
1 ND	$0.50	$1.50	$2.50	£0.30	£0.90	£1.50
2-15 ND	$0.40	$1.20	$2.00	£0.25	£0.75	£1.25
16 ND Russ Heath cover	$0.40	$1.20	$2.00	£0.25	£0.75	£1.25
17 ND Norm Breyfogle cover	$0.40	$1.20	$2.00	£0.25	£0.75	£1.25
18 ND Brian Bolland cover	$0.40	$1.20	$2.00	£0.25	£0.75	£1.25
19 ND Adam Hughes cover	$0.40	$1.20	$2.00	£0.25	£0.75	£1.25
20-23 ND	$0.40	$1.20	$2.00	£0.25	£0.75	£1.25
Title Value:	$9.30	$27.90	$46.50	£5.80	£17.40	£29.00
Trade Paperback, reprints #1-4				£1.20	£3.60	£6.00
Annual 1 (Nov 1990), colour, Ploog cover				£0.35	£1.05	£1.75
Special 1 (1990), colour, Joe Staton art; includes Maze Agency #0 with Alan Davis art				£0.50	£1.50	£2.50

MAZE AGENCY CHRISTMAS SPECIAL, THE
Innovation,OS; 1 Feb 1992

	$Good	$Fine	$N.Mint	£Good	£Fine	£N.Mint
1 ND Adam Hughes cover	$0.40	$1.20	$2.00	£0.25	£0.75	£1.25
Title Value:	$0.40	$1.20	$2.00	£0.25	£0.75	£1.25

MAZING MAN
DC Comics; 1 Jan 1986-12 Dec 1986

	$Good	$Fine	$N.Mint	£Good	£Fine	£N.Mint
1-6	$0.15	$0.45	$0.75	£0.10	£0.35	£0.60
7-8 Hembeck art	$0.15	$0.45	$0.75	£0.10	£0.35	£0.60
9-11	$0.15	$0.45	$0.75	£0.10	£0.35	£0.60
12 part Dark Knight cover by Frank Miller	$0.15	$0.45	$0.75	£0.10	£0.35	£0.60
Title Value:	$1.80	$5.40	$9.00	£1.20	£4.20	£7.20

MAZING MAN SPECIAL
DC Comics; 1 1987-2 Apr 1988; 3 Aug 1990

	$Good	$Fine	$N.Mint	£Good	£Fine	£N.Mint
1 LD in the U.K.	$0.25	$0.75	$1.25	£0.15	£0.45	£0.75
2	$0.15	$0.45	$0.75	£0.10	£0.35	£0.60
3 Kyle Baker/Todd McFarlane art featured	$0.25	$0.75	$1.25	£0.15	£0.45	£0.75
Title Value:	$0.65	$1.95	$3.25	£0.40	£1.25	£2.10

MAZINGER GRAPHIC NOVEL
First; nn 1990

	$Good	$Fine	$N.Mint	£Good	£Fine	£N.Mint
nn ND 64pgs, painted art by Go Nagi	$1.50	$4.50	$7.50	£1.00	£3.00	£5.00
Title Value:	$1.50	$4.50	$7.50	£1.00	£3.00	£5.00

MECHA
Dark Horse; 1 Jun 1987-6 Jan 1989

	$Good	$Fine	$N.Mint	£Good	£Fine	£N.Mint
1-6 ND Fong/Nichols art	$0.40	$1.20	$2.00	£0.25	£0.75	£1.25
Title Value:	$2.40	$7.20	$12.00	£1.50	£4.50	£7.50

MECHA ONE-SHOT SPECIAL
Dark Horse,OS; 1 May 1995

	$Good	$Fine	$N.Mint	£Good	£Fine	£N.Mint
1 ND Comics' Greatest World spin-off; Chris Warner cover	$0.50	$1.50	$2.50	£0.30	£0.90	£1.50
Title Value:	$0.50	$1.50	$2.50	£0.30	£0.90	£1.50

MECHANICS
Fantagraphics; 1 Oct 1985-3 Dec 1985

	$Good	$Fine	$N.Mint	£Good	£Fine	£N.Mint
1-3 ND reprints from Love & Rockets in colour plus new story	$0.60	$1.80	$3.00	£0.40	£1.20	£2.00
Title Value:	$1.80	$5.40	$9.00	£1.20	£3.60	£6.00

MECHANOID INVASION, THE
Caliber Press,MS; 1 Aug 1990-4 1990

	$Good	$Fine	$N.Mint	£Good	£Fine	£N.Mint
1-4 ND 48pgs	$0.40	$1.20	$2.00	£0.25	£0.75	£1.25
Title Value:	$1.60	$4.80	$8.00	£1.00	£3.00	£5.00

MECHANOIDS
Caliber Press; 1 1990-5 1990

	$Good	$Fine	$N.Mint	£Good	£Fine	£N.Mint
1-5 ND 48pgs, based on role-playing game; black and white	$0.40	$1.20	$2.00	£0.25	£0.75	£1.25
Title Value:	$2.00	$6.00	$10.00	£1.25	£3.75	£6.25

MECHOVERSE
Airbrush Comics,MS; 1 Aug 1988-2 1988

	$Good	$Fine	$N.Mint	£Good	£Fine	£N.Mint
1-2 ND	$0.30	$0.90	$1.50	£0.20	£0.60	£1.00
Title Value:	$0.60	$1.80	$3.00	£0.40	£1.20	£2.00

MECHTHINGS
Renegade; 1 Jul 1987-4 Feb 1988

	$Good	$Fine	$N.Mint	£Good	£Fine	£N.Mint
1-4 ND	$0.40	$1.20	$2.00	£0.25	£0.75	£1.25
Title Value:	$1.60	$4.80	$8.00	£1.00	£3.00	£5.00

MEDAL OF HONOUR
Dark Horse,MS; 1 Oct 1994-2 Feb 1995

	$Good	$Fine	$N.Mint	£Good	£Fine	£N.Mint
1-5 ND text anthology of war heroism; Walt Simonson cover	$0.50	$1.50	$2.50	£0.30	£0.90	£1.50
Title Value:	$2.50	$7.50	$12.50	£1.50	£4.50	£7.50

MEDAL OF HONOUR SPECIAL
Dark Horse,OS; 1 Apr 1994

	$Good	$Fine	$N.Mint	£Good	£Fine	£N.Mint
1 ND Joe Kubert cover	$0.50	$1.50	$2.50	£0.30	£0.90	£1.50
Title Value:	$0.50	$1.50	$2.50	£0.30	£0.90	£1.50

MEDIA STARR
Innovation,MS; 1 Jul 1989-3 Oct 1989

	$Good	$Fine	$N.Mint	£Good	£Fine	£N.Mint
1-3 ND	$0.40	$1.20	$2.00	£0.25	£0.75	£1.25
Title Value:	$1.20	$3.60	$6.00	£0.75	£2.25	£3.75

MEDUSA COMICS
Triangle Publications; 1 1986

	$Good	$Fine	$N.Mint	£Good	£Fine	£N.Mint
1 ND	$0.25	$0.75	$1.25	£0.15	£0.45	£0.75
Title Value:	$0.25	$0.75	$1.25	£0.15	£0.45	£0.75

MEET MERTON
I.W. Super; 9 1964

	$Good	$Fine	$N.Mint	£Good	£Fine	£N.Mint
9 reprints from Toby Press title; distributed in the U.K.	$0.65	$2.00	$4.00	£0.40	£1.25	£2.50
Title Value:	$0.65	$2.00	$4.00	£0.40	£1.25	£2.50

MEGALITH
Continuity; 1 Apr 1985-2 1985
(see Revengers featuring Megalith)

	$Good	$Fine	$N.Mint	£Good	£Fine	£N.Mint
1-2 ND Neal Adams art	$0.40	$1.20	$2.00	£0.25	£0.75	£1.25
Title Value:	$0.80	$2.40	$4.00	£0.50	£1.50	£2.50

MEGALITH (2ND SERIES)
Continuity; 1 1989-14 1992

	$Good	$Fine	$N.Mint	£Good	£Fine	£N.Mint
1-2 part Neal Adams art	$0.40	$1.20	$2.00	£0.25	£0.75	£1.25
3 painted issue	$0.40	$1.20	$2.00	£0.25	£0.75	£1.25
4-9	$0.40	$1.20	$2.00	£0.25	£0.75	£1.25
10 Neal Adams painted art, $2.50 cover begins	$0.40	$1.20	$2.00	£0.25	£0.75	£1.25
11 silver embossed cover by Neal Adams	$0.40	$1.20	$2.00	£0.25	£0.75	£1.25
12 painted art by Neal Adams	$0.40	$1.20	$2.00	£0.25	£0.75	£1.25
13-14	$0.40	$1.20	$2.00	£0.25	£0.75	£1.25
Title Value:	$5.60	$16.80	$28.00	£3.50	£10.50	£17.50

Note: all Non-Distributed on the news-stands in the U.K.

MEGALITH (3RD SERIES)
Continuity; 0 Apr 1993; 1 Apr 1993-7 1994

	$Good	$Fine	$N.Mint	£Good	£Fine	£N.Mint
0 Deathwatch 2000 part 1, silver foil embossed cover (originally came pre-bagged as an "incentive pack" with Hybrids (2nd) #0)	$0.80	$2.40	$4.00	£0.50	£1.50	£2.50
0 as above but un-bagged individual issue	$0.40	$1.20	$2.00	£0.25	£0.75	£1.25
1 Deathwatch 2000 part 5, pre-bagged with 2 trading cards, Neal Adams plot; gatefold cover	$0.40	$1.20	$2.00	£0.25	£0.75	£1.25
2 Deathwatch 2000 part 10, pre-bagged with trading card, Neal Adams plot; gatefold cover opening out top and bottom	$0.40	$1.20	$2.00	£0.25	£0.75	£1.25
3 Deathwatch 200 part 16, pre-bagged with trading card; Tyvek indestructible cover	$0.40	$1.20	$2.00	£0.25	£0.75	£1.25
4 Rise of Magic X-over, embossed parchment cover by Neal Adams	$0.40	$1.20	$2.00	£0.25	£0.75	£1.25
5-6 Rise of Magic X-over, embossed parchment cover by Sienkiewicz	$0.40	$1.20	$2.00	£0.25	£0.75	£1.25
7 Rise of Magic X-over, embossed parchment cover by Neal Adams	$0.40	$1.20	$2.00	£0.25	£0.75	£1.25
Title Value:	$4.00	$12.00	$20.00	£2.50	£7.50	£12.50

Note: all Non-Distributed on the news-stands in the U.K.

MEGATON
Megaton Publications; 1 1983-8 1986
(see Graphic Fantasy)

	$Good	$Fine	$N.Mint	£Good	£Fine	£N.Mint
1 black and white, Erik Larsen's 1st pro work, 1st appearance Vanguard	$2.00	$6.00	$10.00	£1.40	£4.20	£7.00
2 black and white, 1st appearance Savage Dragon (cameo), Erik Larsen art	$1.50	$4.50	$7.50	£1.00	£3.00	£5.00
3 black and white, 1st full appearance Savage Dragon, Erik Larsen art	$3.00	$9.00	$15.00	£2.00	£6.00	£10.00
4 black and white, Savage Dragon appears, Erik Larsen art	$2.00	$6.00	$10.00	£1.40	£4.20	£7.00
5 black and white, Rob Liefeld art inside front cover; Angel Medina art (June 1986)	$0.60	$1.80	$3.00	£0.40	£1.20	£2.00
6-7 black and white	$0.60	$1.80	$3.00	£0.40	£1.20	£2.00
8 black and white, Rob Liefeld Youngblood preview (1pg advert)	$0.60	$1.80	$3.00	£0.40	£1.20	£2.00
Title Value:	$10.90	$32.70	$54.50	£7.40	£22.20	£37.00

Note: all Non-Distributed on the news-stands in the U.K.

MEGATON (2ND SERIES)
Megaton Publications; 1 1986-3 1987

	$Good	$Fine	$N.Mint	£Good	£Fine	£N.Mint
1-3 ND colour	$0.30	$0.90	$1.50	£0.20	£0.60	£1.00
Title Value:	$0.90	$2.70	$4.50	£0.60	£1.80	£3.00

MEGATON EXPLOSION
Megaton Publications,OS; 1 Jun 1987

	$Good	$Fine	$N.Mint	£Good	£Fine	£N.Mint
1 very rare in the U.K. and the U.S. 16pgs, self published fanzine by Rob Liefeld and friends featuring the first concept of Youngblood, distributed free around colleges; approximately 200 copies printed	$3.50	$10.50	$17.50	£2.50	£7.50	£12.50
Title Value:	$3.50	$10.50	$17.50	£2.50	£7.50	£12.50

MEGATON MAN
Kitchen Sink; 1 Nov 1984-10 Jun 1986
(see Return of Megaton Man)

	$Good	$Fine	$N.Mint	£Good	£Fine	£N.Mint
1 ND scarce in the U.K.	$0.60	$1.80	$3.00	£0.50	£1.50	£2.50
1 2nd/3rd printing ND						

Marvels #1

The Mask (1st) #1

Master of Kung Fu #17

	$Good	$Fine	$N.Mint	£Good	£Fine	£N.Mint
	$0.50	$1.50	$2.50	£0.30	£0.90	£1.50
2-3 ND	$0.50	$1.50	$2.50	£0.40	£1.20	£2.00
4-5 ND	$0.50	$1.50	$2.50	£0.30	£0.90	£1.50
6-10 ND Borderworlds back-up						
	$0.50	$1.50	$2.50	£0.30	£0.90	£1.50
Title Value:	$6.10	$18.30	$30.50	£4.00	£12.00	£20.00
Volume 1 (Sep 1990), reprints #1-4 softcover				£1.55	£4.65	£7.75
Signed Hardcover				£3.00	£9.00	£15.00
Megaton Man Meets The Uncategorizable X+Thems						
(Apr 1989)				£0.30	£0.60	£0.90

MELODY
Kitchen Sink; 1 May 1988-present

	$Good	$Fine	$N.Mint	£Good	£Fine	£N.Mint
1 ND Sylvie Rancourt and Jacques Boivin; black and white begins						
	$0.60	$1.80	$3.00	£0.40	£1.20	£2.00
1 2nd printing ND	$0.40	$1.20	$2.00	£0.25	£0.75	£1.25
2 ND	$0.50	$1.50	$2.50	£0.30	£0.90	£1.50
2 2nd printing, ND (Jun 1993)						
	$0.60	$1.80	$3.00	£0.40	£1.20	£2.00
3 ND	$0.50	$1.50	$2.50	£0.30	£0.90	£1.50
3 2nd printing, ND (Jun 1993)						
	$0.60	$1.80	$3.00	£0.40	£1.20	£2.00
4-9 ND	$0.40	$1.20	$2.00	£0.25	£0.75	£1.25
10 ND	$0.60	$1.80	$3.00	£0.40	£1.20	£2.00
Title Value:	$6.20	$18.60	$31.00	£3.95	£11.85	£19.75
Melody Book 1 (Jun 1991), reprints #1-4						
Softcover				£1.80	£5.40	£9.00
Hardcover				£3.70	£11.10	£18.50

MELTING POT
Kitchen Sink,MS; 1 Jan 1994-4 Apr 1994

	$Good	$Fine	$N.Mint	£Good	£Fine	£N.Mint
1-3 ND Kevin Eastman, Eric Talbot and Simon Bisley						
	$0.60	$1.80	$3.00	£0.40	£1.20	£2.00
4 ND Kevin Eastman and Simon Bisley						
	$0.60	$1.80	$3.00	£0.40	£1.20	£2.00
Title Value:	$2.40	$7.20	$12.00	£1.60	£4.80	£8.00

MEMORIES
Marvel Comics Group/Epic,OS; 1 Oct 1992

	$Good	$Fine	$N.Mint	£Good	£Fine	£N.Mint
1 ND Katsuhiro Otomo companion piece to Akira						
	$0.40	$1.20	$2.00	£0.25	£0.75	£1.25
Title Value:	$0.40	$1.20	$2.00	£0.25	£0.75	£1.25

MEN IN BLACK, THE
Aircel,MS; 1-3 1991

	$Good	$Fine	$N.Mint	£Good	£Fine	£N.Mint
1-3 ND black and white						
	$0.40	$1.20	$2.00	£0.25	£0.75	£1.25
Title Value:	$1.20	$3.60	$6.00	£0.75	£2.25	£3.75
The Men in Black (Jun 1990)						
80pgs squarebound, black and white, reprints issues #1-3				£1.00	£3.00	£5.00

MEN IN BLACK, THE (2ND SERIES)
Aircel,MS; 1 May 1991-3 Jul 1992

	$Good	$Fine	$N.Mint	£Good	£Fine	£N.Mint
1-3 ND black and white						
	$0.40	$1.20	$2.00	£0.25	£0.75	£1.25
Title Value:	$1.20	$3.60	$6.00	£0.75	£2.25	£3.75

MEN OF WAR
DC Comics; 1 Aug 1977-26 Mar 1980

	$Good	$Fine	$N.Mint	£Good	£Fine	£N.Mint
1 ND origin Gravedigger						
	$0.50	$1.50	$2.50	£0.30	£0.90	£1.50
2 origin continued	$0.25	$0.75	$1.25	£0.15	£0.45	£0.75
3-10	$0.25	$0.75	$1.25	£0.15	£0.45	£0.75
11-26	$0.20	$0.60	$1.00	£0.10	£0.35	£0.60
Title Value:	$5.95	$17.85	$29.75	£3.25	£10.55	£17.85

FEATURES
Dateline: Frontline in 4-6, 9-11, 21-23. Enemy Ace in 1-3, 8-10, 12-14, 19, 20. Gravedigger in 1-26. Rosa, Master Spy in 17, 18, 24, 25.

MEPHISTO VS. FOUR HEROES
Marvel Comics Group,MS; 1 Apr 1987-4 Jul 1987

	$Good	$Fine	$N.Mint	£Good	£Fine	£N.Mint
1 ND Fantastic Four; John Buscema art begins						
	$0.40	$1.20	$2.00	£0.25	£0.75	£1.25
2 ND X-Factor	$0.40	$1.20	$2.00	£0.25	£0.75	£1.25
3 ND X-Men	$0.40	$1.20	$2.00	£0.25	£0.75	£1.25
4 ND Avengers	$0.40	$1.20	$2.00	£0.25	£0.75	£1.25
Title Value:	$1.60	$4.80	$8.00	£1.00	£3.00	£5.00

MERCY
DC Comics,OS; 1 Apr 1993

	$Good	$Fine	$N.Mint	£Good	£Fine	£N.Mint
1 ND 64pgs, Paul Johnson art; under "Vertigo" banner						
	$1.00	$3.00	$5.00	£0.70	£2.10	£3.50
Title Value:	$1.00	$3.00	$5.00	£0.70	£2.10	£3.50

MERLIN
Adventure,MS; 1 Dec 1990-6 May 1991

	$Good	$Fine	$N.Mint	£Good	£Fine	£N.Mint
1-6 ND	$0.40	$1.20	$2.00	£0.25	£0.75	£1.25
Title Value:	$2.40	$7.20	$12.00	£1.50	£4.50	£7.50

MERLIN (2ND SERIES)
Adventure,MS; 1 Dec 1992-2 Jan 1993

	$Good	$Fine	$N.Mint	£Good	£Fine	£N.Mint
1-2 ND	$0.40	$1.20	$2.00	£0.25	£0.75	£1.25
Title Value:	$0.80	$2.40	$4.00	£0.50	£1.50	£2.50

MERLINREALM IN 3-D
Blackthorne; (3-D Series #2) 1 Oct 1985

	$Good	$Fine	$N.Mint	£Good	£Fine	£N.Mint
1 ND reprints, with 3-D glasses (25% less without glasses)						
	$0.40	$1.20	$2.00	£0.25	£0.75	£1.25
Title Value:	$0.40	$1.20	$2.00	£0.25	£0.75	£1.25

MERMAID FOREST
Viz Communications,MS; 1 Feb 1994-4 May 1994

	$Good	$Fine	$N.Mint	£Good	£Fine	£N.Mint
1-4 ND Rumiko Takahashi; black and white						
	$0.50	$1.50	$2.50	£0.30	£0.90	£1.50
Title Value:	$2.00	$6.00	$10.00	£1.20	£3.60	£6.00
Mermaid Forest Graphic Novel (Nov 1994)						
256pgs, nine chapters collected from Animerica and final four						
from above series; black and white				£2.50	£7.50	£12.50

MERMAID'S DREAM
Viz Communications,MS; 1 Dec 1994-3 Feb 1995

	$Good	$Fine	$N.Mint	£Good	£Fine	£N.Mint
1-3 ND Rumiko Takahashi; black and white						
	$0.50	$1.50	$2.50	£0.30	£0.90	£1.50
Title Value:	$1.50	$4.50	$7.50	£0.90	£2.70	£4.50

MERMAID'S GAZE
Viz Communications,MS; 1 Mar 1995-4 Jun 1995

	$Good	$Fine	$N.Mint	£Good	£Fine	£N.Mint
1-4 ND Rumiko Takahashi script and art; black and white						
	$0.50	$1.50	$2.50	£0.30	£0.90	£1.50
Title Value:	$2.00	$6.00	$10.00	£1.20	£3.60	£6.00

MERMAID'S MASK
Viz Communications,MS; 1 Jul 1995-3 Sep 1995

	$Good	$Fine	$N.Mint	£Good	£Fine	£N.Mint
1-3 ND Rumiko Takahashi script and art; black and white						
	$0.50	$1.50	$2.50	£0.30	£0.90	£1.50
Title Value:	$1.50	$4.50	$7.50	£0.90	£2.70	£4.50

MERMAID'S PROMISE
Viz Communications,MS; 1 Aug 1994-4 Nov 1994

	$Good	$Fine	$N.Mint	£Good	£Fine	£N.Mint
1-4 ND Rumiko Takahashi; black and white						
	$0.50	$1.50	$2.50	£0.30	£0.90	£1.50
Title Value:	$2.00	$6.00	$10.00	£1.20	£3.60	£6.00

MERMAID'S SCAR
Viz Communications,MS; 1 Jun 1994-4 Sep 1994

	$Good	$Fine	$N.Mint	£Good	£Fine	£N.Mint
1-4 ND Rumiko Takahashi; black and white						
	$0.50	$1.50	$2.50	£0.30	£0.90	£1.50
Title Value:	$2.00	$6.00	$10.00	£1.20	£3.60	£6.00
Mermaid's Scar Graphic Novel (Oct 1995) 304pgs, reprints				£2.40	£7.20	£12.00

META-4
First,MS; 1 Feb 1991-3 Apr 1991

	$Good	$Fine	$N.Mint	£Good	£Fine	£N.Mint
1 ND 48pgs, Ian Gibson art begins, Gibson cover						
	$0.50	$1.50	$2.50	£0.30	£0.90	£1.50
2-3 ND Whilce Portacio cover						
	$0.50	$1.50	$2.50	£0.30	£0.90	£1.50
Title Value:	$1.50	$4.50	$7.50	£0.90	£2.70	£4.50

METACOPS
Monster Comics; 1 Feb 1991-3 1991

	$Good	$Fine	$N.Mint	£Good	£Fine	£N.Mint
1-3 ND black and white						
	$0.40	$1.20	$2.00	£0.25	£0.75	£1.25
Title Value:	$1.20	$3.60	$6.00	£0.75	£2.25	£3.75

METAL MEN
DC Comics, ; 1 Apr/May 1963-41 Dec/Jan 1969/70; 42 Mar 1973-44 Jul/Aug 1973; 45-Apr/May 1976-56 Feb/Mar 1978

(see Action, Brave and the Bold, DC Comics Presents, Showcase)

	$Good	$Fine	$N.Mint	£Good	£Fine	£N.Mint
1	$55.00	$165.00	$450.00	£26.00	£77.50	£210.00
2	$21.00	$62.50	$150.00	£10.00	£30.00	£70.00
3-5	$15.00	$45.00	$105.00	£7.00	£21.00	£50.00
6	$9.25	$28.00	$65.00	£4.25	£12.50	£30.00
7 scarce in the U.K.	$9.25	$28.00	$65.00	£4.60	£13.50	£32.50
8-10	$9.25	$28.00	$65.00	£4.25	£12.50	£30.00
11-16	$7.00	$21.00	$50.00	£2.85	£8.50	£20.00
17 last Silver Age issue, indicia dated Dec 1965/Jan 1966						
	$7.00	$21.00	$50.00	£2.85	£8.50	£20.00
18-20	$8.25	$25.00	$50.00	£2.90	£8.75	£17.50
21-26	$6.25	$18.50	$37.50	£2.50	£7.50	£15.00
27 scarce in the U.K. origin Metal Men						
	$10.00	$30.00	$60.00	£3.30	£10.00	£20.00
28-30	$6.25	$18.50	$37.50	£2.50	£7.50	£15.00
31-36	$5.25	$16.00	$32.50	£2.05	£6.25	£12.50
37 1st "new" Metal Men; new direction for title						
	$5.25	$16.00	$32.50	£2.05	£6.25	£12.50
38-41	$5.25	$16.00	$32.50	£2.05	£6.25	£12.50
42-44 all reprint	$2.50	$7.50	$15.00	£0.80	£2.50	£5.00
45 Walt Simonson art						
	$2.50	$7.50	$15.00	£0.80	£2.50	£5.00
46 scarce in the U.K. Walt Simonson art						
	$2.50	$7.50	$15.00	£1.00	£3.00	£6.00
47 scarce in the U.K. Walt Simonson art; story titles "The X-Effect"						
	$2.50	$7.50	$15.00	£1.00	£3.00	£6.00
48 Walt Simonson art, Eclipso appears						
	$2.50	$7.50	$15.00	£0.80	£2.50	£5.00
49 Walt Simonson art						
	$2.50	$7.50	$15.00	£0.80	£2.50	£5.00
50 all reprint	$2.50	$7.50	$15.00	£0.65	£2.00	£4.00
51 Walt Simonson cover						
	$2.50	$7.50	$15.00	£0.65	£2.00	£4.00
52-53	$2.50	$7.50	$15.00	£0.65	£2.00	£4.00
54-55 Green Lantern X-over						
	$2.50	$7.50	$15.00	£0.65	£2.00	£4.00
56	$2.50	$7.50	$15.00	£0.65	£2.00	£4.00
Title Value:	$402.50	$1209.50	$2720.00	£166.95	£501.00	£1137.50

METAL MEN (2ND SERIES)
DC Comics,MS; 1 Oct 1993-4 Jan 1994

	$Good	$Fine	$N.Mint	£Good	£Fine	£N.Mint
1 Mike Carlin script, Dan Jurgens and Brett Breeding art begin; foil enhanced cover						
	$0.30	$0.90	$1.50	£0.20	£0.60	£1.00
2 true origin of the Metal Men explored						
	$0.25	$0.75	$1.25	£0.15	£0.45	£0.75
3	$0.25	$0.75	$1.25	£0.15	£0.45	£0.75
4 Dr. Will Magnus becomes a Metal Man						
	$0.25	$0.75	$1.25	£0.15	£0.45	£0.75

	$Good	$Fine	$N.Mint	£Good	£Fine	£N.Mint
Title Value:	$1.05	$3.15	$5.25	£0.65	£1.95	£3.25

METAL MILITIA
Entity Comics,MS; 1 Aug 1995-3 1995

	$Good	$Fine	$N.Mint	£Good	£Fine	£N.Mint
1 ND Hoang Nguyen plot and art, Lam Duy plot and script; Jae Lee cover						
	$0.45	$1.35	$2.25	£0.30	£0.90	£1.50
1 ND Videogame Edition (Aug 1995) – pre-bagged with floppy disk game Sango Fighter						
	$1.40	$4.20	$7.00	£0.90	£2.70	£4.50
2-3 ND	$0.50	$1.50	$2.50	£0.30	£0.90	£1.50
Title Value:	$2.85	$8.55	$14.25	£1.80	£5.40	£9.00

METALLIC MEMORIES HARDCOVER GRAPHIC NOVEL
Marvel Comics,OS; 1 Jan 1993

	$Good	$Fine	$N.Mint	£Good	£Fine	£N.Mint
1 ND 96pgs, companion volume to Chaos by Moebius						
	$3.00	$9.00	$15.00	£2.00	£6.00	£10.00
Title Value:	$3.00	$9.00	$15.00	£2.00	£6.00	£10.00

METAMORPHO
National Periodical Publications; 1 Jul/Aug 1965-17 Mar/Apr 1968
(see Action, Brave and the Bold, First Issue Special, World's Finest)

	$Good	$Fine	$N.Mint	£Good	£Fine	£N.Mint
1	$12.00	$36.00	$85.00	£7.75	£23.50	£55.00
2	$7.75	$23.50	$55.00	£5.00	£15.00	£35.00
3 last Silver Age issue cover dated Nov/Dec 1965						
	$7.00	$21.00	$50.00	£4.25	£12.50	£30.00
4-6	$6.25	$18.50	$37.50	£3.30	£10.00	£20.00
7-9	$5.25	$16.00	$32.50	£2.90	£8.75	£17.50
10 origin and 1st appearance Element Girl						
	$6.25	$18.50	$37.50	£3.30	£10.00	£20.00
11-17	$4.55	$13.50	$27.50	£2.05	£6.25	£12.50
Title Value:	$99.35	$297.00	$630.00	£53.25	£161.00	£340.00

METAMORPHO (LIMITED SERIES)
DC Comics,MS; 1 Aug 1993-4 Nov 1993

	$Good	$Fine	$N.Mint	£Good	£Fine	£N.Mint
1-4 Graham Nolan art						
	$0.25	$0.75	$1.25	£0.15	£0.45	£0.75
Title Value:	$1.00	$3.00	$5.00	£0.60	£1.80	£3.00

METAPHISIQUE
Eclipse,MS; 1 Jun 1992-2 Jul 1992

	$Good	$Fine	$N.Mint	£Good	£Fine	£N.Mint
1-2 ND Norm Breyfogle script and art						
	$0.40	$1.20	$2.00	£0.25	£0.75	£1.25
Title Value:	$0.80	$2.40	$4.00	£0.50	£1.50	£2.50

METAPHYSIQUE
Malibu Bravura,MS; 1 Apr 1995-6 Dec 1995

	$Good	$Fine	$N.Mint	£Good	£Fine	£N.Mint
1 ND Norm Breyfogle script and art begins						
	$0.60	$1.80	$3.00	£0.40	£1.20	£2.00
1 ND Ashcan Edition (Apr 1995) – interviews and articles, black and white						
	$0.30	$0.90	$1.50	£0.20	£0.60	£1.00
1 ND Gold Foil Collector's Edition (Apr 1995) – gold foil embossed cover						
	$1.20	$3.60	$6.00	£0.80	£2.40	£4.00
2-6 ND	$0.60	$1.80	$3.00	£0.40	£1.20	£2.00
Title Value:	$5.10	$15.30	$25.50	£3.40	£10.20	£17.00

METEOR MAN
Marvel Comics Group,MS,Film; 1 Aug 1993-6 Jan 1994

	$Good	$Fine	$N.Mint	£Good	£Fine	£N.Mint
1 based on film	$0.25	$0.75	$1.25	£0.15	£0.45	£0.75
1 ND pre-bagged with copy of "Rap Sheet" magazine and square pin badge						
	$0.40	$1.20	$2.00	£0.25	£0.75	£1.25
2-3	$0.25	$0.75	$1.25	£0.15	£0.45	£0.75
4 Night Thrasher guest-stars						
	$0.25	$0.75	$1.25	£0.15	£0.45	£0.75
5-6	$0.25	$0.75	$1.25	£0.15	£0.45	£0.75
Title Value:	$1.90	$5.70	$9.50	£1.15	£3.45	£5.75

METEOR MAN MOVIE ADAPTATION
Marvel Comics Group,Film; 1 Apr 1993

	$Good	$Fine	$N.Mint	£Good	£Fine	£N.Mint
1 64pgs	$0.40	$1.20	$2.00	£0.25	£0.75	£1.25
Title Value:	$0.40	$1.20	$2.00	£0.25	£0.75	£1.25

METROPOL
Marvel Comics Group/Epic; 1 Mar 1991-12 Feb 1992

	$Good	$Fine	$N.Mint	£Good	£Fine	£N.Mint
1-8 ND Ted McKeever script/art						
	$0.50	$1.50	$2.50	£0.30	£0.90	£1.50
9-12 ND Eddy Current appears; Ted McKeever script/art						
	$0.50	$1.50	$2.50	£0.30	£0.90	£1.50
Title Value:	$6.00	$18.00	$30.00	£3.60	£10.80	£18.00

METROPOL A.D.
Marvel Comics Group/Epic,MS; 1 Oct 1992-3 Dec 1992

	$Good	$Fine	$N.Mint	£Good	£Fine	£N.Mint
1-3 ND Ted McKeever sequel to Metropol						
	$0.60	$1.80	$3.00	£0.40	£1.20	£2.00
Title Value:	$1.80	$5.40	$9.00	£1.20	£3.60	£6.00

METROPOLIS S.C.U.
DC Comics,MS; 1 Nov 1994-4 Feb 1995

	$Good	$Fine	$N.Mint	£Good	£Fine	£N.Mint
1-2 Lois Lane appears						
	$0.30	$0.90	$1.50	£0.20	£0.60	£1.00
3 Superman appears						
	$0.30	$0.90	$1.50	£0.20	£0.60	£1.00
4	$0.30	$0.90	$1.50	£0.20	£0.60	£1.00
Title Value:	$1.20	$3.60	$6.00	£0.80	£2.40	£4.00

MEZZ GALACTIC TOUR
Dark Horse,OS; 1 May 1994

	$Good	$Fine	$N.Mint	£Good	£Fine	£N.Mint
1 ND spin-off from Nexus						
	$0.50	$1.50	$2.50	£0.30	£0.90	£1.50
Title Value:	$0.50	$1.50	$2.50	£0.30	£0.90	£1.50

MGM'S MARVELLOUS WIZARD OF OZ
Marvel Comics Group/DC Comics,Tabloid OS; 1 Nov 1975

	$Good	$Fine	$N.Mint	£Good	£Fine	£N.Mint
1 ND scarce in the U.K. 80pgs, adapts film						
	$1.00	$3.00	$5.00	£0.70	£2.10	£3.50
Title Value:	$1.00	$3.00	$5.00	£0.70	£2.10	£3.50

MIAMI MICE
Rip Off Press; 1 1986-4 1987

	$Good	$Fine	$N.Mint	£Good	£Fine	£N.Mint
1 ND Mark Bode art begins						
	$0.40	$1.20	$2.00	£0.25	£0.75	£1.25
1 2nd printing ND	$0.30	$0.90	$1.50	£0.20	£0.60	£1.00
1 3rd printing ND	$0.40	$0.90	$1.50	£0.20	£0.60	£1.00
2-3 ND	$0.40	$1.20	$2.00	£0.25	£0.75	£1.25
4 ND Teenage Mutant Ninja Turtles by Laird/ Eastman and Cerebus by Sim appear						
	$0.50	$1.50	$2.50	£0.30	£0.90	£1.50
Title Value:	$2.30	$6.90	$11.50	£1.45	£4.35	£7.25

MICHAEL MAUSER, THE NEW CRIME FILES OF
Apple Comics; 1 Aug 1991

	$Good	$Fine	$N.Mint	£Good	£Fine	£N.Mint
1 ND Nicola Cuti, Joe Staton						
	$0.40	$1.20	$2.00	£0.25	£0.75	£1.25
Title Value:	$0.40	$1.20	$2.00	£0.25	£0.75	£1.25

MICHAELANGELO CHRISTMAS SPECIAL
Mirage Studios; nn Feb 1991

	$Good	$Fine	$N.Mint	£Good	£Fine	£N.Mint
1 ND 48pgs, reprints Michaelangelo one-shot (1986) plus 14pgs of new story						
	$0.40	$1.20	$2.00	£0.25	£0.75	£1.25
Title Value:	$0.40	$1.20	$2.00	£0.25	£0.75	£1.25

MICHAELANGELO, TEENAGE MUTANT NINJA TURTLE
Mirage Studios,OS; 1 1986

	$Good	$Fine	$N.Mint	£Good	£Fine	£N.Mint
1 ND	$1.00	$3.00	$5.00	£0.70	£2.10	£3.50
Title Value:	$1.00	$3.00	$5.00	£0.70	£2.10	£3.50

MICKEY & DONALD, WALT DISNEY'S
Gladstone; 1 Mar 1988-18 May 1990

	$Good	$Fine	$N.Mint	£Good	£Fine	£N.Mint
1 ND Mickey, Goofy and Donald Duck begin; 1949 Firestone givaway plus Don Rosa art						
	$0.80	$2.40	$4.00	£0.20	£0.60	£1.00
2 ND	$0.60	$1.80	$3.00	£0.20	£0.60	£1.00
3 ND infinity cover	$0.60	$1.80	$3.00	£0.20	£0.60	£1.00
4-8 ND	$0.40	$1.20	$2.00	£0.20	£0.60	£1.00
9 ND Christmas issue						
	$0.40	$1.20	$2.00	£0.20	£0.60	£1.00
10-13 ND	$0.40	$1.20	$2.00	£0.20	£0.60	£1.00
14 ND patriotic flag cover						
	$0.40	$1.20	$2.00	£0.20	£0.60	£1.00
15-16 ND	$0.40	$1.20	$2.00	£0.20	£0.60	£1.00
17 ND 68pgs, Christmas cover plus Rosa art						
	$0.50	$1.50	$2.50	£0.20	£0.60	£1.00
18 ND 68pgs	$0.50	$1.50	$2.50	£0.20	£0.60	£1.00
Title Value:	$8.20	$24.60	$41.00	£3.60	£10.80	£18.00

Note: Barks reprints in all.

MICKEY MOUSE
Gladstone; 219 1986-256 Apr 1990
(previously published by Whitman)

	$Good	$Fine	$N.Mint	£Good	£Fine	£N.Mint
219 1st Gladstone issue, 75c, Gottfredson newspaper reprints begin						
	$0.80	$2.40	$4.00	£0.20	£0.60	£1.00
220-224 scarce in the U.K.						
	$0.60	$1.80	$3.00	£0.20	£0.60	£1.00
225 1st 95¢ issue	$0.60	$1.80	$3.00	£0.20	£0.60	£1.00
226-243	$0.40	$1.20	$2.00	£0.20	£0.60	£1.00
244 100pgs, 60th anniversary special						
	$0.50	$1.50	$2.50	£0.25	£0.75	£1.25
245-256	$0.40	$1.20	$2.00	£0.20	£0.60	£1.00
Title Value:	$16.90	$50.70	$85.50	£7.65	£22.95	£38.25

Note: all Non-Distributed on the news-stands in the U.K.

MICKEY MOUSE ADVENTURES
Disney; 1 Jun 1990-20 Jan 1992

	$Good	$Fine	$N.Mint	£Good	£Fine	£N.Mint
1 ND part reprint	$0.30	$0.90	$1.50	£0.20	£0.60	£1.00
2-7 ND new stories	$0.30	$0.90	$1.50	£0.20	£0.60	£1.00
8 ND new stories, John Byrne cover						
	$0.30	$0.90	$1.50	£0.20	£0.60	£1.00
9 ND adaptation of "The Sorcerer's Apprentice" from Fantasia film						
	$0.30	$0.90	$1.50	£0.20	£0.60	£1.00
10-20 ND	$0.30	$0.90	$1.50	£0.20	£0.60	£1.00
Title Value:	$6.00	$18.00	$30.00	£4.00	£12.00	£20.00

Note: banned from distribution in UK

MICKEY MOUSE DIGEST
Gladstone; 1 1986-5 1987

	$Good	$Fine	$N.Mint	£Good	£Fine	£N.Mint
1-5 ND scarce in the U.K.						
	$0.30	$0.90	$1.50	£0.20	£0.60	£1.00
Title Value:	$1.50	$4.50	$7.50	£1.00	£3.00	£5.00

MICRONAUTS
Marvel Comics Group; 1 Jan 1979-59 Aug 1984

	$Good	$Fine	$N.Mint	£Good	£Fine	£N.Mint
1 ND Golden's Wrightsonesque art begins						
	$0.50	$1.50	$2.50	£0.30	£0.90	£1.50
2-6 ND Golden art	$0.40	$1.20	$2.00	£0.25	£0.75	£1.25
7 ND Man-Thing appears, Golden art						
	$0.40	$1.20	$2.00	£0.25	£0.75	£1.25
8 ND Captain Universe appears, Golden art						
	$0.40	$1.20	$2.00	£0.25	£0.75	£1.25
9-12 ND Golden art	$0.40	$1.20	$2.00	£0.25	£0.75	£1.25
13-14 ND	$0.30	$0.90	$1.50	£0.20	£0.60	£1.00
15-17 ND Fantastic Four appear						
	$0.30	$0.90	$1.50	£0.20	£0.60	£1.00
18-19 ND	$0.30	$0.90	$1.50	£0.20	£0.60	£1.00
20-21 ND Ant-Man appears						
	$0.30	$0.90	$1.50	£0.20	£0.60	£1.00
22-25 ND	$0.30	$0.90	$1.50	£0.20	£0.60	£1.00
26-29 ND Nick Fury appears						
	$0.30	$0.90	$1.50	£0.20	£0.60	£1.00
30	$0.30	$0.90	$1.50	£0.20	£0.60	£1.00

	$Good	$Fine	$N.Mint	£Good	£Fine	£N.Mint
31-34 Dr. Strange appears						
	$0.25	$0.75	$1.25	£0.15	£0.45	£0.75
35 52pgs, Dr. Strange appears						
	$0.30	$0.90	$1.50	£0.20	£0.60	£1.00
36	$0.25	$0.75	$1.25	£0.15	£0.45	£0.75
37 X-Men appear	$0.40	$1.20	$2.00	£0.25	£0.75	£1.25
38	$0.25	$0.75	$1.25	£0.15	£0.45	£0.75
39 Steve Ditko art	$0.25	$0.75	$1.25	£0.15	£0.45	£0.75
40 Fantastic Four X-over						
	$0.25	$0.75	$1.25	£0.15	£0.45	£0.75
41 Dr. Doom appears; X-over Fantastic Four #236						
	$0.25	$0.75	$1.25	£0.15	£0.45	£0.75
42 Wasp appears	$0.25	$0.75	$1.25	£0.15	£0.45	£0.75
43 Avengers appear						
	$0.25	$0.75	$1.25	£0.15	£0.45	£0.75
44	$0.25	$0.75	$1.25	£0.15	£0.45	£0.75
45 Arcade appears	$0.25	$0.75	$1.25	£0.15	£0.45	£0.75
46-56	$0.25	$0.75	$1.25	£0.15	£0.45	£0.75
57 ND DS	$0.25	$0.75	$1.25	£0.15	£0.45	£0.75
58-59	$0.25	$0.75	$1.25	£0.15	£0.45	£0.75
Title Value:	$17.75	$53.25	$88.75	£11.15	£33.45	£55.75

Note: Chaykin in 13-18, Giffen in 36, 37, Gil Kane 40-45, Butch Guice 48-58. Mike Golden covers on 2-21, 23.

MICRONAUTS ANNUAL
Marvel Comics Group; 1 Dec 1979-2 Oct 1980

	$Good	$Fine	$N.Mint	£Good	£Fine	£N.Mint
1-2 ND Steve Ditko cover/art						
	$0.30	$0.90	$1.50	£0.20	£0.60	£1.00
Title Value:	$0.60	$1.80	$3.00	£0.40	£1.20	£2.00

MICRONAUTS SPECIAL EDITION
Marvel Comics Group; 1 Dec 1983-5 Apr 1984

	$Good	$Fine	$N.Mint	£Good	£Fine	£N.Mint
1 ND reprints from #1 begin						
	$0.40	$1.20	$2.00	£0.25	£0.75	£1.25
2-5 ND reprints	$0.40	$1.20	$2.00	£0.25	£0.75	£1.25
Title Value:	$2.00	$6.00	$10.00	£1.25	£3.75	£6.25

MICRONAUTS: THE NEW VOYAGES
Marvel Comics Group; 1 Oct 1984-20 May 1986

	$Good	$Fine	$N.Mint	£Good	£Fine	£N.Mint
1-15 LD in the U.K.	$0.25	$0.75	$1.25	£0.15	£0.45	£0.75
16 Secret Wars II X-over						
	$0.25	$0.75	$1.25	£0.15	£0.45	£0.75
17-20	$0.25	$0.75	$1.25	£0.15	£0.45	£0.75
Title Value:	$5.00	$15.00	$25.00	£3.00	£9.00	£15.00

MIDNIGHT EYE: GOKU P.I.
Viz Communications,MS; 1 Nov 1991-6 Apr 1992

	$Good	$Fine	$N.Mint	£Good	£Fine	£N.Mint
1-6 ND	$0.90	$2.70	$4.50	£0.60	£1.80	£3.00
Title Value:	$5.40	$16.20	$27.00	£3.60	£10.80	£18.00
Hardcover (1992), reprints #1-6				£4.00	£12.00	£20.00

MIDNIGHT MEN
Marvel Comics Group,MS; 1 Jun 1993-4 Sep 1993

	$Good	$Fine	$N.Mint	£Good	£Fine	£N.Mint
1 ND Howard Chaykin script and art begins, embossed cover with metallic ink						
	$0.40	$1.20	$2.00	£0.25	£0.75	£1.25
2-4 ND	$0.40	$1.20	$2.00	£0.25	£0.75	£1.25
Title Value:	$1.60	$4.80	$8.00	£1.00	£3.00	£5.00

MIDNIGHT MYSTERY
ACG; 1 Jan/Feb 1961-7 Oct 1961

	$Good	$Fine	$N.Mint	£Good	£Fine	£N.Mint
1 distributed in the U.K.						
	$10.50	$33.00	$65.00	£7.50	£22.50	£45.00
2-7 distributed in the U.K.						
	$5.25	$16.00	$32.50	£3.30	£10.00	£20.00
Title Value:	$42.00	$129.00	$260.00	£27.30	£82.50	£165.00

MIDNIGHT SCREAMS
Mystery Graphix Press,MS; 1 Sep 1991-2 Jan 1992

	$Good	$Fine	$N.Mint	£Good	£Fine	£N.Mint
1-2 ND black and white; includes uncut sheet of b/w trading cards						
	$0.40	$1.20	$2.00	£0.25	£0.75	£1.25
Title Value:	$0.80	$2.40	$4.00	£0.50	£1.50	£2.50

MIDNIGHT SONS ASHCAN EDITION
Marvel Comics Group,OS; nn Jul 1994

	$Good	$Fine	$N.Mint	£Good	£Fine	£N.Mint
nn ND 16pgs, previews Blade the Vampire Hunter						
	$0.25	$0.75	$1.25	£0.15	£0.45	£0.75
Title Value:	$0.25	$0.75	$1.25	£0.15	£0.45	£0.75

MIDNIGHT SONS UNLIMITED
Marvel Comics Group; 1 Apr 1993-9 May 1995

	$Good	$Fine	$N.Mint	£Good	£Fine	£N.Mint
1 64pgs, Ghost Rider, Morbius, Nightstalkers and Darkhold appear, Mark Texeira cover						
	$0.60	$1.80	$3.00	£0.40	£1.20	£2.00
2 64pgs, Ghost Rider, Morbius, Nightstalkers and Darkhold appear, Bill Sienkiewicz cover						
	$0.60	$1.80	$3.00	£0.40	£1.20	£2.00
3 64pgs, Ghost Rider, Morbius, Nightstalkers and Darkhold appear; Spiderman guest-stars; cover by John Romita Jnr						
	$0.60	$1.80	$3.00	£0.40	£1.20	£2.00
4 64pgs, Siege of Darkness part 17 (conclusion); spot varnished painted cover						
	$0.60	$1.80	$3.00	£0.40	£1.20	£2.00
5 64pgs, Dr. Strange and Midnight Sons						
	$0.60	$1.80	$3.00	£0.40	£1.20	£2.00
6 64pgs, Dr. Strange						
	$0.60	$1.80	$3.00	£0.40	£1.20	£2.00
7 64pgs, Man Thing						
	$0.60	$1.80	$3.00	£0.40	£1.20	£2.00
8 64pgs, Blade, Man-Thing and Scarlet Witch						
	$0.60	$1.80	$3.00	£0.40	£1.20	£2.00
9 64pgs, Ghost Rider, Legion of Night; Alex Ross painted cover						
	$0.60	$1.80	$3.00	£0.40	£1.20	£2.00
Title Value:	$5.40	$16.20	$27.00	£3.60	£10.80	£18.00

MIDNIGHT TALES
Charlton; 1 Dec 1972-18 May 1976

	$Good	$Fine	$N.Mint	£Good	£Fine	£N.Mint
1 distributed in the U.K.						
	$0.90	$2.70	$4.50	£0.60	£1.80	£3.00
2-10 distributed in the U.K.						
	$0.60	$1.80	$3.00	£0.40	£1.20	£2.00
11 distributed in the U.K.						
	$0.50	$1.50	$2.50	£0.30	£0.90	£1.50
12 reprint; distributed in the U.K.						
	$0.40	$1.20	$2.00	£0.25	£0.75	£1.25
13-16 distributed in the U.K.						
	$0.50	$1.50	$2.50	£0.30	£0.90	£1.50
17 reprint; distributed in the U.K.						
	$0.40	$1.20	$2.00	£0.25	£0.75	£1.25
18 distributed in the U.K.						
	$0.50	$1.50	$2.50	£0.30	£0.90	£1.50
Title Value:	$10.10	$30.30	$50.50	£6.50	£19.50	£32.50

MIDNITE, THE REBEL SKUNK
Blackthorne; 1 Nov 1986-3 Mar 1987

	$Good	$Fine	$N.Mint	£Good	£Fine	£N.Mint
1 ND Reform School Girl parody						
	$0.30	$0.90	$1.50	£0.20	£0.60	£1.00
2-3 ND	$0.30	$0.90	$1.50	£0.20	£0.60	£1.00
Title Value:	$0.90	$2.70	$4.50	£0.60	£1.80	£3.00

MIGHTY COMICS
Archie; 40 Nov 1966-50 Oct 1967
(previously Flyman)

	$Good	$Fine	$N.Mint	£Good	£Fine	£N.Mint
40 distributed in the U.K.						
	$2.90	$8.75	$17.50	£2.00	£6.00	£12.00
41-50 distributed in the U.K.						
	$2.50	$7.50	$15.00	£1.65	£5.00	£10.00
Title Value:	$27.90	$83.75	$167.50	£18.50	£56.00	£112.00

MIGHTY CRUSADERS
Archie; 1 Nov 1965-7 Oct 1966

	$Good	$Fine	$N.Mint	£Good	£Fine	£N.Mint
1 distributed in the U.K.						
	$5.00	$15.00	$30.00	£3.30	£10.00	£20.00
2 distributed in the U.K.						
	$2.90	$8.75	$17.50	£2.05	£6.25	£12.50
3 distributed in the U.K.						
	$2.50	$7.50	$15.00	£1.65	£5.00	£10.00
4 distributed in the U.K.						
	$2.90	$8.75	$17.50	£2.05	£6.25	£12.50
5-7 distributed in the U.K.						
	$2.50	$7.50	$15.00	£1.65	£5.00	£10.00
Title Value:	$20.80	$62.50	$125.00	£14.00	£42.50	£85.00

MIGHTY CRUSADERS (2ND SERIES)
Red Circle (Archie); 1 Mar 1983-13 Sep 1985

	$Good	$Fine	$N.Mint	£Good	£Fine	£N.Mint
1 distributed in the U.K.						
	$0.40	$1.20	$2.00	£0.25	£0.75	£1.25
2-10 distributed in the U.K.						
	$0.30	$0.90	$1.50	£0.20	£0.60	£1.00
11-13 distributed in the U.K.						
	$0.25	$0.75	$1.25	£0.15	£0.45	£0.75
Title Value:	$3.85	$11.55	$19.25	£2.50	£7.50	£12.50

MIGHTY HERCULES, THE
Gold Key; 1 Jul 1963-2 Nov 1963

	$Good	$Fine	$N.Mint	£Good	£Fine	£N.Mint
1 scarce, limited distribution in the U.K.						
	$15.00	$45.00	$90.00	£10.00	£30.00	£60.00
2 scarce, limited distribution in the U.K.						
	$14.00	$43.00	$85.00	£9.00	£28.00	£55.00
Title Value:	$29.00	$88.00	$175.00	£19.00	£58.00	£115.00

MIGHTY MAGNOR, THE
Malibu; 1 Apr 1993-6 1994

	$Good	$Fine	$N.Mint	£Good	£Fine	£N.Mint
1 ND Sergio Aragones art begins						
	$0.50	$1.50	$2.50	£0.30	£0.90	£1.50
1 ND Direct Market edition – pop-up feature						
	$0.80	$2.40	$4.00	£0.50	£1.50	£2.50
2-6	$0.40	$1.20	$2.00	£0.25	£0.75	£1.25
Title Value:	$3.30	$9.90	$16.50	£2.05	£6.15	£10.25

MIGHTY MARVEL WESTERN, THE
Marvel Comics Group; 1 Oct 1968-46 Sep 1976

	$Good	$Fine	$N.Mint	£Good	£Fine	£N.Mint
1 64pgs, Rawhide Kid, Kid Colt Outlaw and Two-Gun Kid reprints begin						
	$1.50	$4.50	$7.50	£1.00	£3.00	£5.00
2-3 64pgs	$0.70	$2.10	$3.50	£0.40	£1.50	£2.50
4-9 64pgs	$0.60	$1.80	$3.00	£0.40	£1.20	£2.00
10 scarce in the U.K. 64pgs						
	$0.60	$1.80	$3.00	£0.45	£1.35	£2.25
11-20 64pgs	$0.50	$1.50	$2.50	£0.30	£0.90	£1.50
21-46 ND	$0.40	$1.20	$2.00	£0.25	£0.75	£1.25
Title Value:	$22.50	$67.50	$112.50	£14.35	£43.05	£71.75

ARTISTS
Williamson reprints in 32, 37.
REPRINT FEATURES
Kid Colt Outlaw in 1-24, 43-46. Rawhide Kid 1-46. Two-Gun Kid 1-46. Matt Slade 25-42.

MIGHTY MITES, THE
Eternity,OS; 1 1986

	$Good	$Fine	$N.Mint	£Good	£Fine	£N.Mint
1 ND X-Men parody (2 cover versions exist)						
	$0.40	$1.20	$2.00	£0.25	£0.75	£1.25
Title Value:	$0.40	$1.20	$2.00	£0.25	£0.75	£1.25

MIGHTY MITES, THE (2ND SERIES)
Continuum Comics; 1 Aug 1993-4 1993

	$Good	$Fine	$N.Mint	£Good	£Fine	£N.Mint
1-4 ND	$0.40	$1.20	$2.00	£0.25	£0.75	£1.25
Title Value:	$1.60	$4.80	$8.00	£1.00	£3.00	£5.00

MIGHTY MORPHIN POWER RANGERS
Hamilton Comics; 1 Nov 1994-6 Apr 1995

VERY GENERAL PERCENTAGE CONVERSION CHART WHICH MAY BE USED TO CALCULATE LOW AND INBETWEEN GRADES:

	$Good	$Fine	$N.Mint	£Good	£Fine	£N.Mint
1 ND Don Markstein script, Gray Morrow art; Brett Blevins and Terry Austin cover	$0.40	$1.20	$2.00	£0.25	£0.75	£1.25
2-6 ND	$0.40	$1.20	$2.00	£0.25	£0.75	£1.25
Title Value:	$2.40	$7.20	$12.00	£1.50	£4.50	£7.50

Mighty Morphin Power Rangers (May 1995)
Trade paperback collects 6 issue series, photo cover				£1.30	£3.90	£6.50

MIGHTY MORPHIN POWER RANGERS (2ND SERIES)
Hamilton Comics,MS; 1 May 1995-4 Aug 1995?
	$Good	$Fine	$N.Mint	£Good	£Fine	£N.Mint
1-3 ND	$0.40	$1.20	$2.00	£0.25	£0.75	£1.25
4 ND Gray Morrow art	$0.40	$1.20	$2.00	£0.25	£0.75	£1.25
Title Value:	$1.60	$4.80	$8.00	£1.00	£3.00	£5.00

MIGHTY MORPHIN POWER RANGERS MAGAZINE, SABAN'S
Marvel Comics Group,Magazine OS; 1 Nov 1995
	$Good	$Fine	$N.Mint	£Good	£Fine	£N.Mint
1 ND articles and features and pull-out poster	$0.40	$1.20	$2.00	£0.25	£0.75	£1.25
Title Value:	$0.40	$1.20	$2.00	£0.25	£0.75	£1.25

MIGHTY MORPHIN POWER RANGERS MOVIE ADAPTATION
Marvel Comics Group,OS; nn Sep 1995
	$Good	$Fine	$N.Mint	£Good	£Fine	£N.Mint
nn ND 48pgs, adaptation of film, Ron Lim art; foil board cover	$0.80	$2.40	$4.00	£0.50	£1.50	£2.50
Title Value:	$0.80	$2.40	$4.00	£0.50	£1.50	£2.50

Mighty Morphin Power Rangers Two Pack (Sep 1995)
ND, film adaptation of above split into two comics, shrink-wrapped with bonus photos and pin-ups				£0.30	£0.90	£1.50

MIGHTY MORPHIN POWER RANGERS SAGA
Hamilton Comics,MS; 1 Jul 1995-6 1995?
	$Good	$Fine	$N.Mint	£Good	£Fine	£N.Mint
1-6 ND Don Markstein script, John Heebink art	$0.40	$1.20	$2.00	£0.25	£0.75	£1.25
Title Value:	$2.40	$7.20	$12.00	£1.50	£4.50	£7.50

MIGHTY MORPHIN POWER RANGERS, SABAN'S
Marvel Comics Group; 1 Nov 1995-present
	$Good	$Fine	$N.Mint	£Good	£Fine	£N.Mint
1 ND Scott Lobdell and Fabian Nicieza script, Ron Lim and Mark McKenna art; 2 stories	$0.40	$1.20	$2.00	£0.25	£0.75	£1.25
2-5 ND	$0.40	$1.20	$2.00	£0.25	£0.75	£1.25
Title Value:	$2.00	$6.00	$9.75	£1.25	£3.75	£6.25

MIGHTY MORPHIN POWER RANGERS: NINJA TROOPERS/VR TROOPERS, SABAN'S
Marvel Comics Group; 1 Dec 1995-present
	$Good	$Fine	$N.Mint	£Good	£Fine	£N.Mint
1 ND flip-book format featuring Ron Lim art	$0.50	$1.50	$2.50	£0.30	£0.90	£1.50
2 ND flip-book format featuring Ron Lim art	$0.40	$1.20	$2.00	£0.25	£0.75	£1.25
3-4 ND	$0.40	$1.20	$2.00	£0.25	£0.75	£1.25
Title Value:	$1.70	$5.10	$8.25	£1.05	£3.15	£5.25

MIGHTY MORPHIN POWER RANGERS: THE MOVIE PHOTO ADAPTATION, SABAN'S
Marvel Comics Group,OS; 1 Nov 1995
	$Good	$Fine	$N.Mint	£Good	£Fine	£N.Mint
1 ND 48pgs, movie adaptation with film stills	$0.60	$1.80	$3.00	£0.40	£1.20	£2.00
Title Value:	$0.60	$1.80	$3.00	£0.40	£1.20	£2.00

MIGHTY MOUSE
Marvel Comics Group; 1 Oct 1990-10 Jul 1991
	$Good	$Fine	$N.Mint	£Good	£Fine	£N.Mint
1-2 Dark Knight parody	$0.15	$0.45	$0.75	£0.10	£0.30	£0.50
3 John Byrne cover; Namor parody	$0.15	$0.45	$0.75	£0.10	£0.30	£0.50
4 George Perez cover; Crisis on Infinite Earths parody	$0.15	$0.45	$0.75	£0.10	£0.30	£0.50
5 Crisis parody continues	$0.15	$0.45	$0.75	£0.10	£0.30	£0.50
6 Todd McFarlane Spiderman parody	$0.15	$0.45	$0.75	£0.10	£0.30	£0.50

	$Good	$Fine	$N.Mint	£Good	£Fine	£N.Mint
7 computer-generated issue	$0.15	$0.45	$0.75	£0.10	£0.30	£0.50
8-10	$0.15	$0.45	$0.75	£0.10	£0.30	£0.50
Title Value:	$1.50	$4.50	$7.50	£1.00	£3.00	£5.00

MIGHTY MOUSE
Spotlight; 1 1987
	$Good	$Fine	$N.Mint	£Good	£Fine	£N.Mint
1 ND Paul Chadwick cover	$0.50	$1.50	$2.50	£0.30	£0.90	£1.50
Title Value:	$0.50	$1.50	$2.50	£0.30	£0.90	£1.50

Note: Buckler art in all.

MIGHTY MOUSE AND FRIENDS HOLIDAY SPECIAL
Spotlight; 1 1987
	$Good	$Fine	$N.Mint	£Good	£Fine	£N.Mint
1 ND Deputy Dawg, Heckle & Jeckle appear	$0.40	$1.20	$2.00	£0.25	£0.75	£1.25
Title Value:	$0.40	$1.20	$2.00	£0.25	£0.75	£1.25

MIGHTY MUTANIMALS
Archie; 1 Mar 1991-3 May 1991
	$Good	$Fine	$N.Mint	£Good	£Fine	£N.Mint
1 ND features Teenage Mutant Ninja Turtles	$0.25	$0.75	$1.25	£0.15	£0.45	£0.75
2-3 ND	$0.25	$0.75	$1.25	£0.15	£0.45	£0.75
Title Value:	$0.75	$2.25	$3.75	£0.45	£1.35	£2.25

MIGHTY MUTANIMALS (2ND SERIES)
Archie; 1 Mar 1992-9 1992
	$Good	$Fine	$N.Mint	£Good	£Fine	£N.Mint
1-9 ND	$0.25	$0.75	$1.25	£0.15	£0.45	£0.75
Title Value:	$2.25	$6.75	$11.25	£1.35	£4.05	£6.75

MIGHTY MUTANIMALS INVASION FROM SPACE, THE
Archie,OS; 1 Jan 1992
	$Good	$Fine	$N.Mint	£Good	£Fine	£N.Mint
1 ND 96pgs	$0.50	$1.50	$2.50	£0.30	£0.90	£1.50
Title Value:	$0.50	$1.50	$2.50	£0.30	£0.90	£1.50

MIGHTY SAMSON
Gold Key; 1 Jul 1964-20 Nov 1969; 21 Sep 1972-31 Mar 1976; 32 Aug 1982
(see Gold Key Champion)
	$Good	$Fine	$N.Mint	£Good	£Fine	£N.Mint
1 origin; painted covers begin (to #32); Frank Thorne art begins	$5.75	$17.50	$35.00	£3.75	£11.00	£22.50
2-5	$2.65	$8.00	$16.00	£1.65	£5.00	£10.00
6-10	$2.05	$6.25	$12.50	£1.30	£4.00	£8.00
11-20	$1.65	$5.00	$10.00	£1.15	£3.50	£7.00
21-31	$1.00	$3.00	$5.00	£0.60	£1.80	£3.00
32	$0.50	$1.50	$2.50	£0.30	£0.90	£1.50
Title Value:	$54.60	$165.25	$319.00	£35.25	£106.70	£207.00

Note: most issues distributed on the news-stands in the U.K.

MIKE DANGER, MICKEY SPILLANE'S
Tekno Comix; 1 Sep 1995-present
	$Good	$Fine	$N.Mint	£Good	£Fine	£N.Mint
1 ND Max Allan Collins script, Eduardo Barreto and Steve Leialoha art	$0.40	$1.20	$2.00	£0.25	£0.75	£1.25
2-5 ND	$0.40	$1.20	$2.00	£0.25	£0.75	£1.25
6 ND	$0.45	$1.35	$2.25	£0.30	£0.90	£1.50
7 ND pre-bagged with Tekno back-issue comic	$0.45	$1.35	$2.25	£0.30	£0.90	£1.50
Title Value:	$2.90	$8.70	$14.50	£1.85	£5.55	£9.25

MIKE GRELL'S SABLE
First; 1 Sep 1989-10 Dec 1990
	$Good	$Fine	$N.Mint	£Good	£Fine	£N.Mint
1-10 ND Mike Grell art	$0.40	$1.20	$2.00	£0.25	£0.75	£1.25
Title Value:	$4.00	$12.00	$20.00	£2.50	£7.50	£12.50

MIKE MIST IN 3-D (MS. TREE'S..)
Eclipse,OS; 1 Aug 1985
	$Good	$Fine	$N.Mint	£Good	£Fine	£N.Mint
1 ND with 3-D glasses (25% less without glasses)	$0.40	$1.20	$2.00	£0.25	£0.75	£1.25
Title Value:	$0.40	$1.20	$2.00	£0.25	£0.75	£1.25

Meet Merton #9

Men of War #26

Metal Men #41

MINT = 100% / NEAR MINT (inc. +/-) = 90–99% / VERY FINE (inc. +/-) = 75–89% / FINE (inc. +/-) = 55–74% / VERY GOOD (inc. +/-) = 35–54% / GOOD (inc. +/-) = 15–34% / FAIR = 5–14% / POOR = 1–4%

463

MIKE MIST MINUTE MYSTERIES
Eclipse,OS; 1 1986

	$Good	$Fine	$N.Mint	£Good	£Fine	£N.Mint
1 ND	$0.40	$1.20	$2.00	£0.25	£0.75	£1.25
Title Value:	$0.40	$1.20	$2.00	£0.25	£0.75	£1.25

MILK & CHEESE 666
Slave Labor,OS; 1 Apr 1995

	$Good	$Fine	$N.Mint	£Good	£Fine	£N.Mint
1 ND Evan Dorkin script and art; black and white	$0.40	$1.20	$2.00	£0.25	£0.75	£1.25
Title Value:	$0.40	$1.20	$2.00	£0.25	£0.75	£1.25

MILK & CHEESE'S FIRST SECOND ISSUE
Slave labor,OS; 1 Mar 1994

	$Good	$Fine	$N.Mint	£Good	£Fine	£N.Mint
1 ND Evan Dorkin script and art	$0.40	$1.20	$2.00	£0.25	£0.75	£1.25
1 2nd printing, ND (Nov 1994)	$0.80	$2.40	$4.00	£0.50	£1.50	£2.50
Title Value:	$0.80	$2.40	$4.00	£0.50	£1.50	£2.50

MILK AND CHEESE SPECIAL
Slave Labor,OS; 1 May 1991

	$Good	$Fine	$N.Mint	£Good	£Fine	£N.Mint
1 ND Evan Dorkin script/art; black and white	$0.50	$1.50	$2.50	£0.30	£0.90	£1.50
1 2nd printing ND	$0.45	$1.35	$2.25	£0.30	£0.90	£1.50
1 3rd/4th printing ND	$0.40	$1.20	$2.00	£0.25	£0.75	£1.25
1 5th printing, ND (Oct 1994)	$0.40	$1.20	$2.00	£0.25	£0.75	£1.25
1 6th printing ND 24pgs	$0.40	$1.20	$2.00	£0.25	£0.75	£1.25
Title Value:	$2.55	$7.65	$12.75	£1.60	£4.80	£8.00

The Milk and Cheese Experience (Mar 1994)

	£Good	£Fine	£N.Mint
Trade paperback reprints all strips in chronological order	£1.30	£3.90	£6.50

MILK AND CHEESE'S FOURTH NUMBER ONE
Slave Labor; 1 Jun 1993

	$Good	$Fine	$N.Mint	£Good	£Fine	£N.Mint
1 ND Evan Dorkin script/art	$0.40	$1.20	$2.00	£0.25	£0.75	£1.25
1 2nd printing, ND (Mar 1995)	$0.40	$1.20	$2.00	£0.25	£0.75	£1.25
Title Value:	$0.80	$2.40	$4.00	£0.50	£1.50	£2.50

Fun With Milk & Cheese (1994) Trade paperback

	£Good	£Fine	£N.Mint
reprints all four "first" issues plus unpublished strips	£1.30	£3.90	£6.50
2nd print – Jan 1995	£1.30	£3.90	£6.50

MILK AND CHEESE'S OTHER
Slave Labor,OS; 1 Jan 1992

	$Good	$Fine	$N.Mint	£Good	£Fine	£N.Mint
1 ND Evan Dorkin script/art	$0.50	$1.50	$2.50	£0.30	£0.90	£1.50
1 2nd printing, ND (Jul 1993)	$0.40	$1.20	$2.00	£0.25	£0.75	£1.25
1 3rd printing ND	$0.40	$1.20	$2.00	£0.25	£0.75	£1.25
Title Value:	$1.30	$3.90	$6.50	£0.80	£2.40	£4.00

MILK AND CHEESE'S THIRD NUMBER ONE
Slave Labor,OS; 1 Oct 1992

	$Good	$Fine	$N.Mint	£Good	£Fine	£N.Mint
1 ND Evan Dorkin script/art	$0.50	$1.50	$2.50	£0.30	£0.90	£1.50
1 2nd printing, ND (Jun 1993)	$0.40	$1.20	$2.00	£0.25	£0.75	£1.25
1 3rd printing ND	$0.40	$1.20	$2.00	£0.25	£0.75	£1.25
Title Value:	$1.30	$3.90	$6.50	£0.80	£2.40	£4.00

MILLENNIUM
Cross-over series at the beginning of 1988 with a number of tie-ins around a core mini-series. The story revolves around the Manhunters, revealed as having been placed on Earth eons ago in order to assume positions of power and importance. The listings below are in alphabetical rather than chronological order.

1) Action Comics #596 – unofficial X-over
2) Adventures of Superman# 436 – unofficial X-over
3) Adventures of Superman #437
4) Batman #415
5) Blue Beetle #20
6) Blue Beetle #21
7) Booster Gold #24
8) Booster Gold #25
9) Captain Atom #11
10) Detective Comics #582
11) Firestorm #67
12) Firestorm #68
13) Flash #8
14) Flash #9
15) Green Lantern #220
16) Green Lantern #221
17) Infinity Inc. #46
18) Infinity Inc. #47
19) Justice League International #9
20) Justice League International #10
21) Legion of Super-Heroes (2nd Series) #42 - unofficial X-over
22) Legion of Super-Heroes (2nd Series) #43
23) Outsiders #27
24) Outsiders #28
25) Secret Origins (2nd Series) #22
26) Secret Origins (2nd Series) #23
27) Spectre (2nd Series) #10
28) Spectre (2nd Series) #11
29) Suicide Squad #9
30) Superman #13
31) Superman #14
32) Teen Titans Spotlight #18
33) Teen Titans Spotlight #19
34) Wonder Woman #12
35) Wonder Woman #13
36) Young All Stars #8
37) Young All Stars #9

Note: unofficial cross-over means that the storyline may be referred to in the comic but not emblazoned on the cover with the "Millenium" logo.

MILLENNIUM (LIMITED SERIES)
DC Comics,MS; 1 Jan 1988-8 Feb 1988

	$Good	$Fine	$N.Mint	£Good	£Fine	£N.Mint
1-8 Staton/Ian Gibson art	$0.25	$0.75	$1.25	£0.15	£0.45	£0.75
Title Value:	$2.00	$6.00	$10.00	£1.20	£3.60	£6.00

Note: multi-cross over series similar to Legends and Crisis on, Infinite Earths

MILLENNIUM FEVER
DC Comics/Vertigo,MS; 1 Oct 1995-4 Jan 1996

	$Good	$Fine	$N.Mint	£Good	£Fine	£N.Mint
1-4 ND Nick Abadzis script, Duncan Fegredo art	$0.45	$1.35	$2.25	£0.30	£0.90	£1.50
Title Value:	$1.80	$5.40	$9.00	£1.20	£3.60	£6.00

MILLENNIUM INDEX
ICG/Eclipse,MS; 1,2 Mar 1988

	$Good	$Fine	$N.Mint	£Good	£Fine	£N.Mint
1 ND scarce in the U.K. information and colour cover reproductions Millennium maxi-series #1-#4 and X-overs weeks 1-4	$0.50	$1.50	$2.50	£0.30	£0.90	£1.50
2 ND scarce in the U.K. information and colour cover reproductions Millennium maxi-series #5-#8 and X-overs weeks 5-8	$0.50	$1.50	$2.50	£0.30	£0.90	£1.50
Title Value:	$1.00	$3.00	$5.00	£0.60	£1.80	£3.00

MILLENNIUM SHOWCASE
Millennium; 1 Jul 1991

	$Good	$Fine	$N.Mint	£Good	£Fine	£N.Mint
1 ND Death Hawk	$0.40	$1.20	$2.00	£0.25	£0.75	£1.25
Title Value:	$0.40	$1.20	$2.00	£0.25	£0.75	£1.25

MILLIE ANNUAL, MAD ABOUT
Marvel Comics Group; 1 Nov 1971

	$Good	$Fine	$N.Mint	£Good	£Fine	£N.Mint
1 very scarce in the U.K., 72pgs	$2.50	$7.50	$12.50	£1.50	£4.50	£7.50
Title Value:	$2.50	$7.50	$12.50	£1.50	£4.50	£7.50

MILLIE THE MODEL
Marvel Comics Group; 79 Jul 1960-207 Dec 1973
(see Modelling with..., A Date with..., Life with..., Mad About..)

	$Good	$Fine	$N.Mint	£Good	£Fine	£N.Mint
79-99 scarce in the U.K.	$3.75	$11.00	$22.50	£2.50	£7.50	£15.00
100 scarce in the U.K.	$5.00	$15.00	$30.00	£3.30	£10.00	£20.00
101-106 scarce in the U.K.	$2.50	$7.50	$15.00	£1.65	£5.00	£10.00
107 scarce in the U.K. Jack Kirby appears in story	$2.50	$7.50	$15.00	£1.65	£5.00	£10.00
108-150	$2.50	$7.50	$15.00	£1.65	£5.00	£10.00
151-153	$2.80	$8.25	$14.00	£1.80	£5.25	£9.00
154 scarce in the U.K. title re-vamped, new Millie	$3.00	$9.00	$15.00	£2.00	£6.00	£10.00
155-160 scarce in the U.K.	$3.00	$9.00	$15.00	£2.00	£6.00	£10.00
161-190 scarce in the U.K.	$2.50	$7.50	$12.50	£1.60	£4.80	£8.00
191 scarce in the U.K.	$2.00	$6.00	$10.00	£1.50	£4.50	£7.50
192 scarce in the U.K. 52pgs	$2.50	$7.50	$12.50	£1.60	£4.80	£8.00
193-207 scarce in the U.K.	$2.00	$6.00	$10.00	£1.50	£4.50	£7.50
Title Value:	$347.65	$1037.25	$1947.00	£231.30	£696.05	£1300.00

MILLIE THE MODEL ANNUAL
Marvel Comics Group; 1 1962-10 Nov 1971

	$Good	$Fine	$N.Mint	£Good	£Fine	£N.Mint
1 very scarce in the U.K.	$17.50	$52.50	$125.00	£12.00	£36.00	£85.00
2 scarce in the U.K.	$16.50	$50.00	$100.00	£11.50	£35.00	£70.00
3-5 scarce in the U.K.	$10.50	$33.00	$65.00	£7.50	£22.50	£45.00
6-8 scarce in the U.K.	$6.50	$20.00	$40.00	£4.55	£13.50	£27.50
9-10 scarce in the U.K.	$6.25	$18.50	$37.50	£4.15	£12.50	£25.00
Title Value:	$97.50	$298.50	$615.00	£67.95	£204.00	£422.50

MILLIE THE MODEL QUEEN SIZE
Marvel Comics Group; 11 Sep 1974-12 1975
(formerly Millie the Model Annual)

	$Good	$Fine	$N.Mint	£Good	£Fine	£N.Mint
11-12 scarce in the U.K.	$5.00	$15.00	$30.00	£3.30	£10.00	£20.00
Title Value:	$10.00	$30.00	$60.00	£6.60	£20.00	£40.00

MILLIE, A DATE WITH
Marvel Comics Group; 1 Oct 1959-7 Oct 1960
(previous series published by Atlas, 1956/1957)

	$Good	$Fine	$N.Mint	£Good	£Fine	£N.Mint
1 ND scarce in the U.K.	$18.50	$55.00	$130.00	£12.00	£36.00	£85.00
2 ND scarce in the U.K.	$10.50	$33.00	$65.00	£7.50	£22.50	£45.00
3-7 ND scarce in the U.K.	$7.50	$22.50	$45.00	£5.00	£15.00	£30.00
Title Value:	$66.50	$200.50	$420.00	£44.50	£133.50	£280.00

MILLIE, LIFE WITH
Marvel Comics Group; 8 Dec 1960-20 Dec 1962

	$Good	$Fine	$N.Mint	£Good	£Fine	£N.Mint

(formerly Date with Millie; becomes Modelling with Millie)

8 ND scarce in the U.K.
| | $7.50 | $22.50 | $45.00 | £5.00 | £15.00 | £30.00 |

9-11 ND scarce in the U.K.
| | $5.75 | $17.50 | $35.00 | £3.75 | £11.00 | £22.50 |

12-20 ND scarce in the U.K.
| | $4.15 | $12.50 | $25.00 | £2.90 | £8.75 | £17.50 |

| Title Value: | $62.10 | $187.50 | $375.00 | £42.35 | £126.75 | £255.00 |

MILLIE, MAD ABOUT
Marvel Comics Group; 1 Apr 1969-17 Dec 1970

1 rare in the U.K. 68pgs
| | $6.25 | $18.50 | $37.50 | £4.15 | £12.50 | £25.00 |

2 rare in the U.K.
| | $4.50 | $13.50 | $22.50 | £3.00 | £9.00 | £15.00 |

3-10 rare in the U.K.
| | $4.00 | $12.00 | $20.00 | £2.50 | £7.50 | £12.50 |

11-15 rare in the U.K.
| | $3.50 | $10.50 | $17.50 | £2.20 | £6.50 | £11.00 |

16-17 rare in the U.K., reprints
| | $3.00 | $9.00 | $15.00 | £2.00 | £6.00 | £10.00 |

| Title Value: | $66.25 | $198.50 | $337.50 | £42.15 | £126.00 | £215.00 |

MILLIE, MODELLING WITH
Marvel Comics Group; 21 Feb 1963-54 Jun 1967

21 very scarce in the U.K.
| | $7.00 | $21.00 | $50.00 | £5.00 | £15.00 | £35.00 |

22-30 scarce in the U.K.
| | $5.75 | $17.50 | $35.00 | £3.30 | £10.00 | £20.00 |

31-50 scarce in the U.K.
| | $4.15 | $12.50 | $25.00 | £2.90 | £8.75 | £17.50 |

51-54 scarce in the U.K.
| | $4.50 | $13.50 | $22.50 | £3.00 | £9.00 | £15.00 |

| Title Value: | $159.75 | $482.50 | $955.00 | £104.70 | £316.00 | £625.00 |

MINDGAME GALLERY, THE
Mindgame Press; 1 Jul 1990-5 1991

1 ND Steve Bissette script, Rick Veitch art
| | $0.40 | $1.20 | $2.00 | £0.25 | £0.75 | £1.25 |

2-4 ND
| | $0.40 | $1.20 | $2.00 | £0.25 | £0.75 | £1.25 |

5 ND new Empire Lanes story
| | $0.40 | $1.20 | $2.00 | £0.25 | £0.75 | £1.25 |

| Title Value: | $2.00 | $6.00 | $10.00 | £1.25 | £3.75 | £6.25 |

MIRACLE SQUAD
Upshot Graphics/Fantagraphics, MS; 1 Aug 1986-4 1987

1-4 ND Tidwell art
| | $0.40 | $1.20 | $2.00 | £0.25 | £0.75 | £1.25 |

| Title Value: | $1.60 | $4.80 | $8.00 | £1.00 | £3.00 | £5.00 |

MIRACLE SQUAD: BLOOD AND DUST
Apple Comics, MS; 1 Jan 1989-4 Jul 1989

1-4 ND
| | $0.40 | $1.20 | $2.00 | £0.25 | £0.75 | £1.25 |

| Title Value: | $1.60 | $4.80 | $8.00 | £1.00 | £3.00 | £5.00 |

Miracle Squad Bargain Pre-Pack (Jun 1991), reprints #1-4 $0.70 £2.10 £3.50

MIRACLEMAN
Eclipse; 1 Aug 1985-24 1993?

1 ND Marvelman reprints from Warrior magazine begin; Alan Moore scripts, Leach and Davis art
| | $0.70 | $2.10 | $3.50 | £0.50 | £1.50 | £2.50 |

1 UK edition, Quality advert on back; distributed in the U.K.
| | $0.60 | $1.80 | $3.00 | £0.40 | £1.20 | £2.00 |

2 ND Leach, Davis art
| | $0.50 | $1.50 | $2.50 | £0.40 | £1.20 | £2.00 |

3-5 ND Davis art
| | $0.50 | $1.50 | $2.50 | £0.40 | £1.20 | £2.00 |

6 ND Davis, Beckum art
| | $0.40 | $1.20 | $2.00 | £0.30 | £0.90 | £1.50 |

7 ND Beckum art
| | $0.40 | $1.20 | $2.00 | £0.30 | £0.90 | £1.50 |

8 ND 50s reprints, New Wave preview
| | $0.40 | $1.20 | $2.00 | £0.30 | £0.90 | £1.50 |

9 ND scarce in the U.K. contraversial birth issue
| | $0.40 | $1.20 | $2.00 | £0.30 | £0.90 | £1.50 |

10 ND
| | $0.40 | $1.20 | $2.00 | £0.30 | £0.90 | £1.50 |

11 ND John Totleben art
| | $0.40 | $1.20 | $2.00 | £0.30 | £0.90 | £1.50 |

12 ND very scarce in the U.K. John Totleben art
| | $0.40 | $1.20 | $2.00 | £0.60 | £1.80 | £3.00 |

13 ND John Totleben art, $1.75 cover price
| | $0.40 | $1.20 | $2.00 | £0.30 | £0.90 | £1.50 |

14-15 ND John Totleben art
| | $0.40 | $1.20 | $2.00 | £0.30 | £0.90 | £1.50 |

16 ND last Alan Moore script
| | $0.40 | $1.20 | $2.00 | £0.30 | £0.90 | £1.50 |

17 ND 1st Neil Gaiman script, Mark Buckingham art
| | $0.40 | $1.20 | $2.00 | £0.40 | £1.20 | £2.00 |

18-22 ND Neil Gaiman script, Mark Buckingham art
| | $0.40 | $1.20 | $2.00 | £0.30 | £0.90 | £1.50 |

23-24 ND Neil Gaiman script, Mark Buckingham art, Barry Windsor-Smith painted covers
| | $0.50 | $1.50 | $2.50 | £0.30 | £0.90 | £1.50 |

| Title Value: | $11.10 | $33.30 | $57.50 | £8.60 | £25.80 | £43.00 |

Note: a Gold and Silver logo edition of #1 is available and each would be priced at 25% more. Issues #25-28 were advertised & solicited but did not come out.

Graphic Album 1 "A Dream Of Flying" (1989),
reprints issues #1-4, Garry Leach painted cover, hardcover £4.00 £12.00 £20.00
(2nd print – Nov 1991) £3.75 £11.25 £18.75
Softcover version £1.20 £3.60 £6.00

Graphic Album 2 "The Red King Syndrome" (1990)
reprints #5-8,9,10 with John Bolton painted cover, hardcover £4.00 £12.00 £20.00
(2nd print – Nov 1991) £3.75 £11.25 £18.75
Softcover version £1.60 £4.80 £8.00

Graphic Album 3 "Olympus" (1991), Softcover version £1.60 £4.80 £8.00
Graphic Album 4 "The Golden Age" (Sep 1993)
reprints #17-22, softcover £1.60 £4.80 £8.00
Hardcover £4.50 £13.50 £22.50

MIRACLEMAN 3-D SPECIAL
Eclipse; 1 Dec 1985

1 ND reprints Marvelman Special (Quality), Alan Moore/Alan Davis framing sequence; glasses included
(25% less if without glasses)
| | $0.40 | $1.20 | $2.00 | £0.40 | £1.20 | £2.00 |

1 ND scarce in the U.K., non-3-D version
| | $0.60 | $1.80 | $3.00 | £0.70 | £2.10 | £3.50 |

| Title Value: | $1.00 | $3.00 | $5.00 | £1.10 | £3.30 | £5.50 |

MIRACLEMAN FAMILY
Eclipse, MS; 1 May 1988-2 Sep 1988

1 ND reprints from Young Marvelman Adventures and Marvelman #361; story and art by the Mick Anglo
Studios, colour; new Garry Leach cover
| | $0.40 | $1.20 | $2.00 | £0.25 | £0.75 | £1.25 |

2 ND reprints from Young Marvelman #347, Marvelman Family #4; story and art by the Mick Anglo Studios,
colour; new Paul Gulacy cover
| | $0.40 | $1.20 | $2.00 | £0.25 | £0.75 | £1.25 |

| Title Value: | $0.80 | $2.40 | $4.00 | £0.50 | £1.50 | £2.50 |

Note: all references to "Marvelman" in original art re-lettered "Miracleman".

MIRACLEMAN TRIUMPHANT
Eclipse; 1 May 1994

1 ND
| | $0.50 | $1.50 | $2.50 | £0.30 | £0.90 | £1.50 |

| Title Value: | $0.50 | $1.50 | $2.50 | £0.30 | £0.90 | £1.50 |

MIRACLEMAN: THE APOCRYPHA
Eclipse, MS; 1 Nov 1991-3 Feb 1992

1 ND features work by Matt Wagner, Norm Breyfogle, Neil Gaiman, Mark Buckingham
| | $0.50 | $1.50 | $2.50 | £0.30 | £0.90 | £1.50 |

2 ND features work by Louise Simonson, Neil Gaiman, Mark Buckingham
| | $0.50 | $1.50 | $2.50 | £0.30 | £0.90 | £1.50 |

3 ND features work by Steve Moore, Val Mayerik, Neil Gaiman, Mark Buckingham
| | $0.50 | $1.50 | $2.50 | £0.30 | £0.90 | £1.50 |

| Title Value: | $1.50 | $4.50 | $7.50 | £0.90 | £2.70 | £4.50 |

Miracleman: The Apocrypha Trade paperback (Feb 1993)
reprints mini-series, new Mark Buckingham cover £2.00 £6.00 £10.00

MISS FURY
Adventure, MS; 1 Jun 1991-4 Feb 1992

1-4 ND
| | $0.40 | $1.20 | $2.00 | £0.25 | £0.75 | £1.25 |

| Title Value: | $1.60 | $4.80 | $8.00 | £1.00 | £3.00 | £5.00 |

MISS FURY QUARTERLY
A Plus Comics; 1 Jan 1992

1 ND 48pgs
| | $0.40 | $1.20 | $2.00 | £0.25 | £0.75 | £1.25 |

| Title Value: | $0.40 | $1.20 | $2.00 | £0.25 | £0.75 | £1.25 |

MISS VICTORY GOLDEN ANNIVERSARY SPECIAL
AC Comics, OS; 1 Nov 1991

1 ND 68pgs, new colour Miss Victory story plus black and white Golden Age reprints
| | $0.70 | $2.10 | $3.50 | £0.50 | £1.50 | £2.50 |

| Title Value: | $0.70 | $2.10 | $3.50 | £0.50 | £1.50 | £2.50 |

MISTER E
DC Comics, MS; 1 May 1991-4 Sep 1991

1 John K. Snyder III art begins
| | $0.40 | $1.20 | $2.00 | £0.25 | £0.75 | £1.25 |

2-3
| | $0.40 | $1.20 | $2.00 | £0.25 | £0.75 | £1.25 |

4 Dr. Fate/Phantom Stranger guest-star
| | $0.40 | $1.20 | $2.00 | £0.25 | £0.75 | £1.25 |

| Title Value: | $1.60 | $4.80 | $8.00 | £1.00 | £3.00 | £5.00 |

Note: spin-off from Books of Magic. Delay between issues #3 and #4.

MISTER MIRACLE
DC Comics; 1 Mar/Apr 1971-18 Feb/Mar 1974; 19 Sep 1977-25 Aug/Sep 1978
(see Brave and the Bold, DC Comics Presents, Justice League)

1 Jack Kirby art begins
| | $5.25 | $16.00 | $32.50 | £2.90 | £8.75 | £17.50 |

2
| | $2.50 | $7.50 | $15.00 | £1.65 | £5.00 | £10.00 |

3
| | $2.05 | $6.25 | $12.50 | £1.25 | £3.75 | £7.50 |

4-8 52pgs, Joe Simon & Jack Kirby Boy Commandos reprints
| | $2.05 | $6.25 | $12.50 | £1.00 | £3.00 | £6.00 |

9 scarce in the U.K. origin Mr. Miracle, Darkseid cameo
| | $1.65 | $5.00 | $10.00 | £0.80 | £2.50 | £5.00 |

10
| | $1.65 | $5.00 | $10.00 | £0.80 | £2.50 | £5.00 |

11-17
| | $1.65 | $5.00 | $10.00 | £0.65 | £2.00 | £4.00 |

18 last Jack Kirby art, Darkseid cameo
| | $1.65 | $5.00 | $10.00 | £0.65 | £2.00 | £4.00 |

19 scarce in the U.K. Rogers and Neal Adams art
| | $1.00 | $3.00 | $5.00 | £0.60 | £1.80 | £3.00 |

20 scarce in the U.K. Rogers art
| | $0.80 | $2.40 | $4.00 | £0.60 | £1.80 | £3.00 |

21-22 Rogers art
| | $0.80 | $2.40 | $4.00 | £0.50 | £1.50 | £2.50 |

23-25 Golden art
| | $0.80 | $2.40 | $4.00 | £0.50 | £1.50 | £2.50 |

| Title Value: | $42.35 | $128.40 | $251.50 | £21.30 | £64.60 | £125.50 |

MISTER MIRACLE (2ND SERIES)
DC Comics; 1 Jan 1989-28 Jun 1991

1-2 Ian Gibson cover/art
| | $0.25 | $0.75 | $1.25 | £0.15 | £0.45 | £0.75 |

3-4 Forever People appear
| | $0.25 | $0.75 | $1.25 | £0.15 | £0.45 | £0.75 |

5
| | $0.25 | $0.75 | $1.25 | £0.15 | £0.45 | £0.75 |

6 G'Nort appears
| | $0.25 | $0.75 | $1.25 | £0.15 | £0.45 | £0.75 |

7-8 Blue Beetle, Booster Gold appear
| | $0.25 | $0.75 | $1.25 | £0.15 | £0.45 | £0.75 |

9-12
| | $0.25 | $0.75 | $1.25 | £0.15 | £0.45 | £0.75 |

	$Good	$Fine	$N.Mint	£Good	£Fine	£N.Mint
13-14 Lobo appears	$0.25	$0.75	$1.25	£0.15	£0.45	£0.75
15-19	$0.25	$0.75	$1.25	£0.15	£0.45	£0.75
20 Ian Gibson art	$0.25	$0.75	$1.25	£0.15	£0.45	£0.75
21	$0.25	$0.75	$1.25	£0.15	£0.45	£0.75
22 new Mister Miracle, Shilo Norman, begins training by Scott Free the existing Mr. Miracle						
	$0.25	$0.75	$1.25	£0.15	£0.45	£0.75
23-28	$0.25	$0.75	$1.25	£0.15	£0.45	£0.75
Title Value:	$7.00	$21.00	$35.00	£4.20	£12.60	£21.00

MISTER MIRACLE (3RD SERIES)
DC Comics; 1 Jan 1996-present

	$Good	$Fine	$N.Mint	£Good	£Fine	£N.Mint
1-3 ND	$0.40	$1.20	$2.00	£0.25	£0.75	£1.25
Title Value:	$1.20	$3.60	$6.00	£0.75	£2.25	£3.75

MISTER MIRACLE SPECIAL
DC Comics; 1 1987

	$Good	$Fine	$N.Mint	£Good	£Fine	£N.Mint
1 52pgs, Steve Rude art, Jack Kirby tribute						
	$0.30	$0.90	$1.50	£0.20	£0.60	£1.00
Title Value:	$0.30	$0.90	$1.50	£0.20	£0.60	£1.00

MISTER X
Vortex; 1 Jun 1984-14 Aug 1988

	$Good	$Fine	$N.Mint	£Good	£Fine	£N.Mint
1 scarce in the U.K. J. Hernandez art						
	$0.80	$2.40	$4.00	£0.50	£1.50	£2.50
2 J. Hernandez art	$0.60	$1.80	$3.00	£0.40	£1.20	£2.00
3-4 J. Hernandez art						
	$0.50	$1.50	$2.50	£0.30	£0.90	£1.50
5 scarce in the U.K.	$0.50	$1.50	$2.50	£0.35	£1.05	£1.75
6-9	$0.50	$1.50	$2.50	£0.30	£0.90	£1.50
10 Dave McKean art	$0.50	$1.50	$2.50	£0.30	£0.90	£1.50
11-14	$0.50	$1.50	$2.50	£0.30	£0.90	£1.50
Title Value:	$7.40	$22.20	$37.00	£4.55	£13.65	£22.75

Note all Non-Distributed on the news-stands in the U.K.

				£Good	£Fine	£N.Mint
Special 1 (Nov 1990), Milligan/Ewins				£0.35	£1.05	£1.75
Trade paperback, Vortex edition, collects #1-4				£1.70	£5.10	£8.50
Titan (UK) Edition				£1.60	£4.80	£8.00
Warner Edition (Dec 1989)				£1.20	£3.60	£6.00
Hardback, Grafitti edition				£4.00	£12.00	£20.00

MISTER X VOLUME TWO
Vortex; 1 Apr 1989-12 Mar 1990

	$Good	$Fine	$N.Mint	£Good	£Fine	£N.Mint
1-12 ND	$0.50	$1.50	$2.50	£0.30	£0.90	£1.50
Title Value:	$6.00	$18.00	$30.00	£3.60	£10.80	£18.00

MISTS OF AVALON, THE
Eclipse,MS; 1 Mar 1994

	$Good	$Fine	$N.Mint	£Good	£Fine	£N.Mint
1 ND 48pgs, Sarah Byam and Steve Parkhouse						
	$1.00	$3.00	$5.00	£0.70	£2.10	£3.50
Title Value:	$1.00	$3.00	$5.00	£0.70	£2.10	£3.50

Note: cancelled mini-series ?

MISTY
Marvel Comics Group/Star; 1 Dec 1985-6 May 1986

	$Good	$Fine	$N.Mint	£Good	£Fine	£N.Mint
1-6 ND Millie's niece						
	$0.15	$0.45	$0.75	£0.10	£0.30	£0.50
Title Value:	$0.90	$2.70	$4.50	£0.60	£1.80	£3.00

MOBFIRE
DC Comics/Vertigo,MS; 1 Dec 1994-6 May 1995

	$Good	$Fine	$N.Mint	£Good	£Fine	£N.Mint
1-6 ND Gary Ushaw and Warren Pleece creative team						
	$0.40	$1.20	$2.00	£0.25	£0.75	£1.25
Title Value:	$2.40	$7.20	$12.00	£1.50	£4.50	£7.50

MOBILE SUIT GUNDAM 0083
Viz Communications,MS; 1 Jan 1994-13 Jan 1995

	$Good	$Fine	$N.Mint	£Good	£Fine	£N.Mint
1-13 ND 48pgs, colour						
	$0.90	$2.70	$4.50	£0.60	£1.80	£3.00
Title Value:	$11.70	$35.10	$58.50	£7.80	£23.40	£39.00

MOD
Kitchen Sink; 1 1981

	$Good	$Fine	$N.Mint	£Good	£Fine	£N.Mint
1 ND 5pgs Bob Burden art						
	$0.60	$1.80	$3.00	£0.40	£1.20	£2.00
Title Value:	$0.60	$1.80	$3.00	£0.40	£1.20	£2.00

MOD SQUAD
Dell; 1 Jan 1969-8 Apr 1971

	$Good	$Fine	$N.Mint	£Good	£Fine	£N.Mint
1 based on TV series, photo cover						
	$7.00	$21.00	$35.00	£5.00	£15.00	£25.00
2 based on TV series, photo cover						
	$4.00	$12.00	$20.00	£2.50	£7.50	£12.50
3 based on TV series, photo cover						
	$3.50	$10.50	$17.50	£2.00	£6.00	£10.00
4-7	$3.50	$10.50	$17.50	£2.00	£6.00	£10.00
8 reprints #2	$3.00	$9.00	$15.00	£1.60	£4.80	£8.00
Title Value:	$31.50	$94.50	$157.50	£19.10	£57.30	£95.50

Note: very limited distribution in the U.K.

MODERN CLASSICS: FREAKS' AMOUR
Dark Horse,MS; 1 Jul 1992-3 Jan 1993

	$Good	$Fine	$N.Mint	£Good	£Fine	£N.Mint
1-3 ND 48pgs, based on Tom DeHaven's cult novel, cover by Charles Burns						
	$0.80	$2.40	$4.00	£0.50	£1.50	£2.50
Title Value:	$2.40	$7.20	$12.00	£1.50	£4.50	£7.50

MODERN PULP
Special Studio; 1 Jan 1991

	$Good	$Fine	$N.Mint	£Good	£Fine	£N.Mint
1 ND black and white						
	$0.40	$1.20	$2.00	£0.25	£0.75	£1.25
Title Value:	$0.40	$1.20	$2.00	£0.25	£0.75	£1.25

MODESTY BLAISE
DC Comics,MS; 1 Mar 1993-3 May 1993

	$Good	$Fine	$N.Mint	£Good	£Fine	£N.Mint
1-3 ND 48pgs, Pete O'Donnell and Dick Giordano						
	$0.70	$2.10	$3.50	£0.50	£1.50	£2.50
Title Value:	$2.10	$6.30	$10.50	£1.50	£4.50	£7.50

MODESTY BLAZE GRAPHIC NOVEL
DC Comics,OS; nn Feb 1995

	$Good	$Fine	$N.Mint	£Good	£Fine	£N.Mint
1 ND 144pgs, Peter O'Donnell script, Dick Giordano art						
	$3.50	$10.50	$17.50	£2.50	£7.50	£12.50
Title Value:	$3.50	$10.50	$17.50	£2.50	£7.50	£12.50

MOEBIUS
Marvel Comics Group/Epic Graphic Novel; 1 Oct 1987-8 1993

(see also The Incal)

		£Good	£Fine	£N.Mint
1 72pgs, Upon A Star		£1.10	£3.30	£5.50
(2nd print, Feb 1990)		£0.90	£2.70	£4.50
2 72pgs, Arzach and Other Fantasy Stories		£1.00	£3.00	£5.00
(2nd print, Apr 1990)		£0.90	£2.70	£4.50
3 120pgs, The Airtight Garage		£1.30	£3.90	£6.50
(2nd print, Apr 1990)		£1.20	£3.60	£6.00
4 72pgs, The Long Tomorrow and other SF Stories		£1.00	£3.00	£5.00
5 72pgs, The Gardens of Aedena		£1.00	£3.00	£5.00
6 72pgs, Pharagonesia and other Strange Stories		£1.00	£3.00	£5.00
7 96pgs, The Goddess, links with Airtight Garage saga in "Elsewhere Prince"		£1.20	£3.60	£6.00
8 Mississippi River		£0.90	£2.70	£4.50

Note: there are also UK (Titan) editions of #5, #6.
Note also: #1-8 U.S. editions are Non Distributed in the U.K.

		£Good	£Fine	£N.Mint
Art of Moebius Collection, text by Lofficier (Jan 1990)		£1.75	£3.50	£7.00

MOEBIUS 0: THE HORNY GOOF
Dark Horse; 0 1991

	$Good	$Fine	$N.Mint	£Good	£Fine	£N.Mint
0 ND sci-fi story with Moebius art originally planned by Marvel Comics						
	$0.60	$1.80	$3.00	£0.40	£1.20	£2.00
Title Value:	$0.60	$1.80	$3.00	£0.40	£1.20	£2.00

MOEBIUS: CHAOS HARDCOVER
Marvel Comics Group,OS; 1 Dec 1991

	$Good	$Fine	$N.Mint	£Good	£Fine	£N.Mint
1 ND rare in the U.K. 96pgs, Moebius material with introduction and new cover by Moebius						
	$3.50	$10.50	$17.50	£2.50	£7.50	£12.50
Title Value:	$3.50	$10.50	$17.50	£2.50	£7.50	£12.50

MOEBIUS: FUSION
Marvel Comics Group,OS; nn Nov 1993

nn ND 128pgs, collects sketches, paintings, poetry and Marvel posters by Moebius

	$Good	$Fine	$N.Mint	£Good	£Fine	£N.Mint
	$4.00	$12.00	$20.00	£2.80	£8.25	£14.00
Title Value:	$4.00	$12.00	$20.00	£2.80	£8.25	£14.00

MOEBIUS: STEL
Marvel Comics Group; nn Jul 1994

nn ND 80pgs, softcover, sequel to Moebius #7: The Goddess

	$Good	$Fine	$N.Mint	£Good	£Fine	£N.Mint
	$3.00	$9.00	$15.00	£2.00	£6.00	£10.00
Title Value:	$3.00	$9.00	$15.00	£2.00	£6.00	£10.00

MONGREL
Northstar; 1 Oct 1994-2 1995

	$Good	$Fine	$N.Mint	£Good	£Fine	£N.Mint
1 ND black and white						
	$0.40	$1.20	$2.00	£0.25	£0.75	£1.25
1 ND Deluxe Edition, with sketches; black and white						
	$0.50	$1.50	$2.50	£0.30	£0.90	£1.50
1 ND Gold Edition (Oct 1994) – signed and numbered						
	$0.80	$2.40	$4.00	£0.50	£1.50	£2.50
2 ND	$0.40	$1.20	$2.00	£0.25	£0.75	£1.25
2 ND Prestige Format – 8pg section on werewolf legends, foil logo on cover						
	$0.50	$1.50	$2.50	£0.30	£0.90	£1.50
Title Value:	$2.60	$7.80	$13.00	£1.60	£4.80	£8.00

MONKEES, THE
Dell, TV; 1 Mar 1967-17 Oct 1969

	$Good	$Fine	$N.Mint	£Good	£Fine	£N.Mint
1 distributed in the U.K.						
	$15.00	$45.00	$90.00	£10.00	£30.00	£60.00
2-3 distributed in the U.K.						
	$10.00	$30.00	$50.00	£7.00	£21.00	£35.00
4-5 distributed in the U.K.						
	$9.50	$29.00	$47.50	£6.50	£19.50	£32.50
6-10 distributed in the U.K.						
	$9.00	$27.00	$45.00	£6.00	£18.00	£30.00
11-17 distributed in the U.K.						
	$8.50	$26.00	$42.50	£5.50	£16.50	£27.50
Title Value:	$158.50	$480.00	$807.50	£105.50	£316.50	£537.50

MONOLITH
Comico,MS; 1 Oct 1991-4 Jan 1992

	$Good	$Fine	$N.Mint	£Good	£Fine	£N.Mint
1-4 ND colour, Kelley Jones covers						
	$0.40	$1.20	$2.00	£0.25	£0.75	£1.25
Title Value:	$1.60	$4.80	$8.00	£1.00	£3.00	£5.00

MONSTER FRAT HOUSE
Eternity,OS; 1 Oct 1989

	$Good	$Fine	$N.Mint	£Good	£Fine	£N.Mint
1 ND Paul O'Conner script, John Grigni, Sandy Carruthers, Mike Roberts art; black and white						
	$0.30	$0.90	$1.50	£0.20	£0.60	£1.00
Title Value:	$0.30	$0.90	$1.50	£0.20	£0.60	£1.00

MONSTER HUNTERS
Charlton; 1 Aug 1975-18 Feb 1979

	$Good	$Fine	$N.Mint	£Good	£Fine	£N.Mint
1	$1.00	$3.00	$5.00	£0.70	£2.10	£3.50
2 Steve Ditko art	$1.00	$3.00	$5.00	£0.70	£2.10	£3.50
3-5	$0.40	$1.20	$2.00	£0.25	£0.75	£1.25
6 Steve Ditko art	$0.50	$1.50	$2.50	£0.30	£0.90	£1.50
7	$0.40	$1.20	$2.00	£0.25	£0.75	£1.25
8 Steve Ditko art	$0.50	$1.50	$2.50	£0.30	£0.90	£1.50
9	$0.40	$1.20	$2.00	£0.25	£0.75	£1.25
10 Steve Ditko art	$0.50	$1.50	$2.50	£0.30	£0.90	£1.50
11-13	$0.40	$1.20	$2.00	£0.25	£0.75	£1.25
14 all Steve Ditko art						

	$Good	$Fine	$N.Mint	£Good	£Fine	£N.Mint
	$0.50	$1.50	$2.50	£0.30	£0.90	£1.50
15-18	$0.40	$1.20	$2.00	£0.25	£0.75	£1.25
Title Value:	$8.80	$26.40	$44.00	£5.60	£16.80	£28.00

Note: reprints in #12-18. Distributed in the U.K.

MONSTER MASSACRE SPECIAL
Blackball Comics; 1 Jan 1994
1 ND 48pgs, features art by Kev O'Neill, Keith Giffen and Simon Bisley; Bisley cover

	$Good	$Fine	$N.Mint	£Good	£Fine	£N.Mint
	$0.40	$1.20	$2.00	£0.25	£0.75	£1.25
Title Value:	$0.40	$1.20	$2.00	£0.25	£0.75	£1.25

MONSTER MASTERWORKS
Marvel Comics Group; nn Feb 1990
(see Marvel Masterworks)
Trade paperback
collection of Marvel pre-Superhero reprints with work by Lee, Kirby, Ditko and Everett. Cover by Walt Simonson

	£Good	£Fine	£N.Mint
	£1.40	£4.20	£7.00

MONSTER MENACE
Marvel Comics Group,MS; 1 Dec 1993-4 Mar 1994
1-4 pre-Marvel super-hero reprints begin featuring classics by Steve Ditko and Jack Kirby

	$Good	$Fine	$N.Mint	£Good	£Fine	£N.Mint
	$0.30	$0.90	$1.50	£0.20	£0.60	£1.00
Title Value:	$1.20	$3.60	$6.00	£0.80	£2.40	£4.00

MONSTER-HUNTER
Night Realm; 1 1990
1 ND black and white

	$Good	$Fine	$N.Mint	£Good	£Fine	£N.Mint
	$0.40	$1.20	$2.00	£0.25	£0.75	£1.25
Title Value:	$0.40	$1.20	$2.00	£0.25	£0.75	£1.25

MONSTERS FROM OUTER SPACE
Adventure,MS; 1 Feb 1993-3 Apr 1993

	$Good	$Fine	$N.Mint	£Good	£Fine	£N.Mint
1-3 ND	$0.40	$1.20	$2.00	£0.25	£0.75	£1.25
Title Value:	$1.20	$3.60	$6.00	£0.75	£2.25	£3.75

MONSTERS ON THE PROWL
Marvel Comics Group; 9 Feb 1971-27 Nov 1973; 28 Jun 1974-30 Oct 1974
(formerly Chamber of Darkness)

	$Good	$Fine	$N.Mint	£Good	£Fine	£N.Mint
9 Barry Smith inks	$0.80	$2.40	$4.00	£0.50	£1.50	£2.50
10-12	$0.40	$1.20	$2.00	£0.25	£0.75	£1.25
13-14 ND 52pgs	$0.50	$1.50	$2.50	£0.30	£0.90	£1.50
15	$0.40	$1.20	$2.00	£0.25	£0.75	£1.25
16 5th appearance Kull, 1st appearance Thulsa Doom, Severin art	$0.50	$1.50	$2.50	£0.30	£0.90	£1.50
17-30 ND	$0.40	$1.20	$2.00	£0.25	£0.75	£1.25
Title Value:	$9.50	$28.50	$47.50	£5.90	£17.70	£29.50

Note: all reprint except one new story in #9-13, 15, 16.

MONSTERS UNLEASHED
Marvel Comics Group,Magazine; 1 Jul 1973-11 Apr 1975
1 ND Frankenstein main feature begins

	$Good	$Fine	$N.Mint	£Good	£Fine	£N.Mint
	$1.00	$3.00	$6.00	£0.65	£2.00	£4.00

2 ND Frankenstein issue; Boris Karloff feature and Frankenstein painted cover by Boris

	$1.00	$3.00	$5.00	£0.70	£2.10	£3.50

3 ND Frankenstein, Man-Thing stories, Son of Satan text story; Gil Kane art with part Neal Adams art (as "The Crusty Bunkers"), Neal Adams cover

	$1.00	$3.00	$5.00	£0.70	£2.10	£3.50

4 scarce in the U.K. Frankenstein story, Gulliver Jones by Dave Cockrum, Ray Harryhausen feature; Werewolf cover

	$0.80	$2.40	$4.00	£0.50	£1.50	£2.50

5 Frankenstein, Werewolf, Man-Thing

	$0.80	$2.40	$4.00	£0.50	£1.50	£2.50

6 Werewolf by Night text story featuring illustrations by Mike Ploog, Frankenstein main feature and painted cover by Boris

	$0.80	$2.40	$4.00	£0.50	£1.50	£2.50

7 Werewolf by Night text story featuring illustrations by Broderick and Janson; Frankenstein main feature

	$0.80	$2.40	$4.00	£0.50	£1.50	£2.50

8 early George Perez work , Neal Adams reprint ("One Hungers"), Frankenstein main feature

	$Good	$Fine	$N.Mint	£Good	£Fine	£N.Mint
	$1.00	$3.00	$5.00	£0.60	£1.80	£3.00

9 Frankenstein, Man-Thing plus Wendigo back-up by Chris Claremont

	$0.80	$2.40	$4.00	£0.50	£1.50	£2.50

10 Frankenstein plus Tigra back-up by Chris Claremont

	$0.80	$2.40	$4.00	£0.50	£1.50	£2.50

11 Gabriel Devil-Hunter, Dave Cockrum Creature pin-up, Frank Brunner cover

	$Good	$Fine	$N.Mint	£Good	£Fine	£N.Mint
	$0.80	$2.40	$4.00	£0.50	£1.50	£2.50
Title Value:	$9.60	$28.80	$49.00	£6.15	£18.50	£31.50

ARTISTS
Adams reprint in 8. Ploog in 6,7. Williamson reprint in 9.
FEATURES
Frankenstein Monster in 2-5, 7-11. Wendigo in 9. Tigra (origin) in 10. Man-Thing in 3 (reprints origin), 4-11.

MONSTERS UNLEASHED ANNUAL
Marvel Comics Group,Magazine; 1 Summer 1975
1 ND 88pgs, squarebound, all reprint featuring Gene Colan and Gil Kane art; Neal Adams inks as part of "The Crusty Bunkers"

	$Good	$Fine	$N.Mint	£Good	£Fine	£N.Mint
	$0.80	$2.40	$4.00	£0.60	£1.80	£3.00
Title Value:	$0.80	$2.40	$4.00	£0.60	£1.80	£3.00

MONSTERS, NO SUCH THING AS
Choral Comics; 1,2 1986

	$Good	$Fine	$N.Mint	£Good	£Fine	£N.Mint
1-2 ND	$0.25	$0.75	$1.25	£0.15	£0.45	£0.75
Title Value:	$0.50	$1.50	$2.50	£0.30	£0.90	£1.50

MOON KNIGHT
Marvel Comics Group; 1 Nov 1980-38 Jul 1984
(see Marvel Preview, Marvel Spotlight, Werewolf By Night #32)
1 Neal Adamsesque art by Bill Sienkiewicz begins, new origin

	$Good	$Fine	$N.Mint	£Good	£Fine	£N.Mint
	$0.80	$2.40	$4.00	£0.50	£1.50	£2.50

2-5 Sienkiewicz art

	$0.50	$1.50	$2.50	£0.30	£0.90	£1.50

6 Sienkiewicz art, Earl Norem painted cover

	$0.40	$1.20	$2.00	£0.25	£0.75	£1.25

7-8 Sienkiewicz art

	$0.40	$1.20	$2.00	£0.25	£0.75	£1.25

9 Sienkiewicz art, Frank Miller cover

	$N.Mint	£Fine	£N.Mint
	$2.00	£0.75	£1.25

10 Sienkiewicz art

	$Good	$Fine	$N.Mint	£Good	£Fine	£N.Mint
	$0.40	$1.20	$2.00	£0.25	£0.75	£1.25

11-12 Sienkiewicz art

	$0.30	$0.90	$1.50	£0.20	£0.60	£1.00

13 Sienkiewicz art, Daredevil appears

	$0.30	$0.90	$1.50	£0.20	£0.60	£1.00

14 Sienkiewicz art

	$0.30	$0.90	$1.50	£0.20	£0.60	£1.00

15 1st Direct Sale issue, Sienkiewicz art, part Frank Miller cover

	$0.30	$0.90	$1.50	£0.20	£0.60	£1.00

16 Thing appears

	$0.30	$0.90	$1.50	£0.20	£0.60	£1.00

17-20 Sienkiewicz art

	$0.30	$0.90	$1.50	£0.20	£0.60	£1.00

21 Brother Voodoo appears, Sienkiewicz cover only

	$0.30	$0.90	$1.50	£0.20	£0.60	£1.00

22 Sienkiewicz cover only

	$0.30	$0.90	$1.50	£0.20	£0.60	£1.00

23 Sienkiewicz art; art style begins to change from Neal Adamsesque to his own distinctive line-work

	$0.30	$0.90	$1.50	£0.20	£0.60	£1.00

24 Sienkiewicz art

	$0.30	$0.90	$1.50	£0.20	£0.60	£1.00

25 52pgs, Sienkiewicz art

	$0.50	$1.50	$2.50	£0.30	£0.90	£1.50

26 Sienkiewicz art

	$0.30	$0.90	$1.50	£0.20	£0.60	£1.00

27 Frank Miller cover

	$0.30	$0.90	$1.50	£0.20	£0.60	£1.00

28 Sienkiewicz art; 5pgs Kevin Nowlan art

	$0.30	$0.90	$1.50	£0.20	£0.60	£1.00

29 Sienkiewicz art

	$0.30	$0.90	$1.50	£0.20	£0.60	£1.00

Miracleman #2

Mod Squad #3

Monsters on the Prowl #11

	$Good	$Fine	$N.Mint	£Good	£Fine	£N.Mint
30 LD in the U.K. Moon Knight battles Werewolf, Sienkiewicz art	$0.30	$0.90	$1.50	£0.25	£0.75	£1.25
31-32 Kevin Nowlan art	$0.30	$0.90	$1.50	£0.20	£0.60	£1.00
33 LD in the U.K. Kevin Nowlan art	$0.30	$0.90	$1.50	£0.25	£0.75	£1.25
34 LD in the U.K. Sienkiewicz art	$0.30	$0.90	$1.50	£0.25	£0.75	£1.25
35 DS X-Men and Fantastic Four appear, Kevin Nowlan art	$0.50	$1.50	$2.50	£0.30	£0.90	£1.50
36 LD in the U.K. Dr. Strange appears, Sienkiewicz art, Mike Kaluta cover	$0.30	$0.90	$1.50	£0.25	£0.75	£1.25
37-38 very LD Scott Hampton art, Mike Kaluta cover	$0.30	$0.90	$1.50	£0.30	£0.90	£1.50
Title Value:	$13.60	$40.80	$68.00	£9.15	£27.45	£45.75

Note: issue #15 onwards ND/LD in the U.K.
ARTISTS
Sienkiewicz in 1-15, 17-36. Hampton in 37, 38.

MOON KNIGHT SPECIAL
Marvel Comics Group,OS; 1 Oct 1992

	$Good	$Fine	$N.Mint	£Good	£Fine	£N.Mint
1 ND 48pgs, Master of Kung Fu appears, pin-up gallery, Doug Moench script	$0.50	$1.50	$2.50	£0.30	£0.90	£1.50
Title Value:	$0.50	$1.50	$2.50	£0.30	£0.90	£1.50

MOON KNIGHT SPECIAL EDITION
Marvel Comics Group; 1 Nov 1983-3 Jan 1984

	$Good	$Fine	$N.Mint	£Good	£Fine	£N.Mint
1 ND Hulk appears	$0.50	$1.50	$2.50	£0.30	£0.90	£1.50
2-3 ND	$0.50	$1.50	$2.50	£0.30	£0.90	£1.50
Title Value:	$1.50	$4.50	$7.50	£0.90	£2.70	£4.50

Note: all reprints of Sienkiewicz's magazine work, on Baxter paper

MOON KNIGHT, MARC SPECTOR
Marvel Comics Group; 1 Jun 1989-60 Mar 1994

	$Good	$Fine	$N.Mint	£Good	£Fine	£N.Mint
1 ND	$0.60	$1.80	$3.00	£0.40	£1.20	£2.00
2 ND Spiderman appears (cameo)	$0.50	$1.50	$2.50	£0.30	£0.90	£1.50
3 ND	$0.50	$1.50	$2.50	£0.30	£0.90	£1.50
4-5 ND Black Cat appears	$0.40	$1.20	$2.00	£0.25	£0.75	£1.25
6-7 ND	$0.40	$1.20	$2.00	£0.25	£0.75	£1.25
8-9 ND Acts of Vengeance tie-in, Punisher appears	$0.50	$1.50	$2.50	£0.30	£0.90	£1.50
10 ND Acts of Vengeance tie-in	$0.40	$1.20	$2.00	£0.25	£0.75	£1.25
11-14 ND	$0.40	$1.20	$2.00	£0.25	£0.75	£1.25
15-18 ND Trial of Marc Spector	$0.40	$1.20	$2.00	£0.25	£0.75	£1.25
19-21 ND Spiderman/Punisher appear	$0.50	$1.50	$2.50	£0.30	£0.90	£1.50
22-24 ND	$0.30	$0.90	$1.50	£0.20	£0.60	£1.00
25 ND DS Ghost Rider guest-stars	$0.50	$1.50	$2.50	£0.30	£0.90	£1.50
26-30 ND Scarlet Redemption story, Bill Sienkiewicz cover	$0.30	$0.90	$1.50	£0.20	£0.60	£1.00
31 ND Scarlet Redemption epilogue	$0.30	$0.90	$1.50	£0.20	£0.60	£1.00
32 ND Hobgoblin appears, Spiderman guset stars	$0.30	$0.90	$1.50	£0.20	£0.60	£1.00
33 ND Hobgoblin appears, Spiderman guest stars	$0.30	$0.90	$1.50	£0.20	£0.60	£1.00
34 ND	$0.30	$0.90	$1.50	£0.20	£0.60	£1.00
35 ND Punisher appears, $1.75 cover begins	$0.30	$0.90	$1.50	£0.20	£0.60	£1.00
36 ND	$0.30	$0.90	$1.50	£0.20	£0.60	£1.00
37 ND Punisher appears	$0.30	$0.90	$1.50	£0.20	£0.60	£1.00
38 ND Punisher appears, new logo	$0.30	$0.90	$1.50	£0.20	£0.60	£1.00
39 ND new direction for title, Dr. Doom appears	$0.30	$0.90	$1.50	£0.20	£0.60	£1.00
40 ND Dr. Doom appears	$0.30	$0.90	$1.50	£0.20	£0.60	£1.00
41-43 ND Infinity War X-over	$0.30	$0.90	$1.50	£0.20	£0.60	£1.00
44 ND Infinity War X-over, Dr. Strange and Mr. Fantastic appear	$0.30	$0.90	$1.50	£0.20	£0.60	£1.00
45-49 ND	$0.30	$0.90	$1.50	£0.20	£0.60	£1.00
50 ND DS die-cut cover	$0.50	$1.50	$2.50	£0.30	£0.90	£1.50
51 ND Gambit appears	$0.30	$0.90	$1.50	£0.20	£0.60	£1.00
52 ND Gambit and Werewolf appear	$0.30	$0.90	$1.50	£0.20	£0.60	£1.00
53-54 ND	$0.30	$0.90	$1.50	£0.20	£0.60	£1.00
55 ND 1st Stephen Platt art on Moon Knight	$2.50	$7.50	$12.50	£1.60	£4.80	£8.00
56 ND Stephen Platt art	$1.50	$4.50	$7.50	£1.00	£3.00	£5.00
57 ND Stephen Platt art, Infinity Crusade epilogue	$1.00	$3.00	$5.00	£0.80	£2.40	£4.00
58-59 ND Stephen Platt cover art	$0.50	$1.50	$2.50	£0.30	£0.90	£1.50
60 ND Stephen Platt cover and art	$0.80	$2.40	$4.00	£0.60	£1.80	£3.00

	$Good	$Fine	$N.Mint	£Good	£Fine	£N.Mint
Title Value:	$26.40	$79.20	$132.00	£17.15	£51.45	£85.75

MOON KNIGHT, THE FIST OF KHONSHU
Marvel Comics Group; 1 Jun 1985-6 Dec 1985

	$Good	$Fine	$N.Mint	£Good	£Fine	£N.Mint
1 DS new costume	$0.40	$1.20	$2.00	£0.25	£0.75	£1.25
2-4	$0.40	$1.20	$2.00	£0.25	£0.75	£1.25
5-6 LD in the U.K.	$0.40	$1.20	$2.00	£0.30	£0.90	£1.50
Title Value:	$2.40	$7.20	$12.00	£1.60	£4.80	£8.00

MOON KNIGHT: DIVIDED WE FALL
Marvel Comics Group,OS; 1 Jun 1992

	$Good	$Fine	$N.Mint	£Good	£Fine	£N.Mint
1 48pgs	$0.80	$2.40	$4.00	£0.50	£1.50	£2.50
Title Value:	$0.80	$2.40	$4.00	£0.50	£1.50	£2.50

MOONSHADOW
Marvel Comics Group/Epic; 1 May 1985-12 Feb 1987

	$Good	$Fine	$N.Mint	£Good	£Fine	£N.Mint
1 ND "origin", Jon J. Muth art begins	$0.80	$2.40	$4.00	£0.50	£1.50	£2.50
2-5 ND	$0.60	$1.80	$3.00	£0.40	£1.20	£2.00
6-12 ND	$0.50	$1.50	$2.50	£0.30	£0.90	£1.50
Title Value:	$6.70	$20.10	$33.50	£4.20	£12.60	£21.00
Trade paperback (Jul 1989)						
Reprints 12 issue series with new ending				£2.00	£6.00	£10.00
2nd printing (Dec 1990)				£1.60	£4.80	£6.00
Hardback (by Graphitti) (1200 copies),						
(Mar 1990). Signed and numbered				£5.00	£15.00	£25.00

MOONSHADOW (2ND SERIES)
DC Comics/Vertigo,MS; 1 Sep 1994-12 Aug 1995

	$Good	$Fine	$N.Mint	£Good	£Fine	£N.Mint
1 ND reprints of the original Marvel Epic series begin with new covers by Jon J. Muth	$0.50	$1.50	$2.50	£0.30	£0.90	£1.50
2-11 ND	$0.50	$1.50	$2.50	£0.30	£0.90	£1.50
12 ND	$0.60	$1.80	$3.00	£0.40	£1.20	£2.00
Title Value:	$6.10	$18.30	$30.50	£3.70	£11.10	£18.50

MOONTRAP
Caliber Press; 1 1988

	$Good	$Fine	$N.Mint	£Good	£Fine	£N.Mint
1 ND adapts film	$0.40	$1.20	$2.00	£0.25	£0.75	£1.25
Title Value:	$0.40	$1.20	$2.00	£0.25	£0.75	£1.25

MOONWALKER IN 3-D
Blackthorne; (3-D Series #75) 1 Summer 1989

	$Good	$Fine	$N.Mint	£Good	£Fine	£N.Mint
1 ND with bound-in 3-D glasses (25% less without glasses); based on Michael Jackson film	$0.40	$1.20	$2.00	£0.25	£0.75	£1.25
Title Value:	$0.40	$1.20	$2.00	£0.25	£0.75	£1.25

MORBID ANGEL: PENANCE
London Night Studios,MS; 1 Oct 1995-2 1995

	$Good	$Fine	$N.Mint	£Good	£Fine	£N.Mint
1-2 ND black and white	$0.60	$1.80	$3.00	£0.40	£1.20	£2.00
Title Value:	$1.20	$3.60	$6.00	£0.80	£2.40	£4.00

MORBIUS
Marvel Comics Group; 1 Sep 1992-32 Apr 1995
(see Adventure Into Fear, Amazing Spiderman #101/102)

	$Good	$Fine	$N.Mint	£Good	£Fine	£N.Mint
1 ND DS Rise of the Midnight Sons part 3, pre-bagged with colour poster	$0.50	$1.50	$2.50	£0.30	£0.90	£1.50
2 ND Rise of the Midnight Sons tie-in, Peter Parker appears	$0.40	$1.20	$2.00	£0.25	£0.75	£1.25
3 ND Spiderman vs. Morbius	$0.40	$1.20	$2.00	£0.25	£0.75	£1.25
4 ND Spiderman cameo	$0.40	$1.20	$2.00	£0.25	£0.75	£1.25
5 ND intro Basilisk II	$0.40	$1.20	$2.00	£0.25	£0.75	£1.25
6-9 ND	$0.30	$0.90	$1.50	£0.20	£0.60	£1.00
10 ND two stories, back-up art by Isaac Cordova	$0.30	$0.90	$1.50	£0.20	£0.60	£1.00
11 ND X-over with Nightstalkers #9	$0.30	$0.90	$1.50	£0.20	£0.60	£1.00
12 ND black parchment outer cover with gold ink, Werewolf By Night appears	$0.40	$1.20	$2.00	£0.25	£0.75	£1.25
13 ND	$0.30	$0.90	$1.50	£0.20	£0.60	£1.00
14 ND Werewolf By Night appears	$0.30	$0.90	$1.50	£0.20	£0.60	£1.00
15 ND Ghost Rider appears	$0.30	$0.90	$1.50	£0.20	£0.60	£1.00
16 ND Siege of Darkness part 5; neon ink/spot varnish cover	$0.30	$0.90	$1.50	£0.20	£0.60	£1.00
17 ND Siege of Darkness part 13; neon ink/spot varnish cover	$0.30	$0.90	$1.50	£0.20	£0.60	£1.00
18-19 ND Deathlok guest-stars	$0.30	$0.90	$1.50	£0.20	£0.60	£1.00
20 ND	$0.30	$0.90	$1.50	£0.20	£0.60	£1.00
21 ND Spiderman appears; with free Spiderman vs. Venom card sheet	$0.30	$0.90	$1.50	£0.20	£0.60	£1.00
22-23 ND Spiderman appears	$0.30	$0.90	$1.50	£0.20	£0.60	£1.00
24 ND	$0.30	$0.90	$1.50	£0.20	£0.60	£1.00
25 ND 48pgs, metallic fifth ink on cover	$0.40	$1.20	$2.00	£0.25	£0.75	£1.25
26-27 ND	$0.30	$0.90	$1.50	£0.20	£0.60	£1.00
28 ND Werewolf by Night appears	$0.30	$0.90	$1.50	£0.20	£0.60	£1.00
29 ND Werewolf by Night, Spiderman, Vengeamce, Dr. Strange and Ghost Rider appear	$0.30	$0.90	$1.50	£0.20	£0.60	£1.00
30-32 ND	$0.30	$0.90	$1.50	£0.20	£0.60	£1.00
Title Value:	$10.40	$31.20	$52.00	£6.80	£20.40	£34.00

MORBIUS REVISITED
Marvel Comics Group,MS; 1 Aug 1993-5 Dec 1993

	$Good	$Fine	$N.Mint	£Good	£Fine	£N.Mint
1 selected reprints from Adventure into Fear #20 onwards begin	$0.40	$1.20	$2.00	£0.25	£0.75	£1.25
2-5	$0.40	$1.20	$2.00	£0.25	£0.75	£1.25
Title Value:	$2.00	$6.00	$10.00	£1.25	£3.75	£6.25

MORE FUN COMICS
National Periodical Publications; 1 Feb 1935-127 Nov/Dec 1947

1 very rare in both U.K. and U.S. 1st published DC comic, titled "New Fun Comics" (to issue #6), almost certainly less than 20 extant copies in any condition
| | $4750.00 | $14200.00 | $47500.00 | £3200.00 | £9600.00 | £32000.00 |

2 extremely rare in both U.K. and U.S; certainly less than 10 known copies, traditionally the rarest DC comic
| | $1925.00 | $5800.00 | $17500.00 | £1325.00 | £4000.00 | £12000.00 |

3 very rare in the U.K., rare in the U.S. about 30 extant copies, possibly the 1st ever sci-fi cover on a comic book (April 1935)
| | $1150.00 | $3500.00 | $10500.00 | £770.00 | £2325.00 | £7000.00 |

4-5 very rare in the U.K., rare in the U.S. about 30 extant copies
| | $1100.00 | $3300.00 | $10000.00 | £750.00 | £2250.00 | £6750.00 |

6 extremely rare in both U.K. and U.S. 1st appearance Dr. Occult by Jerry Siegel and Joe Shuster thought to be a prototype for Superman, less than 20 known copies
| | $2250.00 | $6700.00 | $22500.00 | £1500.00 | £4500.00 | £15000.00 |

(Note that values for Near Mint are theoretical only as no true near mint copies have yet been found. Issues #1-6 can only be considered to exist in up to a Very Fine grade)

7 very rare in both U.K. and U.S. title changed to "More Fun Comics" as New Comics #1 was published in the same month (Dec. 1935). About 25 known copies; significantly none are known in Near Mint condition
| | $620.00 | $1875.00 | $5000.00 | £405.00 | £1200.00 | £3250.00 |

8 very rare in both U.K. and U.S. probably less than 20 known copies
| | $620.00 | $1875.00 | $5000.00 | £375.00 | £1125.00 | £3000.00 |

9 extremely rare in the U.K., very rare in the U.S. 1st comic-sized issue, probably less than 15 known copies
| | $680.00 | $2050.00 | $5500.00 | £435.00 | £1300.00 | £3500.00 |

10 rare in the U.K., very scarce in the U.S.
| | $375.00 | $1125.00 | $3000.00 | £250.00 | £750.00 | £2000.00 |

11 very rare in the U.K., rare in the U.S. last paper cover, about 30 extant copies
| | $375.00 | $1125.00 | $3000.00 | £275.00 | £820.00 | £2200.00 |

12 rare in the U.K., very scarce in the U.S., 1st glossy cover
| | $280.00 | $840.00 | $2250.00 | £185.00 | £560.00 | £1500.00 |

13 rare in the U.K., very scarce in the U.S.
| | $280.00 | $840.00 | $2250.00 | £185.00 | £560.00 | £1500.00 |

14 very rare in the U.K. 1st Dr. Occult in costume (skin-tight with cape – recognisable Superman prototype dated October 1936, 18 months before Action Comics #1); about 10 exant copies
| | $1125.00 | $3400.00 | $10250.00 | £770.00 | £2325.00 | £7000.00 |

15 very rare in the U.K., rare in the U.S. about 30 extant copies
| | $560.00 | $1675.00 | $4500.00 | £375.00 | £1125.00 | £3000.00 |

16 rare in the U.K., very scarce in the U.S., 1st numbering on cover (top left)
| | $560.00 | $1675.00 | $4500.00 | £360.00 | £1075.00 | £2900.00 |

17 rare in the U.K., very scarce in the U.S.
| | $560.00 | $1675.00 | $4500.00 | £360.00 | £1075.00 | £2900.00 |

[please note that the above are approximate values only as copies almost never come onto the UK market and as such prices are dictated by the American market. Also note that it would be more realistic to consider #1-20 ever being available on the market in no more that VFN condition]

18-20 very scarce in the U.K., scarce in the U.S.
| | $250.00 | $750.00 | $1750.00 | £155.00 | £470.00 | £1100.00 |

21-26 very scarce in the U.K.
| | $210.00 | $640.00 | $1500.00 | £140.00 | £425.00 | £1000.00 |

27 very scarce in the U.K. Christmas cover
| | $210.00 | $640.00 | $1500.00 | £140.00 | £425.00 | £1000.00 |

28-29 scarce in the U.K.
| | $210.00 | $640.00 | $1500.00 | £140.00 | £425.00 | £1000.00 |

30 scarce in the U.K. 1st adventure-type cover
| | $210.00 | $640.00 | $1500.00 | £140.00 | £425.00 | £1000.00 |

31-35 | $190.00 | $570.00 | $1350.00 | £125.00 | £385.00 | £900.00 |

36-38 | $185.00 | $550.00 | $1300.00 | £125.00 | £375.00 | £875.00 |

39 Christmas cover
| | $185.00 | $550.00 | $1300.00 | £125.00 | £375.00 | £875.00 |

40 | $185.00 | $550.00 | $1300.00 | £125.00 | £375.00 | £875.00 |

41 last "funnies" cover
| | $150.00 | $450.00 | $1050.00 | £100.00 | £300.00 | £700.00 |

42 adventure-type covers re-start (end #51)
| | $150.00 | $450.00 | $1050.00 | £100.00 | £300.00 | £700.00 |

43-47 | $150.00 | $450.00 | $1050.00 | £100.00 | £300.00 | £700.00 |

48 dinosaur cover
| | $150.00 | $450.00 | $1050.00 | £100.00 | £300.00 | £700.00 |

49-50 | $150.00 | $450.00 | $1050.00 | £100.00 | £300.00 | £700.00 |

51 scarce in the U.K. 1st appearance The Spectre (in costume in one panel announcing his arrival next issue)
| | $500.00 | $1500.00 | $4000.00 | £340.00 | £1025.00 | £2750.00 |

52 rare in the U.K. origin and 1st full appearance The Spectre, in costume for 1 panel only, about 50 copies thought to exist
| | $4500.00 | $13500.00 | $45000.00 | £3000.00 | £9000.00 | £30000.00 |
[Scarce in high grade – Very Fine+ or better]
[Prices may vary widely on this comic]

53 rare in the U.K. origin The Spectre continues, in costume at end of story
| | $3000.00 | $9000.00 | $30000.00 | £2000.00 | £6000.00 | £20000.00 |
[Prices may vary widely on this comic]

54 | $1025.00 | $3100.00 | $7250.00 | £670.00 | £2025.00 | £4750.00 |

55 scarce in the U.K. 1st appearance Dr. Fate, about 90 extant copies
| | $1375.00 | $4100.00 | $11000.00 | £900.00 | £2700.00 | £7250.00 |

56 2nd appearance Dr. Fate and 1st Dr. Fate cover
| | $540.00 | $1625.00 | $3800.00 | £355.00 | £1050.00 | £2500.00 |

57-60 | $370.00 | $1100.00 | $2600.00 | £240.00 | £720.00 | £1700.00 |

61-64 | $285.00 | $850.00 | $2000.00 | £185.00 | £550.00 | £1300.00 |

65 classic Spectre-in-mirror cover
| | $285.00 | $850.00 | $2000.00 | £185.00 | £550.00 | £1300.00 |

66 | $285.00 | $850.00 | $2000.00 | £185.00 | £550.00 | £1300.00 |

67 origin Dr. Fate
| | $680.00 | $2050.00 | $5500.00 | £435.00 | £1300.00 | £3500.00 |

68-70 | $210.00 | $640.00 | $1500.00 | £140.00 | £425.00 | £1000.00 |

71 origin and 1st appearance Johnny Quick
| | $560.00 | $1675.00 | $4500.00 | £375.00 | £1125.00 | £3000.00 |

72 | $200.00 | $600.00 | $1400.00 | £125.00 | £385.00 | £900.00 |

73 scarce in the U.K. origin and 1st appearance Aquaman
| | $1100.00 | $3300.00 | $10000.00 | £720.00 | £2150.00 | £6500.00 |

74 2nd appearance Aquaman
| | $210.00 | $640.00 | $1500.00 | £140.00 | £425.00 | £1000.00 |

75-80 | $200.00 | $600.00 | $1400.00 | £125.00 | £385.00 | £900.00 |

81 | $140.00 | $425.00 | $1000.00 | £92.50 | £275.00 | £650.00 |

82 1st small logo
| | $140.00 | $425.00 | $1000.00 | £92.50 | £275.00 | £650.00 |

83-88 | $140.00 | $425.00 | $1000.00 | £92.50 | £275.00 | £650.00 |

89 origin Green Arrow and Speedy team
| | $155.00 | $470.00 | $1100.00 | £105.00 | £320.00 | £750.00 |

90-97 | $92.50 | $275.00 | $650.00 | £60.00 | £180.00 | £425.00 |

98 scarce in the U.K.
| | $92.50 | $275.00 | $650.00 | £62.50 | £190.00 | £450.00 |

99 | $92.50 | $275.00 | $650.00 | £60.00 | £180.00 | £425.00 |

100 | $140.00 | $385.00 | $900.00 | £85.00 | £255.00 | £600.00 |
[Note: issues pre #100 aregenerally at least scarce in the U.K.]

101 origin and 1st appearance Superboy, last Spectre in title; Jerry Siegel and Joe Shuster not consulted about the creation of Superboy; it was the only part of a long law-suit against DC which they won
| | $560.00 | $1675.00 | $6750.00 | £375.00 | £1125.00 | £4500.00 |
[Scarce in high grade - Very Fine+ or better]

102 2nd appearance Superboy
| | $165.00 | $500.00 | $1175.00 | £110.00 | £330.00 | £775.00 |

103 3rd appearance Superboy
| | $105.00 | $320.00 | $750.00 | £70.00 | £210.00 | £500.00 |

104 1st Superboy cover
| | $100.00 | $300.00 | $700.00 | £62.50 | £190.00 | £450.00 |

105 | $92.50 | $275.00 | $650.00 | £60.00 | £180.00 | £425.00 |

106 "funnies" covers begin again (end #127)
| | $92.50 | $275.00 | $650.00 | £60.00 | £180.00 | £425.00 |

107 last Superboy story (Superboy #1 not set to appear for another 3 years until Mar/Apr 1949)
| | $92.50 | $275.00 | $650.00 | £60.00 | £180.00 | £425.00 |

108-110 | $25.00 | $75.00 | $175.00 | £16.00 | £49.00 | £115.00 |

111-115 | $21.00 | $62.50 | $150.00 | £14.00 | £43.00 | £100.00 |

116-120 | $19.00 | $57.50 | $135.00 | £12.50 | £39.00 | £90.00 |

121-124 | $15.50 | $47.00 | $110.00 | £10.50 | £32.00 | £75.00 |

125 Superman on cover though he does not appear inside (it's almost as if he was stuck on as an accident or after-thought, perhaps to make a failing title sell better)
| | $77.50 | $235.00 | $550.00 | £50.00 | £150.00 | £350.00 |

126 | $15.50 | $47.00 | $110.00 | £10.50 | £32.00 | £75.00 |

127 very scarce in the U.K., scarce in the U.S.
| | $31.00 | $92.50 | $220.00 | £22.50 | £67.50 | £160.00 |

Title Value: $47238.50 $141827.50 $402095.00 £31320.50 £94164.50 £267080.00

Note: the first 8 issues were larger than normal comic size (8"x10"). Issues 1-6 were 10"x15" and issues 7 and 8 were 10"x12".

Note also: all Non-Distributed on the news-stands in the U.K. and while no British pence stamp copies have been recorded, it is probable that some copies came over as ballast on ships or through army personnel in the war.

MORLOCK 2001
Atlas; 1 Feb 1975-3 Jul 1975
1-2 distributed in the U.K.
| | $0.30 | $0.90 | $1.50 | £0.20 | £0.60 | £1.00 |
3 Steve Ditko and Bernie Wrightson art; distributed in the U.K.
| | $0.40 | $1.20 | $2.00 | £0.25 | £0.75 | £1.25 |
Title Value: $1.00 $3.00 $5.00 £0.65 £1.95 £3.25
Note: issue 3 titled "Moorlock 2001 and the Midnight Men"

MORNINGSTAR SPECIAL
DC Comics/Comico,OS; 1 Jun 1990
1 ND | $0.40 | $1.20 | $2.00 | £0.25 | £0.75 | £1.25 |
1 2nd printing, ND (Sep 1991) | $0.40 | $1.20 | $2.00 | £0.25 | £0.75 | £1.25 |
Title Value: $0.80 $2.40 $4.00 £0.50 £1.50 £2.50

MORT THE DEAD TEENAGER
Marvel Comics Group,MS; 1 Dec 1993-4 Mar 1994
1-4 ND Larry Hama script | $0.40 | $1.20 | $2.00 | £0.25 | £0.75 | £1.25 |
Title Value: $1.60 $4.80 $8.00 £1.00 £3.00 £5.00

MORTAL KOMBAT
Malibu; 0 Nov 1994; 1 Jul 1994-6 Dec 1994
0 ND (Nov 1994) | $0.60 | $1.80 | $3.00 | £0.40 | £1.20 | £2.00 |
1 ND | $0.60 | $1.80 | $3.00 | £0.40 | £1.20 | £2.00 |
1 ND Gold Foil Edition (Oct 1994) | $1.50 | $4.50 | $7.50 | £1.00 | £3.00 | £5.00 |
1 ND The Special Edition (Nov 1994), expanded to 40pgs with interviews from the Mortal Kombat film personnel
| | $0.70 | $2.10 | $3.50 | £0.50 | £1.50 | £2.50 |
2-6 ND | $0.60 | $1.80 | $3.00 | £0.40 | £1.20 | £2.00 |
Title Value: $6.40 $19.20 $32.00 £4.30 £12.90 £21.50

Mortal Kombat Kollection (Jul 1995)
Trade Paperback collects 6 issue series, based on video game | $1.70 | | | | £5.10 | £8.50 |

MORTAL KOMBAT: BARAKA
Malibu,OS; 1 Jun 1995
1 ND tie-in with Mortal Kombat: Battlewave
| | $0.60 | $1.80 | $3.00 | £0.40 | £1.20 | £2.00 |
Title Value: $0.60 $1.80 $3.00 £0.40 £1.20 £2.00

MORTAL KOMBAT: BATTLEWAVE
Malibu,MS; 1 Feb 1995-6 Jul 1995

MINT = 100% / NEAR MINT (inc. +/-) = 90–99% / VERY FINE (inc. +/-) = 75–89% / FINE (inc. +/-) = 55–74% / VERY GOOD (inc. +/-) = 35–54% / GOOD (inc. +/-) = 15–34% / FAIR = 5–14% / POOR = 1–4%

469

Columns: *$Good* | *$Fine* | *$N.Mint* | *£Good* | *£Fine* | *£N.Mint*

Item	$Good	$Fine	$N.Mint	£Good	£Fine	£N.Mint
1-6 ND	$0.60	$1.80	$3.00	£0.40	£1.20	£2.00
Title Value:	$3.60	$10.80	$18.00	£2.40	£7.20	£12.00

MORTAL KOMBAT: GORO, PRINCE OF PAIN
Malibu Bravura,MS; 1 Sep 1994-3 Nov 1994

Item	$Good	$Fine	$N.Mint	£Good	£Fine	£N.Mint
1 ND based on video game movie	$0.60	$1.80	$3.00	£0.40	£1.20	£2.00
1 ND Platinum Edition (Apr 1995) – platinum foil embossed cover	$1.50	$4.50	$7.50	£1.00	£3.00	£5.00
2-3 ND based on video game movie	$0.60	$1.80	$3.00	£0.40	£1.20	£2.00
Title Value:	$3.30	$9.90	$16.50	£2.20	£6.60	£11.00

MORTAL KOMBAT: KITANA & MILEENA
Malibu Bravura,OS; 1 Aug 1995

Item	$Good	$Fine	$N.Mint	£Good	£Fine	£N.Mint
1 ND ties into Mortal Kombat: Tournament Edition II #1 and Battlewave series	$0.60	$1.80	$3.00	£0.40	£1.20	£2.00
Title Value:	$0.60	$1.80	$3.00	£0.40	£1.20	£2.00

MORTAL KOMBAT: KUNG LAO
Marvel Comics Group/Malibu Comics,OS; 1 Jul 1995

Item	$Good	$Fine	$N.Mint	£Good	£Fine	£N.Mint
1 ND ties in with Battlewave series	$0.60	$1.80	$3.00	£0.40	£1.20	£2.00
Title Value:	$0.60	$1.80	$3.00	£0.40	£1.20	£2.00

MORTAL KOMBAT: RAYDEN/KANO
Malibu; 1 Mar 1995-3 May 1995

Item	$Good	$Fine	$N.Mint	£Good	£Fine	£N.Mint
1 ND based on video game	$0.60	$1.80	$3.00	£0.40	£1.20	£2.00
1 ND based on video game – foil-stamped cover version	$0.70	$2.10	$3.50	£0.50	£1.50	£2.50
2-3 ND based on video game	$0.60	$1.80	$3.00	£0.40	£1.20	£2.00
Title Value:	$2.50	$7.50	$12.50	£1.70	£5.10	£8.50

MORTAL KOMBAT: TOURNAMENT EDITION BATTLE FINALE
Malibu,OS; 1 Dec 1994

Item	$Good	$Fine	$N.Mint	£Good	£Fine	£N.Mint
1 ND DS	$0.60	$1.80	$3.00	£0.40	£1.20	£2.00
Title Value:	$0.60	$1.80	$3.00	£0.40	£1.20	£2.00

MORTAL KOMBAT: TOURNAMENT EDITION II
Malibu Bravura,OS; 1 Aug 1995

Item	$Good	$Fine	$N.Mint	£Good	£Fine	£N.Mint
1 ND 40pgs	$0.80	$2.40	$4.00	£0.50	£1.50	£2.50
Title Value:	$0.80	$2.40	$4.00	£0.50	£1.50	£2.50

MORTAL KOMBAT: U.S. SPECIAL FORCES
Malibu,MS; 1 Jan 1995-2 Feb 1995

Item	$Good	$Fine	$N.Mint	£Good	£Fine	£N.Mint
1-2 ND 40pgs	$0.60	$1.80	$3.00	£0.40	£1.20	£2.00
Title Value:	$1.20	$3.60	$6.00	£0.80	£2.40	£4.00

MOTORHEAD
Dark Horse; 1 Aug 1995-present

Item	$Good	$Fine	$N.Mint	£Good	£Fine	£N.Mint
1 ND Predator X-over (see Ghost 5, Agents of Law 6 and X 18); Simon Bisley cover	$0.50	$1.50	$2.50	£0.30	£0.90	£1.50
2-5 ND Simon Bisley cover	$0.50	$1.50	$2.50	£0.30	£0.90	£1.50
Title Value:	$2.50	$7.50	$12.50	£1.50	£4.50	£7.50

MOTORHEAD SPECIAL
Dark Horse; 1 Mar 1994

Item	$Good	$Fine	$N.Mint	£Good	£Fine	£N.Mint
1 ND 48pgs, Jae Lee cover; spin-off from Comics Greatest World	$0.80	$2.40	$4.00	£0.50	£1.50	£2.50
Title Value:	$0.80	$2.40	$4.00	£0.50	£1.50	£2.50

MOTORMOUTH
Marvel UK; 1 Jun 1992-13 Jun 1993
(see Overkill in British section)

Item	$Good	$Fine	$N.Mint	£Good	£Fine	£N.Mint
1 Marks, Frank and Lanning script/art	$0.30	$0.90	$1.50	£0.20	£0.60	£1.00
2 Nick Fury and Shield appear	$0.30	$0.90	$1.50	£0.20	£0.60	£1.00
3	$0.30	$0.90	$1.50	£0.20	£0.60	£1.00
4 Nick Fury and Shield appear	$0.30	$0.90	$1.50	£0.20	£0.60	£1.00
5 Excalibur and Archangel appear	$0.30	$0.90	$1.50	£0.20	£0.60	£1.00
6 Cable, Punisher, Badhand and Nick Fury appear	$0.30	$0.90	$1.50	£0.20	£0.60	£1.00
7 Nick Fury and Cable appear	$0.30	$0.90	$1.50	£0.20	£0.60	£1.00
8 Cable appears	$0.30	$0.90	$1.50	£0.20	£0.60	£1.00
9 Nick Fury and Cable appear	$0.30	$0.90	$1.50	£0.20	£0.60	£1.00
10 Red Sonja appears	$0.30	$0.90	$1.50	£0.20	£0.60	£1.00
11	$0.30	$0.90	$1.50	£0.20	£0.60	£1.00
12 Death's Head II appears	$0.30	$0.90	$1.50	£0.20	£0.60	£1.00
13 Death's Head II and Killpower appear	$0.30	$0.90	$1.50	£0.20	£0.60	£1.00
Title Value:	$3.90	$11.70	$19.50	£2.60	£7.80	£13.00

MOTORMOUTH & KILLPOWER
Marvel UK,MS; 1 Nov 1993-2 Dec 1993

Item	$Good	$Fine	$N.Mint	£Good	£Fine	£N.Mint
1 Andrew Cartmel script begins, Death's Head II appears; green foil stamped cover	$0.30	$0.90	$1.50	£0.20	£0.60	£1.00
2 Death's Head II appears	$0.30	$0.90	$1.50	£0.20	£0.60	£1.00
Title Value:	$0.60	$1.80	$3.00	£0.40	£1.20	£2.00

MR. A
Comic Art,Magazine; 1 1973; 2 1975
1 ND Steve Ditko script and art; something of a cult magazine for its satirical and political content; black and white begins

Item	$Good	$Fine	$N.Mint	£Good	£Fine	£N.Mint
	$1.50	$4.50	$7.50	£1.00	£3.00	£5.00
2 ND Steve Ditko script and art	$1.20	$3.60	$6.00	£0.80	£2.40	£4.00
Title Value:	$2.70	$8.10	$13.50	£1.80	£5.40	£9.00

MR. HERO – THE NEWMATIC MAN, NEIL GAIMAN'S
Tekno Comix; 1 Mar 1995-present

Item	$Good	$Fine	$N.Mint	£Good	£Fine	£N.Mint
1 ND James Vance script, Ted Slampyak and Bob McLeod art	$0.40	$1.20	$2.00	£0.25	£0.75	£1.25
2-11 ND	$0.40	$1.20	$2.00	£0.25	£0.75	£1.25
12 ND	$0.45	$1.35	$2.25	£0.30	£0.90	£1.50
13 ND pre-bagged with Tekno back-issue comic	$0.45	$1.35	$2.25	£0.30	£0.90	£1.50
Title Value:	$5.30	$15.90	$26.50	£3.35	£10.05	£16.75

MR. LIZARD 1993 ANNUAL
Now Comics,OS; 1 Sep 1993

Item	$Good	$Fine	$N.Mint	£Good	£Fine	£N.Mint
1 ND pre-bagged with Instant Ralph Snart Action Figure Capsule	$0.50	$1.50	$2.50	£0.30	£0.90	£1.50
Title Value:	$0.50	$1.50	$2.50	£0.30	£0.90	£1.50

MR. LIZARD 3-D SPECIAL
Now Comics,OS; 1 May 1993

Item	$Good	$Fine	$N.Mint	£Good	£Fine	£N.Mint
1 ND pre-bagged with 3-D glasses (25% less without glasses)	$0.50	$1.50	$2.50	£0.30	£0.90	£1.50
Title Value:	$0.50	$1.50	$2.50	£0.30	£0.90	£1.50

MR. LIZARD SPECIAL
Now Comics,OS; 1 Aug 1992

Item	$Good	$Fine	$N.Mint	£Good	£Fine	£N.Mint
1 ND pre-bagged with badge (25% less without badge)	$0.50	$1.50	$2.50	£0.30	£0.90	£1.50
Title Value:	$0.50	$1.50	$2.50	£0.30	£0.90	£1.50

MR. MONSTER (1ST SERIES)
Eclipse; 1 Jan 1985-10 Jun 1987
(see Airboy/Mr.Monster Special, Vanguard Illustrated #7)

Item	$Good	$Fine	$N.Mint	£Good	£Fine	£N.Mint
1 ND scarce in the U.K. Michael T. Gilbert script/layouts begin	$1.00	$3.00	$5.00	£0.70	£2.10	£3.50
2 ND Dave Stevens cover	$0.60	$1.80	$3.00	£0.40	£1.20	£2.00
3 ND scarce in the U.K. Alan Moore script; Steve Bissette cover	$0.50	$1.50	$2.50	£0.70	£2.10	£3.50
4-9 ND	$0.50	$1.50	$2.50	£0.30	£0.90	£1.50
10 ND "6-D" issue	$0.50	$1.50	$2.50	£0.30	£0.90	£1.50
Title Value:	$5.60	$16.80	$28.00	£3.90	£11.70	£19.50

MR. MONSTER (2ND SERIES)
Dark Horse; 1 Feb 1988-8 Sep 1991

Item	$Good	$Fine	$N.Mint	£Good	£Fine	£N.Mint
1 ND origin story; black and white begins	$0.40	$1.20	$2.00	£0.25	£0.75	£1.25
2 ND origin story continues	$0.40	$1.20	$2.00	£0.25	£0.75	£1.25
3-7 ND	$0.40	$1.20	$2.00	£0.25	£0.75	£1.25
8 ND DS squarebound	$0.80	$2.40	$4.00	£0.50	£1.50	£2.50
Title Value:	$3.60	$10.80	$18.00	£2.25	£6.75	£11.25

Note: big delay (nearly 3 years) between issues 7 and 8.

MR. MONSTER SUPER-DUPER SPECIALS
Eclipse; 1 May 1986-8 Jul 1987

Item	$Good	$Fine	$N.Mint	£Good	£Fine	£N.Mint
1 Mr. Monster's 3-D High-Octane Horror #1 includes Wolverton, Evans	$0.50	$1.50	$2.50	£0.30	£0.90	£1.50
2 Mr. Monster's High-Octane Horror #2 includes Kubert, Powell	$0.50	$1.50	$2.50	£0.30	£0.90	£1.50
3-4 Mr. Monster's True Crime #1,2 all Jack Cole	$0.50	$1.50	$2.50	£0.30	£0.90	£1.50
5 Mr. Monster's High-Voltage Super-Science Atom Age Sci-Fi #1, Vic Torry by Powell	$0.50	$1.50	$2.50	£0.30	£0.90	£1.50
6 Mr. Monster's Hi-Shock Schlock #1	$0.50	$1.50	$2.50	£0.30	£0.90	£1.50
7 Mr. Monster's Hi-Shock Schlock #2	$0.50	$1.50	$2.50	£0.30	£0.90	£1.50
8 Mr. Monster's Weird Tales of the Future #1 Wolverton art	$0.50	$1.50	$2.50	£0.30	£0.90	£1.50
Title Value:	$4.00	$12.00	$20.00	£2.40	£7.20	£12.00

Note; all Non-Distributed on the news-stands in the U.K.

MR. MONSTER'S TRIPLE 3-D THREAT
3-D Zone,OS; 1 Sep 1993

Item	$Good	$Fine	$N.Mint	£Good	£Fine	£N.Mint
1 ND features work by Alan Moore, Paul Chadwick, Dave Stevens; with 3-D glasses (25% less without glasses)	$0.60	$1.80	$3.00	£0.40	£1.20	£2.00
Title Value:	$0.60	$1.80	$3.00	£0.40	£1.20	£2.00

MR. PUNCH HARDCOVER GRAPHIC NOVEL
DC Comics,OS; 1 Dec 1994

Item	$Good	$Fine	$N.Mint	£Good	£Fine	£N.Mint
1 ND 96pgs, Neil Gaiman script, Dave McKean art	$5.00	$15.00	$25.00	£3.00	£9.00	£15.00
Title Value:	$5.00	$15.00	$25.00	£3.00	£9.00	£15.00

Mr. Punch Softcover Graphic Novel (Nov 1995)
96pgs, softcover reprint of the above hardcover with the stipulation of "available in North America only" — £2.00 £6.00 £10.00

MR. T AND THE T-FORCE
Now Comics; 1 Jun 1993-14 1994

Item	$Good	$Fine	$N.Mint	£Good	£Fine	£N.Mint
1 pre-bagged with Mr. T trading card, Neal Adams script and art begins	$0.40	$1.20	$2.00	£0.25	£0.75	£1.25
1 Advanced edition, (Jun 1993), gold embossed logo, signed by Mr. T on cover	$1.20	$3.60	$6.00	£0.80	£2.40	£4.00
2-8 pre-bagged with trading card	$0.30	$0.90	$1.50	£0.20	£0.60	£1.00
2-8 pre-bagged with gold foil stamped trading card	$0.40	$1.20	$2.00	£0.25	£0.75	£1.25

	$Good	$Fine	$N.Mint	£Good	£Fine	£N.Mint
9-11	$0.30	$0.90	$1.50	£0.20	£0.60	£1.00
9-11 pre-bagged with trading card	$0.40	$1.20	$2.00	£0.25	£0.75	£1.25
12-14	$0.30	$0.90	$1.50	£0.20	£0.60	£1.00
Title Value:	$9.50	$28.50	$47.50	£6.15	£18.45	£30.75

Note: all Non-Distributed on the news-stands in the U.K.

MR. T AND THE T-FORCE ANNUAL
Now Comics; 1 Jul 1994

	$Good	$Fine	$N.Mint	£Good	£Fine	£N.Mint
1 ND metallic gold cover	$0.50	$1.50	$2.50	£0.30	£0.90	£1.50
Title Value:	$0.50	$1.50	$2.50	£0.30	£0.90	£1.50

MS. CYANIDE & ICE
Blackout Comics; 0 May 1995; 1 1995

	$Good	$Fine	$N.Mint	£Good	£Fine	£N.Mint
0 ND John R. Platt script, Bill Wylie and Scott Elmer art	$0.50	$1.50	$2.50	£0.30	£0.90	£1.50
1 ND	$0.50	$1.50	$2.50	£0.30	£0.90	£1.50
Title Value:	$1.00	$3.00	$5.00	£0.60	£1.80	£3.00

MS. MARVEL
Marvel Comics Group; 1 Jan 1977-23 Apr 1979

	$Good	$Fine	$N.Mint	£Good	£Fine	£N.Mint
1	$0.80	$2.40	$4.00	£0.50	£1.50	£2.50
2 origin	$0.50	$1.50	$2.50	£0.30	£0.90	£1.50
3-4	$0.40	$1.20	$2.50	£0.25	£0.75	£1.25
5 Ms. Marvel battles Vision	$0.40	$1.20	$2.00	£0.25	£0.75	£1.25
6-7	$0.40	$1.20	$2.00	£0.25	£0.75	£1.25
8 1st appearance Deathbird	$0.50	$1.50	$2.50	£0.30	£0.90	£1.50
9-10	$0.40	$1.20	$2.00	£0.25	£0.75	£1.25
11-14	$0.30	$0.90	$1.50	£0.20	£0.60	£1.00
15 Tiger Shark appears	$0.30	$0.90	$1.50	£0.20	£0.60	£1.00
16 Beast and Scarlet Witch appear, 1st appearance Mystique	$1.50	$4.50	$7.50	£0.40	£1.20	£2.00
17	$1.50	$4.50	$7.50	£0.30	£0.90	£1.50
18 1st full appearance Mystique	$2.50	$7.50	$12.50	£0.30	£0.90	£1.50
19 Captain Marvel appears	$0.30	$0.90	$1.50	£0.20	£0.60	£1.00
20 new costume	$0.30	$0.90	$1.50	£0.20	£0.60	£1.00
21	$0.30	$0.90	$1.50	£0.20	£0.60	£1.00
22 Mike Zeck art	$0.30	$0.90	$1.50	£0.20	£0.60	£1.00
23 Vance Astro of Guardians of the Galaxy appears	$0.30	$0.90	$1.50	£0.20	£0.60	£1.00
Title Value:	$13.10	$39.30	$65.50	£5.85	£17.55	£29.25

Note: the intended issues #24 and #25 are published for the first time in Marvel Super-Heroes (2nd Series) 10 and 11.

MS. MYSTIC
Pacific; 1 Oct 1982-2 Feb 1984
(see Captain Victory #3)

	$Good	$Fine	$N.Mint	£Good	£Fine	£N.Mint
1-2 ND Neal Adams art	$0.30	$0.90	$1.50	£0.20	£0.60	£1.00
Title Value:	$0.60	$1.80	$3.00	£0.40	£1.20	£2.00

MS. MYSTIC (2ND SERIES)
Continuity; 1 Oct 1987-9 1992

	$Good	$Fine	$N.Mint	£Good	£Fine	£N.Mint
1 reprints Pacific issue #1	$0.40	$1.20	$2.00	£0.25	£0.75	£1.25
2 reprints Pacific issue #2	$0.40	$1.20	$2.00	£0.25	£0.75	£1.25
3 new material begins, part Neal Adams art	$0.40	$1.20	$2.00	£0.25	£0.75	£1.25
4 Neal Adams and Graham Nolan cover, Adams/Stone script						

	$Good	$Fine	$N.Mint	£Good	£Fine	£N.Mint
	$0.40	$1.20	$2.00	£0.25	£0.75	£1.25
5 Dwayne Turner pencils and Neal Adams inks	$0.40	$1.20	$2.00	£0.25	£0.75	£1.25
6	$0.40	$1.20	$2.00	£0.25	£0.75	£1.25
7-8 Neal Adams cover	$0.40	$1.20	$2.00	£0.25	£0.75	£1.25
9 Dennis Beauvais art	$0.40	$1.20	$2.00	£0.25	£0.75	£1.25
Title Value:	$3.60	$10.80	$18.00	£2.25	£6.75	£11.25

MS. MYSTIC (3RD SERIES)
Continuity; 1 May 1993-3 Aug 1993

	$Good	$Fine	$N.Mint	£Good	£Fine	£N.Mint
1 ND Deathwatch 2000 part 8, pre-bagged with 2 trading cards, "dot-focus" cover; Neal Adams plot and cover	$0.40	$1.20	$2.00	£0.25	£0.75	£1.25
2 ND Deathwatch 2000 part 12, pre-bagged with trading card	$0.40	$1.20	$2.00	£0.25	£0.75	£1.25
3 ND Deathwatch 2000 part 17, pre-bagged with trading card; Tyvek indestructible cover	$0.40	$1.20	$2.00	£0.25	£0.75	£1.25
Title Value:	$1.20	$3.60	$6.00	£0.75	£2.25	£3.75

MS. MYSTIC (4TH SERIES)
Continuity; 1 Oct 1993-4 1994

	$Good	$Fine	$N.Mint	£Good	£Fine	£N.Mint
1 ND Vol.2 No 1 in indicia; Neal Adams co-inks	$0.40	$1.20	$2.00	£0.25	£0.75	£1.25
2 ND	$0.40	$1.20	$2.00	£0.25	£0.75	£1.25
3 ND Rise of Magic X-over; parchment embossed cover	$0.40	$1.20	$2.00	£0.25	£0.75	£1.25
4 ND Rise of Magic X-over; parchment embossed cover by Neal Adams	$0.40	$1.20	$2.00	£0.25	£0.75	£1.25
Title Value:	$1.60	$4.80	$8.00	£1.00	£3.00	£5.00

MS. TREE
Eclipse/Aardvark/Renegade; 1 Feb 1983-50 Jun 1989
(see The PI's)

	$Good	$Fine	$N.Mint	£Good	£Fine	£N.Mint
1 ND Eclipse issues begin; 2pg Frank Miller pin-up	$0.40	$1.20	$2.00	£0.25	£0.75	£1.25
2-9 ND	$0.40	$1.20	$2.00	£0.25	£0.75	£1.25
10 ND Aardvark issues begin	$0.40	$1.20	$2.00	£0.25	£0.75	£1.25
11-18 ND	$0.40	$1.20	$2.00	£0.25	£0.75	£1.25
19 ND Renegade issues begin	$0.40	$1.20	$2.00	£0.25	£0.75	£1.25
20-49 ND	$0.40	$1.20	$2.00	£0.25	£0.75	£1.25
50 ND with flexidisc	$0.60	$1.80	$3.00	£0.40	£1.20	£2.00
Title Value:	$20.20	$60.60	$101.00	£12.65	£37.95	£63.25

Note: called Ms. Tree's Thrilling Detective Adventures on issues #1-3 Files of Ms. Tree:

	£Good	£Fine	£N.Mint
1 reprints #1-3	£1.00	£3.00	£5.00
2 The Cold Dish, reprints #4-8 plus new story	£1.00	£3.00	£5.00
3 Mike Mist's Casebook, collects all appearances	£1.00	£3.00	£5.00

MS. TREE 3-D
Renegade; 1 Aug 1985

	$Good	$Fine	$N.Mint	£Good	£Fine	£N.Mint
1 ND with bound-in 3-D glasses (25% less if without glasses)	$0.50	$1.50	$2.50	£0.30	£0.90	£1.50
Title Value:	$0.50	$1.50	$2.50	£0.30	£0.90	£1.50

MS. TREE QUARTERLY
DC Comics; 1 Jul 1990-8 Apr 1992; 9 Jul 1992-10 Oct 1992

	$Good	$Fine	$N.Mint	£Good	£Fine	£N.Mint
1 ND 80pgs, squarebound, Ms. Tree's origin by Max Allan Collins, Midnight begins with art by Graham Nolan, 11pg Batman illustrated prose story by Mike Grell	$0.60	$1.80	$3.00	£0.40	£1.20	£2.00
2 ND 80pgs, squarebound, John Butcher prose story by Mike Baron begins	$0.60	$1.80	$3.00	£0.40	£1.20	£2.00
3 ND 80pgs, squarebound, Frank Miller pin-up	$0.60	$1.80	$3.00	£0.40	£1.20	£2.00

Morbius #1

More Fun Comics #71

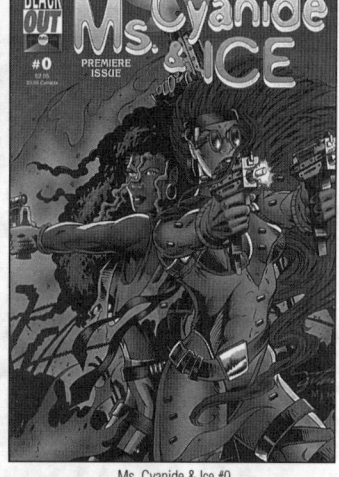

Ms. Cyanide & Ice #0

	$Good	$Fine	$N.Mint	£Good	£Fine	£N.Mint
4 ND 80pgs, cover by George Pratt						
	$0.60	$1.80	$3.00	£0.40	£1.20	£2.00
5-7 ND 80pgs	$0.60	$1.80	$3.00	£0.40	£1.20	£2.00
8-9 ND 64pgs	$0.55	$1.65	$2.75	£0.35	£1.05	£1.75
10 ND 80pgs, titled Ms. Tree Special						
	$0.60	$1.80	$3.00	£0.40	£1.20	£2.00
Title Value:	$5.90	$17.70	$29.50	£3.90	£11.70	£19.50

Note: owing to the binding process, many copies of issues 1-3 have badly crinkled spines/covers.

MS. TREE SUMMER SPECIAL
Renegade; 1 Aug 1986

	$Good	$Fine	$N.Mint	£Good	£Fine	£N.Mint
1 ND	$0.40	$1.20	$2.00	£0.25	£0.75	£1.25
Title Value:	$0.40	$1.20	$2.00	£0.25	£0.75	£1.25

MS. TREE'S 1950S THREE-DIMENSIONAL CRIME
Renegade; 1 Jul 1987

1 ND reprints, new framing sequence; with bound-in 3-D glasses (25% less if without glasses)

	$Good	$Fine	$N.Mint	£Good	£Fine	£N.Mint
	$0.50	$1.50	$2.50	£0.30	£0.90	£1.50
Title Value:	$0.50	$1.50	$2.50	£0.30	£0.90	£1.50

MS. TREE'S CLASSIC CRIME
Renegade; 1 1987

	$Good	$Fine	$N.Mint	£Good	£Fine	£N.Mint
1 ND reprints	$0.40	$1.20	$2.00	£0.25	£0.75	£1.25
Title Value:	$0.40	$1.20	$2.00	£0.25	£0.75	£1.25

MS. TREE'S ROCK & ROLL 3-D SPECIAL
Renegade; 1 1986

	$Good	$Fine	$N.Mint	£Good	£Fine	£N.Mint
1 ND	$0.50	$1.50	$2.50	£0.30	£0.90	£1.50
Title Value:	$0.50	$1.50	$2.50	£0.30	£0.90	£1.50

MS. VICTORY SPECIAL
AC Comics; 1 1985

	$Good	$Fine	$N.Mint	£Good	£Fine	£N.Mint
1 ND	$0.50	$1.50	$2.50	£0.30	£0.90	£1.50
Title Value:	$0.50	$1.50	$2.50	£0.30	£0.90	£1.50

MUDWOG GRAPHIC NOVEL
Continuity; 1 Nov 1991-2 1992

1 ND reprints from Echo of Future Past featuring Arthur Suydam work

	$Good	$Fine	$N.Mint	£Good	£Fine	£N.Mint
	$1.00	$3.00	$5.00	£0.70	£2.10	£3.50
2 ND new material by Arthur Suydam						
	$2.00	$6.00	$10.00	£1.20	£3.60	£6.00
Title Value:	$3.00	$9.00	$15.00	£1.90	£5.70	£9.50

MULLKON EMPIRE, JOHN JAKE'S
Tekno Comix; 1 Sep 1995-present

1 ND Kate Worley script, John Watkiss art and John Higgins colours

	$Good	$Fine	$N.Mint	£Good	£Fine	£N.Mint
	$0.40	$1.20	$2.00	£0.25	£0.75	£1.25
2-5 ND	$0.40	$1.20	$2.00	£0.25	£0.75	£1.25
6 ND	$0.45	$1.35	$2.25	£0.30	£0.90	£1.50
Title Value:	$2.45	$7.35	$12.25	£1.55	£4.65	£7.75

MUMMY ARCHIVES, THE
Millennium,OS; 1 1992

1 ND text and illustrations

	$Good	$Fine	$N.Mint	£Good	£Fine	£N.Mint
	$0.40	$1.20	$2.00	£0.25	£0.75	£1.25
Title Value:	$0.40	$1.20	$2.00	£0.25	£0.75	£1.25

MUMMY'S CURSE
Aircel,MS; 1 Nov 1990-4 Feb 1991

1-4 ND Barry Blair art, black and white

	$Good	$Fine	$N.Mint	£Good	£Fine	£N.Mint
	$0.40	$1.20	$2.00	£0.25	£0.75	£1.25
Title Value:	$1.60	$4.80	$8.00	£1.00	£3.00	£5.00

MUMMY, THE
Dell, Movie; 12-537-211 Sep/Nov 1962

nn limited distribution in the U.K, adaptation of movie; two different back covers are known to exist

	$Good	$Fine	$N.Mint	£Good	£Fine	£N.Mint
	$7.00	$21.00	$35.00	£4.50	£13.50	£22.50
Title Value:	$7.00	$21.00	$35.00	£4.50	£13.50	£22.50

MUMMY, THE (2ND SERIES)
Millennium,MS; 1 Oct 1990-12 Dec 1991

1-12 ND adaptation of Anne Rice novel

	$Good	$Fine	$N.Mint	£Good	£Fine	£N.Mint
	$0.40	$1.20	$2.00	£0.30	£0.90	£1.50
Title Value:	$4.80	$14.40	$24.00	£3.60	£10.80	£18.00

MUMMY, THE (LIMITED SERIES)
Monster Comics,MS; 1 Mar 1991-4 Aug 1991

1-4 ND Scott Beaderstadt adaptation of film

	$Good	$Fine	$N.Mint	£Good	£Fine	£N.Mint
	$0.40	$1.20	$2.00	£0.25	£0.75	£1.25
Title Value:	$1.60	$4.80	$8.00	£1.00	£3.00	£5.00

MUNDEN'S BAR ANNUAL
First; 1 Apr 1988; 2 May 1991

1 ND 48pgs, squarebound, Moncuse art (new Fish Police X-over), Rude, Staton, Ordway, Bolland (9pgs), Feazell reprints

	$Good	$Fine	$N.Mint	£Good	£Fine	£N.Mint
	$0.80	$2.40	$4.00	£0.50	£1.50	£2.50
2 ND 56pgs, squarebound, Reed Waller, Kate Worley, Evan Dorkin, Hilary Barta plus unseen TMNT story by Eastman/Laird						
	$0.80	$2.40	$4.00	£0.70	£2.10	£3.50
Title Value:	$1.60	$4.80	$8.00	£1.20	£3.60	£6.00

MUNSTERS, THE
Gold Key; 1 Jan 1965-16 Jan 1968

	$Good	$Fine	$N.Mint	£Good	£Fine	£N.Mint
1 photo cover	$22.50	$67.50	$160.00	£15.00	£45.00	£105.00
2	$11.00	$34.00	$80.00	£7.75	£23.50	£55.00
3-5	$10.00	$30.00	$60.00	£6.50	£20.00	£40.00
6-16	$10.00	$30.00	$50.00	£7.00	£21.00	£35.00
Title Value:	$173.50	$521.50	$970.00	£119.25	£359.50	£665.00

Note: very limited distribution on the news-stands in the U.K.

MUPPET BABIES, THE
Marvel Comics Group/Star, TV; 1 Aug 1985-26 Jul 1989

	$Good	$Fine	$N.Mint	£Good	£Fine	£N.Mint
1-26 ND	$0.15	$0.45	$0.75	£0.10	£0.30	£0.50
Title Value:	$3.90	$11.70	$19.50	£2.60	£7.80	£13.00

MUPPETS TAKE MANHATTAN, THE
Marvel Comics Group,MS Film; 1 Nov 1984-3 Jan 1985

	$Good	$Fine	$N.Mint	£Good	£Fine	£N.Mint
1-3 ND	$0.15	$0.45	$0.75	£0.10	£0.30	£0.50

	$Good	$Fine	$N.Mint	£Good	£Fine	£N.Mint
Title Value:	$0.45	$1.35	$2.25	£0.30	£0.90	£1.50

MURDER
Renegade; 1 Aug 1986-5 Dec 1986

1-2 ND Dan Day, Steve Ditko, Toth art

	$Good	$Fine	$N.Mint	£Good	£Fine	£N.Mint
	$0.40	$1.20	$2.00	£0.25	£0.75	£1.25
3 ND Dan Day, Steve Ditko, Toth art/cover						
	$0.40	$1.20	$2.00	£0.25	£0.75	£1.25
4-5 ND Dan Day, Steve Ditko, Toth art						
	$0.40	$1.20	$2.00	£0.25	£0.75	£1.25
Title Value:	$2.00	$6.00	$10.00	£1.25	£3.75	£6.25

MURDER CITY
Malibu; 1 1990

1 ND 48pgs, squarebound, reprints newspaper strips

	$Good	$Fine	$N.Mint	£Good	£Fine	£N.Mint
	$0.50	$1.50	$2.50	£0.30	£0.90	£1.50
Title Value:	$0.50	$1.50	$2.50	£0.30	£0.90	£1.50

MUTANT CHRONICLES: GOLGOTHA
Caliber Press,MS; 1 1996-present

	$Good	$Fine	$N.Mint	£Good	£Fine	£N.Mint
1 ND pre-bagged	$0.60	$1.80	$3.00	£0.40	£1.20	£2.00
Title Value:	$0.60	$1.80	$3.00	£0.40	£1.20	£2.00

MUTANT SUMMER FUN
Marvel Comics Group,OS; 1 Aug 1990

(see New Mutants)

1 ND 80pgs, Anne Nocenti script, Brett Blevins art

	$Good	$Fine	$N.Mint	£Good	£Fine	£N.Mint
	$0.40	$1.20	$2.00	£0.25	£0.75	£1.25
Title Value:	$0.40	$1.20	$2.00	£0.25	£0.75	£1.25

MUTANTS VS. ULTRAS: FIRST ENCOUNTERS
Marvel Comics Group/Ultraverse,OS; 1 Jan 1996

1 ND 80pgs, X-Men vs. Exiles, Wolverine vs. Night Man, Prime vs. Hulk

	$Good	$Fine	$N.Mint	£Good	£Fine	£N.Mint
	$1.40	$4.20	$7.00	£0.90	£2.70	£4.50
Title Value:	$1.40	$4.20	$7.00	£0.90	£2.70	£4.50

MUTANTS: GENERATION NEXT, THE
Marvel Comics Group; 1 Mar 1995-4 Jun 1995

(previously Generation X)

1 printing on glossy stock paper begins; Scott Lobdell script and Chris Bachalo art begin

	$Good	$Fine	$N.Mint	£Good	£Fine	£N.Mint
	$1.00	$3.00	$5.00	£0.60	£1.80	£3.00
2-3	$0.60	$1.80	$3.00	£0.30	£0.90	£1.50
4 continued in X-Men: Omega						
	$0.60	$1.80	$3.00	£0.30	£0.90	£1.50
Title Value:	$2.80	$8.40	$14.00	£1.50	£4.50	£7.50
The Ultimate Generation Next (Jul 1995) 96pgs, Bookshelf Edition collects issues #1-4 with etched gold cover				£1.20	£3.60	£6.00

MUTANTS: THE AMAZING X-MEN, THE
Marvel Comics Group; 1 Mar 1995-4 Jun 1995

1 Fabian Nicieza script, Andy Kubert art

	$Good	$Fine	$N.Mint	£Good	£Fine	£N.Mint
	$1.00	$3.00	$5.00	£0.60	£1.80	£3.00
2-3 Fabian Nicieza script, Andy Kubert art						
	$0.60	$1.80	$3.00	£0.30	£0.90	£1.50
4 Fabian Nicieza script, Andy Kubert art; continued in X-Men: Omega						
	$0.60	$1.80	$3.00	£0.30	£0.90	£1.50
Title Value:	$2.80	$8.40	$14.00	£1.50	£4.50	£7.50

Note: this title temporarily replaced the X-Men during the "Age of Apocalypse" storyline

The Ultimate Amazing X-Men (Jul 1995) 96pgs, Bookshelf Edition collects issues #1-4 with etched gold cover — £1.20 / £3.60 / £6.00

MUTANTS: THE ASTONISHING X-MEN, THE
Marvel Comics Group; 1 Mar 1995-4 Jun 1995

1 Scott Lobdell script, Madureira and Green art

	$Good	$Fine	$N.Mint	£Good	£Fine	£N.Mint
	$1.00	$3.00	$5.00	£0.60	£1.80	£3.00
2-3 Scott Lobdell script, Madureira and Green art						
	$0.60	$1.80	$3.00	£0.30	£0.90	£1.50
4 Scott Lobdell script, Madureira and Green art; continued in X-Men: Omega						
	$0.60	$1.80	$3.00	£0.30	£0.90	£1.50
Title Value:	$2.80	$8.40	$14.00	£1.50	£4.50	£7.50

Note: this title temporarily replaced the Uncanny X-Men during the "Age of Apocalypse" storyline

The Ultimate Astonishing X-Men (Jul 1995) 96pgs, Bookshelf Edition collects issues #1-4 with etched gold cover — £1.20 / £3.60 / £6.00

MUTATIS
Marvel Comics Group,MS; 1 Dec 1992-3 Feb 1993

1-3 ND John Higgins cover and art

	$Good	$Fine	$N.Mint	£Good	£Fine	£N.Mint
	$0.40	$1.20	$2.00	£0.25	£0.75	£1.25
Title Value:	$1.20	$3.60	$6.00	£0.75	£2.25	£3.75

MY FAVOURITE MARTIAN
Gold Key; 1 Jan 1964-9 Oct 1966

1 photo covers begin

	$Good	$Fine	$N.Mint	£Good	£Fine	£N.Mint
	$13.50	$41.00	$110.00	£9.25	£28.00	£75.00
2	$9.00	$28.00	$55.00	£5.75	£17.50	£35.00
3-5	$7.50	$22.50	$45.00	£5.00	£15.00	£30.00
6-9	$8.50	$26.00	$42.50	£5.50	£16.50	£27.50
Title Value:	$79.00	$240.50	$470.00	£52.00	£156.50	£310.00

Note: limited distribution on the news-stands in the U.K.

MY GREATEST ADVENTURE
National Periodical Publications; 1 Jan/Feb 1955-85 Feb 1964

(becomes Doom Patrol)

	$Good	$Fine	$N.Mint	£Good	£Fine	£N.Mint
1	$115.00	$350.00	$1050.00	£82.50	£250.00	£750.00
2	$62.50	$185.00	$500.00	£44.00	£130.00	£350.00
3-5	$38.00	$110.00	$300.00	£25.00	£75.00	£200.00
6-10	$31.00	$92.50	$250.00	£21.50	£65.00	£175.00
11-15	$29.00	$85.00	$200.00	£18.50	£55.00	£130.00
16-18 Jack Kirby art						
	$32.00	$95.00	$225.00	£21.00	£62.50	£150.00
19	$21.00	$62.50	$150.00	£14.00	£43.00	£100.00
20-21 Jack Kirby art						
	$25.00	$75.00	$175.00	£16.00	£49.00	£115.00

	$Good	$Fine	$N.Mint	£Good	£Fine	£N.Mint
22-25	$21.00	$62.50	$150.00	£14.00	£43.00	£100.00
26-27	$17.00	$50.00	$120.00	£11.00	£34.00	£80.00
28 Jack Kirby art	$25.00	$75.00	$175.00	£16.00	£49.00	£115.00
29-30	$17.00	$50.00	$120.00	£11.00	£34.00	£80.00
31-36	$14.00	$43.00	$100.00	£10.00	£30.00	£70.00
1st official distribution in the U.K.						
37-40	$14.00	$43.00	$100.00	£9.25	£28.00	£65.00
41-50	$10.50	$32.00	$75.00	£6.25	£19.00	£45.00
51-57	$10.00	$30.00	$70.00	£5.50	£17.00	£40.00
58 Toth art	$10.50	$32.00	$75.00	£6.25	£19.00	£45.00
59	$10.00	$30.00	$70.00	£5.50	£17.00	£40.00
60 Toth art	$10.50	$32.00	$75.00	£5.50	£17.00	£40.00
61 Toth art; last 10 cents issue						
	$10.00	$32.00	$75.00	£5.50	£17.00	£40.00
62-70	$6.25	$19.00	$45.00	£3.55	£10.50	£25.00
71-76	$5.50	$17.00	$40.00	£2.85	£8.50	£20.00
77 Toth art	$5.50	$17.00	$40.00	£3.20	£9.50	£22.50
78-79	$5.50	$17.00	$40.00	£2.85	£8.50	£20.00
80 origin and 1st appearance Doom Patrol (Robotman, Negative Man, Elasti-Girl, The Chief)						
	$47.00	$140.00	$375.00	£31.00	£92.50	£250.00
[Scarce in high grade – Very Fine+ or better]						
81 2nd appearance Doom Patrol, Toth art						
	$21.00	$62.50	$150.00	£12.50	£39.00	£90.00
82 3rd appearance Doom Patrol						
	$20.50	$60.00	$145.00	£12.00	£36.00	£85.00
83-84	$20.00	$60.00	$140.00	£10.50	£32.00	£75.00
85 Toth art	$20.00	$60.00	$140.00	£11.00	£34.00	£80.00
Title Value:	$1546.25	$4627.50	$11520.00	£992.70	£2999.00	£7477.50

FEATURES

Doom Patrol in 80-85. SF stories in 37-79, 81-85.

MY LITTLE MARGIE
Charlton; 1 Jul 1954-54 Nov 1964

	$Good	$Fine	$N.Mint	£Good	£Fine	£N.Mint
1 scarce in the U.K.						
	$22.50	$67.50	$160.00	£15.00	£45.00	£105.00
2 scarce in the U.K.						
	$10.50	$32.00	$75.00	£7.00	£21.00	£50.00
3-5 scarce in the U.K.						
	$7.00	$21.00	$42.50	£4.55	£13.50	£27.50
6-9	$6.50	$20.00	$40.00	£4.30	£13.00	£26.00
1st official distribution in the U.K.						
10	$6.50	$20.00	$40.00	£4.30	£13.00	£26.00
11-15	$5.75	$17.50	$35.00	£3.75	£11.00	£22.50
16-19	$4.55	$13.50	$27.50	£2.90	£8.75	£17.50
20 scarce in the U.K. 100pgs						
	$10.50	$33.00	$65.00	£7.50	£22.50	£45.00
21-40	$3.75	$11.00	$22.50	£2.50	£7.50	£15.00
41-53	$2.50	$7.50	$15.00	£1.65	£5.00	£10.00
54 scarce in the U.K. parody of Beatles and Beatles on front cover						
	$15.00	$45.00	$90.00	£10.00	£30.00	£60.00
Title Value:	$266.45	$799.50	$1647.50	£176.45	£529.00	£1085.00

Note: limited distribution on the news-stands in the U.K.

MY LOVE
Marvel Comics Group; 1 Sep 1969-39 Mar 1976

	$Good	$Fine	$N.Mint	£Good	£Fine	£N.Mint
1 ND scarce in the U.K.						
	$2.50	$7.50	$12.50	£1.50	£4.50	£7.50
2-5 ND	$1.50	$4.50	$7.50	£0.80	£2.40	£4.00
6-9 ND	$1.30	$3.90	$6.50	£0.70	£2.10	£3.50
10 ND Williamson reprint						
	$1.30	$3.90	$6.50	£0.70	£2.10	£3.50
11-13 ND	$0.70	$2.10	$3.50	£0.50	£1.50	£2.50
14 ND Morrow cover/art, part Jack Kirby reprint						
	$0.70	$2.10	$3.50	£0.50	£1.50	£2.50
15-20 ND	$0.70	$2.10	$3.50	£0.50	£1.50	£2.50
21-22 ND	$0.60	$1.80	$3.00	£0.40	£1.20	£2.00
23 ND scarce in the U.K. 7pg Steranko reprint of Our Love Story #5						
	$0.70	$2.10	$3.50	£0.50	£1.50	£2.50
24-37 ND	$0.60	$1.80	$3.00	£0.40	£1.20	£2.00
38-39 ND all reprint						
	$0.60	$1.80	$3.00	£0.40	£1.20	£2.00
Title Value:	$33.50	$100.50	$167.50	£20.90	£62.70	£104.50

MY LOVE SPECIAL
Marvel Comics Group; 1 Dec 1971

	$Good	$Fine	$N.Mint	£Good	£Fine	£N.Mint
1 ND scarce in the U.K. 52pgs						
	$1.00	$3.00	$5.00	£0.60	£1.80	£3.00
Title Value:	$1.00	$3.00	$5.00	£0.60	£1.80	£3.00

MY NAME IS CHAOS
DC Comics,MS; 1 Feb 1992-4 May 1992

	$Good	$Fine	$N.Mint	£Good	£Fine	£N.Mint
1 ND 48pgs, art by John Ridgway begins, script by Tom Veitch						
	$0.70	$2.10	$3.50	£0.50	£1.50	£2.50
2-4 ND 48pgs	$0.70	$2.10	$3.50	£0.50	£1.50	£2.50
Title Value:	$2.80	$8.40	$14.00	£2.00	£6.00	£10.00

MY NAME IS HOLOCAUST
DC Comics/Milestone,MS; 1 May 1995-5 Sep 1995

	$Good	$Fine	$N.Mint	£Good	£Fine	£N.Mint
1-5	$0.40	$1.20	$2.00	£0.25	£0.75	£1.25
Title Value:	$2.00	$6.00	$10.00	£1.25	£3.75	£6.25

MY OWN ROMANCE
Marvel Comics Group; 76 Jul 1960

(previous issues ND)

	$Good	$Fine	$N.Mint	£Good	£Fine	£N.Mint
76 rare in the U.K. though distributed in the U.K.						
	$2.30	$7.00	$14.00	£1.30	£4.00	£8.00
Title Value:	$2.30	$7.00	$14.00	£1.30	£4.00	£8.00

MY SECRET MARRIAGE
IW Super; 9 1964

	$Good	$Fine	$N.Mint	£Good	£Fine	£N.Mint
9 reprints; distributed in the U.K.						
	$0.65	$2.00	$4.00	£0.40	£1.25	£2.50
Title Value:	$0.65	$2.00	$4.00	£0.40	£1.25	£2.50

MYRON MOOSE FUNNIES
Fantagraphics; 1-3 1987

	$Good	$Fine	$N.Mint	£Good	£Fine	£N.Mint
1-3 ND	$0.25	$0.75	$1.25	£0.15	£0.45	£0.75
Title Value:	$0.75	$2.25	$3.75	£0.45	£1.35	£2.25

MYS-TECH WARS
Marvel UK,MS; 1 Mar 1993-4 Jun 1993

	$Good	$Fine	$N.Mint	£Good	£Fine	£N.Mint
1 MysTech Wars cross-over story begins; Nick Fury, Fantastic Four, X-Men, X-Force appear; Bryan Hitch and Jeff Anderson art						
	$0.25	$0.75	$1.25	£0.15	£0.45	£0.75
2 Nick Fury appears						
	$0.25	$0.75	$1.25	£0.15	£0.45	£0.75
3-4 Death's Head II appears						
	$0.25	$0.75	$1.25	£0.15	£0.45	£0.75
Title Value:	$1.00	$3.00	$5.00	£0.60	£1.80	£3.00

Note: story runs through Motormouth #9, Dark Angel #10, Death's Head II #5, Warheads #11, Dark Angel #11, Knights of Pendragon #12.

MYSTERIES OF UNEXPLORED WORLDS
Charlton; 1 Aug 1956-48 Sep 1965

	$Good	$Fine	$N.Mint	£Good	£Fine	£N.Mint
1 scarce in the U.K.	$25.00	$75.00	$175.00	£17.50	£52.50	£125.00
2	$10.50	$33.00	$65.00	£7.50	£22.50	£45.00
3-4 Steve Ditko art						
	$18.00	$55.00	$110.00	£12.50	£38.00	£75.00
5-6 Steve Ditko cover and art						
	$20.00	$60.00	$120.00	£13.00	£40.00	£80.00
7 64pgs, Steve Ditko art featured						
	$20.00	$60.00	$120.00	£13.00	£40.00	£80.00
8-9 Steve Ditko art						
	$18.00	$55.00	$110.00	£12.50	£38.00	£75.00
10-11 Steve Ditko cover and art						
	$20.00	$60.00	$120.00	£13.00	£40.00	£80.00
12 Steve Ditko art						
	$14.00	$43.00	$85.00	£9.00	£28.00	£55.00
13-17	$4.55	$13.50	$27.50	£2.90	£8.75	£17.50
18 1st appearance of The Watcher prototype (May 1960); a discovery courtesy of Jonathan Ross, this prototype appears three years before The Watcher in Fantastic Four #13						
	$5.00	$15.00	$30.00	£3.30	£10.00	£20.00
19 Steve Ditko art						
	$14.00	$43.00	$85.00	£9.00	£28.00	£55.00
20	$4.55	$13.50	$27.50	£2.90	£8.75	£17.50
21-24 Steve Ditko art						
	$14.00	$43.00	$85.00	£9.00	£28.00	£55.00
25	$4.55	$13.50	$27.50	£2.90	£8.75	£17.50
26 Steve Ditko art						
	$14.00	$43.00	$85.00	£9.00	£28.00	£55.00
27-30	$3.30	$10.00	$20.00	£2.05	£6.25	£12.50
31-45	$2.05	$6.25	$12.50	£1.25	£3.75	£7.50
46 origin and 1st appearance Son of Vulcan						
	$3.30	$10.00	$20.00	£2.05	£6.25	£12.50
47-48 Son of Vulcan						
	$2.05	$6.25	$12.50	£1.25	£3.75	£7.50
Title Value:	$393.70	$1194.75	$2410.00	£258.10	£789.25	£1587.50

Note: most issues distributed in the U.K.after 1958

MYSTERIOUS SUSPENSE
Charlton; 1 Oct 1968

	$Good	$Fine	$N.Mint	£Good	£Fine	£N.Mint
1 scarce, distributed in the U.K. The Question appears, Steve Ditko art						
	$5.25	$16.00	$32.50	£3.30	£10.00	£20.00
Title Value:	$5.25	$16.00	$32.50	£3.30	£10.00	£20.00

MYSTERY IN SPACE
National Periodical Publications/DC Comics; 1 Apr/May 1951-110 Sep 1966; 111 Sep 1980-117 Mar 1981

(see Adam Strange)

	$Good	$Fine	$N.Mint	£Good	£Fine	£N.Mint
1 Frazetta art (8pgs)						
	$275.00	$820.00	$2200.00	£180.00	£540.00	£1450.00
[Scarce in high grade – Very Fine+ or better]						
2	$120.00	$360.00	$850.00	£77.50	£235.00	£550.00
3	$100.00	$310.00	$725.00	£67.50	£200.00	£475.00
4-5	$77.50	$235.00	$550.00	£52.50	£160.00	£375.00
6-10	$62.50	$190.00	$450.00	£43.00	£125.00	£300.00
11-15	$43.00	$125.00	$300.00	£29.00	£85.00	£200.00
16-25	$39.00	$115.00	$275.00	£26.00	£77.50	£185.00
26 1st appearance Space Cabbie (ends #47)						
	$34.00	$100.00	$240.00	£22.50	£67.50	£160.00
27-40	$32.00	$95.00	$225.00	£21.00	£62.50	£150.00
41-52	$25.00	$75.00	$175.00	£16.00	£49.00	£115.00
53 Adam Strange series begins (see Showcase #17 for 1st appearance)						
	$140.00	$420.00	$1400.00	£90.00	£270.00	£900.00
1st official distribution in the U.K.						
54	$47.00	$140.00	$375.00	£31.00	£92.50	£250.00
55 Infantino Adam Strange begins; painted grey-tone cover						
	$41.00	$120.00	$320.00	£25.00	£75.00	£200.00
56-60	$22.50	$67.50	$180.00	£15.00	£45.00	£120.00
61 1st appearance Ulthoon						
	$21.00	$62.50	$150.00	£14.00	£43.00	£100.00
62 1st appearance Mortan						
	$21.00	$62.50	$150.00	£14.00	£43.00	£100.00
63 origin Vandor	$21.00	$62.50	$150.00	£14.00	£43.00	£100.00
64-65	$19.00	$57.50	$135.00	£10.50	£32.00	£75.00

	$Good	$Fine	$N.Mint	£Good	£Fine	£N.Mint
66 Star Rovers begin	$19.00	$57.50	$135.00	£10.50	£32.00	£75.00
67-70	$19.00	$57.50	$135.00	£10.50	£32.00	£75.00
71 last 10 cents issue	$19.00	$57.50	$135.00	£10.50	£32.00	£75.00
72-74	$12.50	$39.00	$90.00	£7.75	£23.50	£55.00
75 scarce in the U.K. Justice League of America X-over (story continues from Justice League of America #3)	$28.00	$82.50	$225.00	£18.50	£55.00	£150.00
76-80	$12.50	$39.00	$90.00	£7.00	£21.00	£50.00
81-86	$8.50	$26.00	$60.00	£5.00	£15.00	£35.00
87 Hawkman appears (pre Hawkman #1)	$23.50	$70.00	$190.00	£15.00	£45.00	£120.00
88 Hawkman appears (pre Hawkman #1)	$21.00	$62.50	$150.00	£11.00	£34.00	£80.00
89 Hawkman appears (pre Hawkman #1)	$20.00	$60.00	$140.00	£10.00	£30.00	£70.00
90 Hawkman appears (pre Hawkman #1 by one month), 1st Hawkman and Adam Strange team-up	$20.50	$60.00	$165.00	£12.50	£38.00	£100.00
91 last Infantino art on Adam Strange	$5.00	$15.00	$35.00	£2.85	£8.50	£20.00
92 Space Ranger begins	$5.00	$15.00	$35.00	£2.85	£8.50	£20.00
93	$5.00	$15.00	$35.00	£2.10	£6.25	£15.00
94 Adam Strange/Space Ranger team up	$5.00	$15.00	$35.00	£2.85	£8.50	£20.00
95-97	$5.00	$15.00	$35.00	£2.10	£6.25	£15.00
98 Adam Strange/Space Ranger team up	$5.00	$15.00	$35.00	£2.10	£6.25	£15.00
99-101	$5.00	$15.00	$35.00	£2.10	£6.25	£15.00
102 Adam Strange ends	$5.75	$17.50	$35.00	£2.50	£7.50	£15.00
103 origin Ultra the Multi-Alien, Space Ranger ends	$5.75	$17.50	$35.00	£2.90	£8.75	£17.50
104 last Silver Age issue, indicia-dated December 1965	$2.00	$6.00	$12.00	£1.65	£5.00	£10.00
105-110	$2.00	$6.00	$12.00	£1.00	£3.00	£6.00
111 Rogers art	$0.80	$2.40	$4.00	£0.40	£1.20	£2.00
112	$0.80	$2.40	$4.00	£0.25	£0.75	£1.25
113 Golden art	$0.80	$2.40	$4.00	£0.30	£0.90	£1.50
114 Steve Ditko art	$0.80	$2.40	$4.00	£0.30	£0.90	£1.50
115 Bolland, Cowan, Steve Ditko art	$0.80	$2.40	$4.00	£0.30	£0.90	£1.50
116 Von Eeden, Craig, Steve Ditko art	$0.80	$2.40	$4.00	£0.15	£0.90	£1.50
117	$0.80	$2.40	$4.00	£0.25	£0.75	£1.25
Title Value:	$3255.10	$9741.80	$23912.00	£2101.25	£6286.55	£15479.00

FEATURES

Adam Strange in 55-100, 102. Adam Strange/Space Ranger in 94, 98. Hawkman in 87-90. Space Ranger in 92-103. Ultra, the Multi-Alien in 103-110. Most issues have science fiction back-up features.

MYSTERY MAN, THE
Slave Labor; 1 Jul 1988-5 1988

	$Good	$Fine	$N.Mint	£Good	£Fine	£N.Mint
1-5 ND	$0.25	$0.75	$1.25	£0.15	£0.45	£0.75
Title Value:	$1.25	$3.75	$6.25	£0.75	£2.25	£3.75

MYSTERY PLAY, THE
DC Comics/Vertigo,OS; nn Apr 1994

	$Good	$Fine	$N.Mint	£Good	£Fine	£N.Mint
nn ND 80pgs, Hardcover graphic novel; Grant Morrison script, Jon J. Muth art	$4.00	$12.00	$20.00	£2.50	£7.50	£12.50
Title Value:	$4.00	$12.00	$20.00	£2.50	£7.50	£12.50

The Mystery Play Softcover Graphic Novel (Aug 1995)

				£Good	£Fine	£N.Mint
softcover version of the above with Jon J. Muth painted cover				£1.30	£3.90	£6.50

MYTH ADVENTURES
Warp/Apple; 1 1984-12 1986

	$Good	$Fine	$N.Mint	£Good	£Fine	£N.Mint
1-4 ND magazine size	$0.40	$1.20	$2.00	£0.25	£0.75	£1.25
5-12 ND	$0.40	$1.20	$2.00	£0.25	£0.75	£1.25
Title Value:	$4.80	$14.40	$24.00	£3.00	£9.00	£15.00

MYTH CONCEPTIONS
Apple Comics; 1 Summer 1987-7 1988

	$Good	$Fine	$N.Mint	£Good	£Fine	£N.Mint
1-7 ND	$0.40	$1.20	$2.00	£0.25	£0.75	£1.25
Title Value:	$2.80	$8.40	$14.00	£1.75	£5.25	£8.75

N

NAIVE INTER-DIMENSIONAL COMMANDO KOALAS
Independent Comics Group,OS; 1 Oct 1986

	$Good	$Fine	$N.Mint	£Good	£Fine	£N.Mint
1 ND Black Belt Hamsters cameo; black and white	$0.40	$1.20	$2.00	£0.25	£0.75	£1.25
Title Value:	$0.40	$1.20	$2.00	£0.25	£0.75	£1.25

NAM MAGAZINE, THE
Marvel Comics Group,Magazine; 1 Aug 1988-10 May 1989

	$Good	$Fine	$N.Mint	£Good	£Fine	£N.Mint
1 ND reprints from regular series begin	$0.40	$1.20	$2.00	£0.25	£0.75	£1.25
2-10 ND	$0.40	$1.20	$2.00	£0.25	£0.75	£1.25
Title Value:	$4.00	$12.00	$20.00	£2.50	£7.50	£12.50

Note: black and white reprints

NAM, THE
Marvel Comics Group; 1 Dec 1986-84 Sep 1993

	$Good	$Fine	$N.Mint	£Good	£Fine	£N.Mint
1 1st printing ND	$1.00	$3.00	$5.00	£0.70	£2.10	£3.50
1 2nd printing ND	$0.30	$0.90	$1.50	£0.20	£0.60	£1.00
2-5 ND	$0.60	$1.80	$3.00	£0.40	£1.20	£2.00
6-10 ND	$0.50	$1.50	$2.50	£0.30	£0.90	£1.50
11-48 ND	$0.30	$0.90	$1.50	£0.20	£0.60	£1.00
49-50 ND 3 part story	$0.30	$0.90	$1.50	£0.20	£0.60	£1.00
51 ND 3 part story	$0.25	$0.75	$1.25	£0.15	£0.45	£0.75
52-53 ND Punisher appears	$0.40	$1.20	$2.00	£0.20	£0.60	£1.00
54-58 ND The Death of Joe Hallen story	$0.25	$0.75	$1.25	£0.15	£0.45	£0.75
59-64 ND	$0.25	$0.75	$1.25	£0.15	£0.45	£0.75
65 ND $1.75 cover begins	$0.25	$0.75	$1.25	£0.15	£0.45	£0.75
66 ND	$0.25	$0.75	$1.25	£0.15	£0.45	£0.75
67-69 ND Punisher appears	$0.25	$0.75	$1.25	£0.15	£0.45	£0.75
70-74 ND	$0.25	$0.75	$1.25	£0.15	£0.45	£0.75
75 ND DS story of the My Lai Massacre	$0.25	$0.75	$1.25	£0.15	£0.45	£0.75
76-78 ND	$0.25	$0.75	$1.25	£0.15	£0.45	£0.75
79-81 ND Beginning of the End story; the 1968 TET Offensive, tryptych (ie 3-part) cover by Michael Golden	$0.25	$0.75	$1.25	£0.15	£0.45	£0.75
82-84 ND	$0.25	$0.75	$1.25	£0.15	£0.45	£0.75
Title Value:	$27.00	$81.00	$135.00	£17.20	£51.60	£86.00

Note: Limited series designed to last same length as Vietnam War, ie. about 10 years. It didn't.

Trade paperbacks:

				£Good	£Fine	£N.Mint
1 96pgs, reprints #1-4				£1.00	£3.00	£5.00
2nd print (Apr 1991)				£0.90	£2.70	£4.50
2 96pgs, reprints #5-8				£0.90	£2.70	£4.50
3 96pgs, reprints #9-12				£0.90	£2.70	£4.50

NAMOR
Marvel Comics Group; 1 Apr 1990-62 May 1995

	$Good	$Fine	$N.Mint	£Good	£Fine	£N.Mint
1 ND John Byrne script/art begins	$0.70	$2.10	$3.50	£0.50	£1.50	£2.50
2-3 ND	$0.50	$1.50	$2.50	£0.30	£0.90	£1.50
4 ND	$0.40	$1.20	$2.00	£0.25	£0.75	£1.25
5 ND Iron Man/Mr. Fantastic/Invisible Woman appear	$0.40	$1.20	$2.00	£0.25	£0.75	£1.25
6-7 ND	$0.30	$0.90	$1.50	£0.20	£0.60	£1.00
8 ND Iron Fist returns (cameo: not in costume)	$0.30	$0.90	$1.50	£0.20	£0.60	£1.00
9 ND	$0.30	$0.90	$1.50	£0.20	£0.60	£1.00
10 ND re-intro Iron Fist	$0.30	$0.90	$1.50	£0.20	£0.60	£1.00
11 ND	$0.30	$0.90	$1.50	£0.20	£0.60	£1.00
12 ND DS re-intro Invaders	$0.30	$0.90	$1.50	£0.20	£0.60	£1.00
13 ND Fantastic Four appear	$0.30	$0.90	$1.50	£0.20	£0.60	£1.00
14 ND	$0.30	$0.90	$1.50	£0.20	£0.60	£1.00
15 ND Iron Fist (Skrull in disguise) on last page	$0.30	$0.90	$1.50	£0.20	£0.60	£1.00
16 ND Iron Fist (Skrull) vs. Sub-Mariner	$0.30	$0.90	$1.50	£0.20	£0.60	£1.00
17-18 ND	$0.30	$0.90	$1.50	£0.20	£0.60	£1.00
19 ND Punisher appears	$0.30	$0.90	$1.50	£0.20	£0.60	£1.00
20 ND	$0.30	$0.90	$1.50	£0.20	£0.60	£1.00
21-22 ND Wolverine appears	$0.30	$0.90	$1.50	£0.20	£0.60	£1.00
23 ND Wolverine appears, Iron Fist cameo, $1.25 cover begins	$0.30	$0.90	$1.50	£0.20	£0.60	£1.00
24 ND Namor vs. Wolverine, Iron Fist and Dr. Strange appear	$0.30	$0.90	$1.50	£0.20	£0.60	£1.00
25 ND Wolverine appears	$0.30	$0.90	$1.50	£0.20	£0.60	£1.00
26 ND Iron Fist appears, 1st Jae Lee art	$1.00	$3.00	$5.00	£0.60	£1.80	£3.00
27 ND Jae Lee art	$0.60	$1.80	$3.00	£0.40	£1.20	£2.00
28 ND Jae Lee art	$0.50	$1.50	$2.50	£0.30	£0.90	£1.50
29 ND Iron Fist and Human Torch appear, Jae Lee art	$0.40	$1.20	$2.00	£0.25	£0.75	£1.25
30 ND Jae Lee art	$0.40	$1.20	$2.00	£0.25	£0.75	£1.25
31-32 ND Namor vs. Dr. Doom, Jae Lee art	$0.30	$0.90	$1.50	£0.20	£0.60	£1.00
33 ND Jae Lee art	$0.30	$0.90	$1.50	£0.20	£0.60	£1.00
34 ND Jae Lee art; last John Byrne script	$0.30	$0.90	$1.50	£0.20	£0.60	£1.00
35-36 ND Jae Lee art	$0.30	$0.90	$1.50	£0.20	£0.60	£1.00
37 ND Jae Lee art, holo-grafix foil cover	$0.40	$1.20	$2.00	£0.25	£0.75	£1.25
38-39 ND Jae Lee art	$0.25	$0.75	$1.25	£0.15	£0.45	£0.75
40 ND last Jae Lee art	$0.25	$0.75	$1.25	£0.15	£0.45	£0.75
41 ND Shawn McManus art begins	$0.25	$0.75	$1.25	£0.15	£0.45	£0.75
42 ND	$0.25	$0.75	$1.25	£0.15	£0.45	£0.75
43 ND Namor vs. Stingray	$0.25	$0.75	$1.25	£0.15	£0.45	£0.75
44 ND Glenn Herdling, Geoff Isherwood and Jeff Albrecht as new creative team	$0.25	$0.75	$1.25	£0.15	£0.45	£0.75

	$Good	$Fine	$N.Mint	£Good	£Fine	£N.Mint
45 ND	$0.25	$0.75	$1.25	£0.15	£0.45	£0.75
46-48 ND Starblast X-over						
49 ND Valentine's Day issue; Namorita, Invisible Woman, Andromeda appear						
	$0.25	$0.75	$1.25	£0.15	£0.45	£0.75
50 ND 48pgs, love affair between Namor and Sue Richards (Invisible Woman)						
	$0.40	$1.20	$2.00	£0.25	£0.75	£1.25
50 ND 48pgs, love affair between Namor and Sue Richards (Invisible Woman); silver cover overprinted with transparent inks; with free Spiderman's Amazing Powers card sheet						
	$0.60	$1.80	$3.00	£0.40	£1.20	£2.00
51 X-over Fantastic Four #389 and Fantastic Four Unlimited #6						
	$0.25	$0.75	$1.25	£0.15	£0.45	£0.75
52-53	$0.25	$0.75	$1.25	£0.15	£0.45	£0.75
54 Llyra gives birth to Namor's son						
	$0.25	$0.75	$1.25	£0.15	£0.45	£0.75
55-56	$0.25	$0.75	$1.25	£0.15	£0.45	£0.75
57 Captain America guest-stars						
	$0.25	$0.75	$1.25	£0.15	£0.45	£0.75
58-59 Namor vs. The Abomination						
	$0.25	$0.75	$1.25	£0.15	£0.45	£0.75
60-61	$0.25	$0.75	$1.25	£0.15	£0.45	£0.75
62 Atlantis Rising prelude; Namor vs. Triton						
	$0.25	$0.75	$1.25	£0.15	£0.45	£0.75
Title Value:	$20.60	$61.80	$103.00	£13.10	£39.30	£65.50

NAMOR ANNUAL
Marvel Comics Group; 1 Sep 1991-4 1994

	$Good	$Fine	$N.Mint	£Good	£Fine	£N.Mint
1 ND Subterranean Odyssey part 3, continued in Iron Man Annual #12						
	$0.50	$1.50	$2.50	£0.30	£0.90	£1.50
2 ND Return of the Defenders part 2, continued in Silver Surfer Annual #5						
	$0.50	$1.50	$2.50	£0.30	£0.90	£1.50
3 ND 64pgs, pre-bagged with trading card introducing Assassin						
	$0.60	$1.80	$3.00	£0.35	£1.05	£1.75
4 ND 64pgs	$0.60	$1.80	$3.00	£0.35	£1.05	£1.75
Title Value:	$2.20	$6.60	$11.00	£1.30	£3.90	£6.50

NATHANIEL DUSK
DC Comics,MS; 1 Feb 1984-4 May 1984

	$Good	$Fine	$N.Mint	£Good	£Fine	£N.Mint
1-4 ND Gene Colan art	$0.25	$0.75	$1.25	£0.15	£0.45	£0.75
Title Value:	$1.00	$3.00	$5.00	£0.60	£1.80	£3.00

Note: all Baxter paper

NATHANIEL DUSK II
DC Comics,MS; 1 Oct 1985-4 Jan 1986

	$Good	$Fine	$N.Mint	£Good	£Fine	£N.Mint
1-4 ND scarce in the U.K. Gene Colan art						
	$0.25	$0.75	$1.25	£0.15	£0.45	£0.75
Title Value:	$1.00	$3.00	$5.00	£0.60	£1.80	£3.00

Note: all Baxter paper

NATION OF SNITCHES
DC Comics/Piranha Press,OS; 1 Nov 1990

	$Good	$Fine	$N.Mint	£Good	£Fine	£N.Mint
1 ND Jon Hammer story/concept	$0.60	$1.80	$3.00	£0.40	£1.20	£2.00
Title Value:	$0.60	$1.80	$3.00	£0.40	£1.20	£2.00

NATURE OF THE BEAST
Caliber Press,MS; 1 May 1991-3 1991

	$Good	$Fine	$N.Mint	£Good	£Fine	£N.Mint
1-3 ND black and white	$0.40	$1.20	$2.00	£0.25	£0.75	£1.25
Title Value:	$1.20	$3.60	$6.00	£0.75	£2.25	£3.75

NAUSICAA OF THE VALLEY OF THE WIND
Viz Communications; 1 1988-7 1989

	$Good	$Fine	$N.Mint	£Good	£Fine	£N.Mint
1 ND 64pgs, squarebound begins, Hayau Miyazaki script/art; Moebius bound-in poster at front of book						
	$0.60	$1.80	$3.00	£0.40	£1.20	£2.00
2-7 ND	$0.60	$1.80	$3.00	£0.40	£1.20	£2.00

	$Good	$Fine	$N.Mint	£Good	£Fine	£N.Mint
Title Value:	$4.20	$12.60	$21.00	£2.80	£8.40	£14.00
Graphic Album #1-4 (1990)				£1.55	£4.65	£7.75
Graphic Novel 5 (1993)				£2.00	£6.00	£10.00
Graphic Novel 6 (May 1995)				£2.00	£6.00	£10.00
Nausicaa of the Valley of the Wind Perfect Collection 1 (May 1995) collects the first two volumes in one book				£2.40	£7.20	£12.00

NAUSICAA OF THE VALLEY OF THE WIND VOLUME 2
Viz Communications,MS; 1 1990-5 1991

	$Good	$Fine	$N.Mint	£Good	£Fine	£N.Mint
1-5 ND	$0.60	$1.80	$3.00	£0.40	£1.20	£2.00
Title Value:	$3.00	$9.00	$15.00	£2.00	£6.00	£10.00

NAUSICAA OF THE VALLEY OF THE WIND VOLUME 3
Viz Communications,MS; 1 Feb 1993-3 Apr 1993

	$Good	$Fine	$N.Mint	£Good	£Fine	£N.Mint
1-3 ND	$0.80	$2.40	$4.00	£0.50	£1.50	£2.50
Title Value:	$2.40	$7.20	$12.00	£1.50	£4.50	£7.50
Nausicaa of the Valley of Wind Perfect Collection 2 (Aug 1995) 284pgs, collects volumes 3 and 4				£2.40	£7.20	£12.00

NAUSICAA OF THE VALLEY OF WIND PART 4
Viz Communications,MS; 1 June 1994-5 Oct 1994

	$Good	$Fine	$N.Mint	£Good	£Fine	£N.Mint
1-5 ND Hayao Miyazaki; black and white						
	$0.60	$1.80	$3.00	£0.40	£1.20	£2.00
Title Value:	$3.00	$9.00	$15.00	£2.00	£6.00	£10.00

NAUSICAA VALLEY OF THE WIND PART 5
Viz Communications,MS; 1 Jul 1995-8 Feb 1996

	$Good	$Fine	$N.Mint	£Good	£Fine	£N.Mint
1 ND Hayao Miyazaki script and art; black and white						
	$0.50	$1.50	$2.50	£0.30	£0.90	£1.50
2-8 ND Hiyao Miyazaki script and art; black and white						
	$0.50	$1.50	$2.50	£0.30	£0.90	£1.50
Title Value:	$4.00	$12.00	$20.00	£2.40	£7.20	£12.00

NAVY WAR HEROES
Charlton; 1 Jan 1964-7 Mar/Apr 1965

	$Good	$Fine	$N.Mint	£Good	£Fine	£N.Mint
1 distributed in the U.K.	$1.30	$4.00	$8.00	£0.80	£2.50	£5.00
2-7 distributed in the U.K.	$0.50	$1.50	$3.00	£0.30	£1.00	£2.00
Title Value:	$4.30	$13.00	$26.00	£2.60	£8.50	£17.00

NAZA STONE AGE WARRIOR
Dell; 1 Jan/Mar 1965-9 Mar 1966

	$Good	$Fine	$N.Mint	£Good	£Fine	£N.Mint
1 painted cover	$2.90	$8.75	$17.50	£2.05	£6.25	£12.50
2-4 painted cover	$1.65	$5.00	$10.00	£1.15	£3.50	£7.00
5-8	$1.65	$5.00	$10.00	£1.15	£3.50	£7.00
9 dinosaur cover	$1.65	$5.00	$10.00	£1.15	£3.50	£7.00
Title Value:	$16.10	$48.75	$97.50	£11.25	£34.25	£68.50

Note: limited distribution on the news-stands in the U.K.

NAZRAT
Imperial/Eternity; 1 Dec 1987-6 1988

	$Good	$Fine	$N.Mint	£Good	£Fine	£N.Mint
1-4 ND	$0.30	$0.90	$1.50	£0.20	£0.60	£1.00
5-6 ND Eternity issues	$0.30	$0.90	$1.50	£0.20	£0.60	£1.00
Title Value:	$1.80	$5.40	$9.00	£1.20	£3.60	£6.00

NAZZ, THE
DC Comics,MS; 1 Oct 1990-4 Apr 1991

	$Good	$Fine	$N.Mint	£Good	£Fine	£N.Mint
1-4 ND 48pgs, Bryan Talbot art	$0.80	$2.40	$4.00	£0.50	£1.50	£2.50
Title Value:	$3.20	$9.60	$16.00	£2.00	£6.00	£10.00

Note: Mature Readers, Prestige Format. Delays occurred owing to production problems.

NEAR MYTHS
Rip Off Press,OS; 1 1990

	$Good	$Fine	$N.Mint	£Good	£Fine	£N.Mint
1 ND Trina Robbins script and art	$0.40	$1.20	$2.00	£0.25	£0.75	£1.25
Title Value:	$0.40	$1.20	$2.00	£0.25	£0.75	£1.25

My Greatest Adventure #69

Mystery in Space #76

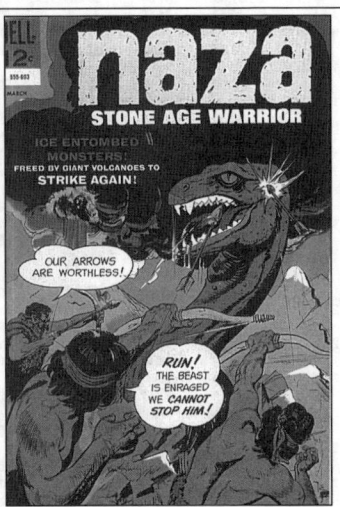

Naza, Stone Age Warrior #9

MINT = 100% / NEAR MINT (inc. +/-) = 90-99% / VERY FINE (inc. +/-) = 75-89% / FINE (inc. +/-) = 55-74%
VERY GOOD (inc. +/-) = 35-54% / GOOD (inc. +/-) = 15-34% / FAIR = 5-14% / POOR = 1-4%

475

NEAT STUFF
Fantagraphics,Magazine; 1 Jul 1985-15 1990

	$Good	$Fine	$N.Mint	£Good	£Fine	£N.Mint
1 ND scarce in the U.K. Bagge story/art begins; 8" x 11" black and white format begins	$1.50	$4.50	$7.50	£1.00	£3.00	£5.00
1 2nd printing ND	$0.60	$1.80	$3.00	£0.40	£1.20	£2.00
2 ND	$1.00	$3.00	$5.00	£0.70	£2.10	£3.50
2 2nd printing ND	$0.40	$1.20	$2.00	£0.25	£0.75	£1.25
3 ND	$0.60	$1.80	$3.00	£0.40	£1.20	£2.00
3 2nd printing, ND (Oct 1991)	$0.40	$1.20	$2.00	£0.25	£0.75	£1.25
4 ND	$0.60	$1.80	$3.00	£0.40	£1.20	£2.00
4 2nd printing, ND (Apr 1992)	$0.40	$1.20	$2.00	£0.25	£0.75	£1.25
5 ND	$0.60	$1.80	$3.00	£0.40	£1.20	£2.00
5 2nd printing, ND (Jul 1992)	$0.40	$1.20	$2.00	£0.25	£0.75	£1.25
6 ND	$0.50	$1.50	$2.50	£0.30	£0.90	£1.50
6 2nd printing, ND (Dec 1992)	$0.40	$1.20	$2.00	£0.25	£0.75	£1.25
7-9 ND	$0.50	$1.50	$2.50	£0.30	£0.90	£1.50
9 2nd printing, ND (Apr 1994)	$0.40	$1.20	$2.00	£0.25	£0.75	£1.25
10-12 ND	$0.50	$1.50	$2.50	£0.30	£0.90	£1.50
12 2nd printing, ND (Jun 1994)	$0.40	$1.20	$2.00	£0.25	£0.75	£1.25
13-15 ND	$0.50	$1.50	$2.50	£0.30	£0.90	£1.50
15 2nd printing, ND (Nov 1994)	$0.40	$1.20	$2.00	£0.25	£0.75	£1.25
Title Value:	$13.10	$39.30	$65.50	£8.30	£24.90	£41.50

Note: all Non-Distributed on the news-stands in the U.K.

	$Good	$Fine	$N.Mint	£Good	£Fine	£N.Mint
Best of Neat Stuff collection from #1-5, 128pgs				£2.00	£6.00	£10.00

NECROMANCER: SEASON OF THE WITCH
Innovation,MS; 1 May 1991-3 Jul 1991

	$Good	$Fine	$N.Mint	£Good	£Fine	£N.Mint
1-3 ND bi-weekly	$0.40	$1.20	$2.00	£0.25	£0.75	£1.25
Title Value:	$1.20	$3.60	$6.00	£0.75	£2.25	£3.75

NECROMANTRA/LORD PUMPKIN
Malibu Ultraverse,MS; 1 Apr 1995-4 Jul 1995

	$Good	$Fine	$N.Mint	£Good	£Fine	£N.Mint
1-4 ND 40pgs, flip-book format with two stories, Gabriel Gecko and Kyle Hotz art; Godwheel tie-in	$2.00	$1.50	$2.50	£0.30	£0.90	£1.50
Title Value:	$2.00	$6.00	$10.00	£1.20	£3.60	£6.00

NECROSCOPE
Malibu,MS; 1 Oct 1992-5 Aug 1993

	$Good	$Fine	$N.Mint	£Good	£Fine	£N.Mint
1 ND painted colour art by Daerick Gross begins	$0.60	$1.80	$3.00	£0.40	£1.20	£2.00
1 2nd printing, ND (Dec 1993) – skull hologram on cover	$0.50	$1.50	$2.50	£0.30	£0.90	£1.50
2-5 ND	$0.50	$1.50	$2.50	£0.30	£0.90	£1.50
Title Value:	$3.10	$9.30	$15.50	£1.90	£5.70	£9.50

Note: all Non-Distributed on the news-stands in the U.K.

	$Good	$Fine	$N.Mint	£Good	£Fine	£N.Mint
Necroscope Collection Softcover (Sep 1994)						
Trade paperback reprints mini-series				2.60	7.80	13.00

NECROSCOPE BOOK II: WAMPHYRI
Malibu,MS; 1 Aug 1993-present

	$Good	$Fine	$N.Mint	£Good	£Fine	£N.Mint
1-5 ND Dave Kendall art begins, 8" x 10" format	$0.50	$1.50	$2.50	£0.30	£0.90	£1.50
Title Value:	$2.50	$7.50	$12.50	£1.50	£4.50	£7.50

NEGATIVE BURN
Caliber Press; 1 1992-present

	$Good	$Fine	$N.Mint	£Good	£Fine	£N.Mint
1 ND black and white anthology begins	$0.50	$1.50	$2.50	£0.30	£0.90	£1.50
2 ND	$0.50	$1.50	$2.50	£0.30	£0.90	£1.50
3 ND Bone appears	$1.50	$4.50	$7.50	£1.00	£3.00	£5.00
4-8 ND	$0.50	$1.50	$2.50	£0.30	£0.90	£1.50
9-10 ND Alan Moore's "Songbook"	$0.50	$1.50	$2.50	£0.30	£0.90	£1.50
11 ND Bolland, Gaiman and Moore work featured; Moebius cover	$0.50	$1.50	$2.50	£0.30	£0.90	£1.50
12 ND Bolland, Gaiman and Moore work featured	$0.50	$1.50	$2.50	£0.30	£0.90	£1.50
13 ND 64pgs, Alan Moore's "Songbook" with Neil Gaiman art (!), Brian Bolland art; Strangers in Paradise story	$1.50	$4.50	$7.50	£1.00	£3.00	£5.00
14 ND 48pgs, Alan Moore's "Songbook", Michael T. Gilbert's Mr. Monster, Brian Bolland's Mr. Mamoulian all continue; Bob Burden Flaming Carrot cover	$0.50	$1.50	$2.50	£0.30	£0.90	£1.50
15-18 ND 48pgs, Alan Moore's "Songbook", Brian Bolland's Mr. Mamoulian both continue	$0.50	$1.50	$2.50	£0.30	£0.90	£1.50
19 ND 48pgs, Alan Moore's "Songbook", Brian Bolland's Mr. Mamoulian both continue and Flaming Carrot appears	$0.50	$1.50	$2.50	£0.30	£0.90	£1.50
20 ND 48pgs, Alan Moore's "Songbook", Brian Bolland's Mr. Mamoulian both continue	$0.50	$1.50	$2.50	£0.30	£0.90	£1.50
21 ND 48pgs, Brian Bolland's Mr. Mamoulian continues plus the return of Trollords	$0.50	$1.50	$2.50	£0.30	£0.90	£1.50
22 ND 48pgs, Brian Bolland's Mr. Mamoulian, Moebius painted cover	$0.50	$1.50	$2.50	£0.30	£0.90	£1.50
23 ND 40pgs, Brian Bolland's Mr. Mamoulian	$0.50	$1.50	$2.50	£0.30	£0.90	£1.50
24 ND 40pgs, Brian Bolland's Mr. Mamoulian, Mike Kaluta cover	$0.50	$1.50	$2.50	£0.30	£0.90	£1.50
25 ND 64pgs, Alan Moore and Dave Gibbons Songbook, Guy Davis' Baker Street and David Mack's Kabuki all feature	$0.60	$1.80	$3.00	£0.40	£1.20	£2.00
26 ND 48pgs, Alan Moore's Songbook and Brian Bolland's Mr. Mamoulian	$0.50	$1.50	$2.50	£0.30	£0.90	£1.50
27-29 ND Brian Bolland's Mr. Mamoulian	$0.50	$1.50	$2.50	£0.30	£0.90	£1.50
Title Value:	$16.60	$49.80	$83.00	£10.20	£30.60	£51.00

Negative Burn: Best of Year One (Feb 1995)

	$Good	$Fine	$N.Mint	£Good	£Fine	£N.Mint
Trade paperback 128pgs, collects best of the stories				£1.30	£3.90	£6.50

NEIL THE HORSE COMICS & STORIES
AV/Renegade; 1 Feb 1983-10 Dec 1984; 11 Apr 1985-15 1987?
(see Charlton Bullseye #2)

	$Good	$Fine	$N.Mint	£Good	£Fine	£N.Mint
1 ND Arn Saba script and art begins; black and white	$0.40	$1.20	$2.00	£0.25	£0.75	£1.25
1 2nd printing ND	$0.30	$0.90	$1.50	£0.20	£0.60	£1.00
2-10 ND	$0.30	$0.90	$1.50	£0.20	£0.60	£1.00
11 ND 1st Renegade issue	$0.30	$0.90	$1.50	£0.20	£0.60	£1.00
12-14 ND	$0.30	$0.90	$1.50	£0.20	£0.60	£1.00
15 ND double size	$0.20	$0.90	$1.50	£0.20	£0.60	£1.00
Title Value:	$5.20	$14.70	$24.50	£3.25	£9.75	£16.25

NEMESIS
A Plus Comics; 1 Sep 1991

	$Good	$Fine	$N.Mint	£Good	£Fine	£N.Mint
1 ND 48pgs, reprints ACG series, new Kurt Schaffenberger cover	$0.40	$1.20	$2.00	£0.25	£0.75	£1.25
Title Value:	$0.40	$1.20	$2.00	£0.25	£0.75	£1.25

NEOMEN
Slave Labor; 1 1987

	$Good	$Fine	$N.Mint	£Good	£Fine	£N.Mint
1 ND Cirocco layouts	$0.40	$1.20	$2.00	£0.25	£0.75	£1.25
Title Value:	$0.40	$1.20	$2.00	£0.25	£0.75	£1.25

NEON CITY
Innovation; 1 May 1991

	$Good	$Fine	$N.Mint	£Good	£Fine	£N.Mint
1 ND black and white	$0.40	$1.20	$2.00	£0.25	£0.75	£1.25
Title Value:	$0.40	$1.20	$2.00	£0.25	£0.75	£1.25

NEON CITY: AFTER THE FALL
Innovation; 1 Sep 1992

	$Good	$Fine	$N.Mint	£Good	£Fine	£N.Mint
1 ND	$0.40	$1.20	$2.00	£0.25	£0.75	£1.25
Title Value:	$0.40	$1.20	$2.00	£0.25	£0.75	£1.25

NEON KNIGHT
Now Comics; 1 Apr 1991

	$Good	$Fine	$N.Mint	£Good	£Fine	£N.Mint
1 ND	$0.40	$1.20	$2.00	£0.25	£0.75	£1.25
Title Value:	$0.40	$1.20	$2.00	£0.25	£0.75	£1.25
Direct Market Special (Apr 1991), reprints				£0.35	£1.05	£1.75

NERVOUS REX
Fantagraphics; 1 1985-10 1986?

	$Good	$Fine	$N.Mint	£Good	£Fine	£N.Mint
1 ND	$0.30	$0.90	$1.50	£0.20	£0.60	£1.00
1 2nd printing ND	$0.30	$0.90	$1.50	£0.20	£0.60	£1.00
2-10 ND	$0.30	$0.90	$1.50	£0.20	£0.60	£1.00
Title Value:	$3.30	$9.90	$16.50	£2.20	£6.60	£11.00
Graphic Novel (1986)				£0.50	£1.50	£2.50

NETHERWORLDS
Adventure; 1 Aug 1988-4 1988

	$Good	$Fine	$N.Mint	£Good	£Fine	£N.Mint
1-4 ND	$0.30	$0.90	$1.50	£0.20	£0.60	£1.00
Title Value:	$1.20	$3.60	$6.00	£0.80	£2.40	£4.00

NEUTRO
Dell; 1 Jan 1967

	$Good	$Fine	$N.Mint	£Good	£Fine	£N.Mint
1 rare in the U.K., though distributed in the U.K.	$3.30	$10.00	$20.00	£2.05	£6.25	£12.50
Title Value:	$3.30	$10.00	$20.00	£2.05	£6.25	£12.50

NEW ADVENTURE COMICS
(see Adventure Comics)

NEW ADVENTURES OF SUPERBOY, THE
(see Superboy)

NEW AMERICA
Eclipse,MS; 1 Nov 1987-4 Mar 1988
(see Scout)

	$Good	$Fine	$N.Mint	£Good	£Fine	£N.Mint
1-4 ND Scout spin-off	$0.40	$1.20	$2.00	£0.25	£0.75	£1.25
Title Value:	$1.60	$4.80	$8.00	£1.00	£3.00	£5.00

NEW COMICS
(see Adventure Comics)

NEW DNAGENTS
(see DNAgents)

NEW FRONTIER, THE
Dark Horse,MS; 1 Dec 1992-3 Feb 1993

	$Good	$Fine	$N.Mint	£Good	£Fine	£N.Mint
1-3 ND spin-off from Heavy Metal magazine	$0.50	$1.50	$2.50	£0.30	£0.90	£1.50
Title Value:	$1.50	$4.50	$7.50	£0.90	£2.70	£4.50

NEW FRONTIERS
Evolution Comics; 1,2 1991

	$Good	$Fine	$N.Mint	£Good	£Fine	£N.Mint
1 ND	$0.40	$1.20	$2.00	£0.25	£0.75	£1.25
1 2nd printing, ND Curt Swan cover	$0.30	$0.90	$1.50	£0.20	£0.60	£1.00
2 ND	$0.40	$1.20	$2.00	£0.25	£0.75	£1.25
2 2nd printing ND	$0.30	$0.90	$1.50	£0.20	£0.60	£1.00
Title Value:	$1.40	$4.20	$7.00	£0.90	£2.70	£4.50

NEW FUN COMICS
(see More Fun Comics)

NEW GODS, THE
DC Comics; 1 Feb/Mar 1971-11 Oct/Nov 1972; 12 Jul 1977-19 Jul/Aug 1978
(see Adventure Comics, First Issue Special, Super-Team Family)

1 Jack Kirby art begins, X-over Forever People #1, 1st full appearance Darkseid (see Forever People #1)

	$Good	$Fine	$N.Mint	£Good	£Fine	£N.Mint
	$7.00	$21.00	$50.00	£3.50	£10.50	£25.00

2 2nd full appearance Darkseid, Darkseid on cover

	$4.55	$13.50	$27.50	£2.50	£7.50	£15.00
3	$3.30	$10.00	$20.00	£2.05	£6.25	£12.50

4-5 52pgs, Joe Simon & Jack Kirby Manhunter reprints

| | $2.50 | $7.50 | $15.00 | £1.65 | £5.00 | £10.00 |

6 52pgs, Joe Simon & Jack Kirby Manhunter reprints

| | $2.50 | $7.50 | $15.00 | £1.25 | £3.75 | £7.50 |

7 52pgs, Joe Simon & Jack Kirby Manhunter reprints, part origin Darkseid

| | $2.50 | $7.50 | $15.00 | £1.25 | £3.75 | £7.50 |

8-9 52pgs, Joe Simon & Jack Kirby Manhunter reprints

	$2.50	$7.50	$15.00	£1.25	£3.75	£7.50
10	$2.05	$6.25	$12.50	£1.00	£3.00	£6.00

11 last Jack Kirby art

| | $2.05 | $6.25 | $12.50 | £1.00 | £3.00 | £6.00 |

12-19 scarce in the U.K.

	$1.50	$4.50	$7.50	£0.50	£1.50	£2.50
Title Value:	$45.95	$138.00	$272.50	£22.35	£67.25	£134.50

Note: 12-19 titled "Return of the New Gods" on cover only.
FEATURES
New Gods in all issues. Young Gods in 5,7,8.

NEW GODS, THE (2ND SERIES)
DC Comics; 1 Feb 1989-28 Jul 1991

| **1-6** | $0.30 | $0.90 | $1.50 | £0.20 | £0.60 | £1.00 |

7-10 Bloodline story

| | $0.30 | $0.90 | $1.50 | £0.20 | £0.60 | £1.00 |

11-12 Bloodline story

	$0.25	$0.75	$1.25	£0.15	£0.45	£0.75
13-24	$0.25	$0.75	$1.25	£0.15	£0.45	£0.75

25 Forever People guest-star

	$0.25	$0.75	$1.25	£0.15	£0.45	£0.75
26-28	$0.25	$0.75	$1.25	£0.15	£0.45	£0.75
Title Value:	$7.50	$22.50	$37.50	£4.70	£14.10	£23.50

Note: New Format

NEW GODS, THE (3RD SERIES)
DC Comics; 1 Oct 1995-present

1 Darkseid appears; Tom Peyer and Rachel Pollack script, Luke Ross and Brian Garvey art begins

| | $0.40 | $1.20 | $2.00 | £0.25 | £0.75 | £1.25 |

2-3 Darkseid appears

	$0.40	$1.20	$2.00	£0.25	£0.75	£1.25
4-6	$0.40	$1.20	$2.00	£0.25	£0.75	£1.25
Title Value:	$2.40	$7.20	$12.00	£1.50	£4.50	£7.50

NEW GODS, THE (LIMITED SERIES)
DC Comics,MS; 1 May 1984-6 Nov 1984

1 ND 48pgs, new Jack Kirby covers begin, reprints New Gods #1, #2; Darkseid cover

| | $0.50 | $1.50 | $2.50 | £0.30 | £0.90 | £1.50 |

2 ND 48pgs, reprints New Gods #3, #4

| | $0.50 | $1.50 | $2.50 | £0.30 | £0.90 | £1.50 |

3 ND 48pgs, reprints New Gods #5, #6

| | $0.50 | $1.50 | $2.50 | £0.30 | £0.90 | £1.50 |

4 ND 48pgs, reprints New Gods #7, #8

| | $0.50 | $1.50 | $2.50 | £0.30 | £0.90 | £1.50 |

5 ND 48pgs, reprints New Gods #9, #10

| | $0.50 | $1.50 | $2.50 | £0.30 | £0.90 | £1.50 |

6 ND 72pgs, scarce, new story and art by Jack Kirby (48pgs); reprints New Gods #11

	$0.50	$1.50	$2.50	£0.40	£1.20	£2.00
Title Value:	$3.00	$9.00	$15.00	£1.90	£5.70	£9.50

Note: all Baxter paper

NEW GUARDIANS, THE
DC Comics; 1 Oct 1988-12 Sep 1989
(see Millennium)

| **1** ND DS | $0.15 | $0.45 | $0.75 | £0.10 | £0.35 | £0.60 |
| **2-5** | $0.15 | $0.45 | $0.75 | £0.10 | £0.35 | £0.60 |

6-7 Invasion X-over

	$0.15	$0.45	$0.75	£0.10	£0.35	£0.60
8-12	$0.15	$0.45	$0.75	£0.10	£0.35	£0.60
Title Value:	$1.80	$5.40	$9.00	£1.20	£4.20	£7.20

Note: Deluxe Format, Mando paper

NEW HUMANS
Pied Piper; 1 Jul 1987-3 1987

1-2 ND Ex-Mutants spin-off, Ron Lim cover and art

| | $0.40 | $1.20 | $2.00 | £0.25 | £0.75 | £1.25 |

3 ND Ex-Mutants spin-off, Jack Snider and Jeff Dee art

	$0.40	$1.20	$2.00	£0.25	£0.75	£1.25
Title Value:	$1.20	$3.60	$6.00	£0.75	£2.25	£3.75

NEW HUMANS (2ND SERIES)
Eternity; 1 Dec 1987-15 1989

1-3 40pgs, reprints Pied Piper material, black and white

| | $0.40 | $1.20 | $2.00 | £0.25 | £0.75 | £1.25 |

4 40pgs, all new material begins; sub-titled "The Shattered Earth Chronicles"

	$0.40	$1.20	$2.00	£0.25	£0.75	£1.25
5-10 40pgs	$0.40	$1.20	$2.00	£0.25	£0.75	£1.25
11-15 40pgs	$0.30	$0.90	$1.50	£0.20	£0.60	£1.00
Title Value:	$5.50	$16.50	$27.50	£3.50	£10.50	£17.50

Note: all Non-Distributed on the news-stands in the U.K.

NEW HUMANS ANNUAL
Eternity; 1 Jan 1989

1 ND 60pgs, squarebound, black and white

	$0.50	$1.50	$2.50	£0.30	£0.90	£1.50
Title Value:	$0.50	$1.50	$2.50	£0.30	£0.90	£1.50

NEW MUTANTS
Marvel Comics Group; 1 Mar 1983-100 Apr 1991

(see Fallen Angels, Marvel Graphic Novel, Marvel Team Up #100 and Annual #6, Mutant Summer Fun, Rom Annual #2, Spellbound #4, Web of Spiderman Annual #2)

1 ND	$1.20	$3.60	$6.00	£0.80	£2.40	£4.00
2-5 very LD	$0.60	$1.80	$3.00	£0.40	£1.20	£2.00
6	$0.50	$1.50	$2.50	£0.30	£0.90	£1.50
7 LD in the U.K.	$0.50	$1.50	$2.50	£0.40	£1.20	£2.00
8-13	$0.50	$1.50	$2.50	£0.30	£0.90	£1.50

14 LD in the U.K. X-over X-Men #180

| | $0.50 | $1.50 | $2.50 | £0.40 | £1.20 | £2.00 |

15-16 LD in the U.K.

| | $0.50 | $1.50 | $2.50 | £0.40 | £1.20 | £2.00 |

17 LD in the U.K. Sienkiewicz cover (with June Brigman)

| | $0.50 | $1.50 | $2.50 | £0.40 | £1.20 | £2.00 |

18 1st Sienkiewicz art (ends #38), 1st New Mutants cybernetic Warlock (no relation to Adam Warlock), 1st full Sienkiewicz cover

| | $1.50 | $4.50 | $7.50 | £0.70 | £2.10 | £3.50 |

19 2nd Sienkiewicz art

| | $0.90 | $2.70 | $4.50 | £0.60 | £1.80 | £3.00 |

20 Sienkiewicz art

| | $0.60 | $1.80 | $3.00 | £0.40 | £1.20 | £2.00 |

21 DS Sienkiewicz art

| | $1.00 | $3.00 | $5.00 | £0.70 | £2.10 | £3.50 |

22 Nightcrawler and Cyclops appear; Sienkiewicz art

| | $0.50 | $1.50 | $2.50 | £0.30 | £0.90 | £1.50 |

23 Cloak & Dagger, Nightcrawler and Cyclops appear, Sienkiewicz art

| | $0.50 | $1.50 | $2.50 | £0.30 | £0.90 | £1.50 |

24 Cloak & Dagger appear, Sienkiewicz art

| | $0.50 | $1.50 | $2.50 | £0.30 | £0.90 | £1.50 |

25 1st appearance Legion (cameo), Sienkiewicz art

| | $1.50 | $4.50 | $7.50 | £0.80 | £2.40 | £4.00 |

26 1st full appearance Legion, Sienkiewicz art

| | $1.60 | $4.80 | $8.00 | £1.00 | £3.00 | £5.00 |

27 1st appearance Legion in costume, Sienkiewicz art

| | $0.90 | $2.70 | $4.50 | £0.60 | £1.80 | £3.00 |

28 origin of Legion, Sienkiewicz art

| | $0.90 | $2.70 | $4.50 | £0.60 | £1.80 | £3.00 |

29 1st appearance Guido, Sienkiewicz art; ties into Secret Wars II #1

| | $0.50 | $1.50 | $2.50 | £0.30 | £0.90 | £1.50 |

30 Secret Wars II X-over, Dazzler appears; Sienkiewicz art

| | $0.50 | $1.50 | $2.50 | £0.30 | £0.90 | £1.50 |

31 LD in the U.K. Sienkiewicz cover

| | $0.50 | $1.50 | $2.50 | £0.30 | £0.90 | £1.50 |

32-33 LD in the U.K. Storm appears

| | $0.40 | $1.20 | $2.00 | £0.25 | £0.75 | £1.25 |

34 LD in the U.K. X-over New Mutants Special Edition, Storm appears

| | $0.40 | $1.20 | $2.00 | £0.25 | £0.75 | £1.25 |

35 LD in the U.K. Sienkiewicz inks

| | $0.40 | $1.20 | $2.00 | £0.25 | £0.75 | £1.25 |

36-37 LD in the U.K. Secret Wars X-over, Sienkiewicz inks

| | $0.40 | $1.20 | $2.00 | £0.30 | £0.90 | £1.50 |

38 LD in the U.K. Sienkiewicz inks

| | $0.40 | $1.20 | $2.00 | £0.25 | £0.75 | £1.25 |

39 LD in the U.K. Sienkiewicz cover

| | $0.40 | $1.20 | $2.00 | £0.25 | £0.75 | £1.25 |

40 LD in the U.K. Magneto vs. Avengers

	$0.40	$1.20	$2.00	£0.30	£0.90	£1.50
41-42	$0.30	$0.90	$1.50	£0.20	£0.60	£1.00

43 Whilce Portacio inks

	$0.30	$0.90	$1.50	£0.20	£0.60	£1.00
44 Legion appears	$0.30	$0.90	$1.50	£0.20	£0.60	£1.00
45	$0.30	$0.90	$1.50	£0.20	£0.60	£1.00

46 X-Men appear, Mutant Massacre tie-in

	$0.40	$1.20	$2.00	£0.25	£0.75	£1.25
47-49	$0.30	$0.90	$1.50	£0.20	£0.60	£1.00
50 DS	$0.50	$1.50	$2.50	£0.30	£0.90	£1.50

51 Kevin Nowlan art

| | $0.40 | $1.20 | $2.00 | £0.25 | £0.75 | £1.25 |

52 Sienkiewicz cover

	$0.30	$0.90	$1.50	£0.20	£0.60	£1.00
53-56	$0.30	$0.90	$1.50	£0.20	£0.60	£1.00

57 Kevin Nowlan art

	$0.30	$0.90	$1.50	£0.20	£0.60	£1.00
58	$0.30	$0.90	$1.50	£0.20	£0.60	£1.00

59 ND Fall of the Mutants begins

| | $0.60 | $1.80 | $3.00 | £0.40 | £1.20 | £2.00 |

60 DS, Fall of the Mutants

| | $0.50 | $1.50 | $2.50 | £0.30 | £0.90 | £1.50 |

61 Fall of the Mutants

| | $0.40 | $1.20 | $2.00 | £0.25 | £0.75 | £1.25 |

62 Jon J. Muth art, Miller cover

| | $0.30 | $0.90 | $1.50 | £0.20 | £0.60 | £1.00 |

63 X-Men/Wolverine appear (clones)

	$0.50	$1.50	$2.50	£0.30	£0.90	£1.50
64-70	$0.30	$0.90	$1.50	£0.20	£0.60	£1.00

71-72 LD in the U.K. Inferno x-over

| | $0.40 | $1.20 | $2.00 | £0.25 | £0.75 | £1.25 |

73 LD in the U.K. DS Inferno x-over

	$0.50	$1.50	$2.50	£0.30	£0.90	£1.50
74	$0.30	$0.90	$1.50	£0.20	£0.60	£1.00

75 Sabretooth appears, John Byrne art

| | $0.50 | $1.50 | $2.50 | £0.25 | £0.75 | £1.25 |

76 X-Factor, X-Terminators appear

| | $0.40 | $1.20 | $2.00 | £0.25 | £0.75 | £1.25 |

	$Good	$Fine	$N.Mint	£Good	£Fine	£N.Mint
77	$0.30	$0.90	$1.50	£0.20	£0.60	£1.00
78 Dr. Strange appears	$0.30	$0.90	$1.50	£0.20	£0.60	£1.00
79-82	$0.30	$0.90	$1.50	£0.20	£0.60	£1.00
83-85 Acts of Vengeance tie-in	$0.30	$0.90	$1.50	£0.20	£0.60	£1.00
86 Acts of Vengeance tie-in, Rob Liefeld art begins, Cable appears in last panel though un-named	$2.00	$6.00	$10.00	£1.20	£3.60	£6.00
87 1st appearance Cable, Rob Liefeld art	$5.00	$15.00	$25.00	£1.50	£4.50	£7.50
87 2nd printing, ND Jan 1991, metallic ink cover	$0.45	$1.35	$2.25	£0.30	£0.90	£1.50
88 Rob Liefeld art, 2nd appearance Cable	$2.40	$7.00	$12.00	£1.00	£3.00	£5.00
89 Rob Liefeld art	$1.50	$4.50	$7.50	£1.00	£3.00	£5.00
90-91 Sabretooth appears, Rob Liefeld art	$1.50	$4.50	$7.50	£1.00	£3.00	£5.00
92 Rob Liefeld cover only (not interior art)	$0.70	$2.10	$3.50	£0.50	£1.50	£2.50
93-94 Wolverine vs. Cable, Rob Liefeld art	$1.50	$4.50	$7.50	£1.00	£3.00	£5.00
95 The X-Tinction Agenda part 2 (see X-Men #270 for start of story), death of New Mutants' Warlock, Rob Liefeld art	$1.50	$4.50	$7.50	£1.00	£3.00	£5.00
95 ND The X-Tinction Agenda part 2 (2nd print – gold cover)	$0.70	$2.10	$3.50	£0.40	£1.20	£2.00
96 The X-Tinction Agenda part 5, Rob Liefeld art	$1.20	$3.60	$6.00	£0.80	£2.40	£4.00
97 The X-Tinction Agenda part 8, Wolverine appears, Rob Liefeld cover	$1.20	$3.60	$6.00	£0.80	£2.40	£4.00
98 1st appearance Deadpool, Rob Liefeld art	$1.50	$4.50	$7.50	£1.00	£3.00	£5.00
99 LD in the U.K. 1st appearance Feral, Rob Liefeld art	$1.50	$4.50	$7.50	£1.00	£3.00	£5.00
100 48pgs, Cable assembles X-Force..(see X-Force #1), Rob Liefeld art	$1.50	$4.50	$7.50	£0.80	£2.40	£4.00
100 ND 48pgs, (2nd print – Aug 1990, gold cover)	$0.60	$1.80	$3.00	£0.40	£1.20	£2.00
100 3rd printing, ND 48pgs, (silver cover)	$0.55	$1.65	$2.75	£0.35	£1.05	£1.75
Title Value:	$68.70	$205.90	$343.50	£42.10	£126.30	£210.50
Demon Bear (1991),						
Trade paperback reprints, new Sienkiewicz cover				£1.00	£3.00	£5.00
2nd print (Sep 1992), new cover by Bill Sienkiewicz				£1.20	£3.60	£6.00

NEW MUTANTS ANNUAL, THE
Marvel Comics Group; 1 1984-7 1991

	$Good	$Fine	$N.Mint	£Good	£Fine	£N.Mint
1 ND	$0.90	$2.70	$4.50	£0.60	£1.80	£3.00
2 ND Captain Britain and Psylocke (1st appearance) by Davis/Neary (pre Excalibur #1)	$1.00	$3.00	$5.00	£0.70	£2.10	£3.50
3 ND Davis/Neary art	$0.50	$1.50	$2.50	£0.30	£0.90	£1.50
4 ND 64pgs, Evolutionary War	$0.50	$1.50	$2.50	£0.30	£0.90	£1.50
5 ND squarebound, Atlantis Attacks part 9, 1st Rob Liefeld art on New Mutants	$1.20	$3.60	$6.00	£0.80	£2.40	£4.00
6 ND Days of Future Past/Present story, Cable appears, Rob Liefeld art; 1st appearance Shatterstar (cameo)	$0.50	$1.50	$2.50	£0.30	£0.90	£1.50
7 ND Kings of Pain part 1, continued in New Warriors Annual #1	$0.50	$1.50	$2.50	£0.30	£0.90	£1.50
Title Value:	$5.10	$15.30	$25.50	£3.30	£9.90	£16.50

NEW MUTANTS ONE-SHOT
Marvel Comics Group,OS; nn Oct 1994

	$Good	$Fine	$N.Mint	£Good	£Fine	£N.Mint
nn ND 48pgs, reprints Marvel Graphic Novel #4	$1.00	$3.00	$5.00	£0.70	£2.10	£3.50
Title Value:	$1.00	$3.00	$5.00	£0.70	£2.10	£3.50

NEW MUTANTS SPECIAL
Marvel Comics Group,OS; 1 1985

	$Good	$Fine	$N.Mint	£Good	£Fine	£N.Mint
1 ND 60pgs, Art Adams art, ties in with X-Men/Alpha Flight MS, X-Men Annual #9	$1.00	$3.00	$5.00	£0.70	£2.10	£3.50
Title Value:	$1.00	$3.00	$5.00	£0.70	£2.10	£3.50

NEW ORDER HANDBOOK
Image,OS; nn Feb 1995

	$Good	$Fine	$N.Mint	£Good	£Fine	£N.Mint
nn ND guide to Image titles cover-dated february 1995; "New Order" is an attempt at tighter continuity and a jumping-on point for new readers	$0.30	$0.90	$1.50	£0.20	£0.60	£1.00
Title Value:	$0.30	$0.90	$1.50	£0.20	£0.60	£1.00

NEW TALENT SHOWCASE
DC Comics; 1 Jan 1984-19 Oct 1985
(Talent Showcase #16 on)

	$Good	$Fine	$N.Mint	£Good	£Fine	£N.Mint
1-3 Scott Hampton art	$0.15	$0.45	$0.75	£0.10	£0.30	£0.50
4-17 features new strips and artists	$0.15	$0.45	$0.75	£0.10	£0.30	£0.50
18 Williamson cover	$0.15	$0.45	$0.75	£0.10	£0.30	£0.50
19 features new strips and artists	$0.15	$0.45	$0.75	£0.10	£0.30	£0.50
Title Value:	$2.85	$8.55	$14.25	£1.90	£5.70	£9.50

Note: Direct Sales only therefore not distributed on the news-stands in the U.K.

NEW TEEN TITANS (1ST SERIES)
DC Comics; 1 Nov 1980-91 Jul 1988
(see Best of DC 18, Tales of the Teen Titans/New Teen Titans, Teen Titans, The New Titans, Marvel and DC present) (becomes Tales of the Teen Titans with issue #41)

	$Good	$Fine	$N.Mint	£Good	£Fine	£N.Mint
1 part origin	$2.00	$6.00	$10.00	£1.20	£3.60	£6.00
2 1st appearance Deathstroke the Terminator	$2.00	$6.00	$10.00	£1.20	£3.60	£6.00
3 scarce in the U.K. origin Starfire	$1.00	$3.00	$5.00	£0.70	£2.10	£3.50
4 scarce in the U.K. origin Starfire, Justice League of America X-over, Batman appears (see note below)	$1.00	$3.00	$5.00	£0.70	£2.10	£3.50
5	$0.60	$1.80	$3.00	£0.40	£1.20	£2.00
6 origin Raven	$0.80	$2.40	$4.00	£0.50	£1.50	£2.50
7 origin Cyborg	$0.80	$2.40	$4.00	£0.50	£1.50	£2.50
8 origin Kid Flash re-told	$0.80	$2.40	$4.00	£0.50	£1.50	£2.50
9 2nd appearance Deathstroke the Terminator	$1.00	$3.00	$5.00	£0.70	£2.10	£3.50
10 origin Changeling re-told, 3rd appearance of Deathstroke	$1.50	$4.50	$7.50	£0.60	£1.80	£3.00
11-12	$0.50	$1.50	$2.50	£0.40	£1.20	£2.00
13 very LD Captain Zahl, Madame Rouge appear, Robotman revived	$0.50	$1.50	$2.50	£0.50	£1.50	£2.50
14 LD in the U.K. origin Doom Patrol retold	$0.50	$1.50	$2.50	£0.30	£0.90	£1.50
15 very LD Captain Zahl, Madam Rouge die	$0.70	$2.10	$3.50	£0.40	£1.20	£2.00
16 52pgs, 1st appearance Captain Carrot in 16pg insert	$0.50	$1.50	$2.50	£0.30	£0.90	£1.50
17-18	$0.50	$1.50	$2.50	£0.30	£0.90	£1.50
19 Hawkman X-over	$0.50	$1.50	$2.50	£0.30	£0.90	£1.50
20	$0.50	$1.50	$2.50	£0.30	£0.90	£1.50
21 1st appearance Brother Blood, 1st appearance of The Monitor from Crisis on Infinite Earths (cameo - see G.I. Combat #274), 1st Night Force in 16pg insert	$0.40	$1.20	$2.00	£0.25	£0.75	£1.25
22	$0.40	$1.20	$2.00	£0.25	£0.75	£1.25
23 1st appearance Vigilante (no costume), Blackfire appears	$0.40	$1.20	$2.00	£0.25	£0.75	£1.25
24 Omega Men X-over	$0.40	$1.20	$2.00	£0.25	£0.75	£1.25
25 Omega Men cameo	$0.40	$1.20	$2.00	£0.25	£0.75	£1.25
26	$0.40	$1.20	$2.00	£0.25	£0.75	£1.25
27 1st appearance Atari Force in 16pg insert	$0.40	$1.20	$2.00	£0.25	£0.75	£1.25
28 1st appearance Terra	$0.50	$1.50	$2.50	£0.30	£0.90	£1.50
29 New Brotherhood of Evil, Speedy appears	$0.40	$1.20	$2.00	£0.25	£0.75	£1.25
30 Terra joins team	$0.40	$1.20	$2.00	£0.25	£0.75	£1.25
31-33	$0.40	$1.20	$2.00	£0.25	£0.75	£1.25
34 Deathstroke appears	$0.45	$1.35	$2.25	£0.30	£0.90	£1.50
35-36	$0.40	$1.20	$2.00	£0.25	£0.75	£1.25
37 X-over Batman and the Outsiders #5	$0.40	$1.20	$2.00	£0.25	£0.75	£1.25
38 origin Wonder Girl	$0.40	$1.20	$2.00	£0.25	£0.75	£1.25
39 last appearance Dick Grayson as Robin the Boy Wonder	$0.40	$1.20	$2.00	£0.25	£0.75	£1.25
40-41	$0.40	$1.20	$2.00	£0.25	£0.75	£1.25
42 "Judas Contract" story	$0.40	$1.20	$2.00	£0.25	£0.75	£1.25
43 "Judas Contract" story (note: some copies badly mis-cut in production process)	$0.40	$1.20	$2.00	£0.25	£0.75	£1.25
44 "Judas Contract" story continues in Annual #3; origin Terminator (see issue #2 for 1st appearance)	$0.40	$1.20	$2.00	£0.25	£0.75	£1.25
45	$0.40	$1.20	$2.00	£0.25	£0.75	£1.25
46 Aqualad, Aquagirl join	$0.40	$1.20	$2.00	£0.25	£0.75	£1.25
47	$0.40	$1.20	$2.00	£0.25	£0.75	£1.25
48 vs "The RECOMbatants" (unofficial DNAgents X-over)	$0.40	$1.20	$2.00	£0.25	£0.75	£1.25
49	$0.40	$1.20	$2.00	£0.25	£0.75	£1.25
50 DS, Wonder Girl (Donna Troy) weds	$0.50	$1.50	$2.50	£0.30	£0.90	£1.50
51-52	$0.30	$0.90	$1.50	£0.20	£0.60	£1.00
53 1st appearance Azreal (not to be confused with the Jean-Paul Valley character who becomes Azrael and dons the Batman costume)	$0.30	$0.90	$1.50	£0.20	£0.60	£1.00
54-55	$0.30	$0.90	$1.50	£0.20	£0.60	£1.00
56 1st appearance Jinx	$0.30	$0.90	$1.50	£0.20	£0.60	£1.00
57-58	$0.30	$0.90	$1.50	£0.20	£0.60	£1.00
59 reprints 1st appearance (from DC Presents #26)	$0.30	$0.90	$1.50	£0.20	£0.60	£1.00
60 reprints from Baxter (2nd) series begin	$0.25	$0.75	$1.25	£0.15	£0.45	£0.75
61-91 all reprints	$0.25	$0.75	$1.25	£0.15	£0.45	£0.75
Title Value:	$39.65	$118.95	$198.25	£24.75	£74.25	£123.75

Note: issue 4 often has ink-marks on the cover; see Batman 208, Superman 207. Perez art 1-4, 6-34, 37-47,49,50.

NEW TEEN TITANS (1ST SERIES) ANNUAL
DC Comics; 1 Nov 1982-4 1985

	$Good	$Fine	$N.Mint	£Good	£Fine	£N.Mint

(becomes Tales of the Teen Titans Annual with issue #3)

1 48pgs, George Perez art; Omega Men X-over
| | $0.40 | $2.00 | | £0.25 | £0.75 | £1.25 |

2 48pgs, George Perez art; 1st Vigilante in costume
| | $0.50 | $2.50 | | £0.30 | £0.90 | £1.50 |

3 LD in the U.K. 48pgs, "Judas Contract" story continues from issue #44 (1st Series)
| | $0.50 | $1.50 | $2.50 | £0.40 | £1.20 | £2.00 |

4 48pgs, reprints New Teen Titans Annual #1
| | $0.50 | $1.50 | $2.50 | £0.30 | £0.90 | £1.50 |

Title Value: | $1.90 | $5.70 | $9.50 | £1.25 | £3.75 | £6.25 |

NEW TEEN TITANS (2ND SERIES)
DC Comics; 1 Aug 1984-49 Nov 1988
(becomes The New Titans)

1 George Perez cover and art
| | $0.90 | $2.70 | $4.50 | £0.60 | £1.80 | £3.00 |

2-3 George Perez cover and art
| | $0.60 | $1.80 | $3.00 | £0.40 | £1.20 | £2.00 |

4-5 George Perez cover and art
| | $0.50 | $1.50 | $2.50 | £0.30 | £0.90 | £1.50 |

6 | $0.40 | $1.20 | $2.00 | £0.25 | £0.75 | £1.25 |

7 origin Lilith | $0.40 | $1.20 | $2.00 | £0.25 | £0.75 | £1.25 |

8 1st appearance Kole (later killed in Crisis on Infinite Earths)
| | $0.40 | $1.20 | $2.00 | £0.25 | £0.75 | £1.25 |

9-12 | $0.40 | $1.20 | $2.00 | £0.25 | £0.75 | £1.25 |

13-14 Crisis X-over
| | $0.40 | $1.20 | $2.00 | £0.25 | £0.75 | £1.25 |

15 | $0.40 | $1.20 | $2.00 | £0.25 | £0.75 | £1.25 |

16 Omega Men X-over
| | $0.40 | $1.20 | $2.00 | £0.25 | £0.75 | £1.25 |

17-18 | $0.40 | $1.20 | $2.00 | £0.25 | £0.75 | £1.25 |

19 George Perez cover
| | $0.40 | $1.20 | $2.00 | £0.25 | £0.75 | £1.25 |

20 George Perez cover; old Titans appear
| | $0.40 | $1.20 | $2.00 | £0.25 | £0.75 | £1.25 |

21-23 George Perez cover
| | $0.40 | $1.20 | $2.00 | £0.25 | £0.75 | £1.25 |

24-36 | $0.40 | $1.20 | $2.00 | £0.25 | £0.75 | £1.25 |

37 1st $1.75 issue | $0.40 | $1.20 | $2.00 | £0.25 | £0.75 | £1.25 |

38 Infinity Inc. appear
| | $0.40 | $1.20 | $2.00 | £0.25 | £0.75 | £1.25 |

39 LD in the U.K. | $0.40 | $1.20 | $2.00 | £0.30 | £0.90 | £1.50 |

40 Mike Collins art
| | $0.40 | $1.20 | $2.00 | £0.25 | £0.75 | £1.25 |

41-43 | $0.40 | $1.20 | $2.00 | £0.25 | £0.75 | £1.25 |

44 old Doom Patrol cameo, Collins art
| | $0.40 | $1.20 | $2.00 | £0.25 | £0.75 | £1.25 |

45-46 | $0.40 | $1.20 | $2.00 | £0.25 | £0.75 | £1.25 |

47 Titans' origins retold
| | $0.40 | $1.20 | $2.00 | £0.25 | £0.75 | £1.25 |

48-49 | $0.40 | $1.20 | $2.00 | £0.25 | £0.75 | £1.25 |

Title Value: | $20.70 | $62.10 | $103.50 | £13.05 | £39.15 | £65.25 |

Note: all Deluxe Format Baxter paper, all ND. Perez art 1-5, 19-23; Dan Jurgens 6; Garcia Lopez 7-11

Trade paperback, reprints The Judas Contract
from issues #42-44, Annual #3. Also reprints issues #39-41. | | | | £1.20 | £3.60 | £6.00 |

NEW TEEN TITANS (2ND SERIES) ANNUAL
DC Comics; 1 Sep 1985-4 1988
(becomes New Titans Annual)

1 ND 48pgs, Superman, new Brainiac appear, 1st appearance Vanguard
| | $0.50 | $1.50 | $2.50 | £0.30 | £0.90 | £1.50 |

2 ND 64pgs, John Byrne cover/art, Jim Baikie, Garcia Lopez art, origin Brother Blood, intro new Dr. Light
| | $0.60 | $1.80 | $3.00 | £0.40 | £1.20 | £2.00 |

3 ND 48pgs, 1st appearance Godiva, Mike Collins art
| | $0.50 | $1.50 | $2.50 | £0.30 | £0.90 | £1.50 |

4 ND 48pgs, George Perez cover
| | $0.50 | $1.50 | $2.50 | £0.30 | £0.90 | £1.50 |

Title Value: | $2.10 | $6.30 | $10.50 | £1.30 | £3.90 | £6.50 |

NEW TEEN TITANS DRUG AWARENESS CAMPAIGN
Keebler/DC Comics; nn Nov 1983-3 1985

nn George Perez art; white cover, Nancy Reagan foreword, intro The Protector (see note below)
| | $0.40 | $1.20 | $2.00 | £0.25 | £0.75 | £1.25 |

2 ND scarce in the U.K. blue cover, Mando paper
| | $0.50 | $1.50 | $2.50 | £0.30 | £0.90 | £1.50 |

3 ND very scarce in the U.K. orange cover, Mando paper
| | $0.50 | $1.50 | $2.50 | £0.40 | £1.20 | £2.00 |

Title Value: | $1.40 | $4.20 | $7.00 | £0.95 | £2.85 | £4.75 |

Note: These drug-propaganda comics were sponsored by Keebler, but after completion of the artwork it was discovered that Robin was licensed to Nabisco, a rival company. He was therefore re-drawn throughout (with no explanation) as "The Protector". Owing to the comics' intended distribution in schools, Starfire's costume was also re-designed to cover her cleavage.

NEW TEEN TITANS, TALES OF THE
DC Comics, MS; 1 Jun 1982-4 Sep 1982

1 origin Cyborg | $0.30 | $0.90 | $1.50 | £0.20 | £0.60 | £1.00 |

2 origin Raven | $0.30 | $0.90 | $1.50 | £0.20 | £0.60 | £1.00 |

3 origin Changeling
| | $0.30 | $0.90 | $1.50 | £0.20 | £0.60 | £1.00 |

4 origin Starfire | $0.30 | $0.90 | $1.50 | £0.20 | £0.60 | £1.00 |

Title Value: | $1.20 | $3.60 | $6.00 | £0.80 | £2.40 | £4.00 |

Note: Perez art in #1,2,4.

NEW TITANS
DC Comics; 0 Oct 1994; 50 Dec 1988-130 Feb 1996
(formerly The New Teen Titans [2nd Series])

0 (Oct 1994) Zero Hour X-over, new team formation
| | $0.40 | $1.20 | $2.00 | £0.25 | £0.75 | £1.25 |

50 LD in the U.K. George Perez art
| | $0.90 | $2.70 | $4.50 | £0.60 | £1.80 | £3.00 |

51 LD in the U.K. George Perez art
| | $0.60 | $1.80 | $3.00 | £0.40 | £1.20 | £2.00 |

52-59 George Perez art
| | $0.50 | $1.50 | $2.50 | £0.30 | £0.90 | £1.50 |

60-61 LD in the U.K. X-over with Batman #440-442 (Tim Drake/new Robin story)
| | $0.80 | $2.40 | $4.00 | £0.40 | £1.20 | £2.00 |

62-64 George Perez art
| | $0.40 | $1.20 | $2.00 | £0.25 | £0.75 | £1.25 |

65 Tim Drake Robin and Batman appear
| | $0.40 | $1.20 | $2.00 | £0.25 | £0.75 | £1.25 |

66-69 | $0.40 | $1.20 | $2.00 | £0.25 | £0.75 | £1.25 |

70 Terminator appears
| | $0.40 | $1.20 | $2.00 | £0.25 | £0.75 | £1.25 |

71 48pgs, New Titans anniversary story begins
| | $0.50 | $1.50 | $2.50 | £0.30 | £0.90 | £1.50 |

72 Aqualad appears; Golden Eagle dies
| | $0.40 | $1.20 | $2.00 | £0.25 | £0.75 | £1.25 |

73-79 | $0.40 | $1.20 | $2.00 | £0.25 | £0.75 | £1.25 |

80 1st new line up from New Titans Annual 7
| | $0.40 | $1.20 | $2.00 | £0.25 | £0.75 | £1.25 |

81 War of the Gods tie-in
| | $0.40 | $1.20 | $2.00 | £0.25 | £0.75 | £1.25 |

82 | $0.40 | $1.20 | $2.00 | £0.25 | £0.75 | £1.25 |

83 Jericho vs. Deathstroke the Terminator; death of Jericho
| | $0.40 | $1.20 | $2.00 | £0.25 | £0.75 | £1.25 |

84 death of Raven | $0.40 | $1.20 | $2.00 | £0.25 | £0.75 | £1.25 |

85 Aquaman guest stars

New Gods (Limited) #6

New Mutants #60

Next Men #1

	$Good	$Fine	$N.Mint	£Good	£Fine	£N.Mint
	$0.40	$1.20	$2.00	£0.25	£0.75	£1.25
86	$0.40	$1.20	$2.00	£0.25	£0.75	£1.25
87 Superman and Deathstroke appear	$0.40	$1.20	$2.00	£0.25	£0.75	£1.25
88-89	$0.40	$1.20	$2.00	£0.25	£0.75	£1.25
90 Total Chaos part 2, continued in Team Titans #1	$0.40	$1.20	$2.00	£0.25	£0.75	£1.25
91 Total Chaos part 5, continued in Team Titans #2	$0.40	$1.20	$2.00	£0.25	£0.75	£1.25
92 Total Chaos part 8, continued in Team Titans #3	$0.40	$1.20	$2.00	£0.25	£0.75	£1.25
93 Titans Sell-Out part 3, continued in Team Titans #4	$0.40	$1.20	$2.00	£0.25	£0.75	£1.25
94-96 Patriot Games story, triptych cover (one part of three that join together)	$0.40	$1.20	$2.00	£0.25	£0.75	£1.25
97 The Darkening part 1	$0.40	$1.20	$2.00	£0.25	£0.75	£1.25
98	$0.40	$1.20	$2.00	£0.25	£0.75	£1.25
99 Nightwing proposes to Starfire	$0.40	$1.20	$2.00	£0.25	£0.75	£1.25
100 48pgs, the wedding of Nightwing and Starfire, foil holografix cover, former Teen Titans guest-star	$0.70	$2.10	$3.50	£0.45	£1.35	£2.25
101 Nightwing and Starfire leave team	$0.40	$1.20	$2.00	£0.25	£0.75	£1.25
102-103	$0.40	$1.20	$2.00	£0.25	£0.75	£1.25
104-107 Terminus: The Fate of Cyborg story, bi-weekly	$0.40	$1.20	$2.00	£0.25	£0.75	£1.25
108 Supergirl, Flash, Lex Luthor and Sarge Steel appear	$0.40	$1.20	$2.00	£0.25	£0.75	£1.25
109	$0.40	$1.20	$2.00	£0.25	£0.75	£1.25
110 Flash and Sarge Steel guest-star	$0.40	$1.20	$2.00	£0.25	£0.75	£1.25
111-113	$0.40	$1.20	$2.00	£0.25	£0.75	£1.25
114 X-over with Damage #6	$0.40	$1.20	$2.00	£0.25	£0.75	£1.25
115 continued in Green Lantern #57	$0.40	$1.20	$2.00	£0.25	£0.75	£1.25
116 continued from Green Lantern #57	$0.40	$1.20	$2.00	£0.25	£0.75	£1.25
117-118	$0.40	$1.20	$2.00	£0.25	£0.75	£1.25
119 continued in Showcase '95 #2	$0.40	$1.20	$2.00	£0.25	£0.75	£1.25
120-121	$0.40	$1.20	$2.00	£0.25	£0.75	£1.25
122 The Crimelord/Syndicate War part 2, continued in Darkstars #32	$0.40	$1.20	$2.00	£0.25	£0.75	£1.25
123	$0.40	$1.20	$2.00	£0.25	£0.75	£1.25
124 The Siege of Zi Charam part 1, continued in Green Lantern #65	$0.40	$1.20	$2.00	£0.25	£0.75	£1.25
125 48pgs, The Siege of Zi Charam part 5 (conclusion); wraparound cover	$0.80	$2.40	$4.00	£0.50	£1.50	£2.50
126-128 Meltdown story	$0.45	$1.35	$2.25	£0.30	£0.90	£1.50
129	$0.45	$1.35	$2.25	£0.30	£0.90	£1.50
130 Meltdown conclusion, George Perez cover	$0.45	$1.35	$2.25	£0.30	£0.90	£1.50
Title Value:	$36.15	$108.45	$179.75	£22.45	£67.35	£112.25

Note: Deluxe Format

NEW TITANS ANNUAL
DC Comics; 5 Aug 1989-11 1996
(formerly New Teen Titans Annual [2nd Series] #1-4)

	$Good	$Fine	$N.Mint	£Good	£Fine	£N.Mint
5 48pgs, George Perez cover	$0.60	$1.80	$3.00	£0.40	£1.20	£2.00
6 48pgs, Grindberg/Cullins/Swan art	$0.60	$1.80	$3.00	£0.40	£1.20	£2.00
7 64pgs, Armageddon: 2001 tie-in	$0.60	$1.80	$3.00	£0.40	£1.20	£2.00
8 64pgs, Eclipso: The Darkness Within tie-in	$0.60	$1.80	$3.00	£0.40	£1.20	£2.00
9 64pgs, Bloodlines part 5, 1st appearance Anima, continued in Superman Annual #5	$0.60	$1.80	$3.00	£0.40	£1.20	£2.00
10 64pgs, Elseworlds story; Marv Wolfman script	$0.60	$1.80	$3.00	£0.40	£1.20	£2.00
11 64pgs, Year One	$0.60	$1.80	$3.00	£0.40	£1.20	£2.00
Title Value:	$4.20	$12.60	$21.00	£2.80	£8.40	£14.00

Note: Deluxe Format

NEW TRIUMPH
Matrix Graphics; 1 Sep 1984-6 1988

	$Good	$Fine	$N.Mint	£Good	£Fine	£N.Mint
1 ND	$0.40	$1.20	$2.00	£0.25	£0.75	£1.25
1 2nd printing, ND ($1.75 cover)	$0.40	$1.20	$2.00	£0.25	£0.75	£1.25
2-6 ND	$0.40	$1.20	$2.00	£0.25	£0.75	£1.25
Title Value:	$2.80	$8.40	$14.00	£1.75	£5.25	£8.75
Annual 1				£0.40	£1.20	£2.00

NEW TRIUMPH FEATURING NORTHGUARD
Matrix Graphics; 1,2 1985

	$Good	$Fine	$N.Mint	£Good	£Fine	£N.Mint
1-2 ND black and white; Canadian independent comic	$0.30	$0.90	$1.50	£0.20	£0.60	£1.00
Title Value:	$0.60	$1.80	$3.00	£0.40	£1.20	£2.00

NEW WARRIORS
Marvel Comics Group; 1 Jul 1990-present

	$Good	$Fine	$N.Mint	£Good	£Fine	£N.Mint
1 ND Night Thrasher, Namorita, Nova, Marvel Boy, Firestar, Speedball begin	$1.20	$3.60	$6.00	£1.50	£4.50	£7.50
1 2nd printing, ND (Jul 1991, gold ink cover)	$0.80	$2.40	$4.00	£0.50	£1.50	£2.50
2 ND	$1.00	$3.00	$5.00	£1.00	£3.00	£5.00
3 ND	$0.80	$2.40	$4.00	£0.80	£2.40	£4.00
4-5 ND	$0.80	$2.40	$4.00	£0.60	£1.80	£3.00
6 ND Inhumans appear	$0.60	$1.80	$3.00	£0.50	£1.50	£2.50
7 ND Punisher appears	$0.60	$1.80	$3.00	£0.50	£1.50	£2.50
8-9 ND Punisher appears	$0.60	$1.80	$3.00	£0.40	£1.20	£2.00
10 ND	$0.60	$1.80	$3.00	£0.40	£1.20	£2.00
11-13 ND Forever Yesterday story	$0.50	$1.50	$2.50	£0.30	£0.90	£1.50
14 Namor and Darkhawk appear	$0.50	$1.50	$2.50	£0.30	£0.90	£1.50
15	$0.50	$1.50	$2.50	£0.30	£0.90	£1.50
16 Fantastic Four appear	$0.30	$0.90	$1.50	£0.20	£0.60	£1.00
17 Silver Surfer, Fantastic Four appear	$0.30	$0.90	$1.50	£0.20	£0.60	£1.00
18	$0.30	$0.90	$1.50	£0.20	£0.60	£1.00
19 New Warriors vs. Gideon, new facts about group's origin	$0.30	$0.90	$1.50	£0.20	£0.60	£1.00
20	$0.30	$0.90	$1.50	£0.20	£0.60	£1.00
21	$0.25	$0.75	$1.25	£0.15	£0.45	£0.75
22 Darkhawk and Rage appear	$0.25	$0.75	$1.25	£0.15	£0.45	£0.75
23-24	$0.25	$0.75	$1.25	£0.15	£0.45	£0.75
25 DS, Rage and Darkhawk appear, die-cut cover	$0.60	$1.80	$3.00	£0.40	£1.20	£2.00
26 Rage joins New Warriors	$0.25	$0.75	$1.25	£0.15	£0.45	£0.75
27 Infinity War X-over	$0.25	$0.75	$1.25	£0.15	£0.45	£0.75
28 1st appearance Turbo	$0.25	$0.75	$1.25	£0.15	£0.45	£0.75
29-30	$0.25	$0.75	$1.25	£0.15	£0.45	£0.75
31 X-Force appear	$0.25	$0.75	$1.25	£0.15	£0.45	£0.75
32 Spiderman, Archangel and Dr. Strange appear	$0.25	$0.75	$1.25	£0.15	£0.45	£0.75
33 Cloak and Dagger, Darkhawk appear	$0.25	$0.75	$1.25	£0.15	£0.45	£0.75
34 Spiderman, Avengers, Thing, Torch and Darkhawk appear; concluded in New Warriors Annual #3	$0.25	$0.75	$1.25	£0.15	£0.45	£0.75
35-37	$0.25	$0.75	$1.25	£0.15	£0.45	£0.75
38 ties in to Night Thrasher #1 (on-going series)	$0.25	$0.75	$1.25	£0.15	£0.45	£0.75
39	$0.25	$0.75	$1.25	£0.15	£0.45	£0.75
40 Firelord, Air-Walker and Super-Nova appear	$0.25	$0.75	$1.25	£0.15	£0.45	£0.75
40 ND Direct Market Edition — gold foil enhanced cover	$0.45	$1.35	$2.25	£0.30	£0.90	£1.50
41-42	$0.25	$0.75	$1.25	£0.15	£0.45	£0.75
43 Marvel Boy returns	$0.25	$0.75	$1.25	£0.15	£0.45	£0.75
44	$0.25	$0.75	$1.25	£0.15	£0.45	£0.75
45 X-over with X-Force #32	$0.25	$0.75	$1.25	£0.15	£0.45	£0.75
46 X-Force appear	$0.25	$0.75	$1.25	£0.15	£0.45	£0.75
47 with free Spiderman vs. Venom card sheet	$0.25	$0.75	$1.25	£0.15	£0.45	£0.75
48-49	$0.25	$0.75	$1.25	£0.15	£0.45	£0.75
50 ND Direct Market Edition — 48pgs, glow-in-the-dark cover	$0.60	$1.80	$3.00	£0.40	£1.20	£2.00
50 Newstand edition 48pgs	$0.40	$1.20	$2.00	£0.25	£0.75	£1.25
51-56	$0.30	$0.90	$1.50	£0.20	£0.60	£1.00
57 Sub-Mariner appears	$0.30	$0.90	$1.50	£0.20	£0.60	£1.00
58-59	$0.30	$0.90	$1.50	£0.20	£0.60	£1.00
60 48pgs, Nova Omega part 2 continued from Nova #18	$0.45	$1.35	$2.25	£0.30	£0.90	£1.50
61 Scarlet Spider joins the team; continued in Spectacular Spiderman #227	$0.30	$0.90	$1.50	£0.20	£0.60	£1.00
62 Maximum Clonage tie-in	$0.30	$0.90	$1.50	£0.20	£0.60	£1.00
63-64 bi-weekly	$0.30	$0.90	$1.50	£0.20	£0.60	£1.00
65 Scarlet Spider appears	$0.30	$0.90	$1.50	£0.20	£0.60	£1.00
66	$0.30	$0.90	$1.50	£0.20	£0.60	£1.00
67 continued from Web of Scarlet Spider #3 and concluded in Web of Scarlet Spider #4	$0.30	$0.90	$1.50	£0.20	£0.60	£1.00
68-69 Future Shock part 1, New Warriors vs. Guardians of the Galaxy	$0.30	$0.90	$1.50	£0.20	£0.60	£1.00
Title Value:	$27.30	$81.90	$136.50	£19.15	£57.45	£95.75
New Warriors Trade paperback (Aug 1992) reprints Thor #411, #412 and New Warriors #1-4, new cover by Mark Bagley				£1.40	£4.20	£7.00

NEW WARRIORS ANNUAL
Marvel Comics Group; 1 Jul 1991-present

1 ND Kings of Pain part 2, feature on origins of New Warriors, Cable and X-force appear

VERY GENERAL PERCENTAGE CONVERSION CHART WHICH MAY BE USED TO CALCULATE LOW AND INBETWEEN GRADES:

	$Good	$Fine	$N.Mint	£Good	£Fine	£N.Mint
	$0.90	$2.70	$4.50	£0.60	£1.80	£3.00

2 ND 64pgs, The Hero Killers part 4, continued from Web of Spiderman Annual #8, Spiderman appears

	$0.50	$1.50	$2.50	£0.30	£0.90	£1.50

3 ND 64pgs, pre-bagged with trading card; Spiderman, Archangel, Cloak & Darkhawk appear

	$0.60	$1.80	$3.00	£0.40	£1.20	£2.00
4 ND 64pgs	$0.60	$1.80	$3.00	£0.40	£1.20	£2.00
Title Value:	$2.60	$7.80	$13.00	£1.70	£5.10	£8.50

NEW WARRIORS ASHCAN EDITION
Marvel Comics Group; nn Aug 1994
nn ND 16pgs, black and white featuring a shorter history of the New Warriors

	$0.25	$0.75	$1.25	£0.15	£0.45	£0.75
Title Value:	$0.25	$0.75	$1.25	£0.15	£0.45	£0.75

NEW WAVE
Eclipse; 1 Jun 1986-14 Apr 1987
1 ND 16pgs, 50¢ cover, bi-weekly; Lee Weeks/Ty Templeton art begins, colour

	$0.25	$0.75	$1.25	£0.15	£0.45	£0.75

1 ND as above with corrected pages that were originally spoiled after printing

	$0.15	$0.45	$0.75	£0.10	£0.30	£0.50
2-4 ND	$0.25	$0.75	$1.25	£0.15	£0.45	£0.75

5 ND origin New Wave Team concludes (begun in #1), Paul Gulacy cover

	$0.25	$0.75	$1.25	£0.15	£0.45	£0.75
6-8 ND	$0.25	$0.75	$1.25	£0.15	£0.45	£0.75

9 ND 1st monthly issue, $1.50 cover

	$0.25	$0.75	$1.25	£0.15	£0.45	£0.75
10-14 ND	$0.25	$0.75	$1.25	£0.15	£0.45	£0.75
Title Value:	$3.65	$10.95	$18.25	£2.20	£6.60	£11.00

NEW WAVE VS THE VOLUNTEERS 3-D
Eclipse; 1 Apr 1987-2 Jun 1987
1-2 ND glasses included (25% less if without glasses)

	$0.40	$1.20	$2.00	£0.25	£0.75	£1.25
Title Value:	$0.80	$2.40	$4.00	£0.50	£1.50	£2.50

NEW YORK WORLD'S FAIR
National Periodical Publications; 1 1939-2 1940
1 very scarce in the U.S. rare in the U.K. produced for the World's Fair; features Superman (only time with blond hair as depicted on cover) and 1st published appearance of the Golden Age Sandman prior to Adventure Comics #40; about 120 extant copies exist

	$2250.00	$6750.00	$22500.00	£1500.00	£4500.00	£15000.00

[Very Rare in high grade – Very Fine+ or better]

2 scarce in the U.K. Superman, Batman and Robin appear (1st time ever together on cover only and can be regarded as a forerunner of World's Best #1 that appeared about 15 months later), Hourman appears

	$1250.00	$3750.00	$12500.00	£850.00	£2550.00	£8500.00
Title Value:	$3500.00	$10450.00	$35000.00	£2350.00	£7050.00	£23500.00

Note: not distributed on the news-stands in the U.K. and no copies known with British pence stamps. It is possible that there are copies to discover in the U.K. as there was a heavy official British presence at the 1939 World's Fair – search those attics!

NEW YORK: YEAR ZERO
Eclipse,MS; 1 Aug 1988-3 Oct 1988

	$Good	$Fine	$N.Mint	£Good	£Fine	£N.Mint
1-3 ND	$0.40	$1.20	$2.00	£0.25	£0.75	£1.25
Title Value:	$1.20	$3.60	$6.00	£0.75	£2.25	£3.75

NEWMAN
Legacy Comics,OS; 1 1991
1 ND black and white

	$0.40	$1.20	$2.00	£0.25	£0.75	£1.25
Title Value:	$0.40	$1.20	$2.00	£0.25	£0.75	£1.25

NEWMEN
Image; 1 Apr 1994-present
1 Rob Liefeld amd Eric Stephenson co-plot, Jeff Matsuda and Jonathan Sibal art; 1st appearance Newmen

	$0.50	$1.50	$2.50	£0.30	£0.90	£1.50
2-3	$0.40	$1.20	$2.00	£0.25	£0.75	£1.25

4 guest-stars Ripclaw

	$0.40	$1.20	$2.00	£0.25	£0.75	£1.25

5 Newmen and Ripclaw vs. Ikonn

	$0.40	$1.20	$2.00	£0.25	£0.75	£1.25
6-7	$0.40	$1.20	$2.00	£0.25	£0.75	£1.25

8-9 New Blood story

	$0.40	$1.20	$2.00	£0.25	£0.75	£1.25

10 Extreme Sacrifice part 4, continued in Team Youngblood #17; pre-bagged with trading card

	$0.40	$1.20	$2.00	£0.25	£0.75	£1.25
11-19	$0.45	$1.35	$2.25	£0.30	£0.90	£1.50

20 Extreme Babewatch

	$0.50	$1.50	$2.50	£0.30	£0.90	£1.50
Title Value:	$8.65	$25.95	$43.25	£5.55	£16.65	£27.75

Note: all Non-Distributed on the news-stands in the U.K.

NEWSTIME – THE LIFE AND DEATH OF THE MAN OF STEEL
DC Comics,Magazine OS; 1 May 1993
1 ND magazine based on Newsweek-type with features and interviews following Superman: Doomsday

	$0.60	$1.80	$3.00	£0.40	£1.20	£2.00
Title Value:	$0.60	$1.80	$3.00	£0.40	£1.20	£2.00

NEWSTRALIA
Innovation; 1 Jul 1989
1 ND 3pgs layouts by Tim Truman

	$0.30	$0.90	$1.50	£0.20	£0.60	£1.00
Title Value:	$0.30	$0.90	$1.50	£0.20	£0.60	£1.00

NEXT MAN
Comico; 1 Mar 1985-5 Oct 1985

	$Good	$Fine	$N.Mint	£Good	£Fine	£N.Mint
1-5 ND	$0.40	$1.20	$2.00	£0.25	£0.75	£1.25
Title Value:	$2.00	$6.00	$10.00	£1.25	£3.75	£6.25

NEXT MEN
Dark Horse; 0 Apr 1992; 1 Jan 1992-30 Dec 1994
0 (Apr 1992), reprints stories in Dark Horse Presents #54-57 in colour, new cover by John Byrne

	$1.00	$3.00	$5.00	£0.70	£2.10	£3.50

1 John Byrne script and art begins, silver foil embossed (red) cover

	$1.00	$3.00	$5.00	£0.70	£2.10	£3.50

1 2nd printing, (blue cover)

	$0.60	$1.80	$3.00	£0.40	£1.20	£2.00
2	$0.60	$1.80	$3.00	£0.40	£1.20	£2.00
3-18	$0.50	$1.50	$2.50	£0.30	£0.90	£1.50
19-22 Faith story	$0.50	$1.50	$2.50	£0.30	£0.90	£1.50
23-26 Power story	$0.50	$1.50	$2.50	£0.30	£0.90	£1.50
27-30 Lies story	$0.50	$1.50	$2.50	£0.30	£0.90	£1.50
Title Value:	$17.20	$51.60	$86.00	£10.60	£31.80	£53.00

Note: all Non-Distributed on the news-stands in the U.K.

John Byrne's Next Men Collection (Mar 1993)

	£Good	£Fine	£N.Mint
Softcover, reprints #0-6 with new painted cover	£2.00	£6.00	£10.00
Hardcover with dust-jacket	£3.50	£10.50	£17.50

John Byrne's Next Men Collection 2 (1993)

	£Good	£Fine	£N.Mint
Trade paperback reprints issues #7-12	£2.00	£6.00	£10.00

John Byrne's Next Men: Fame (Oct 1994)

	£Good	£Fine	£N.Mint
Trade paperback reprints issues #13-18, Gary Cody cover	£2.20	£6.60	£11.00

John Byrne's Next Men: Faith (Jan 1995)

	£Good	£Fine	£N.Mint
Trade paperback reprints issues #19-22, Gary Cody cover	£2.00	£6.00	£10.00

John Byrne's Next Men: Power (Mar 1995) Trade paperback

	£Good	£Fine	£N.Mint
reprints #1-4 of Next Men: Power, Gary Cody painted cover	£2.00	£6.00	£10.00

NEXT NEXUS
First,MS; 1 Jan 1989-4 Apr 1989
1-4 ND Steve Rude art

	$0.40	$1.20	$2.00	£0.25	£0.75	£1.25
Title Value:	$1.60	$4.80	$8.00	£1.00	£3.00	£5.00

NEXUS (1ST SERIES)
Capital,Magazine; 1 Mar 1981-3 Oct 1982
1 ND scarce in the U.K.

	$2.00	$6.00	$10.00	£2.00	£6.00	£10.00

2 ND scarce in the U.K.

	$1.50	$4.50	$7.50	£1.50	£4.50	£7.50

3 ND includes the first flex-disc in comics

	$1.00	$3.00	$5.00	£1.00	£3.00	£5.00
Title Value:	$4.50	$13.50	$22.50	£4.50	£13.50	£22.50

Nexus Book One Trade paperback, reprints #1-3 — £1.50 £4.50 £7.50

NEXUS (2ND SERIES)
Capital/First; 1 May 1983-80 Feb 1991

	$Good	$Fine	$N.Mint	£Good	£Fine	£N.Mint
1	$0.70	$2.10	$3.50	£0.50	£1.50	£2.50
2	$0.50	$1.50	$2.50	£0.40	£1.20	£2.00
3 scarce in the U.K.	$0.50	$1.50	$2.50	£0.50	£1.50	£2.50
4-5	$0.50	$1.50	$2.50	£0.40	£1.20	£2.00
6 last Capital issue	$0.50	$1.50	$2.50	£0.40	£1.20	£2.00
7-10	$0.50	$1.50	$2.50	£0.40	£1.20	£2.00
11-20	$0.40	$1.20	$2.00	£0.30	£0.90	£1.50
21-49	$0.40	$1.20	$2.00	£0.25	£0.75	£1.25

50 bookshelf format, Crossroads X-over

	$0.80	$2.40	$4.00	£0.50	£1.50	£2.50
51-80	$0.40	$1.20	$2.00	£0.25	£0.75	£1.25
Title Value:	$33.60	$100.80	$168.00	£22.45	£67.35	£112.25

Note: all Non-Distributed on the news-stands in the U.K.
Nexus Book One Softcover Collection (Apr 1993)
reprints issues #1-5 plus new matreial and new painted cover — £2.00 £6.00 £10.00
Nexus Book Two Trade Paperback (Sep 1993)
reprints issues #6-10 plus new material — £2.00 £6.00 £10.00

NEXUS LEGENDS
First; 1 May 1988-23 Jan 1991
1-23 ND reprints of original Nexus

	$0.30	$0.90	$1.50	£0.20	£0.60	£1.00
Title Value:	$6.90	$20.70	$34.50	£4.60	£13.80	£23.00

NEXUS THE LIBERATOR
Dark Horse,MS; 1 Oct 1992-4 Jan 1993
1 ND Whilce Portacio cover

	$0.50	$1.50	$2.50	£0.30	£0.90	£1.50

2 ND Adam Hughes cover

	$0.50	$1.50	$2.50	£0.30	£0.90	£1.50

3 ND Whilce Portacio cover

	$0.50	$1.50	$2.50	£0.30	£0.90	£1.50

4 ND Adam Hughes cover

	$0.50	$1.50	$2.50	£0.30	£0.90	£1.50
Title Value:	$2.00	$6.00	$10.00	£1.20	£3.60	£6.00

NEXUS: ALIEN JUSTICE
Dark Horse,MS; 1 Dec 1992-3 Feb 1993
1-3 ND Mike Baron script, Steve Rude covers and art

	$0.70	$2.10	$3.50	£0.40	£1.20	£2.00
Title Value:	$2.10	$6.30	$10.50	£1.20	£3.60	£6.00

NEXUS: OUT OF THE VORTEX
Dark Horse,MS; 1 Feb 1995-5 Jun 1995
1-5 ND Joe Comstock and Brian Kane art

	$0.50	$1.50	$2.50	£0.30	£0.90	£1.50
Title Value:	$2.50	$7.50	$12.50	£1.50	£4.50	£7.50

NEXUS: THE ORIGIN
Dark Horse,OS; 1 Jul 1992
1 ND 48pgs, all new origin story by Mike Baron and Steve Rude

	$0.60	$1.80	$3.00	£0.40	£1.20	£2.00
Title Value:	$0.60	$1.80	$3.00	£0.40	£1.20	£2.00

NEXUS: WAGES OF SIN
Dark Horse,MS; 1 Mar 1995-4 Jun 1995
1-4 ND Mike Baron script, Steve Rude art

	$0.60	$1.80	$3.00	£0.40	£1.20	£2.00
Title Value:	$2.40	$7.20	$12.00	£1.60	£4.80	£8.00

MINT = 100% / NEAR MINT (inc. +/-) = 90-99% / VERY FINE (inc. +/-) = 75-89% / FINE (inc. +/-) = 55-74%
VERY GOOD (inc. +/-) = 35-54% / GOOD (inc. +/-) = 15-34% / FAIR = 5-14% / POOR = 1-4%

481

	$Good	$Fine	$N.Mint	£Good	£Fine	£N.Mint

NFL PRO ACTION
Marvel Comics Group,Magazine OS; 1 Feb 1994
1 ND 64pgs, bound-in sheet of trading cards

	$Good	$Fine	$N.Mint	£Good	£Fine	£N.Mint
	$0.40	$1.20	$2.00	£0.25	£0.75	£1.25
Title Value:	$0.40	$1.20	$2.00	£0.25	£0.75	£1.25

NFL PRO ACTION (2ND SERIES)
Marvel Comics Group,MS; 1 Aug 1994-4 Nov 1994

	$Good	$Fine	$N.Mint	£Good	£Fine	£N.Mint
1-4 ND 48pgs	$0.50	$1.50	$2.50	£0.30	£0.90	£1.50
Title Value:	$2.00	$6.00	$10.00	£1.20	£3.60	£6.00

NFL SUPERPRO
Marvel Comics Group,OS; 1 Mar 1991
1 ND 48pgs, tied in with Superbowl promotion

	$Good	$Fine	$N.Mint	£Good	£Fine	£N.Mint
	$0.50	$1.50	$2.50	£0.30	£0.90	£1.50
Title Value:	$0.50	$1.50	$2.50	£0.30	£0.90	£1.50

NFL SUPERPRO (2ND SERIES)
Marvel Comics Group; 1 Oct 1991-12 1992
1 Spiderman appears

	$Good	$Fine	$N.Mint	£Good	£Fine	£N.Mint
	$0.15	$0.45	$0.75	£0.10	£0.35	£0.60
2-4	$0.15	$0.45	$0.75	£0.10	£0.35	£0.60
5 $1.25 cover begins						
	$0.15	$0.45	$0.75	£0.10	£0.35	£0.60
6-12	$0.15	$0.45	$0.75	£0.10	£0.35	£0.60
Title Value:	$1.80	$5.40	$9.00	£1.20	£4.20	£7.20

NFL SUPERPRO SPECIAL
Marvel Comics Group,OS; 1 Aug 1991
1 ND 48pgs

	$Good	$Fine	$N.Mint	£Good	£Fine	£N.Mint
	$0.40	$1.20	$2.00	£0.25	£0.75	£1.25
Title Value:	$0.40	$1.20	$2.00	£0.25	£0.75	£1.25

NICK FURY AND HIS AGENTS OF SHIELD
Marvel Comics Group; 1 Feb 1973-5 Oct 1973
1 ND less common Steranko cover

	$Good	$Fine	$N.Mint	£Good	£Fine	£N.Mint
	$1.00	$3.00	$5.00	£0.70	£2.10	£3.50
2-5 ND less common Steranko cover						
	$0.70	$2.10	$3.50	£0.50	£1.50	£2.50
Title Value:	$3.80	$11.40	$19.00	£2.70	£8.10	£13.50

Note: all reprints from Strange Tales #146-155

NICK FURY ASHCAN
Marvel Comics Group,OS; nn Apr 1995
1 ND 16pgs, black and white; history of Nick Fury and Shield

	$Good	$Fine	$N.Mint	£Good	£Fine	£N.Mint
	$0.15	$0.45	$0.75	£0.10	£0.30	£0.50
Title Value:	$0.15	$0.45	$0.75	£0.10	£0.30	£0.50

NICK FURY VS SHIELD
Marvel Comics Group,MS; 1 Jun 1988-6 Nov 1988
1 ND Paul Neary art, Steranko cover

	$Good	$Fine	$N.Mint	£Good	£Fine	£N.Mint
	$1.00	$3.00	$5.00	£0.80	£2.40	£4.00
2 ND scarce in the U.K. Paul Neary art, Sienkiewicz cover						
	$0.80	$2.40	$4.00	£0.60	£1.80	£3.00
3 ND Paul Neary art, Joe Jusko cover						
	$0.80	$2.40	$4.00	£0.60	£1.80	£3.00
4-6 ND Paul Neary art						
	$0.80	$2.40	$4.00	£0.60	£1.80	£3.00
Title Value:	$5.00	$15.00	$25.00	£3.80	£11.40	£19.00

Note: all are 48pgs, bookshelf format. All painted covers
Trade paperback (Aug 1989)

276pgs reprints 6 issue limited series				£1.60	£4.80	£8.00

NICK FURY, AGENT OF SHIELD
Marvel Comics Group; 1 Jun 1968-18 Mar 1971
(see Double Edge Omega, Marvel Spotlight #31, Nick Fury Vs Shield, Strange Tales)

	$Good	$Fine	$N.Mint	£Good	£Fine	£N.Mint
1 Steranko art	$8.25	$25.00	$50.00	£5.75	£17.50	£35.00
2 Steranko art	$4.15	$12.50	$25.00	£2.90	£8.75	£17.50
3 Steranko art	$3.75	$11.00	$22.50	£2.50	£7.50	£15.00
4 origin Nick Fury and SHIELD retold						
	$3.30	$10.00	$20.00	£2.05	£6.25	£12.50
5 scarce in the U.K. Steranko art, classic psychedelia cover						
	$5.00	$15.00	$30.00	£2.90	£8.75	£17.50
6 Steranko cover	$2.90	$8.75	$17.50	£1.25	£3.75	£7.50
7 Steranko cover (Salvador Dali imitation)						
	$2.90	$8.75	$17.50	£1.25	£3.75	£7.50
8-9	$1.65	$5.00	$10.00	£0.80	£2.50	£5.00
10 2nd Barry Smith art in comics (3 pgs)						
	$1.65	$5.00	$10.00	£1.00	£3.00	£6.00
11	$1.65	$5.00	$10.00	£0.80	£2.50	£5.00
12 Barry Smith art	$1.65	$5.00	$10.00	£1.00	£3.00	£6.00
13 scarce in the U.K. classic patriotic cover						
	$1.65	$5.00	$10.00	£0.80	£2.50	£5.00
14 ND	$1.25	$3.75	$7.50	£0.80	£2.50	£5.00
15 scarce in the U.K. 1st appearance Bullseye (see Daredevil #131)						
	$5.00	$15.00	$30.00	£2.50	£7.50	£15.00
16 scarce in the U.K. 52pgs, all reprint						
	$0.65	$2.00	$4.00	£0.75	£2.25	£4.50
17-18 very scarce in the U.K. 52pgs, all reprint						
	$0.65	$2.00	$4.00	£0.80	£2.50	£5.00
Title Value:	$48.35	$145.75	$292.00	£29.45	£89.50	£179.00

Note: Steranko covers on #1-7

NICK FURY, AGENT OF SHIELD (2ND SERIES)
Marvel Comics Group; 1 Sep 1989-47 May 1993

	$Good	$Fine	$N.Mint	£Good	£Fine	£N.Mint
1-6 ND	$0.40	$1.20	$2.00	£0.25	£0.75	£1.25
7-9 ND The Chaos Serpent						
	$0.40	$1.20	$2.00	£0.25	£0.75	£1.25
10 ND The Chaos Serpent; Captain America appears						
	$0.40	$1.20	$2.00	£0.25	£0.75	£1.25
11 ND	$0.30	$0.90	$1.50	£0.20	£0.60	£1.00

	$Good	$Fine	$N.Mint	£Good	£Fine	£N.Mint
12-14 ND The Hydra Affair						
	$0.30	$0.90	$1.50	£0.20	£0.60	£1.00
15 ND Fantastic Four appear, Apogee of Disaster begins						
	$0.30	$0.90	$1.50	£0.20	£0.60	£1.00
16-19 ND Apogee of Disaster story						
	$0.30	$0.90	$1.50	£0.20	£0.60	£1.00
20 ND Red Skull appears						
	$0.30	$0.90	$1.50	£0.20	£0.60	£1.00
21-25 ND	$0.30	$0.90	$1.50	£0.20	£0.60	£1.00
26 ND Wolverine cameo, Fantastic Four and Avengers appear						
	$0.30	$0.90	$1.50	£0.20	£0.60	£1.00
27-29 ND Wolverine appears						
	$0.30	$0.90	$1.50	£0.20	£0.60	£1.00
30 ND	$0.30	$0.90	$1.50	£0.20	£0.60	£1.00
31 ND Deathlok appears						
	$0.30	$0.90	$1.50	£0.20	£0.60	£1.00
32 ND $1.75 cover begins						
	$0.30	$0.90	$1.50	£0.20	£0.60	£1.00
33 ND intro New Super Agents of Shield						
	$0.30	$0.90	$1.50	£0.20	£0.60	£1.00
34 ND	$0.30	$0.90	$1.50	£0.20	£0.60	£1.00
35 ND Luke Cage appears						
	$0.30	$0.90	$1.50	£0.20	£0.60	£1.00
36-37 ND	$0.30	$0.90	$1.50	£0.20	£0.60	£1.00
38-41 ND Cold War of Nick Fury story						
	$0.30	$0.90	$1.50	£0.20	£0.60	£1.00
42-43 ND	$0.30	$0.90	$1.50	£0.20	£0.60	£1.00
44 ND Captain America appears						
	$0.30	$0.90	$1.50	£0.20	£0.60	£1.00
45 ND X-Force/Cable tie-in						
	$0.30	$0.90	$1.50	£0.20	£0.60	£1.00
46 ND X-Force tie-in						
	$0.30	$0.90	$1.50	£0.20	£0.60	£1.00
47 ND Nick Fury vs. Baron Strucker						
	$0.30	$0.90	$1.50	£0.20	£0.60	£1.00
Title Value:	$15.10	$45.30	$75.50	£9.90	£29.70	£49.50

NICK FURY, AGENT OF SHIELD SPECIAL EDITION
Marvel Comics Group; 1 Dec 1983-2 Jan 1984
1-2 ND 48pgs, reprints classic Steranko art, new wraparound covers by Steranko, Baxter paper

	$Good	$Fine	$N.Mint	£Good	£Fine	£N.Mint
	$0.50	$1.50	$2.50	£0.30	£0.90	£1.50
Title Value:	$1.00	$3.00	$5.00	£0.60	£1.80	£3.00

NICK FURY/BLACK WIDOW: DEATH DUTY
Marvel Comics Group,OS; 1 Apr 1995
1 ND 48pgs, Cefn Ridout script, Charlie Adlard art

	$Good	$Fine	$N.Mint	£Good	£Fine	£N.Mint
	$1.20	$3.60	$6.00	£0.80	£2.40	£4.00
Title Value:	$1.20	$3.60	$6.00	£0.80	£2.40	£4.00

NICK FURY/CAPTAIN AMERICA BOOKSHELF EDITION
Marvel Comics Group,OS; 1 Apr 1995
1 ND 48pgs, Howard Chaykin script

	$Good	$Fine	$N.Mint	£Good	£Fine	£N.Mint
	$1.20	$3.60	$6.00	£0.80	£2.40	£4.00
Title Value:	$1.20	$3.60	$6.00	£0.80	£2.40	£4.00

NICK RYAN, THE SKULL
Antarctic Press,MS; 1 Dec 1994-3 1995
1-3 ND black and white

	$Good	$Fine	$N.Mint	£Good	£Fine	£N.Mint
	$0.40	$1.20	$2.00	£0.75	£0.75	£1.25
Title Value:	$1.20	$3.60	$6.00	£0.75	£2.25	£3.75

NIGHT BEFORE CHRISTMASK, THE
Dark Horse,OS; 1 Oct 1995
1 ND 32pgs, hardcover; Rick Geary story featuring a boy who discovers the mythical Mask

	$Good	$Fine	$N.Mint	£Good	£Fine	£N.Mint
	$2.00	$6.00	$10.00	£1.20	£3.60	£6.00
Title Value:	$2.00	$6.00	$10.00	£1.20	£3.60	£6.00

NIGHT FEARS
Millennium; 1 Jan 1994
1 ND horror anthology; colour

	$Good	$Fine	$N.Mint	£Good	£Fine	£N.Mint
	$0.40	$1.20	$2.00	£0.25	£0.75	£1.25
Title Value:	$0.40	$1.20	$2.00	£0.25	£0.75	£1.25

NIGHT FORCE, THE
DC Comics; 1 Aug 1982-14 Sep 1983
(see New Teen Titans #21)

	$Good	$Fine	$N.Mint	£Good	£Fine	£N.Mint
1 Gene Colan art begins	$0.15	$0.45	$0.75	£0.10	£0.35	£0.60
2-12	$0.15	$0.45	$0.75	£0.10	£0.35	£0.60
13 origin The Baron	$0.15	$0.45	$0.75	£0.10	£0.35	£0.60
14	$0.15	$0.45	$0.75	£0.10	£0.35	£0.60
Title Value:	$2.10	$6.30	$10.50	£1.40	£4.90	£8.40

Note: all Gene Colan art.

NIGHT GLIDER
Topps,OS; 1 Apr 1993
1 ND pre-bagged with coupon #4 for Secret City Saga #0 plus chrome trading card, Jack Kirby cover

	$Good	$Fine	$N.Mint	£Good	£Fine	£N.Mint
	$0.50	$1.50	$2.50	£0.30	£0.90	£1.50
1 ND without coupon/card						
	$0.40	$1.20	$2.00	£0.25	£0.75	£1.25
Title Value:	$0.90	$2.70	$4.50	£0.55	£1.65	£2.75

NIGHT LIFE
Strawberry Jam; 1 1986-7 1987; Caliber; 8 Jan 1992

	$Good	$Fine	$N.Mint	£Good	£Fine	£N.Mint
1-8 ND	$0.40	$1.20	$2.00	£0.25	£0.75	£1.25
Title Value:	$3.20	$9.60	$16.00	£2.00	£6.00	£10.00

NIGHT MAN
Malibu Ultraverse; 1 Oct 1993-23 Aug 1995
1 40pgs, Rune insert, Steve Englehart script and Darick Robertson art begins

	$Good	$Fine	$N.Mint	£Good	£Fine	£N.Mint
	$0.50	$1.50	$2.50	£0.30	£0.90	£1.50
2-3	$0.40	$1.20	$2.00	£0.25	£0.75	£1.25

	$Good	$Fine	$N.Mint	£Good	£Fine	£N.Mint
4 origin Firearm by Howard Chaykin						
	$0.40	$1.20	$2.00	£0.25	£0.75	£1.25
5-10	$0.40	$1.20	$2.00	£0.25	£0.75	£1.25
11-15	$0.30	$0.90	$1.50	£0.20	£0.60	£1.00
16 flip-book format with Ultraverse Premiere #11						
	$0.50	$1.50	$2.50	£0.30	£0.90	£1.50
17 $2.50 cover begins						
	$0.30	$0.90	$1.50	£0.20	£0.60	£1.00
18-20	$0.30	$0.90	$1.50	£0.20	£0.60	£1.00
21 cover by Mark Pacella and Art Thibert						
	$0.30	$0.90	$1.50	£0.20	£0.60	£1.00
22 Loki appears; 1st issue under Marvel Comics solicitation						
	$0.30	$0.90	$1.50	£0.20	£0.60	£1.00
23	$0.30	$0.90	$1.50	£0.20	£0.60	£1.00
Title Value:	$8.20	$24.60	$41.00	£5.25	£15.75	£26.25

Note: all Non-Distributed on the news-stands in the U.K.

NIGHT MAN (2ND SERIES)
Marvel Comics Group; 1 Dec 1995-4 Mar 1996

	$Good	$Fine	$N.Mint	£Good	£Fine	£N.Mint
1 ND Steve Englehart script, M.C. Wyman art						
	$0.30	$0.90	$1.50	£0.20	£0.60	£1.00
1 ND variant cover, computer painted cover by Chuck Maiden						
	$0.80	$2.40	$4.00	£0.50	£1.50	£2.50
2 ND flip-book format with Phoenix Ressurection chapter						
	$0.30	$0.90	$1.50	£0.20	£0.60	£1.00
3 ND Lord Pumpkin returns						
	$0.30	$0.90	$1.50	£0.20	£0.60	£1.00
4 ND Lord Pumpkin appears						
	$0.30	$0.90	$1.50	£0.20	£0.60	£1.00
Title Value:	$2.00	$6.00	$10.00	£1.30	£3.90	£6.50

NIGHT MAN ANNUAL, THE
Malibu Ultraverse; 1 Dec 1994

	$Good	$Fine	$N.Mint	£Good	£Fine	£N.Mint
1 ND 64pgs, continued in Strangers Annual #1						
	$0.50	$1.50	$2.50	£0.30	£0.90	£1.50
Title Value:	$0.50	$1.50	$2.50	£0.30	£0.90	£1.50

NIGHT MAN: INFINITY, THE
Marvel Comics Group,OS; nn Nov 1995

nn ND Black September tie-in; split by the Reality Gem, two versions of The Night Man are transported to the Marvel and Ultraverse universes

	$Good	$Fine	$N.Mint	£Good	£Fine	£N.Mint
	$0.50	$1.50	$2.50	£0.30	£0.90	£1.50
nn ND Variant cover; 1 copy recieved for every 5 regular copies ordered						
	$0.80	$2.40	$4.00	£0.50	£1.50	£2.50
Title Value:	$1.30	$3.90	$6.50	£0.80	£2.40	£4.00

NIGHT MUSIC
Eclipse; 1 Dec 1984-3 Mar 1985
(see Pelleas & Melisande,Salome,Red Dog)

	$Good	$Fine	$N.Mint	£Good	£Fine	£N.Mint
1-3 ND P. Craig Russell						
	$0.40	$1.20	$2.00	£0.25	£0.75	£1.25
Title Value:	$1.20	$3.60	$6.00	£0.75	£2.25	£3.75

NIGHT NURSE
Marvel Comics Group; 1 Nov 1972-4 May 1973

	$Good	$Fine	$N.Mint	£Good	£Fine	£N.Mint
1-4 ND scarce in the U.K.						
	$0.50	$1.50	$2.50	£0.30	£0.90	£1.50
Title Value:	$2.00	$6.00	$10.00	£1.20	£3.60	£6.00

NIGHT OF THE LIVING DEAD
Fantaco,MS; 1 Nov 1990-4 Jan 1991

	$Good	$Fine	$N.Mint	£Good	£Fine	£N.Mint
1-4 ND 48pgs, Bissette art						
	$0.60	$1.80	$3.00	£0.40	£1.20	£2.00
Title Value:	$2.40	$7.20	$12.00	£1.60	£4.80	£8.00

Note: based on George Romero film
Night of the Living Dead Limited Hardcover #1-#4 (1992)
signed by Carlos Kastro and scripters Skulan and Stanway

	$Good	$Fine	$N.Mint	£Good	£Fine	£N.Mint
200 copies of each only				£25.00	£45.00	£75.00

NIGHT OF THE LIVING DEAD (2ND SERIES)
Fantaco; 1 Mar 1994-3 1994

	$Good	$Fine	$N.Mint	£Good	£Fine	£N.Mint
1-3 ND black and white						
	$0.60	$1.80	$3.00	£0.40	£1.20	£2.00
Title Value:	$1.80	$5.40	$9.00	£1.20	£3.60	£6.00

NIGHT OF THE LIVING DEAD: AFTERMATH
Fantaco,OS; 1 Nov 1992

	$Good	$Fine	$N.Mint	£Good	£Fine	£N.Mint
1 ND black and white						
	$0.40	$1.20	$2.00	£0.25	£0.75	£1.25
Title Value:	$0.40	$1.20	$2.00	£0.25	£0.75	£1.25

NIGHT OF THE LIVING DEAD: LONDON — BLOODLINE
Fantaco,MS; 1 May 1993

	$Good	$Fine	$N.Mint	£Good	£Fine	£N.Mint
1 ND Clive Barker co-script; black and white						
	$0.60	$1.80	$3.00	£0.40	£1.20	£2.00
Title Value:	$0.60	$1.80	$3.00	£0.40	£1.20	£2.00

NIGHT RAVEN: HOUSE OF CARDS
Marvel Comics Group; nn 1991

	$Good	$Fine	$N.Mint	£Good	£Fine	£N.Mint
nn Jamie Delano script/David Lloyd art				£1.20	£3.60	£6.00
nn new format, new cover edition (Jan 1993)				£0.75	£2.25	£3.75

Note: some remaindering in the U.K.

NIGHT THRASHER
Marvel Comics Group; 1 Jul 1993-21 Apr 1995

	$Good	$Fine	$N.Mint	£Good	£Fine	£N.Mint
1 48pgs, holo-grafix foil cover						
	$0.50	$1.50	$2.50	£0.30	£0.90	£1.50
2-9	$0.40	$1.20	$2.00	£0.25	£0.75	£1.25
10 with free Spiderman vs. Venom card sheet						
	$0.40	$1.20	$2.00	£0.25	£0.75	£1.25
11 X-over with Nova #6 and New Warriors #48						
	$0.40	$1.20	$2.00	£0.25	£0.75	£1.25
12 X-over with Nova #7 and New Warriors #49						
	$0.40	$1.20	$2.00	£0.25	£0.75	£1.25
13-14	$0.40	$1.20	$2.00	£0.25	£0.75	£1.25
15 Hulk guest-stars						
	$0.40	$1.20	$2.00	£0.25	£0.75	£1.25
16 The Prowler appears						
	$0.40	$1.20	$2.00	£0.25	£0.75	£1.25
17 War Machine appears						
	$0.40	$1.20	$2.00	£0.25	£0.75	£1.25
18 Nick Fury and Black Panther appear						
	$0.40	$1.20	$2.00	£0.25	£0.75	£1.25
19-21	$0.40	$1.20	$2.00	£0.25	£0.75	£1.25
Title Value:	$8.50	$25.50	$42.50	£5.30	£15.90	£26.50

NIGHT THRASHER: FOUR CONTROL
Marvel Comics Group,MS; 1 Oct 1992-Jan 1993

1 follows on from events in New Warriors #25; issues 1-4 have "themes" respectively of strength/ money /power/ compassion

	$Good	$Fine	$N.Mint	£Good	£Fine	£N.Mint
	$0.50	$1.50	$2.50	£0.30	£0.90	£1.50
2-4	$0.40	$1.20	$2.00	£0.25	£0.75	£1.25
Title Value:	$1.70	$5.10	$8.50	£1.05	£3.15	£5.25

NIGHT'S CHILDREN
Fantaco,MS; 1 May 1991-4 Nov 1991

	$Good	$Fine	$N.Mint	£Good	£Fine	£N.Mint
1-4 ND	$0.60	$1.80	$3.00	£0.40	£1.20	£2.00
Title Value:	$2.40	$7.20	$12.00	£1.60	£4.80	£8.00

NIGHT'S CHILDREN: THE RIPPER
Millennium,MS; 1 Oct 1995-present

	$Good	$Fine	$N.Mint	£Good	£Fine	£N.Mint
1 ND 48pgs, Wendy Snow-Lang script and art; black and white						
	$0.80	$2.40	$4.00	£0.50	£1.50	£2.50
Title Value:	$0.80	$2.40	$4.00	£0.50	£1.50	£2.50

NIGHT'S CHILDREN: THE VAMPIRE
Millennium; 1 Jul 1995-2 1995

Nick Fury, Agent of Shield #18

Nightmark #1

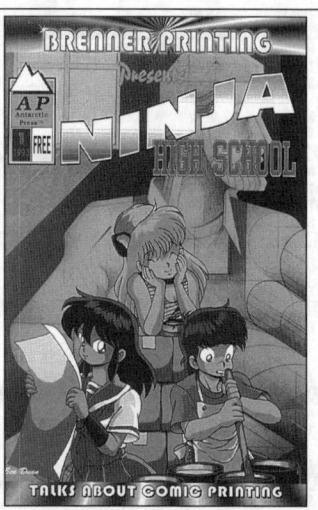

Ninja High School (Brenner Printing) #1

	$Good	$Fine	$N.Mint	£Good	£Fine	£N.Mint

1-2 ND Wendy Snow-Lang script and art; black and white

| | $0.60 | $1.80 | $3.00 | £0.40 | £1.20 | £2.00 |
| Title Value: | $1.20 | $3.60 | $6.00 | £0.80 | £2.40 | £4.00 |

NIGHT'S CHILDREN: VAMPYR
Fantaco,MS; 1 Jan 1993-4 Apr 1993

1-4 ND

| | $0.60 | $1.80 | $3.00 | £0.40 | £1.20 | £2.00 |
| Title Value: | $2.40 | $7.20 | $12.00 | £1.60 | £4.80 | £8.00 |

NIGHTBREED
Marvel Comics Group/Epic; 1 Apr 1990-25 1992

1 ND story by John Wagner/Alan Grant, art by Jim Baikie

| | $0.60 | $1.80 | $3.00 | £0.40 | £1.20 | £2.00 |

2-4 ND

| | $0.50 | $1.50 | $2.50 | £0.30 | £0.90 | £1.50 |

5 ND new story lines based on film begins, Baikie art

| | $0.50 | $1.50 | $2.50 | £0.30 | £0.90 | £1.50 |

6-10 ND Blevins art

| | $0.50 | $1.50 | $2.50 | £0.30 | £0.90 | £1.50 |

11-12 ND Mark Nelson art

| | $0.40 | $1.20 | $2.00 | £0.25 | £0.75 | £1.25 |

13 ND Texeira art

| | $0.40 | $1.20 | $2.00 | £0.25 | £0.75 | £1.25 |

14 ND

| | $0.40 | $1.20 | $2.00 | £0.25 | £0.75 | £1.25 |

15 ND 1st monthly issue

| | $0.40 | $1.20 | $2.00 | £0.25 | £0.75 | £1.25 |

16-25 ND

| | $0.40 | $1.20 | $2.00 | £0.25 | £0.75 | £1.25 |
| Title Value: | $11.10 | $33.30 | $55.50 | £6.85 | £20.55 | £34.25 |

Note: adaptation of horror film by Clive Barker

Nightbreed Chronicles (Titan – 1990), based on film

| | | | | £1.20 | £3.60 | £6.00 |

Trade Paperback (Nov 1991), reprints #1-4

| | | | | £1.10 | £3.30 | £5.50 |

NIGHTCAT
Marvel Comics Group,OS; 1 Apr 1991

1 ND based on American rock singer Jackie Tavar

| | $0.60 | $1.80 | $3.00 | £0.40 | £1.20 | £2.00 |
| Title Value: | $0.60 | $1.80 | $3.00 | £0.40 | £1.20 | £2.00 |

NIGHTCRAWLER
Marvel Comics Group,MS; 1 Nov 1985-4 Feb 1986

(see X-Men)

1-4 ND Cockrum art

| | $0.50 | $1.50 | $2.50 | £0.30 | £0.90 | £1.50 |
| Title Value: | $2.00 | $6.00 | $10.00 | £1.20 | £3.60 | £6.00 |

NIGHTCRY
Visual Anarchy; 1 1994

1 ND 64pgs, Razor story leads off a black and white anthology

| | $0.70 | $2.10 | $3.50 | £0.50 | £1.50 | £2.50 |
| Title Value: | $0.70 | $2.10 | $3.50 | £0.50 | £1.50 | £2.50 |

NIGHTLINGER SPECIAL
Caliber Press; 1 Aug 1994

1 ND black and white

| | $0.50 | $1.50 | $2.50 | £0.30 | £0.90 | £1.50 |
| Title Value: | $0.50 | $1.50 | $2.50 | £0.30 | £0.90 | £1.50 |

NIGHTMARE
Innovation; 1 Dec 1989

1 ND Alex Nino art; colour

| | $0.30 | $0.90 | $1.50 | £0.20 | £0.60 | £1.00 |
| Title Value: | $0.30 | $0.90 | $1.50 | £0.20 | £0.60 | £1.00 |

NIGHTMARE
Marvel Comics Group,MS; 1 Dec 1994-4 Mar 1995

1-4 spin-off from Dr. Strange series

| | $0.40 | $1.20 | $2.00 | £0.25 | £0.75 | £1.25 |
| Title Value: | $1.60 | $4.80 | $8.00 | £1.00 | £3.00 | £5.00 |

NIGHTMARE CIRCUS
Marvel Comics Group; 1 Jan 1996-present

1-3 ND based on Sega video game

| | $0.50 | $1.50 | $2.50 | £0.30 | £0.90 | £1.50 |
| Title Value: | $1.50 | $4.50 | $7.50 | £0.90 | £2.70 | £4.50 |

NIGHTMARE ON ELM STREET
Innovation,MS; 1 Jul 1991-6 Apr 1992

1-2 ND

| | $0.50 | $1.50 | $2.50 | £0.30 | £0.90 | £1.50 |

3 ND prequel to 6th film – Freddy's Dead

| | $0.50 | $1.50 | $2.50 | £0.30 | £0.90 | £1.50 |

4-6 ND

| | $0.50 | $1.50 | $2.50 | £0.30 | £0.90 | £1.50 |
| Title Value: | $3.00 | $9.00 | $15.00 | £1.80 | £5.40 | £9.00 |

NIGHTMARE ON ELM STREET
Marvel Comics Group,MS Film; 1 Oct 1989-2 Nov 1989

1-2 ND 48pgs

| | $0.50 | $1.50 | $2.50 | £0.30 | £0.90 | £1.50 |
| Title Value: | $1.00 | $3.00 | $5.00 | £0.60 | £1.80 | £3.00 |

Note: black and white, based on film of same name

NIGHTMARE ON ELM STREET: THE BEGINNING
Innovation,MS; 1 May 1992-3 Jun 1993

1-3 ND

| | $0.50 | $1.50 | $2.50 | £0.30 | £0.90 | £1.50 |
| Title Value: | $1.50 | $4.50 | $7.50 | £0.90 | £2.70 | £4.50 |

NIGHTMARES
Eclipse; 1,2 May 1985

1-2 ND Moench script, Gulacy art

| | $0.40 | $1.20 | $2.00 | £0.25 | £0.75 | £1.25 |
| Title Value: | $0.80 | $2.40 | $4.00 | £0.50 | £1.50 | £2.50 |

NIGHTMARK
Alpha Productions; 1 1991

1 ND black and white

| | $0.30 | $0.90 | $1.50 | £0.20 | £0.60 | £1.00 |
| Title Value: | $0.30 | $0.90 | $1.50 | £0.20 | £0.60 | £1.00 |

NIGHTMARK: BLOOD & HONOUR
Alpha Productions,MS; 1 Feb 1994-3 Jun 1994

1-3 ND black and white

| | $0.50 | $1.50 | $2.50 | £0.30 | £0.90 | £1.50 |
| Title Value: | $1.50 | $4.50 | $7.50 | £0.90 | £2.70 | £4.50 |

Nightmark: Blood & Honour Pre-Pack (1994)

issues #1-3 in sealed white envelope, ND

| | | | | £1.00 | £3.00 | £5.00 |

NIGHTMASK
Marvel Comics Group/New Universe; 1 Nov 1986-12 Oct 1987

1-12 ND

| | $0.15 | $0.45 | $0.75 | £0.10 | £0.35 | £0.60 |
| Title Value: | $1.80 | $5.40 | $9.00 | £1.20 | £4.20 | £7.20 |

NIGHTRIDER
Marvel Comics Group; 1 Oct 1974-6 Aug 1975

1 ND

| | $0.40 | $1.20 | $2.00 | £0.25 | £0.75 | £1.25 |

2-6 ND

| | $0.30 | $0.90 | $1.50 | £0.20 | £0.60 | £1.00 |
| Title Value: | $1.90 | $5.70 | $9.50 | £1.25 | £3.75 | £6.25 |

Note: re-lettered reprints of (western) Ghost Rider

NIGHTSTALKERS
Marvel Comics Group; 1 Nov 1992-18 Apr 1994

1 ND DS pre-bagged, Rise of the Midnight Sons part 5; Hannibal King, Frank Drake and Blade the Vampire Killer begin, includes fold-out poster

| | $0.50 | $1.50 | $2.50 | £0.30 | £0.90 | £1.50 |

2-4

| | $0.40 | $1.20 | $2.00 | £0.25 | £0.75 | £1.25 |

5-6 Punisher appears

| | $0.40 | $1.20 | $2.00 | £0.25 | £0.75 | £1.25 |

7 Ghost Rider appears

| | $0.40 | $1.20 | $2.00 | £0.25 | £0.75 | £1.25 |

8 Morbius appears

| | $0.40 | $1.20 | $2.00 | £0.25 | £0.75 | £1.25 |

9 Morbius appears, continued in Morbius #11

| | $0.40 | $1.20 | $2.00 | £0.25 | £0.75 | £1.25 |

10 Midnight Massacre part 1, outer cover of black parchment and gold lettering

| | $0.40 | $1.20 | $2.00 | £0.25 | £0.75 | £1.25 |

11

| | $0.30 | $0.90 | $1.50 | £0.20 | £0.60 | £1.00 |

12 gold ink enhanced cover

| | $0.30 | $0.90 | $1.50 | £0.20 | £0.60 | £1.00 |

13

| | $0.30 | $0.90 | $1.50 | £0.20 | £0.60 | £1.00 |

14 Siege of Darkness part 1; Ghost Rider, Blaze, Morbius and the Darkhold Redeemers appear; spot varnish cover

| | $0.30 | $0.90 | $1.50 | £0.20 | £0.60 | £1.00 |

15 Siege of Darkness part 9; spot varnish cover

| | $0.30 | $0.90 | $1.50 | £0.20 | £0.60 | £1.00 |

16-17

| | $0.30 | $0.90 | $1.50 | £0.20 | £0.60 | £1.00 |

18 Nightstalkers vs. Varnae

| | $0.30 | $0.90 | $1.50 | £0.20 | £0.60 | £1.00 |
| Title Value: | $6.50 | $19.50 | $32.50 | £4.15 | £12.45 | £20.75 |

NIGHTSTREETS
Arrow; 1 1986-5 1987

1-5 ND

| | $0.30 | $0.90 | $1.50 | £0.20 | £0.60 | £1.00 |
| Title Value: | $1.50 | $4.50 | $7.50 | £1.00 | £3.00 | £5.00 |

Nightstreets Book I (1991), reprints issues #1-4 plus eight new pages

| | | | | £1.00 | £3.00 | £5.00 |

Nightstreets Book II (1991), reprints issue 5 plus 60 new pages to conclude "Mob Rules" storyline

| | | | | £1.00 | £3.00 | £5.00 |

NIGHTVEIL
AC Comics; 1 1984-7 1987

1-7 ND scarce in the U.K.

| | $0.50 | $1.50 | $2.50 | £0.30 | £0.90 | £1.50 |
| Title Value: | $3.50 | $10.50 | $17.50 | £2.10 | £6.30 | £10.50 |

Special 1

| | | | | £0.30 | £0.90 | £1.50 |

Cauldron of Horror 1 (1989)

| | | | | £0.25 | £0.75 | £1.25 |

Cauldron of Horror 2 (1990), b/w Joe Kubert reprint from Avon's Weird Horrors #9 (1953)

| | | | | £0.30 | £0.90 | £1.50 |

NIGHTVENGER
Axis Comics; 1 May 1994-3 1994

1-3 ND

| | $0.40 | $1.20 | $2.00 | £0.25 | £0.75 | £1.25 |
| Title Value: | $1.20 | $3.60 | $6.00 | £0.75 | £2.25 | £3.75 |

NIGHTVISION
Rebel Studios,MS; 1 Feb 1993-3 1993

1 ND 56pgs, David Quinn script begins, Tim Vigil cover

| | $0.50 | $1.50 | $2.50 | £0.30 | £0.90 | £1.50 |

1 2nd printing, ND (Aug 1994)

| | $0.50 | $1.50 | $2.50 | £0.30 | £0.90 | £1.50 |

2 ND 32pgs, Brian Stelfreeze cover

| | $0.50 | $1.50 | $2.50 | £0.30 | £0.90 | £1.50 |

3 ND

| | $0.50 | $1.50 | $2.50 | £0.30 | £0.90 | £1.50 |
| Title Value: | $2.00 | $6.00 | $10.00 | £1.20 | £3.60 | £6.00 |

NIGHTWATCH
Marvel Comics Group; 1 Apr 1994-12 Mar 1995

1 Ron Lim covers and art begin

| | $0.30 | $0.90 | $1.50 | £0.20 | £0.60 | £1.00 |

1 ND Collector's Edition, prismatic foil cover overlaid with black translucent ink

| | $0.45 | $1.35 | $2.25 | £0.30 | £0.90 | £1.50 |

2 with free Spiderman and his Deadly Foes card sheet

| | $0.30 | $0.90 | $1.50 | £0.20 | £0.60 | £1.00 |

3-5

| | $0.30 | $0.90 | $1.50 | £0.20 | £0.60 | £1.00 |

6 Venom guest-stars

| | $0.30 | $0.90 | $1.50 | £0.20 | £0.60 | £1.00 |

7-8 Cardiac appears

| | $0.30 | $0.90 | $1.50 | £0.20 | £0.60 | £1.00 |

9 origin Nightwatch told in more detail

| | $0.30 | $0.90 | $1.50 | £0.20 | £0.60 | £1.00 |

10-12

| | $0.30 | $0.90 | $1.50 | £0.20 | £0.60 | £1.00 |
| Title Value: | $4.05 | $12.15 | $20.25 | £2.70 | £8.10 | £13.50 |

NIGHTWING
DC Comics,MS; 1 Sep 1995-4 Dec 1995

NIGHTWING (continued)

	$Good	$Fine	$N.Mint	£Good	£Fine	£N.Mint
1 Denny O'Neil script, Greg Land and Mike Sellers art, Brian Stelfreeze covers all begin	$0.50	$1.50	$2.50	£0.30	£0.90	£1.50
2 new Nightwing costume	$0.50	$1.50	$2.50	£0.30	£0.90	£1.50
3-4	$0.50	$1.50	$2.50	£0.30	£0.90	£1.50
Title Value:	$2.00	$6.00	$10.00	£1.20	£3.60	£6.00

NIGHTWING: ALFRED'S RETURN
DC Comics,OS; 1 Aug 1995

	$Good	$Fine	$N.Mint	£Good	£Fine	£N.Mint
1 ND 64pgs, Alan Grant script, Dick Giordano art	$0.80	$2.40	$4.00	£0.50	£1.50	£2.50
Title Value:	$0.80	$2.40	$4.00	£0.50	£1.50	£2.50

1963
Image,MS; 1 Apr 1993-6 Oct 1993

	$Good	$Fine	$N.Mint	£Good	£Fine	£N.Mint
1 ND Mystery Incorporated; Alan Moore script with Rick Veitch and Dave Gibbons art	$0.40	$1.20	$2.00	£0.25	£0.75	£1.25
1 ND Gold Edition - produced in the U.K. by Chaos City Comics; gold outer cover, signed by Dave Gibbons (500 copies)	$4.00	$12.00	$20.00	£1.50	£4.50	£7.50
1 ND Platinum Edition - as above but with Platinum outer cover (100 copies)	$8.00	$24.00	$40.00	£4.00	£12.00	£20.00
1 ND Bronze Edition - as above but with bronze outer cover (20 copies); not signed however	$15.00	$45.00	$75.00	£10.00	£30.00	£50.00
2 ND The Fury; Moore, Veitch, Bissette, Valentino and Gibbons	$0.40	$1.20	$2.00	£0.25	£0.75	£1.25
3 ND Tales of the Uncanny; Moore, Veitch, Bissette, Simpson and Brown	$0.40	$1.20	$2.00	£0.25	£0.75	£1.25
4 ND Tales From Beyond; Moore, Bissette, Totleben, Valentino and Workman	$0.40	$1.20	$2.00	£0.25	£0.75	£1.25
5 ND Horus, Lord of Light; Moore, Veitch, Totleben, Workman and Kilroy	$0.40	$1.20	$2.00	£0.25	£0.75	£1.25
6 ND Tomorrow Syndicate; Moore, Veitch, Gibbons and Kilroy	$0.40	$1.20	$2.00	£0.25	£0.75	£1.25
Title Value:	$29.40	$88.20	$147.00	£17.00	£51.00	£85.00

1984
Warren; 1 May 1978-10 Jan 1980
(becomes 1994)

	$Good	$Fine	$N.Mint	£Good	£Fine	£N.Mint
1 ND	$0.90	$2.70	$4.50	£0.60	£1.80	£3.00
2-10 ND	$0.60	$1.80	$3.00	£0.40	£1.20	£2.00
Title Value:	$6.30	$18.90	$31.50	£4.20	£12.60	£21.00

Note: Corben art in most issues

1994
Warren; 11 Feb 1980-29 1983
(previously 1984)

	$Good	$Fine	$N.Mint	£Good	£Fine	£N.Mint
11-29 ND	$0.60	$1.80	$3.00	£0.40	£1.20	£2.00
Title Value:	$11.40	$34.20	$57.00	£7.60	£22.80	£38.00

NINJA
Eternity; 1 1986-13 1987

	$Good	$Fine	$N.Mint	£Good	£Fine	£N.Mint
1-13 ND	$0.40	$1.20	$2.00	£0.25	£0.75	£1.25
Title Value:	$5.20	$15.60	$26.00	£3.25	£9.75	£16.25
Trade paperback, reprints				£0.85	£2.55	£4.25

NINJA ELITE
Adventure; 1 1987-7 Jul 1988

	$Good	$Fine	$N.Mint	£Good	£Fine	£N.Mint
1-3 ND	$0.30	$0.90	$1.50	£0.20	£0.60	£1.00
4 ND ties into Adventureres	$0.30	$0.90	$1.50	£0.20	£0.60	£1.00
5-7 ND	$0.30	$0.90	$1.50	£0.20	£0.60	£1.00
Title Value:	$2.10	$6.30	$10.50	£1.40	£4.20	£7.00

NINJA FUNNIES
Eternity; 1-5 1987

	$Good	$Fine	$N.Mint	£Good	£Fine	£N.Mint
1-5 ND 16pgs	$0.30	$0.90	$1.50	£0.20	£0.60	£1.00
Title Value:	$1.50	$4.50	$7.50	£1.00	£3.00	£5.00

NINJA HIGH SCHOOL
Antarctic/Eternity; 1 1986-present

	$Good	$Fine	$N.Mint	£Good	£Fine	£N.Mint
0 ND (Jan 1994), foil-enhanced UV card-stock cover	$0.40	$1.20	$2.00	£0.25	£0.75	£1.25
1-3 ND (#1-3 intended as mini-series)	$0.40	$1.20	$2.00	£0.25	£0.75	£1.25
4 ND	$0.40	$1.20	$2.00	£0.25	£0.75	£1.25
5-6 ND Eternity issues	$0.40	$1.20	$2.00	£0.25	£0.75	£1.25
6 2nd printing ND	$0.30	$0.90	$1.50	£0.20	£0.60	£1.00
7-43 ND	$0.40	$1.20	$2.00	£0.25	£0.75	£1.25
44-49 ND	$0.55	$1.65	$2.75	£0.35	£1.05	£1.75
Title Value:	$21.20	$63.60	$105.74	£13.30	£39.90	£66.50
Annual 1 (Aug 1993)				£0.30	£0.90	£1.50
Trade paperback Vol 1, reprints #1-4				£0.90	£2.70	£4.50
Trade paperback, 2nd/3rd print				£0.85	£2.55	£4.25
Trade paperback Vol 1 (4th print – Feb 1992)				£1.00	£3.00	£5.00
Trade paperback Vol 2: A Boy and His Dog Supreme (Aug 1990), reprints #5-7				£1.00	£3.00	£5.00
2nd print				£0.90	£2.70	£4.50
Trade paperback Vol 3 (May 1991), reprints #8-11				£1.00	£3.00	£5.00
2nd print (Aug 1993)				£0.90	£2.70	£4.50
Trade paperback Vol 4: Of Rats and Men (Jul 1991) reprints #12-15				£1.00	£3.00	£5.00
Trade paperback Vol 5 (Dec 1994) reprints #16-18 plus new additional story				£1.00	£3.00	£5.00
Trade paperback Vol 6 (Jul 1995) reprints issues #19-21				£1.00	£3.00	£5.00
Trade paperback Vol 7 (Sep 1995) reprints issues #22-24				£1.00	£3.00	£5.00

NINJA HIGH SCHOOL IN COLOR
Eternity,MS; 1 Aug 1992-14 1993

1-14 ND reprints in colour, new covers by Ben Dunn

	$Good	$Fine	$N.Mint	£Good	£Fine	£N.Mint
	$0.40	$1.20	$2.00	£0.25	£0.75	£1.25
Title Value:	$5.60	$16.80	$28.00	£3.50	£10.50	£17.50

NINJA HIGH SCHOOL YEAR BOOK
Antarctic Press; 1 1989- 7 1991

	$Good	$Fine	$N.Mint	£Good	£Fine	£N.Mint
1-6 ND black and white	$0.60	$1.80	$3.00	£0.40	£1.20	£2.00
7 ND 64pgs, titled Ninja High School Yearbook 1995; black and white	$0.60	$1.80	$3.00	£0.40	£1.20	£2.00
Title Value:	$4.20	$12.60	$21.00	£2.80	£8.40	£14.00

NINJA HIGH SCHOOL, BRENNER PRINTING PRESENTS
Antarctic Press; 1 1993

	$Good	$Fine	$N.Mint	£Good	£Fine	£N.Mint
1 ND scarce in the U.K. promotional comic produced by Brenner and illustrating the process of printing up a comic book; available at 1993 San Diego Comicon	$0.80	$2.40	$4.00	£0.50	£1.50	£2.50
Title Value:	$0.80	$2.40	$4.00	£0.50	£1.50	£2.50

NINJA HIGH SCHOOL/SPEED RACER
Eternity,MS; 1 Jul 1993-2 Aug 1993

	$Good	$Fine	$N.Mint	£Good	£Fine	£N.Mint
1-2 ND	$0.60	$1.80	$3.00	£0.40	£1.20	£2.00
Title Value:	$1.20	$3.60	$6.00	£0.80	£2.40	£4.00

NINJA HIGH SCHOOL: THE PROM FORMULA
Eternity,MS; 1 Jun 1991-2 Jul 1991

	$Good	$Fine	$N.Mint	£Good	£Fine	£N.Mint
1-2 ND	$0.50	$1.50	$2.50	£0.30	£0.90	£1.50
Title Value:	$1.00	$3.00	$5.00	£0.60	£1.80	£3.00

NINJA SPECIAL
Eternity; 1 1987

	$Good	$Fine	$N.Mint	£Good	£Fine	£N.Mint
1 ND	$0.40	$1.20	$2.00	£0.25	£0.75	£1.25
Title Value:	$0.40	$1.20	$2.00	£0.25	£0.75	£1.25

NINJAK
Valiant/Acclaim Comics; 0 and 00 1995; 1 Nov 1993-28 1995

	$Good	$Fine	$N.Mint	£Good	£Fine	£N.Mint
0 ND Mark Moretti script and art; origin of Ninjak	$0.45	$1.35	$2.25	£0.30	£0.90	£1.50
00 ND Mark Moretti script and art; origin of Ninjak	$0.45	$1.35	$2.25	£0.30	£0.90	£1.50
1 Joe Quesada art begins; all foil cover	$0.80	$2.40	$4.00	£0.50	£1.50	£2.50
1 Gold Premium Edition; gold logo, in Valiant logo stamped mylar pro-bag	$2.00	$6.00	$10.00	£1.20	£3.60	£6.00
1 Valiant Validated Signature Series (May 1994), signed by Mark Moretti, Joe Quesada and Jimmy Palmiotti; 5,300 copies with certificate and Mylar sleeve	$2.00	$6.00	$10.00	£1.20	£3.60	£6.00
2-3	$0.45	$1.35	$2.25	£0.30	£0.90	£1.50
4 bound-in Upper Deck trading card	$0.45	$1.35	$2.25	£0.30	£0.90	£1.50
5 guest stars X-O Manowar	$0.45	$1.35	$2.25	£0.30	£0.90	£1.50
6 guest stars X-O Manowar	$0.40	$1.20	$2.00	£0.25	£0.75	£1.25
7	$0.40	$1.20	$2.00	£0.25	£0.75	£1.25
8 Chaos Effect tie-in	$0.40	$1.20	$2.00	£0.25	£0.75	£1.25
9-16	$0.40	$1.20	$2.00	£0.25	£0.75	£1.25
17 1st Acclaim Comics issue, Bart Sears cover; bi-weekly	$0.45	$1.35	$2.25	£0.30	£0.90	£1.50
18 Bart Sears cover; bi-weekly	$0.45	$1.35	$2.25	£0.30	£0.90	£1.50
19-21 Breaking the Web story; bi-weekly	$0.45	$1.35	$2.25	£0.30	£0.90	£1.50
22-28 bi-weekly	$0.45	$1.35	$2.25	£0.30	£0.90	£1.50
Title Value:	$17.30	$51.90	$86.50	£11.05	£33.15	£55.25

Note: all Non-Distributed on the news-stands in the U.K.

NINJAK YEARBOOK
Valiant; 1 Dec 1994

	$Good	$Fine	$N.Mint	£Good	£Fine	£N.Mint
1 ND 1st Valiant work by Brian Hitch	$0.50	$1.50	$2.50	£0.30	£0.90	£1.50
Title Value:	$0.50	$1.50	$2.50	£0.30	£0.90	£1.50

NINJUTSU, ART OF THE NINJA
Solson Publications; 1,2 1986

	$Good	$Fine	$N.Mint	£Good	£Fine	£N.Mint
1-2 ND	$0.30	$0.90	$1.50	£0.20	£0.60	£1.00
Title Value:	$0.60	$1.80	$3.00	£0.40	£1.20	£2.00

NIRA X: CYBERANGEL
Entity Comics,MS; 1 Dec 1994-4 Jun 1995

	$Good	$Fine	$N.Mint	£Good	£Fine	£N.Mint
1 ND Bill Maus script and art – foil stamped cover	$0.60	$1.80	$3.00	£0.40	£1.20	£2.00
1 2nd printing, ND (May 1995) – foil stamped cover	$0.60	$1.80	$3.00	£0.40	£1.20	£2.00
2-4 ND Bill Maus script and art, foil stamped cover	$0.50	$1.50	$2.50	£0.30	£0.90	£1.50
Title Value:	$2.70	$8.10	$13.50	£1.70	£5.10	£8.50
Nira X: Birth of the Cyberangel (Sep 1995) Trade paperback collects four issue mini-series				£1.70	£5.10	£8.50

NIRA X: CYBERANGEL (2ND SERIES)
Entity Comics; 1 Jul 1995-2 1995

	$Good	$Fine	$N.Mint	£Good	£Fine	£N.Mint
1 ND Bill Maus script and art; chromium cover	$0.80	$2.40	$4.00	£0.50	£1.50	£2.50
2 ND	$0.80	$2.40	$4.00	£0.50	£1.50	£2.50
Title Value:	$1.60	$4.80	$8.00	£1.00	£3.00	£5.00

NO ESCAPE
Marvel Comics Group,MS; 1 Jun 1994-3 Aug 1994

	$Good	$Fine	$N.Mint	£Good	£Fine	£N.Mint
1-3 film adaptation	$0.30	$0.90	$1.50	£0.20	£0.60	£1.00
Title Value:	$0.90	$2.70	$4.50	£0.60	£1.80	£3.00

NO GUTS OR GLORY
Fantaco,OS; 1 Aug 1991

	$Good	$Fine	$N.Mint	£Good	£Fine	£N.Mint
1 ND Kevin Eastman script/art	$0.50	$1.50	$2.50	£0.30	£0.90	£1.50
Title Value:	$0.50	$1.50	$2.50	£0.30	£0.90	£1.50

NOCTURNAL EMISSIONS
Vortex; 1 Jun 1991-4 1992

	$Good	$Fine	$N.Mint	£Good	£Fine	£N.Mint
1-4 ND Fiona Smyth script and art, black and white	$0.50	$1.50	$2.50	£0.30	£0.90	£1.50
Title Value:	$2.00	$6.00	$10.00	£1.20	£3.60	£6.00

NOCTURNALS, THE
Malibu Bravura,MS; 1 Jan 1995-6 Jun 1995

	$Good	$Fine	$N.Mint	£Good	£Fine	£N.Mint
1 ND Daniel Brereton script and art	$0.60	$1.80	$3.00	£0.40	£1.20	£2.00
1 ND Glow-in-the-Dark Logo Edition (Jan 1995) – limited to 2,500 copies	$1.50	$4.50	$7.50	£0.80	£2.40	£4.00
1 Newstand edition, ND (Jan 1995) – with same interior but alternative cover	$0.60	$1.80	$3.00	£0.40	£1.20	£2.00
2-6 ND Daniel Brereton script and art	$0.60	$1.80	$3.00	£0.40	£1.20	£2.00
Title Value:	$5.70	$17.10	$28.50	£3.60	£10.80	£18.00

NOCTURNE
Aircel,MS; 1 Jun 1991-3 Aug 1991

	$Good	$Fine	$N.Mint	£Good	£Fine	£N.Mint
1-3 ND Barry Blair art	$0.40	$1.20	$2.00	£0.25	£0.75	£1.25
Title Value:	$1.20	$3.60	$6.00	£0.75	£2.25	£3.75

NOCTURNE
Marvel Comics Group; 1 Jul 1995-4 Sep 1995

	$Good	$Fine	$N.Mint	£Good	£Fine	£N.Mint
1 Dan Abnett script, Joe Fonteriz and John Stokes art all begin; Nocturne inherits the mantle of Night Raven	$0.30	$0.90	$1.50	£0.20	£0.60	£1.00
2	$0.30	$0.90	$1.50	£0.20	£0.60	£1.00
3-4 bi-weekly	$0.30	$0.90	$1.50	£0.20	£0.60	£1.00
Title Value:	$1.20	$3.60	$6.00	£0.80	£2.40	£4.00

NOMAD
Marvel Comics Group; 1 May 1992-25 May 1994

	$Good	$Fine	$N.Mint	£Good	£Fine	£N.Mint
1 ND fold-out cover/map	$0.40	$1.20	$2.00	£0.25	£0.75	£1.25
2 ND	$0.30	$0.90	$1.50	£0.20	£0.60	£1.00
3 ND U.S.Agent appears	$0.30	$0.90	$1.50	£0.20	£0.60	£1.00
4 ND Dead Man's Hand part 2, Daredevil appears, continued in Punisher War Journal #45	$0.30	$0.90	$1.50	£0.20	£0.60	£1.00
5 ND Dead Man's Hand part 5, Punisher appears, continued in Punisher War Journal #46	$0.30	$0.90	$1.50	£0.20	£0.60	£1.00
6 ND Dead Man's Hand part 8, Punisher and Daredevil appear	$0.30	$0.90	$1.50	£0.20	£0.60	£1.00
7 ND Infinity War X-over	$0.30	$0.90	$1.50	£0.20	£0.60	£1.00
8-15	$0.30	$0.90	$1.50	£0.20	£0.60	£1.00
16 Gambit appears	$0.30	$0.90	$1.50	£0.20	£0.60	£1.00
17	$0.30	$0.90	$1.50	£0.20	£0.60	£1.00
18 continued from Captain America #420	$0.30	$0.90	$1.50	£0.20	£0.60	£1.00
19 Nomad vs. Captain America	$0.30	$0.90	$1.50	£0.20	£0.60	£1.00
20	$0.30	$0.90	$1.50	£0.20	£0.60	£1.00
21 Man-Thing appears	$0.30	$0.90	$1.50	£0.20	£0.60	£1.00
22 Zaran the Weapons Master appears	$0.30	$0.90	$1.50	£0.20	£0.60	£1.00
23-24	$0.30	$0.90	$1.50	£0.20	£0.60	£1.00
25 with free Spiderman vs. Venom card sheet	$0.30	$0.90	$1.50	£0.20	£0.60	£1.00
Title Value:	$7.60	$22.80	$38.00	£5.05	£15.15	£25.25

NOMAD (LIMITED SERIES)
Marvel Comics Group,MS; 1 Nov 1990-4 Feb 1991
(see Captain America #180)

	$Good	$Fine	$N.Mint	£Good	£Fine	£N.Mint
1 ND	$0.50	$1.50	$2.50	£0.30	£0.90	£1.50
2 ND	$0.40	$1.20	$2.00	£0.25	£0.75	£1.25
3-4 ND Captain America appears	$0.40	$1.20	$2.00	£0.25	£0.75	£1.25
Title Value:	$1.70	$5.10	$8.50	£1.05	£3.15	£5.25

Note: see Captain America for history of this character as sidekick

NOMAN
Tower; 1 Nov 1966-2 Mar 1967
(see Thunder Agents)

	$Good	$Fine	$N.Mint	£Good	£Fine	£N.Mint
1 distributed in the U.K. Giant	$7.50	$22.50	$45.00	£5.00	£15.00	£30.00
2 distributed in the U.K. Giant	$5.75	$17.50	$35.00	£3.75	£11.00	£22.50
Title Value:	$13.25	$40.00	$80.00	£8.75	£26.00	£52.50

NORMALMAN
Aardvark/Renegade; 1 Jan 1984-12 1987

	$Good	$Fine	$N.Mint	£Good	£Fine	£N.Mint
1 ND Valentino art begins	$0.50	$1.50	$2.50	£0.30	£0.90	£1.50
2-7 ND	$0.40	$1.20	$2.00	£0.25	£0.75	£1.25
8 ND last Aardvark issue	$0.40	$1.20	$2.00	£0.25	£0.75	£1.25
9 ND	$0.40	$1.20	$2.00	£0.25	£0.75	£1.25
10 ND Cerebus cameo	$0.50	$1.50	$2.50	£0.30	£0.90	£1.50
11-12 ND	$0.40	$1.20	$2.00	£0.25	£0.75	£1.25
Title Value:	$5.00	$15.00	$25.00	£3.10	£9.30	£15.50

NORMALMAN 3-D ANNUAL
Renegade; 1 1987

	$Good	$Fine	$N.Mint	£Good	£Fine	£N.Mint
1 ND with 3-D glasses (25% less if without glasses)	$0.50	$1.50	$2.50	£0.30	£0.90	£1.50
Title Value:	$0.50	$1.50	$2.50	£0.30	£0.90	£1.50

NORMALMAN/MEGATON SPECIAL
Image,OS; 1 Aug 1994

	$Good	$Fine	$N.Mint	£Good	£Fine	£N.Mint
1 ND Valentino, Simpson, Burden and Marder	$0.40	$1.20	$2.00	£0.25	£0.75	£1.25
Title Value:	$0.40	$1.20	$2.00	£0.25	£0.75	£1.25

NORMALMAN: THE NOVEL
Slave Labor; nn 1990

	$Good	$Fine	$N.Mint	£Good	£Fine	£N.Mint
nn ND reprints series of 12	$2.00	$6.00	$10.00	£1.50	£4.50	£7.50
Title Value:	$2.00	$6.00	$10.00	£1.50	£4.50	£7.50

NORTHGUARD: THE MANDES CONCLUSION
Caliber Press; 1-3 1989

	$Good	$Fine	$N.Mint	£Good	£Fine	£N.Mint
1-3 ND black and white	$0.30	$0.90	$1.50	£0.20	£0.60	£1.00
Title Value:	$0.90	$2.70	$4.50	£0.60	£1.80	£3.00

NORTHSTAR
Marvel Comics Group,MS; 1 Apr 1994-4 Jul 1994

	$Good	$Fine	$N.Mint	£Good	£Fine	£N.Mint
1 Simon Furman script begins; aftermath following Alpha Flight #130	$0.40	$1.20	$2.00	£0.25	£0.75	£1.25
2-4	$0.40	$1.20	$2.00	£0.25	£0.75	£1.25
Title Value:	$1.60	$4.80	$8.00	£1.00	£3.00	£5.00

NORTHSTAR
Northstar; 1 1988

	$Good	$Fine	$N.Mint	£Good	£Fine	£N.Mint
1 ND rare in the U.K. signed by Tim Vigil, Mort Castle and Mark Bernard, black and white (spot red colour on cover) – 1000 copies	$6.00	$18.00	$30.00	£5.00	£15.00	£25.00
Title Value:	$6.00	$18.00	$30.00	£5.00	£15.00	£25.00

NORTHSTAR 5TH ANNIVERSARY SPECIAL
Northstar,OS; 1 Jan 1995

	$Good	$Fine	$N.Mint	£Good	£Fine	£N.Mint
1 ND black and white collection of greatest hits	$0.40	$1.20	$2.00	£0.25	£0.75	£1.25
Title Value:	$0.40	$1.20	$2.00	£0.25	£0.75	£1.25

NORTHSTAR, BEST OF
Northstar; 1 Aug 1992-3 1993

	$Good	$Fine	$N.Mint	£Good	£Fine	£N.Mint
1 ND Tim Vigil, Mark Nelson art featured	$0.50	$1.50	$2.50	£0.30	£0.90	£1.50
2 ND $2.75 cover	$0.50	$1.50	$2.50	£0.30	£0.90	£1.50
3 ND	$0.50	$1.50	$2.50	£0.30	£0.90	£1.50
Title Value:	$1.50	$4.50	$7.50	£0.90	£2.70	£4.50

NOSFERATU
Dark Horse,OS; 1 May 1991

	$Good	$Fine	$N.Mint	£Good	£Fine	£N.Mint
1 ND 64pgs, Phillipe Druillet script/art	$0.80	$2.40	$4.00	£0.50	£1.50	£2.50
Title Value:	$0.80	$2.40	$4.00	£0.50	£1.50	£2.50

NOSFERATU (2ND SERIES)
Caliber Press,OS; 1 Mar 1995

	$Good	$Fine	$N.Mint	£Good	£Fine	£N.Mint
1 ND 48pgs, Rafael Nieves script and Ken Holewczynski art; film adaptation	$0.80	$2.40	$4.00	£0.50	£1.50	£2.50
Title Value:	$0.80	$2.40	$4.00	£0.50	£1.50	£2.50

NOSFERATU (LIMITED SERIES)
Caliber/Tome Press,MS; 1 Jul 1991-2 Aug 1991

	$Good	$Fine	$N.Mint	£Good	£Fine	£N.Mint
1-2 ND	$0.50	$1.50	$2.50	£0.30	£0.90	£1.50
Title Value:	$1.00	$3.00	$5.00	£0.60	£1.80	£3.00

NOSFERATU: PLAGUE OF TERROR
Millennium,MS; 1 May 1991-4 Aug 1991

	$Good	$Fine	$N.Mint	£Good	£Fine	£N.Mint
1-4 ND Mark Ellis and Rik Levins script/art	$0.40	$1.20	$2.00	£0.25	£0.75	£1.25
Title Value:	$1.60	$4.80	$8.00	£1.00	£3.00	£5.00
Nosferatu: Plague of Darkness (May 1995) collects four issue series with new blood red cover				£1.30	£3.90	£6.50

NOT BRAND ECHH
Marvel Comics Group; 1 Aug 1967-13 May 1969

	$Good	$Fine	$N.Mint	£Good	£Fine	£N.Mint
1	$5.25	$16.00	$32.50	£3.30	£10.00	£20.00
2 scarce in the U.K. "Gnatman & Rotten"	$3.00	$9.00	$15.00	£2.00	£6.00	£10.00
3	$3.00	$9.00	$15.00	£1.80	£5.25	£9.00
4 "The Ecchsmen"	$3.00	$9.00	$15.00	£1.80	£5.25	£9.00
5	$3.00	$9.00	$15.00	£1.80	£5.25	£9.00
6-7	$3.00	$9.00	$15.00	£1.50	£4.50	£7.50
8 "The Ecchsmen"	$3.00	$9.00	$15.00	£1.50	£4.50	£7.50
9-12 68pgs	$3.00	$9.00	$15.00	£1.50	£4.50	£7.50
13 scarce in the U.K. 68pgs	$3.00	$9.00	$15.00	£1.60	£4.80	£8.00
Title Value:	$41.25	$124.00	$212.50	£22.80	£68.05	£117.50

Note: Kirby art in #1, 3, 5-7. Origin of Forbush Man in #5. 10 is all reprint.

NOVA
Marvel Comics Group; 1 Sep 1976-25 May 1979
(The Man Called Nova #22-25)

	$Good	$Fine	$N.Mint	£Good	£Fine	£N.Mint
1 origin	$1.00	$3.00	$5.00	£0.60	£1.80	£3.00
2-3	$0.50	$1.50	$2.50	£0.30	£0.90	£1.50
4 Nova vs. Thor, Jack Kirby cover	$0.50	$1.50	$2.50	£0.30	£0.90	£1.50
5-6	$0.50	$1.50	$2.50	£0.30	£0.90	£1.50
7 Jack Kirby cover	$0.50	$1.50	$2.50	£0.30	£0.90	£1.50
8-11	$0.50	$1.50	$2.50	£0.30	£0.90	£1.50
12 Nova vs. Spiderman, X-over Spiderman #171	$0.60	$1.80	$3.00	£0.40	£1.20	£2.00

VERY GENERAL PERCENTAGE CONVERSION CHART WHICH MAY BE USED TO CALCULATE LOW AND INBETWEEN GRADES:

	$Good	$Fine	$N.Mint	£Good	£Fine	£N.Mint
13 1st appearance Crime-Buster						
	$0.50	$1.50	$2.50	£0.30	£0.90	£1.50
14	$0.50	$1.50	$2.50	£0.30	£0.90	£1.50
15 Spiderman, Iron Man, Hulk, Nick Fury and Captain America appear						
	$0.50	$1.50	$2.50	£0.30	£0.90	£1.50
16-18 Nick Fury appears						
	$0.50	$1.50	$2.50	£0.30	£0.90	£1.50
19-20 ND	$0.50	$1.50	$2.50	£0.30	£0.90	£1.50
21-23	$0.40	$1.20	$2.00	£0.25	£0.75	£1.25
24 1st full appearance new Champions						
	$0.40	$1.20	$2.00	£0.25	£0.75	£1.25
25 ND very scarce in the U.K. new Champions appear						
	$0.40	$1.20	$2.00	£1.00	£3.00	£5.00
Title Value:	$12.60	$37.80	$63.00	£8.40	£25.20	£42.00

Note: story continues in Fantastic Four #208-212.

NOVA (2ND SERIES)

Marvel Comics Group; 1 Jan 1994-18 Jun 1995

	$Good	$Fine	$N.Mint	£Good	£Fine	£N.Mint
1 48pgs, new costume and new powers						
	$0.45	$1.35	$2.25	£0.30	£0.90	£1.50
1 ND 48pgs, Collector's Edition, gold foil cover						
	$0.60	$1.80	$3.00	£0.40	£1.20	£2.00
2	$0.40	$1.20	$2.00	£0.25	£0.75	£1.25
3 Spiderman guest-stars						
	$0.40	$1.20	$2.00	£0.25	£0.75	£1.25
4	$0.40	$1.20	$2.00	£0.25	£0.75	£1.25
5 with free Spiderman and his Deadly Foes card sheet						
	$0.40	$1.20	$2.00	£0.25	£0.75	£1.25
6-10	$0.40	$1.20	$2.00	£0.25	£0.75	£1.25
11 Thing, Ant-Man and Dr. Doom appear						
	$0.40	$1.20	$2.00	£0.25	£0.75	£1.25
12 The Inhumans appear						
	$0.40	$1.20	$2.00	£0.25	£0.75	£1.25
13 Night Thrasher and Firestar appear						
	$0.40	$1.20	$2.00	£0.25	£0.75	£1.25
14 New Warriors appear						
	$0.40	$1.20	$2.00	£0.25	£0.75	£1.25
15-17	$0.40	$1.20	$2.00	£0.25	£0.75	£1.25
18 Nova Omega part 1, continued in New Warriors #60						
	$0.40	$1.20	$2.00	£0.25	£0.75	£1.25
Title Value:	$7.85	$23.55	$39.25	£4.95	£14.85	£24.75

NTH MAN, THE ULTIMATE NINJA

Marvel Comics Group; 1 Aug 1989-16 Sep 1990

(see Marvel Comics Presents #25)

	$Good	$Fine	$N.Mint	£Good	£Fine	£N.Mint
1-7 ND	$0.25	$0.75	$1.25	£0.15	£0.45	£0.75
8 early Dale Keown art						
	$0.40	$1.20	$2.00	£0.25	£0.75	£1.25
9-16	$0.25	$0.75	$1.25	£0.15	£0.45	£0.75
Title Value:	$4.15	$12.45	$20.75	£2.50	£7.50	£12.50

NUKLA

Dell; 1 Oct/Dec 1965-4 Sep 1966

	$Good	$Fine	$N.Mint	£Good	£Fine	£N.Mint
1 origin of Nukla; distributed in the U.K.						
	$4.00	$12.00	$24.00	£2.50	£7.50	£15.00
2-3 distributed in the U.K.						
	$2.05	$6.25	$12.50	£1.25	£3.75	£7.50
4 Steve Ditko art; distributed in the U.K.						
	$4.00	$12.00	$24.00	£2.50	£7.50	£15.00
Title Value:	$12.10	$36.50	$73.00	£7.50	£22.50	£45.00

NURSE BETSY CRANE

Charlton; 12 Sep 1961-27 Mar 1964

	$Good	$Fine	$N.Mint	£Good	£Fine	£N.Mint
12-13 distributed in the U.K.						
	$0.75	$2.25	$4.50	£0.50	£1.50	£3.00

	$Good	$Fine	$N.Mint	£Good	£Fine	£N.Mint
14-20 distributed in the U.K.						
	$0.65	$2.00	$4.00	£0.40	£1.25	£2.50
21-27 distributed in the U.K.						
	$0.55	$1.75	$3.50	£0.30	£1.00	£2.00
Title Value:	$9.90	$30.75	$61.50	£5.90	£18.75	£37.50

NYOKA THE JUNGLE GIRL, THE FURTHER ADVENTURES OF

AC Comics; 1 1988-5 1989

	$Good	$Fine	$N.Mint	£Good	£Fine	£N.Mint
1-5 ND part 50s reprints						
	$0.40	$1.20	$2.00	£0.25	£0.75	£1.25
Title Value:	$2.00	$6.00	$10.00	£1.25	£3.75	£6.25

O

OBLIVION

Comico; 1 Jul 1995-present

	$Good	$Fine	$N.Mint	£Good	£Fine	£N.Mint
1 ND Art Adams cover						
	$0.50	$1.50	$2.50	£0.30	£0.90	£1.50
2 ND pre-bagged with trading card						
	$0.50	$1.50	$2.50	£0.30	£0.90	£1.50
Title Value:	$1.00	$3.00	$5.00	£0.60	£1.80	£3.00

OBLIVION CITY

Slave Labor; 1 Jun 1991-19 1993

	$Good	$Fine	$N.Mint	£Good	£Fine	£N.Mint
1 ND	$0.50	$1.50	$2.50	£0.30	£0.90	£1.50
1 2nd printing, ND (May 1992)						
	$0.40	$1.20	$2.00	£0.25	£0.75	£1.25
2-10 ND	$0.50	$1.50	$2.50	£0.30	£0.90	£1.50
11-19 ND	$0.40	$1.20	$2.00	£0.25	£0.75	£1.25
Title Value:	$9.00	$27.00	$45.00	£5.50	£16.50	£27.50
Oblivion City Starter Set,						
issues #1-4 offered at less than combined retail				£1.00	£3.00	£5.00
Big City: The Complete Oblivion City (Mar 1995)						
250pgs, reprints all 19 issues				£2.70	£8.10	£13.50

OBNOXIO THE CLOWN

Marvel Comics Group, OS; 1 Apr 1983

	$Good	$Fine	$N.Mint	£Good	£Fine	£N.Mint
1 ND X-Men co-star						
	$0.50	$1.50	$2.50	£0.30	£0.90	£1.50
Title Value:	$0.50	$1.50	$2.50	£0.30	£0.90	£1.50

OFFCASTES

Marvel Comics Group/Epic, MS; 1 Jul 1993-3 Sep 1993

	$Good	$Fine	$N.Mint	£Good	£Fine	£N.Mint
1-3 ND Mike Vosburg script and art						
	$0.40	$1.20	$2.00	£0.25	£0.75	£1.25
Title Value:	$1.20	$3.60	$6.00	£0.75	£2.25	£3.75

OFFICIAL BUZ SAWYER

Pioneer; 1 Aug 1988-5 1989

	$Good	$Fine	$N.Mint	£Good	£Fine	£N.Mint
1-5 ND Roy Crane reprints from newspaper strip; black and white						
	$0.40	$1.20	$2.00	£0.25	£0.75	£1.25
Title Value:	$2.00	$6.00	$10.00	£1.25	£3.75	£6.25

OFFICIAL CRISIS ON INFINITE EARTHS CROSSOVER INDEX

I.C.G/Eclipse; 1 Jul 1986

(see Crisis on Infinite Earths)

	$Good	$Fine	$N.Mint	£Good	£Fine	£N.Mint
1 ND very scarce in the U.K. information and colour cover reproductions of Crisis X-overs plus continuity flow charts and character indexes						
	$0.50	$1.50	$2.50	£0.30	£0.90	£1.50
Title Value:	$0.50	$1.50	$2.50	£0.30	£0.90	£1.50

OFFICIAL CRISIS ON INFINITE EARTHS INDEX, THE

I.C.G/Eclipse; 1 Mar 1986

(see Crisis on Infinite Earths)

	$Good	$Fine	$N.Mint	£Good	£Fine	£N.Mint
1 ND scarce in the U.K. George Perez cover, information and colour cover reproductions Crisis on Infinite Earths maxi-series #1-12						
	$0.50	$1.50	$2.50	£0.30	£0.90	£1.50

Nocturnal Emissions #1

Not Brand Echh #12

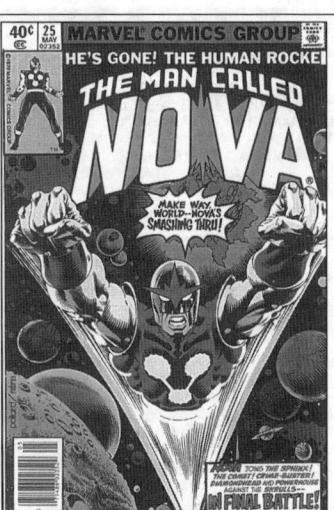

The Man Called Nova #25

MINT = 100% / NEAR MINT (inc. +/-) = 90–99% / VERY FINE (inc. +/-) = 75–89% / FINE (inc. +/-) = 55–74% / VERY GOOD (inc. +/-) = 35–54% / GOOD (inc. +/-) = 15–34% / FAIR = 5–14% / POOR = 1–4%

487

	$Good	$Fine	$N.Mint	£Good	£Fine	£N.Mint
Title Value:	$0.50	$1.50	$2.50	£0.30	£0.90	£1.50

OFFICIAL DOOM PATROL INDEX, THE
I.C.G/Eclipse; 1,2 Feb 1986

1 ND information and colour cover reproductions My Greatest Adventure #80-#85, Doom Patrol #86-#98 plus synopses and character indexes

	$0.50	$1.50	$2.50	£0.30	£0.90	£1.50

2 ND information and colour cover reproductions Doom Patrol #99-#124, Showcase #94-#96, Blue Ribbon Digest #19 plus synopses and character indexes; John Byrne cover

	$0.50	$1.50	$2.50	£0.30	£0.90	£1.50
Title Value:	$1.00	$3.00	$5.00	£0.60	£1.80	£3.00

OFFICIAL HANDBOOK OF THE MARVEL UNIVERSE DELUXE EDITION, THE
Marvel Comics Group,MS; 1 Dec 1985-20 Jul 1986
(see Official Handbook of the Marvel Universe)

	$Good	$Fine	$N.Mint	£Good	£Fine	£N.Mint
1-5 ND	$0.80	$2.40	$4.00	£0.50	£1.50	£2.50
6-10 ND	$0.60	$1.80	$3.00	£0.40	£1.20	£2.00
11-20 ND	$0.50	$1.50	$2.50	£0.30	£0.90	£2.00
Title Value:	$12.00	$36.00	$60.00	£7.50	£22.50	£37.50

Trade paperback

#1-10, 128pgs, reprints 2 of the above issues per book

				£0.90	£2.70	£4.50

Note: covers of #1-15 and #16-20 were intended to fit together into continuous pictures. 2nd prints of #1-3 available (1991)

OFFICIAL HANDBOOK OF THE MARVEL UNIVERSE UPDATE '89
Marvel Comics Group,MS; 1 Jul 1989-6 Nov 1989; 7 Jan 1990-8 Feb 1990

1-8 ND DS

	$0.40	$1.20	$2.00	£0.25	£0.75	£1.25
Title Value:	$3.20	$9.60	$16.00	£2.00	£6.00	£10.00

Note: originally announced as a 6 issue run, extended by 2 further issues. Peter Sanderson text plus various artists.

OFFICIAL HANDBOOK OF THE MARVEL UNIVERSE, THE
Marvel Comics Group,MS; 1 Jan 1983-20 Jul 1986

	$Good	$Fine	$N.Mint	£Good	£Fine	£N.Mint
1 ND (A)	$0.80	$2.40	$4.00	£0.50	£1.50	£2.50
2 ND (B-C)	$0.60	$1.80	$3.00	£0.40	£1.20	£2.00
3-6 ND (B-L)	$0.60	$1.80	$3.00	£0.40	£1.20	£2.00
7-10 ND (M-R)	$0.60	$1.80	$3.00	£0.40	£1.20	£2.00
11-12 ND (R-Z)	$0.50	$1.50	$2.50	£0.30	£0.90	£1.50

13-14 Book of the Dead

	$0.50	$1.50	$2.50	£0.30	£0.90	£1.50

15 Weaponry Catalogue

	$0.50	$1.50	$2.50	£0.30	£0.90	£1.50
Title Value:	$8.70	$26.10	$43.50	£5.60	£16.80	£28.00

Note: alphabetical listing of all Marvel characters. The covers of 1-12 fit together as a poster.

OFFICIAL HAWKMAN INDEX, THE
I.C.G/Eclipse; 1 Nov 1986-2 Dec 1986

1 ND information and colour cover repros Brave and the Bold #34-#36, #42-#44, Mystery in Space #87-#90, Hawkman #1-#16 plus synopses and character indexes

	$0.50	$1.50	$2.50	£0.30	£0.90	£1.50

2 ND information and colour cover repros Hawkman #17-#27, Atom #39-#45, Showcase #101-#103, plus synopses, character indexes and other appearances in Detective and World's Finest, Hawkman 2nd/Shadow War

	$0.50	$1.50	$2.50	£0.30	£0.90	£1.50
Title Value:	$1.00	$3.00	$5.00	£0.60	£1.80	£3.00

OFFICIAL JOHNNY HAZARD
Pioneer; 1 Aug 1988-5 1989

1-5 ND Frank Robbins reprints from newspaper strip; black and white

	$0.40	$1.20	$2.00	£0.25	£0.75	£1.25
Title Value:	$2.00	$6.00	$10.00	£1.25	£3.75	£6.25

OFFICIAL JUNGLE JIM, THE
Pioneer; 1 Jun 1988-16 1989

1-16 ND black and white Alex Raymond reprints from newspaper strip, colour covers

	$0.40	$1.20	$2.00	£0.25	£0.75	£1.25
Title Value:	$6.40	$19.20	$32.00	£4.00	£12.00	£20.00
Annual 1				£0.40	£1.20	£2.00

OFFICIAL JUNGLE JIM ANNUAL
Pioneer,OS; 1 Jan 1989

1 ND 48pgs, black and white reprints, colour cover

	$0.60	$1.80	$3.00	£0.40	£1.20	£2.00
Title Value:	$0.60	$1.80	$3.00	£0.40	£1.20	£2.00

OFFICIAL JUSTICE LEAGUE OF AMERICA INDEX, THE
I.C.G/Eclipse; 1 Apr 1986-8 Mar 1987

1 scarce in the U.K. information and colour cover reproductions Brave and the Bold #28-#30, Justice League of America #1-#19 plus character synopses; George Perez cover

	$0.50	$1.50	$2.50	£0.30	£0.90	£1.50

2 scarce in the U.K. information and colour cover reproductions Justice League of America #20-#56; George Perez cover

	$0.50	$1.50	$2.50	£0.30	£0.90	£1.50

3 scarce in the U.K. information and colour cover reproductions Justice League of America #57-#95

	$0.50	$1.50	$2.50	£0.30	£0.90	£1.50

4 scarce in the U.K. information and colour cover reproductions Justice League of America #96-#130

	$0.50	$1.50	$2.50	£0.30	£0.90	£1.50

5 scarce in the U.K. information and colour cover reproductions Justice League of America #131-#167; Joe Staton cover

	$0.50	$1.50	$2.50	£0.30	£0.90	£1.50

6 scarce in the U.K. information and colour cover reproductions Justice League of America #168-#203; Jerry Ordway cover featuring Darkseid

	$0.50	$1.50	$2.50	£0.30	£0.90	£1.50

7 scarce in the U.K. information and colour cover reproductions Justice League of America #204-#237; Joe Staton cover

	$0.50	$1.50	$2.50	£0.30	£0.90	£1.50

8 scarce in the U.K. information and colour cover reproductions Justice League of America #238-#261, 100pg Spectacular #6,#17, Justice League Digests and Tabloids, Red Tornado mini-series, Zatanna Special

	$0.50	$1.50	$2.50	£0.30	£0.90	£1.50
Title Value:	$4.00	$12.00	$20.00	£2.40	£7.20	£12.00

Note: all Non-Distributed on the news-stands in the U.K.

OFFICIAL LEGION OF SUPER-HEROES INDEX
I.C.G/Eclipse; 1 Dec 1986-5 Apr 1987

1 information and colour cover reproductions of Legion from Adventure #247 up to appearances prior to Adventure Comics #300 plus synopses and character breakdowns

	$0.50	$1.50	$2.50	£0.30	£0.90	£1.50

2 information and colour cover reproductions of Legion appearances in Adventure Comics #301-#323 plus synopses and character breakdowns

	$0.50	$1.50	$2.50	£0.30	£0.90	£1.50

3 information and colour cover reproductions of Legion appearances in Adventure Comics #324-#347 plus synopses and character breakdowns

	$0.50	$1.50	$2.50	£0.30	£0.90	£1.50

4 information and colour cover reproductions of Legion appearances in Adventure Comics #348-#369 and Superboy #147 plus synopses and character breakdowns

	$0.50	$1.50	$2.50	£0.30	£0.90	£1.50

5 information and colour cover reproductions of Legion appearances in Adventure Comics #370-#380 and Action #377-#390 plus synopses and character breakdowns

	$0.50	$1.50	$2.50	£0.30	£0.90	£1.50
Title Value:	$2.50	$7.50	$12.50	£1.50	£4.50	£7.50

Note: all Non-Distributed on the news-stands in the U.K.

OFFICIAL MANDRAKE ANNUAL, THE
Pioneer,OS; 1 Feb 1987

1 ND 48pgs, black and white cover and art, reprinting newspaper strips

	$0.60	$1.80	$3.00	£0.40	£1.20	£2.00
Title Value:	$0.60	$1.80	$3.00	£0.40	£1.20	£2.00

OFFICIAL MANDRAKE KING SIZE, THE
Pioneer,OS; 1 1989

1 ND 48pgs, black and white cover and art, reprinting newspaper strips

	$0.60	$1.80	$3.00	£0.40	£1.20	£2.00
Title Value:	$0.60	$1.80	$3.00	£0.40	£1.20	£2.00

OFFICIAL MANDRAKE MONTHLY, THE
Pioneer; 1-3 1989

1 ND 48pgs, squarebound, also features Buz Sawyer, Secret Agent and Jungle Jim; black and white covers and art

	$0.80	$2.40	$4.00	£0.50	£1.50	£2.50

2-3 ND 48pgs, squarebound, also features Buz Sawyer, Secret Agent and Jungle Jim; black and white card-stock covers and art

	$0.80	$2.40	$4.00	£0.50	£1.50	£2.50
Title-Value:	$2.40	$7.20	$12.00	£1.50	£4.50	£7.50

OFFICIAL MANDRAKE, THE
Pioneer; 1 Jun 1988-15 1989

1-15 ND Falk/Davis reprints from newspaper strip; black and white with colour covers

	$0.40	$1.20	$2.00	£0.25	£0.75	£1.25
Title Value:	$6.00	$18.00	$30.00	£3.75	£11.25	£18.75

Note: #1-9 called The Official Mandrake the Magician

OFFICIAL MANDRAKE, THE (2ND SERIES)
Pioneer,OS; 1 1989

1 ND black and white cover and art, reprinting newspaper strips

	$0.80	$2.40	$4.00	£0.50	£1.50	£2.50
Title Value:	$0.80	$2.40	$4.00	£0.50	£1.50	£2.50

OFFICIAL MARVEL INDEX
Marvel Comics Group; 1 1985-5 1987

The series of five Official Marvel Indexes provide in-depth information on writers, artists, characters and features and was intended as an on-going concern. The titles and issue numbers covered are as follows and more details can be found under these respective titles:

Volume 1 – Amazing Spiderman #1-#9; **Volume 2** – Fantastic Four #1-#12; **Volume 3** – Marvel Team-Up #1-#6; **Volume 4** – X-Men #1-#6; **Volume 5** – Avengers #1-#7

OFFICIAL MODESTY BLAISE
Pioneer; 1 Jul 1988-8 1989

1-8 ND Peter O'Donnell strip reprints; black and white

	$0.40	$1.20	$2.00	£0.25	£0.75	£1.25
Title Value:	$3.20	$9.60	$16.00	£2.00	£6.00	£10.00

OFFICIAL PRINCE VALIANT
Pioneer; 1 Jun 1988-18 1989

1-18 ND Hal Foster reprints from newspaper strip; black and white

	$0.40	$1.20	$2.00	£0.25	£0.75	£1.25
Title Value:	$7.20	$21.60	$36.00	£4.50	£13.50	£22.50
Annual 1, Hal Foster reprints				£0.45	£1.35	£2.25
King Size 1, Hal Foster reprints				£0.45	£1.35	£2.25

OFFICIAL PRINCE VALIANT MONTHLY
Pioneer; 1 1989

1 ND newspaper strip reprints by Hal Foster

	$0.60	$1.80	$3.00	£0.40	£1.20	£2.00
Title Value:	$0.60	$1.80	$3.00	£0.40	£1.20	£2.00

OFFICIAL RIP KIRBY
Pioneer; 1 Jun 1988-5 1989

1-5 ND Alex Raymond reprints from newspaper strip

	$0.40	$1.20	$2.00	£0.25	£0.75	£1.25
Title Value:	$2.00	$6.00	$10.00	£1.25	£3.75	£6.25

OFFICIAL SECRET AGENT
Pioneer; 1 Jun 1988-7 Dec 1988

1-7 ND Archie Goodwin and Al Williamson reprints of newspaper strip; black and white

	$0.40	$1.20	$2.00	£0.25	£0.75	£1.25
Title Value:	$2.80	$8.40	$14.00	£1.75	£5.25	£8.75

OFFICIAL TEEN TITANS INDEX
I.C.G/Eclipse; 1 Aug 1985-5 Dec 1985

1 information and colour cover reproductions Brave and the Bold #54,#60, Showcase #59, Teen Titans (1st) #1-22 plus character synopses

	$0.50	$1.50	$2.50	£0.30	£0.90	£1.50

2 information and colour cover reproductions Teen Titans (1st) #23-53, DC Super Stars #1, Showcase #75, Hawk and the Dove (1st) #1-6

	$0.50	$1.50	$2.50	£0.30	£0.90	£1.50

3 information and colour cover reproductions DC Comics Presents #26, New Teen Titans (1st) #1-25,

	$Good	$Fine	$N.Mint	£Good	£Fine	£N.Mint
Annual #1, Tales of the New Teen Titans #1-4, Marvel and DC Present #1	$0.50	$1.50	$2.50	£0.30	£0.90	£1.50
4 information and colour cover reproductions DC Comics Presents #26, New Teen Titans (1st) #26-50, Annual #2-3, Giveaway #1-3	$0.50	$1.50	$2.50	£0.30	£0.90	£1.50
5 information and colour cover reproductions DC Comics Presents #26, New Teen Titans (1st) #51-62, New Teen Titans (2nd) #1-16, Annual (2nd) #1	$0.50	$1.50	$2.50	£0.30	£0.90	£1.50
Title Value:	$2.50	$7.50	$12.50	£1.50	£4.50	£7.50

Note: all Non-Distributed on the news-stands in the U.K.

OGRE
Black Diamond Publishing,MS; 1 Jan 1994-4 Apr 1994

	$Good	$Fine	$N.Mint	£Good	£Fine	£N.Mint
1-4 ND Phil White script, Pete Ayala art	$0.50	$1.50	$2.50	£0.30	£0.90	£1.50
Title Value:	$2.00	$6.00	$10.00	£1.20	£3.60	£6.00

OH MY GODDESS!
Dark Horse,MS; 1 Aug 1994-6 Jan 1995

	$Good	$Fine	$N.Mint	£Good	£Fine	£N.Mint
1-6 ND Kosuke Fujishima script/art	$0.50	$1.50	$2.50	£0.30	£0.90	£1.50
Title Value:	$3.00	$9.00	$15.00	£1.80	£5.40	£9.00

OH MY GODDESS! PART 2
Dark Horse,MS; 1 Feb 1995-8 Sep 1995

	$Good	$Fine	$N.Mint	£Good	£Fine	£N.Mint
1-8 ND Kosuke Fujishima script and art; black and white	$0.50	$1.50	$2.50	£0.30	£0.90	£1.50
Title Value:	$4.00	$12.00	$20.00	£2.40	£7.20	£12.00

OH MY GODDESS! PART 3
Dark Horse,MS; 1 Nov 1995-present

	$Good	$Fine	$N.Mint	£Good	£Fine	£N.Mint
1-5 ND Kosuke Fujishima script and art; black and white	$0.60	$1.80	$3.00	£0.40	£1.20	£2.00
Title Value:	$3.00	$9.00	$15.00	£2.00	£6.00	£10.00

OKTANE
Dark Horse,MS; 1 Aug 1995-4 Nov 1995

	$Good	$Fine	$N.Mint	£Good	£Fine	£N.Mint
1-4 ND Gerard Jones script, Gene Ha and Andrew Pepoy art	$0.50	$1.50	$2.50	£0.30	£0.90	£1.50
Title Value:	$2.00	$6.00	$10.00	£1.20	£3.60	£6.00

OKTOBERFEST COMICS
Now and Then,OS; 1 1986

	$Good	$Fine	$N.Mint	£Good	£Fine	£N.Mint
1 ND scarce in the U.K. Dave Sim, Gene Day art	$1.20	$3.60	$6.00	£0.80	£2.40	£4.00
Title Value:	$1.20	$3.60	$6.00	£0.80	£2.40	£4.00

OLYMPIANS
Marvel Comics Group/Epic,MS; 1 Jul 1991-2 Mar 1992

	$Good	$Fine	$N.Mint	£Good	£Fine	£N.Mint
1-2 ND super-hero spoof	$0.60	$1.80	$3.00	£0.40	£1.20	£2.00
Title Value:	$1.20	$3.60	$6.00	£0.80	£2.40	£4.00

OMAC
DC Comics; 1 Sep/Oct 1974-8 Nov/Dec 1975
(see Kamandi, Warlord)

	$Good	$Fine	$N.Mint	£Good	£Fine	£N.Mint
1 origin and 1st appearance Omac; Jack Kirby art	$2.05	$6.25	$12.50	£1.00	£3.00	£6.00
2-8 Jack Kirby art	$1.50	$4.50	$7.50	£0.60	£1.80	£3.00
Title Value:	$12.55	$37.75	$65.00	£5.20	£15.60	£27.00

OMAC (2ND SERIES)
DC Comics,MS; 1 Nov 1991-4 Feb 1992

	$Good	$Fine	$N.Mint	£Good	£Fine	£N.Mint
1-4 ND 48pgs, John Byrne two-tone black and white art plus script	$0.80	$2.40	$4.00	£0.50	£1.50	£2.50
Title Value:	$3.20	$9.60	$16.00	£2.00	£6.00	£10.00

Note: Prestige Format

OMAHA THE CAT DANCER
Steeldragon Press/Kitchen Sink; 0 Sep 1990; 1 Jun 1986-20 1994

	$Good	$Fine	$N.Mint	£Good	£Fine	£N.Mint
0 ND originally published as Bizarre Sex #9 redesigned 44pg "origin" (Sep 1990)	$0.40	$1.20	$2.00	£0.25	£0.75	£1.25
0 ND 48pgs, Expanded Edition (Jan 1994), all new art featured in a squarebound format	$0.80	$2.40	$4.00	£0.50	£1.50	£2.50
0 2nd printing, ND of the original #0 (Mar 1995)	$0.40	$1.20	$2.00	£0.25	£0.75	£1.25
1 ND	$0.60	$1.80	$3.00	£0.40	£1.20	£2.00
1 2nd printing ND	$0.40	$1.20	$2.00	£0.25	£0.75	£1.25
2-4 ND	$0.50	$1.50	$2.50	£0.30	£0.90	£1.50
4 2nd printing, (May 1995)	$0.40	$1.20	$2.00	£0.25	£0.75	£1.25
5-11 ND	$0.50	$1.50	$2.50	£0.30	£0.90	£1.50
11 2nd printing, ND (Aug 1994) $2.95 cover	$0.40	$1.20	$2.00	£0.25	£0.75	£1.25
12 ND	$0.50	$1.50	$2.50	£0.30	£0.90	£1.50
12 2nd printing, ND (Oct 1994)	$0.40	$1.20	$2.00	£0.25	£0.75	£1.25
13-20 ND	$0.50	$1.50	$2.50	£0.30	£0.90	£1.50
Title Value:	$13.30	$39.90	$66.50	£8.10	£24.30	£40.50

	£Good	£Fine	£N.Mint
Collected Omaha Book 1, softcover, reprints #1,2 & stories from Snarf, Dope & Bizarre Sex	£2.00	£6.00	£10.00
Book 1 Limited Edition Hardcover	£3.60	£10.80	£18.00
Book 2 reprints #3-6	£1.70	£5.10	£8.50
Book 3 reprints #7-10	£1.70	£5.10	£8.50
2nd print – Feb 1995	£1.70	£5.10	£8.50
Book 4 reprints #11-14 plus new 8pg story	£1.70	£5.10	£8.50
Books #2-4, Hardcover	£3.20	£9.60	£16.00

OMAHA THE CAT DANCER (2ND SERIES)
Fantagraphics; 1 Jun 1994-present

	$Good	$Fine	$N.Mint	£Good	£Fine	£N.Mint
1 ND black and white	$0.50	$1.50	$2.50	£0.30	£0.90	£1.50
1 2nd printing, ND (Sep 1994)						

	$Good	$Fine	$N.Mint	£Good	£Fine	£N.Mint
	$0.40	$1.20	$2.00	£0.25	£0.75	£1.25
2-3 ND black and white	$0.50	$1.50	$2.50	£0.30	£0.90	£1.50
4-5 ND black and white	$0.55	$1.65	$2.75	£0.35	£1.05	£1.75
6 ND	$0.55	$1.65	$2.75	£0.35	£1.05	£1.75
Title Value:	$3.55	$10.65	$17.75	£2.20	£6.60	£11.00

Note: originally announced as being published by Kitchen Sink

OMEGA
Rebel Studios; 1 Aug 1987-2 1987

	$Good	$Fine	$N.Mint	£Good	£Fine	£N.Mint
1 ND rare in the U.K., Tim Vigil art, withdrawn after copyright problems with Marvel's Omega The Unknown, many destroyed, covers 1–3 of future Omen title appear as pin-ups	$10.00	$30.00	$50.00	£7.00	£21.00	£35.00
1 2nd printing, ND yellow cover	$4.50	$13.50	$22.50	£3.00	£9.00	£15.00
2 ND	$0.60	$1.80	$3.00	£0.40	£1.20	£2.00
Title Value:	$15.10	$45.30	$75.50	£10.40	£31.20	£52.00

OMEGA ELITE
Blackthorne; 1 1987

	$Good	$Fine	$N.Mint	£Good	£Fine	£N.Mint
1 ND Jim Starlin cover	$0.30	$0.90	$1.50	£0.20	£0.60	£1.00
Title Value:	$0.30	$0.90	$1.50	£0.20	£0.60	£1.00

OMEGA MEN
DC Comics; 1 Dec 1982-38 May 1986
(see Green Lantern #141,Lobo)

	$Good	$Fine	$N.Mint	£Good	£Fine	£N.Mint
1 ND	$0.40	$1.20	$2.00	£0.25	£0.75	£1.25
2 ND origin Broot, Lobo appears in ad for next issue (no name mentioned)	$0.40	$1.20	$2.00	£0.25	£0.75	£1.25
3 ND 1st appearance Lobo	$2.00	$6.00	$10.00	£1.20	£3.60	£6.00
4 ND	$0.40	$1.20	$2.00	£0.25	£0.75	£1.25
5 ND 2nd Lobo appearance (2pgs)	$0.60	$1.80	$3.00	£0.40	£1.20	£2.00
6-8 ND	$0.40	$1.20	$2.00	£0.25	£0.75	£1.25
9 ND 3rd Lobo appearance (2pgs)	$0.60	$1.80	$3.00	£0.40	£1.20	£2.00
10 ND 1st full Lobo story	$1.50	$4.50	$7.50	£0.80	£2.40	£4.00
11-18 ND	$0.30	$0.90	$1.50	£0.20	£0.60	£1.00
19 ND Lobo appearance	$0.45	$1.35	$2.25	£0.30	£0.90	£1.50
20 ND full Lobo story	$0.60	$1.80	$3.00	£0.40	£1.20	£2.00
21-23 ND	$0.30	$0.90	$1.50	£0.20	£0.60	£1.00
24 ND Kev O'Neill art	$0.30	$0.90	$1.50	£0.20	£0.60	£1.00
25 ND	$0.30	$0.90	$1.50	£0.20	£0.60	£1.00
26 ND McManus art, Alan Moore script	$0.40	$1.20	$2.00	£0.25	£0.75	£1.25
27 ND Alan Moore script	$0.40	$1.20	$2.00	£0.25	£0.75	£1.25
28-30 ND	$0.30	$0.90	$1.50	£0.20	£0.60	£1.00
31 ND Crisis X-over	$0.30	$0.90	$1.50	£0.20	£0.60	£1.00
32 ND	$0.30	$0.90	$1.50	£0.20	£0.60	£1.00
33 ND unofficial Crisis X-over, Dave Gibbons art	$0.30	$0.90	$1.50	£0.20	£0.60	£1.00
34-35 ND Titans X-over	$0.30	$0.90	$1.50	£0.20	£0.60	£1.00
36 ND	$0.30	$0.90	$1.50	£0.20	£0.60	£1.00
37 ND full Lobo story	$0.60	$1.80	$3.00	£0.40	£1.20	£2.00
38 ND	$0.30	$0.90	$1.50	£0.20	£0.60	£1.00
Title Value:	$16.45	$49.35	$82.25	£10.50	£31.50	£52.50

Note: all Deluxe Format Baxter paper

OMEGA MEN ANNUAL
DC Comics; 1 Nov 1984-2 Nov 1985

	$Good	$Fine	$N.Mint	£Good	£Fine	£N.Mint
1 ND 52pgs	$0.40	$1.20	$2.00	£0.25	£0.75	£1.25
2 ND 52pgs, Kev O'Neill art (5pgs)	$0.40	$1.20	$2.00	£0.25	£0.75	£1.25
Title Value:	$0.80	$2.40	$4.00	£0.50	£1.50	£2.50

OMEGA THE UNKNOWN
Marvel Comics Group; 1 Mar 1976-10 Sep 1977

	$Good	$Fine	$N.Mint	£Good	£Fine	£N.Mint
1	$0.40	$1.20	$2.00	£0.25	£0.75	£1.25
2 Omega battles Hulk	$0.30	$0.90	$1.50	£0.20	£0.60	£1.00
3-7	$0.30	$0.90	$1.50	£0.20	£0.60	£1.00
8 ND 1st appearance new Foolkiller (cameo)	$0.50	$1.50	$2.50	£0.30	£0.90	£1.50
9 ND FoolKiller (1st full appearance)	$0.60	$1.80	$3.00	£0.40	£1.20	£2.00
10 ND	$0.30	$0.90	$1.50	£0.20	£0.60	£1.00
Title Value:	$3.60	$10.80	$18.00	£2.35	£7.05	£11.75

Note: storyline completed in The Defenders.

OMEN
Northstar; 1 1987-4 1989

	$Good	$Fine	$N.Mint	£Good	£Fine	£N.Mint
1 ND scarce in the U.K. Tim Vigil co-script and art begins, re-drawn from Omega Premiere Edition 1 (Rebel Studios), letter reprinted from Marvel stating copyright infringement problem	$1.00	$3.00	$5.00	£0.70	£2.10	£3.50
1 ND signed, numbered edition (? copies)	$10.00	$30.00	$50.00	£7.00	£21.00	£35.00
1 2nd printing, ND no letter reprinted	$0.60	$1.80	$3.00	£0.40	£1.20	£2.00

	$Good	$Fine	$N.Mint	£Good	£Fine	£N.Mint
2-4 ND	$0.70	$2.10	$3.50	£0.50	£1.50	£2.50
Title Value:	$13.70	$41.10	$68.50	£9.60	£28.80	£48.00

ON A PALE HORSE
Innovation,MS; 1 Jun 1991-6 Nov 1991
1 ND 48pgs, squarebound, painted art adaptation of Piers Anthony novel begins

	$0.80	$2.40	$4.00	£0.60	£1.80	£3.00
1 2nd printing, ND (Aug 1993), $4.95 cover						
	$0.60	$1.80	$3.00	£0.40	£1.20	£2.00
2 ND 48pgs, squarebound						
	$0.70	$2.10	$3.50	£0.50	£1.50	£2.50
2 2nd printing, ND (Sep 1993)						
	$0.60	$1.80	$3.00	£0.40	£1.20	£2.00
3-6 ND 48pgs, squarebound						
	$0.60	$1.80	$3.00	£0.40	£1.20	£2.00
Title Value:	$5.10	$15.30	$25.50	£3.50	£10.50	£17.50

ONE HUNDRED AND ONE DALMATIANS GRAPHIC NOVEL
Disney,OS; 1 1991
1 ND 48pgs, adaptation of film

	$1.00	$3.00	$5.00	£0.70	£2.10	£3.50
1 Newstand edition, ND 48pgs, without trading cards						
	$0.55	$1.65	$2.75	£0.35	£1.05	£1.75
Title Value:	$1.55	$4.65	$7.75	£1.05	£3.15	£5.25

ONE MILE UP
Eclipse,MS; 1 Feb 1992-2 1992

1-2 ND	$0.40	$1.20	$2.00	£0.25	£0.75	£1.25
Title Value:	$0.80	$2.40	$4.00	£0.50	£1.50	£2.50

ONE SHOT WESTERN
Caliber Press,OS; 1 Feb 1992

1 ND	$0.40	$1.20	$2.00	£0.25	£0.75	£1.25
Title Value:	$0.40	$1.20	$2.00	£0.25	£0.75	£1.25

1,001 NIGHTS OF BACCHUS, THE
Dark Horse,OS; 1 May 1993
1 ND 48pgs, Eddie Campbell script/art

	$0.80	$2.40	$4.00	£0.50	£1.50	£2.50
Title Value:	$0.80	$2.40	$4.00	£0.50	£1.50	£2.50

ONE, THE
Marvel Comics Group/Epic,MS; 1 Jul 1985-6 Feb 1986

1-6 ND	$0.40	$1.20	$2.00	£0.25	£0.75	£1.25
Title Value:	$2.40	$7.20	$12.00	£1.50	£4.50	£7.50
Trade paperback (Dec 1989)						
216pgs, black and white. Intro by Alan Moore			£1.60	£4.80	£8.00	

Note: this trade paperback was re-offered by King Hell Press in Mar 1995

ONYX OVERLORD
Marvel Comics Group,MS; 1 Oct 1992-4 Jan 1993
1 ND Moebius and L'Officier sequel to "Airtight Garage"

	$0.40	$1.20	$2.00	£0.25	£0.75	£1.25
2-4 ND	$0.40	$1.20	$2.00	£0.25	£0.75	£1.25
Title Value:	$1.60	$4.80	$8.00	£1.00	£3.00	£5.00

OPEN SEASON
Renegade/Strawberry Jam; 1 Dec 1986-6 Apr 1988; 7 1988
1 ND story and art by Jim Bricker begins (all issues black and white)

	$0.40	$1.20	$2.00	£0.25	£0.75	£1.25
2-5 ND	$0.40	$1.20	$2.00	£0.25	£0.75	£1.25
6 ND The Black Issue (for mourning the announcement it was being cancelled)						
	$0.40	$1.20	$2.00	£0.25	£0.75	£1.25
7 ND Strawberry Jam issue						
	$0.40	$1.20	$2.00	£0.25	£0.75	£1.25
Title Value:	$2.80	$8.40	$14.00	£1.75	£5.25	£8.75

OPEN SEASON: THE PLAY
Slave Labor,MS; 1 Nov 1990
1 ND based on stage play, intro by Neil Gaiman

	$0.25	$0.75	$1.25	£0.15	£0.45	£0.75
Title Value:	$0.25	$0.75	$1.25	£0.15	£0.45	£0.75

Note: intended mini-series

OPEN SPACE
Marvel Comics Group/Marvel Graphics,MS; 1 Dec 1989-4 Aug 1990

1-4 ND squarebound	$0.60	$1.80	$3.00	£0.40	£1.20	£2.00
Title Value:	$2.40	$7.20	$12.00	£1.60	£4.80	£8.00

Note: collection of SF stories set in a shared universe by a variety of writers/artists inc. Steve Yeowell (#1). Paul Chadwick cover on #3. Bookshelf Format

OPERA
Eclipse,OS; 1 Sep 1991
1 ND 144pgs, collection of opera adaptations by P. Craig Russell

	$2.50	$7.50	$12.50	£1.50	£4.50	£7.50
Title Value:	$2.50	$7.50	$12.50	£1.50	£4.50	£7.50

OPERATION KNIGHTSTRIKE
Image; 1 May 1995-present
1 ND Chapel, Al Simmons, Bravo, Dutch, Battlestone and Cabbot appear; Brian Witten script, Richard Horie and Jon Sibal art

	$0.50	$1.50	$2.50	£0.30	£0.90	£1.50
2-3 ND	$0.50	$1.50	$2.50	£0.30	£0.90	£1.50
Title Value:	$1.50	$4.50	$7.50	£0.90	£2.70	£4.50

OPERATION: URBAN STORM
Image,OS; 1 Jan 1993
1 ND benefit comic for the re-building of Los Angeles after the riots featuring work by Liefeld, Lee, Larsen, Portacio, Silvestri, McFarlane and others

	$0.40	$1.20	$2.00	£0.25	£0.75	£1.25
Title Value:	$0.40	$1.20	$2.00	£0.25	£0.75	£1.25

ORBIT
Eclipse; 1 Aug 1990-3 1990
1 ND 48pgs, Isaac Asimov story adapted by John Bolton, Dave Stevens cover

	$0.70	$2.10	$3.50	£0.50	£1.50	£2.50

2 ND 48pgs, adaptations of Isaac Asimov and other SF writers continue

	$0.70	$2.10	$3.50	£0.50	£1.50	£2.50

3 ND 48pgs, John Bolton art featured plus cover

	$0.70	$2.10	$3.50	£0.50	£1.50	£2.50
Title Value:	$2.10	$6.30	$10.50	£1.50	£4.50	£7.50

Note: owing to scheduling problems, the original contents of issues #1 and #2 were swopped around

ORIENTAL HEROES
Jademan; 1 Aug 1988-56 Mar 1993

1-56 ND	$0.40	$1.20	$2.00	£0.25	£0.75	£1.25
Title Value:	$22.40	$67.20	$112.00	£14.00	£42.00	£70.00

ORIGINAL ASTROBOY
Now Comics; 1 Jul 1987-20 1989
1 ND Ken Steacy art begins

	$0.40	$1.20	$2.00	£0.25	£0.75	£1.25
2-18 ND	$0.40	$1.20	$2.00	£0.25	£0.75	£1.25
19-20 ND Comic Code on cover						
	$0.40	$1.20	$2.00	£0.25	£0.75	£1.25
Title Value:	$8.00	$24.00	$40.00	£5.00	£15.00	£25.00

ORIGINAL SHIELD
Archie; 1 Apr 1984-2 Jun 1984
1-2 ND origin retold, Dick Ayers art

	$0.30	$0.90	$1.50	£0.20	£0.60	£1.00
Title Value:	$0.60	$1.80	$3.00	£0.40	£1.20	£2.00

ORIGINAL SWAMP THING SAGA
(see Swamp Thing)

ORION
Dark Horse,MS; 1 Aug 1992-6 Aug 1993
1 ND 56pgs, Masamune Shirow script/art begins

	$0.60	$1.80	$3.00	£0.40	£1.20	£2.00
2-6 ND 40pgs	$0.60	$1.80	$3.00	£0.40	£1.20	£2.00
Title Value:	$3.60	$10.80	$18.00	£2.40	£7.20	£12.00

Orion Trade paperback reprints mini-series, painted cover by Masamune Shirow

				£2.00	£6.00	£10.00

ORLAK: FLESH AND STEEL
Caliber Press,OS; 1 Jan 1992

1 ND	$0.40	$1.20	$2.00	£0.25	£0.75	£1.25
Title Value:	$0.40	$1.20	$2.00	£0.25	£0.75	£1.25

ORLAK: REDUX
Caliber Press,OS; 1 Sep 1991
1 ND 64pgs, collects story from pages of Caliber Presents

	$0.60	$1.80	$3.00	£0.40	£1.20	£2.00
Title Value:	$0.60	$1.80	$3.00	£0.40	£1.20	£2.00

OTHERS, THE
Image; 0 Mar 1995; 1 Apr 1995-4 Jul 1995
0 ND 16pgs, continuing from Shadowhawk #15 reprinting the stories from Shadowhawk #3 and #4 plus 5 new pages

	$0.25	$0.75	$1.25	£0.15	£0.45	£0.75
1-3 ND Patrick Blaine and Jason Gorder art						
	$0.40	$1.20	$2.00	£0.25	£0.75	£1.25
4 ND	$0.40	$1.20	$2.00	£0.25	£0.75	£1.25
Title Value:	$1.85	$5.55	$9.25	£1.15	£3.45	£5.75

OUR ARMY AT WAR
National Periodical Publications; 1 Aug 1952-301 Feb 1977
(becomes Sgt.Rock)

	$Good	$Fine	$N.Mint	£Good	£Fine	£N.Mint
1	$125.00	$375.00	$1000.00	£82.50	£250.00	£675.00
2	$75.00	$225.00	$525.00	£50.00	£150.00	£350.00
3	$52.50	$160.00	$375.00	£39.00	£115.00	£275.00
4-5	$43.00	$125.00	$300.00	£29.00	£85.00	£200.00
6-10	$39.00	$115.00	$275.00	£26.00	£75.00	£180.00
11-20	$30.00	$90.00	$210.00	£21.00	£62.50	£150.00
21-31	$21.00	$62.50	$150.00	£14.00	£43.00	£100.00
32-50	$17.00	$50.00	$120.00	£11.00	£34.00	£80.00
51-60	$14.00	$43.00	$100.00	£10.50	£32.00	£75.00
61-70	$12.50	$39.00	$90.00	£8.50	£26.00	£60.00
71-80	$10.50	$32.00	$75.00	£7.00	£21.00	£50.00
81 very scarce in the U.K. 1st appearance Sgt. Rock						
	$200.00	$600.00	$1600.00	£125.00	£375.00	£1000.00
[Very scarce in high grade – Very Fine+ or better]						
82 scarce in the U.K. 2nd appearance Sgt. Rock (very brief)						
	$50.00	$150.00	$350.00	£35.00	£105.00	£245.00
83 scarce in the U.K. 1st Joe Kubert art on Sgt. Rock						
	$85.00	$255.00	$600.00	£55.00	£170.00	£400.00
84	$23.50	$70.00	$165.00	£15.50	£47.00	£110.00
85 origin Ice Cream soldier						
	$23.50	$70.00	$165.00	£15.50	£47.00	£110.00
86-87	$23.50	$70.00	$165.00	£15.50	£47.00	£110.00
1st official distribution in the U.K.						
88-90 scarce in the U.K.						
	$23.50	$70.00	$165.00	£15.50	£47.00	£110.00
91 scarce in the U.K. 1st all Sgt. Rock stories issue						
	$52.50	$160.00	$375.00	£36.00	£105.00	£250.00
92-100 scarce in the U.K.						
	$15.00	$45.00	$105.00	£10.50	£32.00	£75.00
101-110 scarce in the U.K.						
	$10.00	$30.00	$60.00	£5.75	£17.50	£35.00
111-120 scarce in the U.K.						
	$10.00	$30.00	$60.00	£5.00	£15.00	£30.00
121-127 scarce in the U.K.						
	$6.25	$18.50	$37.50	£4.15	£12.50	£25.00
128 combat training and partial origin Sgt. Rock shown in some panels only						
	$25.00	$75.00	$150.00	£14.00	£43.00	£85.00

	$Good	$Fine	$N.Mint	£Good	£Fine	£N.Mint
129-130	$6.25	$18.50	$37.50	£4.15	£12.50	£25.00
131-150	$5.75	$17.50	$35.00	£3.30	£10.00	£20.00
151 Kubert art, 1st appearance Enemy Ace	$33.00	$100.00	$200.00	£20.00	£60.00	£120.00
152	$5.25	$16.00	$32.50	£2.50	£7.50	£15.00
153 2nd appearance Enemy Ace	$14.00	$43.00	$85.00	£8.25	£25.00	£50.00
154	$5.25	$16.00	$32.50	£2.50	£7.50	£15.00
155 3rd appearance Enemy Ace	$8.25	$25.00	$50.00	£5.00	£15.00	£30.00
156-157	$5.25	$16.00	$32.50	£2.50	£7.50	£15.00
158 1st appearance Iron Major	$6.25	$18.50	$37.50	£3.30	£10.00	£20.00
159-161	$5.25	$16.00	$32.50	£2.50	£7.50	£15.00
162 scarce in the U.K. Viking Prince guest-stars	$6.50	$19.50	$32.50	£3.50	£10.50	£17.50
163 Viking Prince guest-stars	$6.50	$19.50	$32.50	£3.00	£9.00	£15.00
164 scarce in the U.K. (very scarce?) 80pgs, Giant G-19	$10.00	$30.00	$50.00	£6.00	£18.00	£30.00
165-167 scarce in the U.K.	$6.50	$19.50	$32.50	£3.50	£10.50	£17.50
168-170 ND	$6.50	$19.50	$32.50	£4.00	£12.00	£20.00
171-176 ND	$5.00	$15.00	$25.00	£2.50	£7.50	£12.50
177 ND 80pgs, Giant G-32	$7.00	$21.00	$35.00	£4.00	£12.00	£20.00
178-181 ND	$5.00	$15.00	$25.00	£2.50	£7.50	£12.50
182-183 ND Neal Adams art	$5.00	$15.00	$25.00	£3.00	£9.00	£15.00
184-185 ND	$4.00	$12.00	$20.00	£2.00	£6.00	£10.00
186 ND Neal Adams art	$5.00	$15.00	$25.00	£3.00	£9.00	£15.00
187-189 ND	$4.00	$12.00	$20.00	£2.00	£6.00	£10.00
190 ND 80pgs, Giant G-44	$5.00	$15.00	$25.00	£3.00	£9.00	£15.00
191-199 ND	$4.00	$12.00	$20.00	£2.00	£6.00	£10.00
200 ND	$3.00	$9.00	$15.00	£1.50	£4.50	£7.50
201-202 ND	$1.50	$4.50	$7.50	£0.80	£2.40	£4.00
203 ND 80pgs, Giant G-56	$2.50	$7.50	$12.50	£1.50	£4.50	£7.50
204-205 ND all reprint	$1.50	$4.50	$7.50	£0.80	£2.40	£4.00
206-215 ND	$1.50	$4.50	$7.50	£0.80	£2.40	£4.00
216 ND 68pgs, (Giant G-68)	$2.50	$7.50	$12.50	£1.50	£4.50	£7.50
217-228 ND	$1.20	$3.60	$6.00	£0.60	£1.80	£3.00
229 ND 68pgs, (Giant G-80)	$2.50	$7.50	$12.50	£1.50	£4.50	£7.50
230-239 ND	$1.00	$3.00	$5.00	£0.50	£1.50	£2.50
240 52pgs, Neal Adams art	$1.50	$4.50	$7.50	£1.00	£3.00	£5.00
241 52pgs	$1.00	$3.00	$5.00	£0.50	£1.50	£2.50
242 less common in the U.K. 100pgs, DC-100pg Super Spectacular #9	$1.50	$4.50	$7.50	£1.00	£3.00	£5.00
243-248 52pgs	$1.00	$3.00	$5.00	£0.50	£1.50	£2.50
249 Wood art	$1.00	$3.00	$5.00	£0.50	£1.50	£2.50
250	$1.00	$3.00	$5.00	£0.50	£1.50	£2.50
251-268	$1.00	$3.00	$5.00	£0.40	£1.20	£2.00
269 100pgs	$1.00	$3.00	$5.00	£0.80	£2.40	£4.00
270	$1.00	$3.00	$5.00	£0.40	£1.20	£2.00
271-274	$1.00	$3.00	$5.00	£0.30	£0.90	£1.50
275 100pgs	$1.00	$3.00	$5.00	£0.80	£2.40	£4.00
276-279	$1.00	$3.00	$5.00	£0.30	£0.90	£1.50
280 68pgs, reprints 1st Sgt. Rock story & 1st Sgt. Rock by Kubert to celebrate 200th appearance of character	$1.00	$3.00	$5.00	£0.50	£1.50	£2.50
281-289	$1.00	$3.00	$5.00	£0.30	£0.90	£1.50
290-291 scarce in the U.K.	$1.00	$3.00	$5.00	£0.40	£1.20	£2.00
292	$1.00	$3.00	$5.00	£0.30	£0.90	£1.50
293 scarce in the U.K.	$1.00	$3.00	$5.00	£0.40	£1.20	£2.00
294-299	$1.00	$3.00	$5.00	£0.30	£0.90	£1.50
300 new celebratory Kanigher and Kubert story	$1.00	$3.00	$5.00	£0.30	£0.90	£1.50
301	$1.00	$3.00	$5.00	£0.30	£0.90	£1.50
Title Value:	$3252.90	$9754.20	$22137.00	£2084.00	£6284.80	£14388.00

FEATURES
Sgt.Rock in new stories in 88-163, 165-176, 178-189, 191-202, 206-215, 217-228, 230-239, 241, 234-301.

REPRINT FEATURES
Capt. Storm in 242. Frogman in 164, 177. Gunner & Sarge in 164, 177, 190, 203, 242. Haunted Tank in 164, 177, 190, 203, 216. Hunter's Hellcats in 269. Johnny Cloud in 164, 177, 190, 203, 242, 269. Mlle. Marie in 164, 177, 190, 203, 238. Sgt. Rock in 164, 177, 190, 203, 216, 229, 240, 269, 275, 280

OUR FIGHTING FORCES

National Periodical Publications/DC Comics; 1 Oct/Nov 1954-181 Sep/Oct 1978

	$Good	$Fine	$N.Mint	£Good	£Fine	£N.Mint
1 scarce in the U.K. Jerry Grandenetti art featured	$62.50	$185.00	$500.00	£44.00	£130.00	£350.00
2 scarce in the U.K.	$40.00	$120.00	$280.00	£28.00	£82.50	£196.00
3 scarce in the U.K. Joe Kubert cover	$36.00	$105.00	$252.00	£25.00	£75.00	£175.00
4-9 scarce in the U.K.	$24.00	$70.00	$168.00	£17.50	£52.50	£122.50
10 scarce in the U.K. Wally Wood art featured	$25.00	$75.00	$175.00	£18.00	£52.50	£126.00
11-20	$17.00	$50.00	$119.00	£12.00	£36.00	£84.00
21-40	$11.00	$33.00	$77.00	£8.00	£24.00	£56.00
41-44	$10.00	$30.00	$60.00	£8.00	£24.00	£48.00
45 1st appearance Gunner and Sarge	$33.00	$97.50	$198.00	£24.00	£70.00	£144.00
46-48	$8.00	$24.00	$48.00	£6.00	£18.00	£36.00
49 1st appearance The Pooch	$12.50	$39.00	$77.00	£9.25	£28.00	£56.00
50	$8.00	$24.00	$48.00	£6.00	£18.00	£36.00
1st official distribution in the U.K.						
51-60 scarce in the U.K.	$5.00	$15.00	$30.00	£4.00	£12.00	£24.00
61-71 scarce in the U.K.	$4.00	$12.00	$24.00	£3.00	£9.00	£18.00
72-80	$2.50	$7.50	$15.00	£1.65	£5.00	£10.00
81-90	$2.05	$6.25	$12.50	£1.40	£4.25	£8.50
91-98	$2.00	$6.00	$10.00	£1.30	£3.90	£6.50
99-100 scarce in the U.K.	$2.00	$6.00	$10.00	£1.50	£4.50	£7.50
101-102 scarce in the U.K.	$1.20	$3.60	$6.00	£0.80	£2.40	£4.00
103-105 ND	$1.40	$4.20	$7.00	£0.90	£2.70	£4.50
106-120 ND	$1.10	$3.35	$5.50	£0.75	£2.25	£3.75
121-122 ND	$1.05	$3.15	$5.25	£0.70	£2.10	£3.50
123 ND 1st of Losers series	$1.40	$4.20	$7.00	£0.90	£2.70	£4.50
124-129 ND	$1.05	$3.15	$5.25	£0.70	£2.10	£3.50
130 scarce in the U.K.						

Omen #1

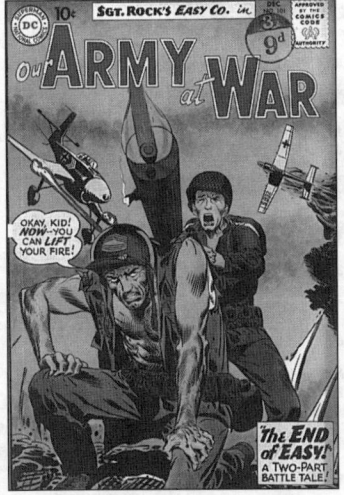

Our Army At War #101

Our Fighting Forces #181

	$Good	$Fine	$N.Mint	£Good	£Fine	£N.Mint
131-132	$0.90	$2.70	$4.50	£0.60	£1.80	£3.00
133-137 52pgs	$0.80	$2.40	$4.00	£0.50	£1.50	£2.50
138-139	$0.90	$2.70	$4.50	£0.60	£1.80	£3.00
140 ND	$0.80	$2.40	$4.00	£0.50	£1.50	£2.50
141-150	$0.90	$2.70	$4.50	£0.60	£1.80	£3.00
151-158 Jack Kirby art	$0.60	$1.80	$3.00	£0.40	£1.20	£2.00
159 scarce in the U.K. Jack Kirby art	$0.60	$1.80	$3.00	£0.40	£1.20	£2.00
160-162 Jack Kirby art	$0.80	$2.40	$4.00	£0.50	£1.50	£2.50
	$0.60	$1.80	$3.00	£0.40	£1.20	£2.00
163-164	$0.45	$1.35	$2.25	£0.30	£0.90	£1.50
165-166 ND	$0.55	$1.65	$2.75	£0.35	£1.05	£1.75
167-170	$0.45	$1.35	$2.25	£0.30	£0.90	£1.50
171	$0.40	$1.20	$2.00	£0.25	£0.75	£1.25
172-174 scarce in the U.K.	$0.45	$1.35	$2.25	£0.30	£0.90	£1.50
175-177	$0.40	$1.20	$2.00	£0.25	£0.75	£1.25
178-180 ND	$0.55	$1.65	$2.75	£0.35	£1.05	£1.75
181 ND 44pgs	$0.60	$1.80	$3.00	£0.40	£1.20	£2.00
Title Value:	$1036.80	$3084.65	$6901.80	£747.50	£2236.70	£4973.00

FEATURES
Captain Hunter in 99-106. Devil-Dog in 95-98. Gunner & Sarge in 51-94. Hunter's Hellcats in 106-122. Losers in 123-181. Super-Spy in 181.

OUR LOVE STORY
Marvel Comics Group; 1 Oct 1969-38 Feb 1976

	$Good	$Fine	$N.Mint	£Good	£Fine	£N.Mint
1 ND	$1.80	$5.25	$9.00	£1.20	£3.60	£6.00
2-4 ND	$0.80	$2.40	$4.00	£0.50	£1.50	£2.50
5 ND scarce in the U.K. 7pg Steranko story in famous psychedelia style						
	$3.00	$9.00	$15.00	£2.00	£6.00	£10.00
6-13 ND	$0.60	$1.80	$3.00	£0.40	£1.20	£2.00
14 ND	$1.20	$3.60	$6.00	£0.80	£2.40	£4.00
15-30 ND	$0.50	$1.50	$2.50	£0.30	£0.90	£1.50
31-38 ND	$0.40	$1.20	$2.00	£0.25	£0.75	£1.25
Title Value:	$24.40	$73.05	$122.00	£15.50	£46.50	£77.50

OUT OF THIS WORLD
Charlton; 1 Aug 1956-16 Dec 1959

	$Good	$Fine	$N.Mint	£Good	£Fine	£N.Mint
1 scarce in the U.K.	$20.50	$62.50	$125.00	£13.00	£40.00	£80.00
2 scarce in the U.K.	$11.50	$35.00	$70.00	£7.50	£22.50	£45.00
3-6 scarce in the U.K. Steve Ditko art	$25.00	$75.00	$150.00	£16.50	£50.00	£100.00
7 very scarce in the U.K. 68pgs, some Steve Ditko art	$25.00	$75.00	$150.00	£16.50	£50.00	£100.00
8 very scarce in the U.K. 68pgs, some Steve Ditko art	$20.50	$62.50	$125.00	£13.00	£40.00	£80.00
9-10 Steve Ditko art	$18.00	$55.00	$110.00	£12.50	£38.00	£75.00
11 Steve Ditko art	$20.50	$62.50	$125.00	£14.00	£43.00	£85.00
12 Steve Ditko art	$18.00	$55.00	$110.00	£12.50	£38.00	£75.00
13-15	$7.50	$22.50	$45.00	£5.00	£15.00	£30.00
16 Steve Ditko art	$18.00	$55.00	$110.00	£12.50	£38.00	£75.00
Title Value:	$292.50	$885.00	$1770.00	£195.00	£592.50	£1180.00

Note: issues #15 and #16 were the only ones officially distributed in the U.K.

OUTBREED 999
Blackout Comics; 1 May 1994-6 1995

	$Good	$Fine	$N.Mint	£Good	£Fine	£N.Mint
1-6 ND Bob Perry pencils and Dave Gutierrez ink	$0.50	$1.50	$2.50	£0.30	£0.90	£1.50
Title Value:	$3.00	$9.00	$15.00	£1.80	£5.40	£9.00

Commemorative Outbreed 999 Series Collection (Aug 1995)

	$Good	$Fine	$N.Mint	£Good	£Fine	£N.Mint
ND, set of issues #1-5, plus limited signed poster				£2.00	£6.00	£10.00

OUTCAST SPECIAL, THE
Acclaim Comics,OS; 1 Aug 1995

	$Good	$Fine	$N.Mint	£Good	£Fine	£N.Mint
1 ND Norm Breyfogle art	$0.50	$1.50	$2.50	£0.30	£0.90	£1.50
Title Value:	$0.50	$1.50	$2.50	£0.30	£0.90	£1.50

OUTCASTS
DC Comics,MS; 1 Oct 1987-12 Sep 1988

	$Good	$Fine	$N.Mint	£Good	£Fine	£N.Mint
1-12 ND	$0.25	$0.75	$1.25	£0.15	£0.45	£0.75
Title Value:	$3.00	$9.00	$15.00	£1.80	£5.40	£9.00

Note: Wagner/Grant scripts; Cam Kennedy/Steve Montano art in all; all Deluxe Format Baxter paper.

OUTER LIMITS, THE
Dell, TV; 1 Jan/Mar 1964-18 Oct 1969

	$Good	$Fine	$N.Mint	£Good	£Fine	£N.Mint
1 distributed in the U.K.	$8.25	$25.00	$50.00	£5.75	£17.50	£35.00
2 distributed in the U.K.	$5.00	$15.00	$30.00	£3.30	£10.00	£20.00
3-5 distributed in the U.K.	$3.30	$10.00	$20.00	£2.05	£6.25	£12.50
6-10 distributed in the U.K.	$2.90	$8.75	$17.50	£1.80	£5.50	£11.00
11-18 distributed in the U.K.	$3.00	$9.00	$15.00	£2.00	£6.00	£10.00
Title Value:	$61.65	$185.75	$347.50	£40.20	£121.75	£227.50

OUTER SPACE
Charlton; 17 May 1958-25 Dec 1959

	$Good	$Fine	$N.Mint	£Good	£Fine	£N.Mint
17	$11.50	$35.00	$70.00	£7.50	£22.50	£45.00
18-20 Steve Ditko art	$16.50	$50.00	$100.00	£10.50	£33.00	£65.00
21 Steve Ditko cover						
	$10.00	$30.00	$60.00	£6.50	£20.00	£40.00
22-24 pence-stamp copies known	$10.00	$30.00	$60.00	£6.50	£20.00	£40.00
1st official distribution in the U.K.						
25	$10.00	$30.00	$60.00	£6.50	£20.00	£40.00
Title Value:	$111.00	$335.00	$670.00	£71.50	£221.50	£440.00

Note: issues #24 and 25 were the only ones officially distributed in the U.K.

OUTER SPACE (2ND SERIES)
Charlton; 1 Nov 1968

	$Good	$Fine	$N.Mint	£Good	£Fine	£N.Mint
1 scarce in the U.K. Steve Ditko art (10pgs), Pat Boyette cover; distributed in the U.K.	$6.00	$18.00	$30.00	£4.00	£12.00	£20.00
Title Value:	$6.00	$18.00	$30.00	£4.00	£12.00	£20.00

OUTLANDER
Malibu/Eternity; 1 Oct 1987-7 Jun 1988

	$Good	$Fine	$N.Mint	£Good	£Fine	£N.Mint
1-7 ND black and white	$0.40	$1.20	$2.00	£0.25	£0.75	£1.25
Title Value:	$2.80	$8.40	$14.00	£1.75	£5.25	£8.75

OUTLANDERS
Dark Horse; 0 May 1992; 1 Jan 1989-33 Nov 1991

	$Good	$Fine	$N.Mint	£Good	£Fine	£N.Mint
0 ND 40pgs, includes fold-out mini-poster	$0.55	$1.65	$2.75	£0.35	£1.05	£1.75
1-25 ND	$0.50	$1.50	$2.50	£0.30	£0.90	£1.50
26 ND 56pgs	$0.50	$1.50	$2.50	£0.35	£1.05	£1.75
27-33 ND	$0.50	$1.50	$2.50	£0.30	£0.90	£1.50
Title Value:	$17.05	$51.15	$85.25	£10.30	£30.90	£51.50

Note: issues #1-7 are black and white

	£Good	£Fine	£N.Mint
Graphic Novel Collection 1, reprints #1-4	£1.40	£4.20	£7.00
Graphic Novel Collection 2 (Nov 1990), reprints issues #5-8 plus 20 new pages	£1.30	£3.90	£6.50
Graphic Novel Collection 3 (1992) reprints issues #9-12	£1.30	£3.90	£6.50
Outlanders Special 1 (Mar 1993), new material	£0.30	£0.90	£1.50
Outlander Volume 4 (Mar 1995) Trade paperback reprints issues #13-16, Ken Macklin painted cover	£1.70	£5.10	£8.50

OUTLANDERS EPILOGUE
Dark Horse,OS; 1 Mar 1994

	$Good	$Fine	$N.Mint	£Good	£Fine	£N.Mint
1 ND black and white	$0.50	$1.50	$2.50	£0.30	£0.90	£1.50
Title Value:	$0.50	$1.50	$2.50	£0.30	£0.90	£1.50

OUTLAW KID, THE
Marvel Comics Group; 1 Aug 1970-30 Oct 1975

	$Good	$Fine	$N.Mint	£Good	£Fine	£N.Mint
1-2	$0.80	$2.40	$4.00	£0.50	£1.50	£2.50
3 Williamson reprint	$0.50	$1.50	$2.50	£0.30	£0.90	£1.50
4-5	$0.50	$1.50	$2.50	£0.30	£0.90	£1.50
6	$0.50	$1.50	$2.50	£0.25	£0.75	£1.25
7-8 ND 52pgs	$0.50	$1.50	$2.50	£0.30	£0.90	£1.50
9 ND scarce in the U.K. Williamson reprint	$0.50	$1.50	$2.50	£0.30	£0.90	£1.50
10 ND scarce in the U.K. origin new Outlaw Kid	$0.50	$1.50	$2.50	£0.30	£0.90	£1.50
11-27 ND	$0.40	$1.20	$2.00	£0.25	£0.75	£1.25
28 ND Williamson reprint	$0.40	$1.20	$2.00	£0.25	£0.75	£1.25
29-30 ND	$0.40	$1.20	$2.00	£0.25	£0.75	£1.25
Title Value:	$13.60	$40.80	$68.00	£8.35	£25.05	£41.75

Note: all issues are reprint apart from one new story each in issues #10-16.

OUTLAWS
DC Comics,MS; 1 Sep 1991-8 Apr 1992

	$Good	$Fine	$N.Mint	£Good	£Fine	£N.Mint
1-8	$0.25	$0.75	$1.25	£0.15	£0.45	£0.75
Title Value:	$1.75	$5.25	$8.75	£1.05	£3.15	£5.25

OUTLAWS OF THE WEST
Charlton; 11 Sep 1957-81 May 1970; 82 Jul 1979-88 Apr 1980

	$Good	$Fine	$N.Mint	£Good	£Fine	£N.Mint
11 scarce in the U.K.	$7.50	$22.50	$45.00	£5.00	£15.00	£30.00
12-13	$3.75	$11.00	$22.50	£2.05	£6.25	£12.50
14 68pgs	$4.55	$13.50	$27.50	£2.90	£8.75	£17.50
15-17	$3.75	$11.00	$22.50	£2.50	£7.50	£15.00
18 Steve Ditko art	$8.25	$25.00	$50.00	£5.75	£17.50	£35.00
19-20	$3.75	$11.00	$22.50	£2.05	£6.25	£12.50
21-27	$2.50	$7.50	$15.00	£1.65	£5.00	£10.00
1st official distribution in the U.K.						
28-30	$2.50	$7.50	$15.00	£1.65	£5.00	£10.00
31-50	$1.50	$4.50	$9.00	£1.00	£3.00	£6.00
51-53	$0.80	$2.50	$5.00	£0.55	£1.75	£3.50
54 Kid Montana appears	$0.80	$2.50	$5.00	£0.55	£1.75	£3.50
55-63	$0.80	$2.50	$5.00	£0.55	£1.75	£3.50
64 1st appearance Captain Doom	$1.00	$3.00	$5.00	£0.70	£2.10	£3.50
65-70	$1.00	$3.00	$5.00	£0.70	£2.10	£3.50
71-72	$0.60	$1.80	$3.00	£0.40	£1.20	£2.00
73 1st appearance The Sharp Shooter	$0.60	$1.80	$3.00	£0.40	£1.20	£2.00
74-79	$0.60	$1.80	$3.00	£0.40	£1.20	£2.00
80-81 Steve Ditko art	$0.80	$2.40	$4.00	£0.50	£1.50	£2.50
82-88	$0.50	$1.50	$2.50	£0.30	£0.90	£1.50
Title Value:	$129.45	$388.00	$762.50	£84.60	£256.30	£501.00

Note: most issues after 1959 distributed on the new-stands in the U.K.

OUTSIDERS ANNUAL
DC Comics; 1 1986

1 ND Kevin Nowlan art featuring Batman

	$Good	$Fine	$N.Mint	£Good	£Fine	£N.Mint
	$0.50	$1.50	$2.50	£0.30	£0.90	£1.50
Title Value:	$0.50	$1.50	$2.50	£0.30	£0.90	£1.50

OUTSIDERS SPECIAL
DC Comics; 1 Jul 1987

	$Good	$Fine	$N.Mint	£Good	£Fine	£N.Mint
1 ND	$0.40	$1.20	$2.00	£0.25	£0.75	£1.25
Title Value:	$0.40	$1.20	$2.00	£0.25	£0.75	£1.25

OUTSIDERS, THE
DC Comics; 1 Nov 1985-28 Feb 1988
(see also Batman and the...)

	$Good	$Fine	$N.Mint	£Good	£Fine	£N.Mint
1-10 ND	$0.40	$1.20	$2.00	£0.25	£0.75	£1.25
11 ND John Byrne art, Bolland pin-up						
	$0.40	$1.20	$2.00	£0.25	£0.75	£1.25
12-17 ND	$0.30	$0.90	$1.50	£0.20	£0.60	£1.00
18-22 ND Batman appears						
	$0.30	$0.90	$1.50	£0.20	£0.60	£1.00
23-26 ND	$0.30	$0.90	$1.50	£0.20	£0.60	£1.00
27-28 ND Millennium X-over, Erik Larsen art						
	$0.30	$0.90	$1.50	£0.20	£0.60	£1.00
Title Value:	$9.50	$28.50	$47.50	£6.15	£18.45	£30.75

Note: all Deluxe Format Baxter paper.

OUTSIDERS, THE (2ND SERIES)
DC Comics; 0 Oct 1994; 1 Nov 1993-24 Nov 1995

	$Good	$Fine	$N.Mint	£Good	£Fine	£N.Mint
0 (Oct 1994) Zero Hour X-over, The Eradicator forms a new team of Outsiders						
	$0.40	$1.20	$2.00	£0.25	£0.75	£1.25
1 Version 1A (alpha) featuring Geo-Force, Technocrat and Faust; each issue has four common pages						
but can be read as stand-alone stories						
	$0.40	$1.20	$2.00	£0.25	£0.75	£1.25
1 Version 1B (omega) featuring Halo, Katana and Looker; each issue has four common pages						
but can be read as stand-alone stories; both comics have Travis Charest covers			£0.75	£1.25		
	$0.40	$1.20	$2.00	£0.25	£0.75	£1.25
2	$0.40	$1.20	$2.00	£0.25	£0.75	£1.25
3-4 The Eradicator appears						
	$0.40	$1.20	$2.00	£0.25	£0.75	£1.25
5-6	$0.40	$1.20	$2.00	£0.25	£0.75	£1.25
7 Batman cameo	$0.40	$1.20	$2.00	£0.25	£0.75	£1.25
8 Batman appears	$0.40	$1.20	$2.00	£0.25	£0.75	£1.25
9-10	$0.40	$1.20	$2.00	£0.25	£0.75	£1.25
11 Zero Hour X-over						
	$0.40	$1.20	$2.00	£0.25	£0.75	£1.25
12-13	$0.40	$1.20	$2.00	£0.25	£0.75	£1.25
14 Lady Shiva appears						
	$0.40	$1.20	$2.00	£0.25	£0.75	£1.25
15	$0.40	$1.20	$2.00	£0.25	£0.75	£1.25
16 ties into Showcase '95 #3						
	$0.40	$1.20	$2.00	£0.25	£0.75	£1.25
17 Green Lantern, Darkstar and Arsenal appear						
	$0.40	$1.20	$2.00	£0.25	£0.75	£1.25
18-19	$0.40	$1.20	$2.00	£0.25	£0.75	£1.25
20 Outsiders vs. Metamorpho						
	$0.40	$1.20	$2.00	£0.25	£0.75	£1.25
21-23	$0.40	$1.20	$2.00	£0.25	£0.75	£1.25
24 Eradicator, Superboy, Supergirl and Steel appear						
	$0.40	$1.20	$2.00	£0.25	£0.75	£1.25
Title Value:	$10.40	$31.20	$52.00	£6.50	£19.50	£32.50

OVER THE EDGE
Marvel Comics Group; 1 Nov 1995-present

	$Good	$Fine	$N.Mint	£Good	£Fine	£N.Mint
1 ND Daredevil vs. Mr. Fear						
	$0.20	$0.60	$1.00	£0.10	£0.35	£0.65
2 ND Dr. Strange appears						
	$0.20	$0.60	$1.00	£0.10	£0.35	£0.65
3 ND Hulk appears	$0.20	$0.60	$1.00	£0.10	£0.35	£0.65
4 ND Ghost Rider appears						
	$0.20	$0.60	$1.00	£0.10	£0.35	£0.65
5 ND The Punisher appears						
	$0.20	$0.60	$1.00	£0.10	£0.35	£0.65
Title Value:	$1.00	$3.00	$5.00	£0.50	£1.75	£3.25

OWL, THE
Gold Key; 1 Apr 1967-2 Apr 1968

	$Good	$Fine	$N.Mint	£Good	£Fine	£N.Mint
1 distributed in the U.K.						
	$3.75	$11.00	$22.50	£2.50	£7.50	£15.00
2 distributed in the U.K.						
	$3.30	$10.00	$20.00	£2.30	£7.00	£14.00
Title Value:	$7.05	$21.00	$42.50	£4.80	£14.50	£29.00

OWLHOOTS
Kitchen Sink; 1,2 1991

	$Good	$Fine	$N.Mint	£Good	£Fine	£N.Mint
1-2 ND James Vance script, John Garcia art; sepia colour						
	$0.30	$0.90	$1.50	£0.20	£0.60	£1.00
Title Value:	$0.60	$1.80	$3.00	£0.40	£1.20	£2.00

OZ-WONDERLAND WAR
DC Comics,MS; 1 Jan 1986-3 Mar 1986
(see also Captain Carrot)

	$Good	$Fine	$N.Mint	£Good	£Fine	£N.Mint
1-2 ND DS	$0.25	$0.75	$1.25	£0.15	£0.45	£0.75
3 ND DS, Doom Patrol cameo						
	$0.25	$0.75	$1.25	£0.15	£0.45	£0.75
Title Value:	$0.75	$2.25	$3.75	£0.45	£1.35	£2.25

P

P.I'S: MICHAEL MAUSER & MR. TREE
First,MS; 1 Jan 1983-3 May 1985

	$Good	$Fine	$N.Mint	£Good	£Fine	£N.Mint
1-3 ND	$0.40	$1.20	$2.00	£0.25	£0.75	£1.25

	$Good	$Fine	$N.Mint	£Good	£Fine	£N.Mint
Title Value:	$1.20	$3.60	$6.00	£0.75	£2.25	£3.75

P.J. WARLOCK
Eclipse; 1 Nov 1986-3 May 1987

	$Good	$Fine	$N.Mint	£Good	£Fine	£N.Mint
1-3 ND Bill Schorr art, black and white						
	$0.40	$1.20	$2.00	£0.25	£0.75	£1.25
Title Value:	$1.20	$3.60	$6.00	£0.75	£2.25	£3.75

PACIFIC PRESENTS
Pacific; 1 Oct 1982-4 Jun 1984

	$Good	$Fine	$N.Mint	£Good	£Fine	£N.Mint
1 ND Rocketeer by Dave Stevens, Missing Man by Steve Ditko						
	$1.00	$3.00	$5.00	£0.70	£2.10	£3.50
2 ND Rocketeer by Dave Stevens, Missing Man by Steve Ditko						
	$0.80	$2.40	$4.00	£0.60	£1.80	£3.00
3-4 ND Tim Conrad art						
	$0.30	$0.90	$1.50	£0.20	£0.60	£1.00
Title Value:	$2.40	$7.20	$12.00	£1.70	£5.10	£8.50

PACT, THE
Image,MS; 1 Feb 1994-3 Jun 1994

	$Good	$Fine	$N.Mint	£Good	£Fine	£N.Mint
1 ND Jim Valentino layout art, Walter McDanial pencils and Matt Banning inks						
	$0.40	$1.20	$2.00	£0.25	£0.75	£1.25
2 ND Youngblood appear						
	$0.40	$1.20	$2.00	£0.25	£0.75	£1.25
3 ND The Pact vs. The Renegades						
	$0.40	$1.20	$2.00	£0.25	£0.75	£1.25
Title Value:	$1.20	$3.60	$6.00	£0.75	£2.25	£3.75

PALADIN
Valiant; 1 Mar 1992

	$Good	$Fine	$N.Mint	£Good	£Fine	£N.Mint
1 ND 28pgs, three-panel gatefold cover, metallic silver ink logo						
	$0.40	$1.20	$2.00	£0.25	£0.75	£1.25
Title Value:	$0.40	$1.20	$2.00	£0.25	£0.75	£1.25

PALADIN ALPHA
Firstlight Comixx; 1 Dec 1994-2 Jan 1995

	$Good	$Fine	$N.Mint	£Good	£Fine	£N.Mint
1 ND Darryl Banks cover						
	$0.50	$1.50	$2.50	£0.30	£0.90	£1.50
2 ND	$0.50	$1.50	$2.50	£0.30	£0.90	£1.50
Title Value:	$1.00	$3.00	$5.00	£0.60	£1.80	£3.00

PARADAX
Vortex; 1 Apr 1987-2 Aug 1987

	$Good	$Fine	$N.Mint	£Good	£Fine	£N.Mint
1 ND Milligan/McCarthy art						
	$0.50	$1.50	$2.50	£0.30	£0.90	£1.50
2 ND reprints from Strange Days #1-3						
	$0.50	$1.50	$2.50	£0.30	£0.90	£1.50
Title Value:	$1.00	$3.00	$5.00	£0.60	£1.80	£3.00

PARADIGM
Gauntlet Comics; 1 1993-4 1994

	$Good	$Fine	$N.Mint	£Good	£Fine	£N.Mint
1-2 ND	$0.50	$1.50	$2.50	£0.30	£0.90	£1.50
2 ND Collector's Edition (Oct 1993) – pre-bagged with limited edition print						
	$0.60	$1.80	$3.00	£0.40	£1.20	£2.00
3-4 ND	$0.50	$1.50	$2.50	£0.30	£0.90	£1.50
Title Value:	$2.60	$7.80	$13.00	£1.60	£4.80	£8.00

PARAGON: DARK APOCALYPSE
AC Comics,MS; 1 Apr 1993-4 Jun 1993

	$Good	$Fine	$N.Mint	£Good	£Fine	£N.Mint
1-4 ND	$0.50	$1.50	$2.50	£0.30	£0.90	£1.50
Title Value:	$2.00	$6.00	$10.00	£1.20	£3.60	£6.00

PARANOIA
Adventure,MS; 1 Nov 1991-6 Apr 1992

	$Good	$Fine	$N.Mint	£Good	£Fine	£N.Mint
1-6 ND colour	$0.50	$1.50	$2.50	£0.30	£0.90	£1.50
Title Value:	$3.00	$9.00	$15.00	£1.80	£5.40	£9.00

PARSIFAL
Star Reach; 1 May 1978

	$Good	$Fine	$N.Mint	£Good	£Fine	£N.Mint
1 ND P. Craig Russell, reprints Star Reach #8, #10						
	$0.40	$1.20	$2.00	£0.25	£0.75	£1.25
Title Value:	$0.40	$1.20	$2.00	£0.25	£0.75	£1.25

PARTICLE DREAMS
Fantagraphics; 1 Aug 1986-6 Jun 1987

	$Good	$Fine	$N.Mint	£Good	£Fine	£N.Mint
1-6 ND Kief Llama by Matt Howarth						
	$0.60	$1.80	$3.00	£0.40	£1.20	£2.00
Title Value:	$3.60	$10.80	$18.00	£2.40	£7.20	£12.00

PARTNERS IN PANDEMONIUM
Caliber Press,MS; 1 Nov 1991-3 1992

	$Good	$Fine	$N.Mint	£Good	£Fine	£N.Mint
1-3 ND	$0.40	$1.20	$2.00	£0.25	£0.75	£1.25
Title Value:	$1.20	$3.60	$6.00	£0.75	£2.25	£3.75

PARTS UNKNOWN
Eclipse/FX Comix,MS; 1 Jul 1992-4 Oct 1992

	$Good	$Fine	$N.Mint	£Good	£Fine	£N.Mint
1-4 ND based on film						
	$0.40	$1.20	$2.00	£0.25	£0.75	£1.25
Title Value:	$1.60	$4.80	$8.00	£1.00	£3.00	£5.00

PARTS UNKNOWN II: THE NEXT INVASION
Eclipse; 1 Dec 1993-3 Feb 1994

	$Good	$Fine	$N.Mint	£Good	£Fine	£N.Mint
1-3 ND Brad Gorby art; black and white						
	$0.50	$1.50	$2.50	£0.30	£0.90	£1.50
Title Value:	$1.50	$4.50	$7.50	£0.90	£2.70	£4.50

PARTS UNKNOWN: DARK INTENTIONS
Knight Press; 0 Aug 1995; 1 1995-present

	$Good	$Fine	$N.Mint	£Good	£Fine	£N.Mint
0 ND Beau Smith script, Brad Gorby and Mark Heike art; black and white						
	$0.50	$1.50	$2.50	£0.30	£0.90	£1.50
1-3 ND Beau Smith script, Brad Gorby art; black and white						
	$0.50	$1.50	$2.50	£0.30	£0.90	£1.50
Title Value:	$2.00	$6.00	$10.00	£1.20	£3.60	£6.00

PAT BOONE
National Periodical Publications, TV; 1 Sep/Oct 1959-5 May/Jun 1960
(see also Lois Lane #9)

	$Good	$Fine	$N.Mint	£Good	£Fine	£N.Mint
1 photo cover	$39.00	$115.00	$275.00	£25.00	£75.00	£175.00

MINT = 100% / NEAR MINT (inc. +/-) = 90–99% / VERY FINE (inc. +/-) = 75–89% / FINE (inc. +/-) = 55–74%
VERY GOOD (inc. +/-) = 35–54% / GOOD (inc. +/-) = 15–34% / FAIR = 5–14% / POOR = 1–4%

493

	$Good	$Fine	$N.Mint	£Good	£Fine	£N.Mint
1st official distribution in the U.K.						
2-5	$32.00	$95.00	$225.00	£21.00	£62.50	£150.00
Title Value:	$167.00	$495.00	$1175.00	£109.00	£325.00	£775.00

PAT SAVAGE: WOMAN OF BRONZE SPECIAL
Millennium,OS; 1 Sep 1992

	$Good	$Fine	$N.Mint	£Good	£Fine	£N.Mint
1 ND the cousin of Doc Savage, cover/art by Brian Stelfreeze with Adam Hughes						
	$0.40	$1.20	$2.00	£0.25	£0.75	£1.25
Title Value:	$0.40	$1.20	$2.00	£0.25	£0.75	£1.25

PATHWAYS TO FANTASY
Pacific; 1 Jul 1984

	$Good	$Fine	$N.Mint	£Good	£Fine	£N.Mint
1 ND John Bolton, Scott Hampton, Jeff Jones, Barry Smith, Leila Dowling art						
	$0.60	$1.80	$3.00	£0.40	£1.20	£2.00
Title Value:	$0.60	$1.80	$3.00	£0.40	£1.20	£2.00

PATSY AND HEDY ANNUAL
Marvel Comics Group; 1 1963

	$Good	$Fine	$N.Mint	£Good	£Fine	£N.Mint
1 scarce in the U.K. 68pgs						
	$6.50	$20.00	$40.00	£4.55	£13.50	£27.50
Title Value:	$6.50	$20.00	$40.00	£4.55	£13.50	£27.50

PATSY AND HEDY CAREER GIRLS
Marvel Comics Group; 70 Jun/Jul 1960-110 Feb 1967
(previous issues ND)

	$Good	$Fine	$N.Mint	£Good	£Fine	£N.Mint
70-110	$1.50	$4.50	$9.00	£1.00	£3.00	£6.00
Title Value:	$61.50	$184.50	$369.00	£41.00	£123.00	£246.00

PATSY WALKER
Marvel Comics Group; 51 Nov 1959-124 Dec 1965
(previous issues ND)

	$Good	$Fine	$N.Mint	£Good	£Fine	£N.Mint
51-60	$3.75	$11.00	$22.50	£2.50	£7.50	£15.00
61-80	$2.90	$8.75	$17.50	£2.05	£6.25	£12.50
81-91	$2.05	$6.25	$12.50	£1.50	£4.50	£9.00
92 Millie X-over	$2.05	$6.25	$12.50	£1.50	£4.50	£9.00
93-97	$2.05	$6.25	$12.50	£1.50	£4.50	£9.00
98 Millie X-over	$2.05	$6.25	$12.50	£1.50	£4.50	£9.00
99	$2.05	$6.25	$12.50	£1.50	£4.50	£9.00
100	$2.50	$7.50	$15.00	£1.65	£5.00	£10.00
101-124	$1.50	$4.50	$9.00	£1.00	£3.00	£6.00
Title Value:	$172.95	$519.25	$1043.50	£120.15	£362.50	£725.00

PATSY WALKER FASHION PARADE
Marvel Comics Group; 1 1966

	$Good	$Fine	$N.Mint	£Good	£Fine	£N.Mint
1 rare in the U.K., 68pgs						
	$6.25	$18.50	$37.50	£4.15	£12.50	£25.00
Title Value:	$6.25	$18.50	$37.50	£4.15	£12.50	£25.00

PAUL THE SAMURAI
New England Comics,MS; 1 Oct 1990-3 Sep 1991

	$Good	$Fine	$N.Mint	£Good	£Fine	£N.Mint
1-3 ND	$0.70	$2.10	$3.50	£0.50	£1.50	£2.50
Title Value:	$2.10	$6.30	$10.50	£1.50	£4.50	£7.50

PAUL THE SAMURAI (2ND SERIES)
New England Comics; 1 Jun 1992-10 Feb 1992

	$Good	$Fine	$N.Mint	£Good	£Fine	£N.Mint
1 ND oversized "Tick" format, more serious treatment of character						
	$0.70	$2.10	$3.50	£0.50	£1.50	£2.50
2-3 ND	$0.60	$1.80	$3.00	£0.40	£1.20	£2.00
4-10 ND	$0.55	$1.65	$2.75	£0.35	£1.05	£1.75
Title Value:	$5.75	$17.25	$28.75	£3.75	£11.25	£18.75

PEACEMAKER
Charlton; 1 Mar 1967-5 Nov 1967

	$Good	$Fine	$N.Mint	£Good	£Fine	£N.Mint
1 distributed in the U.K.						
	$2.90	$8.75	$17.50	£2.05	£6.25	£12.50
2-3 distributed in the U.K.						
	$2.00	$6.00	$10.00	£1.40	£4.20	£7.00
4 origin told; distributed in the U.K.						
	$3.50	$10.50	$17.50	£2.50	£7.50	£12.50
5 distributed in the U.K.						
	$2.00	$6.00	$10.00	£1.40	£4.20	£7.00
Title Value:	$12.40	$37.25	$65.00	£8.75	£26.35	£46.00

PEACEMAKER
DC Comics,MS; 1 Jan 1988-4 Apr 1988

	$Good	$Fine	$N.Mint	£Good	£Fine	£N.Mint
1-4	$0.15	$0.45	$0.75	£0.10	£0.35	£0.60
Title Value:	$0.60	$1.80	$3.00	£0.40	£1.40	£2.40

Note: Deluxe Format

PELLEAS & MELISANDE
Eclipse; (Night Music 4,5); 1,2 1986

	$Good	$Fine	$N.Mint	£Good	£Fine	£N.Mint
1-2 ND P. Craig Russell art						
	$0.40	$1.20	$2.00	£0.25	£0.75	£1.25
Title Value:	$0.80	$2.40	$4.00	£0.50	£1.50	£2.50

PENDULUM
Adventure,MS; 1 Nov 1992-4 Feb 1993

	$Good	$Fine	$N.Mint	£Good	£Fine	£N.Mint
1-4 ND	$0.40	$1.20	$2.00	£0.25	£0.75	£1.25
Title Value:	$1.60	$4.80	$8.00	£1.00	£3.00	£5.00

PENDULUM PRESS CLASSICS
Pendulum Press; 1 Jan 1991-6 1991

	$Good	$Fine	$N.Mint	£Good	£Fine	£N.Mint
1 ND Moby Dick, 64pgs						
	$0.70	$2.10	$3.50	£0.50	£1.50	£2.50
2 ND Treasure Island, 64pgs						
	$0.70	$2.10	$3.50	£0.50	£1.50	£2.50
3 ND Dr. Jekyll and Mr. Hyde						
	$0.70	$2.10	$3.50	£0.50	£1.50	£2.50
4 ND 20,000 Leagues Under The Sea						
	$0.70	$2.10	$3.50	£0.50	£1.50	£2.50
5 ND A Christmas Carol						
	$0.70	$2.10	$3.50	£0.50	£1.50	£2.50
6 ND A Midsummer Night's Dream						
	$0.70	$2.10	$3.50	£0.50	£1.50	£2.50
Title Value:	$4.20	$12.60	$21.00	£3.00	£9.00	£15.00

	$Good	$Fine	$N.Mint	£Good	£Fine	£N.Mint
Pendulum Press Collectors Kit: each of the above comes with a 30 minute audio cassette and illustrated pamphlet				£0.85	£2.55	£4.25

PENTACLE: SIGN OF THE FIVE
Eternity,MS; 1 Jan 1991-4 Apr 1991

	$Good	$Fine	$N.Mint	£Good	£Fine	£N.Mint
1 ND continues story of Warlock 5 (Aircel), black and white						
	$0.40	$1.20	$2.00	£0.25	£0.75	£1.25
2-4 ND black and white	$0.40	$1.20	$2.00	£0.25	£0.75	£1.25
Title Value:	$1.60	$4.80	$8.00	£1.00	£3.00	£5.00

PERG
Lightning Comics; 1 Dec 1993-8 1994

	$Good	$Fine	$N.Mint	£Good	£Fine	£N.Mint
1 ND glow in the dark flip-cover						
	$0.40	$1.20	$2.00	£0.25	£0.75	£1.25
1 ND Platinum Edition (Sep 1994), signed and limited to 2,000 copies						
	$1.20	$3.60	$6.00	£0.80	£2.40	£4.00
2 ND	$0.40	$1.20	$2.00	£0.25	£0.75	£1.25
2 Platinum Edition ND						
	$1.00	$3.00	$5.00	£0.70	£2.10	£3.50
3 ND	$0.40	$1.20	$2.00	£0.25	£0.75	£1.25
3 Platinum Edition ND						
	$1.00	$3.00	$5.00	£0.70	£2.10	£3.50
4 ND 1st appearance Hellina						
	$0.60	$1.80	$3.00	£0.40	£1.20	£2.00
4 ND Platinum Edition (Jan 1995) – metallic ink cover, signed by Joseph Zyskowski, 1,500 copies						
	$2.00	$6.00	$10.00	£1.20	£3.60	£6.00
4 ND Signed and numbered Edition (Jul 1995) – pre-bagged in mylar sleeve, 500 copies						
	$1.50	$4.50	$7.50	£1.00	£3.00	£5.00
5-8 ND	$0.40	$1.20	$2.00	£0.25	£0.75	£1.25
Title Value:	$10.10	$30.30	$50.50	£6.55	£19.65	£32.75

PETER CANNON: THUNDERBOLT
DC Comics; 1 Sep 1992-12 Aug 1993

	$Good	$Fine	$N.Mint	£Good	£Fine	£N.Mint
1 Michael Collins script/art begins						
	$0.25	$0.75	$1.25	£0.15	£0.45	£0.75
2-8	$0.25	$0.75	$1.25	£0.15	£0.45	£0.75
9 Justice League Europe appear, $1.50 cover begins						
	$0.25	$0.75	$1.25	£0.15	£0.45	£0.75
10 Justice League Europe appear						
	$0.25	$0.75	$1.25	£0.15	£0.45	£0.75
11-12	$0.25	$0.75	$1.25	£0.15	£0.45	£0.75
Title Value:	$3.00	$9.00	$15.00	£1.80	£5.40	£9.00

PETER PAN GRAPHIC NOVEL
Disney; nn Nov 1990

	$Good	$Fine	$N.Mint	£Good	£Fine	£N.Mint
nn ND 64pgs, adaptation of film						
	$1.00	$3.00	$5.00	£0.70	£2.10	£3.50
Title Value:	$1.00	$3.00	$5.00	£0.70	£2.10	£3.50

PETER PAN GRAPHIC NOVEL, COMPLETE
Adventure,OS; 1 Feb 1992

	$Good	$Fine	$N.Mint	£Good	£Fine	£N.Mint
1 ND 40pgs, collects 2-part mini-series						
	$1.00	$3.00	$5.00	£0.70	£2.10	£3.50
Title Value:	$1.00	$3.00	$5.00	£0.70	£2.10	£3.50

PETER PAN: RETURN TO NEVER NEVER LAND
Adventure,MS; 1,2 Sep 1991

	$Good	$Fine	$N.Mint	£Good	£Fine	£N.Mint
1-2 ND adaptation of classic story						
	$0.40	$1.20	$2.00	£0.25	£0.75	£1.25
Title Value:	$0.80	$2.40	$4.00	£0.50	£1.50	£2.50

PETER PORKCHOPS
National Periodical Publications; 61 Sep/Nov 1959; 62 Oct/Dec 1960
(Previous issues ND)

	$Good	$Fine	$N.Mint	£Good	£Fine	£N.Mint
61-62 very scarce in the U.K.						
	$8.25	$25.00	$50.00	£5.75	£17.50	£35.00
Title Value:	$16.50	$50.00	$100.00	£11.50	£35.00	£70.00

Note: character becomes Pig-Iron in Captain Carrot

PETER RABBIT 3-D
Eternity,OS; 1 Apr 1990

	$Good	$Fine	$N.Mint	£Good	£Fine	£N.Mint
1 ND reprints by Harrison Cady; with bound-in 3-D glasses (25% less if without glasses)						
	$0.30	$0.90	$1.50	£0.20	£0.60	£1.00
Title Value:	$0.30	$0.90	$1.50	£0.20	£0.60	£1.00

PETER THE LITTLE PEST
Marvel Comics Group; 1 Nov 1969-4 May 1970

	$Good	$Fine	$N.Mint	£Good	£Fine	£N.Mint
1 ND	$1.50	$4.50	$9.00	£1.00	£3.00	£6.00
2-4 ND reprints	$1.00	$3.00	$5.00	£0.70	£2.10	£3.50
Title Value:	$4.50	$13.50	$24.00	£3.10	£9.30	£16.50

PHANTOM
Marvel Comics Group,MS; 1 Feb 1995-3 Apr 1995

	$Good	$Fine	$N.Mint	£Good	£Fine	£N.Mint
1-3 ties in with US animated TV series; Glen Lumsden art						
	$0.60	$1.80	$3.00	£0.40	£1.20	£2.00
Title Value:	$1.80	$5.40	$9.00	£1.20	£3.60	£6.00

PHANTOM
Pioneer,MS; 1 May 1990-4 Aug 1990

	$Good	$Fine	$N.Mint	£Good	£Fine	£N.Mint
1-4 ND material never-before reprinted						
	$0.90	$2.70	$4.50	£0.60	£1.80	£3.00
Title Value:	$3.60	$10.80	$18.00	£2.40	£7.20	£12.00

PHANTOM 2040
Marvel Comics Group,MS; 1 May 1995-4 Aug 1995

	$Good	$Fine	$N.Mint	£Good	£Fine	£N.Mint
1 ND based on US TV cartoon; Steve Ditko art; centrespread poster by Steve Ditko and John Romita (1st time collaboration)						
	$0.30	$0.90	$1.50	£0.20	£0.60	£1.00
2-4 ND based on US TV cartoon; Steve Ditko art						
	$0.30	$0.90	$1.50	£0.20	£0.60	£1.00
Title Value:	$1.20	$3.60	$6.00	£0.80	£2.40	£4.00

PHANTOM FORCE
Image,MS; 1 Dec 1993-2 May 1994; Genesis West; 0 Mar 1994; 3 May 1994-10 1995

	$Good	$Fine	$N.Mint	£Good	£Fine	£N.Mint

0 (Mar 1994) Jack Kirby pencils (8pgs), cover by Jack Kirby and Jim Lee

| | $0.40 | $1.20 | $2.00 | £0.25 | £0.75 | £1.25 |

1 pre-bagged with trading card (5 different); Jack Kirby plot and pencils, inks by Liefeld, Larsen, McFarlane, Williams and Lee

| | $0.40 | $1.20 | $2.00 | £0.25 | £0.75 | £1.25 |

2 64pgs, Jack Kirby pencils (8pgs), inked by Liefeld, Larsen, Gordon, Ordway, Giffen; cover by Kirby and Larsen

| | $0.50 | $1.50 | $2.50 | £0.30 | £0.90 | £1.50 |

3 Jack Kirby pencils (8pgs), inked by Liefeld, Larsen, Thibideaux, Giffen, Ordway and Gordon; cover by Kirby and McFarlane

| | $0.40 | $1.20 | $2.00 | £0.25 | £0.75 | £1.25 |

4 Jack Kirby and Michael Thibodeaux cover, Kirby splash page

| | $0.40 | $1.20 | $2.00 | £0.25 | £0.75 | £1.25 |

5-8 Michael Thibodeaux script

| | $0.40 | $1.20 | $2.00 | £0.25 | £0.75 | £1.25 |

9 Michael Thibodeaux script and art, Jack Kirby cover (one of his last?)

| | $0.40 | $1.20 | $2.00 | £0.25 | £0.75 | £1.25 |

10 Michael Thibodeaux art; origin of Kublak

| | $0.40 | $1.20 | $2.00 | £0.25 | £0.75 | £1.25 |
| **Title Value:** | $4.50 | $13.50 | $22.50 | £2.80 | £8.40 | £14.00 |

Note: all Non-Distributed on the news-stands in the U.K.

PHANTOM OF FEAR CITY

Claypool Comics; 1 May 1993-12 Apr 1994

1 ND Steve Englehart script begins

	$0.40	$1.20	$2.00	£0.25	£0.75	£1.25
2-12 ND	$0.40	$1.20	$2.00	£0.25	£0.75	£1.25
Title Value:	$4.80	$14.40	$24.00	£3.00	£9.00	£15.00

PHANTOM SPECIAL EDITION

Pioneer,MS; 1 May 1990-4 Jul 1990

1-4 ND reprints of Sunday paper strips

| | $2.00 | $6.00 | $10.00 | £1.40 | £4.20 | £7.00 |
| **Title Value:** | $8.00 | $24.00 | $40.00 | £5.60 | £16.80 | £28.00 |

PHANTOM STRANGER

National Periodical Publications; 1 May/Jun 1969-41 Feb/Mar 1976

(see Brave and the Bold, DComics Presents, DC Super-Stars, Saga of Swamp Thing, Showcase #80)

| **1** | $7.75 | $23.50 | $55.00 | £5.00 | £15.00 | £35.00 |
| **2** | $3.30 | $10.00 | $20.00 | £2.05 | £6.25 | £12.50 |

3 Neal Adams cover

| | $3.30 | $10.00 | $20.00 | £2.05 | £6.25 | £12.50 |
| **4** Neal Adams art | $3.75 | $11.00 | $22.50 | £2.50 | £7.50 | £15.00 |

5-10 Neal Adams cover

| | $2.50 | $7.50 | $15.00 | £1.65 | £5.00 | £10.00 |

11-14 Neal Adams cover

| | $2.50 | $7.50 | $12.50 | £1.60 | £4.80 | £8.00 |

15-19 52pgs, Neal Adams cover

| | $1.50 | $4.50 | $7.50 | £1.00 | £3.00 | £5.00 |
| **20-22** | $1.00 | $3.00 | $5.00 | £0.70 | £2.10 | £3.50 |

23 Kaluta art, Spawn of Frankenstein begins (ends #30)

	$1.00	$3.00	$5.00	£0.70	£2.10	£3.50
24-25 Kaluta art	$1.00	$3.00	$5.00	£0.70	£2.10	£3.50
26-30	$1.00	$3.00	$5.00	£0.70	£2.10	£3.50

31 Black Orchid begins

| | $1.00 | $3.00 | $5.00 | £0.60 | £1.80 | £3.00 |
| **32** | $1.00 | $3.00 | $5.00 | £0.60 | £1.80 | £3.00 |

33 Deadman appears

| | $1.00 | $3.00 | $5.00 | £0.60 | £1.80 | £3.00 |
| **34-38** | $1.00 | $3.00 | $5.00 | £0.60 | £1.80 | £3.00 |

39-41 Deadman appears

| | $1.00 | $3.00 | $5.00 | £0.60 | £1.80 | £3.00 |
| **Title Value:** | $72.60 | $218.00 | $405.00 | £47.20 | £142.10 | £263.50 |

FEATURES

Black Orchid in 31, 32, 35, 36, 38-41. Dr.13 in 12-16, 18, 19, 21, 22, 34. Phantom Stranger in 11-25, 27-41.

P.Stranger/Dr.13 in 1-10. P.Stranger/Dr.13/ Spawn of Frankenstein in 26. Spawn of Frankenstein in 23-25, 27-30.

REPRINT FEATURES

Dr.13 in 1-3, 17. Mark Merlin in 16, 18, 19. Phantom Stranger (1950s) in 1-3.

PHANTOM STRANGER (2ND SERIES)

DC Comics,OS; 1 Oct 1993

1 64pgs, Guy Davis art

| | $0.60 | $1.80 | $3.00 | £0.40 | £1.20 | £2.00 |
| **Title Value:** | $0.60 | $1.80 | $3.00 | £0.40 | £1.20 | £2.00 |

PHANTOM STRANGER (LIMITED SERIES)

DC Comics,MS; 1 Oct 1987-4 Jan 1988

1-4 Mike Mignola art, P. Craig Russell inks, Eclipso appears

| | $0.25 | $0.75 | $1.25 | £0.15 | £0.45 | £0.75 |
| **Title Value:** | $1.00 | $3.00 | $5.00 | £0.60 | £1.80 | £3.00 |

PHANTOM ZONE

DC Comics,MS; 1 Jan 1982-4 Apr 1982

1 Superman appears

| | $0.25 | $0.75 | $1.25 | £0.15 | £0.45 | £0.75 |

2-4 Batman, Green Lantern, Wonder Woman, Zatanna and Supergirl appear

| | $0.25 | $0.75 | $1.25 | £0.15 | £0.45 | £0.75 |
| **Title Value:** | $1.00 | $3.00 | $5.00 | £0.60 | £1.80 | £3.00 |

Note: Superman in all, Gene Colan art.

PHANTOM, THE

Gold Key/King; 1 Nov 1962-28 Dec 1967; Charlton; 30 Feb 1969-74 Dec 1976

1 rare in the U.K. Russ Manning art; painted covers begin (end #17)

	$11.50	$35.00	$70.00	£7.50	£22.50	£45.00
2 rare in the U.K.	$5.75	$17.50	$35.00	£4.15	£12.50	£25.00
3-5 rare in the U.K.	$5.00	$15.00	$30.00	£3.30	£10.00	£20.00

6-10 rare in the U.K.

| | $4.55 | $13.50 | $27.50 | £2.90 | £8.75 | £17.50 |

11-17 rare in the U.K.

| | $3.75 | $11.00 | $22.50 | £2.50 | £7.50 | £15.00 |

18 rare in the U.K., Flash Gordon by Wood

| | $4.55 | $13.50 | $27.50 | £2.90 | £8.75 | £17.50 |

19-20 rare in the U.K., Flash Gordon

| | $2.90 | $8.75 | $17.50 | £2.05 | £6.25 | £12.50 |

21 scarce in the U.K.

| | $3.50 | $10.50 | $17.50 | £3.00 | £9.00 | £15.00 |
| **22** | $3.50 | $10.50 | $17.50 | £2.50 | £7.50 | £12.50 |

23 scarce in the U.K.

	$3.50	$10.50	$17.50	£3.00	£9.00	£15.00
24	$3.50	$10.50	$17.50	£2.50	£7.50	£12.50
25 Jeff Jones art	$3.50	$10.50	$17.50	£2.50	£7.50	£12.50
26-27	$3.50	$10.50	$17.50	£2.50	£7.50	£12.50
28-35	$3.00	$9.00	$15.00	£2.00	£6.00	£10.00

36 scarce in the U.K. Steve Ditko art

| | $2.80 | $8.25 | $14.00 | £1.80 | £5.25 | £9.00 |

37-38 scarce in the U.K.

| | $2.40 | $7.00 | $12.00 | £1.60 | £4.80 | £8.00 |

39 scarce in the U.K. Steve Ditko art

| | $2.80 | $8.25 | $14.00 | £1.80 | £5.25 | £9.00 |

40 scarce in the U.K.

| | $2.40 | $7.00 | $12.00 | £1.60 | £4.80 | £8.00 |

41-54 scarce in the U.K.

| | $1.80 | $5.25 | $9.00 | £1.20 | £3.60 | £6.00 |

55-66 scarce in the U.K.

| | $1.50 | $4.50 | $7.50 | £1.00 | £3.00 | £5.00 |

67-69 scarce in the U.K. Newton art

| | $1.50 | $4.50 | $7.50 | £1.00 | £3.00 | £5.00 |

70 scarce in the U.K. Maltese Falcon/Casablanca tribute; Bogart, Bacall, Greenstreet, Lorre appear, Newton art

| | $1.50 | $4.50 | $7.50 | £1.00 | £3.00 | £5.00 |

71 scarce in the U.K. Newton art

| | $1.50 | $4.50 | $7.50 | £1.00 | £3.00 | £5.00 |

Outer Space #17

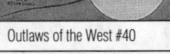

Outlaws of the West #40

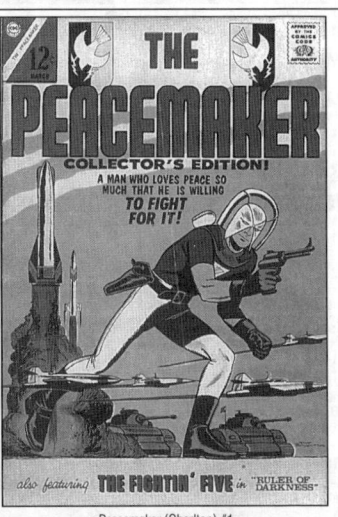

Peacemaker (Charlton) #1

NEAR MINT MEANS NEAR MINT!

	$Good	$Fine	$N.Mint	£Good	£Fine	£N.Mint
72	$1.20	$3.60	$6.00	£0.60	£1.80	£3.00
73 Newton art	$1.20	$3.60	$6.00	£0.60	£1.80	£3.00
74 scarce in the U.K. Newton art	$1.20	$3.60	$6.00	£0.80	£2.40	£4.00
Title Value:	$207.60	$616.80	$1130.50	£139.25	£418.30	£758.50

Note: all distributed in the U.K.

PHANTOM, THE (1ST SERIES)
DC Comics,MS; 1 May 1988-4 Aug 1988

	$Good	$Fine	$N.Mint	£Good	£Fine	£N.Mint
1-4	$0.25	$0.75	$1.25	£0.15	£0.45	£0.75
Title Value:	$1.00	$3.00	$5.00	£0.60	£1.80	£3.00

Note: Deluxe Format

PHANTOM, THE (2ND SERIES)
DC Comics; 1 Mar 1989-13 Mar 1990

	$Good	$Fine	$N.Mint	£Good	£Fine	£N.Mint
1-13	$0.25	$0.75	$1.25	£0.15	£0.45	£0.75
Title Value:	$3.25	$9.75	$16.25	£1.95	£5.85	£9.75

PHAZE
Eclipse; 1 Apr 1988-2 Oct 1988

	$Good	$Fine	$N.Mint	£Good	£Fine	£N.Mint
1 ND Sienkiewicz cover, painted colour art	$0.40	$1.20	$2.00	£0.25	£0.75	£1.25
2 ND Gulacy cover, painted colour art	$0.40	$1.20	$2.00	£0.25	£0.75	£1.25
Title Value:	$0.80	$2.40	$4.00	£0.50	£1.50	£2.50

PHOENIX
Atlas; 1 Jan 1975-4 Oct 1975

	$Good	$Fine	$N.Mint	£Good	£Fine	£N.Mint
1-2 origin; distributed in the U.K.	$0.25	$0.75	$1.25	£0.15	£0.45	£0.75
3 distributed in the U.K.	$0.25	$0.75	$1.25	£0.15	£0.45	£0.75
4 new costume, Estrada art; distributed in the U.K.	$0.25	$0.75	$1.25	£0.15	£0.45	£0.75
Title Value:	$1.00	$3.00	$5.00	£0.60	£1.80	£3.00

PHOENIX – THE UNTOLD STORY
Marvel Comics Group,OS; 1 Apr 1984

	$Good	$Fine	$N.Mint	£Good	£Fine	£N.Mint
1 ND scarce in the U.K. reprints X-Men #137 in unpublished original version, John Byrne art	$2.00	$6.00	$10.00	£1.50	£4.50	£7.50
Title Value:	$2.00	$6.00	$10.00	£1.50	£4.50	£7.50

PHOENIX RESSURRECTION – GENESIS, THE
Marvel Comics Group,OS; 1 Feb 1996

	$Good	$Fine	$N.Mint	£Good	£Fine	£N.Mint
1 ND 48pgs, X-Men appear; art by Bryan Hitch, Mark Pacella, Randy Green and others	$0.80	$2.40	$4.00	£0.50	£1.50	£2.50
Title Value:	$0.80	$2.40	$4.00	£0.50	£1.50	£2.50

PHOENIX RESSURRECTION – REVELATIONS, THE
Marvel Comics Group/Ultraverse,OS; 1 Feb 1996

	$Good	$Fine	$N.Mint	£Good	£Fine	£N.Mint
1 ND 48pgs, X-Men appear; art by John Royle, Jeff Matsuda and others	$0.80	$2.40	$4.00	£0.50	£1.50	£2.50
Title Value:	$0.80	$2.40	$4.00	£0.50	£1.50	£2.50

PHOENIX RESSURRECTION: THE AFTERMATH
Marvel Comics Group,OS; 1 Mar 1996

	$Good	$Fine	$N.Mint	£Good	£Fine	£N.Mint
1 ND 48pgs, intro Foxfire	$0.80	$2.40	$4.00	£0.50	£1.50	£2.50
Title Value:	$0.80	$2.40	$4.00	£0.50	£1.50	£2.50

PHONY PAGES
Renegade,MS; 1 May 1986-2 Jun 1986

	$Good	$Fine	$N.Mint	£Good	£Fine	£N.Mint
1-2 ND Terry Beaty parody reprints	$0.40	$1.20	$2.00	£0.25	£0.75	£1.25
Title Value:	$0.80	$2.40	$4.00	£0.50	£1.50	£2.50

PILGRIM'S PROGRESS, THE
Marvel Comics Group,OS; 1 May 1993

	$Good	$Fine	$N.Mint	£Good	£Fine	£N.Mint
1 ND 96pgs, softcover	$1.50	$4.50	$7.50	£1.00	£3.00	£5.00
Title Value:	$1.50	$4.50	$7.50	£1.00	£3.00	£5.00

PINEAPPLE ARMY
Viz Communications; 1 Dec 1988-10 1989

	$Good	$Fine	$N.Mint	£Good	£Fine	£N.Mint
1-10 ND Naohi Urasawa script/art, black and white; bi-weekly with painted covers	$0.80	$2.40	$4.00	£0.50	£1.50	£2.50
Title Value:	$8.00	$24.00	$40.00	£5.00	£15.00	£25.00
Graphic Novel (Oct 1990), reprints #1-10, softcover				£1.90	£5.70	£9.50

PINHEAD
Marvel Comics Group/Epic; 1 Dec 1993-7 1994

	$Good	$Fine	$N.Mint	£Good	£Fine	£N.Mint
1 ND based on Clive Barker character from Hellraiser films; red foil embossed cover	$0.50	$1.50	$2.50	£0.30	£0.90	£1.50
2-7 ND	$0.50	$1.50	$2.50	£0.30	£0.90	£1.50
Title Value:	$3.50	$10.50	$17.50	£2.10	£6.30	£10.50

PINHEAD/MARSHALL LAW: LAW IN HELL
Marvel Comics Group/Epic,MS; 1 Nov 1993-2 Dec 1993

	$Good	$Fine	$N.Mint	£Good	£Fine	£N.Mint
1 ND Pat Mills and Kev O'Neill	$0.60	$1.80	$3.00	£0.40	£1.20	£2.00
2 ND Pat Mills and Kev O'Neill; silver foil embossed cover	$0.60	$1.80	$3.00	£0.40	£1.20	£2.00
Title Value:	$1.20	$3.60	$6.00	£0.80	£2.40	£4.00

PINK FLOYD EXPERIENCE, THE
Revolutionary Comics,MS; 1 Jan 1991-5 1991

	$Good	$Fine	$N.Mint	£Good	£Fine	£N.Mint
1-5 ND	$0.40	$1.20	$2.00	£0.25	£0.75	£1.25
Title Value:	$2.00	$6.00	$10.00	£1.25	£3.75	£6.25

PINKY AND THE BRAIN CHRISTMAS SPECIAL
DC Comics,OS; 1 Jan 1996

	$Good	$Fine	$N.Mint	£Good	£Fine	£N.Mint
1 ND based on US animated TV show	$0.30	$0.90	$1.50	£0.20	£0.60	£1.00
Title Value:	$0.30	$0.90	$1.50	£0.20	£0.60	£1.00

PINOCCHIO AND THE EMPEROR OF THE NIGHT
Marvel Comics Group,OS; 1 Mar 1986

	$Good	$Fine	$N.Mint	£Good	£Fine	£N.Mint
1	$0.15	$0.45	$0.75	£0.10	£0.35	£0.60
Title Value:	$0.15	$0.45	$0.75	£0.10	£0.35	£0.60

Note: high quality paper.

PIRANHA IS LOOSE
Special Studio; 1 Jan 1991

	$Good	$Fine	$N.Mint	£Good	£Fine	£N.Mint
1 ND black and white	$0.30	$0.90	$1.50	£0.20	£0.60	£1.00
Title Value:	$0.30	$0.90	$1.50	£0.20	£0.60	£1.00

PIRATE CORPS!
Eternity; 1 Jul 1987-4 1988

	$Good	$Fine	$N.Mint	£Good	£Fine	£N.Mint
1-4 ND	$0.30	$0.90	$1.50	£0.20	£0.60	£1.00
Title Value:	$1.20	$3.60	$6.00	£0.80	£2.40	£4.00

PIRATE CORPS! (2ND SERIES)
Slave Labor; 1 1989-5 1990

	$Good	$Fine	$N.Mint	£Good	£Fine	£N.Mint
1 ND Evan Dorkin script/art begins; black and white	$0.40	$1.20	$2.00	£0.25	£0.75	£1.25
1 2nd printing, ND	$0.40	$1.20	$2.00	£0.25	£0.75	£1.25
1 3rd printing, ND (Jul 1995)	$0.30	$0.90	$1.50	£0.20	£0.60	£1.00
2 ND	$0.40	$1.20	$2.00	£0.25	£0.75	£1.25
2 2nd printing, ND (Feb 1993)	$0.40	$1.20	$2.00	£0.25	£0.75	£1.25
2 3rd printing, ND (Jul 1995)	$0.30	$0.90	$1.50	£0.20	£0.60	£1.00
3 ND	$0.40	$1.20	$2.00	£0.25	£0.75	£1.25
3 2nd printing, ND (Feb 1993)	$0.40	$1.20	$2.00	£0.25	£0.75	£1.25
3 3rd printing, ND (Jul 1995)	$0.30	$0.90	$1.50	£0.20	£0.60	£1.00
4 ND	$0.40	$1.20	$2.00	£0.25	£0.75	£1.25
4 2nd printing, ND (Oct 1993)	$0.40	$1.20	$2.00	£0.25	£0.75	£1.25
4 3rd printing, ND (Jul 1995)	$0.30	$0.90	$1.50	£0.20	£0.60	£1.00
5 ND	$0.40	$1.20	$2.00	£0.25	£0.75	£1.25
5 2nd printing, ND (Apr 1994)	$0.40	$1.20	$2.00	£0.25	£0.75	£1.25
Title Value:	$5.20	$15.60	$26.00	£3.30	£9.90	£16.50
Special 1				£0.30	£0.90	£1.50

PIRATE CORPS: THE BLUNDER YEARS
Slave Labor; 1 Jul 1993-2 1993

	$Good	$Fine	$N.Mint	£Good	£Fine	£N.Mint
1 ND 56pgs, reprints Pirate Corps #1 & 2	$0.90	$2.70	$4.50	£0.60	£1.80	£3.00
2 ND 56pgs, reprints Pirate Corps #3 & 4	$0.90	$2.70	$4.50	£0.60	£1.80	£3.00
Title Value:	$1.80	$5.40	$9.00	£1.20	£3.60	£6.00

PIRATES OF DARK WATER, THE
Marvel Comics Group,MS; 1 Nov 1991-9 Jul 1992

	$Good	$Fine	$N.Mint	£Good	£Fine	£N.Mint
1 series adapts first five episodes of U.S. animated show	$0.15	$0.45	$0.75	£0.10	£0.35	£0.60
2-3	$0.15	$0.45	$0.75	£0.10	£0.35	£0.60
4 $1.25 cover begins	$0.15	$0.45	$0.75	£0.10	£0.35	£0.60
5-8	$0.15	$0.45	$0.75	£0.10	£0.35	£0.60
9 Charles Vess cover	$0.15	$0.45	$0.75	£0.10	£0.35	£0.60
Title Value:	$1.35	$4.05	$6.75	£0.90	£3.15	£5.40

PISTOLERO
Eternity,OS; nn Jul 1990

	$Good	$Fine	$N.Mint	£Good	£Fine	£N.Mint
nn, ND , 56pgs	$1.00	$3.00	$5.00	£0.65	£1.95	£3.25
Title Value:	$1.00	$3.00	$5.00	£0.65	£1.95	£3.25

PITT
Image; ½ Jan 1993; 1 Jan 1993-present

	$Good	$Fine	$N.Mint	£Good	£Fine	£N.Mint
½ ND 24pgs; Brian Hotton script, Dale Keown art	$0.30	$0.90	$1.50	£0.20	£0.60	£1.00
1 Brian Hotton script and Dale Keown art begins	$1.50	$4.50	$7.50	£0.70	£2.10	£3.50
1 Ashcan Edition, 8.5" x 5.5" red card cover, black and white interior, limited to 5,500 copies (numbered in silver bottom right of cover), each signed in silver ink on cover by Keown and Hotton	$3.00	$9.00	$15.00	£2.00	£6.00	£10.00
2 ties-in to Youngblood #4	$0.80	$2.40	$4.00	£0.50	£1.50	£2.50
2 Ashcan Edition, 8.5" x 5.5" Platinum card cover, black and white interior	$2.50	$7.50	$12.50	£1.50	£4.50	£7.50
2 Ashcan Edition, 8.5" x 5.5" Black card cover, black and white interior	$2.50	$7.50	$12.50	£1.50	£4.50	£7.50
2 Ashcan Edition, 8.5" x 5.5" Olive card cover, black and white interior	$2.50	$7.50	$12.50	£1.50	£4.50	£7.50
3 scarce in both US and UK	$1.50	$4.50	$7.50	£1.20	£3.60	£6.00
4	$0.80	$2.40	$4.00	£0.70	£2.10	£3.50
5-10	$0.50	$1.50	$2.50	£0.30	£0.90	£1.50
Title Value:	$18.40	$55.20	$92.00	£11.60	£34.80	£58.00

Note: all Non-Distributed on the news-stands in the U.K.

PITT, THE
New Universe; nn 1988

(see The Draft)

	$Good	$Fine	$N.Mint	£Good	£Fine	£N.Mint
nn ND John Byrne story; ties into Starbrand and DP7	$0.70	$2.10	$3.50	£0.50	£1.50	£2.50
Title Value:	$0.70	$2.10	$3.50	£0.50	£1.50	£2.50

Note: 48pgs, Bookshelf Format

PIXY JUNKET
Viz Communications,MS; 1 Sep 1993-6 Feb 1994

	$Good	$Fine	$N.Mint	£Good	£Fine	£N.Mint
1-6 ND	$0.50	$1.50	$2.50	£0.30	£0.90	£1.50
Title Value:	$3.00	$9.00	$15.00	£1.80	£5.40	£9.00

PLAN 9 FRON OUTER SPACE MOVIE ADAPTATION
Eternity,OS; nn May 1990
nn ND 64pgs, squarebound, adapts cult film

	$Good	$Fine	$N.Mint	£Good	£Fine	£N.Mint
	$0.90	$2.70	$4.50	£0.60	£1.80	£3.00
Title Value:	$0.90	$2.70	$4.50	£0.60	£1.80	£3.00
2nd print (1991)				£0.65	£1.95	£3.25

PLANET 29
Caliber Press,MS; 1 Oct 1991-3 1992

	$Good	$Fine	$N.Mint	£Good	£Fine	£N.Mint
1-3 ND	$0.40	$1.20	$2.00	£0.25	£0.75	£1.25
Title Value:	$1.20	$3.60	$6.00	£0.75	£2.25	£3.75

PLANET COMICS
I.W. Comics; 1,8,9 1959-1961
1 rare in the U.K., reprints; distributed in the U.K.

	$Good	$Fine	$N.Mint	£Good	£Fine	£N.Mint
	$6.25	$18.50	$37.50	£4.15	£12.50	£25.00

8-9 rare in the U.K.; reprints; distributed in the U.K.

	$Good	$Fine	$N.Mint	£Good	£Fine	£N.Mint
	$5.75	$17.50	$35.00	£3.75	£11.00	£22.50
Title Value:	$17.75	$53.50	$107.50	£11.65	£34.50	£70.00

PLANET COMICS (2ND SERIES)
Pacific; 1 Jul 1984
1 ND 76pgs, squarebound

	$Good	$Fine	$N.Mint	£Good	£Fine	£N.Mint
	$1.50	$4.50	$7.50	£1.00	£3.00	£5.00
Title Value:	$1.50	$4.50	$7.50	£1.00	£3.00	£5.00

PLANET COMICS (3RD SERIES)
Blackthorne; 1-5 1988
1 ND Dave Stevens cover

	$Good	$Fine	$N.Mint	£Good	£Fine	£N.Mint
	$0.40	$1.20	$2.00	£0.25	£0.75	£1.25
2-3 ND Bill Stout cover						
	$0.40	$1.20	$2.00	£0.25	£0.75	£1.25
4-5 ND	$0.40	$1.20	$2.00	£0.25	£0.75	£1.25
Title Value:	$2.00	$6.00	$10.00	£1.25	£3.75	£6.25

PLANET OF THE APES
Adventure; 1 Apr 1990-24 Jul 1992
1 Charles Marshall script, Kent Burles and Barb Kaalberg art; available with green, pink or yellow wraparound extra half cover

	$Good	$Fine	$N.Mint	£Good	£Fine	£N.Mint
	$0.90	$2.70	$4.50	£0.50	£1.50	£2.50

1 Limited Edition (Apr 1990), gold embossed logo, sponsored by American Entertainment

	$Good	$Fine	$N.Mint	£Good	£Fine	£N.Mint
	$1.20	$3.60	$6.00	£0.80	£2.40	£4.00
1 2nd printing	$0.60	$1.80	$3.00	£0.40	£1.20	£2.00
1 3rd printing	$0.40	$1.20	$2.00	£0.25	£0.75	£1.25
2-5	$0.50	$1.50	$2.50	£0.30	£0.90	£1.50
6-13	$0.40	$1.20	$2.00	£0.25	£0.75	£1.25
14-17 Countdown Zero story						
	$0.40	$1.20	$2.00	£0.25	£0.75	£1.25
18	$0.40	$1.20	$2.00	£0.25	£0.75	£1.25
19 ties in to Conquest of the Planet of the Apes						
	$0.40	$1.20	$2.00	£0.25	£0.75	£1.25
20	$0.40	$1.20	$2.00	£0.25	£0.75	£1.25
21-24 tie-in with Conquest of the Planet of the Apes						
	$0.40	$1.20	$2.00	£0.25	£0.75	£1.25
Title Value:	$12.70	$38.10	$63.50	£7.90	£23.70	£39.50

Note: all Non-Distributed on the news-stands in the U.K.
Annual 1 (Nov 1991) 48pgs, six stories cover by Mark Pennington £0.45 £1.35 £2.25
Graphic Novel (Dec 1990), 144pgs reprints adaptation of film £1.10 £3.30 £5.50

PLANET OF THE APES
Marvel Comics Group,Magazine Film; 1 Aug 1974-29 Feb 1977
(see Adventures on the Planet of the Apes)

	$Good	$Fine	$N.Mint	£Good	£Fine	£N.Mint
1	$1.00	$3.00	$5.00	£0.80	£2.40	£4.00
2-5 ND	$0.70	$2.10	$3.50	£0.50	£1.50	£2.50
6-10 ND	$0.60	$1.80	$3.00	£0.40	£1.20	£2.00
11-15 ND	$0.50	$1.50	$2.50	£0.30	£0.90	£1.50
16-29 ND	$0.40	$1.20	$2.00	£0.25	£0.75	£1.25
Title Value:	$14.90	$44.70	$74.50	£9.80	£29.40	£49.00

Note: issues 1-10 are 84pgs, 11-13 are 76pgs, 14-29 are 52pgs.
ARTISTS
Ploog art in 1-4, 6, 8, 11, 13, 14, 19.

PLANET OF THE APES, TERROR ON
Adventure,MS; 1 Aug 1991-4 Nov 1991
1 ND Doug Moench script, Mike Ploog art begins (from 1970s Marvel magazines)

	$Good	$Fine	$N.Mint	£Good	£Fine	£N.Mint
	$0.40	$1.20	$2.00	£0.25	£0.75	£1.25
2-4 ND	$0.40	$1.20	$2.00	£0.25	£0.75	£1.25
Title Value:	$1.60	$4.80	$8.00	£1.00	£3.00	£5.00

PLANET OF THE APES: FORBIDDEN ZONE
Adventure,MS; 1 Feb 1993-4 May 1993

	$Good	$Fine	$N.Mint	£Good	£Fine	£N.Mint
1-4 ND	$0.40	$1.20	$2.00	£0.25	£0.75	£1.25
Title Value:	$1.60	$4.80	$8.00	£1.00	£3.00	£5.00

PLANET OF THE APES: SINS OF THE FATHERS
Adventure,OS; 1 May 1992
1 ND prequel to Planet of the Apes series

	$Good	$Fine	$N.Mint	£Good	£Fine	£N.Mint
	$0.40	$1.20	$2.00	£0.25	£0.75	£1.25
Title Value:	$0.40	$1.20	$2.00	£0.25	£0.75	£1.25

PLANET OF THE APES: URCHAK'S FOLLY
Adventure,MS; 1 Mar 1991-4 Jun 1991

	$Good	$Fine	$N.Mint	£Good	£Fine	£N.Mint
1-4 ND	$0.40	$1.20	$2.00	£0.25	£0.75	£1.25
Title Value:	$1.60	$4.80	$8.00	£1.00	£3.00	£5.00

PLANET OF VAMPIRES
Atlas; 1 Feb 1975-3 Jun 1975
1-2 part Neal Adams covers; distributed in the U.K.

	$Good	$Fine	$N.Mint	£Good	£Fine	£N.Mint
	$0.30	$0.90	$1.50	£0.20	£0.60	£1.00

3 Russ Heath art; distributed in the U.K.

	$Good	$Fine	$N.Mint	£Good	£Fine	£N.Mint
	$0.30	$0.90	$1.50	£0.20	£0.60	£1.00

	$Good	$Fine	$N.Mint	£Good	£Fine	£N.Mint
Title Value:	$0.90	$2.70	$4.50	£0.60	£1.80	£3.00

PLANET TERRY
Marvel Comics Group/Star; 1 Apr 1985-9 Jan 1986

	$Good	$Fine	$N.Mint	£Good	£Fine	£N.Mint
1-9	$0.15	$0.45	$0.75	£0.10	£0.30	£0.50
Title Value:	$1.35	$4.05	$6.75	£0.90	£2.70	£4.50

PLANET-X
Eternity,OS; 1 Sep 1991
1 ND horror anthology

	$Good	$Fine	$N.Mint	£Good	£Fine	£N.Mint
	$0.40	$1.20	$2.00	£0.25	£0.75	£1.25
Title Value:	$0.40	$1.20	$2.00	£0.25	£0.75	£1.25

PLASMA BABY
Caliber Press; 1 Jan 1992-3 1992

	$Good	$Fine	$N.Mint	£Good	£Fine	£N.Mint
1-3 ND	$0.45	$1.35	$2.25	£0.30	£0.90	£1.50
Title Value:	$1.35	$4.05	$6.75	£0.90	£2.70	£4.50

PLASMER
Marvel UK,MS; 1 Nov 1993-2 Dec 1993
1 pre-bagged with 4 trading cards, Captain America guest-stars

	$Good	$Fine	$N.Mint	£Good	£Fine	£N.Mint
	$0.40	$1.20	$2.00	£0.25	£0.75	£1.25
2 Captain Britain and Black Knight appear						
	$0.40	$1.20	$2.00	£0.25	£0.75	£1.25
Title Value:	$0.80	$2.40	$4.00	£0.50	£1.50	£2.50

PLASTIC FORKS
Marvel Comics Group/Epic,MS; 1 Apr 1990-5 Aug 1990
1-5 ND 64pgs, Ted McKeever art

	$Good	$Fine	$N.Mint	£Good	£Fine	£N.Mint
	$0.90	$2.70	$4.50	£0.60	£1.80	£3.00
Title Value:	$4.50	$13.50	$22.50	£3.00	£9.00	£15.00

Note: Creator owned title.
Hardback (by Graphitti), 1991. Signed. £5.00 £15.00 £25.00

PLASTIC MAN
National Periodical Publications; 1 Nov/Dec 1966-10 May/Jun 1968; 11 Feb/Mar 1976-20 Oct/Nov 1977
(see Action, Adventure, Brave and the Bold, DC Presents, DC Special, Superfriends, World's Finest)
1 Gil Kane cover/art, 1st Silver Age Plastic Man (see House of Mystery #160)

	$Good	$Fine	$N.Mint	£Good	£Fine	£N.Mint
	$8.50	$26.00	$60.00	£5.50	£17.00	£40.00
2 scarce in the U.K.	$5.00	$15.00	$30.00	£3.30	£10.00	£20.00
3-5 scarce in the U.K.						
	$4.55	$13.50	$27.50	£2.90	£8.75	£17.50
6-7 scarce in the U.K.						
	$2.90	$8.75	$17.50	£2.05	£6.25	£12.50
8-10 scarce in the U.K.						
	$2.50	$7.50	$15.00	£1.65	£5.00	£10.00
11-12	$1.00	$3.00	$5.00	£0.60	£1.80	£3.00
13 scarce in the U.K.						
	$1.00	$3.00	$5.00	£0.70	£2.10	£3.50
14	$1.00	$3.00	$5.00	£0.60	£1.80	£3.00
15 scarce in the U.K.						
	$1.00	$3.00	$5.00	£0.70	£2.10	£3.50
16-20	$1.00	$3.00	$5.00	£0.60	£1.80	£3.00
Title Value:	$50.45	$151.50	$302.50	£32.75	£99.35	£198.50

PLASTIC MAN
Super Comics; 11,16,18 1963-1964
11 rare in the U.K., reprint

	$Good	$Fine	$N.Mint	£Good	£Fine	£N.Mint
	$5.75	$17.50	$35.00	£3.75	£11.00	£22.50
16 reprint	$5.25	$16.00	$32.50	£3.30	£10.00	£20.00
18 Spirit appearance, reprint						
	$5.25	$16.00	$32.50	£3.30	£10.00	£20.00
Title Value:	$16.25	$49.50	$100.00	£10.35	£31.00	£62.50

Note: all distributed on the news-stands in the U.K.

PLASTIC MAN (2ND SERIES)
DC Comics,MS; 1 Nov 1988-4 Feb 1989
1-4 part Nowlan art

	$Good	$Fine	$N.Mint	£Good	£Fine	£N.Mint
	$0.25	$0.75	$1.25	£0.15	£0.45	£0.75
Title Value:	$1.00	$3.00	$5.00	£0.60	£1.80	£3.00

PLASTRON CAFE
Mirage Studios; 1 Feb 1993-5 1993
1 ND anthology featuring Eastman, Laird and Rick Veitch

	$Good	$Fine	$N.Mint	£Good	£Fine	£N.Mint
	$0.40	$1.20	$2.00	£0.25	£0.75	£1.25
2-5 ND	$0.40	$1.20	$2.00	£0.25	£0.75	£1.25
Title Value:	$2.00	$6.00	$10.00	£1.25	£3.75	£6.25

PLAYGROUND
Caliber Press,OS; 1 Oct 1990
1 ND black and white

	$Good	$Fine	$N.Mint	£Good	£Fine	£N.Mint
	$0.40	$1.20	$2.00	£0.25	£0.75	£1.25
Title Value:	$0.40	$1.20	$2.00	£0.25	£0.75	£1.25

PLOP!
DC Comics; 1 Sep/Oct 1973-24 Nov/Dec 1976
1 Bernie Wrightson art

	$Good	$Fine	$N.Mint	£Good	£Fine	£N.Mint
	$1.00	$3.00	$5.00	£0.70	£2.10	£3.50
2-4	$0.80	$2.40	$4.00	£0.50	£1.50	£2.50
5 Bernie Wrightson art						
	$0.80	$2.40	$4.00	£0.50	£1.50	£2.50
6-10	$0.80	$2.40	$4.00	£0.50	£1.50	£2.50
11-13	$0.80	$2.40	$4.00	£0.40	£1.20	£2.00
14 Wood art	$0.80	$2.40	$4.00	£0.40	£1.20	£2.00
15	$0.80	$2.40	$4.00	£0.40	£1.20	£2.00
16 ND Steve Ditko/Wally Wood art						
	$0.80	$2.40	$4.00	£0.40	£1.20	£2.00
17-20	$0.80	$2.40	$4.00	£0.40	£1.20	£2.00
21-24 ND 52pgs	$0.80	$2.40	$4.00	£0.50	£1.50	£2.50
Title Value:	$19.40	$58.20	$97.00	£11.20	£33.60	£56.00

POISON ELVES
Sirius Entertainment; 1 1995-present

Description	$Good	$Fine	$N.Mint	£Good	£Fine	£N.Mint
1 ND Drew Hayes script and art begins; 24pgs, black and white	$1.60	$4.80	$8.00	£1.20	£3.60	£6.00
1 ND Commemorative edition - foil enhanced cover; limited to 1000 copies	$2.50	$7.50	$12.50	£1.50	£4.50	£7.50
2 ND	$1.00	$3.00	$5.00	£0.70	£2.10	£3.50
3-5 ND	$0.80	$2.40	$4.00	£0.50	£1.50	£2.50
6-7 ND	$0.50	$1.50	$2.50	£0.30	£0.90	£1.50
Title Value:	$8.50	$25.50	$42.50	£5.50	£16.50	£27.50

POIZON
London Night Studios,OS; ½ Sep 1995

Description	$Good	$Fine	$N.Mint	£Good	£Fine	£N.Mint
½ ND	$0.60	$1.80	$3.00	£0.40	£1.20	£2.00
Title Value:	$0.60	$1.80	$3.00	£0.40	£1.20	£2.00

POLICE ACADEMY
Marvel Comics Group; 1 Nov 1989-9 Jul 1990

Description	$Good	$Fine	$N.Mint	£Good	£Fine	£N.Mint
1-9	$0.15	$0.45	$0.75	£0.10	£0.35	£0.60
Title Value:	$1.35	$4.05	$6.75	£0.90	£3.15	£5.40

POLICE ACTION
Atlas; 1 Feb 1975-3 Jun 1975

Description	$Good	$Fine	$N.Mint	£Good	£Fine	£N.Mint
1-3 Sekowsky/Ploog art; distributed in the U.K.	$0.25	$0.75	$1.25	£0.15	£0.45	£0.75
Title Value:	$0.75	$2.25	$3.75	£0.45	£1.35	£2.25

POPEYE
Charlton; 94 Jul 1969-138 Dec 1976

Description	$Good	$Fine	$N.Mint	£Good	£Fine	£N.Mint
94-100 distributed in the U.K.	$2.50	$7.50	$15.00	£1.65	£5.00	£10.00
101-120 distributed in the U.K.	$2.00	$6.00	$10.00	£1.40	£4.20	£7.00
121-138 distributed in the U.K.	$1.50	$4.50	$7.50	£1.00	£3.00	£5.00
Title Value:	$84.50	$253.50	$440.00	£57.55	£173.00	£300.00

POPEYE SPECIAL
Ocean; 1 Summer 1987-2 Sep 1988

Description	$Good	$Fine	$N.Mint	£Good	£Fine	£N.Mint
1 ND origin	$0.40	$1.20	$2.00	£0.25	£0.75	£1.25
2 ND 60th anniversary special	$0.40	$1.20	$2.00	£0.25	£0.75	£1.25
Title Value:	$0.80	$2.40	$4.00	£0.50	£1.50	£2.50

PORTIA PRINZ OF THE GLAMAZONS
Eclipse; 1 Dec 1986-6 Oct 1987

Description	$Good	$Fine	$N.Mint	£Good	£Fine	£N.Mint
1-6 ND Howell art	$0.40	$1.20	$2.00	£0.25	£0.75	£1.25
Title Value:	$2.40	$7.20	$12.00	£1.50	£4.50	£7.50

POST BROS, THOSE ANNOYING
Vortex/Rip Off Press; 1 Jan 1985-38 Jan 1993; Aeon; 39 Aug 1994-present

Description	$Good	$Fine	$N.Mint	£Good	£Fine	£N.Mint
1 ND	$0.50	$1.50	$2.50	£0.30	£0.90	£1.50
1 2nd printing, ND (Jan 1994)	$0.40	$1.20	$2.00	£0.25	£0.75	£1.25
2-38 ND	$0.40	$1.20	$2.00	£0.25	£0.75	£1.25
39 ND 1st Aeon issue	$0.50	$1.50	$2.50	£0.30	£0.90	£1.50
40-46 ND	$0.50	$1.50	$2.50	£0.30	£0.90	£1.50
Title Value:	$19.70	$59.10	$98.50	£12.20	£36.60	£61.00

Those Annoying Post Bros. In: Das Loot (Aug 1994)
Trade paperback reprints issues #1-5 plus 8pg unpublished story £2.00 £6.00 £10.00

Those Annoying Post Bros.: Disturb the Neighbours
(Sep 1995) reprints issues #6-8 £1.30 £3.90 £6.50

POST BROTHERS ANNUAL, THOSE ANNOYING
Aeon; 1 Aug 1995

Description	$Good	$Fine	$N.Mint	£Good	£Fine	£N.Mint
1 ND 56pgs, Matt Howarth with Nancy Collins; black and white	$0.90	$2.70	$4.50	£0.60	£1.80	£3.00
Title Value:	$0.90	$2.70	$4.50	£0.60	£1.80	£3.00

POST-MORTEM
Brave New Words,OS; 1 1991

Description	$Good	$Fine	$N.Mint	£Good	£Fine	£N.Mint
1 ND 64pgs, squarebound, Matt Howarth script and art, black and white; features Savage Henry and Those Annoying Post Brothers	$0.90	$2.70	$4.50	£0.60	£1.80	£3.00
Title Value:	$0.90	$2.70	$4.50	£0.60	£1.80	£3.00

POWER & GLORY
Malibu Bravura; 1 Feb 1994-4 May 1994

Description	$Good	$Fine	$N.Mint	£Good	£Fine	£N.Mint
1 ND Howard Chaykin script, art and cover; cover version 1A	$0.45	$1.35	$2.25	£0.30	£0.90	£1.50
1 ND Howard Chaykin script, art and cover; cover version 1B (photo collage)	$0.45	$1.35	$2.25	£0.30	£0.90	£1.50
1 ND Blue Foil Edition (Oct 1994) – 10,000 copies	$2.00	$6.00	$10.00	£1.20	£3.60	£6.00
1 ND Serigraph edition (Apr 1994) limited to 3000 copies	$3.00	$9.00	$15.00	£1.50	£4.50	£7.50
2-4 ND	$0.45	$1.35	$2.25	£0.30	£0.90	£1.50
Title Value:	$7.25	$21.75	$36.25	£4.20	£12.60	£21.00

Power & Glory Softcover Collection (Oct 1994)
Trade paperback reprints mini-series with new text/features £1.70 £5.10 £8.50

Power & Glory Sotfcover Collection Signed (Oct 1994)
as above, signed by Howard Chaykin. 500 copies £4.00 £12.00 £20.00

POWER & GLORY WINTER SPECIAL
Malibu,OS; 1 Dec 1994

Description	$Good	$Fine	$N.Mint	£Good	£Fine	£N.Mint
1 ND Howard Chaykin script and art	$0.50	$1.50	$2.50	£0.30	£0.90	£1.50
Title Value:	$0.50	$1.50	$2.50	£0.30	£0.90	£1.50

Note: Non-Distributed on the news-stands in the U.K.

POWER COMICS
Power Comics; 1 1977-5 1979

Description	$Good	$Fine	$N.Mint	£Good	£Fine	£N.Mint
1 ND First Dave Sim Aardvark story	$2.00	$6.00	$10.00	£1.50	£4.50	£7.50

1 ND reprint of above (Mar 1977)

Description	$Good	$Fine	$N.Mint	£Good	£Fine	£N.Mint
(continued)	$0.80	$2.40	$4.00	£0.50	£1.50	£2.50
2 ND Cobalt Blue appears	$0.40	$1.20	$2.00	£0.25	£0.75	£1.25
3-5 ND	$0.40	$1.20	$2.00	£0.25	£0.75	£1.25
Title Value:	$4.40	$13.20	$22.00	£3.00	£9.00	£15.00

POWER COMICS (2ND SERIES)
Eclipse,MS; 1 Mar 1988-4 Sep 1988

Description	$Good	$Fine	$N.Mint	£Good	£Fine	£N.Mint
1-4 ND Brian Bolland and Dave Gibbons reprints	$0.40	$1.20	$2.00	£0.25	£0.75	£1.25
Title Value:	$1.60	$4.80	$8.00	£1.00	£3.00	£5.00

Note: series features black super-hero Powerman (renamed Powerbolt by Eclipse) and reprints early Bolland and Gibbons work that was specially commissioned and published in Nigeria in 1975.

POWER COMPANY
Axis Comics; 1 Jun 1994-2 1994

Description	$Good	$Fine	$N.Mint	£Good	£Fine	£N.Mint
1 ND Crash, Flex, Seizure, Maelstrom, Channel and Rook begin	$0.40	$1.20	$2.00	£0.25	£0.75	£1.25
2 ND	$0.40	$1.20	$2.00	£0.25	£0.75	£1.25
Title Value:	$0.80	$2.40	$4.00	£0.50	£1.50	£2.50

POWER FACTOR
Wonder Color Comics/Pied Piper Comics; 1 May 1987-2 1988

Description	$Good	$Fine	$N.Mint	£Good	£Fine	£N.Mint
1 ND colour	$0.25	$0.75	$1.25	£0.15	£0.45	£0.75
2 ND colour, published by Pied Piper	$0.25	$0.75	$1.25	£0.15	£0.45	£0.75
Title Value:	$0.50	$1.50	$2.50	£0.30	£0.90	£1.50

POWER FACTOR (2ND SERIES)
Innovation; 1 Nov 1990-3 1991

Description	$Good	$Fine	$N.Mint	£Good	£Fine	£N.Mint
1-3 ND colour	$0.40	$1.20	$2.00	£0.25	£0.75	£1.25
Title Value:	$1.20	$3.60	$6.00	£0.75	£2.25	£3.75

POWER GIRL
DC Comics,MS; 1 Jun 1988-4 Sep 1988
(see All Star Comics, Justice League Europe, 1986 Secret Origins #11, Showcase #97-100)

Description	$Good	$Fine	$N.Mint	£Good	£Fine	£N.Mint
1-2	$0.25	$0.75	$1.25	£0.15	£0.45	£0.75
3-4 Phantom Stranger appears	$0.25	$0.75	$1.25	£0.15	£0.45	£0.75
Title Value:	$1.00	$3.00	$5.00	£0.60	£1.80	£3.00

POWER LORDS
DC Comics,MS Toy; 1 Dec 1983-3 Feb 1984

Description	$Good	$Fine	$N.Mint	£Good	£Fine	£N.Mint
1-3 Mark Texeira art	$0.15	$0.45	$0.75	£0.10	£0.35	£0.60
Title Value:	$0.45	$1.35	$2.25	£0.30	£1.05	£1.80

POWER OF MARK, THE
Image; 1 Feb 1995

Description	$Good	$Fine	$N.Mint	£Good	£Fine	£N.Mint
1 ND Dan Miki art	$0.45	$1.35	$2.25	£0.30	£0.90	£1.50
Title Value:	$0.45	$1.35	$2.25	£0.30	£0.90	£1.50

POWER OF THE ATOM
(see Atom)

POWER PACHYDERMS
Marvel Comics Group,OS; 1 Sep 1989

Description	$Good	$Fine	$N.Mint	£Good	£Fine	£N.Mint
1 ND X-Men parody	$0.30	$0.90	$1.50	£0.20	£0.60	£1.00
Title Value:	$0.30	$0.90	$1.50	£0.20	£0.60	£1.00

Note: parody of X-Men characters as elephants

POWER PACK
Marvel Comics Group; 1 Aug 1984-62 Feb 1991

Description	$Good	$Fine	$N.Mint	£Good	£Fine	£N.Mint
1 DS	$0.40	$1.20	$2.00	£0.25	£0.75	£1.25
2-5	$0.30	$0.90	$1.50	£0.20	£0.60	£1.00
6 Spiderman appears	$0.30	$0.90	$1.50	£0.20	£0.60	£1.00
7-8 Cloak & Dagger appear	$0.30	$0.90	$1.50	£0.20	£0.60	£1.00
9 Spiderman appears	$0.30	$0.90	$1.50	£0.20	£0.60	£1.00
10	$0.30	$0.90	$1.50	£0.20	£0.60	£1.00
11	$0.25	$0.75	$1.25	£0.15	£0.45	£0.75
12 Kitty Pryde/Nightcrawler/Leech appear	$0.25	$0.75	$1.25	£0.15	£0.45	£0.75
13-14	$0.25	$0.75	$1.25	£0.15	£0.45	£0.75
15 Thor (Beta Ray Bill) appears	$0.25	$0.75	$1.25	£0.15	£0.45	£0.75
16 painted cover	$0.25	$0.75	$1.25	£0.15	£0.45	£0.75
17	$0.25	$0.75	$1.25	£0.15	£0.45	£0.75
18 LD in the U.K. Secret Wars X-over, ties into Thor #363	$0.25	$0.75	$1.25	£0.15	£0.45	£0.75
19 DS, Cloak and Dagger, Thor (Beta Ray Bill), Wolverine, Kitty Pryde appear; Guice cover	$0.80	$2.40	$4.00	£0.40	£1.20	£2.00
20 New Mutants appear	$0.25	$0.75	$1.25	£0.15	£0.45	£0.75
21 Spiderman cameo	$0.25	$0.75	$1.25	£0.15	£0.45	£0.75
22	$0.25	$0.75	$1.25	£0.15	£0.45	£0.75
23 Fantastic Four cameo	$0.25	$0.75	$1.25	£0.15	£0.45	£0.75
24 Cloak cameo	$0.25	$0.75	$1.25	£0.15	£0.45	£0.75
25 LD in the U.K. DS Fantastic Four cameo	$0.30	$0.90	$1.50	£0.20	£0.60	£1.00
26 ND	$0.25	$0.75	$1.25	£0.15	£0.45	£0.75
27 ND scarce in the U.K. Mutant Massacre, Wolverine and Sabretooth appear	$0.40	$1.20	$2.00	£0.40	£1.20	£2.00
28 ND scarce in the U.K. Avengers and Fantastic Four appear	$0.25	$0.75	$1.25	£0.15	£0.45	£0.75

29 ND Spiderman vs. Hobgoblin

	$Good	$Fine	$N.Mint	£Good	£Fine	£N.Mint
	$0.30	$0.90	$1.50	£0.20	£0.60	£1.00
30-32 ND	$0.25	$0.75	$1.25	£0.15	£0.45	£0.75
33 ND New Mutants appear (some)						
	$0.25	$0.75	$1.25	£0.15	£0.45	£0.75
34 ND	$0.25	$0.75	$1.25	£0.15	£0.45	£0.75
35 ND Fall of Mutants, X-Factor appear						
	$0.25	$0.75	$1.25	£0.15	£0.45	£0.75
36 ND Sentinels story						
	$0.25	$0.75	$1.25	£0.15	£0.45	£0.75
37-38 ND	$0.25	$0.75	$1.25	£0.15	£0.45	£0.75
39 ND 1st format change/slick cover						
	$0.25	$0.75	$1.25	£0.15	£0.45	£0.75
40 ND New Mutants appear						
	$0.25	$0.75	$1.25	£0.15	£0.45	£0.75
41 ND	$0.25	$0.75	$1.25	£0.15	£0.45	£0.75
42-44 ND Inferno tie-in						
	$0.25	$0.75	$1.25	£0.15	£0.45	£0.75
45 ND	$0.25	$0.75	$1.25	£0.15	£0.45	£0.75
46 ND Punisher appears, Whilce Portacio art						
			$1.25	£0.15	£0.45	£0.75
47-49 ND	$0.25	$0.75	$1.25	£0.15	£0.45	£0.75
50 DS	$0.30	$0.90	$1.50	£0.20	£0.60	£1.00
51-52 ND	$0.25	$0.75	$1.25	£0.15	£0.45	£0.75
53 ND Acts of Vengeance tie-in						
	$0.25	$0.75	$1.25	£0.15	£0.45	£0.75
54-62 ND	$0.25	$0.75	$1.25	£0.15	£0.45	£0.75
Title Value:	$17.35	$52.05	$86.75	£10.50	£31.50	£52.50
Note: Format change/slick cover from #39 on						

POWER PACK HOLIDAY SPECIAL
Marvel Comics Group; nn Feb 1992

	$Good	$Fine	$N.Mint	£Good	£Fine	£N.Mint
nn 64pgs	$0.40	$1.20	$2.00	£0.25	£0.75	£1.25
Title Value:	$0.40	$1.20	$2.00	£0.25	£0.75	£1.25

POWER PLAY
Millennium,MS; 1 Feb 1995-4 Aug 1995
1-4 ND black and white

	$Good	$Fine	$N.Mint	£Good	£Fine	£N.Mint
	$0.60	$1.80	$3.00	£0.40	£1.20	£2.00
Title Value:	$2.40	$7.20	$12.00	£1.60	£4.80	£8.00

POWER PLAYS
AC Comics; 1 1987-2 1987

	$Good	$Fine	$N.Mint	£Good	£Fine	£N.Mint
1-2 ND 52pgs	$0.40	$1.20	$2.00	£0.25	£0.75	£1.25
Title Value:	$0.80	$2.40	$4.00	£0.50	£1.50	£2.50

POWER, THE
Aircel,MS; 1 Mar 1991-4 Jun 1991
1-4 ND Barry Blair script, Dave Cooper art, black and white

	$Good	$Fine	$N.Mint	£Good	£Fine	£N.Mint
	$0.30	$0.90	$1.50	£0.20	£0.60	£1.00
Title Value:	$1.20	$3.60	$6.00	£0.80	£2.40	£4.00

POWERLINE
Marvel Comics Group/Epic; 1 May 1988-8 Jul 1989
(see Dr.Zero, St.George)

	$Good	$Fine	$N.Mint	£Good	£Fine	£N.Mint
1-8 ND	$0.40	$1.20	$2.00	£0.25	£0.75	£1.25
Title Value:	$3.20	$9.60	$16.00	£2.00	£6.00	£10.00
Note: art by D. Ross/Williamson/Gray Morrow						

POWERMAN
Marvel Comics Group; 17 Feb 1974-125 Sep 1986
(formerly Hero for Hire; becomes Powerman and Iron Fist with issue #50)
17 ND Iron Man appears

	$Good	$Fine	$N.Mint	£Good	£Fine	£N.Mint
	$2.00	$6.00	$10.00	£1.20	£3.60	£6.00
18-20 ND	$1.20	$3.60	$6.00	£0.80	£2.40	£4.00
21 Luke Cage vs. original Powerman						
	$0.60	$1.80	$3.00	£0.40	£1.20	£2.00
22-23	$0.60	$1.80	$3.00	£0.40	£1.20	£2.00

	$Good	$Fine	$N.Mint	£Good	£Fine	£N.Mint
24 1st appearance Black Goliath						
	$0.80	$2.40	$4.00	£0.50	£1.50	£2.50
25 Black Goliath appears						
	$1.80	$3.00	£0.40	£1.20	£2.00	
26	$0.60	$1.80	$3.00	£0.40	£1.20	£2.00
27 George Perez art						
	$0.60	$1.80	$3.00	£0.40	£1.20	£2.00
28-30	$0.60	$1.80	$3.00	£0.40	£1.20	£2.00
31 Neal Adams inks (credited as "The Crusty Bunkers" which was his art studio team at the time)						
	$0.60	$1.80	$3.00	£0.40	£1.20	£2.00
32-44	$0.50	$1.50	$2.50	£0.30	£0.90	£1.50
45 Jim Starlin cover						
	$0.50	$1.50	$2.50	£0.30	£0.90	£1.50
46-47	$0.50	$1.50	$2.50	£0.30	£0.90	£1.50
48 1st appearance of Iron Fist in title, John Byrne art						
	$0.60	$1.80	$3.00	£0.40	£1.20	£2.00
49 John Byrne art	$0.60	$1.80	$3.00	£0.40	£1.20	£2.00
50 John Byrne art, logo changes to "Powerman and Iron Fist" from here on						
	$0.90	$2.70	$4.50	£0.60	£1.80	£3.00
51-52 Mike Zeck art						
	$0.40	$1.20	$2.00	£0.25	£0.75	£1.25
53-56	$0.40	$1.20	$2.00	£0.25	£0.75	£1.25
57 X-Men appear	$0.90	$2.70	$4.50	£0.60	£1.80	£3.00
58-64 ND	$0.40	$1.20	$2.00	£0.30	£0.90	£1.50
65	$0.40	$1.20	$2.00	£0.25	£0.75	£1.25
66 2nd appearance Sabretooth (see Iron Fist #14)						
	$4.50	$13.50	$22.50	£3.00	£9.00	£15.00
67 ND	$0.45	$1.35	$2.25	£0.30	£0.90	£1.50
68-72	$0.40	$1.20	$2.00	£0.25	£0.75	£1.25
73 Rom X-over, Frank Miller cover						
	$0.40	$1.20	$2.00	£0.25	£0.75	£1.25
74 Frank Miller cover						
	$0.40	$1.20	$2.00	£0.25	£0.75	£1.25
75 52pgs	$0.45	$1.35	$2.25	£0.30	£0.90	£1.50
76 2pgs Frank Miller art						
	$0.40	$1.20	$2.00	£0.25	£0.75	£1.25
77 Daredevil guest-stars (X-over Daredevil #178)						
	$0.40	$1.20	$2.00	£0.25	£0.75	£1.25
78 3rd appearance Sabretooth. Referred to as "The Slasher" and heavily disguised with sacking over his head. Claws exposed in a few panels...						
	$2.00	$6.00	$10.00	£1.00	£3.00	£5.00
79 Dr. Who parody	$0.40	$1.20	$2.00	£0.25	£0.75	£1.25
80-83	$0.40	$1.20	$2.00	£0.25	£0.75	£1.25
84 4th appearance Sabretooth						
	$2.00	$6.00	$10.00	£1.00	£3.00	£5.00
85-86	$0.40	$1.20	$2.00	£0.25	£0.75	£1.25
87 Moon Knight appears						
	$0.40	$1.20	$2.00	£0.25	£0.75	£1.25
88-99	$0.40	$1.20	$2.00	£0.25	£0.75	£1.25
100 52pgs	$0.55	$1.65	$2.75	£0.35	£1.05	£1.75
101-117	$0.30	$0.90	$1.50	£0.20	£0.60	£1.00
118-120 ND	$0.30	$0.90	$1.50	£0.30	£0.90	£1.50
121 ND Secret Wars X-over						
	$0.30	$0.90	$1.50	£0.30	£0.90	£1.50
122-124 ND scarce in the U.K.						
	$0.30	$0.90	$1.50	£0.40	£1.20	£2.00
125 ND DS scarce	$0.50	$1.50	$2.50	£0.60	£1.80	£3.00
Title Value:	$58.25	$174.75	$291.25	£38.35	£115.05	£191.75

ARTISTS
Byrne covers on 104, 106, 107, 113-116.

Phantom Stranger #2

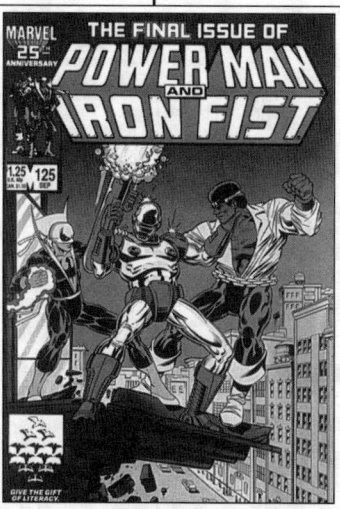

Power Man & Iron Fist #125

Powers That Be #1

MINT = 100% / NEAR MINT (inc. +/-) = 90-99% / VERY FINE (inc. +/-) = 75-89% / FINE (inc. +/-) = 55-74%
VERY GOOD (inc. +/-) = 35-54% / GOOD (inc. +/-) = 15-34% / FAIR = 5-14% / POOR = 1-4%

499

POWERMAN ANNUAL
Marvel Comics Group; 1 Nov 1976
1 ND 52pgs, Punisher appears in a flashback sequence

	$Good	$Fine	$N.Mint	£Good	£Fine	£N.Mint
	$0.80	$2.40	$4.00	£0.60	£1.80	£3.00
Title Value:	$0.80	$2.40	$4.00	£0.60	£1.80	£3.00

POWERMAN GIANT SIZE
Marvel Comics Group; 1 1975
1 ND 68pgs, all reprint

	$Good	$Fine	$N.Mint	£Good	£Fine	£N.Mint
	$1.50	$4.50	$7.50	£1.00	£3.00	£5.00
Title Value:	$1.50	$4.50	$7.50	£1.00	£3.00	£5.00

POWERS THAT BE
Broadway Comics; 1 Nov 1995-present
1 ND intro Star Seed and Fatale, Jim Shooter script

	$Good	$Fine	$N.Mint	£Good	£Fine	£N.Mint
	$0.50	$1.50	$2.50	£0.30	£0.90	£1.50
2-3 ND	$0.50	$1.50	$2.50	£0.30	£0.90	£1.50
Title Value:	$1.50	$4.50	$7.50	£0.90	£2.70	£4.50

PRAIRIE MOON & OTHER STORIES
Dark Horse,OS; 1 Oct 1992
1 ND 48pgs, Rick Geary anthology

	$Good	$Fine	$N.Mint	£Good	£Fine	£N.Mint
	$0.40	$1.20	$2.00	£0.25	£0.75	£1.25
Title Value:	$0.40	$1.20	$2.00	£0.25	£0.75	£1.25

PRE-TEEN DIRTY GENE KUNG-FU KANGAROOS
Blackthorne; 1 Aug 1986
1 ND Teenage Mutant Ninja Turtles appear, Lee Marrs script/art, black and white

	$Good	$Fine	$N.Mint	£Good	£Fine	£N.Mint
	$0.40	$1.20	$2.00	£0.25	£0.75	£1.25
Title Value:	$0.40	$1.20	$2.00	£0.25	£0.75	£1.25

PREACHER
DC Comics/Vertigo; 1 Apr 1995-present

	$Good	$Fine	$N.Mint	£Good	£Fine	£N.Mint
1 Garth Ennis script, Steve Dillon art	$2.00	$6.00	$10.00	£1.50	£4.50	£7.50
2 Garth Ennis script, Steve Dillon art	$1.50	$4.50	$7.50	£1.00	£3.00	£5.00
3 Garth Ennis script, Steve Dillon art	$1.20	$3.60	$6.00	£0.80	£2.40	£4.00
4-5 Garth Ennis script, Steve Dillon art	$1.00	$3.00	$5.00	£0.60	£1.80	£3.00
6-7 Garth Ennis script, Steve Dillon art	$0.60	$1.80	$3.00	£0.40	£1.20	£2.00
8-9 Garth Ennis script, Steve Dillon art	$0.50	$1.50	$2.50	£0.30	£0.90	£1.50
10-12	$0.50	$1.50	$2.50	£0.30	£0.90	£1.50
Title Value:	$11.30	$33.90	$56.50	£6.80	£20.40	£34.00

PREDATOR
Dark Horse,MS; 1 May 1989-4 1990

	$Good	$Fine	$N.Mint	£Good	£Fine	£N.Mint
1 ND	$3.00	$9.00	$15.00	£1.60	£4.80	£8.00
1 2nd printing ND	$0.80	$2.40	$4.00	£0.50	£1.50	£2.50
2 ND	$1.50	$4.50	$7.50	£0.80	£2.40	£4.00
2 2nd printing ND	$0.50	$1.50	$2.50	£0.30	£0.90	£1.50
3 ND	$1.00	$3.00	$5.00	£0.60	£1.80	£3.00
3 2nd printing ND	$0.50	$1.50	$2.50	£0.30	£0.90	£1.50
4 ND	$1.00	$3.00	$5.00	£0.60	£1.80	£3.00
Title Value:	$8.30	$24.90	$41.50	£4.70	£14.10	£23.50

Predator Collection (Sep 1990) reprints issues #1-4, new cover £1.50 £4.50 £7.50
Limited Edition Hardcover (Apr 1991)
signed and numbered, 2500 copies £10.00 £30.00 £50.00

PREDATOR 2
Dark Horse,MS; 1 Feb 1991-2 Mar 1991
1-2 ND adaptation of film, Dan Barry pencils; with 2 trading cards

	$Good	$Fine	$N.Mint	£Good	£Fine	£N.Mint
	$0.50	$1.50	$2.50	£0.30	£0.90	£1.50
Title Value:	$1.00	$3.00	$5.00	£0.60	£1.80	£3.00

PREDATOR VS. MAGNUS ROBOT FIGHTER
Dark Horse,MS; 1 Dec 1992-2 Jan 1993
1 ND Jim Shooter script, Barry Windsor-Smith cover; contains bound-in trading cards

	$Good	$Fine	$N.Mint	£Good	£Fine	£N.Mint
	$0.50	$1.50	$2.50	£0.30	£0.90	£1.50

1 ND Platinum Edtion (Dec 1992) – "Platinum Edtion" banner on bottom of platinum-coloured cover

	$Good	$Fine	$N.Mint	£Good	£Fine	£N.Mint
	$3.00	$9.00	$15.00	£2.00	£6.00	£10.00

2 ND Jim Shooter script, Barry Windsor-Smith cover; contains bound-in trading cards

	$Good	$Fine	$N.Mint	£Good	£Fine	£N.Mint
	$0.50	$1.50	$2.50	£0.30	£0.90	£1.50
Title Value:	$4.00	$12.00	$20.00	£2.60	£7.80	£13.00

Predator vs. Magnus Robot Fighter (Sep 1994)
Trade paperback 64pgs, reprints mini-series £1.00 £3.00 £5.00

PREDATOR: BAD BLOOD
Dark Horse,MS; 1 Dec 1993-4 Mar 1994
1-4 ND Derek Thompson cover and art

	$Good	$Fine	$N.Mint	£Good	£Fine	£N.Mint
	$0.50	$1.50	$2.50	£0.30	£0.90	£1.50
Title Value:	$2.00	$6.00	$10.00	£1.20	£3.60	£6.00

PREDATOR: BIG GAME
Dark Horse,MS; 1 Mar 1991-4 Jun 1991
1-4 ND Evan Dorkin art

	$Good	$Fine	$N.Mint	£Good	£Fine	£N.Mint
	$0.50	$1.50	$2.50	£0.30	£0.90	£1.50
Title Value:	$2.00	$6.00	$10.00	£1.20	£3.60	£6.00

Predator: Big Game Trade paperback (Aug 1992)
reprints issues #1-#4 £1.70 £5.10 £8.50

PREDATOR: BLOODY SANDS OF TIME
Dark Horse,MS; 1 Feb 1992-2 Mar 1992
1-2 ND script/pencils by Dan Barry, inks and covers by Chris Warner

	$Good	$Fine	$N.Mint	£Good	£Fine	£N.Mint
	$0.50	$1.50	$2.50	£0.30	£0.90	£1.50
Title Value:	$1.00	$3.00	$5.00	£0.60	£1.80	£3.00

PREDATOR: COLD WAR
Dark Horse,MS; 1 Nov 1991-4 Feb 1992
1-4 ND Brian Stelfreeze covers

	$Good	$Fine	$N.Mint	£Good	£Fine	£N.Mint
	$0.50	$1.50	$2.50	£0.30	£0.90	£1.50
Title Value:	$2.00	$6.00	$10.00	£1.20	£3.60	£6.00

Predator: Cold War Softcover Collection (May 1993)
reprints mini-series with new cover by Ray Lago £1.65 £4.95 £8.25

PREDATOR: INVADERS FROM THE FOURTH DIMENSION
Dark Horse,OS; 1 Jul 1994

	$Good	$Fine	$N.Mint	£Good	£Fine	£N.Mint
1 ND 48pgs	$0.80	$2.40	$4.00	£0.50	£1.50	£2.50
Title Value:	$0.80	$2.40	$4.00	£0.50	£1.50	£2.50

PREDATOR: JUNGLE TALES
Dark Horse,OS; 1 Mar 1995
1 ND reprints stories from Dark Horse Comics #1,2 and #10-12; Val Mayerik cover

	$Good	$Fine	$N.Mint	£Good	£Fine	£N.Mint
	$0.60	$1.80	$3.00	£0.40	£1.20	£2.00
Title Value:	$0.60	$1.80	$3.00	£0.40	£1.20	£2.00

PREDATOR: RACE WAR
Dark Horse,MS; 0 Apr 1993; 1 Feb 1993-4 Aug 1993
0 ND (Apr 1993), reprints prologue from Dark Horse Presents #67-69

	$Good	$Fine	$N.Mint	£Good	£Fine	£N.Mint
	$0.50	$1.50	$2.50	£0.30	£0.90	£1.50

1-4 ND Dave Dorman covers

	$Good	$Fine	$N.Mint	£Good	£Fine	£N.Mint
	$0.50	$1.50	$2.50	£0.30	£0.90	£1.50
Title Value:	$2.50	$7.50	$12.50	£1.50	£4.50	£7.50

Predator: Race War (Jul 1995) Trade paperback
reprints mini-series with new cover by Ray Lago £2.40 £7.20 £12.00

PRESSBUTTON
Eclipse; 1 1984-6 1985

	$Good	$Fine	$N.Mint	£Good	£Fine	£N.Mint
1-2 ND	$0.40	$1.20	$2.00	£0.30	£0.90	£1.50
3-5 ND	$0.40	$1.20	$2.00	£0.25	£0.75	£1.25

6 ND scarce in the U.K.

	$Good	$Fine	$N.Mint	£Good	£Fine	£N.Mint
	$0.40	$1.20	$2.00	£0.30	£0.90	£1.50
Title Value:	$2.40	$7.20	$12.00	£1.65	£4.95	£8.25

PREZ
DC Comics; 1 Aug/Sep 1973-4 Feb/Mar 1974
(see Supergirl #10)
1 Joe Simon scripts begin, origin and 1st appearance Prez

	$Good	$Fine	$N.Mint	£Good	£Fine	£N.Mint
	$0.25	$0.75	$1.25	£0.15	£0.45	£0.75
2-4	$0.25	$0.75	$1.25	£0.15	£0.45	£0.75
Title Value:	$1.00	$3.00	$5.00	£0.60	£1.80	£3.00

PREZ (2ND SERIES)
DC Comics/Vertigo,OS; 1 Sep 1994
1 ND 64pgs, Ed Brubaker script; Eric Shanower art; photo cover

	$Good	$Fine	$N.Mint	£Good	£Fine	£N.Mint
	$0.80	$2.40	$4.00	£0.50	£1.50	£2.50
Title Value:	$0.80	$2.40	$4.00	£0.50	£1.50	£2.50

PRICE, THE
(see Eclipse Graphic Album Series #5)

PRIMAL
Dark Horse,MS; 1 Oct 1992-2 Nov 1992
1-2 ND continuation from Graphic Novel by Barker and Chichester, photo cover

	$Good	$Fine	$N.Mint	£Good	£Fine	£N.Mint
	$0.50	$1.50	$2.50	£0.30	£0.90	£1.50
Title Value:	$1.00	$3.00	$5.00	£0.60	£1.80	£3.00

PRIMAL FORCE
DC Comics; 0 Oct 1994; 1 Nov 1994-14 Dec 1995
0 (Oct 1994) Zero Hour X-over; Tornado, Jack O'Lantern, Meridian, Golem and Claw begin;
spin-off from Zero Hour

	$Good	$Fine	$N.Mint	£Good	£Fine	£N.Mint
	$0.40	$1.20	$2.00	£0.25	£0.75	£1.25
1-6	$0.40	$1.20	$2.00	£0.25	£0.75	£1.25

7 Superman, Green lantern, Wonder Woman and Batman (Azrael) guest-star

	$Good	$Fine	$N.Mint	£Good	£Fine	£N.Mint
	$0.40	$1.20	$2.00	£0.25	£0.75	£1.25
8-12	$0.40	$1.20	$2.00	£0.25	£0.75	£1.25

13-14 Underworld Unleashed tie-in

	$Good	$Fine	$N.Mint	£Good	£Fine	£N.Mint
	$0.40	$1.20	$2.00	£0.25	£0.75	£1.25
Title Value:	$6.00	$18.00	$30.00	£3.75	£11.25	£18.75

PRIMAL: FROM THE CRADLE TO THE GRAVE
Dark Horse,OS; 1 Oct 1994
1 ND 64pgs, Clive Barker and Dan Chichester

	$Good	$Fine	$N.Mint	£Good	£Fine	£N.Mint
	$1.50	$4.50	$7.50	£1.00	£3.00	£5.00
Title Value:	$1.50	$4.50	$7.50	£1.00	£3.00	£5.00

PRIME
Malibu Ultraverse; ½ May 1994; 1 Jun 1993-26 Aug 1995
½ 24pgs, produced in association with Wizard Press, Norm Breyfogle art,
small Wizard logo hologram on cover; pre-bagged in mylar with certificate

	$Good	$Fine	$N.Mint	£Good	£Fine	£N.Mint
	$0.45	$1.35	$2.25	£0.30	£0.90	£1.50

1 Norm Breyfogle covers and art begin; 1st appearance Prime and Prototype, Ultraverse #0 coupon card

	$Good	$Fine	$N.Mint	£Good	£Fine	£N.Mint
	$1.00	$3.00	$5.00	£0.50	£1.50	£2.50

1 Limited Edition – full hologram cover; 7,500 copies

	$Good	$Fine	$N.Mint	£Good	£Fine	£N.Mint
	$3.00	$9.00	$15.00	£1.50	£4.50	£7.50

2 pre-bagged with trading card

	$Good	$Fine	$N.Mint	£Good	£Fine	£N.Mint
	$1.00	$3.00	$5.00	£0.50	£1.50	£2.50

2 un-bagged/without trading card

	$Good	$Fine	$N.Mint	£Good	£Fine	£N.Mint
	$0.50	$1.50	$2.50	£0.30	£0.90	£1.50
3 origin Prime	$0.60	$1.80	$3.00	£0.40	£1.20	£2.00

4 two covers available; the positions of Prime and Prototype are inter-changed on each cover; Prime vs. Prototype

	$Good	$Fine	$N.Mint	£Good	£Fine	£N.Mint
	$0.50	$1.50	$2.50	£0.30	£0.90	£1.50

5 40pgs, Rune insert

	$Good	$Fine	$N.Mint	£Good	£Fine	£N.Mint
	$0.50	$1.50	$2.50	£0.30	£0.90	£1.50

6 continued in Break-Thru #1; President Bill Clinton appears

	$Good	$Fine	$N.Mint	£Good	£Fine	£N.Mint
	$0.40	$1.20	$2.00	£0.25	£0.75	£1.25

7 Break-Thru X-over

	$Good	$Fine	$N.Mint	£Good	£Fine	£N.Mint
	$0.40	$1.20	$2.00	£0.25	£0.75	£1.25

8 Freex origin by Walt Simonson; Mantra appears

	$Good	$Fine	$N.Mint	£Good	£Fine	£N.Mint
	$0.40	$1.20	$2.00	£0.25	£0.75	£1.25

9 continued in Firearm #6

	$Good	$Fine	$N.Mint	£Good	£Fine	£N.Mint
	$0.40	$1.20	$2.00	£0.25	£0.75	£1.25

10 continued from Firearm #6, new look and costume for Prime

	$Good	$Fine	$N.Mint	£Good	£Fine	£N.Mint
	$0.40	$1.20	$2.00	£0.25	£0.75	£1.25

PRIME (continued)

	$Good	$Fine	$N.Mint	£Good	£Fine	£N.Mint
11	$0.40	$1.20	$2.00	£0.25	£0.75	£1.25
12 64pgs, anniversary issue with silver logos	$0.55	$1.65	$2.75	£0.35	£1.05	£1.75
13 48pgs	$0.50	$1.50	$2.50	£0.30	£0.90	£1.50
14-19	$0.40	$1.20	$2.00	£0.25	£0.75	£1.25
20 reveals identity to Kelly	$0.40	$1.20	$2.00	£0.25	£0.75	£1.25
21	$0.40	$1.20	$2.00	£0.25	£0.75	£1.25
22 Godwheel tie-in; Mark Pacella and Art Thibert cover	$0.40	$1.20	$2.00	£0.25	£0.75	£1.25
23 Pat Broderick guest art, leads into Power of Prime mini-series; bi-weekly	$0.40	$1.20	$2.00	£0.25	£0.75	£1.25
24 leads into Power of Prime mini-series; bi-weekly	$0.40	$1.20	$2.00	£0.25	£0.75	£1.25
25 1st issue under Marvel Comics solicitation; Chelsea Clinton appears	$0.40	$1.20	$2.00	£0.25	£0.75	£1.25
26	$0.40	$1.20	$2.00	£0.25	£0.75	£1.25
Title Value:	$16.20	$48.60	$81.00	£9.50	£28.50	£47.50

Note: all Non-Distributed on the news-stands in the U.K.

Prime Collection Sofcover (Aug 1994)

	$Good	$Fine	$N.Mint	£Good	£Fine	£N.Mint
reprints issues #1-4, Alex Ross painted cover				£1.30	£3.90	£6.50

Prime Collection Hardcover (Aug 1994)

	$Good	$Fine	$N.Mint	£Good	£Fine	£N.Mint
limited to 2,000 copies with signed plate				£3.50	£10.50	£17.50

PRIME (2ND SERIES)
Marvel Comics Group; 1 Dec 1995-present

	$Good	$Fine	$N.Mint	£Good	£Fine	£N.Mint
1 ND Gerard Jones and Len Strazewski script; Kevin West and John Statema art; Spiderman and Spider-Prime vs. The new lizard	$0.30	$0.90	$1.50	£0.20	£0.60	£1.00
1 ND variant cover, computer painted cover by Chuck Maiden	$0.90	$2.70	$4.50	£0.60	£1.80	£3.00
1 ND Signed Limited Edition (Mar 1996) – 2,000 copies with certificate	$1.50	$4.50	$7.50	£1.00	£3.00	£5.00
2 ND flip-book format with Phoenix Ressurrection chapter	$0.30	$0.90	$1.50	£0.20	£0.60	£1.00
3-4 ND	$0.30	$0.90	$1.50	£0.20	£0.60	£1.00
Title Value:	$3.60	$10.80	$18.00	£2.40	£7.20	£12.00

PRIME ANNUAL
Malibu Ultraverse; 1 Oct 1994

	$Good	$Fine	$N.Mint	£Good	£Fine	£N.Mint
1 ND 64pgs, Boris Vallejo painted cover	$0.50	$1.50	$2.50	£0.30	£0.90	£1.50
Title Value:	$0.50	$1.50	$2.50	£0.30	£0.90	£1.50

PRIME CUTS
Fantagraphics,Magazine; 1 Jun 1987-10 1988

	$Good	$Fine	$N.Mint	£Good	£Fine	£N.Mint
1-10 ND	$0.80	$2.40	$4.00	£0.50	£1.50	£2.50
Title Value:	$8.00	$24.00	$40.00	£5.00	£15.00	£25.00

PRIME MONTH ASHCAN
Malibu,OS; nn Oct 1994

	$Good	$Fine	$N.Mint	£Good	£Fine	£N.Mint
nn ND 16pgs, black and white, information and sketches of the character Prime	$0.15	$0.45	$0.75	£0.10	£0.30	£0.50
Title Value:	$0.15	$0.45	$0.75	£0.10	£0.30	£0.50

PRIME SLIME TALES
Mirage/Now Comics; 1 Apr 1986-4 Jan 1987

	$Good	$Fine	$N.Mint	£Good	£Fine	£N.Mint
1-4 ND	$0.40	$1.20	$2.00	£0.25	£0.75	£1.25
Title Value:	$1.60	$4.80	$8.00	£1.00	£3.00	£5.00

PRIME, POWER OF
Marvel Comics Group/Malibu Ultraverse,MS; 1 Jul 1995-4 Oct 1995

	$Good	$Fine	$N.Mint	£Good	£Fine	£N.Mint
1-4 ND Godwheel tie-in	$0.40	$1.20	$2.00	£0.25	£0.75	£1.25
Title Value:	$1.60	$4.80	$8.00	£1.00	£3.00	£5.00

PRIME: INFINITY
Marvel Comics Group,OS; nn Nov 1995

	$Good	$Fine	$N.Mint	£Good	£Fine	£N.Mint
nn ND Black September tie-in; Spiderman and Spider-Prime vs. The new Lizard	$0.50	$1.50	$2.50	£0.30	£0.90	£1.50
nn ND Signed Limited Edition (Dec 1995); 2,000 copies with certificate	$2.50	$7.50	$12.50	£1.50	£4.50	£7.50
nn ND Variant cover; 1 copy recieved for every 5 regular copies ordered	$0.80	$2.40	$4.00	£0.50	£1.50	£2.50
Title Value:	$3.80	$11.40	$19.00	£2.30	£6.90	£11.50

PRIMER
Comico; 1 Oct 1982-6 Feb 1984

	$Good	$Fine	$N.Mint	£Good	£Fine	£N.Mint
1 1st appearances Victor, Slaughterman, Az, Skrog, Mr. Justice; black and white "showcase" comic for "talented amateurs"	$0.90	$2.70	$4.50	£0.60	£1.80	£3.00
2 scarce in the U.K. 1st appearance Grendel by Matt Wagner	$10.50	$33.00	$65.00	£7.50	£22.50	£45.00
3	$1.00	$3.00	$5.00	£0.60	£1.80	£3.00
4 1st Sam Kieth art in comics? (1 preview page announcing feature for next issue)	$1.00	$3.00	$5.00	£0.60	£1.80	£3.00
5 1st appearance The Maxx by Sam Kieth	$3.30	$10.00	$20.00	£1.65	£5.00	£10.00
6 scarce in the U.K. 1st appearance Evangeline	$1.00	$3.00	$5.00	£1.00	£3.00	£5.00
Title Value:	$17.70	$54.70	$104.50	£11.95	£35.90	£69.00

Note: all Non-Distributed on the news-stands in the U.K.

PRIMORTALS ORIGINS, LEONARD NIMOY'S
Tekno Comix; 1 Nov 1995-present

	$Good	$Fine	$N.Mint	£Good	£Fine	£N.Mint
1 ND pre-bagged with copy of Neil Gaiman's Mr. Hero	$0.60	$1.80	$3.00	£0.30	£0.90	£1.50
2 ND	$0.60	$1.80	$3.00	£0.30	£0.90	£1.50
Title Value:	$1.20	$3.60	$6.00	£0.60	£1.80	£3.00

Note: this mini-series replaced issues in the on-going title for two months between issues #12 and #13

PRIMORTALS, LEONARD NIMOY'S
Tekno Comix; 1 Mar 1995-present

	$Good	$Fine	$N.Mint	£Good	£Fine	£N.Mint
1 ND Kate Worley script, Scot Eaton and Mike Barreiro art begins	$0.40	$1.20	$2.00	£0.25	£0.75	£1.25
2-11 ND	$0.40	$1.20	$2.00	£0.25	£0.75	£1.25
12 ND	$0.45	$1.35	$2.25	£0.30	£0.90	£1.50
Title Value:	$4.85	$14.55	$24.25	£3.05	£9.15	£15.25

PRIMUS
Charlton, TV; 1 Feb 1972-7 Oct 1972

	$Good	$Fine	$N.Mint	£Good	£Fine	£N.Mint
1 Joe Staton art; distributed in the U.K.	$1.50	$4.50	$7.50	£1.00	£3.00	£5.00
2-7 Joe Staton art; distributed in the U.K.	$1.00	$3.00	$5.00	£0.60	£1.80	£3.00
Title Value:	$7.50	$22.50	$37.50	£4.60	£13.80	£23.00

PRINCE AND THE PAUPER GRAPHIC NOVEL, THE
Disney; nn Dec 1990

	$Good	$Fine	$N.Mint	£Good	£Fine	£N.Mint
nn ND 64pgs, adaptation of film	$1.00	$3.00	$5.00	£0.60	£1.80	£3.00
Title Value:	$1.00	$3.00	$5.00	£0.60	£1.80	£3.00

PRINCE VALIANT
Marvel Comics Group,MS; 1 Dec 1994-4 Mar 1995

	$Good	$Fine	$N.Mint	£Good	£Fine	£N.Mint
1-4 Charles Vess script, John Ridway art and cover by Mike Kaluta	$0.60	$1.80	$3.00	£0.40	£1.20	£2.00
Title Value:	$2.40	$7.20	$12.00	£1.60	£4.80	£8.00

PRINCE VALIANT
Pioneer; 1 Apr 1990
(see Official Prince Valiant)

	$Good	$Fine	$N.Mint	£Good	£Fine	£N.Mint
1 ND material never-before reprinted	$1.00	$3.00	$5.00	£0.70	£2.10	£3.50
Title Value:	$1.00	$3.00	$5.00	£0.70	£2.10	£3.50

PRINCE VANDAL
Triumphant Comics; 0 Jul 1994; 1 Nov 1993-12 Oct 1994

	$Good	$Fine	$N.Mint	£Good	£Fine	£N.Mint
0 (Jul 1994) origin/life story of Prince Vandal	$0.40	$1.20	$2.00	£0.25	£0.75	£1.25
0 Signed Edition (Oct 1994) – pre-bagged with mini-poster photo-print and backing board	$1.00	$3.00	$5.00	£0.50	£1.50	£2.50
1 serially numbered each time at top of cover; Bobby Rae pencils begin; Unleashed X-over	$0.50	$1.50	$2.50	£0.30	£0.90	£1.50
2-6 serially numbered at top	$0.40	$1.20	$2.00	£0.25	£0.75	£1.25
7	$0.40	$1.20	$2.00	£0.25	£0.75	£1.25
8 dual issue with Chromium Man #11 (Note: there is only the one comic between the two titles)	$0.40	$1.20	$2.00	£0.25	£0.75	£1.25
9 dual issue with Chromium Man #12 (Note: there is only the one comic between the two titles)	$0.40	$1.20	$2.00	£0.25	£0.75	£1.25
10-12	$0.40	$1.20	$2.00	£0.25	£0.75	£1.25
Title Value:	$6.30	$18.90	$31.50	£3.80	£11.40	£19.00

Note: all Non-Distributed on the news-stands in the U.K.

PRINCE: ALTER EGO
DC Comics/Piranha Press,OS; 1 1991

	$Good	$Fine	$N.Mint	£Good	£Fine	£N.Mint
1 ND Brian Bolland cover, Denys Cowan/Kent Williams art, promotional tie-in with album "Diamonds and Pearls"	$1.50	$4.50	$7.50	£1.00	£3.00	£5.00
1 2nd printing ND	$0.80	$2.40	$4.00	£0.50	£1.50	£2.50
1 3rd printing, ND (Aug 1992)	$0.40	$1.20	$2.00	£0.25	£0.75	£1.25
Title Value:	$2.70	$8.10	$13.50	£1.75	£5.25	£8.75

PRINCE: THREE CHAINS OF GOLD
DC Comics/Piranha Press,OS; 1 Jun 1994

	$Good	$Fine	$N.Mint	£Good	£Fine	£N.Mint
1 ND 48pgs, Dwayne McDuffie script, David Williams, Steve Carr and Joe Rubenstein art	$0.60	$1.80	$3.00	£0.40	£1.20	£2.00
Title Value:	$0.60	$1.80	$3.00	£0.40	£1.20	£2.00

PRISONER, THE
DC Comics,MS; 1 Dec 1988-4 Mar 1989

	$Good	$Fine	$N.Mint	£Good	£Fine	£N.Mint
1-4 48pgs, Dean Motter script/art	$0.70	$2.10	$3.50	£0.40	£1.20	£2.00
Title Value:	$2.80	$8.40	$14.00	£1.60	£4.80	£8.00

Note: all Prestige Format,squarebound. Uses concepts from the television series.

Trade paperback (Jul 1990)

	$Good	$Fine	$N.Mint	£Good	£Fine	£N.Mint
208 pgs, new wraparound painted cover by Dean Motter				£1.90	£5.70	£9.50

PRIVATE BEACH
Antarctic Press,MS; 1 Jan 1995-3 1995

	$Good	$Fine	$N.Mint	£Good	£Fine	£N.Mint
1-3 ND David Hahn script and art; black and white	$0.55	$1.65	$2.75	£0.35	£1.05	£1.75
Title Value:	$1.65	$4.95	$8.25	£1.05	£3.15	£5.25

PRIVATEERS
Vanguard; 1 Aug 1987

	$Good	$Fine	$N.Mint	£Good	£Fine	£N.Mint
1 ND	$0.30	$0.90	$1.50	£0.20	£0.60	£1.00
Title Value:	$0.30	$0.90	$1.50	£0.20	£0.60	£1.00

PROFESSIONAL: GOGOL 13, THE
Viz,MS; 1-4 1991

	$Good	$Fine	$N.Mint	£Good	£Fine	£N.Mint
1-4 ND 48pgs, squarebound, Takao Saito material adapted by James Hudnall	$0.90	$2.70	$4.50	£0.60	£1.80	£3.00
Title Value:	$3.60	$10.80	$18.00	£2.40	£7.20	£12.00

PROFESSOR XAVIER AND THE X-MEN
Marvel Comics Group; 1 Oct 1995-present

	$Good	$Fine	$N.Mint	£Good	£Fine	£N.Mint
1 ND Fred Schiller script, Jan Duursema and Rick Magyar art, new stories begin; special cover price of 99 cents	$0.25	$0.75	$1.25	£0.15	£0.45	£0.75
2-3 ND	$0.20	$0.60	$1.00	£0.15	£0.45	£0.75
4 ND Magneto and the Brotherhood of Evil Mutants appear	$0.20	$0.60	$1.00	£0.15	£0.45	£0.75
5 ND Magneto and the Brotherhood of Evil Mutants appear						

	$Good	$Fine	$N.Mint	£Good	£Fine	£N.Mint
	$0.20	$0.60	$1.00	£0.10	£0.35	£0.65
Title Value:	$1.05	$3.15	$5.25	£0.70	£2.15	£3.65

note: originally announced as X-Men Dollar Book

PROJECT A-KO
Malibu,MS; 1,2 Mar 1994; 3,4 Apr 1994
1-4 ND based on Japanese anime series

	$Good	$Fine	$N.Mint	£Good	£Fine	£N.Mint
	$0.60	$1.80	$3.00	£0.40	£1.20	£2.00
Title Value:	$2.40	$7.20	$12.00	£1.60	£4.80	£8.00

Project A-KO Graphic Novel (Mar 1995)
collects four issue mini-series plus new 8pg
battle sequence (Note: published by CPM Comics) £1.30 £3.90 £6.50

PROJECT A-KO 2
CPM Comics,MS; 1 Apr 1995-3 Aug 1995
1-3 ND 24pgs, Tim Eldred art

	$Good	$Fine	$N.Mint	£Good	£Fine	£N.Mint
	$0.60	$1.80	$3.00	£0.40	£1.20	£2.00
Title Value:	$1.80	$5.40	$9.00	£1.20	£3.60	£6.00

PROJECT A-KO: VERSUS
CPM Comics,MS; 1 Oct 1995-present
1 ND 24pgs, John Ott script and Studio Go! art

	$Good	$Fine	$N.Mint	£Good	£Fine	£N.Mint
	$0.60	$1.80	$3.00	£0.40	£1.20	£2.00
Title Value:	$0.60	$1.80	$3.00	£0.40	£1.20	£2.00

PROJECT X
Kitchen Sink; 1 1993
1 ND issue #1 of Thump 'N Guts, poster, trading card and 100 dollar bill flyer in envelope all pre-bagged in gold; Kevin Eastman and Simon Bisley

	$Good	$Fine	$N.Mint	£Good	£Fine	£N.Mint
	$1.00	$3.00	$5.00	£0.60	£1.80	£3.00
Title Value:	$1.00	$3.00	$5.00	£0.60	£1.80	£3.00

PROJECT: NEWMAN
Legacy Comics,OS; 1 1991
1 ND black and white

	$Good	$Fine	$N.Mint	£Good	£Fine	£N.Mint
	$0.15	$0.45	$0.75	£0.10	£0.30	£0.50
Title Value:	$0.15	$0.45	$0.75	£0.10	£0.30	£0.50

PROMISE
Viz,OS; 1 Apr 1994
1 ND 80pgs, Keiko Nishi script and art; black and white

	$Good	$Fine	$N.Mint	£Good	£Fine	£N.Mint
	$1.20	$3.60	$6.00	£0.80	£2.40	£4.00
Title Value:	$1.20	$3.60	$6.00	£0.80	£2.40	£4.00

PROPELLERMAN
Dark Horse,MS; 1 Jan 1993-8 Mar 1994
1-8 ND Matthias Schultheiss script and art

	$Good	$Fine	$N.Mint	£Good	£Fine	£N.Mint
	$0.60	$1.80	$3.00	£0.40	£1.20	£2.00
Title Value:	$4.80	$14.40	$24.00	£3.20	£9.60	£16.00

PROPHET
Image; 0 Jul 1994; 1 Oct 1993-10 Jan 1995

	$Good	$Fine	$N.Mint	£Good	£Fine	£N.Mint
0 Dan Panosian story, cover & art	$2.00	$6.00	$10.00	£1.20	£3.60	£6.00
0 San Diego Edition; released at the 1994 San Diego Comicon	$2.00	$6.00	$10.00	£1.50	£4.50	£7.50
1 Rob Liefeld script/layouts, Dan Panosian pencils/inks	$0.50	$1.50	$2.50	£0.30	£0.90	£1.50
1 Gold Edition, foil embossed cover	$2.00	$6.00	$10.00	£1.20	£3.60	£6.00
2-4	$0.40	$1.20	$2.00	£0.25	£0.75	£1.25
4 scarce in the U.K. Platt cover art	$2.50	$7.50	$12.50	£1.50	£4.50	£7.50
5-7	$0.40	$1.20	$2.00	£0.25	£0.75	£1.25
8 War Games part 2, X-over with Bloodstrike #15/16	$0.40	$1.20	$2.00	£0.25	£0.75	£1.25
9 Extreme Sacrifices prologue	$0.40	$1.20	$2.00	£0.25	£0.75	£1.25
10 Extreme Sacrifice part 6, pre-bagged with trading card	$0.40	$1.20	$2.00	£0.25	£0.75	£1.25
Title Value:	$12.60	$37.80	$63.00	£7.95	£23.85	£39.75

Note: all Non-Distributed on the news-stands in the U.K.

PROPHET (2ND SERIES)
Image; 1 Aug 1995-present

	$Good	$Fine	$N.Mint	£Good	£Fine	£N.Mint
1 ND Chuck Dixon script and Stephen Platt art begins; wraparound chromium cover by Platt	$0.50	$1.50	$2.50	£0.30	£0.90	£1.50
2 ND Chuck Dixon and Stephen Platt	$0.50	$1.50	$2.50	£0.30	£0.90	£1.50
3 ND	$0.50	$1.50	$2.50	£0.30	£0.90	£1.50
4 ND guest-starring The NewMen	$0.50	$1.50	$2.50	£0.30	£0.90	£1.50
Title Value:	$2.00	$6.00	$10.00	£1.20	£3.60	£6.00

PROPHET ANNUAL
Image; 1 Sep 1995-present
1 ND Supreme Apocalypse part 2, continued in Glory 5; Chuck Dixon script, Stephen Platt art

	$Good	$Fine	$N.Mint	£Good	£Fine	£N.Mint
	$0.50	$1.50	$2.50	£0.30	£0.90	£1.50
Title Value:	$0.50	$1.50	$2.50	£0.30	£0.90	£1.50

PROPHET BABEWATCH SPECIAL
Image,OS; 1 Dec 1995

	$Good	$Fine	$N.Mint	£Good	£Fine	£N.Mint
1 ND	$0.50	$1.50	$2.50	£0.30	£0.90	£1.50
Title Value:	$0.50	$1.50	$2.50	£0.30	£0.90	£1.50

PROPHET SOURCEBOOK
Image; 1 Oct 1994
1 ND information on the character featuring Stephen Platt art

	$Good	$Fine	$N.Mint	£Good	£Fine	£N.Mint
	$0.60	$1.80	$3.00	£0.40	£1.20	£2.00
Title Value:	$0.60	$1.80	$3.00	£0.40	£1.20	£2.00

PROTECTORS
New York Comics; 1 1986
1 ND black and white

	$Good	$Fine	$N.Mint	£Good	£Fine	£N.Mint
	$0.15	$0.45	$0.75	£0.10	£0.35	£0.60
Title Value:	$0.15	$0.45	$0.75	£0.10	£0.35	£0.60

PROTECTORS HANDBOOK, THE
Malibu,OS; 1 Dec 1992
1 ND information on the Protectors plus interview with the creators

	$Good	$Fine	$N.Mint	£Good	£Fine	£N.Mint
	$0.40	$1.20	$2.00	£0.25	£0.75	£1.25
Title Value:	$0.40	$1.20	$2.00	£0.25	£0.75	£1.25

PROTECTORS, THE
Malibu; 1 Sep 1992-20 Apr 1994

	$Good	$Fine	$N.Mint	£Good	£Fine	£N.Mint
1-12	$0.30	$0.90	$1.50	£0.20	£0.60	£1.00
1-12 direct market edition with bound-in poster and wraparound protective cover	$0.40	$1.20	$2.00	£0.25	£0.75	£1.25
13 Genesis tie-in; pre-bagged with free Sky-Cap	$0.30	$0.90	$1.50	£0.20	£0.60	£1.00
14-15 Genesis tie-in	$0.30	$0.90	$1.50	£0.20	£0.60	£1.00
16-17	$0.30	$0.90	$1.50	£0.20	£0.60	£1.00
18 Genesis tie-in	$0.30	$0.90	$1.50	£0.20	£0.60	£1.00
19-20	$0.30	$0.90	$1.50	£0.20	£0.60	£1.00
Title Value:	$10.80	$32.40	$54.00	£7.00	£21.00	£35.00

Note: all Non-Distributed on the news-stands in the U.K.

PROTOTYPE
Malibu Ultraverse; 0 Aug 1994; 1 Aug 1993-18 Feb 1995

	$Good	$Fine	$N.Mint	£Good	£Fine	£N.Mint
0 40pgs, Joe Quesada and Jimmy Palmiotti cover	$0.40	$1.20	$2.00	£0.25	£0.75	£1.25
1 pre-bagged with trading card	$0.60	$1.80	$3.00	£0.40	£1.20	£2.00
1 Hologram cover	$3.00	$9.00	$15.00	£1.50	£4.50	£7.50
1 Ultra-Limited foil edition	$2.50	$7.50	$12.50	£1.00	£3.00	£5.00
1 Gold hologram edition	$4.00	$12.00	$20.00	£1.70	£5.00	£8.50
2	$0.50	$1.50	$2.50	£0.30	£0.90	£1.50
3 40pgs, Rune insert	$0.40	$1.20	$2.00	£0.25	£0.75	£1.25
4-5	$0.40	$1.20	$2.00	£0.25	£0.75	£1.25
6 origins month X-over	$0.40	$1.20	$2.00	£0.25	£0.75	£1.25
7-12	$0.40	$1.20	$2.00	£0.25	£0.75	£1.25
13 48pgs, flip-book format with Ultraverse Premiere #6	$0.55	$1.65	$2.75	£0.35	£1.05	£1.75
14-18	$0.40	$1.20	$2.00	£0.25	£0.75	£1.25
Title Value:	$17.55	$52.65	$88.25	£9.25	£27.65	£46.25

Note: all Non-Distributed on the news-stands in the U.K.

PROTOTYPE, GIANT SIZE
Malibu Ultraverse; 1 Sep 1994
1 ND 40pgs, Hostile Takeover part 4 (of 4)

	$Good	$Fine	$N.Mint	£Good	£Fine	£N.Mint
	$0.40	$1.20	$2.00	£0.25	£0.75	£1.25
Title Value:	$0.40	$1.20	$2.00	£0.25	£0.75	£1.25

PROWLER
Eclipse; 1 Jul 1987-4 Oct 1987
(see Revenge of the Prowler)

	$Good	$Fine	$N.Mint	£Good	£Fine	£N.Mint
1 ND Tim Truman script, John K. Snyder III art begins, colour	$0.40	$1.20	$2.00	£0.25	£0.75	£1.25
2-4 ND Graham Nolan back-up detailing origin Prowler	$0.40	$1.20	$2.00	£0.25	£0.75	£1.25
Title Value:	$1.60	$4.80	$8.00	£1.00	£3.00	£5.00

Note: although the next issue was advertised, the series was suddenly cancelled.

PROWLER
Marvel Comics Group,MS; 1 Nov 1994-4 Feb 1995

	$Good	$Fine	$N.Mint	£Good	£Fine	£N.Mint
1-3	$0.30	$0.90	$1.50	£0.20	£0.60	£1.00
4 The Prowler vs. The Vulture	$0.30	$0.90	$1.50	£0.20	£0.60	£1.00
Title Value:	$1.20	$3.60	$6.00	£0.80	£2.40	£4.00

PROWLER IN WHITE ZOMBIE, THE
Eclipse,OS; 1 Oct 1988
1 ND features Graham Nolan art, black and white

	$Good	$Fine	$N.Mint	£Good	£Fine	£N.Mint
	$0.40	$1.20	$2.00	£0.25	£0.75	£1.25
Title Value:	$0.40	$1.20	$2.00	£0.25	£0.75	£1.25

PRUDENCE & CAUTION
Defiant; 1 May 1994-6 Oct 1994

	$Good	$Fine	$N.Mint	£Good	£Fine	£N.Mint
1 ND 48pgs, Chris Claremont script begins	$0.40	$1.20	$2.00	£0.25	£0.75	£1.25
2-3 ND	$0.40	$1.20	$2.00	£0.25	£0.75	£1.25
4 ND Schism X-over	$0.40	$1.20	$2.00	£0.25	£0.75	£1.25
5-6 ND	$0.40	$1.20	$2.00	£0.25	£0.75	£1.25
Title Value:	$2.40	$7.20	$12.00	£1.50	£4.50	£7.50

PSI FORCE
Marvel Comics Group/New Universe; 1 Nov 1986-32 Jun 1989

	$Good	$Fine	$N.Mint	£Good	£Fine	£N.Mint
1-5 ND Mark Texeira art	$0.15	$0.45	$0.75	£0.10	£0.35	£0.60
6-7 ND	$0.15	$0.45	$0.75	£0.10	£0.35	£0.60
8 Mark Texeira art	$0.15	$0.45	$0.75	£0.10	£0.35	£0.60
9-12	$0.15	$0.45	$0.75	£0.10	£0.35	£0.60
13 Williamson inks	$0.15	$0.45	$0.75	£0.10	£0.35	£0.60
14-15	$0.15	$0.45	$0.75	£0.10	£0.35	£0.60
16-22 Ron Lim art	$0.15	$0.45	$0.75	£0.10	£0.35	£0.60
23-32 ND	$0.15	$0.45	$0.75	£0.10	£0.35	£0.60
Title Value:	$4.80	$14.40	$24.00	£3.20	£11.20	£19.20

PSI FORCE ANNUAL
Marvel Comics Group/New Universe; 1 1987

	$Good	$Fine	$N.Mint	£Good	£Fine	£N.Mint
1 ND	$0.25	$0.75	$1.25	£0.15	£0.45	£0.75
Title Value:	$0.25	$0.75	$1.25	£0.15	£0.45	£0.75
PSI-LORDS						
Valiant; 1 Sep 1994-10 Jun 1995						
1 Mike Leeke pencils, Dick Giordano inks, wraparound chrome cover						
	$0.50	$1.50	$2.50	£0.30	£0.90	£1.50
2 Valiant Vision issue (3-D effect)						
	$0.40	$1.20	$2.00	£0.25	£0.75	£1.25
3-10	$0.40	$1.20	$2.00	£0.25	£0.75	£1.25
Title Value:	$4.10	$12.30	$20.50	£2.55	£7.65	£12.75
PSYBA-RATS, THE						
DC Comics,MS; 1 Apr 1995-3 Jun 1995						
1-3 48pgs	$0.40	$1.20	$2.00	£0.25	£0.75	£1.25
Title Value:	$1.20	$3.60	$6.00	£0.75	£2.25	£3.75
PSYCHO						
DC Comics,MS; 1 Sep 1991-3 Nov 1991						
1-3 48pgs, painted art by Dan Brereton						
	$0.80	$2.40	$4.00	£0.50	£1.50	£2.50
Title Value:	$2.40	$7.20	$12.00	£1.50	£4.50	£7.50
Note: Prestige Format						
PSYCHO-PATH						
Greater Mercury Comics; 1 Dec 1990						
1 ND black and white						
	$0.30	$0.90	$1.50	£0.20	£0.60	£1.00
Title Value:	$0.30	$0.90	$1.50	£0.20	£0.60	£1.00
PSYCHOBLAST						
First; 1 Nov 1987-9 Jul 1988						
1-9 ND Steven Grant script						
	$0.40	$1.20	$2.00	£0.25	£0.75	£1.25
Title Value:	$3.60	$10.80	$18.00	£2.25	£6.75	£11.25
PSYCHONAUTS						
Marvel Comics Group/Epic,MS; 1 Oct 1993-4 Jan 1994						
1-4 ND 48pgs, Alan Grant co-script, art by Yasuo Yazaki						
	$0.80	$2.40	$4.00	£0.50	£1.50	£2.50
Title Value:	$3.20	$9.60	$16.00	£2.00	£6.00	£10.00
PTERANO-MAN						
Kitchen Sink; 1 Aug 1990						
1 ND Don Simpson script and art						
	$0.40	$1.20	$2.00	£0.25	£0.75	£1.25
Title Value:	$0.40	$1.20	$2.00	£0.25	£0.75	£1.25
PUBLIC ENEMIES						
Malibu,OS; 1 Nov 1989						
1 ND 48pgs, squarebound; black and white reprints of 40s and 50s crime comics						
	$0.50	$1.50	$2.50	£0.30	£0.90	£1.50
Title Value:	$0.50	$1.50	$2.50	£0.30	£0.90	£1.50
PULP DREAMS						
Eros Comix; 1 May 1991						
1 ND adult pin-ups, black and white						
	$0.30	$0.90	$1.50	£0.20	£0.60	£1.00
Title Value:	$0.30	$0.90	$1.50	£0.20	£0.60	£1.00
PUMA BLUES						
Aardvark/Mirage; 1 Jun 1986-26 1988						
1 ND	$0.50	$1.50	$2.50	£0.30	£0.90	£1.50
1 2nd printing ND	$0.40	$1.20	$2.00	£0.25	£0.75	£1.25
2-19 ND	$0.40	$1.20	$2.00	£0.25	£0.75	£1.25
20 ND features work by Alan Moore, Frank Miller, Mike Grell						
	$0.80	$2.40	$4.00	£0.50	£1.50	£2.50
21 ND 1st Mirage issue						
	$0.40	$1.20	$2.00	£0.25	£0.75	£1.25
22-26 ND	$0.40	$1.20	$2.00	£0.25	£0.75	£1.25
Title Value:	$11.30	$33.90	$56.50	£7.05	£21.15	£35.25

	$Good	$Fine	$N.Mint	£Good	£Fine	£N.Mint
Trade Paperback (1988), reprints				£1.80	£5.40	£9.00
PUMPKINHEAD: THE RITES OF EXORCISM						
Dark Horse,MS; 1 Sep 1993-3 Nov 1993						
1-3 ND	$0.40	$1.20	$2.00	£0.25	£0.75	£1.25
Title Value:	$1.20	$3.60	$6.00	£0.75	£2.25	£3.75
PUNISHER						
Marvel Comics Group; 1 Jul 1987-104 Jul 1995						
1 ND	$2.50	$7.50	$12.50	£1.60	£4.80	£8.00
2 ND	$1.50	$4.50	$7.50	£1.00	£3.00	£5.00
3-5 ND	$1.00	$3.00	$5.00	£0.80	£2.40	£4.00
6 ND Kevin Nowlan inks						
	$0.80	$2.40	$4.00	£0.60	£1.80	£3.00
7 ND	$0.80	$2.40	$4.00	£0.60	£1.80	£3.00
8-9 ND Whilce Portacio art						
	$1.00	$3.00	$5.00	£0.60	£1.80	£3.00
10 ND scarce in the U.K. X-over with Daredevil #257, Whilce Portacio art						
	$2.50	$7.50	$12.50	£1.60	£4.80	£8.00
11 ND Whilce Portacio art						
	$0.80	$2.40	$4.00	£0.50	£1.50	£2.50
12 ND Whilce Portacio art						
	$0.80	$2.40	$4.00	£0.50	£1.50	£2.50
13 LD in the U.K. Whilce Portacio art						
	$0.80	$2.40	$4.00	£0.50	£1.50	£2.50
14 drugs overdose cover, Whilce Portacio art						
	$0.80	$2.40	$4.00	£0.50	£1.50	£2.50
15 Kingpin appears, Whilce Portacio art						
	$0.80	$2.40	$4.00	£0.50	£1.50	£2.50
16-18 Kingpin appears, Whilce Portacio art						
	$0.70	$2.10	$3.50	£0.40	£1.20	£2.00
19 Larry Stroman art						
	$0.70	$2.10	$3.50	£0.40	£1.20	£2.00
20	$0.70	$2.10	$3.50	£0.40	£1.20	£2.00
21 Erik Larsen art	$0.50	$1.50	$2.50	£0.30	£0.90	£1.50
22-23	$0.50	$1.50	$2.50	£0.30	£0.90	£1.50
24 LD in the U.K. 1st appearance Shadowmasters						
	$0.60	$1.80	$3.00	£0.40	£1.20	£2.00
25 LD in the U.K. DS						
	$0.60	$1.80	$3.00	£0.40	£1.20	£2.00
26	$0.40	$1.20	$2.00	£0.25	£0.75	£1.25
27 Acts of Vengeance tie-in						
	$0.40	$1.20	$2.00	£0.25	£0.75	£1.25
28-29 Acts of Vengeance tie-in, Dr. Doom appears						
	$0.40	$1.20	$2.00	£0.25	£0.75	£1.25
30	$0.40	$1.20	$2.00	£0.25	£0.75	£1.25
31-34	$0.30	$0.90	$1.50	£0.20	£0.60	£1.00
35 Jigsaw Puzzle story, bi-weekly						
	$0.30	$0.90	$1.50	£0.20	£0.60	£1.00
36-37 Jigsaw Puzzle story, Mark Texeira, bi-weekly						
	$0.30	$0.90	$1.50	£0.20	£0.60	£1.00
38-40 Jigsaw Puzzle story, bi-weekly						
	$0.30	$0.90	$1.50	£0.20	£0.60	£1.00
41	$0.30	$0.90	$1.50	£0.20	£0.60	£1.00
42 Mark Texeira art						
	$0.30	$0.90	$1.50	£0.20	£0.60	£1.00
43-48	$0.30	$0.90	$1.50	£0.20	£0.60	£1.00
49 Ron Wagner art begins						
	$0.30	$0.90	$1.50	£0.20	£0.60	£1.00
50 48pgs	$0.40	$1.20	$2.00	£0.25	£0.75	£1.25
51-52	$0.30	$0.90	$1.50	£0.20	£0.60	£1.00
53-56 bi-weekly issue						
	$0.30	$0.90	$1.50	£0.20	£0.60	£1.00

Prez #1

Primer #3

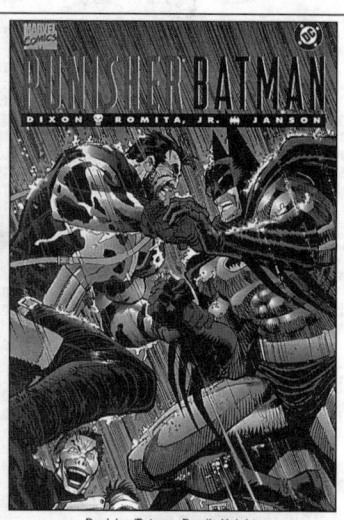
Punisher/Batman: Deadly Knights

	$Good	$Fine	$N.Mint	£Good	£Fine	£N.Mint
57 bi-weekly issue, brown card "wanted poster" outer cover	$0.40	$1.20	$2.00	£0.25	£0.75	£1.25
57 as above but without outer cover	$0.30	$0.90	$1.50	£0.20	£0.60	£1.00
58 painted cover, bi-weekly issue	$0.30	$0.90	$1.50	£0.20	£0.60	£1.00
59 bi-weekly issue, Punisher has skin grafted on and becomes black	$0.30	$0.90	$1.50	£0.20	£0.60	£1.00
60 Luke Cage returns, $1.25 cover begins	$0.30	$0.90	$1.50	£0.20	£0.60	£1.00
61-62 Luke Cage appears	$0.25	$0.75	$1.25	£0.15	£0.45	£0.75
63	$0.25	$0.75	$1.25	£0.15	£0.45	£0.75
64 Eurohit part 1 (ends #70), Dougie Braithwaite pencils begin, Dan Abnett scripts begin, bi-weekly	$0.25	$0.75	$1.25	£0.15	£0.45	£0.75
65-70 bi-weekly	$0.25	$0.75	$1.25	£0.15	£0.45	£0.75
71 new creative team Abnett with Lanning, Braithwaite with Williamson take over	$0.25	$0.75	$1.25	£0.15	£0.45	£0.75
72 LD in the U.K.	$0.25	$0.75	$1.25	£0.20	£0.60	£1.00
73-74	$0.25	$0.75	$1.25	£0.15	£0.45	£0.75
75 DS	$0.40	$1.20	$2.00	£0.25	£0.75	£1.25
76-85	$0.25	$0.75	$1.25	£0.15	£0.45	£0.75
86 48pgs, Suicide Run part 3, foil embossed cover by Michael Golden	$0.40	$1.20	$2.00	£0.25	£0.75	£1.25
87 Suicide Run part 6, continued in Punisher War Journal #63; Michael Golden cover	$0.25	$0.75	$1.25	£0.15	£0.45	£0.75
88 Suicide Run part 9, continued in Punisher War Journal #64; Michael Golden cover	$0.25	$0.75	$1.25	£0.15	£0.45	£0.75
89 Russ Heath art	$0.25	$0.75	$1.25	£0.15	£0.45	£0.75
90 Russ Heath art; with free Spiderman and his Deadly Foes card sheet	$0.25	$0.75	$1.25	£0.15	£0.45	£0.75
91-92 Russ Heath art	$0.25	$0.75	$1.25	£0.15	£0.45	£0.75
93 Bill Sienkiewicz cover	$0.25	$0.75	$1.25	£0.15	£0.45	£0.75
94-99	$0.25	$0.75	$1.25	£0.15	£0.45	£0.75
100 64pgs	$0.40	$1.20	$2.00	£0.25	£0.75	£1.25
100 64pgs, Enhanced Cover Edition – prismatic-foil enhanced cover	$0.50	$1.50	$2.50	£0.30	£0.90	£1.50
101-102 Bullseye appears	$0.25	$0.75	$1.25	£0.15	£0.45	£0.75
103 Countdown: 4, continued in Punisher War Journal #79	$0.25	$0.75	$1.25	£0.15	£0.45	£0.75
104 Countdown:14, continued in Punisher War Journal #80; Kingpin and Bullseye appear; Jae Lee cover	$0.25	$0.75	$1.25	£0.15	£0.45	£0.75
Title Value:	$46.75	$140.25	$233.75	£30.00	£90.00	£150.00

PUNISHER (2ND SERIES)
Marvel Comics Group; 1 Nov 1995-present

	$Good	$Fine	$N.Mint	£Good	£Fine	£N.Mint
1 ND John Ostrander script, Tom Lyle and Chris Ivy art; Doc Samson, Avengers and Bullseye appear, metallic foil-stamped cover	$0.60	$1.80	$3.00	£0.40	£1.20	£2.00
2-3 ND	$0.40	$1.20	$2.00	£0.25	£0.75	£1.25
4 ND Daredevil appears	$0.40	$1.20	$2.00	£0.25	£0.75	£1.25
5 ND	$0.40	$1.20	$2.00	£0.25	£0.75	£1.25
Title Value:	$2.20	$6.60	$11.00	£1.40	£4.20	£7.00

PUNISHER (LIMITED SERIES)
Marvel Comics Group,MS; 1 Jan 1986-5 May 1986
(see Spiderman, Capt.America, Daredevil, Marvel Graphic Novel, Marvel Preview, Marvel Super-Action, Punisher War Journal, Spectacular Spiderman)

	$Good	$Fine	$N.Mint	£Good	£Fine	£N.Mint
1 ND scarce in the U.K. Mike Zeck art	$5.00	$15.00	$25.00	£4.00	£12.00	£20.00
2 ND scarce in the U.K. Mike Zeck art	$3.00	$9.00	$15.00	£2.00	£6.00	£10.00
3 ND Mike Zeck art (75 and 95 cents versions available)	$2.00	$6.00	$10.00	£1.50	£4.50	£7.50
4-5 ND Mike Zeck art	$1.50	$4.50	$7.50	£1.00	£3.00	£5.00
Title Value:	$13.00	$39.00	$65.00	£9.50	£28.50	£47.50

Note: 75 cents and 95 cents cover versions of issue #3 available. No differentiation in value at this time.

	£Good	£Fine	£N.Mint
Hardback, oversize, LD; reprints #1,2 of mini-series	£0.80	£2.40	£4.00
Circle of Blood Trade paperback, 144pgs, ND, reprints #1-5	£1.00	£3.00	£5.00
(2nd print. Sep 1989)	£1.20	£3.60	£6.00
(3rd print. Dec 1990)	£1.10	£3.30	£5.50

Note: #1-4 labelled as 4-issue series, #5 labelled as 5-issue series. Mike Zeck art in #1-4.

PUNISHER 2099
Marvel Comics Group; 1 Feb 1993-34 Nov 1995

	$Good	$Fine	$N.Mint	£Good	£Fine	£N.Mint
1 ND Pat Mills script begins, foil-stamped cover	$0.40	$1.20	$2.00	£0.25	£0.75	£1.25
2-12 ND	$0.30	$0.90	$1.50	£0.20	£0.60	£1.00
13 ND Spiderman 2099 appears	$0.30	$0.90	$1.50	£0.20	£0.60	£1.00
14-15 ND	$0.30	$0.90	$1.50	£0.20	£0.60	£1.00
16 ND with free Spiderman and his Deadly Foes card sheet	$0.30	$0.90	$1.50	£0.20	£0.60	£1.00
17-25 ND	$0.30	$0.90	$1.50	£0.20	£0.60	£1.00
25 ND Enhanced Edition, multi-level foil-enhanced cover	$0.40	$1.20	$2.00	£0.25	£0.75	£1.25
26-29 ND	$0.30	$0.90	$1.50	£0.20	£0.60	£1.00
30-31 ND One Nation Under Doom	$0.30	$0.90	$1.50	£0.20	£0.60	£1.00
32-33 ND One Nation Under Doom; bi-weekly						

	$Good	$Fine	$N.Mint	£Good	£Fine	£N.Mint
(32-33 ND One Nation Under Doom; bi-weekly)	$0.30	$0.90	$1.50	£0.20	£0.60	£1.00
34 ND One Nation Under Doom	$0.30	$0.90	$1.50	£0.20	£0.60	£1.00
Title Value:	$10.70	$32.10	$53.50	£7.10	£21.30	£35.50

PUNISHER AND CAPTAIN AMERICA: BLOOD AND GLORY
Marvel Comics Group,MS; 1 Oct 1992-3 Dec 1992

	$Good	$Fine	$N.Mint	£Good	£Fine	£N.Mint
1 ND 48pgs, embossed cover	$0.90	$2.70	$4.50	£0.60	£1.80	£3.00
2-3 ND 48pgs	$0.90	$2.70	$4.50	£0.60	£1.80	£3.00
Title Value:	$2.70	$8.10	$13.50	£1.80	£5.40	£9.00

PUNISHER ANNIVERSARY MAGAZINE
Marvel Comics Group,OS; 1 Feb 1994

	$Good	$Fine	$N.Mint	£Good	£Fine	£N.Mint
1 ND 48pgs, celebrates 20 years with articles and profiles; Michael Golden cover	$0.80	$2.40	$4.00	£0.50	£1.50	£2.50
Title Value:	$0.80	$2.40	$4.00	£0.50	£1.50	£2.50

PUNISHER ANNUAL
Marvel Comics Group; 1 1988-7 1994

	$Good	$Fine	$N.Mint	£Good	£Fine	£N.Mint
1 ND scarce in the U.K. 64pgs, Evolutionary War, Mark Texeira art	$1.00	$3.00	$5.00	£0.70	£2.10	£3.50
2 ND squarebound, Moon Knight appears, Atlantis Attacks part 5, Jim Lee art	$0.60	$1.80	$3.00	£0.40	£1.20	£2.00
3 ND Lifeform story begins, continues in Daredevil Annual #6, Mark Texeira art	$0.50	$1.50	$2.50	£0.30	£0.90	£1.50
4 ND Baron Strucker story, continued in Captain America Annual #10	$0.40	$1.20	$2.00	£0.25	£0.75	£1.25
5 ND The System Bytes by Peter David	$0.40	$1.20	$2.00	£0.25	£0.75	£1.25
6 ND 64pgs, pre-bagged with trading card, 1st appearance Phalanx	$0.50	$1.50	$2.50	£0.30	£0.90	£1.50
7 ND 64pgs, sequel to "Eurohit" storyline from Punisher #64-70	$0.50	$1.50	$2.50	£0.30	£0.90	£1.50
Title Value:	$3.90	$11.70	$19.50	£2.50	£7.50	£12.50

PUNISHER ARMORY
Marvel Comics Group; 1 Jul 1990-10 1994

	$Good	$Fine	$N.Mint	£Good	£Fine	£N.Mint
1 ND part reprints from Punisher War Journal	$0.50	$1.50	$2.50	£0.30	£0.90	£1.50
2 ND Jim Lee cover	$0.40	$1.20	$2.00	£0.25	£0.75	£1.25
3 ND Joe Jusko painted cover	$0.40	$1.20	$2.00	£0.25	£0.75	£1.25
4 ND Dougie Braithwaite cover	$0.40	$1.20	$2.00	£0.25	£0.75	£1.25
5-6 ND Eliot R. Brown cover	$0.40	$1.20	$2.00	£0.25	£0.75	£1.25
7-8 ND Dougie Braithwaite cover	$0.40	$1.20	$2.00	£0.25	£0.75	£1.25
9-10 ND Michael Golden cover	$0.40	$1.20	$2.00	£0.25	£0.75	£1.25
Title Value:	$4.10	$12.30	$20.50	£2.55	£7.65	£12.75

PUNISHER ASHCAN
Marvel Comics Group,OS; nn Dec 1994

	$Good	$Fine	$N.Mint	£Good	£Fine	£N.Mint
nn ND history of The Punisher	$0.15	$0.45	$0.75	£0.10	£0.30	£0.50
Title Value:	$0.15	$0.45	$0.75	£0.10	£0.30	£0.50

PUNISHER BACK-TO-SCHOOL SPECIAL
Marvel Comics Group; 1 Nov 1992; 2 Oct 1993; 3 Oct 1994

	$Good	$Fine	$N.Mint	£Good	£Fine	£N.Mint
1 ND 64pgs, features John Ridgway art	$0.50	$1.50	$2.50	£0.30	£0.90	£1.50
2 ND 64pgs, Bill Sienkiewicz cover	$0.50	$1.50	$2.50	£0.30	£0.90	£1.50
3 ND 64pgs	$0.50	$1.50	$2.50	£0.30	£0.90	£1.50
Title Value:	$1.50	$4.50	$7.50	£0.90	£2.70	£4.50

PUNISHER CLASSICS
Marvel Comics Group,OS; 1 Dec 1989

	$Good	$Fine	$N.Mint	£Good	£Fine	£N.Mint
1 ND 68pgs, squarebound, reprints black and white Marvel Preview #2 (5th appearance) and Marvel Super Action #1, Larry Stroman cover	$0.90	$2.70	$4.50	£0.60	£1.80	£3.00
Title Value:	$0.90	$2.70	$4.50	£0.60	£1.80	£3.00

Note: originally announced as "Punisher Classics" and appeared with "Classic Punisher" on the cover.

PUNISHER HOLIDAY SPECIAL
Marvel Comics Group; 1 Jan 1993; 2 Jan 1994; 3 Jan 1995

	$Good	$Fine	$N.Mint	£Good	£Fine	£N.Mint
1 ND foil stamped cover	$0.60	$1.80	$3.00	£0.40	£1.20	£2.00
2 ND 64pgs, Bill Sienkiewicz cover	$0.60	$1.80	$3.00	£0.40	£1.20	£2.00
3 ND 64pgs, Dale Eaglesham art	$0.60	$1.80	$3.00	£0.40	£1.20	£2.00
Title Value:	$1.80	$5.40	$9.00	£1.20	£3.60	£6.00

PUNISHER IN NAM: FINAL INVASION
Marvel Comics Group,OS; nn Apr 1994

	$Good	$Fine	$N.Mint	£Good	£Fine	£N.Mint
nn ND 80pgs, Frank Castle (Punisher) and his last mission in Vietnam; Don Lomax script	$1.20	$3.60	$6.00	£0.80	£2.40	£4.00
Title Value:	$1.20	$3.60	$6.00	£0.80	£2.40	£4.00

PUNISHER KILLS THE MARVEL UNIVERSE
Marvel Comics Group,OS; 1 Feb 1996

	$Good	$Fine	$N.Mint	£Good	£Fine	£N.Mint
1 ND 48pgs, Garth Ennis script, Dougie Braithwaite art	$1.20	$3.60	$6.00	£0.80	£2.40	£4.00
Title Value:	$1.20	$3.60	$6.00	£0.80	£2.40	£4.00

PUNISHER MAGAZINE
Marvel Comics Group; 1 Oct 1989-16 1990

	$Good	$Fine	$N.Mint	£Good	£Fine	£N.Mint
1 ND 64pgs, reprints Mini-Series #1/2; black and white begins	$0.70	$2.10	$3.50	£0.40	£1.20	£2.00
2 ND reprints Mini-Series #3/4						

Item	$Good	$Fine	$N.Mint	£Good	£Fine	£N.Mint
(continued from previous page)	$0.50	$1.50	$2.50	£0.30	£0.90	£1.50
3 ND reprints Mini-Series #5, Punisher regular series #1	$0.40	$1.20	$2.00	£0.25	£0.75	£1.25
4 ND reprints issues #2, #3 of Punisher regular series	$0.40	$1.20	$2.00	£0.25	£0.75	£1.25
5 ND reprints issues #4, #5 of Punisher regular series	$0.40	$1.20	$2.00	£0.25	£0.75	£1.25
6 ND reprints issues #6, #7 of Punisher regular series	$0.40	$1.20	$2.00	£0.25	£0.75	£1.25
7 ND reprints issues #8, #9 of Punisher regular series	$0.40	$1.20	$2.00	£0.25	£0.75	£1.25
8-13 ND reprints from regular series	$0.40	$1.20	$2.00	£0.25	£0.75	£1.25
14 ND Punisher War Journal reprints begin	$0.40	$1.20	$2.00	£0.25	£0.75	£1.25
15 ND reprints Punisher War Journal 2, Punisher Annual #2	$0.40	$1.20	$2.00	£0.25	£0.75	£1.25
16 ND reprints Punisher War Journal #3,8	$0.40	$1.20	$2.00	£0.25	£0.75	£1.25
Title Value:	$6.80	$20.40	$34.00	£4.20	£12.60	£21.00

PUNISHER MEETS ARCHIE: WHEN WORLDS COLLIDE
Marvel Comics Group/Archie Comics,OS; 1 Aug 1994

Item	$Good	$Fine	$N.Mint	£Good	£Fine	£N.Mint
1 ND 48pgs, die-cut cover	$0.70	$2.10	$3.50	£0.40	£1.20	£2.00
1 ND 48pgs, regular cover	$0.40	$1.20	$2.00	£0.25	£0.75	£1.25
1 ND 48pgs, Archie version: "Archie Meets the Punisher	$0.50	$1.50	$2.50	£0.30	£0.90	£1.50
Title Value:	$1.60	$4.80	$8.00	£0.95	£2.85	£4.75

PUNISHER MOVIE ADAPTATION
Marvel Comics Group,OS; 1 Aug 1990

Item	$Good	$Fine	$N.Mint	£Good	£Fine	£N.Mint
1 ND 48pgs, adaptation of the movie by Potts/Anderson	$0.90	$2.70	$4.50	£0.60	£1.80	£3.00
Title Value:	$0.90	$2.70	$4.50	£0.60	£1.80	£3.00

Note: Bookshelf Format

PUNISHER SUMMER SPECIAL
Marvel Comics Group; 1 Aug 1991; 2 Aug 1992; 3 Aug 1993; 4 Jul 1994

Item	$Good	$Fine	$N.Mint	£Good	£Fine	£N.Mint
1 ND 48pgs, four new stories featuring scripts by Pat Mills and Peter David, Mark Texeira art	$0.50	$1.50	$2.50	£0.30	£0.90	£1.50
2 ND 48pgs, Pat Mills script, Simon Bisley painted cover	$0.50	$1.50	$2.50	£0.30	£0.90	£1.50
3 ND 48pgs, Brian Stelfreeze cover	$0.50	$1.50	$2.50	£0.30	£0.90	£1.50
4 ND 48pgs, John Romita Jnr. cover	$0.50	$1.50	$2.50	£0.30	£0.90	£1.50
Title Value:	$2.00	$6.00	$10.00	£1.20	£3.60	£6.00

PUNISHER VS WOLVERINE: THE AFRICAN SAGA
Marvel Comics Group,OS; nn 1990

Item	$Good	$Fine	$N.Mint	£Good	£Fine	£N.Mint
nn ND 48pgs, reprints Punisher War Journal #6,7, Jim Lee art	$1.20	$3.60	$6.00	£0.80	£2.40	£4.00
Title Value:	$1.20	$3.60	$6.00	£0.80	£2.40	£4.00

PUNISHER WAR JOURNAL
Marvel Comics Group; 1 Nov 1988-80 Jul 1995

Item	$Good	$Fine	$N.Mint	£Good	£Fine	£N.Mint
1 ND origin retold, Jim Lee art	$2.00	$6.00	$10.00	£1.20	£3.60	£6.00
2 ND scarce in the U.K. Daredevil, Jim Lee art	$1.50	$4.50	$7.50	£0.80	£2.40	£4.00
3 ND scarce in the U.K. Daredevil, Jim Lee art	$1.00	$3.00	$5.00	£0.60	£1.80	£3.00
4-5 ND Jim Lee art	$1.00	$3.00	$5.00	£0.60	£1.80	£3.00
6 ND 1st Punisher/Wolverine story, Jim Lee art	$2.00	$6.00	$10.00	£1.20	£3.60	£6.00
7 ND 2nd Punisher/Wolverine story, Jim Lee art	$1.20	$3.60	$6.00	£0.80	£2.40	£4.00
8 ND Shadowmasters appear, Jim Lee art	$0.60	$1.80	$3.00	£0.40	£1.20	£2.00
9-10 ND Jim Lee art	$0.60	$1.80	$3.00	£0.40	£1.20	£2.00
11 ND Jim Lee art	$0.50	$1.50	$2.50	£0.30	£0.90	£1.50
12 ND Acts of Vengeance tie-in, Jim Lee art	$0.50	$1.50	$2.50	£0.30	£0.90	£1.50
13 ND Acts of Vengeance tie-in, Jim Lee cover	$0.50	$1.50	$2.50	£0.30	£0.90	£1.50
14-15 ND Spiderman appears, Jim Lee cover	$0.50	$1.50	$2.50	£0.30	£0.90	£1.50
16 ND Mark Texeira inks	$0.50	$1.50	$2.50	£0.30	£0.90	£1.50
17-19 ND Jim Lee art	$0.50	$1.50	$2.50	£0.30	£0.90	£1.50
20-24 ND	$0.40	$1.20	$2.00	£0.25	£0.75	£1.25
25-28 ND Texeira inks	$0.40	$1.20	$2.00	£0.25	£0.75	£1.25
29-30 ND Ghost Rider appears, Texeira inks	$0.40	$1.20	$2.00	£0.25	£0.75	£1.25
31-33 ND The Kamchatkan Konspiracy, Andy Kubert and Joe Kubert art	$0.40	$1.20	$2.00	£0.25	£0.75	£1.25
34 ND	$0.40	$1.20	$2.00	£0.25	£0.75	£1.25
35 ND scarce in the U.K.	$0.50	$1.50	$2.50	£0.30	£0.90	£1.50
36 ND photo cover	$0.40	$1.20	$2.00	£0.25	£0.75	£1.25
37-39 ND	$0.40	$1.20	$2.00	£0.25	£0.75	£1.25
40 ND painted cover by Michael Golden	$0.40	$1.20	$2.00	£0.25	£0.75	£1.25
41-44 ND	$0.40	$1.20	$2.00	£0.25	£0.75	£1.25
45 ND Dead Man's Hand part 3, continued in Daredevil 408	$0.40	$1.20	$2.00	£0.25	£0.75	£1.25
46 ND Dead Man's Hand part 6, continued in Daredevil 409	$0.40	$1.20	$2.00	£0.25	£0.75	£1.25
47 ND Dead Man's Hand part 9 (conclusion), Daredevil and Nomad appear	$0.40	$1.20	$2.00	£0.25	£0.75	£1.25
48-49 ND	$0.40	$1.20	$2.00	£0.25	£0.75	£1.25
50 DS embossed cover by Mark Texeira, preview of Punisher 2099	$0.50	$1.50	$2.50	£0.30	£0.90	£1.50
51-56 ND	$0.40	$1.20	$2.00	£0.25	£0.75	£1.25
57-58 ND Ghost Rider and Daredevil appear	$0.40	$1.20	$2.00	£0.25	£0.75	£1.25
59-60 ND	$0.40	$1.20	$2.00	£0.25	£0.75	£1.25
61 ND 48pgs, Suicide Run part 1, embossed foil cover by Michael Golden	$0.80	$2.40	$4.00	£0.50	£1.50	£2.50
62 ND Suicide Run part 4	$0.40	$1.20	$2.00	£0.25	£0.75	£1.25
63 ND Suicide Run part 7	$0.40	$1.20	$2.00	£0.25	£0.75	£1.25
64 ND 48pgs, Suicide Run part 10 (conclusion)	$0.40	$1.20	$2.00	£0.25	£0.75	£1.25
64 ND 48pgs, Suicide Run part 10, die-cut cover by Michael Golden	$0.50	$1.50	$2.50	£0.30	£0.90	£1.50
65 ND Pariah story	$0.40	$1.20	$2.00	£0.25	£0.75	£1.25
66 ND Pariah story, with free Spiderman vs. Venom card sheet	$0.40	$1.20	$2.00	£0.25	£0.75	£1.25
67-74 ND	$0.40	$1.20	$2.00	£0.25	£0.75	£1.25
75 ND 48pgs, new logo and cover design painted by Mark Texeira	$0.50	$1.50	$2.50	£0.30	£0.90	£1.50
76-78 ND	$0.40	$1.20	$2.00	£0.25	£0.75	£1.25
79 ND Countdown: 3, continued in Punisher War Zone #41; Jae Lee cover	$0.40	$1.20	$2.00	£0.25	£0.75	£1.25
80 ND Countdown: 0; Punisher vs. Bullseye, Nick Fury appears	$0.40	$1.20	$2.00	£0.25	£0.75	£1.25
Title Value:	$41.60	$124.80	$208.00	£25.65	£76.95	£128.25

An Eye For An Eye (Feb 1992)

Item	£Good	£Fine	£N.Mint
Trade paperback reprints issues #1-3, new Jim Lee cover	£1.10	£3.30	£5.50

PUNISHER WAR ZONE
Marvel Comics Group; 1 Mar 1992-41 Jul 1995

Item	$Good	$Fine	$N.Mint	£Good	£Fine	£N.Mint
1 ND die-cut cover giving bullet-ridden effect, John Romita Jnr. art begins	$0.60	$1.80	$3.00	£0.40	£1.20	£2.00
2-10 ND	$0.40	$1.20	$2.00	£0.25	£0.75	£1.25
11 ND last John Romita Jnr. art	$0.30	$0.90	$1.50	£0.20	£0.60	£1.00
12 ND Abnett and Lanning script begin, Mike McKone pencils begin	$0.30	$0.90	$1.50	£0.20	£0.60	£1.00
13-18 ND	$0.30	$0.90	$1.50	£0.20	£0.60	£1.00
19 ND Wolverine guest-stars	$0.30	$0.90	$1.50	£0.20	£0.60	£1.00
20-22 ND	$0.30	$0.90	$1.50	£0.20	£0.60	£1.00
23 ND 48pgs, Suicide Run part 2, foil embossed cover by Michael Golden	$0.40	$1.20	$2.00	£0.25	£0.75	£1.25
24 ND Suicide Run part 5, continued in Punisher #87	$0.30	$0.90	$1.50	£0.20	£0.60	£1.00
25 ND 48pgs, Suicide Run part 8, continued in Punisher #88	$0.30	$0.90	$1.50	£0.20	£0.60	£1.00
26 ND John Buscema art	$0.30	$0.90	$1.50	£0.20	£0.60	£1.00
27 ND John Buscema art, with free Spiderman vs. Venom card sheet	$0.30	$0.90	$1.50	£0.20	£0.60	£1.00
28-30 ND John Buscema art	$0.30	$0.90	$1.50	£0.20	£0.60	£1.00
31-36 ND Joe Kubert art	$0.30	$0.90	$1.50	£0.20	£0.60	£1.00
37 ND Mark Texeira art	$0.30	$0.90	$1.50	£0.20	£0.60	£1.00
38-40 ND	$0.30	$0.90	$1.50	£0.20	£0.60	£1.00
41 ND Countdown: 2, continued in Punisher #104; Jae Lee cover	$0.30	$0.90	$1.50	£0.20	£0.60	£1.00
Title Value:	$13.60	$40.80	$68.00	£8.90	£26.70	£44.50

PUNISHER WAR ZONE ANNUAL
Marvel Comics Group; 1 Aug 1993-2 Aug 1994

Item	$Good	$Fine	$N.Mint	£Good	£Fine	£N.Mint
1 ND 64pgs, pre-bagged with trading card introducing Phalanx	$0.50	$1.50	$2.50	£0.30	£0.90	£1.50
2 ND 64pgs	$0.50	$1.50	$2.50	£0.30	£0.90	£1.50
Title Value:	$1.00	$3.00	$5.00	£0.60	£1.80	£3.00

PUNISHER/BATMAN: DEADLY KNIGHTS
Marvel Comics Group/DC Comics,OS; 1 Oct 1994

Item	$Good	$Fine	$N.Mint	£Good	£Fine	£N.Mint
1 ND 48pgs, squarebound, Chuck Dixon, John Romita Jnr and Klaus Janson	$0.90	$2.70	$4.50	£0.60	£1.80	£3.00
Title Value:	$0.90	$2.70	$4.50	£0.60	£1.80	£3.00

PUNISHER: A MAN NAMED FRANK
Marvel Comics Group,OS; 1 Aug 1994

Item	$Good	$Fine	$N.Mint	£Good	£Fine	£N.Mint
1 ND 48pgs, Chuck Dixon and John Buscema	$1.20	$3.60	$6.00	£0.80	£2.40	£4.00
Title Value:	$1.20	$3.60	$6.00	£0.80	£2.40	£4.00

PUNISHER: BLOODLINES
Marvel Comics Group,OS; 1 Feb 1992

Item	$Good	$Fine	$N.Mint	£Good	£Fine	£N.Mint
1 ND 48pgs	$0.90	$2.70	$4.50	£0.60	£1.80	£3.00
Title Value:	$0.90	$2.70	$4.50	£0.60	£1.80	£3.00

MINT = 100% / NEAR MINT (inc. +/-) = 90–99% / VERY FINE (inc. +/-) = 75–89% / FINE (inc. +/-) = 55–74%
VERY GOOD (inc. +/-) = 35–54% / GOOD (inc. +/-) = 15–34% / FAIR = 5–14% / POOR = 1–4%

505

PUNISHER: CRUISE HARD
Marvel Comics Group,OS; 1 Feb 1995
1 ND Dan Abnett and Andy Lanning script

	$Good	$Fine	$N.Mint	£Good	£Fine	£N.Mint
	$0.60	$1.80	$3.00	£0.40	£1.20	£2.00
Title Value:	$0.60	$1.80	$3.00	£0.40	£1.20	£2.00

PUNISHER: DIE HARD IN THE BIG EASY
Marvel Comics Group,OS; 1 Jan 1993
1 ND 48pgs, John Wagner script

	$Good	$Fine	$N.Mint	£Good	£Fine	£N.Mint
	$0.90	$2.70	$4.50	£0.60	£1.80	£3.00
Title Value:	$0.90	$2.70	$4.50	£0.60	£1.80	£3.00

PUNISHER: EMPTY QUARTER
Marvel Comics Group,OS; 1 Jan 1995
1 ND 64pgs, Mike Baron script, Bill Reinhold art

	$Good	$Fine	$N.Mint	£Good	£Fine	£N.Mint
	$1.20	$3.60	$6.00	£0.80	£2.40	£4.00
Title Value:	$1.20	$3.60	$6.00	£0.80	£2.40	£4.00

PUNISHER: FAMILY AFFAIR SPECIAL
Marvel Comics Group,OS; 1 Oct 1991
1 ND 64pgs

	$Good	$Fine	$N.Mint	£Good	£Fine	£N.Mint
	$0.50	$1.50	$2.50	£0.30	£0.90	£1.50
Title Value:	$0.50	$1.50	$2.50	£0.30	£0.90	£1.50

PUNISHER: G-FORCE BOOKSHELF EDITION
Marvel Comics Group,OS; 1 Apr 1992
1 ND 48pgs, Mike Baron script

	$Good	$Fine	$N.Mint	£Good	£Fine	£N.Mint
	$0.90	$2.70	$4.50	£0.60	£1.80	£3.00
Title Value:	$0.90	$2.70	$4.50	£0.60	£1.80	£3.00

PUNISHER: NO ESCAPE
Marvel Comics Group,OS; 1 Aug 1990
1 ND 48pgs, Todd Smith art, The Captain/Paladin appear

	$Good	$Fine	$N.Mint	£Good	£Fine	£N.Mint
	$0.90	$2.70	$4.50	£0.60	£1.80	£3.00
Title Value:	$0.90	$2.70	$4.50	£0.60	£1.80	£3.00

Note: Bookshelf Format

PUNISHER: ORIGIN OF MICRO-CHIP
Marvel Comics Group,MS; 1 Jul 1993-2 Aug 1993
1 Dougie Braithwaite cover

	$Good	$Fine	$N.Mint	£Good	£Fine	£N.Mint
1	$0.40	$1.20	$2.00	£0.25	£0.75	£1.25
2	$0.40	$1.20	$2.00	£0.25	£0.75	£1.25
Title Value:	$0.80	$2.40	$4.00	£0.50	£1.50	£2.50

PUNISHER: P.O.V.
Marvel Comics Group,MS; 1 Jul 1991-4 Oct 1991
1 ND Jim Starlin script/Bernie Wrightson art; Nick Fury co-stars

	$Good	$Fine	$N.Mint	£Good	£Fine	£N.Mint
1	$0.70	$2.10	$3.50	£0.50	£1.50	£2.50
2 ND Kingpin appears	$0.70	$2.10	$3.50	£0.50	£1.50	£2.50
3 ND	$0.70	$2.10	$3.50	£0.50	£1.50	£2.50
4 ND Nick Fury appears	$0.70	$2.10	$3.50	£0.50	£1.50	£2.50
Title Value:	$2.80	$8.40	$14.00	£2.00	£6.00	£10.00

Note: Bookshelf Format

PUNISHER: THE GHOSTS OF INNOCENTS
Marvel Comics Group,MS; 1 Jan 1993-2 Feb 1993
1-2 ND 48pgs, Jim Starlin script

	$Good	$Fine	$N.Mint	£Good	£Fine	£N.Mint
	$0.90	$2.70	$4.50	£0.60	£1.80	£3.00
Title Value:	$1.80	$5.40	$9.00	£1.20	£3.60	£6.00

PUNISHER: THE PRIZE
Marvel Comics Group,OS; 1 Dec 1990
1 ND 64pgs, Iron Man's armour featured

	$Good	$Fine	$N.Mint	£Good	£Fine	£N.Mint
	$0.70	$2.10	$3.50	£0.50	£1.50	£2.50
Title Value:	$0.70	$2.10	$3.50	£0.50	£1.50	£2.50

PUNISHER: YEAR ONE
Marvel Comics Group,MS; 1 Dec 1994-4 Mar 1995
1-4 Dan Abnett and Andy Lanning tell Punisher's origin

	$Good	$Fine	$N.Mint	£Good	£Fine	£N.Mint
	$0.40	$1.20	$2.00	£0.25	£0.75	£1.25
Title Value:	$1.60	$4.80	$8.00	£1.00	£3.00	£5.00

PUNX
Acclaim Comics,MS; 1 Jul 1995-4 Oct 1995
1-4 ND Keith Giffen script and pencil art, Claude St. Aubain inks

	$Good	$Fine	$N.Mint	£Good	£Fine	£N.Mint
	$0.50	$1.50	$2.50	£0.30	£0.90	£1.50
Title Value:	$2.00	$6.00	$10.00	£1.20	£3.60	£6.00

PUNX SPECIAL
Valiant/Acclaim Comics,OS; 1 Nov 1995
1 ND Keith Giffen script and art with Claude St. Aubain

	$Good	$Fine	$N.Mint	£Good	£Fine	£N.Mint
	$0.50	$1.50	$2.50	£0.30	£0.90	£1.50
Title Value:	$0.50	$1.50	$2.50	£0.30	£0.90	£1.50

PUPPET MASTER
Eternity,MS; 1 Dec 1990-4 Mar 1991

	$Good	$Fine	$N.Mint	£Good	£Fine	£N.Mint
1-4 ND	$0.40	$1.20	$2.00	£0.25	£0.75	£1.25
Title Value:	$1.60	$4.80	$8.00	£1.00	£3.00	£5.00
Puppet Master Comic Companion 48pgs, articles and photos (1991)				£0.70	£2.10	£3.50

PUPPET MASTER 2
Eternity,MS Film; 1,2 Oct 1991
1-2 ND film adaptation

	$Good	$Fine	$N.Mint	£Good	£Fine	£N.Mint
	$0.40	$1.20	$2.00	£0.25	£0.75	£1.25
Title Value:	$0.80	$2.40	$4.00	£0.50	£1.50	£2.50

PURE IMAGES
Pure Imagination; 1 Nov 1990-6 1991
1 ND article/unseen artwork on Spiderman detailing how the character originated

	$Good	$Fine	$N.Mint	£Good	£Fine	£N.Mint
1	$0.40	$1.20	$2.00	£0.25	£0.75	£1.25

2 ND article/unseen artwork on The Hulk and The Fantastic Four

	$Good	$Fine	$N.Mint	£Good	£Fine	£N.Mint
2	$0.40	$1.20	$2.00	£0.25	£0.75	£1.25

3-4 ND Monsterama

	$Good	$Fine	$N.Mint	£Good	£Fine	£N.Mint
3-4	$0.40	$1.20	$2.00	£0.25	£0.75	£1.25

5 ND Jack Kirby issue, Dave Gibbons pin-up

	$Good	$Fine	$N.Mint	£Good	£Fine	£N.Mint
5	$0.40	$1.20	$2.00	£0.25	£0.75	£1.25

6 ND Mechanical Dinosaurs

	$Good	$Fine	$N.Mint	£Good	£Fine	£N.Mint
6	$0.40	$1.20	$2.00	£0.25	£0.75	£1.25
Title Value:	$2.40	$7.20	$12.00	£1.50	£4.50	£7.50

PUREHEART THE POWERFUL, ARCHIE AS
Archie; 1 Sep 1966-6 Nov 1967
1 versus The Octopus

	$Good	$Fine	$N.Mint	£Good	£Fine	£N.Mint
1	$10.00	$30.00	$60.00	£6.50	£20.00	£40.00
2	$6.25	$18.50	$37.50	£4.55	£13.50	£27.50
3-6	$5.00	$15.00	$30.00	£3.30	£10.00	£20.00
Title Value:	$36.25	$108.50	$217.50	£24.25	£73.50	£147.50

Note: all distributed on the news-stands in the U.K.

PURPLE CLAW
I.W. Comics; 8 (early 1960s)
8 scarce distributed in the U.K. 50s reprints

	$Good	$Fine	$N.Mint	£Good	£Fine	£N.Mint
	$2.05	$6.25	$12.50	£1.30	£4.00	£8.00
Title Value:	$2.05	$6.25	$12.50	£1.30	£4.00	£8.00

PURPLE CLAW MYSTERIES
AC Comics; 1 Oct 1994
1 ND Bill Black script, Dick Ayers art; black and white

	$Good	$Fine	$N.Mint	£Good	£Fine	£N.Mint
	$0.60	$1.80	$3.00	£0.40	£1.20	£2.00
Title Value:	$0.60	$1.80	$3.00	£0.40	£1.20	£2.00

PURPLE SNIT, THE TWISTED TANTRUMS OF THE
Blackthorne; 1 Oct 1986-2 1986
1-2 ND black and white

	$Good	$Fine	$N.Mint	£Good	£Fine	£N.Mint
	$0.25	$0.75	$1.25	£0.15	£0.45	£0.75
Title Value:	$0.50	$1.50	$2.50	£0.30	£0.90	£1.50

PUSSYCAT
Marvel Comics Group,Magazine OS; 1 1968
1 ND scarce in the U.K. Men's magazine reprint, Wood and Everett art

	$Good	$Fine	$N.Mint	£Good	£Fine	£N.Mint
	$17.50	$52.50	$125.00	£10.50	£32.00	£75.00
Title Value:	$17.50	$52.50	$125.00	£10.50	£32.00	£75.00

Q

QUACK
Star Reach; 1 Jul 1976-6 Dec 1977
1 ND Frank Brunner and Howard Chaykin art

	$Good	$Fine	$N.Mint	£Good	£Fine	£N.Mint
1	$0.90	$2.70	$4.50	£0.60	£1.80	£3.00
2-6 ND	$0.50	$1.50	$2.50	£0.30	£0.90	£1.50
Title Value:	$3.40	$10.20	$17.00	£2.10	£6.30	£10.50

QUADRANT
Quadrant; 1 1983-8 1986
1 ND scarce in the U.K. magazine

	$Good	$Fine	$N.Mint	£Good	£Fine	£N.Mint
	$1.50	$4.50	$7.50	£1.00	£3.00	£5.00

1 ND scarce in the U.K. 1st comic format

	$Good	$Fine	$N.Mint	£Good	£Fine	£N.Mint
	$1.50	$4.50	$7.50	£1.00	£3.00	£5.00

2 ND scarce in the U.K.

	$Good	$Fine	$N.Mint	£Good	£Fine	£N.Mint
	$0.50	$1.50	$2.50	£0.50	£1.50	£2.50

3-8 ND scarce in the U.K.

	$Good	$Fine	$N.Mint	£Good	£Fine	£N.Mint
	$0.50	$1.50	$2.50	£0.40	£1.20	£2.00
Title Value:	$6.50	$19.50	$32.50	£4.90	£14.70	£24.50

Trade Paperback reprints issues #1-8, the "Hellrazor Saga" plus new 8pg story, new cover pre-bagged

	£Good	£Fine	£N.Mint
	£1.85	£5.55	£9.25
2nd printing	£1.65	£4.95	£8.25

QUANTUM LEAP
Innovation; 1 Aug 1991-12 Apr 1993
1 based on TV series

	$Good	$Fine	$N.Mint	£Good	£Fine	£N.Mint
1	$2.00	$6.00	$10.00	£3.50	£10.50	£17.50

1 special edition reprint (Sep 1992) – features 8pgs of articles and photos from Quantum Leap Convention

	$Good	$Fine	$N.Mint	£Good	£Fine	£N.Mint
	$0.50	$1.50	$2.50	£0.60	£1.80	£3.00
2	$1.00	$3.00	$5.00	£2.00	£6.00	£10.00

2 2nd printing, (Oct 1992)

	$Good	$Fine	$N.Mint	£Good	£Fine	£N.Mint
	$0.50	$1.50	$2.50	£0.40	£1.20	£2.00
3	$0.70	$2.10	$3.50	£1.50	£4.50	£7.50
4-5	$0.50	$1.50	$2.50	£1.00	£3.00	£5.00
6-10	$0.50	$1.50	$2.50	£0.80	£2.40	£4.00
11-12	$0.50	$1.50	$2.50	£0.70	£2.10	£3.50
Title Value:	$9.20	$27.60	$46.00	£15.40	£46.20	£77.00

Note: all Non-Distributed on the news-stands in the U.K.

	£Good	£Fine	£N.Mint
Annual 1 (Jun 1993), pin-up gallery included	£0.40	£1.20	£2.00

QUANTUM LEAP TIME AND SPACE SPECIAL
Innovation; 1 Aug 1993
1 ND silver foil logo; number 13 on cover

	$Good	$Fine	$N.Mint	£Good	£Fine	£N.Mint
	$0.50	$1.50	$2.50	£0.80	£2.40	£4.00
Title Value:	$0.50	$1.50	$2.50	£0.80	£2.40	£4.00

QUANTUM LEAP: SECOND CHILDHOOD
Innovation,MS; 1 Mar 1994-3 May 1994

	$Good	$Fine	$N.Mint	£Good	£Fine	£N.Mint
1-3 ND	$0.40	$1.20	$2.00	£0.50	£1.50	£2.50
Title Value:	$1.20	$3.60	$6.00	£1.50	£4.50	£7.50

QUASAR
Marvel Comics Group; 1 Oct 1989-60 Jul 1994
(see Avengers #302)

	$Good	$Fine	$N.Mint	£Good	£Fine	£N.Mint
1 ND origin	$0.40	$1.20	$2.00	£0.25	£0.75	£1.25
2 ND	$0.30	$0.90	$1.50	£0.20	£0.60	£1.00
3 ND Quasar vs. Human Torch	$0.30	$0.90	$1.50	£0.20	£0.60	£1.00
4 ND	$0.30	$0.90	$1.50	£0.20	£0.60	£1.00
5 LD in the U.K. Acts of Vengeance tie-in	$0.30	$0.90	$1.50	£0.20	£0.60	£1.00

6 LD in the U.K. Acts of Vengeance tie-in, Venom cameo (2pgs)

(QUASAR, continued)

Issue	$Good	$Fine	$N.Mint	£Good	£Fine	£N.Mint
	$0.25	$0.75	$1.25	£0.20	£0.60	£1.00
7 Quasar vs. cosmic-powered Spiderman	$0.25	$0.75	$1.25	£0.15	£0.45	£0.75
8 New Mutants appear	$0.25	$0.75	$1.25	£0.15	£0.45	£0.75
9-10	$0.25	$0.75	$1.25	£0.15	£0.45	£0.75
11 Excalibur guest-stars	$0.25	$0.75	$1.25	£0.15	£0.45	£0.75
12	$0.25	$0.75	$1.25	£0.15	£0.45	£0.75
13 Journey Into Mystery story, Squadron Supreme appear	$0.25	$0.75	$1.25	£0.15	£0.45	£0.75
14-15 Journey Into Mystery story	$0.25	$0.75	$1.25	£0.15	£0.45	£0.75
16 DS Journey Into Mystery story concludes, many guest-stars	$0.30	$0.90	$1.50	£0.20	£0.60	£1.00
17 Neal Adams cover, "Speedster" guest-stars (Flash parody ?)	$0.25	$0.75	$1.25	£0.15	£0.45	£0.75
18	$0.25	$0.75	$1.25	£0.15	£0.45	£0.75
19 Cosmos in Collision part 1 (of 7); Quasar vs. Jack of Hearts	$0.25	$0.75	$1.25	£0.15	£0.45	£0.75
20 Fantastic Four guest-star	$0.25	$0.75	$1.25	£0.15	£0.45	£0.75
21-22 ND	$0.25	$0.75	$1.25	£0.15	£0.45	£0.75
23 ND Ghost Rider appears	$0.25	$0.75	$1.25	£0.15	£0.45	£0.75
24 ND Galactus, Thanos and the Celestials appear	$0.25	$0.75	$1.25	£0.15	£0.45	£0.75
25 ND DS Cosmos in Collision conclusion	$0.30	$0.90	$1.50	£0.20	£0.60	£1.00
26 ND Infinity Gauntlet X-over, Thanos appears	$0.25	$0.75	$1.25	£0.15	£0.45	£0.75
27 ND Infinity Gauntlet X-over	$0.25	$0.75	$1.25	£0.15	£0.45	£0.75
28 ND Thor, Wonderman, Captain America, Hulk, Doc Samson, Hercules and others appear	$0.25	$0.75	$1.25	£0.15	£0.45	£0.75
29 ND	$0.25	$0.75	$1.25	£0.15	£0.45	£0.75
30 ND What If? story featuring The Watcher	$0.25	$0.75	$1.25	£0.15	£0.45	£0.75
31 ND Quasar in the New Universe, DP 7 appear	$0.25	$0.75	$1.25	£0.15	£0.45	
32 ND scarce in the U.K. Galactic Storm part 3	$0.25	$0.75	$1.25	£0.20	£0.60	£1.00
33 ND Galactic Storm part 10	$0.25	$0.75	$1.25	£0.15	£0.45	£0.75
34 ND Galactic Storm part 17	$0.25	$0.75	$1.25	£0.15	£0.45	£0.75
35-36 ND Galactic Storm: Aftermath	$0.25	$0.75	$1.25	£0.15	£0.45	£0.75
37 ND Infinity War X-over	$0.25	$0.75	$1.25	£0.15	£0.45	£0.75
38 ND Infinity War X-over, Wolverine, Nova and Hulk appear	$0.25	$0.75	$1.25	£0.15	£0.45	£0.75
39-40 ND Infinity War X-over	$0.25	$0.75	$1.25	£0.15	£0.45	£0.75
41 ND	$0.25	$0.75	$1.25	£0.15	£0.45	£0.75
42-43 ND Quasar vs. Blue Marvel (Marvel Boy)	$0.25	$0.75	$1.25	£0.15	£0.45	£0.75
44-49 ND	$0.25	$0.75	$1.25	£0.15	£0.45	£0.75
50 ND DS gold-holo-grafix foil cover, Silver Surfer appears	$0.40	$1.20	$2.00	£0.25	£0.75	£1.25
51-52 ND Squadron Supreme guest-stars						
	$0.25	$0.75	$1.25	£0.15	£0.45	£0.75
53 ND Warlock appears	$0.25	$0.75	$1.25	£0.15	£0.45	£0.75
54 ND Starblast part 2	$0.25	$0.75	$1.25	£0.15	£0.45	£0.75
55 ND Starblast part 6	$0.25	$0.75	$1.25	£0.15	£0.45	£0.75
56 ND Starblast part 10	$0.25	$0.75	$1.25	£0.15	£0.45	£0.75
57 ND Starblast epilogue	$0.25	$0.75	$1.25	£0.15	£0.45	£0.75
58 ND with free Spiderman and his Deadly Foes card sheet	$0.25	$0.75	$1.25	£0.15	£0.45	£0.75
59 ND	$0.25	$0.75	$1.25	£0.15	£0.45	£0.75
60 ND Nova guest-stars	$0.25	$0.75	$1.25	£0.15	£0.45	£0.75
Title Value:	**$15.60**	**$46.80**	**$78.00**	**£9.60**	**£28.80**	**£48.00**

QUASAR SPECIAL EDITION
Marvel Comics Group, MS; 1 Mar 1992-3 May 1992

Issue	$Good	$Fine	$N.Mint	£Good	£Fine	£N.Mint
1 Galactic Storm part 3, same as issue #32 but news-stand as opposed to Direct Market	$0.25	$0.75	$1.25	£0.15	£0.45	£0.75
2 Galactic Storm part 10 reprinted for news-stand	$0.25	$0.75	$1.25	£0.15	£0.45	£0.75
3 Galactic Storm part 17 reprinted for news-stand	$0.25	$0.75	$1.25	£0.15	£0.45	£0.75
Title Value:	**$0.75**	**$2.25**	**$3.75**	**£0.45**	**£1.35**	**£2.25**

QUEEN OF THE DAMNED
Innovation, MS; 1 Oct 1991-12 Jan 1994

Issue	$Good	$Fine	$N.Mint	£Good	£Fine	£N.Mint
1 ND Vampire Lestat spin-off begins	$0.50	$1.50	$2.50	£0.50	£1.50	£2.50
2-12 ND	$0.50	$1.50	$2.50	£0.40	£1.20	£2.00
Title Value:	**$6.00**	**$18.00**	**$30.00**	**£4.90**	**£14.70**	**£24.50**

QUESTION
DC Comics; 1 Feb 1987-36 Mar 1990

Issue	$Good	$Fine	$N.Mint	£Good	£Fine	£N.Mint
1 ND painted cover	$0.50	$1.50	$2.50	£0.30	£0.90	£1.50
2 ND scarce in the U.K. Batman appears	$0.50	$1.50	$2.50	£0.30	£0.90	£1.50
3-10 ND	$0.50	$1.50	$2.50	£0.30	£0.90	£1.50
11-20 ND	$0.40	$1.20	$2.00	£0.25	£0.75	£1.25
21-25 ND	$0.30	$0.90	$1.50	£0.20	£0.60	£1.00
26 ND Riddler appears	$0.30	$0.90	$1.50	£0.20	£0.60	£1.00
27-35 ND	$0.30	$0.90	$1.50	£0.20	£0.60	£1.00
36 ND ties in with Green Arrow Annual #3	$0.30	$0.90	$1.50	£0.20	£0.60	£1.00
Title Value:	**$13.80**	**$41.40**	**$69.00**	**£8.70**	**£26.10**	**£43.50**

Note: Deluxe Format Baxter paper. For Mature Readers

Question: Thunder Over The Abyss

	$Good	$Fine	$N.Mint	£Good	£Fine	£N.Mint
Trade paperback (Mar 1992), reprints issues #1-5				£1.60	£4.80	£8.00

QUESTION ANNUAL, THE
DC Comics; 1 1988-2 1989

Issue	$Good	$Fine	$N.Mint	£Good	£Fine	£N.Mint
1 ND 48pgs, ties in with Green Arrow Annual #1 and Detective Comics Annual #1 (Batman appears)	$0.50	$1.50	$2.50	£0.30	£0.90	£1.50
2 ND 48pgs, ties in with Green Arrow Annual #2	$0.50	$1.50	$2.50	£0.30	£0.90	£1.50
Title Value:	**$1.00**	**$3.00**	**$5.00**	**£0.60**	**£1.80**	**£3.00**

QUESTION QUARTERLY, THE
DC Comics; 1 Nov 1990-5 Spring 1992

Issue	$Good	$Fine	$N.Mint	£Good	£Fine	£N.Mint
1-5 ND 48pgs	$0.50	$1.50	$2.50	£0.30	£0.90	£1.50
Title Value:	**$2.50**	**$7.50**	**$12.50**	**£1.50**	**£4.50**	**£7.50**

Note: issue 2 delayed owing to production problems. Quarterly frequency.

Pure Images #1

Purple Snit #1

Radical Dreamer #1

QUESTPROBE
Marvel Comics Group,OS; 1 Aug 1984

	$Good	$Fine	$N.Mint	£Good	£Fine	£N.Mint
1 ND	$0.30	$0.90	$1.50	£0.20	£0.60	£1.00
Title Value:	$0.30	$0.90	$1.50	£0.20	£0.60	£1.00

QUESTPROBE (2ND SERIES)
Marvel Comics Group,MS; 1 Sep 1985-3 Nov 1985

	$Good	$Fine	$N.Mint	£Good	£Fine	£N.Mint
1 ND Hulk appears	$0.30	$0.90	$1.50	£0.20	£0.60	£1.00
2 ND Spiderman appears	$0.30	$0.90	$1.50	£0.20	£0.60	£1.00
3 ND Human Torch and Thing appear	$0.30	$0.90	$1.50	£0.20	£0.60	£1.00
Title Value:	$0.90	$2.70	$4.50	£0.60	£1.80	£3.00

Note: issue #4 was announced but it eventually appeared in Marvel Fanfare #33

R

R.A.Z.E.
Firstlight Comixx; 1 Dec 1994-2 1994

	$Good	$Fine	$N.Mint	£Good	£Fine	£N.Mint
1-2 ND	$0.60	$1.80	$3.00	£0.40	£1.20	£2.00
Title Value:	$1.20	$3.60	$6.00	£0.80	£2.40	£4.00

R.E.B.E.L.S. '94-'96
DC Comics; 0 Oct 1994; 1 Nov 1994-17 Mar 1996

	$Good	$Fine	$N.Mint	£Good	£Fine	£N.Mint
0 (Oct 1994) Zero Hour X-over, origin	$0.40	$1.20	$2.00	£0.25	£0.75	£1.25
1-2	$0.40	$1.20	$2.00	£0.25	£0.75	£1.25
3 title becomes R.E.B.E.L.S. '95	$0.40	$1.20	$2.00	£0.25	£0.75	£1.25
4-10	$0.40	$1.20	$2.00	£0.25	£0.75	£1.25
11 Captain Comet appears	$0.40	$1.20	$2.00	£0.25	£0.75	£1.25
12	$0.40	$1.20	$2.00	£0.25	£0.75	£1.25
13 Underworld Unleashed tie-in	$0.40	$1.20	$2.00	£0.25	£0.75	£1.25
14-17	$0.40	$1.20	$2.00	£0.25	£0.75	£1.25
Title Value:	$7.20	$21.60	$36.00	£4.50	£13.50	£22.50

R.I.P. BRASHER, AVENGER OF THE DEAD
TSR; 1 1990-4 1991

	$Good	$Fine	$N.Mint	£Good	£Fine	£N.Mint
1-4 ND role-playing game; Doug Moench script; cover design by George Perez	$0.50	$1.50	$2.50	£0.30	£0.90	£1.50
Title Value:	$2.00	$6.00	$10.00	£1.20	£3.60	£6.00

R.O.B.O.T. BATTALION 2050
Eclipse,OS; 1 Mar 1988

	$Good	$Fine	$N.Mint	£Good	£Fine	£N.Mint
1 ND Bill Sienkiewicz cover; black and white	$0.30	$0.90	$1.50	£0.20	£0.60	£1.00
Title Value:	$0.30	$0.90	$1.50	£0.20	£0.60	£1.00

RACE OF SCORPIONS
Dark Horse; 1 Sep 1991-4 Dec 1991

	$Good	$Fine	$N.Mint	£Good	£Fine	£N.Mint
1-4 ND squarebound	$0.50	$1.50	$2.50	£0.30	£0.90	£1.50
Title Value:	$2.00	$6.00	$10.00	£1.20	£3.60	£6.00
Book 1 (1991) 48pgs squarebound, reprints from Dark Horse Presents				£0.50	£1.50	£2.50
Book 2 (1991), 48pgs, reprints as above				£0.50	£1.50	£2.50

RACER-X
Now Comics; 0 May 1988; 1 Jul 1988-11 Aug 1989

	$Good	$Fine	$N.Mint	£Good	£Fine	£N.Mint
0 ND $3.50 cover	$0.50	$1.50	$2.50	£0.30	£0.90	£1.50
1 ND	$0.50	$1.50	$2.50	£0.30	£0.90	£1.50
2-11 ND	$0.40	$1.20	$2.00	£0.25	£0.75	£1.25
Title Value:	$5.00	$15.00	$25.00	£3.10	£9.30	£15.50

RACER-X VOLUME TWO
Now Comics; 1 Sep 1989-9 1990

	$Good	$Fine	$N.Mint	£Good	£Fine	£N.Mint
1-9 ND	$0.30	$0.90	$1.50	£0.20	£0.60	£1.00
Title Value:	$2.70	$8.10	$13.50	£1.80	£5.40	£9.00

RACK & PAIN
Dark Horse,MS; 1 Feb 1994-4 May 1994

	$Good	$Fine	$N.Mint	£Good	£Fine	£N.Mint
1-4 ND Greg Capullo covers	$0.50	$1.50	$2.50	£0.30	£0.90	£1.50
Title Value:	$2.00	$6.00	$10.00	£1.20	£3.60	£6.00

RADICAL DREAMER
Blackball Comics; -1 Dec 1994; 0 May 1994; 1 Jun 1994-5? 1995

	$Good	$Fine	$N.Mint	£Good	£Fine	£N.Mint
0-1 ND Mark Wheatley script and art	$0.40	$1.20	$2.00	£0.25	£0.75	£1.25
1 ND issue "-1", immediately precedes issue #0; Poster Format	$0.50	$1.50	$2.50	£0.30	£0.90	£1.50
2 ND Mark Wheatley script and art	$0.40	$1.20	$2.00	£0.25	£0.75	£1.25
3-5 ND Mark Wheatley script and art; Poster Format as 16pgs fold out into 2 eight page posters	$0.40	$1.20	$2.00	£0.25	£0.75	£1.25
Title Value:	$2.90	$8.70	$14.50	£1.80	£5.40	£9.00
Radical Dreamer: The Dream Collection (Aug 1994) pre-bagged set of issues #0 and #1; 10,000 sets				£0.50	£1.50	£2.50

RADICAL DREAMER (2ND SERIES)
Mark's Giant Economy Size Comics; 1 Jun 1995-present

	$Good	$Fine	$N.Mint	£Good	£Fine	£N.Mint
1 ND Mark Wheatley script and art begins; utilizes unpublished material from Blackball series plus new art; black and white	$0.60	$1.80	$3.00	£0.40	£1.20	£2.00
2-3 ND	$0.60	$1.80	$3.00	£0.40	£1.20	£2.00
Title Value:	$1.80	$5.40	$9.00	£1.20	£3.60	£6.00

RADIO BOY
Eclipse,OS; 1 Mar 1987

1 ND Japanimation parody

	$Good	$Fine	$N.Mint	£Good	£Fine	£N.Mint
	$0.40	$1.20	$2.00	£0.25	£0.75	£1.25
Title Value:	$0.40	$1.20	$2.00	£0.25	£0.75	£1.25

RADIOACTIVE MAN
Bongo Comics,MS; 1 Dec 1993-6 Oct 1994

	$Good	$Fine	$N.Mint	£Good	£Fine	£N.Mint
1 ND fluorescent red skeleton cover, pull-out poster	$0.70	$2.10	$3.50	£0.50	£1.50	£2.50
2 ND '60s Marvel parody	$0.60	$1.80	$3.00	£0.40	£1.20	£2.00
3 ND 1970s theme issue	$0.50	$1.50	$2.50	£0.30	£0.90	£1.50
4 ND 1980s "dark phoenix" parody	$0.50	$1.50	$2.50	£0.30	£0.90	£1.50
5 ND Watchmen parody	$0.50	$1.50	$2.50	£0.30	£0.90	£1.50
6 ND last issues spoof	$0.50	$1.50	$2.50	£0.30	£0.90	£1.50
Title Value:	$3.30	$9.90	$16.50	£2.10	£6.30	£10.50

RADIOACTIVE MAN 80 PAGE COLOSSAL
Bongo Comics,OS; nn Jul 1995

	$Good	$Fine	$N.Mint	£Good	£Fine	£N.Mint
nn ND 80pgs, contains four stories plus pin-ups	$1.00	$3.00	$5.00	£0.60	£1.80	£3.00
Title Value:	$1.00	$3.00	$5.00	£0.60	£1.80	£3.00

RADIUM AND HIS INTERGALACTIC ODD SQUAD
Fantasy General Comics; 1 1985

	$Good	$Fine	$N.Mint	£Good	£Fine	£N.Mint
1 ND black and white	$0.30	$0.90	$1.50	£0.20	£0.60	£1.00
Title Value:	$0.30	$0.90	$1.50	£0.20	£0.60	£1.00

RAFFERTY ASHCAN
Malibu,OS; nn Nov 1994

	$Good	$Fine	$N.Mint	£Good	£Fine	£N.Mint
nn ND 16pgs, black and white; previews Rafferty cross-over story, Chaykin cover	$0.15	$0.45	$0.75	£0.10	£0.35	£0.60
Title Value:	$0.15	$0.45	$0.75	£0.10	£0.35	£0.60

RAGAMUFFINS
Eclipse,OS; 1 Jan 1985

	$Good	$Fine	$N.Mint	£Good	£Fine	£N.Mint
1 ND Gene Colan reprints	$0.40	$1.20	$2.00	£0.25	£0.75	£1.25
Title Value:	$0.40	$1.20	$2.00	£0.25	£0.75	£1.25

RAGMAN
DC Comics; 1 Aug/Sep 1976-5 Jun/Jul 1977
(see Batman Family #20)

	$Good	$Fine	$N.Mint	£Good	£Fine	£N.Mint
1 scarce in the U.K. origin and 1st appearance Ragman	$0.70	$2.10	$3.50	£0.50	£1.50	£2.50
2 scarce in the U.K. origin	$0.50	$1.50	$2.50	£0.40	£1.20	£2.00
3 ND	$0.50	$1.50	$2.50	£0.40	£1.20	£2.00
4-5 very scarce in the U.K. Kubert art	$0.50	$1.50	$2.50	£0.40	£1.20	£2.00
Title Value:	$2.70	$8.10	$13.50	£2.10	£6.30	£10.50

RAGMAN (2ND SERIES)
DC Comics,MS; 1 Oct 1991-8 May 1992

	$Good	$Fine	$N.Mint	£Good	£Fine	£N.Mint
1-2	$0.25	$0.75	$1.25	£0.15	£0.45	£0.75
3 origin	$0.25	$0.75	$1.25	£0.15	£0.45	£0.75
4-5	$0.25	$0.75	$1.25	£0.15	£0.45	£0.75
6-8 Batman appears	$0.25	$0.75	$1.25	£0.15	£0.45	£0.75
Title Value:	$2.00	$6.00	$10.00	£1.20	£3.60	£6.00

RAGMAN: CRY OF THE DEAD
DC Comics,MS; 1 Aug 1993-6 Jan 1994

	$Good	$Fine	$N.Mint	£Good	£Fine	£N.Mint
1-6 Joe Kubert covers	$0.30	$0.90	$1.50	£0.20	£0.60	£1.00
Title Value:	$1.80	$5.40	$9.00	£1.20	£3.60	£6.00

RAI
Valiant; 0 Oct 1992; 1 Mar 1992-8 Sep 1992; 9 Apr 1993-33 Apr 1995

	$Good	$Fine	$N.Mint	£Good	£Fine	£N.Mint
0 (Oct 1992), origin of Rising Spirit, guest-stars all Valiant heroes; joint 1st appearance (cameo) Bloodshot (see Eternal Warrior #4). Note: shipped before Eternal Warrior #4 though same cover date	$1.50	$4.50	$7.50	£1.00	£3.00	£5.00
0 as above but glossy cover	$2.00	$6.00	$10.00	£1.20	£3.60	£6.00
1	$2.00	$6.00	$10.00	£1.20	£3.60	£6.00
2	$1.50	$4.50	$7.50	£1.00	£3.00	£5.00
3 scarce in the U.K.	$2.00	$6.00	$10.00	£1.20	£3.60	£6.00
4 very scarce in the U.K. (the scarcest Valiant comic)	$2.50	$7.50	$12.50	£1.50	£4.50	£7.50
5	$0.80	$2.40	$4.00	£0.40	£1.20	£2.00
6 Unity: Chapter 7	$0.80	$2.40	$4.00	£0.40	£1.20	£2.00
7 Unity: Chapter 15, Sting appears, Walt Simonson cover; death of Rai	$0.80	$2.40	$4.00	£0.40	£1.20	£2.00
8 Unity aftermath, exploring the consequences of the death of Rai during Unity	$0.80	$2.40	$4.00	£0.40	£1.20	£2.00
9 title returns as "Rai & the Future Force"; story continued from Magnus #24; Magnus now appears throughout	$0.50	$1.50	$2.50	£0.30	£0.90	£1.50
10	$0.50	$1.50	$2.50	£0.30	£0.90	£1.50
11-20	$0.40	$1.20	$2.00	£0.25	£0.75	£1.25
21 with free Upper Deck trading card	$0.40	$1.20	$2.00	£0.25	£0.75	£1.25
22 continued from Magnus #37	$0.40	$1.20	$2.00	£0.25	£0.75	£1.25
23-24	$0.40	$1.20	$2.00	£0.25	£0.75	£1.25
25 sub-titled "The New.."	$0.40	$1.20	$2.00	£0.25	£0.75	£1.25
26 Chaos Effect tie-in	$0.40	$1.20	$2.00	£0.25	£0.75	£1.25

	$Good	$Fine	$N.Mint	£Good	£Fine	£N.Mint

27 ties-in with Magnus Robot Fighter #42

	$0.40	$1.20	$2.00	£0.25	£0.75	£1.25
28-33	$0.40	$1.20	$2.00	£0.25	£0.75	£1.25
Title Value:	$24.90	$74.70	$124.50	£15.05	£45.15	£75.25

Note: all Non-Distributed on the news-stands in the U.K.

| Rai (1994) Trade paperback reprints issues #0-4 | | | | £1.60 | £4.80 | £8.00 |

RAIDERS OF THE LOST ARK
Marvel Comics Group,MS Film; 1 Sep 1981-3 Nov 1981

1-2 ND adapts film, Walt Simonson script

| | $0.25 | $0.75 | $1.25 | £0.15 | £0.45 | £0.75 |

3 ND adapts film, Walt Simonson script and cover art

| | $0.25 | $0.75 | $1.25 | £0.15 | £0.45 | £0.75 |
| Title Value: | $0.75 | $2.25 | $3.75 | £0.45 | £1.35 | £2.25 |

RAIN
Tundra Publishing,MS; 1 May 1991-5 1991

| **1-5** ND | $0.40 | $1.20 | $2.00 | £0.25 | £0.75 | £1.25 |
| Title Value: | $2.00 | $6.00 | $10.00 | £1.25 | £3.75 | £6.25 |

RAINBOW BRITE AND THE STAR STEALER
DC Comics,OS,Toy,Film; nn 1985

nn ND very scarce in the U.K. adapts animated film

| | $0.15 | $0.45 | $0.75 | £0.10 | £0.35 | £0.60 |
| Title Value: | $0.15 | $0.45 | $0.75 | £0.10 | £0.35 | £0.60 |

RALPH SNART – THE LOST ISSUES
Now Comics,MS; 1 Apr 1993-3 Jun 1993

1 ND pre-bagged with trading card; features the issues originally meant to be #27-29 of the 1990 series
  (note: two different trading cards available)

	$0.30	$0.90	$1.50	£0.20	£0.60	£1.00
2-3 ND	$0.30	$0.90	$1.50	£0.20	£0.60	£1.00
Title Value:	$0.90	$2.70	$4.50	£0.60	£1.80	£3.00

RALPH SNART ADVENTURES
Now Comics,MS; 1 Jun 1986-3 Oct 1986

| **1-3** ND | $0.30 | $0.90 | $1.50 | £0.20 | £0.60 | £1.00 |
| Title Value: | $0.90 | $2.70 | $4.50 | £0.60 | £1.80 | £3.00 |

RALPH SNART ADVENTURES (2ND SERIES)
Now Comics; 1 Nov 1986-9 Jul 1987

| **1-7** ND | $0.30 | $0.90 | $1.50 | £0.20 | £0.60 | £1.00 |

8-9 ND 1st colour issues

| | $0.30 | $0.90 | $1.50 | £0.20 | £0.60 | £1.00 |
| Title Value: | $2.70 | $8.10 | $13.50 | £1.80 | £5.40 | £9.00 |

Ralph Snart Adventures (Oct 1992)

| Trade paperback reprints issues #1-3, new cover by Marc Hansen | $1.00 | $3.00 | $5.00 | | | |

Ralph Snart Adventures II

| Trade paperback reprints issues #5-7, new cover by Marc Hansen | $1.00 | $3.00 | $5.00 | | | |

RALPH SNART ADVENTURES (3RD SERIES)
Now Comics; 1 Sep 1988-31 1992

1 ND reprints vol 2 in colour

| | $0.40 | $1.20 | $2.00 | £0.25 | £0.75 | £1.25 |

2-7 ND reprints vol 2 in colour

| | $0.30 | $0.90 | $1.50 | £0.20 | £0.60 | £1.00 |

8-23 ND Comics Code on cover

| | $0.30 | $0.90 | $1.50 | £0.20 | £0.60 | £1.00 |

24 ND Comics Code on cover, 3-D issue with glasses (25% less without glasses)

| | $0.30 | $0.90 | $1.50 | £0.20 | £0.60 | £1.00 |

25-31 ND Comics Code on cover

| | $0.30 | $0.90 | $1.50 | £0.20 | £0.60 | £1.00 |
| Title Value: | $9.40 | $28.20 | $47.00 | £6.25 | £18.75 | £31.25 |

Trade Paperback (1989)

| reprints #1-7, full colour; comic book size | | | | £1.70 | £5.10 | £8.50 |
| black and white paperback size | | | | £0.60 | £1.80 | £3.00 |

RALPH SNART ADVENTURES (4TH SERIES)
Now Comics,MS; 1 May 1992-3 Jul 1992

1-3 ND pre-bagged, 4 different trading cards available in each issue

| | $0.30 | $0.90 | $1.50 | £0.20 | £0.60 | £1.00 |
| Title Value: | $0.90 | $2.70 | $4.50 | £0.60 | £1.80 | £3.00 |

RALPH SNART ADVENTURES (5TH SERIES)
Now Comics; 1 Jul 1993-12 May 1994

1-11 Direct Market Edition – pre-bagged with trading card

| | $0.30 | $0.90 | $1.50 | £0.20 | £0.60 | £1.00 |

1-11 Newstand edition, un-bagged/without card

| | $0.25 | $0.75 | $1.25 | £0.15 | £0.45 | £0.75 |

12 anniversary issue with temporary tattoo

| | $0.30 | $0.90 | $1.50 | £0.20 | £0.60 | £1.00 |
| Title Value: | $6.35 | $19.05 | $31.75 | £4.05 | £12.15 | £20.25 |

Note: all Non-Distributed on the news-stands in the U.K.

RALPH SNART ADVENTURES (6TH SERIES)
Now Comics; 1 Aug 1994

1 ND Marc Hansen script and art; colour

| | $0.30 | $0.90 | $1.50 | £0.20 | £0.60 | £1.00 |
| Title Value: | $0.30 | $0.90 | $1.50 | £0.20 | £0.60 | £1.00 |

RALPH SNART ADVENTURES SUMMER SPECIAL
Now Comics,OS; 1 Jul 1994

1 ND Marc Hansen script and art

| | $0.40 | $1.20 | $2.00 | £0.25 | £0.75 | £1.25 |
| Title Value: | $0.40 | $1.20 | $2.00 | £0.25 | £0.75 | £1.25 |

RALPH SNART ADVENTURES 3-D SPECIAL
Now Comics,OS; 1 Oct 1992

1 ND pre-bagged with glasses (25% less without glasses)

| | $0.40 | $1.20 | $2.00 | £0.25 | £0.75 | £1.25 |

1 ND special edition as above plus 12 trading cards

| | $0.50 | $1.50 | $2.50 | £0.30 | £0.90 | £1.50 |
| Title Value: | $0.90 | $2.70 | $4.50 | £0.55 | £1.65 | £2.75 |

RAMAR OF THE JUNGLE
Charlton; 1 1954; 2 Sep 1955-5 Sep 1956

1 ND scarce in the U.K. based on 1950s TV series starring Jon Hall as a great white hunter

	$14.00	$43.00	$100.00	£9.25	£28.00	£65.00
2-5 ND	$10.00	$30.00	$70.00	£6.25	£19.00	£45.00
Title Value:	$54.00	$163.00	$380.00	£34.25	£104.00	£245.00

Note: all Non-Distributed on the news-stands in the U.K.

RAMBO IN 3-D
Blackthorne; (3-D Series #49) 1 Autumn 1988

1 ND based on Stallone film; with bound-in 3-D glasses (25% less if without glasses)

| | $0.40 | $1.20 | $2.00 | £0.25 | £0.75 | £1.25 |
| Title Value: | $0.40 | $1.20 | $2.00 | £0.25 | £0.75 | £1.25 |

RAMPAGING HULK
Marvel Comics Group,Magazine; 1 Jan 1977-27 Jun 1981
(titled Rampaging Hulk #1-9, becomes The Hulk with #10)

1 LD in the U.K. Walt Simonson art

| | $1.00 | $3.00 | $5.00 | £0.70 | £2.10 | £3.50 |

2 original X-Men appear, X-Men article, Walt Simonson art

| | $1.00 | $3.00 | $5.00 | £0.60 | £1.80 | £3.00 |

3 Iron Man appears in Bloodstone back-up story, Walt Simonson art; Earl Norem painted cover

| | $0.60 | $1.80 | $3.00 | £0.40 | £1.20 | £2.00 |

4 Jim Starlin and Nino art; Giffen art on super-villain histories and Marshall Rogers art on 2pg intro to
  Bloodstone story

| | $0.60 | $1.80 | $3.00 | £0.40 | £1.20 | £2.00 |

5-6 Sub-Mariner vs. Hulk

| | $0.60 | $1.80 | $3.00 | £0.40 | £1.20 | £2.00 |

7 Gerber script and Jim Starlin art on Man-Thing back-up story

| | $0.60 | $1.80 | $3.00 | £0.40 | £1.20 | £2.00 |

8 LD in the U.K. original Avengers appear, George Perez art (1pg)

| | $0.60 | $1.80 | $3.00 | £0.40 | £1.20 | £2.00 |

9 original Avengers appear; Shanna She-Devil ckecklist and portfolio

| | $0.60 | $1.80 | $3.00 | £0.40 | £1.20 | £2.00 |

10 ND

| | $0.60 | $1.80 | $3.00 | £0.40 | £1.20 | £2.00 |

11-12 ND Moon Knight story

| | $0.60 | $1.80 | $3.00 | £0.40 | £1.20 | £2.00 |

13 ND Moon Knight; Sienkiewicz art

| | $0.60 | $1.80 | $3.00 | £0.40 | £1.20 | £2.00 |

14 ND Moon Knight story; Sienkiewicz art

| | $0.60 | $1.80 | $3.00 | £0.40 | £1.20 | £2.00 |

15 ND Moon Knight story; Sienkiewicz art

| | $0.50 | $1.50 | $2.50 | £0.30 | £0.90 | £1.50 |

16 ND Mike Zeck art, Bissette art (1pg)

| | $0.50 | $1.50 | $2.50 | £0.30 | £0.90 | £1.50 |

17-18 ND Moon Knight story; Sienkiewicz art

| | $0.50 | $1.50 | $2.50 | £0.30 | £0.90 | £1.50 |

19 ND

| | $0.50 | $1.50 | $2.50 | £0.30 | £0.90 | £1.50 |

20 ND Moon Knight story; Sienkiewicz art

	$0.50	$1.50	$2.50	£0.30	£0.90	£1.50
21-24 ND	$0.50	$1.50	$2.50	£0.30	£0.90	£1.50
25 ND Chaykin art	$0.50	$1.50	$2.50	£0.30	£0.90	£1.50
26 ND	$0.50	$1.50	$2.50	£0.30	£0.90	£1.50

27 ND Walt Simonson art (1pg)

| | $0.50 | $1.50 | $2.50 | £0.30 | £0.90 | £1.50 |
| Title Value: | $15.70 | $47.10 | $78.50 | £10.00 | £30.00 | £50.00 |

FEATURES

Bloodstone in 1-6,8. Dominic Fortune by Chaykin in 21-25. Hulk in 1-27. Man-Thing in 7. Moon Knight in 11-15,17,18,20. Shanna in 9.

RANMA 1/2
Viz Communications,MS; 1 Jul 1992-7 Jan 1993

1-7 ND Rumiko Takahashi; black and white

| | $0.90 | $2.70 | $4.50 | £0.60 | £1.80 | £3.00 |
| Title Value: | $6.30 | $18.90 | $31.50 | £4.20 | £12.60 | £21.00 |

| Ranma 1/2 Graphic Novel (Jul 1993) reprints series; 300pgs | | | | £2.30 | £6.90 | £11.50 |

RANMA 1/2 PART 2
Viz Communications,MS; 1 Mar 1993-11 Jan 1994

1-11 ND Rumiko Takahashi; black and white

| | $0.50 | $1.50 | $2.50 | £0.30 | £0.90 | £1.50 |
| Title Value: | $5.50 | $16.50 | $27.50 | £3.30 | £9.90 | £16.50 |

Ranma ½ Graphic Novel 2 (June 1994)

| reprints first half of series, black and white | | | | £2.00 | £6.00 | £10.00 |

Ranma ½ Graphic Novel 3 (Aug 1994)

| reprints second half of series, black and white | | | | £2.00 | £6.00 | £10.00 |

RANMA 1/2 PART 3
Viz Communications,MS; 1 Feb 1994-13 Feb 1995

1-13 ND Rumiko Takahashi; black and white

| | $0.50 | $1.50 | $2.50 | £0.30 | £0.90 | £1.50 |
| Title Value: | $6.50 | $19.50 | $32.50 | £3.90 | £11.70 | £19.50 |

| Ranma ½ Volume 4 (Jul 1995) collects the first half of part 3 | | | | £2.10 | £6.30 | £10.50 |
| Ranma ½ Volume 5 (Sep 1995) collects second half of part 3 | | | | £2.10 | £6.30 | £10.50 |

RANMA 1/2 PART 4
Viz Communications,MS; 1 Jan 1995-11 Nov 1995

1-11 ND Rumiko Takahashi; black and white

| | $0.50 | $1.50 | $2.50 | £0.30 | £0.90 | £1.50 |
| Title Value: | $5.50 | $16.50 | $27.50 | £3.30 | £9.90 | £16.50 |

RAPHAEL
Mirage Studios,Oversized; 1 1985
(see Teenage Mutant Ninja Turtles)

1 ND orange/black/white cover, 1st appearance Casey Jones

| | $1.00 | $3.00 | $5.00 | £0.70 | £2.10 | £3.50 |

1 2nd printing, ND new 10 page story, new painted cover (blue)

| | $0.60 | $1.80 | $3.00 | £0.40 | £1.20 | £2.00 |
| Title Value: | $1.60 | $4.80 | $8.00 | £1.10 | £3.30 | £5.50 |

	$Good	$Fine	$N.Mint	£Good	£Fine	£N.Mint

RARE BIT FIENDS
King Hell; 1 Jul 1994-15 1995?
1-15 ND Rick Veitch script and art; black and white

| | $0.60 | $1.80 | $3.00 | £0.40 | £1.20 | £2.00 |
| Title Value: | $9.00 | $27.00 | $45.00 | £6.00 | £18.00 | £30.00 |

RASCALS IN PARADISE
Dark Horse,MS; 1 Jul 1994-3 Nov 1994
1-3 ND Jim Silke script and art; oversize format

| | $0.80 | $2.40 | $4.00 | £0.50 | £1.50 | £2.50 |
| Title Value: | $2.40 | $7.20 | $12.00 | £1.50 | £4.50 | £7.50 |

Rascals in Paradise (Oct 1995) Trade paperback collects issues
#1-3 with Dave Stevens/Geof Darrow introduction

| | | | | £2.30 | £6.90 | £11.50 |

RATMAN: DARK CIRCLE
Comico,MS; 1 Jul 1993-4 Oct 1993
1 ND Elementals spin-off

| | $0.40 | $1.20 | $2.00 | £0.25 | £0.75 | £1.25 |

1 ND Limited Edition – with poster

	$0.50	$1.50	$2.50	£0.30	£0.90	£1.50
2-4 ND	$0.40	$1.20	$2.00	£0.25	£0.75	£1.25
Title Value:	$2.10	$6.30	$10.50	£1.30	£3.90	£6.50

RAVAGE
Fathom Press; 1 Jun 1992
1 ND black and white

| | $0.30 | $0.90 | $1.50 | £0.20 | £0.60 | £1.00 |
| Title Value: | $0.30 | $0.90 | $1.50 | £0.20 | £0.60 | £1.00 |

RAVAGE 2099
Marvel Comics Group; 1 Dec 1992-33 Aug 1995
1 ND Stan Lee script begins, gold foil-stamped cover

| | $0.30 | $0.90 | $1.50 | £0.20 | £0.60 | £1.00 |
| 2-9 ND | $0.25 | $0.75 | $1.25 | £0.15 | £0.45 | £0.75 |

10 ND new direction for title with Pat Mills scripting

| | $0.25 | $0.75 | $1.25 | £0.15 | £0.45 | £0.75 |
| 11-13 ND | $0.25 | $0.75 | $1.25 | £0.15 | £0.45 | £0.75 |

14 ND Punisher 2099 appears

| | $0.25 | $0.75 | $1.25 | £0.15 | £0.45 | £0.75 |

15 ND continued in X-Men 2099 #5

| | $0.25 | $0.75 | $1.25 | £0.15 | £0.45 | £0.75 |
| 16-17 ND | $0.25 | $0.75 | $1.25 | £0.15 | £0.45 | £0.75 |

18 ND with free Spiderman vs. Venom card sheet

	$0.25	$0.75	$1.25	£0.15	£0.45	£0.75
19-24 ND	$0.25	$0.75	$1.25	£0.15	£0.45	£0.75
25 ND 48pgs	$0.30	$0.90	$1.50	£0.20	£0.60	£1.00
26-30 ND	$0.25	$0.75	$1.25	£0.15	£0.45	£0.75

31 ND upgraded paper stock begins

| | $0.25 | $0.75 | $1.25 | £0.15 | £0.45 | £0.75 |
| 32 ND | $0.25 | $0.75 | $1.25 | £0.15 | £0.45 | £0.75 |

33 ND Doom vs. Ravage

| | $0.25 | $0.75 | $1.25 | £0.15 | £0.45 | £0.75 |
| Title Value: | $8.35 | $25.05 | $41.75 | £5.05 | £15.15 | £25.25 |

RAVENS & RAINBOWS
Pacific,OS; 1 1983
1 ND Jeff Jones reprints

| | $0.30 | $0.90 | $1.50 | £0.20 | £0.60 | £1.00 |
| Title Value: | $0.30 | $0.90 | $1.50 | £0.20 | £0.60 | £1.00 |

RAVER
Malibu,MS; 1 Apr 1993-3 Jun 1993
1 Walter Koenig ("Chekov" in Star Trek) script begins, foil-enhanced "oil-slick" cover; Direct Sales Edition

	$0.50	$1.50	$2.50	£0.30	£0.90	£1.50
1 Newsstand edition	$0.40	$1.20	$2.00	£0.25	£0.75	£1.25
2-3	$0.40	$1.20	$2.00	£0.25	£0.75	£1.25
Title Value:	$1.70	$5.10	$8.50	£1.05	£3.15	£5.25

Note: all Non-Distributed on the news-stands in the U.K.

RAVER, WALTER KOENIG'S
Millennium; 0 Dec 1994; 1 Nov 1994
0 ND (Dec 1994) story continues from issue #1

| | $0.40 | $1.20 | $2.00 | £0.25 | £0.75 | £1.25 |
| 1 ND | $0.40 | $1.20 | $2.00 | £0.25 | £0.75 | £1.25 |

1 ND Deluxe Edition with foil cover designed by Walter Koenig

| | $0.50 | $1.50 | $2.50 | £0.30 | £0.90 | £1.50 |
| Title Value: | $1.30 | $3.90 | $6.50 | £0.80 | £2.40 | £4.00 |

RAWHIDE KID
Atlas/Marvel Comics Group; 17 Aug 1960-151 May 1979
(previous issues ND)
17 origin, Jack Kirby art

| | $20.00 | $60.00 | $120.00 | £13.00 | £40.00 | £80.00 |

18-20 rare in the U.K.

| | $10.00 | $30.00 | $60.00 | £6.50 | £20.00 | £40.00 |

21-22 scarce in the U.K.

| | $9.00 | $28.00 | $55.00 | £5.75 | £17.50 | £35.00 |

23 scarce in the U.K. origin retold by Jack Kirby

| | $16.50 | $50.00 | $100.00 | £11.50 | £35.00 | £70.00 |

24-30 scarce in the U.K.

| | $9.00 | $28.00 | $55.00 | £5.75 | £17.50 | £35.00 |
| 31-39 | $7.50 | $22.50 | $45.00 | £5.00 | £15.00 | £30.00 |

40 Two-Gun Kid X-over

	$7.50	$22.50	$45.00	£5.00	£15.00	£30.00
41-42	$6.25	$18.50	$37.50	£4.15	£12.50	£25.00
43 rare in the U.K.	$6.25	$18.50	$37.50	£5.00	£15.00	£30.00
44	$6.25	$18.50	$37.50	£4.15	£12.50	£25.00
45 origin retold	$6.25	$18.50	$37.50	£4.15	£12.50	£25.00
46 Toth art	$4.15	$12.50	$25.00	£2.50	£7.50	£15.00
47-50	$4.15	$12.50	$25.00	£2.50	£7.50	£15.00
51-68	$4.50	$13.50	$22.50	£2.80	£8.25	£14.00
69-70 ND	$4.50	$13.50	$22.50	£3.00	£9.00	£15.00
71-74 ND	$3.00	$9.00	$15.00	£2.00	£6.00	£10.00
75-78	$2.50	$7.50	$12.50	£1.60	£4.80	£8.00

79 Williamson reprints

| | $2.50 | $7.50 | $12.50 | £1.60 | £4.80 | £8.00 |
| 80-85 | $2.50 | $7.50 | $12.50 | £1.60 | £4.80 | £8.00 |

86 Williamson reprints

	$2.00	$6.00	$10.00	£1.20	£3.60	£6.00
87-88	$2.00	$6.00	$10.00	£1.20	£3.60	£6.00
89-92 ND	$2.00	$6.00	$10.00	£1.30	£3.90	£6.50
93 ND 52pgs	$2.50	$7.50	$12.50	£1.40	£4.20	£7.00
94	$2.00	$6.00	$10.00	£1.20	£3.60	£6.00

95 ND Williamson reprint

	$2.00	$6.00	$10.00	£1.30	£3.90	£6.50
96-99	$2.00	$6.00	$10.00	£1.20	£3.60	£6.00
100	$2.50	$7.50	$12.50	£1.60	£4.80	£8.00
101-110	$1.20	$3.60	$6.00	£0.80	£2.40	£4.00

111 ND Williamson reprint

	$1.20	$3.60	$6.00	£0.80	£2.40	£4.00
112-151	$1.20	$3.60	$6.00	£0.70	£2.10	£3.50
Title Value:	$496.20	$1497.10	$2766.00	£317.75	£956.00	£1779.50

Note: Kirby art in 17-32, 34, 42, 43. Most later issues are entirely reprint.

RAWHIDE KID (2ND SERIES)
Marvel Comics Group,MS; 1 Aug 1985-4 Nov 1985

| 1-4 ND | $0.25 | $0.75 | $1.25 | £0.15 | £0.45 | £0.75 |
| Title Value: | $1.00 | $3.00 | $5.00 | £0.60 | £1.80 | £3.00 |

RAWHIDE KID ANNUAL
Marvel Comics Group; 1 Sep 1971
1 ND scarce in the U.K. 72pgs, all reprint

| | $1.50 | $4.50 | $7.50 | £1.00 | £3.00 | £5.00 |
| Title Value: | $1.50 | $4.50 | $7.50 | £1.00 | £3.00 | £5.00 |

RAY
DC Comics,MS; 1 Feb 1992-6 Jul 1992
1 Joe Quesada art begins

	$1.00	$3.00	$5.00	£0.70	£2.10	£3.50
2-3	$0.60	$1.80	$3.00	£0.40	£1.20	£2.00
4-6	$0.50	$1.50	$2.50	£0.30	£0.90	£1.50
Title Value:	$3.70	$11.10	$18.50	£2.40	£7.20	£12.00

The Ray: In A Blaze of Power (May 1994) Trade paperback reprints
mini-series with new cover by Joe Quesada and Brian Stelfreeze

| | | | | £1.30 | £3.90 | £6.50 |

RAY (2ND SERIES)
DC Comics; 0 Oct 1994; 1 May 1994-present
0 (Oct 1994) Zero Hour X-over, origin retold

| | $0.40 | $1.20 | $2.00 | £0.25 | £0.75 | £1.25 |

1 Howard Porter and Robert Jones art, Christopher Priest script, Joe Quesada cover

| | $0.40 | $1.20 | $2.00 | £0.25 | £0.75 | £1.25 |

1 ND Collector's Edition, gold foil embossed cover by Joe Quesada

| | $0.60 | $1.80 | $3.00 | £0.40 | £1.20 | £2.00 |
| 2-5 | $0.40 | $1.20 | $2.00 | £0.25 | £0.75 | £1.25 |

6-7 Black Canary appears

| | $0.40 | $1.20 | $2.00 | £0.25 | £0.75 | £1.25 |

8 Lobo appears

	$0.40	$1.20	$2.00	£0.25	£0.75	£1.25
9-15	$0.40	$1.20	$2.00	£0.25	£0.75	£1.25
16-17	$0.45	$1.35	$2.25	£0.30	£0.90	£1.50

18-19 Underworld Unleashed tie-in

| | $0.45 | $1.35 | $2.25 | £0.30 | £0.90 | £1.50 |

20-21 Black Condor guest-stars

	$0.45	$1.35	$2.25	£0.30	£0.90	£1.50
22	$0.45	$1.35	$2.25	£0.30	£0.90	£1.50
Title Value:	$10.15	$30.45	$50.75	£6.50	£19.50	£32.50

RAY ANNUAL, THE
DC Comics; 1 Jun 1995-present

| 1 64pgs, Year One | $0.80 | $2.40 | $4.00 | £0.50 | £1.50 | £2.50 |
| Title Value: | $0.80 | $2.40 | $4.00 | £0.50 | £1.50 | £2.50 |

RAY BRADBURY COMICS
Topps,MS; 1 Apr 1993-5 Aug 1993
1 pre-bagged with 3 trading cards, all-dinasaur issue with work by Richard Corben and Al Williamson

| | $0.60 | $1.80 | $3.00 | £0.40 | £1.20 | £2.00 |

2 pre-bagged with 3 trading cards, all-horror issue with work by Sean Phillips

| | $0.60 | $1.80 | $3.00 | £0.40 | £1.20 | £2.00 |

3 pre-bagged with 3 trading cards, all-dinasaur issue; Jurassic Park preview

| | $0.60 | $1.80 | $3.00 | £0.40 | £1.20 | £2.00 |

4 pre-bagged with 3 trading cards, all-Mars Attacks issue; Jurassic Park preview

| | $0.60 | $1.80 | $3.00 | £0.40 | £1.20 | £2.00 |

5 pre-bagged with 3 trading cards

| | $0.60 | $1.80 | $3.00 | £0.40 | £1.20 | £2.00 |
| Title Value: | $3.00 | $9.00 | $15.00 | £2.00 | £6.00 | £10.00 |

Note: all Non-Distributed on the news-stands in the U.K.

RAY BRADBURY COMICS SPECIAL: TALES OF HORROR
Topps,OS; 1 May 1994
1 ND adaptations of Bradbury horror stories, Kelley Jones cover

| | $0.40 | $1.20 | $2.00 | £0.25 | £0.75 | £1.25 |
| Title Value: | $0.40 | $1.20 | $2.00 | £0.25 | £0.75 | £1.25 |

RAY BRADBURY COMICS SPECIAL: THE ILLUSTRATED MAN
Topps,OS; 1 Apr 1994
1 ND Ray Bradbury stories adapted by Guy Davis, P. Craig Russell and Michael Lark; foil etched cover

| | $0.60 | $1.80 | $3.00 | £0.40 | £1.20 | £2.00 |
| Title Value: | $0.60 | $1.80 | $3.00 | £0.40 | £1.20 | £2.00 |

RAY BRADBURY'S MARTIAN CHRONICLES SPECIAL EDITION
Topps,OS; 1 Jun 1994
1 ND adaptations of Bradbury's Martian Chronicles; foreword by Mike Kaluta, cover by Jim Steranko

VERY GENERAL PERCENTAGE CONVERSION CHART WHICH MAY BE USED TO CALCULATE LOW AND INBETWEEN GRADES:

	$Good	$Fine	$N.Mint	£Good	£Fine	£N.Mint
	$0.40	$1.20	$2.00	£0.25	£0.75	£1.25
Title Value:	$0.40	$1.20	$2.00	£0.25	£0.75	£1.25

RAZOR
London Night Studios; ½ Apr 1995; 0 May 1992; 1 Sep 1992-present

	$Good	$Fine	$N.Mint	£Good	£Fine	£N.Mint
½ ND 16pgs Joseph Linsner cover art, produced with Fan Magazine; 1st appearance of Poison; colour	$2.50	$7.50	$12.50	£1.50	£4.50	£7.50
0 ND Direct Market Edition (May 1992), 1st appearance of Razor	$13.00	$39.00	$65.00	£10.00	£30.00	£50.00
0 ND 2nd print (Aug 1992)	$0.80	$2.40	$4.00	£0.50	£1.50	£2.50
0 ND London Night Special Edition (May 1995) – features the first Razor story, re-drawn by Richard Pollard; black and white	$0.80	$2.40	$4.00	£0.50	£1.50	£2.50
1 ND Everett Hartsoe script begins; black and white	$11.00	$33.00	$55.00	£8.00	£24.00	£40.00
1 2nd printing ND, photo co ver	$2.00	$6.00	$10.00	£1.50	£4.50	£7.50
2 ND	$5.00	$15.00	$25.00	£3.00	£9.00	£15.00
2 ND Limited Edition – red and blue cover variants	$6.00	$18.00	$30.00	£4.00	£12.00	£20.00
2 ND Platinum Edition – no price box on cover	$6.00	$18.00	$30.00	£4.00	£12.00	£20.00
3 ND Jim Balent cover	$3.00	$9.00	$15.00	£2.00	£6.00	£10.00
3 ND Limited Edition with poster	$4.00	$12.00	$20.00	£2.50	£7.50	£12.50
4 ND Tim Vigil cover	$1.20	$3.60	$6.00	£0.80	£2.40	£4.00
4 ND Limited Edition with poster	$1.20	$3.60	$6.00	£0.80	£2.40	£4.00
5 ND Joseph Michael Linsner cover art; Achilles Storm 4 page preview	$2.50	$7.50	$12.50	£1.50	£4.50	£7.50
5 Platinum edition ND	$4.00	$12.00	$20.00	£2.50	£7.50	£12.50
6 ND origin Razor	$1.20	$3.60	$6.00	£0.80	£2.40	£4.00
7-9 ND	$1.20	$3.60	$6.00	£0.80	£2.40	£4.00
10 ND 1st appearance of Stryke; ties into Razor: The Suffering	$1.20	$3.60	$6.00	£0.80	£2.40	£4.00
11-12 ND more of Razor's origin revealed	$0.60	$1.80	$3.00	£0.40	£1.20	£2.00
12 ND Collector's Edition (Nov 1995) – red foil embossed cover	$0.80	$2.40	$4.00	£0.50	£1.50	£2.50
13 ND	$0.60	$1.80	$3.00	£0.40	£1.20	£2.00
14 ND Kevin Sharpe cover	$0.60	$1.80	$3.00	£0.40	£1.20	£2.00
15 ND title becomes Razor Uncut	$0.60	$1.80	$3.00	£0.40	£1.20	£2.00
16 ND Interview with Death story	$0.60	$1.80	$3.00	£0.40	£1.20	£2.00
17 ND	$0.60	$1.80	$3.00	£0.40	£1.20	£2.00
Title Value:	$74.00	$222.00	$370.00	£50.40	£151.20	£252.00

RAZOR AND SHI SPECIAL
London Night Studios;OS; 1 Aug 1994

	$Good	$Fine	$N.Mint	£Good	£Fine	£N.Mint
1 ND reprints Razor Annual #1 with new artwork and pin-ups	$1.50	$4.50	$7.50	£1.00	£3.00	£5.00
1 ND Platinum Edition, available to retailers for every 10 copies ordered of the above	$1.60	$4.80	$8.00	£1.20	£3.60	£6.00
Title Value:	$3.10	$9.30	$15.50	£2.20	£6.60	£11.00

RAZOR ANNUAL
London Night Studios; 1 1993-present

1 ND 1st appearance of Shi; black and white

	$Good	$Fine	$N.Mint	£Good	£Fine	£N.Mint
	$8.00	$24.00	$40.00	£5.00	£15.00	£25.00
1 Gold Edition, ND 1200 copies printed						
	$8.50	$26.00	$42.50	£5.50	£16.50	£27.50
2 ND more facts about origin; black and white						
	$0.90	$2.70	$4.50	£0.60	£1.80	£3.00
Title Value:	$17.40	$52.70	$87.00	£11.10	£33.30	£55.50

RAZOR SWIMSUIT SPECIAL
London Night Studios,OS; 1 Apr 1995

	$Good	$Fine	$N.Mint	£Good	£Fine	£N.Mint
1 ND pin-ups by Bill Tucci, Everette Hartsoe, Kevin Taylor and others	$0.70	$2.10	$3.50	£0.50	£1.50	£2.50
Title Value:	$0.70	$2.10	$3.50	£0.50	£1.50	£2.50

RAZOR VS. DARK ANGEL
London Night Studios/Boneyard Press,OS; 1 Oct 1994

	$Good	$Fine	$N.Mint	£Good	£Fine	£N.Mint
1 ND reprints The Final Nail #1 plus new art and new ending; pre-bagged with death certificate (randomly inserted)	$1.00	$3.00	$5.00	£0.70	£2.10	£3.50
Title Value:	$1.00	$3.00	$5.00	£0.70	£2.10	£3.50

RAZOR VS. DARK ANGEL TO THE DEATH
Boneyard Press,OS; nn Jun 1995

	$Good	$Fine	$N.Mint	£Good	£Fine	£N.Mint
nn ND reprints Razor vs. Dark Angel with new pages, computer colours and new Kyle Hotz cover; pre-bagged	$0.60	$1.80	$3.00	£0.40	£1.20	£2.00
Title Value:	$0.60	$1.80	$3.00	£0.40	£1.20	£2.00

RAZOR/DARK ANGEL: THE FINAL NAIL
London Night Studios/Boneyard Press; 1 1994-2 1994

	$Good	$Fine	$N.Mint	£Good	£Fine	£N.Mint
1-2 ND inter company X-over	$0.70	$2.10	$3.50	£0.50	£1.50	£2.50
Title Value:	$1.40	$4.20	$7.00	£1.00	£3.00	£5.00

RAZOR: BURN
London Night Studios; 1 Dec 1994-5 Jul 1995

	$Good	$Fine	$N.Mint	£Good	£Fine	£N.Mint
1 ND Everette Hartsoe script, Mike Taylor art; black and white	$1.00	$3.00	$5.00	£0.70	£2.10	£3.50
1 ND Commemorative Edition - signed & limited to 3000 copies with certificate of authenticity	$2.50	$7.50	$12.50	£1.50	£4.50	£7.50
2 ND Everette Hartsoe script, Mike Taylor art; black and white	$0.70	$2.10	$3.50	£0.50	£1.50	£2.50
2 ND Platinum Edition	$2.50	$7.50	$12.50	£1.50	£4.50	£7.50
3-4 ND Everette Hartsoe script, Slick art; black and white	$0.70	$2.10	$3.50	£0.50	£1.50	£2.50
5 ND Everette Hartsoe script, Mike Wolfer art; black and white	$0.70	$2.10	$3.50	£0.50	£1.50	£2.50
Title Value:	$8.80	$26.40	$44.00	£5.70	£17.10	£28.50

RAZOR: FLESH & BLOOD CONVENTION BOOK
London Night Studios,OS; nn Oct 1994

	$Good	$Fine	$N.Mint	£Good	£Fine	£N.Mint
nn ND pin-up book with photo cover; 5,000 copies signed and numbered	$1.60	$4.80	$8.00	£1.20	£3.60	£6.00
Title Value:	$1.60	$4.80	$8.00	£1.20	£3.60	£6.00

RAZOR: THE SUFFERING
London Night Studios,MS; 1 Jun 1994-3 Sep 1994

	$Good	$Fine	$N.Mint	£Good	£Fine	£N.Mint
1 ND Everette Hartsoe script and art; black and white	$0.70	$2.10	$3.50	£0.50	£1.50	£2.50
1 ND The Director's Cut; reprints issue #1 with some new art and new cover by Everette Hartsoe to celebrate publisher's third year	$0.70	$2.10	$3.50	£0.50	£1.50	£2.50
2-3 ND Everette Hartsoe script and art; black and white	$0.70	$2.10	$3.50	£0.50	£1.50	£2.50
Title Value:	$2.80	$8.40	$14.00	£2.00	£6.00	£10.00

RAZORLINE: THE FIRST CUT
Marvel Comics Group,OS; 1 Sep 1993

	$Good	$Fine	$N.Mint	£Good	£Fine	£N.Mint
1 previews of Hyperkind, Ectokid, Hokum & Hex and Saint Sinner; Clive Barker interview	$0.30	$0.90	$1.50	£0.20	£0.60	£1.00

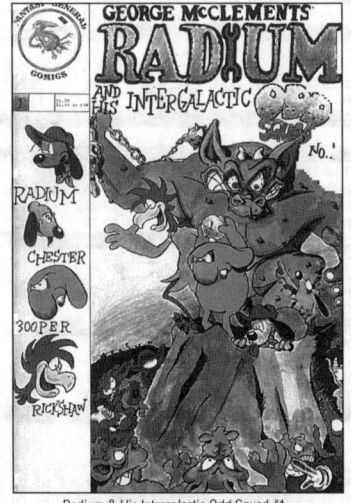

Radium & His Intergalactic Odd Squad #1

Ragman (1st) #2

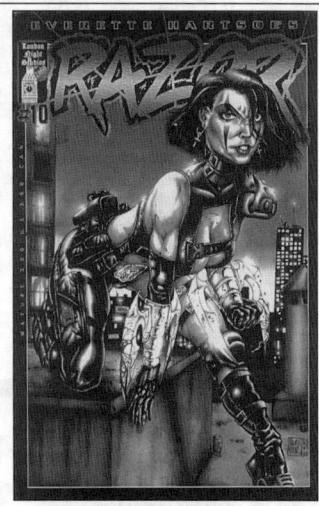

Razor #10

MINT = 100% / NEAR MINT (inc. +/-) = 90–99% / VERY FINE (inc. +/-) = 75–89% / FINE (inc. +/-) = 55–74%
VERY GOOD (inc. +/-) = 35–54% / GOOD (inc. +/-) = 15–34% / FAIR = 5–14% / POOR = 1–4%

511

	$Good	$Fine	$N.Mint	£Good	£Fine	£N.Mint
Title Value:	$0.30	$0.90	$1.50	£0.20	£0.60	£1.00

RE-ANIMATOR
Adventure,MS; 1 Oct 1991-3 Dec 1991
1 ND based on film, colour, Dave Dorman painted covers

	$Good	$Fine	$N.Mint	£Good	£Fine	£N.Mint
	$0.40	$1.20	$2.00	£0.25	£0.75	£1.25
2-3 ND	$0.40	$1.20	$2.00	£0.25	£0.75	£1.25
Title Value:	$1.20	$3.60	$6.00	£0.75	£2.25	£3.75

RE-ANIMATOR, DAWN OF THE
Adventure,MS; 1 Mar 1992-4 Jun 1992
1-4 ND prequel based on film

	$0.40	$1.20	$2.00	£0.25	£0.75	£1.25
Title Value:	$1.60	$4.80	$8.00	£1.00	£3.00	£5.00

RE-ANIMATOR: TALES OF HERBERT WEST
Adventure,OS; 1 Dec 1991
1 ND 48pgs, squarebound, six stories of H.P. Lovecraft

	$0.70	$2.10	$3.50	£0.50	£1.50	£2.50
Title Value:	$0.70	$2.10	$3.50	£0.50	£1.50	£2.50

REACTOMAN
B-Movie; 1 Feb 1987-3 Jun 1987

1-3 ND	$0.30	$0.90	$1.50	£0.20	£0.60	£1.00
Title Value:	$0.90	$2.70	$4.50	£0.60	£1.80	£3.00

REAGAN'S RAIDERS
Solson Productions; 1-3 1986
1-3 ND Rich Buckler art

	$0.25	$0.75	$1.25	£0.15	£0.45	£0.75
Title Value:	$0.75	$2.25	$3.75	£0.45	£1.35	£2.25

REAL GHOSTBUSTERS 3-D HALLOWEEN SPECIAL
Now Comics,OS; 1 Dec 1992
1 ND pre-bagged with 3-D glasses (25% less without glasses)

	$0.40	$1.20	$2.00	£0.25	£0.75	£1.25
Title Value:	$0.40	$1.20	$2.00	£0.25	£0.75	£1.25

REAL GHOSTBUSTERS 3D SLIMER SPECIAL
Now Comics,OS; 1 Jul 1993
1 ND includes 3-D glasses (25% less without glasses)

	$0.40	$1.20	$2.00	£0.25	£0.75	£1.25
Title Value:	$0.40	$1.20	$2.00	£0.25	£0.75	£1.25

REAL GHOSTBUSTERS SUPER 3-D SPECIAL
Now Comics,OS; 1 Oct 1991
1 ND pre-bagged with 3-D glasses (25% less without glasses)

	$0.40	$1.20	$2.00	£0.25	£0.75	£1.25
Title Value:	$0.40	$1.20	$2.00	£0.25	£0.75	£1.25

REAL GHOSTBUSTERS, THE
Now Comics; 1 Jun 1988-28 1990
1-8 ND scarce in the U.K.

	$0.40	$1.20	$2.00	£0.25	£0.75	£1.25
9-10 ND Comics Code on cover	$0.40	$1.20	$2.00	£0.25	£0.75	£1.25
11-28 ND Comics Code on cover	$0.30	$0.90	$1.50	£0.20	£0.60	£1.00
Title Value:	$9.40	$28.20	$47.00	£6.10	£18.30	£30.50

REAL GHOSTBUSTERS, THE (2ND SERIES)
Now Comics; 1 Nov 1991-8 1992

1-8 ND	$0.30	$0.90	$1.50	£0.20	£0.60	£1.00
Title Value:	$2.40	$7.20	$12.00	£1.60	£4.80	£8.00

REAL WAR STORIES
Eclipse; 1 Jul 1987; 2 Dec 1990
1 ND 48pgs, Alan Moore script, Bolland, Bissette, Totleben art; some copies have cutting defects on centre-fold, colour

	$0.60	$1.80	$3.00	£0.40	£1.20	£2.00
1 2nd printing ND	$0.55	$1.65	$2.75	£0.35	£1.05	£1.75

2 ND 48pgs, features work by Sienkiewicz, Badger, Motter, cover by Gulacy, colour

	$0.60	$1.80	$3.00	£0.40	£1.20	£2.00
Title Value:	$1.75	$5.25	$8.75	£1.15	£3.45	£5.75

REALM HANDBOOK, THE
Caliber Press,OS; 1 Sep 1993
1 ND complete reference work on the world of Realm

	$0.50	$1.50	$2.50	£0.30	£0.90	£1.50
Title Value:	$0.50	$1.50	$2.50	£0.30	£0.90	£1.50

REALM OF THE DEAD
Caliber Press,MS; 1 Aug 1993-3 Oct 1993
1 ND Chris Morea art, black and white; cover A featuring Realm characters

	$0.50	$1.50	$2.50	£0.30	£0.90	£1.50

1 ND Chris Morea art, black and white; cover B featuring Deadworld characters

	$0.50	$1.50	$2.50	£0.30	£0.90	£1.50
2 ND	$0.50	$1.50	$2.50	£0.30	£0.90	£1.50

2 ND Limited Edition – 2,500 copies, signed and embossed stamped

	$0.60	$1.80	$3.00	£0.40	£1.20	£2.00
3 ND	$0.50	$1.50	$2.50	£0.30	£0.90	£1.50

3 ND Limited Edition – 2,500 copies, signed and embossed stamped

	$0.60	$1.80	$3.00	£0.40	£1.20	£2.00
Title Value:	$3.20	$9.60	$16.00	£2.00	£6.00	£10.00

Realm of the Dead Graphic Novel (Dec 1994)
reprints mini-series plus free copy of Deadworld Collection that reprints Deadworld #1-7

				£2.00	£6.00	£10.00

REALM, SAGA OF THE
Caliber Press; 1 Dec 1992-5 1993
1 ND reprints of Realm begin

	$0.40	$1.20	$2.00	£0.25	£0.75	£1.25
2-5 ND	$0.40	$1.20	$2.00	£0.25	£0.75	£1.25
Title Value:	$2.00	$6.00	$10.00	£1.25	£3.75	£6.25

REALM, THE
Arrow/Innovation/Caliber; 1 1986-24 1992

1 ND black and white begins

	$0.60	$1.80	$3.00	£0.40	£1.20	£2.00
2-3 ND	$0.50	$1.50	$2.50	£0.30	£0.90	£1.50

4 ND 1st Deadworld story (see Caliber Presents #8)

	$1.00	$3.00	$5.00	£0.60	£1.80	£3.00
5-9 ND	$0.40	$1.20	$2.00	£0.25	£0.75	£1.25
10-13 ND	$0.30	$0.90	$1.50	£0.20	£0.60	£1.00

14 ND 1st Caliber issue ($1.75)

	$0.30	$0.90	$1.50	£0.20	£0.60	£1.00
15-19 ND	$0.30	$0.90	$1.50	£0.20	£0.60	£1.00

20-24 ND Daemonstorm story

	$0.30	$0.90	$1.50	£0.20	£0.60	£1.00
Title Value:	$9.10	$27.30	$45.50	£5.85	£17.55	£29.25
Book 1, reprints #1-4				£0.65	£1.95	£3.25
Book 2, reprints #5-8				£0.90	£2.70	£4.50
Book 3, reprints #9-12				£1.10	£3.30	£5.50
Book 4, reprints #13-15 plus others from Caliber Presents				£1.60	£4.80	£8.00

REALM, THE (2ND SERIES)
Caliber Press; 1 Jun 1993-present
1 ND glossy covers begin; black and white

	$0.40	$1.20	$2.00	£0.25	£0.75	£1.25
2-7 ND	$0.30	$0.90	$1.50	£0.20	£0.60	£1.00

7 ND Limited Edition – signed by one creator with trading card

	$0.50	$1.50	$2.50	£0.30	£0.90	£1.50
8-11 ND	$0.30	$0.90	$1.50	£0.20	£0.60	£1.00

12-13 ND David Mack cover

	$0.30	$0.90	$1.50	£0.20	£0.60	£1.00
Title Value:	$4.50	$13.50	$22.50	£2.95	£8.85	£14.75

REALM, THE: THE SHINDE IMAS
Caliber Press; 1 Sep 1993
1 ND pre-bagged with print, Guy Davis script and art

	$1.50	$4.50	$7.50	£0.90	£2.70	£4.50
Title Value:	$1.50	$4.50	$7.50	£0.90	£2.70	£4.50

REBEL SWORD PART ONE, THE
Dark Horse,MS; 1 Oct 1994-6 Mar 1995
1-6 ND 40pgs, Yoshikazu Yasuhiko script/art; black and white

	$0.60	$1.80	$3.00	£0.40	£1.20	£2.00
Title Value:	$3.60	$10.80	$18.00	£2.40	£7.20	£12.00

REBELS
Warp Graphics; 1 Feb 1995-present

1-8 ND	$0.50	$1.50	$2.50	£0.30	£0.90	£1.50
Title Value:	$4.00	$12.00	$20.00	£2.40	£7.20	£12.00

RED CIRCLE SORCERY
Red Circle (Archie); 6 Apr 1974-11 Feb 1975
(previously Chilling Adventures in Sorcery)

6 Morrow, Chaykin art	$0.40	$1.20	$2.00	£0.25	£0.75	£1.25
7 Morrow, Bruce Jones art; Morrow cover	$0.30	$0.90	$1.50	£0.20	£0.60	£1.00
8 Thorne, Morrow, Toth art; Morrow cover	$0.30	$0.90	$1.50	£0.20	£0.60	£1.00
9 Toth art; Morrow cover	$0.30	$0.90	$1.50	£0.20	£0.60	£1.00
10 Thorne, Morrow, Chaykin, Al Williamson art	$0.30	$0.90	$1.50	£0.20	£0.60	£1.00
11 rare in the U.K.	$0.40	$1.20	$2.00	£0.25	£0.75	£1.25
Title Value:	$2.00	$6.00	$10.00	£1.30	£3.90	£6.50

Note: all distributed on the news-stands in the U.K.

RED DOG
Eclipse; 1 Feb 1988
(Night Music #7)
1 ND Kipling adaptation, P. Craig Russell art

	$0.40	$1.20	$2.00	£0.25	£0.75	£1.25
Title Value:	$0.40	$1.20	$2.00	£0.25	£0.75	£1.25

RED DRAGON
Comico; 1 Oct 1995-present
1 ND Brian Azzarello script, Tony Akins art

	$0.40	$1.20	$2.00	£0.25	£0.75	£1.25
Title Value:	$0.40	$1.20	$2.00	£0.25	£0.75	£1.25

RED FOX
(see British section)

RED HEAT IN 3-D
Blackthorne; (3-D Series #45) 1 Jul 1988
1 ND based on Arnold Schwarzenegger film by Carolco; with bound-in 3-D glasses (25% less without glasses)

	$0.40	$1.20	$2.00	£0.25	£0.75	£1.25
Title Value:	$0.40	$1.20	$2.00	£0.25	£0.75	£1.25

RED MASK OF THE RIO GRANDE
AC Comics,MS; 1-3 1992
1-3 ND Red Mask reprints, art by Frank Bolle; 2,000 copies

	$0.50	$1.50	$2.50	£0.30	£0.90	£1.50
Title Value:	$1.50	$4.50	$7.50	£0.90	£2.70	£4.50

RED MOON
Millennium,MS; 1 Feb 1995-2 Apr 1995
1-2 ND black and white; wraparound cover by John Bolton

	$0.60	$1.80	$3.00	£0.40	£1.20	£2.00
Title Value:	$1.20	$3.60	$6.00	£0.80	£2.40	£4.00

RED RAVEN COMICS
Timely Comics; 1 Aug 1940
(see Human Torch #2)
1 scarce in the U.K. origin & 1st appearance of Red Raven; Jack Kirby cover art (1st cover he ever signed)

	$940.00	$2800.00	$8500.00	£610.00	£1825.00	£5500.00
Title Value:	$940.00	$2800.00	$8500.00	£610.00	£1825.00	£5500.00

TRADE PAPERBACKS, GRAPHIC NOVELS AND OTHER COLLECTIONS ARE PRICED IN POUNDS STERLING ONLY. CONVERT AT 1.5 FOR DOLLARS.

RED SONJA
Marvel Comics Group; 1 Jan 1977-15 May 1979
(see Conan, Marvel Feature, Savage Sword of Conan)

	$Good	$Fine	$N.Mint	£Good	£Fine	£N.Mint
1	$0.40	$1.20	$2.00	£0.25	£0.75	£1.25
2-11 ND	$0.30	$0.90	$1.50	£0.20	£0.60	£1.00
12-14 Brunner cover	$0.30	$0.90	$1.50	£0.20	£0.60	£1.00
15 ND Brunner cover	$0.40	$1.20	$2.00	£0.25	£0.75	£1.25
Title Value:	$4.70	$14.10	$23.50	£3.10	£9.30	£15.50

RED SONJA (2ND SERIES)
Marvel Comics Group; 1 Feb 1983-2 Mar 1983

	$Good	$Fine	$N.Mint	£Good	£Fine	£N.Mint
1-2 ND	$0.30	$0.90	$1.50	£0.20	£0.60	£1.00
Title Value:	$0.60	$1.80	$3.00	£0.40	£1.20	£2.00

RED SONJA (3RD SERIES)
Marvel Comics Group; 1 Aug 1983-13 1986

	$Good	$Fine	$N.Mint	£Good	£Fine	£N.Mint
1 ND	$0.30	$0.90	$1.50	£0.20	£0.60	£1.00
2-3 ND	$0.25	$0.75	$1.25	£0.15	£0.45	£0.75
4 ND	$0.30	$0.90	$1.50	£0.20	£0.60	£1.00
5-13	$0.25	$0.75	$1.25	£0.15	£0.45	£0.75
Title Value:	$3.35	$10.05	$16.75	£2.05	£6.15	£10.25

RED SONJA (4TH SERIES)
Marvel Comics Group,OS; 1 Dec 1995
1 ND Glenn Herdling script, Ken Lashley and Harry Candelario art; painted cover by Brothers Hildebrandt

	$Good	$Fine	$N.Mint	£Good	£Fine	£N.Mint
	$0.50	$1.50	$2.50	£0.30	£0.90	£1.50
Title Value:	$0.50	$1.50	$2.50	£0.30	£0.90	£1.50

RED SONJA IN 3-D
Blackthorne; (3-D Series #53) 1 Autumn 1988-2 1988
1-2 ND with bound-in 3-D glasses (25% less without glasses)

	$Good	$Fine	$N.Mint	£Good	£Fine	£N.Mint
	$0.50	$1.50	$2.50	£0.30	£0.90	£1.50
Title Value:	$1.00	$3.00	$5.00	£0.60	£1.80	£3.00

RED SONJA: SCAVENGER HUNT
Marvel Comics Group,OS; 1 Dec 1995

	$Good	$Fine	$N.Mint	£Good	£Fine	£N.Mint
1 ND 48pgs	$0.50	$1.50	$2.50	£0.30	£0.90	£1.50
Title Value:	$0.50	$1.50	$2.50	£0.30	£0.90	£1.50

RED SONJA: THE MOVIE
Marvel Comics Group,MS; 1 Nov 1985-2 Dec 1985
1-2 ND adapts film, Conan appears

	$Good	$Fine	$N.Mint	£Good	£Fine	£N.Mint
	$0.25	$0.75	$1.25	£0.15	£0.45	£0.75
Title Value:	$0.50	$1.50	$2.50	£0.30	£0.90	£1.50

RED TORNADO
DC Comics; 1 Jul 1985-4 Oct 1985
1 Infantino art, Justice League of America (inc. Superman and Batman) appear

	$Good	$Fine	$N.Mint	£Good	£Fine	£N.Mint
	$0.25	$0.75	$1.25	£0.15	£0.45	£0.75

2 Infantino art, Superman appears

	$Good	$Fine	$N.Mint	£Good	£Fine	£N.Mint
	$0.25	$0.75	$1.25	£0.15	£0.45	£0.75
3-4 Infantino art	$0.25	$0.75	$1.25	£0.15	£0.45	£0.75
Title Value:	$1.00	$3.00	$5.00	£0.60	£1.80	£3.00

RED TRAILS WEST
Millennium,MS; 1 Dec 1994-2 Feb 1995
1-2 ND Wendy Snow-Lang script, black and white

	$Good	$Fine	$N.Mint	£Good	£Fine	£N.Mint
	$0.50	$1.50	$2.50	£0.30	£0.90	£1.50
Title Value:	$1.00	$3.00	$5.00	£0.60	£1.80	£3.00

RED WOLF
Marvel Comics Group; 1 May 1972-9 Sep 1973
(see Avengers #80, Marvel Spotlight #1)

	$Good	$Fine	$N.Mint	£Good	£Fine	£N.Mint
1 ND scarce in the U.K.	$1.00	$3.00	$5.00	£0.50	£1.50	£2.50
2 ND scarce in the U.K. Gil Kane cover	$0.50	$1.50	$2.50	£0.30	£0.90	£1.50
3-4 ND scarce in the U.K.	$0.50	$1.50	$2.50	£0.30	£0.90	£1.50
5 ND scarce in the U.K. Gil Kane cover	$0.50	$1.50	$2.50	£0.30	£0.90	£1.50
6 ND scarce in the U.K.	$0.40	$1.20	$2.00	£0.25	£0.75	£1.25
7 ND scarce in the U.K. story moves to present day	$0.40	$1.20	$2.00	£0.25	£0.75	£1.25
8-9 ND scarce in the U.K.	$0.40	$1.20	$2.00	£0.25	£0.75	£1.25
Title Value:	$4.60	$13.80	$23.00	£2.70	£8.10	£13.50

REDBLADE
Dark Horse,MS; 1 Apr 1993-3 Jun 1993
1-3 ND Vince Garriano script and art

	$Good	$Fine	$N.Mint	£Good	£Fine	£N.Mint
	$0.50	$1.50	$2.50	£0.30	£0.90	£1.50
Title Value:	$1.50	$4.50	$7.50	£0.90	£2.70	£4.50

REESE'S PIECES
Eclipse,MS; 1,2 Oct 1985
1-2 ND Ralph Reese reprints

	$Good	$Fine	$N.Mint	£Good	£Fine	£N.Mint
	$0.40	$1.20	$2.00	£0.25	£0.75	£1.25
Title Value:	$0.80	$2.40	$4.00	£0.50	£1.50	£2.50

REGULATORS
Image; 1 Jun 1995-3 1995
1 ND Kurt Busiek script, Ron Randall and Dan Davis art

	$Good	$Fine	$N.Mint	£Good	£Fine	£N.Mint
	$0.50	$1.50	$2.50	£0.30	£0.90	£1.50
2-3 ND	$0.50	$1.50	$2.50	£0.30	£0.90	£1.50
Title Value:	$1.50	$4.50	$7.50	£0.90	£2.70	£4.50

REID FLEMING, WORLD'S TOUGHEST MILKMAN
David Boswell; 1 Oct 1980
(see Heartbreak Comics) (continued from David Boswell publications)

	$Good	$Fine	$N.Mint	£Good	£Fine	£N.Mint
1 1st printing, ND (Oct '80)	$1.00	$3.00	$5.00	£0.70	£2.10	£3.50
1 2nd printing, ND (Jul '85)	$0.70	$2.10	$3.50	£0.40	£1.20	£2.00
Title Value:	$1.70	$5.10	$8.50	£1.10	£3.30	£5.50

REID FLEMING, WORLD'S TOUGHEST MILKMAN VOLUME TWO
Eclipse; 1 Aug 1986-5 1987
1 ND comic size (4th print of original David Boswell comic)

	$Good	$Fine	$N.Mint	£Good	£Fine	£N.Mint
	$0.50	$1.50	$2.50	£0.30	£0.90	£1.50
1 2nd/3rd printing ND	$0.40	$1.20	$2.00	£0.25	£0.75	£1.25
2 ND	$0.40	$1.20	$2.00	£0.25	£0.75	£1.25
2 2nd/3rd printing ND	$0.40	$1.20	$2.00	£0.25	£0.75	£1.25
3-5 ND	$0.40	$1.20	$2.00	£0.25	£0.75	£1.25
Title Value:	$3.30	$9.90	$16.50	£2.05	£6.15	£10.25

REIGN OF THE DRAGON LORD
Eternity; 1,2 1986

	$Good	$Fine	$N.Mint	£Good	£Fine	£N.Mint
1-2 ND	$0.30	$0.90	$1.50	£0.20	£0.60	£1.00
Title Value:	$0.60	$1.80	$3.00	£0.40	£1.20	£2.00

REIKI WARRIORS
Heroic Publishing; 1 Aug 1993

	$Good	$Fine	$N.Mint	£Good	£Fine	£N.Mint
1 ND	$0.60	$1.80	$3.00	£0.40	£1.20	£2.00
Title Value:	$0.60	$1.80	$3.00	£0.40	£1.20	£2.00

REN & STIMPY
Marvel Comics Group, TV; 1 Dec 1992-present
1 ND pre-bagged, includes free-gift scratch and sniff "air-fouler" card; based on animated US TV series

	$Good	$Fine	$N.Mint	£Good	£Fine	£N.Mint
	$2.00	$6.00	$10.00	£2.50	£7.50	£12.50
2 ND	$1.50	$4.50	$7.50	£1.20	£3.60	£6.00
3 ND	$1.00	$3.00	$5.00	£1.00	£3.00	£5.00
4-5 ND	$0.70	$2.10	$3.50	£0.80	£2.40	£4.00
6-7 ND	$0.60	$1.80	$3.00	£0.40	£1.20	£2.00
8-10 ND	$0.50	$1.50	$2.50	£0.30	£0.90	£1.50
11-12 ND	$0.40	$1.20	$2.00	£0.25	£0.75	£1.25
13 ND Halloween issue	$0.40	$1.20	$2.00	£0.25	£0.75	£1.25
14-24 ND	$0.40	$1.20	$2.00	£0.25	£0.75	£1.25
25 ND die-cut cover	$0.60	$1.80	$3.00	£0.40	£1.20	£2.00
26-40 ND	$0.40	$1.20	$2.00	£0.25	£0.75	£1.25
Title Value:	$20.80	$62.40	$104.00	£15.65	£46.95	£78.25

Ren & Stimpy: Pick of the Litter (Jul 1993)

Trade paperback reprints issues #1-4 plus new material	£1.60	£4.80	£8.00

Ren & Stimpy: Running Joke (Nov 1993)

Trade paperback reprints issues #5-8 plus new material	£1.60	£4.80	£8.00

Ren & Stimpy: Don't Try This At Home

Trade paperback reprints issuies #9-12 plus new material	£1.70	£5.10	£8.50

Ren & Stimpy: Your Pals (Oct 1994)

Trade paperback reprints issues #13-16	£1.70	£5.10	£8.50

Ren & Stimpy: Seeck Little Monkey (Mar 1995)

Trade paperback reprints issues #17-20	£1.70	£5.10	£8.50

REN & STIMPY HOLIDAY SPECIAL
Marvel Comics Group,OS; 1 Feb 1995
1 ND reprints issues #3 and #15 plus new material

	$Good	$Fine	$N.Mint	£Good	£Fine	£N.Mint
	$0.60	$1.80	$3.00	£0.40	£1.20	£2.00
Title Value:	$0.60	$1.80	$3.00	£0.40	£1.20	£2.00

REN & STIMPY SPECIAL: AROUND THE WORLD IN A DAZE
Marvel Comics Group,OS; 1 Jan 1996

	$Good	$Fine	$N.Mint	£Good	£Fine	£N.Mint
1 ND 48pgs	$0.60	$1.80	$3.00	£0.40	£1.20	£2.00
Title Value:	$0.60	$1.80	$3.00	£0.40	£1.20	£2.00

REN & STIMPY SPECIAL: FANTASTIC FOURS
Marvel Comics Group,OS; 1 Jan 1995
1 ND 48pgs, Powdered Toast man appears

	$Good	$Fine	$N.Mint	£Good	£Fine	£N.Mint
	$0.60	$1.80	$3.00	£0.40	£1.20	£2.00
Title Value:	$0.60	$1.80	$3.00	£0.40	£1.20	£2.00

REN & STIMPY SPECIAL: HISTORY OF MUSIC
Marvel Comics Group,OS; 1 Oct 1995

	$Good	$Fine	$N.Mint	£Good	£Fine	£N.Mint
1 ND 48pgs	$0.60	$1.80	$3.00	£0.40	£1.20	£2.00
Title Value:	$0.60	$1.80	$3.00	£0.40	£1.20	£2.00

REN & STIMPY SPECIAL: VIRTUAL STUPIDITY
Marvel Comics Group,OS; 1 Jul 1995

	$Good	$Fine	$N.Mint	£Good	£Fine	£N.Mint
1 ND 48pgs	$0.60	$1.80	$3.00	£0.40	£1.20	£2.00
Title Value:	$0.60	$1.80	$3.00	£0.40	£1.20	£2.00

REN & STIMPY SUMMER JOBS SPECIAL
Marvel Comics Group,OS; 1 Jul 1994

	$Good	$Fine	$N.Mint	£Good	£Fine	£N.Mint
1 ND 48pgs	$0.60	$1.80	$3.00	£0.40	£1.20	£2.00
Title Value:	$0.60	$1.80	$3.00	£0.40	£1.20	£2.00

REN & STIMPY TIME AND SPACE SPECIAL
Marvel Comics Group,OS; 1 Oct 1994

	$Good	$Fine	$N.Mint	£Good	£Fine	£N.Mint
1 ND 48pgs	$0.60	$1.80	$3.00	£0.40	£1.20	£2.00
Title Value:	$0.60	$1.80	$3.00	£0.40	£1.20	£2.00

REN & STIMPY: POWDERED TOAST MAN
Marvel Comics Group,OS; 1 Apr 1994

	$Good	$Fine	$N.Mint	£Good	£Fine	£N.Mint
1 ND 48pgs	$0.60	$1.80	$3.00	£0.40	£1.20	£2.00
Title Value:	$0.60	$1.80	$3.00	£0.40	£1.20	£2.00

REN & STIMPY: POWDERED TOASTMAN'S CEREAL SERIAL SPECIAL
Marvel Comics Group,OS; 1 Apr 1995

	$Good	$Fine	$N.Mint	£Good	£Fine	£N.Mint
1 ND 48pgs	$0.60	$1.80	$3.00	£0.40	£1.20	£2.00
Title Value:	$0.60	$1.80	$3.00	£0.40	£1.20	£2.00

REN & STIMPY: RADIO DAZED & CONFUSED
Marvel Comics Group,OS; 1 Nov 1995
1 ND tie-in with Ren & Stimpy CD and cassette

	$Good	$Fine	$N.Mint	£Good	£Fine	£N.Mint
	$0.40	$1.20	$2.00	£0.25	£0.75	£1.25
Title Value:	$0.40	$1.20	$2.00	£0.25	£0.75	£1.25

	$Good	$Fine	$N.Mint	£Good	£Fine	£N.Mint		$Good	$Fine	$N.Mint	£Good	£Fine	£N.Mint

RENEGADE RABBIT
Printed Matter Comics; 1 Dec 1986-2 1987
1-2 ND 9.5" x 7" format (slightly smaller than normal comic size)

| | $0.30 | $0.90 | $1.50 | £0.20 | £0.60 | £1.00 |
| Title Value: | $0.60 | $1.80 | $3.00 | £0.40 | £1.20 | £2.00 |

RENEGADE ROMANCE
Renegade; 1 Jun 1987-2 1988
1 ND 64pgs, Mary Wilshire, DeStefano, Williamson art, G. Hernandez cover

| | $0.50 | $1.50 | $2.50 | £0.30 | £0.90 | £1.50 |

2 ND 64pgs, Mary Wilshire art, Steve Leialoha art, J. Hernandez cover

| | $0.50 | $1.50 | $2.50 | £0.30 | £0.90 | £1.50 |
| Title Value: | $1.00 | $3.00 | $5.00 | £0.60 | £1.80 | £3.00 |

RENFIELD
Caliber Press,MS; 1 Aug 1994-3 1995
1-3 ND black and white

| | $0.50 | $1.50 | $2.50 | £0.30 | £0.90 | £1.50 |
| Title Value: | $1.50 | $4.50 | $7.50 | £0.90 | £2.70 | £4.50 |

Renfield Graphic Novel (Sep 1995) collects six issue series £1.20 £3.60 £6.00
Note: series cancelled in comic book format after 3 issues. Caliber Press decided to issue the last three instalments as a graphic novel and they then decided to include the first three issues as one publication

REPTILICUS
Charlton; 1 Aug 1961-2 Oct 1961
(becomes Reptisaurus)
1 rare though distributed in the U.K. based on a "B" movie "The Beast from 20,000 Fathoms"

| | $12.50 | $39.00 | $90.00 | £8.50 | £26.00 | £60.00 |

2 scarce, distributed in the U.K.

| | $10.00 | $30.00 | $60.00 | £6.50 | £20.00 | £40.00 |
| Title Value: | $22.50 | $69.00 | $150.00 | £15.00 | £46.00 | £100.00 |

REPTISAURUS
Charlton; 3 Jan 1962-8 Dec 1962
3-8 distributed in the U.K.

	$5.25	$16.00	$32.50	£3.30	£10.00	£20.00
Title Value:	$31.50	$96.00	$195.00	£19.80	£60.00	£120.00
Special 1 (Summer 1963)				£1.40	£5.20	£7.00

RESCUERS DOWN UNDER GRAPHIC NOVEL, THE
Disney; nn Nov 1990
nn ND 64pgs, adaptation of film

| | $0.90 | $2.70 | $4.50 | £0.60 | £1.80 | £3.00 |
| Title Value: | $0.90 | $2.70 | $4.50 | £0.60 | £1.80 | £3.00 |

RESCUERS DOWN UNDER, THE
Disney,OS; 1 Aug 1991
1 ND 64pgs, adaptation of film

| | $0.90 | $2.70 | $4.50 | £0.60 | £1.80 | £3.00 |
| Title Value: | $0.90 | $2.70 | $4.50 | £0.60 | £1.80 | £3.00 |

RESIDENTS: FREAK SHOW
Dark Horse,OS; 1 Jun 1992
1 ND 80pgs, anthology featuring John Bolton, Dave McKean, Matt Howarth and Kyle Baker, cover by Charles Burns

| | $1.50 | $4.50 | $7.50 | £1.00 | £3.00 | £5.00 |
| Title Value: | $1.50 | $4.50 | $7.50 | £1.00 | £3.00 | £5.00 |

RESTAURANT AT THE END OF THE UNIVERSE, THE
DC Comics,MS; 1 Mar 1995-3 May 1995
(see Hitch-Hiker's Guide to the Galaxy)
1-3 ND John Carnell script, Steve Leialoha art. The second book of The Hitch-Hiker's Guide

| | $1.20 | $3.60 | $6.00 | £0.80 | £2.40 | £4.00 |
| Title Value: | $3.60 | $10.80 | $18.00 | £2.40 | £7.20 | £12.00 |

RETALIATOR, THE
Eclipse/FX Comix,MS; 1 Sep 1992-4 Dec 1992
1-4 ND based on film

| | $0.40 | $1.20 | $2.00 | £0.25 | £0.75 | £1.25 |
| Title Value: | $1.60 | $4.80 | $8.00 | £1.00 | £3.00 | £5.00 |

RETIEF
Adventure,MS; 1 Apr 1991-6 Sep 1991
1-6 ND $0.40 $1.20 $2.00 £0.25 £0.75 £1.25
Title Value: $2.40 $7.20 $12.00 £1.50 £4.50 £7.50
Retief Graphic Novel reprints issues #1-6, Bob Fugitake art £1.65 £4.95 £8.25

RETIEF (KEITH LAUMER'S...)
Mad Dog Graphics; 1 Apr 1987-6 Mar 1988
1-6 ND Bob Fugitake art, black and white

| | $0.40 | $1.20 | $2.00 | £0.25 | £0.75 | £1.25 |
| Title Value: | $2.40 | $7.20 | $12.00 | £1.50 | £4.50 | £7.50 |

Retief Graphic Novel (1990)
reprints issues #1-6 with new Bob Fugitake cover £1.65 £4.95 £8.25
Note: the above published by Apple Comics

RETIEF (KEITH LAUMER'S...) (2ND SERIES)
Adventure; 1 Dec 1989-6 May 1990
1-6 ND newsprint paper, black and white

| | $0.40 | $1.20 | $2.00 | £0.25 | £0.75 | £1.25 |
| Title Value: | $2.40 | $7.20 | $12.00 | £1.50 | £4.50 | £7.50 |

RETIEF AND THE WARLORDS
Eternity,MS; 1 Jan 1991-3 Mar 1991
1-3 ND black and white

| | $0.40 | $1.20 | $2.00 | £0.25 | £0.75 | £1.25 |
| Title Value: | $1.20 | $3.60 | $6.00 | £0.75 | £2.25 | £3.75 |

RETIEF OF THE C.D.T.
Mad Dog Graphics,OS; 1 1988
1 ND $0.40 $1.20 $2.00 £0.25 £0.75 £1.25
Title Value: $0.40 $1.20 $2.00 £0.25 £0.75 £1.25

RETIEF: GIANT KILLER
Adventure; 1 Dec 1991
1 ND $0.40 $1.20 $2.00 £0.25 £0.75 £1.25
Title Value: $0.40 $1.20 $2.00 £0.25 £0.75 £1.25

RETIEF: GRIME AND PUNISHMENT
Adventure,OS; 1 Nov 1991
1 ND $0.40 $1.20 $2.00 £0.25 £0.75 £1.25
Title Value: $0.40 $1.20 $2.00 £0.25 £0.75 £1.25

RETIEF: THE GARBAGE INVASION
Adventure,OS; 1 Oct 1991
1 ND $0.40 $1.20 $2.00 £0.25 £0.75 £1.25
Title Value: $0.40 $1.20 $2.00 £0.25 £0.75 £1.25

RETURN OF DR.FATE
(see Dr.Fate)

RETURN OF GORGO, THE
Charlton; 2 Summer 1963-3 Autumn 1964
(previously Gorgo's Revenge)
2-3 scarce, distributed in the U.K. Steve Ditko art

| | $7.50 | $22.50 | $45.00 | £5.00 | £15.00 | £30.00 |
| Title Value: | $15.00 | $45.00 | $90.00 | £10.00 | £30.00 | £60.00 |

RETURN OF KONGA, THE
Charlton; nn 1962
(becomes Konga's Revenge)
nn distributed in the U.K.

| | $8.00 | $24.00 | $56.00 | £6.00 | £18.00 | £36.00 |
| Title Value: | $8.00 | $24.00 | $56.00 | £6.00 | £18.00 | £36.00 |

RETURN OF LUM: URUSEI YATSURA, THE
Viz Communications,MS; 1 Dec 1994-8 Jul 1995
(see Lum)
1-8 ND 40pgs, Rumiko Takahashi; black and white

| | $0.60 | $1.80 | $3.00 | £0.40 | £1.20 | £2.00 |
| Title Value: | $4.80 | $14.40 | $24.00 | £3.20 | £9.60 | £16.00 |

Return of Lum Vol. 1 Graphic Novel (Mar 1995)
collection of self-contained stories £2.00 £6.00 £10.00

RETURN OF LUM: URUSEI YATSURA, THE (PART 2)
Viz Communications,MS; 1 Aug 1995-9 Apr 1996
1-9 ND Rumiko Takahashi script and art; black and white

| | $0.55 | $1.65 | $2.75 | £0.40 | £1.20 | £2.00 |
| Title Value: | $4.95 | $14.85 | $24.75 | £3.60 | £10.80 | £18.00 |

RETURN OF MEGATON MAN
Kitchen Sink; 1 Jul 1988-3 Sep 1988
(see Megaton Man)
1-3 ND $0.40 $1.20 $2.00 £0.25 £0.75 £1.25
Title Value: $1.20 $3.60 $6.00 £0.75 £2.25 £3.75

RETURN OF THE JEDI
Marvel Comics Group,MS Film; 1 Oct 1983-4 Jan 1984
1-4 ND adapts film, Williamson art

| | $0.40 | $1.20 | $2.00 | £0.25 | £0.75 | £1.25 |
| Title Value: | $1.60 | $4.80 | $8.00 | £1.00 | £3.00 | £5.00 |

RETURN OF THE NEW GODS
(see New Gods)

REVENGE OF THE PROWLER
Eclipse; 1 Feb 1988-4 Jun 1988
1 ND Tim Truman script, John K. Snyder III art begins

| | $0.40 | $1.20 | $2.00 | £0.25 | £0.75 | £1.25 |

2 ND Flexi-disk double-sided single attached (25% less if disc missing)

| | $0.40 | $1.50 | $2.50 | £0.30 | £0.90 | £1.50 |

3 ND $0.40 $1.20 $2.00 £0.25 £0.75 £1.25
4 ND continues in Total Eclipse #1

| | $0.40 | $1.20 | $2.00 | £0.25 | £0.75 | £1.25 |
| Title Value: | $1.70 | $5.10 | $8.50 | £1.05 | £3.15 | £5.25 |

REVENGERS
Continuity; 1 Apr 1985-6 1989
1 Neal Adams cover, script, pencil layouts and inks; origin and 1st appearance The Ultimate Man Megalith

| | $0.40 | $1.20 | $2.00 | £0.25 | £0.75 | £1.25 |

2 1st appearance Armor and The Silver Streak, Neal Adams cover, script, pencil layouts and inks; Megalith appears

| | $0.40 | $1.20 | $2.00 | £0.25 | £0.75 | £1.25 |

3 Neal Adams script, cover and pencils; features Megalith, Armor and The Silver Streak

| | $0.40 | $1.20 | $2.00 | £0.25 | £0.75 | £1.25 |

4 Neal Adams part script and pencils; features Megalith, Armor and The Silver Streak; 1st appearance The New Clear Warlock

| | $0.40 | $1.20 | $2.00 | £0.25 | £0.75 | £1.25 |

5 Neal Adams part script and pencils; features Megalith and New Clear Warlock

| | $0.40 | $1.20 | $2.00 | £0.25 | £0.75 | £1.25 |

6 Neal Adams part script, Larry Stroman pencils and cover

| | $0.40 | $1.20 | $2.00 | £0.25 | £0.75 | £1.25 |
| Title Value: | $2.40 | $7.20 | $12.00 | £1.50 | £4.50 | £7.50 |

Note: all Non-Distributed on the news-stands in the U.K.

REVENGERS SPECIAL
Continuity,MS; 1 Jul 1992-2 Aug 1992
1 ND 48pgs, Neal Adams story, features pre-X-Factor Larry Stroman art, previews Hybrids series

| | $0.60 | $1.80 | $3.00 | £0.40 | £1.20 | £2.00 |

1 2nd printing, ND (Nov 1993)

| | $0.50 | $1.50 | $2.50 | £0.30 | £0.90 | £1.50 |

2 ND 48pgs, Larry Stroman art, Neal Adams cover

| | $0.50 | $1.50 | $2.50 | £0.30 | £0.90 | £1.50 |
| Title Value: | $1.60 | $4.80 | $8.00 | £1.00 | £3.00 | £5.00 |

REVOLVER
Renegade; 1 Nov 1985-12 Oct 1986
1 Star Guider, Steve Ditko cover and part art, black and white (all issues)

| | $0.30 | $0.90 | $1.50 | £0.20 | £0.60 | £1.00 |

2 Star Guider, Steve Ditko part art

| | $0.30 | $0.90 | $1.50 | £0.20 | £0.60 | £1.00 |

3 Star Guider, Boyette cover

| | $0.30 | $0.90 | $1.50 | £0.20 | £0.60 | £1.00 |

	$Good	$Fine	$N.Mint	£Good	£Fine	£N.Mint
4 Fantastic Fables, Steve Ditko cover and part art						
	$0.30	$0.90	$1.50	£0.20	£0.60	£1.00
5 Fantastic Fables, Bissette cover	$0.30	$0.90	$1.50	£0.20	£0.60	£1.00
6 Fantastic Fables, Bissette cover						
	$0.30	$0.90	$1.50	£0.20	£0.60	£1.00
7-9 Steve Ditko cover						
	$0.30	$0.90	$1.50	£0.20	£0.60	£1.00
10	$0.30	$0.90	$1.50	£0.20	£0.60	£1.00
11 Carmine Infantino cover						
	$0.30	$0.90	$1.50	£0.20	£0.60	£1.00
12 Alex Toth cover	$0.30	$0.90	$1.50	£0.20	£0.60	£1.00
Title Value:	$3.60	$10.80	$18.00	£2.40	£7.20	£12.00

Note: all Non-Distributed on the news-stands in the U.K.

REVOLVER ANNUAL
Renegade; 1 Nov 1986

1 ND (issue #13 of Revolver) Alex Toth cover, Steve Ditko art featured plus checklist of all Revolver issue credits

	$Good	$Fine	$N.Mint	£Good	£Fine	£N.Mint
	$0.30	$0.90	$1.50	£0.20	£0.60	£1.00
Title Value:	$0.30	$0.90	$1.50	£0.20	£0.60	£1.00

REVOLVING DOORS
Blackthorne; 1 Oct 1986-3 Feb 1987

	$Good	$Fine	$N.Mint	£Good	£Fine	£N.Mint
1-3 ND	$0.30	$0.90	$1.50	£0.20	£0.60	£1.00
Title Value:	$0.90	$2.70	$4.50	£0.60	£1.80	£3.00
Graphic Novel (1987)				£0.50	£1.50	£2.50

REX THE WONDER DOG
National Periodical Publications; 1 Jan/Feb 1952-46 Sep/Oct 1959 (cover-date Nov)

(see DC Comics Presents #35)

	$Good	$Fine	$N.Mint	£Good	£Fine	£N.Mint
1 rare in the U.K., Toth art						
	$92.50	$280.00	$750.00	£62.50	£185.00	£500.00
2 rare in the U.K., Toth art						
	$52.50	$160.00	$375.00	£36.00	£105.00	£250.00
3 rare in the U.K., Toth art						
	$39.00	$115.00	$275.00	£26.00	£75.00	£180.00
4-5 very scarce in the U.K.						
	$29.00	$85.00	$200.00	£17.50	£52.50	£125.00
6-10 very scarce in the U.K.						
	$20.00	$60.00	$140.00	£13.50	£41.00	£95.00
11 very scarce in the U.K.						
	$23.50	$70.00	$165.00	£15.50	£47.00	£110.00
12-19 very scarce in the U.K.						
	$11.00	$34.00	$80.00	£7.75	£23.50	£55.00
20-30 very scarce in the U.K.						
	$9.25	$28.00	$65.00	£6.25	£19.00	£45.00
31-40 very scarce in the U.K.						
	$10.00	$31.00	$62.50	£7.00	£21.00	£42.50
41-45 very scarce in the U.K.						
	$10.00	$30.00	$60.00	£6.50	£20.00	£40.00
1st official distribution in the U.K.						
46 rare in the U.K.						
	$10.00	$30.00	$60.00	£6.50	£20.00	£40.00
Title Value:	$715.25	$2165.00	$5005.00	£482.25	£1449.00	£3365.00

RIBIT!
Comico,MS; 1 Jan 1989-4 Apr 1989

1-4 ND Frank Thorne Red Sonja-esque character/art in colour

	$Good	$Fine	$N.Mint	£Good	£Fine	£N.Mint
	$0.40	$1.20	$2.00	£0.25	£0.75	£1.25
Title Value:	$1.60	$4.80	$8.00	£1.00	£3.00	£5.00

RICH BUCKLER'S SECRETS OF DRAWING COMICS
Showcase Publications; 1-4 1986

1-4 ND black and white; all hints and tips for would-be comic artists

	$Good	$Fine	$N.Mint	£Good	£Fine	£N.Mint
	$0.15	$0.45	$0.75	£0.10	£0.35	£0.60
Title Value:	$0.60	$1.80	$3.00	£0.40	£1.40	£2.40

RICHARD DRAGON KUNG FU FIGHTER
DC Comics; 1 Apr/May 1975-18 Nov/Dec 1977

(see Brave and the Bold, DC Comics Presents #39)

	$Good	$Fine	$N.Mint	£Good	£Fine	£N.Mint
1	$0.40	$1.20	$2.00	£0.25	£0.75	£1.25
2 Jim Starlin art	$0.30	$0.90	$1.50	£0.20	£0.60	£1.00
3 Jack Kirby art	$0.25	$0.75	$1.25	£0.15	£0.45	£0.75
4 Wood inks	$0.25	$0.75	$1.25	£0.15	£0.45	£0.75
5 ND Wood inks	$0.25	$0.75	$1.25	£0.20	£0.60	£1.00
6-7 Wood inks	$0.25	$0.75	$1.25	£0.15	£0.45	£0.75
8 scarce in the U.K. Wood inks						
	$0.25	$0.75	$1.25	£0.20	£0.60	£1.00
9	$0.25	$0.75	$1.25	£0.15	£0.45	£0.75
10 scarce in the U.K.						
	$0.25	$0.75	$1.25	£0.20	£0.60	£1.00
11-18	$0.25	$0.75	$1.25	£0.15	£0.45	£0.75
Title Value:	$4.70	$14.10	$23.50	£3.00	£9.00	£15.00

RICHIE RICH
Harvey; 1 Nov 1960-254 Jan 1991

	$Good	$Fine	$N.Mint	£Good	£Fine	£N.Mint
1 scarce in the U.K.						
	$150.00	$450.00	$1050.00	£100.00	£300.00	£700.00
2 scarce in the U.K.						
	$65.00	$200.00	$400.00	£46.00	£135.00	£275.00
3-5 scarce in the U.K.						
	$38.00	$110.00	$225.00	£25.00	£75.00	£150.00
6-10	$23.00	$70.00	$140.00	£15.50	£48.00	£95.00
11-20	$12.50	$38.00	$75.00	£8.25	£25.00	£50.00
21-30	$8.25	$25.00	$50.00	£5.75	£17.50	£35.00
31-40	$9.50	$29.00	$47.50	£6.50	£19.50	£32.50
41-50	$5.50	$16.50	$27.50	£3.50	£10.50	£17.50
51-60	$5.00	$15.00	$25.00	£3.00	£9.00	£15.00
61-80	$3.00	$9.00	$15.00	£2.00	£6.00	£10.00
81-99	$2.00	$6.00	$10.00	£1.50	£4.50	£7.50
100	$3.00	$9.00	$15.00	£2.00	£6.00	£10.00
101-111	$1.50	$4.50	$7.50	£1.00	£3.00	£5.00
112-116 giant	$1.80	$5.25	$9.00	£1.20	£3.60	£6.00
117-120	$1.50	$4.50	$7.50	£1.00	£3.00	£5.00
121-140	$1.00	$3.00	$5.00	£0.70	£2.10	£3.50
141-160	$0.70	$2.10	$3.50	£0.50	£1.50	£2.50
161-180	$0.50	$1.50	$2.50	£0.40	£1.20	£2.00
181-200	$0.40	$1.20	$2.00	£0.30	£0.90	£1.50
201-225	$0.30	$0.90	$1.50	£0.20	£0.60	£1.00
226-254	$0.25	$0.75	$1.25	£0.15	£0.45	£0.75
Title Value:	$1050.75	$3162.00	$6071.25	£707.35	£2131.55	£4094.25

Note: all distributed on the news-stands in the U.K. though later issues more erratically

RICHIE RICH AND CASPER IN 3-D
Blackthorne; (3-D Series #32) 1 Dec 1987

1 ND colour, with bound-in 3-D glasses (25% less without glasses)

	$Good	$Fine	$N.Mint	£Good	£Fine	£N.Mint
	$0.50	$1.50	$2.50	£0.25	£0.75	£1.25
Title Value:	$0.50	$1.50	$2.50	£0.25	£0.75	£1.25

RICHIE RICH MOVIE ADAPTATION
Marvel Comics Group, Film; 1 Mar 1995

1 ND 48pgs, film adaptation starring Macauley Culkin

	$Good	$Fine	$N.Mint	£Good	£Fine	£N.Mint
	$0.60	$1.80	$3.00	£0.40	£1.20	£2.00
Title Value:	$0.60	$1.80	$3.00	£0.40	£1.20	£2.00

RIFLEMAN, THE
Dell; (Four Color #1009) 1 Sep 1959-20 Oct 1964

	$Good	$Fine	$N.Mint	£Good	£Fine	£N.Mint
1 (Four Color #1009) photo cover Chuck Connors						
	$25.00	$75.00	$150.00	£16.50	£50.00	£100.00
2	$16.50	$50.00	$100.00	£10.50	£33.00	£65.00
3 Alex Toth art featured						
	$18.00	$55.00	$110.00	£12.50	£38.00	£75.00

Red Circle Sorcery #7

Reid Fleming (2nd) #1

Rip Hunter #24

	$Good	$Fine	$N.Mint	£Good	£Fine	£N.Mint
4-5	$14.00	$43.00	$85.00	£9.00	£28.00	£55.00
6 Alex Toth art	$15.00	$45.00	$90.00	£10.00	£30.00	£60.00
7-10	$14.00	$43.00	$85.00	£9.00	£28.00	£55.00
11-20	$11.50	$35.00	$70.00	£7.50	£22.50	£45.00
Title Value:	$273.50	$833.00	$1660.00	£178.50	£544.00	£1080.00

Note: all distributed on the news-stands in the U.K.

RIMA THE JUNGLE GIRL
DC Comics; 1 Apr/May 1974-7 Apr/May 1975

	$Good	$Fine	$N.Mint	£Good	£Fine	£N.Mint
1 ND origin, Alex Nino art begins, Space Voyagers begin	$0.90	$1.50	$2.50	£0.30	£0.90	£1.50
2-4 scarce in the U.K. origin	$0.40	$1.20	$2.00	£0.25	£0.75	£1.25
5 last Nino art, last Space Voyagers	$0.40	$1.20	$2.00	£0.25	£0.75	£1.25
6	$0.40	$1.20	$2.00	£0.25	£0.75	£1.25
7 Space Marshall appears	$0.40	$1.20	$2.00	£0.25	£0.75	£1.25
Title Value:	$2.90	$8.70	$14.50	£1.80	£5.40	£9.00

RING OF ROSES
Dark Horse,MS; 1 Jan 1993-4 Apr 1993

	$Good	$Fine	$N.Mint	£Good	£Fine	£N.Mint
1-4 ND black and white	$0.50	$1.50	$2.50	£0.30	£0.90	£1.50
Title Value:	$2.00	$6.00	$10.00	£1.20	£3.60	£6.00

RING, THE
DC Comics,MS; 1 Jan 1990-4 Apr 1990

	$Good	$Fine	$N.Mint	£Good	£Fine	£N.Mint
1-4 ND squarebound	$0.80	$2.40	$4.00	£0.50	£1.50	£2.50
Title Value:	$3.20	$9.60	$16.00	£2.00	£6.00	£10.00
Trade paperback (Jun 1991), 200pgs				£2.80	£5.60	£11.20

Note: adaptation of Richard Wagner's The Ring by Roy Thomas and Gil Kane. Mature Readers label. Full title: The Ring of Nibelung.

RINGO KID, THE
Marvel Comics Group; 1 Jan 1970-23 Nov 1973; 24 Nov 1975-30 Nov 1976

	$Good	$Fine	$N.Mint	£Good	£Fine	£N.Mint
1 Williamson reprint	$0.80	$2.40	$4.00	£0.50	£1.50	£2.50
2 scarce in the U.K.	$0.40	$1.20	$2.00	£0.30	£0.90	£1.50
3 rare in the U.K.	$0.40	$1.20	$2.00	£0.40	£1.20	£2.00
4-30	$0.40	$1.20	$2.00	£0.25	£0.75	£1.25
Title Value:	$12.40	$37.20	$62.00	£7.95	£23.85	£39.75

Note: all issues are reprint. Williamson reprint in #20.

RIO
Comico; Graphic Novel; nn Jun 1987

	$Good	$Fine	$N.Mint	£Good	£Fine	£N.Mint
nn ND Doug Wildey art	$1.50	$4.50	$7.50	£1.00	£3.00	£5.00
Title Value:	$1.50	$4.50	$7.50	£1.00	£3.00	£5.00

RIO AT BAY
Dark Horse; 1 Jul 1992-2 Oct 1992

	$Good	$Fine	$N.Mint	£Good	£Fine	£N.Mint
1-2 ND Doug Wildey script and art	$0.50	$1.50	$2.50	£0.30	£0.90	£1.50
Title Value:	$1.00	$3.00	$5.00	£0.60	£1.80	£3.00
Rio At Bay Softcover Collection (Jun 1993) reprints mini-series, silver foil embossed logo on cover, 10pg section previously unpublished material				£1.00	£3.00	£5.00

RIO KID
Eternity,MS; 1 Nov 1991-2 1991

	$Good	$Fine	$N.Mint	£Good	£Fine	£N.Mint
1-2 ND	$0.40	$1.20	$2.00	£0.25	£0.75	£1.25
Title Value:	$0.80	$2.40	$4.00	£0.50	£1.50	£2.50

RIOT
Viz Communications,MS; 1 Oct 1995-6 Mar 1996

	$Good	$Fine	$N.Mint	£Good	£Fine	£N.Mint
1-6 ND Satoshi Shiki script and art; black and white	$0.55	$1.65	$2.75	£0.35	£1.05	£1.75
Title Value:	$3.30	$9.90	$16.50	£2.10	£6.30	£10.50

RIOT GEAR
Triumphant Comics; 1 Aug 1993-14 Sep 1994

	$Good	$Fine	$N.Mint	£Good	£Fine	£N.Mint
1 coupon for Riot Gear #0; 25,000 copies with serial number on front cover	$0.40	$1.20	$2.00	£0.25	£0.75	£1.25
1 Limited Edition (Feb 1994) – signed by creators with mini-poster photo-print; pre-bagged with backing board	$0.80	$2.40	$4.00	£0.50	£1.50	£2.50
2	$0.40	$1.20	$2.00	£0.25	£0.75	£1.25
3 Unleashed X-over	$0.40	$1.20	$2.00	£0.25	£0.75	£1.25
4-12	$0.40	$1.20	$2.00	£0.25	£0.75	£1.25
13 Kelley Jones cover	$0.40	$1.20	$2.00	£0.25	£0.75	£1.25
14	$0.40	$1.20	$2.00	£0.25	£0.75	£1.25
Title Value:	$6.40	$19.20	$32.00	£4.00	£12.00	£20.00

Note: all Non-Distributed on the news-stands in the U.K.

RIOT GEAR: VIOLENT PAST
Triumphant Comics,MS; 1,2 Feb 1994

	$Good	$Fine	$N.Mint	£Good	£Fine	£N.Mint
1-2 ND	$0.40	$1.20	$2.00	£0.25	£0.75	£1.25
Title Value:	$0.80	$2.40	$4.00	£0.50	£1.50	£2.50

RIP HUNTER TIME MASTER
National Periodical Publications; 1 Mar/Apr 1961-29 Nov/Dec 1965
(see DC Comics Presents #37, Showcase, Time Masters)

	$Good	$Fine	$N.Mint	£Good	£Fine	£N.Mint
1 dinosaur cover	$55.00	$165.00	$450.00	£38.00	£110.00	£300.00
2	$29.00	$85.00	$200.00	£17.50	£52.50	£125.00
3-5	$17.00	$50.00	$120.00	£11.00	£34.00	£80.00
6-7 Toth art	$12.50	$39.00	$90.00	£8.50	£26.00	£60.00
8 Toth art	$10.50	$32.00	$75.00	£7.00	£21.00	£50.00
9-10	$10.50	$32.00	$75.00	£7.00	£21.00	£50.00
11-15	$10.00	$30.00	$70.00	£6.25	£19.00	£45.00
16-19	$8.50	$26.00	$60.00	£5.50	£17.00	£40.00

	$Good	$Fine	$N.Mint	£Good	£Fine	£N.Mint
20 Hitler on cover	$8.50	$26.00	$60.00	£5.50	£17.00	£40.00
21-28	$7.00	$21.00	$50.00	£5.00	£15.00	£35.00
29 Gil Kane cover	$7.00	$21.00	$50.00	£5.00	£15.00	£35.00
Title Value:	$347.00	$1043.00	$2515.00	£230.25	£694.50	£1675.00

RIP IN TIME
Fantagor,MS; 1 Aug 1986-5 1987

	$Good	$Fine	$N.Mint	£Good	£Fine	£N.Mint
1-5 ND Richard Corben art	$0.40	$1.20	$2.00	£0.25	£0.75	£1.25
Title Value:	$2.00	$6.00	$10.00	£1.25	£3.75	£6.25
Trade Paperback (Oct 1990), reprints #1-5				£1.00	£3.00	£5.00

RIPCLAW
Image,MS; ½ 1995; 1 Apr 1995-4 Jul 1995

	$Good	$Fine	$N.Mint	£Good	£Fine	£N.Mint
½ ND produced in conjunction with Wizard Comics	$2.00	$6.00	$10.00	£1.20	£3.60	£6.00
½ Chicago Edition, ND released at the Chicago comic convention	$2.40	$7.00	$12.00	£1.60	£4.80	£8.00
½ Gold Edition ND	$2.40	$7.00	$12.00	£1.60	£4.80	£8.00
½ San Diego Edition, ND realeased at the 1995 San Diego comic convention; features San Diego Comicon insignia (a parrot) in gold at bottom right of cover	$2.40	$7.00	$12.00	£1.60	£4.80	£8.00
1-2 ND Marc Silvestri script, Brian Peterson and Al Vey art	$0.50	$1.50	$2.50	£0.30	£0.90	£1.50
3-4 ND Cyberforce appear; Marc Silvestri script, Brian Peterson and Al Vey art	$0.50	$1.50	$2.50	£0.30	£0.90	£1.50
Title Value:	$11.20	$33.00	$56.00	£7.20	£21.60	£36.00

RIPCLAW (2ND SERIES)
Image; 1 Dec 1995-3 Feb 1996

	$Good	$Fine	$N.Mint	£Good	£Fine	£N.Mint
1-2 ND	$0.50	$1.50	$2.50	£0.30	£0.90	£1.50
3 ND Cyblade appears	$0.50	$1.50	$2.50	£0.30	£0.90	£1.50
Title Value:	$1.50	$4.50	$7.50	£0.90	£2.70	£4.50

RIPCLAW SPECIAL
Image,OS; 1 Aug 1995

	$Good	$Fine	$N.Mint	£Good	£Fine	£N.Mint
1 ND Marc Silvestri script	$0.60	$1.80	$3.01	£0.40	£1.20	£2.00
Title Value:	$0.60	$1.80	$3.01	£0.40	£1.20	£2.00

RIPFIRE
Malibu; 0 Jan 1995

	$Good	$Fine	$N.Mint	£Good	£Fine	£N.Mint
0 ND 40pgs	$0.40	$1.20	$2.00	£0.25	£0.75	£1.25
Title Value:	$0.40	$1.20	$2.00	£0.25	£0.75	£1.25

RIPLEY'S BELIEVE IT OR NOT
Gold Key; 4 Apr 1967-94 Feb 1980
(True War Stories #1-3)

	$Good	$Fine	$N.Mint	£Good	£Fine	£N.Mint
4	$4.50	$13.50	$22.50	£3.00	£9.00	£15.00
5-10	$3.00	$9.00	$15.00	£2.00	£6.00	£10.00
11-20	$2.00	$6.00	$10.00	£1.50	£4.50	£7.50
21-30	$1.50	$4.50	$7.50	£1.00	£3.00	£5.00
31-50	$1.00	$3.00	$5.00	£0.70	£2.10	£3.50
51-70	$0.90	$2.70	$4.50	£0.60	£1.80	£3.00
71-94	$0.70	$2.10	$3.50	£0.50	£1.50	£2.50
Title Value:	$112.30	$336.90	$561.50	£78.00	£234.00	£390.00

Note: most issues distributed on the news-stands in the U.K.

RIPLEY'S BELIEVE IT OR NOT: ANIMAL ODDITIES
Schanes Products; 1 Sep 1993

	$Good	$Fine	$N.Mint	£Good	£Fine	£N.Mint
1 ND black and white	$0.50	$1.50	$2.50	£0.30	£0.90	£1.50
Title Value:	$0.50	$1.50	$2.50	£0.30	£0.90	£1.50

RIPLEY'S BELIEVE IT OR NOT: BEAUTY & GROOMING
Schanes Products; 1 Aug 1993

	$Good	$Fine	$N.Mint	£Good	£Fine	£N.Mint
1 ND black and white	$0.50	$1.50	$2.50	£0.30	£0.90	£1.50
Title Value:	$0.50	$1.50	$2.50	£0.30	£0.90	£1.50

RIPLEY'S BELIEVE IT OR NOT: CHILD PRODIGIES
Schanes Products; 1 May 1993-2 Jun 1993

	$Good	$Fine	$N.Mint	£Good	£Fine	£N.Mint
1-2 ND Scott Hampton cover; black and white	$0.50	$1.50	$2.50	£0.30	£0.90	£1.50
Title Value:	$1.00	$3.00	$5.00	£0.60	£1.80	£3.00

RIPLEY'S BELIEVE IT OR NOT: COINCIDENCES
Schanes Products; 1 Oct 1993

	$Good	$Fine	$N.Mint	£Good	£Fine	£N.Mint
1 ND black and white	$0.50	$1.50	$2.50	£0.30	£0.90	£1.50
Title Value:	$0.50	$1.50	$2.50	£0.30	£0.90	£1.50

RIPLEY'S BELIEVE IT OR NOT: CRIME & MURDER
Schanes Products; 1 May 1993-2 Jun 1993

	$Good	$Fine	$N.Mint	£Good	£Fine	£N.Mint
1-2 ND Scott Hampton cover; black and white	$0.50	$1.50	$2.50	£0.30	£0.90	£1.50
Title Value:	$1.00	$3.00	$5.00	£0.60	£1.80	£3.00

RIPLEY'S BELIEVE IT OR NOT: CRUELTY
Schanes Products; 1 May 1993-2 Jun 1993

	$Good	$Fine	$N.Mint	£Good	£Fine	£N.Mint
1 ND Scott Hampton cover (says Unusual Deaths in indicia); black and white	$0.50	$1.50	$2.50	£0.30	£0.90	£1.50
2 ND Scott Hampton cover; black and white	$0.50	$1.50	$2.50	£0.30	£0.90	£1.50
Title Value:	$1.00	$3.00	$5.00	£0.60	£1.80	£3.00

RIPLEY'S BELIEVE IT OR NOT: DEATH
Schanes Products; 1 Aug 1993

	$Good	$Fine	$N.Mint	£Good	£Fine	£N.Mint
1 ND black and white	$0.50	$1.50	$2.50	£0.30	£0.90	£1.50
Title Value:	$0.50	$1.50	$2.50	£0.30	£0.90	£1.50

RIPLEY'S BELIEVE IT OR NOT: FAIRY TALES & LITERATURE
Schanes Products; 1 Jun 1993-2 Jul 1993

1-2 ND Scott Hampton design photo cover; black and white

Item	$Good	$Fine	$N.Mint	£Good	£Fine	£N.Mint
	$0.50	$1.50	$2.50	£0.30	£0.90	£1.50
Title Value:	$1.00	$3.00	$5.00	£0.60	£1.80	£3.00

RIPLEY'S BELIEVE IT OR NOT: FEATS OF WONDER
Schanes Products; 1 Jun 1993-2 Jul 1993
1-2 ND Scott Hampton cover; black and white

Item	$Good	$Fine	$N.Mint	£Good	£Fine	£N.Mint
	$0.50	$1.50	$2.50	£0.30	£0.90	£1.50
Title Value:	$1.00	$3.00	$5.00	£0.60	£1.80	£3.00

RIPLEY'S BELIEVE IT OR NOT: MODERN WONDERS
Schanes Products; 1 Sep 1993
1 ND black and white; large cover stamp attached announcing U.S. TV programme on Ripley

Item	$Good	$Fine	$N.Mint	£Good	£Fine	£N.Mint
	$0.50	$1.50	$2.50	£0.30	£0.90	£1.50
Title Value:	$0.50	$1.50	$2.50	£0.30	£0.90	£1.50

RIPLEY'S BELIEVE IT OR NOT: PERSONAL HYGIENE
Schanes Products; 1 Aug 1993
1 ND black and white

Item	$Good	$Fine	$N.Mint	£Good	£Fine	£N.Mint
	$0.50	$1.50	$2.50	£0.30	£0.90	£1.50
Title Value:	$0.50	$1.50	$2.50	£0.30	£0.90	£1.50

RIPLEY'S BELIEVE IT OR NOT: RECORDS
Schanes Products; 1 Jun 1993-2 Jul 1993
1-2 ND black and white

Item	$Good	$Fine	$N.Mint	£Good	£Fine	£N.Mint
	$0.50	$1.50	$2.50	£0.30	£0.90	£1.50
Title Value:	$1.00	$3.00	$5.00	£0.60	£1.80	£3.00

RIPLEY'S BELIEVE IT OR NOT: SPORTS FEATS
Schanes Products; 1 Jun 1993-2 Jul 1993
1-2 ND Scott Hampton cover, black and white

Item	$Good	$Fine	$N.Mint	£Good	£Fine	£N.Mint
	$0.50	$1.50	$2.50	£0.30	£0.90	£1.50
Title Value:	$1.00	$3.00	$5.00	£0.60	£1.80	£3.00

RIPLEY'S BELIEVE IT OR NOT: STRANGE DEATHS
Schanes Products; 1 Jun 1993
1 ND reprints famous newspaper cartoons, black and white; Scott Hampton cover (says Unusual Deaths in indicia)

Item	$Good	$Fine	$N.Mint	£Good	£Fine	£N.Mint
	$0.50	$1.50	$2.50	£0.30	£0.90	£1.50
Title Value:	$0.50	$1.50	$2.50	£0.30	£0.90	£1.50

RIPLEY'S BELIEVE IT OR NOT: STRANGE PEOPLE
Schanes Products; 1 Sep 1993
1 ND black and white

Item	$Good	$Fine	$N.Mint	£Good	£Fine	£N.Mint
	$0.50	$1.50	$2.50	£0.30	£0.90	£1.50
Title Value:	$0.50	$1.50	$2.50	£0.30	£0.90	£1.50

RIPLEY'S BELIEVE IT OR NOT: STRANGE RELIGIONS
Schanes Products; 1 Sep 1993-2 Oct 1993
1-2 ND black and white

Item	$Good	$Fine	$N.Mint	£Good	£Fine	£N.Mint
	$0.50	$1.50	$2.50	£0.30	£0.90	£1.50
Title Value:	$1.00	$3.00	$5.00	£0.60	£1.80	£3.00

RIPLEY'S BELIEVE IT OR NOT: THE MACABRE
Schanes Products; 1 Oct 1993
1 ND black and white

Item	$Good	$Fine	$N.Mint	£Good	£Fine	£N.Mint
	$0.50	$1.50	$2.50	£0.30	£0.90	£1.50
Title Value:	$0.50	$1.50	$2.50	£0.30	£0.90	£1.50

RIPLEY'S BELIEVE IT OR NOT: THE ORIENT
Schanes Products; 1 Sep 1993
1 ND black and white

Item	$Good	$Fine	$N.Mint	£Good	£Fine	£N.Mint
	$0.50	$1.50	$2.50	£0.30	£0.90	£1.50
Title Value:	$0.50	$1.50	$2.50	£0.30	£0.90	£1.50

RIPLEY'S BELIEVE IT OR NOT: WILD ANIMALS
Schanes Products; 1 Aug 1993
1 ND black and white

Item	$Good	$Fine	$N.Mint	£Good	£Fine	£N.Mint
	$0.50	$1.50	$2.50	£0.30	£0.90	£1.50
Title Value:	$0.50	$1.50	$2.50	£0.30	£0.90	£1.50

RIPPER
Aircel,MS; 1 Nov 1989-6 Apr 1990
1 ND Barry Blair script/art begins, black and white

Item	$Good	$Fine	$N.Mint	£Good	£Fine	£N.Mint
	$0.40	$1.20	$2.00	£0.25	£0.75	£1.25
1 2nd printing ND	$0.30	$0.90	$1.50	£0.20	£0.60	£1.00
2 ND	$0.40	$1.20	$2.00	£0.25	£0.75	£1.25
2 2nd printing ND	$0.30	$0.90	$1.50	£0.20	£0.60	£1.00
3-6 ND	$0.40	$1.20	$2.00	£0.25	£0.75	£1.25
Title Value:	$3.00	$9.00	$15.00	£1.90	£5.70	£9.50

Note: owing to the content of extreme violence, issue shipped pre-bagged. Approximately 75% value for un-bagged issues

RIPTIDE
Image,MS; 1 Sep 1995-2 Oct 1995
1-2 ND Rob Liefeld script; origin told

Item	$Good	$Fine	$N.Mint	£Good	£Fine	£N.Mint
	$0.50	$1.50	$2.50	£0.30	£0.90	£1.50
Title Value:	$1.00	$3.00	$5.00	£0.60	£1.80	£3.00

RISK
Maximum Comic Press; 1 May 1996-present
1 ND Robert Napton script, Fabian Ribiero art

Item	$Good	$Fine	$N.Mint	£Good	£Fine	£N.Mint
	$0.50	$1.50	$2.50	£0.30	£0.90	£1.50
Title Value:	$0.50	$1.50	$2.50	£0.30	£0.90	£1.50

ROACHMILL
Blackthorne; 1 Dec 1986-6 Aug 1987

Item	$Good	$Fine	$N.Mint	£Good	£Fine	£N.Mint
1 ND	$0.50	$1.50	$2.50	£0.50	£1.50	£2.50
2 ND	$0.40	$1.20	$2.00	£0.40	£1.20	£2.00
3-6 ND	$0.30	$0.90	$1.50	£0.30	£0.90	£1.50
Title Value:	$2.10	$6.30	$10.50	£2.10	£6.30	£10.50
Trade Paperback (Dark Horse), reprints 1-4				£0.80	£2.40	£4.00

ROACHMILL (2ND SERIES)
Dark Horse; 1 May 1988-10 Dec 1990
(see Dark Horse Presents #17)

Item	$Good	$Fine	$N.Mint	£Good	£Fine	£N.Mint
1 ND	$0.40	$1.20	$2.00	£0.40	£1.20	£2.00
2-10 ND	$0.50	$1.50	$2.50	£0.30	£0.90	£1.50
Title Value:	$4.90	$14.70	$24.50	£3.10	£9.30	£15.50
Collection 1 (1991)				£0.80	£2.40	£4.00

ROADKILL: DEADWORLD CHRONICLES
Caliber Press; 1 Jan 1994
1 ND Direct Market Edition – pre-bagged with trading card

Item	$Good	$Fine	$N.Mint	£Good	£Fine	£N.Mint
	$0.70	$2.10	$3.50	£0.50	£1.50	£2.50

1 Newstand edition ND

Item	$Good	$Fine	$N.Mint	£Good	£Fine	£N.Mint
	$0.60	$1.80	$3.00	£0.40	£1.20	£2.00
Title Value:	$1.30	$3.90	$6.50	£0.90	£2.70	£4.50

ROBIN
DC Comics,MS; 1 Jan 1991-5 May 1991
(see Batman, Detective)
1 Batman, Lady Shiva appearances begin, poster by Neal Adams; covers by Brian Bolland begin

Item	$Good	$Fine	$N.Mint	£Good	£Fine	£N.Mint
	$0.80	$2.40	$4.00	£0.50	£1.50	£2.50

1 2nd printing, Roman numerals in date box

Item	$Good	$Fine	$N.Mint	£Good	£Fine	£N.Mint
	$0.30	$0.90	$1.50	£0.20	£0.60	£1.00
1 3rd printing	$0.25	$0.75	$1.25	£0.15	£0.45	£0.75
2	$0.40	$1.20	$2.00	£0.25	£0.75	£1.25
3-5	$0.30	$0.90	$1.50	£0.20	£0.60	£1.00
Title Value:	$2.65	$7.95	$13.25	£1.70	£5.10	£8.50

Robin: A Hero Reborn (Jul 1991) Trade paperback reprints Batman #455-#457 and Robin mini-series #1-5 new cover by Brian Bolland — £0.70 £2.10 £3.50
Robin: Tragedy and Triumph (Nov 1993) Trade paperback reprints Detective Comics #618-621 & Robin II: Joker's Wild #1-4 — £1.30 £3.90 £6.50

ROBIN (2ND SERIES)
DC Comics; 1 Nov 1993-present
0 (Oct 1994) Zero Hour X-over, origins of all three Robins

Item	$Good	$Fine	$N.Mint	£Good	£Fine	£N.Mint
	$0.40	$1.20	$2.00	£0.25	£0.75	£1.25
1	$0.30	$0.90	$1.50	£0.20	£0.60	£1.00

1 ND Collector's Edition – embossed foil enhanced cover

Item	$Good	$Fine	$N.Mint	£Good	£Fine	£N.Mint
	$0.60	$1.80	$3.00	£0.40	£1.20	£2.00
2-5	$0.30	$0.90	$1.50	£0.20	£0.60	£1.00

6 X-over with Showcase'94 #6/7

Item	$Good	$Fine	$N.Mint	£Good	£Fine	£N.Mint
	$0.30	$0.90	$1.50	£0.20	£0.60	£1.00

7 Knightquest storyline concludes, continued in Batman #509

Item	$Good	$Fine	$N.Mint	£Good	£Fine	£N.Mint
	$0.30	$0.90	$1.50	£0.20	£0.60	£1.00

8 Knightsend part 5, continued in Catwoman #12

Item	$Good	$Fine	$N.Mint	£Good	£Fine	£N.Mint
	$0.30	$0.90	$1.50	£0.20	£0.60	£1.00

9 Knightsend: Aftermath, continued in Catwoman #13

Item	$Good	$Fine	$N.Mint	£Good	£Fine	£N.Mint
	$0.30	$0.90	$1.50	£0.20	£0.60	£1.00

10 Zero Hour X-over

Item	$Good	$Fine	$N.Mint	£Good	£Fine	£N.Mint
	$0.30	$0.90	$1.50	£0.20	£0.60	£1.00

11 Two Face appears

Item	$Good	$Fine	$N.Mint	£Good	£Fine	£N.Mint
	$0.30	$0.90	$1.50	£0.20	£0.60	£1.00
12-13	$0.30	$0.90	$1.50	£0.20	£0.60	£1.00

14 The Troika part 4 (conclusion)

Item	$Good	$Fine	$N.Mint	£Good	£Fine	£N.Mint
	$0.30	$0.90	$1.50	£0.20	£0.60	£1.00

14 ND Collector's Edition, with embossed black cover

Item	$Good	$Fine	$N.Mint	£Good	£Fine	£N.Mint
	$0.50	$1.50	$2.50	£0.30	£0.90	£1.50
15-16	$0.30	$0.90	$1.50	£0.20	£0.60	£1.00

17 upgraded coated paper stock (Miraweb Format) begins

Item	$Good	$Fine	$N.Mint	£Good	£Fine	£N.Mint
	$0.40	$1.20	$2.00	£0.25	£0.75	£1.25
18-22	$0.40	$1.20	$2.00	£0.25	£0.75	£1.25

23 Underworld Unleashed tie-in, Killer Moth appears

Item	$Good	$Fine	$N.Mint	£Good	£Fine	£N.Mint
	$0.40	$1.20	$2.00	£0.25	£0.75	£1.25
24	$0.40	$1.20	$2.00	£0.25	£0.75	£1.25

25 Green Arrow guest-stars

Item	$Good	$Fine	$N.Mint	£Good	£Fine	£N.Mint
	$0.40	$1.20	$2.00	£0.25	£0.75	£1.25
26 bi-monthly	$0.40	$1.20	$2.00	£0.25	£0.75	£1.25

27 Contagion part 3, continued in Catwoman #31

Item	$Good	$Fine	$N.Mint	£Good	£Fine	£N.Mint
	$0.40	$1.20	$2.00	£0.25	£0.75	£1.25
Title Value:	$10.70	$32.10	$53.50	£6.90	£20.70	£34.50

ROBIN 3000
DC Comics,MS; 1,2 Jan 1993
1-2 ND 48pgs, squarebound, P. Craig Russell cover and art

Item	$Good	$Fine	$N.Mint	£Good	£Fine	£N.Mint
	$0.90	$2.70	$4.50	£0.60	£1.80	£3.00
Title Value:	$1.80	$5.40	$9.00	£1.20	£3.60	£6.00

ROBIN ANNUAL
DC Comics; 1 Sep 1992-present
1 64pgs, Sam Kieth cover, Eclipso: The Darkness Within tie-in

Item	$Good	$Fine	$N.Mint	£Good	£Fine	£N.Mint
	$0.50	$1.50	$2.50	£0.30	£0.90	£1.50

2 64pgs, Bloodlines part 10, 1st appearance Razorsharp, continued in Action Comics Annual #5

Item	$Good	$Fine	$N.Mint	£Good	£Fine	£N.Mint
	$0.50	$1.50	$2.50	£0.30	£0.90	£1.50

3 64pgs, Elseworlds

Item	$Good	$Fine	$N.Mint	£Good	£Fine	£N.Mint
	$0.60	$1.80	$3.00	£0.40	£1.20	£2.00
4 64pgs, Year One	$0.60	$1.80	$3.00	£0.40	£1.20	£2.00
Title Value:	$2.20	$6.60	$11.00	£1.40	£4.20	£7.00

ROBIN HOOD
Eclipse,MS; 1 Sep 1991-3 Nov 1991

Item	$Good	$Fine	$N.Mint	£Good	£Fine	£N.Mint
1-3 ND	$0.40	$1.20	$2.00	£0.25	£0.75	£1.25
Title Value:	$1.20	$3.60	$6.00	£0.75	£2.25	£3.75

ROBIN HOOD TALES
National Periodical Publications; 7 Jan/Feb 1957-14 Mar/Apr 1958
(issues #1-6 published by Quality)

Item	$Good	$Fine	$N.Mint	£Good	£Fine	£N.Mint
7 rare in the U.K.	$32.00	$95.00	$225.00	£21.00	£62.50	£150.00

8-14 rare in the U.K.

Item	$Good	$Fine	$N.Mint	£Good	£Fine	£N.Mint
	$26.00	$75.00	$180.00	£17.00	£50.00	£120.00
Title Value:	$214.00	$620.00	$1485.00	£140.00	£412.50	£990.00

ROBIN III – CRY OF THE HUNTRESS
DC Comics,MS; 1 Dec 1992-6 Mar 1993
1-6 Mike Zeck cover

Item	$Good	$Fine	$N.Mint	£Good	£Fine	£N.Mint
	$0.40	$1.20	$2.00	£0.25	£0.75	£1.25

1-6 ND Collector's Edition: pre-bagged with mini-poster and "movement-enhanced" cover

MINT = 100% / NEAR MINT (inc. +/-) = 90–99% / VERY FINE (inc. +/-) = 75–89% / FINE (inc. +/-) = 55–74% / VERY GOOD (inc. +/-) = 35–54% / GOOD (inc. +/-) = 15–34% / FAIR = 5–14% / POOR = 1–4%

517

	$Good	$Fine	$N.Mint	£Good	£Fine	£N.Mint
	$0.45	$1.35	$2.25	£0.30	£0.90	£1.50
Title Value:	$5.10	$15.30	$25.50	£3.30	£9.90	£16.50

Note: bi-weekly frequency

ROBIN MINI-SERIES MULTI-PACK
DC Comics,OS; 1 Oct 1991
1 ND scarce in the U.K., shrink-wrapped set of 5 issue mini-series; issue #1 (3rd print), issue #2 (2nd print), illustrated card titled DC Classic Comics

	$1.00	$3.00	$5.00	£0.70	£2.10	£3.50
Title Value:	$1.00	$3.00	$5.00	£0.70	£2.10	£3.50

ROBIN: THE JOKER'S WILD
DC Comics,MS; 1 Dec 1991-4 Mar 1992
1 sequel to Robin mini-series, Joker appears

	$0.25	$0.75	$1.25	£0.15	£0.45	£0.75

1 ND direct sales edition of the above, four cover variations with same hologram but each on a different part of the cover

	$0.30	$0.90	$1.50	£0.20	£0.60	£1.00
2	$0.25	$0.75	$1.25	£0.15	£0.45	£0.75

2 ND direct sales edition of the above, three cover variations with the same hologram but each on a different part of the cover

	$0.30	$0.90	$1.50	£0.20	£0.60	£1.00
3	$0.25	$0.75	$1.25	£0.15	£0.45	£0.75

3 ND direct sales edition of the above, two cover variations with same hologram but each on a different part of the cover

	$0.30	$0.90	$1.50	£0.20	£0.60	£1.00
4	$0.25	$0.75	$1.25	£0.15	£0.45	£0.75

4 ND direct sales edition of the above, hologram cover

	$0.30	$0.90	$1.50	£0.20	£0.60	£1.00
Title Value:	$2.20	$6.60	$11.00	£1.40	£4.20	£7.00

Robin: The Joker's Wild #1 Collector's Set (Dec 1991)
pre-bagged, contains the news-stand edition plus all four
direct-sale hologram editions with hologram trading card — £1.25 £3.75 £6.25
Robin: The Joker's Wild #2 Collector's Set (Jan 1992)
pre-bagged, contains the news-stand edition plus all three
direct-sale hologram editions with hologram trading card — £1.00 £3.00 £5.00
Robin: The Joker's Wild #3 Collector's Set (Jan 1992)
pre-bagged, contains the news-stand edition plus the direct-sale
hologram edition with hologram trading card — £0.75 £2.25 £3.75
Robin: The Joker's Wild #4 Collector's Set (Feb 1992)
contains the news-stand and Direct sale editions plus hologram
trading card — £0.50 £1.50 £2.50
Robin: The Joker's Wild Deluxe Complete Set (Dec 1991)
pre-bagged, all 14 variant covers from the 4 issue mini-series;
gift certificate (issued in advance) and limited to 25,000
editions, 13.7cm x 15.2cm "R" hologram on slipcase — £5.00 £15.00 £25.00
Robin: The Joker's Wild Multi-Pack (Sep 1992)
contains issues #1-4 direct-sales editions (with holograms),
1st printings — £0.50 £1.50 £2.50

ROBOCOP
Marvel Comics Group; 1 Mar 1990-23 Jan 1992
1 ND Alan Grant script begins

	$0.40	$1.20	$2.00	£0.25	£0.75	£1.25
2-10 ND	$0.30	$0.90	$1.50	£0.20	£0.60	£1.00

11 ND last Alan Grant

	$0.25	$0.75	$1.25	£0.15	£0.45	£0.75

12-15 ND Robocop Army story

	$0.25	$0.75	$1.25	£0.15	£0.45	£0.75
16-20 ND	$0.25	$0.75	$1.25	£0.15	£0.45	£0.75

21-23 ND Beyond The Law story

	$0.25	$0.75	$1.25	£0.15	£0.45	£0.75
Title Value:	$6.35	$19.05	$31.75	£4.00	£12.00	£20.00

Bookshelf Special (Jul 1990), 48pgs — £0.65 £1.95 £3.25
Note: based on Movie character, High quality paper

ROBOCOP 2
Marvel Comics Group,OS Film; 1 Aug 1990
1 48pgs, based on Frank Miller screenplay, Alan Grant script

	$0.80	$2.40	$4.00	£0.50	£1.50	£2.50
Title Value:	$0.80	$2.40	$4.00	£0.50	£1.50	£2.50

Note: Bookshelf Format

ROBOCOP 2 (LIMITED SERIES)
Marvel Comics Group,MS Film; 1 Aug 1990-3 Oct 1990
1-3 ND Alan Grant script based on Frank Miller screenplay

	$0.30	$0.90	$1.50	£0.20	£0.60	£1.00
Title Value:	$0.90	$2.70	$4.50	£0.60	£1.80	£3.00

ROBOCOP 2 BOOKSHELF FORMAT
Marvel Comics Group,OS Film; 1 Aug 1991
1 ND 48pgs, adaptation of film

	$1.00	$3.00	$5.00	£0.70	£2.10	£3.50
Title Value:	$1.00	$3.00	$5.00	£0.70	£2.10	£3.50

ROBOCOP 2 MAGAZINE
Marvel Comics Group,OS Film; 1 Aug 1991
1 ND 48pgs, black and white reprint of the above

	$0.40	$1.20	$2.00	£0.25	£0.75	£1.25
Title Value:	$0.40	$1.20	$2.00	£0.25	£0.75	£1.25

ROBOCOP 3
Dark Horse,MS; 1 Aug 1992-3 Oct 1993
1-3 ND adaptation of film, bi-weekly

	$0.50	$1.50	$2.50	£0.30	£0.90	£1.50
Title Value:	$1.50	$4.50	$7.50	£0.90	£2.70	£4.50

ROBOCOP VERSUS TERMINATOR
Dark Horse,MS; 1 May 1992-4 Aug 1992
1 ND Frank Miller and Walt Simonson script/art begins; contains bound-in trading cards

	$0.50	$1.50	$2.50	£0.30	£0.90	£1.50

1 ND sealed envelope (Dark Horse imprinted) containing Platinum Edition, 2 numbered prints and an un-cut sheet of trading cards

	$3.00	$9.00	$15.00	£2.00	£6.00	£10.00

1 Platinum edition ND

	$2.00	$6.00	$10.00	£1.20	£3.60	£6.00
2-4 ND	$0.50	$1.50	$2.50	£0.30	£0.90	£1.50
Title Value:	$7.00	$21.00	$35.00	£4.40	£13.20	£22.00

Robocop vs. Terminator Compilation (1994)
Trade paperback reprints mini-series, new Walt Simonson cover — £1.70 £5.10 £8.50

ROBOCOP: MORTAL COILS
Dark Horse,MS; 1 Sep 1993-4 Dec 1993

	$0.50	$1.50	$2.50	£0.30	£0.90	£1.50
1-4 ND						
Title Value:	$2.00	$6.00	$10.00	£1.20	£3.60	£6.00

ROBOCOP: PRIME SUSPECT
Dark Horse,MS; 1 Oct 1992-4 Jan 1993

	$0.50	$1.50	$2.50	£0.30	£0.90	£1.50
1-4 ND						
Title Value:	$2.00	$6.00	$10.00	£1.20	£3.60	£6.00

ROBOCOP: ROULETTE
Dark Horse,MS; 1 Jan 1994-4 Apr 1994
1-4 ND Nelson painted covers

	$0.50	$1.50	$2.50	£0.30	£0.90	£1.50
Title Value:	$2.00	$6.00	$10.00	£1.20	£3.60	£6.00

ROBOT COMICS
Renegade; 0 Jun 1987
0 ND Bob Burden script and art

	$0.50	$1.50	$2.50	£0.30	£0.90	£1.50
Title Value:	$0.50	$1.50	$2.50	£0.30	£0.90	£1.50

ROBOTECH
Academy Comics,OS; 0 Sep 1994
0 ND Bill Spangler script, William Jang art; outlines history of characters plus interviews with creators

	$0.40	$1.20	$2.00	£0.25	£0.75	£1.25
Title Value:	$0.40	$1.20	$2.00	£0.25	£0.75	£1.25

ROBOTECH DEFENDERS
DC Comics,MS; 1 Mar 1985-2 Apr 1985
(see Robotech Masters, Macross [Comico])

1-2	$0.15	$0.45	$0.75	£0.10	£0.35	£0.60
Title Value:	$0.30	$0.90	$1.50	£0.20	£0.70	£1.20

ROBOTECH II: THE SENTINELS
Eternity; 1 Nov 1988-16 1990

1-3 ND	$0.40	$1.20	$2.00	£0.25	£0.75	£1.25
3 2nd printing ND	$0.30	$0.90	$1.50	£0.20	£0.60	£1.00
4-10 ND	$0.40	$1.20	$2.00	£0.25	£0.75	£1.25
11-16 ND	$0.30	$0.90	$1.50	£0.20	£0.60	£1.00
Title Value:	$6.10	$18.30	$30.50	£3.90	£11.70	£19.50

The Sentinels Graphic Album (1990) reprints issues #1-4 — £2.20 £6.60 £11.00
Limited Edition, reprints issues #1-4 (850 copies) — £5.50 £16.50 £27.50
The Sentinels Hardcover 2 (Aug 1990)
reprints issues #5,6 plus Wedding Special #1,2 — £2.20 £6.60 £11.00
Softcover, reprints issues #1-4 — £1.05 £3.75 £5.25
Hardcover — £5.50 £16.50 £27.50
Signed and Numbered Edition — £7.00 £21.00 £35.00
Robotech II – The Sentinels: Operation Tirol
reprints issues #7-10 — £1.05 £3.75 £5.25
Robotech II – The Sentinels: Mission Impossible!
reprints issues #11-14 — £1.30 £3.90 £6.50

ROBOTECH II: THE SENTINELS – BOOK 2
Eternity; 1 Jun 1990-21 Jul 1993

1-10 ND	$0.40	$1.20	$2.00	£0.25	£0.75	£1.25
11-21 ND	$0.30	$0.90	$1.50	£0.20	£0.60	£1.00
Title Value:	$7.30	$21.90	$36.50	£4.70	£14.10	£23.50

ROBOTECH II: THE SENTINELS – BOOK 3
Eternity,MS; 1 Aug 1993-8 Mar 1994; Academy Comics; 9 Sep 1994-present

1 ND	$0.50	$1.50	$2.50	£0.30	£0.90	£1.50

1 ND The Untold Story Edition (Dec 1993) – special one-shot edition featuring 8 uncensored pages

	$0.45	$1.35	$2.25	£0.30	£0.90	£1.50
2-15 ND	$0.50	$1.50	$2.50	£0.30	£0.90	£1.50
16-17 ND	$0.60	$1.80	$3.00	£0.40	£1.20	£2.00

18 ND $2.95 cover begins

	$0.60	$1.80	$3.00	£0.40	£1.20	£2.00
19-22 ND	$0.60	$1.80	$3.00	£0.40	£1.20	£2.00
Title Value:	$12.15	$36.45	$60.75	£7.60	£22.80	£38.00

ROBOTECH II: THE SENTINELS – CYBERPIRATES
Eternity,MS; 1 Apr 1991-4 Jul 1991
1-4 ND black and white

	$0.40	$1.20	$2.00	£0.25	£0.75	£1.25
Title Value:	$1.60	$4.80	$8.00	£1.00	£3.00	£5.00

ROBOTECH II: THE SENTINELS – SWIMSUIT SPECTACULAR
Eternity,OS; 1 Jul 1992

1 ND	$0.50	$1.50	$2.50	£0.30	£0.90	£1.50
Title Value:	$0.50	$1.50	$2.50	£0.30	£0.90	£1.50

ROBOTECH II: THE SENTINELS – THE ILLUSTRATED HANDBOOK
Eternity,MS; 1 Jul 1991-3 Sep 1991
1-3 ND black and white

	$0.40	$1.20	$2.00	£0.25	£0.75	£1.25
Title Value:	$1.20	$3.60	$6.00	£0.75	£2.25	£3.75

ROBOTECH II: THE SENTINELS – THE MALCONTENT UPRISINGS
Eternity,MS; 1 Apr 1989-12 Dec 1990
1-12 ND black and white

	$0.40	$1.20	$2.00	£0.25	£0.75	£1.25
Title Value:	$4.80	$14.40	$24.00	£3.00	£9.00	£15.00

ROBOTECH II: THE SENTINELS BOOK 4
Academy Comics,MS; 0 Nov 1995-present

	$Good	$Fine	$N.Mint	£Good	£Fine	£N.Mint
0 ND John Waltrip script and art begins						
	$0.60	$1.80	$3.00	£0.40	£1.20	£2.00
0 ND Signed Edition (Nov 1995)						
	$1.20	$3.60	$6.00	£0.80	£2.40	£4.00
Title Value:	$1.80	$5.40	$9.00	£1.20	£3.60	£6.00

ROBOTECH II: THE SENTINELS SCRIPT BOOK
Eternity; 1 Aug 1991-2 1991

	$Good	$Fine	$N.Mint	£Good	£Fine	£N.Mint
1 ND script of unfilmed TV series, episodes #1-4						
	$1.50	$4.50	$7.50	£1.00	£3.00	£5.00
1 2nd printing, ND (Aug 1992)						
	$1.20	$3.60	$6.00	£0.80	£2.40	£4.00
2 ND script of unfilmed TV series, episodes #5-8						
	$1.50	$4.50	$7.50	£1.00	£3.00	£5.00
Title Value:	$4.20	$12.60	$21.00	£2.80	£8.40	£14.00

ROBOTECH IN 3-D
Comico, OS; 1 Aug 1987

	$Good	$Fine	$N.Mint	£Good	£Fine	£N.Mint
1 ND Ken Steacy wraparound cover; with bound-in 3-D glasses (25% less without glasses)						
	$0.50	$1.50	$2.50	£0.30	£0.90	£1.50
Title Value:	$0.50	$1.50	$2.50	£0.30	£0.90	£1.50

ROBOTECH MASTERS
Comico; 1 1985-23 Apr 1988

	$Good	$Fine	$N.Mint	£Good	£Fine	£N.Mint
1-10 ND colour	$0.40	$1.20	$2.00	£0.25	£0.75	£1.25
11-23 ND colour	$0.30	$0.90	$1.50	£0.20	£0.60	£1.00
Title Value:	$7.90	$23.70	$39.50	£5.10	£15.30	£25.50

ROBOTECH SPECIAL
Comico, OS; 1 May 1988

	$Good	$Fine	$N.Mint	£Good	£Fine	£N.Mint
1 ND 40pgs, sub-titled "Dana's Story"; photo-collage cover						
	$0.50	$1.50	$2.50	£0.30	£0.90	£1.50
Title Value:	$0.50	$1.50	$2.50	£0.30	£0.90	£1.50

ROBOTECH SPECIAL: MACROSS MISSIONS – DESTROID
Academy Comics, OS; 1 Jul 1995

	$Good	$Fine	$N.Mint	£Good	£Fine	£N.Mint
1 ND William Jang script and art; black and white						
	$0.60	$1.80	$3.00	£0.40	£1.20	£2.00
Title Value:	$0.60	$1.80	$3.00	£0.40	£1.20	£2.00

ROBOTECH, THE OFFICIAL HOW TO DRAW
Blackthorne, MS; 1 Jan 1987-2 Mar 1987

	$Good	$Fine	$N.Mint	£Good	£Fine	£N.Mint
1-2 ND black and white						
	$0.25	$0.75	$1.25	£0.15	£0.45	£0.75
Title Value:	$0.50	$1.50	$2.50	£0.30	£0.90	£1.50

ROBOTECH, WORLDS OF
Academy Comics, OS; 1 Sep 1995

	$Good	$Fine	$N.Mint	£Good	£Fine	£N.Mint
0 reprints four classic stories; black and white						
	$2.50	$7.50	$12.50	£1.50	£4.50	£7.50
Title Value:	$2.50	$7.50	$12.50	£1.50	£4.50	£7.50

ROBOTECH: ACADEMY BLUES
Academy Comics, OS; 0 May 1995; 1 Jun 1995-present

	$Good	$Fine	$N.Mint	£Good	£Fine	£N.Mint
0 ND Robert Gibson script, Sean Bishop art begins						
	$0.60	$1.80	$3.00	£0.40	£1.20	£2.00
1-3 ND bi-monthly	$0.60	$1.80	$3.00	£0.40	£1.20	£2.00
Title Value:	$2.40	$7.20	$12.00	£1.60	£4.80	£8.00

ROBOTECH: AMAZON WORLD – ESCAPE FROM PRAXIS
Academy Comics; 1 Nov 1994

	$Good	$Fine	$N.Mint	£Good	£Fine	£N.Mint
1 ND black and white						
	$0.60	$1.80	$3.00	£0.40	£1.20	£2.00
Title Value:	$0.60	$1.80	$3.00	£0.40	£1.20	£2.00

ROBOTECH: CLONE
Academy Comics; 0 Dec 1994; 1 Jan 1995-present

	$Good	$Fine	$N.Mint	£Good	£Fine	£N.Mint
0 ND story continues from Robotech: Invid War: Aftermath #7-9; black and white						
	$0.60	$1.80	$3.00	£0.40	£1.20	£2.00
1 ND black and white						
	$0.60	$1.80	$3.00	£0.40	£1.20	£2.00

	$Good	$Fine	$N.Mint	£Good	£Fine	£N.Mint
1 ND Special Edition (Jun 1995), John Schearman art						
	$0.80	$2.40	$4.00	£0.50	£1.50	£2.50
2-5 ND black and white						
	$0.60	$1.80	$3.00	£0.40	£1.20	£2.00
Title Value:	$4.40	$13.20	$22.00	£2.90	£8.70	£14.50

Robotech: The Threadbare Heart Graphic Novel (Apr 1995)
reprints three issue story arc of Robotech that lead directly
into Robotech: Clone

				£1.30	£3.90	£6.50

ROBOTECH: CYBERWORLD – SECRETS OF HAYDON IV
Academy Comics; 1 Jul 1995

	$Good	$Fine	$N.Mint	£Good	£Fine	£N.Mint
1 ND black and white						
	$0.60	$1.80	$3.00	£0.40	£1.20	£2.00
Title Value:	$0.60	$1.80	$3.00	£0.40	£1.20	£2.00

ROBOTECH: FIREWALKERS
Eternity, OS; 1 Mar 1993

	$Good	$Fine	$N.Mint	£Good	£Fine	£N.Mint
1 ND spin-off from Invid War						
	$0.40	$1.20	$2.00	£0.25	£0.75	£1.25
Title Value:	$0.40	$1.20	$2.00	£0.25	£0.75	£1.25

ROBOTECH: GENESIS
Eternity, MS; 1 Mar 1992-6 Jan 1993

	$Good	$Fine	$N.Mint	£Good	£Fine	£N.Mint
1 ND	$0.50	$1.50	$2.50	£0.30	£0.90	£1.50
1 ND Limited Edition (Mar 1992) – includes two trading cards, 8 extra pages, foil embossed cover. 10,000 copies, sequentially numbered on front cover						
	$0.70	$2.10	$3.50	£0.50	£1.50	£2.50
2-6 ND	$0.50	$1.50	$2.50	£0.30	£0.90	£1.50
Title Value:	$3.70	$11.10	$18.50	£2.30	£6.90	£11.50

ROBOTECH: HOSHQ'S STORY
Academy Comics, OS; 1 Nov 1994

	$Good	$Fine	$N.Mint	£Good	£Fine	£N.Mint
1 ND Bruce Lewis script and art; black and white						
	$0.60	$1.80	$3.00	£0.40	£1.20	£2.00
Title Value:	$0.60	$1.80	$3.00	£0.40	£1.20	£2.00

ROBOTECH: INVID WAR
Eternity, MS; 1 Jul 1992-18 Dec 1993

	$Good	$Fine	$N.Mint	£Good	£Fine	£N.Mint
1-5 ND	$0.50	$1.50	$2.50	£0.30	£0.90	£1.50
6-11 ND	$0.40	$1.20	$2.00	£0.25	£0.75	£1.25
12 ND announced as a continuing series						
	$0.40	$1.20	$2.00	£0.25	£0.75	£1.25
13-18 ND	$0.40	$1.20	$2.00	£0.25	£0.75	£1.25
Title Value:	$7.70	$23.10	$38.50	£4.75	£14.25	£23.75

ROBOTECH: INVID WAR AFTERMATH
Eternity; 1 Jan 1994-6 Jun 1994; Academy Comics; 7 Sep 1994-present

	$Good	$Fine	$N.Mint	£Good	£Fine	£N.Mint
1-5 ND black and white						
	$0.50	$1.50	$2.50	£0.30	£0.90	£1.50
6 ND black and white						
	$0.40	$1.20	$2.00	£0.25	£0.75	£1.25
7-13 ND black and white, $2.95 cover						
	$0.40	$1.20	$2.00	£0.25	£0.75	£1.25
Title Value:	$5.70	$17.10	$28.50	£3.50	£10.50	£17.50

ROBOTECH: MACROSS TEMPEST
Academy Comics, OS; 1 Sep 1995

	$Good	$Fine	$N.Mint	£Good	£Fine	£N.Mint
1 ND Gary Terry script and art; black and white						
	$0.60	$1.80	$3.00	£0.40	£1.20	£2.00
Title Value:	$0.60	$1.80	$3.00	£0.40	£1.20	£2.00

ROBOTECH: MECH ANGEL
Academy Comics, OS; 0 Sep 1994

	$Good	$Fine	$N.Mint	£Good	£Fine	£N.Mint
0 ND Bill Spangler script, Jim Reddington art; black and white						
	$0.60	$1.80	$3.00	£0.40	£1.20	£2.00
Title Value:	$0.60	$1.80	$3.00	£0.40	£1.20	£2.00

ROBOTECH: OPTERA, INVID WAR
Academy Comics, OS; 1 Oct 1994

1 ND information, diagrams and text on Robotech

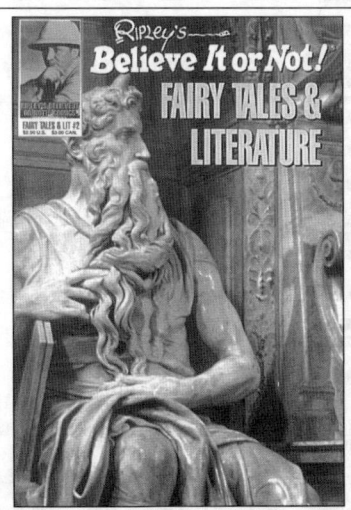
Ripley's Believe It or Not: Fairy Tales & Literature #2

Robin #1 (no cover enhancement)

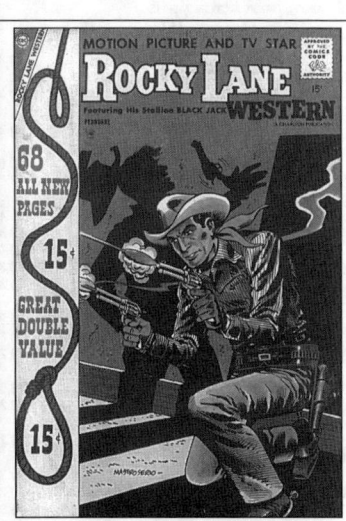
Rocky Lane Western #79

	$Good	$Fine	$N.Mint	£Good	£Fine	£N.Mint
	$0.60	$1.80	$3.00	£0.40	£1.20	£2.00
Title Value:	$0.60	$1.80	$3.00	£0.40	£1.20	£2.00

ROBOTECH: RETURN TO MACROSS
Eternity; 1 May 1993-12 Apr 1994; Academy Comics; 13 Sep 1994-present

	$Good	$Fine	$N.Mint	£Good	£Fine	£N.Mint
1-5 ND black and white						
	$0.50	$1.50	$2.50	£0.30	£0.90	£1.50
6-14 ND black and white						
	$0.40	$1.20	$2.00	£0.25	£0.75	£1.25
15 ND black and white; flip-book format with Robotech Warrior #0						
	$0.40	$1.20	$2.00	£0.25	£0.75	£1.25
16-20 ND	$0.40	$1.20	$2.00	£0.25	£0.75	£1.25
21 ND	$0.50	$1.50	$2.50	£0.30	£0.90	£1.50
22 ND $2.95 cover begins, War of the Believers story						
	$0.50	$1.50	$2.50	£0.30	£0.90	£1.50
23-24 ND War of the Believers story						
	$0.50	$1.50	$2.50	£0.30	£0.90	£1.50
25 ND 40pgs, $3.75 cover, War of the Believers story; silver foil enhanced cover						
	$0.60	$1.80	$3.00	£0.40	£1.20	£2.00
26 ND	$0.60	$1.80	$3.00	£0.40	£1.20	£2.00
Title Value:	$11.70	$35.10	$58.50	£7.25	£21.75	£36.25

ROBOTECH: SMITH WORLD – SABOTAGE ON KARBARRA
Academy Comics,OS; 1 Mar 1995

	$Good	$Fine	$N.Mint	£Good	£Fine	£N.Mint
1 ND black and white						
	$0.60	$1.80	$3.00	£0.40	£1.20	£2.00
Title Value:	$0.60	$1.80	$3.00	£0.40	£1.20	£2.00

ROBOTECH: THE GRAPHIC NOVEL
Comico; 1 Aug 1986

	$Good	$Fine	$N.Mint	£Good	£Fine	£N.Mint
1 ND	$1.00	$3.00	$5.00	£0.70	£2.10	£3.50
Title Value:	$1.00	$3.00	$5.00	£0.70	£2.10	£3.50

ROBOTECH: THE MACROSS SAGA
Comico; 2 Feb 1985-36 Feb 1989
(previously Macross)

	$Good	$Fine	$N.Mint	£Good	£Fine	£N.Mint
2-5 ND	$0.50	$1.50	$2.50	£0.30	£0.90	£1.50
6-36 ND	$0.40	$1.20	$2.00	£0.25	£0.75	£1.25
Title Value:	$14.40	$43.20	$72.00	£8.95	£26.85	£44.75

ROBOTECH: THE NEW GENERATION
Comico; 1 Jul 1985-25 Jul 1988

	$Good	$Fine	$N.Mint	£Good	£Fine	£N.Mint
1-5 ND based on Harmony-Gold TV series, colour						
	$0.50	$1.50	$2.50	£0.30	£0.90	£1.50
6-25 ND based on Harmony-Gold TV series, colour						
	$0.40	$1.20	$2.00	£0.25	£0.75	£1.25
Title Value:	$10.50	$31.50	$52.50	£6.50	£19.50	£32.50

ROBOTECH: WARRIORS
Academy Comics; 1 Feb 1995-3 1995

	$Good	$Fine	$N.Mint	£Good	£Fine	£N.Mint
1-3 ND black and white						
	$0.60	$1.80	$3.00	£0.40	£1.20	£2.00
Title Value:	$1.80	$5.40	$9.00	£1.20	£3.60	£6.00

ROBOTIX
Marvel Comics Group,OS Toy; 1 Feb 1986

	$Good	$Fine	$N.Mint	£Good	£Fine	£N.Mint
1 ND scarce in the U.K.						
	$0.25	$0.75	$1.25	£0.15	£0.45	£0.75
Title Value:	$0.25	$0.75	$1.25	£0.15	£0.45	£0.75

ROCK N' ROLL COMICS
Revolutionary Comics; 1 Jun 1989-71 1994

	$Good	$Fine	$N.Mint	£Good	£Fine	£N.Mint
1 features Guns and Roses						
	$1.80	$5.25	$9.00	£1.20	£3.60	£6.00
1 2nd printing	$1.05	$3.15	$5.25	£0.70	£2.10	£3.50
1 3rd printing	$0.90	$2.70	$4.50	£0.60	£1.80	£3.00
1 4th printing	$0.60	$1.80	$3.00	£0.40	£1.20	£2.00
1 5th printing	$0.45	$1.35	$2.25	£0.30	£0.90	£1.50
1 6th printing	$0.40	$1.20	$2.00	£0.25	£0.75	£1.25
1 7th printing, new group biography/pin-ups						
	$0.40	$1.20	$2.00	£0.25	£0.75	£1.25
2 features Metallica						
	$1.20	$3.60	$6.00	£0.80	£2.40	£4.00
2 2nd printing	$0.60	$1.80	$3.00	£0.40	£1.20	£2.00
2 3rd printing	$0.45	$1.35	$2.25	£0.30	£0.90	£1.50
2 4th/5th/6th printing						
	$0.40	$1.20	$2.00	£0.25	£0.75	£1.25
3 features Bon Jovi						
	$0.90	$2.70	$4.50	£0.60	£1.80	£3.00
3 2nd printing	$0.45	$1.35	$2.25	£0.30	£0.90	£1.50
4 features Motley Crue						
	$0.60	$1.80	$3.00	£0.40	£1.20	£2.00
4 2nd printing	$0.45	$1.35	$2.25	£0.30	£0.90	£1.50
5 Def Leppard	$0.55	$1.65	$2.75	£0.35	£1.05	£1.75
5 2nd printing	$0.45	$1.35	$2.25	£0.30	£0.90	£1.50
6 Rolling Stones	$0.45	$1.35	$2.25	£0.30	£0.90	£1.50
6 2nd/3rd/4th printing						
	$0.40	$1.20	$2.00	£0.25	£0.75	£1.25
7 The Who	$0.45	$1.35	$2.25	£0.30	£0.90	£1.50
7 2nd/3rd printing	$0.40	$1.20	$2.00	£0.25	£0.75	£1.25
8 never published, reason unknown at time of going to press						
	$0.00	$0.00	$0.00	£0.00	£0.00	£0.00
9 Kiss	$0.45	$1.35	$2.25	£0.30	£0.90	£1.50
9 2nd/3rd/4th printing						
	$0.40	$1.20	$2.00	£0.25	£0.75	£1.25
10 Warrant/Whitesnake						
	$0.45	$1.35	$2.25	£0.30	£0.90	£1.50
10 2nd printing	$0.40	$1.20	$2.00	£0.25	£0.75	£1.25
11 Aerosmith	$0.45	$1.35	$2.25	£0.30	£0.90	£1.50
11 2nd printing	$0.40	$1.20	$2.00	£0.25	£0.75	£1.25

	$Good	$Fine	$N.Mint	£Good	£Fine	£N.Mint
12 New Kids on the Block						
	$0.45	$1.35	$2.25	£0.30	£0.90	£1.50
12 2nd/3rd printing	$0.40	$1.20	$2.00	£0.25	£0.75	£1.25
13 Led Zepplin	$0.40	$1.20	$2.00	£0.25	£0.75	£1.25
14 The Sex Pistols	$0.40	$1.20	$2.00	£0.25	£0.75	£1.25
15 Poison	$0.40	$1.20	$2.00	£0.25	£0.75	£1.25
16 Van Halen	$0.40	$1.20	$2.00	£0.25	£0.75	£1.25
17 Madonna/Blondie/Paula Abdul, 1st colour issue						
	$0.40	$1.20	$2.00	£0.25	£0.75	£1.25
18 Alice Cooper	$0.40	$1.20	$2.00	£0.25	£0.75	£1.25
19 Live Crew/Public Enemy						
	$0.40	$1.20	$2.00	£0.25	£0.75	£1.25
20 Queensryche	$0.40	$1.20	$2.00	£0.25	£0.75	£1.25
21 Prince	$0.40	$1.20	$2.00	£0.25	£0.75	£1.25
22 AC/DC	$0.40	$1.20	$2.00	£0.25	£0.75	£1.25
23 Living Color	$0.40	$1.20	$2.00	£0.25	£0.75	£1.25
24 Anthrax	$0.40	$1.20	$2.00	£0.25	£0.75	£1.25
25 ZZ Top	$0.40	$1.20	$2.00	£0.25	£0.75	£1.25
26 The Doors	$0.40	$1.20	$2.00	£0.25	£0.75	£1.25
27-28 Black Sabbath/Ozzy Osbourne						
	$0.40	$1.20	$2.00	£0.25	£0.75	£1.25
29-30 The Cure	$0.40	$1.20	$2.00	£0.25	£0.75	£1.25
31 Vanilla Ice	$0.40	$1.20	$2.00	£0.25	£0.75	£1.25
32 Frank Zappa	$0.40	$1.20	$2.00	£0.25	£0.75	£1.25
33 Guns 'n Roses	$0.40	$1.20	$2.00	£0.25	£0.75	£1.25
34 The Black Crowes						
	$0.40	$1.20	$2.00	£0.25	£0.75	£1.25
35 R.E.M.	$0.40	$1.20	$2.00	£0.25	£0.75	£1.25
36 Michael Jackson						
	$0.40	$1.20	$2.00	£0.25	£0.75	£1.25
37 Ice Cube, Ice T	$0.40	$1.20	$2.00	£0.25	£0.75	£1.25
38 Rod Stewart	$0.40	$1.20	$2.00	£0.25	£0.75	£1.25
39 R 'n R	$0.40	$1.20	$2.00	£0.25	£0.75	£1.25
40 N.W.A., Ice Cube						
	$0.40	$1.20	$2.00	£0.25	£0.75	£1.25
41 Paula Abdul	$0.40	$1.20	$2.00	£0.25	£0.75	£1.25
42 Metallica	$0.40	$1.20	$2.00	£0.25	£0.75	£1.25
43 Guns 'n Roses: Tales from the Tour						
	$0.40	$1.20	$2.00	£0.25	£0.75	£1.25
44 The Skorpions	$0.40	$1.20	$2.00	£0.25	£0.75	£1.25
45 The Grateful Dead						
	$0.40	$1.20	$2.00	£0.25	£0.75	£1.25
46 The Grateful Dead						
	$0.50	$1.50	$2.50	£0.30	£0.90	£1.50
46 2nd printing, (Jan 1994)						
	$0.40	$1.20	$2.00	£0.25	£0.75	£1.25
47 The Grateful Dead						
	$0.40	$1.20	$2.00	£0.25	£0.75	£1.25
48 Queen	$0.40	$1.20	$2.00	£0.25	£0.75	£1.25
49 Rush	$0.40	$1.20	$2.00	£0.25	£0.75	£1.25
50-52 Bob Dylan	$0.40	$1.20	$2.00	£0.25	£0.75	£1.25
53 Bruce Springsteen						
	$0.40	$1.20	$2.00	£0.25	£0.75	£1.25
54 U2	$0.50	$1.50	$2.50	£0.30	£0.90	£1.50
54 U2 2nd print (May 1994)						
	$0.40	$1.20	$2.00	£0.25	£0.75	£1.25
55 U2	$0.40	$1.20	$2.00	£0.25	£0.75	£1.25
56 David Bowie	$0.40	$1.20	$2.00	£0.25	£0.75	£1.25
57 Aerosmith (continues on from #11)						
	$0.40	$1.20	$2.00	£0.25	£0.75	£1.25
58 Kate Bush	$0.40	$1.20	$2.00	£0.25	£0.75	£1.25
59 Eric Clapton	$0.40	$1.20	$2.00	£0.25	£0.75	£1.25
60 Genesis – The '70s						
	$0.40	$1.20	$2.00	£0.25	£0.75	£1.25
61 Yes – The '70s	$0.40	$1.20	$2.00	£0.25	£0.75	£1.25
62 Elton John	$0.40	$1.20	$2.00	£0.25	£0.75	£1.25
63 Janis Joplin	$0.40	$1.20	$2.00	£0.25	£0.75	£1.25
64 San Francisco issue (Grateful Dead, Joplin, Miller, Jefferson Airplane etc)						
	$0.40	$1.20	$2.00	£0.25	£0.75	£1.25
65 Sci-Fi Space Rockers (Marillion, Genesis, Yes etc)						
	$0.40	$1.20	$2.00	£0.25	£0.75	£1.25
66 Allman Bros. and Lynard Skynard						
	$0.40	$1.20	$2.00	£0.25	£0.75	£1.25
67 John Mellencamp						
	$0.40	$1.20	$2.00	£0.25	£0.75	£1.25
68 Tom Petty	$0.40	$1.20	$2.00	£0.25	£0.75	£1.25
69 Neil Young	$0.40	$1.20	$2.00	£0.25	£0.75	£1.25
70 Police/Sting and Iggy Pop						
	$0.40	$1.20	$2.00	£0.25	£0.75	£1.25
71 Meatloaf, Lenny Kravetz, Mozart						
	$0.40	$1.20	$2.00	£0.25	£0.75	£1.25
Title Value:	$44.55	$133.50	$222.75	£28.35	£85.05	£141.75

Note: all Non-Distributed on the news-stands in the U.K.

Annual 1: Encyclopedia Metallica (Dec 1990)

				£Good	£Fine	£N.Mint
reprints, squarebound magazine				0.75	2.25	3.75
Trade Paperback (May 1991)				1.35	4.05	6.75

ROCK N' ROLL COMICS MAGAZINE
Revolutionary Comics; 1 Sep 1990-9 1991

	$Good	$Fine	$N.Mint	£Good	£Fine	£N.Mint
1 ND reprints Rock n' Roll Comics featuring Kiss plus new material						
	$0.40	$1.20	$2.00	£0.25	£0.75	£1.25
2 ND reprints from New Kids on the Block						
	$0.40	$1.20	$2.00	£0.25	£0.75	£1.25

SOME INDEPENDENT COMICS MAY NOT HAVE APPEARED ALTHOUGH THEY WERE ADVERTISED AND SOLICITED.

	$Good	$Fine	$N.Mint	£Good	£Fine	£N.Mint

3 ND reprints Rock n' Roll Comics issue #1 (7th print)

| | $0.40 | $1.20 | $2.00 | £0.25 | £0.75 | £1.25 |

4 ND reprints issue #2 (Metallica)

| | $0.40 | $1.20 | $2.00 | £0.25 | £0.75 | £1.25 |

5 ND reprints issue #11 (Aerosmith)

| | $0.40 | $1.20 | $2.00 | £0.25 | £0.75 | £1.25 |

6 ND reprints issue #15 (Poison)

| | $0.40 | $1.20 | $2.00 | £0.25 | £0.75 | £1.25 |

7 ND reprints issue #17 (Madonna)

| | $0.40 | $1.20 | $2.00 | £0.25 | £0.75 | £1.25 |

8 ND reprints issue #12 (New Kids on the Block)?

| | $0.40 | $1.20 | $2.00 | £0.25 | £0.75 | £1.25 |

9 ND 68pgs, reprints issues #4,15

| | $0.50 | $1.50 | $2.50 | £0.30 | £0.90 | £1.50 |
| **Title Value:** | $3.70 | $11.10 | $18.50 | £2.30 | £6.90 | £11.50 |

Note: issues #1-3 released in same month

ROCKET RACCOON
Marvel Comics Group,MS; 1 May 1985-4 Aug 1985
1-4 ND Mike Mignola art

| | $0.25 | $0.75 | $1.25 | £0.15 | £0.45 | £0.75 |
| **Title Value:** | $1.00 | $3.00 | $5.00 | £0.60 | £1.80 | £3.00 |

ROCKET RANGER
Adventure,MS; 1 Sep 1991-6 Sep 1992
1-6 ND based on computer game

| | $0.50 | $1.50 | $2.50 | £0.30 | £0.90 | £1.50 |
| **Title Value:** | $3.00 | $9.00 | $15.00 | £1.80 | £5.40 | £9.00 |

ROCKETEER
Eclipse; (Graphic Novel 7); nn 1987
nn reprints from Pacific Presents #1 & 2, Starslayer #2 & 3 and Rocketeer Special, Dave Stevens art

| | | | | £1.60 | £5.40 | £8.00 |

nn 2nd print

| | | | | £1.20 | £3.60 | £6.00 |

nn 3rd print (Apr 1991)

| | | | | £1.10 | £3.30 | £5.50 |

nn 3rd print Hardcover (Apr 1991)

| | | | | £4.00 | £12.00 | £20.00 |

Rocketeer Graphic Novel
(Aug 1991) reprints Adventure Magazine #1&2

| | | | | £1.10 | £3.30 | £5.50 |

Rocketeer Graphic Novel Hardcover (Aug 1991)

| | | | | £3.10 | £9.30 | £15.50 |

Rocketeer Graphic Novel
Signed numbered Hardcover (Oct 1991) 1000 copies

| | | | | £6.50 | £19.50 | £32.50 |

ROCKETEER ADVENTURE MAGAZINE
Comico; 1,2 1988; Dark Horse; 3 Jan 1995
1 ND Rocketeer by Stevens, Galactic Girl Guides by Kaluta (see Starstruck); Dave Stevens cover

| | $1.00 | $3.00 | $5.00 | £0.70 | £2.10 | £3.50 |

2 ND Stevens/Kaluta art; Dave Stevens cover

| | $0.60 | $1.80 | $3.00 | £0.40 | £1.20 | £2.00 |

3 ND Dave Stevens, Mike Kaluta, Art Adams art

| | $0.50 | $1.50 | $2.50 | £0.30 | £0.90 | £1.50 |
| **Title Value:** | $2.10 | $6.30 | $10.50 | £1.40 | £4.20 | £7.00 |

Note: issue #3 was originally solicited by Dark Horse cover dated September 1991

ROCKETEER GRAPHIC NOVEL, THE
Disney; OS; 1 Jul 1991
1 ND 64pgs, adaptation of Disney film, Peter David script, Russ Heath art, Dave Stevens cover

| | $1.00 | $3.00 | $5.00 | £0.70 | £2.10 | £3.50 |

1 Newstand edition ND

| | $0.40 | $1.20 | $2.00 | £0.25 | £0.75 | £1.25 |
| **Title Value:** | $1.40 | $4.20 | $7.00 | £0.95 | £2.85 | £4.75 |

ROCKETEER SPECIAL EDITION
Eclipse,OS; 1 Nov 1984
1 ND scarce in the U.K. Chapter 5; intended for Pacific Presents #5; pin-ups by Wildey, Morrow, Anderson, Heath, Stout, Williamson, Jones

| | $1.60 | $4.80 | $8.00 | £1.20 | £3.60 | £6.00 |
| **Title Value:** | $1.60 | $4.80 | $8.00 | £1.20 | £3.60 | £6.00 |

ROCKETMAN ASHCAN EDITION
AC Comics,OS; nn Aug 1995
0 ND 36pgs, reprints classic Rocketman and Jetgirl stories from the 1940s; black and white

| | $1.20 | $3.60 | $6.00 | £0.80 | £2.40 | £4.00 |
| **Title Value:** | $1.20 | $3.60 | $6.00 | £0.80 | £2.40 | £4.00 |

ROCKETMAN: KING OF THE ROCKET MEN
Innovation; 1 Aug 1991-4 Oct 1991
1-4 ND based on 1940s movie serial; Chris Moeller script and painted art

| | $0.40 | $1.20 | $2.00 | £0.25 | £0.75 | £1.25 |
| **Title Value:** | $1.60 | $4.80 | $8.00 | £1.00 | £3.00 | £5.00 |

Graphic Novel (Feb 1992), collects mini-series

| | | | | £1.10 | £3.30 | £5.50 |

Signed Edition by Chris Moeller (May 1993)

| | | | | £1.20 | £3.60 | £6.00 |

ROCKO'S MODERN LIFE
Marvel Comics Group, TV; 1 Jun 1994-7 Dec 1994
1-7 based on TV cartoon

| | $0.40 | $1.20 | $2.00 | £0.25 | £0.75 | £1.25 |
| **Title Value:** | $2.80 | $8.40 | $14.00 | £1.75 | £5.25 | £8.75 |

ROCKOLA
Mirage Studios; 1 May 1987
1 ND

| | $0.30 | $0.90 | $1.50 | £0.20 | £0.60 | £1.00 |
| **Title Value:** | $0.30 | $0.90 | $1.50 | £0.20 | £0.60 | £1.00 |

ROCKY HORROR PICTURE SHOW
Caliber Press,MS; 1 Jul 1990-3 Nov 1990
1 ND 64pgs

| | $0.70 | $2.10 | $3.50 | £0.50 | £1.50 | £2.50 |

1 2nd printing ND

| | $0.50 | $1.50 | $2.50 | £0.30 | £0.90 | £1.50 |

2-3 ND 64pgs

| | $0.60 | $1.80 | $3.00 | £0.40 | £1.20 | £2.00 |
| **Title Value:** | $2.40 | $7.20 | $12.00 | £1.60 | £4.80 | £8.00 |

Note: adaptation of film

Rocky Horror Picture Show Trade Paperback (Feb 1992),
collects mini-series, new photo cover

| | | | | £0.65 | £1.95 | £3.25 |

ROCKY LANE WESTERN
Charlton; 56 Feb 1954-87 Nov 1959
56 1st Charlton issue (previously published by Fawcett)

| | $14.00 | $43.00 | $100.00 | £10.00 | £30.00 | £70.00 |

57 photo cover

| | $9.25 | $28.00 | $65.00 | £6.25 | £19.00 | £45.00 |

58-59

| | $6.25 | $19.00 | $45.00 | £4.25 | £12.50 | £30.00 |

60 photo cover

| | $9.25 | $28.00 | $65.00 | £6.25 | £19.00 | £45.00 |

61-64

| | $6.25 | $19.00 | $45.00 | £4.25 | £12.50 | £30.00 |

65 reprints Fawcett issue #29

| | $6.25 | $19.00 | $45.00 | £4.25 | £12.50 | £30.00 |

66 reprints Fawcett issue #30

| | $7.00 | $21.00 | $42.50 | £4.55 | £13.50 | £27.50 |

67 reprints Fawcett issue #31

| | $7.00 | $21.00 | $42.50 | £4.55 | £13.50 | £27.50 |

68 reprints Fawcett issue #32

| | $7.00 | $21.00 | $42.50 | £4.55 | £13.50 | £27.50 |

69-78

| | $7.00 | $21.00 | $42.50 | £4.55 | £13.50 | £27.50 |

79 scarce in the U.K. 64pgs, squarebound

| | $9.00 | $28.00 | $55.00 | £5.75 | £17.50 | £35.00 |

80-86

| | $6.50 | $20.00 | $40.00 | £4.15 | £12.50 | £25.00 |

87 scarce in the U.K.

| | $7.50 | $22.50 | $45.00 | £4.55 | £13.50 | £27.50 |
| **Title Value:** | $229.25 | $695.50 | $1477.50 | £150.75 | £449.50 | £965.00 |

Note: all Non-Distributed in the U.K. though a few of the last issues may have been just prior to official distribution in November 1959

ROG 2000, THE COMPLETE
Pacific,Magazine; nn Jul 1982
nn ND 40pgs, all reprint; all John Byrne art

| | $0.90 | $2.70 | $4.50 | £0.60 | £1.80 | £3.00 |
| **Title Value:** | $0.90 | $2.70 | $4.50 | £0.60 | £1.80 | £3.00 |

ROGAN GOSH GRAPHIC NOVEL
DC Comics; nn May 1994
nn ND 56pgs, reprints Peter Milligan and Brendan McCarthy story from Revolver magazine

| | $1.40 | $4.20 | $7.00 | £0.90 | £2.70 | £4.50 |
| **Title Value:** | $1.40 | $4.20 | $7.00 | £0.90 | £2.70 | £4.50 |

ROGER RABBIT
Disney; 1 Jul 1990-19 Nov 1991
1-10 ND

| | $0.40 | $1.20 | $2.00 | £0.25 | £0.75 | £1.25 |

11-19 ND

| | $0.30 | $0.90 | $1.50 | £0.20 | £0.60 | £1.00 |
| **Title Value:** | $6.70 | $20.10 | $33.50 | £4.30 | £12.90 | £21.50 |

Note: banned from distibution in UK

ROGER RABBIT'S TOON TOWN
Disney; 1 Jul 1991-6 Jan 1992
1-6 ND

| | $0.30 | $0.90 | $1.50 | £0.20 | £0.60 | £1.00 |
| **Title Value:** | $1.80 | $5.40 | $9.00 | £1.20 | £3.60 | £6.00 |

ROGER WILCO
Adventure,MS; 1 Apr 1992-3 Aug 1992
1-3 ND based on computer game

| | $0.50 | $1.50 | $2.50 | £0.30 | £0.90 | £1.50 |
| **Title Value:** | $1.50 | $4.50 | $7.50 | £0.90 | £2.70 | £4.50 |

ROGUE
Marvel Comics Group,MS; 1 Jan 1995-4 Apr 1995
1-4 foil stamped cover

| | $0.60 | $1.80 | $3.00 | £0.40 | £1.20 | £2.00 |
| **Title Value:** | $2.40 | $7.20 | $12.00 | £1.60 | £4.80 | £8.00 |

Rogue (Jan 1996) Trade paperback reprints mini-series

| | | | | £1.60 | £4.80 | £8.00 |

'ROIDRAGE
Marvel UK; 1 Dec 1993
1

| | $0.30 | $0.90 | $1.50 | £0.20 | £0.60 | £1.00 |
| **Title Value:** | $0.30 | $0.90 | $1.50 | £0.20 | £0.60 | £1.00 |

ROJA FUSION
Antarctic Press; 1 Apr 1995
1 ND 40pgs, black and white

| | $0.60 | $1.80 | $3.00 | £0.40 | £1.20 | £2.00 |
| **Title Value:** | $0.60 | $1.80 | $3.00 | £0.40 | £1.20 | £2.00 |

ROLLING STONES: VOODOO LOUNGE
Marvel Comics Group,OS; nn Nov 1995
nn ND 48pgs, Dave McKean painted art, pull out poster and interactive computer disc

| | $2.00 | $6.00 | $10.00 | £1.30 | £3.90 | £6.50 |
| **Title Value:** | $2.00 | $6.00 | $10.00 | £1.30 | £3.90 | £6.50 |

ROM
Marvel Comics Group; 1 Dec 1979-75 Feb 1986
1 1st appearance Rom

| | $0.30 | $0.90 | $1.50 | £0.25 | £0.75 | £1.25 |

2-3

| | $0.30 | $0.90 | $1.50 | £0.20 | £0.60 | £1.00 |

4-7 ND

| | $0.30 | $0.90 | $1.50 | £0.30 | £0.90 | £1.50 |

8-12 ND Golden cover

| | $0.30 | $0.90 | $1.50 | £0.20 | £0.60 | £1.00 |

13-16 ND

| | $0.30 | $0.90 | $1.50 | £0.20 | £0.60 | £1.00 |

17-19 X-Men appear

| | $0.50 | $1.50 | $2.50 | £0.30 | £0.90 | £1.50 |

19-22

| | $0.25 | $0.75 | $1.25 | £0.15 | £0.45 | £0.75 |

23 ND Luke Cage and Iron Fist appear

| | $0.30 | $0.90 | $1.50 | £0.20 | £0.60 | £1.00 |

24 Nova appears with the new Champions

| | $0.30 | $0.90 | $1.50 | £0.20 | £0.60 | £1.00 |

25 DS

| | $0.30 | $0.90 | $1.50 | £0.20 | £0.60 | £1.00 |

26-27 Galactus appears

| | $0.25 | $0.75 | $1.25 | £0.15 | £0.45 | £0.75 |

28-30

| | $0.25 | $0.75 | $1.25 | £0.15 | £0.45 | £0.75 |

31-32 Rogue appears

| | $0.30 | $0.90 | $1.50 | £0.20 | £0.60 | £1.00 |

	$Good	$Fine	$N.Mint	£Good	£Fine	£N.Mint
33	$0.25	$0.75	$1.25	£0.15	£0.45	£0.75
34-35 Sub-Mariner appears	$0.25	$0.75	$1.25	£0.15	£0.45	£0.75
36-37	$0.25	$0.75	$1.25	£0.15	£0.45	£0.75
38-39 Master of Kung Fu appears	$0.25	$0.75	$1.25	£0.15	£0.45	£0.75
40	$0.25	$0.75	$1.25	£0.15	£0.45	£0.75
41-42 LD in the U.K. Dr. Strange appears	$0.25	$0.75	$1.25	£0.15	£0.45	£0.75
43-49	$0.25	$0.75	$1.25	£0.15	£0.45	£0.75
50 DS Torpedo dies	$0.30	$0.90	$1.50	£0.20	£0.60	£1.00
51	$0.25	$0.75	$1.25	£0.15	£0.45	£0.75
52 Sienkiewicz cover	$0.25	$0.75	$1.25	£0.15	£0.45	£0.75
53 Nick Fury appears, Sienkiewicz cover	$0.25	$0.75	$1.25	£0.15	£0.45	£0.75
54 Nick Fury and Dr. Strange cameos, Sienkiewicz cover	$0.25	$0.75	$1.25	£0.15	£0.45	£0.75
55 Sienkiewicz cover	$0.25	$0.75	$1.25	£0.15	£0.45	£0.75
56 Alpha Flight appears	$0.25	$0.75	$1.25	£0.15	£0.45	£0.75
57 Alpha Flight appears, John Byrne cover	$0.25	$0.75	$1.25	£0.15	£0.45	£0.75
58 Ant-Man and Alpha Flight appear, Guice cover	$0.25	$0.75	$1.25	£0.15	£0.45	£0.75
59 Ant-Man appears; Steve Ditko pencils	$0.25	$0.75	$1.25	£0.15	£0.45	£0.75
60 Ditko pencils, Guice cover	$0.25	$0.75	$1.25	£0.15	£0.45	£0.75
61 Forge appears, Steve Ditko and Jackson Guice art	$0.25	$0.75	$1.25	£0.15	£0.45	£0.75
62 Forge appears, Steve Ditko pencils	$0.25	$0.75	$1.25	£0.15	£0.45	£0.75
63 Forge appears, Steve Ditko pencils, Neary cover	$0.25	$0.75	$1.25	£0.15	£0.45	£0.75
64 Steve Ditko and P.Craig Russell art, Russell cover	$0.25	$0.75	$1.25	£0.15	£0.45	£0.75
65 X-Men, Avengers, West Coast Avengers and Defenders appear; Steve Ditko and Russell art, part Russell cover	$0.25	$0.75	$1.25	£0.15	£0.45	£0.75
66 All Earth's Heroes story; Steve Ditko pencils, Russell cover	$0.30	$0.90	$1.50	£0.20	£0.60	£1.00
67 Steve Ditko and Russell art	$0.25	$0.75	$1.25	£0.15	£0.45	£0.75
68 Steve Ditko pencils, Sienkiewicz cover	$0.25	$0.75	$1.25	£0.15	£0.45	£0.75
69 Steve Ditko and Russell art	$0.25	$0.75	$1.25	£0.15	£0.45	£0.75
70 Steve Ditko pencils, Guice and Ordway cover	$0.25	$0.75	$1.25	£0.15	£0.45	£0.75
71 Steve Ditko and Russell art, Russell and Sienkiewicz cover	$0.25	$0.75	$1.25	£0.15	£0.45	£0.75
72 Secret Wars X-over; Steve Ditko pencils	$0.25	$0.75	$1.25	£0.15	£0.45	£0.75
73 Steve Ditko pencils	$0.25	$0.75	$1.25	£0.15	£0.45	£0.75
74 Steve Ditko pencils, John Byrne inks	$0.25	$0.75	$1.25	£0.15	£0.45	£0.75
75 Steve Ditko and Russell art, Russell cover	$0.25	$0.75	$1.25	£0.15	£0.45	£0.75
Title Value:	$20.40	$61.20	$102.00	£13.15	£39.45	£65.75

FEATURES

Galactus in 26, 27. Jack of Hearts in 12. Nova in 24. Powerman and Iron Fist in 23. Rogue in 31, 32. Tales of the Space Knights in 13, 14, 16, 19-21. Torpedo in 21, 22.

ROM ANNUAL
Marvel Comics Group; 1 Nov 1982-4 1985

	$Good	$Fine	$N.Mint	£Good	£Fine	£N.Mint
1-2	$0.30	$0.90	$1.50	£0.20	£0.60	£1.00
3 ND New Mutants appear	$0.40	$1.20	$2.00	£0.25	£0.75	£1.25
4 ND Gladiator appears	$0.30	$0.90	$1.50	£0.20	£0.60	£1.00
Title Value:	$1.30	$3.90	$6.50	£0.85	£2.55	£4.25

ROMANTIC SECRETS
Charlton; 5 Oct 1955-52 Nov 1964
(issues #1-4 formerly Negro Romances)

	$Good	$Fine	$N.Mint	£Good	£Fine	£N.Mint
5 scarce in the U.K.	$6.50	$20.00	$40.00	£4.15	£12.50	£25.00
6-10	$3.30	$10.00	$20.00	£2.05	£6.25	£12.50
11-20	$1.65	$5.00	$10.00	£1.25	£3.75	£7.50
21-22	$1.25	$3.75	$7.50	£0.80	£2.50	£5.00
1st official distribution in the U.K.						
23-30	$1.25	$3.75	$7.50	£0.80	£2.50	£5.00
31-40	$0.80	$2.50	$5.00	£0.40	£1.75	£3.50
41-52	$0.55	$1.75	$3.50	£0.40	£1.25	£2.50
Title Value:	$66.60	$203.50	$407.00	£45.20	£138.75	£277.50

ROMANTIC STORY
Fawcett; 1 Nov 1949-22 Sum 1953; Charlton; 23 May 1954-27 Dec 1954; 28 Aug 1955-130 Nov 1973

	$Good	$Fine	$N.Mint	£Good	£Fine	£N.Mint
1 scarce in the U.K.	$11.00	$34.00	$80.00	£7.75	£23.50	£55.00
2 scarce in the U.K.	$6.25	$19.00	$45.00	£4.25	£12.50	£30.00
3-5 scarce in the U.K.						

	$Good	$Fine	$N.Mint	£Good	£Fine	£N.Mint
	$5.00	$15.00	$35.00	£3.55	£10.50	£25.00
6-14	$3.55	$10.50	$25.00	£2.50	£7.50	£17.50
15 George Evans art						
	$5.00	$15.00	$35.00	£3.20	£9.50	£22.50
16-34	$2.50	$7.50	$17.50	£1.70	£5.00	£12.00
1st official distribution in the U.K.						
35-39	$2.90	$8.75	$17.50	£2.00	£6.00	£12.00
40 scarce in the U.K. 100pgs						
	$5.75	$17.50	$35.00	£3.75	£11.00	£22.50
41-50	$2.50	$7.50	$15.00	£1.65	£5.00	£10.00
51-60	$1.25	$3.75	$7.50	£0.80	£2.50	£5.00
61-70	$1.25	$3.75	$7.50	£0.65	£2.00	£4.00
71-90	$1.00	$3.00	$5.00	£0.70	£2.10	£3.50
91-110	$0.50	$1.50	$2.50	£0.30	£0.90	£1.50
111-130	$0.40	$1.20	$2.00	£0.25	£0.75	£1.25
Title Value:	$224.95	$675.25	$1435.00	£150.40	£450.50	£965.50

RONIN
DC Comics,MS; 1 Jul 1983-6 Apr 1984

	$Good	$Fine	$N.Mint	£Good	£Fine	£N.Mint
1 ND Frank Miller art; DC's 1st full-process separation comic	$1.00	$3.00	$5.00	£0.60	£1.80	£3.00
2-3 ND Frank Miller art	$0.80	$2.40	$4.00	£0.50	£1.50	£2.50
4-5 ND scarce in the U.K. Frank Miller art	$0.80	$2.40	$4.00	£0.60	£1.80	£3.00
6 ND very scarce in the U.K. Frank Miller art, fold out page of panoramic art ("gatefold")	$1.20	$3.60	$6.00	£1.00	£3.00	£5.00
Title Value:	$5.40	$16.20	$27.00	£3.80	£11.40	£19.00
Trade Paperback, reprints #1-6				£1.40	£4.20	£7.00

ROOK
Warren; 1 Nov 1979-14 Apr 1982
(see Eerie)

	$Good	$Fine	$N.Mint	£Good	£Fine	£N.Mint
1	$0.50	$1.50	$2.50	£0.30	£0.90	£1.50
2-14	$0.40	$1.20	$2.00	£0.25	£0.75	£1.25
Title Value:	$5.70	$17.10	$28.50	£3.55	£10.65	£17.75

Note: distributed in the U.K.

ROOK, THE
Harris Comics; 0 Jun 1995; 1 Aug 1995-present

	$Good	$Fine	$N.Mint	£Good	£Fine	£N.Mint
0 ND (Jun 1995), includes designs and character sketches	$0.60	$1.80	$3.00	£0.40	£1.20	£2.00
1 ND Tom Sniegoski script, Kirk van Wormer and Joe Weems art	$0.60	$1.80	$3.00	£0.40	£1.20	£2.00
2-4 ND	$0.60	$1.80	$3.00	£0.40	£1.20	£2.00
Title Value:	$3.00	$9.00	$15.00	£2.00	£6.00	£10.00

ROOKIE COP
Charlton; 27 Nov 1955-33 Jul 1957
(Crime and Justice #1-26?)

	$Good	$Fine	$N.Mint	£Good	£Fine	£N.Mint
27	$7.50	$22.50	$45.00	£5.00	£15.00	£30.00
28-33 ND	$5.00	$15.00	$30.00	£3.30	£10.00	£20.00
Title Value:	$37.50	$112.50	$225.00	£24.80	£75.00	£150.00

ROOTS OF THE SWAMP THING
DC Comics,MS; 1 Jul 1986-5 Nov 1986

	$Good	$Fine	$N.Mint	£Good	£Fine	£N.Mint
1 ND DS	$0.90	$2.70	$4.50	£0.60	£1.80	£3.00
2-5 ND DS	$0.80	$2.40	$4.00	£0.50	£1.50	£2.50
Title Value:	$4.10	$12.30	$20.50	£2.60	£7.80	£13.00

Note: reprints original Swamp Thing series #1-10, Berni Wrightson art. Deluxe Format Baxter paper.

ROSCOE! THE DAWG DETECTIVE
Renegade; 1 Jul 1987-4 Jan 1988

	$Good	$Fine	$N.Mint	£Good	£Fine	£N.Mint
1-4 ND black and white	$0.30	$0.90	$1.50	£0.20	£0.60	£1.00
Title Value:	$1.20	$3.60	$6.00	£0.80	£2.40	£4.00

ROSE & GUNN
Bishop Press; 1 Jan 1995-present

	$Good	$Fine	$N.Mint	£Good	£Fine	£N.Mint
1 ND features art by Everett Hartsoe and London Night Studios; black and white	$0.60	$1.80	$3.00	£0.40	£1.20	£2.00
2-6 black and white	$0.60	$1.80	$3.00	£0.40	£1.20	£2.00
Title Value:	$3.60	$10.80	$18.00	£2.40	£7.20	£12.00

ROSE, THE
Hero,OS; 1 Dec 1992

	$Good	$Fine	$N.Mint	£Good	£Fine	£N.Mint
1 ND spin-off from The Champions, Mark Beachum art; black and white	$0.30	$0.90	$1.50	£0.20	£0.60	£1.00
Title Value:	$0.30	$0.90	$1.50	£0.20	£0.60	£1.00

ROUGH RAIDERS ANNUAL
Blue Comet Press; 1 1990

	$Good	$Fine	$N.Mint	£Good	£Fine	£N.Mint
1 ND black and white	$0.40	$1.20	$2.00	£0.25	£0.75	£1.25
Title Value:	$0.40	$1.20	$2.00	£0.25	£0.75	£1.25

ROVERS
Malibu; 1 Sep 1987-6 Feb 1988

	$Good	$Fine	$N.Mint	£Good	£Fine	£N.Mint
1-6 ND	$0.30	$0.90	$1.50	£0.20	£0.60	£1.00
Title Value:	$1.80	$5.40	$9.00	£1.20	£3.60	£6.00

ROVERS, THE
Mindgame Corporation; 1 Dec 1990

	$Good	$Fine	$N.Mint	£Good	£Fine	£N.Mint
1 ND 40pgs	$0.40	$1.20	$2.00	£0.25	£0.75	£1.25
Title Value:	$0.40	$1.20	$2.00	£0.25	£0.75	£1.25

ROYAL ROY
Marvel Comics Group/Star; 1 Jun 1985-5 Feb 1986

	$Good	$Fine	$N.Mint	£Good	£Fine	£N.Mint
1-5	$0.15	$0.45	$0.75	£0.10	£0.35	£0.60
Title Value:	$0.75	$2.25	$3.75	£0.50	£1.75	£3.00

RUINS
Marvel Comics Group,MS; 1 Aug 1995-2 Sep 1995

1-2 ND photo-journalist Phil Seldon (from Marvels mini-series) appears; Warren Ellis script,

VERY GENERAL PERCENTAGE CONVERSION CHART WHICH MAY BE USED TO CALCULATE LOW AND INBETWEEN GRADES:

	$Good	$Fine	$N.Mint	£Good	£Fine	£N.Mint
Cliff and Terese Nielsen art; acetate outer cover	$1.00	$3.00	$5.00	£0.65	£1.95	£3.25
Title Value:	$2.00	$6.00	$10.00	£1.30	£3.90	£6.50

RUNE
Malibu Ultraverse; 0 1995; 1 Jan 1994-9 Apr 1995

	$Good	$Fine	$N.Mint	£Good	£Fine	£N.Mint
0 obtained by sending away coupons in 11 Ultraverse issues, came with Solution #0 tattoo card & poster	$1.50	$4.50	$7.50	£1.00	£3.00	£5.00
1 Barry Windsor Smith script and art begins; origin Rune	$0.50	$1.50	$2.50	£0.30	£0.90	£1.50
1 16pgs, Ash Can Edition (Jan 1994) flip sided with Wrath	$0.50	$0.90	$1.50	£0.20	£0.60	£1.00
2	$0.40	$1.20	$2.00	£0.25	£0.75	£1.25
3 64pgs, flip side is Ultraverse Premiere #1 featuring Warstrike and Ripfire	$0.50	$1.50	$2.50	£0.30	£0.90	£1.50
4-8	$0.40	$1.20	$2.00	£0.25	£0.75	£1.25
9 prelude to Godwheel story	$0.40	$1.20	$2.00	£0.25	£0.75	£1.25
Title Value:	$5.60	$16.80	$28.00	£3.55	£10.65	£17.75

Note: all Non-Distributed on the news-stands in the U.K.

Rune: The Awakening (Apr 1995)

				£Good	£Fine	£N.Mint
Trade paperback collects issues #1-5, Barry Windsor-Smith cover				£1.70	£5.10	£8.50

Rune: The Awakening Limited Edition (Apr 1995)

				£Good	£Fine	£N.Mint
as above but with foil-stamped cover, shrink-wrapped with sticker that announces 1,000 copies plus Rune #1 Ultra Limited comic				£4.00	£12.00	£20.00

RUNE (2ND SERIES)
Marvel Comics Group; 1 Dec 1995-present

	$Good	$Fine	$N.Mint	£Good	£Fine	£N.Mint
1 ND Len Kaminski script, Kyle Hotz art, cover by Kyle Hotz and Tim Vigil; Rune vs. Annihilus, Adam Warlock appears	$0.30	$0.90	$1.50	£0.20	£0.60	£1.00
1 ND variant cover, computer painted cover by Chuck Maiden	$0.80	$2.40	$4.00	£0.50	£1.50	£2.50
1 ND Signed Limited Edition (Jan 1996), with certificate; 2,000 copies	$1.50	$4.50	$7.50	£1.00	£3.00	£5.00
2 ND Adam Warlock guest-stars, flip-book format with Phoenix Ressurrection chapter	$0.30	$0.90	$1.50	£0.20	£0.60	£1.00
3 ND Adam Warlock guest-stars	$0.30	$0.90	$1.50	£0.20	£0.60	£1.00
4 ND	$0.30	$0.90	$1.50	£0.20	£0.60	£1.00
Title Value:	$3.50	$10.50	$17.50	£2.30	£6.90	£11.50

RUNE ASHCAN EDITION
Malibu Ultraverse,OS; nn Apr 1994

	$Good	$Fine	$N.Mint	£Good	£Fine	£N.Mint
nn ND 16pgs, black and white	$0.15	$0.45	$0.75	£0.10	£0.30	£0.50
Title Value:	$0.15	$0.45	$0.75	£0.10	£0.30	£0.50

RUNE INDEX
Malibu; 1993

Barry Windsor-Smith's Rune story was available as inserts in particular issues of Malibu comics across certain months. The list in alphabetical order is as follows: Exiles #3, Firearm #2, Freex #4, Hardcase #5, Mantra #4, Night Man #1, Prime #5, Prototype #3, Sludge #1 (part 1), Strangers #5 along with Rune #0 and The Solution #0 which were available direct from Malibu in return for coupons from all the above comics sent back.

RUNE VS. VENOM
Marvel Comics Group,OS; 1 Feb 1996

	$Good	$Fine	$N.Mint	£Good	£Fine	£N.Mint
1 ND 48pgs, Chris Ulm script	$0.90	$2.70	$4.50	£0.60	£1.80	£3.00
1 ND Signed Limited Edition (Feb 1996) – with certificate; 2,000 copies	$2.00	$6.00	$10.00	£1.20	£3.60	£6.00
Title Value:	$2.90	$8.70	$14.50	£1.80	£5.40	£9.00

RUNE, CURSE OF
Malibu Ultraverse,MS; 1 May 1995-4 Jul 1995

	$Good	$Fine	$N.Mint	£Good	£Fine	£N.Mint
1 ND Cover #1A, the left-hand side of a complete poster; Chris Ulm script, Kyle Hotz art; ties into Rune/Silver Surfer #1 and Warlock and the Infinity Watch #42	$0.40	$1.20	$2.00	£0.25	£0.75	£1.25
1 ND Cover #1B, the right-hand side of a complete poster; Chris Ulm script, Kyle Hotz art; ties into Rune/Silver Surfer #1 and Warlock and the Infinity Watch #42	$0.40	$1.20	$2.00	£0.25	£0.75	£1.25
2 ND Rune has Adam Warlock's soul-gem imbedded in his skull	$0.40	$1.20	$2.00	£0.25	£0.75	£1.25
3 ND Loki appears, Gemini vs. Rune	$0.40	$1.20	$2.00	£0.25	£0.75	£1.25
4 ND Rune enters the Negative Zone, Adam Warlock crosses to the Ultraverse	$0.40	$1.20	$2.00	£0.25	£0.75	£1.25
Title Value:	$2.00	$6.00	$10.00	£1.25	£3.75	£6.25

RUNE, GIANT SIZE
Malibu Ultraverse; 1 Sep 1994

	$Good	$Fine	$N.Mint	£Good	£Fine	£N.Mint
1 ND 40pgs, Rune discovers he must exclusively feed on ultrahumans	$0.40	$1.20	$2.00	£0.25	£0.75	£1.25
Title Value:	$0.40	$1.20	$2.00	£0.25	£0.75	£1.25

RUNE/SILVER SURFER
Marvel Comics Group/Malibu Ultraverse,OS; 1 Apr 1995

	$Good	$Fine	$N.Mint	£Good	£Fine	£N.Mint
1 ND 48pgs, Chris Ulm script, Flint Henry art; Barry Windsor-Smith art (flip-book format)	$0.90	$2.70	$4.50	£0.60	£1.80	£3.00
1 ND Collector's Limited Edition (Apr 1995) – foil-stamped cover, limited to 5,000 copies	$1.20	$3.60	$6.00	£0.80	£2.40	£4.00
1 Newstand edition, ND without cover enhancement	$0.60	$1.80	$3.00	£0.40	£1.20	£2.00
Title Value:	$2.70	$8.10	$13.50	£1.80	£5.40	£9.00

RUNE: INFINITY
Marvel Comics Group,OS; nn Nov 1995

	$Good	$Fine	$N.Mint	£Good	£Fine	£N.Mint
nn ND Black September tie-in; Rune vs. Annihilus, Adam Warlock establishes his home in the Ultraverse	$0.50	$1.50	$2.50	£0.30	£0.90	£1.50
nn ND Variant cover; 1 copy recieved for every 5 copies of regular edition ordered	$0.80	$2.40	$4.00	£0.50	£1.50	£2.50
Title Value:	$1.30	$3.90	$6.50	£0.80	£2.40	£4.00

RUNE: THE DARK GOD
Malibu,OS; nn Jan 1995

	$Good	$Fine	$N.Mint	£Good	£Fine	£N.Mint
1 ND originally issued with Spin Magazine; Barry Windsor Smith art	$0.90	$2.70	$4.50	£0.60	£1.80	£3.00
Title Value:	$0.90	$2.70	$4.50	£0.60	£1.80	£3.00

RUST
Now Comics; 1 Jul 1987-13 Sep 1988

	$Good	$Fine	$N.Mint	£Good	£Fine	£N.Mint
1-11 ND	$0.40	$1.20	$2.00	£0.25	£0.75	£1.25
12 ND Terminator preview (5pgs)	$0.80	$2.40	$4.00	£0.50	£1.50	£2.50
13 ND	$0.40	$1.20	$2.00	£0.25	£0.75	£1.25
Title Value:	$5.60	$16.80	$28.00	£3.50	£10.50	£17.50

RUST (2ND SERIES)
Now Comics; 1 Feb 1989-7 Jun 1989

	$Good	$Fine	$N.Mint	£Good	£Fine	£N.Mint
1-7 ND painted artwork	$0.40	$1.20	$2.00	£0.25	£0.75	£1.25
Title Value:	$2.80	$8.40	$14.00	£1.75	£5.25	£8.75

RUST (3RD SERIES)
Adventure; 1 Apr 1992-4 Sep 1992

	$Good	$Fine	$N.Mint	£Good	£Fine	£N.Mint
1 ND painted cover by Dave Dorman	$0.50	$1.50	$2.50	£0.30	£0.90	£1.50
1 ND Limited Edition (Apr 1992) – gold foil-embossed cover and serial numbered on back cover, additional features	$0.70	$2.10	$3.50	£0.50	£1.50	£2.50
2 ND	$0.50	$1.50	$2.50	£0.30	£0.90	£1.50
2 2nd printing, ND (Sep 1992)	$0.40	$1.20	$2.00	£0.25	£0.75	£1.25
3-4 ND	$0.50	$1.50	$2.50	£0.30	£0.90	£1.50
Title Value:	$3.10	$9.30	$15.50	£1.95	£5.85	£9.75

Rook #1

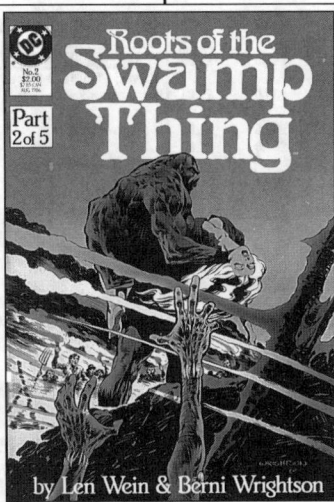

Roots of the Swamp Thing #2

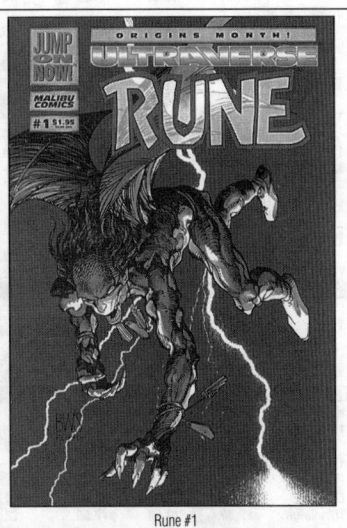

Rune #1

MINT = 100% / NEAR MINT (inc. +/-) = 90–99% / VERY FINE (inc. +/-) = 75–89% / FINE (inc. +/-) = 55–74%
VERY GOOD (inc. +/-) = 35–54% / GOOD (inc. +/-) = 15–34% / FAIR = 5–14% / POOR = 1–4%

523

	$Good	$Fine	$N.Mint	£Good	£Fine	£N.Mint

S

S.T.A.R. CORPS
DC Comics,MS; 1 Nov 1993-6 Apr 1994
1 Superman appears

	$Good	$Fine	$N.Mint	£Good	£Fine	£N.Mint
	$0.30	$0.90	$1.50	£0.20	£0.60	£1.00
2-6	$0.30	$0.90	$1.50	£0.20	£0.60	£1.00
Title Value:	$1.80	$5.40	$9.00	£1.20	£3.60	£6.00

SABER TIGER
Viz,OS; 1 Jul 1991
1 ND 80pgs

	$1.20	$3.60	$6.00	£0.80	£2.40	£4.00
Title Value:	$1.20	$3.60	$6.00	£0.80	£2.40	£4.00

SABLE
First; 1 Mar 1988-27 May 1990
(formerly Jon Sable, Freelance; see also Mike Grell's Sable)
1 ND

	$0.30	$0.90	$1.50	£0.20	£0.60	£1.00

2 ND scarce in the U.K.

	$0.30	$0.90	$1.50	£0.25	£0.75	£1.25
3-27 ND	$0.30	$0.90	$1.50	£0.20	£0.60	£1.00
Title Value:	$8.10	$24.30	$40.50	£5.45	£16.35	£27.25

SABRE
Eclipse; 1 Sep 1982-14 1985
1 ND Don McGregor script begins, Kent Williams covers

	$0.40	$1.20	$2.00	£0.25	£0.75	£1.25
2-14 ND	$0.40	$1.20	$2.00	£0.25	£0.75	£1.25
Title Value:	$5.60	$16.80	$28.00	£3.50	£10.50	£17.50

SABRE (2ND SERIES)
Eclipse; (Graphic Novel) nn Oct 1978
nn ND Don McGregor script, Paul Gulacy art

	$1.50	$4.50	$7.50	£1.00	£3.00	£5.00
Title Value:	$1.50	$4.50	$7.50	£1.00	£3.00	£5.00
nn 2nd print (Jan 1979)				£0.90	£2.70	£4.50
nn 3rd print				£0.65	£2.55	£4.25

SABRETOOTH
Marvel Comics Group,MS; 1 Aug 1993-4 Nov 1993
1 die-cut logo giving "shredded" effect

	$0.80	$2.40	$4.00	£0.60	£1.80	£3.00

1 ND Dynamic Forces Edition, signed by Mark Texeira limited to 10,000 copies

	$3.00	$9.00	$15.00	£2.00	£6.00	£10.00

2 Wolverine appears, card stock cover

	$0.80	$2.40	$4.00	£0.60	£1.80	£3.00
3-4	$0.80	$2.40	$4.00	£0.60	£1.80	£3.00
Title Value:	$6.20	$18.60	$31.00	£4.40	£13.20	£22.00

Sabretooth: Death Hunt (Feb 1995)
Trade paperback reprints four issue mini-series | | | | £1.70 | £5.10 | £8.50

SABRETOOTH CLASSICS
Marvel Comics Group; 1 May 1994-15 Jul 1995
1 reprints Sabretooth's 2nd appearance from Powerman and Iron Fist #66

	$0.30	$0.90	$1.50	£0.20	£0.60	£1.00

2 reprints Sabretooth's 3rd appearance from Powerman and Iron Fist #78

	$0.30	$0.90	$1.50	£0.20	£0.60	£1.00

3 reprints Sabretooth's 4th appearance from Powerman and Iron Fist #84

	$0.30	$0.90	$1.50	£0.20	£0.60	£1.00

4 reprints Sabretooth's 5th appearance from Spectacular Spiderman #116

	$0.30	$0.90	$1.50	£0.20	£0.60	£1.00

5 reprints from Spectacular Spiderman #119

	$0.30	$0.90	$1.50	£0.20	£0.60	£1.00

6 reprints from X-Factor #10

	$0.30	$0.90	$1.50	£0.20	£0.60	£1.00

7 reprints from Thor #374

	$0.30	$0.90	$1.50	£0.20	£0.60	£1.00

8 reprints X-Men #212

	$0.30	$0.90	$1.50	£0.20	£0.60	£1.00

9 reprints X-Men #213

	$0.30	$0.90	$1.50	£0.20	£0.60	£1.00

10 reprints X-Men #214

	$0.30	$0.90	$1.50	£0.20	£0.60	£1.00

11 reprints Daredevil #238

	$0.30	$0.90	$1.50	£0.20	£0.60	£1.00
12	$0.30	$0.90	$1.50	£0.20	£0.60	£1.00

13 reprints X-Men #219

	$0.30	$0.90	$1.50	£0.20	£0.60	£1.00

14 reprints X-Men #220

	$0.30	$0.90	$1.50	£0.20	£0.60	£1.00

15 reprints X-Men #221

	$0.30	$0.90	$1.50	£0.20	£0.60	£1.00
Title Value:	$4.50	$13.50	$22.50	£3.00	£9.00	£15.00

SABRETOOTH SPECIAL
Marvel Comics Group,OS; 1 Jan 1996
1 ND 48pgs, X-Men appear, Gary Frank art; wraparound chromium cover; continued from Uncanny X-Men #328 and X-Men #48

	$1.00	$3.00	$5.00	£0.70	£2.10	£3.50
Title Value:	$1.00	$3.00	$5.00	£0.70	£2.10	£3.50

SACHS & VIOLENS
Marvel Comics Group/Epic,MS; 1 Nov 1993-4 Jul 1994
1 ND Peter David and George Perez art begins; embossed cover and bound-in trading card

	$0.50	$1.50	$2.50	£0.30	£0.90	£1.50

1 ND Silver Premium Edition

	$1.50	$4.50	$7.50	£1.00	£3.00	£5.00
2-4 ND	$0.50	$1.50	$2.50	£0.30	£0.90	£1.50
Title Value:	$3.50	$10.50	$17.50	£2.20	£6.60	£11.00

SAD SACK AND THE SARGE
Harvey; 1 Sep 1957-155 Jun 1982
1 scarce in the U.K.

	$12.50	$39.00	$90.00	£8.50	£26.00	£60.00

2 scarce in the U.K.

	$5.25	$16.00	$37.50	£3.55	£10.50	£25.00

3-5 scarce in the U.K.

	$5.00	$15.00	$35.00	£3.20	£9.50	£22.50
6-10	$5.00	$15.00	$35.00	£2.85	£8.50	£20.00
11-20	$4.15	$12.50	$25.00	£2.50	£7.50	£15.00
21-30	$2.50	$7.50	$15.00	£1.65	£5.00	£10.00
31-40	$1.65	$5.00	$10.00	£1.15	£3.50	£7.00
41-50	$1.50	$4.50	$9.00	£1.00	£3.00	£6.00
51-70	$1.25	$3.75	$7.50	£0.80	£2.50	£5.00
71-90	$1.00	$3.00	$5.00	£0.70	£2.10	£3.50
91-96 48pgs	$1.20	$3.60	$6.00	£0.80	£2.40	£4.00
97-100	$1.00	$3.00	$5.00	£0.70	£2.10	£3.50
101-120	$0.80	$2.40	$4.00	£0.50	£1.50	£2.50
121-155	$0.70	$2.10	$3.50	£0.40	£1.20	£2.00
Title Value:	$252.45	$760.10	$1506.00	£160.50	£484.30	£960.50

Note: although the title is dated well before official distribution in the U.K. (cover dates November 1959, therefore distributed early 1960), it is possible that all issues from #1 came over.

SAD SACK ARMY LIFE (PARADE/TODAY)
Harvey; 1 Oct 1963-60 Nov 1975; 61 May 1976
(...Parade to #57; ...Today from #58 on)
1 scarce in the U.K.

	$5.50	$17.00	$40.00	£3.55	£10.50	£25.00

2 scarce in the U.K. 64pgs

	$4.15	$12.50	$25.00	£2.50	£7.50	£15.00

3 scarce in the U.K. 64pgs

	$3.30	$10.00	$20.00	£2.05	£6.25	£12.50
4-10 64pgs	$2.50	$7.50	$15.00	£1.65	£5.00	£10.00
11-20 64pgs	$1.65	$5.00	$10.00	£1.25	£3.75	£7.50
21-34 64pgs	$1.50	$4.50	$7.50	£1.00	£3.00	£5.00
35-40 48pgs	$1.00	$3.00	$5.00	£0.60	£1.80	£3.00
41-51 48pgs	$0.60	$1.80	$3.00	£0.40	£1.20	£2.00
52 regular 32pgs begins	$0.40	$1.20	$2.00	£0.25	£0.75	£1.25
53-60	$0.40	$1.20	$2.00	£0.25	£0.75	£1.25

61 scarce in the U.K.

	$0.40	$1.20	$2.00	£0.30	£0.90	£1.50
Title Value:	$84.55	$254.80	$478.00	£56.70	£170.40	£320.25

Note: all distributed on the news-stands in the U.K.

SAD SACK IN 3-D
Blackthorne; (3-D Series #49) 1 Autumn 1988
1 ND with bound-in 3-D glasses (25% less without glasses)

	$0.40	$1.20	$2.00	£0.25	£0.75	£1.25
Title Value:	$0.40	$1.20	$2.00	£0.25	£0.75	£1.25

SAD SACK LAUGH SPECIAL
Harvey; 1 Nov 1958-93 Feb 1977
1 scarce in the U.K. 64pgs

	$11.00	$34.00	$80.00	£7.75	£23.50	£55.00

2 scarce in the U.K. 64pgs

	$6.50	$20.00	$40.00	£4.15	£12.50	£25.00
3-5 64pgs	$5.00	$15.00	$30.00	£3.30	£10.00	£20.00
6-10 64pgs	$4.15	$12.50	$25.00	£2.50	£7.50	£15.00
11-30 64pgs	$2.50	$7.50	$15.00	£1.65	£5.00	£10.00
31-50 64pgs	$1.65	$5.00	$10.00	£1.25	£3.75	£7.50
51-60 64pgs	$1.50	$4.50	$7.50	£1.00	£3.00	£5.00
61-76 48pgs	$1.20	$3.60	$6.00	£0.80	£2.40	£4.00
77 regular 32pg issues begin	$1.00	$3.00	$5.00	£0.60	£1.80	£3.00
78-93	$1.00	$3.00	$5.00	£0.60	£1.80	£3.00
Title Value:	$187.45	$565.10	$1091.00	£125.30	£377.50	£730.00

Note: all distributed in the U.K. though more experimentally for the first few issues

SAD SACK WITH SARGE AND SADIE
Harvey; 1 Sep 1972-8 Nov 1973
1 distributed in the U.K. 48pgs

	$1.20	$3.60	$6.00	£0.80	£2.40	£4.00

2 distributed in the U.K.

	$0.80	$2.40	$4.00	£0.50	£1.50	£2.50

3-8 distributed in the U.K.

	$0.50	$1.50	$2.50	£0.30	£0.90	£1.50
Title Value:	$5.00	$15.00	$25.00	£3.10	£9.30	£15.50

SADE
Bishop Press; 1 Nov 1995-present
1 ND black and white

	$0.60	$1.80	$3.00	£0.40	£1.20	£2.00
Title Value:	$0.60	$1.80	$3.00	£0.40	£1.20	£2.00

SAFEST PLACE, THE
Dark Horse,OS; nn Jun 1993
nn ND Steve Ditko script and art

	$0.50	$1.50	$2.50	£0.30	£0.90	£1.50
Title Value:	$0.50	$1.50	$2.50	£0.30	£0.90	£1.50

SAGA OF RA'S AL GHUL
DC Comics,MS; 1 Jan 1988-4 Apr 1988
(see Batman)
1 ND scarce in the U.K. Neal Adams art, reprints 1st appearance in Batman #232

	$0.70	$2.10	$3.50	£0.40	£1.20	£2.00

2 ND scarce in the U.K.

	$0.70	$2.10	$3.50	£0.40	£1.20	£2.00

3 ND scarce in the U.K. Neal Adams art, reprints Batman #243

	$Good	$Fine	$N.Mint	£Good	£Fine	£N.Mint
	$0.70	$2.10	$3.50	£0.40	£1.20	£2.00
4 ND scarce in the U.K. Neal Adams art, reprints Batman #244						
	$0.70	$2.10	$3.50	£0.40	£1.20	£2.00
Title Value:	$2.80	$8.40	$14.00	£1.60	£4.80	£8.00

SAGA OF SWAMP THING
(see Swamp Thing)

SAGE
Fantaco; 1 Oct 1995

	$Good	$Fine	$N.Mint	£Good	£Fine	£N.Mint
1 ND Tom Simonton script and art; black and white						
	$1.00	$3.00	$5.00	£0.60	£1.80	£3.00
Title Value:	$1.00	$3.00	$5.00	£0.60	£1.80	£3.00

SAIGON CHRONICLES, THE
A Plus Comics; 1 Sep 1991-2 1991

	$Good	$Fine	$N.Mint	£Good	£Fine	£N.Mint
1-2 ND 48pgs, new and reprint war stories						
	$0.40	$1.20	$2.00	£0.25	£0.75	£1.25
Title Value:	$0.80	$2.40	$4.00	£0.50	£1.50	£2.50

SAINT SINNER
Marvel Comics Group/Razorline; 1 Oct 1993-7 Apr 1994

	$Good	$Fine	$N.Mint	£Good	£Fine	£N.Mint
1-7 ND based on Clive Barker characters						
	$0.30	$0.90	$1.50	£0.20	£0.60	£1.00
Title Value:	$2.10	$6.30	$10.50	£1.40	£4.20	£7.00

SALIMBA 3-D
Blackthorne,MS; (3-D Series #6,#9); 1 Aug 1986-2 Sep 1986

	$Good	$Fine	$N.Mint	£Good	£Fine	£N.Mint
1-2 ND all Paul Chadwick wraparound cover/art; with 3-D glasses (25% less if without glasses)						
	$0.80	$2.40	$4.00	£0.60	£1.80	£3.00
Title Value:	$1.60	$4.80	$8.00	£1.20	£3.60	£6.00

SALOME
Eclipse; (Night Music 5) 1 1987

	$Good	$Fine	$N.Mint	£Good	£Fine	£N.Mint
1 ND P. Craig Russell art						
	$0.40	$1.20	$2.00	£0.25	£0.75	£1.25
Title Value:	$0.40	$1.20	$2.00	£0.25	£0.75	£1.25

SAM & MAX COLOUR COLLECTION
Marvel Comics Group,OS; 1 Sep 1992

	$Good	$Fine	$N.Mint	£Good	£Fine	£N.Mint
1 ND 64pgs	$0.80	$2.40	$4.00	£0.50	£1.50	£2.50
Title Value:	$0.80	$2.40	$4.00	£0.50	£1.50	£2.50

SAM & MAX FREELANCE POLICE SPECIAL
Comico; 1 Jan 1989

	$Good	$Fine	$N.Mint	£Good	£Fine	£N.Mint
1 ND 40pgs, colour	$0.40	$1.20	$2.00	£0.25	£0.75	£1.25
Title Value:	$0.40	$1.20	$2.00	£0.25	£0.75	£1.25

SAM & MAX FREELANCE POLICE SPECIAL EDITION
Fishwrap Productions; 1 1987

	$Good	$Fine	$N.Mint	£Good	£Fine	£N.Mint
1 ND Steve Purcell script and art, black & white						
	$0.40	$1.20	$2.00	£0.25	£0.75	£1.25
Title Value:	$0.40	$1.20	$2.00	£0.25	£0.75	£1.25

SAM & MAX GO TO THE MOON DIRT BAG SPECIAL
Marvel Comics Group,OS; 1 Jun 1992

	$Good	$Fine	$N.Mint	£Good	£Fine	£N.Mint
1 ND pre-bagged, Sam & Max comic, "Dirt" magazine, pop music cassette						
	$0.70	$2.10	$3.50	£0.40	£1.20	£2.00
Title Value:	$0.70	$2.10	$3.50	£0.40	£1.20	£2.00

SAM & MAX SHOW, THE
Marvel Comics Group,MS; 1 May 1993-3 Jul 1993

	$Good	$Fine	$N.Mint	£Good	£Fine	£N.Mint
1-3 ND Mike Mignola and Art Adams art featured						
	$0.50	$1.50	$2.50	£0.30	£0.90	£1.50
Title Value:	$1.50	$4.50	$7.50	£0.90	£2.70	£4.50

SAMURAI
Aircel; 1 1985-23 1987

	$Good	$Fine	$N.Mint	£Good	£Fine	£N.Mint
1 scarce in the U.K.	$0.80	$2.40	$4.00	£0.50	£1.50	£2.50
1 2nd printing, (1986)						
	$0.40	$1.20	$2.00	£0.25	£0.75	£1.25
1 3rd printing	$0.40	$1.20	$2.00	£0.25	£0.75	£1.25
2	$0.50	$1.50	$2.50	£0.30	£0.90	£1.50
2 2nd printing	$0.40	$1.20	$2.00	£0.25	£0.75	£1.25
3-12	$0.40	$1.20	$2.00	£0.25	£0.75	£1.25
13 Dale Keown cover and art (1st pro work?)						
	$0.80	$2.40	$4.00	£0.40	£1.20	£2.00
14-16 Dale Keown cover and art						
	$0.60	$1.80	$3.00	£0.30	£0.90	£1.50
17-18 Dale Keown inks only						
	$0.50	$1.50	$2.50	£0.30	£0.90	£1.50
19-23	$0.40	$1.20	$2.00	£0.25	£0.75	£1.25
Title Value:	$12.10	$36.30	$60.50	£7.20	£21.60	£36.00

Note: all Non-Distributed on the news-stands in the U.K.

SAMURAI (2ND SERIES)
Aircel; 1 Aug 1988-2 1988

	$Good	$Fine	$N.Mint	£Good	£Fine	£N.Mint
1 ND 1st colour issue						
	$0.40	$1.20	$2.00	£0.25	£0.75	£1.25
2 ND	$0.40	$1.20	$2.00	£0.25	£0.75	£1.25
Title Value:	$0.80	$2.40	$4.00	£0.50	£1.50	£2.50

SAMURAI (3RD SERIES)
Aircel; 1 1989-7 1990?

	$Good	$Fine	$N.Mint	£Good	£Fine	£N.Mint
1-7 ND	$0.40	$1.20	$2.00	£0.25	£0.75	£1.25
Title Value:	$2.80	$8.40	$14.00	£1.75	£5.25	£8.75

SAMURAI CAT
Marvel Comics Group/Epic,MS; 1 Jun 1991-3 Aug 1991

	$Good	$Fine	$N.Mint	£Good	£Fine	£N.Mint
1-3 ND Frank Cirocco art						
	$0.40	$1.20	$2.00	£0.25	£0.75	£1.25
Title Value:	$1.20	$3.60	$6.00	£0.75	£2.25	£3.75

SAMURAI FUNNIES
Solson Publications; 2-3 1987

	$Good	$Fine	$N.Mint	£Good	£Fine	£N.Mint
2 ND Friday 13th film parody ("Samurai the 13th")						
	$0.30	$0.90	$1.50	£0.15	£0.45	£0.75
3 ND scarce in the U.K.						

	$Good	$Fine	$N.Mint	£Good	£Fine	£N.Mint
	$0.30	$0.90	$1.50	£0.20	£0.60	£1.00
Title Value:	$0.60	$1.80	$3.00	£0.35	£1.05	£1.75

SAMURAI PENGUIN
Slave Labor; 1 1986-9 Jun 1988

	$Good	$Fine	$N.Mint	£Good	£Fine	£N.Mint
1 ND	$0.30	$0.90	$1.50	£0.20	£0.60	£1.00
2 ND intro Dr. Radium						
	$0.30	$0.90	$1.50	£0.20	£0.60	£1.00
3 ND	$0.30	$0.90	$1.50	£0.20	£0.60	£1.00
4 ND Boris the Bear parody						
	$0.30	$0.90	$1.50	£0.20	£0.60	£1.00
5 ND	$0.30	$0.90	$1.50	£0.20	£0.60	£1.00
6 ND colour issue; says number 7 in indicia						
	$0.30	$0.90	$1.50	£0.20	£0.60	£1.00
7-9 ND	$0.30	$0.90	$1.50	£0.20	£0.60	£1.00
Title Value:	$2.70	$8.10	$13.50	£1.80	£5.40	£9.00
Food Chain Follies (Jun 1991), 64pgs, reprints #1-3				£0.50	£1.50	£2.50

SAMURAI SANTA
Solson Publications,OS; 1 1987
(becomes Samurai Funnies)

	$Good	$Fine	$N.Mint	£Good	£Fine	£N.Mint
1 ND Jim Lee art, his 1st in comics (black and white)						
	$0.80	$2.40	$4.00	£0.50	£1.50	£2.50
Title Value:	$0.80	$2.40	$4.00	£0.50	£1.50	£2.50

SAMURAI SEVEN
Caliber Press; 1 Jul 1992-4 Jan 1993

	$Good	$Fine	$N.Mint	£Good	£Fine	£N.Mint
1-4 ND	$0.40	$1.20	$2.00	£0.25	£0.75	£1.25
Title Value:	$1.60	$4.80	$8.00	£1.00	£3.00	£5.00

SAMURAI SQUIRREL
Spotlight; 1 1986-2 1987

	$Good	$Fine	$N.Mint	£Good	£Fine	£N.Mint
1-2 ND	$0.40	$1.20	$2.00	£0.25	£0.75	£1.25
Title Value:	$0.80	$2.40	$4.00	£0.50	£1.50	£2.50

SAMURAI, SON OF DEATH
Eclipse; (Graphic Novel 14); nn 1987

	$Good	$Fine	$N.Mint	£Good	£Fine	£N.Mint
nn ND				£0.60	£1.80	£3.00
nn ND 2nd print				£0.55	£1.65	£2.75

SAMURAI: DEATH OF A LEGEND
Night Wynd,MS; 1 Apr 1993-4 Jul 1993

	$Good	$Fine	$N.Mint	£Good	£Fine	£N.Mint
1-4 ND Barry Blair and Dale Keown						
	$0.40	$1.20	$2.00	£0.25	£0.75	£1.25
Title Value:	$1.60	$4.80	$8.00	£1.00	£3.00	£5.00

SAMURAI: DEMON SWORD
Night Wynd,MS; 1 Aug 1993-4 Nov 1993

	$Good	$Fine	$N.Mint	£Good	£Fine	£N.Mint
1-4 ND Barry Blair script and art begins; black and white						
	$0.40	$1.20	$2.00	£0.25	£0.75	£1.25
Title Value:	$1.60	$4.80	$8.00	£1.00	£3.00	£5.00

SAMURAI: MYSTIC CULT
Night Wynd,MS; 1 Nov 1992-4 Mar 1993

	$Good	$Fine	$N.Mint	£Good	£Fine	£N.Mint
1-4 ND Barry Blair script and art						
	$0.40	$1.20	$2.00	£0.25	£0.75	£1.25
Title Value:	$1.60	$4.80	$8.00	£1.00	£3.00	£5.00

SAMURAI: VAMPIRE'S HUNT
Night Wynd,MS; 1 Jul 1992-4 Oct 1992

	$Good	$Fine	$N.Mint	£Good	£Fine	£N.Mint
1-4 ND Barry Blair script and art						
	$0.40	$1.20	$2.00	£0.25	£0.75	£1.25
Title Value:	$1.60	$4.80	$8.00	£1.00	£3.00	£5.00

SAMURAI: YAKUZA'S REVENGE
Night Wynd,MS; 1 Apr 1993-4 Jul 1993

	$Good	$Fine	$N.Mint	£Good	£Fine	£N.Mint
1-4 ND Barry Blair and Patrick McEown						
	$0.40	$1.20	$2.00	£0.25	£0.75	£1.25
Title Value:	$1.60	$4.80	$8.00	£1.00	£3.00	£5.00

SAMUREE
Continuity; 1 May 1987-13 1992

	$Good	$Fine	$N.Mint	£Good	£Fine	£N.Mint
1 Neal Adams script, Mark Beachum art						
	$0.40	$1.20	$2.00	£0.25	£0.75	£1.25
2-3 Neal Adams cover						
	$0.40	$1.20	$2.00	£0.25	£0.75	£1.25
4 Neal Adams part pencils						
	$0.40	$1.20	$2.00	£0.25	£0.75	£1.25
5 Neal Adams plot	$0.40	$1.20	$2.00	£0.25	£0.75	£1.25
6-13	$0.40	$1.20	$2.00	£0.25	£0.75	£1.25
Title Value:	$5.20	$15.60	$26.00	£3.25	£9.75	£16.25

Note: all Non-Distributed on the news-stands in the U.K.

SAMUREE (2ND SERIES)
Continuity; 1 Aug 1993-4 1994

	$Good	$Fine	$N.Mint	£Good	£Fine	£N.Mint
1 ND Rise of Magic X-over, Neal Adams co-plot begins						
	$0.40	$1.20	$2.00	£0.25	£0.75	£1.25
2-4 ND Rise of Magic X-over, embossed parchment cover						
	$0.40	$1.20	$2.00	£0.25	£0.75	£1.25
Title Value:	$1.60	$4.80	$8.00	£1.00	£3.00	£5.00

SAMUREE (3RD SERIES)
Acclaim Comics/Windjammer,MS; 1 Jun 1995-3 Aug 1995

	$Good	$Fine	$N.Mint	£Good	£Fine	£N.Mint
1-3 ND Neal Adams pencils						
	$0.40	$1.20	$2.00	£0.25	£0.75	£1.25
Title Value:	$1.20	$3.60	$6.00	£0.75	£2.25	£3.75

SAN DIEGO COMICON COMICS
Dark Horse,OS; 1 Aug 1992

	$Good	$Fine	$N.Mint	£Good	£Fine	£N.Mint
1 ND special comic-convention jam featuring art by Joe Quesada, John Byrne, Moebius, Paul Chadwick, Steve Rude and many others; Paul Chadwick cover; available only at the convention						
	$0.80	$2.40	$4.00	£0.50	£1.50	£2.50
Title Value:	$0.80	$2.40	$4.00	£0.50	£1.50	£2.50

SANCTUARY
Viz Communications,MS; 1 May 1992-9 Jan 1993
1-9 ND 80pgs, black and white

	$Good	$Fine	$N.Mint	£Good	£Fine	£N.Mint
	$0.90	$2.70	$4.50	£0.60	£1.80	£3.00
Title Value:	$8.10	$24.30	$40.50	£5.40	£16.20	£27.00

Sanctuary Graphic Novel Vol 1 (1993)
reprints from series begin; black and white — £2.40 £7.20 £12.00
Sanctuary Graphic Novel Vol 2 (1994)
reprints from series continue; black and white — £2.40 £7.20 £12.00
Sanctuary Graphic Novel Vol 3 (Jan 1995)
reprints from series continue; black and white — £2.40 £7.20 £12.00
Sanctuary Graphic Novel Vol 4 (Mar 1995)
reprints from series continue; black and white — £2.40 £7.20 £12.00

SANCTUARY PART 2
Viz Communications,MS; 1 Jul 1993-9 Mar 1994
1-9 ND black and white

	$Good	$Fine	$N.Mint	£Good	£Fine	£N.Mint
	$0.90	$2.70	$4.50	£0.60	£1.80	£3.00
Title Value:	$8.10	$24.30	$40.50	£5.40	£16.20	£27.00

SANCTUARY PART 3
Viz Communications,MS; 1 Dec 1994-8 Jul 1995
1-8 ND 48pgs, Sho Fumimura; black and white

	$Good	$Fine	$N.Mint	£Good	£Fine	£N.Mint
	$0.60	$1.80	$3.00	£0.40	£1.20	£2.00
Title Value:	$4.80	$14.40	$24.00	£3.20	£9.60	£16.00

SANCTUARY PART 4
Viz Communications,MS; 1 Aug 1995-7 Feb 1996
1-7 ND Sho Fumimura and Ryoichi Ikegami script and art; black and white

	$Good	$Fine	$N.Mint	£Good	£Fine	£N.Mint
	$0.60	$1.80	$3.00	£0.40	£1.20	£2.00
Title Value:	$4.20	$12.60	$21.00	£2.80	£8.40	£14.00

SANDMAN
DC Comics; 1 Winter 1974; 2 Apr/May 1975-6 Dec/Jan 1975/76

	$Good	$Fine	$N.Mint	£Good	£Fine	£N.Mint
1 ND very scarce in the U.K. Jack Kirby art	$2.00	$6.00	$10.00	£1.30	£3.90	£6.50
2-3 Ernie Chua art	$1.00	$3.00	$5.00	£0.60	£1.80	£3.00
4-5 Jack Kirby art	$1.00	$3.00	$5.00	£0.60	£1.80	£3.00
6 Jack Kirby/Wally Wood art		$3.00	$5.00	£0.60	£1.80	£3.00
Title Value:	$7.00	$21.00	$35.00	£4.30	£12.90	£21.50

SANDMAN (2ND SERIES)
DC Comics/Vertigo; 1 Jan 1989-75 Mar 1996
(see Best of DC #22)

1 LD in the U.K. DS Neil Gaiman scripts, Sam Kieth/Mike Dringenberg art, Dave McKean paint & collage covers begin

	$Good	$Fine	$N.Mint	£Good	£Fine	£N.Mint
	$15.00	$45.00	$75.00	£4.00	£12.00	£20.00

2 very LD Sam Kieth art — $8.00 $24.00 $40.00 £2.00 £6.00 £10.00
3 LD in the U.K. Sam Kieth art — $7.00 $21.00 $35.00 £1.40 £4.20 £7.00
4-5 LD in the U.K. Sam Kieth art — $6.00 $18.00 $30.00 £1.20 £3.60 £6.00
6-7 LD in the U.K. $5.00 $15.00 $25.00 £1.00 £3.00 £5.00
8 LD in the U.K. (see note below), 1st appearance Death (Sandman's sister) — $10.00 $30.00 $50.00 £1.80 £5.25 £9.00
8 Variant edition ND (see notes below the Trade paperbacks) — $35.00 $105.00 $175.00 £20.00 £60.00 £100.00
9-10 LD in the U.K. — $3.00 $9.00 $15.00 £0.80 £2.40 £4.00
11-13 LD in the U.K. — $3.00 $9.00 $15.00 £0.70 £2.10 £3.50
14 LD in the U.K. DS — $3.00 $9.00 $15.00 £0.80 £2.40 £4.00
15-18 ND $2.00 $6.00 $10.00 £0.60 £1.80 £3.00
18 Misprint, ND first 3 panels on page 1 are coloured in blue ink — $6.00 $18.00 $30.00 £3.00 £9.00 £15.00
19 ND $2.00 $6.00 $10.00 £0.60 £1.80 £3.00
20 ND Element Girl appears and "dies" — $2.00 $6.00 $10.00 £0.60 £1.80 £3.00
21 ND Season of Mists story begins (part 0) — $2.00 $6.00 $10.00 £1.20 £3.60 £6.00
22 ND previews World Without End series, Season of Mists part 1 (ends #28); 1st appearance of Daniel later becomes the new Sandman — $3.00 $9.00 $15.00 £0.80 £2.40 £4.00
23 ND $2.00 $6.00 $10.00 £0.60 £1.80 £3.00
24 ND Phantom Stranger appears — $2.00 $6.00 $10.00 £0.60 £1.80 £3.00
25 ND $2.00 $6.00 $10.00 £0.60 £1.80 £3.00
26-29 ND $1.50 $4.50 $7.50 £0.50 £1.50 £2.50
30 ND Bryan Talbot art, Dave McKean cover — $1.50 $4.50 $7.50 £0.50 £1.50 £2.50
31 ND $1.00 $3.00 $5.00 £0.40 £1.20 £2.00
32 ND The Game of You part 1 — $1.00 $3.00 $5.00 £0.40 £1.20 £2.00
33-36 ND $1.00 $3.00 $5.00 £0.40 £1.20 £2.00
37 ND The Game of You part 6 (conclusion) — $0.70 $2.10 $3.50 £0.30 £0.90 £1.50
38 ND Duncan Eagleson/Vince Locke art — $0.70 $2.10 $3.50 £0.30 £0.90 £1.50
39 ND $0.70 $2.10 $3.50 £0.30 £0.90 £1.50
40 ND Jill Thompson art begins — $0.70 $2.10 $3.50 £0.30 £0.90 £1.50
41 ND $0.60 $1.80 $3.00 £0.30 £0.90 £1.50
42 ND Dave McKean painted covers begin — $0.60 $1.80 $3.00 £0.30 £0.90 £1.50
43-44 ND $0.60 $1.80 $3.00 £0.30 £0.90 £1.50
45 ND $1.75 cover begins — $0.60 $1.80 $3.00 £0.30 £0.90 £1.50

	$Good	$Fine	$N.Mint	£Good	£Fine	£N.Mint

46 ND Gaiman and McKean AIDS awareness back-up story — $0.60 $1.80 $3.00 £0.30 £0.90 £1.50
47 ND 1st issue under the "Vertigo" banner — $0.60 $1.80 $3.00 £0.30 £0.90 £1.50
48-49 ND $0.60 $1.80 $3.00 £0.30 £0.90 £1.50
50 ND 48pgs, anniversary issue with pin-ups by McFarlane, McKean, Kaluta and many others; wraparound black cover with gold metallic inks — $0.80 $2.40 $4.00 £0.40 £1.20 £2.00
50 ND Limited Edition - all black cover with gold titles — $10.00 $30.00 $50.00 £6.00 £18.00 £30.00
51-56 ND Bryan Talbot art featured — $0.50 $1.50 $2.50 £0.30 £0.90 £1.50
57 ND Marc Hempel art; American Freak preview; The Kindly Ones story — $0.50 $1.50 $2.50 £0.30 £0.90 £1.50
58-63 ND Marc Hempel art; The Kindly Ones story — $0.50 $1.50 $2.50 £0.30 £0.90 £1.50
64-68 ND $0.50 $1.50 $2.50 £0.30 £0.90 £1.50
69 ND The Kindly Ones storyline concludes, death of Sandman (Morpheus), Daniel takes over as the new Sandman — $1.00 $3.00 $5.00 £0.60 £1.80 £3.00
70-72 ND The Wake, Michael Zulli art — $0.50 $1.50 $2.50 £0.30 £0.90 £1.50
73 ND The Wake epilogue, Michael Zulli art — $0.50 $1.50 $2.50 £0.30 £0.90 £1.50
74 ND $0.50 $1.50 $2.50 £0.30 £0.90 £1.50
75 ND 48pgs, Charles Vess art plus 2pg "farewell" by Neil Gaiman — $0.80 $2.40 $4.00 £0.50 £1.50 £2.50

	$Good	$Fine	$N.Mint	£Good	£Fine	£N.Mint
Title Value:	$189.80	$569.40	$948.00	£71.70	£214.95	£358.50

Note: New Format, Mature Readers label
Preludes and Nocturnes (1991) reprints issues #1-8, 240pgs — £1.85 £5.55 £9.25
Preludes and Nocturnes hardcover (Oct 1995)
reprints issues #1-8 with new cover design by Dave McKean — £4.00 £12.00 £20.00
The Doll's House (1990) reprints issues #8-16, 256pgs — £1.60 £4.80 £8.00
The Doll's House hardcover (Dec 1995)
reprints issues #8-16 with new cover design by Dave McKean — £4.00 £12.00 £20.00
Dream Country (1991) reprints issuesd #17-27, 160pgs — £1.85 £5.55 £9.25
Dream Country Hardcover (Feb 1996)
new cover and slipcase designed by Dave McKean — £4.00 £12.00 £20.00
Sandman Slipcase Package (Nov 1991) designed for the above three trade paperbacks though this package only included Preludes and Dream Country - room available for Doll's House — £3.75 £11.25 £18.75
Seasons of Mists Hardcover (Sep 1992)
reprints issues #22-28, 224pgs painted cover by Dave McKean — £3.75 £11.25 £18.75
Seasons of Mists Softcover (Sep 1992)
reprints issues #22-28, 224pgs new cover painting by Dave McKean — £2.50 £7.50 £12.50
A Game of You Hardcover (Jun 1993)
reprints issues #32-37, 192pgs contributions from Dave McKean, Dick Giordano, George Pratt, Bryan Talbot — £3.75 £11.25 £18.75
A Game of You) Softcover (Sep 1993)
reprints issues #32-37, 192pgs — £2.50 £7.50 £12.50
Fables and Reflections Hardcover (Oct 1993)
reprints #29-31, #38-40, #50, Sandman Special #1 and Vertigo Preview — £3.75 £11.25 £18.75
Fables and Reflections Softcover (Feb 1994)
reprints #29-31, #38-40, #50, Sandman Special #1 and Vertigo Preview; new Dave McKean cover — £2.50 £7.50 £12.50
Brief Lives Hardcover (Aug 1994)
reprints #41-49, 256pgs — £4.00 £12.00 £20.00
Brief Lives Softcover (Jan 1995) reprints issues #41-49 — £2.70 £8.10 £13.50
World's End softcover (Jun 1995) Trade paperback
reprints issues #51-56 with new Dave McKean cover — £2.70 £8.10 £13.50
World's End hardcover (Dec 1995)
reprints issues #51-56 with new Dave McKean cover — £3.75 £11.25 £18.75
The Kindly Ones hardcover (Mar 1996)
reprints issues #57-69 and The Castle story from Vertigo Jam, new cover and dust-jacket by Dave McKean — £4.70 £14.10 £23.50
Note also: #8 accidentally had two separate printings: a 1st printing with regular DC inside front and back covers and a 2nd print which used an editorial by Karen Berger on the inside front cover and a pin up/ad for the next issue drawn by Mike Dringenberg. About 600 copies of the 2nd print were run off when DC asked for such copies for copyright purposes.

SANDMAN MIDNIGHT THEATRE
DC Comics,OS; nn Sep 1995
nn ND Neil Gaiman and Matt Wagner script; Teddy Kristiansen art; the Golden Age Sandman meets the current Sandman/Dream/Morpheus

	$Good	$Fine	$N.Mint	£Good	£Fine	£N.Mint
	$1.40	$4.20	$7.00	£0.90	£2.70	£4.50
Title Value:	$1.40	$4.20	$7.00	£0.90	£2.70	£4.50

SANDMAN MYSTERY THEATRE
DC Comics/Vertigo; 1 Apr 1993-present
1 Matt Wagner script/art, Golden Age Sandman (Wesley Dodds) begins; painted collage photo covers begin

	$Good	$Fine	$N.Mint	£Good	£Fine	£N.Mint
	$0.40	$1.20	$2.00	£0.25	£0.75	£1.25
2-24	$0.40	$1.20	$2.00	£0.25	£0.75	£1.25

25 The Butcher story — $0.40 $1.20 $2.00 £0.25 £0.75 £1.25
26-28 The Butcher story — $0.45 $1.35 $2.25 £0.30 £0.90 £1.50
29-32 Golden Age Hourman features — $0.45 $1.35 $2.25 £0.30 £0.90 £1.50
33-36 $0.45 $1.35 $2.25 £0.30 £0.90 £1.50

	$Good	$Fine	$N.Mint	£Good	£Fine	£N.Mint
Title Value:	$14.95	$44.85	$74.75	£9.55	£28.65	£47.75

Sandman Mystery Theatre: The Tarantula (May 1995)
Trade paperback reprints issues #1-4 with new painted cover — £2.00 £6.00 £10.00

	$Good	$Fine	$N.Mint	£Good	£Fine	£N.Mint

SANDMAN MYSTERY THEATRE ANNUAL
DC Comics/Vertigo; 1 Oct 1994-present

	$Good	$Fine	$N.Mint	£Good	£Fine	£N.Mint
1 64pgs, features work by Alex Ross, John Bolton, George Pratt, David Lloyd	$0.60	$1.80	$3.00	£0.40	£1.20	£2.00
Title Value:	$0.60	$1.80	$3.00	£0.40	£1.20	£2.00

SANDMAN SPECIAL
DC Comics,OS; 1 Nov 1991

	$Good	$Fine	$N.Mint	£Good	£Fine	£N.Mint
1 ND script by Neil Gaiman, art by Talbot and Buckingham, pin-ups by other artists including P. Craig Russell, white spot varnish face cover	$1.50	$4.50	$7.50	£0.60	£1.80	£3.00
Title Value:	$1.50	$4.50	$7.50	£0.60	£1.80	£3.00

SANTA CLAWS
Eternity,OS; 1 Dec 1991

	$Good	$Fine	$N.Mint	£Good	£Fine	£N.Mint
1 ND black and white	$0.50	$1.50	$2.50	£0.30	£0.90	£1.50
Title Value:	$0.50	$1.50	$2.50	£0.30	£0.90	£1.50

SAPPHIRE
Aircel; 1 Feb 1990-10 1991

	$Good	$Fine	$N.Mint	£Good	£Fine	£N.Mint
1 ND Barry Blair script/art begins, black and white	$0.60	$1.80	$3.00	£0.40	£1.20	£2.00
1 2nd printing ND	$0.40	$1.20	$2.00	£0.25	£0.75	£1.25
2 ND	$0.50	$1.50	$2.50	£0.30	£0.90	£1.50
2 2nd printing ND	$0.40	$1.20	$2.00	£0.25	£0.75	£1.25
3 ND	$0.50	$1.50	$2.50	£0.30	£0.90	£1.50
3 2nd printing ND	$0.40	$1.20	$2.00	£0.25	£0.75	£1.25
4 ND	$0.50	$1.50	$2.50	£0.30	£0.90	£1.50
4 2nd printing ND	$0.40	$1.20	$2.00	£0.25	£0.75	£1.25
5-10 ND	$0.40	$1.20	$2.00	£0.25	£0.75	£1.25
Title Value:	$6.10	$18.30	$30.50	£3.80	£11.40	£19.00

Note: shipped pre-bagged owing to sexual content

	$Good	$Fine	$N.Mint	£Good	£Fine	£N.Mint
Graphic Novel: War of the Elves (Nov 1990)						
pre-bagged, reprints #1-4				£1.10	£3.30	£5.50
Graphic Novel: A Wizard's Quest (Aug 1991) reprints #5-8				£1.10	£3.30	£5.50

SARGE SNORKEL, BEETLE BAILEY FEATURING
Charlton; 1 Oct 1973-17 Dec 1976

	$Good	$Fine	$N.Mint	£Good	£Fine	£N.Mint
1 distributed in the U.K.	$1.00	$3.00	$5.00	£0.70	£2.10	£3.50
2 distributed in the U.K.	$0.60	$1.80	$3.00	£0.40	£1.20	£2.00
3 distributed in the U.K.	$0.50	$1.50	$2.50	£0.30	£0.90	£1.50
4-17 distributed in the U.K.	$0.40	$1.20	$2.00	£0.25	£0.75	£1.25
Title Value:	$7.70	$23.10	$38.50	£4.90	£14.70	£24.50

SARGE STEEL
Charlton; 1 Dec 1964-8 Mar/Apr 1966
(becomes Secret Agent)

	$Good	$Fine	$N.Mint	£Good	£Fine	£N.Mint
1 Giordano art	$2.05	$6.25	$12.50	£1.30	£4.00	£8.00
2-5 Giordano art	$1.25	$3.75	$7.50	£0.80	£2.50	£5.00
6 rare in the U.K. Giordano art, Judomaster appears	$1.65	$5.00	$10.00	£1.15	£3.50	£7.00
7-8 Giordano art	$1.50	$4.50	$7.50	£1.00	£3.00	£5.00
Title Value:	$11.70	$35.25	$67.50	£7.65	£23.50	£45.00

Note: all distributed in the U.K.

SATAN'S SIX
Topps,MS; 1 Apr 1993-4 July 1993

	$Good	$Fine	$N.Mint	£Good	£Fine	£N.Mint
1 pre-bagged with coupon #1 for Secret City Saga #0 plus chrome trading card; Jack Kirby and Todd McFarlane	$0.40	$1.20	$2.00	£0.25	£0.75	£1.25
1 without coupon/card	$0.30	$0.90	$1.50	£0.20	£0.60	£1.00
2-4 pre-bagged with 3 trading cards	$0.40	$1.20	$2.00	£0.25	£0.75	£1.25
Title Value:	$1.90	$5.70	$9.50	£1.20	£3.60	£6.00

Note: all Non-Distributed on the news-stands in the U.K.

SATAN'S SIX: HELLSPAWN
Topps,MS; 1 Jun 1994-4 Sep 1994

	$Good	$Fine	$N.Mint	£Good	£Fine	£N.Mint
1-4 ND	$0.40	$1.20	$2.00	£0.25	£0.75	£1.25
Title Value:	$1.60	$4.80	$8.00	£1.00	£3.00	£5.00

SATANIKA
Verotik; 0 Jun 1995-present

	$Good	$Fine	$N.Mint	£Good	£Fine	£N.Mint
0 ND Glenn Danzig script, Simon Bisley art	$1.50	$4.50	$7.50	£1.00	£3.00	£5.00
1 ND Glenn Danzig script, Duke Mighten art	$2.00	$6.00	$10.00	£1.50	£4.50	£7.50
2 ND Glenn Danzig script, Duke Mighten art	$1.40	$4.20	$7.00	£1.00	£3.00	£5.00
3 ND	$0.80	$2.40	$4.00	£0.80	£2.40	£4.00
Title Value:	$5.70	$17.10	$28.50	£4.30	£12.90	£21.50
Satanika (Oct 1995)						
Trade paperback collects mini-series , new Simon Bisley cover				£1.30	£3.90	£6.50

SAVAGE COMBAT TALES
Atlas; 1 Feb 1975-3 Jul 1975

	$Good	$Fine	$N.Mint	£Good	£Fine	£N.Mint
1-3 distributed in the U.K.	$0.25	$0.75	$1.25	£0.15	£0.45	£0.75
Title Value:	$0.75	$2.25	$3.75	£0.45	£1.35	£2.25

SAVAGE DRAGON
Image,MS; 1 Jul 1992-3 Dec 1992

	$Good	$Fine	$N.Mint	£Good	£Fine	£N.Mint
1 Erik Larsen script/art begins, bound-in poster (4 variants)	$1.00	$3.00	$5.00	£0.70	£2.10	£3.50
2	$0.80	$2.40	$4.00	£0.50	£1.50	£2.50
3 Savage Dragon vs. Bedrock; contains Image #0 coupon 6 and bound-in poster (25% less without coupon)	$0.80	$2.40	$4.00	£0.50	£1.50	£2.50
Title Value:	$2.60	$7.80	$13.00	£1.70	£5.10	£8.50

Note: all Non-Distributed on the news-stands in the U.K.

	$Good	$Fine	$N.Mint	£Good	£Fine	£N.Mint
Savage Dragon Trade paperback (Jul 1993)						
reprints mini-series plus material from Image #0				£1.30	£3.90	£6.50

SAVAGE DRAGON (2ND SERIES)
Image; 1 Jun 1993-present

	$Good	$Fine	$N.Mint	£Good	£Fine	£N.Mint
1 Erik Larsen script and art begins	$0.50	$1.50	$2.50	£0.30	£0.90	£1.50
2 48pgs, Savage Dragon vs. Teenage Mutant Ninja Turtles; flip-book with Vanguard #0	$0.50	$1.50	$2.50	£0.30	£0.90	£1.50
3-11	$0.40	$1.20	$2.00	£0.25	£0.75	£1.25
12 pull out poster by Joe Quesada and Jimmy Palmiotti	$0.40	$1.20	$2.00	£0.25	£0.75	£1.25
13 Image X Month tie-in	$0.40	$1.20	$2.00	£0.25	£0.75	£1.25
13 2nd version by Erik Larsen (May 1995) - Star, Mighty Man, Overpower, Rapture and the 1st appearance of Widow	$0.40	$1.20	$2.00	£0.25	£0.75	£1.25
14-16 Possessed story	$0.50	$1.50	$2.50	£0.30	£0.90	£1.50
17-21	$0.50	$1.50	$2.50	£0.30	£0.90	£1.50
22 Teenage Mutant Ninja Turtles appear	$0.50	$1.50	$2.50	£0.30	£0.90	£1.50
23	$0.50	$1.50	$2.50	£0.30	£0.90	£1.50
24 Gang War story	$0.50	$1.50	$2.50	£0.30	£0.90	£1.50
25 ND 48pgs, Freak Force and Super Patriot appear; 2 stories	$0.80	$2.40	$4.00	£0.50	£1.50	£2.50
Title Value:	$12.10	$36.30	$60.50	£7.40	£22.20	£37.00

Note: all Non-Distributed on the news-stands iin the U.K.

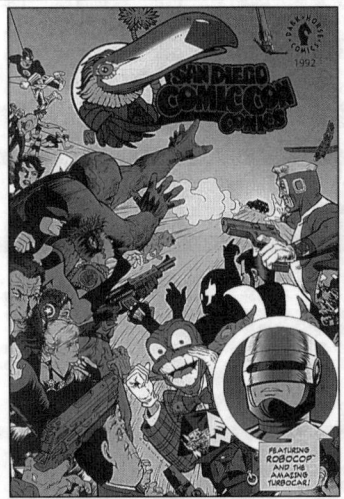

San Diego Comicon Comics 1992

Sandman (1st) #6

Satanika #2

	$Good	$Fine	$N.Mint	£Good	£Fine	£N.Mint

SAVAGE DRAGON VS. THE SAVAGE MEGATON MAN
Image, OS; 1 Apr 1993
1 ND Erik Larsen and Don Simpson script/art

| | $0.40 | $1.20 | $2.00 | £0.25 | £0.75 | £1.25 |

1 ND Gold Edition - foiled embossed cover

| | $3.00 | $9.00 | $15.00 | £1.50 | £4.50 | £7.50 |
| Title Value: | $3.40 | $10.20 | $17.00 | £1.75 | £5.25 | £8.75 |

SAVAGE DRAGON/TEENAGE MUTANT NINJA TURTLES CROSSOVER
Image; OS; 1 Sep 1993
1 ND Michael Dooney script and art

| | $0.50 | $1.50 | $2.50 | £0.30 | £0.90 | £1.50 |
| Title Value: | $0.50 | $1.50 | $2.50 | £0.30 | £0.90 | £1.50 |

SAVAGE HENRY
Vortex/Rip Off Press; 1 Jan 1987-31 1993
1 ND Matt Howarth script and art begins; black and white

| | $0.40 | $1.20 | $2.00 | £0.25 | £0.75 | £1.25 |

1 2nd printing, ND (Feb 1994), new painted cover

| | $0.30 | $0.90 | $1.50 | £0.20 | £0.60 | £1.00 |

2-14 ND

| | $0.40 | $1.20 | $2.00 | £0.25 | £0.75 | £1.25 |

14 2nd printing, ND (Apr 1994)

| | $0.30 | $0.90 | $1.50 | £0.20 | £0.60 | £1.00 |

15-31 ND

| | $0.40 | $1.20 | $2.00 | £0.25 | £0.75 | £1.25 |
| Title Value: | $13.00 | $39.00 | $65.00 | £8.15 | £24.45 | £40.75 |

SAVAGE HENRY (2ND SERIES)
Caliber Press; 1 Jul 1994-3 Oct 1994
1-3 ND Matt Howarth script and art; black and white

| | $0.60 | $1.80 | $3.00 | £0.40 | £1.20 | £2.00 |
| Title Value: | $1.80 | $5.40 | $9.00 | £1.20 | £3.60 | £6.00 |

SAVAGE HENRY: HEAD STRONG
Caliber Press; 1 Feb 1995-present
1-3 ND Matt Howarth script and art; black and white

| | $0.60 | $1.80 | $3.00 | £0.40 | £1.20 | £2.00 |
| Title Value: | $1.80 | $5.40 | $9.00 | £1.20 | £3.60 | £6.00 |

SAVAGE HULK
Marvel Comics Group, OS; 1 Jan 1996
1 ND 64pgs, features work by Peter David, Dave Gibbons, Mike Golden, Sam Kieth, Scott Lobdell, Matt Wagner and others; painted cover by Adam Kubert and Simon Bisley

| | $1.40 | $4.20 | $7.00 | £0.90 | £2.70 | £4.50 |
| Title Value: | $1.40 | $4.20 | $7.00 | £0.90 | £2.70 | £4.50 |

SAVAGE TALES
Marvel Comics Group, Magazine; 1 May 1971; 2 Oct 1973; 3 Feb 1974-11 Jul 1975; 12 Summer 1975
1 ND Conan by Barry Smith, 1st appearance of Man-Thing

| | $21.50 | $65.00 | $130.00 | £10.00 | £30.00 | £60.00 |

2 ND Smith, Morrow, Brunner, Williamson art

| | $5.75 | $17.50 | $35.00 | £4.15 | £12.50 | £25.00 |

3 scarce in the U.K. Williamson, Steranko, Brunner, Smith art

| | $5.00 | $15.00 | $30.00 | £3.30 | £10.00 | £20.00 |

4 becomes Savage Tales Featuring Conan; part Neal Adams art, Barry Smith, Williamson reprints

| | $3.30 | $10.00 | $20.00 | £1.65 | £5.00 | £10.00 |

5 Jim Starlin art

| | $3.30 | $10.00 | $20.00 | £1.65 | £5.00 | £10.00 |

6 becomes Savage Tales Featuring Ka-Zar; Williamson reprint; Neal Adams cover

| | $1.25 | $3.75 | $7.50 | £0.80 | £2.50 | £5.00 |

7 Neal Adams inks, Boris painted cover

| | $1.00 | $3.00 | $6.00 | £0.65 | £2.00 | £4.00 |

8 scarce in the U.K. Shanna She-Devil back-up

| | $1.00 | $3.00 | $6.00 | £0.65 | £2.00 | £4.00 |

9 Shanna She-Devil back-up

| | $0.75 | $2.25 | $4.50 | £0.50 | £1.50 | £3.00 |

10 Russ Heath art, Neal Adams inks; Boris painted cover and Shanna She-Devil back-up

| | $0.75 | $2.25 | $4.50 | £0.50 | £1.50 | £3.00 |

11 Heath art on back-up story ("Intruder!")

| | $0.75 | $2.25 | $4.50 | £0.50 | £1.50 | £3.00 |

12 ND 88pgs, squarebound, all reprint, titled Savage Tales Annual #1 on cover, Gil Kane/BarrySmith/Gray Morrow art

| | $1.00 | $3.00 | $6.00 | £0.65 | £2.00 | £4.00 |
| Title Value: | $45.35 | $137.00 | $274.00 | £25.00 | £75.50 | £151.00 |

FEATURES
Brak the Barbarian in 5-8. Conan in 1-5. Ka-Zar in 6-12. Shanna in 9,10.
REPRINT FEATURES
Jann of the Jungle in 6-8. Ka-Zar in 1, 5. Kull by Wrightson in 2. Femizons in 1-3.

SAVAGE TALES (2ND SERIES)
Marvel Comics Group, Magazine; 1 Nov 1985-9 Mar 1987
1 Larry Hama script, Michael Golden art begins on 'Nam try-out

| | $0.50 | $1.50 | $2.50 | £0.30 | £0.90 | £1.50 |

2-9

| | $0.30 | $0.90 | $1.50 | £0.20 | £0.60 | £1.00 |
| Title Value: | $2.90 | $8.70 | $14.50 | £1.90 | £5.70 | £9.50 |

SAVIOUR
(see British section)

SCARAB
DC Comics/Vertigo, MS; 1 Nov 1993-8 Jun 1994
1 Scot Eaton pencils begin, painted covers by Glenn Fabry begin

| | $0.40 | $1.20 | $2.00 | £0.25 | £0.75 | £1.25 |

2-8

| | $0.40 | $1.20 | $2.00 | £0.25 | £0.75 | £1.25 |
| Title Value: | $3.20 | $9.60 | $16.00 | £2.00 | £6.00 | £10.00 |

SCARAMOUCH
Innovation; 1 Dec 1990-2 Jan 1991
1-2 ND black and white

| | $0.40 | $1.20 | $2.00 | £0.25 | £0.75 | £1.25 |
| Title Value: | $0.80 | $2.40 | $4.00 | £0.50 | £1.50 | £2.50 |

SCARLET IN GASLIGHT
Eternity; 1 Nov 1987-4 Jun 1988

1-4 ND Sherlock Holmes vs. Dracula; black and white

	$0.40	$1.20	$2.00	£0.25	£0.75	£1.25
Title Value:	$1.60	$4.80	$8.00	£1.00	£3.00	£5.00
Graphic Novel Collection (1988)				£0.90	£2.70	£4.50

SCARLET SCORPION/DARKSHADE
AC Comics; 1 Apr 1995-2 1995
1 ND black and white; flip-book format begins

| | $0.80 | $2.40 | $4.00 | £0.50 | £1.50 | £2.50 |

1 ND pre-bagged with trading card by Jerry Ordway

| | $1.00 | $3.00 | $5.00 | £0.70 | £2.10 | £3.50 |

2 ND black and white

| | $0.80 | $2.40 | $4.00 | £0.50 | £1.50 | £2.50 |
| Title Value: | $2.60 | $7.80 | $13.00 | £1.70 | £5.10 | £8.50 |

SCARLET SPIDER
Marvel Comics Group; 1 Nov 1995-2 Dec 1995
1 ND Howard Mackie script, Gil Kane and Tom Palmer art, continued in Spectacular Scarlet Spider #1; metallic ink cover

| | $0.40 | $1.20 | $2.00 | £0.25 | £0.75 | £1.25 |

2 ND continued in Spectacular Scarlet Spider #2

| | $0.40 | $1.20 | $2.00 | £0.25 | £0.75 | £1.25 |
| Title Value: | $0.80 | $2.40 | $4.00 | £0.50 | £1.50 | £2.50 |

SCARLET SPIDER UNLIMITED
Marvel Comics Group; 1 Nov 1995
1 ND 64pgs, Glenn Herdling script, Tod Smith and John Nyberg art; metallic ink cover

| | $0.80 | $2.40 | $4.00 | £0.50 | £1.50 | £2.50 |
| Title Value: | $0.80 | $2.40 | $4.00 | £0.50 | £1.50 | £2.50 |

SCARLET WITCH
Marvel Comics Group, MS; 1 Jan 1994-4 Apr 1994
1 John Higgins art begins

| | $0.40 | $1.20 | $2.00 | £0.25 | £0.75 | £1.25 |

2-3 West Coast Avengers appear

| | $0.40 | $1.20 | $2.00 | £0.25 | £0.75 | £1.25 |

4 Spiderwoman and Iron Man appear

| | $0.40 | $1.20 | $2.00 | £0.25 | £0.75 | £1.25 |
| Title Value: | $1.60 | $4.80 | $8.00 | £1.00 | £3.00 | £5.00 |

SCARLETT
DC Comics; 1 Jan 1993-14 Feb 1994
1 spin-off from Batman: Legends of the Dark Knight

| | $0.25 | $0.75 | $1.25 | £0.15 | £0.45 | £0.75 |

2-4

| | $0.25 | $0.75 | $1.25 | £0.15 | £0.45 | £0.75 |

5 Gray Morrow art

| | $0.25 | $0.75 | $1.25 | £0.15 | £0.45 | £0.75 |

6-14

| | $0.25 | $0.75 | $1.25 | £0.15 | £0.45 | £0.75 |
| Title Value: | $3.50 | $10.50 | $17.50 | £2.10 | £6.30 | £10.50 |

SCARY BOOK, THE
Caliber Press; 1 Jul 1992-4 1992
1-4 ND

| | $0.40 | $1.20 | $2.00 | £0.25 | £0.75 | £1.25 |
| Title Value: | $1.60 | $4.80 | $8.00 | £1.00 | £3.00 | £5.00 |

SCARY TALES
Charlton; 1 Aug 1975-9 Jan 1977; 10 Oct 1977-20 Jun 1979; 21 Aug 1980-46 Oct 1984
1 distributed in the U.K. Joe Staton painted cover

| | $0.60 | $1.80 | $3.00 | £0.40 | £1.20 | £2.00 |

2-10 distributed in the U.K.

| | $0.40 | $1.20 | $2.00 | £0.25 | £0.75 | £1.25 |

11-46 distributed in the U.K.

| | $0.30 | $0.90 | $1.50 | £0.20 | £0.60 | £1.00 |
| Title Value: | $15.00 | $45.00 | $75.00 | £9.85 | £29.55 | £49.25 |

Note: many later issues all reprint

SCAVENGERS
Triumphant Comics; 0 Mar 1994; 1 Sep 1993-16 Dec 1994
0 (Mar 1994) serial numbered at top of cover

| | $0.40 | $1.20 | $2.00 | £0.25 | £0.75 | £1.25 |

1-2 20,000 copies, serial numbering begins at top of cover

| | $0.40 | $1.20 | $2.00 | £0.25 | £0.75 | £1.25 |

2 Limited Edition - signed by creators with mini-poster photo-print; pre-bagged with backing board

| | $1.00 | $3.00 | $5.00 | £0.50 | £1.50 | £2.50 |

3-4

| | $0.40 | $1.20 | $2.00 | £0.25 | £0.75 | £1.25 |

5 Unleashed X-over

| | $0.40 | $1.20 | $2.00 | £0.25 | £0.75 | £1.25 |

6-16

| | $0.40 | $1.20 | $2.00 | £0.25 | £0.75 | £1.25 |
| Title Value: | $7.80 | $23.40 | $39.00 | £4.75 | £14.25 | £23.75 |

Note: all Non-Distributed on the news-stands in the U.K.

SCHISM
Defiant Comics; 1,2 Jul 1994; 3,4 Aug 1994
1-4 ND 48pgs, Jim Shooter script, David Lapham art

| | $0.40 | $1.20 | $2.00 | £0.25 | £0.75 | £1.25 |
| Title Value: | $1.60 | $4.80 | $8.00 | £1.00 | £3.00 | £5.00 |

SCIMIDAR
Eternity, MS; 1 Dec 1988-4 Mar 1989
1 ND (2 cover versions exist)

| | $0.50 | $1.50 | $2.50 | £0.30 | £0.90 | £1.50 |

2-3 ND

| | $0.50 | $1.50 | $2.50 | £0.30 | £0.90 | £1.50 |

4 ND "hot" cover

| | $0.50 | $1.50 | $2.50 | £0.30 | £0.90 | £1.50 |

4 ND "mild" cover

	$0.50	$1.50	$2.50	£0.30	£0.90	£1.50
Title Value:	$2.50	$7.50	$12.50	£1.50	£4.50	£7.50
Book I: Pleasure and Pain				£1.20	£3.60	£6.00
2nd print (1990), new cover				£1.10	£3.30	£5.50

Note: pre-bagged owing to sexual content. Unsealed copies would bring 25% less

SCIMIDAR (2ND SERIES)
CFD Productions; 1 Oct 1995
1 ND 24pgs, Tom Derenick art; black and white

| | $0.55 | $1.65 | $2.75 | £0.35 | £1.05 | £1.75 |
| Title Value: | $0.55 | $1.65 | $2.75 | £0.35 | £1.05 | £1.75 |

VERY GENERAL PERCENTAGE CONVERSION CHART WHICH MAY BE USED TO CALCULATE LOW AND INBETWEEN GRADES:

	$Good	$Fine	$N.Mint	£Good	£Fine	£N.Mint

SCIMIDAR II
Eternity,MS; 1 May 1989-4 Aug 1989

	$Good	$Fine	$N.Mint	£Good	£Fine	£N.Mint
1 ND	$0.40	$1.20	$2.00	£0.25	£0.75	£1.25
1 2nd printing ND	$0.30	$0.90	$1.50	£0.20	£0.60	£1.00
2-4 ND	$0.40	$1.20	$2.00	£0.25	£0.75	£1.25
Title Value:	$1.90	$5.70	$9.50	£1.20	£3.60	£6.00
Trade paperback: Feast and Famine, reprints #1-4				£1.15	£3.45	£5.75
(2nd print - 1991)				£1.10	£3.30	£5.50

Note: sealed in plastic bags. Unsealed copies would bring 25% less

SCIMIDAR III
Eternity,MS; 1 Jan 1990-4 Apr 1990

1 ND	$0.40	$1.20	$2.00	£0.25	£0.75	£1.25
1 2nd printing ND	$0.30	$0.90	$1.50	£0.20	£0.60	£1.00
2-4 ND	$0.40	$1.20	$2.00	£0.25	£0.75	£1.25
Title Value:	$1.90	$5.70	$9.50	£1.20	£3.60	£6.00

Note: pre-bagged owing to sexual content

| Trade Paperback# (Jun 1991), reprints #1-4 | | | | £1.00 | £3.00 | £5.00 |

SCIMIDAR IV: WILD THING
Eternity,MS; 1 Aug 1990-4 Nov 1990
1 ND nude cover; has black and white wraparound outer cover advising content

	$0.40	$1.20	$2.00	£0.25	£0.75	£1.25
1 ND clothed cover	$0.40	$1.20	$2.00	£0.25	£0.75	£1.25
2-4 ND	$0.40	$1.20	$2.00	£0.25	£0.75	£1.25
Title Value:	$2.00	$6.00	$10.00	£1.25	£3.75	£6.25

Note: pre-bagged owing to sexual content

SCIMIDAR PIN-UP BOOK
Eternity,OS; 1 Oct 1990
1 ND seven loose pin-ups (no staples)

	$0.50	$1.50	$2.50	£0.30	£0.90	£1.50
Title Value:	$0.50	$1.50	$2.50	£0.30	£0.90	£1.50

SCIMIDAR V: LIVING COLOUR
Eternity,MS; 1 Apr 1991-4 Jul 1991

1 ND regular cover	$0.40	$1.20	$2.00	£0.25	£0.75	£1.25

1 ND nude cover; has black and white wraparound outer cover advising content

	$0.40	$1.20	$2.00	£0.25	£0.75	£1.25
2-4 ND	$0.40	$1.20	$2.00	£0.25	£0.75	£1.25
Title Value:	$2.00	$6.00	$10.00	£1.25	£3.75	£6.25

Note: all Non-Distributed on the news-stands in the U.K.

SCIMIDAR VI: SLASHDANCE
Aircel,MS; 1 Oct 1992-4 Jan 1993

1 ND	$0.40	$1.20	$2.00	£0.25	£0.75	£1.25

1 ND Deluxe Edition - extra story, sketches and pin-ups

	$0.50	$1.50	$2.50	£0.30	£0.90	£1.50
2-4 ND	$0.40	$1.20	$2.00	£0.25	£0.75	£1.25
Title Value:	$2.10	$6.30	$10.50	£1.30	£3.90	£6.50

SCOOBY-DOO, HANNA-BARBERA'S
Marvel Comics Group, TV; 1 Oct 1977-9 Feb 1979

1 ND	$0.40	$1.20	$2.00	£0.20	£0.60	£1.00
2-9 ND	$0.25	$0.75	$1.25	£0.15	£0.45	£0.75
Title Value:	$2.40	$7.20	$12.00	£1.40	£4.20	£7.00

SCORCHED EARTH
Tundra Publishing,MS; 1 May 1991-4 1991
1-4 ND ecology/S.F. theme

	$0.50	$1.50	$2.50	£0.30	£0.90	£1.50
Title Value:	$2.00	$6.00	$10.00	£1.20	£3.60	£6.00

SCORE, THE
DC Comics/Piranha Press,MS; 1-4 1990
1-4 ND 48pgs, squarebound, Gerard Jones/Mark Badger

	$0.80	$2.40	$4.00	£0.50	£1.50	£2.50
Title Value:	$3.20	$9.60	$16.00	£2.00	£6.00	£10.00

SCORPIO ROSE
Eclipse; 1 Jan 1983-2 Oct 1983
1-2 ND Steve Englehart scripts, Marshall Rogers art; Dr. Orient backup by Rogers & Adam Kubert

	$0.40	$1.20	$2.00	£0.25	£0.75	£1.25
Title Value:	$0.80	$2.40	$4.00	£0.50	£1.50	£2.50

SCORPION
Atlas; 1 Feb 1975-3 Jul 1975
1 Chaykin story/art (Dominic Fortune prototype); distributed in the U.K.

	$0.50	$1.50	$2.50	£0.30	£0.90	£1.50

2 Chaykin story/art;Kaluta/Wrightson part inks; distributed in the U.K.

	$0.50	$1.50	$2.50	£0.30	£0.90	£1.50

3 new costume, no Chaykin; distributed in the U.K.

	$0.50	$1.50	$2.50	£0.30	£0.90	£1.50
Title Value:	$1.50	$4.50	$7.50	£0.90	£2.70	£4.50

SCORPION CORPS
Dagger Comics; 1 Dec 1993-11 1994

1-11 ND	$0.40	$1.20	$2.00	£0.25	£0.75	£1.25
Title Value:	$4.40	$13.20	$22.00	£2.75	£8.25	£13.75

SCOUT
Eclipse; 1 Sep 1985-24 Oct 1987
(see New America, Scout: War Shaman, Swords of Texas)
1 ND scarce in the U.K. Tim Truman art begins

	$0.50	$1.50	$2.50	£0.30	£0.90	£1.50

2 ND scarce in the U.K.

	$0.40	$1.20	$2.00	£0.30	£0.90	£1.50
3-8 ND	$0.40	$1.20	$2.00	£0.25	£0.75	£1.25

9 ND ($1.25) Airboy preview

	$0.40	$1.20	$2.00	£0.25	£0.75	£1.25
10-15 ND	$0.40	$1.20	$2.00	£0.25	£0.75	£1.25

16 ND 3-D issue (Eclipse 3-D Special #16), with bound-in 3-D glasses (25% less without glasses)

	$0.50	$1.50	$2.50	£0.30	£0.90	£1.50

17 ND Beanworld X-over, Larry Marder part art

	$0.40	$1.20	$2.00	£0.25	£0.75	£1.25
18 ND	$0.40	$1.20	$2.00	£0.25	£0.75	£1.25

19 ND with flexi-disc

	$0.40	$1.20	$2.00	£0.25	£0.75	£1.25
20-24 ND	$0.40	$1.20	$2.00	£0.25	£0.75	£1.25
Title Value:	$9.80	$29.40	$49.00	£6.15	£18.45	£30.75
Trade Paperback, reprints #1-7				£2.00	£6.00	£10.00

SCOUT HANDBOOK
Eclipse; 1 Aug 1987
1 ND maps, weapons, personal data etc; Tim Truman cover

	$0.40	$1.20	$2.00	£0.25	£0.75	£1.25
Title Value:	$0.40	$1.20	$2.00	£0.25	£0.75	£1.25

SCOUT WAR SHAMAN
Eclipse; 1 Mar 1988-16 Oct 1989

1-16 ND	$0.40	$1.20	$2.00	£0.25	£0.75	£1.25
Title Value:	$6.40	$19.20	$32.00	£4.00	£12.00	£20.00

SCREEN PLAY
Slave Labor; 1 Jun 1989-3 1989

1-3 ND	$0.30	$0.90	$1.50	£0.20	£0.60	£1.00
Title Value:	$0.90	$2.70	$4.50	£0.60	£1.80	£3.00

SCREWTAPE LETTERS, THE
Marvel Comics Group,OS; 1 Oct 1993
1 ND 96pgs, adaptation of C.S. Lewis work by Charles E. Hall and Pat Redding

	$1.50	$4.50	$7.50	£1.00	£3.00	£5.00
Title Value:	$1.50	$4.50	$7.50	£1.00	£3.00	£5.00

SEA DEVILS
National Periodical Publications; 1 Sep/Oct 1961-35 May/Jun 1967
(see Showcase #27-29)

1 Russ Heath art	$55.00	$170.00	$400.00	£39.00	£115.00	£275.00
2 Russ Heath art	$29.00	$85.00	$200.00	£17.50	£52.50	£125.00
3 Russ Heath art	$19.00	$57.50	$135.00	£12.50	£39.00	£90.00
4-5 Russ Heath art						
	$17.50	$52.50	$125.00	£12.00	£36.00	£85.00
6-10 Russ Heath art						
	$10.00	$30.00	$70.00	£6.25	£19.00	£45.00
11-12	$7.75	$23.50	$55.00	£5.00	£15.00	£35.00
13 Joe Kubert and Gene Colan art						
	$7.75	$23.50	$55.00	£5.00	£15.00	£35.00
14-20	$7.75	$23.50	$55.00	£5.00	£15.00	£35.00
21-30	$5.50	$17.00	$40.00	£3.90	£11.50	£27.50
31-35	$5.00	$15.00	$35.00	£3.55	£10.50	£25.00
Title Value:	$345.50	$1047.50	$2460.00	£231.00	£691.00	£1635.00

SEADRAGON
Elite Comics; 1 May 1986-8 Dec 1986
1 ND Butch Burcham inks begin

	$0.30	$0.90	$1.50	£0.20	£0.60	£1.00
1 2nd printing ND	$0.30	$0.90	$1.50	£0.20	£0.60	£1.00
2-8 ND	$0.30	$0.90	$1.50	£0.20	£0.60	£1.00
Title Value:	$2.70	$8.10	$13.50	£1.80	£5.40	£9.00

SEAQUEST DSV
Nemesis; 1 Mar 1994-4 1994
1-4 ND Keith Pollard and Alfredo Alcala art; based on TV series starring Roy Scheider

	$0.40	$1.20	$2.00	£0.25	£0.75	£1.25
Title Value:	$1.60	$4.80	$8.00	£1.00	£3.00	£5.00

SEBASTIAN O
DC Comics/Vertigo,MS; 1 May 1993-3 Jul 1993
1-3 Grant Morrison script, Steve Yeowell art

	$0.40	$1.20	$2.00	£0.25	£0.75	£1.25
Title Value:	$1.20	$3.60	$6.00	£0.75	£2.25	£3.75

SECRET AGENT
Charlton; 9 Oct 1966-10 Oct 1967
(previously Sarge Steel)
9 distributed in the U.K.

	$1.65	$5.00	$10.00	£1.00	£3.00	£6.00

10 distributed in the U.K.

	$0.80	$2.50	$5.00	£0.55	£1.75	£3.50
Title Value:	$2.45	$7.50	$15.00	£1.55	£4.75	£9.50

Note: from the Danger Man TV series.

SECRET AGENT (2ND SERIES)
Gold Key; 1 Nov 1966-2 Jan 1968
1 rare, distributed in the U.K.

	$15.00	$45.00	$105.00	£10.00	£30.00	£70.00

2 rare, distributed in the U.K.

	$7.75	$23.50	$55.00	£5.00	£15.00	£35.00
Title Value:	$22.75	$68.50	$160.00	£15.00	£45.00	£105.00

SECRET CITY SAGA, JACK KIRBY'S
Topps,MS; 0 Apr 1993; 1 May 1993-4 Aug 1993
0 Walt Simonson cover - originally available free from Topps with the 8 coupons from this series and the four other Jack Kirby titles

	$0.40	$1.20	$2.00	£0.25	£0.75	£1.25
0 Gold Edition	$1.50	$4.50	$7.50	£0.80	£2.40	£4.00

1 pre-bagged with coupon #5 for Secret City Saga #0 plus 3 trading cards, Steve Ditko art and cover

	$0.40	$1.20	$2.00	£0.25	£0.75	£1.25

1 without coupon/cards

	$0.30	$0.90	$1.50	£0.20	£0.60	£1.00

2 pre-bagged with 3 trading cards inked by John Byrne, Sienkiewicz and Gibbons; cover by Steve Ditko and John Byrne

	$0.40	$1.20	$2.00	£0.25	£0.75	£1.25

2 without coupon/cards

	$0.30	$0.90	$1.50	£0.20	£0.60	£1.00

3 pre-bagged with 3 trading cards inked by John Byrne, Sienkiewicz and Gibbons; cover by Steve Ditko and John Byrne

MINT = 100% / NEAR MINT (inc. +/-) = 90-99% / VERY FINE (inc. +/-) = 75-89% / FINE (inc. +/-) = 55-74% / VERY GOOD (inc. +/-) = 35-54% / GOOD (inc. +/-) = 15-34% / FAIR = 5-14% / POOR = 1-4%

529

	$Good	$Fine	$N.Mint	£Good	£Fine	£N.Mint
	$0.40	$1.20	$2.00	£0.25	£0.75	£1.25
3 without coupon/cards						
	$0.30	$0.90	$1.50	£0.20	£0.60	£1.00
4 pre-bagged with 3 trading cards inked by Hughes, Steve Ditko/Art Adams and Jim Valentino; cover by Steve Ditko and George Perez						
	$0.40	$1.20	$2.00	£0.25	£0.75	£1.25
4 without coupon/cards						
	$0.30	$0.90	$1.50	£0.20	£0.60	£1.00
Title Value:	$4.70	$14.10	$23.50	£2.85	£8.55	£14.25

Note: all Non-Distributed on the news-stands in the U.K.

SECRET DEFENDERS
Marvel Comics Group; 1 Mar 1993-25 Mar 1995

	$Good	$Fine	$N.Mint	£Good	£Fine	£N.Mint
1 Dr. Strange assembles rotating teams: Nomad, Darkhawk, Wolverine, Spiderwoman begin; red foil cover, Roy Thomas script begins						
	$0.40	$1.20	$2.00	£0.25	£0.75	£1.25
2-3	$0.30	$0.90	$1.50	£0.20	£0.60	£1.00
4 new team of Ghost Rider, Namorita and Sleepwalker						
	$0.30	$0.90	$1.50	£0.20	£0.60	£1.00
5	$0.30	$0.90	$1.50	£0.20	£0.60	£1.00
6 new team of Scarlet Witch, Spiderman and Captain America						
	$0.30	$0.90	$1.50	£0.20	£0.60	£1.00
7-8	$0.30	$0.90	$1.50	£0.20	£0.60	£1.00
9 new team of War Machine, Thunderstrike and Silver Surfer						
	$0.30	$0.90	$1.50	£0.20	£0.60	£1.00
10	$0.30	$0.90	$1.50	£0.20	£0.60	£1.00
11 Starblast part 3	$0.30	$0.90	$1.50	£0.20	£0.60	£1.00
12 Thanos appears, prismatic foil cover						
	$0.30	$0.90	$1.50	£0.20	£0.60	£1.00
13-14 Thanos appears						
	$0.30	$0.90	$1.50	£0.20	£0.60	£1.00
15 Thanos and Silver Surfer appear; with free Spiderman vs. Venom card sheet						
	$0.30	$0.90	$1.50	£0.20	£0.60	£1.00
16-17	$0.30	$0.90	$1.50	£0.20	£0.60	£1.00
18-19 Archangel and Iceman appear						
	$0.30	$0.90	$1.50	£0.20	£0.60	£1.00
20 Venom appears	$0.30	$0.90	$1.50	£0.20	£0.60	£1.00
21-23	$0.30	$0.90	$1.50	£0.20	£0.60	£1.00
24 the original Defenders vs. The Secret Defenders						
	$0.30	$0.90	$1.50	£0.20	£0.60	£1.00
25 48pgs, Secret Defenders Sepulchre, Cadaver, Deathlok, Dagger and Drax team with Hulk, Namor and Silver Surfer against Dr. Druid						
	$0.40	$1.20	$2.00	£0.25	£0.75	£1.25
Title Value:	$7.70	$23.10	$38.50	£5.10	£15.30	£25.50

SECRET HEARTS
National Periodical Publications/DC Comics; 40 Jun/Jul 1957-153 Jul 1971
(previous issues ND)

	$Good	$Fine	$N.Mint	£Good	£Fine	£N.Mint
40-50 scarce in the U.K.						
	$5.00	$15.00	$30.00	£2.90	£8.75	£17.50
51-58 scarce in the U.K.						
	$4.15	$12.50	$25.00	£2.50	£7.50	£15.00
1st official distribution in the U.K.						
59-60 scarce in the U.K.						
	$4.15	$12.50	$25.00	£2.50	£7.50	£15.00
61-70 scarce in the U.K.						
	$2.90	$8.75	$17.50	£2.05	£6.25	£12.50
71-74	$2.50	$7.50	$15.00	£1.65	£5.00	£10.00
75 last 10 cents issue	$2.50	$7.50	$15.00	£1.65	£5.00	£10.00
76-80	$2.50	$7.50	$15.00	£1.65	£5.00	£10.00
81-100	$2.05	$6.25	$12.50	£1.30	£4.00	£8.00
101-110	$2.00	$6.00	$10.00	£1.30	£3.90	£6.50
111-119	$1.50	$4.50	$7.50	£1.00	£3.00	£5.00
120 Neal Adams cover						
	$1.80	$5.25	$9.00	£1.20	£3.60	£6.00
121-133	$1.30	$3.90	$6.50	£0.90	£2.70	£4.50
134 Neal Adams cover						
	$1.80	$5.25	$9.00	£1.20	£3.60	£6.00
135-140	$1.30	$3.90	$6.50	£0.90	£2.70	£4.50
141-142 Toth art	$1.30	$3.90	$6.50	£0.90	£2.70	£4.50
143	$1.30	$3.90	$6.50	£0.90	£2.70	£4.50
144 Morrow art	$1.30	$3.90	$6.50	£0.90	£2.70	£4.50
145-148	$1.30	$3.90	$6.50	£0.90	£2.70	£4.50
149 Toth art	$1.50	$4.50	$7.50	£1.00	£3.00	£5.00
150-153	$1.30	$3.90	$6.50	£0.90	£2.70	£4.50
Title Value:	$270.40	$813.90	$1549.50	£173.20	£523.65	£994.00

Note: issues pre #40 not included as yet, as the author doesn't have them (as yet!)

SECRET OF THE DWARFS
Comico,OS; 1 Dec 1992

	$Good	$Fine	$N.Mint	£Good	£Fine	£N.Mint
1 ND 48pgs	$0.80	$2.40	$4.00	£0.50	£1.50	£2.50
Title Value:	$0.80	$2.40	$4.00	£0.50	£1.50	£2.50

SECRET OF THE SALAMANDER, THE
Dark Horse, OS; 1 Mar 1992

	$Good	$Fine	$N.Mint	£Good	£Fine	£N.Mint
1 ND 48pgs, Jacques Tardi script, art and cover						
	$0.50	$1.50	$2.50	£0.30	£0.90	£1.50
Title Value:	$0.50	$1.50	$2.50	£0.30	£0.90	£1.50

SECRET ORIGINS (1ST SERIES)
National Periodical Publications; 1 1961
(see Eighty Page Giant Magazine)

	$Good	$Fine	$N.Mint	£Good	£Fine	£N.Mint
1 scarce in the U.K. 80pgs, reprints Green Lantern #1, Detective #225 (Jonn Jonzz), Showcase #4, Showcase #6 (part), Showcase #17, Wonder Woman #105, World's Finest #94						
	$48.00	$140.00	$475.00	£25.00	£75.00	£250.00
Title Value:	$48.00	$140.00	$475.00	£25.00	£75.00	£250.00

REPRINT FEATURES
Origins of the Superman/Batman team, Adam Strange, Green Lantern, Challengers of the Unknown, Wonder Woman, The Flash, Manhunter from Mars

SECRET ORIGINS (2ND SERIES)
DC Comics; 1 Feb/Mar 1973-6 Jan/Feb 1974; 7 Oct/Nov 1974

	$Good	$Fine	$N.Mint	£Good	£Fine	£N.Mint
1 origin of Superman (from Action No #1), Batman (from Detective Comics #33), The Ghost, Silver Age Flash from Showcase #4						
	$2.30	$7.00	$14.00	£1.15	£3.50	£7.00
2 origin Silver Age Atom from Showcase #34, Green Lantern from Showcase #22, Supergirl from Action #252						
	$1.20	$3.60	$6.00	£0.80	£2.40	£4.00
3 origin Wonder Woman from Wonder Woman #1, Wildcat from Sensation Comics #1						
	$1.20	$3.60	$6.00	£0.80	£2.40	£4.00
4 origin Vigilante from Action Comics #42, Kid Eternity from Hit Comics #25						
	$1.20	$3.60	$6.00	£0.80	£2.40	£4.00
5 origin The Spectre from More Fun #52-53						
	$1.20	$3.60	$6.00	£0.80	£2.40	£4.00
6 origin Blackhawk from Military Comics #1, Legion of Super-Heroes from Adventure Comics #247						
	$1.20	$3.60	$6.00	£0.80	£2.40	£4.00
7 origin Robin from Detective Comics #38, Aquaman from More Fun Comics #73						
	$1.20	$3.60	$6.00	£0.80	£2.40	£4.00
Title Value:	$9.50	$28.60	$50.00	£5.95	£17.90	£31.00

SECRET ORIGINS (3RD SERIES)
DC Comics; 1 Apr 1986-50 Aug 1990

	$Good	$Fine	$N.Mint	£Good	£Fine	£N.Mint
1 LD in the U.K. Jerry Ordway art, Superman						
	$0.50	$1.50	$2.50	£0.30	£0.90	£1.50
2 Gil Kane art, Blue Beetle						
	$0.30	$0.90	$1.50	£0.20	£0.60	£1.00
3 Captain Marvel	$0.30	$0.90	$1.50	£0.20	£0.60	£1.00
4 Firestorm	$0.30	$0.90	$1.50	£0.20	£0.60	£1.00
5 Crimson Avenger	$0.30	$0.90	$1.50	£0.20	£0.60	£1.00
6 Rogers/Alan Davis art, Batman						
	$0.50	$1.50	$2.50	£0.30	£0.90	£1.50
7 Bolland cover, Green Lantern, Golden Age Sandman						
	$0.30	$0.90	$1.50	£0.20	£0.60	£1.00
8 Dollman	$0.30	$0.90	$1.50	£0.20	£0.60	£1.00
9 Flash, Skyman	$0.30	$0.90	$1.50	£0.20	£0.60	£1.00
10 part Garcia Lopez art, part Moore script, Phantom Stranger; Legends X-over						
	$0.30	$0.90	$1.50	£0.20	£0.60	£1.00
11 Hawkman, Power Girl						
	$0.25	$0.75	$1.25	£0.15	£0.45	£0.75
12 Challengers of the Unknown, Golden Age Fury						
	$0.25	$0.75	$1.25	£0.15	£0.45	£0.75
13 Nightwing, Johnny Thunder						
	$0.25	$0.75	$1.25	£0.15	£0.45	£0.75
14 Suicide Squad	$0.25	$0.75	$1.25	£0.15	£0.45	£0.75
15 Kevin Maguire art, Spectre, Deadman						
	$0.25	$0.75	$1.25	£0.15	£0.45	£0.75
16 Golden Age Hourman, Warlord, 'Mazing Man						
	$0.25	$0.75	$1.25	£0.15	£0.45	£0.75
17 Kevin Nowlan cover, Adam Strange, Dr. Occult						
	$0.25	$0.75	$1.25	£0.15	£0.45	£0.75
18 The Creeper by Giffen, Golden Age Green Lantern						
	$0.25	$0.75	$1.25	£0.15	£0.45	£0.75
19 Uncle Sam, The Guardian						
	$0.25	$0.75	$1.25	£0.15	£0.45	£0.75
20 Batgirl, Golden Age Dr.Mid-Nite						
	$0.25	$0.75	$1.25	£0.15	£0.45	£0.75
21 Gray Morrow art, Jonah Hex, Black Condor						
	$0.25	$0.75	$1.25	£0.15	£0.45	£0.75
22 Manhunters, Millennium X-over						
	$0.25	$0.75	$1.25	£0.15	£0.45	£0.75
23 Brett Ewins art, Floronic Man, Guardians of the Universe; Millennium X-over						
	$0.25	$0.75	$1.25	£0.15	£0.45	£0.75
24 Ty Templeton art, Blue Devil, Dr.Fate						
	$0.25	$0.75	$1.25	£0.15	£0.45	£0.75
25 Legion of Super-Heroes, Golden Age Atom						
	$0.25	$0.75	$1.25	£0.15	£0.45	£0.75
26 Black Lightning, Miss America, Hourman appears, X-over with Young All Stars #12						
	$0.25	$0.75	$1.25	£0.15	£0.45	£0.75
27 Zatara, Zatanna	$0.25	$0.75	$1.25	£0.15	£0.45	£0.75
28 Rob Liefeld art, Midnight, Nightshade						
	$0.30	$0.90	$1.50	£0.20	£0.60	£1.00
29 Power of the Atom, Mr. America, Golden Age Red Tornado						
	$0.25	$0.75	$1.25	£0.15	£0.45	£0.75
30 Ty Templeton art, Plastic Man, Elongated Man						
	$0.25	$0.75	$1.25	£0.15	£0.45	£0.75
31 Justice Society of America						
	$0.25	$0.75	$1.25	£0.15	£0.45	£0.75
32 Justice League of America						
	$0.25	$0.75	$1.25	£0.15	£0.45	£0.75
33 Art Adams part inks, Justice League of America						
	$0.25	$0.75	$1.25	£0.15	£0.45	£0.75
34 Giffen art featured, Justice League International; covers fit together as poster						
	$0.25	$0.75	$1.25	£0.15	£0.45	£0.75
35 Justice League International; covers fit together as poster						
	$0.25	$0.75	$1.25	£0.15	£0.45	£0.75
36 Poison Ivy by Neil Gaiman, Green Lantern						
	$0.25	$0.75	$1.25	£0.15	£0.45	£0.75
37 Ty Templeton art, Legion of Substitute Heroes, Dr.Light						
	$0.25	$0.75	$1.25	£0.15	£0.45	£0.75
38 Green Arrow, Speedy						
	$0.25	$0.75	$1.25	£0.15	£0.45	£0.75

	$Good	$Fine	$N.Mint	£Good	£Fine	£N.Mint
39 Animal Man by Grant Morrison, Man-Bat	$0.40	$1.20	$2.00	£0.20	£0.60	£1.00
40 Infantino art, Gorilla City, Detective Chimp, Congorilla	$0.25	$0.75	$1.25	£0.15	£0.45	£0.75
41 Flash's Rogues Gallery (Captain Cold/Heat Wave/Pied Piper/Trickster/Weather Wizard), cover based on Flash #174	$0.25	$0.75	$1.25	£0.15	£0.45	£0.75
42 Phantom Girl, Grim Ghost	$0.25	$0.75	$1.25	£0.15	£0.45	£0.75
43 Hawk and the Dove, Cave Carson	$0.25	$0.75	$1.25	£0.15	£0.45	£0.75
44 The Four Clay Faces	$0.25	$0.75	$1.25	£0.15	£0.45	£0.75
45 Blackhawk, El Diablo	$0.25	$0.75	$1.25	£0.15	£0.45	£0.75
46 Justice League/Teen Titans/Legion of Super Heroes Headquarters	$0.25	$0.75	$1.25	£0.15	£0.45	£0.75
47 Curt Swan/Mark Badger art, Ferro Lad, Chemical King, Karate Kid	$0.25	$0.75	$1.25	£0.15	£0.45	£0.75
48 Ambush Bug (Giffen art)/Rex the WonderDog/Stanley and his Monster	$0.25	$0.75	$1.25	£0.15	£0.45	£0.75
49 Cadmus Project/Silent Knight/Legion of Super-Heroes (2 pgs)	$0.25	$0.75	$1.25	£0.15	£0.45	£0.75
50 96pgs, Batman by O'Neil/George Perez, Flash story by Grant Morrison, Black Canary/Dolphin/ Johnny Thunder, Space Museum drawn by Infantino/George Perez	$0.60	$1.80	$3.00	£0.40	£1.20	£2.00
Title Value:	$13.95	$41.85	$69.75	£8.55	£25.65	£42.75

Note: all 48pgs from #6-49

Trade paperback (Mar 1990)
new origin of Batman by O'Neill and Giordano, reprints new origins of Flash, Green Lantern, JLA, Martian Manhunter and Superman; Brian Bolland cover

	$Good	$Fine	$N.Mint	£Good	£Fine	£N.Mint
				£0.60	£1.80	£3.00

SECRET ORIGINS ANNUAL
DC Comics; 1 Aug 1987-3 1989

	$Good	$Fine	$N.Mint	£Good	£Fine	£N.Mint
1 Doom Patrol, John Byrne cover and art	$0.40	$1.20	$2.00	£0.25	£0.75	£1.25
2 48pgs, Flash II, Flash III, Infantino/Murphy Anderson art	$0.40	$1.20	$2.00	£0.25	£0.75	£1.25
3 64pgs, Teen Titans, George Perez art	$0.50	$1.50	$2.50	£0.30	£0.90	£1.50
Title Value:	$1.30	$3.90	$6.50	£0.80	£2.40	£4.00

SECRET ORIGINS OF SUPER-HEROES
DC Comics; nn Autumn 1979
(DC Special Series #19)

	$Good	$Fine	$N.Mint	£Good	£Fine	£N.Mint
nn ND 100pgs	$0.60	$1.80	$3.00	£0.40	£1.20	£2.00
Title Value:	$0.60	$1.80	$3.00	£0.40	£1.20	£2.00

FEATURES
Wonder Woman
REPRINT FEATURES
Superman/Batman, Elongated Man, Hawkman, Robin, Supergirl, Aquaman, Lightning Lad/Lass.

SECRET ORIGINS OF SUPER-HEROES SPECIAL
DC Comics; nn 1978
(DC Special Series #10)

	$Good	$Fine	$N.Mint	£Good	£Fine	£N.Mint
nn ND 52pgs, Dr. Fate, Lightray and Black Canary, Joe Staton and Mike Nasser art	$0.60	$1.80	$3.00	£0.40	£1.20	£2.00
Title Value:	$0.60	$1.80	$3.00	£0.40	£1.20	£2.00

SECRET ORIGINS SPECIAL
DC Comics; 1 Aug 1989

	$Good	$Fine	$N.Mint	£Good	£Fine	£N.Mint
1 LD in the U.K. 64pgs, squarebound, Sam Kieth art featured, Brian Bolland cover, Neil Gaiman/Alan Grant story, origins of Two Face, Penguin and The Riddler	$0.80	$2.40	$4.00	£0.50	£1.50	£2.50

	$Good	$Fine	$N.Mint	£Good	£Fine	£N.Mint
Title Value:	$0.80	$2.40	$4.00	£0.50	£1.50	£2.50

SECRET SIX
National Periodical Publications; 1 Apr/May 1968-7 Apr/May 1969

	$Good	$Fine	$N.Mint	£Good	£Fine	£N.Mint
1 origin and 1st appearance of Secret Six	$6.25	$19.00	$45.00	£3.55	£10.50	£25.00
2-7	$3.90	$11.50	$27.50	£2.10	£6.25	£15.00
Title Value:	$29.65	$88.00	$210.00	£16.15	£48.00	£115.00

SECRET SOCIETY OF SUPER-VILLAINS
DC Comics; 1 May/Jun 1976-15 Jun/Jul 1978

	$Good	$Fine	$N.Mint	£Good	£Fine	£N.Mint
1	$0.80	$2.40	$4.00	£0.50	£1.50	£2.50
2 ND	$0.60	$1.80	$3.00	£0.40	£1.20	£2.00
3 scarce in the U.K.	$0.50	$1.50	$2.50	£0.30	£0.90	£1.50
4	$0.50	$1.50	$2.50	£0.25	£0.75	£1.25
5 Green Lantern appears	$0.50	$1.50	$2.50	£0.25	£0.75	£1.25
6-8	$0.40	$1.20	$2.00	£0.25	£0.75	£1.25
9 scarce in the U.K.	$0.40	$1.20	$2.00	£0.30	£0.90	£1.50
10 Creeper appears	$0.30	$0.90	$1.50	£0.20	£0.60	£1.00
11 Captain Comet appears	$0.40	$1.20	$2.00	£0.25	£0.75	£1.25
12-14	$0.40	$1.20	$2.00	£0.25	£0.75	£1.25
15 Justice Society of America appear	$0.40	$1.20	$2.00	£0.25	£0.75	£1.25
Title Value:	$6.80	$20.40	$34.00	£4.20	£12.60	£21.00

Note: features Gorilla Grodd/ Mirror Master/ Sinestro/ Star Sapphire/ Captain Cold/ Captain Boomerang/ Copperhead/ Manhunter

SECRET SOCIETY OF SUPER-VILLAINS SPECIAL
DC Comics; nn 1977
(DC Special Series #6)

	$Good	$Fine	$N.Mint	£Good	£Fine	£N.Mint
nn ND 52pgs	$0.60	$1.80	$3.00	£0.40	£1.20	£2.00
Title Value:	$0.60	$1.80	$3.00	£0.40	£1.20	£2.00

SECRET WARS II
Marvel Comics Group,MS; 1 Jul 1985-9 Mar 1986

	$Good	$Fine	$N.Mint	£Good	£Fine	£N.Mint
1 ND 1st appearance The Beyonder	$0.25	$0.75	$1.25	£0.25	£0.75	£1.25
2-7 LD in the U.K.	$0.25	$0.75	$1.25	£0.20	£0.60	£1.00
8 LD in the U.K. Spiderman in black costume	$0.25	$0.75	$1.25	£0.20	£0.60	£1.00
9 LD in the U.K. DS	$0.25	$0.75	$11.25	£0.25	£0.75	£1.25
Title Value:	$2.25	$6.75	$11.25	£1.90	£5.70	£9.50

Note: similar to 1st Secret Wars series but with greater character involvement in cross-over titles.

SECRET WEAPONS
Valiant; 1 Sep 1993-23 Aug 1995

	$Good	$Fine	$N.Mint	£Good	£Fine	£N.Mint
1 The Coming of the Darque Age part 1; X-O, Bloodshot, Eternal Warrior, Livewire and Stronghold vs. Dr. Eclipse	$0.30	$0.90	$1.50	£0.20	£0.60	£1.00
2 The Coming of the Darque Age story concludes	$0.30	$0.90	$1.50	£0.20	£0.60	£1.00
3 Empirircal Dynasty part 1, continued in Bloodshot #11	$0.30	$0.90	$1.50	£0.20	£0.60	£1.00
4	$0.30	$0.90	$1.50	£0.20	£0.60	£1.00
5 Ninjak featured	$0.30	$0.90	$1.50	£0.20	£0.60	£1.00
6-8	$0.30	$0.90	$1.50	£0.20	£0.60	£1.00
9 with free Upper Deck trading card	$0.30	$0.90	$1.50	£0.20	£0.60	£1.00
10	$0.30	$0.90	$1.50	£0.20	£0.60	£1.00
11 pre-bagged in brown wrapper marked Top Secret Eyes Only; new direction for title	$0.30	$0.90	$1.50	£0.20	£0.60	£1.00
12 Bloodshot appears						

Sebastian O #1

Secret Hearts #59

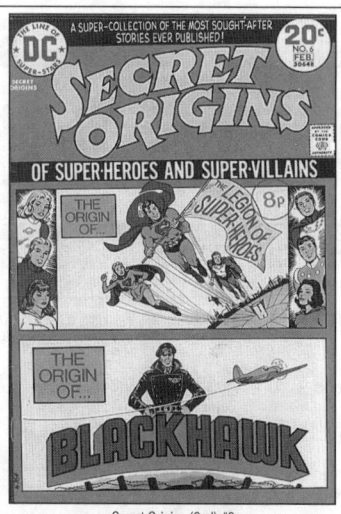

Secret Origins (2nd) #6

	$Good	$Fine	$N.Mint	£Good	£Fine	£N.Mint
	$0.30	$0.90	$1.50	£0.20	£0.60	£1.00
13 Chaos Effect tie-in	$0.30	$0.90	$1.50	£0.20	£0.60	£1.00
14-23	$0.30	$0.90	$1.50	£0.20	£0.60	£1.00
Title Value:	$6.90	$20.70	$34.50	£4.60	£13.80	£23.00

Note: all Non-Distributed on the news-stands in the U.K.

SECRET WEAPONS: PLAYING WITH FIRE
Valiant/Acclaim Comics,MS; 1,2 Nov 1995

	$Good	$Fine	$N.Mint	£Good	£Fine	£N.Mint
1-2 ND	$0.40	$1.20	$2.00	£0.25	£0.75	£1.25
Title Value:	$0.80	$2.40	$4.00	£0.50	£1.50	£2.50

SECRETS OF HAUNTED HOUSE
DC Comics; 1 Apr/May 1975-5 Dec/Jan 1975/76; 6 Jun/Jul 1977-14 Oct/Nov 1978; 15 Aug 1979-46 Mar 1982

	$Good	$Fine	$N.Mint	£Good	£Fine	£N.Mint
1 Cain and Abel appear	$0.60	$1.80	$3.00	£0.40	£1.20	£2.00
2-9	$0.50	$1.50	$2.50	£0.30	£0.90	£1.50
10 Golden art	$0.50	$1.50	$2.50	£0.30	£0.90	£1.50
11-13	$0.40	$1.20	$2.00	£0.25	£0.75	£1.25
14-19 scarce in the U.K. 44pgs	$0.40	$1.20	$2.00	£0.30	£0.90	£1.50
20-23	$0.40	$1.20	$2.00	£0.25	£0.75	£1.25
24 Nasser art	$0.40	$1.20	$2.00	£0.25	£0.75	£1.25
25-30	$0.40	$1.20	$2.00	£0.25	£0.75	£1.25
31-41 Mister E stars	$0.40	$1.20	$2.00	£0.25	£0.75	£1.25
42-46	$0.40	$1.20	$2.00	£0.25	£0.75	£1.25
Title Value:	$19.50	$58.50	$97.50	£12.40	£37.20	£62.00

ARTISTS
Ditko in 9, 12, 41, 45. Nino in 1, 13, 19.

SECRETS OF HAUNTED HOUSE SPECIAL
DC Comics; nn Spring 1978
(DC Special Series #12)

	$Good	$Fine	$N.Mint	£Good	£Fine	£N.Mint
nn ND scarce in the U.K. 52pgs	$0.60	$1.80	$3.00	£0.40	£1.20	£2.00
Title Value:	$0.60	$1.80	$3.00	£0.40	£1.20	£2.00

SECRETS OF SINISTER HOUSE
DC Comics; 5 Jun/Jul 1972-18 Jun/Jul 1974
(previously Sinister House of Secret Love)

	$Good	$Fine	$N.Mint	£Good	£Fine	£N.Mint
5 ND 52pgs	$0.50	$1.50	$2.50	£0.30	£0.90	£1.50
6-9 ND	$0.50	$1.50	$2.50	£0.25	£0.75	£1.25
10 ND Neal Adams inks	$1.00	$3.00	$5.00	£0.70	£2.10	£3.50
11-18 ND	$0.40	$1.20	$2.00	£0.25	£0.75	£1.25
Title Value:	$6.70	$20.10	$33.50	£4.00	£12.00	£20.00

ARTISTS
Nino art in 8, 11-13

SECRETS OF THE LEGION OF SUPER-HEROES
DC Comics,MS; 1 Jan 1981-3 Mar 1981
(see Legion of Super-Heroes)

	$Good	$Fine	$N.Mint	£Good	£Fine	£N.Mint
1 Legion origin retold	$0.30	$0.90	$1.50	£0.20	£0.60	£1.00
2 Braniac 5, Bouncing Boy, Dream Girl, Sun Boy, Karate Kid, Matter-Eater Lad, Shrinking Violet, Mon-El origins retold	$0.30	$0.90	$1.50	£0.20	£0.60	£1.00
3	$0.30	$0.90	$1.50	£0.20	£0.60	£1.00
Title Value:	$0.90	$2.70	$4.50	£0.60	£1.80	£3.00

SECRETS OF THE VALIANT UNIVERSE
Valiant; 1 Sep 1994-3 Nov 1994

	$Good	$Fine	$N.Mint	£Good	£Fine	£N.Mint
1 ND available with Wizard's "Valiant Universe Special"	$0.30	$0.90	$1.50	£0.20	£0.60	£1.00
2 ND Chaos Effect tie-in	$0.30	$0.90	$1.50	£0.20	£0.60	£1.00
3 ND features Sho Sugino the 2nd Rai	$0.30	$0.90	$1.50	£0.20	£0.60	£1.00
Title Value:	$0.90	$2.70	$4.50	£0.60	£1.80	£3.00

SECTAURS
Marvel Comics Group, Toy; 1 Jun 1985-8 1986

	$Good	$Fine	$N.Mint	£Good	£Fine	£N.Mint
1 ND Mark Texeira art	$0.15	$0.45	$0.75	£0.10	£0.30	£0.50
1 ND rare in the U.K. 1985 Coleco Toys Giveaway (banner across bottom left corner)	$0.30	$0.90	$1.50	£0.20	£0.60	£1.00
2 ND Mark Texeira art	$0.15	$0.45	$0.75	£0.10	£0.30	£0.50
3-8 ND	$0.15	$0.45	$0.75	£0.10	£0.30	£0.50
Title Value:	$1.50	$4.50	$7.50	£1.00	£3.00	£5.00

SEDUCTION OF THE INNOCENT
Eclipse,MS; 1 Nov 1985-6 Apr 1986
(see Three-Dimensional Seduction of the Innocent) (#1-3 marked as 3-issue mini-series)

	$Good	$Fine	$N.Mint	£Good	£Fine	£N.Mint
1 all pre-code horror reprints	$0.40	$1.20	$2.00	£0.25	£0.75	£1.25
1 3-D issue (Oct 1985), Dave Stevens cover; with bound-in 3-D glasses (25% less without glasses)	$0.50	$1.50	$2.50	£0.30	£0.90	£1.50
2 all pre-code horror reprints	$0.40	$1.20	$2.00	£0.25	£0.75	£1.25
2 3-D issue (Apr 1986), Berni Wrightson cover, Alex Toth reprint; with bound-in 3-D glasses (25% less without glasses)	$0.50	$1.50	$2.50	£0.30	£0.90	£1.50
3-6 all pre-code horror reprints	$0.40	$1.20	$2.00	£0.25	£0.75	£1.25
Title Value:	$3.40	$10.20	$17.00	£2.10	£6.30	£10.50

Note: all Non-Distributed on the news-stands in the U.K.

SEEKER, JOE MARTIN'S
Sky Comics,OS; 1 Apr 1994

	$Good	$Fine	$N.Mint	£Good	£Fine	£N.Mint
1 ND plastic acetate cover	$0.40	$1.20	$2.00	£0.25	£0.75	£1.25
Title Value:	$0.40	$1.20	$2.00	£0.25	£0.75	£1.25

SEEKERS: INTO THE MYSTERY
DC Comics/Vertigo; 1 Jan 1996-present

	$Good	$Fine	$N.Mint	£Good	£Fine	£N.Mint
1-3 ND J.M. DeMatteis script, Glen Barr art	$0.50	$1.50	$2.50	£0.30	£0.90	£1.50
Title Value:	$1.50	$4.50	$7.50	£0.90	£2.70	£4.50

SEMPER FI
Marvel Comics Group; 1 Dec 1988-9 Aug 1989

	$Good	$Fine	$N.Mint	£Good	£Fine	£N.Mint
1-9 ND	$0.25	$0.75	$1.25	£0.15	£0.45	£0.75
Title Value:	$2.25	$6.75	$11.25	£1.35	£4.05	£6.75

SENSATION COMICS
National Periodical Publications; 1 Jan 1942-116 Jul/Aug 1953

	$Good	$Fine	$N.Mint	£Good	£Fine	£N.Mint
1 Wonder Woman's adventures continue from All Star Comics #8, origin/1st appearance Mr. Terrific, 1st appearance Wildcat	$1950.00	$5800.00	$19500.00	£1300.00	£3900.00	£13000.00
2	$340.00	$1025.00	$2750.00	£225.00	£670.00	£1800.00
3	$175.00	$520.00	$1400.00	£115.00	£355.00	£950.00
4	$135.00	$410.00	$1100.00	£92.50	£280.00	£750.00
5	$110.00	$335.00	$900.00	£75.00	£225.00	£600.00
6 origin and 1st appearance the magic lasso (used on cover)	$110.00	$335.00	$900.00	£77.50	£230.00	£625.00
7-10	$82.50	$250.00	$675.00	£55.00	£165.00	£450.00
11-12	$80.00	$245.00	$575.00	£55.00	£165.00	£385.00
13 Hitler, Mussolini and Emperor Tojo parody cover	$100.00	$300.00	$700.00	£67.50	£200.00	£475.00
14-20	$80.00	$245.00	$575.00	£55.00	£165.00	£385.00
21-30	$60.00	$180.00	$425.00	£41.00	£120.00	£285.00
31-33	$46.00	$135.00	$325.00	£31.00	£90.00	£215.00
34-36 Sargon the Sorcerer back-up	$46.00	$135.00	$325.00	£31.00	£90.00	£215.00
37	$46.00	$135.00	$325.00	£31.00	£90.00	£215.00
38 Christmas cover	$46.00	$135.00	$325.00	£31.00	£90.00	£215.00
39-40	$46.00	$135.00	$325.00	£31.00	£90.00	£215.00
41 Red Cross cover	$36.00	$105.00	$250.00	£25.00	£75.00	£175.00
42-50	$36.00	$105.00	$250.00	£25.00	£75.00	£175.00
51-60	$31.00	$90.00	$215.00	£21.00	£62.50	£150.00
61-67	$29.00	$85.00	$200.00	£18.50	£55.00	£130.00
68 origin and 1st appearance of the Huntress	$32.00	$95.00	$225.00	£21.00	£62.50	£150.00
69-80	$29.00	$85.00	$200.00	£18.50	£55.00	£130.00
81 B. Krigstein art	$29.00	$85.00	$200.00	£18.50	£55.00	£130.00
82	$22.50	$67.50	$160.00	£15.50	£47.00	£110.00
83 scarce in the U.S, very scarce in the U.K. B. Krigstein art	$25.00	$75.00	$200.00	£16.00	£49.00	£130.00
84-93	$22.50	$67.50	$160.00	£15.50	£47.00	£110.00
94 cover logo change, new features announced including Dr. Pat and other romance-orientated stories	$32.00	$95.00	$225.00	£21.00	£62.50	£150.00
95-99	$32.00	$95.00	$225.00	£21.00	£62.50	£150.00
100 scarce in the U.K.	$46.00	$135.00	$325.00	£32.00	£95.00	£225.00
101-105 scarce in the U.K.	$32.00	$95.00	$225.00	£21.00	£62.50	£150.00
106 scarce in the U.K. last Wonder Woman in title and on cover	$32.00	$95.00	$225.00	£21.00	£62.50	£150.00
107 scarce in the U.S, very scarce in the U.K. title becomes mystery anthology	$47.00	$140.00	$375.00	£31.00	£92.50	£250.00
108-109 scarce in the U.S, very scarce in the U.K.	$47.00	$140.00	$375.00	£31.00	£92.50	£250.00
110 very scarce in the U.K. title becomes "Sensation Mystery" on cover	$35.00	$105.00	$245.00	£21.00	£62.50	£150.00
111-116 very scarce in the U.K.	$30.00	$90.00	$210.00	£21.00	£62.50	£150.00
Title Value:	$7370.50	$21982.50	$59115.00	£4949.00	£14768.50	£39630.00

Note: in common with all Golden Age material, this title was not officially distributed on the news-stands in the U.K. but copies may have found their way over through personnel movements during the war or as cheap ballast on ships after the war. No reports of copies with British pence stamps on as yet.

SENSATIONAL SPIDERMAN
Marvel Comics Group; 0 Jan 1996; 1 Feb 1996-present

	$Good	$Fine	$N.Mint	£Good	£Fine	£N.Mint
0 ND 48pgs, The Return of Spiderman part 1, continued in Amazing Spiderman #407; 1st new costume; "moving image" lenticular cover	$1.00	$3.00	$5.00	£0.65	£1.95	£3.25
1 ND Media Blizzard part 1, continued in Amazing Spiderman #408; new Spiderman vs. new Mysterio	$0.40	$1.20	$2.00	£0.30	£0.90	£1.50
2 ND The Return of Kaine part 2, continued in Amazing Spiderman #409	$0.40	$1.20	$2.00	£0.30	£0.90	£1.50
Title Value:	$1.80	$5.40	$9.00	£1.25	£3.75	£6.25

SENSEI
First,MS; 1 Sep 1989-4 Dec 1989
(see Squalor, Twilight Man)

	$Good	$Fine	$N.Mint	£Good	£Fine	£N.Mint
1 ND Val Mayerik cover and art begins, sub-titled "First Fiction Volume 2"; glossy heavier stock paper covers begin	$0.40	$1.20	$2.00	£0.25	£0.75	£1.25
2-4 ND	$0.40	$1.20	$2.00	£0.25	£0.75	£1.25
Title Value:	$1.60	$4.80	$8.00	£1.00	£3.00	£5.00

SENTAI
Antarctic Press; 1 Mar 1994-5 1995

	$Good	$Fine	$N.Mint	£Good	£Fine	£N.Mint
1-5 ND information and features on Asian sci-fi and fantasy	$0.50	$1.50	$2.50	£0.30	£0.90	£1.50
Title Value:	$2.50	$7.50	$12.50	£1.50	£4.50	£7.50

SENTINELS OF JUSTICE
AC Comics; 1 1985-5 1986

	$Good	$Fine	$N.Mint	£Good	£Fine	£N.Mint
1-5 ND	$0.40	$1.20	$2.00	£0.25	£0.75	£1.25
Title Value:	$2.00	$6.00	$10.00	£1.25	£3.75	£6.25

SENTRY SPECIAL
Innovation,OS; 1 Jun 1991

	$Good	$Fine	$N.Mint	£Good	£Fine	£N.Mint
1 ND spin-off from Hero Alliance, black and white	$0.40	$1.20	$2.00	£0.25	£0.75	£1.25
Title Value:	$0.40	$1.20	$2.00	£0.25	£0.75	£1.25

SERAPHIM
Innovation,MS; 1 May 1990-2 Jun 1990

	$Good	$Fine	$N.Mint	£Good	£Fine	£N.Mint
1-2 ND painted art by Doug Talalla	$0.40	$1.20	$2.00	£0.25	£0.75	£1.25
Title Value:	$0.80	$2.40	$4.00	£0.50	£1.50	£2.50

SERGEANT BILKO
National Periodical Publications, TV; 1 May/Jun 1957-18 Mar/Apr 1960

	$Good	$Fine	$N.Mint	£Good	£Fine	£N.Mint
1 scarce in the U.K.	$62.50	$185.00	$500.00	£44.00	£130.00	£350.00
2 scarce in the U.K.	$36.00	$105.00	$250.00	£25.00	£75.00	£175.00
3-5 scarce in the U.K.	$30.00	$90.00	$210.00	£20.00	£60.00	£140.00
6-15	$25.00	$75.00	$175.00	£16.00	£49.00	£115.00
1st official distribution in the U.K.						
16-18	$25.00	$75.00	$175.00	£16.00	£49.00	£115.00
Title Value:	$513.50	$1535.00	$3655.00	£337.00	£1022.00	£2440.00

SERGIO ARAGONES MASSACRES MARVEL
Marvel Comics Group,OS; 1 Feb 1996

	$Good	$Fine	$N.Mint	£Good	£Fine	£N.Mint
1 ND 48pgs, Sergio Aragones draws Spiderman, X-Men, Fantastic Four and others	$1.00	$3.00	$5.00	£0.65	£1.95	£3.25
Title Value:	$1.00	$3.00	$5.00	£0.65	£1.95	£3.25

SERPENT RISING
Caliber Press,OS; 1 Jul 1992

	$Good	$Fine	$N.Mint	£Good	£Fine	£N.Mint
1 ND ecological theme; black and white	$0.40	$1.20	$2.00	£0.25	£0.75	£1.25
Title Value:	$0.40	$1.20	$2.00	£0.25	£0.75	£1.25

SERPENTYNE
Night Wynd,MS; 1 Apr 1992-3 Jun 1992

	$Good	$Fine	$N.Mint	£Good	£Fine	£N.Mint
1-3 ND Barry Blair; black and white	$0.40	$1.20	$2.00	£0.25	£0.75	£1.25
Title Value:	$1.20	$3.60	$6.00	£0.75	£2.25	£3.75

SEVEN BLOCK BOOKSHELF EDITION
Marvel Comics Group/Epic,OS; 1 Oct 1990

	$Good	$Fine	$N.Mint	£Good	£Fine	£N.Mint
1 ND 48pgs, Dixon script, Zaffino art	$0.50	$1.50	$2.50	£0.30	£0.90	£1.50
Title Value:	$0.50	$1.50	$2.50	£0.30	£0.90	£1.50

77 SUNSET STRIP
Gold Key; 1 Nov 1962-2 Feb 1963
(see Four Colour #1066, #1106, #1211, #1263, #1291)

	$Good	$Fine	$N.Mint	£Good	£Fine	£N.Mint
1-2 Russ Manning art; distributed in the U.K.	$10.00	$30.00	$60.00	£6.50	£20.00	£40.00
Title Value:	$20.00	$60.00	$120.00	£13.00	£40.00	£80.00

SEX WARRIOR
Dark Horse,MS; 1 Apr 1993-2 May 1993

	$Good	$Fine	$N.Mint	£Good	£Fine	£N.Mint
1-2 ND Mills and Skinner, McKone and Erasmus	$0.50	$1.50	$2.50	£0.30	£0.90	£1.50
Title Value:	$1.00	$3.00	$5.00	£0.60	£1.80	£3.00

SF SHORT STORIES
Webb Graphics; 1 1991

	$Good	$Fine	$N.Mint	£Good	£Fine	£N.Mint
1 ND black and white	$0.25	$0.75	$1.25	£0.15	£0.45	£0.75
Title Value:	$0.25	$0.75	$1.25	£0.15	£0.45	£0.75

SGT. BILKO'S PVT. DOBERMAN
National Periodical Publications, TV; 1 Jun/Jul 1958-11 Feb/Mar 1960

	$Good	$Fine	$N.Mint	£Good	£Fine	£N.Mint
1 scarce in the U.K.	$39.00	$115.00	$275.00	£25.00	£75.00	£175.00
2	$22.50	$67.50	$160.00	£15.00	£45.00	£105.00
3-5	$17.00	$50.00	$120.00	£11.00	£34.00	£80.00
6-8	$12.50	$39.00	$90.00	£8.50	£26.00	£60.00
1st official distribution in the U.K.						
9-11	$12.50	$39.00	$90.00	£8.50	£26.00	£60.00
Title Value:	$187.50	$566.50	$1335.00	£124.00	£378.00	£880.00

SGT. FURY AND HIS HOWLING COMMANDOS
Marvel Comics Group; 1 May 1963-167 Dec 1981

	$Good	$Fine	$N.Mint	£Good	£Fine	£N.Mint
1 scarce in the U.K. 1st appearance Sgt. Fury, Jack Kirby art begins, Dick Ayers inks	$100.00	$305.00	$825.00	£55.00	£165.00	£450.00
2 scarce in the U.K. Jack Kirby art	$39.00	$115.00	$275.00	£26.00	£75.00	£180.00
3 scarce in the U.K. Jack Kirby art, Reed Richards appears	$21.00	$62.50	$150.00	£14.00	£43.00	£100.00
4 Jack Kirby art	$21.00	$62.50	$150.00	£13.50	£41.00	£95.00
5 1st appearance Baron Strucker, Jack Kirby art	$21.00	$62.50	$150.00	£13.50	£41.00	£95.00
6-7 Jack Kirby art	$14.00	$43.00	$100.00	£9.25	£28.00	£65.00
8-9	$14.00	$43.00	$100.00	£9.25	£28.00	£65.00
10 1st appearance Captain Savage	$14.00	$43.00	$100.00	£9.25	£28.00	£65.00
11 rare in the U.K.	$9.00	$28.00	$55.00	£6.50	£20.00	£40.00
12 scarce in the U.K.	$9.00	$28.00	$55.00	£6.25	£18.50	£37.50
13 Captain America guest-stars, classic cover, Jack Kirby art	$31.00	$92.50	$250.00	£18.50	£55.00	£150.00
14	$8.25	$25.00	$50.00	£5.75	£17.50	£35.00
15 Steve Ditko art	$8.25	$25.00	$50.00	£5.75	£17.50	£35.00
16-20	$8.25	$25.00	$50.00	£5.75	£17.50	£35.00
21-24	$6.50	$20.00	$40.00	£4.15	£12.50	£25.00
25 Red Skull appears	$6.50	$20.00	$40.00	£4.15	£12.50	£25.00
26	$6.50	$20.00	$40.00	£4.15	£12.50	£25.00
27 origin Fury's eye-patch	$6.50	$20.00	$40.00	£4.15	£12.50	£25.00
28-30	$6.50	$20.00	$40.00	£4.15	£12.50	£25.00
31-33	$4.15	$12.50	$25.00	£2.90	£8.75	£17.50
34 origin Howling Commandoes	$4.15	$12.50	$25.00	£2.90	£8.75	£17.50
35-40	$4.15	$12.50	$25.00	£2.90	£8.75	£17.50
41-42	$3.75	$11.00	$22.50	£2.50	£7.50	£15.00
43 Bob Hope, Glen Miller cameos	$3.75	$11.00	$22.50	£2.50	£7.50	£15.00
44-50	$3.75	$11.00	$22.50	£2.50	£7.50	£15.00
51 Churchill, Roosevelt, Stalin cameos	$3.50	$10.50	$17.50	£2.50	£7.50	£12.50
52-60	$3.50	$10.50	$17.50	£2.50	£7.50	£12.50
61-63	$3.00	$9.00	$15.00	£2.00	£6.00	£10.00
64 Captain Savage X-over	$3.00	$9.00	$15.00	£2.00	£6.00	£10.00
65-68	$3.00	$9.00	$15.00	£2.00	£6.00	£10.00
69 scarce in the U.K.	$3.00	$9.00	$15.00	£2.20	£6.50	£11.00
70	$3.00	$9.00	$15.00	£2.00	£6.00	£10.00
71 scarce in the U.K.	$3.00	$9.00	$15.00	£2.20	£6.50	£11.00
72-80	$2.40	$7.00	$12.00	£1.60	£4.80	£8.00
81-88	$2.00	$6.00	$10.00	£1.40	£4.20	£7.00
89-91 ND	$2.00	$6.00	$10.00	£1.50	£4.50	£7.50
92 ND 48pgs, squarebound	$2.40	$7.00	$12.00	£1.60	£4.80	£8.00
93-99 ND	$2.00	$6.00	$10.00	£1.50	£4.50	£7.50
100 ND Captain America, Fantastic Four, Stan Lee cameos plus scripter and artist Gary Friedrich and Dick Ayers cameos	$2.40	$7.00	$12.00	£2.00	£6.00	£10.00
101 ND origin retold	$1.50	$4.50	$7.50	£1.20	£3.60	£6.00
102-106 ND	$1.50	$4.50	$7.50	£1.20	£3.60	£6.00
107-117 ND	$1.50	$4.50	$7.50	£0.80	£2.40	£4.00
118-120 ND	$1.50	$4.50	$7.50	£0.90	£2.70	£4.50
121-127 ND	$1.20	$3.60	$6.00	£0.70	£2.10	£3.50
128	$1.20	$3.60	$6.00	£0.60	£1.80	£3.00
129-131 ND	$1.20	$3.60	$6.00	£0.70	£2.10	£3.50
132	$1.20	$3.60	$6.00	£0.60	£1.80	£3.00
133-140 ND	$1.20	$3.60	$6.00	£0.70	£2.10	£3.50
141-151 ND	$1.00	$3.00	$5.00	£0.60	£1.80	£3.00
152	$1.00	$3.00	$5.00	£0.50	£1.50	£2.50
153-162 ND	$1.00	$3.00	$5.00	£0.60	£1.80	£3.00
163-166	$1.00	$3.00	$5.00	£0.50	£1.50	£2.50
167 scarce in the U.K. reprints issue #1	$1.00	$3.00	$5.00	£0.60	£1.80	£3.00
Title Value:	$734.15	$2213.00	$4692.00	£475.05	£1427.70	£2991.50

Note: Ditko inks in #15. Most issues from #80-120 are reprint. All issues from 121 on are reprint.

SGT. FURY ANNUAL
Marvel Comics Group; 1 1965-7 1971

	$Good	$Fine	$N.Mint	£Good	£Fine	£N.Mint
1 scarce in the U.K. 72pgs, one new story plus reprints of #4, #5	$14.00	$43.00	$100.00	£10.00	£30.00	£70.00
2 72pgs	$7.00	$21.00	$50.00	£5.00	£15.00	£35.00
3 72pgs	$5.00	$15.00	$30.00	£3.30	£10.00	£20.00
4 72pgs	$2.90	$8.75	$17.50	£2.05	£6.25	£12.50
5-6 64pgs, all reprint	$1.65	$5.00	$10.00	£1.25	£3.75	£7.50
7 ND scarce in the U.K. 48pgs, all reprint (Note: almost all copies ink-stained)	$1.65	$5.00	$10.00	£1.25	£3.75	£7.50
Title Value:	$33.85	$102.75	$227.50	£24.10	£72.50	£160.00

SGT. ROCK
DC Comics; 302 Mar 1977-422 Jul 1988
(see Brave and the Bold, Brave and Bold Special, DC Comics Presents, DC Super Stars, One-Hundred Page Super Spectacular, Sgt. Rock Special, Showcase) (previously Our Army At War)

	$Good	$Fine	$N.Mint	£Good	£Fine	£N.Mint
302	$2.05	$6.25	$12.50	£0.80	£2.50	£5.00
303-310	$1.65	$5.00	$10.00	£0.55	£1.75	£3.50
311-312	$1.25	$3.75	$7.50	£0.40	£1.25	£2.50
313-317 ND	$1.25	$3.75	$7.50	£0.50	£1.50	£3.00
318 ND all reprint	$1.25	$3.75	$7.50	£0.50	£1.50	£3.00
319-322 ND	$1.25	$3.75	$7.50	£0.50	£1.50	£3.00
323-350	$1.20	$3.60	$6.00	£0.50	£1.50	£2.50
351-370	$0.80	$2.40	$4.00	£0.40	£1.20	£2.00
371-400	$0.80	$2.40	$4.00	£0.30	£0.90	£1.50
401-422	$0.80	$2.40	$4.00	£0.25	£0.75	£1.25
Title Value:	$121.45	$364.85	$635.50	£47.50	£143.50	£250.50

SGT. ROCK ANNUAL
DC Comics; 2 1982-4 1984

	$Good	$Fine	$N.Mint	£Good	£Fine	£N.Mint
(previously Sgt. Rock's Prize Battle Tales)						
2-4 ND 52pgs	$0.70	$2.10	$3.50	£0.30	£0.90	£1.50
Title Value:	$2.10	$6.30	$10.50	£0.90	£2.70	£4.50

SGT. ROCK SPECIAL
DC Comics; nn 1977, 2 1988, 3 1989-21 Jan 1992

	$Good	$Fine	$N.Mint	£Good	£Fine	£N.Mint
nn ND 52pgs, reprints begin	$0.50	$1.50	$2.50	£0.30	£0.90	£1.50
2 ND 48pgs, Chaykin cover, Chaykin reprint from Weird War Tales	$0.40	$1.20	$2.00	£0.25	£0.75	£1.25
3 48pgs	$0.40	$1.20	$2.00	£0.25	£0.75	£1.25
4 48pgs, Walt Simonson cover	$0.40	$1.20	$2.00	£0.25	£0.75	£1.25
5 48pgs	$0.40	$1.20	$2.00	£0.25	£0.75	£1.25
6 48pgs, Frank Miller reprint	$0.50	$1.50	$2.50	£0.30	£0.90	£1.50
7 48pgs, Jack Kirby reprint	$0.30	$0.90	$1.50	£0.20	£0.60	£1.00
8 48pgs, Neal Adams/Toth reprints	$0.30	$0.90	$1.50	£0.20	£0.60	£1.00
9-10 48pgs	$0.30	$0.90	$1.50	£0.20	£0.60	£1.00
11 48pgs, new Kubert cover	$0.30	$0.90	$1.50	£0.20	£0.60	£1.00
12-15 48pgs	$0.30	$0.90	$1.50	£0.20	£0.60	£1.00
16 48pgs, 1st monthly issue	$0.30	$0.90	$1.50	£0.20	£0.60	£1.00
17 48pgs, Kubert, Russ Heath art	$0.30	$0.90	$1.50	£0.20	£0.60	£1.00
18 48pgs, new Joe Kubert cover	$0.30	$0.90	$1.50	£0.20	£0.60	£1.00
19 48pgs, classic Batman and Sgt. Rock team-up reprinted, new Batman/Sgt. Rock cover by Kubert	$0.30	$0.90	$1.50	£0.20	£0.60	£1.00
20 48pgs, 50th anniversary of attack on Pearl Harbour commemorated	$0.30	$0.90	$1.50	£0.20	£0.60	£1.00
21 48pgs, Kubert, Heath art	$0.30	$0.90	$1.50	£0.20	£0.60	£1.00
Title Value:	$7.10	$21.30	$35.50	£4.60	£13.80	£23.00

Note: issued monthly as of issue #12.

SGT. ROCK SPECIAL (2ND SERIES)
DC Comics; 1 Nov 1992; 2 Dec 1994

	$Good	$Fine	$N.Mint	£Good	£Fine	£N.Mint
1 previously unseen Kanigher/Kubert story plus new stories by P. Craig Russell, Matt Wagner, George Pratt, Mike Golden, Tim Truman; Walt Simonson cover	$0.60	$1.80	$3.00	£0.40	£1.20	£2.00
2 features art by Russ Heath, Howard Chaykin, Brian Bolland, Eduardo Barreto, Graham Nolan	$0.60	$1.80	$3.00	£0.40	£1.20	£2.00
Title Value:	$1.20	$3.60	$6.00	£0.80	£2.40	£4.00

SGT. ROCK SPECTACULAR
DC Comics; nn Spring 1978
(DC Special Series #13)

	$Good	$Fine	$N.Mint	£Good	£Fine	£N.Mint
nn ND 80pgs	$0.60	$1.80	$3.00	£0.40	£1.20	£2.00
Title Value:	$0.60	$1.80	$3.00	£0.40	£1.20	£2.00

SGT. ROCK'S PRIZE BATTLE TALES
National Periodical Publications; 1 Winter 1964
(becomes Sgt. Rock Annual)

	$Good	$Fine	$N.Mint	£Good	£Fine	£N.Mint
1 rare in the U.K. 80pgs, new Kubert cover, Sgt. Rock, Unknown Soldier, Enemy Ace reprints	$23.50	$70.00	$190.00	£15.50	£47.00	£125.00
Title Value:	$23.50	$70.00	$190.00	£15.50	£47.00	£125.00

SGT. ROCK'S PRIZE BATTLE TALES (2ND SERIES)
DC Comics, Digest; nn Fall 1979
(DC Special Series #18)

	$Good	$Fine	$N.Mint	£Good	£Fine	£N.Mint
nn ND 100pgs, digest size	$0.60	$1.80	$3.00	£0.40	£1.20	£2.00
Title Value:	$0.60	$1.80	$3.00	£0.40	£1.20	£2.00

SHADE SPECIAL
AC Comics, OS; nn 1985

	$Good	$Fine	$N.Mint	£Good	£Fine	£N.Mint
nn ND 52pgs, black and white	$0.40	$1.20	$2.00	£0.25	£0.75	£1.25
Title Value:	$0.40	$1.20	$2.00	£0.25	£0.75	£1.25

SHADE, THE CHANGING MAN
DC Comics; 1 Jun/Jul 1977-8 Aug/Sep 1978

	$Good	$Fine	$N.Mint	£Good	£Fine	£N.Mint
1 ND Steve Ditko art	$0.90	$2.70	$4.50	£0.60	£1.80	£3.00
2-8 Steve Ditko art	$0.60	$1.80	$3.00	£0.40	£1.20	£2.00
Title Value:	$5.10	$15.30	$25.50	£3.40	£10.20	£17.00

SHADE, THE CHANGING MAN (2ND SERIES)
DC Comics; 1 Jul 1990-present

	$Good	$Fine	$N.Mint	£Good	£Fine	£N.Mint
1 LD in the U.K. 48pgs, scripts by Pete Milligan, painted covers by Brendan McCarthy begin	$0.70	$2.10	$3.50	£0.50	£1.50	£2.50
2-3 LD in the U.K.	$0.50	$1.50	$2.50	£0.30	£0.90	£1.50
4-5	$0.40	$1.20	$2.00	£0.25	£0.75	£1.25
6 previews World Without End series	$0.40	$1.20	$2.00	£0.25	£0.75	£1.25
7-14	$0.40	$1.20	$2.00	£0.25	£0.75	£1.25
15 Jamie Hewlett cover	$0.40	$1.20	$2.00	£0.25	£0.75	£1.25
16-17	$0.40	$1.20	$2.00	£0.25	£0.75	£1.25
18 American Scream concludes	$0.40	$1.20	$2.00	£0.25	£0.75	£1.25
19	$0.40	$1.20	$2.00	£0.25	£0.75	£1.25
20 Off The Road story begins, painted cover by Jamie Hewlett	$0.40	$1.20	$2.00	£0.25	£0.75	£1.25

	$Good	$Fine	$N.Mint	£Good	£Fine	£N.Mint
21-25 painted cover by Jamie Hewlett	$0.40	$1.20	$2.00	£0.25	£0.75	£1.25
26	$0.40	$1.20	$2.00	£0.25	£0.75	£1.25
27-29 Shade the Changing Woman story	$0.40	$1.20	$2.00	£0.25	£0.75	£1.25
30 Duncan Eagleson guest art	$0.40	$1.20	$2.00	£0.25	£0.75	£1.25
31-32 Ernest & Jim story	$0.40	$1.20	$2.00	£0.25	£0.75	£1.25
33 Birth Pains part 1, Shade reborn; 1st issue under "Vertigo" line of comics	$0.40	$1.20	$2.00	£0.25	£0.75	£1.25
34-41	$0.40	$1.20	$2.00	£0.25	£0.75	£1.25
42-44 John Constantine appears	$0.40	$1.20	$2.00	£0.25	£0.75	£1.25
45-49	$0.40	$1.20	$2.00	£0.25	£0.75	£1.25
50 48pgs, with pin-up gallery featuring Brian Bolland	$0.60	$1.80	$3.00	£0.40	£1.20	£2.00
51-53 Sean Philips art	$0.40	$1.20	$2.00	£0.25	£0.75	£1.25
54-60	$0.40	$1.20	$2.00	£0.25	£0.75	£1.25
61-64	$0.45	$1.35	$2.25	£0.30	£0.90	£1.50
65 Richard Case art begins	$0.45	$1.35	$2.25	£0.30	£0.90	£1.50
66-69	$0.45	$1.35	$2.25	£0.30	£0.90	£1.50
Title Value:	$28.75	$86.25	$143.75	£18.20	£54.60	£91.00

Note: New Format

SHADO: SONG OF THE DRAGON
DC Comics, MS; 1 Mar 1991-4 Jun 1992

	$Good	$Fine	$N.Mint	£Good	£Fine	£N.Mint
1-4 ND 48pgs	$0.80	$2.40	$4.00	£0.50	£1.50	£2.50
Title Value:	$3.20	$9.60	$16.00	£2.00	£6.00	£10.00

Note: Prestige Format

SHADOW & THE MYSTERIOUS THREE, THE
Dark Horse, OS; 1 Sep 1994

	$Good	$Fine	$N.Mint	£Good	£Fine	£N.Mint
1 ND three stories; features Mike Kaluta art	$0.60	$1.80	$3.00	£0.40	£1.20	£2.00
Title Value:	$0.60	$1.80	$3.00	£0.40	£1.20	£2.00

SHADOW AND DOC SAVAGE, THE
Dark Horse, MS; 1 Jul 1995-2 Aug 1995

	$Good	$Fine	$N.Mint	£Good	£Fine	£N.Mint
1-2 ND Steve Vance script, Stan Manoukian and Vince Roucher art	$0.60	$1.80	$3.00	£0.40	£1.20	£2.00
Title Value:	$1.20	$3.60	$6.00	£0.80	£2.40	£4.00

SHADO ANNUAL, THE
DC Comics; 1 Dec 1987-2 Dec 1988

	$Good	$Fine	$N.Mint	£Good	£Fine	£N.Mint
1-2 ND	$0.50	$1.50	$2.50	£0.30	£0.90	£1.50
Title Value:	$1.00	$3.00	$5.00	£0.60	£1.80	£3.00

SHADOW CABINET
DC Comics/Milestone; 0 Jan 1994; 1 Jun 1994-17 Oct 1995

	$Good	$Fine	$N.Mint	£Good	£Fine	£N.Mint
0 48pgs, (Jan 1994) spot-varnished cover by Walt Simonson, conclusion of Milestone cross-over story Shadow War (see Static #8)	$0.45	$1.35	$2.25	£0.30	£0.90	£1.50
1 John Byrne cover	$0.40	$1.20	$2.00	£0.25	£0.75	£1.25
2-17	$0.30	$0.90	$1.50	£0.20	£0.60	£1.00
Title Value:	$5.65	$16.95	$28.25	£3.75	£11.25	£18.75

SHADOW EMPIRES: FAITH CONQUERS
Dark Horse, MS; 1 Jul 1994-4 Oct 1994

	$Good	$Fine	$N.Mint	£Good	£Fine	£N.Mint
1-4 ND Chris Moeller script and painted art	$0.60	$1.80	$3.00	£0.40	£1.20	£2.00
Title Value:	$2.40	$7.20	$12.00	£1.60	£4.80	£8.00

SHADOW MOVIE ADAPTATION, THE
Dark Horse, MS Film; 1 Jun 1994-2 Jul 1994

	$Good	$Fine	$N.Mint	£Good	£Fine	£N.Mint
1-2 ND Mike Kaluta's adaptation of the film starring Alec Baldwin	$0.50	$1.50	$2.50	£0.30	£0.90	£1.50
Title Value:	$1.00	$3.00	$5.00	£0.60	£1.80	£3.00

SHADOW OF THE BATMAN
(see Batman: Shadow of the Bat)

SHADOW OF THE TORTURER, THE
Innovation, MS; 1 Jul 1991-6 Dec 1991

	$Good	$Fine	$N.Mint	£Good	£Fine	£N.Mint
1-6 ND colour	$0.40	$1.20	$2.00	£0.25	£0.75	£1.25
Title Value:	$2.40	$7.20	$12.00	£1.50	£4.50	£7.50

SHADOW RIDERS
Marvel UK, MS; 1 Jun 1993-4 Sep 1993

	$Good	$Fine	$N.Mint	£Good	£Fine	£N.Mint
1 Cable and Ghost Rider appear, Ross Dearsley art begins	$0.30	$0.90	$1.50	£0.20	£0.60	£1.00
2 Ghost Rider appears	$0.30	$0.90	$1.50	£0.20	£0.60	£1.00
3-4 Cable appears	$0.30	$0.90	$1.50	£0.20	£0.60	£1.00
Title Value:	$1.20	$3.60	$6.00	£0.80	£2.40	£4.00

SHADOW SLASHER
Pocket Change Comics; 1 1995-present

	$Good	$Fine	$N.Mint	£Good	£Fine	£N.Mint
1-7 ND 24pgs, Bob Dixon script, Scott Shriver art; black and white	$0.50	$1.50	$2.50	£0.30	£0.90	£1.50
Title Value:	$3.50	$10.50	$17.50	£2.10	£6.30	£10.50

SHADOW STRIKES! ANNUAL, THE
DC Comics; 1 Dec 1989

	$Good	$Fine	$N.Mint	£Good	£Fine	£N.Mint
1 ND	$0.50	$1.50	$2.50	£0.30	£0.90	£1.50
Title Value:	$0.50	$1.50	$2.50	£0.30	£0.90	£1.50

SHADOW STRIKES!, THE
DC Comics; 1 Sep 1989-31 May 1992

	$Good	$Fine	$N.Mint	£Good	£Fine	£N.Mint
1-4 ND	$0.40	$1.20	$2.00	£0.25	£0.75	£1.25
5-6 ND X-over with Doc Savage #17, #18	$0.40	$1.20	$2.00	£0.25	£0.75	£1.25

	$Good	$Fine	$N.Mint	£Good	£Fine	£N.Mint
7-10 ND	$0.40	$1.20	$2.00	£0.25	£0.75	£1.25
11-17 ND	$0.30	$0.90	$1.50	£0.20	£0.60	£1.00
18-19 ND Mark Badger art						
	$0.30	$0.90	$1.50	£0.20	£0.60	£1.00
20-29 ND	$0.30	$0.90	$1.50	£0.20	£0.60	£1.00
30 ND The Shadow: Year One part 1, bi-weekly						
	$0.30	$0.90	$1.50	£0.20	£0.60	£1.00
31 ND The Shadow: Year One part 2, bi-weekly						
	$0.30	$0.90	$1.50	£0.20	£0.60	£1.00
Title Value:	$10.30	$30.90	$51.50	£6.70	£20.10	£33.50

SHADOW WAR OF HAWKMAN
(see Hawkman, Shadow War of the)

SHADOW, THE
Archie; 1 Aug 1964-8 Sep 1965

	$Good	$Fine	$N.Mint	£Good	£Fine	£N.Mint
1 scarce, distributed in the U.K.						
	$5.00	$15.00	$30.00	£3.30	£10.00	£20.00
2-7 distributed in the U.K.						
	$3.30	$10.00	$20.00	£2.30	£7.00	£14.00
8 scarce, distributed in the U.K.						
	$3.30	$10.00	$20.00	£2.50	£7.50	£15.00
Title Value:	$28.10	$85.00	$170.00	£19.60	£59.50	£119.00

SHADOW, THE
DC Comics; 1 Oct/Nov 1973-12 Apr/May 1975

	$Good	$Fine	$N.Mint	£Good	£Fine	£N.Mint
1 scarce in the U.K. Kaluta art						
	$4.15	$12.50	$25.00	£2.50	£7.50	£15.00
2 Kaluta art	$2.50	$7.50	$15.00	£1.50	£4.50	£7.50
3 Kaluta/Wrightson art						
	$2.50	$7.50	$15.00	£1.50	£4.50	£7.50
4 Kaluta art	$2.05	$6.25	$12.50	£1.00	£3.00	£5.00
5	$1.00	$3.00	$6.00	£0.80	£2.40	£4.00
6 Kaluta art	$2.05	$6.25	$12.50	£1.00	£3.00	£5.00
7-10	$0.80	$2.50	$5.00	£0.60	£1.80	£3.00
11 The Shadow vs. The Avenger						
	$0.80	$2.50	$5.00	£0.60	£1.80	£3.00
12	$0.80	$2.50	$5.00	£0.60	£1.80	£3.00
Title Value:	$19.05	$58.00	$116.00	£11.90	£35.70	£62.00

SHADOW, THE (2ND SERIES)
DC Comics; 1 Aug 1987-19 Jan 1989
(becomes revamped into The Shadow Strikes!)

	$Good	$Fine	$N.Mint	£Good	£Fine	£N.Mint
1-6 ND Sienkiewicz art						
	$0.30	$0.90	$1.50	£0.20	£0.60	£1.00
7 ND Marshall Rogers art						
	$0.30	$0.90	$1.50	£0.20	£0.60	£1.00
8-12 ND Kyle Baker art						
	$0.30	$0.90	$1.50	£0.20	£0.60	£1.00
13 ND Kyle Baker art, Shadow dies						
	$0.30	$0.90	$1.50	£0.20	£0.60	£1.00
14-19 ND Kyle Baker art						
	$0.30	$0.90	$1.50	£0.20	£0.60	£1.00
Title Value:	$5.70	$17.10	$28.50	£3.80	£11.40	£19.00

Note: Deluxe Format. Sienkiewicz painted covers on #1-6.

SHADOW, THE (LIMITED SERIES)
DC Comics,MS; 1 May 1986-4 Aug 1986

	$Good	$Fine	$N.Mint	£Good	£Fine	£N.Mint
1 ND scarce in the U.K. Chaykin art						
	$0.50	$1.50	$2.50	£0.30	£0.90	£1.50
2-4 ND Chaykin art						
	$0.50	$1.50	$2.50	£0.25	£0.75	£1.25
Title Value:	$2.00	$6.00	$10.00	£1.05	£3.15	£5.25

Note: Deluxe Format, Baxter paper. Mature Readers label
Trade paperback reprints #1-4 plus eight new pages | | | | £1.40 | £4.20 | £7.00 |

SHADOW, THE PRIVATE FILES OF THE
DC Comics; nn Apr 1989
nn ND Hardcover reprint of issues #1-4 and 6 of 1970s Kaluta series; new story in b/w by Kaluta, new essay by Denny O'Neil

	$Good	$Fine	$N.Mint	£Good	£Fine	£N.Mint
	$4.50	$13.50	$22.50	£3.00	£9.00	£15.00
Title Value:	$4.50	$13.50	$22.50	£3.00	£9.00	£15.00

SHADOW: HELL'S HEAT WAVE, THE
Dark Horse,MS; 1 Apr 1995-3 Jun 1995

	$Good	$Fine	$N.Mint	£Good	£Fine	£N.Mint
1-3 ND Mike Kaluta script, Joel Goss and Gary Gianni art						
	$0.60	$1.80	$3.00	£0.40	£1.20	£2.00
Title Value:	$1.80	$5.40	$9.00	£1.20	£3.60	£6.00

SHADOW: IN THE COILS OF THE LEVIATHAN, THE
Dark Horse,MS; 1 Oct 1993-4 Apr 1994

	$Good	$Fine	$N.Mint	£Good	£Fine	£N.Mint
1-4 ND Mike Kaluta script and Gary Gianni art						
	$0.60	$1.80	$3.00	£0.40	£1.20	£2.00
Title Value:	$2.40	$7.20	$12.00	£1.60	£4.80	£8.00
The Shadow: In The Coils of the Leviathan (Sep 1993)						
Trade paperback reprints mini-series with painted cover by Mike Kaluta				£1.75	£5.25	£8.75

SHADOWALKER
Aircel; 1 Aug 1988-3 1991

	$Good	$Fine	$N.Mint	£Good	£Fine	£N.Mint
1-3 ND	$0.30	$0.90	$1.50	£0.20	£0.60	£1.00
Title Value:	$0.90	$2.70	$4.50	£0.60	£1.80	£3.00

SHADOWALKER CHRONICLES, THE
Ground Zero Graphics,MS; 1 Sep 1991-5 May 1992

	$Good	$Fine	$N.Mint	£Good	£Fine	£N.Mint
1-5 ND	$0.40	$1.20	$2.00	£0.25	£0.75	£1.25
Title Value:	$2.00	$6.00	$10.00	£1.25	£3.75	£6.25

SHADOWBLADE
Hot Comics; 1-4 1987

	$Good	$Fine	$N.Mint	£Good	£Fine	£N.Mint
1-4 ND	$0.25	$0.75	$1.25	£0.15	£0.45	£0.75
Title Value:	$1.00	$3.00	$5.00	£0.60	£1.80	£3.00

SHADOWDRAGON ANNUAL
DC Comics,OS; 1 Oct 1995

	$Good	$Fine	$N.Mint	£Good	£Fine	£N.Mint
1 ND Year One story						
	$0.80	$2.40	$4.00	£0.50	£1.50	£2.50
Title Value:	$0.80	$2.40	$4.00	£0.50	£1.50	£2.50

SHADOWHAWK
Image,MS; 1 Oct 1992-4 Mar 1993

	$Good	$Fine	$N.Mint	£Good	£Fine	£N.Mint
1 Jim Valentino script/art begins, black cover with silver embossed logo and character figure; 1st of the series of coupons to send away for Image Comics #0						
	$1.20	$3.60	$6.00	£0.70	£2.10	£3.50
1 as above, without coupon						
	$0.60	$1.80	$3.00	£0.40	£1.20	£2.00
2 wraparound cover with silver ink highlights plus poster inked by McFarlane						
	$0.60	$1.80	$3.00	£0.40	£1.20	£2.00
3 glow-in-dark cover						
	$0.50	$1.50	$2.50	£0.30	£0.90	£1.50
4 Savage Dragon guest-stars						
	$0.50	$1.50	$2.50	£0.30	£0.90	£1.50
Title Value:	$3.40	$10.20	$17.00	£2.10	£6.30	£10.50

Note: all Non-Distributed on the news-stands in the U.K.
Shadowhawk: Out of the Shadows (1994)
Trade paperback reprints mini-series plus stories in Youngblood #2 and Image #0 | | | | £2.60 | £7.80 | £13.00 |

SHADOWHAWK GALLERY
Image,OS; 1 Apr 1994

	$Good	$Fine	$N.Mint	£Good	£Fine	£N.Mint
1 ND pin-ups by various Image artists						
	$0.40	$1.20	$2.00	£0.25	£0.75	£1.25
Title Value:	$0.40	$1.20	$2.00	£0.25	£0.75	£1.25

SHADOWHAWK II
Image,MS; 1 May 1993-3 Aug 1993

Secrets of Haunted House #1

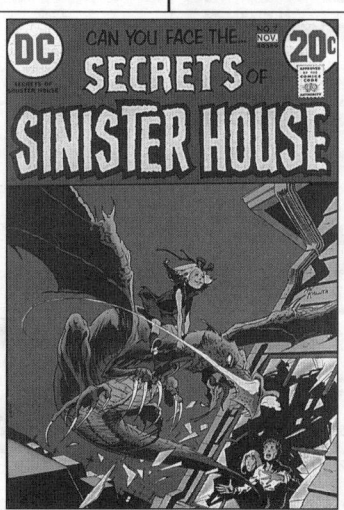

Secrets of Sinister House #7

Sensation Comics #2

MINT = 100% / NEAR MINT (inc. +/-) = 90-99% / VERY FINE (inc. +/-) = 75-89% / FINE (inc. +/-) = 55-74%
VERY GOOD (inc. +/-) = 35-54% / GOOD (inc. +/-) = 15-34% / FAIR = 5-14% / POOR = 1-4%

	$Good	$Fine	$N.Mint	£Good	£Fine	£N.Mint
1 all black embossed outer cover which is die-cut to reveal silver foil beneath; Jim Valentino script and art begins	$0.60	$1.80	$3.00	£0.40	£1.20	£2.00
2	$0.50	$1.50	$2.50	£0.30	£0.90	£1.50
2 Limited Edition - gold embossed logo	$3.00	$9.00	$15.00	£1.50	£4.50	£7.50
3 fold-out poster cover	$0.50	$1.50	$2.50	£0.30	£0.90	£1.50
Title Value:	$4.60	$13.80	$23.00	£2.50	£7.50	£12.50

Note: all Non-Distributed on the news-stands in the U.K.
Shadowhawk: Secret Revealed/Fact File (1994)
Trade paperback flip-book format reprinting mini-series with fact file revealing untold facts £1.70 £5.10 £8.50

SHADOWHAWK III
Image; 0 Sep 1994; 1 Nov 1993-4 Mar 1994; 12 Aug 1994-18 Mar 1995

	$Good	$Fine	$N.Mint	£Good	£Fine	£N.Mint
0 Image X tie-in	$0.40	$1.20	$2.00	£0.25	£0.75	£1.25
1 Jim Valentino script and art begins; red foil enhanced logo	$0.40	$1.20	$2.00	£0.25	£0.75	£1.25
2-4	$0.40	$1.20	$2.00	£0.25	£0.75	£1.25
12 the 5th issue of the series, numbered as 12. The Monster Within story begins, Chapel guest-stars	$0.40	$1.20	$2.00	£0.25	£0.75	£1.25
13 WildC.A.T.S. guest-star	$0.40	$1.20	$2.00	£0.25	£0.75	£1.25
14 1963 characters guest-star	$0.40	$1.20	$2.00	£0.25	£0.75	£1.25
15	$0.40	$1.20	$2.00	£0.25	£0.75	£1.25
16 Shadowhawk vs. Supreme	$0.40	$1.20	$2.00	£0.25	£0.75	£1.25
17 Spawn guest-stars	$0.40	$1.20	$2.00	£0.25	£0.75	£1.25
18	$0.40	$1.20	$2.00	£0.25	£0.75	£1.25
Title Value:	$4.80	$14.40	$24.00	£3.00	£9.00	£15.00

Note: all Non-Distributed on the news-stands in the U.K.

SHADOWHAWK SPECIAL
Image,OS; 1 Dec 1994

	$Good	$Fine	$N.Mint	£Good	£Fine	£N.Mint
1 ND 48pgs, flip-book format showing the Shadowhawks of both past and future	$0.50	$1.50	$2.50	£0.30	£0.90	£1.50
Title Value:	$0.50	$1.50	$2.50	£0.30	£0.90	£1.50

SHADOWHAWK, IMAGES OF
Image,MS; 1 Sep 1993-3 1994

	$Good	$Fine	$N.Mint	£Good	£Fine	£N.Mint
1 ND Alan Grant and Keith Giffen script, Keith Giffen art begins	$0.40	$1.20	$2.00	£0.25	£0.75	£1.25
2-3 ND	$0.40	$1.20	$2.00	£0.25	£0.75	£1.25
Title Value:	$1.20	$3.60	$6.00	£0.75	£2.25	£3.75

SHADOWHAWK, THE NEW
Image; 1 Jun 1995-present

	$Good	$Fine	$N.Mint	£Good	£Fine	£N.Mint
1 ND Kurt Busiek script, James Fry and Andrew Pepoy art	$0.50	$1.50	$2.50	£0.30	£0.90	£1.50
2-5 ND	$0.50	$1.50	$2.50	£0.30	£0.90	£1.50
Title Value:	$2.50	$7.50	$12.50	£1.50	£4.50	£7.50

SHADOWHAWK/VAMPIRELLA
Image/Harris Comics,MS; 1,2 Feb 1995

	$Good	$Fine	$N.Mint	£Good	£Fine	£N.Mint
1 ND 48pgs, Jim Valentino script and art; fully painted cover by Joe Jusko	$1.00	$3.00	$5.00	£0.60	£1.80	£3.00
2 ND 48pgs, Jim Valentino script and art; fully painted cover by Mark Texeira	$1.00	$3.00	$5.00	£0.60	£1.80	£3.00
Title Value:	$2.00	$6.00	$10.00	£1.20	£3.60	£6.00

SHADOWHAWKS OF LEGEND
Image,OS; 1 Nov 1995

	$Good	$Fine	$N.Mint	£Good	£Fine	£N.Mint
1 ND 48pgs, four stories featuring work by Alan Moore, Kurt Busiek, Stan Sakai and Jim Valentino among others	$1.00	$3.00	$5.00	£0.60	£1.80	£3.00
Title Value:	$1.00	$3.00	$5.00	£0.60	£1.80	£3.00

SHADOWLAND
Fantagraphics; 1 Oct 1989-2 1990?

	$Good	$Fine	$N.Mint	£Good	£Fine	£N.Mint
1-2 ND adult material	$0.40	$1.20	$2.00	£0.25	£0.75	£1.25
Title Value:	$0.80	$2.40	$4.00	£0.50	£1.50	£2.50

SHADOWMAN
Valiant/Acclaim Comics; 0 Apr 1994; 1 May 1992-43 1995

	$Good	$Fine	$N.Mint	£Good	£Fine	£N.Mint
0 Deluxe Edition, origin of Shadowman, Master D'Arque appears; all foil cover	$0.50	$1.50	$2.50	£0.30	£0.90	£1.50
0 Regular Edition	$0.30	$0.90	$1.50	£0.20	£0.60	£1.00
0 Valiant Validated Signature Series Edition (Jun 1994), signed by at least one creator; 5,300 copies with certificate and Mylar sleeve	$1.50	$4.50	$7.50	£1.00	£3.00	£5.00
1 scarce in the U.K. Steve Engelhart script begins	$1.60	$4.80	$8.00	£1.00	£3.00	£5.00
2	$1.00	$3.00	$5.00	£0.60	£1.80	£3.00
3	$0.80	$2.40	$4.00	£0.40	£1.20	£2.00
4 Unity: Chapter 6, team-up with Solar Man of the Atom	$0.60	$1.80	$3.00	£0.30	£0.90	£1.50
5 Unity: Chapter 14, Eternal Warrior and Magnus Robot Fighter appear, Walt Simonson cover	$0.60	$1.80	$3.00	£0.30	£0.90	£1.50
6-7	$0.60	$1.80	$3.00	£0.30	£0.90	£1.50
8 1st appearance Master D'Arque	$0.80	$2.40	$4.00	£0.50	£1.50	£2.50
9-10	$0.40	$1.20	$2.00	£0.25	£0.75	£1.25
11 new costume	$0.40	$1.20	$2.00	£0.25	£0.75	£1.25
12-15	$0.40	$1.20	$2.00	£0.25	£0.75	£1.25
16 1st appearance of Dr. Mirage	$0.50	$1.50	$2.50	£0.30	£0.90	£1.50
17-18 Archer & Armstrong appear	$0.40	$1.20	$2.00	£0.25	£0.75	£1.25
19 Aerosmith rock group appear	$0.40	$1.20	$2.00	£0.25	£0.75	£1.25
20-22 Master D'Arque appears	$0.40	$1.20	$2.00	£0.25	£0.75	£1.25
23 Doctor Mirage guest-stars; Shadowman vs. Master D'Arque	$0.40	$1.20	$2.00	£0.25	£0.75	£1.25
24	$0.40	$1.20	$2.00	£0.25	£0.75	£1.25
25 with free Valiant Upper Deck card bound-in at centre-fold	$0.40	$1.20	$2.00	£0.25	£0.75	£1.25
26-27	$0.40	$1.20	$2.00	£0.25	£0.75	£1.25
28 Shadowman vs. Master D'Arque	$0.40	$1.20	$2.00	£0.25	£0.75	£1.25
29 Chaos Effect X-over	$0.40	$1.20	$2.00	£0.25	£0.75	£1.25
30-36	$0.40	$1.20	$2.00	£0.25	£0.75	£1.25
37 X-O Manowar appears	$0.40	$1.20	$2.00	£0.25	£0.75	£1.25
38 1st Acclaim Comics issue	$0.40	$1.20	$2.00	£0.25	£0.75	£1.25
39-43	$0.40	$1.20	$2.00	£0.25	£0.75	£1.25
Title Value:	$23.00	$69.00	$115.00	£14.00	£42.00	£70.00

Note: all Non-Distributed on the news-stands in the U.K.
Shadowman (1994)
Trade paperback reprints issues #1-3 & 6 £1.30 £3.90 £6.50

SHADOWMAN YEARBOOK
Valiant; 1 Jan 1995

	$Good	$Fine	$N.Mint	£Good	£Fine	£N.Mint
1 ND story set in Edwardian London starring the turn-of-the-century Shadowman	$0.50	$1.50	$2.50	£0.30	£0.90	£1.50
Title Value:	$0.50	$1.50	$2.50	£0.30	£0.90	£1.50

SHADOWMASTERS
Marvel Comics Group,MS; 1 Oct 1989-4 Jan 1990

	$Good	$Fine	$N.Mint	£Good	£Fine	£N.Mint
1 ND 48pgs, squarebound, Russ Heath inks, part Jim Lee covers begin	$0.60	$1.80	$3.00	£0.40	£1.20	£2.00
2-4 ND squarebound	$0.60	$1.80	$3.00	£0.40	£1.20	£2.00
Title Value:	$2.40	$7.20	$12.00	£1.60	£4.80	£8.00

Note: ties in with Punisher and Punisher War Journal

SHADOWS FALL
DC Comics,MS; 1 Nov 1994-6 Apr 1995

	$Good	$Fine	$N.Mint	£Good	£Fine	£N.Mint
1-6	$0.60	$1.80	$3.00	£0.40	£1.20	£2.00
Title Value:	$3.60	$10.80	$18.00	£2.40	£7.20	£12.00

SHADOWS FROM THE GRAVE
Renegade,MS; 1 May 1987-2 Mar 1988

	$Good	$Fine	$N.Mint	£Good	£Fine	£N.Mint
1-2 ND	$0.30	$0.90	$1.50	£0.20	£0.60	£1.00
Title Value:	$0.60	$1.80	$3.00	£0.40	£1.20	£2.00

SHAIANA
Entity Comics,MS; 1 Jul 1995-2 1995

	$Good	$Fine	$N.Mint	£Good	£Fine	£N.Mint
1 ND chromium cover	$0.80	$2.40	$4.00	£0.50	£1.50	£2.50
2 ND	$0.80	$2.40	$4.00	£0.50	£1.50	£2.50
Title Value:	$1.60	$4.80	$8.00	£1.00	£3.00	£5.00

SHAMAN GRAPHIC NOVEL
Continuity,OS; 1 Aug 1992

	$Good	$Fine	$N.Mint	£Good	£Fine	£N.Mint
1 ND 48pgs	$0.60	$1.80	$3.00	£0.40	£1.20	£2.00
Title Value:	$0.60	$1.80	$3.00	£0.40	£1.20	£2.00

SHAMAN'S TEARS
Image; 0 Nov 1995; 1 May 1993-2 Aug 1993; 3 Jun 1994-present

	$Good	$Fine	$N.Mint	£Good	£Fine	£N.Mint
0 origin of Shaman	$0.50	$1.50	$2.50	£0.30	£0.90	£1.50
1 Mike Grell script and art begins, red foil embossed cover	$0.50	$1.50	$2.50	£0.30	£0.90	£1.50
2 double gate-fold poster cover	$0.50	$1.50	$2.50	£0.30	£0.90	£1.50
3	$0.40	$1.20	$2.00	£0.25	£0.75	£1.25
4 Jon Sable returns	$0.40	$1.20	$2.00	£0.25	£0.75	£1.25
5-8 Jon Sable appears	$0.40	$1.20	$2.00	£0.25	£0.75	£1.25
9 The Becoming of Broadarrow story	$0.40	$1.20	$2.00	£0.25	£0.75	£1.25
10-11 The Becoming of Broadarrow story	$0.45	$1.35	$2.25	£0.30	£0.90	£1.50
12 ND	$0.45	$1.35	$2.25	£0.30	£0.90	£1.50
13 ND The Offspring story	$0.45	$1.35	$2.25	£0.30	£0.90	£1.50
Title Value:	$6.10	$18.30	$30.50	£3.85	£11.55	£19.25

Note: all Non-Distributed on the news-stands in the U.K.
Note also: issues #3 and #4 were solicited by Axis but never appeared

SHANDA
Antarctic Press; 1 Jul 1994-present

	$Good	$Fine	$N.Mint	£Good	£Fine	£N.Mint
1-11 ND black and white	$0.50	$1.50	$2.50	£0.30	£0.90	£1.50
Title Value:	$5.50	$16.50	$27.50	£3.30	£9.90	£16.50

SHANNA THE SHE-DEVIL
Marvel Comics Group; 1 Dec 1972-5 Aug 1973
(see Ka-Zar, Marvel Fanfare, Savage Tales)

	$Good	$Fine	$N.Mint	£Good	£Fine	£N.Mint
1 ND Steranko cover	$0.90	$2.70	$4.50	£0.60	£1.80	£3.00
2 ND Steranko cover	$0.60	$1.80	$3.00	£0.40	£1.20	£2.00

	$Good	$Fine	$N.Mint	£Good	£Fine	£N.Mint
3-5 ND	$0.50	$1.50	$2.50	£0.30	£0.90	£1.50
Title Value:	$3.00	$9.00	$15.00	£1.90	£5.70	£9.50

SHATTER
First; 1 Jun 1985-14 Apr 1988

	$Good	$Fine	$N.Mint	£Good	£Fine	£N.Mint
1-14 ND scarce in the U.K. computer generated art						
	$0.40	$1.20	$2.00	£0.25	£0.75	£1.25
Title Value:	$5.60	$16.80	$28.00	£3.50	£10.50	£17.50

SHATTER POINT
Eternity,MS; 1 Dec 1990-4 Mar 1991

	$Good	$Fine	$N.Mint	£Good	£Fine	£N.Mint
1-4 ND black and white						
	$0.40	$1.20	$2.00	£0.25	£0.75	£1.25
Title Value:	$1.60	$4.80	$8.00	£1.00	£3.00	£5.00

SHATTER SPECIAL
First; 1 Jun 1985
(see Jon Sable #25-31)

	$Good	$Fine	$N.Mint	£Good	£Fine	£N.Mint
1 ND 1st computer generated comic						
	$0.50	$1.50	$2.50	£0.30	£0.90	£1.50
1 2nd printing ND	$0.40	$1.20	$2.00	£0.25	£0.75	£1.25
Title Value:	$0.90	$2.70	$4.50	£0.55	£1.65	£2.75

SHAZAM!
DC Comics; 1 Feb 1973-35 May/Jun 1978
(see All-New Collector's Edition, Limited Collector's Edition, Shazam: The New Beginning, World's Finest)

	$Good	$Fine	$N.Mint	£Good	£Fine	£N.Mint
1 origin Captain Marvel retold						
	$0.80	$2.40	$4.00	£0.50	£1.50	£2.50
2 photo cover	$0.50	$1.50	$2.50	£0.30	£0.90	£1.50
3	$0.50	$1.50	$2.50	£0.30	£0.90	£1.50
4-5	$0.40	$1.20	$2.00	£0.25	£0.75	£1.25
6 photo cover	$0.40	$1.20	$2.00	£0.25	£0.75	£1.25
7	$0.40	$1.20	$2.00	£0.25	£0.75	£1.25
8 100pgs	$0.60	$1.80	$3.00	£0.40	£1.20	£2.00
9-11	$0.40	$1.20	$2.00	£0.25	£0.75	£1.25
12-14 100pgs	$0.60	$1.80	$3.00	£0.40	£1.20	£2.00
15 100pgs, Lex Luthor appears, Superman cameo						
	$0.60	$1.80	$3.00	£0.40	£1.20	£2.00
16-17 100pgs	$0.60	$1.80	$3.00	£0.40	£1.20	£2.00
18-19	$0.40	$1.20	$2.00	£0.25	£0.75	£1.25
20 ND	$0.40	$1.20	$2.00	£0.30	£0.90	£1.50
21	$0.40	$1.20	$2.00	£0.25	£0.75	£1.25
22 scarce in the U.K.						
	$0.40	$1.20	$2.00	£0.30	£0.90	£1.50
23	$0.40	$1.20	$2.00	£0.25	£0.75	£1.25
24 ND	$0.40	$1.20	$2.00	£0.30	£0.90	£1.50
25 1st appearance Isis						
	$0.40	$1.20	$2.00	£0.25	£0.75	£1.25
26	$0.40	$1.20	$2.00	£0.25	£0.75	£1.25
27-28 scarce in the U.K.						
	$0.40	$1.20	$2.00	£0.30	£0.90	£1.50
29	$0.40	$1.20	$2.00	£0.25	£0.75	£1.25
30-31 scarce in the U.K.						
	$0.40	$1.20	$2.00	£0.30	£0.90	£1.50
32-34	$0.40	$1.20	$2.00	£0.25	£0.75	£1.25
35 story continued in World's Finest Comics #253, Newton art						
	$0.40	$1.20	$2.00	£0.25	£0.75	£1.25
Title Value:	$16.00	$48.00	$80.00	£10.50	£31.50	£52.50

Note: issues 8, 21-24 are all reprint.
ARTISTS
New C.C.Beck art in 1-7, 9, 10.
FEATURES
Captain Marvel in 1-7, 9-13, 15, 16, 18, 19, 26-33. Cap. Marvel/Captain Marvel Jr. in 34. Cap. Marvel Jr. in 9, 12, 15, 18. Isis in 25. Mary Marvel in 10, 13, 16, 19. Marvel Family in 11,14, 17, 20, 35.
REPRINT FEATURES
Captain Marvel in 1, 2, 4, 8, 12-17, 21, 22, 24, 25. Capt. Marvel Jr. in 5, 8, 13, 14, 16, 17, 21, 24. Marvel Family in 3, 6-8, 12, 13, 15, 16, 23. Mary Marvel in 8, 12, 14,17, 22.

SHAZAM! ARCHIVES, THE
DC Comics; nn Nov 1992
nn ND 208pgs, Hardcover; reprints the very rare Flash Comics ash-can issue plus Whiz Comics #2-15 with covers and ads

	$Good	$Fine	$N.Mint	£Good	£Fine	£N.Mint
	$8.00	$24.00	$40.00	£5.50	£16.50	£27.50
Title Value:	$8.00	$24.00	$40.00	£5.50	£16.50	£27.50

SHAZAM, THE POWER OF
DC Comics; nn Mar 1994
nn ND 96pgs, Hardcover; Jerry Ordway script, art and painted cover

	$Good	$Fine	$N.Mint	£Good	£Fine	£N.Mint
	$4.50	$13.50	$22.50	£3.00	£9.00	£15.00
Title Value:	$4.50	$13.50	$22.50	£3.00	£9.00	£15.00
The Power of Shazam Softcover Graphic Novel (Feb 1995)						
96pgs, Jerry Ordway cover and art				£1.30	£3.90	£6.50

SHAZAM, THE POWER OF (2ND SERIES)
DC Comics; 1 Mar 1995-present

	$Good	$Fine	$N.Mint	£Good	£Fine	£N.Mint
1 Jerry Ordway scripts and painted covers begin						
	$0.35	$1.05	$1.75	£0.25	£0.75	£1.25
2-13	$0.35	$1.05	$1.75	£0.25	£0.75	£1.25
Title Value:	$4.55	$13.65	$22.75	£3.25	£9.75	£16.25

SHAZAM: THE NEW BEGINNING
DC Comics,MS; 1 Apr 1987-4 Jul 1987

	$Good	$Fine	$N.Mint	£Good	£Fine	£N.Mint
1-4 Legends tie-in						
	$0.25	$0.75	$1.25	£0.15	£0.45	£0.75
Title Value:	$1.00	$3.00	$5.00	£0.60	£1.80	£3.00

SHE-CAT
AC Comics; 1 Mar 1990-4 1990; 5 Sep 1994

	$Good	$Fine	$N.Mint	£Good	£Fine	£N.Mint
1 ND black and white begins						
	$0.40	$1.20	$2.00	£0.25	£0.75	£1.25
2 ND	$0.40	$1.20	$2.00	£0.25	£0.75	£1.25

	$Good	$Fine	$N.Mint	£Good	£Fine	£N.Mint
3 ND Colt of Femforce appears						
	$0.40	$1.20	$2.00	£0.25	£0.75	£1.25
4 ND	$0.40	$1.20	$2.00	£0.25	£0.75	£1.25
5 ND very scarce in the U.K. as most copies were mis-cut at the printing stage and destroyed by the publisher						
	$0.40	$1.20	$2.00	£0.30	£0.90	£1.50
5 ND 48pgs, reprinted issue (Mar 1995) with new cover by Brad Gorby and an 8pg origin recap; 1,500 copies only						
	$0.50	$1.50	$2.50	£0.30	£0.90	£1.50
Title Value:	$2.50	$7.50	$12.50	£1.60	£4.80	£8.00
She-Cat Chronicles (Jul 1995) Trade paperback						
reprints issues #1-4, signed by Bill Marimon; 400 copies				£1.60	£4.80	£8.00

SHE-HULK, THE SAVAGE
Marvel Comics Group; 1 Feb 1980-25 Feb 1982

	$Good	$Fine	$N.Mint	£Good	£Fine	£N.Mint
1 ND origin and 1st appearance, written by Stan Lee						
	$0.80	$2.40	$4.00	£0.50	£1.50	£2.50
2-3 ND	$0.50	$1.50	$2.50	£0.30	£0.90	£1.50
4-5 ND	$0.40	$1.20	$2.00	£0.25	£0.75	£1.25
6 ND Iron Man appears						
	$0.40	$1.20	$2.00	£0.25	£0.75	£1.25
7 ND	$0.40	$1.20	$2.00	£0.25	£0.75	£1.25
8 ND Man-Thing appears, Golden cover						
	$0.40	$1.20	$2.00	£0.25	£0.75	£1.25
9 Morbius appears						
	$0.40	$1.20	$2.00	£0.25	£0.75	£1.25
10	$0.30	$0.90	$1.50	£0.20	£0.60	£1.00
11-12 ND Morbius appears						
	$0.30	$0.90	$1.50	£0.20	£0.60	£1.00
13-14 ND Man-Wolf and Hell Cat appear						
	$0.30	$0.90	$1.50	£0.20	£0.60	£1.00
15-24 ND	$0.30	$0.90	$1.50	£0.20	£0.60	£1.00
25 ND scarce in the U.K. 52pgs						
	$0.30	$1.50	$2.50	£0.30	£0.90	£1.50
Title Value:	$9.20	$27.60	$46.00	£5.90	£17.70	£29.50

SHE-HULK, THE SENSATIONAL
Marvel Comics Group; 1 May 1989-60 Feb 1994

	$Good	$Fine	$N.Mint	£Good	£Fine	£N.Mint
1 ND John Byrne story/art						
	$0.50	$1.50	$2.50	£0.30	£0.90	£1.50
2 ND John Byrne story/art						
	$0.40	$1.20	$2.00	£0.25	£0.75	£1.25
3 ND Spiderman appears, John Byrne story/art						
	$0.40	$1.20	$2.00	£0.25	£0.75	£1.25
4-8 ND John Byrne story/art						
	$0.40	$1.20	$2.00	£0.25	£0.75	£1.25
9-10 ND	$0.40	$1.20	$2.00	£0.25	£0.75	£1.25
11 ND	$0.30	$0.90	$1.50	£0.20	£0.60	£1.00
12 ND Peter David script, Leialoha/Trina Robbins art						
	$0.30	$0.90	$1.50	£0.20	£0.60	£1.00
13 ND	$0.30	$0.90	$1.50	£0.20	£0.60	£1.00
14 ND The Cosmic Squish Principle part 1, Bolland cover announced but did not appear: issued separately (with re-ordered issues of comic) explaining the delay; Howard the Duck appears						
	$0.30	$0.90	$1.50	£0.20	£0.60	£1.00
15 ND part 2, Bolland cover, Howard the Duck						
	$0.30	$0.90	$1.50	£0.20	£0.60	£1.00
16 ND part 3, Howard the Duck appears						
	$0.30	$0.90	$1.50	£0.20	£0.60	£1.00
17 ND part 4, Howard the Duck appears						
	$0.30	$0.90	$1.50	£0.20	£0.60	£1.00
18-20 ND	$0.30	$0.90	$1.50	£0.20	£0.60	£1.00
21-23 ND Return of the Blonde Phantom, featuring 1940s Timely super-heroes						
	$0.30	$0.90	$1.50	£0.20	£0.60	£1.00
24 ND Death's Head appears						
	$0.30	$0.90	$1.50	£0.20	£0.60	£1.00
25 ND Hercules appears						
	$0.30	$0.90	$1.50	£0.20	£0.60	£1.00
26-28 ND	$0.30	$0.90	$1.50	£0.20	£0.60	£1.00
29 ND Wolverine, Hulk, Spiderman appear						
	$0.30	$0.90	$1.50	£0.20	£0.60	£1.00
30 ND a host of Marvel character cameos						
	$0.30	$0.90	$1.50	£0.20	£0.60	£1.00
31 ND John Byrne script/pencils begin (again), John Byrne on cover						
	$0.30	$0.90	$1.50	£0.20	£0.60	£1.00
32-35 ND	$0.30	$0.90	$1.50	£0.20	£0.60	£1.00
36 ND $1.75 cover begins						
	$0.30	$0.90	$1.50	£0.20	£0.60	£1.00
37-49 ND	$0.30	$0.90	$1.50	£0.20	£0.60	£1.00
50 ND 48pgs, anniversary issue, green foil-stamped cover, last John Byrne script/art; features work by Gibbons, Simonson, Chaykin, Austin, Hughes						
	$0.50	$1.50	$2.50	£0.30	£0.90	£1.50
51 ND Scott Benshaw and Tom Morgan guest creative team						
	$0.30	$0.90	$1.50	£0.20	£0.60	£1.00
52 ND Mr. Fantastic and The Thing appear, cover by Adam Hughes						
	$0.30	$0.90	$1.50	£0.20	£0.60	£1.00
53 ND cover by Adam Hughes						
	$0.30	$0.90	$1.50	£0.20	£0.60	£1.00
54 ND cover by Michael Golden						
	$0.30	$0.90	$1.50	£0.20	£0.60	£1.00
55-60 ND	$0.30	$0.90	$1.50	£0.20	£0.60	£1.00
Title Value:	$19.30	$57.90	$96.50	£12.65	£37.95	£63.25
She-Hulk Trade paperback (May 1992)						
reprints issues #1-8, new cover by John Byrne				£1.40	£4.20	£7.00

SHE-HULK: CEREMONY
Marvel Comics Group,MS; 1 Apr 1990-2 May 1990
1-2 ND 48pgs, She-Hulk proposes to Wyatt Wingfoot

	$Good	$Fine	$N.Mint	£Good	£Fine	£N.Mint
	$0.80	$2.40	$4.00	£0.50	£1.50	£2.50
Title Value:	$1.60	$4.80	$8.00	£1.00	£3.00	£5.00

Note: bi-weekly frequency

SHEENA
IW Comics; 9 1963
9 scarce distributed in the U.K. 1950s reprints

	$Good	$Fine	$N.Mint	£Good	£Fine	£N.Mint
	$5.00	$15.00	$30.00	£3.30	£10.00	£20.00
Title Value:	$5.00	$15.00	$30.00	£3.30	£10.00	£20.00

SHEENA 3-D SPECIAL
Blackthorne; (3-D Series #1) 1 May 1985
1 ND all reprint, Dave Stevens cover; with 3-D glasses (25% less without glasses)

	$Good	$Fine	$N.Mint	£Good	£Fine	£N.Mint
	$0.60	$1.80	$3.00	£0.40	£1.20	£2.00

1 ND scarce in the U.K., non-3-D issue

	$Good	$Fine	$N.Mint	£Good	£Fine	£N.Mint
	$0.60	$1.80	$3.00	£0.40	£1.20	£2.00
Title Value:	$1.20	$3.60	$6.00	£0.80	£2.40	£4.00

SHEENA, QUEEN OF THE JUNGLE
Marvel Comics Group,MS Film; 1 Dec 1984-2 Feb 1985

	$Good	$Fine	$N.Mint	£Good	£Fine	£N.Mint
1-2 ND adapts film	$0.25	$0.75	$1.25	£0.15	£0.45	£0.75
Title Value:	$0.50	$1.50	$2.50	£0.30	£0.90	£1.50

SHELTER
Axis Comics; 1 Jul 1994?

	$Good	$Fine	$N.Mint	£Good	£Fine	£N.Mint
1 ND	$0.45	$1.35	$2.25	£0.30	£0.90	£1.50
Title Value:	$0.45	$1.35	$2.25	£0.30	£0.90	£1.50

SHERLOCK HOLMES
DC Comics; 1 Sep/Oct 1975
1 ND Walt Simonson cover

	$Good	$Fine	$N.Mint	£Good	£Fine	£N.Mint
	$0.40	$1.20	$2.00	£0.25	£0.75	£1.25
Title Value:	$0.40	$1.20	$2.00	£0.25	£0.75	£1.25

SHERLOCK HOLMES
Eternity; 1 Jun 1988-22 1990
(see Cases of...)
1-22 ND newspaper strip reprints

	$Good	$Fine	$N.Mint	£Good	£Fine	£N.Mint
	$0.40	$1.20	$2.00	£0.25	£0.75	£1.25
Title Value:	$8.80	$26.40	$44.00	£5.50	£16.50	£27.50
Book I, reprints				£0.40	£1.20	£2.00

SHERLOCK HOLMES IN THE CASE OF THE MISSING MARTIAN
Eternity,MS; 1 Sep 1990-4 Dec 1990

	$Good	$Fine	$N.Mint	£Good	£Fine	£N.Mint
1-4 ND	$0.40	$1.20	$2.00	£0.25	£0.75	£1.25
Title Value:	$1.60	$4.80	$8.00	£1.00	£3.00	£5.00

Note: bi-weekly

SHERLOCK HOLMES IN THE CURIOUS CASE OF THE VANISHING VILLAIN
Tundra,OS; 1 Aug 1992

	$Good	$Fine	$N.Mint	£Good	£Fine	£N.Mint
1 ND	$0.60	$1.80	$3.00	£0.40	£1.20	£2.00
Title Value:	$0.60	$1.80	$3.00	£0.40	£1.20	£2.00

SHERLOCK HOLMES OF THE '30s
Eternity,MS; 1 Mar 1990-7 Sep 1990

	$Good	$Fine	$N.Mint	£Good	£Fine	£N.Mint
1-7 ND	$0.40	$1.20	$2.00	£0.25	£0.75	£1.25
Title Value:	$2.80	$8.40	$14.00	£1.75	£5.25	£8.75

SHERLOCK HOLMES, NEW ADVENTURES OF
Dell; 1169,1245 1961-1962
1169 scarce though distributed in the U.K. (Four Colour #1169)

	$Good	$Fine	$N.Mint	£Good	£Fine	£N.Mint
	$22.00	$65.00	$132.00	£14.50	£44.00	£87.50

1245 scarce though distributed in the U.K. (Four Colour #1245)

	$Good	$Fine	$N.Mint	£Good	£Fine	£N.Mint
	$22.00	$65.00	$132.00	£14.50	£44.00	£87.50
Title Value:	$44.00	$130.00	$264.00	£29.00	£88.00	£175.00

SHERLOCK HOLMES: A CASE OF BLIND FEAR
Eternity; nn Jul 1990

	£Good	£Fine	£N.Mint
Trade Paperback (Jul 1990), reprints	£1.10	£3.30	£5.50

SHERLOCK HOLMES: A STUDY IN SCARLET
Innovation; nn 1990

	$Good	$Fine	$N.Mint	£Good	£Fine	£N.Mint
1 ND reprints	$1.20	$3.60	$6.00	£0.80	£2.40	£4.00
Title Value:	$1.20	$3.60	$6.00	£0.80	£2.40	£4.00

SHERLOCK HOLMES: ADVENTURES OF THE OPERA GHOST
Caliber Press,MS; 1,2 Oct 1994
1-2 ND Steven Jones script, Aldin Baroza art; black and white

	$Good	$Fine	$N.Mint	£Good	£Fine	£N.Mint
	$0.50	$1.50	$2.50	£0.30	£0.90	£1.50
Title Value:	$1.00	$3.00	$5.00	£0.60	£1.80	£3.00

SHERLOCK HOLMES: CHRONICLES OF CRIME & MYSTERY
Northstar; 1 Mar 1992-3 1992
1 ND The Speckled Band

	$Good	$Fine	$N.Mint	£Good	£Fine	£N.Mint
	$0.40	$1.20	$2.00	£0.25	£0.75	£1.25

1 2nd printing, ND (May 1993)

	$Good	$Fine	$N.Mint	£Good	£Fine	£N.Mint
	$0.40	$1.20	$2.00	£0.25	£0.75	£1.25
2-3 ND	$0.40	$1.20	$2.00	£0.25	£0.75	£1.25
Title Value:	$1.60	$4.80	$8.00	£1.00	£3.00	£5.00

SHERLOCK HOLMES: HOUND OF THE BASKERVILLES GRAPHIC NOVEL
Innovation,OS; nn Apr 1993
nn ND 68pgs, squarebound, painted cover by Jim Steranko

	$Good	$Fine	$N.Mint	£Good	£Fine	£N.Mint
	$1.20	$3.60	$6.00	£0.80	£2.40	£4.00
Title Value:	$1.20	$3.60	$6.00	£0.80	£2.40	£4.00

SHERLOCK HOLMES: RETURN OF THE DEVIL
Adventure,MS; 1 Nov 1992-2 Dec 1992

	$Good	$Fine	$N.Mint	£Good	£Fine	£N.Mint
1-2 ND	$0.40	$1.20	$2.00	£0.25	£0.75	£1.25
Title Value:	$0.80	$2.40	$4.00	£0.50	£1.50	£2.50

SHERLOCK HOLMES: TALES OF MYSTERY & SUSPENSE
Northstar; 1 Aug 1992-4 1993; 5 Oct 1994
1-3 ND black and white

	$Good	$Fine	$N.Mint	£Good	£Fine	£N.Mint
	$0.40	$1.20	$2.00	£0.25	£0.75	£1.25
3 ND with poster	$0.50	$1.50	$2.50	£0.30	£0.90	£1.50

4 ND black and white

	$Good	$Fine	$N.Mint	£Good	£Fine	£N.Mint
	$0.40	$1.20	$2.00	£0.25	£0.75	£1.25

5 ND black and white; cover by Jon J. Muth

	$Good	$Fine	$N.Mint	£Good	£Fine	£N.Mint
	$0.40	$1.20	$2.00	£0.25	£0.75	£1.25
Title Value:	$2.50	$7.50	$12.50	£1.55	£4.65	£7.75

SHERLOCK HOLMES: THE MUSGRAVE RITUAL
Caliber/Tome Press; 1 1992
1 ND black and white

	$Good	$Fine	$N.Mint	£Good	£Fine	£N.Mint
	$0.40	$1.20	$2.00	£0.25	£0.75	£1.25
Title Value:	$0.40	$1.20	$2.00	£0.25	£0.75	£1.25

SHERLOCK HOLMES: THE RED-HEADED LEAGUE AND OTHER STORIES
Eternity; nn Aug 1990
nn ND 6 stories reprinted from 1950s U.S. newspaper strips

	$Good	$Fine	$N.Mint	£Good	£Fine	£N.Mint
	$2.50	$7.50	$12.50	£1.50	£4.50	£7.50
Title Value:	$2.50	$7.50	$12.50	£1.50	£4.50	£7.50

SHERLOCK JNR.
Eternity,MS; 1 Oct 1990-3 Nov 1990

	$Good	$Fine	$N.Mint	£Good	£Fine	£N.Mint
1-3 ND reprints	$0.40	$1.20	$2.00	£0.25	£0.75	£1.25
Title Value:	$1.20	$3.60	$6.00	£0.75	£2.25	£3.75

Note: first two issues bi-weekly

SHI/CYBLADE SPECIAL - THE BATTLE FOR INDEPENDENTS
Crusade Comics,OS; nn Aug 1995
nn ND co-written and co-pencilled by Marc Silvestri and William Tucci; cover by William Tucci

	$Good	$Fine	$N.Mint	£Good	£Fine	£N.Mint
	$0.60	$1.80	$3.00	£0.40	£1.20	£2.00

nn Variant cover, ND Marc Silvestri cover art, Shi on left of cover back to back with Cyblade

	$Good	$Fine	$N.Mint	£Good	£Fine	£N.Mint
	$1.00	$3.00	$5.00	£0.70	£2.10	£3.50
Title Value:	$1.60	$4.80	$8.00	£1.10	£3.30	£5.50

SHI: SENRYAKU
Crusade Comics,MS; 1 Aug 1995-3 Nov 1995
1 ND William Tucci cover art, backgrounds and philosophies on Shi

	$Good	$Fine	$N.Mint	£Good	£Fine	£N.Mint
	$0.60	$1.80	$3.00	£0.40	£1.20	£2.00

1 Variant cover, ND cover as regular but with no Crusade logo

	$Good	$Fine	$N.Mint	£Good	£Fine	£N.Mint
	$1.50	$4.50	$7.50	£0.80	£2.40	£4.00

2 ND William Tucci cover art, backgrounds and philosophies on Shi

	$Good	$Fine	$N.Mint	£Good	£Fine	£N.Mint
	$0.60	$1.80	$3.00	£0.40	£1.20	£2.00

3 ND Joe Jusko cover art, backgrounds and philosophies on Shi

	$Good	$Fine	$N.Mint	£Good	£Fine	£N.Mint
	$0.60	$1.80	$3.00	£0.40	£1.20	£2.00
Title Value:	$3.30	$9.90	$16.50	£2.00	£6.00	£10.00

SHI: THE WAY OF THE WARRIOR
Crusade Comics; 1 Mar 1994-present
1 ND William Tucci script and art; colour

	$Good	$Fine	$N.Mint	£Good	£Fine	£N.Mint
	$7.00	$21.00	$35.00	£5.00	£15.00	£25.00

1 ND Commemorative Edition avaialble at the 1994 San Diego Comic convention

	$Good	$Fine	$N.Mint	£Good	£Fine	£N.Mint
	$8.00	$24.00	$40.00	£6.00	£18.00	£30.00

1 ND Fan Appreciation Edition (Apr 1995) - reprints issue #1 with new cover by William Tucci with poster at centrefold

	$Good	$Fine	$N.Mint	£Good	£Fine	£N.Mint
	$0.80	$2.40	$4.00	£0.50	£1.50	£2.50

1 Gold Variant Fan Appreciation Edition, ND as regular issue but with gold Crusade Comics logo on cover

	$Good	$Fine	$N.Mint	£Good	£Fine	£N.Mint
	$6.00	$18.00	$30.00	£4.00	£12.00	£20.00

1 Variant cover Fan Appreciation Edition, ND as regular issue but with no Crusade Comics logo on cover

	$Good	$Fine	$N.Mint	£Good	£Fine	£N.Mint
	$1.60	$4.80	$8.00	£1.20	£3.60	£6.00

2 Ashcan, ND contains never seen before Shi prototype

	$Good	$Fine	$N.Mint	£Good	£Fine	£N.Mint
	$5.00	$15.00	$25.00	£3.00	£9.00	£15.00

2 Commemorative Edition, ND available at the San Diego comic convention, limited to 3,000 copies signed by William Tucci; black and white

	$Good	$Fine	$N.Mint	£Good	£Fine	£N.Mint
	$3.00	$9.00	$15.00	£2.00	£6.00	£10.00

2 Fan Appreciation Edition, ND reprints issue #2 with new cover by William Tucci

	$Good	$Fine	$N.Mint	£Good	£Fine	£N.Mint
	$5.00	$15.00	$25.00	£3.00	£9.00	£15.00

3 ND

	$Good	$Fine	$N.Mint	£Good	£Fine	£N.Mint
	$0.60	$1.80	$3.00	£0.40	£1.20	£2.00

4 ND 1st appearance Tomoe

	$Good	$Fine	$N.Mint	£Good	£Fine	£N.Mint
	$3.00	$9.00	$15.00	£2.00	£6.00	£10.00

4 Ashcan Edition, ND white cover composed of rice paper, signed by William Tucci

	$Good	$Fine	$N.Mint	£Good	£Fine	£N.Mint
	$1.20	$3.60	$6.00	£0.80	£2.40	£4.00

5 ND

	$Good	$Fine	$N.Mint	£Good	£Fine	£N.Mint
	$8.00	$24.00	$40.00	£5.00	£15.00	£25.00

5 Variant cover, ND Marc Silvestri cover art

	$Good	$Fine	$N.Mint	£Good	£Fine	£N.Mint
	$0.60	$1.80	$3.00	£0.40	£1.20	£2.00

6 ND

	$Good	$Fine	$N.Mint	£Good	£Fine	£N.Mint
	$3.00	$9.00	$15.00	£2.00	£6.00	£10.00

7 ND part 1 of two part story, x-over in Funnytime Features #7

	$Good	$Fine	$N.Mint	£Good	£Fine	£N.Mint
	$0.70	$2.10	$3.50	£1.00	£3.00	£5.00
	$0.60	$1.80	$3.00	£0.40	£1.20	£2.00
Title Value:	$54.10	$162.30	$270.50	£36.70	£110.10	£183.50

Shi - The Way of the Warrior (Dec 1994)

	£Good	£Fine	£N.Mint
Trade paperback reprints issues #1-4 plus unpublished artwork	£1.70	£5.10	£8.50

SHIELD
Red Circle (Archie); 1 Jun 1983-7 Jul 1984
(see Original Shield)
1 ND titled Lancelot Strong, the...

	$Good	$Fine	$N.Mint	£Good	£Fine	£N.Mint
	$0.30	$0.90	$1.50	£0.20	£0.60	£1.00

2 ND Rudy Nebres art

	$Good	$Fine	$N.Mint	£Good	£Fine	£N.Mint
	$0.30	$0.90	$1.50	£0.20	£0.60	£1.00

3 ND titled Shield - Steel Sterling, Alex Nino art

	$Good	$Fine	$N.Mint	£Good	£Fine	£N.Mint
	$0.30	$0.90	$1.50	£0.20	£0.60	£1.00

4 ND title becomes Steel Sterling (Jan 1984), Kaniger script and Barreto art

	$Good	$Fine	$N.Mint	£Good	£Fine	£N.Mint
	$0.30	$0.90	$1.50	£0.20	£0.60	£1.00
5 ND	$0.30	$0.90	$1.50	£0.20	£0.60	£1.00

6 ND Infantino/Barreto art

	$Good	$Fine	$N.Mint	£Good	£Fine	£N.Mint
	$0.30	$0.90	$1.50	£0.20	£0.60	£1.00
7 ND	$0.30	$0.90	$1.50	£0.20	£0.60	£1.00
Title Value:	$2.10	$6.30	$10.50	£1.40	£4.20	£7.00

SHIELD ANNUAL, LEGEND OF THE
DC Comics/Impact; 1 May 1992
1 Neal Adams cover, leads into Crusaders #1 (see other Impact annuals), includes trading cards

	$Good	$Fine	$N.Mint	£Good	£Fine	£N.Mint
	$0.25	$0.75	$1.25	£0.15	£0.45	£0.75
Title Value:	$0.25	$0.75	$1.25	£0.15	£0.45	£0.75

	$Good	$Fine	$N.Mint	£Good	£Fine	£N.Mint

SHIELD, LEGEND OF THE

DC Comics/Impact; 1 Jul 1991-16 Oct 1992
(see The Comet/Fly/Jaguar/Web)

	$Good	$Fine	$N.Mint	£Good	£Fine	£N.Mint
1-10	$0.15	$0.45	$0.75	£0.10	£0.35	£0.60
11 previews Crusaders #1 (see Jaguar #9), includes trading cards						
	$0.15	$0.45	$0.75	£0.10	£0.35	£0.60
12-16	$0.15	$0.45	$0.75	£0.10	£0.35	£0.60
Title Value:	$2.40	$7.20	$12.00	£1.60	£5.60	£9.60

Note: Archie character acquired by DC though events takes place outside DC Universe continuity

SHOCK SUSPENSTORIES (1ST SERIES)

E.C. Comics; 1 Feb/Mar 1952-18 Dec/Jan 1954/1955

	$Good	$Fine	$N.Mint	£Good	£Fine	£N.Mint
1 scarce in the U.K.						
	$67.50	$205.00	$550.00	£47.00	£140.00	£375.00
2	$43.00	$125.00	$300.00	£29.00	£85.00	£200.00
3	$32.00	$95.00	$225.00	£21.00	£62.50	£150.00
4	$29.00	$85.00	$200.00	£19.00	£57.50	£135.00
5	$27.00	$80.00	$190.00	£18.50	£55.00	£130.00
6 classic bondage cover						
	$36.00	$105.00	$250.00	£24.00	£72.50	£170.00
7 classic "melting face" cover, Ray Bradbury adaptation						
	$34.00	$100.00	$240.00	£22.50	£67.50	£160.00
8 classic "knife-to-girl's-throat" cover						
	$27.00	$80.00	$190.00	£18.50	£55.00	£130.00
9 Ray Bradbury adaptation						
	$25.00	$75.00	$175.00	£17.00	£50.00	£120.00
10-11	$25.00	$75.00	$175.00	£17.00	£50.00	£120.00
12 drug story/cover						
	$25.00	$75.00	$175.00	£17.00	£50.00	£120.00
13 Frazetta story						
	$36.00	$105.00	$250.00	£24.00	£72.50	£170.00
14-18	$17.50	$52.50	$125.00	£12.00	£36.00	£85.00
Title Value:	$519.00	$1542.50	$3720.00	£351.50	£1047.50	£2525.00

Note: all Non-Distributed on the news-stands in the U.K.

SHOCK SUSPENSTORIES (2ND SERIES)

Russ Cochran/EC Comics; 1 Sep 1991-2 1991

	$Good	$Fine	$N.Mint	£Good	£Fine	£N.Mint
1 ND reprints Shock Suspense Stories #1,2						
	$0.60	$1.80	$3.00	£0.40	£1.20	£2.00
2 ND	$0.30	$0.90	$1.50	£0.20	£0.60	£1.00
Title Value:	$0.90	$2.70	$4.50	£0.60	£1.80	£3.00

SHOCK SUSPENSTORIES (3RD SERIES)

Russ Cochran/EC Comics; 1 Sep 1992-present

	$Good	$Fine	$N.Mint	£Good	£Fine	£N.Mint
1 ND reprints begin from original 1950s EC series with exact cover and interior reproduction						
	$0.40	$1.20	$2.00	£0.25	£0.75	£1.25
2-14 ND	$0.40	$1.20	$2.00	£0.25	£0.75	£1.25
Title Value:	$5.60	$16.80	$28.00	£3.50	£10.50	£17.50
Shock Suspenstories Annual 1 (Aug 1994)						
reprints five stories with covers, softcover			£1.20	£3.60	£6.00	
Shock Suspenstories Annual 2 (Dec 1994)						
reprints five stories with covers, softcover			£1.20	£3.60	£6.00	

SHOCKING TALES DIGEST

Harvey; 1 Oct 1981

	$Good	$Fine	$N.Mint	£Good	£Fine	£N.Mint
1 ND all reprint	$0.40	$1.20	$2.00	£0.25	£0.75	£1.25
Title Value:	$0.40	$1.20	$2.00	£0.25	£0.75	£1.25

SHOGUN WARRIORS

Marvel Comics Group; 1 Feb 1979-20 Sep 1980

	$Good	$Fine	$N.Mint	£Good	£Fine	£N.Mint
1 ND	$0.30	$0.90	$1.50	£0.20	£0.60	£1.00
2-18 ND	$0.25	$0.75	$1.25	£0.15	£0.45	£0.75
19-20 Fantastic Four appear						
	$0.25	$0.75	$1.25	£0.15	£0.45	£0.75
Title Value:	$5.05	$15.15	$25.25	£3.05	£9.15	£15.25

SHOGUNAUT

Firstlight Comixx; 1 Dec 1994-2 1995

	$Good	$Fine	$N.Mint	£Good	£Fine	£N.Mint
1-2 ND	$0.50	$1.50	$2.50	£0.30	£0.90	£1.50
Title Value:	$1.00	$3.00	$5.00	£0.60	£1.80	£3.00

SHOTGUN MARY

Antarctic Press,MS; 1 Sep 1995-3 Jan 1996

	$Good	$Fine	$N.Mint	£Good	£Fine	£N.Mint
1 ND Warrior Nun Areala tie-in; Herb Mallette and Joseph Wight						
	$0.60	$1.80	$3.00	£0.40	£1.20	£2.00
1 ND Variant Cover Edition (Sep 1995) - pre-baaged with CD soundtrack by Pink Filth						
	$1.80	$5.25	$9.00	£1.20	£3.60	£6.00
2-3 ND	$0.60	$1.80	$3.00	£0.40	£1.20	£2.00
Title Value:	$3.60	$10.65	$18.00	£2.40	£7.20	£12.00

SHOWCASE

National Periodical Publications/DC Comics; 1 Mar/Apr 1956-93 Sep 1970; 94 Aug/Sep 1977-104 Sep 1978

	$Good	$Fine	$N.Mint	£Good	£Fine	£N.Mint
1 Fire Fighters starring Fireman Farrell						
	$250.00	$750.00	$2500.00	£175.00	£520.00	£1750.00
2 King of the Wild; Jack Kirby art						
	$87.50	$260.00	$700.00	£57.50	£175.00	£475.00
3 The Frogmen; Robert Kanigher script, Russ Heath art featuring a painted (grey-tone) cover						
	$82.50	$250.00	$675.00	£55.00	£165.00	£450.00
4 origin and 1st appearance of Silver Age Flash: generally regarded as the comic that started the Silver Age (Sep/Oct 1956)						
	$1650.00	$5000.00	$25000.00	£1150.00	£3500.00	£17500.00
[Prices may vary widely on this comic]						
[Rare in high grade - Very Fine+ or better]						
4 ND Silver Age Classic reprint (Mar 1992)						
	$0.25	$0.75	$1.25	£0.15	£0.45	£0.80
5 Manhunters	$100.00	$305.00	$825.00	£70.00	£215.00	£575.00
6 origin and 1st appearance Challengers of the Unknown by Jack Kirby (1st DC Silver Age super-hero team)						
	$225.00	$680.00	$2750.00	£150.00	£460.00	£1850.00
7 2nd appearance Challengers of the Unknown; Jack Kirby art						
	$150.00	$450.00	$1500.00	£100.00	£300.00	£1000.00
8 scarce in the U.K. 2nd Silver Age Flash, origin and 1st appearance Captain Cold						
	$900.00	$2700.00	$14500.00	£600.00	£1825.00	£9750.00
[Prices vary widely on this comic. Scarcer than Showcase #4]						
9 rare in the U.K. 1st Lois Lane solo comic (pre-dates Lois Lane #1)						
	$475.00	$1425.00	$4750.00	£325.00	£970.00	£3250.00
[Very rare in high grade - Very Fine+ or better]						
10 scarce in the U.K. 2nd Lois Lane solo comic (pre-dates Lois Lane #1); Jor-El appears						
	$200.00	$600.00	$2000.00	£135.00	£405.00	£1350.00
11 3rd appearance Challengers of the Unknown, Jack Kirby art						
	$135.00	$405.00	$1350.00	£90.00	£270.00	£900.00
12 4th appearance Challengers of the Unknown, Jack Kirby art						
	$125.00	$375.00	$1200.00	£85.00	£255.00	£850.00
13 3rd Silver Age Flash, 1st appearance Mr. Element						
	$300.00	$900.00	$3000.00	£200.00	£600.00	£2000.00
14 4th Silver Age Flash, Mr. Element becomes Dr. Alchemy (1st appearance)						
	$360.00	$1075.00	$3600.00	£240.00	£720.00	£2400.00
[Note: this issue is scarcer than #13]						
[Scarce in high grade - Very Fine+ or better]						
15 1st appearance Space Ranger						
	$125.00	$375.00	$1250.00	£85.00	£255.00	£850.00
[Scarce in high grade - Very Fine+ or better]						
16 2nd appearance Space Ranger						
	$77.50	$230.00	$700.00	£52.50	£155.00	£475.00
17 origin and 1st appearance of Adam Strange (see Mystery in Space #53); sub-titled Adventures on Other Worlds						
	$175.00	$520.00	$1750.00	£120.00	£360.00	£1200.00
[Scarce in high grade - Very Fine+ or better]						
18 2nd appearance Adam Strange; sub-titled Adventures on Other Worlds						

The Shadow (Archie) #6

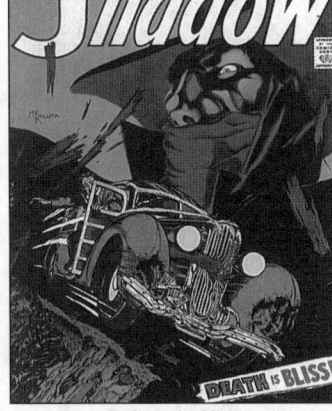

The Shadow (1st DC) #4

Shi #6

	$Good	$Fine	$N.Mint	£Good	£Fine	£N.Mint
	$110.00	$335.00	$900.00	£75.00	£225.00	£600.00
19 3rd appearance Adam Strange	$100.00	$305.00	$825.00	£67.50	£205.00	£550.00
20 scarce in the U.K. 1st appearance Rip Hunter Time Master	$70.00	$215.00	$650.00	£48.00	£145.00	£435.00
21 2nd appearance Rip Hunter Time Master	$45.00	$135.00	$360.00	£30.00	£90.00	£240.00
22 origin and 1st appearance of Silver Age Green Lantern	$365.00	$1100.00	$4400.00	£250.00	£750.00	£3000.00
1st official distribution in the U.K.						
22 ND Silver Age Classic reprint (Mar 1992)	$0.25	$0.75	$1.25	£0.15	£0.45	£0.80
23 2nd appearance Green Lantern, nuclear explosion cover	$150.00	$450.00	$1500.00	£100.00	£300.00	£1000.00
24 3rd appearance Green Lantern	$140.00	$420.00	$1400.00	£95.00	£285.00	£950.00
25 3rd appearance Rip Hunter; painted (grey-tone) cover	$31.00	$92.50	$250.00	£21.00	£62.50	£170.00
26 4th appearance Rip Hunter	$34.00	$100.00	$240.00	£21.00	£62.50	£150.00
27 1st appearance Sea Devils; painted (grey-tone) cover; Russ Heath art	$75.00	$225.00	$600.00	£50.00	£150.00	£400.00
28 2nd appearance Sea Devils; painted (grey-tone) cover; Russ heath art	$44.00	$130.00	$350.00	£29.00	£87.50	£235.00
29 3rd appearance Sea Devils; painted (grey-tone) cover; Russ Heath art	$43.00	$125.00	$340.00	£29.00	£85.00	£230.00
30 Aquaman appears, origin retold (see Adventure Comics #260 for 1st Silver Age appearance)	$70.00	$215.00	$650.00	£44.00	£130.00	£400.00
31-33 Aquaman	$52.50	$155.00	$425.00	£28.00	£82.50	£225.00
34 origin & 1st appearance Silver Age Atom; Gil Kane and Murphy Anderson art	$140.00	$430.00	$1300.00	£87.50	£265.00	£800.00
35 2nd appearance Silver Age Atom; last 10 cents issue	$92.50	$275.00	$740.00	£55.00	£170.00	£455.00
36 3rd appearance Silver Age Atom (pre Atom #1)	$70.00	$215.00	$575.00	£44.00	£130.00	£350.00
37 1st appearance the Metal Men	$65.00	$195.00	$525.00	£39.00	£115.00	£315.00
38 2nd appearance the Metal Men	$52.50	$155.00	$420.00	£28.00	£82.50	£225.00
39 3rd appearance the Metal Men	$41.00	$120.00	$325.00	£22.50	£67.50	£180.00
40 4th appearance the Metal Men	$41.00	$120.00	$325.00	£22.50	£67.50	£180.00
41-42 Tommy Tomorrow	$21.00	$62.50	$150.00	£9.25	£28.00	£65.00
43 Dr. No (film adaptation), no ads, originally published as British Classics Illustrated 158A, 1st major Silver Age film adaptation	$44.00	$130.00	$350.00	£26.00	£77.50	£210.00
44 Tommy Tomorrow	$14.00	$43.00	$100.00	£6.25	£19.00	£45.00
45 rare in the U.K. Sgt. Rock; origin retold; Russ Heath cover	$25.00	$75.00	$200.00	£15.50	£47.00	£125.00
46-47 Tommy Tomorrow	$12.00	$36.00	$85.00	£6.00	£18.00	£42.50
48-49 Cave Carson	$8.00	$24.00	$65.00	£3.40	£10.00	£27.50
50 I-Spy	$8.50	$26.00	$60.00	£4.25	£12.50	£30.00
51 I-Spy	$8.50	$26.00	$60.00	£3.55	£10.50	£25.00
52 Cave Carson	$6.25	$18.50	$50.00	£3.00	£9.00	£24.00
53-54 scarce in the U.K. G.I.Joe; Russ Heath art	$7.50	$22.50	$60.00	£3.50	£10.50	£28.00
55 Dr. Fate/Hourman, 1st solo (ie. not part of a team) Golden Age Green Lantern in Silver Age (see Green Lantern [1st Series] #40), 1st Silver Age Solomon Grundy	$25.00	$75.00	$225.00	£13.00	£40.00	£120.00
56 Dr. Fate/Hourman	$10.00	$30.00	$80.00	£5.00	£15.00	£40.00
57 scarce in the U.K. Enemy Ace by Joe Kubert (see Our Army at War #155)	$15.00	$45.00	$120.00	£7.50	£22.50	£60.00
58 scarce in the U.K. Enemy Ace by Kubert	$13.50	$41.00	$110.00	£6.75	£20.50	£55.00
59 3rd Teen Titans (see Brave and the Bold #54, #60)	$12.50	$38.00	$100.00	£7.50	£22.50	£60.00
60 1st Silver Age appearance The Spectre (last seen 20 years before in More Fun Comics #101 dated February 1945)	$26.00	$77.50	$210.00	£10.50	£32.00	£84.00
61 2nd Silver Age appearance The Spectre, Murphy Anderson art	$15.50	$47.00	$125.00	£7.50	£22.50	£60.00
62 1st appearance Inferior Five	$9.25	$28.00	$75.00	£4.35	£13.00	£35.00
63 2nd appearance Inferior Five; Incredible Hulk parody	$6.25	$18.50	$50.00	£3.00	£9.00	£24.00
64 The Spectre by Murphy Anderson	$13.50	$41.00	$110.00	£6.75	£20.50	£55.00
65 Inferior Five, X-Men parody	$5.00	$15.00	$40.00	£2.50	£7.50	£20.00
66 1st appearance B'wana Beast	$4.35	$13.00	$35.00	£1.55	£4.65	£12.50
67 B'wana Beast	$4.35	$13.00	$35.00	£1.25	£3.75	£10.00
68 Maniaks (1st appearance)	$3.75	$11.00	$30.00	£1.25	£3.75	£10.00
69 Maniaks	$3.75	$11.00	$30.00	£1.25	£3.75	£10.00
70 rare in the U.K. Binky						

	$Good	$Fine	$N.Mint	£Good	£Fine	£N.Mint
	$3.75	$11.00	$30.00	£2.15	£6.50	£17.50
71 scarce in the U.K. Maniaks (Woody Allen appears)	$3.75	$11.00	$30.00	£1.55	£4.65	£12.50
72 Top Gun; Alex Toth art	$3.75	$11.00	$30.00	£1.25	£3.75	£10.00
73 origin & 1st appearance of the Creeper; Steve Ditko art	$13.00	$40.00	$120.00	£6.50	£20.00	£60.00
74 1st appearance Anthro	$9.25	$28.00	$75.00	£4.35	£13.00	£35.00
75 1st appearance Hawk and the Dove; Steve Ditko art	$12.50	$38.00	$100.00	£6.25	£18.50	£50.00
76 1st appearance Bat Lash	$6.75	$20.50	$55.00	£3.50	£10.50	£28.00
77 1st appearance Angel and the Ape	$6.25	$18.50	$50.00	£3.25	£9.75	£26.00
78 1st appearance Johnny Double	$3.75	$11.00	$30.00	£1.85	£5.50	£15.00
79 1st appearance Dolphin; Aqualad origin reprint	$6.75	$20.50	$55.00	£2.50	£7.50	£20.00
80 Phantom Stranger (part reprint); Neal Adams cover	$4.25	$12.50	$30.00	£1.50	£4.50	£10.50
81 rare in the U.K. Windy & Willy	$3.55	$10.50	$25.00	£2.50	£7.50	£17.50
82 1st appearance Nightmaster by Jerry Grandenetti	$8.50	$26.00	$60.00	£4.25	£12.50	£30.00
83 Nightmaster; Wrightson, Jones and Kaluta art	$7.00	$21.00	$50.00	£3.20	£9.50	£22.50
84 Nightmaster; Wrightson, Jones & Kaluta art	$7.00	$21.00	$50.00	£3.20	£9.50	£22.50
85-87 Firehair byJoe Kubert	$3.55	$10.50	$25.00	£1.05	£3.20	£7.50
88-90 Jason's Quest	$2.85	$8.50	$20.00	£0.50	£1.50	£3.50
91-93 Manhunter (science-fiction character, not to be confused with super-hero)	$1.40	$4.25	$10.00	£0.50	£1.50	£3.50
94 1st appearance New Doom Patrol	$1.50	$4.50	$7.50	£1.00	£3.00	£5.00
95 2nd appearance New Doom Patrol	$1.05	$3.15	$5.25	£0.90	£2.10	£3.50
96 Doom Patrol	$0.90	$2.70	$4.50	£0.60	£1.80	£3.00
97 origin Power Girl, "headlights" cover (love that cleavage!)	$0.80	$2.40	$4.00	£0.50	£1.50	£2.50
98 origin Power Girl	$0.80	$2.40	$4.00	£0.40	£1.20	£2.00
99 scarce in the U.K. Power Girl	$0.80	$2.40	$4.00	£0.50	£1.50	£2.50
100 scarce in the U.K. 52pgs, features almost every character ever to appear in title	$1.20	$3.60	$6.00	£0.70	£2.10	£3.50
101-103 Hawkman	$0.80	$2.40	$4.00	£0.40	£1.20	£2.00
104 ND 44pgs, OSS Spies at War	$0.80	$2.40	$4.00	£0.60	£1.80	£4.00
Title Value:	$7858.90	$23637.50	$89973.75	£5174.95	£15603.15	£60058.60

REPRINT FEATURES
(50, 51, 70, 72, 81 are entirely reprint, 79, 80 are partly reprint), Aquaman in 79. Binky in 70. Johnny Thunder, Trigger Twins in 72. King Faraday in 50, 51. Part 1950s Phantom Stranger in 80. 1950s/1960s humour title with some art changes in 81.

The Essential Showcase Volume 1 (Jan 1993)

	$Good	$Fine	$N.Mint	£Good	£Fine	£N.Mint
Softcover, 192pgs, reprints selected issues from #1–#19				£2.50	£7.50	£12.50

SHOWCASE '93
DC Comics,MS; 1 Jan 1993-12 Dec 1993

	$Good	$Fine	$N.Mint	£Good	£Fine	£N.Mint
1 Arthur Adams and Terry Austin cover; features Catwoman, Blue Devil, Cyborg stories	$0.40	$1.20	$2.00	£0.25	£0.75	£1.25
2 Kevin Maguire and Terry Austin cover; features Catwoman (Robin cameo), Blue Devil, Cyborg stories	$0.40	$1.20	$2.00	£0.25	£0.75	£1.25
3 Brian Bolland cover; features Catwoman, Blue Devil plus Flash by Travis Charest	$0.40	$1.20	$2.00	£0.25	£0.75	£1.25
4 Michael Golden cover; features Catwoman, Blue Devil plus Geo-Force	$0.40	$1.20	$2.00	£0.25	£0.75	£1.25
5 features Robin, Blue Devil and Geo-Force	$0.40	$1.20	$2.00	£0.25	£0.75	£1.25
6 Mike Zeck cover; features Robin, Blue Devil and Deathstroke the Terminator	$0.40	$1.20	$2.00	£0.25	£0.75	£1.25
7 Knightfall part 13 - Batman vs. Two-Face; also features Kobra, Deathstroke, Peacemaker, Jade and Obsidian, bi-weekly	$0.50	$1.50	$2.50	£0.30	£0.90	£1.50
8 Knightfall part 14 - Batman vs. Two-Face; also features Kobra, Deathstroke, Peacemaker, Fire and Ice, bi-weekly; continued in Batman #498	$0.50	$1.50	$2.50	£0.30	£0.90	£1.50
9 Howard Chaykin cover; features Huntress, Kobra, Shining Knight	$0.40	$1.20	$2.00	£0.25	£0.75	£1.25
10 Paul Gulacy cover; features Huntress, Kobra, Martian Manhunter	$0.40	$1.20	$2.00	£0.25	£0.75	£1.25
11 George Perez cover; features Robin and Nightwing, Kobra, Wonder Woman	$0.40	$1.20	$2.00	£0.25	£0.75	£1.25
12 Alan Davis and Mark Farmer cover; features Robin And Nightwing, Green Lantern, The Creeper	$0.40	$1.20	$2.00	£0.25	£0.75	£1.25
Title Value:	$5.00	$15.00	$25.00	£3.10	£9.30	£15.50

SHOWCASE '94
DC Comics,MS; 1 Jan 1994-12 Dec 1994

	$Good	$Fine	$N.Mint	£Good	£Fine	£N.Mint
1 48pgs, Graham Nolan cover; features Joker, Gunfire, Orion & Metron	$0.40	$1.20	$2.00	£0.25	£0.75	£1.25

VERY GENERAL PERCENTAGE CONVERSION CHART WHICH MAY BE USED TO CALCULATE LOW AND INBETWEEN GRADES:

	$Good	$Fine	$N.Mint	£Good	£Fine	£N.Mint
2 48pgs, Kevin O'Neill cover; features Joker, Gunfire, Blue Beetle	$0.40	$1.20	$2.00	£0.25	£0.75	£1.25
3 48pgs, Mike Mignola cover; features Two-Face, Riddler, Scarecrow and Mad Hatter, Blue Beetle	$0.40	$1.20	$2.00	£0.25	£0.75	£1.25
4 48pgs, Kyle Baker cover; features Two-Face, Riddler, Scarecrow and Mad Hatter, Razorsharpe, Blue Beetle	$0.40	$1.20	$2.00	£0.25	£0.75	£1.25
5 48pgs, Robin and The Huntress; Bloodwynd, Loose Cannon; continued in Robin #7; bi-weekly	$0.40	$1.20	$2.00	£0.25	£0.75	£1.25
6 48pgs, Robin and The Huntress; Bloodwynd, Loose Cannon; continued from Robin #7; bi-weekly	$0.40	$1.20	$2.00	£0.25	£0.75	£1.25
7 48pgs, Penguin by Peter David with art by P. Craig Russell and Michael T. Gilbert; Terrorsmith, Arsenal	$0.40	$1.20	$2.00	£0.25	£0.75	£1.25
8 48pgs, Origin of Scarface by Alan Grant & John Wagner, Ted McKeever art; Wildcat, Zero Hour prelude	$0.40	$1.20	$2.00	£0.25	£0.75	£1.25
9 48pgs, Origin of Scarface by Alan Grant & John Wagner; Zero Hour prelude featuring Waverider and Monarch	$0.40	$1.20	$2.00	£0.25	£0.75	£1.25
10 48pgs, Azrael, Black Condor; Zero Hour X-over; Joe Quesada cover	$0.40	$1.20	$2.00	£0.25	£0.75	£1.25
11 48pgs, Man-Bat, Condor, Starfire; Geof Darrow cover	$0.40	$1.20	$2.00	£0.25	£0.75	£1.25
12 48pgs, Barbara Gordon/Oracle, Ballistic, Triumph				£0.25	£0.75	£1.25
Title Value:	$4.80	$14.40	$24.00	£3.00	£9.00	£15.00

SHOWCASE '95
DC Comics,MS; 1 Jan 1995-12 Dec 1995

	$Good	$Fine	$N.Mint	£Good	£Fine	£N.Mint
1 Supergirl, Argus and the Golden Age Green Lantern	$0.50	$1.50	$2.50	£0.30	£0.90	£1.50
2 Supergirl, Argus and the Metal Men	$0.50	$1.50	$2.50	£0.30	£0.90	£1.50
3 The Eradicator, Claw of Primal Force and The Question	$0.50	$1.50	$2.50	£0.30	£0.90	£1.50
4 Thorn, Catwoman and Green Arrow	$0.50	$1.50	$2.50	£0.30	£0.90	£1.50
5 48pgs, Thorn, The Spoiler, Firehawk	$0.50	$1.50	$2.50	£0.30	£0.90	£1.50
6 48pgs, Lobo, Leviathan, Andromeda	$0.50	$1.50	$2.50	£0.30	£0.90	£1.50
7 48pgs, Mongul, Arion, New Gods	$0.60	$1.80	$3.00	£0.40	£1.20	£2.00
8 48pgs, Mongul, Spectre, Arsenal	$0.50	$1.50	$2.50	£0.30	£0.90	£1.50
9 48pgs, Lois Lane, Lobo, Martian Manhunter	$0.50	$1.50	$2.50	£0.30	£0.90	£1.50
10 48pgs, Gangbuster, Darkstars, Hi-Tech; bi-weekly	$0.50	$1.50	$2.50	£0.30	£0.90	£1.50
11 48pgs, Agent Liberty, Arkham Asylum, Hi-Tech	$0.50	$1.50	$2.50	£0.30	£0.90	£1.50
12 48pgs, Supergirl, Maitresse, The Shade (an Underworld Unleashed story)	$0.50	$1.50	$2.50	£0.30	£0.90	£1.50
Title Value:	$6.10	$18.30	$30.50	£3.70	£11.10	£18.50

SHOWCASE '96
DC Comics,MS; 1 Jan 1996-present

	$Good	$Fine	$N.Mint	£Good	£Fine	£N.Mint
1 ND 48pgs, Steel and Warrior team-up, Aqualad and Metropolis S.C.U. feature in separate stories	$0.60	$1.80	$3.00	£0.40	£1.20	£2.00
2 ND Steel and Warrior team-up, Circe vs. Ares	$0.60	$1.80	$3.00	£0.40	£1.20	£2.00
3 ND Black Canary, Oracle and Lois Lane team, Lightray and Deadman	$0.60	$1.80	$3.00	£0.40	£1.20	£2.00
Title Value:	$1.80	$5.40	$9.00	£1.20	£3.60	£6.00

SHRIEK
Fantaco; 1 1989

	$Good	$Fine	$N.Mint	£Good	£Fine	£N.Mint
1 ND 48pgs, magazine size; features work by Gurchain Singh, Kevin Eastman and Steve Bisette; black and white	$1.50	$4.50	$7.50	£1.00	£3.00	£5.00
Title Value:	$0.25	$0.75	$1.25	£0.15	£0.45	£0.75

SHRIKE
Cat Wild; 1 Jan 1991

	$Good	$Fine	$N.Mint	£Good	£Fine	£N.Mint
1 ND black and white	$0.25	$0.75	$1.25	£0.15	£0.45	£0.75
Title Value:	$0.25	$0.75	$1.25	£0.15	£0.45	£0.75

SHROUD, THE
Marvel Comics Group,MS; 1 Mar 1994-4 Jun 1994

	$Good	$Fine	$N.Mint	£Good	£Fine	£N.Mint
1-3	$0.30	$0.90	$1.50	£0.20	£0.60	£1.00
4 Spiderman guest-stars	$0.30	$0.90	$1.50	£0.20	£0.60	£1.00
Title Value:	$1.20	$3.60	$6.00	£0.80	£2.40	£4.00

SHURIKEN
Victory; 1 1985-10 May 1987
(see Blade of Shuriken)

	$Good	$Fine	$N.Mint	£Good	£Fine	£N.Mint
1 ND black and white begins	$0.30	$0.90	$1.50	£0.20	£0.60	£1.00
1 2nd printing ND	$0.25	$0.75	$1.25	£0.15	£0.45	£0.75
2-10 ND	$0.30	$0.90	$1.50	£0.20	£0.60	£1.00
Title Value:	$3.25	$9.75	$16.25	£2.15	£6.45	£10.75
Graphic Novel (Blackthorne), reprints				£1.10	£3.30	£5.50

SHURIKEN (2ND SERIES)
Eternity,MS; 1 Aug 1991-6 Jan 1992

	$Good	$Fine	$N.Mint	£Good	£Fine	£N.Mint
1-6 ND	$0.40	$1.20	$2.00	£0.25	£0.75	£1.25
Title Value:	$2.40	$7.20	$12.00	£1.50	£4.50	£7.50

SHURIKEN: COLD STEEL
Eternity; 1-4 1987

	$Good	$Fine	$N.Mint	£Good	£Fine	£N.Mint
1-4 ND 16pgs	$0.40	$1.20	$2.00	£0.25	£0.75	£1.25
Title Value:	$1.60	$4.80	$8.00	£1.00	£3.00	£5.00

SIDNEY MELLON'S THUNDERSKULL!
Slave Labor; 1 1989

	$Good	$Fine	$N.Mint	£Good	£Fine	£N.Mint
1 ND black and white	$0.40	$1.20	$2.00	£0.25	£0.75	£1.25
Title Value:	$0.40	$1.20	$2.00	£0.25	£0.75	£1.25

SIEGEL & SHUSTER: DATELINE 1930S
Eclipse; 1 Nov 1984-2 1985

	$Good	$Fine	$N.Mint	£Good	£Fine	£N.Mint
1 ND pre-Superman reprints, includes interview	$0.40	$1.20	$2.00	£0.25	£0.75	£1.25
2 ND reprints	$0.40	$1.20	$2.00	£0.25	£0.75	£1.25
Title Value:	$0.80	$2.40	$4.00	£0.50	£1.50	£2.50

SIGNAL TO NOISE GRAPHIC NOVEL
Dark Horse,OS; nn Dec 1992
nn ND 80pgs, Neil Gaiman script, Dave McKean art; originally published in the U.K.

	$Good	$Fine	$N.Mint	£Good	£Fine	£N.Mint
	$3.00	$9.00	$15.00	£2.00	£6.00	£10.00
Title Value:	$3.00	$9.00	$15.00	£2.00	£6.00	£10.00

SILBUSTER
Antarctic Press; 1 Jan 1994-present

	$Good	$Fine	$N.Mint	£Good	£Fine	£N.Mint
1-4 ND 40pgs, Kazumitsu Sahara; black and white	$0.60	$1.80	$3.00	£0.40	£1.20	£2.00
5-10 ND 40pgs, Ikkou Sahara; black and white	$0.60	$1.80	$3.00	£0.40	£1.20	£2.00
11-12 ND	$0.60	$1.80	$3.00	£0.40	£1.20	£2.00
Title Value:	$7.20	$21.60	$36.00	£4.80	£14.40	£24.00
Collected Silbuster (Aug 1995) 136pgs, collects issues #1-4, black and white				£1.50	£4.50	£7.50

SILENCERS, THE
Caliber Press,MS; 1 Sep 1991-4 Dec 1991

	$Good	$Fine	$N.Mint	£Good	£Fine	£N.Mint
1-4 ND	$0.40	$1.20	$2.00	£0.25	£0.75	£1.25
Title Value:	$1.60	$4.80	$8.00	£1.00	£3.00	£5.00

SILENT INVASION
Renegade; 1 Jul 1986-12 1988

	$Good	$Fine	$N.Mint	£Good	£Fine	£N.Mint
1-12 ND	$0.40	$1.20	$2.00	£0.25	£0.75	£1.25
Title Value:	$4.80	$14.40	$24.00	£3.00	£9.00	£15.00
Book 1, reprints #1-4				£1.20	£3.60	£6.00
Book 2, reprints #5-8				£1.20	£3.60	£6.00

SILENT MOBIUS
Viz Communications,MS; 1 Aug 1991-6 Jan 1992

	$Good	$Fine	$N.Mint	£Good	£Fine	£N.Mint
1 ND 40pgs, Japanese material begins; Kia Asamiya script and art, black and white	$1.00	$3.00	$5.00	£0.60	£1.80	£3.00
2-6 ND	$1.00	$3.00	$5.00	£0.60	£1.80	£3.00
Title Value:	$6.00	$18.00	$30.00	£3.60	£10.80	£18.00
Silent Mobius Graphic Novel Vol 1 (Oct 1992) 120pgs, reprints mini-series				£2.00	£6.00	£10.00

SILENT MOBIUS PART 2
Viz Communications,MS; 1 Feb 1992-5 Jun 1992

	$Good	$Fine	$N.Mint	£Good	£Fine	£N.Mint
1 ND Kia Asamiya script and art begins, black and white	$0.90	$2.70	$4.50	£0.60	£1.80	£3.00
2-5 ND	$0.90	$2.70	$4.50	£0.60	£1.80	£3.00
Title Value:	$4.50	$13.50	$22.50	£3.00	£9.00	£15.00
Silent Mobius Graphic Novel Vol 2 (Nov 1992) 120pgs, reprints mini-series				£2.00	£6.00	£10.00

SILENT MOBIUS PART 3
Viz Communications,MS; 1 Oct 1992-5 Feb 1993

	$Good	$Fine	$N.Mint	£Good	£Fine	£N.Mint
1 ND Kia Asamiya script and art begins, black and white	$0.60	$1.80	$3.00	£0.40	£1.20	£2.00
2-5 ND	$0.60	$1.80	$3.00	£0.40	£1.20	£2.00
Title Value:	$3.00	$9.00	$15.00	£2.00	£6.00	£10.00

SILENT MOBIUS PART 4
Viz Communications,MS; 1 Sep 1993-5 Jan 1994

	$Good	$Fine	$N.Mint	£Good	£Fine	£N.Mint
1 ND Kia Asamiya script and art, black and white	$0.60	$1.80	$3.00	£0.40	£1.20	£2.00
2-5 ND	$0.60	$1.80	$3.00	£0.40	£1.20	£2.00
Title Value:	$3.00	$9.00	$15.00	£2.00	£6.00	£10.00

SILENT MOBIUS PART 5
Viz Communications,MS; 1 Feb 1994-5 Jun 1994

	$Good	$Fine	$N.Mint	£Good	£Fine	£N.Mint
1-5 ND	$0.60	$1.80	$3.00	£0.40	£1.20	£2.00
Title Value:	$3.00	$9.00	$15.00	£2.00	£6.00	£10.00

SILVER SABLE
Marvel Comics Group; 1 Jun 1992-35 Apr 1995

	$Good	$Fine	$N.Mint	£Good	£Fine	£N.Mint
1 ND silver foil-stamped embossed cover, Peter Parker appears	$0.30	$0.90	$1.50	£0.20	£0.60	£1.00
2-3 ND	$0.25	$0.75	$1.25	£0.15	£0.45	£0.75
4-5 ND Infinity War X-over, Dr. Doom appears	$0.25	$0.75	$1.25	£0.15	£0.45	£0.75
6-7 ND Deathlok appears	$0.25	$0.75	$1.25	£0.15	£0.45	£0.75
8 ND	$0.25	$0.75	$1.25	£0.15	£0.45	£0.75
9 ND origin Silver Sable	$0.25	$0.75	$1.25	£0.15	£0.45	£0.75
10 ND Punisher appears	$0.25	$0.75	$1.25	£0.15	£0.45	£0.75
11 ND back-up feature begins	$0.25	$0.75	$1.25	£0.15	£0.45	£0.75
12 ND	$0.25	$0.75	$1.25	£0.15	£0.45	£0.75
13 ND Cage appears, continued in Terror Inc. #12	$0.25	$0.75	$1.25	£0.15	£0.45	£0.75
14 ND Cage and Terror appear	$0.25	$0.75	$1.25	£0.15	£0.45	£0.75
15 ND Captain America appears	$0.25	$0.75	$1.25	£0.15	£0.45	£0.75
16-17 ND Infinity Crusade X-over						

	$Good	$Fine	$N.Mint	£Good	£Fine	£N.Mint
	$0.25	$0.75	$1.25	£0.15	£0.45	£0.75
18 ND Venom appears						
	$0.25	$0.75	$1.25	£0.15	£0.45	£0.75
19 ND Siege of Darkness tie-in						
	$0.25	$0.75	$1.25	£0.15	£0.45	£0.75
20-23 ND						
	$0.25	$0.75	$1.25	£0.15	£0.45	£0.75
24 ND with free Spiderman vs. Venom card sheet						
	$0.25	$0.75	$1.25	£0.15	£0.45	£0.75
25 ND 48pgs						
	$0.30	$0.90	$1.50	£0.20	£0.60	£1.00
26 ND Sandman and Trapster appear						
	$0.25	$0.75	$1.25	£0.15	£0.45	£0.75
27 ND Sandman appears						
	$0.25	$0.75	$1.25	£0.15	£0.45	£0.75
28-35 ND						
Title Value:	$8.85	$26.55	$44.25	£5.35	£16.05	£26.75

SILVER SCREAM, THE
Lorne-Harvey Publications/Recollections; 1 Jun 1991-3 Nov 1991

	$Good	$Fine	$N.Mint	£Good	£Fine	£N.Mint
1-3 ND horror reprints; black and white						
	$0.30	$0.90	$1.50	£0.20	£0.60	£1.00
Title Value:	$0.90	$2.70	$4.50	£0.60	£1.80	£3.00

SILVER STAR
Pacific; 1 Feb 1983-6 Jul 1983

	$Good	$Fine	$N.Mint	£Good	£Fine	£N.Mint
1 ND Jack Kirby art, Last of the Viking Heroes backup						
	$0.30	$0.90	$1.50	£0.20	£0.60	£1.00
2 ND Jack Kirby art; Steve Ditko art on back-up						
	$0.30	$0.90	$1.50	£0.20	£0.60	£1.00
3 ND Jack Kirby art, Flynn backup						
	$0.30	$0.90	$1.50	£0.20	£0.60	£1.00
4-6 ND Jack Kirby art						
	$0.30	$0.90	$1.50	£0.20	£0.60	£1.00
Title Value:	$1.80	$5.40	$9.00	£1.20	£3.60	£6.00

SILVER STAR (2ND SERIES)
Topps,MS; 1 Oct 1993; 2 Jul 1994-4 Sep 1994

	$Good	$Fine	$N.Mint	£Good	£Fine	£N.Mint
1 ND pre-bagged with 3 trading cards; James Fry and Terry Austin art						
	$0.40	$1.20	$2.00	£0.25	£0.75	£1.25
2-4 ND James Fry and Terry Austin art						
	$0.40	$1.20	$2.00	£0.25	£0.75	£1.25
Title Value:	$1.60	$4.80	$8.00	£1.00	£3.00	£5.00

SILVER SURFER (1ST SERIES)
Marvel Comics Group; 1 Aug 1968-18 Sep 1970
(see Fantastic Four, Fantasy Masterpieces, Marvel Graphic Novel, Marvel Presents #8, Marvel's Greatest Comics, Tales to Astonish)

	$Good	$Fine	$N.Mint	£Good	£Fine	£N.Mint
1 72pgs, squarebound, origin Silver Surfer, Watcher begins (origin)						
	$55.00	$165.00	$450.00	£38.00	£110.00	£300.00
2 72pgs, squarebound						
	$20.50	$60.00	$165.00	£12.50	£38.00	£100.00
3 72pgs, squarebound, 1st appearance Mephisto						
	$17.50	$52.50	$140.00	£11.00	£34.00	£90.00
4 scarce in the U.K. 72pgs, squarebound, Thor appears						
	$50.00	$150.00	$400.00	£34.00	£100.00	£275.00
5 scarce in the U.K. 72pgs, squarebound, The Stranger appears, Fantastic Four cameo						
	$10.50	$32.00	$85.00	£6.75	£20.50	£55.00
6 72pgs, squarebound, Brunner inks						
	$10.00	$30.00	$80.00	£6.25	£18.50	£50.00
7 72pgs, squarebound, Brunner cover						
	$10.00	$30.00	$80.00	£6.25	£18.50	£50.00
8-10	$8.50	$26.00	$60.00	£5.50	£17.00	£40.00
11-13	$6.25	$19.00	$45.00	£4.25	£12.50	£30.00
14 Spiderman X-over						
	$10.00	$30.00	$70.00	£5.50	£17.00	£40.00
15 scarce in the U.K. Human Torch X-over						
	$6.25	$19.00	$45.00	£4.60	£13.50	£32.50
16-17	$6.25	$19.00	$45.00	£4.25	£12.50	£30.00
18 very scarce in the U.K. Inhumans appear, Jack Kirby cover/art						
	$6.25	$19.00	$45.00	£5.00	£15.00	£35.00
Title Value:	$252.75	$760.50	$1965.00	£167.60	£498.50	£1297.50

Note: #1-17 John Buscema pencils

SILVER SURFER (2ND SERIES)
Marvel Comics Group,OS; 1 Jun 1982

	$Good	$Fine	$N.Mint	£Good	£Fine	£N.Mint
1 ND scarce in the U.K. 52pgs, John Byrne art, Stan Lee script						
	$1.50	$4.50	$9.00	£1.15	£3.50	£7.00
Title Value:	$1.50	$4.50	$9.00	£1.15	£3.50	£7.00

SILVER SURFER (3RD SERIES)
Marvel Comics Group; 1 Jul 1987-present

	$Good	$Fine	$N.Mint	£Good	£Fine	£N.Mint
1 ND DS, Marshall Rogers art begins, ends #12, Englehart scripts						
	$1.60	$4.80	$8.00	£1.20	£3.60	£6.00
2 ND	$0.80	$2.40	$4.00	£0.50	£1.50	£2.50
3-5	$0.50	$1.50	$2.50	£0.30	£0.90	£1.50
6	$0.40	$1.20	$2.00	£0.25	£0.75	£1.25
7 LD in the U.K.	$0.40	$1.20	$2.00	£0.30	£0.90	£1.50
8	$0.40	$1.20	$2.00	£0.25	£0.75	£1.25
9-10 Galactus appears						
	$0.40	$1.20	$2.00	£0.25	£0.75	£1.25
11 Galactus appears						
	$0.30	$0.90	$1.50	£0.20	£0.60	£1.00
12	$0.30	$0.90	$1.50	£0.20	£0.60	£1.00
13 Staton art	$0.30	$0.90	$1.50	£0.20	£0.60	£1.00
14 Staton art, Surfer battles Surfer; ties into Silver Surfer Annual #1						
	$0.30	$0.90	$1.50	£0.20	£0.60	£1.00
15 1st Ron Lim art on series, Fantastic Four appear						
	$0.80	$2.40	$4.00	£0.50	£1.50	£2.50
16 2nd Ron Lim art on series						
	$0.70	$2.10	$3.50	£0.40	£1.20	£2.00
17 Ron Lim art	$0.60	$1.80	$3.00	£0.40	£1.20	£2.00
18 Ron Lim art, Galactus vs. The In-Betweener						
	$0.60	$1.80	$3.00	£0.40	£1.20	£2.00
19 LD in the U.K. Surfer battles Firelord, Ron Lim art						
	$0.60	$1.80	$3.00	£0.40	£1.20	£2.00
20 Ron Lim art	$0.40	$1.20	$2.00	£0.25	£0.75	£1.25
21 Rogers art	$0.40	$1.20	$2.00	£0.25	£0.75	£1.25
22-24 Ron Lim art	$0.40	$1.20	$2.00	£0.25	£0.75	£1.25
25 LD in the U.K. DS Ron Lim art						
	$0.50	$1.50	$2.50	£0.30	£0.90	£1.50
26-30 Ron Lim art	$0.40	$1.20	$2.00	£0.25	£0.75	£1.25
31 LD in the U.K. DS Ron Lim art						
	$0.50	$1.50	$2.50	£0.30	£0.90	£1.50
32 Ron Frenz art	$0.40	$1.20	$2.00	£0.25	£0.75	£1.25
33 Impossible Man appears, Ron Lim art						
	$0.40	$1.20	$2.00	£0.25	£0.75	£1.25
34 Thanos returns (cover and cameo), (1st) Starlin script/Ron Lim art begins						
	$1.20	$3.60	$6.00	£0.80	£2.40	£4.00
35 Ron Lim art, 1st full re-appearance Thanos, Drax the Destroyer re-introduced on last page						
	$1.50	$4.50	$7.50	£1.00	£3.00	£5.00
36 Ron Lim art, history of Thanos						
	$1.00	$3.00	$5.00	£0.70	£2.10	£3.50
37 Ron Lim art	$0.60	$1.80	$3.00	£0.40	£1.20	£2.00
38 Ron Lim art, Silver Surfer vs. Thanos						
	$1.00	$3.00	$5.00	£0.70	£2.10	£3.50
39 Alan Grant script (no Jim Starlin/Ron Lim)						
	$0.40	$1.20	$2.00	£0.25	£0.75	£1.25
40-43 Jim Starlin script, Ron Lim art						
	$0.40	$1.20	$2.00	£0.25	£0.75	£1.25

Showcase #97

Silver Surfer (mini-series) #1

Silver Surfer Annual #1

Issue	Description	$Good	$Fine	$N.Mint	£Good	£Fine	£N.Mint
44-45	Jim Starlin script, Ron Lim art, Thanos appears	$0.40	$1.20	$2.00	£0.25	£0.75	£1.25
46	Warlock returns, Jim Starlin script, Ron Lim art	$0.90	$2.70	$4.50	£0.60	£1.80	£3.00
47	Warlock appears, Jim Starlin script, Ron Lim art	$0.80	$2.40	$4.00	£0.50	£1.50	£2.50
48	Jim Starlin script, Ron Lim art	$0.40	$1.20	$2.00	£0.25	£0.75	£1.25
49	Jim Starlin script, Ron Lim art, Thanos appears	$0.50	$1.50	$2.50	£0.30	£0.90	£1.50
50	Silver Surfer vs. Thanos, special silver-embossed cover, Ron Lim art	$1.00	$3.00	$5.00	£0.60	£1.80	£3.00
50	2nd printing, scarce in the U.K. Silver Surfer vs. Thanos, Ron Lim art	$0.50	$1.50	$2.50	£0.30	£0.90	£1.50
50	3rd printing, very scarce in the U.K. not embossed	$0.50	$1.50	$2.50	£0.30	£0.90	£1.50
50	rare in the U.K. misprint; silver over-lay production problem resulting in a pure all white Silver Surfer and logo (other misprints have only part of silver foil missing)	$1.50	$4.50	$7.50	£2.00	£6.00	£10.00
51	Infinity Gauntlet X-over, Ron Lim art	$0.50	$1.50	$2.50	£0.30	£0.90	£1.50
52-53	Infinity Gauntlet X-over, Ron Lim art, bi-weekly	$0.50	$1.50	$2.50	£0.30	£0.90	£1.50
54	Infinity Gauntlet X-over, Ron Lim art, bi-weekly; Silver Surfer vs. Rhino	$0.50	$1.50	$2.50	£0.30	£0.90	£1.50
55	Infinity Gauntlet X-over, Ron Lim art, bi-weekly; Thanos appears	$0.50	$1.50	$2.50	£0.30	£0.90	£1.50
56-57	Infinity Gauntlet X-over, Ron Lim art, bi-weekly; Thanos appears	$0.40	$1.20	$2.00	£0.25	£0.75	£1.25
58	Infinity Gauntlet X-over, Dr. Strange and Hulk appear (return of the old Defenders), Ron Lim art, bi-weekly issue	$0.50	$1.50	$2.50	£0.30	£0.90	£1.50
59	Infinity Gauntlet X-over, Dr. Strange, Warlock appear, Ron Lim art, bi-weekly issue	$0.50	$1.50	$2.50	£0.30	£0.90	£1.50
60	Infinity Gauntlet epilogue, Ron Lim art, bi-weekly issue	$0.40	$1.20	$2.00	£0.25	£0.75	£1.25
61	Ron Lim art	$0.30	$0.90	$1.50	£0.20	£0.60	£1.00
62	$1.25 cover begins, Ron Lim art	$0.30	$0.90	$1.50	£0.20	£0.60	£1.00
63	Captain Marvel "returns", Ron Lim art	$0.30	$0.90	$1.50	£0.20	£0.60	£1.00
64	Silver Surfer vs. Dark Silver Surfer, Ron Lim art	$0.30	$0.90	$1.50	£0.20	£0.60	£1.00
65-66	Ron Lim art	$0.30	$0.90	$1.50	£0.20	£0.60	£1.00
67-69	Infinity War X-over, Galactus appears, Ron Lim cover, bi-weekly	$0.30	$0.90	$1.50	£0.20	£0.60	£1.00
70	The Herald War begins, bi-weekly	$0.30	$0.90	$1.50	£0.20	£0.60	£1.00
71	Firelord appears, bi-weekly; 1st appearance Morg	$0.25	$0.75	$1.25	£0.15	£0.45	£0.75
72-73	Firelord appears, bi-weekly	$0.25	$0.75	$1.25	£0.15	£0.45	£0.75
74	Firelord and Nova appear	$0.25	$0.75	$1.25	£0.15	£0.45	£0.75
75	conclusion to The Herald Ordeal, foil embossed cover	$0.40	$1.20	$2.00	£0.25	£0.75	£1.25
76-78	Jack of Hearts appears	$0.25	$0.75	$1.25	£0.15	£0.45	£0.75
79		$0.25	$0.75	$1.25	£0.15	£0.45	£0.75
80	1st appearance Ganymede	$0.25	$0.75	$1.25	£0.15	£0.45	£0.75
81		$0.25	$0.75	$1.25	£0.15	£0.45	£0.75
82	Jack of Hearts and Beta Ray Bill appear	$0.25	$0.75	$1.25	£0.15	£0.45	£0.75
83-85	Infinity Crusade X-over	$0.25	$0.75	$1.25	£0.15	£0.45	£0.75
85	ND pre-bagged with Dirt Magazine and sticker	$0.60	$1.80	$3.00	£0.40	£1.20	£2.00
86	Blood and Thunder part 6; Dr. Strange, Warlock and the Infinity Watch appear	$0.25	$0.75	$1.25	£0.15	£0.45	£0.75
87		$0.25	$0.75	$1.25	£0.15	£0.45	£0.75
88	Blood and Thunder part 10; Silver Surfer and Thanos team-up	$0.25	$0.75	$1.25	£0.15	£0.45	£0.75
89-90		$0.25	$0.75	$1.25	£0.15	£0.45	£0.75
91	Ron Lim cover and art	$0.25	$0.75	$1.25	£0.15	£0.45	£0.75
92	Ron Lim cover and art; with free Spiderman and his Deadly Foes card sheet	$0.25	$0.75	$1.25	£0.15	£0.45	£0.75
93	Down to Earth story begins as Silver Surfer returns to Earth...	$0.25	$0.75	$1.25	£0.15	£0.45	£0.75
94	Adam Warlock and Fantastic Four appear	$0.25	$0.75	$1.25	£0.15	£0.45	£0.75
95		$0.25	$0.75	$1.25	£0.15	£0.45	£0.75
96	Fantastic Four appear	$0.25	$0.75	$1.25	£0.15	£0.45	£0.75
97-99		$0.25	$0.75	$1.25	£0.15	£0.45	£0.75
100	48pgs, Silver Surfer vs. Mephisto	$0.50	$1.50	$2.50	£0.30	£0.90	£1.50
100	48pgs, Hologram cover	$0.80	$2.40	$4.00	£0.50	£1.50	£2.50
101-104		$0.30	$0.90	$1.50	£0.20	£0.60	£1.00
105	Silver Surfer vs. Skrull						

Issue	Description	$Good	$Fine	$N.Mint	£Good	£Fine	£N.Mint
		$0.30	$0.90	$1.50	£0.20	£0.60	£1.00
106	Legacy and Morg guest-star	$0.30	$0.90	$1.50	£0.20	£0.60	£1.00
107	Galactus, Morg and Tyrant appear	$0.30	$0.90	$1.50	£0.20	£0.60	£1.00
108-109	Galactus vs. Tyrant; bi-weekly	$0.30	$0.90	$1.50	£0.20	£0.60	£1.00
110	Nebula appears, John Buscema art	$0.30	$0.90	$1.50	£0.20	£0.60	£1.00
111-114	George Perez scripts begin; $1.95 cover begins	$0.40	$1.20	$2.00	£0.25	£0.75	£1.25
Title Value:		$52.00	$156.00	$260.00	£34.10	£102.30	£170.50

Silver Surfer: Rebirth of Thanos (Jun 1993)

Description	$Good	$Fine	$N.Mint	£Good	£Fine	£N.Mint
Trade paperback reprints issues #34-38				£1.60	£4.80	£8.00

SILVER SURFER (3RD SERIES) ANNUAL

Marvel Comics Group; 1 1988-present

Issue	Description	$Good	$Fine	$N.Mint	£Good	£Fine	£N.Mint
1	ND scarce in the U.K. squarebound, Evolutionary War; 1st Ron Lim art on the Silver Surfer	$0.80	$2.40	$4.00	£0.50	£1.50	£2.50
2	ND squarebound Atlantis Attacks part 1	$0.50	$1.50	$2.50	£0.30	£0.90	£1.50
3	ND Lifeform story conclusion	$0.50	$1.50	$2.50	£0.30	£0.90	£1.50
4	ND story continues in Guardians of the Galaxy Annual #1 (many copies have crinkled spine owing to production process)	$0.50	$1.50	$2.50	£0.30	£0.90	£1.50
5	ND Return of the Defenders part 3, guest stars Dr. Strange, Hulk, Sub-Mariner, continued in Dr. Strange Annual #2	$0.50	$1.50	$2.50	£0.30	£0.90	£1.50
6	ND 64pgs, pre-bagged with trading card, 1st appearance Legacy	$0.60	$1.80	$3.00	£0.40	£1.20	£2.00
7	ND 64pgs, Firelord, Air-Walker and Galactus appear	$0.60	$1.80	$3.00	£0.40	£1.20	£2.00
Title Value:		$4.00	$12.00	$20.00	£2.50	£7.50	£12.50

SILVER SURFER (LIMITED SERIES)

Marvel Comics Group,MS; 1 Dec 1988-2 Jan 1989

Issue	Description	$Good	$Fine	$N.Mint	£Good	£Fine	£N.Mint
1-2	ND scarce in the U.K. Stan Lee script, Moebius art	$0.60	$1.80	$3.00	£0.40	£1.20	£2.00
Title Value:		$1.20	$3.60	$6.00	£0.80	£2.40	£4.00

Silver Surfer: Parable Hardback

Description	$Good	$Fine	$N.Mint	£Good	£Fine	£N.Mint
(Apr 1989). Reprints 2 issue mini-series				£2.40	£7.20	£12.00

Silver Surfer: Parable Softback (Jul 1991)

Description	$Good	$Fine	$N.Mint	£Good	£Fine	£N.Mint
reprints mini-series plus new material				£1.20	£3.60	£6.00

SILVER SURFER ASHCAN EDITION

Marvel Comics Group,OS; nn May 1995

Issue	Description	$Good	$Fine	$N.Mint	£Good	£Fine	£N.Mint
nn	ND 16pgs, black and white	$0.15	$0.45	$0.75	£0.10	£0.30	£0.50
Title Value:		$0.15	$0.45	$0.75	£0.10	£0.30	£0.50

SILVER SURFER VS. DRACULA

Marvel Comics Group,OS; 1 Feb 1994

Issue	Description	$Good	$Fine	$N.Mint	£Good	£Fine	£N.Mint
1	ND reprints Tomb of Dracula #50, new Ron Lim cover	$0.30	$0.90	$1.50	£0.20	£0.60	£1.00
Title Value:		$0.30	$0.90	$1.50	£0.20	£0.60	£1.00

SILVER SURFER/WARLOCK: RESURRECTION

Marvel Comics Group,MS; 1 Mar 1993-4 Jun 1993

Issue	Description	$Good	$Fine	$N.Mint	£Good	£Fine	£N.Mint
1-4	Jim Starlin script and art with Terry Austin	$0.40	$1.20	$2.00	£0.25	£0.75	£1.25
Title Value:		$1.60	$4.80	$8.00	£1.00	£3.00	£5.00

SILVER SURFER: THE FIRST COMING OF GALACTUS

Marvel Comics Group,OS; 1 Feb 1993

Issue	Description	$Good	$Fine	$N.Mint	£Good	£Fine	£N.Mint
1	ND 64pgs, reprints Fantastic Four #48-#50, Ron Lim cover	$1.00	$3.00	$5.00	£0.70	£2.10	£3.50
Title Value:		$1.00	$3.00	$5.00	£0.70	£2.10	£3.50

SILVER SURFER: THE ULTIMATE COSMIC EXPERIENCE

Marvel Comics Group; nn 1978

Issue	Description	$Good	$Fine	$N.Mint	£Good	£Fine	£N.Mint
nn	ND rare in the U.K. 114pgs, Stan Lee script Jack Kirby art, Earl Norem cover	$21.00	$62.50	$150.00	£14.00	£43.00	£100.00
Title Value:		$21.00	$62.50	$150.00	£14.00	£43.00	£100.00

SILVERBACK

Comico,MS; 1 Oct 1989-3 Dec 1989

Issue	Description	$Good	$Fine	$N.Mint	£Good	£Fine	£N.Mint
1-3	ND Matt Wagner plot, John Beck art	$0.40	$1.20	$2.00	£0.25	£0.75	£1.25
Title Value:		$1.20	$3.60	$6.00	£0.75	£2.25	£3.75

SILVERBLADE

DC Comics,MS; 1 Sep 1987-12 Aug 1988

Issue	Description	$Good	$Fine	$N.Mint	£Good	£Fine	£N.Mint
1	Gene Colan art begins; includes bound-in poster	$0.15	$0.45	$0.75	£0.10	£0.35	£0.60
2-12		$0.15	$0.45	$0.75	£0.10	£0.35	£0.60
Title Value:		$1.80	$5.40	$9.00	£1.20	£4.20	£7.20

SILVERHAWKS

Marvel Comics Group,Star; 1 Aug 1987-6 Jun 1988

Issue	Description	$Good	$Fine	$N.Mint	£Good	£Fine	£N.Mint
1-6	ND	$0.15	$0.45	$0.75	£0.10	£0.35	£0.60
Title Value:		$0.90	$2.70	$4.50	£0.60	£2.10	£3.60

SILVERHEELS

Pacific; 1 Dec 1983-3 May 1984

Issue	Description	$Good	$Fine	$N.Mint	£Good	£Fine	£N.Mint
1	ND Bruce Jones script, Scott Hampton, Ken Steacy art	$0.40	$1.20	$2.00	£0.25	£0.75	£1.25
2	ND Scott Hampton, Ken Steacy art	$0.40	$1.20	$2.00	£0.25	£0.75	£1.25
3	ND Scott Hampton art, Ken Steacy, J. Hernandez back-ups	$0.40	$1.20	$2.00	£0.25	£0.75	£1.25
Title Value:		$1.20	$3.60	$6.00	£0.75	£2.25	£3.75

BACK ISSUES!

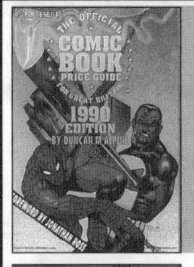

Nº 2 (1990)

Simon Bisley cover featuring Spiderman and the Punisher! Interior pin-ups by Ewins & Lloyd, Kitson and Ridgeway; first typeset Guide in the new familiar format. The days when Iron Man #55 was £4.00 and New Mutants #87 wasn't even out yet! £6.95

Special signed and hand-stamped edition £7.95

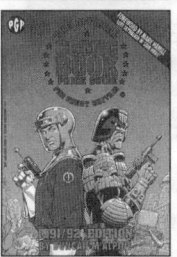

Nº 3 (1991)

Dave Gibbons cover featuring Judge Dredd and Dan Dare. New features include the famous First Appearance Index and Artist Gallery featuring Philips & Kane, Higgins & Hughes. £7.95

Special signed and hand-stamped edition £8.95

Signed and numbered Limited Edition. Only 250 of these were produced and some very low numbers (25-100) have been kept back for a first come, first served basis £9.95

Numbers #1–#10 also available . . . . please enquire

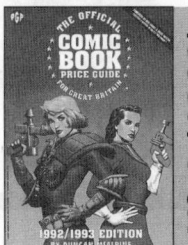

Nº 4 (1992)

Sean Philips cover featuring the "girlfriends" of Dredd and Dare— Judge Anderson and Dr. Jocelyn Peabody! Special colour section for the first time and many new features £8.95

Signed by author and cover artist £9.95

Special signed and hand-stamped edition £9.95

Signed and numbered Limited Edition. Only 50 of these were produced, signed by the author and cover artist £10.95

Numbers #1–#5 available . . . . please enquire

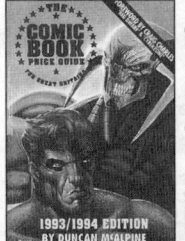

Nº 5 (1993)

Liam Sharpe cover featuring the unlikely team-up of Death's Head (a robot) and Magnus Robot Fighter £9.95

Signed by author and cover artist £10.95

Special signed and hand-stamped edition £10.95

Signed and numbered Limited Edition. Only 50 of these were produced, signed by the author and cover artist £11.95

Numbers #1–#5 available . . . . please enquire

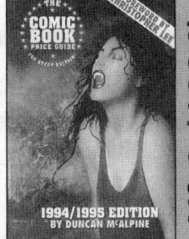

Nº 6 (1994)

John Bolton cover featuring a specially created character called "Liliana", one in a long line of vampiresses from the depths of the artist's imagination £10.95

Signed by author and cover artist £11.95

Special signed and hand-stamped edition £11.95

Signed and numbered Limited Edition. Only 50 of these were produced, signed by the author and cover artist £12.95

Numbers #1–#5 available . . . . please enquire

	$Good	$Fine	$N.Mint	£Good	£Fine	£N.Mint

SILVERHEELS (2ND SERIES)
Eclipse; (Graphic Novel 12); 1 1987
1 ND Jones/Campbell/Scott Hampton; completes story

	$Good	$Fine	$N.Mint	£Good	£Fine	£N.Mint
	$2.00	$6.00	$10.00	£1.40	£4.20	£7.00
Title Value:	$2.00	$6.00	$10.00	£1.40	£4.20	£7.00

SILVERSTORM
Aircel; 1 Jul 1990-4 1990
1-4 ND Steven Butler art

	$Good	$Fine	$N.Mint	£Good	£Fine	£N.Mint
	$0.40	$1.20	$2.00	£0.25	£0.75	£1.25
Title Value:	$1.60	$4.80	$8.00	£1.00	£3.00	£5.00

Silverstorm Collection (1991), reprints issues #1-4, new cover by Dave Dorman £1.05 £3.15 £5.25

SIMONSON, THE ART OF WALTER
DC Comics; nn Aug 1989
nn ND 208pgs, Trade paperback; reprints include Detective Comics #450, new intro by Howard Chaykin

	$Good	$Fine	$N.Mint	£Good	£Fine	£N.Mint
	$4.00	$12.00	$20.00	£2.50	£7.50	£12.50
Title Value:	$4.00	$12.00	$20.00	£2.50	£7.50	£12.50

SIMPSONS COMICS
Bongo Comics; 1 Dec 1993-present
1 ND pull-out poster; cover parody of Fantastic Four #1

	$Good	$Fine	$N.Mint	£Good	£Fine	£N.Mint
1	$0.80	$2.40	$4.00	£0.50	£1.50	£2.50
2-10 ND	$0.50	$1.50	$2.50	£0.30	£0.90	£1.50
11 ND 1st monthly issue	$0.45	$1.35	$2.25	£0.30	£0.90	£1.50
12-14 ND	$0.45	$1.35	$2.25	£0.30	£0.90	£1.50
Title Value:	$7.10	$21.30	$35.50	£4.40	£13.20	£22.00

Simpsons Comics Spectacular Vol. 1 (1995) 128pgs, selected reprints £1.30 £3.90 £6.50
Simpsons Comics Spectacular Vol. 2 (Jun 1995) selected reprints £1.30 £3.90 £6.50

SIMPSONS COMICS AND STORIES
Welsh Publishing,OS; 1 Apr 1993
1 ND pre-bagged with poster

	$Good	$Fine	$N.Mint	£Good	£Fine	£N.Mint
	$0.90	$2.70	$4.50	£0.60	£1.80	£3.00
Title Value:	$0.90	$2.70	$4.50	£0.60	£1.80	£3.00

SIMPSONS ILLUSTRATED 1992 ANNUAL
Marvel Comics Group,Magazine OS; 1 Apr 1992
1 ND pre-bagged with 3-D glasses

	$Good	$Fine	$N.Mint	£Good	£Fine	£N.Mint
	$0.60	$1.80	$3.00	£0.40	£1.20	£2.00
Title Value:	$0.60	$1.80	$3.00	£0.40	£1.20	£2.00

SIN CITY: A DAME TO KILL FOR
Dark Horse,MS; 1 Nov 1993-6 Apr 1994

	$Good	$Fine	$N.Mint	£Good	£Fine	£N.Mint
1 ND Frank Miller script and art	$0.80	$2.40	$4.00	£0.60	£1.80	£3.00
1 2nd printing, ND (Jul 1994)	$0.60	$1.80	$3.00	£0.40	£1.20	£2.00
2 ND Frank Miller script and art	$0.70	$2.10	$3.50	£0.50	£1.50	£2.50
2 2nd printing, ND (Jul 1994)	$0.60	$1.80	$3.00	£0.40	£1.20	£2.00
3 ND Frank Miller script and art	$0.60	$1.80	$3.00	£0.40	£1.20	£2.00
3 2nd printing, ND (Jul 1994)	$0.60	$1.80	$3.00	£0.40	£1.20	£2.00
4-6 ND Frank Miller script and art	$0.60	$1.80	$3.00	£0.40	£1.20	£2.00
Title Value:	$5.70	$17.10	$28.50	£3.90	£11.70	£19.50

Sin City: A Dame To Kill For Collection (Oct 1994) Trade paperback reprints mini-series with extra new pages by Frank Miller
Softcover £2.00 £6.00 £10.00
Hardcover £3.50 £10.50 £17.50
Signed, Limited Edition (Nov 1994) £12.00 £36.00 £60.00

SIN CITY: SILENT NIGHT
Dark Horse,OS; 1 Nov 1995
1 ND Frank Miller's wordless tale; black and white; card-stock cover

	$Good	$Fine	$N.Mint	£Good	£Fine	£N.Mint
	$0.60	$1.80	$3.00	£0.40	£1.20	£2.00
Title Value:	$0.60	$1.80	$3.00	£0.40	£1.20	£2.00

SIN CITY: THE BABE WORE RED & OTHER STORIES
Dark Horse,OS; 1 Nov 1994
1 ND Frank Miller script and art; black and white

	$Good	$Fine	$N.Mint	£Good	£Fine	£N.Mint
	$0.60	$1.80	$3.00	£0.40	£1.20	£2.00
Title Value:	$0.60	$1.80	$3.00	£0.40	£1.20	£2.00

SIN CITY: THE BIG FAT KILL
Dark Horse,MS; 1 Nov 1994-5 Mar 1995
1-5 ND Frank Miller script and art, black and white

	$Good	$Fine	$N.Mint	£Good	£Fine	£N.Mint
	$0.60	$1.80	$3.00	£0.40	£1.20	£2.00
Title Value:	$3.00	$9.00	$15.00	£2.00	£6.00	£10.00

SINBAD
Adventure,MS; 1 Feb 1990-4 May 1990

	$Good	$Fine	$N.Mint	£Good	£Fine	£N.Mint
1-4 ND	$0.40	$1.20	$2.00	£0.25	£0.75	£1.25
Title Value:	$1.60	$4.80	$8.00	£1.00	£3.00	£5.00

SINBAD: HOUSE OF GOD
Adventure,MS; 1 Mar 1991-4 Jun 1991

	$Good	$Fine	$N.Mint	£Good	£Fine	£N.Mint
1-4 ND	$0.40	$1.20	$2.00	£0.25	£0.75	£1.25
Title Value:	$1.60	$4.80	$8.00	£1.00	£3.00	£5.00

SINERGY
Caliber Press; 1 Apr 1993-5 Oct 1993

	$Good	$Fine	$N.Mint	£Good	£Fine	£N.Mint
1 ND	$0.50	$1.50	$2.50	£0.30	£0.90	£1.50
1 ND Signed, Numbered Edition - 2,000 copies	$0.80	$2.40	$4.00	£0.50	£1.50	£2.50
2 ND	$0.50	$1.50	$2.50	£0.30	£0.90	£1.50
2 ND Limited Edition, signed by different creators; 2,000 copies	$0.60	$1.80	$3.00	£0.40	£1.20	£2.00
3 ND	$0.50	$1.50	$2.50	£0.30	£0.90	£1.50
3 ND Limited Edition, signed by different creators; 2,000 copies	$0.60	$1.80	$3.00	£0.40	£1.20	£2.00
4 ND	$0.50	$1.50	$2.50	£0.30	£0.90	£1.50
4 ND Limited Edition, signed by different creators; 2,000 copies	$0.60	$1.80	$3.00	£0.40	£1.20	£2.00
5 ND	$0.50	$1.50	$2.50	£0.30	£0.90	£1.50
5 ND Limited Edition, signed by different creators; 2,000 copies	$0.60	$1.80	$3.00	£0.40	£1.20	£2.00
Title Value:	$5.70	$17.10	$28.50	£3.60	£10.80	£18.00

Sinergy Graphic Novel (Jul 1994) 176pgs collects mini-series £2.00 £6.00 £10.00
Deluxe Edition, signed with print £2.70 £8.10 £13.50

SINISTER HOUSE OF SECRET LOVE
DC Comics; 1 Oct/Nov 1971-4 Apr/May 1972
(becomes Secrets of Sinister House)

	$Good	$Fine	$N.Mint	£Good	£Fine	£N.Mint
1 ND 52pgs, gothic romance/mysteries begin	$1.50	$4.50	$7.50	£1.00	£3.00	£5.00
2 ND 52pgs	$0.80	$2.40	$4.00	£0.50	£1.50	£2.50
3-4 ND 52pgs	$0.60	$1.80	$3.00	£0.40	£1.20	£2.00
Title Value:	$3.50	$10.50	$17.50	£2.30	£6.90	£11.50

SINKING GRAPHIC NOVEL
Marvel Comics Group,OS; nn Dec 1992
nn ND 80pgs, James Hudnall script, Rob Ortelezah art

	$Good	$Fine	$N.Mint	£Good	£Fine	£N.Mint
	$3.00	$9.00	$15.00	£2.00	£6.00	£10.00
Title Value:	$3.00	$9.00	$15.00	£2.00	£6.00	£10.00

SINNER
Fantagraphics,Magazine; 1 Spring 1987-7 1990?

	$Good	$Fine	$N.Mint	£Good	£Fine	£N.Mint
1-7 ND Munoz art	$0.60	$1.80	$3.00	£0.40	£1.20	£2.00
Title Value:	$4.20	$12.60	$21.00	£2.80	£8.40	£14.00

SIREN
Marvel Comics Group; 1 Dec 1995-3 Feb 1996

	$Good	$Fine	$N.Mint	£Good	£Fine	£N.Mint
1 ND Hank Kanaiz script, Kevin West and Bob Almond art; Siren and Diamondback vs. War Machine	$0.30	$0.90	$1.50	£0.20	£0.60	£1.00
1 ND variant cover, computer painted cover by Chuck Maiden	$0.80	$2.40	$4.00	£0.50	£1.50	£2.50
1 ND Signed Limited Edition (Jan 1996), with certificate; 2,000 copies	$1.50	$4.50	$7.50	£1.00	£3.00	£5.00
2 ND flip-book format with Phoenix Ressurrection chapter	$0.30	$0.90	$1.50	£0.20	£0.60	£1.00
3 ND	$0.30	$0.90	$1.50	£0.20	£0.60	£1.00
Title Value:	$3.20	$9.60	$16.00	£2.10	£6.30	£10.50

SIREN: INFINITY
Marvel Comics Group,OS; nn Nov 1995

	$Good	$Fine	$N.Mint	£Good	£Fine	£N.Mint
nn ND Black September tie-in; spin-off from Ultraforce/Avengers X-over, War Machine appears	$0.50	$1.50	$2.50	£0.30	£0.90	£1.50
nn Variant cover, ND 1 copy received for every 5 copies of the regular issue ordered	$0.80	$2.40	$4.00	£0.50	£1.50	£2.50
Title Value:	$1.30	$3.90	$6.50	£0.80	£2.40	£4.00

SISTERHOOD OF STEEL
Eclipse; (Graphic Novel 13); 1 1987
(see Marvel series)
nn ND Christy Marx, Pete Ledger

	$Good	$Fine	$N.Mint	£Good	£Fine	£N.Mint
	$1.50	$4.50	$7.50	£1.00	£3.00	£5.00
Title Value:	$1.50	$4.50	$7.50	£1.00	£3.00	£5.00

SISTERHOOD OF STEEL, THE
Marvel Comics Group/Epic; 1 Dec 1984-8 Apr 1986
(see Marvel Graphic Novel)

	$Good	$Fine	$N.Mint	£Good	£Fine	£N.Mint
1-8 ND Baxter paper	$0.30	$0.90	$1.50	£0.20	£0.60	£1.00
Title Value:	$2.40	$7.20	$12.00	£1.60	£4.80	£8.00

SIX FROM SIRIUS
Marvel Comics Group/Epic,MS; 1 Jul 1984-4 Oct 1984

	$Good	$Fine	$N.Mint	£Good	£Fine	£N.Mint
1-4 ND Gulacy art	$0.40	$1.20	$2.00	£0.25	£0.75	£1.25
Title Value:	$1.60	$4.80	$8.00	£1.00	£3.00	£5.00

Trade paperback, reprints #1-4 £1.00 £3.00 £5.00

SIX FROM SIRIUS II
Marvel Comics Group/Epic,MS; 1 Feb 1986-4 May 1986

	$Good	$Fine	$N.Mint	£Good	£Fine	£N.Mint
1-4 ND Gulacy art	$0.40	$1.20	$2.00	£0.25	£0.75	£1.25
Title Value:	$1.60	$4.80	$8.00	£1.00	£3.00	£5.00

SIX GUN HEROES
A Plus Comics; 1 Jul 1991
1 ND 48pgs, western reprints including Steve Ditko art

	$Good	$Fine	$N.Mint	£Good	£Fine	£N.Mint
	$0.40	$1.20	$2.00	£0.25	£0.75	£1.25
Title Value:	$0.40	$1.20	$2.00	£0.25	£0.75	£1.25

SIX MILLION DOLLAR MAN
Charlton; 1 Jun 1976-9 Jul 1978

	$Good	$Fine	$N.Mint	£Good	£Fine	£N.Mint
1 scarce in the U.K. Joe Staton art begins, Staton painted cover	$0.60	$1.80	$3.00	£0.40	£1.20	£2.00
2 scarce in the U.K. Neal Adams cover	$0.50	$1.50	$2.50	£0.30	£0.90	£1.50
3 scarce in the U.K.	$0.40	$1.20	$2.00	£0.25	£0.75	£1.25
4-6	$0.30	$0.90	$1.50	£0.20	£0.60	£1.00
7-9 scarce in the U.K.	$0.30	$0.90	$1.50	£0.25	£0.75	£1.25
Title Value:	$3.30	$9.90	$16.50	£2.30	£6.90	£11.50

Note: all distributed in the U.K. Note also: irregularly published

SIX MILLION DOLLAR MAN (MAGAZINE)
Charlton,Magazine; 1 Jun 1976-8 Mar 1978

	$Good	$Fine	$N.Mint	£Good	£Fine	£N.Mint
1 ND Neal Adams art						
	$0.60	$1.80	$3.00	£0.60	£1.80	£3.00
2-8 ND	$0.40	$1.20	$2.00	£0.40	£1.20	£2.00
Title Value:	$3.40	$10.20	$17.00	£3.40	£10.20	£17.00

SIX-GUN HEROES
Charlton; 24 Jan 1954-83 Apr 1965

	$Good	$Fine	$N.Mint	£Good	£Fine	£N.Mint
24 scarce in the U.K.						
	$15.50	$47.00	$110.00	£10.50	£32.00	£75.00
25 scarce in the U.K.						
	$9.00	$28.00	$55.00	£5.75	£17.50	£35.00
26-30	$7.50	$22.50	$45.00	£5.00	£15.00	£30.00
31-40	$6.25	$18.50	$37.50	£4.15	£12.50	£25.00
41-50	$5.75	$17.50	$35.00	£3.75	£11.00	£22.50
51-56	$3.75	$11.00	$22.50	£2.50	£7.50	£15.00
57 1st appearance Gunmaster						
	$5.00	$15.00	$30.00	£3.30	£10.00	£20.00
58-60	$3.75	$11.00	$22.50	£2.50	£7.50	£15.00
61-70	$2.90	$8.75	$17.50	£2.05	£6.25	£12.50
71-83	$2.50	$7.50	$15.00	£1.65	£5.00	£10.00
Title Value:	$282.25	$846.50	$1717.50	£188.00	£564.50	£1145.00

Note: reasonable distribution of issues in the U.K. after 1959/60

SIXTY SEVEN SECONDS GRAPHIC NOVEL
Marvel Comics Group,OS; nn Dec 1992

	$Good	$Fine	$N.Mint	£Good	£Fine	£N.Mint
nn ND 80pgs, Robinson script, Steve Yeowell art						
	$3.00	$9.00	$15.00	£2.00	£6.00	£10.00
Title Value:	$3.00	$9.00	$15.00	£2.00	£6.00	£10.00

SKATEMAN
Pacific; 1 Nov 1983

	$Good	$Fine	$N.Mint	£Good	£Fine	£N.Mint
1 ND Neal Adams story and art						
	$0.30	$0.90	$1.50	£0.20	£0.60	£1.00
Title Value:	$0.30	$0.90	$1.50	£0.20	£0.60	£1.00

SKELETON WARRIORS
Marvel Comics Group,MS; 1 Apr 1995-4 Jul 1995

	$Good	$Fine	$N.Mint	£Good	£Fine	£N.Mint
1-4 ND based on US animated series						
	$0.25	$0.75	$1.25	£0.15	£0.45	£0.75
Title Value:	$1.00	$3.00	$5.00	£0.60	£1.80	£3.00

SKIDMARKS
Tundra,MS; 1 Aug 1992

	$Good	$Fine	$N.Mint	£Good	£Fine	£N.Mint
1 ND reprints British independent comic from the '80s						
	$0.50	$1.50	$2.50	£0.30	£0.90	£1.50
Title Value:	$0.50	$1.50	$2.50	£0.30	£0.90	£1.50

SKIN GRAFT
DC Comics/Vertigo,MS; 1 Jul 1993-4 Oct 1993

	$Good	$Fine	$N.Mint	£Good	£Fine	£N.Mint
1 Warren Pleece art begins, photo covers begin; sub-titled "The Adventures of a Tattooed Man"						
(Note: The Tattooed Man - a Green Lantern villain)						
	$0.50	$1.50	$2.50	£0.30	£0.90	£1.50
2-4	$0.50	$1.50	$2.50	£0.30	£0.90	£1.50
Title Value:	$2.00	$6.00	$10.00	£1.20	£3.60	£6.00

SKREEMER
DC Comics,MS; 1 May 1989-6 Oct 1989

	$Good	$Fine	$N.Mint	£Good	£Fine	£N.Mint
1-6 ND	$0.25	$0.75	$1.25	£0.15	£0.45	£0.75
Title Value:	$1.50	$4.50	$7.50	£0.90	£2.70	£4.50

Note: Mature Readers label. 1st DC creator-owned project (see Tempus Fugitives); Peter Milligan script/Brett Ewins art

SKROG
Comico; 1 1984

	$Good	$Fine	$N.Mint	£Good	£Fine	£N.Mint
1 ND black and white						
	$0.40	$1.20	$2.00	£0.25	£0.75	£1.25
Title Value:	$0.40	$1.20	$2.00	£0.25	£0.75	£1.25

SKROG (YIP YIP YAY) SPECIAL
Crystal; 1 Dec 1987

	$Good	$Fine	$N.Mint	£Good	£Fine	£N.Mint
1 ND 64pgs, black and white						
	$0.40	$1.20	$2.00	£0.25	£0.75	£1.25
Title Value:	$0.40	$1.20	$2.00	£0.25	£0.75	£1.25

SKRULL KILL KREW
Marvel Comics Group,MS; 1 Sep 1995-5 Jan 1996

	$Good	$Fine	$N.Mint	£Good	£Fine	£N.Mint
1-5 ND Grant Morrison and Mark Millar script, Steve Yeowell and Chris Ivy art						
	$0.60	$1.80	$3.00	£0.40	£1.20	£2.00
Title Value:	$3.00	$9.00	$15.00	£2.00	£6.00	£10.00

SKULL AND BONES
DC Comics,MS; 1 Feb 1992-3 Apr 1992

	$Good	$Fine	$N.Mint	£Good	£Fine	£N.Mint
1-3 ND 48pgs	$0.80	$2.40	$4.00	£0.50	£1.50	£2.50
Title Value:	$2.40	$7.20	$12.00	£1.50	£4.50	£7.50

SKULL THE SLAYER
Marvel Comics Group; 1 Aug 1975-8 Nov 1976

	$Good	$Fine	$N.Mint	£Good	£Fine	£N.Mint
1 ND 1st appearance of Skull The Slayer; Marv Wolfman script begins						
	$0.40	$1.20	$2.00	£0.25	£0.75	£1.25
2-3	$0.30	$0.90	$1.50	£0.20	£0.60	£1.00
4-5 Black Knight appears						
	$0.30	$0.90	$1.50	£0.20	£0.60	£1.00
6-8	$0.30	$0.90	$1.50	£0.20	£0.60	£1.00
Title Value:	$2.50	$7.50	$12.50	£1.65	£4.95	£8.25

SKY GAL
AC Comics; 1 Sep 1993-3 1994

	$Good	$Fine	$N.Mint	£Good	£Fine	£N.Mint
1 ND pre-bagged with trading card						
	$0.60	$1.80	$3.00	£0.40	£1.20	£2.00
2-3 ND	$0.60	$1.80	$3.00	£0.40	£1.20	£2.00
Title Value:	$1.80	$5.40	$9.00	£1.20	£3.60	£6.00

SKY WOLF
Eclipse,MS; 1 Mar 1988-3 Oct 1988
(see Airboy)

	$Good	$Fine	$N.Mint	£Good	£Fine	£N.Mint
1-3 ND Tom Lyle cover and art; colour						
	$0.40	$1.20	$2.00	£0.25	£0.75	£1.25
Title Value:	$1.20	$3.60	$6.00	£0.75	£2.25	£3.75

SKY-HOPPER
Illuminated Comics; 1 Feb 1991

	$Good	$Fine	$N.Mint	£Good	£Fine	£N.Mint
1 ND black and white						
	$0.15	$0.45	$0.75	£0.10	£0.30	£0.50
Title Value:	$0.15	$0.45	$0.75	£0.10	£0.30	£0.50

SLAPSTICK
Marvel Comics Group,MS; 1 Nov 1992-4 Feb 1993

	$Good	$Fine	$N.Mint	£Good	£Fine	£N.Mint
1-3	$0.25	$0.75	$1.25	£0.15	£0.45	£0.75
4 Ghost Rider, Daredevil, Captain America, Fantastic Four and Speedball appear						
	$0.25	$0.75	$1.25	£0.15	£0.45	£0.75
Title Value:	$1.00	$3.00	$5.00	£0.60	£1.80	£3.00

SLASH
Northstar; 1 Aug 1992-7 1993?

	$Good	$Fine	$N.Mint	£Good	£Fine	£N.Mint
1 ND horror anthology						
	$0.50	$1.50	$2.50	£0.30	£0.90	£1.50
1 ND red embossed cover						
	$0.80	$2.40	$4.00	£0.50	£1.50	£2.50
2-6 ND	$0.50	$1.50	$2.50	£0.30	£0.90	£1.50
7 ND $2.95 cover	$0.60	$1.80	$3.00	£0.40	£1.20	£2.00
Title Value:	$4.40	$13.20	$22.00	£2.70	£8.10	£13.50

SLASH ANNUAL
Northstar; 1 Jan 1994

	$Good	$Fine	$N.Mint	£Good	£Fine	£N.Mint
1 ND 48pgs, black and white						
	$0.90	$2.70	$4.50	£0.60	£1.80	£3.00
Title Value:	$0.90	$2.70	$4.50	£0.60	£1.80	£3.00

SLASH MARAUD
DC Comics,MS; 1 Nov 1987-6 Apr 1988

	$Good	$Fine	$N.Mint	£Good	£Fine	£N.Mint
1-6 ND Gulacy art	$0.25	$0.75	$1.25	£0.15	£0.45	£0.75

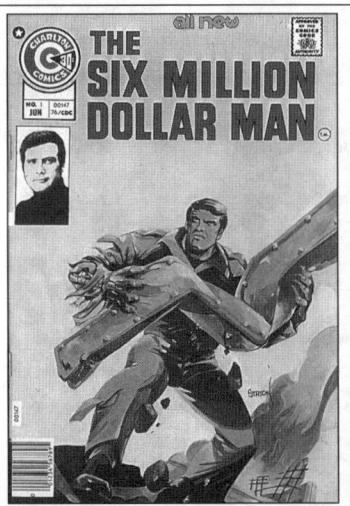

Six Million Dollar Man #1

Skate Man #1

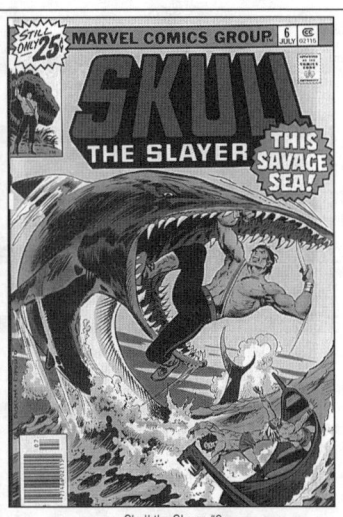

Skull the Slayer #6

MINT = 100% / NEAR MINT (inc. +/-) = 90–99% / VERY FINE (inc. +/-) = 75–89% / FINE (inc. +/-) = 55–74%
VERY GOOD (inc. +/-) = 35–54% / GOOD (inc. +/-) = 15–34% / FAIR = 5–14% / POOR = 1–4%

547

	$Good	$Fine	$N.Mint	£Good	£Fine	£N.Mint
Title Value:	$1.50	$4.50	$7.50	£0.90	£2.70	£4.50

Note: Mature Readers, Deluxe Format.

SLAUGHTERHOUSE USA

Innovation,OS; 1 Jun 1991

	$Good	$Fine	$N.Mint	£Good	£Fine	£N.Mint
1 ND	$0.40	$1.20	$2.00	£0.25	£0.75	£1.25
Title Value:	$0.40	$1.20	$2.00	£0.25	£0.75	£1.25

SLAUGHTERMAN

Comico; 1 Feb 1983-2 1983

	$Good	$Fine	$N.Mint	£Good	£Fine	£N.Mint
1-2 ND	$0.40	$1.20	$2.00	£0.25	£0.75	£1.25
Title Value:	$0.80	$2.40	$4.00	£0.50	£1.50	£2.50

SLEDGE HAMMER

Marvel Comics Group,MS TV; 1 Feb 1988-2 Mar 1988

	$Good	$Fine	$N.Mint	£Good	£Fine	£N.Mint
1 Satana appears	$0.25	$0.75	$1.25	£0.15	£0.45	£0.75
2 "Spiderman" appears	$0.25	$0.75	$1.25	£0.15	£0.45	£0.75
Title Value:	$0.50	$1.50	$2.50	£0.30	£0.90	£1.50

SLEEPWALKER

Marvel Comics Group; 1 Jun 1991-33 Mar 1994

	$Good	$Fine	$N.Mint	£Good	£Fine	£N.Mint
1 ND Blevins art begins	$0.30	$0.90	$1.50	£0.20	£0.60	£1.00
2 ND Blevins art	$0.25	$0.75	$1.25	£0.15	£0.45	£0.75
3 ND X-Factor/X-Men/Fantastic Four/Avengers appear in dream sequence, Blevins art	$0.25	$0.75	$1.25	£0.15	£0.45	£0.75
4 ND Leonardi art	$0.25	$0.75	$1.25	£0.15	£0.45	£0.75
5 ND Blevins art, Spiderman, Kingpin appear	$0.25	$0.75	$1.25	£0.15	£0.45	£0.75
6 ND Blevins art, Infinity Gauntlet X-over, Spiderman appears	$0.25	$0.75	$1.25	£0.15	£0.45	£0.75
7 ND Infinity Gauntlet X-over	$0.25	$0.75	$1.25	£0.15	£0.45	£0.75
8 ND Deathlok appears	$0.25	$0.75	$1.25	£0.15	£0.45	£0.75
9 $1.25 cover begins	$0.25	$0.75	$1.25	£0.15	£0.45	£0.75
10	$0.25	$0.75	$1.25	£0.15	£0.45	£0.75
11 Sleepwalker vs. Ghost Rider	$0.25	$0.75	$1.25	£0.15	£0.45	£0.75
12 Nightmare appears, upside down logo	$0.25	$0.75	$1.25	£0.15	£0.45	£0.75
13	$0.25	$0.75	$1.25	£0.15	£0.45	£0.75
14 intro Spectra	$0.25	$0.75	$1.25	£0.15	£0.45	£0.75
15 Fantastic Four guest star	$0.25	$0.75	$1.25	£0.15	£0.45	£0.75
16 Mr. Fantastic and The Thing appear	$0.25	$0.75	$1.25	£0.15	£0.45	£0.75
17 X-over Darkhawk #20, Darkhawk and Spiderman appear	$0.25	$0.75	$1.25	£0.15	£0.45	£0.75
18 Infinity War X-over, Professor Xavier appears, Joe Quesada cover	$0.25	$0.75	$1.25	£0.15	£0.45	£0.75
19 Halloween issue with pop-out mask on cover	$0.30	$0.90	$1.50	£0.20	£0.60	£1.00
20 Sam Kieth cover	$0.25	$0.75	$1.25	£0.15	£0.45	£0.75
21 Hobgoblin appears, Sam Kieth cover	$0.25	$0.75	$1.25	£0.15	£0.45	£0.75
22 Hobgoblin appears	$0.25	$0.75	$1.25	£0.15	£0.45	£0.75
23-24	$0.25	$0.75	$1.25	£0.15	£0.45	£0.75
25 48pgs, "oil-slick" holo-grafix cover; new direction for title	$0.30	$0.90	$1.50	£0.20	£0.60	£1.00
26	$0.25	$0.75	$1.25	£0.15	£0.45	£0.75
27 Avengers guest-star	$0.25	$0.75	$1.25	£0.15	£0.45	£0.75
28-33	$0.25	$0.75	$1.25	£0.15	£0.45	£0.75
Title Value:	$8.40	$25.20	$42.00	£5.10	£15.30	£25.50

SLEEPWALKER HOLIDAY SPECIAL

Marvel Comics Group,OS; 1 Jan 1993

	$Good	$Fine	$N.Mint	£Good	£Fine	£N.Mint
1 ND 48pgs	$0.30	$0.90	$1.50	£0.20	£0.60	£1.00
Title Value:	$0.30	$0.90	$1.50	£0.20	£0.60	£1.00

SLEEZE BROTHERS

Marvel Comics Group/Epic,MS; 1 Aug 1989-6 Jan 1990

	$Good	$Fine	$N.Mint	£Good	£Fine	£N.Mint
1 ND Andy Lanning pencils begin	$0.25	$0.75	$1.25	£0.15	£0.45	£0.75
2-6 ND	$0.25	$0.75	$1.25	£0.15	£0.45	£0.75
Title Value:	$1.50	$4.50	$7.50	£0.90	£2.70	£4.50
Trade paperback reprints issues #1-6 plus 8pgs new material				£1.90	£5.70	£9.50

SLEEZE BROTHERS SPECIAL

Marvel Comics Group,OS; 1 Nov 1991

	$Good	$Fine	$N.Mint	£Good	£Fine	£N.Mint
1 ND 48pgs	$0.60	$1.80	$3.00	£0.40	£1.20	£2.00
Title Value:	$0.60	$1.80	$3.00	£0.40	£1.20	£2.00

SLOW DANCE WITH DEATH

Comico,OS; 1 May 1992

	$Good	$Fine	$N.Mint	£Good	£Fine	£N.Mint
1 ND 48pgs, duo-tone art	$0.80	$2.40	$4.00	£0.50	£1.50	£2.50
Title Value:	$0.80	$2.40	$4.00	£0.50	£1.50	£2.50

SLUDGE

Malibu Ultraverse; 1 Oct 1993-13 Nov 1994

	$Good	$Fine	$N.Mint	£Good	£Fine	£N.Mint
1 40pgs, Rune part 1, Steve Gerber script begins	$0.50	$1.50	$2.50	£0.30	£0.90	£1.50
2	$0.40	$1.20	$2.00	£0.25	£0.75	£1.25
3 Break Thru tie-in	$0.40	$1.20	$2.00	£0.25	£0.75	£1.25

(continued — right column)

	$Good	$Fine	$N.Mint	£Good	£Fine	£N.Mint
4 origin of Mantra	$0.40	$1.20	$2.00	£0.25	£0.75	£1.25
5-8	$0.40	$1.20	$2.00	£0.25	£0.75	£1.25
9-10 origin of Sludge	$0.40	$1.20	$2.00	£0.25	£0.75	£1.25
11	$0.40	$1.20	$2.00	£0.25	£0.75	£1.25
12 64pgs, flip-book format with Ultraverse Premiere #8	$0.50	$1.50	$2.50	£0.30	£0.90	£1.50
13	$0.40	$1.20	$2.00	£0.25	£0.75	£1.25
Title Value:	$5.40	$16.20	$27.00	£3.35	£10.05	£16.75

Note: all Non-Distributed on the news-stands in the U.K.

SLUDGE: RED XMAS

Malibu Ultraverse,OS; 1 Dec 1994

	$Good	$Fine	$N.Mint	£Good	£Fine	£N.Mint
1 ND Steve Gerber script, Mike Ploog art	$0.40	$1.20	$2.00	£0.25	£0.75	£1.25
Title Value:	$0.40	$1.20	$2.00	£0.25	£0.75	£1.25

SMURFS

Marvel Comics Group, TV; 1 Dec 1982-3 Feb 1983

	$Good	$Fine	$N.Mint	£Good	£Fine	£N.Mint
1-3 ND	$0.15	$0.45	$0.75	£0.10	£0.35	£0.60
Title Value:	$0.45	$1.35	$2.25	£0.30	£1.05	£1.80

SNAKE EYES

Fantagraphics,OS; nn Feb 1991

	$Good	$Fine	$N.Mint	£Good	£Fine	£N.Mint
nn 2nd printing, ND (Oct 1992)	$1.00	$3.00	$5.00	£0.70	£2.10	£3.50
nn ND 80pgs, anthology featuring Charles Burns and David Mazzuchelli	$1.20	$3.60	$6.00	£0.80	£2.40	£4.00
Title Value:	$2.20	$6.60	$11.00	£1.50	£4.50	£7.50

SNAKE, THE

Anubis Press; 0 Jan 1994; 1 Mar 1994

	$Good	$Fine	$N.Mint	£Good	£Fine	£N.Mint
0 ND black and white	$0.40	$1.20	$2.00	£0.25	£0.75	£1.25
0 ND Ashcan Edition (Feb 1994), 10,000 copies; black and white	$0.50	$1.50	$2.50	£0.30	£0.90	£1.50
1 ND Edward Morges script and art	$0.40	$1.20	$2.00	£0.25	£0.75	£1.25
1 ND Ashcan Edition (Sep 1994) - 5,000 copies, black and white	$0.50	$1.50	$2.50	£0.30	£0.90	£1.50
Title Value:	$1.80	$5.40	$9.00	£1.10	£3.30	£5.50

SNARF

Kitchen Sink; 1 1988-25 ?

	$Good	$Fine	$N.Mint	£Good	£Fine	£N.Mint
1-25 ND black and white	$0.25	$0.75	$1.25	£0.15	£0.45	£0.75
Title Value:	$6.25	$18.75	$31.25	£3.75	£11.25	£18.75

SNOW WHITE AND THE SEVEN DWARFS

Gladstone,Magazine OS; 1 1987

	$Good	$Fine	$N.Mint	£Good	£Fine	£N.Mint
1 ND 50th anniversary; adapts film	$0.80	$2.40	$4.00	£0.50	£1.50	£2.50
Title Value:	$0.80	$2.40	$4.00	£0.50	£1.50	£2.50

SNOW WHITE SPECIAL EDITION

Marvel Comics Group, Film; nn Jan 1995

	$Good	$Fine	$N.Mint	£Good	£Fine	£N.Mint
nn ND 48pgs, uses original artwork from 1937	$0.40	$1.20	$2.00	£0.25	£0.75	£1.25
Title Value:	$0.40	$1.20	$2.00	£0.25	£0.75	£1.25

SOAP OPERA ROMANCES

Charlton; 1 Jul 1982-5 Mar 1983

	$Good	$Fine	$N.Mint	£Good	£Fine	£N.Mint
1 Nurse Betsy Crane reprints from the early 60s begin; distributed in the U.K.	$0.25	$0.75	$1.25	£0.15	£0.45	£0.75
2-5 distributed in the U.K.	$0.25	$0.75	$1.25	£0.15	£0.45	£0.75
Title Value:	$1.25	$3.75	$6.25	£0.75	£2.25	£3.75

SOJOURN

White Cliffs Publishing Co.,Tabloid; 1 1977-2 Sep 1977

	$Good	$Fine	$N.Mint	£Good	£Fine	£N.Mint
1-2 ND John Severin, Sergio Aragones, Doug Wildey, Steve Bissette, Joe Kubert art; black and white	$0.40	$1.20	$2.00	£0.25	£0.75	£1.25
Title Value:	$0.80	$2.40	$4.00	£0.50	£1.50	£2.50

Note: magazine size which folds out to what can best be described as tabloid size. Joe Kubert covers

SOLAR, MAN OF THE ATOM

Valiant/Acclaim Comics; 1 Sep 1991-60 Mar 1996

(see Doctor Solar)

	$Good	$Fine	$N.Mint	£Good	£Fine	£N.Mint
1 return of the first Gold Key hero, script by Jim Shooter telling origin Solar	$2.00	$6.00	$10.00	£1.40	£4.20	£7.00
2	$1.40	$4.20	$7.00	£0.80	£2.40	£4.00
3 scarce in the U.K. 1st appearance Harada	$2.00	$6.00	$10.00	£1.40	£4.20	£7.00
4-5	$1.00	$3.00	$5.00	£0.60	£1.80	£3.00
6	$0.80	$2.40	$4.00	£0.40	£1.20	£2.00
7 X-O Manowar armour appears	$0.80	$2.40	$4.00	£0.40	£1.20	£2.00
8	$0.80	$2.40	$4.00	£0.40	£1.20	£2.00
9 Solar vs. God-Child	$0.80	$2.40	$4.00	£0.40	£1.20	£2.00
10 48pgs, black cover, title-embossed on heavier stock paper, Alpha & Omega by Barry Windsor-Smith concludes, 1st appearance Eternal Warrior, leads into Unity	$2.50	$7.50	$12.50	£1.50	£4.50	£7.50
10 2nd printing, Oct 1992	$0.50	$1.50	$2.50	£0.30	£0.90	£1.50
11 Unity prelude, Eternal Warrior (1st full appearance) vs. Harbinger	$0.50	$1.50	$2.50	£0.30	£0.90	£1.50
12 Unity: Chapter 9, Frank Miller cover	$0.50	$1.50	$2.50	£0.30	£0.90	£1.50
13 Unity: Chapter 17, the conclusion guest-starring all Valiant characters, Walt Simonson cover	$0.50	$1.50	$2.50	£0.30	£0.90	£1.50

TRADE PAPERBACKS, GRAPHIC NOVELS AND OTHER COLLECTIONS ARE PRICED IN POUNDS STERLING ONLY. CONVERT AT 1.5 FOR DOLLARS.

	$Good	$Fine	$N.Mint	£Good	£Fine	£N.Mint
14 1st appearence of Fred Bender a.k.a. Dr. Eclipse	$0.80	$2.40	$4.00	£0.50	£1.50	£2.50
15	$0.50	$1.50	$2.50	£0.30	£0.90	£1.50
16 Bob Layton scripts begin	$0.50	$1.50	$2.50	£0.30	£0.90	£1.50
17 continued from X-O Manowar #12	$0.50	$1.50	$2.50	£0.30	£0.90	£1.50
18 X-O Manowar appears	$0.50	$1.50	$2.50	£0.30	£0.90	£1.50
19-20	$0.50	$1.50	$2.50	£0.30	£0.90	£1.50
21-22 Master Darque appears	$0.40	$1.20	$2.00	£0.25	£0.75	£1.25
23 1st appearance of Solar the Destroyer as Solar splits into two beings	$0.40	$1.20	$2.00	£0.25	£0.75	£1.25
24	$0.40	$1.20	$2.00	£0.25	£0.75	£1.25
25 The Coming of the Darque Age story; Solar vs. Dr. Eclipse, continued in Secret Weapons #2	$0.40	$1.20	$2.00	£0.25	£0.75	£1.25
26-28	$0.40	$1.20	$2.00	£0.25	£0.75	£1.25
29 produced in Valiant Vision (3-D effect without altering basic art of comic)	$0.40	$1.20	$2.00	£0.25	£0.75	£1.25
30-32	$0.40	$1.20	$2.00	£0.25	£0.75	£1.25
33 with free Upper Deck trading card; in Valiant Vision (no glasses included)	$0.40	$1.20	$2.00	£0.25	£0.75	£1.25
34-35 in Valiant Vision (no glasses included)	$0.40	$1.20	$2.00	£0.25	£0.75	£1.25
36 Dr. Eclipse appears	$0.40	$1.20	$2.00	£0.25	£0.75	£1.25
37	$0.40	$1.20	$2.00	£0.25	£0.75	£1.25
38 Chaos Effect tie-in	$0.40	$1.20	$2.00	£0.25	£0.75	£1.25
39-40	$0.40	$1.20	$2.00	£0.25	£0.75	£1.25
41 Solar vs. Harada	$0.40	$1.20	$2.00	£0.25	£0.75	£1.25
42-45	$0.40	$1.20	$2.00	£0.25	£0.75	£1.25
46 1st Acclaim Comics issue, Dan Jurgens script and art begin; Brave New Worlds story	$0.40	$1.20	$2.00	£0.25	£0.75	£1.25
47 Brave New Worlds story	$0.40	$1.20	$2.00	£0.25	£0.75	£1.25
48-49 Brave New Worlds story; bi-weekly	$0.40	$1.20	$2.00	£0.25	£0.75	£1.25
50 DS, Brave New Worlds story conclusion	$0.50	$1.50	$2.50	£0.30	£0.90	£1.50
51-59 bi-weekly	$0.40	$1.20	$2.00	£0.25	£0.75	£1.25
60	$0.40	$1.20	$2.00	£0.25	£0.75	£1.25
Title Value:	$35.00	$105.00	$175.00	£21.45	£64.35	£107.25

Note: all Non-Distributed on the news-stands in the U.K.

Solar, Man of the Atom #0 (1994)

Trade paperback reprints 8pgs inserts from issues #1-10				£1.30	£3.90	£6.50

Solar, Man of the Atom #1 (Jan 1995)

Trade paperback reprints issues #1-4				£1.30	£3.90	£6.50

SOLARMAN
Marvel Comics Group; 1 Jan 1989; 2 May 1990

	$Good	$Fine	$N.Mint	£Good	£Fine	£N.Mint
1 Jim Mooney art, Stan Lee script	$0.25	$0.75	$1.25	£0.15	£0.45	£0.75
2 Stan Lee script, Mike Zeck art	$0.25	$0.75	$1.25	£0.15	£0.45	£0.75
Title Value:	$0.50	$1.50	$2.50	£0.30	£0.90	£1.50

SOLD OUT
Fantaco; 1,2 1986

	$Good	$Fine	$N.Mint	£Good	£Fine	£N.Mint
1-2 ND	$0.30	$0.90	$1.50	£0.20	£0.60	£1.00
Title Value:	$0.60	$1.80	$3.00	£0.40	£1.20	£2.00

SOLITAIRE
Malibu Ultraverse; 1 Nov 1993-12 Nov 1994

	$Good	$Fine	$N.Mint	£Good	£Fine	£N.Mint
1 Gerard Jones script and Jeff Johnson art begin	$0.40	$1.20	$2.00	£0.25	£0.75	£1.25
1 Collector's Edition - pre-bagged in black with a special edition playing card (Ace of Spades one being the rarest)	$0.50	$1.50	$2.50	£0.30	£0.90	£1.50
2	$0.40	$1.20	$2.00	£0.25	£0.75	£1.25
3 Night Man origin by Kevin Maguire	$0.40	$1.20	$2.00	£0.25	£0.75	£1.25
4-12	$0.40	$1.20	$2.00	£0.25	£0.75	£1.25
Title Value:	$5.30	$15.90	$26.50	£3.30	£9.90	£16.50

Note: all Non-Distributed on the news-stands in the U.K.

SOLO
Marvel Comics Group,MS; 1 Sep 1994-4 Dec 1994

	$Good	$Fine	$N.Mint	£Good	£Fine	£N.Mint
1-4 Spiderman guest-stars	$0.30	$0.90	$1.50	£0.20	£0.60	£1.00
Title Value:	$1.20	$3.60	$6.00	£0.80	£2.40	£4.00

SOLO AVENGERS (AVENGERS SPOTLIGHT)
Marvel Comics Group; 1 Dec 1987-40 Jan 1991

(becomes Avengers Spotlight 21 on)

	$Good	$Fine	$N.Mint	£Good	£Fine	£N.Mint
1 ND 2nd Jim Lee art for Marvel (see Alpha Flight #51)	$0.80	$2.40	$4.00	£0.30	£0.90	£1.50
2-3 ND	$0.30	$0.90	$1.50	£0.20	£0.60	£1.00
4 ND Ron Lim art	$0.30	$0.90	$1.50	£0.20	£0.60	£1.00
5-7 LD in the U.K.	$0.30	$0.90	$1.50	£0.20	£0.60	£1.00
8-11	$0.25	$0.75	$1.25	£0.15	£0.45	£0.75
12-13 Ron Lim art	$0.25	$0.75	$1.25	£0.15	£0.45	£0.75
14 Alan Davis She Hulk	$0.25	$0.75	$1.25	£0.15	£0.45	£0.75
15-20	$0.25	$0.75	$1.25	£0.15	£0.45	£0.75
21 title becomes Avengers Spotlight	$0.25	$0.75	$1.25	£0.15	£0.45	£0.75
22-24	$0.25	$0.75	$1.25	£0.15	£0.45	£0.75
25 Acts of Vengeance part 1	$0.25	$0.75	$1.25	£0.15	£0.45	£0.75
26-28 ND Acts of Vengeance tie-in	$0.25	$0.75	$1.25	£0.15	£0.45	£0.75
29 ND Acts of Vengeance epilogue	$0.25	$0.75	$1.25	£0.15	£0.45	£0.75
30 LD in the U.K. new costume/direction for Hawkeye	$0.25	$0.75	$1.25	£0.15	£0.45	£0.75
31-34 LD in the U.K. back-up story U.S.Agent	$0.25	$0.75	$1.25	£0.15	£0.45	£0.75
35 LD in the U.K. Tigra back-up begins (ends #37)	$0.25	$0.75	$1.25	£0.15	£0.45	£0.75
36-39 LD in the U.K. Avengers Re-Born story; Gilgamesh/Dr. Druid/Tigra/Black Knight featured	$0.25	$0.75	$1.25	£0.15	£0.45	£0.75
40 LD in the U.K. Avengers Re-Born epilogue	$0.25	$0.75	$1.25	£0.15	£0.45	£0.75
Title Value:	$10.85	$32.55	$53.75	£6.45	£19.35	£32.25

ARTISTS

Grindberg in 6. Guice in 7, 13. Ron Lim in 4, 13. John Ridgway in 5.

FEATURES

Black Knight in 4. Black Widow in 7, 14. Captain Marvel in 2. Dr.Druid in 10. Falcon in 6. Hawkeye in all. Hellcat in 9. Hercules in 11. Mockingbird in 1. Moondragon in 16. Moonknight in 3. Scarlet Witch in 5. Sub-Mariner in 17. Wasp in 15. Wonder man in 13. Yellowjacket in 12.

SOLO EX-MUTANTS
Eternity; 1 Jan 1988-6 1989

(see Ex-Mutants)

	$Good	$Fine	$N.Mint	£Good	£Fine	£N.Mint
1 ND reprints Ex-Mutants #1 (Pied Piper issue) with new Ron Lim cover	$0.40	$1.20	$2.00	£0.25	£0.75	£1.25
2-6 ND	$0.40	$1.20	$2.00	£0.25	£0.75	£1.25
Title Value:	$2.40	$7.20	$12.00	£1.50	£4.50	£7.50

Note: black and white

SOLOMON KANE IN 3-D
Blackthorne; (3-D Series #60) 1 Winter 1988

	$Good	$Fine	$N.Mint	£Good	£Fine	£N.Mint
1 ND with bound-in 3-D glasses (25% less without glasses)	$0.50	$1.50	$2.50	£0.30	£0.90	£1.50
Title Value:	$0.50	$1.50	$2.50	£0.30	£0.90	£1.50

SOLOMON KANE, THE SWORD OF
Marvel Comics Group,MS; 1 Sep 1985-6 Mar 1986

	$Good	$Fine	$N.Mint	£Good	£Fine	£N.Mint
1 ND DS	$0.30	$0.90	$1.50	£0.20	£0.60	£1.00
2-6 ND	$0.25	$0.75	$1.25	£0.15	£0.45	£0.75
Title Value:	$1.55	$4.65	$7.75	£0.95	£2.85	£4.75

ARTISTS

Mignola in 3. Nowlan cover on 4. Ridgway in 6. Williamson in 3, 4.

SOLUTION, THE
Malibu Ultraverse; 1 Sep 1993-17 Feb 1995

	$Good	$Fine	$N.Mint	£Good	£Fine	£N.Mint
0 ND obtained with Rune #0 by sending off coupons contained within 11 Ultraverse issues	$1.50	$4.50	$7.50	£1.00	£3.00	£5.00
1 Darick Robertson/John Lowe art begins	$0.50	$1.50	$2.50	£0.30	£0.90	£1.50
1 Limited Edition, full hologram cover, 5,000 copies produced	$3.00	$9.00	$15.00	£1.50	£4.50	£7.50
2 40pgs, Rune insert	$0.50	$1.50	$2.50	£0.30	£0.90	£1.50
3	$0.40	$1.20	$2.00	£0.25	£0.75	£1.25
4 Break-Thru X-over; gatefold cover	$0.40	$1.20	$2.00	£0.25	£0.75	£1.25
5 origin The Strangers by Adam Hughes	$0.40	$1.20	$2.00	£0.25	£0.75	£1.25
6 origin of Tech	$0.40	$1.20	$2.00	£0.25	£0.75	£1.25
7-8 origin of The Solution	$0.40	$1.20	$2.00	£0.25	£0.75	£1.25
9-12	$0.40	$1.20	$2.00	£0.25	£0.75	£1.25
13 Hostile Takeover part 3	$0.40	$1.20	$2.00	£0.25	£0.75	£1.25
14-15	$0.40	$1.20	$2.00	£0.25	£0.75	£1.25
16 64pgs, flip-book format with Ultraverse Premiere #10	$0.50	$1.50	$2.50	£0.30	£0.90	£1.50
17	$0.40	$1.20	$2.00	£0.25	£0.75	£1.25
Title Value:	$11.60	$34.80	$58.00	£6.90	£20.70	£34.50

Note: all Non-Distributed on the news-stands in the U.K.

SOMERSET HOLMES
Pacific; 1 Sep 1983-4 Apr 1984; Eclipse; 5 Nov 1984-6 Dec 1985

	$Good	$Fine	$N.Mint	£Good	£Fine	£N.Mint
1-5 ND Jones/Campbell/Brent Anderson begin, Cliff Hanger by Williamson	$0.40	$1.20	$2.00	£0.25	£0.75	£1.25
6 ND scarce in the U.K. Jones/Campbell/Brent Anderson begin, Cliff Hanger by Williamson	$0.40	$1.20	$2.00	£0.30	£0.90	£1.50
Title Value:	$2.40	$7.20	$12.00	£1.55	£4.65	£7.75

SOMERSET HOLMES (2ND SERIES)
Eclipse; Graphic Novel 10; 1986

	$Good	$Fine	$N.Mint	£Good	£Fine	£N.Mint
1 ND reprints issues #1-6, new cover	$2.50	$7.50	$12.50	£1.50	£4.50	£7.50
Title Value:	$2.50	$7.50	$12.50	£1.50	£4.50	£7.50

SON OF AMBUSH BUG
(see Ambush Bug)

SON OF CELLULOID
Eclipse,OS; nn 1991

nn ND 64pgs, Hardcover, adaptation of Clive Barker material by Steve Niles, painted art by Les Edwards

	$Good	$Fine	$N.Mint	£Good	£Fine	£N.Mint
	$4.50	$13.50	$22.50	£3.00	£9.00	£15.00
Title Value:	$4.50	$13.50	$22.50	£3.00	£9.00	£15.00

SON OF MUTANT WORLD
Fantagor,MS; 1 Summer 1990-5 Feb 1991
1-5 ND Richard Corben/Bruce Jones art, Richard Corben cover

	$0.40	$1.20	$2.00	£0.25	£0.75	£1.25
Title Value:	$2.00	$6.00	$10.00	£1.25	£3.75	£6.25

Note: bi-monthly frequency

SON OF SATAN
Marvel Comics Group; 1 Dec 1975-8 Feb 1977
(see Marvel Spotlight)
1 splash page by Jim Starlin

	$1.80	$5.25	$9.00	£1.20	£3.60	£6.00
2	$1.20	$3.60	$6.00	£0.60	£1.80	£3.00
3-7	$1.00	$3.00	$5.00	£0.50	£1.50	£2.50

8 ND Russ Heath art

	$1.00	$3.00	$5.00	£0.50	£1.50	£2.50
Title Value:	$9.00	$26.85	$45.00	£4.80	£14.40	£24.00

ARTISTS
Part P.Craig Russell art in 4, 5. Russ Heath in 8.

SON OF VULCAN
Charlton; 49 Nov 1965-50 Jan 1966
(becomes Thunderbolt)
49-50 distributed in the U.K.

	$2.50	$7.50	$15.00	£1.65	£5.00	£10.00
Title Value:	$5.00	$15.00	$30.00	£3.30	£10.00	£20.00

SONG OF THE CID
Caliber/Tome Press,MS; 1 Jul 1991-2 Aug 1991

1-2 ND	$0.40	$1.20	$2.00	£0.25	£0.75	£1.25
Title Value:	$0.80	$2.40	$4.00	£0.50	£1.50	£2.50

SONIC DISRUPTERS
DC Comics,MS; 1 Dec 1987-7 Jul 1988

1-7 ND	$0.15	$0.45	$0.75	£0.10	£0.35	£0.60
Title Value:	$1.05	$3.15	$5.25	£0.70	£2.45	£4.20

Note: Mike Baron story, Mature Readers, Deluxe format (planned 12-issue series, cancelled with #7).

SOULQUEST
Innovation; 1 Apr 1989
1 ND 48pgs, squarebound, based on role playing game

	$0.40	$1.20	$2.00	£0.25	£0.75	£1.25
Title Value:	$0.40	$1.20	$2.00	£0.25	£0.75	£1.25

SOULSEARCHERS AND COMPANY
Claypool Comics; 1 Jun 1993-14 Jul 1994
1-14 ND Peter David script

	$0.50	$1.50	$2.50	£0.30	£0.90	£1.50
Title Value:	$7.00	$21.00	$35.00	£4.20	£12.60	£21.00

SOUTHERN KNIGHTS
Guild/Comics Interview; 2 Jan 1983-35 1987?
(previously Crusaders)
2 ND scarce in the U.K. magazine size, black and white begins

	$0.40	$1.20	$2.00	£0.40	£1.20	£2.00

3-7 ND scarce in the U.K.

	$0.30	$0.90	$1.50	£0.30	£0.90	£1.50

8 ND 1st Comics Interview issue

	$0.30	$0.90	$1.50	£0.25	£0.75	£1.25

9-33 ND

	$0.30	$0.90	$1.50	£0.25	£0.75	£1.25

34 ND Christmas issue

	$0.30	$0.90	$1.50	£0.25	£0.75	£1.25

35 ND 100pgs, squarebound, actually bound-together copies of Champions #1 and Eternity Smith; George Perez cover

	$0.40	$1.20	$2.00	£0.30	£0.90	£1.50
Title Value:	$10.40	$31.20	$52.00	£8.95	£26.85	£44.75
Dread Halloween Special 1				£0.40	£1.20	£2.00
Special 1 (1989), reprints				£0.25	£0.75	£1.25
Graphic Novel #1-4 (more?)				£0.65	£1.95	£3.25

SOUTHERN SQUADRON
Aircel,MS; 1 Jul 1990-4 Oct 1990
1 ND Mike Grell cover and introduction; David de Vries script, Gary Chaloner and Glenn Lumsden art; black and white

	$0.40	$1.20	$2.00	£0.25	£0.75	£1.25
2 ND	$0.40	$1.20	$2.00	£0.25	£0.75	£1.25

3 ND Jerry Ordway introduction and cover

	$0.40	$1.20	$2.00	£0.25	£0.75	£1.25
4 ND	$0.40	$1.20	$2.00	£0.25	£0.75	£1.25
Title Value:	$1.60	$4.80	$8.00	£1.00	£3.00	£5.00

SOUTHERN SQUADRON: FREEDOM OF INFORMATION ACT
Eternity,MS; 1 Jan 1992-4 Apr 1992

1-4 ND	$0.40	$1.20	$2.00	£0.25	£0.75	£1.25
Title Value:	$1.60	$4.80	$8.00	£1.00	£3.00	£5.00

SOVEREIGN SEVEN
DC Comics; 1 Jul 1995-present
1 Cascade, Network, Reflex, Rampart, Finale, Indigo and Cruiser begin and Darkseid appears; script by Chris Claremont, art by Dwayne Turner

	$0.40	$1.20	$2.00	£0.30	£0.90	£1.50
1 Gold Edition ND	$2.00	$6.00	$10.00	£1.50	£4.50	£7.50
2 Cascade dies	$0.40	$1.20	$2.00	£0.25	£0.75	£1.25
3-9	$0.40	$1.20	$2.00	£0.25	£0.75	£1.25
Title Value:	$5.60	$16.80	$28.00	£3.o0	£11.40	£19.00

SOVEREIGN SEVEN ANNUAL
DC Comics; 1 Dec 1995-present
1 56pgs, Year One story, Lobo appears

	$0.80	$2.40	$4.00	£0.50	£1.50	£2.50
Title Value:	$0.80	$2.40	$4.00	£0.50	£1.50	£2.50

SOVIET SUPER SOLDIERS
Marvel Comics Group,OS; 1 Nov 1992

1	$0.40	$1.20	$2.00	£0.25	£0.75	£1.25
Title Value:	$0.40	$1.20	$2.00	£0.25	£0.75	£1.25

SPACE 1999
Charlton; 1 Nov 1975-7 Nov 1976

1	$0.60	$1.80	$3.00	£0.40	£1.20	£2.00
2	$0.50	$1.50	$2.50	£0.30	£0.90	£1.50

3-7 John Byrne art

	$0.80	$2.40	$4.00	£0.50	£1.50	£2.50
Title Value:	$5.10	$15.30	$25.50	£3.20	£9.60	£16.00

Note: all distributed in the U.K.

SPACE 1999 (MAGAZINE)
Charlton,Magazine; 1 Nov 1975-8 Nov 1976

1 ND	$0.80	$2.40	$4.00	£0.60	£1.80	£3.00
2-8 ND	$0.60	$1.80	$3.00	£0.50	£1.50	£2.50
Title Value:	$5.00	$15.00	$25.00	£4.10	£12.30	£20.50

SPACE ADVENTURES
Charlton; 1 Jul 1952-59 Nov 1964; 60 Oct 1967
1 scarce in the U.K.

	$40.00	$120.00	$280.00	£26.00	£77.50	£185.00
2	$20.00	$60.00	$140.00	£12.50	£39.00	£90.00
3-9	$14.00	$43.00	$100.00	£10.50	£32.00	£75.00

10-11 Steve Ditko cover and art

	$34.00	$100.00	$240.00	£22.50	£67.50	£160.00

12 rare in the U.K. Steve Ditko cover

	$39.00	$115.00	$275.00	£26.00	£75.00	£180.00

13-14 Blue Beetle reprint from Fox title

	$14.00	$43.00	$100.00	£10.00	£30.00	£70.00
15	$14.00	$43.00	$100.00	£10.00	£30.00	£70.00

16 Krigstein art

	$17.00	$50.00	$120.00	£11.00	£34.00	£80.00
17-18	$14.00	$43.00	$100.00	£10.00	£30.00	£70.00
19	$10.00	$30.00	$70.00	£6.25	£19.00	£45.00

20 reprints Destination Moon from Fawcett title

	$23.50	$70.00	$165.00	£15.50	£47.00	£110.00
21	$10.00	$30.00	$70.00	£6.25	£19.00	£45.00

22 titled "War At Sea"

	$10.00	$30.00	$70.00	£6.25	£19.00	£45.00

23 reprints Destination Moon from Fawcett title

	$19.00	$57.50	$135.00	£12.50	£39.00	£90.00

24-27 Steve Ditko art

	$14.00	$43.00	$100.00	£10.00	£30.00	£70.00
28-30	$5.50	$17.00	$40.00	£3.55	£10.50	£25.00

1st official distribution in the U.K.

31-32 Steve Ditko art

	$14.00	$43.00	$100.00	£10.00	£30.00	£70.00

33 1st appearance of Captain Atom by Steve Ditko

	$36.00	$105.00	$250.00	£22.50	£67.50	£160.00

34-40 Captain Atom by Steve Ditko

	$13.50	$41.00	$95.00	£9.25	£28.00	£65.00

41 1st appearance Mercury Man

	$3.00	$9.00	$18.00	£2.00	£6.00	£12.00

42 Captain Atom by Steve Ditko

	$13.50	$41.00	$95.00	£9.25	£28.00	£65.00
43	$3.00	$9.00	$18.00	£2.00	£6.00	£12.00

44-45 Mercury Man

	$3.00	$9.00	$18.00	£2.00	£6.00	£12.00
46-59	$3.00	$9.00	$18.00	£2.00	£6.00	£12.00

60 1st Paul Mann and the Saucers from the Future

	$5.00	$15.00	$25.00	£3.50	£10.50	£17.50
Title Value:	$728.00	$2197.50	$5084.00	£497.40	£1499.00	£3473.50

Note: most issues distributed in the U.K. after 1959

SPACE ARK
AC/Apple; 1 1985-5 1988

1-2 ND	$0.40	$1.20	$2.00	£0.25	£0.75	£1.25

3 ND 1st Apple issue

	$0.40	$1.20	$2.00	£0.25	£0.75	£1.25
4-5 ND	$0.40	$1.20	$2.00	£0.25	£0.75	£1.25
Title Value:	$2.00	$6.00	$10.00	£1.25	£3.75	£6.25

SPACE BEAVER
Ten Buck Comics; 1 Oct 1986-11 1988

1-11 ND	$0.30	$0.90	$1.50	£0.20	£0.60	£1.00
Title Value:	$3.30	$9.90	$16.50	£2.20	£6.60	£11.00

SPACE FAMILY ROBINSON
Gold Key; 1 Dec 1962-36 Oct 1969
(becomes Lost in Space #37 onwards)
1 rare in the U.K. painted covers begin

	$33.00	$100.00	$200.00	£23.00	£70.00	£140.00

2 scarce in the U.K.

	$14.00	$43.00	$85.00	£9.00	£28.00	£55.00

3-5 scarce in the U.K.

	$8.25	$25.00	$50.00	£5.75	£17.50	£35.00

6-10 scarce in the U.K.

	$7.50	$22.50	$45.00	£5.25	£16.00	£32.50

11-20 scarce in the U.K.

	$5.00	$15.00	$30.00	£3.30	£10.00	£20.00

21-36 scarce in the U.K.

	$4.00	$12.00	$20.00	£2.50	£7.50	£12.50
Title Value:	$223.25	$672.50	$1280.00	£148.50	£450.50	£862.50

Note: all distributed in the U.K.

SPACE GHOST
Gold Key,OS; 1 Mar 1967

	$Good	$Fine	$N.Mint	£Good	£Fine	£N.Mint

1 rare though distributed in the U.K.

| | $46.00 | $135.00 | $275.00 | £29.00 | £87.50 | £175.00 |
| Title Value: | $46.00 | $135.00 | $275.00 | £29.00 | £87.50 | £175.00 |

SPACE GHOST
Comico, OS; 1 Sep 1987
1 ND bookshelf format, Steve Rude art

| | $0.80 | $2.40 | $4.00 | £0.50 | £1.50 | £2.50 |
| Title Value: | $0.80 | $2.40 | $4.00 | £0.50 | £1.50 | £2.50 |

SPACE MAN
Dell; 1253 Jan/Mar 1962; Gold Key; 2 Apr/Jun 1962-8 Mar/May 1964; 9 Jul 1972-10 Oct 1972
1 very scarce in the U.K., limited distribution in the U.K. (Four Color #1253)

| | $10.00 | $30.00 | $60.00 | £6.50 | £20.00 | £40.00 |

2 scarce though distributed in the U.K. painted cover

| | $5.00 | $15.00 | $30.00 | £3.30 | £10.00 | £20.00 |

3 scarce though distributed in the U.K. painted cover

| | $4.55 | $13.50 | $27.50 | £2.90 | £8.75 | £17.50 |

4-8 scarce though distributed in the U.K. painted cover

| | $3.30 | $10.00 | $20.00 | £2.05 | £6.25 | £12.50 |

9-10 limited distribution in the U.K. reprints issue #1

| | $1.30 | $3.90 | $6.50 | £0.90 | £2.70 | £4.50 |
| Title Value: | $38.65 | $116.30 | $230.50 | £24.75 | £75.40 | £149.00 |

SPACE PATROL
Adventure, MS; 1 Jan 1993-3 Mar 1993
1-3 ND

| | $0.40 | $1.20 | $2.00 | £0.25 | £0.75 | £1.25 |
| Title Value: | $1.20 | $3.60 | $6.00 | £0.75 | £2.25 | £3.75 |

SPACE USAGI
Mirage Studios, MS; 1 Aug 1992-3 Oct 1992
1-3 ND features Usagi Yojimbo by Stan Sakai

| | $0.40 | $1.20 | $2.00 | £0.25 | £0.75 | £1.25 |
| Title Value: | $1.20 | $3.60 | $6.00 | £0.75 | £2.25 | £3.75 |

SPACE USAGI II
Mirage Studios, MS; 1 Jan 1994-3 Mar 1994
1-3 ND Stan Sakai with Mary Woodring

| | $0.40 | $1.20 | $2.00 | £0.25 | £0.75 | £1.25 |
| Title Value: | $1.20 | $3.60 | $6.00 | £0.75 | £2.25 | £3.75 |

SPACE WAR
Charlton; 1 Oct 1959-27 Mar 1964; 28 Mar 1978-34 Mar 1979
1 ND

| | $13.50 | $41.00 | $95.00 | £9.25 | £28.00 | £65.00 |

2-3 distributed in the U.K.

| | $7.00 | $21.00 | $50.00 | £5.00 | £15.00 | £35.00 |

4-6 distributed in the U.K. Steve Ditko art

| | $12.50 | $39.00 | $90.00 | £8.50 | £26.00 | £60.00 |

7 distributed in the U.K.

| | $3.55 | $10.50 | $25.00 | £2.50 | £7.50 | £17.50 |

8 distributed in the U.K. Steve Ditko art

| | $12.50 | $39.00 | $90.00 | £8.50 | £26.00 | £60.00 |

9 distributed in the U.K.

| | $3.55 | $10.50 | $25.00 | £2.50 | £7.50 | £17.50 |

10 distributed in the U.K. Steve Ditko art

| | $12.50 | $39.00 | $90.00 | £8.50 | £26.00 | £60.00 |

11-20 distributed in the U.K.

| | $3.75 | $11.00 | $22.50 | £2.50 | £7.50 | £15.00 |

21-27 distributed in the U.K.

| | $3.30 | $10.00 | $20.00 | £2.05 | £6.25 | £12.50 |

28-29 distributed in the U.K. Steve Ditko reprint

| | $7.50 | $22.50 | $37.50 | £5.00 | £15.00 | £25.00 |

30 distributed in the U.K. Steve Ditko reprint and Wally Wood art

| | $7.50 | $22.50 | $37.50 | £5.00 | £15.00 | £25.00 |

31 distributed in the U.K. Steve Ditko reprint, atomic bomb cover

| | $7.50 | $22.50 | $37.50 | £5.00 | £15.00 | £25.00 |

32 distributed in the U.K.

| | $0.90 | $2.70 | $4.50 | £0.60 | £1.80 | £3.00 |

33-34 distributed in the U.K. Steve Ditko reprint

| | $7.00 | $21.00 | $35.00 | £4.50 | £13.50 | £22.50 |
| Title Value: | $202.60 | $613.70 | $1284.50 | £135.70 | £410.55 | £855.50 |

SPACED
Unbridled Ambition/Eclipse; 1 1985-13 1988
1 ND scarce in the U.K.

| | $3.00 | $9.00 | $15.00 | £2.00 | £6.00 | £10.00 |

2 ND scarce in the U.K.

| | $2.00 | $6.00 | $10.00 | £1.20 | £3.60 | £6.00 |

3 ND scarce in the U.K.

| | $1.20 | $3.60 | $6.00 | £0.80 | £2.40 | £4.00 |

4 ND scarce in the U.K.

| | $1.00 | $3.00 | $5.00 | £0.60 | £1.80 | £3.00 |

5 ND

| | $0.60 | $1.80 | $3.00 | £0.40 | £1.20 | £2.00 |

6-7 ND

| | $0.50 | $1.50 | $2.50 | £0.30 | £0.90 | £1.50 |

8-13 ND

| | $0.40 | $1.20 | $2.00 | £0.25 | £0.75 | £1.25 |
| Title Value: | $11.20 | $33.60 | $56.00 | £7.10 | £21.30 | £35.50 |

SPANNER'S GALAXY
DC Comics, MS; 1 Dec 1984-6 May 1985
1-6

| | $0.15 | $0.45 | $0.75 | £0.10 | £0.35 | £0.60 |
| Title Value: | $0.90 | $2.70 | $4.50 | £0.60 | £2.10 | £3.60 |

Note: flexographically-printed DC comic.

SPARKPLUG
Hero, MS; 1 Mar 1993-3 1993
1-3 ND

| | $0.50 | $1.50 | $2.50 | £0.30 | £0.90 | £1.50 |
| Title Value: | $1.50 | $4.50 | $7.50 | £0.90 | £2.70 | £4.50 |

SPARROW
DC Comics/Piranha Press, OS; 1 Mar 1990
1 ND 104pgs, Alison Marek script/art; black and white

| | $1.50 | $4.50 | $7.50 | £1.00 | £3.00 | £5.00 |
| Title Value: | $1.50 | $4.50 | $7.50 | £1.00 | £3.00 | £5.00 |

SPARTAN: WARRIOR SPIRIT
Image, MS; 1 Aug 1995-4 Nov 1995
1-4 ND Kurt Busiek script

| | $0.50 | $1.50 | $2.50 | £0.30 | £0.90 | £1.50 |
| Title Value: | $2.00 | $6.00 | $10.00 | £1.20 | £3.60 | £6.00 |

SPAWN
Image; 1 May 1992-present
1 Todd McFarlane script/art begins; 1st appearance Spawn and 1st appearance Pitt (as a pin-up)

| | $3.00 | $9.00 | $15.00 | £1.50 | £4.50 | £7.50 |

2 1st appearance Violator

| | $2.50 | $7.50 | $12.50 | £1.50 | £4.50 | £7.50 |

3 some details of origin told

| | $2.50 | $7.50 | $12.50 | £1.20 | £3.60 | £6.00 |

4 scarce in the U.K. contains Image #0 coupon 2; new powers detailed

| | $3.00 | $9.00 | $15.00 | £1.50 | £4.50 | £7.50 |

4 without coupon

| | $1.00 | $3.00 | $5.00 | £0.70 | £2.10 | £3.50 |

5 scarce in the U.K.

| | $1.50 | $4.50 | $7.50 | £1.00 | £3.00 | £5.00 |

6 1st appearance Overkill

| | $1.20 | $3.60 | $6.00 | £0.80 | £2.40 | £4.00 |

7

| | $1.20 | $3.60 | $6.00 | £0.70 | £2.10 | £3.50 |

8 features Alan Moore's 1st super-hero script for some years plus poster by Frank Miller; cover in classic Spiderman #1 pose

| | $1.20 | $3.60 | $6.00 | £0.70 | £2.10 | £3.50 |

9 Neil Gaiman script, 1st appearance Angela

| | $1.50 | $4.50 | $7.50 | £0.80 | £2.40 | £4.00 |

10 Dave Sim script, Cerebus the Aardvark appears

| | $1.00 | $3.00 | $5.00 | £0.50 | £1.50 | £2.50 |

11 Frank Miller script, Geoff Darrow poster

Space Family Robinson #6

Space War #19

Special Marvel Edition #2

	$Good	$Fine	$N.Mint	£Good	£Fine	£N.Mint
	$0.80	$2.40	$4.00	£0.40	£1.20	£2.00
12 the conclusion to Spawn's origin and Spawn's killer revealed to be Chapel						
	$0.80	$2.40	$4.00	£0.40	£1.20	£2.00
13 Spawn vs. Chapel						
	$0.80	$2.40	$4.00	£0.40	£1.20	£2.00
14 Violator appears						
	$0.80	$2.40	$4.00	£0.40	£1.20	£2.00
15 1st appearance Medieval Spawn, Violator appears						
	$0.60	$1.80	$3.00	£1.00	£3.00	£5.00
16 1st Greg Capullo Spawn						
	$0.60	$1.80	$3.00	£1.00	£3.00	£5.00
17 1st appearance Redeemer						
	$0.60	$1.80	$3.00	£0.80	£2.40	£4.00
18	$1.20	$3.60	$6.00	£0.80	£2.40	£4.00
19-20 issued Oct 1994 after issue #24						
	$1.20	$3.60	$6.00	£0.80	£2.40	£4.00
21	$1.20	$3.60	$6.00	£0.80	£2.40	£4.00
22-23	$0.60	$1.80	$3.00	£0.40	£1.20	£2.00
24 leads into Angela mini-series						
	$0.60	$1.80	$3.00	£0.40	£1.20	£2.00
25 Image X Month tie-in						
	$0.60	$1.80	$3.00	£0.40	£1.20	£2.00
26-30	$0.60	$1.80	$3.00	£0.40	£1.20	£2.00
31	$0.50	$1.50	$2.50	£0.30	£0.90	£1.50
32 new costume and 6pg preview of Spawn mini-series						
	$0.50	$1.50	$2.50	£0.30	£0.90	£1.50
33-34 Spawn vs. Violator						
	$0.50	$1.50	$2.50	£0.30	£0.90	£1.50
35 Violator appears						
	$0.50	$1.50	$2.50	£0.30	£0.90	£1.50
36	$0.40	$1.20	$2.00	£0.25	£0.75	£1.25
37 intro The Freak; Alan Moore script						
	$0.40	$1.20	$2.00	£0.25	£0.75	£1.25
38 bi-weekly	$0.40	$1.20	$2.00	£0.25	£0.75	£1.25
39 Christmas story special; bi-weekly						
	$0.40	$1.20	$2.00	£0.25	£0.75	£1.25
40-41 bi-weekly	$0.40	$1.20	$2.00	£0.25	£0.75	£1.25
Title Value:	$39.70	$119.10	$198.50	£25.10	£75.30	£125.50

Note: all Non-Distributed on the news-stands in the U.K.
Spawn (May 1995)
Trade paperback reprints issues #1-5,
new cover by Todd McFarlane £1.30 £3.90 £6.50

SPAWN/BATMAN
Image,OS; 1 May 1994

	$Good	$Fine	$N.Mint	£Good	£Fine	£N.Mint
1 ND 48pgs Frank Miller script, Todd McFarlane art						
	$1.00	$3.00	$5.00	£0.70	£2.10	£3.50
Title Value:	$1.00	$3.00	$5.00	£0.70	£2.10	£3.50

SPAWN: BLOOD FEUD
Image,MS; 1 Jun 1995-4 Sep 1995

	$Good	$Fine	$N.Mint	£Good	£Fine	£N.Mint
1 ND Alan Moore script, Tony Daniel and Kevin Conrad art						
	$0.60	$1.80	$3.00	£0.40	£1.20	£2.00
2-4 ND Alan Moore script, Tony Daniel and Kevin Conrad art						
	$0.50	$1.50	$2.50	£0.30	£0.90	£1.50
Title Value:	$2.10	$6.30	$10.50	£1.30	£3.90	£6.50

SPECIAL MARVEL EDITION
Marvel Comics Group; 1 Jan 1971-16 Feb 1974
(becomes Master of Kung Fu)

	$Good	$Fine	$N.Mint	£Good	£Fine	£N.Mint
1 68pgs, Jack Kirby Thor reprints begin (continued from Marvel Tales #27) from Journey Into Mystery #117 onwards (3 per issue)						
	$1.50	$4.50	$7.50	£1.00	£3.00	£5.00
2-4 ND 68pgs, Thor reprints						
	$0.90	$2.70	$4.50	£0.60	£1.80	£3.00
5 ND Jack Kirby Sgt. Fury reprints begin from Sgt. Fury #3 onwards						
	$0.70	$2.10	$3.50	£0.40	£1.20	£2.00
6-10 ND Sgt. Fury reprints						
	$0.70	$2.10	$3.50	£0.40	£1.20	£2.00
11 ND reprints Sgt. Fury #13 (Captain America)						
	$0.70	$2.10	$3.50	£0.40	£1.20	£2.00
12-14 ND Sgt.Fury reprints						
	$0.70	$2.10	$3.50	£0.40	£1.20	£2.00
15 ND scarce in the U.K. 1st appearance Master of Kung Fu, Jim Starlin art						
	$6.25	$18.50	$37.50	£4.15	£12.50	£25.00
16 ND 2nd appearance Master of Kung Fu, Jim Starlin art						
	$4.15	$12.50	$25.00	£2.90	£8.75	£17.50
Title Value:	$21.60	$64.60	$118.50	£13.85	£41.65	£76.50

SPECIAL WAR SERIES
Charlton; 1 Aug 1965-4 Nov 1965

	$Good	$Fine	$N.Mint	£Good	£Fine	£N.Mint
1 distributed in the U.K.						
	$1.65	$5.00	$10.00	£1.15	£3.50	£7.00
2-3 distributed in the U.K.						
	$1.25	$3.75	$7.50	£0.80	£2.50	£5.00
4 distributed in the U.K. 1st appearance of Judo Master						
	$4.15	$12.50	$25.00	£2.90	£8.75	£17.50
Title Value:	$8.30	$25.00	$50.00	£5.65	£17.25	£34.50

SPECIES
Dark Horse,MS; 1 Jun 1995-4 Sep 1995

	$Good	$Fine	$N.Mint	£Good	£Fine	£N.Mint
1-4 ND adaption of film by Dennis Feldman, John Bolton painted covers						
	$0.50	$1.50	$2.50	£0.30	£0.90	£1.50
Title Value:	$2.00	$6.00	$10.00	£1.20	£3.60	£6.00

SPECTACULAR SCARLET SPIDERMAN
Marvel Comics Group; 1 Nov 1995-2 Dec 1995

1 ND Todd Dezago script, Sal Buscema and Bill Sienkiewicz art; metallic ink cover

	$Good	$Fine	$N.Mint	£Good	£Fine	£N.Mint
	$0.40	$1.20	$2.00	£0.25	£0.75	£1.25
2 ND Ben Reilly ends his career as The Scarlet Spider						
	$0.40	$1.20	$2.00	£0.25	£0.75	£1.25
Title Value:	$0.80	$2.40	$4.00	£0.50	£1.50	£2.50

SPECTACULAR SPIDERMAN
Marvel Comics Group; 1 Dec 1976-229 Oct 1995; 230 Jan 1996-present

	$Good	$Fine	$N.Mint	£Good	£Fine	£N.Mint
1 origin retold, Tarantula appears						
	$9.00	$28.00	$55.00	£5.00	£15.00	£30.00
2 ND Kraven the Hunter appears						
	$3.30	$10.00	$20.00	£2.05	£6.25	£12.50
3 ND 1st appearance Lightmaster						
	$2.05	$6.25	$12.50	£1.25	£3.75	£7.50
4-5 ND	$1.65	$5.00	$10.00	£1.00	£3.00	£6.00
6 ND part reprint Marvel Team Up #4 with X-Men and Morbius						
	$2.05	$6.25	$12.50	£1.15	£3.50	£7.00
7 ND Morbius appears						
	$2.05	$6.25	$12.50	£1.15	£3.50	£7.00
8 ND Morbius appears, Gulacy cover						
	$2.05	$6.25	$12.50	£1.15	£3.50	£7.00
9 ND 1st appearance White Tiger						
	$1.25	$3.75	$7.50	£0.80	£2.50	£5.00
10 ND George Perez cover						
	$1.25	$3.75	$7.50	£0.80	£2.50	£5.00
11 ND Inhumans appear						
	$1.20	$3.60	$6.00	£0.80	£2.40	£4.00
12 ND scarce in the U.K.						
	$1.20	$3.60	$6.00	£1.00	£3.00	£5.00
13-16 ND	$1.20	$3.60	$6.00	£0.80	£2.40	£4.00
17 ND scarce in the U.K. Angel and X-Men appear, The Champions appear						
	$1.50	$4.50	$7.50	£1.50	£4.50	£7.50
18 ND Angel, Iceman and X-Men appear, Champions disband						
	$1.50	$4.50	$7.50	£1.30	£3.90	£6.50
19-21 ND	$1.20	$3.60	$6.00	£0.80	£2.40	£4.00
22 ND Moon Knight appears, Zeck art						
	$1.60	$4.80	$8.00	£1.10	£3.30	£5.50
23 ND Moon Knight appears						
	$1.60	$4.80	$8.00	£1.00	£3.00	£5.00
24-25 ND	$1.20	$3.60	$6.00	£0.80	£2.40	£4.00
26 ND Daredevil appears						
	$1.40	$4.20	$7.00	£0.90	£2.70	£4.50
27 ND 1st Frank Miller art on Daredevil						
	$3.00	$9.00	$15.00	£1.60	£4.80	£8.00
28 ND Frank Miller Daredevil						
	$2.50	$7.50	$12.50	£1.40	£4.20	£7.00
29-35 ND	$1.00	$3.00	$5.00	£0.70	£2.10	£3.50
36 ND 1st appearance Swarm						
	$1.00	$3.00	$5.00	£0.70	£2.10	£3.50
37 ND	$1.00	$3.00	$5.00	£0.70	£2.10	£3.50
38 ND Morbius appears						
	$1.00	$3.00	$5.00	£0.70	£2.10	£3.50
39 ND Morbius appears (flashback), Bingham cover						
	$1.00	$3.00	$5.00	£0.70	£2.10	£3.50
40-52 ND	$1.00	$3.00	$5.00	£0.70	£2.10	£3.50
53	$0.80	$2.40	$4.00	£0.50	£1.50	£2.50
54 Frank Miller cover						
	$0.80	$2.40	$4.00	£0.50	£1.50	£2.50
55	$0.80	$2.40	$4.00	£0.50	£1.50	£2.50
56 2nd appearance Jack O'Lantern, 1st battle between Spiderman and Jack O'Lantern, Miller cover						
	$1.50	$4.50	$7.50	£0.80	£2.40	£4.00
57 Frank Miller cover						
	$0.80	$2.40	$4.00	£0.50	£1.50	£2.50
58 John Byrne art	$1.00	$3.00	$5.00	£0.60	£1.80	£3.00
59	$0.80	$2.40	$4.00	£0.50	£1.50	£2.50
60 DS, origin retold with new facts, Miller cover						
	$1.00	$3.00	$5.00	£0.70	£2.10	£3.50
61-63	$0.60	$1.80	$3.00	£0.40	£1.20	£2.00
64 1st appearance Cloak and Dagger						
	$2.00	$6.00	$10.00	£1.20	£3.60	£6.00
65-68	$0.60	$1.80	$3.00	£0.40	£1.20	£2.00
69 2nd appearance Cloak and Dagger						
	$1.50	$4.50	$7.50	£0.80	£2.40	£4.00
70 3rd appearance Cloak and Dagger						
	$1.20	$3.60	$6.00	£0.70	£2.10	£3.50
71-74	$0.60	$1.80	$3.00	£0.40	£1.20	£2.00
75 DS	$0.80	$2.40	$4.00	£0.50	£1.50	£2.50
76 LD in the U.K.	$0.60	$1.80	$3.00	£0.50	£1.50	£2.50
77 very LD rare	$0.60	$1.80	$3.00	£0.60	£1.80	£3.00
78-80 LD in the U.K.						
	$0.60	$1.80	$3.00	£0.50	£1.50	£2.50
81-82 Punisher, Cloak & Dagger appear						
	$1.50	$4.50	$7.50	£1.00	£3.00	£5.00
83 origin Punisher retold						
	$2.00	$6.00	$10.00	£1.50	£4.50	£7.50
84	$0.60	$1.80	$3.00	£0.40	£1.20	£2.00
85 1st Hobgoblin (Ned Leeds) origin						
	$4.00	$12.00	$20.00	£1.50	£4.50	£7.50
86-88	$0.60	$1.80	$3.00	£0.40	£1.20	£2.00
89 Fantastic Four and Captain America cameos						
	$0.60	$1.80	$3.00	£0.40	£1.20	£2.00
90 LD in the U.K. Avengers cameo						
	$0.60	$1.80	$3.00	£0.40	£1.20	£2.00
91-93 LD in the U.K.						

Issue / Description	$Good	$Fine	$N.Mint	£Good	£Fine	£N.Mint
	$0.60	$1.80	$3.00	£0.40	£1.20	£2.00
94-96 Cloak & Dagger	$0.60	$1.80	$3.00	£0.40	£1.20	£2.00
97-99	$0.60	$1.80	$3.00	£0.30	£0.90	£1.50
100 DS	$0.70	$2.10	$3.50	£0.40	£1.20	£2.00
101-102 John Byrne cover	$0.50	$1.50	$2.50	£0.30	£0.90	£1.50
103 Human Torch appears; Peter David's 1st commissioned script for Marvel Comics (see Spiderman #266)	$0.50	$1.50	$2.50	£0.30	£0.90	£1.50
104-106	$0.50	$1.50	$2.50	£0.30	£0.90	£1.50
107-110 LD in the U.K. Death of Jean DeWolff story, Daredevil appears	$0.50	$1.50	$2.50	£0.35	£1.05	£1.75
111 LD in the U.K. Secret Wars X-over	$0.50	$1.50	$2.50	£0.35	£1.05	£1.75
112 LD in the U.K. Beechum art	$0.50	$1.50	$2.50	£0.35	£1.05	£1.75
113-114 LD in the U.K.	$0.50	$1.50	$2.50	£0.35	£1.05	£1.75
115 LD in the U.K. Dr. Strange appears, Beechum art	$0.50	$1.50	$2.50	£0.35	£1.05	£1.75
116 5th appearance Sabretooth	$1.20	$3.60	$6.00	£0.80	£2.40	£4.00
117 LD in the U.K. Dr. Strange appears	$0.50	$1.50	$2.50	£0.35	£1.05	£1.75
118 LD in the U.K. Mike Zeck layouts	$0.50	$1.50	$2.50	£0.35	£1.05	£1.75
119 Sabretooth appears	$1.00	$3.00	$5.00	£0.60	£1.80	£3.00
120	$0.40	$1.20	$2.00	£0.25	£0.75	£1.25
121-129	$0.50	$1.50	$2.50	£0.30	£0.90	£1.50
130 Hobgoblin story and cover	$0.50	$1.50	$2.50	£0.30	£0.90	£1.50
131-132 Kraven Saga, Zeck art	$1.00	$3.00	$5.00	£0.60	£1.80	£3.00
133 very LD, Sienkiewicz cover	$0.50	$1.50	$2.50	£0.35	£1.05	£1.75
134 LD scarce in the U.K.	$0.50	$1.50	$2.50	£0.35	£1.05	£1.75
135-138 LD in the U.K.	$0.50	$1.50	$2.50	£0.30	£0.90	£1.50
139 LD in the U.K. origin Tombstone	$0.50	$1.50	$2.50	£0.30	£0.90	£1.50
140 1pg Punisher appearance	$0.50	$1.50	$2.50	£0.30	£0.90	£1.50
141 Punisher appears	$0.80	$2.40	$4.00	£0.50	£1.50	£2.50
142 1pg Punisher	$0.50	$1.50	$2.50	£0.30	£0.90	£1.50
143 Punisher appears	$0.80	$2.40	$4.00	£0.50	£1.50	£2.50
144 LD in the U.K.	$0.50	$1.50	$2.50	£0.30	£0.90	£1.50
145	$0.50	$1.50	$2.50	£0.25	£0.75	£1.25
146 Inferno X-over, Hobgoblin appears (cameo)	$0.50	$1.50	$2.50	£0.30	£0.90	£1.50
147 Inferno X-over, Hobgoblin appears, 1st appearance demonic Hobgoblin	$4.00	$12.00	$20.00	£0.70	£2.10	£3.50
148 Inferno X-over	$0.50	$1.50	$2.50	£0.25	£0.75	£1.25
149 story continues from Annual #7	$0.50	$1.50	$2.50	£0.25	£0.75	£1.25
150-157	$0.50	$1.50	$2.50	£0.25	£0.75	£1.25
158 LD in the U.K. Spiderman acquires the powers of Captain Universe to become the strongest hero in the Marvel Universe; Acts of Vengeance tie-in	$2.00	$6.00	$10.00	£0.80	£2.40	£4.00
159 Acts of Vengeance tie-in, Cosmic Spiderman	$1.50	$4.50	$7.50	£0.60	£1.80	£3.00
160 Acts of Vengeance tie-in, Cosmic Spiderman	$1.20	$3.60	$6.00	£0.40	£1.20	£2.00
161-164 Hobgoblin appears	$0.40	$1.20	$2.00	£0.25	£0.75	£1.25
165-167	$0.40	$1.20	$2.00	£0.25	£0.75	£1.25
168 LD in the U.K. Thor, Captain America appear	$0.40	$1.20	$2.00	£0.25	£0.75	£1.25
169 LD in the U.K. Thor, Iron Man and Captain America appear	$0.40	$1.20	$2.00	£0.25	£0.75	£1.25
170 ND Thor, Captain America, She-Hulk, Quasar and Sersi appear; conclusion of Spiderman's refusal to join Avengers (3 part)	$0.40	$1.20	$2.00	£0.25	£0.75	£1.25
171-173 ND	$0.30	$0.90	$1.50	£0.20	£0.60	£1.00
174	$0.30	$0.90	$1.50	£0.15	£0.45	£0.75
175-177 LD in the U.K.	$0.30	$0.90	$1.50	£0.20	£0.60	£1.00
178 LD in the U.K. The Child Within story; The Green Goblin returns	$0.30	$0.90	$1.50	£0.20	£0.60	£1.00
179 LD in the U.K. The Child Within story; The Green Goblin appears	$0.30	$0.90	$1.50	£0.20	£0.60	£1.00
180 The Child Within story, Vermin, Green Goblin appear	$0.30	$0.90	$1.50	£0.20	£0.60	£1.00
181-183 The Child Within story, Vermin, Green Goblin appear	$0.25	$0.75	$1.25	£0.15	£0.45	£0.75
184 The Child Within epilogue, Green Goblin, Vermin, Molten Man appear	$0.25	$0.75	$1.25	£0.15	£0.45	£0.75
185 Frog Man appears, $1.25 cover begins						

Issue / Description	$Good	$Fine	$N.Mint	£Good	£Fine	£N.Mint
	$0.25	$0.75	$1.25	£0.15	£0.45	£0.75
186-188 Funeral Arrangements story, Vulture appears	$0.25	$0.75	$1.25	£0.15	£0.45	£0.75
189 48pgs, 30th anniversary issue, origin retold thru' Aunt May's eyes, Green Goblin appears, card cover with Spiderman hologram (scarcest of the 4 hologram anniversary covers)	$1.50	$4.50	$7.50	£0.80	£2.40	£4.00
189 2nd printing, (Nov 1992) - gold foil hologram cover	$0.60	$1.80	$3.00	£0.40	£1.20	£2.00
190-193	$0.25	$0.75	$1.25	£0.15	£0.45	£0.75
194-195 Death of Vermin story	$0.25	$0.75	$1.25	£0.15	£0.45	£0.75
195 ND pre-bagged with copy of Dirt magazine and audio cassette	$0.55	$1.65	$2.75	£0.35	£1.05	£1.75
196 Death of Vermin story	$0.25	$0.75	$1.25	£0.15	£0.45	£0.75
197-198 Cyclops, Iceman, Beast and Archangel (original X-Men) appear	$0.25	$0.75	$1.25	£0.15	£0.45	£0.75
199 X-Men and Green Goblin appear	$0.25	$0.75	$1.25	£0.15	£0.45	£0.75
200 card-stock holo-grafix cover, death of Harry Osborn (Green Goblin II)	$0.60	$1.80	$3.00	£0.40	£1.20	£2.00
201 Maximum Carnage part 5, continued in Amazing Spiderman #379	$0.25	$0.75	$1.25	£0.15	£0.45	£0.75
202 Maximum Carnage part 9, continued in Web of Spiderman #102	$0.25	$0.75	$1.25	£0.15	£0.45	£0.75
203 Maximum Carnage part 13, continued in Spiderman Unlimited #2	$0.25	$0.75	$1.25	£0.15	£0.45	£0.75
204-206	$0.25	$0.75	$1.25	£0.15	£0.45	£0.75
207 Siege of Darkness tie-in, Ghost Rider appears	$0.25	$0.75	$1.25	£0.15	£0.45	£0.75
208 Siege of Darkness tie-in, Black Cat back-up story	$0.25	$0.75	$1.25	£0.15	£0.45	£0.75
209	$0.25	$0.75	$1.25	£0.15	£0.45	£0.75
210 Black Cat appears	$0.25	$0.75	$1.25	£0.15	£0.45	£0.75
211 Pursuit part 2	$0.25	$0.75	$1.25	£0.15	£0.45	£0.75
212 with free Spiderman vs. Venom card sheet	$0.25	$0.75	$1.25	£0.15	£0.45	£0.75
213	$0.25	$0.75	$1.25	£0.15	£0.45	£0.75
213 ND Collector's Edition. pre-bagged with 16pg preview and animation cel from Spiderman animated TV series; metallic ink cover	$0.60	$1.80	$3.00	£0.40	£1.20	£2.00
214 Typhoid Mary appears	$0.25	$0.75	$1.25	£0.15	£0.45	£0.75
215-216	$0.25	$0.75	$1.25	£0.15	£0.45	£0.75
217 Power and Responsibility part 4	$0.25	$0.75	$1.25	£0.15	£0.45	£0.75
217 Power and Responsibility part 4, foil stamped cover, incorporates 16pg flip-book and second foil stamped cover	$0.60	$1.80	$3.00	£0.40	£1.20	£2.00
218 Puma appears	$0.25	$0.75	$1.25	£0.15	£0.45	£0.75
219 Spiderman and Daredevil vs. The Vulture and The Owl (see Spiderman #396)	$0.30	$0.90	$1.50	£0.15	£0.45	£0.75
220 48pgs, Web of Death part 2, continued in Spiderman #398	$0.60	$1.80	$3.00	£0.40	£1.20	£2.00
221 Web of Death part 4; Dr. Octopus dies	$0.30	$0.90	$1.50	£0.20	£0.60	£1.00
222 The Jackal appears; leads into Spiderman #400	$0.30	$0.90	$1.50	£0.20	£0.60	£1.00
223 48pgs, Aftershocks part 2 (see Spiderman 2nd Series #57)	$0.50	$1.50	$2.50	£0.30	£0.90	£1.50
223 ND 48pgs, Enhanced Edition - multi-level debossed cover	$0.60	$1.80	$3.00	£0.40	£1.20	£2.00
224 The Mark of Kaine part 4, continued in Spiderman Unlimited #9	$0.30	$0.90	$1.50	£0.20	£0.60	£1.00
225 48pgs, 1st appearance all new Green Goblin	$0.60	$1.80	$3.00	£0.40	£1.20	£2.00
225 ND 48pgs, 3-D holodisk cover, 1st new green Goblin	$0.80	$2.40	$4.00	£0.50	£1.50	£2.50
226 The Trial of Peter Parker part 4 (conclusion), Peter Parker/Spiderman revealed to be a clone	$0.30	$0.90	$1.50	£0.20	£0.60	£1.00
227 Maximum Clonage part 5, continued in Spiderman: Maximum Clonage Omega	$0.30	$0.90	$1.50	£0.20	£0.60	£1.00
228 Timebomb part 1, continued in Web of Spiderman #129; Bill Sienkiewicz inks and cover art; bi-weekly	$0.30	$0.90	$1.50	£0.20	£0.60	£1.00
229 ND continued from Spiderman #63; Peter Parker gives up being Spiderman; wraparound acetate cover; bi-weekly	$0.80	$2.40	$4.00	£0.50	£1.50	£2.50
229 Newstand edition, ND no cover enhancements	$0.45	$1.35	$2.25	£0.30	£0.90	£1.50
230 ND The Return of Spiderman part 4 (conclusion)	$0.30	$0.90	$1.50	£0.20	£0.60	£1.00
231 ND The Return of Kaine part 1, continued in Sensational Spiderman #2	$0.30	$0.90	$1.50	£0.20	£0.60	£1.00
232 ND	$0.30	$0.90	$1.50	£0.20	£0.60	£1.00
Title Value:	$185.10	$556.90	$948.50	£114.35	£343.50	£588.00

Spiderman and Daredevil Special Edition

	$Good	$Fine	$N.Mint	£Good	£Fine	£N.Mint
ND, reprints #26-28 (1st Miller Daredevil)				£0.35	£1.05	£1.75

Note: Black Cat appears in 75, 76, 82, 83, 85-90, 93, 95, 112, 113, 115, 116, 117, 119.

SPECTACULAR SPIDERMAN ANNUAL

Marvel Comics Group; 1 1980-present

1 ND 52pgs, Dr. Octopus appears

MINT = 100% / NEAR MINT (inc. +/-) = 90–99% / VERY FINE (inc. +/-) = 75–89% / FINE (inc. +/-) = 55–74%
VERY GOOD (inc. +/-) = 35–54% / GOOD (inc. +/-) = 15–34% / FAIR = 5–14% / POOR = 1–4%

553

	$Good	$Fine	$N.Mint	£Good	£Fine	£N.Mint
	$1.40	$4.20	$7.00	£1.00	£3.00	£5.00
2 ND 52pgs	$1.00	$3.00	$5.00	£0.70	£2.10	£3.50
3 ND 52pgs, Man-Wolf gemstone destroyed	$1.00	$3.00	$5.00	£0.70	£2.10	£3.50
4 ND 52pgs, more background details of Aunt May	$0.80	$2.40	$4.00	£0.60	£1.80	£3.00
5 ND Beechum art	$0.80	$2.40	$4.00	£0.60	£1.80	£3.00
6 ND Beechum art	$0.70	$2.10	$3.50	£0.50	£1.50	£2.50
7 ND	$0.60	$1.80	$3.00	£0.40	£1.20	£2.00
8 ND 64pgs, squarebound, Evolutionary War, 1st appearance Speedball	$0.60	$1.80	$3.00	£0.40	£1.20	£2.00
9 ND squarebound, Atlantis Attacks part 6, Cloak and Dagger appear	$0.60	$1.80	$3.00	£0.40	£1.20	£2.00
10 ND Spiderman's Totally Tiny Adventure part 2 continued from Spiderman Annual #24, solo Prowler story by Todd McFarlane	$0.60	$1.80	$3.00	£0.40	£1.20	£2.00
11 ND The Vibranium Vendetta part 2, continued in Web of Spiderman Annual #7	$0.50	$1.50	$2.50	£0.30	£0.90	£1.50
12 ND The Hero Killers part 2, New Warriors appear, Venom appears, continued in Web of Spiderman Annual #8	$0.50	$1.50	$2.50	£0.30	£0.90	£1.50
13 ND 64pgs, pre-bagged with trading card introducing Nocturne	$0.60	$1.80	$3.00	£0.40	£1.20	£2.00
14 ND	$0.60	$1.80	$3.00	£0.40	£1.20	£2.00
Title Value:	$10.30	$30.90	$51.50	£7.10	£21.30	£35.50

SPECTACULAR SPIDERMAN SUPER-SIZE SPECIAL
Marvel Comics Group,OS; 1 Sep 1995

	$Good	$Fine	$N.Mint	£Good	£Fine	£N.Mint
1 ND 64pgs, Planet of Symbiotes part 4, continued in Web of Spiderman Super-Size Special #1; metallic ink cover	$0.80	$2.40	$4.00	£0.50	£1.50	£2.50
Title Value:	$0.80	$2.40	$4.00	£0.50	£1.50	£2.50

SPECTACULAR SPIDERMAN, THE
Marvel Comics Group,Magazine; 1 Jul 1968-2 Nov 1968

	$Good	$Fine	$N.Mint	£Good	£Fine	£N.Mint
1 scarce in the U.K. John Romita art, origin re-told and up-dated, black and white	$10.00	$33.00	$85.00	£7.50	£22.50	£45.00
2 scarce in the U.K. Green Goblin appears in full length story, colour throughout	$14.00	$43.00	$85.00	£10.00	£28.00	£55.00
Title Value:	$24.50	$76.00	$150.00	£16.50	£50.50	£100.00

Note: Very Limited distribution on the news-stands in the U.K.

SPECTRE, THE
National Periodical Publications; 1 Nov/Dec 1967-10 May/Jun 1969
(see Adventure, Brave and the Bold, DC Comics Presents, Showcase, Wrath of the Spectre)

	$Good	$Fine	$N.Mint	£Good	£Fine	£N.Mint
1	$12.50	$39.00	$90.00	£7.00	£21.00	£50.00
2 Neal Adams cover and art	$10.00	$30.00	$70.00	£4.25	£12.50	£30.00
3-4 Neal Adams cover and art	$9.25	$28.00	$65.00	£3.85	£11.50	£27.00
5 Neal Adams cover and art	$9.25	$28.00	$65.00	£3.55	£10.50	£25.00
6	$6.50	$20.00	$40.00	£2.90	£8.75	£17.50
7 Hourman appears	$6.50	$20.00	$40.00	£2.90	£8.75	£17.50
8	$6.50	$20.00	$40.00	£2.90	£8.75	£17.50
9 Bernie Wrightson art	$6.50	$20.00	$40.00	£3.30	£10.00	£20.00
10	$6.50	$20.00	$40.00	£2.90	£8.75	£17.50
Title Value:	$82.75	$253.00	$555.00	£37.40	£112.00	£249.00

SPECTRE, THE (2ND SERIES)
DC Comics; 1 Apr 1987-31 Oct 1989

	$Good	$Fine	$N.Mint	£Good	£Fine	£N.Mint
1-3 Gene Colan art, Mike Kaluta cover	$0.25	$0.75	$1.25	£0.15	£0.45	£0.75
4-6 Colan art	$0.25	$0.75	$1.25	£0.15	£0.45	£0.75
7-8 Cam Kennedy art, Mignola cover	$0.25	$0.75	$1.25	£0.15	£0.45	£0.75
9 Gray Morrow art, Mike Mignola cover; 1st DC comic featuring nudity without Mature Readers label (production error)	$0.25	$0.75	$1.25	£0.15	£0.45	£0.75
10-11 Millennium X-over	$0.25	$0.75	$1.25	£0.15	£0.45	£0.75
12	$0.25	$0.75	$1.25	£0.15	£0.45	£0.75
13 Charles Vess cover	$0.25	$0.75	$1.25	£0.15	£0.45	£0.75
14-22	$0.25	$0.75	$1.25	£0.15	£0.45	£0.75
23 Invasion X-over	$0.25	$0.75	$1.25	£0.15	£0.45	£0.75
24-29 Ghost in the Machine story	$0.25	$0.75	$1.25	£0.15	£0.45	£0.75
30	$0.25	$0.75	$1.25	£0.15	£0.45	£0.75
31 LD in the U.K.	$0.25	$0.75	$1.25	£0.20	£0.60	£1.00
Title Value:	$7.75	$23.25	$38.75	£4.70	£14.10	£23.50

Note: Kaluta covers #1-3, Garcia Lopez covers #5, #6, Mignola covers #7-9

SPECTRE, THE (2ND SERIES) ANNUAL
DC Comics; 1 1988

	$Good	$Fine	$N.Mint	£Good	£Fine	£N.Mint
1 ND 48pgs, Baikie art, Art Adams cover includes Marvel/Indie character cameos	$0.40	$1.20	$2.00	£0.25	£0.75	£1.25
Title Value:	$0.40	$1.20	$2.00	£0.25	£0.75	£1.25

SPECTRE, THE (3RD SERIES)
DC Comics; 0 Oct 1994; 1 Dec 1992-present

	$Good	$Fine	$N.Mint	£Good	£Fine	£N.Mint
0 (Oct 1994) Zero Hour X-over, origin retold	$0.40	$1.20	$2.00	£0.25	£0.75	£1.25
1 Tom Mandrake art begins; glow-in-the-dark cover	$1.20	$3.60	$6.00	£0.60	£1.80	£3.00
2	$0.80	$2.40	$4.00	£0.30	£0.90	£1.50
3 Madame Xanadu appears	$0.80	$2.40	$4.00	£0.30	£0.90	£1.50
4	$0.40	$1.20	$2.00	£0.25	£0.75	£1.25
5 Charles Vess cover	$0.40	$1.20	$2.00	£0.25	£0.75	£1.25
6 Garry Leach cover	$0.40	$1.20	$2.00	£0.25	£0.75	£1.25
7 Madame Xanadu becomes The Spectre (temporarily)	$0.40	$1.20	$2.00	£0.25	£0.75	£1.25
8 glow-in-the-dark cover	$0.80	$2.40	$4.00	£0.40	£1.20	£2.00
9 Matt Wagner cover	$0.40	$1.20	$2.00	£0.25	£0.75	£1.25
10 Kaluta cover	$0.40	$1.20	$2.00	£0.25	£0.75	£1.25
11-12	$0.40	$1.20	$2.00	£0.25	£0.75	£1.25
13 glow-in-the-dark cover	$0.80	$2.40	$4.00	£0.40	£1.20	£2.00
14 Phantom Stranger appears	$0.40	$1.20	$2.00	£0.25	£0.75	£1.25
15 Phantom Stranger, Demon, Dr. Fate and John Constantine appear	$0.40	$1.20	$2.00	£0.25	£0.75	£1.25
16-21	$0.40	$1.20	$2.00	£0.25	£0.75	£1.25
22 Superman guest-stars; painted cover by Alex Ross	$0.40	$1.20	$2.00	£0.25	£0.75	£1.25
23-26	$0.40	$1.20	$2.00	£0.25	£0.75	£1.25
27 Simon Bisley painted cover	$0.40	$1.20	$2.00	£0.25	£0.75	£1.25
28-29	$0.40	$1.20	$2.00	£0.25	£0.75	£1.25
30-34	$0.45	$1.35	$2.25	£0.30	£0.90	£1.50
35-36 Underworld Unleashed tie-in	$0.45	$1.35	$2.25	£0.30	£0.90	£1.50
37-38	$0.45	$1.35	$2.25	£0.30	£0.90	£1.50
39 painted cover by Kev O'Neill	$0.45	$1.35	$2.25	£0.30	£0.90	£1.50
Title Value:	$18.90	$56.70	$94.50	£11.25	£33.75	£56.25

The Spectre: Crimes & Punishments (Dec 1993)
Trade paperback reprints issues #1-4 with new glow-in-the-dark cover

				£Good	£Fine	£N.Mint
				£1.30	£3.90	£6.50

SPECTRE, THE (3RD SERIES) ANNUAL
DC Comics; 1 Nov 1995-present

	$Good	$Fine	$N.Mint	£Good	£Fine	£N.Mint
1 56pgs, Year One, Dr. Fate appears	$0.80	$2.40	$4.00	£0.50	£1.50	£2.50
Title Value:	$0.80	$2.40	$4.00	£0.50	£1.50	£2.50

SPECTRE, WRATH OF THE
DC Comics,MS; 1 May 1988-4 Aug 1988

	$Good	$Fine	$N.Mint	£Good	£Fine	£N.Mint
1-3 ND 48pgs, reprints Adventure #431-440	$0.50	$1.50	$2.50	£0.30	£0.90	£1.50
4 ND 48pgs, 3 new stories originally intended for Adventure Comics #441-443	$0.50	$1.50	$2.50	£0.30	£0.90	£1.50
Title Value:	$2.00	$6.00	$10.00	£1.20	£3.60	£6.00

SPEED RACER
Now Comics; 1 Aug 1987-42 1992

	$Good	$Fine	$N.Mint	£Good	£Fine	£N.Mint
1 ND	$0.40	$1.20	$2.00	£0.25	£0.75	£1.25
1 2nd printing ND	$0.30	$0.90	$1.50	£0.20	£0.60	£1.00
2-19 ND	$0.40	$1.20	$2.00	£0.25	£0.75	£1.25
20-42 ND Comics Code on cover	$0.40	$1.20	$2.00	£0.25	£0.75	£1.25
Title Value:	$17.10	$51.30	$85.50	£10.70	£32.10	£53.50

SPEED RACER (2ND SERIES)
Now Comics,MS; 1 Jul 1992-3 Sep 1992

	$Good	$Fine	$N.Mint	£Good	£Fine	£N.Mint
1 ND includes cut-out model	$0.40	$1.20	$2.00	£0.25	£0.75	£1.25
1 ND Prestige Edition, pre-bagged with badge, 16 extra pages, 500 copies signed and numbered by creators, numbered neon label on front cover	$0.50	$1.50	$2.50	£0.30	£0.90	£1.50
1 Newsstand edition, ND pre-bagged with badge, signed and numbered by creators	$0.50	$1.50	$2.50	£0.30	£0.90	£1.50
2-3 ND	$0.40	$1.20	$2.00	£0.25	£0.75	£1.25
Title Value:	$2.20	$6.60	$11.00	£1.35	£4.05	£6.75

SPEED RACER 3-D SPECIAL
Now Comics; 1 Jan 1993-2 1993

	$Good	$Fine	$N.Mint	£Good	£Fine	£N.Mint
1-2 ND pre-bagged with glasses (25% less without glasses)	$0.50	$1.50	$2.50	£0.30	£0.90	£1.50
Title Value:	$1.00	$3.00	$5.00	£0.60	£1.80	£3.00

SPEED RACER FEATURING NINJA HIGH SCHOOL
Now Comics,MS; 1 Aug 1993-2 1994

	$Good	$Fine	$N.Mint	£Good	£Fine	£N.Mint
1 ND	$0.50	$1.50	$2.50	£0.30	£0.90	£1.50
2 ND pre-bagged with trading card; part 3 - part 4 published by Eternity the same month	$0.50	$1.50	$2.50	£0.30	£0.90	£1.50
Title Value:	$1.00	$3.00	$5.00	£0.60	£1.80	£3.00

SPEED RACER SPECIAL
Now Comics; 1 1987-2 1988

	$Good	$Fine	$N.Mint	£Good	£Fine	£N.Mint
1 ND $2 cover	$0.40	$1.20	$2.00	£0.25	£0.75	£1.25
2 ND	$0.60	$1.80	$3.00	£0.40	£1.20	£2.00
Title Value:	$1.00	$3.00	$5.00	£0.65	£1.95	£3.25

SPEED RACER, THE NEW ADVENTURES OF
Now Comics; 0 Nov 1993; 1 Dec 1993-11 1994?

	$Good	$Fine	$N.Mint	£Good	£Fine	£N.Mint
0 ND pre-bagged with trading card	$0.50	$1.50	$2.50	£0.30	£0.90	£1.50
1-11 ND	$0.40	$1.20	$2.00	£0.25	£0.75	£1.25
Title Value:	$4.90	$14.70	$24.50	£3.05	£9.15	£15.25

SPEEDBALL THE MASKED MARVEL
Marvel Comics Group; 1 Sep 1988-11 Jul 1989
(see New Warriors)

	$Good	$Fine	$N.Mint	£Good	£Fine	£N.Mint
1 ND Steve Ditko story/art begins	$0.30	$0.90	$1.50	£0.20	£0.60	£1.00
2-11	$0.25	$0.75	$1.25	£0.15	£0.45	£0.75
Title Value:	$2.80	$8.40	$14.00	£1.70	£5.10	£8.50

SPELLBOUND
Marvel Comics Group,MS; 1 Jan 1988-6 Mar 1988

	$Good	$Fine	$N.Mint	£Good	£Fine	£N.Mint
1-3 ND	$0.25	$0.75	$1.25	£0.15	£0.45	£0.75
4 ND New Mutants appear	$0.25	$0.75	$1.25	£0.15	£0.45	£0.75
5-6 ND	$0.25	$0.75	$1.25	£0.15	£0.45	£0.75
Title Value:	$1.50	$4.50	$7.50	£0.90	£2.70	£4.50

Note: all high quality paper, bi-weekly frequency

SPELLJAMMER COMICS
DC Comics; 1 Sep 1990-18 Feb 1992

	$Good	$Fine	$N.Mint	£Good	£Fine	£N.Mint
1-7 ND	$0.40	$1.20	$2.00	£0.25	£0.75	£1.25
8 ND Joe Quesada (1st professional work?)	$0.60	$1.80	$3.00	£0.40	£1.20	£2.00
9 ND Joe Quesada art	$0.50	$1.50	$2.50	£0.30	£0.90	£1.50
10 ND part prose, Joe Quesada art	$0.40	$1.20	$2.00	£0.25	£0.75	£1.25
11-13 ND Joe Quesada art	$0.40	$1.20	$2.00	£0.25	£0.75	£1.25
14-18 ND	$0.40	$1.20	$2.00	£0.25	£0.75	£1.25
Title Value:	$7.50	$22.50	$37.50	£4.70	£14.10	£23.50

Note: New Format

SPENCER SPOOK, THE ADVENTURES OF
Ace; 1 Oct 1986-4 1987

	$Good	$Fine	$N.Mint	£Good	£Fine	£N.Mint
1-4 ND Pat Boyette art	$0.30	$0.90	$1.50	£0.20	£0.60	£1.00
Title Value:	$1.20	$3.60	$6.00	£0.80	£2.40	£4.00

SPICY DETECTIVE STORIES
Eternity; nn 1987

	$Good	$Fine	$N.Mint	£Good	£Fine	£N.Mint
nn ND 1930s detective pulp reprints	$1.20	$3.60	$6.00	£0.80	£2.40	£4.00
Title Value:	$1.20	$3.60	$6.00	£0.80	£2.40	£4.00
2nd print (1990)				£0.85	£2.55	£4.25

SPICY HORROR STORIES
Eternity; nn Oct 1990

	$Good	$Fine	$N.Mint	£Good	£Fine	£N.Mint
nn ND 1930s/1940s horror pulp reprints	$1.50	$4.50	$7.50	£1.00	£3.00	£5.00
Title Value:	$1.50	$4.50	$7.50	£1.00	£3.00	£5.00

SPICY MYSTERY STORIES TRADE PAPERBACK
Eternity; nn Jun 1990

	$Good	$Fine	$N.Mint	£Good	£Fine	£N.Mint
nn ND 10 classic pulp tales from the 1930s	$1.50	$4.50	$7.50	£1.00	£3.00	£5.00
Title Value:	$1.50	$4.50	$7.50	£1.00	£3.00	£5.00

SPICY TALES
Eternity; 1 Feb 1989-17 1991

	$Good	$Fine	$N.Mint	£Good	£Fine	£N.Mint
1 ND reprint detective anthology begins	$0.40	$1.20	$2.00	£0.25	£0.75	£1.25
2-17 ND	$0.40	$1.20	$2.00	£0.25	£0.75	£1.25
Title Value:	$6.80	$20.40	$34.00	£4.25	£12.75	£21.25
Special 1,2				£0.30	£0.90	£1.50
Collection (1990), reprints				£1.10	£3.30	£5.50
Graphic Album, new reprints (1990)				£1.10	£3.30	£5.50

SPICY WESTERN STORIES TRADE PAPERBACK
Eternity; nn Jul 1990

	$Good	$Fine	$N.Mint	£Good	£Fine	£N.Mint
nn ND reprints 1930s western pulps	$1.50	$4.50	$7.50	£1.00	£3.00	£5.00
Title Value:	$1.50	$4.50	$7.50	£1.00	£3.00	£5.00

SPIDER, THE
Eclipse,MS; 1 Jun 1991-3 Oct 1991
(see DC's Hawkworld)

	$Good	$Fine	$N.Mint	£Good	£Fine	£N.Mint
1-3 ND 48pgs, Tim Truman and Alcatena	$0.80	$2.40	$4.00	£0.50	£1.50	£2.50
Title Value:	$2.40	$7.20	$12.00	£1.50	£4.50	£7.50

SPIDER: REIGN OF THE VAMPIRE KING, THE
Eclipse,MS; 1 Aug 1992-3 Oct 1992

	$Good	$Fine	$N.Mint	£Good	£Fine	£N.Mint
1-3 ND 48pgs, Truman and Alcatena	$0.80	$2.40	$4.00	£0.50	£1.50	£2.50
Title Value:	$2.40	$7.20	$12.00	£1.50	£4.50	£7.50

SPIDERMAN
Marvel Comics Group; 1 Aug 1990-63 Oct 1995; 64 Jan 1996-present

	$Good	$Fine	$N.Mint	£Good	£Fine	£N.Mint
1 ND Todd McFarlane art begins, green cover/white logo, Lizard appears	$0.90	$2.70	$4.50	£0.60	£1.80	£3.00
1 ND as above, pre-bagged with Spidey Face in bottom left hand corner	$1.80	$5.25	$9.00	£1.20	£3.60	£6.00
1 ND as above, pre-bagged with bar-code lines in bottom left hand corner	$1.20	$3.60	$6.00	£0.80	£2.40	£4.00
1 ND silver/black cover edition, Direct Sales only to comic shops	$1.20	$3.60	$6.00	£0.80	£2.40	£4.00
1 ND as above, pre-bagged	$2.00	$6.00	$10.00	£1.40	£4.20	£7.00
1 ND gold cover edition, Direct Sales only, 2nd print in indicia but there is only this one (Note: Marvel have stated no bagged copies)	$0.90	$2.70	$4.50	£0.60	£1.80	£3.00
1 ND green cover/white logo signed by McFarlane with letter of authenticity (20,000 copies)	$4.50	$13.50	$22.50	£3.00	£9.00	£15.00
1 ND silver/black cover signed by McFarlane with letter of authenticity (20,000 copies)	$4.50	$13.50	$22.50	£3.00	£9.00	£15.00
1 ND Platinum Edition, 10,000 copies sent by Marvel to distributors in U.S. and U.K. as "thankyou". (Most copies damaged through the mail, however...)	$40.00	$120.00	$200.00	£25.00	£75.00	£125.00
2 ND Lizard appears	$0.90	$2.70	$4.50	£0.60	£1.80	£3.00
3 ND Lizard appears, origin Spiderman retold	$0.90	$2.70	$4.50	£0.60	£1.80	£3.00
4-5 ND Lizard appears	$0.80	$2.40	$4.00	£0.50	£1.50	£2.50
6 ND Ghost Rider appears	$0.90	$2.70	$4.50	£0.60	£1.80	£3.00
6 ND Ghost Rider appears (2nd print)	$0.30	$0.90	$1.50	£0.20	£0.60	£1.00
7 ND Ghost Rider appears	$0.80	$2.40	$4.00	£0.50	£1.50	£2.50
8 ND Perceptions story; Wolverine appears last page	$0.60	$1.80	$3.00	£0.40	£1.20	£2.00
9-12 ND Perceptions story, Wolverine/Wendigo appear	$0.60	$1.80	$3.00	£0.40	£1.20	£2.00
13-14 ND Morbius the Living Vampire appears	$0.80	$2.40	$4.00	£0.50	£1.50	£2.50
15 ND Impossible Man appears	$0.40	$1.20	$2.00	£0.25	£0.75	£1.25
16 ND X-over with X-Force #4; entire issue printed sideways, last McFarlane art	$0.40	$1.20	$2.00	£0.25	£0.75	£1.25
17 ND Thanos appears, Nocenti script, Leonardi and Austin art	$0.40	$1.20	$2.00	£0.25	£0.75	£1.25
18 ND Erik Larsen script and art begins, Sinister Six appear						

Spectacular Spiderman #17

The Spectre (3rd) #22

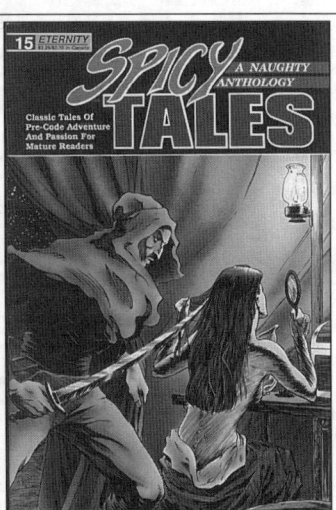

Spicy Tales #15

	$Good	$Fine	$N.Mint	£Good	£Fine	£N.Mint
	$0.40	$1.20	$2.00	£0.25	£0.75	£1.25
19 ND Erik Larsen script and art, Deathlok, Hulk, Sinister Six appear	$0.40	$1.20	$2.00	£0.25	£0.75	£1.25
20 ND Erik Larsen script and art, Sinister Six appear	$0.40	$1.20	$2.00	£0.25	£0.75	£1.25
21 ND Erik Larsen script and art, Sinister Six appear, Deathlok and Hulk appear	$0.40	$1.20	$2.00	£0.25	£0.75	£1.25
22 ND Erik Larsen script and art, Sinister Six appear, Deathlok, Ghost Rider and Sleepwalker appear	$0.40	$1.20	$2.00	£0.25	£0.75	£1.25
23 ND Erik Larsen script and art, Sinister Six appear plus Ghost Rider, Solo, Deathlok, Hulk, Nova, Fantastic Four, gatefold cover	$0.40	$1.20	$2.00	£0.25	£0.75	£1.25
24 ND Infinity War X-over	$0.40	$1.20	$2.00	£0.25	£0.75	£1.25
25 ND Excalibur appear	$0.40	$1.20	$2.00	£0.25	£0.75	£1.25
26 ND 30th anniversary issue, hologram cover, gatefold centre-spread, Spiderman's origin as seen through the eyes of Peter Parker, Larsen art	$0.80	$2.40	$4.00	£0.50	£1.50	£2.50
27-31 ND	$0.40	$1.20	$2.00	£0.25	£0.75	£1.25
32-34 ND Punisher guest-stars	$0.40	$1.20	$2.00	£0.25	£0.75	£1.25
35 ND Maximum Carnage part 4, continued in Spectacular Spiderman #201	$0.40	$1.20	$2.00	£0.25	£0.75	£1.25
36 ND Maximum Carnage part 8, continued in Spectacular Spiderman #202	$0.40	$1.20	$2.00	£0.25	£0.75	£1.25
37 ND Maximum Carnage part 12, continued in Spectacular Spiderman #203	$0.40	$1.20	$2.00	£0.25	£0.75	£1.25
38-40 ND Electro appears	$0.40	$1.20	$2.00	£0.25	£0.75	£1.25
41-43 ND Iron Fist appears; Jae Lee art	$0.30	$0.90	$1.50	£0.20	£0.60	£1.00
44 ND Howard Mackie, Tom Lyle and Scott Hanna creative team begins	$0.30	$0.90	$1.50	£0.20	£0.60	£1.00
45 ND Pursuit part 1, continued in Spectacular Spiderman #211	$0.30	$0.90	$1.50	£0.20	£0.60	£1.00
46 ND Hobgoblin and Demogoblin appear	$0.30	$0.90	$1.50	£0.20	£0.60	£1.00
46 ND Collector's Edition, pre-bagged with 16pg preview and animation cel from the Spiderman animated TV series, metallic ink cover	$0.60	$1.80	$3.00	£0.40	£1.20	£2.00
47 ND Hobgoblin and Demogoblin appear	$0.30	$0.90	$1.50	£0.20	£0.60	£1.00
48-49	$0.30	$0.90	$1.50	£0.20	£0.60	£1.00
50 48pgs, holo-grafix foil cover	$0.80	$2.40	$4.00	£0.50	£1.50	£2.50
51 Power and responsibility part 3	$0.30	$0.90	$1.50	£0.20	£0.60	£1.00
51 Power and responsibility part 3, foil stamped cover, incorporates 16pg flip-book with second foil stamped cover; continued in Spectacular Spiderman #217	$0.60	$1.80	$3.00	£0.40	£1.20	£2.00
52 Venom appears	$0.30	$0.90	$1.50	£0.20	£0.60	£1.00
53 Venom appears	$0.40	$1.20	$2.00	£0.25	£0.75	£1.25
54 48pgs, Web of Life part 2, continued in Web of Spiderman #121	$0.55	$1.65	$2.75	£0.35	£1.05	£1.75
55 Web of Life part 4 (conclusion)	$0.40	$1.20	$2.00	£0.25	£0.75	£1.25
56 The Jackal appears	$0.40	$1.20	$2.00	£0.25	£0.75	£1.25
57 48pgs, Aftershocks part 1, continued in Spectacular Spiderman #223	$0.50	$1.50	$2.50	£0.30	£0.90	£1.50
57 ND 48pgs, Enhanced Edition - multi-level debossed cover	$0.60	$1.80	$3.00	£0.40	£1.20	£2.00
58 The Mark of Kaine part 3, continued in Spectacular Spiderman #224; Spiderman and The Scarlet Spider vs. Kaine	$0.40	$1.20	$2.00	£0.25	£0.75	£1.25
59 continued from Amazing Spiderman #402	$0.40	$1.20	$2.00	£0.25	£0.75	£1.25
60 The Trial of Peter Parker part 3, continued in Spectacular Spiderman #226	$0.40	$1.20	$2.00	£0.25	£0.75	£1.25
61 Maximum Clonage part 4, continued in Spectacular Spiderman #227	$0.40	$1.20	$2.00	£0.25	£0.75	£1.25
62 Exiled part 3, continued in Spiderman Unlimited #10	$0.40	$1.20	$2.00	£0.25	£0.75	£1.25
63 The Great Responsibility part 2, continued in Spectacular Spiderman #229	$0.40	$1.20	$2.00	£0.25	£0.75	£1.25
64 The Return of Spiderman part 3, continued in Spectacular Spiderman #230	$0.40	$1.20	$2.00	£0.25	£0.75	£1.25
65 Media Blizzard part 3 (conclusion), continued from Amazing Spiderman #408	$0.40	$1.20	$2.00	£0.25	£0.75	£1.25
66 The Return of Kaine part 4 (conclusion from Spiderman #409)	$0.40	$1.20	$2.00	£0.25	£0.75	£1.25
Title Value:	**$89.55**	**$268.50**	**$447.5**	**£57.20**	**£171.60**	**£286.00**

Note: a print run of over 2.5 million copies makes this one of the best selling comics of modern times.

The Blue Lizard Spiderman:

Note also that a printing defect on the silver ink/black cover unbagged (and possibly bagged) editions that came to this country (apparently only to the North of England) shows a blue-coloured Lizard in a couple of panels. The number of copies is alledged to be anything from 200-1,500 but more are suspected. This anomaly is duly noted but no firmly established value can be given for it even though isolated copies have been sold at a wide range of premium prices. An average now seems to be **£5.00-**

£10.00.

Note also that pre-bagged copies of the gold edition have been sighted but these have been constructed outside Marvel Comics as they never officially designed this package.

Note also that up to 40,000 copies of the regular green and silver editions were officially signed by Todd McFarlane in gold ink on the cover. They would have an added value though counterfeits have been known. Genuine copies should be accompanied by a signed letter of authentication and a red spider-web seal on the back.

The Platinum Edition: this is a special edition of Spiderman #1 with no ads + 10 pages of sketches and pin-ups. They were made available by Marvel in the Spring of 1991 to (mostly US) retailers only. 10,000 were officially printed. It has very glossy cardstock (stiffer) covers.

AS MANY OF THESE WERE MAILED THROUGH THE POST, MOST SUFFER FROM SCRATCHES OR CRUMPLED CORNERS. ABSOLUTELY NEAR MINT COPIES ARE VERY RARE

Spiderman Mini-Masterpiece (Dec 1995)
boxed set collecting Spiderman #45 & #50,
Spectacular Spiderman #211, Web of Spiderman #112,

	$Good	$Fine	$N.Mint	£Good	£Fine	£N.Mint
Amazing Spiderman #389, ND				£1.30	£3.90	£6.50

SPIDERMAN 2099

Marvel Comics Group; 1 Nov 1992-present
(see Doom 2099, Ghost Rider 2099, Hulk 2099, Punisher 2099, Ravage 2099, X-Men 2099)

	$Good	$Fine	$N.Mint	£Good	£Fine	£N.Mint
1 ND Peter David script, Leonardi/Williamson art begins, red-foil border cover on heavier stock paper; origin begins	$0.60	$1.80	$3.00	£0.40	£1.20	£2.00
2 ND origin continues	$0.50	$1.50	$2.50	£0.30	£0.90	£1.50
3 ND origin concludes	$0.30	$0.90	$1.50	£0.20	£0.60	£1.00
4 ND Doom 2099 appears	$0.25	$0.75	$1.25	£0.15	£0.45	£0.75
5-7 ND	$0.25	$0.75	$1.25	£0.15	£0.45	£0.75
8 ND 1st appearance Vulture 2099	$0.25	$0.75	$1.25	£0.15	£0.45	£0.75
9-15 ND	$0.25	$0.75	$1.25	£0.15	£0.45	£0.75
16 ND Peter David script, continued in Ravage 2099 #15	$0.25	$0.75	$1.25	£0.15	£0.45	£0.75
17-18 ND	$0.25	$0.75	$1.25	£0.15	£0.45	£0.75
19 ND with free Spiderman's Amazing Powers card sheet	$0.25	$0.75	$1.25	£0.15	£0.45	£0.75
20-25 ND	$0.25	$0.75	$1.25	£0.15	£0.45	£0.75
25 ND multi-level embossed foil stamped cover; 8pg Hulk 2099 preview	$0.60	$1.80	$3.00	£0.40	£1.20	£2.00
26-31 ND	$0.30	$0.90	$1.50	£0.20	£0.60	£1.00
32 ND $1.95 begin	$0.40	$1.20	$2.00	£0.25	£0.75	£1.25
33 ND	$0.40	$1.20	$2.00	£0.25	£0.75	£1.25
34-35 ND One Nation Under Doom	$0.40	$1.20	$2.00	£0.25	£0.75	£1.25
36 ND One Nation Under Doom; Cover A high-lighting Spiderman 2099 that joins to Cover B	$0.40	$1.20	$2.00	£0.25	£0.75	£1.25
36 ND One Nation Under Doom; Cover B high-lighting Venom 2099 that joins to Cover A	$0.40	$1.20	$2.00	£0.25	£0.75	£1.25
37 ND One Nation Under Doom; Cover A high-lighting Spiderman 2099 being attacked by Venom 2099	$0.40	$1.20	$2.00	£0.25	£0.75	£1.25
37 ND One Nation Under Doom; Cover B high-lighting Venom 2099 in the classic "Amazing Fantasy #15 pose"	$0.40	$1.20	$2.00	£0.25	£0.75	£1.25
38 ND Venom 2099 saga concludes; Cover A shows Spiderman 2099	$0.40	$1.20	$2.00	£0.25	£0.75	£1.25
38 ND Venom 2099 saga concludes; Cover B shows Venom 2099	$0.40	$1.20	$2.00	£0.25	£0.75	£1.25
39 ND intro Goblin 2099, ties into 2099 Genesis	$0.40	$1.20	$2.00	£0.25	£0.75	£1.25
40 ND	$0.40	$1.20	$2.00	£0.25	£0.75	£1.25
41 ND Goblin 2099 vs. Vulture 2099	$0.40	$1.20	$2.00	£0.25	£0.75	£1.25
Title Value:	**$14.50**	**$43.50**	**$72.50**	**£9.05**	**£27.15**	**£45.25**

SPIDERMAN 2099 ANNUAL

Marvel Comics Group; 1 Sep 1994-present

	$Good	$Fine	$N.Mint	£Good	£Fine	£N.Mint
1 ND Peter David Script	$0.60	$1.80	$3.00	£0.40	£1.20	£2.00
Title Value:	**$0.60**	**$1.80**	**$3.00**	**£0.40**	**£1.20**	**£2.00**

SPIDERMAN 2099 SPECIAL

Marvel Comics Group; 1 Nov 1995

	$Good	$Fine	$N.Mint	£Good	£Fine	£N.Mint
1 ND 64pgs, One Nation Under Doom, painted cover by the Brothers Hildebrandt	$0.80	$2.40	$4.00	£0.50	£1.50	£2.50
Title Value:	**$0.80**	**$2.40**	**$4.00**	**£0.50**	**£1.50**	**£2.50**

SPIDERMAN ADVENTURES

Marvel Comics Group; 1 Dec 1994-present

	$Good	$Fine	$N.Mint	£Good	£Fine	£N.Mint
1 based on newest animated series, foil stamped and embossed cover	$0.60	$1.80	$3.00	£0.40	£1.20	£2.00
2 The Scorpion appears	$0.30	$0.90	$1.50	£0.20	£0.60	£1.00
3-4 Spider-Slayer appears	$0.30	$0.90	$1.50	£0.20	£0.60	£1.00
5 Mysterio appears	$0.30	$0.90	$1.50	£0.20	£0.60	£1.00
6 Kraven the Hunter appears	$0.30	$0.90	$1.50	£0.20	£0.60	£1.00
7 Dr. Octopus origin retold	$0.30	$0.90	$1.50	£0.20	£0.60	£1.00
8-9 origin of Venom retold	$0.30	$0.90	$1.50	£0.20	£0.60	£1.00
10 Spiderman vs. Venom; bi-weekly						

	$Good	$Fine	$N.Mint	£Good	£Fine	£N.Mint
	$0.30	$0.90	$1.50	£0.20	£0.60	£1.00
11 Spiderman vs. Hobgoblin; bi-weekly	$0.30	$0.90	$1.50	£0.20	£0.60	£1.00
12 Hobgoblin and Kingpin appear	$0.30	$0.90	$1.50	£0.20	£0.60	£1.00
13 Chameleon appears	$0.30	$0.90	$1.50	£0.20	£0.60	£1.00
14 origin of Spiderman retold as brand new adventures not seen on the animated show begin	$0.30	$0.90	$1.50	£0.20	£0.60	£1.00
15 The Lizard appears	$0.30	$0.90	$1.50	£0.20	£0.60	£1.00
Title Value:	$4.80	$14.40	$24.00	£3.20	£9.60	£16.00

Spiderman Adventures (Nov 1995) Trade paperback
112pgs, collects issues #1-5, computer animated cel cover — £1.20 £3.60 £6.00

SPIDERMAN AND HIS AMAZING FRIENDS
Marvel Comics Group,OS TV; 1 Dec 1981

	$Good	$Fine	$N.Mint	£Good	£Fine	£N.Mint
1 ND adapts TV cartoon, 1st appearance of Firestar but outside Marvel continuity	$0.60	$1.80	$3.00	£0.40	£1.20	£2.00
Title Value:	$0.60	$1.80	$3.00	£0.40	£1.20	£2.00

SPIDERMAN ASHCAN, AMAZING
Marvel Comics Group; nn Jun 1994

	$Good	$Fine	$N.Mint	£Good	£Fine	£N.Mint
nn ND 16pgs, origin retold and profiles on Spiderman villains	$0.30	$0.90	$1.50	£0.20	£0.60	£1.00
Title Value:	$0.30	$0.90	$1.50	£0.20	£0.60	£1.00

SPIDERMAN BOOK AND RECORD SET
Power Records; PR-24 1974

	$Good	$Fine	$N.Mint	£Good	£Fine	£N.Mint
24 ND scarce in the U.K. 20pg booklet with 45 rpm record	$3.00	$9.00	$15.00	£2.00	£6.00	£10.00
24 as above but without record	$1.50	$4.50	$7.50	£1.00	£3.00	£5.00
Title Value:	$4.50	$13.50	$22.50	£3.00	£9.00	£15.00

SPIDERMAN CLASSICS
Marvel Comics Group; 1 Apr 1993-16 Jul 1994

	$Good	$Fine	$N.Mint	£Good	£Fine	£N.Mint
1 reprints Amazing Fantasy #15 and Strange Tales #115	$0.25	$0.75	$1.25	£0.15	£0.45	£0.75
2 reprints Amazing Spiderman #1	$0.25	$0.75	$1.25	£0.15	£0.45	£0.75
3 reprints Amazing Spiderman #2	$0.25	$0.75	$1.25	£0.15	£0.45	£0.75
4 reprints Amazing Spiderman #3, Ron Lim cover	$0.25	$0.75	$1.25	£0.15	£0.45	£0.75
5 reprints Amazing Spiderman #4	$0.25	$0.75	$1.25	£0.15	£0.45	£0.75
6 reprints Amazing Spiderman #5	$0.25	$0.75	$1.25	£0.15	£0.45	£0.75
7 reprints Amazing Spiderman #6	$0.25	$0.75	$1.25	£0.15	£0.45	£0.75
8 reprints Amazing Spiderman #7	$0.25	$0.75	$1.25	£0.15	£0.45	£0.75
9 reprints Amazing Spiderman #8	$0.25	$0.75	$1.25	£0.15	£0.45	£0.75
10 reprints Amazing Spiderman #9	$0.25	$0.75	$1.25	£0.15	£0.45	£0.75
11 reprints Amazing Spiderman #10	$0.25	$0.75	$1.25	£0.15	£0.45	£0.75
12-15	$0.25	$0.75	$1.25	£0.15	£0.45	£0.75
15 ND Collector's Edition, pre-bagged with animation cel from Spiderman TV series; reprints Amazing Spiderman #14; metallic ink cover	$0.60	$1.80	$3.00	£0.40	£1.20	£2.00
16	$0.25	$0.75	$1.25	£0.15	£0.45	£0.75
Title Value:	$4.60	$13.80	$23.00	£2.80	£8.40	£14.00

SPIDERMAN COLLECTORS' PREVIEW
Marvel Comics Group,OS; 1 Dec 1994

	$Good	$Fine	$N.Mint	£Good	£Fine	£N.Mint
1 ND previews the storylines leading up to Spiderman #400 plus news and features	$0.30	$0.90	$1.50	£0.20	£0.60	£1.00
Title Value:	$0.30	$0.90	$1.50	£0.20	£0.60	£1.00

SPIDERMAN COMICS DIGEST
Marvel Comics Group,Digest; 1 Jan 1987-10 Oct 1987

	$Good	$Fine	$N.Mint	£Good	£Fine	£N.Mint
1-10 ND scarce in the U.K., all reprints	$0.30	$0.90	$1.50	£0.20	£0.60	£1.00
Title Value:	$3.00	$9.00	$15.00	£2.00	£6.00	£10.00

SPIDERMAN GIANT SIZE
Marvel Comics Group; 1 Jul 1974-6 Sep 1975

	$Good	$Fine	$N.Mint	£Good	£Fine	£N.Mint
1 ND 68pgs, Spiderman vs. Dracula; reprints Spiderman/Human Torch from Strange Tales Annual #2	$4.15	$12.50	$25.00	£2.50	£7.50	£15.00
2-3 ND 68pgs	$1.65	$5.00	$10.00	£1.15	£3.50	£7.00
4 ND 68pgs, 3rd full appearance of the Punisher	$10.00	$30.00	$60.00	£6.50	£20.00	£40.00
5-6 ND 68pgs	$1.50	$4.50	$9.00	£1.00	£3.00	£6.00
Title Value:	$20.45	$61.50	$123.00	£13.30	£40.50	£81.00

SPIDERMAN GIVEAWAY
Marvel Comics Group; 1980-1984
(all Non Distributed on the news-stands in the U.K.)

	£Good	£Fine	£N.Mint
nn 1979 32pgs, All Detergent Promotion; reprints Amazing Spiderman #23 and origin re-told	£0.50	£1.50	£3.00
nn 1979 16pgs, Columbus Despatch Spiderman and Hulk Giveaway	£0.30	£0.90	£1.50
nn 1980 32pgs, Aim Toothpaste Promotion, Green Goblin appears	£0.30	£0.90	£1.50
nn 1980 16pgs, Chicago Tribune Spiderman and Hulk Giveaway; origin re-told	£0.25	£0.75	£1.25
nn 1981 32pgs, Dallas Times Herald Spiderman and Hulk Giveaway; Kingpin and Sandman appear	£0.30	£0.90	£1.50
nn 1982 16pgs, Aim Toothpaste Promotion, Dr. Octopus appears	£0.25	£0.75	£1.25
nn 1982 16pgs, American Cancer Society; Storm and Powerman appear	£0.25	£0.75	£1.25
nn 1983 32pgs, Dallas Times Herald Giveaway, Kingpin appears	£0.30	£0.90	£1.50
nn 1983 32pgs, Dallas Times Herald Giveaway, Dallas Cowboys/ Ringmaster/Crime Circus appear	£0.30	£0.90	£1.50
nn 1983 32pgs, Dallas Times Herald Giveaway; Firestar and Iceman appear	£0.30	£0.90	£1.50
nn 1984 16pgs, National Education Association; Power Pack appear, highlights problem of Child Abuse	£0.25	£0.75	£1.25

SPIDERMAN HOLIDAY SPECIAL '95
Marvel Comics Group,OS; 1 Feb 1996

	$Good	$Fine	$N.Mint	£Good	£Fine	£N.Mint
1 ND four stories featuring Venom and Human Torch among others; cover by Adam Kubert	$0.60	$1.80	$3.00	£0.40	£1.20	£2.00
Title Value:	$0.60	$1.80	$3.00	£0.40	£1.20	£2.00

SPIDERMAN MAGAZINE
Marvel Comics Group,Magazine; 1 Mar 1994-15 May 1995

	$Good	$Fine	$N.Mint	£Good	£Fine	£N.Mint
1 puzzles and games magazine for a younger audience; bound-in sheet of 8 trading cards; cover by John Romita Jnr. Characters and stories are not considered part of the Marvel Universe continuity	$0.40	$1.20	$2.00	£0.25	£0.75	£1.25
2-7 ND	$0.40	$1.20	$2.00	£0.25	£0.75	£1.25
8 ND bound-in trading cards	$0.40	$1.20	$2.00	£0.25	£0.75	£1.25
9-13 ND	$0.40	$1.20	$2.00	£0.25	£0.75	£1.25
14-15 ND with bound-in trading cards	$0.40	$1.20	$2.00	£0.25	£0.75	£1.25
Title Value:	$6.00	$18.00	$30.00	£3.75	£11.25	£18.75

SPIDERMAN MAGAZINE (2ND SERIES)
Marvel Comics Group,Magazine; 1 Nov 1995-present

	$Good	$Fine	$N.Mint	£Good	£Fine	£N.Mint
1 ND revamped series with quarterly frequency; painted cover by Brothers Hildebrandt	$0.45	$1.35	$2.25	£0.30	£0.90	£1.50
Title Value:	$0.45	$1.35	$2.25	£0.30	£0.90	£1.50

SPIDERMAN MEGAZINE
Marvel Comics Group; 1 Oct 1994-6 Mar 1995

	$Good	$Fine	$N.Mint	£Good	£Fine	£N.Mint
1 96pgs, reprints Amazing Spiderman #15, #220-223 and Marvel Team Up #1	$0.60	$1.80	$3.00	£0.40	£1.20	£2.00
2 96pgs, reprints featuring Black Cat, Green Goblin and Human Torch	$0.60	$1.80	$3.00	£0.40	£1.20	£2.00
3 96pgs, reprints featuring Juggernaut, Human Torch, Morbius and Sandman	$0.60	$1.80	$3.00	£0.40	£1.20	£2.00
4 96pgs, reprints featuring X-Men, Morbius, Human Torch and Sandman	$0.60	$1.80	$3.00	£0.40	£1.20	£2.00
5 96pgs, reprints featuring Vision, Tarantula and Puppet Master	$0.60	$1.80	$3.00	£0.40	£1.20	£2.00
6 96pgs, reprints featuring Thing, Human Torch and Tarantula	$0.60	$1.80	$3.00	£0.40	£1.20	£2.00
Title Value:	$3.60	$10.80	$18.00	£2.40	£7.20	£12.00

SPIDERMAN SAGA
Marvel Comics Group,MS; 1 Nov 1991-4 Feb 1992

	$Good	$Fine	$N.Mint	£Good	£Fine	£N.Mint
1 ND scarce in the U.K. history of Spiderman using panels from Amazing Fantasy #15 onwards, McFarlane cover	$0.50	$1.50	$2.50	£0.30	£0.90	£1.50
2 ND scarce in the U.K. covers Spiderman issues #101-175	$0.50	$1.50	$2.50	£0.30	£0.90	£1.50
3 ND scarce in the U.K. covers Spiderman issues #176-238	$0.50	$1.50	$2.50	£0.30	£0.90	£1.50
4 ND scarce in the U.K. covers Spiderman issues #239-300	$0.50	$1.50	$2.50	£0.30	£0.90	£1.50
Title Value:	$2.00	$6.00	$10.00	£1.20	£3.60	£6.00

Note: series delayed from original solicitation

SPIDERMAN SPECIAL EDITION - TRIAL OF VENOM
Marvel Comics Group/Unicef,OS; 1 Nov 1992

	$Good	$Fine	$N.Mint	£Good	£Fine	£N.Mint
1 ND scarce in the U.K. Peter David script, card stock glossy cover, bound-in poster; comes with certificate and black commemorative card plaque	$2.00	$6.00	$10.00	£1.40	£4.20	£7.00
Title Value:	$2.00	$6.00	$10.00	£1.40	£4.20	£7.00

Note: special promotional giveaway obtained by sending $5 to Unicef (the International Children's Fund). Estimated 10,000 print run and therefore scarce in this country, particularly as Unicef would only send copies to American postal addresses and not UK or European ones.

SPIDERMAN SUPER SIZE SPECIAL
Marvel Comics Group,OS; 1 Jul 1995

	$Good	$Fine	$N.Mint	£Good	£Fine	£N.Mint
1 ND Planet of the Symbiotes part 2, continued in Venom Super Size Special; Phil Gosier art	$0.80	$2.40	$4.00	£0.50	£1.50	£2.50
Title Value:	$0.80	$2.40	$4.00	£0.50	£1.50	£2.50

SPIDERMAN TEAM-UP
Marvel Comics Group; 1 Dec 1995-present

	$Good	$Fine	$N.Mint	£Good	£Fine	£N.Mint
1 ND 48pgs, Mark Waid script, Ken Lashley art; Cyclops, Phoenix, Beast, Psylocke and Archangel appear	$0.60	$1.80	$3.00	£0.40	£1.20	£2.00
2 ND Silver Surfer	$0.60	$1.80	$3.00	£0.40	£1.20	£2.00
Title Value:	$1.20	$3.60	$6.00	£0.80	£2.40	£4.00

SPIDERMAN UNLIMITED
Marvel Comics Group; 1 May 1993-present

	$Good	$Fine	$N.Mint	£Good	£Fine	£N.Mint
1 ND 64pgs, Maximum Carnage part 1, continued in Web of Spiderman #101; Ron Lim cover and art begins	$0.80	$2.40	$4.00	£0.50	£1.50	£2.50
2 ND 64pgs, Maximum Carnage part 14 (conclusion), Ron Lim cover and art	$0.80	$2.40	$4.00	£0.50	£1.50	£2.50
3 ND 64pgs, Dr. Octopus origin explored in more detail, Ron Lim cover and art	$0.80	$2.40	$4.00	£0.50	£1.50	£2.50
4 ND 64pgs, Mysterio and Rhino appear	$0.80	$2.40	$4.00	£0.50	£1.50	£2.50
5 ND 64pgs, Human Torch appears	$0.80	$2.40	$4.00	£0.50	£1.50	£2.50

	$Good	$Fine	$N.Mint	£Good	£Fine	£N.Mint

6 ND 64pgs, Thunderstrike appears

| | $0.80 | $2.40 | $4.00 | £0.50 | £1.50 | £2.50 |

7-8 ND 64pgs

| | $0.80 | $2.40 | $4.00 | £0.50 | £1.50 | £2.50 |

9 ND 64pgs, The Mark of Kaine part 5 (conclusion)

| | $0.80 | $2.40 | $4.00 | £0.50 | £1.50 | £2.50 |

10 ND 64pgs, Exiled part 4 (conclusion)

| | $0.80 | $2.40 | $4.00 | £0.50 | £1.50 | £2.50 |

11 ND The Black Cat appears (and introduces Ben Reilly the new Spiderman for 1st time)

| | $0.80 | $2.40 | $4.00 | £0.50 | £1.50 | £2.50 |
| **Title Value:** | $8.80 | $26.40 | $44.00 | £5.50 | £16.50 | £27.50 |

Note: quarterly frequency

SPIDERMAN VS. DRACULA
Marvel Comics Group,OS; 1 Jan 1994
1 ND 48pgs, reprints Spiderman Giant Size #1

| | $0.30 | $0.90 | $1.50 | £0.20 | £0.60 | £1.00 |
| **Title Value:** | $0.30 | $0.90 | $1.50 | £0.20 | £0.60 | £1.00 |

SPIDERMAN VS. WOLVERINE
Marvel Comics Group,OS; 1 Feb 1987
1 ND 64pgs, Japanese Connection story in which Spiderman kills, Bright/Williamson art

| | $3.00 | $9.00 | $15.00 | £2.00 | £6.00 | £10.00 |
| **Title Value:** | $3.00 | $9.00 | $15.00 | £2.00 | £6.00 | £10.00 |

Bookshelf Special (Aug 1990),
reprints the above with new Mark Bright cover £0.75 £2.25 £3.75
(2nd printing - May 1991) £0.70 £2.10 £3.50

SPIDERMAN, ADVENTURES IN READING
Marvel Comics Group,OS; 1 Dec 1990
1 ND promotional comic exploring illiteracy in America

| | $0.30 | $0.90 | $1.50 | £0.20 | £0.60 | £1.00 |
| **Title Value:** | $0.30 | $0.90 | $1.50 | £0.20 | £0.60 | £1.00 |

SPIDERMAN, DEADLY FOES OF
Marvel Comics Group,MS; 1 May 1991-4 Aug 1991
1 ND scarce in the U.K. Beetle, Rhino, Hydroman, Boomerang, Speed Demon featured

| | $0.40 | $1.20 | $2.00 | £0.25 | £0.75 | £1.25 |

2-3 ND scarce in the U.K.

| | $0.40 | $1.20 | $2.00 | £0.25 | £0.75 | £1.25 |

4 ND scarce in the U.K. Kingpin appears

| | $0.40 | $1.20 | $2.00 | £0.25 | £0.75 | £1.25 |
| **Title Value:** | $1.60 | $4.80 | $8.00 | £1.00 | £3.00 | £5.00 |

Deadly Foes of Spiderman (Apr 1994)
Trade paperback reprints issues #1~4 with new cover £1.70 £5.10 £8.50

SPIDERMAN, LETHAL FOES OF
Marvel Comics Group,MS; 1 Sep 1993-4 Dec 1993
1 ND origin of Dr. Octopus explored

| | $0.40 | $1.20 | $2.00 | £0.25 | £0.75 | £1.25 |

2-4 ND Dr. Octopus appears

| | $0.40 | $1.20 | $2.00 | £0.25 | £0.75 | £1.25 |
| **Title Value:** | $1.60 | $4.80 | $8.00 | £1.00 | £3.00 | £5.00 |

SPIDERMAN, THE BEST OF
Marvel Comics Group/Ballantine,OS; nn 1986
nn ND Trade paperback, oversize; reprints newspaper strip

| | $1.80 | $5.25 | $5.25 | £1.20 | £3.60 | £6.00 |
| **Title Value:** | $1.80 | $5.25 | $5.25 | £1.20 | £3.60 | £6.00 |

SPIDERMAN, THE OFFICIAL MARVEL INDEX TO
Marvel Comics Group,MS; 1 Apr 1985-9 Dec 1985
1 ND information and colour cover repros Amazing Fantasy #15, Amazing Spiderman #1-#29, King Size Annual #1,#2; Byrne cover

| | $0.50 | $1.50 | $2.50 | £0.30 | £0.90 | £1.50 |

2 ND information and colour cover repros Amazing Spiderman #30-#58, King Size Annual #3,#4; Romita Snr. cover

| | $0.50 | $1.50 | $2.50 | £0.30 | £0.90 | £1.50 |

3 ND information and colour cover repros Amazing Spiderman #59-#84, King Size Annual #5, Spectacular Spiderman (magazine) #1,#2; Paul Neary cover

| | $0.50 | $1.50 | $2.50 | £0.30 | £0.90 | £1.50 |

4 ND information and colour cover repros Amazing Spiderman #85-#112, King Size Annual #7,#8

| | $0.50 | $1.50 | $2.50 | £0.30 | £0.90 | £1.50 |

5 ND information and colour cover repros Amazing Spiderman #114-#137, King Size Annual #9, Giant Size Super-Heroes #1

| | $0.50 | $1.50 | $2.50 | £0.30 | £0.90 | £1.50 |

6 ND information and colour cover repros Amazing Spiderman #138-#155, Giant Size Annual #1-#6

| | $0.50 | $1.50 | $2.50 | £0.30 | £0.90 | £1.50 |

7 ND information and colour cover repros Amazing Spiderman #156-#174, Annuals #10,#11

| | $0.50 | $1.50 | $2.50 | £0.30 | £0.90 | £1.50 |

8 ND information and colour cover repros Amazing Spiderman #175-#195, Annuals #12

| | $0.50 | $1.50 | $2.50 | £0.30 | £0.90 | £1.50 |

9 ND information and colour cover repros Amazing Spiderman #196-#215, Annuals #13,#14

| | $0.50 | $1.50 | $2.50 | £0.30 | £0.90 | £1.50 |
| **Title Value:** | $4.50 | $13.50 | $22.50 | £2.70 | £8.10 | £13.50 |

Note: Volume 1 in Official Marvel Index Series of 5.

SPIDERMAN, UNTOLD TALES OF
Marvel Comics Group; 1 Sep 1995-present
1 ND Kurt Busiek script, Pat Olliffe and Al Vey art begins; Spiderman's adventures in the early days; cover priced at 99 cents

| | $0.20 | $0.60 | $1.00 | £0.15 | £0.45 | £0.75 |

2 ND

| | $0.20 | $0.60 | $1.00 | £0.15 | £0.45 | £0.75 |

3 ND Sandman appears

| | $0.20 | $0.60 | $1.00 | £0.15 | £0.45 | £0.75 |

4 ND

| | $0.20 | $0.60 | $1.00 | £0.15 | £0.45 | £0.75 |

5 ND The Vulture appears

| | $0.20 | $0.60 | $1.00 | £0.15 | £0.45 | £0.75 |

6 ND Human Torch appears

| | $0.20 | $0.60 | $1.00 | £0.15 | £0.45 | £0.75 |

7 ND

| | $0.20 | $0.60 | $1.00 | £0.15 | £0.45 | £0.75 |

	$Good	$Fine	$N.Mint	£Good	£Fine	£N.Mint
Title Value:	$1.40	$4.20	$7.00	£1.05	£3.15	£5.25

SPIDERMAN/BATMAN
Marvel Comics Group/DC Comics,OS; 1 Nov 1995
1 ND 48pgs, J.M. DeMatteis script, Mark Bagley and Mark Farmer art; Carnage and The Joker appear; card-stock embossed cover

| | $1.20 | $3.60 | $6.00 | £0.80 | £2.40 | £4.00 |
| **Title Value:** | $1.20 | $3.60 | $6.00 | £0.80 | £2.40 | £4.00 |

SPIDERMAN/DR. STRANGE: THE WAY TO DUSTY DEATH
Marvel Comics Group,OS; 1 Feb 1993
1 ND 64pgs

| | $1.00 | $3.00 | $5.00 | £0.70 | £2.10 | £3.50 |
| **Title Value:** | $1.00 | $3.00 | $5.00 | £0.70 | £2.10 | £3.50 |

SPIDERMAN/PUNISHER
Marvel Comics Group,MS; 1,2 Feb 1996
1-2 ND Tom Lyle script, Shawn McManus art; bi-weekly

| | $0.60 | $1.80 | $3.00 | £0.40 | £1.20 | £2.00 |
| **Title Value:** | $1.20 | $3.60 | $6.00 | £0.80 | £2.40 | £4.00 |

SPIDERMAN/PUNISHER/SABRETOOTH: DESIGNER GENES
Marvel Comics Group,OS; 1 Jun 1993
1 ND 64pgs, bookshelf format, McDaniel and Williams art

| | $1.50 | $4.50 | $7.50 | £1.00 | £3.00 | £5.00 |
| **Title Value:** | $1.50 | $4.50 | $7.50 | £1.00 | £3.00 | £5.00 |

SPIDERMAN/SPIDERMAN 2099
Marvel Comics Group,OS; nn Jan 1996
nn ND 48pgs, Peter David script, Rick Leonardi and Al Williamson art

| | $1.20 | $3.60 | $6.00 | £0.80 | £2.40 | £4.00 |
| **Title Value:** | $1.20 | $3.60 | $6.00 | £0.80 | £2.40 | £4.00 |

SPIDERMAN/ULTRAFORCE
Marvel Comics Group,OS; 1 Mar 1996
1 Version 1A, ND 48pgs, features half of Ultraforce with Green Goblin

| | $0.80 | $2.40 | $4.00 | £0.50 | £1.50 | £2.50 |

1 Version 1B, ND 48pgs, features other half of Ultraforce with Spiderman

| | $0.80 | $2.40 | $4.00 | £0.50 | £1.50 | £2.50 |
| **Title Value:** | $1.60 | $4.80 | $8.00 | £1.00 | £3.00 | £5.00 |

SPIDERMAN/X-FACTOR: SHADOWGAMES
Marvel Comics Group,MS; 1 May 1994-3 Jul 1994
1-3 ND Pat Broderick art

| | $0.40 | $1.20 | $2.00 | £0.25 | £0.75 | £1.25 |
| **Title Value:** | $1.20 | $3.60 | $6.00 | £0.75 | £2.25 | £3.75 |

SPIDERMAN: CHAOS IN CALGARY
Marvel Comics Group,OS; 4 1990; 4 Feb 1993
4 ND distributed in Canada (not in U.S. or U.K.), safety-conscious story for motorcyclists

| | $2.50 | $7.50 | $12.50 | £1.50 | £4.50 | £7.50 |

4 ND reprint of Canadian giveaway

| | $0.40 | $1.20 | $2.00 | £0.25 | £0.75 | £1.25 |
| **Title Value:** | $2.90 | $8.70 | $14.50 | £1.75 | £5.25 | £8.75 |

SPIDERMAN: DOUBLE TROUBLE
Marvel Comics Group,OS; 2 1990; 2 Feb 1993
2 ND only distributed in Canada (not U.S. or U.K.), anti-drugs

| | $2.50 | $7.50 | $12.50 | £1.50 | £4.50 | £7.50 |

2 ND reprint of Canadian giveaway

| | $0.40 | $1.20 | $2.00 | £0.25 | £0.75 | £1.25 |
| **Title Value:** | $2.90 | $8.70 | $14.50 | £1.75 | £5.25 | £8.75 |

SPIDERMAN: FRIENDS & ENEMIES
Marvel Comics Group,MS; 1 Jan 1995-4 Apr 1995
1-4 ND Spiderman, Darkhawk, Nova and Speedball appear; Ron Lim art

| | $0.40 | $1.20 | $2.00 | £0.25 | £0.75 | £1.25 |
| **Title Value:** | $1.60 | $4.80 | $8.00 | £1.00 | £3.00 | £5.00 |

SPIDERMAN: FUNERAL FOR AN OCTOPUS
Marvel Comics Group,MS; 1 Mar 1995-3 May 1995
1 ND spin-off from Spectacular Spiderman #221; Scarlet Spider and Sinister Six appear

| | $0.40 | $1.20 | $2.00 | £0.25 | £0.75 | £1.25 |

2 ND

| | $0.40 | $1.20 | $2.00 | £0.25 | £0.75 | £1.25 |

3 ND Mark of Kaine tie-in (see Spiderman Unlimited #9)

| | $0.40 | $1.20 | $2.00 | £0.25 | £0.75 | £1.25 |
| **Title Value:** | $1.20 | $3.60 | $6.00 | £0.75 | £2.25 | £3.75 |

SPIDERMAN: HIT AND RUN
Marvel Comics Group,OS; 3 1990; 3 Feb 1993
3 ND only distributed in Canada (not in U.S. or U.K.), anti-hit and run drivers, Ghost Rider appears

| | $2.50 | $7.50 | $12.50 | £1.50 | £4.50 | £7.50 |

3 ND reprint of Canadian giveaway, Ghost Rider appears

| | $0.40 | $1.20 | $2.00 | £0.25 | £0.75 | £1.25 |
| **Title Value:** | $2.90 | $8.70 | $14.50 | £1.75 | £5.25 | £8.75 |

SPIDERMAN: MAXIMUM CLONAGE ALPHA
Marvel Comics Group,OS; 1 Aug 1995
1 ND 48pgs, Maximum Clonage part 1, continued in Web of Spiderman #127; clear chromium cover

| | $1.00 | $3.00 | $5.00 | £0.70 | £2.10 | £3.50 |

SPIDERMAN: MAXIMUM CLONAGE OMEGA
Marvel Comics Group,OS; 1 1995
1 ND 48pgs, Maximum Clonage part 6 (conclusion) with Scarlet Spider and Spiderman vs. The Jackal and his Clone Assassin; chromium cover

| | $1.00 | $3.00 | $5.00 | £0.70 | £2.10 | £3.50 |
| **Title Value:** | $1.00 | $3.00 | $5.00 | £0.70 | £2.10 | £3.50 |

SPIDERMAN: MUTANT AGENDA
Marvel Comics Group,MS; 0 Feb 1994-3 May 1994
0-3 ND 48pgs, sections allocated to paste in Spiderman newspaper strip (Note: item would be valued more if the strips were neatly pasted in)

| | $0.30 | $0.90 | $1.50 | £0.20 | £0.60 | £1.00 |
| **Title Value:** | $1.20 | $3.60 | $6.00 | £0.80 | £2.40 | £4.00 |

SPIDERMAN: SKATING ON THIN ICE
Marvel Comics Group,OS; 1 1990; 1 Feb 1993
1 ND only distributed in Canada, (not in U.S. or in U.K.), Todd McFarlane cover, anti-drug issue

	$Good	$Fine	$N.Mint	£Good	£Fine	£N.Mint
	$2.50	$7.50	$12.50	£1.50	£4.50	£7.50

1 ND reprint of Canadian giveaway

| | $0.40 | $1.20 | $2.00 | £0.25 | £0.75 | £1.25 |
| Title Value: | $2.90 | $8.70 | $14.50 | £1.75 | £5.25 | £8.75 |

SPIDERMAN: SOUL OF THE HUNTER
Marvel Comics Group; 1 Oct 1992
1 ND 48pgs, Spiderman vs. the ghost of Kraven, Mike Zeck art

| | $1.00 | $3.00 | $5.00 | £0.70 | £2.10 | £3.50 |
| Title Value: | $1.00 | $3.00 | $5.00 | £0.70 | £2.10 | £3.50 |

SPIDERMAN: THE ARACHNIS PROJECT
Marvel Comics Group,MS; 1 Aug 1994-6 Jan 1995
1 ND series tied in with Smithsonian Institute exhibition on Spiderman

| | $0.30 | $0.90 | $1.50 | £0.20 | £0.60 | £1.00 |
| 2-5 ND | $0.30 | $0.90 | $1.50 | £0.20 | £0.60 | £1.00 |

6 ND Venom appears

| | $0.30 | $0.90 | $1.50 | £0.20 | £0.60 | £1.00 |
| Title Value: | $1.80 | $5.40 | $9.00 | £1.20 | £3.60 | £6.00 |

SPIDERMAN: THE CLONE JOURNALS
Marvel Comics Group,OS; 1 Mar 1995
1 ND edited reprints deatailing the story of the Spiderman clones plus new material

| | $0.40 | $1.20 | $2.00 | £0.25 | £0.75 | £1.25 |
| Title Value: | $0.40 | $1.20 | $2.00 | £0.25 | £0.75 | £1.25 |

SPIDERMAN: THE FINAL ADVENTURE
Marvel Comics Group,MS; 1 Dec 1995-4 Mar 1996
1-3 ND Fabian Nicieza script, Darick Robertson and Chris Ivy art; foil stamped cover

| | $0.60 | $1.80 | $3.00 | | £1.20 | £2.00 |

4 ND Fabian Nicieza script, Darick Robertson and Jeff Albrecht art; foil stamped cover

| | $0.60 | $1.80 | $3.00 | £0.40 | £1.20 | £2.00 |
| Title Value: | $2.40 | $7.20 | $12.00 | £1.60 | £4.80 | £8.00 |

SPIDERMAN: THE JACKAL FILES
Marvel Comics Group,OS; 1 Aug 1995
1 ND The Jackal appears, Maximum Clonage tie-in

| | $0.40 | $1.20 | $2.00 | £0.25 | £0.75 | £1.25 |
| Title Value: | $0.40 | $1.20 | $2.00 | £0.25 | £0.75 | £1.25 |

SPIDERMAN: THE LOST YEARS
Marvel Comics Group,MS; 0 Jan 1996; 1 Aug 1995-3 Oct 1995
0 ND 64pgs, reprints the 4-part "Birth of Spiderman" and 3-part "Parker Legacy"

| | $0.80 | $2.40 | $4.00 | | £1.50 | £2.50 |

1-2 ND J.M. DeMatteis script, John Romita Jnr. art

| | $0.60 | $1.80 | $3.00 | £0.40 | £1.20 | £2.00 |

3 ND Ben (Scarlet Spider) Reilly vs. Kaine; J.M. DeMatteis script, John Romita Jnr. art

| | $0.60 | $1.80 | $3.00 | £0.40 | £1.20 | £2.00 |
| Title Value: | $2.60 | $7.80 | $13.00 | £1.70 | £5.10 | £8.50 |

SPIDERMAN: THE PARKER YEARS
Marvel Comics Group,OS; 1 Nov 1995
1 ND Evan Skolnick script, Joe St. Pierre art, wraparound cover by John Romita Jnr. with no ads; Venom and Carnage appear

| | $0.50 | $1.50 | $2.50 | £0.30 | £0.90 | £1.50 |
| Title Value: | $0.50 | $1.50 | $2.50 | £0.30 | £0.90 | £1.50 |

SPIDERMAN: THE POWER OF TERROR
Marvel Comics Group,MS; 1 Jan 1995-4 Apr 1995
1-3 ND Silvermane and Deathlok appear

| | $0.40 | $1.20 | $2.00 | £0.25 | £0.75 | £1.25 |

4 ND Silvermane, Deathlok, Daredevil and Punisher appear

| | $0.40 | $1.20 | $2.00 | £0.25 | £0.75 | £1.25 |
| Title Value: | $1.60 | $4.80 | $8.00 | £1.00 | £3.00 | £5.00 |

SPIDERMAN: WEB OF DOOM
Marvel Comics Group,MS; 1 Aug 1994-3 Oct 1994
1-3 ND

| | $0.30 | $0.90 | $1.50 | £0.20 | £0.60 | £1.00 |
| Title Value: | $0.90 | $2.70 | $4.50 | £0.60 | £1.80 | £3.00 |

SPIDERWOMAN
Marvel Comics Group; 1 Apr 1978-50 Jun 1983
(see Marvel Spotlight #32)
1 ND new origin

	$0.80	$2.40	$4.00	£0.40	£1.20	£2.00
2-4 ND	$0.40	$1.20	$2.00	£0.25	£0.75	£1.25
5	$0.30	$0.90	$1.50	£0.20	£0.60	£1.00

6 Werewolf By Night appears

| | $0.30 | $0.90 | $1.50 | £0.20 | £0.60 | £1.00 |
| 7-18 ND | $0.30 | $0.90 | $1.50 | £0.20 | £0.60 | £1.00 |

19 Werewolf By Night appears

| | $0.30 | $0.90 | $1.50 | £0.20 | £0.60 | £1.00 |

20 Spiderman appears

| | $0.30 | $0.90 | $1.50 | £0.20 | £0.60 | £1.00 |
| 21-25 | $0.25 | $0.75 | $1.25 | £0.15 | £0.45 | £0.75 |

26 Spiderman cameo

| | $0.25 | $0.75 | $1.25 | £0.15 | £0.45 | £0.75 |
| 27 | $0.25 | $0.75 | $1.25 | £0.15 | £0.45 | £0.75 |

28-29 Spiderman appears

| | $0.25 | $0.75 | $1.25 | £0.15 | £0.45 | £0.75 |
| 30-31 | $0.25 | $0.75 | $1.25 | £0.15 | £0.45 | £0.75 |

32 Werewolf By Night appears, photo montage cover

	$0.30	$0.90	$1.50	£0.20	£0.60	£1.00
33-34	$0.25	$0.75	$1.25	£0.15	£0.45	£0.75
35-36 ND	$0.30	$0.90	$1.50	£0.20	£0.60	£1.00

37 1st appearance Syrin, X-Men cameo appearance, origin retold

| | $0.60 | $1.80 | $3.00 | £0.40 | £1.20 | £2.00 |

38 scarce in the U.K. X-Men appear

| | $0.80 | $2.40 | $4.00 | £0.50 | £1.50 | £2.50 |

39 ND Storm, Angel, Colossus appear; leads into X-Men #148

| | $0.60 | $1.80 | $3.00 | £0.40 | £1.20 | £2.00 |
| 40 | $0.25 | $0.75 | $1.25 | £0.15 | £0.45 | £0.75 |

41-44 scarce in the U.K.

| | $0.25 | $0.75 | $1.25 | £0.20 | £0.60 | £1.00 |

45 scarce in the U.K. Impossible Man appears

| | $0.25 | $0.75 | $1.25 | £0.20 | £0.60 | £1.00 |

46-48 scarce in the U.K.

| | $0.25 | $0.75 | $1.25 | £0.20 | £0.60 | £1.00 |

49 scarce in the U.K. Tigra and Werewolf By Night appear

| | $0.25 | $0.75 | $1.25 | £0.20 | £0.60 | £1.00 |

50 DS scarce in the U.K.

| | $0.60 | $1.80 | $3.00 | £0.40 | £1.20 | £2.00 |
| Title Value: | $15.95 | $47.85 | $79.75 | £10.55 | £31.65 | £52.75 |

ARTISTS
Miller cover on 32. Sienkiewicz covers on 16, 27. Von Eeden art in 23, 24.

SPIDERWOMAN (2ND SERIES)
Marvel Comics Group,MS; 1 Nov 1993-4 Feb 1994

| 1 | $0.40 | $1.20 | $2.00 | £0.25 | £0.75 | £1.25 |

2 origin re-explored in more detail

| | $0.40 | $1.20 | $2.00 | £0.25 | £0.75 | £1.25 |
| 3 | $0.40 | $1.20 | $2.00 | £0.25 | £0.75 | £1.25 |

4 U.S.Agent guest-stars

| | $0.40 | $1.20 | $2.00 | £0.25 | £0.75 | £1.25 |
| Title Value: | $1.60 | $4.80 | $8.00 | £1.00 | £3.00 | £5.00 |

SPIDEY SUPER STORIES
Marvel Comics Group, TV; 1 Oct 1974-57 Mar 1982
1 ND origin retold

	$0.60	$1.80	$3.00	£0.40	£1.20	£2.00
2 ND	$0.50	$1.50	$2.50	£0.30	£0.90	£1.50
3-4 ND	$0.30	$0.90	$1.50	£0.20	£0.60	£1.00

5 ND Iceman appears

| | $0.30 | $0.90 | $1.50 | £0.20 | £0.60 | £1.00 |

Spiderman & Power Pack

Spiderman Classics #1

Spiderman Special Edition

MINT = 100% / NEAR MINT (inc. +/-) = 90-99% / VERY FINE (inc. +/-) = 75-89% / FINE (inc. +/-) = 55-74%
VERY GOOD (inc. +/-) = 35-54% / GOOD (inc. +/-) = 15-34% / FAIR = 5-14% / POOR = 1-4%

559

	$Good	$Fine	$N.Mint	£Good	£Fine	£N.Mint
6-14 ND	$0.30	$0.90	$1.50	£0.20	£0.60	£1.00
15 ND Storm appears						
	$0.30	$0.90	$1.50	£0.20	£0.60	£1.00
16-22 ND	$0.30	$0.90	$1.50	£0.20	£0.60	£1.00
23 ND Green Goblin appears						
	$0.30	$0.90	$1.50	£0.20	£0.60	£1.00
24 ND Thundra appears						
	$0.30	$0.90	$1.50	£0.20	£0.60	£1.00
25 ND Dr. Doom appears						
	$0.30	$0.90	$1.50	£0.20	£0.60	£1.00
26 ND	$0.30	$0.90	$1.50	£0.20	£0.60	£1.00
27 ND Thor and Loki appear						
	$0.30	$0.90	$1.50	£0.20	£0.60	£1.00
28 ND	$0.30	$0.90	$1.50	£0.20	£0.60	£1.00
29 ND Kingpin appears						
	$0.30	$0.90	$1.50	£0.20	£0.60	£1.00
30 ND Kang appears						
	$0.30	$0.90	$1.50	£0.20	£0.60	£1.00
31-33 ND	$0.30	$0.90	$1.50	£0.20	£0.60	£1.00
34 ND Sub-Mariner appears						
	$0.30	$0.90	$1.50	£0.20	£0.60	£1.00
35-38 ND	$0.30	$0.90	$1.50	£0.20	£0.60	£1.00
39 ND Thanos appears in back-up story (outside Marvel continuity)						
	$0.40	$1.20	$2.00	£0.25	£0.75	£1.25
40-57 ND	$0.30	$0.90	$1.50	£0.20	£0.60	£1.00
Title Value:	$17.70	$53.10	$88.50	£11.75	£35.25	£58.75

Note: contains simplified Spiderman stories for young children; published in association with Children's Television Workshop.

SPINE-TINGLING TALES, DR. SPEKTOR PRESENTS

Gold Key; 1 May 1975-4 Jan 1976

	$Good	$Fine	$N.Mint	£Good	£Fine	£N.Mint
1 scarce in the U.K. painted covers begin; all distributed in the U.K.						
	$0.30	$0.90	$1.50	£0.25	£0.75	£1.25
2-3	$0.30	$0.90	$1.50	£0.20	£0.60	£1.00
4 features Baron Tibor - Vampire						
	$0.30	$0.90	$1.50	£0.20	£0.60	£1.00
Title Value:	$1.20	$3.60	$6.00	£0.85	£2.55	£4.25

SPIRAL PATH

Eclipse,MS; 1,2 Jul 1986

	$Good	$Fine	$N.Mint	£Good	£Fine	£N.Mint
1-2 ND reprints from Warrior in colour; Steve Parkhouse script/John Ridgway art						
	$0.40	$1.20	$2.00	£0.25	£0.75	£1.25
Title Value:	$0.80	$2.40	$4.00	£0.50	£1.50	£2.50

SPIRAL ZONE

DC Comics,Magazine MS Toy; 1 Oct 1987-4 Jan 1988

	$Good	$Fine	$N.Mint	£Good	£Fine	£N.Mint
1-4	$0.15	$0.45	$0.75	£0.10	£0.30	£0.50
Title Value:	$0.60	$1.80	$3.00	£0.40	£1.20	£2.00

SPIRIT

Kitchen Sink; 1 Oct 1983-87 Mar 1992

(see Will Eisner's 3-D Classics)

	$Good	$Fine	$N.Mint	£Good	£Fine	£N.Mint
1 ND	$0.60	$1.80	$3.00	£0.40	£1.20	£2.00
2-9 ND	$0.50	$1.50	$2.50	£0.30	£0.90	£1.50
10 ND last colour issue						
	$0.50	$1.50	$2.50	£0.30	£0.90	£1.50
11-40 ND	$0.40	$1.20	$2.00	£0.25	£0.75	£1.25
41 ND Frederick Wertham parody						
	$0.40	$1.20	$2.00	£0.25	£0.75	£1.25
42-76 ND	$0.40	$1.20	$2.00	£0.25	£0.75	£1.25
77-87 ND new Eisner cover						
	$0.40	$1.20	$2.00	£0.25	£0.75	£1.25
Title Value:	$35.90	$107.70	$179.50	£22.35	£67.05	£111.75

SPIRIT DAILYS

Ken Pierce; 1-4 1980

	$Good	$Fine	$N.Mint	£Good	£Fine	£N.Mint
1-4 ND	$1.00	$3.00	$5.00	£0.70	£2.10	£3.50
Title Value:	$4.00	$12.00	$20.00	£2.80	£8.40	£14.00

Note: reprints all 738 Daily strips.

SPIRIT MAGAZINE, THE

Warren; 1 Apr 1974-16 Oct 1976; Kitchen Sink; 17 Winter 1977-41 1983

	$Good	$Fine	$N.Mint	£Good	£Fine	£N.Mint
1	$1.20	$3.60	$6.00	£1.00	£3.00	£5.00
2	$0.80	$2.40	$4.00	£0.80	£2.40	£4.00
3-5	$0.60	$1.80	$3.00	£0.60	£1.80	£3.00
6-9	$0.50	$1.50	$2.50	£0.50	£1.50	£2.50
10 origin	$0.50	$1.50	$2.50	£0.50	£1.50	£2.50
11-17	$0.50	$1.50	$2.50	£0.40	£1.20	£2.00
18 scarce in the U.K.						
	$0.50	$1.50	$2.50	£0.60	£1.80	£3.00
19-20	$0.50	$1.50	$2.50	£0.40	£1.20	£2.00
21-29	$0.40	$1.20	$2.00	£0.30	£0.90	£1.50
30 Eisner, Canniff, Kurtzman, Corben, John Byrne, Frank Miller, Austin, Rogers art						
	$0.80	$2.40	$4.00	£0.50	£1.50	£2.50
31-35	$0.40	$1.20	$2.00	£0.30	£0.90	£1.50
36-41	$0.60	$1.80	$3.00	£0.40	£1.20	£2.00
Title Value:	$21.30	$63.90	$106.50	£17.40	£52.20	£87.00

Note: all Non-Distributed on the news-stands in the U.K.

Spirit Color Special

scarce in the U.K. reprints colour sections

				£1.40	£4.20	£7.00

SPIRIT SPECIAL, THE

Warren; nn 1975

nn ND scarce in the U.K. Will Eisner art

	$Good	$Fine	$N.Mint	£Good	£Fine	£N.Mint
	$1.00	$3.00	$5.00	£1.00	£3.00	£5.00
Title Value:	$1.00	$3.00	$5.00	£1.00	£3.00	£5.00

SPIRIT WORLD

Hampshire/DC,Magazine; 1 Fall 1971

(see In the Days of the Mob)

	$Good	$Fine	$N.Mint	£Good	£Fine	£N.Mint
1 ND Jack Kirby art, includes poster						
	$1.50	$4.50	$7.50	£1.00	£3.00	£5.00
Title Value:	$1.50	$4.50	$7.50	£1.00	£3.00	£5.00

SPIRIT, THE

I.W. Super; 11 1963-12 1964

	$Good	$Fine	$N.Mint	£Good	£Fine	£N.Mint
11 rare, distributed in the U.K. 40s/50s Will Eisner reprints						
	$3.30	$10.00	$20.00	£2.05	£6.25	£12.50
12 rare, distributed in the U.K. 40s/50s Will Eisner reprints						
	$2.90	$8.75	$17.50	£1.65	£5.00	£10.00
Title Value:	$6.20	$18.75	$37.50	£3.70	£11.25	£22.50

Note: all reprint except one new story in each issue.

SPIRIT, THE (2ND SERIES)

Harvey; 1 Oct 1966-2 Mar 1967

	$Good	$Fine	$N.Mint	£Good	£Fine	£N.Mint
1 scarce in the U.K. giant, Will Eisner art; distributed in the U.K.						
	$7.00	$21.00	$50.00	£5.00	£15.00	£35.00
2 giant, Will Eisner art; distributed in the U.K.						
	$6.25	$19.00	$45.00	£4.25	£12.50	£30.00
Title Value:	$13.25	$40.00	$95.00	£9.25	£27.50	£65.00

SPIRIT, THE (3RD SERIES)

Kitchen Sink; 1 Jan 1973-2 Sep 1973

	$Good	$Fine	$N.Mint	£Good	£Fine	£N.Mint
1-2 ND Will Eisner art						
	$2.00	$6.00	$10.00	£1.40	£4.20	£7.00
Title Value:	$4.00	$12.00	$20.00	£2.80	£8.40	£14.00

SPIRIT: THE ORIGIN YEARS

Kitchen Sink; 1 Jul 1992-6 1993

	$Good	$Fine	$N.Mint	£Good	£Fine	£N.Mint
1 ND new cover designs by Will Eisner begin						
	$0.50	$1.50	$2.50	£0.30	£0.90	£1.50
2-6 ND	$0.50	$1.50	$2.50	£0.30	£0.90	£1.50
Title Value:	$3.00	$9.00	$15.00	£1.80	£5.40	£9.00

SPITFIRE AND THE TROUBLESHOOTERS

Marvel Comics Group/New Universe; 1 Oct 1986-13 Oct 1987

	$Good	$Fine	$N.Mint	£Good	£Fine	£N.Mint
1-3 ND	$0.15	$0.45	$0.75	£0.10	£0.35	£0.60
4 ND Todd McFarlane art						
	$0.15	$0.45	$0.75	£0.10	£0.35	£0.60
5-9 ND	$0.15	$0.45	$0.75	£0.10	£0.35	£0.60
10 title becomes Codename: Spitfire						
	$0.15	$0.45	$0.75	£0.10	£0.35	£0.60
11-13	$0.15	$0.45	$0.75	£0.10	£0.35	£0.60
Title Value:	$1.95	$5.85	$9.75	£1.30	£4.55	£7.80

SPLAT!

Mad Dog Graphics; 1 Feb 1987-3 Aug 1987

	$Good	$Fine	$N.Mint	£Good	£Fine	£N.Mint
1 ND features Peter Bagge and Hunt Emerson art						
	$0.40	$1.20	$2.00	£0.25	£0.75	£1.25
2 ND	$0.40	$1.20	$2.00	£0.25	£0.75	£1.25
3 ND 1st appearance Eddy Current by Ted McKeever, Lone Wolf parody by Fujitake						
	$0.80	$2.40	$4.00	£0.50	£1.50	£2.50
Title Value:	$1.60	$4.80	$8.00	£1.00	£3.00	£5.00

SPLATTER

Arpad Publishing/Northstar; 1 May 1991-9 1993

	$Good	$Fine	$N.Mint	£Good	£Fine	£N.Mint
1 horror anthology, Tim Vigil art featured; black and white						
	$0.60	$1.80	$3.00	£0.40	£1.20	£2.00
1 Gold Edition - (Feb 1993); 3,000 copies						
	$1.00	$3.00	$5.00	£0.60	£1.80	£3.00
1 2nd printing	$0.50	$1.50	$2.50	£0.30	£0.90	£1.50
1 3rd printing	$0.50	$1.50	$2.50	£0.30	£0.90	£1.50
2-4 Tim Vigil art; black and white						
	$0.50	$1.50	$2.50	£0.30	£0.90	£1.50
5 black and white	$0.50	$1.50	$2.50	£0.30	£0.90	£1.50
6-9	$0.50	$1.50	$2.50	£0.30	£0.90	£1.50
Title Value:	$6.60	$19.80	$33.00	£4.00	£12.00	£20.00

Note: all Non-Distributed on the news-stands in the U.K.

The Splatter Collection (Apr 1993)

reprints #2-5

				£1.50	£4.50	£7.50

SPLATTER ANNUAL

Northstar; 1 1993-2 1994

	$Good	$Fine	$N.Mint	£Good	£Fine	£N.Mint
1-2 ND 48pgs, black and white						
	$0.80	$2.40	$4.00	£0.50	£1.50	£2.50
Title Value:	$1.60	$4.80	$8.00	£1.00	£3.00	£5.00

SPLATTER: HOLIDAY IN HELL

Northstar,OS; 1 Nov 1994

	$Good	$Fine	$N.Mint	£Good	£Fine	£N.Mint
1 ND 48pgs, black and white						
	$0.80	$2.40	$4.00	£0.50	£1.50	£2.50
Title Value:	$0.80	$2.40	$4.00	£0.50	£1.50	£2.50

SPLITTING IMAGE

Image; 1 Jan 1993-2 Apr 1993

	$Good	$Fine	$N.Mint	£Good	£Fine	£N.Mint
1-2 ND parodies of Image characters by Valentino and Liefeld plus covers by other Image artists						
	$0.40	$1.20	$2.00	£0.25	£0.75	£1.25
Title Value:	$0.80	$2.40	$4.00	£0.50	£1.50	£2.50

SPOOF

Marvel Comics Group; 1 Oct 1970; 2 Nov 1972-5 May 1973

	$Good	$Fine	$N.Mint	£Good	£Fine	£N.Mint
1 ND scarce in the U.K. Marie Severin art						
	$0.90	$2.70	$4.50	£0.60	£1.80	£3.00
2-5 ND scarce in the U.K.						
	$0.50	$1.50	$2.50	£0.30	£0.90	£1.50
Title Value:	$2.90	$8.70	$14.50	£1.80	£5.40	£9.00

Note: TV and film parodies.

SPOOKY

Harvey; 1 Nov 1955-161 Sep 1980

	$Good	$Fine	$N.Mint	£Good	£Fine	£N.Mint
1	$28.00	$82.50	$225.00	£18.50	£55.00	£150.00
2	$15.50	$47.00	$110.00	£10.50	£32.00	£75.00
3-5	$8.50	$26.00	$60.00	£5.50	£17.00	£40.00
6-10	$7.00	$21.00	$50.00	£5.00	£15.00	£35.00

	$Good	$Fine	$N.Mint	£Good	£Fine	£N.Mint

(continued from previous)

Issue	$Good	$Fine	$N.Mint	£Good	£Fine	£N.Mint
11-20	$4.25	$12.50	$30.00	£2.85	£8.50	£20.00
21-40	$2.50	$7.50	$17.50	£1.75	£5.25	£12.50
41-60	$2.00	$6.00	$12.00	£1.25	£3.75	£7.50
61-80	$1.50	$4.50	$7.50	£1.00	£3.00	£5.00
81-100	$1.00	$3.00	$5.00	£0.70	£2.10	£3.50
101-120	$0.90	$2.70	$4.50	£0.60	£1.80	£3.00
121-140	$0.50	$1.50	$2.50	£0.40	£1.20	£2.00
141-161	$0.40	$1.20	$2.00	£0.25	£0.75	£1.25
Title Value:	$322.90	$966.70	$2087.00	£218.25	£655.75	£1416.25

Note: some issues distributed in the U.K. after 1959/60

SPOTLIGHT
Heroic Publishing; 0 Aug 1993

	$Good	$Fine	$N.Mint	£Good	£Fine	£N.Mint
0 ND pre-bagged with trading card and signed by creators	$0.50	$1.50	$2.50	£0.30	£0.90	£1.50
Title Value:	$0.50	$1.50	$2.50	£0.30	£0.90	£1.50

SPRING-HEEL JACK
Dark Horse,MS; 1, 2 1991

	$Good	$Fine	$N.Mint	£Good	£Fine	£N.Mint
1-2 ND David Barbour and Wayne Tanaka script/art	$0.40	$1.20	$2.00	£0.25	£0.75	£1.25
Title Value:	$0.80	$2.40	$4.00	£0.50	£1.50	£2.50

SPRING-HEEL JACK: REVENGE OF THE RIPPER
Rebel Studios,MS; 1 May 1993-3 Feb 1994

	$Good	$Fine	$N.Mint	£Good	£Fine	£N.Mint
1-3 ND Wayne Tanaka art	$0.40	$1.20	$2.00	£0.25	£0.75	£1.25
Title Value:	$1.20	$3.60	$6.00	£0.75	£2.25	£3.75

SPUMCO COMIC BOOK
Marvel Comics Group; 1 Oct 1995-present

	$Good	$Fine	$N.Mint	£Good	£Fine	£N.Mint
1-4 ND 64pgs, cartoon adventures from the Ren & Stimpy studio; 9" x 12" format	$1.40	$4.20	$7.00	£0.90	£2.70	£4.50
Title Value:	$5.60	$16.80	$28.00	£3.60	£10.80	£18.00
Spumco (Feb 1996)						
Trade paperback 256pgs, reprints mini-series				£3.30	£9.90	£16.50

SPYKE
Marvel Comics Group/Epic,MS; 1 Jul 1993-4 Oct 1993

	$Good	$Fine	$N.Mint	£Good	£Fine	£N.Mint
1 ND Mike Baron script begins, embossed cover with metallic ink	$0.40	$1.20	$2.00	£0.25	£0.75	£1.25
2-4 ND	$0.40	$1.20	$2.00	£0.25	£0.75	£1.25
Title Value:	$1.60	$4.80	$8.00	£1.00	£3.00	£5.00

SPYMAN
Harvey; 1 Sep 1966-3 Feb 1967

	$Good	$Fine	$N.Mint	£Good	£Fine	£N.Mint
1 distributed in the U.K. Jim Steranko art	$5.75	$17.50	$35.00	£4.15	£12.50	£25.00
2 distributed in the U.K. Jim Steranko art	$4.15	$12.50	$25.00	£2.50	£7.50	£15.00
3 distributed in the U.K.	$4.15	$12.50	$25.00	£2.50	£7.50	£15.00
Title Value:	$14.05	$42.50	$85.00	£9.15	£27.50	£55.00

SQUAD: A HARDCASE MINI-SERIES, THE
Malibu Ultraverse; 0 Nov 1994-2 Jan 1995

	$Good	$Fine	$N.Mint	£Good	£Fine	£N.Mint
0 ND numbered #0-A	$0.40	$1.20	$2.00	£0.25	£0.75	£1.25
1 ND numbered #0-B	$0.40	$1.20	$2.00	£0.25	£0.75	£1.25
2 ND numbered #0-C	$0.40	$1.20	$2.00	£0.25	£0.75	£1.25
Title Value:	$1.20	$3.60	$6.00	£0.75	£2.25	£3.75

SQUADRON SUPREME
Marvel Comics Group,MS; 1 Sep 1985-12 Aug 1986
(see Avengers #69, Quasar)

	$Good	$Fine	$N.Mint	£Good	£Fine	£N.Mint
1 ND	$0.40	$1.20	$2.00	£0.25	£0.75	£1.25
2-11 ND	$0.30	$0.90	$1.50	£0.20	£0.60	£1.00
12 ND DS	$0.40	$1.20	$2.00	£0.25	£0.75	£1.25
Title Value:	$3.80	$11.40	$19.00	£2.50	£7.50	£12.50

SQUALOR
First,MS; 1 Dec 1989-4 Aug 1990
(see Sensei, Twilight Man)

	$Good	$Fine	$N.Mint	£Good	£Fine	£N.Mint
1 ND sub-titled "First Fiction Volume Three"; glossy heavier stock paper covers	$0.40	$1.20	$2.00	£0.25	£0.75	£1.25
2-4 ND	$0.40	$1.20	$2.00	£0.25	£0.75	£1.25
Title Value:	$1.60	$4.80	$8.00	£1.00	£3.00	£5.00

ST. GEORGE
Marvel Comics Group/Epic; 1 Jun 1988-8 Aug 1989

	$Good	$Fine	$N.Mint	£Good	£Fine	£N.Mint
1 ND Klaus Janson art begins, Sienkiewicz cover	$0.30	$0.90	$1.50	£0.20	£0.60	£1.00
2 ND Jon Muth cover	$0.30	$0.90	$1.50	£0.20	£0.60	£1.00
3 ND Nowlan cover	$0.30	$0.90	$1.50	£0.20	£0.60	£1.00
4 ND Chiarello cover	$0.30	$0.90	$1.50	£0.20	£0.60	£1.00
5 ND Kev O'Neill cover	$0.30	$0.90	$1.50	£0.20	£0.60	£1.00
6-7 ND	$0.30	$0.90	$1.50	£0.20	£0.60	£1.00
8 ND Jim Lee art	$0.40	$1.20	$2.00	£0.25	£0.75	£1.25
Title Value:	$2.50	$7.50	$12.50	£1.65	£4.95	£8.25

Note: all painted covers

STAINLESS STEEL ARMADILLO
Antarctic Press,MS; 1 Feb 1995-6 Dec 1995

	$Good	$Fine	$N.Mint	£Good	£Fine	£N.Mint
1-6 ND Ryukihei script and art; black and white	$0.60	$1.80	$3.00	£0.40	£1.20	£2.00
Title Value:	$3.60	$10.80	$18.00	£2.40	£7.20	£12.00

STALKER
DC Comics; 1 Jun/Jul 1975-4 Dec/Jan 1975

	$Good	$Fine	$N.Mint	£Good	£Fine	£N.Mint
1 origin and 1st appearance of Stalker, Steve Ditko/Wally Wood art	$0.60	$1.80	$3.00	£0.40	£1.20	£2.00
2-4 Steve Ditko/Wally Wood art	$0.50	$1.50	$2.50	£0.30	£0.90	£1.50
Title Value:	$2.10	$6.30	$10.50	£1.30	£3.90	£6.50

STALKERS
Marvel Comics Group/Epic,MS; 1 Apr 1990-12 Mar 1991

	$Good	$Fine	$N.Mint	£Good	£Fine	£N.Mint
1 ND Chadwick cover, Mark Texeira art begins (ends #7)	$0.30	$0.90	$1.50	£0.20	£0.60	£1.00
2 ND	$0.30	$0.90	$1.50	£0.20	£0.60	£1.00
3-6 ND two stories per issue	$0.30	$0.90	$1.50	£0.20	£0.60	£1.00
7 ND two stories, last Texeira art	$0.30	$0.90	$1.50	£0.20	£0.60	£1.00
8-12 ND two stories per issue	$0.30	$0.90	$1.50	£0.20	£0.60	£1.00
Title Value:	$3.60	$10.80	$18.00	£2.40	£7.20	£12.00

STAN SHAW'S BEAUTY & THE BEAST
Dark Horse,OS; 1 Nov 1993

	$Good	$Fine	$N.Mint	£Good	£Fine	£N.Mint
1 ND 48pgs	$0.90	$2.70	$4.50	£0.60	£1.80	£3.00
Title Value:	$0.90	$2.70	$4.50	£0.60	£1.80	£3.00

STANLEY AND HIS MONSTER
National Periodical Publications; 109 Apr/May 1968-112 Oct/Nov 1968
(formerly The Fox and the Crow; see Secret Origins #48)

	$Good	$Fine	$N.Mint	£Good	£Fine	£N.Mint
109-112 scarce in the U.K.	$2.90	$8.75	$17.50	£2.05	£6.25	£12.50
Title Value:	$11.60	$35.00	$70.00	£8.20	£25.00	£50.00

STANLEY AND HIS MONSTER (2ND SERIES)
DC Comics,MS; 1 Feb 1993-4 May 1993

	$Good	$Fine	$N.Mint	£Good	£Fine	£N.Mint
1-4	$0.25	$0.75	$1.25	£0.15	£0.45	£0.75
Title Value:	$1.00	$3.00	$5.00	£0.60	£1.80	£3.00

STAR
Image,MS; 1 Jun 1995-4 Sep 1995

	$Good	$Fine	$N.Mint	£Good	£Fine	£N.Mint
1-4 ND Tom and Mary Bierbaum script, Ben Herrera art	$0.50	$1.50	$2.50	£0.30	£0.90	£1.50
Title Value:	$2.00	$6.00	$10.00	£1.20	£3.60	£6.00

STAR BLAZERS
Argo Press; 1 Aug 1995-2 1995

	$Good	$Fine	$N.Mint	£Good	£Fine	£N.Mint
1 ND sub-titled "The Magazine of the Battleship Yamato"	$0.60	$1.80	$3.00	£0.40	£1.20	£2.00
2 ND	$0.60	$1.80	$3.00	£0.40	£1.20	£2.00
Title Value:	$1.20	$3.60	$6.00	£0.80	£2.40	£4.00

STAR BRAND, THE
Marvel Comics Group/New Universe; 1 Oct 1986-19 May 1989

	$Good	$Fine	$N.Mint	£Good	£Fine	£N.Mint
1-6 Romita Jr./Williamson art	$0.25	$0.75	$1.25	£0.15	£0.45	£0.75
7-9	$0.25	$0.75	$1.25	£0.15	£0.45	£0.75
10 ND John Byrne art	$0.25	$0.75	$1.25	£0.20	£0.60	£1.00
11 ND John Byrne art	$0.25	$0.75	$1.25	£0.15	£0.45	£0.75
12 ND John Byrne art, The Pitt begins, Byrne self-cameo	$0.25	$0.75	$1.25	£0.15	£0.45	£0.75
13 ND John Byrne art, Pitt X-over	$0.25	$0.75	$1.25	£0.15	£0.45	£0.75
14-19 ND John Byrne art	$0.25	$0.75	$1.25	£0.15	£0.45	£0.75
Title Value:	$4.75	$14.25	$23.75	£2.90	£8.70	£14.50

STAR BRAND, THE ANNUAL
Marvel Comics Group/New Universe; 1 Oct 1987

	$Good	$Fine	$N.Mint	£Good	£Fine	£N.Mint
1 ND	$0.30	$0.90	$1.50	£0.20	£0.60	£1.00
Title Value:	$0.30	$0.90	$1.50	£0.20	£0.60	£1.00

STAR FEMS
AC Comics,OS; nn 1987

	$Good	$Fine	$N.Mint	£Good	£Fine	£N.Mint
nn ND Black Blaze appears; Paul Gulacy cover	$0.40	$1.20	$2.00	£0.25	£0.75	£1.25
Title Value:	$0.40	$1.20	$2.00	£0.25	£0.75	£1.25

STAR HUNTERS
DC Comics; 1 Oct/Nov 1977-7 Oct/Nov 1978
(see DC Super-Stars #16)

	$Good	$Fine	$N.Mint	£Good	£Fine	£N.Mint
1 scarce in the U.K.	$0.30	$0.90	$1.50	£0.20	£0.60	£1.00
2-6	$0.25	$0.75	$1.25	£0.15	£0.45	£0.75
7 ND 44pgs	$0.30	$0.90	$1.50	£0.20	£0.60	£1.00
Title Value:	$1.85	$5.55	$9.25	£1.15	£3.45	£5.75

STAR MASTERS
AC Comics; 1 Mar 1984

	$Good	$Fine	$N.Mint	£Good	£Fine	£N.Mint
1 ND Tom Lyle script and art	$0.30	$0.90	$1.50	£0.20	£0.60	£1.00
Title Value:	$0.30	$0.90	$1.50	£0.20	£0.60	£1.00

STAR MASTERS
Marvel Comics Group; 1 Dec 1995-3 Feb 1996

	$Good	$Fine	$N.Mint	£Good	£Fine	£N.Mint
1 ND Silver Surfer, Beta Ray Thor and Quasar begin	$0.40	$1.20	$2.00	£0.25	£0.75	£1.25
2 ND ties into Thor #494	$0.40	$1.20	$2.00	£0.25	£0.75	£1.25
3 ND concludes in Cosmic Powers Unlimited #4	$0.40	$1.20	$2.00	£0.25	£0.75	£1.25
Title Value:	$1.20	$3.60	$6.00	£0.75	£2.25	£3.75

	$Good	$Fine	$N.Mint	£Good	£Fine	£N.Mint

STAR POLICE
Sky Comics; 1 Jul 1994
1 ND Michael Brown script

	$Good	$Fine	$N.Mint	£Good	£Fine	£N.Mint
	$0.40	$1.20	$2.00	£0.25	£0.75	£1.25
Title Value:	$0.40	$1.20	$2.00	£0.25	£0.75	£1.25

STAR RANGERS
Adventure; 1 Oct 1987-4 Feb 1988
1 ND Jim Mooney art

	$0.40	$1.20	$2.00	£0.25	£0.75	£1.25

2-3 ND Adam Hughes art

	$0.40	$1.20	$2.00	£0.25	£0.75	£1.25

4 ND Dave Dorman cover

	$0.40	$1.20	$2.00	£0.25	£0.75	£1.25
Title Value:	$1.60	$4.80	$8.00	£1.00	£3.00	£5.00

STAR REACH
Star Reach; 1 Apr 1974-18 Oct 1979
1 ND Cody Starbuck by Chaykin, Jim Starlin art

	$1.00	$3.00	$5.00	£0.70	£2.10	£3.50

1 2nd printing, ND (Nov 1975)

	$0.60	$1.80	$3.00	£0.40	£1.20	£2.00

1 3rd/4th printing ND

	$0.40	$1.20	$2.00	£0.25	£0.75	£1.25

2 ND Jim Starlin, Workman art, Stephanie Star by Friedrich/Giordano; Neal Adams cover

	$0.80	$2.40	$4.00	£0.50	£1.50	£2.50
2 2nd printing ND	$0.50	$1.50	$2.50	£0.30	£0.90	£1.50
2 3rd printing ND	$0.40	$1.20	$2.00	£0.25	£0.75	£1.25
3 ND Brunner art	$0.60	$1.80	$3.00	£0.40	£1.20	£2.00
3 2nd printing ND	$0.50	$1.50	$2.50	£0.30	£0.90	£1.50
3 3rd printing ND	$0.40	$1.20	$2.00	£0.25	£0.75	£1.25
4 ND Chaykin art	$0.60	$1.80	$3.00	£0.40	£1.20	£2.00
4 2nd printing ND	$0.50	$1.50	$2.50	£0.30	£0.90	£1.50
4 3rd printing ND	$0.40	$1.20	$2.00	£0.25	£0.75	£1.25
5 ND Chaykin art	$0.60	$1.80	$3.00	£0.40	£1.20	£2.00
5 2nd printing ND	$0.50	$1.50	$2.50	£0.30	£0.90	£1.50
5 3rd printing ND	$0.40	$1.20	$2.00	£0.25	£0.75	£1.25
6 ND Jeff Jones art						
	$0.55	$1.65	$2.75	£0.35	£1.05	£1.75
6 2nd printing ND	$0.50	$1.50	$2.50	£0.30	£0.90	£1.50
6 3rd printing ND	$0.40	$1.20	$2.00	£0.25	£0.75	£1.25

7 ND Dave Sim script, Bonivert, Staton art, Barry Smith cover

	$0.50	$1.50	$2.50	£0.30	£0.90	£1.50
7 2nd printing ND	$0.40	$1.20	$2.00	£0.25	£0.75	£1.25

8 ND P. Craig Russell, Gene Day art

	$0.50	$1.50	$2.50	£0.30	£0.90	£1.50
8 2nd printing ND	$0.40	$1.20	$2.00	£0.25	£0.75	£1.25
9 ND	$0.50	$1.50	$2.50	£0.30	£0.90	£1.50
9 2nd printing ND	$0.40	$1.20	$2.00	£0.25	£0.75	£1.25
10 Brunner art	$0.50	$1.50	$2.50	£0.30	£0.90	£1.50
10 2nd printing ND						
	$0.40	$1.20	$2.00	£0.25	£0.75	£1.25
11-15 ND	$0.40	$1.20	$2.00	£0.25	£0.75	£1.25
16-18 ND magazine size						
	$0.50	$1.50	$2.50	£0.30	£0.90	£1.50
Title Value:	$17.15	$51.45	$85.75	£10.75	£32.25	£53.75
Greatest Hits Graphic Novel (1979) 124pgs				£1.20	£3.60	£6.00

STAR REACH CLASSICS
Eclipse; 1 Mar 1984-6 Aug 1984
1 ND Jim Starlin and Dave Sim reprints; Starlin cover

	$0.40	$1.20	$2.00	£0.25	£0.75	£1.25

2 ND Sergio Aragones reprints

	$0.40	$1.20	$2.00	£0.25	£0.75	£1.25

3 ND P. Craig Russell reprint/cover

	$0.40	$1.20	$2.00	£0.25	£0.75	£1.25

4 ND Frank Brunner reprint/cover

	$0.40	$1.20	$2.00	£0.25	£0.75	£1.25

5 ND Ditko reprint, Chaykin cover

	$0.40	$1.20	$2.00	£0.25	£0.75	£1.25

6 ND P. Craig Russell reprint/cover

	$0.40	$1.20	$2.00	£0.25	£0.75	£1.25
Title Value:	$2.40	$7.20	$12.00	£1.50	£4.50	£7.50

Note: reprints from Star Reach & Quack!

STAR SLAMMERS
Malibu Bravura,MS; 1 May 1994-5 Nov 1994
1-5 ND Walter Simonson script and art

	$2.00	$6.00	$10.00	£1.25	£3.75	£6.25
Title Value:	$2.00	$6.00	$10.00	£1.25	£3.75	£6.25

STAR TREK
Gold Key; 1 Jul 1967-61 Mar 1979

	$Good	$Fine	$N.Mint	£Good	£Fine	£N.Mint
1 photo cover	$55.00	$165.00	$450.00	£38.00	£110.00	£300.00
2 photo cover	$37.00	$110.00	$260.00	£25.00	£75.00	£175.00
3-5 photo cover	$27.00	$80.00	$190.00	£18.50	£55.00	£130.00
6-9 photo cover	$21.00	$62.50	$150.00	£14.00	£43.00	£100.00
10 painted covers begin (ends #59)						
	$12.50	$38.00	$75.00	£9.00	£28.00	£55.00
11-14	$12.50	$38.00	$75.00	£9.00	£28.00	£55.00
15-20 distributed in the U.K.						
	$12.50	$38.00	$75.00	£8.25	£25.00	£50.00
21 scarce though distributed in the U.K.						
	$9.00	$28.00	$55.00	£6.25	£18.50	£37.50
22-23 distributed in the U.K.						
	$9.00	$28.00	$55.00	£5.75	£17.50	£35.00
24 scarce though distributed in the U.K.						

	$Good	$Fine	$N.Mint	£Good	£Fine	£N.Mint
	$9.00	$28.00	$55.00	£6.25	£18.50	£37.50
25-26 distributed in the U.K.						
	$9.00	$28.00	$55.00	£5.75	£17.50	£35.00
27 scarce though distributed in the U.K.						
	$9.00	$28.00	$55.00	£6.25	£18.50	£37.50
28-29 distributed in the U.K.						
	$9.00	$28.00	$55.00	£5.75	£17.50	£35.00
30 scarce though distributed in the U.K.						
	$9.00	$28.00	$55.00	£6.25	£18.50	£37.50
31-35 distributed in the U.K.						
	$6.25	$18.50	$37.50	£4.15	£12.50	£25.00
36	$6.75	$20.00	$33.75	£4.50	£13.50	£22.50
37-40	$6.25	$18.50	$37.50	£4.55	£13.50	£27.50
41-44	$4.15	$12.50	$25.00	£2.90	£8.75	£17.50
45 same photo cover as #7						
	$4.15	$12.50	$25.00	£2.90	£8.75	£17.50
46-50	$4.15	$12.50	$25.00	£2.90	£8.75	£17.50
51-59	$4.15	$12.50	$25.00	£2.50	£7.50	£15.00
60 scarce in the U.K. line drawn cover						
	$4.15	$12.50	$25.00	£2.90	£8.75	£17.50
61 scarce in the U.K. line-drawn cover						
	$4.15	$12.50	$25.00	£2.90	£8.75	£17.50
Title Value:	$634.65	$1912.00	$4151.25	£429.25	£1293.50	£2802.50

Note: irregular distribution in the U.K.

STAR TREK
Marvel Comics Group; 1 Apr 1980-18 Feb 1982
1 ND reprints movie adaptation from Super Special #15

	$1.00	$3.00	$5.00	£0.70	£2.10	£3.50

2 ND reprints movie adaptation from Super Special #15

	$0.80	$2.40	$4.00	£0.50	£1.50	£2.50

3 ND reprints movie adaptation from Super Special #15

	$0.60	$1.80	$3.00	£0.40	£1.20	£2.00
4-12 ND	$0.60	$1.80	$3.00	£0.40	£1.20	£2.00
13-14	$0.60	$1.80	$3.00	£0.30	£0.90	£1.50
15 ND	$0.60	$1.80	$3.00	£0.40	£1.20	£2.00
16-17	$0.60	$1.80	$3.00	£0.30	£0.90	£1.50
18 ND	$0.60	$1.80	$3.00	£0.40	£1.20	£2.00
Title Value:	$11.40	$34.20	$57.00	£7.20	£21.60	£36.00

STAR TREK (1ST SERIES)
DC Comics; 1 Feb 1984-56 Nov 1988
1 George Perez cover art, Mando paper begins

	$2.00	$6.00	$10.00	£1.30	£3.90	£6.50
2	$1.50	$4.50	$7.50	£0.80	£2.40	£4.00
3-5	$1.20	$3.60	$6.00	£0.60	£1.80	£3.00
6-10	$1.00	$3.00	$5.00	£0.50	£1.50	£2.50
11-20	$0.60	$1.80	$3.00	£0.40	£1.20	£2.00
21-32	$0.50	$1.50	$2.50	£0.30	£0.90	£1.50
33 DS anniversary issue						
	$0.80	$2.40	$4.00	£0.50	£1.50	£2.50
34-48	$0.50	$1.50	$2.50	£0.30	£0.90	£1.50
49 Who Killed Captain Kirk story begins by Peter David (ends #55)						
	$0.50	$1.50	$2.50	£0.30	£0.90	£1.50
50 DS painted cover						
	$0.60	$1.80	$3.00	£0.40	£1.20	£2.00
51-55	$0.40	$1.20	$2.00	£0.25	£0.75	£1.25
56 Gray Morrow art						
	$0.40	$1.20	$2.00	£0.25	£0.75	£1.25
Title Value:	$35.90	$107.70	$179.50	£21.20	£63.60	£106.00

Star Trek: The Mirror Universe
Trade paperback (Jun 1991)
reprints issues #9-16, new painted cover £2.40 £7.20 £12.00

The Best of Star Trek
Trade paperback (Dec 1991), 240pgs £2.50 £7.50 £12.50

Star Trek: Who Killed Captain Kirk (Aug 1993)
Trade paperback reprints issues #49-55 by Peter David,
new painted cover by Jason Palmer £2.10 £6.30 £10.50

STAR TREK (1ST SERIES) ANNUAL
DC Comics; 1 Oct 1985-3 1988

	$0.60	$1.80	$3.00	£0.40	£1.20	£2.00
1-3						
Title Value:	$1.80	$5.40	$9.00	£1.20	£3.60	£6.00

STAR TREK (2ND SERIES)
DC Comics; 1 Oct 1989-present

	$1.40	$4.20	$7.00	£0.80	£2.40	£4.00
1						
2	$0.80	$2.40	$4.00	£0.50	£1.50	£2.50
3	$0.60	$1.80	$3.00	£0.40	£1.20	£2.00
4-12	$0.50	$1.50	$2.50	£0.30	£0.90	£1.50
13 Return of the Worthy story, part written by Billy Mumy						
	$0.50	$1.50	$2.50	£0.30	£0.90	£1.50
14 Return of the Worthy story, part written by Billy Mumy						
	$0.50	$1.50	$2.50	£0.30	£0.90	£1.50
15 Return of the Worthy story, part written by Billy Mumy						
	$0.50	$1.50	$2.50	£0.30	£0.90	£1.50
16-23	$0.50	$1.50	$2.50	£0.30	£0.90	£1.50
24 DS 25th anniversary salute						
	$0.60	$1.80	$3.00	£0.40	£1.20	£2.00
25-29	$0.50	$1.50	$2.50	£0.30	£0.90	£1.50
30-33 Veritas story						
	$0.50	$1.50	$2.50	£0.30	£0.90	£1.50
34	$0.50	$1.50	$2.50	£0.30	£0.90	£1.50
35-40 The Tabukan Syndrome, bi-weekly						
	$0.50	$1.50	$2.50	£0.30	£0.90	£1.50
41-45	$0.50	$1.50	$2.50	£0.30	£0.90	£1.50

	$Good	$Fine	$N.Mint	£Good	£Fine	£N.Mint
46-49 bi-weekly	$0.50	$1.50	$2.50	£0.30	£0.90	£1.50
50 64pgs	$0.80	$2.40	$4.00	£0.50	£1.50	£2.50
51-70	$0.40	$1.20	$2.00	£0.25	£0.75	£1.25
71 $2.50 begin	$0.50	$1.50	$2.50	£0.30	£0.90	£1.50
72-74	$0.50	$1.50	$2.50	£0.30	£0.90	£1.50
75 56pgs	$0.80	$2.40	$4.00	£0.50	£1.50	£2.50
76-80	$0.50	$1.50	$2.50	£0.30	£0.90	£1.50
Title Value:	$40.00	$120.00	$200.00	£24.30	£72.90	£121.50

Note: New Format
Star Trek: Tests of Courage (Oct 1994)

	$Good	$Fine	$N.Mint	£Good	£Fine	£N.Mint
Trade paperback reprints issues #35-40				£2.40	£7.20	£12.00

STAR TREK (2ND SERIES) ANNUAL
DC Comics; 1 Jun 1990-present

	$Good	$Fine	$N.Mint	£Good	£Fine	£N.Mint
1 48pgs, Gray Morrow art, script by Peter David/George Takei	$0.60	$1.80	$3.00	£0.40	£1.20	£2.00
2 LD in the U.K. 64pgs	$0.60	$1.80	$3.00	£0.50	£1.50	£2.50
3-5 64pgs	$0.60	$1.80	$3.00	£0.40	£1.20	£2.00
6 64pgs, Convergence part 1, continued in Star Trek: The Next Generation Annual #6	$0.80	$2.40	$4.00	£0.50	£1.50	£2.50
Title Value:	$3.80	$11.40	$19.00	£2.60	£7.80	£13.00

STAR TREK DYNABRITE COMICS
Whitman; 11357, 11358 1978

	$Good	$Fine	$N.Mint	£Good	£Fine	£N.Mint
11357 scarce in the U.K. 48pgs, reprints Gold Key Star Trek issues #33, #41	$1.00	$3.00	$5.00	£1.50	£4.50	£7.50
11358 scarce in the U.K. 48pgs, reprints Gold Key Star Trek issues #34, #36	$1.00	$3.00	$5.00	£1.50	£4.50	£7.50
Title Value:	$2.00	$6.00	$10.00	£3.00	£9.00	£15.00

STAR TREK MOVIE SPECIAL
DC Comics; 1 1984; 2 1987

	$Good	$Fine	$N.Mint	£Good	£Fine	£N.Mint
1 68pgs, adapts Star Trek III	$0.50	$1.50	$2.50	£0.30	£0.90	£1.50
2 68pgs, adapts Star Trek IV	$0.50	$1.50	$2.50	£0.30	£0.90	£1.50
Title Value:	$1.00	$3.00	$5.00	£0.60	£1.80	£3.00

STAR TREK SPECIAL
DC Comics; 1 May 1994-present

	$Good	$Fine	$N.Mint	£Good	£Fine	£N.Mint
1 64pgs, Peter David script; also features script and art by Mike Collins; painted cover by Bill Sienkiewicz	$0.80	$2.40	$4.00	£0.50	£1.50	£2.50
2 64pgs, painted cover by Dan Curry	$0.80	$2.40	$4.00	£0.50	£1.50	£2.50
3 64pgs	$0.80	$2.40	$4.00	£0.50	£1.50	£2.50
Title Value:	$2.40	$7.20	$12.00	£1.50	£4.50	£7.50

STAR TREK V MOVIE ADAPTATION
DC Comics; nn Aug 1989

	$Good	$Fine	$N.Mint	£Good	£Fine	£N.Mint
nn adapts Star Trek V film	$0.50	$1.50	$2.50	£0.30	£0.90	£1.50
Title Value:	$0.50	$1.50	$2.50	£0.30	£0.90	£1.50

STAR TREK VI MOVIE ADAPTATION
DC Comics; 1 Feb 1992

	$Good	$Fine	$N.Mint	£Good	£Fine	£N.Mint
1 64pgs, Peter David script	$0.60	$1.80	$3.00	£0.40	£1.20	£2.00
1 ND Direct Sales Edition - 64pgs, Peter David script, photo gallery of stills from the film	$1.00	$3.00	$5.00	£0.70	£2.10	£3.50
Title Value:	$1.60	$4.80	$8.00	£1.10	£3.30	£5.50

STAR TREK: ASHES OF EDEN
DC Comics,OS; nn Jul 1995

	$Good	$Fine	$N.Mint	£Good	£Fine	£N.Mint
nn ND adaptation of William Shatner novel	$3.00	$9.00	$15.00	£2.00	£6.00	£10.00
Title Value:	$3.00	$9.00	$15.00	£2.00	£6.00	£10.00

STAR TREK: DEBT OF HONOUR
DC Comics,OS; 1 Aug 1992

	$Good	$Fine	$N.Mint	£Good	£Fine	£N.Mint
1 ND 96pgs, Adam Hughes art, Chris Claremont script; 25th anniversary celebration, painted cover by Dave Dorman	$4.50	$13.50	$22.50	£3.00	£9.00	£15.00
Title Value:	$4.50	$13.50	$22.50	£3.00	£9.00	£15.00

Softcover Graphic Novel (Dec 1992)

	$Good	$Fine	$N.Mint	£Good	£Fine	£N.Mint
96pgs, new painted cover by Jason Palmer				£2.00	£6.00	£10.00

STAR TREK: DEEP SPACE NINE
Malibu/Marvel Comics Group; 0 Jan 1995, 1 Sep 1993-present

	$Good	$Fine	$N.Mint	£Good	£Fine	£N.Mint
0 ND fully painted art by Trevor Goring	$0.60	$1.80	$3.00	£0.40	£1.20	£2.00
1 ND	$0.60	$1.80	$3.00	£0.60	£1.80	£3.00
1 ND Limited Edition - all black cover	$2.50	$7.50	$12.50	£1.50	£4.50	£7.50
1 ND Gold Edition (May 1994) - gold foil cover, limited to 2,400 copies	$3.00	$9.00	$15.00	£2.00	£6.00	£10.00
1 ND Dual Foil Edition (May 1994) - gold and silver foil logo on black matte finish	$3.00	$9.00	$15.00	£2.00	£6.00	£10.00
1 Newsstand edition, ND photo cover	$0.60	$1.80	$3.00	£0.60	£1.80	£3.00
2 ND pre-bagged with trading card	$0.50	$1.50	$2.50	£0.30	£0.90	£1.50
3-21 ND	$0.50	$1.50	$2.50	£0.30	£0.90	£1.50
22-23 ND bi-weekly	$0.50	$1.50	$2.50	£0.30	£0.90	£1.50
24 ND	$0.50	$1.50	$2.50	£0.30	£0.90	£1.50
25 ND 48pgs, bi-weekly	$0.80	$2.40	$4.00	£0.50	£1.50	£2.50
26-27 ND	$0.50	$1.50	$2.50	£0.30	£0.90	£1.50
28 ND 1st issue solicited under Marvel Comics banner	$0.50	$1.50	$2.50	£0.30	£0.90	£1.50
29-30 ND	$0.50	$1.50	$2.50	£0.30	£0.90	£1.50
31 ND 48pgs	$0.80	$2.40	$4.00	£0.50	£1.50	£2.50
32 ND	$0.50	$1.50	$2.50	£0.30	£0.90	£1.50
Title Value:	$26.40	$79.20	$132.00	£16.80	£50.40	£84.00

STAR TREK: DEEP SPACE NINE - BLOOD AND HONOUR
Malibu,OS; 1 May 1995

	$Good	$Fine	$N.Mint	£Good	£Fine	£N.Mint
1 ND Mark Lenard (Sarek in Star Trek) script, Ken Penders art	$0.60	$1.80	$3.00	£0.40	£1.20	£2.00
1 ND Signed Limited Edition (Jun 1995) - 500 copies signed by Mark Lenard with certificate	$2.50	$7.50	$12.50	£1.50	£4.50	£7.50
Title Value:	$3.10	$9.30	$15.50	£1.90	£5.70	£9.50

STAR TREK: DEEP SPACE NINE - THE RULES OF DIPLOMACY
Malibu,OS; 1 Aug 1995

	$Good	$Fine	$N.Mint	£Good	£Fine	£N.Mint
1 ND script by Aron Eisenberg (Nog in DS9)	$0.60	$1.80	$3.00	£0.40	£1.20	£2.00
1 ND Signed Limited Edition; 1,000 copies with certificate	$2.50	$7.50	$12.50	£1.50	£4.50	£7.50
Title Value:	$3.10	$9.30	$15.50	£1.90	£5.70	£9.50

STAR TREK: DEEP SPACE NINE - WORF
Marvel Comics Group,OS; 0 Feb 1996

	$Good	$Fine	$N.Mint	£Good	£Fine	£N.Mint
0 ND 48pgs, biography and pin-up section to tie in with Worf joining the series on television	$0.80	$2.40	$4.00	£0.50	£1.50	£2.50
Title Value:	$0.80	$2.40	$4.00	£0.50	£1.50	£2.50

STAR TREK: DEEP SPACE NINE ANNUAL
Malibu; 1 Dec 1994-present

	$Good	$Fine	$N.Mint	£Good	£Fine	£N.Mint
1 ND	$0.60	$1.80	$3.00	£0.40	£1.20	£2.00
1 ND Gold Edition (Mar 1996)	$2.50	$7.50	$12.50	£1.50	£4.50	£7.50
Title Value:	$3.10	$9.30	$15.50	£1.90	£5.70	£9.50

Splatter #1

Starstream #1

Star Trek (Gold Key) #35

	$Good	$Fine	$N.Mint	£Good	£Fine	£N.Mint

STAR TREK: DEEP SPACE NINE HEARTS AND MINDS

Malibu,MS; 1 June 1994-4 Sep 1994

	$Good	$Fine	$N.Mint	£Good	£Fine	£N.Mint
1 ND	$0.50	$1.50	$2.50	£0.30	£0.90	£1.50
1 ND Deluxe Edition, holographic cover (Nov 1994)						
	$1.20	$3.60	$6.00	£0.80	£2.40	£4.00
2-4 ND	$0.50	$1.50	$2.50	£0.30	£0.90	£1.50
Title Value:	$3.20	$9.60	$16.00	£2.00	£6.00	£10.00

Note: the Holographic Edition of #1 was re-solicited by Marvel Comics Group cover date Feb 1996 at $14.95 with specific information that the issue would not be available outside the U.S and Canada

STAR TREK: DEEP SPACE NINE SPECIAL

Malibu,OS; 1 Jun 1995

	$Good	$Fine	$N.Mint	£Good	£Fine	£N.Mint
1 ND 48pgs, five complete stories						
	$0.80	$2.40	$4.00	£0.50	£1.50	£2.50
Title Value:	$0.80	$2.40	$4.00	£0.50	£1.50	£2.50

STAR TREK: DEEP SPACE NINE THE MAQUIS

Malibu,MS; 1 Feb 1995-3 Apr 1995

	$Good	$Fine	$N.Mint	£Good	£Fine	£N.Mint
1 ND	$0.50	$1.50	$2.50	£0.30	£0.90	£1.50
1 ND Photo Cover Edition (Feb 1995)						
	$0.50	$1.50	$2.50	£0.30	£0.90	£1.50
2-3 ND	$0.50	$1.50	$2.50	£0.30	£0.90	£1.50
Title Value:	$2.00	$6.00	$10.00	£1.20	£3.60	£6.00

STAR TREK: DEEP SPACE NINE/STAR TREK: NEXT GENERATION

Malibu/DC Comics,MS; 1 Oct 1994-2 Nov 1994

	$Good	$Fine	$N.Mint	£Good	£Fine	£N.Mint
1 ND	$0.50	$1.50	$2.50	£0.30	£0.90	£1.50
1 ND Gold Foil Edition						
	$2.50	$7.50	$12.50	£1.50	£4.50	£7.50
2 ND	$0.50	$1.50	$2.50	£0.30	£0.90	£1.50
Title Value:	$3.50	$10.50	$17.50	£2.10	£6.30	£10.50

Note: a cross collaboration between DC and Malibu. Both companies published issues #1 and 2 though the story is structured over 4 parts

STAR TREK: DEEP SPACE NINE/STAR TREK: NEXT GENERATION

DC Comics/Malibu,MS; 1 Oct 1994-2 Nov 1994

	$Good	$Fine	$N.Mint	£Good	£Fine	£N.Mint
1 ND	$0.50	$1.50	$2.50	£0.30	£0.90	£1.50
1 ND Gold Foil Edition						
	$2.50	$7.50	$12.50	£1.50	£4.50	£7.50
2 ND	$0.50	$1.50	$2.50	£0.30	£0.90	£1.50
Title Value:	$3.50	$10.50	$17.50	£2.10	£6.30	£10.50

Note: a cross collaboration between DC and Malibu. Both companies published issues #1 and 2 though the story is structured over 4 parts

STAR TREK: DEEP SPACE NINE: LIGHTSTORM

Malibu,OS; 1 Nov 1994

	$Good	$Fine	$N.Mint	£Good	£Fine	£N.Mint
1 ND sequel to Star Trek: Deep Space Nine Hearts and Minds						
	$0.80	$2.40	$4.00	£0.50	£1.50	£2.50
1 ND Silver Foil Logo Edition (Nov 1994) - limited to 2,500 copies						
	$2.50	$7.50	$12.50	£1.50	£4.50	£7.50
Title Value:	$3.30	$9.90	$16.50	£2.00	£6.00	£10.00

STAR TREK: GENERATIONS

DC Comics,OS Film; 1 Jan 1995

	$Good	$Fine	$N.Mint	£Good	£Fine	£N.Mint
1 LD 64pgs, adaptation of the seventh Star Trek film						
	$0.80	$2.40	$4.00	£0.50	£1.50	£2.50
1 LD 64pgs, Prestige Format						
	$1.20	$3.60	$6.00	£0.80	£2.40	£4.00
Title Value:	$2.00	$6.00	$10.00	£1.30	£3.90	£6.50

STAR TREK: THE MODALA IMPERATIVE

DC Comics,MS; 1 Jul 1991-4 Aug 1991

	$Good	$Fine	$N.Mint	£Good	£Fine	£N.Mint
1-4 LD in the U.K. bi-weekly 25th anniversary series						
	$0.50	$1.50	$2.50	£0.30	£0.90	£1.50
Title Value:	$2.00	$6.00	$10.00	£1.20	£3.60	£6.00

STAR TREK: THE NEXT GENERATION

DC Comics,MS TV; 1 Feb 1988-6 Jul 1988

	$Good	$Fine	$N.Mint	£Good	£Fine	£N.Mint
1 DS	$1.60	$4.80	$8.00	£1.00	£3.00	£5.00
2-6	$1.20	$3.60	$6.00	£0.60	£1.80	£3.00
Title Value:	$7.60	$22.80	$38.00	£4.00	£12.00	£20.00

Note: New Format

Star Trek: The Next Generation - Beginnings (Jul 1995)
Trade paperback
reprints mini-series with new Bill Sienkiewicz cover | | | | £2.70 | £8.10 | £13.50

STAR TREK: THE NEXT GENERATION (2ND SERIES)

DC Comics; 1 Oct 1989-present

	$Good	$Fine	$N.Mint	£Good	£Fine	£N.Mint
1	$2.00	$6.00	$10.00	£1.20	£3.60	£6.00
2	$1.50	$4.50	$7.50	£0.80	£2.40	£4.00
3	$1.20	$3.60	$6.00	£0.60	£1.80	£3.00
4-10	$0.80	$2.40	$4.00	£0.50	£1.50	£2.50
11-12	$0.60	$1.80	$3.00	£0.40	£1.20	£2.00
13 written by Peter David/Billy Mumy						
	$0.60	$1.80	$3.00	£0.40	£1.20	£2.00
14-20	$0.60	$1.80	$3.00	£0.40	£1.20	£2.00
21-23	$0.50	$1.50	$2.50	£0.30	£0.90	£1.50
24 DS	$0.60	$1.80	$3.00	£0.40	£1.20	£2.00
25-29	$0.50	$1.50	$2.50	£0.30	£0.90	£1.50
30 The Rift part 1	$0.50	$1.50	$2.50	£0.30	£0.90	£1.50
31 The Rift part 2	$0.50	$1.50	$2.50	£0.30	£0.90	£1.50
32	$0.50	$1.50	$2.50	£0.30	£0.90	£1.50
33-38 bi-weekly	$0.50	$1.50	$2.50	£0.30	£0.90	£1.50
39 Divergence story						
	$0.50	$1.50	$2.50	£0.30	£0.90	£1.50
40	$0.50	$1.50	$2.50	£0.30	£0.90	£1.50
41-49	$0.40	$1.20	$2.00	£0.25	£0.75	£1.25
50 64pgs	$0.80	$2.40	$4.00	£0.50	£1.50	£2.50
51-58	$0.40	$1.20	$2.00	£0.25	£0.75	£1.25
59-61 Children of Chaos story						
	$0.40	$1.20	$2.00	£0.25	£0.75	£1.25

	$Good	$Fine	$N.Mint	£Good	£Fine	£N.Mint
62-70	$0.40	$1.20	$2.00	£0.25	£0.75	£1.25
71 $2.50 begin	$0.50	$1.50	$2.50	£0.30	£0.90	£1.50
72-74	$0.50	$1.50	$2.50	£0.30	£0.90	£1.50
75 56pgs	$0.80	$2.40	$4.00	£0.50	£1.50	£2.50
76-80	$0.50	$1.50	$2.50	£0.30	£0.90	£1.50
Title Value:	$44.10	$132.30	$220.50	£27.15	£81.45	£135.75

The Star Lost (Apr 1993)
Trade paperback
reprints issues #20-24, introduction by Ron Moore,
producer of Star Trek: The Next Generation | | | | £1.90 | £5.70 | £9.50
The Best of Star Trek: The Next Generation (Mar 1994)
Trade paperback reprints issues #5,6,19 and Annual #2 | | | | £2.70 | £8.10 | £13.50
Star Trek: Revisitations (Dec 1995) Trade paperback
reprints issues #22-24 and #49-50, painted cover | | | | £2.70 | £8.10 | £13.50

STAR TREK: THE NEXT GENERATION (2ND SERIES) ANNUAL

DC Comics; 1 Aug 1990-present

	$Good	$Fine	$N.Mint	£Good	£Fine	£N.Mint
1 ND 48pgs, script by John de Lancie ("Q") from TV series						
	$0.80	$2.40	$4.00	£0.50	£1.50	£2.50
2-5 ND 64pgs	$0.80	$2.40	$4.00	£0.50	£1.50	£2.50
6 ND 56pgs, Convergence part 2 continued from Star Trek Annual #6						
	$0.80	$2.40	$4.00	£0.50	£1.50	£2.50
Title Value:	$4.80	$14.40	$24.00	£3.00	£9.00	£15.00

Note: New Format

STAR TREK: THE NEXT GENERATION - ILL WIND

DC Comics,MS; 1 Nov 1995-4 Feb 1996

	$Good	$Fine	$N.Mint	£Good	£Fine	£N.Mint
1-4 ND painted covers by Hugh Fleming						
	$0.50	$1.50	$2.50	£0.30	£0.90	£1.50
Title Value:	$2.00	$6.00	$10.00	£1.20	£3.60	£6.00

STAR TREK: THE NEXT GENERATION - SEASON FINALE

DC Comics,OS; 1 Aug 1994

	$Good	$Fine	$N.Mint	£Good	£Fine	£N.Mint
1 ND 64pgs, adaptation of the last ever episode						
	$0.80	$2.40	$4.00	£0.50	£1.50	£2.50
Title Value:	$0.80	$2.40	$4.00	£0.50	£1.50	£2.50

STAR TREK: THE NEXT GENERATION - SHADOWHEART

DC Comics,MS; 1 Dec 1994-4 Mar 1995

	$Good	$Fine	$N.Mint	£Good	£Fine	£N.Mint
1-4 ND	$0.50	$1.50	$2.50	£0.30	£0.90	£1.50
Title Value:	$2.00	$6.00	$10.00	£1.20	£3.60	£6.00

STAR TREK: THE NEXT GENERATION SPECIAL

DC Comics; 1 Nov 1993; 2 Sep 1994; 3 Oct 1995

	$Good	$Fine	$N.Mint	£Good	£Fine	£N.Mint
1 ND 64pgs, three stories						
	$0.80	$2.40	$4.00	£0.50	£1.50	£2.50
2 ND 64pgs, three stories featuring a Chris Claremont script						
	$0.80	$2.40	$4.00	£0.50	£1.50	£2.50
3 ND 64pgs, one story based on unused plot from TV series						
	$0.80	$2.40	$4.00	£0.50	£1.50	£2.50
Title Value:	$2.40	$7.20	$12.00	£1.50	£4.50	£7.50

STAR TREK: THE NEXT GENERATION/STAR TREK: DEEP SPACE NINE

DC Comics,MS; 1 Dec 1994-2 Jan 1995

	$Good	$Fine	$N.Mint	£Good	£Fine	£N.Mint
1-2 ND inter-company X-over with Malibu Comics						
	$0.50	$1.50	$2.50	£0.30	£0.90	£1.50
Title Value:	$1.00	$3.00	$5.00	£0.60	£1.80	£3.00

STAR TREK: THE NEXT GENERATION: THE MODALA IMPERATIVE

DC Comics,MS; 1 Sep 1991-4 Oct 1991

	$Good	$Fine	$N.Mint	£Good	£Fine	£N.Mint
1-4 bi-weekly	$0.50	$1.50	$2.50	£0.30	£0.90	£1.50
Title Value:	$2.00	$6.00	$10.00	£1.20	£3.60	£6.00

Note: story continued from The Modala Imperative mini-series

STAR TREK: VOYAGER PREMIERE EPISODE ADAPTATION

Malibu,MS; 1,2 Jan 1995

	$Good	$Fine	$N.Mint	£Good	£Fine	£N.Mint
1 ND cover numbered "A"; Mike Barr script, Rob Davis and Terry Pallot art begin						
	$0.50	$1.50	$2.50	£0.30	£0.90	£1.50
1 ND cover numbered "A" News-stand Edition, same interior but with photo cover						
	$0.50	$1.50	$2.50	£0.30	£0.90	£1.50
2 ND cover numbered "B"						
	$0.50	$1.50	$2.50	£0.30	£0.90	£1.50
2 ND cover numbered "B" News-stand Edition, same interior but with photo cover						
	$0.50	$1.50	$2.50	£0.30	£0.90	£1.50
Title Value:	$2.00	$6.00	$10.00	£1.20	£3.60	£6.00

STAR WARS

Marvel Comics Group; 1 Jul 1977-107 Sep 1986
(see Droids, Ewoks, Marvel Movie Showcase, Marvel Special Edition)

	$Good	$Fine	$N.Mint	£Good	£Fine	£N.Mint
1 ND 30¢ cover price (three variants with/without UPC code?)						
	$7.00	$21.00	$50.00	£4.25	£12.50	£30.00
1 very rare in the U.K. 35c cover price variant with UPC code on cover						
	$52.50	$160.00	$375.00	£36.00	£105.00	£250.00
2	$4.00	$12.00	$20.00	£2.50	£7.50	£12.50
3	$3.00	$9.00	$15.00	£2.00	£6.00	£10.00
4-5	$3.00	$9.00	$15.00	£1.50	£4.50	£7.50
6 ND	$1.50	$4.50	$7.50	£1.00	£3.00	£5.00
7 ND new stories begin						
	$1.50	$4.50	$7.50	£1.00	£3.00	£5.00
8-10 ND	$1.50	$4.50	$7.50	£1.00	£3.00	£5.00
11-12 ND	$1.20	$3.60	$6.00	£0.80	£2.40	£4.00
13 ND John Byrne cover						
	$1.20	$3.60	$6.00	£0.80	£2.40	£4.00
14-15 ND	$1.20	$3.60	$6.00	£0.80	£2.40	£4.00
16 ND Walt Simonson art						
	$1.20	$3.60	$6.00	£0.80	£2.40	£4.00
17-20 ND	$1.20	$3.60	$6.00	£0.80	£2.40	£4.00
21-37 ND	$1.00	$3.00	$5.00	£0.60	£1.80	£3.00
38 ND Golden art	$1.00	$3.00	$5.00	£0.60	£1.80	£3.00
39-44 ND reprints Empire Strikes Back from Super Special #16, Williamson art						
	$1.50	$4.50	$7.50	£0.70	£2.10	£3.50

VERY GENERAL PERCENTAGE CONVERSION CHART WHICH MAY BE USED TO CALCULATE LOW AND INBETWEEN GRADES:

	$Good	$Fine	$N.Mint	£Good	£Fine	£N.Mint
45-48 ND	$1.00	$3.00	$5.00	£0.60	£1.80	£3.00
49 ND Walt Simonson art	$1.00	$3.00	$5.00	£0.60	£1.80	£3.00
50 ND 52pgs, Williamson art	$1.00	$3.00	$5.00	£0.70	£2.10	£3.50
51-63 ND Walt Simonson art	$1.00	$3.00	$5.00	£0.50	£1.50	£2.50
64 ND no Simonson	$1.00	$3.00	$5.00	£0.50	£1.50	£2.50
65-66 ND Walt Simonson art	$1.00	$3.00	$5.00	£0.50	£1.50	£2.50
67-91 ND	$1.00	$3.00	$5.00	£0.50	£1.50	£2.50
92 ND Sienkiewicz cover (with Cynthia Martin)	$1.00	$3.00	$5.00	£0.50	£1.50	£2.50
93-99 ND	$1.00	$3.00	$5.00	£0.50	£1.50	£2.50
100 ND scarce in the U.K. DS	$1.00	$3.00	$5.00	£0.50	£1.50	£2.50
101-106 ND scarce in the U.K.	$1.00	$3.00	$5.00	£1.00	£3.00	£5.00
107 ND very scarce in the U.K. Whilce Portacio inks	$6.00	$18.00	$30.00	£4.00	£12.00	£20.00
Title Value:	$187.00	$563.50	$1062.50	£114.45	£340.10	£651.00

Note: #1-6 adapt Star Wars movie. 2nd prints of #1-6 have "Reprint" printed on the covers.
ARTISTS
Chaykin in 1-10. Infantino/Gene Day in 18, 21, 25. Simonson art in 16, 49, 51, 52, 55-66.

STAR WARS ANNUAL
Marvel Comics Group; 1 1979; 2 1982-3 Dec 1983

	$Good	$Fine	$N.Mint	£Good	£Fine	£N.Mint
1 ND 52pgs	$1.50	$4.50	$7.50	£1.00	£3.00	£5.00
2-3 ND 52pgs	$1.20	$3.60	$6.00	£0.80	£2.40	£4.00
Title Value:	$3.90	$11.70	$19.50	£2.60	£7.80	£13.00

STAR WARS GALAXY MAGAZINE
Topps,Magazine; 1 Oct 1994-present

	$Good	$Fine	$N.Mint	£Good	£Fine	£N.Mint
1 ND news, features and articles on Star Wars	$0.80	$2.40	$4.00	£0.50	£1.50	£2.50
1 ND Direct Market Edition (Oct 1994) - pre-bagged with trading card, poster and ashcan edition of Star Wars: Dark Lords of Sith #1	$0.90	$2.70	$4.50	£0.60	£1.80	£3.00
2 ND news, features and articles on Star Wars	$0.80	$2.40	$4.00	£0.50	£1.50	£2.50
2 ND Direct Market Edition (Jan 1995) - pre-bagged with X-Files #1 ashcan edition, Star Wars poster and Mastervision card, Star Wars trading card	$5.00	$15.00	$25.00	£3.00	£9.00	£15.00
3 ND pre-bagged with Star Wars trading card and Skycap	$0.80	$2.40	$4.00	£0.50	£1.50	£2.50
4 ND pre-bagged with three trading cards	$0.80	$2.40	$4.00	£0.50	£1.50	£2.50
5 ND pre-bagged with three trading cards	$1.00	$3.00	$5.00	£0.70	£2.10	£3.50
Title Value:	$10.10	$30.30	$50.50	£6.30	£18.90	£31.50

STAR WARS IN 3-D
Blackthorne; (3-D Series #30,#47,#48); 1 Winter 1987-4 1988

	$Good	$Fine	$N.Mint	£Good	£Fine	£N.Mint
1 ND all with bound-in 3-D glasses (25% less without glasses)	$0.80	$2.40	$4.00	£0.60	£1.80	£3.00
2-4 ND	$0.60	$1.80	$3.00	£0.40	£1.20	£2.00
Title Value:	$2.60	$7.80	$13.00	£1.80	£5.40	£9.00

STAR WARS: BOBA FETT - BOUNTY ON BAR-KOODA
Dark Horse,OS; 1 Dec 1995

	$Good	$Fine	$N.Mint	£Good	£Fine	£N.Mint
1 ND 48pgs, John Wagner script, Cam Kennedy art	$1.00	$3.00	$5.00	£0.65	£1.95	£3.25
Title Value:	$1.00	$3.00	$5.00	£0.65	£1.95	£3.25

STAR WARS: DARK EMPIRE
Dark Horse,MS; 1 Feb 1992-6 Dec 1992

	$Good	$Fine	$N.Mint	£Good	£Fine	£N.Mint
1 Tom Veitch script, Cam Kennedy art begins, cover paintings by Dave Dorman begin	$5.50	$16.50	$27.50	£2.00	£6.00	£10.00
1 2nd printing, Aug 1992	$0.80	$2.40	$4.00	£0.50	£1.50	£2.50
2 scarce in the U.K.	$5.50	$16.50	$27.50	£2.00	£6.00	£10.00
2 2nd printing, Aug 1992	$0.80	$2.40	$4.00	£0.50	£1.50	£2.50
3	$2.00	$6.00	$10.00	£1.20	£3.60	£6.00
3 2nd printing, Oct 1992	$0.60	$1.80	$3.00	£0.40	£1.20	£2.00
4	$1.20	$3.60	$6.00	£0.80	£2.40	£4.00
5-6	$1.00	$3.00	$5.00	£0.60	£1.80	£3.00
Title Value:	$18.40	$55.20	$92.00	£8.60	£25.80	£43.00

Note: all Non-Distributed on the news-stands in the U.K.
Star Wars: Dark Empire Softcover Collection (Apr 1993)

				£Good	£Fine	£N.Mint
reprints mini-series with text and sketch pages				£2.40	£7.20	£12.00
(2nd print - Jul 1994)				£2.20	£6.60	£11.00
Signed, Limited Hardcover Edition (May 1993), gold foil embossed cover, 1000 copies				£15.00	£45.00	£75.00

STAR WARS: DARK EMPIRE II
Dark Horse,MS; 1 Dec 1994-6 May 1995

	$Good	$Fine	$N.Mint	£Good	£Fine	£N.Mint
1-6 ND Tom Veitch script, Cam Kennedy art; painted covers by Dave Dorman	$0.60	$1.80	$3.00	£0.40	£1.20	£2.00
Title Value:	$3.60	$10.80	$18.00	£2.40	£7.20	£12.00

Star Wars: Dark Empire II (Aug 1995)

				£Good	£Fine	£N.Mint
Trade paperback reprints issues #1-6 plus cover paintings				£2.40	£7.20	£12.00

STAR WARS: DROIDS
Dark Horse,MS; 1 Apr 1994-6 Sep 1994

	$Good	$Fine	$N.Mint	£Good	£Fine	£N.Mint
1 ND	$0.80	$2.40	$4.00	£0.50	£1.50	£2.50
2-6 ND	$0.50	$1.50	$2.50	£0.30	£0.90	£1.50
Title Value:	$3.30	$9.90	$16.50	£2.00	£6.00	£10.00
Special (Jan 1995)				£0.30	£0.90	£1.50

Star Wars: Droids (Apr 1995)

				£Good	£Fine	£N.Mint
Trade paperback collects story from Dark Horse Comics #17-19, Star Wars: Droids #1-6 and 8pg story from Star Wars Galaxy Magazine				£2.40	£7.20	£12.00

STAR WARS: DROIDS (2ND SERIES)
Dark Horse,MS; 1 Apr 1995-present

	$Good	$Fine	$N.Mint	£Good	£Fine	£N.Mint
1-7 ND Ian Gibson art	$0.50	$1.50	$2.50	£0.30	£0.90	£1.50
8 ND	$0.50	$1.50	$2.50	£0.30	£0.90	£1.50
Title Value:	$4.00	$12.00	$20.00	£2.40	£7.20	£12.00

STAR WARS: EMPIRE'S END
Dark Horse,MS; 1 Oct 1995-2 Nov 1995

	$Good	$Fine	$N.Mint	£Good	£Fine	£N.Mint
1-2 ND Tom Veitch script, Jim Baikie art; painted covers by Dave Dorman	$0.60	$1.80	$3.00	£0.40	£1.20	£2.00
Title Value:	$1.20	$3.60	$6.00	£0.80	£2.40	£4.00

STAR WARS: HEIR TO THE EMPIRE
Dark Horse,MS; 1 Oct 1995-6 Mar 1996

	$Good	$Fine	$N.Mint	£Good	£Fine	£N.Mint
1 ND Mike Baron script, Olivier Vatine and Fred Blanchard art begins	$0.60	$1.80	$3.00	£0.40	£1.20	£2.00
2-6 ND	$0.60	$1.80	$3.00	£0.40	£1.20	£2.00
Title Value:	$3.60	$10.80	$18.00	£2.40	£7.20	£12.00

STAR WARS: JABBA THE HUTT
Dark Horse,OS; 1 Mar 1995

	$Good	$Fine	$N.Mint	£Good	£Fine	£N.Mint
1 ND Jim Woodring script, Art Wetherell art; cover by Steve Bissette and Cam Kennedy	$0.50	$1.50	$2.50	£0.30	£0.90	£1.50
Title Value:	$0.50	$1.50	$2.50	£0.30	£0.90	£1.50

STAR WARS: JABBA THE HUTT - THE DYNASTY TRAP
Dark Horse,OS; 1 Aug 1995

	$Good	$Fine	$N.Mint	£Good	£Fine	£N.Mint
1 ND	$0.50	$1.50	$2.50	£0.30	£0.90	£1.50
Title Value:	$0.50	$1.50	$2.50	£0.30	£0.90	£1.50

STAR WARS: JABBA THE HUTT: THE HUNGER OF PRINCESS NAMPI
Dark Horse,OS; 1 Jun 1995

	$Good	$Fine	$N.Mint	£Good	£Fine	£N.Mint
1 ND Jim Woodring script, Art Wetherell art	$0.50	$1.50	$2.50	£0.30	£0.90	£1.50
Title Value:	$0.50	$1.50	$2.50	£0.30	£0.90	£1.50

STAR WARS: RIVER OF CHAOS
Dark Horse,MS; 1 May 1995-4 Aug 1995

	$Good	$Fine	$N.Mint	£Good	£Fine	£N.Mint
1-4 ND June Brigman and Roy Richardson art	$0.50	$1.50	$2.50	£0.30	£0.90	£1.50
Title Value:	$2.00	$6.00	$10.00	£1.20	£3.60	£6.00

STAR WARS: SPLINTER OF THE MIND'S EYE
Dark Horse,MS; 1 Dec 1995-present

	$Good	$Fine	$N.Mint	£Good	£Fine	£N.Mint
1,2 ND Terry Austin script, Chris Sprouse art	$0.50	$1.50	$2.50	£0.30	£0.90	£1.50
Title Value:	$1.00	$3.00	$5.00	£0.60	£1.80	£3.00

STAR WARS: TALES OF THE JEDI
Dark Horse,MS; 1 Oct 1993-5 Feb 1994

	$Good	$Fine	$N.Mint	£Good	£Fine	£N.Mint
1 ND	$0.80	$2.40	$4.00	£0.50	£1.50	£2.50
2-5 ND	$0.60	$1.80	$3.00	£0.40	£1.20	£2.00
Title Value:	$3.20	$9.60	$16.00	£2.10	£6.30	£10.50

Star Wars: Tales of the Jedi (Jul 1994)

				£Good	£Fine	£N.Mint
Trade paperback reprints mini-series, painted cover by Dave Dorman				£2.00	£6.00	£10.00

STAR WARS: TALES OF THE JEDI - DARK LORDS OF SITH BOOK 1
Dark Horse,MS; 1 Oct 1994-6 Mar 1995

	$Good	$Fine	$N.Mint	£Good	£Fine	£N.Mint
1-6 ND Tom Veitch script, Kevin Anderson art; pre-bagged with trading card	$0.50	$1.50	$2.50	£0.30	£0.90	£1.50
Title Value:	$3.00	$9.00	$15.00	£1.80	£5.40	£9.00

STAR WARS: TALES OF THE JEDI - THE FREEDON NADD UPRISING
Dark Horse,MS; 1 Jul 1994-2 Aug 1994

	$Good	$Fine	$N.Mint	£Good	£Fine	£N.Mint
1-2 ND Dave Dorman painted cover	$0.50	$1.50	$2.50	£0.30	£0.90	£1.50
Title Value:	$1.00	$3.00	$5.00	£0.60	£1.80	£3.00

STAR WARS: TALES OF THE JEDI - THE SITH WAR
Dark Horse,MS; 1 Aug 1995-6 Jan 1996

	$Good	$Fine	$N.Mint	£Good	£Fine	£N.Mint
1-6 ND Kevin Anderson script, Dario Carrasco and Jordi Ensign art	$0.50	$1.50	$2.50	£0.30	£0.90	£1.50
Title Value:	$3.00	$9.00	$15.00	£1.80	£5.40	£9.00

STAR WARS: X-WING - ROGUE SQUADRON: THE PHANTOM AFFAIR
Dark Horse,MS; 1 Nov 1995-4 Feb 1996

	$Good	$Fine	$N.Mint	£Good	£Fine	£N.Mint
1-4 ND	$0.60	$1.80	$3.00	£0.40	£1.20	£2.00
Title Value:	$2.40	$7.20	$12.00	£1.60	£4.80	£8.00

STAR WARS: X-WING ROGUE SQUADRON
Dark Horse,MS; 1 Jul 1995-4 Oct 1995

	$Good	$Fine	$N.Mint	£Good	£Fine	£N.Mint
1 ND Mike Baron script, Allen Nunis and Andy Mushynsky art begins; Dave Dorman painted covers	$0.60	$1.80	$3.00	£0.40	£1.20	£2.00
2-4 ND	$0.60	$1.80	$3.00	£0.40	£1.20	£2.00
Title Value:	$2.40	$7.20	$12.00	£1.60	£4.80	£8.00

STAR-SPANGLED WAR STORIES
National Periodical Publications/DC Comics; 1 (#131) Aug 1952-204 Feb/Mar 1977
(issues #1 & #2 called Star Spangled Comics, numbered #131 & #132)
(becomes Unknown Soldier)

	$Good	$Fine	$N.Mint	£Good	£Fine	£N.Mint
1 scarce in the U.K. number 131 on cover, continuing the numbering of Star Spangled Comics	$80.00	$240.00	$650.00	£52.50	£155.00	£425.00
2 scarce in the U.K. number 132 on cover	$57.50	$175.00	$475.00	£41.00	£120.00	£325.00
3 scarce in the U.K. number 133 on cover	$55.00	$165.00	$450.00	£38.00	£110.00	£300.00
3 scarce in the U.K. no number on cover						

MINT = 100% / NEAR MINT (inc. +/-) = 90–99% / VERY FINE (inc. +/-) = 75–89% / FINE (inc. +/-) = 55–74%
VERY GOOD (inc. +/-) = 35–54% / GOOD (inc. +/-) = 15–34% / FAIR = 5–14% / POOR = 1–4%

565

	$Good	$Fine	$N.Mint	£Good	£Fine	£N.Mint
	$28.00	$82.50	$225.00	£18.50	£55.00	£150.00
4 no number on cover						
	$28.00	$82.50	$225.00	£18.50	£55.00	£150.00
5 numbers on cover begin						
	$28.00	$82.50	$225.00	£18.50	£55.00	£150.00
6-10	$21.50	$65.00	$175.00	£15.00	£45.00	£120.00
11-20	$22.00	$65.00	$155.00	£15.00	£45.00	£105.00
21-30	$19.00	$57.50	$135.00	£12.50	£39.00	£90.00
31 1st Code approved issue						
	$12.50	$39.00	$90.00	£8.50	£26.00	£60.00
32-40	$12.50	$39.00	$90.00	£8.50	£26.00	£60.00
41-44	$11.00	$34.00	$80.00	£7.75	£23.50	£55.00
45 1st painted (grey-tone) cover by DC, starting a long collectible line that lasted into the 1960s						
	$14.00	$43.00	$100.00	£9.25	£28.00	£65.00
46-50	$11.00	$34.00	$80.00	£7.75	£23.50	£55.00
51-70	$8.50	$26.00	$60.00	£5.50	£17.00	£40.00
71-83	$7.75	$23.50	$55.00	£5.00	£15.00	£35.00
84 origin Mlle. Marie						
	$17.00	$50.00	$120.00	£11.00	£34.00	£80.00
85-86 Mille. Marie						
	$9.25	$28.00	$65.00	£6.25	£19.00	£45.00
1st official distribution in the U.K.						
87-89 scarce in the U.K. Mille. Marie						
	$9.25	$28.00	$65.00	£7.00	£21.00	£50.00
90 scarce in the U.K. 1st War That Time Forgot (ends #137), classic dinosaur covers begin						
	$38.00	$110.00	$265.00	£25.00	£75.00	£175.00
91 scarce in the U.K.						
	$8.25	$25.00	$50.00	£5.75	£17.50	£35.00
92 scarce in the U.K. 2nd dinosaur cover						
	$18.00	$55.00	$110.00	£12.50	£38.00	£75.00
93 scarce in the U.K.						
	$8.25	$25.00	$50.00	£5.75	£17.50	£35.00
94-99 scarce in the U.K. dinosaur covers						
	$18.00	$55.00	$110.00	£12.50	£38.00	£75.00
100 very scarce in the U.K. dinosaur cover						
	$21.50	$65.00	$130.00	£14.00	£43.00	£85.00
101-106 scarce in the U.K. dinosaur covers						
	$13.00	$40.00	$80.00	£9.00	£28.00	£55.00
107-110	$13.00	$40.00	$80.00	£8.25	£25.00	£50.00
111-125	$11.50	$35.00	$70.00	£7.50	£22.50	£45.00
126	$7.50	$22.50	$45.00	£5.00	£15.00	£30.00
127-133 ND	$11.50	$35.00	$70.00	£7.50	£22.50	£45.00
134 ND Neal Adams art						
	$13.00	$40.00	$80.00	£8.25	£25.00	£50.00
135-136 ND	$11.50	$35.00	$70.00	£7.50	£22.50	£45.00
137 ND last dinosaur cover						
	$11.50	$35.00	$70.00	£7.50	£22.50	£45.00
138 ND 1st appearance Enemy Ace (series ends #150), Kubert art						
	$11.50	$35.00	$70.00	£7.50	£22.50	£45.00
139 ND 2nd appearance Enemy Ace						
	$10.50	$33.00	$65.00	£7.50	£22.50	£45.00
140-143 ND Enemy Ace						
	$7.50	$22.50	$45.00	£5.00	£15.00	£30.00
144 ND Enemy Ace, Neal Adams and Kubert art						
	$7.50	$22.50	$45.00	£5.00	£15.00	£30.00
145 ND Enemy Ace						
	$7.50	$22.50	$45.00	£5.00	£15.00	£30.00
146-150 ND Enemy Ace						
	$6.50	$20.00	$40.00	£4.15	£12.50	£25.00
151 ND 1st appearance Unknown Soldier; Enemy Ace reprints begin (to #161)						
	$8.25	$25.00	$50.00	£5.75	£17.50	£35.00
152-153 ND	$2.50	$7.50	$15.00	£1.65	£5.00	£10.00
154 ND origin Unknown Soldier						
	$5.00	$15.00	$30.00	£3.30	£10.00	£20.00
155 ND	$2.50	$7.50	$15.00	£1.65	£5.00	£10.00
156 scarce in the U.K.						
	$1.50	$4.50	$7.50	£1.00	£3.00	£5.00
157	$1.50	$4.50	$7.50	£0.80	£2.40	£4.00
158-164 52pgs	$1.50	$4.50	$7.50	£1.00	£3.00	£5.00
165-167	$1.50	$4.50	$7.50	£0.80	£2.40	£4.00
168 scarce in the U.K.						
	$1.50	$4.50	$7.50	£1.00	£3.00	£5.00
169-170	$1.50	$4.50	$7.50	£0.80	£2.40	£4.00
171-180	$0.80	$2.40	$4.00	£0.50	£1.50	£2.50
181-183 Enemy Ace vs. The Balloon Buster						
	$0.80	$2.40	$4.00	£0.50	£1.50	£2.50
184-191	$0.80	$2.40	$4.00	£0.50	£1.50	£2.50
192-195	$0.80	$2.40	$4.00	£0.40	£1.20	£2.00
196 scarce in the U.K.						
	$0.80	$2.40	$4.00	£0.50	£1.50	£2.50
197 scarce in the U.K. Kaluta inks						
	$0.80	$2.40	$4.00	£0.50	£1.50	£2.50
198-199	$0.80	$2.40	$4.00	£0.40	£1.20	£2.00
200 scarce in the U.K.						
	$0.80	$2.40	$4.00	£0.50	£1.50	£2.50
201-203	$0.80	$2.40	$4.00	£0.40	£1.20	£2.00
204 scarce in the U.K.						
	$0.80	$2.40	$4.00	£0.50	£1.50	£2.50
Title Value: $2175.95	$6594.10	$15023.50	£1455.90	£4403.70	£10004.50	

FEATURES

Enemy Ace in 138-150 (2pgs only in 146, remainder reprint), 181-183, 200. Mlle.Marie in 84-91. Suicide Squadron in 110, 116-121, 125, 127, 128. Unknown Soldier in 151-204. War That Time Forgot in 90, 92,

94-137.

REPRINT FEATURES

Ballon Buster in 160, 163. Enemy Ace in 151-159, 161. Viking Prince in 149, 150.

STARBLAST	$Good	$Fine	$N.Mint	£Good	£Fine	£N.Mint
Marvel Comics Group,MS; 1 Jan 1994-4 Apr 1994						
1 48pgs, Starblast part 1, Nova, Quasar, Hyperion, Black Bolt appear						
	$0.40	$1.20	$2.00	£0.25	£0.75	£1.25
2 Starblast part 4	$0.40	$1.20	$2.00	£0.25	£0.75	£1.25
3 Starblast part 8	$0.40	$1.20	$2.00	£0.25	£0.75	£1.25
4 Starblast part 12	$0.40	$1.20	$2.00	£0.25	£0.75	£1.25
Title Value:	$1.60	$4.80	$8.00	£1.00	£3.00	£5.00

STARBLAZERS (1ST SERIES)						
Comico,MS; 1 Apr 1987-4 Jul 1987						
1-4 ND	$0.40	$1.20	$2.00	£0.25	£0.75	£1.25
Title Value:	$1.60	$4.80	$8.00	£1.00	£3.00	£5.00
Trade paperback (Sep 1991);						
reprints series with new Ken Steacy cover				£2.20	£6.60	£11.00

STARBLAZERS (2ND SERIES)						
Comico,MS; 1 1989-5 1989						
1-5 ND Steacy wraparound covers; colour						
	$0.40	$1.20	$2.00	£0.25	£0.75	£1.25
Title Value:	$2.00	$6.00	$10.00	£1.25	£3.75	£6.25

STARDUSTERS						
Night Wynd,MS; 1 Dec 1991-4 Mar 1992						
1-4 ND	$0.40	$1.20	$2.00	£0.25	£0.75	£1.25
Title Value:	$1.60	$4.80	$8.00	£1.00	£3.00	£5.00

STARFIRE						
DC Comics; 1 Aug/Sep 1976-8 Oct/Nov 1977						
1 scarce in the U.K. origin and 1st appearance Starfire (not to be confused with Teen Titans Starfire)						
	$0.30	$0.90	$1.50	£0.20	£0.60	£1.00
2-8	$0.25	$0.75	$1.25	£0.15	£0.45	£0.75
Title Value:	$2.05	$6.15	$10.25	£1.25	£3.75	£6.25

STARFORCE SIX SPECIAL						
AC Comics,OS; nn 1985						
nn ND	$0.40	$1.20	$2.00	£0.25	£0.75	£1.25
Title Value:	$0.40	$1.20	$2.00	£0.25	£0.75	£1.25

STARJAMMERS						
Marvel Comics Group,MS; 1 Oct 1995-4 Jan 1996						
1-4 ND Warren Ellis script, Carlos Pacheco and Cam Smith art; foil stamped cover						
	$0.60	$1.80	$3.00	£0.40	£1.20	£2.00
Title Value:	$2.40	$7.20	$12.00	£1.60	£4.80	£8.00

STARK: FUTURE						
Aircel; 1 1986-17 1987						
1-17 ND	$0.40	$1.20	$2.00	£0.25	£0.75	£1.25
Title Value:	$6.80	$20.40	$34.00	£4.25	£12.75	£21.25

STARLIGHT AGENCY						
Antarctic Press,MS; 1 Sep 1991-3 Nov 1991						
1-3 ND	$0.40	$1.20	$2.00	£0.25	£0.75	£1.25
Title Value:	$1.20	$3.60	$6.00	£0.75	£2.25	£3.75

STARLORD, THE SPECIAL EDITION						
Marvel Comics Group,OS; 1 Feb 1982						
(see Marvel Comics Super Special #10, Marvel Premiere, Marvel Preview, Marvel Spotlight #6, #7)						
1 ND John Byrne art reprinted from Marvel Preview, additional pages by Golden; Gibbons Dr.Who back-up reprint						
	$1.00	$3.00	$5.00	£0.70	£2.10	£3.50
Title Value:	$1.00	$3.00	$5.00	£0.70	£2.10	£3.50
Note: Direct Sales; 1st Marvel Baxter paper comic.						

STARMAN						
DC Comics; 1 Oct 1988-46 May 1992						
(see First Issue Special #12)						
1	$0.30	$0.90	$1.50	£0.20	£0.60	£1.00
2-4	$0.25	$0.75	$1.25	£0.15	£0.45	£0.75
5-6 Invasion X-over						
	$0.25	$0.75	$1.25	£0.15	£0.45	£0.75
7-8	$0.25	$0.75	$1.25	£0.15	£0.45	£0.75
9 Batman appears	$0.25	$0.75	$1.25	£0.15	£0.45	£0.75
10 Blockbuster appears						
	$0.25	$0.75	$1.25	£0.15	£0.45	£0.75
11-13	$0.25	$0.75	$1.25	£0.15	£0.45	£0.75
14 Superman appears						
	$0.25	$0.75	$1.25	£0.15	£0.45	£0.75
15-16	$0.25	$0.75	$1.25	£0.15	£0.45	£0.75
17-18 Power Girl appears						
	$0.25	$0.75	$1.25	£0.15	£0.45	£0.75
19-27	$0.25	$0.75	$1.25	£0.15	£0.45	£0.75
28 LD in the U.K. "Superman" appears, ties in with Superman #50						
	$0.25	$0.75	$1.25	£0.20	£0.60	£1.00
29	$0.25	$0.75	$1.25	£0.15	£0.45	£0.75
30-33 The Seduction of Starman story						
	$0.25	$0.75	$1.25	£0.15	£0.45	£0.75
34-37	$0.25	$0.75	$1.25	£0.15	£0.45	£0.75
38 War of the Gods tie-in						
	$0.25	$0.75	$1.25	£0.15	£0.45	£0.75
39-41	$0.25	$0.75	$1.25	£0.15	£0.45	£0.75
42 origin Starman begins, Eclipso appears						
	$0.25	$0.75	$1.25	£0.15	£0.45	£0.75
43 origin Starman continued, Eclipso, Lobo appear						
	$0.25	$0.75	$1.25	£0.15	£0.45	£0.75
44 Starman and Eclipso vs. Lobo						
	$0.25	$0.75	$1.25	£0.15	£0.45	£0.75
45 Power Girl appears						
	$0.25	$0.75	$1.25	£0.15	£0.45	£0.75

	$Good	$Fine	$N.Mint	£Good	£Fine	£N.Mint
46	$0.25	$0.75	$1.25	£0.15	£0.45	£0.75
Title Value:	$11.55	$34.65	$57.75	£7.00	£21.00	£35.00

Note: 18 has free 16pg insert (see Batman #443, Superman #39)

STARMAN (2ND SERIES)
DC Comics; 0 Oct 1994; 1 Nov 1994-present

	$Good	$Fine	$N.Mint	£Good	£Fine	£N.Mint
0 (Oct 1994) Zero Hour X-over, origin	$1.20	$3.60	$6.00	£0.50	£1.50	£2.50
1	$1.20	$3.60	$6.00	£0.60	£1.80	£3.00
2	$0.80	$2.40	$4.00	£0.40	£1.20	£2.00
3-4	$0.50	$1.50	$2.50	£0.30	£0.90	£1.50
5 Starman vs. Starman	$0.50	$1.50	$2.50	£0.30	£0.90	£1.50
6 guest artist Teddy Kristiansen on a one-off story	$0.50	$1.50	$2.50	£0.30	£0.90	£1.50
7	$0.50	$1.50	$2.50	£0.30	£0.90	£1.50
8 becomes a Vertigo title	$0.50	$1.50	$2.50	£0.30	£0.90	£1.50
9-12	$0.50	$1.50	$2.50	£0.30	£0.90	£1.50
13 Underworld Unleashed	$0.45	$1.35	$2.25	£0.30	£0.90	£1.50
14-17	$0.45	$1.35	$2.25	£0.30	£0.90	£1.50
Title Value:	$10.45	$31.35	$51.50	£6.00	£18.00	£30.00

Starman: Sins of the Father (Jan 1996)

	$Good	$Fine	$N.Mint	£Good	£Fine	£N.Mint
Trade paperback collects issues #0-5, new painted cover by Tony Harris				£1.70	£5.10	£8.50

STARRIORS
Marvel Comics Group,MS Toy; 1 Aug 1984-4 Feb 1985

	$Good	$Fine	$N.Mint	£Good	£Fine	£N.Mint
1-4 ND	$0.15	$0.45	$0.75	£0.10	£0.30	£0.50
Title Value:	$0.60	$1.80	$3.00	£0.40	£1.20	£2.00

STARSLAYER
Pacific/First; 1 Feb 1982-34 Nov 1985

	$Good	$Fine	$N.Mint	£Good	£Fine	£N.Mint
1 Grell art begins	$0.60	$1.80	$3.00	£0.40	£1.20	£2.00
2 scarce in the U.K. origin and 1st appearance Rocketeer by Dave Stevens	$1.50	$4.50	$7.50	£1.00	£3.00	£5.00
3 2nd appearance Rocketeer by Stevens	$1.20	$3.60	$6.00	£0.80	£2.40	£4.00
4	$0.60	$1.80	$3.00	£0.40	£1.20	£2.00
5 2nd appearance Groo	$1.50	$4.50	$7.50	£1.00	£3.00	£5.00
6 last Pacific issue	$0.50	$1.50	$2.50	£0.30	£0.90	£1.50
7 1st First issue, last Grell art	$0.50	$1.50	$2.50	£0.30	£0.90	£1.50
8-9	$0.30	$0.90	$1.50	£0.20	£0.60	£1.00
10 1st appearance Grimjack	$0.50	$1.50	$2.50	£0.30	£0.90	£1.50
11-17	$0.30	$0.90	$1.50	£0.20	£0.60	£1.00
18 Starslayer meets Grimjack	$0.30	$0.90	$1.50	£0.20	£0.60	£1.00
19-34	$0.30	$0.90	$1.50	£0.20	£0.60	£1.00
Title Value:	$14.70	$44.10	$73.50	£9.70	£29.10	£48.50

Note: all Non-Distributed on the news-stands in the U.K.

STARSLAYER: THE DIRECTOR'S CUT
Valiant/Windjammer,MS; 1 Jun 1995-8 Oct 1995

	$Good	$Fine	$N.Mint	£Good	£Fine	£N.Mint
1-8 ND new story, pencil art and cover by Mike Grell; bi-weekly	$0.50	$1.50	$2.50	£0.30	£0.90	£1.50
Title Value:	$4.00	$12.00	$20.00	£2.40	£7.20	£12.00

STARSTREAM
Whitman; 1-4 1976

1 ND scarce in the U.K. adaptations of sci-fi classics begins: "Who Goes There?" adapted by John W. Campbell Jnr. plus other stories featuring Frank Bolle and Garcia Lopez art; heavy stock paper covers begin

	$Good	$Fine	$N.Mint	£Good	£Fine	£N.Mint
	$0.50	$1.50	$2.50	£0.30	£0.90	£1.50
2-4 ND scarce in the U.K. Bolle and McWilliams art	$0.50	$1.50	$2.50	£0.30	£0.90	£1.50
Title Value:	$2.00	$6.00	$10.00	£1.20	£3.60	£6.00

STARSTRUCK
Dark Horse,MS; 1 Aug 1990-4 Mar 1991
(sub-titled "The Expanding Universe")

	$Good	$Fine	$N.Mint	£Good	£Fine	£N.Mint
1-3 ND 48pgs, reprints Marvel mini-series, Mike Kaluta art, black and white	$0.60	$1.80	$3.00	£0.40	£1.20	£2.00
4 ND 64pgs, reprints Marvel mini-series, Mike Kaluta art, black and white; includes two bound-in trading cards at centre-fold	$0.90	$2.70	$4.50	£0.60	£1.80	£3.00
Title Value:	$2.70	$8.10	$13.50	£1.80	£5.40	£9.00

STARSTRUCK
Marvel Comics Group/Epic,MS; 1 Mar 1985-6 Feb 1986
(see Marvel Graphic Novel; Rocketeer Adventure Magazine [Comico])

	$Good	$Fine	$N.Mint	£Good	£Fine	£N.Mint
1-6 ND Kaluta art and cover	$0.50	$1.50	$2.50	£0.30	£0.90	£1.50
Title Value:	$3.00	$9.00	$15.00	£1.80	£5.40	£9.00

STARTLING CRIME ILLUSTRATED
Arts Industria; 1 Jan 1991

	$Good	$Fine	$N.Mint	£Good	£Fine	£N.Mint
1 ND black and white, photo cover	$0.25	$0.75	$1.25	£0.15	£0.45	£0.75
Title Value:	$0.25	$0.75	$1.25	£0.15	£0.45	£0.75

STARWATCHERS
Valiant; 1 Sep 1994-3 Nov 1994

	$Good	$Fine	$N.Mint	£Good	£Fine	£N.Mint
1-2 ND Mike Leeke and Dick Giordano art	$0.40	$1.20	$2.00	£0.25	£0.75	£1.25
3 ND Chaos Effect tie-in; Mike Leeke and Dick Giordano art	$0.40	$1.20	$2.00	£0.25	£0.75	£1.25
Title Value:	$1.20	$3.60	$6.00	£0.75	£2.25	£3.75

STATE
Majestic Entertainment; 1 Dec 1993

	$Good	$Fine	$N.Mint	£Good	£Fine	£N.Mint
1 ND Phil Hester and Mike Sellers art begins	$0.40	$1.20	$2.00	£0.25	£0.75	£1.25
Title Value:	$0.40	$1.20	$2.00	£0.25	£0.75	£1.25

STATIC
DC Comics/Milestone; 1 Jun 1993-present

	$Good	$Fine	$N.Mint	£Good	£Fine	£N.Mint
1	$0.30	$0.90	$1.50	£0.20	£0.60	£1.00
1 ND Direct Market Edition - pre-bagged with poster and the 4th set of jigsaw puzzle pieces	$0.50	$1.50	$2.50	£0.30	£0.90	£1.50
1 ND Platinum Edition - platinum logo	$1.20	$3.60	$6.00	£0.80	£2.40	£4.00
2-7	$0.30	$0.90	$1.50	£0.20	£0.60	£1.00
8 spot varnished cover by Walt Simonson, continued in Shadow Cabinet #0	$0.30	$0.90	$1.50	£0.20	£0.60	£1.00
9-12	$0.30	$0.90	$1.50	£0.20	£0.60	£1.00
13 John Byrne cover	$0.30	$0.90	$1.50	£0.20	£0.60	£1.00
14 48pgs, Worlds Collide part 14 (conclusion)	$0.45	$1.35	$2.25	£0.30	£0.90	£1.50
15-20	$0.30	$0.90	$1.50	£0.20	£0.60	£1.00
21 The Blood Syndicate appear	$0.30	$0.90	$1.50	£0.20	£0.60	£1.00
22-24	$0.30	$0.90	$1.50	£0.20	£0.60	£1.00
25 48pgs, Hardware guest-stars	$0.55	$1.65	$2.75	£0.35	£1.05	£1.75
26	$0.50	$1.50	$2.50	£0.30	£0.90	£1.50
27 special 99 cents issue	$0.20	$0.60	$1.00	£0.15	£0.45	£0.75

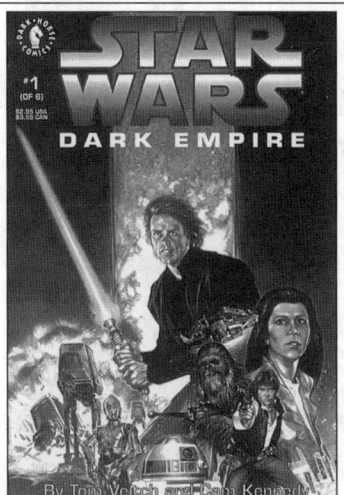

Star Wars: Dark Empire #1

Strange Adventures #226

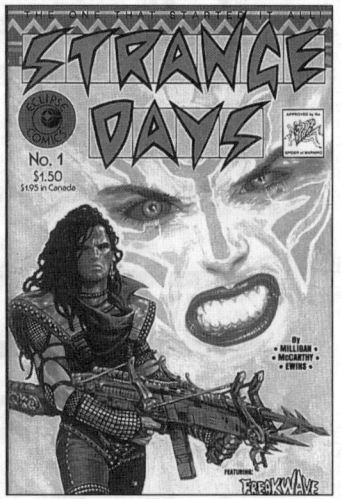

Strange Days #1

NEAR MINT MEANS NEAR MINT!

	$Good	$Fine	$N.Mint	£Good	£Fine	£N.Mint
28	$0.50	$1.50	$2.50	£0.30	£0.90	£1.50
29 Howard Chaykin cover	$0.50	$1.50	$2.50	£0.30	£0.90	£1.50
30	$0.50	$1.50	$2.50	£0.30	£0.90	£1.50
31	$0.20	$0.60	$1.00	£0.15	£0.45	£0.75
32-33	$0.50	$1.50	$2.50	£0.30	£0.90	£1.50
Title Value:	$13.00	$39.00	$65.00	£8.45	£25.35	£42.25

STATIC, CHARLTON ACTION FEATURING
Charlton; 11 Oct 1985-12 Dec 1985

	$Good	$Fine	$N.Mint	£Good	£Fine	£N.Mint
11-12 Steve Ditko cover and art	$0.40	$1.20	$2.00	£0.25	£0.75	£1.25
Title Value:	$0.80	$2.40	$4.00	£0.50	£1.50	£2.50

Note: very Limited Distribution in the U.K.

STEALTH FORCE
Malibu/Eternity; 1 Jul 1987-8 Apr 1988

	$Good	$Fine	$N.Mint	£Good	£Fine	£N.Mint
1-7 ND	$0.40	$1.20	$2.00	£0.25	£0.75	£1.25
8 ND 1st Eternity issue	$0.40	$1.20	$2.00	£0.25	£0.75	£1.25
Title Value:	$3.20	$9.60	$16.00	£2.00	£6.00	£10.00

STEED AND MRS. PEEL
Eclipse,MS; 1 Dec 1990-3 Jun 1991
(see Avengers Gold Key)

	$Good	$Fine	$N.Mint	£Good	£Fine	£N.Mint
1-3 ND 48pgs, Grant Morrison script, Ian Gibson art	$1.00	$3.00	$5.00	£0.70	£2.10	£3.50
Title Value:	$3.00	$9.00	$15.00	£2.10	£6.30	£10.50

STEEL
DC Comics; 0 Oct 1994; 1 Feb 1994-present

	$Good	$Fine	$N.Mint	£Good	£Fine	£N.Mint
0 (Oct 1994), Zero Hour X-over, Steel's armour takes on new capabilities	$0.40	$1.20	$2.00	£0.25	£0.75	£1.25
1 spin-off from The Reign of the Supermen; Louise Simonson script and Jon Bogdanove art begin	$0.30	$0.90	$1.50	£0.20	£0.60	£1.00
2-5	$0.30	$0.90	$1.50	£0.20	£0.60	£1.00
6 Worlds Collide X-over, continued in Blood Syndicate #16	$0.30	$0.90	$1.50	£0.20	£0.60	£1.00
7 Worlds Collide X-over, continued in Blood Syndicate #17	$0.30	$0.90	$1.50	£0.20	£0.60	£1.00
8 Zero Hour X-over	$0.30	$0.90	$1.50	£0.20	£0.60	£1.00
9-13	$0.30	$0.90	$1.50	£0.20	£0.60	£1.00
14 story continued from Superman #99 and continued in Adventures of Superman #522	$0.30	$0.90	$1.50	£0.20	£0.60	£1.00
15	$0.30	$0.90	$1.50	£0.20	£0.60	£1.00
16 upgraded coated paper stock (Miraweb Format) begins	$0.40	$1.20	$2.00	£0.25	£0.75	£1.25
17-20	$0.40	$1.20	$2.00	£0.25	£0.75	£1.25
21 Underworld Unleashed tie-in, Steel vs. Metallo	$0.40	$1.20	$2.00	£0.25	£0.75	£1.25
22-25	$0.40	$1.20	$2.00	£0.25	£0.75	£1.25
Title Value:	$8.90	$26.70	$44.50	£5.75	£17.25	£28.75

STEEL ANGEL
Caliber Press,MS; 1 Sep 1992-3 Jan 1993

	$Good	$Fine	$N.Mint	£Good	£Fine	£N.Mint
1-3 ND	$0.40	$1.20	$2.00	£0.25	£0.75	£1.25
Title Value:	$1.20	$3.60	$6.00	£0.75	£2.25	£3.75

STEEL ANNUAL
DC Comics; 1 Jul 1994-present

	$Good	$Fine	$N.Mint	£Good	£Fine	£N.Mint
1 64pgs, Elseworlds	$0.60	$1.80	$3.00	£0.40	£1.20	£2.00
2 64pgs, Year One	$0.80	$2.40	$4.00	£0.50	£1.50	£2.50
Title Value:	$1.40	$4.20	$7.00	£0.90	£2.70	£4.50

STEEL PULSE
True Fiction Publications; 1 Spring 1986

	$Good	$Fine	$N.Mint	£Good	£Fine	£N.Mint
1 ND	$0.30	$0.90	$1.50	£0.20	£0.60	£1.00
Title Value:	$0.30	$0.90	$1.50	£0.20	£0.60	£1.00

STEEL STERLING
(see Shield)

STEEL, THE INDESTRUCTIBLE MAN
DC Comics; 1 Mar 1978-5 Oct/Nov 1978
(see Justice League of America)

	$Good	$Fine	$N.Mint	£Good	£Fine	£N.Mint
1	$0.30	$0.90	$1.50	£0.20	£0.60	£1.00
2-4	$0.25	$0.75	$1.25	£0.15	£0.45	£0.75
5 ND 44pgs	$0.30	$0.90	$1.50	£0.20	£0.60	£1.00
Title Value:	$1.35	$4.05	$6.75	£0.85	£2.55	£4.25

STEELGRIP STARKEY
Marvel Comics Group/Epic,MS; 1 Jul 1986-6 Jun 1987

	$Good	$Fine	$N.Mint	£Good	£Fine	£N.Mint
1-6 ND Baxter paper	$0.30	$0.90	$1.50	£0.20	£0.60	£1.00
Title Value:	$1.80	$5.40	$9.00	£1.20	£3.60	£6.00

STEELTOWN ROCKERS
Marvel Comics Group,MS; 1 Apr 1990-6 Sep 1990

	$Good	$Fine	$N.Mint	£Good	£Fine	£N.Mint
1-6	$0.15	$0.45	$0.75	£0.10	£0.35	£0.60
Title Value:	$0.90	$2.70	$4.50	£0.60	£2.10	£3.60

STEVE CANYON 3-D
Kitchen Sink; 1 Jun 1986

	$Good	$Fine	$N.Mint	£Good	£Fine	£N.Mint
1 ND Milton Caniff reprints; with bound-in 3-D glasses (25% less without glasses)	$0.60	$1.80	$3.00	£0.40	£1.20	£2.00
Title Value:	$0.60	$1.80	$3.00	£0.40	£1.20	£2.00

STEVE CANYON MAGAZINE
Kitchen Sink; 1 1986-24 1987?

	$Good	$Fine	$N.Mint	£Good	£Fine	£N.Mint
1-18 ND	$1.00	$3.00	$5.00	£0.70	£2.10	£3.50
19 ND DS,40th Anniversary Special	$1.50	$4.50	$7.50	£1.00	£3.00	£5.00
20-21 ND	$1.50	$4.50	$7.50	£1.00	£3.00	£5.00
22-24 ND book form	$2.50	$7.50	$12.50	£1.50	£4.50	£7.50
Title Value:	$30.00	$90.00	$150.00	£20.10	£60.30	£100.50

STEVE ZODIAC AND THE FIREBALL XL-5
Gold Key; 1 Jan 1964

	$Good	$Fine	$N.Mint	£Good	£Fine	£N.Mint
1 rare, distributed in the U.K.	$9.00	$28.00	$55.00	£5.75	£17.50	£35.00
Title Value:	$9.00	$28.00	$55.00	£5.75	£17.50	£35.00

STICKBOY
Revolutionary Comics/Fantagraphics; 1 1990-6 May 1993

	$Good	$Fine	$N.Mint	£Good	£Fine	£N.Mint
1 ND	$0.40	$1.20	$2.00	£0.25	£0.75	£1.25
1 2nd printing ND	$0.30	$0.90	$1.50	£0.20	£0.60	£1.00
2-5 ND	$0.40	$1.20	$2.00	£0.25	£0.75	£1.25
6 ND 1st Fantagraphics issue (May 1993)	$0.40	$1.20	$2.00	£0.25	£0.75	£1.25
Title Value:	$2.70	$8.10	$13.50	£1.70	£5.10	£8.50

STIG'S INFERNO
Vortex/Eclipse; 1 May 1984-7 Mar 1987

	$Good	$Fine	$N.Mint	£Good	£Fine	£N.Mint
1 ND scarce in the U.K. Ty Templeton art begins; black and white	$0.40	$1.20	$2.00	£0.40	£1.20	£2.00
2 ND scarce in the U.K.	$0.40	$1.20	$2.00	£0.30	£0.90	£1.50
3 ND	$0.40	$1.20	$2.00	£0.25	£0.75	£1.25
4 ND says number 5 in indicia	$0.40	$1.20	$2.00	£0.25	£0.75	£1.25
5 ND last Vortex issue	$0.40	$1.20	$2.00	£0.25	£0.75	£1.25
6-7 ND	$0.40	$1.20	$2.00	£0.25	£0.75	£1.25
Title Value:	$2.80	$8.40	$14.00	£1.95	£5.85	£9.75
Trade paperback (1988), reprints #1-5				£0.85	£2.55	£4.25

STORM
Marvel Comics Group,MS; 1 Feb 1996-present

	$Good	$Fine	$N.Mint	£Good	£Fine	£N.Mint
1-2 ND Warren Ellis script, Terry Dodson and Karl Story art; foil stamped cover	$0.60	$1.80	$3.00	£0.40	£1.20	£2.00
Title Value:	$1.20	$3.60	$6.00	£0.80	£2.40	£4.00

STORMQUEST
Caliber Press; 1 Nov 1994-6 Jun 1995

	$Good	$Fine	$N.Mint	£Good	£Fine	£N.Mint
1 ND Barricade, Soulfire, Time-Stepper, Shalimar, Tremblor, Shrike and Brightblade begin	$0.40	$1.20	$2.00	£0.25	£0.75	£1.25
2-6 ND	$0.40	$1.20	$2.00	£0.25	£0.75	£1.25
Title Value:	$2.40	$7.20	$12.00	£1.50	£4.50	£7.50

STORMWATCH
Image; 0 Jun 1993; 1 Mar 1993-present

	$Good	$Fine	$N.Mint	£Good	£Fine	£N.Mint
0 ND pre-bagged with trading card	$0.50	$1.50	$2.50	£0.30	£0.90	£1.50
1 Jim Lee and Brandon Choi script begins, Jim Lee covers begin; includes coupon (send all three) for limited edition Stormwatch trading card	$0.60	$1.80	$3.00	£0.40	£1.20	£2.00
2 1st appearance Cannon and Farenheit	$0.50	$1.50	$2.50	£0.30	£0.90	£1.50
3 1st appearance Backlash	$1.00	$3.00	$5.00	£0.60	£1.80	£3.00
4-7	$0.50	$1.50	$2.50	£0.30	£0.90	£1.50
8 1st appearance Sarah Rainmaker (later joins Gen 13), Ripclaw appears	$0.50	$1.50	$2.50	£0.30	£0.90	£1.50
9 1st appearance Defile	$0.60	$1.80	$3.00	£0.40	£1.20	£2.00
10	$0.50	$1.50	$2.50	£0.30	£0.90	£1.50
10 Variant cover, ND cover forms larger picture when combined with variant covers of Deathblow #5, Gen 13 #5, Kindred #3, Team 7 #1, Union #0, Wetworks #2, Wildc.a.t.s. #11	$1.50	$4.50	$7.50	£1.00	£3.00	£5.00
11	$0.50	$1.50	$2.50	£0.30	£0.90	£1.50
12 Stormwatch vs. Hellstrike	$0.50	$1.50	$2.50	£0.30	£0.90	£1.50
13-16	$0.50	$1.50	$2.50	£0.30	£0.90	£1.50
17 team mourn the death of their leader Battalion	$0.50	$1.50	$2.50	£0.30	£0.90	£1.50
18-20	$0.50	$1.50	$2.50	£0.30	£0.90	£1.50
21 Stormwatch vs. WildC.A.T.S.	$0.50	$1.50	$2.50	£0.30	£0.90	£1.50
22 Wildstorm Rising part 9, continued in Wildstorm Rising #10; with two foil-bagged painted trading cards; cover by Barry Windsor-Smith	$0.50	$1.50	$2.50	£0.30	£0.90	£1.50
22 Newstand edition, without trading cards	$0.40	$1.20	$2.00	£0.25	£0.75	£1.25
23-24 bi-weekly	$0.50	$1.50	$2.50	£0.30	£0.90	£1.50
25 cover-dated May 1994, issued between #9 and 10 as part of "Images of Tomorrow" previewing the 25th issue and how it reads/looks	$0.50	$1.50	$2.50	£0.30	£0.90	£1.50
25 2nd printing, (Aug 1995)	$0.50	$1.50	$2.50	£0.30	£0.90	£1.50
26 bi-weekly	$0.50	$1.50	$2.50	£0.30	£0.90	£1.50
27-31	$0.50	$1.50	$2.50	£0.30	£0.90	£1.50
Title Value:	$19.10	$57.30	$95.50	£11.65	£34.95	£58.25

Note: all Non-Distributed on the news-stands in the U.K.

STORMWATCH SPECIAL
Image; 1 Jan 1994-present

	$Good	$Fine	$N.Mint	£Good	£Fine	£N.Mint
1 ND Dwayne Turner, Richard Johnson and Kevin Nowlan art	$0.80	$2.40	$4.00	£0.50	£1.50	£2.50
2 ND Ron Marz script, Cully Hamner art	$0.80	$2.40	$4.00	£0.50	£1.50	£2.50

	$Good	$Fine	$N.Mint	£Good	£Fine	£N.Mint
Title Value:	$1.60	$4.80	$8.00	£1.00	£3.00	£5.00

STORMWATCHER
(see British section)

STRANGE ADVENTURES
National Periodical Publications/DC Comics; 1 Aug/Sep 1950-244 Nov 1973

	$Good	$Fine	$N.Mint	£Good	£Fine	£N.Mint
1 52pgs, cover and adaptation of film "Destination Moon", part painted cover						
	$265.00	$800.00	$2150.00	£180.00	£540.00	£1450.00
[Scarce in high grade - Very Fine+ or better]						
2 52pgs	$140.00	$425.00	$1000.00	£95.00	£285.00	£675.00
3 52pgs	$105.00	$320.00	$750.00	£70.00	£210.00	£500.00
4 52pgs	$92.50	$275.00	$650.00	£60.00	£180.00	£425.00
5-8 52pgs	$77.50	$235.00	$550.00	£52.50	£160.00	£375.00
9 52pgs, origin and 1st appearance Captain Comet						
	$150.00	$450.00	$1200.00	£100.00	£305.00	£825.00
10 52pgs, Captain Comet cover						
	$77.50	$235.00	$550.00	£52.50	£160.00	£375.00
11-12 52pgs, Captain Comet cover						
	$55.00	$170.00	$400.00	£39.00	£115.00	£275.00
13-14 Captain Comet covers						
	$52.50	$160.00	$375.00	£36.00	£105.00	£250.00
15-17	$52.50	$160.00	$375.00	£36.00	£105.00	£250.00
18-19 Captain Comet covers						
	$52.50	$160.00	$375.00	£36.00	£105.00	£250.00
20	$52.50	$160.00	$375.00	£36.00	£105.00	£250.00
21-25	$43.00	$125.00	$300.00	£29.00	£85.00	£200.00
26-27 Captain Comet covers						
	$43.00	$125.00	$300.00	£29.00	£85.00	£200.00
28-30	$43.00	$125.00	$300.00	£29.00	£85.00	£200.00
31-34	$37.00	$110.00	$260.00	£25.00	£75.00	£175.00
35 Captain Comet cover						
	$37.00	$110.00	$260.00	£25.00	£75.00	£175.00
36-40	$37.00	$110.00	$260.00	£25.00	£75.00	£175.00
41-50	$34.00	$100.00	$240.00	£22.50	£67.50	£160.00
51-52	$26.00	$77.50	$185.00	£17.50	£52.50	£125.00
53 last pre Comic Code issue						
	$26.00	$77.50	$185.00	£17.50	£52.50	£125.00
54-60	$21.00	$62.50	$150.00	£14.00	£43.00	£100.00
61-70	$17.50	$52.50	$125.00	£12.00	£36.00	£85.00
71-80	$14.00	$43.00	$100.00	£9.25	£28.00	£65.00
81-90	$12.50	$39.00	$90.00	£8.50	£26.00	£60.00
91-99	$11.00	$34.00	$80.00	£7.75	£23.50	£55.00
100	$14.00	$43.00	$100.00	£9.25	£28.00	£65.00
101-109	$11.00	$34.00	$80.00	£5.50	£17.00	£40.00

1st official distribution in the U.K.

	$Good	$Fine	$N.Mint	£Good	£Fine	£N.Mint
110	$11.50	$35.00	$70.00	£5.75	£17.50	£35.00
111-113	$11.50	$35.00	$70.00	£5.00	£15.00	£30.00
114 Star Hawkins begins (ends #185), Heath art						
	$11.50	$35.00	$70.00	£5.00	£15.00	£30.00
115-116	$11.50	$35.00	$70.00	£5.00	£15.00	£30.00
117 origin and 1st appearance Atomic Knights (ends #160)						
	$50.00	$150.00	$450.00	£33.00	£100.00	£300.00
118-119	$11.50	$35.00	$70.00	£5.00	£15.00	£30.00
120 2nd appearance Atomic Knights						
	$22.00	$65.00	$200.00	£13.50	£42.00	£125.00
121-122	$10.00	$30.00	$60.00	£4.15	£12.50	£25.00
123 3rd appearance Atomic Knights						
	$13.00	$40.00	$120.00	£7.75	£23.00	£70.00
124 1st appearance Faceless Creature						
	$10.00	$30.00	$60.00	£4.15	£12.50	£25.00
125	$10.00	$30.00	$60.00	£4.15	£12.50	£25.00
126 Atomic Knights appear						
	$13.00	$40.00	$120.00	£6.50	£20.00	£60.00
127-128	$10.00	$30.00	$60.00	£4.15	£12.50	£25.00
129 Atomic Knights appear						
	$12.50	$38.00	$75.00	£5.00	£15.00	£30.00
130-131	$10.00	$30.00	$60.00	£4.15	£12.50	£25.00
132 Atomic Knights appear						
	$12.50	$38.00	$75.00	£3.30	£10.00	£20.00
133-134	$10.00	$30.00	$60.00	£3.30	£10.00	£20.00
135 Atomic Knights appear						
	$12.50	$38.00	$75.00	£4.15	£12.50	£25.00
136-137	$8.25	$25.00	$50.00	£3.30	£10.00	£20.00
138 Atomic Knights appear						
	$12.50	$38.00	$75.00	£4.15	£12.50	£25.00
139-140	$8.25	$25.00	$50.00	£3.30	£10.00	£20.00
141 Atomic Knights appear						
	$12.50	$38.00	$75.00	£3.75	£11.00	£22.50
142 return of the Faceless Creature						
	$8.25	$25.00	$50.00	£2.90	£8.75	£17.50
143	$8.25	$25.00	$50.00	£2.90	£8.75	£17.50
144 Atomic Knights appear						
	$12.50	$38.00	$75.00	£3.75	£11.00	£22.50
145-146	$8.25	$25.00	$50.00	£2.90	£8.75	£17.50
147 Atomic Knights appear						
	$12.50	$38.00	$75.00	£3.75	£11.00	£22.50
148-149	$8.25	$25.00	$50.00	£2.90	£8.75	£17.50
150 Atomic Knights appear, painted cover						
	$10.00	$30.00	$60.00	£3.75	£11.00	£22.50
151-152	$8.25	$25.00	$50.00	£2.90	£8.75	£17.50
153 Atomic Knights appear						
	$10.00	$30.00	$60.00	£3.75	£11.00	£22.50
154-155	$8.25	$25.00	$50.00	£2.90	£8.75	£17.50
156 Atomic Knights appear						
	$10.00	$30.00	$60.00	£3.75	£11.00	£22.50
157-158	$8.25	$25.00	$50.00	£2.90	£8.75	£17.50
159 Star Rovers	$8.25	$25.00	$50.00	£2.90	£8.75	£17.50
160 last Atomic Knights						
	$9.00	$28.00	$55.00	£3.75	£11.00	£22.50
161 last Space Museum						
	$6.50	$20.00	$40.00	£2.50	£7.50	£15.00
162	$6.50	$20.00	$40.00	£2.50	£7.50	£15.00
163 Star Rovers	$6.50	$20.00	$40.00	£2.50	£7.50	£15.00
164-170	$6.50	$20.00	$40.00	£2.50	£7.50	£15.00
171-179	$5.75	$17.50	$35.00	£1.65	£5.00	£10.00
180 origin and 1st appearance Animal Man, Carmine Infantino art						
	$29.00	$85.00	$200.00	£17.00	£50.00	£120.00
181-182	$3.30	$10.00	$20.00	£1.25	£3.75	£7.50
183 last Silver Age issue, indicia-dated December 1965						
	$3.30	$10.00	$20.00	£1.25	£3.75	£7.50
184 2nd appearance Animal Man, Gil Kane art						
	$20.00	$60.00	$140.00	£8.50	£26.00	£60.00
185-188	$4.00	$12.00	$20.00	£1.50	£4.50	£7.50
189 Steve Ditko art featured						
	$4.00	$12.00	$20.00	£1.50	£4.50	£7.50
190 1st Animal Man in costume, 3rd appearance						
	$22.50	$67.50	$160.00	£11.00	£34.00	£80.00
191-194	$3.00	$9.00	$15.00	£1.00	£3.00	£5.00
195 1st full Animal Man story						
	$14.00	$43.00	$100.00	£6.25	£19.00	£45.00
196-200	$3.00	$9.00	$15.00	£1.00	£3.00	£5.00
201 last Animal Man in title (full length story)						
	$5.75	$17.50	$35.00	£0.80	£2.50	£5.00
202-204	$2.00	$6.00	$10.00	£0.80	£2.40	£4.00
205 origin and 1st appearance Deadman, Carmine Infantino art						
	$10.00	$30.00	$70.00	£5.00	£15.00	£35.00
206 Deadman, Neal Adams art						
	$8.25	$25.00	$50.00	£3.30	£10.00	£20.00
207-210 Deadman, Neal Adams art						
	$6.50	$20.00	$40.00	£2.50	£7.50	£15.00
211-215 Deadman, Neal Adams art						
	$5.75	$17.50	$35.00	£2.05	£6.25	£12.50
216 scarce in the U.K. Deadman, Neal Adams art						
	$5.75	$17.50	$35.00	£2.50	£7.50	£15.00
217 Adam Strange and Atomic Knights reprints begin						
	$1.20	$3.60	$6.00	£0.50	£1.50	£2.50
218-221	$1.20	$3.60	$6.00	£0.50	£1.50	£2.50
222 new Adam Strange story by Gil Kane and Murphy Anderson						
	$2.00	$6.00	$10.00	£0.80	£2.40	£4.00
223-225	$1.20	$3.60	$6.00	£0.50	£1.50	£2.50
226 scarce in the U.K. 64pgs, squarebound, new 8pg illustrated Adam Strange text story; rest reprints including Adam Strange and Atomic Knights						
	$1.20	$3.60	$6.00	£0.60	£1.80	£3.00
227 64pgs, new 6pg sci-fi illustrated text story by O'Neil and Anderson; rest reprint including Adam Strange and Atomic Knights						
	$1.20	$3.60	$6.00	£0.40	£1.20	£2.00
228-231 64pgs, seven reprint stories including Adam Strange and Atomic Knights						
	$1.20	$3.60	$6.00	£0.40	£1.20	£2.00
232-233 48pgs, four reprint stories including Adam Strange						
	$0.80	$2.40	$4.00	£0.40	£1.20	£2.00
234 48pgs, four reprint stories including Adam Strange, Kubert cover						
	$0.80	$2.40	$4.00	£0.40	£1.20	£2.00
235 48pgs, reprints Mystery in Space #75 (co-starring Justice League of America) plus two reprint stories						
	$0.80	$2.40	$4.00	£0.60	£1.80	£3.00
236 48pgs, four reprint stories including Adam Strange						
	$0.80	$2.40	$4.00	£0.40	£1.20	£2.00
237-244 scarce in the U.K.						
	$0.80	$2.40	$4.00	£0.40	£1.20	£2.00
Title Value:	$4634.10	$13951.10	$32676.00	£2864.95	£8590.85	£20303.50

FEATURES
Adam Strange in 222, 226 (text story with illustrations). Animal Man in 180, 184, 190, 195, 201. Atomic Knights in 117, 120, 123, 126, 129, 132, 135, 138, 141, 144, 147, 150, 153, 156, 160. Darwin Jones in 149, 160. Deadman in 205-216. Enchantress in 187, 191, 200. Immortal Man in 177, 185, 190, 198. Space Museum in 112, 115, 118, 121, 124, 127, 130, 133, 136, 139, 142, 145, 148, 151, 154, 157, 161. Star Hawkins in 114, 116, 119, 122, 125, 128, 131, 134, 137, 140, 143, 146, 149, 152, 155, 158, 162, 173, 176, 179, 182, 185. Star Rovers in 159, 163.

REPRINT FEATURES
Adam Strange in 217-221, 223-244. Atomic Knights in 217-231.

STRANGE BREW
Aardvark-Vanaheim; 1 Dec 1982

	$Good	$Fine	$N.Mint	£Good	£Fine	£N.Mint
1 ND (Jan 1983 in indicia)						
	$0.60	$1.80	$3.00	£0.40	£1.20	£2.00
Title Value:	$0.60	$1.80	$3.00	£0.40	£1.20	£2.00

STRANGE COMBAT TALES
Marvel Comics Group/Epic,MS; 1 Oct 1993-4 Jan 1994

	$Good	$Fine	$N.Mint	£Good	£Fine	£N.Mint
1-4 ND	$0.40	$1.20	$2.00	£0.25	£0.75	£1.25
Title Value:	$1.60	$4.80	$8.00	£1.00	£3.00	£5.00

STRANGE DAYS
Eclipse; 1 Oct 1984-3 Apr 1985

	$Good	$Fine	$N.Mint	£Good	£Fine	£N.Mint
1 ND Johnny Nemo, Freakwave by Milligan, Ewins, McCarthy begin						
	$1.20	$3.60	$6.00	£0.80	£2.40	£4.00
2 ND scarce in the U.K.						
	$1.20	$3.60	$6.00	£0.90	£2.70	£4.50
3 ND	$1.20	$3.60	$6.00	£0.80	£2.40	£4.00
Title Value:	$3.60	$10.80	$18.00	£2.50	£7.50	£12.50

	$Good	$Fine	$N.Mint	£Good	£Fine	£N.Mint

STRANGE DAYS MOVIE ADAPTATION
Marvel Comics Group,OS; 1 Jan 1996
1 ND film adaptation of Jim Cameron film by Dan Chichester and Bill Reinhold

	$1.20	$3.60	$6.00	£0.80	£2.40	£4.00
Title Value:	$1.20	$3.60	$6.00	£0.80	£2.40	£4.00

STRANGE MYSTERIES
I.W. Super; 9 1963-18 1964
9-18 scarce in the U.K. reprint; distributed in the U.K.

	$2.05	$6.25	$12.50	£1.25	£3.75	£7.50
Title Value:	$16.40	$50.00	$100.00	£10.00	£30.00	£60.00

STRANGE PLANETS
I.W. Super; 1,8-12,15-18 1958-1964
1 scarce in the U.K. reprints Incredible Science Fiction #8 (EC)

	$7.50	$22.50	$45.00	£5.00	£15.00	£30.00

8 very scarce in the U.K.

	$3.30	$10.00	$20.00	£2.05	£6.25	£12.50

9 scarce in the U.K. Wood art

	$10.50	$33.00	$65.00	£7.50	£22.50	£45.00

10 scarce in the U.K. Wood art

	$10.00	$30.00	$60.00	£6.50	£20.00	£40.00

11 scarce in the U.K. reprints An Earthman on Venus, Wood art

	$12.50	$38.00	$75.00	£8.25	£25.00	£50.00

12 scarce in the U.K. reprints Rocket to the Moon

	$10.00	$30.00	$60.00	£6.50	£20.00	£40.00

15 scarce in the U.K.

	$3.30	$10.00	$20.00	£2.05	£6.25	£12.50

16 scarce in the U.K. reprints Strange Worlds #6

	$3.75	$11.00	$22.50	£2.50	£7.50	£15.00

17 scarce in the U.K.

	$2.05	$6.25	$12.50	£1.25	£3.75	£7.50

18 scarce in the U.K. reprints Daring Adventures #6

	$3.30	$10.00	$20.00	£2.05	£6.25	£12.50
Title Value:	$66.20	$200.75	$400.00	£43.65	£132.50	£265.00

Note: all distributed in the U.K.

STRANGE SPORTS STORIES
Adventure; 1 May 1992-3 Jul 1992
1-3 ND includes two trading cards bound on outside

	$0.40	$1.20	$2.00	£0.25	£0.75	£1.25
Title Value:	$1.20	$3.60	$6.00	£0.75	£2.25	£3.75

STRANGE SPORTS STORIES
DC Comics; 1 Sep/Oct 1973-6 Jul/Aug 1974
(see Brave and the Bold, DC Special, DC Special Blue Ribbon Digest, DC Super Stars)

1	$1.50	$4.50	$7.50	£0.50	£1.50	£2.50
2-6	$1.00	$3.00	$5.00	£0.30	£0.90	£1.50
Title Value:	$6.50	$19.50	$32.50	£2.00	£6.00	£10.00

STRANGE SUSPENSE STORIES
Fawcett/Charlton; 1 Jun 1952-77 Oct 1965
(becomes Captain Atom)
1 scarce in the U.K.

	$55.00	$170.00	$400.00	£36.00	£105.00	£250.00

2 scarce in the U.K.

	$36.00	$105.00	$250.00	£23.50	£70.00	£165.00

3-5 scarce in the U.K.

	$32.00	$95.00	$225.00	£21.00	£62.50	£150.00
6-9	$20.00	$60.00*	$140.00	£11.00	£34.00	£80.00

10 titled Lawbreaker's Suspense Stories

	$20.00	$60.00	$140.00	£11.00	£34.00	£80.00

11 scarce in the U.K. titled Lawbreaker's Suspense Stories; famous severed tongue panel

	$43.00	$125.00	$300.00	£29.00	£85.00	£200.00

12-14 titled Lawbreaker's Suspense Stories

	$7.75	$22.50	$55.00	£5.00	£15.00	£35.00

15 scarce in the U.K. titled Lawbreaker's Suspense Stories; famous acid thrown in face story

	$23.50	$70.00	$165.00	£15.50	£47.00	£110.00
16	$17.50	$52.50	$125.00	£12.00	£36.00	£85.00
17	$12.50	$39.00	$90.00	£8.50	£26.00	£60.00

18 Steve Ditko art

	$25.00	$75.00	$175.00	£17.00	£50.00	£120.00

19 Steve Ditko art; famous electric chair cover

	$33.00	$100.00	$200.00	£21.50	£65.00	£130.00

20 Steve Ditko art

	$23.50	$70.00	$165.00	£15.50	£47.00	£110.00
21	$12.50	$39.00	$90.00	£8.50	£26.00	£60.00

22 titled This Is Suspense, Steve Ditko cover

	$23.00	$70.00	$140.00	£15.50	£48.00	£95.00

23 titled This Is Suspense, Wood art

	$22.50	$67.50	$135.00	£15.00	£45.00	£90.00

24 titled This Is Suspense, Evans art

	$11.50	$35.00	$70.00	£7.50	£22.50	£45.00

25-26 titled This Is Suspense

	$8.25	$25.00	$50.00	£5.75	£17.50	£35.00
27	$10.00	$30.00	$60.00	£6.50	£20.00	£40.00
28-30	$7.50	$22.50	$45.00	£5.00	£15.00	£30.00

31-37 Steve Ditko art

	$16.50	$50.00	$100.00	£12.50	£38.00	£75.00
38	$7.50	$22.50	$45.00	£5.00	£15.00	£30.00

39-40 Steve Ditko art

	$16.50	$50.00	$100.00	£12.50	£38.00	£75.00

41 Steve Ditko art

	$15.50	$48.00	$95.00	£11.50	£35.00	£70.00
42-44	$5.00	$15.00	$30.00	£3.30	£10.00	£20.00

45 Steve Ditko art

	$11.50	$35.00	$70.00	£7.50	£22.50	£45.00

46	$5.00	$15.00	$30.00	£3.30	£10.00	£20.00

47-48 Steve Ditko art

	$11.50	$35.00	$70.00	£7.50	£22.50	£45.00
49	$5.00	$15.00	$30.00	£3.30	£10.00	£20.00

1st official distribution in the U.K.

50-53 Steve Ditko art

	$11.50	$35.00	$70.00	£7.50	£22.50	£45.00
54-60	$5.00	$15.00	$30.00	£3.30	£10.00	£20.00
61-74	$2.50	$7.50	$15.00	£1.65	£5.00	£10.00
75	$15.00	$45.00	$90.00	£10.00	£30.00	£60.00
76-77	$5.00	$15.00	$30.00	£3.30	£10.00	£20.00
Title Value:	$978.75	$2946.50	$6390.00	£651.80	£1964.50	£4245.00

Note: most issues distributed in the U.K.after 1958/59

STRANGE TALES
Atlas/Marvel Comics Group; 1 Jun 1951-168 May 1968; 169 Sep 1973-188 Nov 1976
(becomes Dr.Strange)
1 scarce in the U.K.

	$200.00	$600.00	$2000.00	£135.00	£405.00	£1350.00
2	$82.50	$250.00	$675.00	£57.50	£175.00	£475.00
3-5	$62.50	$185.00	$500.00	£44.00	£130.00	£350.00
6-9	$44.00	$130.00	$350.00	£31.00	£92.50	£250.00
10 Krigstein art	$44.00	$130.00	$350.00	£31.00	£92.50	£250.00
11-14	$28.00	$82.50	$225.00	£20.00	£60.00	£160.00
15 Krigstein art	$28.00	$82.50	$225.00	£20.00	£60.00	£160.00
16-20	$28.00	$82.50	$225.00	£18.50	£55.00	£150.00
21-25	$25.00	$75.00	$200.00	£17.50	£52.50	£140.00
26-34	$21.50	$65.00	$175.00	£15.50	£47.00	£125.00
35-40	$17.50	$52.50	$140.00	£11.50	£36.00	£95.00
41-50	$15.50	$47.00	$125.00	£10.50	£33.00	£87.50
51-60	$15.50	$47.00	$125.00	£10.00	£31.00	£82.50
61-66	$13.50	$41.00	$110.00	£9.25	£28.00	£75.00

67 possible Quicksilver prototype; Ditko and Kirby art

	$16.50	$50.00	$135.00	£11.00	£34.00	£90.00

68 Ditko and Kirby art

	$15.50	$47.00	$125.00	£11.00	£34.00	£90.00

69 possible Professor X prototype; Ditko and Kirby art

	$15.50	$47.00	$125.00	£11.00	£34.00	£90.00

70 possible Giant Man prototype; Ditko and Kirby art

	$15.50	$47.00	$125.00	£11.00	£34.00	£90.00

71-72 Ditko and Kirby art

	$15.50	$47.00	$125.00	£11.00	£34.00	£90.00

73 possible Ant-Man prototype; Ditko and Kirby art

	$15.50	$47.00	$125.00	£11.00	£34.00	£90.00

74 Ditko and Kirby art

	$15.50	$47.00	$125.00	£11.00	£34.00	£90.00

1st official distribution in the U.K.

75 possible Iron Man prototype; Ditko and Kirby art

	$15.50	$47.00	$125.00	£10.50	£32.00	£85.00

76 possible Human Torch prototype; Ditko and Kirby art

	$17.50	$52.50	$125.00	£12.00	£36.00	£85.00

77 scarce in the U.K. Ditko and Kirby art

	$15.50	$47.00	$125.00	£11.00	£34.00	£90.00

78 rare in the U.K. possible Ant-Man prototype; Ditko and Kirby art

	$15.50	$47.00	$125.00	£13.00	£39.00	£105.00

79 features an early Marvel sorcerer fashioned in the tradition of Dr. Strange (see Journey Into Mystery #78), Ditko and Kirby art

	$18.50	$55.00	$150.00	£13.00	£39.00	£105.00

80 Ditko and Kirby art

	$15.50	$47.00	$125.00	£10.50	£32.00	£85.00

81-83 Ditko and Kirby art

	$13.00	$39.00	$105.00	£8.75	£26.00	£70.00

84 Magneto prototype? It's a monster not a mutant man..; Ditko and Kirby art

	$18.50	$55.00	$150.00	£8.75	£26.00	£70.00

85 Ditko and Kirby art

	$13.00	$39.00	$105.00	£8.75	£26.00	£70.00

86-88 Ditko and Kirby art

	$13.00	$39.00	$105.00	£8.00	£24.00	£65.00

89 1st appearance Fin Fang Foom, classic Jack Kirby monster art and cover, Ditko art also

	$36.00	$105.00	$325.00	£21.00	£62.50	£190.00

90-91 Ditko and Kirby art

	$13.00	$39.00	$105.00	£7.50	£22.50	£60.00

92 (Jan 1962), last 10 cents issue

	$13.00	$39.00	$105.00	£7.50	£22.50	£60.00

93-96 Jack Kirby art

	$13.00	$39.00	$105.00	£6.75	£20.50	£55.00

97 early Aunt May/Uncle Ben (Spiderman's foster parents) prototypes, three months prior to the publication of Amazing Fantasy #15

	$34.00	$100.00	$275.00	£18.50	£55.00	£150.00

98-99 Jack Kirby art

	$13.00	$39.00	$105.00	£6.75	£20.50	£55.00

100 Jack Kirby art

	$15.00	$45.00	$120.00	£7.50	£22.50	£60.00

101 scarce in the U.K. 1st of Human Torch series by Jack Kirby; origin of Fantastic Four briefly re-told

	$92.50	$280.00	$750.00	£55.00	£165.00	£450.00

102 1st appearance The Wizard (later leader of The Frightful Four)

	$46.00	$135.00	$275.00	£25.00	£75.00	£150.00
103	$39.00	$115.00	$235.00	£20.50	£62.50	£125.00

104 (Jan 1963), 1st appearance Paste-Pot Pete (later The Trapster)

	$36.00	$105.00	$215.00	£20.00	£60.00	£120.00
105	$36.00	$105.00	$215.00	£20.00	£60.00	£120.00

106 less common in the U.K. Fantastic Four appear

	$27.00	$80.00	$160.00	£15.00	£45.00	£90.00

VERY GENERAL PERCENTAGE CONVERSION CHART WHICH MAY BE USED TO CALCULATE LOW AND INBETWEEN GRADES:

# / Description	$Good	$Fine	$N.Mint	£Good	£Fine	£N.Mint
107 Human Torch/Sub-Mariner battle; 4th Age Sub-Mariner appearance	$30.00	$90.00	$180.00	£17.50	£52.50	£105.00
108-109 less common in the U.K.	$27.00	$80.00	$160.00	£15.00	£45.00	£90.00
110 1st appearance Dr. Strange by Steve Ditko; as a back-up story only (with no mention on cover!)	$120.00	$360.00	$850.00	£70.00	£210.00	£500.00
110 ND Marvel Milestone Edition (Apr 1995) - metallic ink cover	$0.60	$1.80	$3.00	£0.40	£1.20	£2.00
111 scarce in the U.K. 2nd appearance Dr. Strange	$50.00	$150.00	$300.00	£29.00	£87.50	£175.00
112-113	$15.00	$45.00	$90.00	£10.00	£30.00	£60.00
114 The Acrobat appears, disguised as Captain America; the first appearance of Captain America since the 1950s, 3rd appearance Dr. Strange as his regular back-up stories begin	$52.50	$155.00	$315.00	£30.00	£90.00	£180.00
115 origin Dr. Strange, Spiderman appears, 2nd appearance and origin Sandman	$55.00	$170.00	$340.00	£35.00	£105.00	£245.00
116 less common in the U.K. (Jan 1964), Human Torch battles The Thing; painted (grey-tone) cover	$15.50	$48.00	$95.00	£9.00	£28.00	£55.00
117 less common in the U.K.	$11.50	$35.00	$70.00	£6.50	£20.00	£40.00
118 less common in the U.K. Fantastic Four guest-star	$11.50	$35.00	$70.00	£6.50	£20.00	£40.00
119 less common in the U.K. Spiderman appears	$15.50	$48.00	$95.00	£9.00	£28.00	£55.00
120 less common in the U.K. Iceman appears, Angel, Marvel Girl, Professor X cameos	$11.50	$35.00	$70.00	£6.50	£20.00	£40.00
121 less common in the U.K. Human Torch and Dr. Strange team up	$10.00	$30.00	$60.00	£5.00	£15.00	£30.00
122 less common in the U.K.	$10.00	$30.00	$60.00	£5.00	£15.00	£30.00
123 less common in the U.K. 1st appearance The Beetle; Thor appears (1st outside own magazine); Loki and Odin also appear	$10.50	$33.00	$65.00	£5.00	£15.00	£30.00
124 less common in the U.K. 1st Human Torch and Thing team-up (ends #134)	$9.00	$28.00	$55.00	£5.00	£15.00	£30.00
125 less common in the U.K. Sub-Mariner vs. Thing and The Human Torch	$9.00	$28.00	$55.00	£5.00	£15.00	£30.00
126 scarce in the U.K. 1st appearance Clea	$9.00	$28.00	$55.00	£5.00	£15.00	£30.00
127 rare in the U.K.	$9.00	$28.00	$55.00	£5.25	£16.00	£32.50
128 scarce in the U.K. (Jan 1965), Scarlet Witch and Quicksilver appear	$9.00	$28.00	$55.00	£4.15	£12.50	£25.00
129	$9.00	$28.00	$55.00	£3.30	£10.00	£20.00
130 very scarce in the U.K. Beatles cameo	$9.00	$28.00	$55.00	£5.00	£15.00	£30.00
131-133	$8.25	$25.00	$50.00	£3.30	£10.00	£20.00
134 The Watcher appears	$8.25	$25.00	$50.00	£3.30	£10.00	£20.00
135 origin and 1st appearance Nick Fury, Agent of Shield	$14.00	$43.00	$100.00	£7.00	£21.00	£50.00
136 2nd appearance Nick Fury, Agent of Shield	$6.50	$20.00	$40.00	£3.30	£10.00	£20.00
137 less common in the U.K.	$6.50	$20.00	$40.00	£3.30	£10.00	£20.00
138	$6.50	$20.00	$40.00	£2.50	£7.50	£15.00
139 last Silver Age issue indicia-dated December 1965	$6.50	$20.00	$40.00	£2.50	£7.50	£15.00
140 (Jan 1966)	$6.50	$20.00	$40.00	£2.50	£7.50	£15.00
141-145	$5.75	$17.50	$35.00	£2.05	£6.25	£12.50
146 Steve Ditko cover	$5.75	$17.50	$35.00	£2.05	£6.25	£12.50
147	$5.75	$17.50	$35.00	£2.05	£6.25	£12.50
148 origin The Ancient One	$10.00	$30.00	$60.00	£3.30	£10.00	£20.00
149	$5.75	$17.50	$35.00	£2.05	£6.25	£12.50
150 John Buscema's 1st work for Marvel	$5.75	$17.50	$35.00	£2.05	£6.25	£12.50
151 scarce in the U.K. Jim Steranko art on Shield, his first Marvel work	$6.50	$20.00	$40.00	£3.30	£10.00	£20.00
152 (Jan 1967), Steranko art	$5.00	$15.00	$30.00	£2.50	£7.50	£15.00
153-156 Steranko art	$5.00	$15.00	$30.00	£2.50	£7.50	£15.00
157 Steranko art, Living Tribunal appears (cameo)	$5.00	$15.00	$30.00	£2.50	£7.50	£15.00
158 Steranko art, 1st full appearance Living Tribunal	$5.00	$15.00	$30.00	£2.50	£7.50	£15.00
159 origin Nick Fury retold, Nick Fury vs. Captain America, Steranko art	$5.75	$17.50	$35.00	£2.50	£7.50	£15.00
160 classic Steranko art	$5.00	$15.00	$30.00	£2.50	£7.50	£15.00
161-163 classic Steranko art	$4.55	$13.50	$27.50	£2.05	£6.25	£12.50
164 (Jan 1968), classic Steranko art	$4.55	$13.50	$27.50	£2.05	£6.25	£12.50
165-166 classic Steranko art	$4.55	$13.50	$27.50	£2.05	£6.25	£12.50
167 classic Steranko art, classic patriotic cover	$5.75	$17.50	$35.00	£2.50	£7.50	£15.00
168 classic Steranko art	$4.55	$13.50	$27.50	£2.05	£6.25	£12.50
169 ND origin and 1st appearance Brother Voodoo	$0.80	$2.40	$4.00	£0.60	£1.80	£3.00
170 ND origin Brother Voodoo continued	$0.60	$1.80	$3.00	£0.40	£1.20	£2.00
171 ND	$0.60	$1.80	$3.00	£0.40	£1.20	£2.00
172 ND (Feb 1974)	$0.60	$1.80	$3.00	£0.40	£1.20	£2.00
173 ND	$0.60	$1.80	$3.00	£0.40	£1.20	£2.00
174 ND 1st appearance Golem II (origin); see Hulk #134	$0.60	$1.80	$3.00	£0.50	£1.50	£2.50
175 scarce in the U.K. monster reprints from Amazing Aventures (1st Series) #1	$0.50	$1.50	$2.50	£0.30	£0.90	£1.50
176-177 Golem	$0.50	$1.50	$2.50	£0.25	£0.75	£1.25
178 (Feb 1975), Warlock by Jim Starlin begins, 1st appearance Magus	$3.30	$10.00	$20.00	£1.65	£5.00	£10.00
179-181 Warlock, Jim Starlin art	$2.00	$6.00	$10.00	£1.00	£3.00	£5.00
182 reprints Dr. Strange	$0.50	$1.50	$2.50	£0.30	£0.90	£1.50
183 (Jan 1976), reprints Dr. Strange	$0.50	$1.50	$2.50	£0.30	£0.90	£1.50
184-187 reprints Dr. Strange	$0.50	$1.50	$2.50	£0.30	£0.90	£1.50
188 ND reprint Dr. Strange	$0.50	$1.50	$2.50	£0.50	£1.50	£2.50
Title Value:	$3395.80	$10185.70	$25964.50	£2146.00	£6486.60	£16688.50

ARTISTS
Kirby in 75-105, 108, 109, 114, 120, 135-150, 151-153 with Steranko. Ditko in 75-146.
FEATURES
Brother Voodoo in 169-173. Dr. Strange in 114-134. Golem in 174, 176, 177. Human Torch in 101-

Strange Suspense Stories #62

Strange Tales #136

Sub-Mariner Special #2

MINT = 100% / NEAR MINT (inc. +/-) = 90–99% / VERY FINE (inc. +/-) = 75–89% / FINE (inc. +/-) = 55–74%
VERY GOOD (inc. +/-) = 35–54% / GOOD (inc. +/-) = 15–34% / FAIR = 5–14% / POOR = 1–4%

571

123. Human Torch/Thing in 124-134. Nick Fury, Agent of Shield in 135-168. Warlock in 178-181 (series continues in Warlock 9). Monster/Fantasy stories in 75-109, 111, 112 (back-ups only in 101-109, 111, 112).

REPRINT FEATURES

Monster/fantasy in 175. Dr. Strange in 182-188.

STRANGE TALES (2ND SERIES)

Marvel Comics Group; 1 Apr 1987-19 Oct 1988

	$Good	$Fine	$N.Mint	£Good	£Fine	£N.Mint
1 ND Cloak & Dagger/Dr Strange in separate stories begin						
	$0.30	$0.90	$1.50	£0.20	£0.60	£1.00
2 ND	$0.25	$0.75	$1.25	£0.20	£0.60	£1.00
3-8	$0.25	$0.75	$1.25	£0.15	£0.45	£0.75
9 Dazzler appears	$0.25	$0.75	$1.25	£0.15	£0.45	£0.75
10 Black Cat appears						
	$0.25	$0.75	$1.25	£0.15	£0.45	£0.75
11-12	$0.25	$0.75	$1.25	£0.15	£0.45	£0.75
13-14 Punisher appears						
	$0.25	$0.75	$1.25	£0.15	£0.45	£0.75
15-17	$0.25	$0.75	$1.25	£0.15	£0.45	£0.75
18 X-Factor appears, Kevin Nowlan inks			$1.25	£0.15	£0.45	£0.75
	$0.25	$0.75				
19	$0.25	$0.75	$1.25	£0.15	£0.45	£0.75
Title Value:	$4.80	$14.40	$24.00	£2.95	£8.85	£14.75

STRANGE TALES (3RD SERIES)

Marvel Comics Group,OS; 1 Feb 1995

	$Good	$Fine	$N.Mint	£Good	£Fine	£N.Mint
1 ND 64pgs, The Thing, Dr. Strange, Nick Fury, Human Torch feature, painted art by Ricardo Villagran; card-stock cover with protective acetate over-lay						
	$1.40	$4.20	$7.00	£0.90	£2.70	£4.50
Title Value:	$1.40	$4.20	$7.00	£0.90	£2.70	£4.50

STRANGE TALES ANNUAL

Marvel Comics Group; 1 1962-2 1963

1 very rare in the U.K. 72pgs, '50s/60s monster/fantasy reprints including Strange Tales #73 ("Grottu"), #92 ("Serpent Creature"), Tales To Astonish #7 ("Shadow Thing"), #9 ("Diablo"); Kirby, Ditko art

	$Good	$Fine	$N.Mint	£Good	£Fine	£N.Mint
	$50.00	$150.00	$400.00	£38.00	£110.00	£300.00

[Very rare in high grade - Very Fine+ or better]

2 rare in the U.K. 72pgs, Spiderman vs. Human Torch, (joint 4th appearance of Spiderman with Spiderman #3 dated July 1963) by Jack Kirby/Steve Ditko, monster/fantasy reprints

	$Good	$Fine	$N.Mint	£Good	£Fine	£N.Mint
	$55.00	$165.00	$450.00	£40.00	£120.00	£325.00

[Very scarce in high grade - Very Fine+ or better]

	$Good	$Fine	$N.Mint	£Good	£Fine	£N.Mint
Title Value:	$105.00	$315.00	$850.00	£79.00	£230.00	£625.00

Note: Annual #2 occasionally turns up with a blank back and inside front covers (see Fantastic Four Annual #1-3, Spiderman Annual #1,2 and Sgt. Fury Annual #1). These were subscription copies sent over to this country as left-overs and are very scarce. With their white back covers which show soiling and wear that much more easily, they are **very rare** in near mint condition.

STRANGE WORLDS

Atlas; 1 Dec 1958-5 Aug 1959

	$Good	$Fine	$N.Mint	£Good	£Fine	£N.Mint
1 ND scarce in the U.K. classic flying saucer cover, Jack Kirby, Steve Ditko art						
	$50.00	$150.00	$400.00	£34.00	£100.00	£275.00
2 ND scarce in the U.K. Steve Ditko cover and art						
	$31.00	$92.50	$250.00	£21.50	£65.00	£175.00
3 ND scarce in the U.K. part Jack Kirby art						
	$25.00	$75.00	$200.00	£15.50	£47.00	£125.00
4 ND scarce in the U.K. Williamson art						
	$23.50	$70.00	$190.00	£15.00	£45.00	£120.00
5 ND scarce in the U.K. Steve Ditko art						
	$20.50	$60.00	$165.00	£13.50	£41.00	£110.00
Title Value:	$150.00	$447.50	$1205.00	£99.50	£298.00	£805.00

STRANGE WORLDS

Eternity; 1 Apr 1990

	$Good	$Fine	$N.Mint	£Good	£Fine	£N.Mint
1 ND 60pgs. squarebound anthology of 1950s sci-fi reprints						
	$0.60	$1.80	$3.00	£0.40	£1.20	£2.00
Title Value:	$0.60	$1.80	$3.00	£0.40	£1.20	£2.00

STRANGELOVE

Entity Comics; 1 Aug 1995-present

	$Good	$Fine	$N.Mint	£Good	£Fine	£N.Mint
1 ND Stacy Freeman script, Tatsuya Ishida art; black and white						
	$0.50	$1.50	$2.50	£0.30	£0.90	£1.50
2-3 ND	$0.50	$1.50	$2.50	£0.30	£0.90	£1.50
Title Value:	$1.50	$4.50	$7.50	£0.90	£2.70	£4.50

STRANGERS ANNUAL, THE

Malibu Ultraverse; 1 Dec 1994

	$Good	$Fine	$N.Mint	£Good	£Fine	£N.Mint
1 ND 64pgs, continued from Night Man Annual #1						
	$0.60	$1.80	$3.00	£0.40	£1.20	£2.00
Title Value:	$0.60	$1.80	$3.00	£0.40	£1.20	£2.00

STRANGERS IN PARADISE

Antarctic Press; 1 Nov 1993-3 Feb 1994

	$Good	$Fine	$N.Mint	£Good	£Fine	£N.Mint
1 ND Terry Moore art						
	$6.00	$18.00	$30.00	£4.00	£12.00	£20.00
1 2nd printing ND	$1.50	$4.50	$7.50	£1.00	£3.00	£5.00
1 3rd printing, ND (Apr 1994)						
	$1.00	$3.00	$5.00	£0.70	£2.10	£3.50
2 ND	$5.00	$15.00	$25.00	£3.00	£9.00	£15.00
3 ND	$3.50	$10.50	$17.50	£2.50	£7.50	£12.50
Title Value:	$17.00	$51.00	$85.00	£11.20	£33.60	£56.00

STRANGERS IN PARADISE (2ND SERIES)

Abstract Studios; 1 Sep 1994-8 1995?

	$Good	$Fine	$N.Mint	£Good	£Fine	£N.Mint
1 ND	$1.50	$4.50	$7.50	£1.00	£3.00	£5.00
1 2nd printing ND	$0.60	$1.80	$3.00	£0.40	£1.20	£2.00
2 ND	$0.90	$2.70	$4.50	£0.60	£1.80	£3.00
2 2nd printing ND	$0.60	$1.80	$3.00	£0.40	£1.20	£2.00
3 ND	$0.90	$2.70	$4.50	£0.60	£1.80	£3.00
3 2nd printing ND	$0.55	$1.65	$2.75	£0.35	£1.05	£1.75
4 ND	$0.60	$1.80	$3.00	£0.40	£1.20	£2.00
4 2nd printing ND	$0.55	$1.65	$2.75	£0.35	£1.05	£1.75
5 ND	$0.60	$1.80	$3.00	£0.40	£1.20	£2.00
5 2nd printing ND	$0.55	$1.65	$2.75	£0.35	£1.05	£1.75
6 ND	$0.60	$1.80	$3.00	£0.40	£1.20	£2.00
6 2nd printing ND	$0.55	$1.65	$2.75	£0.35	£1.05	£1.75
7-8 ND	$0.60	$1.80	$3.00	£0.40	£1.20	£2.00
Title Value:	$9.70	$29.10	$48.50	£6.40	£19.20	£32.00

STRANGERS, THE

Malibu Ultraverse; 1 Jun 1993-26 May 1995

	$Good	$Fine	$N.Mint	£Good	£Fine	£N.Mint
1 1st appearance Atom Bob, Electrocute, Grenade, Lady Killer, Spectral, Zip Zap and Yrial						
	$1.00	$3.00	$5.00	£0.50	£1.50	£2.50
1 Limited Edition (Jun 1993) - full hologram cover; 7,500 copies (offered again by Marvel Comics in Sep 1995)						
	$3.00	$9.00	$15.00	£1.50	£4.50	£7.50
2 pre-bagged with trading card						
	$1.00	$3.00	$5.00	£0.50	£1.50	£2.50
2 un-bagged/without card						
	$0.60	$1.80	$3.00	£0.40	£1.20	£2.00
3	$0.60	$1.80	$3.00	£0.40	£1.20	£2.00
4 Hardcase appears						
	$0.50	$1.50	$2.50	£0.30	£0.90	£1.50
5 40pgs, Rune insert						
	$0.50	$1.50	$2.50	£0.30	£0.90	£1.50
6	$0.40	$1.20	$2.00	£0.25	£0.75	£1.25
7 Prototype appears						
	$0.40	$1.20	$2.00	£0.25	£0.75	£1.25
8 origin Solution by Art Nichols						
	$0.40	$1.20	$2.00	£0.25	£0.75	£1.25
9-11	$0.40	$1.20	$2.00	£0.25	£0.75	£1.25
12 anniversary issue with silver logos						
	$0.40	$1.20	$2.00	£0.25	£0.75	£1.25
13 64pgs, flip-book format with Ultraverse Premiere #4; Strangers team up with Mantra						
	$0.55	$1.65	$2.75	£0.35	£1.05	£1.75
14-24	$0.40	$1.20	$2.00	£0.25	£0.75	£1.25
25 Godwheel tie-in						
	$0.40	$1.20	$2.00	£0.25	£0.75	£1.25
26 1st issue under Marvel Comics solicitation; Godwheel tie-in						
	$0.40	$1.20	$2.00	£0.25	£0.75	£1.25
Title Value:	$15.75	$47.25	$78.75	£9.25	£27.75	£46.25

Note: all Non-Distributed on the news-stands in the U.K.

The Strangers Collection: Jumpstart Softcover (Oct 1994)

	£Good	£Fine	£N.Mint
Trade paperback reprints issues #1-4	£1.30	£3.90	£6.50

The Strangers Collection: Jumpstart Signed Edition

(Oct 1994) as above, signed by Steve Englehart and Rick Hoberg, 500 copies £4.00 £12.00 £20.00

STRATA

Renegade; 1 Jan 1986-6 Apr 1987

	$Good	$Fine	$N.Mint	£Good	£Fine	£N.Mint
1-6 ND	$0.40	$1.20	$2.00	£0.25	£0.75	£1.25
Title Value:	$2.40	$7.20	$12.00	£1.50	£4.50	£7.50

STRATONAUT

Night Wynd,MS; 1 Jan 1992-4 Apr 1992

	$Good	$Fine	$N.Mint	£Good	£Fine	£N.Mint
1-4 ND Barry Blair script/art; black and white						
	$0.40	$1.20	$2.00	£0.25	£0.75	£1.25
Title Value:	$1.60	$4.80	$8.00	£1.00	£3.00	£5.00

STRAW MEN

All American Comics; 1 1989-8 1990

	$Good	$Fine	$N.Mint	£Good	£Fine	£N.Mint
1-8 ND	$0.30	$0.90	$1.50	£0.20	£0.60	£1.00
Title Value:	$2.40	$7.20	$12.00	£1.60	£4.80	£8.00

STRAWBERRY SHORTCAKE

Marvel Comics Group/Star; 1 Jun 1985-7 Apr 1986

	$Good	$Fine	$N.Mint	£Good	£Fine	£N.Mint
1-7 ND	$0.15	$0.45	$0.75	£0.10	£0.35	£0.60
Title Value:	$1.05	$3.15	$5.25	£0.70	£2.45	£4.20

STRAY BULLETS

El Capitan Books; 1 1995-present

	$Good	$Fine	$N.Mint	£Good	£Fine	£N.Mint
1 ND David Lapham art						
	$2.00	$6.00	$10.00	£4.00	£12.00	£20.00
1 2nd/3rd/4th printings ND						
	$0.60	$1.80	$3.00	£0.40	£1.20	£2.00
2 ND	$1.50	$4.50	$7.50	£2.50	£7.50	£12.50
3 ND	$1.20	$3.60	$6.00	£1.20	£3.60	£6.00
4-5 ND	$0.80	$2.40	$4.00	£0.60	£1.80	£3.00
6-7 ND	$0.70	$2.10	$3.50	£0.50	£1.50	£2.50
Title Value:	$8.30	$24.90	$41.50	£10.30	£30.90	£51.50

STRAY TOASTERS

Marvel Comics Group/Epic,MS; 1 1988-4 Apr 1989

	$Good	$Fine	$N.Mint	£Good	£Fine	£N.Mint
1 ND Sienkiewicz story/painted art begins						
	$0.80	$2.40	$4.00	£0.50	£1.50	£2.50
2 ND scarce in the U.K. Sienkiewicz art						
	$0.80	$2.40	$4.00	£0.60	£1.80	£3.00
3-4 ND Sienkiewicz art						
	$0.80	$2.40	$4.00	£0.50	£1.50	£2.50
Title Value:	$3.20	$9.60	$16.00	£2.10	£6.30	£10.50

Trade paperback (May 1991), reprints mini-series £2.00 £6.00 £10.00

Note: all 48pg squarebound Bookshelf Format

STREET FIGHTER

Malibu; 1 Aug 1993-3 1994

	$Good	$Fine	$N.Mint	£Good	£Fine	£N.Mint
1 ND	$0.50	$1.50	$2.50	£0.30	£0.90	£1.50
1 ND Gold Edition (Oct 1994)						
	$2.00	$6.00	$10.00	£1.00	£3.00	£5.00
2 ND bound-in poster at centrefold						
	$0.50	$1.50	$2.50	£0.30	£0.90	£1.50
2 ND Gold Edition (Oct 1994)						

TRADE PAPERBACKS, GRAPHIC NOVELS AND OTHER COLLECTIONS ARE PRICED IN POUNDS STERLING ONLY. CONVERT AT 1.5 FOR DOLLARS.

	$Good	$Fine	$N.Mint	£Good	£Fine	£N.Mint
	$1.50	$4.50	$7.50	£1.00	£3.00	£5.00
3 ND	$0.50	$1.50	$2.50	£0.30	£0.90	£1.50
3 ND Gold Edition (Oct 1994)						
	$1.50	$4.50	$7.50	£1.00	£3.00	£5.00
Title Value:	$6.50	$19.50	$32.50	£3.90	£11.70	£19.50

Note: based on video game

STREET FIGHTER II
Viz Communications,MS; 1 Jun 1994-8 Jan 1995

	$Good	$Fine	$N.Mint	£Good	£Fine	£N.Mint
1-8 ND Masaomi Kanzaki	$0.60	$1.80	$3.00	£0.40	£1.20	£2.00
Title Value:	$4.80	$14.40	$24.00	£3.20	£9.60	£16.00

STREET MUSIC
Fantagraphics,Magazine; 1 1988-6 1989?

1-6 ND	$0.50	$1.50	$2.50	£0.30	£0.90	£1.50
Title Value:	$3.00	$9.00	$15.00	£1.80	£5.40	£9.00

STREET POET-RAY
Marvel Comics Group/Epic; 1 Apr 1990-5 Dec 1990

1 ND Michael Redmond rap-poetry/Junko Hoshizawa art begins

	$0.40	$1.20	$2.00	£0.25	£0.75	£1.25
2 ND 20th International Earth Day special						
	$0.40	$1.20	$2.00	£0.25	£0.75	£1.25
3 ND Amnesty International special						
	$0.40	$1.20	$2.00	£0.25	£0.75	£1.25
4 ND Rock and Roll Hall of Fame						
	$0.40	$1.20	$2.00	£0.25	£0.75	£1.25
5 ND Amnesty International						
	$0.40	$1.20	$2.00	£0.25	£0.75	£1.25
Title Value:	$2.00	$6.00	$10.00	£1.25	£3.75	£6.25

Note: bi-monthly frequency Bookshelf Format

STREET SHADOWS
Caliber Press,MS; 1 Apr 1992-2 1992

1 ND spin-off from Caliber Presents

	$0.50	$1.50	$2.50	£0.30	£0.90	£1.50
2 ND	$0.50	$1.50	$2.50	£0.30	£0.90	£1.50
Title Value:	$1.00	$3.00	$5.00	£0.60	£1.80	£3.00

STREET WOLF
Blackthorne; 1 Jul 1986-3 Dec 1986

1-3 ND	$0.40	$1.20	$2.00	£0.25	£0.75	£1.25
Title Value:	$1.20	$3.60	$6.00	£0.75	£2.25	£3.75

STREETFIGHTER: THE BATTLE FOR SHADALOO
DC Comics, Film; 1 Feb 1995

1 ND 64pgs, adaptation of film based on Nintendo game starring Jean Claude Van Damme

	$0.80	$2.40	$4.00	£0.50	£1.50	£2.50
Title Value:	$0.80	$2.40	$4.00	£0.50	£1.50	£2.50

STREETS
DC Comics,MS; 1 Oct 1993-3 Dec 1993

1-3 ND 48pgs, painted art	$0.80	$2.40	$4.00	£0.50	£1.50	£2.50
Title Value:	$2.40	$7.20	$12.00	£1.50	£4.50	£7.50

STRIKE
Eclipse; 1 Aug 1987-6 Feb 1988

1-6 ND	$0.40	$1.20	$2.00	£0.25	£0.75	£1.25
Title Value:	$2.40	$7.20	$12.00	£1.50	£4.50	£7.50

STRIKE FORCE AMERICA
Comico; 1 May 1992-5 1992

1 ND Sam Kieth cover

	$0.40	$1.20	$2.00	£0.25	£0.75	£1.25
2 ND pin-up gallery included						
	$0.40	$1.20	$2.00	£0.25	£0.75	£1.25
3-5 ND	$0.40	$1.20	$2.00	£0.25	£0.75	£1.25
Title Value:	$2.00	$6.00	$10.00	£1.25	£3.75	£6.25
The Strike Force Files (Feb 1993)						
shrink-wrapped pack of issues #1 & #2 and Elementals #16		£1.60	£4.80	£8.00

STRIKE FORCE LEGACY
Comico; 1 Oct 1993

1 ND 48pgs, gold embossed logo; Mike Leeke and Mike Chen art

	$0.60	$1.80	$3.00	£0.40	£1.20	£2.00
Title Value:	$0.60	$1.80	$3.00	£0.40	£1.20	£2.00

STRIKE VS. SGT. STRIKE SPECIAL
Eclipse,OS; 1 May 1988

1 ND Tom Lyle art, colour

	$0.40	$1.20	$2.00	£0.25	£0.75	£1.25
Title Value:	$0.40	$1.20	$2.00	£0.25	£0.75	£1.25

STRIKEBACK!
Malibu Bravura,MS; 1 Oct 1994-3 Dec 1994

1 ND Kevin Maguire art

	$0.60	$1.80	$3.00	£0.40	£1.20	£2.00
1 ND Gold Foil Collector's Edition (Feb 1995)						
	$1.50	$4.50	$7.50	£1.00	£3.00	£5.00
2-3 ND Kevin Maguire art						
	$0.60	$1.80	$3.00	£0.40	£1.20	£2.00
Title Value:	$3.30	$9.90	$16.50	£2.20	£6.60	£11.00

STRIKEFORCE: MORITURI
Marvel Comics Group; 1 Dec 1986-31 Jul 1989

1 ND Brent Anderson art begins, 3pgs Whilce Portacio art

	$0.25	$0.75	$1.25	£0.15	£0.45	£0.75
2-9 ND	$0.25	$0.75	$1.25	£0.15	£0.45	£0.75
10 ND Whilce Portacio inks						
	$0.25	$0.75	$1.25	£0.15	£0.45	£0.75
11-12 ND	$0.25	$0.75	$1.25	£0.15	£0.45	£0.75
13 ND DS	$0.25	$0.75	$1.25	£0.15	£0.45	£0.75
14-15 ND	$0.25	$0.75	$1.25	£0.15	£0.45	£0.75

	$Good	$Fine	$N.Mint	£Good	£Fine	£N.Mint
16 ND Whilce Portacio inks						
	$0.25	$0.75	$1.25	£0.15	£0.45	£0.75
17-20 ND	$0.25	$0.75	$1.25	£0.15	£0.45	£0.75
21 ND format change to higher quality paper						
	$0.25	$0.75	$1.25	£0.15	£0.45	£0.75
22-31 ND	$0.25	$0.75	$1.25	£0.15	£0.45	£0.75
Title Value:	$7.75	$23.25	$38.75	£4.65	£13.95	£23.25

STRIKER: SECRET OF THE BERSERKER
Viz Communications,MS; 1 Apr 1995-4 Jul 1995

1-4 ND Takashige & Mingawa script and art; black and white	$0.50	$1.50	$2.50	£0.30	£0.90	£1.50
Title Value:	$2.00	$6.00	$10.00	£1.20	£3.60	£6.00

STRIKER: THE ARMOURED WARRIOR
Viz Communications,MS; 1 Jun 1992-4 Sep 1992

1-4 ND	$0.50	$1.50	$2.50	£0.30	£0.90	£1.50
Title Value:	$2.00	$6.00	$10.00	£1.20	£3.60	£6.00

STRIKER: THE ARMOURED WARRIOR (2ND SERIES)
Viz Communications,MS; 1 Dec 1992

1 ND	$0.50	$1.50	$2.50	£0.30	£0.90	£1.50
Title Value:	$0.50	$1.50	$2.50	£0.30	£0.90	£1.50

STRONG MAN, THE POWER OF
AC Comics; 1 1989

1 ND 40pgs, (16 in colour), Cave Girl and Thun'da appear	$0.50	$1.50	$2.50	£0.30	£0.90	£1.50
Title Value:	$0.50	$1.50	$2.50	£0.30	£0.90	£1.50

STRYFE'S STRIKE FILE
Marvel Comics Group,OS; 1 Jan 1993

1 ND information on the mutant heroes and villains, metallic ink cover; Larry Stroman, Andy Kubert and Greg Capullo art featured

	$0.50	$1.50	$2.50	£0.30	£0.90	£1.50
1 2nd printing, ND Jul 1993; gold and silver metallic cover						
	$0.40	$1.20	$2.00	£0.25	£0.75	£1.25
Title Value:	$0.90	$2.70	$4.50	£0.55	£1.65	£2.75

STRYKE
London Night Studios; 0 Mar 1995

½ ND Everette Hartsoe script, Jude Millien art, pre-bagged with tarot card

	$0.60	$1.80	$3.00	£0.40	£1.20	£2.00
0 ND Everette Hartsoe script, Keith Pollard art						
	$0.90	$2.70	$4.50	£0.60	£1.80	£3.00
0 Commemorative Edition, ND with certificate of authenticity						
	$3.00	$9.00	$15.00	£2.00	£6.00	£10.00
0 Variant cover ND	$1.00	$3.00	$5.00	£0.70	£2.10	£3.50
Title Value:	$5.50	$16.50	$27.50	£3.70	£11.10	£18.50

STRYKE: NATURAL BORN KILLER
London Night Studios,MS; 1 Jun 1995

1 ND Everette Hartsoe script, Jude Millien art	$0.60	$1.80	$3.00	£0.40	£1.20	£2.00
Title Value:	$0.60	$1.80	$3.00	£0.40	£1.20	£2.00

STUCK RUBBER BABY GRAPHIC NOVEL
DC Comics/Paradox Press,OS; nn Oct 1995

nn ND 224pgs, Hardcover, Howard Cruse script and art	$4.50	$13.50	$22.50	£3.00	£9.00	£15.00
Title Value:	$4.50	$13.50	$22.50	£3.00	£9.00	£15.00

STUPID
Image; 1 Jul 1993

1 ND Hilary Barta and Doug Rice; Spawn parody

	$0.40	$1.20	$2.00	£0.25	£0.75	£1.25
1 ND Ash Can Edition (Oct 1993)						
	$1.50	$4.50	$7.50	£0.80	£2.40	£4.00
Title Value:	$1.90	$5.70	$9.50	£1.05	£3.15	£5.25

STUPID HEROES
Mirage/Next Comics; 1 Aug 1994-3 1994

1 ND Peter Laird script and art

	$0.40	$1.20	$2.00	£0.25	£0.75	£1.25
2 ND	$0.40	$1.20	$2.00	£0.25	£0.75	£1.25
3 ND with two bound-in trading cards						
	$0.40	$1.20	$2.00	£0.25	£0.75	£1.25
Title Value:	$1.20	$3.60	$6.00	£0.75	£2.25	£3.75

STYGMATA
Entity Comics; 0 Apr 1994; 1 Jul 1994-3 Sep 1994

0 ND foil-stamped cover	$0.60	$1.80	$3.00	£0.40	£1.20	£2.00
1 ND foil enhanced logo						
	$0.60	$1.80	$3.00	£0.40	£1.20	£2.00
1 ND Gold Signed and Numbered Edition (Jul 1994)						
	$1.50	$4.50	$7.50	£1.00	£3.00	£5.00
2 ND	$0.60	$1.80	$3.00	£0.40	£1.20	£2.00
3 ND foil-stamped cover						
	$0.60	$1.80	$3.00	£0.40	£1.20	£2.00
Title Value:	$3.90	$11.70	$19.50	£2.60	£7.80	£13.00
Stygmata: Dragon Prophet (Mar 1995)						
Trade paperback reprints mini-series, gold foil enhanced cover				£0.90	£2.70	£4.50

STYGMATA YEARBOOK
Entity Comics; 1 Dec 1994

1 ND foil-stamped enhanced cover	$0.60	$1.80	$3.00	£0.40	£1.20	£2.00
Title Value:	$0.60	$1.80	$3.00	£0.40	£1.20	£2.00

SUB-MARINER (1ST) COMICS
Timely/Atlas; 1 Spring 1941-25 Spring 1948; 26 Jun 1948-32 Jun 1949; 33 Apr 1954-42 Oct 1955

1 Sub-Mariner begins, 20pg Angel back-up story begins (ends #21)

	$Good	$Fine	$N.Mint	£Good	£Fine	£N.Mint
	$1700.00	$5100.00	$17000.00	£1150.00	£3450.00	£11500.00
2	$500.00	$1500.00	$4000.00	£340.00	£1025.00	£2750.00
3	$310.00	$930.00	$2500.00	£215.00	£650.00	£1750.00
4	$260.00	$780.00	$2100.00	£175.00	£520.00	£1400.00
5	$185.00	$560.00	$1500.00	£125.00	£375.00	£1000.00
6-10	$170.00	$510.00	$1200.00	£110.00	£340.00	£800.00
11-16	$110.00	$340.00	$800.00	£77.50	£235.00	£550.00
17 1st war theme cover						
	$110.00	$340.00	$800.00	£77.50	£235.00	£550.00
18-20	$110.00	$340.00	$800.00	£77.50	£235.00	£550.00
21-23	$92.50	$275.00	$650.00	£60.00	£180.00	£425.00
24 Namora appears (cover)						
	$92.50	$275.00	$650.00	£60.00	£180.00	£425.00
25 Namora appears (cover), The Blonde Phantom begins						
	$105.00	$320.00	$750.00	£70.00	£210.00	£500.00
26-28 Namora appears (cover)						
	$92.50	$275.00	$650.00	£60.00	£180.00	£425.00
29 Namora appears (cover) and shares co-title (only time)						
	$92.50	$275.00	$650.00	£60.00	£180.00	£425.00
30-31	$92.50	$275.00	$650.00	£60.00	£180.00	£425.00
32 scarce in the U.S, very scarce in the U.K: origin Sub-Mariner re-told						
	$150.00	$450.00	$1050.00	£105.00	£320.00	£750.00
33 scarce in the U.K: 1st Atlas issue, origin re-told						
	$85.00	$255.00	$600.00	£55.00	£170.00	£400.00
34-37	$62.50	$190.00	$450.00	£43.00	£125.00	£300.00
38	$77.50	$235.00	$550.00	£52.50	£160.00	£375.00
39-41	$62.50	$190.00	$450.00	£43.00	£125.00	£300.00
42 scarce in the U.K.						
	$77.50	$235.00	$550.00	£52.50	£160.00	£375.00
Title Value:	$6762.50	$20395.00	$54250.00	£4566.00	£13765.00	£36650.00

Note: all Non-Distributed on the news-stands in the U.K. though it is possible that copies came over via American G.I.'s or U.S. relatives of U.K. citizens.

SUB-MARINER (2ND SERIES)
Marvel Comics Group; 1 May 1968-72 Sep 1974
(see Namor, The Sub-Mariner, Tales to Astonish and Sub-Mariner Comics)

	$Good	$Fine	$N.Mint	£Good	£Fine	£N.Mint
1 origin retold, Fantastic Four appear						
	$21.00	$62.50	$150.00	£13.50	£41.00	£95.00
2 scarce in the U.K: Inhumans appear						
	$8.25	$25.00	$50.00	£5.00	£15.00	£30.00
3 Triton appears	$5.75	$17.50	$35.00	£2.90	£8.75	£17.50
4	$5.75	$17.50	$35.00	£2.50	£7.50	£15.00
5 1st appearance Tiger Shark						
	$5.75	$17.50	$35.00	£2.90	£8.75	£17.50
6	$5.25	$16.00	$32.50	£2.05	£6.25	£12.50
7 photo cover (Sub-Mariner in flight across cityscape)						
	$5.25	$16.00	$32.50	£2.05	£6.25	£12.50
8 scarce in the U.K: Thing vs Sub-Mariner						
	$5.75	$17.50	$35.00	£3.30	£10.00	£20.00
9 1st Serpent Crown						
	$5.25	$16.00	$32.50	£2.05	£6.25	£12.50
10	$5.25	$16.00	$32.50	£2.05	£6.25	£12.50
11-13	$3.75	$11.00	$22.50	£1.65	£5.00	£10.00
14 Sub-Mariner vs. Golden Age Human Torch, Toro dies						
	$5.75	$17.50	$35.00	£2.50	£7.50	£15.00
15	$3.75	$11.00	$22.50	£1.65	£5.00	£10.00
16-17	$2.05	$6.25	$12.50	£1.15	£3.50	£7.00
18 Triton appears	$2.05	$6.25	$12.50	£1.15	£3.50	£7.00
19 1st appearance Sting Ray						
	$2.05	$6.25	$12.50	£1.15	£3.50	£7.00
20 Sub-Mariner vs. Dr. Doom						
	$2.05	$6.25	$12.50	£1.15	£3.50	£7.00
21	$1.60	$4.80	$8.00	£1.00	£3.00	£5.00
22 Dr. Strange (as masked super-hero) appears						
	$1.60	$4.80	$8.00	£1.00	£3.00	£5.00
23 1st appearance Orka						
	$1.60	$4.80	$8.00	£1.00	£3.00	£5.00
24-25	$1.60	$4.80	$8.00	£1.00	£3.00	£5.00
26 Sub-Mariner vs. Red Raven						
	$1.50	$4.50	$7.50	£0.80	£2.40	£4.00
27 1st appearance Commander Kraken						
	$1.50	$4.50	$7.50	£0.80	£2.40	£4.00
28	$1.50	$4.50	$7.50	£0.80	£2.40	£4.00
29 Sub-Mariner vs. Hercules						
	$1.50	$4.50	$7.50	£0.80	£2.40	£4.00
30 Sub-Mariner vs. Captain Marvel						
	$1.50	$4.50	$7.50	£0.80	£2.40	£4.00
31-33	$1.50	$4.50	$7.50	£0.80	£2.40	£4.00
34 Hulk, Silver Surfer, Sub-Mariner team-up: 1st Defenders, though not yet named						
	$4.00	$12.00	$20.00	£2.00	£6.00	£10.00
35 Hulk, Silver Surfer, Sub-Mariner team-up: 2nd Defenders, though not yet named						
	$3.50	$10.50	$17.50	£1.60	£4.80	£8.00
36 Berni Wrightson inks						
	$1.50	$4.50	$7.50	£0.80	£2.40	£4.00
37 death of Lady Dorma						
	$1.50	$4.50	$7.50	£0.80	£2.40	£4.00
38 origin retold	$1.50	$4.50	$7.50	£0.80	£2.40	£4.00
39	$1.50	$4.50	$7.50	£0.80	£2.40	£4.00
40 Spiderman appears						
	$1.50	$4.50	$7.50	£0.80	£2.40	£4.00
41	$1.20	$3.60	$6.00	£0.70	£2.10	£3.50
42 last 15 cents issue						
	$1.20	$3.60	$6.00	£0.70	£2.10	£3.50

	$Good	$Fine	$N.Mint	£Good	£Fine	£N.Mint
43 scarce in the U.K. 52pgs, (almost all copies ink-stained)						
	$1.20	$3.60	$6.00	£1.00	£3.00	£5.00
44 Sub-Mariner vs. Human Torch						
	$1.20	$3.60	$6.00	£0.70	£2.10	£3.50
45 Human Torch appears						
	$1.20	$3.60	$6.00	£0.70	£2.10	£3.50
46 Namor's father appears						
	$1.20	$3.60	$6.00	£0.70	£2.10	£3.50
47-48 Dr. Doom appears						
	$1.20	$3.60	$6.00	£0.70	£2.10	£3.50
49 Dr. Doom appears with the Cosmic Cube						
	$1.20	$3.60	$6.00	£0.70	£2.10	£3.50
50 1st appearance Namorita (later Nita in New Warriors), Bill Everett art						
	$1.50	$4.50	$7.50	£1.00	£3.00	£5.00
51 scarce in the U.K. Bill Everett art						
	$1.00	$3.00	$5.00	£0.70	£2.10	£3.50
52 scarce in the U.K.						
	$1.00	$3.00	$5.00	£0.70	£2.10	£3.50
53 scarce in the U.K. Bill Everett Sub-Mariner reprint from 1950s						
	$1.00	$3.00	$5.00	£0.70	£2.10	£3.50
54-56	$1.00	$3.00	$5.00	£0.60	£1.80	£3.00
57 Bill Everett art; classic cover with bondage thrown in for good measure						
	$1.00	$3.00	$5.00	£0.70	£2.10	£3.50
58 Bill Everett art (with Sam Kweskin); part Gil Kane cover						
	$1.00	$3.00	$5.00	£0.60	£1.80	£3.00
59 Sub-Mariner vs. Thor (no Everett art)						
	$1.00	$3.00	$5.00	£0.70	£2.10	£3.50
60 Bill Everett art	$1.00	$3.00	$5.00	£0.60	£1.80	£3.00
61 part Everett art (last ever original work?)						
	$1.00	$3.00	$5.00	£0.60	£1.80	£3.00
62-63 Everett script, Chaykin art on back-up						
	$1.00	$3.00	$5.00	£0.60	£1.80	£3.00
64 Chaykin art on back-up						
	$1.00	$3.00	$5.00	£0.60	£1.80	£3.00
65-66	$1.00	$3.00	$5.00	£0.60	£1.80	£3.00
67 Fantastic Four and Triton appear; 1st new costume						
	$1.00	$3.00	$5.00	£0.60	£1.80	£3.00
68	$1.00	$3.00	$5.00	£0.60	£1.80	£3.00
69 Sub-Mariner vs. Spiderman, Dr. Strange appears						
	$1.00	$3.00	$5.00	£0.60	£1.80	£3.00
70-72 ND	$1.00	$3.00	$5.00	£0.60	£1.80	£3.00
Title Value:	$173.55	$522.15	$1004.00	£93.45	£281.90	£536.50

Note: Everett art in #49-55, #57, #60. Tales of Atlantis in #62-66.

SUB-MARINER (2ND SERIES) ANNUAL
Marvel Comics Group; 1 1971-2 1972

	$Good	$Fine	$N.Mint	£Good	£Fine	£N.Mint
1 scarce in the U.K. 68pgs, reprints Tales to Astonish #70-73						
	$1.50	$4.50	$7.50	£1.20	£3.60	£6.00
2 ND scarce in the U.K. 68pgs, reprints Tales to Astonish #74-75						
	$1.40	$4.20	$7.00	£1.00	£3.00	£5.00
Title Value:	$2.90	$8.70	$14.50	£2.20	£6.60	£11.00

SUB-MARINER (LIMITED SERIES)
Marvel Comics Group,MS; 1 Sep 1984-4 Dec 1984

	$Good	$Fine	$N.Mint	£Good	£Fine	£N.Mint
1-4 ND	$0.30	$0.90	$1.50	£0.20	£0.60	£1.00
Title Value:	$1.20	$3.60	$6.00	£0.80	£2.40	£4.00

SUB-MARINER, SAGA OF THE
Marvel Comics Group,MS; 1 Nov 1988-12 Oct 1989

	$Good	$Fine	$N.Mint	£Good	£Fine	£N.Mint
1-4 ND	$0.30	$0.90	$1.50	£0.20	£0.60	£1.00
5 ND Invaders appear						
	$0.30	$0.90	$1.50	£0.20	£0.60	£1.00
6 ND	$0.30	$0.90	$1.50	£0.20	£0.60	£1.00
7 ND Fantastic Four appear						
	$0.30	$0.90	$1.50	£0.20	£0.60	£1.00
8 ND Avengers appear						
	$0.30	$0.90	$1.50	£0.20	£0.60	£1.00
9 ND original X-Men appear						
	$0.30	$0.90	$1.50	£0.20	£0.60	£1.00
10-12 ND	$0.30	$0.90	$1.50	£0.20	£0.60	£1.00
Title Value:	$3.60	$10.80	$18.00	£2.40	£7.20	£12.00

SUBMARINE ATTACK
Charlton; 11 May 1958-54 Feb/Mar 1966
(previously Speed Demons)

	$Good	$Fine	$N.Mint	£Good	£Fine	£N.Mint
11	$3.75	$11.00	$22.50	£2.50	£7.50	£15.00
12-20	$2.50	$7.50	$15.00	£1.65	£5.00	£10.00
21-40	$1.65	$5.00	$10.00	£1.15	£3.50	£7.00
41-54	$1.50	$4.50	$9.00	£1.00	£3.00	£6.00
Title Value:	$80.25	$241.50	$483.50	£54.35	£164.50	£329.00

Note: all distributed on the news-stands in the U.K. including the first few issues that technically fall outside official distribution

SUBSPECIES
Eternity,MS; 1 May 1991-4 Aug 1991

	$Good	$Fine	$N.Mint	£Good	£Fine	£N.Mint
1-4 ND based on film, colour						
	$0.40	$1.20	$2.00	£0.25	£0.75	£1.25
Title Value:	$1.60	$4.80	$8.00	£1.00	£3.00	£5.00

SUBURBAN HIGH LIFE
Slave Labor; 1 Jun 1987-3 1988

	$Good	$Fine	$N.Mint	£Good	£Fine	£N.Mint
1 ND Frank Cirocco, Mark Martin, Rick Geary, Trina Robbins art						
	$0.40	$1.20	$2.00	£0.25	£0.75	£1.25
1 2nd printing, ND (Jun 1987)						
	$0.30	$0.90	$1.50	£0.20	£0.60	£1.00
2-3 ND	$0.40	$1.20	$2.00	£0.25	£0.75	£1.25
Title Value:	$1.50	$4.50	$7.50	£0.95	£2.85	£4.75
Trade paperback, reprints				£0.65	£1.95	£3.25

SUBURBAN NIGHTMARES
Renegade,MS; 1 May 1988-4 Aug 1988

	$Good	$Fine	$N.Mint	£Good	£Fine	£N.Mint
1-4 ND	$0.40	$1.20	$2.00	£0.25	£0.75	£1.25
Title Value:	$1.60	$4.80	$8.00	£1.00	£3.00	£5.00

SUBURBAN NINJA SHE-DEVILS, THE
Marvel Comics Group,OS; 1 Jan 1992

	$Good	$Fine	$N.Mint	£Good	£Fine	£N.Mint
1 ND Turtles parody by Steve Gerber	$0.30	$0.90	$1.50	£0.20	£0.60	£1.00
Title Value:	$0.30	$0.90	$1.50	£0.20	£0.60	£1.00

SUE AND SALLY SMITH, FLYING NURSES
Charlton; 48 Nov 1962-54 Nov 1963

	$Good	$Fine	$N.Mint	£Good	£Fine	£N.Mint
48-54 distributed in the U.K.	$1.00	$3.00	$6.00	£0.65	£2.00	£4.00
Title Value:	$7.00	$21.00	$42.00	£4.55	£14.00	£28.00

SUGAR AND SPIKE
National Periodical Publications/DC Comics; 15 Oct/Nov 1959-98 Oct/Nov 1971; 99 Mar 1992
(see also The Best of DC)
(previous issues ND)

	$Good	$Fine	$N.Mint	£Good	£Fine	£N.Mint
15-20 scarce in the U.K.	$33.00	$100.00	$200.00	£22.50	£67.50	£135.00
21-29 rare in the U.K.	$18.00	$55.00	$110.00	£12.50	£38.00	£75.00
30 rare in the U.K. Scribbly guest stars	$18.00	$55.00	$110.00	£12.50	£38.00	£75.00
31-40 rare in the U.K.	$18.00	$55.00	$110.00	£12.50	£38.00	£75.00
41-60 rare in the U.K.	$10.50	$33.00	$65.00	£7.50	£22.50	£45.00
61-71 rare in the U.K.	$9.00	$27.00	$45.00	£5.00	£15.00	£25.00
72 rare in the U.K. 1st Bernie the Brain	$9.00	$27.00	$45.00	£5.00	£15.00	£25.00
73-80 rare in the U.K.	$9.00	$27.00	$45.00	£5.00	£15.00	£25.00
81-84 rare in the U.K.	$7.00	$21.00	$35.00	£3.50	£10.50	£17.50
85 very scarce in the U.K. 68pgs	$7.00	$21.00	$35.00	£3.00	£9.00	£15.00
86-95 rare in the U.K.	$7.00	$21.00	$35.00	£3.50	£10.50	£17.50
96 very scarce in the U.K. 68pgs	$7.00	$21.00	$35.00	£3.00	£9.00	£15.00
97-98 scarce in the U.K. 52pgs	$7.00	$21.00	$35.00	£2.50	£7.50	£12.50
99 ND Silver Age Classic series (Mar 1992) featuring material originally intended for this issue before the series was cancelled	$0.25	$0.75	$1.25	£0.15	£0.45	£0.75
Title Value:	$1074.25	$3278.75	$6231.25	£695.15	£2095.45	£4010.75

Note: all issues by Sheldon Mayer.

SUICIDE SQUAD
DC Comics; 1 May 1987-66 Jun 1992
(see Deadshot)

	$Good	$Fine	$N.Mint	£Good	£Fine	£N.Mint
1 Howard Chaykin cover	$0.25	$0.75	$1.25	£0.15	£0.45	£0.75
2-8	$0.25	$0.75	$1.25	£0.15	£0.45	£0.75
9 Millennium X-over	$0.25	$0.75	$1.25	£0.15	£0.45	£0.75
10	$0.25	$0.75	$1.25	£0.15	£0.45	£0.75
11 Speedy and The Vixen appear	$0.25	$0.75	$1.25	£0.15	£0.45	£0.75
12	$0.25	$0.75	$1.25	£0.15	£0.45	£0.75
13 X-over with Justice League International #13	$0.25	$0.75	$1.25	£0.15	£0.45	£0.75
14-15	$0.25	$0.75	$1.25	£0.15	£0.45	£0.75
16 Shade the Changing Man returns	$0.25	$0.75	$1.25	£0.15	£0.45	£0.75
17-20	$0.25	$0.75	$1.25	£0.15	£0.45	£0.75
21 Bonus Book 16pg insert featuring The Bronze Tiger	$0.25	$0.75	$1.25	£0.15	£0.45	£0.75
22-25	$0.25	$0.75	$1.25	£0.15	£0.45	£0.75
26-28 The Janus Directive X-over with Checkmate #15, #16	$0.25	$0.75	$1.25	£0.15	£0.45	£0.75
29-30 Janus Directive	$0.25	$0.75	$1.25	£0.15	£0.45	£0.75
31-39	$0.25	$0.75	$1.25	£0.15	£0.45	£0.75
40 part 1 The Phoenix Gambit, Batman guest-stars, features free poster, one year gap in storyline after #39	$0.25	$0.75	$1.25	£0.15	£0.45	£0.75
41-43 parts 2-4 The Phoenix Gambit, Batman guest-stars	$0.25	$0.75	$1.25	£0.15	£0.45	£0.75
44-47	$0.25	$0.75	$1.25	£0.15	£0.45	£0.75
48-49 ties into The Killing Joke; Joker appears	$0.25	$0.75	$1.25	£0.15	£0.45	£0.75
50 48pgs, 50 year history of Suicide Squad	$0.30	$0.90	$1.50	£0.20	£0.60	£1.00
51-52	$0.25	$0.75	$1.25	£0.15	£0.45	£0.75
53 The Dragon's Horde part 1, Katana/Manhunter guest-star	$0.25	$0.75	$1.25	£0.15	£0.45	£0.75
54-57 The Dragon's Horde story	$0.25	$0.75	$1.25	£0.15	£0.45	£0.75
58 War of the Gods tie-in	$0.25	$0.75	$1.25	£0.15	£0.45	£0.75
59 Mystery of the Atom begins, Superman, Batman, Aquaman appear	$0.25	$0.75	$1.25	£0.15	£0.45	£0.75
60 Superman, Batman, Aquaman appear	$0.25	$0.75	$1.25	£0.15	£0.45	£0.75
61 Superman, Batman, Aquaman appear, intro Adam Cray the new Atom	$0.25	$0.75	$1.25	£0.15	£0.45	£0.75
62 Superman, Batman, Aquaman appear, Adam Cray dies, Ray Palmer (the Atom) returns	$0.25	$0.75	$1.25	£0.15	£0.45	£0.75
63-66	$0.25	$0.75	$1.25	£0.15	£0.45	£0.75
Title Value:	$16.55	$49.65	$82.75	£9.95	£29.85	£49.75

SUICIDE SQUAD ANNUAL
DC Comics; 1 1988

	$Good	$Fine	$N.Mint	£Good	£Fine	£N.Mint
1 ND Keith Giffen backup, new Manhunter appears	$0.30	$0.90	$1.50	£0.20	£0.60	£1.00
Title Value:	$0.30	$0.90	$1.50	£0.20	£0.60	£1.00

SULTRY TEENAGE SUPER FOXES
Solson Publications; 1 1987

	$Good	$Fine	$N.Mint	£Good	£Fine	£N.Mint
1 ND	$0.30	$0.90	$1.50	£0.20	£0.60	£1.00
Title Value:	$0.30	$0.90	$1.50	£0.20	£0.60	£1.00

SUN DEVILS
DC Comics,MS; 1 Jul 1984-12 Jun 1985

	$Good	$Fine	$N.Mint	£Good	£Fine	£N.Mint
1-12 ND	$0.20	$0.60	$1.00	£0.15	£0.45	£0.75
Title Value:	$2.40	$7.20	$12.00	£1.80	£5.40	£9.00

Note: high quality paper

SUN RUNNERS
Pacific/Eclipse; 1 Feb 1984-7 Dec 1985

	$Good	$Fine	$N.Mint	£Good	£Fine	£N.Mint
1 ND Pat Broderick cover and art, colour	$0.30	$0.90	$1.50	£0.20	£0.60	£1.00
2-4 ND Pat Broderick cover and art, colour; Mike Mahoney back-up strip by Roger McKenzie and Paul Smith	$0.30	$0.90	$1.50	£0.20	£0.60	£1.00
5 ND Pat Broderick cover and art, colour						

Sugar & Spike #97

Suicide Squad #66

Super DC Giant #14

	$Good	$Fine	$N.Mint	£Good	£Fine	£N.Mint
6-7 ND	$0.30	$0.90	$1.50	£0.20	£0.60	£1.00
	$0.30	$0.90	$1.50	£0.20	£0.60	£1.00
Title Value:	$2.10	$6.30	$10.50	£1.40	£4.20	£7.00

Note: although the next issue was advertised, the series was suddenly cancelled.

SUN RUNNERS CHRISTMAS SPECIAL
Amazing Comics; 1 1987

	$Good	$Fine	$N.Mint	£Good	£Fine	£N.Mint
1 ND	$0.40	$1.20	$2.00	£0.25	£0.75	£1.25
Title Value:	$0.40	$1.20	$2.00	£0.25	£0.75	£1.25

SUNGLASSES AFTER DARK
Verotik,OS; 1 Nov 1995
1 ND Nancy Collins script, Stan Shaw art

	$Good	$Fine	$N.Mint	£Good	£Fine	£N.Mint
	$0.60	$1.80	$3.00	£0.40	£1.20	£2.00
Title Value:	$0.60	$1.80	$3.00	£0.40	£1.20	£2.00

SUPER COPS
Red Circle (Archie), Film; 1 Jul 1974
1 Gray Morrow and Frank Thorne art; distributed in the U.K.

	$Good	$Fine	$N.Mint	£Good	£Fine	£N.Mint
	$0.50	$1.50	$2.50	£0.30	£0.90	£1.50
Title Value:	$0.50	$1.50	$2.50	£0.30	£0.90	£1.50

SUPER DC GIANT
DC Comics; 13 Sep/Oct 1970-26 Jul/Aug 1971; 27 Summer 1976
(No issues numbered #1-12 were published)

	$Good	$Fine	$N.Mint	£Good	£Fine	£N.Mint
13 ND Binky	$0.80	$2.40	$4.00	£0.60	£1.80	£3.00
14 Top Guns of the West, Joe Kubert cover						
	$0.80	$2.40	$4.00	£0.40	£1.20	£2.00
15 Western Comics; new Warrior Breed story, Joe Kubert cover						
	$1.00	$3.00	$5.00	£0.40	£1.20	£2.00
16 Best of The Brave and the Bold; 2 new framing pages featuring Batman and Flash; reprints Brave and the Bold #58, #67						
	$1.00	$3.00	$5.00	£0.80	£2.40	£4.00
17 ND scarce in the U.K, scarce in the U.S. Love 1970						
	$0.80	$2.40	$4.00	£0.50	£1.50	£2.50
18 ND Three Mousketeers						
	$0.80	$2.40	$4.00	£0.40	£1.20	£2.00
19 ND scarce in the U.K. Neal Adams reprint, Jerry Lewis						
	$0.80	$2.40	$4.00	£0.80	£2.40	£4.00
20 House of Mystery						
	$1.00	$3.00	$5.00	£0.40	£1.20	£2.00
21 ND scarce in the U.K, scarce in the U.S. Love 1971						
	$0.80	$2.40	$4.00	£0.50	£1.50	£2.50
22 Top Guns of the West, features Batlash/Johnny Thunder/Night Hawk/Matt Savage; Joe Kubert cover						
	$0.80	$2.40	$4.00	£0.40	£1.20	£2.00
23 Unexpected	$0.80	$2.40	$4.00	£0.40	£1.20	£2.00
24 Supergirl; reprints back-up stories from Action Comics #295-298						
	$0.80	$2.40	$4.00	£0.50	£1.50	£2.50
25 scarce in the U.K. Challengers of the Unknown						
	$0.80	$2.40	$4.00	£0.80	£2.40	£4.00
26 Aquaman	$0.80	$2.40	$4.00	£0.60	£1.80	£3.00
27 ND 48pgs, and scarce in the U.K., Strange Flying Saucer Stories						
	$0.80	$2.40	$4.00	£0.60	£1.80	£3.00
Title Value:	$12.60	$37.80	$63.00	£8.10	£24.30	£40.50

Note: Issues 13-26 are 68pgs. S-13, 14, 16-27 are all reprint.
ARTISTS
Kirby reprints in 20, 25.
REPRINT FEATURES
Bat Lash in 22. Batman/Flash in 16. Buffalo Bill in 15. Johnny Thunder in 14, 22. Matt Savage in 14, 22. Metamorpho in 16. Nighthawk in 14, 22. Pow-Wow Smith in 15. Trigger Twins in 14. Vigilante in 15. Wyoming Kid in 14.

SUPER FRIENDS
DC Comics, TV; 1 Nov 1975-47 Aug 1981
(900 Best of DC Limited Collector's Edition)
1 scarce in the U.K. Superman, Batman, Robin, Wonder Woman, Aquaman plus Zan and Jayna the Wonder Twins begin; based on Saturday morning cartoon show

	$Good	$Fine	$N.Mint	£Good	£Fine	£N.Mint
	$0.60	$1.80	$3.00	£0.40	£1.20	£2.00
2-3 scarce in the U.K.						
	$0.50	$1.50	$2.50	£0.30	£0.90	£1.50
4 scarce in the U.K. Riddler appears						
	$0.50	$1.50	$2.50	£0.30	£0.90	£1.50
5-7	$0.50	$1.50	$2.50	£0.25	£0.75	£1.25
8 Red Tornado appears; dinosaur cover						
	$0.40	$1.20	$2.00	£0.25	£0.75	£1.25
9 1st appearance Ice (though outside DC continuity)						
	$0.40	$1.20	$2.00	£0.25	£0.75	£1.25
10	$0.40	$1.20	$2.00	£0.25	£0.75	£1.25
11-13	$0.30	$0.90	$1.50	£0.20	£0.60	£1.00
14 scarce in the U.K. 44pgs						
	$0.30	$0.90	$1.50	£0.25	£0.75	£1.25
15-21	$0.30	$0.90	$1.50	£0.20	£0.60	£1.00
22 Chronos appears						
	$0.30	$0.90	$1.50	£0.20	£0.60	£1.00
23 Mirror Master appears						
	$0.30	$0.90	$1.50	£0.20	£0.60	£1.00
24	$0.30	$0.90	$1.50	£0.20	£0.60	£1.00
25 1st appearance Fire (though outside DC continuity)						
	$0.30	$0.90	$1.50	£0.20	£0.60	£1.00
26-27	$0.30	$0.90	$1.50	£0.20	£0.60	£1.00
28 Bizarro, Demon, Man-Bat, Solomon Grundy and Swamp Thing appear						
	$0.30	$0.90	$1.50	£0.20	£0.60	£1.00
29	$0.30	$0.90	$1.50	£0.20	£0.60	£1.00
30 Gorilla Grodd appears						
	$0.30	$0.90	$1.50	£0.20	£0.60	£1.00
31 Black Orchid guest-stars						
	$0.30	$0.90	$1.50	£0.20	£0.60	£1.00

	$Good	$Fine	$N.Mint	£Good	£Fine	£N.Mint
32 The Scarecrow appears						
	$0.30	$0.90	$1.50	£0.20	£0.60	£1.00
33 Hawkman appears						
	$0.30	$0.90	$1.50	£0.20	£0.60	£1.00
34-36	$0.30	$0.90	$1.50	£0.20	£0.60	£1.00
37 Supergirl appears						
	$0.30	$0.90	$1.50	£0.20	£0.60	£1.00
38-40	$0.30	$0.90	$1.50	£0.20	£0.60	£1.00
41 The Toyman appears						
	$0.30	$0.90	$1.50	£0.20	£0.60	£1.00
42	$0.30	$0.90	$1.50	£0.20	£0.60	£1.00
43 Plastic Man back-up						
	$0.30	$0.90	$1.50	£0.20	£0.60	£1.00
44	$0.30	$0.90	$1.50	£0.20	£0.60	£1.00
45 Sinestro appears; Plastic Man back-up						
	$0.30	$0.90	$1.50	£0.20	£0.60	£1.00
46-47	$0.30	$0.90	$1.50	£0.20	£0.60	£1.00
Title Value:	$15.90	$47.70	$78.50	£10.25	£30.75	£51.25

FEATURES
Super Friends (Superman, Batman, Robin, Wonder Woman, Aquaman) in all issues. Jack O'Lantern in 37, 40, 44. Plastic Man in 43, 45. The Seraph in 38, 41, 46. Wonder Twins in 14, 29, 34, 36, 39, 42.

SUPER FRIENDS SPECIAL, THE
DC Comics,OS; 1 1981
1 ND scarce in the U.K.

	$Good	$Fine	$N.Mint	£Good	£Fine	£N.Mint
	$0.40	$1.20	$2.00	£0.30	£0.90	£1.50
Title Value:	$0.40	$1.20	$2.00	£0.30	£0.90	£1.50

SUPER GREEN BERET (TED HOLTON..)
Milson Publishing; 1 Apr 1967-2 Jun 1967

	$Good	$Fine	$N.Mint	£Good	£Fine	£N.Mint
1-2 ND	$4.00	$12.00	$20.00	£2.50	£7.50	£12.50
Title Value:	$8.00	$24.00	$40.00	£5.00	£15.00	£25.00

SUPER HEROES
Dell; 1 Jan 1967-4 Jun 1967
1 1st appearance The Fab Four (Marvel rip-off!); distributed in the U.K.

	$Good	$Fine	$N.Mint	£Good	£Fine	£N.Mint
	$4.00	$12.00	$20.00	£2.80	£8.25	£14.00
2-4 distributed in the U.K.						
	$3.00	$9.00	$15.00	£2.00	£6.00	£10.00
Title Value:	$13.00	$39.00	$65.00	£8.80	£26.25	£44.00

SUPER POWERS
DC Comics,MS; 1 Jul 1984-5 Nov 1984
1 Jack Kirby plot and covers begin; Joker, Luthor, Penguin cover; Batman appears

	$Good	$Fine	$N.Mint	£Good	£Fine	£N.Mint
	$0.40	$1.20	$2.00	£0.25	£0.75	£1.25
2 Batman, Joker, Penguin, Luthor appear						
	$0.40	$1.20	$2.00	£0.25	£0.75	£1.25
3-4 Batman, Joker, Penguin, Luthor appear; Darkseid appears						
	$0.40	$1.20	$2.00	£0.25	£0.75	£1.25
5 Jack Kirby art and script (not just plot); Batman, Joker, Pengiun, Luthor and Darkseid appear						
	$0.40	$1.20	$2.00	£0.25	£0.75	£1.25
Title Value:	$2.00	$6.00	$10.00	£1.25	£3.75	£6.25

SUPER POWERS (2ND SERIES)
DC Comics,MS; 1 Sep 1985-6 Feb 1986
1 Jack Kirby cover and art; Darkseid appears (and on cover), Justice League of America inc. Batman appear

	$Good	$Fine	$N.Mint	£Good	£Fine	£N.Mint
	$0.40	$1.20	$2.00	£0.25	£0.75	£1.25
2-3 Jack Kirby cover and art						
	$0.40	$1.20	$2.00	£0.25	£0.75	£1.25
4-6 Jack Kirby cover and art, Batman appears						
	$0.40	$1.20	$2.00	£0.25	£0.75	£1.25
Title Value:	$2.40	$7.20	$12.00	£1.50	£4.50	£7.50

SUPER POWERS (3RD SERIES)
DC Comics,MS; 1 Sep 1986-4 Dec 1986
1 Infantino art, Batman appears

	$Good	$Fine	$N.Mint	£Good	£Fine	£N.Mint
	$0.30	$0.90	$1.50	£0.20	£0.60	£1.00
2-3 Infantino art, Batman and Darkseid appear						
	$0.30	$0.90	$1.50	£0.20	£0.60	£1.00
4 Infantino art, Batman appears						
	$0.30	$0.90	$1.50	£0.20	£0.60	£1.00
Title Value:	$1.20	$3.60	$6.00	£0.80	£2.40	£4.00

SUPER SOLDIERS
Marvel UK; 1 Apr 1993-10 Jan 1994
1 Bennet/Stevens and Currie/Ramos, USAgent appears; silver-embossed logo

	$Good	$Fine	$N.Mint	£Good	£Fine	£N.Mint
	$0.40	$1.20	$2.00	£0.25	£0.75	£1.25
2-3	$0.30	$0.90	$1.50	£0.20	£0.60	£1.00
4 Avengers, USAgent and Captain America appear						
	$0.30	$0.90	$1.50	£0.20	£0.60	£1.00
5 Captain America and West Coast Anengers appear						
	$0.30	$0.90	$1.50	£0.20	£0.60	£1.00
6 origin Hauer, Nick Fury appears; day-glow cover						
	$0.30	$0.90	$1.50	£0.20	£0.60	£1.00
7 Nick Fury and X-Men appear						
	$0.30	$0.90	$1.50	£0.20	£0.60	£1.00
8-9 Punisher appears						
	$0.30	$0.90	$1.50	£0.20	£0.60	£1.00
10	$0.30	$0.90	$1.50	£0.20	£0.60	£1.00
Title Value:	$3.10	$9.30	$15.50	£2.05	£6.15	£10.25

SUPER VILLAIN CLASSICS
Marvel Comics Group,OS; 1 May 1983
1 ND Galactus the Origin by Kirby, extra art by John Byrne

	$Good	$Fine	$N.Mint	£Good	£Fine	£N.Mint
	$0.60	$1.80	$3.00	£0.40	£1.20	£2.00
1 2nd printing, ND (Feb 1996), with new colour separations and extra pin-ups						
	$0.50	$1.50	$2.50	£0.30	£0.90	£1.50
Title Value:	$1.10	$3.30	$5.50	£0.70	£2.10	£3.50

SUPER-HEROES BATTLE SUPER-GORILLAS
DC Comics,OS; 1 Winter 1976

VERY GENERAL PERCENTAGE CONVERSION CHART WHICH MAY BE USED TO CALCULATE LOW AND INBETWEEN GRADES:

	$Good	$Fine	$N.Mint	£Good	£Fine	£N.Mint
(see DC Special #16)						
1 ND 52pgs, Superman, Batman, Flash reprints	$0.40	$1.20	$2.00	£0.25	£0.75	£1.25
Title Value:	$0.40	$1.20	$2.00	£0.25	£0.75	£1.25

SUPER-HEROES GIANT SIZE
Marvel Comics Group; 1 Jun 1974

	$Good	$Fine	$N.Mint	£Good	£Fine	£N.Mint
1 ND 52pgs, Spiderman vs. Man-Wolf, Morbius appears, Gil Kane art	$9.00	$27.00	$45.00	£5.00	£15.00	£25.00
Title Value:	$9.00	$27.00	$45.00	£5.00	£15.00	£25.00

SUPER-HEROES PUZZLES AND GAMES
Marvel Comics Group; nn 1979

	$Good	$Fine	$N.Mint	£Good	£Fine	£N.Mint
nn ND 32pgs, cereal giveaway; features origins of Spiderman, Spiderwoman, Hulk and Captain America	$0.40	$1.20	$2.00	£0.25	£0.75	£1.25
Title Value:	$0.40	$1.20	$2.00	£0.25	£0.75	£1.25

SUPER-STAR HOLIDAY SPECIAL
DC Comics; nn Spring 1980
(DC Special Series #21)

	$Good	$Fine	$N.Mint	£Good	£Fine	£N.Mint
nn ND 64pgs, new Batman story by Frank Miller (1st Frank Miller Batman – see Batman: The Dark Knight Returns), House of Mystery, Sgt. Rock, Superboy/Legion of Super-Heroes	$2.00	$6.00	$10.00	£1.50	£4.50	£7.50
Title Value:	$2.00	$6.00	$10.00	£1.50	£4.50	£7.50

SUPER-STARS GIANT SIZE
Marvel Comics Group; 1 May 1974
(becomes Fantastic Four Giant Size)

	$Good	$Fine	$N.Mint	£Good	£Fine	£N.Mint
1 ND 52pgs, features Fantastic Four; Thing vs. Hulk	$3.00	$9.00	$15.00	£2.00	£6.00	£10.00
Title Value:	$3.00	$9.00	$15.00	£2.00	£6.00	£10.00

SUPER-TEAM FAMILY
DC Comics; 1 Oct Nov 1975-15 Mar Apr 1978

	$Good	$Fine	$N.Mint	£Good	£Fine	£N.Mint
1 68pgs, new Teen Titans story o/w reprints inc. a Neal Adams reprint	$0.60	$1.80	$3.00	£0.60	£1.80	£3.00
2 68pgs, new Creeper/Wildcat story o/w reprints inc. Neal Adams reprints	$0.40	$1.20	$2.00	£0.50	£1.50	£2.50
3 68pgs, new Flash/Hawkman story o/w reprints inc. Neal Adams reprints	$0.40	$1.20	$2.00	£0.40	£1.20	£2.00
4 68pgs, all reprint begins	$0.40	$1.20	$2.00	£0.30	£0.90	£1.50
5 52pgs, Batman/Eclipso reprint from Brave and the Bold #64, new 1pg origin Eclipso	$0.40	$1.20	$2.00	£0.40	£1.20	£2.00
6 scarce in the U.K. 52pgs	$0.30	$0.90	$1.50	£0.30	£0.90	£1.50
7 52pgs	$0.30	$0.90	$1.50	£0.25	£0.75	£1.25
8 52pgs, new Challengers of the Unknown story, Doom patrol origin sequence reprinted from Doom Patrol #86, Doom Patrol #87 reprinted	$0.50	$1.50	$2.50	£0.25	£0.75	£1.25
9 ND 52pgs, new Challengers of the Unknown story	$0.50	$1.50	$2.50	£0.35	£1.05	£1.75
10 52pgs, new Challengers of the Unknown story	$0.50	$1.50	$2.50	£0.25	£0.75	£1.25
11 52pgs	$0.30	$0.90	$1.50	£0.25	£0.75	£1.25
12-15 ND 52pgs	$0.30	$0.90	$1.50	£0.35	£1.05	£1.75
Title Value:	$5.80	$17.40	$29.00	£5.25	£15.75	£26.25

FEATURES
Aquaman/Captain Comet/Atom in 13. Creeper/Wildcat in 2. Challengers of the Unknown in 8-10. Flash/Hawkman in 3. Flash/New Gods in 15. Green Lantern/Hawkman/Atom in 12. Wonder Woman/Atom in 14.
REPRINT FEATURES
Aquaman/Green Arrow, Batman/Deadman, Green Arrow in 2. Batman/Eclipso, Superboy in 5. Doom Patrol in 7-10. Flash in 1. Justice Society of America in 4. Marvel Family in 6. Superman/Batman in 1, 3, 4, 6. Teen Titans in 1, 7.

SUPER-VILLAIN TEAM-UP
Marvel Comics Group; 1 Aug 1975-14 Oct 1977; 15 Nov 1978

	$Good	$Fine	$N.Mint	£Good	£Fine	£N.Mint
1 ND	$3.00	$5.00		£0.70	£2.10	£3.50
2 ND	$0.60	$1.80	$3.00	£0.40	£1.20	£2.00
3-4	$0.60	$1.80	$3.00	£0.25	£0.75	£1.25
5-7 Fantastic Four appear	$0.60	$1.80	$3.00	£0.25	£0.75	£1.25
8 Giffen art	$0.60	$1.80	$3.00	£0.25	£0.75	£1.25
9 Avengers tie-in to #155	$0.60	$1.80	$3.00	£0.40	£1.20	£2.00
10 ND Avengers appear	$0.60	$1.80	$3.00	£0.40	£1.20	£2.00
11-12 ND Captain America appears	$0.50	$1.50	$2.50	£0.40	£1.20	£2.00
13 ND	$0.50	$1.50	$2.50	£0.35	£1.05	£1.75
14 ND X-Men cameo, Magneto appears; The Champions guest-star (tie-in to Champions #16), John Byrne cover	$0.50	$1.50	$2.50	£0.40	£1.20	£2.00
15 ND rare in the U.K. reprint	$0.50	$1.50	$2.50	£0.50	£1.50	£2.50
16-17 ND	$0.50	$1.50	$2.50	£0.30	£0.90	£1.50
Title Value:	$9.90	$29.70	$49.50	£6.05	£18.15	£30.25

FEATURES
Dr.Doom/Sub-Mariner in 1-15. Red Skull/Hate Monger in 16, 17. Avengers tie-in issue 9.

SUPER-VILLAIN TEAM-UP GIANT SIZE
Marvel Comics Group; 1 Oct 1974-2 Jul 1975

	$Good	$Fine	$N.Mint	£Good	£Fine	£N.Mint
1 ND 68pgs, pre-dates Super-Villain Team Up #1	$1.50	$4.50	$7.50	£1.00	£3.00	£5.00
2 ND 68pgs	$1.20	$3.60	$6.00	£0.80	£2.40	£4.00
Title Value:	$2.70	$8.10	$13.50	£1.80	£5.40	£9.00

Note: Dr. Doom and Sub-Mariner in both.

SUPERBOY
National Periodical Publications/DC Comics; 1 Mar/Apr 1949-354 Dec 1987
(see Action, Adventure, DC Superstars, Legion of Super-Heroes)
(becomes Superboy and the Legion of Super-Heroes with #231)
(becomes The Legion of Super-Heroes with #259) (becomes Tales of the Legion with #314)

	$Good	$Fine	$N.Mint	£Good	£Fine	£N.Mint
1 scarce in the U.K. Superman appears on cover; cover "illusion" of page being turned back	$550.00	$1650.00	$5500.00	£375.00	£1125.00	£3750.00
[Prices may vary widely on this comic]						
2	$165.00	$500.00	$1350.00	£110.00	£335.00	£900.00
3	$125.00	$375.00	$1000.00	£82.50	£250.00	£675.00
4	$90.00	$270.00	$725.00	£57.50	£175.00	£475.00
5	$100.00	$300.00	$700.00	£62.50	£190.00	£450.00
6 (Jan/Feb 1950)	$70.00	$215.00	$575.00	£47.00	£140.00	£375.00
7	$70.00	$215.00	$575.00	£47.00	£140.00	£375.00
8 1st appearance of Superman as Superbaby	$70.00	$215.00	$575.00	£47.00	£140.00	£375.00
9	$70.00	$215.00	$575.00	£47.00	£140.00	£375.00
10 1st appearance Lana Lang	$75.00	$225.00	$600.00	£50.00	£150.00	£400.00
11	$62.50	$190.00	$450.00	£43.00	£125.00	£300.00
12 (Jan/Feb 1951)	$62.50	$190.00	$450.00	£43.00	£125.00	£300.00
13-15	$62.50	$190.00	$450.00	£43.00	£125.00	£300.00
16-17	$40.00	$120.00	$280.00	£27.00	£80.00	£190.00
18 (Feb/Mar 1952)	$40.00	$120.00	$280.00	£27.00	£80.00	£190.00
19-20	$40.00	$120.00	$280.00	£27.00	£80.00	£190.00
21-23	$35.00	$105.00	$245.00	£23.50	£70.00	£165.00
24 (Feb/Mar 1953)	$35.00	$105.00	$245.00	£23.50	£70.00	£165.00
25-26	$35.00	$105.00	$245.00	£23.50	£70.00	£165.00
27 scarce in the U.S, very scarce in the U.K.	$39.00	$115.00	$275.00	£29.00	£85.00	£200.00
28-29	$35.00	$105.00	$245.00	£23.50	£70.00	£165.00
30 (Jan 1954)	$35.00	$105.00	$245.00	£23.50	£70.00	£165.00
31-37	$25.00	$75.00	$175.00	£17.00	£50.00	£120.00
38 (Jan 1955)	$25.00	$75.00	$175.00	£17.00	£50.00	£120.00
39-40	$25.00	$75.00	$175.00	£17.00	£50.00	£120.00
41-45	$20.50	$60.00	$145.00	£13.50	£41.00	£95.00
46 (Jan 1956)	$20.50	$60.00	$145.00	£13.50	£41.00	£95.00
47-48	$20.50	$60.00	$145.00	£13.50	£41.00	£95.00
49 1st appearance Metallo (robot guardian of Kal-El on Krypton)	$20.50	$60.00	$145.00	£13.50	£41.00	£95.00
50	$20.50	$60.00	$145.00	£13.50	£41.00	£95.00
51-53	$15.50	$47.00	$110.00	£10.50	£32.00	£75.00
54 (Jan 1957)	$15.50	$47.00	$110.00	£10.50	£32.00	£75.00
55-60	$15.50	$47.00	$110.00	£10.50	£32.00	£75.00
61	$14.00	$43.00	$100.00	£9.25	£28.00	£65.00
62 (Jan 1958)	$14.00	$43.00	$100.00	£9.25	£28.00	£65.00
63-67	$14.00	$43.00	$100.00	£9.25	£28.00	£65.00
68 origin and 1st appearance original Bizarro	$55.00	$165.00	$450.00	£38.00	£110.00	£300.00
69	$10.50	$32.00	$75.00	£7.00	£21.00	£50.00
70 (Jan 1959)	$10.50	$32.00	$75.00	£7.00	£21.00	£50.00
71-75	$10.50	$32.00	$75.00	£7.00	£21.00	£50.00
76 1st appearance Beppo the Super Monkey; copies known with distribution stamps	$10.50	$32.00	$75.00	£7.00	£21.00	£50.00
1st official distribution in the U.K.						
77	$10.50	$32.00	$75.00	£7.00	£21.00	£50.00
78 (Jan 1960), origin Mr. Mxyzptlk re-told (see Superman #30 for 1st appearance)	$16.00	$49.00	$130.00	£11.00	£34.00	£90.00
79	$10.50	$32.00	$75.00	£7.00	£21.00	£50.00
80 Superboy and Supergirl meet for the first time, chronologically	$16.00	$49.00	$115.00	£11.00	£34.00	£80.00
81	$9.25	$28.00	$65.00	£6.25	£19.00	£45.00
82 1st appearance Bizarro Krypto	$9.25	$28.00	$65.00	£6.25	£19.00	£45.00
83 1st appearance Kryptonite Kid	$9.25	$28.00	$65.00	£6.25	£19.00	£45.00
84-85	$9.25	$28.00	$65.00	£6.25	£19.00	£45.00
86 (Jan 1961), 4th appearance of Legion, 1st appearance Pete Ross	$13.50	$41.00	$110.00	£9.25	£28.00	£75.00
87-88	$9.25	$28.00	$65.00	£6.25	£19.00	£45.00
89 1st appearance Mon-El	$25.00	$75.00	$200.00	£16.50	£50.00	£135.00
90 Peter Ross discovers Superboy's identity, while sharing a tent (!)	$9.25	$28.00	$65.00	£6.25	£19.00	£45.00
91	$9.25	$28.00	$65.00	£6.25	£19.00	£45.00
92 last 10 cents issue	$9.25	$28.00	$65.00	£6.25	£19.00	£45.00
93 11th Legion appearance	$9.25	$28.00	$65.00	£6.25	£19.00	£45.00
94 (Jan 1962)	$5.25	$16.00	$37.50	£3.55	£10.50	£25.00
95-97	$5.25	$16.00	$37.50	£3.55	£10.50	£25.00
98 19th Legion; origin and 1st appearance Ultra Boy	$6.25	$19.00	$45.00	£4.25	£12.50	£30.00
99	$5.25	$16.00	$37.50	£3.55	£10.50	£25.00
100 origin of Superboy retold, Ultra Boy appears, Pete Ross in Legion	$25.00	$75.00	$175.00	£14.00	£43.00	£100.00
101	$4.55	$13.50	$27.50	£3.00	£9.00	£18.00
102 (Jan 1963)	$4.55	$13.50	$27.50	£3.00	£9.00	£18.00

MINT = 100% / NEAR MINT (inc. +/-) = 90–99% / VERY FINE (inc. +/-) = 75–89% / FINE (inc. +/-) = 55–74%
VERY GOOD (inc. +/-) = 35–54% / GOOD (inc. +/-) = 15–34% / FAIR = 5–14% / POOR = 1–4%

577

Issue / Notes	$Good	$Fine	$N.Mint	£Good	£Fine	£N.Mint
103-109	$4.55	$13.50	$27.50	£3.00	£9.00	£18.00
110 (Jan 1964)	$4.55	$13.50	$27.50	£3.00	£9.00	£18.00
111-116	$4.15	$12.50	$25.00	£2.50	£7.50	£15.00
117 Legion of Super-Heroes appears	$4.15	$12.50	$25.00	£2.50	£7.50	£15.00
118 (Jan 1965)	$4.15	$12.50	$25.00	£2.50	£7.50	£15.00
119-120	$4.15	$12.50	$25.00	£2.50	£7.50	£15.00
121-124	$3.75	$11.00	$22.50	£2.05	£6.25	£12.50
125 last Silver Age issue, indicia dated December 1965	$3.75	$11.00	$22.50	£2.05	£6.25	£12.50
126 (Jan 1966), origin Krypto	$4.50	$13.50	$22.50	£2.50	£7.50	£12.50
127-128	$4.50	$13.50	$22.50	£2.50	£7.50	£12.50
129 80pgs, Giant G-22, reprints Superboy #89 (1st Mon-El)	$4.55	$13.50	$27.50	£2.50	£7.50	£15.00
130	$4.50	$13.50	$22.50	£2.50	£7.50	£12.50
131-134	$3.00	$9.00	$15.00	£1.50	£4.50	£7.50
135 (Jan 1967)	$3.00	$9.00	$15.00	£1.50	£4.50	£7.50
136-137	$3.00	$9.00	$15.00	£1.50	£4.50	£7.50
138 80pgs, Giant G-35	$5.50	$16.50	$27.50	£3.00	£9.00	£15.00
139-140	$3.00	$9.00	$15.00	£1.50	£4.50	£7.50
141-142	$2.50	$7.50	$12.50	£1.20	£3.60	£6.00
143 Neal Adams cover	$2.50	$7.50	$12.50	£1.20	£3.60	£6.00
144 (Jan 1968)	$2.50	$7.50	$12.50	£1.20	£3.60	£6.00
145	$2.50	$7.50	$12.50	£1.20	£3.60	£6.00
146 2pg Superboy Legend at centrefold (often missing!)	$2.50	$7.50	$12.50	£1.20	£3.60	£6.00
147 80pgs, Giant G-47, Legion origin retold in new story, reprints Superman #147, Adventure Comics #290 (origin Sun Boy and 9th Legion appearance)	$3.00	$9.00	$15.00	£2.00	£6.00	£10.00
148-149 Neal Adams cover	$2.50	$7.50	$12.50	£1.20	£3.60	£6.00
150	$2.50	$7.50	$12.50	£1.20	£3.60	£6.00
151-152 Neal Adams cover	$2.00	$6.00	$10.00	£1.00	£3.00	£5.00
153 (Jan 1969), Neal Adams cover	$2.00	$6.00	$10.00	£1.00	£3.00	£5.00
154	$2.00	$6.00	$10.00	£1.00	£3.00	£5.00
155 Neal Adams cover	$2.00	$6.00	$10.00	£1.00	£3.00	£5.00
156 80pgs, Giant G-59	$2.50	$7.50	$12.50	£1.50	£4.50	£7.50
157	$2.00	$6.00	$10.00	£1.00	£3.00	£5.00
158 Wood inks	$2.00	$6.00	$10.00	£1.00	£3.00	£5.00
159-161	$2.00	$6.00	$10.00	£1.00	£3.00	£5.00
162 (Jan 1970)	$2.00	$6.00	$10.00	£1.00	£3.00	£5.00
163-164 Neal Adams cover	$2.00	$6.00	$10.00	£1.00	£3.00	£5.00
165 80pgs, Giant G-71, reprints Adventure Comics #210 (1st Krypto)	$2.50	$7.50	$12.50	£1.50	£4.50	£7.50
166-168 Neal Adams cover	$2.00	$6.00	$10.00	£1.00	£3.00	£5.00
169-170	$2.00	$6.00	$10.00	£1.00	£3.00	£5.00
171 (Jan 1971), 1st appearance Aquaboy	$1.50	$4.50	$7.50	£0.80	£2.40	£4.00
172 new Legion stories	$1.50	$4.50	$7.50	£0.80	£2.40	£4.00
173 Neal Adams cover, new Legion stories	$1.50	$4.50	$7.50	£0.80	£2.40	£4.00
174 80pgs, Giant G-83	$2.50	$7.50	$12.50	£1.50	£4.50	£7.50
175 Neal Adams cover	$1.50	$4.50	$7.50	£0.80	£2.40	£4.00
176 Neal Adams cover, new Legion stories	$1.50	$4.50	$7.50	£0.80	£2.40	£4.00
177 48pgs, (the Americans count the covers and make it 52pgs!)	$1.50	$4.50	$7.50	£0.80	£2.40	£4.00
178 48pgs, Neal Adams cover	$1.50	$4.50	$7.50	£0.80	£2.40	£4.00
179-180 48pgs	$1.50	$4.50	$7.50	£0.80	£2.40	£4.00
181 48pgs, (Jan 1972)	$1.00	$3.00	$5.00	£0.70	£2.10	£3.50
182 48pgs, Superboy meets young Bruce Wayne (Batman)	$1.00	$3.00	$5.00	£0.70	£2.10	£3.50
183-184 48pgs, new Legion stories	$1.00	$3.00	$5.00	£0.70	£2.10	£3.50
185 100pgs, DC-100pg Super Spectacular #12; Legion reprints, reprints Brave and Bold #60 (2nd Teen Titans)	$1.50	$4.50	$7.50	£1.00	£3.00	£5.00
186-187 48pgs	$1.00	$3.00	$5.00	£0.70	£2.10	£3.50
188 new Legion stories	$0.60	$1.80	$3.00	£0.50	£1.50	£2.50
189	$0.60	$1.80	$3.00	£0.40	£1.20	£2.00
190 new Legion stories	$0.60	$1.80	$3.00	£0.60	£1.80	£3.00
191 origin Sun Boy retold	$0.60	$1.80	$3.00	£0.60	£1.80	£3.00
192	$0.60	$1.80	$3.00	£0.40	£1.20	£2.00
193 (Jan 1973), new Legion stories	$0.60	$1.80	$3.00	£0.60	£1.80	£3.00
194	$0.60	$1.80	$3.00	£0.40	£1.20	£2.00

Issue / Notes	$Good	$Fine	$N.Mint	£Good	£Fine	£N.Mint
195 new Legion stories	$0.60	$1.80	$3.00	£0.60	£1.80	£3.00
196	$0.60	$1.80	$3.00	£0.40	£1.20	£2.00
197 scarce in the U.K. 1st of new Legion series	$1.50	$4.50	$7.50	£1.40	£4.20	£7.00
198-199 scarce in the U.K.	$1.00	$3.00	$5.00	£1.20	£3.60	£6.00
200 scarce in the U.K. (Jan 1974), Bouncing Boy, Duo Damsel wed	$1.50	$4.50	$7.50	£1.20	£3.60	£6.00
201	$0.60	$1.80	$3.00	£0.60	£1.80	£3.00
202 100pgs, squarebound	$1.00	$3.00	$5.00	£1.00	£3.00	£5.00
203 original Invisible Kid dies	$0.60	$1.80	$3.00	£0.60	£1.80	£3.00
204	$0.60	$1.80	$3.00	£0.60	£1.80	£3.00
205 100pgs, squarebound	$1.00	$3.00	$5.00	£1.00	£3.00	£5.00
206 (Jan 1975)	$0.60	$1.80	$3.00	£0.60	£1.80	£3.00
207	$0.60	$1.80	$3.00	£0.60	£1.80	£3.00
208 scarce in the U.K. 68pgs, squarebound	$1.00	$3.00	$5.00	£0.90	£2.70	£4.50
209	$0.60	$1.80	$3.00	£0.60	£1.80	£3.00
210 origin Karate Kid	$0.60	$1.80	$3.00	£0.60	£1.80	£3.00
211 ND	$0.50	$1.50	$2.50	£1.00	£3.00	£5.00
212-213 scarce in the U.K.	$0.50	$1.50	$2.50	£0.70	£2.10	£3.50
214 (Jan 1976)	$0.50	$1.50	$2.50	£0.50	£1.50	£2.50
215-216	$0.50	$1.50	$2.50	£0.50	£1.50	£2.50
217	$0.50	$1.50	$2.50	£0.40	£1.20	£2.00
218 ND	$0.50	$1.50	$2.50	£0.70	£2.10	£3.50
219-222 scarce in the U.K.	$0.50	$1.50	$2.50	£0.60	£1.80	£3.00
223 scarce in the U.K. (Jan 1977)	$0.40	$1.20	$2.00	£0.60	£1.80	£3.00
224-226 scarce in the U.K.	$0.40	$1.20	$2.00	£0.60	£1.80	£3.00
227 ND	$0.40	$1.20	$2.00	£0.70	£2.10	£3.50
228-229	$0.40	$1.20	$2.00	£0.40	£1.20	£2.00
230 scarce in the U.K.	$0.40	$1.20	$2.00	£0.60	£1.80	£3.00
231 52pgs	$0.40	$1.20	$2.00	£0.40	£1.20	£2.00
232 ND 52pgs	$0.40	$1.20	$2.00	£0.50	£1.50	£2.50
233-234 52pgs	$0.40	$1.20	$2.00	£0.40	£1.20	£2.00
235 scarce in the U.K. 52pgs, (Jan 1978)	$0.40	$1.20	$2.00	£0.50	£1.50	£2.50
236-238 52pgs	$0.40	$1.20	$2.00	£0.30	£0.90	£1.50
239 52pgs, Jim Starlin script/layouts	$0.40	$1.20	$2.00	£0.35	£1.05	£1.75
240 scarce in the U.K. 52pgs, Chaykin art	$0.40	$1.20	$2.00	£0.35	£1.05	£1.75
241-242 52pgs	$0.40	$1.20	$2.00	£0.25	£0.75	£1.25
243-245 ND 44pgs	$0.40	$1.20	$2.00	£0.30	£0.90	£1.50
246	$0.30	$0.90	$1.50	£0.20	£0.60	£1.00
247 (Jan 1979)	$0.30	$0.90	$1.50	£0.20	£0.60	£1.00
248-249	$0.30	$0.90	$1.50	£0.20	£0.60	£1.00
250-251 Jim Starlin layouts	$0.40	$1.20	$2.00	£0.25	£0.75	£1.25
252	$0.30	$0.90	$1.50	£0.20	£0.60	£1.00
253 1st appearance Blok	$0.30	$0.90	$1.50	£0.20	£0.60	£1.00
254 LD in the U.K.	$0.30	$0.90	$1.50	£0.25	£0.75	£1.25
255-258	$0.30	$0.90	$1.50	£0.20	£0.60	£1.00
259 (Jan 1980), title becomes The Legion of Super-Heroes, Superboy leaves the Legion	$0.40	$1.20	$2.00	£0.25	£0.75	£1.25
260-264	$0.40	$1.20	$2.00	£0.25	£0.75	£1.25
265 68pgs, Jim Starlin art on free insert	$0.50	$1.50	$2.50	£0.30	£0.90	£1.50
266	$0.30	$0.90	$1.50	£0.20	£0.60	£1.00
267 LD in the U.K.	$0.30	$0.90	$1.50	£0.25	£0.75	£1.25
268-270	$0.30	$0.90	$1.50	£0.20	£0.60	£1.00
271 (Jan 1981)	$0.30	$0.90	$1.50	£0.20	£0.60	£1.00
272 48pgs, Dial H for Hero insert	$0.40	$1.20	$2.00	£0.25	£0.75	£1.25
273-279	$0.30	$0.90	$1.50	£0.20	£0.60	£1.00
280 Superboy re-joins the Legion	$0.30	$0.90	$1.50	£0.20	£0.60	£1.00
281-282	$0.30	$0.90	$1.50	£0.20	£0.60	£1.00
283 (Jan 1982)	$0.30	$0.90	$1.50	£0.20	£0.60	£1.00
284	$0.30	$0.90	$1.50	£0.20	£0.60	£1.00
285-287 Giffen art	$0.40	$1.20	$2.00	£0.40	£1.20	£2.00
288-289	$0.40	$1.20	$2.00	£0.25	£0.75	£1.25
290 The Great Darkness Saga begins; Darkseid appears	$0.40	$1.20	$2.00	£0.25	£0.75	£1.25
291-293	$0.40	$1.20	$2.00	£0.25	£0.75	£1.25
294 LD in the U.K. 48pgs, Giffen art	$0.50	$1.50	$2.50	£0.50	£1.50	£2.50
295 (Jan 1983)	$0.30	$0.90	$1.50	£0.20	£0.60	£1.00
296-297	$0.30	$0.90	$1.50	£0.20	£0.60	£1.00
298 free 16pg insert Amethyst, Princess of Gemworld (1st appearance)	$0.30	$0.90	$1.50	£0.20	£0.60	£1.00

	$Good	$Fine	$N.Mint	£Good	£Fine	£N.Mint
299	$0.30	$0.90	$1.50	£0.20	£0.60	£1.00
300 64pgs, anniversary issue, features work by many Legion artists	$0.40	$1.20	$2.00	£0.30	£0.90	£1.50
301-303	$0.30	$0.90	$1.50	£0.20	£0.60	£1.00
304 Karate Kid and Princess Projectra resign from Legion	$0.30	$0.90	$1.50	£0.20	£0.60	£1.00
305-306	$0.30	$0.90	$1.50	£0.20	£0.60	£1.00
307 (Jan 1984)	$0.30	$0.90	$1.50	£0.20	£0.60	£1.00
308-313	$0.30	$0.90	$1.50	£0.20	£0.60	£1.00
314 title becomes Tales of the Legion	$0.25	$0.75	$1.25	£0.15	£0.45	£0.75
315-318	$0.25	$0.75	$1.25	£0.15	£0.45	£0.75
319 (Jan 1985)	$0.25	$0.75	$1.25	£0.15	£0.45	£0.75
320-324	$0.25	$0.75	$1.25	£0.15	£0.45	£0.75
325 LD in the U.K.	$0.25	$0.75	$1.25	£0.20	£0.60	£1.00
326 reprints from Baxter (2nd) series begin (ends #354)	$0.25	$0.75	$1.25	£0.15	£0.45	£0.75
327-330	$0.25	$0.75	$1.25	£0.15	£0.45	£0.75
331 (Jan 1986)	$0.25	$0.75	$1.25	£0.15	£0.45	£0.75
332-336	$0.25	$0.75	$1.25	£0.15	£0.45	£0.75
337-338 LD in the U.K.		$0.75	$1.25	£0.20	£0.60	£1.00
339	$0.25	$0.75	$1.25	£0.15	£0.45	£0.75
340 LD in the U.K.	$0.25	$0.75	$1.25	£0.20	£0.60	£1.00
341-342	$0.25	$0.75	$1.25	£0.15	£0.45	£0.75
343 LD in the U.K. (Jan 1987)		$0.75	$1.25	£0.20	£0.60	£1.00
344-354	$0.25	$0.75	$1.25	£0.15	£0.45	£0.75
Title Value:	$3665.80	$11039.25	$27877.75	£2448.85	£7327.30	£18626.75
The Great Darkness Saga (Nov 1989) Trade paperback reprints #290-294, Annual #2, Darkseid appears; also with fold-out poster which is a reprint of the original Keith Giffen one				£2.40	£7.20	£12.00

ARTISTS
Ditko art in 257, 267, 268, 272, 274, 276, 281 Nasser art in 222, 225, 226, 230, 233, 236. Wood inks in 153-155, 157-161.

FEATURES
Legion of Super-Heroes 147, 172, 173, 176, 183, 184, 188, 190, 191, 193, 195, 197-354. Superboy in 1-128, 130-137, 139-146, 148-155, 157-164, 166- 173, 175-184, 186-197.

REPRINT FEATURES
Dial H for Hero in 184, 186, 187. Legion in 177, 178, 181, 185. Star Spangled Kid, Teen Titans, Kid Eternity, Little Boy Blue in 185. Superboy in 129, 138, 156, 165, 174, 179, 182, 183, 185. Superboy/Legion in 147, 202 205, 208. Superman in 147.

SUPERBOY (2ND SERIES)
DC Comics, TV; 1 Feb 1990-22 Feb 1992

	$Good	$Fine	$N.Mint	£Good	£Fine	£N.Mint
1 photocover of Gerard Christopher, 1st TV series Superboy	$0.25	$0.75	$1.25	£0.15	£0.45	£0.75
2-12	$0.25	$0.75	$1.25	£0.15	£0.45	£0.75
13 Mr. Mxyzptlk appears	$0.25	$0.75	$1.25	£0.15	£0.45	£0.75
14-21	$0.25	$0.75	$1.25	£0.15	£0.45	£0.75
22 Metallo appears	$0.25	$0.75	$1.25	£0.15	£0.45	£0.75
Title Value:	$5.50	$16.50	$27.50	£3.30	£9.90	£16.50

Note: continuity takes place outside DC Comics universe.

SUPERBOY (3RD SERIES)
DC Comics; 0 Oct 1994; 1 Feb 1994-present

	$Good	$Fine	$N.Mint	£Good	£Fine	£N.Mint
0 (Oct 1994) Zero Hour X-over, origin retold	$0.30	$0.90	$1.50	£0.20	£0.60	£1.00
1 new series set in Hawaii by Karl Kesel, Tom Grummett and Doug Hazelwood	$0.30	$0.90	$1.50	£0.20	£0.60	£1.00
2-5	$0.30	$0.90	$1.50	£0.20	£0.60	£1.00
6 Worlds Collide X-over, continued in Icon #15	$0.30	$0.90	$1.50	£0.20	£0.60	£1.00
7 Worlds Collide X-over, continued in Hardware #18	$0.30	$0.90	$1.50	£0.20	£0.60	£1.00
8 Zero Hour X-over	$0.30	$0.90	$1.50	£0.20	£0.60	£1.00
9-15	$0.30	$0.90	$1.50	£0.20	£0.60	£1.00
16 Loose Cannon guest-stars; upgraded coated paper (Miraweb Format) begins	$0.40	$1.20	$2.00	£0.25	£0.75	£1.25
17-20	$0.40	$1.20	$2.00	£0.25	£0.75	£1.25
21 Future Tense part 1; the new Superboy meets The Legion of Super-Heroes and the original Superboy for the 1st time	$0.40	$1.20	$2.00	£0.25	£0.75	£1.25
22 Underworld Unleashed tie-in	$0.40	$1.20	$2.00	£0.25	£0.75	£1.25
23-24	$0.40	$1.20	$2.00	£0.25	£0.75	£1.25
25 48pgs, origin Knockout	$0.60	$1.80	$3.00	£0.40	£1.20	£2.00
Title Value:	$9.00	$27.00	$45.00	£5.85	£17.55	£29.25

SUPERBOY (3RD SERIES) ANNUAL
DC Comics; 1 1994-present

	$Good	$Fine	$N.Mint	£Good	£Fine	£N.Mint
1 64pgs, squarebound, Elseworlds story continued from Adventures of Superman Annual #6	$0.60	$1.80	$3.00	£0.40	£1.20	£2.00
2 56pgs, Year One, Superboy learns who he was cloned from	$0.80	$2.40	$4.00	£0.50	£1.50	£2.50
Title Value:	$1.40	$4.20	$7.00	£0.90	£2.70	£4.50

SUPERBOY ANNUAL
National Periodical Publications; 1 Summer 1964

	$Good	$Fine	$N.Mint	£Good	£Fine	£N.Mint
1 80pgs, reprints including part origin Krypto from Adventure Comics #259	$15.00	$45.00	$135.00	£10.00	£30.00	£90.00
Title Value:	$15.00	$45.00	$135.00	£10.00	£30.00	£90.00

SUPERBOY SPECIAL
DC Comics, OS; 1 Jun 1992

	$Good	$Fine	$N.Mint	£Good	£Fine	£N.Mint
1 ties up plot lines from Superboy (2nd Series)	$0.25	$0.75	$1.25	£0.15	£0.45	£0.75
Title Value:	$0.25	$0.75	$1.25	£0.15	£0.45	£0.75

SUPERBOY SPECTACULAR
DC Comics; 1 1980

	$Good	$Fine	$N.Mint	£Good	£Fine	£N.Mint
1 ND 68pgs, new 8pg story with six Silver Age reprints	$0.40	$1.20	$2.00	£0.40	£1.20	£2.00
Title Value:	$0.40	$1.20	$2.00	£0.40	£1.20	£2.00

Note: All reprint apart from one new story. This comic was only distributed via specialist comic shops and related outlets - it was not put on general news-stand sale. This was the first direct-sales only comic by either DC or Marvel.

SUPERBOY, THE NEW ADVENTURES OF
DC Comics; 1 Jan 1980-54 Jun 1984

	$Good	$Fine	$N.Mint	£Good	£Fine	£N.Mint
1-6	$0.15	$0.45	$0.75	£0.10	£0.35	£0.60
7 68pgs, Jim Starlin art on insert	$0.15	$0.45	$0.75	£0.10	£0.35	£0.60
8-14	$0.15	$0.45	$0.75	£0.10	£0.35	£0.60
15 intro Superboy's new parents	$0.15	$0.45	$0.75	£0.10	£0.35	£0.60
16-27	$0.15	$0.45	$0.75	£0.10	£0.35	£0.60
28 Dial H for Hero begins (ends 49)	$0.15	$0.45	$0.75	£0.10	£0.35	£0.60
29-44	$0.15	$0.45	$0.75	£0.10	£0.35	£0.60
45 1st appearance Sunburst	$0.15	$0.45	$0.75	£0.10	£0.35	£0.60
46-49	$0.15	$0.45	$0.75	£0.10	£0.35	£0.60
50 52pgs, Giffen art, Legion co-stars	$0.20	$0.60	$1.00	£0.15	£0.45	£0.75
51-54	$0.15	$0.45	$0.75	£0.10	£0.35	£0.60

Superboy #70

Superboy (3rd) #0

Supercops #1

	$Good	$Fine	$N.Mint	£Good	£Fine	£N.Mint
Title Value:	$8.15	$24.45	$40.75	£5.45	£19.00	£32.55

FEATURES
Dial H for Hero in 28-49. Krypto in 10, 17, 22. Misadventures of Superbaby in 11, 14, 19, 24. Superboy's Secret Diary 9, 12, 18, 23.

SUPERCAR
Gold Key; 1 Nov 1962-4 Aug 1963

	$Good	$Fine	$N.Mint	£Good	£Fine	£N.Mint
1 rare though distributed in the U.K.						
	$26.00	$77.50	$210.00	£17.50	£52.50	£140.00
2-3 rare though distributed in the U.K.						
	$13.00	$39.00	$105.00	£9.25	£28.00	£75.00
4 very rare though distributed in the U.K.						
	$18.00	$52.50	$145.00	£11.50	£36.00	£95.00
Title Value:	$70.00	$208.00	$565.00	£47.50	£144.50	£385.00

SUPERCOPS
Now Comics; 1 Sep 1990-4 Dec 1990

	$Good	$Fine	$N.Mint	£Good	£Fine	£N.Mint
1 ND 48pgs, Chuck Dixon script, Peter Grau art; Dave Dorman painted cover	$0.30	$1.20	$2.00	£0.25	£0.75	£1.25
1 2nd printing ND	$0.30	$0.90	$1.50	£0.20	£0.60	£1.00
2-4 ND	$0.40	$1.20	$2.00	£0.25	£0.75	£1.25
Title Value:	$1.90	$5.70	$9.50	£1.20	£3.60	£6.00

SUPERGIRL
DC Comics; 1 Nov 1972-9 Dec/Jan 1973/74; 10 Sep 1974
(see Action, Adventure, Best of DC, Brave and the Bold, Crisis, DC Comics Presents, Super DC Giant, Superman Family, Secret Origins of Super-Heroes, Super-Team Family)

	$Good	$Fine	$N.Mint	£Good	£Fine	£N.Mint
1 Zatanna back-up begins	$1.00	$3.00	$5.00	£0.60	£1.80	£3.00
2-3	$0.80	$2.40	$4.00	£0.40	£1.20	£2.00
4 last Zatanna back-up	$0.80	$2.40	$4.00	£0.40	£1.20	£2.00
5	$0.80	$2.40	$4.00	£0.40	£1.20	£2.00
6	$0.60	$1.80	$3.00	£0.30	£0.90	£1.50
7 Zatanna guest-stars	$0.60	$1.80	$3.00	£0.30	£0.90	£1.50
8 Batman, Hawkman and Green Lantern appear	$0.60	$1.80	$3.00	£0.30	£0.90	£1.50
9	$0.60	$1.80	$3.00	£0.30	£0.90	£1.50
10 Prez appears	$0.60	$1.80	$3.00	£0.30	£0.90	£1.50
Title Value:	$7.20	$21.60	$36.00	£3.70	£11.10	£18.50

Note: Hawkman Zatanna reprint in 5. Melba in 6.

SUPERGIRL (2ND SERIES)
DC Comics; 1 Nov 1982-23 Sep 1984
(titled Daring New Adventures of Supergirl #1-13)

	$Good	$Fine	$N.Mint	£Good	£Fine	£N.Mint
1 origin retold	$0.50	$1.50	$2.50	£0.30	£0.90	£1.50
2-12	$0.40	$1.20	$2.00	£0.20	£0.60	£1.00
13 new costume	$0.40	$1.20	$2.00	£0.20	£0.60	£1.00
14-15	$0.40	$1.20	$2.00	£0.20	£0.60	£1.00
16 Ambush Bug X-over	$0.40	$1.20	$2.00	£0.20	£0.60	£1.00
17-19	$0.40	$1.20	$2.00	£0.20	£0.60	£1.00
20 New Titans appear	$0.40	$1.20	$2.00	£0.20	£0.60	£1.00
21-23	$0.40	$1.20	$2.00	£0.20	£0.60	£1.00
Title Value:	$9.30	$27.90	$46.50	£4.70	£14.10	£23.50

SUPERGIRL (3RD SERIES)
DC Comics,MS; 1 Feb 1994-4 May 1994;
1 June Brigman pencils, Jackson Guice inks begin; The Matrix Supergirl orgin retold

	$Good	$Fine	$N.Mint	£Good	£Fine	£N.Mint
1	$0.30	$0.90	$1.50	£0.20	£0.60	£1.00
2-3	$0.30	$0.90	$1.50	£0.20	£0.60	£1.00
4 Superman appoars	$0.30	$0.90	$1.50	£0.20	£0.60	£1.00
Title Value:	$1.20	$3.60	$6.00	£0.80	£2.40	£4.00

SUPERGIRL MOVIE SPECIAL
DC Comics,OS; 1 1985

	$Good	$Fine	$N.Mint	£Good	£Fine	£N.Mint
1 Gray Morrow art, adaptation of film starring Helen Slater	$0.30	$0.90	$1.50	£0.20	£0.60	£1.00
Title Value:	$0.30	$0.90	$1.50	£0.20	£0.60	£1.00

SUPERGIRL/TEAM LUTHOR SPECIAL
DC Comics,OS; 1 Apr 1993

	$Good	$Fine	$N.Mint	£Good	£Fine	£N.Mint
1 64pgs	$0.50	$1.50	$2.50	£0.30	£0.90	£1.50
Title Value:	$0.50	$1.50	$2.50	£0.30	£0.90	£1.50

SUPERHEROES VS SUPERVILLAINS
Archie; 1 1966

	$Good	$Fine	$N.Mint	£Good	£Fine	£N.Mint
1 giant, all reprint; distributed in the U.K.	$6.25	$19.00	$45.00	£4.25	£12.50	£30.00
Title Value:	$6.25	$19.00	$45.00	£4.25	£12.50	£30.00

SUPERHUMAN SAMURAI CYBER SQUAD
Hamilton Comics; 0 Oct 1995

	$Good	$Fine	$N.Mint	£Good	£Fine	£N.Mint
0 ND Jack C. Harris script, Joe Staton art	$0.60	$1.80	$3.00	£0.40	£1.20	£2.00
Title Value:	$0.60	$1.80	$3.00	£0.40	£1.20	£2.00

SUPERMAN (1ST SERIES) (ADVENTURES OF SUPERMAN)
National Periodical Publications/DC Comics; 0 Oct 1994; 1 Summer 1939-423 Sep 1986; 424 Jan 1987-499 Feb 1993; 500 Jun 1993-present
(see Action Comics, All-New Collector's Edition, Best of DC, DC Comics Presents, Eighty Page Giant Magazine, Famous First Edition, Limited Collector's Edition, One Hundred Page Super Spectacular,Super-Heroes Battle Super-Gorillas, Super Powers, Superman Family, Super Team Family, World's Finest Comics) (becomes Adventures of Superman with #424)

	$Good	$Fine	$N.Mint	£Good	£Fine	£N.Mint
0 (Oct 1994) Zero Hour X-over, origin retold; concluded in Action Comics #0	$0.40	$1.20	$2.00	£0.25	£0.75	£1.25
1 stories from Action Comics #1-4 reprinted with 4 new preceding pages, new 2 page origin of Superman; around 200 extant copies in any condition	$9700.00	$29200.00	$97500.00	£6500.00	£19500.00	£65000.00

	$Good	$Fine	$N.Mint	£Good	£Fine	£N.Mint
	[Prices may vary widely on this comic]					
2	$1125.00	$3350.00	$9000.00	£750.00	£2250.00	£6000.00
3	$750.00	$2250.00	$6000.00	£500.00	£1500.00	£4000.00
4 (Spring 1940), 2nd appearance Lex Luthor (suddenly bald! see Action Comics #23 for 1st appearance), 1st Luthor on cover (see Action Comics #47)						
	$640.00	$1925.00	$4500.00	£425.00	£1275.00	£3000.00
5	$375.00	$1125.00	$3000.00	£250.00	£750.00	£2000.00
6	$280.00	$840.00	$2250.00	£185.00	£560.00	£1500.00
7 1st war cover	$280.00	$840.00	$2250.00	£185.00	£560.00	£1500.00
8 (Jan/Feb 1941)	$235.00	$710.00	$1900.00	£160.00	£485.00	£1300.00
9	$235.00	$710.00	$1900.00	£160.00	£485.00	£1300.00
10 Lex Luthor appears	$235.00	$710.00	$1900.00	£160.00	£485.00	£1300.00
11-12	$185.00	$550.00	$1300.00	£125.00	£375.00	£875.00
13 early appearance Jimmy Olsen (as office boy - see Action Comics #6)						
	$185.00	$550.00	$1300.00	£125.00	£375.00	£875.00
14 (Jan/Feb 1942), classic patriotic cover: Superman and American Eagle; cover concept re-used on issue #424						
	$375.00	$1125.00	$3000.00	£250.00	£750.00	£2000.00
	[Scarce in high grade - Very Fine+ or better]					
15	$185.00	$550.00	$1300.00	£125.00	£375.00	£875.00
16	$155.00	$470.00	$1100.00	£110.00	£330.00	£775.00
17 Emperor Hirohito and Adolf Hitler on cover; Superman loses powers for the 1st time as he battles Luthor and the Powerstone (see Action Comics #47)						
	$155.00	$470.00	$1100.00	£110.00	£330.00	£775.00
18 patriotic cover: "Do The Job On The Japanazis!"						
	$155.00	$470.00	$1100.00	£110.00	£330.00	£775.00
19	$155.00	$470.00	$1100.00	£110.00	£330.00	£775.00
20 (Jan/Feb 1943)	$155.00	$470.00	$1100.00	£110.00	£330.00	£775.00
21-23	$125.00	$375.00	$875.00	£80.00	£245.00	£575.00
24 classic patriotic flag cover	$180.00	$540.00	$1250.00	£120.00	£365.00	£850.00
25	$125.00	$375.00	$875.00	£80.00	£245.00	£575.00
26 (Jan/Feb 1944)	$110.00	$340.00	$800.00	£75.00	£225.00	£525.00
27	$110.00	$340.00	$800.00	£75.00	£225.00	£525.00
28	$115.00	$345.00	$805.00	£77.50	£235.00	£550.00
28 scarce in the U.K. Armed Forces edition						
29	$120.00	$360.00	$850.00	£80.00	£245.00	£575.00
	$110.00	$340.00	$800.00	£75.00	£225.00	£525.00
30 1st appearance Mr. Mxyztplk (the "t" and the "p" became reversed in spelling in the Silver Age)						
	$155.00	$465.00	$1250.00	£100.00	£305.00	£825.00
31	$100.00	$300.00	$700.00	£65.00	£195.00	£465.00
32 (Jan/Feb 1945)	$100.00	$300.00	$700.00	£65.00	£195.00	£465.00
33 3rd appearance Mr. Mxyztplk	$110.00	$330.00	$770.00	£72.50	£220.00	£515.00
34-36	$100.00	$300.00	$700.00	£65.00	£195.00	£465.00
37 Prankster cover and story	$100.00	$300.00	$700.00	£65.00	£195.00	£465.00
38 (Jan/Feb 1946), contraversial Atom Bomb story						
	$100.00	$300.00	$700.00	£65.00	£195.00	£465.00
39	$100.00	$300.00	$700.00	£65.00	£195.00	£465.00
40 Mr. Mxyztplk cover and story	$100.00	$300.00	$700.00	£65.00	£195.00	£465.00
41-43	$75.00	$225.00	$525.00	£50.00	£150.00	£350.00
44 (Jan/Feb 1947), Toyman cover and story	$75.00	$225.00	$625.00	£50.00	£150.00	£350.00
45 Lois Lane as Superwoman (see Action Comics #60 for 1st appearance of this plus Action #156 and Superman #123)						
	$80.00	$240.00	$560.00	£52.50	£160.00	£380.00
46-49	$75.00	$225.00	$525.00	£50.00	£150.00	£350.00
50 (Jan/Feb 1948)	$75.00	$225.00	$525.00	£50.00	£150.00	£350.00
51-52	$60.00	$180.00	$425.00	£40.00	£120.00	£280.00
53 10th anniversay issue, origin Superman retold in new detail	$215.00	$640.00	$1720.00	£140.00	£430.00	£1150.00
54-55	$60.00	$180.00	$425.00	£40.00	£120.00	£280.00
56 (Jan/Feb 1949)	$60.00	$180.00	$425.00	£40.00	£120.00	£280.00
57 Lois Lane as Superwoman (see Action Comics #60, Superman #45)	$62.50	$190.00	$450.00	£44.00	£130.00	£310.00
58-60	$60.00	$180.00	$425.00	£40.00	£120.00	£280.00
61 1st appearance Green Kryptonite, Superman 1st learns he's from Krypton	$145.00	$430.00	$1000.00	£100.00	£300.00	£700.00
	[Scarce in high grade - Very Fine+ or better]					
62 (Jan/Feb 1950), Orsen Welles on cover, his famous Martian Invasion broadcast featured	$62.50	$190.00	$450.00	£44.00	£130.00	£310.00
63-64	$60.00	$180.00	$425.00	£40.00	£120.00	£280.00
65 1st foes to come from Krypton (see Action Comics #194)	$62.50	$190.00	$450.00	£44.00	£130.00	£310.00
66	$60.00	$180.00	$425.00	£40.00	£120.00	£280.00
67 singer Perry Como appears	$60.00	$180.00	$425.00	£40.00	£120.00	£280.00
68 (Jan/Feb 1951), Lex Luthor cover and story	$60.00	$180.00	$425.00	£40.00	£120.00	£280.00
69 Prankster cover and story	$60.00	$180.00	$425.00	£40.00	£120.00	£280.00
70-72	$60.00	$180.00	$425.00	£40.00	£120.00	£280.00
72 rare in both U.S. and U.K. giveaway issue with cover banner and price blacked out						

# / Description	$Good	$Fine	$N.Mint	£Good	£Fine	£N.Mint
	$75.00	$225.00	$525.00	£50.00	£150.00	£350.00
73	$60.00	$180.00	$425.00	£40.00	£120.00	£280.00
74 (Jan/Feb 1952), Lex Luthor cover and story						
	$60.00	$180.00	$425.00	£40.00	£120.00	£280.00
75 unknown percentage have number 74 on cover						
	$60.00	$180.00	$425.00	£40.00	£120.00	£280.00
76 1st Superman Batman team-up story, Batman on cover						
	$170.00	$510.00	$1200.00	£110.00	£340.00	£800.00
77-78	$55.00	$165.00	$385.00	£37.00	£110.00	£260.00
79 Lex Luthor cover and story						
	$55.00	$165.00	$385.00	£37.00	£110.00	£260.00
80 (Jan/Feb 1953)	$55.00	$165.00	$385.00	£37.00	£110.00	£260.00
81	$50.00	$150.00	$350.00	£32.00	£95.00	£225.00
82 Mr. Mxyztplk appears						
	$50.00	$150.00	$350.00	£32.00	£95.00	£225.00
83-84	$50.00	$150.00	$350.00	£32.00	£95.00	£225.00
85 Lex Luthor story						
	$50.00	$150.00	$350.00	£32.00	£95.00	£225.00
86 (Jan 1954)	$50.00	$150.00	$350.00	£32.00	£95.00	£225.00
87	$50.00	$150.00	$350.00	£32.00	£95.00	£225.00
88 Lex Luthor, Prankster, Toyman cover and story						
	$50.00	$150.00	$360.00	£33.00	£97.50	£230.00
89-90	$50.00	$150.00	$350.00	£32.00	£95.00	£225.00
91-93	$43.00	$125.00	$300.00	£29.00	£85.00	£200.00
94 (Jan 1955)	$43.00	$125.00	$300.00	£29.00	£85.00	£200.00
95	$43.00	$125.00	$300.00	£29.00	£85.00	£200.00
96 Mr. Mxyztplk cover and story						
	$43.00	$125.00	$300.00	£29.00	£85.00	£200.00
97-99	$43.00	$125.00	$300.00	£29.00	£85.00	£200.00
100 scarce in the U.K. cover has reproductions of issues #1, #25, #50, #75 (see Batman #100)						
	$185.00	$560.00	$1500.00	£125.00	£375.00	£1000.00
101 scarce in the U.K.						
	$32.00	$95.00	$225.00	£21.00	£62.50	£150.00
102 scarce in the U.K. (Jan 1956)						
	$32.00	$95.00	$225.00	£21.00	£62.50	£150.00
103-105 scarce in the U.K.						
	$32.00	$95.00	$225.00	£21.00	£62.50	£150.00
106 scarce in the U.K. Lex Luthor cover and story						
	$32.00	$95.00	$225.00	£21.00	£62.50	£150.00
107-109	$32.00	$95.00	$225.00	£20.00	£60.00	£140.00
110 (Jan 1957)	$32.00	$95.00	$225.00	£20.00	£60.00	£140.00
111-112	$28.00	$82.50	$195.00	£18.50	£55.00	£130.00
113 1st full length 3-part story						
	$28.00	$82.50	$195.00	£18.50	£55.00	£130.00
114-117	$28.00	$82.50	$195.00	£18.50	£55.00	£130.00
118 (Jan 1958)	$28.00	$82.50	$195.00	£18.50	£55.00	£130.00
119-120	$28.00	$82.50	$195.00	£18.50	£55.00	£130.00
121-122	$24.00	$72.50	$170.00	£16.00	£49.00	£115.00
123 Supergirl try-out (blonde on cover, brunette inside - see Action Comics #156), 3 part story						
	$25.00	$75.00	$175.00	£17.00	£50.00	£120.00
124-125	$24.00	$72.50	$170.00	£16.00	£49.00	£115.00
126 (Jan 1959)	$24.00	$72.50	$170.00	£16.00	£49.00	£115.00
127 1st appearance Lori Lemaris, 1st appearance Titano the Super-Ape						
	$25.00	$75.00	$175.00	£17.00	£50.00	£120.00
128-130	$24.00	$72.50	$170.00	£16.00	£49.00	£115.00
131	$21.00	$62.50	$150.00	£14.00	£43.00	£100.00
1st official distribution in the U.K.						
132 Batman and Robin cameo						
	$19.00	$57.50	$135.00	£12.50	£39.00	£90.00
133	$19.00	$57.50	$135.00	£12.50	£39.00	£90.00
134 (Jan 1960)	$19.00	$57.50	$135.00	£12.50	£39.00	£90.00
135-137	$19.00	$57.50	$135.00	£12.50	£39.00	£90.00
138 Aquaman appears						
	$19.00	$57.50	$135.00	£12.50	£39.00	£90.00
139	$19.00	$57.50	$135.00	£12.50	£39.00	£90.00
140 1st appearance Blue Kryptonite, 1st appearance Bizarro Supergirl, 1st appearance Bizarro Junior						
	$21.00	$62.50	$150.00	£14.00	£43.00	£100.00
141 classic story: Superman's Return to Krypton						
	$15.50	$47.00	$110.00	£10.50	£32.00	£75.00
142 (Jan 1961), Batman appears (1st time since issue #76)						
	$15.50	$47.00	$110.00	£10.50	£32.00	£75.00
143-145	$15.50	$47.00	$110.00	£10.50	£32.00	£75.00
146 scarce in the U.K. Superman's life story						
	$18.50	$55.00	$130.00	£12.00	£36.00	£85.00
147 7th appearance of Legion of Super-Heroes, 1st Legion of Super Villains, Adult Legion appear; Krypto vs. Titano						
	$18.50	$55.00	$130.00	£12.00	£36.00	£85.00
148	$15.50	$47.00	$110.00	£10.50	£32.00	£75.00
149 10th Legion, classic Death of Superman story, last 10 cents issue; answers to Great Superman Boo Boo Contest!						
	$15.50	$47.00	$110.00	£10.50	£32.00	£75.00
150 (Jan 1962), Superman, Supergirl and Krypto origins briefly retold, Bizarros and Brainiac cameo appearances; creation of artificial Krypton						
	$8.50	$26.00	$60.00	£5.50	£17.00	£40.00
151	$8.50	$26.00	$60.00	£5.50	£17.00	£40.00
152 16th Legion appearance						
	$9.25	$28.00	$65.00	£6.25	£19.00	£45.00
153-154	$8.50	$26.00	$60.00	£5.50	£17.00	£40.00
155 20th Legion appearance						
	$8.50	$26.00	$60.00	£6.25	£19.00	£45.00
156 Legion appears						
	$8.50	$26.00	$60.00	£5.50	£17.00	£40.00
157 Mon-El, Lightning Lad cameo						
	$8.50	$26.00	$60.00	£5.50	£17.00	£40.00
158 (Jan 1963), 1st appearance Flamebird and Nightwing (Jimmy Olsen and Superman as crime-fighters in Kandor)						
	$8.50	$26.00	$60.00	£5.50	£17.00	£40.00
159-160	$8.50	$26.00	$60.00	£5.50	£17.00	£40.00
161 Ma & Pa Kent death 1st told						
	$6.25	$19.00	$45.00	£4.25	£12.50	£30.00
162 Legion appears						
	$7.00	$21.00	$50.00	£5.00	£15.00	£35.00
163-165	$6.25	$19.00	$45.00	£4.25	£12.50	£30.00
166 (Jan 1964)	$6.25	$19.00	$45.00	£4.25	£12.50	£30.00
167 Luthor and Brainiac team-up						
	$10.50	$32.00	$75.00	£7.00	£21.00	£50.00
168	$6.25	$19.00	$45.00	£4.25	£12.50	£30.00
169 Batman appears; The Great DC Contest (answers in #174)						
	$6.25	$19.00	$45.00	£4.25	£12.50	£30.00
170 President Kennedy story originally prepared for #168						
	$6.25	$19.00	$45.00	£4.25	£12.50	£30.00
171	$6.00	$18.00	$42.50	£3.90	£11.50	£27.50
172 Luthor and Brainiac team-up, Legion cameo						
	$6.00	$18.00	$42.50	£3.90	£11.50	£27.50
173 Luthor and Brainiac team-up, Legion cameo and Batman cameo (with wierd chest emblem and eyes seen through mask!); Tales of Green Kryptonite begin (also #176,#177,#179)						
	$6.00	$18.00	$42.50	£3.90	£11.50	£27.50
174 (Jan 1965), Bizarro appears and Batman cameo (with another weird chest emblem!)						
	$6.00	$18.00	$42.50	£3.90	£11.50	£27.50
175	$6.00	$18.00	$42.50	£3.90	£11.50	£27.50
176 Green Kryptonite deadly to humans (1st and only appearance)						
	$6.00	$18.00	$42.50	£3.90	£11.50	£27.50
177-180	$6.00	$18.00	$42.50	£3.90	£11.50	£27.50
181 1st appearance Superman 2965; last Silver Age issue, indicia-dated November 1965						
	$5.75	$17.50	$35.00	£3.75	£11.00	£22.50
182 (Jan 1966)	$5.75	$17.50	$35.00	£3.75	£11.00	£22.50
183 80pgs, Giant G-18, rare Golden Age reprints inc. Superman #30 (1st Golden Age Mr. Mxyztplk)						
	$6.25	$18.50	$37.50	£4.15	£12.50	£25.00
184 Fortress of Solitude feature at centre-spread (often missing!)						
	$5.75	$17.50	$35.00	£3.75	£11.00	£22.50
185	$5.75	$17.50	$35.00	£3.75	£11.00	£22.50
186 Batman cameo						
	$5.75	$17.50	$35.00	£3.75	£11.00	£22.50
187 80pgs, Giant G-23						
	$6.25	$18.50	$37.50	£4.15	£12.50	£25.00
188	$5.75	$17.50	$35.00	£3.75	£11.00	£22.50
189 Batman cameo, Supergirl origin briefly retold						
	$5.75	$17.50	$35.00	£3.75	£11.00	£22.50
190	$5.75	$17.50	$35.00	£3.75	£11.00	£22.50
191	$5.00	$15.00	$30.00	£3.30	£10.00	£20.00
192 (Jan 1967), Justice League of America appear						
	$5.00	$15.00	$30.00	£3.30	£10.00	£20.00
193 80pgs, Giant G-31, reprints #149						
	$5.75	$17.50	$35.00	£4.15	£12.50	£25.00
194-195	$5.00	$15.00	$30.00	£3.30	£10.00	£20.00
196 classic The Thing From 40,000AD (reprint of #87), Superman vs. Superman cover						
	$5.00	$15.00	$30.00	£3.30	£10.00	£20.00
197 80pgs, Giant G-36						
	$5.75	$17.50	$35.00	£4.15	£12.50	£25.00
198	$5.00	$15.00	$30.00	£3.30	£10.00	£20.00
199 1st Superman/Flash race (see Flash #175, World's Finest #198/199; see also Adv. of Superman #463 for updated version of the race)						
	$24.00	$72.50	$195.00	£12.50	£38.00	£100.00
[Scarce in high grade - Very Fine+ or better]						
200 Krypton history						
	$5.00	$15.00	$30.00	£3.30	£10.00	£20.00
201	$4.15	$12.50	$25.00	£2.50	£7.50	£15.00
202 scarce in the U.K. 80pgs, Giant G-42, all Bizarro reprints						
	$5.00	$15.00	$30.00	£3.30	£10.00	£20.00
203 (Jan 1968)	$4.15	$12.50	$25.00	£2.50	£7.50	£15.00
204 Neal Adams cover art, 1st appearance Q-Energy, lethal to Superman						
	$4.15	$12.50	$25.00	£2.50	£7.50	£15.00
205 Neal Adams cover art, more facts about the destruction of Krypton						
	$4.15	$12.50	$25.00	£2.50	£7.50	£15.00
206 Neal Adams cover						
	$4.15	$12.50	$25.00	£2.50	£7.50	£15.00
207 80pgs, Giant G-48, 30th anniversary with classic reprints						
	$5.00	$15.00	$30.00	£3.30	£10.00	£20.00
208 Neal Adams cover						
	$4.15	$12.50	$25.00	£2.50	£7.50	£15.00
209-210	$4.15	$12.50	$25.00	£2.50	£7.50	£15.00
211	$4.15	$12.50	$25.00	£2.05	£6.25	£12.50
212 80pgs, Giant G-54						
	$4.55	$13.50	$27.50	£2.50	£7.50	£15.00
213 (Jan 1969)	$4.15	$12.50	$25.00	£2.05	£6.25	£12.50
214-215 Neal Adams cover						
	$4.15	$12.50	$25.00	£2.05	£6.25	£12.50
216	$4.15	$12.50	$25.00	£2.05	£6.25	£12.50
217 80pgs, Giant G-60, reprints #123						
	$4.55	$13.50	$27.50	£2.50	£7.50	£15.00
218-220	$4.15	$12.50	$25.00	£2.05	£6.25	£12.50
221	$2.50	$7.50	$15.00	£1.65	£5.00	£10.00
222 80pgs, Giant G-66						

	$Good	$Fine	$N.Mint	£Good	£Fine	£N.Mint
	$3.30	$10.00	$20.00	£2.05	£6.25	£12.50
223 (Jan 1970)	$2.50	$7.50	$15.00	£1.65	£5.00	£10.00
224	$2.50	$7.50	$15.00	£1.65	£5.00	£10.00
225 2pgs text: The Superman Legend						
	$2.50	$7.50	$15.00	£1.65	£5.00	£10.00
226	$2.50	$7.50	$15.00	£1.65	£5.00	£10.00
227 80pgs, Giant G-72, all kryptonite issue						
	$3.30	$10.00	$20.00	£2.05	£6.25	£12.50
228-230	$2.50	$7.50	$15.00	£1.65	£5.00	£10.00
231	$2.05	$6.25	$12.50	£1.25	£3.75	£7.50
232 scarce in the U.K. 80pgs, Giant G-78, reprints #141						
	$2.50	$7.50	$15.00	£1.65	£5.00	£10.00
233 (Jan 1971), 1st new look: Clark Kent becomes TV reporter, "Kryptonite No More" - all kryptonite turned to lead; 1st appearance Sand Creature Superman						
	$2.05	$6.25	$12.50	£1.25	£3.75	£7.50
234 Neal Adams cover						
	$2.05	$6.25	$12.50	£1.25	£3.75	£7.50
235-236	$2.05	$6.25	$12.50	£1.25	£3.75	£7.50
237 Neal Adams cover						
	$2.05	$6.25	$12.50	£1.25	£3.75	£7.50
238 Gray Morrow art						
	$2.05	$6.25	$12.50	£1.25	£3.75	£7.50
239 scarce in the U.K. 80pgs, Giant G-84, reprints #127 (1st Titano)						
	$2.50	$7.50	$15.00	£1.65	£5.00	£10.00
240 Kaluta art	$1.25	$3.75	$7.50	£0.80	£2.50	£5.00
241 52pgs	$1.50	$4.50	$7.50	£1.00	£3.00	£5.00
242 52pgs, Neal Adams cover						
	$1.50	$4.50	$7.50	£1.00	£3.00	£5.00
243-244 52pgs	$1.50	$4.50	$7.50	£1.00	£3.00	£5.00
245 scarce in the U.K. DC 100pg Super Spectacular #7						
	$1.80	$5.25	$9.00	£1.20	£3.60	£6.00
246 52pgs	$1.50	$4.50	$7.50	£1.00	£3.00	£5.00
247 52pgs, (Jan 1972)	$1.50	$4.50	$7.50	£1.00	£3.00	£5.00
248 52pgs, Cockrum art						
	$1.50	$4.50	$7.50	£1.00	£3.00	£5.00
249 52pgs, Neal Adams inks, origin and 1st appearance Terra-Man						
	$1.80	$5.25	$9.00	£1.20	£3.60	£6.00
250 52pgs	$1.50	$4.50	$7.50	£1.00	£3.00	£5.00
251 52pgs	$1.20	$3.60	$6.00	£0.80	£2.40	£4.00
252 scarce in the U.S, very scarce in the U.K. 100pgs, DC-100pg Super Spectacular #13; reprints Superman #17 and Action Comics #47						
	$1.80	$5.25	$9.00	£1.70	£5.10	£8.50
253 52pgs	$1.20	$3.60	$6.00	£0.80	£2.40	£4.00
254 scarce in the U.K. Neal Adams art						
	$1.50	$4.50	$7.50	£1.00	£3.00	£5.00
255-259	$0.60	$1.80	$3.00	£0.40	£1.20	£2.00
260 (Jan 1973)	$0.60	$1.80	$3.00	£0.40	£1.20	£2.00
261-262	$0.60	$1.80	$3.00	£0.40	£1.20	£2.00
263 photo cover	$0.60	$1.80	$3.00	£0.40	£1.20	£2.00
264 1st appearance Steve Lombard, Cockrum art						
	$0.60	$1.80	$3.00	£0.40	£1.20	£2.00
265-267	$0.60	$1.80	$3.00	£0.40	£1.20	£2.00
268 Batgirl co-stars						
	$0.60	$1.80	$3.00	£0.40	£1.20	£2.00
269-270	$0.60	$1.80	$3.00	£0.40	£1.20	£2.00
271 (Jan 1974)	$0.55	$1.65	$2.75	£0.35	£1.05	£1.75
272 100pgs	$1.00	$3.00	$5.00	£0.70	£2.10	£3.50
273-277	$0.55	$1.65	$2.75	£0.35	£1.05	£1.75
278 100pgs	$1.00	$3.00	$5.00	£0.70	£2.10	£3.50
279-282	$0.50	$1.50	$2.50	£0.30	£0.90	£1.50
283 (Jan 1975)	$0.50	$1.50	$2.50	£0.30	£0.90	£1.50
284 100pgs	$1.00	$3.00	$5.00	£0.70	£2.10	£3.50
285-289	$0.50	$1.50	$2.50	£0.30	£0.90	£1.50
290-293 scarce in the U.K.						
	$0.50	$1.50	$2.50	£0.40	£1.20	£2.00
294	$0.50	$1.50	$2.50	£0.30	£0.90	£1.50
295 (Jan 1976)	$0.50	$1.50	$2.50	£0.30	£0.90	£1.50
296-299	$0.50	$1.50	$2.50	£0.30	£0.90	£1.50
300 origin Superman 2001						
	$0.90	$2.70	$4.50	£0.60	£1.80	£3.00
301-304 scarce in the U.K.						
	$0.50	$1.50	$2.50	£0.35	£1.05	£1.75
305 scarce in the U.K. Bizarro appears						
	$0.50	$1.50	$2.50	£0.35	£1.05	£1.75
306 scarce in the U.K.						
	$0.50	$1.50	$2.50	£0.35	£1.05	£1.75
307 scarce in the U.K. (Jan 1977)						
	$0.50	$1.50	$2.50	£0.35	£1.05	£1.75
308-312 scarce in the U.K.						
	$0.50	$1.50	$2.50	£0.35	£1.05	£1.75
313-314 scarce in the U.K. Neal Adams covers						
	$0.50	$1.50	$2.50	£0.35	£1.05	£1.75
315-316 scarce in the U.K.						
	$0.50	$1.50	$2.50	£0.35	£1.05	£1.75
317 scarce in the U.K. Neal Adams cover						
	$0.50	$1.50	$2.50	£0.35	£1.05	£1.75
318 scarce in the U.K.						
	$0.50	$1.50	$2.50	£0.35	£1.05	£1.75
319 scarce in the U.K. (Jan 1978)						
	$0.50	$1.50	$2.50	£0.35	£1.05	£1.75

	$Good	$Fine	$N.Mint	£Good	£Fine	£N.Mint
320 scarce in the U.K.						
	$0.50	$1.50	$2.50	£0.35	£1.05	£1.75
321-326	$0.50	$1.50	$2.50	£0.30	£0.90	£1.50
327-329 ND 44pgs	$0.50	$1.50	$2.50	£0.35	£1.05	£1.75
330	$0.50	$1.50	$2.50	£0.30	£0.90	£1.50
331 (Jan 1979)	$0.40	$1.20	$2.00	£0.25	£0.75	£1.25
332	$0.40	$1.20	$2.00	£0.25	£0.75	£1.25
333 Bizarro appears						
	$0.40	$1.20	$2.00	£0.25	£0.75	£1.25
334-337	$0.40	$1.20	$2.00	£0.25	£0.75	£1.25
338 40th anniversary issue						
	$0.40	$1.20	$2.00	£0.25	£0.75	£1.25
339-342	$0.40	$1.20	$2.00	£0.25	£0.75	£1.25
343 (Jan 1980)	$0.40	$1.20	$2.00	£0.25	£0.75	£1.25
344-353	$0.40	$1.20	$2.00	£0.25	£0.75	£1.25
354 1st appearance Superman 2020						
	$0.40	$1.20	$2.00	£0.25	£0.75	£1.25
355 (Jan 1981)	$0.40	$1.20	$2.00	£0.25	£0.75	£1.25
356-363	$0.40	$1.20	$2.00	£0.25	£0.75	£1.25
364 George Perez cover						
	$0.40	$1.20	$2.00	£0.25	£0.75	£1.25
365-366	$0.40	$1.20	$2.00	£0.25	£0.75	£1.25
367 (Jan 1982)	$0.40	$1.20	$2.00	£0.25	£0.75	£1.25
368-375	$0.40	$1.20	$2.00	£0.25	£0.75	£1.25
376 X-over Supergirl (2nd Series) #1						
	$0.30	$0.90	$1.50	£0.20	£0.60	£1.00
377 Masters of the Universe insert						
	$0.30	$0.90	$1.50	£0.20	£0.60	£1.00
378	$0.30	$0.90	$1.50	£0.20	£0.60	£1.00
379 (Jan 1983), Bizarro appears						
	$0.30	$0.90	$1.50	£0.20	£0.60	£1.00
380 X-over Superboy (2nd Series) #38						
	$0.40	$1.20	$2.00	£0.25	£0.75	£1.25
381-386	$0.30	$0.90	$1.50	£0.20	£0.60	£1.00
387 X-over Action Comics #547						
	$0.30	$0.90	$1.50	£0.20	£0.60	£1.00
388-390	$0.30	$0.90	$1.50	£0.20	£0.60	£1.00
391 (Jan 1984)	$0.30	$0.90	$1.50	£0.20	£0.60	£1.00
392-399	$0.30	$0.90	$1.50	£0.20	£0.60	£1.00
400 scarce in the U.K. 68pgs, top artists' tributes inc. 10pgs of new Steranko art, 1pg John Byrne art						
	$1.20	$3.60	$6.00	£0.80	£2.40	£4.00
401-402	$0.30	$0.90	$1.50	£0.20	£0.60	£1.00
403 (Jan 1985)	$0.30	$0.90	$1.50	£0.20	£0.60	£1.00
404-410	$0.30	$0.90	$1.50	£0.20	£0.60	£1.00
411 tribute to Julius Schwartz issue						
	$0.30	$0.90	$1.50	£0.20	£0.60	£1.00
412	$0.30	$0.90	$1.50	£0.20	£0.60	£1.00
413 unofficial Crisis X-over						
	$0.30	$0.90	$1.50	£0.20	£0.60	£1.00
414 Crisis X-overs						
	$0.30	$0.90	$1.50	£0.20	£0.60	£1.00
415 (Jan 1986), Crisis X-overs						
	$0.30	$0.90	$1.50	£0.20	£0.60	£1.00
416-422	$0.30	$0.90	$1.50	£0.20	£0.60	£1.00
423 George Perez and Curt Swan art, Alan Moore story, ties in with Action #583 last pre-John Byrne Superman						
	$1.20	$3.60	$6.00	£0.60	£1.80	£3.00
424 LD in the U.K. (Jan 1987), title becomes The Adventures of Superman, patriotic cover based on issue #14						
	$0.45	$1.35	$2.25	£0.30	£0.90	£1.50
425	$0.25	$0.75	$1.25	£0.15	£0.45	£0.75
426 Legends X-over						
	$0.25	$0.75	$1.25	£0.15	£0.45	£0.75
427-435	$0.25	$0.75	$1.25	£0.15	£0.45	£0.75
436 (Jan 1988), Millennium X-over						
	$0.25	$0.75	$1.25	£0.15	£0.45	£0.75
437-440 John Byrne scripts						
	$0.25	$0.75	$1.25	£0.15	£0.45	£0.75
441 John Byrne script and art						
	$0.25	$0.75	$1.25	£0.15	£0.45	£0.75
442 John Byrne script and cover art						
	$0.25	$0.75	$1.25	£0.15	£0.45	£0.75
443-448	$0.25	$0.75	$1.25	£0.15	£0.45	£0.75
449 (Jan 1989), Invasion X-over, Captain Atom, Guardians, Newsboy Legion appear						
	$0.25	$0.75	$1.25	£0.15	£0.45	£0.75
450-461	$0.25	$0.75	$1.25	£0.15	£0.45	£0.75
462 (Jan 1990), George Perez art						
	$0.25	$0.75	$1.25	£0.15	£0.45	£0.75
463 4th Superman/Flash race (see Superman #199, Flash #175, World's Finest Comics #198/199)						
	$0.50	$1.50	$2.50	£0.20	£0.60	£1.00
464 X-over with Superman #41, Lobo appears						
	$0.50	$1.50	$2.50	£0.20	£0.60	£1.00
465 Art Thilbert inks; X-over with Superman #42, Action Comics #652						
	$0.25	$0.75	$1.25	£0.15	£0.45	£0.75
466 "Fantastic Four" type story; 1st appearance Hank Henshaw later The Cyborg Superman						
	$0.50	$1.50	$2.50	£0.30	£0.90	£1.50
467 Dark Knight Over Metropolis, Batman appears, continued in Action Comics #654, bi-weekly						
	$0.25	$0.75	$1.25	£0.15	£0.45	£0.75
468 Art Thilbert co-artist, 8pg insert re-telling origin						
	$0.25	$0.75	$1.25	£0.15	£0.45	£0.75
469 Art Thibert co-artist						
	$0.25	$0.75	$1.25	£0.15	£0.45	£0.75
470 Art Thibert co-artist, continued from Superman #47						
	$0.25	$0.75	$1.25	£0.15	£0.45	£0.75

VERY GENERAL PERCENTAGE CONVERSION CHART WHICH MAY BE USED TO CALCULATE LOW AND INBETWEEN GRADES:

	$Good	$Fine	$N.Mint	£Good	£Fine	£N.Mint
471 The Sinbad Contract part 2, continued in Action Comics #658						
	$0.25	$0.75	$1.25	£0.15	£0.45	£0.75
472 Krisis of the Krimson Kryptonite part 2, continued in Action Comics #659						
	$0.25	$0.75	$1.25	£0.15	£0.45	£0.75
473 Art Thilbert inks, Green Lantern(s) guest-star						
	$0.25	$0.75	$1.25	£0.15	£0.45	£0.75
474 (Jan 1991), Art Thilbert inks						
	$0.25	$0.75	$1.25	£0.15	£0.45	£0.75
475	$0.25	$0.75	$1.25	£0.15	£0.45	£0.75
476 Time and Time Again part 1, Booster Gold appears, continued in Action Comics #663						
	$0.25	$0.75	$1.25	£0.15	£0.45	£0.75
477 Time and Time Again part 4, guest-stars "middle period" Legion of Super-Heroes						
	$0.25	$0.75	$1.25	£0.15	£0.45	£0.75
478 Time and Time Again part 7 (conclusion)						
	$0.25	$0.75	$1.25	£0.15	£0.45	£0.75
479 The Red Glass trilogy part 2						
	$0.25	$0.75	$1.25	£0.15	£0.45	£0.75
480-481	$0.25	$0.75	$1.25	£0.15	£0.45	£0.75
482 The Parasite appears, cover based on Action Comics #360						
	$0.25	$0.75	$1.25	£0.15	£0.45	£0.75
483 The Parasite appears						
	$0.25	$0.75	$1.25	£0.15	£0.45	£0.75
484 Blackout part 1, continues in Action Comics #671						
	$0.25	$0.75	$1.25	£0.15	£0.45	£0.75
485 Blackout part 5 (conclusion)						
	$0.25	$0.75	$1.25	£0.15	£0.45	£0.75
486 (Jan 1992)	$0.25	$0.75	$1.25	£0.15	£0.45	£0.75
487	$0.25	$0.75	$1.25	£0.15	£0.45	£0.75
488 Panic in the Sky part 3, continued in Action Comics #675						
	$0.25	$0.75	$1.25	£0.15	£0.45	£0.75
489 Panic in the Sky epilogue, continued in Action Comics #676						
	$0.25	$0.75	$1.25	£0.15	£0.45	£0.75
490	$0.25	$0.75	$1.25	£0.15	£0.45	£0.75
491 Metallo returns						
	$0.25	$0.75	$1.25	£0.15	£0.45	£0.75
492 continued from Superman #69, Agent Liberty appears						
	$0.25	$0.75	$1.25	£0.15	£0.45	£0.75
493 The Blaze/Satanus War part 1, continued in Action Comics #680						
	$0.25	$0.75	$1.25	£0.15	£0.45	£0.75
494 The Blaze/Satanus War epilogue						
	$0.25	$0.75	$1.25	£0.15	£0.45	£0.75
495 Forever People appear						
	$0.25	$0.75	$1.25	£0.15	£0.45	£0.75
496 Doomsday cameo						
	$0.70	$2.10	$3.50	£0.30	£0.90	£1.50
497 Superman: Doomsday part 3						
	$1.00	$3.00	$5.00	£0.40	£1.20	£2.00
498 (Jan 1993), Funeral for a Friend part 1, continued in Action Comics #685						
	$0.60	$1.80	$3.00	£0.30	£0.90	£1.50
498 2nd printing, (II in date/number box)						
	$0.25	$0.75	$1.25	£0.15	£0.45	£0.75
498 3rd printing	$0.25	$0.75	$1.25	£0.15	£0.45	£0.75
499 Funeral for a Friend part 5, continued in Action Comics #686						
	$0.60	$1.80	$3.00	£0.15	£0.45	£0.75
500 64pgs, squarebound, the return of Superman (though in four variations), 1st appearance of the new Superboy; bi-weekly						
	$0.30	$0.90	$1.50	£0.20	£0.60	£1.00
500 ND 64pgs, squarebound, translucent cover panel, extra 8pg section; pre-bagged in white plastic; bi-weekly						
	$0.60	$1.80	$3.00	£0.40	£1.20	£2.00
500 ND Platinum Edition, pre-bagged in black with "S" emblem in platinum on front						
	$6.00	$18.00	$30.00	£5.00	£15.00	£25.00
501 Reign of the Supermen part 2, bi-weekly						
	$3.00	$9.00	$15.00	£1.50	£4.50	£7.50
501 ND Reign of the Supermen part 2, die-cut outer cover, bound-in mini-poster; bi-weekly						
	$0.45	$1.35	$2.25	£0.30	£0.90	£1.50
501 ND Dynamic Forces Edition, signed by Kesel and Grummett; 10,000 copies						
	$3.00	$9.00	$15.00	£2.00	£6.00	£10.00
502 Reign of the Supermen part 8, Supergirl appears						
	$0.30	$0.90	$1.50	£0.20	£0.60	£1.00
503 Reign of the Supermen part 12, continued in Action Comics #690						
	$0.30	$0.90	$1.50	£0.20	£0.60	£1.00
504 Reign of the Supermen part 16, continued in Action Comics #691						
	$0.30	$0.90	$1.50	£0.20	£0.60	£1.00
505 Superman returns! (ties in with Green Lantern #46 and Superman #82)						
	$0.30	$0.90	$1.50	£0.20	£0.60	£1.00
505 ND Collector's Edition - foil enhanced cover, continued in Action Comics #691						
	$0.45	$1.35	$2.25	£0.30	£0.90	£1.50
506	$0.30	$0.90	$1.50	£0.20	£0.60	£1.00
507 Barry Kitson pencils begin; story continued in Action Comics #494						
	$0.30	$0.90	$1.50	£0.20	£0.60	£1.00
508 (Jan 1994), Challengers of the Unknown appear						
	$0.30	$0.90	$1.50	£0.20	£0.60	£1.00
509 death of Auron						
	$0.30	$0.90	$1.50	£0.20	£0.60	£1.00
510 Bizarro appears, continued in Action Comics #697						
	$0.30	$0.90	$1.50	£0.20	£0.60	£1.00
511	$0.30	$0.90	$1.50	£0.20	£0.60	£1.00
512 Parasite appears						
	$0.30	$0.90	$1.50	£0.20	£0.60	£1.00
513 The Battle for Metropolis part 4 (conclusion)						
	$0.30	$0.90	$1.50	£0.20	£0.60	£1.00
514 concluded in Action Comics #701						
	$0.30	$0.90	$1.50	£0.20	£0.60	£1.00
515	$0.30	$0.90	$1.50	£0.20	£0.60	£1.00
516 Zero Hour X-over						
	$0.30	$0.90	$1.50	£0.20	£0.60	£1.00
517-518	$0.30	$0.90	$1.50	£0.20	£0.60	£1.00
519 (Jan 1995)	$0.30	$0.90	$1.50	£0.20	£0.60	£1.00
520-521	$0.30	$0.90	$1.50	£0.20	£0.60	£1.00
522 story continued from Steel #14						
	$0.30	$0.90	$1.50	£0.20	£0.60	£1.00
523 The Death of Clark Kent part 2, continued in Action Comics #710						
	$0.30	$0.90	$1.50	£0.20	£0.60	£1.00
524 The Death of Clark Kent part 6, continued in Action Comics #711; upgraded coated paper stock (Miraweb Format) begins						
	$0.40	$1.20	$2.00	£0.25	£0.75	£1.25
525-526	$0.40	$1.20	$2.00	£0.25	£0.75	£1.25
527 The Joker appears on the last page						
	$0.40	$1.20	$2.00	£0.25	£0.75	£1.25
528	$0.40	$1.20	$2.00	£0.25	£0.75	£1.25
529 The Trial of Superman, continued in Action Comics #716						
	$0.40	$1.20	$2.00	£0.25	£0.75	£1.25
530 The Trial of Superman, continued in Superman: The Man of Tomorrow #3; Underworld Unleashed tie-in						
	$0.40	$1.20	$2.00	£0.25	£0.75	£1.25
531 (Jan 1996), The Trial of Superman concluded from Superman #108						
	$0.40	$1.20	$2.00	£0.25	£0.75	£1.25
532 Lori Lemaris returns						
	$0.40	$1.20	$2.00	£0.25	£0.75	£1.25
533 Impulse guest-stars						
	$0.40	$1.20	$2.00	£0.25	£0.75	£1.25
Title Value:	$24004.00	$72104.20	$202102.75	£16118.20	£48147.80	£134851.75

Note: #207 is often found with printing ink smears on cover (see Batman #208, New Teen Titans #4).

Superman #5

Superman #30

Superman #146

MINT = 100% / NEAR MINT (inc. +/-) = 90–99% / VERY FINE (inc. +/-) = 75–89% / FINE (inc. +/-) = 55–74%
VERY GOOD (inc. +/-) = 35–54% / GOOD (inc. +/-) = 15–34% / FAIR = 5–14% / POOR = 1–4%

583

	$Good	$Fine	$N.Mint	£Good	£Fine	£N.Mint

FEATURES

Bruce (Superman) Wayne in 353, 358, 363. Mr & Mrs Superman in 327, 329. Private Life of Clark Kent in 247, 254, 356, 258, 260, 262, 267, 270, 273, 277, 280, 285, 287, 289, 292, 294, 328, 371, 373. Superman: The In-Between Years in 359, 362, 365, 366, 370, 374. Superman 2020/1 in 354, 355, 357, 361, 364, 368, 372. Terra-Man in 249. World of Krypton in 233, 234, 236, 238, 240, 243, 246, 248, 251, 255, 257, 263, 264, 266, 268, 271, 275, 279, 282, 352, 356, 360, 367.

REPRINT FEATURES

Bizarro World in 193, 202. Captain Comet in 244. Dr. Fate, Hawkman, Black Condor, Spectre in 252. Jimmy Olsen, Green Lantern in 272. Kid Eternity, Atom, Super-Chief, Air Wave, Hawkman in 245. Lois Lane in 207, 212. Starman The Ray in 252. Superboy 212, 222, 227, 232. Supergirl in 212. Superman in 183, 187, 193, 197, 207, 212, 222, 227, 229-232, 239, 241-253, 272, 278, 284.

SUPERMAN (1ST SERIES) ANNUAL

National Periodical Publications/DC Comics; 1 1960-8 Winter 1963/64; 9 Sep 1983-12 Aug 1986

1 rare in the U.K. 80pgs

	$77.50	$230.00	$700.00	£52.50	£155.00	£475.00

[Scarce in high grade - Very Fine+ or better]

2 80pgs, Villains issue, reprints Action #242 (1st Brainiac), origin Metallo (Action #252), origin Bizarro (Superboy #68), Titano (Superman #127)

	$44.00	$130.00	$350.00	£28.00	£82.50	£225.00

3 80pgs

	$30.00	$90.00	$240.00	£20.50	£60.00	£165.00

4 scarce in the U.K. 80pgs, 12th Legion of Super-Heroes (2pgs of portraits and powers - debateable as to being a full Legion story appearance)

	$30.00	$90.00	$240.00	£20.50	£60.00	£165.00

5 80pgs, Krypton issue

	$21.50	$65.00	$175.00	£13.50	£41.00	£110.00

6 80pgs, Monsters, reprints Adventure #247 (1st Legion), reprints Superman #123

	$18.50	$55.00	$150.00	£12.50	£38.00	£100.00

7 80pgs, Silver anniversary issue, Batman appears

	$15.00	$45.00	$120.00	£10.00	£30.00	£80.00

8 scarce in the U.K. 80pgs

	$13.50	$41.00	$110.00	£9.25	£28.00	£75.00

9 Toth and Austin art, Batman appears; Curt Swan self-appearance back-up story

	$1.00	$3.00	$5.00	£0.60	£1.80	£3.00

10

	$1.00	$3.00	$5.00	£0.40	£1.20	£2.00

11 Alan Moore script, Dave Gibbons art

	$1.00	$3.00	$5.00	£0.70	£2.10	£3.50

12 Bolland cover

	$1.00	$3.00	$5.00	£0.40	£1.20	£2.00

Title Value:	$254.00	$758.00	$2105.00	£168.85	£500.80	£1405.50

SUPERMAN (2ND SERIES)

DC Comics; 1 Jan 1987-77 Mar 1993; 78 Jun 1993-present

0 (Oct 1994) Zero Hour X-over, origin retold; continued in Adventures of Superman #0

	$0.40	$1.20	$2.00	£0.25	£0.75	£1.25

1 John Byrne art

	$0.40	$1.20	$2.00	£0.25	£0.75	£1.25

2-3 John Byrne art

	$0.30	$0.90	$1.50	£0.20	£0.60	£1.00

4 John Byrne art, 1st appearance Bloodsport

	$0.30	$0.90	$1.50	£0.20	£0.60	£1.00

5-7 John Byrne art

	$0.30	$0.90	$1.50	£0.20	£0.60	£1.00

8 John Byrne art, Legion of Super-Heroes appear

	$0.30	$0.90	$1.50	£0.20	£0.60	£1.00

9 John Byrne art, Joker appears

	$0.40	$1.20	$2.00	£0.25	£0.75	£1.25

10 John Byrne art

	$0.30	$0.90	$1.50	£0.20	£0.60	£1.00

11 John Byrne art, "Beyonder" appears (Ben DeRoy)

	$0.30	$0.90	$1.50	£0.20	£0.60	£1.00

12 John Byrne art

	$0.30	$0.90	$1.50	£0.20	£0.60	£1.00

13-14 John Byrne art, Millennium X-over

	$0.30	$0.90	$1.50	£0.20	£0.60	£1.00

15-17 John Byrne art

	$0.30	$0.90	$1.50	£0.20	£0.60	£1.00

18 Mike Mignola art, Hawkman appears

	$0.30	$0.90	$1.50	£0.20	£0.60	£1.00

19-21 John Byrne art

	$0.30	$0.90	$1.50	£0.20	£0.60	£1.00

22 John Byrne art, Superman kills! Condemns to death General Zod, Quex-Ul and Zaora

	$0.30	$0.90	$1.50	£0.20	£0.60	£1.00

23 Mike Mignola art, Batman X-over

	$0.30	$0.90	$1.50	£0.20	£0.60	£1.00

24-25

	$0.30	$0.90	$1.50	£0.20	£0.60	£1.00

26-27 Invasion X-over

	$0.30	$0.90	$1.50	£0.20	£0.60	£1.00

28-36

	$0.30	$0.90	$1.50	£0.20	£0.60	£1.00

37 Guardian and Newsboy Legion appear, cover based on Jack Kirby's Jimmy Olsen #133

	$0.30	$0.90	$1.50	£0.20	£0.60	£1.00

38

	$0.30	$0.90	$1.50	£0.20	£0.60	£1.00

39 free 16pg insert (see Batman #443, Starman #18)

	$0.30	$0.90	$1.50	£0.20	£0.60	£1.00

40

	$0.30	$0.90	$1.50	£0.20	£0.60	£1.00

41 LD in the U.K. X-over with Adventures of Superman #464, Lobo appears

	$0.30	$0.90	$1.50	£0.25	£0.75	£1.25

42 X-over Adventures of Superman #465/Action Comics #652

	$0.30	$0.90	$1.50	£0.20	£0.60	£1.00

43

	$0.30	$0.90	$1.50	£0.20	£0.60	£1.00

44 part 1 Dark Knight Over Metropolis, X-over Adventures of Superman #467/Action #654

	$0.30	$0.90	$1.50	£0.20	£0.60	£1.00

45 free 8pg insert

	$0.30	$0.90	$1.50	£0.20	£0.60	£1.00

46 Jade/Obsidian guest-star

	$0.30	$0.90	$1.50	£0.20	£0.60	£1.00

47 continues in Adventures of Superman #470

	$0.30	$0.90	$1.50	£0.20	£0.60	£1.00

48 continues in Adventures of Superman #471

	$0.30	$0.90	$1.50	£0.20	£0.60	£1.00

49 Krisis of the Krimson Kryptonite part 1continues in Adventures of Superman #472

	$0.30	$0.90	$1.50	£0.20	£0.60	£1.00

50 48pgs, Krisis of the Krimson Kryptonite part 4; Clark Kent proposes to Lois Lane; Byrne co-artist and inks

	$0.60	$1.80	$3.00	£0.40	£1.20	£2.00

50 2nd printing, (many copies were mis-cut), has "Historic Engagement Issue" on front cover

	$0.30	$0.90	$1.50	£0.20	£0.60	£1.00

51-52

	$0.30	$0.90	$1.50	£0.20	£0.60	£1.00

53 Superman reveals identity to Lois Lane

	$0.50	$1.50	$2.50	£0.30	£0.90	£1.50

53 2nd printing

	$0.25	$0.75	$1.25	£0.15	£0.45	£0.75

54 Time and Time Again part 3, Newsboy Legion back-up stories begin

	$0.30	$0.90	$1.50	£0.20	£0.60	£1.00

55 Time and Time Again part 6

	$0.30	$0.90	$1.50	£0.20	£0.60	£1.00

56 The Red Glass Trilogy part 1

	$0.30	$0.90	$1.50	£0.20	£0.60	£1.00

57 48pgs, Revenge of the Krypton Man part 2, continues in Adventures of Superman #480

	$0.30	$0.90	$1.50	£0.20	£0.60	£1.00

58-59

	$0.30	$0.90	$1.50	£0.20	£0.60	£1.00

60 continued from Man of Steel #4, intro Agent Liberty

	$0.30	$0.90	$1.50	£0.20	£0.60	£1.00

61 Armageddon: 2001 epilogue, Metal Men appear

	$0.30	$0.90	$1.50	£0.20	£0.60	£1.00

62 Blackout part 4, continues in Adventures of Superman #485

	$0.30	$0.90	$1.50	£0.20	£0.60	£1.00

63 Aquaman appears

	$0.30	$0.90	$1.50	£0.20	£0.60	£1.00

64 Christmas issue

	$0.30	$0.90	$1.50	£0.20	£0.60	£1.00

65 Panic in the Sky part 2, continues in Adventures of Superman #488

	$0.30	$0.90	$1.50	£0.20	£0.60	£1.00

66 Panic in the Sky part 6, continues in Adventures of Superman #489; Doomsday device launched

	$0.30	$0.90	$1.50	£0.20	£0.60	£1.00

67

	$0.30	$0.90	$1.50	£0.20	£0.60	£1.00

68 X-over with Deathstroke the Terminator #12/13

	$0.30	$0.90	$1.50	£0.20	£0.60	£1.00

69 Agent Liberty appears

	$0.30	$0.90	$1.50	£0.20	£0.60	£1.00

70 Robin appears, continues from Superman The Man of Steel #14

	$0.30	$0.90	$1.50	£0.20	£0.60	£1.00

71 The Blaze/Satanus War part 4 (conclusion), continued from Superman: The Man of Steel #15

	$0.30	$0.90	$1.50	£0.20	£0.60	£1.00

72 Crisis at Hand part 2, continued from Superman: The Man of Steel #16

	$0.30	$0.90	$1.50	£0.20	£0.60	£1.00

73 Doomsday cameo

	$0.60	$1.80	$3.00	£0.30	£0.90	£1.50

74 Superman: Doomsday part 2, continued in Adventures of Superman #497

	$0.80	$2.40	$4.00	£0.50	£1.50	£2.50

74 2nd printing

	$0.25	$0.75	$1.25	£0.15	£0.45	£0.75

75 Superman: Doomsday part 6 (conclusion), the death of Superman drawn in full splash pages with special fold-out last page, continued in Adventures of Superman #498

	$0.60	$1.80	$3.00	£0.40	£1.20	£2.00

75 2nd-4th printings

	$0.25	$0.75	$1.25	£0.15	£0.45	£0.75

75 ND Collector's Edition: pre-bagged in black with satin Superman arm-band, Daily Planet obituary page and commemorative Superman stamp

	$2.50	$7.50	$12.50	£1.50	£4.50	£7.50

75 as above but un-ooglod, contents complete

	$0.90	$2.70	$4.50	£0.60	£1.80	£3.00

75 ND Platinum Edition (Apr 1993) - 10,000 copies, pre-bagged in black with trading card

	$10.00	$30.00	$50.00	£7.00	£21.00	£35.00

76 Funeral for a Friend part 4, continued in Adventures of Superman #499

	$0.30	$0.90	$1.50	£0.20	£0.60	£1.00

77 Funeral for a Friend part 8 (conclusion)

	$0.30	$0.90	$1.50	£0.20	£0.60	£1.00

78 Reign of the Supermen part 3

	$0.30	$0.90	$1.50	£0.20	£0.60	£1.00

78 ND Reign of the Supermen part 3, die-cut outer cover, bound-in mini-poster

	$0.40	$1.20	$2.00	£0.25	£0.75	£1.25

78 ND Dynamic Forces Edition, signed by Jurgens and Breeding; 10,000 copies

	$2.50	$7.50	$12.50	£1.50	£4.50	£7.50

79 Reign of the Supermen part 7

	$0.30	$0.90	$1.50	£0.20	£0.60	£1.00

80 Reign of the Supermen part 11, continued in Adventures of Superman #503

	$0.30	$0.90	$1.50	£0.20	£0.60	£1.00

81 Reign of the Supermen part 15, continued in Adventures of Superman #504

	$0.30	$0.90	$1.50	£0.20	£0.60	£1.00

82 Reign of the Supermen part 20 - the one, true Superman revealed!

	$0.30	$0.90	$1.50	£0.20	£0.60	£1.00

82 ND Collector's Edition - chromium cover and no ads

	$0.60	$1.80	$3.00	£0.40	£1.20	£2.00

83 Justice League America appear

	$0.30	$0.90	$1.50	£0.20	£0.60	£1.00

84-85 The (new) Toyman appears

	$0.30	$0.90	$1.50	£0.20	£0.60	£1.00

86 Superman's powers increase including the ability to travel through space (again! In the good old days of the Silver Age, unlimited space and time travel was dead easy)

	$0.30	$0.90	$1.50	£0.20	£0.60	£1.00

87 Bizarro World part 1; Bizarro appears, continued in Superman (1st Series) #510

	$0.30	$0.90	$1.50	£0.20	£0.60	£1.00

88 Bizaro World part 5 (conclusion), Bizarro appears; continued from Superman: The Man of Steel #31

TRADE PAPERBACKS, GRAPHIC NOVELS AND OTHER COLLECTIONS ARE PRICED IN POUNDS STERLING ONLY. CONVERT AT 1.5 FOR DOLLARS.

	$Good	$Fine	$N.Mint	£Good	£Fine	£N.Mint
	$0.30	$0.90	$1.50	£0.20	£0.60	£1.00
89	$0.30	$0.90	$1.50	£0.20	£0.60	£1.00
90 The Battle for Metropolis part 3, continued in Superman (1st Series) #513	$0.30	$0.90	$1.50	£0.20	£0.60	£1.00
91 continued in Superman (1st series) #514	$0.30	$0.90	$1.50	£0.20	£0.60	£1.00
92 continued in Superman (1st series) #515	$0.30	$0.90	$1.50	£0.20	£0.60	£1.00
93 Zero Hour X-over	$0.30	$0.90	$1.50	£0.20	£0.60	£1.00
94-97	$0.30	$0.90	$1.50	£0.20	£0.60	£1.00
98 The Toyman appears	$0.30	$0.90	$1.50	£0.20	£0.60	£1.00
99 tie-in with Steel #15, Gil Kane guest art	$0.30	$0.90	$1.50	£0.20	£0.60	£1.00
100 64pgs, The Death of Clark Kent part 1, continued in Superman [2nd Series] #523; Standard Edition	$0.60	$1.80	$3.00	£0.40	£1.20	£2.00
100 64pgs, The Death of Clark Kent part 1, continued in Superman [2nd Series] #523; Collector's Edition with holographic foil-enhanced cover	$0.80	$2.40	$4.00	£0.50	£1.50	£2.50
101 The Death of Clark Kent part 5, continued in Superman [2nd Series] #524. Upgraded coated paper stock (Miraweb Format) begins	$0.40	$1.20	$2.00	£0.25	£0.75	£1.25
102 Captain Marvel guest-stars	$0.40	$1.20	$2.00	£0.25	£0.75	£1.25
103-104	$0.40	$1.20	$2.00	£0.25	£0.75	£1.25
105 Green Lantern guest-stars; Superman's origin retold in part	$0.40	$1.20	$2.00	£0.25	£0.75	£1.25
106 The Trial of Superman, continued in Superman [1st Series] #529; Ron Frenz art begins	$0.40	$1.20	$2.00	£0.25	£0.75	£1.25
107	$0.40	$1.20	$2.00	£0.25	£0.75	£1.25
108 The Trial of Superman, concluded in Superman [1st series] #531	$0.40	$1.20	$2.00	£0.25	£0.75	£1.25
109	$0.40	$1.20	$2.00	£0.25	£0.75	£1.25
110 Plastic Man guest-stars	$0.40	$1.20	$2.00	£0.25	£0.75	£1.25
Title Value:	$55.25	$165.75	$276.25	£36.40	£109.20	£182.00

Multi-Pack (1990)

Three issues from #19-#21 or #20-#22 pre-bagged with illustrated header card, ND £0.30 £0.90 £1.50

Superman: The Death of Superman (1993)

Trade paperback reprints Superman: The Man of Steel #17-19, Superman #73-75, Adventures of Superman #496-497, Action Comics #683-684 £0.65 £1.95 £3.25

Signed, Numbered Edition (1993)

Trade paperback, as above though signed by Dan Jurgens, Brett Breeding and Jon Bogdanove; limited to 5,000 copies £3.00 £9.00 £15.00

Platinum Edition (Jun 1993) - available to Retailers only who responded to a questionnaire from DC. Same content as Trade paperback but with platinum strip on cover, scarce in the U.K. £3.00 £9.00 £15.00

Superman: Panic in the Sky (May 1993)

Trade paperback 192pgs, reprints Action Comics #674/675, Superman: The Man of Steel #9/10, Superman #65/66, Adventures of Superman #488/489 £1.30 £3.90 £6.50

World Without a Superman

Trade paperback (Jul 1993) reprints Funeral For A Friend storyline from Adventures of Superman #498-500, Action Comics #685,686, Superman: The Man of Steel #20,21, Superman #76,77 £1.00 £3.00 £5.00

Superman: The Return of Superman (Mar 1994)

Trade paperback 480pgs, reprints The Reign of the Supermen storyline from the four Superman titles £2.00 £6.00 £10.00

Superman: Time & Time Again (Sep 1994)

Trade paperback reprints Action #663-665, Adventures of Superman #476-478 and Superman #54,55,61 and #63 £1.00 £3.00 £5.00

Superman: Eradication! The Origin of the Eradicator (Jan 1996)

Trade paperback reprints Adventures of Superman #460, 464,465, Superman #41,42 and Action Comics #651 £1.70 £5.10 £8.50

SUPERMAN (2ND SERIES) ANNUAL
DC Comics; 1 Aug 1987-2 1988; 3 Jun 1991-present

	$Good	$Fine	$N.Mint	£Good	£Fine	£N.Mint
1 48pgs, (no John Byrne art)	$0.40	$1.20	$2.00	£0.25	£0.75	£1.25
2 48pgs, John Byrne back-up	$0.40	$1.20	$2.00	£0.25	£0.75	£1.25
3 64pgs, Armageddon: 2001 tie-in, Batman appears	$0.40	$1.20	$2.00	£0.25	£0.75	£1.25
3 2nd printing	$0.40	$1.20	$2.00	£0.25	£0.75	£1.25
3 3rd printing	$0.40	$1.20	$2.00	£0.25	£0.75	£1.25
4 64pgs, Eclipso: The Darkness Within tie-in, Joe Quesada cover	$0.50	$1.50	$2.50	£0.30	£0.90	£1.50
5 64pgs, Bloodlines part 6, 1st appearance Myriad, continued in Green Lantern Annual #2	$0.50	$1.50	$2.50	£0.30	£0.90	£1.50
6 64pgs, Elseworlds story, Mike Mignola cover	$0.60	$1.80	$3.00	£0.40	£1.20	£2.00
7 64pgs, Year One, Superman's first encounter with magic	$0.80	$2.40	$4.00	£0.50	£1.50	£2.50
Title Value:	$4.40	$13.20	$22.00	£2.75	£8.25	£13.75

SUPERMAN AND HIS INCREDIBLE FORTRESS OF SOLITUDE
DC Comics,Tabloid; (DC Special Series 26); nn Summer 1981

	$Good	$Fine	$N.Mint	£Good	£Fine	£N.Mint
nn ND 64pgs, all new stories featuring Supergirl and Green Lantern cameo appearances	$1.00	$3.00	$5.00	£0.70	£2.10	£3.50
	$1.00	$3.00	$5.00	£0.70	£2.10	£3.50

SUPERMAN AND SPIDERMAN
Marvel Comics Group/DC Comics,Tabloid; nn (Marvel Treasury Edition #28) 1981

	$Good	$Fine	$N.Mint	£Good	£Fine	£N.Mint
nn ND 68pgs, Parasite and Dr. Doom appear (not to be confused with Superman vs. The Amazing Spiderman)	$2.50	$7.50	$15.00	£1.65	£5.00	£10.00
Title Value:	$2.50	$7.50	$15.00	£1.65	£5.00	£10.00

Note: A British has also been published, which is worth around 50%

SUPERMAN ANNUAL, THE ADVENTURES OF
DC Comics; 1 Sep 1987; 2 Aug 1990-present

	$Good	$Fine	$N.Mint	£Good	£Fine	£N.Mint
1 48pgs, Jim Starlin script	$0.40	$1.20	$2.00	£0.25	£0.75	£1.25
2 48pgs, Legion '90 appear	$0.40	$1.20	$2.00	£0.25	£0.75	£1.25
3 64pgs, Armageddon: 2001 tie-in	$0.40	$1.20	$2.00	£0.25	£0.75	£1.25
4 64pgs, Eclipso: The Darkness Within tie-in, Lobo and Guy Gardner appear	$0.50	$1.50	$2.50	£0.30	£0.90	£1.50
5 64pgs, Bloodlines (Wave Two) part 16, 1st appearance Sparx; continued in Hawkman Annual #1	$0.50	$1.50	$2.50	£0.30	£0.90	£1.50
6 64pgs, Elseworlds, continued in Superboy Annual #1	$0.60	$1.80	$3.00	£0.40	£1.20	£2.00
7 64pgs, Year One, Superman and Maggie Sawyer first meet	$0.80	$2.40	$4.00	£0.50	£1.50	£2.50
Title Value:	$3.60	$10.80	$18.00	£2.25	£6.75	£11.25

SUPERMAN ARCHIVES
DC Comics; 1 Dec 1989; 2 Nov 1990; 3 Nov 1991; 4 Jun 1994

	$Good	$Fine	$N.Mint	£Good	£Fine	£N.Mint
1 ND reprints Superman #1-#4 by Siegel and Shuster plus covers and ads. Intro by Jim Steranko. Hardcover.	$7.50	$22.50	$37.50	£5.00	£15.00	£25.00
1 2nd printing, ND (Dec 1991)	$7.50	$22.50	$37.50	£5.00	£15.00	£25.00
2 ND reprints Superman #5-#8 by Siegel and Shuster plus covers and ads. Intro by Ron Goulart. Hardcover	$7.50	$22.50	$37.50	£5.00	£15.00	£25.00
2 2nd printing, ND (Dec 1990)	$7.50	$22.50	$37.50	£5.00	£15.00	£25.00
3 ND reprints Superman #9-#12 by Siegel and Shuster plus covers and ads. Intro by Golden Age artist Jack Burnley	$7.50	$22.50	$37.50	£5.00	£15.00	£25.00
4 ND reprints Superman #13-#16 by Siegel and Shuster plus covers and ads. Intro by Golden Age artist Jack Burnley	$7.50	$22.50	$37.50	£5.00	£15.00	£25.00
Title Value:	$45.00	$135.00	$225.00	£30.00	£90.00	£150.00

SUPERMAN BOOK AND RECORD SET
Power Records; PR-28, PR-33 1974

	$Good	$Fine	$N.Mint	£Good	£Fine	£N.Mint
28,33 scarce in the U.K. 20pg booklet with 45 rpm record	$1.65	$5.00	$10.00	£1.25	£3.75	£7.50
Title Value:	$3.30	$10.00	$20.00	£2.50	£7.50	£15.00

Note: item would be valued at 50% less without record.

SUPERMAN FAMILY
DC Comics; 164 Apr May 1974-222 Sep 1982
(previously Jimmy Olsen)

	$Good	$Fine	$N.Mint	£Good	£Fine	£N.Mint
164 100pgs	$0.80	$2.40	$4.00	£0.50	£1.50	£2.50
165-169 100pgs	$0.70	$2.10	$3.50	£0.45	£1.35	£2.25
170 68pgs	$0.60	$1.80	$3.00	£0.40	£1.20	£2.00
171 68pgs, Batgirl and Justice League of America appear	$0.60	$1.80	$3.00	£0.40	£1.20	£2.00
172-173 scarce in the U.K. 68pgs	$0.60	$1.80	$3.00	£0.50	£1.50	£2.50
174-175 68pgs	$0.60	$1.80	$3.00	£0.40	£1.20	£2.00
176 ND 68pgs	$0.60	$1.80	$3.00	£0.60	£1.80	£3.00
177-179 scarce in the U.K. 52pgs	$0.60	$1.80	$3.00	£0.50	£1.50	£2.50
180-181 52pgs	$0.60	$1.80	$3.00	£0.35	£1.05	£1.75
182 ND 80pgs, Rogers art	$0.60	$1.80	$3.00	£0.70	£2.10	£3.50
183 80pgs	$0.50	$1.50	$2.50	£0.35	£1.05	£1.75
184 ND scarce in the U.K. 80pgs	$0.50	$1.50	$2.50	£0.50	£1.50	£2.50
185-187 ND 80pgs	$0.50	$1.50	$2.50	£0.40	£1.20	£2.00
188 ND 80pgs, Nightwing and Flamebird appear	$0.50	$1.50	$2.50	£0.40	£1.20	£2.00
189-190 ND 80pgs	$0.50	$1.50	$2.50	£0.40	£1.20	£2.00
191-193 scarce in the U.K. 68pgs	$0.50	$1.50	$2.50	£0.35	£1.05	£1.75
194 ND 68pgs, Rogers art	$0.60	$1.80	$3.00	£0.60	£1.80	£3.00
195-204 ND 68pgs	$0.50	$1.50	$2.50	£0.35	£1.05	£1.75
205-210 ND 52pgs	$0.50	$1.50	$2.50	£0.30	£0.90	£1.50
211 52pgs, Earth 2 Batman and Catwoman marry (see Adventure Comics #462)	$0.50	$1.50	$2.50	£0.30	£0.90	£1.50
212-222 52pgs	$0.40	$1.20	$2.00	£0.25	£0.75	£1.25
Title Value:	$31.20	$93.60	$155.50	£22.30	£66.90	£111.50

FEATURES

Clark Kent in 195-197, 199-222. Jimmy Olsen in 164, 167, 170, 173, 176, 179 182-222. Krypto in 182-192. Lois Lane in 166, 169, 172, 175, 178, 181-222. Mr. and Mrs. Superman in 195, 196, 198-222. Nightwing & Flamebird in 183-194. Perry White in 183. Superbaby in 182, 216. Superboy in 191-198.

	$Good	$Fine	$N.Mint	£Good	£Fine	£N.Mint

Super-girl in 165, 168, 171, 177, 180, 182-199, 200 (Superwoman), 210-222. Superman in 184-193. World of Krypton in 182.

REPRINT FEATURES

Bizarro World in 166, 169. Jimmy Olsen in 164-169, 171, 172, 174, 175, 177, 178, 180, 181. Lois Lane in 164, 165, 167, 168, 170, 171, 173, 174, 176, 177, 179, 180. Superbaby in 165-167. Superboy in 164-170, 173, 176. Supergirl in 164, 166, 167, 169, 170, 172, 173, 175, 176, 178, 179. Superman in 165, 168, 174, 175.

SUPERMAN GALLERY, THE

DC Comics,OS; 1 Apr 1993

1 ND pin-ups by Frank Miller, Todd McFarlane, Steve Rude, George Perez, Jerry Ordway, John Byrne, Mike Zeck and others

	$Good	$Fine	$N.Mint	£Good	£Fine	£N.Mint
	$0.50	$1.50	$2.50	£0.30	£0.90	£1.50
Title Value:	$0.50	$1.50	$2.50	£0.30	£0.90	£1.50

SUPERMAN II THE ADVENTURE CONTINUES

DC Comics,Tabloid; nn Summer 1981

(DC Special Series #25)

nn ND 64pgs, mainly film stills and interviews with the stars

	$1.00	$3.00	$5.00	£0.70	£2.10	£3.50
Title Value:	$1.00	$3.00	$5.00	£0.70	£2.10	£3.50

SUPERMAN III MOVIE SPECIAL

DC Comics,OS; 1 Sep 1983

1 48pgs, adapts film

	$0.40	$1.20	$2.00	£0.25	£0.75	£1.25
Title Value:	$0.40	$1.20	$2.00	£0.25	£0.75	£1.25

SUPERMAN IV MOVIE SPECIAL

DC Comics,OS; nn Oct 1987

nn 64pgs

	$0.40	$1.20	$2.00	£0.25	£0.75	£1.25
Title Value:	$0.40	$1.20	$2.00	£0.25	£0.75	£1.25

SUPERMAN MEETS THE QUIK BUNNY

DC Comics,OS; nn 1987

nn ND Infantino and Giordano art, Mike Carlin script; promotional giveaway from Nestle

	$0.30	$0.90	$1.50	£0.20	£0.60	£1.00
Title Value:	$0.30	$0.90	$1.50	£0.20	£0.60	£1.00

SUPERMAN METROPOLIS EDITION, THE AMAZING WORLD OF

DC Comics,Tabloid; nn 1973

nn ND 64pgs, includes photo-features and poster (map of Krypton), reprints origin from #300 and classic story "Superman in Superman Land" from Action Comics #210

	$1.50	$4.50	$7.50	£1.00	£3.00	£5.00
Title Value:	$1.50	$4.50	$7.50	£1.00	£3.00	£5.00

SUPERMAN PIZZA HUT GIVEAWAYS

DC Comics/Pizza Hut; 97, 113 1977

(see Batman, Wonder Woman)

97 ND original issue #97 reprinted in its entirety but with different ads and Pizza Hut banner on the cover

	$1.50	$4.50	$7.50	£1.00	£3.00	£5.00

113 ND original issue #113 reprinted in its entirety but with different ads and Pizza Hut banner on the cover

	$1.50	$4.50	$7.50	£1.00	£3.00	£5.00
Title Value:	$3.00	$9.00	$15.00	£2.00	£6.00	£10.00

SUPERMAN RADIO SHACK

DC Comics/Radio Shack; nn Jul 1980-nn Jul 1982

nn ND 32pgs, "The Computers That Saved Metropolis" appeared as an insert in Action Comics #509, Superboy (New Adventures) #7, Superboy #265, House of Mystery #282

	$0.30	$0.90	$1.50	£0.20	£0.60	£1.00

nn ND 32pgs, "Victory By Computer" guest-stars Supergirl

	$0.30	$0.90	$1.50	£0.20	£0.60	£1.00

nn ND 32pgs, "Computer Masters of Metropolis"

	$0.30	$0.90	$1.50	£0.20	£0.60	£1.00
Title Value:	$0.90	$2.70	$4.50	£0.60	£1.80	£3.00

SUPERMAN RECORD COMIC

DC Comics; nn 1966

nn ND scarce in the U.K. set contains iron-on patch, decoder, membership card and badge plus 45 rpm record reading origin

	$20.00	$60.00	$140.00	£13.50	£41.00	£95.00
Title Value:	$20.00	$60.00	$140.00	£13.50	£41.00	£95.00

Note: set would be devalued by any of the above missing; at least 50% if the record was missing.

SUPERMAN SPECIAL

DC Comics; 1 1983-3 1985

1 48pgs, Gil Kane story and art

	$0.50	$1.50	$2.50	£0.30	£0.90	£1.50
2-3 48pgs	$0.50	$1.50	$2.50	£0.30	£0.90	£1.50
Title Value:	$1.50	$4.50	$7.50	£0.90	£2.70	£4.50

SUPERMAN SPECIAL (2ND SERIES)

DC Comics; 1 Oct 1992

1 64pgs, Walt Simonson script and art, a re-working of "Kryptonite No More" from Superman #233

	$0.70	$2.10	$3.50	£0.40	£1.20	£2.00
Title Value:	$0.70	$2.10	$3.50	£0.40	£1.20	£2.00

Note: originally meant for the 1991 Superman Annual (No. 3)

SUPERMAN SPECTACULAR

DC Comics; nn 1977

(DC Special Series #5)

nn ND, 80pgs

	$0.50	$1.50	$2.50	£0.30	£0.90	£1.50
Title Value:	$0.50	$1.50	$2.50	£0.30	£0.90	£1.50

SUPERMAN VS. ALIENS

Dark Horse/DC Comics,MS; 1 May 1995-3 Jul 1995

1-3 ND 48pgs, squarebound, Dan Jurgens script and Kevin Nowlan art

	$1.00	$3.00	$5.00	£0.70	£2.10	£3.50
Title Value:	$3.00	$9.00	$15.00	£2.10	£6.30	£10.50

SUPERMAN VS. THE AMAZING SPIDERMAN

Marvel Comics Group/DC Comics,Tabloid; nn 1976

(see Superman and Spiderman)

nn 96pgs, Ross Andru art, Doc Octopus, Parasite, Wonder Woman and Lex Luthor appear; distributed in the U.K.

	$3.00	$9.00	$15.00	£2.50	£7.50	£12.50

Title Value:	$3.00	$9.00	$15.00	£2.50	£7.50	£12.50

SUPERMAN'S GIRL FRIEND, LOIS LANE

(see Lois Lane)

SUPERMAN'S PAL, JIMMY OLSEN

(see Jimmy Olsen)

SUPERMAN, THE ADVENTURES OF

(see Superman #424 onwards)

SUPERMAN, THE LEGACY OF

DC Comics; 1 Mar 1993

1 64pgs, anthology by such as Jerry Ordway, Roger Stern, Curt Swan, Walt Simonson, Karl Kesel, William Messner-Loebs and Art Adams, Art Adams cover

	$0.50	$1.50	$2.50	£0.30	£0.90	£1.50
Title Value:	$0.50	$1.50	$2.50	£0.30	£0.90	£1.50

SUPERMAN/DOOMSDAY: HUNTER/PREY

DC Comics,MS; 1 Mar 1994-3 Jul 1994

1 48pgs, Dan Jurgens and Brett Breeding; bi-weekly, set 1 year after Doomsday "killed" by Superman

	$1.00	$3.00	$5.00	£0.70	£2.10	£3.50

2 48pgs, Dan Jurgens and Brett Breeding; bi-weekly, origin of Doomsday explored

	$1.00	$3.00	$5.00	£0.70	£2.10	£3.50

3 48pgs, Dan Jurgens and Brett Breeding; bi-weekly

	$1.00	$3.00	$5.00	£0.70	£2.10	£3.50
Title Value:	$3.00	$9.00	$15.00	£2.10	£6.30	£10.50

Superman/Doomsday: Hunter/Prey (Oct 1995)

Trade paperback reprints mini-series, new cover

				£2.00	£6.00	£10.00

SUPERMAN/TOYMAN

DC Comics; 1 Jan 1996

1 ND tie-in with the release of Superman figures by Kenner

	$0.40	$1.20	$2.00	£0.25	£0.75	£1.25
Title Value:	$0.40	$1.20	$2.00	£0.25	£0.75	£1.25

SUPERMAN: AT EARTH'S END

DC Comics; 1 Nov 1995

1 ND Tom Veitch script, Frank Gomez art

	$1.00	$3.00	$5.00	£0.70	£2.10	£3.50
Title Value:	$1.00	$3.00	$5.00	£0.70	£2.10	£3.50

SUPERMAN: DOOMSDAY

The multi-part story that lead up to the death of Superman and record sales of Superman titles and Superman #75 becoming one of the biggest selling comics of all time at 4 million copies. The parts of the story are as follows:

Part 1 - Superman, The Man of Steel #18

X-over 1 - Justice League of America #69

Part 2 - Superman #74

Part 3 - Adventures of Superman #497

Part 4 - Action Comics #684

Part 5 - Superman, The Man of Steel #19

Part 6 - Superman #75

The aftermath continues as Funeral For A Friend in the following:

X-over 1 - Justice League of America #70

Part 1 - Adventures of Superman #498

Part 2 - Action Comics #685

Part 3 - Superman, The Man of Steel #20

Part 4 - Superman #76

Part 5 - Adventures of Superman #499

Part 6 - Action Comics #686

Part 7 - Superman, The Man of Steel #21

Part 8 - Superman #77

SUPERMAN: FOR EARTH

DC Comics,OS; 1 May 1991

1 48pgs, ecology theme

	$0.90	$2.70	$4.50	£0.60	£1.80	£3.00
Title Value:	$0.90	$2.70	$4.50	£0.60	£1.80	£3.00

Note: Prestige Format. Originally announced as Superman: Earth Day 1991. Printed on re-cycled paper

SUPERMAN: GREATEST STORIES EVER TOLD

DC Comics; nn 1987; nn Mar 1993

nn Softcover version of the above

	$3.00	$9.00	$15.00	£2.00	£6.00	£10.00

nn Hardcover, classic reprints including Superman #30, #53, #123, #149

	$6.00	$18.00	$30.00	£4.00	£12.00	£20.00
Title Value:	$9.00	$27.00	$45.00	£6.00	£18.00	£30.00

SUPERMAN: KAL

DC Comics,OS; 1 Mar 1995

1 ND 48pgs squarebound, Dave Gibbons script, Jose Garcia Lopez art

	$1.20	$3.60	$6.00	£0.80	£2.40	£4.00
Title Value:	$1.20	$3.60	$6.00	£0.80	£2.40	£4.00

SUPERMAN: SPEEDING BULLETS

DC Comics/Elseworlds,OS; 1 Nov 1993

1 ND 48pgs, Superman adopted by Thomas and Martha Wayne to become Batman

	$1.00	$3.00	$5.00	£0.70	£2.10	£3.50
Title Value:	$1.00	$3.00	$5.00	£0.70	£2.10	£3.50

SUPERMAN: THE EARTH STEALERS

DC Comics,OS; 1 Feb 1988; nn Jun 1989

1 ND 48pgs, squarebound, John Byrne script, Curt Swan and Jerry Ordway art

	$0.80	$2.40	$4.00	£0.50	£1.50	£2.50
1 2nd printing ND	$0.60	$1.80	$3.00	£0.40	£1.20	£2.00
Title Value:	$1.40	$4.20	$7.00	£0.90	£2.70	£4.50

SUPERMAN: THE MAN OF STEEL (1ST SERIES)

DC Comics,MS; 1 Jun 1986-6 Aug 1986

1 re-vamped origin, "rocket" cover

	$0.25	$0.75	$1.25	£0.15	£0.45	£0.75

1 ND direct sales only, "S" emblem cover

	$0.40	$1.20	$2.00	£0.25	£0.75	£1.25

1 ND Silver Edition (1993), silver border around cover

	$0.30	$0.90	$1.50	£0.20	£0.60	£1.00

	$Good	$Fine	$N.Mint	£Good	£Fine	£N.Mint
2 intro new Lois Lane	$0.25	$0.75	$1.25	£0.15	£0.45	£0.75
2 ND Silver Edition (1993), silver border around cover	$0.30	$0.90	$1.50	£0.20	£0.60	£1.00
3 Batman appears	$0.25	$0.75	$1.25	£0.15	£0.45	£0.75
4 intro new Lex Luthor	$0.25	$0.75	$1.25	£0.15	£0.45	£0.75
5 intro new Bizarro	$0.25	$0.75	$1.25	£0.15	£0.45	£0.75
6 intro new Lana Lang	$0.25	$0.75	$1.25	£0.15	£0.45	£0.75
Title Value:	$2.50	$7.50	$12.50	£1.55	£4.65	£7.75

Note: a very small quantity of the Non-Distributed "S" emblem-cover first issues did appear in UK newsagents.

MPI Audio Edition (1986), same issues with stiffer card covers featuring Superman and Action Silver Age covers.
Each comic came with a 30 minute audio cassette of that particular part of the story. Smaller than standard comic size.

	$Good	$Fine	$N.Mint	£Good	£Fine	£N.Mint
ND and very scarce in the U.K.				£1.00	£3.00	£5.00

Superman: The Man of Steel
Trade paperback reprints #1-6 with new story and art

				£Good	£Fine	£N.Mint
				£1.60	£4.80	£8.00

Limited Edition, as above, very scarce in the U.K.

				£Good	£Fine	£N.Mint
				£5.00	£15.00	£25.00

Superman: The Man of Steel (Aug 1993)
Trade paperback reprints issues #1-6 with new format and new cover, intro by Ray Bradbury

				£Good	£Fine	£N.Mint
				£1.00	£3.00	£5.00

Note: all John Byrne story/art, updates entire Superman legend.

SUPERMAN: THE MAN OF STEEL (2ND SERIES)
DC Comics; 0 Oct 1994; 1 Jul 1991-21 Mar 1993; 22 Jun 1993-present

	$Good	$Fine	$N.Mint	£Good	£Fine	£N.Mint
0 (Oct 1994) Zero Hour X-over, origin retold; continued in Superman #0	$0.40	$1.20	$2.00	£0.25	£0.75	£1.25
1 48pgs, Revenge of the Krypton Man part 1, continued in Superman #57	$0.40	$1.20	$2.00	£0.25	£0.75	£1.25
2	$0.30	$0.90	$1.50	£0.20	£0.60	£1.00
3 War of the Gods tie-in	$0.30	$0.90	$1.50	£0.20	£0.60	£1.00
4	$0.25	$0.75	$1.25	£0.15	£0.45	£0.75
5 continued from Action Comics #670, issue reads sideways	$0.25	$0.75	$1.25	£0.15	£0.45	£0.75
6 Blackout part 3, continues in Superman #62	$0.30	$0.75	$1.25	£0.15	£0.45	£0.75
7-8	$0.25	$0.75	$1.25	£0.15	£0.45	£0.75
9 Panic in the Sky part 1, continues in Superman #65	$0.25	$0.75	$1.25	£0.15	£0.45	£0.75
10 Panic in the Sky part 5, continues in Superman #66	$0.25	$0.75	$1.25	£0.15	£0.45	£0.75
11-13	$0.25	$0.75	$1.25	£0.15	£0.45	£0.75
14 Robin guest-stars, continues in Superman #70	$0.25	$0.75	$1.25	£0.15	£0.45	£0.75
15 The Blaze/Satanus War part 3, continued in Superman #71	$0.25	$0.75	$1.25	£0.15	£0.45	£0.75
16 Crisis at Hand part 1, continued in Superman #72	$0.25	$0.75	$1.25	£0.15	£0.45	£0.75
17 cameo appearance Doomsday, continued in Superman #73	$0.60	$1.80	$3.00	£0.40	£1.20	£2.00
18 1st full appearance Doomsday, Superman: Doomsday part 1, continued in Justice League America #69	$0.80	$2.40	$4.00	£0.50	£1.50	£2.50
18 2nd/3rd printing	$0.25	$0.75	$1.25	£0.15	£0.45	£0.75
19 Superman: Doomsday part 5, continued in Superman #75	$0.50	$1.50	$2.50	£0.30	£0.90	£1.50
20 Funeral for a Friend part 3, continued in Superman #76	$0.30	$0.90	$1.50	£0.20	£0.60	£1.00
21 Funeral for a Friend part 7, continued in Superman #77	$0.30	$0.90	$1.50	£0.20	£0.60	£1.00
22 Reign of the Supermen part 4	$0.30	$0.90	$1.50	£0.20	£0.60	£1.00
22 ND Reign of the Supermen part 4, die-cut outer cover, bound-in mini-poster	$0.40	$1.20	$2.00	£0.25	£0.75	£1.25
22 ND Dynamic Forces Edition, signed by Simonson and Bogdanove; 10,000 copies	$3.00	$9.00	$15.00	£1.50	£4.50	£7.50
23 Reign of the Supermen part 6	$0.30	$0.90	$1.50	£0.20	£0.60	£1.00
24 Reign of the Supermen part 10, continued in Superman #80	$0.30	$0.90	$1.50	£0.20	£0.60	£1.00
25 Reign of the Supermen part 14, continued in Superman #81	$0.30	$0.90	$1.50	£0.20	£0.60	£1.00
26 Reign of the Supermen epilogue (part 18), continued finally in Superman #82 (and X-over with Green Lantern #46)	$0.30	$0.90	$1.50	£0.20	£0.60	£1.00
27-28	$0.30	$0.90	$1.50	£0.20	£0.60	£1.00
29 continued from Action Comics #694	$0.30	$0.90	$1.50	£0.20	£0.60	£1.00
30 Superman vs. Lobo	$0.30	$0.90	$1.50	£0.20	£0.60	£1.00
30 ND pre-bagged with sheet of "vinyl clings" of Superman and Lobo to make your own cover - great fun!	$0.50	$1.50	$2.50	£0.30	£0.90	£1.50
31	$0.30	$0.90	$1.50	£0.20	£0.60	£1.00
32 Bizarro appears, concluded in Superman (2nd Series) #88	$0.30	$0.90	$1.50	£0.20	£0.60	£1.00
33 Parasite appears	$0.30	$0.90	$1.50	£0.20	£0.60	£1.00
34 The Battle for Metropolis, continued in Superman (2nd Series) #90	$0.30	$0.90	$1.50	£0.20	£0.60	£1.00
35 Worlds Collide X-over, continued in Hardware #17	$0.30	$0.90	$1.50	£0.20	£0.60	£1.00
36 Worlds Collide X-over, continued in Ilcon #16	$0.30	$0.90	$1.50	£0.20	£0.60	£1.00
37 Zero Hour X-over, Batman appears	$0.30	$0.90	$1.50	£0.20	£0.60	£1.00
38-42	$0.30	$0.90	$1.50	£0.20	£0.60	£1.00
43 Mister Miracle appears	$0.30	$0.90	$1.50	£0.20	£0.60	£1.00
44 prologue to The Death of Clark Kent (see Superman [2nd Series] #100)	$0.30	$0.90	$1.50	£0.20	£0.60	£1.00
45 The Death of Clark Kent part 4, continued in Superman #101; upgraded coated paper stock (Miraweb Format) begins	$0.40	$1.20	$2.00	£0.25	£0.75	£1.25
46-47	$0.40	$1.20	$2.00	£0.25	£0.75	£1.25
48 Aquaman guest-stars	$0.40	$1.20	$2.00	£0.25	£0.75	£1.25
49	$0.40	$1.20	$2.00	£0.25	£0.75	£1.25
50 The Trial of Superman begins, continued in Superman #106	$0.60	$1.80	$3.00	£0.40	£1.20	£2.00
51 The Trial of Superman, continued in Superman #107	$0.40	$1.20	$2.00	£0.25	£0.75	£1.25
52 The Trial of Superman, continued in Superman #108	$0.40	$1.20	$2.00	£0.25	£0.75	£1.25
53	$0.40	$1.20	$2.00	£0.25	£0.75	£1.25
54 Spectre guest-stars	$0.40	$1.20	$2.00	£0.25	£0.75	£1.25
Title Value:	$22.65	$67.95	$113.25	£14.05	£42.15	£70.25

SUPERMAN: THE MAN OF STEEL ANNUAL
DC Comics; 1 Jul 1992-present

Superman (2nd) #0

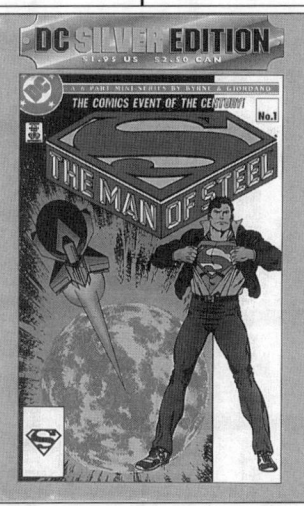

Superman: The Man of Steel #1 (Silver Edition)

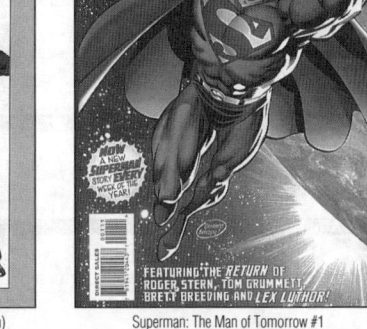

Superman: The Man of Tomorrow #1

	$Good	$Fine	$N.Mint	£Good	£Fine	£N.Mint
1 64pgs, Eclipso: The Darkness Within tie-in, Starman appears	$0.50	$1.50	$2.50	£0.30	£0.90	£1.50
2 64pgs, Bloodlines part 2, 1st appearance Edge, continued in Batman: Shadow of the Bat Anual #1	$0.50	$1.50	$2.50	£0.30	£0.90	£1.50
3 64pgs, Elseworlds story	$0.50	$1.50	$2.50	£0.30	£0.90	£1.50
4 64pgs, Year One story, how Superman met members of the Justice League of America; Walt Simonson cover	$0.60	$1.80	$3.00	£0.40	£1.20	£2.00
Title Value:	$2.10	$6.30	$10.50	£1.30	£3.90	£6.50

SUPERMAN: THE MAN OF STEEL GALLERY
DC Comics,OS; 1 Dec 1995

	$Good	$Fine	$N.Mint	£Good	£Fine	£N.Mint
1 ND pin-ups by various artists including Alan Davis, Dave Gibbons, Michael Golden, Curt Swan	$0.80	$2.40	$4.00	£0.50	£1.50	£2.50
Title Value:	$0.80	$2.40	$4.00	£0.50	£1.50	£2.50

SUPERMAN: THE MAN OF TOMORROW
DC Comics; 1 Summer 1995-present

	$Good	$Fine	$N.Mint	£Good	£Fine	£N.Mint
1 Lex Luthor returns; Roger Stern script, Tom Grummett and Brett Breeding art	$0.40	$1.20	$2.00	£0.25	£0.75	£1.25
2	$0.40	$1.20	$2.00	£0.25	£0.75	£1.25
3 Underworld Unleashed tie-in, continued in Action Comics #717	$0.40	$1.20	$2.00	£0.25	£0.75	£1.25
4 Captain Marvel guest-stars	$0.40	$1.20	$2.00	£0.25	£0.75	£1.25
Title Value:	$1.60	$4.80	$8.00	£1.00	£3.00	£5.00

Note: quarterly frequency

SUPERMAN: THE REIGN OF THE SUPERMEN
Multi-part storyline that re-introduces Superman, back from the dead, in four incarnations. The parts of the story are as follows:

Part 1 - Action Comics #687
Part 2 - Superman (1st) #501
Part 3 - Superman (2nd) #78
Part 4 - Superman: The Man of Steel #22
Part 5 - Action Comics #688
Part 6 - Superman: The Man of Steel #23
Part 7 - Superman (2nd) #79
Part 8 - Superman (1st) #502
Part 9 - Action Comics #689
Part 10 - Superman: The Man of Steel #24
Part 11 - Superman (2nd) #80
Part 12 - Superman (1st) #503
Part 13 - Action Comics #690
Part 14 - Superman: The Man of Steel #25
Part 15 - Superman (2nd) #81
Part 16 - Superman (1st) #504
Part 17 - Action Comics #691
Part 18 - Superman: The Man of Steel #26
Part 19 - Green Lantern (2nd) #46
Part 20 - Superman #82

SUPERMAN: THE SECRET YEARS
DC Comics,MS; 1 Feb 1985-4 May 1985

	$Good	$Fine	$N.Mint	£Good	£Fine	£N.Mint
1-4 Frank Miller cover art	$0.30	$0.90	$1.50	£0.20	£0.60	£1.00
Title Value:	$1.20	$3.60	$6.00	£0.80	£2.40	£4.00

SUPERMAN: UNDER A YELLOW SUN
DC Comics,OS; nn Mar 1994

	$Good	$Fine	$N.Mint	£Good	£Fine	£N.Mint
nn ND 64pgs, squarebound, J.F. Moore script, Barreto and Gammill art	$1.00	$3.00	$5.00	£0.70	£2.10	£3.50
Title Value:	$1.00	$3.00	$5.00	£0.70	£2.10	£3.50

SUPERNATURAL THRILLERS
Marvel Comics Group; 1 Dec 1972-6 Nov 1973; 7 Jul 1974-15 Oct 1975

	$Good	$Fine	$N.Mint	£Good	£Fine	£N.Mint
1 ND Theodore Sturgeon adaptation	$0.60	$1.80	$3.00	£0.40	£1.20	£2.00
2 ND The Invisible Man adapted by Ron Goulart	$0.50	$1.50	$2.50	£0.30	£0.90	£1.50
3 ND Valley of the Worm by Robert E. Howard, Gil Kane art and cover	$0.50	$1.50	$2.50	£0.30	£0.90	£1.50
4 ND Dr. Jekyll and Mr. Hyde adaptation	$0.50	$1.50	$2.50	£0.30	£0.90	£1.50
5 ND The Living Mummy begins (ends #15)	$0.50	$1.50	$2.50	£0.30	£0.90	£1.50
6 ND The Headless Horseman	$0.50	$1.50	$2.50	£0.30	£0.90	£1.50
7-12 ND	$0.50	$1.50	$2.50	£0.30	£0.90	£1.50
13	$0.50	$1.50	$2.50	£0.25	£0.75	£1.25
14 ND	$0.50	$1.50	$2.50	£0.30	£0.90	£1.50
15	$0.50	$1.50	$2.50	£0.25	£0.75	£1.25
Title Value:	$7.60	$22.80	$38.00	£4.50	£13.50	£22.50

Note: Steranko covers on 1, 2
FEATURES
Dr. Jekyll and Mr. Hyde in 4. Headless Horseman in 6. Invisible Man in 2. It! in 1. Living Mummy in 7-15.

SUPERPATRIOT
Image,MS; 1 Jul 1993-4 Oct 1995

	$Good	$Fine	$N.Mint	£Good	£Fine	£N.Mint
1 ND Erik Larsen script, Keith Giffen plot begins	$0.40	$1.20	$2.00	£0.25	£0.75	£1.25
2-4 ND	$0.40	$1.20	$2.00	£0.25	£0.75	£1.25
Title Value:	$1.60	$4.80	$8.00	£1.00	£3.00	£5.00

SUPERPATRIOT: LIBERTY & JUSTICE
Image,MS; 1 Jun 1995-4 Sep 1995

	$Good	$Fine	$N.Mint	£Good	£Fine	£N.Mint
1-4 ND Dave Johnson art	$0.50	$1.50	$2.50	£0.30	£0.90	£1.50
Title Value:	$2.00	$6.00	$10.00	£1.20	£3.60	£6.00

SUPREME
Image; 0 Aug 1995; 1 Nov 1992-present

	$Good	$Fine	$N.Mint	£Good	£Fine	£N.Mint
0 origin of Supreme	$0.50	$1.50	$2.50	£0.30	£0.90	£1.50
1 Rob Liefeld and Brian Murray script/art begins, silver embossed cover	$0.50	$1.50	$2.50	£0.30	£0.90	£1.50
1 Gold Edition	$2.50	$7.50	$12.50	£1.50	£4.50	£7.50
2-4	$0.40	$1.20	$2.00	£0.25	£0.75	£1.25
5 Supreme vs. Krome	$0.40	$1.20	$2.00	£0.25	£0.75	£1.25
6-10	$0.40	$1.20	$2.00	£0.25	£0.75	£1.25
11 Extreme Prejudice part 4	$0.40	$1.20	$2.00	£0.25	£0.75	£1.25
12 Aftermath of Extreme Prejudice	$0.40	$1.20	$2.00	£0.25	£0.75	£1.25
13 Supreme Madness story begins; guest-stars Pitt, Spawn, Stormwatch and Union	$0.50	$1.50	$2.50	£0.30	£0.90	£1.50
14 Supreme Madness story, Supreme vs. Union	$0.50	$1.50	$2.50	£0.30	£0.90	£1.50
15 Supreme Madness story, Spawn appears	$0.50	$1.50	$2.50	£0.30	£0.90	£1.50
16 Supreme Madness story, Supreme vs. Stormwatch	$0.50	$1.50	$2.50	£0.30	£0.90	£1.50
17 Supreme Madness story, Supreme vs. Pitt	$0.50	$1.50	$2.50	£0.30	£0.90	£1.50
18 Supreme Madness story, Pitt appears	$0.50	$1.50	$2.50	£0.30	£0.90	£1.50
19-22	$0.50	$1.50	$2.50	£0.30	£0.90	£1.50
23 Extreme Sacrifice part 1, continued in Bloodstrike #18; pre-bagged with trading card	$0.50	$1.50	$2.50	£0.30	£0.90	£1.50
24	$0.50	$1.50	$2.50	£0.30	£0.90	£1.50
25 cover-dated May 1994, issued between #12 and #13 as part of "Images of Tomorrow" previewing the 25th issue and how it reads/looks	$0.50	$1.50	$2.50	£0.30	£0.90	£1.50
26-27	$0.50	$1.50	$2.50	£0.30	£0.90	£1.50
28 A Supreme Apocalypse - Prelude	$0.50	$1.50	$2.50	£0.30	£0.90	£1.50
28 Variant cover, Joe Quesada/Jimmy Palmiotti cover art	$0.60	$1.80	$3.00	£0.60	£1.80	£3.00
29 Supreme Apocalypse part 1, continued in Brigade #22	$0.50	$1.50	$2.50	£0.30	£0.90	£1.50
30 Supreme Apocalypse part 5	$0.50	$1.50	$2.50	£1.50	£4.50	£7.50
31-32	$0.50	$1.50	$2.50	£0.30	£0.90	£1.50
33 Extreme Babewatch	$0.50	$1.50	$2.50	£0.30	£0.90	£1.50
34 She-Supreme begins	$0.50	$1.50	$2.50	£0.30	£0.90	£1.50
Title Value:	$19.50	$58.50	$97.50	£13.25	£39.75	£66.25

Note: all Non-Distributed on the news-stands in the U.K.

SUPREME ANNUAL
Image; 1 May 1995-present

	$Good	$Fine	$N.Mint	£Good	£Fine	£N.Mint
1 ND Keith Giffen co-plot and pencil art, Charlie Adlard inks	$0.60	$1.80	$3.00	£0.40	£1.20	£2.00
Title Value:	$0.60	$1.80	$3.00	£0.40	£1.20	£2.00

SUPREME, LEGEND OF
Image,MS; 1 Dec 1994-3 Feb 1995

	$Good	$Fine	$N.Mint	£Good	£Fine	£N.Mint
1-3 ND	$0.50	$1.50	$2.50	£0.30	£0.90	£1.50
Title Value:	$1.50	$4.50	$7.50	£0.90	£2.70	£4.50

SUPREME: GLORY DAYS
Image,MS; 1 Oct 1994-2 Nov 1994

	$Good	$Fine	$N.Mint	£Good	£Fine	£N.Mint
1-2 ND Supreme in World War II, Rob Liefeld script	$0.60	$1.80	$3.00	£0.40	£1.20	£2.00
Title Value:	$1.20	$3.60	$6.00	£0.80	£2.40	£4.00

SURGE
Eclipse,MS; 1 Jul 1984-4 Jan 1985

	$Good	$Fine	$N.Mint	£Good	£Fine	£N.Mint
1-4 ND DNAgents spin-off series, Mark Evanier script, Rick Hoberg art, colour	$0.30	$0.90	$1.50	£0.20	£0.60	£1.00
Title Value:	$1.20	$3.60	$6.00	£0.80	£2.40	£4.00

SURVIVE!
Apple Comics; 1 Oct 1991

	$Good	$Fine	$N.Mint	£Good	£Fine	£N.Mint
1 ND Don Lomax script and art	$0.40	$1.20	$2.00	£0.25	£0.75	£1.25
Title Value:	$0.40	$1.20	$2.00	£0.25	£0.75	£1.25

SUSHI
Shunga Comix; 1 Feb 1990-2 1990

	$Good	$Fine	$N.Mint	£Good	£Fine	£N.Mint
1-2 ND adult material, black and white	$0.40	$1.20	$2.00	£0.25	£0.75	£1.25
Title Value:	$0.80	$2.40	$4.00	£0.50	£1.50	£2.50

SWAMP THING
DC Comics; 1 Oct/Nov 1972-24 Aug/Sep 1976
(see Brave and the Bold, DC Comics Presents, House of Secrets #92, Original Swamp Thing Saga, Saga of the Swamp Thing)

	$Good	$Fine	$N.Mint	£Good	£Fine	£N.Mint
1 scarce in the U.K. 2nd appearance Swamp Thing (see House of Secrets #92), Berni Wrightson art begins	$10.00	$30.00	$60.00	£5.75	£17.50	£35.00
2 3rd appearance Swamp Thing, Wrightson art	$5.75	$17.50	$35.00	£3.30	£10.00	£20.00
3 Wrightson art	$3.30	$10.00	$20.00	£2.05	£6.25	£12.50
4 Wrightson art	$2.50	$7.50	$15.00	£1.65	£5.00	£10.00
5-6 Wrightson art	$2.50	$7.50	$15.00	£1.25	£3.75	£7.50
7 Wrightson art, Batman X-over	$2.90	$8.75	$17.50	£1.65	£5.00	£10.00

	$Good	$Fine	$N.Mint	£Good	£Fine	£N.Mint
8 Wrightson art	$2.50	$7.50	$15.00	£1.25	£3.75	£7.50
9-10 ND Wrightson art	$2.50	$7.50	$15.00	£1.30	£4.00	£8.00
11-12 scarce in the U.K.	$0.80	$2.40	$4.00	£0.50	£1.50	£2.50
13-19	$0.80	$2.40	$4.00	£0.40	£1.20	£2.00
20-21 scarce in the U.K.	$0.80	$2.40	$4.00	£0.50	£1.50	£2.50
22 ND scarce in the U.K.	$0.80	$2.40	$4.00	£0.70	£2.10	£3.50
23 very scarce in the U.K.	$0.80	$2.40	$4.00	£0.60	£1.80	£3.00
24 ND scarce in the U.K.	$0.80	$2.40	$4.00	£0.70	£2.10	£3.50
Title Value:	$48.15	$144.85	$278.50	£27.55	£83.40	£160.00

Note: Kaluta inks in 9.

SWAMP THING (2ND SERIES)

DC Comics/Vertigo; 1 May 1982-present
(sub-titled "Saga of the...") (see Challengers of the Unknown, DC Comics Presents, House of Secrets #92, Original Swamp Thing Saga, Roots of the Swamp Thing, Swamp Thing)

	$Good	$Fine	$N.Mint	£Good	£Fine	£N.Mint
1 origin retold, Phantom Stranger series begins (ends #13)	$0.60	$1.80	$3.00	£0.40	£1.20	£2.00
2 photo cover from movie	$0.50	$1.50	$2.50	£0.30	£0.90	£1.50
3-10	$0.50	$1.50	$2.50	£0.30	£0.90	£1.50
11-14 LD in the U.K.	$0.40	$1.20	$2.00	£0.50	£1.50	£2.50
15-16 LD in the U.K. Bissette art	$0.40	$1.20	$2.00	£0.80	£2.40	£4.00
17-19 LD in the U.K. Bissette art	$0.40	$1.20	$2.00	£0.60	£1.80	£3.00
20 1st Alan Moore script	$3.30	$10.00	$20.00	£2.50	£7.50	£15.00
21 new origin	$2.50	$7.50	$15.00	£2.05	£6.25	£12.50
22	$1.65	$5.00	$10.00	£1.65	£5.00	£10.00
23-24 scarce in the U.K.	$1.50	$4.50	$7.50	£1.50	£4.50	£7.50
25 scarce in the U.K. Demon trilogy begins	$1.50	$4.50	$7.50	£1.50	£4.50	£7.50
26-27 Demon trilogy	$1.00	$3.00	$5.00	£1.30	£3.90	£6.50
28-30 last code-approved issues	$1.00	$3.00	$5.00	£1.10	£3.30	£5.50
31 title changes to Swamp Thing, no code	$0.80	$2.40	$4.00	£0.70	£2.10	£3.50
32	$0.80	$2.40	$4.00	£0.70	£2.10	£3.50
33 mostly reprints House of Secrets #92	$0.80	$2.40	$4.00	£0.70	£2.10	£3.50
34	$1.50	$4.50	$7.50	£1.00	£3.00	£5.00
35-36	$0.80	$2.40	$4.00	£0.60	£1.80	£3.00
37 1st appearance John Constantine	$3.00	$9.00	$15.00	£1.50	£4.50	£7.50
38 2nd appearance John Constantine	$1.20	$3.60	$6.00	£0.80	£2.40	£4.00
39-40 John Constantine appears	$0.90	$2.70	$4.50	£0.60	£1.80	£3.00
41-43	$0.60	$1.80	$3.00	£0.40	£1.20	£2.00
44 American Gothic story begins (ends 50), unofficial Crisis X-over; John Constantine appears (thru' to #51)	$0.60	$1.80	$3.00	£0.40	£1.20	£2.00
45	$0.60	$1.80	$3.00	£0.40	£1.20	£2.00
46 Crisis X-over featuring Batman, Hawkman and Phantom Stranger	$0.60	$1.80	$3.00	£0.40	£1.20	£2.00
47-49	$0.50	$1.50	$2.50	£0.30	£0.90	£1.50
50 DS	$0.60	$1.80	$3.00	£0.50	£1.50	£2.50
51	$0.50	$1.50	$2.50	£0.30	£0.90	£1.50
52 Batman last page, 1 panel Joker	$0.60	$1.80	$3.00	£0.40	£1.20	£2.00
53 DS Batman appears, Arkham Asylum	$0.80	$2.40	$4.00	£0.60	£1.80	£3.00
54 Batman 1 panel	$0.60	$1.80	$3.00	£0.40	£1.20	£2.00
55-59	$0.50	$1.50	$2.50	£0.30	£0.90	£1.50
60 1st New Format	$0.50	$1.50	$2.50	£0.30	£0.90	£1.50
61-63	$0.40	$1.20	$2.00	£0.25	£0.75	£1.25
64 last Alan Moore script	$0.40	$1.20	$2.00	£0.25	£0.75	£1.25
65 Batman 2 panels, Arkham Asylum	$0.40	$1.20	$2.00	£0.25	£0.75	£1.25
66 Batman, Arkham Asylum	$0.40	$1.20	$2.00	£0.25	£0.75	£1.25
67 Hellblazer preview, Arkham Asylum	$0.60	$1.80	$3.00	£0.40	£1.20	£2.00
68-69	$0.40	$1.20	$2.00	£0.25	£0.75	£1.25
70 Rick Veitch/Brett Ewins art, Hellblazer	$0.40	$1.20	$2.00	£0.25	£0.75	£1.25
71-75 LD in the U.K.	$0.40	$1.20	$2.00	£0.30	£0.90	£1.50
76 LD in the U.K. X-over with Hellblazer #10	$0.40	$1.20	$2.00	£0.30	£0.90	£1.50
77-78 LD in the U.K.	$0.40	$1.20	$2.00	£0.30	£0.90	£1.50

	$Good	$Fine	$N.Mint	£Good	£Fine	£N.Mint
79 Superman appears	$0.40	$1.20	$2.00	£0.25	£0.75	£1.25
80	$0.40	$1.20	$2.00	£0.25	£0.75	£1.25
81 Invasion X-over	$0.40	$1.20	$2.00	£0.25	£0.75	£1.25
82 Sgt. Rock X-over	$0.40	$1.20	$2.00	£0.25	£0.75	£1.25
83 Enemy Ace appears	$0.40	$1.20	$2.00	£0.25	£0.75	£1.25
84 modern Sandman appears (3rd ever?)	$1.00	$3.00	$5.00	£0.40	£1.20	£2.00
85 DC Western Heroes appear	$0.30	$0.90	$1.50	£0.20	£0.60	£1.00
86 Tomahawk appears	$0.30	$0.90	$1.50	£0.20	£0.60	£1.00
87 Demon appears	$0.30	$0.90	$1.50	£0.20	£0.60	£1.00
88-99	$0.30	$0.90	$1.50	£0.20	£0.60	£1.00
100 48pgs	$0.50	$1.50	$2.50	£0.30	£0.90	£1.50
101	$0.30	$0.90	$1.50	£0.20	£0.60	£1.00
102 previews World Without End series	$0.30	$0.90	$1.50	£0.20	£0.60	£1.00
103	$0.30	$0.90	$1.50	£0.20	£0.60	£1.00
104-109 Quest for the Elementals story	$0.30	$0.90	$1.50	£0.20	£0.60	£1.00
110-113	$0.30	$0.90	$1.50	£0.20	£0.60	£1.00
114-115 John Constantine appears	$0.30	$0.90	$1.50	£0.20	£0.60	£1.00
116 Dick Foreman guest writer, photo cover	$0.30	$0.90	$1.50	£0.20	£0.60	£1.00
117-118 John Higgins cover	$0.30	$0.90	$1.50	£0.20	£0.60	£1.00
119-120 John Higgins cover	$0.30	$0.90	$1.50	£0.20	£0.60	£1.00
121-124 John Higgins cover	$0.30	$0.90	$1.50	£0.20	£0.60	£1.00
125 DS Arcane returns, John Higgins painted cover	$0.60	$1.80	$3.00	£0.40	£1.20	£2.00
126 Dick Foreman script, John Higgins painted cover	$0.30	$0.90	$1.50	£0.20	£0.60	£1.00
127-128 Project Proteus	$0.30	$0.90	$1.50	£0.20	£0.60	£1.00
129 Swamp Fever part 1, 1st issue under the "Vertigo" banner, painted covers by Charles Vess begin	$0.40	$1.20	$2.00	£0.25	£0.75	£1.25
130 Swamp Fever part 2 (conclusion)	$0.40	$1.20	$2.00	£0.25	£0.75	£1.25
131 Swamp Thing changes in appearance	$0.40	$1.20	$2.00	£0.25	£0.75	£1.25
132	$0.40	$1.20	$2.00	£0.25	£0.75	£1.25
133 pin-up by Paul Chadwick	$0.40	$1.20	$2.00	£0.25	£0.75	£1.25
134-135	$0.40	$1.20	$2.00	£0.25	£0.75	£1.25
136-138 painted covers by Charles Vess	$0.40	$1.20	$2.00	£0.25	£0.75	£1.25
139 Black Orchid appears, continued from Black Orchid #5; painted cover by Charles Vess	$0.40	$1.20	$2.00	£0.25	£0.75	£1.25
140 Grant Morrison and Mark Millar scripts begin; Alec Holland awakes thinking being the Swamp Thing was all a dream...(like that bit in Dallas!)	$0.40	$1.20	$2.00	£0.25	£0.75	£1.25
141-147	$0.40	$1.20	$2.00	£0.25	£0.75	£1.25
148-149 Sargon the Sorceror appears	$0.40	$1.20	$2.00	£0.25	£0.75	£1.25
150 48pgs, Swamp Thing vs. Sargon the Sorceror	$0.60	$1.80	$3.00	£0.40	£1.20	£2.00
151-153 Brian Bolland painted cover	$0.40	$1.20	$2.00	£0.25	£0.75	£1.25
154	$0.40	$1.20	$2.00	£0.25	£0.75	£1.25
155 $2.25 cover begin	$0.45	$1.35	$2.25	£0.30	£0.90	£1.50
156-164	$0.45	$1.35	$2.25	£0.30	£0.90	£1.50
Title Value:	$87.25	$261.90	$441.50	£65.45	£196.50	£333.75

Note: most distributed copies of issues #60, #61 have large white Co-Mag distribution labels. Issues #30 on are Mature Readers in content though only labelled as such from #57.

Trade paperback DC Edition,
ND, colour, Ramsey Campbell foreword,

	£Good	£Fine	£N.Mint
reprints #21-27 plus 15 pages of new material	£2.00	£6.00	£10.00

Trade paperback Warner Books Edition,

	£Good	£Fine	£N.Mint
as above, ND scarce	£2.25	£6.75	£11.25

Swamp Thing: Love and Death (Nov 1990)

	£Good	£Fine	£N.Mint
Trade paperback reprints #28-34 and Annual #2, all recoloured	£1.80	£5.40	£9.00

Trade paperback Titan (UK) Edition
Books #1-11, all black and white, as follows:

	£Good	£Fine	£N.Mint
1) James Herbert foreword (reprints #21-24)	£1.40	£4.20	£7.00
2) Clive Barker foreword (reprints #25-28)	£2.50	£7.50	£12.50
3) (reprints #29-31, Annual #2)	£1.40	£4.20	£7.00
4) (reprints #32-36)	£1.30	£3.90	£6.50
5) (reprints #37-40)	£1.10	£3.30	£5.50
6) (reprints #41-44)	£1.10	£3.30	£5.50
7) (reprints #45-47)	£1.00	£3.00	£5.00
8) (reprints #48-51)	£1.10	£3.30	£5.50
9) (reprints #52-55)	£1.10	£3.30	£5.50
10) (reprints #56-59)	£1.10	£3.30	£5.50
11) (reprints #60-64)	£1.30	£3.90	£6.50

MINT = 100% / NEAR MINT (inc. +/-) = 90–99% / VERY FINE (inc. +/-) = 75–89% / FINE (inc. +/-) = 55–74%
VERY GOOD (inc. +/-) = 35–54% / GOOD (inc. +/-) = 15–34% / FAIR = 5–14% / POOR = 1–4%

589

	$Good	$Fine	$N.Mint	£Good	£Fine	£N.Mint

Swamp Thing: Dark Genesis, Trade paperback (Mar 1992), reprints Swamp Thing (1st Series) #1-10, House of Secrets #92, cover painting by Berni Wrightson

| | | | | £2.50 | £7.50 | £12.50 |

SWAMP THING (2ND SERIES) ANNUAL
DC Comics; 1 Nov 1982-present
(sub-titled "Saga of the...")

	$Good	$Fine	$N.Mint	£Good	£Fine	£N.Mint
1 52pgs, adapts film	$0.40	$1.20	$2.00	£0.30	£0.90	£1.50
2 LD in the U.K. continues from Saga of Swamp Thing #31, Moore script, title changes to Swamp Thing Annual	$1.00	$3.00	$5.00	£0.80	£2.40	£4.00
3	$0.40	$1.20	$2.00	£0.30	£0.90	£1.50
4 LD in the U.K. Batman appears cover and story	$0.60	$1.80	$3.00	£0.40	£1.20	£2.00
5 Neil Gaiman story, Floronic Man and Brother Power The Geek appear, Batman cameo	$0.60	$1.80	$3.00	£0.40	£1.20	£2.00
6 ND 64pgs, Nancy Collins script, John Higgins cover	$0.60	$1.80	$3.00	£0.40	£1.20	£2.00
7 ND 64pgs, The Children's Crusade part 4, painted cover by Charles Vess	$0.80	$2.40	$4.00	£0.50	£1.50	£2.50
Title Value:	$4.40	$13.20	$22.00	£3.10	£9.30	£15.50

Note: some copies of Annual 2 have a pin-sized burn-mark in the cover. All Mature Readers label.

SWAMP THING SAGA, ORIGINAL
DC Comics; 2 1977; 14 Summer 1978; 17 Sep 1979; 20 Feb 1980
(DC Special Series #2, #14, #17, #20)

	$Good	$Fine	$N.Mint	£Good	£Fine	£N.Mint
2,14,17,20 ND 52pgs	$1.00	$3.00	$5.00	£0.60	£1.80	£3.00
Title Value:	$4.00	$12.00	$20.00	£2.40	£7.20	£12.00

REPRINT FEATURES
All are Wrightson reprints. 2 reprints Swamp Thing 1, 2. 14 reprints Swamp Thing 3, 4. 17 reprints ST 5, 6, 7. 20 reprints ST 8, 9, 10.

SWEET XVI
Marvel Comics Group,MS; 1 Apr 1991-6 Sep 1991

	$Good	$Fine	$N.Mint	£Good	£Fine	£N.Mint
1 Barbara Slate script/art begins	$0.15	$0.45	$0.75	£0.10	£0.35	£0.60
2-6	$0.15	$0.45	$0.75	£0.10	£0.35	£0.60
Title Value:	$0.90	$2.70	$4.50	£0.60	£2.10	£3.60

SWEET XVI BACK-TO-SCHOOL SPECIAL
Marvel Comics Group,OS; 1 Nov 1992

	$Good	$Fine	$N.Mint	£Good	£Fine	£N.Mint
1 64pgs, Barbarar Slate script/art	$0.40	$1.20	$2.00	£0.25	£0.75	£1.25
Title Value:	$0.40	$1.20	$2.00	£0.25	£0.75	£1.25

SWING WITH SCOOTER
National Periodical Publications/DC Comics; 1 Jun/Jul 1966-35 Aug/Sep 1971; 36 Oct/Nov 1972

	$Good	$Fine	$N.Mint	£Good	£Fine	£N.Mint
1	$3.30	$10.00	$20.00	£2.05	£6.25	£12.50
2-3	$2.05	$6.25	$12.50	£1.25	£3.75	£7.50
4-10	$1.65	$5.00	$10.00	£1.00	£3.00	£6.00
11-20	$1.50	$4.50	$7.50	£1.00	£3.00	£5.00
21-36	$1.20	$3.60	$6.00	£0.80	£2.40	£4.00
Title Value:	$53.15	$160.10	$286.00	£34.35	£103.15	£183.50

SWORD OF SORCERY
DC Comics; 1 Feb/Mar 1973-5 Nov/Dec 1973
(see Wonder Woman #202)

	$Good	$Fine	$N.Mint	£Good	£Fine	£N.Mint
1 scarce in the U.K. Howard Chaykin art, some Neal Adams inks, (credited as The Crusty Bunkers); Fafhrd and Grey Mouser begin	$0.60	$1.80	$3.00	£0.40	£1.20	£2.00
2 part Neal Adams inks	$0.50	$1.50	$2.50	£0.30	£0.90	£1.50
3 Bernie Wrightson art (5 pages)	$0.50	$1.50	$2.50	£0.30	£0.90	£1.50
4 Howard Chaykin art	$0.60	$1.80	$3.00	£0.40	£1.20	£2.00
5 Jim Starlin and Walt Simonson art	$0.60	$1.80	$3.00	£0.40	£1.20	£2.00
Title Value:	$2.80	$8.40	$14.00	£1.80	£5.40	£9.00

SWORD OF THE ATOM
(see Atom)

SWORDS OF CEREBUS
(see Cerebus)

SWORDS OF SHA-PEI
Caliber Press,MS; 1 Apr 1991-3 Sep 1991

	$Good	$Fine	$N.Mint	£Good	£Fine	£N.Mint
1-3 ND	$0.40	$1.20	$2.00	£0.25	£0.75	£1.25
Title Value:	$1.20	$3.60	$6.00	£0.75	£2.25	£3.75

Swords of Shar-Pei Compilation (Feb 1992), collects 3 issue mini-series 3 issue mini-series plus intro story from Caliber Presents

| | | | | £0.65 | £1.95 | £3.25 |

SWORDS OF TEXAS
Eclipse,MS; 1 Oct 1987-4 Jan 1988

	$Good	$Fine	$N.Mint	£Good	£Fine	£N.Mint
1 ND Scout spin-off	$0.40	$1.20	$2.00	£0.25	£0.75	£1.25
2-4 ND	$0.40	$1.20	$2.00	£0.25	£0.75	£1.25
Title Value:	$1.60	$4.80	$8.00	£1.00	£3.00	£5.00

SWORDS OF THE SWASHBUCKLERS
Marvel Comics Group/Epic,MS; 1 Apr 1985-12 Jun 1987
(see Marvel Graphic Novel)

	$Good	$Fine	$N.Mint	£Good	£Fine	£N.Mint
1-12 ND Jackson Guice art	$0.40	$1.20	$2.00	£0.25	£0.75	£1.25
Title Value:	$4.80	$14.40	$24.00	£3.00	£9.00	£15.00

SWORDS OF VALOR
A Plus Comics,OS; 1 Sep 1991

	$Good	$Fine	$N.Mint	£Good	£Fine	£N.Mint
1 ND 48pgs, Robin Hood reprints from Charlton comics, black and white	$0.40	$1.20	$2.00	£0.25	£0.75	£1.25

	$Good	$Fine	$N.Mint	£Good	£Fine	£N.Mint
Title Value:	$0.40	$1.20	$2.00	£0.25	£0.75	£1.25

SYMBOLS OF JUSTICE
High Impact Studios; 1 May 1995-present

	$Good	$Fine	$N.Mint	£Good	£Fine	£N.Mint
1 ND Rick Lyon script and Ricky Carralero art	$0.60	$1.80	$3.00	£0.40	£1.20	£2.00
2 ND black and white	$0.60	$1.80	$3.00	£0.40	£1.20	£2.00
3 ND	$0.60	$1.80	$3.00	£0.40	£1.20	£2.00
Title Value:	$1.80	$5.40	$9.00	£1.20	£3.60	£6.00

SYPHONS
Now Comics; 1 Jul 1986-7 1987

	$Good	$Fine	$N.Mint	£Good	£Fine	£N.Mint
1 ND Caputo cover	$0.30	$0.90	$1.50	£0.20	£0.60	£1.00
2-7 ND	$0.30	$0.90	$1.50	£0.20	£0.60	£1.00
Title Value:	$2.10	$6.30	$10.50	£1.40	£4.20	£7.00

SYPHONS (2ND SERIES)
Now Comics,MS; 1 Mar 1994-3 May 1994

	$Good	$Fine	$N.Mint	£Good	£Fine	£N.Mint
1-3 ND Allen Curtis script, Mark Beachum art	$0.40	$1.20	$2.00	£0.25	£0.75	£1.25
Title Value:	$1.20	$3.60	$6.00	£0.75	£2.25	£3.75

Syphons (Aug 1994)
Trade paperback reprints issues #1-3, new cover

| | | | | £0.80 | £2.40 | £4.00 |

SYPHONS ANNUAL
Now Comics; 1 1995

	$Good	$Fine	$N.Mint	£Good	£Fine	£N.Mint
1 ND Rich Buckler art	$0.50	$1.50	$2.50	£0.30	£0.90	£1.50
Title Value:	$0.50	$1.50	$2.50	£0.30	£0.90	£1.50

SYPHONS: COUNTDOWN TO ARMAGEDDON
Now Comics,MS; 1 Feb 1995-3 Apr 1995

	$Good	$Fine	$N.Mint	£Good	£Fine	£N.Mint
1-3 ND Rick Buckler art	$0.50	$1.50	$2.50	£0.30	£0.90	£1.50
Title Value:	$1.50	$4.50	$7.50	£0.90	£2.70	£4.50

SYPHONS: THE SYGATE STRATAGEM
Now Comics; 1 Oct 1994-3 Dec 1994

	$Good	$Fine	$N.Mint	£Good	£Fine	£N.Mint
1-3 ND	$0.50	$1.50	$2.50	£0.30	£0.90	£1.50
Title Value:	$1.50	$4.50	$7.50	£0.90	£2.70	£4.50

T

T MINUS 1
Renegade; 1,2 Sep 1988

	$Good	$Fine	$N.Mint	£Good	£Fine	£N.Mint
1-2 ND bi-weekly	$0.40	$1.20	$2.00	£0.25	£0.75	£1.25
Title Value:	$0.80	$2.40	$4.00	£0.50	£1.50	£2.50

T.H.U.N.D.E.R.
Solson Publications; 1 1987

	$Good	$Fine	$N.Mint	£Good	£Fine	£N.Mint
1 ND black and white	$0.30	$0.90	$1.50	£0.20	£0.60	£1.00
Title Value:	$0.30	$0.90	$1.50	£0.20	£0.60	£1.00

TABOO
Spiderbaby Grafix; 1 Autumn 1988-5 1992; Tundra Publishing; 6 1993; King Hell Press; 7,8 1994; Kitchen Sink Press; 9 1995-10 Sep 1995

	$Good	$Fine	$N.Mint	£Good	£Fine	£N.Mint
1 Stephen Bissette, S. Clay Wilson, Paul Chadwick plus others; adult horror stories begin; 144pgs	$1.50	$4.50	$7.50	£1.00	£3.00	£5.00
1 2nd printing	$1.20	$3.60	$6.00	£0.80	£2.40	£4.00
2	$1.50	$4.50	$7.50	£1.00	£3.00	£5.00
2 2nd printing	$1.20	$3.60	$6.00	£0.80	£2.40	£4.00
3	$1.50	$4.50	$7.50	£1.00	£3.00	£5.00
3 2nd printing	$1.20	$3.60	$6.00	£0.80	£2.40	£4.00
4 160pgs, Moebius art featured, part 3 From Hell by Alan Moore/Eddie Campbell, also Charles Vess, Neil Gaiman	$2.00	$6.00	$10.00	£1.50	£4.50	£7.50
5 130pgs, part 4 From Hell featured	$2.00	$6.00	$10.00	£1.50	£4.50	£7.50
6 122pgs, 1st Tundra issue, part 5 From Hell featured plus Neil Gaiman's Sweeny Todd Penny Dreadful (16pgs)	$2.00	$6.00	$10.00	£1.50	£4.50	£7.50
7 128pgs, part 6 From Hell	$2.50	$7.50	$12.50	£1.80	£5.25	£9.00
8 128pgs, work by David Lloyd, P. Craig Russell, Greg Capullo	$2.50	$7.50	$12.50	£1.80	£5.25	£9.00
9 ND stories by Tim Truman and Matt Howarth; introduction by Steve Bissette	$3.00	$9.00	$15.00	£2.00	£6.00	£10.00
10 ND	$3.00	$9.00	$15.00	£2.00	£6.00	£10.00
Title Value:	$25.10	$75.30	$125.30	£17.50	£52.20	£87.50

Note: all Non-Distributed on the news-stands in the U.K.

TAILGUNNER JO
DC Comics,MS; 1 Sep 1988-6 Feb 1989

	$Good	$Fine	$N.Mint	£Good	£Fine	£N.Mint
1	$0.15	$0.45	$0.75	£0.10	£0.35	£0.60
2 LD in the U.K.	$0.15	$0.45	$0.75	£0.15	£0.45	£0.75
3-6	$0.15	$0.45	$0.75	£0.10	£0.35	£0.60
Title Value:	$0.90	$2.70	$4.50	£0.65	£2.20	£3.75

Note: New Format

TAINTED
DC Comics/Vertigo,OS; 1 Feb 1995

	$Good	$Fine	$N.Mint	£Good	£Fine	£N.Mint
1 ND Jamie Delano script, Al Davison art	$0.90	$2.70	$4.50	£0.60	£1.80	£3.00
Title Value:	$0.90	$2.70	$4.50	£0.60	£1.80	£3.00

TAKEN UNDER
Caliber Press; 1 Apr 1992

	$Good	$Fine	$N.Mint	£Good	£Fine	£N.Mint
1 ND spin-off from Caliber Presents	$0.50	$1.50	$2.50	£0.30	£0.90	£1.50
Title Value:	$0.50	$1.50	$2.50	£0.30	£0.90	£1.50

TRADE PAPERBACKS, GRAPHIC NOVELS AND OTHER COLLECTIONS ARE PRICED IN POUNDS STERLING ONLY. CONVERT AT 1.5 FOR DOLLARS.

	$Good	$Fine	$N.Mint	£Good	£Fine	£N.Mint
TALE OF ONE BAD RAT						
Dark Horse,MS; 1 Oct 1994-4 Jan 1995						
1 ND Bryan Talbot script and art begin						
	$0.60	$1.80	$3.00	£0.50	£1.50	£2.50
2-4 ND	$0.60	$1.80	$3.00	£0.40	£1.20	£2.00
Title Value:	$2.40	$7.20	$12.00	£1.70	£5.10	£8.50
The Tale of One Bad Rat (Sep 1995)						
Trade paperback reprints issues #1-4 with new painted cover				£2.00	£6.00	£10.00
TALES FROM THE ANIVERSE (1ST SERIES)						
Arrow; 1 Apr 1985-6 Feb 1986						
1-6 ND black and white						
	$0.30	$0.90	$1.50	£0.20	£0.60	£1.00
Title Value:	$1.80	$5.40	$9.00	£1.20	£3.60	£6.00
TALES FROM THE ANIVERSE (2ND SERIES)						
Massive Comics Group; 1 Sep 1991-5 1992						
1 ND	$0.40	$1.20	$2.00	£0.25	£0.75	£1.25
2 ND 48pgs	$0.50	$1.50	$2.50	£0.30	£0.90	£1.50
3-5 ND	$0.40	$1.20	$2.00	£0.25	£0.75	£1.25
Title Value:	$2.10	$6.30	$10.50	£1.30	£3.90	£6.50
TALES FROM THE CRYPT						
E.C. Comics; 20 Oct/Nov 1950-46 Feb/Mar 1955						
(formerly International Comics #1-5, becomes International Crime Patrol #6, becomes Crime Patrol #7-16, becomes Crypt of Terror #17-19)						
20	$100.00	$305.00	$825.00	£67.50	£205.00	£550.00
21	$92.50	$275.00	$650.00	£60.00	£185.00	£435.00
22	$75.00	$225.00	$525.00	£50.00	£150.00	£350.00
23-25	$55.00	$170.00	$400.00	£39.00	£115.00	£275.00
26-30	$46.00	$135.00	$325.00	£30.00	£90.00	£210.00
31 1st ever Williamson art at E.C.						
	$50.00	$150.00	$350.00	£32.00	£95.00	£225.00
32	$39.00	$115.00	$275.00	£26.00	£77.50	£185.00
33 origin Crypt Keeper						
	$57.50	$175.00	$475.00	£39.00	£115.00	£310.00
34 Ray Bradbury adaptation						
	$39.00	$115.00	$275.00	£26.00	£77.50	£185.00
35-40	$39.00	$115.00	$275.00	£26.00	£77.50	£185.00
41-45	$36.00	$105.00	$250.00	£25.00	£75.00	£175.00
46 scarce in both US and UK						
	$43.00	$125.00	$300.00	£29.00	£85.00	£200.00
Title Value:	$1305.00	$3885.00	$9400.00	£877.50	£2625.00	£6300.00
Note: all Non-Distributed on the news-stands in the U.K.						
TALES FROM THE CRYPT (2ND SERIES)						
Gladstone; 1 Jul 1990-6 Jan 1992						
1-6 DS	$0.50	$1.50	$2.50	£0.30	£0.90	£1.50
Title Value:	$3.00	$9.00	$15.00	£1.80	£5.40	£9.00
Note: reprints from classic 1950s EC material featuring such artists as Wally Wood, Jack Davis and Harvey Kurtzman. Note also: issue #7 was advertised but never appeared.						
TALES FROM THE CRYPT (3RD SERIES)						
Russ Cochran/EC Comics; 1 Sep 1991-6 1992						
1 64pgs, reprints Tales from the Crypt #31 and Crime Suspense Stories 12; published in extra-large format rather than normal comic size						
	$0.50	$1.50	$2.50	£0.30	£0.90	£1.50
2 64pgs, reprints Tales from the Crypt #34, Crime Suspense Stories #15						
	$0.50	$1.50	$2.50	£0.30	£0.90	£1.50
3 64pgs, reprints Tales from the Crypt #24, Crime Suspense Stories #21						
	$0.50	$1.50	$2.50	£0.30	£0.90	£1.50
4 64pgs, reprints Tales from the Crypt #43, Crime Suspense Stories #18						
	$0.50	$1.50	$2.50	£0.30	£0.90	£1.50
5 64pgs, reprints Tales from the Crypt #22, Crime Suspense Stories #23						
	$0.50	$1.50	$2.50	£0.30	£0.90	£1.50
6 64pgs, reprints Tales from the Crypt #36, Crime Suspense Stories #6						

	$Good	$Fine	$N.Mint	£Good	£Fine	£N.Mint
	$0.50	$1.50	$2.50	£0.30	£0.90	£1.50
Title Value:	$3.00	$9.00	$15.00	£1.80	£5.40	£9.00
Note: issues #7-9 were advertised but never appeared.						
TALES FROM THE CRYPT (4TH SERIES)						
Russ Cochran/EC Comics; 1 Sep 1992-present						
1 ND reprints from the original 1950s EC series begin with exact cover and interior reproduction						
	$0.40	$1.20	$2.00	£0.25	£0.75	£1.25
2-14 ND	$0.40	$1.20	$2.00	£0.25	£0.75	£1.25
Title Value:	$5.60	$16.80	$28.00	£3.50	£10.50	£17.50
Tales from the Crypt Annual 1 (Aug 1994)						
reprints issues #1-5 with covers, softcover				£1.20	£3.60	£6.00
Tales from the Crypt Annual 2 (Dec 1994)						
reprints issues #6-10 with covers, softcover				£1.20	£3.60	£6.00
TALES FROM THE HEART						
Slave Labor; 1 1987-6 1989; 7 Nov 1990-9 1991						
1-6 ND	$0.40	$1.20	$2.00	£0.25	£0.75	£1.25
7 ND Matt Wagner cover						
	$0.40	$1.20	$2.00	£0.25	£0.75	£1.25
8 ND	$0.40	$1.20	$2.00	£0.25	£0.75	£1.25
9 ND $2.95 cover begins						
	$0.60	$1.80	$3.00	£0.40	£1.20	£2.00
Title Value:	$3.80	$11.40	$19.00	£2.40	£7.20	£12.00
Note: #1,2 published by Entropy						
TALES FROM THE HEART OF AFRICA - TEMPORARY NATIVES						
Marvel Comics Group/Epic,OS; 1 Aug 1990						
1 ND 48pgs	$0.60	$1.80	$3.00	£0.40	£1.20	£2.00
Title Value:	$0.60	$1.80	$3.00	£0.40	£1.20	£2.00
TALES FROM THE MUMMY'S TOMB						
Millennium,OS; 1 Jul 1991						
1 ND 48pgs, Frank Frazetta cover						
	$0.60	$1.80	$3.00	£0.40	£1.20	£2.00
Title Value:	$0.60	$1.80	$3.00	£0.40	£1.20	£2.00
TALES OF ASGARD						
Marvel Comics Group,OS; 1 Oct 1968						
1 scarce in the U.K. 72pgs, classic Jack Kirby reprints from Journey into Mystery back-ups in issues #97-106						
	$5.00	$15.00	$30.00	£3.75	£11.25	£22.50
Title Value:	$5.00	$15.00	$30.00	£3.75	£11.25	£22.50
TALES OF ASGARD (2ND SERIES)						
Marvel Comics Group,OS; 1 Feb 1984						
1 ND 48pgs, Thor reprints, Simonson cover						
	$0.40	$1.20	$2.00	£0.25	£0.75	£1.25
Title Value:	$0.40	$1.20	$2.00	£0.25	£0.75	£1.25
TALES OF EVIL						
Atlas; 1 Feb 1975-3 Jul 1975						
1-2 distributed in the U.K.						
	$0.25	$0.75	$1.25	£0.15	£0.45	£0.75
3 origin Man Monster, Buckler/Vosburg art; distributed in the U.K.						
	$0.25	$0.75	$1.25	£0.15	£0.45	£0.75
Title Value:	$0.75	$2.25	$3.75	£0.45	£1.35	£2.25
TALES OF GHOST CASTLE						
DC Comics; 1 May/Jun 1975-3 Sep/Oct 1975						
1-3	$0.25	$0.75	$1.25	£0.15	£0.45	£0.75
Title Value:	$0.75	$2.25	$3.75	£0.45	£1.35	£2.25
TALES OF LETHARGY						
Alpha Productions,MS; 1 Oct 1993-3 Dec 1993						
1-3 ND	$0.40	$1.20	$2.00	£0.25	£0.75	£1.25
Title Value:	$1.20	$3.60	$6.00	£0.75	£2.25	£3.75
TALES OF ORDINARY MADNESS						
Dark Horse,MS; 1 Jan 1992-4 Apr 1992						
1-4 ND Malcolm Bourne script, painted covers by John Bolton						
	$0.50	$1.50	$2.50	£0.30	£0.90	£1.50

Supernatural Thrillers #2

Swing With Scooter #3

Sword of Sorcery #1

	$Good	$Fine	$N.Mint	£Good	£Fine	£N.Mint		$Good	$Fine	$N.Mint	£Good	£Fine	£N.Mint
Title Value:	$2.00	$6.00	$10.00	£1.20	£3.60	£6.00		$39.00	$115.00	$270.00	£20.00	£60.00	£140.00

TALES OF SUSPENSE

Atlas/Marvel Comics Group; 1 Jan 1959-99 Mar 1968
(becomes Captain America)

1 scarce in the U.K. part Williamson art
$150.00 $450.00 $1350.00 £105.00 £315.00 £950.00

2 Steve Ditko cover
$62.50 $185.00 $500.00 £44.00 £130.00 £350.00

3 flying saucer cover
$57.50 $175.00 $475.00 £41.00 £120.00 £325.00

4 Williamson/Jack Kirby/Bill Everett art
$55.00 $165.00 $440.00 £36.00 £105.00 £285.00

5 the 1st in a long line of Jack Kirby monster covers
$38.00 $110.00 $300.00 £25.00 £75.00 £200.00

6 $38.00 $110.00 $300.00 £25.00 £75.00 £200.00

7 possible Lava Man prototype in the story "I Fought the Molten Man-Thing", pre-figuring Journey into Mystery #97. Note that the two cover layouts are remarkably similar
$38.00 $110.00 $300.00 £25.00 £75.00 £200.00

8 $38.00 $110.00 $300.00 £25.00 £75.00 £200.00

9 possible Iron Man prototype
$38.00 $110.00 $300.00 £25.00 £75.00 £200.00

1st official distribution in the U.K.

10 $38.00 $110.00 $300.00 £25.00 £75.00 £200.00

11-12 ND scarce in the U.K.
$28.00 $82.50 $225.00 £21.50 £65.00 £175.00

13-15 $28.00 $82.50 $225.00 £18.50 £55.00 £150.00

16 1st appearance Metallo (see DC's Action #252); Iron Man prototype? Metallo here is actually a gigantic robot used by a criminal who becomes trapped inside forever
$31.00 $92.50 $250.00 £20.50 £60.00 £165.00

17-20 $28.00 $82.50 $225.00 £18.50 £55.00 £150.00

21-24 $21.50 $65.00 $175.00 £13.00 £39.00 £105.00

25 (Jan 1962), last 10 cents issue
$21.50 $65.00 $175.00 £13.00 £39.00 £105.00

26-27 $21.50 $65.00 $175.00 £13.00 £39.00 £105.00

28 possible Stone Men from Saturn prototype
$21.50 $65.00 $175.00 £13.00 £39.00 £105.00

29-30 $21.50 $65.00 $175.00 £13.00 £39.00 £105.00

31 Dr. Doom prototype? "The Monster in the Iron Mask" is exactly that, not a disfigured man/ruler turned evil
$21.50 $65.00 $175.00 £13.00 £39.00 £105.00

32 1st Sazzik the Sorcerer, prototype of Dr. Strange? debateable as Sazzik is 15th century, evil and grotesque-looking! (see also Strange Tales #79 and Journey Into Mystery #78). Ant-Man prototype more in keeping with the cover story "The Man in the Bee-Hive"
$21.50 $65.00 $175.00 £13.00 £39.00 £105.00

33-34 $18.50 $55.00 $150.00 £11.50 £36.00 £95.00

35 Watcher prototype? More possible than other "prototypes"! Zarkorr is a humanoid alien who wears a Watcher-like disguise to preach world peace to humanity
$18.50 $55.00 $150.00 £11.50 £36.00 £95.00

36 $18.50 $55.00 $150.00 £11.50 £36.00 £95.00

37 (Jan 1963) $18.50 $55.00 $150.00 £11.50 £36.00 £95.00

38 $18.50 $55.00 $150.00 £11.50 £36.00 £95.00

39 origin & 1st appearance Iron Man, part Kirby art
$370.00 $1100.00 $3350.00 £240.00 £730.00 £2200.00
[Prices may vary widely on this comic]

39 ND Marvel Milestone Edition (Oct 1994) - silver border around cover
$0.60 $1.80 $3.00 £0.40 £1.20 £2.00

40 scarce in the U.K. 2nd Iron Man and new Iron Man armour (gold rather than grey)
$135.00 $415.00 $1250.00 £80.00 £240.00 £725.00

41 features villain called Dr. Strange, two months before Strange Tales #110 (Jul 1963) with 1st appearance of the hero Dr. Strange
$85.00 $255.00 $600.00 £52.50 £160.00 £375.00

42 $43.00 $125.00 $300.00 £25.00 £75.00 £175.00

43 less common in the U.K.
$43.00 $125.00 $300.00 £26.00 £77.50 £185.00

44 scarce in the U.K. "Pharaoh" mis-spelt on cover
$43.00 $125.00 $300.00 £29.00 £85.00 £200.00

45 less common in the U.K.
$43.00 $125.00 $300.00 £26.00 £77.50 £185.00

46 less common in the U.K. 1st appearance Crimson Dynamo
$26.00 $75.00 $180.00 £17.00 £50.00 £120.00

47 $26.00 $75.00 $180.00 £15.00 £45.00 £105.00

48 Iron Man's new armour (red and gold)
$32.00 $95.00 $225.00 £19.00 £57.50 £135.00

49 (Jan 1964), joint 3rd appearance X-Men; came out same month (Jan. 1964) as X-Men #3 and Avengers #3; The Watcher back-up story (2nd appearance)
$28.00 $82.50 $195.00 £16.00 £49.00 £115.00

50 1st appearance Mandarin
$15.50 $47.00 $110.00 £10.00 £30.00 £70.00

51 1st appearance Scarecrow (note: not DC's long-time villain)
$14.00 $43.00 $100.00 £9.25 £28.00 £65.00

52 1st appearance Black Widow
$18.50 $55.00 $130.00 £10.50 £32.00 £75.00

53 2nd appearance Black Widow, origin and 3rd appearance The Watcher
$15.50 $47.00 $110.00 £8.50 £26.00 £60.00

54 The Mandarin returns
$10.50 $32.00 $75.00 £6.25 £19.00 £45.00

55 extra 5 page section on inside information about Iron Man
$10.50 $32.00 $75.00 £6.25 £19.00 £45.00

56 1st appearance Unicorn
$10.50 $32.00 $75.00 £6.25 £19.00 £45.00

57 scarce in the U.K. origin and 1st appearance of Hawkeye, Black Widow appears
$21.00 $62.50 $150.00 £12.50 £39.00 £90.00

58 scarce in the U.K. Captain America vs. Iron Man

59 scarce in the U.K. 1st solo Silver Age Captain America series begins
$37.00 $110.00 $260.00 £20.00 £60.00 £140.00

60 very scarce in the U.K. 2nd appearance Hawkeye
$17.00 $50.00 $120.00 £10.50 £32.00 £75.00

61 less common in the U.K. (Jan 1965)
$10.50 $32.00 $75.00 £6.25 £19.00 £45.00

62 less common in the U.K. origin Mandarin
$10.50 $32.00 $75.00 £6.25 £19.00 £45.00

63 1st Silver Age origin Captain America
$29.00 $85.00 $200.00 £15.00 £45.00 £105.00

64 1st new Black Widow (1st costume)
$10.50 $32.00 $75.00 £6.25 £19.00 £45.00

65 1st appearance Silver Age Red Skull (since Captain America Comics #74 in 1949)
$16.00 $49.00 $115.00 £7.75 £23.50 £55.00

66 2nd Silver Age Red Skull, origin retold
$15.50 $47.00 $110.00 £6.25 £19.00 £45.00

67-68 $7.75 $23.50 $55.00 £3.90 £11.50 £27.50

69 1st appearance Titanium Man
$7.75 $23.50 $55.00 £3.90 £11.50 £27.50

70 $7.75 $23.50 $55.00 £3.90 £11.50 £27.50

71 $7.75 $23.50 $55.00 £3.20 £9.50 £22.50

72 Quicksilver and Scarlet Witch appear; last Silver Age issue cover dated December 1965
$7.75 $23.50 $55.00 £3.20 £9.50 £22.50

73 (Jan 1966) $7.75 $23.50 $55.00 £3.20 £9.50 £22.50

74-75 $7.75 $23.50 $55.00 £3.20 £9.50 £22.50

76-77 $7.75 $23.50 $55.00 £2.50 £7.50 £17.50

78 Nick Fury appears
$7.75 $23.50 $55.00 £2.50 £7.50 £17.50

79 Iron Man battles Sub-Mariner; 1st appearance of the Cosmic Cube
$7.75 $23.50 $55.00 £2.50 £7.50 £17.50

80 Iron Man battles Sub-Mariner, X-over with Tales to Astonish #82
$9.25 $28.00 $65.00 £2.50 £7.50 £17.50

81-83 $7.00 $21.00 $50.00 £2.50 £7.50 £17.50

84 scarce in the U.K.
$7.00 $21.00 $50.00 £2.85 £8.50 £20.00

85 scarce in the U.K. (Jan 1967)
$7.00 $21.00 $50.00 £2.85 £8.50 £20.00

86-94 $7.00 $21.00 $50.00 £2.50 £7.50 £17.50

95 Iron Man vs. Grey Gargoyle
$7.00 $21.00 $50.00 £2.50 £7.50 £17.50

96 $7.00 $21.00 $50.00 £2.50 £7.50 £17.50

97 (Jan 1968), Black Panther appears, 1st appearance Whiplash
$7.00 $21.00 $50.00 £2.50 £7.50 £17.50

98 Captain America battles Black Panther
$7.00 $21.00 $50.00 £2.50 £7.50 £17.50

99 less common in the U.K. leads into Captain America #100 and Iron Man #1
$10.00 $30.00 $70.00 £3.90 £11.50 £27.50

Title Value: $2626.60 $7823.30 $20898.00 £1601.70 £4815.70 £12877.00

ARTISTS
Ditko in 10-15, 17-44, 46, 48, 49. Kirby in 10-35, 40, 41, 43, 59-68, 78-86, 92-99.

FEATURES
Captain America in 59-99. Iron Man in 39-99. Tales of the Watcher in 48-58. Monster/fantasy stories in 10-47 (as back-ups in 39-47).

TALES OF SUSPENSE (2ND SERIES)

Marvel Comics Group, OS; 1 Jan 1995

1 ND 64pgs, Iron Man and Captain America appear, Colin MacNeil painted art; card-stock cover with protective acettate overlay
$1.40 $4.20 $7.00 £0.90 £2.70 £4.50

Title Value: $1.40 $4.20 $7.00 £0.90 £2.70 £4.50

TALES OF TERROR

Eclipse; 1 Aug 1985-13 Jul 1987

1-4 ND $0.40 $1.20 $2.00 £0.25 £0.75 £1.25

5 ND Dowling, Weeks art, Conrad cover
$0.40 $1.20 $2.00 £0.25 £0.75 £1.25

6 ND $0.40 $1.20 $2.00 £0.25 £0.75 £1.25

7 ND David Lloyd, Bolton art
$0.40 $1.20 $2.00 £0.25 £0.75 £1.25

8 ND $0.40 $1.20 $2.00 £0.25 £0.75 £1.25

9 ND Bolton, Geary, Ridgway art
$0.40 $1.20 $2.00 £0.25 £0.75 £1.25

10-13 ND $0.40 $1.20 $2.00 £0.25 £0.75 £1.25

Title Value: $5.20 $15.60 $26.00 £3.25 £9.75 £16.25

TALES OF THE BEANWORLD

Beanworld/Eclipse; 1 Feb 1985-21 1993
(see Scout #17)

1 ND scarce in the U.K. Larry Marder story/art begins; black and white
$0.80 $2.40 $4.00 £0.50 £1.50 £2.50

2-3 ND scarce in the U.K.
$0.60 $1.80 $3.00 £0.40 £1.20 £2.00

4 ND scarce in the U.K.
$0.50 $1.50 $2.50 £0.35 £1.05 £1.75

5 ND $0.50 $1.50 $2.50 £0.30 £0.90 £1.50

6-19 ND $0.40 $1.20 $2.00 £0.25 £0.75 £1.25

20 ND $2.50 cover $0.50 $1.50 $2.50 £0.30 £0.90 £1.50

21 ND $2.95 cover $0.60 $1.80 $3.00 £0.40 £1.20 £2.00

Title Value: $9.70 $29.10 $48.50 £6.15 £18.45 £30.75

Book 1
Trade paperback (reprints #1-4) £1.20 £3.60 £6.00
2nd printing (1990) £1.10 £3.30 £5.50
Book 2
Trade paperback (Dec 1992), reprints #5-7

	$Good	$Fine	$N.Mint	£Good	£Fine	£N.Mint
Softcover				£1.10	£3.30	£5.50
Hardcover				£4.00	£12.00	£20.00

Larry Marder's Beanworld: Book One (Mar 1995)
reprints issues #1-4; introduction by Scott McCloud | | | £1.30 | £3.90 | £6.50

TALES OF THE FEHNNIK
Antarctic Press; 1 Aug 1995
1 ND Elin Winkler script, Pat Kelley art; black and white

	$Good	$Fine	$N.Mint	£Good	£Fine	£N.Mint
	$0.55	$1.65	$2.75	£0.35	£1.05	£1.75
Title Value:	$0.55	$1.65	$2.75	£0.35	£1.05	£1.75

TALES OF THE GREEN LANTERN CORPS
(see Green Lantern Corps, Tales of The)

TALES OF THE JACKALOPE
Blackthorne; 1 Feb 1986-8 Dec 1986
1-8 ND Bob Crabb art; black and white

	$Good	$Fine	$N.Mint	£Good	£Fine	£N.Mint
	$0.40	$1.20	$2.00	£0.25	£0.75	£1.25
Title Value:	$3.20	$9.60	$16.00	£2.00	£6.00	£10.00

TALES OF THE LEGION
(see Legion)

TALES OF THE MARVELS: BLOCKBUSTER
Marvel Comics Group,OS; nn Jun 1995
nn ND 48pgs, Mike Baron script, Shawn Martinbrough art; story stems from F.F. #260 with battle between Silver Surfer and Terrax; acetate outer cover

	$Good	$Fine	$N.Mint	£Good	£Fine	£N.Mint
	$1.20	$3.60	$6.00	£0.80	£2.40	£4.00
Title Value:	$1.20	$3.60	$6.00	£0.80	£2.40	£4.00

TALES OF THE MARVELS: INNER DEMONS
Marvel Comics Group,OS; 1 Feb 1996
1 ND 48pgs, Human Torch, Sub-Mariner (origin re-examined) and The Enforcers appear; painted art by Bob Wakelin

	$Good	$Fine	$N.Mint	£Good	£Fine	£N.Mint
	$1.20	$3.60	$6.00	£0.80	£2.40	£4.00
Title Value:	$1.20	$3.60	$6.00	£0.80	£2.40	£4.00

TALES OF THE MARVELS: WONDER YEARS
Marvel Comics Group,MS; 1 Oct 1995-2 Nov 1995
1-2 ND Dan Abnett and Andy Lanning script, painted art by Igor Kordey, Wonder Man stars; acetate outer cover

	$Good	$Fine	$N.Mint	£Good	£Fine	£N.Mint
	$1.00	$3.00	$5.00	£0.70	£2.10	£3.50
Title Value:	$2.00	$6.00	$10.00	£1.40	£4.20	£7.00

TALES OF THE MYSTERIOUS TRAVELLER
Charlton; 1 Aug 1956-13 Jun 1959; 14 Oct 1985-15 Dec 1985

	$Good	$Fine	$N.Mint	£Good	£Fine	£N.Mint
1 ND scarce in the U.K.	$36.00	$105.00	$250.00	£25.00	£75.00	£175.00
2 ND scarce in the U.K. part Steve Ditko art	$30.00	$90.00	$210.00	£20.00	£60.00	£140.00
3 ND scarce in the U.K. Steve Ditko cover and part art	$27.00	$80.00	$190.00	£17.50	£52.50	£125.00
4-5 ND scarce in the U.K. Steve Ditko cover and art	$34.00	$100.00	$240.00	£22.50	£67.50	£160.00
6-10 ND scarce in the U.K. Steve Ditko cover and art	$29.00	$85.00	$200.00	£19.00	£57.50	£135.00

11 distributed in the U.K. (note: cover date of February 1959, before official distribution in early 1960 with cover dates of November 1959) Steve Ditko cover and art: $29.00 | $85.00 | $200.00 | £19.00 | £57.50 | £135.00

12 distributed in the U.K. (note cover date of April 1959, before official distribution in early 1960 with cover dates of November 1959: $11.00 | $34.00 | $80.00 | £7.75 | £23.50 | £55.00

13 distributed in the U.K. (note cover date of June 1959, before official distribution in early 1960 with cover dates of November 1959: $11.00 | $34.00 | $80.00 | £7.75 | £23.50 | £55.00

14-15 LD in the U.K. Steve Ditko cover and art (reprints): $0.40 | $1.20 | $2.00 | £0.25 | £0.75 | £1.25

Title Value: $357.80 | $1055.40 | $2494.00 | £237.50 | £716.00 | £1682.50

TALES OF THE SUN RUNNERS
Sirius/Amazing; 1 Jul 1986-3 Jan 1987
1-3 ND black and white

	$Good	$Fine	$N.Mint	£Good	£Fine	£N.Mint
	$0.40	$1.20	$2.00	£0.25	£0.75	£1.25
Title Value:	$1.20	$3.60	$6.00	£0.75	£2.25	£3.75

TALES OF THE TEEN TITANS
(see New Teen Titans)

TALES OF THE TEEN TITANS ANNUAL
(see New Teen Titans Annual)

TALES OF THE TEENAGE MUTANT NINJA TURTLES
Mirage Studios; 1 May 1987-7 Apr 1989
(merges with Teenage Mutant Ninja Turtles)

	$Good	$Fine	$N.Mint	£Good	£Fine	£N.Mint
1 ND	$0.60	$1.80	$3.00	£0.40	£1.20	£2.00
1 2nd printing ND	$0.50	$1.50	$2.50	£0.30	£0.90	£1.50
2-7 ND	$0.50	$1.50	$2.50	£0.30	£0.90	£1.50
Title Value:	$4.10	$12.30	$20.50	£2.50	£7.50	£12.50
Collected Edition (1990), reprints #1-7				£1.60	£4.80	£8.00

TALES OF THE UNEXPECTED
National Periodical Publications; 1 Feb/Mar 1956-104 Dec/Jan 1967/68
(becomes The Unexpected)

	$Good	$Fine	$N.Mint	£Good	£Fine	£N.Mint
1 scarce in the U.K.	$100.00	$300.00	$900.00	£65.00	£200.00	£600.00
2 scarce in the U.K.	$52.50	$155.00	$425.00	£36.00	£105.00	£285.00
3-5 scarce in the U.K.	$38.00	$110.00	$300.00	£25.00	£75.00	£200.00
6-10	$31.00	$92.50	$250.00	£21.50	£65.00	£175.00
11	$20.00	$60.00	$160.00	£13.00	£39.00	£105.00
12-13 Jack Kirby art	$21.00	$62.50	$170.00	£14.00	£43.00	£115.00
14	$20.00	$60.00	$160.00	£13.00	£39.00	£105.00
15-18 Jack Kirby art	$21.00	$62.50	$170.00	£14.00	£43.00	£115.00
19-20	$20.00	$60.00	$160.00	£13.00	£39.00	£105.00
21-24 Jack Kirby art	$20.50	$60.00	$165.00	£13.50	£41.00	£110.00
25-30	$16.00	$49.00	$130.00	£11.00	£34.00	£90.00
31-39	$14.00	$43.00	$115.00	£10.00	£30.00	£80.00

40 1st of Space Ranger series (see Showcase #15/16) - no mention on the cover: $87.50 | $265.00 | $800.00 | £60.00 | £180.00 | £540.00

41-42 Space Ranger: $33.00 | $97.50 | $260.00 | £21.50 | £65.00 | £175.00

1st official distribution in the U.K.

43 1st Space Ranger series cover; painted (grey-tone) cover: $65.00 | $195.00 | $585.00 | £42.00 | £125.00 | £375.00

	$Good	$Fine	$N.Mint	£Good	£Fine	£N.Mint
44-46	$26.00	$77.50	$185.00	£15.00	£45.00	£105.00
47-50	$19.00	$57.50	$135.00	£12.00	£36.00	£85.00
51-60	$17.00	$50.00	$120.00	£11.00	£34.00	£80.00
61-66	$14.00	$43.00	$100.00	£8.50	£26.00	£60.00
67 last 10 cents issue	$14.00	$43.00	$100.00	£8.50	£26.00	£60.00
68-70	$8.50	$26.00	$60.00	£5.00	£15.00	£35.00
71-81	$7.75	$23.50	$55.00	£4.25	£12.50	£30.00
82 last Space Ranger	$7.75	$23.50	$55.00	£4.25	£12.50	£30.00
83-90	$6.25	$19.00	$45.00	£2.85	£8.50	£20.00
91	$6.25	$19.00	$45.00	£2.50	£7.50	£17.50
92 last Silver Age issue indicia dated Dec 1965/Jan 1966	$6.25	$19.00	$45.00	£2.50	£7.50	£17.50
93-100	$6.25	$19.00	$45.00	£2.50	£7.50	£17.50
101-104	$5.00	$15.00	$35.00	£1.75	£5.25	£12.50
Title Value:	$1823.00	$5464.00	$14300.00	£1157.80	£3502.00	£9160.00

TALES OF THE VOYAGER
White Wolf; 1 Aug 1991

	$Good	$Fine	$N.Mint	£Good	£Fine	£N.Mint
1 ND	$0.40	$1.20	$2.00	£0.25	£0.75	£1.25
Title Value:	$0.40	$1.20	$2.00	£0.25	£0.75	£1.25

TALES OF THE ZOMBIE
Marvel Comics Group,Magazine; 1 Aug 1973-10 Mar 1975

1 ND scarce in the U.K. 72pgs, The Zombie by Steve Gerber and Pablo Marcos begins; back-up stories begin with Voodoo themes, all black and white: $2.50 | $7.50 | $15.00 | £1.25 | £3.75 | £7.50

	$Good	$Fine	$N.Mint	£Good	£Fine	£N.Mint
2 ND 72pgs, Boris painted cover	$1.65	$5.00	$10.00	£0.80	£2.50	£5.00
3 ND 72pgs, Boris painted cover	$1.25	$3.75	$7.50	£0.65	£2.00	£4.00
4 64pgs, James Bond feature (v2 #1 in indicia)	$1.25	$3.75	$7.50	£0.65	£2.00	£4.00
5 64pgs	$1.25	$3.75	$7.50	£0.65	£2.00	£4.00
6 64pgs, Brother Voodoo back-up with Gene Colan art	$1.25	$3.75	$7.50	£0.50	£1.50	£3.00
7-8 64pgs	$1.25	$3.75	$7.50	£0.50	£1.50	£3.00
9 scarce in the U.K. 64pgs, double-length Zombie story	$1.25	$3.75	$7.50	£0.50	£1.50	£3.00
10 64pgs, Brother Voodoo main feature	$1.25	$3.75	$7.50	£0.50	£1.50	£3.00
Title Value:	$14.15	$42.50	$85.00	£6.50	£19.75	£39.50

ARTISTS
Kaluta art in 8.
FEATURES
Brother Voodoo in 5 (text only), 6, 10. Zombie in 1-9. Photos and text of Bond movie Live and Let Die in 4.
Note: a next issue was advertised but never appeared.

TALES OF THE ZOMBIE ANNUAL
Marvel Comics Group,Magazine; 1 Summer 1975
1 ND 88pgs, squarebound, all reprint

	$Good	$Fine	$N.Mint	£Good	£Fine	£N.Mint
	$1.25	$3.75	$7.50	£0.80	£2.50	£5.00
Title Value:	$1.25	$3.75	$7.50	£0.80	£2.50	£5.00

TALES TO ASTONISH
Atlas/Marvel Comics Group; 1 Jan 1959-101 Mar 1968
(becomes The Incredible Hulk)

	$Good	$Fine	$N.Mint	£Good	£Fine	£N.Mint
1 scarce in the U.K. Jack Davis art	$150.00	$450.00	$1350.00	£105.00	£315.00	£950.00
2 Steve Ditko flying saucer cover	$67.50	$205.00	$550.00	£47.00	£140.00	£375.00
3-4	$47.00	$140.00	$375.00	£31.00	£92.50	£250.00

5 possible Stone Men from Saturn prototypes in the story "The Things on Easter Island", part Williamson art: $47.00 | $140.00 | $375.00 | £31.00 | £92.50 | £250.00

6 lead story called "I Saw the Invasion of the Stone Men" but their appearance does not suggest prototypes for The Stone Men from Saturn: $35.00 | $105.00 | $280.00 | £23.50 | £70.00 | £190.00

7 possible Toad Men prototypes in the story "We Met In The Swamp", pre-figuring Hulk #2: $35.00 | $105.00 | $280.00 | £23.50 | £70.00 | £190.00

8-9: $35.00 | $105.00 | $280.00 | £23.50 | £70.00 | £190.00

1st official distribution in the U.K.

10: $35.00 | $105.00 | $280.00 | £23.50 | £70.00 | £190.00

11-13 ND scarce in the U.K.: $28.00 | $82.50 | $220.00 | £21.50 | £65.00 | £175.00

14: $28.00 | $82.50 | $220.00 | £18.50 | £55.00 | £150.00

15 Electro prototype?? More like a prototype for the Hulk villain/monster Zzaxx (see Tales of Suspense #13 for a monster called "Elektro"): $28.00 | $82.50 | $220.00 | £18.50 | £55.00 | £150.00

16 lead story "Thorr the Unbelievable" has characters that pre-figure The Stone Men from Saturn who appeared in Thor's first adventure in Journey into Mystery #83. Also Mole Men prototypes pre-figuring their appearance in Fantastic Four #1: $29.00 | $85.00 | $280.00 | £19.00 | £57.50 | £155.00

17-20: $28.00 | $82.50 | $220.00 | £18.50 | £55.00 | £150.00

	$Good	$Fine	$N.Mint	£Good	£Fine	£N.Mint

21-26 | $20.50 | $60.00 | $165.00 | £13.00 | £39.00 | £105.00

27 very scarce in the U.K. (Jan 1962), origin and 1st appearance of Ant-Man (in fantasy/horror story; no costume); last 10 cents issue. It is traditionally the hardest key Marvel to find in high grade
| | $300.00 | $900.00 | $3000.00 | £200.00 | £600.00 | £2000.00 |
[Prices may vary widely on this comic]
[Very rare in high grade - Very Fine+ or better]

28 possible Stone Men from Saturn prototypes appear in the story "Back From The Dead" and refer to themselves as "stone men"
| | $20.50 | $60.00 | $165.00 | £13.00 | £39.00 | £105.00 |
29-30 | $20.50 | $60.00 | $165.00 | £13.00 | £39.00 | £105.00
31-34 | $18.50 | $55.00 | $150.00 | £12.50 | £38.00 | £100.00
35 1st costumed Ant-Man, series begins
| | $150.00 | $455.00 | $1375.00 | £87.50 | £265.00 | £800.00 |
36 2nd costumed Ant-Man
| | $70.00 | $215.00 | $575.00 | £44.00 | £130.00 | £350.00 |
37 less common in the U.K. 1st appearance Egghead
| | $46.00 | $135.00 | $325.00 | £22.50 | £67.50 | £160.00 |
38 less common in the U.K. 1st appearance Egghead
| | $50.00 | $150.00 | $350.00 | £25.00 | £75.00 | £175.00 |
39 less common in the U.K. (Jan 1963)
| | $46.00 | $135.00 | $325.00 | £25.00 | £75.00 | £175.00 |
40 | $46.00 | $135.00 | $325.00 | £22.50 | £67.50 | £160.00
41-43 | $29.00 | $85.00 | $200.00 | £16.00 | £49.00 | £115.00
44 origin and 1st appearance of The Wasp
| | $33.00 | $97.50 | $230.00 | £18.50 | £55.00 | £130.00 |
45-48 | $18.50 | $55.00 | $130.00 | £10.50 | £32.00 | £75.00
49 Ant-Man becomes Giant-Man
| | $22.50 | $67.50 | $160.00 | £12.50 | £39.00 | £90.00 |
50 1st origin and appearance Human Top
| | $13.50 | $41.00 | $95.00 | £7.00 | £21.00 | £50.00 |
51 (Jan 1964), Giant Man vs. Human Top
| | $13.50 | $41.00 | $95.00 | £6.25 | £19.00 | £45.00 |
52 origin and 1st appearance Black Knight
| | $13.50 | $41.00 | $95.00 | £7.00 | £21.00 | £50.00 |
53-54 | $13.50 | $41.00 | $95.00 | £6.25 | £19.00 | £45.00
55 less common in the U.K.
| | $13.50 | $41.00 | $95.00 | £6.75 | £20.00 | £47.50 |
56 | $13.50 | $41.00 | $95.00 | £6.00 | £18.00 | £42.50
57 scarce in the U.K. Spiderman appears (early X-over)
| | $17.50 | $52.50 | $140.00 | £10.00 | £30.00 | £80.00 |
58 | $13.50 | $41.00 | $95.00 | £6.00 | £18.00 | £42.50
59 Giant Man vs. Hulk, Avengers cameo
| | $20.00 | $60.00 | $140.00 | £10.50 | £32.00 | £75.00 |
60 Hulk series begins, Giant-Man series continues
| | $21.00 | $62.50 | $150.00 | £12.50 | £39.00 | £90.00 |
61 scarce in the U.K. Steve Ditko cover and art
| | $9.25 | $28.00 | $65.00 | £6.25 | £19.00 | £45.00 |
62 rare in the U.K. 1st appearance The Leader (cameo)
| | $9.25 | $28.00 | $65.00 | £7.75 | £23.50 | £55.00 |
63 (Jan 1965), 1st full appearance The Leader (see Incredible Hulk #400)
| | $9.25 | $28.00 | $65.00 | £6.00 | £18.00 | £42.50 |
64 | $9.25 | $28.00 | $65.00 | £4.60 | £13.50 | £32.50
65 1st new Giant Man (new costume)
| | $9.25 | $28.00 | $65.00 | £5.25 | £16.00 | £37.50 |
66 | $9.25 | $28.00 | $65.00 | £4.60 | £13.50 | £32.50
67 one of those great Marvel story titles: "Where Strides The Behemoth"
| | $9.25 | $28.00 | $65.00 | £4.25 | £12.50 | £30.00 |
68 | $9.25 | $28.00 | $65.00 | £3.90 | £11.50 | £27.50
69 last of Giant-Man series
| | $9.25 | $20.00 | $66.00 | £3.90 | £11.50 | £27.50 |
70 Sub-Mariner series begins
| | $12.50 | $39.00 | $90.00 | £6.25 | £19.00 | £45.00 |
71-73 | $7.00 | $21.00 | $50.00 | £3.20 | £9.50 | £22.50
74 last Silver Age issue cover dated December 1965
| | $7.00 | $21.00 | $50.00 | £3.20 | £9.50 | £22.50 |
75 (Jan 1966) | $7.00 | $21.00 | $50.00 | £2.85 | £8.50 | £20.00
76-78 | $7.00 | $21.00 | $50.00 | £2.85 | £8.50 | £20.00
79 Hulk vs Hercules (1st Hulk/Hercules battle)
| | $7.00 | $21.00 | $50.00 | £3.20 | £9.50 | £22.50 |
80 | $7.00 | $21.00 | $50.00 | £2.85 | £8.50 | £20.00
81 | $7.00 | $21.00 | $50.00 | £2.50 | £7.50 | £17.50
82 Sub-Mariner battles Iron Man, X-over with Tales of Suspense #79/80
| | $9.25 | $28.00 | $65.00 | £3.20 | £9.50 | £22.50 |
83-84 | $7.00 | $21.00 | $50.00 | £2.50 | £7.50 | £17.50
85-86 scarce in the U.K.
| | $7.00 | $21.00 | $50.00 | £2.85 | £8.50 | £20.00 |
87 (Jan 1967) | $7.00 | $21.00 | $50.00 | £2.50 | £7.50 | £17.50
88-89 | $7.00 | $21.00 | $50.00 | £2.50 | £7.50 | £17.50
90 1st appearance The Abomination
| | $8.50 | $26.00 | $60.00 | £3.20 | £9.50 | £22.50 |
91 | $6.25 | $19.00 | $45.00 | £2.50 | £7.50 | £17.50
92 4th appearance Silver Surfer, cameo only (pre-dates Silver Surfer #1)
| | $9.25 | $28.00 | $65.00 | £3.55 | £10.50 | £25.00 |
93 5th appearance Silver Surfer (pre-dates Silver Surfer #1), battles Hulk, classic cover
| | $10.50 | $32.00 | $75.00 | £5.00 | £15.00 | £35.00 |
94-96 High Evolutionary appears
| | $6.25 | $19.00 | $45.00 | £2.50 | £7.50 | £17.50 |
97-98 scarce in the U.K.
| | $6.25 | $19.00 | $45.00 | £2.85 | £8.50 | £20.00 |
99 scarce in the U.K. (Jan 1968)
| | $6.25 | $19.00 | $45.00 | £2.85 | £8.50 | £20.00 |
100 scarce in the U.K. Hulk vs. Sub-Mariner
| | $9.25 | $28.00 | $65.00 | £3.20 | £9.50 | £22.50 |

101 scarce in the U.K. lead into Hulk #102 and Iron Man/Sub-Mariner #1
| | $11.00 | $34.00 | $80.00 | £5.00 | £15.00 | £35.00 |
Title Value: | $2487.25 | $7433.50 | $19995.00 | £1501.40 | £4507.50 | £12272.50

Note: Kirby art in 10-40, 44, 49-51, 68-70, 82, 83. Everett art in 78-84, 87-91, 94-96.
ARTISTS
Ditko art in 10-48, 60-67; inks in 50. Kirby art in 10-40, 44, 49-51, 68-70, 82, 83.
FEATURES
Ant-Man in 27, 35-48. Giant-Man in 49-69. Hulk in 60-101. Sub-Mariner in 70-101. Hulk vs Sub-Mariner in 100. Monster/fantasy stories in 10-59 (as back-ups in 35-59).

TALES TO ASTONISH (2ND SERIES)
Marvel Comics Group; 1 Dec 1979-14 Jan 1981
1 ND reprints Sub-Mariner from issue #1
| | $0.50 | $1.50 | $2.50 | £0.30 | £0.90 | £1.50 |
2-3 ND | $0.40 | $1.20 | $2.00 | £0.25 | £0.75 | £1.25
4-14 ND | $0.30 | $0.90 | $1.50 | £0.20 | £0.60 | £1.00
Title Value: | $4.60 | $13.80 | $23.00 | £3.00 | £9.00 | £15.00

TALES TO ASTONISH (3RD SERIES)
Marvel Comics Group, OS; 1 Dec 1994
1 64pgs, squarebound. Peter David script, John Estes art. The Hulk, Hank Pym and The Wasp appear; painted cover with protective acetate outer cover
| | $1.40 | $4.20 | $7.00 | £0.90 | £2.70 | £4.50 |
Title Value: | $1.40 | $4.20 | $7.00 | £0.90 | £2.70 | £4.50

TALES TOO TERRIBLE TO TELL
New England Comics; 1 Winter 1989-12 1993
(becomes Terrology with #12)
1 pre-Code horror reprints
| | $0.80 | $2.40 | $4.00 | £0.50 | £1.50 | £2.50 |
1 2nd printing, Jun 1993
| | $0.60 | $1.80 | $3.00 | £0.40 | £1.20 | £2.00 |
2 pre-Code horror reprints
| | $0.60 | $1.80 | $3.00 | £0.40 | £1.20 | £2.00 |
3 pre-Code horror reprints, Bissette cover
| | $0.60 | $1.80 | $3.00 | £0.40 | £1.20 | £2.00 |
4-8 pre Code horror reprints
| | $0.60 | $1.80 | $3.00 | £0.40 | £1.20 | £2.00 |
9 pre Code horror reprints, $3.95 cover
| | $0.80 | $2.40 | $4.00 | £0.50 | £1.50 | £2.50 |
10-11 pre Code horror reprints
| | $0.60 | $1.80 | $3.00 | £0.40 | £1.20 | £2.00 |
12 pre Code horror reprints; title becomes "Terrology"
| | $0.60 | $1.80 | $3.00 | £0.40 | £1.20 | £2.00 |
Title Value: | $8.20 | $24.60 | $41.00 | £5.40 | £16.20 | £27.00

Note: reprints of 1950s horror stories plus articles, cover gallery and new material. Quarterly frequency. Non-Distributed in the U.K.

TALESPIN
Disney, MS; 1 Dec 1990-4 Mar 1991
1-4 ND | $0.30 | $0.90 | $1.50 | £0.20 | £0.60 | £1.00

TALESPIN (2ND SERIES)
Disney; 1 May 1991-9 Jan 1992
1-9 ND | $0.30 | $0.90 | $1.50 | £0.20 | £0.60 | £1.00
Title Value: | $2.70 | $8.10 | $13.50 | £1.80 | £5.40 | £9.00

TALOS OF THE WILDERNESS SEA
DC Comics, OS; 1 Jun 1987
1 48pgs, Gil Kane art, no adverts
| | $0.30 | $0.90 | $1.50 | £0.20 | £0.60 | £1.00 |
Title Value: | $0.30 | $0.90 | $1.50 | £0.20 | £0.60 | £1.00

TANK GIRL
Dark Horse, MS; 1 Jul 1991-4 Oct 1991
1 ND reprints from U.K.'s Deadline magazine, Jamie Hewlett art
| | $0.60 | $1.80 | $3.00 | £0.40 | £1.20 | £2.00 |
2-4 ND reprints from U.K.'s Deadline magazine, Jamie Hewlett art
| | $0.50 | $1.50 | $2.50 | £0.30 | £0.90 | £1.50 |
Title Value: | $2.10 | $6.30 | $10.50 | £1.30 | £3.90 | £6.50
Tank Girl Volume One (1994) Trade paperback reprints mini-series, painted cover by Jamie Hewlett
| | | | | £2.00 | £6.00 | £10.00 |

TANK GIRL II
Dark Horse, MS; 1 Jun 1993-4 Sep 1993
1-4 ND Alan Martin and Jamie Hewlett
| | $0.50 | $1.50 | $2.50 | £0.30 | £0.90 | £1.50 |
Title Value: | $2.00 | $6.00 | $10.00 | £1.20 | £3.60 | £6.00
Tank Girl II (Jan 1995) Trade paperback reprints mini-series, Jamie Hewlett painted cover
| | | | | £2.40 | £7.20 | £12.00 |

TANK GIRL MOVIE ADAPTATION
DC Comics, OS; 1 May 1995
1 ND 64pgs, Peter Milligan and Andy Pritchett adaptation of film, John Bolton cover
| | $1.00 | $3.00 | $5.00 | £0.70 | £2.10 | £3.50 |
Title Value: | $1.00 | $3.00 | $5.00 | £0.70 | £2.10 | £3.50

TANK GIRL: APOCALYPSE
DC Comics, MS; 1 Nov 1995-4 Feb 1996
1-4 ND Alan Grant script, Brian Bolland covers
| | $0.50 | $1.50 | $2.50 | £0.30 | £0.90 | £1.50 |
Title Value: | $2.00 | $6.00 | $10.00 | £1.20 | £3.60 | £6.00

TANK GIRL: THE ODYSSEY
DC Comics/Vertigo, MS; 1 Jun 1995-4 Sep 1995
1-4 ND Peter Milligan script, Jamie Hewlett art; painted cover by Brian Bolland
| | $0.50 | $1.50 | $2.50 | £0.30 | £0.90 | £1.50 |
Title Value: | $2.00 | $6.00 | $10.00 | £1.20 | £3.60 | £6.00

TAPPING THE VEIN
(see Clive Barker's...)

TARGET: AIRBOY
Eclipse; 1 Mar 1988

	$Good	$Fine	$N.Mint	£Good	£Fine	£N.Mint
1 ND Sam Kieth cover and art, Clint of the Radioactive Hamsters appears, card covers; continuity ties in these events before Airboy #37						
	$0.80	$2.40	$4.00	£0.50	£1.50	£2.50
Title Value:	$0.80	$2.40	$4.00	£0.50	£1.50	£2.50

TARGITT
Atlas; 1 Mar 1975-2 Jul 1975

	$Good	$Fine	$N.Mint	£Good	£Fine	£N.Mint
1-3 distributed in the U.K. "John Targitt, Man-Stalker" on cover						
	$0.25	$0.75	$1.25	£0.15	£0.45	£0.75
Title Value:	$0.75	$2.25	$3.75	£0.45	£1.35	£2.25

TARZAN
DC Comics; 207 Apr 1972-258 Feb 1977
(see Limited Collector's Edition, One Hundred Page Super Spectacular) (previously published by Gold Key)

	$Good	$Fine	$N.Mint	£Good	£Fine	£N.Mint
207 52pgs, origin begins						
	$2.05	$6.25	$12.50	£1.00	£3.00	£6.00
208-209 52pgs, origin						
	$1.65	$5.00	$10.00	£0.80	£2.50	£5.00
210 ND origin ends						
	$1.30	$4.00	$8.00	£0.65	£2.00	£4.00
211-215 ND	$1.30	$4.00	$8.00	£0.65	£2.00	£4.00
216 ND Chaykin back-up						
	$1.30	$4.00	$8.00	£0.65	£2.00	£4.00
217-220 ND	$1.30	$4.00	$8.00	£0.65	£2.00	£4.00
221-229 ND	$1.30	$3.75	$7.50	£0.55	£1.75	£3.50
230 ND 100pgs, Kaluta art						
	$1.30	$4.00	$8.00	£0.65	£2.00	£4.00
231-234 ND 100pgs, Nino art						
	$1.30	$4.00	$8.00	£0.65	£2.00	£4.00
235 very LD 100pgs						
	$1.30	$4.00	$8.00	£0.65	£2.00	£4.00
236-237 ND	$1.25	$3.75	$7.50	£0.55	£1.75	£3.50
238 ND 68pgs	$1.30	$4.00	$8.00	£0.65	£2.00	£4.00
239-240 ND	$1.25	$3.75	$7.50	£0.55	£1.75	£3.50
241-250 ND	$1.25	$3.75	$7.50	£0.50	£1.50	£3.00
251-258 ND	$1.25	$3.75	$7.50	£0.40	£1.25	£2.50
Title Value:	$67.50	$204.50	$409.00	£29.65	£91.75	£183.50

FEATURES
Beyond the Furthest Star in 213-218. Carson of Venus in 230. John Carter in 207-209. Korak in 230-234. Tarzan in 207-225, 227-236, 239-256.
REPRINT FEATURES
Congo Bill in 230-235. Detective Chimp in 230-235. Rex the Wonder Dog in 232, 233. Tarzan by Hal Foster in 207-209, 211, 215, 221. Tarzan by Hogarth in 211. Tarzan by Manning in 226, 230-235, 237, 238. Tarzan in 252, 253, 257, 258. Simba (Bomba re-titled) in 230, 231.

TARZAN
Dell/Gold Key; 1 Feb 1948-131 Aug 1962; Gold Key; 132 Nov 1962-206 Feb 1972
(transfers to DC Comics #207 on)

	$Good	$Fine	$N.Mint	£Good	£Fine	£N.Mint
1 Jesse Marsh art begins						
	$105.00	$315.00	$850.00	£67.50	£205.00	£550.00
2	$67.50	$200.00	$475.00	£46.00	£135.00	£325.00
3-5	$50.00	$150.00	$350.00	£33.00	£97.50	£230.00
6-10	$39.00	$115.00	$275.00	£25.00	£75.00	£175.00
11-12	$34.00	$100.00	$240.00	£22.50	£67.50	£160.00
13 1st photo cover (Lex Barker)						
	$34.00	$100.00	$240.00	£22.50	£67.50	£160.00
14-15	$34.00	$100.00	$240.00	£22.50	£67.50	£160.00
16-20	$25.00	$75.00	$175.00	£16.00	£49.00	£115.00
21-24	$20.00	$60.00	$140.00	£13.50	£41.00	£95.00
25 1st appearance Brothers of the Spear (see their own title)						
	$23.50	$70.00	$165.00	£15.50	£47.00	£110.00
26-30	$20.00	$60.00	$140.00	£13.50	£41.00	£95.00
31-38	$12.50	$39.00	$90.00	£8.50	£26.00	£60.00
39 1st Russ Manning art on Brothers of the Spear						
	$13.50	$41.00	$95.00	£9.25	£28.00	£65.00
40	$12.50	$39.00	$90.00	£8.50	£26.00	£60.00
41-53	$9.25	$28.00	$65.00	£6.25	£19.00	£45.00
54 last Lex Barker photo cover						
	$9.25	$28.00	$65.00	£6.25	£19.00	£45.00
55 painted covers restart						
	$6.25	$19.00	$45.00	£4.25	£12.50	£30.00
56-60	$6.25	$19.00	$45.00	£4.25	£12.50	£30.00
61-70	$5.00	$15.00	$35.00	£3.20	£9.50	£22.50
71-78	$3.90	$11.50	$27.50	£2.50	£7.50	£17.50
79 last painted cover						
	$3.90	$11.50	$27.50	£2.50	£7.50	£17.50
80 Gordon Scott photo covers begin						
	$4.25	$12.50	$30.00	£2.85	£8.50	£20.00
81-90	$4.25	$12.50	$30.00	£2.85	£8.50	£20.00
91-99	$3.90	$11.50	$27.50	£2.50	£7.50	£17.50
100	$5.00	$15.00	$35.00	£3.20	£9.50	£22.50
101-109	$3.20	$9.50	$22.50	£2.10	£6.25	£15.00
110 scarce in both US and UK last photo cover						
	$4.25	$12.50	$30.00	£2.85	£8.50	£20.00
111 painted covers restart						
	$2.85	$8.50	$20.00	£2.00	£6.00	£14.00
112-114	$2.85	$8.50	$20.00	£2.00	£6.00	£14.00
1st official distribution in the U.K.						
115-120	$2.85	$8.50	$20.00	£2.00	£6.00	£14.00
121-130	$2.10	$6.25	$15.00	£1.40	£4.25	£10.00
131 last Dell issue						
	$2.10	$6.25	$15.00	£1.40	£4.25	£10.00
132 1st Gold Key issue						
	$3.20	$9.50	$22.50	£2.10	£6.25	£15.00
133-137	$2.50	$7.50	$17.50	£1.75	£5.25	£12.50
138 title becomes "Tarzan of the Apes"						
	$2.50	$7.50	$17.50	£1.75	£5.25	£12.50
139-140	$2.50	$7.50	$17.50	£1.75	£5.25	£12.50
141-150	$2.10	$6.25	$15.00	£1.40	£4.25	£10.00
151-154	$2.00	$6.00	$12.00	£1.30	£4.00	£8.00
155 origin	$3.75	$11.00	$22.50	£2.50	£7.50	£15.00
156-160	$2.00	$6.00	$12.00	£1.30	£4.00	£8.00
161-177	$1.65	$5.00	$10.00	£1.15	£3.50	£7.00
178 origin, reprints #155						
	$2.40	$7.00	$12.00	£1.60	£4.80	£8.00
179-180	$2.00	$6.00	$10.00	£1.40	£4.20	£7.00
181-199	$1.25	$3.75	$7.50	£0.80	£2.50	£5.00
200 scarce in both US and UK						
	$2.05	$6.25	$12.50	£1.25	£3.75	£7.50
201-205	$1.25	$3.75	$7.50	£0.80	£2.50	£5.00
206 numbering continued in DC title						
	$1.25	$3.75	$7.50	£0.80	£2.50	£5.00
Title Value:	$1699.30	$5085.25	$11987.50	£1123.95	£3386.70	£7958.00

Note: issues from about 1958 distributed on the news-stands in the U.K. and then officially distributed from early 1960 with cover dates of November 1959

TARZAN
Marvel Comics Group; 1 Jun 1977-29 Oct 1979

	$Good	$Fine	$N.Mint	£Good	£Fine	£N.Mint
1 ND John Buscema art begins						
	$0.60	$1.80	$3.00	£0.40	£1.20	£2.00
2-5 ND	$0.50	$1.50	$2.50	£0.30	£0.90	£1.50
6-29 ND	$0.40	$1.20	$2.00	£0.25	£0.75	£1.25
Title Value:	$12.20	$36.60	$61.00	£7.60	£22.80	£38.00

TARZAN ANNUAL
Marvel Comics Group; 1 1977-3 1979

	$Good	$Fine	$N.Mint	£Good	£Fine	£N.Mint
1-3 ND 52pgs	$0.40	$1.20	$2.00	£0.25	£0.75	£1.25

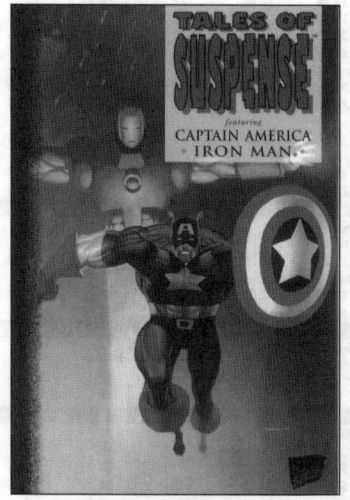

Tales of Suspense (2nd) #1

Tales of the Unexpected #31

Tarzan #158

MINT = 100% / NEAR MINT (inc. +/-) = 90–99% / VERY FINE (inc. +/-) = 75–89% / FINE (inc. +/-) = 55–74% / VERY GOOD (inc. +/-) = 35–54% / GOOD (inc. +/-) = 15–34% / FAIR = 5–14% / POOR = 1–4%

595

	$Good	$Fine	$N.Mint	£Good	£Fine	£N.Mint
Title Value:	$1.20	$3.60	$6.00	£0.75	£2.25	£3.75

TARZAN DIGEST
DC Comics,Digest; 1 Autumn 1972
1 ND 160pgs, reprints

	$Good	$Fine	$N.Mint	£Good	£Fine	£N.Mint
	$1.25	$3.75	$7.50	£0.80	£2.50	£5.00
Title Value:	$1.25	$3.75	$7.50	£0.80	£2.50	£5.00

TARZAN FAMILY
DC Comics; 60 Nov/Dec 1975-66 Nov/Dec 1976
(previously Korak, Son of Tarzan)

	$Good	$Fine	$N.Mint	£Good	£Fine	£N.Mint
60-62 ND 68pgs	$0.50	$1.50	$2.50	£0.30	£0.90	£1.50
63-66 ND 52pgs	$0.40	$1.20	$2.00	£0.25	£0.75	£1.25
Title Value:	$3.10	$9.30	$15.50	£1.90	£5.70	£9.50

ARTISTS
Kaluta reprints in 60-65.
FEATURES
Korak in 60-66. John Carter in 62-64. Pellucidar in 66.
REPRINT FEATURES
Carson of Venus in 60-65. John Carter in 65, 66. Tarzan in 60-64.

TARZAN OF THE APES
Marvel Comics Group,MS; 1 Jul 1984-2 Aug 1984
1-2 ND reprints Marvel Super Special #29

	$Good	$Fine	$N.Mint	£Good	£Fine	£N.Mint
	$0.30	$0.90	$1.50	£0.20	£0.60	£1.00
Title Value:	$0.60	$1.80	$3.00	£0.40	£1.20	£2.00

TARZAN THE WARRIOR
Malibu,MS; 1 Apr 1992-5 Aug 1992
1 ND Simon Bisley cover

	$Good	$Fine	$N.Mint	£Good	£Fine	£N.Mint
	$0.50	$1.50	$2.50	£0.30	£0.90	£1.50

1 2nd printing, ND Nov 1992

	$Good	$Fine	$N.Mint	£Good	£Fine	£N.Mint
	$0.40	$1.20	$2.00	£0.25	£0.75	£1.25
2-5 ND	$0.50	$1.50	$2.50	£0.30	£0.90	£1.50
Title Value:	$2.90	$8.70	$14.50	£1.75	£5.25	£8.75

TARZAN VS. PREDATOR: AT EARTH'S CORE
Dark Horse,MS; 1 Jun 1995-4 Sep 1995
1-4 ND Walt Simonson script, Lee Weeks art

	$Good	$Fine	$N.Mint	£Good	£Fine	£N.Mint
	$0.50	$1.50	$2.50	£0.30	£0.90	£1.50
Title Value:	$2.00	$6.00	$10.00	£1.20	£3.60	£6.00

TARZAN, LORD OF THE JUNGLE
Gold Key; 1 Sep 1965
1 rare in the U.K. giant size reprint

	$Good	$Fine	$N.Mint	£Good	£Fine	£N.Mint
	$7.75	$23.50	$55.00	£5.00	£15.00	£35.00
Title Value:	$7.75	$23.50	$55.00	£5.00	£15.00	£35.00

TARZAN/JOHN CARTER: WARLORDS OF MARS
Dark Horse,MS; 1 Dec 1995-present
1,2 ND Bruce Jones script, Bret Blevins art

	$Good	$Fine	$N.Mint	£Good	£Fine	£N.Mint
	$0.50	$1.50	$2.50	£0.30	£0.90	£1.50
Title Value:	$1.00	$3.00	$5.00	£0.60	£1.80	£3.00

TARZAN: LOVE, LIES AND THE LOST CITY
Malibu,MS; 1 Aug 1992-3 Dec 1992

	$Good	$Fine	$N.Mint	£Good	£Fine	£N.Mint
1-3 ND	$0.50	$1.50	$2.50	£0.30	£0.90	£1.50
Title Value:	$1.50	$4.50	$7.50	£0.90	£2.70	£4.50

TARZAN: MUGAMBI, EDGAR RICE BURROUGHS'
Dark Horse,OS; 1 May 1995
1 ND Darko Macan script, Igor Kordej art

	$Good	$Fine	$N.Mint	£Good	£Fine	£N.Mint
	$0.60	$1.80	$3.00	£0.40	£1.20	£2.00
Title Value:	$0.60	$1.80	$3.00	£0.40	£1.20	£2.00

TARZAN: THE BECKONING
Malibu,MS; 1 Nov 1992-7 May 1993
1-7 ND Tom Yeates art

	$Good	$Fine	$N.Mint	£Good	£Fine	£N.Mint
	$0.50	$1.50	$2.50	£0.30	£0.90	£1.50
Title Value:	$3.50	$10.50	$17.50	£2.10	£6.30	£10.50

TARZAN: THE LOST ADVENTURE, EDGAR RICE BURROUGHS'
Dark Horse,MS; 1 Jan 1995-4 Apr 1995
1 ND 64pgs, Joe R. Lansdale script, Tom Yeates art

	$Good	$Fine	$N.Mint	£Good	£Fine	£N.Mint
	$0.60	$1.80	$3.00	£0.40	£1.20	£2.00

2 ND 64pgs, Joe R. Lansdale script, Charles Vess art

	$Good	$Fine	$N.Mint	£Good	£Fine	£N.Mint
	$0.60	$1.80	$3.00	£0.40	£1.20	£2.00

3 ND 64pgs, Joe R. Lansdale script, Gary Gianni art

	$Good	$Fine	$N.Mint	£Good	£Fine	£N.Mint
	$0.60	$1.80	$3.00	£0.40	£1.20	£2.00

4 ND 64pgs, Joe R. Lansdale script, Mike Kaluta art

	$Good	$Fine	$N.Mint	£Good	£Fine	£N.Mint
	$0.60	$1.80	$3.00	£0.40	£1.20	£2.00
Title Value:	$2.40	$7.20	$12.00	£1.60	£4.80	£8.00

Note: unusual 6.5" x 9.5" pulp magazine size format. Painted covers by Arthur Suydam

TASK FORCE ALPHA: FORGED IN FIRE
Alpha Productions,MS; 1 Jan 1995-2 Feb 1995
1-2 ND 48pgs, Paul Pelletier flip-covers

	$Good	$Fine	$N.Mint	£Good	£Fine	£N.Mint
	$0.40	$1.20	$2.00	£0.25	£0.75	£1.25
Title Value:	$0.80	$2.40	$4.00	£0.50	£1.50	£2.50

TEAM 1: STORMWATCH
Image,MS; 1 Jul 1995-2 Aug 1995
1-2 ND Steven Seagle script, Tom Raney art

	$Good	$Fine	$N.Mint	£Good	£Fine	£N.Mint
	$0.50	$1.50	$2.50	£0.30	£0.90	£1.50
Title Value:	$1.00	$3.00	$5.00	£0.60	£1.80	£3.00

TEAM 1: WILDC.A.T.S.
Image,MS; 1 Jul 1995-2 Aug 1995
1-2 ND James Robinson script, Rich Johnson art

	$Good	$Fine	$N.Mint	£Good	£Fine	£N.Mint
	$0.50	$1.50	$2.50	£0.30	£0.90	£1.50
Title Value:	$1.00	$3.00	$5.00	£0.60	£1.80	£3.00

TEAM 7
Image,MS; 1 Oct 1994-4 Jan 1995
1 ND Grifter, Backlash, Deathblow, Lynch and Dane

	$Good	$Fine	$N.Mint	£Good	£Fine	£N.Mint
	$1.00	$3.00	$5.00	£0.70	£2.10	£3.50

1 Variant cover, ND cover forms larger picture when combined with variant covers of Deathblow #5, Gen 13 #5, Kindred #3, Stormwatch #10, Wetworks #2, WildC.A.T.S. #11

	$Good	$Fine	$N.Mint	£Good	£Fine	£N.Mint
	$1.50	$4.50	$7.50	£1.00	£3.00	£5.00

2-4 ND Grifter, Backlash, Deathblow, Lynch and Dane

	$Good	$Fine	$N.Mint	£Good	£Fine	£N.Mint
	$0.60	$1.80	$3.00	£0.40	£1.20	£2.00
Title Value:	$4.30	$12.90	$21.50	£2.90	£8.70	£14.50

Team 7 (Jun 1995)
Trade paperback collects mini-series

	$Good	$Fine	$N.Mint	£Good	£Fine	£N.Mint
				£1.30	£3.90	£6.50

TEAM 7 (2ND SERIES)
Image; 1 Jan 1996-present

	$Good	$Fine	$N.Mint	£Good	£Fine	£N.Mint
1 ND	$0.50	$1.50	$2.50	£0.30	£0.90	£1.50
Title Value:	$0.50	$1.50	$2.50	£0.30	£0.90	£1.50

TEAM 7 - OBJECTIVE HELL
Image,MS; 1 May 1995-3 Jul 1995
1 ND Wildstorm Rising Prologue, continued in Wildstorm Rising #1; with two foil-bagged painted trading cards; cover by Barry Windsor-Smith

	$Good	$Fine	$N.Mint	£Good	£Fine	£N.Mint
	$0.50	$1.50	$2.50	£0.30	£0.90	£1.50

1 Newstand edition, ND without trading cards

	$Good	$Fine	$N.Mint	£Good	£Fine	£N.Mint
	$0.40	$1.20	$2.00	£0.25	£0.75	£1.50
2-3 ND	$0.50	$1.50	$2.50	£0.30	£0.90	£1.50
Title Value:	$1.90	$5.70	$9.50	£1.15	£3.45	£5.75

TEAM AMERICA
Marvel Comics Group, Toy; 1 Jun 1982-12 May 1983
(see Captain America #269)

	$Good	$Fine	$N.Mint	£Good	£Fine	£N.Mint
1 ND origin	$0.15	$0.45	$0.75	£0.10	£0.30	£0.50
2-8 ND	$0.15	$0.45	$0.75	£0.10	£0.30	£0.50

9 ND Iron Man appears

	$Good	$Fine	$N.Mint	£Good	£Fine	£N.Mint
	$0.15	$0.45	$0.75	£0.10	£0.30	£0.50
10 ND	$0.15	$0.45	$0.75	£0.10	£0.30	£0.50

11 ND Team America vs. Ghost Rider

	$Good	$Fine	$N.Mint	£Good	£Fine	£N.Mint
	$0.60	$1.80	$3.00	£0.10	£0.35	£0.60
12 ND	$0.15	$0.45	$0.75	£0.10	£0.30	£0.50
Title Value:	$2.25	$6.75	$11.25	£1.20	£3.65	£6.10

TEAM ANARCHY
Dagger Enterprises; 1 Oct 1993-12 Sep 1994
1-11 ND Rick Buckler Jnr. art

	$Good	$Fine	$N.Mint	£Good	£Fine	£N.Mint
	$0.40	$1.20	$2.00	£0.25	£0.75	£1.25
12 ND	$0.40	$1.20	$2.00	£0.25	£0.75	£1.25
Title Value:	$4.80	$14.40	$24.00	£3.00	£9.00	£15.00

TEAM HELIX
Marvel UK,MS; 1 Jan 1993-4 Apr 1993
1-2 Wolverine appears

	$Good	$Fine	$N.Mint	£Good	£Fine	£N.Mint
	$0.30	$0.90	$1.50	£0.20	£0.60	£1.00

3-4 Wolverine and Ka-Zar appear; re-titled "Codename: Genetix"

	$Good	$Fine	$N.Mint	£Good	£Fine	£N.Mint
	$0.30	$0.90	$1.50	£0.20	£0.60	£1.00
Title Value:	$1.20	$3.60	$6.00	£0.80	£2.40	£4.00

TEAM TITANS
DC Comics; 1 Sep 1992-24 Sep 1994
1 48pgs, Total Chaos part 3, Terra origin plus bonus 21pg story

	$Good	$Fine	$N.Mint	£Good	£Fine	£N.Mint
	$0.40	$1.20	$2.00	£0.25	£0.75	£1.25

1 48pgs, Total Chaos part 3, Mirage origin plus bonus 21pg story

	$Good	$Fine	$N.Mint	£Good	£Fine	£N.Mint
	$0.40	$1.20	$2.00	£0.25	£0.75	£1.25

1 48pgs, Total Chaos part 3, Nightrider origin plus bonus 21pg story

	$Good	$Fine	$N.Mint	£Good	£Fine	£N.Mint
	$0.40	$1.20	$2.00	£0.25	£0.75	£1.25

1 48pgs, Total Chaos part 3, Redwing origin plus bonus 21pg story

	$Good	$Fine	$N.Mint	£Good	£Fine	£N.Mint
	$0.40	$1.20	$2.00	£0.25	£0.75	£1.25

1 48pgs, Total Chaos part 3, Killowat origin plus bonus 21pg story

	$Good	$Fine	$N.Mint	£Good	£Fine	£N.Mint
	$0.40	$1.20	$2.00	£0.25	£0.75	£1.25

2 Total Chaos part 6, continued in Deathstroke the Terminator #16

	$Good	$Fine	$N.Mint	£Good	£Fine	£N.Mint
	$0.40	$1.20	$2.00	£0.25	£0.75	£1.25

3 Total Chaos part 9 (conclusion)

	$Good	$Fine	$N.Mint	£Good	£Fine	£N.Mint
	$0.40	$1.20	$2.00	£0.25	£0.75	£1.25

4 Titans Sell-Out part 4 (conclusion)

	$Good	$Fine	$N.Mint	£Good	£Fine	£N.Mint
	$0.40	$1.20	$2.00	£0.25	£0.75	£1.25
5	$0.40	$1.20	$2.00	£0.25	£0.75	£1.25
6 Christmas issue	$0.30	$0.90	$1.50	£0.20	£0.60	£1.00
7-9	$0.30	$0.90	$1.50	£0.20	£0.60	£1.00

10 The Darkening part 4 (conclusion), continued from New Titans #100

	$Good	$Fine	$N.Mint	£Good	£Fine	£N.Mint
	$0.30	$0.90	$1.50	£0.20	£0.60	£1.00
11-19	$0.30	$0.90	$1.50	£0.20	£0.60	£1.00

20-23 prelude to Zero Hour

	$Good	$Fine	$N.Mint	£Good	£Fine	£N.Mint
	$0.30	$0.90	$1.50	£0.20	£0.60	£1.00

24 Zero Hour X-over

	$Good	$Fine	$N.Mint	£Good	£Fine	£N.Mint
	$0.30	$0.90	$1.50	£0.20	£0.60	£1.00
Title Value:	$9.30	$27.90	$46.50	£6.05	£18.15	£30.25

TEAM TITANS ANNUAL
DC Comics; 1 Nov 1993-2 1994
1 64pgs, Bloodlines (Wave Two) part 22, 1st appearance Chimera, continued in Legion '93 Annual #4

	$Good	$Fine	$N.Mint	£Good	£Fine	£N.Mint
	$0.60	$1.80	$3.00	£0.40	£1.20	£2.00

2 64pgs, Luke Ross and Kevin Conrad art; Elseworlds story

	$Good	$Fine	$N.Mint	£Good	£Fine	£N.Mint
	$0.60	$1.80	$3.00	£0.40	£1.20	£2.00
Title Value:	$1.20	$3.60	$6.00	£0.80	£2.40	£4.00

TEAM YANKEE
First,MS; 1 Jan 1989-6 Feb 1989

	$Good	$Fine	$N.Mint	£Good	£Fine	£N.Mint
1-6 ND	$0.40	$1.20	$2.00	£0.25	£0.75	£1.25
Title Value:	$2.40	$7.20	$12.00	£1.50	£4.50	£7.50
Trade Paperback				£1.70	£5.10	£8.50

TEAM YOUNGBLOOD
Image; 1 Sep 1993-21 Aug 1995
1 Rob Liefeld script, Chap Yaep pencils and Norm Rapmund inks begin

	$Good	$Fine	$N.Mint	£Good	£Fine	£N.Mint
	$0.40	$1.20	$2.00	£0.25	£0.75	£1.25
2-8	$0.40	$1.20	$2.00	£0.25	£0.75	£1.25

9 Rob Liefeld returns to Extreme Studios work with this issue; Liefeld script and wraparound cover

	$Good	$Fine	$N.Mint	£Good	£Fine	£N.Mint
	$0.50	$1.50	$2.50	£0.30	£0.90	£1.50
10 $2.50 cover begin	$0.45	$1.35	$2.25	£0.30	£0.90	£1.50
11 story continued from Team Youngblood #10 and Youngblood #7	$0.50	$1.50	$2.50	£0.30	£0.90	£1.50
12 story continued from Youngblood #7 and Team Youngblood #11	$0.50	$1.50	$2.50	£0.30	£0.90	£1.50
13 Riptide poses nude in a men's magazine	$0.50	$1.50	$2.50	£0.30	£0.90	£1.50
14	$0.50	$1.50	$2.50	£0.30	£0.90	£1.50
15 New Blood story, continued from Newmen #8	$0.50	$1.50	$2.50	£0.30	£0.90	£1.50
16 guest-stars Bloodpool	$0.50	$1.50	$2.50	£0.30	£0.90	£1.50
17 Extreme Sacrifice part 5, continued in Prophet #10; pre-bagged with trading card	$0.50	$1.50	$2.50	£0.30	£0.90	£1.50
18 team line-up changes begin decided by reader poll	$0.50	$1.50	$2.50	£0.30	£0.90	£1.50
19	$0.50	$1.50	$2.50	£0.30	£0.90	£1.50
20 Contact part 1, Extreme 3000 prologue	$0.50	$1.50	$2.50	£0.30	£0.90	£1.50
21 Contact part 2, Extreme 3000 tie-in; leads directly into Youngblood 2nd series #1						
Title Value:	$9.65	$28.95	$48.25	£5.90	£17.70	£29.50

Note: all Non-Distributed on the news-stands in the U.K.

TEEN BEAM

National Periodical Publications; 2 Jan/Feb 1968
(previously Teen Beat)

	$Good	$Fine	$N.Mint	£Good	£Fine	£N.Mint
2 rare in the U.K. Monkees photo cover	$2.90	$8.75	$17.50	£2.05	£6.25	£12.50
Title Value:	$2.90	$8.75	$17.50	£2.05	£6.25	£12.50

Note: Pop star photos, features, cartoons.

TEEN BEAT

National Periodical Publications; 1 Nov/Dec 1967
(becomes Teen Beam)

	$Good	$Fine	$N.Mint	£Good	£Fine	£N.Mint
1 rare in the U.K. Monkees photo cover	$4.15	$12.50	$25.00	£2.65	£8.00	£16.00
Title Value:	$4.15	$12.50	$25.00	£2.65	£8.00	£16.00

Note: Pop star photos, features, cartoons.

TEEN TITANS

National Periodical Publications/DC Comics; 1 Jan/Feb 1966-43 Jan/Feb 1973; 44 Nov 1976-53 Feb 1978
(see Brave and the Bold, DC Super-Stars, New Teen Titans, Showcase, Tales of the New Teen Titans, World's Finest)

	$Good	$Fine	$N.Mint	£Good	£Fine	£N.Mint
1 Batman, Flash, Aquaman, Wonder Woman cameos	$24.00	$72.50	$170.00	£15.50	£47.00	£110.00
2	$12.50	$39.00	$90.00	£7.00	£21.00	£50.00
3	$7.00	$21.00	$50.00	£4.25	£12.50	£30.00
4 Speedy appears	$7.00	$21.00	$50.00	£4.25	£12.50	£30.00
5	$7.00	$21.00	$50.00	£4.25	£12.50	£30.00
6-10	$6.25	$19.00	$45.00	£2.85	£8.50	£20.00
11 Speedy appears	$4.25	$12.50	$30.00	£2.10	£6.25	£15.00
12-18	$4.25	$12.50	$30.00	£2.10	£6.25	£15.00
19 Wood inks, Speedy joins	$4.25	$12.50	$30.00	£2.10	£6.25	£15.00
20 Neal Adams art	$5.00	$15.00	$35.00	£2.50	£7.50	£17.50
21 Neal Adams art, Hawk & Dove X-over	$5.00	$15.00	$35.00	£2.50	£7.50	£17.50
22 Neal Adams art, origin Wonder Girl	$5.00	$15.00	$35.00	£2.50	£7.50	£17.50
23 Wonder Girl dons new costume	$2.50	$7.50	$15.00	£1.30	£4.00	£8.00
24	$2.50	$7.50	$15.00	£1.30	£4.00	£8.00
25 Hawk & Dove, Flash, Green Arrow, Green Lantern, Aquaman, Batman, Superman X-over	$2.50	$7.50	$15.00	£1.30	£4.00	£8.00
26-28	$2.50	$7.50	$15.00	£1.30	£4.00	£8.00
29 Hawk & Dove X-over	$2.50	$7.50	$15.00	£1.30	£4.00	£8.00
30 Aquagirl appears	$2.50	$7.50	$15.00	£1.30	£4.00	£8.00
31 Hawk & Dove X-over	$1.50	$4.50	$9.00	£1.00	£3.00	£6.00
32-39	$1.50	$4.50	$9.00	£1.00	£3.00	£6.00
40-43	$1.30	$4.00	$8.00	£0.80	£2.50	£5.00
44 1st appearance Guardian	$0.80	$2.50	$5.00	£0.50	£1.50	£3.00
45 scarce in the U.K.	$0.80	$2.50	$5.00	£0.55	£1.75	£3.50
46 ND 1st appearance Joker's daughter	$1.80	$5.25	$9.00	£1.00	£3.00	£5.00
47 Joker's daughter appears	$1.50	$4.50	$7.50	£0.80	£2.40	£4.00
48 1st Bumblebee, Joker's daughter becomes Harlequin	$1.80	$5.25	$9.00	£0.80	£2.40	£4.00
49 scarce in the U.K.	$1.00	$3.00	$5.00	£0.70	£2.10	£3.50
50 1st Teen Titans West, 1st return original Bat-Girl (see Batman #139)	$1.80	$5.25	$9.00	£0.90	£2.70	£4.50
51-52	$1.00	$3.00	$5.00	£0.50	£1.50	£2.50
53 origin retold	$1.00	$3.00	$5.00	£0.60	£1.80	£3.00
Title Value:	$193.20	$580.75	$1307.50	£105.35	£316.40	£711.00

FEATURES
Aqualad in 30, 36. Hawk and the Dove in 31. Lilith in 36, 38.
REPRINT FEATURES
Aquaman/Aqualad in 35, 38. Green Arrow/Speedy in 35, 38. Hawk and the Dove in 39. Superboy in 36, 37.

TEEN TITANS SPOTLIGHT

DC Comics; 1 Aug 1986-21 Apr 1988

	$Good	$Fine	$N.Mint	£Good	£Fine	£N.Mint
1-2 Starfire, Apartheid story	$0.25	$0.75	$1.25	£0.15	£0.45	£0.75
3-6	$0.25	$0.75	$1.25	£0.15	£0.45	£0.75
7 1st Jackson Guice's art for DC, Hawk appears	$0.25	$0.75	$1.25	£0.15	£0.45	£0.75
8 Hawk appears	$0.25	$0.75	$1.25	£0.15	£0.45	£0.75
9	$0.25	$0.75	$1.25	£0.15	£0.45	£0.75
10 Erik Larsen art	$0.25	$0.75	$1.25	£0.15	£0.45	£0.75
11 "Asterix" issue	$0.25	$0.75	$1.25	£0.15	£0.45	£0.75
12-13	$0.25	$0.75	$1.25	£0.15	£0.45	£0.75
14 Batman appears	$0.25	$0.75	$1.25	£0.15	£0.45	£0.75
15 Erik Larsen art	$0.25	$0.75	$1.25	£0.15	£0.45	£0.75
16-17	$0.25	$0.75	$1.25	£0.15	£0.45	£0.75
18 Art Thibert cover and art (1st in comics?); Millennium X-over	$0.25	$0.75	$1.25	£0.15	£0.45	£0.75
19 Millennium X-over		$0.75	$1.25	£0.15	£0.45	£0.75
20-21	$0.25	$0.75	$1.25	£0.15	£0.45	£0.75
Title Value:	$5.25	$15.75	$26.25	£3.15	£9.45	£15.75

Note: Aqualad in 10,18. Brotherhood of Evil in 11. Changeling in 9. Cyborg in 13,20. Hawk in 7,8. Jericho in 3-6. Magenta in 17. Nightwing in 14. Omega Men in 15. Starfire in 1,2 19. Teen Titans (old) in 21. Thunder and Lightning in 16. Wonder Girl in 12.

TEEN-AGE ROMANCE

Atlas/Marvel Comics Group; 77 Sep 1960-86 Mar 1962
(formerly My Own Romance)

	$Good	$Fine	$N.Mint	£Good	£Fine	£N.Mint
77-86 scarce in the U.K.	$2.50	$7.50	$15.00	£1.65	£5.00	£10.00
Title Value:	$25.00	$75.00	$150.00	£16.50	£50.00	£100.00

TEENAGE MUTANT NINJA TURTLES

Mirage Studios; 1 1984-62 Sep 1993
(see Donatello, Fugitoid, Grimjack #26, Grunts, Gobbledeygook, How to Draw TMNT Leonardo, Michaelangelo, Raphael, Turtle Soup, TMNT Martial Arts Training Manual)

	$Good	$Fine	$N.Mint	£Good	£Fine	£N.Mint
1 scarce in the U.K. magazine size, red and white cover (see Warning below)	$30.00	$90.00	$180.00	£20.00	£60.00	£120.00
1 2nd printing, scarce in the U.K. (6,000 copies)	$3.30	$10.00	$20.00	£1.65	£5.00	£10.00
1 3rd printing	$1.00	$3.00	$6.00	£0.65	£2.00	£4.00
1 4th printing	$0.80	$2.40	$4.00	£0.50	£1.50	£2.50
1 5th printing, new back-up with two pages out of sequence	$0.40	$1.20	$2.00	£0.25	£0.75	£1.25
2 scarce in the U.K. blue/black and white cover, magazine size	$10.00	$30.00	$60.00	£6.50	£20.00	£40.00
2 2nd printing, scarce in the U.K.	$1.50	$4.50	$7.50	£1.00	£3.00	£5.00
2 3rd printing	$0.80	$2.40	$4.00	£0.50	£1.50	£2.50
3 scarce in the U.K. 1st Party Wagon, magazine size	$4.15	$12.50	$25.00	£2.50	£7.50	£15.00
3 2nd printing, new back-up, new cover	$0.90	$2.70	$4.50	£0.60	£1.80	£3.00
4 1st Triceratons, magazine size	$2.05	$6.25	$12.50	£1.25	£3.75	£7.50
4 2nd printing, new back-up, new cover	$0.40	$1.20	$2.00	£0.25	£0.75	£1.25
5	$1.25	$3.75	$7.50	£0.80	£2.50	£5.00
5 2nd printing, new back-up, new cover	$0.40	$1.20	$2.00	£0.25	£0.75	£1.25
6	$1.20	$3.60	$6.00	£0.80	£2.40	£4.00
6 2nd printing, new back-up	$0.40	$1.20	$2.00	£0.25	£0.75	£1.25
7 4 page colour insert by Corben, 1st Bade Biker by Lawson	$1.20	$3.60	$6.00	£0.80	£2.40	£4.00
7 2nd printing	$0.40	$1.20	$2.00	£0.25	£0.75	£1.25
8 Cerebus by Sim X-over	$1.20	$3.60	$6.00	£0.80	£2.40	£4.00
9 Rip in Time preview by Corben	$1.00	$3.00	$5.00	£0.70	£2.10	£3.50
10	$1.00	$3.00	$5.00	£0.70	£2.10	£3.50
11-14	$0.80	$2.40	$4.00	£0.50	£1.50	£2.50
15 Golden Age Parody cover, printed to appear damaged and worn	$0.80	$2.40	$4.00	£0.50	£1.50	£2.50
16 (published before issue #15)	$0.60	$1.80	$3.00	£0.40	£1.20	£2.00
17-20	$0.60	$1.80	$3.00	£0.40	£1.20	£2.00
21	$0.50	$1.50	$2.50	£0.30	£0.90	£1.50
22-23 Mark Martin art	$0.50	$1.50	$2.50	£0.30	£0.90	£1.50
24-25 Rick Veitch art	$0.50	$1.50	$2.50	£0.30	£0.90	£1.50
26 Rick Veitch art	$0.40	$1.20	$2.00	£0.25	£0.75	£1.25
27-32	$0.40	$1.20	$2.00	£0.25	£0.75	£1.25
32 2nd printing, (Jul 1992) - in colour with wraparound cover	$0.50	$1.50	$2.50	£0.30	£0.90	£1.50
33	$0.40	$1.20	$2.00	£0.25	£0.75	£1.25

	$Good	$Fine	$N.Mint	£Good	£Fine	£N.Mint
34-36 The Soul's Triad						
	$0.40	$1.20	$2.00	£0.25	£0.75	£1.25
37 The Twilight of the Rings						
	$0.40	$1.20	$2.00	£0.25	£0.75	£1.25
38 George Bush appears						
	$0.40	$1.20	$2.00	£0.25	£0.75	£1.25
39-40						
	$0.40	$1.20	$2.00	£0.25	£0.75	£1.25
41 Matt Howarth script/art						
	$0.40	$1.20	$2.00	£0.25	£0.75	£1.25
42-47						
	$0.40	$1.20	$2.00	£0.25	£0.75	£1.25
48 Shades of Gray part 1, plotted by Eastman and Laird						
	$0.40	$1.20	$2.00	£0.25	£0.75	£1.25
49 Shades of Gray part 2, plotted by Eastman and Laird						
	$0.40	$1.20	$2.00	£0.25	£0.75	£1.25
50 48pgs, City at War part 1, pin-ups by Larsen, Todd McFarlane and Walt Simonson						
	$0.40	$1.20	$2.00	£0.25	£0.75	£1.25
50 2nd printing, (Aug 1993)						
	$0.40	$1.20	$2.00	£0.25	£0.75	£1.25
51						
	$0.40	$1.20	$2.00	£0.25	£0.75	£1.25
51 2nd printing, (Sep 1993)						
	$0.40	$1.20	$2.00	£0.25	£0.75	£1.25
52 $2.25 cover begins						
	$0.40	$1.20	$2.00	£0.25	£0.75	£1.25
53-62	$0.40	$1.20	$2.00	£0.25	£0.75	£1.25
Title Value:	$88.95	$267.10	$497.00	£57.05	£171.85	£320.00

Note: all Non-Distributed on the news-stands in the U.K.

WARNING: there are counterfeit copies of issues #1 and 2 available. The cover is blue/black instead of solid black and the pages are unusually white. Issue #2 has a glossy cover instead of the original matt coating. In this instance the Guide does not give a value for either of these and thereby promote forgery.

Books published by First/Penguin:

				£Good	£Fine	£N.Mint
Book 1, reprints #1-3 plus 2 new stories, colour				£1.50	£4.50	£7.50
Book 2, reprints #4-6 plus 3 new pages, colour				£1.40	£4.20	£7.00
Book 3, reprints #7-9 plus 12 new pages, colour				£1.40	£4.20	£7.00
Book 4, reprints #10,11 plus Leonardo OS, gatefold, colour				£1.40	£4.20	£7.00

Trade paperbacks published by Mirage:

				£Good	£Fine	£N.Mint
Limited Edition hardback (1,000 copies), reprints #1-11 plus all 4 micro series				£7.00	£21.00	£35.00
Limited Edition softback (5,000 copies), as above				£2.50	£7.50	£12.50
Movie Adaptation (Jun 1990), 64pgs plus 10pg commentary by Eastman/Laird				£0.50	£1.50	£2.50
The Collected TMNT 1 (May 1990), reprints issues #9-11				£0.80	£2.40	£4.00
The Collected TMNT 2 (Jun 1990), reprints issues #12-14				£0.80	£2.40	£4.00
The Collected TMNT 3 (Jul 1990), reprints issues #15,#17,#18				£0.80	£2.40	£4.00
The Collected TMNT 4 (Aug 1990), reprints issues #19-21				£0.80	£2.40	£4.00
The Collected TMNT 5 (Sep 1990), reprints issues #16,#22,#23				£0.80	£2.40	£4.00
The Collected TMNT 6: The River (Sep 1991) reprints issues #24-26				£0.80	£2.40	£4.00
The Collected TMNT 7 (1991), reprints issues #27-29				£0.80	£2.40	£4.00
Challenges Graphic Novel (Nov 1991), six all-new stories, origin retold				£0.80	£2.40	£4.00
Deluxe TMNT Book 1 (Oct 1992) Facsimile Edition of #1, in duo-shade, introduction by Harlan Ellison				£0.75	£2.25	£3.75

TEENAGE MUTANT NINJA TURTLES (2ND SERIES)
Mirage Studios; 1 Oct 1993-present

	$Good	$Fine	$N.Mint	£Good	£Fine	£N.Mint
1 ND Jim Lawson story and pencils begin						
	$0.50	$1.50	$2.50	£0.30	£0.90	£1.50
2-12 ND	$0.50	$1.50	$2.50	£0.30	£0.90	£1.50
13 ND	$0.55	$1.85	$2.75	£0.35	£1.05	£1.75
Title Value:	$6.55	$19.65	$32.75	£3.95	£11.85	£19.75

TEENAGE MUTANT NINJA TURTLES ADVENTURES
Archie; 1 Dec 1988-74 Nov 1995

	$Good	$Fine	$N.Mint	£Good	£Fine	£N.Mint
1 ND	$0.50	$1.50	$2.50	£0.30	£0.90	£1.50
2-5 ND	$0.40	$1.20	$2.00	£0.25	£0.75	£1.25
6-10 ND	$0.30	$0.90	$1.50	£0.20	£0.60	£1.00
11-31 ND	$0.25	$0.75	$1.25	£0.15	£0.45	£0.75
32 ND Peter Laird cover						
	$0.25	$0.75	$1.25	£0.15	£0.45	£0.75
33-47 ND	$0.25	$0.75	$1.25	£0.15	£0.45	£0.75
48-50 ND The Black Hole Trilogy						
	$0.25	$0.75	$1.25	£0.15	£0.45	£0.75
51-61 ND	$0.25	$0.75	$1.25	£0.15	£0.45	£0.75
62-66 ND Dreamland story						
	$0.25	$0.75	$1.25	£0.15	£0.45	£0.75
67-74 ND	$0.25	$0.75	$1.25	£0.15	£0.45	£0.75
Title Value:	$19.60	$58.80	$98.00	£11.90	£35.70	£59.50
Spring Special, 64pgs				£0.35	£1.05	£1.75

TEENAGE MUTANT NINJA TURTLES ADVENTURES (LIMITED SERIES)
Archie,MS; 1 Sep 1988-3 Nov 1988

	$Good	$Fine	$N.Mint	£Good	£Fine	£N.Mint
1-3 ND	$0.50	$1.50	$2.50	£0.30	£0.90	£1.50
Title Value:	$1.50	$4.50	$7.50	£0.90	£2.70	£4.50

Note: all colour
Nestle Nespray drink version, no cover price, same indicia dates and valued the same as printings #2-5.

TEENAGE MUTANT NINJA TURTLES ADVENTURES SPECIAL
Archie; 1 Jun 1992-11 1993

	$Good	$Fine	$N.Mint	£Good	£Fine	£N.Mint
1 ND 64pgs	$0.40	$1.20	$2.00	£0.25	£0.75	£1.25
2 64pgs, Peter Laird cover						
	$0.40	$1.20	$2.00	£0.25	£0.75	£1.25
3-11 64pgs	$0.40	$1.20	$2.00	£0.25	£0.75	£1.25
Title Value:	$4.40	$13.20	$22.00	£2.75	£8.25	£13.75

TEENAGE MUTANT NINJA TURTLES II MOVIE ADAPTATION
Tundra Publishing,OS; 1 Jul 1991

	$Good	$Fine	$N.Mint	£Good	£Fine	£N.Mint
1 ND includes four pages of material not available in Archie version						
	$1.00	$3.00	$5.00	£0.60	£1.80	£3.00
Title Value:	$1.00	$3.00	$5.00	£0.60	£1.80	£3.00

TEENAGE MUTANT NINJA TURTLES III MOVIE ADAPTATION
Archie,OS; 1 May 1993

	$Good	$Fine	$N.Mint	£Good	£Fine	£N.Mint
1 ND 48pgs, Direct Market Edition						
	$0.60	$1.80	$3.00	£0.40	£1.20	£2.00
1 Newstand edition, ND 48pgs						
	$0.50	$1.50	$2.50	£0.30	£0.90	£1.50
Title Value:	$1.10	$3.30	$5.50	£0.70	£2.10	£3.50

TEENAGE MUTANT NINJA TURTLES MARTIAL ARTS TRAINING MANUAL
Solson Publications; 1-4 1986

	$Good	$Fine	$N.Mint	£Good	£Fine	£N.Mint
1-4 ND	$0.80	$2.40	$4.00	£0.50	£1.50	£2.50
Title Value:	$3.20	$9.60	$16.00	£2.00	£6.00	£10.00

TEENAGE MUTANT NINJA TURTLES MOVIE ADAPTATION
Archie; nn Jun 1990

				£Good	£Fine	£N.Mint
nn 48pgs, perfect-bound Direct Sales issue				£0.70	£2.10	£3.50
nn 64pgs news-stand issue with ads				£0.30	£0.90	£1.50

TEENAGE MUTANT NINJA TURTLES MOVIE PARODY
Mirage Studios; nn Jul 1990

	$Good	$Fine	$N.Mint	£Good	£Fine	£N.Mint
nn ND Mark Martin script and art						
	$0.50	$1.50	$2.50	£0.30	£0.90	£1.50
Title Value:	$0.50	$1.50	$2.50	£0.30	£0.90	£1.50

TEENAGE MUTANT NINJA TURTLES MOVIE SPECIAL 2
Archie; 1 May 1991

	$Good	$Fine	$N.Mint	£Good	£Fine	£N.Mint
1 ND adaptation of The Secret of the Ooze						
	$0.40	$1.20	$2.00	£0.25	£0.75	£1.25
Title Value:	$0.40	$1.20	$2.00	£0.25	£0.75	£1.25

TEENAGE MUTANT NINJA TURTLES VOLUMES
Tundra Publishing; 1 Feb 1991

	$Good	$Fine	$N.Mint	£Good	£Fine	£N.Mint
1 ND 150pgs, reprints Teenage Mutant Ninja Turtles Adventures #1-4 recoloured plus adaptation of first Teenage Mutant Ninja Turtles animated episode						
	$1.50	$4.50	$7.50	£1.00	£3.00	£5.00
Title Value:	$1.50	$4.50	$7.50	£1.00	£3.00	£5.00

TEENAGE MUTANT NINJA TURTLES VOLUMES (2ND SERIES)
Tundra Publishing; 1-4 Jul 1991

	$Good	$Fine	$N.Mint	£Good	£Fine	£N.Mint
1-4 ND reprints Archie issues #5-16; each volume has a different Turtle on cover						
	$1.00	$3.00	$5.00	£0.70	£2.10	£3.50
Title Value:	$4.00	$12.00	$20.00	£2.80	£8.40	£14.00

TEENAGE MUTANT NINJA TURTLES WINTER SPECIAL
Archie; 1 Jan 1991

	$Good	$Fine	$N.Mint	£Good	£Fine	£N.Mint
1 ND	$0.40	$1.20	$2.00	£0.25	£0.75	£1.25
	$0.40	$1.20	$2.00	£0.25	£0.75	£1.25

TEENAGE MUTANT NINJA TURTLES/SAVAGE DRAGON CROSSOVER
Mirage Studios,OS; 1 Aug 1995

	$Good	$Fine	$N.Mint	£Good	£Fine	£N.Mint
1 ND Mike Dooney script, Erik Lasen art; continued in Savage Dragon #22						
	$0.50	$1.50	$2.50	£0.30	£0.90	£1.50
Title Value:	$0.50	$1.50	$2.50	£0.30	£0.90	£1.50

TEENAGE MUTANT NINJA TURTLES: HAUNTED PIZZA
Mirage Studios,OS; 1 Dec 1992

	$Good	$Fine	$N.Mint	£Good	£Fine	£N.Mint
1 ND Matt Howarth script/art						
	$0.40	$1.20	$2.00	£0.25	£0.75	£1.25
Title Value:	$0.40	$1.20	$2.00	£0.25	£0.75	£1.25

TEENAGE MUTANT NINJA TURTLES: THE COMIC STRIP
Express Press; 1 Aug 1991

	$Good	$Fine	$N.Mint	£Good	£Fine	£N.Mint
1 ND 24pgs, reprints from U.K. Daily Express newspaper						
	$0.40	$1.20	$2.00	£0.25	£0.75	£1.25
Title Value:	$0.40	$1.20	$2.00	£0.25	£0.75	£1.25
Special Edition 1, printed in green inks				£0.30	£0.90	£1.50

TEENAGE MUTANT NINJA TURTLES: THE MALTESE TURTLE
Mirage Studios,OS; 1 Mar 1993

	$Good	$Fine	$N.Mint	£Good	£Fine	£N.Mint
1 ND 48pgs	$0.40	$1.20	$2.00	£0.25	£0.75	£1.25
Title Value:	$0.40	$1.20	$2.00	£0.25	£0.75	£1.25

TEENAGE MUTANT NINJA TURTLES: YEAR OF THE TURTLE
Archie Comics,MS; 1 Oct 1995-3 Dec 1995

	$Good	$Fine	$N.Mint	£Good	£Fine	£N.Mint
1-3 ND Dan Slott script, Hugh Haynes art						
	$0.30	$0.90	$1.50	£0.20	£0.60	£1.00
Title Value:	$0.90	$2.70	$4.50	£0.60	£1.80	£3.00

TEKNOPHAGE, NEIL GAIMAN'S
Tekno Comix; 1 Aug 1995-present

	$Good	$Fine	$N.Mint	£Good	£Fine	£N.Mint
1 ND Rick Veitch script, Bryan Talbot and Angus McKie art						
	$0.40	$1.20	$2.00	£0.25	£0.75	£1.25
1 ND Steel Edition (Dec 1995) - silver embossed card-stock cover; 25,000 copies						
	$1.50	$4.50	$7.50	£1.00	£3.00	£5.00
2-5 ND	$0.40	$1.20	$2.00	£0.25	£0.75	£1.25
6 ND (non-Code approved issue)						
	$0.40	$1.20	$2.00	£0.25	£0.75	£1.25
7 ND (non-Code approved issue)						
	$0.45	$1.35	$2.25	£0.30	£0.90	£1.50
8 ND pre-bagged with Tekno back- issue comic						
	$0.45	$1.35	$2.25	£0.30	£0.90	£1.50
Title Value:	$4.80	$14.40	$24.00	£3.10	£9.30	£15.50

TEKO
Caliber Press,MS; 1 Jul 1992-3 1992

	$Good	$Fine	$N.Mint	£Good	£Fine	£N.Mint
1-3 ND	$0.50	$1.50	$2.50	£0.30	£0.90	£1.50
Title Value:	$1.50	$4.50	$7.50	£0.90	£2.70	£4.50

TEKWORLD, WILLIAM SHATNER'S
Marvel Comics Group/Epic; 1 Sep 1992-24 Aug 1994

	$Good	$Fine	$N.Mint	£Good	£Fine	£N.Mint
1-24 ND based on Tekworld novels						
	$0.30	$0.90	$1.50	£0.20	£0.60	£1.00
Title Value:	$7.20	$21.60	$36.00	£4.80	£14.40	£24.00

SOME INDEPENDENT COMICS MAY NOT HAVE APPEARED ALTHOUGH THEY WERE ADVERTISED AND SOLICITED.

TELL ME DARK HARDCOVER GRAPHIC NOVEL
DC Comics,OS; nn Dec 1992
nn - 80pgs, Hardcover; script by Karl Edward Wagner,
painted cover and art by Kent Williams

	$Good	$Fine	$N.Mint	£Good	£Fine	£N.Mint
nn - 80pgs, Hardcover				£3.75	£11.25	£18.75
nn - 80pgs, Softcover (Jul 1993), as above				£1.85	£5.55	£9.25

TEMPUS FUGITIVE
DC Comics,MS; 1 Apr 1990-4 Sep 1991

	$Good	$Fine	$N.Mint	£Good	£Fine	£N.Mint
1-4 ND 48pgs	$0.90	$2.70	$4.50	£0.60	£1.80	£3.00
Title Value:	$3.60	$10.80	$18.00	£2.40	£7.20	£12.00

Note: Prestige Format, painted art by Ken Steacy. Creator-owned project (see Skreemer). Publication delays as series went on.

TERMINAL POINT
Dark Horse,MS; 1 Feb 1993-3 Apr 1993

	$Good	$Fine	$N.Mint	£Good	£Fine	£N.Mint
1-3 ND Bruce Zick script and art	$0.50	$1.50	$2.50	£0.30	£0.90	£1.50
Title Value:	$1.50	$4.50	$7.50	£0.90	£2.70	£4.50

TERMINATOR
Now Comics; 1 Sep 1988-17 Feb 1990

	$Good	$Fine	$N.Mint	£Good	£Fine	£N.Mint
1 movie tie-in begins, sub-titled "Tempest"	$2.50	$7.50	$12.50	£1.50	£4.50	£7.50
2 scarce in the U.K.	$1.50	$4.50	$7.50	£1.00	£3.00	£5.00
3 scarce in the U.K.	$1.20	$3.60	$6.00	£0.80	£2.40	£4.00
4	$1.00	$3.00	$5.00	£0.70	£2.10	£3.50
5 scarce in the U.K.	$1.00	$3.00	$5.00	£0.80	£2.40	£4.00
6-9	$0.80	$2.40	$4.00	£0.60	£1.80	£3.00
10 scarce in the U.K.	$0.80	$2.40	$4.00	£0.70	£2.10	£3.50
11	$0.60	$1.80	$3.00	£0.40	£1.20	£2.00
12 52pgs	$0.80	$2.40	$4.00	£0.50	£1.50	£2.50
13-15	$0.60	$1.80	$3.00	£0.40	£1.20	£2.00
16 52pgs	$0.60	$1.80	$3.00	£0.45	£1.35	£2.25
17	$0.60	$1.80	$3.00	£0.40	£1.20	£2.00
Title Value:	$15.60	$46.80	$78.00	£10.85	£32.55	£54.25

Note: Comics Code on cover from issue #8. All Non-Distributed on the news-stands in the U.K.
The Terminator: Tempest Collection (1994)
Trade paperback reprints issues #1-4, John Bolton cover £1.70 £5.10 £8.50

TERMINATOR (LIMITED SERIES)
Dark Horse,MS; 1 Aug 1990-4 Nov 1990

	$Good	$Fine	$N.Mint	£Good	£Fine	£N.Mint
1 ND Chris Warner pencils	$0.80	$2.40	$4.00	£0.60	£1.80	£3.00
2-4 ND Chris Warner pencils	$0.60	$1.80	$3.00	£0.40	£1.20	£2.00
Title Value:	$2.60	$7.80	$13.00	£1.80	£5.40	£9.00

The Terminator Collection (Aug 1991),
reprints #1-4, new John Bolton cover £0.75 £2.25 £3.75
Limited Hardcover (Nov 1991),
signed and numbered (2,000 copies) £9.00 £27.00 £45.00

TERMINATOR 2
Marvel Comics Group,MS; 1 Sep 1991-3 Oct 1991

	$Good	$Fine	$N.Mint	£Good	£Fine	£N.Mint
1 based on Arnold Schwarzenegger film, bi-weekly	$0.15	$0.45	$0.75	£0.10	£0.35	£0.60
2-3 bi-weekly	$0.15	$0.45	$0.75	£0.10	£0.35	£0.60
Title Value:	$0.45	$1.35	$2.25	£0.30	£1.05	£1.80

TERMINATOR 2: FUTURE WAR - NUCLEAR TWILIGHT
Marvel Comics Group,MS; 1 Jan 1996-present

	$Good	$Fine	$N.Mint	£Good	£Fine	£N.Mint
1-3 ND Mark Paniccia script, Gary Erskine art	$0.50	$1.50	$2.50	£0.30	£0.90	£1.50
Title Value:	$1.50	$4.50	$7.50	£0.90	£2.70	£4.50

TERMINATOR 2 MOVIE ADAPTATION BOOKSHELF FORMAT
Marvel Comics Group,OS; 1 Sep 1991
1 ND based on Arnold Schwarzenegger film screenplay, photo cover

	$Good	$Fine	$N.Mint	£Good	£Fine	£N.Mint
	$0.80	$2.40	$4.00	£0.50	£1.50	£2.50
Title Value:	$0.80	$2.40	$4.00	£0.50	£1.50	£2.50

TERMINATOR 2 MOVIE ADAPTATION MAGAZINE
Marvel Comics Group,OS; 1 Sep 1991
1 ND based on Arnold Schwarzenegger film screenplay

	$Good	$Fine	$N.Mint	£Good	£Fine	£N.Mint
	$0.40	$1.20	$2.00	£0.25	£0.75	£1.25
Title Value:	$0.40	$1.20	$2.00	£0.25	£0.75	£1.25

TERMINATOR 2: PRESENT WAR - CYBERNETIC DAWN
Marvel Comics Group,MS; 1 Jan 1996-present
1-3 ND Dan Abnett script, Keith Conroy and Jack Snider art

	$Good	$Fine	$N.Mint	£Good	£Fine	£N.Mint
	$0.50	$1.50	$2.50	£0.30	£0.90	£1.50
Title Value:	$1.50	$4.50	$7.50	£0.90	£2.70	£4.50

TERMINATOR ONE SHOT, THE
Dark Horse,OS; 1 Jul 1991
1 ND 48pgs, Matt Wagner art, pop-up section

	$Good	$Fine	$N.Mint	£Good	£Fine	£N.Mint
	$1.20	$3.60	$6.00	£0.80	£2.40	£4.00
Title Value:	$1.20	$3.60	$6.00	£0.80	£2.40	£4.00

TERMINATOR: END GAME
Dark Horse,MS; 1 Sep 1992-3 Dec 1992
1-3 ND Jackson Guice art, John Higgins cover

	$Good	$Fine	$N.Mint	£Good	£Fine	£N.Mint
	$0.50	$1.50	$2.50	£0.30	£0.90	£1.50
Title Value:	$1.50	$4.50	$7.50	£0.90	£2.70	£4.50

Terminator: Endgame (1994)
Trade paperback reprints mini-series £1.30 £3.90 £6.50

TERMINATOR: ENEMY WITHIN, THE
Dark Horse,MS; 1 Jan 1992-4 Apr 1992
1-4 ND Simon Bisley covers

	$Good	$Fine	$N.Mint	£Good	£Fine	£N.Mint
	$0.50	$1.50	$2.50	£0.30	£0.90	£1.50
Title Value:	$2.00	$6.00	$10.00	£1.20	£3.60	£6.00

The Terminator: The Enemy Within (1994)
Trade paperback reprints mini-series, Simon Bisley cover £2.00 £6.00 £10.00

TERMINATOR: HUNTERS & KILLERS, THE
Dark Horse,MS; 1 Mar 1992-3 May 1992

	$Good	$Fine	$N.Mint	£Good	£Fine	£N.Mint
1-3 ND	$0.50	$1.50	$2.50	£0.30	£0.90	£1.50
Title Value:	$1.50	$4.50	$7.50	£0.90	£2.70	£4.50

Terminator: Hunters and Killers (1994)
Trade paperback reprints mini-series £1.30 £3.90 £6.50

TERMINATOR: SECONDARY OBJECTIVES
Dark Horse,MS; 1 Sep 1991-4 Dec 1991

	$Good	$Fine	$N.Mint	£Good	£Fine	£N.Mint
1-4 ND	$0.50	$1.50	$2.50	£0.30	£0.90	£1.50
Title Value:	$2.00	$6.00	$10.00	£1.20	£3.60	£6.00

The Terminator: Secondary Objectives Collection (Oct 1992)
reprints issues #1-4 with new cover painting by Paul Gulacy £1.70 £5.10 £8.50

TERMINATOR: SPECIAL MINI-SERIES
Now Comics; 1 Jun 1990-2 Jul 1990
1-2 ND sub-titled All My Futures Past

	$Good	$Fine	$N.Mint	£Good	£Fine	£N.Mint
	$0.50	$1.50	$2.50	£0.30	£0.90	£1.50
Title Value:	$1.00	$3.00	$5.00	£0.60	£1.80	£3.00

TERMINATOR: THE BURNING EARTH
Now Comics,MS; 1 Mar 1990-5 Jul 1990

	$Good	$Fine	$N.Mint	£Good	£Fine	£N.Mint
1 ND	$0.60	$1.80	$3.00	£1.00	£3.00	£5.00
2 ND	$0.40	$1.20	$2.00	£0.80	£2.40	£4.00
3-5 ND	$0.40	$1.20	$2.00	£0.60	£1.80	£3.00
Title Value:	$2.20	$6.60	$11.00	£3.60	£10.80	£18.00

TERRAFORMERS
Wonder Color Comics; 1 Apr 1987-2 May 1987

	$Good	$Fine	$N.Mint	£Good	£Fine	£N.Mint
1-2 ND Kelley Jones art	$0.40	$1.20	$2.00	£0.25	£0.75	£1.25
Title Value:	$0.80	$2.40	$4.00	£0.50	£1.50	£2.50

TERRARISTS
Marvel Comics Group,MS; 1 Nov 1993-4 Feb 1994

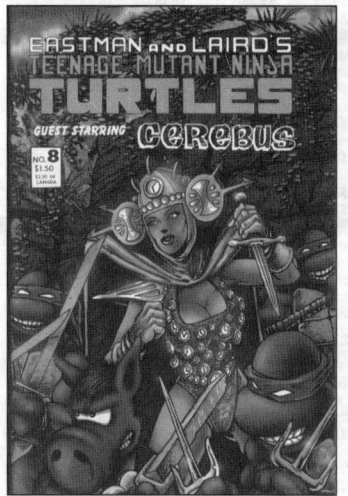

Teenage Mutant Ninja Turtles #8

Teen Titans #3

Tek World #1

	$Good	$Fine	$N.Mint	£Good	£Fine	£N.Mint
1 ND Pat Mills and Tony Skinner script; bound-in trading card						
	$0.40	$1.20	$2.00	£0.25	£0.75	£1.25
2-4 ND bound-in trading card						
	$0.40	$1.20	$2.00	£0.25	£0.75	£1.25
Title Value:	$1.60	$4.80	$8.00	£1.00	£3.00	£5.00

TERROR INC.
Marvel Comics Group; 1 Jul 1992-13 Jul 1993

	$Good	$Fine	$N.Mint	£Good	£Fine	£N.Mint
1-3 ND	$0.25	$0.75	$1.25	£0.15	£0.45	£0.75
4-5 ND Dr. Strange guest-stars						
	$0.25	$0.75	$1.25	£0.15	£0.45	£0.75
6-7 ND Terror vs. Punisher						
	$0.25	$0.75	$1.25	£0.15	£0.45	£0.75
8-11 ND	$0.25	$0.75	$1.25	£0.15	£0.45	£0.75
12 ND Cage and Silver Sable appear; X-over Cage #16 and Silver Sable #14						
	$0.25	$0.75	$1.25	£0.15	£0.45	£0.75
13 ND Infinity Crusade X-over						
	$0.25	$0.75	$1.25	£0.15	£0.45	£0.75
Title Value:	$3.25	$9.75	$16.25	£1.95	£5.85	£9.75

TERROR TALES
Eternity; 1 Jun 1991

	$Good	$Fine	$N.Mint	£Good	£Fine	£N.Mint
1 ND	$0.40	$1.20	$2.00	£0.25	£0.75	£1.25
Title Value:	$0.40	$1.20	$2.00	£0.25	£0.75	£1.25

TERRORESS
Anger Helps; 1 Dec 1990

	$Good	$Fine	$N.Mint	£Good	£Fine	£N.Mint
1 ND black and white						
	$0.15	$0.45	$0.75	£0.10	£0.30	£0.50
Title Value:	$0.15	$0.45	$0.75	£0.10	£0.30	£0.50

TEX AVERY'S SCREWBALL SQUIRREL
Dark Horse,MS; 1 Jul 1995-3 Sep 1995

	$Good	$Fine	$N.Mint	£Good	£Fine	£N.Mint
1-3 ND	$0.50	$1.50	$2.50	£0.30	£0.90	£1.50
Title Value:	$1.50	$4.50	$7.50	£0.90	£2.70	£4.50

TEX BENSON
Metro Comics,MS; 1 Nov 1986-4 Feb 1987

	$Good	$Fine	$N.Mint	£Good	£Fine	£N.Mint
1-4 ND	$0.40	$1.20	$2.00	£0.25	£0.75	£1.25
Title Value:	$1.60	$4.80	$8.00	£1.00	£3.00	£5.00

TEX DAWSON, GUNSLINGER
Marvel Comics Group; 1 Jan 1973-3 Jun 1973
(#2, #3 titled Gunslinger)

	$Good	$Fine	$N.Mint	£Good	£Fine	£N.Mint
1 ND Williamson reprint, Steranko cover						
	$0.50	$1.50	$2.50	£0.30	£0.90	£1.50
2-3 ND reprints	$0.50	$1.50	$2.50	£0.30	£0.90	£1.50
Title Value:	$1.50	$4.50	$7.50	£0.90	£2.70	£4.50

TEXAS CHAINSAW MASSACRE
Northstar,MS; 1 Apr 1992-3 1992

	$Good	$Fine	$N.Mint	£Good	£Fine	£N.Mint
1-3 ND based on film	$0.50	$1.50	$2.50	£0.30	£0.90	£1.50
Title Value:	$1.50	$4.50	$7.50	£0.90	£2.70	£4.50

THANATOS SYNDROME: THE JACKAL, THE
Boneyard Press; 1 Mar 1992

	$Good	$Fine	$N.Mint	£Good	£Fine	£N.Mint
1 ND black and white; smaller than regular comic size						
	$0.25	$0.75	$1.25	£0.15	£0.45	£0.75
Title Value:	$0.25	$0.75	$1.25	£0.15	£0.45	£0.75

THANOS QUEST
Marvel Comics Group,MS; 1 Sep 1990-2 Oct 1990
(see Captain Marvel, Silver Surfer)

	$Good	$Fine	$N.Mint	£Good	£Fine	£N.Mint
1 ND 48pgs, Jim Starlin script, Ron Lim art						
	$1.50	$4.50	$7.50	£1.00	£3.00	£5.00
1 2nd printing ND 48pgs						
	$0.90	$2.70	$4.50	£0.60	£1.80	£3.00
2 ND 48pgs, Jim Starlin script, Ron Lim art; 1st appearance Infinty Gauntlet						
	$1.50	$4.50	$7.50	£1.00	£3.00	£5.00
Title Value:	$3.90	$11.70	$19.50	£2.60	£7.80	£13.00

THE MIGHTY I
Image; 1 May 1995

	$Good	$Fine	$N.Mint	£Good	£Fine	£N.Mint
1 ND 48pgs, interviews and articles on Image product						
	$0.30	$0.90	$1.50	£0.20	£0.60	£1.00
Title Value:	$0.30	$0.90	$1.50	£0.20	£0.60	£1.00

THE PRICE
Eclipse; Graphic Novel 5, Oct 1981

	$Good	$Fine	$N.Mint	£Good	£Fine	£N.Mint
nn ND Jim Starlin art, Dreadstar featured						
	$1.20	$3.60	$6.00	£0.80	£2.40	£4.00
Title Value:	$1.20	$3.60	$6.00	£0.80	£2.40	£4.00

THE STARS MY DESTINATION
Epic Graphic Novel; nn Jul 1992

	$Good	$Fine	$N.Mint	£Good	£Fine	£N.Mint
nn ND 160pgs, Howard Chaykin art						
	$3.00	$9.00	$15.00	£2.00	£6.00	£10.00
Title Value:	$3.00	$9.00	$15.00	£2.00	£6.00	£10.00

THEY CAME FROM THE '50s
Eternity; nn Sep 1990

	$Good	$Fine	$N.Mint	£Good	£Fine	£N.Mint
nn ND collection of pre-Code horror stories						
	$1.50	$4.50	$7.50	£1.00	£3.00	£5.00
Title Value:	$1.50	$4.50	$7.50	£1.00	£3.00	£5.00

THEY WERE ELEVEN
Viz Communications,MS; 1 Feb 1995-4 May 1995

	$Good	$Fine	$N.Mint	£Good	£Fine	£N.Mint
1-4 ND Moto Hagio script and art; black and white						
	$0.50	$1.50	$2.50	£0.30	£0.90	£1.50
Title Value:	$2.00	$6.00	$10.00	£1.20	£3.60	£6.00

THIEF OF SHERWOOD, THE
A Plus Comics,MS; 1 Aug 1991-3 Oct 1991

	$Good	$Fine	$N.Mint	£Good	£Fine	£N.Mint
1-3 ND Sam Glanzman art						
	$0.40	$1.20	$2.00	£0.25	£0.75	£1.25
Title Value:	$1.20	$3.60	$6.00	£0.75	£2.25	£3.75

THING FROM ANOTHER WORLD
Dark Horse,MS; 1 Feb 1992-2 May 1992

	$Good	$Fine	$N.Mint	£Good	£Fine	£N.Mint
1-2 ND John Higgins painted art, based on John Carpenter film						
	$0.60	$1.80	$3.00	£0.40	£1.20	£2.00
Title Value:	$1.20	$3.60	$6.00	£0.80	£2.40	£4.00

THING FROM ANOTHER WORLD: CLIMATE OF FEAR
Dark Horse; 1 Sep 1992-4 Dec 1992

	$Good	$Fine	$N.Mint	£Good	£Fine	£N.Mint
1-4 ND based on John Carpenter's "The Thing", painted cover by John Higgins						
	$0.50	$1.50	$2.50	£0.30	£0.90	£1.50
Title Value:	$2.00	$6.00	$10.00	£1.20	£3.60	£6.00

THING FROM ANOTHER WORLD: ETERNAL VOWS
Dark Horse,MS; 1 Dec 1993-4 Mar 1994

	$Good	$Fine	$N.Mint	£Good	£Fine	£N.Mint
1-4 ND Paul Gulacy cover and art						
	$0.50	$1.50	$2.50	£0.30	£0.90	£1.50
Title Value:	$2.00	$6.00	$10.00	£1.20	£3.60	£6.00

THING, THE
Marvel Comics Group; 1 Jul 1983-36 Jun 1986
(see Fantastic Four, Marvel Fanfare, Marvel Graphic Novel, Marvel Two-In-One)

	$Good	$Fine	$N.Mint	£Good	£Fine	£N.Mint
1 ND John Byrne story						
	$0.30	$0.90	$1.50	£0.20	£0.60	£1.00
2 John Byrne inks/story						
	$0.25	$0.75	$1.25	£0.15	£0.45	£0.75
3-4 Inhumans appear, John Byrne story						
	$0.25	$0.75	$1.25	£0.15	£0.45	£0.75
5 Spiderman, Wonderman, She-Hulk appear, John Byrne story						
	$0.25	$0.75	$1.25	£0.15	£0.45	£0.75
6 John Byrne story						
	$0.25	$0.75	$1.25	£0.15	£0.45	£0.75
7 John Byrne art on back-up story, Byrne script on Thing story						
	$0.25	$0.75	$1.25	£0.15	£0.45	£0.75
8-9 She-Hulk appears, John Byrne scripts						
	$0.25	$0.75	$1.25	£0.15	£0.45	£0.75
10 Fantastic Four appear, John Byrne script						
	$0.25	$0.75	$1.25	£0.15	£0.45	£0.75
11 John Byrne script						
	$0.25	$0.75	$1.25	£0.15	£0.45	£0.75
12 Dr. Doom appears, John Byrne script						
	$0.25	$0.75	$1.25	£0.15	£0.45	£0.75
13 John Byrne script						
	$0.25	$0.75	$1.25	£0.15	£0.45	£0.75
14-18	$0.25	$0.75	$1.25	£0.15	£0.45	£0.75
19-22 John Byrne scripts						
	$0.25	$0.75	$1.25	£0.15	£0.45	£0.75
23 Fantastic Four appear, Mike Carlin scripts begin						
	$0.25	$0.75	$1.25	£0.15	£0.45	£0.75
24 Thing vs. Rhino						
	$0.25	$0.75	$1.25	£0.15	£0.45	£0.75
25	$0.25	$0.75	$1.25	£0.15	£0.45	£0.75
26 Vance Astro (as a young boy) appears						
	$0.25	$0.75	$1.25	£0.15	£0.45	£0.75
27-29	$0.25	$0.75	$1.25	£0.15	£0.45	£0.75
30 Secret Wars X-over						
	$0.25	$0.75	$1.25	£0.15	£0.45	£0.75
31	$0.25	$0.75	$1.25	£0.15	£0.45	£0.75
32 Vance Astro of Guardians of the Galaxy appears						
	$0.25	$0.75	$1.25	£0.15	£0.45	£0.75
33	$0.25	$0.75	$1.25	£0.15	£0.45	£0.75
34 last Carlin script, Neary art						
	$0.25	$0.75	$1.25	£0.15	£0.45	£0.75
35 1st new Ms. Marvel, Byrne script, Neary art						
	$0.25	$0.75	$1.25	£0.15	£0.45	£0.75
36 She-Hulk vs. new Ms. Marvel, John Byrne script, Neary art; story completed in West Coast Avengers #10						
	$0.25	$0.75	$1.25	£0.15	£0.45	£0.75
Title Value:	$9.05	$27.15	$45.25	£5.45	£16.35	£27.25

THING, THE (2ND SERIES)
Marvel Comics Group,MS; 1 Apr 1992-4 Jul 1992

	$Good	$Fine	$N.Mint	£Good	£Fine	£N.Mint
1 reprints Marvel Two-In-One #8 featuring Ghost Rider						
	$0.25	$0.75	$1.25	£0.15	£0.45	£0.75
2 reprints Marvel Two-In-One #80 featuring Ghost Rider						
	$0.25	$0.75	$1.25	£0.15	£0.45	£0.75
3 reprints Marvel Two-In-One #51 featuring Beast, Nick Fury, Wonderman and Ms. Marvel, Frank Miller art						
	$0.25	$0.75	$1.25	£0.15	£0.45	£0.75
4 reprints Marvel Two In One #77 featuring Man-Thing and Nick Fury						
	$0.25	$0.75	$1.25	£0.15	£0.45	£0.75
Title Value:	$1.00	$3.00	$5.00	£0.60	£1.80	£3.00

THOR
Marvel Comics Group; 126 Mar 1966-present
(formerly Journey into Mystery) (see Marvel Graphic Novel, Marvel Preview, Marvel Special, Marvel Treasury Edition, Special Marvel Edition, Tales of Asgard)

	$Good	$Fine	$N.Mint	£Good	£Fine	£N.Mint
126 Thor vs. Hercules; story continued from Journey Into Mystery #125						
	$17.00	$50.00	$120.00	£10.00	£30.00	£70.00
127-130	$7.00	$21.00	$50.00	£3.55	£10.50	£25.00
131-133	$6.25	$19.00	$45.00	£3.20	£9.50	£22.50
134 scarce in the U.K. 1st appearance High Evolutionary, Quicksilver and Scarlet Witch appear						
	$8.50	$26.00	$60.00	£4.25	£12.50	£30.00
135-140 scarce in the U.K.						
	$6.25	$19.00	$45.00	£3.20	£9.50	£22.50
141	$5.00	$15.00	$35.00	£2.50	£7.50	£17.50
142 Thor battles Super-Skrull						
	$5.00	$15.00	$35.00	£2.50	£7.50	£17.50
143	$5.00	$15.00	$35.00	£2.50	£7.50	£17.50
144 scarce in the U.K.						

VERY GENERAL PERCENTAGE CONVERSION CHART WHICH MAY BE USED TO CALCULATE LOW AND INBETWEEN GRADES:

Issue	$Good	$Fine	$N.Mint	£Good	£Fine	£N.Mint
145	$5.00	$15.00	$35.00	£2.85	£8.50	£20.00
146-147 The Inhumans origin told	$5.00	$15.00	$35.00	£2.50	£7.50	£17.50
148 start origin Black Bolt, 1st appearance The Wrecker	$5.00	$15.00	$35.00	£2.50	£7.50	£17.50
149 origins Black Bolt, Medusa, Crystal, Maximus, Gorgon, Karnak	$5.00	$15.00	$35.00	£2.50	£7.50	£17.50
150	$5.00	$15.00	$35.00	£2.50	£7.50	£17.50
151-157	$5.25	$16.00	$32.50	£2.50	£7.50	£15.00
158 origin reprinted in part from Journey into Mystery #83	$10.00	$30.00	$60.00	£5.00	£15.00	£30.00
159 more details of Thor's origin and secret identity of Don Blake	$5.25	$16.00	$32.50	£2.50	£7.50	£15.00
160 Galactus appears	$5.25	$16.00	$32.50	£2.50	£7.50	£15.00
161-162 Galactus appears	$4.15	$12.50	$25.00	£2.05	£6.25	£12.50
163	$4.15	$12.50	$25.00	£2.05	£6.25	£12.50
164 coccoon seen in last panel	$4.15	$12.50	$25.00	£2.05	£6.25	£12.50
165 1st full appearance "Him" - later Warlock (see Fantastic Four #66/67)	$7.50	$22.50	$45.00	£5.00	£15.00	£30.00
166 2nd full appearance "Him" - later Warlock; Thor vs. "Him"	$6.50	$20.00	$40.00	£4.55	£13.50	£27.50
167-169 Galactus appears	$4.15	$12.50	$25.00	£2.05	£6.25	£12.50
170	$4.15	$12.50	$25.00	£2.05	£6.25	£12.50
171-179	$3.75	$11.00	$22.50	£1.65	£5.00	£10.00
180-181 Neal Adams art	$2.50	$7.50	$15.00	£1.65	£5.00	£10.00
182 Dr. Doom appears	$1.25	$3.75	$7.50	£1.00	£3.00	£6.00
183 Thor vs. Dr. Doom	$1.25	$3.75	$7.50	£1.00	£3.00	£6.00
184-186	$1.25	$3.75	$7.50	£1.00	£3.00	£6.00
187-191 scarce in the U.K.	$1.25	$3.75	$7.50	£1.05	£3.25	£6.50
192 scarce in the U.K. Silver Surfer appears at end of story (cameo)	$1.25	$3.75	$7.50	£1.05	£3.25	£6.50
193 very scarce in the U.K. 52pgs, Silver Surfer appears; 25 cents cover price	$5.75	$17.50	$35.00	£4.15	£12.50	£25.00
194-199 scarce in the U.K.	$1.25	$3.75	$7.50	£0.90	£2.75	£5.50
200 very scarce in the U.K. Thor vs. Loki	$1.25	$3.75	$7.50	£1.25	£3.75	£7.50
201-204 scarce in the U.K.	$1.00	$3.00	$5.00	£0.90	£2.70	£4.50
205 scarce in the U.K. Mephisto appears	$1.00	$3.00	$5.00	£0.90	£2.70	£4.50
206 scarce in the U.K. Thor vs. Absorbing Man	$1.00	$3.00	$5.00	£0.90	£2.70	£4.50
207-209 scarce in the U.K.	$1.00	$3.00	$5.00	£0.90	£2.70	£4.50
210-216	$1.00	$3.00	$5.00	£0.70	£2.10	£3.50
217 Thor vs. Odin	$1.00	$3.00	$5.00	£0.70	£2.10	£3.50
218-220	$1.00	$3.00	$5.00	£0.70	£2.10	£3.50
221 Thor vs. Hercules	$1.00	$3.00	$5.00	£0.70	£2.10	£3.50
222-224 ND	$1.00	$3.00	$5.00	£0.90	£2.70	£4.50
225 ND 1st appearance Firelord	$1.50	$4.50	$7.50	£1.00	£3.00	£5.00
226 Galactus appears	$0.80	$2.40	$4.00	£0.60	£1.80	£3.00
227-228 Galactus appears, Rich Buckler's Kirbyesque art	$0.80	$2.40	$4.00	£0.50	£1.50	£2.50
229 Buckler's Kirbyesque art	$0.80	$2.40	$4.00	£0.50	£1.50	£2.50
230 Iron Man cameo, Buckler's Kirbyesque art	$0.80	$2.40	$4.00	£0.50	£1.50	£2.50
231	$0.80	$2.40	$4.00	£0.40	£1.20	£2.00
232 Thor vs. Firelord, Iron Man appears	$0.80	$2.40	$4.00	£0.40	£1.20	£2.00
233	$0.80	$2.40	$4.00	£0.40	£1.20	£2.00
234 Firelord appears	$0.80	$2.40	$4.00	£0.40	£1.20	£2.00
235-245	$0.80	$2.40	$4.00	£0.40	£1.20	£2.00
246 Thor vs. Firelord	$0.80	$2.40	$4.00	£0.40	£1.20	£2.00
247 Firelord appears	$0.80	$2.40	$4.00	£0.40	£1.20	£2.00
248-250	$0.80	$2.40	$4.00	£0.40	£1.20	£2.00
251-253	$0.60	$1.80	$3.00	£0.30	£0.90	£1.50
254 reprints issue #159	$0.60	$1.80	$3.00	£0.30	£0.90	£1.50
255-258	$0.60	$1.80	$3.00	£0.30	£0.90	£1.50
259 Walt Simonson layouts/pencils begin (ends #271)	$0.60	$1.80	$3.00	£0.30	£0.90	£1.50
260-270	$0.60	$1.80	$3.00	£0.30	£0.90	£1.50
271 Iron Man, Beast, Vision, Scarlet Witch and Nick Fury appear; last Walt Simonson layouts/pencils	$0.60	$1.80	$3.00	£0.30	£0.90	£1.50
272-282	$0.60	$1.80	$3.00	£0.30	£0.90	£1.50
283-284 ND Eternals appear	$0.50	$1.50	$2.50	£0.35	£1.05	£1.75
285-289 Eternals appear	$0.50	$1.50	$2.50	£0.30	£0.90	£1.50
290	$0.50	$1.50	$2.50	£0.30	£0.90	£1.50
291-292 Eternals appear	$0.50	$1.50	$2.50	£0.30	£0.90	£1.50
293	$0.50	$1.50	$2.50	£0.30	£0.90	£1.50
294 origin Odin/Asgard retold	$0.50	$1.50	$2.50	£0.30	£0.90	£1.50
295-299	$0.50	$1.50	$2.50	£0.30	£0.90	£1.50
300 ND 52pgs, end of Asgard (origin Odin retold)	$1.00	$3.00	$5.00	£1.00	£3.00	£5.00
301-303	$0.40	$1.20	$2.00	£0.25	£0.75	£1.25
304 ND	$0.40	$1.20	$2.00	£0.30	£0.90	£1.50
305 ND Gabriel the Air-Walker appears	$0.40	$1.20	$2.00	£0.30	£0.90	£1.50
306 Firelord appears	$0.40	$1.20	$2.00	£0.25	£0.75	£1.25
307-315	$0.40	$1.20	$2.00	£0.25	£0.75	£1.25
316 Iron Man appears	$0.40	$1.20	$2.00	£0.25	£0.75	£1.25
317-332	$0.40	$1.20	$2.00	£0.25	£0.75	£1.25
333 Dracula and Dr. Strange appear	$0.40	$1.20	$2.00	£0.25	£0.75	£1.25
334-336	$0.40	$1.20	$2.00	£0.25	£0.75	£1.25
337 1st issue of classic Walt Simonson run, Beta Ray Bill becomes new Thor	$1.00	$3.00	$5.00	£0.70	£2.10	£3.50
338 2nd Walt Simonson art	$0.60	$1.80	$3.00	£0.40	£1.20	£2.00
339 3rd Walt Simonson art	$0.30	$0.90	$1.50	£0.30	£0.90	£1.50
340-350 Walt Simonson art	$0.40	$1.20	$2.00	£0.25	£0.75	£1.25
351 Walt Simonson art	$0.30	$0.90	$1.50	£0.20	£0.60	£1.00
352 Walt Simonson art, Fantastic Four appear	$0.30	$0.90	$1.50	£0.20	£0.60	£1.00
353-354 Walt Simonson art	$0.30	$0.90	$1.50	£0.20	£0.60	£1.00
355 Walt Simonson story	$0.30	$0.90	$1.50	£0.20	£0.60	£1.00
356 Guice cover and art	$0.30	$0.90	$1.50	£0.20	£0.60	£1.00
357-362 Walt Simonson art	$0.30	$0.90	$1.50	£0.20	£0.60	£1.00
363 Secret Wars II X-over, Walt Simonson art	$0.30	$0.90	$1.50	£0.20	£0.60	£1.00
364 Walt Simonson art	$0.30	$0.90	$1.50	£0.20	£0.60	£1.00
365 Walt Simonson art, new secret identity	$0.30	$0.90	$1.50	£0.20	£0.60	£1.00
366-367 Walt Simonson art	$0.30	$0.90	$1.50	£0.20	£0.60	£1.00
368-369 Walt Simonson story	$0.30	$0.90	$1.50	£0.20	£0.60	£1.00
370 P. Craig Russell inks	$0.30	$0.90	$1.50	£0.20	£0.60	£1.00
371-372 Judge Dredd parody, Simonson story	$0.30	$0.90	$1.50	£0.20	£0.60	£1.00
373 LD in the U.K. Mutant Massacre, Simonson story	$0.80	$2.40	$4.00	£0.50	£1.50	£2.50
374 LD in the U.K. Mutant Massacre, X-Factor X-over, Simonson story	$1.50	$4.50	$7.50	£0.80	£2.40	£4.00
375-376 Simonson story	$0.25	$0.75	$1.25	£0.15	£0.45	£0.75
377 X-Factor cameo, Simonson story	$0.25	$0.75	$1.25	£0.15	£0.45	£0.75
378-380 Simonson story	$0.25	$0.75	$1.25	£0.15	£0.45	£0.75
381 Avengers appear, Simonson story	$0.25	$0.75	$1.25	£0.15	£0.45	£0.75
382 LD in the U.K. 52pgs, last Simonson, 300th Thor anniversary	$0.50	$1.50	$2.50	£0.30	£0.90	£1.50
383 Secret Wars X-over	$0.25	$0.75	$1.25	£0.15	£0.45	£0.75
384 1st appearance Dargo, new (future) Thor	$0.25	$0.75	$1.25	£0.15	£0.45	£0.75
385 Thor vs. Hulk, Erik Larsen art	$0.25	$0.75	$1.25	£0.15	£0.45	£0.75
386-390	$0.25	$0.75	$1.25	£0.15	£0.45	£0.75
391 Spiderman appears	$0.25	$0.75	$1.25	£0.15	£0.45	£0.75
392-393 Daredevil appears	$0.25	$0.75	$1.25	£0.15	£0.45	£0.75
394-395	$0.25	$0.75	$1.25	£0.15	£0.45	£0.75
396 Black Knight appears	$0.25	$0.75	$1.25	£0.15	£0.45	£0.75
397-399	$0.25	$0.75	$1.25	£0.15	£0.45	£0.75
400 LD in the U.K. 64pgs, Charles Vess art	$0.50	$1.50	$2.50	£0.35	£1.05	£1.75
401-406	$0.25	$0.75	$1.25	£0.15	£0.45	£0.75

MINT = 100% / NEAR MINT (inc. +/-) = 90–99% / VERY FINE (inc. +/-) = 75–89% / FINE (inc. +/-) = 55–74% / VERY GOOD (inc. +/-) = 35–54% / GOOD (inc. +/-) = 15–34% / FAIR = 5–14% / POOR = 1–4%

601

	$Good	$Fine	$N.Mint	£Good	£Fine	£N.Mint
407-410 Tales of Asgard back-up	$0.25	$0.75	$1.25	£0.15	£0.45	£0.75
411 Acts of Vengeance tie-in, 1st appearanceThe New Warriors (cameo), Thor vs. Juggernaut, Ron Lim art	$0.80	$2.40	$4.00	£0.50	£1.50	£2.50
412 LD in the U.K. Acts of Vengeance tie-in, 1st full appearance The New Warriors, Ron Lim art in back-up story	$2.00	$6.00	$10.00	£1.40	£4.20	£7.00
413 Ron Lim art	$0.25	$0.75	$1.25	£0.15	£0.45	£0.75
414	$0.25	$0.75	$1.25	£0.15	£0.45	£0.75
415 true origin Thor's identity as Don Blake	$0.25	$0.75	$1.25	£0.15	£0.45	£0.75
416 Texiera art	$0.25	$0.75	$1.25	£0.15	£0.45	£0.75
417-418	$0.25	$0.75	$1.25	£0.15	£0.45	£0.75
419-424 The Black Galaxy Saga, bi-weekly issue	$0.25	$0.75	$1.25	£0.15	£0.45	£0.75
425 The Black Galaxy Saga epilogue	$0.25	$0.75	$1.25	£0.15	£0.45	£0.75
426 Lost Asgard storyline resolved	$0.25	$0.75	$1.25	£0.15	£0.45	£0.75
427-428 Captain Britain and Excalibur guest-star	$0.25	$0.75	$1.25	£0.15	£0.45	£0.75
429 Ghost Rider guest stars (and some of Excalibur)	$0.30	$0.90	$1.50	£0.15	£0.45	£0.75
430 Ghost Rider guest stars	$0.30	$0.90	$1.50	£0.15	£0.45	£0.75
431 Enchantress appears	$0.25	$0.75	$1.25	£0.15	£0.45	£0.75
432 LD in the U.K. DS, 350th appearance of Thor, Loki killed and Thor banished; Eric Masterson becomes new Thor; Journey into Mystery #83 reprinted	$0.50	$1.50	$2.50	£0.30	£0.90	£1.50
433 new Thor begins	$0.80	$2.40	$4.00	£0.40	£1.20	£2.00
434 Captain America, Balder, Sif, Warriors Three appear	$0.25	$0.75	$1.25	£0.15	£0.45	£0.75
435 Warriors Three appear	$0.25	$0.75	$1.25	£0.15	£0.45	£0.75
436 Titania/Absorbing Man appear	$0.25	$0.75	$1.25	£0.15	£0.45	£0.75
437 Thor vs. Quasar	$0.25	$0.75	$1.25	£0.15	£0.45	£0.75
438 Dargo the Thor of the Future appears, bi-weekly issue, 1st Thor Corps	$0.25	$0.75	$1.25	£0.15	£0.45	£0.75
439 Dargo the Future Thor vs. new Thor, bi-weekly issue	$0.25	$0.75	$1.25	£0.15	£0.45	£0.75
440 bi-weekly issue	$0.25	$0.75	$1.25	£0.15	£0.45	£0.75
441 Thor vs. Ego, Celestials appear, bi-weekly issue	$0.25	$0.75	$1.25	£0.15	£0.45	£0.75
442 bi-weekly issue	$0.25	$0.75	$1.25	£0.15	£0.45	£0.75
443 Silver Surfer, Dr. Strange appear, bi-weekly	$0.25	$0.75	$1.25	£0.15	£0.45	£0.75
444 $1.25 cover begins	$0.25	$0.75	$1.25	£0.15	£0.45	£0.75
445 Galactic Storm part 7	$0.25	$0.75	$1.25	£0.15	£0.45	£0.75
446 Galactic Storm part 14	$0.25	$0.75	$1.25	£0.15	£0.45	£0.75
447	$0.25	$0.75	$1.25	£0.15	£0.45	£0.75
448 Spiderman guest stars	$0.25	$0.75	$1.25	£0.15	£0.45	£0.75
449	$0.25	$0.75	$1.25	£0.15	£0.45	£0.75
450 64pgs, double gatefold cover	$0.50	$1.50	$2.50	£0.30	£0.90	£1.50
451-452	$0.30	$0.90	$1.50	£0.20	£0.60	£1.00
453-454 bi-weekly	$0.30	$0.90	$1.50	£0.20	£0.60	£1.00
455 Dr. Strange guest-stars, bi-weekly	$0.30	$0.90	$1.50	£0.20	£0.60	£1.00
456 bi-weekly	$0.30	$0.90	$1.50	£0.20	£0.60	£1.00
457 original Thor returns, bi-weekly	$0.30	$0.90	$1.50	£0.20	£0.60	£1.00
458 original Thor vs. Eric Masterson Thor, bi-weekly	$0.30	$0.90	$1.50	£0.20	£0.60	£1.00
459 last Tom DeFalco/Ron Frenz creative team; intro Thunderstrike	$0.50	$1.50	$2.50	£0.30	£0.90	£1.50
460 Jim Starlin script begins, intro new Valkyrie	$0.30	$0.90	$1.50	£0.20	£0.60	£1.00
461 Thor vs. Beta Ray Bill	$0.30	$0.90	$1.50	£0.20	£0.60	£1.00
462	$0.30	$0.90	$1.50	£0.20	£0.60	£1.00
463 Infinity Crusade X-over	$0.30	$0.90	$1.50	£0.20	£0.60	£1.00
464 Infinity Crusade X-over; Loki returns	$0.30	$0.90	$1.50	£0.20	£0.60	£1.00
465-467 Infinity Crusade X-over	$0.30	$0.90	$1.50	£0.20	£0.60	£1.00
468 Blood and Thunder part 1, Silver Surfer and Warlock appear	$0.30	$0.90	$1.50	£0.20	£0.60	£1.00
468 ND pre-bagged with audio cassette and copy of "Dirt" Magazine	$0.60	$1.80	$3.00	£0.40	£1.20	£2.00
469 Blood and Thunder part 5, Warlock and Silver Surfer appear	$0.30	$0.90	$1.50	£0.20	£0.60	£1.00
470 Blood and Thunder part 9, Dr. Strange, Warlock and Silver Surfer appear	$0.30	$0.90	$1.50	£0.20	£0.60	£1.00
471 Blood and Thunder part 13 (conclusion), Warlock and Silver Surfer appear	$0.30	$0.90	$1.50	£0.20	£0.60	£1.00
472	$0.30	$0.90	$1.50	£0.20	£0.60	£1.00
473 Loki returns	$0.30	$0.90	$1.50	£0.20	£0.60	£1.00
474 Loki appears; with free Spiderman and his Deadly Foes card sheet	$0.30	$0.90	$1.50	£0.20	£0.60	£1.00
475 48pgs, new costume	$0.40	$1.20	$2.00	£0.25	£0.75	£1.25
475 ND Collector's Edition, new costume, foil stamped embossed cover	$0.45	$1.35	$2.25	£0.30	£0.90	£1.50
476	$0.30	$0.90	$1.50	£0.20	£0.60	£1.00
477 Thunderstrike appears	$0.30	$0.90	$1.50	£0.20	£0.60	£1.00
478-479	$0.30	$0.90	$1.50	£0.20	£0.60	£1.00
480 High Evolutionary appears	$0.30	$0.90	$1.50	£0.20	£0.60	£1.00
481	$0.30	$0.90	$1.50	£0.20	£0.60	£1.00
482-483 Loki appears	$0.30	$0.90	$1.50	£0.20	£0.60	£1.00
484	$0.30	$0.90	$1.50	£0.20	£0.60	£1.00
485 Thor vs. The Thing	$0.30	$0.90	$1.50	£0.20	£0.60	£1.00
486-487	$0.30	$0.90	$1.50	£0.20	£0.60	£1.00
488 Thor and Lady Sif separate	$0.30	$0.90	$1.50	£0.20	£0.60	£1.00
489 Hulk appears; bi-weekly	$0.30	$0.90	$1.50	£0.20	£0.60	£1.00
490 bi-weekly	$0.30	$0.90	$1.50	£0.20	£0.60	£1.00
491 Warren Ellis scripts and Mike Deodato art (ends #494); new costume	$1.20	$3.60	$6.00	£0.80	£2.40	£4.00
492	$1.20	$3.60	$6.00	£0.80	£2.40	£4.00
493	$0.60	$1.80	$3.00	£0.50	£1.50	£2.50
494	$0.60	$1.80	$3.00	£0.40	£1.20	£2.00
495 Avengers: Timeslide tie-in	$0.30	$0.90	$1.50	£0.20	£0.60	£1.00
496 The First Sign part 2, continued in Iron Man #326	$0.30	$0.90	$1.50	£0.20	£0.60	£1.00
Title Value:	**$475.50**	**$1429.40**	**$2881.25**	**£267.50**	**£802.85**	**£1603.00**

Note: #194 has back-up reprint. #254 is a reprint.
Note also: Hercules appears in #128, 221, 229-231, 235-239, 289, 356, 400. Inhumans appear in #146-152.

Trade paperback (Apr 1990)

	£Good	£Fine	£N.Mint
Reprints #337-#340, new cover by Simonson	£1.00	£3.00	£5.00

ARTISTS
Buckler art in 227-230. Gene Day art in 300, 310-315 (mainly inks).

THOR ANNUAL
Marvel Comics Group; 2 1966-3 1967; 4 Dec 1971; 5 1976-8 1979; 9 1981-present
(formerly Journey into Mystery Annual)

	$Good	$Fine	$N.Mint	£Good	£Fine	£N.Mint
2 scarce in the U.K. 68pgs, back up reprint	$8.25	$25.00	$50.00	£5.00	£15.00	£30.00
3 scarce in the U.K. 68pgs, all reprint	$2.05	$6.25	$12.50	£1.25	£3.75	£7.50
4 ND very scarce in the U.K. 68pgs, all reprint	$2.05	$6.25	$12.50	£1.40	£4.25	£8.50
5 ND 52pgs, Hercules appears	$1.50	$4.50	$7.50	£0.90	£2.70	£4.50
6 ND 52pgs, Guardians of the Galaxy appear	$1.50	$4.50	$7.50	£0.90	£2.70	£4.50
7 ND 52pgs, Walt Simonson art	$1.00	$3.00	$5.00	£0.60	£1.80	£3.00
8 ND 52pgs, Thor vs. Zeus	$1.00	$3.00	$5.00	£0.60	£1.80	£3.00
9 ND 52pgs	$0.60	$1.80	$3.00	£0.40	£1.20	£2.00
10 ND 52pgs, map of Asgard	$0.60	$1.80	$3.00	£0.40	£1.20	£2.00
11 ND	$0.60	$1.80	$3.00	£0.40	£1.20	£2.00
12-13 ND	$0.50	$1.50	$2.50	£0.30	£0.90	£1.50
14 ND Atlantis Attacks part 13, continues in Fantastic Four Annual #22	$0.50	$1.50	$2.50	£0.30	£0.90	£1.50
15 ND The Terminus Factor part 3, continued in West Coast Avengers Annual #5, Dr. Strange, Quasar and Thing appear	$0.50	$1.50	$2.50	£0.30	£0.90	£1.50
16 ND Korvac Quest, Guardians of the Galaxy appear	$0.50	$1.50	$2.50	£0.30	£0.90	£1.50
17 ND 64pgs, Citizen Kang part 2, Avengers appear, continued in Fantastic Four Annual #25	$0.50	$1.50	$2.50	£0.30	£0.90	£1.50
18 ND 64pgs, pre-bagged with trading card introducing The Flame	$0.60	$1.80	$3.00	£0.40	£1.20	£2.00
19 ND 64pgs, Thor vs. Pluto	$0.60	$1.80	$3.00	£0.40	£1.20	£2.00
Title Value:	**$23.35**	**$70.50**	**$130.00**	**£14.45**	**£43.40**	**£80.00**

THOR CORPS, THE
Marvel Comics Group,MS; 1 Sep 1993-4 Dec 1993

	$Good	$Fine	$N.Mint	£Good	£Fine	£N.Mint
1	$0.40	$1.20	$2.00	£0.25	£0.75	£1.25
2 Franklin Richards appears	$0.40	$1.20	$2.00	£0.25	£0.75	£1.25
3 Spiderman 2099, Guardians of the Galaxy, Rawhide Kid, Two-Gun Kid and Kid Colt Outlaw appear	$0.40	$1.20	$2.00	£0.25	£0.75	£1.25
4	$0.40	$1.20	$2.00	£0.25	£0.75	£1.25
Title Value:	**$1.60**	**$4.80**	**$8.00**	**£1.00**	**£3.00**	**£5.00**

	$Good	$Fine	$N.Mint	£Good	£Fine	£N.Mint
THOR GIANT SIZE						
Marvel Comics Group; 1 1975						
1 ND very scarce in the U.K. 68pgs, all reprint (Jack Kirby)						
	$1.25	$3.75	$7.50	£1.25	£3.75	£7.50
Title Value:	$1.25	$3.75	$7.50	£1.25	£3.75	£7.50
THOR: ALONE AGAINST THE CELESTIALS						
Marvel Comics Group,OS; 1 Aug 1992						
1 64pgs, reprints Thor #387-389						
	$1.00	$3.00	$5.00	£0.70	£2.10	£3.50
Title Value:	$1.00	$3.00	$5.00	£0.70	£2.10	£3.50
THORR-SVERD, THE SWORD OF THOR						
Vincent Creations; 1-3 1987						
1 ND	$0.30	$0.90	$1.50	£0.20	£0.60	£1.00
1 2nd printing ND	$0.25	$0.75	$1.25	£0.15	£0.45	£0.75
2-3 ND	$0.30	$0.90	$1.50	£0.20	£0.60	£1.00
Title Value:	$1.15	$3.45	$5.75	£0.75	£2.25	£3.75
THOSE ANNOYING POST BROTHERS						
(see Post Bros)						
THREAT						
Fantagraphics,Magazine; 1 1985-10 1987						
1-10 ND	$0.50	$1.50	$2.50	£0.30	£0.90	£1.50
Title Value:	$5.00	$15.00	$25.00	£3.00	£9.00	£15.00
THREE MOUSEKETEERS, THE						
National Periodical Publications; 25 Aug/Sep 1960-26 Oct/Nov 1960						
(previous issues ND)						
25-26 very scarce in the U.K.						
	$7.00	$21.00	$50.00	£5.00	£15.00	£35.00
Title Value:	$14.00	$42.00	$100.00	£10.00	£30.00	£70.00
THREE MOUSEKETEERS, THE (2ND SERIES)						
DC Comics; 1 May/Jun 1970-7 May/Jun 1971						
1 very scarce in the U.K.						
	$2.05	$6.25	$12.50	£1.25	£3.75	£7.50
2-7 very scarce in the U.K.						
	$1.50	$4.50	$7.50	£1.00	£3.00	£5.00
Title Value:	$11.05	$33.25	$57.50	£7.25	£21.75	£37.50
THREE MUSKETEERS						
Eternity; 1 Dec 1988-3 1989						
1-3 ND	$0.40	$1.20	$2.00	£0.25	£0.75	£1.25
Title Value:	$1.20	$3.60	$6.00	£0.75	£2.25	£3.75
Graphic Album, reprints				£1.10	£3.30	£5.50
THREE MUSKETEERS GRAPHIC ALBUM, THE						
Malibu,OS; 1 1990						
1 ND 100pgs, squarebound, black and white						
	$1.50	$4.50	$7.50	£1.00	£3.00	£5.00
Title Value:	$1.50	$4.50	$7.50	£1.00	£3.00	£5.00
THREE MUSKETEERS, THE						
Marvel Comics Group,MS; 1,2 Feb 1994						
1-2 ND adaptation of Disney film						
	$0.30	$0.90	$1.50	£0.20	£0.60	£1.00
Title Value:	$0.60	$1.80	$3.00	£0.40	£1.20	£2.00
THREE STOOGES, THE						
Gold Key; 10 Oct 1962-55 Jun 1972						
(previous issues ND)						
10 scarce in the U.K.						
	$10.00	$30.00	$70.00	£6.25	£19.00	£45.00
11-20	$7.00	$21.00	$50.00	£5.00	£15.00	£35.00
21-30	$6.25	$19.00	$45.00	£4.25	£12.50	£30.00
31-40	$5.50	$17.00	$40.00	£3.90	£11.50	£27.50
41-55	$5.75	$17.50	$35.00	£4.15	£12.50	£25.00
Title Value:	$283.75	$862.50	$1945.00	£200.00	£596.50	£1345.00
Note: all distributed in the U.K.						

	$Good	$Fine	$N.Mint	£Good	£Fine	£N.Mint
3-D ADVENTURE COMICS						
Stats Etc; 1 Aug 1986						
1 ND promotional material, with bound-in 3-D glasses (25% less without glasses); smaller size (5"x7")						
	$0.45	$1.35	$2.25	£0.30	£0.90	£1.50
Title Value:	$0.45	$1.35	$2.25	£0.30	£0.90	£1.50
3-D ALIEN TERROR						
Eclipse; 1 Jun 1986						
1 ND Pound, Castrillo, Morrow art; Tom Yeates cover. Issued with bound-in 3-D glasses						
(25% less without glasses)						
	$0.55	$1.65	$2.75	£0.35	£1.05	£1.75
1 ND scarce in the U.K. non-3-D						
	$0.60	$1.80	$3.00	£0.40	£1.20	£2.00
Title Value:	$1.15	$3.45	$5.75	£0.75	£2.25	£3.75
3-D EXOTIC BEAUTIES						
3-D Zone,OS; 1 1990						
1 ND illustrations and story featuring belly-dancers and other such sordid stuff!						
	$0.30	$0.90	$1.50	£0.20	£0.60	£1.00
Title Value:	$0.30	$0.90	$1.50	£0.20	£0.60	£1.00
3-D HEAVY METAL MONSTERS						
3-D Zone,OS; 1 Sep 1993						
1 ND with 3-D glasses (25% less without glasses)						
	$0.80	$2.40	$4.00	£0.50	£1.50	£2.50
Title Value:	$0.80	$2.40	$4.00	£0.50	£1.50	£2.50
3-D HEROES						
Blackthorne; (3-D Series #3) 1 Feb 1986						
1 ND Steve Huston painted cover and art						
	$0.45	$1.35	$2.25	£0.30	£0.90	£1.50
Title Value:	$0.45	$1.35	$2.25	£0.30	£0.90	£1.50
3-D LASER ERASER AND PRESSBUTTON						
Eclipse; 1 Aug 1986						
1 ND Mike Collins and Mark Farmer art, Jerry Paris/Garry Leach cover; with 3-D glasses						
(25% less without glasses)						
	$0.60	$1.80	$3.00	£0.40	£1.20	£2.00
1 ND scarce in the U.K. non-3-D						
	$0.90	$2.70	$4.50	£0.60	£1.80	£3.00
Title Value:	$1.50	$4.50	$7.50	£1.00	£3.00	£5.00
3-D SUBSTANCE						
The 3-D Zone; nn 1990; 2 Dec 1991						
nn ND Steve Ditko art, with 3-D glasses (25% less without glasses)						
	$0.60	$1.80	$3.00	£0.40	£1.20	£2.00
2 ND Steve Ditko art featured, with 3-D glasses (25% less without glasses)						
	$0.80	$2.40	$4.00	£0.50	£1.50	£2.50
Title Value:	$1.40	$4.20	$7.00	£0.90	£2.70	£4.50
3-D THREE STOOGES						
Eclipse; (3-D Special 11,14,19); 1 Sep 1986-3 Oct 1987						
1 ND reprints 3 Stooges #2 (St.John); all issues with bound-in 3-D glasses (25% less without glasses)						
	$0.55	$1.65	$2.75	£0.35	£1.05	£1.75
1 ND scarce in the U.K. non-3-D						
	$0.60	$1.80	$3.00	£0.40	£1.20	£2.00
2 ND reprints 3 Stooges #3 (St.John)						
	$0.55	$1.65	$2.75	£0.35	£1.05	£1.75
3 ND reprints 3 Stooges #1 (Jubilee)						
	$0.55	$1.65	$2.75	£0.35	£1.05	£1.75
Title Value:	$2.25	$6.75	$11.25	£1.45	£4.35	£7.25
3-D TRUE CRIME						
3-D Zone,OS; 1 Jun 1992						
1 ND three classic stories by Jack Cole that Dr. Frederick Wertham referred to in "Seduction of the Innocent", with 3-D glasses (25% less without glasses)						
	$0.80	$2.40	$4.00	£0.50	£1.50	£2.50
Title Value:	$0.80	$2.40	$4.00	£0.50	£1.50	£2.50

Teknophage #1

Terminator (one-shot) #1

Terroress #1

NEAR MINT MEANS NEAR MINT!

3-D ZONE PRESENTS
The 3-D Zone; 1 Feb 1987-21 Jun 1989

Item	$Good	$Fine	$N.Mint	£Good	£Fine	£N.Mint
1 Wally Wood reprints from 1950s featuring Dr. Jekyll and Mr. Hyde; all issues come with bound-in 3-D glasses (25% less without glasses)	$0.45	$1.35	$2.25	£0.30	£0.90	£1.50
2 Weird Tales of Basil Wolverton	$0.45	$1.35	$2.25	£0.30	£0.90	£1.50
3 Picturescope Jungle Adventures, L.B. Cole reprint	$0.45	$1.35	$2.25	£0.30	£0.90	£1.50
4 Electric Fear by Brian Swift	$0.45	$1.35	$2.25	£0.30	£0.90	£1.50
5 Krazy Kat by George Herriman	$0.45	$1.35	$2.25	£0.30	£0.90	£1.50
6 Rat Fink by Ed Roth	$0.45	$1.35	$2.25	£0.30	£0.90	£1.50
7 Hollywood, colour 3-D photo-cover; photos of Jayne Mansfield, Jane Russell and other buxom beauties!	$0.55	$1.65	$2.75	£0.35	£1.05	£1.75
8 High Seas by Joe Kubert	$0.45	$1.35	$2.25	£0.30	£0.90	£1.50
9 Red Mask by Frank Bolle	$0.45	$1.35	$2.25	£0.30	£0.90	£1.50
10 Jet; Bob Powell and Al Williamson reprints	$0.45	$1.35	$2.25	£0.30	£0.90	£1.50
11 Danse Macabre, Matt Fox art	$0.45	$1.35	$2.25	£0.30	£0.90	£1.50
12 Presidents; oversize issue (8"x10") with photos	$0.55	$1.65	$2.75	£0.35	£1.05	£1.75
13 Flash Gordon, oversize issue (8"x10"), Raymond reprints	$0.60	$1.80	$3.00	£0.40	£1.20	£2.00
14 Tyranostar	$0.45	$1.35	$2.25	£0.30	£0.90	£1.50
15 3-Dementia Comics; Kurtzman, Kubert, Engel, Foster, Scott Shaw art	$0.55	$1.65	$2.75	£0.35	£1.05	£1.75
16 Space Vixens, Dave Stevens cover	$0.45	$1.35	$2.25	£0.30	£0.90	£1.50
17 Thrilling Love; features Kamen, Feldstein, Wood, Frazetta art	$0.45	$1.35	$2.25	£0.30	£0.90	£1.50
18 Spacehawk by Basil Wolverton	$0.45	$1.35	$2.25	£0.30	£0.90	£1.50
19 Cracked Classics	$0.45	$1.35	$2.25	£0.30	£0.90	£1.50
20 Commander Battle & His Atomic Submarine by Michael Vance	$0.45	$1.35	$2.25	£0.30	£0.90	£1.50
21 The Deep, Deep Sleep by Steve Vance	$0.45	$1.35	$2.25	£0.30	£0.90	£1.50
Title Value:	$9.90	$29.70	$49.50	£6.55	£19.65	£32.75

Note: all the above came with bound-in 3-D glasses. Values would be approximately 25% less for copies without glasses. Note also that all are Non-Distributed on the news-stands in the U.K.

THREE-DIMENSIONAL ALIEN WORLDS
Pacific; 1 Jul 1984

Item	$Good	$Fine	$N.Mint	£Good	£Fine	£N.Mint
1 ND Bolton, Dave Stevens art; 1st published Art Adams art (5pgs); with bound-in 3-D glasses (25% less without glasses)	$1.00	$3.00	$5.00	£0.70	£2.10	£3.50
1 2nd printing ND	$0.90	$2.70	$4.50	£0.60	£1.80	£3.00
Title Value:	$1.90	$5.70	$9.50	£1.30	£3.90	£6.50

THREE-DIMENSIONAL DNAGENTS
Eclipse; 1 Jan 1986

Item	$Good	$Fine	$N.Mint	£Good	£Fine	£N.Mint
1 ND Mark Evanier script, features art by Jerry Ordway; glasses included (25% less without glasses)	$0.50	$1.50	$2.50	£0.30	£0.90	£1.50
Title Value:	$0.50	$1.50	$2.50	£0.30	£0.90	£1.50

THREE-DIMENSIONAL SEDUCTION OF THE INNOCENT
Eclipse; 1 Oct 1985-2 Apr 1986

Item	$Good	$Fine	$N.Mint	£Good	£Fine	£N.Mint
1 ND pre-code reprints, Dave Stevens cover	$0.50	$1.50	$2.50	£0.30	£0.90	£1.50
1 ND scarce in the U.K. non-3-D issue	$0.60	$1.80	$3.00	£0.40	£1.20	£2.00
2 ND pre-code reprints	$0.50	$1.50	$2.50	£0.30	£0.90	£1.50
2 ND scarce in the U.K. non-3-D issue	$0.60	$1.80	$3.00	£0.40	£1.20	£2.00
Title Value:	$2.20	$6.60	$11.00	£1.40	£4.20	£7.00

3X3 EYES
Innovation,MS; 1 Aug 1991-5 Feb 1992

Item	$Good	$Fine	$N.Mint	£Good	£Fine	£N.Mint
1 ND	$0.55	$1.65	$2.75	£0.35	£1.05	£1.75
1 2nd printing, ND (Mar 1992)	$0.45	$1.35	$2.25	£0.30	£0.90	£1.50
2-5 ND	$0.40	$1.20	$2.00	£0.25	£0.75	£1.25
Title Value:	$2.60	$7.80	$13.00	£1.65	£4.95	£8.25
3 x 3 Eyes (Feb 1995)						
Trade paperback reprints mini-series, black and white				£1.70	£5.10	£8.50

Note: this edition published by Dark Horse Comics

3X3 EYES (2ND SERIES)
Dark Horse,MS; 1 Oct 1995-5 Feb 1996

Item	$Good	$Fine	$N.Mint	£Good	£Fine	£N.Mint
1-5 ND Yuzo Takada script and art; black and white	$0.60	$1.80	$3.00	£0.40	£1.20	£2.00
Title Value:	$3.00	$9.00	$15.00	£2.00	£6.00	£10.00

THRESHERZ
Firstlight Comixx,MS; 1 Aug 1994-5 Dec 1994

Item	$Good	$Fine	$N.Mint	£Good	£Fine	£N.Mint
1 ND holo-foil enhanced cover by Andy Smith	$0.50	$1.50	$2.50	£0.30	£0.90	£1.50
1 ND Gold Edition available to retailers with every 15 copies of #1	$1.00	$3.00	$5.00	£0.60	£1.80	£3.00
2-5 ND	$0.50	$1.50	$2.50	£0.30	£0.90	£1.50
Title Value:	$3.50	$10.50	$17.50	£2.10	£6.30	£10.50

THRILL-O-RAMA
Harvey; 1 Oct 1965-3 Dec 1966

Item	$Good	$Fine	$N.Mint	£Good	£Fine	£N.Mint
1 rare in the U.K. "Man in Black Called Fate"	$2.50	$7.50	$17.50	£1.75	£5.25	£12.50
2 rare in the U.K. Pirana, Williamson art	$2.10	$6.25	$15.00	£1.40	£4.25	£10.00
3 scarce in the U.K. Pirana	$1.75	$5.25	$12.50	£1.05	£3.20	£7.50
Title Value:	$6.35	$19.00	$45.00	£4.20	£12.70	£30.00

THRILLER
DC Comics; 1 Nov 1983-12 Nov 1984

Item	$Good	$Fine	$N.Mint	£Good	£Fine	£N.Mint
1 ND 1st appearance "7 Seconds"	$0.25	$0.75	$1.25	£0.15	£0.45	£0.75
2-12 ND	$0.25	$0.75	$1.25	£0.15	£0.45	£0.75
Title Value:	$3.00	$9.00	$15.00	£1.80	£5.40	£9.00

Note: all Deluxe Format Baxter paper.

THRILLING PLANET TALES
AC Comics,OS; 1 Jun 1991

Item	$Good	$Fine	$N.Mint	£Good	£Fine	£N.Mint
1 ND 68pgs, reprints of classic Fiction House Planet Tales series, Murphy Anderson, Lee Elias, George Evans art featured (1000 copies)	$1.50	$4.50	$7.50	£1.00	£3.00	£5.00
Title Value:	$1.50	$4.50	$7.50	£1.00	£3.00	£5.00

THRILLING WONDER TALES
AC Comics; nn May 1991

Item	$Good	$Fine	$N.Mint	£Good	£Fine	£N.Mint
nn ND classic sci-fi reprints featuring Kirby, Wood and Ayers art	$0.50	$1.50	$2.50	£0.30	£0.90	£1.50
Title Value:	$0.50	$1.50	$2.50	£0.30	£0.90	£1.50

THRILLGY
Pacific; 1 Jan 1984

Item	$Good	$Fine	$N.Mint	£Good	£Fine	£N.Mint
1 ND Tim Conrad art	$0.30	$0.90	$1.50	£0.20	£0.60	£1.00
Title Value:	$0.30	$0.90	$1.50	£0.20	£0.60	£1.00

THUMBSCREWS
Caliber Press; 1 Sep 1992-3 1992

Item	$Good	$Fine	$N.Mint	£Good	£Fine	£N.Mint
1 ND 64pgs, horror anthology begins	$0.50	$1.50	$2.50	£0.30	£0.90	£1.50
2-3 ND 64pgs	$0.50	$1.50	$2.50	£0.30	£0.90	£1.50
Title Value:	$1.50	$4.50	$7.50	£0.90	£2.70	£4.50

THUN'DA TALES
Fantagraphics; 1 1987
(see Untamed Love)

Item	$Good	$Fine	$N.Mint	£Good	£Fine	£N.Mint
1 ND Frank Frazetta reprint	$0.50	$1.50	$2.50	£0.30	£0.90	£1.50
Title Value:	$0.50	$1.50	$2.50	£0.30	£0.90	£1.50

THUNDER AGENTS
Tower; 1 Nov 1965-19 Nov 1968; 20 Nov 1969

Item	$Good	$Fine	$N.Mint	£Good	£Fine	£N.Mint
1 Giant	$14.00	$43.00	$100.00	£9.25	£28.00	£65.00
2 Giant	$10.00	$30.00	$60.00	£6.50	£20.00	£40.00
3-5 Giant	$6.50	$20.00	$40.00	£4.55	£13.50	£27.50
6-10 Giant	$5.00	$15.00	$30.00	£3.30	£10.00	£20.00
11-15 Giant	$4.15	$12.50	$25.00	£2.90	£8.75	£17.50
16-17 Giant	$3.30	$10.00	$20.00	£2.05	£6.25	£12.50
18-19 rare, distributed in the U.K. Giant	$3.30	$10.00	$20.00	£2.50	£7.50	£15.00
20 Giant, all reprint	$3.30	$10.00	$20.00	£2.05	£6.25	£12.50
Title Value:	$105.75	$320.50	$655.00	£71.55	£216.00	£442.50

Note: Steve Ditko art in 6,7,12,16,18. Wally Wood art in most issues

THUNDER AGENTS (2ND SERIES)
JC Comics Group,Magazine OS; 1 Feb 1982

Item	$Good	$Fine	$N.Mint	£Good	£Fine	£N.Mint
1 scarce in the U.K. 48pgs, reprints 1st appearance of The Fly from Double Life of Private Strong #1(Jun 1959) by Joe Simon & Jack Kirby, 1st professional work by Mark Texeira, Neal Adams reprint art (10pgs)	$1.50	$4.50	$7.50	£1.00	£3.00	£5.00
Title Value:	$1.50	$4.50	$7.50	£1.00	£3.00	£5.00

Note: Non-Distributed on the news-stands in the U.K.

THUNDER AGENTS (3RD SERIES)
JC Comics; 1 May 1983-2 Jan 1984

Item	$Good	$Fine	$N.Mint	£Good	£Fine	£N.Mint
1 ND reprints of Wally Wood and Reed Crandall material; sub-titled "Hall of Fame featuring..."	$0.50	$1.50	$2.50	£0.30	£0.90	£1.50
2 ND new stories, intro Agent Vulcan; Murphy Anderson pin-up	$0.50	$1.50	$2.50	£0.30	£0.90	£1.50
Title Value:	$1.00	$3.00	$5.00	£0.60	£1.80	£3.00

THUNDER AGENTS, WALLY WOOD'S
Deluxe Comics; 1 Nov 1984-5 Oct 1986

Item	$Good	$Fine	$N.Mint	£Good	£Fine	£N.Mint
1 ND 48pgs, part Keith Giffen art	$0.50	$1.50	$2.50	£0.30	£0.90	£1.50
2 ND 48pgs, part George Perez art	$0.50	$1.50	$2.50	£0.30	£0.90	£1.50
3 ND 48pgs, Dave Cockrum, Keith Giffen, Steve Ditko art featured, George Perez cover	$0.50	$1.50	$2.50	£0.30	£0.90	£1.50
4 ND 48pgs	$0.50	$1.50	$2.50	£0.30	£0.90	£1.50
5 ND 48pgs, Jerry Ordway cover	$0.50	$1.50	$2.50	£0.30	£0.90	£1.50
Title Value:	$2.50	$7.50	$12.50	£1.50	£4.50	£7.50

THUNDERBOLT, PETER CANNON
Charlton; 1 Jan 1966; 51 Mar/Apr 1966-60 Nov 1967
(previously Son of Vulcan)

Item	$Good	$Fine	$N.Mint	£Good	£Fine	£N.Mint
1 rare, distributed in the U.K. origin told	$2.05	$6.25	$12.50	£1.25	£3.75	£7.50
51-60 distributed in the U.K.	$1.25	$3.75	$7.50	£0.80	£2.50	£5.00

	$Good	$Fine	$N.Mint	£Good	£Fine	£N.Mint
Title Value:	$14.55	$43.75	$87.50	£9.25	£28.75	£57.50

THUNDERBUNNY
Red Circle; 1 Jan 1984

	$Good	$Fine	$N.Mint	£Good	£Fine	£N.Mint
1 ND	$0.40	$1.20	$2.00	£0.25	£0.75	£1.25
Title Value:	$0.40	$1.20	$2.00	£0.25	£0.75	£1.25

THUNDERBUNNY (2ND SERIES)
Warp/Apple; 1 Jun 1985-12 1989

	$Good	$Fine	$N.Mint	£Good	£Fine	£N.Mint
1 ND origin retold	$0.30	$0.90	$1.50	£0.20	£0.60	£1.00
2-5 ND	$0.30	$0.90	$1.50	£0.20	£0.60	£1.00
6 ND last Warp issue	$0.30	$0.90	$1.50	£0.20	£0.60	£1.00
7-10 ND	$0.30	$0.90	$1.50	£0.20	£0.60	£1.00
11 ND THUNDER Agents appear	$0.30	$0.90	$1.50	£0.20	£0.60	£1.00
12 ND	$0.30	$0.90	$1.50	£0.20	£0.60	£1.00
Title Value:	$3.60	$10.80	$18.00	£2.40	£7.20	£12.00

THUNDERCATS
Marvel Comics Group/Star, TV; 1 Dec 1985-24 Jun 1988

	$Good	$Fine	$N.Mint	£Good	£Fine	£N.Mint
1 ND	$0.15	$0.45	$0.75	£0.10	£0.30	£0.50
2 ND 65 and 75 cent covers are known to exist	$0.15	$0.45	$0.75	£0.10	£0.30	£0.50
3-24 ND	$0.15	$0.45	$0.75	£0.10	£0.30	£0.50
Title Value:	$3.60	$10.80	$18.00	£2.40	£7.20	£12.00

THUNDERSTRIKE
Marvel Comics Group; 1 Jun 1993-24 Sep 1995

	$Good	$Fine	$N.Mint	£Good	£Fine	£N.Mint
1 ND 48pgs, lightning pattern foil enhanced cover	$0.60	$1.80	$3.00	£0.40	£1.20	£2.00
2 ND Juggernaut appears	$0.30	$0.90	$1.50	£0.20	£0.60	£1.00
3	$0.30	$0.90	$1.50	£0.20	£0.60	£1.00
4 ND Spiderman appears	$0.30	$0.90	$1.50	£0.20	£0.60	£1.00
5 ND Nick Fury and Shield appear	$0.30	$0.90	$1.50	£0.20	£0.60	£1.00
6-7 ND	$0.30	$0.90	$1.50	£0.20	£0.60	£1.00
8 ND with free Spiderman and his Deadly Foes card sheet	$0.30	$0.90	$1.50	£0.20	£0.60	£1.00
9 ND	$0.30	$0.90	$1.50	£0.20	£0.60	£1.00
10 ND Thor appears	$0.30	$0.90	$1.50	£0.20	£0.60	£1.00
11-19 ND	$0.30	$0.90	$1.50	£0.20	£0.60	£1.00
20 ND Black Panther guest-stars	$0.30	$0.90	$1.50	£0.20	£0.60	£1.00
21 ND War Machine, Ant-Man and She-Hulk appear	$0.30	$0.90	$1.50	£0.20	£0.60	£1.00
22 ND	$0.30	$0.90	$1.50	£0.20	£0.60	£1.00
23 ND The Avengers and Thor guest-star	$0.30	$0.90	$1.50	£0.20	£0.60	£1.00
24 ND Thunderstrike vs. Bloodaxe	$0.30	$0.90	$1.50	£0.20	£0.60	£1.00
Title Value:	$7.50	$22.50	$37.50	£5.00	£15.00	£25.00

THUNDERSTRIKE DOUBLE FEATURE
Marvel Comics Group, MS; 1 Oct 1994-4 Jan 1995

	$Good	$Fine	$N.Mint	£Good	£Fine	£N.Mint
1 ND 48pgs, flip-book format; features Thunderstrike #13 plus Code: Blue	$0.50	$1.50	$2.50	£0.30	£0.90	£1.50
2 ND 48pgs, flip-book format; features Thunderstrike #14 plus Code: Blue	$0.50	$1.50	$2.50	£0.30	£0.90	£1.50
3 ND 48pgs, flip-book format; features Thunderstrike #15 plus Code: Blue	$0.50	$1.50	$2.50	£0.30	£0.90	£1.50
4 ND 48pgs, flip-book format; features Thunderstrike #16 plus Code: Blue	$0.50	$1.50	$2.50	£0.30	£0.90	£1.50
Title Value:	$2.00	$6.00	$10.00	£1.20	£3.60	£6.00

TICK SPECIAL EDITION, THE
New England Comics; 1,2 1988

	$Good	$Fine	$N.Mint	£Good	£Fine	£N.Mint
1 ND 1st appearance The Tick	$8.25	$25.00	$50.00	£5.75	£17.50	£35.00
2 ND	$7.50	$22.50	$45.00	£5.00	£15.00	£30.00
Title Value:	$15.75	$47.50	$95.00	£10.75	£32.50	£65.00

TICK'S GIANT CIRCUS OF THE MIGHTY, THE
New England Comics; 1 Apr 1992-3 1992

	$Good	$Fine	$N.Mint	£Good	£Fine	£N.Mint
1-3 ND	$0.50	$1.50	$2.50	£0.30	£0.90	£1.50
Title Value:	$1.50	$4.50	$7.50	£0.90	£2.70	£4.50

TICK, THE
New England Comics; 1 Jun 1988-12 1993

	$Good	$Fine	$N.Mint	£Good	£Fine	£N.Mint
1 black and white, reprints Special Edition 1 with minor changes; Ben Edlund script and art; slightly larger format 7.5" x 10.5"	$5.75	$17.50	$35.00	£3.30	£10.00	£20.00
1 2nd printing	$0.90	$2.70	$4.50	£0.60	£1.80	£3.00
1 3rd printing	$0.60	$1.80	$3.00	£0.40	£1.20	£2.00
1 4th printing	$0.50	$1.50	$2.50	£0.30	£0.90	£1.50
1 5th printing, (Apr 1991)	$0.50	$1.50	$2.50	£0.30	£0.90	£1.50
1 6th printing, (Apr 1995)	$0.50	$1.50	$2.50	£0.30	£0.90	£1.50
2 reprints Special Edition #2 with minor changes	$5.50	$16.50	$27.50	£2.00	£6.00	£10.00
2 very rare in the U.K., rare in the U.S. un-cut edition available from New England Comics	$12.00	$36.00	$60.00	£8.00	£24.00	£40.00
2 2nd printing	$0.60	$1.80	$3.00	£0.40	£1.20	£2.00
2 3rd printing	$0.50	$1.50	$2.50	£0.30	£0.90	£1.50
2 4th printing	$0.50	$1.50	$2.50	£0.30	£0.90	£1.50
2 5th printing, (Jul 1991)	$0.50	$1.50	$2.50	£0.30	£0.90	£1.50
3	$1.00	$3.00	$5.00	£0.70	£2.10	£3.50
3 2nd printing	$0.60	$1.80	$3.00	£0.40	£1.20	£2.00
3 3rd printing	$0.50	$1.50	$2.50	£0.30	£0.90	£1.50
3 4th printing	$0.50	$1.50	$2.50	£0.30	£0.90	£1.50
3 5th printing, (Oct 1993)	$0.50	$1.50	$2.50	£0.30	£0.90	£1.50
3 6th printing, (Apr 1995)	$0.50	$1.50	$2.50	£0.30	£0.90	£1.50
4	$1.00	$3.00	$5.00	£0.70	£2.10	£3.50
4 2nd printing	$0.60	$1.80	$3.00	£0.40	£1.20	£2.00
4 3rd printing	$0.50	$1.50	$2.50	£0.30	£0.90	£1.50
4 4th printing	$0.50	$1.50	$2.50	£0.30	£0.90	£1.50
4 5th printing, (Apr 1992)	$0.50	$1.50	$2.50	£0.30	£0.90	£1.50
5	$1.00	$3.00	$5.00	£0.70	£2.10	£3.50
5 2nd printing, (Aug 1992)	$0.50	$1.50	$2.50	£0.30	£0.90	£1.50
6	$0.80	$2.40	$4.00	£0.50	£1.50	£2.50
6 2nd printing, (Aug 1991)	$0.50	$1.50	$2.50	£0.30	£0.90	£1.50
6 3rd printing	$0.50	$1.50	$2.50	£0.30	£0.90	£1.50
6 4th printing ND	$0.50	$1.50	$2.50	£0.30	£0.90	£1.50
7 1st appearance Man-Eating Cow	$0.80	$2.40	$4.00	£0.50	£1.50	£2.50
7 2nd printing, (Nov 1991)	$0.50	$1.50	$2.50	£0.30	£0.90	£1.50
7 3rd printing ND	$0.50	$1.50	$2.50	£0.30	£0.90	£1.50
8	$0.80	$2.40	$4.00	£0.50	£1.50	£2.50
8 2nd printing, (Apr 1992)	$0.50	$1.50	$2.50	£0.30	£0.90	£1.50
8 3rd printing ND	$0.50	$1.50	$2.50	£0.30	£0.90	£1.50
8 scarce in the U.K. printed without title logo	$1.20	$3.60	$6.00	£0.80	£2.40	£4.00
9	$0.60	$1.80	$3.00	£0.40	£1.20	£2.00
9 2nd printing ND	$0.50	$1.50	$2.50	£0.30	£0.90	£1.50
10-11	$0.60	$1.80	$3.00	£0.40	£1.20	£2.00
11 2nd printing ND	$0.50	$1.50	$2.50	£0.30	£0.90	£1.50
12	$0.60	$1.80	$3.00	£0.40	£1.20	£2.00
Title Value:	$47.05	$141.40	$241.50	£28.40	£85.30	£145.50

Note: all Non-Distributed on the news-stands in the U.K.

	$Good	$Fine	$N.Mint	£Good	£Fine	£N.Mint
Tick Omnibus: Sunday Through Wednesday, reprints #1-6 plus new story				£1.45	£4.35	£7.25
Tick Omnibus Limited Edition, signed				£2.20	£6.60	£11.00

Note: number 8 issued by New England Comics without a logo as a special issue for distributors and retailers

TICK, THE NEW (KARMA TORNADO)
New England Comics; 1 Aug 1993-9 1995?

	$Good	$Fine	$N.Mint	£Good	£Fine	£N.Mint
1 ND pre-bagged with trading card; black and white begins	$0.70	$2.10	$3.50	£0.50	£1.50	£2.50
2 ND	$0.60	$1.80	$3.00	£0.40	£1.20	£2.00
3 ND title becomes "The Tick: Karma Tornado"	$0.60	$1.80	$3.00	£0.40	£1.20	£2.00
4-8 ND	$0.60	$1.80	$3.00	£0.40	£1.20	£2.00
9 ND	$0.55	$1.65	$2.75	£0.35	£1.05	£1.75
Title Value:	$5.45	$16.35	$27.25	£3.65	£10.95	£18.25
Tick Karma Tornado (Sep 1995)						
Trade paperback collects issues #1-5 with new Ben Edlund cover				£1.80	£5.40	£9.00

TIGER GIRL
Gold Key; 1 Sep 1968

	$Good	$Fine	$N.Mint	£Good	£Fine	£N.Mint
1 scarce, distributed in the U.K.	$3.75	$11.00	$22.50	£2.50	£7.50	£15.00
Title Value:	$3.75	$11.00	$22.50	£2.50	£7.50	£15.00

TIGER WOMAN, QUEST OF
Millennium, OS; 1 Apr 1995

	$Good	$Fine	$N.Mint	£Good	£Fine	£N.Mint
1 ND Donald Marquez script and art	$0.50	$1.50	$2.50	£0.30	£0.90	£1.50
Title Value:	$0.50	$1.50	$2.50	£0.30	£0.90	£1.50

TIGER WOMAN, THE
Millennium; 1 Sep 1994-2 1994

	$Good	$Fine	$N.Mint	£Good	£Fine	£N.Mint
1-2 ND Donald Marquez script, Brian Buniak art	$0.50	$1.50	$2.50	£0.30	£0.90	£1.50
Title Value:	$1.00	$3.00	$5.00	£0.60	£1.80	£3.00

TIGER-MAN
Atlas; 1 Apr 1975-3 Sep 1975

	$Good	$Fine	$N.Mint	£Good	£Fine	£N.Mint
1	$0.25	$0.75	$1.25	£0.15	£0.45	£0.75
2-3 Steve Ditko art	$0.30	$0.90	$1.50	£0.20	£0.60	£1.00
Title Value:	$0.85	$2.55	$4.25	£0.55	£1.65	£2.75

TIGER-X
Eternity; 1 Jun 1988-3 1989

	$Good	$Fine	$N.Mint	£Good	£Fine	£N.Mint
1-3 ND	$0.40	$1.20	$2.00	£0.25	£0.75	£1.25
Title Value:	$1.20	$3.60	$6.00	£0.75	£2.25	£3.75
Trade Paperback, reprints				£1.00	£3.00	£5.00

TIGER-X II
Eternity; 1 1989-4 1990

	$Good	$Fine	$N.Mint	£Good	£Fine	£N.Mint
1-4 ND	$0.40	$1.20	$2.00	£0.25	£0.75	£1.25
Title Value:	$1.60	$4.80	$8.00	£1.00	£3.00	£5.00

TIGER-X SPECIAL
Eternity; 1 1988

	$Good	$Fine	$N.Mint	£Good	£Fine	£N.Mint
1 ND	$0.40	$1.20	$2.00	£0.25	£0.75	£1.25
Title Value:	$0.40	$1.20	$2.00	£0.25	£0.75	£1.25

	$Good	$Fine	$N.Mint	£Good	£Fine	£N.Mint

TIGERS OF TERRA
Antarctic Press; 1 Jun 1994-present
1-15 ND Ted Nomura script and art; black and white

	$0.50	$1.50	$2.50	£0.30	£0.90	£1.50

16-17 ND Ted Nomura script and art; black and white

	$0.55	$1.65	$2.75	£0.35	£1.05	£1.75
Title Value:	$8.60	$25.80	$43.00	£5.20	£15.60	£26.00

Tigers of Terra Book 1 (Aug 1995)
104pgs, collects issues #1,2; black and white

				£1.30	£3.90	£6.50

TIGERS OF TERRA COLOR SPECIAL
Antarctic Press,OS; 1 Aug 1993
1 ND black and white

	$0.60	$1.80	$3.00	£0.40	£1.20	£2.00
Title Value:	$0.60	$1.80	$3.00	£0.40	£1.20	£2.00

TIGRESS, THE
Hero; 1 Aug 1992-7 1993
1-5 ND black and white

	$0.40	$1.20	$2.00	£0.25	£0.75	£1.25

6-7 ND 44pgs, black and white

	$0.50	$1.50	$2.50	£0.30	£0.90	£1.50
Title Value:	$3.00	$9.00	$15.00	£1.85	£5.55	£9.25

TIM HOLT WESTERN ANNUAL
AC Comics,OS; 1 1991
1 ND 52pgs, black and white photo cover and black and white reprint art by Frank Bolle, scripted by Gardner Fox; Limited Collectors Edition blazon on cover

	$0.50	$1.50	$2.50	£0.30	£0.90	£1.50
Title Value:	$0.50	$1.50	$2.50	£0.30	£0.90	£1.50

TIMBER WOLF
DC Comics,MS; 1 Nov 1992-5 Mar 1993
(see Adventure Comics #327)
1-5 ND

	$0.25	$0.75	$1.25	£0.15	£0.45	£0.75
Title Value:	$1.25	$3.75	$6.25	£0.75	£2.25	£3.75

TIME BANDITS
Marvel Comics Group,OS Film; 1 1982
1 ND 52pgs, adapts film

	$0.30	$0.90	$1.50	£0.20	£0.60	£1.00
Title Value:	$0.30	$0.90	$1.50	£0.20	£0.60	£1.00

TIME BEAVERS
First, Graphic Novel; nn 1985
nn ND Tim Truman art

	$1.50	$4.50	$7.50	£1.00	£3.00	£5.00
Title Value:	$1.50	$4.50	$7.50	£1.00	£3.00	£5.00

TIME COP MOVIE ADAPTATION
Dark Horse,MS Film; 1,2 Sep 1994
1-2 ND Ron Randall art, Denis Beauvais painted cover

	$0.50	$1.50	$2.50	£0.30	£0.90	£1.50
Title Value:	$1.00	$3.00	$5.00	£0.60	£1.80	£3.00

TIME GATES
Double Edge; 1 May 1991-4 Oct 1991
1 ND dinosaur issue; black and white begins

	$0.30	$0.90	$1.50	£0.20	£0.60	£1.00

2-4 ND

	$0.30	$0.90	$1.50	£0.20	£0.60	£1.00
Title Value:	$1.20	$3.60	$6.00	£0.75	£2.40	£4.00

TIME MACHINE GRAPHIC NOVEL, THE
Eternity,OS; 1 Aug 1991
1 ND adaptation of classic sci-fi book

	$1.50	$4.50	$7.50	£1.00	£3.00	£5.00
Title Value:	$1.50	$4.50	$7.50	£1.00	£3.00	£5.00

TIME MACHINE, THE
Eternity,MS; 1 Apr 1990-3 May 1990
1-3 ND adaptation of H.G. Wells classic; Bill Spangler black and white art

	$0.40	$1.20	$2.00	£0.25	£0.75	£1.25
Title Value:	$1.20	$3.60	$6.00	£0.75	£2.25	£3.75

Note: issues 1,2 bi-weekly

TIME MASTERS
DC Comics,MS; 1 Feb 1990-8 Sep 1990
(see Rip Hunter)
1 Art Thibert art begins, Rip Hunter appears throughout

	$0.25	$0.75	$1.25	£0.15	£0.45	£0.75

2 Superman appears

	$0.25	$0.75	$1.25	£0.15	£0.45	£0.75

3 Jonah Hex appears

	$0.25	$0.75	$1.25	£0.15	£0.45	£0.75

4 Tomahawk appears

	$0.25	$0.75	$1.25	£0.15	£0.45	£0.75

5 Cave Carson appears

	$0.25	$0.75	$1.25	£0.15	£0.45	£0.75

6 Dr. Fate appears

	$0.25	$0.75	$1.25	£0.15	£0.45	£0.75

7 Arion appears

	$0.25	$0.75	$1.25	£0.15	£0.45	£0.75

8 Vandal Savage appears

	$0.25	$0.75	$1.25	£0.15	£0.45	£0.75
Title Value:	$2.00	$6.00	$10.00	£1.20	£3.60	£6.00

Note: Deluxe Format; series re-evaluates time-travel in the DC Universe.

TIME TRIPPERS
Snyder Inkworks; 1-3 Winter 1990
1-3 ND black and white

	$0.15	$0.45	$0.75	£0.10	£0.30	£0.50
Title Value:	$0.45	$1.35	$2.25	£0.30	£0.90	£1.50

TIME TWISTERS
Quality Comics; 1 Sep 1987-21 May 1989
1 LD in the U.K. reprints from 2000 AD begin; early issues feature Alan Moore scripts

	$0.25	$0.75	$1.25	£0.15	£0.45	£0.75

2-13 LD in the U.K.

	$0.25	$0.75	$1.25	£0.15	£0.45	£0.75

14 LD in the U.K. Brian Bolland art (3pgs)

	$0.30	$0.90	$1.50	£0.20	£0.60	£1.00

15-16 LD in the U.K. Jackson Guice cover

	$0.25	$0.75	$1.25	£0.15	£0.45	£0.75

17-21 LD in the U.K.

	$0.25	$0.75	$1.25	£0.15	£0.45	£0.75
Title Value:	$5.30	$15.90	$26.50	£3.20	£9.60	£16.00

TIME WARP
DC Comics; 1 Oct/Nov 1979-5 Jun/Jul 1980
1-5 ND scarce in the U.K. 68pgs

	$0.40	$1.20	$2.00	£0.25	£0.75	£1.25
Title Value:	$2.00	$6.00	$10.00	£1.25	£3.75	£6.25

ARTISTS
Ditko art in 1-4. Nasser art in 4.

TIMEDRIFTER
Innovation; 1 Dec 1990-3 Feb 1991
1-3 ND Gerard Jones script/art; black and white

	$0.40	$1.20	$2.00	£0.25	£0.75	£1.25
Title Value:	$1.20	$3.60	$6.00	£0.75	£2.25	£3.75

TIMESPIRITS
Marvel Comics Group/Epic,MS; 1 Jan 1985-8 Mar 1986
1-8 ND

	$0.40	$1.20	$2.00	£0.25	£0.75	£1.25
Title Value:	$3.20	$9.60	$16.00	£2.00	£6.00	£10.00

Note: all on Baxter paper, Mature Readers label. Williamson art in 4.

TIMESTRYKE
Marvel UK,MS; 1 Dec 1993
1 red foil enhanced cover (cancelled after 1 issue)

	$0.40	$1.20	$2.00	£0.25	£0.75	£1.25
Title Value:	$0.40	$1.20	$2.00	£0.25	£0.75	£1.25

TIMEWALKER
Valiant/Acclaim Comics; 0 Apr 1994; 1 Dec 1994-15 Jun 1995
0 origin told

	$0.40	$1.20	$2.00	£0.25	£0.75	£1.25

1 spin-off from The Chaos Effect storyline

	$0.40	$1.20	$2.00	£0.25	£0.75	£1.25

2-5

	$0.40	$1.20	$2.00	£0.25	£0.75	£1.25

6-7 Harbinger Wars story

	$0.40	$1.20	$2.00	£0.25	£0.75	£1.25

8 1st Acclaim Comics issue, Harbinger Wars story; bi-weekly

	$0.40	$1.20	$2.00	£0.25	£0.75	£1.25

9 bi-weekly, leads into Timewalker #0

	$0.40	$1.20	$2.00	£0.25	£0.75	£1.25

10-15 bi-weekly

	$0.40	$1.20	$2.00	£0.25	£0.75	£1.25
Title Value:	$6.40	$19.20	$32.00	£4.00	£12.00	£20.00

Note: all Non-Distributed on the news-stands in the U.K.

Timewalker (May 1995)
Trade paperback reprints early appearances from Archer & Armstrong #8, 10, 11 and Magnus #33

				£1.30	£3.90	£6.50

TIMEWALKER YEARBOOK
Valiant; 1 May 1995
1 ND story continues from Magnus Robot Fighter #33

	$0.50	$1.50	$2.50	£0.30	£0.90	£1.50
Title Value:	$0.50	$1.50	$2.50	£0.30	£0.90	£1.50

TINY TOON ADVENTURES
DC Comics,Magazine; 1 Oct 1990-5 1991
1 ND 32pgs, Bugs Bunny, Daffy Duck and other MGM cartoon characters

	$0.30	$0.90	$1.50	£0.20	£0.60	£1.00

2 ND 32pgs, Winter theme

	$0.30	$0.90	$1.50	£0.20	£0.60	£1.00

3-5 ND 32pgs

	$0.30	$0.90	$1.50	£0.20	£0.60	£1.00
Title Value:	$1.50	$4.50	$7.50	£1.00	£3.00	£5.00

TION
Pink Egg Publishing; 1,2 1990
1-2 ND black and white

	$0.40	$1.20	$2.00	£0.25	£0.75	£1.25
Title Value:	$0.80	$2.40	$4.00	£0.50	£1.50	£2.50

TITAN GRAPHIC NOVEL
Continuity,OS; 1 Jul 1992
1 ND 48pgs, Neal Adams cover

	$0.80	$2.40	$4.00	£0.50	£1.50	£2.50
Title Value:	$0.80	$2.40	$4.00	£0.50	£1.50	£2.50

TITAN SPECIAL
Dark Horse/Comics Greatest World,OS; 1 May 1994
1 ND 48pgs, Bart Sears cover

	$0.80	$2.40	$4.00	£0.50	£1.50	£2.50
Title Value:	$0.80	$2.40	$4.00	£0.50	£1.50	£2.50

TITANS SELL-OUT SPECIAL, THE
DC Comics,OS; 1 Dec 1992
1 ND 48pgs, Titans Sell-Out part 1, X-over Deathstroke the Terminator #17, (continuation of "Total Chaos" storyline); bound-in Nightwing poster

	$0.60	$1.80	$3.00	£0.40	£1.20	£2.00
Title Value:	$0.60	$1.80	$3.00	£0.40	£1.20	£2.00

TMNT MUTANT UNIVERSE SOURCEBOOK
Archie,OS; 1 Jan 1993
1 ND 48pgs

	$0.40	$1.20	$2.00	£0.25	£0.75	£1.25
Title Value:	$0.40	$1.20	$2.00	£0.25	£0.75	£1.25

TMNT PRESENT: DONATELLO & LEATHERHEAD
Archie,MS; 1 Jun 1993-3 Aug 1993
1-3 ND

	$0.25	$0.75	$1.25	£0.15	£0.45	£0.75
Title Value:	$0.75	$2.25	$3.75	£0.45	£1.35	£2.25

	$Good	$Fine	$N.Mint	£Good	£Fine	£N.Mint

TMNT PRESENTS: APRIL O'NEIL - THE MAY EAST SAGA
Archie,MS; 1 Mar 1993-3 May 1993

	$Good	$Fine	$N.Mint	£Good	£Fine	£N.Mint
1-3 ND	$0.25	$0.75	$1.25	£0.15	£0.45	£0.75
Title Value:	$0.75	$2.25	$3.75	£0.45	£1.35	£2.25

TMNT PRESENTS: MERDUDE & MICHAELANGELO
Archie,MS; 1 Aug 1993-3 Nov 1993

1-3 ND	$0.25	$0.75	$1.25	£0.15	£0.45	£0.75
Title Value:	$0.75	$2.25	$3.75	£0.45	£1.35	£2.25

TMNT/SAVAGE DRAGON CROSS-OVER SPECIAL
Mirage Studios,OS; 1 Nov 1993
1 ND X-over with Savage Dragon #2, part Erik Larsen cover

	$0.50	$1.50	$2.50	£0.30	£0.90	£1.50
Title Value:	$0.50	$1.50	$2.50	£0.30	£0.90	£1.50

TMNT\FLAMING CARROT CROSS-OVER: LAND OF GREEN FIRE
Mirage Studios,MS; 1 Jan 1994-4 Apr 1994
1-4 ND Bob Burden script

	$0.50	$1.50	$2.50	£0.30	£0.90	£1.50
Title Value:	$2.00	$6.00	$10.00	£1.20	£3.60	£6.00

TO BE ANNOUNCED
Strawberry Jam; 1 1985-7 Jun 1987

1-7 ND	$0.30	$0.90	$1.50	£0.20	£0.60	£1.00
Title Value:	$2.10	$6.30	$10.50	£1.40	£4.20	£7.00

TO DIE FOR IN 3-D
Blackthorne; (3-D Series #64) 1 Spring 1989
1 ND

	$0.50	$1.50	$2.50	£0.30	£0.90	£1.50

1 ND non 3-D version

	$0.40	$1.20	$2.00	£0.25	£0.75	£1.25
Title Value:	$0.90	$2.70	$4.50	£0.55	£1.65	£2.75

TOKA JUNGLE KING
Dell; 1 Aug/Oct 1964-10 Jan 1967

1 painted cover	$2.90	$8.75	$17.50	£2.05	£6.25	£12.50
2 painted cover	$1.65	$5.00	$10.00	£1.25	£3.75	£7.50

3 Frank Springer covers and art begin

	$1.25	$3.75	$7.50	£0.80	£2.50	£5.00
4-5	$1.25	$3.75	$7.50	£0.80	£2.50	£5.00
6-10	$1.50	$4.50	$7.50	£0.80	£2.50	£4.00
Title Value:	$15.80	$47.50	$87.50	£9.70	£29.50	£55.00

Note: all Limited Distribution in the U.K.

TOM CORBETT, SPACE CADET
Eternity,MS; 1 Mar 1990-4 Jun 1990

1-4 ND	$0.40	$1.20	$2.00	£0.25	£0.75	£1.25
Title Value:	$1.60	$4.80	$8.00	£1.00	£3.00	£5.00

Graphic Album: The Reconstructed Man,
reprints issues Book I #1-4   £1.10   £3.30   £5.50

TOM CORBETT, SPACE CADET BOOK TWO
Eternity,MS; 1 Sep 1990-4 Dec 1990
1 ND new adventures based on 1950s CBS television series begin

	$0.40	$1.20	$2.00	£0.25	£0.75	£1.25
2-4 ND	$0.40	$1.20	$2.00	£0.25	£0.75	£1.25
Title Value:	$1.60	$4.80	$8.00	£1.00	£3.00	£5.00

TOM CORBETT, THE ORIGINAL
Eternity,MS; 1 Sep 1990-5 Jan 1991
1 ND bi-weekly issues, reprints 1950s newspaper strip of popular TV series

	$0.50	$1.50	$2.50	£0.30	£0.90	£1.50
2-5 ND	$0.50	$1.50	$2.50	£0.30	£0.90	£1.50
Title Value:	$2.50	$7.50	$12.50	£1.50	£4.50	£7.50

TOM KATZ
Sun Comic Publishing; 1 May 1993

1 ND	$0.40	$1.20	$2.00	£0.25	£0.75	£1.25
Title Value:	$0.40	$1.20	$2.00	£0.25	£0.75	£1.25

TOMAHAWK
National Periodical Publications; 65 Nov/Dec 1959-140 May/Jun 1972
(see Limited Collector's Edition #47, Unknown Soldier) (previous issues ND)
65-70 scarce in the U.K.

	$Good	$Fine	$N.Mint	£Good	£Fine	£N.Mint
	$6.50	$20.00	$40.00	£4.55	£13.50	£27.50

71-76 scarce in the U.K.

	$6.25	$18.50	$37.50	£4.15	£12.50	£25.00

77 last 10 cents issue

	$6.25	$18.50	$37.50	£3.75	£11.00	£22.50
78-80	$5.00	$15.00	$30.00	£3.75	£11.00	£22.50
81-90	$4.55	$13.50	$27.50	£2.90	£8.75	£17.50
91-100	$3.30	$10.00	$20.00	£2.05	£6.25	£12.50

101 becomes Tomahawk and his Rip Roaring Rangers

	$2.05	$6.25	$12.50	£1.25	£3.75	£7.50
102-110	$2.05	$6.25	$12.50	£1.25	£3.75	£7.50
111-113	$1.25	$3.75	$7.50	£0.80	£2.50	£5.00

114 scarce in the U.K.

	$1.25	$3.75	$7.50	£1.00	£3.00	£6.00
115	$1.25	$3.75	$7.50	£0.80	£2.50	£5.00

116 scarce in the U.K. Neal Adams cover

	$1.25	$3.75	$7.50	£1.00	£3.00	£6.00

117-119 Neal Adams covers

	$1.25	$3.75	$7.50	£0.80	£2.50	£5.00
120	$1.25	$3.75	$7.50	£0.80	£2.50	£5.00

121 Neal Adams cover

	$1.00	$3.00	$6.00	£0.65	£2.00	£4.00
122	$1.00	$3.00	$6.00	£0.65	£2.00	£4.00

123-130 Neal Adams covers

	$1.00	$3.00	$6.00	£0.65	£2.00	£4.00

131 Frazetta reprint, becomes Son of Tomahawk on cover only

	$1.25	$3.75	$7.50	£0.80	£2.50	£5.00
132-138	$1.00	$3.00	$6.00	£0.65	£2.00	£4.00

139 scarce in the U.K. 52pgs, Frazetta reprint

	$1.00	$3.00	$6.00	£0.65	£2.00	£4.00

140 scarce in the U.K. 52pgs

	$1.00	$3.00	$6.00	£0.65	£2.00	£4.00
Title Value:	$229.50	$690.25	$1389.00	£150.75	£454.00	£913.00

FEATURES
Firehair in 131 (2pgs), 132, 134, 136.

TOMB OF DARKNESS
Marvel Comics Group; 9 Jul 1974-23 Nov 1976
(formerly Beware)
9 ND early '60s horror reprints begin

	$0.40	$1.20	$2.00	£0.30	£0.90	£1.50
10-20	$0.40	$1.20	$2.00	£0.25	£0.75	£1.25
21-22 ND	$0.40	$1.20	$2.00	£0.30	£0.90	£1.50
23	$0.40	$1.20	$2.00	£0.25	£0.75	£1.25
Title Value:	$6.00	$18.00	$30.00	£3.90	£11.70	£19.50

TOMB OF DRACULA
Marvel Comics Group; 1 Apr 1972-70 Aug 1979

1 ND	$11.50	$35.00	$70.00	£6.50	£20.00	£40.00
2 ND	$6.50	$20.00	$40.00	£3.30	£10.00	£20.00
3 ND	$5.00	$15.00	$30.00	£2.50	£7.50	£15.00
4-5 ND	$3.30	$10.00	$20.00	£1.65	£5.00	£10.00

6 ND Neal Adams cover

	$2.90	$8.75	$17.50	£1.65	£5.00	£10.00
7-9	$2.90	$8.75	$17.50	£1.25	£3.75	£7.50

10 1st Blade the Vampire Slayer

	$3.30	$10.00	$20.00	£1.50	£4.50	£9.00
11	$2.05	$6.25	$12.50	£0.80	£2.50	£5.00

12 scarce in the U.K. Brunner cover

Thunder Agents #2

Toka, Jungle King #10

Tomahawk #125

MINT = 100% / NEAR MINT (inc. +/-) = 90-99% / VERY FINE (inc. +/-) = 75-89% / FINE (inc. +/-) = 55-74%
VERY GOOD (inc. +/-) = 35-54% / GOOD (inc. +/-) = 15-34% / FAIR = 5-14% / POOR = 1-4%

607

	$Good	$Fine	$N.Mint	£Good	£Fine	£N.Mint
	$2.05	$6.25	$12.50	£1.00	£3.00	£6.00
13 origin Blade	$2.05	$6.25	$12.50	£0.80	£2.50	£5.00
14-17	$2.05	$6.25	$12.50	£0.80	£2.50	£5.00
18 Werewolf By Night appears						
	$2.05	$6.25	$12.50	£0.80	£2.50	£5.00
19-20 ND	$2.05	$6.25	$12.50	£1.00	£3.00	£6.00
21-22 ND	$1.65	$5.00	$10.00	£0.65	£2.00	£4.00
23-28	$1.65	$5.00	$10.00	£0.55	£1.75	£3.50
29-30 ND	$1.65	$5.00	$10.00	£0.65	£2.00	£4.00
31-34 ND	$1.25	$3.75	$7.50	£0.55	£1.75	£3.50
35 ND Brother Voodoo appears						
	$1.25	$3.75	$7.50	£0.55	£1.75	£3.50
36-40 ND	$1.25	$3.75	$7.50	£0.55	£1.75	£3.50
41-42 ND	$1.00	$3.00	$6.00	£0.50	£1.50	£3.00
43 ND Bernie Wrightson cover art						
	$1.00	$3.00	$6.00	£0.50	£1.50	£3.00
44-49 ND	$1.00	$3.00	$6.00	£0.50	£1.50	£3.00
50 ND Silver Surfer appears						
	$1.65	$5.00	$10.00	£0.65	£2.00	£4.00
51-54 ND	$1.00	$3.00	$6.00	£0.50	£1.50	£3.00
55-62	$1.00	$3.00	$6.00	£0.40	£1.25	£2.50
63-66 ND	$0.80	$2.50	$5.00	£0.50	£1.50	£3.00
67 ND Lilith appears						
	$0.80	$2.50	$5.00	£0.50	£1.50	£3.00
68-69 ND	$0.80	$2.50	$5.00	£0.50	£1.50	£3.00
70 ND scarce in the U.K. 52pgs						
	$1.00	$3.00	$6.00	£0.55	£1.75	£3.50
Title Value:	$123.25	$373.50	$745.00	£56.90	£174.50	£349.00

TOMB OF DRACULA (2ND SERIES)
Marvel Comics Group,Magazine; 1 Nov 1979-6 Sep 1980

	$Good	$Fine	$N.Mint	£Good	£Fine	£N.Mint
1 ND Gene Colan art begins						
	$0.80	$2.40	$4.00	£0.50	£1.50	£2.50
2 ND Steve Ditko art						
	$0.80	$2.40	$4.00	£0.50	£1.50	£2.50
3 ND 2pgs Frank Miller art						
	$0.80	$2.40	$4.00	£0.50	£1.50	£2.50
4 ND Stephen King feature						
	$0.60	$1.80	$3.00	£0.40	£1.20	£2.00
5 ND	$0.60	$1.80	$3.00	£0.40	£1.20	£2.00
6 ND 12pgs Sienkiewicz art						
	$0.80	$2.40	$4.00	£0.50	£1.50	£2.50
Title Value:	$4.40	$13.20	$22.00	£2.80	£8.40	£14.00

TOMB OF DRACULA (LIMITED SERIES)
Marvel Comics Group/Epic,MS; 1 Nov 1991-4 Feb 1992

1-4 ND Marv Wolfman script, Gene Colan art						
	$1.00	$3.00	$5.00	£0.60	£1.80	£3.00
Title Value:	$4.00	$12.00	$20.00	£2.40	£7.20	£12.00

TOMOE
Crusade Comics; 0 Feb 1996; 1 Jul 1995

0 ND	$0.50	$1.50	$2.50	£0.30	£0.90	£1.50
0 Variant cover ND	$1.50	$4.50	$7.50	£1.00	£3.00	£5.00
1 ND orders of Shi #6 split to contain an even number of Tomoe #1; same interior as Shi #6 but with cover featuring Tomoe						
	$1.00	$3.00	$5.00	£0.60	£1.80	£6.00
1 Commemorative Edition, ND features Tomoe on right of cover holding a fan, no logo or title, limited to 5,000 copies; black and white						
	$4.00	$12.00	$20.00	£2.50	£7.50	£12.50
Title Value:	$7.00	$21.00	$35.00	£5.00	£15.00	£25.00

TOMORROW KNIGHTS
Marvel Comics Group/Epic,MS; 1 Jun 1990-6 Mar 1991

1-6 ND DS	$0.40	$1.20	$2.00	£0.25	£0.75	£1.25
Title Value:	$2.40	$7.20	$12.00	£1.50	£4.50	£7.50
Note: bi-monthly						

TOMORROW MAN
Antarctic Press,OS; 1 Aug 1993

1 ND 48pgs	$0.50	$1.50	$2.50	£0.30	£0.90	£1.50
Title Value:	$0.50	$1.50	$2.50	£0.30	£0.90	£1.50

TOMORROW MAN/KNIGHT HUNTER: LAST RITES
Antarctic Press,MS; 1 Aug 1994-6 Jun 1995

1-6 ND Jochen Weltjens script, Bobby Padilla art						
	$0.50	$1.50	$2.50	£0.30	£0.90	£1.50
Title Value:	$3.00	$9.00	$15.00	£1.80	£5.40	£9.00

TOP CAT
Charlton; 1 Nov 1970-20 Nov 1973

1 Ray Dirgo art begins						
	$5.75	$17.50	$35.00	£3.30	£10.00	£20.00
2-3	$3.30	$10.00	$20.00	£2.05	£6.25	£12.50
4-10	$2.90	$8.75	$17.50	£1.65	£5.00	£10.00
11-20	$2.50	$7.50	$15.00	£1.25	£3.75	£7.50
Title Value:	$57.65	$173.75	$347.50	£31.45	£95.00	£190.00

TOP COW/BALLISTIC STUDIOS SWIMSUIT SPECIAL
Image,OS; 1 May 1995

1 ND Marc Silvestri and co. and their pin-ups for Top Cow						
	$0.60	$1.80	$3.00	£0.40	£1.20	£2.00
Title Value:	$0.60	$1.80	$3.00	£0.40	£1.20	£2.00

TOP DOG, THE SECRET LIFE OF
Marvel Comics Group/Star; 1 Apr 1985-10 Oct 1986

1-9 scarce in the U.K.						
	$0.15	$0.45	$0.75	£0.10	£0.30	£0.50
10 scarce in the U.K., Spiderman appears						
	$0.15	$0.45	$0.75	£0.10	£0.30	£0.50
Title Value:	$1.50	$4.50	$7.50	£1.00	£3.00	£5.00

TOPPS COMICS PRESENTS
Topps; 0 Aug 1993

0 ND preview comic featuring Dracula vs. Zorro, Jack Kirby's Teenagents, Silver Star and Bill The Galactic Hero; available for free from 1993 San Diego Comicon

	$0.25	$0.75	$1.25	£0.15	£0.45	£0.75
Title Value:	$0.25	$0.75	$1.25	£0.15	£0.45	£0.75

TOR
DC Comics; 1 May/Jun 1975-6 Mar/Apr 1976

1 new origin by Kubert						
	$0.25	$0.75	$1.25	£0.15	£0.45	£0.75
2 reprints original 1950s #1						
	$0.25	$0.75	$1.25	£0.15	£0.45	£0.75
3-6 all reprint	$0.25	$0.75	$1.25	£0.15	£0.45	£0.75
Title Value:	$1.50	$4.50	$7.50	£0.90	£2.70	£4.50

TOR
Marvel Comics Group, Magazine MS; 1 Jun 1993-4 Sep 1993

1-4 ND Joe Kubert script and art						
	$1.00	$3.00	$5.00	£0.70	£2.10	£3.50
Title Value:	$4.00	$12.00	$20.00	£2.80	£8.40	£14.00

TOR 3-D
Eclipse; 1 Jul 1986-2 Aug 1986

1 ND reprints 3-D Comics #1,#2 (St.John) by Joe Kubert; with bound-in 3-D glasses (25% less without glasses)						
	$0.50	$1.50	$2.50	£0.30	£0.90	£1.50
1 ND non 3-D issue						
	$0.60	$1.80	$3.00	£0.40	£1.20	£2.00
2 ND reprints 3-D Comics #1,#2 (St.John) by Joe Kubert; with bound-in 3-D glasses (25% less without glasses)						
	$0.50	$1.50	$2.50	£0.30	£0.90	£1.50
2 ND scarce in the U.K. non 3-D issue						
	$0.60	$1.80	$3.00	£0.40	£1.20	£2.00
Title Value:	$2.20	$6.60	$11.00	£1.40	£4.20	£7.00

TORCH OF LIBERTY SPECIAL, THE
Dark Horse,OS; 1 Dec 1994

1 ND John Byrne script, Kieron Dwyer art; spin-off from Danger Unlimited						
	$0.50	$1.50	$2.50	£0.30	£0.90	£1.50
Title Value:	$0.50	$1.50	$2.50	£0.30	£0.90	£1.50

TORCHY
Innovation; 1 Spring 1991-4 Winter 1991

1 ND Bill Ward reprints begin, black and white; quarterly frequency; Olivia de Berardinis painted cover						
	$0.40	$1.20	$2.00	£0.25	£0.75	£1.25
2 ND Matt Thompson painted cover						
	$0.40	$1.20	$2.00	£0.25	£0.75	£1.25
3 ND Olivia de Berardinis painted cover						
	$0.40	$1.20	$2.00	£0.25	£0.75	£1.25
4 ND Brian Stelfreeze pianted cover						
	$0.40	$1.20	$2.00	£0.25	£0.75	£1.25
Title Value:	$1.60	$4.80	$8.00	£1.00	£3.00	£5.00

Torchy the Blonde Bombshell Book One (Jan 1992)
reprints issues #1-4, new cover by Olivia de Berardinis — £0.90 / £2.70 / £4.50

TORG: REALITY STORM!
Adventure,MS; 1 Feb 1992-4 May 1992

1-4 ND based on role-playing game						
	$0.40	$1.20	$2.00	£0.25	£0.75	£1.25
Title Value:	$1.60	$4.80	$8.00	£1.00	£3.00	£5.00

TORMENT
Aircel,MS; 1 Aug 1991-3 Oct 1991

1-3 ND black and white						
	$0.40	$1.20	$2.00	£0.25	£0.75	£1.25
Title Value:	$1.20	$3.60	$6.00	£0.75	£2.25	£3.75

TORRID AFFAIRS
Eternity; 1 1988-5 1989

1 ND 1950s romance reprints						
	$0.40	$1.20	$2.00	£0.25	£0.75	£1.25
2 ND "hot" cover	$0.40	$1.20	$2.00	£0.25	£0.75	£1.25
2 ND "tame" cover	$0.40	$1.20	$2.00	£0.25	£0.75	£1.25
3-5 ND	$0.40	$1.20	$2.00	£0.25	£0.75	£1.25
Title Value:	$2.40	$7.20	$12.00	£1.50	£4.50	£7.50

TORTURE
Cat Wild; 1 Jan 1991

1 ND black and white						
	$0.40	$1.20	$2.00	£0.25	£0.75	£1.25
Title Value:	$0.40	$1.20	$2.00	£0.25	£0.75	£1.25

TOTAL CARNAGE
Dark Horse,OS; 1 Dec 1993

1 ND 48pgs	$0.80	$2.40	$4.00	£0.50	£1.50	£2.50
Title Value:	$0.80	$2.40	$4.00	£0.50	£1.50	£2.50

TOTAL ECLIPSE
Eclipse; 1 May 1988-5 1989

1-5 ND	$0.60	$1.80	$3.00	£0.40	£1.20	£2.00
Title Value:	$3.00	$9.00	$15.00	£2.00	£6.00	£10.00

TOTAL ECLIPSE: THE SERAPHIM OBJECTIVE
Eclipse,OS; 1 Nov 1988

1 ND scarce in the U.K. Airboy, Valkyrie, Misery and The Heap appear; also features The Liberty Project						
	$0.60	$1.80	$3.00	£0.50	£1.50	£2.50
Title Value:	$0.60	$1.80	$3.00	£0.50	£1.50	£2.50

TOTAL RECALL MOVIE ADAPTATION
DC Comics,OS; nn Aug 1990
nn based on Arnold Schwarzenegger film

	$0.40	$1.20	$2.00	£0.25	£0.75	£1.25
Title Value:	$0.40	$1.20	$2.00	£0.25	£0.75	£1.25

TRADE PAPERBACKS, GRAPHIC NOVELS AND OTHER COLLECTIONS ARE PRICED IN POUNDS STERLING ONLY. CONVERT AT 1.5 FOR DOLLARS.

	$Good	$Fine	$N.Mint	£Good	£Fine	£N.Mint

TOTAL WAR
Gold Key; 1 Jul 1965-2 Oct 1965
(becomes Mars Patrol Total War)
1 scarce in the U.K. Wally Wood art and painted cover; distributed in the U.K.

	$Good	$Fine	$N.Mint	£Good	£Fine	£N.Mint
1	$5.00	$15.00	$35.00	£3.20	£9.50	£22.50

2 scarce in the U.K. Wally Wood art and painted cover; distributed in the U.K.

	$Good	$Fine	$N.Mint	£Good	£Fine	£N.Mint
2	$4.25	$12.50	$30.00	£2.85	£8.50	£20.00
Title Value:	$9.25	$27.50	$65.00	£6.05	£18.00	£42.50

TOTEM: SIGN OF THE WARDOG
Alpha Productions; 1 Jun 1991-5 1991

	$Good	$Fine	$N.Mint	£Good	£Fine	£N.Mint
1-5 ND black and white	$0.40	$1.20	$2.00	£0.25	£0.75	£1.25
Title Value:	$2.00	$6.00	$10.00	£1.25	£3.75	£6.25
Annual 1 (May 1994) 48pgs, black and white				£0.50	£1.50	£2.50

TOTEM: THE STEEL MOSQUITO
Alpha Productions; 1 Jul 1993

	$Good	$Fine	$N.Mint	£Good	£Fine	£N.Mint
1 ND	$0.40	$1.20	$2.00	£0.25	£0.75	£1.25
Title Value:	$0.40	$1.20	$2.00	£0.25	£0.75	£1.25

TOWER OF SHADOWS
Marvel Comics Group; 1 Sep 1969-9 Jan 1971
(becomes Creatures on the Loose)

	$Good	$Fine	$N.Mint	£Good	£Fine	£N.Mint
1 scarce in the U.K. Steranko art	$3.30	$10.00	$20.00	£1.65	£5.00	£10.00
2 Neal Adams art (7pgs)	$1.65	$5.00	$10.00	£1.00	£3.00	£6.00
3 Barry Smith art (7pgs)	$1.65	$5.00	$10.00	£1.00	£3.00	£6.00
4 ND Gene Colan art	$1.25	$3.75	$7.50	£0.65	£2.00	£4.00
5 ND Barry Smith art, Wood inks	$1.50	$4.50	$9.00	£0.80	£2.50	£5.00
6 ND Wood art	$1.25	$3.75	$7.50	£0.65	£2.00	£4.00
7 ND Barry Smith art, Wood inks	$1.50	$4.50	$9.00	£0.80	£2.50	£5.00
8 ND Wood art	$1.25	$3.75	$7.50	£0.65	£2.00	£4.00
9 ND Wrightson cover	$1.15	$3.50	$7.00	£0.55	£1.75	£3.50
Title Value:	$14.50	$43.75	$87.50	£7.75	£23.75	£47.50

Note: back-up reprints in 6-9.

TOWER OF SHADOWS ANNUAL
Marvel Comics Group; 1 Dec 1971
1 ND scarce in the U.K. all reprint including Neal Adams

	$Good	$Fine	$N.Mint	£Good	£Fine	£N.Mint
1	$1.00	$3.00	$6.00	£0.65	£2.00	£4.00
Title Value:	$1.00	$3.00	$6.00	£0.65	£2.00	£4.00

TOXIC AVENGER
Marvel Comics Group; 1 Apr 1991-11 Feb 1992

	$Good	$Fine	$N.Mint	£Good	£Fine	£N.Mint
1 based on the cult Troma film series	$0.25	$0.75	$1.25	£0.15	£0.45	£0.75
2-10	$0.25	$0.75	$1.25	£0.15	£0.45	£0.75
11 nuclear explosion photo cover	$0.25	$0.75	$1.25	£0.15	£0.45	£0.75
Title Value:	$2.75	$8.25	$13.75	£1.65	£4.95	£8.25

TOXIC CRUSADERS
Marvel Comics Group; 1 May 1992-8 Dec 1992
1 anthology based on cartoon series featuring writing by Stan Lee and Steve Gerber, Sam Kieth cover

	$Good	$Fine	$N.Mint	£Good	£Fine	£N.Mint
1	$0.25	$0.75	$1.25	£0.15	£0.45	£0.75
2-3 Sam Kieth cover	$0.25	$0.75	$1.25	£0.15	£0.45	£0.75
4 three stories	$0.25	$0.75	$1.25	£0.15	£0.45	£0.75
5	$0.25	$0.75	$1.25	£0.15	£0.45	£0.75
6 Captain Planet parody	$0.25	$0.75	$1.25	£0.15	£0.45	£0.75
7-8	$0.25	$0.75	$1.25	£0.15	£0.45	£0.75
Title Value:	$2.00	$6.00	$10.00	£1.20	£3.60	£6.00

TOXIC CRUSADERS (2ND SERIES)
Marvel Comics Group,MS; 1 Mar 1993-3 May 1993

	$Good	$Fine	$N.Mint	£Good	£Fine	£N.Mint
1 Steve Gerber script, based on US TV series	$0.25	$0.75	$1.25	£0.15	£0.45	£0.75
2-3 Jeremy Banx script	$0.25	$0.75	$1.25	£0.15	£0.45	£0.75
Title Value:	$0.75	$2.25	$3.75	£0.45	£1.35	£2.25

TOYBOY, JASON KRITER
Continuity; 1 Oct 1986-7 Mar 1989

	$Good	$Fine	$N.Mint	£Good	£Fine	£N.Mint
1 ND Neal Adams script and part pencils	$0.40	$1.20	$2.00	£0.25	£0.75	£1.25
2-3 ND Neal Adams cover	$0.40	$1.20	$2.00	£0.25	£0.75	£1.25
4-5 ND Neal Adams script and part art	$0.40	$1.20	$2.00	£0.25	£0.75	£1.25
6 ND	$0.40	$1.20	$2.00	£0.25	£0.75	£1.25
7 ND Neal Adams script, Michael Golden cover and art	$0.40	$1.20	$2.00	£0.25	£0.75	£1.25
Title Value:	$2.80	$8.40	$14.00	£1.75	£5.25	£8.75

TRACKER
Blackthorne,MS; 1 May 1988-4 Sep 1988

	$Good	$Fine	$N.Mint	£Good	£Fine	£N.Mint
1-4 ND	$0.40	$1.20	$2.00	£0.25	£0.75	£1.25
Title Value:	$1.60	$4.80	$8.00	£1.00	£3.00	£5.00

TRAGG AND THE SKY GODS
Gold Key; 1 Jun 1975-8 Feb 1977; Whitman; 9 May 1982
1 scarce in the U.K. line-drawn and water-colour cover (most covers feature dinosaurs); origin and 1st appearance Tragg the Caveman

	$Good	$Fine	$N.Mint	£Good	£Fine	£N.Mint
1	$0.60	$1.80	$3.00	£0.40	£1.20	£2.00

2 scarce in the U.K. line-drawn and water-colour cover

	$Good	$Fine	$N.Mint	£Good	£Fine	£N.Mint
2	$0.40	$1.20	$2.00	£0.30	£0.90	£1.50

3 1st painted cover (ends #8)

	$Good	$Fine	$N.Mint	£Good	£Fine	£N.Mint
3	$0.40	$1.20	$2.00	£0.25	£0.75	£1.25
4	$0.30	$0.90	$1.50	£0.25	£0.75	£1.25
5-8 Dan Spiegle art	$0.30	$0.90	$1.50	£0.25	£0.75	£1.25

9 scarce in the U.K. line-drawn cover

	$Good	$Fine	$N.Mint	£Good	£Fine	£N.Mint
9	$0.30	$0.90	$1.50	£0.30	£0.90	£1.50
Title Value:	$3.20	$9.60	$16.00	£2.50	£7.50	£12.50

Note: all Limited Distribution in the U.K.

TRANCERS
Eternity; 1 Aug 1991-2 Sep 1991

	$Good	$Fine	$N.Mint	£Good	£Fine	£N.Mint
1-2 ND film adaptation; sub-titled "The Adventures of Jack Deth"	$0.40	$1.20	$2.00	£0.25	£0.75	£1.25
Title Value:	$0.80	$2.40	$4.00	£0.50	£1.50	£2.50
Prestige Edition (Nov 1991), collects first 2 issues squarebound				£0.65	£1.95	£3.25

TRANSFORMERS COMIC MAGAZINE, THE
Marvel Comics Group,Digest; 1 Oct 1986-11 Aug 1988

	$Good	$Fine	$N.Mint	£Good	£Fine	£N.Mint
1-11 ND	$0.25	$0.75	$1.25	£0.15	£0.45	£0.75
Title Value:	$2.75	$8.25	$13.75	£1.65	£4.95	£8.25

TRANSFORMERS IN 3-D
Blackthorne; (3-D Series #25,#29,#37); 1 1987-3 Apr 1988

	$Good	$Fine	$N.Mint	£Good	£Fine	£N.Mint
1 ND all with bound-in 3-D glasses (25% less without glasses)	$0.50	$1.50	$2.50	£0.30	£0.90	£1.50
2-3 ND	$0.50	$1.50	$2.50	£0.30	£0.90	£1.50
Title Value:	$1.50	$4.50	$7.50	£0.90	£2.70	£4.50

TRANSFORMERS UNIVERSE, THE
Marvel Comics Group,MS; 1 Dec 1986-4 Mar 1987

	$Good	$Fine	$N.Mint	£Good	£Fine	£N.Mint
1-4 ND guide to all the characters	$0.25	$0.75	$1.25	£0.15	£0.45	£0.75
Title Value:	$1.00	$3.00	$5.00	£0.60	£1.80	£3.00
Trade Paperback, 128pgs, reprints #1-4				£0.60	£1.80	£3.00

TRANSFORMERS, THE
Marvel Comics Group, TV Toy; 1 Sep 1984-80 Jul 1991

	$Good	$Fine	$N.Mint	£Good	£Fine	£N.Mint
1 ND	$0.60	$1.80	$3.00	£0.40	£1.20	£2.00
2 ND	$0.50	$1.50	$2.50	£0.30	£0.90	£1.50
3 ND Spiderman guest-stars	$0.50	$1.50	$2.50	£0.30	£0.90	£1.50
4-5	$0.30	$0.90	$1.50	£0.20	£0.60	£1.00
6	$0.25	$0.75	$1.25	£0.15	£0.45	£0.75
7-8 ND Kyle Baker inks	$0.25	$0.75	$1.25	£0.15	£0.45	£0.75
9-49	$0.25	$0.75	$1.25	£0.15	£0.45	£0.75
50 DS	$0.30	$0.90	$1.50	£0.20	£0.60	£1.00
51-61 ND	$0.25	$0.75	$1.25	£0.15	£0.45	£0.75
62-66 ND Matrix Quest story	$0.25	$0.75	$1.25	£0.15	£0.45	£0.75
67-74 ND	$0.25	$0.75	$1.25	£0.15	£0.45	£0.75
75 ND DS	$0.30	$0.90	$1.50	£0.20	£0.60	£1.00
76-80 ND	$0.25	$0.75	$1.25	£0.15	£0.45	£0.75
Title Value:	$21.05	$63.15	$105.25	£12.75	£38.25	£63.75

Note: first 4 issues titled "Limited Mini Series"; series carried on in order after 3 month gap. 2nd and 3rd prints of most early issues available (priced at about 60% of the above)

TRANSFORMERS: GENERATION 2
Marvel Comics Group; 1 Nov 1993-12 Oct 1994

	$Good	$Fine	$N.Mint	£Good	£Fine	£N.Mint
1 48pgs, Simon Furman and Derek Yaniger	$0.50	$1.50	$2.50	£0.30	£0.90	£1.50
1 48pgs, Direct Market Edition, foil stamped gatefold cover	$0.80	$2.40	$4.00	£0.50	£1.50	£2.50
2	$0.45	$1.35	$2.25	£0.30	£0.90	£1.50
3-11	$0.40	$1.20	$2.00	£0.25	£0.75	£1.25
12 48pgs	$0.50	$1.50	$2.50	£0.30	£0.90	£1.50
Title Value:	$5.85	$17.55	$29.25	£3.65	£10.95	£18.25

TRANSFORMERS: HEADMASTERS
Marvel Comics Group,MS; 1 Jul 1987-4 Oct 1987

	$Good	$Fine	$N.Mint	£Good	£Fine	£N.Mint
1-4 ND	$0.25	$0.75	$1.25	£0.15	£0.45	£0.75
Title Value:	$1.00	$3.00	$5.00	£0.60	£1.80	£3.00

TRANSFORMERS: THE MOVIE
Marvel Comics Group,MS; 1 Dec 1986-3 Feb 1987

	$Good	$Fine	$N.Mint	£Good	£Fine	£N.Mint
1-3 ND adapts animated film	$0.25	$0.75	$1.25	£0.15	£0.45	£0.75
Title Value:	$0.75	$2.25	$3.75	£0.45	£1.35	£2.25

TRANSIT
Vortex; 1 Apr 1987-5 1989

	$Good	$Fine	$N.Mint	£Good	£Fine	£N.Mint
1 ND Ted McKeever script and art begins; black and white	$0.50	$1.50	$2.50	£0.30	£0.90	£1.50
2-5 ND	$0.50	$1.50	$2.50	£0.30	£0.90	£1.50
Title Value:	$2.50	$7.50	$12.50	£1.50	£4.50	£7.50

TRANSYLVANIA SPECIAL EDITION
Continuity,OS; 1 Sep 1991
1 ND 36pgs, Neal Adams script/art featuring Dracula, Frankenstein and Werewolf, originally serialized in Echo of Future Past

	$Good	$Fine	$N.Mint	£Good	£Fine	£N.Mint
1	$1.00	$3.00	$5.00	£0.70	£2.10	£3.50
Title Value:	$1.00	$3.00	$5.00	£0.70	£2.10	£3.50

TRAPPED
Eclipse,OS; (Graphic Novel) 1 1993
1 ND 80pgs, squarebound, based on Dean R. Koontz novel, painted art Anthony Bilau

	$Good	$Fine	$N.Mint	£Good	£Fine	£N.Mint
1	$2.00	$6.00	$10.00	£1.40	£4.20	£7.00
Title Value:	$2.00	$6.00	$10.00	£1.40	£4.20	£7.00

	$Good	$Fine	$N.Mint	£Good	£Fine	£N.Mint

TRAUMA CORPS
Anubis Press; 0 Jan 1994-2 1994
0 ND black and white

	$Good	$Fine	$N.Mint	£Good	£Fine	£N.Mint
	$0.50	$1.50	$2.50	£0.30	£0.90	£1.50

1 ND foil enhanced cover

	$0.50	$1.50	$2.50	£0.30	£0.90	£1.50

1 ND Ashcan Edition (Nov 1994) - black and white; 5,000 copies

	$0.50	$1.50	$2.50	£0.30	£0.90	£1.50
2 ND	$0.50	$1.50	$2.50	£0.30	£0.90	£1.50
Title Value:	$2.00	$6.00	$10.00	£1.20	£3.60	£6.00

TREKKER
Dark Horse; 1 May 1987-9 1988
1-9 ND Ron Randall art

	$0.50	$1.50	$2.50	£0.30	£0.90	£1.50
Title Value:	$4.50	$13.50	$22.50	£2.70	£8.10	£13.50
Trekker Collection (1988), reprints #1–4				£0.80	£2.40	£4.00
Trekker Color Special (1989)				£0.30	£0.90	£1.50

TRENCHER
Image; 1 May 1993-4 Oct 1993
1 ND Keith Giffen script and art begins

	$0.40	$1.20	$2.00	£0.25	£0.75	£1.25
2-4 ND	$0.40	$1.20	$2.00	£0.25	£0.75	£1.25
Title Value:	$1.60	$4.80	$8.00	£1.00	£3.00	£5.00

TRENCHER X-MAS BITES HOLIDAY BLOW-OUT
Image,OS; 1 Dec 1993
1 ND Keith Giffen script and art

	$0.40	$1.20	$2.00	£0.25	£0.75	£1.25
Title Value:	$0.40	$1.20	$2.00	£0.25	£0.75	£1.25

TRIAD UNIVERSE
Triad Publishing; 1 Jul 1994
1 ND Laurence Richardson art

	$0.40	$1.20	$2.00	£0.25	£0.75	£1.25
Title Value:	$0.40	$1.20	$2.00	£0.25	£0.75	£1.25

TRIAL RUN
Miller Publishing; 1,2 1990
1-2 ND smaller than regular comic size, black and white

	$0.30	$0.90	$1.50	£0.20	£0.60	£1.00
Title Value:	$0.60	$1.80	$3.00	£0.40	£1.20	£2.00

TRIARCH
Caliber Press; 1 Jan 1991-4 1991
1-4 ND

	$0.40	$1.20	$2.00	£0.25	£0.75	£1.25
Title Value:	$1.60	$4.80	$8.00	£1.00	£3.00	£5.00

TRIBE
Image; 1 Apr 1993; Axis Comics; 2 Sep 1993-3 1994
1 ND Larry Stroman art begins

	$0.50	$1.50	$2.50	£0.30	£0.90	£1.50

1 ND Ivory Edition - signed by Stroman and Johnson; 10,000 copies

	$0.80	$2.40	$4.00	£0.50	£1.50	£2.50
2-3 ND	$0.40	$1.20	$2.00	£0.25	£0.75	£1.25
Title Value:	$2.10	$6.30	$10.50	£1.30	£3.90	£6.50
Tribe, The Book (Feb 1994)						
Graphic Novel 112pgs, reprints 3 issue series				£2.00	£6.00	£10.00

TRICKSTER KING MONKEY
Eastern; 1 May 1988
1 ND scarce in the U.K.

	$0.40	$1.20	$2.00	£0.25	£0.75	£1.25
Title Value:	$0.40	$1.20	$2.00	£0.25	£0.75	£1.25

TRIGGER TWINS
DC Comics; 1 Mar/Apr 1973
1 scarce in the U.K. reprints

	$0.30	$0.90	$1.50	£0.20	£0.60	£1.00
Title Value:	$0.30	$0.90	$1.50	£0.20	£0.60	£1.00

TRIPLE-X
Dark Horse,MS; 1 Dec 1994-7 Jun 1995
1-7 ND 48pgs, Arnold and Jacob Pander script/art; black and white

	$0.80	$2.40	$4.00	£0.50	£1.50	£2.50
Title Value:	$5.60	$16.80	$28.00	£3.50	£10.50	£17.50

TRIUMPH
DC Comics,MS; 1 Jun 1995-4 Sep 1995
1-4 Chris Priest script, Mike Miller art

	$0.40	$1.20	$2.00	£0.25	£0.75	£1.25
Title Value:	$1.60	$4.80	$8.00	£1.00	£3.00	£5.00

TRIUMPHANT UNLEASHED
Triumphant Comics; 0 Nov 1993
0 ND

	$0.40	$1.20	$2.00	£0.25	£0.75	£1.25
Title Value:	$0.40	$1.20	$2.00	£0.25	£0.75	£1.25

TROLL
Image,OS; 1 Dec 1993
1 ND Rob Liefeld script and Jeff Matsuda art begins

	$0.50	$1.50	$2.50	£0.30	£0.90	£1.50
Title Value:	$0.50	$1.50	$2.50	£0.30	£0.90	£1.50

TROLL HALLOWEEN SPECIAL
Image,OS; 1 Oct 1994
1 ND

	$0.60	$1.80	$3.00	£0.40	£1.20	£2.00
Title Value:	$0.60	$1.80	$3.00	£0.40	£1.20	£2.00

TROLL II
Image; 1 Jul 1994
1 ND 48pgs, squarebound, created by Rob Liefeld; Badrock guest-stars

	$0.60	$1.80	$3.00	£0.40	£1.20	£2.00
Title Value:	$0.60	$1.80	$3.00	£0.40	£1.20	£2.00

TROLL STOCKING STUFFER
Image,OS; 1 Dec 1994

1 ND Giffen, Fleming and Nauck creative team

	$0.60	$1.80	$3.00	£0.40	£1.20	£2.00
Title Value:	$0.60	$1.80	$3.00	£0.40	£1.20	£2.00

TROLL THANKSGIVING SPECIAL
Image,OS; 1 Nov 1994
1 ND Robert Loren Fleming and Jeff Matsuda

	$0.60	$1.80	$3.00	£0.40	£1.20	£2.00
Title Value:	$0.60	$1.80	$3.00	£0.40	£1.20	£2.00

TROLL: ONCE A HERO
Image,OS; 1 Aug 1994
1 ND 48pgs, Troll in World War II

	$0.50	$1.50	$2.50	£0.30	£0.90	£1.50
Title Value:	$0.50	$1.50	$2.50	£0.30	£0.90	£1.50

TROLLORDS (1ST SERIES)
Tru Studios; 1 Feb 1986-15 1988
1 ND black and white begins

	$0.30	$0.90	$1.50	£0.20	£0.60	£1.00
1 2nd printing ND	$0.25	$0.75	$1.25	£0.15	£0.45	£0.75
2-15 ND	$0.30	$0.90	$1.50	£0.20	£0.60	£1.00
Title Value:	$4.75	$14.25	$23.75	£3.15	£9.45	£15.75
Special 1 (Feb 1987)				£0.30	£0.90	£1.50

TROLLORDS (2ND SERIES)
Comico; 1 Nov 1988-4 May 1989
1-4 ND colour

	$0.30	$0.90	$1.50	£0.20	£0.60	£1.00
Title Value:	$1.20	$3.60	$6.00	£0.80	£2.40	£4.00

TROLLORDS SPECIAL
Tru Studios; 1 Feb 1987
1 ND sub-titled "Jerry's Big Fun Book"

	$0.30	$0.90	$1.50	£0.20	£0.60	£1.00
Title Value:	$0.30	$0.90	$1.50	£0.20	£0.60	£1.00

TROLLORDS: DEATH AND KISSES
Apple Comics; 1 Jun 1989-6 Apr 1990
1-6 ND black and white

	$0.40	$1.20	$2.00	£0.25	£0.75	£1.25
Title Value:	$2.40	$7.20	$12.00	£1.50	£4.50	£7.50

TROUBLE WITH GIRLS
Malibu/Eternity; 1 Aug 1987-14 Jan 1989
1 black and white begins

	$0.50	$1.50	$2.50	£0.30	£0.90	£1.50
2 scarce in the U.K.	$0.40	$1.20	$2.00	£0.30	£0.90	£1.50
3-4	$0.40	$1.20	$2.00	£0.25	£0.75	£1.25

5 1st Eternity issue

	$0.40	$1.20	$2.00	£0.25	£0.75	£1.25
6-14	$0.30	$0.90	$1.50	£0.20	£0.60	£1.00
Title Value:	$4.80	$14.40	$24.00	£3.15	£9.45	£15.75

Note: all Non-Distributed on the news-stands in the U.K.

Graphic Novel 1 (Sep 1988), reprints #1-3				£0.90	£2.70	£4.50
Graphic Novel 2 (1989), reprints #4-6, new Gulacy cover				£0.90	£2.70	£4.50

TROUBLE WITH GIRLS (2ND SERIES)
Comico/Eternity; 1 Feb 1989-23 May 1991
1-4 colour issues

	$0.30	$0.90	$1.50	£0.20	£0.60	£1.00

5 1st Eternity issue, black and white begins

	$0.30	$0.90	$1.50	£0.20	£0.60	£1.00
6-23	$0.30	$0.90	$1.50	£0.20	£0.60	£1.00
Title Value:	$6.90	$20.70	$34.50	£4.60	£13.80	£23.00

Note: all Non-Distributed on the news-stands in the U.K.

TROUBLE WITH GIRLS ANNUAL
Eternity; 1 1988
1 ND 60pgs

	$0.50	$1.50	$2.50	£0.30	£0.90	£1.50
Title Value:	$0.50	$1.50	$2.50	£0.30	£0.90	£1.50

TROUBLE WITH GIRLS XMAS SPECIAL
Eternity,OS; 1 Feb 1992
1 ND 40pgs

	$0.50	$1.50	$2.50	£0.30	£0.90	£1.50
Title Value:	$0.50	$1.50	$2.50	£0.30	£0.90	£1.50

TROUBLE WITH GIRLS, THE
Marvel Comics Group,MS; 1 Jun 1993-4 Sep 1993
(see Eternity titles)
1 ND embossed cover with metallic ink; all new stories

	$0.40	$1.20	$2.00	£0.25	£0.75	£1.25
2-4 ND	$0.30	$0.90	$1.50	£0.20	£0.60	£1.00
Title Value:	$1.30	$3.90	$6.50	£0.85	£2.55	£4.25

TROUBLE WITH TIGERS
Antarctic Press; 1,2 1992
1-2 ND Ninja High School/Tigers of Terra X-over

	$0.40	$1.20	$2.00	£0.25	£0.75	£1.25
Title Value:	$0.80	$2.40	$4.00	£0.50	£1.50	£2.50

TRUE 3-D
Harvey; 1 Dec 1953-2 Feb 1954
1 ND Powell art, with bound-in glasses (25% less without glasses)

	$6.25	$19.00	$45.00	£4.25	£12.50	£30.00

2 very scarce in the U.K. Powell art, with bound-in glasses (25% less without glasses)

	$6.25	$19.00	$45.00	£5.00	£15.00	£35.00
Title Value:	$12.50	$38.00	$90.00	£9.25	£27.50	£65.00

TRUE LOVE
Eclipse; 1,2 Jan 1986
1 ND 50s reprints, Dave Stevens cover

	$0.40	$1.20	$2.00	£0.25	£0.75	£1.25

2 ND reprints, Brent Anderson cover

	$0.40	$1.20	$2.00	£0.25	£0.75	£1.25
Title Value:	$0.80	$2.40	$4.00	£0.50	£1.50	£2.50

TRULY TASTELESS AND TACKY
Caliber Press; 1 1992

1 ND features cartoon jokes in the "Far Side" vein, black and white

	$Good	$Fine	$N.Mint	£Good	£Fine	£N.Mint
	$0.15	$0.45	$0.75	£0.10	£0.30	£0.50
Title Value:	$0.15	$0.45	$0.75	£0.10	£0.30	£0.50

TSR WORLDS ANNUAL
DC Comics,OS; 1 Aug 1990

	$Good	$Fine	$N.Mint	£Good	£Fine	£N.Mint
1 ND intro Spelljammers	$0.40	$1.20	$2.00	£0.25	£0.75	£1.25
Title Value:	$0.40	$1.20	$2.00	£0.25	£0.75	£1.25

Note: ties in with Advanced Dugeons and Dragons, Forgotten Realms and Dragonlance.

TUROK SON OF STONE
Dell/Gold Key; 1 (Four Color #596) Dec 1954; 2 (Four Color #656) Oct 1955-130 Apr 1982
(issues prior to "1st official distribution" all ND otherwise all distributed after that)

	$Good	$Fine	$N.Mint	£Good	£Fine	£N.Mint
1 very scarce in the U.K. (Four Color #596) 1st appearance Turok Son of Stone; painted covers begin	$85.00	$255.00	$595.00	£55.00	£165.00	£395.00
2 very scarce in the U.K. (Four Color #656) (Oct 1955)	$50.00	$150.00	$350.00	£34.00	£100.00	£235.00
3 scarce in the U.K. (Mar 1956)	$32.00	$95.00	$225.00	£21.00	£62.50	£150.00
4 scarce in the U.K. (Apr 1956)	$32.00	$95.00	$225.00	£21.00	£62.50	£150.00
5 scarce in the U.K.	$32.00	$95.00	$225.00	£21.00	£62.50	£150.00
6-10	$21.00	$62.50	$150.00	£14.00	£43.00	£100.00
11-16	$12.50	$39.00	$90.00	£8.50	£26.00	£60.00
1st official distribution in the U.K.						
17-20	$12.50	$39.00	$90.00	£7.75	£23.50	£55.00
21-30	$8.50	$26.00	$60.00	£5.50	£17.00	£40.00
31-40	$7.00	$21.00	$50.00	£5.00	£15.00	£35.00
41-50	$5.50	$17.00	$40.00	£3.55	£10.50	£25.00
51-60	$5.75	$17.50	$35.00	£3.30	£10.00	£20.00
61-62	$4.15	$12.50	$25.00	£2.50	£7.50	£15.00
63 line drawn cover	$4.15	$12.50	$25.00	£2.50	£7.50	£15.00
64-70	$4.15	$12.50	$25.00	£2.50	£7.50	£15.00
71-80	$2.90	$8.75	$17.50	£1.65	£5.00	£10.00
81-90	$2.05	$6.25	$12.50	£1.25	£3.75	£7.50
91-110	$1.65	$5.00	$10.00	£0.80	£2.50	£5.00
111-113	$1.25	$3.75	$7.50	£0.65	£2.00	£4.00
114-115 48pgs	$1.25	$3.75	$7.50	£0.80	£2.50	£5.00
116-129	$1.25	$3.75	$7.50	£0.65	£2.00	£4.00
130 scarce in the U.K. line drawn cover	$1.25	$3.75	$7.50	£0.65	£2.00	£5.00
Title Value:	$877.50	$2657.50	$6020.00	£560.95	£1696.50	£3868.00

Note: most scripts by Paul S. Newman and art by Jack Sparling and Alberto Giolitti.

TUROK SON OF STONE, THE ORIGINAL
Valiant/Western Publishing; 1 Apr 1995-4 Jul 1995

	$Good	$Fine	$N.Mint	£Good	£Fine	£N.Mint
1-4 ND reprints from the original Gold Key series featuring artwork by Alberto Gioletti	$0.50	$1.50	$2.50	£0.30	£0.90	£1.50
Title Value:	$2.00	$6.00	$10.00	£1.20	£3.60	£6.00

TUROK THE HUNTED
Valiant/Acclaim Comics,MS; 1 Mar 1996-2 April 1996

	$Good	$Fine	$N.Mint	£Good	£Fine	£N.Mint
1,2 ND Mike Grell and Simon Furman script, Mike Deodato and Mozart Couto art	$0.50	$1.50	$2.50	£0.30	£0.90	£1.50
Title Value:	$1.00	$3.00	$5.00	£0.60	£1.80	£3.00

TUROK, DINOSAUR HUNTER
Valiant/Acclaim Comics; 0 Jul 1995; 1 Jun 1993-present

	$Good	$Fine	$N.Mint	£Good	£Fine	£N.Mint
0 origin Turok and Andar	$0.40	$1.20	$2.00	£0.25	£0.75	£1.25
1 chromium embossed cover (care! the glue attaching the chromium plate has been known to leak out), Bart Sears art begins	$0.60	$1.80	$3.00	£0.40	£1.20	£2.00
1 Limited Gold Edition	$2.50	$7.50	$12.50	£1.20	£3.60	£6.00
1 Valiant Validated Signature Series Edition (Feb 1994), signed by Randy Elliot and Bart Sears; 5,300 copies with certificate and Mylar sleeve	$2.50	$7.50	$12.50	£1.20	£3.60	£6.00
2-3	$0.40	$1.20	$2.00	£0.25	£0.75	£1.25
4 Tim Truman script	$0.40	$1.20	$2.00	£0.25	£0.75	£1.25
5-6	$0.40	$1.20	$2.00	£0.25	£0.75	£1.25
7 Tim Truman script/art begins	$0.40	$1.20	$2.00	£0.25	£0.75	£1.25
8-10	$0.40	$1.20	$2.00	£0.25	£0.75	£1.25
11 with free Upper Deck card bound-in at centre-fold	$0.40	$1.20	$2.00	£0.25	£0.75	£1.25
12-15	$0.40	$1.20	$2.00	£0.25	£0.75	£1.25
16 Chaos Effect X-over	$0.40	$1.20	$2.00	£0.25	£0.75	£1.25
17-18	$0.40	$1.20	$2.00	£0.25	£0.75	£1.25
19 X-O Manowar appears	$0.40	$1.20	$2.00	£0.25	£0.75	£1.25
20-24	$0.40	$1.20	$2.00	£0.25	£0.75	£1.25
25 1st Acclaim Comics issue; bi-weekly	$0.40	$1.20	$2.00	£0.25	£0.75	£1.25
26-28 bi-weekly	$0.40	$1.20	$2.00	£0.25	£0.75	£1.25
29-30 Mike Deodato Jnr. art; bi-weekly	$0.50	$1.50	$2.50	£0.30	£0.90	£1.50
31-33 Paul Gulacy art; bi-weekly	$0.50	$1.50	$2.50	£0.30	£0.90	£1.50
34-40 bi-weekly	$0.50	$1.50	$2.50	£0.30	£0.90	£1.50
Title Value:	$22.80	$68.40	$114.00	£13.40	£40.20	£67.00

Note: all Non-Distributed on the news-stands in the U.K.

TUROK, DINOSAUR HUNTER YEARBOOK
Valiant; 1 Sep 1994; 2 Apr 1995

	$Good	$Fine	$N.Mint	£Good	£Fine	£N.Mint
1 ND Mike Baron script, Dave Cockrum pencils, Ganzalo Mayo inks; painted cover by Eric Hope	$0.60	$1.80	$3.00	£0.40	£1.20	£2.00
2 ND Mike Grell script, Mike Deodato Jnr. art; cover by Paul Smith and Bob Layton	$0.50	$1.50	$2.50	£0.30	£0.90	£1.50
Title Value:	$1.10	$3.30	$5.50	£0.70	£2.10	£3.50

TUROK, DINOSAUR HUNTER/SHAMAN'S TEARS
Acclaim Comics,MS; 1 Apr 1995-1 Jun 1995

	$Good	$Fine	$N.Mint	£Good	£Fine	£N.Mint
1-3 ND Mike Grell script and art with inks by Clarke Hawbaker	$0.50	$1.50	$2.50	£0.30	£0.90	£1.50
Title Value:	$1.50	$4.50	$7.50	£0.90	£2.70	£4.50

TURTLE SOUP
Mirage Studios,OS; 1 Sep 1987
(see Teenage Mutant Ninja Turtles)

	$Good	$Fine	$N.Mint	£Good	£Fine	£N.Mint
1 ND	$0.50	$1.50	$2.50	£0.30	£0.90	£1.50
Title Value:	$0.50	$1.50	$2.50	£0.30	£0.90	£1.50

TURTLE SOUP (2ND SERIES)
Mirage Studios,MS; 1 Nov 1991-4 Feb 1992

	$Good	$Fine	$N.Mint	£Good	£Fine	£N.Mint
1-4 ND colour	$0.40	$1.20	$2.00	£0.25	£0.75	£1.25
Title Value:	$1.60	$4.80	$8.00	£1.00	£3.00	£5.00
Turtle Soup Book I (1991), six stories by a variety of creators				£0.30	£0.90	£1.50

TV SCREEN CARTOONS
National Periodical Publications; 131 Nov/Dec 1959-138 Jan/Feb 1961
(previous issues ND as first official distribution in the U.K. was early 1960, cover date November 1959)

	$Good	$Fine	$N.Mint	£Good	£Fine	£N.Mint
131-138 rare in the U.K. Fox and The Crow featured	$9.25	$28.00	$65.00	£6.25	£19.00	£45.00
Title Value:	$74.00	$224.00	$520.00	£50.00	£152.00	£360.00

TV STARS
Marvel Comics Group, TV; 1 Aug 1978-4 Feb 1979

Tragg and the Sky Gods #6

True 3-D #1

Turok, Son of Stone #63

	$Good	$Fine	$N.Mint	£Good	£Fine	£N.Mint
1 ND scarce in the U.K. features Hanna-Barbera characters such as CB Bears and Undercover Elephant						
	$0.75	$2.25	$4.50	£0.30	£1.00	£2.00
2-4 ND scarce in the U.K.						
	$0.50	$1.50	$3.00	£0.25	£0.75	£1.50
Title Value:	$2.25	$6.75	$13.50	£1.05	£3.25	£6.50

TWILIGHT
DC Comics,MS; 1 May 1991-3 Jul 1991

	$Good	$Fine	$N.Mint	£Good	£Fine	£N.Mint
1-3 ND 48pgs, features DC Space Heroes: Tommy Tomorrow, Star Rovers, Star Hawkins, Manhunter 2070, Ironwolf, Space Cabbie						
	$0.80	$2.40	$4.00	£0.50	£1.50	£2.50
Title Value:	$2.40	$7.20	$12.00	£1.50	£4.50	£7.50
Note: Prestige Format. Publication delayed from original solicitation.						

TWILIGHT AVENGER
Elite; 1 Jul 1986-2 1987

	$Good	$Fine	$N.Mint	£Good	£Fine	£N.Mint
1-2 ND	$0.40	$1.20	$2.00	£0.25	£0.75	£1.25
Title Value:	$0.80	$2.40	$4.00	£0.50	£1.50	£2.50

TWILIGHT AVENGER (2ND SERIES)
Eternity; 1 1988-8 1989

	$Good	$Fine	$N.Mint	£Good	£Fine	£N.Mint
1-8 ND	$0.40	$1.20	$2.00	£0.25	£0.75	£1.25
Title Value:	$3.20	$9.60	$16.00	£2.00	£6.00	£10.00

TWILIGHT MAN
First,MS; 1 Feb 1989-4 May 1989
(see Sensei, Squalor)

	$Good	$Fine	$N.Mint	£Good	£Fine	£N.Mint
1 ND sub-titled "First Fiction Volume One"; glossy heavier stock paper covers						
	$0.40	$1.20	$2.00	£0.25	£0.75	£1.25
2-4 ND	$0.40	$1.20	$2.00	£0.25	£0.75	£1.25
Title Value:	$1.60	$4.80	$8.00	£1.00	£3.00	£5.00

TWILIGHT ZONE
Gold Key; 1 Nov 1962-91 Jun 1979; 92 May 1982

	$Good	$Fine	$N.Mint	£Good	£Fine	£N.Mint
1 scarce in the U.K.	$10.00	$30.00	$70.00	£6.25	£19.00	£45.00
2	$8.25	$25.00	$50.00	£5.75	£17.50	£35.00
3-4 Toth art	$6.25	$18.50	$37.50	£4.15	£12.50	£25.00
5	$6.25	$18.50	$37.50	£4.15	£12.50	£25.00
6-8	$5.75	$17.50	$35.00	£3.75	£11.00	£22.50
9 Toth art	$6.25	$18.50	$37.50	£4.15	£12.50	£25.00
10	$5.75	$17.50	$35.00	£3.75	£11.00	£22.50
11-15	$4.15	$12.50	$25.00	£2.90	£8.75	£17.50
16-20	$3.30	$10.00	$20.00	£2.05	£6.25	£12.50
21-30	$2.05	$6.25	$12.50	£1.25	£3.75	£7.50
31-40	$1.25	$3.75	$7.50	£0.80	£2.50	£5.00
41-50	$1.00	$3.00	$5.00	£0.70	£2.10	£3.50
51-60	$0.80	$2.40	$4.00	£0.50	£1.50	£2.50
61-70	$0.60	$1.80	$3.00	£0.40	£1.20	£2.00
71 reprint	$0.50	$1.50	$2.50	£0.30	£0.90	£1.50
72-80	$0.50	$1.50	$2.50	£0.30	£0.90	£1.50
81-82	$0.40	$1.20	$2.00	£0.25	£0.75	£1.25
83 48pgs	$0.40	$1.20	$2.00	£0.30	£0.90	£1.50
84 48pgs, new logo begins						
	$0.40	$1.20	$2.00	£0.30	£0.90	£1.50
85-91 48pgs	$0.40	$1.20	$2.00	£0.30	£0.90	£1.50
92	$0.30	$0.90	$1.50	£0.20	£0.60	£1.00
Title Value:	$170.20	$512.60	$1003.50	£111.25	£335.20	£657.00
Note: most issues distributed on the news-stands in the U.K.						

TWILIGHT ZONE 3-D WINTER SPECIAL
Now Comics,OS; 1 May 1993

	$Good	$Fine	$N.Mint	£Good	£Fine	£N.Mint
1 ND pre-bagged with 3-D glasses (25% less without glasses)						
	$0.50	$1.50	$2.50	£0.30	£0.90	£1.50
Title Value:	$0.50	$1.50	$2.50	£0.30	£0.90	£1.50

TWILIGHT ZONE ANNIVERSARY SPECIAL
Now Comics,OS; 1 Nov 1992

	$Good	$Fine	$N.Mint	£Good	£Fine	£N.Mint
1 ND	$0.50	$1.50	$2.50	£0.30	£0.90	£1.50
Title Value:	$0.50	$1.50	$2.50	£0.30	£0.90	£1.50

TWILIGHT ZONE ANNUAL
Now Comics,OS; 1 Apr 1993

	$Good	$Fine	$N.Mint	£Good	£Fine	£N.Mint
1 ND two complete stories, no ads						
	$0.50	$1.50	$2.50	£0.30	£0.90	£1.50
Title Value:	$0.50	$1.50	$2.50	£0.30	£0.90	£1.50

TWILIGHT ZONE SCIENCE FICTION SPECIAL
Now Comics,OS; 1 Mar 1993

	$Good	$Fine	$N.Mint	£Good	£Fine	£N.Mint
1 ND 64pgs, pre-bagged with hologram badge						
	$0.60	$1.80	$3.00	£0.40	£1.20	£2.00
Title Value:	$0.60	$1.80	$3.00	£0.40	£1.20	£2.00

TWILIGHT ZONE WINTER SPECIAL
Now Comics,OS; 1 Apr 1993

	$Good	$Fine	$N.Mint	£Good	£Fine	£N.Mint
1 ND pre-bagged with 3-D glasses (25% less without glasses)						
	$0.60	$1.80	$3.00	£0.40	£1.20	£2.00
Title Value:	$0.60	$1.80	$3.00	£0.40	£1.20	£2.00

TWILIGHT ZONE, THE
Now Comics,MS; 1 Nov 1990; 1 Oct 1991

	$Good	$Fine	$N.Mint	£Good	£Fine	£N.Mint
1 48pgs, Direct Sales Edition - Neal Adams art, Bill Sienkiewicz collage cover						
	$0.50	$1.50	$2.50	£0.30	£0.90	£1.50
1 Direct Sales Edition, reprints 1990 one-shot with Neal Adams art and Sienkiewicz cover						
	$0.40	$1.20	$2.00	£0.25	£0.75	£1.25
1 48pgs, Premiere/Prestige Edition, squarebound with extra Harlan Ellison text story, Neal Adams art and wraparound cover						
	$0.80	$2.40	$4.00	£0.50	£1.50	£2.50
1 32pgs, Premiere Collector's Edition - pre-bagged, card cover with gold logo/upper and lower borders; Harlan Ellison interview, Neal Adams art and wraparound cover (25% less if un-bagged)						
	$0.60	$1.80	$3.00	£0.40	£1.20	£2.00
1 Newstand edition, reprints 1990 one-shot with Neal Adams cover						
	$0.50	$1.50	$2.50	£0.30	£0.90	£1.50

	$Good	$Fine	$N.Mint	£Good	£Fine	£N.Mint
Title Value:	$2.80	$8.40	$14.00	£1.75	£5.25	£8.75
Note: all Non-Distributed on the new-stands in the U.K.						

TWILIGHT ZONE, THE (2ND SERIES)
Now Comics; 1 Nov 1991-16 1993

	$Good	$Fine	$N.Mint	£Good	£Fine	£N.Mint
1 Direct Sale Edition - non-code, Bruce Jones story						
	$0.40	$1.20	$2.00	£0.25	£0.75	£1.25
1 Newstand edition, code-approved, Bruce Jones story						
	$0.40	$1.20	$2.00	£0.25	£0.75	£1.25
2	$0.40	$1.20	$2.00	£0.25	£0.75	£1.25
3 dinosaur cover	$0.40	$1.20	$2.00	£0.25	£0.75	£1.25
4-8	$0.40	$1.20	$2.00	£0.25	£0.75	£1.25
9 3-D Special (Jul 1992) - pre-bagged with glasses and small hologram on cover (25 % less without glasses)						
	$0.60	$1.80	$3.00	£0.40	£1.20	£2.00
9 48pgs, Prestige Edition (Jul 1992) - squarebound, pre-bagged with 3-D glasses, 2 extra stories with different small hologram on cover (25% less without glasses)						
	$1.00	$3.00	$5.00	£0.70	£2.10	£3.50
10-16	$0.40	$1.20	$2.00	£0.25	£0.75	£1.25
Title Value:	$8.00	$24.00	$40.00	£5.10	£15.30	£25.50
Note: all Non-Distributed on the news-stands in the U.K.						

TWILIGHT ZONE, THE (3RD SERIES)
Now Comics; 1 May 1993-6 1993

	$Good	$Fine	$N.Mint	£Good	£Fine	£N.Mint
1	$0.50	$1.50	$2.50	£0.30	£0.90	£1.50
2 computer-generated art, cover by Val Mayerik						
	$0.50	$1.50	$2.50	£0.30	£0.90	£1.50
2 titled "The Twilight Zone Computer Special" with computer-generated cover art by John Picha						
	$0.50	$1.50	$2.50	£0.30	£0.90	£1.50
3-6	$0.50	$1.50	$2.50	£0.30	£0.90	£1.50
Title Value:	$3.50	$10.50	$17.50	£2.10	£6.30	£10.50
Note: all Non-Distributed on the news-stands in the U.K.						

TWIST
Kitchen Sink; 1 Sep 1987-3 1989

	$Good	$Fine	$N.Mint	£Good	£Fine	£N.Mint
1 ND Wolverton, Clowes, Bagge, J.D.King art						
	$0.40	$1.20	$2.00	£0.25	£0.75	£1.25
2 ND Clowes, J.D.King, Bagge art						
	$0.40	$1.20	$2.00	£0.25	£0.75	£1.25
3 ND	$0.40	$1.20	$2.00	£0.25	£0.75	£1.25
Title Value:	$1.20	$3.60	$6.00	£0.75	£2.25	£3.75

TWISTED
Alchemy Studios; 1 Dec 1990

	$Good	$Fine	$N.Mint	£Good	£Fine	£N.Mint
1 ND horror/sci-fi/mystery anthology						
	$0.60	$1.80	$3.00	£0.40	£1.20	£2.00
Title Value:	$0.60	$1.80	$3.00	£0.40	£1.20	£2.00

TWISTED TALES
Pacific/Eclipse; 1 November 1982-10 Dec 1984

	$Good	$Fine	$N.Mint	£Good	£Fine	£N.Mint
1 Richard Corben, Bret Blevins, Tim Conrad art						
	$0.60	$1.80	$3.00	£0.40	£1.20	£2.00
2 Mike Ploog, Ken Steacy art; Berni Wrightson cover						
	$0.60	$1.80	$3.00	£0.40	£1.20	£2.00
3 Richard Corben, Doug Wildey, Bret Blevins art; Corben dinosaur cover						
	$0.50	$1.50	$2.50	£0.30	£0.90	£1.50
4 John Bolton, Don Lomax, Bruce Jones art; Bolton cover						
	$0.50	$1.50	$2.50	£0.30	£0.90	£1.50
5 Richard Corben, Bill Wray, Val Mayerik art; Corben cover						
	$0.50	$1.50	$2.50	£0.30	£0.90	£1.50
6 John Bolton, John Totleben art; Bolton cover						
	$0.50	$1.50	$2.50	£0.30	£0.90	£1.50
7	$0.50	$1.50	$2.50	£0.30	£0.90	£1.50
8 Butch Guice art	$0.50	$1.50	$2.50	£0.30	£0.90	£1.50
10 scarce in the U.K. 1st Eclipse issue; Berni Wrightson, Gray Morrrow, Rick Geary art						
	$0.60	$1.80	$3.00	£0.40	£1.20	£2.00
Title Value:	$5.30	$15.90	$26.50	£3.30	£9.90	£16.50
Note: all Non-Distributed on the news-stands in the U.K.						

TWISTED TALES (2ND SERIES)
Eclipse; Graphic Novel 15; Nov 1987

	$Good	$Fine	$N.Mint	£Good	£Fine	£N.Mint
nn ND Dave Stevens cover						
	$1.00	$3.00	$5.00	£0.70	£2.10	£3.50
Title Value:	$1.00	$3.00	$5.00	£0.70	£2.10	£3.50

TWISTED TALES 3-D
Blackthorne; (3-D Series #7) 1 Aug 1986

	$Good	$Fine	$N.Mint	£Good	£Fine	£N.Mint
1 ND Corben, Totleben, Bolton art; with bound-in 3-D glasses (25% less without glasses)						
	$0.60	$1.80	$3.00	£0.40	£1.20	£2.00
Title Value:	$0.60	$1.80	$3.00	£0.40	£1.20	£2.00

TWISTED TALES OF BRUCE JONES
Eclipse,MS; 1 Feb 1986-4 May 1986

	$Good	$Fine	$N.Mint	£Good	£Fine	£N.Mint
1-4 ND Warren reprints in colour						
	$0.40	$1.20	$2.00	£0.25	£0.75	£1.25
Title Value:	$1.60	$4.80	$8.00	£1.00	£3.00	£5.00

TWISTER
Dark Horse/Harris Publications,MS; 1 Jan 1992-4 Apr 1992

	$Good	$Fine	$N.Mint	£Good	£Fine	£N.Mint
1 ND pre-bagged with "newspaper"						
	$0.60	$1.80	$3.00	£0.40	£1.20	£2.00
2-4 ND	$0.60	$1.80	$3.00	£0.40	£1.20	£2.00
Title Value:	$2.40	$7.20	$12.00	£1.60	£4.80	£8.00

2001: A SPACE ODYSSEY
Marvel Comics Group; 1 Dec 1976-10 Sep 1977

	$Good	$Fine	$N.Mint	£Good	£Fine	£N.Mint
1 Jack Kirby art	$0.50	$1.50	$2.50	£0.30	£0.90	£1.50
2-7 Jack Kirby art	$0.40	$1.20	$2.00	£0.25	£0.75	£1.25
8 origin and 1st appearance Mr. Machine (later Machine Man), Jack Kirby art						
	$0.50	$1.50	$2.50	£0.30	£0.90	£1.50
9-10 Mr. Machine appears, Jack Kirby art						
	$0.40	$1.20	$2.00	£0.25	£0.75	£1.25

	$Good	$Fine	$N.Mint	£Good	£Fine	£N.Mint
Title Value:	$4.20	$12.60	$21.00	£2.60	£7.80	£13.00

2001: A SPACE ODYSSEY (TABLOID)
Marvel Comics Group,Tabloid OS; 1 Oct 1976
(see Marvel Treasury Special)

	$Good	$Fine	$N.Mint	£Good	£Fine	£N.Mint
1 Jack Kirby art	$0.50	$1.50	$2.50	£0.30	£0.90	£1.50
Title Value:	$0.50	$1.50	$2.50	£0.30	£0.90	£1.50

2001 NIGHTS
Viz,MS; 1 Oct 1990-10 1991
1-10 ND 64pgs, reprints Japanese material

	$Good	$Fine	$N.Mint	£Good	£Fine	£N.Mint
	$0.70	$2.10	$3.50	£0.50	£1.50	£2.50
Title Value:	$7.00	$21.00	$35.00	£5.00	£15.00	£25.00

Note: Premiere Format

2010
Marvel Comics Group,MS Film; 1 Apr 1985-2 May 1985
1-2 ND reprints Marvel Super Special #37

	$Good	$Fine	$N.Mint	£Good	£Fine	£N.Mint
	$0.25	$0.75	$1.25	£0.15	£0.45	£0.75
Title Value:	$0.50	$1.50	$2.50	£0.30	£0.90	£1.50

2099 A.D.
Marvel Comics Group,OS; 1 May 1995
1 ND 48pgs, Spiderman, Punisher, Ghost Rider and X-Men appear; clear chromium cover

	$Good	$Fine	$N.Mint	£Good	£Fine	£N.Mint
	$0.80	$2.40	$4.00	£0.50	£1.50	£2.50
Title Value:	$0.80	$2.40	$4.00	£0.50	£1.50	£2.50

2099 APOCALYPSE
Marvel Comics Group,OS; 1 Dec 1995
1 ND 48pgs, the conclusion of One Nation Under Doom, leads into X-Nation 2099 Genesis

	$Good	$Fine	$N.Mint	£Good	£Fine	£N.Mint
	$1.00	$3.00	$5.00	£0.65	£1.95	£3.25
Title Value:	$1.00	$3.00	$5.00	£0.65	£1.95	£3.25

2099 GENESIS
Marvel Comics Group,OS; 1 Jan 1996
1 ND 48pgs, continued from X-Men 2099 #28 and introducing Fantastic Four 2099; continued in Fantastic Four 2099 #1; Warren Ellis script, Dale Eaglesham and Scott Koblish art, chromium cover by Humberto Ramos

	$Good	$Fine	$N.Mint	£Good	£Fine	£N.Mint
	$1.00	$3.00	$5.00	£0.65	£1.95	£3.25
Title Value:	$1.00	$3.00	$5.00	£0.65	£1.95	£3.25

2099 MEGAHITS
Marvel Comics Group,OS; nn Dec 1995
nn ND boxed set of Doom , Punisher, Ravage, Spiderman and X-Men 2099 #1's

	$Good	$Fine	$N.Mint	£Good	£Fine	£N.Mint
	$1.80	$5.25	$9.00	£1.20	£3.60	£6.00
Title Value:	$1.80	$5.25	$9.00	£1.20	£3.60	£6.00

2099 SPECIAL: THE WORLD OF DOOM
Marvel Comics Group,OS; 1 May 1995
1 ND information and interviews concerning all aspects of the 2099 universe; painted cover by the Brothers Hildebrandt

	$Good	$Fine	$N.Mint	£Good	£Fine	£N.Mint
	$0.45	$1.35	$2.25	£0.30	£0.90	£1.50
Title Value:	$0.45	$1.35	$2.25	£0.30	£0.90	£1.50

2099 UNLIMITED
Marvel Comics Group; 1 Jul 1993-10 1996

	$Good	$Fine	$N.Mint	£Good	£Fine	£N.Mint
1 ND 64pgs, introduces The Hulk of 2099; Spiderman 2099 back-ups begin	$0.80	$2.40	$4.00	£0.50	£1.50	£2.50
2-8 ND 64pgs	$0.80	$2.40	$4.00	£0.50	£1.50	£2.50
9 ND 64pgs, Joe Kubert cover	$0.80	$2.40	$4.00	£0.50	£1.50	£2.50
10 ND 64pgs	$0.80	$2.40	$4.00	£0.50	£1.50	£2.50
Title Value:	$8.00	$24.00	$40.00	£5.00	£15.00	£25.00

TWO THOUSAND MANIACS
Aircel,MS; 1 Sep 1991-3 Nov 1991
1-3 ND based on Herschell Gordon Lewis film, black and white

	$Good	$Fine	$N.Mint	£Good	£Fine	£N.Mint
	$0.25	$0.75	$1.25	£0.15	£0.45	£0.75
Title Value:	$0.75	$2.25	$3.75	£0.45	£1.35	£2.25

TWO-FISTED ANNUAL
E.C. Comics; 1 1952-2 1953

	$Good	$Fine	$N.Mint	£Good	£Fine	£N.Mint
1 scarce in the U.K. 128pgs, Kurtzman cover and art	$75.00	$225.00	$525.00	£50.00	£150.00	£350.00
2 very scarce in the U.K. 128pgs, Jack Davis cover and art	$55.00	$170.00	$400.00	£39.00	£115.00	£275.00
Title Value:	$130.00	$395.00	$925.00	£89.00	£265.00	£625.00

Note: both Non-Distributed on the news-stands in the U.K.

TWO-FISTED TALES
E.C. Comics; 18 Nov/Dec 1950-41 Feb/Mar 1955

	$Good	$Fine	$N.Mint	£Good	£Fine	£N.Mint
18 Harvey Kurtzman covers begin (to #29); classic conflict covers begin	$85.00	$255.00	$600.00	£55.00	£170.00	£400.00
19	$62.50	$190.00	$450.00	£43.00	£125.00	£300.00
20	$39.00	$115.00	$275.00	£27.00	£80.00	£190.00
21 Kurtzman art	$29.00	$87.50	$205.00	£19.00	£57.50	£135.00
22	$29.00	$87.50	$205.00	£19.00	£57.50	£135.00
23-25	$23.50	$70.00	$165.00	£16.00	£49.00	£115.00
26-29	$17.00	$50.00	$120.00	£11.00	£34.00	£80.00
30 Jack Davis cover	$17.00	$50.00	$120.00	£11.00	£34.00	£80.00
31 Civil War issue, Kurtzman cover	$15.50	$47.00	$110.00	£10.50	£32.00	£75.00
32-33 Wood cover, Kubert art	$15.50	$47.00	$110.00	£10.50	£32.00	£75.00
34 Jack Davis cover	$15.50	$47.00	$110.00	£10.50	£32.00	£75.00
35 Civil War issue, Jack Davis cover	$15.50	$47.00	$110.00	£10.50	£32.00	£75.00
36-38	$12.50	$39.00	$90.00	£8.50	£26.00	£60.00
39 John Severin cover	$12.50	$39.00	$90.00	£8.50	£26.00	£60.00
40 George Evans cover	$12.50	$39.00	$90.00	£8.50	£26.00	£60.00
41	$12.50	$39.00	$90.00	£8.50	£26.00	£60.00

	$Good	$Fine	$N.Mint	£Good	£Fine	£N.Mint
Title Value:	$552.50	$1664.00	$3920.00	£369.50	£1123.00	£2640.00

Note: all Non-Distributed on the news-stands in the U.K.

TWO-FISTED TALES (2ND SERIES)
Russ Cochran/EC Comics; 1 Oct 1992-present
1 ND reprints begin from original 1950s EC series with exact cover and interior reproduction

	$Good	$Fine	$N.Mint	£Good	£Fine	£N.Mint
	$0.40	$1.20	$2.00	£0.25	£0.75	£1.25
2-13 ND	$0.40	$1.20	$2.00	£0.25	£0.75	£1.25
Title Value:	$5.20	$15.60	$26.00	£3.25	£9.75	£16.25

Two-Fisted Tales Annual #1 (Sep 1994)

				£Good	£Fine	£N.Mint
reprints issues #1-5 with covers				£1.20	£3.60	£6.00

Two-Fisted tales Annual #2 (Jan 1995)

				£Good	£Fine	£N.Mint
reprints issues #6-10 with covers				£1.20	£3.60	£6.00

TWO-FISTED TALES SPECIAL, THE NEW
Dark Horse,OS; 1 Aug 1994
1 ND 48pgs, new Kurtzman story plus reprints

	$Good	$Fine	$N.Mint	£Good	£Fine	£N.Mint
	$0.90	$2.70	$4.50	£0.60	£1.80	£3.00
Title Value:	$0.90	$2.70	$4.50	£0.60	£1.80	£3.00

TWO-GUN KID
Atlas/Marvel Comics Group; 54 Aug 1960-59 Apr 1961; 60 Nov 1962-92 Mar 1968; 93 Jul 1970-136 Apr 1977
(previous issues ND)

	$Good	$Fine	$N.Mint	£Good	£Fine	£N.Mint
54	$6.50	$20.00	$40.00	£4.15	£12.50	£25.00
55-57	$5.75	$17.50	$35.00	£3.30	£10.00	£20.00
58 rare in the U.K. Jack Kirby art	$3.75	$11.00	$22.50	£2.50	£7.50	£15.00
59 rare in the U.K. last 10 cents issue	$3.75	$11.00	$22.50	£2.50	£7.50	£15.00
60 origin and 1st appearance of new Two-Gun Kid by Jack Kirby	$3.30	$10.00	$20.00	£2.05	£6.25	£12.50
61-70	$1.65	$5.00	$10.00	£1.25	£3.75	£7.50
71-72 rare in the U.K.	$1.65	$5.00	$10.00	£1.50	£4.50	£9.00
73-80	$1.65	$5.00	$10.00	£1.25	£3.75	£7.50
81-91	$1.15	$3.50	$7.00	£0.75	£2.25	£4.50
92 last new material	$1.15	$3.50	$7.00	£0.75	£2.25	£4.50
93-100	$0.80	$2.40	$4.00	£0.50	£1.50	£2.50
101 ND origin retold	$0.80	$2.40	$4.00	£0.50	£1.50	£2.50
102-109 ND	$0.40	$1.20	$2.00	£0.40	£1.20	£2.00
110 ND Williamson reprint	$0.40	$1.20	$2.00	£0.40	£1.20	£2.00
111-136 ND	$0.30	$0.90	$1.50	£0.30	£0.90	£1.50
Title Value:	$99.95	$302.30	$587.00	£71.50	£214.95	£414.00

Note: Kirby art in #54, 55, 57-62, 75-77.

TWO-GUN KID: SUNSET RIDERS
Marvel Comics Group,MS; 1 Nov 1995-2 Dec 1995
1-2 ND 64pgs, parchment paper cover

	$Good	$Fine	$N.Mint	£Good	£Fine	£N.Mint
	$1.40	$4.20	$7.00	£0.90	£2.70	£4.50
Title Value:	$2.80	$8.40	$14.00	£1.80	£5.40	£9.00

TYPHOID
Marvel Comics Group,MS; 1 Nov 1995-4 Feb 1996
1-4 ND Ann Nocenti script, John van Fleet art; UV coated covers

	$Good	$Fine	$N.Mint	£Good	£Fine	£N.Mint
	$0.80	$2.40	$4.00	£0.50	£1.50	£2.50
Title Value:	$3.20	$9.60	$16.00	£2.00	£6.00	£10.00

TYRANNOSAURUS REX
Monster Comics; 1 Jul 1991-3 1991

	$Good	$Fine	$N.Mint	£Good	£Fine	£N.Mint
1-3 ND	$0.40	$1.20	$2.00	£0.25	£0.75	£1.25
Title Value:	$1.20	$3.60	$6.00	£0.75	£2.25	£3.75

TYRANT, S.R. BISSETTE'S
Spiderbaby Graphix; 1 Sep 1994-present

	$Good	$Fine	$N.Mint	£Good	£Fine	£N.Mint
1 ND black and white; Steve Bissette script and art on a dinosaur world epic	$0.80	$2.40	$4.00	£0.50	£1.50	£2.50
2-3 ND	$0.60	$1.80	$3.00	£0.40	£1.20	£2.00
3 Gold Edition ND	$2.50	$7.50	$12.50	£1.50	£4.50	£7.50
4-5 ND	$0.60	$1.80	$3.00	£0.40	£1.20	£2.00
Title Value:	$5.70	$17.10	$28.50	£3.60	£10.80	£18.00

U

UFO AND OUTER SPACE
Gold Key; 14 Jun 1978-25 Feb 1980
(previously UFO Flying Saucers)

	$Good	$Fine	$N.Mint	£Good	£Fine	£N.Mint
14 painted covers continue	$0.40	$1.20	$2.00	£0.25	£0.75	£1.25
15-25	$0.40	$1.20	$2.00	£0.25	£0.75	£1.25
Title Value:	$4.80	$14.40	$24.00	£3.00	£9.00	£15.00

Note: some issues are reprint. Limited Distribution in the U.K.

UFO FLYING SAUCERS
Gold Key; 1 Oct 1968-13 Jan 1977
(becomes UFO and Outer Space)

	$Good	$Fine	$N.Mint	£Good	£Fine	£N.Mint
1 scarce in the U.K. giant; painted covers begin	$3.00	$9.00	$15.00	£2.00	£6.00	£10.00
2-3	$1.50	$4.50	$7.50	£1.00	£3.00	£5.00
4-5	$1.00	$3.00	$5.00	£0.70	£2.10	£3.50
6-13	$0.90	$2.70	$4.50	£0.60	£1.80	£3.00
Title Value:	$15.20	$45.60	$76.00	£10.20	£30.60	£51.00

Note: some issues distributed in the U.K. and then only sporadically

ULTRA KLUTZ
Onward; 1 Jun 1986-31 1993
1-30 ND black and white

MINT = 100% / NEAR MINT (inc. +/-) = 90–99% / VERY FINE (inc. +/-) = 75–89% / FINE (inc. +/-) = 55–74%
VERY GOOD (inc. +/-) = 35–54% / GOOD (inc. +/-) = 15–34% / FAIR = 5–14% / POOR = 1–4%

613

	$Good	$Fine	$N.Mint	£Good	£Fine	£N.Mint
	$0.30	$0.90	$1.50	£0.20	£0.60	£1.00
31 ND 48pgs, black and white	$0.40	$1.20	$2.00	£0.25	£0.75	£1.25
Title Value:	$9.40	$28.20	$47.00	£6.25	£18.75	£31.25

ULTRA KLUTZ (2ND SERIES)
Parody Press; 1 Aug 1993-11 1994

	$Good	$Fine	$N.Mint	£Good	£Fine	£N.Mint
1 ND reprints from first series begin (presumably parodying Ultraman from Archie Comics)	$0.40	$1.20	$2.00	£0.25	£0.75	£1.25
1 ND Deluxe Edition - silver foil embossed cover	$0.50	$1.50	$2.50	£0.30	£0.90	£1.50
2-11 ND	$0.40	$1.20	$2.00	£0.25	£0.75	£1.25
Title Value:	$4.90	$14.70	$24.50	£3.05	£9.15	£15.25

ULTRA X-MEN COLLECTION
Marvel Comics Group,MS; 1 Dec 1994-5 Apr 1995

	$Good	$Fine	$N.Mint	£Good	£Fine	£N.Mint
1-5 ND collects the set of Fleer Ultra X-Men trading cards, bound by a metallic ink gatefold cover	$0.60	$1.80	$3.00	£0.40	£1.20	£2.00
Title Value:	$3.00	$9.00	$15.00	£2.00	£6.00	£10.00

ULTRAFORCE
Malibu Ultraverse; 0 Sep/Oct 1994; 1 Aug 1994-10 Aug 1995

	$Good	$Fine	$N.Mint	£Good	£Fine	£N.Mint
0 reprints ashcan editions released with Wizard #35 and #36; prequel to Ultraforce #1	$0.50	$1.50	$2.50	£0.30	£0.90	£1.50
1 40pgs, Prime, Prototype, Hardcase, Contrary, Topaz, Ghoul and Pixx begin; bound-in Prime/Ultraforce trading card, George Perez art	$0.50	$1.50	$2.50	£0.30	£0.90	£1.50
1 Gold Hologram Cover Edition (Aug 1994)	$3.00	$9.00	$15.00	£2.00	£6.00	£10.00
1 Ashcan Edition (Jun 1994) - 16pgs interviews and sketches; black and white, limited to 25,000 copies	$0.30	$0.90	$1.50	£0.20	£0.60	£1.00
1 Newstand edition, ND less common variant cover; pre-bagged with Skybox trading card	$0.50	$1.50	$2.50	£0.40	£1.20	£2.00
2	$0.50	$1.50	$2.50	£0.30	£0.90	£1.50
2 Variant cover, ND white cover featuring Prime; limited edition stamp on cover	$1.00	$3.00	$5.00	£0.80	£2.40	£4.00
3-5	$0.50	$1.50	$2.50	£0.30	£0.90	£1.50
6-7 George Perez cover	$0.50	$1.50	$2.50	£0.30	£0.90	£1.50
8 Marvel's Black Knight appears, George Perez cover	$0.50	$1.50	$2.50	£0.30	£0.90	£1.50
9 Marvel's Black Knight appears, George Perez cover and art	$0.50	$1.50	$2.50	£0.30	£0.90	£1.50
10 1st issue under Marvel Comics solicitation; Sersi (from Marvel's Avengers) appears, Eliminator appears; leads into Ultraforce/Avengers Prelude #1; George Perez cover	$0.50	$1.50	$2.50	£0.30	£0.90	£1.50
Title Value:	$10.40	$31.20	$52.00	£6.70	£20.10	£33.50

Note: all Non-Distributed on the news-stands in the U.K.

ULTRAFORCE (2ND SERIES)
Marvel Comics Group; 1 Dec 1995-present

	$Good	$Fine	$N.Mint	£Good	£Fine	£N.Mint
1 ND Warren Ellis script, Steve Butler and Dennis Jensen art, cover by Steve Butler and George Perez	$0.30	$0.90	$1.50	£0.20	£0.60	£1.00
1 ND variant cover, computer painted art by Chuck Maiden	$0.80	$2.40	$4.00	£0.50	£1.50	£2.50
1 ND Signed Limited Edition (Mar 1996) - 2,000 copies with certificate	$1.50	$4.50	$7.50	£1.00	£3.00	£5.00
2 ND 1st appearance of Lament, flip-book format with Phoenix Ressurrection chapter	$0.30	$0.90	$1.50	£0.20	£0.60	£1.00
3 ND origin Wreckage	$0.30	$0.90	$1.50	£0.20	£0.60	£1.00
4 ND cover by Darick Robertson and George Perez	$0.30	$0.90	$1.50	£0.20	£0.60	£1.00
Title Value:	$3.50	$10.50	$17.50	£2.30	£6.90	£11.50

ULTRAFORCE/AVENGERS
Malibu Ultraverse/Marvel Comics Group,OS; 1 Oct 1995
(see Avengers/Ultraforce)

	$Good	$Fine	$N.Mint	£Good	£Fine	£N.Mint
1 ND 48pgs, Warren Ellis script, George Perez wraparound cover and art; Loki appears	$0.80	$2.40	$4.00	£0.50	£1.50	£2.50
Title Value:	$0.80	$2.40	$4.00	£0.50	£1.50	£2.50

ULTRAFORCE/AVENGERS PRELUDE
Marvel Comics Group/Malibu Ultraverse,OS; 1 Sep 1995

	$Good	$Fine	$N.Mint	£Good	£Fine	£N.Mint
1 ND Ultraforce, Avengers, Loki and Adam Warlock appear	$0.50	$1.50	$2.50	£0.30	£0.90	£1.50
Title Value:	$0.50	$1.50	$2.50	£0.30	£0.90	£1.50

ULTRAFORCE: INFINITY
Marvel Comics Group,OS; nn Nov 1995

	$Good	$Fine	$N.Mint	£Good	£Fine	£N.Mint
nn ND Black September tie-in, intro the Fantastic Ultraforce Four	$0.50	$1.50	$2.50	£0.30	£0.90	£1.50
nn Variant cover, ND 1 copy received for every 5 copies of the regular issue ordered	$0.80	$2.40	$4.00	£0.50	£1.50	£2.50
Title Value:	$1.30	$3.90	$6.50	£0.80	£2.40	£4.00

ULTRAMAN
Harvey/Ultracomics; 1 Jul 1993-3 Sep 1993

	$Good	$Fine	$N.Mint	£Good	£Fine	£N.Mint
1-3 Direct Market Edition: pre-bagged with trading card; logo and all other cover deatails printed on the polybag; Ken Steacy painted cover	$0.40	$1.20	$2.00	£0.25	£0.75	£1.25
1-3 Newstand edition, un-bagged/without trading card	$0.30	$0.90	$1.50	£0.20	£0.60	£1.00
Title Value:	$2.10	$6.30	$10.50	£1.35	£4.05	£6.75

Note: all Non-Distributed on the news-stands in the U.K.

ULTRAMAN (2ND SERIES)
Nemesis Comics; -1 Mar 1994; 1 Apr 1994-5 1994

	$Good	$Fine	$N.Mint	£Good	£Fine	£N.Mint
-1 ND (issue #1 in indicia) Ernie Colon art begins	$0.30	$0.90	$1.50	£0.20	£0.60	£1.00
-1 ND Collector's Edition - card-stock embossed cover	$0.40	$1.20	$2.00	£0.25	£0.75	£1.25
1 ND protective half-outer cover	$0.40	$1.20	$2.00	£0.25	£0.75	£1.25
2-5 ND	$0.40	$1.20	$2.00	£0.25	£0.75	£1.25
Title Value:	$2.70	$8.10	$13.50	£1.70	£5.10	£8.50

ULTRAMAN 3-D SPECIAL
Now Comics,OS; 1 Jul 1993

	$Good	$Fine	$N.Mint	£Good	£Fine	£N.Mint
1 ND hologravure process that does not need 3-D glasses	$0.50	$1.50	$2.50	£0.30	£0.90	£1.50
Title Value:	$0.50	$1.50	$2.50	£0.30	£0.90	£1.50

ULTRAMAN CLASSIC: BATTLE OF THE ULTRA-BROTHERS
Viz Communications,MS; 1 Feb 1994-5 Jul 1994

	$Good	$Fine	$N.Mint	£Good	£Fine	£N.Mint
1 ND 64pgs, squarebound, black and white	$0.80	$2.40	$4.00	£0.50	£1.50	£2.50
2-5 ND 64pgs, black and white	$0.80	$2.40	$4.00	£0.50	£1.50	£2.50
Title Value:	$4.00	$12.00	$20.00	£2.50	£7.50	£12.50

ULTRAVERSE DOUBLE FEATURE
Malibu Ultraverse; 1 Jan 1995

	$Good	$Fine	$N.Mint	£Good	£Fine	£N.Mint
1 ND 64pgs, Prime and Solitaire in separate stories	$0.60	$1.80	$3.00	£0.40	£1.20	£2.00
Title Value:	$0.60	$1.80	$3.00	£0.40	£1.20	£2.00

ULTRAVERSE ORIGINS
Malibu Ultraverse,OS; 1 Jan 1994

	$Good	$Fine	$N.Mint	£Good	£Fine	£N.Mint
1 ND origins of Ultraverse characters featuring art by Maguire, Bogdanove, Mike Zeck, Barry Windsor-Smith, George Perez, Hughes, Chaykin, Walt Simonson; gatefold cover by Joe Quesada	$0.30	$0.90	$1.50	£0.20	£0.60	£1.00
Title Value:	$0.30	$0.90	$1.50	£0.20	£0.60	£1.00

ULTRAVERSE PREMIERE
Malibu Ultraverse,OS; 0 Nov 1993

	$Good	$Fine	$N.Mint	£Good	£Fine	£N.Mint
0 ND collection of short stories featuring Prime, Strangers, Hardcase, Rune, Mantra and Freex; available through mail only with coupons sent in	$1.00	$3.00	$5.00	£0.60	£1.80	£3.00
Title Value:	$1.00	$3.00	$5.00	£0.60	£1.80	£3.00

ULTRAVERSE YEAR ONE
Malibu Ultraverse,OS; nn Sep 1994

	$Good	$Fine	$N.Mint	£Good	£Fine	£N.Mint
1 ND 48pgs, information and cover reproductions of Ultraverse characters and titles	$0.60	$1.80	$3.00	£0.40	£1.20	£2.00
Title Value:	$0.60	$1.80	$3.00	£0.40	£1.20	£2.00

ULTRAVERSE YEAR TWO
Marvel Comics Group/Malibu Ultraverse,OS; 1 Oct 1995

	$Good	$Fine	$N.Mint	£Good	£Fine	£N.Mint
1 ND 48pgs, information and cover reproductions concerning the inter-locking of Marvel and Ultraverse characters	$0.60	$1.80	$3.00	£0.40	£1.20	£2.00
Title Value:	$0.60	$1.80	$3.00	£0.40	£1.20	£2.00

ULTRAVERSE YEAR ZERO: THE DEATH OF THE SQUAD
Malibu Ultraverse,MS; 1 Apr 1995-4 Jul 1995

	$Good	$Fine	$N.Mint	£Good	£Fine	£N.Mint
1 ND chronicles events before Prime #1; Mantra back-up feature	$0.50	$1.50	$2.50	£0.30	£0.90	£1.50
2 ND chronicles events before Prime #1; Rune back-up feature	$0.50	$1.50	$2.50	£0.30	£0.90	£1.50
3 ND chronicles events before Prime #1; Codename: Firearm back-up feature	$0.50	$1.50	$2.50	£0.30	£0.90	£1.50
Title Value:	$1.50	$4.50	$7.50	£0.90	£2.70	£4.50

ULTRAVERSE/MARVEL DREAM TEAM
Marvel Comics Group/Malibu Ultraverse,OS; 1 Sep 1995

	$Good	$Fine	$N.Mint	£Good	£Fine	£N.Mint
1 ND 48pgs, pin-ups of Marvel and Ultraverse characters; Shi by William Tucci also appears	$0.80	$2.40	$4.00	£0.50	£1.50	£2.50
Title Value:	$0.80	$2.40	$4.00	£0.50	£1.50	£2.50

UNCANNY TALES
Marvel Comics Group; 1 Dec 1973-12 Oct 1975

	$Good	$Fine	$N.Mint	£Good	£Fine	£N.Mint
1 ND 50s/60s horror reprints begin	$0.50	$1.50	$2.50	£0.30	£0.90	£1.50
2-12 ND	$0.50	$1.50	$2.50	£0.30	£0.90	£1.50
Title Value:	$6.00	$18.00	$30.00	£3.60	£10.80	£18.00

UNCENSORED MOUSE
Eternity; 1,2 Apr 1989

	$Good	$Fine	$N.Mint	£Good	£Fine	£N.Mint
1 ND	$0.60	$1.80	$3.00	£0.40	£1.20	£2.00
2 ND scarce in both the U.S. and the U.K.	$0.60	$1.80	$3.00	£0.50	£1.50	£2.50
Title Value:	$1.20	$3.60	$6.00	£0.90	£2.70	£4.50

Note: previously unpublished Mickey Mouse material with satirical or racist overtones. Sealed in plastic bags. Opened examples will bring 50% of the above values. Issue #2 is scarcer owing to legal problems with Disney at the time and as such less were distributed in both the US and UK. Planned as an on-going series, it finished after just two issues.

UNCLE SCROOGE
Gladstone; 210 Oct 1986-242 1989; Disney; 243 Jun 1990-280 Jun 1993; Gladstone; 281 Jul 1993-present

	$Good	$Fine	$N.Mint	£Good	£Fine	£N.Mint
210 1st Gladstone issue, 75¢, Barks reprints begin	$3.00	$9.00	$15.00	£1.00	£3.00	£5.00
211 scarce in the U.K. Prize of Pizarro	$2.00	$6.00	$10.00	£0.70	£2.10	£3.50
212-215	$2.00	$6.00	$10.00	£0.60	£1.80	£3.00
216 1st 95¢ issue	$2.00	$6.00	$10.00	£0.60	£1.80	£3.00
217-218	$2.00	$6.00	$10.00	£0.60	£1.80	£3.00
219 Son of the Sun by Rosa	$3.00	$9.00	$15.00	£1.00	£3.00	£5.00
220 Rosa 10pg story	$1.00	$3.00	$5.00	£0.60	£1.80	£3.00
221	$0.60	$1.80	$3.00	£0.40	£1.20	£2.00
222 Mysterious Island by Barks, includes restored panels & article						

	$Good	$Fine	$N.Mint	£Good	£Fine	£N.Mint
	$0.60	$1.80	$3.00	£0.40	£1.20	£2.00
223	$0.60	$1.80	$3.00	£0.40	£1.20	£2.00
224 Cash Flow by Rosa						
	$0.60	$1.80	$3.00	£0.40	£1.20	£2.00
225	$0.60	$1.80	$3.00	£0.40	£1.20	£2.00
226 Paper Chase by Rosa						
	$0.60	$1.80	$3.00	£0.40	£1.20	£2.00
227 Fiscal Fitness by Rosa						
	$0.60	$1.80	$3.00	£0.40	£1.20	£2.00
228-230	$0.60	$1.80	$3.00	£0.40	£1.20	£2.00
231-240	$0.50	$1.50	$2.50	£0.30	£0.90	£1.50
241-242 68pgs	$0.60	$1.80	$3.00	£0.40	£1.20	£2.00
243 all new material begins						
	$0.50	$1.50	$2.50	£0.30	£0.90	£1.50
244-249	$0.50	$1.50	$2.50	£0.30	£0.90	£1.50
250 anniversary issue						
	$0.60	$1.80	$3.00	£0.40	£1.20	£2.00
251-254	$0.50	$1.50	$2.50	£0.30	£0.90	£1.50
255 classic The Flying Dutchman by Carl Barks						
	$0.50	$1.50	$2.50	£0.30	£0.90	£1.50
256-260	$0.50	$1.50	$2.50	£0.30	£0.90	£1.50
261-262 Return to Xanadu by Don Rosa						
	$0.50	$1.50	$2.50	£0.30	£0.90	£1.50
263-267	$0.50	$1.50	$2.50	£0.30	£0.90	£1.50
268 Carl Barks reprint						
	$0.50	$1.50	$2.50	£0.30	£0.90	£1.50
269-272	$0.50	$1.50	$2.50	£0.30	£0.90	£1.50
273-274 all Carl Barks issue						
	$0.50	$1.50	$2.50	£0.30	£0.90	£1.50
275 all Carl Barks issue plus Don Rosa poster						
	$0.50	$1.50	$2.50	£0.30	£0.90	£1.50
276-280 Carl Barks reprint						
	$0.50	$1.50	$2.50	£0.30	£0.90	£1.50
281 Carl Barks reprint; title noe re-published by Gladstone						
	$0.50	$1.50	$2.50	£0.30	£0.90	£1.50
282-284 Carl Barks reprint						
	$0.50	$1.50	$2.50	£0.30	£0.90	£1.50
285 The Life and Times of Scrooge McDuck begin (ends #297)						
	$0.80	$2.40	$4.00	£0.50	£1.50	£2.50
286-287	$0.50	$1.50	$2.50	£0.30	£0.90	£1.50
288 64pgs, Land Beneath the Ground by Barks						
	$0.60	$1.80	$3.00	£0.40	£1.20	£2.00
289-295	$0.50	$1.50	$2.50	£0.30	£0.90	£1.50
Title Value:	$62.20	$186.60	$311.00	£31.60	£94.80	£158.00

Note: all Non-Distributed on the news-stands in the U.K.

UNCLE SCROOGE ADVENTURES
Gladstone; 1 Nov 1987-21 May 1990; Gladstone/Disney; 22 Aug 1993-present
(formerly Gladstone title)

	$Good	$Fine	$N.Mint	£Good	£Fine	£N.Mint
1 McDuck of Arabia, Barks reprints begin						
	$1.00	$3.00	$5.00	£0.50	£1.50	£2.50
2-3	$0.50	$1.50	$2.50	£0.30	£0.90	£1.50
4 Golden River by Barks						
	$0.50	$1.50	$2.50	£0.30	£0.90	£1.50
5 Last Sled to Dawson by Rosa						
	$0.50	$1.50	$2.50	£0.30	£0.90	£1.50
6-8	$0.50	$1.50	$2.50	£0.30	£0.90	£1.50
9 Fortune on the Rocks by Rosa						
	$0.50	$1.50	$2.50	£0.30	£0.90	£1.50
10	$0.50	$1.50	$2.50	£0.30	£0.90	£1.50
11-19	$0.40	$1.20	$2.00	£0.25	£0.75	£1.25
20-21 64pgs	$0.50	$1.50	$2.50	£0.30	£0.90	£1.50

	$Good	$Fine	$N.Mint	£Good	£Fine	£N.Mint
22 Carl Barks' "Prize of Pizarro" reprint						
	$0.40	$1.20	$2.00	£0.25	£0.75	£1.25
23 64pgs	$0.50	$1.50	$2.50	£0.30	£0.90	£1.50
24-25	$0.40	$1.20	$2.00	£0.25	£0.75	£1.25
26 64pgs, Back to Klondike reprinted						
	$0.60	$1.80	$3.00	£0.40	£1.20	£2.00
27-29	$0.40	$1.20	$2.00	£0.25	£0.75	£1.25
30 64pgs, Ramona Scarpa's "The Lentils of Babylon" begins						
	$0.60	$1.80	$3.00	£0.40	£1.20	£2.00
31-32	$0.40	$1.20	$2.00	£0.25	£0.75	£1.25
33 64pgs, new story called "Horsing Around With History" written by Carl Barks						
	$0.60	$1.80	$3.00	£0.40	£1.20	£2.00
34-36	$0.40	$1.20	$2.00	£0.25	£0.75	£1.25
Title Value:	$16.80	$50.40	$84.00	£10.30	£30.90	£51.50

Note: all Non-Distributed on the news-stands in the U.K.

UNCLE SCROOGE DIGEST
Gladstone; 1 1986-5 1987

	$Good	$Fine	$N.Mint	£Good	£Fine	£N.Mint
1 ND	$0.30	$0.90	$1.50	£0.20	£0.60	£1.00
2 ND Second Richest Duck by Barks						
	$0.40	$1.20	$2.00	£0.25	£0.75	£1.25
3-5 ND	$0.30	$0.90	$1.50	£0.20	£0.60	£1.00
Title Value:	$1.60	$4.80	$8.00	£1.05	£3.15	£5.25

UNCLE SCROOGE GOES TO DISNEYLAND
Gladstone; 1 1985

	$Good	$Fine	$N.Mint	£Good	£Fine	£N.Mint
1 ND 100pgs, 20pgs Carl Barks						
	$0.80	$2.40	$4.00	£0.50	£1.50	£2.50
Title Value:	$0.80	$2.40	$4.00	£0.50	£1.50	£2.50

UNCLE WALT'S COLLECTORY
Gladstone/Disney; 1 Jun 1995

	$Good	$Fine	$N.Mint	£Good	£Fine	£N.Mint
1 ND 48pgs, Don Rosa art						
	$0.50	$1.50	$2.50	£0.30	£0.90	£1.50
Title Value:	$0.50	$1.50	$2.50	£0.30	£0.90	£1.50

UNDERDOG
Charlton; 1 Nov 1970-10 Jan 1972

	$Good	$Fine	$N.Mint	£Good	£Fine	£N.Mint
1 scarce in the U.K. Frank Johnson art begins						
	$10.00	$30.00	$60.00	£5.00	£15.00	£30.00
2-3 scarce in the U.K.						
	$6.50	$20.00	$40.00	£3.30	£10.00	£20.00
4-10	$5.75	$17.50	$35.00	£2.50	£7.50	£15.00
Title Value:	$63.25	$192.50	$385.00	£29.10	£87.50	£175.00

Note: some issues distributed on the news-stands in the U.K.

UNDERDOG (2ND SERIES)
Gold Key/Whitman; 1 Mar 1975-23 Feb 1979

	$Good	$Fine	$N.Mint	£Good	£Fine	£N.Mint
1	$7.50	$22.50	$45.00	£3.30	£10.00	£20.00
2-3	$4.15	$12.50	$25.00	£2.05	£6.25	£12.50
4-10	$3.30	$10.00	$20.00	£1.65	£5.00	£10.00
11-23	$2.50	$7.50	$15.00	£1.25	£3.75	£7.50
Title Value:	$71.40	$215.00	$430.00	£35.20	£106.25	£212.50

Note: some issues distributed on the news-stands in the U.K.

UNDERDOG IN 3-D
Blackthorne; (3-D Series #43) 1 Jun 1988

	$Good	$Fine	$N.Mint	£Good	£Fine	£N.Mint
1 ND with bound-in 3-D glasses (25% less without glasses)						
	$0.30	$0.90	$1.50	£0.20	£0.60	£1.00
Title Value:	$0.30	$0.90	$1.50	£0.20	£0.60	£1.00

UNDERGROUND
Aircel,Magazine OS; 1 1987

	$Good	$Fine	$N.Mint	£Good	£Fine	£N.Mint
1 ND	$0.40	$1.20	$2.00	£0.25	£0.75	£1.25
Title Value:	$0.40	$1.20	$2.00	£0.25	£0.75	£1.25

UNDERSEA AGENT
Tower; 1 Jan 1966-6 Mar 1967
1 distributed in the U.K. Giant

TV Stars #1

UFO Flying Saucers #4

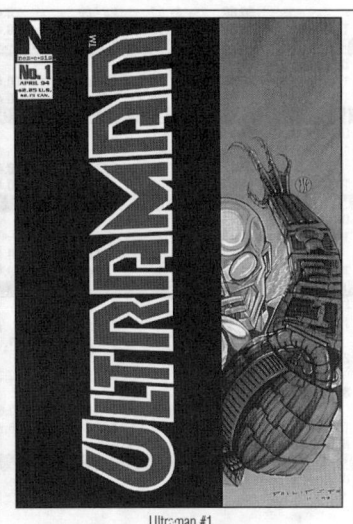

Ultraman #1

	$Good	$Fine	$N.Mint	£Good	£Fine	£N.Mint
	$7.50	$22.50	$45.00	£5.00	£15.00	£30.00
2-6 distributed in the U.K. Giant						
	$4.55	$13.50	$27.50	£3.00	£9.00	£18.00
Title Value:	$30.25	$90.00	$182.50	£20.00	£60.00	£120.00

UNDERWORLD
DC Comics,MS; 1 Dec 1987-4 Mar 1988

	$Good	$Fine	$N.Mint	£Good	£Fine	£N.Mint
1-4	$0.15	$0.45	$0.75	£0.10	£0.35	£0.60
Title Value:	$0.60	$1.80	$3.00	£0.40	£1.40	£2.40

UNDERWORLD UNLEASHED
DC Comics,MS; 1 Nov 1995-3 Jan 1996

1-3 ND 48pgs, Neron and DC villains have their day; fluorescent ink covers

	$Good	$Fine	$N.Mint	£Good	£Fine	£N.Mint
	$0.60	$1.80	$3.00	£0.40	£1.20	£2.00
Title Value:	$1.80	$5.40	$9.00	£1.20	£3.60	£6.00

UNDERWORLD UNLEASHED TIE-INS –

1995

Below is a list in chronological order of Underworld Unleashed tie-ins:
Aquaman #14
Azrael #10
Damage #18
Green Arrow #102
Guy Gardner: Warrior #36
Manhunter #12
Extreme Justice #10
Flash #107
Primal Force #13
The Spectre #35
Green Lantern #68
Hawkman #26
Justice League America #105
R.E.B.E.L.S. '95 #13
Starman #13
Detective Comics #691
Fate #13
Impulse #8
The Ray #18
Steel #21
Catwoman #27
Damage #19
Green Arrow #103
Guy Gardner: Warrior #37
Robin #23
Batman #525
Extreme Justice #11
Legion of Super-Heroes #75
Primal Force #14
Superboy #22
The Spectre #36
Green Lantern #69
Hawkman #27
Justice League America #106
R.E.B.E.L.S. '95 #14
Adventures of Superman #530
Detective Comics #692
Fate #14
Justice League Task Force #30
Legionnaires #32
Superman: The Man of Tomorrow #3
The Ray #19

UNDERWORLD UNLEASHED: ABYSS - HELL'S SENTINEL
DC Comics,OS; 1 Dec 1995

1 ND 48pgs, Spectre, Fate, Zatanna, Deadman and Phantom Stranger appear with Sentinel
(formerly the Golden Age Green Lantern)

	$Good	$Fine	$N.Mint	£Good	£Fine	£N.Mint
	$0.60	$1.80	$3.00	£0.40	£1.20	£2.00
Title Value:	$0.60	$1.80	$3.00	£0.40	£1.20	£2.00

UNDERWORLD UNLEASHED: APOKOLIPS - DARK UPRISING
DC Comics,OS; 1 Nov 1995

	$Good	$Fine	$N.Mint	£Good	£Fine	£N.Mint
1 ND 48pgs	$0.60	$1.80	$3.00	£0.40	£1.20	£2.00
Title Value:	$0.60	$1.80	$3.00	£0.40	£1.20	£2.00

UNDERWORLD UNLEASHED: BATMAN - DEVIL'S ASYLUM
DC Comics,OS; 1 Dec 1995

1 ND Alan Grant script, Brian Stelfreeze art

	$Good	$Fine	$N.Mint	£Good	£Fine	£N.Mint
	$0.60	$1.80	$3.00	£0.40	£1.20	£2.00
Title Value:	$0.60	$1.80	$3.00	£0.40	£1.20	£2.00

UNDERWORLD UNLEASHED: PATTERNS OF FEAR
DC Comics,OS; 1 Dec 1995

1 ND 48pgs, Barbara Gordon as Oracle assesses the new threat from DC villains as a result of Neron's work

	$Good	$Fine	$N.Mint	£Good	£Fine	£N.Mint
	$0.60	$1.80	$3.00	£0.40	£1.20	£2.00
Title Value:	$0.60	$1.80	$3.00	£0.40	£1.20	£2.00

UNEARTHLY SPECTACULARS
Harvey; 1 Oct 1965-3 Mar 1967

1 rare in the U.K. Jack Quick Frost and Miracles Inc. begin

	$Good	$Fine	$N.Mint	£Good	£Fine	£N.Mint
	$2.50	$7.50	$15.00	£1.65	£5.00	£10.00

2 rare in the U.K. Giant, Wood art, Williamson art, Adams art on advert

	$3.75	$11.00	$22.50	£2.50	£7.50	£15.00

3 scarce in the U.K. Giant, Williamson art

	$3.75	$11.00	$22.50	£2.50	£7.50	£15.00
Title Value:	$10.00	$29.50	$60.00	£6.65	£20.00	£40.00

Note: all distributed on the news-stands in the U.K.

UNEXPECTED SPECIAL, THE
DC Comics; nn 1977
(DC Special Series #4)
nn ND 52pgs, Alex Nino art

	$Good	$Fine	$N.Mint	£Good	£Fine	£N.Mint
	$0.50	$1.50	$2.50	£0.30	£0.90	£1.50
Title Value:	$0.50	$1.50	$2.50	£0.30	£0.90	£1.50

UNEXPECTED, THE
National Periodical Publications; 105 Feb/Mar 1968-222 May 1982
(see Super DC Giant) (previously Tales of the Unexpected)

	$Good	$Fine	$N.Mint	£Good	£Fine	£N.Mint
105	$3.30	$10.00	$20.00	£1.65	£5.00	£10.00
106-112	$2.05	$6.25	$12.50	£1.25	£3.75	£7.50
113 last 12 cent issue						
	$2.05	$6.25	$12.50	£1.25	£3.75	£7.50
114-115	$1.00	$3.00	$6.00	£0.65	£2.00	£4.00
116 Wrightson art	$1.50	$4.50	$7.50	£1.00	£3.00	£5.00
117-118	$1.20	$3.60	$6.00	£0.80	£2.40	£4.00
119 Wrightson art	$1.50	$4.50	$7.50	£1.00	£3.00	£5.00
120	$1.20	$3.60	$6.00	£0.80	£2.40	£4.00
121 Wrightson art	$1.50	$4.50	$7.50	£1.00	£3.00	£5.00
122-125	$1.20	$3.60	$6.00	£0.80	£2.40	£4.00
126 52pgs	$1.40	$4.20	$7.00	£0.90	£2.70	£4.50
127 52pgs	$1.20	$3.60	$6.00	£0.80	£2.40	£4.00
128 52pgs, Wrightson art						
	$1.50	$4.50	$7.50	£1.00	£3.00	£5.00
129-132 52pgs	$1.00	$3.00	$5.00	£0.70	£2.10	£3.50
133 scarce in the U.K. 52pgs						
	$1.00	$3.00	$5.00	£0.80	£2.40	£4.00
134-136 52pgs	$1.00	$3.00	$5.00	£0.70	£2.10	£3.50
137-139	$0.80	$2.40	$4.00	£0.50	£1.50	£2.50
140 ND	$0.80	$2.40	$4.00	£0.60	£1.80	£3.00
141-156	$0.80	$2.40	$4.00	£0.40	£1.20	£2.00
157-162 100pgs	$0.80	$2.40	$4.00	£0.50	£1.50	£2.50
163-186	$0.40	$1.20	$2.00	£0.30	£0.90	£1.50
187-188 ND 44pgs						
	$0.50	$1.50	$2.50	£0.35	£1.05	£1.75
189-190 ND 68pgs						
	$0.60	$1.80	$3.00	£0.40	£1.20	£2.00
191 68pgs, Rogers art						
	$0.55	$1.65	$2.75	£0.35	£1.05	£1.75
192-195 ND 68pgs						
	$0.60	$1.80	$3.00	£0.40	£1.20	£2.00
196-200	$0.40	$1.20	$2.00	£0.25	£0.75	£1.25
201-202	$0.30	$0.90	$1.50	£0.20	£0.60	£1.00
203 Kaluta cover	$0.30	$0.90	$1.50	£0.20	£0.60	£1.00
204-222	$0.30	$0.90	$1.50	£0.20	£0.60	£1.00
Title Value:	$90.85	$273.45	$471.75	£57.75	£173.40	£302.00

ARTISTS
Ditko art in 189, 221. Kirby reprints in 127, 162. Nino art in 152, 159, 162. Wood art in 122 (inks), 137 (inks), 138. Wrightson reprint in 161.
FEATURES
Johnny Peril in 106-114, 117, 200, 205-213. Madame Xanadu in 190, 192, 194, 195.
REPRINT FEATURES
Johnny Peril in 127, 158. Various reprints in 126-136, 157-162.

UNICORN ISLE
Warp/Apple; 1 1986-5 1988

	$Good	$Fine	$N.Mint	£Good	£Fine	£N.Mint
1-5 ND	$0.40	$1.20	$2.00	£0.25	£0.75	£1.25
Title Value:	$2.00	$6.00	$10.00	£1.25	£3.75	£6.25

UNION
Image,MS; 0 Jul 1994; 1 Jun 1993-4 Feb 1994

	$Good	$Fine	$N.Mint	£Good	£Fine	£N.Mint
0 ND (Jul 1994)	$0.50	$1.50	$2.50	£0.30	£0.90	£1.50

0 Variant cover, ND Whilce Portacio cover art; cover forms larger picture when combined with the variant covers of Deathblow #5, Gen 13 #5, Kindred #3, Stormwatch #10, Team 7 #1, Wetworks #2, WildC.A.T.S #11

	$1.50	$4.50	$7.50	£1.00	£3.00	£5.00

1 ND Direct Market Edition, Mark Texeira art begins, foil embossed cover

	$0.50	$1.50	$2.50	£0.30	£0.90	£1.50

1 Newstand edition, ND (no cover enhancement)

	$0.40	$1.20	$2.00	£0.25	£0.75	£1.25
2-4 ND	$0.40	$1.20	$2.00	£0.25	£0.75	£1.25
Title Value:	$4.10	$12.30	$20.50	£2.60	£7.80	£13.00

Note: all Non-Distributed on the news-stands in the U.K.

UNION (2ND SERIES)
Image; 1 Feb 1995-present

1-3 ND Mike Heisler script and Ryan Benjamin art

	$Good	$Fine	$N.Mint	£Good	£Fine	£N.Mint
	$0.50	$1.50	$2.50	£0.30	£0.90	£1.50

4 ND Wildstorm Rising part 3, continued in Gen 13 #2; with two foil-bagged painted trading cards. Cover by Barry Windsor-Smith

	$0.50	$1.50	$2.50	£0.30	£0.90	£1.50

4 Newstand edition, ND without trading cards

	$0.40	$1.20	$2.00	£0.25	£0.75	£1.25
5-7 ND	$0.50	$1.50	$2.50	£0.30	£0.90	£1.50
8-9 ND Regal Vengeance story						
	$0.50	$1.50	$2.50	£0.30	£0.90	£1.50
10 ND Regal Vengeance story; Michael Golden cover						
	$0.50	$1.50	$2.50	£0.30	£0.90	£1.50
Title Value:	$5.40	$16.20	$27.00	£3.25	£9.75	£16.25

UNITY
The Unity series as written by Jim Shooter and drawn by Barry Windsor-Smith and Bob Layton defines the Valiant universe and how and where the titles and characters are related. Unity #0 was given away free by the distribution companies: retailers received 2 copies for every set of Unity chapters ordered. All 8 Valiant titles cover dated May and June 1992 had these chapters and the order is set out below. Unity #1 then concluded the 18 part story cover dated July 1992.

Chapter 1 - Unity #0
Chapter 2 - Eternal Warrior #1
Chapter 3 - Archer & Armstrong #1
Chapter 4 - Magnus Robot Fighter #15
Chapter 5 - X-O Manowar #7

	$Good	$Fine	$N.Mint	£Good	£Fine	£N.Mint

Chapter 6 - Shadowman #4
Chapter 7 - Rai #6
Chapter 8 - Harbinger #8
Chapter 9 - Solar Man of the Atom #12
Chapter 10 - Eternal Warrior #2
Chapter 11 - Archer & Armstrong #2
Chapter 12 - Magnus Robot Fighter #16
Chapter 13 - X-O Manowar #8
Chapter 14 - Shadowman #5
Chapter 15 - Rai #7
Chapter 16 - Harbinger #9
Chapter 17 - Solar Man of the Atom #13
Chapter 18 - Unity #1

UNITY (LIMITED SERIES)
Valiant; 0 May 1992-1 Oct 1992

0 ND scarce in the U.K. 16pgs, originally given away free to retailers depending on the minimum order of all Valiant titles solicited for May cover date, Barry Windsor-Smith art
$0.60 $1.80 $3.00 £0.40 £1.20 £2.00

0 ND rare in the U.K. Red logo edition, giveaway to U.S. retailers only
$1.50 $4.50 $7.50 £1.00 £3.00 £5.00

0 Gold Edition, ND retailer's "thankyou" from Valiant
$1.50 $4.50 $7.50 £1.00 £3.00 £5.00

1 ND very scarce in the U.K. 16pgs, Unity: Epilogue; retailers quantities limited, depending on half the minimum order of all Valiant titles solicited for June cover date; cover/art by Barry Windsor-Smith
$0.60 $1.80 $3.00 £0.40 £1.20 £2.00

1 ND Gold Logo Premium - retailer's "thankyou" from Valiant
$1.50 $4.50 $7.50 £1.00 £3.00 £5.00

1 ND Platinum Logo Premium - retailer's "thankyou" from Valiant
$2.00 $6.00 $10.00 £1.20 £3.60 £6.00

Title Value: $7.70 $23.10 $38.50 £5.00 £15.00 £25.00

Unity Collection 1 (Jul 1992)
very scarce in the U.K., collects the first set of Unity chapters with Unity #0,Eternal Warrior #1,Archer & Armstrong #1, Magnus #15,X-O #6,Shadowman #4,Rai #5, Harbinger #8 and Solar #12. Frank Miller cover, signed by Jim Shooter and Bob Layton £5.00 £15.00 £25.00

Unity Trade paperback 1 (1993)
as above collects first four chapters of the Unity story but unsigned £1.30 £3.90 £6.50

Unity Collection 2 (Aug 1992)
very scarce in the U.K., collects the second set of Unity chapters with Walt Simonson covers: Eternal Warrior #2,Archer & Armstrong #2,Magnus #16,X-O #8, Shadowman #5,Rai #7,Harbinger #9, Solar #13 and Unity #1. Frank Miller cover, signed by Jim Shooter and Bob Layton £5.00 £15.00 £25.00

Unity Trade paperback 2 (Oct 1994)
as above collects chapters #5-9 of Unity story but unsigned £1.30 £3.90 £6.50

Unity Trade paperback 3 (Nov 1994)
collects chapters #10-14 of Unity story £1.30 £3.90 £6.50

Unity Trade paperback 4 (Dec 1994)
collects chapters #15-18 of Unity story £1.30 £3.90 £6.50

UNITY: THE LOST CHAPTERS
Valiant,OS; 1 Feb 1995
1 ND 48pgs, features X-O Manowar
$0.50 $1.50 $2.50 £0.30 £0.90 £1.50
Title Value: $0.50 $1.50 $2.50 £0.30 £0.90 £1.50

UNIVERSAL INTERGALACTIC DISCOVERY CO.
Comico; 1 Apr 1992
1 ND $0.40 $1.20 $2.00 £0.25 £0.75 £1.25
Title Value: $0.40 $1.20 $2.00 £0.25 £0.75 £1.25

UNIVERSAL MONSTERS
Dark Horse; 1 Jun 1993-4 Sep 1993
1 ND 48pgs, squarebound, Frankenstein; adapted and painted by Denis Beauvais
$1.00 $3.00 $5.00 £0.70 £2.10 £3.50
2 ND 48pgs, squarebound, Creature From The Black Lagoon; Art Adams and Terry Austin art
$1.00 $3.00 $5.00 £0.70 £2.10 £3.50
3 ND 48pgs, squarebound, Dracula; Dan Vado script and Jonathan D. Smith art
$1.00 $3.00 $5.00 £0.70 £2.10 £3.50
4 ND 48pgs, squarebound, The Mummy; Dan Jolley script and Tony Harris art
$1.00 $3.00 $5.00 £0.70 £2.10 £3.50
Title Value: $4.00 $12.00 $20.00 £2.80 £8.40 £14.00

UNIVERSAL PRESENTS DRACULA, THE MUMMY/OTHER STORIES
Dell,OS; nn 02-530-311 Sep/Nov 1963
1 scarce in the U.K. 80pgs, all reprint from Dell Giants; distributed in some areas in the U.K.
$30.00 $90.00 $210.00 £20.00 £60.00 £140.00
Title Value: $30.00 $90.00 $210.00 £20.00 £60.00 £140.00

UNIVERSAL SOLDIER
Now Comics,MS; 1 Sep 1992-3 Nov 1992
1 ND based on film, pre-bagged with hologram cover
$0.40 $1.20 $2.00 £0.25 £0.75 £1.25
1 Newsstand edition, ND based on film, toned down version, photo cover
$0.30 $0.90 $1.50 £0.20 £0.60 £1.00
2 ND pre-bagged $0.40 $1.20 $2.00 £0.25 £0.75 £1.25
2 Newsstand edition ND $0.30 $0.90 $1.50 £0.20 £0.60 £1.00
3 ND pre-bagged $0.40 $1.20 $2.00 £0.25 £0.75 £1.25
3 Newsstand edition ND $0.30 $0.90 $1.50 £0.20 £0.60 £1.00
Title Value: $2.10 $6.30 $10.50 £1.35 £4.05 £6.75

UNKNOWN SOLDIER
DC Comics; 205 Apr/May 1977-268 Oct 1982
(see Brave and the Bold, DC Super-Stars) (previously Star-Spangled War Stories)

205 $0.30 $0.90 $1.50 £0.20 £0.60 £1.00
206-211 $0.30 $0.90 $1.50 £0.15 £0.45 £0.75
212-218 ND $0.30 $0.90 $1.50 £0.20 £0.60 £1.00
219 ND 44pgs, Frank Miller art
$0.50 $1.50 $2.50 £0.30 £0.90 £1.50
220-221 ND 44pgs
$0.40 $1.20 $2.00 £0.25 £0.75 £1.25
222-250 $0.25 $0.75 $1.25 £0.15 £0.45 £0.75
251-253 Enemy Ace stories
$0.25 $0.75 $1.25 £0.15 £0.45 £0.75
254-256 Walt Simonson art, Capt. Fear
$0.25 $0.75 $1.25 £0.15 £0.45 £0.75
257-259 $0.25 $0.75 $1.25 £0.15 £0.45 £0.75
260-261 Enemy Ace stories
$0.25 $0.75 $1.25 £0.15 £0.45 £0.75
262-264 $0.25 $0.75 $1.25 £0.15 £0.45 £0.75
265-267 Enemy Ace stories
$0.25 $0.75 $1.25 £0.15 £0.45 £0.75
268 $0.25 $0.75 $1.25 £0.15 £0.45 £0.75
Title Value: $17.25 $51.75 $86.25 £10.35 £31.05 £51.75

FEATURES
Andy Stewart Combat Nurse in 227, 228. Balloon Buster in 262-264. Captain Fear in 254-256. Capt. Storm in 257-259. Dateline: Frontline in 243-245, 254-256. Enemy Ace in 251-253, 260, 261, 265-267. Frogman (Robert Starr) in 219-221. Losers in 265. Lt. Larry Rock in 205-207. Mlle. Marie in 249. Ruptured Duck in 246-248. Tomahawk in 262-264. Unknown Soldier in all issues. Viking Commandos in 266, 267.

UNKNOWN SOLDIER (2ND SERIES)
DC Comics,MS; 1 Dec 1988-12 Nov 1989
1 LD in the U.K., origin re-told
$0.25 $0.75 $1.25 £0.15 £0.45 £0.75
2-12 LD in the U.K.
$0.25 $0.75 $1.25 £0.15 £0.45 £0.75
Title Value: $3.00 $9.00 $15.00 £1.80 £5.40 £9.00
Note: Mature Readers label

UNKNOWN WORLDS
ACG; 1 Aug 1960-57 Aug 1967
(all distributed in the U.K.)
1 $17.00 $50.00 $120.00 £11.00 £34.00 £80.00
2 $11.50 $35.00 $70.00 £7.50 £22.50 £45.00
3-5 $10.00 $30.00 $60.00 £6.50 £20.00 £40.00
6-10 $8.25 $25.00 $50.00 £5.75 £17.50 £35.00
11-20 $6.50 $20.00 $40.00 £4.15 £12.50 £25.00
21-40 $4.15 $12.50 $25.00 £2.50 £7.50 £15.00
41-57 $3.30 $10.00 $20.00 £2.05 £6.25 £12.50
Title Value: $303.85 $920.00 $1835.00 £193.10 £585.25 £1182.50
Note: Magic Agent in #35,36,48,50,52,54,56

UNKNOWN WORLDS OF FRANK BRUNNER
Eclipse,MS; 1,2 Aug 1985
1-2 ND reprints in colour
$0.40 $1.20 $2.00 £0.25 £0.75 £1.25
Title Value: $0.80 $2.40 $4.00 £0.50 £1.50 £2.50

UNKNOWN WORLDS OF SCIENCE FICTION
Marvel Comics Group,Magazine; 1 Jan 1975-6 Nov 1975
1 ND 80pgs, squarebound, scarce; Neal Adams, Williamson, Wood, Kaluta, Brunner reprints
$1.00 $3.00 $5.00 £0.80 £2.40 £4.00
2 ND 80pgs, squarebound, George Perez and Mike Kaluta art featured, Kaluta cover ("Two Jima" theme)
$0.80 $2.40 $4.00 £0.50 £1.50 £2.50
3 ND 80pgs, squarebound, George Perez and Alex Nino art featured
$0.80 $2.40 $4.00 £0.50 £1.50 £2.50
4 ND 80pgs, squarebound, Corben art featured, Frank Brunner cover
$0.80 $2.40 $4.00 £0.50 £1.50 £2.50
5 ND 72pgs, Howard Chaykin and Gray Morrow art featured
$0.80 $2.40 $4.00 £0.50 £1.50 £2.50
6 ND 72pgs, Alex Nino and Gene Colan art featured, Frank Brunner cover
$0.80 $2.40 $4.00 £0.50 £1.50 £2.50
Title Value: $5.00 $15.00 $25.00 £3.30 £9.90 £16.50
ARTISTS
Brunner art in 2-4. Nino art in 3-6. Perez art in 2, 3.

UNKNOWN WORLDS OF SCIENCE FICTION SPECIAL
Marvel Comics Group,Magazine; 1 1976
1 ND scarce in the U.K. 96pgs, all reprint featuring Buscema, Giordano, Nino art
$0.80 $2.40 $4.00 £0.50 £1.50 £2.50
Title Value: $0.80 $2.40 $4.00 £0.50 £1.50 £2.50

UNLEASHED
Triumphant Comics,OS; 1 Nov 1993
1 ND serially numbered at top of page; promotional giveaway to introduce the "Unleashed" X-over story
$0.40 $1.20 $2.00 £0.25 £0.75 £1.25
1 ND $0.40 $1.20 $2.00 £0.25 £0.75 £1.25
Title Value: $0.80 $2.40 $4.00 £0.50 £1.50 £2.50

UNSUPERVISED EXISTENCE
Fantagraphics; 1 1990-7 1992?
1-7 ND $0.50 $1.50 $2.50 £0.30 £0.90 £1.50
Title Value: $3.50 $10.50 $17.50 £2.10 £6.30 £10.50

UNTAMED
Marvel Comics Group/Epic,MS; 1 Jun 1993-3 Aug 1993
1-3 ND Neil Hansen script and art
$0.40 $1.20 $2.00 £0.25 £0.75 £1.25
Title Value: $1.20 $3.60 $6.00 £0.75 £2.25 £3.75

UNTAMED LOVE
Fantagraphics; 1 Nov 1987
(see Thun'da Tales)
1 ND Frank Frazetta reprints

	$Good	$Fine	$N.Mint	£Good	£Fine	£N.Mint
Title Value:	$0.40	$1.20	$2.00	£0.25	£0.75	£1.25
Title Value:	$0.40	$1.20	$2.00	£0.25	£0.75	£1.25

UNTOLD LEGEND OF THE BATMAN
(see Batman: Untold Legend of The)

UNTOUCHABLES
Eastern; 1 1988-8 1988

	$Good	$Fine	$N.Mint	£Good	£Fine	£N.Mint
1-8 ND 20pgs	$0.25	$0.75	$1.25	£0.15	£0.45	£0.75
Title Value:	$2.00	$6.00	$10.00	£1.20	£3.60	£6.00

UNUSUAL TALES
Charlton; 1 Nov 1955-49 Mar/Apr 1965
(becomes Blue Beetle #50-54)

	$Good	$Fine	$N.Mint	£Good	£Fine	£N.Mint
1 scarce in the U.K.	$18.50	$55.00	$130.00	£12.50	£39.00	£90.00
2 scarce in the U.K.	$10.00	$30.00	$70.00	£6.25	£19.00	£45.00
3-5 scarce in the U.K.	$5.50	$17.00	$40.00	£3.55	£10.50	£25.00
6 Steve Ditko cover art	$8.50	$26.00	$60.00	£5.50	£17.00	£40.00
7-10 Steve Ditko art	$17.00	$50.00	$120.00	£11.00	£34.00	£80.00
11 scarce in the U.K. 68pgs, Steve Ditko art	$18.50	$55.00	$130.00	£12.00	£36.00	£85.00
12 Steve Ditko art	$12.50	$39.00	$90.00	£8.50	£26.00	£60.00
13	$4.25	$12.50	$30.00	£2.85	£8.50	£20.00
14-15 Steve Ditko art	$12.50	$39.00	$90.00	£8.50	£26.00	£60.00
16-17	$4.25	$12.50	$30.00	£2.85	£8.50	£20.00
1st official distribution in the U.K.						
18-20	$4.25	$12.50	$30.00	£2.85	£8.50	£20.00
21	$3.55	$10.50	$25.00	£2.10	£6.25	£15.00
22 Steve Ditko art	$8.50	$26.00	$60.00	£5.50	£17.00	£40.00
23 Steve Ditko cover art	$6.25	$19.00	$45.00	£4.25	£12.50	£30.00
24	$3.55	$10.50	$25.00	£2.10	£6.25	£15.00
25-27 Steve Ditko art	$8.50	$26.00	$60.00	£5.50	£17.00	£40.00
28	$3.55	$10.50	$25.00	£2.10	£6.25	£15.00
29 Steve Ditko art	$8.50	$26.00	$60.00	£5.50	£17.00	£40.00
30	$3.55	$10.50	$25.00	£2.10	£6.25	£15.00
31-49	$3.20	$9.50	$22.50	£1.75	£5.25	£12.50
Title Value:	$326.75	$980.50	$2290.00	£206.90	£629.75	£1482.50

URBAN DECAY
Anubis Press,MS; 0 Jul 1994; 1 Jan 1994-4 Apr 1994

	$Good	$Fine	$N.Mint	£Good	£Fine	£N.Mint
0 ND (Jul 1994) chromatix enhanced cover	$0.50	$1.50	$2.50	£0.30	£0.90	£1.50
0 ND Ashcan Edition (Sep 1994) - 5,000 copies, black and white	$0.60	$1.80	$3.00	£0.40	£1.20	£2.00
1 ND Mark Texeira painted cover; b/w poster at centre-fold	$0.50	$1.50	$2.50	£0.30	£0.90	£1.50
1 ND Ash Can Edition (Jan 1994)	$0.60	$1.80	$3.00	£0.40	£1.20	£2.00
2-4 ND	$0.50	$1.50	$2.50	£0.30	£0.90	£1.50
Title Value:	$3.70	$11.10	$18.50	£2.30	£6.90	£11.50

URBAN DECAY: CYBERJOCK
Anubis Press,OS; 1 Jul 1994

	$Good	$Fine	$N.Mint	£Good	£Fine	£N.Mint
1 ND black and white	$0.40	$1.20	$2.00	£0.25	£0.75	£1.25
Title Value:	$0.40	$1.20	$2.00	£0.25	£0.75	£1.25

URBAN DECAY: FORK
Anubis Press; 0 Oct 1994; 1 Dec 1994

	$Good	$Fine	$N.Mint	£Good	£Fine	£N.Mint
0 ND black and white	$0.50	$1.50	$2.50	£0.30	£0.90	£1.50
1 ND black and white	$0.40	$1.20	$2.00	£0.25	£0.75	£1.25
Title Value:	$0.90	$2.70	$4.50	£0.55	£1.65	£2.75

URBAN DECAY: KILLZONE
Anubis Press,OS; 1 Jan 1995

	$Good	$Fine	$N.Mint	£Good	£Fine	£N.Mint
1 ND black and white	$0.40	$1.20	$2.00	£0.25	£0.75	£1.25
Title Value:	$0.40	$1.20	$2.00	£0.25	£0.75	£1.25

URBAN DECAY: KILLZONE ASHCAN EDITION
Anubis Press,OS; nn Aug 1994

	$Good	$Fine	$N.Mint	£Good	£Fine	£N.Mint
1 ND black and white	$0.50	$1.50	$2.50	£0.30	£0.90	£1.50
Title Value:	$0.50	$1.50	$2.50	£0.30	£0.90	£1.50

URBAN DECAY: ZERO JOE
Anubis Press; 0 Feb 1995

	$Good	$Fine	$N.Mint	£Good	£Fine	£N.Mint
0 ND black and white	$0.50	$1.50	$2.50	£0.30	£0.90	£1.50
Title Value:	$0.50	$1.50	$2.50	£0.30	£0.90	£1.50

URBAN LEGENDS
Dark Horse; 1 Jun 1993

	$Good	$Fine	$N.Mint	£Good	£Fine	£N.Mint
1 ND humour anthology, Dan Clowes cover	$0.60	$1.80	$3.00	£0.40	£1.20	£2.00
Title Value:	$0.60	$1.80	$3.00	£0.40	£1.20	£2.00

URTH 4
Continuity; 1 1990-7 1991

	$Good	$Fine	$N.Mint	£Good	£Fine	£N.Mint
1-7 ND	$0.30	$0.90	$1.50	£0.20	£0.60	£1.00

	$Good	$Fine	$N.Mint	£Good	£Fine	£N.Mint
Title Value:	$2.10	$6.30	$10.50	£1.40	£4.20	£7.00

URTH 4 (2ND SERIES)
Continuity; 1 Sep 1992-4 1993
(see Earth 4)

	$Good	$Fine	$N.Mint	£Good	£Fine	£N.Mint
1 ND Neal Adams cover	$0.40	$1.20	$2.00	£0.25	£0.75	£1.25
2-4 ND	$0.40	$1.20	$2.00	£0.25	£0.75	£1.25
Title Value:	$1.60	$4.80	$8.00	£1.00	£3.00	£5.00

US 1
Marvel Comics Group,Toy; 1 May 1983-12 Oct 1984

	$Good	$Fine	$N.Mint	£Good	£Fine	£N.Mint
1-12 ND	$0.15	$0.45	$0.75	£0.10	£0.35	£0.60
Title Value:	$1.80	$5.40	$9.00	£1.20	£4.20	£7.20

US AIR FORCE COMICS
Charlton; 1 Oct 1958-37 Mar/Apr 1965
(becomes Army Attack 2nd Series)

	$Good	$Fine	$N.Mint	£Good	£Fine	£N.Mint
1 scarce in the U.K.	$5.00	$15.00	$35.00	£3.55	£10.50	£25.00
2	$2.55	$7.50	$18.00	£1.75	£5.25	£12.50
3-4	$2.10	$6.25	$15.00	£1.40	£4.25	£10.00
5-10	$1.75	$5.25	$12.50	£1.10	£3.40	£8.00
11-20	$1.05	$3.20	$7.50	£0.70	£2.10	£5.00
21-37	$0.80	$2.50	$5.00	£0.55	£1.75	£3.50
Title Value:	$46.35	$141.00	$318.00	£31.05	£95.40	£215.00

Note: all distributed on the newsstand in the U.K.

US FIGHTING AIR FORCE
IW Super; 9 1964

	$Good	$Fine	$N.Mint	£Good	£Fine	£N.Mint
9 reprints; distributed in the U.K.	$0.75	$2.25	$4.50	£0.50	£1.50	£3.00
Title Value:	$0.75	$2.25	$4.50	£0.50	£1.50	£3.00

USAGI YOJIMBO
Fantagraphics; 1 Jun 1987-38 1993
(see Critters)

	$Good	$Fine	$N.Mint	£Good	£Fine	£N.Mint
1 continues from Critters #14; black and white begins	$0.60	$1.80	$3.00	£0.40	£1.20	£2.00
1 2nd printing	$0.50	$1.50	$2.50	£0.30	£0.90	£1.50
2-9	$0.50	$1.50	$2.50	£0.30	£0.90	£1.50
10 Teenage Mutant Ninja Turtles appear	$0.50	$1.50	$2.50	£0.30	£0.90	£1.50
10 2nd printing	$0.40	$1.20	$2.00	£0.25	£0.75	£1.25
11-23	$0.40	$1.20	$2.00	£0.25	£0.75	£1.25
24 Lone Goat and Kid	$0.40	$1.20	$2.00	£0.25	£0.75	£1.25
25-32	$0.40	$1.20	$2.00	£0.25	£0.75	£1.25
33 Sergio Aragones script	$0.40	$1.20	$2.00	£0.25	£0.75	£1.25
34 $2.25 cover begins	$0.40	$1.20	$2.00	£0.25	£0.75	£1.25
35-38	$0.40	$1.20	$2.00	£0.25	£0.75	£1.25
Title Value:	$17.20	$51.60	$86.00	£10.65	£31.95	£53.25

Note: all Non-Distributed on the news-stands in the U.K.

	£Good	£Fine	£N.Mint
Book 1, reprints appearances prior to Usagi Yojimbo #1	£2.40	£7.20	£12.00
Book 1, 2nd,3rd prints	£2.00	£5.00	£10.00
4th print - Mar 1993	£1.60	£4.80	£8.00
Book 1 Hardcover	£5.00	£15.00	£25.00
Book 2, reprints issues #1-6	£1.30	£3.90	£6.50
Book 2 (2nd print - Nov 1991)	£1.25	£3.75	£6.25
Book 2 Hardcover (Nov 1991), signed and numbered (1,000 copies)	£4.50	£13.50	£22.50
Book 3, reprints issues #7-12	£1.30	£3.90	£6.50
2nd print (May 1995)	£1.80	£5.40	£9.00
Book 3 Hardcover (May 1995), signed and numbered (500 copies)	£5.00	£15.00	£25.00
Book 4, reprints issues #13-18	£1.30	£3.90	£6.50
Book 5 (Nov 1992), reprints issues #19-24	£1.30	£3.90	£6.50
Book 6, (Jul 1994), softcover	£1.70	£5.10	£8.50
Book 6, (Jul 1994), signed	£5.00	£15.00	£25.00
Color Special 1	£0.35	£1.05	£1.75
Color Special 1 - Special Edition (Jun 1990). New cover. 2,000 copies	£0.55	£1.65	£2.75

USAGI YOJIMBO COLOUR SPECIAL
Fantagraphics; 1 Nov 1989-3 1991

	$Good	$Fine	$N.Mint	£Good	£Fine	£N.Mint
1-3 ND 48pgs	$0.50	$1.50	$2.50	£0.30	£0.90	£1.50
Title Value:	$1.50	$4.50	$7.50	£0.90	£2.70	£4.50

USAGI YOJIMBO SUMMER SPECIAL
Fantagraphics; 1 Spring 1987

	$Good	$Fine	$N.Mint	£Good	£Fine	£N.Mint
1 ND scarce in the U.K. reprints from Albedo	$1.00	$3.00	$5.00	£0.60	£1.80	£3.00
Title Value:	$1.00	$3.00	$5.00	£0.60	£1.80	£3.00

USAGI YOJIMBO VOLUME TWO
Mirage Studios; 1 May 1993-present

	$Good	$Fine	$N.Mint	£Good	£Fine	£N.Mint
1-2 ND Teenage Mutant Ninja Turtles appear	$0.55	$1.65	$2.75	£0.35	£1.05	£1.75
3-16 ND	$0.55	$1.65	$2.75	£0.35	£1.05	£1.75
Title Value:	$8.80	$26.40	$44.00	£5.60	£16.80	£28.00

V

V
DC Comics, TV; 1 Feb 1985-18 Jul 1986

	$Good	$Fine	$N.Mint	£Good	£Fine	£N.Mint
1-18 based upon TV movie and series	$0.25	$0.75	$1.25	£0.15	£0.45	£0.75

	$Good	$Fine	$N.Mint	£Good	£Fine	£N.Mint
Title Value:	$4.50	$13.50	$22.50	£2.70	£8.10	£13.50

V FOR VENDETTA
DC Comics,MS; 1 Sep 1988-10 Apr 1989
1 ND David Lloyd art begins, Alan Moore script; reprints from British Warrior magazine

	$0.80	$2.40	$4.00	£0.50	£1.50	£2.50
2-3 very LD	$0.60	$1.80	$3.00	£0.40	£1.20	£2.00
4-6 ND	$0.50	$1.50	$2.50	£0.30	£0.90	£1.50

7 ND contains previously-unpublished story intended for cancelled Warrior magazine issue #27

	$0.50	$1.50	$2.50	£0.30	£0.90	£1.50

8-10 ND all new material

	$0.50	$1.50	$2.50	£0.30	£0.90	£1.50
Title Value:	$5.50	$16.50	$27.50	£3.40	£10.20	£17.00

Note: all Deluxe Format, Mature Readers
Trade paperback (Jul 1990),
288pgs, new cover painting and introduction by David Lloyd

				£1.90	£5.70	£9.50

VALENTINO
Renegade; 1 1985
1 ND

	$0.40	$1.20	$2.00	£0.25	£0.75	£1.25
Title Value:	$0.40	$1.20	$2.00	£0.25	£0.75	£1.25

VALENTINO TOO
Renegade,OS; 1 1987
1 ND

	$0.30	$0.90	$1.50	£0.20	£0.60	£1.00
Title Value:	$0.30	$0.90	$1.50	£0.20	£0.60	£1.00

VALERIA THE SHE-BAT
Continuity; 1 May 1993; 5 Nov 1993
1 ND script and art by Neal Adams, plastic acetate covers; available only to retailers ordering sufficient quantities of Deathwatch 2000 titles for May cover date

	$3.00	$9.00	$15.00	£2.00	£6.00	£10.00

5 ND parchment embossed cover

	$0.60	$1.80	$3.00	£0.40	£1.20	£2.00
Title Value:	$3.60	$10.80	$18.00	£2.40	£7.20	£12.00

Note: issues #2-4 do not exist

VALERIA, THE SHE-BAT (2ND SERIES)
Acclaim Comics/Windjammer,MS; 1,2 Sep 1995
1-2 ND Neal Adams script and art with Peter Stone; reprints original series

	$0.50	$1.50	$2.50	£0.30	£0.90	£1.50
Title Value:	$1.00	$3.00	$5.00	£0.60	£1.80	£3.00

VALIANT ERA COLLECTION
Valiant,OS; nn 1994
1 ND Trade paperback reprinting Magnus #12, Shadowman #8, Solar #10,11, Eternal Warrior #4, 5. Pre-bagged with 8pg Valiant Era Special Edition

	$2.50	$7.50	$12.50	£1.50	£4.50	£7.50
Title Value:	$2.50	$7.50	$12.50	£1.50	£4.50	£7.50

VALIANT READER - A GUIDE TO THE VALIANT UNIVERSE
Valiant; 1 Sep 1993; 2 Oct 1994
1 ND a who's who of Valiant characters

	$0.25	$0.75	$1.25	£0.15	£0.45	£0.75

2 ND details title histories from the beginning

	$0.25	$0.75	$1.25	£0.15	£0.45	£0.75
Title Value:	$0.50	$1.50	$2.50	£0.30	£0.90	£1.50

VALIANT VISION STARTER KIT
Valiant,OS; 1 Jan 1994
1 ND 8pg comic, poster and glasses; a 3-D effect on a comic that can be read quite normally without the glasses

	$0.30	$0.90	$1.50	£0.20	£0.60	£1.00
Title Value:	$0.30	$0.90	$1.50	£0.20	£0.60	£1.00

VALIANT ZERO COLLECTION
Valiant; nn Apr 1995
1 ND Trade paperback, 112pgs. Reprints Magnus, Harbinger, X-O, Archer & Armstrong and Armorines #0 issues

	$2.00	$6.00	$10.00	£1.30	£3.90	£6.50
Title Value:	$2.00	$6.00	$10.00	£1.30	£3.90	£6.50

VALKYRIE
Eclipse,MS; 1 May 1987-3 Aug 1987
1 ND scarce in the U.K. Gulacy covers and art begin, colour; Air Fighters spin-off series

	$0.50	$1.50	$2.50	£0.30	£0.90	£1.50
2-3 ND	$0.40	$1.20	$2.00	£0.25	£0.75	£1.25
Title Value:	$1.30	$3.90	$6.50	£0.80	£2.40	£4.00

Prisoner of the Past (Dec 1987)
Trade paperback, reprints #1-3

				£1.10	£3.30	£5.50

VALKYRIE (2ND SERIES)
Eclipse,MS; 1 Jul 1988-3 Sep 1988
1-3 ND Brent Anderson art; Air Fighters spin-off series, colour

	$0.40	$1.20	$2.00	£0.25	£0.75	£1.25
Title Value:	$1.20	$3.60	$6.00	£0.75	£2.25	£3.75

VALKYRIE!
Ken Pierce; nn 1982
nn ND 84pgs, Trade paperback; Golden Age reprints from Airfighters and Airboy

	$1.50	$4.50	$7.50	£1.00	£3.00	£5.00
Title Value:	$1.50	$4.50	$7.50	£1.00	£3.00	£5.00

VALLEY OF THE GWANGI
Dell; 01-880-912 Dec 1969
01-880-912 photo cover from film; distributed in the U.K. though thought to be sporadic in areas

	$12.50	$38.00	$75.00	£8.25	£25.00	£50.00
Title Value:	$12.50	$38.00	$75.00	£8.25	£25.00	£50.00

VALOR
DC Comics; 1 Nov 1992-23 Sep 1994
1 Eclipso: The Darkness Within spin-off begins with the former Mon-El

	$0.25	$0.75	$1.25	£0.15	£0.45	£0.75

2 Supergirl appears

	$0.25	$0.75	$1.25	£0.15	£0.45	£0.75
3-4 Lobo appears	$0.25	$0.75	$1.25	£0.15	£0.45	£0.75
5-7	$0.25	$0.75	$1.25	£0.15	£0.45	£0.75

8 Adam Hughes cover

	$0.25	$0.75	$1.25	£0.15	£0.45	£0.75

9 Adam Hughes cover, Darkstar appears

	$0.25	$0.75	$1.25	£0.15	£0.45	£0.75

10 Adam Hughes cover

	$0.25	$0.75	$1.25	£0.15	£0.45	£0.75

11 Adam Hughes cover, new direction for title

	$0.25	$0.75	$1.25	£0.15	£0.45	£0.75

12 Adam Hughes cover

	$0.25	$0.75	$1.25	£0.15	£0.45	£0.75
13-16	$0.25	$0.75	$1.25	£0.15	£0.45	£0.75
17 Valor "dies"; prelude to Zero Hour mini-series						
	$0.25	$0.75	$1.25	£0.15	£0.45	£0.75
18-21	$0.25	$0.75	$1.25	£0.15	£0.45	£0.75

22 End of an Era part 2, continued in Legion of Super-Heroes #60

	$0.25	$0.75	$1.25	£0.15	£0.45	£0.75

23 Zero Hour X-over; End of an Era part 5, continued in Legion of Super-Heroes #61

	$0.30	$0.90	$1.50	£0.20	£0.60	£1.00
Title Value:	$5.80	$17.40	$29.00	£3.50	£10.50	£17.50

VAMPEROTICA
Brainstorm Comics; 1 1995-present
1 ND adult material; black and white

	$1.20	$3.60	$6.00	£0.80	£2.40	£4.00

2 ND adult material; black and white

	$1.00	$3.00	$5.00	£0.60	£1.80	£3.00

3-6 ND adult material; black and white

	$0.60	$1.80	$3.00	£0.40	£1.20	£2.00
Title Value:	$4.60	$13.80	$23.00	£3.00	£9.00	£15.00

VAMPIRE COMPANION, THE
Innovation; 1 Jan 1991-4 1992

Unknown Worlds #56

Urban Decay #1

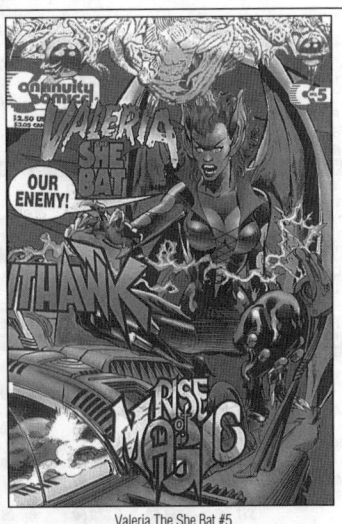

Valeria The She Bat #5

MINT = 100% / NEAR MINT (inc. +/-) = 90–99% / VERY FINE (inc. +/-) = 75–89% / FINE (inc. +/-) = 55–74%
VERY GOOD (inc. +/-) = 35–54% / GOOD (inc. +/-) = 15–34% / FAIR = 5–14% / POOR = 1–4%

619

	$Good	$Fine	$N.Mint	£Good	£Fine	£N.Mint
1 ND articles/interview with Anne Rice						
	$0.60	$1.80	$3.00	£0.40	£1.20	£2.00
2-3 ND	$0.60	$1.80	$3.00	£0.40	£1.20	£2.00
4 ND John Bolton cover						
	$0.60	$1.80	$3.00	£0.40	£1.20	£2.00
Title Value:	$2.40	$7.20	$12.00	£1.60	£4.80	£8.00

VAMPIRE LESTAT, THE
Innovation,MS; 1 Jan 1990-12 Aug 1991
(see The Mummy)

	$Good	$Fine	$N.Mint	£Good	£Fine	£N.Mint
1 ND John Bolton covers begin						
	$4.50	$13.50	$22.50	£3.00	£9.00	£15.00
1 2nd printing ND	$0.80	$2.40	$4.00	£0.50	£1.50	£2.50
1 3rd printing ND	$0.60	$1.80	$3.00	£0.40	£1.20	£2.00
1 4th printing ND	$0.40	$1.20	$2.00	£0.25	£0.75	£1.25
2 ND	$3.00	$9.00	$15.00	£2.00	£6.00	£10.00
2 2nd printing ND	$0.80	$2.40	$4.00	£0.50	£1.50	£2.50
2 3rd printing ND	$0.40	$1.20	$2.00	£0.25	£0.75	£1.25
3 ND	$1.50	$4.50	$7.50	£1.00	£3.00	£5.00
3 2nd printing ND	$0.60	$1.80	$3.00	£0.40	£1.20	£2.00
4 ND	$1.20	$3.60	$6.00	£0.80	£2.40	£4.00
4 2nd printing ND	$0.50	$1.50	$2.50	£0.30	£0.90	£1.50
5 ND	$1.00	$3.00	$5.00	£0.70	£2.10	£3.50
5 2nd printing ND	$0.50	$1.50	$2.50	£0.30	£0.90	£1.50
6-8 ND	$0.90	$2.70	$4.50	£0.60	£1.80	£3.00
9 ND many copies were damaged at the time of printing hence a 2nd print was issued						
	$0.90	$2.70	$4.50	£0.60	£1.80	£3.00
9 2nd printing, ND (Jan 1992)						
	$0.50	$1.50	$2.50	£0.30	£0.90	£1.50
10-12 ND	$0.90	$2.70	$4.50	£0.60	£1.80	£3.00
Title Value:	$22.60	$67.80	$113.00	£14.90	£44.70	£74.50

Note: John Bolton covers

	£Good	£Fine	£N.Mint
Vampire Lestat Softcover (Nov 1991), reprints maxi-series	£3.10	£9.30	15.50
Signed Edition (May 1993), signed in gold ink by Faye Perozich	£3.50	£10.50	17.50
Vampire Lestat Hardcover (Jan 1992), reprints maxi-series, (4,500 copies)	£5.00	£15.00	£25.00
Signed Edition (May 1993), signed in gold ink by Faye Perozich	£6.00	£18.00	£30.00
Slipcase Set (Oct 1991), 12 issues plus 2 Vampire Companions in gold-embossed slipcase (2,000)	£7.00	£21.00	£35.00

VAMPIRE MIYU
Antarctic Press,MS; 1 Oct 1995

	$Good	$Fine	$N.Mint	£Good	£Fine	£N.Mint
1 ND Narumi Kakinouchi script and art; black and white						
	$0.60	$1.80	$3.00	£0.40	£1.20	£2.00
Title Value:	$0.60	$1.80	$3.00	£0.40	£1.20	£2.00

VAMPIRE TALES
Marvel Comics Group,Magazine; 1 Aug 1973-11 Jun 1975

	$Good	$Fine	$N.Mint	£Good	£Fine	£N.Mint
1 ND 72pgs, Morbius begins by Don McGregor						
	$3.30	$10.00	$20.00	£1.65	£5.00	£10.00
2 ND 72pgs, Steranko reprint						
	$1.65	$5.00	$10.00	£1.00	£3.00	£6.00
3 scarce in the U.K. 72pgs, Satana appears, Infantino reprint						
	$1.00	$3.00	$6.00	£0.55	£1.75	£3.50
4 72pgs, Boris painted cover						
	$1.00	$3.00	$6.00	£0.50	£1.50	£3.00
5 scarce in the U.K. 72pgs, Gulacy and Chaykin art, origin Morbius retold with Gil Kane art						
	$1.25	$3.75	$7.50	£0.80	£2.50	£5.00
6 72pgs, Boris painted cover, Lilith Daughter of Dracula appears, Steve Gerber script						
	$0.80	$2.50	$5.00	£0.50	£1.50	£3.00
7 72pgs, Gulacy and Chaykin art featured						
	$0.80	$2.50	$5.00	£0.50	£1.50	£3.00
8 72pgs, 1st Joe Staton art for Marvel on a short story ("The Vendetta"), Blade the Vampire-Slayer appears						
	$0.80	$2.50	$5.00	£0.50	£1.50	£3.00
9 72pgs, Blade the Vampire-Slayer appears, Jesus Blasco art on a short story, Russ Heath art (5pgs)						
	$0.80	$2.50	$5.00	£0.50	£1.50	£3.00
10 72pgs, Gulacy art (1pg)						
	$0.80	$2.50	$5.00	£0.50	£1.50	£3.00
11 72pgs	$0.80	$2.50	$5.00	£0.50	£1.50	£3.00
Title Value:	$13.00	$39.75	$79.50	£7.50	£22.75	£45.50

FEATURES
Blade in 8,9,10. Lilith in 6. Morbius in 1-5, 7, 8, 10, 11.
Note: a next issue was advertised but never appeared.

VAMPIRE TALES ANNUAL
Marvel Comics Group,Magazine; 1 Summer 1975

	$Good	$Fine	$N.Mint	£Good	£Fine	£N.Mint
1 ND 88pgs, squarebound, all reprint featuring Russ Heath art						
	$0.80	$2.50	$5.00	£0.55	£1.75	£3.50
Title Value:	$0.80	$2.50	$5.00	£0.55	£1.75	£3.50

VAMPIRE VERSES
Cry For Dawn; 1 Aug 1995

	$Good	$Fine	$N.Mint	£Good	£Fine	£N.Mint
1 ND 40pgs, Mike Bliss script, Frank Forte art; black and white						
	$0.60	$1.80	$3.00	£0.40	£1.20	£2.00
Title Value:	$0.60	$1.80	$3.00	£0.40	£1.20	£2.00

VAMPIRELLA
Warren; 1 Sep 1969-112 Sep 1983; 113 Jan 1988

	$Good	$Fine	$N.Mint	£Good	£Fine	£N.Mint
1 ND Neal Adams art						
	$50.00	$150.00	$350.00	£29.00	£85.00	£200.00
2 distributed in the U.K.						
	$21.00	$62.50	$150.00	£12.50	£39.00	£90.00
3 ND rare in the U.K.						
	$50.00	$150.00	$300.00	£30.00	£90.00	£180.00
4-5 ND	$12.00	$36.00	$85.00	£7.00	£21.00	£50.00
6 distributed in the U.K.						
	$11.00	$34.00	$80.00	£6.25	£19.00	£45.00
7 ND	$12.00	$36.00	$85.00	£7.00	£21.00	£50.00
8 ND Vampirella begins						
	$12.00	$36.00	$85.00	£7.00	£21.00	£50.00
9 ND Barry Windsor Smith art						
	$10.00	$30.00	$70.00	£6.25	£19.00	£45.00
10 ND Neal Adams art, no Vampirella story						
	$5.75	$17.50	$35.00	£4.15	£12.50	£25.00
11-15 ND	$8.25	$25.00	$50.00	£5.00	£15.00	£30.00
16-18 ND	$5.75	$17.50	$35.00	£4.15	£12.50	£25.00
19 ND 1973 Annual						
	$7.50	$22.50	$45.00	£5.00	£15.00	£30.00
20 ND	$5.75	$17.50	$35.00	£4.15	£12.50	£25.00
21-25 ND	$5.00	$15.00	$30.00	£3.30	£10.00	£20.00
26 ND	$4.15	$12.50	$25.00	£2.90	£8.75	£17.50
27 ND 1974 Annual						
	$5.00	$15.00	$30.00	£3.30	£10.00	£20.00
28-30 ND	$4.15	$12.50	$25.00	£2.90	£8.75	£17.50
31-36 ND	$3.75	$11.00	$22.50	£2.50	£7.50	£15.00
37 ND 1975 Annual						
	$4.15	$12.50	$25.00	£2.90	£8.75	£17.50
38-40 ND	$3.75	$11.00	$22.50	£2.50	£7.50	£15.00
41-45 ND	$3.30	$10.00	$20.00	£2.05	£6.25	£12.50
46 ND origin retold						
	$3.75	$11.00	$22.50	£2.50	£7.50	£15.00
47-49 ND	$3.30	$10.00	$20.00	£2.05	£6.25	£12.50
50 ND Spirit appears						
	$3.30	$10.00	$20.00	£2.05	£6.25	£12.50
51-60 ND	$2.50	$7.50	$15.00	£1.65	£5.00	£10.00
61-70 ND	$2.05	$6.25	$12.50	£1.25	£3.75	£7.50
71-99 ND	$1.65	$5.00	$10.00	£0.80	£2.50	£5.00
100 ND origin retold						
	$5.00	$15.00	$30.00	£1.65	£5.00	£10.00
101-112 ND	$3.30	$10.00	$20.00	£0.80	£2.50	£5.00
113 very scarce in the U.K., scarce in the U.S.						
	$20.00	$60.00	$120.00	£11.50	£35.00	£70.00
Title Value:	$543.40	$1635.50	$3425.00	£315.45	£953.50	£1995.00

Note also: while it is known for sure that issues #2 and #6 were distributed on the news-stands in the U.K. it could be that some or many more issues were, even if in limited quantities

VAMPIRELLA (2ND SERIES)
Harris Publications/Dark Horse,MS; 1 Nov 1991-4 Jun 1992

	$Good	$Fine	$N.Mint	£Good	£Fine	£N.Mint
1-4 ND Mike Kaluta covers						
	$1.00	$3.00	$5.00	£0.70	£2.10	£3.50
Title Value:	$4.00	$12.00	$20.00	£2.80	£8.40	£14.00
Vampirella (Feb 1994)						
Trade paperback reprints issues #1-4				£0.80	£2.40	£4.00

VAMPIRELLA (3RD SERIES)
Harris Comics,MS; 0 Dec 1994; 1 Nov 1992-5 Nov 1993

	$Good	$Fine	$N.Mint	£Good	£Fine	£N.Mint
0 ND story bridges the gap between "Morning in America" and "Dracula War"						
	$0.90	$2.70	$4.50	£0.60	£1.80	£3.00
0 ND (May 1995) Signed and Numbered Edition - pre-bagged in mylar with certificate; 2,500 copies						
	$3.00	$9.00	$15.00	£2.00	£6.00	£10.00
0 Gold Edition ND	$8.00	$24.00	$40.00	£4.00	£12.00	£20.00
1 ND Adam Hughes cover; coupons begin for limited poster (ends #6)						
	$8.00	$24.00	$40.00	£5.00	£15.00	£25.00
1 2nd printing, ND Jun 1993						
	$1.50	$4.50	$7.50	£1.00	£3.00	£5.00
2 ND Adam Hughes cover						
	$6.00	$18.00	$30.00	£3.50	£10.50	£17.50
3 ND	$3.00	$9.00	$15.00	£2.50	£7.50	£12.50
4-5 ND	$2.50	$7.50	$12.50	£2.00	£6.00	£10.00
Title Value:	$35.40	$106.20	$174.50	£22.60	£67.80	£113.00

VAMPIRELLA ANNUAL
Warren; 1 1972

	$Good	$Fine	$N.Mint	£Good	£Fine	£N.Mint
1 scarce in the U.K. partly reprint; thought to be distributed in the U.K.						
	$26.00	$75.00	$180.00	£14.00	£43.00	£100.00
Title Value:	$26.00	$75.00	$180.00	£14.00	£43.00	£100.00

VAMPIRELLA CLASSIC
Harris Comics; 1 Feb 1995-5 Nov 1995

	$Good	$Fine	$N.Mint	£Good	£Fine	£N.Mint
1 ND classic Vampirella stories reprinted in colour; reprint of Frank Frazetta's cover to the original Vampirella Magazine #1						
	$0.60	$1.80	$3.00	£0.40	£1.20	£2.00
2-5 ND	$0.60	$1.80	$3.00	£0.40	£1.20	£2.00
Title Value:	$3.00	$9.00	$15.00	£2.00	£6.00	£10.00

VAMPIRELLA SPECIAL
Warren; nn 1977

	$Good	$Fine	$N.Mint	£Good	£Fine	£N.Mint
nn ND reprints in colour; thought to be distributed in the U.K.						
	$5.00	$15.00	$30.00	£3.30	£10.00	£20.00
Title Value:	$5.00	$15.00	$30.00	£3.30	£10.00	£20.00

VAMPIRELLA STRIKES
Harris Comics; 1 Oct 1995-present

	$Good	$Fine	$N.Mint	£Good	£Fine	£N.Mint
1 ND photo cover	$0.60	$1.80	$3.00	£0.40	£1.20	£2.00
1 ND Signed, Numbered Edition (Oct 1995); pre-bagged with certificate - 1,500 copies						
	$4.00	$12.00	$20.00	£2.50	£7.50	£12.50
1 Variant cover, ND features a different photo cover of Vampirella						
	$2.50	$7.50	$12.50	£1.50	£4.50	£7.50
2 ND Mike Deodato Jnr cover art						
	$0.60	$1.80	$3.00	£0.40	£1.20	£2.00
Title Value:	$7.70	$23.10	$38.50	£4.80	£14.40	£24.00

VAMPIRELLA'S SUMMER NIGHTS
Dark Horse/Harris Publications,OS; 1 Oct 1992

	$Good	$Fine	$N.Mint	£Good	£Fine	£N.Mint
1 ND 48pgs	$0.80	$2.40	$4.00	£0.50	£1.50	£2.50
Title Value:	$0.80	$2.40	$4.00	£0.50	£1.50	£2.50

	$Good	$Fine	$N.Mint	£Good	£Fine	£N.Mint

VAMPIRELLA, VENGEANCE OF
Harris Comics; 1 Feb 1994-25 Apr 1996
1 ND Joe Quesada and Jimmy Palmiotti wraparound foil cover

	$5.00	$15.00	$25.00	£3.00	£9.00	£15.00

1 2nd printing, ND Joe Quesada and Jimmy Palmiotti wraparound foil cover (Jun 1994)

	$2.00	$6.00	$10.00	£1.40	£4.20	£7.00
1 Gold Edition ND	$8.00	$24.00	$40.00	£4.50	£13.50	£22.50
2 ND	$2.50	$7.50	$12.50	£1.60	£4.80	£8.00
3-4 ND	$1.50	$4.50	$7.50	£1.00	£3.00	£5.00
5 ND	$1.20	$3.60	$6.00	£0.80	£2.40	£4.00
6 ND	$1.00	$3.00	$5.00	£0.70	£2.10	£3.50
7 ND	$0.90	$2.70	$4.50	£0.60	£1.80	£3.00

8 ND pre-bagged with Vampirella trading card

| | $0.90 | $2.70 | $4.50 | £0.60 | £1.80 | £3.00 |
| 9-10 ND | $0.80 | $2.40 | $4.00 | £0.50 | £1.50 | £2.50 |

11 ND pre-bagged with chase card

| | $0.60 | $1.80 | $3.00 | £0.40 | £1.20 | £2.00 |
| 12-13 ND | $0.60 | $1.80 | $3.00 | £0.40 | £1.20 | £2.00 |

14 ND The Mystery Walk; Vampirella's "secret" origin story begins; giant pull-out poster

| | $0.60 | $1.80 | $3.00 | £0.40 | £1.20 | £2.00 |

14 Variant cover, ND Buzz art on cover, received for every 25 copies of the regular issue ordered

| | $5.00 | $15.00 | $25.00 | £3.00 | £9.00 | £15.00 |
| 15 ND | $0.60 | $1.80 | $3.00 | £0.40 | £1.20 | £2.00 |

15 Variant cover, ND Buzz art on cover, received for every 25 copies of the regular issue ordered

| | $5.00 | $15.00 | $25.00 | £3.00 | £9.00 | £15.00 |
| 16 ND | $0.60 | $1.80 | $3.00 | £0.40 | £1.20 | £2.00 |

16 Variant cover, ND Buzz art on cover, received for every 25 copies of the regular issue ordered

| | $5.00 | $15.00 | $25.00 | £3.00 | £9.00 | £15.00 |
| 17 ND | $0.60 | $1.80 | $3.00 | £0.40 | £1.20 | £2.00 |

17 Variant cover, ND Buzz art on cover, received for every 25 copies of the regular issue ordered

| | $5.00 | $15.00 | $25.00 | £3.00 | £9.00 | £15.00 |
| 18 ND | $0.60 | $1.80 | $3.00 | £0.40 | £1.20 | £2.00 |

18 Variant cover, ND Buzz art on cover, received for every 25 copies of the regular issue ordered

| | $5.00 | $15.00 | $25.00 | £3.00 | £9.00 | £15.00 |
| 19 ND | $0.60 | $1.80 | $3.00 | £0.40 | £1.20 | £2.00 |

19 Variant cover, ND Buzz art on cover, received for every 25 copies of the regular issue ordered

	$5.00	$15.00	$25.00	£3.00	£9.00	£15.00
20-22 ND	$0.60	$1.80	$3.00	£0.40	£1.20	£2.00
Title Value:	$63.30	$189.90	$316.50	£39.00	£117.00	£195.00

VAMPIRELLA/SHADOWHAWK
(see Shadowhawk/Vampirella)

VAMPIRELLA: THE CULT OF CHAOS TRADE PAPERBACK
Dark Horse,OS; 1 Sep 1991
1 ND 142pgs, all reprint, new cover by Jim Steranko

| | $2.50 | $7.50 | $12.50 | £1.50 | £4.50 | £7.50 |
| Title Value: | $2.50 | $7.50 | $12.50 | £1.50 | £4.50 | £7.50 |

VAMPIRELLA: TRANSCENDING TIME & SPACE TRADE PAPERBACK
Harris Comics,OS; nn 1994
nn ND 148pgs, black and white; reprints from original Vampirella series issues #17-23 with new cover by Dave Stevens

| | $2.50 | $7.50 | $12.50 | £1.70 | £5.00 | £8.50 |

nn 2nd printing, ND (Jan 1995)

| | $2.50 | $7.50 | $12.50 | £1.70 | £5.00 | £8.50 |
| Title Value: | $5.00 | $15.00 | $25.00 | £3.40 | £10.00 | £17.00 |

VAMPS
DC Comics/Vertigo,MS; 1 Aug 1994-6 Jan 1995
1 Brian Bolland covers begin

	$0.80	$2.40	$4.00	£0.50	£1.50	£2.50
2-6	$0.60	$1.80	$3.00	£0.40	£1.20	£2.00
Title Value:	$3.80	$11.40	$19.00	£2.50	£7.50	£12.50

Vamps (Feb 1996) Trade paperback
reprints mini-series, new cover by William Simpson

| | | | | £1.30 | £3.90 | £6.50 |

VAMPS: HOLLYWOOD & VEIN
DC Comics/Vertigo,MS; 1 Feb 1996-present
1-2 ND Elaine Lee script, William Simpson art

| | $0.45 | $1.35 | $2.25 | £0.30 | £0.90 | £1.50 |
| Title Value: | $0.90 | $2.70 | $4.50 | £0.60 | £1.80 | £3.00 |

VAMPYRE'S KISS BOOK 1
Aircel,MS; 1 Jun 1990-4 Sep 1990
1-4 ND Barry Blair script/art; black and white

| | $0.50 | $1.50 | $2.50 | £0.30 | £0.90 | £1.50 |
| Title Value: | $2.00 | $6.00 | $10.00 | £1.20 | £3.60 | £6.00 |

Note: shipped pre-bagged. Issues 1,2 bi-weekly

| Book I Set (Jun 1991), issues 1-4 pre-bagged | | | | £1.10 | £3.30 | £5.50 |

VAMPYRE'S KISS BOOK 2
Aircel,MS; 1 Dec 1990-4 Mar 1991
1-4 ND Barry Blair script and art; black and white

| | $0.40 | $1.20 | $2.00 | £0.25 | £0.75 | £1.25 |
| Title Value: | $1.60 | $4.80 | $8.00 | £1.00 | £3.00 | £5.00 |

VAMPYRE'S KISS BOOK 3
Aircel/Blair Grafix Productions,MS; 1 Oct 1991-4 Jan 1992
1-4 ND Barry Blair script and art; black and white

| | $0.40 | $1.20 | $2.00 | £0.25 | £0.75 | £1.25 |
| Title Value: | $1.60 | $4.80 | $8.00 | £1.00 | £3.00 | £5.00 |

VAMPYRES
Eternity,MS; 1 Dec 1988-4 1989
1-4 ND black and white

| | $0.40 | $1.20 | $2.00 | £0.25 | £0.75 | £1.25 |
| Title Value: | $1.60 | $4.80 | $8.00 | £1.00 | £3.00 | £5.00 |

VAMPYRES GRAPHIC NOVEL
Eternity,OS; 1 Aug 1991
1 ND anthology of tales

| | $1.50 | $4.50 | $7.50 | £1.00 | £3.00 | £5.00 |
| Title Value: | $1.50 | $4.50 | $7.50 | £1.00 | £3.00 | £5.00 |

VANGUARD
Image; 1 Oct 1993-6 1994
(see Savage Dragon #2)
1 Erik Larsen co-creator; Tom Coker pencils, Jim Sinclair inks begin; gatefold cover. Supreme appears

| | $0.40 | $1.20 | $2.00 | £0.25 | £0.75 | £1.25 |
| 2-3 | $0.40 | $1.20 | $2.00 | £0.25 | £0.75 | £1.25 |

4 Berzerker back-up

| | $0.40 | $1.20 | $2.00 | £0.25 | £0.75 | £1.25 |

5 part Angel Medina art

	$0.40	$1.20	$2.00	£0.25	£0.75	£1.25
6	$0.40	$1.20	$2.00	£0.25	£0.75	£1.25
Title Value:	$2.40	$7.20	$12.00	£1.50	£4.50	£7.50

Note: all Non-Distributed on the news-stands in the U.K.

VANGUARD (2ND SERIES)
Image,MS; 1 Sep 1995-4 Dec 1995
1 ND intro Amok, Scot Eaton art

| | $0.50 | $1.50 | $2.50 | £0.30 | £0.90 | £1.50 |
| 2-3 ND | $0.50 | $1.50 | $2.50 | £0.30 | £0.90 | £1.50 |

4 ND most Image characters appear

| | $0.50 | $1.50 | $2.50 | £0.30 | £0.90 | £1.50 |
| Title Value: | $2.00 | $6.00 | $10.00 | £1.20 | £3.60 | £6.00 |

VANGUARD ILLUSTRATED
Pacific; 1 Nov 1983-7 Jul 1984
1 Legends of the Stargrazers with Tom Yeates art and cover; Mike Baron and Steve Rude back-up, Freakwave back-up by Milligan/McCarthy

| | $0.50 | $1.50 | $2.50 | £0.30 | £0.90 | £1.50 |

2 Legends of the Stargrazers with Tom Yeates art and cover; Mike Baron and Steve Rude back-up, Freakwave back-up by Milligan/McCarthy; Dave Stevens cover

| | $0.50 | $1.50 | $2.50 | £0.30 | £0.90 | £1.50 |

3 Mike Baron and Steve Rude story continues, Freakwave back-up by Milligan/McCarthy; Al Williamson cover

| | $0.50 | $1.50 | $2.50 | £0.30 | £0.90 | £1.50 |

4 Geary, Rude art, Paul Neary back-up/inks, Missing Man by Ditko pin-up page; Steve Rude cover

| | $0.50 | $1.50 | $2.50 | £0.30 | £0.90 | £1.50 |

5 Burchett, Geary art; Kaluta cover

| | $0.50 | $1.50 | $2.50 | £0.30 | £0.90 | £1.50 |

6 Peter Milligan story with George Freeman art, Perez art (4pg lead story)

| | $0.50 | $1.50 | $2.50 | £0.30 | £0.90 | £1.50 |

7 1st appearance Mr. Monster by Gilbert, Goldyn appears; Kaluta cover

| | $1.00 | $3.00 | $5.00 | £0.70 | £2.10 | £3.50 |
| Title Value: | $4.00 | $12.00 | $20.00 | £2.50 | £7.50 | £12.50 |

Note: all Non-Distributed on the news-stands in the U.K.

VANITY
Pacific; 1 Jun 1984-2 Aug 1984

| 1-2 ND colour | $0.30 | $0.90 | $1.50 | £0.20 | £0.60 | £1.00 |
| Title Value: | $0.60 | $1.80 | $3.00 | £0.40 | £1.20 | £2.00 |

VARMINTS
Blue Comet Press; 1 1987

| 1 ND | $0.40 | $1.20 | $2.00 | £0.25 | £0.75 | £1.25 |
| Title Value: | $0.40 | $1.20 | $2.00 | £0.25 | £0.75 | £1.25 |

VAULT OF EVIL
Marvel Comics Group; 1 Feb 1973-23 Nov 1975
1 ND horror reprints begin; Werewolf cover by Gil Kane

	$0.60	$1.80	$3.00	£0.40	£1.20	£2.00
2-22 ND	$0.50	$1.50	$2.50	£0.30	£0.90	£1.50
23	$0.50	$1.50	$2.50	£0.25	£0.75	£1.25
Title Value:	$11.60	$34.80	$58.00	£6.95	£20.85	£34.75

Note: Brunner covers on 3, 4.

VAULT OF HORROR
E.C. Comics; 12 Apr/May 1950-40 Dec/Jan 1954/55
(formerly War Against Crime #1-11)
12 very scarce in the U.K.

| | $425.00 | $1275.00 | $3400.00 | £280.00 | £840.00 | £2250.00 |

13 scarce in the U.K.

	$100.00	$300.00	$700.00	£67.50	£200.00	£475.00
14	$87.50	$265.00	$625.00	£60.00	£180.00	£425.00
15	$70.00	$210.00	$500.00	£48.00	£140.00	£335.00
16	$52.50	$160.00	$375.00	£36.00	£105.00	£250.00
17-20	$43.00	$125.00	$300.00	£29.00	£85.00	£200.00
21-26	$36.00	$105.00	$250.00	£25.00	£75.00	£175.00
27-28	$25.00	$75.00	$175.00	£17.00	£50.00	£120.00

29 Ray Bradbury adaptation

| | $25.00 | $75.00 | $175.00 | £17.00 | £50.00 | £120.00 |
| 30 | $25.00 | $75.00 | $175.00 | £17.00 | £50.00 | £120.00 |

31 Ray Bradbury adaptation

| | $25.00 | $75.00 | $175.00 | £17.00 | £50.00 | £120.00 |
| 32-36 | $25.00 | $75.00 | $175.00 | £17.00 | £50.00 | £120.00 |

37 1st appearance of Drusilla (Vampirella clone!)

| | $29.00 | $85.00 | $200.00 | £19.00 | £57.50 | £135.00 |
| 38-39 | $21.00 | $62.50 | $150.00 | £14.00 | £43.00 | £100.00 |

40 scarce in both US and UK

| | $29.00 | $85.00 | $200.00 | £19.00 | £57.50 | £135.00 |
| Title Value: | $1473.00 | $4385.00 | $10750.00 | £993.50 | £2956.00 | £7255.00 |

Note: all Non-Distributed on the news-stands in the U.K.

VAULT OF HORROR (2ND SERIES)
Gladstone; 1 Aug 1990-6 Jun 1991
1 DS reprints Vault of Horror #34, Haunt of Fear #1

| | $0.50 | $1.50 | $2.50 | £0.30 | £0.90 | £1.50 |

2 DS reprints Vault of Horror #27, Haunt of Fear #18

| | $0.50 | $1.50 | $2.50 | £0.30 | £0.90 | £1.50 |

3 DS reprints Vault of Horror #13, Haunt of Fear #22

	$Good	$Fine	$N.Mint	£Good	£Fine	£N.Mint
	$0.50	$1.50	$2.50	£0.30	£0.90	£1.50

4 DS reprints Vault of Horror #23, Haunt of Fear #13

	$0.50	$1.50	$2.50	£0.30	£0.90	£1.50

5 DS reprints Vault of Horror #19, Haunt of Fear #5

	$0.50	$1.50	$2.50	£0.30	£0.90	£1.50

6 DS reprints Vault of Horror #32, Weird Fantasy #6

	$0.50	$1.50	$2.50	£0.30	£0.90	£1.50
Title Value:	$3.00	$9.00	$15.00	£1.80	£5.40	£9.00

Note: issue #7 was advertised but never published.
Note also: all Non-Distributed on the news-stands in the U.K.

VAULT OF HORROR (3RD SERIES)
Russ Cochran/EC Comics; 1 Sep 1991-5 May 1992
1 reprints Vault of Horror #28, Weird Science #18

	$0.50	$1.50	$2.50	£0.30	£0.90	£1.50

2 reprints Vault of Horror #33, Weird Science #20

	$0.50	$1.50	$2.50	£0.30	£0.90	£1.50

3 reprints Vault of Horror #26, Weird Science #7

	$0.50	$1.50	$2.50	£0.30	£0.90	£1.50

4 reprints Vault of Horror #35, Weird Science #15

	$0.50	$1.50	$2.50	£0.30	£0.90	£1.50

5 reprints Vault of Horror #18, Weird Science #11

	$0.50	$1.50	$2.50	£0.30	£0.90	£1.50
Title Value:	$2.50	$7.50	$12.50	£1.50	£4.50	£7.50

Note: issues # 6 and 7 were advertised but never published.
Note also: all Non-Distributed on the news-stands in the U.K.

VAULT OF HORROR (4TH SERIES)
Russ Cochran/EC Comics; 1 Oct 1992-present
1 ND reprints begin from original 1950s EC series with exact cover and interior reproduction

	$0.40	$1.20	$2.00	£0.25	£0.75	£1.25
2-13 ND	$0.40	$1.20	$2.00	£0.25	£0.75	£1.25
Title Value:	$5.20	$15.60	$26.00	£3.25	£9.75	£16.25

Vault of Horror Annual #1 (Sep 1994)
reprints issues #1-5 with covers

				£1.20	£3.60	£6.00

Vault of Horror Annual #2 (Jan 1995)
reprints issues #6-10 with covers

				£1.20	£3.60	£6.00

VAULT OF SCREAMING HORROR
Fantaco; 1 Oct 1993
1 ND Gurchain Singh script and art

	$0.60	$1.80	$3.00	£0.40	£1.20	£2.00
Title Value:	$0.60	$1.80	$3.00	£0.40	£1.20	£2.00

VECTOR
Now Comics; 1 Jul 1986-3 Nov 1986
1-3 ND computer artwork

	$0.30	$0.90	$1.50	£0.20	£0.60	£1.00
Title Value:	$0.90	$2.70	$4.50	£0.60	£1.80	£3.00

VELOCITY
Eclipse; 1 1991-6 1991
1-6 ND Gary and Warren Pleece script/art

	$0.50	$1.50	$2.50	£0.30	£0.90	£1.50
Title Value:	$3.00	$9.00	$15.00	£1.80	£5.40	£9.00

VELOCITY
Image,MS; 1 Sep 1995-4 Dec 1995
1-3 ND Kurt Busiek script, Anthony Chun and Aaron Sowd art

	$0.50	$1.50	$2.50	£0.30	£0.90	£1.50
4 ND	$0.50	$1.50	$2.50	£0.30	£0.90	£1.50
Title Value:	$2.00	$6.00	$10.00	£1.20	£3.60	£6.00

VELVET
Adventure,MS; 1 Mar 1993-4 Jun 1993
1-4 ND	$0.40	$1.20	$2.00	£0.25	£0.75	£1.25
Title Value:	$1.60	$4.80	$8.00	£1.00	£3.00	£5.00

VENGEANCE SQUAD
Charlton; 1 Jul 1975-6 May 1976
1 distributed in the U.K.

	$0.40	$1.20	$2.00	£0.25	£0.75	£1.25

2 distributed in the U.K.

	$0.30	$0.90	$1.50	£0.20	£0.60	£1.00

3 scarce, distributed in the U.K.

	$0.30	$0.90	$1.50	£0.20	£0.75	£1.25

4-6 distributed in the U.K.

	$0.30	$0.90	$1.50	£0.20	£0.60	£1.00
Title Value:	$1.90	$5.70	$9.50	£1.30	£3.90	£6.50

Note: Michael Mauser backups by Staton in all

VENGER ROBO
Viz Communications,MS; 1 Jan 1994-7 Jul 1994
1-7 ND Go Nagi and Ken Ishikawa; black and white

	$0.50	$1.50	$2.50	£0.30	£0.90	£1.50
Title Value:	$3.50	$10.50	$17.50	£2.10	£6.30	£10.50

VENOM SUPER SIZE SPECIAL
Marvel Comics Group,OS; 1 Aug 1995
1 ND Planet of the Symbiotes part 3, continued in Spectacular Spiderman Super Size Special #1

	$0.80	$2.40	$4.00	£0.50	£1.50	£2.50
Title Value:	$0.80	$2.40	$4.00	£0.50	£1.50	£2.50

VENOM-DEATHTRAP: THE VAULT
Marvel Comics Group,OS; 1 May 1993
1 ND 64pgs, bookshelf format, Ron Lim cover and art; reprints Marvel Graphic Novel

	$1.40	$4.20	$7.00	£0.90	£2.70	£4.50
Title Value:	$1.40	$4.20	$7.00	£0.90	£2.70	£4.50

VENOM: ALONG CAME A SPIDER
Marvel Comics Group,MS; 1 Jan 1996-4 Apr 1996
1 ND 48pgs, Venom vs. the new Spiderman (Ben Reilly); Larry Hama script, Greg Luzniak art

	$0.60	$1.80	$3.00	£0.40	£1.20	£2.00
2-4 ND	$0.60	$1.80	$3.00	£0.40	£1.20	£2.00

Title Value:	$2.40	$7.20	$12.00	£1.60	£4.80	£8.00

VENOM: CARNAGE UNLEASHED
Marvel Comics Group,MS; 1 Apr 1995-4 Jul 1995
1-4 ND Venom vs. Carnage; card-stock cover

	$0.60	$1.80	$3.00	£0.40	£1.20	£2.00
Title Value:	$2.40	$7.20	$12.00	£1.60	£4.80	£8.00

VENOM: FUNERAL PYRE
Marvel Comics Group,MS; 1 Aug 1993-3 Oct 1993
1 ND Punisher guest-stars, bronze "flaming foil" holo-grafix cover

	$0.60	$1.80	$3.00	£0.40	£1.20	£2.00

2-3 ND Punisher guest-stars, card stock cover

	$0.60	$1.80	$3.00	£0.40	£1.20	£2.00
Title Value:	$1.80	$5.40	$9.00	£1.20	£3.60	£6.00

VENOM: LETHAL PROTECTOR
Marvel Comics Group,MS; 1 Feb 1993-6 Jul 1993
1 ND Spiderman appears, holo-grafix cover

	$1.00	$3.00	$5.00	£0.50	£1.50	£2.50

1 ND Gold Edition - gold foil cover, available from Diamond Distributors for every 100 copies ordered of #1

	$3.00	$9.00	$15.00	£2.00	£6.00	£10.00

1 ND Black Edition - a misprint of the regular edition; approx. 650 copies in circulation but forgeries are known. Value given here is a best an estimate rather than based on actual sales

	$20.00	$60.00	$100.00	£6.00	£18.00	£30.00

2-6 ND Spiderman appears

	$0.60	$1.80	$3.00	£0.40	£1.20	£2.00
Title Value:	$27.00	$81.00	$135.00	£10.50	£31.50	£52.50

Venom: Lethal Protector (Jul 1995)
Trade paperback reprints mini-series

				£2.00	£6.00	£10.00

VENOM: NIGHTS OF VENGEANCE
Marvel Comics Group,MS; 1 Aug 1994-4 Nov 1994
1 ND foil stamped neon ink cover, Ron Lim cover and art

	$0.60	$1.80	$3.00	£0.40	£1.20	£2.00
2-4 ND	$0.60	$1.80	$3.00	£0.40	£1.20	£2.00
Title Value:	$2.40	$7.20	$12.00	£1.60	£4.80	£8.00

VENOM: SEPARATION ANXIETY
Marvel Comics Group,MS; 1 Dec 1994-4 Mar 1995
1 ND multi-level embossed cover

	$0.60	$1.80	$3.00	£0.40	£1.20	£2.00

2-4 ND card-stock cover

	$0.60	$1.80	$3.00	£0.40	£1.20	£2.00
Title Value:	$2.40	$7.20	$12.00	£1.60	£4.80	£8.00

Venom: Separation Anxiety (Jan 1996)
Trade paperback reprints mini-series

				£1.30	£3.90	£6.50

VENOM: SINNER TAKES ALL
Marvel Comics Group,MS; 1 Sep 1995-5 Dec 1995
1-5 ND 48pgs, Larry Hama script, Greg Luzniak art; Venom vs. the new Sin-Eater

	$0.60	$1.80	$3.00	£0.40	£1.20	£2.00
Title Value:	$3.00	$9.00	$15.00	£2.00	£6.00	£10.00

VENOM: THE ENEMY WITHIN
Marvel Comics Group,MS; 1 Feb 1994-4 Apr 1994
1-3 ND Morbius and Demogoblin appear	$0.60	$1.80	$3.00	£0.40	£1.20	£2.00
Title Value:	$1.80	$5.40	$9.00	£1.20	£3.60	£6.00

VENOM: THE MACE
Marvel Comics Group,MS; 1 May 1994-3 Jul 1994
1-3 ND Carl Potts script and Liam Sharp art	$0.60	$1.80	$3.00	£0.40	£1.20	£2.00
Title Value:	$1.80	$5.40	$9.00	£1.20	£3.60	£6.00

VENOM: THE MADNESS
Marvel Comics Group,MS; 1 Nov 1993-3 Jan 1994
1 ND Ann Nocenti script and Kelley Jones art begin; embossed cover

	$0.60	$1.80	$3.00	£0.40	£1.20	£2.00
2-3	$0.60	$1.80	$3.00	£0.40	£1.20	£2.00
Title Value:	$1.80	$5.40	$9.00	£1.20	£3.60	£6.00

VENTURE
AC Comics; 1 1986-5 1987
1-4 ND	$0.40	$1.20	$2.00	£0.25	£0.75	£1.25

5 ND Cirocco, Nino art, Neal Adams cover

	$0.40	$1.20	$2.00	£0.25	£0.75	£1.25
Title Value:	$2.00	$6.00	$10.00	£1.25	£3.75	£6.25

VENUS WARS
Dark Horse; 1 Apr 1991-14 Apr 1992
1 ND Yoshikazu Yashuiko script/art begins, translated into English, black and white; 2 bound-in trading cards

	$0.40	$1.20	$2.00	£0.25	£0.75	£1.25
2-11 ND	$0.40	$1.20	$2.00	£0.25	£0.75	£1.25
12 ND 48pgs	$0.50	$1.50	$2.50	£0.30	£0.90	£1.50
13-14 ND	$0.40	$1.20	$2.00	£0.25	£0.75	£1.25
Title Value:	$5.70	$17.10	$28.50	£3.55	£10.65	£17.75

Venus Wars Vol. 1 (Sep 1993) Trade paperback
reprints series with painted cover by Yoshikazu Yashuiko

				£1.85	£5.55	£9.25

VENUS WARS II, THE
Dark Horse; 1 Jun 1992-15 Aug 1993
1 ND 48pgs	$0.50	$1.50	$2.50	£0.30	£0.90	£1.50
2-8 ND	$0.40	$1.20	$2.00	£0.25	£0.75	£1.25
9-12 ND 40pgs	$0.45	$1.35	$2.25	£0.30	£0.90	£1.50
13-15 ND 32pgs	$0.40	$1.20	$2.00	£0.25	£0.75	£1.25
Title Value:	$6.30	$18.90	$32.25	£4.00	£12.00	£20.00

VERDICT: THE ACOLYTE
Caliber Press,OS; 1 Aug 1992
1 ND reprints from Caliber Presents

	$0.60	$1.80	$3.00	£0.40	£1.20	£2.00
Title Value:	$0.60	$1.80	$3.00	£0.40	£1.20	£2.00

	$Good	$Fine	$N.Mint	£Good	£Fine	£N.Mint
VEROTIKA						
Verotik; 1 1995-present						
1 ND adult material						
	$2.00	$6.00	$10.00	£1.50	£4.50	£7.50
2 ND adult material						
	$1.40	$4.20	$7.00	£1.00	£3.00	£5.00
3-6 ND adult material						
	$0.80	$2.40	$4.00	£0.80	£2.40	£4.00
Title Value:	$6.60	$19.80	$33.00	£5.70	£17.10	£28.50
VERSION #1						
Dark Horse,MS; 1 Dec 1992-8 Jul 1993						
1-3 ND	$0.50	$1.50	$2.50	£0.30	£0.90	£1.50
4 ND 40pgs	$0.50	$1.50	$2.50	£0.35	£1.05	£1.75
5-8 ND	$0.50	$1.50	$2.50	£0.30	£0.90	£1.50
Title Value:	$4.00	$12.00	$20.00	£2.45	£7.35	£12.25
VERSION #2						
Dark Horse,MS; 1 Aug 1993-7 Feb 1994						
1-7 ND Hisashi Sakaguchi script and art						
	$0.50	$1.50	$2.50	£0.30	£0.90	£1.50
Title Value:	$3.50	$10.50	$17.50	£2.10	£6.30	£10.50
VERTIGO GALLERY: DREAMS AND NIGHTMARES						
DC Comics/Vertigo,OS; 1 Oct 1995						
1 ND pin-ups featuring past Vertigo characters, Dave McKean cover						
	$0.80	$2.40	$4.00	£0.50	£1.50	£2.50
Title Value:	$0.80	$2.40	$4.00	£0.50	£1.50	£2.50
VERTIGO JAM						
DC Comics/Vertigo,OS; 1 Aug 1993						
1 ND Sandman, Hellblazer, Shade, Animal Man, Doom Patrol, Kid Eternity stories						
	$0.80	$2.40	$4.00	£0.50	£1.50	£2.50
Title Value:	$0.80	$2.40	$4.00	£0.50	£1.50	£2.50
VERTIGO PREVIEW						
DC Comics,OS; 1 Jan 1993						
1 ND promo of Vertigo line of titles Sandman Mystery Theatre, Doom Patrol, Swamp Thing, Animal Man, Hellblazer and Shade						
	$0.30	$0.90	$1.50	£0.20	£0.60	£1.00
Title Value:	$0.30	$0.90	$1.50	£0.20	£0.60	£1.00
VERTIGO RAVE						
DC Comics,OS; 1 Nov 1994						
1 ND previews upcoming Vertigo titles for 1995						
	$0.25	$0.75	$1.25	£0.15	£0.45	£0.75
Title Value:	$0.25	$0.75	$1.25	£0.15	£0.45	£0.75
VERTIGO VOICES: THE EATERS						
DC Comics/Vertigo,OS; 1 Nov 1995						
1 ND 64pgs, Peter Milligan script, Dean Ormston cover and art						
	$1.00	$3.00	$5.00	£0.60	£1.80	£3.00
Title Value:	$1.00	$3.00	$5.00	£0.60	£1.80	£3.00
VERY BEST OF DENNIS THE MENACE, THE						
Marvel Comics Group,Digest; 1 Apr 1982-3 Aug 1982						
1-3 ND reprints	$0.25	$0.75	$1.25	£0.15	£0.45	£0.75
Title Value:	$0.75	$2.25	$3.75	£0.45	£1.35	£2.25
VERY BEST OF MARVEL TRADE PAPERBACK, THE						
Marvel Comics Group; nn Sep 1991						
nn reprints selected classic stories including Fantastic Four #5, Daredevil #7 and Spiderman #39/40						
	$2.50	$7.50	$12.50	£1.70	£5.00	£8.50
nn 2nd printing, Sep 1992						
	$2.40	$7.00	$12.00	£1.60	£4.80	£8.00
Title Value:	$4.90	$14.50	$24.50	£3.30	£9.80	£16.50
VIC AND BLOOD						
Mad Dog Graphics,MS; 1 Oct 1987-2 Feb 1988						
1-2 ND Harlan Ellison script, Richard Corben art						
	$0.50	$1.50	$2.50	£0.30	£0.90	£1.50

	$Good	$Fine	$N.Mint	£Good	£Fine	£N.Mint
Title Value:	$1.00	$3.00	$5.00	£0.60	£1.80	£3.00
VICKI						
Atlas; 1 Feb 1975-4 Jul 1975						
1 LD in the U.K.	$0.60	$1.80	$3.00	£0.40	£1.20	£2.00
2-4 LD in the U.K.	$0.50	$1.50	$2.50	£0.30	£0.90	£1.50
Title Value:	$2.10	$6.30	$10.50	£1.30	£3.90	£6.50
VICKI VALENTINE						
Renegade; 1 Jul 1985-4 1986						
1 ND Ellen Dolan, Mam'selle Poupee, Sophisticated Lady, Ms.Tree, Mike Mist, Rainbow, Amber cameos (1pg by Eisner, Valentino, Beatty, Meugniot); Deni Loubert appears						
	$0.30	$0.90	$1.50	£0.20	£0.60	£1.00
2-4 ND	$0.30	$0.90	$1.50	£0.20	£0.60	£1.00
Title Value:	$1.20	$3.60	$6.00	£0.80	£2.40	£4.00
VICTIMS						
Eternity; 1 Dec 1988-5 1989						
1-5 ND black and white reprints						
	$0.40	$1.20	$2.00	£0.25	£0.75	£1.25
Title Value:	$2.00	$6.00	$10.00	£1.25	£3.75	£6.25
VICTOR VECTOR & YONDO						
Fractal Comics; 1 Jul 1994-3 Sep 1994						
1-3 ND Ken Steacy script and art; based on CD-Rom characters						
	$0.40	$1.20	$2.00	£0.25	£0.75	£1.25
Title Value:	$1.20	$3.60	$6.00	£0.75	£2.25	£3.75
VICTORY						
Topps,MS; 1 Jun 1994-5 Oct 1994						
1-5 ND Jack Kirby characters return! Captain Victory, Lady Lightning, Lord Ghoast, Silverstar, Teenagants and Satan's Six						
	$0.40	$1.20	$2.00	£0.25	£0.75	£1.25
Title Value:	$2.00	$6.00	$10.00	£1.25	£3.75	£6.25
VIDEO JACK						
Marvel Comics Group/Epic,MS; 1 Nov 1987-6 Nov 1988						
1-6 ND Giffen art	$0.30	$0.90	$1.50	£0.20	£0.60	£1.00
Title Value:	$1.80	$5.40	$9.00	£1.20	£3.60	£6.00
VIETNAM JOURNAL						
Apple Comics; 1 Nov 1987-16 1989						
1 ND Don Lomax script/art begins						
	$0.40	$1.20	$2.00	£0.25	£0.75	£1.25
1 2nd printing ND	$0.30	$0.90	$1.50	£0.20	£0.60	£1.00
2-16 ND	$0.40	$1.20	$2.00	£0.25	£0.75	£1.25
Title Value:	$6.70	$20.10	$33.50	£4.20	£12.60	£21.00
Indian Country						
Trade paperback reprints issues #1-4 plus new story				£1.45	£4.35	£7.25
The Iron Triangle (Jan 1992)						
Trade paperback reprints issues #5-8				£1.40	£4.20	£7.00
VIETNAM JOURNAL: TET '68						
Apple Comics,MS; 1 Sep 1991-5 1992						
1-5 ND Don Lomax script/art						
	$0.40	$1.20	$2.00	£0.25	£0.75	£1.25
Title Value:	$2.00	$6.00	$10.00	£1.25	£3.75	£6.25
VIETNAM JOURNAL: VALLEY OF DEATH						
Apple Comics; 1 Mar 1994-2 1994						
1-2 ND Don Lomax script and art; black and white						
	$0.40	$1.20	$2.00	£0.25	£0.75	£1.25
Title Value:	$0.80	$2.40	$4.00	£0.50	£1.50	£2.50
VIGIL: DESERT FOXES						
Millennium,MS; 1 Jul 1995-2 Aug 1995						
1-2 ND black and white						
	$0.60	$1.80	$3.00	£0.40	£1.20	£2.00
Title Value:	$1.20	$3.60	$6.00	£0.80	£2.40	£4.00
VIGIL: FALL FROM GRACE						
Innovation,MS; 1 Winter 1991-2 Spring 1992						

Vampirella (Dark Horse) #1

Vamps #2

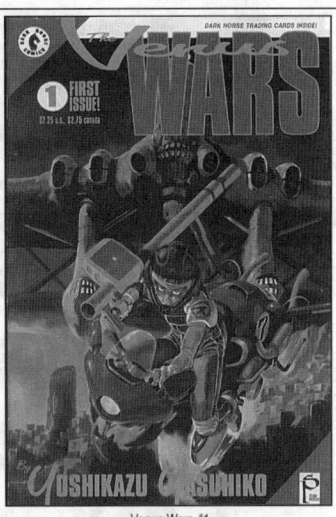

Venus Wars #1

	$Good	$Fine	$N.Mint	£Good	£Fine	£N.Mint
1-2 ND 48pgs, black and white						
	$0.50	$1.50	$2.50	£0.30	£0.90	£1.50
Title Value:	$1.00	$3.00	$5.00	£0.60	£1.80	£3.00
VIGIL: REBIRTH						
Millennium; 1 Nov 1994-2 May 1995						
1-2 ND 48pgs, black and white						
	$0.60	$1.80	$3.00	£0.40	£1.20	£2.00
Title Value:	$1.20	$3.60	$6.00	£0.80	£2.40	£4.00
VIGIL: THE GOLDEN PARTS						
Innovation,OS; 1 1992						
1 ND 48pgs, black and white						
	$0.50	$1.50	$2.50	£0.30	£0.90	£1.50
Title Value:	$0.50	$1.50	$2.50	£0.30	£0.90	£1.50
VIGILANTE ANNUAL, THE						
DC Comics; 1 Oct 1985-2 Nov 1986						
1-2 ND	$0.40	$1.20	$2.00	£0.25	£0.75	£1.25
Title Value:	$0.80	$2.40	$4.00	£0.50	£1.50	£2.50
VIGILANTE, THE						
DC Comics; 1 Oct 1983-50 Feb 1988						
1 ND origin	$0.60	$1.80	$3.00	£0.40	£1.20	£2.00
2 ND	$0.50	$1.50	$2.50	£0.30	£0.90	£1.50
3 ND Cyborg X-over						
	$0.40	$1.20	$2.00	£0.25	£0.75	£1.25
4-5 ND	$0.40	$1.20	$2.00	£0.25	£0.75	£1.25
6-7 ND origin	$0.40	$1.20	$2.00	£0.25	£0.75	£1.25
8-16 ND	$0.40	$1.20	$2.00	£0.25	£0.75	£1.25
17 ND Baikie art, Alan Moore script						
	$0.80	$2.40	$4.00	£0.50	£1.50	£2.50
18 ND Baikie art, Alan Moore script						
	$0.60	$1.80	$3.00	£0.40	£1.20	£2.00
19 ND	$0.40	$1.20	$2.00	£0.25	£0.75	£1.25
20 ND Nightwing X-over						
	$0.40	$1.20	$2.00	£0.25	£0.75	£1.25
21 ND Nightwing X-over						
	$0.30	$0.90	$1.50	£0.20	£0.60	£1.00
22-34 ND	$0.30	$0.90	$1.50	£0.20	£0.60	£1.00
35 ND John Byrne cover						
	$0.30	$0.90	$1.50	£0.20	£0.60	£1.00
36-46 ND	$0.30	$0.90	$1.50	£0.20	£0.60	£1.00
47 ND Batman appears						
	$0.30	$0.90	$1.50	£0.20	£0.60	£1.00
48-49 ND	$0.30	$0.90	$1.50	£0.20	£0.60	£1.00
50 ND scarce in the U.K. death (by suicide - 1st in comics?) of Vigilante						
	$0.30	$0.90	$1.50	£0.40	£1.20	£2.00
Title Value:	$17.90	$53.70	$89.50	£11.80	£35.40	£59.00
VIGILANTE: CITY LIGHTS, PRAIRIE JUSTICE						
DC Comics; 1 Nov 1995-4 Feb 1996						
1-4 ND Golden Age Vigilante appears, painted covers by Mark Chiarello						
	$0.50	$1.50	$2.50	£0.30	£0.90	£1.50
Title Value:	$2.00	$6.00	$10.00	£1.20	£3.60	£6.00
VIKING PRINCE GRAPHIC NOVEL						
DC Comics; nn Aug 1991						
nn ND 128pgs, Hardcover, Bo Hampton painted art, Lee Marrs script						
Introduction by Will Eisner				£3.00	£9.00	£15.00
nn ND 128pgs, Softcover (Aug 1992)				£1.90	£5.70	£9.50
VILLAINS & VIGILANTES						
Eclipse,MS; 1 Feb 1987-4 Jul 1987						
1-4 ND Jeff Dee pencils, colour						
	$0.40	$1.20	$2.00	£0.25	£0.75	£1.25
Title Value:	$1.60	$4.80	$8.00	£1.00	£3.00	£5.00
VIOLATOR						
Image,MS; 1 May 1994-3 Jul 1994						
1 ND Alan Moore script, Bart Sears pencils and Mark Pennington inks						
	$0.80	$2.40	$4.00	£0.50	£1.50	£2.50
2 ND Alan Moore script, Bart Sears pencils and Mark Pennington inks; Spawn appears						
	$0.60	$1.80	$3.00	£0.40	£1.20	£2.00
3 ND Alan Moore script, Bart Sears pencils and Mark Pennington inks; Violator vs. Spawn						
	$0.60	$1.80	$3.00	£0.40	£1.20	£2.00
Title Value:	$2.00	$6.00	$10.00	£1.30	£3.90	£6.50
VIOLATOR/BADROCK						
Image,MS; 1 May 1995-4 Aug 1995						
1-4 ND Alan Moore script, Brian Denham and Jonathan Sibal art						
	$0.50	$1.50	$2.50	£0.30	£0.90	£1.50
Title Value:	$2.00	$6.00	$10.00	£1.20	£3.60	£6.00
VIOLENCE						
London Night Studios; 1 Nov 1995-present						
1 ND	$0.60	$1.80	$3.00	£0.40	£1.20	£2.00
Title Value:	$0.60	$1.80	$3.00	£0.40	£1.20	£2.00
VIOLENT CASES - AMERICAN EDITION						
Tundra Publishing,OS; 1 Sep 1991						
1 ND Neil Gaiman script, Dave McKean art						
	$1.50	$4.50	$7.50	£1.00	£3.00	£5.00
Title Value:	$1.50	$4.50	$7.50	£1.00	£3.00	£5.00
VIPER						
DC Comics,MS; 1 Sep 1994-4 Oct 1994						
1-4 ND based on US TV series; Howard Chaykin cover; bi-weekly						
	$0.40	$1.20	$2.00	£0.25	£0.75	£1.25
Title Value:	$1.60	$4.80	$8.00	£1.00	£3.00	£5.00
VIRTUA FIGHTER						
Marvel Comics Group/Malibu Comics; 1 Aug 1995						
1 ND based on Sega video game featuring Sarah						
	$0.60	$1.80	$3.00	£0.40	£1.20	£2.00

	$Good	$Fine	$N.Mint	£Good	£Fine	£N.Mint
Title Value:	$0.60	$1.80	$3.00	£0.40	£1.20	£2.00
VIRUS						
Dark Horse,MS; 1 Dec 1992-4 Mar 1994						
1 ND Mike Ploog cover						
	$0.50	$1.50	$2.50	£0.30	£0.90	£1.50
2-4 ND	$0.50	$1.50	$2.50	£0.30	£0.90	£1.50
Title Value:	$2.00	$6.00	$10.00	£1.20	£3.60	£6.00
Virus (May 1995)						
Trade paperback collects four issue series with new cover			£2.30	£6.90	£11.50
VISION AND SCARLET WITCH, THE						
Marvel Comics Group,MS; 1 Nov 1982-4 Feb 1983						
(see Avengers, Marvel Fanfare, X-Men)						
1-3 ND	$0.30	$0.90	$1.50	£0.20	£0.60	£1.00
4 ND Magneto confirmed as Scarlet Witch's and Quicksilver's father (see Avengers #187-#189 and X-Men #125)						
	$0.40	$1.20	$2.00	£0.25	£0.75	£1.25
Title Value:	$1.30	$3.90	$6.50	£0.85	£2.55	£4.25
VISION AND SCARLET WITCH, THE (2ND SERIES)						
Marvel Comics Group,MS; 1 Oct 1985-12 Sep 1986						
1 ND DS	$0.30	$0.90	$1.50	£0.20	£0.60	£1.00
2 ND West Coast Avengers X-over						
	$0.30	$0.90	$1.50	£0.20	£0.60	£1.00
3-11 ND	$0.25	$0.75	$1.25	£0.15	£0.45	£0.75
12 ND DS	$0.30	$0.90	$1.50	£0.20	£0.60	£1.00
Title Value:	$3.15	$9.45	$15.75	£1.95	£5.85	£9.75
VISION, THE						
Marvel Comics Group,MS; 1 Nov 1994-4 Feb 1995						
1-4 ND	$0.40	$1.20	$2.00	£0.25	£0.75	£1.25
Title Value:	$1.60	$4.80	$8.00	£1.00	£3.00	£5.00
VISIONARIES						
Marvel Comics Group/Star; 1 Nov 1987-6 Nov 1988						
1-6 ND	$0.15	$0.45	$0.75	£0.10	£0.35	£0.60
Title Value:	$0.90	$2.70	$4.50	£0.60	£2.10	£3.60
VISIONS						
Visions,Fanzine; 1 1979-5 1981						
1 ND scarce in the U.K. 1st appearance Flaming Carrot						
	$10.00	$30.00	$60.00	£6.50	£20.00	£40.00
2 ND scarce in the U.K. Flaming Carrot						
	$5.00	$15.00	$30.00	£3.30	£10.00	£20.00
3 ND scarce in the U.K. Flaming Carrot						
	$2.90	$8.75	$17.50	£2.05	£6.25	£12.50
4 ND scarce in the U.K. Flaming Carrot cover only						
	$2.90	$8.75	$17.50	£2.05	£6.25	£12.50
5 ND scarce in the U.K. 1pg Flaming Carrot						
	$1.25	$3.75	$7.50	£0.80	£2.50	£5.00
Title Value:	$22.05	$66.25	$132.50	£14.70	£45.00	£90.00
VISIONS: THE ART OF ARTHUR SUYDAM						
Dark Horse,OS; nn May 1995						
nn ND 128pgs, collection of illustrations with new Aliens cover painting						
	$6.00	$18.00	$30.00	£4.00	£12.00	£20.00
Title Value:	$6.00	$18.00	$30.00	£4.00	£12.00	£20.00
VISITOR VS. THE VALIANT UNIVERSE						
Valiant,MS; 1,2 Mar 1995						
1 ND Solar and Harada appear						
	$0.40	$1.20	$2.00	£0.25	£0.75	£1.25
2 ND X-O, Eternal Warrior, Geomancer and Magnus appear						
	$0.40	$1.20	$2.00	£0.25	£0.75	£1.25
Title Value:	$0.80	$2.40	$4.00	£0.50	£1.50	£2.50
VISITOR, THE						
Valiant/Acclaim Comics; 1 Apr 1995-13 Nov 1995						
1-3 ND Bernard Chang art						
	$0.40	$1.20	$2.00	£0.25	£0.75	£1.25
4 ND 1st Acclaim Comics issue, Bernard Chand art; bi-weekly						
	$0.40	$1.20	$2.00	£0.25	£0.75	£1.25
5 ND Bernard Chang art; bi-weekly						
	$0.40	$1.20	$2.00	£0.25	£0.75	£1.25
6-7 ND John Ross and Mike DeCarlo art; bi-weekly						
	$0.40	$1.20	$2.00	£0.25	£0.75	£1.25
8 ND John Ross art; The Visitor vs. The Harbinger; bi-weekly						
	$0.40	$1.20	$2.00	£0.25	£0.75	£1.25
9 ND John Ross art, The Harbinger appears; bi-weekly						
	$0.40	$1.20	$2.00	£0.25	£0.75	£1.25
10-11 ND bi-weekly						
	$0.40	$1.20	$2.00	£0.25	£0.75	£1.25
12 ND John Ross art; bi-weekly						
	$0.40	$1.20	$2.00	£0.25	£0.75	£1.25
13 ND bi-weekly	$0.40	$1.20	$2.00	£0.25	£0.75	£1.25
Title Value:	$5.20	$15.60	$26.00	£3.25	£9.75	£16.25
VOGUE						
Image,MS; 1 Oct 1995-3 Dec 1995						
1-3 ND	$0.50	$1.50	$2.50	£0.30	£0.90	£1.50
1 ND Variant cover	$1.00	$3.00	$5.00	£1.00	£3.00	£5.00
2-3 ND	$0.50	$1.50	$2.50	£0.30	£0.90	£1.50
Title Value:	$2.50	$7.50	$12.50	£1.90	£5.70	£9.50
VOID INDIGO						
Marvel Comics Group/Epic,MS; 1 Nov 1984-2 Mar 1985						
(see Marvel Graphic Novel)						
1-2 ND	$0.40	$1.20	$2.00	£0.25	£0.75	£1.25
Title Value:	$0.80	$2.40	$4.00	£0.50	£1.50	£2.50
Note: Mature Readers label						
VOLTAR						
A Plus Comics; 1 Jan 1992						

	$Good	$Fine	$N.Mint	£Good	£Fine	£N.Mint
1 ND Alfredo Alcala art, reprint	$0.40	$1.20	$2.00	£0.25	£0.75	£1.25
Title Value:	$0.40	$1.20	$2.00	£0.25	£0.75	£1.25

VOLTRON
Modern,MS; 1-3 1984

	$Good	$Fine	$N.Mint	£Good	£Fine	£N.Mint
1-3 ND Dick Ayers art	$0.15	$0.45	$0.75	£0.10	£0.30	£0.50
Title Value:	$0.45	$1.35	$2.25	£0.30	£0.90	£1.50

VOODOO/ZEALOT: SKIN TRADE
Image,OS; nn Sep 1995

	$Good	$Fine	$N.Mint	£Good	£Fine	£N.Mint
nn ND 48pgs, Steve Seagle script, Michael Lopez art	$1.00	$3.00	$5.00	£0.70	£2.10	£3.50
Title Value:	$1.00	$3.00	$5.00	£0.70	£2.10	£3.50

VORTEX
Vortex; 1 Nov 1982-15 1988

	$Good	$Fine	$N.Mint	£Good	£Fine	£N.Mint
1 ND scarce in the U.K.	$1.60	$4.80	$8.00	£1.00	£3.00	£5.00
2 ND 1st comic appearance Mr. X	$0.80	$2.40	$4.00	£0.50	£1.50	£2.50
3 ND	$0.60	$1.80	$3.00	£0.40	£1.20	£2.00
4-6 ND	$0.50	$1.50	$2.50	£0.30	£0.90	£1.50
7 ND Gilbert Hernandez story, Jaimie Hernandez cover	$0.50	$1.50	$2.50	£0.30	£0.90	£1.50
8-15 ND	$0.50	$1.50	$2.50	£0.30	£0.90	£1.50
Title Value:	$9.00	$27.00	$45.00	£5.50	£16.50	£27.50

VORTEX LIMITED SERIES
Comico,MS; 1 Sep 1991-4 Aug 1993

	$Good	$Fine	$N.Mint	£Good	£Fine	£N.Mint
1-4 ND	$0.40	$1.20	$2.00	£0.25	£0.75	£1.25
Title Value:	$1.60	$4.80	$8.00	£1.00	£3.00	£5.00

VORTEX, OUT OF THE
Dark Horse/Comics Greatest World; 1 Oct 1993-12 Oct 1994

	$Good	$Fine	$N.Mint	£Good	£Fine	£N.Mint
1 ND John Ostrander script begins; foil stamped cover	$0.40	$1.20	$2.00	£0.25	£0.75	£1.25
2-12 ND	$0.40	$1.20	$2.00	£0.25	£0.75	£1.25
Title Value:	$4.80	$14.40	$24.00	£3.00	£9.00	£15.00

VOYAGE TO THE BOTTOM OF THE SEA
Dell; 1 (Four Color 1230) 1961; 2 (10133-412) Gold Key 1961-16 Sep 1969

	$Good	$Fine	$N.Mint	£Good	£Fine	£N.Mint
1 scarce in the U.K. (Four Color #1230) adapts film	$11.00	$34.00	$67.50	£7.50	£22.50	£45.00
1 issue #1 in indicia, Dell cover number 10133-12	$7.50	$22.50	$45.00	£5.00	£15.00	£30.00
2	$5.75	$17.50	$35.00	£3.75	£11.00	£22.50
3 Alberto Gioletti art begins	$5.00	$15.00	$30.00	£3.30	£10.00	£20.00
4-5	$5.00	$15.00	$30.00	£3.30	£10.00	£20.00
6-10	$3.75	$11.00	$22.50	£2.50	£7.50	£15.00
11-14	$3.30	$10.00	$20.00	£2.30	£7.00	£14.00
15-16 all reprint	$2.50	$7.50	$15.00	£1.65	£5.00	£10.00
Title Value:	$76.20	$229.00	$460.00	£51.15	£154.00	£308.50

Note: all distributed on the news-stands in the U.K.

W

WACKY SQUIRREL
Dark Horse; 1 Oct 1987-4 1988

	$Good	$Fine	$N.Mint	£Good	£Fine	£N.Mint
1-4 ND	$0.40	$1.20	$2.00	£0.25	£0.75	£1.25
Title Value:	$1.60	$4.80	$8.00	£1.00	£3.00	£5.00

WACKY SQUIRREL'S HALLOWEEN ADVENTURE SPECIAL
Dark Horse,OS; nn 1987

	$Good	$Fine	$N.Mint	£Good	£Fine	£N.Mint
nn ND Mr. Monster by Michael T. Gilbert appears	$0.40	$1.20	$2.00	£0.25	£0.75	£1.25
Title Value:	$0.40	$1.20	$2.00	£0.25	£0.75	£1.25

WACKY SQUIRREL'S SUMMER FUN SPECIAL
Dark Horse,OS; 1 Jul 1987

	$Good	$Fine	$N.Mint	£Good	£Fine	£N.Mint
1 ND	$0.40	$1.20	$2.00	£0.25	£0.75	£1.25
Title Value:	$0.40	$1.20	$2.00	£0.25	£0.75	£1.25

WAGON TRAIN
Dell; 1 (Four Color #895) Mar 1958; 2 (Four Color #971); 3 (Four Color #1019) -13 Jun 1962

	$Good	$Fine	$N.Mint	£Good	£Fine	£N.Mint
1 photo cover	$14.00	$43.00	$85.00	£9.00	£28.00	£55.00
2-3 photo cover	$7.00	$21.00	$42.00	£4.65	£14.00	£28.00
4	$5.25	$16.00	$32.50	£3.75	£11.00	£22.50
5 Alex Toth art	$5.75	$17.50	$35.00	£4.00	£12.00	£24.00
6-13	$5.25	$16.00	$32.50	£3.75	£11.00	£22.50
Title Value:	$81.00	$246.50	$496.50	£56.05	£167.00	£337.50

Note: all distributed on the news-stands in the U.K.

WAGON TRAIN (2ND SERIES)
Gold Key; 1 Jan 1964-4 Oct 1964

	$Good	$Fine	$N.Mint	£Good	£Fine	£N.Mint
1 LD in the U.K.	$5.00	$15.00	$30.00	£3.30	£10.00	£20.00
2-4 LD in the U.K.	$3.30	$10.00	$20.00	£2.30	£7.00	£14.00
Title Value:	$14.90	$45.00	$90.00	£10.20	£31.00	£62.00

WALLY THE WIZARD
Marvel Comics Group/Star; 1 Apr 1985-12 Mar 1986

	$Good	$Fine	$N.Mint	£Good	£Fine	£N.Mint
1-12 ND scarce in the U.K.	$0.15	$0.45	$0.75	£0.10	£0.35	£0.60
Title Value:	$1.80	$5.40	$9.00	£1.20	£4.20	£7.20

WALLY WOOD'S WAR
ACG,OS; nn Jul 1995

	$Good	$Fine	$N.Mint	£Good	£Fine	£N.Mint
nn ND reprints Wally Wood's rare D-Day stories from the 1960s	$0.50	$1.50	$2.50	£0.30	£0.90	£1.50
Title Value:	$0.50	$1.50	$2.50	£0.30	£0.90	£1.50

WALT DISNEY GIANT
Gladstone; 1 1995-present

	$Good	$Fine	$N.Mint	£Good	£Fine	£N.Mint
1 ND 48pgs, Carl Barks reprints begin	$0.50	$1.50	$2.50	£0.30	£0.90	£1.50
2-3 ND	$0.50	$1.50	$2.50	£0.30	£0.90	£1.50
Title Value:	$1.50	$4.50	$7.50	£0.90	£2.70	£4.50

WALT DISNEY SPRING FEVER
Disney,OS; 1 Apr 1991

	$Good	$Fine	$N.Mint	£Good	£Fine	£N.Mint
1 ND 64pgs, features Donald Duck by Barks, Chip 'N Dale, Mickey Mouse, Goofy	$0.50	$1.50	$2.50	£0.30	£0.90	£1.50
Title Value:	$0.50	$1.50	$2.50	£0.30	£0.90	£1.50

WALT DISNEY'S AUTUMN ADVENTURES
Disney; 1 Oct 1990

	$Good	$Fine	$N.Mint	£Good	£Fine	£N.Mint
1 ND 64pgs, Donald Duck, Pluto, Mickey Mouse, Goofy and others	$0.60	$1.80	$3.00	£0.40	£1.20	£2.00
Title Value:	$0.60	$1.80	$3.00	£0.40	£1.20	£2.00

Note: quarterly frequency

WALT DISNEY'S CHRISTMAS PARADE
Gladstone; 1 Winter 1988; 2 Winter 1989

	$Good	$Fine	$N.Mint	£Good	£Fine	£N.Mint
1 ND 100pgs, squarebound, Barks reprint, painted Barks cover	$0.60	$1.80	$3.00	£0.40	£1.20	£2.00
2 ND 100pgs, squarebound	$0.60	$1.80	$3.00	£0.40	£1.20	£2.00
Title Value:	$1.20	$3.60	$6.00	£0.80	£2.40	£4.00

WALT DISNEY'S COMICS AND STORIES
Dell Publishing Company, Dell 1 Oct 1940-263 Aug 1962; Gold Key/Whitman; 264 Oct 1962- 510 1984; Gladstone; 511 Nov 1986-547 1989; Disney; 548 Jun 1990-585 Jun 1993; Gladstone; 586 Aug 1993-present

	$Good	$Fine	$N.Mint	£Good	£Fine	£N.Mint
1 Donald Duck reprints by Al Taliaferro and Mickey Mouse reprints by Gottfredson begin; about 220 copies exist in any condition	$1350.00	$4050.00	$13500.00	£900.00	£2700.00	£9000.00
2	$600.00	$1800.00	$5400.00	£400.00	£1200.00	£3600.00
3	$235.00	$700.00	$1880.00	£160.00	£480.00	£1280.00
4 Christmas cover	$165.00	$495.00	$1320.00	£110.00	£330.00	£880.00
5	$125.00	$375.00	$1000.00	£85.00	£255.00	£680.00
6-10	$100.00	$300.00	$800.00	£65.00	£200.00	£535.00
11	$90.00	$270.00	$720.00	£60.00	£180.00	£480.00
12-14	$85.00	$255.00	$680.00	£55.00	£170.00	£455.00
15-17	$80.00	$240.00	$640.00	£55.00	£165.00	£440.00
18-21	$65.00	$195.00	$520.00	£45.00	£135.00	£360.00
22-30	$60.00	$180.00	$480.00	£40.00	£120.00	£320.00
31 original Donald Duck stories by Carl Barks begin (see Four Colour #9)	$325.00	$980.00	$2950.00	£215.00	£650.00	£1975.00
32 Carl Barks art	$165.00	$495.00	$1325.00	£105.00	£325.00	£875.00
33 Carl Barks art	$115.00	$345.00	$925.00	£75.00	£230.00	£615.00
34 Carl Barks art, Gremlins by Walt Kelly	$100.00	$300.00	$800.00	£65.00	£200.00	£535.00
35-36 Carl Barks art	$87.50	$260.00	$700.00	£57.50	£175.00	£470.00
37 Donald Duck by Jack Hannah	$44.00	$130.00	$350.00	£30.00	£90.00	£240.00
38 Carl Barks art	$72.50	$215.00	$585.00	£49.00	£145.00	£390.00
39 Christmas cover, Carl Barks art	$72.50	$215.00	$585.00	£49.00	£145.00	£390.00
40 no Carl Barks art; Walt Kelly art	$72.50	$215.00	$585.00	£49.00	£145.00	£390.00
41-50 Carl Barks art	$50.00	$150.00	$400.00	£34.00	£100.00	£270.00
51-60 Carl Barks art	$33.00	$97.50	$260.00	£21.50	£65.00	£175.00
61-68 Carl Barks art	$30.00	$90.00	$240.00	£20.00	£60.00	£160.00
69 Carl Barks art; my favourite cover	$30.00	$90.00	$240.00	£20.00	£60.00	£160.00
70 Carl Barks art	$30.00	$90.00	$240.00	£20.00	£60.00	£160.00
71-80 Carl Barks art	$21.50	$65.00	$175.00	£15.00	£45.00	£120.00
81-87 Carl Barks art	$20.00	$60.00	$160.00	£13.50	£41.00	£110.00
88 1st appearance Gladstone Gander, Carl Barks art	$25.00	$75.00	$200.00	£16.50	£50.00	£135.00
89-90 Carl Barks art	$20.00	$60.00	$160.00	£13.50	£41.00	£110.00
91-97 Carl Barks art	$15.00	$45.00	$120.00	£10.00	£30.00	£80.00
98 1st appearance of Uncle Scrooge in title, Carl Barks art	$35.00	$105.00	$280.00	£25.00	£75.00	£200.00
99 Carl Barks art	$15.00	$45.00	$120.00	£10.00	£30.00	£80.00
100 Carl Barks art	$22.50	$67.50	$180.00	£15.00	£45.00	£120.00
101-110 Carl Barks art	$14.00	$42.00	$112.00	£9.25	£28.00	£75.00
111 Carl Barks art	$12.00	$36.00	$96.00	£8.00	£24.00	£64.00
112 "drugs issue" (mentions ether), Carl Barks art	$12.00	$36.00	$96.00	£8.00	£24.00	£64.00

MINT = 100% / NEAR MINT (inc. +/-) = 90–99% / VERY FINE (inc. +/-) = 75–89% / FINE (inc. +/-) = 55–74%
VERY GOOD (inc. +/-) = 35–54% / GOOD (inc. +/-) = 15–34% / FAIR = 5–14% / POOR = 1–4%

625

Issue	$Good	$Fine	$N.Mint	£Good	£Fine	£N.Mint
113 no Barks art	$6.00	$18.00	$48.00	£4.00	£12.00	£32.00
114 Carl Barks art	$12.00	$36.00	$96.00	£8.00	£24.00	£65.00
115-116 no Barks	$6.00	$18.00	$48.00	£4.00	£12.00	£32.00
117 Carl Barks art	$12.00	$36.00	$96.00	£8.00	£24.00	£65.00
118-123 no Barks	$6.00	$18.00	$48.00	£4.00	£12.00	£32.00
124 Carl Barks art	$11.00	$33.00	$88.00	£7.00	£21.50	£57.50
125 1st appearance Junior Woodchucks, Carl Barks art	$15.00	$45.00	$120.00	£10.00	£30.00	£80.00
126-130 Carl Barks art	$11.00	$33.00	$88.00	£7.00	£21.50	£57.50
131 Carl Barks art	$10.00	$30.00	$80.00	£6.50	£19.50	£52.50
132 Daisy Duck and Grandma Duck appear, Carl Barks art	$10.00	$30.00	$80.00	£6.50	£19.50	£52.50
133 Carl Barks art	$10.00	$30.00	$80.00	£6.50	£19.50	£52.50
134 1st appearance of The Beagle Boys, Carl Barks art	$22.50	$67.50	$180.00	£15.00	£45.00	£120.00
135-139 Carl Barks art	$10.00	$30.00	$80.00	£6.50	£19.50	£52.50
140 1st appearance Gyro Gearloose, Carl Barks art	$25.00	$75.00	$200.00	£17.00	£50.00	£138.25
141-150 Carl Barks art	$8.75	$26.00	$70.00	£5.75	£17.50	£47.00
151-170 Carl Barks art	$6.00	$18.00	$48.00	£4.00	£12.00	£32.00
171-199 Carl Barks art	$5.00	$15.00	$40.00	£3.35	£10.00	£27.00
200 Carl Barks art	$8.00	$24.00	$65.00	£5.25	£16.00	£43.00
201-240 Carl Barks art	$5.00	$15.00	$35.00	£3.35	£10.00	£23.50
241-266 Carl Barks art	$4.00	$12.00	$28.00	£2.60	£7.75	£18.50
267-268 Carl Bark art	$4.00	$12.00	$28.00	£2.60	£7.75	£18.50
269-283 Carl Barks art	$4.00	$12.00	$28.00	£2.60	£7.75	£18.50
284-285 no Barks	$2.50	$7.50	$17.50	£1.60	£4.90	£11.50
286 Barks stories	$3.00	$9.00	$21.00	£2.00	£6.00	£14.00
287 no Barks	$2.50	$7.50	$17.50	£1.60	£4.90	£11.50
288-289 Barks stories	$3.00	$9.00	$21.00	£2.00	£6.00	£14.00
290-294 Barks stories	$2.50	$7.50	$17.50	£1.60	£4.90	£11.50
295-296 no Barks	$2.00	$6.00	$14.00	£1.30	£3.95	£9.25
297-298 Barks stories	$2.50	$7.50	$17.50	£1.60	£4.90	£11.50
299-307 early Barks reprints	$3.00	$9.00	$21.00	£2.00	£6.00	£14.00
308 Barks stories	$3.50	$10.50	$17.50	£2.30	£6.75	£11.50
309-311 no Barks	$2.80	$8.25	$14.00	£1.85	£5.50	£9.25
312 last original stories	$4.20	$12.50	$21.00	£2.80	£8.25	£14.00
313-315 Barks reprints	$1.20	$3.60	$6.00	£0.80	£2.40	£4.00
316 Barks reprints; apparently the last issue published during the lifetime of Walt Disney	$1.40	$4.20	$7.00	£0.90	£2.70	£4.50
317-350 Barks reprints	$1.20	$3.60	$6.00	£0.80	£2.40	£4.00
351-360 Barks reprints (with poster - 50% less without)	$2.25	$6.75	$11.25	£1.50	£4.50	£7.50
361-379 Barks reprint	$1.20	$3.60	$6.00	£0.80	£2.40	£4.00
380-400 Barks reprint	$1.05	$3.15	$5.25	£0.70	£2.10	£3.50
401-415 Barks reprint	$0.90	$2.70	$4.50	£0.60	£1.80	£3.00
416-429 Barks reprint	$0.60	$1.80	$3.00	£0.40	£1.20	£2.00
430 no Barks	$0.40	$1.20	$2.00	£0.25	£0.75	£1.25
431 Barks reprint	$0.45	$1.35	$2.25	£0.30	£0.90	£1.50
432 no Barks	$0.40	$1.20	$2.00	£0.25	£0.75	£1.25
434-436 Barks reprint	$0.45	$1.35	$2.25	£0.30	£0.90	£1.50
437-438 no Barks art	$0.40	$1.20	$2.00	£0.25	£0.75	£1.25
439-440 Barks reprint	$0.45	$1.35	$2.25	£0.30	£0.90	£1.50
441 no Barks	$0.40	$1.20	$2.00	£0.25	£0.75	£1.25
442-443 Barks reprint	$0.45	$1.35	$2.25	£0.30	£0.90	£1.50
444-445 no Barks	$0.30	$0.90	$1.50	£0.20	£0.60	£1.00
446-465 Barks reprint	$0.40	$1.20	$2.00	£0.25	£0.75	£1.25

Issue	$Good	$Fine	$N.Mint	£Good	£Fine	£N.Mint
466 no Barks	$0.30	$0.90	$1.50	£0.20	£0.60	£1.00
467-499 Barks reprint	$0.40	$1.20	$2.00	£0.25	£0.75	£1.25
500 Barks reprint	$0.45	$1.35	$2.25	£0.30	£0.90	£1.50
501-505 Barks reprint	$0.40	$1.20	$2.00	£0.25	£0.75	£1.25
506 no Barks	$0.30	$0.90	$1.50	£0.20	£0.60	£1.00
507-510 Barks reprint	$0.40	$1.20	$2.00	£0.25	£0.75	£1.25
511 1st Gladstone issue, 75c cover begins	$1.20	$3.60	$6.00	£0.80	£2.40	£4.00
512	$0.60	$1.80	$3.00	£0.40	£1.20	£2.00
513-516	$0.50	$1.50	$2.50	£0.30	£0.90	£1.50
517 1st 95¢ issue	$0.50	$1.50	$2.50	£0.30	£0.90	£1.50
518-520	$0.50	$1.50	$2.50	£0.30	£0.90	£1.50
521	$0.40	$1.20	$2.00	£0.25	£0.75	£1.25
522 reprints 1st appearance Huey, Dewey & Louie	$0.40	$1.20	$2.00	£0.25	£0.75	£1.25
523-524 Donald Duck by Rosa	$0.40	$1.20	$2.00	£0.25	£0.75	£1.25
525	$0.40	$1.20	$2.00	£0.25	£0.75	£1.25
526 Donald Duck by Rosa	$0.40	$1.20	$2.00	£0.25	£0.75	£1.25
527	$0.40	$1.20	$2.00	£0.25	£0.75	£1.25
528 Donald Duck by Rosa	$0.40	$1.20	$2.00	£0.25	£0.75	£1.25
529-530	$0.40	$1.20	$2.00	£0.25	£0.75	£1.25
531 Donald Duck by Rosa	$0.40	$1.20	$2.00	£0.25	£0.75	£1.25
532-545	$0.40	$1.20	$2.00	£0.25	£0.75	£1.25
546-547 98pgs	$0.50	$1.50	$2.50	£0.30	£0.90	£1.50
548 new material begins	$0.40	$1.20	$2.00	£0.25	£0.75	£1.25
549	$0.40	$1.20	$2.00	£0.25	£0.75	£1.25
550 48pgs, "new" Carl Barks story, un-published for 30 years	$0.55	$1.65	$2.75	£0.35	£1.05	£1.75
551-560	$0.40	$1.20	$2.00	£0.25	£0.75	£1.25
561 early Barks illustrations feature begins	$0.40	$1.20	$2.00	£0.25	£0.75	£1.25
562-570	$0.40	$1.20	$2.00	£0.25	£0.75	£1.25
571 64pgs, Barks reprints, photo feature on Disney Legends Awards	$0.60	$1.80	$3.00	£0.40	£1.20	£2.00
572-573	$0.40	$1.20	$2.00	£0.25	£0.75	£1.25
574 64pgs, Barks reprints plus Disney Sunday pages	$0.60	$1.80	$3.00	£0.40	£1.20	£2.00
575-577 64pgs, Carl Barks reprints	$0.60	$1.80	$3.00	£0.40	£1.20	£2.00
578-579 Carl Barks reprints	$0.40	$1.20	$2.00	£0.25	£0.75	£1.25
580 64pgs, reprints Donald Duck's first appearance in the Silly Symphonies comic strip in 1934	$0.60	$1.80	$3.00	£0.40	£1.20	£2.00
581 Carl Barks reprints	$0.40	$1.20	$2.00	£0.25	£0.75	£1.25
582-583 64pgs, reprints "Three Caballeros" from Four Color #71	$0.60	$1.80	$3.00	£0.40	£1.20	£2.00
584 Carl Barks reprint	$0.40	$1.20	$2.00	£0.25	£0.75	£1.25
585 48pgs, "Mickey Mouse, Circus Roustabout" by Gottfredson and Taliaferro reprinted	$0.50	$1.50	$2.50	£0.30	£0.90	£1.50
586 Carl Barks reprint; title now re-published by Gladstone; part 1 of Gottfredson's "Lair of the Wolf Barker"	$0.40	$1.20	$2.00	£0.25	£0.75	£1.25
587 new 10pg story plus conclusion to Gottfredson's "Lair of the Wolf Barker"	$0.40	$1.20	$2.00	£0.25	£0.75	£1.25
588-592	$0.40	$1.20	$2.00	£0.25	£0.75	£1.25
593	$0.50	$1.50	$2.50	£0.30	£0.90	£1.50
594-598	$0.40	$1.20	$2.00	£0.25	£0.75	£1.25
599 ND $1.95 cover begins	$0.40	$1.20	$2.00	£0.25	£0.75	£1.25
600 ND 48pgs, special reprints including Carl Barks' first ten page Duck story	$0.60	$1.80	$3.00	£0.40	£1.20	£2.00
Title Value:	**$8699.45**	**$26070.80**	**$72155.25**	**£5795.35**	**£17442.35**	**£48385.00**

Note: all Non-Distributed on the news-stands in the U.K.

WALT DISNEY'S COMICS DIGEST
Gladstone; 1 1986-7 1987
(formerly Gladstone title)

Issue	$Good	$Fine	$N.Mint	£Good	£Fine	£N.Mint
1 ND Three Caballeros	$0.40	$1.20	$2.00	£0.25	£0.75	£1.25
2-7 ND	$0.40	$1.20	$2.00	£0.25	£0.75	£1.25
Title Value:	**$2.80**	**$8.40**	**$14.00**	**£1.75**	**£5.25**	**£8.75**

WALT DISNEY'S SUMMER FUN
Disney,OS; 1 Jul 1991

Issue	$Good	$Fine	$N.Mint	£Good	£Fine	£N.Mint
1 ND 64pgs, new stories plus Donald Duck by Barks reprint	$0.50	$1.50	$2.50	£0.30	£0.90	£1.50
Title Value:	**$0.50**	**$1.50**	**$2.50**	**£0.30**	**£0.90**	**£1.50**

WALT KELLY'S CHRISTMAS CLASSICS
Eclipse,OS; 1 Dec 1987
(Seduction of the Innocent #8)

Issue	$Good	$Fine	$N.Mint	£Good	£Fine	£N.Mint
1 ND Steve Leiloha cover (in Walt Kelly style), colour	$0.40	$1.20	$2.00	£0.25	£0.75	£1.25
Title Value:	**$0.40**	**$1.20**	**$2.00**	**£0.25**	**£0.75**	**£1.25**

	$Good	$Fine	$N.Mint	£Good	£Fine	£N.Mint

WALT KELLY'S SANTA CLAUS ADVENTURES
Innovation,OS; 1 Dec 1990
1 ND 64pgs, squarebound

	$1.40	$4.20	$7.00	£0.90	£2.70	£4.50
Title Value:	$1.40	$4.20	$7.00	£0.90	£2.70	£4.50

WALT KELLY'S SPRINGTIME TALES
Eclipse,OS; 1 Apr 1988
(Seduction of the Innocent #10)
1 ND

	$0.50	$1.50	$2.50	£0.30	£0.90	£1.50
Title Value:	$0.50	$1.50	$2.50	£0.30	£0.90	£1.50

WANDERERS, THE
DC Comics; 1 Jun 1988-13 Apr 1989
(see Adventure Comics #375)
1 LD in the U.K. origin & 1st appearance new team: Dartalon, Elvar, Psyche, Quantum Queen, Re-Animage, Aviax

	$0.25	$0.75	$1.25	£0.20	£0.60	£1.00
2	$0.25	$0.75	$1.25	£0.15	£0.45	£0.75

3 Legion of Super-Heroes guest-star

	$0.25	$0.75	$1.25	£0.15	£0.45	£0.75
4-13	$0.25	$0.75	$1.25	£0.15	£0.45	£0.75
Title Value:	$3.25	$9.75	$16.25	£2.00	£6.00	£10.00

Note: spin-off series from Legion of Super-Heroes, all Deluxe Format.

WANDERING STARS
Fantagraphics,OS; 1 Sep 1987
1 ND Sam Keith cover and art

	$0.50	$1.50	$2.50	£0.30	£0.90	£1.50
Title Value:	$0.50	$1.50	$2.50	£0.30	£0.90	£1.50

WANTED: THE WORLD'S MOST DANGEROUS VILLAINS
DC Comics; 1 Jul/Aug 1972-9 Aug/Sep 1973
(see DC Special)
1 reprints Green Lantern #1

	$1.20	$3.60	$6.00	£0.80	£2.40	£4.00

2 features 1940s Batman and Joker in reprint of Batman #25

	$1.20	$3.60	$6.00	£0.80	£2.40	£4.00
3-8	$0.80	$2.40	$4.00	£0.50	£1.50	£2.50

9 Jack Kirby reprint

	$0.80	$2.40	$4.00	£0.50	£1.50	£2.50
Title Value:	$8.00	$24.00	$40.00	£5.10	£15.30	£25.50

REPRINT FEATURES
Batman in 1, 2. Doll Man in 5. Dr.Fate in 3, 8. Green Arrow in 1. Green Lantern in 1, 5; GA Green Lantern in 4. Flash in 2, 8. GA Hawkman, Vigilante in 3. Kid Eternity in 4. Johnny Quick, Hourman in 7. Starman, Wildcat in 6. Superman, GA Sandman in 9.

WAR (1ST SERIES)
Charlton; 1 Jul 1975-48 Dec 1984
1 distributed in the U.K.

	$0.40	$1.20	$2.00	£0.25	£0.75	£1.25
2-48 distributed in the U.K.						
	$0.30	$0.90	$1.50	£0.20	£0.60	£1.00
Title Value:	$14.50	$43.50	$72.50	£9.65	£28.95	£48.25

WAR (2ND SERIES)
A Plus Comics; 1 May 1991
1 ND 48pgs, ACG and Charlton war reprints, Wood and Glanzman art

	$0.40	$1.20	$2.00	£0.25	£0.75	£1.25
Title Value:	$0.40	$1.20	$2.00	£0.25	£0.75	£1.25

WAR DANCER
Defiant; 1 Feb 1994-9 Oct 1994
1 ND Jim Shooter and Alan Weiss script, Alan Weiss art

	$0.40	$1.20	$2.00	£0.25	£0.75	£1.25
2-6 ND	$0.40	$1.20	$2.00	£0.25	£0.75	£1.25

7 ND Schism X-over; continued from Charlemagne #6

	$0.40	$1.20	$2.00	£0.25	£0.75	£1.25

8-9 ND	$0.40	$1.20	$2.00	£0.25	£0.75	£1.25
Title Value:	$3.60	$10.80	$18.00	£2.25	£6.75	£11.25

WAR HEROES
Charlton; 1 Feb 1963-27 Nov 1967
1 distributed in the U.K.

	$2.50	$7.50	$15.00	£1.65	£5.00	£10.00
2-3 distributed in the U.K.						
	$1.65	$5.00	$10.00	£1.15	£3.50	£7.00
4-10 distributed in the U.K.						
	$1.25	$3.75	$7.50	£0.80	£2.50	£5.00
11-20 distributed in the U.K.						
	$1.20	$3.60	$6.00	£0.80	£2.40	£4.00
21-27 distributed in the U.K.						
	$1.00	$3.00	$5.00	£0.70	£2.10	£3.50
Title Value:	$33.55	$100.75	$182.50	£22.45	£68.20	£123.50

WAR HEROES CLASSICS
Lorne Harvey Publications/Recollections,OS; 1 Jun 1991
1 ND features Black Cat and Girl Commandoes, Paul Pelletier cover; black and white

	$0.40	$1.20	$2.00	£0.25	£0.75	£1.25
Title Value:	$0.40	$1.20	$2.00	£0.25	£0.75	£1.25

WAR IS HELL
Marvel Comics Group; 1 Jan 1973-15 Oct 1975
1 ND '50s reprints begin; Al Williamson reprint

	$0.50	$1.50	$2.50	£0.30	£0.90	£1.50
2-6 ND	$0.40	$1.20	$2.00	£0.25	£0.75	£1.25

7-8 ND Sgt. Fury reprints

	$0.40	$1.20	$2.00	£0.25	£0.75	£1.25

9-15 ND new stories

	$0.40	$1.20	$2.00	£0.25	£0.75	£1.25
Title Value:	$6.10	$18.30	$30.50	£3.80	£11.40	£19.00

WAR MACHINE
Marvel Comics Group; 1 Feb 1994-present
1 spin-off from Iron Man series: Jim Rhodes as War Machine

	$0.30	$0.90	$1.50	£0.20	£0.60	£1.00

1 ND Collector's Edition, silver-etched foil image on black embossed cover

	$0.60	$1.80	$3.00	£0.40	£1.20	£2.00

1 ND Ashcan Edition (Apr 1994), 12pgs black and white; 75 cents sticker price on back cover

	$0.30	$0.90	$1.50	£0.20	£0.60	£1.00

2 with free Spiderman's Amazing Powers card sheet

	$0.30	$0.90	$1.50	£0.20	£0.60	£1.00

3 Nick Fury vs. War Machine

	$0.30	$0.90	$1.50	£0.20	£0.60	£1.00
4-6	$0.30	$0.90	$1.50	£0.20	£0.60	£1.00

7 Hawkeye guest-stars

	$0.30	$0.90	$1.50	£0.20	£0.60	£1.00
8	$0.30	$0.90	$1.50	£0.20	£0.60	£1.00

8 ND pre-bagged with acetate print from Marvel Action Hour TV series; neon ink cover; X-over Iron Man #310

	$0.60	$1.80	$3.00	£0.40	£1.20	£2.00

9 Hands of the Mandarin part 2, continued in Iron Man #311

	$0.30	$0.90	$1.50	£0.20	£0.60	£1.00

10 Hands of the Mandarin part 5, continued in Iron Man #312

	$0.30	$0.90	$1.50	£0.20	£0.60	£1.00
11-13	$0.30	$0.90	$1.50	£0.20	£0.60	£1.00

14 Force Works appear

	$0.30	$0.90	$1.50	£0.20	£0.60	£1.00

15 48pgs, flip-book format, Captain America, Bucky and Nick Fury appear; continued in Iron Man #317

	$0.50	$1.50	$2.50	£0.30	£0.90	£1.50

16 Captain America, Bucky and Nick Fury appear

	$0.30	$0.90	$1.50	£0.20	£0.60	£1.00
17	$0.30	$0.90	$1.50	£0.20	£0.60	£1.00

18 Avengers: The Crossing tie-in

Vogue #2

Wanted #1

War Is Hell #1

	$Good	$Fine	$N.Mint	£Good	£Fine	£N.Mint
	$0.30	$0.90	$1.50	£0.20	£0.60	£1.00

19 Avengers: The Crossing tie-in, new armour, Hawkeye guest-stars

	$0.30	$0.90	$1.50	£0.20	£0.60	£1.00

20-21 Avengers: The Crossing tie-in

	$0.30	$0.90	$1.50	£0.20	£0.60	£1.00

22 new War Machine vs. new Iron Man

	$0.30	$0.90	$1.50	£0.20	£0.60	£1.00

23 Avengers: Timeslide tie-in, continues in Iron Man #325

	$0.30	$0.90	$1.50	£0.20	£0.60	£1.00

24 guest-starring The Avengers

	$0.30	$0.90	$1.50	£0.20	£0.60	£1.00
Title Value:	$8.90	$26.70	$44.50	£5.90	£17.70	£29.50

WAR MAN
Marvel Comics Group,MS; 1 Nov 1993-2 Dec 1993

	$Good	$Fine	$N.Mint	£Good	£Fine	£N.Mint
1-2 Chuck Dixon and Juan Zanotto						
	$0.40	$1.20	$2.00	£0.25	£0.75	£1.25
Title Value:	$0.80	$2.40	$4.00	£0.50	£1.50	£2.50

WAR OF THE GODS
Cross-over series featuring the major DC characters in battle against the classical Gods brought to Earth under the spell of Circe. The cross-overs are listed below in chronological order around the core mini-series.

1) War of the Gods 1
2) Man of Steel 3
3) Wonder Woman (2nd Series) 58
4) Hawkworld 15
5) Legion '91 31
6) Starman 38
7) Captain Atom 57
8) Dr. Fate 32
9) War of the Gods 2
10) Flash 55
11) Wonder Woman (2nd Series) 59
12) Hawkworld 16
13) Batman 470
14) Dr. Fate 33
15) Animal Man 40
16) Suicide Squad 58
17) War of the Gods 3
18) Wonder Woman (2nd Series) 60
19) Demon (2nd Series) 17
20) New Titans 81
21) War of the Gods 4
22) Wonder Woman (2nd Series) 61

WAR OF THE GODS (LIMITED SERIES)
DC Comics,MS; 1 Sep 1991-4 Jan 1992

	$Good	$Fine	$N.Mint	£Good	£Fine	£N.Mint
1 George Perez script and art						
	$0.25	$0.75	$1.25	£0.15	£0.45	£0.75

1 ND direct sales edition of the above ("Collector's Edition" on cover of all direct sales editions), mini-posters included

	$0.30	$0.90	$1.50	£0.20	£0.60	£1.00

2 George Perez script and art, Superman, Batman, Flash and many others heroes appear

	$0.25	$0.75	$1.25	£0.15	£0.45	£0.75

2 ND direct sales edition of the above, yellow border cover, four glossy pin-up posters included

	$0.30	$0.90	$1.50	£0.20	£0.60	£1.00

3 George Perez script and art, Lobo featured

	$0.25	$0.75	$1.25	£0.15	£0.45	£0.75

3 ND direct sales edition of the above, four glossy pin-up posters included

	$0.30	$0.90	$1.50	£0.20	£0.60	£1.00

4 George Perez script and art

	$0.25	$0.75	$1.25	£0.15	£0.45	£0.75

4 ND direct sales edition of the above, four glossy pin-up posters included

	$0.30	$0.90	$1.50	£0.20	£0.60	£1.00
Title Value:	$2.20	$6.60	$11.00	£1.40	£4.20	£7.00

Note: cross-over series with tie-ins across other DC titles

WAR PARTY
Lightning Comics; 1 Oct 1994-2 1994

	$Good	$Fine	$N.Mint	£Good	£Fine	£N.Mint
1-2 ND	$0.60	$1.80	$3.00	£0.40	£1.20	£2.00
Title Value:	$1.20	$3.60	$6.00	£0.80	£2.40	£4.00

WAR PARTY VS. DEATHMARK
Lightning Comics; 1 Mar 1995

	$Good	$Fine	$N.Mint	£Good	£Fine	£N.Mint
1 ND black and white						
	$0.50	$1.50	$2.50	£0.30	£0.90	£1.50
Title Value:	$0.50	$1.50	$2.50	£0.30	£0.90	£1.50

WAR SIRENS & LIBERTY BELLES
Lorne-Harvey Publications/Recollectios,OS; nn 1991

nn ND 100pgs, squarebound, black and white Golden Age reprints featuring Black Cat, Rocket Girl and Girl Commandoes

	$0.90	$2.70	$4.50	£0.60	£1.80	£3.00
Title Value:	$0.90	$2.70	$4.50	£0.60	£1.80	£3.00

WAR, THE
DC Comics,MS; 1 Jun 1989-4 Sep 1989

	$Good	$Fine	$N.Mint	£Good	£Fine	£N.Mint
1-4 ND 48pgs	$0.60	$1.80	$3.00	£0.40	£1.20	£2.00
Title Value:	$2.40	$7.20	$12.00	£1.60	£4.80	£8.00

Note: squarebound bookshelf format. The climax to all the New Universe stories

WARBLADE: ENDANGERED SPECIES
Image; 1 Jan 1995-4 Apr 1995

	$Good	$Fine	$N.Mint	£Good	£Fine	£N.Mint
1 ND Warblade and Ripclaw, tri-fold cover						
	$0.60	$1.80	$3.00	£0.40	£1.20	£2.00
2-4 ND Warblade and Ripclaw						
	$0.50	$1.50	$2.50	£0.30	£0.90	£1.50
Title Value:	$2.10	$6.30	$10.50	£1.30	£3.90	£6.50

WARCAT SPECIAL
Entity Comics; 1 May 1995

	$Good	$Fine	$N.Mint	£Good	£Fine	£N.Mint
1 ND Jason Raschack script, Raff lenco art, foil-stamped cover						
	$0.50	$1.50	$2.50	£0.30	£0.90	£1.50
Title Value:	$0.50	$1.50	$2.50	£0.30	£0.90	£1.50

WARCHILD
Maximum Comic Press,MS; 0 Jul 1995; 1 Jan 1995-4 Oct 1995

	$Good	$Fine	$N.Mint	£Good	£Fine	£N.Mint
0 ND features work by Liefeld, Stephenson, Platt, Yaep and Matsuda						
	$0.50	$1.50	$2.50	£0.30	£0.90	£1.50
1-2 ND Rob Liefeld script, Eric Stephenson art (2 alternate covers)						
	$0.50	$1.50	$2.50	£0.30	£0.90	£1.50
3 ND Rob Liefeld script, Eric Stephenson art (3 alternate covers)						
	$0.50	$1.50	$2.50	£0.30	£0.90	£1.50
4 ND Rob Liefeld script, Eric Stephenson art (2 alternate covers)						
	$0.50	$1.50	$2.50	£0.30	£0.90	£1.50
Title Value:	$2.50	$7.50	$12.50	£1.50	£4.50	£7.50

WARDRUMS
(see Journey: Wardrums)

WARHEADS
Marvel UK; 1 Jun 1992-14 Aug 1993
(see Overkill in British section)

	$Good	$Fine	$N.Mint	£Good	£Fine	£N.Mint
1 Wolverine guest-star, Nick Vince script and Gary Erskine art						
	$0.25	$0.75	$1.25	£0.15	£0.45	£0.75
2 Nick Fury and Shield appear						
	$0.25	$0.75	$1.25	£0.15	£0.45	£0.75
3 Nick Fury, Shield and Iron Man appear						
	$0.25	$0.75	$1.25	£0.15	£0.45	£0.75
4 X-Force appear	$0.25	$0.75	$1.25	£0.15	£0.45	£0.75
5 X-Force appear, Death's Head II cameo						
	$0.25	$0.75	$1.25	£0.15	£0.45	£0.75
6 Death's Head II appears						
	$0.25	$0.75	$1.25	£0.15	£0.45	£0.75
7 Death's Head II and Silver Surfer appear						
	$0.25	$0.75	$1.25	£0.15	£0.45	£0.75
8 X-Men and Silver Surfer appear						
	$0.25	$0.75	$1.25	£0.15	£0.45	£0.75
9-10	$0.25	$0.75	$1.25	£0.15	£0.45	£0.75
11 Mys-Tech Wars X-over, Death's Head II appears						
	$0.25	$0.75	$1.25	£0.15	£0.45	£0.75
12-14	$0.25	$0.75	$1.25	£0.15	£0.45	£0.75
Title Value:	$3.50	$10.50	$17.50	£2.10	£6.30	£10.50

WARHEADS: BLACK DAWN
Marvel UK,MS; 1 Jul 1993-2 Aug 1993

	$Good	$Fine	$N.Mint	£Good	£Fine	£N.Mint
1 David Hine art, red metallic cover and embossed logo						
	$0.40	$1.20	$2.00	£0.25	£0.75	£1.25
2	$0.25	$0.75	$1.25	£0.15	£0.45	£0.75
Title Value:	$0.65	$1.95	$3.25	£0.40	£1.20	£2.00

WARLASH
CFD Productions; 1 Oct 1995-present

	$Good	$Fine	$N.Mint	£Good	£Fine	£N.Mint
1-2 ND Frank Forte script, Rob Murdock art; black and white						
	$0.60	$1.80	$3.00	£0.40	£1.20	£2.00
Title Value:	$1.20	$3.60	$6.00	£0.80	£2.40	£4.00

WARLASH ASHCAN EDITION
Anubis Press; nn Sep 1994

	$Good	$Fine	$N.Mint	£Good	£Fine	£N.Mint
nn ND black and white						
	$0.50	$1.50	$2.50	£0.30	£0.90	£1.50
Title Value:	$0.50	$1.50	$2.50	£0.30	£0.90	£1.50

WARLOCK (1ST SERIES)
Marvel Comics Group; 1 Aug 1972-8 Oct 1973; 9 Oct 1975-15 Nov 1976
(see Fantastic Four #67, Strange Tales, Marvel Premiere)

	$Good	$Fine	$N.Mint	£Good	£Fine	£N.Mint
1 ND origin retold by Gil Kane						
	$5.00	$15.00	$30.00	£3.30	£10.00	£20.00
2-3 ND	$2.05	$6.25	$12.50	£1.25	£3.75	£7.50
4 scarce in the U.K. Dr. Doom cameo						
	$1.30	$4.00	$8.00	£1.00	£3.00	£6.00
5 scarce in the U.K.	$1.30	$4.00	$8.00	£1.00	£3.00	£6.00
6-8	$1.25	$3.75	$7.50	£0.80	£2.50	£5.00
9 2nd Thanos saga begins, Starlin story/art, continues from Strange Tales #181, Thanos cameo						
	$1.50	$4.50	$9.00	£1.00	£3.00	£6.00
10 Jim Starlin art, origin Thanos retold						
	$4.15	$12.50	$25.00	£2.05	£6.25	£12.50
11 Jim Starlin art, Thanos appears, Warlock "dies"						
	$3.30	$10.00	$20.00	£1.65	£5.00	£10.00
12-14 Jim Starlin art						
	$1.25	$3.75	$7.50	£0.80	£2.50	£5.00
15 origin Soul-Gem, Jim Starlin art, Thanos cover						
	$2.50	$7.50	$15.00	£1.65	£5.00	£10.00
Title Value:	$30.65	$92.50	$185.00	£18.95	£57.75	£115.50

WARLOCK (2ND SERIES)
Marvel Comics Group,MS; 1 Dec 1982-6 May 1983

	$Good	$Fine	$N.Mint	£Good	£Fine	£N.Mint
1 ND reprints begin						
	$0.80	$2.40	$4.00	£0.50	£1.50	£2.50
2-6 ND	$0.80	$2.40	$4.00	£0.50	£1.50	£2.50
Title Value:	$4.80	$14.40	$24.00	£3.00	£9.00	£15.00

Note: reprints from Strange Tales #178-181, Warlock #9-15 by Starlin

WARLOCK (3RD SERIES)
Marvel Comics Group,MS; 1 May 1992-6 Oct 1992

	$Good	$Fine	$N.Mint	£Good	£Fine	£N.Mint
1 ND reprints from Warlock Special Edition begin (1982/83 series)						
	$0.50	$1.50	$2.50	£0.30	£0.90	£1.50
2-5 ND	$0.50	$1.50	$2.50	£0.30	£0.90	£1.50
6 ND Warlock vs. Thanos, Avengers, Thing and Spiderman appear						
	$0.50	$1.50	$2.50	£0.30	£0.90	£1.50

WARLOCK 5

Aircel; 1 Nov 1986-22 1989

	$Good	$Fine	$N.Mint	£Good	£Fine	£N.Mint
Title Value:	$3.00	$9.00	$15.00	£1.80	£5.40	£9.00
1 ND scarce in the U.K.	$0.40	$1.20	$2.00	£0.50	£1.50	£2.50
2 ND	$0.40	$1.20	$2.00	£0.40	£1.20	£2.00
3 ND very scarce in the U.K.	$0.40	$1.20	$2.00	£0.50	£1.50	£2.50
4 ND scarce in the U.K.	$0.40	$1.20	$2.00	£0.40	£1.20	£2.00
5 ND scarce in the U.K. robot skull cover	$0.40	$1.20	$2.00	£0.40	£1.20	£2.00
6 ND scarce in the U.K. misnumbered "5", woman on cover	$0.40	$1.20	$2.00	£0.40	£1.20	£2.00
7-9 ND scarce in the U.K.	$0.40	$1.20	$2.00	£0.40	£1.20	£2.00
10-15 ND	$0.40	$1.20	$2.00	£0.25	£0.75	£1.25
16-17 ND Dale Keown pencils	$0.50	$1.50	$2.50	£0.30	£0.90	£1.50
18-22 ND	$0.40	$1.20	$2.00	£0.25	£0.75	£1.25
Title Value:	$9.00	$27.00	$45.00	£7.15	£21.45	£35.75
Trade paperback 1, reprints issues #1-5				£0.80	£2.40	£4.00
Trade paperback 2, reprints issues #6-9				£0.80	£2.40	£4.00

WARLOCK 5 BOOK II

Aircel; 1 Jun 1989-7 1990

	$Good	$Fine	$N.Mint	£Good	£Fine	£N.Mint
1-7 ND black and white	$0.40	$1.20	$2.00	£0.25	£0.75	£1.25
Title Value:	$2.80	$8.40	$14.00	£1.75	£5.25	£8.75
Graphic Album				£0.80	£2.40	£4.00

WARLOCK 5: THE GATHERING

Night Wynd; 1 Oct 1994-2 Jan 1994

	$Good	$Fine	$N.Mint	£Good	£Fine	£N.Mint
1-2 ND Barry Blair script and art	$0.40	$1.20	$2.00	£0.25	£0.75	£1.25
Title Value:	$0.80	$2.40	$4.00	£0.50	£1.50	£2.50

WARLOCK AND THE INFINITY WATCH

Marvel Comics Group; 1 Feb 1992-42 Jul 1995

	$Good	$Fine	$N.Mint	£Good	£Fine	£N.Mint
1 ND script by Jim Starlin, sequel to Infinity Gauntlet	$0.50	$1.50	$2.50	£0.30	£0.90	£1.50
2 ND	$0.40	$1.20	$2.00	£0.25	£0.75	£1.25
3-4 ND High Evolutionary appears	$0.40	$1.20	$2.00	£0.25	£0.75	£1.25
5-7 ND	$0.40	$1.20	$2.00	£0.25	£0.75	£1.25
8 ND Infinity War X-over, Thanos appears	$0.40	$1.20	$2.00	£0.25	£0.75	£1.25
9 ND Infinity War X-over, Galactus appears	$0.40	$1.20	$2.00	£0.25	£0.75	£1.25
10 ND Infinity War X-over, Thanos appears	$0.40	$1.20	$2.00	£0.25	£0.75	£1.25
11 ND	$0.30	$0.90	$1.50	£0.20	£0.60	£1.00
12-13 ND Hulk appears	$0.30	$0.90	$1.50	£0.20	£0.60	£1.00
14-17 ND	$0.30	$0.90	$1.50	£0.20	£0.60	£1.00
18 ND Reed Richards guest-stars	$0.30	$0.90	$1.50	£0.20	£0.60	£1.00
19-22 ND Infinity Crusade tie-in	$0.30	$0.90	$1.50	£0.20	£0.60	£1.00
23 ND Blood and Thunder part 4, Silver Surfer and Thor appear	$0.30	$0.90	$1.50	£0.20	£0.60	£1.00
24 ND Blood and Thunder part 8, Silver Surfer, Dr. Strange and Thor appear	$0.30	$0.90	$1.50	£0.20	£0.60	£1.00
25 ND Blood and Thunder part 12, Silver Surfer, Dr. Strange and Thor appear; embossed die-cut cover	$0.50	$1.50	$2.50	£0.30	£0.90	£1.50
26-27 ND	$0.30	$0.90	$1.50	£0.20	£0.60	£1.00
28 ND Giant Man, Black Widow, Thunderstrike, Hercules, Captain America and Vision appear	$0.30	$0.90	$1.50	£0.20	£0.60	£1.00
29-36 ND	$0.30	$0.90	$1.50	£0.20	£0.60	£1.00
37-39 ND Firelord appears	$0.30	$0.90	$1.50	£0.20	£0.60	£1.00
40 ND Thanos appears	$0.30	$0.90	$1.50	£0.20	£0.60	£1.00
41 ND Atlantis Rising tie-in	$0.30	$0.90	$1.50	£0.20	£0.60	£1.00
42 ND Atlantis Rising tie-in; ties into Curse of Rune #1 published by Malibu	$0.30	$0.90	$1.50	£0.20	£0.60	£1.00
Title Value:	$13.90	$41.70	$69.50	£9.05	£27.15	£45.25

WARLOCK CHRONICLES, THE

Marvel Comics Group; 1 Jul 1993-8 Feb 1994

	$Good	$Fine	$N.Mint	£Good	£Fine	£N.Mint
1 Jim Starlin script begins, holo-grafix foil cover	$0.50	$1.50	$2.50	£0.30	£0.90	£1.50
2-5 Infinity Crusade X-over	$0.40	$1.20	$2.00	£0.25	£0.75	£1.25
6 Blood and Thunder part 3	$0.40	$1.20	$2.00	£0.25	£0.75	£1.25
7 Blood and Thunder part 7	$0.40	$1.20	$2.00	£0.25	£0.75	£1.25
8 Blood and Thunder part 11	$0.40	$1.20	$2.00	£0.25	£0.75	£1.25
Title Value:	$3.30	$9.90	$16.50	£2.05	£6.15	£10.25

WARLOCKS

Aircel; 1 Nov 1988-12 Oct 1989

	$Good	$Fine	$N.Mint	£Good	£Fine	£N.Mint
1-12 ND Barry Blair script and art, black and white	$0.40	$1.20	$2.00	£0.25	£0.75	£1.25

	$Good	$Fine	$N.Mint	£Good	£Fine	£N.Mint
Title Value:	$4.80	$14.40	$24.00	£3.00	£9.00	£15.00
Special Edition 1 (1989) 40pgs, reprints				£0.25	£0.75	£1.25

WARLORD

DC Comics; 1 Jan/Feb 1976-2 Mar/Apr 1976; 3 Oct/Nov 1976-133 Winter 1988

(see DC Special Blue Ribbon Digest #10, First Issue Special #8)

	$Good	$Fine	$N.Mint	£Good	£Fine	£N.Mint
1 scarce in the U.K. Mike Grell art, continues from First Issue Special #8	$2.50	$7.50	$15.00	£1.65	£5.00	£10.00
2 scarce in the U.K. 1st appearance Machiste	$1.50	$4.50	$7.50	£1.00	£3.00	£5.00
3-4 scarce in the U.K.	$1.00	$3.00	$5.00	£0.60	£1.80	£3.00
5 ND scarce in the U.K.	$1.00	$3.00	$5.00	£0.70	£2.10	£3.50
6-8 scarce in the U.K.	$0.80	$2.40	$4.00	£0.50	£1.50	£2.50
9 scarce in the U.K. new costume	$0.80	$2.40	$4.00	£0.50	£1.50	£2.50
10 ND	$0.80	$2.40	$4.00	£0.60	£1.80	£3.00
11 ND origin retold from First Issue Special #8	$0.60	$1.80	$3.00	£0.40	£1.20	£2.00
12-14 ND	$0.60	$1.80	$3.00	£0.40	£1.20	£2.00
15 ND 44pgs, Tara returns, birth of Warlord's son	$0.70	$2.10	$3.50	£0.45	£1.35	£2.25
16-20 ND	$0.50	$1.50	$2.50	£0.30	£0.90	£1.50
21-27 ND	$0.40	$1.20	$2.00	£0.25	£0.75	£1.25
28 ND 1st Wizard World	$0.40	$1.20	$2.00	£0.25	£0.75	£1.25
29-30 ND	$0.40	$1.20	$2.00	£0.25	£0.75	£1.25
31 ND	$0.30	$0.90	$1.50	£0.20	£0.60	£1.00
32 ND 1st appearance Shakira	$0.30	$0.90	$1.50	£0.20	£0.60	£1.00
33-36 ND	$0.30	$0.90	$1.50	£0.20	£0.60	£1.00
37-39 ND Jim Starlin art on Omac back-up	$0.40	$1.20	$2.00	£0.25	£0.75	£1.25
40 ND new costume	$0.30	$0.90	$1.50	£0.20	£0.60	£1.00
41-47 ND	$0.30	$0.90	$1.50	£0.20	£0.60	£1.00
48 ND 52pgs, Arak Son of Thunder insert, Claw back-up	$0.40	$1.20	$2.00	£0.25	£0.75	£1.25
49 ND Claw back-up	$0.30	$0.90	$1.50	£0.20	£0.60	£1.00
50 ND	$0.30	$0.90	$1.50	£0.20	£0.60	£1.00
51 ND reprints #1	$0.25	$0.75	$1.25	£0.15	£0.45	£0.75
52 ND Dragonsword back-up	$0.25	$0.75	$1.25	£0.15	£0.45	£0.75
53 ND Mark Texeira art (1st pro work?), Dragonsword back-up	$0.25	$0.75	$1.25	£0.15	£0.45	£0.75
54 ND Mark Texeira art, Dragonsword back-up	$0.25	$0.75	$1.25	£0.15	£0.45	£0.75
55 ND Mark Texeira art, Arion back-up begins	$0.25	$0.75	$1.25	£0.15	£0.45	£0.75
56-58 ND Mark Texeira art	$0.25	$0.75	$1.25	£0.15	£0.45	£0.75
59 ND last Mike Grell art	$0.25	$0.75	$1.25	£0.15	£0.45	£0.75
60-62 ND	$0.25	$0.75	$1.25	£0.15	£0.45	£0.75
63 ND Barren Earth back-up starts, 16pg Masters of the Universe insert	$0.25	$0.75	$1.25	£0.15	£0.45	£0.75
64-70 ND	$0.25	$0.75	$1.25	£0.15	£0.45	£0.75
71 ND last Grell script	$0.25	$0.75	$1.25	£0.15	£0.45	£0.75
72-90 ND	$0.25	$0.75	$1.25	£0.15	£0.45	£0.75
91 ND origin retold	$0.25	$0.75	$1.25	£0.15	£0.45	£0.75
92-99 ND	$0.25	$0.75	$1.25	£0.15	£0.45	£0.75
100 ND DS painted cover	$0.30	$0.90	$1.50	£0.20	£0.60	£1.00
101-113 ND	$0.25	$0.75	$1.25	£0.15	£0.45	£0.75
114-115 ND Legends X-overs	$0.25	$0.75	$1.25	£0.15	£0.45	£0.75
116-119 ND	$0.25	$0.75	$1.25	£0.15	£0.45	£0.75
120-122 ND Art Thibert co-artist	$0.25	$0.75	$1.25	£0.15	£0.45	£0.75
123-130 ND	$0.25	$0.75	$1.25	£0.15	£0.45	£0.75
131 ND Rob Liefeld art on insert story, 1st work at DC	$0.50	$1.50	$2.50	£0.30	£0.90	£1.50
132 ND	$0.25	$0.75	$1.25	£0.15	£0.45	£0.75
133 ND DS	$0.30	$0.90	$1.50	£0.20	£0.60	£1.00
Title Value:	$48.10	$144.30	$243.00	£30.10	£90.35	£152.25
Warlord Trade paperback (Jan 1992), reprints plus 9 new pages of story/art by Mike Grell				£2.50	£7.50	£12.50

FEATURES

Arion, Lord of Atlantis in 55-62. Claw in 48, 49. Dragonsword in 51-54. Omac in 37-39, 42-47. Wizard World in 28, 29, 40, 41.

WARLORD (2ND SERIES)

DC Comics, MS; 1 Jan 1992-6 Jun 1992

	$Good	$Fine	$N.Mint	£Good	£Fine	£N.Mint
1-6 Mike Grell covers	$0.30	$0.90	$1.50	£0.20	£0.60	£1.00
Title Value:	$1.80	$5.40	$9.00	£1.20	£3.60	£6.00

WARLORD ANNUAL

DC Comics; 1 Nov 1982-6 Nov 1987

	$Good	$Fine	$N.Mint	£Good	£Fine	£N.Mint
1 ND 52pgs, Mike Grell cover	$0.30	$0.90	$1.50	£0.20	£0.60	£1.00

	$Good	$Fine	$N.Mint	£Good	£Fine	£N.Mint
2-5 ND	$0.30	$0.90	$1.50	£0.20	£0.60	£1.00
6 ND New Gods X-over						
	$0.30	$0.90	$1.50	£0.20	£0.60	£1.00
Title Value:	$1.80	$5.40	$9.00	£1.20	£3.60	£6.00

WARP
First; 1 Mar 1983-19 1985

	$Good	$Fine	$N.Mint	£Good	£Fine	£N.Mint
1-16 ND Frank Brunner art						
	$0.25	$0.75	$1.25	£0.15	£0.45	£0.75
17-19 ND scarce in the U.K.						
	$0.25	$0.75	$1.25	£0.15	£0.45	£0.75
Title Value:	$4.75	$14.25	$23.75	£2.85	£8.55	£14.25

WARP GRAPHICS ANNUAL
Warp; 1 1986

	$Good	$Fine	$N.Mint	£Good	£Fine	£N.Mint
1 ND 64pgs squarebound, includes new Elfquest story plus Mythadventures, A Distant Soil, Thunderbunny, Panda Khan, Blood of the Innocent, Captain Obese and Unicorn Isle; all colour						
	$0.60	$1.80	$3.00	£0.40	£1.20	£2.00
1 2nd printing ND	$0.50	$1.50	$2.50	£0.30	£0.90	£1.50
Title Value:	$1.10	$3.30	$5.50	£0.70	£2.10	£3.50

WARP SPECIAL
First; 1 Jul 1983-3 Jun 1984

	$Good	$Fine	$N.Mint	£Good	£Fine	£N.Mint
1 ND Chaykin art, features Chaos Prince of Madness origin						
	$0.25	$0.75	$1.25	£0.15	£0.45	£0.75
2 ND Silvestri/Gustovich art						
	$0.25	$0.75	$1.25	£0.15	£0.45	£0.75
3 ND Freeman art	$0.25	$0.75	$1.25	£0.15	£0.45	£0.75
Title Value:	$0.75	$2.25	$3.75	£0.45	£1.35	£2.25

WARPWALKING
Caliber Press,MS; 1 Jan 1992-4 Apr 1992

	$Good	$Fine	$N.Mint	£Good	£Fine	£N.Mint
1-4 ND	$0.40	$1.20	$2.00	£0.25	£0.75	£1.25
Title Value:	$1.60	$4.80	$8.00	£1.00	£3.00	£5.00

WARREN PRESENTS
Warren; 1 Jan 1979-12 1982

	$Good	$Fine	$N.Mint	£Good	£Fine	£N.Mint
1-12 ND	$0.50	$1.50	$2.50	£0.30	£0.90	£1.50
Title Value:	$6.00	$18.00	$30.00	£3.60	£10.80	£18.00

Note: most issues are reprint but not distributed in the U.K.

WARRIOR NUN AREALA
Antarctic Press,MS; 1 Dec 1994-3 Apr 1995

	$Good	$Fine	$N.Mint	£Good	£Fine	£N.Mint
1 ND Ben Dunn script and art						
	$0.90	$2.70	$4.50	£0.60	£1.80	£3.00
1 ND Signed Limited Edition (May 1995) - 5,000 copies						
	$2.50	$7.50	$12.50	£1.50	£4.50	£7.50
2-3 ND Ben Dunn script and art						
	$0.60	$1.80	$3.00	£0.40	£1.20	£2.00
Title Value:	$4.60	$13.80	$23.00	£2.90	£8.70	£14.50
Warrior Nun Areala (Jun 1995)						
Trade paperback reprints mini-series				£1.30	£3.90	£6.50

WARRIOR NUN AREALA BOOK TWO
Antarctic Press,MS; 1 Aug 1995-6 Jan 1996

	$Good	$Fine	$N.Mint	£Good	£Fine	£N.Mint
1-6 ND Ben Dunn script and art						
	$0.60	$1.80	$3.00	£0.40	£1.20	£2.00
Title Value:	$3.60	$10.80	$18.00	£2.40	£7.20	£12.00

WARRIORS
Adventure; 1 Nov 1987-7 1988?

	$Good	$Fine	$N.Mint	£Good	£Fine	£N.Mint
1 ND Adam Hughes art						
	$0.40	$1.20	$2.00	£0.25	£0.75	£1.25
2-7 ND	$0.40	$1.20	$2.00	£0.25	£0.75	£1.25
Title Value:	$2.80	$8.40	$14.00	£1.75	£5.25	£8.75

WARRIORS OF PLASM
Defiant; 1 Aug 1993-15 Oct 1994

	$Good	$Fine	$N.Mint	£Good	£Fine	£N.Mint
1 ND Jim Shooter script and David Lapham art begins						
	$0.40	$1.20	$2.00	£0.25	£0.75	£1.25
2-9 ND	$0.40	$1.20	$2.00	£0.25	£0.75	£1.25
10-12 ND	$0.30	$0.90	$1.50	£0.20	£0.60	£1.00
13 ND Schism X-over						
	$0.30	$0.90	$1.50	£0.20	£0.60	£1.00
14-15 ND	$0.30	$0.90	$1.50	£0.20	£0.60	£1.00
Title Value:	$5.40	$16.20	$27.00	£3.45	£10.35	£17.25
Warriors of Plasm (Feb 1994)						
Trade paperback reprints issues #1-4 and #0 plus sketches				£1.30	£3.90	£6.50

WARRIORS OF PLASM GRAPHIC NOVEL
Defiant; 1 Nov 1993

	$Good	$Fine	$N.Mint	£Good	£Fine	£N.Mint
1 ND 48pgs, squarebound; Len Wein and Dave Cockrum						
	$0.80	$2.40	$4.00	£0.50	£1.50	£2.50
Title Value:	$0.80	$2.40	$4.00	£0.50	£1.50	£2.50

WARSTRIKE
Malibu Ultraverse; 1 May 1994-7 Nov 1994

	$Good	$Fine	$N.Mint	£Good	£Fine	£N.Mint
1 ND Walt Simonson cover						
	$0.40	$1.20	$2.00	£0.25	£0.75	£1.25
2-7 ND	$0.40	$1.20	$2.00	£0.25	£0.75	£1.25
Title Value:	$2.80	$8.40	$14.00	£1.75	£5.25	£8.75

Note: all Non-Distributed on the news-stands in the U.K.

WARWORLD
Dark Horse,OS; 1 Feb 1989

	$Good	$Fine	$N.Mint	£Good	£Fine	£N.Mint
1 ND black and white						
	$0.40	$1.20	$2.00	£0.25	£0.75	£1.25
Title Value:	$0.40	$1.20	$2.00	£0.25	£0.75	£1.25

WARZONE
Entity Comics,MS; 1 Feb 1995-3 1995

	$Good	$Fine	$N.Mint	£Good	£Fine	£N.Mint
1-3 ND black and white						
	$0.60	$1.80	$3.00	£0.40	£1.20	£2.00
Title Value:	$1.80	$5.40	$9.00	£1.20	£3.60	£6.00

WASTELAND
DC Comics; 1 Dec 1987-18 Mar 1989

	$Good	$Fine	$N.Mint	£Good	£Fine	£N.Mint
1 LD in the U.K. David Lloyd art						
	$0.30	$0.90	$1.50	£0.20	£0.60	£1.00
2-4	$0.30	$0.90	$1.50	£0.20	£0.60	£1.00
5 George Freeman cover						
	$0.30	$0.90	$1.50	£0.20	£0.60	£1.00
5 (same story and art as above, cover numbered 6), Donald Simpson cover						
	$0.30	$0.90	$1.50	£0.20	£0.60	£1.00
6 ("The Real Number 6" on cover)						
	$0.30	$0.90	$1.50	£0.20	£0.60	£1.00
7-10	$0.30	$0.90	$1.50	£0.20	£0.60	£1.00
11 David Lloyd art						
	$0.30	$0.90	$1.50	£0.20	£0.60	£1.00
12-18	$0.30	$0.90	$1.50	£0.20	£0.60	£1.00
Title Value:	$5.70	$17.10	$28.50	£3.80	£11.40	£19.00

Note: Mature Readers, Deluxe Format. David Lloyd art featured.

WATCHMEN
DC Comics,MS; 1 May 1986-12 Aug 1987
(publication of last issue delayed)

	$Good	$Fine	$N.Mint	£Good	£Fine	£N.Mint
1 ND Dave Gibbons art begins, Alan Moore script						
	$1.00		$5.00	£0.60	£1.80	£3.00
2-11 ND	$0.60	$1.80	$3.00	£0.40	£1.20	£2.00
12 ND	$0.70	$2.10	$3.50	£0.50	£1.50	£2.50
Title Value:	$7.70	$23.10	$38.50	£5.10	£15.30	£25.50

Note: all are Deluxe Format, Baxter Paper. All have Dave Gibbons art/Alan Moore script.
Note also that in September 1990 DC announced that they had "uncovered" a quantity of issue #2 for re-release at cover price of $1.50.

	$Good	$Fine	$N.Mint	£Good	£Fine	£N.Mint
DC Trade paperback ND, reprints #1-12, new cover				£2.00	£6.00	£10.00
Warner Books Edition ND, cover as above				£2.00	£6.00	£10.00
Titan UK Edition, Yellow Smiley cover				£1.80	£5.40	£9.00
(Note: 2nd printings available of all the above at 90% value)						
Limited Edition Hardback, with slipcase; ND				£6.00	£18.00	£30.00

WAVEMAKERS
Blind Bat Press; 1 Jan 1990

	$Good	$Fine	$N.Mint	£Good	£Fine	£N.Mint
1 ND black and white						
	$0.50	$1.50	$2.50	£0.30	£0.90	£1.50
Title Value:	$0.50	$1.50	$2.50	£0.30	£0.90	£1.50

WAXWORK
Blackthorne; (3-D Series #55) 1 1988

	$Good	$Fine	$N.Mint	£Good	£Fine	£N.Mint
1 ND	$0.50	$1.50	$2.50	£0.30	£0.90	£1.50
1 ND non 3-D version						
	$0.40	$1.20	$2.00	£0.25	£0.75	£1.25
Title Value:	$0.90	$2.70	$4.50	£0.55	£1.65	£2.75

WAY OUT STRIPS
Fantagraphics; 1 Feb 1994

	$Good	$Fine	$N.Mint	£Good	£Fine	£N.Mint
1 ND Carol Swain script and art; black and white						
	$0.40	$1.20	$2.00	£0.25	£0.75	£1.25
Title Value:	$0.40	$1.20	$2.00	£0.25	£0.75	£1.25

WEAPON X
Marvel Comics Group; 1 Mar 1995-4 Jun 1995

	$Good	$Fine	$N.Mint	£Good	£Fine	£N.Mint
1 ND Larry Hama script, Adam Kubert art						
	$1.00	$3.00	$5.00	£0.60	£1.80	£3.00
2-3 ND Larry Hama script, Adam Kubert art						
	$0.60	$1.80	$3.00	£0.40	£1.20	£2.00
4 ND Larry Hama script, Adam Kubert art; continued in X-Men: Omega						
	$0.60	$1.80	$3.00	£0.40	£1.20	£2.00
Title Value:	$2.80	$8.40	$14.00	£1.75	£5.40	£9.00

Note: this title temporarily replaced Wolverine during the "Age of Apocalypse" storyline
The Ultimate Weapon X (Jul 1995)

	$Good	$Fine	$N.Mint	£Good	£Fine	£N.Mint
96pgs, Bookshelf Edtion collects issues #1-4 with etched gold cover				£1.20	£3.60	£6.00

WEAPON ZERO
Image; 0 Oct 1995-present

	$Good	$Fine	$N.Mint	£Good	£Fine	£N.Mint
0 ND Walt Simonson script, Joe Benitez art						
	$0.50	$1.50	$2.50	£0.30	£0.90	£1.50
1 ND	$0.50	$1.50	$2.50	£0.30	£0.90	£1.50
Title Value:	$1.00	$3.00	$5.00	£0.60	£1.80	£3.00

WEAPON ZERO T-MINUS
Image,MS; 4 May 1995-1 Aug 1995

	$Good	$Fine	$N.Mint	£Good	£Fine	£N.Mint
4-1 ND Walt Simonson script, Joe Benitez and Batt art						
	$0.50	$1.50	$2.50	£0.30	£0.90	£1.50
Title Value:	$2.00	$6.00	$10.00	£1.20	£3.60	£6.00

WEASEL PATROL
Eclipse,OS; 1 Apr 1989

	$Good	$Fine	$N.Mint	£Good	£Fine	£N.Mint
1 ND	$0.40	$1.20	$2.00	£0.25	£0.75	£1.25
Title Value:	$0.40	$1.20	$2.00	£0.25	£0.75	£1.25

WEAVEWORLD
Marvel Comics Group/Epic,MS; 1 Dec 1991-3 Mar 1992

	$Good	$Fine	$N.Mint	£Good	£Fine	£N.Mint
1-3 ND 48pgs, squarebound; adapts Clive Barker novel						
	$0.80	$2.40	$4.00	£0.50	£1.50	£2.50
Title Value:	$2.40	$7.20	$12.00	£1.50	£4.50	£7.50

WEB
DC Comics/Impact; 1 Sep 1991-14 Oct 1992
(see Comet, Fly, Jaguar, Shield)

	$Good	$Fine	$N.Mint	£Good	£Fine	£N.Mint
1-8	$0.15	$0.45	$0.75	£0.10	£0.35	£0.60
9 previews Crusaders #1 (see Jaguar #9), trading cards included						
	$0.15	$0.45	$0.75	£0.10	£0.35	£0.60
10	$0.15	$0.45	$0.75	£0.10	£0.35	£0.60
11 $1.25 covers begin						
	$0.15	$0.45	$0.75	£0.10	£0.35	£0.60
12-14	$0.15	$0.45	$0.75	£0.10	£0.35	£0.60

	$Good	$Fine	$N.Mint	£Good	£Fine	£N.Mint
Title Value:	$2.10	$6.30	$10.50	£1.40	£4.90	£8.40

Note: Archie character acquired by DC though events take place outside DC Universe continuity

WEB ANNUAL, THE
DC Comics/Impact; 1 May 1992

	$Good	$Fine	$N.Mint	£Good	£Fine	£N.Mint
1 48pgs, Earthquest part 1, leads into Crusaders #1 (see other Impact annuals), includes trading cards						
	$0.30	$0.90	$1.50	£0.20	£0.60	£1.00
Title Value:	$0.30	$0.90	$1.50	£0.20	£0.60	£1.00

WEB OF HORROR
Major; 1 Dec 1969-3 Apr 1970

	$Good	$Fine	$N.Mint	£Good	£Fine	£N.Mint
1 scarce in the U.K. Wrightson, Kaluta art						
	$5.75	$17.50	$35.00	£3.75	£11.00	£22.50
2 scarce in the U.K. Wrightson, Kaluta art						
	$4.15	$12.50	$25.00	£2.90	£8.75	£17.50
3 scarce in the U.K. Wrightson, Kaluta, Brunner						
	$4.15	$12.50	$25.00	£2.90	£8.75	£17.50
Title Value:	$14.05	$42.50	$85.00	£9.55	£28.50	£57.50

Note: all distributed on the news-stands in the U.K.

WEB OF SCARLET SPIDER
Marvel Comics Group; 1 Nov 1995-4 Jan 1996

	$Good	$Fine	$N.Mint	£Good	£Fine	£N.Mint
1 ND Tom DeFalco script, Paris Karounos and Randy Emberlin art, continued in Amazing Scarlet Spider #1; metallic ink cover						
	$0.40	$1.20	$2.00	£0.25	£0.75	£1.25
2 ND continued in Amazing Scarlet Spider #2						
	$0.40	$1.20	$2.00	£0.25	£0.75	£1.25
3 ND continued in New Warriors #67						
	$0.40	$1.20	$2.00	£0.25	£0.75	£1.25
4 ND Nightmare in Scarlet part 3 (conclusion)						
	$0.40	$1.20	$2.00	£0.25	£0.75	£1.25
Title Value:	$1.60	$4.80	$8.00	£1.00	£3.00	£5.00

WEB OF SPIDERMAN SUPER-SIZE SPECIAL
Marvel Comics Group,OS; 1 Oct 1995

	$Good	$Fine	$N.Mint	£Good	£Fine	£N.Mint
1 ND 64pgs, Planet of Symbiotes part 5 (conclusion); metallic ink cover						
	$0.80	$2.40	$4.00	£0.50	£1.50	£2.50
Title Value:	$0.80	$2.40	$4.00	£0.50	£1.50	£2.50

WEB OF SPIDERMAN, THE
Marvel Comics Group; 1 Apr 1985-129 Oct 1995

	$Good	$Fine	$N.Mint	£Good	£Fine	£N.Mint
1 LD in the U.K. Charles Vess cover						
	$3.30	$10.00	$20.00	£1.30	£4.00	£8.00
2-3	$1.50	$4.50	$7.50	£0.80	£2.40	£4.00
4-5	$1.00	$3.00	$5.00	£0.60	£1.80	£3.00
6 Secret Wars X-over, Zeck art						
	$1.00	$3.00	$5.00	£0.60	£1.80	£3.00
7	$1.00	$3.00	$5.00	£0.60	£1.80	£3.00
8 Charles Vess cover						
	$1.00	$3.00	$5.00	£0.60	£1.80	£3.00
9	$1.00	$3.00	$5.00	£0.60	£1.80	£3.00
10 Dominic Fortune appears						
	$1.00	$3.00	$5.00	£0.60	£1.80	£3.00
11	$0.80	$2.40	$4.00	£0.50	£1.50	£2.50
12 Peter David story						
	$0.80	$2.40	$4.00	£0.50	£1.50	£2.50
13 Peter David story, Byrne cover						
	$0.80	$2.40	$4.00	£0.50	£1.50	£2.50
14-15 red costume returns						
	$0.80	$2.40	$4.00	£0.50	£1.50	£2.50
16-17 red costume returns						
	$0.80	$2.40	$4.00	£0.40	£1.20	£2.00
18 "Venom's hand appears"						
	$0.80	$2.40	$4.00	£0.40	£1.20	£2.00
19 1st appearance Solo						
	$0.80	$2.40	$4.00	£0.40	£1.20	£2.00
20-25	$0.80	$2.40	$4.00	£0.35	£1.05	£1.75
26 Charles Vess cover						
	$0.80	$2.40	$4.00	£0.35	£1.05	£1.75
27-28	$0.80	$2.40	$4.00	£0.35	£1.05	£1.75
29 Wolverine and Hobgoblin appear						
	$2.50	$7.50	$12.50	£1.40	£4.20	£7.00
30 origin Hobgoblin and The Rose						
	$2.00	$6.00	$10.00	£1.20	£3.60	£6.00
31-32 Kraven saga, Zeck art						
	$1.50	$4.50	$7.50	£0.80	£2.40	£4.00
33 very LD	$0.60	$1.80	$3.00	£0.50	£1.50	£2.50
34 LD in the U.K.	$0.60	$1.80	$3.00	£0.35	£1.05	£1.75
35 LD in the U.K. 1st appearance Tarantula II						
	$0.60	$1.80	$3.00	£0.35	£1.05	£1.75
36 LD in the U.K. 1st appearance Tombstone						
	$0.60	$1.80	$3.00	£0.35	£1.05	£1.75
37	$0.60	$1.80	$3.00	£0.30	£0.90	£1.50
38 Hobgoblin appears						
	$1.00	$3.00	$5.00	£0.60	£1.80	£3.00
39	$0.50	$1.50	$2.50	£0.30	£0.90	£1.50
40 LD in the U.K.	$0.50	$1.50	$2.50	£0.35	£1.05	£1.75
41-45	$0.50	$1.50	$2.50	£0.30	£0.90	£1.50
46 Hulk appears	$0.50	$1.50	$2.50	£0.35	£1.05	£1.75
47 Inferno X-over, Hobgoblin II appears						
	$0.50	$1.50	$2.50	£0.40	£1.20	£2.00
48 Inferno X-over, origin Hobgoblin II (formerly Jack O'Lantern); X-over Spectacular Spiderman #147						
	$3.00	$9.00	$15.00	£0.90	£2.70	£4.50
49	$0.50	$1.50	$2.50	£0.30	£0.90	£1.50
50 DS Puma, Prowler, Rocket Racer, Sandman, Silver Sable, Will O' The Wisp appear						
	$0.50	$1.50	$2.50	£0.30	£0.90	£1.50
51-58	$0.40	$1.20	$2.00	£0.25	£0.75	£1.25
59 Dr. Doom appears; Acts of Vengeance tie-in (2nd part of Super Spiderman Saga – see Spectacular Spiderman #158)						
	$1.40	$4.20	$7.00	£0.60	£1.80	£3.00
60 LD in the U.K. Goliath appears; Acts of Vengeance tie-in, Cosmic Spiderman						
	$0.60	$1.80	$3.00	£0.40	£1.20	£2.00
61 LD in the U.K. Wizard and Dragon Man appear; Acts of Vengeance tie-in, Cosmic Spiderman						
	$0.40	$1.20	$2.00	£0.30	£0.90	£1.50
62-63	$0.40	$1.20	$2.00	£0.20	£0.60	£1.00
64 Acts of Vengeance aftermath						
	$0.40	$1.20	$2.00	£0.20	£0.60	£1.00
65 Super Spidey Saga epilogue						
	$0.40	$1.20	$2.00	£0.20	£0.60	£1.00
66 Green Goblin appears						
	$0.50	$1.50	$2.50	£0.25	£0.75	£1.25
67 LD in the U.K. Green Goblin appears						
	$0.50	$1.50	$2.50	£0.30	£0.90	£1.50
68 ND	$0.40	$1.20	$2.00	£0.20	£0.60	£1.00
69 ND Spiderman vs Hulk						
	$0.40	$1.20	$2.00	£0.25	£0.75	£1.25
70 ND	$0.40	$1.20	$2.00	£0.20	£0.60	£1.00
71-72 ND Dominic Fortune appears						
	$0.30	$0.90	$1.50	£0.20	£0.60	£1.00
73 ND Human Torch/Sub-Mariner appear, John Byrne script						
	$0.30	$0.90	$1.50	£0.20	£0.60	£1.00
74-75 ND Colossus appears						
	$0.30	$0.90	$1.50	£0.20	£0.60	£1.00
76-77 ND	$0.30	$0.90	$1.50	£0.20	£0.60	£1.00
78 ND Cloak and Dagger appear						
	$0.30	$0.90	$1.50	£0.20	£0.60	£1.00
79 ND	$0.30	$0.90	$1.50	£0.20	£0.60	£1.00

Warp Graphics Annual #1

Watchcats #1

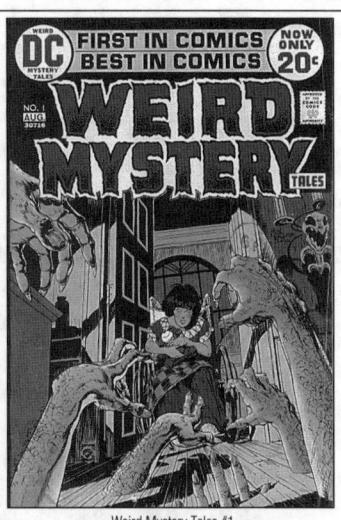

Weird Mystery Tales #1

MINT = 100% / NEAR MINT (inc. +/-) = 90–99% / VERY FINE (inc. +/-) = 75–89% / FINE (inc. +/-) = 55–74%
VERY GOOD (inc. +/-) = 35–54% / GOOD (inc. +/-) = 15–34% / FAIR = 5–14% / POOR = 1–4%

631

	$Good	$Fine	$N.Mint	£Good	£Fine	£N.Mint
80 ND Silvermane appears	$0.30	$0.90	$1.50	£0.20	£0.60	£1.00
81-83 ND	$0.30	$0.90	$1.50	£0.20	£0.60	£1.00
84-88 ND Name of the Rose story, Hobgoblin appears	$0.30	$0.90	$1.50	£0.20	£0.60	£1.00
89 ND Name of the Rose story, The Rose becomes Blood Rose, Richard Fisk becomes the new Kingpin	$0.30	$0.90	$1.50	£0.20	£0.60	£1.00
90 ND pre-bagged 30th anniversary issue, hologram cover, gatefold poster	$0.90	$2.70	$4.50	£0.60	£1.80	£3.00
90 2nd printing, ND (Nov 1992) - gold foil hologram cover	$0.60	$1.80	$3.00	£0.40	£1.20	£2.00
91-92 ND	$0.30	$0.90	$1.50	£0.20	£0.60	£1.00
93 ND Moon Knight guest-stars	$0.30	$0.90	$1.50	£0.20	£0.60	£1.00
94 ND Infinity War X-over, Spiderman vs. Hobgoblin	$0.30	$0.90	$1.50	£0.20	£0.60	£1.00
95 ND Spirits of Venom part 1, continued in Spirits of Vengeance #5	$0.30	$0.90	$1.50	£0.20	£0.60	£1.00
96 ND Spirits of Venom part 3, Ghost Rider, John Blaze and Hobgoblin appear, concludes in Spirits of Vengeance #6; painted cover by Mark Texeira	$0.30	$0.90	$1.50	£0.20	£0.60	£1.00
97-99 ND	$0.30	$0.90	$1.50	£0.20	£0.60	£1.00
100 ND 48pgs, holo-grafix foil cover, 1st appearance Spider-armour	$0.60	$1.80	$3.00	£0.40	£1.20	£2.00
101 Maximum Carnage part 2, continued in Amazing Spiderman #378	$0.30	$0.90	$1.50	£0.20	£0.60	£1.00
102 Maximum Carnage part 6, continued in Amazing Spiderman #379	$0.30	$0.90	$1.50	£0.20	£0.60	£1.00
103 Maximum Carnage part 10, continued in Amazing Spiderman #380	$0.30	$0.90	$1.50	£0.20	£0.60	£1.00
104-106 Infinity Crusade X-over	$0.30	$0.90	$1.50	£0.20	£0.60	£1.00
106 ND pre-bagged with copy of Dirt Magazine and audio cassette	$0.60	$1.80	$3.00	£0.40	£1.20	£2.00
107-108 Sandman appears	$0.30	$0.90	$1.50	£0.20	£0.60	£1.00
109-111 Lizard appears	$0.30	$0.90	$1.50	£0.20	£0.60	£1.00
112 Pursuit story, concluded in Spiderman #389	$0.30	$0.90	$1.50	£0.20	£0.60	£1.00
113 Gambit and Black Cat appear	$0.30	$0.90	$1.50	£0.20	£0.60	£1.00
113 ND Collector's Edition, pre-bagged with 16pg preview and animation cel from Spiderman TV series; metallic ink cover	$0.60	$1.80	$3.00	£0.40	£1.20	£2.00
114-116	$0.30	$0.90	$1.50	£0.20	£0.60	£1.00
117 Power and Responsibility part 1	$0.30	$0.90	$1.50	£0.20	£0.60	£1.00
117 Power and Responsibility part 1, foil stamped cover; incorporates 16pg flip book with second foil stamped cover; continued in Spiderman #394	$0.60	$1.80	$3.00	£0.40	£1.20	£2.00
118-119 Venom appears	$0.30	$0.90	$1.50	£0.20	£0.60	£1.00
119 ND pre-bagged with copy of Marvel Milestone Edition of Amazing Spiderman #150	$0.60	$1.80	$3.00	£0.40	£1.20	£2.00
120 48pgs, Web of Life part 1, continued in Spiderman #54	$0.50	$1.50	$2.50	£0.30	£0.90	£1.50
121 Web of Life part 3, continued in Spiderman #55	$0.30	$0.90	$1.50	£0.20	£0.60	£1.00
122-123 The Jackal appears	$0.30	$0.90	$1.50	£0.20	£0.60	£1.00
124 The Mark of Kaine part 1, continued in Amazing Spiderman #401	$0.30	$0.90	$1.50	£0.20	£0.60	£1.00
125 48pgs, the return of the Gwen Stacy clone	$0.60	$1.80	$3.00	£0.40	£1.20	£2.00
125 ND 48pgs, 3-D holodisk cover, Gwen Stacy clone	$0.80	$2.40	$4.00	£0.50	£1.50	£2.50
126 The Trial of Peter Parker part 1, continued in Amazing Spiderman #403	$0.30	$0.90	$1.50	£0.20	£0.60	£1.00
127 Maximum Clonage part 2, continued in Amazing Spiderman #404	$0.30	$0.90	$1.50	£0.20	£0.60	£1.00
128 Exiled part 1, continued in Amazing Spiderman #405	$0.30	$0.90	$1.50	£0.20	£0.60	£1.00
129 Timebomb part 2, continues in Amazing Spiderman #406	$0.30	$0.90	$1.50	£0.20	£0.60	£1.00
Title Value:	$80.00	$240.10	$403.50	£45.90	£137.80	£231.00

WEB OF THE SPIDERMAN ANNUAL, THE
Marvel Comics Group; 1 Sep 1985-10 1994

	$Good	$Fine	$N.Mint	£Good	£Fine	£N.Mint
1 ND	$0.80	$2.40	$4.00	£0.50	£1.50	£2.50
2 ND Arthur Adams art, New Mutants X-over	$1.20	$3.60	$6.00	£0.60	£1.80	£3.00
3 ND scarce in the U.K. all poster issue	$0.60	$1.80	$3.00	£0.50	£1.50	£2.50
4 ND squarebound, Evolutionary War, Ron Lim art	$0.60	$1.80	$3.00	£0.40	£1.20	£2.00
5 ND squarebound, Atlantis Attacks part 11, Fantastic Four appear	$0.50	$1.50	$2.50	£0.30	£0.90	£1.50
6 ND Spiderman's Totally Tiny Adventure part 3 Punisher appears	$0.50	$1.50	$2.50	£0.30	£0.90	£1.50
7 ND The Vibranium Vendetta part 3 (conclusion), Iron Man, Black Panther, Kingpin appear, origins retold of Green Goblin I & II plus Hobgoblin I & II and Venom	$0.50	$1.50	$2.50	£0.30	£0.90	£1.50
8 ND The Hero Killers part 3, New Warriors appear, Venom appears	$0.50	$1.50	$2.50	£0.30	£0.90	£1.50
9 ND 64pgs, pre-bagged with trading card introducing Cadre	$0.60	$1.80	$3.00	£0.40	£1.20	£2.00
10 ND 64pgs, Spiderman vs. Shriek	$0.60	$1.80	$3.00	£0.40	£1.20	£2.00
Title Value:	$6.40	$19.20	$32.00	£4.00	£12.00	£20.00

WEIRD FALL
Antarctic Press; 1 Jul 1995

	$Good	$Fine	$N.Mint	£Good	£Fine	£N.Mint
1 ND Matt Howarth script and art; black and white	$0.50	$1.50	$2.50	£0.30	£0.90	£1.50
Title Value:	$0.50	$1.50	$2.50	£0.30	£0.90	£1.50

WEIRD FANTASY
E.C. Comics; 13 May/Jun 1950-22 Nov/Dec 1953
(formerly A Moon, A Girl, A Romance; becomes Weird Science Fantasy #23 on)

	$Good	$Fine	$N.Mint	£Good	£Fine	£N.Mint
1 number #13 on cover	$105.00	$325.00	$875.00	£75.00	£225.00	£600.00
2 number #14 on cover	$67.50	$205.00	$480.00	£46.00	£135.00	£325.00
3 number #15 on cover	$55.00	$170.00	$400.00	£39.00	£115.00	£270.00
4 number #16 on cover	$52.50	$160.00	$375.00	£36.00	£105.00	£250.00
5 number #17 on cover, Wally Wood art	$50.00	$150.00	$350.00	£34.00	£100.00	£235.00
6-10	$34.00	$100.00	$240.00	£22.50	£67.50	£160.00
11-13	$29.00	$85.00	$200.00	£19.00	£57.50	£135.00
14 Frazetta and Williamson art - 1st time at E.C.	$43.00	$125.00	$300.00	£29.00	£85.00	£200.00
15-16 Williamson art	$29.00	$85.00	$200.00	£19.00	£57.50	£135.00
17-19 Ray Bradbury adaptation	$29.00	$85.00	$200.00	£19.00	£57.50	£135.00
20 Frazetta and Williamson art	$29.00	$85.00	$200.00	£19.00	£57.50	£135.00
21 classic space girl-and-space monster cover by Frazetta and Williamson	$43.00	$125.00	$300.00	£29.00	£85.00	£200.00
22	$21.00	$62.50	$150.00	£14.00	£43.00	£100.00
Title Value:	$868.00	$2587.50	$6230.00	£585.50	£1748.00	£4195.00

Note: all Non-Distributed on the news-stands in the U.K.

WEIRD FANTASY (2ND SERIES)
Russ Cochran/EC Comics; 1 Oct 1992-present

	$Good	$Fine	$N.Mint	£Good	£Fine	£N.Mint
1 ND reprints begin from original 1950s EC series with exact cover and interior reproduction	$0.40	$1.20	$2.00	£0.25	£0.75	£1.25
2-13 ND	$0.40	$1.20	$2.00	£0.25	£0.75	£1.25
Title Value:	$5.20	$15.60	$26.00	£3.25	£9.75	£16.25

Weird Fantasy Annual #1 (Sep 1994)
reprints issues #1-5 with covers — £1.20 / £3.60 / £6.00

Weird Fantasy Annual #2 (Jan 1995)
reprints issues #6-10 with covers — £1.20 / £3.60 / £6.00

WEIRD MYSTERY TALES
DC Comics; 1 Jul/Aug 1972-24 Nov 1975
(see DC 100 Page Super-Spectacular)

	$Good	$Fine	$N.Mint	£Good	£Fine	£N.Mint
1 scarce in the U.K. Jack Kirby art	$1.50	$4.50	$7.50	£1.00	£3.00	£5.00
2-3 Jack Kirby art	$0.80	$2.40	$4.00	£0.50	£1.50	£2.50
4 2pgs Jim Starlin art	$0.80	$2.40	$4.00	£0.50	£1.50	£2.50
5-10	$0.80	$2.40	$4.00	£0.50	£1.50	£2.50
11-20	$0.60	$1.80	$3.00	£0.40	£1.20	£2.00
21-23 scarce in the U.K.	$0.60	$1.80	$3.00	£0.50	£1.50	£2.50
24 Kaluta art	$0.60	$1.80	$3.00	£0.50	£1.50	£2.50
Title Value:	$17.10	$51.30	$85.50	£11.50	£34.50	£57.50

ARTISTS
Nino art in 5, 6, 9, 13, 16, 21. Wood art in 23.

WEIRD ROMANCE
Eclipse; 1 Feb 1988
(Seduction of the Innocent #9)

	$Good	$Fine	$N.Mint	£Good	£Fine	£N.Mint
1 ND	$0.40	$1.20	$2.00	£0.25	£0.75	£1.25
Title Value:	$0.40	$1.20	$2.00	£0.25	£0.75	£1.25

WEIRD SCIENCE
E.C. Comics; 1 May/Jun 1950-22 Nov/Dec 1953
(formerly Saddle Romances #1-11; becomes Weird Science-Fantasy #23 on)

	$Good	$Fine	$N.Mint	£Good	£Fine	£N.Mint
1 scarce in the U.K. has #12 on cover	$110.00	$335.00	$900.00	£75.00	£225.00	£600.00
2 scarce in the U.K. has #13 on cover; classic Feldstein flying saucer cover	$70.00	$210.00	$500.00	£48.00	£140.00	£335.00
3 scarce in the U.K. has #14 on cover	$62.50	$190.00	$450.00	£43.00	£125.00	£300.00
4 scarce in the U.K. has #15 on cover	$60.00	$180.00	$425.00	£41.00	£120.00	£285.00
5-10	$39.00	$115.00	$275.00	£26.00	£77.50	£185.00
11-14	$30.00	$90.00	$210.00	£20.00	£60.00	£140.00
15-16 Williamson art	$32.00	$95.00	$225.00	£21.00	£62.50	£150.00
17-18 Williamson art; Ray Bradbury adaptation	$32.00	$95.00	$225.00	£21.00	£62.50	£150.00
19-20 Ray Bradbury adaptation	$43.00	$125.00	$300.00	£29.00	£85.00	£200.00
21-22 Frazetta, Williamson, Wood art	$43.00	$125.00	$300.00	£29.00	£85.00	£200.00

	$Good	$Fine	$N.Mint	£Good	£Fine	£N.Mint
Title Value:	$956.50	$2845.00	$6865.00	£643.00	£1905.00	£4590.00
Note: all Non-Distributed on the news-stands in the U.K.						

WEIRD SCIENCE (2ND SERIES)
Gladstone; 1 Sep 1990-4 Mar 1991

	$Good	$Fine	$N.Mint	£Good	£Fine	£N.Mint
1 ND 64pgs, reprints Weird Science #22, Weird Fantasy #1						
	$0.50	$1.50	$2.50	£0.30	£0.90	£1.50
2 ND 64pgs, reprints Weird Science #16, Weird Fantasy #7						
	$0.50	$1.50	$2.50	£0.30	£0.90	£1.50
3 ND 64pgs, reprints Weird Science #9						
	$0.50	$1.50	$2.50	£0.30	£0.90	£1.50
4 ND 64pgs, reprints						
	$0.50	$1.50	$2.50	£0.30	£0.90	£1.50
Title Value:	$2.00	$6.00	$10.00	£1.20	£3.60	£6.00

Note: reprints of 1950s sci-fi material featuring art by Wood, Feldstein, Kamen, Kurtzman and others. Bi-monthly

WEIRD SCIENCE (3RD SERIES)
Russ Cochran/EC Comics; 1 Sep 1992-present

	$Good	$Fine	$N.Mint	£Good	£Fine	£N.Mint
1 ND reprints begin from original 1950s EC series with exact cover and interior reproduction						
	$0.40	$1.20	$2.00	£0.25	£0.75	£1.25
2-14 ND	$0.40	$1.20	$2.00	£0.25	£0.75	£1.25
Title Value:	$5.60	$16.80	$28.00	£3.50	£10.50	£17.50
Weird Science Annual #1 (Aug 1994)						
reprints five stories with covers, softcover				£1.20	£3.60	£6.00
Weird Science Annual #2						
reprints five stories with covers, softcover				£1.20	£3.60	£6.00

WEIRD SCIENCE-FANTASY
EC Comics; 23 Mar 1954-29 Jun 1955
(formerly Weird Science. Becomes Incredible Science Fiction)

	$Good	$Fine	$N.Mint	£Good	£Fine	£N.Mint
23-24 Williamson, Wood art						
	$32.00	$95.00	$225.00	£21.00	£62.50	£150.00
25 Williamson, Wood art; Ray Bradbury adaptation						
	$32.00	$95.00	$225.00	£21.00	£62.50	£150.00
26 flying saucer special issue						
	$32.00	$95.00	$225.00	£21.00	£62.50	£150.00
27	$32.00	$95.00	$225.00	£21.00	£62.50	£150.00
28 Williamson, Wood art						
	$32.00	$95.00	$225.00	£21.00	£62.50	£150.00
29 Williamson, Wood art, Frazetta cover						
	$52.50	$160.00	$375.00	£36.00	£105.00	£250.00
Title Value:	$244.50	$730.00	$1725.00	£162.00	£480.00	£1150.00
Note: all Non-Distributed on the news-stands in the U.K.						

WEIRD SCIENCE-FANTASY (2ND SERIES)
Russ Cochran/EC Comics; 1 Nov 1992-present

	$Good	$Fine	$N.Mint	£Good	£Fine	£N.Mint
1 ND reprints begin from original 1950s EC series with exact cover and interior reproduction						
	$0.30	$0.90	$1.50	£0.20	£0.60	£1.00
2-7 ND	$0.30	$0.90	$1.50	£0.20	£0.60	£1.00
Title Value:	$2.10	$6.30	$10.50	£1.40	£4.20	£7.00
Weird-Science Fantasy Annual #1 (Oct 1994)						
reprints issues #1-5 with covers				£1.20	£3.60	£6.00
Weird-Science Fantasy Annual #2 (Jul 1995)						
reprints issues #6-11 with covers				£1.70	£5.10	£8.50

WEIRD SCIENCE-FANTASY ANNUAL
E.C. Comics; 1 1952-2 1953

	$Good	$Fine	$N.Mint	£Good	£Fine	£N.Mint
1 very scarce in the U.K.						
	$155.00	$465.00	$1250.00	£105.00	£325.00	£875.00
2 very scarce in the U.K.						
	$100.00	$310.00	$725.00	£70.00	£210.00	£500.00
Title Value:	$255.00	$775.00	$1975.00	£175.00	£535.00	£1375.00

WEIRD SUSPENSE
Atlas; 1 Feb 1975-3 Jul 1975

	$Good	$Fine	$N.Mint	£Good	£Fine	£N.Mint
1-3 Tarantula appears; distributed in the U.K.						
	$0.25	$0.75	$1.25	£0.15	£0.45	£0.75
Title Value:	$0.75	$2.25	$3.75	£0.45	£1.35	£2.25

WEIRD TALES ILLUSTRATED
Millennium; 1 May 1992-2 1992

	$Good	$Fine	$N.Mint	£Good	£Fine	£N.Mint
1 ND John Bolton and Kelley Jones art featured						
	$0.50	$1.50	$2.50	£0.30	£0.90	£1.50
1 ND Deluxe Edition, squarebound; as above plus art by Tim Vigil and P. Craig Russell, back cover also by John Bolton						
	$0.60	$1.80	$3.00	£0.40	£1.20	£2.00
2 ND John Bolton, Mike Mignola and P. Craig Russell art featured						
	$0.50	$1.50	$2.50	£0.30	£0.90	£1.50
Title Value:	$1.60	$4.80	$8.00	£1.00	£3.00	£5.00

WEIRD WAR TALES
DC Comics; 1 Sep/Oct 1971-124 Jun 1983

	$Good	$Fine	$N.Mint	£Good	£Fine	£N.Mint
1 48pgs	$1.25	$3.75	$7.50	£0.80	£2.50	£5.00
2-3 48pgs	$1.00	$3.00	$5.00	£0.70	£2.10	£3.50
4-5 48pgs	$0.90	$2.70	$4.50	£0.60	£1.80	£3.00
6-7	$0.80	$2.40	$4.00	£0.50	£1.50	£2.50
8 Neal Adams inks						
	$1.00	$3.00	$5.00	£0.60	£1.80	£3.00
9-10	$0.80	$2.40	$4.00	£0.50	£1.50	£2.50
11-20	$0.60	$1.80	$3.00	£0.40	£1.20	£2.00
21-35	$0.50	$1.50	$2.50	£0.30	£0.90	£1.50
36 64pgs	$0.60	$1.80	$3.00	£0.40	£1.20	£2.00
37-42	$0.50	$1.50	$2.50	£0.30	£0.90	£1.50
43 ND	$0.50	$1.50	$2.50	£0.35	£1.05	£1.75
44-50	$0.50	$1.50	$2.50	£0.30	£0.90	£1.50
51-52 scarce in the U.K. Rogers art						
	$0.40	$1.20	$2.00	£0.30	£0.90	£1.50
53-56	$0.40	$1.20	$2.00	£0.25	£0.75	£1.25
57 scarce in the U.K.						

	$Good	$Fine	$N.Mint	£Good	£Fine	£N.Mint
	$0.40	$1.20	$2.00	£0.30	£0.90	£1.50
58-60	$0.40	$1.20	$2.00	£0.25	£0.75	£1.25
61 ND science-fiction special						
	$0.40	$1.20	$2.00	£0.25	£0.75	£1.25
62-63 ND	$0.40	$1.20	$2.00	£0.25	£0.75	£1.25
64 ND Frank Miller art						
	$0.80	$2.40	$4.00	£0.50	£1.50	£2.50
65-66 ND	$0.40	$1.20	$2.00	£0.25	£0.75	£1.25
67 ND 44pgs	$0.50	$1.50	$2.50	£0.30	£0.90	£1.50
68 ND 44pgs, Frank Miller art						
	$0.80	$2.40	$4.00	£0.50	£1.50	£2.50
69 ND 44pgs, science-fiction special						
	$0.50	$1.50	$2.50	£0.30	£0.90	£1.50
70-92	$0.30	$0.90	$1.50	£0.20	£0.60	£1.00
93 1st appearance Creature Commandoes						
	$0.30	$0.90	$1.50	£0.20	£0.60	£1.00
94-96	$0.30	$0.90	$1.50	£0.20	£0.60	£1.00
97 2nd appearance Creature Commandoes						
	$0.30	$0.90	$1.50	£0.20	£0.60	£1.00
98	$0.30	$0.90	$1.50	£0.20	£0.60	£1.00
99 dinosaur issue	$0.30	$0.90	$1.50	£0.20	£0.60	£1.00
100 Creature Commandoes full length story						
	$0.30	$0.90	$1.50	£0.20	£0.60	£1.00
101	$0.30	$0.90	$1.50	£0.20	£0.60	£1.00
102 Creature Commandoes						
	$0.30	$0.90	$1.50	£0.20	£0.60	£1.00
103-104	$0.30	$0.90	$1.50	£0.20	£0.60	£1.00
105 Creature Commandoes						
	$0.30	$0.90	$1.50	£0.20	£0.60	£1.00
106-107	$0.30	$0.90	$1.50	£0.20	£0.60	£1.00
108 Creature Commandoes become cover feature						
	$0.30	$0.90	$1.50	£0.20	£0.60	£1.00
109-110	$0.30	$0.90	$1.50	£0.20	£0.60	£1.00
111 G.I. Robot joins Creature Commandoes						
	$0.30	$0.90	$1.50	£0.20	£0.60	£1.00
112	$0.30	$0.90	$1.50	£0.20	£0.60	£1.00
113 G.I. Robot as cover feature						
	$0.30	$0.90	$1.50	£0.20	£0.60	£1.00
114	$0.30	$0.90	$1.50	£0.20	£0.60	£1.00
115-116 Gil Kane covers						
	$0.30	$0.90	$1.50	£0.20	£0.60	£1.00
117	$0.30	$0.90	$1.50	£0.20	£0.60	£1.00
118 Gil Kane cover						
	$0.30	$0.90	$1.50	£0.20	£0.60	£1.00
119	$0.30	$0.90	$1.50	£0.20	£0.60	£1.00
120 G.I. Robot as cover feature						
	$0.30	$0.90	$1.50	£0.20	£0.60	£1.00
121 last Creature Commandoes						
	$0.30	$0.90	$1.50	£0.20	£0.60	£1.00
122 G.I. Robot as cover feature (last appearance)						
	$0.30	$0.90	$1.50	£0.20	£0.60	£1.00
123-124	$0.30	$0.90	$1.50	£0.20	£0.60	£1.00
Title Value:	$55.45	$166.35	$278.50	£35.65	£107.05	£179.25

ARTISTS
Ditko art in 46, 49, 95, 99, 104, 105, 106. Nino art in 9, 11, 13, 16, 23, 24, 25, 31, 36, 55, 61, 69, 70.

FEATURES
Creature Commandos in 93, 97, 102, 105, 108-110, 112, 114, 116. Creature Commandos/War That Time Forgot in 100. Creature Commandos/G.I.Robot in 111, 115. G.I.Robot in 108, 113, 116. War That Time Forgot in 94, 99, 103.

Note: Issues #1-7 and #36 are partly reprint.

WEIRD WESTERN TALES
DC Comics; 12 Jun/Jul 1972-70 Aug 1980
(previously All-Star Western)

	$Good	$Fine	$N.Mint	£Good	£Fine	£N.Mint
12 52pgs, Neal Adams/Wrightson art, 3rd appearance Jonah Hex						
	$3.75	$11.00	$22.50	£2.50	£7.50	£15.00
13 Neal Adams art, 4th appearance Jonah Hex						
	$2.50	$7.50	$15.00	£1.65	£5.00	£10.00
14 Toth art	$1.25	$3.75	$7.50	£0.80	£2.50	£5.00
15 Neal Adams art						
	$1.25	$3.75	$7.50	£0.80	£2.50	£5.00
16-17	$0.60	$1.80	$3.00	£0.40	£1.20	£2.00
18 Jonah Hex series begins						
	$1.00	$3.00	$5.00	£0.70	£2.10	£3.50
19-28	$0.60	$1.80	$3.00	£0.40	£1.20	£2.00
29 origin Jonah Hex						
	$1.50	$4.50	$7.50	£1.00	£3.00	£5.00
30-31	$0.60	$1.80	$3.00	£0.40	£1.20	£2.00
32 scarce in the U.K.						
	$0.60	$1.80	$3.00	£0.40	£1.20	£2.50
33-34	$0.60	$1.80	$3.00	£0.40	£1.20	£2.00
35 ND	$0.60	$1.80	$3.00	£0.50	£1.50	£2.50
36 scarce in the U.K.						
	$0.60	$1.80	$3.00	£0.40	£1.20	£2.00
37 scarce in the U.K.						
	$0.60	$1.80	$3.00	£0.50	£1.50	£2.50
38 scarce in the U.K. last Jonah Hex feature						
	$0.60	$1.80	$3.00	£0.50	£1.50	£2.50
39 origin and 1st appearance Scalp-Hunter						
	$0.50	$1.50	$2.50	£0.30	£0.90	£1.50
40-47	$0.50	$1.50	$2.50	£0.30	£0.90	£1.50
48-49 ND 44pgs	$0.55	$1.65	$2.75	£0.35	£1.05	£1.75
50	$0.50	$1.50	$2.50	£0.30	£0.90	£1.50

	$Good	$Fine	$N.Mint	£Good	£Fine	£N.Mint
51-70	$0.40	$1.20	$2.00	£0.25	£0.75	£1.25
Title Value:	$37.95	$113.60	$198.50	£24.95	£75.10	£131.00

FEATURES
Cinnamon in 48, 49. El Diablo 12, 13, 15-17. Jonah Hex 12-14, 16-38. Scalphunter in 39-70.
REPRINT FEATURES
Bat Lash, Pow-Wow Smith in 12.

WEIRD WONDER TALES
Marvel Comics Group; 1 Dec 1973-22 May 1977

	$Good	$Fine	$N.Mint	£Good	£Fine	£N.Mint
1 ND horror/fantasy reprints begin	$0.50	$1.50	$2.50	£0.30	£0.90	£1.50
2-4 ND	$0.40	$1.20	$2.00	£0.30	£0.90	£1.50
5-16	$0.40	$1.20	$2.00	£0.25	£0.75	£1.25
17 ND Jack Kirby cover	$0.40	$1.20	$2.00	£0.25	£0.75	£1.25
18 ND	$0.40	$1.20	$2.00	£0.25	£0.75	£1.25
19 ND reprints Dr. Droom origin and 1st appearance from Amazing Adventures (1st) #1 though re-named Dr. Druid; Jack Kirby and Steve Ditko back-up reprints; new Kirby cover	$0.50	$1.50	$2.50	£0.30	£0.90	£1.50
20 ND Dr. Druid (Droom) reprint by Kirby; new Jack Kirby cover	$0.50	$1.50	$2.50	£0.30	£0.90	£1.50
21 ND Dr. Druid (Droom) reprint	$0.40	$1.20	$2.00	£0.25	£0.75	£1.25
22 ND Dr. Druid (Droom) back-up reprints by Jack Kirby, with new Jack Kirby and John Byrne splash-page; Kubert back-up reprint	$0.50	$1.50	$2.50	£0.30	£0.90	£1.50
Title Value:	$9.20	$27.60	$46.00	£5.85	£17.55	£29.25

REPRINT FEATURES
Dr. Droom (re-named Dr.Druid) in 19-22. Venus in 16-18.

WEIRD WORLDS
DC Comics; 1 Sep 1972-9 Jan/Feb 1974; 10 Oct/Nov 1974

	$Good	$Fine	$N.Mint	£Good	£Fine	£N.Mint
1 ND	$1.00	$3.00	$5.00	£0.70	£2.10	£3.50
2-3 part Neal Adams inks	$0.60	$1.80	$3.00	£0.40	£1.20	£2.00
4 Kaluta art	$0.60	$1.80	$3.00	£0.40	£1.20	£2.00
5-7	$0.60	$1.80	$3.00	£0.40	£1.20	£2.00
8-10 Chaykin art, Ironwolf	$0.50	$1.50	$2.50	£0.30	£0.90	£1.50
Title Value:	$6.10	$18.30	$30.50	£4.00	£12.00	£20.00

FEATURES
Iron Wolf in 8-10. John Carter of Mars in 1-7. Pellucidar in 1-7.

WEIRD, THE
DC Comics,MS; 1 Apr 1988-4 Jul 1988

	$Good	$Fine	$N.Mint	£Good	£Fine	£N.Mint
1-4 LD in the U.K. Justice League X-over	$0.50	$1.50	$2.50	£0.30	£0.90	£1.50
Title Value:	$2.00	$6.00	$10.00	£1.20	£3.60	£6.00

Note: all 48pgs, Starlin scripts, Wrightson art

WELCOME BACK KOTTER
DC Comics, TV; 1 Nov 1976-10 Mar/Apr 1978
(see Limited Collector's Edition C-57)

	$Good	$Fine	$N.Mint	£Good	£Fine	£N.Mint
1-10 scarce in the U.K.	$0.25	$0.75	$1.25	£0.15	£0.45	£0.75
Title Value:	$2.50	$7.50	$12.50	£1.50	£4.50	£7.50

Note: from US TV series.

WENDIGO, THE
Caliber Press,OS; 1 Dec 1991

	$Good	$Fine	$N.Mint	£Good	£Fine	£N.Mint
1 ND film adaptation	$0.50	$1.50	$2.50	£0.30	£0.90	£1.50
Title Value:	$0.50	$1.50	$2.50	£0.30	£0.90	£1.50

WEREWOLF
Dell; 1 Dec 1966-3 Apr 1967

	$Good	$Fine	$N.Mint	£Good	£Fine	£N.Mint
1 Werewolf as secret agent begins; distributed in the U.K.	$0.80	$2.50	$5.00	£0.55	£1.75	£3.50
2 origin; distributed in the U.K.	$0.65	$2.00	$4.00	£0.40	£1.25	£2.50
3 distributed in the U.K.	$0.65	$2.00	$4.00	£0.40	£1.25	£2.50
Title Value:	$2.10	$6.50	$13.00	£1.35	£4.25	£8.50

WEREWOLF BY NIGHT
Marvel Comics Group; 1 Sep 1972-43 Mar 1977
(see Marvel Spotlight)

	$Good	$Fine	$N.Mint	£Good	£Fine	£N.Mint
1 ND scarce in the U.K. Ploog art	$6.50	$20.00	$40.00	£4.15	£12.50	£25.00
2 ND Ploog art	$3.30	$10.00	$20.00	£1.65	£5.00	£10.00
3-5 ND Ploog art	$2.50	$7.50	$15.00	£1.25	£3.75	£7.50
6-7 Ploog art	$1.65	$5.00	$10.00	£0.80	£2.50	£5.00
8-10	$1.25	$3.75	$7.50	£0.65	£2.00	£4.00
11-12	$1.25	$3.75	$7.50	£0.50	£1.50	£3.00
13-14 Ploog art	$1.25	$3.75	$7.50	£0.55	£1.75	£3.50
15 ND Werewolf vs. Dracula, Ploog art	$1.25	$3.75	$7.50	£0.65	£2.00	£4.00
16 ND Ploog art	$1.25	$3.75	$7.50	£0.55	£1.75	£3.50
17-18 ND	$1.25	$3.75	$7.50	£0.50	£1.50	£3.00
19 ND Werewolf vs. Dracula	$1.25	$3.75	$7.50	£0.50	£1.50	£3.00
20-31	$1.00	$3.00	$5.00	£0.50	£1.50	£2.50
32 1st appearance Moon Knight	$7.50	$22.50	$45.00	£2.50	£7.50	£15.00
33 2nd appearance Moon Knight	$5.00	$15.00	$30.00	£1.25	£3.75	£7.50
34-36	$0.60	$1.80	$3.00	£0.40	£1.20	£2.00
37 Moon Knight appears	$1.00	$3.00	$5.00	£0.70	£2.10	£3.50
38	$0.60	$1.80	$3.00	£0.40	£1.20	£2.00
39 Brother Voodoo appears	$0.60	$1.80	$3.00	£0.40	£1.20	£2.00
40 ND Brother Voodoo appears	$0.60	$1.80	$3.00	£0.50	£1.50	£2.50
41 Brother Voodoo appears	$0.60	$1.80	$3.00	£0.40	£1.20	£2.00
42-43 ND Iron Man appears	$0.80	$2.40	$4.00	£0.50	£1.50	£2.50
Title Value:	$66.90	$201.40	$384.00	£32.30	£97.80	£185.00

WEREWOLF GIANT SIZE
Marvel Comics Group; 2 Oct 1974-5 Jul 1975
(formerly Giant Size Creatures)

	$Good	$Fine	$N.Mint	£Good	£Fine	£N.Mint
2 ND 68pgs, Frankenstein appears, Steve Ditko reprint	$1.20	$3.60	$6.00	£0.80	£2.40	£4.00
3 ND 68pgs	$1.00	$3.00	$5.00	£0.70	£2.10	£3.50
4 ND 68pgs, Morbius appears	$1.40	$4.20	$7.00	£0.90	£2.70	£4.50
5 ND 68pgs	$1.00	$3.00	$5.00	£0.70	£2.10	£3.50
Title Value:	$4.60	$13.80	$23.00	£3.10	£9.30	£15.50

WEREWOLF IN 3-D
Blackthorne; (3-D Series #61) 1 1988

	$Good	$Fine	$N.Mint	£Good	£Fine	£N.Mint
1 ND with 3-D glasses (25% less without glasses)	$0.50	$1.50	$2.50	£0.30	£0.90	£1.50
Title Value:	$0.50	$1.50	$2.50	£0.30	£0.90	£1.50

WEST COAST AVENGERS
Marvel Comics Group; 1 Oct 1985-102 Jan 1994

	$Good	$Fine	$N.Mint	£Good	£Fine	£N.Mint
1 ND DS	$0.50	$1.50	$2.50	£0.60	£1.80	£3.00
2-9 ND	$0.40	$1.20	$2.00	£0.40	£1.20	£2.00
10 very LD Thing appears, X-over with Thing #36	$0.40	$1.20	$2.00	£0.40	£1.20	£2.00
11 LD in the U.K.	$0.30	$0.90	$1.50	£0.30	£0.90	£1.50
12-13	$0.30	$0.90	$1.50	£0.20	£0.60	£1.00
14 Daimon Hellstrom 1st called "Hellstorm"	$0.30	$0.90	$1.50	£0.25	£0.75	£1.25
15-19	$0.30	$0.90	$1.50	£0.20	£0.60	£1.00
20 Dr. Strange appears	$0.30	$0.90	$1.50	£0.20	£0.60	£1.00
21	$0.30	$0.90	$1.50	£0.20	£0.60	£1.00
22-23 Dr. Strange and Fantastic Four appear	$0.30	$0.90	$1.50	£0.20	£0.60	£1.00
24-26	$0.30	$0.90	$1.50	£0.20	£0.60	£1.00
27 LD in the U.K. Nick Fury appears	$0.30	$0.90	$1.50	£0.25	£0.75	£1.25
28 LD in the U.K.	$0.30	$0.90	$1.50	£0.25	£0.75	£1.25
29	$0.30	$0.90	$1.50	£0.20	£0.60	£1.00
30 LD in the U.K.	$0.30	$0.90	$1.50	£0.25	£0.75	£1.25
31-41	$0.30	$0.90	$1.50	£0.20	£0.60	£1.00
42 1st John Byrne art on West Coast Avengers; Visionquest begins	$0.40	$1.20	$2.00	£0.25	£0.75	£1.25
43-44 John Byrne art, Visionquest	$0.30	$0.90	$1.50	£0.20	£0.60	£1.00
45 John Byrne art, Visionquest; 1st appearance new Vision	$0.30	$0.90	$1.50	£0.20	£0.60	£1.00
46 John Byrne art; 1st Great Lakes Avengers	$0.30	$0.90	$1.50	£0.20	£0.60	£1.00
47 John Byrne art; title becomes "Avengers West Coast"	$0.30	$0.90	$1.50	£0.20	£0.60	£1.00
48-49 John Byrne art	$0.30	$0.90	$1.50	£0.20	£0.60	£1.00
50 John Byrne art, original Human Torch appears	$0.30	$0.90	$1.50	£0.20	£0.60	£1.00
51-52 John Byrne art	$0.30	$0.90	$1.50	£0.20	£0.60	£1.00
53-54 Acts of Vengeance tie-in, John Byrne art	$0.30	$0.90	$1.50	£0.20	£0.60	£1.00
55 LD in the U.K. Acts of Vengeance tie-in, John Byrne art	$0.30	$0.90	$1.50	£0.25	£0.75	£1.25
56-57 John Byrne art	$0.30	$0.90	$1.50	£0.20	£0.60	£1.00
58-59	$0.30	$0.90	$1.50	£0.15	£0.45	£0.75
60-70 LD in the U.K.	$0.30	$0.90	$1.50	£0.20	£0.60	£1.00
71 ND Spiderwoman joins team	$0.30	$0.90	$1.50	£0.20	£0.60	£1.00
72-74 ND	$0.30	$0.90	$1.50	£0.20	£0.60	£1.00
75 ND DS Fantastic Four guest-star	$0.40	$1.20	$2.00	£0.25	£0.75	£1.25
76-78 ND	$0.30	$0.90	$1.50	£0.20	£0.60	£1.00
79 Dr. Strange appears; $1.25 cover begins	$0.25	$0.75	$1.25	£0.15	£0.45	£0.75
80 Galactic Storm part 2; Captain America, Rick Jones and Quasar appear	$0.25	$0.75	$1.25	£0.15	£0.45	£0.75
81 Galactic Storm part 9; Quasar appears	$0.25	$0.75	$1.25	£0.15	£0.45	£0.75
82 Galactic Storm part 16	$0.25	$0.75	$1.25	£0.15	£0.45	£0.75
83	$0.25	$0.75	$1.25	£0.15	£0.45	£0.75
84 Spiderman appears, origin Spiderwoman retold	$0.25	$0.75	$1.25	£0.15	£0.45	£0.75
85-86 Spiderman appears	$0.25	$0.75	$1.25	£0.15	£0.45	£0.75

	$Good	$Fine	$N.Mint	£Good	£Fine	£N.Mint
87-88 Wolverine appears	$0.25	$0.75	$1.25	£0.15	£0.45	£0.75
89-93	$0.25	$0.75	$1.25	£0.15	£0.45	£0.75
94 Jim Rhodes as War Machine joins	$0.25	$0.75	$1.25	£0.15	£0.45	£0.75
95 Darkhawk guest-stars	$0.25	$0.75	$1.25	£0.15	£0.45	£0.75
96-97 Infinity Crusade tie-in	$0.25	$0.75	$1.25	£0.15	£0.45	£0.75
98-99	$0.25	$0.75	$1.25	£0.15	£0.45	£0.75
100 64pgs, red foil embossed cover, Mockingbird dies	$0.80	$2.40	$4.00	£0.50	£1.50	£2.50
101 Blood Ties part 3, X-Men and Magneto appear	$0.60	$1.80	$3.00	£0.70	£2.10	£3.50
102 leads into Force Works #1	$0.60	$1.20	$2.00	£0.40	£1.20	£2.00
Title Value:	$31.75	$95.25	$158.75	£22.90	£68.70	£114.50

WEST COAST AVENGERS ANNUAL
Marvel Comics Group; 1 Oct 1986-8 1993

	$Good	$Fine	$N.Mint	£Good	£Fine	£N.Mint
1 ND	$0.50	$1.50	$2.50	£0.40	£1.20	£2.00
2 ND Silver Surfer X-over	$0.50	$1.50	$2.50	£0.40	£1.20	£2.00
3 ND 64pgs, squarebound, Evolutionary War, new Giant Man appears, Ron Lim art	$0.50	$1.50	$2.50	£0.30	£0.90	£1.50
4 ND squarebound, Atlantis Attacks part 12	$0.50	$1.50	$2.50	£0.30	£0.90	£1.50
5 ND The Terminus Factor part 4, continues in Avengers Annual #19	$0.50	$1.50	$2.50	£0.30	£0.90	£1.50
6 ND The Subterranean Odyssey part 5 (conclusion)	$0.50	$1.50	$2.50	£0.30	£0.90	£1.50
7 ND Assault On Armor City part 2, continues in Iron Man Annual #13, Darkhawk appears	$0.50	$1.50	$2.50	£0.30	£0.90	£1.50
8 ND 64pgs, pre-bagged with trading card introducing Raptor	$0.60	$1.80	$3.00	£0.40	£1.20	£2.00
Title Value:	$4.10	$12.30	$20.50	£2.70	£8.10	£13.50

WEST COAST AVENGERS, THE
Marvel Comics Group,MS; 1 Sep 1984-4 Dec 1984

	$Good	$Fine	$N.Mint	£Good	£Fine	£N.Mint
1 ND Hawkeye, Mockingbird, Iron Man, Tigra, begin	$0.70	$2.10	$3.50	£0.50	£1.50	£2.50
2 ND	$0.40	$1.20	$2.00	£0.40	£1.20	£2.00
3 ND scarce in the U.K.	$0.40	$1.20	$2.00	£0.50	£1.50	£2.50
4 ND	$0.40	$1.20	$2.00	£0.40	£1.20	£2.00
Title Value:	$1.90	$5.70	$9.50	£1.80	£5.40	£9.00

WESTERN COMICS
National Periodical Publications; 78 Nov/Dec 1959-85 Jan/Feb 1961
(see Super DC Giant) (previous issues ND)

	$Good	$Fine	$N.Mint	£Good	£Fine	£N.Mint
78-85 rare in the U.K. Matt Savage appears	$7.00	$21.00	$50.00	£5.00	£15.00	£35.00
Title Value:	$56.00	$168.00	$400.00	£40.00	£120.00	£280.00

WESTERN GUNFIGHTERS
Marvel Comics Group; 1 Aug 1970-33 Nov 1975

	$Good	$Fine	$N.Mint	£Good	£Fine	£N.Mint
1 64pgs, Ghost Rider and Apache Kid plus other western heroes begin (all reprint)	$1.00	$3.00	$5.00	£0.60	£1.80	£3.00
2-3 64pgs	$0.60	$1.80	$3.00	£0.40	£1.20	£2.00
4 64pgs, Barry Windsor Smith art	$1.00	$3.00	$5.00	£0.60	£1.80	£3.00
5 64pgs	$0.60	$1.80	$3.00	£0.40	£1.20	£2.00
6-7 ND 64pgs	$0.50	$1.50	$2.50	£0.30	£0.90	£1.50
8-13 ND all reprint	$0.50	$1.50	$2.50	£0.30	£0.90	£1.50
14 ND all reprint, Steranko cover	$0.50	$1.50	$2.50	£0.30	£0.90	£1.50
15-33 ND all reprint	$0.50	$1.50	$2.50	£0.30	£0.90	£1.50
Title Value:	$17.80	$53.40	$89.00	£10.80	£32.40	£54.00
ARTISTS						

Steranko cover on 14. Williamson reprint in 18.

WESTERN KID, THE
Marvel Comics Group; 1 Dec 1971-5 Aug 1972

	$Good	$Fine	$N.Mint	£Good	£Fine	£N.Mint
1 ND	$0.60	$1.80	$3.00	£0.40	£1.20	£2.00
2 ND	$0.40	$1.20	$2.00	£0.25	£0.75	£1.25
3 Williamson reprint	$0.40	$1.20	$2.00	£0.25	£0.75	£1.25
4-5 ND	$0.40	$1.20	$2.00	£0.25	£0.75	£1.25
Title Value:	$2.20	$6.60	$11.00	£1.40	£4.20	£7.00

WESTERN TEAM-UP
Marvel Comics Group; 1 Nov 1973

	$Good	$Fine	$N.Mint	£Good	£Fine	£N.Mint
1 ND scarce in the U.K. origin/1st appearance The Dakota Kid, rest reprint	$0.40	$1.20	$2.00	£0.40	£1.20	£2.00
Title Value:	$0.40	$1.20	$2.00	£0.40	£1.20	£2.00

WESTERNER, THE
I.W. Super; 15-17 1964

	$Good	$Fine	$N.Mint	£Good	£Fine	£N.Mint
15-17 reprints; distributed in the U.K.	$0.65	$2.00	$4.00	£0.40	£1.25	£2.50
Title Value:	$1.95	$6.00	$12.00	£1.20	£3.75	£7.50

WETWORKS
Image; 1 Jul 1994-present

	$Good	$Fine	$N.Mint	£Good	£Fine	£N.Mint
1 ND Whilce Portacio with Brandon Choi	$1.00	$3.00	$5.00	£0.60	£1.80	£3.00
2 ND Whilce Portacio with Brandon Choi	$0.80	$2.40	$4.00	£0.50	£1.50	£2.50
2 Variant cover, ND cover forms larger picture when combined with variant covers of Deathblow #5, Gen 13 #5, Kindred #3, Stormwatch #10, Team 7 #1, Union #0, WildC.A.T.S. #11	$1.50	$4.50	$7.50	£1.00	£3.00	£5.00
3 ND Whilce Portacio with Brandon Choi	$0.50	$1.50	$2.50	£0.30	£0.90	£1.50
4-7 ND Whilce Portacio script and art	$0.50	$1.50	$2.50	£0.30	£0.90	£1.50
8 ND Wildstorm Rising part 7, continued in Backlash #8; with two foil-bagged painted trading cards. Cover by Barry-Windsor Smith.	$0.50	$1.50	$2.50	£0.30	£0.90	£1.50
8 Newstand edition, ND without trading cards	$0.40	$1.20	$2.00	£0.25	£0.75	£1.25
9-10 ND Whilce Portacio script and art	$0.50	$1.50	$2.50	£0.30	£0.90	£1.50
11-13 ND	$0.50	$1.50	$2.50	£0.30	£0.90	£1.50
Title Value:	$9.20	$27.60	$46.00	£5.65	£16.95	£28.25

WETWORKS SOURCEBOOK
Image; 1 Sep 1994

	$Good	$Fine	$N.Mint	£Good	£Fine	£N.Mint
1 ND information and statistics about Wetworks characters	$0.50	$1.50	$2.50	£0.30	£0.90	£1.50
Title Value:	$0.50	$1.50	$2.50	£0.30	£0.90	£1.50

WHAT IF SPECIAL
Marvel Comics Group,OS; 1 Jun 1988

	$Good	$Fine	$N.Mint	£Good	£Fine	£N.Mint
1 features Iron Man	$0.40	$1.20	$2.00	£0.25	£0.75	£1.25
Title Value:	$0.40	$1.20	$2.00	£0.25	£0.75	£1.25

WHAT IF...?
Marvel Comics Group; 1 Feb 1977-47 Oct 1985

	$Good	$Fine	$N.Mint	£Good	£Fine	£N.Mint
1 ND Spiderman, Fantastic Four	$2.50	$7.50	$15.00	£1.65	£5.00	£10.00
2 ND Hulk, origin Hulk retold						

Weird Western Tales #26

Western Gunfighters #2

Wetworks #1

	$Good	$Fine	$N.Mint	£Good	£Fine	£N.Mint
	$1.50	$4.50	$9.00	£1.00	£3.00	£6.00
3 ND Avengers (vs. Hulk), Gil Kane/Janson art						
	$1.25	$3.75	$7.50	£0.65	£2.00	£4.00
4 ND Invaders						
5 ND Captain America						
	$1.25	$3.75	$7.50	£0.65	£2.00	£4.00
6 ND Fantastic Four						
	$1.20	$3.60	$6.00	£0.70	£2.10	£3.50
7 ND Spiderman						
8 ND Daredevil	$1.20	$3.60	$6.00	£0.70	£2.10	£3.50
9 ND Avengers	$1.20	$3.60	$6.00	£0.70	£2.10	£3.50
10 ND Thor	$1.20	$3.60	$6.00	£0.70	£2.10	£3.50
11 ND Jack Kirby art, Fantastic Four						
	$1.00	$3.00	$5.00	£0.70	£2.10	£3.50
12 ND Hulk	$1.00	$2.70	$4.50	£0.60	£1.80	£3.00
13 ND scarce in the U.K. Conan						
	$0.90	$2.70	$4.50	£0.70	£2.10	£3.50
14 ND Sgt. Fury	$0.90	$2.70	$4.50	£0.60	£1.80	£3.00
15 ND Nova	$0.90	$2.70	$4.50	£0.60	£1.80	£3.00
16 ND Master of Kung Fu						
	$0.90	$2.70	$4.50	£0.60	£1.80	£3.00
17 ND Captain Marvel, Spiderwoman, Ghost Rider						
	$1.20	$3.60	$6.00	£0.80	£2.40	£4.00
18 ND Dr. Strange	$0.90	$2.70	$4.50	£0.60	£1.80	£3.00
19 ND Spiderman	$0.90	$2.70	$4.50	£0.60	£1.80	£3.00
20 ND Avengers	$0.90	$2.70	$4.50	£0.60	£1.80	£3.00
21 Fantastic Four	$0.80	$2.40	$4.00	£0.50	£1.50	£2.50
22 ND Dr.Doom, origin retold						
	$0.80	$2.40	$4.00	£0.50	£1.50	£2.50
23 ND Hulk	$0.80	$2.40	$4.00	£0.50	£1.50	£2.50
24 ND Spiderman	$0.80	$2.40	$4.00	£0.50	£1.50	£2.50
25 ND Avengers	$0.80	$2.40	$4.00	£0.50	£1.50	£2.50
26 ND Captain America						
	$0.80	$2.40	$4.00	£0.50	£1.50	£2.50
27 ND X-Men "If Phoenix Had Not Died"; alternative to X-Men #137						
	$2.00	$6.00	$10.00	£0.80	£2.40	£4.00
28 ND Daredevil, Frank Miller art, Ghost Rider						
	$2.00	$6.00	$10.00	£1.00	£3.00	£5.00
29 ND Avengers, old X-Men appear, alternative to Avengers Annual #2, Golden cover						
	$0.80	$2.40	$4.00	£0.50	£1.50	£2.50
30 ND Spiderman	$2.00	$6.00	$10.00	£0.80	£2.40	£4.00
31 ND Wolverine/Hulk, X-Men/Magneto appear						
	$2.00	$6.00	$10.00	£1.00	£3.00	£5.00
32 ND Avengers	$0.60	$1.80	$3.00	£0.40	£1.20	£2.00
33 ND Galactus/Dazzler, Iron Man						
	$0.60	$1.80	$3.00	£0.40	£1.20	£2.00
34 ND Humour issue, Marvel crew each draw themselves, Frank Miller/Sienkiewicz art featured						
	$0.60	$1.80	$3.00	£0.40	£1.20	£2.00
35 ND Frank Miller art, Daredevil/Elektra						
	$0.80	$2.40	$4.00	£0.50	£1.50	£2.50
36 ND Fantastic Four, John Byrne art that reworks F.F. #1						
	$0.60	$1.80	$3.00	£0.40	£1.20	£2.00
37 ND The Beast/The Thing, Silver Surfer, old X-Men appear						
	$0.80	$2.40	$4.00	£0.50	£1.50	£2.50
38 ND Daredevil/Captain America, Vision/Scarlet Witch						
	$0.60	$1.80	$3.00	£0.40	£1.20	£2.00
39 ND Thor/Conan	$0.60	$1.80	$3.00	£0.40	£1.20	£2.00
40 ND Dr. Strange	$0.60	$1.80	$3.00	£0.40	£1.20	£2.00
41 ND Sub-Mariner						
	$0.50	$1.50	$2.50	£0.30	£0.90	£1.50
42 ND Invisible Girl, Fantastic Four						
	$0.50	$1.50	$2.50	£0.30	£0.90	£1.50
43 ND Conan	$0.50	$1.50	$2.50	£0.30	£0.90	£1.50
44 ND Captain America						
	$0.50	$1.50	$2.50	£0.30	£0.90	£1.50
45 ND Hulk	$0.50	$1.50	$2.50	£0.30	£0.90	£1.50
46 ND Spiderman	$0.50	$1.50	$2.50	£0.30	£0.90	£1.50
47 ND Thor	$0.50	$1.50	$2.50	£0.30	£0.90	£1.50
Title Value:	$46.05	$138.15	$238.00	£27.50	£82.70	£142.50

Note: all 52pgs.

Best of What If Trade paperback (Jan 1992), reprints seven stories 192pgs — £1.60 £4.80 £8.00

WHAT IF...? (2ND SERIES)

Marvel Comics Group; 1 Jul 1989-present

	$Good	$Fine	$N.Mint	£Good	£Fine	£N.Mint
1 ND Avengers/Evolutionary War						
	$0.80	$2.40	$4.00	£0.50	£1.50	£2.50
2 ND scarce in the U.K. Daredevil/Kingpin						
	$0.60	$1.80	$3.00	£0.40	£1.20	£2.00
3 ND Captain America						
	$0.50	$1.50	$2.50	£0.30	£0.90	£1.50
4 ND Spiderman's black costume						
	$0.50	$1.50	$2.50	£0.35	£1.05	£1.75
5 ND Wonderman/Vision/Avengers						
	$0.50	$1.50	$2.50	£0.30	£0.90	£1.50
6 ND X-Men, Ron Lim art						
	$0.70	$2.10	$3.50	£0.40	£1.20	£2.00
7 ND Wolverine, Rob Liefeld art						
	$1.00	$3.00	$5.00	£0.70	£2.10	£3.50
8 ND Iron Man	$0.40	$1.20	$2.00	£0.25	£0.75	£1.25
9 ND X-Men	$0.40	$1.20	$2.00	£0.30	£0.90	£1.50
10 ND Punisher	$0.60	$1.80	$3.00	£0.40	£1.20	£2.00
11 ND Fantastic Four						
	$0.40	$1.20	$2.00	£0.25	£0.75	£1.25
12 ND X-Men/Asgard						
	$0.40	$1.20	$2.00	£0.25	£0.75	£1.25
13 ND Professor Xavier						
	$0.40	$1.20	$2.00	£0.25	£0.75	£1.25
14 ND Captain Marvel						
	$0.40	$1.20	$2.00	£0.25	£0.75	£1.25
15 ND Fantastic Four						
	$0.40	$1.20	$2.00	£0.25	£0.75	£1.25
16 ND Wolverine/Conan						
	$0.60	$1.80	$3.00	£0.30	£0.90	£1.50
17 ND Kraven/Spiderman						
	$0.30	$0.90	$1.50	£0.20	£0.60	£1.00
18 ND Fantastic Four/Dr. Doom						
	$0.30	$0.90	$1.50	£0.20	£0.60	£1.00
19 ND The Vision	$0.30	$0.90	$1.50	£0.20	£0.60	£1.00
20-21 ND Spiderman/Mary-Jane Watson/Black Cat						
	$0.30	$0.90	$1.50	£0.20	£0.60	£1.00
22 ND Silver Surfer, Ron Lim art						
	$0.40	$1.20	$2.00	£0.25	£0.75	£1.25
23 ND X-Men	$0.40	$1.20	$2.00	£0.25	£0.75	£1.25
24 ND Wolverine as vampire, Dr. Strange's soul in Punisher						
	$0.40	$1.20	$2.00	£0.25	£0.75	£1.25
25 ND 40pgs, Atlantis Attacks						
	$0.40	$1.20	$2.00	£0.25	£0.75	£1.25
26 ND Punisher/Daredevil, guest-starring Spiderman, Kingpin, Cloak and Dagger						
	$0.40	$1.20	$2.00	£0.25	£0.75	£1.25
27 ND Sub-Mariner/Fantastic Four						
	$0.30	$0.90	$1.50	£0.20	£0.60	£1.00
28 ND DS Captain America, "Iwo Jima" cover (go and look it up)						
	$0.30	$0.90	$1.50	£0.20	£0.60	£1.00
29 ND Captain America/Avengers, continued from What If #28						
	$0.30	$0.90	$1.50	£0.20	£0.60	£1.00
30 ND 52pgs, Sue Richards						
	$0.40	$1.20	$2.00	£0.25	£0.75	£1.25
31 ND Spiderman	$0.30	$0.90	$1.50	£0.20	£0.60	£1.00
32 ND Phoenix, ties in with Days of Future Past story						
	$0.30	$0.90	$1.50	£0.20	£0.60	£1.00
33 ND Phoenix	$0.30	$0.90	$1.50	£0.20	£0.60	£1.00
34 ND all humour issue featuring The Watcher						
	$0.30	$0.90	$1.50	£0.20	£0.60	£1.00
35 ND Fantastic Four, ties in with What If (1st series) #1						
	$0.30	$0.90	$1.50	£0.20	£0.60	£1.00
36 ND Cosmic Avengers vs. Guardians of the Galaxy						
	$0.30	$0.90	$1.50	£0.20	£0.60	£1.00
37 ND X-Vampires vs. Dormammu						
	$0.30	$0.90	$1.50	£0.20	£0.60	£1.00
38 ND Thor, ties in to Thor #400						
	$0.30	$0.90	$1.50	£0.20	£0.60	£1.00
39 ND The Watcher						
	$0.30	$0.90	$1.50	£0.20	£0.60	£1.00
40 ND Storm, X-Men						
	$0.30	$0.90	$1.50	£0.20	£0.60	£1.00
41 ND Avengers vs. Galactus						
	$0.30	$0.90	$1.50	£0.20	£0.60	£1.00
42 ND follow-up to Amazing Spiderman #100-#102, Morbius appears						
	$0.30	$0.90	$1.50	£0.20	£0.60	£1.00
43 ND Wolverine marrying Mariko						
	$0.30	$0.90	$1.50	£0.20	£0.60	£1.00
44 ND Punisher Possessed By Venom						
	$0.30	$0.90	$1.50	£0.20	£0.60	£1.00
45 ND Barbara Ketch as Ghost Rider, Spiderman and Dr. Strange appear						
	$0.30	$0.90	$1.50	£0.20	£0.60	£1.00
46 ND Cable destroys the X-Men						
	$0.30	$0.90	$1.50	£0.20	£0.60	£1.00
47 ND X-Men, Avengers and Fantastic Four vs. Magneto						
	$0.30	$0.90	$1.50	£0.20	£0.60	£1.00
48 ND Daredevil saves Nuke						
	$0.30	$0.90	$1.50	£0.20	£0.60	£1.00
49 ND Silver Surfer and Infinity Gauntlet						
	$0.30	$0.90	$1.50	£0.20	£0.60	£1.00
50 ND DS Hulk kills Wolverine, silver-embossed logo						
	$0.60	$1.80	$3.00	£0.40	£1.20	£2.00
51 ND Punisher as Captain America						
	$0.30	$0.90	$1.50	£0.20	£0.60	£1.00
52 ND Wolverine and Alpha Flight						
	$0.30	$0.90	$1.50	£0.20	£0.60	£1.00
53 ND Dr. Doom as Dr. Strange						
	$0.30	$0.90	$1.50	£0.20	£0.60	£1.00
54 ND Death's Head I & II; Fantastic Four and Captain America appear						
	$0.30	$0.90	$1.50	£0.20	£0.60	£1.00
55-56 ND Avengers/Galactic Storm						
	$0.30	$0.90	$1.50	£0.20	£0.60	£1.00
57 ND Punisher/SHIELD						
	$0.30	$0.90	$1.50	£0.20	£0.60	£1.00
58 ND Punisher/Spiderman						
	$0.30	$0.90	$1.50	£0.20	£0.60	£1.00
59 ND Wolverine and Alpha Flight; Bryan Hitch art						
	$0.30	$0.90	$1.50	£0.20	£0.60	£1.00
60 ND three alternatives on the wedding of Scott Summers and Jean Grey; Bryan Hitch art						
	$0.30	$0.90	$1.50	£0.20	£0.60	£1.00
61 ND Spiderman; with free Spiderman and his Deadly Foes card sheet						

VERY GENERAL PERCENTAGE CONVERSION CHART WHICH MAY BE USED TO CALCULATE LOW AND INBETWEEN GRADES:

	$Good	$Fine	$N.Mint	£Good	£Fine	£N.Mint
	$0.30	$0.90	$1.50	£0.20	£0.60	£1.00
62 ND Wolverine vs. Weapon X						
	$0.30	$0.90	$1.50	£0.20	£0.60	£1.00
63 ND Iron Man and War Machine						
	$0.30	$0.90	$1.50	£0.20	£0.60	£1.00
64 ND Iron Man with Magneto, Rhino and Electro						
	$0.30	$0.90	$1.50	£0.20	£0.60	£1.00
65 ND Captain America						
	$0.30	$0.90	$1.50	£0.20	£0.60	£1.00
66 ND Rogue and Avengers						
	$0.30	$0.90	$1.50	£0.20	£0.60	£1.00
67-68 ND Captain America						
	$0.30	$0.90	$1.50	£0.20	£0.60	£1.00
69 ND Stryfe/X-Men						
	$0.30	$0.90	$1.50	£0.20	£0.60	£1.00
70 ND Silver Surfer/Galactus						
	$0.30	$0.90	$1.50	£0.20	£0.60	£1.00
71 ND Hulk and Red Skull						
	$0.30	$0.90	$1.50	£0.20	£0.60	£1.00
72 ND Spiderman (alternate origin)						
	$0.30	$0.90	$1.50	£0.20	£0.60	£1.00
73 ND Daredevil/Kingpin						
	$0.30	$0.90	$1.50	£0.20	£0.60	£1.00
74 ND X-Men/Mr. Sinister						
	$0.30	$0.90	$1.50	£0.20	£0.60	£1.00
75 ND Generation X						
	$0.30	$0.90	$1.50	£0.20	£0.60	£1.00
76 ND Peter Parker/Spiderman						
	$0.30	$0.90	$1.50	£0.20	£0.60	£1.00
77 ND Legion/Magneto						
	$0.30	$0.90	$1.50	£0.20	£0.60	£1.00
78 ND Hulk, Spiderman, Ghost Rider and Wolverine						
	$0.30	$0.90	$1.50	£0.20	£0.60	£1.00
79 ND Storm as Phoenix; Wolverine, Black Panther and Dr. Doom appear						
	$0.30	$0.90	$1.50	£0.20	£0.60	£1.00
80 ND Hulk	$0.30	$0.90	$1.50	£0.20	£0.60	£1.00
81 ND X-Men and Galactus in the Age of Apocalypse						
	$0.30	$0.90	$1.50	£0.20	£0.60	£1.00
82 ND J. Jonah Jameson adopts Spiderman						
	$0.30	$0.90	$1.50	£0.20	£0.60	£1.00
83 ND Daredevil a disciple of Dr. Strange						
	$0.30	$0.90	$1.50	£0.20	£0.60	£1.00
Title Value:	$29.60	$88.80	$148.00	£19.35	£58.05	£96.75

WHAT THE -?!

Marvel Comics Group; 1 Aug 1988-4 Nov 1988; 5 1989-24 Dec 1992

	$Good	$Fine	$N.Mint	£Good	£Fine	£N.Mint
1 ND Punisher	$0.50	$1.50	$2.50	£0.30	£0.90	£1.50
2 ND Superman/Fantastic Four by John Byrne, Wolverine by Mignola						
	$0.40	$1.20	$2.00	£0.25	£0.75	£1.25
3 ND 2pgs Batman/Joker by Todd McFarlane, X-Men/New Mutants/X-Factor by Kyle Baker						
	$0.50	$1.50	$2.50	£0.30	£0.90	£1.50
4 ND Archie, Lone Wolf						
	$0.40	$1.20	$2.00	£0.25	£0.75	£1.25
5 ND Hulk/Punisher/Wolverine, Erik Larsen art						
	$0.40	$1.20	$2.00	£0.25	£0.75	£1.25
6 ND Alpha Flight/Punisher by John Byrne						
	$0.30	$0.90	$1.50	£0.20	£0.60	£1.00
7 ND J.L.A./Alpha Flight/Hell-Cat						
	$0.30	$0.90	$1.50	£0.20	£0.60	£1.00
8 ND Forbush Man						
	$0.30	$0.90	$1.50	£0.20	£0.60	£1.00
9 ND Marvel Comics Presents featuring Wolverine/ Galactus; John Byrne cover						
	$0.30	$0.90	$1.50	£0.20	£0.60	£1.00
10 ND X-Men/Akira/Silver Surfer/Vision/Scarlet Witch						
	$0.30	$0.90	$1.50	£0.20	£0.60	£1.00
11 ND Daredevil/She-Hulk						
	$0.25	$0.75	$1.25	£0.15	£0.45	£0.75
12 ND Moanin' the Bavarian, John Byrne cover						
	$0.25	$0.75	$1.25	£0.15	£0.45	£0.75
13 ND Silver Burper, John Byrne cover						
	$0.25	$0.75	$1.25	£0.15	£0.45	£0.75
14 ND Spittle-Man						
	$0.25	$0.75	$1.25	£0.15	£0.45	£0.75
15 ND Wolverina, John Byrne cover						
	$0.25	$0.75	$1.25	£0.15	£0.45	£0.75
16 ND Dr. Octopus, The Watcher						
	$0.25	$0.75	$1.25	£0.15	£0.45	£0.75
17 ND Punisher and Wolverine parodies						
	$0.25	$0.75	$1.25	£0.15	£0.45	£0.75
18 ND Captain America and Star Trek parodies						
	$0.25	$0.75	$1.25	£0.15	£0.45	£0.75
19 ND Nick Fury parody						
	$0.25	$0.75	$1.25	£0.15	£0.45	£0.75
20 ND "Infinity Wart" X-over						
	$0.25	$0.75	$1.25	£0.15	£0.45	£0.75
21 ND Wolverine, She-Hulk, Ghost Rider parodies						
	$0.25	$0.75	$1.25	£0.15	£0.45	£0.75
22 ND X-Men	$0.25	$0.75	$1.25	£0.15	£0.45	£0.75
23 ND Super-Pro football parody						
	$0.25	$0.75	$1.25	£0.15	£0.45	£0.75
24 ND Halloween issue						
	$0.25	$0.75	$1.25	£0.15	£0.45	£0.75
Title Value:	$7.20	$21.60	$36.00	£4.45	£13.35	£22.25

Note: parody series like Not Brand Echh, originally announced as a mini-series. Published irregularly from #5 on not settling into bi-monthly frequency.

WHAT THE FALL SPECIAL

Marvel Comics Group,OS; 1 Sep 1993

	$Good	$Fine	$N.Mint	£Good	£Fine	£N.Mint
1 ND 64pgs	$0.40	$1.20	$2.00	£0.25	£0.75	£1.25
Title Value:	$0.40	$1.20	$2.00	£0.25	£0.75	£1.25

WHAT THE SUMMER SPECIAL

Marvel Comics Group,OS; 1 Jun 1993

	$Good	$Fine	$N.Mint	£Good	£Fine	£N.Mint
1 ND 64pgs, all X-Men parody issue						
	$0.40	$1.20	$2.00	£0.25	£0.75	£1.25
Title Value:	$0.40	$1.20	$2.00	£0.25	£0.75	£1.25

WHEEL OF WORLDS, NEIL GAIMAN'S

Tekno Comix; 0 Jul 1995

	$Good	$Fine	$N.Mint	£Good	£Fine	£N.Mint
0 ND 48pgs, featuring Teknophage, Lady Justice, Mr. Hero and Adam Cain; featuring art by Bryan Talbot, Alan Craddock and Angus McKie						
0 ND 48pgs, Direct Market Edition (Jul 1995) - with double-sided poster and wraparound cover						
	$0.60	$1.80	$3.00	£0.40	£1.20	£2.00
Title Value:	$1.00	$3.00	$5.00	£0.65	£1.95	£3.25

WHEELIE AND THE CHOPPER BUNCH

Charlton; 1 Jul 1975-7 Jul 1976

	$Good	$Fine	$N.Mint	£Good	£Fine	£N.Mint
1 John Byrne art	$1.50	$4.50	$7.50	£1.00	£3.00	£5.00
2 John Byrne art	$1.20	$3.60	$6.00	£0.80	£2.40	£4.00
3-7 John Byrne art	$0.90	$2.70	$4.50	£0.60	£1.80	£3.00
Title Value:	$7.20	$21.60	$36.00	£4.80	£14.40	£24.00

Note: irregularly distributed on the news-stands in the U.K. Early John Byrne art.

WHERE CREATURES ROAM

Marvel Comics Group; 1 Jul 1970-8 Sep 1971

	$Good	$Fine	$N.Mint	£Good	£Fine	£N.Mint
1 ND reprints from pre-superhero Marvels begin; Steve Ditko and Jack Kirby reprints featured						
	$0.90	$2.70	$4.50	£0.60	£1.80	£3.00
2-4 ND	$0.60	$1.80	$3.00	£0.40	£1.20	£2.00
5	$0.60	$1.80	$3.00	£0.30	£0.90	£1.50
6-8	$0.60	$1.80	$3.00	£0.40	£1.20	£2.00
Title Value:	$5.10	$15.30	$25.50	£3.30	£9.90	£16.50

Note: all horror/fantasy reprints. Kirby/Ditko art in most issues.

WHERE MONSTERS DWELL

Marvel Comics Group; 1 Jan 1970-38 Oct 1975

	$Good	$Fine	$N.Mint	£Good	£Fine	£N.Mint
1 ND horror/fantasy reprints from pre-superhero Marvels begin						
	$0.90	$2.70	$4.50	£0.60	£1.80	£3.00
2 ND	$0.60	$1.80	$3.00	£0.40	£1.20	£2.00
3-10	$0.50	$1.50	$2.50	£0.30	£0.90	£1.50
11	$0.40	$1.20	$2.00	£0.25	£0.75	£1.25
12 scarce in the U.K. 48pgs, squarebound						
	$0.50	$1.50	$2.50	£0.30	£0.90	£1.50
13 Gil Kane cover	$0.40	$1.20	$2.00	£0.25	£0.75	£1.25
14-15 Severin cover						
	$0.40	$1.20	$2.00	£0.25	£0.75	£1.25
16-20	$0.40	$1.20	$2.00	£0.25	£0.75	£1.25
21 reprints Strange Tales #89 - Fin Fang Foom						
	$0.40	$1.20	$2.00	£0.25	£0.75	£1.25
22-23	$0.40	$1.20	$2.00	£0.25	£0.75	£1.25
24 ND	$0.40	$1.20	$2.00	£0.30	£0.90	£1.50
25-27	$0.40	$1.20	$2.00	£0.25	£0.75	£1.25
28-29 ND	$0.40	$1.20	$2.00	£0.30	£0.90	£1.50
30	$0.40	$1.20	$2.00	£0.25	£0.75	£1.25
31 ND	$0.40	$1.20	$2.00	£0.30	£0.90	£1.50
32-37	$0.40	$1.20	$2.00	£0.25	£0.75	£1.25
38 ND Williamson art						
	$0.50	$1.50	$2.50	£0.30	£0.90	£1.50
Title Value:	$16.90	$50.70	$84.50	£10.70	£32.10	£53.50

Note: Kirby/Ditko art in most.

WHISPER (1ST SERIES)

Capital; 1 Dec 1983-2 Mar 1984

	$Good	$Fine	$N.Mint	£Good	£Fine	£N.Mint
1 ND scarce in the U.K.						
	$0.60	$1.80	$3.00	£0.40	£1.20	£2.00
2 ND scarce in the U.K.						
	$0.50	$1.50	$2.50	£0.30	£0.90	£1.50
Title Value:	$1.10	$3.30	$5.50	£0.70	£2.10	£3.50

Note: Norm Breyfogle art

WHISPER (2ND SERIES)

First; 1 Jun 1986-37 Jun 1990

	$Good	$Fine	$N.Mint	£Good	£Fine	£N.Mint
1 $1.25 cover begins						
	$0.30	$0.90	$1.50	£0.20	£0.60	£1.00
2	$0.30	$0.90	$1.50	£0.20	£0.60	£1.00
3-9 Norm Breyfogle cover and pencil art						
	$0.30	$0.90	$1.50	£0.20	£0.60	£1.00
10 Norm Breyfogle cover and pencil art; $1.75 cover begins						
	$0.30	$0.90	$1.50	£0.20	£0.60	£1.00
11 Norm Breyfogle cover and pencil art						
	$0.30	$0.90	$1.50	£0.20	£0.60	£1.00
12-17	$0.30	$0.90	$1.50	£0.20	£0.60	£1.00
18 $1.95 cover begins						
	$0.30	$0.90	$1.50	£0.20	£0.60	£1.00
19-37	$0.30	$0.90	$1.50	£0.20	£0.60	£1.00
Title Value:	$11.10	$33.30	$55.50	£7.40	£22.20	£37.00

Note: all Non-Distributed on the news-stands in the U.K.

WHISPER SPECIAL

First; 1 Nov 1985

	$Good	$Fine	$N.Mint	£Good	£Fine	£N.Mint
1 ND 64pgs, Steven Grant script, Rich Larson art						
	$0.50	$1.50	$2.50	£0.30	£0.90	£1.50
Title Value:	$0.50	$1.50	$2.50	£0.30	£0.90	£1.50

MINT = 100% / NEAR MINT (inc. +/-) = 90-99% / VERY FINE (inc. +/-) = 75-89% / FINE (inc. +/-) = 55-74%
VERY GOOD (inc. +/-) = 35-54% / GOOD (inc. +/-) = 15-34% / FAIR = 5-14% / POOR = 1-4%

637

	$Good	$Fine	$N.Mint	£Good	£Fine	£N.Mint

WHITE DEVIL

Eternity,MS; 1 Aug 1990-6 1991

1-6 ND pre-bagged owing to sexual/violent content

| | $0.40 | $1.20 | $2.00 | £0.25 | £0.75 | £1.25 |
| Title Value: | $2.40 | $7.20 | $12.00 | £1.50 | £4.50 | £7.50 |

WHITE FANG MOVIE ADAPTATION

Disney,OS; nn Feb 1991

| nn ND, 64pgs | $1.20 | $3.60 | $6.00 | £0.80 | £2.40 | £4.00 |
| Title Value: | $1.20 | $3.60 | $6.00 | £0.80 | £2.40 | £4.00 |

Note: banned from sale in U.K.

WHITE LIKE SHE

Dark Horse,MS; 1 May 1994-4 Aug 1994

1-4 ND Bob Fingerman script/art; black and white

| | $0.60 | $1.80 | $3.00 | £0.40 | £1.20 | £2.00 |
| Title Value: | $2.40 | $7.20 | $12.00 | £1.60 | £4.80 | £8.00 |

WHIZ COMICS

Fawcett; 1 (#2) Feb 1940-155 Jun 1953

(see Thrill Comics #1 and Flash Comics #1 in Top 50 Rarest section)

1 origin and 1st appearance (in general distribution) Captain Marvel; no number on cover, number 2 listed inside

| | $5400.00 | $16200.00 | $54000.00 | £3600.00 | £10800.00 | £36000.00 |

2 no number on cover, number 3 listed inside

| | $465.00 | $1400.00 | $3750.00 | £310.00 | £930.00 | £2500.00 |

3 no number on cover, number 4 listed inside

| | $280.00 | $840.00 | $2250.00 | £185.00 | £560.00 | £1500.00 |

4 scarce in the U.K. no number on cover, number 5 listed inside

| | $230.00 | $690.00 | $1850.00 | £155.00 | £465.00 | £1250.00 |

5 scarce in the U.K.

	$180.00	$540.00	$1450.00	£120.00	£365.00	£975.00
6-10	$155.00	$470.00	$1100.00	£105.00	£320.00	£750.00
11-14	$110.00	$340.00	$800.00	£77.50	£235.00	£550.00

15 origin Sivana

| | $125.00 | $385.00 | $900.00 | £85.00 | £255.00 | £600.00 |
| 16-20 | $110.00 | $340.00 | $800.00 | £77.50 | £235.00 | £550.00 |

21 1st appearance the Lieutenant Marvels

| | $85.00 | $255.00 | $600.00 | £55.00 | £170.00 | £400.00 |
| 22-24 | $67.50 | $200.00 | $475.00 | £45.00 | £135.00 | £315.00 |

25 origin and 1st appearance Captain Marvel Jnr. (no mention on cover)

	$455.00	$1350.00	$3650.00	£300.00	£900.00	£2400.00
26-30	$57.50	$175.00	$410.00	£39.00	£115.00	£275.00
31-32	$50.00	$150.00	$350.00	£34.00	£100.00	£235.00

33 Captain Marvel and Spy Smasher team up (and on cover)

| | $50.00 | $150.00 | $350.00 | £34.00 | £100.00 | £235.00 |
| 34 | $39.00 | $115.00 | $275.00 | £25.00 | £75.00 | £175.00 |

35 Captain Marvel and Spy Smasher team up (and on cover)

| | $39.00 | $115.00 | $275.00 | £25.00 | £75.00 | £175.00 |
| 36-40 | $39.00 | $115.00 | $275.00 | £25.00 | £75.00 | £175.00 |

41 time travel story

| | $29.00 | $85.00 | $200.00 | £18.50 | £55.00 | £130.00 |
| 42 | $29.00 | $85.00 | $200.00 | £18.50 | £55.00 | £130.00 |

43 Captain Marvel and Spy Smasher team up (and on cover)

| | $29.00 | $85.00 | $200.00 | £18.50 | £55.00 | £130.00 |

44 patriotic cover, features The Life Story of Captain Marvel

	$29.00	$85.00	$200.00	£18.50	£55.00	£130.00
45-50	$29.00	$85.00	$200.00	£18.50	£55.00	£130.00
51-60	$23.50	$70.00	$165.00	£15.00	£45.00	£105.00
61-70	$21.00	$62.50	$150.00	£13.50	£41.00	£95.00
71-90	$17.50	$52.50	$125.00	£12.00	£36.00	£85.00

91 infinity cover

| | $17.50 | $52.50 | $125.00 | £12.00 | £36.00 | £85.00 |
| 92-99 | $17.50 | $52.50 | $125.00 | £12.00 | £36.00 | £85.00 |

100 anniversary issue

| | $22.50 | $67.50 | $160.00 | £14.00 | £43.00 | £100.00 |
| 101-106 | $17.00 | $50.00 | $120.00 | £11.00 | £34.00 | £80.00 |

107 photo cover

| | $17.00 | $50.00 | $120.00 | £11.00 | £34.00 | £80.00 |
| 108-130 | $17.00 | $50.00 | $120.00 | £11.00 | £34.00 | £80.00 |

131 dinosaur cover

| | $16.00 | $49.00 | $115.00 | £10.50 | £32.00 | £75.00 |
| 132-152 | $16.00 | $49.00 | $115.00 | £10.50 | £32.00 | £75.00 |

153-155 very scarce in the U.K.

| | $23.50 | $70.00 | $165.00 | £15.00 | £45.00 | £105.00 |
| Title Value: | $12095.50 | $36353.00 | $103160.00 | £8077.50 | £24321.00 | £68805.00 |

Note: like all Golden Age comics, these were not officially distributed on the news-stands in the U.K. but some came over with personnel movements during the Second World War and more regularly as bulk shipments through the news trade. There are many reports of the last 20 or so issues being available at coastal towns/seaside resorts like Blackpool and Brighton and copies have been known with British pence stamps

WHO'S WHO

DC Comics,MS; 1 Mar 1985-26 1987

1 LD in the U.K. George Perez cover

| | $0.25 | $0.75 | $1.25 | £0.20 | £0.60 | £1.00 |

2 LD scarce in the U.K. George Perez cover, Batman feature

| | $0.25 | $0.75 | $1.25 | £0.25 | £0.75 | £1.25 |

3-10 LD in the U.K.

| | $0.25 | $0.75 | $1.25 | £0.15 | £0.45 | £0.75 |

11 LD in the U.K. Joker feature

| | $0.25 | $0.75 | $1.25 | £0.20 | £0.60 | £1.00 |

12-26 LD in the U.K.

| | $0.25 | $0.75 | $1.25 | £0.15 | £0.45 | £0.75 |
| Title Value: | $6.50 | $19.50 | $32.50 | £4.10 | £12.30 | £20.50 |

Note: Issue #1 & #2 were printed from flexographic plates which tended to become clogged with paper-dust; many copies, especially of issue 1, have heavy ink blotches in the fine tints. All have wraparound covers.

WHO'S WHO (2ND SERIES)

DC Comics,MS; 1 Aug 1990-16 Feb 1992

1 ND 48pgs, Superman cover by Jerry Ordway, features pull-out poster of Atlantis

| | $1.00 | $3.00 | $5.00 | £0.60 | £1.80 | £3.00 |

2 ND 48pgs, art by Arthur Adams/Adam Hughes featured, Flash cover

| | $1.00 | $3.00 | $5.00 | £0.60 | £1.80 | £3.00 |

3 ND 48pgs, Arthur Adams/Adam Hughes featured, Green Lantern cover

| | $1.00 | $3.00 | $5.00 | £0.60 | £1.80 | £3.00 |

4 ND 48pgs, George Perez/Arthur Adams/Jerry Ordway art featured, Wonder Woman cover

| | $1.00 | $3.00 | $5.00 | £0.60 | £1.80 | £3.00 |

5 ND 48pgs, Batmobile cover, Penguin/Riddler/Poison Ivy entries

| | $1.00 | $3.00 | $5.00 | £0.60 | £1.80 | £3.00 |

6 ND 48pgs, Barbara Gordon/Huntress entries

| | $1.00 | $3.00 | $5.00 | £0.60 | £1.80 | £3.00 |

7 ND 48pgs, Justice League of America cover, Captain Atom/Shade entries

| | $1.00 | $3.00 | $5.00 | £0.60 | £1.80 | £3.00 |

8 ND 48pgs, Aqualad/Butcher/Spectre entries

| | $1.00 | $3.00 | $5.00 | £0.60 | £1.80 | £3.00 |

9 ND 48pgs, Legion of Super-Heroes cover/entries plus Firehawk by Barry Kitson and Hugo Strange by George Perez

| | $1.00 | $3.00 | $5.00 | £0.60 | £1.80 | £3.00 |

10 ND 48pgs, Robin cover, Flash entry by Carmine Infantino

| | $1.00 | $3.00 | $5.00 | £0.60 | £1.80 | £3.00 |

11 ND 48pgs, Guy Gardner cover plus Legion '91

| | $1.00 | $3.00 | $5.00 | £0.60 | £1.80 | £3.00 |

12 ND 48pgs, Aquaman cover plus Mera/Metal Men/Hawkwoman

| | $1.00 | $3.00 | $5.00 | £0.60 | £1.80 | £3.00 |

13 ND 48pgs, Giffen and Stelfreeze art featured, Joker by Brian Bolland

| | $1.00 | $3.00 | $5.00 | £0.60 | £1.80 | £3.00 |

14 ND 48pgs, New Teen Titans cover, Animal Man by Bolland

| | $1.00 | $3.00 | $5.00 | £0.60 | £1.80 | £3.00 |

15 ND 48pgs, Swamp Thing by John Higgins, Doom Patrol

| | $1.00 | $3.00 | $5.00 | £0.60 | £1.80 | £3.00 |

16 ND 56pgs, Catwoman by Brian Stelfreeze (Todd McFarlane missed the deadline), Legion of Super-Heroes

| | $1.00 | $3.00 | $5.00 | £0.60 | £1.80 | £3.00 |
| Title Value: | $16.00 | $48.00 | $80.00 | £9.60 | £28.80 | £48.00 |

Note: all 48pgs graphic novel size, loose-leaf format featuring all statistical information on dozens of characters.

Note: Binder issued separately in Nov 1990, features cover illustration by George Perez. Binder 2 issued in April 1991 with the cover by Brian Bolland in larger size to contain more leaves

WHO'S WHO IN STAR TREK

DC Comics,MS; 1 Mar 1987-2 Apr 1987

1-2 scarce in the U.K.

| | $0.60 | $1.80 | $3.00 | £0.30 | £0.90 | £1.50 |
| Title Value: | $1.20 | $3.60 | $6.00 | £0.60 | £1.80 | £3.00 |

Note: all wraparound covers

WHO'S WHO IN THE LEGION

DC Comics,MS; 1 May 1988-7 Nov 1988

| 1-7 | $0.30 | $0.90 | $1.50 | £0.20 | £0.60 | £1.00 |
| Title Value: | $2.10 | $6.30 | $10.50 | £1.40 | £4.20 | £7.00 |

Note: all wraparound covers

WHO'S WHO UPDATE '87

DC Comics,MS; 1 Aug 1987-5 Dec 1987

1 Batgirl/Batman feature

	$0.25	$0.75	$1.25	£0.15	£0.45	£0.75
2-5	$0.25	$0.75	$1.25	£0.15	£0.45	£0.75
Title Value:	$1.25	$3.75	$6.25	£0.75	£2.25	£3.75

Note: all wraparound covers

WHO'S WHO UPDATE '88

DC Comics,MS; 1 Aug 1988-4 Nov 1988

1	$0.25	$0.75	$1.25	£0.15	£0.45	£0.75
2 Joker feature	$0.25	$0.75	$1.25	£0.15	£0.45	£0.75
3-4	$0.25	$0.75	$1.25	£0.15	£0.45	£0.75
Title Value:	$1.00	$3.00	$5.00	£0.60	£1.80	£3.00

Note: all wraparound covers

WHO'S WHO UPDATE '93

DC Comics; 1,2 Jan 1993

1-2 ND 48pgs, loose-leaf format, Travis Charest cover

| | $1.00 | $3.00 | $5.00 | £0.60 | £1.80 | £3.00 |
| Title Value: | $2.00 | $6.00 | $10.00 | £1.20 | £3.60 | £6.00 |

WHODUNNIT?

Eclipse; 1 Jun 1986-3 Jan 1987

| 1-3 ND | $0.40 | $1.20 | $2.00 | £0.25 | £0.75 | £1.25 |
| Title Value: | $1.20 | $3.60 | $6.00 | £0.75 | £2.25 | £3.75 |

WHY I HATE SATURN GRAPHIC ALBUM

DC Comics/Piranha Press,OS; 1 Jul 1990

1 ND 208pgs, script/art by Kyle Baker

| | $2.50 | $7.50 | $12.50 | £1.70 | £5.00 | £8.50 |

1 2nd printing, ND (Oct 1991), new cover by Kyle Baker

| | $2.40 | $7.00 | $12.00 | £1.60 | £4.80 | £8.00 |
| Title Value: | $4.90 | $14.50 | $24.50 | £3.30 | £9.80 | £16.50 |

WICKED

Millennium,MS; 1 Nov 1994-4 Jun 1995

1-4 ND Sean Shaw script and art; black and white

| | $0.40 | $1.20 | $2.00 | £0.25 | £0.75 | £1.25 |
| Title Value: | $1.60 | $4.80 | $8.00 | £1.00 | £3.00 | £5.00 |

WICKED: THE RECKONING

Millennium,MS; 1 Aug 1995-2 Sep 1995

1-2 ND Sean Shaw script and art; black and white

| | $0.50 | $1.50 | $2.50 | £0.30 | £0.90 | £1.50 |
| Title Value: | $1.00 | $3.00 | $5.00 | £0.60 | £1.80 | £3.00 |

TRADE PAPERBACKS, GRAPHIC NOVELS AND OTHER COLLECTIONS ARE PRICED IN POUNDS STERLING ONLY. CONVERT AT 1.5 FOR DOLLARS.

	$Good	$Fine	$N.Mint	£Good	£Fine	£N.Mint

WIDOW: METAL GYPSIES
London Night Studios,MS; 1 Aug 1995-present
1-3 ND Mike Wolfer script and art

	$0.60	$1.80	$3.00	£0.40	£1.20	£2.00
Title Value:	$1.80	$5.40	$9.00	£1.20	£3.60	£6.00

WILD ANIMALS
Pacific; 1 Dec 1982
1 ND Scott Shaw, Larry Gonick, Sergio Aragones art

	$0.50	$1.50	$2.50	£0.30	£0.90	£1.50
Title Value:	$0.50	$1.50	$2.50	£0.30	£0.90	£1.50

WILD CARDS
Marvel Comics Group/Epic,MS; 1 Sep 1990-4 Dec 1990
1-4 ND 48pgs, Barry Kitson/Jackson Guice art

	$0.50	$1.50	$2.50	£0.30	£0.90	£1.50
Title Value:	$0.50	$6.00	$10.00	£1.20	£3.60	£6.00

Note: Bookshelf Format

Trade paperback (Oct 1991), reprints mini-series				£1.80	£5.40	£9.00

WILD DOG
DC Comics,MS; 1 Sep 1987-4 Dec 1987
(see Action Comics)

1-4	$0.15	$0.45	$0.75	£0.10	£0.35	£0.60
Title Value:	$0.60	$1.80	$3.00	£0.40	£1.40	£2.40

WILD DOG SPECIAL
DC Comics,OS; 1 Nov 1989

1 48pgs	$0.25	$0.75	$1.25	£0.15	£0.45	£0.75
Title Value:	$0.25	$0.75	$1.25	£0.15	£0.45	£0.75

WILD KNIGHTS
Eternity; 1 Aug 1988-10 May 1989
1-10 ND Evan Dorkin script, black and white

	$0.40	$1.20	$2.00	£0.25	£0.75	£1.25
Title Value:	$4.00	$12.00	$20.00	£2.50	£7.50	£12.50

WILD THING
Marvel UK; 1 Apr 1993-9 Dec 1993

1 embossed cover	$0.30	$0.90	$1.50	£0.20	£0.60	£1.00
2	$0.25	$0.75	$1.25	£0.15	£0.45	£0.75
3 Shield appear	$0.25	$0.75	$1.25	£0.15	£0.45	£0.75
4-5	$0.25	$0.75	$1.25	£0.15	£0.45	£0.75

6 classic Spiderman villains appear including Dr. Octopus, Kraven, Electro and The Vulture

	$0.25	$0.75	$1.25	£0.15	£0.45	£0.75
7-9	$0.25	$0.75	$1.25	£0.15	£0.45	£0.75
Title Value:	$2.30	$6.90	$11.50	£1.40	£4.20	£7.00

WILD THINGS
Metro Comics; 1,2 1986
1-2 ND John Workman art

	$0.40	$1.20	$2.00	£0.25	£0.75	£1.25
Title Value:	$0.80	$2.40	$4.00	£0.50	£1.50	£2.50

WILD, THE
Eastern; 1 Oct 1988-4 1988

1-4 ND bi-weekly	$0.30	$0.90	$1.50	£0.20	£0.60	£1.00
Title Value:	$1.20	$3.60	$6.00	£0.80	£2.40	£4.00

WILD, WILD WEST, THE
Gold Key; 1 Jun 1966-7 Oct 1969
1 LD scarce in the U.K.

	$15.50	$47.00	$110.00	£10.00	£30.00	£70.00
2 LD in the U.K.	$11.00	$34.00	$80.00	£7.00	£21.00	£50.00

3-7 LD in the U.K.

	$8.50	$26.00	$60.00	£5.50	£17.00	£40.00
Title Value:	$69.00	$211.00	$490.00	£44.50	£136.00	£320.00

WILD, WILD WEST, THE (2ND SERIES)
Millennium,MS; 1 Oct 1990-4 Jan 1991
1-4 ND Adam Hughes cover, colour

	$0.50	$1.50	$2.50	£0.30	£0.90	£1.50
Title Value:	$2.00	$6.00	$10.00	£1.20	£3.60	£6.00

WILDBRATS
Fantagraphics,OS; 1 Sep 1992
1 ND parody of Jim Lee's Wildc.a.t.s (Image)

	$0.40	$1.20	$2.00	£0.25	£0.75	£1.25
Title Value:	$0.40	$1.20	$2.00	£0.25	£0.75	£1.25

WILDC.A.T.S
Image; 1 Aug 1992-present
1 Jim Lee script/art, includes two trading cards; first appearance WildC.A.T.S.

	$1.20	$3.60	$6.00	£0.60	£1.80	£3.00

1 gold embossed cover

	$3.00	$9.00	$15.00	£2.00	£6.00	£10.00

1 gold embossed cover, signed by Jim Lee

	$5.00	$15.00	$25.00	£3.00	£9.00	£15.00

2 1st appearance WetWorks in back-up feature; Jim Lee script/art, includes two trading cards, silver "prism" cover, contains Image #0 coupon 5

	$1.50	$4.50	$7.50	£0.80	£2.40	£4.00
2 without coupon	$0.60	$1.80	$3.00	£0.40	£1.20	£2.00

2 Newstand edition, white background and black logo, with coupon

	$0.60	$1.80	$3.00	£0.40	£1.20	£2.00

3 previews Whilce Portacio's "Wetworks"

	$0.80	$2.40	$4.00	£0.40	£1.20	£2.00

4 pre-bagged with trading card by Jim Lee; 1st appearance Tribe by Larry Stroman

	$0.80	$2.40	$4.00	£0.40	£1.20	£2.00

4 pre-bagged with extra trading card, limited to 2.5% of the total print run

	$1.20	$3.60	$6.00	£0.80	£2.40	£4.00

5 two double gatefold pages

	$0.80	$2.40	$4.00	£0.50	£1.50	£2.50

6-7 Killer Instinct story

	$0.80	$2.40	$4.00	£0.50	£1.50	£2.50

7 Limited Edition - as above with additional silver outer card cover

	$3.00	$9.00	$15.00	£2.00	£6.00	£10.00

8 unauthorised (?) cameos by Clark Kent and Lois Lane, Scott Summers and Jean Grey

	$0.80	$2.40	$4.00	£0.50	£1.50	£2.50
9	$0.80	$2.40	$4.00	£0.50	£1.50	£2.50

10 1st appearance Huntsman

	$0.80	$2.40	$4.00	£0.50	£1.50	£2.50

11 Huntsman appears

	$0.60	$1.80	$3.00	£0.40	£1.20	£2.00

11 Variant cover, ND cover forms larger picture when combined with variant covers of Deathblow #5, Gen 13 #5, Kindred #3, Stormwatch #10, Team 7 #1, Wetworks #2

	$1.50	$4.50	$7.50	£1.00	£3.00	£5.00

12-13 Huntsman appears

	$0.60	$1.80	$3.00	£0.40	£1.20	£2.00

14 Image X Month tie-in

	$0.60	$1.80	$3.00	£0.40	£1.20	£2.00

15 Travis Charest art

	$0.60	$1.80	$3.00	£0.40	£1.20	£2.00

16-19 Travis Charest art

	$0.50	$1.50	$2.50	£0.30	£0.90	£1.50

20 Wildstorm Rising part 2, continued in Union #4; with two foil-bagged painted trading cards. Cover by Barry Windsor-Smith, art by Travis Charest

	$0.50	$1.50	$2.50	£0.30	£0.90	£1.50

20 Newstand edition, without trading cards

	$0.40	$1.20	$2.00	£0.25	£0.75	£1.25

21 Travis Charest art

	$0.50	$1.50	$2.50	£0.30	£0.90	£1.50

22-24 Alan Moore script, Travis Charest art

	$0.50	$1.50	$2.50	£0.30	£0.90	£1.50

25 48pgs, Alan Moore script, Travis Charest art; wraparound chromium cover

Where Creatures Roam #1

Where Monsters Dwell #1

The Witching Hour #2

	$Good	$Fine	$N.Mint	£Good	£Fine	£N.Mint
	$1.00	$3.00	$5.00	£0.65	£1.95	£3.25
Title Value:	$32.90	$98.70	$164.50	£20.40	£61.20	£102.00

Note: all Non-Distributed on the news-stands in the U.K.

WildC.A.T.S (1994)
Trade paperback
112pgs, reprints #1-4 pre-bagged with an issue #0

				£1.30	£3.90	£6.50

WildC.A.T.S. #10-12: The Director's Cut (Aug 1994)
ND three 64pg perfect bound editions, signed and
numbered by Chris Claremont. 5,000 sets

				£12.00	£36.00	£60.00

WILDC.A.T.S ADVENTURES
Image; 1 Sep 1994-10 Jun 1995
1-10 ND based on US animated show

	$0.40	$1.20	$2.00	£0.25	£0.75	£1.25
Title Value:	$4.00	$12.00	$20.00	£2.50	£7.50	£12.50

WILDC.A.T.S ADVENTURES SOURCEBOOK
Image; 1 Jan 1995
1 ND information and statistics on the characters from the animated series; Jeff Smith cover

	$0.50	$1.50	$2.50	£0.30	£0.90	£1.50
Title Value:	$0.50	$1.50	$2.50	£0.30	£0.90	£1.50

WILDC.A.T.S SOURCEBOOK
Image; 1 Sep 1993; 2 Oct 1994
1-2 ND information and statistics about the WildC.A.T.S. team

	$0.50	$1.50	$2.50	£0.30	£0.90	£1.50
Title Value:	$1.00	$3.00	$5.00	£0.60	£1.80	£3.00

WILDC.A.T.S SPECIAL
Image,OS; 1 Nov 1993
1 ND Steve Gerber script, Travis Charest art

	$0.80	$2.40	$4.00	£0.50	£1.50	£2.50
Title Value:	$0.80	$2.40	$4.00	£0.50	£1.50	£2.50

WILDC.A.T.S: TRILOGY
Image,MS; 1 Jun 1993-3 Aug 1993
1-3 ND Jae Lee and Brandon Choi script/art

	$0.50	$1.50	$2.50	£0.30	£0.90	£1.50
Title Value:	$1.50	$4.50	$7.50	£0.90	£2.70	£4.50

WILDSTAR
Image; 1 Sep 1995-present
1-3 ND Al Gordon script, Chris Marrinan art

	$0.50	$1.50	$2.50	£0.30	£0.90	£1.50
Title Value:	$1.50	$4.50	$7.50	£0.90	£2.70	£4.50

WILDSTAR: SKY ZERO
Image,MS; 1 Mar 1993-4 Nov 1993
1 Jerry Ordway script and art begins

	$0.50	$1.50	$2.50	£0.30	£0.90	£1.50

1 Gold Edition (Mar 1993) - approx. 5,000 copies, embossed cover with gold logo and gold number/date box

	$2.50	$7.50	$12.50	£1.50	£4.50	£7.50
2	$0.40	$1.20	$2.00	£0.25	£0.75	£1.25

3 Savage Dragon appears

	$0.40	$1.20	$2.00	£0.25	£0.75	£1.25
Title Value:	$3.80	$11.40	$19.00	£2.30	£6.90	£11.50

Note: all Non-Distributed on the news-stands in the U.K.

Wildstar: Sky Zero (Aug 1994)
Trade paperback reprints mini-series with 2 extra story pages

				£1.70	£5.10	£8.50

WILDSTAR: THE SERIES - ASHCAN
Image,OS; nn Aug 1995
nn ND 16pgs, black and white

	$0.20	$0.60	$1.00	£0.15	£0.45	£0.75
Title Value:	$0.20	$0.60	$1.00	£0.15	£0.45	£0.75

WILDSTORM
Image,MS; 1 Aug 1995-4 Nov 1995
1-4 ND

	$0.50	$1.50	$2.50	£0.30	£0.90	£1.50
Title Value:	$2.00	$6.00	$10.00	£1.20	£3.60	£6.00

WILDSTORM RARITIES
Image,OS; 1 Dec 1994
1 ND Gen 13 appear

	$1.00	$3.00	$5.00	£0.70	£2.10	£3.50
Title Value:	$1.00	$3.00	$5.00	£0.70	£2.10	£3.50

WILDSTORM RISING
Image,MS; 1,10 May 1995
1 ND James Robinson script, Barry Windsor-Smith cover and art; with two foil-bagged painted trading cards; story continued in WildC.A.T.S #20

	$0.50	$1.50	$2.50	£0.30	£0.90	£1.50

1 Newstand edition, ND without trading cards

	$0.40	$1.20	$2.00	£0.25	£0.75	£1.25

10 ND James Robinson script, Barry Windsor-Smith cover and art; with two foil-bagged painted trading cards

	$0.50	$1.50	$2.50	£0.30	£0.90	£1.50

10 Newstand edition, ND without trading cards

	$0.40	$1.20	$2.00	£0.25	£0.75	£1.25
Title Value:	$1.80	$5.40	$9.00	£1.10	£3.30	£5.50

WILDSTORM RISING CHECKLIST
Cross-over series from Image by James Robison and Barry Windsor-Smith. The issue story order is as follows:
Prologue - Team 7 - Objective Hell #1
Part 1 - Wildstorm Rising Part 1
Part 2 - WildC.A.T.S. #20
Part 3 - Union #4
Part 4 - Gen 13 #2
Part 5 - Grifter #1
Part 6 - Deathblow #16
Part 7 - Wetworks #8
Part 8 - Backlash #8
Part 9 - Stormwatch #22
Part 10 - Wildstorm Rising Part 10

WILDSTORM RISING TRADE PAPERBACK
Image,OS; nn Oct 1995
nn ND

	$3.00	$9.00	$15.00	£2.00	£6.00	£10.00
Title Value:	$3.00	$9.00	$15.00	£2.00	£6.00	£10.00

WILDSTORM SOURCEBOOK
Image,OS; 1 May 1995
1 ND guide to the Wildstorm Rising cross-over story

	$0.50	$1.50	$2.50	£0.30	£0.90	£1.50
Title Value:	$0.50	$1.50	$2.50	£0.30	£0.90	£1.50

WILDSTORM SWIMSUIT SPECIAL
Image,OS; 1 Dec 1994; 2 Aug 1995
1 ND Jim Lee art featured

	$0.60	$1.80	$3.00	£0.40	£1.20	£2.00

2 ND Jim Lee cover and featured in art

	$0.50	$1.50	$2.50	£0.30	£0.90	£1.50
Title Value:	$1.10	$3.30	$5.50	£0.70	£2.10	£3.50

WILDSTORM'S CHAMBER OF HORRORS
Image,OS; 1 Oct 1995
1 ND 48pgs, Simon Bisley cover

	$0.70	$2.10	$3.50	£0.50	£1.50	£2.50
Title Value:	$0.70	$2.10	$3.50	£0.50	£1.50	£2.50

WILL EISNER'S 3-D CLASSICS FEATURING THE SPIRIT
Kitchen Sink,OS; 1 Dec 1985
1 ND Spirit reprints, with 3-D glasses

	$0.60	$1.80	$3.00	£0.40	£1.20	£2.00
Title Value:	$0.60	$1.80	$3.00	£0.40	£1.20	£2.00

WILL EISNER'S QUARTERLY
Kitchen Sink,Magazine; 1 1984-8 1986
1 ND

	$1.20	$3.60	$6.00	£0.80	£2.40	£4.00
2-3 ND	$0.90	$2.70	$4.50	£0.60	£1.80	£3.00

4-6 ND giants, squarebound

	$1.20	$3.60	$6.00	£0.80	£2.40	£4.00
7-8 ND	$0.60	$1.80	$3.00	£0.40	£1.20	£2.00
Title Value:	$7.80	$23.40	$39.00	£5.20	£15.60	£26.00

WILLOW
Marvel Comics Group,MS Film; 1 Aug 1988-3 Oct 1988
(see Marvel Graphic Novel)
1-3 ND reprints Graphic Novel

	$0.15	$0.45	$0.75	£0.10	£0.35	£0.60
Title Value:	$0.45	$1.35	$2.25	£0.30	£1.05	£1.80

WIN A PRIZE COMICS
Charlton; 1 Feb 1955-2 Apr 1955
1 Edgar Allen Poe adaptation featured; lead story by Joe Simon and Jack Kirby (9pgs)

	$62.50	$190.00	$450.00	£43.00	£125.00	£300.00

2 Joe Simon and Jack Kirby art (4pgs)

	$43.00	$125.00	$300.00	£29.00	£85.00	£200.00
Title Value:	$105.50	$315.00	$750.00	£72.00	£210.00	£500.00

Note: both issues not distributed on the news-stands in the U.K.

WINDY AND WILLY
DC Comics; 1 May/Jun 1969-4 Nov/Dec 1969
(see Showcase #81)
1-4 very scarce in the U.K.

	$0.80	$2.40	$4.00	£0.50	£1.50	£2.50
Title Value:	$3.20	$9.60	$16.00	£2.00	£6.00	£10.00

Note: reprints from 1950s/60s humour title with some art changes.

WINTER WORLD
Eclipse,MS; 1 Sep 1987-3 Mar 1988
1 ND George Zaffino art begins, colour

	$0.40	$1.20	$2.00	£0.25	£0.75	£1.25

2-3 ND scarce in the U.K.

	$0.40	$1.20	$2.00	£0.25	£0.75	£1.25
Title Value:	$1.20	$3.60	$6.00	£0.75	£2.25	£3.75

Graphic Novel - Limited Edition,
reprints issues #1-3, signed and numbered

				£4.00	£12.00	£20.00

WITCHBLADE
Image; 1 Oct 1995-present
1 ND Mike Turner art

	$1.40	$4.20	$7.00	£1.40	£4.20	£7.00

2 ND Mike Turner art

	$1.00	$3.00	$5.00	£0.80	£2.40	£4.00
3 ND	$0.50	$1.50	$2.50	£0.30	£0.90	£1.50
Title Value:	$2.90	$8.70	$14.50	£2.50	£7.50	£12.50

WITCHCRAFT
DC Comics/Vertigo,MS; 1 Jun 1994-3 Aug 1994
1-3 48pgs, painted cover by Mike Kaluta; The Three Witches from Sandman (Mildred, Morganna and Cynthia)

	$0.60	$1.80	$3.00	£0.40	£1.20	£2.00
Title Value:	$1.80	$5.40	$9.00	£1.20	£3.60	£6.00

WITCHING HOUR
National Periodical Publications/DC Comics; 1 Feb/Mar 1969-85 Oct 1978
1 Neal Adams art (2pgs), part Toth art

	$4.15	$12.50	$25.00	£2.50	£7.50	£15.00
2 Toth art	$2.50	$7.50	$12.50	£1.50	£4.50	£7.50
3 Wrightson art	$1.80	$5.25	$9.00	£1.20	£3.60	£6.00
4	$1.50	$4.50	$7.50	£1.00	£3.00	£5.00
5 Wrightson art	$1.80	$5.25	$9.00	£1.20	£3.60	£6.00
6 Toth art	$1.80	$5.25	$9.00	£1.20	£3.60	£6.00
7 2pgs Kaluta art	$1.20	$3.60	$6.00	£0.80	£2.40	£4.00
8 Neal Adams art	$1.80	$5.25	$9.00	£1.20	£3.60	£6.00
9-10	$1.20	$3.60	$6.00	£0.80	£2.40	£4.00
11-12	$1.00	$3.00	$5.00	£0.70	£2.10	£3.50
13 Neal Adams art						
	$1.20	$3.60	$6.00	£0.80	£2.40	£4.00

Issue	$Good	$Fine	$N.Mint	£Good	£Fine	£N.Mint
14 Williamson, Jones art	$1.00	$3.00	$5.00	£0.70	£2.10	£3.50
15	$0.50	$1.50	$2.50	£0.35	£1.05	£1.75
16-21 52pgs	$0.60	$1.80	$3.00	£0.40	£1.20	£2.00
22-25	$0.50	$1.50	$2.50	£0.30	£0.90	£1.50
26 ND	$0.50	$1.50	$2.50	£0.35	£1.05	£1.75
27-30	$0.50	$1.50	$2.50	£0.30	£0.90	£1.50
31-37	$0.30	$0.90	$1.50	£0.20	£0.60	£1.00
38 100pgs	$0.50	$1.50	$2.50	£0.30	£0.90	£1.50
39-40	$0.30	$0.90	$1.50	£0.20	£0.60	£1.00
41-60	$0.25	$0.75	$1.25	£0.15	£0.45	£0.75
61 scarce in the U.K.	$0.25	$0.75	$1.25	£0.20	£0.60	£1.00
62-65	$0.25	$0.75	$1.25	£0.15	£0.45	£0.75
66-70 scarce in the U.K.	$0.25	$0.75	$1.25	£0.20	£0.60	£1.00
71-83	$0.25	$0.75	$1.25	£0.15	£0.45	£0.75
84-85 ND 44pgs	$0.30	$0.90	$1.50	£0.20	£0.60	£1.00
Title Value:	$46.30	$138.35	$235.90	£29.85	£89.55	£151.75

ARTISTS
Nino art in 31, 40, 45, 47. Wood art in 15.

WITCHING HOUR, ANNE RICE'S
Millennium,MS; 1 1992-8 1993?

Issue	$Good	$Fine	$N.Mint	£Good	£Fine	£N.Mint
1 ND Duncan Eagleson script/art, John Bolton covers begin	$1.00	$3.00	$5.00	£0.60	£1.80	£3.00
1 Platinum edition ND	$2.50	$7.50	$12.50	£1.50	£4.50	£7.50
2-8 ND	$0.60	$1.80	$3.00	£0.40	£1.20	£2.00
Title Value:	$7.70	$23.10	$38.50	£4.90	£14.70	£24.50

Anne Rice's The Witching Hour: The Beginning (Nov 1994)

Issue	$Good	$Fine	$N.Mint	£Good	£Fine	£N.Mint
reprints issues #1-3, wraparound cover by John Bolton				£1.40	£4.20	£7.00

WITHIN OUR REACH
Marvel Comics Group; nn Jan 1991

Issue	$Good	$Fine	$N.Mint	£Good	£Fine	£N.Mint
nn ND 80pgs, charity anthology including stories featuring Spiderman, Concrete (by Chadwick), Sherlock Holmes, Spiderman/Santa Claus cover by Norm Breyfogle	$1.00	$3.00	$5.00	£0.60	£1.80	£3.00
Title Value:	$1.00	$3.00	$5.00	£0.60	£1.80	£3.00

WIZARD OF FOURTH STREET
Dark Horse,MS; 1 Dec 1987-2 Mar 1988

Issue	$Good	$Fine	$N.Mint	£Good	£Fine	£N.Mint
1 ND	$0.30	$0.90	$1.50	£0.20	£0.60	£1.00
2 ND scarce in the U.K.	$0.30	$0.90	$1.50	£0.25	£0.75	£1.25
Title Value:	$0.60	$1.80	$3.00	£0.45	£1.35	£2.25

Note: originally announced as a 6 issue mini-series

WIZARD'S TALE, THE
Eclipse,MS; 1 Dec 1993-3 Feb 1994

Issue	$Good	$Fine	$N.Mint	£Good	£Fine	£N.Mint
1-3 ND 48pgs	$1.00	$3.00	$5.00	£0.60	£1.80	£3.00
Title Value:	$3.00	$9.00	$15.00	£1.80	£5.40	£9.00

WOLF & RED
Dark Horse,MS; 1 Apr 1995-3 Jun 1995

Issue	$Good	$Fine	$N.Mint	£Good	£Fine	£N.Mint
1-3 ND based on Tex Avery cartoon characters	$0.50	$1.50	$2.50	£0.30	£0.90	£1.50
Title Value:	$1.50	$4.50	$7.50	£0.90	£2.70	£4.50

WOLFMAN
Dell; 12-922-308 Jun/Aug 1963

Issue	$Good	$Fine	$N.Mint	£Good	£Fine	£N.Mint
12-922-308 scarce, distributed in the U.K. adapts film	$3.75	$11.00	$22.50	£2.50	£7.50	£15.00
Title Value:	$3.75	$11.00	$22.50	£2.50	£7.50	£15.00

WOLFPACK
Marvel Comics Group,MS; 1 Feb 1988-12 Jul 1989
(see Marvel Graphic Novel)

Issue	$Good	$Fine	$N.Mint	£Good	£Fine	£N.Mint
1-12 ND	$0.25	$0.75	$1.25	£0.15	£0.45	£0.75
Title Value:	$3.00	$9.00	$15.00	£1.80	£5.40	£9.00

WOLPH
Blackthorne,MS; 1 Jul 1987-4 Oct 1987

Issue	$Good	$Fine	$N.Mint	£Good	£Fine	£N.Mint
1-4 ND	$0.40	$1.20	$2.00	£0.25	£0.75	£1.25
Title Value:	$1.60	$4.80	$8.00	£1.00	£3.00	£5.00

WOLVERINE
Marvel Comics Group; 1 Nov 1988-90 Feb 1995; 91 Jul 1995-present
(see Captain America Annual #8, Havok and...,Hulk and.., Kitty and.., Marvel Comics Presents, Marvel Fanfare, Marvel Team Up, Power Pack, Punisher War Journal #6,#7, Spiderman and.., X-Men)
(see Weapon X)

Issue	$Good	$Fine	$N.Mint	£Good	£Fine	£N.Mint
1 ND	$7.00	$21.00	$35.00	£2.50	£7.50	£12.50
2 ND	$3.00	$9.00	$15.00	£1.00	£3.00	£5.00
3 ND	$2.00	$6.00	$10.00	£0.90	£2.70	£4.50
4 ND 1st appearance Roughouse and Bloodsport	$2.00	$6.00	$10.00	£0.90	£2.70	£4.50
5 ND	$2.00	$6.00	$10.00	£0.80	£2.40	£4.00
6 ND	$1.60	$4.80	$8.00	£0.70	£2.10	£3.50
7-8 ND Hulk appears	$1.60	$4.80	$8.00	£0.70	£2.10	£3.50
9 ND Peter David script	$1.60	$4.80	$8.00	£0.70	£2.10	£3.50
10 ND scarce in the U.K. Sabretooth vs. Wolverine (chronologically their 1st battle)	$6.00	$18.00	$30.00	£3.00	£9.00	£15.00
11 ND bi-weekly issue, The Gehenna Stone story by Peter David begins	$1.50	$4.50	$7.50	£0.60	£1.80	£3.00
12-15 ND bi-weekly issue, The Gehenna Stone story	$1.50	$4.50	$7.50	£0.60	£1.80	£3.00
16 ND bi-weekly issue, The Gehenna Stone story	$1.00	$3.00	$5.00	£0.50	£1.50	£2.50
17 ND John Byrne co-art begins (to #23)	$1.00	$3.00	$5.00	£0.50	£1.50	£2.50
18 ND John Byrne art	$1.00	$3.00	$5.00	£0.40	£1.20	£2.00
19-20 ND Acts of Vengeance tie-in, John Byrne art	$1.00	$3.00	$5.00	£0.40	£1.20	£2.00
21-23 ND John Byrne art	$0.80	$2.40	$4.00	£0.40	£1.20	£2.00
24 ND Peter David script	$0.80	$2.40	$4.00	£0.40	£1.20	£2.00
25 ND	$0.80	$2.40	$4.00	£0.40	£1.20	£2.00
26 ND bi-weekly issues begin (end #31)	$0.80	$2.40	$4.00	£0.40	£1.20	£2.00
27-30 ND The Lazarus Project story, bi-weekly	$0.80	$2.40	$4.00	£0.40	£1.20	£2.00
31 ND bi-weekly	$0.60	$1.80	$3.00	£0.40	£1.20	£2.00
32-38 ND	$0.60	$1.80	$3.00	£0.40	£1.20	£2.00
39 ND Storm guest-stars	$0.60	$1.80	$3.00	£0.40	£1.20	£2.00
40 ND Wolverine vs. Wolverine clone	$0.60	$1.80	$3.00	£0.40	£1.20	£2.00
41 ND Sabretooth announces he's Wolverine's father, Cable appears, bi-weekly issue	$1.50	$4.50	$7.50	£1.00	£3.00	£5.00
41 2nd printing, ND Oct 1991, gold ink cover	$0.60	$1.80	$3.00	£0.40	£1.20	£2.00
42 ND Sabretooth proven not to be Wolverine's father, Cable appears, bi-weekly issue	$1.00	$3.00	$5.00	£0.70	£2.10	£3.50
42 2nd printing, ND (Dec 1991, gold ink cover)	$0.40	$1.20	$2.00	£0.25	£0.75	£1.25
43 ND Sabretooth father-saga concludes, bi-weekly issue	$0.90	$2.70	$4.50	£0.60	£1.80	£3.00
44 ND bi-weekly issue	$0.60	$1.80	$3.00	£0.40	£1.20	£2.00
45 ND Sabretooth appears, bi-weekly issue	$0.60	$1.80	$3.00	£0.40	£1.20	£2.00
46 ND Hunter in the Darkness story with Sabretooth concludes, bi-weekly issue	$0.60	$1.80	$3.00	£0.40	£1.20	£2.00
47 ND Hunter in the Darkness story epilogue	$0.60	$1.80	$3.00	£0.40	£1.20	£2.00
48 ND Weapon X sequel begins	$0.60	$1.80	$3.00	£0.40	£1.20	£2.00
49 ND Weapon X sequel; lead into true origin of Wolverine	$0.60	$1.80	$3.00	£0.40	£1.20	£2.00
50 ND die-cut cover (as if claws are ripping through), true origin of Wolverine revealed, Professor X, Nick Fury appear	$0.80	$2.40	$4.00	£0.50	£1.50	£2.50
51 ND Sabretooth appears, Andy Kubert art	$0.50	$1.50	$2.50	£0.30	£0.90	£1.50
52 ND	$0.50	$1.50	$2.50	£0.30	£0.90	£1.50
53 ND Spiral and Mystique appear	$0.50	$1.50	$2.50	£0.30	£0.90	£1.50
54 ND The Thing, Nick Fury and Gambit appear	$0.50	$1.50	$2.50	£0.30	£0.90	£1.50
55 ND Gambit appears	$0.50	$1.50	$2.50	£0.30	£0.90	£1.50
56 ND Sunfire guest stars, bi-weekly	$0.50	$1.50	$2.50	£0.30	£0.90	£1.50
57 ND Mariko dies, bi-weekly	$0.50	$1.50	$2.50	£0.30	£0.90	£1.50
58-59 ND Terror Inc., bi-weekly	$0.50	$1.50	$2.50	£0.30	£0.90	£1.50
60 ND Sabretooth appears, bi-weekly	$0.50	$1.50	$2.50	£0.30	£0.90	£1.50
61 ND bi-weekly	$0.40	$1.20	$2.00	£0.30	£0.90	£1.50
62-63 ND Sabretooth appears	$0.40	$1.20	$2.00	£0.30	£0.90	£1.50
64 ND	$0.40	$1.20	$2.00	£0.30	£0.90	£1.50
65 ND Professor X appears	$0.40	$1.20	$2.00	£0.30	£0.90	£1.50
66-68 ND X-Men appear, Texeira art	$0.40	$1.20	$2.00	£0.30	£0.90	£1.50
69 ND X-Men appear, Texeira art (tie-in to X-Men #300)	$0.40	$1.20	$2.00	£0.30	£0.90	£1.50
70-72 ND	$0.40	$1.20	$2.00	£0.30	£0.90	£1.50
73 ND Wolverine and Gambit vs. X-Cutioner	$0.40	$1.20	$2.00	£0.30	£0.90	£1.50
74 ND	$0.40	$1.20	$2.00	£0.30	£0.90	£1.50
75 ND 48pgs, hologram cover, Wolverine loses his Adamantium skeleton	$1.50	$4.50	$7.50	£0.80	£2.40	£4.00
76 ND	$0.50	$1.50	$2.50	£0.30	£0.90	£1.50
77 ND Alpha Flight appears	$0.50	$1.50	$2.50	£0.30	£0.90	£1.50
78 ND	$0.50	$1.50	$2.50	£0.30	£0.90	£1.50
79 ND Wolverine now without his exo-skeleton..	$0.50	$1.50	$2.50	£0.30	£0.90	£1.50
80 ND Nightcrawler appears	$0.50	$1.50	$2.50	£0.30	£0.90	£1.50
81 ND Nightcrawler and Kitty Pryde appear	$0.50	$1.50	$2.50	£0.30	£0.90	£1.50
82-84 ND	$0.50	$1.50	$2.50	£0.30	£0.90	£1.50
85 Deluxe Edition - foil stamped cover; Cable appears	$0.80	$2.40	$4.00	£0.50	£1.50	£2.50

	$Good	$Fine	$N.Mint	£Good	£Fine	£N.Mint

85 Regular Edition; Cable appears
| | $0.50 | $1.50 | $2.50 | £0.35 | £1.05 | £1.75 |

86-87
| | $0.50 | $1.50 | $2.50 | £0.30 | £0.90 | £1.50 |

87 Deluxe Edition – printed on glossy stock paper
| | $0.50 | $1.50 | $2.50 | £0.30 | £0.90 | £1.50 |

88
| | $0.40 | $1.20 | $2.00 | £0.25 | £0.75 | £1.25 |

88 Deluxe Edition – printed on glossy stock paper; X-over with Ghost Rider #57
| | $0.50 | $1.50 | $2.50 | £0.30 | £0.90 | £1.50 |

89
| | $0.40 | $1.20 | $2.00 | £0.25 | £0.75 | £1.25 |

89 Deluxe Edition – printed on glossy stock paper with bound-in Fleer trading card
| | $0.50 | $1.50 | $2.50 | £0.30 | £0.90 | £1.50 |

90 Wolverine vs. Sabretooth
| | $0.40 | $1.20 | $2.00 | £0.25 | £0.75 | £1.25 |

90 Deluxe Edition – printed on glossy paper with bound-in Fleer trading card; see Weapon X #1
| | $0.50 | $1.50 | $2.50 | £0.30 | £0.90 | £1.50 |

91 continued from X-Men: Prime; Larry Hama script, Steve Skroce and Al Green art
| | $0.40 | $1.20 | $2.00 | £0.30 | £0.90 | £1.50 |

92 Sabretooth appears, continued in X-Force #45
| | $0.40 | $1.20 | $2.00 | £0.30 | £0.90 | £1.50 |

93-94 bi-weekly
| | $0.40 | $1.20 | $2.00 | £0.30 | £0.90 | £1.50 |

95-99
| | $0.40 | $1.20 | $2.00 | £0.30 | £0.90 | £1.50 |

Title Value:
| | $89.40 | $268.20 | $447.00 | £47.75 | £143.25 | £238.75 |

Note: all high quality paper. John Byrne art from #17-23. Peter David script in #24.

Wolverine: Weapon X Graphic Novel
Hardcover, 128pgs, reprints Marvel Comics Presents
#72-#84 by Barry Windsor-Smith
| | | | | £2.50 | £7.50 | £12.50 |

Wolverine: Weapon X (Mar 1995)
Trade paperback Softcover version of the above
| | | | | £1.70 | £5.10 | £8.50 |

Wolverine: triumphs & Tragedies (Dec 1995)
Trade paperback 176pgs, reprints Wolverine's father saga
| | | | | £2.20 | £6.60 | £11.00 |

WOLVERINE '95
Marvel Comics Group,OS; nn Sep 1995
nn ND 64pgs, Nightcrawler, Deadpool and Maverick appear; Larry Hama script, J.H. Williams art
| | $0.80 | $2.40 | $4.00 | £0.50 | £1.50 | £2.50 |

Title Value:
| | $0.80 | $2.40 | $4.00 | £0.50 | £1.50 | £2.50 |

WOLVERINE (LIMITED SERIES)
Marvel Comics Group,MS; 1 Sep 1982-4 Dec 1982
(see Kitty Pryde and.., Marvel Comics Presents, Spiderman vs.., X-Men)
1 ND Frank Miller art
| | $5.75 | $17.50 | $35.00 | £2.05 | £6.25 | £12.50 |

2-3 ND Frank Miller art
| | $3.30 | $10.00 | $20.00 | £1.30 | £4.00 | £8.00 |

4 ND scarce in the U.K. Frank Miller art
| | $4.15 | $12.50 | $25.00 | £1.65 | £5.00 | £10.00 |

Title Value:
| | $16.50 | $50.00 | $100.00 | £6.30 | £19.25 | £38.50 |

Wolverine
Trade paperback, reprints mini-series; Chris Claremont foreword, new Frank Miller cover
| | | | | £1.00 | £3.00 | £5.00 |
(2nd print)
| | | | | £0.80 | £2.40 | £4.00 |

WOLVERINE IN GLOBAL JEOPARDY
Marvel Comics Group,OS; 1 Dec 1993
1 ND co-produced with World Wildlife Fund featuring Ka-Zar, Namor and Shanna with Wolverine; card stock cover enhanced with separate colour ink
| | $0.60 | $1.80 | $3.00 | £0.40 | £1.20 | £2.00 |

Title Value:
| | $0.60 | $1.80 | $3.00 | £0.40 | £1.20 | £2.00 |

WOLVERINE SAGA, THE
Marvel Comics Group,MS; 1 Sep 1989-4 Dec 1989
1 ND 48pgs, Liefeld cover
| | $0.80 | $2.40 | $4.00 | £0.50 | £1.50 | £2.50 |

2-3 ND 48pgs
| | $0.80 | $2.40 | $4.00 | £0.50 | £1.50 | £2.50 |

4 ND 48pgs, Kaluta cover
| | $0.80 | $2.40 | $4.00 | £0.50 | £1.50 | £2.50 |

Title Value:
| | $3.20 | $9.60 | $16.00 | £2.00 | £6.00 | £10.00 |

Note: all squarebound Bookshelf Format, uses text and art

WOLVERINE SPECIAL EDITION: THE JUNGLE ADVENTURE
Marvel Comics Group,OS; 1 Jan 1990
1 ND 48pgs, Walt Simonson script, Mike Mignola art
| | $1.00 | $3.00 | $5.00 | £0.70 | £2.10 | £3.50 |

Title Value:
| | $1.00 | $3.00 | $5.00 | £0.70 | £2.10 | £3.50 |

Note: Bookshelf Format

WOLVERINE VS. SPIDERMAN
Marvel Comics Group,OS; 1 Mar 1995
1 ND reprints Marvel Comics Presents #48-50 with Erik Larsen art
| | $0.50 | $1.50 | $2.50 | £0.30 | £0.90 | £1.50 |

Title Value:
| | $0.50 | $1.50 | $2.50 | £0.30 | £0.90 | £1.50 |

WOLVERINE/FURY: SCORPIO RISING
Marvel Comics Group,OS; 1 Dec 1994
1 ND 48pgs, Howard Chaykin and Shawn McManus creative team
| | $1.20 | $3.60 | $6.00 | £0.80 | £2.40 | £4.00 |

Title Value:
| | $1.20 | $3.60 | $6.00 | £0.80 | £2.40 | £4.00 |

WOLVERINE/GAMBIT: VICTIMS
Marvel Comics Group,MS; 1 Sep 1995-4 Dec 1995
1-4 ND Jeph Loeb script, Tim Sale art
| | $0.80 | $2.40 | $4.00 | | £1.50 | £2.50 |

Title Value:
| | $3.20 | $9.60 | $16.00 | £2.00 | £6.00 | £10.00 |

WOLVERINE/PUNISHER: DAMAGING EVIDENCE
Marvel Comics Group,MS; 1 Oct 1993-3 Dec 1993
1-3 ND
| | $0.40 | $1.20 | $2.00 | £0.25 | £0.75 | £1.25 |

Title Value:
| | $1.20 | $3.60 | $6.00 | £0.75 | £2.25 | £3.75 |

WOLVERINE/TYPHOID MARY: TYPHOID'S KISS
Marvel Comics Group,OS; 1 Jul 1994
1 ND 64pgs, reprints Marvel Comics Presents #108-116

| | $1.40 | $4.20 | $7.00 | £0.90 | £2.70 | £4.50 |

Title Value:
| | $1.40 | $4.20 | $7.00 | £0.90 | £2.70 | £4.50 |

WOLVERINE: BLOOD HUNGRY
Marvel Comics Group,OS; 1 Feb 1994
1 ND 64pgs, Peter David script, Sam Kieth art and cover
| | $1.40 | $4.20 | $7.00 | £0.90 | £2.70 | £4.50 |

Title Value:
| | $1.40 | $4.20 | $7.00 | £0.90 | £2.70 | £4.50 |

WOLVERINE: BLOODLUST
Marvel Comics Group,OS; nn Jan 1991
nn ND 48pgs, Alan Davis and Paul Neary script/art
| | $0.90 | $2.70 | $4.50 | £0.60 | £1.80 | £3.00 |

Title Value:
| | $0.90 | $2.70 | $4.50 | £0.60 | £1.80 | £3.00 |

WOLVERINE: BLOODY CHOICES
Marvel Comics Group,OS; 1 Jan 1994
1 ND 64pgs, reprints Marvel Graphic Novel; Nick Fury appears
| | $1.50 | $4.50 | $7.50 | £1.00 | £3.00 | £5.00 |

Title Value:
| | $1.50 | $4.50 | $7.50 | £1.00 | £3.00 | £5.00 |

WOLVERINE: EVILUTION
Marvel Comics Group,OS; 1 Nov 1994
1 ND 48pgs, Anne Nocenti script, Mark Texeira art
| | $1.20 | $3.60 | $6.00 | £0.80 | £2.40 | £4.00 |

Title Value:
| | $1.20 | $3.60 | $6.00 | £0.80 | £2.40 | £4.00 |

WOLVERINE: INNER FURY
Marvel Comics Group,OS; 1 Feb 1993
1 ND 48pgs, Bill Sienkiewicz art
| | $1.20 | $3.60 | $6.00 | £0.80 | £2.40 | £4.00 |

Title Value:
| | $1.20 | $3.60 | $6.00 | £0.80 | £2.40 | £4.00 |

WOLVERINE: KILLING
Marvel Comics Group,OS; 1 Nov 1993
1 ND 48pgs, John Reiber and Kent Williams
| | $1.20 | $3.60 | $6.00 | £0.80 | £2.40 | £4.00 |

Title Value:
| | $1.20 | $3.60 | $6.00 | £0.80 | £2.40 | £4.00 |

WOLVERINE: MARVEL COLLECTOR'S EDITION
Marvel Comics Group/Charleston Chew,OS; 1 Sep 1992
1 ND scarce in the U.K. features solo stories of Wolverine and Ghost Rider backed on the flip-side with Spiderman and Silver Surfer, Sam Kieth cover and art featured;
| | $2.00 | $6.00 | $10.00 | £1.20 | £3.60 | £6.00 |

Title Value:
| | $2.00 | $6.00 | $10.00 | £1.20 | £3.60 | £6.00 |

Note: this comic only distributed in U.S., made available by sending one wrapper from Charleston Chew Bar back to the confectionary company.

WOLVERINE: RAHNE FALL
Marvel Comics Group,OS; 1 Aug 1995
1 ND 64pgs, Wolverine and Wolfsbane vs. Sabretooth
| | $1.40 | $4.20 | $7.00 | £0.90 | £2.70 | £4.50 |

Title Value:
| | $1.40 | $4.20 | $7.00 | £0.90 | £2.70 | £4.50 |

WOLVERINE: RAHNE OF TERRA
Marvel Comics Group,OS; 1 Nov 1991
1 ND Peter David script, Andy Kubert art
| | $1.20 | $3.60 | $6.00 | £0.80 | £2.40 | £4.00 |

1 2nd printing, ND Sep 1992
| | $1.00 | $3.00 | $5.00 | £0.70 | £2.10 | £3.50 |

Title Value:
| | $2.20 | $6.60 | $11.00 | £1.50 | £4.50 | £7.50 |

WOLVERINE: SAVE THE TIGER
Marvel Comics Group,OS; 1 Jul 1992
1 ND 80pgs, reprints Marvel Comics Presents #1-10, new Sam Kieth cover
| | $0.60 | $1.80 | $3.00 | £0.40 | £1.20 | £2.00 |

Title Value:
| | $0.60 | $1.80 | $3.00 | £0.40 | £1.20 | £2.00 |

WONDER MAN
Marvel Comics Group,OS; 1 Mar 1986
1 ND DS
| | $0.40 | $1.20 | $2.00 | £0.25 | £0.75 | £1.25 |

Title Value:
| | $0.40 | $1.20 | $2.00 | £0.25 | £0.75 | £1.25 |

WONDER MAN (2ND SERIES)
Marvel Comics Group; 1 Sep 1991-30 1994
1 ND Gerard Jones' 1st Marvel work; bound-in gate-fold poster at centre-fold
| | $0.30 | $0.90 | $1.50 | £0.20 | £0.60 | £1.00 |

2 ND Avengers West Coast appear
| | $0.25 | $0.75 | $1.25 | £0.15 | £0.45 | £0.75 |

3-4 ND
| | $0.25 | $0.75 | $1.25 | £0.15 | £0.45 | £0.75 |

5 ND Beast appears
| | $0.25 | $0.75 | $1.25 | £0.15 | £0.45 | £0.75 |

6 ND Beast appears, $1.25 cover begins
| | $0.25 | $0.75 | $1.25 | £0.15 | £0.45 | £0.75 |

7 ND Galactic Storm part 4, Hulk and Rick Jones appear
| | $0.25 | $0.75 | $1.25 | £0.15 | £0.45 | £0.75 |

8 ND Galactic Storm part 11, Vision appears
| | $0.25 | $0.75 | $1.25 | £0.15 | £0.45 | £0.75 |

9 ND Galactic Storm part 18
| | $0.25 | $0.75 | $1.25 | £0.15 | £0.45 | £0.75 |

10 ND Galactic Storm: Aftermath, Avengers appear
| | $0.25 | $0.75 | $1.25 | £0.15 | £0.45 | £0.75 |

11-12 ND
| | $0.25 | $0.75 | $1.25 | £0.15 | £0.45 | £0.75 |

13 ND Infinity War X-over, Hercules and Thor appear
| | $0.25 | $0.75 | $1.25 | £0.15 | £0.45 | £0.75 |

14 ND Infinity War X-over, Warlock and Thanos appear
| | $0.25 | $0.75 | $1.25 | £0.15 | £0.45 | £0.75 |

15 ND Infinity War X-over, many Marvel characters appear
| | $0.25 | $0.75 | $1.25 | £0.15 | £0.45 | £0.75 |

16-17 ND West Coast Avengers appear
| | $0.25 | $0.75 | $1.25 | £0.15 | £0.45 | £0.75 |

18 ND Wonder Man vs. West Coast Avengers
| | $0.25 | $0.75 | $1.25 | £0.15 | £0.45 | £0.75 |

19-21 ND
| | $0.25 | $0.75 | $1.25 | £0.15 | £0.45 | £0.75 |

VERY GENERAL PERCENTAGE CONVERSION CHART WHICH MAY BE USED TO CALCULATE LOW AND INBETWEEN GRADES:

	$Good	$Fine	$N.Mint	£Good	£Fine	£N.Mint
22 new direction for title; covers of #22-25 fit together as one image						
	$0.25	$0.75	$1.25	£0.15	£0.45	£0.75
23-24 ND	$0.25	$0.75	$1.25	£0.15	£0.45	£0.75
25 ND 48pgs, new costume; Scarlet Witch and Beast appear; embossed cover						
	$0.30	$0.90	$1.50	£0.20	£0.60	£1.00
26-27 ND Hulk appears						
	$0.25	$0.75	$1.25	£0.15	£0.45	£0.75
28 ND Thor and Asgard appear						
	$0.25	$0.75	$1.25	£0.15	£0.45	£0.75
29 ND Spiderman guest-stars						
	$0.25	$0.75	$1.25	£0.15	£0.45	£0.75
30 ND Iron Man appears						
	$0.25	$0.75	$1.25	£0.15	£0.45	£0.75
Title Value:	$7.60	$22.80	$38.00	£4.60	£13.80	£23.00

WONDER MAN ANNUAL

Marvel Comics Group; 1 Jul 1992-2 1993

	$Good	$Fine	$N.Mint	£Good	£Fine	£N.Mint
1 ND The System Bytes part 3, continued in Guardians of the Galaxy Annual #2						
	$0.30	$0.90	$1.50	£0.20	£0.60	£1.00
2 ND 64pgs, pre-bagged with trading card introducing Hit-Maker						
	$0.30	$0.90	$1.50	£0.20	£0.60	£1.00
Title Value:	$0.60	$1.80	$3.00	£0.40	£1.20	£2.00

WONDER WOMAN

National Periodical Publications/DC Comics; 1 Summer 1942-329 Feb 1986

(see Adventure, All New Collector's Edition, Best of DC #20, Brave and the Bold, DC Comics Presents, Famous First Edition, Justice League of America, Legend of Wonder Woman, Secret Origins, Secret Origins of Heroes, Super-Team Family, World's Finest Comics)

	$Good	$Fine	$N.Mint	£Good	£Fine	£N.Mint
1 origin retold from All Star Comics #8						
	$1500.00	$4500.00	$15000.00	£1000.00	£3000.00	£10000.00
2 1st appearance Mars, God of War						
	$250.00	$750.00	$2000.00	£165.00	£500.00	£1350.00
3	$150.00	$450.00	$1200.00	£100.00	£300.00	£800.00
4-5	$105.00	$325.00	$875.00	£75.00	£225.00	£600.00
6 1st appearance The Cheetah, Cheetah cover						
	$92.50	$280.00	$750.00	£62.50	£185.00	£500.00
7-10	$87.50	$265.00	$710.00	£57.50	£175.00	£475.00
11-20	$75.00	$225.00	$525.00	£50.00	£150.00	£350.00
21-30	$67.50	$205.00	$485.00	£46.00	£135.00	£320.00
31-40	$50.00	$150.00	$350.00	£32.00	£95.00	£225.00
41-44	$36.00	$105.00	$250.00	£26.00	£77.50	£185.00
45 origin retold in more detail						
	$67.50	$205.00	$485.00	£46.00	£135.00	£325.00
46-47	$36.00	$105.00	$250.00	£26.00	£77.50	£185.00
48 Wonder Woman vs. Wonder Woman (robot)						
	$36.00	$105.00	$250.00	£26.00	£77.50	£185.00
49-50	$36.00	$105.00	$250.00	£26.00	£77.50	£185.00
51-58	$25.00	$75.00	$175.00	£17.50	£52.50	£125.00
59 last Golden Age logo						
	$25.00	$75.00	$175.00	£17.50	£52.50	£125.00
60	$25.00	$75.00	$175.00	£17.50	£52.50	£125.00
61-63	$19.00	$57.50	$135.00	£12.50	£39.00	£90.00
64 dinosaur cover						
	$19.00	$57.50	$135.00	£12.50	£39.00	£90.00
65-69	$19.00	$57.50	$135.00	£12.50	£39.00	£90.00
70 1st appearance Angle Man						
	$19.00	$57.50	$135.00	£12.50	£39.00	£90.00
71-79	$18.50	$55.00	$130.00	£12.00	£36.00	£85.00
80 1st appearance Invisible Plane						
	$19.00	$57.50	$135.00	£12.50	£39.00	£90.00
81-90	$17.50	$52.50	$125.00	£12.00	£36.00	£85.00
91-93	$14.00	$43.00	$100.00	£10.00	£30.00	£70.00
94 Robin Hood appears						

	$Good	$Fine	$N.Mint	£Good	£Fine	£N.Mint
	$14.00	$43.00	$100.00	£10.00	£30.00	£70.00
95 atom bomb cover						
	$14.00	$43.00	$100.00	£10.00	£30.00	£70.00
96	$14.00	$43.00	$100.00	£10.00	£30.00	£70.00
97 dinosaur cover						
	$14.00	$43.00	$100.00	£10.00	£30.00	£70.00
98 new details regarding Wonder Woman's origin revealed; classic art team of Ross Andru and Mike Esposito begins						
	$15.50	$47.00	$110.00	£10.50	£32.00	£75.00
99	$14.00	$43.00	$100.00	£10.00	£30.00	£70.00
100	$13.50	$41.00	$110.00	£9.25	£28.00	£75.00
101-104	$13.00	$40.00	$80.00	£9.00	£28.00	£55.00
105 very scarce in the U.K., scarce in the U.S. origin retold with new facts						
	$46.00	$135.00	$325.00	£30.00	£90.00	£210.00
106	$13.00	$40.00	$80.00	£9.00	£28.00	£55.00
107 1st Adventures of Wonder Girl, 1st Merboy, origin Wonder Woman's costume						
	$13.00	$40.00	$80.00	£9.00	£28.00	£55.00
108-109	$13.00	$40.00	$80.00	£9.00	£28.00	£55.00
		1st official distribution in the U.K.				
110-120	$10.00	$30.00	$60.00	£6.50	£20.00	£40.00
121	$7.50	$22.50	$45.00	£5.00	£15.00	£30.00
122 1st appearance Wonder Tot						
	$7.75	$23.50	$47.50	£5.25	£16.00	£32.50
123	$7.50	$22.50	$45.00	£5.00	£15.00	£30.00
124 1st appearance Wonder Woman family						
	$7.75	$23.50	$47.50	£5.25	£16.00	£32.50
125	$7.50	$22.50	$45.00	£5.00	£15.00	£30.00
126 last 10 cents issue						
	$7.50	$22.50	$45.00	£5.00	£15.00	£30.00
127	$5.00	$15.00	$30.00	£3.30	£10.00	£20.00
128 origin Robot Plane						
	$5.00	$15.00	$30.00	£3.30	£10.00	£20.00
129-130	$5.00	$15.00	$30.00	£3.30	£10.00	£20.00
131-140	$4.15	$12.50	$25.00	£2.50	£7.50	£15.00
141-150	$3.30	$10.00	$20.00	£2.05	£6.25	£12.50
151-157	$2.90	$8.75	$17.50	£1.65	£5.00	£10.00
158 last Silver Age issue, indicia dated November 1965						
	$2.90	$8.75	$17.50	£1.65	£5.00	£10.00
159 origin retold	$3.30	$10.00	$20.00	£2.05	£6.25	£12.50
160-170	$2.50	$7.50	$15.00	£1.25	£3.75	£7.50
171-174	$1.65	$5.00	$10.00	£0.80	£2.50	£5.00
175 scarce in the U.K.						
	$1.65	$5.00	$10.00	£1.00	£3.00	£6.00
176-178	$1.65	$5.00	$10.00	£0.80	£2.50	£5.00
179 Wonder Woman loses powers, 1st appearance I-Ching						
	$1.65	$5.00	$10.00	£0.80	£2.50	£5.00
180 death Steve Trevor						
	$1.65	$5.00	$10.00	£0.80	£2.50	£5.00
181-190	$1.25	$3.75	$7.50	£0.55	£1.75	£3.50
191-195	$0.80	$2.50	$5.00	£0.50	£1.50	£3.00
196 52pgs, origin and 1st appearance retold from All-Star Comics #8; extraordinary bondage cover featuring hot pants and sado-masochism!						
	$0.80	$2.50	$5.00	£0.55	£1.75	£3.50
197-198 52pgs	$0.80	$2.50	$5.00	£0.55	£1.75	£3.50
199-200 52pgs, Jeff Jones covers						
	$0.80	$2.50	$5.00	£0.55	£1.75	£3.50
201 scarce in the U.K. Catwoman appears						
	$0.50	$1.50	$2.50	£0.40	£1.20	£2.00
202 1st appearance Fafhrd & the Grey Mouser						
	$0.50	$1.50	$2.50	£0.60	£1.80	£3.00
203	$0.50	$1.50	$2.50	£0.30	£0.90	£1.50

Wolverine vs. Spiderman

Wonder Woman #6

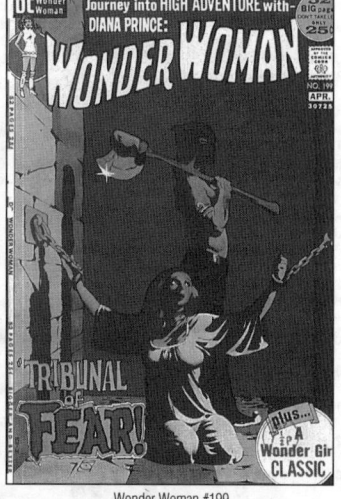

Wonder Woman #199

MINT = 100% / NEAR MINT (inc. +/-) = 90-99% / VERY FINE (inc. +/-) = 75-89% / FINE (inc. +/-) = 55-74%
VERY GOOD (inc. +/-) = 35-54% / GOOD (inc. +/-) = 15-34% / FAIR = 5-14% / POOR = 1-4%

643

Issue / Note	$Good	$Fine	$N.Mint	£Good	£Fine	£N.Mint
204 scarce in the U.K. Wonder Woman regains powers/costume, I-Ching reprints	$0.50	$1.50	$2.50	£0.40	£1.20	£2.00
205-210	$0.50	$1.50	$2.50	£0.30	£0.90	£1.50
211 100pgs	$0.80	$2.40	$4.00	£0.50	£1.50	£2.50
212-213 Justice League of America guest-star	$0.40	$1.20	$2.00	£0.30	£0.90	£1.50
214 100pgs, Justice League of America guest-star	$0.60	$1.80	$3.00	£0.60	£1.80	£3.00
215-216 Justice League of America guest-star	$0.40	$1.20	$2.00	£0.30	£0.90	£1.50
217 68pgs, Justice League of America guest-star	$0.50	$1.50	$2.50	£0.40	£1.20	£2.00
218-219 Justice League of America guest-star	$0.40	$1.20	$2.00	£0.30	£0.90	£1.50
220 ND Neal Adams inks, Justice League of America guest-star	$0.50	$1.50	$2.50	£0.50	£1.50	£2.50
221-222 Justice League of America guest-star	$0.40	$1.20	$2.00	£0.30	£0.90	£1.50
223	$0.40	$1.20	$2.00	£0.30	£0.90	£1.50
224 ND	$0.40	$1.20	$2.00	£0.35	£1.05	£1.75
225-227	$0.40	$1.20	$2.00	£0.30	£0.90	£1.50
228 scarce in the U.K. both Wonder Women team-up, new WWII begins (ends #243)	$0.40	$1.20	$2.00	£0.40	£1.20	£2.00
229-230	$0.40	$1.20	$2.00	£0.30	£0.90	£1.50
231 scarce in the U.K.	$0.40	$1.20	$2.00	£0.35	£1.05	£1.75
232-236	$0.40	$1.20	$2.00	£0.30	£0.90	£1.50
237 origin retold	$0.40	$1.20	$2.00	£0.30	£0.90	£1.50
238-240	$0.40	$1.20	$2.00	£0.30	£0.90	£1.50
241 Spectre appears	$0.40	$1.20	$2.00	£0.30	£0.90	£1.50
242-246	$0.40	$1.20	$2.00	£0.30	£0.90	£1.50
247 scarce in the U.K. 44pgs, Tales of the Amazons back-up	$0.40	$1.20	$2.00	£0.40	£1.20	£2.00
248-249 ND 44pgs	$0.50	$1.50	$2.50	£0.40	£1.20	£2.00
250	$0.40	$1.20	$2.00	£0.30	£0.90	£1.50
251-264	$0.30	$0.90	$1.50	£0.25	£0.75	£1.25
265-266 Wonder Girl back-ups	$0.30	$0.90	$1.50	£0.25	£0.75	£1.25
267 Animal Man guest-stars, 1st Modern Age appearance	$2.00	$6.00	$10.00	£0.60	£1.80	£3.00
268 Animal Man guest-stars, 2nd Modern Age appearance	$1.80	$5.25	$9.00	£0.50	£1.50	£2.50
269 Wood part inks	$0.30	$0.90	$1.50	£0.25	£0.75	£1.25
270	$0.30	$0.90	$1.50	£0.25	£0.75	£1.25
271 1st Huntress back-up	$0.30	$0.90	$1.50	£0.25	£0.75	£1.25
272-279	$0.30	$0.90	$1.50	£0.25	£0.75	£1.25
280 Demon X-over	$0.30	$0.90	$1.50	£0.25	£0.75	£1.25
281-283 Joker appears	$0.50	$1.50	$2.50	£0.30	£0.90	£1.50
284-286	$0.30	$0.90	$1.50	£0.25	£0.75	£1.25
287 New Teen Titans X-over	$0.30	$0.90	$1.50	£0.25	£0.75	£1.25
288-290	$0.30	$0.90	$1.50	£0.25	£0.75	£1.25
291-293 3-part story; Huntress, Wonder Girl, Raven, Power Girl, Starfire, Black Canary, Supergirl, Phantom Lady, Madame Xanadu, Batgirl, Zatanna, Lois Lane guest-star	$0.30	$0.90	$1.50	£0.25	£0.75	£1.25
294-296	$0.30	$0.90	$1.50	£0.25	£0.75	£1.25
297 Kaluta cover	$0.30	$0.90	$1.50	£0.25	£0.75	£1.25
298-299	$0.30	$0.90	$1.50	£0.25	£0.75	£1.25
300 LD in the U.K. 76pgs, Giffen art, anniversary issue, Justice League of America/New Teen Titans appear	$0.50	$1.50	$2.50	£0.35	£1.05	£1.75
301-326	$0.30	$0.90	$1.50	£0.20	£0.60	£1.00
327-328 LD in the U.K. Crisis X-over	$0.30	$0.90	$1.50	£0.20	£0.60	£1.00
329 DS Crisis X-over	$0.50	$1.50	$2.50	£0.30	£0.90	£1.50
Title Value:	**$6351.40**	**$19106.05**	**$49819.50**	**£4254.45**	**£12763.90**	**£33358.75**

Note: Golden Age issues, that is 1940s/50s issues, were not available on the news-stand in the U.K. but some may have come over through personnel movement during the Second World War or as cheap ballast on ships, perhaps most likely in the late 1940s.

ARTISTS
Wood inks in 195,269.

FEATURES
Huntress in 271-287,289,290,294. Tales of the Amazons in 247-249. Wonder Woman in all "new look" Wonder Woman (without powers) in 178-203. Wonder Girl solo in 265,266.
Note: #191,196,199,200,211,214,217 are partially reprint. #197 and #198 are entirely reprint. #196 reprints origin from All-Star Comics 8 with alterations and text additions.

WONDER WOMAN (2ND SERIES)
DC Comics; 0 Oct 1994; 1 Feb 1987-present

Issue / Note	$Good	$Fine	$N.Mint	£Good	£Fine	£N.Mint
0 (Oct 1994), Zero Hour X-over, origin retold	$1.00	$3.00	$5.00	£0.60	£1.80	£3.00
1 LD in the u.k. new origin by George Perez	$0.60	$1.80	$3.00	£0.40	£1.20	£2.00
2 George Perez art	$0.50	$1.50	$2.50	£0.30	£0.90	£1.50
3 George Perez art	$0.40	$1.20	$2.00	£0.25	£0.75	£1.25
4-7 George Perez art	$0.30	$0.90	$1.50	£0.20	£0.60	£1.00
8 George Perez art, Superman X-over	$0.30	$0.90	$1.50	£0.20	£0.60	£1.00
9 George Perez art	$0.30	$0.90	$1.50	£0.20	£0.60	£1.00
10 George Perez art; with triple foldout cover, Trial of the Gods begins	$0.30	$0.90	$1.50	£0.20	£0.60	£1.00
11 George Perez art, Trial of the Gods	$0.30	$0.90	$1.50	£0.20	£0.60	£1.00
12-13 George Perez art, Millennium X-over	$0.30	$0.90	$1.50	£0.20	£0.60	£1.00
14-24 George Perez art	$0.30	$0.90	$1.50	£0.20	£0.60	£1.00
25 George Perez cover and script, Invasion X-over	$0.30	$0.90	$1.50	£0.20	£0.60	£1.00
26 George Perez cover, Invasion X-over, 16pg Bonus Book	$0.30	$0.90	$1.50	£0.20	£0.60	£1.00
27-48 George Perez covers	$0.30	$0.90	$1.50	£0.20	£0.60	£1.00
49 George Perez cover; guest-stars Superman, Guy Gardner, Captain Atom, Black Canary, Troia, Martian Manhunter in a retrospective on Wonder Woman	$0.30	$0.90	$1.50	£0.20	£0.60	£1.00
50 LD in the U.K. DS, George Perez cover; Superman, New Titans, Justice League appear	$0.40	$1.20	$2.00	£0.25	£0.75	£1.25
51 George Perez cover, Arkham Asylum featured	$0.30	$0.90	$1.50	£0.20	£0.60	£1.00
52-57 George Perez covers	$0.30	$0.90	$1.50	£0.20	£0.60	£1.00
58-61 War of the Gods tie-in	$0.30	$0.90	$1.50	£0.20	£0.60	£1.00
62 last George Perez script and cover	$0.30	$0.90	$1.50	£0.20	£0.60	£1.00
63 Brian Bolland covers begin; continued from Wonder Woman special	$0.30	$0.90	$1.50	£0.20	£0.60	£1.00
64-65	$0.30	$0.90	$1.50	£0.20	£0.60	£1.00
66-70 Exodus Into Space story	$0.30	$0.90	$1.50	£0.20	£0.60	£1.00
71 Wonder Woman returns to Earth after a year's absence	$0.30	$0.90	$1.50	£0.20	£0.60	£1.00
72 Wonder Woman's origin re-told	$0.30	$0.90	$1.50	£0.20	£0.60	£1.00
73-75	$0.30	$0.90	$1.50	£0.20	£0.60	£1.00
76 Dr. Fate guest-stars	$0.30	$0.90	$1.50	£0.20	£0.60	£1.00
77-84	$0.30	$0.90	$1.50	£0.20	£0.60	£1.00
85 1st Mike Deodato Wonder Woman	$2.00	$6.00	$10.00	£1.00	£3.00	£5.00
86-87	$0.50	$1.50	$2.50	£0.30	£0.90	£1.50
88 1st Christopher Priest script, Superman appears	$1.00	$3.00	$5.00	£0.70	£2.10	£3.50
89	$0.80	$2.40	$4.00	£0.50	£1.50	£2.50
90 1st appearance Artemis	$1.50	$4.50	$7.50	£0.80	£2.40	£4.00
91	$0.80	$2.40	$4.00	£0.50	£1.50	£2.50
92 Artemis becomes the new Wonder Woman	$0.80	$2.40	$4.00	£0.50	£1.50	£2.50
93 tie-in with Justice League America #95	$0.80	$2.40	$4.00	£0.50	£1.50	£2.50
94-95	$0.60	$1.80	$3.00	£0.40	£1.20	£2.00
96 The Joker appears	$0.60	$1.80	$3.00	£0.40	£1.20	£2.00
97-99	$0.60	$1.80	$3.00	£0.40	£1.20	£2.00
100 48pgs, Brian Bolland cover; Standard Edition, death of Artemis	$0.70	$2.10	$3.50	£0.50	£1.50	£2.50
100 48pgs, Brian Bolland cover; Collector's Edition with holographic foil-stamped cover	$0.90	$2.70	$4.50	£0.60	£1.80	£3.00
101 John Byrne script and art begins and new direction for title	$0.40	$1.20	$2.00	£0.25	£0.75	£1.25
102-103 Darkseid appears	$0.40	$1.20	$2.00	£0.25	£0.75	£1.25
104-105	$0.40	$1.20	$2.00	£0.25	£0.75	£1.25
106 Demon and Phantom Stranger guest-stars	$0.40	$1.20	$2.00	£0.25	£0.75	£1.25
107 Demon, Arion and Phantom Stranger guest-stars	$0.40	$1.20	$2.00	£0.25	£0.75	£1.25
Title Value:	**$43.60**	**$130.80**	**$218.00**	**£28.15**	**£84.45**	**£140.75**
Multi-Pack (1990)						
Three issues from #10-12 or #22-24 pre-bagged with illustrated header card; ND rare in the U.K.				£0.30	£0.90	£1.50
Wonder Woman: The Contest (1995)						
Trade paperback reprints issues #90, #0 and #91-93, new Mike Deodato cover				£1.30	£3.90	£6.50

WONDER WOMAN ANNUAL
DC Comics; 1 1988-2 1989; 3-1992; 4 1995-present

Issue / Note	$Good	$Fine	$N.Mint	£Good	£Fine	£N.Mint
1 48pgs, George Perez, Art Adams, Brian Bolland, John Bolton, Garcia Lopez, Ross Andru, Curt Swan art						
2 48pgs, part George Perez story and cover art Women writers/artists inc. Trina Robbins, Collen Doran and Lee Mars	$0.50	$1.50	$2.50	£0.30	£0.90	£1.50
3 64pgs, Eclipso: The Darkness Within tie-in	$0.50	$1.50	$2.50	£0.30	£0.90	£1.50

	$Good	$Fine	$N.Mint	£Good	£Fine	£N.Mint
4 64pgs, Year One, script by Kate Worley, art by Brent Anderson	$0.80	$2.40	$4.00	£0.50	£1.50	£2.50
Title Value:	$2.30	$6.90	$11.50	£1.40	£4.20	£7.00

WONDER WOMAN BOOK AND RECORD SET
Power Records; PR-35 1974

	$Good	$Fine	$N.Mint	£Good	£Fine	£N.Mint
PR-35 scarce, 20pg booklet with 45 rpm record				£1.00	£3.00	£5.00

Note: Item would be value at 50% less without record

WONDER WOMAN PIZZA HUT GIVEAWAYS
DC Comics/Pizza Hut; 60, 62 Dec 1977
(see Batman, Superman)

	$Good	$Fine	$N.Mint	£Good	£Fine	£N.Mint
60 ND original issue #60 reprinted in its entirety apart from different ads and Pizza Hut banner at top; scarce in the U.K.	$1.50	$4.50	$7.50	£1.00	£3.00	£5.00
62 ND original issue #62 reprinted in its entirety apart from different ads and Pizza Hut banner at top; scarce in the U.K.	$1.50	$4.50	$7.50	£1.00	£3.00	£5.00
Title Value:	$3.00	$9.00	$15.00	£2.00	£6.00	£10.00

WONDER WOMAN SPECIAL
DC Comics, OS; 1 May 1992

	$Good	$Fine	$N.Mint	£Good	£Fine	£N.Mint
1 Deathstroke the Terminator appears, continued in Wonder Woman #63	$0.50	$1.50	$2.50	£0.30	£0.90	£1.50
Title Value:	$0.50	$1.50	$2.50	£0.30	£0.90	£1.50

WONDER WOMAN SPECTACULAR
DC Comics; nn 1978
(DC Special Series #9)

	$Good	$Fine	$N.Mint	£Good	£Fine	£N.Mint
nn ND 80pgs	$0.90	$2.70	$4.50	£0.60	£1.80	£3.00
Title Value:	$0.90	$2.70	$4.50	£0.60	£1.80	£3.00

WONDER WOMAN, THE LEGEND OF
DC Comics, MS; 1 May 1986-4 Aug 1986

	$Good	$Fine	$N.Mint	£Good	£Fine	£N.Mint
1-4 Trina Robbins art, Kurt Busiek script	$0.25	$0.75	$1.25	£0.15	£0.45	£0.75
Title Value:	$1.00	$3.00	$5.00	£0.60	£1.80	£3.00

WONDERWORLDS
Innovation, OS; 1 Feb 1992

	$Good	$Fine	$N.Mint	£Good	£Fine	£N.Mint
1 ND 100pgs, reprints	$0.60	$1.80	$3.00	£0.40	£1.20	£2.00
Title Value:	$0.60	$1.80	$3.00	£0.40	£1.20	£2.00

WORDSMITH
Renegade; 1 Aug 1985-12 Jan 1988

	$Good	$Fine	$N.Mint	£Good	£Fine	£N.Mint
1-12 ND	$0.30	$0.90	$1.50	£0.20	£0.60	£1.00
Title Value:	$3.60	$10.80	$18.00	£2.40	£7.20	£12.00
Collection 1, reprints issues #1-6				£1.65	£4.95	£8.25
Collection 2, reprints issues #7-12				£1.65	£4.95	£8.25

WORLD CHAMPION WRESTLING
Marvel Comics Group; 1 Apr 1992-12 Mar 1993

	$Good	$Fine	$N.Mint	£Good	£Fine	£N.Mint
1 based on WCW television wrestling stars, photo cover	$0.25	$0.75	$1.25	£0.15	£0.45	£0.75
2-12	$0.25	$0.75	$1.25	£0.15	£0.45	£0.75
Title Value:	$3.00	$9.00	$15.00	£1.80	£5.40	£9.00

WORLD OF GINGER FOX
Comico; Graphic Novel; nn Nov 1986
(see Ginger Fox)

	$Good	$Fine	$N.Mint	£Good	£Fine	£N.Mint
nn - Mike Baron script, Mich O'Connell art				£1.10	£3.30	£5.50
Limited Edition Hardback				£3.70	£11.10	£18.50

WORLD OF KRYPTON
DC Comics, MS; 1 Jul 1979-3 Sep 1979

	$Good	$Fine	$N.Mint	£Good	£Fine	£N.Mint
1 ND Howard Chaykin pencils	$0.40	$1.20	$2.00	£0.25	£0.75	£1.25
2-3 ND	$0.40	$1.20	$2.00	£0.25	£0.75	£1.25
Title Value:	$1.20	$3.60	$6.00	£0.75	£2.25	£3.75

Note: 1st DC mini-series.

WORLD OF KRYPTON
DC Comics, MS; 1 Dec 1987-4 Mar 1988

	$Good	$Fine	$N.Mint	£Good	£Fine	£N.Mint
1-2 John Byrne script and cover art, Mike Mignola art	$0.25	$0.75	$1.25	£0.15	£0.45	£0.75
3 ND John Byrne script and cover art, Mike Mignola art	$0.25	$0.75	$1.25	£0.20	£0.60	£1.00
4 John Byrne script and cover art, Mike Mignola art	$0.25	$0.75	$1.25	£0.15	£0.45	£0.75
Title Value:	$1.00	$3.00	$5.00	£0.65	£1.95	£3.25

WORLD OF METROPOLIS
DC Comics, MS; 1 Jun 1988-4 Sep 1988

	$Good	$Fine	$N.Mint	£Good	£Fine	£N.Mint
1-4 John Byrne cover art and script	$0.25	$0.75	$1.25	£0.15	£0.45	£0.75
Title Value:	$1.00	$3.00	$5.00	£0.60	£1.80	£3.00

Note: see World of Krypton (2nd), World of Smallville.

WORLD OF SMALLVILLE
DC Comics, MS; 1 Apr 1988-4 Jul 1988

	$Good	$Fine	$N.Mint	£Good	£Fine	£N.Mint
1-4 John Byrne cover art and script	$0.25	$0.75	$1.25	£0.15	£0.45	£0.75
Title Value:	$1.00	$3.00	$5.00	£0.60	£1.80	£3.00

Note: see World of Krypton (2nd Series), World of Metropolis.

WORLD OF WOOD
Eclipse, MS; 1 May 1986-4 Jun 1986; 5,6 1987

	$Good	$Fine	$N.Mint	£Good	£Fine	£N.Mint
1 ND wrongly printed indicia, Dave Stevens cover	$0.40	$1.20	$2.00	£0.25	£0.75	£1.25
2 ND scarce in the U.K. Wood/Stevens cover	$0.40	$1.20	$2.00	£0.25	£0.75	£1.25
3 ND Wood, Blevins, Williamson cover	$0.40	$1.20	$2.00	£0.25	£0.75	£1.25
4-6 ND	$0.40	$1.20	$2.00	£0.25	£0.75	£1.25
Title Value:	$2.40	$7.20	$12.00	£1.50	£4.50	£7.50

WORLD OF YOUNG MASTER
New Comics Group; 1 Mar 1989

	$Good	$Fine	$N.Mint	£Good	£Fine	£N.Mint
1 ND intro The Demonblade	$0.40	$1.20	$2.00	£0.25	£0.75	£1.25
Title Value:	$0.40	$1.20	$2.00	£0.25	£0.75	£1.25

WORLD WITHOUT END
DC Comics, MS; 1 Dec 1990-6 Jun 1991

	$Good	$Fine	$N.Mint	£Good	£Fine	£N.Mint
1-6 ND 48pgs, Delano and Higgins script/art	$0.50	$1.50	$2.50	£0.30	£0.90	£1.50
Title Value:	$3.00	$9.00	$15.00	£1.80	£5.40	£9.00

Note: production delays between issue #4 and #5

WORLD WRESTLING FEDERATION BATTLEMANIA
Valiant, Magazine; 1 Sep 1991-9 Apr 1992

	$Good	$Fine	$N.Mint	£Good	£Fine	£N.Mint
1-9 ND	$0.40	$1.20	$2.00	£0.25	£0.75	£1.25
Title Value:	$3.60	$10.80	$18.00	£2.25	£6.75	£11.25

WORLD'S BEST COMICS
(see World's Finest Comics)

WORLD'S FINEST COMICS
National Periodical Publications/DC Comics; 1 Spring 1941-323 Jan 1986

	$Good	$Fine	$N.Mint	£Good	£Fine	£N.Mint
1 titled "World's Best Comics", Superman and Batman begin in separate stories though they share the covers; the early covers are highly patriotic	$1200.00	$3600.00	$12000.00	£850.00	£2550.00	£8500.00
2	$465.00	$1400.00	$3750.00	£310.00	£930.00	£2500.00
3 origin and 1st appearance The Scarecrow	$300.00	$900.00	$2400.00	£200.00	£600.00	£1600.00
4	$225.00	$670.00	$1800.00	£150.00	£450.00	£1200.00
5	$210.00	$630.00	$1700.00	£140.00	£430.00	£1150.00
6-7 Joe Simon & Jack Kirby art	$150.00	$450.00	$1200.00	£100.00	£300.00	£800.00
8	$130.00	$390.00	$1050.00	£87.50	£260.00	£700.00
9 Hitler/Mussolini cover	$135.00	$410.00	$1100.00	£92.50	£280.00	£750.00
10	$97.50	$290.00	$975.00	£65.00	£195.00	£650.00
11-16	$125.00	$385.00	$900.00	£85.00	£255.00	£600.00
17 last card covers	$125.00	$385.00	$900.00	£85.00	£255.00	£600.00
[All the above are scarce in high grade - Very Fine+ or better]						
18-20	$105.00	$320.00	$750.00	£70.00	£210.00	£500.00
21-29	$85.00	$255.00	$600.00	£55.00	£170.00	£400.00
30 origin giant penny trophy in Batcave	$85.00	$255.00	$600.00	£55.00	£170.00	£400.00
31-40	$70.00	$210.00	$500.00	£49.00	£145.00	£340.00
41-47	$52.50	$160.00	$375.00	£36.00	£105.00	£250.00
48 last square-bound	$52.50	$160.00	$375.00	£36.00	£105.00	£250.00
49-50	$50.00	$150.00	$350.00	£34.00	£100.00	£235.00
51 scarce in both US and UK	$55.00	$165.00	$385.00	£37.00	£110.00	£260.00
52-60	$50.00	$150.00	$350.00	£34.00	£100.00	£235.00
61-64	$36.00	$105.00	$250.00	£24.00	£75.00	£175.00
65 scarce in both US and UK Tomahawk begins (end #101), origin of Superman briefly retold	$52.50	$155.00	$425.00	£34.00	£100.00	£275.00
66-69 scarce in the U.S, very scarce in the U.K.	$43.00	$125.00	$340.00	£28.00	£82.50	£225.00
70 scarce in the U.S, very scarce in the U.K. last 68pg issue	$43.00	$125.00	$340.00	£28.00	£82.50	£225.00
71 rare in the U.K., very scarce in the U.S. Superman and Batman regular team ups begin although they had always shared the cover	$95.00	$280.00	$750.00	£70.00	£205.00	£550.00
72-73 scarce in the U.S, very scarce in the U.K.	$65.00	$195.00	$525.00	£47.00	£140.00	£375.00
74-75 scarce in the U.S, very scarce in the U.K.	$52.50	$155.00	$425.00	£38.00	£110.00	£300.00
76 scarce in the U.K.	$39.00	$115.00	$275.00	£26.00	£75.00	£180.00
77 scarce in the U.K. The Super Batman	$39.00	$115.00	$275.00	£26.00	£75.00	£180.00
78-80 scarce in the U.K.	$39.00	$115.00	$275.00	£26.00	£75.00	£180.00
81-87	$32.00	$95.00	$225.00	£21.00	£62.50	£150.00
88 1st Luthor-Joker team-up	$34.00	$100.00	$240.00	£22.50	£67.50	£160.00
89	$32.00	$95.00	$225.00	£21.00	£62.50	£150.00
90 The Super Batwoman	$34.00	$100.00	$240.00	£22.50	£67.50	£160.00
91-93	$22.50	$67.50	$160.00	£15.50	£47.00	£110.00
94 scarce in the U.K. origin Superman/Batman team	$55.00	$165.00	$450.00	£38.00	£110.00	£300.00
95	$22.50	$67.50	$160.00	£15.50	£47.00	£110.00
96-99 Jack Kirby Green Arrow	$22.50	$67.50	$160.00	£15.50	£47.00	£110.00
100	$39.00	$115.00	$275.00	£25.00	£75.00	£175.00
101-104	$15.50	$47.00	$110.00	£10.50	£32.00	£75.00
1st official distribution in the U.K.						
105-110	$15.50	$47.00	$110.00	£10.00	£30.00	£70.00
111-120	$12.00	$36.00	$85.00	£6.25	£19.00	£45.00
121 last 10 cents issue	$12.00	$36.00	$85.00	£6.25	£19.00	£45.00
122-128	$6.25	$19.00	$45.00	£3.55	£10.50	£25.00
129 Joker cover/story	$8.50	$26.00	$60.00	£4.25	£12.50	£30.00
130	$6.25	$19.00	$45.00	£3.55	£10.50	£25.00

	$Good	$Fine	$N.Mint	£Good	£Fine	£N.Mint
131-139	$5.50	$17.00	$40.00	£2.85	£8.50	£20.00
140 Clayface appears	$5.50	$17.00	$40.00	£2.85	£8.50	£20.00
141	$5.00	$15.00	$35.00	£2.10	£6.25	£15.00
142 origin and 1st appearance Composite Superman	$5.50	$17.00	$40.00	£2.85	£8.50	£20.00
143	$5.00	$15.00	$35.00	£2.10	£6.25	£15.00
144 Clayface appears	$5.00	$15.00	$35.00	£2.10	£6.25	£15.00
145-150	$5.00	$15.00	$35.00	£2.10	£6.25	£15.00
151-153	$4.15	$12.50	$25.00	£1.65	£5.00	£10.00
154 1st Sons of Superman/Batman; last Silver Age issue, indicia dated December 1965	$4.15	$12.50	$25.00	£1.65	£5.00	£10.00
155	$4.15	$12.50	$25.00	£1.65	£5.00	£10.00
156 Joker cover/story; 1st appearance Bizarro Batman	$15.00	$45.00	$90.00	£6.50	£20.00	£40.00
157	$4.15	$12.50	$25.00	£1.65	£5.00	£10.00
158 Brainiac appears, origin Bottle City of Kandor retold	$4.15	$12.50	$25.00	£1.65	£5.00	£10.00
159-160	$4.15	$12.50	$25.00	£1.65	£5.00	£10.00
161 80pgs, Giant G-28	$5.00	$15.00	$30.00	£2.05	£6.25	£12.50
162-163	$3.30	$10.00	$20.00	£1.25	£3.75	£7.50
164 Brainiac appears	$3.30	$10.00	$20.00	£1.25	£3.75	£7.50
165	$3.30	$10.00	$20.00	£1.25	£3.75	£7.50
166 Joker cover/story	$3.75	$11.00	$22.50	£1.65	£5.00	£10.00
167 Brainiac and Supergirl appear	$3.30	$10.00	$20.00	£1.25	£3.75	£7.50
168 return and death of the Composite Superman	$3.30	$10.00	$20.00	£1.25	£3.75	£7.50
169 Batgirl/Supergirl appear (also in #176)	$3.30	$10.00	$20.00	£1.25	£3.75	£7.50
170 80pgs, Giant G-40	$4.15	$12.50	$25.00	£2.05	£6.25	£12.50
171	$2.90	$8.75	$17.50	£1.25	£3.75	£7.50
172 Adult Legion appear	$2.90	$8.75	$17.50	£1.25	£3.75	£7.50
173-174	$2.90	$8.75	$17.50	£1.25	£3.75	£7.50
175-176 Neal Adams art, reprints John Jonzz origin from Detective #225, #226	$3.30	$10.00	$20.00	£1.50	£4.50	£9.00
177 Joker cover/story	$3.30	$10.00	$20.00	£1.50	£4.50	£9.00
178	$2.90	$8.75	$17.50	£1.25	£3.75	£7.50
179 80pgs, Giant G-52, reprints #94 and Superman #76	$3.30	$10.00	$20.00	£2.05	£6.25	£12.50
180	$2.90	$8.75	$17.50	£1.25	£3.75	£7.50
181-187	$1.65	$5.00	$10.00	£0.80	£2.50	£5.00
188 scarce in the U.K. 80pgs, Giant G-64	$2.50	$7.50	$15.00	£1.65	£5.00	£10.00
189-190	$1.65	$5.00	$10.00	£0.80	£2.50	£5.00
191-196	$1.25	$3.75	$7.50	£0.65	£2.00	£4.00
197 80pgs, Giant G-76	$2.50	$7.50	$15.00	£1.25	£3.75	£7.50
198 Neal Adams cover, 3rd Superman/Flash race (see Superman #199, Flash #175, Adv. Superman #463)	$12.50	$38.00	$75.00	£5.75	£17.50	£35.00
199 3rd Superman/Flash race continued (see Superman #199, Flash #175, Adv. Superman #463)	$12.50	$38.00	$75.00	£5.00	£15.00	£30.00
200 Neal Adams cover art, Superman/Batman regular team-ups end, Superman/Robin co-star	$1.25	$3.75	$7.50	£0.65	£2.00	£4.00
201 Neal Adams cover art, Green Lantern appears	$0.80	$2.40	$4.00	£0.50	£1.50	£2.50
202 Neal Adams cover art, Batman appears	$0.80	$2.40	$4.00	£0.50	£1.50	£2.50
203 Neal Adams cover art, Aquaman appears	$0.80	$2.40	$4.00	£0.50	£1.50	£2.50
204 52pgs, Neal Adams cover art, Hawkman appears	$1.00	$3.00	$5.00	£0.70	£2.10	£3.50
205 52pgs, Neal Adams cover art, Frazetta Shining Knight reprint, Teen Titans X-over	$1.00	$3.00	$5.00	£0.70	£2.10	£3.50
206 80pgs, Giant G-88	$1.50	$4.50	$7.50	£0.80	£2.40	£4.00
207 52pgs	$1.00	$3.00	$5.00	£0.70	£2.10	£3.50
208-211 52pgs, Neal Adams cover	$1.00	$3.00	$5.00	£0.70	£2.10	£3.50
212 52pgs	$1.00	$3.00	$5.00	£0.70	£2.10	£3.50
213-222	$0.80	$2.40	$4.00	£0.40	£1.20	£2.00
223-226 100pgs	$1.20	$3.60	$6.00	£0.80	£2.40	£4.00
227 100pgs, Joker appears (cameo)	$1.20	$3.60	$6.00	£0.80	£2.40	£4.00
228 100pgs	$1.20	$3.60	$6.00	£0.80	£2.40	£4.00
229	$0.80	$2.40	$4.00	£0.40	£1.20	£2.00
230 scarce in the U.K. 68pgs, Neal Adams reprint	$1.00	$3.00	$5.00	£0.70	£2.10	£3.50
231 Green Arrow and Flash appear	$0.80	$2.40	$4.00	£0.40	£1.20	£2.00
232-233 scarce in the U.K.	$0.80	$2.40	$4.00	£0.50	£1.50	£2.50
234-243 LD in the U.K.	$0.80	$2.40	$4.00	£0.40	£1.20	£2.00
244 ND 80pgs, Neal Adams cover						

	$Good	$Fine	$N.Mint	£Good	£Fine	£N.Mint
244 ND 80pgs, Neal Adams cover	$0.90	$2.70	$4.50	£0.60	£1.80	£3.00
245 80pgs, Neal Adams cover art, no Comics Code Authority stamp (alledgedly for violence)	$0.90	$2.70	$4.50	£0.50	£1.50	£2.50
246 ND 80pgs, Neal Adams cover	$0.90	$2.70	$4.50	£0.60	£1.80	£3.00
247-252 ND 80pgs	$0.90	$2.70	$4.50	£0.50	£1.50	£3.00
253 68pgs	$0.80	$2.40	$4.00	£0.40	£1.20	£2.00
254 scarce in the U.K. 68pgs	$0.80	$2.40	$4.00	£0.45	£1.35	£2.25
255-256 ND 68pgs	$0.80	$2.40	$4.00	£0.50	£1.50	£2.50
257 scarce in the U.K. 68pgs	$0.80	$2.40	$4.00	£0.45	£1.35	£2.25
258 ND 68pgs, Neal Adams cover	$0.80	$2.40	$4.00	£0.50	£1.50	£2.50
259 ND 68pgs, Rogers/Nasser art	$0.80	$2.40	$4.00	£0.45	£1.35	£2.25
260-265 ND 68pgs	$0.80	$2.40	$4.00	£0.50	£1.50	£2.50
266-269 ND 52pgs	$0.60	$1.80	$3.00	£0.40	£1.20	£2.00
270 ND 52pgs, Neal Adams cover	$0.60	$1.80	$3.00	£0.40	£1.20	£2.00
271 ND 52pgs, George Perez cover art, new origin Superman/Batman team	$0.80	$2.40	$4.00	£0.50	£1.50	£2.50
272-275 52pgs	$0.50	$1.50	$2.50	£0.30	£0.90	£1.50
276-278 52pgs, George Perez cover	$0.50	$1.50	$2.50	£0.30	£0.90	£1.50
279-282 52pgs	$0.50	$1.50	$2.50	£0.30	£0.90	£1.50
283 Composite Superman returns	$0.40	$1.20	$2.00	£0.25	£0.75	£1.25
284 Legion of Super-Heroes appears, Composite Superman appears	$0.40	$1.20	$2.00	£0.25	£0.75	£1.25
285-299	$0.40	$1.20	$2.00	£0.25	£0.75	£1.25
300 52pgs, Mark Texeira lead story, Teen Titans back-up by George Perez	$0.60	$1.80	$3.00	£0.40	£1.20	£2.00
301	$0.30	$0.90	$1.50	£0.20	£0.60	£1.00
302 Neal Adams reprint from World's Finest Comics #176	$0.30	$0.90	$1.50	£0.20	£0.60	£1.00
303-321	$0.30	$0.90	$1.50	£0.20	£0.60	£1.00
322 Giffen art	$0.30	$0.90	$1.50	£0.20	£0.60	£1.00
323	$0.30	$0.90	$1.50	£0.20	£0.60	£1.00
Title Value:	**$9066.95**	**$27255.95**	**$70052.00**	**£6061.75**	**£18139.90**	**£46876.50**

Note: like all Golden Age material, these comics were not available on the news-stands in the U.K. until cover date November 1959 but some Golden Age issues may have come to England as a result of personnel movements during the Second World War or as cheap ballast on ships. **Note:** Joker covers and stories-129, 156, 166, 177. Bruce Wayne's older brother Thomas appears in 223, 227

ARTISTS
Ditko art in 249-255. Kirby reprints in 187, 197. Nasser art in 244-246, 259, 260.

FEATURES
Adam Strange in 263. Aquaman in 125-133, 135, 137, 139, 263, 264. Atom in 260. Black Canary in 244-249, 251-256, 262, 267. Black Lightning in 257-261. Captain Marvel/Marvel Family in 253-270, 272-282. Creeper in 249-255. Green Arrow in 107-134, 136, 138, 140, 244-249, 251-258, 261-266, 268-270, 272-282. Green Arrow/Hawkman in 259. Hawkman in 256-258, 261, 262, 264-270, 272-277, 279-282. Metamorpho in 218-220, 229. Plastic Man in 273. Red Tornado in 265-270, 272. Superman/Batman in 71-160, 162-169, 171-178, 180-187, 189-196, 202, 207, 211, 215-228, 230-249, 250 (guest starring Wonder Woman, Green Arrow, Black Canary), 251-282. Tommy Tomorrow in 107-124. Vigilante in 244-248. Wonder Woman in 244-249, 251, 252. Zatanna in 274-278.
Superman team-ups as follows: Flash in 198, 199; Robin in 200; Green Lantern in 201; Aquaman in 203; Wonder Woman in 204; Teen Titans in 205; Dr.Fate in 208; Hawkman in 209; Green Arrow in 210; Manhunter From Mars in 212; Atom in 213; Vigilante in 214.
REPRINT FEATURES
Aquaman in 144, 146, 223, 228, 230. Batman in 209. Bizarro in 181 (origin). Black Canary in 225. Black Pirate, The King in 210. Captain Comet in 204. Challengers of the Unknown in 230. Congo Bill in 195. Congorilla in 148-151. Deadman in 223, 226. Eclipso in 226, 228. Ghost Patrol in 208. Green Arrow in 143, 145, 154, 159, 187, 204. Green Lantern in 174. Grim Ghost, Air Wave in 212. Harlequin in 211. Johnny Quick in 186, 198, 224. Lois Lane 141. Martian Manhunter in 175 (origin), 176, 184, 226, 227. Metamorpho in 224, 228. Rip Hunter in 225, 227. Robin in 190-193. Robotman 168, 208, 223, 226. Roy Raymond in 158, 166, 189. GA Sandman in 226. Silent Knight in 182, 205. Superboy in 146, 171. Superman in 142, 173, 178. Superman/Batman in 161, 170, 179, 180, 188, 205, 223-225, 228, 229. Superman/Batman/Green Arrow in 197. Tommy Tomorrow in 156, 162, 185. Tarantula in 207. Vigilante in 225, 227, 228.

WORLD'S FINEST COMICS (2ND SERIES)
DC Comics,MS; 1 Aug 1990-3 Oct 1990

	$Good	$Fine	$N.Mint	£Good	£Fine	£N.Mint
1 ND 48pgs, art by Steve Rude begins, script by Dave Gibbons	$0.90	$2.70	$4.50	£0.60	£1.80	£3.00
2-3 ND 48pgs	$0.90	$2.70	$4.50	£0.60	£1.80	£3.00
Title Value:	**$2.70**	**$8.10**	**$13.50**	**£1.80**	**£5.40**	**£9.00**

Multi-Pack (Nov 1991)

	£Good	£Fine	£N.Mint
ND, pre-bagged mini-series with illustrated header card	£1.50	£4.50	£7.50

Trade paperback (Jan 1993)

	£Good	£Fine	£N.Mint
160pgs, reprints mini-series plus sketches by Steve Rude	£2.50	£7.50	£12.50

WORLD'S FINEST COMICS DIGEST
DC Comics,Digest; nn Feb 1981
(DC Special series #23)

	$Good	$Fine	$N.Mint	£Good	£Fine	£N.Mint
nn ND 68pgs	$0.80	$2.40	$4.00	£0.50	£1.50	£2.50
Title Value:	**$0.80**	**$2.40**	**$4.00**	**£0.50**	**£1.50**	**£2.50**

WORLD'S GREATEST SUPER HEROES
(see DC 100 Page Super Spectacular #6)

WORLD'S WORST COMICS AWARDS
Kitchen Sink,MS; 1 Feb 1991-2 Mar 1991

	$Good	$Fine	$N.Mint	£Good	£Fine	£N.Mint
1 ND scarce in the U.K. a look at the worst comics published in the last 25 years	$0.50	$1.50	$2.50	£0.35	£1.05	£1.75

	$Good	$Fine	$N.Mint	£Good	£Fine	£N.Mint
2 ND	$0.50	$1.50	$2.50	£0.30	£0.90	£1.50
Title Value:	$1.00	$3.00	$5.00	£0.65	£1.95	£3.25

WORLDS COLLIDE
DC Comics/Milestone; 1 Jul 1994

	$Good	$Fine	$N.Mint	£Good	£Fine	£N.Mint
1 ND 48pgs, Collector's Edition - pre-bagged with sheet of vinyl clings; X-over between the regular DC universe and the Milestone universe; continued in Superboy #7	$0.60	$1.80	$3.00	£0.40	£1.20	£2.00
1 48pgs, Regular Edition	$0.40	$1.20	$2.00	£0.25	£0.75	£1.25
Title Value:	$1.00	$3.00	$5.00	£0.65	£1.95	£3.25

WORLDS OF H.P. LOVECRAFT, THE
Caliber Press; 1 1993

	$Good	$Fine	$N.Mint	£Good	£Fine	£N.Mint
1 ND Rob Davis art, black and white; adapts The Picture in the House	$0.50	$1.50	$2.50	£0.30	£0.90	£1.50
Title Value:	$0.50	$1.50	$2.50	£0.30	£0.90	£1.50

WORLDS UNKNOWN
Marvel Comics Group; 1 May 1973-8 Aug 1974

	$Good	$Fine	$N.Mint	£Good	£Fine	£N.Mint
1 ND scarce in the U.K. Harlan Ellison story with art by Ralph Reese; also features Gil Kane art plus 1950s reprint	$0.50	$1.50	$2.50	£0.30	£0.90	£1.50
2 ND scarce in the U.K. features Gil Kane art; dinosaur cover	$0.50	$1.50	$2.50	£0.30	£0.90	£1.50
3 ND scarce in the U.K. full length adaptation of "Farewell To The Master" by Harry Bates which was to become the classic SF film "The Day The Earth Stood Still"	$0.50	$1.50	$2.50	£0.30	£0.90	£1.50
4 ND scarce in the U.K. adaptation of Fredric Brown story "Arena" by Buscema and Giordano plus 1950s reprint	$0.50	$1.50	$2.50	£0.30	£0.90	£1.50
5 ND scarce in the U.K. adaptation of A.E. Van Vogt's "Black Destroyer"	$0.50	$1.50	$2.50	£0.30	£0.90	£1.50
6 ND scarce in the U.K. adaptation of Theodore Sturgeon's "Killdozer"	$0.50	$1.50	$2.50	£0.30	£0.90	£1.50
7 ND adaptation of The Golden Voyage of Sinbad	$0.40	$1.20	$2.00	£0.25	£0.75	£1.25
8 adaptation of The Golden Voyage of Sinbad, classic Vince Coletta art	$0.30	$0.90	$1.50	£0.20	£0.60	£1.00
Title Value:	$3.70	$11.10	$18.50	£2.25	£6.75	£11.25

FEATURES
Science-fiction adaptations in 1-6. Sinbad in 7, 8. Back-up reprints in 1, 4.

WRATH
Malibu Ultraverse; 1 Jan 1994-9 Nov 1994

	$Good	$Fine	$N.Mint	£Good	£Fine	£N.Mint
1 ND Mike Barr script, James Pascoe art		$1.20	$2.00	£0.25	£0.75	£1.25
2 ND Mantra guest-stars	$0.40	$1.20	$2.00	£0.25	£0.75	£1.25
3-4 ND	$0.40	$1.20	$2.00	£0.25	£0.75	£1.25
5 ND guest-starring Freex	$0.40	$1.20	$2.00	£0.25	£0.75	£1.25
6-7 ND	$0.40	$1.20	$2.00	£0.25	£0.75	£1.25
8 ND Warstrike and Mantra appear	$0.40	$1.20	$2.00	£0.25	£0.75	£1.25
9 ND Prime appears	$0.40	$1.20	$2.00	£0.25	£0.75	£1.25
Title Value:	$3.60	$10.80	$18.00	£2.25	£6.75	£11.25

WRATH OF THE SPECTRE
(see Spectre)

WRATH, GIANT SIZE
Malibu Ultraverse; 1 Aug 1994

	$Good	$Fine	$N.Mint	£Good	£Fine	£N.Mint
1 ND 40pgs, Warstrike and Mantra appear	$0.40	$1.20	$2.00	£0.25	£0.75	£1.25
Title Value:	$0.40	$1.20	$2.00	£0.25	£0.75	£1.25

WULF THE BARBARIAN
Atlas; 1 Feb 1975-4 Sep 1975

	$Good	$Fine	$N.Mint	£Good	£Fine	£N.Mint
1 distributed in the U.K.	$0.30	$0.90	$1.50	£0.20	£0.60	£1.00
2 distributed in the U.K. Hama/Janson art	$0.30	$0.90	$1.50	£0.20	£0.60	£1.00
3 distributed in the U.K. Leo Summer art	$0.30	$0.90	$1.50	£0.20	£0.60	£1.00
4 distributed in the U.K.	$0.30	$0.90	$1.50	£0.20	£0.60	£1.00
Title Value:	$1.20	$3.60	$6.00	£0.80	£2.40	£4.00

WYATT EARP
Atlas/Marvel Comics Group; 29 Jun 1960; 30 Oct 1972-34 Jun 1973
(previous issues ND)

	$Good	$Fine	$N.Mint	£Good	£Fine	£N.Mint
29 Jack Kirby art	$3.75	$11.00	$22.50	£2.50	£7.50	£15.00
30-34 ND all reprints	$0.60	$1.80	$3.00	£0.40	£1.20	£2.00
Title Value:	$6.75	$20.00	$37.50	£4.50	£13.50	£25.00

Note: Williamson reprint in 30.

WYATT EARP, FRONTIER MARSHAL
Charlton; 12 Jan 1956-2 Dec 1967

	$Good	$Fine	$N.Mint	£Good	£Fine	£N.Mint
12 scarce in the U.K.	$6.25	$18.50	$37.50	£4.15	£12.50	£25.00
13-19	$3.30	$10.00	$20.00	£2.30	£7.00	£14.00
20 64pgs, Williamson art	$7.50	$22.50	$45.00	£5.00	£15.00	£30.00
21-26	$2.50	$7.50	$15.00	£1.65	£5.00	£10.00
1st official distribution in the U.K.						
27-30	$2.50	$7.50	$15.00	£1.65	£5.00	£10.00
31-50	$1.65	$5.00	$10.00	£1.25	£3.75	£7.50
51-72	$1.25	$3.75	$7.50	£0.80	£2.50	£5.00
Title Value:	$122.35	$368.50	$737.50	£84.35	£256.50	£513.00

Note: issues after about 1958 came to be distributed on the news-stands in the U.K.

X

X
Dark Horse; 1 Jan 1994-present

	$Good	$Fine	$N.Mint	£Good	£Fine	£N.Mint
1 ND Alan Grant script begins, red foil stamped logo	$0.50	$1.50	$2.50	£0.30	£0.90	£1.50
2-17 ND	$0.50	$1.50	$2.50	£0.30	£0.90	£1.50
18-20 ND Predator X-over	$0.50	$1.50	$2.50	£0.30	£0.90	£1.50
21 ND Frank Miller cover	$0.50	$1.50	$2.50	£0.30	£0.90	£1.50
Title Value:	$10.50	$31.50	$52.50	£6.30	£18.90	£31.50

X-1999
Viz Communications,MS; 1 May 1995-6 Oct 1995

	$Good	$Fine	$N.Mint	£Good	£Fine	£N.Mint
1-6 ND Clamp script and art; black and white	$0.50	$1.50	$2.50	£0.30	£0.90	£1.50
Title Value:	$3.00	$9.00	$15.00	£1.80	£5.40	£9.00

X-CALIBRE
Marvel Comics Group; 1 Mar 1995-4 Jun 1995

	$Good	$Fine	$N.Mint	£Good	£Fine	£N.Mint
1 Warren Ellis script, Lashley and Wegrzyn art	$1.00	$3.00	$5.00	£0.60	£1.80	£3.00
2-3 Warren Ellis script, Lashley and Wegrzyn art	$0.50	$1.50	$2.50	£0.30	£0.90	£1.50
4 Warren Ellis script, Lashley and Wegrzyn art; continued in X-Men: Omega	$0.50	$1.50	$2.50	£0.30	£0.90	£1.50
Title Value:	$2.50	$7.50	$12.50	£1.50	£4.50	£7.50

World's Finest Comics #2

World's Finest Comics #158

X-Files #5

	$Good	$Fine	$N.Mint	£Good	£Fine	£N.Mint

Note: this title temporarily replaced Excalibur during the "Age of Apocalypse" storyline

The Ultimate X-Calibre (Jul 1995)
96pgs, Bookshelf Edition collects issues #1-4
with etched gold cover — £1.20 | £3.60 | £6.00

X-FACTOR

Marvel Comics Group; 1 Feb 1986-111 Feb 1995; 112 Jul 1995-present
(see Avengers #263, Cloak and Dagger #18, Fantastic Four #286, Hulk #336, #337, Mephisto)
(title becomes Factor X)

1 LD in the U.K. DS Guice art begins (ends #7)
| | $2.50 | $7.50 | $12.50 | £1.40 | £4.20 | £7.00 |

2 LD in the U.K. Mike Zeck cover
| | $1.50 | $4.50 | $7.50 | £0.70 | £2.10 | £3.50 |

3-4
| | $1.00 | $3.00 | $5.00 | £0.60 | £1.80 | £3.00 |

5 LD in the U.K. 1st appearance Apocalypse
| | $1.50 | $4.50 | $7.50 | £0.70 | £2.10 | £3.50 |

6 LD in the U.K. 1st full appearance Apocalypse
| | $2.00 | $6.00 | $10.00 | £0.80 | £2.40 | £4.00 |

7 LD in the U.K.
| | $0.80 | $2.40 | $4.00 | £0.50 | £1.50 | £2.50 |

8
| | $0.80 | $2.40 | $4.00 | £0.40 | £1.20 | £2.00 |

9 Mutant Massacre tie-in
| | $0.80 | $2.40 | $4.00 | £0.40 | £1.20 | £2.00 |

10 Mutant Massacre tie-in, Walt Simonson art begins, Sabretooth appears
| | $0.80 | $2.40 | $4.00 | £0.50 | £1.50 | £2.50 |

11 Mutant Massacre tie-in, Walt Simonson art
| | $0.60 | $1.80 | $3.00 | £0.40 | £1.20 | £2.00 |

12 Mutant Massacre tie-in, Walt Simonson cover only (Silvestri art)
| | $0.60 | $1.80 | $3.00 | £0.40 | £1.20 | £2.00 |

13-15 Walt Simonson art
| | $0.50 | $1.50 | $2.50 | £0.30 | £0.90 | £1.50 |

16 Mazzucchelli art
| | $0.50 | $1.50 | $2.50 | £0.30 | £0.90 | £1.50 |

17 Thor appears, Walt Simonson art
| | $0.50 | $1.50 | $2.50 | £0.30 | £0.90 | £1.50 |

18-19 Walt Simonson art
| | $0.50 | $1.50 | $2.50 | £0.30 | £0.90 | £1.50 |

20
| | $0.50 | $1.50 | $2.50 | £0.30 | £0.90 | £1.50 |

21 Walt Simonson art
| | $0.45 | $1.35 | $2.25 | £0.30 | £0.90 | £1.50 |

22
| | $0.50 | $1.50 | $2.50 | £0.30 | £0.90 | £1.50 |

23 Fall of the Mutants, Walt Simonson art, Archangel cameo (1st appearance)
| | $0.60 | $1.80 | $3.00 | £0.40 | £1.20 | £2.00 |

24 LD in the U.K. Walt Simonson art, Fall of the Mutants, 1st full appearance Archangel (formerly Angel of the X-Men); Apocalypse origin
| | $2.50 | $7.50 | $12.50 | £1.00 | £3.00 | £5.00 |

25 DS Walt Simonson art, Fall of the Mutants
| | $0.90 | $2.70 | $4.50 | £0.60 | £1.80 | £3.00 |

26 Walt Simonson art, Fall of the Mutants
| | $0.80 | $2.40 | $4.00 | £0.50 | £1.50 | £2.50 |

27 LD in the U.K. Walt Simonson art
| | $0.50 | $1.50 | $2.50 | £0.35 | £1.05 | £1.75 |

28-30 Walt Simonson art
| | $0.50 | $1.50 | $2.50 | £0.30 | £0.90 | £1.50 |

31 Walt Simonson art
| | $0.40 | $1.20 | $2.00 | £0.25 | £0.75 | £1.25 |

32 Avengers tie-in by Steve Lightle
| | $0.40 | $1.20 | $2.00 | £0.25 | £0.75 | £1.25 |

33-34 Walt Simonson art
| | $0.40 | $1.20 | $2.00 | £0.25 | £0.75 | £1.25 |

35
| | $0.40 | $1.20 | $2.00 | £0.25 | £0.75 | £1.25 |

36-37 LD in the U.K. Inferno X-over, Walt Simonson art
| | $0.45 | $1.35 | $2.25 | £0.30 | £0.90 | £1.50 |

38 LD in the U.K. DS Inferno X-over, X-Men appear, Walt Simonson art
| | $0.80 | $2.40 | $4.00 | £0.50 | £1.50 | £2.50 |

39 LD in the U.K. Inferno X-over, X-Men appear, Walt Simonson art
| | $0.50 | $1.50 | $2.50 | £0.30 | £0.90 | £1.50 |

40 Rob Liefeld cover and art
| | $1.00 | $3.00 | $5.00 | £0.60 | £1.80 | £3.00 |

41-42 Arthur Adams art
| | $0.40 | $1.20 | $2.00 | £0.25 | £0.75 | £1.25 |

43 Judgement story begins (ends #50 with #47 as an interlude), Paul Smith art
| | $0.40 | $1.20 | $2.00 | £0.25 | £0.75 | £1.25 |

44-46 Paul Smith art
| | $0.40 | $1.20 | $2.00 | £0.25 | £0.75 | £1.25 |

47
| | $0.40 | $1.20 | $2.00 | £0.25 | £0.75 | £1.25 |

48 Paul Smith art | $0.40 | $1.20 | $2.00 | £0.25 | £0.75 | £1.25 |

49 Acts of Vengeance tie-in, Paul Smith art
| | $0.40 | $1.20 | $2.00 | £0.25 | £0.75 | £1.25 |

50 LD in the U.K. DS Acts of Vengeance tie-in, McFarlane art, Liefeld cover
| | $0.60 | $1.80 | $3.00 | £0.40 | £1.20 | £2.00 |

51-52 Sabretooth appears
| | $0.60 | $1.80 | $3.00 | £0.40 | £1.20 | £2.00 |

53 Sabretooth appears, Cyclops proposes (and gets turned down)
| | $0.60 | $1.80 | $3.00 | £0.40 | £1.20 | £2.00 |

54 1st appearance Crimson, Colossus appears
| | $0.30 | $0.90 | $1.50 | £0.20 | £0.60 | £1.00 |

55 Peter David script
| | $0.30 | $0.90 | $1.50 | £0.20 | £0.60 | £1.00 |

56
| | $0.30 | $0.90 | $1.50 | £0.20 | £0.60 | £1.00 |

57 Andy Kubert art
| | $0.30 | $0.90 | $1.50 | £0.20 | £0.60 | £1.00 |

58 Jon Bogdanove art
| | $0.30 | $0.90 | $1.50 | £0.20 | £0.60 | £1.00 |

59
| | $0.30 | $0.90 | $1.50 | £0.20 | £0.60 | £1.00 |

60 The X-Tinction Agenda part 3 (see Uncanny X-Men #270 for start of story), Cable appears, Jon Bogdanove art
| | $1.50 | $4.50 | $7.50 | £1.00 | £3.00 | £5.00 |

60 ND The X-Tinction Agenda part 3 (2nd print - gold cover)
| | $0.60 | $1.80 | $3.00 | £0.40 | £1.20 | £2.00 |

61 The X-Tinction Agenda part 6, Cable appears, Jon Bogdanove art
| | $1.00 | $3.00 | $5.00 | £0.70 | £2.10 | £3.50 |

62 The X-Tinction Agenda part 9 (of 9), Cable appears, last Jon Bogdanove art
| | $1.00 | $3.00 | $5.00 | £0.70 | £2.10 | £3.50 |

63 ND Whilce Portacio art begins
| | $1.20 | $3.60 | $6.00 | £0.80 | £2.40 | £4.00 |

64-67 Whilce Portacio art
| | $0.80 | $2.40 | $4.00 | £0.50 | £1.50 | £2.50 |

68 Nathan Summers appears, Whilce Portacio art
| | $0.80 | $2.40 | $4.00 | £0.50 | £1.50 | £2.50 |

69 Whilce Portacio art
| | $0.30 | $0.90 | $1.50 | £0.20 | £0.60 | £1.00 |

70 last "old" X-Factor, Peter David scripts begin
| | $0.30 | $0.90 | $1.50 | £0.20 | £0.60 | £1.00 |

71 1st new X-Factor, Peter David script, 1st Larry Stroman art on title
| | $1.00 | $3.00 | $5.00 | £0.50 | £1.50 | £2.50 |

71 2nd printing, ND Feb 1992
| | $0.40 | $1.20 | $2.00 | £0.25 | £0.75 | £1.25 |

72-73 Peter David script, Larry Stroman art
| | $0.30 | $0.90 | $1.50 | £0.20 | £0.60 | £1.00 |

74 Peter David script
| | $0.30 | $0.90 | $1.50 | £0.20 | £0.60 | £1.00 |

75 LD in the U.K. DS, intro The Nasty Boys, Peter David script
| | $0.40 | $1.20 | $2.00 | £0.25 | £0.75 | £1.25 |

76 Hulk appears, $1.25 cover begins
| | $0.30 | $0.90 | $1.50 | £0.20 | £0.60 | £1.00 |

77
| | $0.30 | $0.90 | $1.50 | £0.20 | £0.60 | £1.00 |

78 (see note below)
| | $0.30 | $0.90 | $1.50 | £0.20 | £0.60 | £1.00 |

79-80
| | $0.30 | $0.90 | $1.50 | £0.20 | £0.60 | £1.00 |

81 Brotherhood of Evil Mutants appear
| | $0.30 | $0.90 | $1.50 | £0.20 | £0.60 | £1.00 |

82-83
| | $0.30 | $0.90 | $1.50 | £0.20 | £0.60 | £1.00 |

84 X-Cutioner's Song part 2, pre-bagged with trading card, continued in X-Men #14
| | $0.40 | $1.20 | $2.00 | £0.25 | £0.75 | £1.25 |

85 X-Cutioner's Song part 5, pre-bagged with trading card, continued in X-Men #15
| | $0.40 | $1.20 | $2.00 | £0.25 | £0.75 | £1.25 |

86 X-Cutioner's Song part 10, pre-bagged with trading card, continued in X-Men #16
| | $0.30 | $0.90 | $1.50 | £0.20 | £0.60 | £1.00 |

87-91 Joe Quesada art
| | $0.30 | $0.90 | $1.50 | £0.20 | £0.60 | £1.00 |

92 DS, Joe Quesada art; hologram cover, Return of Magneto story begins
| | $0.90 | $2.70 | $4.50 | £0.60 | £1.80 | £3.00 |

92 2nd printing, ND (Sep 1993)
| | $0.70 | $2.10 | $3.50 | £0.45 | £1.35 | £2.25 |

93-94 Joe Quesada art
| | $0.30 | $0.90 | $1.50 | £0.20 | £0.60 | £1.00 |

95-99
| | $0.30 | $0.90 | $1.50 | £0.20 | £0.60 | £1.00 |

100 48pgs, death of Jaimie
| | $0.40 | $1.20 | $2.00 | £0.25 | £0.75 | £1.25 |

100 48pgs, red foil embossed cover, death of Jamie
| | $0.70 | $2.10 | $3.50 | £0.45 | £1.35 | £2.25 |

101
| | $0.30 | $0.90 | $1.50 | £0.20 | £0.60 | £1.00 |

102 with free Spiderman vs. Venom card sheet
| | $0.30 | $0.90 | $1.50 | £0.20 | £0.60 | £1.00 |

103-105
| | $0.30 | $0.90 | $1.50 | £0.20 | £0.60 | £1.00 |

106 ND Deluxe Edition - foil stamped cover; Generation X tie-in
| | $0.60 | $1.80 | $3.00 | £0.40 | £1.20 | £2.00 |

106 Regular Edition
| | $0.30 | $0.90 | $1.50 | £0.25 | £0.75 | £1.25 |

107-108
| | $0.30 | $0.90 | $1.50 | £0.20 | £0.60 | £1.00 |

108 ND Deluxe Edition - printed on glossy stock paper
| | $0.40 | $1.20 | $2.00 | £0.25 | £0.75 | £1.25 |

109
| | $0.30 | $0.90 | $1.50 | £0.20 | £0.60 | £1.00 |

109 ND Deluxe Edition - printed on glossy stock paper
| | $0.40 | $1.20 | $2.00 | £0.25 | £0.75 | £1.25 |

110
| | $0.30 | $0.90 | $1.50 | £0.20 | £0.60 | £1.00 |

110 ND Deluxe Edition - printed on glossy stock paper
| | $0.40 | $1.20 | $2.00 | £0.25 | £0.75 | £1.25 |

111
| | $0.30 | $0.90 | $1.50 | £0.20 | £0.60 | £1.00 |

111 ND Deluxe Edition - printed on glossy stock paper plus bound-in Fleer trading card
| | $0.40 | $1.20 | $2.00 | £0.25 | £0.75 | £1.25 |

112 continued from X-Men: Prime; J.F. Moore script, Steve Epting and Al Milgrom art
| | $0.40 | $1.20 | $2.00 | £0.25 | £0.75 | £1.25 |

113 Mystique guest-stars
| | $0.40 | $1.20 | $2.00 | £0.25 | £0.75 | £1.25 |

114-116
| | $0.40 | $1.20 | $2.00 | £0.25 | £0.75 | £1.25 |

117 Cyclops appears, Havok leaves the team
| | $0.40 | $1.20 | $2.00 | £0.25 | £0.75 | £1.25 |

118
| | $0.40 | $1.20 | $2.00 | £0.25 | £0.75 | £1.25 |

119 Sabretooth appears
| | $0.40 | $1.20 | $2.00 | £0.25 | £0.75 | £1.25 |

120
| | $0.40 | $1.20 | $2.00 | £0.25 | £0.75 | £1.25 |

| **Title Value:** | $70.25 | $210.75 | $351.25 | £42.90 | £128.70 | £214.50 |

Note: a cover-priced 70p edition of issue #78 has been reported as well as the regular 80p version. It is unknown how many copies there are but reports suggest it is very scarce in the U.K.

VERY GENERAL PERCENTAGE CONVERSION CHART WHICH MAY BE USED TO CALCULATE LOW AND INBETWEEN GRADES:

X-Men: Wrath of Apocalypse (Feb 1996)

	$Good	$Fine	$N.Mint	£Good	£Fine	£N.Mint
Trade paperback 96pgs, reprints X-Factor #65-68				£0.65	£1.95	£3.25

X-FACTOR ANNUAL
Marvel Comics Group; 1 Oct 1986-present

	$Good	$Fine	$N.Mint	£Good	£Fine	£N.Mint
1 ND	$0.60	$1.80	$3.00	£0.40	£1.20	£2.00
2 ND Adamsesque art by Grindberg	$0.50	$1.50	$2.50	£0.30	£0.90	£1.50
3 ND 64pgs, squarebound, Evolutionary War; Louise Simonson script	$0.50	$1.50	$2.50	£0.30	£0.90	£1.50
4 ND 64pgs, squarebound, Atlantis Attacks part 10, John Byrne art	$0.50	$1.50	$2.50	£0.30	£0.90	£1.50
5 ND 64pgs, squarebound, Days of Future Present part 2, continued in New Mutants Annual #6	$0.50	$1.50	$2.50	£0.30	£0.90	£1.50
6 ND 64pgs, squarebound, King of Pain part 4 (conclusion), Cable appears	$0.50	$1.50	$2.50	£0.30	£0.90	£1.50
7 ND 64pgs, squarebound, Shattershot part 3, continued in X-Force Annual #1	$0.50	$1.50	$2.50	£0.30	£0.90	£1.50
8 ND 64pgs, squarebound, pre-bagged with trading card introducing Charon	$0.60	$1.80	$3.00	£0.40	£1.20	£2.00
9 ND 64pgs, Professor X vs. Haven	$0.60	$1.80	$3.00	£0.40	£1.20	£2.00
Title Value:	$4.80	$14.40	$24.00	£3.00	£9.00	£15.00

X-FACTOR: PRISONER OF LOVE
Marvel Comics Group,OS; 1 Sep 1990

	$Good	$Fine	$N.Mint	£Good	£Fine	£N.Mint
1 ND 48pgs, The Beast in love by Jim Starlin/Jackson Guice	$0.90	$2.70	$4.50	£0.60	£1.80	£3.00
Title Value:	$0.90	$2.70	$4.50	£0.60	£1.80	£3.00

Note: Bookshelf Format

X-FILES
Topps; ½ 1996; 1 Jan 1995-present

	$Good	$Fine	$N.Mint	£Good	£Fine	£N.Mint
½ ND produced in conjunction with Wizard; with certificate	$4.00	$12.00	$20.00	£4.00	£12.00	£20.00
1 ND Stefan Petrucha script and Charlie Adlard art begins; based on hit US (and UK!) TV show	$10.00	$30.00	$50.00	£7.00	£21.00	£35.00
1 2nd printing, ND serial number along top of comic	$1.00	$3.00	$5.00	£1.00	£3.00	£5.00
2 ND	$4.50	$13.50	$22.50	£3.00	£9.00	£15.00
2 2nd printing, ND serial number along top of comic	$0.60	$1.80	$3.00	£0.60	£1.80	£3.00
3 ND	$3.00	$9.00	$15.00	£1.50	£4.50	£7.50
3 2nd printing, ND serial number along top of comic	$0.60	$1.80	$3.00	£0.40	£1.20	£2.00
4 ND Direct Market Edition	$1.80	$5.25	$9.00	£1.20	£3.60	£6.00
4 ND Newstand Edition	$1.00	$3.00	$5.00	£1.00	£3.00	£5.00
5 ND	$1.20	$3.60	$6.00	£0.80	£2.40	£4.00
6 ND $2.95 cover begins	$1.00	$3.00	$5.00	£0.60	£1.80	£3.00
7-8 ND	$0.80	$2.40	$4.00	£0.50	£1.50	£2.50
9 ND	$0.60	$1.80	$3.00	£0.40	£1.20	£2.00
10-11 ND Feelings of Unreality story; bi-weekly	$0.60	$1.80	$3.00	£0.40	£1.20	£2.00
12 ND Feelings of Unreality story	$0.60	$1.80	$3.00	£0.40	£1.20	£2.00
13 ND	$0.60	$1.80	$3.00	£0.40	£1.20	£2.00
Title Value:	$33.30	$99.75	$166.50	£24.10	£72.30	£120.50

X-Files (Jul 1995)

	$Good	$Fine	$N.Mint	£Good	£Fine	£N.Mint
Trade paperback reprints issues #1-6				£2.70	£8.10	£13.50

X-FILES ANNUAL
Topps; 1 Aug 1995-present

	$Good	$Fine	$N.Mint	£Good	£Fine	£N.Mint
1 ND 48pgs, Stefan Petrucha script, Charlie Adlard art	$0.90	$2.70	$4.50	£0.60	£1.80	£3.00
Title Value:	$0.90	$2.70	$4.50	£0.60	£1.80	£3.00

X-FILES COMICS DIGEST, THE
Topps,Digest; 1 Sep 1995-present

	$Good	$Fine	$N.Mint	£Good	£Fine	£N.Mint
1 ND 96pgs, Stefan Petrucha script, Charlie Adlard art; painted covers by Miran Kim begin	$0.70	$2.10	$3.50	£0.50	£1.50	£2.50
1 ND 96pgs, variant cover	$1.50	$4.50	$7.50	£1.50	£4.50	£7.50
Title Value:	$2.20	$6.60	$11.00	£2.00	£6.00	£10.00

X-FILES SPECIAL EDITION
Topps,OS; 1 Jun 1995

	$Good	$Fine	$N.Mint	£Good	£Fine	£N.Mint
1 ND reprints issues #1-3, new cover by Miran Kim	$1.20	$3.60	$6.00	£0.70	£2.10	£3.50
Title Value:	$1.20	$3.60	$6.00	£0.70	£2.10	£3.50

X-FORCE
Marvel Comics Group; 1 Aug 1991-43 Feb 1995; 44 Jul 1995-present
(see Gambit & The X-Ternals)

	$Good	$Fine	$N.Mint	£Good	£Fine	£N.Mint
1 LD in the U.K. pre-bagged with one of the following trading cards: Cable, Shatterstar, Deadpool, Gideon/Sunspot, X-Force Team, Rob Liefeld art. (Note: all issues with trading cards sell for approximately the same price. Cable card is no longer special)	$0.60	$1.80	$3.00	£0.40	£1.20	£2.00
1 2nd printing, LD in the U.K. Aug 1991 - gold metallic ink cover	$0.40	$1.20	$2.00	£0.25	£0.75	£1.25
2 LD in the U.K. Juggernaut appears, Rob Liefeld art	$0.50	$1.50	$2.50	£0.30	£0.90	£1.50
3 LD in the U.K. Spiderman and Juggernaut appear, Rob Liefeld art	$0.40	$1.20	$2.00	£0.25	£0.75	£1.25
4 LD in the U.K. continued from Spiderman #16, entire issue printed sideways, Rob Liefeld art	$0.40	$1.20	$2.00	£0.25	£0.75	£1.25
5 LD in the U.K. Brotherhood of Evil Mutants appear, Rob Liefeld art	$0.40	$1.20	$2.00	£0.25	£0.75	£1.25
6 LD in the U.K. New Brotherhood of Evil Mutants appear, Rob Liefeld art	$0.30	$0.90	$1.50	£0.20	£0.60	£1.00
7 LD in the U.K. $1.25 cover begins, Rob Liefeld art	$0.30	$0.90	$1.50	£0.20	£0.60	£1.00
8 LD in the U.K. Rob Liefeld art on framing sequence, Mike Mignola art; part Cable origin	$0.30	$0.90	$1.50	£0.20	£0.60	£1.00
9-14 LD in the U.K. Rob Liefeld art	$0.30	$0.90	$1.50	£0.20	£0.60	£1.00
15 LD in the U.K. Cable leaves X-Force, Greg Capullo art begins	$0.30	$0.90	$1.50	£0.20	£0.60	£1.00
16 LD in the U.K. X-Cutioner's Song part 4, pre-bagged with trading card, continued in Uncanny X-Men #295	$0.30	$0.90	$1.50	£0.20	£0.60	£1.00
17 LD in the U.K. X-Cutioner's Song part 8, pre-bagged with trading card, continued in Uncanny X-Men #296	$0.30	$0.90	$1.50	£0.20	£0.60	£1.00
18 LD in the U.K. X-Cutioner's Song part 12 (conclusion), pre-bagged with trading card	$0.30	$0.90	$1.50	£0.20	£0.60	£1.00
19-20 LD in the U.K.	$0.30	$0.90	$1.50	£0.20	£0.60	£1.00
21 LD in the U.K. X-Force vs. Iron Man	$0.30	$0.90	$1.50	£0.20	£0.60	£1.00
22-24 LD in the U.K.	$0.30	$0.90	$1.50	£0.20	£0.60	£1.00
25 LD in the U.K. 48pgs, wraparound cover with Cable hologram	$0.80	$2.40	$4.00	£0.50	£1.50	£2.50
26-30 LD in the U.K.	$0.30	$0.90	$1.50	£0.20	£0.60	£1.00
31	$0.30	$0.90	$1.50	£0.15	£0.45	£0.75
32 continued in New Warriors #45	$0.30	$0.90	$1.50	£0.15	£0.45	£0.75
33 continued in New Warriors #46	$0.30	$0.90	$1.50	£0.15	£0.45	£0.75
34 with free Spiderman and his Deadly Foes card sheet	$0.30	$0.90	$1.50	£0.15	£0.45	£0.75
35-37	$0.30	$0.90	$1.50	£0.15	£0.45	£0.75
38 ND Deluxe Edition - foil stamped cover; leads into the creation of Generation X	$0.60	$1.80	$3.00	£0.40	£1.20	£2.00
38 Regular Edition	$0.40	$1.20	$2.00	£0.25	£0.75	£1.25
39-40	$0.30	$0.90	$1.50	£0.20	£0.60	£1.00
40 ND Deluxe Edition - printed on glossy stock paper	$0.40	$1.20	$2.00	£0.25	£0.75	£1.25
41	$0.30	$0.90	$1.50	£0.20	£0.60	£1.00
41 ND Deluxe Edition - printed on glossy stock paper	$0.40	$1.20	$2.00	£0.25	£0.75	£1.25
42	$0.30	$0.90	$1.50	£0.20	£0.60	£1.00
42 ND Deluxe Edition - printed on glossy stock paper	$0.40	$1.20	$2.00	£0.25	£0.75	£1.25
43	$0.30	$0.90	$1.50	£0.20	£0.60	£1.00
43 ND Deluxe Edition - printed on glossy stock paper plus bound-in Fleer trading card; see Gambit & The X-Ternals #1	$0.40	$1.20	$2.00	£0.25	£0.75	£1.25
44 continued from X-Men: Prime; Jeph Loeb script, Adam Pollina art	$0.40	$1.20	$2.00	£0.25	£0.75	£1.25
45	$0.40	$1.20	$2.00	£0.25	£0.75	£1.25
46 bi-weekly	$0.40	$1.20	$2.00	£0.25	£0.75	£1.25
47 Sabretooth appears, bi-weekly	$0.40	$1.20	$2.00	£0.25	£0.75	£1.25
48-49	$0.40	$1.20	$2.00	£0.25	£0.75	£1.25
50 48pgs, double gatefold prismatic foil cover	$0.80	$2.40	$4.00	£0.50	£1.50	£2.50
50 news-stand edition without cover enhancement	$0.60	$1.80	$3.00	£0.40	£1.20	£2.00
50 Variant cover, ND Rob Liefeld cover art; double gatefold prismatic foil cover	$1.00	$3.00	$5.00	£0.70	£2.10	£3.50
51-52	$0.40	$1.20	$2.00	£0.25	£0.75	£1.25
Title Value:	$22.50	$67.50	$112.50	£14.30	£42.90	£71.50

Note: The vast majority of distributed copies of issue #1 (possibly all issues) are defaced by a large white bar code sticker on the bag added by the distributor at a later date and are notoriously difficult to remove. Direct Sales issues do not have this.

Note also: black on white and white on black logos available on issue #1 have been reported but subject to confirmation.

X-Force & Spiderman: Sabotage
Trade paperback (Jan 1993)
64pgs, reprints X-Force #4, Spiderman #16

	$Good	$Fine	$N.Mint	£Good	£Fine	£N.Mint
printed-sideways issues				£0.85	£2.55	£4.25

X-FORCE ANNUAL
Marvel Comics Group; 1 May 1992-present

	$Good	$Fine	$N.Mint	£Good	£Fine	£N.Mint
1 ND Shattershot part 4 (conclusion), continued from X-Factor Annual #7	$0.50	$1.50	$2.50	£0.30	£0.90	£1.50
2 ND 64pgs, pre-bagged with trading card, 1st appearance X-treme	$0.60	$1.80	$3.00	£0.40	£1.20	£2.00
3 ND 64pgs	$0.60	$1.80	$3.00	£0.40	£1.20	£2.00
Title Value:	$1.70	$5.10	$8.50	£1.10	£3.30	£5.50

X-MAN
Marvel Comics Group; 1 Mar 1995-present

	$Good	$Fine	$N.Mint	£Good	£Fine	£N.Mint
1 ND Jeph Loeb script, Steve Skroce art	$1.00	$3.00	$5.00	£0.60	£1.80	£3.00
1 2nd printing ND	$0.50	$1.50	$2.50	£0.30	£0.90	£1.50
2-3 ND Jeph Loeb script, Steve Skroce art	$0.60	$1.80	$3.00	£0.40	£1.20	£2.00
4 ND Jeph Loeb script, Steve Skroce art; continued in X-Men: Omega	$0.50	$1.50	$2.50	£0.30	£0.90	£1.50

MINT = 100% / NEAR MINT (inc. +/-) = 90-99% / VERY FINE (inc. +/-) = 75-89% / FINE (inc. +/-) = 55-74%
VERY GOOD (inc. +/-) = 35-54% / GOOD (inc. +/-) = 15-34% / FAIR = 5-14% / POOR = 1-4%

649

Item	$Good	$Fine	$N.Mint	£Good	£Fine	£N.Mint
5 ND the character from the "After Xavier" alternate worlds storyline crosses over into the Marvel Universe						
	$0.40	$1.20	$2.00	£0.25	£0.75	£1.25
6-11 ND	$0.40	$1.20	$2.00	£0.25	£0.75	£1.25
12 ND Excalibur guest-star						
	$0.40	$1.20	$2.00	£0.25	£0.75	£1.25
13 ND	$0.40	$1.20	$2.00	£0.25	£0.75	£1.25
Title Value:	$6.80	$20.40	$34.00	£4.25	£12.75	£21.25

Note: this title temporarily replaced Cable during the "Age of Apocalypse" storyline

The Ultimate X-Man (Jul 1995)
96pgs, Bookshelf Edition

Item	$Good	$Fine	$N.Mint	£Good	£Fine	£N.Mint
collects issues #1-4 with etched gold cover				£1.20	£3.60	£6.00

X-MEN

Marvel Comics Group; 1 Oct 1991-41 Feb 1995; 42 Jul 1995-present
(see The Mutants: The Amazing X-Men)

Item	$Good	$Fine	$N.Mint	£Good	£Fine	£N.Mint
1 cover "A" featuring Storm, Jim Lee art						
	$0.50	$1.50	$2.50	£0.30	£0.90	£1.50
1 cover "B" featuring Colossus, Jim Lee art						
	$0.50	$1.50	$2.50	£0.30	£0.90	£1.50
1 cover "C" featuring Wolverine, Jim Lee art						
	$0.50	$1.50	$2.50	£0.30	£0.90	£1.50
1 cover "D" featuring Magneto, Jim Lee art						
	$0.50	$1.50	$2.50	£0.30	£0.90	£1.50
1 cover "E" double gatefold featuring all four covers as poster plus all pin-ups, heavier stock paper, Jim Lee art						
	$0.80	$2.40	$4.00	£0.50	£1.50	£2.50
2 Jim Lee art, Magneto story reference ties in with Defenders #16						
	$0.80	$2.40	$4.00	£0.30	£0.90	£1.50
3 Jim Lee art, last Claremont script						
	$0.80	$2.40	$4.00	£0.30	£0.90	£1.50
4 John Byrne script, Jim Lee plot and art, 1st appearance Omega Red						
	$0.80	$2.40	$4.00	£0.30	£0.90	£1.50
5 Longshot returns, John Byrne script, Jim Lee plot and art, 1st appearance Maverick						
	$0.80	$2.40	$4.00	£0.30	£0.90	£1.50
6 Sabretooth appears, Maverick appears						
	$0.60	$1.80	$3.00	£0.30	£0.90	£1.50
7	$0.60	$1.80	$3.00	£0.30	£0.90	£1.50
8 last Jim Lee art, Ghost Rider appears						
	$0.60	$1.80	$3.00	£0.30	£0.90	£1.50
9 X-over with Ghost Rider #26, Wolverine vs. Ghost Rider						
	$0.60	$1.80	$3.00	£0.30	£0.90	£1.50
10 Longshot returns						
	$0.60	$1.80	$3.00	£0.30	£0.90	£1.50
11 Longshot vs. Mojo						
	$0.40	$1.20	$2.00	£0.25	£0.75	£1.25
11 ND scarce in the U.K. silver ink cover variant issued with computer game						
	$3.00	$9.00	$15.00	£1.00	£3.00	£5.00
12-13 Thibert art	$0.40	$1.20	$2.00	£0.25	£0.75	£1.25
14 X-Cutioner's Song part 3, pre-bagged with trading card, continued in X-Force #16						
	$0.40	$1.20	$2.00	£0.25	£0.75	£1.25
15 X-Cutioner's Song part 6, pre-bagged with trading card, continued in X-Force #17						
	$0.40	$1.20	$2.00	£0.25	£0.75	£1.25
16 X-Cutioner's Song part 11, pre-bagged with trading card, continued in X-Force #18						
	$0.40	$1.20	$2.00	£0.25	£0.75	£1.25
17-19 Omega Red appears						
	$0.40	$1.20	$2.00	£0.25	£0.75	£1.25
20	$0.40	$1.20	$2.00	£0.25	£0.75	£1.25
21-24	$0.30	$0.90	$1.50	£0.20	£0.60	£1.00
25 48pgs, hologram cover, Wolverine vs. Magneto						
	$0.90	$2.70	$4.50	£0.60	£1.80	£3.00
25 ND Premium Edition - black and white cover, no date and price, Magneto figure in colour (produced in place of advertised Magneto Gold #0)						
	$4.50	$13.50	$22.50	£3.00	£9.00	£15.00
25 Gold Edition ND	$4.50	$13.50	$22.50	£3.00	£9.00	£15.00
26 Bloodties part 2	$0.30	$0.90	$1.50	£0.20	£0.60	£1.00
27	$0.30	$0.90	$1.50	£0.20	£0.60	£1.00
28-29 Sabretooth appears						
	$0.30	$0.90	$1.50	£0.20	£0.60	£1.00
30 wedding of Scott Summers and Jean Grey; with 3 card insert						
	$0.50	$1.50	$2.50	£0.30	£0.90	£1.50
31	$0.30	$0.90	$1.50	£0.20	£0.60	£1.00
32 with free Spiderman's Amazing Powers card sheet						
	$0.30	$0.90	$1.50	£0.20	£0.60	£1.00
33-35	$0.30	$0.90	$1.50	£0.20	£0.60	£1.00
36 ND Deluxe Edition - foil stamped cover; leads into the creation of Generation X						
	$0.60	$1.80	$3.00	£0.40	£1.20	£2.00
36 Regular Edition						
	$0.40	$1.20	$2.00	£0.25	£0.75	£1.25
37 Andy Kubert art						
	$0.40	$1.20	$2.00	£0.25	£0.75	£1.25
37 ND Deluxe Edition - foil stamped cover						
	$0.60	$1.80	$3.00	£0.40	£1.20	£2.00
38 ND	$0.30	$0.90	$1.50	£0.20	£0.60	£1.00
38 ND Deluxe Edition - printed on glossy stock paper						
	$0.40	$1.20	$2.00	£0.25	£0.75	£1.25
39	$0.30	$0.90	$1.50	£0.20	£0.60	£1.00
39 ND Deluxe Edition - printed on glossy stock paper						
	$0.40	$1.20	$2.00	£0.25	£0.75	£1.25
40	$0.30	$0.90	$1.50	£0.20	£0.60	£1.00
40 ND Deluxe Edition - printed on glossy stock paper						
	$0.40	$1.20	$2.00	£0.25	£0.75	£1.25
41	$0.30	$0.90	$1.50	£0.20	£0.60	£1.00

41 ND Deluxe Edition - printed on glossy stock paper plus bound-in Fleer trading card

Item	$Good	$Fine	$N.Mint	£Good	£Fine	£N.Mint
	$0.40	$1.20	$2.00	£0.25	£0.75	£1.25
42 continued from X-Men: Prime; Fabian Nicieza script and Paul Smith art begins						
	$0.40	$1.20	$2.00	£0.25	£0.75	£1.25
43-44	$0.40	$1.20	$2.00	£0.25	£0.75	£1.25
45 48pgs, Rogue vs. Gambit; double gate-fold prismatic foil cover						
	$0.80	$2.40	$4.00	£0.50	£1.50	£2.50
46	$0.40	$1.20	$2.00	£0.25	£0.75	£1.25
47 Dazzler guest stars						
	$0.40	$1.20	$2.00	£0.25	£0.75	£1.25
48 Sabretooth appears, continued in Sabretooth Special						
	$0.40	$1.20	$2.00	£0.25	£0.75	£1.25
49	$0.40	$1.20	$2.00	£0.25	£0.75	£1.25
50 48pgs	$0.60	$1.80	$3.00	£0.40	£1.20	£2.00
50 ND 48pgs, prismatic foil board cover						
	$0.80	$2.40	$4.00	£0.50	£1.50	£2.50
Title Value:	$40.10	$120.30	$200.50	£23.65	£70.95	£118.25

X-Men/Ghost Rider Trade paperback (Nov 1993)

Item	$Good	$Fine	$N.Mint	£Good	£Fine	£N.Mint
reprints X-Men #8,9 and Ghost Rider #26,27				£0.90	£1.80	£4.50

Magneto Returns (Oct 1995)

Item	£Good	£Fine	£N.Mint
Trade paperback reprints issues #1-7 featuring Jim Lee art	£2.00	£6.00	£10.00

X-Men Milestone (Nov 1995)

Item	£Good	£Fine	£N.Mint
boxed set collecting X-Men #25, Wolverine #75 and Excalibur #71 (all hologram covers), ND	£1.50	£4.50	£7.50

X-Men Collection (Dec 1995)

Item	£Good	£Fine	£N.Mint
boxed set collecting X-Men #27, X-Force #26-28, X-Men Annual #2; ND	£1.00	£3.00	£5.00

X-Men Greatest (Dec 1995)

Item	£Good	£Fine	£N.Mint
boxed set collecting Avengers #368/369, X-Men #26, Avengers West Coast #101 and Uncanny X-Men #307; ND	£1.00	£3.00	£5.00

X-MEN '95

Marvel Comics Group; OS; nn Oct 1995

Item	$Good	$Fine	$N.Mint	£Good	£Fine	£N.Mint
nn ND 64pgs, J.M. DeMatteis script, Terry Dodson art spotlighting Mr. Sinister						
	$0.80	$2.40	$4.00	£0.50	£1.50	£2.50
Title Value:	$0.80	$2.40	$4.00	£0.50	£1.50	£2.50

X-MEN 2099

Marvel Comics Group; 1 Oct 1993-present

Item	$Good	$Fine	$N.Mint	£Good	£Fine	£N.Mint
1 ND blue foil embossed cover, Ron Lim and Adam Kubert art begins						
	$0.40	$1.20	$2.00	£0.25	£0.75	£1.25
1 ND Gold Edition (Jan 1994) - 10 new pages, gold foil cover; limited to 15,000 copies						
	$4.00	$12.00	$20.00	£2.50	£7.50	£12.50
2-7 ND	$0.30	$0.90	$1.50	£0.20	£0.60	£1.00
8 ND with free Spiderman's Amazing Powers card sheet; $1.50 cover begin						
	$0.30	$0.90	$1.50	£0.20	£0.60	£1.00
9-13 ND	$0.30	$0.90	$1.50	£0.20	£0.60	£1.00
14 ND Loki appears						
	$0.30	$0.90	$1.50	£0.20	£0.60	£1.00
15-19 ND	$0.30	$0.90	$1.50	£0.20	£0.60	£1.00
20-22 ND	$0.40	$1.20	$2.00	£0.25	£0.75	£1.25
23-24 ND One Nation Under Doom						
	$0.40	$1.20	$2.00	£0.25	£0.75	£1.25
25 ND 48pgs, One Nation Under Doom						
	$0.50	$1.50	$2.50	£0.30	£0.90	£1.50
25 ND 48pgs, One Nation Under Doom; enhanced cover						
	$0.80	$2.40	$4.00	£0.50	£1.50	£2.50
26 ND One Nation Under Doom						
	$0.40	$1.20	$2.00	£0.25	£0.75	£1.25
27 ND X-Nation, continued from 2099 Apocalypse and Doom 2099 #36						
	$0.40	$1.20	$2.00	£0.25	£0.75	£1.25
28 ND X-Nation, leads into 2099 Genesis						
	$0.40	$1.20	$2.00	£0.25	£0.75	£1.25
29 ND ties into X-Nation						
	$0.40	$1.20	$2.00	£0.25	£0.75	£1.25
30 X-Nation tie-in, continued from Doon 2099 #39						
	$0.40	$1.20	$2.00	£0.25	£0.75	£1.25
Title Value:	$15.10	$45.30	$75.50	£9.65	£28.95	£48.25

X-MEN 2099 SPECIAL

Marvel Comics Group; 1 Oct 1995

Item	$Good	$Fine	$N.Mint	£Good	£Fine	£N.Mint
1 ND 64pgs, painted cover by Brothers Hildebrandt						
	$0.80	$2.40	$4.00	£0.50	£1.50	£2.50
Title Value:	$0.80	$2.40	$4.00	£0.50	£1.50	£2.50

X-MEN 2099: OASIS

Marvel Comics Group; OS; 1 Mar 1996

Item	$Good	$Fine	$N.Mint	£Good	£Fine	£N.Mint
1 ND 48pgs, John Francis Moore script, fully painted art by The Brothers Hildebrandt						
	$1.20	$3.60	$6.00	£0.80	£2.40	£4.00
Title Value:	$1.20	$3.60	$6.00	£0.80	£2.40	£4.00

X-MEN ADVENTURES SEASON II

Marvel Comics Group; 1 Feb 1994-13 Feb 1995
(see X-Men: The Animated Series)

Item	$Good	$Fine	$N.Mint	£Good	£Fine	£N.Mint
1 ND based on the 2nd season of Fox TV's animated series						
	$0.30	$0.90	$1.50	£0.20	£0.60	£1.00
2-13 ND	$0.30	$0.90	$1.50	£0.20	£0.60	£1.00
Title Value:	$3.90	$11.70	$19.50	£2.60	£7.80	£13.00

X-MEN ADVENTURES SEASON III

Marvel Comics Group; 1 Mar 1995-present

Item	$Good	$Fine	$N.Mint	£Good	£Fine	£N.Mint
1-9 ND	$0.30	$0.90	$1.50	£0.20	£0.60	£1.00
10-13 ND The Dark Phoenix Saga						
	$0.30	$0.90	$1.50	£0.20	£0.60	£1.00
Title Value:	$3.90	$11.70	$19.50	£2.60	£7.80	£13.00

X-MEN AND ALPHA FLIGHT

Marvel Comics Group; MS; 1 Jan 1986-2 Feb 1986
(see X-Men Annual #9)

1-2 ND DS, Paul Smith art

	$Good	$Fine	$N.Mint	£Good	£Fine	£N.Mint

Left Column

	$Good	$Fine	$N.Mint	£Good	£Fine	£N.Mint
	$0.60	$1.80	$3.00	£0.40	£1.20	£2.00
Title Value:	$1.20	$3.60	$6.00	£0.80	£2.40	£4.00

X-MEN AND THE MICRONAUTS, THE
Marvel Comics Group,MS; 1 Jan 1984-4 Apr 1984

	$Good	$Fine	$N.Mint	£Good	£Fine	£N.Mint
1-3 ND Guice art	$0.50	$1.50	$2.50	£0.30	£0.90	£1.50
4 ND	$0.50	$1.50	$2.50	£0.30	£0.90	£1.50
Title Value:	$2.00	$6.00	$10.00	£1.20	£3.60	£6.00

X-MEN ANNIVERSARY MAGAZINE
Marvel Comics Group,Magazine OS; 1 Sep 1993
1 ND 48pgs, cover inter-locks with Avengers Anniversary Magazine

	$Good	$Fine	$N.Mint	£Good	£Fine	£N.Mint
	$0.80	$2.40	$4.00	£0.50	£1.50	£2.50
Title Value:	$0.80	$2.40	$4.00	£0.50	£1.50	£2.50

X-MEN ANNUAL
Marvel Comics Group; 1 May 1992-present

1 ND Shattershot part 1, continued in Uncanny X-Men Annual #16, Jim Lee cover and art layouts

	$Good	$Fine	$N.Mint	£Good	£Fine	£N.Mint
	$0.50	$1.50	$2.50	£0.30	£0.90	£1.50

2 ND 64pgs, pre-bagged with trading card, 1st appearance Empyrean

	$Good	$Fine	$N.Mint	£Good	£Fine	£N.Mint
	$0.60	$1.80	$3.00	£0.40	£1.20	£2.00
3 ND 64pgs	$0.60	$1.80	$3.00	£0.40	£1.20	£2.00
Title Value:	$1.70	$5.10	$8.50	£1.10	£3.30	£5.50

X-MEN ARCHIVES: CAPTAIN BRITAIN
Marvel Comics Group,MS; 1 Jul 1995-7 Jan 1996

1 ND 48pgs, reprints; Dave Thorpe script, Alan Davis art; new Alan Davis covers

	$Good	$Fine	$N.Mint	£Good	£Fine	£N.Mint
	$1.00	$3.00	$5.00	£0.70	£2.10	£3.50

2 ND 48pgs, reprints; Dave Thorpe script, Alan Davis art; new Alan Davis covers

	$Good	$Fine	$N.Mint	£Good	£Fine	£N.Mint
	$0.60	$1.80	$3.00	£0.40	£1.20	£2.00

3-7 ND 48pgs, reprints; Dave Thorpe script, Alan Davis art; new Alan Davis covers

	$Good	$Fine	$N.Mint	£Good	£Fine	£N.Mint
	$0.50	$1.50	$2.50	£0.30	£0.90	£1.50
Title Value:	$4.10	$12.30	$20.50	£2.60	£7.80	£13.00

X-MEN ASHCAN
Marvel Comics Group,OS; nn Jan 1995
nn ND previews the major title changes for all the X-Men books for 1995

	$Good	$Fine	$N.Mint	£Good	£Fine	£N.Mint
	$0.15	$0.45	$0.75	£0.10	£0.30	£0.50
Title Value:	$0.15	$0.45	$0.75	£0.10	£0.30	£0.50

X-MEN ASHCAN EDITION
Marvel Comics Group,OS; nn Aug 1994
nn ND 16pgs, black and white, shorter history of the X-Men

	$Good	$Fine	$N.Mint	£Good	£Fine	£N.Mint
	$0.25	$0.75	$1.25	£0.15	£0.45	£0.75
Title Value:	$0.25	$0.75	$1.25	£0.15	£0.45	£0.75

X-MEN AT THE STATE FAIR OF TEXAS
Marvel Comics Group; nn Oct 1983
nn ND very scarce in the U.K. Dallas Times Herald Giveaway, paper cover

	$Good	$Fine	$N.Mint	£Good	£Fine	£N.Mint
	$4.00	$12.00	$20.00	£5.00	£15.00	£25.00
Title Value:	$4.00	$12.00	$20.00	£5.00	£15.00	£25.00

X-MEN CHRONICLES
Fantaco; 1 Jul 1981
1 ND story synopses and character details on early X-Men issue; intended as an on-going series

	$Good	$Fine	$N.Mint	£Good	£Fine	£N.Mint
	$0.60	$1.80	$3.00	£0.40	£1.20	£2.00
Title Value:	$0.60	$1.80	$3.00	£0.40	£1.20	£2.00

X-MEN CHRONICLES (2ND SERIES)
Marvel Comics Group; 1 Mar 1995-2 Apr 1995
1 ND Howard Mackie script, Ian Churchill art begins

	$Good	$Fine	$N.Mint	£Good	£Fine	£N.Mint
	$0.80	$2.40	$4.00	£0.50	£1.50	£2.50
2 ND	$0.80	$2.40	$4.00	£0.50	£1.50	£2.50
Title Value:	$1.60	$4.80	$8.00	£1.00	£3.00	£5.00

Note: this title temporarily replaced X-Men Unlimited during the "Age of Apocalypse" storyline

X-MEN CLASSICS
Marvel Comics Group; 1 Dec 1983-3 Feb 1984

1-3 ND Neal Adams reprints, Baxter paper

	$Good	$Fine	$N.Mint	£Good	£Fine	£N.Mint
	$1.00	$3.00	$5.00	£0.70	£2.10	£3.50
Title Value:	$3.00	$9.00	$15.00	£2.10	£6.30	£10.50

X-MEN FIRSTS
Marvel Comics Group,OS; 1 Feb 1996
1 ND 96pgs, reprints 1st appearances of Wolverine, Rogue, Gambit and Mr. Sinister

	$Good	$Fine	$N.Mint	£Good	£Fine	£N.Mint
	$1.00	$3.00	$5.00	£0.70	£2.10	£3.50
Title Value:	$1.00	$3.00	$5.00	£0.70	£2.10	£3.50

X-MEN GIANT SIZE
Marvel Comics Group; 1 Summer 1975-2 Nov 1975
1 ND 64pgs, 1st appearance of the new X-Men, 2nd full appearance Wolverine; back-up reprints X-Men #43, #47, #57. Gil Kane cover

	$Good	$Fine	$N.Mint	£Good	£Fine	£N.Mint
	$44.00	$130.00	$350.00	£28.00	£82.50	£225.00

1 ND Marvel Milestone Edition (Oct 1991), reprints original issue with ads, silver border around cover

	$Good	$Fine	$N.Mint	£Good	£Fine	£N.Mint
	$0.90	$2.70	$4.50	£0.60	£1.80	£3.00

2 ND 64pgs, all Neal Adams reprints from X-Men #57-59

	$Good	$Fine	$N.Mint	£Good	£Fine	£N.Mint
	$6.50	$20.00	$40.00	£4.15	£12.50	£25.00
Title Value:	$51.40	$152.70	$394.50	£32.75	£96.80	£253.00

X-MEN RARITIES
Marvel Comics Group,OS; nn Oct 1995
nn ND 64pgs, reprints "The Boy Who Could Fly" from Amazing Adult Fantasy #14 (1st reference to mutants), Classic X-Men #1 and Marvel Fanfare #40 to celebrate 20th anniversary of the new X-Men

	$Good	$Fine	$N.Mint	£Good	£Fine	£N.Mint
	$1.20	$3.60	$6.00	£0.80	£2.40	£4.00
Title Value:	$1.20	$3.60	$6.00	£0.80	£2.40	£4.00

X-MEN SPECIAL EDITION
Marvel Comics Group; 1 Feb 1983
1 ND scarce in the U.K. reprints Giant Size #1 plus one new Kitty Pryde story, Baxter paper

	$Good	$Fine	$N.Mint	£Good	£Fine	£N.Mint
	$2.00	$6.00	$10.00	£1.50	£4.50	£7.50
Title Value:	$2.00	$6.00	$10.00	£1.50	£4.50	£7.50

X-MEN SPECTACULAR
Marvel Comics Group,MS; 1-4 Jan 1995

1-4 ND reprints from New Mutants #26-28 and X-Men #161; weekly issues

	$Good	$Fine	$N.Mint	£Good	£Fine	£N.Mint
	$0.50	$1.50	$2.50	£0.30	£0.90	£1.50
Title Value:	$2.00	$6.00	$10.00	£1.20	£3.60	£6.00

X-MEN SPOTLIGHT: THE STARJAMMERS
Marvel Comics Group,MS; 1 May 1990-2 Jun 1990
1 ND 48pgs, squarebound; Dave Cockrum art begins

	$Good	$Fine	$N.Mint	£Good	£Fine	£N.Mint
	$0.90	$2.70	$4.50	£0.60	£1.80	£3.00

2 ND 48pgs, squarebound; Excalibur/X-Factor appear

	$Good	$Fine	$N.Mint	£Good	£Fine	£N.Mint
	$0.90	$2.70	$4.50	£0.60	£1.80	£3.00
Title Value:	$1.80	$5.40	$9.00	£1.20	£3.60	£6.00

X-MEN SURVIVAL GUIDE TO THE MANSION
Marvel Comics Group,OS; 1 Aug 1993
1 ND scarce in the U.K. 48pgs, spiral-bound technical guide to the X-Men's mansion, Andy Kubert cover

	$Good	$Fine	$N.Mint	£Good	£Fine	£N.Mint
	$1.50	$4.50	$7.50	£1.50	£4.50	£7.50
Title Value:	$1.50	$4.50	$7.50	£1.50	£4.50	£7.50

X-MEN UNLIMITED
Marvel Comics Group; 1 Jun 1993-7 Dec 1994; 8 Oct 1995-present
(see X-Men Chronicles 2nd series)
1 ND 64pgs, high quality paper; Scott Lobdell script, Bachalo and Panosian art begins

	$Good	$Fine	$N.Mint	£Good	£Fine	£N.Mint
	$1.20	$3.60	$6.00	£0.70	£2.10	£3.50
2 ND 64pgs	$1.00	$3.00	$5.00	£0.60	£1.80	£3.00

3 ND 64pgs, Sabretooth appears

	$Good	$Fine	$N.Mint	£Good	£Fine	£N.Mint
	$1.20	$3.60	$6.00	£0.70	£2.10	£3.50
4 ND 64pgs	$0.80	$2.40	$4.00	£0.50	£1.50	£2.50

5 ND 64pgs, Liam Sharp art

	$Good	$Fine	$N.Mint	£Good	£Fine	£N.Mint
	$0.80	$2.40	$4.00	£0.50	£1.50	£2.50

6 ND 64pgs, Paul Smith art

	$Good	$Fine	$N.Mint	£Good	£Fine	£N.Mint
	$0.80	$2.40	$4.00	£0.50	£1.50	£2.50

7 ND 64pgs, John Romita Jnr. art

	$Good	$Fine	$N.Mint	£Good	£Fine	£N.Mint
	$0.80	$2.40	$4.00	£0.50	£1.50	£2.50

8 ND 64pgs, Gambit, Ice Man, Professor X and Jean Grey appear; Tom Grummett and Dan Lawlis art

	$Good	$Fine	$N.Mint	£Good	£Fine	£N.Mint
	$0.80	$2.40	$4.00	£0.50	£1.50	£2.50

9 ND Wolverine and Psylocke appear

	$Good	$Fine	$N.Mint	£Good	£Fine	£N.Mint
	$0.80	$2.40	$4.00	£0.50	£1.50	£2.50
10 ND	$0.80	$2.40	$4.00	£0.50	£1.50	£2.50
Title Value:	$9.00	$27.00	$45.00	£5.50	£16.50	£27.50

X-MEN VISIONAIRES: ART OF ANDY & ADAM KUBERT
Marvel Comics Group,OS; nn Dec 1995
nn ND 96pgs, four stories collected into one trade paperback

	$Good	$Fine	$N.Mint	£Good	£Fine	£N.Mint
	$1.80	$5.25	$9.00	£1.20	£3.60	£6.00
Title Value:	$1.80	$5.25	$9.00	£1.20	£3.60	£6.00

X-MEN VS. DRACULA
Marvel Comics Group,OS; 1 Dec 1993
1 ND 48pgs, reprints X-Men Annual #6, new cover by Chris Sprouse/Terry Austin

	$Good	$Fine	$N.Mint	£Good	£Fine	£N.Mint
	$0.40	$1.20	$2.00	£0.25	£0.75	£1.25
Title Value:	$0.40	$1.20	$2.00	£0.25	£0.75	£1.25

X-MEN VS. THE AVENGERS
Marvel Comics Group,MS; 1 Apr 1987-4 Jul 1987

	$Good	$Fine	$N.Mint	£Good	£Fine	£N.Mint
1 ND	$0.60	$1.80	$3.00	£0.40	£1.20	£2.00
2-4 ND	$0.50	$1.50	$2.50	£0.30	£0.90	£1.50
Title Value:	$2.10	$6.30	$10.50	£1.30	£3.90	£6.50

X-MEN X-PLANATIONS
As part of a storyline called "The Age of Apocalypse", all the X-titles changed, causing some confusion for collectors and retailers alike. The basis of the change came about in X-Men: Alpha, which told of Professor Xavier's mutant son, Legion, going back in time and murdering him. Thus the X-Men were never formed and all the familiar X-titles ceased to exist for the four month duration of the story, culminating in X-Men: Omega. Below is a list of the pre X-Men: Alpha titles and their changes.

CABLE becomes **X-MAN**
EXCALIBUR becomes **X-CALIBRE**
GENERATION X becomes **THE MUTANTS: GENERATION NEXT**
UNCANNY X-MEN becomes **THE MUTANTS: THE ASTONISHING X-MEN**
WOLVERINE becomes **WEAPON X**
X-FACTOR becomes **FACTOR X**
X-FORCE becomes **GAMBIT & THE X-TERNALS**
X-MEN becomes **THE MUTANTS: THE AMAZING X-MEN**
X-MEN UNLIMITED becomes **X-MEN CHRONICLES**

X-MEN, THE OFFICIAL MARVEL INDEX
Marvel Comics Group,MS; 1 May 1987-7 Jul 1988
(see also The X-Men Chronicles)
1 ND 48pgs, squarebound; information and colour cover reproductions X-Men #1-#23

	$Good	$Fine	$N.Mint	£Good	£Fine	£N.Mint
	$0.60	$1.80	$3.00	£0.40	£1.20	£2.00

2 ND 48pgs, squarebound; information and colour cover reproductions X-Men #24-#46, new Simonson cover

	$Good	$Fine	$N.Mint	£Good	£Fine	£N.Mint
	$0.60	$1.80	$3.00	£0.40	£1.20	£2.00

3 ND 48pgs, squarebound; information and colour cover reproductions X-Men #47-#66 plus Ka-Zar #2,#3 and Marvel Tales #30 (Angel appearances)

	$Good	$Fine	$N.Mint	£Good	£Fine	£N.Mint
	$0.60	$1.80	$3.00	£0.40	£1.20	£2.00

4 ND 48pgs, squarebound; information/colour cover repros X-Men #67-#96, Giant Size X-Men #1,#2, Annuals #1,#2, Amazing Adventures #11-#17, X-Men Classics and Classic X-Men #1-#3, Hulk vs. Wolverine #1

	$Good	$Fine	$N.Mint	£Good	£Fine	£N.Mint
	$0.60	$1.80	$3.00	£0.40	£1.20	£2.00

5 ND 48pgs, squarebound; information and colour cover reproductions X-Men #97-#108 and Classic X-Men #4-#14

	$Good	$Fine	$N.Mint	£Good	£Fine	£N.Mint
	$0.60	$1.80	$3.00	£0.40	£1.20	£2.00

6 ND 48pgs, squarebound; information and colour cover repros X-Men #109-#124, Classic X-Men #15-#19 and Marvel Treasury Edition #26

	$Good	$Fine	$N.Mint	£Good	£Fine	£N.Mint
	$0.60	$1.80	$3.00	£0.40	£1.20	£2.00

7 ND scarce in the U.K. 48pgs, squarebound; information and colour cover repros X-Men #125-#138, Amazing Adventures (3rd) #1-#14, Classic X-Men #20,#21, Marvel Treasury #27, Bizarre Adventures #27

	$Good	$Fine	$N.Mint	£Good	£Fine	£N.Mint
	$0.60	$1.80	$3.00	£0.50	£1.50	£2.50
Title Value:	$4.20	$12.60	$21.00	£2.90	£8.70	£14.50

Note: Volume 4 in Official Marvel Index series of 5.

X-MEN, THE OFFICIAL MARVEL INDEX
Marvel Comics Group,MS; 1 Apr 1994-5 Aug 1994
1 ND information and indexes on X-Men [1st Series] #1-51

Description	$Good	$Fine	$N.Mint	£Good	£Fine	£N.Mint
	$0.40	$1.20	$2.00	£0.25	£0.75	£1.25
2 ND information and indexes on issues #52-122						
	$0.40	$1.20	$2.00	£0.25	£0.75	£1.25
3 ND information and indexes on issues #123-177						
	$0.40	$1.20	$2.00	£0.25	£0.75	£1.25
4 ND information and indexes on issues #178-234						
	$0.40	$1.20	$2.00	£0.25	£0.75	£1.25
5 ND information and indexes on issues #235-287						
	$0.40	$1.20	$2.00	£0.25	£0.75	£1.25
Title Value:	$2.00	$6.00	$10.00	£1.25	£3.75	£6.25

X-MEN, THE UNCANNY

Marvel Comics Group; 1 Sep 1963-66 Mar 1970; 67 Dec 1970-93 Apr 1975; 94 Aug 1975-321 Feb 1995; 322 Jul 1995-present
(see The Mutants: The Astonishing X-Men) (title prefixed with "The Uncanny..." with issue #142)
(see Amazing Adventures, Bizarre Adventures 27, Classic X-Men, Heroes for Hope, Kitty Pryde, Marvel and DC Present, Marvel Fanfare, Marvel Graphic Novel, Marvel Team-Up, Marvel Triple Action, Nightcrawler, Official Marvel Index to..., Special Edition)

Description	$Good	$Fine	$N.Mint	£Good	£Fine	£N.Mint
1 origin and 1st appearance of the X-Men (Angel, Beast, Cyclops, Iceman, Marvel Girl), 1st appearance Magneto						
	$510.00	$1525.00	$4600.00	£305.00	£910.00	£2750.00
[Scarce in high grade - Very Fine+ or better]						
1 ND Marvel Milestone Edition (Sep 1991), reprints original issue with ads, silver border around cover						
	$0.60	$1.80	$3.00	£0.40	£1.20	£2.00
2 1st appearance The Vanisher						
	$165.00	$500.00	$1350.00	£100.00	£300.00	£800.00
3 (Jan 1964), 1st appearance The Blob						
	$77.50	$230.00	$625.00	£47.00	£140.00	£375.00
4 1st appearance of Quicksilver and the Scarlet Witch, 1st Brotherhood of Evil Mutants and 2nd appearance Magneto						
	$67.50	$205.00	$550.00	£44.00	£130.00	£350.00
5 less common in the U.K. 3rd appearance Magneto						
	$50.00	$150.00	$400.00	£33.00	£97.50	£265.00
6 scarce in the U.K. Sub-Mariner appears						
	$34.00	$100.00	$275.00	£22.50	£67.50	£180.00
7 scarce in the U.K. 1st appearance Cerebro, Magneto appears						
	$31.00	$92.50	$250.00	£21.50	£65.00	£175.00
8 rare in the U.K. 1st appearance Unus the untouchable						
	$31.00	$92.50	$250.00	£25.00	£75.00	£200.00
9 scarce in the U.K. (Jan 1965), Avengers X-over, 1st appearance Lucifer						
	$31.00	$92.50	$250.00	£21.50	£65.00	£175.00
9 ND Marvel Milestone Edition (Oct 1993)						
	$0.60	$1.80	$3.00	£0.40	£1.20	£2.00
10 1st Silver Age appearance Ka-Zar (unusually common in the U.K.!)						
	$32.00	$95.00	$225.00	£17.50	£52.50	£125.00
11 less common in the U.K. 1st appearance The Stranger						
	$25.00	$75.00	$200.00	£16.50	£50.00	£135.00
12 origin Professor X, origin and 1st appearance Juggernaut						
	$42.00	$125.00	$295.00	£20.00	£60.00	£140.00
13 Human Torch X-over, 1st full appearance Juggernaut						
	$25.00	$75.00	$200.00	£13.50	£41.00	£110.00
14 1st appearance Sentinels, 1st monthly issue						
	$28.00	$82.50	$225.00	£13.50	£41.00	£110.00
15 2nd appearance Sentinels, origin The Beast; last Silver Age issue indicia-dated December 1965						
	$29.00	$85.00	$200.00	£15.50	£47.00	£110.00
16 (Jan 1966), 3rd appearance Sentinels						
	$12.50	$38.00	$100.00	£6.75	£20.50	£55.00
17-18 Magneto appears						
	$12.50	$38.00	$100.00	£6.75	£18.50	£50.00
19 1st appearance Mimic (see Incredible Hulk #161)						
	$12.50	$38.00	$100.00	£6.75	£20.50	£55.00
20 explains how Professor X was crippled						
	$12.50	$38.00	$100.00	£6.25	£18.50	£50.00
21 Lucifer appears						
	$10.50	$32.00	$75.00	£5.50	£17.00	£40.00
22 Count Nefaria appears						
	$10.50	$32.00	$75.00	£5.50	£17.00	£40.00
23 Porcupine and Scarecrow appear						
	$10.50	$32.00	$75.00	£5.50	£17.00	£40.00
24 1st appearance The Locust						
	$10.50	$32.00	$75.00	£5.50	£17.00	£40.00
25-26 scarce in the U.K.						
	$10.50	$32.00	$75.00	£6.00	£18.00	£42.50
27 Spiderman appears						
	$10.50	$32.00	$75.00	£5.50	£17.00	£40.00
28 (Jan 1967), 1st appearance Banshee						
	$17.00	$50.00	$120.00	£7.00	£21.00	£50.00
28 ND Marvel Milestone Edition (Nov 1994) - metallic ink cover						
	$0.60	$1.80	$3.00	£0.40	£1.20	£2.00
29 Mimic appears						
	$10.50	$32.00	$75.00	£5.00	£15.00	£35.00
30						
	$10.50	$32.00	$75.00	£5.00	£15.00	£35.00
31 1st appearance Cobalt Man						
	$7.75	$23.50	$55.00	£3.90	£11.50	£27.50
32 Juggernaut appears						
	$7.75	$23.50	$55.00	£3.90	£11.50	£27.50
33 Dr. Strange appears						
	$8.50	$26.00	$60.00	£4.25	£12.50	£30.00
34						
	$7.75	$23.50	$55.00	£3.90	£11.50	£27.50
35 Spiderman appears						
	$12.50	$39.00	$90.00	£5.50	£17.00	£40.00
36 1st appearance Mekano						
	$7.75	$23.50	$55.00	£3.90	£11.50	£27.50
37						
	$7.75	$23.50	$55.00	£3.90	£11.50	£27.50
38 X-Men origin feature begins (ends #57)						
	$10.00	$30.00	$70.00	£4.60	£13.50	£32.50
39 new costumes (3rd)						
	$7.75	$23.50	$55.00	£3.90	£11.50	£27.50
40 (Jan 1968)						
	$7.75	$23.50	$55.00	£3.90	£11.50	£27.50
41						
	$7.00	$21.00	$50.00	£3.55	£10.50	£25.00
42 death of Professor X (later revealed as Changeling disguised as Professor X)						
	$7.00	$21.00	$50.00	£3.55	£10.50	£25.00
43						
	$7.00	$21.00	$50.00	£3.55	£10.50	£25.00
44 GA Red Raven appears (1st time since Golden Age)						
	$7.00	$21.00	$50.00	£3.55	£10.50	£25.00
45 story continues in Avengers #53						
	$7.00	$21.00	$50.00	£3.55	£10.50	£25.00
46-48						
	$7.00	$21.00	$50.00	£3.20	£9.50	£22.50
49 Steranko cover, 1st appearance Lorna Dane						
	$7.00	$21.00	$50.00	£3.55	£10.50	£25.00
50 scarce in the U.K. Jim Steranko art						
	$8.50	$26.00	$60.00	£4.25	£12.50	£30.00
51 Jim Steranko art						
	$7.75	$23.50	$55.00	£3.90	£11.50	£27.50
52 (Jan 1969)						
	$4.70	$14.00	$33.00	£2.50	£7.50	£17.50
53 Barry Windsor Smith art, his first in comic books						
	$6.75	$20.00	$47.50	£3.90	£11.50	£27.50
54 1st Living Pharaoh, Barry Smith cover, 1st Alex Summers (later Havok)						
	$7.00	$21.00	$50.00	£3.40	£10.00	£24.00
55 Barry Smith cover						
	$7.00	$21.00	$50.00	£2.50	£7.50	£17.50
56 Neal Adams art, Pharaoh becomes Living Monolith, 1st appearance Havok						
	$6.75	$20.00	$47.50	£3.00	£9.00	£21.00
57 Neal Adams art, Sentinels story						
	$6.75	$20.00	$47.50	£3.00	£9.00	£21.00
58 Neal Adams art, Sentinels story, Havok appears						
	$10.00	$30.00	$70.00	£3.40	£10.00	£24.00
59 Neal Adams art, Sentinels story, Havok appears						
	$6.75	$20.00	$47.50	£3.00	£9.00	£21.00
60 Neal Adams art, 1st appearance Sauron						
	$6.75	$20.00	$47.50	£3.00	£9.00	£21.00
61 Neal Adams art						
	$6.75	$20.00	$47.50	£3.00	£9.00	£21.00
62-63 Neal Adams art, Ka-Zar X-over						
	$6.75	$20.00	$47.50	£3.00	£9.00	£21.00
64 (Jan 1970), 1st appearance Sunfire						
	$7.00	$21.00	$50.00	£2.50	£7.50	£17.50
65 Neal Adams art, Professor X returns						
	$6.75	$20.00	$47.50	£3.00	£9.00	£21.00
66 scarce in the U.K. X-Men vs. Hulk, last new story						
	$5.50	$17.00	$40.00	£2.50	£7.50	£17.50
67 52pgs, scarce in the U.K., reprints #12,13						
	$3.55	$10.50	$25.00	£1.75	£5.25	£12.50
68 52pgs, (Feb 1971), scarce in the U.K., reprints #14,15						
	$3.55	$10.50	$25.00	£1.75	£5.25	£12.50
69 52pgs, reprints #16,19						
	$3.55	$10.50	$25.00	£1.75	£5.25	£12.50
70 52pgs, reprints #17,18						
	$3.55	$10.50	$25.00	£1.75	£5.25	£12.50
71 ND reprints #20						
	$2.50	$7.50	$17.50	£2.05	£6.00	£14.50
72 ND 52pgs, reprints #21,24						
	$2.85	$8.50	$20.00	£2.35	£7.00	£16.50
73 scarce in the U.K. reprints #25						
	$2.50	$7.50	$17.50	£1.75	£5.25	£12.50
74 scarce in the U.K. (Feb 1972), reprints #26						
	$2.50	$7.50	$17.50	£1.75	£5.25	£12.50
75 scarce in the U.K. reprints #27						
	$2.50	$7.50	$17.50	£1.75	£5.25	£12.50
76 scarce in the U.K. reprints #28						
	$2.50	$7.50	$17.50	£1.75	£5.25	£12.50
77 scarce in the U.K. reprints #29						
	$2.50	$7.50	$17.50	£1.75	£5.25	£12.50
78 scarce in the U.K. reprints #30						
	$2.50	$7.50	$17.50	£1.75	£5.25	£12.50
79 scarce in the U.K. reprints #31						
	$2.50	$7.50	$17.50	£1.75	£5.25	£12.50
80 (Feb 1973), reprints #32						
	$2.50	$7.50	$17.50	£1.75	£5.25	£12.50
81 reprints #33	$2.50	$7.50	$17.50	£1.40	£4.25	£10.00
82 reprints #34	$2.50	$7.50	$17.50	£1.40	£4.25	£10.00
83 reprints #35 (Spiderman appearance)						
	$2.50	$7.50	$17.50	£1.40	£4.25	£10.00
84 reprints #36	$2.50	$7.50	$17.50	£1.40	£4.25	£10.00
85 reprints #37	$2.50	$7.50	$17.50	£1.40	£4.25	£10.00
86 (Feb 1974), reprints #38						
	$2.50	$7.50	$17.50	£1.40	£4.25	£10.00
87 ND rare in the U.K. reprints #39						
	$2.50	$7.50	$17.50	£2.10	£6.25	£15.00
88 ND rare in the U.K. reprints #40						
	$2.50	$7.50	$17.50	£2.10	£6.25	£15.00
89 reprints #41	$2.50	$7.50	$17.50	£1.20	£3.60	£8.50
90 reprints #42	$2.50	$7.50	$17.50	£1.20	£3.60	£8.50
91 reprints #43	$2.50	$7.50	$17.50	£1.20	£3.60	£8.50
92 (Feb 1975), reprints #44						

Issue / Notes	$Good	$Fine	$N.Mint	£Good	£Fine	£N.Mint
(continued)	$2.50	$7.50	$17.50	£1.05	£3.20	£7.50
93 reprints #45	$2.50	$7.50	$17.50	£1.05	£3.20	£7.50
94 ND New X-Men begin; Banshee, Colossus, Nightcrawler, Storm, Thunderbird, Wolverine become members; Gil Kane cover, story continues from Giant Size #1	$45.00	$135.00	$360.00	£28.00	£82.50	£225.00
95 ND Thunderbird dies	$8.50	$26.00	$60.00	£7.75	£23.50	£55.00
96 1st appearance Moira McTaggart	$7.00	$21.00	$50.00	£2.10	£6.25	£15.00
97 (Feb 1976), 1st appearance Lilandra	$6.25	$19.00	$45.00	£2.10	£6.25	£15.00
98 Sentinels; Stan Lee & Jack Kirby cameo	$7.00	$21.00	$50.00	£1.90	£5.75	£13.50
98 scarce in the U.K. 30 cents cover version	$7.00	$21.00	$50.00	£2.10	£6.25	£15.00
99 Sentinels appear	$7.00	$21.00	$50.00	£1.90	£5.75	£13.50
99 scarce in the U.K. 30 cents cover version	$7.00	$21.00	$50.00	£2.10	£6.25	£15.00
100 New X-Men vs Old X-Men, part origin Phoenix	$7.75	$23.50	$55.00	£2.10	£6.25	£15.00
101 1st appearance Phoenix	$7.75	$23.50	$47.50	£2.25	£6.75	£13.50
102 LD in the U.K. origin Storm	$4.00	$12.00	$24.00	£2.00	£6.00	£12.00
103 ND	$4.00	$12.00	$24.00	£2.25	£6.75	£13.50
104 ND Magneto re-appears (see Defenders #15, #16)	$4.00	$12.00	$24.00	£2.50	£7.50	£15.00
105 ND scarce in the U.K.	$4.00	$12.00	$24.00	£2.50	£7.50	£15.00
106-107 ND	$4.00	$12.00	$24.00	£2.00	£6.00	£12.00
108 1st John Byrne X-Men; Corbeau, Fantastic Four, Avengers, Beast cameos	$7.50	$22.50	$45.00	£2.50	£7.50	£15.00
109 (Feb 1978), 1st appearance Vindicator (Alpha Flight), John Byrne art	$6.00	$18.00	$36.00	£2.00	£6.00	£12.00
110 Phoenix joins team, no John Byrne art	$3.75	$11.00	$22.50	£1.00	£3.00	£6.00
111 John Byrne art	$3.75	$11.00	$22.50	£1.00	£3.00	£6.00
112 John Byrne art, George Perez cover	$3.00	$9.00	$18.00	£1.00	£3.00	£6.00
113 John Byrne art	$3.00	$9.00	$18.00	£1.00	£3.00	£6.00
114-116 Ka-Zar, Savage Land appear, John Byrne art	$3.00	$9.00	$18.00	£1.00	£3.00	£6.00
117 (Jan 1979), origin Professor X retold, John Byrne art	$3.00	$9.00	$18.00	£1.00	£3.00	£6.00
118-119 John Byrne art	$3.00	$9.00	$18.00	£1.00	£3.00	£6.00
120 1st appearance Alpha Flight (cameo), John Byrne art	$6.50	$20.00	$40.00	£2.50	£7.50	£15.00
121 ND John Byrne art, 1st full Alpha Flight story, Byrne cameo	$7.50	$22.50	$45.00	£5.00	£15.00	£30.00
122 ND John Byrne art	$3.00	$9.00	$18.00	£1.65	£5.00	£10.00
123 Colossus becomes Proletarian (for seven pages only!), John Byrne art	$3.00	$9.00	$18.00	£1.00	£3.00	£6.00
124-126 John Byrne art	$3.00	$9.00	$18.00	£1.00	£3.00	£6.00
127 1st appearance Proteus, John Byrne art	$3.00	$9.00	$18.00	£1.00	£3.00	£6.00
128 John Byrne art	$3.00	$9.00	$18.00	£1.00	£3.00	£6.00
129 (Jan 1980), 1st appearance Kitty Pryde, John Byrne art	$4.00	$12.00	$24.00	£1.25	£3.75	£7.50
130 1st appearance Dazzler, John Byrne art	$3.50	$10.50	$21.00	£1.25	£3.75	£7.50
131-132 John Byrne art	$3.00	$9.00	$18.00	£0.80	£2.50	£5.00
133 Wolverine goes solo, John Byrne art	$3.00	$9.00	$18.00	£1.30	£4.00	£8.00
134 John Byrne art	$3.00	$9.00	$18.00	£0.80	£2.50	£5.00
135 Dr. Strange, Spiderman, Silver Surfer cameos, John Byrne art	$3.00	$9.00	$18.00	£0.80	£2.50	£5.00
136 John Byrne art	$2.50	$7.50	$15.00	£0.80	£2.50	£5.00
137 ND DS, death of Phoenix; Recorder, Watcher appear, John Byrne art	$2.90	$8.75	$17.50	£1.30	£4.00	£8.00
138 X-Men's history re-capped, John Byrne art	$2.50	$7.50	$15.00	£1.25	£3.75	£7.50
139 Alpha Flight appears, Kitty Pryde joins, Wolverine's new costume, John Byrne art	$5.00	$15.00	$30.00	£1.25	£3.75	£7.50
140 Alpha Flight, Pierre Trudeau appear, brief uncited Wolverine, John Byrne art	$4.50	$13.50	$27.00	£1.30	£4.00	£8.00
141 (Jan 1981), Days Of Future Past story, 1st new Phoenix (Rachel Summers), John Byrne art	$4.50	$13.50	$27.00	£1.50	£4.50	£9.00
142 ND Days Of Future Past story, X-Men all "die", John Byrne art; this is the first issue of "The Uncanny X-Men"	$3.30	$10.00	$20.00	£1.30	£4.00	£8.00
143 ND John Byrne art, "Alien" type story	$2.00	$6.00	$12.00	£0.80	£2.50	£5.00

Issue / Notes	$Good	$Fine	$N.Mint	£Good	£Fine	£N.Mint
(continued)	$1.50	$4.50	$9.00	£0.50	£1.50	£3.00
144 Brent Anderson art (see note below)	$1.50	$4.50	$9.00	£0.50	£1.50	£3.00
145 old X-Men appear	$1.50	$4.50	$9.00	£0.50	£1.50	£3.00
146-147	$1.50	$4.50	$9.00	£0.50	£1.50	£3.00
148 Spiderwoman, Dazzler appear	$1.50	$4.50	$9.00	£0.50	£1.50	£3.00
149	$1.50	$4.50	$9.00	£0.50	£1.50	£3.00
150 DS Magneto appears	$1.50	$4.50	$9.00	£0.50	£1.50	£3.00
151-152	$1.60	$4.80	$8.00	£0.50	£1.50	£2.50
153 (Jan 1982)	$1.60	$4.80	$8.00	£0.50	£1.50	£2.50
154-156	$1.60	$4.80	$8.00	£0.50	£1.50	£2.50
157 Phoenix reborn	$1.60	$4.80	$8.00	£0.50	£1.50	£2.50
158 1st appearance Rogue in X-Men (see Avengers Annual #10)	$2.50	$7.50	$12.50	£0.80	£2.40	£4.00
159 Dracula vs. X-Men, Sienkiewicz art	$1.20	$3.60	$6.00	£0.60	£1.80	£3.00
160 Anderson art	$1.20	$3.60	$6.00	£0.50	£1.50	£2.50
161 origin Magneto	$1.20	$3.60	$6.00	£0.80	£2.40	£4.00
162 scarce in the U.K. Wolverine solo story	$2.40	$7.00	$12.00	£0.80	£2.40	£4.00
163 scarce in the U.K. 1st appearance Binary	$1.20	$3.60	$6.00	£0.80	£2.40	£4.00
164 scarce in the U.K. Carol Danvers as Binary	$1.20	$3.60	$6.00	£0.80	£2.40	£4.00
165 (Jan 1983), 1st Paul Smith art	$2.00	$6.00	$10.00	£0.90	£2.70	£4.50
166 DS, Paul Smith art	$1.60	$4.80	$8.00	£1.00	£3.00	£5.00
167 New Mutants X-over, Paul Smith art	$1.20	$3.60	$6.00	£0.90	£2.70	£4.50
168 1st Madelyne Pryor (see Avengers Annual #10), Paul Smith art	$1.20	$3.60	$6.00	£0.90	£2.70	£4.50
169-170 Paul Smith art	$1.20	$3.60	$6.00	£0.80	£2.40	£4.00
171 Rogue joins X-Men, Walt Simonson art	$2.40	$7.00	$12.00	£1.00	£3.00	£5.00
172 LD in the U.K. spotlight on Wolverine, Paul Smith art	$1.20	$3.60	$6.00	£1.10	£3.30	£5.50
173 Paul Smith art, Wolverine cover	$1.20	$3.60	$6.00	£1.10	£3.30	£5.50
174 "Phoenix" cameo, Paul Smith art	$1.20	$3.60	$6.00	£0.80	£2.40	£4.00
175 DS, anniversary, "Phoenix" returns, part Paul Smith cover/art (rest Romita)	$2.00	$6.00	$10.00	£1.10	£3.30	£5.50
176 LD in the U.K.	$1.20	$3.60	$6.00	£0.60	£1.80	£3.00
177 LD in the U.K. (Jan 1984)	$1.20	$3.60	$6.00	£0.60	£1.80	£3.00
178-183 LD in the U.K.	$1.20	$3.60	$6.00	£0.60	£1.80	£3.00
184 LD in the U.K. 1st appearance Forge	$1.50	$4.50	$7.50	£0.60	£1.80	£3.00
185 LD in the U.K. Storm loses powers, Rogue appears	$1.20	$3.60	$6.00	£0.80	£2.40	£4.00
186 DS Barry Smith art	$1.20	$3.60	$6.00	£0.50	£1.50	£2.50
187-188	$1.00	$3.00	$5.00	£0.40	£1.20	£2.00
189 (Jan 1985)	$1.00	$3.00	$5.00	£0.40	£1.20	£2.00
190-192	$1.00	$3.00	$5.00	£0.40	£1.20	£2.00
193 DS 100th anniversary issue	$1.80	$5.25	$9.00	£0.70	£2.10	£3.50
194 Juggernaut appears, John Romita Jnr. art	$1.00	$3.00	$5.00	£0.50	£1.50	£2.50
195 Power Pack X-over	$1.00	$3.00	$5.00	£0.50	£1.50	£2.50
196 LD in the U.K. Secret Wars X-over	$1.00	$3.00	$5.00	£0.60	£1.80	£3.00
197 LD in the U.K. Juggernaut appears, John Romita Jnr. art	$1.00	$3.00	$5.00	£0.60	£1.80	£3.00
198 Barry Smith art	$1.00	$3.00	$5.00	£0.50	£1.50	£2.50
199 very LD	$1.00	$3.00	$5.00	£0.80	£2.40	£4.00
200 LD in the U.K. DS Magneto on trial	$2.00	$6.00	$10.00	£1.00	£3.00	£5.00
201 very LD (Jan 1986), 1st appearance Cyclop's son Nathan Summers; Whilce Portacio inks (1st work on X-Men)	$5.00	$15.00	$25.00	£1.50	£4.50	£7.50
202-203 LD in the U.K. Secret Wars X-over	$1.60	$4.80	$8.00	£0.80	£2.40	£4.00
204	$1.60	$4.80	$8.00	£0.60	£1.80	£3.00
205 Barry Smith art, solo Wolverine story	$4.00	$12.00	$20.00	£1.50	£4.50	£7.50
206	$1.60	$4.80	$8.00	£0.60	£1.80	£3.00
207 Wolverine cover/story	$1.60	$4.80	$8.00	£0.70	£2.10	£3.50
208-209	$1.60	$4.80	$8.00	£0.60	£1.80	£3.00
210 Mutant Massacre tie-in	$4.00	$12.00	$20.00	£1.70	£5.00	£8.50
211 Mutant Massacre tie-in, Colossus kills						

	$Good	$Fine	$N.Mint	£Good	£Fine	£N.Mint
	$4.00	$12.00	$20.00	£1.70	£5.00	£8.50
212 Mutant Massacre tie-in, Wolverine and Sabretooth battle						
	$5.50	$16.50	$27.50	£2.00	£6.00	£10.00
213 (Jan 1987), Mutant Massacre tie-in, Davis/Neary art, Wolverine and Sabretooth battle						
	$5.50	$16.50	$27.50	£2.20	£6.50	£11.00
214 Barry Smith art						
	$1.20	$3.60	$6.00	£0.60	£1.80	£3.00
215 Alan Davis art	$1.20	$3.60	$6.00	£0.50	£1.50	£2.50
216-217	$1.20	$3.60	$6.00	£0.30	£0.90	£1.50
218 Art Adams cover						
	$1.20	$3.60	$6.00	£0.30	£0.90	£1.50
219 Havok joins the X-Men, Sabretooth appears						
	$1.20	$3.60	$6.00	£0.40	£1.20	£2.00
220-221	$1.20	$3.60	$6.00	£0.30	£0.90	£1.50
222 Wolverine battles Sabretooth cover and story						
	$3.00	$9.00	$15.00	£0.80	£2.40	£4.00
223	$1.20	$3.60	$6.00	£0.40	£1.20	£2.00
224 LD in the U.K.	$1.20	$3.60	$6.00	£0.50	£1.50	£2.50
225 (Jan 1988), Fall of the Mutants						
	$2.00	$6.00	$10.00	£0.65	£1.95	£3.25
226 LD in the U.K. DS Fall of Mutants						
	$2.00	$6.00	$10.00	£0.70	£2.10	£3.50
227 Fall of the Mutants						
	$2.00	$6.00	$10.00	£0.65	£1.95	£3.25
228-232	$1.20	$3.60	$6.00	£0.40	£1.20	£2.00
233 LD in the U.K. Wolverine temporarily transformed into alien Brood member						
	$1.20	$3.60	$6.00	£0.50	£1.50	£2.50
234 Wolverine temporarily transformed into alien Brood member						
	$1.20	$3.60	$6.00	£0.40	£1.20	£2.00
235-238	$1.20	$3.60	$6.00	£0.35	£1.05	£1.75
239 Inferno X-over	$1.20	$3.60	$6.00	£0.40	£1.20	£2.00
240 (Jan 1989), Inferno X-over, Sabretooth appears						
	$1.60	$4.80	$8.00	£0.40	£1.20	£2.00
241 Inferno X-over						
	$1.20	$3.60	$6.00	£0.35	£1.05	£1.75
242 LD in the U.K. DS Inferno X-over, X-Factor appear						
	$1.20	$3.60	$6.00	£0.50	£1.50	£2.50
243 Inferno X-over, Sabretooth appears						
	$1.00	$3.00	$5.00	£0.45	£1.35	£2.25
244 1st appearance Jubilee						
	$4.00	$12.00	$20.00	£0.60	£1.80	£3.00
245 Rob Liefeld's 2nd X-book, only part art						
	$0.80	$2.40	$4.00	£0.60	£1.80	£3.00
246-247	$1.00	$3.00	$5.00	£0.30	£0.90	£1.50
248 1st Jim Lee art on X-Men						
	$4.50	$13.50	$22.50	£1.00	£3.00	£5.00
248 2nd printing, ND (Jun 1992) - gold cover						
	$0.50	$1.50	$2.50	£0.30	£0.90	£1.50
249	$0.60	$1.80	$3.00	£0.30	£0.90	£1.50
250 Ka-Zar appears						
	$0.60	$1.80	$3.00	£0.30	£0.90	£1.50
251-252 bi-weekly issue						
	$0.60	$1.80	$3.00	£0.30	£0.90	£1.50
253-255 bi-weekly issue						
	$1.00	$3.00	$5.00	£0.40	£1.20	£2.00
256 Acts of Vengeance tie-in, Jim Lee art						
	$2.80	$8.25	$14.00	£1.00	£3.00	£5.00
257 (Jan 1990), Acts of Vengeance tie-in, Jim Lee art						
	$2.50	$7.50	$12.50	£1.00	£3.00	£5.00
258 Acts of Vengeance tie-in, Wolverine cover and story, Jim Lee art						
	$2.80	$8.25	$14.00	£1.20	£3.60	£6.00

	$Good	$Fine	$N.Mint	£Good	£Fine	£N.Mint
259 LD in the U.K.	$1.00	$3.00	$5.00	£0.40	£1.20	£2.00
260-262	$0.60	$1.80	$3.00	£0.30	£0.90	£1.50
263-265 bi-weekly issue						
	$0.60	$1.80	$3.00	£0.30	£0.90	£1.50
266 1st full appearance Gambit (see Annual #14), bi-weekly issue						
	$8.00	$24.00	$40.00	£2.50	£7.50	£12.50
267 LD in the U.K. Jim Lee art run begins						
	$3.20	$9.50	$16.00	£1.20	£3.60	£6.00
268 Captain America/Black Widow appear, Jim Lee/Scott Williams art begins, Wolverine cover, last bi-weekly issue						
	$4.00	$12.00	$20.00	£1.40	£4.20	£7.00
269 LD in the U.K. Jim Lee art						
	$1.60	$4.80	$8.00	£1.20	£3.60	£6.00
270 LD in the U.K. The X-Tinction Agenda part 1 (of 9; see New Mutants/X-Factor), Jim Lee art						
	$2.00	$6.00	$10.00	£0.90	£2.70	£4.50
270 ND The X-Tinction Agenda part 1 (2nd print - gold ink cover)						
	$0.80	$2.40	$4.00	£0.50	£1.50	£2.50
271 The X-Tinction Agenda part 4, Jim Lee art						
	$2.00	$6.00	$10.00	£0.70	£2.10	£3.50
272 (Jan 1991), The X-Tinction Agenda part 7, Jim Lee art						
	$2.00	$6.00	$10.00	£0.70	£2.10	£3.50
273 X-Factor/New Mutants appear, many artists including Jim Lee and John Byrne						
	$1.60	$4.80	$8.00	£0.65	£1.95	£3.25
274 Jim Lee art	$1.60	$4.80	$8.00	£0.55	£1.65	£2.75
275 DS Jim Lee art, gatefold cover						
	$1.50	$4.50	$7.50	£0.70	£2.10	£3.50
275 2nd printing, ND gold ink cover						
	$0.50	$1.50	$2.50	£0.30	£0.90	£1.50
276-277 Jim Lee art						
	$0.60	$1.80	$3.00	£0.50	£1.50	£2.50
278 Paul Smith art	$0.60	$1.80	$3.00	£0.25	£0.75	£1.25
279 this leads into the new X-Men #1						
	$0.60	$1.80	$3.00	£0.25	£0.75	£1.25
280 X-over X-Factor #70, Andy Kubert art						
	$0.60	$1.80	$3.00	£0.25	£0.75	£1.25
281 ties into X-Men #1, new line-up revealed: Storm, Marvel Girl, Archangel, Ice man, Colossus, Whilce Portacio pencils, Thibert inks, John Byrne scripts begin						
	$1.60	$4.80	$8.00	£0.60	£1.80	£3.00
281 2nd printing, ND scarce in the U.K. red ink cover						
	$0.55	$1.65	$2.75	£0.35	£1.05	£1.75
282 John Byrne script, 1st appearance Bishop (on last page), Whilce Portacio pencils, Thibert inks						
	$2.00	$6.00	$10.00	£0.60	£1.80	£3.00
282 2nd printing, ND Gold cover. Inside back cover shows how 2nd print #281 should have originally been presented, a combination of gold and red)						
	$0.60	$1.80	$3.00	£0.60	£1.80	£3.00
283 1st full appearance Bishop, John Byrne script, Whilce Portacio pencils, Thibert inks						
	$2.40	$7.00	$12.00	£0.60	£1.80	£3.00
284 John Byrne script, Portacio pencils, Thibert inks						
	$0.50	$1.50	$2.50	£0.30	£0.90	£1.50
285 John Byrne script, Portacio art, $1.25 cover begins						
	$0.50	$1.50	$2.50	£0.20	£0.60	£1.00
286 John Byrne script, Lee and Portacio plot and pencils, Thibert co-pencils						
	$0.50	$1.50	$2.50	£0.20	£0.60	£1.00
287-288 John Byrne script, Portacio art, Bishop appears						
	$0.50	$1.50	$2.50	£0.20	£0.60	£1.00
289 John Byrne script, Portacio art, Bishop appears and joins team						
	$0.50	$1.50	$2.50	£0.20	£0.60	£1.00
290-292 Whilce Portacio art						
	$0.50	$1.50	$2.50	£0.20	£0.60	£1.00
293	$0.50	$1.50	$2.50	£0.20	£0.60	£1.00
294 X-Cutioner's Song part #1, pre-bagged and includes Marvel trading card, continues in X-Factor #84						

Uncanny X-Men #61

Uncanny X-Men #315

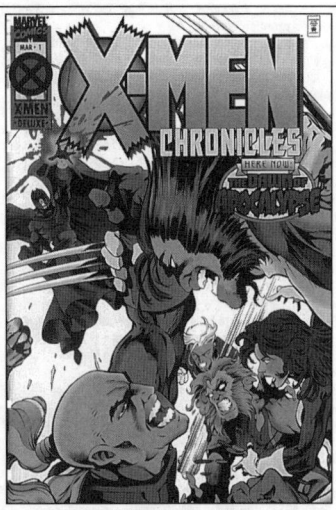

X-Men Chronicles #1

MINT = 100% / NEAR MINT (inc. +/-) = 90–99% / VERY FINE (inc. +/-) = 75–89% / FINE (inc. +/-) = 55–74%
VERY GOOD (inc. +/-) = 35–54% / GOOD (inc. +/-) = 15–34% / FAIR = 5–14% / POOR = 1–4%

	$Good	$Fine	$N.Mint	£Good	£Fine	£N.Mint
	$0.50	$1.50	$2.50	£0.30	£0.90	£1.50
295 X-Cutioner's Song part 5, pre-bagged and includes Marvel trading card, continues in X-Factor #85						
	$0.50	$1.50	$2.50	£0.25	£0.75	£1.25
296 X-Cutioner's Song part 9, pre-bagged and includes Marvel trading card, continues in X-Factor #86						
	$0.40	$1.20	$2.00	£0.20	£0.60	£1.00
297-299	$0.40	$1.20	$2.00	£0.20	£0.60	£1.00
300 64pgs, squarebound, anniversary issue, silver holo-grafix foil cover						
	$1.00	$3.00	$5.00	£0.50	£1.50	£2.50
301-303	$0.30	$0.90	$1.50	£0.20	£0.60	£1.00
304 LD in the U.K. 64pgs, 30th anniversary issue; Magneto returns, Magneto hologram cover						
	$1.00	$3.00	$5.00	£0.60	£1.80	£3.00
305	$0.30	$0.90	$1.50	£0.20	£0.60	£1.00
306 X-Cutioner vs. Archangel						
	$0.30	$0.90	$1.50	£0.20	£0.60	£1.00
307 Bloodties part 4; Spiderwoman, Crystal and Quicksilver appear						
	$0.30	$0.90	$1.50	£0.20	£0.60	£1.00
308 Jean Grey proposes to Scott Summers (see X-Men 2nd Series #30)						
	$0.30	$0.90	$1.50	£0.20	£0.60	£1.00
309 Magneto cameo						
	$0.30	$0.90	$1.50	£0.20	£0.60	£1.00
310 Sabretooth and Cable appear; 3 bound-in trading cards						
	$0.60	$1.80	$3.00	£0.30	£0.90	£1.50
311	$0.30	$0.90	$1.50	£0.20	£0.60	£1.00
312 with free Spiderman's Amazing Powers card sheet						
	$0.30	$0.90	$1.50	£0.20	£0.60	£1.00
313-316	$0.30	$0.90	$1.50	£0.20	£0.60	£1.00
316 LD in the U.K. Deluxe Edition - foil stamped cover						
	$0.60	$1.80	$3.00	£0.40	£1.20	£2.00
317	$0.30	$0.90	$1.50	£0.20	£0.60	£1.00
317 ND Deluxe Edition - foil stamped cover						
	$0.60	$1.80	$3.00	£0.40	£1.20	£2.00
318	$0.30	$0.90	$1.50	£0.20	£0.60	£1.00
318 ND Deluxe Edition - printed on glossy stock paper						
	$0.40	$1.20	$2.00	£0.25	£0.75	£1.25
319	$0.30	$0.90	$1.50	£0.20	£0.60	£1.00
319 ND Deluxe Edition - printed on glossy stock paper						
	$0.40	$1.20	$2.00	£0.25	£0.75	£1.25
320 (Jan 1995)	$0.30	$0.90	$1.50	£0.20	£0.60	£1.00
320 ND Deluxe Edition - printed on glossy stock paper						
	$0.40	$1.20	$2.00	£0.25	£0.75	£1.25
321	$0.30	$0.90	$1.50	£0.20	£0.60	£1.00
321 ND Deluxe Edition - printed on glossy stock paper plus bound-in Fleer trading card						
	$0.40	$1.20	$2.00	£0.25	£0.75	£1.25
322 continued from X-Men: Prime; Scott Lobdell script, Tom Grummett art						
	$0.40	$1.20	$2.00	£0.25	£0.75	£1.25
323-324	$0.40	$1.20	$2.00	£0.25	£0.75	£1.25
325 48pgs, 20th anniversary of the new X-Men; double gate-fold prismatic foil cover						
	$0.80	$2.40	$4.00	£0.50	£1.50	£2.50
326 Sabretooth appears						
	$0.40	$1.20	$2.00	£0.30	£0.90	£1.50
327 Magneto appears						
	$0.40	$1.20	$2.00	£0.30	£0.90	£1.50
328 Sabretooth appears, continued in X-Men #48						
	$0.40	$1.20	$2.00	£0.30	£0.90	£1.50
329 Dr. Strange appears						
	$0.40	$1.20	$2.00	£0.30	£0.90	£1.50
330	$0.40	$1.20	$2.00	£0.30	£0.90	£1.50
Title Value:	**$2205.70**	**$6616.35**	**$16593.25**	**£1192.90**	**£3570.20**	**£9155.50**

Note: issue 144 often turns up ink-smudged: near mint copies are scarce in both the U.S. and U.K.

ARTISTS
Kirby art in 1-11, lay-outs in 12-17. Cockrum art in 94-105, 107, 145-158.

FEATURES
Origins as follows: Angel in 54-56; Beast in 48-53; Cyclops in 39-43; Iceman in 44-47; Marvel Girl in 57.

	£Good	£Fine	£N.Mint
X-Men: Asgardian Wars (Apr 1989) Trade paperback reprints X-Men Annual #9, X-Men/Alpha Flight mini-series, New Mutants Special #1 with Art Adams and Paul Smith art	£1.80	£5.40	£9.00
X-Men: Phoenix Saga Trade paperback 192pgs, reprints #129-137	£1.40	£4.20	£7.00
(2nd - 5th printings)	£1.25	£3.75	£6.25
(6th printing - Nov 1990)	£1.20	£3.60	£6.00
(7th printing - Nov 1994)	£1.20	£3.60	£6.00
X-Men: Savage Land Trade paperback reprints X-Men Fanfare #1-4	£1.00	£3.00	£5.00
(2nd print that emphasizes "X-Men" more. Oct 1989)	£0.90	£2.70	£4.50
X-Men: Days of Future Past 48pgs, reprints X-Men #141,#142 featuring Claremont script, Byrne/Austin art	£0.60	£1.80	£3.00
(2nd print - Nov 1990)	£0.50	£1.50	£2.50
(3rd print - Mar 1995)	£0.80	£2.40	£4.00
X-Men: Days of Future Present Trade paperback 160pgs, reprints storyline from Fantastic Four Annual #23, X-Men Annual #14, X-Factor Annual #5, New Mutants Annual #10. Mike Mignola cover	£1.80	£5.40	£9.00
(2nd print - Mar 1995)	£2.00	£6.00	£10.00
X-Men: From The Ashes Trade paperback reprints X-Men #165-175	£1.80	£5.40	£9.00
(2nd print - May 1993)	£1.75	£5.25	£8.75
(3rd print - Nov 1994)	£1.70	£5.10	£8.50
X-Men: X-Tinction Agenda Trade paperback (Dec 1992) reprints X-Men #270-272, X-Factor #60-62, New Mutants #95-97 special "enhanced" cover	£3.00	£9.00	£15.00

	$Good	$Fine	$N.Mint	£Good	£Fine	£N.Mint
(2nd print - Jun 1993)				£2.80	£8.40	£14.00
(3rd print - Nov 1994)				£2.75	£8.25	£13.75
X-Men: The X-Cutioner's Song (Jun 1994) Trade paperback reprints X-Cutioner's Song storyline, metal foil stamped cover				£3.20	£9.60	£16.00
Greatest Battles of the X-Men (Oct 1994) Trade paperback 176pgs, reprints				£2.00	£6.00	£10.00
Marvel Limited: The Best of Chris Claremont X-Men (Dec 1994) 230pgs, leather-bound hardcover with foil stamping; classic reprints				£3.00	£9.00	£15.00
X-Men: Fatal Attractions (Feb 1995) Trade paperback 160pgs, reprints "Fatal Attractions" story from 1993				£2.40	£7.20	£12.00
X-Men: The Coming of Bishop (Apr 1995) Trade paperback reprints origin and 1st appearance of Bishop				£1.70	£5.10	£8.50
X-Men Spotlight (Nov 1995) boxed set collecting Uncanny X-Men #304, X-Force #25 and X-Factor #92 (all hologram covers)				£1.50	£4.50	£7.50
X-Men: Legion Quest (Jan 1996) Trade paperback 88pgs, reprints Legion Quest saga; gold foil etched cover				£1.20	£3.60	£6.00
X-Men: Dawn of the Age of Apocalypse (Jan 1996) Trade paperback 96pgs, reprints Cable #20 and X-Men: Alpha				£1.20	£3.60	£6.00
X-Men: Twilight of the Age of Apocalypse (Feb 1996) Trade paperback 96pgs, reprints X-Universe #1,2 and X-Men: Omega				£1.20	£3.60	£6.00

X-MEN, THE UNCANNY '95
Marvel Comics Group,OS; nn Nov 1995

	$Good	$Fine	$N.Mint	£Good	£Fine	£N.Mint
nn ND 64pgs, Terry Kavanagh script, Bryan Hitch art; Cannonball and Husk appear	$0.80	$2.40	$4.00	£0.50	£1.50	£2.50
Title Value:	**$0.80**	**$2.40**	**$4.00**	**£0.50**	**£1.50**	**£2.50**

X-MEN, THE UNCANNY ANNUAL
Marvel Comics Group; 1 1970-2 1971; 3 1979-present

	$Good	$Fine	$N.Mint	£Good	£Fine	£N.Mint
1 52pgs, scarce, reprints X-Men #9, #11	$8.50	$26.00	$60.00	£5.50	£17.00	£40.00
2 ND 52pgs, scarce, reprints X-Men #22, #23	$7.00	$21.00	$50.00	£5.00	£15.00	£35.00
3 ND 52pgs, Arkon appears, George Perez art	$2.50	$7.50	$15.00	£1.25	£3.75	£7.50
4 ND 52pgs, Dr.Strange appears, John Romita Jnr art	$1.50	$4.50	$7.50	£1.00	£3.00	£5.00
5 ND 52pgs, Anderson art	$1.20	$3.60	$6.00	£0.80	£2.40	£4.00
6 ND Dracula, Lilith appear, Sienkiewicz art	$0.90	$2.70	$4.50	£0.60	£1.80	£3.00
7 ND Golden art	$0.80	$2.40	$4.00	£0.50	£1.50	£2.50
8 ND	$0.80	$2.40	$4.00	£0.50	£1.50	£2.50
9 ND Arthur Adams art (see X-Men/Alpha Flight #1 & #2)	$2.50	$7.50	$12.50	£1.00	£3.00	£5.00
10 ND Arthur Adams art, Longshot joins X-Men	$2.00	$6.00	$10.00	£1.00	£3.00	£5.00
11 ND Davis/Neary art, Captain Britain, Meggan, Psylocke (Excalibur) appear	$0.80	$2.40	$4.00	£0.60	£1.80	£3.00
12 ND squarebound, Evolutionary War, Art Adams art	$0.60	$1.80	$3.00	£0.40	£1.20	£2.00
13 ND squarebound, Atlantis Attacks part 3	$0.60	$1.80	$3.00	£0.40	£1.20	£2.00
14 ND Days of Future Present conclusion, continued from New Mutants Annual #6, Cable appears, 1st appearance Gambit (cameo - chronologically his 2nd appearance) - see Uncanny X-Men #266	$2.00	$6.00	$10.00	£0.80	£2.40	£4.00
15 ND King of Pain part 3, continued in X-Factor Annual #6; origin retold	$0.60	$1.80	$3.00	£0.40	£1.20	£2.00
16 ND Shattershot part 2, continued in X-Factor Annual #7, Jae Lee art	$0.60	$1.80	$3.00	£0.40	£1.20	£2.00
17 ND 64pgs, pre-bagged with trading card introducing X-Cutioner	$0.60	$1.80	$3.00	£0.40	£1.20	£2.00
18 ND 64pgs, Sabretooth and Caliban appear	$0.60	$1.80	$3.00	£0.40	£1.20	£2.00
Title Value:	**$34.30**	**$103.40**	**$206.50**	**£20.95**	**£63.35**	**£128.50**

X-MEN: ALPHA
Marvel Comics Group,OS; 1 Feb 1995

	$Good	$Fine	$N.Mint	£Good	£Fine	£N.Mint
1 ND 48pgs, the death of Professor X; chromium cover	$1.50	$4.50	$7.50	£1.00	£3.00	£5.00
1 ND 48pgs, Gold Edition (Apr 1995) - gold chromium wraparound cover	$8.00	$24.00	$40.00	£5.00	£15.00	£25.00
Title Value:	**$9.50**	**$28.50**	**$47.50**	**£6.00**	**£18.00**	**£30.00**

X-MEN: ASKANI'S SON
Marvel Comics Group,MS; 1 Jan 1996-present

	$Good	$Fine	$N.Mint	£Good	£Fine	£N.Mint
1 ND Scott Lobdell script, Gene Ha art; the sequel to The Adventures of Cyclops & Phoenix, UV coated cover	$0.60	$1.80	$3.00	£0.40	£1.20	£2.00
2 ND UV coated cover	$0.60	$1.80	$3.00	£0.40	£1.20	£2.00
Title Value:	**$1.20**	**$3.60**	**$6.00**	**£0.80**	**£2.40**	**£4.00**

X-MEN: BOOKS OF ASKANI
Marvel Comics Group,OS; 1 Feb 1996

	$Good	$Fine	$N.Mint	£Good	£Fine	£N.Mint
1 ND painted portraits by John Bolton, Bill Sienkiewicz and others	$0.60	$1.80	$3.00	£0.40	£1.20	£2.00
Title Value:	**$0.60**	**$1.80**	**$3.00**	**£0.40**	**£1.20**	**£2.00**

X-MEN: GOD LOVES, MAN KILLS
Marvel Comics Group,OS; 1 Oct 1994

	$Good	$Fine	$N.Mint	£Good	£Fine	£N.Mint
1 ND 64pgs, reprints Marvel Graphic Novel #5	$1.20	$3.60	$6.00	£0.80	£2.40	£4.00
Title Value:	**$1.20**	**$3.60**	**$6.00**	**£0.80**	**£2.40**	**£4.00**

X-MEN: MARVEL COLLECTOR'S EDITION
Marvel Comics Group,OS; 1 Oct 1993
1 ND scarce in the U.K. 16pgs, Magneto appears; available in conjunction with Stridex Acne Medication

	$Good	$Fine	$N.Mint	£Good	£Fine	£N.Mint
	$2.00	$6.00	$10.00	£1.50	£4.50	£7.50
Title Value:	$2.00	$6.00	$10.00	£1.50	£4.50	£7.50

X-MEN: OMEGA
Marvel Comics Group,OS; 1 Jun 1995
1 ND 48pgs, the conclusion to The Age of Xavier storyline; chromium cover

	$1.50	$4.50	$7.50	£1.00	£3.00	£5.00

1 ND 48pgs, (Jul 1995) gold variant cover with limited print run

	$8.00	$24.00	$40.00	£5.00	£15.00	£25.00
Title Value:	$9.50	$28.50	$47.50	£6.00	£18.00	£30.00

X-MEN: PRIME
Marvel Comics Group,OS; 1 Jul 1995
1 ND 48pgs, all the plotlines of the current X-titles converge and re-start here; Scott Lobdell and Fabian Nicieza script; Bryan Hitch art

	$1.50	$4.50	$7.50	£1.00	£3.00	£5.00
Title Value:	$1.50	$4.50	$7.50	£1.00	£3.00	£5.00

X-MEN: THE ANIMATED SERIES
Marvel Comics Group; 1 Nov 1992-15 Jan 1994
(see X-Men Adventures Season II)
1 based on US cartoon series, styled in the image of the original new X-Men from Uncanny X-Men #94

	$0.80	$2.40	$4.00	£0.50	£1.50	£2.50
2	$0.60	$1.80	$3.00	£0.40	£1.20	£2.00

3 title changed to "X-Men Adventures"; Magneto appears

	$0.50	$1.50	$2.50	£0.30	£0.90	£1.50
4 Magneto appears	$0.50	$1.50	$2.50	£0.30	£0.90	£1.50
5	$0.50	$1.50	$2.50	£0.30	£0.90	£1.50
6	$0.40	$1.20	$2.00	£0.25	£0.75	£1.25
7 Cable appears	$0.40	$1.20	$2.00	£0.25	£0.75	£1.25
8-9	$0.40	$1.20	$2.00	£0.25	£0.75	£1.25

10 Archangel guest-stars

	$0.40	$1.20	$2.00	£0.25	£0.75	£1.25
11-14	$0.40	$1.20	$2.00	£0.25	£0.75	£1.25

15 48pgs, eight page pin-up gallery

	$0.50	$1.50	$2.50	£0.30	£0.90	£1.50
Title Value:	$7.00	$21.00	$35.00	£4.35	£13.05	£21.75

X-Men Adventures Vol. 1 (Feb 1994)
Trade paperback 96pgs, reprints issues #1-4

				£0.60	£1.80	£3.00

X-Men Adventures Volume 2 (Jul 1994)
Trade paperback reprints issues #5-8

				£0.60	£1.80	£3.00

X-Men Adventures Volume 3 (Dec 1994)
Trade paperback reprints issues #9-12

				£0.80	£2.40	£4.00

X-Men Adventures Volume 4 (Jul 1995)
Trade paperback reprints issues #13-16

				£0.80	£2.40	£4.00

X-MEN: THE EARLY YEARS
Marvel Comics Group; 1 May 1994-17 Sep 1995
1 ND reprints begin from Uncanny X-Men #1 by Stan Lee and Jack Kirby

	$0.30	$0.90	$1.50	£0.20	£0.60	£1.00
2-16 ND	$0.30	$0.90	$1.50	£0.20	£0.60	£1.00

17 ND 48pgs, reprints Uncanny X-Men #17 and #18

	$0.50	$1.50	$2.50	£0.30	£0.90	£1.50
Title Value:	$5.30	$15.90	$26.50	£3.50	£10.50	£17.50

X-MEN: THE MANY LOVES OF JEAN & SCOTT
Marvel Comics Group,Magazine OS; 1 Mar 1994
1 ND wedding album issue with new stories, reprints and pin-ups

	$0.60	$1.80	$3.00	£0.40	£1.20	£2.00
Title Value:	$0.60	$1.80	$3.00	£0.40	£1.20	£2.00

X-MEN: YEAR OF THE MUTANTS COLLECTORS' REVIEW
Marvel Comics Group,OS; 1 Feb 1995
1 ND 48pgs, flip-book format; information on current creators and characters

	$0.40	$1.20	$2.00	£0.25	£0.75	£1.25
Title Value:	$0.40	$1.20	$2.00	£0.25	£0.75	£1.25

X-O MANOWAR
Valiant/Acclaim Comics; 0 Jul 1993; ½ 1994; 1 Feb 1992-present
½ ND produced in conjunction with Wizard Comics; issued in a Wizard protective Mylar with certificate of authenticity

	$1.00	$3.00	$5.00	£1.00	£3.00	£5.00

½ Gold Edition, ND as above, but with gold logo

	$1.50	$4.50	$7.50	£1.50	£4.50	£7.50

0 (Jul 1993), origin re-told and expanded, part Joe Quesada completely foil cover enhanced with metallic inks

	$0.60	$1.80	$3.00	£0.40	£1.20	£2.00

0 Limited Gold Edition

	$3.00	$9.00	$15.00	£1.50	£4.50	£7.50

0 Valiant Validated Signature Series Edition (Feb 1994), signed by Joe Quesada and Jimmy Palmiotti; 5,300 copies with certificate in Mylar sleeve

	$3.00	$9.00	$15.00	£1.50	£4.50	£7.50
1 origin	$2.00	$6.00	$10.00	£1.40	£4.20	£7.00
2 origin	$1.50	$4.50	$7.50	£1.00	£3.00	£5.00
3 Harada appears	$1.50	$4.50	$7.50	£1.00	£3.00	£5.00

4 Harbinger appears; 1st appearance (cameo) Jack Boniface (later Shadowman)

	$1.50	$4.50	$7.50	£1.00	£3.00	£5.00
5	$1.00	$3.00	$5.00	£0.60	£1.80	£3.00

6 part Steve Ditko art

	$1.00	$3.00	$5.00	£0.60	£1.80	£3.00
7 Unity: Chapter 5	$0.60	$1.80	$3.00	£0.40	£1.20	£2.00

8 Unity: Chapter 13, Harbinger appears, Walt Simonson cover

	$0.60	$1.80	$3.00	£0.40	£1.20	£2.00
9-10	$0.50	$1.50	$2.50	£0.30	£0.90	£1.50
11 Solar appears	$0.50	$1.50	$2.50	£0.30	£0.90	£1.50

12 continues in Solar, Man of the Atom #17

	$0.50	$1.50	$2.50	£0.30	£0.90	£1.50
13	$0.50	$1.50	$2.50	£0.30	£0.90	£1.50
14 Turok appears	$0.60	$1.80	$3.00	£0.40	£1.20	£2.00

14 Valiant Signature Series (Dec 1993) - signed set of issues #14 and #15, limited to 5,000 sets;

signed in gold ink on cover by Bart Sears

	$2.50	$7.50	$12.50	£1.50	£4.50	£7.50
15 Turok appears	$0.60	$1.80	$3.00	£0.40	£1.20	£2.00

15 Pink Logo variant - issued free with a box of Ultra-Pro mylar comic sleeves (Jul 1993)

	$1.00	$3.00	$5.00	£0.70	£2.10	£3.50
16-18	$0.50	$1.50	$2.50	£0.30	£0.90	£1.50

19 Randy Cartier becomes X-O, She God of War

	$0.50	$1.50	$2.50	£0.30	£0.90	£1.50
20	$0.50	$1.50	$2.50	£0.30	£0.90	£1.50
21-23	$0.40	$1.20	$2.00	£0.25	£0.75	£1.25

24 Cameo appearance of Armorines, the real X-O returns...

	$0.40	$1.20	$2.00	£0.25	£0.75	£1.25

25 Armorines #0 insert included

	$0.40	$1.20	$2.00	£0.25	£0.75	£1.25

27 Turok guest-stars

	$0.40	$1.20	$2.00	£0.25	£0.75	£1.25
28	$0.40	$1.20	$2.00	£0.25	£0.75	£1.25

29 Turok guest-stars

	$0.40	$1.20	$2.00	£0.25	£0.75	£1.25
30 Solar appears	$0.40	$1.20	$2.00	£0.25	£0.75	£1.25
31-32	$0.40	$1.20	$2.00	£0.25	£0.75	£1.25

33 Chaos Effect tie-in

	$0.40	$1.20	$2.00	£0.25	£0.75	£1.25
34-36	$0.40	$1.20	$2.00	£0.25	£0.75	£1.25

37-40 The Wolfbridge Affair, weekly issue

	$0.40	$1.20	$2.00	£0.25	£0.75	£1.25
41-43	$0.40	$1.20	$2.00	£0.25	£0.75	£1.25

44 1st Acclaim Comics issue, Bart Sears art; bi-weekly

	$0.40	$1.20	$2.00	£0.25	£0.75	£1.25

45 Bart Sears art; bi-weekly

	$0.40	$1.20	$2.00	£0.25	£0.75	£1.25
46-47 bi-weekly	$0.40	$1.20	$2.00	£0.25	£0.75	£1.25

48 Bart Sears art; bi-weekly

	$0.40	$1.20	$2.00	£0.25	£0.75	£1.25
49 bi-weekly	$0.40	$1.20	$2.00	£0.25	£0.75	£1.25

50 issue 50-X, story continued in #50-O

	$0.50	$1.50	$2.50	£0.30	£0.90	£1.50
50 issue 50-O	$0.50	$1.50	$2.50	£0.30	£0.90	£1.50
51-60 bi-weekly	$0.50	$1.50	$2.50	£0.30	£0.90	£1.50
Title Value:	$46.10	$138.30	$230.50	£29.15	£87.45	£145.75

Note: all Non-Distributed at the news-stands in the U.K.

X-O Manowar (Jul 1993) Trade paperback reprints issues #1-4 with new 8pg X-O Manowar Sourcebook, new cover by Bob Layton

				£1.35	£4.05	£6.75

Bart Sears' X-O Manowar Hardcover (Apr 1995)
collects all Bart Sears' work on the title including special issues

				£2.40	£7.20	£12.00

X-O MANOWAR YEARBOOK
Valiant/Acclaim Comics; 1 Apr 1995
1 ND Brian Hitch cover

	$0.60	$1.80	$3.00	£0.40	£1.20	£2.00
Title Value:	$0.60	$1.80	$3.00	£0.40	£1.20	£2.00

X-TERMINATORS
Marvel Comics Group,MS; 1 Oct 1988-4 Jan 1989
1 ND 1st appearance N'astirh; Inferno tie-in

	$0.60	$1.80	$3.00	£0.30	£0.90	£1.50
2-3 Inferno tie-in	$0.40	$1.20	$2.00	£0.25	£0.75	£1.25

4 co-stars New Mutants, Inferno tie-in

	$0.60	$1.80	$3.00	£0.25	£0.75	£1.25
Title Value:	$1.80	$5.40	$9.00	£1.05	£3.15	£5.25

X-THIEVES
Fictioneer; 7 Apr 1988-9 Jun 1988
(previously Aristocratic...)

7-9 ND	$0.40	$1.20	$2.00	£0.25	£0.75	£1.25
Title Value:	$1.20	$3.60	$6.00	£0.75	£2.25	£3.75

X-UNIVERSE
Marvel Comics Group,MS; 1 May 1995-2 Jun 1995
1-2 ND Ben Grimm, Sue Storm, Bruce Banner and Gwen Stacy appear; foil-stamped card-stock cover

	$0.60	$1.80	$3.00	£0.50	£1.50	£2.50
Title Value:	$1.60	$4.80	$8.00	£1.00	£3.00	£5.00

X: ONE SHOT TO THE HEAD
Dark Horse,OS; 1 Aug 1994
1 ND collects the early appearances from Dark Horse Comics #8-10

	$0.50	$1.50	$2.50	£0.30	£0.90	£1.50
Title Value:	$0.50	$1.50	$2.50	£0.30	£0.90	£1.50

XANADU: HELIA'S TALE
Eclipse; 1 1988
1 ND

	$0.40	$1.20	$2.00	£0.25	£0.75	£1.25
Title Value:	$0.40	$1.20	$2.00	£0.25	£0.75	£1.25

XANDER IN LOST UNIVERSE, GENE RODDENBURY'S
Tekno Comix; 1 Dec 1995-present
1 ND Jae Lee covers begin

	$0.45	$1.35	$2.25	£0.30	£0.90	£1.50
2 ND	$0.45	$1.35	$2.25	£0.30	£0.90	£1.50
3 ND Jae Lee cover	$0.45	$1.35	$2.25	£0.30	£0.90	£1.50

4 ND pre-bagged with back-issue Tekno comic; Jae Lee cover

	$0.45	$1.35	$2.25	£0.30	£0.90	£1.50
Title Value:	$1.80	$5.40	$9.00	£1.20	£3.60	£6.00

XENOBROOD
DC Comics,MS; 0 Oct 1994; 1 Nov 1994-6 Apr 1995
0 (Oct 1994) Zero Hour X-over, origin

	$0.40	$1.20	$2.00	£0.25	£0.75	£1.25

	$Good	$Fine	$N.Mint	£Good	£Fine	£N.Mint
1-2	$0.30	$0.90	$1.50	£0.20	£0.60	£1.00
3-4 Superman appears						
	$0.30	$0.90	$1.50	£0.20	£0.60	£1.00
5-6	$0.30	$0.90	$1.50	£0.20	£0.60	£1.00
Title Value:	$2.20	$6.60	$11.00	£1.45	£4.35	£7.25

XENON
Eclipse; 1 Dec 1987-23 1989

	$Good	$Fine	$N.Mint	£Good	£Fine	£N.Mint
1 ND Masaomi Kamzaki script/art (translated Japanese reprint); black and white						
	$0.30	$0.90	$1.50	£0.20	£0.60	£1.00
2-23 ND	$0.30	$0.90	$1.50	£0.20	£0.60	£1.00
Title Value:	$6.90	$20.70	$34.50	£4.60	£13.80	£23.00
Heavy Metal Warrior Part 1 (Aug 1991), reprints				£1.60	£4.80	£8.00
Heavy Metal Warrior Part 2 (Oct 1992), reprints				£1.85	£5.55	£9.25
Heavy Metal Warrior Part 3 (Dec 1992) reprints				£1.85	£5.55	£9.25
Heavy Metal Warrior Part 4 (Feb 1993) reprints				£1.85	£5.55	£9.25

XENOTECH
Mirage/Next Comics; 1 Aug 1994-3 1994

	$Good	$Fine	$N.Mint	£Good	£Fine	£N.Mint
1 ND Michael Doohey script, Robert Jones art begins						
	$0.50	$1.50	$2.50	£0.30	£0.90	£1.50
2 ND	$0.50	$1.50	$2.50	£0.30	£0.90	£1.50
3 ND with two bound-in trading cards						
	$0.50	$1.50	$2.50	£0.30	£0.90	£1.50
Title Value:	$1.50	$4.50	$7.50	£0.90	£2.70	£4.50

XENOZOIC TALES
Kitchen Sink; 1 Feb 1987-12 1990; 13 Dec 1994
(see Death Rattle #7)

	$Good	$Fine	$N.Mint	£Good	£Fine	£N.Mint
1 ND Mark Schultz script and art begins; black and white						
	$0.30	$0.90	$1.50	£0.20	£0.60	£1.00
1 2nd printing, ND (Jan 1989)						
	$0.25	$0.75	$1.25	£0.15	£0.45	£0.75
2 ND	$0.30	$0.90	$1.50	£0.20	£0.60	£1.00
2 2nd printing ND	$0.25	$0.75	$1.25	£0.15	£0.45	£0.75
3-11 ND	$0.30	$0.90	$1.50	£0.20	£0.60	£1.00
12 ND delayed issue with new format paper stock and heavier stock cover						
	$0.40	$1.20	$2.00	£0.25	£0.75	£1.25
13 ND Mark Schultz script and art returns; black and white						
	$0.50	$1.50	$2.50	£0.30	£0.90	£1.50
Title Value:	$4.70	$14.10	$23.50	£3.05	£9.15	£15.25

Xenozoic Tales: Cadillacs and Dinosaurs
Trade paperback reprints Xenozoic Tales #1-4 plus first story
from Death Rattle #8. 136pgs, black and white £2.00 £6.00 £10.00
Note: five printings are available that sell for about the same value

XIMOS
Triumphant Comics; 1 Feb 1994-2 1994

	$Good	$Fine	$N.Mint	£Good	£Fine	£N.Mint
1-2 ND	$0.40	$1.20	$2.00	£0.25	£0.75	£1.25
Title Value:	$0.80	$2.40	$4.00	£0.50	£1.50	£2.50

XIMOS: VIOLENT PAST
Triumphant Comics,MS; 1,2 Mar 1994

	$Good	$Fine	$N.Mint	£Good	£Fine	£N.Mint
1-2 ND	$0.40	$1.20	$2.00	£0.25	£0.75	£1.25
Title Value:	$0.80	$2.40	$4.00	£0.50	£1.50	£2.50

XOMBI
DC Comics/Milestone; 0 Jan 1994; 1 Jun 1994-21 Feb 1996

	$Good	$Fine	$N.Mint	£Good	£Fine	£N.Mint
0 (Jan 1994) Denys Cowan and Jimmy Palmiotti art begins; spot varnished cover by Walt Simonson						
	$0.40	$1.20	$2.00	£0.25	£0.75	£1.25
1 John Byrne cover						
	$0.40	$1.20	$2.00	£0.25	£0.75	£1.25
2-12	$0.40	$1.20	$2.00	£0.25	£0.75	£1.25
13 becomes a Mature Readers title						
	$0.40	$1.20	$2.00	£0.25	£0.75	£1.25
14-16	$0.40	$1.20	$2.00	£0.25	£0.75	£1.25
17 special price of 99 cents						
	$0.20	$0.60	$1.00	£0.10	£0.35	£0.65
18 Howard Chaykin cover						
	$0.40	$1.20	$2.00	£0.25	£0.75	£1.25
19-21	$0.40	$1.20	$2.00	£0.25	£0.75	£1.25
Title Value:	$8.60	$25.80	$43.00	£5.35	£16.10	£26.90

Y

YAKUZA
Eternity; 1 Sep 1987-5 1988

	$Good	$Fine	$N.Mint	£Good	£Fine	£N.Mint
1-5 ND	$0.40	$1.20	$2.00	£0.25	£0.75	£1.25
Title Value:	$2.00	$6.00	$10.00	£1.25	£3.75	£6.25

YANG
Charlton; 1 Nov 1973-13 May 1976; 14 Sep 1985-17 Jan 1986
(see House of Yang)

	$Good	$Fine	$N.Mint	£Good	£Fine	£N.Mint
1 distributed in the U.K.						
	$0.90	$2.70	$4.50	£0.60	£1.80	£3.00
2 distributed in the U.K.						
	$0.60	$1.80	$3.00	£0.40	£1.20	£2.00
3-10 distributed in the U.K.						
	$0.50	$1.50	$2.50	£0.30	£0.90	£1.50
11-17 distributed in the U.K.						
	$0.40	$1.20	$2.00	£0.25	£0.75	£1.25
Title Value:	$8.30	$24.90	$41.50	£5.15	£15.45	£25.75

YARN MAN
Kitchen Sink; 1 Oct 1989

	$Good	$Fine	$N.Mint	£Good	£Fine	£N.Mint
1 ND	$0.40	$1.20	$2.00	£0.25	£0.75	£1.25
Title Value:	$0.40	$1.20	$2.00	£0.25	£0.75	£1.25

YATTERING AND JACK HARDCOVER, THE
Eclipse,OS; 1 Feb 1992

	$Good	$Fine	$N.Mint	£Good	£Fine	£N.Mint
1 ND 64pgs, adaptation of Clive Barker story by Steve Niles and John Bolton						
	$4.50	$13.50	$22.50	£3.00	£9.00	£15.00
Title Value:	$4.50	$13.50	$22.50	£3.00	£9.00	£15.00

YELLOW SUBMARINE
Gold Key; 35000-902 1969

	$Good	$Fine	$N.Mint	£Good	£Fine	£N.Mint
nn LD scarce in the U.K. 64pgs, adapts film						
	$26.00	$77.50	$185.00	£17.50	£52.50	£125.00
Title Value:	$26.00	$77.50	$185.00	£17.50	£52.50	£125.00

Note: comes with pull-out poster that would lose up to 50% of the value if missing

YOGI BEAR
Charlton; 1 Nov 1970-35 Jan 1976

	$Good	$Fine	$N.Mint	£Good	£Fine	£N.Mint
1 scarce, distributed in the U.K. Ray Dirgo art						
	$3.75	$11.00	$22.50	£2.50	£7.50	£15.00
2	$2.05	$6.25	$12.50	£1.25	£3.75	£7.50
3-6	$1.65	$5.00	$10.00	£0.80	£2.50	£5.00
7 Summer Fun Giant						
	$2.05	$6.25	$12.50	£1.25	£3.75	£7.50
8-10	$1.65	$5.00	$10.00	£0.80	£2.50	£5.00
11-30	$1.50	$4.50	$7.50	£0.80	£2.40	£4.00
31-35	$1.20	$3.60	$6.00	£0.60	£1.80	£3.00
Title Value:	$55.40	$166.50	$297.50	£29.60	£89.50	£160.00

YOGI BEAR, HANNA-BARBERA'S
Marvel Comics Group; 1 Nov 1977-9 Mar 1979

	$Good	$Fine	$N.Mint	£Good	£Fine	£N.Mint
1 ND	$0.50	$1.50	$2.50	£0.30	£0.90	£1.50
2-9 ND	$0.40	$1.20	$2.00	£0.25	£0.75	£1.25
Title Value:	$3.70	$11.10	$18.50	£2.30	£6.90	£11.50

YOU'RE UNDER ARREST
Dark Horse,MS; 1 Dec 1995-present

	$Good	$Fine	$N.Mint	£Good	£Fine	£N.Mint
1-4 ND Kosuke Fujishima script and art; black and white						
	$0.60	$1.80	$3.00	£0.40	£1.20	£2.00
Title Value:	$2.40	$7.20	$12.00	£1.60	£4.80	£8.00

YOUNG ALL-STARS
DC Comics; 1 Jun 1987-31 Oct 1989

	$Good	$Fine	$N.Mint	£Good	£Fine	£N.Mint
1-7	$0.25	$0.75	$1.25	£0.15	£0.45	£0.75
8 unofficial Millennium X-over						
	$0.25	$0.75	$1.25	£0.15	£0.45	£0.75
9 Millennium X-over						
	$0.25	$0.75	$1.25	£0.15	£0.45	£0.75
10-14	$0.25	$0.75	$1.25	£0.15	£0.45	£0.75
15 LD in the U.K.	$0.25	$0.75	$1.25	£0.20	£0.60	£1.00
16-22	$0.25	$0.75	$1.25	£0.15	£0.45	£0.75
23 intro The Squire, Phantasmo, Fireball and Kuei the Man Demon						
	$0.25	$0.75	$1.25	£0.15	£0.45	£0.75
24-31	$0.25	$0.75	$1.25	£0.15	£0.45	£0.75
Title Value:	$7.75	$23.25	$38.75	£4.70	£14.10	£23.50

Note: Deluxe Format Baxter paper

YOUNG ALL-STARS ANNUAL
DC Comics; 1 1988

	$Good	$Fine	$N.Mint	£Good	£Fine	£N.Mint
1 48pgs	$0.30	$0.90	$1.50	£0.20	£0.60	£1.00
Title Value:	$0.30	$0.90	$1.50	£0.20	£0.60	£1.00

YOUNG DRACULA: DIARY OF A VAMPIRE
Caliber Press,MS; 1 Mar 1993-3 Jul 1993

	$Good	$Fine	$N.Mint	£Good	£Fine	£N.Mint
1-3 ND 48pgs	$0.60	$1.80	$3.00	£0.40	£1.20	£2.00
Title Value:	$1.80	$5.40	$9.00	£1.20	£3.60	£6.00

YOUNG GUN
AC Comics,OS; 1 1992

	$Good	$Fine	$N.Mint	£Good	£Fine	£N.Mint
1 ND black and white						
	$0.40	$1.20	$2.00	£0.25	£0.75	£1.25
Title Value:	$0.40	$1.20	$2.00	£0.25	£0.75	£1.25

YOUNG INDIANA JONES CHRONICLES, THE
Dark Horse; 1 Feb 1992-12 Jan 1993

	$Good	$Fine	$N.Mint	£Good	£Fine	£N.Mint
1 ND based on TV series, Dan Barry script/pencils, Frank Springer inks begin						
	$0.50	$1.50	$2.50	£0.30	£0.90	£1.50
2 ND Dan Barry script/art/cover						
	$0.50	$1.50	$2.50	£0.30	£0.90	£1.50
3-4 ND Dan Barry and Gray Morrow script/art						
	$0.50	$1.50	$2.50	£0.30	£0.90	£1.50
5-12 ND Dan Barry script/art/cover						
	$0.50	$1.50	$2.50	£0.30	£0.90	£1.50
Title Value:	$6.00	$18.00	$30.00	£3.60	£10.80	£18.00

YOUNG LOVE
National Periodical Publications/DC Comics; 39 Sep/Oct 1963-120 Winter 1975/6; 121 Oct 1976-126 Jul 1977
(#1-38 published by Prize Features)

	$Good	$Fine	$N.Mint	£Good	£Fine	£N.Mint
39 scarce in the U.K.						
	$3.75	$11.00	$22.50	£2.50	£7.50	£15.00
40-50 scarce in the U.K.						
	$2.50	$7.50	$15.00	£1.65	£5.00	£10.00
51-60	$2.05	$6.25	$12.50	£1.25	£3.75	£7.50
61-63	$1.65	$5.00	$10.00	£1.15	£3.50	£7.00
64 Joe Simon & Jack Kirby art						
	$2.05	$6.25	$12.50	£1.25	£3.75	£7.50
65-70	$1.65	$5.00	$10.00	£1.15	£3.50	£7.00
71-72	$1.25	$3.75	$7.50	£0.80	£2.50	£5.00
73 Alex Toth art	$1.50	$4.50	$9.00	£1.00	£3.00	£6.00
74-77	$1.25	$3.75	$7.50	£0.80	£2.50	£5.00
78-79 Alex Toth art						
	$1.50	$4.50	$9.00	£1.00	£3.00	£6.00
80	$1.25	$3.75	$7.50	£0.80	£2.50	£5.00
81-90	$1.00	$3.00	$5.00	£0.70	£2.10	£3.50
91-100	$0.80	$2.40	$4.00	£0.50	£1.50	£2.50
101-106	$0.60	$1.80	$3.00	£0.40	£1.20	£2.00

	$Good	$Fine	$N.Mint	£Good	£Fine	£N.Mint
107-114 scarce in the U.K. 100pgs						
	$0.80	$2.40	$4.00	£0.50	£1.50	£2.50
115-121	$0.60	$1.80	$3.00	£0.40	£1.20	£2.00
122 Alex Toth art	$0.60	$1.80	$3.00	£0.40	£1.20	£2.00
123-126	$0.60	$1.80	$3.00	£0.40	£1.20	£2.00
Title Value:	$117.10	$352.60	$670.50	£76.55	£231.35	£439.50

YOUNG MASTER
New Comics Group; 1 Nov 1987-9 1989
(becomes The Master)

	$Good	$Fine	$N.Mint	£Good	£Fine	£N.Mint
1 ND Hama script/Meyerick art begins						
	$0.40	$1.20	$2.00	£0.25	£0.75	£1.25
2-9 ND	$0.40	$1.20	$2.00	£0.25	£0.75	£1.25
Title Value:	$3.60	$10.80	$18.00	£2.25	£6.75	£11.25

YOUNG ROMANCE COMICS
National Periodical Publications; 125 Aug/Sep 1963/1964-208 Nov/Dec 1975
(previous issues published by Prize/Headline and ND)

	$Good	$Fine	$N.Mint	£Good	£Fine	£N.Mint
125 scarce in the U.K.						
	$4.15	$12.50	$25.00	£2.90	£8.75	£17.50
126-130 scarce in the U.K.						
	$2.50	$7.50	$15.00	£1.65	£5.00	£10.00
131-135 scarce in the U.K.						
	$2.05	$6.25	$12.50	£1.40	£4.25	£8.50
136-150	$2.05	$6.25	$12.50	£1.25	£3.75	£7.50
151-160	$1.80	$5.25	$9.00	£1.20	£3.60	£6.00
161-170	$1.50	$4.50	$7.50	£1.00	£3.00	£5.00
171-190	$1.00	$3.00	$5.00	£0.70	£2.10	£3.50
191-196	$0.80	$2.40	$4.00	£0.50	£1.50	£2.50
197-204 less common in the U.K. 100pgs						
	$0.90	$2.70	$4.50	£0.60	£1.80	£3.00
205-208	$0.80	$2.40	$4.00	£0.50	£1.50	£2.50
Title Value:	$125.85	$378.10	$691.00	£82.70	£248.65	£451.50

YOUNG ZEN INTERGALACTIC NINJA SPECIAL: CITY OF DEATH
Entity Comics,OS; 1 1994

	$Good	$Fine	$N.Mint	£Good	£Fine	£N.Mint
1 ND gold foil stamped cover						
	$0.80	$2.40	$4.00	£0.50	£1.50	£2.50
Title Value:	$0.80	$2.40	$4.00	£0.50	£1.50	£2.50

YOUNGBLOOD
Image; 0 Dec 1992; 1 Apr 1992-10 1995

	$Good	$Fine	$N.Mint	£Good	£Fine	£N.Mint
0 (Dec 1992), origin Youngblood team, includes two trading cards and Image #0 coupon 7						
	$0.60	$1.80	$3.00	£0.40	£1.20	£2.00
0 without coupon	$0.50	$1.50	$2.50	£0.30	£0.90	£1.50
0 Gold cover Edition						
	$3.00	$9.00	$15.00	£2.00	£6.00	£10.00
0 Gold Cover Signed Edition						
	$4.00	$12.00	$20.00	£2.80	£8.25	£14.00
1 Rob Liefeld script/art, includes two trading cards; 1st appearance Youngblood						
	$1.20	$3.60	$6.00	£0.70	£2.10	£3.50
1 The Silent Edition (Jun 1994), without word balloons; card-stock cover						
	$1.50	$4.50	$7.50	£1.00	£3.00	£5.00
1 2nd printing, no trading cards						
	$0.60	$1.80	$3.00	£0.40	£1.20	£2.00
2 Rob Liefeld script/art, includes two trading cards; 1st appearance Shadowhawk						
	$0.90	$2.70	$4.50	£0.60	£1.80	£3.00
3 Rob Liefeld script/art, includes two trading cards; 1st appearance Supreme						
	$0.60	$1.80	$3.00	£0.40	£1.20	£2.00
4 Rob Liefeld script/art, includes two trading cards, glow-in-the-dark cover; 1st appearance Pitt						
	$0.60	$1.80	$3.00	£0.40	£1.20	£2.00
5	$0.60	$1.80	$3.00	£0.40	£1.20	£2.00
6 48pgs, story continued from Team Youngblood #9						
	$0.80	$2.40	$4.00	£0.50	£1.50	£2.50
7	$0.50	$1.50	$2.50	£0.30	£0.90	£1.50

	$Good	$Fine	$N.Mint	£Good	£Fine	£N.Mint
8 Chapel vs. Spawn						
	$0.50	$1.50	$2.50	£0.30	£0.90	£1.50
9 Image X Month tie-in						
	$0.50	$1.50	$2.50	£0.30	£0.90	£1.50
10 Chapel commits suicide						
	$0.50	$1.50	$2.50	£0.30	£0.90	£1.50
Title Value:	$16.90	$50.70	$84.50	£11.10	£33.15	£55.50

Note: originally a 3 issue series was expanded into 4. The new issue 3 has expanded contents from issue 2 and the new issue 4 contains what was originally issue 3. All Non-Distributed on the news-stands in the U.K.

	$Good	$Fine	$N.Mint	£Good	£Fine	£N.Mint
Youngblood (Jan 1995)						
Trade paperback reprints issues #1-5, re-dialogued			£2.20	£6.60	£11.00

YOUNGBLOOD
Image; 1 Sep 1995-present

	$Good	$Fine	$N.Mint	£Good	£Fine	£N.Mint
1-2 ND Rob Liefeld and Eric Stephenson script, Roger Cruz and Danny Miki art						
	$0.50	$1.50	$2.50	£0.30	£0.90	£1.50
3 ND Extreme Babewatch tie-in; 4 alternate covers available (distributed in equal quantities)						
	$0.50	$1.50	$2.50	£0.30	£0.90	£1.50
Title Value:	$1.50	$4.50	$7.50	£0.90	£2.70	£4.50

YOUNGBLOOD YEAR ONE
Image; 1 Nov 1994-2 1995

	$Good	$Fine	$N.Mint	£Good	£Fine	£N.Mint
1 ND Rob Liefeld script, Danny Miki art, cover by George Perez						
	$0.50	$1.50	$2.50	£0.30	£0.90	£1.50
2 ND Liefeld and Miki						
	$0.50	$1.50	$2.50	£0.30	£0.90	£1.50
Title Value:	$1.00	$3.00	$5.00	£0.60	£1.80	£3.00

YOUNGBLOOD YEARBOOK
Image,OS; 1 Jul 1993

	$Good	$Fine	$N.Mint	£Good	£Fine	£N.Mint
1 ND Chap Yaep and Norm Rapmund art; four-page fold-out						
	$0.50	$1.50	$2.50	£0.30	£0.90	£1.50
Title Value:	$0.50	$1.50	$2.50	£0.30	£0.90	£1.50

YOUNGBLOOD: BATTLEZONE
Image; 1 May 1993; 2 Jul 1993

	$Good	$Fine	$N.Mint	£Good	£Fine	£N.Mint
1-2 ND information and specifications of Youngblood weaponry and vehicles etc; Liefeld cover						
	$0.50	$1.50	$2.50	£0.30	£0.90	£1.50
Title Value:	$1.00	$3.00	$5.00	£0.60	£1.80	£3.00

YOUNGBLOOD: STRIKE FILE
Image; 1 Apr 1993-11 Feb 1995

	$Good	$Fine	$N.Mint	£Good	£Fine	£N.Mint
1 ND Rob Liefeld script and art begins, 1st appearance Glory						
	$0.60	$1.80	$3.00	£0.40	£1.20	£2.00
1 ND Gold Edition	$1.20	$3.60	$6.00	£0.80	£2.40	£4.00
2-5 ND	$0.40	$1.20	$2.00	£0.25	£0.75	£1.25
6 ND flip-book format featuring two stories with Badrock and Masada						
	$0.50	$1.50	$2.50	£0.30	£0.90	£1.50
7 ND flip-book format featuring two stories with Troll and Die Hard						
	$0.50	$1.50	$2.50	£0.30	£0.90	£1.50
8 ND flip-book format featuring two stories with Shaft and Dutch						
	$0.50	$1.50	$2.50	£0.30	£0.90	£1.50
9 ND	$0.50	$1.50	$2.50	£0.30	£0.90	£1.50
10 ND 1st appearance the Bloodpool						
	$0.50	$1.50	$2.50	£0.30	£0.90	£1.50
11 ND Extreme Sacrifice tie-in; origins of Link and Crypt						
	$0.50	$1.50	$2.50	£0.30	£0.90	£1.50
Title Value:	$6.40	$19.20	$32.00	£4.00	£12.00	£20.00

YUMMY FUR
Vortex/Drawn & Quarterly, ; 1 Dec 1986-32 1994?

	$Good	$Fine	$N.Mint	£Good	£Fine	£N.Mint
1 reprints Chester Brown mini-comics #1 (originally published from July 1983 to September 1985)						
	$0.80	$2.40	$4.00	£0.50	£1.50	£2.50
2 reprints Chester Brown mini-comics #2 (originally published from July 1983 to September 1985)						
	$0.60	$1.80	$3.00	£0.40	£1.20	£2.00
3 reprints Chester Brown mini-comics #3 (originally published from July 1983 to September 1985)						
	$0.60	$1.80	$3.00	£0.40	£1.20	£2.00

Yang #1

Young Love #8

Zen Intergalactic Ninja (2nd) #1

	$Good	$Fine	$N.Mint	£Good	£Fine	£N.Mint
4 new material begins						
	$0.50	$1.50	$2.50	£0.30	£0.90	£1.50
5-8	$0.50	$1.50	$2.50	£0.30	£0.90	£1.50
9 very scarce in the U.K.						
	$0.50	$1.50	$2.50	£0.50	£1.50	£2.50
10-26	$0.50	$1.50	$2.50	£0.30	£0.90	£1.50
27 last Vortex issue						
	$0.50	$1.50	$2.50	£0.30	£0.90	£1.50
28-31	$0.50	$1.50	$2.50	£0.30	£0.90	£1.50
32 $2.95 cover	$0.60	$1.80	$3.00	£0.40	£1.20	£2.00
Title Value:	$16.60	$49.80	$83.00	£10.30	£30.90	£51.50
Note: all Non-Distributed on the news-stands in the U.K.						
Book 1 (Aug 1990), reprints issues #1-12 plus new story		£1.00	£3.00	£5.00		

YUPPIES FROM HELL
Marvel Comics Group,OS; 1 Feb 1989
1 ND black and white social satire by Barbara Slate

	$Good	$Fine	$N.Mint	£Good	£Fine	£N.Mint
	$0.70	$2.10	$3.50	£0.50	£1.50	£2.50
1 ND black and white social satire by Barbara Slate (2nd print - Jan 1991)						
	$0.60	$1.80	$3.00	£0.40	£1.20	£2.00
Title Value:	$1.30	$3.90	$6.50	£0.90	£2.70	£4.50

YUPPIES FROM HELL
Marvel Comics Group,OS; 1 Apr 1992
1 ND Barbara Slate script/art

	$Good	$Fine	$N.Mint	£Good	£Fine	£N.Mint
	$0.50	$1.50	$2.50	£0.30	£0.90	£1.50
Title Value:	$0.50	$1.50	$2.50	£0.30	£0.90	£1.50

YUPPIES FROM HELL, SON OF
Marvel Comics Group; 1 Jan 1991
1 ND Barbara Slate continues the satire

	$Good	$Fine	$N.Mint	£Good	£Fine	£N.Mint
	$0.50	$1.50	$2.50	£0.30	£0.90	£1.50
Title Value:	$0.50	$1.50	$2.50	£0.30	£0.90	£1.50

Z

ZAMINDAR
Innovation; 1 Jan 1994-2 Feb 1994
1-2 ND adaptation of sci-fi film

	$Good	$Fine	$N.Mint	£Good	£Fine	£N.Mint
	$0.50	$1.50	$2.50	£0.30	£0.90	£1.50
Title Value:	$1.00	$3.00	$5.00	£0.60	£1.80	£3.00

ZAP
Last Gasp; 1 1990-12 1990
1-12 reprints of 1960s comics inc. covers featuring "underground" material by Robert Crumb et al.

	$Good	$Fine	$N.Mint	£Good	£Fine	£N.Mint
	$0.40	$1.20	$2.00	£0.25	£0.75	£1.25
Title Value:	$4.80	$14.40	$24.00	£3.00	£9.00	£15.00
Note: all Non-Distributed on the news-stands in the U.K.						

ZATANNA
DC Comics,MS; 1 Jul 1993-4 Oct 1993

	$Good	$Fine	$N.Mint	£Good	£Fine	£N.Mint
1	$0.40	$1.20	$2.00	£0.25	£0.75	£1.25
2 new costume	$0.40	$1.20	$2.00	£0.25	£0.75	£1.25
3-4	$0.40	$1.20	$2.00	£0.25	£0.75	£1.25
Title Value:	$1.60	$4.80	$8.00	£1.00	£3.00	£5.00

ZATANNA SPECIAL
DC Comics,OS; 1 Apr 1987
1 64pgs, Gray Morrow art, no ads

	$Good	$Fine	$N.Mint	£Good	£Fine	£N.Mint
	$0.30	$0.90	$1.50	£0.20	£0.60	£1.00
Title Value:	$0.30	$0.90	$1.50	£0.20	£0.60	£1.00

ZEALOT
Image,MS; 1 Aug 1995-3 Oct 1995
1 ND Ron Marz script, Terry Shoemaker and Jon Holdredge art

	$Good	$Fine	$N.Mint	£Good	£Fine	£N.Mint
	$0.60	$1.80	$3.00	£0.40	£1.20	£2.00
2-3 ND	$0.50	$1.50	$2.50	£0.30	£0.90	£1.50
Title Value:	$1.60	$4.80	$8.00	£1.00	£3.00	£5.00

ZELL, SWORDANCER
Thoughts and Images; 1 1986
1 ND

	$Good	$Fine	$N.Mint	£Good	£Fine	£N.Mint
	$0.40	$1.20	$2.00	£0.25	£0.75	£1.25
Title Value:	$0.40	$1.20	$2.00	£0.25	£0.75	£1.25

ZEN INTERGALACTIC NINJA
Archie; 1 May 1992-3 Jul 1992

	$Good	$Fine	$N.Mint	£Good	£Fine	£N.Mint
1-3 ND	$0.50	$1.50	$2.50	£0.30	£0.90	£1.50
Title Value:	$1.50	$4.50	$7.50	£0.90	£2.70	£4.50

ZEN INTERGALACTIC NINJA
Zen Comics; 0 Jun/Jul 1993; 1 Aug 1993-5 1994
0 ND (Jun/Jul 1993) - available direct only from publishers; gold embossed cover, black and white interior

	$Good	$Fine	$N.Mint	£Good	£Fine	£N.Mint
	$1.50	$4.50	$7.50	£1.00	£3.00	£5.00
1 ND Stern, Andru and Eposito begin						
	$0.50	$1.50	$2.50	£0.30	£0.90	£1.50
1 2nd printing, ND (1992)						
	$0.30	$0.90	$1.50	£0.20	£0.60	£1.00
2 ND	$0.50	$1.50	$2.50	£0.30	£0.90	£1.50
2 2nd printing, ND (1992)						
	$0.30	$0.90	$1.50	£0.20	£0.60	£1.00
3 ND	$0.50	$1.50	$2.50	£0.30	£0.90	£1.50
3 2nd printing ND	$0.30	$0.90	$1.50	£0.20	£0.60	£1.00
4-5 ND	$0.50	$1.50	$2.50	£0.30	£0.90	£1.50
Title Value:	$4.90	$14.70	$24.50	£3.10	£9.30	£15.50

ZEN INTERGALACTIC NINJA - MILESTONE
Entity Comics,MS; 1 Mar 1994-3 Jul 1994
1 ND features Mike Esposito and Ross Andru art

	$Good	$Fine	$N.Mint	£Good	£Fine	£N.Mint
	$0.50	$1.50	$2.50	£0.30	£0.90	£1.50
1 ND Gold Edition (Mar 1994) with new gold foil stamped cover						
	$0.60	$1.80	$3.00	£0.40	£1.20	£2.00
2-3 ND features Mike Esposito and Ross Andru art						

	$Good	$Fine	$N.Mint	£Good	£Fine	£N.Mint
	$0.50	$1.50	$2.50	£0.30	£0.90	£1.50
Title Value:	$2.10	$6.30	$10.50	£1.30	£3.90	£6.50
Note: reprints "Defend the Earth" series originally published by Archie						

ZEN INTERGALACTIC NINJA APRIL FOOL'S SPECIAL
Entity Comics,OS; 1 Apr 1994
1 ND black and white

	$Good	$Fine	$N.Mint	£Good	£Fine	£N.Mint
	$0.50	$1.50	$2.50	£0.30	£0.90	£1.50
Title Value:	$0.50	$1.50	$2.50	£0.30	£0.90	£1.50

ZEN INTERGALACTIC NINJA COLOUR DELUXE
Entity Comics; 0 1994; 1 Mar 1994-7 Feb 1995
0 ND Jae Lee cover art

	$Good	$Fine	$N.Mint	£Good	£Fine	£N.Mint
	$0.50	$1.50	$2.50	£0.30	£0.90	£1.50
1 ND	$0.50	$1.50	$2.50	£0.30	£0.90	£1.50
1 ND pre-bagged with chromium trading card						
	$0.80	$2.40	$4.00	£0.50	£1.50	£2.50
2 ND	$0.50	$1.50	$2.50	£0.30	£0.90	£1.50
2 ND pre-bagged with chromium trading card						
	$0.80	$2.40	$4.00	£0.50	£1.50	£2.50
3 ND 3-part Fire Upon The Earth story concludes						
	$0.50	$1.50	$2.50	£0.30	£0.90	£1.50
4-6 ND Battle Beyond the Ozone story						
	$0.50	$1.50	$2.50	£0.30	£0.90	£1.50
7 ND Battle Beyond the Ozone story; foil-enhanced cover						
	$0.50	$1.50	$2.50	£0.30	£0.90	£1.50
Title Value:	$5.60	$16.80	$28.00	£3.40	£10.20	£17.00
Zen Intergalactic Ninja: A Fire Upon The Earth (Dec 1994)						
Trade paperback reprints issues #0-3, foil-stamped cover				£1.70	£5.10	£8.50

ZEN INTERGALACTIC NINJA COLOUR DELUXE (2ND SERIES)
Entity Comics; 1 Mar 1995-present
1-2 ND Roger Stern script, Joe Orbeta art

	$Good	$Fine	$N.Mint	£Good	£Fine	£N.Mint
	$0.50	$1.50	$2.50	£0.30	£0.90	£1.50
2 ND Deluxe Edition (May 1995) - pre-bagged with interactive plactic phone card						
	$1.00	$3.00	$5.00	£0.65	£1.95	£3.25
3-4 ND Roger Stern script, Joe Orbeta art						
	$0.50	$1.50	$2.50	£0.30	£0.90	£1.50
5 ND	$0.50	$1.50	$2.50	£0.30	£0.90	£1.50
Title Value:	$3.50	$10.50	$17.50	£2.15	£6.45	£10.75

ZEN INTERGALACTIC NINJA EARTH-DAY ANNUAL
Zen Comics; 1 Jun 1993
1 ND metallic cover by Sam Kieth

	$Good	$Fine	$N.Mint	£Good	£Fine	£N.Mint
	$0.60	$1.80	$3.00	£0.40	£1.20	£2.00
Title Value:	$0.60	$1.80	$3.00	£0.40	£1.20	£2.00

ZEN INTERGALACTIC NINJA SPECIAL, THE ART OF
Entity Comics,OS; 1 Jun 1994
1 ND pin-ups collection; part Frank Brunner cover

	$Good	$Fine	$N.Mint	£Good	£Fine	£N.Mint
	$0.60	$1.80	$3.00	£0.40	£1.20	£2.00
1 2nd printing, ND (Jan 1995)						
	$0.60	$1.80	$3.00	£0.40	£1.20	£2.00
Title Value:	$1.20	$3.60	$6.00	£0.80	£2.40	£4.00

ZEN INTERGALACTIC NINJA SPRING SPECTACULAR
Entity Comics,OS; 1 Apr 1994
1 ND Hearn Cho script/art; black and white

	$Good	$Fine	$N.Mint	£Good	£Fine	£N.Mint
	$0.50	$1.50	$2.50	£0.30	£0.90	£1.50
Title Value:	$0.50	$1.50	$2.50	£0.30	£0.90	£1.50

ZEN INTERGALACTIC NINJA SUMMER SPECIAL: VIDEO WARRIOR
Entity Comics; 1 Jun 1994
1 ND prismatic vortex holo-foil enhanced cover (!)

	$Good	$Fine	$N.Mint	£Good	£Fine	£N.Mint
	$0.60	$1.80	$3.00	£0.40	£1.20	£2.00
Title Value:	$0.60	$1.80	$3.00	£0.40	£1.20	£2.00

ZEN INTERGALACTIC NINJA XMAS SPECIAL
Zen Comics,OS; 1 Feb 1993
1 ND

	$Good	$Fine	$N.Mint	£Good	£Fine	£N.Mint
1 ND	$0.50	$1.50	$2.50	£0.30	£0.90	£1.50
1 ND foil-stamped cover limited to 1,000 copies						
	$0.80	$2.40	$4.00	£0.50	£1.50	£2.50
Title Value:	$1.30	$3.90	$6.50	£0.80	£2.40	£4.00

ZEN INTERGALACTIC NINJA: MISTRESS OF CHAOS
Entity Comics,OS; 1 May 1994
1 ND Steve Stern text with Bill Maus illustrations; card stock cover

	$Good	$Fine	$N.Mint	£Good	£Fine	£N.Mint
	$0.50	$1.50	$2.50	£0.30	£0.90	£1.50
Title Value:	$0.50	$1.50	$2.50	£0.30	£0.90	£1.50

ZEN INTERGALACTIC NINJA: STAR QUEST
Entity Comics; 1 Mar 1994-present
1-11 ND gold foil enhanced cover

	$Good	$Fine	$N.Mint	£Good	£Fine	£N.Mint
	$0.60	$1.80	$3.00	£0.40	£1.20	£2.00
Title Value:	$6.60	$19.80	$33.00	£4.40	£13.20	£22.00
Zen Intergalactic Ninja: Starquest (Jan 1995)						
Trade paperback reprints issues #1-4 with foil-stamped cover				£0.90	£2.70	£4.50

ZEN INTERGALACTIC NINJA: THE HUNTED
Entity Comics,MS; 1 Nov 1993-3 Jan 1994
1 ND Bill Maus script and art, silver foil stamped cover

	$Good	$Fine	$N.Mint	£Good	£Fine	£N.Mint
	$0.60	$1.80	$3.00	£0.40	£1.20	£2.00
1 ND Bill Maus script and art, silver foil stamped cover; pre-bagged with chromium trading card by Sam Kieth						
	$0.80	$2.40	$4.00	£0.50	£1.50	£2.50
2-3 ND Bill Maus script and art, silver foil stamped cover						
	$0.60	$1.80	$3.00	£0.40	£1.20	£2.00
Title Value:	$2.60	$7.80	$13.00	£1.70	£5.10	£8.50
Zen Intergalactic Ninja: The Hunted (Oct 1994)						
Trade paperback collects mini-series plus Nira X preview				£0.90	£2.70	£4.50
Signed & Numbered Hardcover (Oct 1994)				£4.00	£12.00	£20.00

ZEN YEARBOOK: HAZARDOUS DUTY
Entity Comics; 1 Dec 1994
1 ND foil-stamped enhanced cover

	$Good	$Fine	$N.Mint	£Good	£Fine	£N.Mint
	$0.60	$1.80	$3.00	£0.40	£1.20	£2.00
Title Value:	$0.60	$1.80	$3.00	£0.40	£1.20	£2.00

ZERO HOUR

DC Comics,MS; 0 Sep 1994-4 Sep 1994
(see Zero Issues in 40 individual DC titles)

	$Good	$Fine	$N.Mint	£Good	£Fine	£N.Mint
4 Zero Hour: Crisis in Time part 1; Dan Jurgens and Jerry Ordway creative team						
	$0.30	$0.90	$1.50	£0.20	£0.60	£1.00
3 Zero Hour: Crisis in Time part 2						
	$0.30	$0.90	$1.50	£0.20	£0.60	£1.00
2 Zero Hour: Crisis in Time part 3, birth of Power Girl's child						
	$0.30	$0.90	$1.50	£0.20	£0.60	£1.00
1 Zero Hour: Crisis in Time part 4; 25th and 30th centuries are removed from DC continuity						
	$0.30	$0.90	$1.50	£0.20	£0.60	£1.00
0 gatefold Time-line chart; birth of a new DC Universe						
	$0.30	$0.90	$1.50	£0.20	£0.60	£1.00
Title Value:	$1.50	$4.50	$7.50	£1.00	£3.00	£5.00

ZERO ISSUES

As part of DC Comics "Zero Hour" mini-series, most of the main DC titles of the time had special "0" issues, usually re-telling origins and acting as jumping-on points for new readers. Distinguished by some excellent cover art, the Zero Isuues are as follows in alphabetical order:

Action Comics #0
Adventures of Superman #0
Anima #0
Aquaman #0
Batman #0
Batman: Legends of the Dark Knight #0
Batman: Shadow of the Bat #0
Catwoman #0
Damage #0
Darkstars #0
Deathstroke the Hunted #0
Demon #0
Detective Comics #0
Fate #0
Flash #0
Green Arrow #0
Green Lantern #0
Gunfire #0
Guy Gardner, Warrior #0
Hawkman #0
Justice League of America #0
Justice League Task Force #0
Legionnaires #0
Legion of Super-Heroes #0
Lobo #0
Manhunter #0
New Titans #0
Outsiders #0
Primal Force #0
Ray #0
Rebels '94 #0
Robin #0
Spectre #0
Starman #0
Steel #0
Superboy #0
Superman #0
Superman: The Man of Steel #0
Wonder Woman #0
Xenobrood #0

ZERO PATROL

Continuity; 1 Nov 1984-10 1992

	$Good	$Fine	$N.Mint	£Good	£Fine	£N.Mint
1-2 Neal Adams script, cover and part art, Megalith backup						
	$0.30	$0.90	$1.50	£0.20	£0.60	£1.00
3 part Neal Adams art						
	$0.30	$0.90	$1.50	£0.20	£0.60	£1.00
4 part Neal Adams script, art and cover						
	$0.30	$0.90	$1.50	£0.20	£0.60	£1.00
5 part Neal Adams art						
	$0.30	$0.90	$1.50	£0.20	£0.60	£1.00
6-10	$0.30	$0.90	$1.50	£0.20	£0.60	£1.00
Title Value:	$3.00	$9.00	$15.00	£2.00	£6.00	£10.00

Note: all Non-Distributed on the news-stands in the U.K.

ZERO TOLERANCE

First,MS; 1 Oct 1990-4 Jan 1991

	$Good	$Fine	$N.Mint	£Good	£Fine	£N.Mint
1-4 ND Tim Vigil pencils, Tim Tyler inks						
	$0.40	$1.20	$2.00	£0.25	£0.75	£1.25
Title Value:	$1.60	$4.80	$8.00	£1.00	£3.00	£5.00

ZETRAMAN

Antarctic Press,MS; 1 Sep 1991-3 Feb 1992

	$Good	$Fine	$N.Mint	£Good	£Fine	£N.Mint
1-3 ND	$0.40	$1.20	$2.00	£0.25	£0.75	£1.25
Title Value:	$1.20	$3.60	$6.00	£0.75	£2.25	£3.75

ZETRAMAN 2

Antarctic Press,MS; 1 Oct 1993-2 Dec 1994; 3 Aug 1995

	$Good	$Fine	$N.Mint	£Good	£Fine	£N.Mint
1-3 ND	$0.40	$1.20	$2.00	£0.25	£0.75	£1.25
Title Value:	$1.20	$3.60	$6.00	£0.75	£2.25	£3.75

ZILLION

Eternity; 1 Apr 1993-6 Sep 1993

	$Good	$Fine	$N.Mint	£Good	£Fine	£N.Mint
1 ND Tom Mason script and Harrison Fong art begins, plastic coated covers; black and white						
	$0.40	$1.20	$2.00	£0.25	£0.75	£1.25
2-6 ND	$0.40	$1.20	$2.00	£0.25	£0.75	£1.25
Title Value:	$2.40	$7.20	$12.00	£1.50	£4.50	£7.50

ZIPPY QUARTERLY

Fantagraphics,Magazine; 1 Mar 1993-present

	$Good	$Fine	$N.Mint	£Good	£Fine	£N.Mint
1-3 ND 48pgs	$0.90	$2.70	$4.50	£0.60	£1.80	£3.00
4-9 ND 32pgs	$0.80	$2.40	$4.00	£0.50	£1.50	£2.50
10 ND 40pgs	$0.90	$2.70	$4.50	£0.60	£1.80	£3.00
11 ND 32pgs	$0.80	$2.40	$4.00	£0.50	£1.50	£2.50
Title Value:	$9.20	$27.60	$46.00	£5.90	£17.70	£29.50

ZOMBIE WAR

Fantaco/Tundra,MS; 1 Jun 1992-2 Aug 1992

	$Good	$Fine	$N.Mint	£Good	£Fine	£N.Mint
1-2 ND co-scripted by Kevin Eastman						
	$0.50	$1.50	$2.50	£0.30	£0.90	£1.50
Title Value:	$1.00	$3.00	$5.00	£0.60	£1.80	£3.00

ZONE

Dark Horse,OS; 1 Jun 1990

	$Good	$Fine	$N.Mint	£Good	£Fine	£N.Mint
1 ND ties up plot from Dark Horse Presents						
	$0.40	$1.20	$2.00	£0.25	£0.75	£1.25
Title Value:	$0.40	$1.20	$2.00	£0.25	£0.75	£1.25

ZONE CONTINUUM

Caliber Press,MS; 1 Aug 1992-4 Nov 1992

	$Good	$Fine	$N.Mint	£Good	£Fine	£N.Mint
1-4 ND Bruce Zick script/art, black and white						
	$0.40	$1.20	$2.00	£0.25	£0.75	£1.25
Title Value:	$1.60	$4.80	$8.00	£1.00	£3.00	£5.00

ZONE CONTINUUM (2ND SERIES)

Caliber Press; 1 Mar 1994-2 Dec 1994

	$Good	$Fine	$N.Mint	£Good	£Fine	£N.Mint
1-2 ND Bruce Zick script and art, black and white						
	$0.50	$1.50	$2.50	£0.30	£0.90	£1.50
Title Value:	$1.00	$3.00	$5.00	£0.60	£1.80	£3.00

ZOONIVERSE

Eclipse,MS; 1 Aug 1986-6 Jun 1987

	$Good	$Fine	$N.Mint	£Good	£Fine	£N.Mint
1-4 ND	$0.30	$0.90	$1.50	£0.20	£0.60	£1.00
5 ND rare in the U.K. (never imported into U.K. comic shops)						
	$0.30	$0.90	$1.50	£0.25	£0.75	£1.25
6 ND	$0.30	$0.90	$1.50	£0.20	£0.60	£1.00
Title Value:	$1.80	$5.40	$9.00	£1.25	£3.75	£6.25

ZORRO

Marvel Comics Group,MS; 1 Dec 1990-12 Dec 1991

	$Good	$Fine	$N.Mint	£Good	£Fine	£N.Mint
1-11 based on US TV series						
	$0.25	$0.75	$1.25	£0.15	£0.45	£0.75
12 based on US TV series, Alex Toth cover						
	$0.25	$0.75	$1.25	£0.15	£0.45	£0.75
Title Value:	$3.00	$9.00	$15.00	£1.80	£5.40	£9.00

Note: produced by Marvel UK but printed in America, based on televsion show.

ZORRO

Topps; 0 Jan 1994; 1 Jan 1994-11 Dec 1994

	$Good	$Fine	$N.Mint	£Good	£Fine	£N.Mint
0 (Jan 1994) Don McGregor and Mike Mayhew; Brian Stelfreeze cover; promotional free issue						
	$0.25	$0.75	$1.25	£0.15	£0.45	£0.75
1 Frank Miller cover						
	$0.50	$1.50	$2.50	£0.30	£0.90	£1.50
2 1st appearance Lady Rawhide (not in costume), Jae Lee cover						
	$0.50	$1.50	$2.50	£0.30	£0.90	£1.50
3 1st appearance Lady Rawhide, Adam Hughes cover						
	$3.00	$9.00	$15.00	£1.40	£4.20	£7.00
4 Mike Grell cover						
	$0.50	$1.50	$2.50	£0.30	£0.90	£1.50
5 Lady Rawhide appears, Keith Giffen/Joe Sinnott cover						
	$1.20	$3.60	$6.00	£0.80	£2.40	£4.00
6 Mike Mignola cover						
	$0.50	$1.50	$2.50	£0.30	£0.90	£1.50
7 Paul Gulacy cover						
	$0.50	$1.50	$2.50	£0.30	£0.90	£1.50
8 George Perez cover						
	$0.50	$1.50	$2.50	£0.30	£0.90	£1.50
9 Lady Rawhide appears (and on cover)						
	$0.80	$2.40	$4.00	£0.50	£1.50	£2.50
10 Lady Rawhide appears						
	$0.80	$2.40	$4.00	£0.50	£1.50	£2.50
11 Joseph Michael Linsner cover art, Lady Rawhide appears (and on cover)						
	$0.80	$2.40	$4.00	£0.50	£1.50	£2.50
Title Value:	$9.85	$29.55	$49.25	£5.65	£16.95	£28.25

Note: all Non-Distributed on the news-stands in the U.K.

ZOT IN DIMENSION 10 AND A HALF

Not Available,Mini-comic; 1 Jun 1986

	$Good	$Fine	$N.Mint	£Good	£Fine	£N.Mint
1 ND 8pgs, orange paper, Matt Feazell art						
	$0.30	$0.90	$1.50	£0.20	£0.60	£1.00
1 2nd printing ND	$0.25	$0.75	$1.25	£0.15	£0.45	£0.75
Title Value:	$0.55	$1.65	$2.75	£0.35	£1.05	£1.75

ZOT!

Eclipse; 1 Apr 1984-36 Jul 1991

	$Good	$Fine	$N.Mint	£Good	£Fine	£N.Mint
1 ND Scott McLoud story/art begins						
	$0.60	$1.80	$3.00	£0.40	£1.20	£2.00
2-9 ND	$0.50	$1.50	$2.50	£0.30	£0.90	£1.50
10 ND last colour issue						
	$0.50	$1.50	$2.50	£0.30	£0.90	£1.50
11 ND black and white begins						
	$0.40	$1.20	$2.00	£0.25	£0.75	£1.25
12-14 ND	$0.40	$1.20	$2.00	£0.25	£0.75	£1.25
14 ½ ND Zot by Matt Feazell						
	$0.40	$1.20	$2.00	£0.25	£0.75	£1.25
15-35 ND	$0.40	$1.20	$2.00	£0.25	£0.75	£1.25
36 ND 48pgs	$0.50	$1.50	$2.50	£0.30	£0.90	£1.50
Title Value:	$16.00	$48.00	$80.00	£9.90	£29.70	£49.50

MINT = 100% / NEAR MINT (inc. +/-) = 90–99% / VERY FINE (inc. +/-) = 75–89% / FINE (inc. +/-) = 55–74%
VERY GOOD (inc. +/-) = 35–54% / GOOD (inc. +/-) = 15–34% / FAIR = 5–14% / POOR = 1–4%

661

THE RAINBOW 1ᴰ

No. 1. Vol. 1.   PRICE ONE PENNY.   February 14, 1914.

THE JOLLY ADVENTURES OF THE BRUIN BOYS.—THEIR SNOW-MAN HAS A WARM TIME.

1. There was a great surprise awaiting the boys at Mrs. Bruin's Boarding-School when they awoke the other morning. "Look!" cried Tiger Tim excitedly. "It has been snowing in the night! Isn't it grand!" "I wish we could go out," grumbled Willie Ostrich. "It will all have melted away by the time we've finished our lessons."

2. "I know!" exclaimed Tim. "Let's dress and go up on the roof before Mrs. Bruin gets up! We can have some fine fun up there." The other boys thought it a jolly fine idea, too, and in less than half a minute they were climbing through the roof door. "Come along, boys!" piped Joey, the parrot. "Who'll take me on for a snowball fight?"

3. But Tiger Tim had a better idea than that. "Let's make a snow-man," he said. "He'll look fine sitting up here on the chimney!" So they all set to work, and this is the beauty they made. "Now, that's what I call a real work of art!" cried Jumbo, as Tim put on the finishing touch. "Well done, sir! You ought to get a medal for that!" "Bravo, Tim!" chimed in Joey. "That's the coolest piece of work I've seen for a long time!"

4. But while all this was going on Mrs. Bruin was busy down in the kitchen below, preparing breakfast for her pupils, and as soon as the fire began to burn up, down the chimney came a great heap of snow—plomp!—which put the fire out. "Goodness me!" she exclaimed, with a start. "I've never known it to snow such large flakes as this before! What ever can be the cause of it all?"

5. And she promptly went up on to the roof to find out. Meanwhile, the naughty boys were wondering what had become of their snow-man. "He needn't have left us in such a hurry," cried Georgie Giraffe, who was looking down the chimney for him. "He has done the disappearing trick, if you ask me!" "I wish I could do the same," groaned Jumbo, who just then spotted their teacher. "Oh dear! We're in for it now, I can see!"

6. And Jumbo had guessed quite right, for Mrs. Bruin pretty quickly had them downstairs again, and they had to put up with a cold breakfast. "Isn't she cool to us this morning!" remarked Jacko. "Yes, and so is everything else," agreed Fido. "Cold tea, eh! Bur-r-h!" Anyway, Mrs. Bruin made up for it by giving them all a good dinner, because they promised to be good in future. Do you think they will be? We shall see next week!

British Comics Guide

AN INTRODUCTION TO
BRITISH COMICS

Cut a collector of British comics and you will find nostalgia flowing in his veins: the memory of a scene, or a certain character, or the excellence of an anonymous artist are all spurs that will turn a reader into a collector. Traditionally, British comics have been aimed at a young audience up to the age of fourteen and the influence of comics in those formative years is incalculable; that such disposable ephemera would be of any interest to you after that age (or whatever age you gave up reading comics, after all, it's kid's stuff, isn't it?) is difficult to imagine, yet the past few years have seen a change towards comics and to comic collecting.

A combination of events have given the public a greater awareness of comics: the arrival of graphic novels such as **The Dark Knight Returns** (1986) and **Watchmen** (1988), neither of which were available through general retailers in their original formats, caused a stir in the British media. Comics, it was said, were not necessarily 'kid's stuff' any longer, and the publicity machine which rolled in their wake spotlighted the adult direction comics can take. The emphasis was on the very differences between recent titles such as **Crisis** and **Revolver** and the traditional British comic, yet the collecting of the latter also took an upswing around the same time, probably due to the interest in, and the coverage given to, the anniversaries of **The Dandy**, **The Beano** and **Eagle** in that period (1987-90). For a change these comics received a great deal of serious attention in the press, where comics only seem to be mentioned when they are the target of some pressure group trying to get them banned for promoting violence and sado-masochism.

A history of British comics would require a book in itself: an albeit short but representative history by Lew Stringer appeared in **The Comics Journal 122**, June 1988 (an issue which covered many aspects of British comics). Rather than repeat the information available there, this introduction will try to cover some of the various collectable aspects of British comics.

The direction of collecting has changed greatly over the years. There will always be the hard-core of fans who will collect the comics they read as a child, but as time marches on, comics published early in the century drift into obscurity, the realm of specialists and completists. The British 'Golden Age' comics of the thirties, with the advent of the 1d provincial comics and the ever present comics of the Amalgamated Press such as **Comic Cuts**, **Illustrated Chips** and **Puck** still attract collectors. The thirties also saw the first photogravure comic in the shape of **Mickey Mouse Weekly 1936** and the birth of **The**

Dandy (1937) and **The Beano** (1938). Pre-War comics such as these are very rare and probably command the highest prices of all British comics; who can tell how many copies were pulped during the War-time when paper was at a premium.

Perhaps the greatest nostalgia generator of them all appeared in 1950 to herald the arrival of the 'Silver Age' – **Eagle**. The brainchild of Marcus Morris and artist Frank Hampson, **Eagle** introduced 'Dan Dare' in its first issue. Hampson's perfectionist attitude to the strip assured Dare a place in the history books as Britain's most fondly remembered hero. His other strips were drawn with the same loving care for detail, making them equally collectable.

Hampson spearheads the group of artists whose every page is collected rather than specific characters they may have worked on, although (as with Hampson) they may be remembered for one strip above all others. In this group would be such artists as Frank Bellamy whose work for **Eagle** included biographical strips such as 'The Happy Warrior' (Winston Churchill) and 'Montgomery of Alamein', adventure strips 'Fraser of Africa' and 'Heros the Spartan', and 'Dan Dare' himself. Bellamy also did numerous other notable strips such as 'Thunderbirds' in **TV Century 21** and 'Garth' in the **Daily Mirror** newspaper.

Don Lawrence is best remembered for 'The Rise and Fall of the Trigan Empire' which first appeared in **Ranger** and later in the educational weekly **Look and Learn**. His earlier work on 'Olac the Gladiator' in **Tiger** and 'Karl the Viking' in Lion continue to prove popular, particularly in Europe where Lawrence has chronicled the adventures of 'Storm' for the past fourteen years.

Ron Embleton's career ranged from the one-off comics of the late forties, through classic strips such as 'Wrath of the Gods' in **Boys' World** and 'Wulf the Briton' in **Express Weekly**, 'Stingray' and 'Captain Scarlet' in **TV Century 21**, all the way to 'Oh Wicked Wanda' and 'Sweet Chastity' in **Penthouse**.

Also in the group of particularly collected artists would be the classic artists of the early days such as Tom Browne, Percy Cocking, Bertie Brown and Roy Wilson; the artists who made D.C. Thomson's comics amongst the most widely read by children, Dudley D. Watkins, Paddy Brennan and the stars of the fifties funny strips, Leo Baxendale and Ken Reid; the great adventure artists of Amalgamated Press, Eric Parker, H.M. Brock, Hugh McNeil, Derek Eyles, and later Joe Colquhoun and Denis McLoughlin. The traditional anonymity of British comics has meant that many names are still unknown, and the use of European and South American artists (amongst the most

notable being Hugo Pratt, Jesus Blasco, Alberto Breccia, Esteban Maroto, Enric Sio and Solano Lopez) via agencies has further complicated the issue of who did which strip. The re-introduction of credits in **2000AD** has led to greater interest in the artists themselves, and the work of Brian Bolland, Dave Gibbons, Simon Bisley and others who have found work and wider recognition in America, have built up followers in great numbers.

Nostalgia isn't limited to the comics themselves. Film, radio and TV have all created memorable characters which have made the translation into strip form. **Film Fun**, **Radio Fun** and later **TV Comic** all plundered their respective media for inspiration and not only for particular characters: the artists and actors themselves were often the heroes of the strips, ranging from Harold Lloyd (under the guise of 'Winkle') to Big Daddy (the wrestler). Most of the characters starred in humour strips, but adventure strips based on TV shows are particularly sought after. The Gerry Anderson puppet shows inspired their own comic in **TV Century 21**, whilst The Avengers, The Man From U.N.C.L.E., Danger Man and many others continue to grow in popularity long after their respective shows have ceased production. Dr Who has had one of the longest and varied careers in British comics and still appears today.

One area in which British and American comics have differed greatly is in the genre of the costumed superhero. Whilst the heroes and supergroups have crossed the Atlantic, notable in the Power Comics of the sixties, **Smash!**, **Pow!**, **Terrific** and **Fantastic**, and via the British end of Marvel Comics, there have been few home-grown successes. The earliest weekly costumed hero was 'The Amazing Mr X' in **Dandy 1944**, although there had been occasional short lived strips earlier, an example being William Ward's macabre, Batman inspired, 'The Bat' who appeared in **Thrill Comics** and **Extra Fun** in 1940. The most successful was Marvelman, produced by Mick Anglo's Gower Street Studios between 1954 and 1963, although he was a derivative of the American character Captain Marvel. 'Marvelman' was revived in 1982 in **Warrior** with writer Alan Moore at the helm. Moore was also writing Captain Britain for Marvel UK (at various times in **Marvel Super-heroes**, **The Daredevils** and **The Mighty World of Marvel**), another strip which had American origins, albeit that it was created and originally written and drawn by Americans for the British market. Both characters subsequently made successful moves to America in **Miracleman** and **Excalibur**.

The British comic at its conception was

designed for adults, using the strips to caricature and satirise popular figures of the time, yet it is now predominantly a form of children's entertainment. That doesn't mean that adult comics ceased to exist, for in the early seventies there was a thriving underground movement led by **Cyclops**, **Nasty Tales**, **Cozmic Comix** and the many other comix that were published by the Ar-Zak group. These and the adult orientated comics that followed such as **Graphixus**, **Near Myths** and more recently **Knockabout** nurtured the talents of many new artists, amongst them Brian Bolland, Dave Gibbons, Bryan Talbot and Hunt Emerson.

Also aimed at the more adult end of the market (with varying degrees of success) were the independents which sprung up in the recent past. These have been helped by the distribution services and specialist shops which have grown up around the comics industry. Amongst the more notable titles to appear in the past ten years was **Deadface** from Harrier, **Redfox** and **The Adventures of Luther Arkwright** from Valkyrie and the graphic novel Violent Cases from Escape. The Fast Fiction group published and distributed numerous small-press comics, whilst the (admittedly patchy) growth of the graphic novel may lead to more appearances of comics in regular retail outlets and booksellers which have previously only carried juvenile material to any great extent.

1994-95: TWO YEARS IN REVIEW

What has gone before:
The year is 1995. The British comics industry existed, but in turmoil, a world of declining sales and falling hope. However, one man stood tall and strong, his task: to single-handedly save the industry. His name: Judge Dredd.
Now read on...

Our recap panel may be jokey, the past twenty-four months of British comics have been the most worthy of a comic strip themselves ever. 1995 was dominated by news of big-budget movies based on comic properties, most of them new to the screen, the biggest news of all being the coming of **Judge Dredd** to the silver screen. It was the Cursed Earth saga in real life: Dredd, the only Icon in British comics now worth using as a metaphor, was to ride out across the Cursed turmoil of the British Comics Industry carrying his life-saving serum, taking comics to the roving, disinterested hoards outside the sheltering walls of fandom.

On Dredd's broad shoulders rested the fate of British comics. The Stallone PR department dispensed rapid fire news releases like bullets from a Lawgiver. Like heatseekers they found their target, and no lawless tabloid escaped the reports. Early news from the set was promising, and the budget took a substantial leap in pre-production. With Fleetway planning to blitz the marketplace with Dredd material in the wake of the movie, no industry watcher could deny that the movie was going to revive the idea of comics in the minds of the masses.

John Wagner would have been proud to have written the true outcome. Who else would have

typed the words "the serum was a dud"? The long haul was for nothing, the end results critically slaughtered in the States where the film opened in the blockbuster Independence Day weekend slot. Stallone's "Let them eat celluloid" attitude summed up his feelings as he backed away from publicising the movie on its release. The debate raged: released in the wake of **Batman Forever** comparisons were inevitable, and where the latter was a brash, outrageous flight of multi-coloured, over-the-top performance art, **Judge Dredd** seemed seriously slow, colourless in both acting and plot in comparison. The pros of choosing a young British director – because he would understand the character and be able to bring out the line of dark humour that typifies Dredd – became buried by the cons of his inexperience.

Simply put, **Judge Dredd** was a badly conceived movie. The plot was only an average one for Dredd and the faults in the movie could not be covered by a wallpaper of wonderful designs and grandiose backdrops. The meter of the film was wrong, climaxing in the middle and running on empty by the end.

Why should we concentrate on the merits – or demerits – of one film?

Because few comics these days will be released unless they are part of a multi-media event. Where the **Judge Dredd Megazine** was launched in 1990 without the bruhaha of a film release, British comics have become accessories to the world of media entertainment – just part of the package deal. **Judge Dredd: Lawman of the Future** was launched to co-incide with the film, the **Megazine** was relaunched, and serious thought was put into renumbering **2000AD** so it too could be relaunched. Dredd was always the skeleton of **2000AD** on which other strips are hung like limbs, but it has to be said that for too many years those limbs have been withered and unsupportive, bending and almost breaking the papers' spine. The movie was seen as a steroid boost to put the paper back on its feet; unfortunately the 'steroids' were no more than an Anadin, curing the symptoms and not the disease.

In critical terms, both **2000AD** and the **Megazine** benefited from having more direction and more balls than they'd had in years but sadly that didn't translate into sales. The **Megazine** has since gone monthly, and **Lawman of the Future** folded. In a effort to force an editorial change, the **Megazine**'s long-time editor David Bishop and **2000AD**'s John Tomlinson have recently switched places. As this has only just occurred at the time of writing, whether this has the desired effect is still in the lap of the Gods.

The same story could be told for the **Tank Girl** movie, on which was pinned the hopes of **Deadline**, Britain's most overground underground comic. The tanking of **Tank Girl: The Movie** has finally buried **Deadline**. The movie industry isn't always a white dove holding an olive branch in its beak. Sometimes it's a vulture and it will eat you. What amazed

and dismayed most fans was the departure of Tank Girl herself from **Deadline**, heading off for pastures new; although packaged by the same team, **Tank Girl: The Comic** (get used to these 'The Movie' and 'The Comic' dogtags – you'll need them to tell one grunt from another in the multimedia age) was published by Manga Publishing for all of eight issues. From riding high in the turret of **Deadline**, TG has become a sad victim of her disastrous franchise. And the film will be how she is remembered: petulant and squeaky. The evil that men do lives after them, wrote Shakespeare. The good is oft interred with their bones. The film built high upon its comic strip foundations didn't die alone. It collapsed and suffocated its Caesar, damning her with the praise and high promise offered before the opening credits rolled.

Why should it surprise us? For every brilliant **Batman** movie there has been a dozen poisonous **Punishers**, for every single **Superman** and score of **Superman IV**s. The promise of reasonable adaptations like **The Crow** and **The Mask** – both worth the merit the film industry held them in – led to a gluttonous feeding frenzy, film companies picking up rights to films with little idea of how they were to translate them off the page. Stallone and Schwarzenegger are superstars not superheroes. You cannot equate the two.

Let's examine some of the comic releases over the past couple of years. The most successful launches in the past eighteen months have been adaptations not from film but from elsewhere, mostly from television: **The X-Files** has been a phenomenal success, reprinting the Topps comic strip with a smattering of background features. Low costs and high sales have guaranteed it a Price Guide 'Success' merit badge. Tailcoating on a cult TV show which continues to draw more fans each season by word of mouth means that the natural attrition comics tend to suffer – no new fans replacing those that drift off into other areas – may not happen for some time. Boom issues, those twice-a-year promoted editions with the tacky free gift taped to the cover, only run for three issues at the most. All publishing companies dream of the free advertising a 26-week run on television offers and the awareness that brings to the crowds thronging W.H. Smiths on a Saturday.

The most successful comic launches in many years were not aimed at the same age group: while sales of pre-movie **2000AD** were sliding below 60,000, Fleetway's **Tots TV** launched at over 200,000 copies, and settled at a figure well in the 100,000s, making it and **Budgie** – based on the Duchess of York's chatty baby helicopter, and itself backed up with a successful children's TV slot – their best-selling titles.

Not that television makes for instant success. Fallers in the mid-nineties warzone included **Look-In** which, in the past decade, had turned from a comic with features into a **Smash Hits** clone with a couple of cartoons, and the Anderson franchise comics, which had switched from Fleetway to an independent publisher in early 1995, but failed to take off once the shows were off the air. The junior comic market has suffered its own downswing, with Buster slipping to fortnightly and the restructuring in 1994 of the Fleetway humour department which pulled a number of reprint titles into one big value comic called the **BVC** (of course!).

The only recent launch of note in the junior market has been Manga Publishing's **Space Precinct**, a live action Anderson series which – shock! – hasn't been an instant hit; sadly, the poor viewing figures for its terrestrial slot on BBC2 were also reflected in poor sales figures for the comic and, as one insider put it, it bombed. **Space Precinct** aside, Manga Publishing have been one of the few success stories in British comics these past two years. Founded out of the ashes of Dark Horse International in 1994, the company is a spin-off from Manga Video whose release of **Akira** in 1991 heralded a wave of japanese animated cartoon (anime) releases. Taking over **Manga Mania** and **Jurassic Park** at first (although the dinosaur reprints soon went the way of their jurassic originals), Manga Publishing have carved out a slice of the market pie with strong releases: **X-Files**, **Streetfighter** and **Mortal Kombat** and a line of graphic novels reprinting material from Dark Horse and Viz Communications. The anime boom – slowing but still maintaining a good head of steam – has carried **Manga Mania** into the top-selling (comics, that is) category. Attractively priced, and having revamped with added colour in 1994, it offers one of the most value-for-money packages around. A further revamp, probably to coincide with the completion of 'Akira', could give the title another kick start.

The other end of the scale was the launches of Tower Comics, which achieved the worst press of any new launch possible; produced by Northern & Shell, best known for their X-rated porn titles, the company attracted a number of ex-Marvel UK employees over the months they operated. Their first launch ("Ai, ai, ai. If this isn't the comic you've all been waiting for, then I must be a monkey's auntie" said the intro) was based on **Mighty Morphin Power Rangers** which looked suspiciously like it had been put together by a monkey's auntie. An equally poor **Action Man** title helped burn Tower Comics' rickety bridge, with sales poor at one end and support from professionals collapsing at the other amidst threats of court action. Ex-Marvel UK employees rapidly became ex-Northern & Shell employees also.

Marvel UK itself became something of a shadow land; their parent company had purchased the Panini sticker company, based in Rome but with British offices in Tunbridge Wells. An immediate cost-cutting round saw the folding of almost all Marvel's magazine division, the exception being the long-running **Dr Who Magazine**: **Hammer Horror**; newcomers **Bizarre**, **Playback** and Clive Barker's **Hellraiser** all folded immediately, and changes within Marvel's juvenile comics saw a number of planned launches canned. The **VR**

Troopers tie-in lasted a scant few issues before Marvel UK shut down their Arundel House offices and relocated to Tunbridge Wells, downsizing at the same time.

The move comes as no surprise when you consider the extreme changes that Marvel UK's parent company went through in the same period. The loss of the Americanized Marvel UK titles was summed up by Marvel UK's Paul Neary in **Comics Buyer's Guide #1081** (August 5, 1994) thus: "Think of Marvel UK as a studio, producing comics by talented people in our area. Our location gives us another pool of talent and a slightly different take on things..." and then listed Pino Rinaldi, Fonteriz, Carlos Pacheco and Sal Larroca as his top artists. All Spanish. Not British. But, ignoring that:

"Because we're from a slightly different culture, if we aimed dead-on mainstream we'd be slightly off. And I think that's the way to do it because of what we've done in the past, when we published under our own imprint. We've aimed well off mainstream to start with, and, by the time we finish with all of our different cultural stuff, it's been so far off that it's been hard to see where it fits in." The results: comics that were unattractive to both American and British audiences. They folded.

Realigning the company to concentrate on the UK did not work, although perhaps the writing was already on the wall a year before when Lou Bank told retailers on September 17, 1993, "Every once in a while you're going to have an artist on a title that may really increase it's sales, but for the most part, you're not getting new launches with hot new artists on them. Certainly not from Marvel UK. Boy, now there's a quote...You've got to understand we're not aiming at most of you [the retailers] as part of our target audience. Marvel's target audience is 12-18 year old males...Marvel isn't the one that has to publish to every single audience. That's not what we specialise in...we want to expand our audience; we don't expand upwards, we expand downwards. Make all the jokes you want, we're looking for the younger readers, that's what Marvel is, plain and simple." Soon after, Bank left the UK for Dark Horse.

The shuffling and reshuffling of companies has left the UK market with its lowest comic output in 100 years. Marvel's streamlining has pushed it back into third place for number of titles, second place now reverting to Dundee's D.C. Thomson who rise from third position by dint of a steady output of 11 titles. Just ahead of them are Fleetway Editions, although how long their parents – Gutenberghus, the Denmark publishing giants – will maintain an output in Britain in the face of eroding sales is down more to the success of titles abroad than in Britain. There is a possibility that Fleetway will become a studio for talent, supplying comics to countries where they will sell...not such a far fetched notion when you know that this is precisely what has happened with D.C. Thomson, who employ staff to create comics which are only published abroad.

Over the past two years the number of

original graphic novels has just about fallen to zero, with only two titles appearing in 1994-95 – **Mr Punch** by Neil Gaiman & Dave McKean and **Playing the Game** by Doris Lessing and Charlie Adlard. Both Titan and Boxtree maintained a steady schedule, reprinting from DC, Dark Horse and Marvel; Manga launched a new line of manga reprints in late 1995 which have solid backing through their own titles; although given a high profile launch, the Mandarin manga graphic novels launched in January 1995 turned out to be a one-off dip of the toe into the market. Gollancz are unlikely to issue any more original graphic novels in the near future and HarperCollins are waiting to see whether **Playing the Game** succeeds, and since it slid onto the market without any publicity through the trade press, sales will probably follow the same pattern as James Herbert's **The City** released in early 1994 which proved that Herbert's followers did not move in droves to take the illustrated story to their hearts. With that in mind, it can be said with some certainty that the next two years will almost certainly see no more original graphic novels from the established publishers who have all now played their hands and lost.

Strangely, two comic related areas did very well: Bantam sold 7,500 copies of the hardcover **Death & Life of Superman** by Roger Stern, and direct-mailed Superman fans to promote the paperback. Denny O'Neil's **Knightfall** was another strong-seller, and the story even warranted a junior edition by Alan Grant. 10 original Dredd novels were published by Virgin over the eighteen months between August 1993 and February 1995, led by David Bishop's **The Savage Amusement**. More comic characters made the transition to paperback than ever before, ranging from **The Mask** movie novelisation to an original Tintin novel by Frederic Tuten. A proposed series of Marvel character novelisations failed to get off the ground, but the continued interest in comics as source material in Hollywood and by games companies itself guarantees more crossover ventures.

The most successful adaptations came from radio where Dirk Maggs continued a series of shows that captured the essence of comics wonderfully – fun and thrills served up with a cliffhanger ending. A hilarious reworking of the origins of Spider-Man in early 1995 was followed by a 16 week run of Judge Dredd on Radio 1 during the summer, the lead role suitably gritted out by voice actor Gary Martin. If only all adaptations could have been so well presented.

Comics have continued their battle with the establishment with both Savoy and Knockabout in court to defend their wares. Whilst the decision went against Savoy, who failed to overturn a ruling and save their comics from being destroyed under the Obscene Publications Act, the fight to save copies of Robert Crumb's **My Trouble With Women**, seized by H.M. Customs in January 1995 on the grounds that two panels were obscene despite the fact that the book has been openly on sale in this country for many years, was aided by a number of charity parachute jumps performed by high-profile industry supporters including Paul Hudson, Dez Skinn and Frank Plowright. The outcome of the case was a pleasant surprise for Knockabout's Tony and Carol Bennett, the magistrates in Uxbridge ruling in January 1996 that the books were not obscene under the provision of the 1959 Obscene Publications Act and the Customs Consolidation Act of 1876 (which allows H.M. Customs to have anything else seized alongside the obscene material burnt whether it is itself obscene or not). Although Knockabout were awarded £6,000 in costs, it was not all good news as they estimated their losses over the one-year period to be over £30,000; and H.M. Customs seems to be continuing its war of attrition against publishers, and are now refusing to preview samples of imported titles – a publisher now has to import and hope for the best.

The shame of this case was that Knockabout have a consistently high track record for quality of titles, and it would be to a great loss for them to close. That their case was not being supported by larger, more financially stable companies shows how blinkered they are to the question of censorship, which is not simply something that happens to other people: it is happening with random imprecision, a clear example of rules being made up on the hoof, or – if you're completely cynical – on the jackboot.

Pity us if we have to add free expression to our necrology. We have lost many fine talents these past eighteen months, more than can be fully covered here. On December 2, 1994, Tony Weare took his own life at the age of 82, in a typically expressive fashion, asking not to be mourned. Weare was the artist of 'Matt Marriott' in the **Evening News** for 22 years, a master of using shade to build up the impression of shape. Hugo Pratt, the Italian artist whose work graced a number of British war comics in the late 1950s and early 1960s died on August 20, 1995, aged 68, followed by Carl Giles on August 27th. Giles was without doubt the most widely known cartoonist working in Britain, a favourite of royalty and the common man alike, whose annual collections regularly sold half a million copies. Three months later, Pat Nicolle, whose western and historical strips began to appear in 1950, died at the age of 87. Nicolle was probably best known for his superbly drawn – and accurate in every detail – historical adaptations of both movies and the classics. November was a bad month, as it also marked the death of Desmond Walduck whose illustrations filled numerous annuals in the 1950s-60s. His name will be forever linked with Frank Hampson, as it was often Walduck who took over the finished art for 'Dan Dare' when Hampson was ill, drawing much of the artwork on 'Operation Saturn', 'Prisoners of Space' and 'The Phantom Fleet'. Although Jerry Siegel, who died on January 28, 1996, aged 81, was best known for co-creating Superman, he was also responsible for one of Britain's most enduring

characters: The Spider, originally created for **Lion** by Ted Cowan. Siegel wrote the supervillain strip between 1966-69, and created the superhero duo, Gadgetman and Gimmick Kid for the same paper in 1968. January also saw the death of Jesus Blasco, the Barcelona-based artist of countless British comic strips; probably best known for his work on 'The Steel Claw', Blasco in fact drew strips prolifically and almost non-stop for the UK market between 1954 and 1977, influencing the likes of Brian Bolland with his realism, and use of chiaroscuro and camera-angle POVs.

All this negativity has to be tempered with good news. Where modern British comics are in serious trouble, the back issue market is undergoing something of a renaissance. Much of this can be put down to the attention high profile sales have garnered. Of particular note, a copy of the first issue of **Beano** became the highest priced British comic when it sold, in September 1995, for £4,200 at postal auction. Whilst the price is an isolated case at the moment, it is worth noting that the sale brought in several serious bids over £3,000, and further sales of **Beano #1** in the future may consolidate the asking price somewhere between £3-4,000. The sale of issue #2 in December for £1,275 – only the third comic (along with **Dandy #1**, which sold at auction for £2,300 in 1995) to pass the four-figure barrier is also a good indicator that early copies of **Beano** beyond #1 are now attracting serious collector interest.

The postal auction format established by Malcolm Phillips of Comic Book Postal Auctions has attracted furious bidding for other British comics, and notable sales include **Smash! #1** for £115, **Valiant #1**, **Hurricane #1** and **Champion #1** for £66, **Pow!** for £55 and **Terrific** for £50. Individually they are remarkable (as yet one off) prices even for very fine condition comics, often with their free gifts still attached; combined, they show a growing interest in British comics from the 1960s. Other Amalgamated Press titles have all shown a steady growth, from **Radio Fun** (a copy with rusty staples) at £390 to **TV Fun** at £66. #2 of **Knockout** (a tricky issue to get hold of) went recently for £132. Prices on even high profile titles which are not that uncommon have also started to take a hike, including the recent sales of **Eagle #1** for £200 and **TV Century 21** (with free gift) for £190.

The back issue market has also been stimulated by a series of facsimile reprints which have included a number of scarce science fiction titles from the 1940s and 1950s. These could well have an effect on prices in the future, weeding out the 'readers' from the die-hard 'collectors' and, perhaps, stimulating interest in an area notoriously difficult to collect in. Many new readers will be seeing these comics for the first time, and it is impossible to imagine that they will not return for the real thing if it should become available from dealers.

Like the eye of a storm, nostalgia moves slowly across the comics landscape; the kids

growing up in the 1960s are now the late thirty-somethings of the 1990s, and that is the age that nostalgia bites, when life has settled somewhat and forty approaches. We assume this to be true although empirical data is hard to come by; however, the disinterest nowadays in comics of the 1920s and early 1930s is compelling evidence, and further proof that age isn't necessarily an important factor in the pricing of comics. If Mystic Meg were to look into the future of British comics she may see luck befalling anyone who kept their old sixties comics in pristine condition with the free gifts attached. Of the modern British comic industry, she may have less to say and maybe we should conclude that its a rollover year and whilst there were no jackpot winner this time, that just means the prize is going to be greater than ever next time round.

ACKNOWLEDGMENTS

This year has seen our biggest expansion in some years, not only because of its two years worth of additional coverage; over 15,000 words of additional information has been added since the previous edition and once again I have to thank my colleagues and fellow collectors who have helped the section grow in both size and accuracy. My sincere thanks go to everyone who has helped in the past and whilst singling out names seems a little unfair, the annual list was getting too long, so I'd like to particularly thank David Ashford, Mike Bentley, Howard Corn of *Eagle Times*, Bill Lofts, Ray Moore, Lance Rickman, and Bryon Whitworth of *The Comic Journal*. Research isn't done in isolation, and I have to thank all those other historians, researchers, dealers and retailers who have, by their previous efforts, made my job somewhat easier. This is particularly true of Denis Gifford, whose own guides pointed the way and proved that tackling of project of this size was possible. As ever, I save my final thanks for John and Sue Allen-Clark; there are some traditions that are just too hard to break.

PRICING

British comics are often graded differently to American comics and many American comic grades will have little meaning. We have listed only one price corresponding to an American grade of Very Fine: complete, clean, with no major defects, sometimes referred to as British Grade A.

As ever, we leave you with this very important note: the prices listed here are just a guide based upon averages of sales we have noted from dealers. They were not issued to us on tablets of stone, and this is not a bible. The person who decides on whether a price is right is you, the buyer, and a combination of opportunity, desire and cashflow.

When selling comics, the rule of thumb is: don't presume that two contemporary papers have the same value to a collector. Prices depend on two things: supply and *demand*. You may be able to supply the rarest comic in the world, but it's only 'worth' what you're asking if somebody wants to buy it at that price.

Steve Holland, Colchester, Mar 1996

BRITISH COMICS
POINTS TO REMEMBER

- THIS BOOK IS ONLY A GUIDE AND SHOULD BE TREATED AS ONLY A GUIDE.

- COMICS SHOULD BE VERY STRICTLY GRADED, EVEN UNDER-GRADED, TO ENSURE CORRECT VALUATION

- WHEN GRADING A COMIC, THE WHOLE COMIC MUST BE GRADED, NOT JUST THE COVER. START FROM THE INSIDE AND WORK OUT.

- FOR THE BRITISH COMICS SECTION, A SINGLE NEAR MINT PRICE HAS BEEN GIVEN. HOWEVER, BRITISH COMICS ARE OFTEN GRADED DIFFERENTLY FROM AMERICAN COMICS AND THE TOP GRADE OF BRITISH COMIC IS GENERALLY REFERRED TO AS "GRADE A" IN BRITISH COLLECTING TERMS, THAT IS COMPLETE, FLAT, CLEAN AND WITH NO MAJOR DEFECTS. PLEASE THEN REFER TO PERCENTAGE CHARTS AT THE BOTTOM OF EACH PAGE. OWING TO PAPER QUALITY AND AN ASSORTMENT OF SHAPES AND SIZES BRITISH COMICS AND ANNUALS IN PERFECT NEAR MINT CONDITION ARE EXTREMELY UNUSUAL. THIS PARTICULAR GRADE IS SOMETIMES REFERRED TO IN BRITISH TERMS AS "EXCELLENT".

- PRICES OF COMICS ARE CALCULATED AND SET AT TIME OF GOING TO PRESS ONLY. PLEASE ALLOW FOR A PERCENTAGE INCREASE AT LEAST IN LINE WITH INFLATION THROUGHOUT THE YEAR. THIS PERCENTAGE MAY BE MUCH HIGHER FOR OLDER, SCARCER OR IMPORTANT ISSUES.

- SOME COMICS, PARTICULARLY RARE AND "KEY" ISSUES, MAY FETCH PREMIUM PRICES IN HIGH GRADE CONDITION, IN EXCEPTIONAL CIRCUMSTANCES THESE MAY BE CALCULATED IN MULTIPLES OF GUIDE (1.25, 1.5, 2.0 times Guide – SEE RELEVANT SECTION IN THE INTRODUCTION). FOR THOSE NEW TO COLLECTING, IT IS ADVISED TO SEEK PROFESSIONAL OPINIONS

- SCARCE, RARE AND VERY RARE HAVE BEEN USED SPARINGLY. THEY MUST NOT BE OVER-USED OR USED CASUALLY.

- THIS BOOK MUST AT ALL TIMES BE USED WITH COMMON SENSE AND FLEXIBILITY OF INTERPRETATION WITH REGARD TO PRICES.

N.MINT

A

A1
Atomeka Press; 1 May 1989-6a, Mar 1992

1 96pgs; Moore, Gaiman, Milligan scripts, Windsor-Smith, Leach, Campbell, Bolton, McKeever, Bolland, Parkhouse, Sienkiewicz, McKean, Motter, Gibbons, McCarthy, Fabry art; strips include Warpsmith, Deadface, Bojeffries Saga, Mr X, Flaming Carrot	£5.00
2 128pgs; Moore, Milligan scripts, Pedro Henry text, Lloyd, Hewlett, Parkhouse, Bolton, Michael T. Gilbert, Fabry, Bond, Windsor-Smith, Bisley, McKeever, Campbell art; strips include Mr Monster, Deadface, Mr X (montage), Bojeffries, Pressbutton text	£5.00
3 80pgs; Morrison, Moore scripts, Campbell, Bolland, McKean, Fabry, Bond, Bolton, Parkhouse, Moebius art	£3.50
4 96pgs; James Robinson, Moore scripts, Hewlett, Fabry, Moebius, Sienkiewicz, Bolton, Parkhouse art	£3.50
5 96pgs; Gaiman, Milligan scripts, Fabry, Ewins, Joe Kubert, Lloyd art, Jeff Hawke by Sydney Jordan & Goring/Rich	£4.50
6a 72pgs; Tank Girl by Hewlett, Campbell, Fabry art	£3.00
The A1 True Life Bikini Confidential No.1 (1990) A.Moore, S.Moore scripts, Milligan text, Gilbert, Bolland, Hewlett, Jackson, Parkhouse, Leach art	£4.00
Note: Issue 6b was announced but not released.	

A1 COMIC
D.R.Burnside; 1946, 3 unnumbered issues

nn - 16pgs 6d price; John Turner art	£4.00
nn - 16pgs 4d price; John Turner art	£4.00
nn - 20pgs; John Turner art	£4.00

A1 COMICS
P.M. Productions; nn May 1945

nn - 8pgs; small, printed on folded beige card or one-sided blue paper; Gifford art	£5.00

AARDVARK
Aardvark Publications; 1 1974

1 underground	£1.00

AARGH!
Mad Love; nn Oct 1988

nn - Anti Clause 28 benefit comic; Moore, Gaiman scripts, Talbot, O'Neill, Sim/Gerhardt, Spiegelman, Bissette, Emerson, Gibbons, Leach, Sienkiewicz, Miller art, McKean cover	£3.50

A.B.C. WARRIORS
Fleetway-Quality; 1 1990-8 1991

1 2000AD reprints begin	£1.25
2-8	£1.00

A.B.C. WARRIORS, THE
Titan (Best of 2000AD); 1983-1988; 1991

Book One	£4.50
Book Two	£4.50
Book Three Bisley, S.M.S. art	£5.00
Book Four Bisley S.M.S. art	£5.00
The Black Hole (Oct 1991) reprints books 3 & 4	£8.00

A.B.C. WARRIORS (2000AD BOOKS)
Mandarin; Sep 1992

Khronicles of Khaos 2000AD reprints, Kevin Walker art	£7.00

ABRAHAM FOUNDER OF A NATION
Lion/Fleurus; nn 1979

nn - 52pgs; French reprint	£1.00

ABSLOM DAAK: DALEK KILLER
Marvel; nn 1990

nn - reprints from Dr Who Weekly, Dillon, Lloyd art newly coloured	£6.00

ACCIDENT MAN
Apocalypse (Apocalypse Presents); Jun 1991-Aug 1991

nn - reprints from Toxic #1-6, Emond art	£2.50
nn - reprints from Toxic, Mighton art	£2.50
Note: new series later published by Dark Horse (USA)	

ACE
Hamilton; nn 1947

nn - 16pgs; Bob Wilkin art	£4.00

ACE
Harrier; 1 1987

1 Eddie Campbell art	£1.00

ACE ADVENTURE ALBUM, THE
Moring; nn 1956?

nn - hardback; McLoughlin cover (from Okay Adventure Annual)	£8.00

ACE BOOK OF COMICS
Odhams; nn Sep 1952

nn - 188pgs; hardback	£6.00

ACE COMIC, THE
Valentine & Sons; nn 1948

nn - 16pgs; Sam Fair, Nat Brand art	£4.00

ACE HIGH WESTERN COMIC
Gould-Light; 1-5 1953

1-5 Ron Embleton, Norman Light art	£12.00

ACE-HIGH WESTERN COMICS
International; nn Jun 1945

nn - 8pgs; Gifford art	£4.00

ACE MALLOY OF THE SPECIAL SQUADRON
Arnold Book Co.; 50 Aug 1952-65 Nov 1952, 16 issues

50 Ace Malloy by Kirk Logan begins	£10.00
51-65	£6.00

THE ACE OF COMICS
(see The Ace of Fun Comic)
William Foster; 1 Oct 1947

1 8pgs; Bob Wilkin art	£4.00

THE ACE OF FUN COMIC
Estuary; nn 1947-2 1947

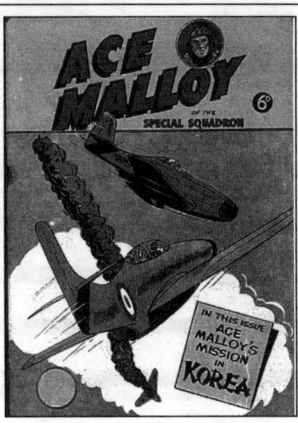

Ace Malloy of the Special Squadron

Action #1

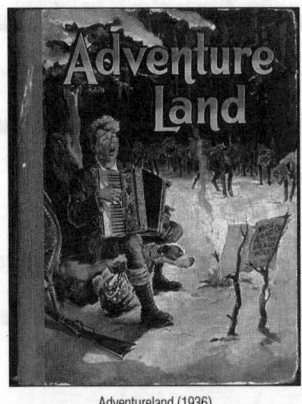

Adventureland (1936)

N.MINT

nn - 8pgs; printed on blue paper; Bob Wilkin art	£4.00
2 8pgs; printed on white paper; Wilkin art	£4.00
Note: all characters continued from The Ace of Comics	

ACES
Acme Press; 1 Apr 1988-5 Dec 1988 (continued as Point Blank)

1 Airmail by Micheluzzi, Hollywood Eye by Riviere/Bocquet & Berthet, Morgan by Segura & Ortiz (ends 3) European reprints begin	£2.50
2-3,5	£2.00
4 Dieter Lumpen by Zenter & Pellejero European reprint begins	£2.00

ACE WESTERN COMIC ANNUAL
L. Miller; Sep 1953

1954 softcover	£8.00

ACID-HEAD ARNIE
Knockabout; nn 1994

nn - Anthony Smith art	£2.00

ACOMIC BOMBSHELL
Cartoon Art; nn 1947

nn - 16pgs; Dennis Reader art	£4.00

ACTION
Pictorial Art; nn Sep 1948

nn - 8pgs; M.M.M. art	£4.00

ACTION
IPC; 14th Feb 1976-16th Oct 1976, 36 unnumbered issues; 23rd Oct 1976 (not distributed)

14 Feb 1976 Dredger by Horacio Altuna, Hellman of Hammer Force by Mike Dorey, Blackjack by Leopoldo Sanchez, Play Till You Drop by Barrie Mitchell, Hook Jaw by Ramon Sola, Sport's Not For Losers by Dudley Wynn, The Coffin Sub by Angelo Todaro, The Running Man by Lalia all begin	£4.00
14 Feb 1976 with free gift (Red Arrow plane)	£5.00
21 Feb-9 Oct 1976	£2.00
16 Oct 1976 last issue of original run	£3.00
23 Oct 1976 rare; withdrawn from sale because of violent content, some copies printed for editorial checking	£25.00

FREE GIFT ISSUES
14 Feb 1976 Red Arrow plane 21 Feb 1976 Hook Jaw Transfer, 28 Feb 1976 16 Soccer Cards, 29 Mar 1976 Invasion (game).

CHRONOLOGY
3 Apr 1976 last Coffin Sub. 24 Apr 1976 last Play Till You Drop, Green's Grudge War by Belardinelli starts. 1 May 1976 last Sport's Not For Losers, no Hook Jaw, Look Out For Lefty by Barrie Mitchell starts. 8 May 1976 Death Game 1999 by Costa begins, no Hook Jaw. 12 Jun 1976 last Running Man. 19 Jun 1976 Hell's Highway by Mike White begins. 4 Sep 1976 last Blackjack. 11 Sep 1976 Kid's Rule OK by Mike White begins. 25 Sep 1976 Probationer by Tom Hirst begins.

ARTISTS/FEATURES
Horacio Altuna in 14 Feb-9 May 1976. Massimo Belardinelli in 24 Apr-18 Sep 1976. Ricardo Villagran in 19 Jun, 17 Jul, 14 Aug-21 Aug, 4 Sep, 18 Sep-25 Sep, 16 Oct 1976.

ACTION (NEW SERIES)
IPC; 4th Dec 1976-12th Nov 1977, 50 unnumbered issues (joins Battle Action)

4 Dec 1976 Dredger by Ricardo Villagran, Spinball (ex-Death Game 1999) by Costa, Look Out For Lefty by Tony Harding, Hookjaw by John Stokes, Hell's Highway by Mike White revived	£2.00
11 Dec-10 Sep 1977	£0.75
17 Sep 1977 Spinball retitled The Spinball Slaves	£0.75
24 Sep-12 Nov 1977	£0.75

ARTISTS/FEATURES
Massimo Belardinelli in 4 Dec-18 Dec 1976. Jesus Blasco in 29 Jan-5 Feb 1977, 19 Feb-26 Feb 1977. Ron Turner in 17 Sep-12 Nov 1977. Ricardo Villagran in 4 Dec-11 Dec 1976, 8 Jan 1977, 22 Jan 1977.

ACTION ALBUM
Moring; nn 1956?

nn - softcover; McLoughlin Swift Morgan, Roy Carson, Buffalo Bill reprints (9,6,29,45,49,31)	£8.00

ACTION ANNUAL
IPC; 1977-1985

1977-1978	£2.50
1979 Spinball by Bolland	£3.00
1980-1985	£2.00

ACTION BOOK FOR BOYS
Purnell; 1967

1967 scarce, mostly text stories with some strips	£3.00

ACTION COMICS
Miller; 1 1958-2 1958

1-2 68pgs; reprints from A1 Comics (Magazine Enterprises) 2 features Ghost Rider	£3.00

ACTION DOUBLE DOUBLE COMICS
Thorpe & Porter; 1 1967-4 1968

1 bound-together remaindered copies of selected DC and Marvel comics, some with new line drawn covers	£2.50
2-3	£2.00
4 reprints Action Comics #350, Fantastic Four #65, Avengers #47	£2.00

ACTION FORCE
Marvel; 1 7th Mar 1987-50 13th Feb 1988 (joins Transformers)

1 Action Force based on toy-line begins	£1.00
2-13,16,18-22,24-43,47-50	£0.50
14-15 Steve Yeowell art	£0.50
17 Masters of Kung Fu by Grant Morrison and Steve Yeowell	£0.50
23 Brett Ewins art	£0.50
44-46 Mike Collins art	£0.50

ACTION FORCE ANNUAL
Marvel; 1988

1989 GI Joe reprints; original text story by Abnett/J. Paris	£2.50

ACTION FORCE MINI-COMIC
IPC/CPG Products; 1 16th Jul 1983-5 10th Sep 1983 (givaway in Battle, Eagle, Tiger)

1,5 8pgs; Ron Turner art	£0.50
2-4 Vano art	£0.30

N.MINT

ACTION FORCE MONTHLY
Marvel; 1 Jun 1988-15 Aug 1989

1	£1.20
2,4-15	£0.80
3 Grant Morrison script	£0.80

ACTION MAN
Northern & Shell; 1 29th Jun 1995-6 1995

1 24pgs; Mike McKone, Simon Fraser art	£0.75
2-6	£0.50

ACTION PICTURE LIBRARY
IPC; 1 Aug 1969-30 Oct 1970

1 60pgs pocket size	£3.00
2-14	£1.00
15-30 68pgs; back-up stories begin	£1.00

ARTISTS/FEATURES
1 Wildcat by Redondo. 2 The Doom Machine. 3 Tiger Trap. 4 At Gunpoint. 5 Voodoo!. 6 Taken For A Ride. 7 Wall of Death. 8 Terror of the Deep by Carlos Pino. 9 Atom Pirates. 10 Frontier Fury. 11 Back From the Dead. 12 Scorpion Island. 13 Hunter!. 14 Blood Heat by Carlos Pino. 15 The Destroyer. 16 Sabotage!. 17 Scoop!. 18 Gang-Buster by Henares. 19 Cue For Murder. 20 The Supermen. 21 Mob Rule. 22 Sky-Jack!. 23 Rats of London. 24 The Bandit. 25 Time Fuse. 26 Sea Hunt. 27 The Mercenaries. 28 Salvage. 29 The Shore-Busters. 30 The Faceless Ones by Eustaquio Segrelles.

ACTION SERIES
Miller; 1-12 1958

1 68pgs; Ghost Riders, Magazine Enterprises reprints begin	£6.00
2 Prairie Guns	£4.00
3 B-Bar-B Riders	£4.00
4 Red Mask	£4.00
5 Thunda	£4.00
6,8 Cave Girl	£4.00
9 Lone Vigilante	£4.00
10 Kid Cowboy	£4.00
11,12 Dan Adams, Fawcett reprints (from Gene Autrey)	£5.00

ACTION SERIES
Young World; 1 Jul 1964-12 Sep 1964

1,8 Secret Agent X9, US newspaper reprints begin	£3.00
2 Big Ben Bolt	£2.00
3,10 Flash Gordon	£3.00
4 Tim Tyler	£2.00
5,12 Brick Bradford	£2.00
6 Mandrake the Magician	£2.00
7,11 Ripcord	£2.00

ACTION SPECIAL
IPC; May 1976-May 1980

1976-1978 titled Action Summer Special	£1.50
1979 titled Action Holiday Special	£1.50
1980 titled Action Holiday Special; Erik the Viking reprint by Lawrence	£1.75

ACTION STREAMLINE COMICS
Streamline; nn 1950s

nn - 68pgs; US reprints	£5.00

ACTION 21
Engale; 1 Jul 1988-10 Oct 1989

1 Stingray by Ron Embleton, Captain Scarlet by Embleton, Thunderbirds by Bellamy, Fireball XL5 by Mike Noble, Lady Penelope by Eric Eden, Zero-X by Mike Noble - all TV Century 21 reprints begin	£2.50
2 Secret Agent X by Rab Hamilton reprints begin	£2.00
3-7	£2.00
8 Angels by Jon Davis reprints from Lady Penelope begin	£2.00
9-10	£2.00

ACTION WAR PICTURE LIBRARY
MV Features; 1 1965-? (24+ issues)

1-? 68pgs pocket size	£0.50

AD POLICE
Manga; September 1995

nn - Tony Takezaki manga reprints	£8.00

ADAM THE GARDENER
Express Books

- (1946) reprints Cyril Cowell newspaper strip from Sunday Express	£2.00
- (1978)	£1.00
- (1984)	£1.00

ADVENTURE
D.C. Thomson; 1 17th Sep 1921-1878 14th Jan 1961 (joins Rover)

1 scarce	£60.00
1 facsimile	£3.00
2	£30.00
1921-29 issues	£12.50
1930-39 issues	£10.00
1940-46 issues	£7.50
1947-49 issues	£5.00
1950-55 issues	£4.00
1956-61 issues	£3.00
Note: Story paper, one of Thomson's Big Five	

ADVENTURE ALBUM, THE
G.T. Ltd; nn 1959?

nn - card cover; McLoughlin Buffalo Bill reprints and cover	£8.00

ADVENTURE ANNUAL, THE
Boardman; 1953

1953 Swift Morgan, Roy Carson by Denis McLoughlin	£10.00

ADVENTURE DOUBLE DOUBLE COMICS
Thorpe & Porter; 1-3 1967

1 bound-together remainders of DC and Marvel comics, some with new line drawn covers	£2.50
2	£2.00
3 reprints Adventure Comics #355, World's Finest #163, Wonder Woman #163, Aquaman #28	£2.00

	N.MINT

ADVENTURE HERO
Scion; 1 1952
| 1 24pgs; King-Ganteaurne art | £6.00 |

ADVENTURE KNOWLEDGE
Macdonald/Sackett; 1-4 1979
1 Lost in the Amazon by Gerry Embleton	£1.00
2 Mystery of the Pharaoh	£1.00
3 Death in the Arctic	£1.00
4 Danger on the Red Planet	£1.00

ADVENTURE LAND
D.C. Thomson; 1923-1940
(1924) (Aut 1923) (Barefoot castaway on beach attracting ship with fire)	£30.00
(1925) (Aut 1924) (Boy in open-neck red shirt with alsation in mountains)	£20.00
(1926) (Aut 1925) (Boy in open-neck yellow shirt in south-seas)	£17.50
(1927) (Aut 1926) (Boy in red-check shirt by campfire)	£15.00
(1928) (Aut 1927) (Elk pulling sleigh and trapper through snow)	£15.00
(1929) (Aut 1928) (Trapper in check shirt in bough of tree looking down at river)	£15.00
(1930) (Aut 1929) (Young man standing in boat guiding it to shore)	£15.00
(1931) (Aut 1930) (Biplane diving down from sky)	£12.50
(1932) (Aut 1931) (Three men operating radio and two huskies in snow)	£12.50
(1933) (Aut 1932) (White man and native on raft with red shirt as flag)	£12.50
(1934) (Aut 1933) (Man with earphones, kite-like aerial in canoe)	£12.50
(1935) (Aut 1934) (Hiking boy, waving card reading Bill Jones First Up)	£12.50
(1936) (Aut 1935) (Boy playing Who's Afraid of the Big Bad Wolf on accordian)	£10.00
(1937) (Aut 1936) (Man in racing car with leaping tiger on front)	£10.00
(1938) (Aut 1937) (Man with pistol entering cave on edge of cliff)	£10.00
(1939) (Aut 1938) (Man in loin cloth hitting rock-carved hand with sledgehammer)	£10.00
(1940) (Aut 1939) (Man in topee holding gun leading leopard on a chain)	£10.00
(1941) (Aut 1940) (Indian rowing white man in canoe, attacked by natives from bank)	£10.00

ADVENTURE PICTURE LIBRARY
Famepress; 1 1960s-(53+)
| 1 pocket size | £1.00 |
| 2-53+ | £0.75 |

ADVENTURE STORIES OF WORLD FAMOUS EXPLORERS
Elders & Fyffes; 1-2 1946?
| 1-2 44pgs oblong; promo, Tony Weare art | £10.00 |

ADVENTURE STORY COMICS
Odhams; Nov 1951
| nn - 52pgs | £3.00 |

ADVENTURE STREAMLINE COMICS
Streamline; nn 1950s
| nn - 68pgs; US reprints | £4.00 |

ADVENTURES IN 3.D.
United Anglo-American; 1-2 1954?
| 1 36pgs; reprints from Harvey; Nostrand/Powell art | £12.00 |
| 2 Powell art | £10.00 |

ADVENTURES IN WONDERLAND
Miller; 1-2 1955
| 1-2 36pgs; reprints from Lev Gleason | £4.00 |

ADVENTURES INTO THE UNKNOWN
Arnold Book Co./Thorpe & Porter; 1 1950-?
1 68pgs; very scarce; American Comics Group reprints	£12.50
2-5	£5.00
6-?	£2.50

ADVENTURES INTO WEIRD WORLDS
Thorpe & Porter; 1 1952-?
1 68pgs; rare; Marvel reprints	£20.00
2-5 very scarce	£10.00
6-20 scarce	£5.00
21-?	£2.50

ADVENTURES OF BIGGLES, THE
Strato; 1-9 1950s
| 1 68pgs; Biggles by Albert Devine Australian reprints; very scarce | £15.00 |
| 2-9 some incl. reprints from Tim Valour, Crimson Comet | £7.50 |

ADVENTURES OF BLONDIE AND DAGWOOD
Associated Newspapers; nn Feb 1957
| nn - 84pgs; reprints American newspaper strip by Chic Young | £5.00 |

ADVENTURES OF CHARLIE CHICK, THE
(no publisher); nn 1946?
| nn - 8pgs; newspaper strip reprints, Fred Robinson art | £3.00 |

ADVENTURES OF DILLY DUCKLING, THE
Brockhampton; nn 1948
| nn - 68pgs; Ken Reid art | £12.00 |

ADVENTURES OF DINKY AND DOO, THE
Walthamstow Guardian; nn 1940s; 1-2 1940s
| nn - folds to give 6pgs small; Fred Robinson newspaper strip reprints | £3.00 |
| 1-2 8pgs small | £3.00 |

ADVENTURES OF DOCTOR DOOLITTLE, THE
(see Doctor Doolittle)

ADVENTURES OF ELMO THE LION, THE
(see also The Further Adventures of Elmo)
Kingsbury; nn 1942
| nn - 20pgs; reprints newspaper strip by Charles Cole | £3.00 |

ADVENTURES OF FAT FREDDY'S CAT
Hassle Free Press; 1 1978-5 1979
| 1-5 reprints US underground strips by Gilbert Shelton | £4.00 |

ADVENTURES OF GOOD DEED DANNY, THE
(see also The Daily Deeds of Sammy the Scout)
W.H.Allen; nn Feb 1946
| nn - 16pgs; reprints Sammy the Scout newspaper strip by Ern Shaw | £3.00 |

ADVENTURES OF JASPER, THE
Ellison Hawks; nn 1940s

	N.MINT

| nn - 28pgs; reprints The Dog Owner newspaper strip by Walkden Fisher | £3.00 |

ADVENTURES OF LUTHER ARKWRIGHT, THE
Book 1: Rat Trap (Never Ltd, Dec 1982) Bryan Talbot script/art begins, most copies have binding defects and loose pages	£8.00
Book 1: Rat Trap (Valkyrie, Nov 1989)	£4.50
Book 2: Transfiguration (Valkyrie, Dec 1987)	£6.00
Book 3: Gotterdammerung (Valkyrie, Jun 1989)	£6.00

ADVENTURES OF LUTHER ARKWRIGHT, THE
Valkyrie; 1 Oct 1987-10 Apr 1989
1 Bryan Talbot script/art begins	£2.50
2-7	£1.50
8-9 all new material (first publication of Book 3)	£1.75
10 ARKeology; contributions by Talbot, Gaiman & McKean, Morrison	£2.00

ADVENTURES OF P.C. FRANK, THE
Heavy Tripp Rock 'n' Roll Kartoon Korp; 1-2 1969
| 1-2 1pg newspaper sheet, printed one side; underground | £1.50 |

ADVENTURES OF ROBIN HOOD
Ward Lock; nn 1938?
| nn - 128pgs; hardcover; full length text story adapting Erroll Flynn movie | £15.00 |
| nn as above; softcover | £10.00 |

ADVENTURES OF ROBIN HOOD, THE
Publicity Productions; Nov 1954
| 1954 70pgs; Eleanor Graham Vance text, illus by Jay Hyde Barnum | £8.00 |

ADVENTURES OF ROBIN HOOD, THE
C.A. Pearson (TV Picture Stories); 1 Apr 1959-3 Aug 1959
| 1 68pgs pocket size | £6.00 |
| 2-3 | £4.00 |
ARTISTS/FEATURES
1 The Moneylender. 2 Friar Tuck. 3 A Husband for Marion.

ADVENTURES OF ROBIN HOOD ANNUAL, THE
(see also Robin Hood Annual)
Adprint; nn 1956-3 1958
| nn text/photo | £6.00 |
| 2-3 illus. by Ron Embleton | £6.00 |

ADVENTURES OF SIM, THE
Brockhampton; nn Mar 1953
| nn - 68pgs; small oblong; Tim (William Tymym) art | £3.00 |

ADVENTURES OF STEVE
P.J.Press; nn 1947
| nn - reprints Come on Steve newspaper strip by Roland Davies | £6.00 |

ADVENTURES OF SUPERMAN, THE
(see Superman)

AERONAUTS
World; 1985
| 1985 96pgs; reprints French strip by Charlier & Jije | £2.50 |

AIR ACE PICTURE LIBRARY
Fleetway/IPC; 1 Jan 1960-545 Nov 1970
1 60pgs pocket size; Target Top Secret by Solano Lopez	£12.50
2	£5.00
3-50	£2.00
51-199	£1.00
200-399	£0.75
400 mostly reprints from hereon	£0.50
401-545 68pgs from 492, most have back-up strips	£0.50
ARTISTS/FEATURES
1 Target Top Secret by Solano Lopez. 2 Out of the Sun. 3 Torpedo Strike by Luis Ramos?. 4 Mission Completed. 5 Sky High by Solano Lopez. 6 MacGregor's Crew by Solano Lopez. 7 Seek and Strike by Mike Western. 8 Hurribombers. 9 Endless Battle by Solano Lopez. 10 Objective Destroyed by Ian Kennedy. 11 Scramble! by Ferdinando Tacconi. 12 Tiger in the Sky by Solano Lopez. Other issues incl. art by Luis Bermejo. Kurt Caesar. Joe Colquhoun in 35. Fernando Fernandez. Ian Kennedy. Solano Lopez. Jose Ortiz. Ferdinando Tacconi. Ron Turner in 141,450. Mike Western in 7,23,46.

AIR ACE PICTURE LIBRARY HOLIDAY SPECIAL
Fleetway/IPC; May 1969-1979?
| 1969 224pgs; reprints from Air Ace Picture Library begin | £2.00 |
| 1970-1979 later issues 192pgs | £1.00 |

AIR FLIGHTS OF FLYER HART, THE
D.C. Thomson; 27th Jan 1962
| - 28pgs; giveaway with New Hotspur 119 | £2.00 |

AIR WAR PICTURE LIBRARY
M.V. Features; 1 1965-?
| 1-? 68pgs pocket size | £0.50 |

AIR WAR PICTURE STORIES
C.A. Pearson; 1 Feb 1961-42? 1962
| 1 68pgs pocket size; Mission of No Return | £2.00 |
| 2-42? | £1.00 |

AIRBOY COMICS
Streamline/United Anglo-American; 1951 (5+ issues)
nn - 28pgs; reprints from Hillman	£9.00
nn 36pgs	£9.00
3-5	£6.00

AIRBOY COMICS
Thorpe & Porter; 1 1953
| 1 68pgs; reprints from Hillman | £8.00 |

AJAX ADVENTURE ANNUAL
Popular Press Ltd; nn 1950s
| nn - features Dollman and Plastic Man by L.B. Cole reprints; McLoughlin cover | £7.50 |

AKIRA
Mandarin; Jan 1995
| Book 1 320pgs; Katsuhiro Otomo reprints | £11.00 |

ALAN MOORE'S SHOCKING FUTURES
Titan (Best of 2000AD); Nov 1986
| - 2000AD reprints by Alan Moore | £5.00 |

	N.MINT		N.MINT

ALAN MOORE'S TWISTED TIMES

Titan (Best of 2000AD); Jan 1987

- 2000AD reprints by Alan Moore	£4.50

ALEC

Escape; Jul 1984-Sep 1986/ Acme; Jun 1990

Episodes in the Life of Alec McGarry 36pgs (1,000 copies)	£5.00
Love and Beerglasses	£3.00
Doggie in the Window	£2.50
The Complete Alec (Acme) 144pgs	£8.00
Note: all Eddie Campbell script/art. Later episodes published by Fantagraphics and Dark Horse (USA)	

ALEX

Heineman/Penguin/Headline; 1987-present

Alex (1987) reprints newspaper strip from Independent by Russell Taylor & Charles Pettie	£3.00
The Unabashed Alex (1988)	£2.00
Alex 3-5	£1.50
Alex Calls the Shots (Headline, Oct 1993) Daily Telegraph reprints	£6.00

ALIAS SMITH AND JONES

World; 1976-1977

1976 64pgs; 4 strips + 2 text stories	£3.00
1977 64pgs; 3 strips + 6 text stories	£2.50

ALICE IN WONDERLAND

Miller; nn Nov 1941

nn - 20pgs small square; reprints from US newspaper strip redrawn by British artist	£3.00

ALIEN 3

Dark Horse; 1 Aug 1992-3 Sep 1992

1-3 reprints US movie adaptation with new text features	£1.50

ALIENS

Titan; 1990-present

Aliens Book 1 (1990) Dark Horse reprints begin	£7.00
Aliens Book 2 (1990)	£7.50
Aliens: Earth War (1992)	£9.00
Aliens versus Predator (1992)	£10.00
Aliens: Genocide (Apr 1993)	£9.00
Aliens: Hive (1993) Kelley Jones art	£9.00
Aliens: Newt's Tale (Nov 1994) retells Aliens movie from Newt's perspective	£7.00
Aliens: Rogue (Nov 1994) Will Simpson art	£9.00

ALIENS

Trident/Dark Horse; 1 Feb 1991-17 Jun 1992

1 Aliens, Predator, Aliens vs Predator reprints begin	£1.75
2-16	£1.50
17 pubd. by Dark Horse; Bisley art	£1.50

ALIENS (NEW SERIES)

Dark Horse; v2:1 Jul 1992-22 Apr 1994

1 Aliens: Hive (ends 9), Predator: Cold War (ends 8) reprints begin, Bolton cover	£1.50
2-8 Newt's Tale reprints	£1.50
9 Aliens: Sacrifice by Milligan & Johnson begins, Colonial Marines reprints begin, free Aliens: Countdown comic pt.1	£1.50
10 Aliens: Countdown comic pt.2, Tribes reprints begin (ends 16), Johnson art	£1.50
11-12 Johnson art ends	£1.50
12 Aliens: Horror Show begins (ends 14), Roach art	£1.50
13 Aliens: Holy War by Mike Cook & Christian Gorny begins, Roach art	£1.50
14 Roach art ends	£1.50
15 Aliens: Backsplash begins (ends 16)	£1.50
16-17	£1.50
18 Renegade by Chris Claremont	£1.50
19-22	£1.50

ALIENS VS PREDATOR: THE DEADLIEST OF THE SPECIES

Boxtree; Apr-Nov 1995

Aliens vs Predator Book 1 (Apr 1995) Dark Horse reprints by Chris Claremont, Jackson Guice, Eduardo Barreto	£10.00
Aliens vs Predator Book 2 (Nov 1995)	£10.00

ALL ACTION COMIC

Moring; nn 1956?

nn - softcover 68pgs; McLoughlin, Turner, Embleton reprints	£10.00

ALL FAVOURITES

(see Mighty Comic)

K.G. Murray Ltd; 1 mid 1950s-31? early 1960s

1 rare, 100pgs squarebound begin; b/w reprints from National Periodical Publications incl. Tomahawk, Tommy Tomorrow, Mr. District Attorney, Congo Bill, Johnny Thunder, Wonder Woman (later issues incl. Atom, Viking Prince and Adam Strange among others); priced at 2 shillings	£75.00
2 rare	£50.00
3-5 very scarce	£40.00
6-10 scarce	£35.00
11-31 scarce	£30.00
Note: more issues beyond #31 thought to exist. A second series was published late 1960s/early 1970s, with black & white reprints, but no more information is available at time of going to press.	

ALL FUN ANNUAL

A. Soloway; nn 1945

nn annual, Nat Brand art	£9.00

ALL FUN COMIC

A. Soloway; v.1 n.1 1940-v.7 n.2 1949, 27 issues

Vol 1:1-5 8pgs tabloid	£6.00
Vol 2:1-Vol 7:1 16pgs, half-tabloid	£4.00
Vol 7:2 16pgs, full colour	£5.00

ALL PICTURE COMIC, THE

Sphinx; 12th Mar 1921-25th Jun 1921, 16 unnumbered issues

12 Mar 1921	£12.00
19 Mar-25 Jun 1921 first entirely pictorial British comic	£8.00
The All Picture Comic (J.F. Perrott, 193?) reprints 1st issue with minor differences	£8.00

ALL-SORTS COMIC

Scion; nn 1948

nn - 8pgs; Plummer, Jukes art	£4.00

ALL STAR ANNUAL

A. Soloway; nn 1945

nn - Nat Brand art	£9.00

ALL STAR COMIC

A. Soloway; v.1 n.1 1940-v.7 n.2 1949, 27 issues

Vol 1:1-5 8pgs, tabloid	£6.00
Vol 2:1-Vol 7:1 16pgs, half-tabloid	£4.00
Vol 7:2 16pgs, full colour	£5.00

ALL STAR WESTERN

(see Giant Comic)

ALL TOP COMICS

Streamline/United Anglo-American; nn 1949

nn - 28pgs; reprints from Fox	£6.00

ALL WORLDS ALBUM

Moring; nn 1956?

nn - softcover; incl. new McLoughlin Swift Morgan from uncorrected artwork	£12.00

ALLEYCAT

CM Comics; 1 1993-2 Jan 1994

1 Chris Morgan art, intro. Alleycat	£1.00
2 Russell Leach art, intro. Vampyra	£0.75

'ALLO 'ALLO ANNUAL

Grandreams; 1988

1988 Based on TV series, mostly text; Alan Hunt art	£2.00

ALLY SLOPER

Judy Office; 1873-1888

Ally Sloper: A Moral Lesson (1873) 220pgs; Ally Sloper by C.H. Ross	£50.00
Ally Sloper's Book of Beauty (1877)	£25.00
Ally Sloper's Guide to the Paris Exhibition (1878)	£20.00
The Eastern Question Tackled (1878)	£15.00
Ally Sloper's Sentimental Journey (1880)	£12.50
The Ups and Downs of Ally Sloper (1882)	£12.50
The Ups and Downs of Ally Sloper (1887) reprint of above in magazine format	£12.50
Ally Sloper's Comic Crackers (1883)	£12.50
True Story of Ally Sloper and the Paint Pot (1887) full colour	£20.00
Fifty Sloper Cartoons (1888) W.G. Baxter memorial volume, hardback	£20.00

ALLY SLOPER

(previously Ally Sloper's Half Holiday)

The Sloperies; 1571 6th Jun 1914-1679 9th Sep 1916 (109 issues; joins London Society)

1571 24pgs; magazine, Ally Sloper by W.F. Thomas	£15.00
1572-1679	£5.00

ALLY SLOPER

D. McKenzie; 1 1948

1 8pgs; Ally Sloper by T.D.Reid, common	£1.50

ALLY SLOPER

Alan Class; 1 Oct 1976-4 Jan 1977

1 Swade by Frank Bellamy, Emerson art	£2.50
2 The Wrangler by Harry Bishop, O'Neill art	£1.50
3 Dawn O'Dare by Frank Hampson, Raymond Briggs art	£2.50
4 Pagan by John Richardson, Emerson art	£1.50

ALLY SLOPER'S CHRISTMAS HOLIDAYS

W.J. Sinkins/ Dalziel/The Sloperies; Dec 1884-Dec 1913, 30 unnumbered issues

1884 16pgs; Ally Sloper by W.G. Baxter	£40.00
1885-1913 W.G. Baxter art	£25.00

ALLY SLOPER'S COMIC KALENDER

Judy Office; Dec 1875-Dec 1887, 13 unnumbered issues

1875 24pgs; Ally Sloper by C.H. Ross	£45.00
1876-1807 Ally Sloper by Mario Duval	£30.00

ALLY SLOPER'S COMIC VOLUME

The Sloperies; 1913?-?

- remainder copies of Ally Sloper's Half-Holiday in colour covers	£12.50

ALLY SLOPER'S HALF-HOLIDAY

W.J. Sinkins/Dalziel/The Sloperies; 1 3rd May 1884-1570 30th May 1914 (becomes Ally Sloper)

1 8pgs tabloid; C.H. Ross/Marie Duval Ally Sloper reprints from Judy begin	£100.00
2-1570 incl. Ally Sloper by W.G. Baxter, later by W.F. Thomas	£27.50

ALLY SLOPER'S HALF-HOLIDAY (NEW SERIES)

The Sloperies; 1 5th Nov 1922-23 14th Apr 1923 (becomes Half Holiday)

1 16pgs; Ally Sloper by W.F. Thomas	£40.00
2-23	£7.50

ALLY SLOPER'S HALF-HOLIDAY

Ally Sloper Publications; 1 1949

1 8pgs; Ally Sloper by A.R.G.	£5.00

ALLY SLOPER'S HA'PORTH

Gilbert Dalziel; 1 23rd Jan 1899-10 21st Mar 1899

1 8pp tabloid; miscellaneous strips and cartoons	£45.00
2-10	£10.00

ALLY SLOPER'S QUARTERLY

Gilbert Dalziel; no date

- 12 issues of Ally Sloper's Half-Holiday rebound each	£7.50

ALLY SLOPER'S SUMMER NUMBER

Judy Offices; Jun 1880-Jun 1887, 8 issues

1880 24pgs; Ally Sloper by C.H. Ross/Marie Duval	£55.00
1881-1887	£22.50

AMAZING ADVENTURES OF CAPTAIN KRUNCH

KP Foods; nn 1977

nn - 20pgs; giveaway, Alf Saporito art	£0.25

AMAZING COMICS

Modern Fiction; nn Oct 1949

nn - 8pgs; Captain Night by Denis Gifford, Mick Anglo, Bob Monkhouse art	£9.00

AMAZING EXPLOITS OF JEREMY BEAR

Golden Press; nn 1971

nn - 20pgs; 3-D giveaway with Sugar Puffs	£0.10

	N.MINT
AMAZING ROCK & ROLL ADVENTURES	
(see Brainstorm Comix)	
AMAZING STORIES	
Alan Class; nn 196?-?	
nn - very scarce, 68pgs; reprints from American Comics Group	£12.00
2-10 scarce	£5.00
11-?	£2.50
AMAZING STORIES OF SUSPENSE	
Alan Class; 1 196?-?	
1-? 68pgs; incl. Ditko Captain Atom art	£2.50
AMAZING WORLD OF DOCTOR WHO	
PBS; 1976	
- reprints stories from Dr. Who Annual 1976, Daleks from TV21	£10.00
AMERICA	
Fleetway; 1991	
- 64pgs; Judge Dredd Megazine reprints by John Wagner & Colin MacNeil	£5.00
AMERICAN COMIC ANNUAL	
Miller; nn 1943	
nn - 68pgs; reprints US newspaper strips	£5.00
AMERICAN EAGLE	
Strato; 1954?	
1 US reprints	£4.00
ANDERSON PSI DIVISION	
(see Judge Anderson)	
Fleetway; 1991	
Shamballa (1991) 64pgs; 2000AD reprints by Alan Grant & Arthur Ranson	£3.00
Note: heavily remaindered in 1994	
ANDY CAPP	
(see also Laugh Again with Andy Capp)	
Mirror; 1958-present	
(1) The Andy Capp Book (1958) reprints Daily Mirror strip by Reg Smythe	£15.00
(2) Andy Capp's Spring Tonic (1959) bottle shaped	£7.50
(3) Life With Andy Capp (1959)	£7.50
(4) Andy Capp's Spring Collection (1960)	£6.00
(5) Best of Andy Capp (1960) 1st oblong	£5.00
(6) Laugh With Andy Capp (1961)	£5.00
(7) World of Andy Capp (1961)	£4.00
(8) More Andy Capp (1962)	£4.00
(9) Andy Capp, I Must Be Dreaming (1962)	£4.00
(10) Andy Capp Picks His Favourites (1963)	£4.00
(11) Happy Days With Andy Capp (1963)	£4.00
(12) Laugh At Life With Andy Capp (1964)	£4.00
(13) Andy Capp and Florrie (1964)	£3.00
(14) All the Best From Andy Capp (1965)	£3.00
(15) (Andy in wash-tub)	£3.00
(16) (Carving on tree)	£3.00
(17) (Andy heading goal)	£3.00
18-20 numbered inside	£2.50
21-46	£2.50
47-49,51-53 copyright dated annually, cy1983 onwards	£2.50
50 Andy Capp Strikes Gold!	£2.50
The World of Andy Capp (1980-1986) magazine format	£3.00
This Is Your Life Andy Capp (1986)	£3.00
The Cream of Andy Capp (Mirror, 1965) hardcover, issued with dust-jacket	£10.00
You're A Star Andy Capp (Mirror, Mar 1988)	£2.00
The World of Andy Capp (Titan, Oct 1990)	£9.00
Don't Wait Up (Ravette, Apr 1992)	£3.00
After A Few (Ravette, Apr 1992)	£3.00
ANDY DEVINE	
Miller; 50 1950-?	
50 reprints from Fawcett	£5.00
51-?	£2.50
ANDY PANDY HOLIDAY SPECIAL	
Polystyle; nn May 1980	
nn - 48pgs; reprints	£0.35
ANGELS ANNUAL, THE	
Century 21; 1967	
1967 scarce	£12.00
ANGELS STORYBOOK, THE	
Century 21; A2 1968	
A2	£9.00
ANIMAL WEIRDNESS	
H. Bunch (Cozmic); nn Oct 1974	
nn - 36pgs; Petagno art	£2.00
ANNIE	
Seymour; nn Jul 1982	
nn - 68pgs; US reprint, based on film	£0.75
ANNIE OAKLEY	
Miller; 1 Jun 1957-17? 1958	
1 28pgs; Annie Oakley by Arthur Baker begins	£6.00
2-17?	£3.00
ANNIE OAKLEY AND TAGG	
World Distributors; 1 1955-10 1956	
1 reprints from Dell	£4.00
2-10 photocovers	£2.50
APACHE KID	
Streamline; 1951, 10+ issues	
nn,**2-10** 28pgs; reprints from Atlas	£2.50
APACHE PICTURE AND STORY ALBUM	
Mellifont; W1 1950s	
W1 96pgs	£3.00

All Favourites #9

Ally Sloper's Half Holiday #1

Avengers #1 (22/9/73)

	N.MINT
APPLESEED	
Manga; Sep 1995-present	
Vol.1: The Promethean Challenge Masamune Shirow manga reprints begin	£8.00
APULHEAD LIVES	
Apulhead Productions; nn 1976	
nn - Peter Kennedy art, underground	£1.00
ARCHIE	
Gerald Swan; 1950-1953	
1-? 36pgs; reprints from Archie	£3.00
ARCHIE COMICS	
Thorpe & Porter; 1953-?	
1-? reprints from Archie	£3.00
ARIZONA KID, THE	
Streamline/United Anglo-American; 1 1952	
1 28pgs; reprints from Marvel	£3.00
ARROWHEAD	
Streamline; 1954, 2 unnumbered issues	
nn-nn 28pgs; reprints from Atlas; Sinnott art	£3.00
'ARRY'S BUDGET	
Guy Rayner; 1 26th Jun 1886-21 6th Nov 1886 (becomes 'Arry's Illustrated Budget)	
1 8pgs tabloid	£30.00
2-21	£15.00
ART ATTACK	
Visual Records; nn Aug 1977	
nn - underground	£1.00
ARTHUR ASKEY'S ANNUAL	
D.C. Thomson; 1940	
(1940) very scarce	£40.00
Note: no more issued, although more were planned	
ASPECT	
Steve Moore; 1 1969-2 Mar 1970	
1 Parkhouse art	£1.00
2 Baikie, Alan Hunter, Neary, Parkhouse, Windsor-Smith art	£2.00
ASTERIX	
Brockhampton Press/ Hodder & Stoughton; 1969-present	
Asterix the Gaul (Brockhampton, 1969) French reprints begin	£10.00
Asterix and Cleopatra (Brockhampton, 1969)	£10.00
Asterix the Gladiator (Brockhampton, 1969)	£10.00
Asterix in Britain (Brockhampton, 1970)	£8.00
Asterix the Legionnaire (Brockhampton, 1970)	£8.00
Asterix in Spain (Brockhampton, 1971)	£5.00
Asterix and the Big Fight (Brockhampton, 1971)	£5.00
Asterix and the Roman Agent (Brockhampton, 1972)	£5.00
Asterix and the Olympic Games (Brockhampton, 1972)	£5.00
Asterix in Switzerland (Brockhampton, 1973)	£5.00
The Mansions of the Gods (Brockhampton, 1973)	£5.00
Asterix and the Laurel Wreath (Brockhampton, 1974)	£5.00
Asterix and the Goths (Brockhampton, 1974)	£5.00
Asterix and the Soothsayer (Brockhampton, 1975)	£5.00
Asterix and the Golden Sickle (Hodder, 1975)	£3.00
Asterix and the Great Crossing (Hodder, 1976)	£3.00
Asterix and the Cauldron (Hodder, 1976)	£3.00
Asterix and the Chieftain's Shield (Hodder, 1977)	£3.00
Asterix and Caesar's Gift (Hodder, 1977)	£3.00
Asterix and the Normans (Hodder, 1978)	£3.00
The Twelve Tasks of Asterix (Hodder, 1978) based on the film	£3.00
Obelix and Co. (Hodder, 1979)	£3.00
Asterix and the Banquet (Hodder, 1979)	£3.00
Asterix in Corsica (Hodder, 1979)	£3.00
Asterix in Belgium (Hodder, 1980)	£3.00
Asterix and the Black Gold (Hodder, 1982)	£3.00
Asterix and Son (Hodder, 1983)	£3.00
Asterix versus Caesar (Hodder, 1986) based on the film	£3.00
Asterix and the Magic Carpet (Hodder, 1988)	£3.00
How Obelix Fell into the Magic Potion When He was a Little Boy (Hodder, 1989)	£3.00
Asterix and the Secret Weapon (Hodder, 1992) cased	£6.00
Asterix and the Secret Weapon (Hodder, 1993) softcover	£4.00
Operation Getafix: Book of the Film (Hodder, 1990)	£1.50
Asterix the Gaul (contains: Asterix in Britain, Asterix in Switzerland, Asterix the Gaul)	£4.00
Asterix and the Romans (contains: Asterix the Legionary, Asterix & the Chieftain's Shield, The Mansions of the Gods, Asterix in Belgium) (Hodder, 1986)	£4.00
Asterix the Brave (contains: Asterix and the Golden Sickle, Asterix and the Cauldron, Asterix and the Normans, Asterix and the Great Crossing) (Hodder, 1987)	£4.00
Note: omnibus editions heavily remaindered in 1995	
ASTERIX ADVENTURE GAMES BOOKS	
Hodder & Stoughton; 1986-present	
Asterix to the Rescue (1986)	£2.00
The Meeting of the Chieftains (1989)	£2.00
Idol of the Gauls (Apr 1990)	£2.00
ASTONISHING STORIES	
Alan Class; nn 1967-?	
nn rare, 68pgs; reprints from American Comics Group, Atlas	£10.00
2-5 scarce	£5.00
6-?	£2.50
ASTOUNDING COMIC ADVENTURES	
(see Super Duper Comics)	
ASTOUNDING STORIES	
Alan Class; 1 Feb 1966-195 Apr 1989	
1 68pgs; reprints from Marvel, American Comics Group, Archie	£5.00
2	£2.50
3-5	£1.50
6-195	£1.00

	N.MINT
A-TEAM ANNUAL, THE	
World; 1984-1988	
1984-1988 mainly text stories by Nick Pemberton	£1.50
A-TEAM SPECIALS	
Marvel; Jun 1985-Mar 1986	
Summer Special	£0.60
Special No.2	£0.60
ATOM, THE	
Buchanon Books; nn 1947	
nn - 12pgs; Rex Hart art	£4.00
ATOMIC AGE COMIC, THE	
Algar/L. Burn; nn 1947	
nn - 36pgs; H. Stanley White, Basil Reynolds art	£5.00
ATOMIC COMIC	
Fudge; nn Sep 1947	
nn - 8pgs; Bob Wilkin art	£3.00
Note: printed in alternate green/purple and released in two forms, half with green cover, half with purple.	
ATOMIC COMIC SERIES	
(see Science Service, Sam Bronx and the Robots)	
ATOMIC COMICS	
Mutant Enterprises; 1 1975	
1 underground	£1.00
ATOMIC MOUSE	
Miller; 1 1953-4 1953	
1-4 28pgs; reprints from Charlton; Al Fago art	£2.50
ATOMIC SPY RING	
(see Secret Service Series)	
Hotspur Publishing Co.; 6 1949	
6 Bob Wilkin, Walter Booth art	£3.00
ATTACK!	
Famepress/ Award/ White; 1 1962-?	
1 68pgs pocket size; Hill 70, Italian reprints begin	£1.00
2-?	£0.60
ATTACK PICTURE LIBRARY HOLIDAY SPECIAL	
I.P.C. Magazines; May 1982-May 1984, 3 unnumbered issues	
1982-1984 192pgs pocket; reprints from picture libraries	£1.00
AUGUSTA	
Barrie & Jenkins; 1977-1978	
Augusta the Great 76pgs; newspaper reprints by Domenic Poelsma from Evening Standard	£2.00
I, Augusta	£2.00
AUTHENTIC POLICE CASES	
R. & L. Locker; nn 1949	
nn - 36pgs; reprints from St. John Publishing (some stories used in Seduction Of The Innocent)	£12.00
AVALON	
Harrier; 1 Oct 1986-14 Mar 1988	
1 Phil Elliott art	£1.00
2-14	£0.60
AVENGERS	
(see also New Avengers Annual, TV Crimebusters)	
Souvenir/Atlas; 1967-1969	
1967 Diana Rigg	£20.00
1968 Linda Thorson	£12.50
1969 Linda Thorson, scarce	£15.00
AVENGERS, THE	
Thorpe & Porter; 1 1966	
1 68pgs, Diana Rigg; Mick Anglo art, very scarce	£50.00
Note: an American comic **John Steed - Emma Peel** (Gold Key, 1968) is given inside as Avengers No 1, the title changed to avoid copyright problems with Marvel; this has nothing to do with the above title, the strips being coloured reprints from TV Comic (qv).	
AVENGERS, THE	
Marvel; 1 22nd Sep 1973-147 14th Jul 1976 (joins Mighty World of Marvel)	
1 36pgs; The Avengers, Doctor Strange reprints begin	£2.00
1 with free gift (sheet of transfers)	£4.00
2	£1.50
2 with free gift (Avengers Wonder Weapon)	£3.00
3-27,29-94	£1.00
28 1st "Avengers & Master of Kung Fu"	£1.25
95 1st "Avengers & Savage Sword of Conan"	£1.25
96-147	£1.00
AVENGERS ANNUAL, THE	
Marvel/World Distributors; 1974-1977	
1975 80pgs; reprints #110-112; colour	£6.00
1976 64pgs; reprints #83-85; colour	£5.00
1977 80pgs; reprints #143, Giant Size Conan #1, Conan #39,57; colour	£4.00
1978 reprints #59-60, Conan #24; colour	£3.50
AVENGERS TREASURY	
Marvel; nn 1982	
nn - 56pgs; US reprints, Dave Gibbons cover	£1.50
AVENGERS WINTER SPECIAL	
Marvel; nn Nov 1982	
nn - US reprints	£1.25

B

	N.MINT
BAD COMPANY	
Titan (Best of 2000AD); Aug 1987-Dec 1988	
Book One 2000AD reprints by Milligan & Ewins/McCarthy begin	£4.50
Book Two	£4.50
Book Three The Bewilderness	£4.50
Book Four The Krool Heart	£4.50

	N.MINT
BANG ON COMIC	
Philmar; nn 1948	
nn - 8pgs; Wally Robertson, Jack Pamby art	£4.00
BANG-ON-COMIC, THE	
Fudge; nn 1947	
nn - 8pgs; David Williams art	£4.00
BANTAM COMICS	
P.M. Productions; nn 1944	
nn - 8pgs, small; printed on beige card; Glyn Protheroe art	£5.00
BARBARA CARTLAND PICTURE ROMANCES	
Macmillan; nn 1982	
nn - 132pgs oblong; reprints US newspaper strip	£0.35
BARBARIENNE	
(see Cuirass)	
Harrier; 1 Mar 1987-8 Nov 1988	
1-5 28pgs; Nick Neocleous art 1-4, John Marshall art 5	£0.60
6-8 36pgs titled Barbarienne Versus Cuirass; John Marshall art	£0.50
BAREFOOT GEN	
Penguin; 1989, 1990	
Barefoot Gen reprints Hadashi no Gen by Keiji Nakazawa	£5.00
Barefoot Gen, new edition (1995) with intro by Art Spiegelman	£8.00
Barefoot Gen: The Day After	£4.00
Barefoot Gen: The Day After new edition (1995)	£8.00
BARETTA ANNUAL	
Brown Watson; 1977	
1977 based on TV series; Ron Tiner art	£2.00
BARKER, THE	
Locker; 1949	
1 36pgs; reprints from Quality	£4.00
BARRY MCKENZIE	
Macdonald/ Private Eye; 1968-1972	
Wonderful World of Barrie McKenzie reprints Private Eye strip by Nicholas Garland	£2.00
Bazza Pulls It Off	£2.00
BASH STREET KIDS BOOK	
D.C. Thomson; Sep 1979-present (bi-annual at first, now annual)	
1980	£10.00
1982	£7.50
1984	£7.50
1986	£6.00
1989	£5.00
1990-1996	£3.00
BAT MAGAZINE	
Cartoon Art; 1-2 1952	
1 68pgs	£8.00
2 cited in NUT "Spotlight on Comics" film	£12.00
BATMAN	
Atlas; 1 1950?-125? 1962?	
1 very rare; b/w reprints of original Batman and Detective Comics	£125.00
2 very rare	£75.00
3-5 rare	£30.00
6-10 very scarce	£20.00
11-50	£15.00
51-125?	£12.50
BATMAN	
Four Square Books (NEL); 1966	
Batman paperback format reprints, origin by Bob Kane	£5.00
Batman versus The Penguin	£5.00
Batman versus The Joker	£5.00
Batman versus The Catwoman	£5.00
BATMAN (TRADE PAPERBACKS)	
Titan Books; 1986-present	
The Dark Knight Returns (1986) Miller story/art	£9.00
Year One (1988) Miller story, Mazzuchelli art	£6.00
The Killing Joke (1988) by Moore & Bolland	£2.50
Year Two (1989) Davis/McFarlane art	£6.00
Vow From the Grave (1989)	£6.00
Gotham By Gaslight (1989)	£2.50
The Joker's Revenge (1989)	£6.00
Challenge of the Man-Bat (1989)	£6.00
A Death in the Family (1989) Death of Robin	£2.50
The Demon Awakes (1989)	£6.00
Arkham Asylum (1989) hardback, by Morrison & McKean	£15.00
Arkham Asylum (1990) softcover	£9.00
Digital Justice (1990) hardback	£15.00
The Frightened City (1990)	£6.00
Red Water, Crimson Death (1990)	£6.00
Batman 3-D (1990)	£5.50
The Cult (1991)	£8.50
Gothic (Aug 1991) Legends of the Dark Knight 6-10 reprints	£8.50
Batman versus Predator (Jul 1992) by Gibbons & Kubert/Kubert	£8.00
Red Rain (Jul 1992) Moench/Jones/Jones III	£6.00
Shaman (Feb 1993) Legends of the Dark Knight reprints	£8.00
Sword of Azrael (1993) Joe Quesada art	£6.00
Venom (Sep 1993) Legends of the Dark Knight reprints	£6.50
Knightfall: Broken Bat (Nov 1993) 288pgs; Batman, Detective reprints	£8.00
Knightfall: Who Rules the Night (Nov 1993) 296pgs; Batman, Detective, Showcase, Shadow of the Bat reprints	£8.00
Collected Legends of the Dark Knight (Apr 1994) Legends/Dark Knight reprints	£8.50
Ten Nights of the Beast (Aug 1994) reprints Batman 417-420, Jim Aparo art	£4.00
Dark Joker - The Wild (Sep 1994) Elseworlds novel, Kelley Jones art	£6.00
The Last Angel (Nov 1994) Lee Moder/Scott Hanna art	£8.00
Castle of the Bat (Dec 1994) Bo Hampton art	£4.00

	N.MINT
Batman featuring Two-Face and The Ridder (Aug 1995) Bob Kane, Sam Kieth art	£9.00
Batman vs Predator II: Bloodmatch (Dec 1995) Paul Gulacy art	£5.00
BATMAN ADVENTURES	
(see Batman: The Collected Adventures)	
Fleetway Editions; 1 Mar 1993-?	
1 DC reprints begin	£1.20
2-?	£0.50
BATMAN AND ROBIN	
Brown Watson; 1972	
1 scarce, reprints Detective #404, Neal Adams art; new text stories	£10.00
BATMAN AND SUPERMAN	
Fleetway Editions; 1 Mar 1994-? 1995? (definitely ended)	
1 Batman, Superman reprints begin, Who's Who in Superman booklet	£1.20
2 Knightfall continued from Batman Special #4	£1.00
3-?	£0.75
BATMAN ANNUAL/BATMAN OFFICIAL ANNUAL	
Atlas/Top Sellers/London Editions/World/Fleetway; 1960-1995	
1960-61 scarce, b/w reprints also featuring John Jones and Kit Carson	£75.00
1961-62	£40.00
1962-63 also features Roy Raymond and Congorilla	£25.00
1963-64	£20.00
1964-65	£15.00
1965-66 Atlas; 80pgs, monochrome colour throughout	£12.00
1967 Atlas; features John Jones	£12.50
(1968?) Top Sellers; purple cover; reprints incl. Detective #345	£12.00
(1969?) light blue cover; 1960s DC reprints	£10.00
1970 titled Batman Bumper Book; incl. text stories	£7.50
1971-1978	£5.00
1979 Egmont; entitled Batman Official Annual (to 1985?); incl. origin of Batman by Kane	£5.00
1980 Egmont; reprints Team-Up, plus from 1950s	£5.00
1981 Egmont; reprints Batman/Swamp Thing x-over (Swamp Thing #7), Wrightson art	£5.00
1982 London Editions; 78pgs; Bolland cover, Arthur Ranson end-papers	£6.00
1983, 1986-1988	£4.00
1984 London Editions; 64pgs; Dave Gibbons cover	£5.00
1985 London Editions; 64pgs; Alan Moore + Jamie Delano text stories, Alan Davis illos, Talbot cover	£6.00
1989 London Editions; reprints Detective #570, Alan Davis art	£3.50
1990,1992,1994-1995	£3.00
1991 World; reprints Detective #474-476	£3.00
1993 Fleetway; reprints Batman #460-461, plus classic from 1945	£3.00
BATMAN BUMPER BOOK	
Top Sellers; 1971	
1971 64pgs; reprints from 1950s/60s; incl. Bob Kane art, Avengers TV featured	£10.00
BATMAN DOUBLE DOUBLE COMICS	
Thorpe & Porter; nn 1967	
nn bound-together remaindered copies of Batman #188, #189, #196 with new line-drawn cover	£5.00
BATMAN/JUDGE DREDD	
(see Judgement on Gotham, Vendetta in Gotham)	
Fleetway; 1995	
The Ultimate Riddle magazine sized DC reprint by Wagner/Grant, Critchlow & Power	£3.00
BATMAN MONTHLY	
London Editions/Fleetway Editions; 1 Aug 1990-55 Feb 1993; (becomes Batman Monthly (New Series))	
1 US reprints begin	£2.00
2-3	£1.25
4-10,12-23	£1.00
11 Batman 50th Anniversary issue	£1.25
24-29	£0.85
30-55	£0.85
BATMAN MONTHLY (NEW SERIES)	
Fleetway Editions; Vol 2. No.1 Mar 1993-11 Jan 1994 (becomes Batman & Superman)	
1 Batman: Year One by Miller reprints	£1.25
2 Miller art, Year One concludes	£1.00
3-11	£1.00
BATMAN POCKET BOOK	
Egmont/Methuen; 1 1978-9? 1980	
1 100pgs; pocket size; US reprints begin; colour	£1.25
2 Joker cover, Marshal Rogers art	£1.25
3-9	£1.00
BATMAN SPECIAL EDITION	
Fleetway Editions; 4 Spr 1994-5?	
4 Knightfall reprints begin, continued in Batman & Superman	£1.25
5 features Joker reprints	£1.00
BATMAN STORY BOOK ANNUAL	
World Distributirs; 1967-1970	
1967 6 text stories	£10.00
1968 11 text stories	£10.00
1969 Batmobile cover, 13 text stories	£8.00
1970 11 text stories	£8.00
BATMAN: THE COLLECTED ADVENTURES	
Titan; Dec 1993-Jul 1994	
Volume 1 144pgs; reprints Batman Adventures #1-6	£4.00
Volume 2 reprints Batman Adventures #7-12	£4.00
BATMAN WITH ROBIN THE BOY WONDER STORY BOOK ANNUAL	
World Distributors; 1966-1969	
1966 96pgs; 6 stories, all text	£8.00
1967 11 stories by Douglas Enefer, illus. by John Leeder	£7.50
1968-1969 13/11 stories, all text	£6.00
BATMAN WORLD ADVENTURE LIBRARY	
World Distributors; 1 Nov 1966-10 Aug 1967	
1 68pgs pocket size; text stories	£5.00
2-10	£3.50

	N.MINT
BATTLE	
Mick Anglo/Atlas; Nov 1960-Jul 1961, 9 issues	
Nov 1960-Jun 1961 28pgs; Roy Castle, Denis Gifford art	£1.00
BATTLE ACTION	
(see Battle Picture Weekly)	
BATTLE ACTION COMIC	
Cartoon Art; nn 1952	
nn - 28pgs; US reprints	£2.00
BATTLE ACTION FORCE	
(see Battle Picture Weekly)	
BATTLE ACTION IN PICTURES	
Miller; 1-3 1959	
1-3 68pgs pocket size; US reprints	£1.50
BATTLE ATTACK	
Streamline/United Anglo-American; nn 1953	
nn - 28pgs; reprints from Stanmor	£2.00
BATTLE CRY	
Streamline/United Anglo-American; 1953, 2 unnumbered issues	
nn - 28pgs; reprints from Stanmor begin	£2.00
nn - 68pgs	£3.00
BATTLE FIRE	
Streamline; nn 1955	
nn - 28pgs; reprints from Stanmor	£2.00
BATTLE GROUND	
Streamline/United Anglo-American; nn 1955	
nn - 28pgs; reprints from Atlas	£2.00
BATTLE GROUND	
Miller; 1 1960-11 1961	
1-11 68pgs; reprints from Fawcett	£3.00
BATTLE PICTURE LIBRARY	
Fleetway/IPC; 1 Jan 1961-1706 Dec 1984	
1 The Rats of Tobruk; 60pgs pocket size	£12.50
2	£8.00
3-20	£5.00
21-50	£2.50
51-350	£1.00
351-528 mostly reprints from hereon	£0.75
529-1706 68pgs	£0.60
ARTISTS/FEATURES	
1 The Rats of Tobruk by Renzo Calegari. 2 Devils' Cauldron by Luis Bermejo. 3 Trained To Kill by Fred T. Holmes. 4 Island of Guilt. 5 The Ghost Battalion by Aldoma Puig.6 The Silver Plated Luger by Roberto Diso. 7 Killer At Large by Jose Bielsa. 8 Tough Company by Annibale Casabianca. 9 Crack-Up! by John Severin. 10 Achtung - Kommando by Fred T. Holmes. 11 Battle Shock. 12 Blood on the Sand by Leo Duranona. Other issues incl. art by Luis Bermejo, Gino D'Antonio, Victor de la Fuente, Ian Kennedy, Solano Lopez, Jorge Moliterni, Jose Ortiz, Aldomo Puig, Ferdinando Tacconi, et al. Hugo Pratt in 62. Ron Turner in 869, 875-876, 987, 1041, 1086, 1161, 1415, 1487, 1536, 1566, 1630, 1639, 1640-1642, 1655.	
BATTLE PICTURE LIBRARY HOLIDAY SPECIAL	
Fleetway/IPC; 1964-1982?	
1964 224pgs; reprints from picture libraries	£3.50
1965-1974	£2.00
1975-1982 later issues 192pgs	£1.00
BATTLE PICTURE WEEKLY	
IPC; 8th Mar 1975-23rd Jan 1988, 673 unnumbered issues (joins Eagle)	
No.1 D-Day Dawson by Casabianca, Rat Pack by Ezquerra, Day of the Eagle by Pat Wright begin	£2.50
No.1 with free gift (Combat Stickers)	£5.00
No.2 - 15 Mar 1975	£1.25
No.2 with free gift (30" x 20" poster)	£3.00
No.3 - 22 Mar 1975	£1.00
No.3 with free gift (20 Battle Swap Cards)	£2.00
29 Mar 1975-16 Oct 1976	£0.75
23 Oct 1976 1st Battle Picture Weekly and Valiant	£1.00
30 Oct 1976-12 Nov 1977	£0.75
19 Nov 1977 1st Battle Action; Dredger, Spinball Wars by Ron Turner begin	£0.75
26 Nov 1977-16 Dec 1978	£0.75
199 (23 Dec 1978) last Colquhoun Johnny Red	£0.75
200 (6 Jan 1979) Charley's War by Pat Mills & Joe Colquhoun, H.M.S. Nightshade by John Wagner & Mike Western begin, 1st John Cooper Johnny Red	£1.25
13 Jan 1979-1 Oct 1983	£0.75
8 Oct 1983 Action Force toy tie-in begins	£0.55
15 Oct 1983-19 Jan 1985	£0.55
26 Jan 1985 last WWI Charley's War by Mills & Colquhoun	£0.55
2 Feb 1985 1st WWII Charley's War by Scott Goodall & Colquhoun	£0.45
9 Feb 1985-26 Jul 1986, 23 Aug-28 Sep 1986, 8 Nov 1986	£0.45
2 Aug-16 Aug 1986 Manhatten Transfer by Pete Milligan & E.B. Romero	£0.45
4 Oct 1986 last Charley's War	£0.45
11 Oct 1986 censored Charley's War reprints begin	£0.40
18 Oct-1 Nov 1986, 15 Nov-22 Nov 1986 Milligan scripts	£0.45
29 Nov 1986 Action Force end, Milligan script	£0.45
6 Dec 1986-17 Jan 1987, 31 Jan 1987-23 Jan 1988	£0.40
24 Jan 1987 1st Battle With Storm Force, Storm Force begins	£0.40
ARTISTS/FEATURES	
Belardinelli in various 1975-1977 (Rat Pack). Joe Colquhoun in 23 Oct 1976-22 Jan 1977 (Soldier Sharp), 29 Jan-23 Dec 1978 (Johnny Red), 6 Jan 1979-4 Oct 1986 (Charley's War), plus various features. Carlos Ezquerra in 8 Mar-15 Mar 1975, 19 Jul 1975, 23 Aug 1975, 27 Sep 1975, 18 Oct 1975, 22 Nov 1975, 20 Dec 1975 (Rat Pack), 10 Jan-27 Mar 1976, 15 May 1976-23 Apr 1977, 29 Jan-23 Apr 1977, 19 Nov 1977-10 Jun 1978 (Major Eazy), 4 Jun-17 Sep 1977 (El Mestizo), plus various short features. Ron Turner 19 Nov 1977-3 Nov 1979 (Spinball Wars), 8 Dec 1979-28 Jan 1984 (numerous short stories), 3 Dec 1983-7 Jan 1984 (Codename: Sky Raider), 24 Mar-21 Apr 1984 (Sea Fury), 30 Jun-4 Aug 1984 (Death Castle).	
Note: no issue dated 30 Dec 1978.	
BATTLE PICTURE WEEKLY ANNUAL	
Fleetway, 1976-1988	
1976-1982	£2.50

	N.MINT
1983-1986 becomes Battle Annual	£2.00
1987 becomes Battle Action Force Annual	£2.00
1988 becomes Battle Annual	£1.50
ARTISTS/FEATURES	
Joe Colquhoun (Charley's War) in 1982-1983. Cam Kennedy in 1981,1983,1984.	
BATTLE SQUADRON	
Streamline/United Anglo-American; 1956, 2 unnumbered issues	
nn - 28pgs; reprints from Stanmor begin	£2.00
nn - 68pgs	£3.00
BATTLE STORIES	
Miller; 1 1952-9 1953	
1 28pgs; reprints from Fawcett	£5.00
2-9 68pgs	£3.50
BATTLECRY PICTURE LIBRARY	
Famepress; 1 1965-(14+)	
1 68pgs pocket size; foreign reprints begin	£1.00
2-14+	£0.50
BATTLEFIELD	
Brugeditor; 1 1962-?	
1 68pgs pocket size; Spanish reprints begin	£1.00
2-?	£0.50
BATTLEGROUND	
Famepress/Alex White; 1 1965-(137+)	
1 68pgs pocket size; Italian reprints begin	£1.00
2-137+	£0.50
BATTLER BRITTON	
Fleetway; 1960-1961	
1960 hardcover, with dust-jacket	£5.00
1960 without dust-jacket	£2.00
Book Two (1961) hardcover, with dust-jacket	£5.00
Book Two without dust-jacket	£2.00
BATTLER BRITTON PICTURE LIBRARY HOLIDAY SPECIAL	
IPC; 1978-1982; Ron Phillips 1988	
1978 192pgs; Air Ace Picture Library reprints begin	£1.50
1979-1982	£1.25
1988	£1.00
BATTLESTAR GALACTICA	
Granddreams; 1978	
- hardback, John Higgins art	£2.50
BATTLETIDE	
(see main American comics section) (see also Death's Head II, Motormouth)	
BATTLETIDE II: DEATH'S HEAD II & KILLPOWER	
(see main American comics section)	
BEANO BOOK, THE	
D.C. Thomson; Sep 1939-present	
(1940) (Big Eggo and others on see-saw supported by Pansy Potter)	£800.00
(1941) (Large eggs with characters emerging; Big Eggo's head peering through)	£475.00
(1942) (Lord Snooty playing bagpipes)	£350.00
(1943) becomes Magic Beano Book (Big Eggo and Koko lead in three-legged race)	£300.00
(1944) (Eggo and Koko in pillow fight on a pole)	£250.00
(1945) (Big Eggo and other characters playing leap-frog)	£250.00
(1946) (Big Eggo pulling other characters in cart)	£200.00
(1947) (Hairy Dan on Pansy Potters shoulders looking into Big Eggo's mouth)	£150.00
(1948) (Big Eggo and other characters playing musical instruments)	£150.00
(1949) (Biffo, Big Eggo and others gathered around Maxy's Taxi)	£110.00
(1950) (Biffo painting portraits of others, Big Eggo peering round canvas)	£90.00
(1951) reverts to Beano Book (Biffo riding a mechanical horse)	£75.00
(1952) (Biffo nailing pictures of characters to cover)	£60.00
(1953) (Jack Flash carry characters on trips to moon)	£55.00
(1954) (Biffo hanging from tree, monkey sawing branch, Dennis with lobster)	£50.00
(1955) (Policeman falling in river where Biffo and Dennis are fishing)	£50.00
(1956) (Biffo in captains hat watching other characters, Dennis in plane)	£45.00
(1957) (Dennis scoring goal, with ball rebounding off of other characters)	£42.50
(1958) (Biffo juggling, Dennis releasing bees from hive)	£40.00
(1959) (Dennis playing leapfrog with goat about to butt him)	£40.00
(1960) (Biffo doing jigsaw puzzle of other characters)	£35.00
(1961) (Beano in large letters, characters at top/bottom of cover)	£27.50
(1962) (Jonah dancing on mast of sinking ship with S.O.S. flag)	£25.00
(1963) (Bash Street Kids on large swing tied to Beano logo)	£22.50
(1964) (Biffo in circus ring with bar-bells, tickled by Buster with feather)	£20.00
(1965) (Minnie & Little Plum blowing up balloon shaped like Biffo's head)	£20.00
1966 1st dated on cover	£17.50
1967	£12.50
1968,1969	£10.00
1970	£7.00
1971-1975	£5.00
1976-1979	£4.00
1980-1989	£3.50
1990-1996	£3.00
BEANO COMIC, THE	
D.C. Thomson; 1 30th Jul 1938-present (2789 to 30th Dec 1995)	
1	£2500.00
Note: a copy sold at auction September 1995 for £4,200 representing the highest price paid for a British comic. As there have been no further sales recorded at this price, it must be considered a one-off sale price rather than a "going rate". Having said that, the company responsible for the auction has stated that there were several serious bidders over the £3,000 mark. The position of the Guide at this point is healthy caution	
1 facsimile	£25.00
2	£650.00
3	£475.00
4	£350.00
1938 remaining issues	£125.00
1939 issues	£80.00

	N.MINT
1940 issues	£60.00
1941-1943 issues	£50.00
1944-1945 issues	£45.00
1946-1948 issues	£32.50
1949-1951 issues	£22.50
1952-1954 issues	£12.50
1955-1958 issues	£8.00
1959-1960 issues	£5.00
1961-1963 issues	£4.00
1964-1966 issues	£3.00
1967-1969 issues	£2.00
1970-1975 issues	£1.25
1976-1980 issues	£0.85
1981-1990 issues	£0.60
1991-1995 issues	£0.30

Note: issue 1660 (11 May 1974) was accidentally misnumbered 1659.

CHRONOLOGY
1 1st Lord Snooty by Watkins. 21 (17 Dec 1938) 1st Pansy Potter by McNeill. 130 (18 Jan 1941) 1st Tom Thumb by Watkins. 200 (27 Feb 1943) 1st Shipwrecked Circus by Watkins. 222 (1 Jan 1944) 1st Jimmy and his Magic Patch by Watkins. 240 (9 Sep 1944) 1st Strang the Terrible by Watkins. 327 (24 Jan 1948) 1st Biffo the Bear by Watkins. 413 (17 Jun 1950) title shortened to Beano. 452 (17 Mar 1951) 1st Dennis the Menace by David Law. 561 (18 Apr 1953) 1st Roger the Dodger by Ken Reid. 583 (19 Sep 1953) 1st General Jumbo by Paddy Brennan. 586 (10 Oct 1953) 1st Little Plum by Leo Baxendale. 596 (19 Dec 1953) 1st Minnie the Minx by Baxendale. 604 (13 Feb 1954) 1st When the Bell Rings by Baxendale (becomes The Bash Street Kids from 1 Dec 1956). 680 (30 Jul 1955) 1st Grandpa by Reid. 817 (15 Mar 1958) 1st Jonah by Reid. 881 (6 Jun 1959) 1st Three Bears by Baxendale. 1139 (16 May 1964) 1st Billy Whizz by Malcolm Judge. 1289 (1 Apr 1967) 1st Billy the Cat by David Sutherland. 1363 (31 Aug 1968) 1st Grasher (in Dennis the Menace). 1553 (22 Apr 1972) 1st Babyface Finlayson by Ron Spencer. 1678 (14 Sep 1974) 1st Dennis the Menace front cover. 2674 (16 Oct 1993) 1st all colour issue.

ARTISTS
Leo Baxendale in 586-1045. Paddy Brennan in 400-505,516-536,553-567,583-599,642-654,664-683,701-723,740-768,789-801,891-903,1068-1094. David Law in 452-1462. Allan Morley in 1-35,69-335,337-475. Ken Reid in 561-1152. Dudley D.Watkins in 1-1422.

BEANO COMIC LIBRARY
D.C. Thomson; 1 Apr 1982-present (332 to Dec 1995)

1 pocket; King Dennis the Menace by David Gudgeon	£5.00
2-10	£2.00
11-100	£1.00
101-332	£0.50

BEANO SUMMER SPECIAL, THE
D.C. Thomson; Jun 1964-present (See also Dandy-Beano Summer Special)

1964	£35.00
1965	£20.00
1966-1969	£12.50
1970-1975	£7.50
1976-1979	£5.50
1980-1989	£3.00
1990-1995	£1.25

BEANO SUPER STARS, THE
D.C. Thomson; 1 1992-present (48 to Dec 1995)

1 Dennis the Menace	£1.25
2 The Bash Street Kids	£1.10
3 Minnie the Minx	£1.10
4 Roger the Dodger	£1.10
5-45	£1.00

BEAVIS AND BUTT-HEAD
Titan

Greatest Hits	£6.00
Trashcan Edition	£7.00
Holidazed and Confused (Jul 1995)	£7.00
Wanted (March 1996)	£7.00

BEAVIS AND BUTT-HEAD
Marvel; 1 1994-present (19 issues to Dec 1995)

1 reprints US strips based on TV show	£1.00
2-20	£0.35

BEEM
Eddie Campbell; nn 1974

nn - Roland Bunn (Campbell) art	£1.00

BEEZER, THE
D.C. Thomson; 1 21st Jan 1956-1809 15th Sep 1990 (becomes The Beezer and Topper)

1 tabloid size	£125.00
1 with free gift (The Whiz Bang)	£175.00
2	£40.00
3	£15.00
1956 issues	£12.50
8 Sep 1956 with free gift (Hilly Billy Banger)	£25.00
1957-1959 issues	£6.00
1960-1965 issues	£3.50
1966-1969 issues	£2.50
1970-1977 issues	£1.25
1978-1981 issues	£0.75
1981-1990 small size issues	£0.50

CHRONOLOGY
1 1st Ginger by Watkins, Lone Wolfe by Ron Smith, Pop, Dick and Harry by Tom Bannister, Nosey Parker by Allan Morley, Banana Bunch by Baxendale. 34 (8 Sep 1956) 1st Baby Crockett by Bill Ritchie. 103 (4 Jan 1958) 1st Cap'n'Hand by David Law. 148 (15 Nov 1958) 1st Colonel Blink by Tom Bannister. 171 (25 Apr 1959) 1st Showboat Circus by Paddy Brennan. 210 (23 Jan 1960) 1st The Badd Lads by Malcolm Judge. 322 (17 Mar 1962) 1st Numbskulls by Malcolm Judge. 577 (4 Feb 1967) 1st Smiffy by Bill Ritchie. 788 (20 Feb 1971) 1st Barny's Barmy Army by Ken Hunter. 1079 (18 Sep 1976) 1st "Beezer and Cracker". 1207 (3 Mar 1979) 1st "Beezer and Plug". 1315 (28 Mar 1981) 1st small size.

ARTISTS
Leo Baxendale in 1-436. Paddy Brennan in 171-211,726-760,1079-1206. David Law in 103-147. Allan

Battle #1

Beano Book 1960

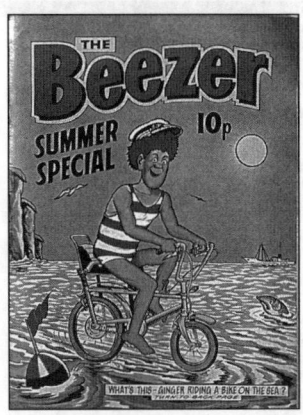

Beezer Summer Special #1

	N.MINT		N.MINT
Morley in 1-13. Ron Smith in 103-147,165-169,284-329,445-557,584-605,1044-1099. Dudley D.Watkins in 1-718 (719-737 contain Watkins Ginger reprints).		**65** Rogue Trooper, Halo Jones	£1.20
BEEZER AND TOPPER, THE		**66** Halo Jones	£1.20
D.C. Thomson; 1 22nd Sep 1990-21st August 1993, 153 issues		**67-74,77-80**	£1.20
1	£1.00	**75-76** Robo-Hunter	£1.20
2-15	£0.35	**81** Slaine the King, new Fabry cover	£1.75
16-67	£0.25	**82-83** Skizz Book 1. 83 A.B.C. Warriors	£1.50
68-153	£0.20	**84** Ace Trucking Co.	£1.20
BEEZER AND TOPPER SUMMER SPECIAL, THE		**85** Robo-Hunter, free poster	£1.20
(see Beezer Summer Special)		**86** Robo-Hunter	£1.10
BEEZER BOOK, THE		**87-88** Strontium Dog	£1.10
D.C. Thomson; Sep 1957-1994		**89,92** Ace Trucking Co	£1.10
(1958) (Characters climbing up steep stairway)	£100.00	**90** Rogue Trooper	£1.10
(1959) (Stepladder, balloon, bicycle holding up logo)	£40.00	**91** The Dead	£1.10
(1960) (Head and shoulders of Baby Crockett)	£30.00	**93** Slaine, Ace Trucking	£1.20
(1961) (Globe wearing a school cap, characters in corners)	£25.00	**94-95** Rogue Trooper	£1.00
(1962) (Old locomotive with characters)	£20.00	**96-98** Strontium Dog	£1.00
(1963) (Two pirates in the logo, aeroplane at top of cover)	£17.50	**99** Zenith	£1.20
(1964) (Large head/shoulders of decorated man, logo on hat)	£15.00	**100-119**	£1.25
(1965) (Colonel Blink with drum about to walk into manhole)	£12.50	**BESTOFALL COMICS**	
1966 1st dated on cover	£10.00	**Cartoon Art; nn Oct 1948**	
1967-1969	£8.00	**nn** - 20pgs; Paddy Brennan, Dennis Reader art	£6.00
1970-1979	£5.00	**BEVERLY HILLBILLIES ANNUAL, THE**	
1980-1989	£3.00	**World Distributors; 1964-1966**	
1990-1994	£2.00	**1964** based on TV series	£5.00
BEEZER COMIC, THE		**1965**	£4.00
Scoop Books; nn 1946		**1966**	£3.00
nn - 8pgs; Alf Farningham, William McCail art	£3.00	**BIBLE ILLUSTRATED, THE**	
BEEZER SUMMER SPECIAL, THE		**Bible Pictures/Thorpe and Porter; 1 1947-8 1948**	
D.C. Thomson; Jun 1973-present		**1** 52pgs; EC reprints from Picture Stories From the Bible, Old Testament	£10.00
1973	£5.00	**2-5** Old Testament	£10.00
1974-1979	£3.00	**6-8** New Testament	£10.50
1980-1989	£1.50	**BIBLE TALES FOR YOUNG PEOPLE**	
1990-1992	£1.00	**Miller; 1-5 1954**	
BEEZER & TOPPER SUMMER SPECIAL		**1-5** reprints from Atlas, including Everett, Krigstein art	£6.00
DC Thompson; 1993-1995		Note: becomes Illustrated Bible Tales which featured new material	
1993 - 1995	£0.90	**BIC**	
BEHOLD THE HAMSTER		(see Skidmarks)	
Bob Comics; nn 1991		**Ovo Comic; 1 Jul 1987-7 Jan 1990**	
nn - 64pgs; Bob Lynch art	£1.50	**1** 12pgs, Ed Hillyer art	£1.50
BELINDA		**1** reprint	£0.75
Dunlop/ Mirror Features; 1940s		**2-7**	£1.00
Belinda and the Bomb Alley Boys (1946) reprints Daily Mirror strip by Tony Royle	£5.00	**BIG...COMIC**	
Belinda in Shooting Star (194?)	£5.00	(see also Kang the Mighty)	
BEN BOWIE AND HIS MOUNTAIN MEN		**Scion; 1948-1949. Variously titled, unnumbered**	
World Distributors; 1 1955-? (8+ issues)		**Big Atlantis Comic** (1949) Ron Turner, Walter Booth art	£10.00
1-8 28pgs; reprints from Dell	£2.00	**Big Boy Comic** (1948) Embleton art	£10.00
BENEFIT		**Big Castle Comic** (1948) F.A.Philpott art	£7.50
Gemsanders; nn 1973		**The Big Cheer Comic** (1948) Serge Drigin, Frank Minnitt art	£8.00
nn - free comic	£0.35	**Big Chief Comic** (1948) R.W.Plummer art	£7.50
BERYL THE PERIL		**Big Chuckle Comic** (1949) Minnitt, Booth art	£9.00
D.C. Thomson; Sep 1958-Sep 1987 (bi-annual to 1979, irregular thereon)		**Big Combat Comic** (1949) Turner art	£10.00
(1959) (Beryl appears out of hole she has cut in cover with saw)	£100.00	**The Big Cowboy Comic** (1949) Embleton, Minnitt art	£10.00
(1961) (Beryl dressed as a cowboy, riding a pneumatic drill)	£40.00	**Big Dip Comic** (1948) Plummer, Minnitt art	£8.00
(1963) (Beryl wearing boxing gloves, attacking teacher shaped punch bag)	£30.00	**The Big Dynamo Comic** (1948) Drigin, Minnitt art, Maskman story	£8.00
(1965) (Beryl pulling tiger by rope away from circus)	£25.00	**Big Eagle Comic** (1949) Embleton, Minnitt art	£10.00
1907-1969 dated on cover	£15.00	**Big Flame Wonder Comic** (1948) Embleton, Bill Holroyd, Minnitt art	£10.00
1971-1979	£7.50	**Big Game Comic** (1948) Plummer art	£7.50
1981-1988	£3.00	**The Big Game Comic: Maskman** (1948) Booth, Minnitt art, Maskman story	£8.00
BEST OF BILLY'S BOOTS HOLIDAY SPECIAL, THE		**Big Hit Comic** (1948) Embleton, John Jukes, Plummer art	£10.00
Fleetway; 1990-1991		**Big Idea Comic** (1948) Embleton, Plummer art	£10.00
1990 reprints Billy's Boots	£0.60	**Big Indian Comic** (1948) Embleton art	£10.00
1991 Ron Turner reprints	£0.60	**Big Jungle Comic** (1948) Embleton, Minnitt art	£10.00
BEST OF THE WEST		**The Big Laugh Comic** (1949) Minnitt art	£8.00
Cartoon Art; 1-3 1951?		**Big Mounty Comic** (1949) Turner art	£10.00
1 32pgs; reprints from Magazine Enterprises begin	£3.00	**Big Noise Wonder Comic** (1948) Embleton, Plummer art	£10.00
2-3 68pgs	£4.00	**Big Pirate Comic** (1948) Embleton, Minnitt art	£10.00
BEST OF 2000AD		**Big Racer Comic** (1948) Drigin, Minnitt art	£8.00
IPC/Fleetway; 1 Oct 1985-119 Aug 1995 (becomes Classic 2000AD)		**Big Ranch Comic** (1949) Turner art	£10.00
1 Strontium Dog, Judge Dredd; 2000AD reprints begin	£8.00	**Big Sahara Comic** (1949) Plummer, Minnitt art	£8.00
2	£5.00	**Big Scoop Comic** (1949) Turner, Minnitt art	£10.00
3,5 Nemesis	£3.50	**Big Shot Comic** (1948) Plummer, Jukes art	£7.50
4	£3.25	**Big Show Comic** (1948) Plummer, Jukes art	£7.50
6-8 Nemesis; 8 D.R. & Quinch	£2.50	**Big Slide Comic** (1948) Embleton, Holroyd art	£10.00
9-11 Robo-Hunter	£2.00	**The Big Star Comic** (1948) Drigin, Jukes art	£7.50
12 Robo-Hunter	£2.50	**The Big Thrill Comic** (1948) Drigin, Minnitt art	£8.00
13-14 A.B.C. Warriors	£1.75	**Big Tong Comic** (1949) Embleton, Holroyd art	£10.00
15-16 Strontium Dog	£1.75	**The Big Top** (1949) Plummer, Booth, Minnitt art	£8.00
17-18 D.R. & Quinch	£2.00	**Big Trail Comic** (1949) Minnitt art	£8.00
19 D.R. & Quinch, Slaine	£2.00	**Big Train Comic** (1949) Booth, Minnitt art	£8.00
20-22 Slaine	£1.50	**Big Treasure** (see Kang the Mighty)	
23-25,29-32	£1.25	**Big Treat Comic** (1948) Plummer, Minnitt, Jukes art	£8.00
26 Robo-Hunter	£1.25	**Big Win Comic** (1948) Embleton, Jukes art	£10.00
27-28 Harry 20	£1.25	**BIG ADVENTURE BOOK**	
33-34,36-37 Slaine	£1.50	**Fleetway; 1984**	
35,41,46-47,49,53-55	£1.25	**1984** 224pgs hardcover; Hook Jaw, Dredger, Steel Claw by Blasco reprints	£2.50
38-39,43-45,48,56 Nemesis	£1.25	**BIG BOOK OF EVERYTHING, THE**	
40,42 Halo Jones	£2.00	**Knockabout; nn 1983**	
50,57 Strontium Dog	£1.25	**nn** - 100pgs; Hunt Emerson art	£5.00
51-52 Robo-Hunter	£1.20	**BIG COMIC BOOK ANNUAL**	
58,60-64	£1.20	**Fleetway; 1991**	
59 Slaine	£1.20	**1991** 250pgs; reprints	£2.50

	N.MINT
BIG COMIC HOLIDAY SPECIAL	
Fleetway; 1990-present?	
1990-1994 132pgs; reprints	£1.00
BIG EARS	
Big Ears; nn 1971	
nn - amateur comic	£0.35
BIG LITTLE COMIC, THE	
P.M. Productions; nn Sep 1945	
nn - 8pgs, printed on beige card; Denis Gifford art	£4.00
BIG NUMBERS	
Mad Love; 1 Apr 1990-2 Aug 1990	
1 44pgs large square; Alan Moore & Bill Sienkiewicz	£3.50
2	£3.50
BIG ONE, THE	
Fleetway; 17th Oct 1964-20th Feb 1965, 19 unnumbered issues (joins Buster)	
17 Oct 1964 12pgs, large (14.5x21.5"); various retitled humour strips by Eric Roberts, Reg Parlett, Hugh McNeill, Roy Wilson, etc. begin	£40.00
24 Oct 1964	£15.00
1 Nov 1964	£7.50
8 Nov 1964-20 Feb 1965 scarce	£5.00
BIG PARADE COMIC	
Grant Hughes; Sep 1947	
nn - 16pgs; Bob Wilkin art	£4.00
BIG SHOT	
Streamline/United Anglo-American; 1949, 2 unnumbered issues	
nn - 36pgs; reprints from Columbia	£4.00
nn - 28pgs	£3.50
BIG SIX	
Apulhead Productions; Sum nn 1976	
nn	£1.00
BIG SURPRISE COMIC	
Tower Press; 1-3 1950	
1-2 6pgs; Wally Robertson art	£4.00
3 10pgs; Futureman by Denis Gifford	£6.00
BIG-TIME! COMIC	
Apex Publicity Service; nn 1947	
nn - 8pgs; R.W.Plummer, John Jukes art	£6.00
BIG TOP COMIC, THE	
Martin & Reid; nn 1949	
nn - 8pgs; E.H.Banger art	£4.00
BIGGLES	
(see Adventures of Biggles, Express Weekly)	
BIGGLES	
Brockhampton; Sep 1952	
Biggles Breaks the Silence 52pgs; hardback, small	£10.00
Biggles Hunts Big Game 52pgs	£10.00
BIGGLES	
Hodder & Stoughton; 1 1978-6 1984	
1 Biggles & the Saragasso Triangle (1978) scarce (copies withdrawn from sale due to text difficulties); Bjorn Karlstrom art begins	£7.50
2 Biggles & the Golden Bird (1978)	£5.00
3 Biggles & the Tiger (1981)	£5.00
4 Biggles & the Menace From Outer Space (1981)	£5.00
5 Biggles in the Kalahari (1983)	£5.00
6 Biggles and the Gibraltar Bomb (1984)	£5.00
Note: all Swedish reprints, 52pgs	
BIGGLES	
Redfox; 1993	
Spitfire Parade 56pgs; French reprint by Francis Bergese	£1.00
BIGGLES IN THE CRUISE OF THE CONDOR	
Juvenile Productions; nn May 1955	
nn - 44pgs hardback, Pat Williams art	£5.00
BIJOU FUNNIES	
H.Bunch/Cozmic Comix; 1 Mar 1974	
1 36pgs; Skip Williamson reprints	£1.50
BILL BOYD WESTERN	
Miller; 1-? 1950?; 50-? 1955?	
1-? 24pgs; reprints from Fawcett	£5.00
50-? 36pgs	£3.00
Note: Two seperate runs, first starting at No.1, the second starting with No.50; there were at least 15 issues published in total	
BILL BOYD WESTERN ANNUAL	
Miller; nn 1956-5 1960	
nn (1956) 1st story - "The Diamond Horseshoe!"	£7.50
nn	£6.00
3-5	£5.00
BILL CARTER	
Foldes Press; 1-3 1947	
1 titled Calling Bill Carter; 12pgs; Rex Hart art	£5.00
2-3	£4.00
BILLY AND BUNNY BOOK, THE	
John Leng; Autumn 1921-Autumn 1948	
(1922) (B&B pulling log with pixie sitting on it)	£27.50
(1923) dated Xmas 1922 on cover	£25.00
(1924) (B&B welcome pixies on the steps of a castle)	£22.50
(1925) (B&B on flying broomsticks with snowman and dog)	£20.00
(1926) (B&B trying to put salt on tail of turkey)	£20.00
(1927) (B&B in masks holding up Father Christmas in snow)	£20.00
(1928) (B&B riding downhill with dog on sledge)	£20.00
(1929) (B&B in circus ring, Bunny dressed as clown)	£20.00
(1930) (B&B on skies, Bunny falling over)	£20.00
(1931) (B&B playing blind man's bluff)	£15.00

	N.MINT
(1932) (B&B on toy train pushing toy soldier, dog, golliwog away)	£15.00
(1933) (Billy in pirate costume, Bunny in green blazer in sailing boat) first larger size	£15.00
(1934) (B&B looking into large trick mirror which makes them giants)	£15.00
(1935) (Billy on chair, Bunny jumping through hoop)	£15.00
(1936) (B&B watching Punch & Judy show)	£10.00
(1937) (Billy banging drum, Bunny playing bagpipes)	£10.00
(1938) (Billy driving car with big L-plate following ducklings)	£10.00
(1939) (B&B posing before camera)	£10.00
(1940) (B&B in a hot-air balloon)	£10.00
(1941) (Billy pedalling tandem, Bunny on back with feet up)	£7.50
(1947) cover details not known, 4/- price	£7.50
(1948) cover details not known, 4/- price	£7.50
(1949) (B&B in old tin bath pulled through water by goose)	£7.50
BILLY BUCKSKIN WESTERN	
Miller; 1-2 1956	
1-2 28pgs; reprints from Atlas; Mort Drucker art	£3.00
BILLY THE KID (MASKED RAIDER PRESENTS...)	
Miller; 50 1956-?? 1957	
50-? 28pgs; reprints from Charlton	£3.00
BILLY THE KID ADVENTURE MAGAZINE	
World Distributors; 1 1953-76 1959	
1 36pgs; reprints from Toby	£5.00
2-10	£4.00
11-76 36pgs/68pgs; incl. Williamson, Frazetta art	£3.00
BILLY THE KID BOOK OF PICTURE STORIES	
Amalgamated; 1958-1959	
1958 Matania art, reprints Billy the Kid, Buffalo Bill, Wyatt Earp from Sun, Comet	£6.00
1959 Matania, Blasco art	£6.00
BILLY THE KID WESTERN ANNUAL	
World Distributors; 1953-1961	
1953 Based on TV series	£4.00
1954 1st story - "The Streets of Laredo" by Jesse Allard; incl. Pot Shot Pete by Harvey Kurtzman	£3.00
1955 1st story - "The Battle of Coyote Pass" by Jeff Delmar	£3.00
(1956) 1st story - "Stagecoach Showdown" by Duke Manton	£3.00
cy1957 1st story - "A Man Called Wyatt Earp" by Hart Cooper; incl. Durango Kid by Fred Guardineer	£3.00
1958 1st story - "The Black Rider of Sunset Pass" by Tex Bland	£3.00
1959-1961	£3.00
BILLY'S BOOTS HOLIDAY SPECIAL	
(See The Best of Billy's Boots Holiday Special)	
BINKY' GUIDE TO LOVE	
HarperCollins; nn Jan 1995	
nn - reprints Life in Hell by Matt Groening	£13.00
BIONIC WOMAN ANNUAL	
Granddreams; 1977-1978	
1977-1978 Ian Gibson art	£3.00
BIRTHDAY BOOK FOR BOYS	
Fleetway; 1972	
- hardback; strips from Buster, Valiant and Tiger including Fishboy and Galaxus - The Thing from Outer Space	£4.00
BIRTHRITE	
Congress Press; 1 1989-4 1991	
1 Birthrite by Scott Blatchley & Patrick Farncombe begins	£1.25
2-4	£1.25
BISLEY'S SCRAPBOOK	
Atomeka; 1 Sep 1993	
1 with double cover	£3.00
1 with single cover	£2.50
BIZARRO COMIC	
Troll Publications; 1 1972-2 1974	
1-2 12pgs/15pgs; amateur comic	£1.00
BJ AND THE BEAR ANNUAL	
Grandreams; 1981	
1981 Steve Moore stories, Alan Moore illus.	£2.00
BLAAM!	
Willyprods; preview 1988; 1 Sep 1988-3 Feb 1989	
Preview free with Heartbreak Hotel No.5, Duncan Fegredo art	£0.75
1 Neil Gaiman script (10,000 copies)	£1.50
2-3	£0.30
BLACK AXE	
(see main American comics section)	
BLACK BOB BOOK	
D.C. Thomson; 1950-1965 (irregular)	
1950 oblong format begins; Jack Prout art (bc: Bob on top of mountain with shepherd coming up hill towards him)	£40.00
1951 (bc: on hilltop with small boy looking down at sheep)	£27.50
1953 (bc: Bob with two birds perched on foodbowl)	£25.00
1955 (bc: oval inset of Bob pulling girl and puppy in bath tub through snow)	£25.00
1957 (bc: Bob on mountain being patted on head)	£20.00
1959 (bc: Bob with three other dogs)	£15.00
1961 (fc: six evenly spaced heads)	£7.50
1965 regular format (Bob surrounded by silver cups)	£7.50
Note: fc of all but 1961 is single head shot of Bob, so bc descriptions are given.	
BLACK CAT WESTERN	
Streamline/United Anglo-American; 1 1950	
1 28pgs; reprints from Harvey	£4.00
BLACK DIAMOND WESTERN	
Pemberton; nn 1951-33 1954	
nn 36pgs; reprints from Lev Gleason begin	£5.00
2-33 28pgs; incl. Dick Rockwell, Charles Biro, Al Luster, Basil Wolverton reprints	£3.00
BLACK DOG	
Knuller Ltd; nn 1969	
nn - Mal Dean art	£1.00

	N.MINT
BLACK DRAGON, THE	
Titan; Dec 1995	
- 208pgs; reprints Marvel series by Chris Claremont & John Bolton in b&w	£9.00
BLACK FURY	
World Distributors; 1 Jun 1955-8 1956	
1 28pgs; reprints from Charlton	£4.00
2-8	£3.00
BLACK FURY	
Miller; 50 1957-61 1958, 12 issues	
50 28pgs; reprints from Charlton	£4.00
51-61	£3.00
BLACKHAWK	
Boardman/Popular; 11 1949-61 1953, 15 issues variously numbered	
11,18,20,21,25,27,28,32,40,42,44 12pgs; reprints from Quality, incl. Reed Crandell art	£8.00
15 second strip redrawn by Denis McLoughlin	£12.00
47,57,59,61 28pgs	£6.00
BLACKHAWK	
Strato; 1 1956-36 1958	
1 68pgs; reprints from Quality begin	£6.00
2-36 68pgs	£4.00
BLACK JACK (ROCKY LANE'S...)	
Miller; 1 1956-11 1957	
1 28pgs; reprints from Charlton	£5.00
2-11	£3.00
BLACK KNIGHT, THE	
Miller; 1-5 1956?	
1-5 28pgs; reprints from Atlas	£3.00
BLACK MAGIC	
Arnold Book Co.; 1 1952-16 1954	
1-14,16 68pgs; reprints from Prize Publishing	£6.00
15 reprints stories from Eerie & Crime SuspenStories cited in US and UK horror campaign	£15.00
BLACK MAGIC ALBUM	
Arnold Book Co; 1 1954	
1 reprints from Prize, cited in UK horror campaign	£18.00
BLACK ORCHID	
Titan; Aug 1991	
- reprints Black Orchid #1-3 by Neil Gaiman & Dave McKean	£11.00
BLACK RIDER (WESTERN TALES OF...)	
Miller; 1 1955-4 1956	
1-4 28pgs; reprints from Atlas	£3.00
BLACK STALLION	
Hodder & Stoughton; 1983	
The Black Stallion French reprints by Robert Genia & Michel Faure	£1.50
The Black Stallion and Satan	£1.50
The Black Stallion Returns	£1.50
BLAKE THE TRAPPER	
Miller; 1-3? 1950s	
1-3 reprints	£3.00
BLAKE'S SEVEN	
Marvel; 1 Oct 1981-23 Aug 1983	
1 Blake's 7 by Ian Kennedy begins	£10.00
1 with free gift (iron on transfer)	£15.00
2	£5.00
3-20,22	£3.50
21 no Blake's 7 strip	£3.50
23 double sized issue	£5.00
ARTISTS/FEATURES	
Artists include Ian Kennedy, David Lloyd, Steve Dillon, Mick Austin, Phil Gascoine.	
BLAKE'S SEVEN ANNUAL	
World Distributors; 1978-1979, 1981	
1978-1979	£5.00
1981 smaller print run	£7.00
BLAKE'S SEVEN SPECIALS	
Marvel; May 1981-Nov 1982, 1994	
Summer Special 1981	£4.00
Summer Special 1982	£3.00
Winter Special 1982	£2.50
Winter Special 1994	£2.50
BLAST!	
(see also Lazerus Churchyard, Sherlock Holmes, White Trash)	
John Brown; 1 Jun 1991-7 Dec 1991	
1 Mr Monster by Gilbert & Bisley, Concrete by Paul Chadwick, Torpedo reprints by Abuli & Bernet, Axel Pressbutton by Henry & Dillon, Junior by Bagge, Lazarus Churchyard by Warren Ellis & D'Isreali begins	£2.00
2 Big Berta by Yan Shimony begins, Concrete, Mr. Monster reprints	£1.50
3-6	£1.50
7 White Trash by Gordon Rennie & Martin Emond, Sherlock Holmes by Rennie & Woodrow Phoenix begin	£1.50
BLAZER COMIC, THE	
Philmar; nn 1949	
nn - 16pgs; Frank Minnett, George Parlett art	£4.00
BLAZING TRAILS	
Class; nn 1960s	
nn - 68pgs; reprints from Charlton	£3.00
BLAZING WEST	
Streamline/United Anglo-American; nn 1951	
nn - 28pgs; reprints from American Comic Group	£2.50
BLAZING WEST/BOYS' RANCH	
Streamline/United Anglo-American; nn 1951	
nn - 68pgs; two comics in one, Blazing West (front) reprints from American Comic Group, Boys' Ranch (rear) reprints from Harvey	£4.00
BLOCKBUSTER	
Marvel; 1 Jun 1981-9 Feb 1982	

	N.MINT
1 Iron Fist, The Inhumans, Omega reprints begin	£1.50
2-9	£1.00
BLOCKBUSTER WINTER SPECIAL	
Marvel; nn Nov 1980	
nn - 52pgs; reprints	£1.75
BLOODSEED	
(see main American comics section)	
BLOOD SEX AND TERROR	
BST Comics; 1 Jan 1977-2 May 1977	
1-2 2 incl. Dave Huxley art	£1.25
BLUDGEON FUNNIES	
(Publisher?); nn 1968	
nn - Gilbert Shelton, S. Clay Wilson reprints	£2.00
BLUE BEETLE	
Streamline/United Anglo-American; 1-nn 1950, 2 issues	
1 28pgs; reprints from Fox	£8.50
nn - 28pgs	£6.00
BLUE BEETLE	
Miller; 1-3? 1950s	
1-3 28pgs; reprints from Fox	£5.00
BLUE BOLT ADVENTURES	
(see also Blue Bolt Series)	
Miller; 1-2 1951	
1-2 28pgs; reprints from Novelty	£4.00
BLUE BOLT SERIES	
Swan; 1 Aug 1952-22 May 1954	
1 Indian Warriors (see also 6 below)	£7.50
2 White Rider	£5.00
3 Young King Cole	£3.50
4,9,13,15,17-22 Blue Bolt	£5.00
5 Super Horse	£3.50
6 Indian Warhawks (Indian Warriors)	£3.50
7 Spacehawks	£5.00
8,10 Dick Cole	£3.50
11,14 Target	£3.50
12,16 Outlaws	£3.50
Note: all titles reprints from Novelty, although some original material appears in 20-22	
BLUE CIRCLE	
Streamline; 1 1953	
1 28pgs; reprints from Fox	£4.00
BLUE PETER ANNUAL	
IPC/BBC; 1 1965-present	
1 scarce	£90.00
2	£30.00
3-5	£15.00
6-10	£7.00
11-20	£5.00
21-31	£3.00
BLUE PETER HOLIDAY SPECIAL	
IPC/BBC; 1976	
1976 40pgs	£2.00
BOB COLT	
Miller; 50 1951-58 1952	
50 36pgs; reprints from Fawcett begin	£6.00
51-58 28pgs	£4.00
BOB COMIC BOOK	
P.M. Productions; nn 1949	
nn - 24pgs; Colin Merritt art	£4.00
BOBBY BENSON'S B-BAR-B RIDERS	
(see also Action Series)	
World Distributors; 1 1950-12 1951	
1 36pgs; reprints from Magazine Enterprises	£6.00
2-12 incl. Powell art	£3.00
BOG STANDARD KOMIX	
Bonk & Talbot; nn Jul 1977	
nn - Talbot art	£4.00
BOGEY	
Vicar's Raw Balls Co Ltd; nn 1975	
nn - Antonio Ghura art	£1.00
BOGIE MAN, THE	
(see also Toxic)	
Fat Man Press; 1 Sep 1989-4 Sep 1990 (released late)	
1 Bogie Man by John Wagner/Alan Grant & Robin Smith begins	£2.00
2-4	£1.50
The Bogie Man (1991) trade paperback, collects 1-4	£3.50
The Bogie Man (Apocalypse Presents, Jul 1991) Toxic reprints, Kennedy art	£1.50
The Manhatten Project (Apocalypse Presents, Sep 1991) Toxic reprints, Smith art	£1.50
The Manhatten Project (Tundra, Jul 1992) revised version	£3.00
BOGIE MAN, THE: CHINATOON	
Atomeka; 1 Mar 1993-4 Jun 1993	
1 by John Wagner/Alan Grant & Robin Smith	£1.80
2-4	£1.50
Chinatoon (Atomeka, Oct 1993) collects 1-4	£3.50
BOINGY BAXTER	
(Publisher?); nn 1969	
nn - Robert Crumb reprints	£2.00
BONANZA	
Top Sellers; 1970-1971 (8+ issues)	
1 36pgs; reprints from Dell	£3.00
2-? US reprints, later issues feature original material	£1.00
BONANZA	
Purnell; 1962-1969	

	N.MINT
1962 Text stories, illus. by Desmond Walduck & Eric Dadswell	£4.00
1963 Text stories, illus. by Leo Rawlings & R. Simonette	£3.50
1964 Stories by Basil Deakin, illus. by Leo Rawlings & R. Walker	£3.50
1965,1967	£3.00
1966,1968 Stories by Basil Deakin, illus. by Barrie Mitchell	£2.50
1969 Stories by Basil Deakin, illus by Barrie Mitchell, McLoughlin cover	£3.00
Note: the 1966 annual appears to have 2 variant editions with identical contents but two different covers, the first showing 4 characters on horseback, the second 3 characters standing	

BONANZA
World Distributors; 1963-1969
1963 Dell/Gold Key reprints	£5.00
1964-1966	£3.50
1967 Stories and features by J.L. Morrissey, M. Broadley, and J.W. Elliott	£3.00
1968 illus by Walt Howarth	£3.00
1969	£3.00

BONANZA COMIC ALBUM
World Distributors; 1 1965
1 softcover; reprints incl. Dell Bonanza #7	£4.00

BONANZA WORLD ADVENTURE LIBRARY
World Distributors; 1 Jun 1967-3 Aug 1967
1 68pgs; The Ponderosa Ranch, reprints from Dell	£3.00
2-3	£2.50

BONZA COMIC
W. Forshaw/ Ensign; 1-4 1947
1 8pgs; W.Forshaw art	£6.00
2 first Ensign issue; Bryan Berry art	£5.00
3-4 4 incl. Frank Minnitt art	£5.00

BOOK OF REDFOX, THE
Harrier/Valkyrie; 1986-1989
Book 1 (Harrier) reprints Redfox 1-4, Bolland cover	£3.00
Book 1 (Valkyrie) recoloured cover	£4.00
Book 2 (Valkyrie) reprints Redfox 5-10, Fabry cover	£4.00

BOOKS OF MAGIC, THE
Titan; Feb 1993, Mar 1995
The Books of Magic (Feb 1993) reprints The Books of Magic 1-4 by Neil Gaiman	£13.00
Bindings (Mar 1995) reprints ongoing series 1-4 by John Ney Rieber	£8.00

BOOMERANG COMIC
Scion; nn 1948
nn - 8pgs; Bob Wilkin art	£4.00

BOUNCER COMIC
P.M.Productions; nn 1949
nn - 8pgs; full colour photogravure; Wally Roberton, Frank Minnitt, George Parlett art	£4.00

BOY COMICS
Miller; 1 1950-8 1951
1-8 28pgs; reprints from Lev Gleason	£3.00

BOY DETECTIVE COMICS
Hermitage/Thorpe & Porter; 1 1952
1 68pgs; reprints from Avon	£4.00

BOYS DUX
Cartoon Art; 1 1948
1 8pgs; Dennis Reader art	£3.00

BOYS HOLIDAY BOOK, THE
D.C. Thomson; nn May 1927
nn - paperback annual containing 21 stories	

BOYS' RANCH
(see also Blazing West/Boys' Ranch)
Streamline/United Anglo-American; 1951, 4+ issues
nn - 28pgs; reprint from Harvey with some panels censored	£5.00
2-4	£4.00

BOYS' WORLD
Longacre; v1,1 26th Jan 1963-v2,40 3rd Oct 1964, 89 issues (joins Eagle)
Vol 1,1 Pike Mason by Tom Tully & Luis Bermejo, John Brody by Colin Andrew, Wrath of the Gods by Michael Moorcock & Ron Embleton all begin	£12.50
1 with free gift (Pathfinder Watch compass)	£25.00
2	£7.50
3-10, 12-23,25-45,47-49	£5.00
11 1st Merlo the Magician text story by Harry Harrison	£5.00
24 1st Iron Man by Gerry Embleton (later by Martin Salvador), Brett Million (The Angry Planet, partly based on Deathworld by Harry Harrison) by H.K. Bulmer & Frank Langford, 1st Merlo the Magician picture strip by Garcia Pizarro, 1st John Burns Wrath of the Gods, 1st Brian Lewis John Brody	£5.50
46 1st Frank Bellamy Brett Million (The Ghost World)	£5.00
Vol 2,1-17	£3.50
18 1st Raff Regan	£2.50
19-40	£2.50

BOYS' WORLD ANNUAL
Odhams; 1963-1972
1964 Don Harley, Brian Lewis art	£6.00
1965 John Burns, Gerry Embleton art, Ron Embleton, Don Harley, Bellamy illos	£5.00
1966 Ron Embleton, Don Harley art, Bellamy illos	£4.00
1967 John Burns art, R.Embleton, Lawrence illos	£3.00
1968 Don Lawrence art	£3.00
1969 Lawrence, Kieth Watson, Frank Humphris illos	£3.00
1970 larger size; Don Harley art, R.Embleton illos	£3.50
1971 Lawrence art, Bellamy illos	£3.50
1972 Lawrence, Humphris illos	£3.00

BRAINSTORM!
Alchemy Publications; nn Dec 1982
nn - Bryan Talbot art, Chester P. Hackenbush reprints	£15.00

BRAINSTORM COMIX
Alchemy; Nov 1975-Sum 1977
1-2 Chester Hackenbush by Talbot	£12.00
3 titled Mixed Bunch No.1; "The Papist Affair" (early version of Luther Arkwright) by Talbot, Emerson art	£15.00

Bunty #1

Buster 6/11/65

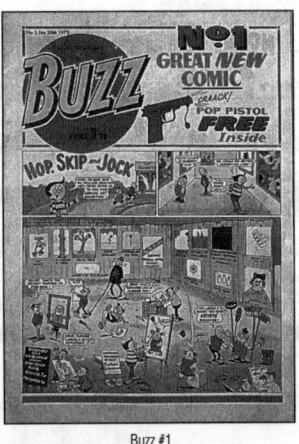

Buzz #1

	N.MINT
4 titled Brainstorm Cornix No 3; Hackenbush by Talbot	£12.00
5 titled Brainstorm Fantasy Comix No.1; Higgins, Talbot art	£10.00
6 titled Amazing Rock & Roll Adventures; "The Omega Report" by Talbot	£10.00
BRANDED PICTURE AND STORY ALBUM	
Mellifont; W7 1950s	
W7 96pgs	£3.00
BRAVE AND THE BOLD ANNUAL, THE	
Thorpe & Porter; 1967	
1967 scarce; bound-together remaindered copies of selected DC comics incl. Brave & Bold #56	£25.00
BREEZY COMIC	
P.M. Productions; nn 1946	
nn - 12pgs; reprints from Cheery Comic	£3.00
BREEZY COMIC	
G & C Productions; nn 1947	
nn - 8pgs; Alf Farningham, Sam Fair art	£3.00
BRICK BRADFORD	
(see also Action Series)	
World Distributors; 1-6 1959	
1-6 68pgs reprints US newspaper strip	£2.50
BRICKMAN	
Harrier; 1 Dec 1986	
1 Lew Stringer, Gibbons, O'Neill, Collins/Farmer art	£1.50
BRIGHT AND BREEZY	
P.M. Productions; nn 1948	
nn - 8pgs; George Parlett, Frank Minnitt art	£3.00
BRIT FORCE	
C.M. Comics; 1 Feb 1993-4? Jan 1994)	
1 28pgs; Chris Morgan story/art	£1.00
2-4?	£0.75
BRITISH CARTOONISTS YEAR BOOK	
Anthony Gibbs & Phillips; Nov 1963	
1964 reprints newspaper cartoons and strips	£4.00
BRITISH HEROES	
Sporting Cartoons; 1 Jun 1953-8 1954	
1 28pgs	£4.00
2-8	£2.00
BRONC SADDLER	
Miller; 1-2 1959	
1-2 68pgs small; US reprints	£3.00
BRONCO BILL COMIC	
Donald Peters; 23/2 1950	
23/2 36pgs; reprints US newspaper strip by Harry O'Neill	£3.50
BRONCO BILL WESTERN COMIC	
Donald Peters; 1 1951-17 1952?	
1-17 28pgs; reprints US newspaper strip by Harry O'Neill	£3.00
BRONCO LAYNE	
World Distributors; 1959-1964	
1959 Stories by Joe Morrissey	£4.00
1960 Stories by Joe Morrissey, illus. by Walt Howarth	£3.50
1961-1962,1964	£3.00
1963 Stories by Joe Morrissey; incl. Dell reprints	£3.00
BRONCO! PICTURE AND STORY ALBUM	
Mellifont Press; W8 1950s	
W8	£3.00
BROONS, THE	
D.C. Thomson; Sep 1940-present (bi-annual)	
1940 (Faces of family, each named) Dudley D. Watkins art begins	£500.00
1942 (head/shoulders of Maw/Paw in oval with family around them, yellow b/g)	£325.00
1948 (Paw reading newspaper, Maw with tea tray, yellow b/g)	£100.00
1952 (Family sitting round table smiling at reader)	£80.00
1954 (Maw/Paw doing Highland Fling, tartan b/g)	£50.00
1956 (Family looking out of large window)	£50.00
1958 (Family playing board games on table and floor, tartan b/g)	£35.00
1960 (Family at dinner table, calander reads 25 Jan, tartan b/g)	£30.00
1962 (Family at home, woman reading story to child on lap, tartan b/g)	£30.00
1964 (Family perched on mountain top waving, tartan b/g)	£30.00
1966-1970 (copyright dated, e.g. cover year 1965 for 1966)	£15.00
1972-1980 last Watkins	£7.50
1982-1989	£4.50
1992	£3.00
1994	£2.50
BRUCE THE BARBARIAN	
Quartet; nn 1973	
nn - 132pgs; reprints Labour Weekly strip by Murray Ball	£1.00
BUBBLEGUM CRISIS	
Manga; Sep 1995	
Bubblegum Crisis: Grand Mal by Adam Warren; Dark Horse reprint	£10.00
BUCCANEERS	
Popular; 4 May 1951	
4 36pgs; reprints from Quality	£3.00
BUCCANEERS, THE	
(see TV Photo Stories)	
C.A. Pearson (TV Picture Stories); 1 Feb 1959-2 Apr 1959	
1 68pgs pocket size; The Wasp	£5.00
2 The Gunpowder Plot	£3.00
BUCK JONES	
World Distributors; 1 1953-11 1954	
1 36pgs; reprints from Dell	£6.00
2-11	£3.50
BUCK JONES ANNUAL	
Amalgamated; 1957-1958	
1957,1958	£6.00

	N.MINT
BUCK RYAN	
(see also Super Detective Library)	
Mirror Features; 1946	
The Case of the Oblong Thistle 32pgs oblong; reprints Daily Mirror strip by Jack Monk	£8.00
BUCKY O'HARE	
D.C. Thomson; 20th Mar 1992-20 10th/24th Dec 1992	
1 Continuity reprints	£0.75
2-20	£0.35
BUDDY	
D.C. Thomson; 1 14th Feb 1981-130 6th Aug 1983 (joins Victor)	
1 Limp-Along Leslie, The Wolf of Kabul, Hammer by Denis McLoughlin, Billy the Cat begin, Jonah by Ken Reid reprints begin	£1.50
2	£1.00
3-19,21-46,48-98	£0.45
20 General Jumbo by Sandy Calder begins	£0.45
47 The Fighting Frazers by McLoughlin begins	£0.45
99 The Winged Warriors of Flame Island by Ian Kennedy begins	£0.45
100-102,104-123,125-130	£0.35
103 Jasper Sly by Alcatena begins	£0.35
124 Frontline UK by Kennedy, Midshipman Coward by Alcatena begin	£0.35
ARTISTS	
Alcatena in 103-113,124-129. Ian Kennedy, Bill Lacey, Denis McLoughlin in various.Ken Reid reprints in 1-130.	
BUFFALO BILL	
(see Buffalo Bill Comic, Swift Morgan, Roy Carson)	
Boardman/Popular; Oct 1948-1951	
(8) nn, 12pgs	£6.00
10,14,22,24,26,29,31 foreign reprints, McLoughlin covers	£5.00
19,33,35,37,41,43 McLoughlin art	£10.00
39 Ron Embleton art	£10.00
Note: numbering is tied in with other Boardman titles, e.g Swift Morgan, Roy Carson	
BUFFALO BILL	
Streamline/United Anglo-American; 1952, 2 unnumbered issues	
nn - 28pgs; reprints from Youthful Magazines; Doug Wildey art	£4.00
nn - 68pgs	£5.00
BUFFALO BILL ALBUM	
Moring; nn c1956)	
nn - reprints Boardman Buffalo Bill (8,33,22,45,49,39,10,43)	£8.00
BUFFALO BILL CODY	
Miller; 1-19 1950s	
1 28pgs; Buffalo Bill by Harry Cunningham begins	£7.00
2-19	£4.50
BUFFALO BILL COMIC	
(series contines from Buffalo Bill)	
Popular/Moring; 45 Jan 1953, 49 Mar 1953, nn 1955	
45,49 28pgs; McLoughlin art	£10.00
nn (Moring) 68pgs; reprints	£7.50
BUFFALO BILL WILD WEST ANNUAL	
Popular/Dean; 1949-1961	
1	£12.50
2-12	£7.50
13 retitled "Buffalo Bill's True West Annual", scarce	£20.00
BUGS BUNNY	
Thorpe & Porter; 1-4? 1953	
1-4 28pgs; reprints from Dell	£3.50
BUGS BUNNY	
Top Sellers; 1 1972-? 1973	
1-? 36pgs; reprints from Dell	£1.00
BUGS BUNNY ANNUAL	
World Distributors; 1964-1982	
1965-1972 96pgs	£3.00
1973-1975 80pgs	£2.50
1976-1980,1983 64pgs	£2.00
1981-1982 entitled Bugs Bunny Cartoon Annual	£2.00
BUGS BUNNY CARTOON ANNUAL	
World Distributors; 1970	
1971 softcover	£3.00
Note: published in 1970 with 1971 cover date	
BULLDOG BRITTAIN COMMANDO!	
Miller; 1-3 1952	
1 Bulldog Brittain by Colin Andrew begins	£5.00
2-3	£2.50
BULLET	
D.C.Thomson; 1 14th Feb 1976-147 2nd Dec 1978 (joins Warlord)	
1 Fireball by Neville Wilson, The Smasher, Twisty by Barrie Mitchell all begin	£2.50
1 with free gift (Secret Sign ring plus 16 stick-on symbols)	£5.00
2 Wonder Mann begins	£0.75
3-147	£0.45
BULLET SPORTS SPECIAL	
D.C.Thomson; nn Apr 1977	
nn - 32pgs	£0.75
BULLETMAN	
Arnold; 10 1951, 1 issue	
10 24pgs; reprints from Fawcett	£10.00
BUMPER COMIC ALBUM	
Robert Edwards; nn 1950s	
nn - 96pgs; reprints from various Paget comics, Banger art	£6.00
BUMPER NEW FUNNIES	
(see New Funnies)	
BUMPER STORY BOOK FOR BOYS	
Fleetway; 1975	
1975 mostly text	£2.50

	N.MINT		N.MINT

BUMPER SUPER MAG
Young World; 1 Jun 1964
1 80pgs; Walt Disney reprints	£1.50

BUNTY
(see The Girl of the Islands)
D.C. Thomson; 1 18th Jan 1958-present (1981 issues to 30th Dec 1995)
1 The Four Mary's by Bill Holroyd, Uncle Tom's Cabin by Paddy Brennan, The Dancing Life of Moira Kent by Ron Smith all begin	£5.00
1 with free gift (Ladybird ring)	£7.50
2	£2.50
3-50	£1.25
51-1000	£0.60
1001-1981	£0.25

BUNTY BOOK FOR GIRLS
D.C. Thomson; 1959-present
(1960) (Silent Night, Holy Night)	£7.50
(1961) (The Songs We Sing At Christmas)	£5.00
(1962) (A Little Town of Bethlehem)	£5.00
(1963) (January/February depicted by illustrations)	£5.00
(1964) (Girls in various ballet poses)	£5.00
1965 1st dated	£4.00
1966-1969	£3.00
1970-1979	£2.75
1980-1989	£2.25
1990-1994	£2.00

BUNTY PICTURE LIBRARY
D.C. Thomson; 1 1963-present (409 to Dec 1995)
1 68pgs	£2.00
2-10	£1.00
11-100	£0.35
101-409	£0.15

BURGLAR BILL
Trident; 1 Dec 1990
1 Paul Grist art and script	£1.00

BUSTER
Fleetway/IPC/Fleetway; 28th May 1960-present
No.1 - 28 May 1960 Buster by Bill Titcombe, Phantom Force Five by Eric Bradbury, Sea Hawk by Eric Parker begin	£45.00
No.1 with free gift (Buster's Balloon Beeper)	£75.00
No 2 - 4 Jun 1960	£20.00
No 2 - with free gift (Zoomer Jet)	£35.00
No 3 - 11 Jun 1960	£10.00
No 3 - with free gift (Dodger Kit)	£17.50
18 Jun 1960-18 Feb 1961	£5.00
25 Feb 1961 1st Buster & Radio Fun; Superman newspaper strip reprint begins; and Wagon Train also begins	£7.50
4 Mar 1961-18 Mar 1961	£2.50
18 Mar 1961 with free gift (3 Men of Danger Photocards)	£5.00
25 Mar 1961-8 Sep 1962	£2.50
15 Sep 1962 1st Buster & Film Fun; Nick Shannon (Johnny Winco reprints from Knockout) by Mike Western begins	£4.00
22 Sep 1962-20 Feb 1965	£2.50
27 Feb 1965 1st Buster & Big One; The Toys of Doom by Solano Lopez begins	£4.00
6 Mar 1965-29 May 1965	£2.50
5 Jun 1965 1st smaller size issue	£2.00
12 Jun 1965-6 Nov 1965	£2.00
6 Nov 1965 with free gift (The Buster Guy Fawkes Banger)	£5.00
13 Nov 1965-5 Nov 1966	£1.50
12 Nov 1966 1st Galaxus, The Thing from Outer Space by Solano Lopez	£2.00
19 Nov 1966-13 Jan 1968	£1.50
20 Jan 1968 1st Buster & Giggle; Fishboy by John Stokes begins	£2.00
27 Jan 1968-26 Sep 1971	£1.50
2 Oct 1971 1st Buster & Jet; Faceache by Ken Reid begins	£1.50
9 Oct 1971-15 Jun 1974	£0.75
22 Jun 1974-7 Apr 1990	£0.50
14 Apr 1990-13 Jan 1995	£0.30
20 Jan 1995-present fortnightly	£0.40

CHRONOLOGY
20 Oct 1960 Maxwell Hawke by Bradbury begins. 22 Jun 1974 1st "Buster and Cor!!". 6 Nov 1976 1st "Buster and Monster Fun". 6 Feb 1982 1st "Buster and Jackpot". 2 Jan 1984 1st "Buster and School Fun". 19 Sep 1987 1st "Buster and Nipper". 29 Oct 1988 1st "Buster and Oink!" (not given on cover). 14 Apr 1990 1st full colour. 3 Nov 1990 1st "Buster and Whizzer & Chips". 25 Dec 1993/1 Jan 1994 Double Number. 17 Dec/29 Dec 1995 Double Number.
Note: no issues dated 29 Jun-3 Aug 1974

BUSTER ADVENTURE LIBRARY
Fleetway; 1 Jul 1966-36 Dec 1967
1 John Steel reprints begin (odd numbers to 25)	£3.50
2 Robin Hood reprints begin (all even numbers)	£2.50
3-26,28,30,32,34,36	£2.00
27,29,31,33,35 Rick Random reprints	£3.00

ARTISTS/FEATURES
1 Dateline for Danger (TPL355) by Lopez Espi. 2 Robin Hood's Challenge. 3 Catch Me A Killer (TPL363) by Luis Bermejo. 4 Robin Hood's Peril. 5 Showdown (TPL367) by Reg Bunn. 6 Robin Hood At Bay (TPL122, 2 stories) by Reg Bunn, Pat Nicolle. 7 Death Deals A Joker. 8 Sword of Robin Hood (TPL287, 2 stories) by Nadir Quinto, Martin Salvador. 9 Terror Calls the Tune (TPL371) by Luis Bermejo. 10 Robin Hood and the Beast of Rockspur. 11 Tomorrow You Die! (TPL379) by Luis Bermejo. 12 Robin Hood the Valiant (TPL275, 3 stories) by Guido Buzzelli, Nadir Quinto. 13 Death Shadows the Hunter (TPL395) by Luis Bermejo. 14 Robin Hood and the Seal of Doom (TPL226?) by Luis Bermejo. 15 Savage Waterfront (TPL403) by Luis Bermejo. 16 Prince of Sherwood (TPL170, 3 stories) by Reg Bunn, Angel Pardo. 17 Dead Man's Tale (TPL399) by Alberto Breccia. 18 Robin Hood and the Hunted Thief. 19 The Big Fix (TPL431) by Luis Bermejo. 20 Robin Hood the Bold. 21 Who Is My Enemy? (TPL431) by Erio Nicolo. 22 Robin Hood & the Castle of Fear. 23 Invitation to Death (TPL427). 24 Courage of Robin Hood (TPL303, 2 stories) incl. Martin Salvador. 25 The Devil of Antiga by Erio Nicolo. 26 Rally to Robin Hood (TPL186,134, 3 stories) by Angel Pardo, Reg Bunn. 27 Terror From Space (SDL143) by Ron Turner. 28 Ho For Robin Hood (TPL174, 3 stories) by Arthur Horowicz, Guido Buzzelli. 29 Killer in Space (SDL44) by Ron Turner. 30 Robin Hood, Freedom Fighter. 31 Kidnappers From Mars (SDL31) by Ron Turner. 32 Robin Hood the Magnificent. 33 Death Planet (SDL48) by Bill Lacey. 34 Vengeance Arrow (TPL198, 3 stories) by Angel Pardo, Nadir Quinto, Reg Bunn. 35 Emperor of the Moon (SDL49) by Ron Turner. 36 The Justice of Robin Hood.

BUSTER AND MONSTER FUN HOLIDAY BOOK
Fleetway; 1990-1994
1990-1994	£1.00

BUSTER BOOK
(see also Buster Book of Thrills)
Fleetway; 1962-1994
1962 softback	£20.00
1963 softback	£12.50
1964-1965 softback	£7.50
1966-1969	£6.00
1970-1973	£4.00
1974-1979	£3.50
1980-1989	£3.00
1990-1994	£2.50

BUSTER BOOK OF GAGS
Fleetway; 1969
1969 very scarce	£10.00

BUSTER BOOK OF SPOOKY STORIES
Fleetway; 1975-1976
1975-1976 Eric Bradbury, Carlos Cruz reprints; scarce, softcover	£4.00

BUSTER BOOK OF THRILLS
Fleetway; 1962
1962 softback, scarce; Ron Turner Rick Random reprint	£25.00

BUSTER COMIC
Philipp Marx; nn 1946
nn - 8pgs; reprints	£3.00

BUSTER COMICS
Cartoon Art; nn 1947
nn - 16pgs; Dennis Reader art	£2.50

BUZZ
D.C. Thomson; 1 20th Jan 1973-103 4th Jan 1995 (joins Topper)
1 tabloid size	£5.00
2-10	£1.00
11-103	£0.50

BY THE TIME I GET TO WAGGA WAGGA
Harrier; 1 May 1987
1 Eddie Campbell art	£1.00

C

CAIN'S HUNDRED
Thorpe & Porter; 1 1962
1 68pgs; reprints from Dell, together with reprints from Mr District Attorney (National Periodical Publications)	£3.00

CALCULUS CAT: DEATH TO TELEVISION
Knockabout; nn 1987
nn - Hunt Emerson reprints	£5.00

CALIMERO
Top Sellers; 1 1973-? 1974
1 36pgs; reprints Italian strip, based on animated cartoon by Nino & Tony Pagot	£1.00
2-?	£0.50

CALLING MATT HARDY
Foldes Modern Printing; nn 1947
nn - Rex Hart art	£4.00

CALVIN AND HOBBES
Sphere/Warner; 1988-present
Calvin & Hobbes (1988) newspaper strip reprints by Bill Watterson begin	£3.50
Something Under the Bed is Drooling (1989)	£4.00
Yukon Ho! (1989)	£4.00
The Essential Calving & Hobbes (1990)	£5.00
Weirdos From Another Planet (1990)	£4.00
The Calvin & Hobbes Lazy Sunday Book (1990)	£5.00
The Revenge of the Baby-Sat (1991)	£5.00
The Authoritative Calvin & Hobbes (1991)	£6.00
Scientific Progress goes "Boink" (1991)	£5.00
Attack of the Deranged Mutant Killer Monster Snow Goons (Warner, 1992)	£4.00
The Indespensible Calvin & Hobbes (Warner, 1992)	£7.00
The Days Are Just Packed (Warner, Oct 1993) large landscape size	£7.00
Homicidal Psycho Jungle Cat (Warner, 1994)	£8.00
The Calvin & Hobbes Tenth Anniversary Book (Warner, 1995)	£9.00

CALVIN AND HOBBES
Warner; Apr 1992
1: Thereby Hangs A Tail paperback size series	£3.00
2: One Day the Wind Will Change	£3.00
3: In the Shadow of the Night	£3.00

CAMBERWICK GREEN HOLIDAY SPECIAL
Polystyle; nn May 1981
nn - 48pgs; reprints, based on TV series	£0.25

CANARDO
Fleetway (Xpresso Books); 1991
A Shabby Dog Story (Jul 1991) reprint from Belgium, Sokal art	£2.50
Blue Angel (Sep 1991) reprint from Belgium, Sokal art	£2.50
Note: Both titles were widely remaindered in 1994	

CANCELLED
Bob Comics; nn 1991

	N.MINT
nn - Phil 'n' Phyl, Jimmy Hero reprints by Bob Lynch	£0.50
CANDIDA THE MARCHESA	
Top Sellers; 1-3 1974	
1-3 132pgs pocket; adult, reprints Italian strip	£0.75
CANDY	
City; 1 21st Jan 1967-154 27th December 1969 (joins Jack & Jill)	
1 11.25x9.75" oblong; Candy & the Magic Toyshop photostrip based on Gerry Anderson, Thunderbirds, Bengo by Tymym begins	£7.50
2	£5.00
3-154	£3.00
Note: changes to upright format during 1968	
CANDY AND ANDY ANNUAL	
Century 21; 1967-1969	
1967-1969 scarce	£4.00
CANDY COMIC	
Philmar; 1 Sep 1947-3 1948	
1-3 8pgs; 2 including Wally Robertson	£3.00
CAPTAIN, THE	
Alexander Hamilton; v.1:1 1949	
Vol.1:1 16pgs; Reg Parlett art	£3.00
CAPTAIN AMERICA	
Miller; 1 1954-?	
1-? 28pgs; reprints from Marvel	£6.00
CAPTAIN AMERICA	
Marvel; 1 25th Feb 1981-59 3rd Apr 1982	
1 32pgs; Captain America, Iron Man, Defenders, Dazzler reprints begin	£1.50
1 with free gift (Superhero sticker)	£3.00
2	£1.25
2 with free gift (Superhero sticker)	£2.50
3-5	£1.00
6-20,22-36	£0.75
21 1st "Captain America and Marvel Action"; Captain America, Thor, Iron Man, Dazzler, Fantastic Four	£0.75
37 1st "Captain America and Marvel Super Adventures"; glossy cover, 8pgs colour	£1.25
37 with free gift (Captain Britain mask)	£2.50
38-49,51-59	£0.75
50 reprints Captain America #241	£1.00
CAPTAIN AMERICA SUMMER SPECIAL	
Marvel; nn May 1981	
nn - 52pgs; reprints	£0.40
CAPTAIN AMERICA COLLECTORS EDITION	
Marvel/Grandreams; 1981	
1981 US reprints, Steranko colour art from Captain America #110-111, 113	£3.00
CAPTAIN AND THE KIDS, THE	
Miller; nn 1942	
nn - 12pgs small oblong; reprints American newspaper strip	£4.00
CAPTAIN BRITAIN	
Marvel; 1 13th Oct 1976-39 6th Jul 1977 (joins Super Spider-Man)	
1 Captain Britain by Chris Claremont & Herbe Trimpe/Fred Kida begins	£2.50
1 with free gift (Captain Britain mask)	£4.00
2	£1.25
3-6,8-10	£1.00
7 Howard the Duck pull-out comic	£1.25
11-16,19-23 Gary Friedrich scripts	£0.75
17 free comic insert; some pages from issue 18 printed in error	£1.25
18 colour pages reprinted from 17	£1.00
24-39 glossy cover issues, various creators	£1.00
CAPTAIN BRITAIN	
Marvel; nn 1986	
nn - 192pgs; Jamie Delano & Alan Davis reprints	£6.00
CAPTAIN BRITAIN ANNUAL	
Marvel; 1978	
1978	£2.50
CAPTAIN BRITAIN MONTHLY	
Marvel; 1 Jan 1985-14 Feb 1986	
1 Captain Britain by Jamie Delano & Alan Davis, Freefall Warriors by Steve Parkhouse begin, Abslom Daak, Nightraven reprints begin	£5.00
2,4	£3.50
3 Mike Collins Captain Britain script	£3.50
5 Space Thieves by David Harper & Barry Kitson begins	£3.50
6-10,13	£3.00
11 The Cherubin by Mike Collins & Mark Farmer	£3.00
12 Black Knight reprints begin	£3.00
14 including Morrison text story	£3.00
CAPTAIN BRITAIN SUMMER SPECIAL	
Marvel; Jun 1980-May 1983, Oct 1992	
1980 52pgs, reprints	£1.50
1981 52pgs, reprints	£1.50
1983	£1.50
Autumn Special 1992 Alan Davis reprints	£1.00
CAPTAIN FIGHT	
Cartoon Art; 1 1950	
1 28pgs; Fiction House reprints	£4.00
CAPTAIN FLASH	
Miller; 1-2 1955	
1-2 28pgs; Sterling reprints	£4.00
CAPTAIN GALLANT	
Miller; 1-4 1956	
1-4 28pgs; Charlton reprints, based on TV series	£4.00
CAPTAIN KREMMEN AND THE KRELLS	
Corgi/Transworld; nn 1977	
nn - 68pgs; Roger Walker art	£1.25

	N.MINT
CAPTAIN MAGNET	
Cartoon Art; 1 1947-2 1948	
1 8pgs	£4.00
2 16pgs	£4.00
CAPTAIN MARVEL	
Miller; nn Dec 1944	
nn - 68pgs; Fawcett reprints	£50.00
CAPTAIN MARVEL ADVENTURES	
Miller; 1946-27th Jan 1954 (becomes Marvelman)	
Note: Miller published a number of different series of Captain Marvel, all based on the Fawcett comics; variations in format are listed below:	
54 16pgs, photogravure	£20.00
55-58 16pgs, photogravure	£12.00
- 16pgs, red/blue letterpress (15? issues)	£8.00
50 (Apr 1950)-84 36/24pgs	£7.50
v1:1 (19 Aug 1953)-24 (27 Jan 1954) 28pgs	£6.00
Captain Marvel Colouring Book (Miller, 1948)	£12.00
CAPTAIN MARVEL JR	
Miller; 1945-27th Jan 1954 (becomes Young Marvelman)	
Note: Miller published a number of different series of Captain Marvel Jr., all based on the Fawcett comics; variations in format are listed below:	
nn,3,37,50 16pgs, photogravure (4+ issues)	£10.00
80 (May 1950)-83 24pgs	£7.00
v1:1 (19 Aug 1953)-24 (27 Jan 1954) 28pgs	£6.00
CAPTAIN MIDNIGHT	
Miller/Arnold Book Co.; 1946-Jul 1963 (54? issues)	
Note: Miller published a number of different series of Captain Midnight, all based on the Fawcett comics; variations in format are listed below:	
42 16pgs, photogravure	£10.00
43 68pgs, photogravure	£10.00
100-139 28pgs	£6.00
1 (Aug 1962)-12 (Jul 1963) 28pgs	£5.00
CAPTAIN MIRACLE	
Anglo; 1 Oct 1960-9 Jun 1961	
1 28pgs; rejigged Marvelman reprints	£4.00
2-5,7-9 Don Lawrence art	£3.50
6 title given as Invincible on cover; Don Lawrence art	£4.00
CAPTAIN SCARLET	
Ravette; Oct 1993	
Spectrum is Green TV21 reprints	£3.00
Indestructable TV21 reprints	£3.00
CAPTAIN SCARLET AND THE MYSTERONS	
Fleetway; 1 23rd Oct 1993-14 6th May 1994 (joins Thunderbirds)	
1 Captain Scarlet TV21 reprints and original material begins, Angels, Zero X reprints begin	£1.00
2-14	£0.85
CAPTAIN SCARLET AND THE MYSTERONS STORYBOOK	
Century 21; 1967	
1967	£20.00
CAPTAIN SCARLET ANNUAL	
City; 1967-1968	
1967 Ron Turner art	£15.00
1968 Ron Turner art	£10.00
CAPTAIN SCARLET ANNUAL, THE OFFICIAL	
Grandreams; 1993	
1993	£5.00
CAPTAIN SCARLET/THUNDERBIRDS ANNUAL	
City, 1969	
1969	£20.00
CAPTAIN SCIENCE	
Cartoon Art; nn 1951	
nn - 28pgs; Youthful Magazines reprints	£4.00
CAPTAIN STARLITE IN ROBBERY UNDER ARMS	
Miller; 1 1957	
1 28pgs; King Studios art	£4.00
Note: Subtitled "The Book of the Film", but has no connection with "Robbery Under Arms" movie.	
CAPTAIN 3.D.	
United Anglo-American; nn 1954	
nn - 36pgs; reprints from Harvey, Kirby/Ditko art, issued with 3D glasses	£18.00
nn - without glasses	£10.00
CAPTAIN TORNADO	
S.N.P.I./ Mundial; 50 Feb 1952-91? 1955?, 42? issues	
50 24pgs; Captain Tornado (French reprint) begins	£4.00
51-91?	£2.00
CAPTAIN UNIVERSE	
Arnold Book Co.; 1,2 1954	
1,2 28pgs; Colin Dudley-Page art	£8.00
CAPTAIN VALIANT	
(see Space Comics)	
CAPTAIN VIDEO	
Miller; 1 Apr 1951-5 1952	
1 36pgs; reprints from Fawcett	£8.00
2-5	£5.00
CAPTAIN VIGOUR	
Sports Cartoons; 1 Dec 1952-17 Apr 1954 (joins Steve Sampson)	
1 Captain Vigour by Philip Mendoza begins	£4.00
2-17	£2.00
CAPTAIN ZENITH COMIC	
Martin & Reid; nn 1950	
nn - 8pgs; Captain Zenith by Mick Anglo	£8.00
CARELESS NIPPERS	
White; 1 1948-2 1950	
1 20pgs oblong; road safety promo, Brian White art	£2.00

	N.MINT
2 4pgs tabloid	£1.00
CARNIVAL COMIC, THE	
Martin & Reid; nn 1949	
nn - 8pgs; Frank Minnett, E.H.Banger, Wally Robertson art	£3.00
CARNOSAUR CARNAGE	
(see Monster Massacre)	
CARTOON CAPERS COMIC	
Martin & Reid; nn 1949	
nn - 8pgs, E.H.Banger, Wally Robertson, Mick Anglo art	£3.00
CARTOONS AND SKETCHES	
James Henderson; 571 13th Jul 1901-612 26th Apr 1902	
571 special 'Club Edition' of Snap-Shots	£20.00
572-612	£4.00
CARY COLT	
Miller; 1-8 1954	
1-8 28pgs; Spanish (?) reprints, some Fawcett reprints	£2.00
CASANOVA'S LAST STAND	
Knockabout (Crack); nn Nov 1993	
nn - 64pgs; Hunt Emerson art	£7.00
CASEY RUGGLES COMIC	
Donald F. Peters; 1 1951-47 1955	
1,4 36pgs; reprints American newspaper strip; common	£1.00
2-3,5-47 scarcer	£5.00
CASPER THE FRIENDLY GHOST	
Streamline/United Anglo-American; 1 1953	
1 28pgs; reprints from Harvey	£2.50
CASPER THE FRIENDLY GHOST	
Top Sellers; 1 1973-? 1974	
1-? 36pgs; reprints from Harvey	£1.00
CASTLE OF HORROR	
Portman; 1 Sep 1978-?	
1-? 68pgs; reprints from Marvel	£1.50
CAVE GIRL	
(see Action Series)	
CEASEFIRE	
Knockabout (Fanny); 1991	
1 32pgs; Julie Hollings, Jackie Smith, Carol Swain, Trina Robbins art	£2.80
CENTURY COMIC	
(see All Favouites, Five-Score Comic Monthly, Mighty Comic)	
K.G. Murray Ltd; 1 late 1950s-92? mid 1960s	
1 rare 100pgs, squarebound begins; b/w reprints from National Periodical Publications incl. Pow-Wow Smith, Congo Bill, Tomahawk, Rex the Wonder Dog, Binky, Superman, Aquaman (later issues feature Wonder Woman, Batman, Lois Lane, Tommy Tomorrow among others); priced at 2 shillings	£75.00
2 rare	£50.00
3-5 very scarce	£40.00
6-10 very scarce	£35.00
11-92? scarce	£30.00
Note: more issues thought to exist	
CHALLENGER ALBUM, THE	
P.M. Productions; 1949?	
1949? 52pgs; reprints The Challenger 1-2, Starflash Comic 1-2 with new text story	£8.00
CHALLENGER COMIC, THE	
P.M. Productions; 1 Sep 1948-2 1948	
1-2 8pgs; Frank Minnitt, Eric Roberts art	£4.00
CHALLENGERS OF THE UNKNOWN	
Strato; 1-4 1960	
1-4 reprints from National Periodical Publications	£3.00
CHAMP	
D.C. Thomson; 1 25th Feb 1984-87 19th Oct 1985 (joins Victor)	
1 We Are United by Peter Foster, The Sinister World of Mr. Pendragon by Alcatena begin	£1.00
1 with free gift (Soccer Slide Guide)	£2.00
2	£0.50
2 with free gift (Soccer Star pictures + wallet)	£1.00
3	£0.50
3 with free gift (Soccer Star pictures)	£1.00
4-87	£0.20
ARTISTS	
Alcatena in 1,11-12,19-24,32,44-46.	
CHAMPION	
Fleetway; 26th Feb 1966-4th Jun 1966, 15 unnumbered issues (joins Lion)	
No.1 - 26 Feb 1966 Jet Jordan, School For Spacemen, Return of the Stormtroopers by Eric Bradbury, When the Sky Turned Green by Carlos Cruz begin	£10.00
No.1 with free gift (Screamer Balloon)	£15.00
No. 2 - 5 Mar 1966	£7.50
12 Mar 1966-4 Jun 1966	£5.00
CHAMPION COMIC, THE	
The Joker; 1 9th Jan 1894-106 11th Jan 1896 (becomes Joker, New Series)	
1 8pgs tabloid size	£35.00
2	£25.00
3-5	£20.00
6-50	£15.00
51-106	£10.00
Note: contains mostly joke cartoons	
CHAMPION THE WONDER HORSE	
World Distributors; undated-1954	
"Trail to Danger" (1st story)	£4.00
1954 Dell reprints	£3.50
CHAMPION THE WONDER HORSE	
Daily Mirror; 1957-1962	
1957 scarce	£6.00
1958 Stories by Arthur Groom, illus. by John Pollack	£4.00
1959 Stories by Arthur Groom, illus. by John Burns	£4.00

Century Comic #30

Chick's Own #1

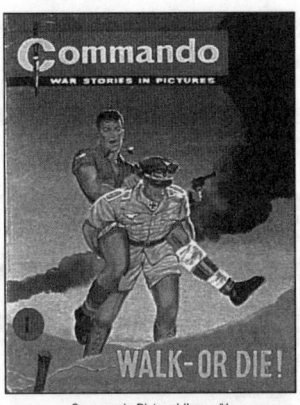

Commando Picture Library #1

N.MINT | N.MINT

	N.MINT
1960 Stories by Arthur Groom, illus. by Michael Godfrey	£3.50
1961 Stories by Arthur Groom, illus. by Michael Godfrey	£3.50
1962	£3.00

CHAMPION THE WONDER HORSE
Purnell; 1959
| **1959** Text stories, John Burns frontis | £4.00 |

CHANNEL 33 1/3 SUMMER SPECIAL
Marvel; nn May 1983
| nn - Dickie Howett art | £1.25 |

CHARLES RAND
Thorpe & Porter; 1 1966
| **1** 68pgs; Charles Rand by Mick Anglo | £5.00 |

CHARLIE CHAN
(see New Adventures of Charlie Chan)

CHARLIE CHAN
Strea:nline/United Anglo-American; 1 1950
| **1** 28pgs; reprints from Charlton | £6.00 |

CHARLIE CHAN
Miller; 1-2 1955
| **1-2** 28pgs; reprints from Charlton | £4.00 |

CHARLIE CHAPLIN
Top Sellers; Dec 1973-1974
| **1** 36pgs; Charlie Chaplin by Torregrosa | £2.00 |
| **2-?** | £1.00 |

CHARLIE CHAPLIN FUN BOOK
Amalgamated Press; nn 1915
| nn - 44pgs; Funny Wonder reprints | £35.00 |

CHARLIE CHICK'S PAPER
F.W. Woolworth; 1 Feb 1934
| **1** 8pgs; Alan Fraser art | £3.00 |

CHARLIE'S ANGELS ANNUAL
Stafford Pemberton; 1978-1981
| **1978-1981** | £2.00 |

CHEEKY SUMMER SPECIAL
IPC; Jun 1978-May 1982
| **1978-1979,1981-1982** | £0.50 |
| **1980** titled Holiday Special | £0.50 |

CHEEKY WEEKLY
IPC; 1 22nd Oct 1977-120 2nd Feb 1980 (joins Whoopee)
| **1** Cheeky by Frank McDiarmid | £1.50 |
| **2-120** | £0.35 |

CHEERFUL COMIC, THE
C.A. Ransom; 1 17th Sep 1928-28 20th Apr 1929
| **1** 8pgs tabloid; reprints from Monster Comic begin, Reg Carter art | £10.00 |
| **2-28** Reg Carter art | £4.00 |

CHEERIE COMIC
Homer McCrickrick; 1 1946
| **1** 8pgs; John Turner art | £4.00 |

CHEERY CHICKS CHUMMY COMIC
Aida Reubens; 1 Jun 1947-12 Jun 1948
| **1** 8pgs; titled Cheery Chicks Comic, Dennis Childs art | £3.00 |
| **2-12** becomes Cheery Chicks Chummy Comic | £1.00 |

CHEERY COMIC
P.M. Productions; nn Aug 1944
| nn - 16pgs; Reg Carter art | £3.00 |

CHEERY TIME COMIC
Philmar; nn 1948
| nn - 8pgs; Jack Pamby, Wally Robertson art | £3.00 |

CHEYENNE ANNUAL
World Distributors; 1960-1964
1960 stories by Joe Morrissey; "Trial by Water" (1st story)	£5.00
1961 stories by Joe Morrissey; "Bounty Hunter" (1st story)	£4.00
1962 (blue background) stories by Joe Morrissey, Dell/Gold Key reprints	£4.00
1962 (orange background)	£4.00
1963 Dell reprints	£3.50
1964 Dell reprints	£3.50

CHEYENNE ADVENTURE STORIES
Adprint; 1961
| **1961** stories by John Stanstead, illus. by Desmond Walduck | £5.00 |

CHEYENNE COMIC ALBUM
World Distributors; 1 1958,1964
| **1** "The Captives" (1st story) | £5.00 |
| **1964** Dell/Gold Key reprints | £4.00 |
Note: Other editions probably exist

CHEYENNE: A TELEVISION STORY BOOK
New Town Printers; 1961-1963
1961 "Moose Jaw Trail" (1st story)	£5.00
1962 "The Kiowa Trial" (1st story)	£4.00
1963	£4.00

CHEYENNE KID
Miller; 1 1957-18 1958
| **1** 28pgs; Charlton reprints, incl. Williamson/Torres art in some issues | £4.00 |
| **2-18** | £2.50 |

CHEYENNE WESTERN ALBUM
G.T. Ltd.; 1959?
| - reprints Kit Carson, Lucky Logan, Davy Crockett, Buck Jones | £5.00 |

CHICKS' OWN, THE
Amalgamated Press; 1 25th Sep 1920-1605 9th May 1957 (joins Playbox)
1 12pgs tabloid; Dicky the Duck by Arthur White begins	£50.00
1920 issues	£15.00
1921-1939 incl. White, Hugh O'Neill, Philip Swinnerton art	£5.00
1940-1951 8pgs; becomes fortnightly	£2.50

	N.MINT
1952-1957 12pgs, reverts to weekly	£2.00

CHRONOLOGY
21 Apr 1934 1st "Chicks' Own & Bo Peep". 12 Aug 1939 1st "Chicks' Own & Happy Days". 31 May 1941 1st "Chicks' Own & Bubbles". 27 Oct 1951 reverts to weekly schedule. 9 Jun 1956 becomes all picture.

CHICKS' OWN ANNUAL
Amalgamated Press; 1924-1957
1924 scarce	£50.00
1925	£40.00
1926-1930	£30.00
1931-1940	£20.00
1941-1950	£15.00
1951-1957	£10.00
Note: the early annuals are tabloid size

CHIEF ANNUAL, THE
P.M. Productions; 1947
| **1947** Minnitt, Wally Robertson art | £5.00 |

CHILDREN OF THE VOYAGER
(see main American comics section)

CHILDREN'S FAIRY, THE
(previously The Childrens' Sunday Fairy)
Amalgamated Press; 1 1st Nov 1919-76 9th Apr 1921 (becomes Bubbles and the Children's Fairy)
1 12pgs; Julius Baker, Herbert Foxwell art	£25.00
2	£10.00
3-76	£5.00

CHILDREN'S HAPPY TRAVEL COMIC
Elliott-Sinclair Books; 1946, 4 issues
| **1-4** 2pgs; supplement to Children's Happy Travel Magazine | £1.50 |

CHILDREN'S HOLIDAY FUN
John Leng; nn May 1937-May 1940, 4 undated issues
| nn 84pgs oblong; George Jones, Cyril Cowell art | £5.00 |
| nn-nn | £4.00 |
Note: annual extra edition of Fairyland Tales

CHILDREN'S OWN FAVOURITE
World Service; 15th Oct 1938-10th Dec 1938, 9 issues
| **15 Oct 1938** 8pgs; Norman Ward art | £6.00 |
| **22 Oct-10 Dec 1938** | £3.00 |
Note: free comic supplement to The Favourite Weekly. 4pgs, folds to give 8pgs.

CHILDREN'S OWN SUNDAY PICTORIAL, THE
Sunday Pictorial; 6th Aug 1933-4th Feb 1934, 27 issues
6 Aug 1933 4pgs; supplement to Sunday Pictorial, Pip Squeak & Wilfred by A.B.Payne, Tich by Steve Dowling begin	£8.00
13 Aug-5 Nov 1933	£2.00
12 Nov 1933-4 Feb 1934 reduced to 3pgs	£1.50
Note: continues as single sheet.

CHILDREN'S ROCKET BOOK, THE
(continuation of The Planet)
J.B. Allen; nn May 1949
| nn 12pgs, photogravure; Bill Holroyd, E.H.Banger art | £5.00 |

CHILDREN'S SOUTH WALES ECHO & EXPRESS, THE
(see South Wales Echo & Express Children's Supplement)

CHILDREN'S SUNDAY FAIRY, THE
(previously The Sunday Fairy)
Amalgamated Press; 23 11th Oct 1919-25 25th Oct 1919 (becomes The Children's Fairy)
| **23** 12pgs; Julius Baker art | £5.00 |
| **24-25** | £5.00 |

CHILDSPLAY
Atlas; 1-? 1980
| **1** 36pgs; Dell reprints | £1.00 |
| **2-?** | £0.40 |

CHILLER POCKET BOOK
Marvel; 1 Mar 1980-28 Jul 1982
1 52pgs small size; Dracula, Satana reprints begin	£1.00
2-8,10-19,21-28	£0.40
9,20 100pgs; Xmas double numbers	£0.80

CHILLING TALES OF HORROR
Portman; 1 1979-4 1980
| **1-4** 52pgs; Stanley reprints | £1.00 |

CHIPPER HOLIDAY SPECIAL
Birmingham Evening Mail; nn 7th July 1980
| nn - 20pgs tabloid; Jack Bell art | £0.35 |

CHIPS
(see Illustrated Chips)

"CHIPS" ANNUAL
World; 1980-1981
| **1980-1981** based on TV series | £1.00 |

CHIPS COMIC
IPC; 1 12th Mar 1983-21 30th Jul 1983 (joins Playhour)
| **1** 16pgs; based on TV series | £1.00 |
| **2-21** | £0.35 |

CHIPS COMIC BOOK
IPC; 1 Oct 1984
| **1** with story cassette | £0.50 |

CHOPPER
Fleetway; Aug 1990
| Song of the Surfer 2000AD reprints by John Wagner & Colin MacNeil | £6.00 |

CHRISTMAS COMIC, THE
Trapps Holmes; 1899-1904
| **1899-1904** 16pgs; annual double number of The Halfpenny Comic | £30.00 |

CHRISTMAS COMIC
C.A. Pearson; Dec 1931-Nov 1933 (becomes Jolly Jumbo's Christmas Comic)
| **1931-1933** 12pgs; annual, Walter Bell art | £15.00 |

	N.MINT

CHRISTMAS HOLIDAY COMIC
(previously Christmas Comic, Jolly Jumbo's Christmas Comic)
C.A. Pearson; Nov 1936-Nov 1939

1936-1939 12pgs	£18.00

CHRISTMAS STORYTELLER
(see Storyteller)
Marshall Cavendish; Nov 1983-Nov 1984

1983,1984 64pgs; with cassette	£0.50

CHRONICLES OF GENGHIS GRIMTOAD, THE
Marvel; nn Oct 1990

nn - reprints from Strip by Wagner/Grant & Gibson	£6.00

CHRONICLES OF JUDGE DREDD, THE
(see The Complete Judge Dredd)
Titan; 1981-1990

1 Judge Dredd, 2000AD reprints begin, Bolland art	£6.00
1 hardback	£12.00
2-3 The Cursed Earth Part One/Two	£5.00
2-3 hardback	£10.00
4-5 Judge Caligula Book One/Two	£5.00
4-5 hardback	£10.00
6 Judge Dredd 2 McMahon art	£5.00
6 hardback	£10.00
7 Judge Death, Bolland art	£5.00
7 hardback	£10.00
8-10 Judge Child Book One/Two/Three	£5.00
11 Judge Dredd 3, McMahon art	£5.00
12 Block Mania	£4.50
13-14 Apocalypse War Book One/Two	£5.00
15-23 Judge Dredd 4-12	£4.50
24 City of the Damned	£5.00
25-34 Judge Dredd 13-22	£4.50
35-37 Judge Dredd in Oz Book One/Two/Three	£5.00
38-40 Judge Dredd 23-25	£5.00
41-42 Judge Dredd 26-27	£5.50
43-45 Mega-City Vice 1,2,3	£5.50
46 Destiny's Angels	£5.50

Note: numbering comes from Titan adverts and was dropped on later issues.

CHRONICLES OF ULLAH, THE
Magpie Graphics; 1 Apr 1992-7 Sep 1993

1 Of Beggars & Kings begins	£1.00
2-7	£0.75

CHUCKLER
Target Publications; 1 31st Mar 1934-238 15th Oct 1938 (becomes Rattler & Chuckler)

1 12pgs tabloid orange paper; Edward Banger art, incl. 4-page supplement	£20.00
2 12pgs	£6.00
3-29 12pgs	£4.00
30-158 8pgs	£3.00
159-238 8pgs white paper	£3.00

CHUCKLES
Amalgamated Press; 1 10th Jan 1914-517 1st Dec 1923 (becomes Jungle Jinks & Chuckles)

1 8pgs tabloid; Tom Wilkinson, H. O'Neill, W. Radford art	£45.00
2	£12.50
3-5	£7.50
6-300	£4.00
301-517	£2.50

CHRONOLOGY
21 April 1917 size reduced. 5 May-2 Jun 1917 page count increased to 12. 22 Sep 1917 size restored.
Note: in 1919 became a nursery comic.

CHUMMY COMIC
P.M. Productions; nn 1944

nn 8pgs; Reg Carter art	£4.00

CHUMMY COMIC
H. Jeffrey; nn Jan 1948

nn - 8pgs; John Turner art	£3.00

CIRCUS BOY
A Daily Mirror Book; 1958-1960

1958 all text, stories by Gordon Grimsley, illus. by John Pollack	£3.00
1959	£3.00
cy1960 all text, stories by Gordon Grimsley, illus. by John Pollack	£3.00

CIRCUS COMIC
P.M. Productions; nn 1945

nn - 8pgs; Reg Carter art	£4.00

CIRCUS COMICS
Hotspur Publishing Co.; 1 1949

1 8pgs; Denis Gifford art	£4.00

CISCO KID, THE
World Distributors; 1 1952-51 1955

1 36pgs; reprints from Dell begin	£10.00
2-48	
49-51 28pgs	£5.00

THE CISCO KID COMIC ALBUM
World Distributors; 1 1953?-3 1955?

1	£5.00
2-3	£4.00

CLASH OF THE TITANS
Independant Television; nn Jul 1981

nn - 64pgs; Look-In Special, reprints US strip based on film	£1.00

CLASS WAR COMIX
Epic Productions; 1 Jul 1974

1: New Times 36pgs, hardbound	£2.50

CLASSIC ACTION HOLIDAY SPECIAL
Fleetway; nn Jun 1990

nn - new stories featuring classic Fleetway characters incl. Kelley's Eye by John Cooper, Robot Archie by Sandy James, The Steel Claw by Vano, Jet Ace Logan by John Gillatt, Johnny Cougar by Sandy James £0.75

CLASSIC COMICS
Hawk Books; 1990

- 36pgs; unnumbered series of hardbacks adapted by Dr. Marion Kimberly, Spanish reprints (each)	£1.50

ARTISTS/FEATURES
Call of the Wild, Davy Crockett, Hound of the Baskervilles by Jose Casanovas Sr., Huckleberry Finn, Hunchback of Notre Dame, Journey of Marco Polo by Jesus Blasco, Moby Dick, Robin Hood, Swiss Family Robinson, The Three Musketeers.

A CLASSIC IN PICTURES
Amex; 1-12 1949

1-12 each	£8.00

ARTISTS/FEATURES
1 Oliver Twist by C.L. Doughty. 2 Ivanhoe by F.A. Philpott. 3 Macbeth by F.A. Philpott. 4 Westward Ho by Colin Merritt. 5 Treasure Island by Colin Merritt. 6 A Tale of Two Cities. 7 The Three Musketeers. 8 Lorna Doone by C.L. Doughty. 9 Henry V by F.A. Philpott. 10 Barnaby Rudge. 11 Mutiny on the Bounty by Colin Merritt. 12 Julius Caesar by F.A. Philpott.
Note: this series was reprinted by Philipp Marx under their Bairns Books imprint as Famous Stories In Pictures (qv)

CLASSIC JUDGE DREDD
(see The Complete Judge Dredd)
Fleetway; 1 Aug 1995-present (5 to Dec 1995)

1 2000AD reprints begin, Midnight Surfer	£1.50
2-5	£1.25

CLASSIC 2000AD
(previously The Best of 2000AD)
Fleetway Editions; 1 Sep 1995-present

1 reprints America by Wagner & McNeil	£1.50
2,4	£1.50
3 reprints Shambala by Grant & Ranson	£1.50

CLASSICS ILLUSTRATED
(see Double Duo, Illustrated Library of..., World Illustrated)
Thorpe and Porter; 1 1953-163 1962 (167 issues - see special Classics Illustrated section below)
The Price Guide is pleased to welcome Mr. Dan Malan, the acknowledged foremost expert on Classics Illustrated and his extended article dealing with the peculiar and unique problems with British Classics Illustrated. Any additional information is most welcome and should be sent to the editorial address.

BRITISH CLASSICS ILLUSTRATED & RELATED SERIES
INTRODUCTION, BY DAN MALAN
The worldwide success of the CLASSICS ILLUSTRATED series is legendary. Albert L.Kanter, a self-taught Russian Jewish immigrant to America, launched the CLASSIC COMICS series in 1941. Others had serialized comic-strip adaptations of literary works, but Al Kanter believed that a full comic-book could be devoted to one literary title, that a series of such titles could be successful, and that a company publishing only to such a series could prosper. He could never have dreamed that he would live to see over a billion copies published worldwide.

An entire generation was raised on CLASSICS ILLUSTRATED, which was not really a "series," but individual titles connected only by the now famous black-&-yellow logo. Many titles had to be reprinted every year. What other series could compare with that long-term popularity? In the U.S. CI series between 1941-71, there were 1400 editions of 169 titles. The logo CLASSIC COMICS became CLASSICS ILLUSTRATED in 1947. In 1951, they changed from line-drawn covers to painted covers. Many of the titles got new covers and internal art along the way. They were so popular in the 1950s that they began related series: JUNIORS, SPECIALS, and WORLD AROUND US.

CLASSICS ILLUSTRATED were published in at least 22 languages in 30 countries.Many countries put new covers on their editions, and some produced completely new titles. There were three large groups of new foreign CI titles. There were 88 new Greek CI "History & Mythology" titles. There were 60 new Brazilian CI titles from works by Brazilian authors. But the major new thrust in foreign CI titles was the joint European CI series, which ran simultaneously in about 10 European countries from 1956-76. When the U.S. CI series stopped producing new titles in 1962, this European operation picked up the baton and produced 82 new titles from 1962-76.

1996 BRITISH CLASSICS ILLUSTRATED UPDATE BY DAN MALAN
Since the last edition, many new CI editions have been reported, but little new input on pricing. I did hear about a British dealer holding out for £200 for a Doctor No. But the most significant discovery was two hardback deluxe ed. covers on softcover editions, with (121) reorder lists, but no cover price, indicia or printing information. For new edition prices, see other editions of the same title and cover.

PUBLICATIONS AVAILABLE
CLASSICS COLLECTOR magazine
(4-issue air mail subscription to England: $20)
Dan Malan's **THE COMPLETE GUIDE TO CLASSICS ILLUSTRATED**:
(each volume has 112 pages with 800 colour photos of CI; V1: U.S. CI, V2: Foreign CI; each $25)
Dan Malan bio/bibliography: **GUSTAVE DORÉ – ADRIFT ON DREAMS OF SPLENDOUR**
(352 pages, 500 illustrations): $40
+ coming in 1996: Dickens' **CHRISTMAS CAROL**,
with 45 lost Doré engravings & other Victorian illustrations: $20.

MALAN CLASSICAL ENTERPRISES,
7519 Lindbergh Dr., St.Louis, MO 63117, USA
Telephone: (314) 781–2319 Fax: (314) 781–0699

The British CLASSICS ILLUSTRATED series was by far the most complicated, or as we like to say, the most challenging. Back in the 1970s, American collectors were able to research and compile information on nearly 1400 U.S. CI editions. That is now included in the U.S. Overstreet Comic Book Price Guide. Now we are doing the same for British CI. Please use this current listing as a starting point to write down additional edition info, and sent it to Malan Classical Enterprises. We want the British CI listing to shortly be as comprehensive as the U.S. list. This list is also the first attempt at comprehensive pricing of British CI. We welcome your inputs on actual selling prices for various British CI editions. Thank you.

The British CI series was published from 10/51-6/63. That ending date is our educated guess. The first ten chronological titles are the only ones with listed dates. But we have many ways to calculate CI dates within a couple months. But we need to explain why the British series is so complicated. There are many reasons:
1) British CI were not issued in numerical order. At first the title numbers were issued randomly, then missing numbers were filled in. On the next page there is a comprehensive list of the chronological

order in which British CI titles and cover/art variations were issued. It represents eight years of research.

2) In 1953, British CI added prices for South Africa and Australia, and added New Zealand in 1955. In 1956, they separated and began individual country series. We are including the Australian and New Zealand editions, and treat them sort of like variations of British editions. Few collectors make a distinction be- tween British/Australian/New Zealand CI. But we are not including here the very different 1947-1953 Australian series. Those 72 titles had paper covers, b&w interior art, many new covers, different logos, and came in various sizes and shapes. A very odd series. We will cover them in volume two of our book series. There are only rumors of South African CI, in English or Afrikaaner.

3) British CI from 1951-56 used U.S. CI numbers, but then began using non-U.S. CI numbers. Much of the later numbering came from the joint European CI series, including 15 new titles and 11 new covers. There were many printing errors of title numbers on the front covers or reorder lists, printing the American or European numbering instead of the (correct) British numbering. See 5).

4) Many British CI were later reissued with different covers or internal artwork. Altogether, there were 167 titles and 227 cover/art variations. Most of them were U.S. Line Drawn Covers with old art (LDC/A1, or L/1), replaced by U.S. painted covers with new art (PC/A2, or P/2), or by new British covers (NP).

5) Four numbers (2/13/18/40) were each used for two different titles. Three early titles got new numbers: #2 became #20, #13 became #85, #18 became #56. But #40 Poe's Mysteries) was simply terminated. Then four titles had A or B suffixes: (56A/139A/139B/158A). Also, at least six titles were misprinted with the wrong number: #12 misprinted as #132, #65 misprinted as #127, #93 misprinted as #152, #111 misprinted as #16, #127 misprinted as #153, and #139A misprinted as #139. All of these misprints were later corrected, except for #139A, which exists as #139A only on reorder lists.

6) We are very confident that British #51.LORD JIM never existed. In all our vast research, we have never seen one, or known anyone who ever had one. If you can confirm the existence of a copy of British CI#51, please let me know. But I do insist on photocopy verification. So here is how we arrived at the 167 British CI titles: #1-163 + 4 A/Bs + #40 said twice - #51 never existed.

7) British CI were published with five different cover prices: 1/0: 1953-55 editions (HRNs between 82-123); many also list AU/NZ/SA price. 1/3: British price for 1951-52 (10 titles) and 1956-63 (from HRN 124 on). 1/6: all New Zealand editions, + five 1952 British editions: 13/14/25/40/74. 2/0: all Australian editions, + four 1952 British 64-page editions: 2/6/7/10. 2/6: ten 1953-54 CI hardback DELUXE editions, all with new painted covers.

8) Brit.CI were printed in eight different countries, shown here by date and HRN: England, Ireland, Denmark, Sweden, U.S.A., Poland, Netherlands and France.

```
1951-2-3--4--5--6---7----8--9-----60--1-2-3
       U
    S    1 1 1 1 1 1 1                  1 1 1 1
1
HRN:8 7 8 0 1 1 2 2 2 2 2 1 1 2 3 3 4 5 6 7 8 8 9 3 3 4 5
5
    2 7 2 6 2 5 0 3 4 5 9 9 3 9 5 2 6 5 6 3 5 5 4 6 1 6
7
ENG:E-E--E-E--E-E-E-E-E-E       E-E-E--E
IRE:   I         I-I-I-I-I-I-I-I-I---I-I-I-I
DMK:       D-D-D-D-D-D-D-D-D-D                D
SWE:                          S--S--S-S-S
USA:                          U---U+
POL:                          P---P--P
NTH:N-N (4)
FRN:              F (4)
```

The British CI series began in October 1951, reprinting two random U.S. titles per month. Ten titles (49/68/16/60/64/77/37/22/17/58) were issued between October 1951 and March 1952. All had U.S. line drawn covers (LDC). The first six editions contained U.S. reorder lists with the highest reorder number (HRN) of 82. Four of these scarce early (1/3 price) issues were printed in the Netherlands. One interesting feature about these early editions was the outside back cover (obc) ads for multi-title Giant editions (Adventure/Indian/Mystery). Details kept changing: name (Giant/Omnibus/Monster/Companion), price (6/0, 7/6, 6/7), schedule (shortly/September/Autumn), and contents (Indian: -#4, +#58; Adventure: -#8, then -#6 +#2; Mystery:deleted). The INDIAN (17/22/37/58) and ADVENTURE (2/7/10) Giants finally came out about October 1952, and are now very rare/valuable. CI#s 40 & 74 list them as available, plus a gift box (49/60/68/77), probably never published.

Getting back to the CI themselves, after the first ten titles they decided to diversify with more valuable editions. During 1952 they issued five 1/6 editions (13/14/25/40/74) with stiff covers, and four 2/0 editions (2/6/7/10) which had 64 pages each and were bound instead of stapled. Evidently the more expensive titles did not sell well, because they then dropped the price to 1/0 (15/18/78/82) right away at the beginning of 1953. Those four 1/0 editions also list a 1/6 price for South Africa and a 1/9 price for Australia. We list these as 1/16/19 to show all three prices. The 1/9 Australian price quickly changed to 2/0. We mentioned above the earlier Australian CI series. They had no dates or title numbers, but we were able to calculate that the 72 titles ran monthly from 7/47-6/53, when they joined the British series. The last Australian b&w CI (US#104) has an illustrated ad for the new series "with full-color artwork." Many early British CI can be found with "2/0 Australia" stickers over the price. We do not count stickers as variations.

The other major development of 1953 was the introduction of the 2/6 Hardback Deluxe edition. They were hardback books with new wraparound painted covers, and a small CI logo at the bottom. They had neither numbers nor reorder lists. We did not list them in the regular CI editions, but in a special category. They are all rare and valuable. In early 1953, the regular CI editions began announcing Deluxe editions, first 4, then 8, 10, 12, 14, and then back down to 10. We are confident that they only issued ten (CIs 15/18/78/82/89/ 104/106/107/108/112). Most of these copies which now turn up have spines all torn up. The last Deluxe ad was in 1955.

There were also Bible Comics ads. These were British hardback reprints of the 1940s U.S. EC Picture Stories from the Bible. At this time the random CI U.S. titles jumped up to the 100+ range, with many western stories, which were then popular. Towards the end of 1955, the schedule increased to two new titles per month, and the first ad for CI Juniors appeared. Also, the first cover/art change appeared, with #13 changing from LDC/A1 to PC/A1, later changing to A2. Plus, New Zealand was added, at 1/6. We list that cover pricing as 1/16/16/2 for GB/SA/NZ/AU. Then each country began 'its own individual country series, but all printed together.

In 1956, the joint European CI series began, with two new CI titles monthly in 10 languages simultaneously. This answers many British questions, such as why are there coming-next ads in over 30 titles, in the middle of the British series? Or where did all those new covers and titles come from? It also enables us to go rather precise dating on years and years of undated British CI. It even allows us to predict as-yet undiscovered British CI editions.

There are 34 British CI editions with ibc coming-next ads, coinciding exactly with #1-34 in the joint European series, while the British numbering was random. Many of these titles were new to the British series, some were unchanged reprints, while some were reprints, but changed to PCs or A2

(49/78/77/64/6/10/15). You can find them in 1/3, 1/6 & 2/0 editions. They also issued other new titles which do no have coming-next ads. So 1956 was one busy year, between British, Australian, and New Zealand editions, with and without ads, they published about 130 editions.

This was also when the British CI series began to fill in the missing numbers from the random numbering schedule previously employed. They issued random CI titles from 1951-56 up to #129. Then from 1956-60 they filled in the missing numbers. So for the next five years all editions had HRNs of 126 or 129. How can we tell all those editions apart? We use a dual HRN, with the second number being the highest filled-in-number. If an HRN is 126 or 129, look for #1. If there is no #1 on the list, then 126 or 129 is the correct HRN. If there is a #1, then look through the list for these numbers: 12/19/28/33/39/45/52/56/65/76/83/85/95. Those are the HRN filled-in numbers. A first edition of CI#1. HUCKLEBERRY FINN would have an HRN of 129/12. That means that the highest number on the reorder list is 129, and of the filled-in numbers, there is a #12 but not a #19. The next edition of CI#1 has the filled-in numbers up to #76, so it has an HRN of 129/76. It may seem complicated, but with a little practice, you can master the technique. Any dealer's list with British CIs for sale is full of HRNs 126 and 129. This allows for precise edition identification. Why is this so important? One particular edition may have a very rare cover or artwork variation, and be worth much more. British #1 was also the point at which non-U.S. numbering began. After five years, they finally published #1, which is U.S. CI#19. So in this list we will refer to it as #1(US#19).

By 1960 they had filled in all the missing numbers. But just as things began getting too simple again, there was another major development in America. In 1961 (thru circumstances way too complicated to cover here - see my Classics book V1), the American publisher William Kanter (son of the founder) was influenced to stop the production of new CI titles in America. This influence was primarily exerted by the distributor, the Curtis Co. By this time the European operation was going great. So William decided to basically shift the entire operation overseas, and actually moved to England. So in 1961, behind the scenes, both Thorpe & Porter in England and another Swedish company began production of new CI titles. So by the beginning of 1962, the CI baton had completely shifted to Europe. Some of the new titles actually had artwork already prepared in the U.S., but never published. It really is a shame there was not more communication back then, because American CI enthusiasts would have jumped at the chance to get the new European CI titles.

By 1960, the U.S. CI publisher Gilberton had the largest European distribution of any American publication, not just comics. Not only were 10 countries issuing two CI monthly apiece, but by then all those countries were publishing the three spin-off series: CI JUNIORS, SPECIALS, and WORLD ILLUSTRATED. There were also all those reprint editions of CI and Juniors. Counting all editions of all CI series, in 1960 nearly 1,000 editions of CI were published in Europe! In the U.S., CI Juniors began in 1953, Specials in 1955, and World Around Us in 1958. British Juniors began in 1955, and the highest was 501-513 and 516. But it is uncertain if they were all issued. British Juniors used the "CI-Junior" logo are quite scarce. They ended in 1957. In 1959 the series began again as PIXI TALES, with non-U.S. numbering. The first ad for British SPECIALs was in 1957 for 10 Commandments. The British WORLD ILLUSTRATED series began in 1959. There were 88 Pixi, 8 Specials, and 34 WI, of which 11 Pixi and 8 WI were new British titles.

BRITISH CLASSICS ILLUSTRATED

FIRST APPEARANCE IN CHRONOLOGICAL ORDER-OF-PUBLICATION, GROUPED BY HIGHEST-NUMBER-ON-REORDER-LIST
(L/1=Line Drawn Cover/1st Art; P/2=Painted Cover/2nd Art; NP=New British cover)

#	C/A	HRN	DATE	#	C/A	HRN	DATE
49	L	US82	10/51	53	L	124	
68	L/1			91	P		
16	L		11/51	98	P		
60	L/1			105	P		(1955)
64	L		1/52	E1-34/AD		(1956)	NO AD
77	L			*49	P	125	23.L/1
37	L	77-10T	2/52	(105)	R		125.P
22	L			(112)	R		32.L
17	L		3/52	99	P		119.P
2	L/1	77-16T		*96	R		71.L/1
6	L/1			(124)	R		69.L
7	L/1			(104)	R		31.L
10	L/1			(101)	R		122.P
13	L/1			(100)	R		
14	L			(115)	R		
25	L					126	90.P1
40	L	77-19T					126.P
74	L		(1952)	*78	P	129	79.L
15	L	82	(1953)	129	P		113.P
18	L/1			*77	NP		94.P
78	L			(114)	R		80.P
82	P			(106)	R		
89	P	106		(111)	R		
101.	P			5	P/2		
104	P			29	P		
106	P			1/19	P/2	126/12	
108	P			2/47	P		
112	P			3/34	P		11/133.P
42	L/1	112		4/128	P		12/132.P
97	P		(1953)	*64	P		
107	P		(1954)	(108	R		(1956)
111	P			8/81	P		(1957)
48	P	115		(97	R		
57	L			(121	R		
86	P			9/130	P		
88	P			(123)	R		
114	P			*6.	P/2		
115	P			*10	P/2	126/19	
73	L	120		19/131	P		
120	P			*15.P			*7.P/2
72	L	121		13/134.P			*42.P/1
96	P		(1954)	18/135	P		
100	P		(1955)	*72	P		
121	P						
*13	P/1	123					
118	P						
123	P						
46	L						
103	P1						
124	P						

#	C/A	HRN	DATE
20/2	P/2		
*58	P	126/28	
21/3	P/2		
24/138	P		
27/51	P		
28/75	P		
26/137	P	126/33	
34/85	P		
36/54	P		
*69	P		(1957)
41/70.L			(1958)
30/24	P	126/39	
33/50	P/1		
*46	P		
35/39	P	126/45	
38/52	P/2		
39/67	P		
40/65	P		
43/87	P		
44/93	P1		
45/116	P		
*73	NP		
*103	P2		
47/139	P	126/52	
50/141	P		
51/136	???		
52/144	P	126/55	
*55	P	126/56	
56A/20	L	129/65	
*7	P/1		
*23	P/1		(1958)
*31	P		(1959)
54/146	P		
59/147	P		
61/148	P		
62	P		
65/127	P		
*77	P		
84	P		
135:	HRNERROR		
138:	HRNERROR		
*17	NP	129/76	
*32	P		
*37	NP		
56/18	P1/1		
*57	P		
63/149	P		
66/4	P2		
67/1	P2		
70/150	P		
75/140	P		
76/12	P/2		
83/151	P		
*109	P		
*42	P/2	129/83	
93/152	P		
127/153	P		
*16	NP	129/85	
81/27	P		

#	C/A	HRN	DATE
*82	NP		
85/13	P/2		(1959)
87/142	P		(1960)
95/145	P		
102/30	P	129/95	
110/28	P		
116/36	P		
132/154	P		
133/155	P		
134/156	P		
*14	NP	134	
*22	NP		
*53	NP		
*56A.20	NP		
*56/18	P2/2		
*60	P/2		
*68	P/2		
92/9	P/2		
128/59	P		
*25	P	136	
*41/70	P		
*68	P/1		
117/41	P		
130/61	P		
131/63	P/1		(1960)
136/157	P		(1961)
137/158	P		
139/159	P	139	
139A/160	P	141	
139B/161	P	139B	
140/162	P	140	
141/163	P	141	
142/164	P	142	
*23.P/2		141	
*33/50	P/2		
*35/39	P/2		
*44/93	P2		
*71	P/2		
*74	NP		
*90	P2		
*116/36	P/N	A2	
*131/63	P/2		(1961)
143	DEVIL		(1962)
144/165	P		
145/166	P		
146	MUNCH		
147	ALICE		
148	NIGHTS		
*84	NP/NA2		
149	GORILLA		
150	GHOST		
151/45	P/2		
152/56	P/2		
153/35	P/2		
154/8	P/2		
155/38	P/2		
156	DOG	156	
157	QUEEN		
158/167	P		(1962)

#	C/A	HRN	DATE
158A	DR.NO		(1963)
159	MASTER		
160/168	P		
161	AENEID	157	
162	NORTH	156	
163	ARGO	157	

Classics Illustrated #16

Classics Illustrated #18

But the most significant new British titles are in the regular CI series. The British CI series contains 12 new covers and 15 new titles. The new covers are #s 14, 16(redrawn), 17, 20, 22, 37, 53, 73, 74, 77, 82 & 135 (US#43), of which three are quite valuable (53/74/135). Of the 15 new "titles," two are actually new art. #84.THE GOLD BUG has a second edition with HRN 141 with new cover & interior art. #116.TYPEE has a second edition with HRN 141 with the same cover but all-new art. The other 13 new British titles are 143, 146-150, 156, 157, 158A, 159, & 161-163. #158A.DR.NO may be the most sought-after of all the new British titles, but #163. THE ARGONAUTS is the rarest.

You can see from the list that there is only the 2/0 edition of #163. It appears that the "British" branch of the series was actually cutting back early. You may notice from the list that we have yet to find any 1/3 editions of many late titles: 135/138/142/151/152/153/154/155/158A/163. There was a collector who wrote to Thorpe & Porter in 1963 and got the official order list, and all those titles are omitted from the list, plus #51 and 20+ other titles. It lists #152 as Wild Animals. The British series never corrected that misprint. One issue we have wrestled with here is that many British editions are worth more in the U.S. than they are in England. American comics are quite expensive. A Mint set of British CI (1st editions) would be worth about US$5,000 (in England). A Mint set of U.S. CI (1st eds) is worth about US$28,000. American collectors are simply used to paying large amounts for comics, especially rare items. There is a great demand in America for British CI of new titles or covers, plus new Juniors, W.I., the ten hardback Deluxe, the two Giants, any Double Duos, or related items. So we are here caught in a dilemma. Should we list the value in England or should we list the "international" value? Is it fair for Americans to buy up all the new British titles so there are hardly any left for British collectors? Since this is the "British" comic book price guide, it seemed only fair to list current market value in England, not in America. But in our classics collectibles book series we address this international pricing dilemma in a comprehensive way. A great deal of research has been done on the artists who did the CI series.

The early U.S. artists were of little note, until Jerry Iger in 1945 took over as Art Director. His

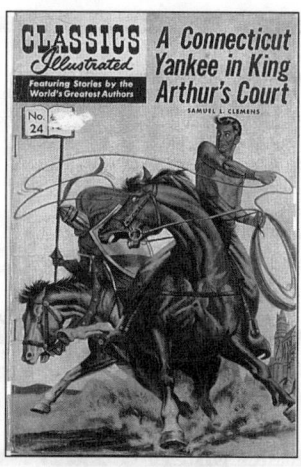

Classics Illustrated #24

N.MINT   N.MINT

brought in his "shop" of artists. Two of his artists became the most prominent CI artists - Henry C. Kiefer and Alex Blum. But by the mid-1950s, they were gone, and a new artist group (primarily former EC artists) had arrived. The most prominent later artists were Norman Nadel, George Evans & Gerald McCann. When CI production moved to Europe in 1962, British artists dominated: Norman Light (143 & 156), Mick Anglo (84, 148 & 150), Denis Gifford (146), and Jennifer Robertson (147 + Juniors). The art for #158.DR.NO was by Norman Nodel, originally done for a never-published U.S. Dell Movie Classic. The new art for 116.TYPEE was by American artist Luis Dominguez, to be the U.S. CI A2 version, but never issued here. The artist for 162.SAGA OF THE NORTH was Tomas Porto, from a Spanish artist group which became prominent in later CI titles.

Can anyone help us with artist info on other new British titles, such as THE AENEID and THE ARGONAUTS? British CI series ended about June of 1963. But the European CI operation, directed by a man named "Bo All" in Sweden, published another 67 CI titles from 1963 to 1976. In the early 1970s, a British publisher, Top Sellers, Ltd., published 24 more of those new European CI titles Double Duos (see below). Many British CI collectors are interested in the U.S. CI titles never issued in the British series. Here are those U.S. titles, with the British Pounds cost in GOOD-FINE-NEAR MINT for the cheapest edition of each title:

	Good	Fine	N.Mint
#21.3 FAMOUS MYSTERIES	£7.00	£22.00	£50.00
#92.COURTSHIP OF MILES STANDISH	£1.00	£2.00	£3.00
#26.FRANKENSTEIN	£1.00	£2.00	£3.00
#95.ALL QUIET ON-WESTERN FRONT	£2.00	£4.00	£7.00
#33.SHERLOCK HOLMES	£13.00	£38.00	£90.00
#102.THE WHITE COMPANY	£3.00	£6.00	£10.00
#44.MYSTERIES OF PARIS	£11.00	£32.00	£75.00
#110.A STUDY IN SCARLET	£4.00	£10.00	£22.00
#66.CLOISTER & THE HEARTH	£11.00	£32.00	£75.00
#117.CAPTAINS COURAGEOUS	£1.00	£2.00	£3.00
#76.THE PRISONER OF ZENDA	£1.00	£2.00	£3.00
#143.KIM	£1.00	£2.00	£3.00
#83.THE JUNGLE BOOK	£1.00	£2.00	£3.00
#169.NEGRO AMERICANS-EARLY YEARS	£4.00	£9.00	£18.00

Besides these new titles, there were also about 70 U.S. CI covers never issued in England, plus about 15 more internal art variations, plus the 34 titles with the CLASSIC COMICS logo. So there is a veritable CI collectibles pathway through the ocean between the U.S. and British series.

CLASSICS ILLUSTRATED - TERMINOLOGY

"HRN" =	highest number on reorder list (for HRNs of 126 or 129, also include the highest filled-in number: 12/19/28/33/39/45/52/65/76/83/85/95)
"price" =	front cover price (all "1/0" & "1/3": British; "1/6" = New Zealand, except for CI#s 13/14/25/40/74 = British; "2/0" = Australia, except for CI 2/6/7/10 = British; "1/16/2" = British/South Africa/Australia)
"prtd" =	printed in England/ USA/ Ireland/ France/ Netherlands/ Denmark/ Sweden/ Poland
"detail" =	identifying details ("ad-#2" = coming-next ad; "(r)" = reprint edit.)
"c/a" =	cover & interior ("L" = U.S. line drawn cover; "P" = U.S. painted cover; "NP" = new British painted cover; "/1" or "/2" = interior art version)
"NM" =	British Pounds value in NEAR MINT condition (GOOD-FINE-N.MINT ratio 1-3-5)

CI GIANT EDITIONS ("Illustrated Library of Great ... Stories")
- no dates (Fall 1952), no numbers, no CI reorder lists, hardback (RARE) (Mystery Giant and Gift Box also advertised but never issued)
nn. INDIAN (contained CI titles - 17, 22, 37, and 58) NM - 195
nn. ADVENTURE (contained CI titles - 2, 6, and 10) NM - 195

CLASSICS ILLUSTRATED DELUXE EDITIONS
(HARDBACK: WITH NEW WRAPAROUND COVERS)

- no dates (1953-1955), no numbers, no CI reorder lists, individual titles
(four others advertised but never issued; spines usually damaged)

NN (CI#15) UNCLE TOM'S CABIN	£65.00
NN (CI#104) BRING 'EM BACK ALIVE	£65.00
NN (CI#18) HUNCHBACK-NOTRE DAME	£65.00
NN (CI#106) BUFFALO BILL	£65.00
NN (CI#78) JOAN OF ARC	£65.00
NN (CI#107) KING OF-KHYBER RIFLES	£75.00
NN (CI#82) MASTER OF BALLANTRAE	£65.00
NN (CI#108) KNIGHTS OF-ROUND TABLE	£65.00
NN (CI#89) CRIME & PUNISHMENT	£65.00
NN (CI#112) KIT CARSON	£65.00

DOUBLE DUOS

(New European CI titles published by Top Sellers, Ltd., early 1970s) (digest-size b&w artwork, two 32-page titles in each volume)
(SCARCE - NEAR-MINT VALUE FOR EACH VOLUME ABOUT £35)

(1) VOYAGE TO THE FAR EAST, Fernao M.Pinto / THE BRIGANDS, Marie-Henri de Stendhal
(2) ATTACK ON THE MILL, Emile Zola / ESCAPE OF THE INCAS, William Prescott
(3) MARCH OF THE 10,000, Xenophon / SHIP FROM BUENOS AIRES, Herman Melville
(4) THE OPEN BOAT, Stephen Crane / THE DENVER EXPRESS, A.A.Hayes
(5) SAILING UNCHARTED WATERS, John Fiske / THE BURMA ROAD, Al Sundel
(6) CONQUEST OF PERU, William Prescott / THE WANDERING HORSEMEN, Nicolai Leskov
(7) THE BLUE HOTEL, Stephen Crane / A TERRIBLE REVENGE, Nicolai Gogol
(8) THE BATTLE FOR JERUSALEM, Josephus / CASTLE OF OTRANTO, Horace Walpole
9. DEATH OF CAPTAIN COOK, Jms.Cook/Jms.King / YOUNG CARTHAGINIAN, G.A.Henty
10. QUEST FOR THE GRAIL, W.von Eschenbach / SEVEN WHO WERE HANGED, Leonid Andreyev
11. WRECK OF THE SAO JOAO, Juan Fernandez / WARLORD OF MEXICO, Fr.Diego Duran
12. MARTIN EDEN, Jack London / THE APOSTLE OF THE INDIES, John Fiske

#	BACKNO	COVERNO	PRINT	DETAILS	COVERART	N.M
1(US#19) HUCKLEBERRY FINN, MARK TWAIN						
1a)	129	2/0	Dmk	E19:ad-#2	P/2	£7.00
1b)	129/12	1/3	Ire	E19:ad-#2	"	£7.00
2a)	129/76	1/3	Ire	(r)	"	£3.00
2b)	129/76	2/0	Ire	(r)	"	£3.00
3)	129/85	1/3	Swe	(r)	"	£3.00
4)	141	1/3	Pol	(r)	"	£3.00
2.IVANHOE, SIR WALTER SCOTT (#20-P/2)						
1)	77-16T	2/(B)	Eng	stf.cvr-LOGO	L/1	£17.00

	BACKNO	COVERNO	PRINT	DETAILS	COVERART	N.MINT
2 (US#47) 20,000 LEAGUES UNDER-SEA, VERNE						
1a)	129	2/0	Dmk	E20:ad-#3-LOGO	P	£7.00
1b)	129	1/6	Dmk	E20:ad-#3	"	£7.00
1c)	129/12	1/3	Ire	E20:ad-#3	"	£7.00
2a)	126/39	2/0	Eng	(r)	"	£3.00
2b)	126/39	1/3	Eng	(r)	"	£3.00
2c)	126/39	1/3	Ire	(r)	"	£3.00
	126/19	**1/6**	**Dmk**	**PC**		
3a)	129/65	2/0	Eng	(r)	"	£3.00
3b)	129/65	1/3	Eng	(r)	"	£3.00
4a)	134	1/3	Pol	(r)	"	£3.00
4b)	134	1/3	Swe	(r)	"	£3.00
3. (US#34) MYSTERIOUS ISLAND, JULES VERNE						
1a)	129/11	1/6	Dmk	E21:ad-#4	P	£7.00
1b)	129/11	1/6	Dmk	E21:ad-#4	"	£7.00
1c)	129/12	1/3	Ire	E21:ad-#4	"	£7.00
2)	129/85	1/3	Swe	(r)	"	£3.00
3a)	136	1/3	USA	(r)	"	£3.00
3b)	136	2/0	USA	(r)	"	£3.00
4a)	141	1/6	Swe	(r)	"	£3.00
4b)	141	1/3	Pol	(r)	"	£3.00
	141	**1/5**	**Swe**	**PC**		
4. (US#128) MACBETH, WILLIAM SHAKESPEARE						
1a)	129/11	1/6	Dmk	E22:ad-#64	P	£7.00
1b)	129/11	1/6	Dmk	E22:ad-#64	"	£7.00
1c)	129/12	1/3	Ire	E22:ad-#64	"	£7.00
2)	134	1/3	Swe	(r)	"	£3.00
3)	141	1/3	Pol	(r)	"	£3.00
5. MOBY DICK, HERMAN MELVILLE						
1a)	129	2/0	Dmk	E17:ad-#29	P/2	£7.00
1b)	129	1/3	Ire	E17:ad-#29	"	£7.00
2)	126/33	1/3	Frn	(r)	"	£3.00
3)	129/65	1/3	Eng	(r)	"	£3.00
4a)	129/76	2/0	Ire	(r)	"	£3.00
4b)	129/76	1/3	Ire	(r)	"	£3.00
5a)	134	1/6	Swe	(r)	"	£3.00
5b)	134	1/3	Swe	(r)	"	£3.00
	134	**1/3**	**Swe**	**PC-A2**		
6)	157	2/0	Pol	(r)	"	£3.00
6. A TALE OF TWO CITIES, CHARLES DICKENS						
1)	77-16T	2/(B)	Eng	stiff cover	L/1	£17.00
2)	121	1/16/16/2	Eng	GB/SA/NA/AU	"	£9.00
	121	**1/16/16/2**	**Eng**	**LDC-A1**		
3a)	126/12	2/0	Dmk	E30:ad-#10	P/2	£6.00
3b)	126/12	1/3	Dmk	E30:ad-#10	"	£6.00
4a)	129/65	2/0	Eng	(r)	"	£3.00
4b)	129/65	1/3	Eng	(r)	"	£3.00
4c)	129/65	1/3	none	(r)	"	£3.00
	141	**1/6**	**Swe**	**PC-A2**		
5)	157	2/0	Pol	(r)	"	£3.00
7. ROBIN HOOD (ANONYMOUS)						
1)	77-16T	2/(B)	Eng	stiff cover	L/1	£17.00
2a)	126/19	1/3	Ire	1st SPCL ad	P/2	£5.00
2b)	126/19	1/3	Ire	(r)	"	£5.00
3)	126/28	1/3	Dmk	(E41-no ad)	"	£3.00
4)	126/45	1/6	Ire	(r)	"	£3.00
5a)	129/65	none		A1 or A2?	P/?	£5.00
5b)	129/65	1/3	none	A1!	P/1	£5.00
6)	129/83	1/6	Ire	HRN:153error	P/2	£3.00
7a)	134	1/6	Swe	(r)	P/2	£3.00
7b)	134	1/3	Swe	(r)	"	£3.00
	156	**1/3**	**Swe**	**PC-A2**		
8. (US#81) THE ODYSSEY, HOMER						
1a)	129/12	2/0	Dmk	E25:ad-#97	P	£7.00
1b)	129/12	1/6	Dmk	E25:ad-#97	"	£7.00
1c)	126/12	1/3	Dmk	E25:ad-#97	"	£7.00
2a)	134	1/3	Swe	(r)	"	£3.00
2b)	134	1/3	Pol	(r)	"	£3.00
3)	141	1/3	Pol	(r)	"	£3.00
9(US#130) CAESAR'S CONQUESTS, J.CAESAR						
1a)	126/12	2/0	Dmk	E28:ad-#123	P	£7.00
1b)	126/12	1/6	Dmk	E28:ad-#123	"	£7.00
1c)	126/12	1/6	Dmk	E28:ad-#123	"	£7.00
2a)	129/83	2/0	Ire	HRN:154error	"	£3.00
2b)	129/83	1/3	Ire	HRN:154error	"	£3.00
3)	134	1/6	Swe	(r)	"	£3.00
10.ROBINSON CRUSOE, DANIEL DEFOE						
1)	77-16T	2/(B)	Eng	stiff cover	L/1	£17.00
2a)	126/19	2/0	Dmk	E31:ad-#19	P/2	£6.00
2b)	126/19	1/3	Dmk	E31:ad-#19	"	£6.00
3)	126/39	1/3	Ire	(r)	"	£3.00
4a)	126/45	2/0	Ire	(r)	"	£3.00
4b)	126/45	1/6	Ire	(r)	"	£3.00
4c)	126/45	1/3	Ire	(r)	"	£3.00
5)	129/83	1/3	Ire	HRN:153error	"	£3.00
6a)	134	1/6	Swe	(r)	"	£3.00
6b)	134	1/3	Swe	(r)	"	£3.00
11.(US#133) THE TIME MACHINE, H.G.WELLS						
1a)	129/12	2/0	Eng	(no ad)	P	£6.00
1b)	129/12	1/3	Eng	(no ad)	"	£6.00
2a)	126/45	2/0	Ire	(r)	"	£3.00
2b)	126/45	1/3	Ire	(r)	"	£3.00

12(US#132) THE DARK FRIGATE, C.B.HAWES

						N.MINT
1a)	129/12	2/0	Eng	(no ad)	P	£6.00
1b)	129/12	1/3	Eng	(no ad)	"	£6.00
2a)	129/65	2/0	Eng	Title:132error	"	£5.00
2b)	129/65	1/3	Eng	Title:132error	"	£5.00
3)	129/76	1/3	Ire	(r)	"	£3.00
4)	134	1/3	Pol	(r)	"	£3.00
5a)	141	2/0	Swe	(r)	"	£3.00
5b)	141	1/6	Swe	(r)	"	£3.00

13.DR.JEKYLL/MR.HYDE,STEVENSON (#85-P/2)

1)	77-16T	1/6(B)	Eng	stiff cover	L/1	£17.00
2)	121	1/16/16/2	Eng	GB/SA/NZ/AU	P/1	£8.00

13.(US#134) ROMEO & JULIET, SHAKESPEARE

1a)	126/19	2/0	Dmk	E34:ad-#18	P	£7.00
1b)	126/19	1/6	Dmk	E34:ad-#18	"	£7.00
1c)	126/19	1/3	Dmk	E34:ad-#18	"	£7.00
2)	134	1/3	Swe	(r)	"	£3.00

14.WESTWARD HO!, CHARLES KINGSLEY

1a)	77-16T	1/6(B)	Nth	indicia:ifc	L	£30.00
1b)	77-16T	1/6(B)	Nth	indicia:obc	"	£30.00
2)	112	1/16/2	Eng	GB/SA/AU	"	£25.00
3a)	134	2/0	Pol	NEW BRIT.CVR.	NP	£40.00
3b)	134	1/3	Pol	(r)	"	£40.00
4a)	141	2/0	Dmk	(r)	"	£40.00
4b)	141	1/6	Dmk	(r)	"	£40.00
4c)	141	1/3	Dmk	(r)	"	£40.00

15.UNCLE TOM'S CABIN, HARRIET B.STOWE

1a)	82	1/16/19	Ire	no DLX ad	L	£14.00
1b)	82	1/16/19	Ire	ad:4-DLX	"	£14.00
2a)	126/19	2/0	Dmk	E33:ad-#13	P	£6.00
2b)	126/19	1/6	Dmk	E33:ad-#13	"	£6.00
2c)	126/19	1/3	Dmk	E33:ad-#13	"	£6.00
3a)	129/65	2/0	Ire	(r)	"	£3.00
3b)	129/65	1/3	Ire	(r)	"	£3.00
3c)	129/65	1/3	none	(r)	"	£3.00
	129/76	**1/3**	**none**	**PC**		
4)	134	1/3	Swe	(r)	"	£3.00

16.GULLIVER'S TRAVELS, JONATHAN SWIFT
(#16.THE TALISMAN - error!, see #111)

1)	82(US)	1/3	Nth	"11/51"	L	£19.00
2a)	129/85	2/0	Swe	REDRAWN CVR.	RP	£9.00
2b)	129/85	1/3	Swe	(r)	"	£9.00
3a)	141	1/6	Dmk	(r)	"	£9.00
3b)	141	1/3	Dmk	(r)	"	£9.00

17.THE DEERSLAYER, JAMES FENIMORE COOPER

1)	77-10T	1/3	Eng	"3/52"	L	£19.00
2a)	129/76	2/0	Eng	NEW BRIT.CVR.	NP	£30.00
2b)	129/76	1/3	Eng	(r)	"	£30.00
3)	129/85	1/3	Swe	(r)	"	£30.00
4a)	134	2/0	Pol	(r)	"	£30.00
4b)	134	1/3	Pol	(r)	"	£30.00
5)	141	2/0	Swe	(r)	"	£30.00

18.HUNCHBACK-NOTRE DAME,V.HUGO (#56-P/2)

1a)	82	1/16/19	Ire	no DLX ad	L/1	£14.00
1b)	82	1/16/19	Ire	ad:4-DLX	"	£14.00
	121	**Soft.Dlx**	**NPC**			

18(US#135) WATERLOO, ERCKMANN-CHATRIAN

1a)	126/19	2/0	Dmk	(E35-no ad)	P	£6.00
1b)	126/19	1/6	Dmk	(E35-no ad)	"	£6.00
1c)	126/19	1/3	Dmk	(E35-no ad)	"	£6.00
2a)	134	2/0	Pol	(r)	"	£3.00
2b)	134	1/3	Pol	(r)	"	£3.00
2c)	134	1/3	Swe	(r)	"	£3.00
	134	**1/3**	**Pol**			
	134	**1/3**	**Swe**			

19 (US#130) COVERED WAGON, EMERSON HOUGH

1a)	126/19	2/0	Dmk	E32:ad-#15	P	£7.00
1b)	126/19	1/3	Dmk	E32:ad-#15	"	£7.00
2)	126/33	1/3	Ire	(r)	"	£3.00
3a)	126/45	2/0	Ire	(r)	"	£3.00
3b)	126/45	1/3	Ire	(r)	"	£3.00
4a)	129/65	2/0	Eng	(r)	"	£3.00
4b)	129/65	1/3	Eng	(r)	"	£3.00
5)	129/85	2/0	Eng	(r)	"	£3.00
6)	141	1/3	Swe	(r)	"	£9.00
7)	156	2/0	Swe	(r)	"	£9.00

20 (US#2) IVANHOE, WALTER SCOTT (#2-L/1)

1a)	126/19	2/0	Dmk	(E38-no ad)	P/2	£6.00
1b)	126/19	1/6	Dmk	(E38-no ad)	"	£3.00
1c)	126/19	1/3	Dmk	(E38-no ad)	"	£3.00
2a)	129/83	2/0	Ire	HRN:153error	"	£3.00
2b)	129/83	1/3	Ire	HRN:153error	"	£3.00
3)	157	2/0	Swe	(r)	"	£3.00

21(US#3) COUNT-MONTE CRISTO, ALEX.DUMAS

1a)	126/28	2/0	Dmk	(E40-no ad)	P/2	£6.00
1b)	126/28	1/6	Dmk	(E40-no ad)	"	£6.00
1c)	126/28	1/3	Dmk	(E40-no ad)	"	£6.00
	126/28	**1/6**	**Dmk**	**PC-A2**		
2a)	129/65	2/0	Eng	(r)	"	£3.00
2b)	129/65	1/3	Eng	(r)	"	£3.00

22.THE PATHFINDER, JAMES FENIMORE COOPER

1)	77-10T	1/3	Eng	"2/52"	L	£19.00

						N.MINT
2a)	126/45	2/0	Dmk	(r)	"	£5.00
2b)	126/45	1/6	Dmk	(r)	"	£5.00
2c)	126/45	1/3	Dmk	(r)	"	£5.00
3a)	129/65	2/0	Ire	(r)	"	£5.00
3b)	129/65	1/3	Ire	(r)	"	£5.00
4a)	129/76	2/0	Eng	(r)	"	£5.00
4b)	129/76	1/3	Eng	(r)	"	£5.00
5)	134	1/3	Pol	NEW BRIT.CVR.	NP	£40.00
6)	141	1/6	Swe	(r)	"	£40.00

23.OLIVER TWIST, CHARLES DICKENS

1a)	125	2/0	Eng	(no ad)	L/1	£8.00
1b)	125	1/6	Eng	(no ad)	"	£8.00
1c)	125	1/3	Eng	(no ad)	"	£8.00
	125	**1/6**	**Eng**	**LDC-A1**		
2a)	129/65	2/0	Eng	(r)	P/1	£5.00
2b)	129/65	1/3	Eng	(r)	"	£5.00
3)	129/76	1/3	Eng	(r)	P/?	£4.00
4)	141	1/3	Swe	MIRROR CVR.	P/2	£6.00

24(US#138) JOURNEY-CENTER-EARTH, J.VERNE

1a)	126/28	2/0	Dmk	HRN:138error	P	£6.00
1b)	126/28	1/3	Dmk	HRN:138error	"	£6.00
2)	141	1/6	Swe	(r)	"	£3.00

25.TWO YEARS BEFORE-MAST, RICHARD H.DANA

1)	77-16T	1/6(B)	Eng	stiff cover	L	£14.00
2)	112	1/16/2	Eng	GB/SA/AU	"	£8.00
3a)	136	2/0	USA	(r)	P	£4.00
3b)	136	1/3	USA	(r)	"	£4.00
4a)	141	1/3	Dmk	(r)	"	£3.00
4b)	141	1/3	Pol	(r)	"	£3.00
	141	**1/6**	**Dmk**	**PC**		

26(US#137) A LITTLE SAVAGE, FRED.MARRYAT

1a)	126/33	2/0	Dmk	obc-list	P	£6.00
1b)	126/33	1/3	Dmk	obc-list	"	£6.00
2)	129/76	1/3	Ire	(r)	"	£3.00
3a)	134	2/0	Swe	(r)	"	£3.00
3b)	134	1/3	Swe	(r)	"	£3.00

27(US#51) THE SPY, JAMES FENIMORE COOPER

1a)	126/28	2/0	Ire	(0)	P	£6.00
1b)	126/28	1/6	Ire	(0)	"	£6.00
1b)	126/28	1/3	Ire	(0)	"	£6.00
2a)	129/65	2/0	Eng	(r)	"	£3.00
2b)	129/76	1/3	Eng	(r)	"	£3.00
3)	129/76	1/3	none	(r)	"	£3.00
4a)	141	1/6	Swe	(r)	"	£3.00
4b)	141	1/3	Swe	(r)	"	£3.00
	141	**1/3**	**Pol**	**PC**		

28(US#75) LADY OF THE LAKE, WALTER SCOTT

1a)	126/28	2/0	Ire	(0)	P	£6.00
1b)	126/28	1/6	Ire	(0)	"	£6.00
1b)	126/28	1/3	Ire	(0)	"	£6.00
2)	129/95	1/3	USA	(r)	"	£3.00

29.PRINCE & THE PAUPER, MARK TWAIN

1a)	129	2/0	Ire	E18:ad-#1	P	£6.00
1b)	129	1/6	Dmk	E18:ad-#1	"	£6.00
1c)	129	1/3	Ire	E18:ad-#1	"	£6.00
2a)	129/76	1/3	Eng	(r)	"	£3.00
2b)	129/76	1/3	Ire	(r)	"	£3.00
2c)	129/76	1/3	none	(r)	"	£3.00
3)	141	1/6	Swe	(r)	"	£3.00

30(US#24) A CONNECTICUT YANKEE IN KING ARTHUR'S COURT, MARK TWAIN

1a)	126/39	2/0	Ire	(0)	P/2	£6.00
1b)	126/39	1/6	Ire	(0)	"	£6.00
1c)	129/76	1/3	Ire	(0)	"	£6.00
2)	129/76	1/3	Eng	(r)	"	£3.00
3)	129/85	1/3	Swe	(r)	"	£3.00
4)	141	1/6	Swe	(r)	"	£3.00

31.THE BLACK ARROW, R.L.STEVENSON

1a)	125	2/0	Eng	(no ad)	L	£8.00
1b)	125	1/3	Eng	(no ad)	"	£8.00
2a)	129/65	2/0	Pol	(r)	P	£4.00
2b)	129/65	1/3	Pol	(r)	"	£4.00
3a)	129/76	2/0	Ire	(r)	"	£3.00
3b)	129/76	1/3	Ire	(r)	"	£3.00

32.LORNA DOONE, RICHARD D.BLACKMORE

1a)	125	2/0	Eng	(no ad)	L	£8.00
1b)	125	1/6	Eng	(no ad)	"	£8.00
1c)	125	1/3	Eng	(no ad)	"	£8.00
2)	129/76	1/3	Ire	(r)	P	£4.00
3)	134	1/3	Pol	(r)	"	£3.00
4)	141	2/0	Pol	(r)	"	£3.00

33(US#50) TOM SAWYER, MARK TWAIN

1a)	126/39	2/0	Ire	(0)	P/1	£6.00
1b)	126/39	1/6	Ire	(0)	"	£6.00
1c)	126/39	1/3	Ire	(0)	"	£6.00
2)	129/76	1/3	none	(r)	"	£3.00
3)	141	2/0	Swe	(r)	P/2	£4.00
4)	157	2/0	Pol	(r)	"	£3.00

34(US#85) THE SEA WOLF, JACK LONDON

1a)	126/34	2/0	Dmk	(0)	P	£6.00
1b)	126/33	1/6	Dmk	(0)	"	£6.00
1c)	126/34	1/3	Dmk	(0) LOGO var.	"	£6.00
	126/33	**1/3**	**Dmk**	**PC**		

N.MINT   N.MINT

Ref	Issue	Grade	Pub	Note	Code	"	N.MINT
	126/33	1/6	Dmk	PC			
	126/33	2/0	Dmk	PC			
	126/34	1/3	Dmk	PC			
	126/34	1/6	Dmk	PC			
	126/34	2/0	Dmk	PC			
2a)	126/39	2/0	Ire	(r)		"	£4.00
2b)	126/39	1/6	Ire	(r)		"	£4.00
2c)	126/39	1/3	Ire	(r)		"	£4.00
3)	129/65	1/3	Eng	(r)		"	£3.00
4a)	134	1/6	Swe	(r)		"	£3.00
4b)	134	1/3	Swe	(r)		"	£3.00

35(US#39) JANE EYRE, CHARLOTTE BRONTE

Ref	Issue	Grade	Pub	Note	Code	"	N.MINT
1a)	126/45	2/0	Ire	(0)	P/1		£6.00
1b)	126/45	1/3	Ire	(0)	"		£6.00
2a)	129/76	2/0	Eng	(r)	"		£3.00
2b)	129/76	1/3	Eng	(r)	"		£3.00
3a)	129/95	2/0	USA	(r)	"		£3.00
3b)	129/95	1/3	USA	(r)	"		£3.00
4)	141	2/0	Swe	(r)	P/2		£5.00

36(US#54) MAN IN-IRON MASK, ALEX.DUMAS

Ref	Issue	Grade	Pub	Note	Code	"	N.MINT
1a)	126/33	2/0	Dmk	(0)	P/2		£6.00
1b)	126/33	1/6	Dmk	(0)	"		£6.00
1c)	126/33	1/3	Dmk	(0)	"		£6.00
2)	129/65	1/3	Eng	(r)	"		£3.00
3)	129/85	1/3	Eng	(r)	"		£3.00
4a)	134	1/3	Pol	(r)	"		£3.00
4b)	134	1/3	Swe	(r)	"		£3.00

37.THE PIONEERS, JAMES FENIMORE COOPER

Ref	Issue	Grade	Pub	Note	Code	"	N.MINT
1)	77-10T	1/3	Eng	"2/52"	L		£19.00
2)	129/65	1/3	Eng	(r)	"		£7.00
3a)	129/76	2/0	Eng	NEW BRIT.CVR.	NP		£30.00
3b)	129/76	1/3	Eng	(r)	"		£30.00
3c)	129/76	1/3	Eng	(r)	"		£30.00

38.(US#52) HOUSE-7 GABLES, N.HAWTHORNE

Ref	Issue	Grade	Pub	Note	Code	"	N.MINT
1a)	126/45	2/0	Ire	(0)	P/2		£6.00
1b)	126/45	1/3	Ire	(0)	"		£6.00
2a)	129/85	2/0	Swe	(r)	"		£3.00
2b)	129/85	1/3	none	(r)	"		£3.00
3)	141	1/3	Pol	(r)	"		£3.00

39(US#67) SCOTTISH CHIEFS, JANE PORTER

Ref	Issue	Grade	Pub	Note	Code	"	N.MINT
1a)	126/45	2/0	Dmk	(0)	P		£6.00
1b)	126/45	1/6	Dmk	(0)	"		£6.00
1c)	126/45	1/3	Dmk	(0)	"		£6.00
2a)	129/65	2/0	Eng	(r)	"		£3.00
2b)	129/65	1/3	Eng	(r)	"		£3.00
3)	129/85	2/0	Swe	(r)	"		£3.00
4a)	134	1/6	Swe	(r)	"		£3.00
4b)	134	1/3	Swe	(r)	"		£3.00

40.POE'S MYSTERIES (ONLY ONE EDITION)

Ref	Issue	Grade	Pub	Note	Code	"	N.MINT
1)	77-19T	1/6(B)	Eng	stiff cover	L		£30.00

40.BENJAMIN FRANKLIN (AUTOBIOGRAPHY)

Ref	Issue	Grade	Pub	Note	Code	"	N.MINT
1)	126/33	1/3	Dmk	(0)	P		£8.00
2a)	126/45	2/0	Dmk	(r)	"		£5.00
2b)	126/45	1/6	Dmk	(r)	"		£5.00
2c)	126/45	1/3	Dmk	(r)	"		£5.00
3)	129/76	1/3	none	(r)	"		£3.00
4)	129/95	1/3	USA	(r)	"		£3.00
5a)	141	1/3	Swe	(r)	"		£3.00
5b)	141	1/3	Pol	(r)	"		£3.00

41.THE PILOT, JAMES FENIMORE COOPER

Ref	Issue	Grade	Pub	Note	Code	"	N.MINT
1)	126/33	1/3	Dmk	(0)	L		£9.00
2a)	126/45	2/0	Dmk	(r)	"		£6.00
2b)	126/45	1/6	Dmk	(r)	"		£6.00
2c)	126/45	1/3	Dmk	(r)	"		£6.00
3a)	136	2/0	USA	(r)	P		£4.00
3b)	136	1/3	USA	(r)	"		£4.00
4a)	141	1/6	Swe	(r)	"		£3.00
4b)	141	1/3	Pol	(r)	"		£3.00

42.SWISS FAMILY ROBINSON, JOHANN WYSS

Ref	Issue	Grade	Pub	Note	Code	"	N.MINT
1)	112	1/16/2	Eng	ad:13-DLX	L/1		£10.00
2)	121	1/16/2	Eng	GB/SA/AU	"		£8.00
3a)	126/19	2/0	Ire	(no ad)	P/1		£6.00
3b)	126/19	1/3	Ire	(no ad)	"		£6.00
4)	126/33	1/3	Ire	(r)	"		£4.00
5)	126/56	1/3	Eng	(r)	"		£4.00
6)	129/65	1/3	Eng	(A1 or A2?)	P/?		£4.00
	129/65	1/3	Eng	PC-A1?			
	129/76	1/3	none	PC-A1?			
7)	129/83	1/3	Ire	(r)	P/2		£4.00
8)	129/85	1/3	Swe	(r)	"		£4.00

43(US#87) A MIDSUMMER NIGHT'S DREAM, WILLIAM SHAKESPEARE

Ref	Issue	Grade	Pub	Note	Code	"	N.MINT
1a)	126/45	1/3	Dmk	(0)	P		£6.00
1b)	126/45	1/3	Dmk	(0)	"		£6.00
2a)	129/52	2/0	Dmk	(r)	"		£4.00
2b)	129/52	1/3	Dmk	(r)	"		£4.00
	129/52	2/0	Dmk	PC			
3)	129/76	1/3	none	(r)	"		£4.00

44(US#93) PUDD'NHEAD WILSON, MARK TWAIN

Ref	Issue	Grade	Pub	Note	Code	"	N.MINT
1a)	126/45	2/0	Dmk	(0)	P1		£6.00
1b)	126/45	1/6	Dmk	(0)	"		£6.00
1c)	126/45	1/3	Dmk	(0)	"		£6.00
2a)	141	1/6	Dmk	(r)	P2		£5.00

Ref	Issue	Grade	Pub	Note	Code	"	N.MINT
2b)	141	1/3	Dmk	(r)		"	£5.00

45(US#116) THE BOTTLE IMP, R.L.STEVENSON

Ref	Issue	Grade	Pub	Note	Code	"	N.MINT
1a)	126/45	2/0	Dmk	(0)	P		£6.00
1b)	126/45	1/6	Dmk	(0)	"		£6.00
1c)	126/45	1/3	Dmk	(0)	"		£6.00
	126/45	1/6	Dmk	PC			
2a)	126/52	2/0	Dmk	(r)	"		£5.00
2b)	129/52	1/3	Dmk	(r)	"		£5.00
3)	134	1/3	Pol	(r)	"		£3.00
4)	141	1/6	Swe	(r)	"		£3.00

46.KIDNAPPED, ROBERT LOUIS STEVENSON

Ref	Issue	Grade	Pub	Note	Code	"	N.MINT
1a)	123	2/0	Eng	(0)	L		£8.00
1b)	123	1/0	Eng	(0)	"		£8.00
2a)	126/39	2/0	Ire	(r)	P		£5.00
2b)	126/39	1/6	Ire	(r)	"		£5.00
2c)	126/39	1/3	Ire	(r)	"		£5.00
3a)	129/76	1/3	Ire	(r)	"		£3.00
3b)	129/76	1/3	Eng	(r)	"		£3.00
4a)	134	2/0	Pol	(r)	"		£3.00
4b)	134	1/3	Pol	(r)	"		£3.00
5)	141	1/6	Swe	(r)	"		£3.00

47(US#139) IN-REIGN OF TERROR, G.A.HENTY

Ref	Issue	Grade	Pub	Note	Code	"	N.MINT
1a)	129/52	2/0	Dmk	(0)	P		£6.00
1b)	129/52	1/3	Dmk	(0)	"		£6.00
2)	129/95	1/3	USA	(r)	"		£3.00
3)	141	1/6	Swe	(r)	"		£3.00

48.DAVID COPPERFIELD, CHARLES DICKENS

Ref	Issue	Grade	Pub	Note	Code	"	N.MINT
1)	115	1/16/2	Eng	ad:14-DLX	P		£7.00
2a)	126/39	2/0	Ire	(r)	"		£3.00
2b)	126/39	2/0	Ire	(r)	"		£3.00
2c)	126/39	1/6	Ire	(r)	"		£3.00
2d)	126/39	1/3	Ire	(r)	"		£3.00
3)	126/56	1/3	Eng	(r)	"		£3.00
4a)	129/76	1/3	Ire	(r)	"		£3.00
4b)	129/76	1/3	Eng	(r)	"		£3.00
5)	157	2/0	Pol	(r)	"		£3.00

49.ALICE IN WONDERLAND, LEWIS CARROLL

Ref	Issue	Grade	Pub	Note	Code	"	N.MINT
1)	82(US)	1/3	Eng	"10/51"	L		£25.00
2a)	124	2/0	Dmk	E1:ad-#105	P		£8.00
2b)	125	1/3	Ire	E1:ad-#105-LOGO	"		£8.00
3)	129/65	1/3	Eng	(r)	"		£4.00
4)	129/76	?	?		"		£4.00
5)	141	?	Pol	(r)	"		£4.00

50(US#141) CASTLE DANGEROUS, W.SCOTT

Ref	Issue	Grade	Pub	Note	Code	"	N.MINT
1a)	129/52	2/0	Dmk	(0)	P		£6.00
1b)	129/52	1/3	Dmk	(0)	"		£6.00
2a)	129/83	2/0	Ire	HRN:154error	"		£3.00
2b)	129/83	1/3	Ire	HRN:154error	"		£3.00
3)	134	1/3	Pol	(r)	"		£3.00
4a)	141	1/3	Dmk	(r)	"		£3.00
4b)	141	1/3	Dmk	(r)	"		£3.00

51(US#136) LORD JIM, JOSEPH CONRAD

(we believe that #51 does not exist!)

52(US#144) FIRST MEN IN-MOON, H.G.WELLS

Ref	Issue	Grade	Pub	Note	Code	"	N.MINT
1a)	126/55	2/0	Ire	(0)	P		£6.00
1b)	126/55	1/3	Ire	(0)	"		£6.00
2a)	129/85	2/0	Swe	(r)	"		£3.00
2b)	129/85	1/3	Swe	(r)	"		£3.00
3)	141	1/6	Swe	(r)	"		£3.00

53.A CHRISTMAS CAROL, CHARLES DICKENS

Ref	Issue	Grade	Pub	Note	Code	"	N.MINT
1a)	124	2/0	Eng	(no ad)	L		£18.00
1b)	124	1/6	Eng	(no ad)	"		£18.00
1c)	124	1/3	Eng	(no ad)	"		£18.00
	124	1/6	Eng	LDC			
2)	134	1/3	Pol	NEW BRIT.CVR.	NP		£100.00
3)	141	2/0	Pol	(r)	"		£100.00

54(US#146) WITH FIRE & SWORD, SIENKIEWICZ

Ref	Issue	Grade	Pub	Note	Code	"	N.MINT
1a)	126/65	2/0	Ire	(0)	P		£6.00
1b)	126/65	1/3	Ire	(0)	"		£6.00
1c)	126/65	1/3	none	(0)	"		£6.00
2a)	129/85	2/0	Swe	(r)	"		£3.00
2b)	129/85	1/3	Swe	(r)	"		£3.00

55.SILAS MARNER, GEORGE ELIOT

Ref	Issue	Grade	Pub	Note	Code	"	N.MINT
1)	126/56	1/3	Eng	(0)	P		£6.00
2a)	129/95	2/0	USA	(r)	"		£3.00
2b)	129/95	1/3	USA	(r)	"		£3.00
3)	141	1/6	Swe	(r)	"		£3.00

56(US#18) HUNCHBACK-NOTRE DAME (+ SEE #18)

Ref	Issue	Grade	Pub	Note	Code	"	N.MINT
1)	129/76	1/3	none	(L/1-#18)	P1/1		8.00
2a)	134	2/0	Swe	(r)	P2/2		5.00
2b)	134	1/3	Swe	(r)	"		£5.00

56A (US#20) CORSICAN BROTHERS, A.DUMAS

Ref	Issue	Grade	Pub	Note	Code	"	N.MINT
1)	129/65	1/3	Eng	(0)	L		£20.00
2a)	134	2/0	Pol	NEW BRIT.CVR.	NP		£25.00
2b)	134	1/3	Pol	(r)	"		£25.00
3a)	141	1/6	Dmk	(r)	"		£25.00
3b)	141	1/3	Dmk	(r)	"		£25.00

57.SONG OF HIAWATHA, HENRY W.LONGFELLOW

Ref	Issue	Grade	Pub	Note	Code	"	N.MINT
1)	115	1/16/2	Eng	(ad:12-DLX)	L		£9.00
2)	121	1/16/2	Eng	(r)	"		£6.00
3a)	129/76	2/0	Eng	(r)	P		£4.00
3b)	129/76	1/3	Eng	(r)	"		£4.00

N.MINT

4)	129/95	1/3	USA	(r)	"	£3.00

58.THE PRAIRIE, JAMES FENIMORE COOPER

1)	77-10T	1/3	Eng	"3/52"	L	£19.00
2a)	126/28	2/0	Dmk	(E39-no ad)	P	£5.00
2b)	126/28	1/6	Dmk	(r)	"	£5.00
2c)	126/28	1/3	Dmk	(r)	"	£5.00
3a)	129/65	2/0	Ire	(r)	"	£3.00
3b)	129/65	1/3	Ire	(r)	"	£3.00
4)	141	1/3	Swe	(r)	"	£3.00
	141	**1/6**	**Swe**	**PC**		
5)	156	2/0	Swe	(r)	"	£3.00

59(US#147) BEN-HUR, LEW WALLACE

1a)	129/65	2/0	Ire	(0)	P	£6.00
1b)	129/65	1/3	Ire	(0)	"	£6.00
2)	129/85	1/3	Swe	(r)	"	£3.00
3)	157	2/0	Pol	(r)	"	£3.00

60.BLACK BEAUTY, ANNA SEWELL

1)	82(US)	1/3	Eng	"11/51"	L/1	£19.00
2)	134	2/0	Swe	(E122)	P/2	£7.00

61(US#148) THE BUCCANEER (MOVIE)

1a)	126/65	1/3	Ire	(0)	P	£6.00
1b)	126/65	1/6	Ire	(0)	"	£6.00
1c)	126/65	1/3	Ire	(0)	"	£6.00
2)	141	1/6	Swe	(r)	"	£3.00

62.WESTERN STORIES, BRET HARTE

1)	129/65	1/3	Eng	(0)	P	£6.00
2)	129/83	1/3	Ire	HRN:153error	"	£3.00
3a)	134	2/0	Pol	(r)	"	£3.00
3b)	134	1/3	Pol	(r)	"	£3.00

63(US#149) OFF ON A COMET, JULES VERNE

1a)	129/76	2/0	Ire	(0)	P	£6.00
1b)	129/76	1/3	Ire	(0)	"	£6.00
2)	141	1/6	Swe	(r)	"	£3.00

64.TREASURE ISLAND, ROBERT L.STEVENSON

1)	82(US)	1/3	Nth	"1/52"	L	£19.00
2a)	129/12	2/0	Dmk	E23:ad-#108	P	£5.00
2b)	129/12	1/6	Dmk	E23:ad-#108	"	£5.00
2c)	126/12	1/3	Dmk	E23:ad-#108	"	£5.00
3a)	129/65	2/0	Ire	(r)	"	£3.00
3b)	129/65	1/6	Ire	(r)	"	£3.00
3c)	129/65	1/3	Ire	(r)	"	£3.00
3d)	129/65	1/3	Eng	(r)	"	£3.00
	129/65	**1/3**	**Ire**	**PC**		
4)	134	1/6	Swe	(r)	"	£3.00

65(US#127) KING OF-MOUNTAINS, EDM.ABOUT

1a)	129/65	2/0	Eng	TITLE#127error	P	£6.00
1b)	129/65	1/3	Eng	TITLE#127error	"	£6.00
2a)	134	2/0	Pol	correct title#	"	£3.00
2b)	134	1/3	Pol	(r)	"	£3.00
3)	141	1/6	Swe	(r)	"	£3.00

66(US#4) LAST OF-MOHICANS, JMS.F.COOPER

1a)	129/76	2/0	Ire	(0)	P/2	£6.00
1b)	129/76	1/6	Ire	(0)	"	£6.00
1c)	129/76	1/3	Ire	(0)	"	£6.00
2)	129/85	1/3	none	(r)	"	£3.00
3)	141	1/6	Swe	(r)	"	£3.00

67(US#1) THE THREE MUSKETEERS, A.DUMAS

1a)	129/76	2/0	Ire	(0)	P/2	£6.00
1b)	129/76	1/6	Ire	(0)	"	£6.00
1c)	129/76	1/3	Ire	(0)	"	£6.00

68.JULIUS CAESAR, WILLIAM SHAKESPEARE

1)	82(US)	1/3	Eng	"10/51"	L/1	£20.00
2a)	134	2/0	Pol	(r)	P/2	£5.00
2b)	134	1/6	Swe	(r)	"	£5.00
2c)	134	1/3	Pol	(r)	"	£5.00
3a)	136	2/0	USA	(note:A1!)	P/1	£4.00
3b)	136	1/3	USA	(r)	"	£4.00

69.AROUND-WORLD IN 80 DAYS, JULES VERNE

1a)	125	2/0	Eng	(no ad)	L	£7.00
1b)	125	1/3	Eng	(no ad)	"	£7.00
2a)	126/33	2/0	Dmk	(r)	P	£5.00
2b)	126/33	1/6	Dmk	(r)	"	£5.00
2c)	126/33	1/3	Dmk	(r)	"	£5.00
3a)	129/65	2/0	Ire	(r)	"	£3.00
3b)	129/65	1/3	Ire	(r)	"	£3.00
4)	129/83	1/3	Ire	(r)	"	£3.00
5)	141	1/6	Swe	(r)	"	£3.00

70(US#150) THE VIRGINIAN, OWEN WISTER

1a)	129/76	2/0	Ire	(0)	P	£6.00
1b)	129/76	1/3	Ire	(0)	"	£6.00
2)	141	1/6	Swe	(r)	"	£3.00

71.THE MAN WHO LAUGHS, VICTOR HUGO

1a)	125	2/0	Eng	(no ad)	L/1	£12.00
1b)	125	1/3	Eng	(no ad)	"	£12.00
2a)	141	1/6	Swe	MIRROR CVR.	P/2	£9.00
2b)	141	1/3	Swe	(r)	"	£9.00

72.THE OREGON TRAIL, FRANCIS PARKMAN

1)	121	1/16/2	Eng	(ad:10-DLX)	L	£9.00
2a)	126/19	2/0	Dmk	(E36-no ad)	P	£5.00
2b)	126/19	1/3	Dmk	(r)	"	£5.00
3)	129/65	1/3	Eng	(r)	"	£3.00
4a)	129/76	2/0	Ire	(r)	"	£3.00

Classics Illustrated #34

Classics Illustrated #71

Classics Illustrated #146

						N.MINT
4b)	129/76	1/3	Ire	(r)	"	£3.00

73.THE BLACK TULIP, ALEXANDRE DUMAS

						N.MINT
1)	120	1/16/2	Eng	(ad:10-DLX)	L	£25.00
2a)	126/45	2/0	Dmk	NEW BRIT.CVR.	NP	£35.00
2b)	126/45	1/6	Dmk	(r)	"	£35.00
2c)	129/45	1/3	Eng	(r)	"	£35.00
3a)	129/85	2/0	Ire	(r)	"	£30.00
3b)	129/85	1/3	Ire	(r)	"	£30.00
4)	141	1/6	Swe	(r)	"	£30.00
	141	**1/3**	**Pol**	**NPC**		

74.MIDSHIPMAN EASY, FREDERICK MARRYAT

1)	77-16T	1/6(B) Eng		(stiff cvr.)	L	£30.00
2a)	129/65	2/0	Eng	(soft cover)	"	£25.00
2b)	129/65	1/6	Eng	(r)	"	£25.00
2c)	129/65	1/3	Eng	(r)	"	£25.00
3a)	141	2/0	Pol	NEW BRIT.CVR.	NP	£125.00
3b)	141	1/3	Pol	(logo var.)	"	£125.00

75(US#140) ON JUNGLE TRAILS, FRANK BUCK

1a)	129/76	2/0	Ire	(0)	P	£6.00
1b)	129/76	1/3	Ire	(0)	"	£6.00
2)	129/85	1/3	Swe	(r)	"	£4.00

76(US#12) RIP VAN WINKLE, WASH.IRVING

1a)	129/76	2/0	Ire	(0)	P/2	£6.00
1b)	129/76	1/3	Ire	(0)	"	£6.00
2a)	129/85	2/0	Swe	(r)	"	£3.00
2b)	129/85	1/6	Swe	(r)	"	£3.00
2c)	129/85	1/3	Swe	(r)	"	£3.00
3)	141	1/6	Swe	(r)	"	£3.00

77.THE ILIAD, HOMER

1)	82(US)	1/3	Eng	"1/52"	L	£19.00
2a)	129	2/0	Dmk	NEW BRIT.CVR.	NP	£25.00
2b)	129	1/6	Dmk	(E13:ad-#114)	"	£25.00
2c)	129	1/3	Ire	(E13:ad-#114)	"	£25.00
3a)	129/65	2/0	Eng	U.S.COVER	P	£7.00
3b)	129/85	1/3	Eng	(r)	"	£7.00
4a)	129/85	2/0	Swe	SAME AS ED#2	NP	£23.00
4b)	129/85	1/3	Swe	(r)	"	£23.00
4c)	129/85	1/3	none	(r)	"	£23.00

78.JOAN OF ARC (ANONYMOUS)

1a)	82	1/16/19	Ire	(no DLX ad)	L	£14.00
1b)	82	1/16/19	Eng	(ad:4-DLX)	"	£14.00
2a)	129	2/0	Dmk	E11:ad-#129	P	£6.00
2b)	129	1/3	Ire	E11:ad-#129	"	£6.00
3)	126/39	1/3	Ire	(r)	"	£3.00
4a)	129/65	2/0	Eng	(r)	"	£3.00
4b)	129/65	1/3	Eng	(r)	"	£3.00
5)	134	1/3	Swe	(r)	"	£3.00

79.CYRANO DE BERGERAC, EDMOND ROSTAND

1a)	129	2/0	Eng	(no ad)	L	£10.00
1b)	129	1/3	Eng	(no ad)	"	£10.00

80.WHITE FANG, JACK LONDON

1a)	129	2/0	Eng	(no ad)	P	£6.00
1b)	129	1/3	Eng	(no ad)	"	£6.00
2)	126/39	2/0	Eng	(r)	"	£3.00
3)	**126/56**	**1/3**	**Eng**	**PC**		
4)	129/76	1/3	Eng	(r)	"	£3.00
5)	129/83	1/3	Ire	HRN:153error	"	£3.00
	129/83	**1/3**	**Ire**	**HRN:153 error**		
	129/83	**1/6**	**Ire**	**HRN:153 error**		
6a)	141	1/3	Swe	(r)	"	
6b)	141	1/3	Pol	(r)	"	£3.00

81(US#27) MARCO POLO (ANONYMOUS)

1)	129/85	1/3	Swe	(0)	P	£7.00
2a)	129/95	2/0	USA	(r)	"	£4.00
2b)	129/95	1/3	USA	(r)	"	£4.00

82.MASTER OF BALLANTRAE, R.L.STEVENSON

1a)	82	1/16/19	Ire	(no DLX ad)	P	£10.00
1b)	82	1/16/19	Eng	(ad:4-DLX)	"	£10.00
	121	**none**	**none**	**Soft Dlx.NPC**		
2a)	126/45	2/0	Dmk	(r)	"	£4.00
2b)	126/45	1/6	Dmk	(r)	"	£4.00
2c)	126/45	1/3	Dmk	(r)	"	£4.00
3a)	129/65	2/0	Eng	(r)	"	£3.00
3b)	129/65	1/3	Eng	(r)	"	£3.00
4a)	129/85	2/0	Swe	NEW BRIT.CVR.	NP	£25.00
4b)	129/85	1/3	Swe	(r)	"	£25.00
5)	134	1/3	Swe	(r)	"	£22.00
6a)	141	1/3	Swe	(r)	"	£22.00
6b)	141	1/3	Swe	(r)	"	£22.00
6c)	141	1/3	Pol	(r)	"	£22.00

83(US#151) WON BY THE SWORD, G.A.HENTY

1)	129/76	1/3	Ire	(0)	P	£7.00
2a)	129/85	2/0	Ire	(r)	"	£4.00
2b)	129/85	1/3	Ire	(r)	"	£4.00

84.THE GOLD BUG, EDGAR ALLAN POE

1a)	129/65	2/0	Eng	(U.S.PC/A)	(P/1)	£14.00
1b)	129/65	1/3	Eng	(0)	"	£14.00
2)	141	1/3	Swe	NEW CVR/ART	NP/2	£85.00

85(US#13) DR.JEKYLL & MR.HYDE (SEE #13)

1a)	129/85	1/3	none	(1st PIXI ad)	P/2	£7.00
1b)	129/85	1/6	none		"	£7.00
1c)	129/85	1/3	none		"	£7.00
1d)	129/85	1/3	Swe		"	£7.00

86.UNDER TWO FLAGS, OUIDA

1)	115	1/16/2	Eng	(ad:14-DLX)	P	£7.00
2a)	129/65	2/0	Eng	(r)	"	£3.00
2b)	129/65	1/3	Eng	(r)	"	£3.00
3)	157	2/0	Pol	(LOGO var.)	"	£3.00

87(US#142) ABRAHAM LINCOLN (ANONYMOUS)

1a)	129/85	2/0	Eng	(0)	P	£6.00
1b)	129/85	2/0	Swe	(0)	"	£6.00
1c)	129/85	1/3	Eng	(0)	"	£6.00
1d)	129/85	1/3	Swe	(0)	"	£6.00

88.MEN OF IRON, HOWARD PYLE

1)	115	1/16/2	Eng	(ad:14-DLX)	P	£7.00
2a)	126/45	1/6	Dmk	(r)	"	£3.00
2b)	126/45	1/3	Dmk	(r)	"	£3.00
3a)	141	2/0	Pol	(r)	"	£3.00
3b)	141	1/3	Pol	(r)	"	£3.00

89.CRIME & PUNISHMENT, FEODOR DOSTOEVSKY

1)	106	1/0	Eng	(ad:8-DLX)	P	£8.00
2)	123	1/16/2	Eng	(GB/SA/AU)	"	£6.00
3)	129/65	1/6	none	(r)	"	£3.00
4)	129/83	1/3	Ire	(r)	"	£3.00

90.GREEN MANSIONS, WILLIAM HENRY HUDSON

1a)	126	2/0	Eng	(no ad)	P1	£7.00
1b)	126	1/3	Eng	(no ad)	"	£7.00
2)	141	2/0	Pol	(U.S.-PC2)	P2	£6.00

91.CALL OF THE WILD, JACK LONDON

1a)	124	2/0	Eng	(0)	P	£7.00
1b)	124	1/3	Eng	(0)	"	£7.00
2a)	126/34	2/0	Dmk	(r)	"	£3.00
2b)	126/34	1/6	Dmk	(r)	"	£3.00
2c)	126/34	1/3	Dmk	(r)	"	£3.00
3a)	129/65	2/0	Eng	(r)	"	£3.00
3b)	129/65	1/3	Eng	(r)	"	£3.00
4)	129/85	1/3	Swe	(r)	"	£3.00
5a)	134	1/6	Swe	(r)	"	£3.00
5b)	134	1/3	Swe	(r)	"	£3.00
	134	**1/3**	**Swe**	**PC**		

92(US#9) LES MISERABLES, VICTOR HUGO

1a)	134	1/3	Swe	(0)	P/2	£8.00
1b)	134	1/6	Swe	(0)	"	£8.00

93(US#152) WILD ANIMALS I'VE KNOWN.SETON

1a)	129/83	2/0	Ire	TITLE#152error	P	£6.00
1b)	129/83	1/3	Ire	+ HRN#154error	"	£6.00
2)	141	1/6	Swe	both corrected	"	£4.00

94.DAVID BALFOUR, ROBERT L.STEVENSON

1a)	129	2/0	Eng	(no ad)	P	£7.00
1b)	129	1/3	Eng	(no ad)	"	£7.00
2a)	129/65	2/0	Eng	(r)	"	£3.00
2b)	129/65	1/3	Eng	(r)	"	£3.00
3)	141	1/6	Swe	(r)	"	£3.00

95(US#145) THE CRISIS, WINSTON CHURCHILL

1)	129/85	1/3	Swe	(0)	P	£8.00

96.DANIEL BOONE, JOHN BAKELESS

1)	121	1/16/2	Eng (ad:10-DLX)		P	£7.00
2a)	125	2/0	Dmk	E5:ad-#124	"	£5.00
2b)	125	1/6	Dmk	E5:ad-#124	"	£5.00
2c)	125	1/3	Ire	E5:ad-#124	"	£5.00
3a)	126/33	2/0	Frn	(r)	"	£3.00
3b)	126/33	1/6	Frn	(r)	"	£3.00
4)	129/65	1/3	Eng	(r)	"	£3.00
5)	157	2/0	Pol	(r)	"	£3.00

97.KING SOLOMON'S MINES, H.R.HAGGARD

1)	112	1/16/2	Eng	(ad:13-DLX)	P	£7.00
2)	121	1/16/2	Eng	(no ad)	"	£5.00
3a)	129/12	2/0	Dmk	E26:ad-#121	"	£5.00
3b)	129/12	1/6	Dmk	E26:ad-#121	"	£5.00
3c)	129/12	1/3	Dmk	E26:ad-#121	"	£5.00
4)	126/39	1/3	Ire	(r)	"	£3.00
5)	126/56	1/3	Eng	(r)	"	£3.00
	126/56	**2/0**	**Eng**	**PC**		
6a)	129/65	2/0	Eng	(r)	"	£3.00
6b)	129/65	1/3	Eng	(r)	"	£3.00
7)	129/85	1/3	Swe	(r)	"	£3.00
8)	141	1/6	Swe	(r)	"	£3.00

98.RED BADGE OF COURAGE, STEPHEN CRANE

1a)	124	2/0	Eng	(0)	P	£6.00
1b)	124	1/3	Eng	(0)	"	£6.00
2a)	126/45	2/0	Ire	(r)	"	£3.00
2b)	126/45	1/3	Ire	(r)	"	£3.00
3)	129/76	1/3	Eng	(r)	"	£3.00
4)	129/83	1/3	Ire	(r)	"	£3.00

99.HAMLET, WILLIAM SHAKESPEARE

1a)	125	2/0	Dmk	E4:ad-#96	P	£7.00
1b)	125	1/6	Dmk	E4:ad-#96	"	£7.00
1c)	125	1/3	Ire	E4:ad-#96	"	£7.00
2)	129/76	1/3	Eng	(r)	"	£3.00
3)	134	1/3	Swe	(r)	"	£3.00

100.MUTINY ON THE BOUNTY, NORDHOFF/HALL

1)	121	1/16/2	Eng	(ad:10-DLX)	P	£7.00
2a)	125	2/0	Dmk	E9:ad-#115	"	£5.00

#	No.	Grd	Ctry	Note	Pub	N.MINT
2b)	125	1/6	Dmk	E9:ad-#115	"	£5.00
2c)	125	1/3	Ire	E9:ad-#115	"	£5.00
3)	129/76	1/3	Eng	(r)	"	£3.00
4)	141	1/3	Pol	(LOGO var.)	"	£3.00

101.WILLIAM TELL, FREDERICK SCHILLER

#	No.	Grd	Ctry	Note	Pub	N.MINT
1)	106	1/0	Eng	(ad:8-DLX)	P	£7.00
2a)	121	2/0	Eng	(r)	"	£5.00
2b)	121	1/0	Eng	(r)	"	£5.00
3a)	125	2/0	Dmk	E5:ad-#124	"	£5.00
3b)	125	1/6	Dmk	E5:ad-#124	"	£5.00
3c)	125	1/3	Ire	E5:ad-#124	"	£5.00
4a)	141	1/6	Dmk	(r)	"	£3.00
4b)	141	1/3	Pol	(r)	"	£3.00

102(US#30) THE MOONSTONE, WM.W.COLLINS

#	No.	Grd	Ctry	Note	Pub	N.MINT
1a)	129/95	2/0	USA	(0)	P	£7.00
1b)	129/95	1/3	USA	(0)	"	£7.00

103.MEN AGAINST THE SEA, NORDHOFF/HALL

#	No.	Grd	Ctry	Note	Pub	N.MINT
1a)	123	2/0	Eng	(0)	P1	£7.00
1b)	123	1/0	Eng	(0)	P2	£7.00
2a)	126/45	2/0	Dmk	(U.S.-PC2)	P2	£5.00
2b)	126/45	1/6	Dmk	(r)	"	£5.00
2c)	126/45	1/3	Eng	(r)	"	£5.00
3a)	129/65	2/0	Eng	(r)	"	£3.00
3b)	129/65	1/3	Eng	(r)	"	£3.00
	129/65	**2/0**	**Eng**	**PC2**		
4)	134	1/6	Swe	(r)	"	£3.00

104.BRING 'EM BACK ALIVE, FRANK BUCK

#	No.	Grd	Ctry	Note	Pub	N.MINT
1)	106	1/0	Eng	(ad:8-DLX)	P	£7.00
2)	121	1/16/2	Eng	(GB/SA/AU)	"	£5.00
3a)	125	2/0	Dmk	E7:ad-#101	"	£5.00
3b)	125	1/6	Dmk	E7:ad-#101	"	£5.00
3c)	125	1/3	Ire	E7:ad-#101	"	£5.00
4)	129/65	1/3	Eng	(r)	"	£3.00

105.FROM-EARTH TO-MOON, JULES VERNE

#	No.	Grd	Ctry	Note	Pub	N.MINT
1a)	124	2/0	Eng	(no ad)	P	£7.00
1b)	124	1/3	Eng	(no ad)	"	£7.00
1c)	124	2/0	Dmk	E2:ad-#112	"	£7.00
1d)	124	1/6	Dmk	E2:ad-#112	"	£7.00
1e)	125	1/3	Ire	E2:ad-#112	"	£7.00
2)	129/85	1/3	Swe	(r)	"	£3.00
3)	134	1/3	Swe	(r)	"	£3.00

106.BUFFALO BILL (ANONYMOUS)

#	No.	Grd	Ctry	Note	Pub	N.MINT
1)	106	1/0	Eng	(ad:8-DLX)	P	£7.00
2)	121	1/16/2	Eng	(GB/SA/AU)	"	£5.00
3a)	129	2/0	Dmk	E15:ad-#111	"	£5.00
3b)	129	1/6	Dmk	E15:ad-#111	"	£5.00
3c)	129	1/3	Ire	E15:ad-#111	"	£5.00
4a)	126/45	2/0	Ire	(r)	"	£3.00
4b)	126/45	1/3	Ire	(r)	"	£3.00
5)	129/76	1/3	Eng	(r)	"	£3.00
6a)	129/85	2/0	Swe	(r)	"	£3.00
6b)	129/85	1/3	Swe	(r)	"	£3.00

107.KING OF-KHYBER RIFLES, TALBOT MUNDY

#	No.	Grd	Ctry	Note	Pub	N.MINT
1)	112	1/16/2	Eng	(ad:12-DLX)	P	£7.00
2)	121	1/16/2	Eng	(GB/SA/AU)	"	£5.00
3)	129/65	1/3	Ire	(r)	"	£3.00
4)	129/76	2/0	none	(r)	"	£3.00
	129/76	**2/0**	**none**	**PC**		
5a)	129/85	1/3	Swe	(r)	"	£3.00
5b)	129/85	1/3	Swe	(r)	"	£3.00

108.KNIGHTS OF THE ROUND TABLE (ANON.)

#	No.	Grd	Ctry	Note	Pub	N.MINT
1)	106	1/16/2	Eng	(ad:8-DLX)	P	£7.00
2)	121	1/16/2	Eng	(ad:10-DLX)	"	£5.00
3a)	129/12	2/0	Dmk	E24:ad-#8	"	£5.00
3b)	129/12	1/6	Dmk	E24:ad-#8	"	£5.00
3c)	126/12	1/3	Dmk	E24:ad-#8	"	£5.00
4)	134	1/3	Swe	(r)	"	£3.00
5a)	141	2/0	Pol	(r)	"	£3.00
5b)	141	1/3	Pol	(r)	"	£3.00

109.PITCAIRN'S ISLAND, NORDHOFF & HALL

#	No.	Grd	Ctry	Note	Pub	N.MINT
1)	129/76	1/3	Eng	(0)	P	£7.00
2)	141	1/3	Pol	(r)	"	£4.00

110.(US#28) MICHAEL STROGOFF, JLS.VERNE

#	No.	Grd	Ctry	Note	Pub	N.MINT
1a)	129/95	2/0	USA	(0)	P	£7.00
1b)	129/95	1/3	USA	(0)	"	£7.00
2)	141	1/3	Pol	(LOGO var.)	"	£4.00

111.THE TALISMAN, SIR WALTER SCOTT

#	No.	Grd	Ctry	Note	Pub	N.MINT
1)	112	1/16/2	Eng	(ad:12-DLX)	P	£7.00
2a)	129	2/0	Dmk	E16:ad-#5-LOGO	"	£5.00
2b)	129	1/6	Dmk	E16:ad-#5	"	£5.00
2c)	129	1/3	Ire	E16:ad-#5	"	£5.00
3)	129/76	1/3	Eng	(r)	"	£3.00
4)	134	1/3	Swe	(r)	"	£3.00
5)	141	1/3	Pol	Title#16-LOGO	"	£4.00

112.KIT CARSON (ANONYMOUS)

#	No.	Grd	Ctry	Note	Pub	N.MINT
1)	106	1/16/2	Eng	(ad:8-DLX)	P	£7.00
2)	121	1/16/2	Eng	(r)	"	£5.00
3a)	124	2/0	Dmk	E3:ad-#99	"	£5.00
3b)	124	1/6	Dmk	E3:ad-#99	"	£5.00
3c)	125	1/3	Ire	E3:ad-#99	"	£5.00
4)	126/39	1/3	Ire	(r)	"	£3.00
5)	129/65	1/3	Eng	(r)	"	£3.00
6a)	129/76	2/0	Eng	(r)	"	£3.00
6b)	129/76	1/3	Eng	(r)	"	£3.00

113.THE 45 GUARDSMEN, ALEXANDRE DUMAS

#	No.	Grd	Ctry	Note	Pub	N.MINT
1a)	129	2/0	Eng	(no ad)	P	£7.00
1b)	129	1/6	Eng	(no ad)	"	£7.00
1c)	129	1/3	Eng	(no ad)	"	£7.00
2a)	134	2/0	Pol	(orange top)	"	£3.00
2b)	134	1/3	Pol	(orange top)	"	£3.00
2c)	134	1/3	Swe	(orange top)	"	£3.00

114.THE RED ROVER, JAMES FEN.COOPER

#	No.	Grd	Ctry	Note	Pub	N.MINT
1)	115	1/16/2	Eng	(ad:12-DLX)	P	£7.00
2)	121	1/16/2	Eng	(heavy paper)	"	£5.00
3a)	129	2/0	Dmk	E14:ad-#106	"	£5.00
3b)	129	1/6	Dmk	E14:ad-#106	"	£5.00
3c)	129	1/3	Ire	E14:ad-#106	"	£5.00
4a)	126/33	2/0	Frn	(r)	"	£3.00
4b)	126/33	1/6	Frn	(r)	"	£3.00
5)	129/76	1/3	Eng	(r)	"	£3.00
6a)	141	2/0	Pol	(Logo var.)	"	£3.00
6b)	141	1/3	Pol	(Logo var.)	"	£3.00

115.HOW I FOUND LIVINGSTONE, H.STANLEY

#	No.	Grd	Ctry	Note	Pub	N.MINT
1)	115	1/16/2	Eng	(ad:12-DLX)	P	£7.00
2)	121	1/16/2	Eng	(GB/SA/AU)	"	£5.00
3a)	125	2/0	Dmk	E10:ad-#78	"	£5.00
3b)	125	1/6	Dmk	E10:ad-#78	"	£5.00
3c)	125	1/3	Ire	E10:ad-#78	"	£5.00
4)	129/85	1/3	Swe	(r)	"	£3.00
5a)	134	1/3	Swe	(r)	"	£3.00
5b)	134	1/3	Swe	(r)	"	£3.00
6a)	141	2/0	Pol	(color var.)	"	£3.00
6b)	141	1/3	Pol	(r)	"	£3.00

116(US#36) TYPEE, HERMAN MELVILLE

#	No.	Grd	Ctry	Note	Pub	N.MINT
1a)	129/95	2/0	USA	(U.S.PC/A)	P/1	£7.00
1b)	129/95	1/3	USA	(0)	"	£7.00
2a)	141	1/3	Swe	NEW BRIT.ART	P/2	£40.00
2b)	141	1/3	Swe	(E137)	"	£40.00

117(US#41) 20 YEARS AFTER, ALEX.DUMAS

#	No.	Grd	Ctry	Note	Pub	N.MINT
1a)	136	1/3	USA	(0)	P	£7.00
1b)	136	1/6	USA	(0)	"	£7.00
1c)	136	1/3	USA	(0)	"	£7.00

118.ROB ROY, SIR WALTER SCOTT

#	No.	Grd	Ctry	Note	Pub	N.MINT
1)	123	1/16/16/2	Eng	(GB/SA/NZ/AU)	P	£7.00
2a)	126/19	2/0	Dmk	(E37-no ad)	"	£4.00
2b)	126/19	1/6	Dmk	(E37-no ad)	"	£4.00
2c)	126/19	1/3	Ire	(E37-no ad)	"	£4.00
3)	129/65	1/3	Eng	(r)	"	£3.00
4a)	134	2/0	Pol	(r)	"	£3.00
4b)	134	1/3	Pol	(r)	"	£3.00
	134	**1/3**	**Swe**	**PC**		

119.SOLDIERS OF FORTUNE, RICH.H.DAVIS

#	No.	Grd	Ctry	Note	Pub	N.MINT
1a)	125	2/0	Eng	(no ad)	P	£7.00
1b)	125	1/6	Eng	(no ad)	"	£7.00
1c)	125	1/3	Eng	(no ad)	"	£7.00
2a)	126/45	1/3	Dmk	(r)	"	£3.00
2b)	126/45	1/3	Dmk	(r)	"	£3.00
3)	129/76	1/3	Eng	(r)	"	£3.00
4a)	134	2/0	Pol	(r)	"	£3.00
4b)	134	1/3	Pol	(r)	"	£3.00
4c)	134	1/3	Swe	(r)	"	£3.00

120.THE HURRICANE, C.NORDHOFF & J.HALL

#	No.	Grd	Ctry	Note	Pub	N.MINT
1)	120	1/16/2	Eng	(ad:10-DLX)	P	£7.00
2)	126/28	1/3	Dmk	HRN:138error	"	£4.00
3)	129/76	1/3	Eng	(r)	"	£3.00
4a)	134	1/3	Pol	(r)	"	£3.00
4b)	134	1/3	Pol	(r)	"	£3.00
	134	**1/3**	**Pol**	**PC**		
5)	141	1/3	Swe	(r)	"	£3.00

121.WILD BILL HICKOK (ANONYMOUS)

#	No.	Grd	Ctry	Note	Pub	N.MINT
1)	121	1/16/2	Eng	(1st.Jr.ad)	P	£7.00
2a)	126/12	2/0	Dmk	E27:ad-#9	"	£5.00
2b)	126/12	1/6	Dmk	E27:ad-#9	"	£5.00
2c)	126/12	1/3	Dmk	E27:ad-#9	"	£5.00
3)	126/45	1/3	Ire	(r)	"	£3.00
4)	129/76	1/3	Eng	(r)	"	£3.00
5)	129/95	1/3	USA	(r)	"	£3.00
6)	141	1/3	Swe	(r)	"	£3.00

122.THE MUTINEERS, CHARLES B.HAWES

#	No.	Grd	Ctry	Note	Pub	N.MINT
1a)	125	2/0	Eng	(no ad)	P	£7.00
1b)	125	1/3	Eng	(no ad)	"	£7.00
2a)	129/52	2/0	Dmk	(r)	"	£3.00
2b)	129/52	1/3	Dmk	(r)	"	£3.00
	129/52	**2/0**	**Dmk**	**PC**		
3a)	129/65	1/3	Ire	(r)	"	£3.00
3b)	129/65	1/3	Eng	(r)	"	£3.00
	129/76	**1/3**	**Eng**	**PC**		

123.FANG & CLAW, FRANK BUCK

#	No.	Grd	Ctry	Note	Pub	N.MINT
1)	123	1/16/16/2	Eng	(GB/SA/NZ/AU)	P	£7.00
2a)	126/12	2/0	Dmk	E29:ad-#6	"	£5.00
2b)	126/12	1/6	Dmk	E29:ad-#6	"	£5.00
2c)	126/12	1/3	Dmk	E29:ad-#6	"	£5.00
3)	126/45	1/3	Ire	HRN:133error	"	£3.00
4a)	129/95	2/0	USA	(r)	P	£3.00

N.MINT

						N.MINT
4b)	129/95	1/3	USA	(r)	"	£3.00
5)	141	1/6	Swe	(r)	"	£3.00

124.WAR OF THE WORLDS, H.G.WELLS

1a)	123	2/0	Eng	(0)	P	£7.00
1b)	123	1/6	Eng	(0)	"	£7.00
1c)	123	1/0	Eng	(0)	"	£7.00
	123	**1/6**	**Eng**	**PC**		
2a)	125	2/0	Dmk	E6:ad-#104	"	£5.00
2b)	125	1/6	Dmk	E6:ad-#104	"	£5.00
2c)	125	1/3	Ire	E6:ad-#104	"	£5.00
3)	129/65	1/3	Ire	(r)	"	£3.00

125.THE OX-BOW INCIDENT,WALTER V.T.CLARK

1a)	125	2/0	Eng	(no ad)	P	£7.00
1b)	125	1/3	Eng	(no ad)	"	£7.00
2a)	126/45	2/0	Ire	(r)	"	£3.00
2b)	126/45	1/3	Ire	(r)	"	£3.00
3)	129/83	1/3	Ire	HRN:153error	"	£3.00

126.THE DOWNFALL, EMILE ZOLA

1a)	126	2/0	Eng	(no ad)	P	£7.00
1b)	126	1/6	Eng	(no ad)	"	£7.00
1c)	126	1/3	Eng	(no ad)	"	£7.00
2a)	129/85	2/0	Swe	(r)	"	£3.00
2b)	129/85	1/3	Swe	(r)	"	£3.00
3a)	141	1/6	Swe	(r)	"	£3.00
3b)	141	1/3	Pol	(r)	"	£3.00

127(US#153) INVISIBLE MAN, H.G.WELLS
(127.KING OF-MNTNS. - error! see #65)

1)	129/83	1/3	Ire	Title/HRN:153error	P	£7.00
2)	141	1/6	Swe	Title# corrected		£6.00

128(US#59) WUTHERING HTS., EMILY BRONTE

1a)	134	1/3	Pol	(r)	P	£7.00
2a)	136	2/0	USA	(r)	"	£6.00
2b)	136	1/3	USA	(r)	"	£6.00

129.DAVY CROCKETT (ANONYMOUS)

1a)	129	2/0	Dmk	E12:ad-#77	P	£7.00
1b)	129	1/3	Ire	E12:ad-#77	"	£7.00
2a)	126/33	2/0	Frn	(r)	"	£4.00
2b)	126/33	1/3	Frn	(r)	"	£4.00
3)	134	1/3	Swe	(r)	"	£4.00

130(US#61)WOMAN IN WHITE, WM.W.COLLINS

1a)	136	2/0	USA	(E127)	P	£6.00
1b)	136	1/3	USA	(0)	"	£6.00
2)	141	1/3	Pol	(Logo var.)	"	£5.00

131(US#63) MAN WITHOUT-COUNTRY, E.E.HALE

1a)	136	2/0	USA	(0)	P/1	£6.00
1b)	136	1/6	USA	(0)	"	£6.00
1c)	136	1/3	USA	(0)	"	£6.00
2)	141	1/3	Swe	(E139)	P/2	£7.00

132(US#154) CONSPIRACY-PONTIAC, PARKMAN
(#132.DARK FRIGATE - error! see #12)

1a)	129/95	2/0	USA	(E102)	P	£6.00
1b)	129/95	1/3	USA	(r)	"	£6.00
2)	141	1/6	Swe	(r)	"	£3.00

133(US#155) LION OF-NORTH, G.A.HENTY

1a)	129/95	2/0	USA	(E104)	P	£6.00
1b)	129/95	1/3	USA	(0)	"	£6.00
2a)	141	1/6	Swe	(r)	"	£3.00
2b)	141	1/3	Pol	(r)	"	£3.00

134 (US#156)CONQUEST-MEXICO,B.D.CASTILLO

1a)	129/95	2/0	USA	(E108)	P	£6.00
1b)	129/95	1/3	USA	(0)	"	£6.00
2)	134	1/3	Pol	(r)	"	£3.00
3)	**141**	**1/6**	**Swe**	**PC**		

135 (US#43) GREAT EXPECTATIONS, DICKENS

1)	129/65	2/0	Pol	(E114) HRN=134	NP	£90.00
2)	141	?	?	NEW BRIT.CVR.	"	£90.00

136 (US#157) LIVES OF-HUNTED,E.T.SETON

1a)	136	2/0	USA	(E112)	P	£6.00
1b)	136	1/3	USA	(0)	"	£6.00

137 (US#158) THE CONSPIRATORS, A.DUMAS

1a)	136	2/0	USA	(E116)	P	£6.00
1b)	136	1/6	USA	(0)	"	£6.00
1c)	136	1/3	USA	(0)	"	£6.00

138(US#11) DON QUIXOTE, M.CERVANTES

1)	129/65	2/0	Pol	(E117) HRN=134	P	£8.00

139 (US#159) THE OCTOPUS, FRANK NORRIS

1a)	139	2/0	USA	(E120)	P	£6.00
1b)	139	1/3	USA	(0)	"	£6.00
	139	**1/6**	**USA**	**PC**		

139(A) (US#160) FOOD OF-GODS, H.G.WELLS
(listed as #139A on reorder list only)

1a)	141	2/0	Swe	(E124)	P	£6.00
1b)	141	1/3	Swe	(0)	"	£6.00

139B (US#161) CLEOPATRA, H.R.HAGGARD

1a)	139B	2/0	USA	(E131)	P	£6.00
1b)	139B	1/3	USA	(0)	"	£6.00

140 (US#162) ROBUR THE CONQUEROR, VERNE

1a)	139	1/3	USA	(E129)	P	£7.00
1b)	140	2/0	USA	(0)	"	£6.00
1c)	140	1/6	USA	(0)	"	£6.00
1d)	140	1/3	USA	(0)	"	£6.00

141 (US#163) MASTER OF-WORLD, J.VERNE

1a)	141	2/0	USA	(E136)	P	£7.00
1b)	141	1/3	USA	(0)	"	£7.00

142 (US#164) COSSACK CHIEF, NIC.GOGOL

1)	142	2/0	USA	(E138)	P	£7.00

143 (NEW) SAIL WITH-DEVIL, DANIEL DEFOE

1a)	141	2/0	Swe	E145-	NEW TITLE	75.00
1b)	141	1/3	Swe	(0)	"	£75.00

144 (US#165) QUEEN'S NECKLACE, A.DUMAS

1a)	141	2/0	USA	(E144)	P	£7.00
1b)	141	1/3	Swe	(0)	"	£7.00

145 (US#166) TIGERS & TRAIORS, J.VERNE

1a)	141	2/0	Swe	(E146)	P	£9.00
1b)	141	1/3	Swe	(0)	"	£9.00

146 (NEW) BARON MUNCHAUSEN, R.E.RASPE

1a)	141	2/0	Swe	E147-	NEW TITLE	75.00
1b)	141	1/3	Swe	(0)	"	£75.00

147 (NEW) THRU-LOOKING GLASS, L.CARROLL

1a)	141	2/0	Swe	E148-	NEW TITLE	75.00
1b)	141	1/3	Swe	(0)	"	£75.00

148 (NEW) NIGHTS-TERROR,COLLINS/DICKENS

1a)	141	2/0	Swe	E149-	NEW TITLE	75.00
1b)	141	1/3	Swe	(0)	"	£75.00

149 (NEW) GORILLA HUNTERS, BALLANTYNE

1a)	141	2/0	Swe	E151-	NEW TITLE	75.00
1b)	141	1/3	Swe	(0)	"	£75.00

150 (NEW) CANTERVILLE GHOST, O.WILDE

1a)	141	2/0	Swe	E152-	NEW TITLE	75.00
1b)	141	1/3	Swe	(0)	"	£75.00

151(US#45)TOM BROWN'S SCHOOL DAYS,HUGHES

1)	141	2/0	Swe	(E128)	P/2	£9.00

152 (US#56) TOILERS OF THE SEA, V.HUGO
(152.WILD ANIMALS-KNOWN-error! see #93)

1)	141	2/0	Swe	(E130-mirror)	P/2	£9.00

153(US#35)LAST DAYS-POMPEII,BLWR-LYTTON
(153.INVISIBLE MAN - error! see #127)

1)	141	2/0	Swe	(E132)	P/2	£9.00

154 (US#8) ARABIAN NIGHTS (ANONYMOUS)

1)	141	2/0	Swe	(E135-mirror)	P/2	£20.00

155(US#38)ADV.-CELLINI, BENVENUTO CELLINI

1a)	141	2/0	USA	(E141)	P/2	£9.00
1b)	141	2/0	none		"	£9.00

156(NEW) DOG CRUSOE,ROBT.M.BALLANTYNE

1a)	156	2/0	Swe	E153-	NEW TITLE	£75.00
1b)	156	1/6	Swe	(0)	"	£75.00
1c)	156	1/3	Swe	(0)	"	£75.00

157(NEW) QUEEN OF SPADES,ALEX.PUSHKIN

1a)	156	2/0	Swe	E155-	NEW TITLE	£75.00
1b)	156	1/6	Swe	(0)	"	£75.00
1c)	156	1/3	Swe	(0)	"	£75.00

158 (US#167) FAUST, JOHANN W.VON GOETHE

1a)	156	2/0	Swe	(E156-mirror)	P	£12.00
1b)	156	1/6	Swe	(0)	"	£12.00
1c)	156	1/3	Swe	(0)	"	£12.00

158A (NEW) DR.NO, IAN FLEMING

1a)	156	2/0	Swe	(0)	NEW TITLE	£175.00
1b)	156	1/6	Swe	(not in E series)	"	£175.00

159 (NEW) MASTER & MAN, LEO TOLSTOY

1a)	156	2/0	Swe	(E160)	NEW TITLE	£75.00
1b)	156	1/6	Swe	(0)	"	£75.00
1c)	156	1/3	Swe	(0)	"	£75.00

160 (US#168) IN FREEDOM'S CAUSE, G.A.HENTY

1a)	156	2/0	Swe	(E158)	P	30.00
1b)	156	1/6	Swe	(0)	"	£30.00
1c)	156	1/3	Swe	(0)	"	£30.00

161 (NEW) THE AENEID, VIRGIL

1a)	157	2/0	Swe	E162-	NEW TITLE	£125.00
1b)	157	1/6	Swe	(0)	"	£125.00
1c)	157	1/3	Swe	(0)	"	£125.00

162(NEW) SAGA OF THE NORTH,PIERRE LOTI

1a)	156	2/0	Swe	E163-	NEW TITLE	£80.00
1b)	156	1/6	Swe	(0)	"	£80.00
1c)	156	1/3	Swe	(0)	"	£80.00

163(NEW) THE ARGONAUTS, APPOLONIUS

1)	157	2/0	Swe	E164-	NEW TITLE	£185.00

C.I.-JUNIORS

Brief & rare early series (1955-6) with U.S.numbering. Some listed titles were not published. They are low-cost due to low interest.

501	SNOW WHITE-7 DWARFS	£10.00
502	THE UGLY DUCKLING	£8.00
503	CINDERELLA	£7.00
504	THE PIED PIPER	£7.00
505	SLEEPING BEAUTY	£7.00
506	THREE LITTLE PIGS	£7.00
507	JACK-&-BEANSTALK	£7.00
508	GOLDILOCKS	£7.00
509	BEAUTY &-BEAST	£7.00
510	LTL.RED RIDING HOOD	£7.00
511	PUSS IN BOOTS	£7.00
512	RUMPELSTILTSKIN	£7.00
513	PINNOCHIO	£7.00
516	ALADDIN & HIS LAMP	£7.00

N.MINT

PIXI TALES (1959-63)
Did not follow U.S.or European numbering. They issued all 77 U.S. Junior titles, and 11 new European Juniors: #s 71-72,78,80-83 & 85-88. There are also Australian editions and reprints. All are NM:3 Pounds, except as noted. (#) = U.S. number.

1	THE QUEEN BEE (551)	£7.00
2.3	LITTLE DWARFS (552)	£5.00
3.	KING THRUSHBEARD (553)	£3.00
4.	ENCHANTED DEER (554)	£3.00
5.3	GOLDEN APPLES (555)	£3.00
6.	THE ELF MOUND (556)	£3.00
7.	SILLY WILLY (557)	£3.00
8.	PUSS IN BOOTS (511)	£3.00
9.	JOHNNY APPLESEED (515)	£3.00
10.	EMPEROR'S-CLOTHES (517)	£3.00
11.	GALLANT TAILOR (523)	£3.00
12.	GOLDEN-HAIR GIANT (527)	£3.00
13.	RAPUNZEL (531)	£3.00
14.	WIZARD OF OZ (535)	£7.00
15.	PAUL BUNYAN (519)	£3.00
16.	PENNY PRINCE (528)	£3.00
17.	THE MAGIC DISH (558)	£3.00
18.	UGLY DUCKLING (502)	£3.00
19.	THE PIED PIPER (504)	£3.00
20	SLEEPING BEAUTY (505)	£3.00
21	JACK &-BEANSTALK (507)	£3.00
22	GOLDILOCKS (508)	£3.00
23	BEAUTY &-BEAST (509)	£3.00
24	STEADFAST-SOLDIER (514)	£3.00
25.	THE NIGHTINGALE (522)	£3.00
26.	THE WILD SWANS (524)	£3.00
27.	THE GOLDEN BIRD (530)	£3.00
28.	DANCING PRINCESSES(532)	£3.00
29.	THE TINDER BOX (540)	£3.00
30	THREE LITTLE PIGS (506)	£3.00
31	RUMPELSTILTSKIN (512)	£3.00
32	THE MAGIC SERVANTS (529)	£3.00
33	THE THREE FAIRIES (537)	£3.00
34	ALADDIN & HIS LAMP (516)	£3.00
35.	THE GOLDEN GOOSE (518)	£3.00
36.	THUMBELINA (520)	£3.00
37.	KING-GOLDEN RIVER (521)	£3.00
38.	THE FROG PRINCE (526)	£3.00
39.	SNOW WHITE-7 DWARFS (501)	£3.00
40.	CINDERELLA (503)	£3.00
41.	RED RIDING HOOD (510)	£3.00
42.	PINOCCHIO (513)	£3.00
43.	MAGIC FOUNTAIN (533)	£3.00
44.	GOLDEN TOUCH (534)	£3.00
45.	JAPANESE LANTERN (559)	£3.00
46.	DOLL PRINCESS (560)	£3.00
47.	LITTLE MERMAID (525)	£3.00
48.	ENCHANTED FISH (539)	£3.00
49.	SNOW WHITE/ROSE RED (541)	£3.00
50.	THE CHIMNEY SWEEP (536)	£3.00
51.	THE DONKEY'S TALE (542)	£3.00
52.	THE GOLDEN FLEECE (544)	£3.00
53.	THE WISHING TABLE (547)	£3.00
54.	THE SINGING DONKEY (550)	£3.00
55.	THE MAGIC PITCHER (548)	£3.00
56.	SIMPLE KATE (549)	£3.00
57.	SILLY HANS (538)	£3.00
58.	HOUSE IN THE WOODS (543)	£3.00
59.	THE GLASS MOUNTAIN (545)	£3.00
60.	ELVES & SHOEMAKER (546)	£3.00
61.	HANDS HUMDRUM (561)	£3.00
62.	THE ENCHANTED PONY (562)	£3.00
63.	THE WISHING WELL (563)	£3.00
64.	THE SALT MOUNTAIN (564)	£3.00
65.	THE SILLY PRINCESS (565)	£3.00
66.	CLUMSY HANS (566)	£3.00
67.	FIRE CAME TO-INDIANS(571)	£3.00
68.	THE DRUMMER BOY (572)	£3.00
69.	THE CRYSTAL BALL (573)	£3.00
70	BRIGHTBOOTS (574)	£3.00
71	THE HAPPY PRINCE (NEW)	£15.00
72	THE STAR CHILD (NEW)	£15.00
73	BEARSKIN SOLDIER(567)	£3.00
74	HAPPY HEDGEHOG (568)	£3.00
75	THREE GIANTS (569)	£3.00
76.	PEARL PRINCESS (570)	£3.00
77.	FEARLESS PRINCE (575)	£5.00
78.	ARCHER & THE DOVE (NEW)	£15.00
79.	PRINCESS WHO SAW EVERYTHING (576)	£6.00
80	THE BAD TROLL (NEW)	£15.00
81	THE SELFISH GIANT (NEW)	£15.00
82	BOY-WOULD BE KING (NEW)	£15.00
83	THE MOON PRINCESS (NEW)	£15.00
84	RUNAWAY DUMPLING(577)	£7.00
85.	POTMAKER GENERAL (NEW)	£15.00
86.	BINNY THE BEAVER (NEW)	£19.00
87.	THE FISH PRINCE (NEW)	£22.00
88.	THE GOLDEN SOUP (NEW)	£25.00

Classics Illustrated #147

Classics Illustrated #150

Classics in Pictures #1

	N.MINT
(#86-88 ARE VERY RARE)	

SPECIAL EDITIONS:
8 of the 16 U.S.titles. No dates or numbers (we calculated the dates). There were Australian eds. The 1970 ed. was by Top Sellers, Ltd. Value in NM about 9 Pound each.

THE 10 COMMANDMENTS (6/57)	£9.00
JESUS (12/57)	£9.00
THE ROUGH RIDER (6/58)	£9.00
BLAZING TRAILS WEST(12/58)	£9.00
CROSSING THE ROCKIES(6/59)	£9.00
ROYAL CANADIAN MOUNTED POLICE (12/59)	£9.00
MEN, GUNS & CATTLE (6/60)	£9.00
WORLD WAR II (1970)	£9.00

WORLD ILLUSTRATED:
British followed exactly the joint European series (1956-63), issuing 26 of the 36 U.S. titles (3 new covers) plus eight new titles, although #s 26/28/30/33 are mainly U.S. art. (#)=U.S.title#.

1.	FLIGHT (8)(NPC)	£14.00
2.	PIRATES (7)	£10.00
3.	HORSES (3)	£7.00
4.	PREHIST.ANIMALS (15)	£8.00
5.	SPACE (5)	£7.00
6.	DOGS (1)	£7.00
7.	THE F.B.I. (6)	£7.00
8.	THE CRUSADES (16)	£7.00
9.	SCIENTISTS (18)	£7.00
10	FRENCH REVOLUTION(14)	£8.00
11	THE JUNGLE (19)	£8.00
12	COMMUNICATIONS (20)	£7.00
13	GHOSTS (24)	£7.00
14	GREAT EXPLORERS(23)	£7.00
15.	MAGIC (25)	£8.00
16.	HIGH ADVENTURE (27)	£7.00
17.	WHALING (28)	£7.00
18.	THE VIKINGS (29)	£7.00
19.	UNDERWATER ADV.(30)	£7.00
20	HUNTING (31)(NPC)	£9.00
21	GOLD/GLORY(32)(NPC)	£9.00
22	SPIES (35)	£7.00
23	FISHING (34)	£7.00
24	FAMOUS TEENS (33)	£7.00
25.	FIGHT FOR LIFE (36)	£7.00
26.	DAY OF FURY (NEW)	£25.00
27.	BOATING (22)	£7.00
28.	THE SEA (NEW)	£15.00
29.	GREAT ESCAPES (NEW)	£15.00
30	LIFE-BEYOND THE EARTH (NEW)	£15.00
31	N.W.PASSAGE (NEW)	£15.00
32	GOLDEN HORDE (NEW)	£15.00
33	THE COSSACKS (NEW)	£15.00
34	DISASTERS (NEW)	£20.00

CLICKY
Brockhampton Press; Oct 1953-1961

Clicky the Clockwork Clown 64pgs small oblong; by Enid Blyton, Molly Brett art	£2.00
Clicky the Clown at the Circus	£2.00
Clicky Goes To Toyland	£2.00
Clicky & Father Christmas	£2.00
Clicky & the Flying Horse	£2.00
Clicky Gets Into Trouble	£2.00
Clicky & Tiptoe	£2.00
Happy Holiday Clicky	£2.00

CLIVE
Michael Joseph/ W.H.Allen; 1968-1971

Clive (Michael Joseph) reprints Evening Standard strip by Dominic Poelsma	£1.00
Clive in Love (W.H.Allen)	£1.00
Clive and Augusta (W.H.Allen)	£1.00

CLOGGIES, THE
Private Eye/Andre Deutsh

The Cloggies (Private Eye, 1969) reprints Private Eye strip by Bill Tidy	£1.00
The Cloggies Dance Again (Andre Deutsch, 1973)	£1.00

CLUB LIBRARY: SECRET SERVICE
Med/New English Library; 1 1976-?

1 68pgs pocket size; Shadow Strikes, Spanish reprints	£1.00
2-?	£0.35

CLUB LIBRARY: WAR
Med/New English Library; 1 1976-?

1 68pgs pocket size; Spanish reprints	£1.00
2-?	£0.35

CLUB LIBRARY: WESTERN
Med/New English Library; 1 1976-?

1 68pgs pocket size; Fugitive, Spanish reprints	£1.00
2-?	£0.35

CLUMSY BOY CRUSOE
(full title is Surprising Adventures of Clumsy Boy Crusoe)
Griffith & Farron; nn 1877

nn - 16pgs oblong; Charles Ross art	£45.00

CODENAME: GENETIX
(see main American comics section)

COLLECTED ADVENTURES OF FAT FREDDY'S CAT
(no imprint); nn 1975

nn - 36pgs; Shelton reprints	£3.00

COLLECTED JUDGE CALIGULA, THE
(see The Chronicles of Judge Dredd; The Complete Judge Dredd)
Titan; nn 1991

	N.MINT
nn - 144pgs; 2000AD reprints by Wagner, Bolland & McMahon	£6.00

COLONEL PEWTER
Pall Mall/ Penguin; 1957-1979

Colonel Pewter in Ironicus 68pgs, reprints News Chronicle strip by Arthur Horner	£3.00
Sirius Dog Star 94pgs	£2.00
Penguin Colonel Pewter 148pgs	£4.00
Book of Uriel 150pgs	£2.00

COLORADO KID, THE
Miller; 50 May 1954-84 1959

50 28pgs; Colorado Kid by John Wheeler begins	£4.00
51-84	£2.50

COLOUR OF MAGIC, THE
(see The Light Fantastic)
Corgi; nn Nov 1992

nn - based on Terry Pratchett novel, reprints Innovation series	£7.00

COLOURED COMIC
Trapps Holmes; 1 21st May 1898-415 28th April 1906 (joins Smiles)

1 8pgs tabloid; first weekly comic with full colour cover	£35.00
2	£12.50
3-72	£10.00
73-403 printed in blue	£6.00
404-415 16pgs	£4.00

COLOURED SLICK FUN
Gerald Swan; 20 1945-88 1951 (continuation of Slick Fun)

20 16pgs; 2 colour photogravure; John McCail, William Ward, E.H.Banger art	£8.00
21-47 irregular publication; full colour from 35	£6.00
48 (May 1949)-51 (Aug 1949) monthly	£6.00
52 (1 Sep 1949)-65 (18 Mar 1950) fortnightly	£6.00
66 (1 Apr 1950)-73 (20 May 1950) weekly; blue/red photogravure from 68	£6.00
74 (27 May 1950)-86 (11 Nov 1950) fortnightly	£6.00
87-88 undated	£6.00

COLOURED SLICK FUN BUDGET
Gerald Swan; Jun 1950-1952, 3 issues

1 132pgs; 8 back issues of Coloured Slick Fun in a new cover	£8.00
2 44,53,67,74,48,65,46,63 rebound	£8.00
3 87,77,85,68,82,84,80 + Scramble 50 rebound	£8.00

COMBAT COMIC ALBUM
World Distributors; 1 1965

1 64pgs, Dell reprints in colour	£4.00

COMBAT PICTURE ANNUAL
Micron; 1961

1961 254pgs; reprints from Combat Picture Library plus new text	£2.50
Note: issued in dust jacket which will double price if intact	

COMBAT PICTURE LIBRARY
Micron/Smith; 1 Mar 1959-1212 Jun 1985

1 68pgs pocket size; Sea Hunt	£6.00
2	£2.50
3-5	£1.25
6-250	£1.00
251-1212	£0.50

COMET, THE
(previously The Big Budget)
C.A. Pearson; 1 27th Jun 1909-14 26th Jun 1909

1 16pgs tabloid size; mainly jokes and text	£35.00
2-5 16pgs tabloid size	£15.00
6-14 32pgs smaller size	£10.00

COMET, THE
(titled The Comet/Comet Comic/The Comet Adventure Weekly/Comet Weekly)
Allen/Amalgamated; 1 20th Sep 1946-17th Oct 1959, 580 issues, numbered to 566 (joins Tiger)

1	£40.00
2	£15.00
3-5	£10.00
6-14	£7.50
15 (4 Apr 1947) 1st photogravure issue	£6.00
16-75,77-112	£6.00
76 (13 Aug 1949) Thunderbolt Jaxon begins	£6.00
113 (16 Sep 1950) Kit Carson begins	£6.00
114-192	£6.00
193 (29 Mar 1952) 1st comic-book format issue	£5.00
194-246,248-263,265-269,271-273	£5.00
247 (11 Apr 1953) Dick Barton begins (ends 273)	£5.00
264 (8 Aug 1953) Strongbow the Mighty begins	£5.00
270 (19 Sep 1953) Claude Duval begins	£5.00
274-518	£4.00
519 1st letterpress issue	£3.00
520-564	£3.00
16 May 1959 1st unnumbered issue	£3.00
23 May-17 Oct 1959	£3.00
Note: one un-numbered/undated issue appeared between 27 Jun-15 Aug 1959.	

COMIC ADVENTURES
A. Soloway; v.1:1 1940-v.7:2 1949, 27 issues

Vol 1:1-5 8pgs, tabloid size	£6.00
Vol 2:1-7:1 16pgs, half-tabloid size	£4.00
Vol 7:2 16pgs, full colour	£5.00

COMIC ALBUM OF FOLLY AND FASHION
Judy Office; nn 1870

nn - 48pgs; C.H.Ross reprints	£45.00

COMIC ALMANAC
Fortey; 1879

1879 16pgs; cartoons	£40.00

	N.MINT
COMIC BITS	
Unity; 1 19th Feb 1898-10 12th Apr 1898	
1 12pgs tabloid size	£45.00
2-6 12pgs	£15.00
7-10 8pgs	£10.00
COMIC CAPERS	
A. Soloway; v.1:1 1940-v.7:2 1949, 27 issues	
Vol 1:1-5 8pgs, tabloid size	£6.00
Vol 2:1-7:1 16pgs, half-tabloid	£4.00
Vol 7:2 16pgs, full colour	£5.00
COMIC CARTOON ANNUAL	
Purnell; 1967	
1968 64pgs; reprints incl. Mandrake, Popeye, Phantom, Flash Gordon, Prince Valiant, Secret Agent X9, Ripley	£8.00
Note: published in 1967 with 1968 cover date	
COMIC CHUCKLES	
Martin & Reid; nn 1944	
nn - 16pgs, H.Pease art	£3.00
COMIC COMPANION	
Odhams; 3rd Oct 1908-13th Feb 1909, 20 issues	
3 Oct 1908 4pgs supplement to You and I magazine; George Wakefield art	£30.00
10 Oct 1908-13 Feb 1909	£10.00
COMIC CUTS	
Harmsworth/Amalgamated; 1 17th May 1890-12th Sep 1953 (joins Knockout)	
1 8pgs tabloid; reprints cartoons from American magazines	£250.00
1890-1895	£60.00
1896-1900	£30.00
1901-1920	£8.00
1921-1940	£6.00
1941-1950	£5.00
1951-1953	£2.50
CHRONOLOGY	
331 (Sep 1896) first full colour British comic. 4 Feb 1928 1st "Comic Cuts & Golden Penny". 4 Nov 1939 1st "Comic Cuts & Jolly Comic. 25 May 1940 1st "Comic Cuts & Larks".	
ARTISTS/FEATURES	
Early artists include Jack Yeats, Tom Browne, Percy Cocking, etc. Later artists incl. Ron Embleton (Forgotten City, Mohawk Trails, Tom O'London). James Holdaway (Cal McCord). Ken Reid (Super Sam, Foxy, Billy Boffin).	
COMIC CUTS	
Crawley News; 1 14th Sep 1983-?	
14 Sep 1983 4pgs; supplement to Crawley News	£0.50
21 Sep 1983-?	£0.10
COMIC FUN	
Martin & Reid; nn 1948	
nn - Wally Robertson, Bob Monkhouse art	£4.00
COMIC HOLIDAY ANNUAL	
Ward Lock; nn Aug 1877	
nn - 132pgs; C.H.Ross reprints	£30.00
COMIC HOME JOURNAL, THE	
(previously The Boys' Home Journal, a story paper)	
Harmsworth; 1 11th May 1895-488 10th Sep 1904 (becomes Butterfly)	
1 8pgs tabloid size; Frank Holland, Jack Yeats art	£45.00
2	£20.00
3-5	£15.00
6-488 some issues entitled War Comic Home Journal; some incl. Tom Browne art	£10.00
COMIC LEDGER, THE	
Martin & Reid; 1 1949	
1 8pgs tabloid; Mick Anglo art	£3.00
COMIC LIFE	
(previously Pictorial Comic-Life)	
James Henderson/Amalgamated; 79 30th Dec 1899-1543 21st Jan 1928 (joins My Favourite)	
79 8pgs tabloid size	£50.00
1900-1909	£15.00
1909-1915 with colour cover	£10.00
1916-1919 incl. Roy Wilson art	£10.00
1920-1928 incl. Roy Wilson art	£10.00
CHRONOLOGY	
25 Sep 1909 1st full colour cover. 1916 size reduced during wartime. 13 Mar 1920 1st Amalgamated Press issue. 30 Sep 1922 increases to 12pgs.	
COMIC MOVIES FLICKER BOOKS	
Books & Pictures; 1949	
1-10	£5.00
FEATURES	
1 Bimbo Catches the Big Bad Bear. 2 Red Riding Hood & Wicked Wolf. 3 Cowboy Joe & the Bandit. 4 Flick & Slip the Circus Clowns. 5 Jokey Jumpy the Winner. 6 Blacky & Whitythe Boxers by Walter Booth. 7 Punch & Judy by E.Williams. 8 Brumas by Bill Mevin. 9 Jack & Jill by E.Williams. 10 Cinderella by Walter Booth.	
COMIC MUPPET BOOK	
Fontana/Collins; nn 1979	
nn - 36pgs; Graham Thompson art	£1.00
COMIC PICTORIAL NUGGETS	
James Henderson; 7th May 1892-19th Nov 1892, 29 issues (becomes Nuggets)	
1 16pgs; reprints cartoons & strips from American magazines	£35.00
2-29	£12.50
COMIC PICTORIAL SHEET	
James Henderson; 1 29th Sep 1891-1601 28th Sep 1904 (joins Snap-Shots)	
1 broadsheet; reprints cartoons & strips from American magazines	£35.00
2	£15.00
3-90	£12.50
91-1601	£10.00
COMIC RELIEF COMIC, THE	
Fleetway; nn Mar 1991	
nn - 56pgs; Benefit comic, Baikie, Bisley, Bond, Dillon, Emerson, Gibbons, Hewlett, Lloyd,	

	N.MINT
Parkhouse, Phillips, Pleece, Ranson, Ridgway, Talbot, Viz team, Yeowell et al art; features Lenny Henry, Jonathan Ross, Griff Rees-Jones, Rowan Atkinson	£1.50
COMIC SHOTS	
John W. Fisher; nn May 1946-Jul 1946	
nn - 12pgs, printed red/green; W.Forshaw art	£3.00
nn - 12pgs, printed blue	£3.00
nn - 16pgs, printed brown	£3.00
nn - 16pgs, printed dark brown	£3.00
COMIC WONDER, THE	
Paget; 1 1948-7 1949; 1 1949	
1 8pgs; Alan Fraser art	£5.00
2-7	£3.00
1 8pp; larger size; Wally Robertson art	£4.00
COMICAL COMIC, THE	
Philipp Marx; nn 1945	
nn - Reg Carter art	£4.00
COMICAL CRACKS	
Ensign/W. Forshaw; 1-4 1947	
1 8pp; Charles Ross art	£4.00
2 Ross, W. Forshaw, Bryan Berry art	£4.00
3-4 published by W. Forshaw; 4 incl. Frank Minnitt art	£4.00
COMICAL PRANKS	
Ensign; 1-3 1947	
1-2 Forshaw, Berry art	£5.00
3 Frank Minnitt art	£5.00
COMICAL SNIPS	
Modern Fiction; nn 1947	
nn - Dick Brook art	£4.00
COMICOLOUR	
(see Comicute Budget)	
Gerald Swan; 1 1946-11 1949	
1 8pgs; E.H.Banger, David Williams, John McCail art	£8.00
2-8 5 in full colour photogravure; 3,5,6 incl. Frank Minnitt art	£5.00
9-10 full colour gravure	£5.00
11 12pgs, full colour gravure	£5.00
COMICOLOUR (NEW SERIES)	
Gerald Swan; 1-3 1953	
1-3 28pgs	£5.00
COMICS ON PARADE	
Miller; 3 Feb 1941-13 1943, 11 issues; 1944, 4 unnumbered issues	
3 32pgs gravure; United Features reprints begin	£12.00
4,6-13	£6.00
5 full colour cover	£6.00
CoP: Iron Vic 16pgs gravure issues begin	£6.00
CoP: Captain & the Kids	£6.00
Cynical Susie & others from CoP	£6.00
Joe Jinks, Broncho Bill, Frankie Doodle & others from CoP	£6.00
Five-in-One Comic Annual (Miller, 1943?) 9-13 rebound	£10.00
COMICS ON PARADE	
(previously Sparkler Comic Book Series)	
Donald F. Peters; 17-18 1950, 2 issues (becomes Spark Man)	
17-18 16pgs; United Features reprints	£4.00
COMICS TO HOLD YOU SPELLBOUND	
(see Spellbound)	
Thorpe & Porter; 1 Mar 1953-?	
1 68pgs; titled Stories to Hold You Spellbound, Marvel reprints begin	£5.00
2-?	£1.00
COMICUTE BUDGET	
Gerald Swan; 1951-1952	
1 back issues of Cute Fun 34,35,37,39,38,26, Comicolour 8,6, and Kiddyfun 3,9,4 bound together in new cover	£8.00
2 Cute Fun 34,35,36,37,39,38, Comicolour 8,7, and Kiddyfun 3,9,4 bound together in new cover	£8.00
COMMANDER BATTLE AND THE ATOMIC SUB	
Streamline; 1-3 1955	
1-3 28pgs; ACG reprints	£6.00
COMMANDER COMIC, THE	
G.W.Pearce/Ensign; 1947, 2 unnumbered issues	
nn - 8pgs red/blue gravure; Frank Minnitt art	£3.00
nn - 8pgs green/orange gravure; Frank Minnitt art	£3.00
COMMANDER EARTH	
Gulf Oil; nn 1980	
nn - 4pgs promo; Geoff Jones art	£0.30
COMMANDO CRAIG	
Scion; 1 Jun 1950-3 Aug 1950	
1-3 Norman Light, Ron Turner art	£8.00
COMMANDO LIBRARY	
D.C. Thomson; 1 Jul 1961-present (2914 to Dec 1995)	
1 68pgs pocket size; Walk or Die	£10.00
2	£5.00
3-5	£3.00
5-100	£2.00
101-250	£1.00
251-500	£0.75
501-1000	£0.50
1001-2914	£0.25
ARTISTS/FEATURES	
1 Walk or Die by Amador Garcia. 2 They Called Him Coward by Armando Banato. 3 A Guy Needs Guts by C.T. Rigby. 4 Mercy For None by Gordon Livingstone. 5 Hellfire Landing by Ortiz. 6 They Came By Night by Ros. 7 The Ship They Couldn't Sink by Savi. 8 Red Runs the River by Rafael Auraleon. 9 Jungle Fury! by Madaigan. 10 Hun Bait by Gordon Livingstone. 11 Closer Than Brothers by Ortiz. 12 The Desperate Days by Gordon Livingstone. Cam Kennedy in 417, 604, 642, 666, 702, 729, 825, 878, 2172. John Ridgway in 546, 572, 748, 818, 833, 1021, 1054, 1134, 1385, 1448, 1604, 1698. Saichann in 2247.	

	N.MINT

COMMITTED COMIX
Birmingham Arts Lab; nn 1977
| nn - 28pgs; adult, Chris Welch art | £1.00 |

COMPLETE COMICS
Newton Wickham; nn 1944
| nn - John Turner, Denis Gifford art | £4.00 |

COMPLETE FANTASTIC FOUR, THE
Marvel; 1 28th Sep 1977-53 8th Jun 1979 (joins Mighty World of Marvel)
1 36pgs, reprints origin from F.F. #1	£1.50
1 with free gift (plastic model Boeing 747)	£2.00
2	£1.25
2 with free gift (Maze Game)	£1.50
3-53	£0.75

COMPLETE JUDGE DREDD, THE
Fleetway; 1 Feb 1992-42 Jul 1995 (becomes Classic Judge Dredd)
1 Judge Dredd reprints from 2000AD begin	£5.00
2	£3.00
3	£2.50
4-5	£2.25
6-15	£2.00
16-25	£1.75
26-42	£1.50

COMPLETE JUDGE DREDD, THE
(see The Collected Judge Caligula)
Titan; 1994-1995
The Complete Judge Dredd in Oz (Jun 1994) 240pgs; by Wagner/Grant, Robinson, Dillon, Simpson, etc.	£11.00
The Complete Judge Dredd in the Cursed Earth (Jul 1994) 160pgs; by Mills, McMahon, Bolland	£10.00
The Complete Apocalypse War (Apr 1995) by Wagner/Grant, Ezquerra, McMahon, Bolland etc.	£11.00
Classic Judge Dredd (Jul 1995) by Wagner & Bolland	£10.00
The Complete Judge Child Quest (Jul 1995) by Wagner/Grant, Bolland, McMahon, Smith	£11.00
Judge Dredd and the Angel Gang (Jul 1995) by Wagner/Grant, Ezquerra, McMahon, Smith	£10.00

COMPLETE JUDGE DREDD SPECIAL EDITION, THE
Fleetway Editions; 1 1994-2 1995
| 1 132pgs; 2000AD group reprints | £2.50 |
| 2 | £2.50 |

COMPLETE SPIDER-MAN, THE
Marvel; 1 1990-24 Sep 1992 (continued as The Exploits of Spider-Man)
1 Spider-Man reprints begin, all four US titles	£2.50
1 with free gift (iron-on Spider-Man patch)	£4.00
2	£1.50
3-24 incl. Erik Larsen art	£1.00

CONAN THE BARBARIAN POCKET BOOK
Marvel; 1 Sep 1980-13 12th Nov 1981
1 52pgs small size; Conan by Barry Windsor-Smith reprints begin	£1.00
2,4-13	£0.50
3 100pgs double issue	£1.00

CONAN WINTER SPECIAL
Marvel; nn Nov 1982
| nn - Conan reprints | £1.00 |

CONFESSIONS LIBRARY
Amalgamated; 1 Feb 1959-44 Dec 1960 (becomes Romantic Confessions Picture Library)
| 1 68pgs pocket size; Men Could Not Resist Me | £2.00 |
| 2-44 | £0.75 |

CONFESSIONS OF LOVE
Gerald Swan; 1 1954-14 1955
| 1 68pgs; Star Publications reprints begin | £3.00 |
| 2-14 | £1.00 |

CONFIDENTIAL STORIES
Miller; 1-9 1957
| 1-9 68pgs; US reprints | £1.50 |

CONFLICT PICTURE LIBRARY
Brown Watson; 1 1959-? 1963
| 1 68pgs pocket size | £1.00 |
| 2-? | £0.35 |

CONQUEROR
Harrier; Preview Jun 1984; 1 Aug 1984-9 Dec 1985 (joins Swiftsure)
Preview Dave Harwood art begins (in all issues)	£0.75
1 Harwood/Bolland cover	£0.60
2 Eddie Campbell art, Gibbons cover	£0.50
3 Collins/Farmer art	£0.50
4 Eddie Campbell script	£0.50
5-9	£0.50

CONQUEROR COMIC
Scion; nn 1952
| nn - 20pgs; King-Ganteaume art | £3.00 |

CONQUEROR SPECIAL
Harrier; 1 Feb 1987
| 1 Harwood art | £0.75 |

CONQUEROR UNIVERSE
Harrier; 1 Dec 1985
| 1 Collins/Roach, Harwood, O'Donnell art | £1.00 |

CONTINENTAL FILM PHOTO STORIES
C.A. Pearson; 1 Jan 1960-?
| 1 36pgs pocket size; Harbour of Love, fumetti | £4.00 |
| 2-? | £2.00 |

COOPER KIDS, THE
Pendock Press; nn 1943
| nn - 20pgs; reprints Sunday Pictorial strip by Robert St John Cooper | £4.00 |

COR!!
IPC; 6th Jun 1970-15th Jun 1974 (196? issues)

	N.MINT

No.1 - 6 Jun 1970 Gus Gorilla by Alf Saporito, Tomboy by Brian Lewis, Ivor Lott & Tony Broke by Reg Parlett begin	£5.00
No.1 with free gift (fruit juice sachet)	£10.00
No. 2 - 13 Jun 1970	£2.50
2 with free gift (2 instant picture sheets/Super Anglo Bubble Gum)	£5.00
20 Jun 1970-15 Jun 1974	£0.75

ARTISTS/FEATURES
Joe Colquhoun (The Chameleon, The Goodies). Ron Turner (Robby Hood).

COR!! ANNUAL
Fleetway; 1972-1976
| 1972 | £3.50 |
| 1973-1976 | £3.00 |

COR!! BOOK OF GAGS
IPC; 1977
| 1977 scarce, softcover | £10.00 |

COR!! SUMMER SPECIAL
IPC; 1972-1974
| 1972-1974 | £2.00 |

CORKER COMIC
International; nn Jun 1946
| nn - 8pgs; Denis Gifford art | £4.00 |
| nn - reprint edition, John Turner strip replaces one of the originals | £3.00 |

CORKER COMIC, THE
Philmar; nn 1949
| nn - 16pgs; George Parlett, Wally Robertson, Frank Minnitt, Colin Merritt art | £3.00 |

CORONATION SPECIAL
Sports Cartoons; nn 1953
| nn - 20pgs; special issue to celebrate the Coronation of Queen Elizabeth II | £10.00 |

COSMIC TALES
Northern Light Press/Titan Books; nn 1982
| nn - Angus McKie art | £2.00 |
| nn - (hardback) | £3.50 |

COUNTDOWN
Polystyle; 1 20th Feb 1971-58 24th Mar 1972 (becomes TV Action)
1 24pgs numbered in reverse; Dr Who by Harry Lindfield, Thunderbirds, Capt. Scarlet, UFO begin, 1st Countdown by John Burns	£25.00
1 with free gift (Space wall chart)	£40.00
2 Joe 90, Secret Service begin	£10.00
3 Jon Pertwee cover	£15.00
4-8	£7.50
9-15	£5.00
16-30	£4.00
31-34,36-43,45-58	£4.00
35 Persuaders by Lindfield begins	£4.00
44 Thunderbirds by Don Harley begins (original material)	£4.00

ARTISTS/FEATURES
Features and artists rotated regularly; artists included Harry Lindfield, Frank Langford, John Burns, Gerry Haylock, Jon Davis, Brian Lewis, Martin Asbury, Don Harley in various issues; some Gerry Anderson material was reprinted from TV Century 21, including Thunderbirds, Stingray, Fireball XL5.

COUNTDOWN ANNUAL
Polystyle; 1972-1973
| 1972 features include UFO, Thunderbirds, Captain Scarlet, Countdown, The Secret Service, Joe 90, Dr Who by Jim Baikie | £12.50 |
| 1973 titled "Countdown for TV Action"; features include UFO, Thunderbirds by Ron Turner, The Persuaders, Captain Scarlet, Dr Who by Frank Langford | £8.50 |

COUNTDOWN HOLIDAY SPECIAL
Polystyle; nn 1971
| nn - 48pgs; Hampson Fireball XL5 reprints, scarce | £8.00 |

COUNTDOWN WITH TV ACTION HOLIDAY SPECIAL
Polystyle; nn Mar 1972
| nn - 48pgs | £6.00 |

COUPLES
Workshop; nn 1972
| nn - oblong; reprints newspaper strip from Sunday Times | £0.75 |

COWBOY ACTION
Miller; 1 1956-18 1957
| 1 28pgs; Atlas reprints begin | £5.00 |
| 2-18 | £2.50 |

COWBOY ADVENTURE LIBRARY
Micron; 1 1964-1026 Jun 1985
1 68pgs pocket size; foreign reprints	£1.00
2-5	£0.60
6-1026	£0.35

COWBOY COMIC ALBUM
World Distributors; nn 1955-1958
nn - (Sep 1955); "The Human Scarecrow" (1st story)	£5.00
2 (Sep 1956); "The Traitor of El Nuevo" (1st story)	£4.00
3 (Aug 1957)	£4.00
4 (1958); "The Sea Rustlers" (1st story)	£4.00

COWBOY COMICS/COWBOY PICTURE LIBRARY
Amalgamated Press; 1 Apr 1950-468 Sep 1962
1 Buck Jones - the Fighting Sheriff by Geoff Campion	£75.00
2	£35.00
3-5	£25.00
6-20	£20.00
21-50	£15.00
51-204	£8.00
205-468 titled Cowboy Picture Library	£4.00

ARTISTS/FEATURES
Jesus Blasco in 265, 276, 300, 305, 316, 318, 329, 341, 353, 357, 377, 386, 389, 401, 413, 446, 457, Reg Bunn. Alberto Breccia in 402, 410, 439, 450, 468. Steve Chapman. Arturo Del Castillo in 455, 463, 467. Gerry Embleton. Ron Embleton in 104, 106, 107, 109, 115, 121, 127, 137, 143, 245. Eric Parker.

N.MINT

Carlos V. Roume in 358, 378, 388, 398, 404, 405, 412, 424, 432, 451, 459. Jose Luis Salinas (Cisco Kid reprint) in 55. Tony Weare in 83, 129, 144.

COWBOY HERO ANNUAL
Miller; 1957-1960

1-4	£5.00

COWBOY WESTERN COMICS
Miller; 1-6 1956

1 28pgs; Charlton reprints	£4.00
2-6	£3.00

COZMIC COMICS
H. Bunch; 1 May 1972-6 Mar 1974

1-2 mostly US reprints, Crumb art	£2.50
3 The Firm, Weller art	£1.50
4-5	£1.50
6 Little Nympho by Bolland	£5.00

CRACK ACTION
Archer (King Comic Series); 1-5 1953

1-5 68pgs; reprints various American comics incl. Phantom Lady by Matt Baker, Voodoo, etc	£3.50

CRACK COMICS
R.& L.Locker; 1 1950

1 36pgs; Quality reprints	£4.00

CRACK SHOTS
John W. Fisher; 1 Jul 1946-2 Sep 1946

1-2 16pgs; Denis Gifford art	£4.00

CRACK WESTERN
Popular; Mar 1951-1952, 5 issues, variously numbered

1,3 36pgs	£5.00
48,51,55 28pgs; Quality reprints	£4.00

CRACKER
D.C. Thomson; 1 18th Jan 1975-87 11th Sep 1976 (joins Topper)

1 32pgs	£2.00
1 with free gift (Squeeze'n'Squeak balloon)	£4.00
2	£1.00
3-87 reduces to 28pgs during run	£0.35

CRACKER JACK COMIC
Philmar; nn 1947

nn - 16pgs; Frank Jupo art	£3.00

CRACKER JACK COMIC
Rayburn Productions; 1948

nn - 8pgs; Bob Wilkin art	£3.00

CRACKERJACK WESTERN ALBUM
Children's Press; 1959

1959 stories by Jeff Jefferies et al; Roger Hall painted cover	£4.00

CRACKERS
(previously Lot-O'-Fun)
Amalgamated; 1 22nd Feb 1929-615 31st May 1941 (joins Jingles)

1 12pgs tabloid size; Wally Robertson art	£35.00
2	£15.00
3-5	£12.50
6-177	£10.00
179-615	£5.00
CHRONOLOGY	
3 Feb 1940 1st half-tabloid size.	

CRASH!! COMIC BOOK
Children of God; nn 1975

nn - 16pgs small; religious promo	£0.20

CRASH COMICS
Rayburn Productions; 1 Jun 1948

1 John McCail, Bob Monkhouse, Denis Gifford art	£3.00

CRASHER COMIC, THE
Kayebon Press; 1 1946-10 1947

1-2 8pgs	£3.00
3-5 smaller size, 4 has 12pgs	£3.00
6-10	£2.00

CRASHO COMIC
Cardal/W.Daly; nn 1947

nn - 28pgs; Crewe Davies art	£3.00

CRAZY COMIC, THE
Philipp Marx; nn 1945

nn - 16pgs; Reg Carter art	£3.00

CREEPY WORLDS
Alan Class; 1 Aug 1962-249 Apr 1989

1 very scarce, 64pgs; US reprints begin	£15.00
2	£7.50
3-5	£5.00
6-50	£2.50
51-249	£1.50

CRIME AND PUNISHMENT
Pemberton; 1-3 1951

1-3 36pgs; Lev Gleason reprints	£5.00

CRIMEBUSTER
World Distributors; 1-6 1959

1-6 68pgs; reprints Johnny Hazard newspaper strip by Frank Robbins	£3.50

CRIME DETECTIVE COMICS
Streamline; nn-7 1951

nn - 28pgs; Hillman reprints, incl. issue cited in UK horror campaign	£8.00
2-7	£4.00

CRIME DOES NOT PAY
Arnold Book Co.; 1950, 2 unnumbered issues

nn - 12pgs green/orange gravure; Lev Gleason reprints	£8.00
nn - 36pgs full colour cover	£8.00

Comic Cuts #1

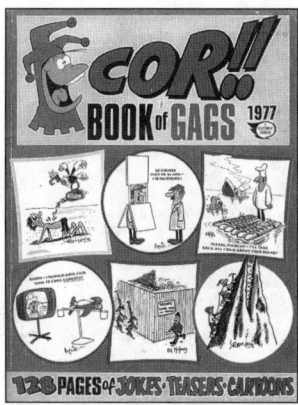
Cor Book of Gags 1977

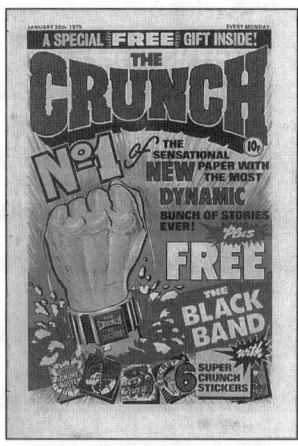
Crunch #1

	N.MINT		N.MINT

CRIME DOES NOT PAY
Pemberton; 1-6 1951
| 1-6 36pgs; Lev Gleason reprints | £6.00 |

CRIMEFIGHTER COMICS
Scion; nn May 1951
| nn - 24pgs; King-Ganteaume art | £5.00 |

CRIME FILES
Cartoon Art; 1 1952
| 1 Standard reprints | £4.00 |

CRIME PATROL
Archer (King Comics Series); 1-5 1953
| 1-5 68pgs; reprints various American comics incl. Ken Shannon, Red Rocket, etc | £6.00 |

CRIME REPORTER
Streamline; 1 1954
| 1 28pgs; Fox reprints | £3.50 |

CRIME SYNDICATE, THE
(see Secret Service Series)
Hotspur; 3 1948
| 3 Bob Wilkin art | £3.00 |

CRISIS
(see For A Few Troubles More, New Statesmen, Third World War, Troubled Souls, True Faith)
Fleetway; 1 17th Sep 1987-63 Oct 1991
1 Third World War by Pat Mills & Carlos Ezquerra, New Statesmen by John Smith	
& Jim Baikie begin	£1.75
2-3	£1.00
4-10	£0.90
11-13,16-20	£0.80
14 New Statesmen ends	£0.80
15 Troubled Souls by Garth Ennis & John McCrea, Sticky Fingers by Myra Hancock	
& David Hine begin	£0.90
21 no Troubled Souls	£0.75
22 no Sticky Fingers	£0.75
23-26	£0.75
27 Troubled Souls. Sticky Fingers both end	£0.75
28 New Statesman Prologue, Angels Amongst Us by Philip Bond begins	£0.80
29 True Faith by Garth Ennis & Warren Pleece begins	£0.80
30 more scarce, new strip Skin advertised but did not appear	£1.00
31-38	£0.80
39 Amnesty International issue	£1.00
40 Third World War Book 3, For A Few Troubles More by Ennis & McCrea,	
Reflexions by Oscar Zarate begin	£1.00
41,43	£1.00
42,45 China in Crisis by Tony Allen & David Hine	£1.00
44 David Lloyd art	£1.00
46-49 The New Adventures of Hitler by Grant Morrison & Steve Yeowell	£1.00
50 1st monthly; Straightgate by Smith & Phillips, Milo Manara art	£1.75
51 Alberto Breccia art	£1.75
52 Amnesty International followup, Fabry art, Sinner by Sampayo & Munoz reprints begin	£1.75
53 Straightgate, Third World War both end	£1.75
54 Insider by Mark Miller & Paul Grist, The General & the Priest by Igor Goldkind	
& Jim Baikie begin	£1.75
55 First Crisis & Revolver, Dan Dare by Morrison & Rian Hughes	£1.75
55-59	£1.75
60 1st magazine size; Trip to Tulum by Fellini & Manara begins	£1.75
61-63 Manara art, 63 incl. Operation Massacre by Solano Lopez	£1.75

ARTISTS/FEATURES
Jim Baikie in 1-4,9-12,28,54-55. Philip Bond in 28-37. Alberto Breccia reprint in 51. Al Davison in 34,62. Gary Erskine in 56-61. Carlos Ezquerra in 1-6,9-14,17-18,20-21. Glenn Fabry in 39,52. Duncan Fegredo in 7-8,19,26. John Hicklenton in 16,25,29,35,53. Paul Johnson in 51,54. David Lloyd in 37,44. Brendan McCarthy in 15-24. John McCrea in 15-20,22-27,31,40-43,45-46. Jose Munoz reprint in 52-55. Sean Phillips in 5-6,13-14, 22-24,27,31,33-34,39,50-53. Warren Pleece in 29-38,41,49. Richard Piers Rayner in 30,38. Steve Yeowell in 46-49. Oscar Zarate in 40-63.

CRUNCH, THE
D.C. Thomson; 1 20th Jan 1979-54 26th Jan 1980 (joins Hotspur)
1 Arena by Alcatena, The Mantracker by Alberto Salinas, The Walking Bombs by Denis	
McLoughlin, Hitler Lives by Pat Wright begin	£1.50
1 with free gift (Black wristband and six stickers)	£3.00
2	£0.75
2 with free gift (Barry Sheene poster)	£1.50
3-54	£0.35

CRYING FREEMAN
Manga; Sep 1995-present
| Vol.1: Portrait of a Killer Kazuo Koike & Ryoichi Ikegami reprints begin | £8.00 |
| Vol.2 (Jan 1996) | £8.00 |

CUBA FOR BEGINNERS
Writers Cooperative; 1 1975
| 1 76pgs oblong | £1.00 |

CUBBY AND THE CHRISTMAS STAR
R.& L.Locker; nn Jun 1946
| nn - 20pgs; comic/tracing book; Bob Monkhouse art | £2.50 |

CUIRASS
(see also Barbarienne)
Harrier; 1 May 1988
| 1 36pgs; John Marshall art | £1.00 |

CURLY KAYOE COMIC
Donald F. Peters; 1950, 2 unnumbered issues
| nn - 12pgs green/orange gravure; reprints American newspaper strip by Sam Leff | £2.00 |
| nn 20pgs full colour gravure | £1.50 |

CURLY'S COMIC
B.B. Ltd; 702 1950
| 702 16pp; Waring art | £2.00 |

CUTE COMIC
Philipp Marx; nn 1945
| nn - Reg Carter art | £2.50 |

CUTE FUN
(see Comicute Budget)
Gerald Swan; 1 Jun 1946-43 Sep 1951
1 8pgs, small size; E.H.Banger, D. Lovern West art	£8.00
2-4	£5.00
5-29 larger size	£5.00
30-43 larger size, 2 colour printing, monthly from 33 (Mar 1950)	£5.00

CUTTING EDGE, THE
(see Legends of Larian)

CYBERSPACE 3000
(see main American comics section)

CYCLONE ILLUSTRATED COMIC, THE
R.& L.Locker; nn Jan 1946
| nn - 16pgs; R.Beaumont art | £4.00 |

CYCLOPS
Innocence and Experience; 1 Jul 1970-4 Oct 1970
| 1,4 adult material; Edward Barker art | £1.50 |
| 2-3 Mal Dean, Barker art | £1.00 |

D

DAD'S ARMY
Pan (Piccolo); nn 1973
| nn - 20pgs; reprints from TV Comic by Bill Titcombe | £1.00 |

DAD'S OWN ANNUAL
Fleetway; 1993
| 1993 | £2.00 |
| Note: Non-fiction look at British boys' comics, but full of factual errors, mis-spelling of artists' names etc. | |

DAFFY DUCK
Top Sellers; 1972-?
| 1 36pgs; reprints from Western Publishing begin | £1.00 |
| 2-? | £0.35 |

DAILY DEEDS OF SAMMY THE SCOUT, THE
(see also The Adventures of Good Deed Danny)
Readers Library; nn-3 1946
| nn - 20pgs, full colour gravure; reprints newspaper strip by Ern Shaw | £3.00 |
| 2-3 Ern Shaw reprints | £2.00 |

DAILY EXPRESS CHILDREN'S OWN
Express Newspapers; 20th May 1933-15th July 1933 (8? issues)
20 May 1933 8pg supplement to Daily Express; George Parlett, Walter Bell,	
Roland Davies, A.W.Brown art	£15.00
27 May-15 Jul 1933	£7.00
Note: issues for 17 June and 24 June may not have appeared	

DAILY MIRROR BOOK FOR BOYS
Daily Mirror; 1970-1972
1970 Garth in Double Diamonds by John Allard	£3.00
1971 Garth in Space by Steve Dowling/John Allard	£3.00
1972 Ron Turner art	£2.00

DAILY MIRROR BOOK OF GARTH
IPC; 1975-1976
| 1975 annual size, Bellamy art | £3.50 |
| 1976 small oblong; Bellamy art | £4.50 |

DAILY MIRROR REFLECTIONS
Pictorial Newspaper/Daily Mirror; 1908-1935, 28 issues
| 1908 112pgs; reprints strips by W.Haselden from Daily Mirror | £5.00 |
| 1909-1935 | £3.00 |

DAILY STRIPS
see Garth, Romeo Brown)

THE DAKOTAS
Purnell; 1963-1964
| 1963 Stories by John Challis, illus. by Denis McLoughlin and R. Wilson | £4.00 |
| 1964 illus by Denis McLoughlin and R. Wilson | £4.00 |

DAKTARI ANNUAL
World Distributors; 1967-1968
| 1967-1968 | £2.00 |

DALE EVANS QUEEN OF THE WEST
World Distributors; 1-12 1955
| 1 28pgs; reprints from Dell begin | £5.00 |
| 2-12 | £2.50 |

DALEK ANNUAL
World Distributors; 1976-1979
| 1976,1977 | £10.00 |
| 1978,1979 | £6.00 |

DALEK BOOK, THE
Souvenir; 1964
| 1964 very scarce | £50.00 |

DALEK OUTER SPACE BOOK, THE
Souvenir; 1965
| 1965 very scarce | £60.00 |

DALEK WORLD, THE
Souvenir; 1966
| 1966 scarce | £40.00 |

DAN ADAMS
(see Action Series)

DAN DARE ANNUAL
Fleetway; 1974, 1979-1980, 1987, 1991
| 1974 Red Moon Mystery/Safari in Space edited Hampson reprints, scarce | £7.50 |
| 1979,1980 includes Judge Dredd strips | £4.00 |

	N.MINT
1987 Ian Kennedy, Ron Turner, Garry Leach art	£2.00
1991 Don Harley, Keith Page art	£3.50
DAN DARE HOLIDAY SPECIAL	
Fleetway; nn May 1990	
nn - Dan Dare by John Ridgway, Ian Kennedy, Mekon by Alan Langford	£1.00
DAN DARE, PILOT OF THE FUTURE	
Dragon's Dream; 1979-1982	
Vol 1 The Man From Nowhere additional art by Don Harley	£5.00
Vol 2 Rogue Planet	£4.50
Vol 3 Reign of the Robots	£4.00
Vol 1-3 hardback editions, scarce (each)	£10.00
DAN DARE, PILOT OF THE FUTURE	
Hamlyn; 1981	
- Dan Dare reprints from Eagle Annual	£5.00
DAN DARE, PILOT OF THE FUTURE DELUXE COLLECTOR'S EDITION	
Hawk; 1 1987-12 Dec 1995	
Vol 1 (1987) hardback	£20.00
Vol 1 (1988) softback	£10.00
Vol 2 (1988) Red Moon Mystery/Marooned on Mercury hardback	£20.00
Vol 2 reprint (1995)	£18.00
Vol 3 (1989) Operation Saturn/The Double Headed Eagle	£18.00
Vol 4 (1990) Prisoners of Space/Operation Triceratops	£16.00
Vol 5 (1991) The Man From Nowhere	£13.00
Vol 6 (1992) Rogue Planet	£18.00
Vol 7 (1993) Reign of the Robots/The Ship That Lived	£19.00
Vol 10 (Nov 1994) Project Nimbus, Frank Bellamy art	£19.00
Vol 11 (1995) The Solid Space Mystery, Keith Watson art	£19.00
Vol 12 (Dec 1995) The Final Volume, Watson art	£25.00
DAN DARE POSTER MAGAZINE	
IPC; 1 Jun 1977	
1 Dave Gibbons art	£1.50
DAN DARE SPACE ANNUAL	
Longacre; 1963	
1963 Eric Eden art	£15.00
DAN DARE SPACE BOOK	
Hulton; 1953	
- scarce; ed. by Marcus Morris & Frank Hampson, Hampson, Cornwell art	£50.00
DAN LENO'S COMIC JOURNAL	
C.A. Pearson; 1 26th Feb 1898-93 2nd Dec 1899	
1 8pgs; first UK comic to feature a real person, music hall comedian Dan Leno by Tom Browne	£45.00
2-93	£10.00
DANCES WITH DEMONS	
(see main American comics listing)	
DANDY BOOK, THE	
D.C. Thomson; Sep 1938-present	
1939 titled Dandy Monster Comic (Korky in foreground pointing to other characters each named, Jimmy/Grockle in right bottom corner)	£950.00
1940 (Korky hanging from trapeze in circus)	£525.00
1941 (Korky leading musical procession of other characters)	£350.00
1942 (Desperate Dan towing other characters in boat)	£250.00
1943 (Characters all riding bikes, Dan in steamroller)	£225.00
1944 (Korky sailing through net on ball kicked by Dan)	£175.00
1945 (Korky ski-ing, Dan using two tree trunks as skis)	£150.00
1946 (Characters in star-shaped frames watched by bellboy)	£125.00
1947 (Korky being tossed in blanket by other characters)	£100.00
1948 (Korky as puppeteer using other characters as puppets)	£100.00
1949 (Korky in top hat smoking cigar, with Dan carrying luggage)	£80.00
1950 (Korky in bathing costume on beach pouring hot water into sea)	£80.00
1951 (Korky as ringmaster in circus, Dan holding up elephant)	£80.00
1952 (Korky painting clockwork model, model Dan pushing paint off shelf)	£80.00
1953 becomes Dandy Book (6 frames, Korky tricks mice out of a feed)	£50.00
1954 (4 frame, Korky conceals stolen fish under his top hat)	£45.00
1955 (4 frame, Korky uses tail to fish under No Fishing sign)	£45.00
1956 (4 frame, Korky painting sign over Korky's Joke Shop)	£40.00
1957 (3 frame, Korky with four anglers in railway carriage)	£35.00
1958 (3 frame, Korky feeds fish iron filings then catches them with magnet)	£35.00
1959 (3 frame, Korky sailing in canoe then in umbrella)	£35.00
1960 (3 frame, Korky uses chained piller box to keep food safe from mice)	£30.00
1961 (3 frame, Korky balancing egg on nose), less common	£27.50
1962 (3 frame, Korky frying bacon & egg under lamp-post)	£25.00
1963 (4 frame, Korky looking through porthole, wearing sailor suit)	£20.00
1964 (3 frame, Korky sitting in deck chair eating a pie)	£20.00
1965 (2 frame, Korky pouring itching powder on pantomime horse)	£15.00
1966 1st dated on cover	£15.00
1967	£10.00
1968,1969	£7.00
1970-1975	£5.00
1976-1979	£3.00
1980-1989	£2.00
1990-1996	£1.50
DANDY COMIC, THE	
D.C. Thomson; 1 4th Dec 1937-present (2823 issues to 30th Dec 1995)	
1 very rare (believed only 30/40 copies exist in any condition)	£1750.00
Note: An issue was sold by postal auction recently for £2,300, but as no further sales have been made at this price it must be considered a one-off sales price rather than the "going rate". The company concerned have stated that if another issue came along in the same condition, they would have no problem in selling for the same price region.	
2 rare	£600.00
3 scarce	£450.00
4	£325.00
5-10	£150.00
1938 remaining issues	£100.00

	N.MINT
1939 issues	£60.00
1940 issues	£40.00
1941-1943 issues	£30.00
1944-1945 issues	£25.00
1946-1948 issues	£12.00
1949-1951 issues	£8.00
1952-1954 issues	£5.00
1955-1958 issues	£3.50
1959-1960 issues	£3.00
1961-1963 issues	£2.50
1964-1966 issues	£2.00
1967-1969 issues	£1.50
1970-1975 issues	£1.00
1976-1980 issues	£0.60
1981-1990 issues	£0.40
1991-1995 issues	£0.35

CHRONOLOGY

1 1st Korky the Cat by James Crichton, Keyhole Kate by Allan Morley Desperate Dan by Dudley Watkins, Jimmy and his Grockle by James Clark, Smarty Grandpa by Watkins. 207 (7 Feb 1942) 1st Peter Pye by Watkins. 227 (14 Nov 1942) 1st Dick Whittington by Watkins. 272 (12 Aug 1944) 1st The Amazing Mr X by Jack Glass (1st British costumed crimefighter serial). 280 (25 Nov 1944) 1st Black Bob text story. 285 (3 Feb 1945) 1st Danny Longlegs by Watkins. 447 (17 Jun 1950) title shortened to Dandy. 603 (13 Jun 1953) 1st Westward Ho by Paddy Brennan. 721 (17 Sep 1955) 1st all-picture issue. 754 (5 May 1956) 1st Black Bob picture strip by Jack Prout. 990 (12 Nov 1960) 1st Corporal Clott by David Law. 1000 (21 Jan 1961) Special issue. 1455 (11 Oct 1960) Dudley Watkins Desperate Dan reprints begin. 2000 (22 Mar 1980) Special issue. 2287 (21 Sep 1985) 1st "Dandy and Nutty". 2345 (1 Nov 1986) 1st "Dandy and Hoot". 2704 (18 Sep 1993) 1st all colour issue.

ARTISTS

Paddy Brennan in 408-437,445-675,707-735,750-773,861-880,967-1076,1087-1103,1310-1319,1451-1493,1529-1544,1590-1617,1662-1679,1976-2031. David Law in 990-1496. Allan Morley in 1-860. Ken Reid in 676-731,760-1187. Ron Smith in 665-728. Dudley D. Watkins in 1-1454 (1455-2148 contain Watkins Desperate Dan reprints with occasional originals by others, notably in 2000.

DANDY-BEANO SUMMER SPECIAL	
D.C. Thomson; 1963	
1963 32pgs, scarce (Desperate Dan eating pie, Dennis about to hit him over the head with a banjo)	£50.00
Note: This was the first British summer special title to be published and started a grand tradition followed by most other titles. Split to become Beano Summer Special and Dandy Summer Special	
DANDY COMIC LIBRARY	
D.C. Thomson; 1 Apr 1983-present (306 to 1995)	
1 64pgs pocket; Rodeo Round-Up (Desperate Dan) by Ken Harrison	£3.00
2-5	£1.25
6-306	£0.50
DANDY SUMMER SPECIAL	
D.C. Thomson; 1964-present	
1964 32pgs; (Korky riding a red/white polka dot inflatable horse)	£25.00
1965	£15.00
1966	£10.00
1967-1969	£7.50
1970-1975	£4.00
1976-1985	£2.50
1986-1999	£1.25
DANGER AND ADVENTURE	
Miller; 1-3? 1955	
1-3? 28pgs; Charlton reprints begin	£3.00
DANGER MAN	
Thorpe & Porter; 1 1966	
1 68pgs; Mick Anglo art	£12.00
DANGER MAN	
Young World Productions (Top TV Series); 1-2 1965	
1 Kingdom of Fear 48pgs, hardback	£15.00
2 War Against the Mafia 48pgs, hardback	£12.50
DANGER MAN ANNUAL	
Atlas/World Distributors; 1964-1966	
1964 (Atlas)	£12.00
1965,1966 (World Distributors)	£8.00
DANGER MAN TELEVISION STORY BOOK	
PBS; 1965	
1965 hardback	£9.00
DANGER MOUSE ANNUAL	
Cosgrove Hall; 1983	
1983	£2.00
DANGER TRAIL	
Bairns Books; nn May 1946	
nn - 16pgs; Ern Shaw, Denis Gifford art	£3.00
DANIEL BOONE	
Miller; 1 Feb 1957-35 1959	
1 28pgs; Daniel Boone by Fernando Castells begins	£5.00
2-35 some incl. Don Lawrence, Norman Light art	£3.00
Note: some issues entitled Exploits of Daniel Boone and feature US reprints from Charlton comics	
DARE	
Fleetway; nn Oct 1991	
nn - Morrison & Hughes reprints from Revolver/Crisis	£2.50
Note: Common; widely remaindered in 1994	
DAREDEVIL	
Pemberton; 1 1951-7 1952	
1 28pgs; Lev Gleason Daredevil Comics reprints begin	£10.00
2-7	£6.00
DAREDEVIL	
Miller; 1-3? 1953	
1-3? 36pgs; Lev Gleason Daredevil Comics reprints begin	£5.00
DAREDEVIL WESTERN COMICS	
Cartoon Art; 1 1949	

	N.MINT
1 28pgs; Fiction House reprints begin	£3.50
DAREDEVIL WINTER SPECIAL	
Marvel; nn Nov 1982	
nn - 52pgs; Marvel reprints, John Higgins cover	£1.25
DAREDEVILS, THE	
Marvel; 1 Jan 1983-11 Nov 1983 (joins Mighty World of Marvel)	
1 Captain Britain by Alan Moore & Alan Davis begins, Spider-Man,	
Miller Daredevil reprints begin	£6.00
1 with free gift (metal Daredevils badge) - attached to front cover with sellotape	
(often causing damage/yellowing)	£7.50
2-5 last Spider-Man	£4.00
6 incorporated Marvel Super-Heroes; Night Raven text stories by Moore,	
Dr. Who back-up reprints by Moore begin	£4.00
7,9	£3.50
8 Grit (Daredevil satire) by Moore & Collins/Farmer	£3.50
10 scarcer; Crusader reprint by Alan Davis (1st professional strip)	£5.00
11 scarcer; Night Raven text by Jamie Delano	£4.00
Note: 1,2,4-11 had pull-out posters, if intact issues are worth 10-20% more. 5,7,10, 11 by Alan Davis.	
Alan Moore articles in 1,3-6	
DARING HERO COMIC	
Scion; 1951-1952, 4 issues, 1,3-4 un-numbered	
nn (1,3-4) 20pgs; King-Ganteaume art	£4.00
2 20pgs, full colour on alternate pages; King Ganteaume art	£4.00
DARK ANGEL	
(see Hell's Angel in main American comics section)	
DARK GUARD	
(see main American comics section)	
DARK STAR HEROES	
Anti-Matter; 1 1984	
1 20pgs; HMS Conqueror by Eddie Campbell & Dave Harwood	£1.00
DARK TALES	
Darryl Cunningham; nn 1992	
nn - stories by Darryl Cunningham	£1.75
DARLING ROMANCE	
Gerald Swan; 1 1950-?	
1-? 36pgs; Close-Up (US) reprints	£1.50
DAVID THE SOLDIER KING	
Lion/Fleurus; nn 1979	
nn - 52pgs; French reprint	£1.00
DAVY CROCKETT	
Miller; 1 Oct 1956-50 Jan 1960	
1 28pgs; Davy Crockett by Don Lawrence begins	£7.50
2-50 some incl. Lawrence art	£3.50
DAZZLE COMIC	
International; nn 1946-5 1948	
nn - 8pgs, tabloid; John Turner art	£4.00
2-4 20pgs, small; Turner, Monkhouse, Gifford art	£3.00
5 4pgs, tabloid; Turner art, Hap Hazard reprint	£3.00
DAZZLER	
Target Publications; 1 19th Aug 1933-294 8th Apr 1939 (joins Golden)	
1 12pgs tabloid; Bert Hill, Louis Diamond art	£15.00
2	£6.00
3-60	£4.00
61-84 8pgs	£3.00
85-87 12pgs	£3.00
88-270 8pgs hereon	£3.00
271, 273-284, 286-294	£3.00
272 first blue paper	£3.00
285 first white paper	£3.00
DC ACTION	
London Editions; 1 Jan 1990-6 Nov 1990	
1 New Teen Titans, Animal Man by Morrison DC reprints begin	£2.00
2-6	£1.75
DEAD-EYE WESTERN	
Streamline/United Anglo American; 1950-1951, 7 unnumbered issues	
nn - 36pgs; Hillman reprints begin	£4.00
nn-nn 36/28pgs	£3.00
DEAD-EYE WESTERN COMIC	
Thorpe & Porter; 1 Feb 1953-?	
1 68pgs; Hillman reprints	£3.50
2-?	£2.50
DEADFACE	
Harrier; 1 Apr 1987-8 Oct 1988	
1 Eddie Campbell story/art begins	£1.50
2-3	£1.25
4-8 Campbell/Hillyer art	£1.00
Note: A collected edition was issued by Dark Horse (US).	
DEADLINE	
Portobello Project; v1:1 1987	
v1:1 Nick Abadzis art	£0.75
DEADLINE	
Tom Astor; 1 Oct 1988-71 Oct/Nov 1995	
1 Tank Girl by Alan Martin & Jamie Hewlett, Sharp by Steve Dillon, Beryl the Bitch by	
Julie Hollings, Wired World by Philip Bond, Johnny nemo by Pete Milligan &	
Brett Ewins all begin, Milligan text	£3.00
2 Hugo Tate by Nick Abadzis, Milligan text	£2.50
3 Double number; B-Bop and Lula by Steve Dillon begins	£2.75
4	£2.00
5 Johnny Nemo text story	£2.00
6 Hot Triggers by Philip Bond, Timulo by D'Israeli begin,	£2.00
7 Temptation by Glenn Dakin begins	£2.00
8-12	£1.80

	N.MINT
13 Atomic Baby by Rob Moran begins	£1.80
14 Double number	£2.50
15-18	£1.60
19 1st 76pgs & colour strips, Fabry art	£1.80
20-22	£1.80
23 Halloween number; last Wired World	£1.80
24 last Timulo, Planet Swerve by Alan Martin & Glyn Dillon begins	£1.70
25 Double number; fold-out cover; Bond art	£2.00
26 Fireball by Jamie Hewlett begins, numbering on cover becomes irregular	£1.70
Feb-May 1991, Aug-Nov 1991	£1.70
Jul 1991 Cheekie Wee Budgie Boy by Glynn Dillon begins	£1.70
Dec 1991/Jan 1992 Double number, Hugo Tate returns	£2.50
Feb-Mar 1992	£2.00
Apr 1992 free tape, Tank Girl returns	£2.00
May 1992 Love & Rockets reprints begin	£2.00
Jun-Nov 1992	£2.00
Dec/Jan 1992/93 (47) Double number	£2.50
Feb-Mar 1993	£2.00
Apr 1993 50th issue, Tank Girl, Wired World, Johnny Nemo, Hugo Tate,	
Several Colours Later by Pleece Brother begins	£2.00
May-Aug 1993 Several Colours Later	£2.00
Sep-Nov 1993 Oct. cover by Glenn Fabry, Nov. cover by John Bolton	£2.00
Dec 1993/Jan 1994 Double number, Brian Bolland cover & poster	£2.50
Feb-Apr 1994	£2.50
May 1994 Exit by Nabiel Kanan reprints begin	£2.50
Jun/Jul 1994 1st bi-monthly issue	£2.50
Aug/Sep 1994-Oct/Nov 1995	£2.50
DEADSHOT DICK WESTERN COMIC	
Foldes Press; nn 1948	
nn - 12pgs; Rex Hart art	£3.00
DEATH OF SUPERMAN, THE	
(see Superman in main American comics section)	
DEATH METAL	
(see main American comics section)	
DEATH METAL VS GENETIX	
(see main American comics section)	
DEATH: THE HIGH COST OF LIVING	
Titan; Jun 1994	
- reprints Vertigo series by Neil Gaiman, Chris Bachalo & Mark Buckingham	£8.00
DEATH 3	
(see main American comics section)	
DEATH WRECK	
(see main American comics section)	
DEATH'S HEAD	
(see also The Incomplete Death's Head, Strip)	
Marvel; 1 Dec 1988-10 Sep 1989	
1 Death's Head by Simon Furman & Bryan Hitch/Mark Farmer begins	£3.00
2 Dragon's Claws guest star	£2.50
3-4	£2.00
5 John Higgins art	£1.50
6-7	£1.50
8 Dr. Who guests	£1.50
9 Fantastic Four guest	£1.50
10 Iron Man guests	£1.50
DEATH'S HEAD	
Marvel; 1990	
The Body In Question Strip reprints	£7.00
DEATH'S HEAD II (LIMITED SERIES)	
(see Overkill) (see main American comics section)	
DEATH'S HEAD II (ONGOING SERIES)	
(see Battletide, Overkill) (see main American comics section)	
Marvel; 1 Dec 1992-16 Apr 1994	
1 X-Men guest, Liam Sharp art begins	£2.00
2-4 Lotus FX storyline, Sharp art; 3. X-Men	£1.50
5 MyS-TECH Wars x-over, Dell Barras art	£1.50
6-7,9,11-13 Simon Coleby art	£1.20
8 Anthony Williams art	£1.20
10 Dougie Braithwaite art	£1.20
14 Sal Larocca art, incl. Death's Head Gold #0 8pg prologue	£1.35
15-16	£1.20
Note: Issue 5 not reprinted in Overkill	
DEATH'S HEAD II AND DIE CUT	
(see main American comics section)	
DEATH'S HEAD II AND KILLPOWER	
(see Battletide II: Death's Head II & Killpower in main American comics section)	
DEATH'S HEAD II GOLD	
(see main American comics section)	
DEATHSHEART	
CM Comics; 1 Jan 1994	
1 Deathsheart by Gary Smith & Andrew Radbourne	£1.50
DEATHWATCH	
Harrier; 1 Jul 1987	
1 28pgs; Art Wetherell art	£0.60
DEBBIE	
D.C. Thomson; 1 17th Feb 1973-518 15th Jan 1983 (joins Mandy)	
1	£1.00
2-518 Debbie & Spellbound from 21 Jan 1978	£0.25
DEBBIE PICTURE STORY LIBRARY	
D.C. Thomson; 1 Apr 1978-present?	
1 68pgs pocket size; Lost on Planet X	£0.80
2-?	£0.25

N.MINT

DEEPSEA
Scion; nn 1952
nn - 24pgs; Terence Patrick art £3.00

DEEP SPACE NINE
Boxtree; Jul 1994-present
Deep Space Nine: Stowaway/Old Wounds (Jul 1994) reprints Malibu series £8.00
Deep Space Nine: Emancipation and Beyond (Aug 1994) Malibu reprints £8.00
Deep Space Nine: Requiem (Apr 1995) Malibu reprints £8.00

DEMON
Portman; 1 1978-?
1 68pgs; Satana by Esteban Moroto reprints begin, Romita, Colan, Infantino, Blasco reprints £1.25
2-? £1.00

DELUXE ALBUM SERIES
Williams/Top Sellers; 1 May 1973-12 Apr 1974
1 52pgs; Tarzan of the Apes reprints £2.50
2-12 reprints £1.00
Note: reprints from America, Britain and Europe: 1 Tarzan of the Apes. 2 Buffalo Bill. 3 Casper the Friendly Ghost. 4 Richie Rich & the Gang. 5 Boom-Boom the White Dolphin. 6 Laurel and Hardy. 7 Dastardly and Muttley by Tony Goffe. 8 Motormouse and Autocat. 9 Calimero. 10 Mr Sandman. 11 Doctor Doolittle by Tony Goffe. 12 Boom-Boom the White Dolphin.

DEMPSEY AND MAKEPEACE ANNUAL
World; 1986
1986 illus. Walt Howarth £2.00

DENNIS THE MENACE BOOK
D.C. Thomson; Sep 1955-present (bi-annual, later annual)
1956 (Dennis holding tin of paint) £110.00
1958 (Dennis whizzing downhill on a go-kart flooring people on the way) £60.00
1960 (Dennis underwater in flippers using pincers on swimmer's toe) £40.00
1962 (Dennis holding giant caricature head of himself over his own head) £25.00
1964 (Dennis bursting through black/red sheet) £20.00
1966,1968 dated on cover £15.00
1970-1978 £7.50
1980-1990 £3.00
1991-1994 £2.50

DEPUTY DAWG PICTURE BOOK
PBS/Total; nn 1973
nn - 36pgs; promo, reprints from Western Comics (US) £0.50

DESPERATE DAN BOOK
D.C. Thomson; 1954, 1978, 1990-1992
1954 scarce, Dudley Watkins art £125.00
1979 £5.00
1991-1993 £3.00

DETECTIVE COMIC
Miller 1-8 1959
1 68pgs; ACG/Fawcett reprints begin £8.00
2-8 reprints incl. Mike Barnett, Man Against Crime £5.00

DETECTIVE COMICS
Kosmos International Agency; nn Feb 1947
nn - 16pgs; reprints Dutch newspaper strip by Piet Van Elk £4.00

DETECTIVE HERO COMIC
Scion; 1 1952
1 24pgs; King-Ganteaume art £6.00

DEVLIN WAUGH: SWIMMING IN BLOOD
Mandarin (2000AD Books); nn Mar 1993
nn - Judge Dredd Megazine reprint by John Smith & Sean Phillips £7.00

DIAL 999
(see TV Photo Stories)

DIAMOND ADVENTURE COMIC
Atlas; 1 Jul 1960-31 1963
1 28pgs; Fiction House reprints begin £5.00
2-31 £3.00

DIANA
D.C. Thomson; 1 23th Feb 1963-720 4th Dec 1976 (joins Jackie)
1 24pgs tabloid; MacGillivray art £2.50
2 £1.50
3-5 £1.00
6-50 £0.50
2-720 some incl. John Burns art, titled Diana & Romeo from 21 Sep 1974 £0.25
Note: Some issues (c1967) contain Avengers which generally raise price to £5.00

DICE MAN
IPC; 1 Jan 1986-5 Oct 1986
1 Judge Dredd by Talbot, Nemesis by O'Neill, Slaine by David Lloyd £2.50
2 ABC Warriors by Dillon, Diceman by Graham Manley, Slaine by Nik Williams £2.00
3 Rogue Trooper by Collins/Farmer, Diceman by Ridgway, Torquemada by Talbot, more scarce £2.25
4 Diceman by Dillon, Slaine by Collins/Farmer £2.00
5 Rogue Trooper by Collins, Ronald Reagan by Hunt Emerson, Diceman by Dillon £1.75

DICK BARTON SPECIAL AGENT ANNUAL
Brown Watson; 1978
1978 David Lloyd art £2.00

DICK BOSS
Literary Press; 1947
Adventures of Dick Boss Mazure art £3.50
Dick Boss in Texas Mazure art £3.50

DICK COLE
(see Blue Bolt Series)

DICK HERCULES OF ST. MARKHAM'S
Sports Cartoons; 1 Dec 1952-17 Apr 1954 (joins Steve Sampson)
1 Dick Hercules by Sydney Jordan begins £5.00
2-17 £3.00

DICK TRACY
Streamline/United Anglo-American; 1 1953-?
1 28pgs; reprints American newspaper strip £8.00

Dandy #250

Dandy Book 1961

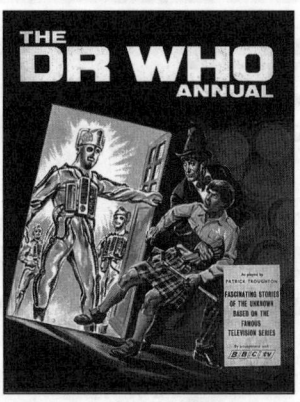
Dr Who Annual 1968

	N.MINT
2-?	£5.00

DICK TURPIN ANNUAL
Grandreams; 1980
1980 Felix Carrion art	£1.50

DICKORY DOCK
IPC; 1 1st Mar 1980-30 20th Sep 1980 (joins Jack & Jill)
1 nursury comic, Peter Woolcock art	£0.75
2-30	£0.20

DICKORY DOCK SUMMER SPECIAL
IPC; nn Jul 1980
nn - 40pgs; Peter Woolcock art	£0.40

DIE CUT VS G-FORCE
(see main American comics section)

DIGITEK
(see Overkill) (see main American comics section)

DINGBATS COMIC
Philmar; 1948
1 8pgs; The Dingbats reprints by Ern Shaw	£2.00

DINGDONGS COMIC
Philmar; nn 1948
nn - 8pgs; Ern Shaw art	£2.00

DIRTY PAIR
Manga; Sep 1995-present
Biohazards (Sep 1995) Toren Smith & Adam Warren Dark Horse reprints	£8.00
Dangerous Acquaintances (Jan 1996)	£8.00

DISCORDIA
London Cartoon Centre; nn Aug 1991
nn - 40pgs; LCC benefit comic	£1.00

DISNEY MAGAZINE
House of Grolier; 1-4? 1978
1-4? 32pgs giveaway; US reprints	£1.25

DISNEY MAGAZINE
London Editions/Fleetway; 1 Feb 1982-12 Feb 1983 (provincial); 1 Mar 1983-?
1-12 32pgs; European reprints, provincial release	£0.50
1-? national release	£0.25

DISNEY MIRROR
Daily Mirror; 1 2nd Mar 1991-162? 2nd Apr 1994
1-98,100-113 8pgs half tabloid giveaway with Daily Mirror	£0.20
99 (16 Jan 1993) printed tabloid size as part of TV weekly supplement	£0.20
114 (1 May 1993) first regular tabloid, loose	£0.20
115-162 ?	£0.10

DISNEY TIME
IPC; 1 29th Jan 1977-21 18th Jun 1977
1 16pgs	£1.50
2-21	£1.25

DISNEY TIME SPECIALS
IPC; May 1977-Aug 1977
Funtime Special	£1.50
Holiday Special	£1.25
Summer Special	£1.00

DISNEYLAND
IPC; 1 27th Feb 1971-298 13th Nov 1976 (joins Mickey Mouse)
1 20pgs; Basil Reynolds, Roland Davies art, various Disney characters	£3.50
1 with free gift (Merry-Go-Round toy)	£6.00
2	£1.50
2-298 incl. Hugh McNeil art	£0.75
Note: incorporates Sunny Stories (26 Jun 1971), Once Upon A Time (29 Apr 1972), Now I Know (20 Oct 1973)	

DISNEYLAND SPECIALS
IPC; 1971-1980
Fun Time Special 1971-1978	£0.75
Christmas Special 1971-1976	£0.75
Springtime Special 1972-1978	£0.75
Holiday Special 1972-1980	£0.75
Summer Special 1972-1980	£0.75
Autumn Special 1973	£0.75
Fun Time Spring Special 1979	£0.75

DIXIE COMIC
Ensign; nn 1947
nn - 8pgs; Frank Minnitt art	£3.00

DIXIE DUGAN
United Anglo-American; nn 1950-2 1951
nn - 36pgs; Columbia Publications reprint of American newspaper strip by J.H.Striebel & J.P.McEvoy	£5.00
2	£3.00

DIXON OF DOCK GREEN
C.A. Pearson (TV Picture Stories); 1 Nov 1959-6 Mar 1960
1 68pgs pocket size	£6.00
2-6	£4.00

ARTISTS/FEATURES
1 A Whiff of Garlic. 2 Bracelets for the Groom. 3 The Hell. 4 The Gent From Siberia. 5 A Little Bit of French. 6 The Case of Mrs. X.

DIZZLING COMIC
Co-ordination Press; nn Sep 1947
nn - 20pgs; reprints Dutch newspaper strips, Piet van Elk art	£2.50

DOC CHAOS
Hydra/Anti-Matter; 1 1984-4 1985; Escape; 1-2 1988?
1 (Hydra) 24pgs, Phil Elliott art	£2.00
2 (Anti-Matter) Elliott art	£2.00
3-4 (Anti-Matter) untoned Elliott art	£1.25
1 (Escape) 44pgs, reprints 1-2, pink cover, rare (all but 50 copies destroyed)	£3.50
1 (Escape) second print, red cover	£2.25

	N.MINT
2 (Escape) 56pgs, reprints 3-4 (art toned) with new material, yellow cover	£2.00

DOC CHAOS: THE CHERNOBLE EFFECT
Hooligan Press; nn Jul 1988
nn - Dave Thorpe text, Bisley, Bolland, Ewins, Fegredo, McKean, Talbot illos	£2.50

DOCTOR DOOLITTLE
Top Sellers; 1 1973-? 1974
1 36pgs; Doctor Doolittle by V.V.Artists begins	£0.75
2-?	£0.25

DOCTOR KILDARE ANNUAL
World Distributors; 1962
1962 based on TV programme	£3.00

DOCTOR SNUGGLES HOLIDAY SPECIAL
Polystyle; May 1981-May 1982, 2 unnumbered issues
1981-1982 48pgs; reprints, based on TV series	£0.25

DOCTOR WHO
(see also The Mark of Mandragora)

DOCTOR WHO AND THE INVASION FROM SPACE
World Distributors; 1965
1965 scarce	£50.00

DOCTOR WHO ANNUAL/YEARBOOK
(see also K-9 Annual)
World Distributors/Marvel; 1965-present
1965 Hartnell	£20.00
1966 Hartnell, scarce	£35.00
1967 1st Troughton	£40.00
1968 Troughton, scarce	£50.00
1969 Troughton	£30.00
1970 1st Pertwee, white and pink spines known	£30.00
1973 1st coverdated; Pertwee	£10.00
1974,1975 Pertwee	£7.50
1976 1st Tom Baker	£4.00
1977-1980 Tom Baker	£3.50
1981 Tom Baker, some issued without coverdate	£3.00
1982 Tom Baker/Davidson	£2.75
1983,1984 Davidson	£2.75
1985-1987 Colin Baker	£2.75
1991-1996 (Marvel) becomes Dr. Who Yearbook	£2.50
Note: The classic Annuals 1965-1970 are mostly text stories with one or two strips.	

DOCTOR WHO CLASSIC COMICS
Marvel; 1 9th Dec 1992-27 7th Dec 1994
1 52pgs; reprints from TV Comic, Countdown & TV Century 21 begin	£2.50
2-8	£2.50
9 reprints Dell movie adaptation Dr. Who and the Daleks, Giordano/Trapini art, Gibbons art	£2.50
10-11 Tides of Time by Gibbons reprint	£2.50
12-27	£2.50

DOCTOR WHO CLASSIC COMICS AUTUMN HOLIDAY SPECIAL
Marvel; Sep 1993
(1993) Evening's Empire, Richard Piers Raynor art	£2.50

DOCTOR WHO COMIC
(see Mighty Midget)

DOCTOR WHO MONTHLY
(see Doctor Who Weekly)

DOCTOR WHO SPECIALS
Polystyle/Marvel; May 1974-1989
Holiday 1974 48pgs	£5.00
Winter 1977	£3.50
Summer 1980 52pgs; Gibbons reprints	£3.00
Very Best of Doctor Who (1981) all reprints, Moore script, Neary art	£3.00
Winter 1981	£2.50
Summer 1982 incl. poster	£2.50
Winter 1982 Pertwee interview, incl. poster	£2.25
Summer 1983 McMahon, Dillon reprints, incl. poster	£2.00
Winter 1983 producers special	£2.00
Summer 1984 merchandise special	£2.00
Winter 1984 archives special	£2.00
Summer 1985	£1.50
Winter 1985	£1.50
Summer 1986 historical stories	£1.25
Autumn 1986 Tom Baker special	£1.50
Autumn 1987 designers special	£1.25
25th Anniversary Special (Nov 1988)	£2.00
It's Bigger on the Inside (Nov 1988)	£2.00
DWM 10th Anniversary Special (1989)	£2.00
Summer 1991 (Jul 1991) location listings	£2.25
Winter 1991 (Nov 1991) UNIT special	£2.25
Holiday 1992 Sarah Jane Smith special	£2.25
Summer 1993 Daleks special	£2.25

DOCTOR WHO SPECIAL: JOURNEY THROUGH TIME
Galley Press; 1986?
- 192pgs, hardback	£7.50

DOCTOR WHO, THE AMAZING WORLD OF
BBC; 1976
1976	£6.00

DOCTOR WHO: VOYAGER
Marvel; nn 1989
nn - Steve Parkhouse & John Ridgeway reprints	£5.00

DOCTOR WHO WEEKLY/MONTHLY/MAGAZINE
Marvel; Dr. Who Weekly 1 17th Oct 1979-43 6th Aug 1980; Dr. Who Monthly 44 Sep 1980-present (232 issues to Dec 1995)
1 Dr. Who by Dave Gibbons begins	£5.00
1 with free gift (transfers)	£7.50
2	£3.50

	N.MINT		N.MINT
2 with free gift (transfers)	£6.00	**DON'T RUSH ME**	
3-16,19-25	£2.50	Wandsworth Council; nn Mar 1975	
17 Paul Neary art, 1st Abslom Daak back-up by Steve Moore & Steve Dillon	£3.00	nn - 4pgs giveaway; race relations promo	£0.10
18 Neary art	£3.00	**DOPE FIEND FUNNIES**	
26-34 Gibbons art, covers not numbered	£2.00	H. Bunch (Cozmic); nn Sep 1974	
35-38,40-43 Alan Moore back-up scripts, Gibbons art	£2.00	nn - Chris Welch, Edward Barker art	£1.50
39 Gibbons art	£2.00	**DOT AND CARRIE**	
44 becomes Dr. Who Monthly, Gibbons art	£4.00	Daily News; 1923-1925	
45-46 Gibbons art	£2.50	**Dot and Carrie** 68pgs oblong; reprints The Star newspaper strip by J.F.Horrabin	£10.00
47,51,57 Gibbons art, A.Moore back-up scripts	£2.00	**Dot and Carrie and Adolphus**	£8.00
48-49,52-55,60 Gibbons art	£2.00	**Dot and Carrie Not Forgetting Adolphus**	£8.00
50,61,68-69 Gibbons art, incl. poster	£2.00	**DOUBLE BILL**	
56 1st Freefall Warriors (in Dr. Who strip) by Gibbons	£2.00	Bob Comics; nn 1992	
58-59 McMahon art	£2.00	nn - 28pgs; Bob Lynch art	£0.60
62-67 Gibbons art	£2.00	**DOUBLE DUO**	
70-73,75-83 incl. poster	£1.50	Williams; nn 1976-12 1977, numbered from 9 onwards	
74,76-82	£1.50	(1) 68pgs; The Open Boat/The Denver Express, reprints Classics Illustrated (European issues)	£14.00
84 Freefall Warriors back-up by Gibbons	£1.50	(2) March of 10,000/Ship to Buenos Aires	£14.00
85 incl. poster, no Dr. Who main strip	£1.50	(3) Voyage to the Far East/The Brigands	£14.00
86 Steve Dillon art	£1.50	(4) Attack on Mill/Escape of Incas	£14.00
87 Dillon art, incl. poster	£1.50	(5) Conquest-Peru/Wandering Horsemen	£14.00
88-99 Ridgway art	£1.25	(6) The Blue Hotel/A Terrible Revenge	£14.00
100 Ridgway art	£1.75	(7) Battle-Jerusalem/Castle Ontranto	£14.00
101-102,104-110 Ridgway art	£1.25	(8) Uncharted Waters/The Burma Road	£14.00
103,111,118,120,123,130 Ridgway art, incl. poster	£1.50	9 Death-Capt. Cook/Young Carthaginian	£14.00
112-117,119,121-122,124,127-129,131-135 Ridgway art	£1.25	10 Quest for the Holy Grail/Seven Who Were Hanged	£14.00
122-123 Berni Resaurant giveaways ("Free" corner flash on cover)	£1.10	11 Wreck of Sao Joao/Warlord-Mexico	£14.00
125-126 Ridgway art	£1.40	12 Martin Eden/Apostle of the Indies	£14.00
136-138	£1.20	**DOUBLE TROUBLE**	
139-144 140 Higgins art, 143-144 Ridgway art	£1.25	Star Publications; nn 1950	
145-146	£1.25	nn - 68pgs oblong; reprints American newspaper strip by Bill Maclean	£3.00
147 Sleeze Brothers in Dr. Who strip	£1.25	**DOWN WITH CRIME**	
148-153	£1.25	Arnold Book Co.; 50-56 1952	
154-166 157-161 incl. Ridgway art, 164-166 incl. Arthur Ranson art	£1.50	50-56 28pgs; Fawcett reprints, incl. material cited in POP & UK campaign	£10.00
167 double issue; free Flexi-Disc	£2.00	**DOWNSIDE**	
168-173	£1.75	Macnamara & Ketley; 1 May 1988-6 Jan 1991	
174-179	£2.00	1	£1.50
180 52pgs; Rayner art, Daleks reprints from TV21 begin	£2.25	2-6	£1.00
181-183	£2.25	**D.R. & QUINCH'S TOTALLY AWESOME GUIDE TO LIFE**	
184-189 free postcards	£2.50	Titan (Best of 2000AD); 1986	
190,193-199	£2.50	- 2000AD reprints by Moore & Davis	£5.00
191-192 Ridgway art	£2.50	**DRACULA**	
200 Anniversary issue, fold out, wraparound cover	£2.50	Top Sellers; nn 1962	
201-206	£2.50	nn - 68pgs; Dell Movie Classics reprint, adapts Dracula film	£2.50
207 30th Anniversary issue, Ridgway art, wraparound cover	£2.50	**DRACULA**	
208-233	£2.50	New English Library; 1 30th Sep 1972-12 24th Feb 1973	
234	£2.95	1 24pgs; Spanish reprints	£1.50
Doctor Who Adventure Comics (1986) 145mm x 105mm reprints		2-12	£0.60
(free with Golden Wonder Crisps) 1-6, each	£0.75	**DRACULA**	
Doctor Who Collected Comics (1986) reprints 87-88,95-97	£1.25	Titan; Jan 1993	
ARTISTS/FEATURES		- reprints Topps Dracula 1-4, movie adaptation, Mignola art	£8.00
(Dr. Who) Colin Andrew in 193-196,203-206. Dave Gibbons in 1-16,19-57,60-69. John Higgins in 140.		**DRACULA**	
Mike McMahon (pencils) in 58-59. Paul Neary in 17-18. Arthur Ranson in 164-166. John Ridgway in 88-		Dark Horse; 1 19th Jan 1993-9 Aug 1993	
126,143-144,157-161,191-192,207 (pencils in 127-132). Jamie Delano script in 114-116,123-126. Steve		1 Bram Stoker's Dracula movie adaptation reprint begins, Mignola art	£1.25
Moore script in 35-55. Grant Morrison script in 118-119,127-129,139. Steve Parkhouse script in 56-		2-5 movie adaptation. 4 - 1st Vampirella reprints	£1.25
84,86-99. (back-ups) Steve Dillon in 6,7,9-11,13-14,17-20,23-24,27-29. David Lloyd in 15-16,21-22,25-		6-9 Vlad the Impaler reprints, Maroto art	£1.25
26,30-46,51,57,59,184 (rpt). Mike McMahon in 56. Paul Neary/David Lloyd in 1-4. Paul Neary in 5,8,12.		**DRACULA COMICS SPECIAL**	
TV21 Dalek reprints in 33-42,180-193 (Richard Jennings), 53-56,58-66,68 (Turner).		Quality; 1 Apr 1974	
DOLLMAN		1 reprints Paul Neary, John Bolton strips from House of Hammer	£2.00
R.& L.Locker; nn Aug 1949		**DRACULA LIVES**	
nn - 36pgs; Quality reprint	£5.00	Marvel; 1 26th Oct 1974-87 16th Jun 1976 (joins Planet of the Apes)	
DOLLMAN		1 36pgs; Dracula, Werewolf By Night reprints begin	£1.50
Popular; 6 Sep 1951, 1 issue		2	£1.25
6 36pgs; Quality reprint	£5.00	3-5	£1.00
DOMU		4-59	£0.60
Mandarin; nn Jan 1995		60-87 title becomes Dracula Lives featuring the Legion of Monsters	£0.50
nn - Katsuhiro Otomo manga reprints	£9.00	**DRACULA LIVES SPECIAL**	
DON WINSLOWE OF THE NAVY		World Distributors; 1 1976	
Miller; nn 1947; 50 1950-61 1952; 100 1952-149 1953 (63 issues in all)		1 68pgs; Marvel reprints	£1.50
nn - 12pgs gravure; Fawcett reprints begin	£5.00	**DRACULA SUMMER SPECIAL**	
50-61 24pgs	£3.50	Marvel; nn May 1982	
100-149 28pgs	£2.50	nn - 48pgs; reprints	£1.25
DONALD AND MICKEY		**DRACULA'S SPINECHILLERS ANNUAL**	
IPC; 1 4th Mar 1972-182 29th Aug 1974 (becomes Mickey & Donald)		World International; 1982	
1 24pgs; American Disney reprints	£2.00	1982 reprints Paul Neary Dracula, Blas Gallego Twins of Evil strips from House of Hammer	£2.00
2-182 titled Donald & Mickey & Goofy from 18 May 1974	£0.50	**DRAGON'S CLAWS**	
DONALD AND MICKEY SPECIALS		(see also Death's Head) (see main American comics section)	
IPC; Jun 1972-Jun 1975		**DRAGONSLAYER**	
Holiday Special 1972-1975	£0.75	Marvel; nn 1982	
Fun Time Extra 1972-1975	£0.75	nn - 52pgs; reprints adaptation of Disney film	£1.25
Christmas Special 1972-1974	£0.75	**DUCK SOUP**	
DONALD DUCK		Duck Soup; 1-3 1979	
IPC; 1 27th Sep 1975-18 24th Jan 1976 (joins Mickey Mouse)		1 24pgs adult material, Steve Bell art	£1.00
1 32pgs; American Disney reprints	£1.25	2-3 Bell art	£0.50
2-18	£0.50	**DUMMY**	
DONALD DUCK CHRISTMAS SPECIAL		New Musical Express; nn 6th Dec 1975	
IPC; nn Nov 1975		nn - 4pgs tabloid supplement; Tony Benyon art	£0.25
nn - 48pgs; American Disney reprints	£0.75	**DURANGO KID**	
DONALD DUCK FUN LIBRARY		Streamline; 1 1951-?	
Egmont/Purnell 1 Apr 1978-?		1 28pgs; Magazine Enterprises reprints begin	£3.50
1 100pgs small size; foreign reprints	£0.75	2-?	£2.00
2-?	£0.50		

N.MINT

DURANGO KID
Compix; 1 1952-20 1953
1 20pgs; Magazine Enterprises reprints begin	£5.00
2-20	£2.50

DUSTY BEAR MONTHLY
New English Library; 1 1975-?
1 24pgs	£0.75
2-?	£0.35

DUSTY BEAR SUMMER FUN BOOK
New English Library; nn 1976
nn - 48pgs	£0.75

DYKE'S DELIGHT
Knockabout (Fanny); 1 1993-2 1994
1 Lesbian anthology ed. by Kate Charlsworth	£2.50
2	£2.50

DYNAMIC
(see also Wonderman)
Paget; nn Feb 1949
nn - 16pgs; Gail Garrity, Captain Justice (Wonderman) by Mick Anglo	£4.00

DYNAMIC COMICS
International; nn Jun 1945
nn - 8pgs; Denis Gifford art	£4.00

DYNAMIC THRILLS
Gerald Swan; 1 Jan 1951-10 1952
1-3,6-7	£7.50
4-5,8-10 Ron Embleton art	£10.00

DYNAMITE DUNN
Miller; nn 1944
nn - 16pgs; United Features reprint from Comics on Parade	£4.00

E

EAGLE
Hulton/Longacre/Odhams/IPC; v1:1 14th Apr 1950-v20:17 26th Apr 1969 (987 issues; joins Lion)
Vol 1:1 Dan Dare by Hampson, PC 49 by Alan Stranks & Strom Gould, Rob Conway, Tommy Walls, The Great Adventurer all by Hampson all begin	£200.00
2	£50.00
3	£25.00
4-5	£20.00
6-10	£15.00
11-35	£10.00
36,38-52	£7.50
37 Riders of the Range by Charles Chilton & Jack Daniel begins	£7.50
Vol 2:1-10	£6.00
11-52	£5.00
Vol 3:1-4,6-52	£5.00
5 Luck of the Legion by Geoffrey Bond & Martin Aitchison begins	£5.00
Vol 4:1-25,27-38	£4.00
26 Storm Nelson by Edward Trice & Richard Jennings begins	£4.00
Vol 5:1-53	£3.50
Vol 6:1-3,5-52	£3.50
4 Jack O'Lantern by George Beardmore & Robert Ayton begins	£3.50
Vol 7:1-52	£3.50
Vol 8:1-10,13-52	£3.50
11 last PC 49	£3.50
12 Mark Question by Stranks & Harry Lindfield begins	£3.50
Vol 9:1-29,32-52	£3.50
30 last Mark Question	£3.50
31 Cavendish Brown MS by Bill Wellings & Pat Williams	£3.50
Vol 10:1,2,5-26,29-45	£3.50
3 last Cavendish Brown	£3.50
4 They Showed The Way by Peter Simpson & Pat Williams begins	£3.50
27 undated; last Hampson Dan Dare, no speech balloons on cover	£3.50
28 1st Bellamy Dan Dare	£3.50
Vol 11:1-10,13-27	£3.00
11 They Showed The Way ends	£3.00
12 Knights of the Road by George Beardmore & Gerald Haylock begins	£3.00
28 last Bellamy Dan Dare	£3.00
29 1st Harley/Cornwell Dare	£3.00
30,33-53	£2.00
31 last Jack O'Lantern	£2.00
32 Fraser of Africa by Bellamy begins	£2.00
Vol 12:1-31	£2.00
32 last Fraser of Africa	£2.00
33 Danger Unlimited by Aitchison begins	£1.75
34-36,38-52	£1.75
37 last Luck of the Legion	£1.75
Vol 13:1-8,11-27,29-32,34-41,44-52	£1.75
9 Riders of the Range, Knights of the Road, Danger Unlimited, Storm Nelson end	£1.75
10 Montgomery of Alemein by Bellamy, Vengeance Trail by Jesus Blasco, Sgt. Bruce CID by Jim Edgar & Paul Travillion, Keith Watson Dan Dare begin	£1.75
28 Lt.Hornblower by Aitchison begins	£1.75
30 Island of Fire by Jennings begins	£1.75
33 Hornblower strip title changes to Captain...	£1.75
42 Mann of Battle by Brian Lewis, Island of Fire ends	£1.75
43 Heros the Spartan by Bellamy begins, Sgt.Bruce becomes Can You Catch a Crook?	£1.75
Vol 14:1-8	£1.75
9 last Hornblower	£1.75
10 1st "Eagle and Swift"; Blackbow the Cheyenne by Victor de la Fuente, Beast in Loch Craggon by John McClusky begin	£1.50

N.MINT

11-52	£1.50
Vol 15:1-4,7-40,42-52	£1.50
5 last Mann of Battle	£1.50
6 Johnny Frog by Ron Embleton begins	£1.50
23 Cornelius Dimworthy by Sam Fair begins	£1.50
41 1st "Eagle and Boys' World"; Iron Man by Martin Salvador, Raff Regan, Wrath of the Gods by Moorcock and John Burns begin	£2.00
41 with free gift (4 Olympic Medals in packet)	£5.00
Vol 16:1-52, Vol 17:1-53	£1.50
Vol 18:1 last original Dan Dare (except v18,52-v19,3)	£1.50
2 Hampson Dan Dare reprints begin (from v5,22)	£1.50
3-52	£1.50
Vol 19:1-52, Vol 20:1-17	£1.50
The Best of Eagle Ed. by Marcus Morris (Michael Joseph/Edbury Press, 1977)	£5.00
The Eagle Book of Cutaways Ed. by Denis Gifford (Webb & Bower/Michael Joseph, 1988)	£2.50

ARTISTS/FEATURES

Martin Aitchison in v3:5-v12:37 (Luck of the Legion), v12:33-v13:9 (Danger Unlimited), v13:10-29 (The Lost World), v13:28-v14:9 (Lt./Capt.Hornblower). Frank Bellamy in v8:40-v9:36 (The Happy Warrior), v9:37-v10:15 (The Shepherd King), v10:16-23 (The Travels of Marco Polo), v10:28-v11:28 (Dan Dare; some pages by Harley/ Cornwell, Gerald Palmer), v11:32-v12:32 (Fraser of Africa), v13:10-27 (Montgomery of Alemein), v13:43-v14:43, v15:23-42, v16:9-30 (Heros the Spartan). Jesus Blasco in v13:10-28 (Venegance Trail). Ron Embleton in v15:6-39 (Johnny Frog). Frank Hampson in v1:1-v10:27 (Dan Dare: note that assistants included Don Harley, Bruce Cornwell, Eric Eden and Keith Watson; some issues have finished art by Harold Johns, Desmond Walduck, based on Hampson roughs. Dan Dare reprints by Hampson in v18:2-v18:51, v19:4-v20:17), v1:1-43 (The Great Adventurer; some assisted by Joscelyn Thomas), v1:1-2 (Rob Conway), v1:1-7 (Tommy Walls; some episodes assisted or wholly by Bruce Cornwell), v11:10-v12:14 (The Road Of Courage; assisted by Joan Porter). Frank Humphris in v3:7-v4:22, v4:38-v7:35, v7:45-v8:50, v8:52-v12:18, v12:21-v13:9 (Riders of the Range), v13:35-41 (The Devil's Henchman), v14:24-v17:35, v17:39-v20:17 (Blackbow the Cheyenne). Don Lawrence in v17:35-38 (Blackbow the Cheyenne). Norman Williams in v2:7-v8:11 (numerous back-cover biographies).

EAGLE (NEW SERIES)
IPC/Fleetway; 1 27th Mar 1982-Jan 1994, 506 issues; 1-3,99,100,127-158,163-344 numbered, all others dated only)
1 mostly photo-strips; Doomlord, Dan Dare picture strip by Gerry Embleton, The Tower King picture strip by Jose Ortiz all begin	£2.00
1 with free gift (Space Spinner)	£3.00
2-4 Sep 1982,18 Sep 1982-19 Feb 1983	£0.75
11 Sep 1982 House of Daemon by Ortiz begins	£0.75
26 Feb 1983 The Fifth Horseman by Ortiz begins	£0.50
5 Mar-17 Sep 1983	£0.50
24 Sep 1983 1st all-picture strip issue, Doomlord continues by Heinzl, Fists of Danny Pike by John Burns begins	£0.30
1 Oct 1983-2 Jun 1984	£0.30
9 Jun 1984 Bloodfang by Baikie begins	£0.30
16 Jun 1984-127 (25th Aug 1984)	£0.30
128 (1 Sep 1984) 1st "Eagle and Scream"; Thirteenth Floor by Ortiz begins	£0.30
129-30 Mar 1985	£0.30
6 Apr 1985 1st "Eagle and Tiger"; Death Wish by Vanyo begins	£0.30
13 Apr 1985-216,218-220,222-231	£0.30
217 (17 May 1986) Ant Wars (2000AD reprints) begins	£0.30
233-258,260-284,286-305	£0.30
259 (7 Mar 1987) new look; Comrade Bronski by Carlos Ezquerra, Survival by Ortiz begin	£0.30
285 (5 Sep 1987) Mach Zero (2000AD reprints) begins	£0.30
306 (30 Jan 1988) 1st Eagle and Battle; Charley's War (censored Battle Action reprints) by Mills and Colquhoun begins	£0.30
307-344 (22 Oct 1988)	£0.30
29 Oct 1988 1st "Eagle and Mask"	£0.30
6 Nov 1988-1 Apr 1989,15 Apr-19 Aug 1989,21 Oct 1989-21 Apr 1990	£0.30
8 Apr 1989 1st "Eagle and Wildcat"	£0.30
26 Aug-14 Oct 1989 old look Dan Dare by Keith Watson begins	£0.75
28 Apr 1990 new look; Ghost World by Eric Bradbury, Dark Angels by Solano Lopez begin	£0.40
5 May 1990-1 Sep 1990, 15 Sep-8 Dec 1990	£0.30
8 Sep 1990 Beast by Eric Bradbury begins	£0.30
15 Dec 1990-19 Jan 1991 John Burns Dan Dare	£0.30
26 Jan 1991-6 Apr 1991	£0.30
May 1991-Jan 1994 becomes monthly, mostly reprints	£0.40

ARTISTS/FEATURES

Jim Baikie in 9 Jun 1984-127 (Bloodfang). Massimo Belardinelli in 206-210 (1pg Alien art feature), 251,252 (Mach 1 reprints). John Burns in 24 Sep 1983-21 Jul 1984, 18 Aug 1984-151 (Fists of Danny Pike), 221-257 (Dole Busters), 15 Dec 90-19 Jan 1991. Carlos Ezquerra in 259-262,264,267-268,272-275. Frank Hampson in 4 Dec-11 Dec 1982 (Dan Dare reprints). Cam Kennedy in 15 Oct 1983-7 Jan 1984, 7 Apr 1984, 18 Aug 1984, 145 (Amstor Computer). Jose Ortiz in 27 Mar-4 Sep 1982 (The Tower King), 11 Sep 1982-12 Feb 1983 (House of Daemon), 26 Feb-16 Jul 1983 (Fifth Horseman), 24 Sep 1983, 17 Dec 1983, 99 (11 Feb 1984) (The Amstor Computer), 18 Feb-31 Mar 1984 (News Team), 8 Dec 1984 (Bloodfang), 128-258 (The Thirteenth Floor), 259-319 (Survival), 332-343 (Kid Cops), 8 Apr-22 Apr 1989, 13 Jun-12 Aug 1989 (Kitten Magee). Keith Watson 26 Aug-14 Oct 1989, 3 Feb-10 Mar 1990, 9 Jun-16 Jun 1990 (Dan Dare).

EAGLE ANNUAL
Hulton/Longacre/Odhams/Fleetway; 1 (Sep 1951)-1975, 1983-1994?
1 scarce, Dan Dare by Frank Hampson/Harold Johns	£45.00
2 Dare by Harold Johns/Greta Tomlinson	£15.00
2 with dust wrapper	£25.00
3 Dare by Don Harley	£10.00
3 with dust wrapper	£15.00
4 Dare by Harold Johns	£10.00
4 with dust wrapper	£12.50
5-7,9	£7.50
8 by Hampson/Harley	£7.50
10 1st with date on cover	£6.00
11,12 last numbered, last with dust jackets	£5.00
1964-1965	£5.00
1966 Heros the Spartan by Bellarny	£5.00

	N.MINT
1967-1969	£3.50
1970 larger size, scarcer; Don Lawrence art	£5.00
1971,1972,1974,1975	£3.00
1973 Don Lawrence art	£4.00
1983-1994? some incl. Ron Turner art	£2.50
Best of Eagle Annual edited by Denis Gifford (Webb & Bower, 1989)	£10.00
Note: copies of 5-12 with dustwrappers command £2.00-3.00 higher. Also note that there was no dustwrapper on the first annual.	

EAGLE BOOKS

Eagle Book of Adventure Stories (Hulton, Dec 1950)	£15.00
Eagle Book of Adventure Stories (Hulton, Sep 1951) 2nd edition	£6.00
Eagle Book of Aircraft by John W.R. Taylor (Hulton, Oct 1953)	£10.00
Eagle Book of Aircraft revised (Aug 1957)	£6.00
Eagle New Book of Aircraft 3rd edition (1960)	£4.00
Eagle Book of Amazing Stories 1973 (1972)	£3.00
Eagle Book of Amazing Stories 1974 (1973)	£3.00
Eagle Book of Balsa Models by Bill Dean (Hulton, Oct 1954)	£8.00
Eagle Book of Cars and Motor Sport	£10.00
Eagle Book of Exploring the Arts (Longacre, 1961) dust wrapper	£25.00
Eagle Book of Exploring the Universe (Hulton, 1960) dust wrapper	£25.00
Eagle Book of Fighting Services (1962)	£8.00
Eagle Book of Hobbies (1958)	£10.00
Eagle Book of How It Works (1962)	£10.00
Eagle Book of Magic (Hulton, 1955) landscape, incl. press-outs	£35.00
Eagle Book of Model Aircraft (1959)	£10.00
Eagle Book of Model Boats (1960)	£8.00
Eagle Book of Model Cars (1961)	£8.00
Eagle Book of Modern Adventurers (Hulton, Oct 1952)	£10.00
Eagle Book of Modern Adventurers (Apr 1957) 2nd edition	£5.00
Eagle Book of Modern Wonders (Hulton, Sep 1955)	£10.00
Eagle Book of Modern Wonders revised (Aug 1957)	£6.00
Eagle Book of Police and Detection (1960)	£10.00
Eagle Book of Records and Champions (Hulton, Oct 1950) scarce	£30.00
Eagle Book of Records and Champions revised (1959)	£15.00
Eagle Book of Rockets and Space Travel (1961)	£15.00
Eagle Book of Ships and Boats (1959)	£12.50
Eagle Book of Spacecraft Models (1960)	£10.00
Eagle Book of Trains by Cecil J. Allen (Hulton, Oct 1953)	£10.00
Eagle Book of Trains revised (Aug 1957)	£6.00
Eagle Book of Trains 3rd edition (1960)	£5.00
Eagle New Book of Trains 4th edition (1963)	£4.00
Eagle/Girl Book of Exploring the Arts	£7.50
Eagle/Girl Book of the Universe	£7.50
I Want To Be…: An Eagle Book of Careers (Hulton, Jul 1957)	£4.00

EAGLE CLASSICS

(see Fraser of Africa, Harris Tweed, P.C. 49, Riders of the Range)

EAGLE EXTRA

Hulton; 11th Sep 1953-13th Nov 1953 (10 issues)

11 Sep 1953-13 Nov 1953 4pg supplement in Eagle	£3.00

EAGLE HOLIDAY SPECIAL

IPC/Fleetway; 1983-1992

1983-1992 Ron Turner Dan Dare in 1985-86	£1.00

EAGLE PICTURE LIBRARY

IPC; 1 May 1985-14 Nov 1985

1 Talisman of Doom by Joe Colquhoun (reprints Saber from Tiger)	£1.00
2-14 reprints	£0.25

ARTISTS/FEATURES

1 Talisman of Doom (Saber) by Joe Colquhoun. 2 Murder in Space (Jet Ace Logan) by Brian Lewis. 3 The Black Archer by Eric Bradbury. 4 Rebels of Rome (Olac) by Ruggero Giovannini. 5 Terror of the Deep. 6 Black Archer vs The Weatherman by John Gillatt. 7 Public Enemy No.1 (Thesbius) by John Gillatt. 8 The Schoolboy Commandos. 9 The Red Knight of Morda (Maroc the Mighty) by Don Lawrence. 10 Company of Thieves (Thesbius) by John Gillatt. 11 The Asssassins (Olac) by Ruggero Giovannini. 12 Janus Stark. 13 Hunter's Moon by Graham Coton. 13 The Metal Monsters. All stories are adapted reprints from Tiger, Lion and Valiant.

EAGLE SPECIAL

Odhams; 1962, 1966

1962 Holiday Extra, 48pgs, Dan Dare by Harold Johns	£15.00
1966 Summer Special, 48pgs, Dan Dare by Bruce Maraffa	£10.00

EAGLE SPORTS ANNUAL

Hulton; 1 Oct 1952-1973

1 (Oct 1952)	£15.00
1 with dust wrapper	£20.00
2 (Sep 1953)	£8.00
3-5	£7.50
6-8	£6.00
1961-1965	£5.00
1966-1970	£4.00
1971-1973	£2.50

EARLY LIFE OF WINSTON CHURCHILL

Burrow; nn 1940s

nn - 60pgs oblong; reprints Philip Mendoza newspaper strip	£6.00

ECHO CHILDREN'S CHRISTMAS SUPPLEMENT

Liverpool Echo; nn 20th Dec 1957

nn - 4pgs; supplement to Liverpool Echo	£0.50

ECLIPSE GRAPHIC NOVELS

HarperCollins/Eclipse Publishing; Jan 1993-1994

The Yattering and Jack (Jan 1993) Clive Barker adaptation, Bolton art	£7.00
Dragonflight (Jan 1993) Anne McCaffrey adaptation	£8.00
Trapped (Apr 1993) Dean R. Koontz adaptation	£7.00
Revelations (May 1993) Clive Barker adaptation	£7.00
Dread (Jun 1993) Clive Barker adaptation, Dan Brereton art	£7.00
Miracleman: The Golden Age by Neil Gaiman & Mark Buckingham, reprints Miracleman 17-22	£9.00

Eagle #37

Eagle Annual 1971

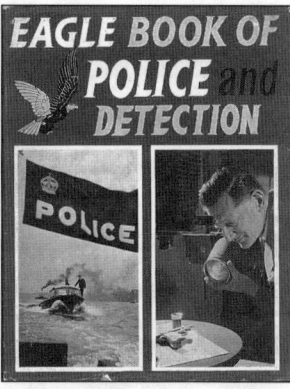

Eagle Book of Police and Detection (1960)

	N.MINT
The Life of Death Clive Barker adaptation	£7.00
EDWARD'S HEAVE COMICS	
H. Bunch (Cozmic); nn Apr 1973	
nn - 36pgs; adult material; Edward Barker art	£1.00
EERIE	
Gold Star; 1-4 1972	
1-4 52pgs; Warren reprints	£1.00
EERIE COMICS	
Thorpe & Porter; 1 Oct 1951-2? 1952	
1 68pgs; Avon reprints begin, incl. strips from Out of This World, cited in UK horror campaign	£20.00
2	£12.50
EERIE TALES	
Alan Class; 1 1962-?	
1 very scarce, 68pgs; American reprints begin	£12.50
2 scarce	£6.00
3-5	£4.00
6-?	£1.50
87TH PRECINCT	
Top Sellers; 1-2 1962	
1 reprints 87th Precinct (Western), Mr District Attorney (National)	£3.00
2	£2.50
ELECTROMAN COMICS	
Scion; May 1951-1952 (6 issues, only 3,4 numbered)	
nn-nn King-Ganteaume art	£6.00
ELLA CINDERS	
Miller; nn 1942	
nn - 12pgs; reprints American newspaper strip	£3.00
ELMO'S OWN	
Chascol; 1 1946?-v3:9? 1949 (becomes Sheriff & Elmo's Own)	
1-v3:9 Charles Cole art	£1.50
EMERGENCY WARD 10	
C.A. Pearson (TV Picture Stories); 1 Jun 1958-21 May 1960	
1 68pgs pocket size	£5.00
2-21	£2.50
ARTISTS/FEATURES	
1 Calling Nurse Roberts. 2 Calling Nurse Young. 3 A Date For Carole. 4 O'Meara Makes Amends. 5 The Cocktail Party. 6 Trouble For Simon. 7 Coming Sister. 8 Night Duty. 9 The Casting Vote. 10 The Daily Round. 11 The Rivals. 12 Checkmate. 13 The Contract. 15 Night Falls on Oxbridge. 16 Carole's Dilemma. 18 A Very Special Baby. 19 Nurse Roberts' Evening Out. 21 Two Lives On His Hands.	
EMMA	
D.C. Thomson; 1 25th Feb 1978-81 8th Sep 1979 (joins Judy)	
1	£1.00
2-81	£0.20
ENID BLYTON'S NODDY AND HIS FRIENDS	
(see Noddy and His Friends)	
ENIGMA	
Titan; Nov 1995	
- 192pgs; reprints Vertigo series by Pete Milligan & Duncan Fegredo	£12.50
ENSIGN COMIC	
Ensign; 1947 (4 un-numbered issues)	
nn - green/red photogravure; W.Forshaw art	£5.00
nn - blue/red photogravure; Charles Ross art	£5.00
nn - blue/red photogravure; Frank Minnitt art	£5.00
nn - black/red on alternate pages; Frank Minnitt art	£5.00
EPIC	
(see Lion Summer Spectacular: Epic)	
ESCAPE	
Escape/Titan; 1 Mar 1983-19 Sep 1990	
1 scarce (1,000 copies) issued with postcards & badge; digest size	£5.00
2 (2,000 copies) 8pg 3-D section & glasses	£3.00
3,4	£2.00
5-7 last digest issues	£1.50
8,9 magazine size	£2.00
10 1st Titan issue, squarebound; 20pg Munoz	£2.50
11 1st Mr Mamoulian by Bolland	£2.25
12-14,17,19 Bolland art	£2.25
18 Bolland, Chaykin, Eisner, Sienkiewicz art	£2.25
15-16 more scarce	£2.50
ARTISTS	
Steve Bissette in 17. Simon Bisley in 15. Brian Bolland in 11-19. Philip Bond in 14-15. Eddie Campbell in 1-4,6-11. Howard Chaykin in 18. Steve Ditko in 17. Will Eisner in 18. Hernandez Bros in 16. Jamie Hewlett in 15. Ted McKeever in 16. Bill Sienkiewicz in 18.	
ESCAPE EXHIBITION SUPPLEMENTS	
Escape/Titan; 1987-1991	
Cosmic Iconoclasm (1987)	£0.95
The Black Island (Mar 1988) Britain in Bandes Dessinees 12pgs	£0.75
Strip Search (1989)	£1.50
Strip Search 2 (Feb 1991) 64pgs	£1.00
ESMERALDA	
Gresham/IPC; 1 12th Jun 1971-33 29th Jan 1972 (joins Bobo Bunny)	
1	£0.80
2-33	£0.20
ESPIONAGE	
Brugeditor; 1-8 1967	
1-8 68pgs pocket size; foreign reprints	£0.50
EULALIE'S FUNNIES	
Apollo Fine Art; 1 Dec 1949-2 Jan 1950	
1-2 8pgs	£0.80
EUREKA	
Ron Tiner; v3:1 1972	
v3:1 Dave Gibbons, Ron Tiner art; Jeff Hawke by Sydney Jordan reprint	£2.00

	N.MINT
EVENING GAZETTE FAMILY CARTOONS	
Colchester Evening Gazette; 21st Mar 1982-?	
21 Mar 1982-? 4pgs; supplement to Colchester Evening News, American reprints	£0.20
EVERYBODY'S ALBUM AND CARICATURE MAGAZINE	
Kendrick; 1 1st Jan 1834-37 27th Jul 1835	
1-37 1pg tabloid	£25.00
EVERYDAY NOVELS AND COMICS	
Popular Fiction; 1940	
nn - 8pgs, large; Jack Greenall, Serge Drigin art	£6.00
EVIL EYE THRILLER, THE	
Bernard Kaye/Art Publicity; 1947 (2 un-numbered issues)	
nn - 8pgs, printed red/black; Evil Eye by Les Barton begins	£4.00
nn - printed red/blue, smaller size	£4.00
EXCITING ROMANCES	
World Distributors; 1-2 1952	
1-2 36pgs; Fawcett reprints	£5.00
EXCITING WAR	
Cartoon Art; 1 1952	
1 Standard reprints	£3.50
EXIT	
N.Khan; 1 1992-8 1994	
1 Exit by Nabiel Khan begins	£3.50
2-8	£2.00
Note: reprinted in Deadline	
EXPLOITS OF SPIDER-MAN, THE	
Marvel; 1 21st Oct 1992-40 1995	
1 Spider-Man, Motormouth reprints begin	£2.00
2-3	£1.00
4-40	£0.75
EXPRESS ANNUAL	
Beaverbrook; 1 (1956)-1960 (becomes TV Express Annual)	
1 undated (1956) Jet Morgan by Tacconi, Biggles text by W.E. Johns	£10.00
nn undated (1957) Wulf the Briton by Embleton	£7.50
1959,1960 Wulf the Briton by Embleton	£6.00
EXPRESS WEEKLY	
Beaverbrook; first appeared in 1954 as a newspaper for children, converted to a comic with issue 39; Junior Express Weekly: 39 18th Jun 1955-73 11th Feb 1956 (35 issues); Express Weekly: 74 18th Feb 1956-285 20th Apr 1960 (212 issues) (becomes TV Express)	
39 Wyatt Earp by Harry Bishop, Mark Fury by Raffaele Paparella begin	£35.00
40	£12.50
41	£7.50
42-49,51-73	£5.00
50 Jeff Hawke by Ferdinando Tacconi begins	£5.00
74 becomes Express Weekly; Rex Keene by Bishop begins, 1st full-colour Mark Fury by Peter Jackson	£15.00
74 with free gift (Super Book of Racing Cars)	£25.00
75-83,85-107,109-114,116-119,121-139	£5.00
84 Jet Morgan by Charles Chilton & Tacconi begins	£7.50
108 Freedom is the Prize by Giovannini begins (1st appearance of Wulf the Briton)	£5.00
115 1st "Express and Rocket"	£5.00
120 1st Wulf the Briton strip	£7.50
140-285 Ron Embleton Wulf the Briton	£3.00
EXPRESS THRILLER COMIC, THE	
William Foster; nn Jul 1946	
nn - 16pgs; Bob Wilkin art	£3.00
EXTRA FUN	
Gerald Swan; 1 Aug 1940-4 Nov 1940	
1 36pgs; John McCail, William Ward, E.H.Banger art	£10.00
2-4	£6.00
EXTRA FUN (NEW SERIES)	
Gerald Swan; 1-2 1952	
1-2 36pgs	£4.00

F

	N.MINT
FABULOUS FURRY FREAK BROTHERS	
Hassle Free Press/Knockabout; 1 1976-12 1992	
1 44pgs; Gilbert Shelton u/g reprints	£3.00
2-4	£2.00
5-12	£1.50
FAIRY FUN COMIC	
P.M. Productions; nn 1948	
nn - 8pgs; Frank Minnitt art	£2.00
FAIRY TIME COMIC	
David Jones; nn 1948	
nn - 8pgs	£2.00
FALCON COMICS	
Hutchinson; 1979-1980	
Tram Fury	£0.75
Rollin' Through	£0.75
Adventures of Moven Marven	£0.75
THE FALL GUY ANNUAL	
Grandreams; 1981-1983	
1981 (blue cover, 1981 for 1982)	£1.50
1981 (red cover, 1982 for 1983) David Lloyd art	£1.50
1981 (yellow cover, 1983 for 1984) David Lloyd art	£1.50
FALLING IN LOVE	
Trent; 1-8 1955	
1 68pgs; National Periodical Publications reprints	£2.50
2-8	£1.50

	N.MINT

FAMILY FAVOURITES COMIC WEEKLY
Miller; 24th Feb 1954-13th Oct 1954 (34 issues)

24 Feb 1954 28pgs; reprints Chicago Tribune-New York News Syndicate newspaper strips	£3.00
3 Mar-13 Oct 1954	£1.50

FAMILY FUN
Pentland Productions; nn 1953

nn - 8pgs giveaway; Gifford art	£0.50

FAMOUS CRIMES
Streamline; 1-2 1951

1-2 28pgs; Fox reprints	£3.00

FAMOUS FIVE
Hodder & Stoughton; 1983

Famous Five & the Golden Galleon 52pgs; French reprints by Serge Rosenzweig & Bernard Dufosse	£1.25
Famous Five & the Inca God	£1.25

FAMOUS ROMANCE LIBRARY
Amalgamated Press; 1 Jan 1958-?

1 68pgs pocket size	£1.50
2-?	£0.50

FAMOUS STORIES IN PICTURES
Bairns Books; 1-12 1955?

1-12 reprints of A Classic in Pictures series with new covers	£4.00

FAMOUS TALES OF FAT FREDDY'S CAT
Knockabout; nn Nov 1994

nn - hardcover; Gilbert Shelton Fat Freddy's Cat reprints	£8.00

FANCY FREE
Scion; nn 1951

nn - R.W.Plummer, John Jukes art	£4.00

FANNY
(see Ceasefire, Dyke's Delight, Immaculate Deception, Night Fruits, Voyeuse)

FANTASTIC
(see Terrific)

Odhams; 1 18th Feb 1967-89 26th Oct 1968

1 Thor (from Journey Into Mystery #83), X-Men (from X-Men #1), Iron Man (from Tales of Suspense #39) reprints begin, Missing Link by Luis Bermejo begins	£7.50
1 with free gift (plastic pennant/wallet)	£12.50
2	£5.00
2 with free gift (Stick-on scars)	£7.50
3	£3.00
3 with free gift (Fantastic Bubble Gum)	£6.00
4-10,12-15,17-30	£2.50
11 no X-Men story	£1.50
16 Missing Link becomes Johnny Future	£1.50
31-50,53-69,71-89	£1.00
51 Iron Man reprints, Johnny Future end	£1.00
52 1st "Fantastic and Terrific"; Avengers (from Avengers #26), Dr. Strange (from Strange Tales #151) reprints begin	£1.00
70 Hulk (from Hulk #1) reprints begin	£2.00

FANTASTIC ANNUAL
Odhams; 1968-1970

1968 reprints Journey Into Mystery #109, X-Men #3, Tales of Suspense #41 (Dr Strange)	£6.00
1969 reprints X-Men #24, Tales of Suspense #68 (Iron Man), Journey Into Mystery #112 (Thor vs Hulk)	£4.00
1970 reprints X-Men #40, FF Ann #2, Tales of Suspense #60 (Iron Man)	£3.50
Note: reprints usually recoloured	

FANTASTIC FOUR
Marvel; 1 6th Oct 1982-29 20th Apr 1983

1 24pgs; FF reprints begin	£1.50
1 with free gift (Fantastic Four press-out boomerang)	£2.50
2	£1.25
2 with free gift (Part 1 of cut-out Fantasti-Car)	£2.50
3-4	£1.00
3-4 with free gift (Parts 2-3 of cut-out Fantasti-Car)	£2.00
5-29 18-19 incl. Spider-Man origin	£0.75
Note: some issues include posters by British artists, namely Mick Austin in 8,10,12, Alan Davis in 2,7,12,14, Paul Neary in 15.	

FANTASTIC FOUR ANNUAL
Grandreams; 1979-1981

1979 reprints FF Annual #4,11, Jack Kirby art	£4.00
1980 reprints FF #185-186	£3.00
1981 reprints incl. FF #26 (with X-Men), Giant Size #4	£3.00

FANTASTIC FOUR COMIC ANNUAL
World Distributors; 1969-1970

1970 reprints FF #22-24,81	£5.00
1971 reprints FF #84-87	£5.00

FANTASTIC FOUR FULL COLOUR COMIC ALBUM
World Distributors; 1970

1 64pgs; reprints FF #51,53,60	£4.00

FANTASTIC FOUR POCKET BOOK
Marvel; 1 Apr 1980-28 Jul 1982

1 52pgs small size; FF reprints begin from #43	£1.00
2-3,5-19,21-28	£0.60
4 reprints F.F. #48 (1st Silver Surfer)	£1.00
20 100pgs double number	£1.25

FANTASTIC FOUR SPECIALS
Marvel; Oct 1981-Oct 1983

Winter Special 1981,1983	£1.25
Summer Special 1982	£1.00

FANTASTIC FOUR TELEVISION PICTURE STORY BOOK, THE
P.B.S.; 1969

1969 scarce, reprints FF #54,56,59	£5.00

FANTASTIC FOUR, THE COMPLETE
Marvel; 1 28th Sep 1977-53 8th Jun 1979 (joins Mighty World of Marvel)

1 36pgs; reprints incl. FF origin from #1	£1.25
1 with free gift (plastic Boeing 747 model)	£2.00
2	£1.00
2 with free gift (Maze game)	£1.50
3-53	£0.75

FANTASTIC SERIES/STUPENDOUS SERIES
Fleetway (A Fleetway Super Library); 1 Jan 1967-26 Jan 1968

1 132pgs, Steel Claw by Carlos Cruz (in all odd numbers)	£6.00
2 The Spider (in all even numbers)	£4.00
3-26 title becomes Stupendous Series	£3.00

ARTISTS/FEATURES
1 The Raiders of Fear by Carlos Cruz. 2 The Professor of Power by Marcuzzi. 3 The Waves of Peril by Massimo Belardinelli. 4 Crime Unlimited by Giorgio Trevisan. 5 The Cold Trail by Jesus Blasco. 6 The Bubbles of Doom by Ogeras. 7 Snake Island. 8 The Man Who Stole New York by Marcuzzi. 9 Forbidden Territory by Massimo Belardinelli. 10 The Chessman by Marcuzzi. 11 The Blinding Light. 12 The Animator by Romagnoli. 13 City Beneath the Sand by Jesus Blasco. 14 The Scarecrow's Revenge by Francisco Cueto. 15 The Formula of Fear by Massimo Belardinelli. 16 Mr Stonehart by Ogeras. 17 Treason By Request. 18 Dr Argo's Challenge by Marcuzzi. 19 The March of the Guerillas. 20 The Immortals by Francisco Cueto. 21 Operation Floodtide by Carlos Cruz. 22 The Shriveller by Marcuzzi. 23 The Torum Experiment by Carlos Cruz. 24 The Melody of Crime by Giorgio Trevisan. 25 The Phantom Pirate. 26 Child's Play by Francisco Cueto.

FANTASTIC SUMMER SPECIAL
Odhams; 1968

1968 56pgs; reprints	£6.00
Note: full title is Smash! Pow! Its Fantastic Summer Special	

FANTASTIC TALES
Top Sellers; 1-20 1963

1 68pgs; American reprints	£2.50
2-20	£1.50

FANTASTIC WORLDS
Cartoon Art; 1 1952

1 Standard reprints	£4.00

FANTASY STORIES
John Spencer; 1-6? 1967?

1-6? 52pgs; some incl. Michael Jay, Mick Anglo art	£1.00

FAREWELL TO JANE
(see Jane)

FARGO KID
Strato; 1959

1 68pgs; Prize Publications reprints, Severin art	£3.00

FAST ACTION WESTERN COMIC
(see Giant Comic)

FAT CAT
Express Books; nn 1979

nn - 100pgs oblong; reprints Sunday Express newspaper strip by Mike Atkinson	£1.00

FAT FREDDY'S COMICS AND STORIES
(see Famous Tales of Fat Freddy's Cat)

Knockabout; nn 1984

nn - 36pgs; Gilbert Shelton u/g reprints	£2.00

FATMAN
Rochdale Alternative Paper; nn 1978

nn - 76pgs oblong; reprints newspaper strip by Tony Smart	£0.75

FAVOURITE COMIC, THE
Amalgamated Press; 1 21st Jan 1911-324 31st Mar 1917 (joins Merry & Bright)

1 8pgs tabloid; G.M.Payne, Tom Radford art	£25.00
2-324 incl. George Wakefield, Herbert Foxwell, Bertie Brown art	£5.00

FAWCETT MOVIE COMIC
Miller; 50 1951-62 1952 (13 issues)

50 36pgs; Monte Hale in The Old Frontier by Bob Powell (9), adapts film	£10.00
51-62	£7.50

FAWCETT'S FUNNY ANIMALS
(see Funny Animals)

F.B.I. COMIC
Streamline; 1-2 1951

1-2 28pgs; Fox reprints	£6.00

FEATURE COMICS
T.V. Boardman; 29 1940-33 1941 (5 issues)

29 36pgs; Quality reprints	£8.00
30-33 20pgs	£5.00

FEATURE STORIES MAGAZINE
Streamline; 1 1951

1 28pgs; Fox reprints	£4.00

FELIX THE CAT
S.G. Bruce; nn May 1949-nn Dec 1949 (5 issues, 2-4 numbered)

nn - Felix the Cat 8pgs; American and Australian reprints	£6.00
2-4 Felix Funnies	£6.00
nn - Felix the Cat Christmas Book	£6.00

FELIX THE CAT
Paladin; 1-9 1953

1-9 28pgs; Toby reprints, Messmer art	£4.00

FELIX THE CAT LITTLE PICTURE BOOKS
S.G. Bruce; 1948 (6 unnumbered issues)

nn (1) 28pgs; Ancient Times, Dell reprints	£4.00
nn (2-6)	£4.00

FEN CRITTUR COMICAL BOOKS
Oblique Angle Publications; nn 1952

nn - 16pgs; amateur comic by Walt Willis and Bob Shaw	£2.50

FIDO
Hotspur Publishing Co.; 1950 (4 un-numbered issues)

nn - Fido the Pup	£2.50

	N.MINT
nn - Fido's Fun	£2.50
nn - Fido at the Fair	£2.50
nn - Fido at the Seaside	£2.50
FIESTA COMIC STRIP	
Galaxy; 1 1989-Vol 3:3 1991	
1-v3:3 adult material	£1.00
FIGHT COMICS	
Streamline; 1 1949	
1 36pgs; Fiction House reprints	£4.00
FIGHT COMICS	
Cartoon Art; 1 1950	
1 36pgs; Fiction House reprints	£4.00
FIGHT COMICS	
Trent; 1-2 1960	
1-2 68pgs; Fiction House reprints	£3.00
FIGHT COMICS - ATTACK	
Cartoon Art; 1 1951	
1 68pgs; Fiction House reprints	£4.00
FIGHTIN' AIR FORCE	
Miller; 1-3 1956	
1-3 28pgs; Charlton reprints	£3.50
FIGHTIN' NAVY	
Miller; 1-3 1956	
1-3 28pgs; Charlton reprints	£3.50
FIGHTING BRIT, THE	
(Cartoon Art); nn 1948	
nn - large (22.5x17.5") single sheet; reprints from Super Duper	£2.50
FIGHTING OUTLAWS	
Streamline; 1-10 1950s	
1-10 reprints	£3.50
FILM FUN	
Amalgamated Press/Fleetway; 1 17th Jan 1920-8th Sep 1962 (2225 issues, numbered to 2052, joins Buster)	
1 Winkle by Tom Radford begins	£400.00
2	£175.00
3-10	£120.00
11-100	£45.00
101-999	£22.50
1000-1300	£10.00
1301-2052	£6.50
23 May 1959 1st unnumbered	£5.00
30 May 1959-6 Jun 1959	£3.00
13 Jun 1959 title changes to Film Fun and Thrills; Scoop Donovan by Geoff Campion begins	£3.00
20 Jun 1959-8 Sep 1962	£2.50
ARTISTS/FEATURES	
Early artists include Tom Radford, George Wakefield, Alex Akerbladh, etc. Later artists incl. Arturo Del Castillo (Ringo, Three Musketeers) 5 Mar 1960-27 May 1961. Ron Turner (Scoop Donovan).	
FILM FUN ANNUAL	
Amalgamated Press; 1938-1961	
1938	£175.00
1939	£110.00
1940-1944	£75.00
1945-1950	£40.00
1951-1955	£20.00
1956-1958	£15.00
1959-1961	£7.50
FILM PICTURE LIBRARY	
C.A. Pearson; 1 Jul 1959-3 Nov 1959	
1 Warlock by Terry Aspin	£5.00
2-3	£3.00
FILM PICTURE STORIES	
Amalgamated Press; 1 28th Jul 1934-30 16th Feb 1935	
1 George Wakefield, J.H.Valda, Jos Walker art	£25.00
2-11 incl. Wakefield, Valda, Walker art	£12.50
12-16 incl. Wakefield, Valda, Walker, Serge Drigin art	£12.50
17-30 incl. Valda, Walker art	£12.50
Note: adaptations of films	
FILM SHOTS	
(see Shots from the Films)	
D. McKenzie; nn 1948	
nn - 8pgs; uses film stills with captions	£6.00
FINAL FRONTIER	
(see Star Trek)	
FIREBALL XL5 ANNUAL	
Century 21; 1963-1966	
1963 scarce	£35.00
1964	£25.00
1965-1966	£15.00
FIREBALL XL5: A LITTLE GOLDEN BOOK	
Golden Press; 1964	
1964	£15.00
FIREFLY, THE	
(previously Fun and Fiction, story paper)	
Amalgamated Press; 1 28th Feb 1914-51 13th Feb 1915 (becomes The Firefly, New Series)	
1 20pgs; George Wakefield, Tom Radford art	£25.00
2-51	£5.00
FIREFLY, THE (NEW SERIES)	
Amalgamated Press; 1 20th Feb 1915-111 31st Mar 1917 (joins Butterfly)	
1 8pgs; G.M.Payne, Bertie Brown, Tom Radford art	£20.00
2-111	£4.50
FIREHAIR COMICS	
Streamline; 1 1950	

	N.MINT
1 28pgs; Fiction House reprints	£4.00
FIRES	
Penguin; nn 1991	
nn - European reprint, Lorenzo Mattotti art	£6.00
FIRKIN	
Virgin; nn Oct 1985	
nn - 100pgs; Hunt Emerson art, reprints The Firkin Version from Fiesta	£5.00
FIRKIN	
Knockabout; 1 Oct 1989-7?	
1 Firkin reprints by Tym Manley & Hunt Emerson	£1.50
2	£1.50
3-7	£1.95
FIRST	
Interstellar Rat; 1 1981	
1 40pgs	£0.75
FIRST LOVE	
Strato; 1 1959-18 1961?	
1-18 68pgs; Harvey reprints	£1.50
FIRST LOVE	
Virago (Upstarts); nn Oct 1988	
nn - 96pgs; edited by Phillip Boys & Corrine Pearlman; Emerson, Campbell, Hollings, Charlesworth art	£3.00
FITNESS AND SUN	
(see Sun)	
FITS	
C.Morris Books; nn Xmas 1946?	
nn - (Xmas) 8pgs	£3.00
FIVE-SCORE COMIC MONTHLY	
(see All Favourites)	
K.G. Murray Ltd; 1 late 1950s-83? early 1960s	
1 rare 100pgs, squarebound begin; b/w reprints from National Periodical Publications incl. Doom Patrol, Superboy, Jimmy Olsen, Straight Arrow, Pow-Wow Smith; priced at 2 shillings	£75.00
2 rare	£50.00
3-5 very scarce	£40.00
6-10 scarce	£35.00
11-83? scarce	£30.00
Note: more issues thought to exist	
FIVE STAR WESTERN	
Scion; nn May 1951-nn 1952 (only 3-4 numbered)	
nn (1) 24pgs; Five Star Gentry by Norman Light begins, Embleton art	£8.00
nn (2) 24pgs; Light, Embleton art	£8.00
3-4 numbered issues; Light art; 4. Ron Embleton art	£8.00
nn-nn (5-6) 20pgs; Light art	£8.00
nn (7) 24pgs; Holdaway cover	£8.00
nn (8) 24pgs; Embleton art	£8.00
FIZZ	
Modern Fiction; 1 Apr 1949	
1 16pgs; Frank Minnitt, Wally Robertson art	£4.00
FIZZER	
Corona Soft Drinks; 1 1978-nn Spr 1981 (5 issues)	
1 8pgs; giveaway	£0.25
2	£0.20
nn Holiday 1979	£0.20
nn Christmas 1979	£0.20
nn Spring 1981	£0.20
FLAG COMIC, THE	
Reynard Press; nn 1946?	
nn - 8pgs; Tom Cottrell art	£3.00
FLASH	
Amex; 1 Jul 1948-11 Dec 1949	
1 8pgs, small size; Kangy the Bush Boy by Colin Merritt, Frank Minnitt art	£7.50
2-3	£5.00
4 1st larger size; Flashback by Colin Merritt begins	£4.00
5-11	£4.00
FLASH, THE	
Top Sellers; 1-5 1962	
1 68pgs; The Flash, Wonder Woman reprints	£10.00
2-5	£5.00
FLASH-BANG COMICS ADVENTURE	
Cartoon Art; nn Oct 1948	
nn - 36pgs; Paddy Brennan art	£8.00
FLASH COMICS	
Camden Magazine Co.; 1 (Feb) 1940-16 1941	
1 32pgs	£6.00
2-16	£4.00
FLASH FEARLESS	
Chrysalis; nn 1975	
nn - 12pgs; New Musical Express supplement, record promo	£0.50
FLASH FILSTRUP	
Arrow/Hutchinson; nn 1981	
nn - 100pgs oblong; American newspaper reprints	£1.00
FLASH GORDON	
World Distributors; 1-3 1953	
1 36pgs; US reprints	£10.00
2-3	£4.00
FLASH GORDON	
World Distributors; 1-6 1959	
1 68pgs; American newspaper strip reprints by Dan Barry	£8.00
2-6	£4.00
FLASH GORDON	
Miller; 1-5 1962	
1 68pgs; American newspaper strip reprints by Dan Barry	£7.50

	N.MINT
2-5	£3.00

FLASH GORDON ANNUAL
World Distributors/Brown Watson/World; 1966-1967, 1976-1977, 1980

1966,1967	£5.00
1976 Charlton reprints, plus John Bolton, Pat Boyette art	£4.00
1977 Pat Boyette art	£3.50
1978 John Bolton art	£3.00
1980 Charlton reprints by Reed Crandall	£2.00

FLASH GORDON WORLD ADVENTURE LIBRARY
World Distributors; 1 Jan 1967-8 Aug 1967

1 68pgs pocket size; American newspaper strip reprints by Dan Barry	£3.50
2-8	£3.00

FLASH STREAMLINE COMICS
Streamline; nn 1951?

nn - 68pg; US reprints	£3.00

FLASHER GORDON
Tabor Publications; nn 1974

nn - 32pgs; adult material; Flasher Gordon by Jeremy Brent	£0.90

FLEETWAY SUPER LIBRARY, A
(see Fantastic Series, Front Line, Secret Agent)

FLICKER FUN
Philman; nn 1948

nn - Frank Minnitt art	£3.50

FLINTSTONES MINI-COMIC
City; nn 6th Mar 1965

nn - supplement to Huckleberry Hound Weekly	£0.35

FLOOK
Associated Newspapers

Amazing Adventures of Rufus and Flook (1949) Daily Mail newspaper reprints by Trog (Wally Fawkes) begin	£10.00
Rufus and Flook v Moses Maggot (1950)	£7.50
Rufus and Flook at School (1951)	£7.50
Flook (1970)	£5.00
Flook & the Peasants Revolt (1975)	£3.00

FLYING A'S RANGE RIDER
World Distributors; 1 1954-16 1955

1 28pgs; Dell reprints, based on TV series	£10.00
2-16	£5.00

FLYING A'S RANGE RIDER TV BUMPER BOOK
New Town Press; 1959

1959 Stories by Joe Morrissey	£4.00

FLYING ACES
Streamline; 1956 (2 unnumbered issues)

nn 28pgs; Key Publications reprint	£5.00
nn 68pgs	£4.00

FOCUS ON FACT
W.H.Allen/Star Books; 1977-1978

1: The World of Invention 132pgs oblong; Daily Mail reprints, Gary Keane art	£0.50
2: The Story of Sport	£0.50
3: The Psychic World	£0.50
4: The Story of Christmas	£0.50
5: Unsolved Mysteries	£0.50
6: The Story of Flight (Spr 1978)	£0.50
7: The Story of Travel (Spr 1978)	£0.50

FOLLYFOOT ANNUAL
World Distributors; 1973

1973	£1.50

FOOD FIRST
Third World/New Internationalist; nn 1980

nn - 24pgs promo; US reprints	£0.20

FOOD FOR THOUGHT
Flying Pig; nn Apr 1985

nn - Band Aid benefit comic, Cold Snap by Moore & Talbot, Nemesis by Mills & O'Neil, Alec by Campbell, Slaine by Mills & Pugh, Emerson, Gibbons, Davis, Elliott, Gibson, Lloyd, Baikie art	£2.50

FOOTBALL COMIC, THE
Sports Cartoons; 1 Jan 1953-11 Nov 1953 (continues as Super-sonic)

1 Power Peters begins	£4.00
2-11 some incl. James Holdaway art	£2.50

FOOTBALL FUN BOOK
D.C. Thomson; nn 3rd Nov 1934

nn - 32pgs giveaway with Skipper, Dudley Watkins art	£2.00

FOOTBALL PICTURE STORY LIBRARY
D.C. Thomson; 1 Jun 1986-present (230 to Dec 1995)

1 Stark...Mission to Mexico	£1.00
2-10	£0.35
11-230	£0.15

FOR A FEW TROUBLES MORE
(see also Troubled Souls)
Fleetway; nn Oct 1990

nn - trade paperback; Crisis reprints by Garth Ennis & John McCrea	£4.00

FOR YOUR EYES ONLY
Marvel; nn Jul 1981

nn - 64pgs; movie adaptation by Steve Moore & Paul Neary	£1.50

FOR YOUR EYES ONLY SPECIAL
Granddreams; 1981

1981	£2.50

FORBIDDEN WORLDS
Strato; 1 1952?-145 196?

1 very scarce, 68pgs; ACG reprints	£15.00
2 scarce	£8.00
3-5 scarce	£5.00
6-10	£3.50

Fantastic #1

Fantastic Annual 1970

Film Fun #1

	N.MINT
2-145	£2.50

FORCES IN COMBAT
Marvel; 1 15th May 1980-37 21st Jan 1981 (joins Future Tense)

1 32pgs; Sgt Fury, Rom (from #1), Rawhide Kid, Machine Man (Ditko art), Kull, Master of Kung Fu reprints begin	£1.25
1 with free gift (Matilda tank sticker)	£2.00
2	£1.00
2 with free gift (Hurricane sticker)	£1.50
3	£1.00
3 with free gift (King George V Battleship sticker)	£1.50
4-37	£0.75

Note: issues 1-13 reprint Embleton's Wulf the Briton from Express Weekly

FOREIGN INTRIGUES
Miller 1-2 1956

1-2 28pgs; Charlton reprints	£4.00

FORGERS, THE
(see Secret Service Series)
Hotspur Publishing Co.; 4 1948

4 8pgs; Bob Wilkin art	£3.00

FORTY YEARS
Marshall Pickering; nn 1991

nn - by Donny Fort (reprints US edition from Zondervan Publishing, 1989)	£2.00

FOSDYKE SAGA, THE
Wolfe/Mirror; 1972

The Fosdyke Saga 196pgs; reprints Daily Mirror strip by Bill Tidy	£2.50

FOUR ACES
Newton Wickham; nn 1945

nn - 8pgs; Alf Farningham, Glyn Protheroe art	£4.00

FOUR ACES COMIC
Miller; 1-6 1954

1 28pgs; Flash Gordon, Mandrake the Magician, The Phantom, Secret Agent X9 reprints begin	£10.00
2-6	£4.00

FOUR DEUCES COMICS
Transatlantic Press; nn 1947

nn - 8pgs; Dennis Reader art	£4.00

FOUR FEATHER FALLS
Collins; 1960-1962

1960 entitled Television's Four Feather Falls	£25.00
1961 entitled Tex Tucker's Four Feather Falls	£15.00
1962 entitled Four Feather Falls	£12.50

FOUR JOLLY MILLER COMIC STRIPS FOR CHILDREN OF ALL AGES
Miller; nn 1943

nn - 4 comic booklets, folded to give 8pgs	£8.00

FOX AND CROW
Top Sellers; 1 1970-?

1-? 36pgs; DC Comics reprints	£2.00

FRANK BUCK
Streamline; 1 1950

1 28pgs; Fox reprints, Wood art	£8.00

FRANK FAZAKERLY
Preston SF Group; nn Jul 1991

nn - 24pgs; Bryan Talbot reprints from Ad Astra; signed/numbered 1000 copies	£2.00

FRANKENSTEIN
Top Sellers; nn 1963

nn - 68pgs; Dell reprints	£12.50

FRANKENSTEIN COMICS
Arnold Book Co.; 1-5 1951

1 68pgs; reprints various US strips incl. Airboy Comics	£12.50
2-5	£6.00

FRANKIE STEIN'S MINI-MONSTER COMIC BOOK
IPC; 9th Mar 1974-30th Mar 1974

- 4 weekly supplements with Shiver & Shake which make up 32pg mini-comic	£0.20

FRANTIC
Marvel; 1 Mar 1980-18 Jul 1981 (joins Marvel Madhouse)

1 36pgs; Marvel reprints	£1.25
2-18	£0.60

FRANTIC SPECIALS
Marvel; May 1979-Oct 1979

Summer Special 52pgs; Mork & Mindy, Superman, M.A.S.H., Bionic Woman	£0.75
Winter Special	£0.60

FRASER OF AFRICA
Hawk (Eagle Classics); nn 1990

nn - 64pgs; reprints Frank Bellamy strip from Eagle	£4.00

FREAKY FABLES
Sphere; nn 1979

nn - 68pgs oblong; Punch reprints by J. Handelsman	£1.00

FRED BASSETT
Associated Newspapers; 1 1966-present

1 84pgs oblong; Daily Mail reprints by Alex Graham begin	£10.00
2	£5.00
3-35	£3.00
36-39	£2.00
40 25th Anniversary	£2.00
41-42?	£1.50

FRED LESLIE'S JOURNAL COMIC BUDGET
Charles Strong; 8th Jul 1902-30th Aug 1902 (7 issues)

8 Jul 1902 8pgs; supplement to Fred Leslie's Journal No's 14-20	£5.00
15 Jul-30 Aug 1902	£3.00

FREDDIE'S LAST DANCE
MSB Publishing (Mindbenders Presents); 1 Sep/Oct 1993-2 Jan/Feb 1994

1 Mindbenders reprints by Steve Donovan & Eric Bradbury	£1.50
2	£1.00

FREDDY'S NIGHTMARES
Trident; 1 (Jan 1992)-?

1 based on movies; Nightmare on Elm Street reprints from Innovation, Marvel	£1.50
2-?	£1.25

FRESH FUN
Gerald Swan; 1 Apr 1940-32 Jan 1951

1 36pgs; William Ward, E.H.Banger, John McCail art	£12.00
2-10 36pgs; William Ward, E.H.Banger, John McCail art	£8.00
11,12 28pgs; E.H.Banger, Glyn Protheroe art	£5.00
13-18,31 20pgs	£5.00
19-30 16pgs	£5.00
32 20pgs; Embleton art	£5.00
Double (1941) William McCail, William Ward art	£8.00
Winter (1942) William Ward, Glyn Protheroe art	£8.00

Note: supposedly joined Laughitoff (1943), Scramble (1947).

FRIENDLY BEACON
ROSPA; nn 1951

nn - 8pgs giveaway; Bob Wilkin art	£2.00

FRITZ THE CAT
Heavy Duty Comics; 1 1972-2 1973

1 28pgs; US underground reprints, Robert Crumb, Gilbert Shelton art	£3.00
2 32pgs	£3.00

FRIZZ AND FRIENDS
Egmont/Methuen; 1 1977

1 100pgs small size; Brazilian reprints	£0.75

FROGMAN COMICS
Thorpe & Porter; 1-4 1952

1 68pgs; Hillman reprints	£7.50
2-4	£5.00

FROLICOMIC, THE
Martin & Reid; 1-4 1949

1-4 8pgs, full colour photogravure on alternate pages, Frank Minnitt art	£3.00

FROLIX
A.J. Barton; 1 Aug 1928-46 9th May 1930

1 16pgs; Murdock Stimpson art	£8.00
2-14	£4.00
15 (4th Oct 1929) 1st weekly issue	£4.00
16-46 weekly issues	£3.00

FRONT LINE
Fleetway (A Fleetway Super Library); 1 Jan 1967-26 Jan 1968

1 132pgs; Maddock's Marauders (in all odd numbers)	£2.50
2 Ironside (in all even numbers)	£1.50
3-26	£1.00

ARTISTS/FEATURES
1 Maddock's Marauders. 2 Ironside - Top Sergeant. 3 Valley of Silence. 4 Trouble Shooter. 5 Blueprint for Treason. 6 Bazooka King. 7 Broken Swastika. 8 Assault. 9 Fight for the Crown. 10 Yesterday's Heroes. 11 The Invisible Shield. 12 Stronghold of Darkness. 13 Forbidden Zone. 14 Break-Out by Ferdinando Tacconi. 15 The Hornet's Nest. 16 Dead Or Alive! 17 Operation Chaos. 18 The War-Makers. 19 Missile Menace. 20 Hit the Silk. 21 Eagles of War. 22 For Freedom. 23 The Gladiators. 24 Courage Alone. 25 Robot Army. 26 Flank Attack.

FRONT LINE COMBAT
Miller; 1-4 1959

1 28pgs; Test of Courage by Alan Willow	£3.50
2-4	£2.50

FRONTIER CIRCUS
Purnell; 1962-1963

1962 Stories by Arthur Groom, illus. by John Burns	£3.00
1963 illus. by John Burns	£3.00

FRONTIER TRAIL
Miller; 50 1958-?

50 28pgs; Ajax reprints begin	£5.00
51-?	£2.50

FRONTIER WESTERN
Miller; 1 1956-13 1957

1 28pgs; Atlas reprints begin	£5.00
2-13	£2.50

FUDGE COMIC, THE
Fudge; nn 1947

nn - 8pgs; David Williams art	£3.00

FUDGE THE ELF
Hodder & Stoughton/London University Press/Savoy; 1939-1951

The Adventures of Fudge the Elf (1939) 9" x 7" clothbound, 1 colour plate	£50.00
Frolics with Fudge (1941) 10" x 7.5" size begins, 4 colour plates with dustjacket; adapted and abridged reprints from Manchester Evening Post begin	£30.00
Fudge's Trip to the Moon (1947) 136pgs	£25.00
Fudge and the Dragon (1948)	£22.00
Fudge and the Dragon (Savoy, 1981) softback reprint	£3.50
Fudge in Bubbleville (1949)	£22.00
Fudge in Bubbleville (Savoy, 1981) softback reprint	£3.50
Fudge in Toffeetown (1950) 96pgs	£25.00
Fudge Turns Detective (1951) 8.5" x 6.5"; 1 colour plate	£20.00

Note: all contain Ken Reid art & script.

FULL O' FUN
Philmar/ P.M. Productions; 1-3 1949

1-3 8pgs; Frank Minnitt art, 2 incl. Colin Merritt art	£3.00

FUN AND FROLIC
International; nn 1945

nn - 8pgs; John Turner art	£3.00

FUN FAIR COMIC
Philmar; nn 1948

nn - 8pgs; Jack Pamby, Wally Robertson art	£3.00

	N.MINT

FUN FARE
Martin & Reid; 1 1946
| 1 8pgs; H.Pease art | £3.00 |

FUN FOR THE FAMILY
Associated Scottish Newspapers; 21st Jul 1940-6th Apr 1941 (38 issues)
| 21 Jul 1940 2pgs supplement to Glasgow Sunday Mail; incl. US reprints e.g.
Flash Gordon, and original UK art by Ern Shaw, etc. | £4.00 |
| 28 Jul-6 Apr 1940 | £2.50 |

FUN-IN
Williams Publishing; 1 1973-26 1974
| 1 36pgs; Motormouse & Autocat; based on Hanna-Babera characters | £1.25 |
| 2-26 incl. Dick Dastardly & Muttley, Scooby-Doo | £0.50 |

FUN PARADE
Hotspur Publishing Co.; 1 1949
| 1 8pgs; Denis Gifford art | £3.00 |

FUN TIME
Williams Publishing; 3rd Nov 1972-19th Jan 1973 (13 issues)
| 3 Nov 1972 16pgs; Boss Cat, Yogi Bear, Huckleberry Hound begin, all strips
based on Hanna-Barbera cartoons | £1.25 |
| 10 Nov 1972-19 Jan 1973 | £0.60 |

FUN'S FUNNY SCRAPBOOK
Fun Office; 1 Aug 1892-2 Sep 1892
| 1 68pgs; reprints strips and cartoons from Fun magazine | £10.00 |
| 2 | £8.00 |

FUNBEAM
P.M. Productions; nn 1949
| nn - 8pgs; Frank Minnitt, George Parlett art | £3.00 |

FUNDAY MERCURY
Birmingham Sunday Mercury; 3rd Sep 1978-?
| 3 Sep 1978 4pgs tabloid; supplement to Sunday Mercury | £0.20 |
| 10th Sep 1978-? | £0.10 |

FUNDERGROUND COMIC
London Transport; nn Aug 1984
| nn - 8pgs; promo; Ron Tiner art | £0.10 |

FUNFAIR
(McKenzie, Vincent); nn 1948
| nn - 12pgs; A.R.G. art | £2.50 |

FUNFAIR COMIC
Phillip Marx; nn 1946
| nn - 8pgs; reprints from Mighty, and Monster | £3.00 |

FUNFAIR COMIC, THE
Martin & Reid; nn 1949
| nn - 8pgs; Wally Robertson, Frank Minnitt art | £3.00 |

FUNNIES BUDGET
Gerald Swan; nn Jun 1950
| nn - 132pgs; bound copies of New Funnies and Topical Funnies in new cover | £8.00 |

FUNNY ANIMALS
(full title: Fawcett's Funny Animals)
Miller; nn Dec 1945-1952
nn - 68pgs photogravure; subtitled American Comic Annual, Fawcett reprints	£8.00
28,39,etc 16/12pgs red/green photogravure	£6.00
P448 16pgs red/green letterpress	£5.00
50-56 (1951-52) 28pgs	£5.00

FUNNY COMIC
P.M. Productions; 1 1948-2 1949
| 1 8pgs; Wally Robertson, Frank Minnitt, Colin Merritt art | £4.00 |
| 2 Robertson art | £4.00 |

FUNNY COMICS
A. Halle; nn 1948
| nn - 8pgs; reprints from Comic Capers and All Fun | £3.00 |

FUNNY CUTS
Trapps Holmes; 1 12th Jul 1890-958 10th Nov 1908
(becomes Funny Cuts the Boys Companion)
1 8pgs tabloid; reprints from American magazines	£45.00
2	£15.00
3-958 original material introduced later	£6.00
CHRONOLOGY
Xmas 1908: special edition with full colour cover. 5 Jan 1906: 1st Funny Cuts & The Halfpenny Comic. 17 Oct 1908: 1st Funny Cuts & The World's Comic.

FUNNY CUTS
Paget; 1-2 1948
| 1-2 8pgs; Mack Earl art | £3.00 |

FUNNY CUTS AND BOYS COMPANION
(previously Funny Cuts)
Trapps Holmes; 1 17th Nov 1908-608 3rd Jul 1920 (joins Funny Wonder)
1 16pgs tabloid	£40.00
2	£10.00
3-5	£6.00
6-50	£5.00
51-608	£4.00
CHRONOLOGY
23 Sep 1913: features colour strips; 3 Feb 1914: reduced to 8pgs.

FUNNY CUTS COMIC
(see Paget's Funny Cuts Comic)

FUNNY FEATURES
Martin & Reid; 1 1944?
| 1 16pgs; H.E.Pease art | £3.00 |

FUNNY FOLK
Hamilton; nn 1947
| nn - Alan Fraser art | £4.00 |

FUNNY FORTNIGHTLY/MONTHLY HOLIDAY SPECIAL
Fleetway; 1990-present

	N.MINT

1990-present
| | £1.00 |

FUNNY PIPS
C.A. Pearson; 12th Sep 1903-26th Dec 1903 (16 issues)
| 12 Sep 1903 8pgs tabloid; supplement to Boys' Leader, Uncle Ebeneezer by George Studdy begins | £30.00 |
| 19 Sep-26 Dec 1903 | £8.00 |

FUNNY STUFF
Holland Press; nn 1947?
| nn - 8pgs; Alan Fraser art | £3.00 |

FUNNY 3-D
United Anglo-American; 1 1954
| 1 36pgs; Harvey reprint, issued with 3-D glasses | £8.00 |

FUNNY TUPPENNY
John Matthew; 1-4 1947
| 1-4 8pgs; H.E.Pease art | £3.00 |

FUNNY WONDER, THE
Harmsworth Brothers; 1 4th Feb 1893-325 22nd Apr 1899; 1 29th Apr 1899-109 25th May 1901 (becomes The Wonder)
1 8pgs tabloid; black on green printing	£75.00
2-202,204-325 incl. Jack Yeats, Tom Browne art	£10.00
203 (19th Dec 1896) Xmas Number, printed full colour on 4pgs	£20.00
1 new series	£15.00
2-109 incl. Yeats, Browne, H.O'Neill art	£6.00

FUNNY WONDER, THE
(previously The Halfpenny Wonder)
Amalgamated Press; 40 26th Dec 1914-1443 16th May 1942 (1404 issues; becomes The Wonder)
40 8pgs tabloid; Bertie Brown, Percy Cocking art	£40.00
41-499 incl. Brown, Don Newhouse & Roy Wilson, Tom Radford art	£8.00
500-999 incl. Roy Wilson art	£6.00
1000-1443 Roy Wilson, George Heath art	£4.00
CHRONOLOGY
7 Aug 1915: Charlie Chaplin by Bertie Brown begins. 1917: blue printing begins. 1918: captions dropped until 1919 (dropped again in 1937 except for page 1). 10 Jul 1920: 1st "Funny Wonder & Funny Cuts". 22 Oct 1922: Pitch & Toss by Roy Wilson begins. 1 Jun 1940: 1st "Funny Wonder & Jester". 26 Apr 1941: 2 col printing begins.

FUNNY WONDER ANNUAL
Amalgamated Press; 1935-1941
1935 scarce	£50.00
1936	£30.00
1937-1938	£20.00
1939-1940	£15.00
1941	£30.00

FUNNYLAND COMICS
Martin & Reid; nn 1948
| nn - Wally Robertson art | £3.00 |

FUNSTAR COMIC, THE
Martin & Reid; nn 1949
| nn - 8pgs, tabloid; Frank Minnitt art | £3.00 |

FUNTOWN
Modern Fiction; nn Dec 1948
| nn - Wally Robertson art | £3.00 |

FURTHER ADVENTURES OF ELMO, THE
(see The Adventures of Elmo the Lion)
Kingsbury Press; nn 1943
| nn - 16pgs, small size; reprints Charles Cole newspaper strip | £2.50 |

FURTHER ADVENTURES OF ROBINSON CRUSOE, THE
Grosvenor Associates; nn 1971
| nn - 16pgs; promotional reprint of US comicbook pubd. in 1952 by Pictorial Media Inc | £1.50 |

FURY
Marvel; 1 16th Mar 1977-25 31st Aug 1977 (joins Mighty World of Marvel)
| 1 Sgt. Fury reprints begin, Williamson art | £1.00 |
| 2-25 | £0.50 |

FUTURE TENSE
Marvel; 1 5th Nov 1980-41 Jan 1982
1 Micronauts, Paladin, Warlock and Starlord reprints begin	£1.25
2-3	£1.00
4-5	£0.75
6 Star Trek: The Motion Picture adaptation reprints begin	£1.00
7-12 Star Trek adaptation	£0.75
13 1st Future Tense & Forces in Combat; non-movie Star Trek reprints (to 33)	£0.60
14-19	£0.50
20 1st Future Tense & Valour; Conan the Barbarian begins	£0.60
21-34	£0.50
35 last weekly issue (1st Jul 1981); Conan ends	£0.50
36 1st monthly issue (Aug 1981), 52pgs; Star Trek returns	£1.25
37-41	£0.75
Note: 1-3 have cut-out parts to build a spaceship with instructions in #3. Add 50% to value if these gifts are present.

G

G-BOY COMICS
Funnibook Co.; nn Nov 1947
| nn - 20pgs; Dennis Reader art | £4.00 |

GABBY HAYES WESTERN
Miller; 50 1951-111 1955 (72 issues)
| 50 28pgs; Fawcett reprints begin | £6.00 |
| 51-111 | £4.00 |

!GAG!
Gag; 1 Dec 1984; Harrier; 1 Jan 1987-7 1989
| 1 A4, 8pgs; Elliott, Dakin, Campbell art | £0.80 |

N.MINT

	N.MINT
1-3 1st Harrier issues, 28pgs; Campbell art	£0.60
4-7 magazine format	£0.80

GAG-MAG, THE
Cartoon Art; nn 1946

nn - 8pgs	£3.00

GALLANT ADVENTURE COMIC
Scion; nn-nn 1952 (4 issues, only 2-3 numbered)

nn (1) 24pgs; Captain Courage by Ron Embleton, Patrick/Bleach art	£8.00
2-3 Embleton art	£8.00
nn (4) Bleach art, Holdaway cover	£6.00

GALLANT DETECTIVE COMIC
Scion; 1952 (2 unnumbered issues)

nn (1) 24pgs; Ron Embleton, James Holdaway art	£8.00
nn (2) James Holdaway, Norman Light art	£8.00

GALLANT SCIENCE COMIC
Scion; 1-2 1952

1-2 24pgs; Ron Embleton art	£8.00

GALLANT WESTERN COMIC
Scion; 1-3 1953

1 24pgs; Patrick/Bleach art	£6.00
2-3 Ron Embleton art	£8.00

GAMBOLS, THE
Daily Express/Beaverbrook; 1952-present?

nn Daily Express newspaper strip reprints by Barry Appleby begin	£75.00
2	£40.00
3	£25.00
4 larger size	£10.00
5-10	£10.00
11-20	£5.00
21-30	£3.00
31-40?	£2.50

GANNETS
Francis Boyle/Southwark Development; nn 1981

nn - 12pgs; Francis Boyle art	£0.50

GARTH
(see also Daily Mirror Book For Boys, Daily Mirror Book of Garth)
Titan; 1 Jan 1985-2 Aug 1985

Book One: The Cloud of Balthus newspaper strip reprints by Edgar & Bellamy	£5.00
Book Two: The Women of Galba Bellamy art	£5.00

GARTH (DAILY STRIPS)
(see also Romeo Brown)
John Dakin; 1979-1981

1 The Bride of Jenghis Khan, Bellamy art; A5 size	£1.00
3 The Spanish Lady, Bellamy art; first A4 size	£1.00
4 Sapphire, Martin Asbury art	£1.00
5 Night of the Knives, Dowling art	£2.00
7 The Doomsmen, Bellamy art	£1.00
nn Mr. Rubio Calls, Asbury art	£1.00

GARTH - MAN OF MYSTERY
Daily Mirror; nn 1946

nn - 36pgs small oblong; Steve Dowling art	£30.00

GARTH/ROMEO BROWN
Daily Mirror; nn 1958

nn - 128pgs oblong flip-book; Garth and the Last Goddess by Dowling; two	
Romeo Brown stories by O'Donnell & Holdaway	£15.00

GAY COMIC, THE
P.M. Productions; nn 1945

nn - 8pgs	£3.00

GEE-WHIZ COMIC
International; nn 1948

nn - 20pgs; John Turner art	£3.00

GEMINI MAN ANNUAL
Granddreams; 1977

1977 Ian Gibson art	£2.00

GEMINI 2000 PICTURE LIBRARY
Famepress; 1 1966-?

1 68pgs pocket size; Hell on Astra 6; foreign reprints begin	£1.00
2-?	£0.50

GENE AUTRY ADVENTURES
Birn Brothers Ltd.; 1958

1958 (all text), illus. by Reg Wilson, "The Masked Rider" (1st story)	£3.00

GENE AUTRY ANNUAL
World Distributors; nn 1958

nn "Stampede" (1st story)	£5.00

GENE AUTRY AND CHAMPION
World Distributors; 1 1956-34 1958

1 28pgs; Dell reprints begin	£5.00
2-29	£3.00
30-34 68pgs	£5.00

GENE AUTRY COMICS
Cartoon Art; 1 1950-19 1952

1 28pgs; Dell reprints begin	£5.00
2-19	£3.00

GENE AUTRY COMICS
Strato Publications; 1 1952-?

1 68pgs; Dell reprints begin	£5.00
2-?	£3.00

GENE AUTRY COMICS
Thorpe & Porter; 1 Apr 1953-14 1954

1 68pgs; Dell reprints begin	£6.00
2-14	£3.00

GENE AUTRY STORIES
Adprint; 1 1954-4 1957

1-4 2 incl. illus by Lance Cattermole	£5.00

GENE DOGS
(see main American comics section)

GENETIX
(see Codename: Genetix) (see main American comics section)

GENGHIS GRIMTOAD
(see The Chronicles of Genghis Grimtoad, Strip)

GERRY ANDERSON'S THUNDERBIRDS
(see Thunderbirds Specials)

GHOST RIDER
Compix (Cartoon Art); 1-3 1952

1 28pgs; Western Enterprises reprints begin	£8.00
2-3	£6.00

GHOST RIDER
Boxtree; Mar 1995

Ghost Rider/Wolverine/Punisher: The Dark Design Marvel reprints	£8.00

GHOST RIDER SPECIAL
Marvel; Oct 1992

nn 36pgs; reprints Ghost Rider 4, Marvel Holiday Special 1	£1.00

GHOST RIDERS
(see Action Series)

GHOST SQUADRON COMICS
United Anglo-American; nn 1950

nn - 28pgs; reprints from Wings Comics (Fiction House)	£5.00

GHOST STORIES COMIC ALBUM
World Distributors; 1 1965

1 64pgs, Dell reprints in colour	£4.00

GHOSTLY WEIRD STORIES
Arnold Book Co.; 1 1953

1 68pgs; Star reprints, cited in UK horror campaign	£10.00

GHOUL TALES
Portman; 1 1979-5 1980

1 Stanley Publications reprints, themselves pre-code reprints	£3.00
2-5 incl. material cited in Seduction of the Innocent	£2.00

GIANT CLASSICS ILLUSTRATED
(see Classics Illustrated)

GIANT COMIC
World Distributors; 1 1956-20 1957

1,5,13,17 Black Diamond Western, Lev Gleason reprints	£5.00
2,6,10,14,18 All Star Western, National Periodical reprints	£5.00
3,7,9,11,15,19 Turok, Son of Stone, Dell reprints	£6.50
4,8,12,16,20 Fast Action Western	£5.00
Note: 68pgs; reprints of American and Australian comicbooks	

GIANT HOLIDAY ADVENTURE COMIC ALBUM, THE
Hawk Books; 1990

- 228pgs; reprints Robin Hood (from TPL), Sexton Blake, Zip Nolan, Dick Barton	
(from SDL), Dick Turpin (from TPL), The Island of Fu Manchu (from SDL), etc	£1.50

GIANT HOLIDAY FANTASY COMIC ALBUM, THE
Hawk Books; 1990

- 288pgs; reprints Thunderbolt Jaxon, Robot Archie, The Men from the Stars	
(from SDL), Maxwell Hawke, The Return of the Claw, etc	£1.50

GIANT SUPER MAG
Young World Productions; 1 Jun 1964-4 Sep 1964

1 80pgs; reprints Walt Disney's Donald Duck & His Friends from Gold Key	£2.00
2-4	£1.50

GIANT WAR PICTURE LIBRARY
Fleetway; 1 Jun 1964-76 Dec 1965

1 68pgs, 13.5" tall format	£10.00
2	**£6**.00
3-50	£4.00
51-76	£3.00

GIDEON
Knight Books/Hodder & Stoughton; 1979

Gideon 52pgs; French reprints	£1.50
Gideon and his Friends	£1.00
Gideon's House	£1.00
Gideon on the River Bank	£1.00

GIFT COMICS
Miller; 1952-1953 (2 issues)

1-2 6 remaindered US comics bound in card covers	£6.00

GIGGLE
Fleetway; 29th Apr 1967-13th Jan 1968 (38 issues, joins Buster)

No. 1 - 29 Apr 1967 Giggle by Alf Saporito, Buck Bingo (Lucky Luke) reprints begin, Captain Swoop £5.00	
No. 1 with free gift (Giggle Balloon)	£10.00
6 May 1967	£2.50
13 May 1967	£1.50
20 May-9 Sep 1967	£0.75
16 Sep 1967-13 Jan 1968 smaller size	£0.50

GIGGLES
(no publisher); nn 1948

nn - 8pgs	£3.00

GILES ANNUAL
Express; 1 1946-44 1992

1 reprints Giles cartoons from Sunday Express (later from Daily Express)	£250.00
2	£180.00
3	£150.00
4,5	£125.00
6	£50.00
7 1st laminated cover	£25.00
8,9 laminated covers	£18.00

	N.MINT
10-13	£15.00
14-19	£10.00
20-24	£5.00
25-29	£4.00
30-34	£3.00
35-39	£2.00
40-43	£1.50
44 all reprints from earlier editions	£1.50
Giles Nurse Special (1975)	£12.50
The Giles Family (Headline, Oct 1993) edited by Peter Tory	£14.00
Giles Classics '94 (1993) reprints	£3.00
GIRL	
Hulton/Longacre; Vol 1:1 2nd Nov 1951-Vol 13:14 3rd Oct 1964	
(643 issues, joins Princess)	
Vol 1:1 Kitty Hawke by Ray Bailey, Penny Wise by Norman Pett, Lettice Leefe by John Ryan begin	£35.00
Vol 1:2	£10.00
Vol 1:3-52	£3.50
Vol 2:1-62	£2.50
Vol 3:1-Vol 6:52	£2.50
Vol 7:1-Vol 9:11	£2.00
Vol 9:12-Vol 12:5 Longacre issues	£1.75
Vol 12:6-Vol 13:14 smaller size	£1.00
GIRL ANNUAL	
Hulton/Longacre; 1 1952-1964	
1 published 1952 for 1953, undated	£10.00
2-10	£5.00
1963-1965	£3.00
The Best of Girl Annual 1952-1959, edited by Denis Gifford (Webb & Bower, 1990)	£3.00
GIRL FROM U.N.C.L.E. ANNUAL, THE	
World Distributors; 1967-1969	
1967	£6.00
1968-1969	£5.00
GIRL OF THE ISLANDS, THE	
D.C. Thomson; nn 4th Oct 1958	
nn - 28pgs; free gift with Bunty featuring Marina, Girl from the Sea	£1.00
GIRL PICTURE LIBRARY	
IPC; 1 Aug 1984-?	
1 68pgs pocket size; Patty's World by Purita Campos	£0.75
2-?	£0.25
GIRLS' CRYSTAL	
(continuation of story paper which ran 899 issues between 28th Oct 1935 and 14th Mar 1953)	
Amalgamated Press; 1 21st Mar 1953-529 18th May 1963	
1 Rivals for the Captaincy by Robert McGillivray begins	£8.00
2-5	£4.00
6-523	£2.50
GIRLS' CRYSTAL ANNUAL	
Amalgamated Press; 1953-1963	
1953 girl skier on cover	£10.00
1954-1959	£5.00
1960-1963	£2.50
GIRLS' DIARY	
Famepress; 1 1964-22 1965	
1 68pgs pocket size; Italian reprints	£0.75
2-22	£0.35
GIRLS DUX	
Cartoon Art; nn 1948	
nn - 8pgs; Dennis Reader art	£3.00
GIVE ME LIBERTY	
Penguin; nn 1991	
nn - Frank Miller & Dave Gibbons, hardcover	£15.00
nn - softcover	£9.00
GLADIATORS COMIC STRIP ADVENTURES	
Century 22; 1 (15th Sep 1993)-2 (30 Sep 1993)	
1 Gladiators based on TV characters, Kev Sutherland art begins	£0.75
2	£0.50
GLEAM, THE	
Frank Shaw/Bedford Publishing; 1 3rd Aug 1901-147 21st May 1904	
1 16pgs; Frank Holland plate	£45.00
2	£12.50
3-5	£7.50
6-20	£5.00
21-147	£2.50
Note: Began as a comic for adults featuring cartoons by Tom Browne, Robert Bromley, etc., later featuring miscellaneous strips by Will Spurier etc. Became a story paper from issue 21, but continued to feature cartoons.	
GLEE COMIC, THE	
Philmar; nn 1948	
nn - 8pgs, small; Harry Parlett, Jack Pamby, Wally Robertson art	£4.00
GLEE CUB COMIC, THE	
Globe Fiction; nn 1946	
nn - 8pgs	£2.00
GLOOPS	
W.C. Leng/Sheffield Telegraph/Star	
The Book of Gloops (1928) Evening Chronicle newspaper reprints by "Cousin Ken"	£5.00
Gloops Club First Anniversary (1929)	£4.00
Gloops Club Second Anniversary (1930)	£4.00
Christmas Book of Gloops (1930) 44pgs; orange paper	£3.00
Gloops Club Third Birthday Number (1931) 36pgs; blue paper	£3.00
Second Gloopers Annual (1931) 44pgs; yellow paper	£3.00
Fourth Birthday Book of Gloops (1932)	£3.00
Gloops Christmas Annual (1932) 36pgs; yellow paper	£3.00
Fifth Birthday of Gloops (1933)	£3.00

Gene Autry and Champion #1

Ghost Stories Comic Album

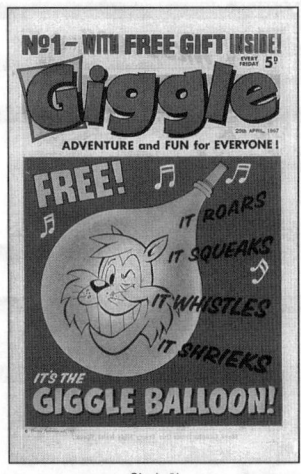
Giggle #1

N.MINT
N.MINT

Gloops Children's Comic Christmas Annual (1933) 36pgs; yellow paper	£3.00
Gloops the Laughter Cat Birthday Number (1934)	£3.00
Gloops the Laughter Cat Xmas Annual (1934) 36pgs; blue paper	£3.00
Gloops the Comic Cat Jubilee Number (1935) 36pgs; white paper	£3.00
Gloops Comic Cat Xmas Annual (1935-37) 36pgs; white paper	£3.00
Gloops Comic Cat Birthday Number (1936-37) 36pgs; white paper	£3.00
Gloops Childrens Comic Birthday Number (1938-40) 36pgs; white paper	£3.00
Gloops Childrens Comic Xmas Annual (1938)	£3.00
Gloops Christmas Annual (1939) 24pgs	£2.50
Gloops Christmas Annual Childrens Comic (1940)	£2.50

GOBO STRIP BOOKS
Sampson Low Marston; 1953-1955	
Gobo and Mr Fierce (1953) Enid Blyton story	£2.00
Gobo in Land of Dreams (1955)	£2.00

GOLDEN
Amalgamated Press; 1 23rd Oct 1937-135 18th May 1940 (joins Jingles)	
1 Roy Wilson, Reg Perrott art begins	£60.00
2	£25.00
3-5	£20.00
6-135 incl. Wilson, Perrott, Ray Bailey art	£15.00

GOLDEN FUN AND STORY BOOK
Amalgamated Press; 1939-1940	
1939 scarce	£25.00
1940	£15.00

GOLDEN ARROW WESTERN
Arnold Book Co./Miller; 10 1951-13 1951	
10 (Arnold) 24pgs; Fawcett reprints	£5.00
11-13 (Miller) 28pgs	£3.00

GOLDEN HEART LOVE STORIES
D.C. Thomson; 1 1960s-?	
1 68pgs pocket size; No Other Man	£0.75
2-?	£0.40

GOLDEN HOURS
Selbourne/Williams; 1 Jan 1972-31 Dec 1972 (joins Sleepytime Stories)	
1-31	£0.35

GOLDEN PENNY COMIC
Fleetway Press/Amalgamated Press; 1 14th Oct 1922-276 28th Jan 1928 (joins Comic Cuts)	
1 8pgs tabloid; Reg Carter, Walter Bell art	£50.00
2	£25.00
3-5	£15.00
6-274 incl. H.C.Milburn, Walter Booth art	£10.00
275-276 Amalgamated issues	£6.00

GOLDEN WEST ANNUAL
Brown Watson; Nov 1954	
1954 text stories by Mullaney, Weston, Took, Daner, Overland, Barton, Gasrland, Hughes; illus J. Abbey; edited by Peter Collins	£4.00

GOLLIWOG COMIC
Philmar; nn 1948	
nn - 8pgs; Wally Robertson art	£3.00

GON
Mandarin; nn Jan 1995	
nn - Masashi Tanaka manga reprints	£9.00

GOOD DOG CAESAR
Brockhampton Press; nn 1953	
nn - 36pgs oblong; Caesar by Tim (William Tymym)	£2.00

GOOFY
IPC; 20th Oct 1973-11th May 1974 (29? issues; joins Donald and Mickey)	
20 Oct 1973 Dell/Western Printing reprints begin	£1.00
27 Oct 1973-11 May 1974	£0.30

GOSPORT COURIER
J.B.Allen; 1 1st Mar 1947 (joins Comet)	
1 8pgs; reprints from Home Review; contents identical to Stretford Courier	£2.00
Note: pre-War newspaper revived as comic to obtain paper quota	

GRAND ADVENTURE COMIC, THE
Martin & Reid; nn 1946	
nn - 16pgs; R. Beaumont art	£4.00

GRANDSTAND COMIC, THE
Martin & Reid; nn 1949	
nn - 8pgs; Minnett, Banger, Robertson art	£4.00

GRAPHIXUS
Graphic Eye; 1 Feb 1977-6 Mar 1979, 5b Spr 1979	
1 Matthews art, Higgins cover	£5.00
2 Matthews, Emerson, Leach art	£4.00
3 Matthews, Whitaker art, Little Nympho by Bolland	£6.00
4,6	£4.00
5 Bolland, Higgins art	£6.00
5b (Alternative Series Imprint 1)	£1.50

GREAT FUN COMIC
Paget; nn 1950	
nn - 16pgs; Banger art	£3.00

GREEN HORNET ANNUAL, THE
World Distributors; 1966-1967	
1966	£15.00
1967	£10.00

GREENHOUSE WARRIORS
Tundra Publishing UK/Phil Elliott; 1 Jun 1992-present (4 to date)	
1 LD, by Glenn Dakin & Phil Elliott	£3.00
2 (Mar 1993) first self-published	£2.00
3-4	£2.00
Note: 6 issue MS, cancelled after one issue, subsequently self-published by Elliott	

GREEN LANTERN ANNUAL
Thorpe & Porter (?); 1967	
1967 very scarce; bound-together remaindered copies of Green Lantern #51, Tales of the Unexpected #96, Lois Lane #72, House of Secrets #78, Batman #190, Superboy #136	£25.00

GREMLINS
Marvel; nn Nov 1984	
nn - 68pgs; American reprint based on film	£1.00

GRUN
Harrier; 1 Jun 1987-4 Dec 1987	
1-4 Paul Marshall art	£0.65

GUILTY
(see Justice Traps the Guilty)

GUMMY
Maynards; 1-12 1954	
1-12 8pgs; giveaway to advertise sweets	£0.10

GUNFLASH WESTERN
Scion; 1 Sep 1951-2 Oct 1951	
1-2 24pgs; Ron Embleton art	£5.00

GUNHAWK, THE
Streamline; nn-2 1951	
nn - 28pgs; Marvel reprints	£3.00
2	£2.50

GUNHAWKS WESTERN
Anglo; 1 Oct 1960-10 Jun 1961	
1 28pgs	£2.00
2-10 some issues incl. Don Lawrence Daniel Boone reprints	£1.50

GUNRUNNER
(see main American comics section)

GUNS OF FACT AND FICTION
United Anglo-American; nn 1951	
nn - 28pgs; reprints A.1 #13 (Magazine Enterprises); cited in Seduction of the Innocent & UK horror campaign	£12.00

GUNSMOKE
Top Sellers; 1 1970-? 1971	
1 36pgs; Dell reprints; based on TV series	£1.00
2-?	£0.50

GUNSMOKE PICTURE AND STORY ALBUM
Mellifont; W3 1950s	
W3 96pgs	£3.00

GUNSMOKE TRAIL
Miller; 1-4 1957	
1-4 28pgs; Ajax-Farrell Publishing Co. reprints	£4.00

GUNSMOKE WESTERN
Miller; 1 1955-23 1956	
1 28pgs; Atlas/Marvel reprints	£6.00
2-23	£4.00

H

HAGAR THE HORRIBLE
Egmont/Eyre Methuen	
Hagar the Horrible (1979) 52pgs; Dik Browne reprints	£1.00
Hagar and the Basilisk (1979)	£1.00

HAGAR THE HORRIBLE WINTER SPECIAL
Polystyle; nn 1976	
nn - 48pgs; Dik Browne reprints	£0.80

HALCON COMICS
A. Halle; nn 1948	
nn - 8pgs; reprints from Comic Capers (Soloway)	£2.50

HALF ASSED FUNNIES
H. Bunch (Cozmic); 1 1973	
1 Edward Barker art	£1.00

HALF-HOLIDAY
(Previously Ally Sloper's Half-Holiday)
The Sloperies (Milford); 24 21st Apr 1923-47 29th Sep 1923 (24 issues; joins London Life)	
24-47	£3.00

HALFPENNY COMIC, THE
Newnes/Trapps Holmes; 1 22nd Jan 1898-467 29th Dec 1906 (joins Funny Cuts)	
1 12pgs tabloid; Tom Browne art	£60.00
2	**£30.00**
3-26 12pgs	£20.00
27-467 8pgs 12x16"; incl. Browne, Jack Yeats, Frank Holland art	£6.00
The Christmas Comic title change for double size christmas editions (1d)	£10.00
CHRONOLOGY	
23 Jul 1898: 1st larger size. 10 Sep 1898 and 5 Nov 1898: full colour issues. 4 Feb 1889: 1st Trapps Holmes issue.	

HALFPENNY WONDER, THE
(previously The Wonder, story paper)
Amalgamated Press; 1 28th Mar 1914-39 19th Dec 1914 (becomes Funny Wonder)	
1 8pgs tabloid; Bertie Brown, Percy Cocking art	£35.00
2	£10.00
3	£7.50
4-39	£5.00

HALLS OF HORROR
(see House of Hammer; for Halls of Horror Winter Special see HoH No.24)

HALO JONES
Titan (Best of 2000AD); Aug 1986-Oct 1986, 1992	
Book One 2000AD reprints by Moore & Gibson begin	£5.00
Book Two	£5.00
Book Three	£5.00
The Complete Halo Jones	£10.00

	N.MINT

HANS KRESSE
Methuen; 1975
1 Masters of Thunder 48pgs; European strip reprints by Hans Kresse begin — £2.00
2 Riders of the Wind — £1.00
3 Sons of the Chief — £1.00
4 Song of the Coyote — £1.00

HAPPIJACK, THE
Scottish Book Distributors; nn 1945
nn - 16pgs small; Frank Jupo art — £2.50

HAPPY COMIC, THE
C.A. Ransom; 1 17th Sep 1928-28 20th Apr 1929
1 8pgs tabloid; contains reprints from The Golden Penny Comic — £30.00
2 incl. Joseph Walker, Reg Carter reprints — £10.00
3 — £7.50
4-26 — £4.00

HAPPY DAYS
Amalgamated Press; 1 8th Oct 1938-45 5th August 1939 (joins Chicks' Own)
1 12pgs tabloid; At Chimpo's Circus by Roy Wilson, Sons of the Sword by Reg Perrott begin — £100.00
2 — £40.00
3-45 incl. Walter Booth, Fred Robinson art — £12.50

HAPPY FAMILIES
Alfred Bird; 1 1938-nn 1939 (4 issues)
1 8 pgs tabloid; giveaway from Birds Custard; Ben Somers art — £1.00
nn - red/black printing — £0.35
nn - (Xmas 1938) full colour on alternate pages — £0.35
nn - (Easter 1939) H.S.Foxwell art — £0.50

HAPPY GANG
Children's Press; nn 1947
nn - 12pgs; Hugh McNeill art — £3.00

HAPPY HIGHWAY, THE
ROSPA; nn 1947
nn - 8pgs giveaway produced by Royal Society of Prevention of Accidents, Bob Wilkin art — £1.50

HAPPY MOMENTS
John Matthew; 1946
1 8pgs; Mick Anglo art — £3.00

HAPPY TIMES FAMILY COMIC, THE
Algar 1 1946-5 1947 (continued as Jolly Times)
1 16pgs; Stanley White, Walter Booth art — £5.00
2-4 — £4.00
5 Basil Reynolds art — £4.00

HAPPY TUPPENY
Rayburn; 1-2 1947
1-2 8pgs; H.E. Pease art — £2.50

HAPPY WARRIOR, THE
Hulton; nn 1958
nn - hardcover; reprints Winston Churchill biog by Frank Bellamy from Eagle — £10.00

HAPPY WORLD
Martin & Reid; nn 1949
nn - 8pgs; Frank Minnitt, Wally Robertson art — £4.00

HAPPY YANK
Rayburn; 1 1948-4 Oct 1949
1 8pgs; Mick Anglo art — £4.00
2-4 — £3.00

HARD BOILED DEFECTIVE STORIES
Penguin; nn Mar 1990
nn - reprints Charles Burns strips from Raw — £8.00

HARD CORE HORROR
(see Lord Horror)

HARD TO SWALLOW
Knockabout (Crack); nn Aug 1988
nn - 80pgs; text by John Dowie, Emerson art — £5.00

HARDY BOYS/NANCY DREW MYSTERIES ANNUAL
Grandreams; 1979
1979 — £1.50

HAROLD HARE'S OWN PAPER
Fleetway; 14th Nov 1959-4th Apr 1964 (230 issues; joins Playhour)
No. 1 - 14 Nov 1959 Harold Hare by Hugh McNeill begins — £25.00
No. 1 with free gift (Mask and Balloon) — £35.00
21 Nov 1959 — £5.00
27 Nov-4 Apr 1964 incl. Philip Mendoza art — £1.00
Note: a collector recently paid over £100 by postal auction for a lot including issue #1, not being particularly interested in the rest
CHRONOLOGY
29 Apr 1961: incorporates Walt Disney's Weekly. Title later changed to Harold Hare, and drops to smaller size.

HARRIER PREVIEW
Harrier; 1 Mar 1988
1 previews of Cuirass and Night Bird — £0.30

HARRIS TWEED
Hawk (Eagle Classics); nn 1990
nn - reprints John Ryan strip from Eagle — £3.00

HAUNT OF FEAR
Strato; 1 1952
1 EC reprints — £15.00

HAUNT OF FEAR, THE
Arnold Book Co.; 1 1954
1 68pgs; Haunt of Fear 23, Crime SuspenStories 14 reprints, widely cited in UK horror campaign — £25.00

HAVOC
Marvel; 1 13th Jul 1991-9 7th Sep 1991
1 36pgs; Robocop, Ghost Rider, Deathlok, Conan, Starslammers reprints begin — £1.25
2-9 — £0.75

HAWKEYE AND THE LAST OF THE MOHICANS
C.A. Pearson (TV Picture Stories); 1 Jun 1958-6 May 1959

	N.MINT

1 68pgs pocket size — £5.00
2-6 — £3.00
ARTISTS/FEATURES
1 The Long Rifles. 2 The Renegade. 3 La Salle's Treasure by Terry Aspin. 4 Revenge by Terry Aspin. 5 The Wild One. 6 The Reckoning.

HAWKEYE AND THE LAST OF THE MOHICANS ANNUAL
Adprint; 1 1958-nn 1959
1 (1958) text stories by Michael Holt; illus. by George Shaw — £5.00
nn (1959) text stories by David Roberts; illus. by Ron Embleton — £5.00

HAYSEEDS
Macmillan; 1971-1972 (2 issues)
nn-nn reprints Harry Hargreaves newspaper strip from Evening News — £1.00

HEARTBREAK HOTEL
Willyprods; 1 Jan 1988-6 Nov/Dec 1988
1 LD, Trina Robbins text, Alan Moore, Gibbons art, flexidisc (1,000) — £2.50
1 LD, no flexidisc (9,000) — £1.75
2 LD, scarce, O'Neill, Talbot, Emerson art, flexidisc (1,000) — £2.50
2 LD, scarce, no flexidisc — £2.00
3 LD, Fabry, Elliott art, flexidisc — £1.75
3 LD, no flexidisc — £1.50
4 Clive Barker text, Grant Morrison, Elliott art, flexidisc — £1.75
4 no flexidisc — £1.50
5 Trina Robbins art, 8pg Blaam! preview — £1.50
6 Dave McKean art — £1.50

HEART THROBS
Fleetway (Xpresso); nn Aug 1991
nn - 83pgs; European reprints by Max Cabanes — £3.50

HEART TO HEART
(see Magic Moment Romances, Twin Hearts)
K.G. Murray Ltd; 1 1958-?
1 very rare 100pgs, squarebound begin; b/w romance reprints from National Periodical Publications; priced at one shilling — £75.00
2-? — £40.00

HEAVY PERIODS
Grass Roots; nn 1980
nn - 36pgs oblong; underground — £1.00

HELL-FIRE RAIDERS
Alan Class; nn 1966
nn - 68pgs; Fawcett reprints featuring Tom Mix, Tex Ritter and Lash LaRue — £2.50

HELL'S ANGEL
(see Overkill) (see main American comics section)

HENRY
Brockhampton Press; 1961-1964
Henry's Exciting Flight 36pgs small oblong; by Dora Thatcher & R. Paul Hoye — £1.50
Henry's Mountain Adventure — £1.00
Henry Goes to Town — £1.00

HERE COME THE PERISHERS
(see The Perishers)
Daily Mirror; nn Jul 1979
nn - Daily Mirror reprints by Dennis Collins — £1.50

HERMAN AND HIS PALS
Bazooka Joe/Graperoo; nn 1970-?
nn - 1pg; reprints of American strip giveaway with Graperoo Bubble Gum — £0.25

HERO
Premier; 1 1975
1 — £0.50

HEROES OF THE SKY
G.T. Ltd; nn c1959
nn - 72pgs, softcover; Norman Light, Joe Colquhoun reprints — £6.00

HEROES OF THE WEST
Miller; 150-158 1959
150 28pgs; Fawcett reprints — £5.00
151-158 incl. Bobby Benson, Presto Kid reprints — £3.00

HEROIC ADVENTURE LIBRARY
C.A. Pearson; 1 Apr 1964-?
1 68pgs pocket size; The Gallant Crusaders — £1.00
2-? — £0.60

HEROINE
Birmingham Arts Lab; 1978
1 36pgs; adult material (feminist) — £1.00

HEWLIGAN'S HAIRCUT
Fleetway; nn Jul 1991
nn - 2000AD reprints by Pete Milligan & Jamie Hewlett — £3.50

HEY DIDDLE DIDDLE
IPC; 25th Mar 1972-15th Sep 1973 (78 issues; joins Playhour)
25 Mar 1972 24pgs; nursery comic — £0.60
1 Apr 1972-27 Jan 1973, 10 Feb-15 Sep 1973 — £0.20
3 Feb 1973 1st "Hey Diddle Diddle and Bobo Bunny" — £0.20

HEY DIDDLE DIDDLE HOLIDAY SPECIAL
IPC; 1972-1973 (2 issues)
1972,1973 48pgs — £0.40

HI-YO SILVER
World Distributors; 1-9 1953
1 36pgs; Dell reprints — £6.00
2-9 — £4.00

HIGH CHAPARRAL ANNUAL, THE
World Distributors
1969-1972 mainly text stories — £4.00
1973 — £3.00

HIGH COMMAND
Dragon's Dream; nn 1981
nn - 100pgs hardback reprint Bellamy strips from Eagle — £7.50

N.MINT | N.MINT

HIGH JINKS COMICS
Hamilton; nn 1947
nn - 8pgs £4.00

HIGH SEAS COMIC
Scion; 1 1952
1 20pgs; King-Ganteaume art £4.00

HIGH SPEED COMIC
Scion; 1 Aug 1951
1 24pgs; King-Ganteaume art £4.00

HIGHWAY PATROL
C.A. Pearson (TV Picture Stories); 1 Jun 1959-8 Jan 1960
1 68pgs pocket size £5.00
2-8 £3.00
ARTISTS/FEATURES
1 Double Cross. 2 The Reckless Driver. 3 The Bank Robbers. 4 The Stolen Brain by Cosmoartis. 5 The Man Who Drove Away. 6 The Larchmont Mystery. 7 The Disappearing Casino. 8 Search Party.

HIP HIP HOORAY COMIC, THE
Philmar; 1 1948
1 8pgs; Jack Pamby, Wally Roberton, Eric Roberts art £4.00

HITLER
Morcrim; 1-2 1977
1-2 132pgs oblong; Hitler's Last Days, Spanish reprint £1.00

HOLIDAY COMIC, THE
(see also The Christmas Comic, The Summer Comic, Summer Holiday Comic, Summer Comic)
C.A. Pearson; 1931-1939 (7 issues)
Jun 1931 12pgs; Walter Bell art £12.00
Jun 1933 Walter Bell art £8.00
Jun 1934 Walter Bell art £8.00
May 1936 Sidney Stanley, G.Larkman art £6.00
Jun 1937 G.Larkman, R.Plummer art £6.00
Jun 1938 Frank Minnitt art £5.00
Jun 1939 Norman Ward art £5.00

HOLLYWOOD ACES
Cartoon Art; 1 1950
1 Fiction House reprints £6.00

HOMER THE HAPPY GHOST
Miller; 1 1955
1 28pgs; Atlas reprints (colophon gives Charlton) £3.00

HONK
Brockhampton Press; 1950-1960
Honk Runs Away 36pgs small oblong; Joy K. Seddon art £1.50
Honk and Tonk £1.00
Happy Christmas Honk £1.00
Fun With Honk £1.00
Honk and the Donkey £1.00
A Holiday for Honk £1.00
Honk for Sale £1.00
Happy-go-lucky Honk £1.00
Honk and Gypsy Rose £1.00

HOODED HORSEMAN, THE
Streamline; nn 1953 (2 issues)
nn - 28pgs; American Comic Group reprints £5.00
nn - 48pgs £5.00

HOOKS DEVLIN
Cartoon Art; 1 1950
1 16pgs; Fiction House reprints £3.00

HOORAY!
Modern Fiction; Dec 1949
1 8pgs; Arthur Martin, Wally Robertson art £4.00

HOOT GIBSON
Streamline/United Anglo-American; 1-6 1950
1-6 28pgs; Fox reprints, incl. Wood art £7.50

HOPALONG CASSIDY COMIC
Miller; 5 Feb 1948; nn 1949; 50 1950-153 1958
5 16pgs gravure; Fawcett reprints £5.00
nn - 68pgs £5.00
50-153 32pgs/24pgs £3.00

HOPALONG CASSIDY JUMP-UP BOOK
Adprint; nn 1950s
nn - 16pgs; text story by Jim Roberts; 5 x pop-ups £8.00

HOPALONG CASSIDY STORIES
Adprint; 1 Jul 1953-6 1958
1 text stories by Elizabeth Beech, Sahula Dycke, Pete Alvarado £4.00
2 text stories by Edmund Collier, Ursula Koering £3.00
3 text stories by Charles Hitchcock; illus by Facey £3.00
4 text stories by Charles Hitchcock; illus by George Shaw, Charles Bourbe £3.00
5 text and photo stories £6.00
6 titled Hopalong Cassidy Adventures £2.50

HOPALONG CASSIDY WESTERN COMIC ANNUAL
Miller; 1 1959-2 1960
1 US reprints incl. Dan Spiegle art £5.00
2 (1960) US reprints incl. Dan Spiegle art £3.00

HORNET, THE
D.C. Thomson; 1 14th Sep 1963-648 7th Feb 1975 (joins The Hotspur)
1 £20.00
1 with free gift (balsa wood Kestrel glider) £40.00
2 £7.50
3 £4.00
4-5 £1.25
6-52,54-98,100-648 £0.50
53 The Truth About Wilson begins £0.50
99 V For Vengeance (Deathless Men) begins by F.A. Philpott begins £0.50

HOSPITAL NURSE PICTURE LIBRARY
C.A. Pearson; 1 Feb 1964-?
1 68pgs pocket size; Nurse in Love, foreign reprints £1.00
2-? £0.50

HOT NADS
Ghura; 1980
1 Antonio Ghura art (adult material) £1.00

HOT ROD AND SPEEDWAY COMICS
United Anglo-American; 1 1953
1 28pgs; Hillman reprints £3.00

HOT ROD COMICS
Arnold Book Co.; 1-4 1951
1-4 28pgs; Fawcett reprints, Bob Powell art £4.00

HOT RODS AND RACING CARS
Miller; 50-51 1953
50-51 28pgs; Charlton reprints £3.00

HOTCH-POTCH
Judy Office; nn 1870s?
nn - James Brown reprints £8.00

HOTSPUR, THE
D.C. Thomson; 1 2nd Sep 1933-1197 17th Oct 1959 (becomes The New Hotspur, below)
1 scarce £75.00
1 facsimile £5.00
2 scarce £50.00
3 £25.00
1933 issues £20.00
1934-1940 issues £12.50
1941-1950 issues £7.50
1951-1955 issues £5.00
1956-1959 issues £3.00

HOTSPUR, THE
(titled The New Hotspur/The Hotspur; see The Air Flights of Flyer Hart)
D.C. Thomson; 1 24th Oct 1959-1110 24th Jan 1981 (joins Victor)
1 Johnny Jett the Super Boy by Dudley Watkins reprints, Coral Island by Bill Holroyd begin £20.00
1 with free gift (Jumping frog) £30.00
2 £6.00
3 £3.00
4-101,103-173 £1.00
102 The Wolf of Kabul by J.T. Higson begins £0.60
174 1st "The Hotspur"; Limpalong Leslie by Bert van de Put begins £1.00
175-299,301-335,337-779,781-851 £0.40
300 Zigimar - the Master Spy by Terry Patrick begins £0.40
336 Spring Heeled Jack by Steve Chapman begins £0.40
780 Nick Jolly by Ron Smith begins £0.40
852 1st "Hotspur & Hornet"; King Cobra by Ron Smith begins £0.40
853-1058 £0.25
1059 1st "Hotspur & The Crunch"; Starhawk begins £0.25
1060-1071,1073-1110 £0.25
1072 The Doom Wardens by Alcatena begins £0.25
ARTISTS/FEATURES
Alcatena in 1072-1083,1095,1100,1102. Dave Gibbons in 882-889,941-949.

HOTSPUR BOOK FOR BOYS, THE
D.C. Thomson; 1935-1949, 1965-1980
(1935) scarce, (Teacher (Big Stiff) showing boys seated on ground a sum on blackboard) £75.00
(1936) (Teacher with three Eskimo boys sitting on ground) £50.00
(1937) (Teacher & boys from Westmore Academy shipwrecked on island) £25.00
(1938) (Teacher tied to a post, Chinese attacking in foreground with boys coming
    to rescue with cricket bats) £20.00
(1939) (Teacher tied up - is there a theme developing here? - by two indians,
    one on horseback) £20.00
(1940) (Young boy on a scrambling bike (No.26) in race) £20.00
(1941) (Young Indian boy with a tiger alarming teacher) £15.00
(1943) (Teacher on ladder painting red wall in a room where a sweep's brush is
    coming down the chimney) £15.00
(1949) (Iron Teacher being held by a tank with a flexible claw) £10.00 -
1966 first dated £6.00
1967-1969 £4.00
1970-1974 £3.00
1975-1981 £2.50
Note: no annuals issued 1942, 1944-48.

HOTSPUR CHRISTMAS SPECIAL
D.C. Thomson; nn 22nd Dec 1963
nn - 8pg supplement to Hotspur £4.00

HOUSE OF HAMMER/HALLS OF HORROR
(see also Dracula's Spinechillers Annual)
General Book Distribution/Top Sellers/Quality; 1 Oct 1976-30 Nov 1984
(joins Warrior)
1 Dracula by Neary, 1st Captain Kronos by Gibson £5.00
2-3 Curse of Frankenstein by Cuyas, Gibson art, rare £6.00
4 Legend of the Seven Golden Vampires by Brian Lewis, Bolton art, very rare £10.00
5 Moon Zero Two by Neary, very rare £10.00
6 Dracula, Prince of Darkness by Bolton, v rare £12.00
7 Twins of Evil by Blas Gallego, 1pg Gibbons art £3.00
8 Quatermass Xperiment by Lewis, Father Shandor by Bolton £4.00
9 Quatermass Xperiment by Lewis £3.00
10 Curse of the Werewolf by Bolton £5.00
11,12 The Gorgon by Trev Goring/Cuyas £4.00
13 Plague of Zombies by Goring/Bolland £5.00
14 Million Years BC by Bolton £4.00
15 Mummy's Shroud by Dave Jackson, Gibbons reprint £2.00
16 Star Wars issue; Shandor by Bolton, Pat Wright art £4.00
17 title becomes Halls of Horror; Vampire Circus by Bolland £6.00

N.MINT

18 Frankenstein, Dracula, Werewolf by Neal Adams, rare	£5.00
19 Reptile by Lewis	£2.00
20 Captain Kronos, Vampire Hunter	£3.00
21 Shandor by Bolton, Berni Wrightson back-up	£2.00
22 The Mummy by Dave Jackson	£2.00
23 Quatermass 2 by David Lloyd, Gibbons back-up	£2.00
Winter Special 1982 (24) Brian Lewis art	£4.00
25 Monster Club reprint by Bolton, pull out poster	£5.00
26 Monster Club by Bolton, Lloyd	£2.00
27-28 Bride of Dracula by John Stokes	£1.50
29 Night Holds Terror by Lewis	£1.50
30 no strips	£2.00

HOW THE WEST WAS WON
Grandreams; 1978

1978	£3.00

HOW T'MAKE IT AS A ROCK STAR
IPC/New Musical Express; nn 1977

nn - 36pgs; Tony Benyon art	£0.80

HOW TO PICK WINNERS
Norfil; nn 1971

nn - 112pgs; reprints Judy and the Colonel by Harry Bishop from Evening Standard	£1.00

HUBBA-HUBBA COMIC BOOK
Transatlantic; nn 1947

1 8pgs; Dennis Reader art	£3.00

HUCKLEBERRY HOUND AND YOGI BEAR EXTRA
City Magazines; 1963

Summer Extra 48pgs	£2.00
Winter Extra	£2.00

HUCKLEBERRY HOUND MINI-COMIC
City Magazines; nn 20th Feb 1965

nn - 16pgs; supplement to Huckleberry Hound Weekly	£1.00

HUCKLEBERRY HOUND EXTRA
City Magaines; 1964-1965

Winter Extra (1964) 48pgs	£2.00
Summer Extra (1965) 40pgs	£2.00

HUCKLEBERRY HOUND WEEKLY
(see Flintstones Mini-Comic, Huckleberry Hound Mini-Comic)
City Magazines/Robert Hayward; 1 7th Oct 1961-308 28th Aug 1967

1 Hanna-Barbera characters, incl. Huckleberry Hound, Mr Jinks, Pixie & Dixie, Yogi Bear, Flintstones, etc	£5.00
2-283 some incl. Top Cat	£1.50
284-308 (Hayward) some incl. Space Ghost	£1.00

HULK ANNUAL/INCREDIBLE HULK ANNUAL
Marvel/Grandreams; 1977-1984

1977 reprints origin from Hulk #1, Hulk #6 (Ditko art), Tales to Astonish #62 (1st Leader); colour	£5.00
1978 64pgs; reprints Hulk/Sub-Mariner from Ann #1; colour	£4.00
1979 1st Grandreams; Bill Bixby cover, strips & stories based on tv show, b/w reprint from Hulk #1, John Higgins art, titled Incredible Hulk Annual	£3.00
1980 1st Marvel/Grandreams; Lou Ferrigno cover, strips & stories based on tv show, b/w reprint from Hulk #3, David Lloyd art, titled Hulk Annual	£3.00
1981	£3.00
(1982) reprints Hulk #127,129,184	£3.00
1983 reprints Hulk Ann #5	£3.00
1984 reprints What If #12, Hulk #104	£3.00

HULK COMIC
Marvel; 1 7th Mar 1979-63 15th May 1980 (joins Spiderman Weekly)

1 Hulk by Dave Gibbons, Black Knight by Steve Parkhouse & John Stokes, Nick Fury by Steve Moore & Steve Dillon (1st pro work), Night Raven by Steve Parkhouse & David Lloyd all begin	£3.50
1 with free gift (Hulk sticker album)	£6.00
2	£1.50
2 with free gift (Hulk stickers)	£3.00
3-14	£2.00
15-19 John Bolton Night Raven	£2.50
20-30	£1.00
31 Captain Britain origin reprinted	£1.25
32-41 incl. Black Knight origin reprints	£1.00
42-46 original Black Knight stories returns	£1.00
47 title becomes The Incredible Hulk Weekly	£0.75
48 UK Antman strip by Steve Moore & Steve Dillon	£0.95
49-63	£0.75

HULK POCKET BOOK
Marvel; 1 Sep 1980-13 Nov 1981

1 52pgs, small size; Incredible Hulk reprints begin from Hulk #1 (origin); b/w	£1.25
1 reprints Incredible Hulk #3-4	£1.00
3 100pgs double-number	£1.25
4-13	£0.75

HULK POP-UP BOOK
Piccolo; nn 1981

nn - 12pgs	£4.00

HUMAN SOUP COMICS
Szostek; 1 1981-3 1983

1 32pgs; J.H. Szostek (adult)	£0.80
2-3	£0.50

HUMPHREY
(see Joe Palooka's Humphrey)

HUNDRED COMIC MONTHLY
(see All Favourites, Five-Score Comic Monthly, Century Comic)
K.G. Murray Ltd; 1 mid 1950s-100? mid 1960s

1 rare 100pgs, squarebound begin; b/w reprints from National Periodical Publications incl. Tommy Tomorrow, Flash, Buzzy, Congo Bill, John Jones Manhunter from Mars, Flash, Buzzy, Congo Bill, Vigilante (later issues feature Wonder Woman, Challengers of the Unknown among others); priced at 2 shillings	£75.00

Hotspur, The New #1

Hundred Comic Monthly #4

Hurricane #1

	N.MINT
2 rare	£50.00
3-5 very scarce	£40.00
6-10 scarce	£35.00
11-100? scarce	£30.00
Note: more issues thought to exist	
HURRICANE	
Fleetway; 29th Feb 1964-8th May 1965 (63 unnumbered issues)	
No.1 - 29 Feb 1964 Typhoon Tracy, Skid Solo, Sword for hire by Alberto Giolitti all begin	£15.00
No.1 with free gift (T.S.R.2 flying model)	£30.00
No. 2 - 7 Mar 1964	£7.50
No. 3 - 14 Mar 1964	£4.00
21 Mar-27 Jun 1964	£2.00
4 Jul 1964 Black Avenger (reprints Billy the Kid from Sun) by Campion, "Hurry" of the Hammers	
(reprints "Roy of the Rovers" from Tiger) by Colquhoun begin	£1.00
11 Jul 1964-8 May 1965	£1.00
HURRICANE ADVENTURE COMIC, THE	
R & L Locker; nn Jan 1946	
nn - 16pgs; R.Beaumont art	£4.00

I

	N.MINT
I LOVE LUCY	
World Distributors; 1-16 1954	
1-16 28pgs; Dell reprints	£5.00
I LOVE YOU	
Miller; 1 1955-23 1956	
1-23 68pgs; Charlton reprints	£3.00
I WANTED BOTH MEN	
Streamline; 1950s	
nn - 28pgs; Fox reprints	£4.00
I WAS A CHEAT	
Streamline; nn 1950s	
nn - US reprints	£4.00
IBIS THE INVINCIBLE	
Miller; nn 1950	
nn - 16pgs; Fawcett reprints	£2.00
IF	
Methuen	
If Chronicles (1983) 164pgs; Steve Bell reprints from The Guardian	£1.50
If Only Again (1984)	£1.00
ILLUSTRATED BIBLE TALES	
(Bible Tales for Young People on imprint)	
Miller; 1 1953-8 1954?	
1-8 28pgs; incl. Don Lawrence art	£2.00
ILLUSTRATED CHIPS	
Harmsworth/Amalgamated Press; (1) 1 26th Jul 1890-6 30th Aug 1890;	
(2) 1 6th Sep 1890-2997 12th Sep 1953 (joins Film Fun)	
1 16pgs half-tabloid	£150.00
2	£80.00
3-6	£50.00
1 (New Series) 8pgs tabloid	£80.00
1890-1899	£35.00
1900-1920	£20.00
1921-1939	£10.00
1940-1950	£5.00
1951-1953	£2.50
CHRONOLOGY	
6 Jun 1891: 1st printed on pink paper. 3 Nov 1939: reverts to white paper. 6 Sep 1941: page size reduced, frequency dropped to fortnightly. 25 May 1940 1st "Illustrated Chip and The Joker". 6 Dec 1947: page size reduced again. 11 Aug 1951: page count raised, reverts to pink paper. 1 Nov 1952: resumes weekly publication. 6 Sep 1952: title becomes "Chips".	
ILLUSTRATED LIBRARY OF GREAT..., AN	
(see Classics Illustrated)	
Thorpe (Classics Companion); 1952	
Indian Stories hardcover CI reprints 17,22,37,58	£75.00
Adventure Stories hardcover CI reprints 2,7,10	£75.00
Note: Exciting Mystery Stories advertised but not published.	
ILLUSTRATED ROMANCE LIBRARY	
World Distributors; 1-? 1960s	
1-? 68pgs pocket size; American reprints	£0.50
IMAGES	
Anti-Matter; 1 1984	
1 8pgs; Eddie Campbell art	£1.00
IMMACULATE DECEPTION - DISSENTING WOMEN	
Knockabout (Fanny 3); 1992	
3 36pgs; Carol Swain, Suzy Varty, Kate Charlesworth art	£2.50
IMMORTALIS	
(see main American comics section)	
IMPRESSIONS OF PAPA AND SON	
Daily Sketch; nn 1923?	
nn - 32pgs; reprints Daily Sketch strip by A.E. Morton	£3.00
INCOMPLETE DEATH'S HEAD, THE	
(see main American comics section)	
INCREDIBLE HULK!, THE	
Marvel; 1 21st Mar 1982-27 29th Sep 1982 (joins Spiderman)	
1 32pgs; Hulk reprints begin, Wolverine (What If) reprint, Brian Bolland centre-fold poster; b/w with 8pgs colour	£1.50
1 with free gift (cut-out walking Hulk)	£3.00
2-3	£1.00
2-3 with free gift (Lou Ferrigno poster)	£2.00
4-17,22-26	£0.75

	N.MINT
18-21 4-part X-Men poster as centre-fold	£1.00
27 repro of Hulk #1 cover as centre-fold poster	£1.00
INCREDIBLE HULK ANNUAL, THE	
(see Hulk Annual)	
INCREDIBLE HULK PRESENTS, THE	
Marvel; 1-12 1980s	
1 Hulk, Dr. Who, Action Force, Indiana Jones begin	£1.20
2-12	£1.00
INCREDIBLE HULK SPECIALS	
Marvel; 1982	
Summer Special reprints Hulk vs Sasquatch, Lou Ferrigno centre-fold poster	£1.50
Winter Special Steve Ditko art, Earl Norem painted cover	£1.25
INDIAN CHIEF	
World Distributors; 1 1953-31 1954	
1 36pgs; Dell reprints	£5.00
2-31	£2.50
INDIAN FIGHTER	
Streamline; 1951 (2 unnumbered issues)	
nn - 28pgs; Youthful Magazines reprints, censored by removal of panels	£4.00
nn - 68pgs	£3.00
INDIAN WARHAWKS	
(see Blue Bolt series)	
INDIAN WARRIORS	
(see also Blue Bolt series)	
Streamline; 1951	
nn - 28pgs; Star Publications reprints	£2.00
INDIANA JONES	
Marvel; 1 Oct 1984-11 Aug 1985 (joins Spiderman)	
1 Temple of Doom based on Spielberg & Lucas film; US reprints	£1.00
2-11	£0.50
INDIANA JONES WINTER SPECIAL	
Marvel; nn Nov 1984	
nn - reprints	£1.00
INDIANS	
Cartoon Art; 1 1951	
1 20pgs; Fiction House reprints	£3.00
INDIANS	
Streamline; 1-25? 1953	
1 28pgs; Fiction House reprints	£3.00
2-25	£2.50
INDIANS ON THE WARPATH	
(see Warpath)	
IN ORBIT	
George Turton & Co; 1-? 1959?	
1-? 80pgs, squarebound	£2.00
INTIMATE LOVE	
World Distributors; 1-6 1953	
1-6 28pgs; Standard Comics reprints	£1.50
INTRODUCTION TO CHILE	
Bolivar; nn 1976	
nn - 100pgs; Chris Welch art	£1.00
INVINCIBLE	
(see Captain Miracle)	
IRONFIST CHINMI	
Bloomsbury; Jul 1995-present	
Kung-Fu Boy (Jul 1995) Takeshi Maekawa manga reprint begins	£4.00
Journey to Mount Shen (Jul 1995)	£4.00
Victory for the Spirit (Sep 1995)	£4.00
Leap of Faith (Sep 1995)	£4.00
Attack of the Black Flame (Dec 1995)	£4.00
Blind Fury (Dec 1995)	£4.00
IS THIS ROMANCE?	
Myra Hancock; nn 1983	
nn - 12pgs; Myra Hancock art	£1.00
IT'S ALL LIES	
Gemsanders; 1 Oct 1973-6 Dec 1973	
1 20pgs; M.Freeth art	£1.00
2-3 20pgs; 3, Parkhouse art	£1.25
4 24pgs; McMahon art	£1.50
5 36pgs	£1.00
6 Parkhouse, Ghura art	£1.25
IT'S ONLY ROCK & ROLL COMIX	
Petagno; nn 1975	
nn - 32pgs; J.J.Petagno art	£1.00

J

	N.MINT
JACE PEARSON OF THE TEXAS RANGERS	
World Distributors; 1 1953-21 1954	
1 36pgs; Dell reprints begin	£5.00
2-21	£2.50
JACK AND JILL	
(see Harold Hare)	
Amalgamated/Fleetway/IPC; 1 27th Feb 1954-?	
1 Jack & Jill by Hugh McNeill, Harold Hare by McNeill, Fred Robinson art	£10.00
2 Sep E. Scott, Philip Mendoza art	£3.00
3- some incl. Sep E. Scott, Philip Mendoza art	£1.00
CHRONOLOGY	
11 Jun 1955: 1st "Jack and Jill & Playbox". 3 Jan 1970: 1st "Jack and Jill & Candy". 22 Sep 1973: 1st "Jack and Jill & Teddy Bear". 7 Oct 1978: 1st "Jack and Jill & Toby". 27 Sep 1980: 1st "Jack and Jill & Dickory Dock". 31 Oct 1981: 1st "Jack and Jill & Teddy Bear's Playtime". 16 Oct 1982: 1st "Jack and Jill &	

	N.MINT

Playbox".

JACK AND JILL SUMMER SPECIAL
Fleetway/IPC; 1961-1973?

1961-1964 48pgs; incl. Harold Hare	£2.00
1965-1970, 1973 becomes "Jack and Jill Holiday Special"	£0.40
1971-1972 becomes "Jack and Jill & Bobo Bunny Holiday Special"	£0.40

JACKPOT
IPC; 5th May 1979-30th Jan 1982, 141 unnumbered issues (joins Buster)

5 May 1979	£1.25
11 May 1979-30 Jan 1982	£0.25

JACKPOT, THE
Swinnerton's; 1 Nov 1946

1 8pgs	£2.00

JACK-POT COMIC, THE
Grant Hughes; nn May 1947

nn - 16pgs; Bob Wilkin art	£3.00

JAG
Fleetway/IPC; 4th May 1968-29th Mar 1969 (48 unnumbered issues; joins Tiger)

No.1 - 4 May 1968 16pgs large size; The Mouse Patrol by Eric Bradbury, The Indestructable Man by Jesus Blasco, Custer by Geoff Campion begin; slightly oversized at 11.5"x15"	£10.00
No.1 with free gift (Bobby Moore's Book of the F.A. Cup)	£20.00
No.2 - 11 May 1968	£5.00
No.2 with free gift (Soccer '68 wall chart Part 1)	£10.00
No.3 - 18 May 1968	£5.00
No.3 with free gift (Soccer '68 wall chart Part 2)	£10.00
25 May 1968 - 15 Feb 1969	£3.00
22 Feb-29 Mar 1969 32pgs smaller size	£2.50

JAG ANNUAL
Fleetway; 1969-1973

1969 scarce	£3.50
1970-1973	£2.50

JAG SOCCER SPECIAL
Fleetway; 1970?

1970 ? scarce	£3.00

JAMES BOND
Titan; Jun 1987-Jul 1990

The Living Daylights (Jun 1987) newspaper reprints by Jim Lawrence & Yaroslav Horak	£5.00
Octopussy (Mar 1988)	£5.00
The Spy Who Loved Me (1989)	£5.50
Casino Royale (Jul 1990) by Anthony Hearne & John McClusky	£5.50

JAMES BOND 007 ANNUAL
World Distributors; 1966

1966 scarce; photo features on Thunderball	£15.00

JAMES BOND: LICENCE TO KILL
Acme/Eclipse; 1992

Licence to Kill adapts movie, Mike Grell art	£2.50

JAMES BOND: PERMISSION TO DIE
Acme/Eclipse; 1 1989-3 1991

1-3 Mike Grell art	£2.50
Permission to Die softcover collection	£9.50
Permission to Die hardcover collection	£21.00

JAMES BOND: SERPENT'S TOOTH
(see main American comics section)

JAMES BOND: A SILENT ARMAGEDDON
(see main American comics section)

JANE
Thomas/Rylee/Mirror/Wolfe/Pelham; 1944-1983

Jane's Journal (Thomas, 1944) 68pgs	£15.00
Pett's Annual (Thomas, 1944) 80pgs	£12.50
Another Jane's Journal (Thomas, 1945)	£10.00
Jane's Summer Idle (Mirror, Jun 1946) 36pgs; Pett reprints	£10.00
Jane's Journal (Rylee, Nov 1946) 84pgs	£10.00
Jane on Sawdust Trail (Mirror, 1947) 36pgs; Pett reprints	£10.00
Another Journal (Rylee, 1948) 68pgs	£7.50
Another Journal (Rylee, Jun 1950) 68pgs	£7.50
Farewell to Jane (Mirror, 1960) 100pgs; Hubbard reprints	£7.50
Jane At War (Wolfe, 1976) 386pgs; Pett reprints	£10.00
Jane (Pelham/Rainbird, 1983) 100pgs oblong; Pett/Hubbard reprints	£2.00

JAPHET BOOK, THE
Daily News; 1924-1925

1924 68pgs oblong; reprints J.F. Horrabin strip from Daily News	£12.00
1925	£10.00

JAPHET HOLIDAY BOOK, THE
News Chronicle; Jul 1936-Jul 1940

1936 68pgs; reprints The Arkubs by J.F. Horrabin from News Chronicle	£8.00
1937-1940	£6.00

JAZZ FUNNIES
Knockabout (Crack); nn 1986

nn - Max Zillion by Hunt Emerson reprints	£5.00

JEFF HAWKE
Titan; 1 Jun 1986-2 Apr 1987

Book One: Overlord newspaper reprints by Willie Patterson & Sydney Jordan	£5.00
Book Two: Council For the Defence	£5.00

JESSE JAMES COMICS
Thorpe & Porter; 1-6 1952

1-6 68pgs; Avon Periodicals reprints, incl. Joe Kubert, E.R.Kinstler art	£6.00

JESTER, THE
(previously The Jester and Wonder)
Amalgamated; 534 27th Jan 1912-998 18th Dec 1920 (becomes The Jolly Jester)

534 G.M.Payne, Tom Radford, Bertie Brown, Austin Payne art	£20.00
535-998 some incl. Alex Akerbladh, Vincent Daniel, Don Newhouse art	£6.00

	N.MINT

JESTER, THE
(previously The Jolly Jester)
Amalgamated; 1164 23rd Feb 1924-2010 18th May 1940 (joins The Funny Wonder)

1164 Don Newhouse, Bertie Brown, Wally Robertson art	£15.00
1165-2010 incl. Roy Wilson, Allan Morley, Frank Minnitt art	£5.00

JESTER AND WONDER, THE
(previously The Wonder and Jester)
Amalgamated; 28 24th May 1902-533 20th Jan 1912 (becomes The Jester)

28 Leonard Shields, Tom Wilkinson art	£45.00
29	£12.50
30,32-54,56-506 incl. George Studdy, Julius Baker, Frank Holland, J.B.Yeats, Percy Cocking art	£6.00
31 (14 Jun 1902) Special Coronation Number, colour	£10.00
55 (29 Nov 1902) Christmas Double Number, colour	£10.00

JESTER ANNUAL
Amalgamated; 1936-1940

1936 scarce	£40.00
1937	£30.00
1938-1940	£25.00

JET
IPC; 1st May 1971-25th Sep 1971 (22 unnumbered issues; joins Buster)

No. 1- 1st May 1971 Von hoffman's Invasion by Eric Bradbury, The Sludgemouth Sloggers by Douglas Maxted, Bala the Briton, Carno's Cadets by Solano Lopez, The Kids From Stalag 41 by Tony Goffe, Faceache by Ken Reid begin	£6.00
No. 1 with free gift (Monster Wasp)	£10.00
8 May-25 Sep 1971	£2.00

JET COMIC, THE
Hamilton; nn 1953

nn - 28pgs; Ron Embleton art	£6.00

JET PLANE RAIDERS, THE
Hotspur Publishing (Secret Service No.1); 1948

1 8pgs; Bob Wilkin art	£3.00

JEWEL IN THE SKULL, THE
Big O/Savoy; nn Oct 1978

nn - Michael Moorcock adaptation, James Cawthorn art	£5.00

JIM BOWIE
(some issues titled Brave Jim Bowie or Adventures of Brave Jim Bowie)
Miller; 1 Mar 1957-24 1959

1-4 28pgs; reprints US strips from Charlton	£2.50
5-24 original British strips	£3.50

JIM BRIDGER MOUNTAIN MAN
(see Western Picture Library)

JIMMY
Brockhampton Press; 1948-1958

Jimmy and the Little Old Engine (1948) 36pgs; Neville Main art	£3.00
Jimmy at the Seaside (1949)	£3.00
Jimmy Goes to a Party (1950)	£2.00
Jimmy at the Fair (1951)	£2.00
Jimmy Goes Sailing (1951)	£2.00
Jimmy at the Zoo (1953)	£2.00
Jimmy and the Redskins (1954)	£2.00
Jimmy and the Space Ship (1956)	£1.50
Jimmy and the Pirates (1958)	£1.50

JIMMY BRINDLE
Jimmy Brindle; 1 1948

1 16pgs; Bob Wilkin art	£2.00

JIMMY DURANTE COMICS
United Anglo-American; 1950, 2 unnumbered issues

nn - 36pgs; full colour, Magazine Enterprises reprints	£3.00
nn - 28pgs; incl. material from Prize Western	£2.00

JINGLE BELLS COMIC
Philmar; nn Sep 1947

nn - 8pgs; Walter Bell, Wally Robertson art	£2.50

JINGLES
Amalgamated; 1 13th Jan 1934-741 29th May 1954 (joins TV Comic)

1 Roy Wilson, George Heath art	£35.00
2	£10.00
3-5	£6.00
6-741 incl. George Parlett, Reg Parlett, Bertie Brown art	£4.00

CHRONOLOGY
6 Jan 1940: first colour cover. 8 Jun 1940: 1st "Jingles & Golden", drops to fortnightly publication. 7 Jun 1941: incorporates Crackers. 25 Oct 1952: returns to weekly publication.

JINGLES ANNUAL
Amalgamated; 1936-1941

1936 scarce (piles of Jingles Annuals being dropped from aeroplane)	£50.00
1937	£30.00
1938-1941	£25.00

JINGO COMIC
W.Forshaw/Ensign Publishing; 1946-1947, 4 issues, mostly unnumbered

nn - 8pgs, green; W.Forshaw art	£3.00
nn - blue; Charles Ross art	£2.50
3 brown; Ross art	£2.50
nn - red/blue gravure; Frank Minnitt art	£2.50

J.J. IT'S ONLY MONEY!
Beaverbrook; nn 1972

nn - 100pgs; reprints Roy Dewar newspaper strip from Sunday Express	£1.00

JOE LOUIS COMICS
Miller; 1 Nov 1950-2 Jan 1951

1-2 36pgs; Fawcett reprints	£3.00

JOE 90
Fleetway; 1 29 July 1994-7 21st October 1994 (joins Thunderbirds)

1 Joe 90: Top Secret reprints begin	£1.50
2-7	£0.75

	N.MINT
JOE 90 ANNUAL	
(see also Joe 90: Top Secret Comic Annual)	
City; 1968-1969	
1968 Ron Turner art	£12.00
1969 white cover	£8.00
JOE 90 STORYBOOK	
City; 1968-1969 (4 issues, unnumbered)	
Joseph Nineski (1968)	£5.00
Appointment with Death (1968)	£4.50
Double Agent (1968)	£4.50
The Cracksman (1969)	£4.00
JOE 90: TOP SECRET	
City; 1 18th Jan 1969-34 6th Sep 1969 (joins TV 21 & Joe 90)	
1 scarce, Joe 90 by Keith Watson, Star Trek by Harry Lindfield, The Champions by Jon Davis, Land of the Giants by Gerry Haylock begin	£20.00
1 with free gift (Mac's Jet Car Kit)	£50.00
2	£10.00
3	£6.00
4,5	£4.00
6-34	£2.50
JOE 90: TOP SECRET COMIC ANNUAL	
(see also Joe 90 Annual)	
City; 1969	
1969 red cover; Joe 90, Star Trek, Land of the Giants, Champions, Ron Turner art	£10.00
JOE PALOOKA	
Streamline; 1 Mar 1953-?	
1 28pgs; Harvey Publications reprints	£4.00
2-?	£2.00
JOE PALOOKA'S HUMPHREY	
United Anglo-American; 1 1950-13 1951	
1 28pgs; Harvey Publications reprints	£3.00
2-13	£1.50
JOE YANK	
Cartoon Arts; 1 1954?	
1 Magazine Enterprises reprints	£4.00
JOHN CARTER OF MARS	
World Distributors; 1-2 1953	
1-2 28pgs; Dell 4-colour reprints	£6.00
JOHN WAYNE ADVENTURE ANNUAL	
World Distributors; Sep 1953-1959	
1953	£10.00
1954-1959	£6.00
JOHN WAYNE ADVENTURE COMICS	
Pemberton/World Distributors; 1 Aug 1952-82 1958	
1 28pgs; Toby Press reprints	£10.00
2	£5.00
3-77 incl. Williamson,Frazetta art	£3.00
78-82 68pgs	£4.00
JOHN WESLEY	
Amalgamated Press; nn May 1953	
nn - reprints Sunday Companion newspaper strip	£1.50
JOHNNY COUGAR'S WRESTLING MONTHLY	
Fleetway Editions; Oct 1992-Mar 1993, 6 issues	
Oct '92 52pgs; Johnny Cougar reprints from Tiger by John Gillatt	£1.00
Nov 1992-Mar 1993	£0.80
JOHNNY HAZARD	
(see also Crimebuster)	
Miller; 1 1954	
1 28pgs; reprints American newspaper strip by Frank Robbins	£8.00
JOHNNY LAW SKY RANGERS ADVENTURES	
World Distributors; 1-4 1955	
1-4 28pgs; Good Comics (Lev Gleason) reprints	£6.00
JOHNNY MACK BROWN	
World Distributors; 1 1954-21 1955	
1 28pgs; Dell 4-colour reprints	£12.00
2-21	£7.50
JO-JO CONGO KING	
Streamline; 1 1950	
1 28pgs; Fox Syndicate reprints	£4.00
JOKER, THE	
Fleetway Press/Amalgamated Press; 1 5th Nov 1927-655 18th May 1940 (joins Illustrated Chips)	
1 Fleetway Press; S.K.Perkins art	£35.00
2-11 Fleetway issues	£10.00
12-655 incl. Percy Cocking, Frank Minnitt, John Jukes, Bertie Brown, Reg Perrott art	£5.00
CHRONOLOGY	
21 Jan 1928: 1st Amalgamated Press issue. 1 Feb 1930: 1st "The Joker & Monster Comic".	
JOKER COMIC	
Bairns Books; nn 1946	
nn - 12pgs; reprints from Star Comics and Super Comics	£2.50
JOKER SPECIAL	
London Editions; nn 1990	
nn – US reprints	£1.50
JOLIDAY COMIC, THE	
D.McKenzie; 1-2 1948	
1-2 8pgs; Mack Earl art	£2.00
JOLLY ADVENTURES	
Martin & Reid; 1 1946-9 1949	
1 8pgs; H.E.Pease, R. Beaumont art	£3.00
2-9 4. incl. Mick Anglo art	£2.50
JOLLY ARROW	
John Matthew; 1-2 1948	

	N.MINT
1-2 16pgs; 2. incl. Frank Minnitt art	£2.50
JOLLY CHUCKLES	
Martin & Reid; 1 1946-11 1949	
1 8pgs; H.E.Pease art	£3.00
2-11 5. incl. Mick Anglo art	£2.50
JOLLY COMIC	
P.M. Productions; nn 1946	
nn - 6pgs folded beige card; reprints from Pigmy and Pocket comics	£2.50
JOLLY COMIC, THE	
Amalgamated Press; 1 19th Jan 1935-250 28th Oct 1939 (joins Comic Cuts)	
1 Roy Wilson art	£25.00
2	£10.00
3-250 incl. Bertie Brown, Frank Minnitt, Reg Perrott, Walter Booth art	£6.00
JOLLY COWBOY	
Martin & Reid; 1 1948	
1 8pgs; Wally Robertson, Bob Monkhouse art	£3.00
JOLLY FUN	
Martin & Reid; 1-2 1946	
1-2 8pgs; H.E.Pease art	£3.00
JOLLY FUN-RAY COMIC, THE	
Philmar; 1 Sep 1947	
1 8pgs; Tony Speer, Stanley White art	£2.50
JOLLY GIANT COMIC, THE	
Philmar; 1 1946	
1 8pgs; Tony Speer art	£2.50
JOLLY JACK IN THE BOX COMIC	
P.M. Productions; 1 1949	
1 8pgs; Frank Minnitt, Walter Bell art	£3.00
JOLLY JACK'S WEEKLY	
Associated Newspapers; 20th Aug 1933-16th Dec 1934, 70 issues	
20 Aug 1933 giveaway with Sunday Dispatch, folds to give 8 pgs; Herbert Foxwell art	£15.00
27 Aug 1933-22 Jul 1934	£5.00
29 Jul-16 Dec 1934 reduced to 4pgs	£2.00
JOLLY JACK'S ANNUAL	
Associated Newspapers; 1935-1941	
1935 scarce	£55.00
1936	£40.00
1937	£30.00
1938-1941	£25.00
JOLLY JESTER, THE	
(previously The Jester)	
Amalgamated Press; 999 25th Dec 1920-1163 16th Feb 1924 (continued as The Jester)	
999 Roy Wilson, Bertie Brown art	£25.00
1000-1163 incl. Wally Robertson, Allan Morley, Walter Bell art	£7.50
JOLLY JESTER COMIC	
Philmar/P.M. Productions; 1-2 1948	
1 Harry Parlett, Wally Robertson art	£3.00
2 Walter Bell, Frank Minnitt, Colin Merritt art	£3.00
JOLLY JINKS	
John Leng; nn Dec 1938	
nn - 84pgs oblong; Christmas extra edition of Fairyland Tales	£5.00
JOLLY JINKS COMIC	
Martin & Reid; nn 1944?	
nn - 8pgs; H.E.Pease art	£3.00
JOLLY JUMBO'S CHRISTMAS COMIC	
(previously The Christmas Comic)	
C.A. Pearson; Nov 1934-Nov 1935 (becomes Christmas Holiday Comic)	
1934-1935 12pgs; features characters from Home Notes, incl. Jolly Jumbo by A.W.Browne	£4.00
JOLLY MILLER CHILDRENS' BOOK, THE	
Miller; nn 1944?	
nn - 12pgs; American reprints from Sparkler Comics and Tip Top Comics	£5.00
JOLLY ROGER	
(see Super Jolly Roger)	
JOLLY TIMES	
(previously Happy Times Family Comic)	
L.Burn; 1 Aug 1947	
1 Walter Booth, Stanley White art	£3.00
JOLLY WESTERN	
Martin & Reid; 1 1947-9 1949 (becomes Rangeland Western)	
1 8pgs; Norman Light art	£6.00
2-8 some incl. Mick Anglo art	£3.00
9 Paddy Brennan art	£4.00
JOLLYBOYS AND GIRLS COMIC	
Philmar; 1 1949	
1 8pgs; Wally Robertson, Frank Minnitt art	£2.50
JOURNEY INTO DANGER	
Miller; 1-8 1957	
1 68pgs; Atlas reprints	£5.00
2-8	£3.00
JOY WHEEL, THE	
Children's Press; nn 1947	
nn - 12pgs; Serge Drigin art	£4.00
JOYRIDE COMIC, THE	
W.Foster; nn-5 1946	
nn - 8pgs; Bob Wilkin art	£3.00
2-5 Wilkin art	£2.50
JRF PRESENTS	
(see Nick Hazard)	
John Lawrence & Philip Harbottle; 1 Sep/Oct 1985-4 Aug 1986; (see also Nick Hazard)	
1 Nick Hazard by Ron Turner, Space Ace reprints by Turner begin	£3.00
2-3 Turner art	£2.00
4 Space Ace special, Turner art	£2.00

N.MINT

JUDGE ANDERSON
(see also Anderson Psi Division)
Titan (Best of 2000AD); Oct 1987-Feb 1990, Jul 1995

Book 1 Ewins art	£4.50
Book 2 Ewins art	£4.50
Book 3 Kitson art	£4.50
Book 4 Roach art	£5.50
Book 5 Austin, Ranson art	£5.50
The Collected Judge Anderson (Jul 1995) reprints Books 1-3	£10.00

JUDGE ANDERSON
Mandarin; May 1995

Childhood's End Megazine reprint by Alan Grant & Kevin Walker	£7.00

JUDGE DREDD
(see also America, The Chronicles of Judge Dredd, The Complete Judge Dredd, Judgement on Gotham, 2000AD, Vendetta in Gotham)

JUDGE DREDD
Eagle/Quality; 1 Sep 1983-35 Sep 1986
(see American Comic section)

1 2000AD reprints begin	£6.00
2	£3.00
3	£2.50
4-5,9-10	£1.75
6-8	£1.50
11-14	£1.25
15-33	£1.00
34-35 Quality issues	£1.00

Note: Bolland, McMahon, Kennedy covers

JUDGE DREDD
Fleetway; Apr 1990-1991

Curse of the Spider Woman (Apr 1990) 2000AD reprints in full colour begin	£4.50
Judge Child Quest (Jan 1991) 160pgs; newly coloured Bolland, McMahon reprints	£8.00
Tale of the Dead Man (1991)	£6.00

JUDGE DREDD (DEFINITIVE EDITIONS)
Fleetway; Oct 1990-1991

Future Crime (Oct 1990) incl. Bolland reprints	£4.50
Bad Science (1990) incl. McMahon reprints	£4.50
Hall of Justice (1991) incl. Gibson reprints	£4.50
Metal Fatigue (1991) incl. Ranson reprints	£4.50

JUDGE DREDD (OFFICIAL MOVIE ADAPTATION)
Fleetway Editions; nn Jul 1995

nn - 64pgs; movie adapted by Andrew Helfer & Carlos Ezquerra	£3.00

JUDGE DREDD (2000AD BOOKS)
Mandarin; Sep 1992-present

Democracy Now! (Sep 1992) 2000AD reprints, Jeff Anderson, John Burns art	£5.00
Raptaur (Sep 1992) Megazine reprints, Dean Ormston art	£6.00
Top Dog (Mar 1993) JD Annual, 2000AD reprints, Colin MacNeil, Burns art	£6.00
Heavy Metal Dredd (Mar 1993) Rock Power reprints, Bisley art	£5.00
Tales of the Damned (Sep 1993) 2000AD, Megazine reprints, Burns, Sean Phillips art	£6.00
Mechanismo (Sep 1993) Megazine reprints, McNeil, Doherty art	£8.00
Book of the Dead (May 1995) 2000AD reprints by Morrison/Millar & Power	£6.00
Babes in Arms (May 1995) 2000AD reprints, Greg Staples art	£8.00

JUDGE DREDD ANNUAL/YEARBOOK
Fleetway; 1981-1994

1981 Mike McMahon art, 1st Dredd story (previously unused) by Ezquerra	£10.00
1982 McMahon art	£8.00
1983 Ezquerra art	£5.00
1984 Ezquerra art	£5.00
1985 Ezquerra art	£4.00
1986	£4.00
1987 Gibson, McCarthy/Riot, Talbot art	£4.50
1988 Higgins art	£4.50
1989 Ezquerra art	£4.50
1990 Arthur Ranson art	£4.00
1991 Sean Phillips, Gibson art	£3.50
1992 becomes Judge Dredd Yearbook, Geoff Senior art	£5.00
1993 Steve Yeowell, Simon Hunter art	£6.00
1994 McMahon, Dean Ormston, Peart art	£6.00
1995 Sean Phillips, Chris Halls, Trevor Hairsine art	£4.00

JUDGE DREDD COLLECTION, THE
IPC/Fleetway nn 1985-5 1989

nn - reprints Wagner/Grant & Smith newspaper strip from the Star begin	£2.95
2-4	£2.25
5 Fat City	£2.50
Judge Dredd Mega Collection (Oct 1990); hardcover	£7.00

JUDGE DREDD CRIME FILES
Titan; 1 Jul 1989-4 Oct 1989

1-4 2000AD Annual, Judge Dredd Annual reprints	£3.50

JUDGE DREDD: LAWMAN OF THE FUTURE
Fleetway Editions; 1 28th Jul 1995-present (13 to date)

1 Dredd for younger audience in movie costume begins; 3 x Dredd stories	£1.00
2-13	£1.00

JUDGE DREDD MEGA-SPECIAL
Fleetway; 1 1988-present (8 to date)

1 John Higgins, Casanovas, Will Simpson art, Bolland cover	£2.75
2 Kev Hopgood, Mick Austin art, McCarthy cover	£2.50
3 Cliff Robinson, David Roach, Ron Smith art	£1.00
4 Glyn Dillon, John McCrae, Ian Gibson, Shaky Kane, Phillips art	£1.75
5 Steve Yeowell art	£1.75
6 Paul Grist, Siku, Shaky Kane art	£1.75
7 Adrian Salmon/Jim Vickers Sin City parody, Steve Sampson art	£1.75
8 Raptour by Grant, Sammy Martini & John Cromer (Ormston/Luke)	£2.00

Jack and Jill #1

Jag #1

Joe 90 #1

	N.MINT

JUDGE DREDD MEGAZINE
(see America, Young Death)
Fleetway; 1 Oct 1990-20 May 1992 (continued as New Series)

1 Judge Dredd by Alan Grant & Jim Baikie, Chopper by Garth Ennis & John McCrea, Young Death by Brian Skuter & Peter Doherty, America by John Wagner & Colin MacNeil, Beyond Our Kenny by Wagner & Cam Kennedy	£6.00
2-3	£4.00
4 Al's Baby by Wagner & Ezquerra begins	£3.75
5-6	£3.50
7 Sean Phillips art	£3.50
8 Red Razers by Mark Miller & Steve Yeowell begins, Phillips art	£2.50
9 Armitage by Dave Stone & Sean Phillips begins	£2.50
10-13	£2.50
14 Judge Dredd (Rock Power) Bisley reprints, free poster	£2.00
15 free Dredd poster by Bisley, Middenface McNulty by McCrea begins	£2.00
16 Brit-Cit Babes by Wagner & Steve Sampson begins, Bisley art	£2.00
17 Bisley art	£2.00
18-20 19 incl. Bisley art, 20 incl. Sam Kieth Judge Dredd	£2.00

ARTISTS/FEATURES
Jim Baikie in 1-5. Simon Bisley reprints in 14,16,19. Peter Doherty in 1-12. Carlos Ezquerra in 4-15. Glen Fabry reprint in 17. John Hicklenton in 7-9,17. Sam Kieth in 20. Cam Kennedy in 1-3. John McCrea in 1-6,15-20. Colin MacNeil in 1-7,18. Dean Ormston in 6,11-17. Sean Phillips in 7-14. Steve Sampson in 16-20. Will Simpson in 10. Steve Yeowell in 8-15.

JUDGE DREDD MEGAZINE (2ND SERIES, FORTNIGHTLY)
(see Devlin Waugh: Swimming in Blood)
Fleetway; 1 2nd May 1992-83 7 Jul 1995 (continued as new series)

1 Armageddon by Grant & Ezquerra, Devlin Waugh by Smith & Phillips begin	£4.00
2	£3.00
3-9 Judgement Day crossover with 2000AD	£2.25
10 first new size, Calhab Justice by Ridgway, Judge Anderson by Ranson	£2.00
11-12	£2.00
13 Mechanismo by Wagner & MacNeil begins (ends 17)	£2.00
14 Judge Anderson by Ranson	£2.00
15,17-21	£2.00
16 Blood on the Bib by Wagner & Ezquerra begins (ends 24)	£2.00
22 Mechanismo returns, Doherty art, Judge Anderson by Ranson	£1.75
23-25	£1.75
26 Devlin Waugh meets Dredd, Phillips art	£1.75
27 Anderson by Kev Walker begins (to 34)	£1.75
28 Harke & Burr by Si Spencer & Dean Ormston begins	£1.75
29 Missionary Man by Gordon Rennie & Frank Quitely begins	£1.75
30,32-34	£1.75
31 Brit-Cit Brute by Robbie Morrison & Nick Percival, Armitage Flashback by Stone & Adlard begin, Calhab Justice returns	£1.75
35 Hershey & Steel by Stone & Adlard begins	£1.75
36 Chopper by Ennis & Martin Emond	£1.75
37 Mechanismo: Body Count by Wagner & Manuel Benet (ends 43), Shimura by Robbie Morrison & Quitely, Return of the Taxidermist by Wagner & Ian Gibson all begin, free poster featuring Judge Anderson story by Mark Harrison	£2.50
37 without poster	£1.50
38-40	£1.75
41 The Creep by Si Spencer & Kevin Cullen begins	£1.75
42-43 43 incl. Missionary Man	£1.75
44 Calhab Justice returns, Pan-African Judges begins	£1.75
45-49	£1.75
50 Judge Anderson: Postcards from the Edge (ends 60), Shimura by Colin McNeil (ends 55), Missionary Man by Quitely (ends 55) return	£1.75
51-52	£1.50
53-54 Mike McMahon Dredd	£1.50
55 Harmony by Chris Standley & Trevor Hairsine begins, McMahon Dredd, Missionary Man continues (ends 59)	£1.50
56 Karyn by John Freeman & Adrian Salmon begins; McMahon Dredd	£1.50
57 Dredd: Wilderlands Prologue by Wagner & Peter Doherty	£1.50
58 Dredd: The Tenth Planet by Wagner & Ezquerra begins (ends 62)	£1.50
59-60	£1.50
61 Brit-Cit Brute, O'Rork begin, Bisley Heavy Metal Dredd reprint	£1.50
62 Bisley Heavy Metal Dredd reprint	£1.50
63 Dredd: Wilderlands by Wagner & Hairsine begins (ends 27; 2000AD x-over), Missionary Man (to 66) and Armitage (to 71) return, Son of Mean Machine begins by Wagner & Carl Critchlow begins (ends 72)	£1.50
64 Free Femme Fatale pin-up booklet	£1.50
65-69,71	£1.50
70 68pgs; 2 x Dredd	£2.25
72 Shimura returns (to 77)	£1.60
73 Maelstrom by Robbie Morrison & Colin McNeil begins (ends 80), Anderson Psi (to 80), Harmony (to 76) return	£1.60
74-80	£1.60
81 Missionary Man returns (to 83)	£1.60
82-83	£1.60

ARTISTS/FEATURES
Charlie Adlard in 10-21,31-33,35-36. Carl Critchlow in 63-72. Martin Emond in 36. Carlos Ezquerra in 1-7,10-11,16-24,58-62. Charlie Gillespie in 52,58,64-71,77-80,82-83. Trevor Hairsine in 55-60,63-67. Chris Halls in 7. Shaky Kane in 2-9. Mike McMahon 53-56. Colin McNeil in 12-17,44-45,50-55,63,73-80. Dean Ormston in 4-6,8-9,13,28,40-42,47-49,70. Frank Quitely in 29-30,37-39,50-55. Sean Phillips in 1-9,26. Arthur Ranson in 10,14,22-24,53. John Ridgway in 10-13,18,64-66. David Roach in 8. Steve Sampson in 50,59,73-77,83.

JUDGE DREDD MEGAZINE (3RD SERIES, FORTNIGHTLY)
Fleetway; 1 21 July 1995-present

1 Dredd by Paul Johnson, Harmony by Sampson (to 6), Missionary Man (to 3), Anderson Psi (to 7) by Ranson return	£2.00
2 Dredd: Three Amigos by Wagner & Hairsine begins	£1.80
3-5,7-8,10-13	£1.80

	N.MINT
6 5th Anniversary issue; Pan-African Judges return	£1.80
9 Judge Hershey returns	£1.80
14 1st monthly issue; Anderson by Ranson, Shimura returns	£2.00

ARTISTS/FEATURES
Trevor Hairsine in 2-7. Paul Johnson in 1. Mike McMahon in 3. Dean Ormston in 4-7. Arthur Ranson in 1-7,14. Steve Sampson in 1-6,8-10.

JUDGE DREDD: THE EARLY CASES
Eagle; 1 Feb 1986-6 Jul 1986

1-6 2000AD reprints, Bolland covers	£1.50

JUDGE DREDD: THE JUDGE CHILD QUEST
(see The Chronicles of Judge Dredd)
Eagle; 1 Aug 1984-5 Dec 1985

1-5 2000AD reprints, Bolland covers	£1.35

JUDGE DREDD/LOBO: PSYCHO BIKERS VS MUTANTS FROM HELL
Fleetway Editions; nn Dec 1995

nn – 48pgs; by Alan Grant/Val Semeiks/John Dell; Bisley cover	£3.00

JUDGE DREDD'S CRIME FILES
Eagle; 1 Aug 1986-6 Jan 1987

1-6 2000AD reprints	£1.50

JUDGE DREDD'S HARDCASE PAPERS
Fleetway; 1 May 1991-4 Aug 1991

1-4 2000AD reprints	£4.00

JUDGEMENT ON GOTHAM
(see Vendetta in Gotham)
Fleetway/DC, Mandarin (2000AD Books); nn 1991, 1992

nn – (Dec 1991) 64pgs softback; Batman vs Judge Dredd by Wagner/Grant & Bisley	£5.00
nn – (Jan 1992) news-stand magazine edition	£3.00
nn – (Mandarin, Sep 1992)	£6.00

JUDY
D.C. Thomson; 1 16th Jan 1960-1991 (becomes Mandy and Judy)

1 Sandra of the Secret Ballet by Paddy Brennan begins	£5.00
2	£2.50
3-5	£1.25
6-499 incl. Brennan, Ron Smith art	£0.50
500-?	£0.20

JUDY PICTURE LIBRARY FOR GIRLS
D.C. Thomson; 1 May 1963-?

1 68pgs pocket size; Dixie of Dude Ranch	£1.25
2-	£0.20

JUGHEAD
Thorpe & Porter; 1 1950s-?

1 Archie reprints	£3.00
2-	£1.50

JULIETTE PICTURE LIBRARY
Famepress; 1 Jan 1966-?

1 68pgs pocket size; One Starlit Night, foreign reprints begin	£1.00
2-?	£0.20

JUMBO COMICS
Hotspur Publishing; 1 1949

1 8pgs; Denis Gifford, Wally Robertson art	£3.00

JUMBO COMICS
Cartoon Art; nn-2 1950

nn – 68pgs; Fiction House reprints	£3.00
2	£2.00

JUMBO COMICS
R. & L.Locker; 1 1951-?

1 Fiction House reprints	£3.00
2-?	£2.00

JUMBO COMICS
Thorpe & Porter; 1 1952-28? 1954?

1 Fiction House reprints	£3.00
2-28?	£2.00

JUMPIN' JACK FLASH
(no imprint); 1 1972

1 36pgs; American underground reprints, Robert Crumb, S.Clay Wilson art	£2.00

JUNE
Fleetway/IPC; 18th Mar 1961-15th Jun 1974, 638? issues (joins Tammy)

18 Mar 1961 Roy Wilson art	£3.50
25 Mar 1961	£1.25
1 Apr 1961-1969 incl. Michael Hubbard art	£0.60
1970-1974 incl. Jim Baikie art	£0.35

CHRONOLOGY
18 Jul 1964: 1st June & Poppet. 30 Jan 1965: 1st June & School Friend. 20 Jan 1973: 1st June & Pixie.

JUNE AND SCHOOLFRIEND PICTURE LIBRARY
(previously School Friend Picture Library)
Fleetway; 328 Oct 1965-579 Jan 1971

328-363 68pgs pocket size	£0.50
364-579 becomes June and School Friend and Princess Picture Library	£0.35

JUNE AND SCHOOLFRIEND PICTURE LIBRARY HOLIDAY SPECIAL
Fleetway; 1966-1971?

1966-1970 228pgs; reprints	£0.75
1971 becomes June Picture Library Holiday Special	£0.60

JUNGLE
Streamline; nn 1950

nn – 28pgs; Fox reprints	£4.00

JUNGLE COMICS
Streamline; 1 1949-4 1950

1-4 36pgs; Fiction House reprints	£3.00

JUNGLE COMICS
Thorpe & Porter; 1 1952-?

1 28pgs; Fiction House reprints	£3.00
2-?	£2.50

	N.MINT		N.MINT
JUNGLE HERO		**KANG THE MIGHTY**	
Scion; nn 1951		Scion; nn 1950	
nn - 24pgs; King-Ganteaume art	£4.00	nn - 16pgs Cornell, Minnitt art	£10.00
JUNGLE JIM		Note: Big Treasure Comic featured as the second half of this comic (See Big...Comic);	
World Distributors; 1-10 1955		not issued seperately	
1 28pgs; Dell 4-colour reprints	£5.00	**KA-POW**	
2-10	£3.00	Phil Clarke & Steve Moore; 1 Jul 1967-3 Aug 1968	
JUNGLE JINKS		1-2 Ken Simpson, Steve Moore art	£1.00
(Title Jungle Jinks and Chuckles/ Jungle Jinks from 5)		3 Mike Higgs art	£0.75
Amalgamated Press; 1 8th Dec 1923-62 7th Feb 1925 (joins Playbox)		Note: first British strip-zine	
1 Tom Wilkinson art	£35.00	**KAYO KIRBY**	
2	£12.50	Cartoon Art; 1 1950	
3-5	£6.00	1 16pgs; Fiction House reprints	£3.00
6-62 incl. W. Radford, B.O.Wymer art	£4.00	**KELTIK KOMIX**	
JUNGLE LIL		Aberdeen People's Press; 1 1979-2 1982	
Streamline; nn 1951		1 28pgs; adult material	£0.80
nn - 28pgs; Fox Publishing reprints	£4.00	2 36pgs	£0.50
JUNGLE THRILLS		**KEN MAYNARD WESTERN**	
Streamline; nn 1952		Miller; nn 1950; 1-8 1951; 1-3 1959	
nn - 28pgs; Fox Publishing reprints	£4.00	nn - large format gravure; Fawcett reprints	£10.00
JUNGLE TRAILS		1-8 28pgs	£5.00
Scion; nn Jul 1951-nn 1952 (3 issues)		1-3 68pgs; incl. reprints from Golden Arrow (Fawcett), Young Eagle (Charlton)	£7.50
nn (1) 24pgs	£5.00	**KENNEDY**	
2 20pgs; Jim Farrell by Ron Embleton	£8.00	Morcrim; 1-2 1977	
nn (3) 20pgs	£5.00	1-2 132pgs; The President Must Die, Spanish reprints	£1.00
JUNIOR EXPRESS WEEKLY		**KID COLT OUTLAW**	
(see Express Weekly)		Miller; 50-52 1951	
JUNIOR MIRROR		50-52 28pgs; Atlas reprints	£5.00
Daily Mirror; 1st Sep 1954-29th Feb 1956, 75 issues		**KID COLT OUTLAW**	
1 Sep 1954 Space Captain Jim Stalwart by C. Bannerman/Bruce Cornwall,		Strato/Top Sellers; 1-58 1950s	
Fighting Tomahawk by Richard Jennings, Flash by Jack Dunkley,		1 68pgs; Atlas reprints	£6.00
Pip Squeak & Wilfred, Junior Mirror all begin	£12.50	2-58	£4.00
8 Sep-3 Nov 1954	£6.00	**KID COLT WESTERN COMICS**	
10 Nov 1954-29 Feb 1956	£3.00	Thorpe & Porter; 1-7 1952	
JUNIOR SPIDER-MAN SUMMER SPECIAL		1-7 68pgs; Atlas reprints	£5.00
Marvel; nn May 1983		**KID COWBOY**	
nn reprints	£1.00	(see Action Series)	
JUNIORS' MAGAZINE		**KID DYNAMITE WESTERN COMIC/ KID DYNAMITE**	
G.W.Pearce; 1 1947		Miller; 1 1954-65 1960	
1 W.Forshaw art	£3.00	1 28pgs; Kid Dynamite by John Wheeler begins	£5.00
JUPITER ADVENTURE COMIC		2-65	£2.50
Scoop Books; nn 1946		**KID ETERNITY**	
nn - George Blow, Alf Farningham art	£4.00	T.V. Boardman; 1-3 1949	
JURASSIC PARK		1-3 36pgs; Quality reprints	£8.00
Dark Horse; 1 (8 Jul 1993)-15 Oct 1994		**KID MONTANA**	
1-5 36pgs; Topps reprints of Spielberg movie adaptation, Kane/Perez art	£1.25	Miller; 50-59 1959	
6 Raptor by Englehart & Gil, Age of Reptiles by Richard Delgado reprints begin	£1.00	50-59 36pgs; Charlton Comics reprints	£3.50
7-9	£1.00	**KID SLADE GUNFIGHTER**	
10 (May 1994)	£0.95	Strato/Top Sellers; 1-7 1957	
11 28pgs (released Jun 1994)	£0.95	1-7 Atlas reprints from Kid Slade Gunfighter and Kid Colt Outlaw	£3.00
12-15	£0.95	**KIDDYFUN**	
JURASSIC PARK		(see Comicute Budget)	
Titan; nn Nov 1993		Gerald Swan; 1 1945-12 1951 (joins Girls' Fun)	
nn - Topps reprints of Spielberg movie adaptation, Kane/Perez art	£6.00	1 8pgs; William Ward, Edward Banger, John McCail art	£5.00
JURASSIC PARK ANNUAL		2-12	£3.00
Grandreams; 1993		**KILLER KOMIX**	
1993 film tie-in	£4.75	Headpress; nn Nov 1992	
JUST DENNIS		nn - 116pgs	£3.00
Alan Class; 1 1965		**KILLING TIME**	
1 68pgs; Hallden reprints	£3.00	Mandarin (2000AD Books); nn Sep 1992	
JUSTICE TRAPS THE GUILTY		nn - 2000AD reprints, Chris Weston art	£7.00
United Anglo-American; 1 1949		**KILLPOWER: THE EARLY YEARS**	
1 Prize Publications reprint	£5.00	(see Motormouth) (see main American comics section)	
JUSTICE TRAPS THE GUILTY		**KINEMA COMIC, THE**	
Arnold Book Co./Thorpe & Porter; 1 1951-43 1954		Amalgamated Press; 1 24th Apr 1920-651 15th Oct 1932 (joins Film Fun)	
1 68pgs; Prize Publications reprints	£8.00	1 George Wakefield, Herbert Foxwell, G.M.Payne art	£45.00
2-28	£5.00	2	£15.00
29-43 Thorpe & Porter issues	£4.00	3-5	£9.00
JUSTICE TRAPS THE GUILTY		6-651 some incl. J.H.Valda art	£6.00
Top Sellers; 1-8 1960s		**KING COMIC**	
1-8 Prize Publications reprints	£3.00	Ensign/G.W.Pearce; 1947, 4 issues, mostly unnumbered	
		nn - 8pgs green/orange gravure; W.Forshaw art	£3.00
		2 (G.W.Pearce) blue/red gravure; Charles Ross art	£2.00
# K		nn - blue/red gravure; Frank Minnitt art	£2.00
		nn - green/orange gravure; Frank Minnitt art	£2.00
K.O. KNOCKOUT		**KING COMIC**	
Cartoon Art; nn 1947		Miller; 1 5th May 1954-14 7th Aug 1954	
nn - 20pgs; two 8pg comics with 4pg wraparound cover; contains Acromaid		1-8 28pgs printed gravure; King-Features newspaper strip reprints	£5.00
Comics by Dennis Reader, Commando Comics by Crewe Davies	£4.00	9-14 litho printed	£2.50
KAANGA		**KING COMIC SERIES**	
Thorpe & Porter; 1 1952-?		(see Crack Action, Crime Patrol, Police Comic, T-Man)	
1 28pgs; Fiction House reprints	£4.00	**KING KONG**	
2-?	£2.50	Top Sellers; nn 1970	
KALGAN THE GOLDEN		nn - 68pgs; Giant Classics Album reprint from Western Publishing; based on film	£2.00
Harrier; 1 Mar 1988		**KING OF THE ROYAL MOUNTED (ZANE GREY'S...)**	
1 Ron Turner art	£0.75	World Distributors; 1-21 1953	
KANE		1-21 28pgs; Dell reprints	£4.00
Dancing Elephant Press; 1 Apr 1993-present (10 to Jul 1995)		**KING OF THE ROYAL MOUNTED**	
1 28pgs; Paul Grist art	£3.00	Miller; 1 1962-15 1963	
1 second printing; different cover	£1.80	1-15 68pgs; reprints American comic strip by Jim Gary	£3.00
2	£2.00	**KISS OF DEATH**	
3-10 32pgs	£1.80	(see also Last Kiss)	

N.MINT

Acme Press; 1 Apr 1987-2 Jun 1987 (3 not issued)
1 John Watkiss art begins	£0.75
2	£0.60

Note: 3 issue mini-series, third issue later appeared as The Last Kiss

KIT CARSON COMICS
Thorpe & Porter; 1 1952
1 68pgs; Avon reprints	£5.00

KIT CARSON'S COWBOY ANNUAL
Amalgamated/Fleetway; 1954-1960
1954 D.C.Eyles art	£10.00
1955-1959 D.C.Eyles art	£7.50
1960 1st Fleetway	£5.00

KIT COWBOY
Miller; 1 Jun 1957-10 1958
1 28pgs; Spanish (?) reprints	£5.00
2-10 incl. Fawcett reprints	£3.00

KIT MORAIN
Martin & Reid; nn 1949
nn - 8pgs tabloid; Mick Anglo, Frank Minnitt, Wally Robertson art	£4.00

KLING KLANG KLATCH
Victor Gollancz; nn Nov 1992
nn - graphic novel by Ian McDonald & David Lyttleton, hardback	£15.00
nn - paperback	£10.00

KLONDIKE
Purnell & Sons; 1962
1962 strip and text stories by George Anderson; illus by Pat Williams, Eric Dadswell	£4.00

KNIGHT RIDER ANNUAL
Grandreams; 1982-1983 (both cover year 1982)
1982 David Lloyd art	£2.00
1982 Jim Eldridge art	£1.50

KNIGHTS OF PENDRAGON, THE
Marvel; 1 July 1990-18 December 1991
1 Gary Erskine/Andy Lanning art begins, Captain Britain cameo	£1.00
2-6	£0.95
7-18	£0.95

KNIGHTS OF PENDRAGON
(see Overkill) (see main American comics section)

K-9 ANNUAL
World; 1983
1983 scarce	£5.00

KNOCKABOUT COMICS
Knockabout; nn 1980-14 1987
nn - Emerson, Graham Manley art	£3.00
2 Talbot, Manley, Emerson art	£2.50
3-5	£1.50
6 Dan Maniac by Mike Matthews begins	£3.50
7,9-11	£3.00
8 Peter Pank by Max begins	£3.00
12 Jack Alarum by Graham Higgins begins	£4.00
13	£4.00
14	£4.50

KNOCKABOUT TRIAL SPECIAL
Knockabout; nn 1984
nn - hardback; Moore text, Emerson, Bolland, Gibbons, Talbot art	£5.00

KNOCKOUT
Amalgamated/Fleetway; 1 4th Mar 1939-16th Feb 1963 (1231 issues, numbered to 1054, joins Valiant)
1 titled The Knock-Out Comic; Billy Bunter by Charles E. Chapman, Sexton Blake by Jos Walker, Deed-a-Day Danny by Hugh McNeill, Our Ernie by C.E. Holt begin	£300.00
2	£150.00
3-5	£100.00
6-11	£75.00
12 1st McNeill Our Ernie, 1st Frank Minnitt Billy Bunter	£75.00
13-65	£50.00
66 1st "Knock-Out and Magnet"	£35.00
67-193	£25.00
194 Gulliver's Travels by Eric Parker begins	£20.00
195-213,215-269,271-308,310-349	£20.00
214 Arabian Nights by Parker begins	£20.00
270 Mr. Midshipman Easy by Parker begins	£20.00
309 Children of the New Forrest by Parker begins	£20.00
350 Kidnapped by Parker begins	£20.00
351-387,389-408,410-430,432-460	£15.00
388 Three Musketeers by Parker begins	£15.00
409 Westward Ho! by Parker begins	£15.00
431 The Phantom Sheriff by Parker begins (later by D.C. Eyles)	£15.00
461 Tough Tod and Happy Annie by McNeill begins	£15.00
462-473,475-489,491-505,507-532,534-561	£10.00
474 Black Arrow by Parker begins	£10.00
490 Dick Turpin's Ride to York by Eyles begins	£10.00
506 Capt. Flame by Sep E. Scott begins	£10.00
533 Captain Kidd by T. Heath-Robinson begins	£10.00
562 Kit Carson by Parker begins (later by Ian Kennedy, Don Lawrence, etc)	£5.00
563	£5.00
564 Breed of the Brudenells by H.M.Brock begins	£5.00
565-606	£4.00
607-610 jointly numbered issue	£4.00
611-615 un-dated issues (1950)	£4.00
616-617 jointly numbered issue	£4.00
618-759,761-814,816-868	£3.50
760 1st "Knockout and Comic Cuts"	£3.50
815 Johnny Winco by Mike Western begins	£3.50

N.MINT

869 Davy Crockett by Kennedy and others begins	£3.50
870-887,895-1053	£3.00
888-894 combined issue dated 3rd Mar-14th Apr 1956	£3.00
1054 last numbered issue	£3.00
16 May 1959-20 Jun 1959,nn,22 Aug 1959-3 Jun 1961	£3.00
10 Jun 1961 title becomes Billy Bunter's Knockout	£3.00
17 Jun 1961-14 Jul 1962	£3.00
21 Jul 1962 1st new look; Kelly's Eye by Solano Lopez begins	£2.50
28 Jul 1962-16 Feb 1963	£2.50

Note: no issues dated 14 Oct-23 Dec 1950 (numbered 607-617), one un-numbered/undated issue published between 27 Jun-15 Aug 1959.

KNOCKOUT
IPC; 12th Jun 1971-23rd Jun 1973, 106 issues (joins Whizzer and Chips)
12 Jun 1971 Mike Lacey, Reg Parlett, Sid Burgon art	£1.00
19 Jun 1971-23 Jun 1973	£0.35

KNOCKOUT FUN BOOK/ ANNUAL
Amalgamated/Fleetway; 1941-1962,1978
1941	£150.00
1942	£100.00
1943	£80.00
1944,1945	£60.00
1946-1948	£30.00
1949-1951	£20.00
1952-1956	£10.00
1957-1959 becomes Knockout Annual	£8.00
1960-1962	£7.50
1978	£2.50

KNOCKOUTS
Longman; 1980
Cave Rescue	£0.50
Undersea Adventure	£0.50
Maiden Flight	£0.50
Haunted Castle	£0.50
Danger at Sea	£0.50

KOMIC FUN
Reynard Press; nn 1948
nn - 8pgs; Alan Fraser art	£3.00

KOMIC KRACKERS
Hamilton & Co.; nn 1949
nn - 8pgs	£4.00

KONA COMIC ALBUM
World Distributors; 1 1965
1 64pgs, Dell reprints in colour	£4.00

KORAK SON OF TARZAN
Williams; 1 1971-44? 1974
1 36pgs; Dell reprints	£3.00
2-44	£2.00

KORAK SON OF TARZAN BUMPER ALBUM
Top Sellers; nn 1973
nn - 52pgs; National Periodicals reprints	£2.50

KRACKER COMIC
Reynard Press; 1-6 1947
1 16pgs; Tom Cottrell art	£4.00
2-6 8pgs	£3.00

KRAZY
IPC; 16th Oct 1976-15th Apr 1978, 79 issues (joins Whizzer and Chips)
16 Oct 1976	£1.00
23 Oct 1976-15 Apr 1978	£0.60

KRAZY HOLIDAY SPECIAL
IPC; May 1977-Jun 1983
1977-1983	£0.75

KUNG FU
Brown Watson; 1974
1974 Stories by Steve Moore, illus. by Desmond Walduck, Melvyn Powell	£3.50

L

LADY CHATTERLEY'S LOVER
Knockabout (Crack); nn 1986
nn - Hunt Emerson art, based on D.H. Lawrence	£5.00

LADY PENELOPE
City; 1 22nd Jan 1966-122 18th May 1968; becomes Penelope 123 25th May 1968-204 13th Dec 1969 (joins Princess Tina)
1 scarce, Perils of Parker by Peter Ford, Man From UNCLE, Lady Penelope by Frank Langford, Space Family Robinson by John Burns begin	£35.00
1 with free gift (Signet Ring)	£50.00
2	£15.00
3-5	£7.50
3-50	£5.00
51-122	£2.50
123 title becomes Penelope	£1.00
124-204	£0.50

ARTISTS/FEATURES
John Burns in 1-52,60-65. Ron Embleton in 39-52.

LADY PENELOPE ANNUAL
City; 1966-1968 (becomes Penelope Annual)
1966	£12.50
1967-1968	£7.50

LADY PENELOPE SUMMER EXTRA
City; 1966
1966 very scarce	£20.00

N.MINT

LANCE O'CASEY
Arnold Book Co.; 10 1951
10 Fawcett reprints incl. strips from Funny Animals — £3.00

LANCER ANNUAL
World Distributors; 1970
1970 96pgs; Dell strip reprints plus text stories — £3.00

LAND OF THE GIANTS ANNUAL
World Distributors; 1968-1969
1969 "Crash Into the Unknown" (1st story) — £10.00
1970 "Two in a Trap" (1st story) — £7.50

LAND OF THE GIANTS TELEVISION STORY BOOK
PBS; 1969
1969 "Countdown to Escape" (1st story) — £5.00

LARAMIE ANNUAL/ LARAMIE
World Distributors/ Dean; 1961-1964
1961 Stories by Alex Gifford, illus. by Patrick Williams — £5.00
1962 Stories by Gordon Grimsley, illus. by Alex Henderson — £4.00
1963 Stories by Gordon Grimsley, illus. by John Burns — £3.00
1964 Dean; illus. by John Burns — £3.00

LARADO ANNUAL
World Distributors; 1966
1966 96pgs; Western/Dell strip reprints, plus text stories — £3.00

LAREDO CROCKETT, RANGER
Donald F. Peters; 1 1953-44 1955 (becomes The Ranger Western Comic)
1 28pgs; American newspaper strip reprints — £5.00
2-44 — £3.00

LARGE COW COMIX
Arts Lab Press; 1 1972-5 1973
1 Hunt Emerson art — £2.50
2 titled Outer Space Comix; Hunt Emerson art — £2.50
3 titled Mr. Spoonbiscuit; Hunt Emerson art — £2.50
4 titled Pholk Comix; Hunt Emerson art — £2.50
5 titled Zomix Comix; Hunt Emerson art — £2.50

LARIAT, THE
Martin & Reid; nn Jul 1950
nn - 16pgs; Mick Anglo art — £2.50

LARKS
Amalgamated Press; 1 29th Oct 1927-656 18th May 1940 (joins Comic Cuts)
1 Bertie Brown, Roy Wilson, Harry Parlett art — £35.00
2 — £12.50
3-5 — £6.00
6-656 incl. George Heath art — £4.00

LASH LARUE WESTERN
Miller; 50 Sep 1950-125 1959, 76 issues
50 36pgs; Fawcett reprints — £5.00
51-125 reduced to 28pgs, later issues reprinted from Charlton — £3.00

LASSIE (M.G.M.'S...)
World Distributors; 1 Oct 1952-18 1954
1 36pgs; Dell reprints — £2.50
2-18 later issues 28pgs — £1.50

LAST KISS
(see also Kiss of Death)
Acme Press/Eclipse International; nn Mar 1989
nn - 52pgs; John Watkiss art — £2.00

LAST OF THE SUMMER WINE
Daily Star; nn Dec 1983
nn - 128pgs; reprints Roger Mahoney strip from Daily Star — £1.00

LAST PLANET, THE
MBS Publishing (Mindbenders Presents); 1 Oct/Nov 1993-2, Jan/Feb 1994
1 Mindbenders reprints by Simon Davies & David Pugh — £1.50
2 — £1.00

LAUGH AGAIN WITH ANDY CAPP
Hamlyn; 1968-1980 (23 issues)
1 132pgs; paperback reprints from Andy Capp series by Reg Smythe — £3.00
2-23 — £1.00

LAUGH FUN BOOK
P.M. Productions; nn Jan 1947
nn - 16pgs; Denis Gifford art — £3.00

LAUGH WITH MURRAY BALL
Leader; nn 1974
nn - reprints Stanley by Murray Ball from Punch — £1.00

LAUREL AND HARDY (LARRY HARMON'S...)
Top Sellers/Williams; 1 Mar 1979-23? 1981?
1 52pgs — £1.50
2-23 — £0.75

LAUREL AND HARDY
Byblos; Mar 1981-Mar 1982, 13 issues
Mar 1981 52pgs; reprints — £1.25
Apr 1981-Mar 1982 — £0.50

LAUREL AND HARDY EXTRA
Top Sellers; 1 Mar 1969-4 1970
1-3 52pgs; Gold Key reprints — £2.50
4 Gold Key reprints — £1.50

LAUREL AND HARDY SPECIAL
Byblos; Aug 1979-Nov 1981
Summer Special 1979,1980,1981 — £0.50
Autumn Special 1979,1980 — £0.50
Winter Special 1979,1980,1981 — £0.50
Spring Special 1980 — £0.50

LAZARUS CHURCHYARD
Tundra; 1 Jun 1992-3 Nov 1992
1 The Virtual Kiss by Warren Ellis & D'Israeli, Blast reprints — £2.50

Lady Penelope #1

Lion #1

Look And Learn Book 1969

	N.MINT
2 Goodnight Ladies mostly original material	£2.25
3 Inspector Sleep new material	£2.25
LAZARUS LAMB IN THE RIDDLE OF THE SPHINCTER	
Pluto Press; nn 1983	
nn - 96pgs; adult material, Ralph Edney art	£1.00
LEA	
Acme; 1989	
The Confessions of Julius Antoine Vol.1 Le Tendre & Rossi European reprint	£4.50
LEGEND	
Random House/Legend; nn Oct 1993	
nn - 96pgs; based on novel by David Gemmell, adapted by Stan Nicholls & Fangorn,	
limited edition hardcover	£20.00
nn - softcover	£10.00
LEGEND HORROR CLASSICS	
John Shier/Associated Magazine Distributors; 1 May 1975-9 Jan 1976	
1 Dracula by Kevin O'Neill	£4.00
2-5,7-9	£3.00
6 1st edited by Kev O'Neill	£3.00
FEATURES	
1 Dracula. 2 Frankenstein. 3 The 7th Voyage of Sinbad. 4 Blood Lust of the Zombies. 5 Dracula Must Be Destroyed. 6 Terror From Space. 7 Beowulf and the Monster from Hell. 8 Killer Jaws. 9 The Jokers.	
LEGENDS OF LARIAN	
Lion Publishing; Sep 1992-present	
The Shadow's Edge (Sep 1992) 48pgs; Jeff Anderson art	£4.00
The Cutting Edge (Mar 1993)	£4.00
LIEUTENANT BLUEBERRY	
Egmont/Methuen; 1977-1978	
1 Fort Navajo 52pgs; Jean Giraud reprints	£3.00
2 Thunder in the West	£3.00
3 Lone Eagle	£3.00
4 Mission to Mexico	£3.00
LIFE AND TIMES OF THE SHMOO	
(see also Li'l Abner)	
Convoy; nn 1949	
nn - 100pgs; reprints Li'l Abner by Al Capp	£4.00
LIFE IS ONE BIG BED OF NAILS	
Papas; nn 1968	
nn - 68pgs oblong; Bill Papas reprints from Guardian	£1.00
LIFE OF CHRIST	
Darton Longman & Todd; nn 1977	
nn - 100pgs oblong; Eric Fraser art	£1.00
LIFE STORY	
Miller; 1-24 1959	
1-24 Fawcett reprints	£1.25
LIFE WITH THE LARKS	
Mirror; nn Sep 1978	
nn - 100pgs oblong; reprints Jack Dunkley newspaper strip from Daily Mirror	£3.00
LIGHT FANTASTIC, THE	
(see The Colour of Magic)	
Corgi; nn Nov 1993	
nn - 128pgs; based on novel by Terry Pratchett, reprints Innovation series,	
Steven Ross/Joe Bennett art	£8.00
LIGHTNING COMICS, THE	
Kangaroo; nn 1946	
nn - 8pgs; Denis McLoughlin art	£20.00
LI'L ABNER	
(see also Life and Times of the Shmoo)	
Miller; nn 1945	
nn - 16pgs; reprints from Comics on Parade	£6.00
LINUS	
Milano Libri; nn May 1970	
nn - 86pgs; foreign reprints	£0.75
LION	
Amalgamated/Fleetway/IPC; 1 23rd Feb 1952-18th May 1974 (1136 issues, numbered to 378; joins Valiant)	
1 Captain Condor by Frank S. Pepper & Ronald Forbes, Sandy Dean, Jungle Robot (early Robot Archie) by F.A. Philpott	£60.00
2	£25.00
3-5	£15.00
6-30	£7.50
31-100	£4.00
101-212,218-256	£3.00
213-217 jointly numbered issue dated 17 Mar-14 Apr 1956	£3.00
257 1st Archie the Robot	£4.00
258-283	£3.00
284 Paddy Payne begins	£2.50
285-17 Oct 1959	£2.50
24 Oct 1959 1st "Lion and Sun"	£3.50
24 Oct 1959 with free gift (two football team photos)	£7.00
[Note: issues dated from 31 Oct 1959-5 Dec 1959 also came with free gift of two football team photos. See corresponding issues of Tiger]	£5.00
29 Oct 1960 Sword of Eingar (1st Karl the Viking story) by Don Lawrence begins	£2.50
2 Nov 1959-22 Oct 1960	£2.50
5 Nov 1960-26 Sep 1964,10 Oct 1964-19 Jun 1965,3 Jul 1965-4 Jun 1966	£2.50
3 Oct 1964 Hand of Zar (1st Maroc the Mighty story) by Don Lawrence begins	£2.50
26 Jun 1965 The Spider by Reg Bunn begins (created by Jerry Siegel)	£2.50
11 Jun 1966 1st "Lion and Champion"; Danger Man by Jesus Blasco begins	£2.00
18 Jun 1966-26 Apr 1969	£2.00
3 May 1969 1st "Lion and Eagle"; Hampson Dan Dare reprints begin	£1.50
10 May 1969-13 Mar 1971	£1.00
20 Mar 1971 1st "Lion and Thunder"; Fury's Family by McLoughlin begins	£0.75
27 Mar 1971-18 May 1974	£0.75

	N.MINT
ARTISTS	
Jesus Blasco in 11 Jun-3 Sep 1966. Joe Colquhoun in ?? Mar 1959-7 Mar 1964, 15 May-18 Sep 1965. Don Lawrence in 28 Oct 1960-10 Aug 1963, 23 Nov 1963-3 Jul 1965. Denis McLoughlin in 20 Mar-21 Oct 1971.	
Note: two un-numbered/undated issues published between 27 Jun-29 Aug 1959, no issues dated 21 Nov 1970-30 Jan 1971, 26 Jan 1974, 9 Feb 1974, 23 Feb 1974, 9 Mar 1974, 23 Mar 1974.	
LION ANNUAL	
Amalgamated/Fleetway; 1954-1983	
1954	£20.00
1955	£15.00
1956-1958	£9.00
1959-1964	£5.00
1965 Karl the Viking by Don Lawrence	£4.00
1966-1968	£4.00
1969-1975	£3.00
1976-1983	£2.50
LION BOOK OF...	
Fleetway; 1961-1969	
War Adventures 1962	£4.00
Speed 1963	£3.50
How It Works 1968	£3.00
Great Conquerors 1970	£3.00
Motor Racing 1970	£3.00
LION PICTURE LIBRARY	
Fleetway/IPC; 1 Oct 1963-136 May 1969	
1 60pgs; Paddy Payne: Rocket Buster (reprint from Lion)	£5.00
2-50	£2.50
51-136 reprints from Air Ace, Battle, War Picture Libraries	£1.00
ARTISTS/FEATURES	
Robot Archie in 2,4,8. Captain Condor by Frank Pepper & Ron Forbes in 6,9. Joe Colquhoun art in 11,13,15,17,20,27,31.	
LION SUMMER SPECIAL	
Fleetway; 1968-1980	
1968-1970 96pgs	£5.00
1971-1973 title becomes Lion and Thunder Summer Special	£3.00
1974-1980 80pgs, title becomes Lion Holiday Special	£2.00
LION SUMMER SPECTACULAR: EPIC	
Fleetway; nn 1967	
nn - movie adaptions incl. Tobruk, Run of the Arrow, Quo Vadis, The Lost World, The Four Feathers, reprints from Film Fun, Thriller Picture Library; Batman, You Only Live Twice and Thunderbirds Are Go! photo features	£7.50
LIONHEART	
CM Comics; 1 Feb 1994	
1	£1.50
LITTLE ASPIRIN	
United Anglo-American; 1 1950	
1 28pgs; Atlas reprints	£2.00
LITTLE LENNY	
United Anglo-American; 1 1950	
1 28pgs; Atlas reprints	£2.00
LITTLE LULU	
World Distributors; 1-3 1955	
1-3 28pgs; Dell reprints	£1.25
LITTLE MARVEL COMIC	
R.& L.Locker; nn Jan 1946	
nn - 8pgs; R.Beaumont art	£4.00
LITTLE MAX COMICS	
United Anglo-American; 1-4 1953	
1-4 28pgs; Harvey Publications reprints	£2.50
LITTLE SHERIFF WESTERN COMIC	
Donald Peters/Westworld; v1:1 Jul 1951-v7:12 1958, 96 issues	
v1:1-12 32pgs; French reprints	£4.00
v2:1-24	£2.00
v3:1-v7:12 later issues 20pgs	£1.75
LITTLE SPARKS	
(previously Sparks)	
Amalgamated Press; (1) 328 24th Apr 1920-331 15th May 1920, 4 issues; (2) 1 22nd May 1920-124 30th Sep 1922 (becomes The Sunbeam)	
328-331 Walter Booth art	£10.00
1 12pgs tabloid; Walter Booth, Don Newhouse, A.B.Payne art	£25.00
2	£9.00
3-5	£6.00
6-124	£4.50
LITTLE STAR	
D.C. Thomson; 1 29th Jan 1972-209 24th Jan 1976 (joins Twinkle)	
1 Tom Kerr art	£1.25
2	£0.75
3-5	£0.50
6-209 incl. Bob Dewar art	£0.20
LITTLE WONDER COMIC	
R.& L.Locker; nn Jan 1946	
nn - 8pgs; R.Beaumont art	£4.00
LOAD RUNNER	
ECC Publications; 1 23rd Jun 1983-13 8th Dec 1983	
1 Load Runner by Peter Dennis, Andy Royd by John Stokes art	£1.50
2-13	£0.50
LOAD O'FUN	
Holland Press; nn 1947	
nn - 8pgs; Alan Fraser art	£3.00
LOBO: THE LAST CZARNIAN	
Titan; nn 1992	
nn - reprints DC series by Alan Grant & Simon Bisley	£6.00

	N.MINT
LOGAN'S RUN ANNUAL	
Brown Watson; 1978	
1978 David Lloyd art; based on film	£3.50
LOLLIPOPS COMIC	
Philmar; 1-3 1949	
1-3 8pgs; 2-3. incl. Frank Minnitt	£3.00
LONDON EXPLORER	
Associated Newspapers; nn 1952	
nn - 68pgs; reprints from Evening News, Peter Jackson art	£5.00
LONDON IS STRANGER THAN FICTION	
Associated Newspapers; nn 1951	
nn - 84pgs; reprints from Evening News, Peter Jackson art	£5.00
LONDON'S DARK	
Escape/Titan; nn Apr 1989	
nn - James Robinson & Paul Johnson	£4.00
LONE EAGLE	
Miller; 1 1956	
1 28pgs; Farrell Publications reprints	£4.00
LONE GROOVER	
Benyon/Eel Pie	
Lone Groover Express (1976) 24pgs tabloid; Tony Benyon art	£2.00
Lone Groover's Little Read Book (1981) 100pgs	£1.00
LONE RANGER	
World Distributors; 1 Jan 1953-66 Jun 1958	
1 36pgs; Dell reprints	£5.00
2-61	£3.00
62-66 68pg issues	£4.00
LONE RANGER	
Top Sellers; 1 1970-?	
1 36pgs; Dell reprints	£1.50
2-?	£1.00
LONE RANGER	
Egmont-Methuen; 1-2 1977	
1-2 100pgs; Dell reprints	£1.00
LONE RANGER, THE	
World Distributors; Aug 1964-1969	
1964 Stories by Douglas Enefer, J.L. Morrissey, M. Broadley, J.W. Elliott, illus. by Walter J. Howarth, "Enter Lone Ranger and Tonto" (1st story)	£4.00
(1965-1967) some issues undated	£4.00
1968 1st - "The Silver Bullet" (1st story)	£3.00
1969 1st - "The Deserted Stage Station" (1st story)	£2.00
LONE RANGER, THE	
Brown Watson; 1975	
1975 "The Story of the Lone Ranger" (1st story)	£2.00
LONE RANGER ADVENTURE STORIES	
Adprint; 1957-1960	
1957 text/photos, Lone Ranger movie adapted by Arthur Groom	£6.00
2 (1958) all text, stories by Richard Lewis, illus. by Don Lawrence	£3.00
1959 all text, stories by Richard Lewis, illus. by Don Lawrence	£3.00
1960 all text, stories by David Roberts, illus. by Eric Dadswell	£3.50
LONE RANGER COMIC ALBUM, THE/ LONE RANGER ALBUM	
World Distributors; 1 1950-5 1954; 1 Mar 1957	
1-5	£5.00
(1957) The Lone Ranger Album	£4.00
LONE RANGER TELEVISION STORY BOOK, THE	
PBS; 1963, 1967	
1963 "Silver Bullets" (1st story)	£5.00
1967 The Lone Range Television Picture Story Book, "The Trap" (1st story)	£3.00
LONE RIDER	
Pemberton; 1-3 1951	
1 36pgs; Farrell Publishing reprints	£5.00
2-3 28pgs	£3.00
LONE RIDER PICTURE LIBRARY	
Fleetway; 1 Jul 1961-16 Feb 1962	
1 The Pay Off by Arturo Del Castillo; 68pgs pocket	£7.50
2-16	£3.00
ARTISTS/FEATURES	
1 The Pay Off by Arturo Del Castillo. 2 Manhunt. 3 Scar of Hate. 4 Born to Kill. 5 Violence in the Sun. 6 The Hungry Gun. 7 The Gunslinger. 8 Son of Texas by Robert Forrest. 9 Troubled Town by Arturo Del Castillo. 10 Mantrap. 11 Saddle of Death by Alberto Breccia. 12 The Killer Breed. 15 Lash. 16 Game of Chance.	
LONE STAR MAGAZINE	
DCMT/Atlas; v1:1 (Nov 1952?)-99 Apr 1963	
Vol 1:1 undated, Steve Larabee, Rocky Stone, Ace Hart begin	£15.00
2 Rocky Stone by Ron Embleton, 3D Ace Hart story	£7.50
3 Rocky Stone by Terence Patrick	£5.00
4 Ace Hart becomes Space Ace by Terence Patrick	£5.00
5 1st John Compari Steve Larabee, Lore of the West by Embleton begins	£4.00
6-7,9-10,12-16,18-34	£4.00
8 1st Embleton cover	£4.00
11 1st Embleton Steve Larabee, Sgt. Rip McCoy by Terrence Patrick begins	£4.00
17 1st Ron Turner Space Ace, Sgt. Rip McCoy by James Holdaway	£4.00
Vol 2:1-5,7-12	£3.00
6 1st Colin Andrew art	£3.00
Vol 3:1 1st Atlas issue	£2.50
2-12	£2.50
Vol 4:1-12	£2.50
Vol 5:1-3,5-12	£2.00
4 Brian Lewis art	£2.00
Vol 6;1-12	£2.00
Vol 7:1-12 last volume numbering. 7:1 1st dated (Feb 1961)	£2.00
85-99 numbered	£2.00

	N.MINT
LONE VIGILANTE	
(see Action Series)	
LONG BOW	
Atlas Publishing; 1 Sep 1960-31 1964	
1 28pgs; Fiction House reprints	£2.50
2-31	£1.50
LONG JOHN SILVER	
Miller; 1-2 1956	
1-2 28pgs; Charlton Comics reprints	£4.00
LOOK ALIVE	
IPC; 1 18th Sep 1982-5 15th Oct 1982	
1 The Chronicles of Genghis Grimtoad by Alan Grant & Angus McBride begins	£1.00
2-5	£0.75
Note: intended as successor to Look & Learn but sadly short-lived	
LOOK AND LAUGH	
Philmar; nn 1948-2 1949	
nn - 16pgs; Reg Perrott, Ern Shaw art	£4.00
2 Frank Minnitt, Wally Robertson, Colin Merritt art	£4.00
LOOK AND LEARN	
(see Picture Classics)	
Fleetway/IPC; 1 20th Jan 1962-1049 17th Apr 1982	
1 Prince Charles cover	£3.00
2	£2.00
3-30	£1.50
31-176,178-231	£1.00
177 article about Gerry Anderson	£2.00
232 scarce, 1st "Look and Learn and Ranger"; Trigan Empire by Mike Butterworth & Don Lawrence begins	£3.00
233-382 Lawrence art	£1.50
383-390 Ron Embleton Trigan Empire	£1.25
391-752 Lawrence art	£0.50
753 1st Oliver Frey Trigan Empire	£0.25
754-853,855-1049	£0.25
854 1st Gerry Wood Trigan Empire	£0.25
Note: many text features were illustrated by notable artists including Frank Bellamy, Luis Bermejo, C.L. Doughty, Ron Embleton, Peter Jackson, Eric Parker, Ferdinando Tacconi, etc	
LOOK AND LEARN BOOK FOR BOYS	
Amalgamated Press/Fleetway; 1962-?(1980s)	
1962 scarce	£7.50
1962 with dust wrapper	£10.00
1963-1965	£5.00
1966-1969	£4.00
1970s	£3.00
1980s	£2.00
LOOK AND LEARN BOOK OF THE TRIGAN EMPIRE	
(see also Tales of the Trigan Empire, The Trigan Empire)	
Fleetway; nn 1973	
nn - reprints Trigan Empire by Don Lawrence from Ranger/Look & Learn	£5.00
LOOK AND LEARN BOOKS	
IPC/Fleetway; 1967-1978	
1001 Questions and Answers (5 editions, 1968-1972), each	£2.50
The Wonders of Nature (5 editions, 1967-1971), each	£2.50
Railway Wonders of the World (1974)	£2.50
Speed & Power (1978)	£2.50
LOOK AND LEARN HOLIDAY SPECIAL	
IPC; nn Apr 1976	
nn - 52pgs	£0.75
LOOK AND LEARN SUMMER EXTRA	
IPC; 1963	
1963 scarce; subtitled On Your Holidays	£7.50
LOOK-IN	
Independent Television; 9th Jan 1971-1994	
9 Jan 71 Leslie Crowther by Tom Kerr, Freewheelers by Vincente Alcazar, Timeslip by Mike Noble begin	£5.00
1971-1973	£1.50
1974-1977	£0.75
1978-1982	£0.50
1982-1994	£0.35
ARTISTS	
Martin Asbury (Kung Fu, Six-Million Dollar Man, Dick Turpin, Battlestar Galactica, Buck Rogers in the 25th Century). Jim Baikie (Chips, Charlie's Angels, Terrahawks, The Fall Guy). John Bolton (The Bionic Woman, 18 Mar 1978-19 May 1979). John Burns (The Tomorrow People, The Bionic Woman, How the West was Won). Ian Gibson (Bionic Action). Tom Kerr (Crowther in Trouble, Doctor in Charge, The Fenn Street Gang). Brian Lewis (Mark Strong, Les Dawson is Superflop, Jason King, The Marked Man). Mike Noble (Timeslip, Follyfoot, The Tomorrow People, Black Beauty, Space 1999, Man From Atlantis, Enid Blyton's Famous Five, Worzel Gummidge, Star Fleet, Robin of Sherwood). Harry North (Doctor on the Go, No.73). Arthur Ranson (Les Dawson, Michael Bentine's Potty Time, Just William, The Bionic Woman, Logan's Run, Worzel Gummidge, Chips, Sapphire and Steel, Further Adventures of Oliver Twist, Elvis the Story, The Story of the Beatles, Danger Mouse, Alias the Jester).	
LOOK-IN SPECIALS	
(see also Clash of the Titans)	
Independant Television; 1973-1984	
Follyfoot Special (1973) Mike Noble art	£1.00
Danger Mouse Special (1982)	£0.50
Madabout Special (1984)	£0.35
LOOK-IN SUMMER EXTRA	
Independant Television; 1974-?	
1974-?	£0.50
LOONEY TUNES	
World Distributors; 1 1953	
1 28pgs; Dell reprints	£2.00

	N.MINT

LORDS OF MISRULE, THE
Atomeka; nn Mar 1993
| nn - by John Tomlinson & Gary Erskine, Bisley cover | £4.50 |

LORNA THE JUNGLE GIRL
Miller; 1-9 1952
| 1-9 28pgs; Atlas reprints | £4.00 |

LORD HORROR
(see Meng & Ecker)
Savoy; 1 1989-7 1991; 1 Mar 1993-4 May 1995
1 Lord Horror by Dave Britton & Kris Guido begins, copies siezed in	
Manchester by James Anderton	£1.00
2 Kris Guido script/art	£1.00
3 "Hard Core Horror No.1" The Romance of Lord horror and Jessie Matthews	£1.25
4 "Hard Core Horror No.2" Churchill's Tick-Tock Men	£1.25
5 "Hard Core Horror No.3" Horror Time For Hitler	£1.25
6 "Hard Core Horror No.4" Entropy: Going Down Slow	£1.25
7 "Hard Core Horror No.5" King Horror: Zero John Coulthart art	£1.25
Reverbstorm 1 (Mar 1993), issued with Reverbstorm CD, John Coulthart art	£1.50
Reverbstorm 2 John Coulthart art	£3.00
Reverbstorm 3 Coulthart art	£3.00
Reverbstorm 4 (May 1995) Coulthart art	£3.50

LOST WORLD COMICS
Cartoon Art; 1 1950
| 1 84pgs; Ficton House reprints | £4.00 |

LOT-O'-FUN
James Henderson/Amalgamated; 1 17th Mar 1906-1196 16th Feb 1929 (joins Crackers)
17 Mar 1906 8pgs; Pip Martin, George Davey art	£60.00
1906	£15.00
1907-1909 incl. H. O'Neil art	£10.00
1910-1919 incl. Desperate Desmond American reprints, Walter Booth, Don Newhouse art	£6.00
1920-1929 incl. Julius Baker, Bertie Brown, Roy Wilson, Vincent Daniel art	£5.00
CHRONOLOGY
13 Mar 1920: 1st Amalgamated issue. 1922: pages increased to 12. 7th Feb 1925: 1st colour rear cover.

LOVE AFFAIR
Miller; 1-3 1950s
| 1-3 68pgs; Fawcett (?) reprints | £1.50 |

LOVE ROMANCE
Amalgamated Press; 1-2 May 1950
| 1-2 28pgs | £1.00 |

LOVE STORY OF CHARLES AND DIANA
IPC; nn Jul 1982
| nn - 40pgs | £1.00 |

LOVE STORY PICTURE LIBRARY
Amalgamated Press/Fleetway/IPC; 1 Aug 1952-?
| 1 68pgs pocket size; Dancing Heart | £1.00 |
| 2-? | £0.50 |

LOVE STORY PICTURE LIBRARY HOLIDAY SPECIAL
IPC; 1972-?
| 1972-? 224pgs; reprints | £0.50 |

LOVERS
Miller; 1-12 1956
| 1-12 28pgs; Marvel reprints | £1.50 |

LUCIFER
Trident; 1 Jul 1990-3 Sep 1990
| 1 Lucifer by Eddie Campbell & Paul Grist begins | £1.25 |
| 2-3 | £1.10 |

LUCK IN THE HEAD, THE
Gollancz; nn Sep 1991
| nn - (hardback) M. John Harrison & Ian Miller | £15.00 |
| nn - (paperback) | £9.00 |

LUCKY CHARM
D.C. Thomson; 1 Oct 1979-20 Jun 1984
| 1 68pgs; Valda reprints from Mandy | £0.75 |
| 2-20 | £0.35 |

LUCKY COMIC, THE
Martin & Reid; nn 1948
| nn - 8pgs; Edward Banger art | £2.50 |

LUCKY DICE COMIC
Funnibook Co.; 1 1946
| 1 8pgs; Dennis Reader art | £5.00 |

LUCKY DIP
Children's Press; nn Apr 1948
| nn - 12pgs; C.M.Montford, Denis Gifford art | £3.00 |

LUCKY DIP COMIC
Philmar; nn 1948
| nn - 8pgs; Jack Pamby, Wally Robertson art | £3.00 |

LUCKY LUKE
Hodder & Stoughton; 1972-1985
Jesse James (1972) Rene Goscinny & Morris European reprints begin	£5.00
The Stage Coach (1972)	£5.00
Dalton City (1973)	£5.00
The Tenderfoot (1974)	£5.00
Western Circus (1974)	£5.00
Apache Canyon (1974)	£5.00
Ma Dalton (1980)	£4.00
The Dashing White Cowboy (1982)	£3.00
Curing the Daltons (1985)	£3.00

M

	N.MINT

MACABRE STORIES
John Spencer; 1-6? 1967?
| 1-6 ? | £1.50 |

MAD MAGAZINE
Thorpe & Porter/Suron Enterprises/Fleetway; 1 Oct 1959-381 Jan 1994
1 32pgs; classic satire magazine begins featuring Alfred E. Neuman character on cover;	
reprints material beginning from about issue #22 or 23 of the American edition	£100.00
2	£50.00
3-5	£30.00
6-9	£15.00
10 2/- cover price begins	£15.00
11-20	£10.00
21-50	£5.00
51-100	£2.50
101-200	£2.00
201-300	£1.50
301-381	£1.50

MAGGIE'S FARM
Penguin; 1981-1982
| Maggie's Farm 96pgs oblong; Steve Bell reprints from Time Out | £1.00 |
| Further Down on Maggie's Farm | £1.00 |

MAGIC
D.C. Thomson; 1 31st Jan 1976-161 24th Feb 1979 (joins Twinkle)
| 1 Bob Dewar art | £2.00 |
| 2-161 | £0.50 |

MAGIC COMIC
Martin & Reid; nn 1948
| nn - 8pgs; Frank Minnitt, Wally Robertson art | £4.00 |

MAGIC COMIC, THE
D.C. Thomson; 1 22nd Jul 1939-80 25th Jan 1941
1 Koko the Pup by E.H. Banger, Dolly Dimple by Allan Morley, Peter Piper by Dudley Watkins	£350.00
1 facsimile	£2.50
2	£175.00
3-10	£85.00
11-30	£45.00
31-47,49-60,62-70,72-80	£22.50
48 Dirty Dick by Morley begins	£22.50
61 Gulliver by Watkins begins	£22.50
71 Bandy Legs by Roland Davies begins	£22.50
ARTISTS/FEATURES
Roland Davies in 71-80. Allan Morley in 1-80. Dudley D. Watkins in 1-80.

MAGIC FUN BOOK
D.C. Thomson; Sep 1939-Sep 1940 (joined Magic Beano Book)
| 1940 (Koko leading other characters skating across icy pond), very scarce | £800.00 |
| 1941 (Koko doing strongman act with Tootsy McTurk on his shoulders), very scarce | £700.00 |

MAGIC MOMENT ROMANCES
(see Heart To Heart, Twin Hearts)
K.G. Murray Ltd; 1 1958-?
1 very rare 100pgs, squarebound begins; b/w romance reprints from National Periodical	
Publications; priced at 2 shillings and sixpence	£75.00
2-?	**£40.00**
Note: very little information available at time of going to press

MAGIC WHEEL, THE
ROSPA; nn 1949
| nn - 8pgs; Bob Wilkin art; promo for Royal Society for the Prevention of Accidents | £1.50 |

MAGNO COMIC
International; nn 1946
| nn - 20pgs; Paddy Brennan art | £6.00 |

MAKABRE
Apocalypse (Apocalypse Presents); nn Oct 1991
| nn - Toxic reprints, Alcatena art | £1.50 |

MAN ELF
(see The Saga of the Man Elf)

MAN FROM U.N.C.L.E. ALL COLOUR COMIC ALBUM, THE
World Distributors; 1 1966
| 1 softcover | £5.00 |

MAN FROM U.N.C.L.E. ANNUAL, THE
World Distributors; 1966-1969
| 1966 | £5.00 |
| 1967,1969 | £4.00 |

MAN FROM U.N.C.L.E. TELEVISION STORYBOOK, THE
PBS; 1967-1968
| 1967,1968 | £5.00 |

MAN FROM U.N.C.L.E. WORLD ADVENTURE LIBRARY, THE
World Distributors; 1-14 1966
| 1-4 US reprints | £2.50 |
| 5-14 UK originals by Mick Anglo, etc | £5.00 |

MANS WORLD COMIC LIBRARY
(see Speed Kings, Strange Worlds, Super Sonic, Thrilling Hero, True Life Adventures)

MANDRAKE THE MAGICIAN
(see also Action Series)
Miller; 1 1961-24 1962
| 1 68pgs; reprints American newspaper strip by Lee Falk & Phil Davis | £3.00 |
| 2-24 | £1.50 |

MANDRAKE THE MAGICIAN WORLD ADVENTURE LIBRARY
World Distributors; 1 Jan 1967-8 Aug 1967
| 1 68pgs pocket size; Aftermath, reprints American newspaper strip by Lee Falk & Phil Davis | £2.50 |
| 2-8 | £1.50 |

MANDY
D.C. Thomson; 1 21st Jan 1967-1991 (becomes Mandy & Judy)
| 1 George Parlett art | £1.00 |
| 2-? incl. Dudley Wynn, Robert MacGillivray art | £0.20 |

N.MINT

CHRONOLOGY	
22 Jan 1983: 1st "Mandy & Debbie".	
MANDY AND JUDY	
D.C. Thomson; 1 1991-present (241 issues to 30th Dec 1995)	
1	£1.00
2-241	£0.15
MANDY MOPS AND CUBBY	
Sampson Low Marston; 1952-1955	
Mandy Mops and Cubby Find a House (1952) Enid Blyton story	£1.25
Mandy Mops and Cubby Again (1952)	£1.25
Mandy Makes Cubby a Hat (1953)	£1.25
Mandy Mops and Cubby and the Whitewash (1955)	£1.25
MANDY PICTURE STORY LIBRARY/ MANDY AND JUDY PICTURE STORY LIBRARY	
D.C. Thomson; 1 Apr 1978-present (231 to Dec 1995)	
1 68pgs pocket size; Driving Into Danger	£0.80
2-231	£0.15
MANGA HEROES	
Manga Publishing; 1 Feb 1995-4 May 1995	
1 Timecop, reprints Dark Horse movie adaptation	£2.00
2-3 Appleseed; reprints Book 2 by Masamune Shirow	£2.00
4 GenoCyber; manga reprint by Tony Takezaki	£2.00
MANGA MANIA	
Dark Horse/Manga Publishing; v1:1 Jul 1993-present (29 to Dec 1995)	
v1:1 Godzilla, Akira, Appleseed reprints begin	£2.25
v1:2-8,10	£2.00
v1:9 Dirty Pair, Demon reprints begin	£2.00
v1:11 1st Manga Entertainment issue; with free Skyblazer Comic	£2.00
v1:12 Dominion by Masamune Shirow reprints begin	£2.00
v1:13,15	£2.00
v1:14 Hellhounds by Maroru Oshi & Kamui Fujiwara reprints begin	£2.00
16 New Look; Bubblegum Crisis by Adam Warren reprints begin	£2.00
17-19,21,23-24	£2.00
20 Silent Mobius by Kia Asamiya reprints begin	£2.00
22 Firetripper by Rumiko Takahashi reprints begin	£2.00
25 1st larger size; Free Dirty Pair poster mag; Dirty Pair by Adam Warren reprints begin	£3.00
25 without poster mag	£1.25
26-28	£2.50
29 Appleseed: Side Story reprints begin	£2.50
MANHUNT	
Streamline; 1-4 1951	
1-4 36pgs; reprints Secret Agent X9 from American newspaper, cited in UK horror campaign	£10.00
MANHUNT	
World Distributors; 1-6 1959	
1-6 28pgs; reprints Secret Agent X9 from American newspaper	£6.00
MANHUNTER	
Miller; 50 1950s	
50 28pgs; reprints American comic	£4.00
MARILYN	
Amalgamated Press; 1 19th Mar 1955-547 18th Sep 1965 (joins Valentine)	
1	£1.00
2-547	£0.35
MARINES IN ACTION	
Streamline; nn 1955	
nn - 28pgs; Atlas reprints	£2.50
MARINES IN BATTLE	
Streamline; nn 1955	
nn - 28pgs; Atlas reprints	£2.50
MARK CONWAY	
Miller; 1 1959	
1 68pgs pocket size; Murder by Phone by Paul Trevillion	£3.00
MARK OF MANDRAGORA, THE	
Virgin; nn May 1993	
nn - reprints Dr Who from Dr Who Magazine, Ranson art	£7.00
MARK TYME	
John Spencer; 1-2 1967	
1-2 Michael Jay art	£1.00
MARKED FOR MURDER	
Top Sellers; 1-3 1960s	
1 52pgs; One Body Too Many, foreign reprints	£1.00
2 The Rat	£0.75
3	£0.75
MARMADUKE	
Brockhampton Press; 1962-1964	
Marmaduke's Great Day (1962) 36pgs oblong; Elizabeth Chapman art	£1.00
A Week With Marmaduke (1964) Elizabeth Chapman art	£1.00
MARRIED BLISS	
Martin & Reid (Humerous Cartoon Series); 1 1946	
1 12pgs; Styx art	£2.00
MARS COMICS	
Streamline; nn 1950	
nn - 28pgs; reprints Planet Comics from Fiction House	£8.00
MARSHAL LAW	
Apocalypse; 1 Nov 1990, nn Mar 1991	
1 48pgs; Kingdom of the Blind by Pat Mills & Kev O'Neill	£1.50
nn - 48pgs; Marshal Law Takes Manhattan	£1.50
Note: Available in U.K. and American size	
MARSMAN COMICS	
Cartoon Art; 1 Dec 1948	
1 20pgs; Powerman by Dennis Reader, Marsman by Paddy Brennan	£10.00
MARTIAL AWE	
John W. Fisher; nn 1946	

Magic Comic #1

Mandy #1

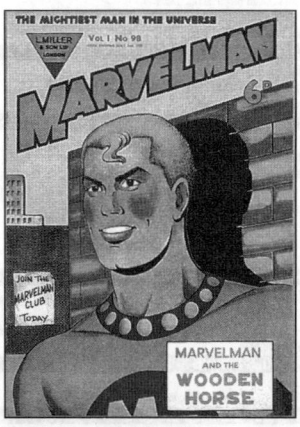

Marvelman #98

	N.MINT
nn - 16pgs; W.Forshaw art	£2.50

MARVEL ACTION
Marvel; 1 1st Apr 1981-15 8th Jul 1981 (joins Captain America)

1 Thor, Dr. Strange, Fantastic Four reprints begin	£1.50
1 with free gift (Fantastic Four Super-Hero sticker)	£3.00
2	£1.00
2 with free gift (Thor Super-Hero sticker)	£2.00
3	£0.75
3 with free gift (Dr Strange Super-Hero sticker)	£1.50
4-15	£0.60

MARVEL ANNUAL
Fleetway/World Distributors; 1972-1975,1978

1973 128pgs; reprints Hulk #2,5, Conan #5, Spider-Man #2,20 Secrets of Spider-Man (Ann #1), FF #7,	£6.00
1974 128pgs; origins of Daredevil (#1), Hulk (#1), and Giant Man, reprints Spider-Man #8, Fantastic Four #12	£5.00
1975 80pgs; 1st World Distributors; reprints Hulk #164-166, Tales To Astonish #93, Silver Surfer	£4.00
1976 64pgs; reprints Hulk (MTU #27), Hulk/Surfer/Namor (Submariner #34-35)	£4.00
1978 64pgs; reprints Daredevil/Black Panther team-up	£3.50

MARVEL CLASSICS COMICS
Marvel; 1 Oct 1981-12 Mar 1982

1-12 52pgs; Marvel reprints	£0.75

MARVEL COMIC
(previously Mighty World of Marvel)
Marvel; 330 24th Jan 1979-352 25th Jul 1979
(joins Spider-Man, see also Marvel Super Heroes)

330 X-Men reprints	£1.25
331-352	£0.75

MARVEL COMIC ANNUAL
World Distributors; 1969-1971

1969 scarce; reprints Journey Into Mystery #98, Hulk #4, Spider-Man #27, plus GA Captain America and Sub-Mariner	£7.50
1970 reprints Journey Into Mystery #105, Hulk #4, Spider-Man #23, plus Captain America, Sub-Mariner, Thor, Iron Man	£6.00
1971 reprints Thor #165, Captain America #100, TOS #98-99, plus Inhumans, Hulk (from Tales to Astonish)	£6.00

MARVEL FAMILY, THE
Miller; nn (3 issues) 1949; 50 1950-89 1953 (30 issues)

nn-nn 16pgs 2-tone gravure	£12.00
50-70 32pgs 2-tone gravure	£8.00
71-89 28pgs smaller size	£6.00

MARVEL MADHOUSE
Marvel; 1 Jun 1981-17 Oct 1982

1 36pgs	£1.00
2-17 Dicky Howett art	£0.40

MARVEL STORYBOOK ANNUAL
World Distributors; 1968

1968 scarce; text stories featuring Captain America, Spider-Man, Thor, Hulk, Sub-Mariner, Iron Man, Ant Man, Doctor Strange and Fantastic Four by Enefer, Tyson, Elliott	£5.00

MARVEL SUPER ADVENTURE
Marvel; 1 6th May 1981-26 28th Oct 1981 (joins Captain America)

1 32pgs; Daredevil (from DD #42), Black Panther (Kirby art) reprints begin	£1.50
1 with free gift (Daredevil iron-on transfer)	£3.00
2-7,9-26	£0.75
8 reprints Daredevil #53 (origin retold)	£1.00

MARVEL SUPER ADVENTURE WINTER SPECIAL
Marvel; nn Dec 1980

nn - 52pgs; reprints featuring The Defenders (origin retold), Iron Fist and GA Sub-Mariner; b/w	£1.25

MARVEL SUPER HEROES
(previously Marvel Comic)
Marvel 353 Sep 1979-397 May 1983 (joins Daredevil)

353-372 52pgs; X-Men, Ms Marvel, Avengers reprints begin	£1.50
373 1st new look issue	£1.50
374-376	£1.25
377 1st new look Captain Britain by Alan Davis	£7.50
378-386 Davis art	£5.00
387-388 1st Alan Moore Captain Britain script, Davis art	£6.00
389-397	£3.00
Note: some issues have Alan Moore Night Raven text stories	

MARVEL SUPER HEROES AND THE OCCULT
Marvel; nn Nov 1980

nn - 64pgs; reprints featuring Human Torch, Dr. Doom, Iron Man, Dr. Strange; b/w with 6pgs colour	£1.00

MARVEL SUPERHEROES ANNUAL
(see also The Superheroes Annual)
Marvel/Granddreams; 1980,1990-1992

1980 64pgs; reprints X-Men #1, Ms Marvel #5, Avengers #157; colour	£4.00
1990 Marvel; 96pgs; reprints Spider-Man & His Amazing Friends #1, FF #232, X-Men, Hulk #340; McFarlane, Byrne art	£3.50
1991 64pgs; reprints Hulk #314, Spider-Man vs Dr. Octopus; Breyfogle art	£3.00
1992 64pgs; reprints Iron Man, FF, X-Men stories	£3.00
1993 64pgs; reprints X-Men, She Hulk, DD, Iron Man stories	£3.00

MARVEL SUPERHEROES OMNIBUS
Marvel; 1986-1987

1986 Spider-Man, Iron Man, Hulk, Captain America, X-Men reprints	£3.00
1987 Amazing Spider-Man 282, Iron Man 217, Incredible Hulk 314, Captain America 291, Uncanny X-Men 213 reprints	£3.50

MARVEL SUPER HEROES SPRING SPECIAL
Marvel; nn Feb 1994

nn - 32pgs; Iron Man, Thing, Black Widow, Daredevil reprints; colour	£1.25

MARVEL SUPER HEROES SUMMER SPECIAL
Marvel; nn May 1979

	N.MINT
nn - 52pgs; reprints from Fantastic Four, Silver Surfer, Dr. Strange; b/w	£1.25

MARVEL TALES
Miller; 1-2 1959

1-2 68pgs; Atlas reprints	£4.00

MARVEL TEAM-UP
Marvel; 1 11th Sep 1980-25 4th Mar 1981 (joins Spider-Man)

1 32pgs; Spider-Man & Daredevil, Ms. Marvel, Morbius the Living Vampire, Fantastic Four reprints begin	£1.25
1 with free gift (Spider-Man & Daredevil Super-Hero stickers)	£2.50
2	£1.00
2 with free gift (Ms. Marvel & Spider-Man Super-Hero stickers)	£2.00
3	£0.75
3 with free gift (Fantastic Four Super-Hero stickers)	£1.50
4-25	£0.60

MARVEL TEAM-UP WINTER SPECIAL
Marvel; nn Nov 1980

nn - 52pgs; reprints featuring Fantastic Four, Red Sonja, Storm/Black Panther; b/w	£1.25

MARVELMAN
(previously Captain Marvel)
Miller; 25 3rd Feb 1954-370 Feb 1963 (346 issues)

25 Marvelman by Mick Anglo & Roy Parker begins	£25.00
26-30	£12.50
31 1st James Bleach Marvelman	£7.50
32 1st Don Lawrence Marvelman	£15.00
33-50	£6.00
51-100	£5.00
101,103-335	£3.00
102 Kid Marvelman by Don Lawrence begins	£3.00
336-370 monthly issues, mostly reprints	£2.50

MARVELMAN ANNUAL
Miller; 1954-1961, 1963

1954 softcover, rare; Marvelman standing on cover	£50.00
1955 softcover, very rare; Marvelman flying on cover	£75.00
1956	£30.00
1957-1960 hardback	£20.00
1961 title becomes Marvelman Adventures; card cover, Marvelman appears with Captain Marvel's face and cape	£15.00
1963 scarce, card cover	£25.00

MARVELMAN FAMILY
Miller; 1 Oct 1956-30 Nov 1959

1 Marvelman Family by Don Lawrence, Marvelman by Kurt (James Bleach), Young Marvelman by Leo Rawlings begin	£15.00
2-11	£7.50
12 1st George Parlett Young Marvelman	£6.50
13 1st Norman Light Marvelman	£5.50
14 1st Arthur Whitworth Marvelman	£5.50
15 1st Bill Merrill reprint by Ron Embleton	£5.50
16-30	£4.50

MARVELMAN FAMILY ANNUAL
Miller; 1963

1963 scarce	£30.00

MARVELMAN JR., ANNUAL
(see also Young Marvelman Annual)
Miller; 1963

1963 scarce, features Young Marvelman	£27.50

MARVELMAN SPECIAL
Quality; 1 May 1984

1 reprints Anglo Marvelman with new framing sequence by Alan Moore & Alan Davis, Big Ben by Ian Gibson	£1.75

MARY MARVEL
Miller; nn 1947?

nn - 16pgs gravure; Fawcett reprints	£10.00

MARY MOUSE
Brockhampton Press; 1942-1964 (22 titles)

(Mary Mouse and the Doll's House, More Adventures of Mary Mouse, Little Mary Mouse Again, Hallo Little Mary Mouse, Mary Mouse and Her Family, Here Comes Mary Mouse Again, How Do You Do Mary Mouse, Hurrah for Mary Mouse, We Do Love Mary Mouse, Welcome Mary Mouse, A Prize for Mary Mouse, Mary Mouse and Her Bicycle, Mary Mouse and the Noah's Ark, Mary Mouse to the Rescue, Mary Mouse in Nursey Rhymme Land, A Day with Mary Mouse, Mary Mouse and the Garden Party, Mary Mouse Goes to the Fair, Mary Mouse has a Wonderful Idea, Mary Mouse Goes to the Sea, Fun With Mary Mouse, Mary Mouse and the Little Donkey)	
nn all by Enid Blyton & Olive Openshaw 36pgs oblong (each)	£1.00

MASK, THE
various; 1994

The Mask (Titan) UK distribution of Dark Horse GN	£9.00
The Mask Returns (Titan) UK distribution of Dark Horse GN	£8.00
The Mask: Official Movie Adaptation (Boxtree) reprints Dark Horse series	£7.00

MASKED RAIDER
World Distributors; 1-4 1955

1-4 28pgs; Charlton Comics reprints	£5.00

MASKED RAIDER
Miller; 50 1957-66 1958

50 28pgs; Charlton Comics reprints	£5.00
51-66	£3.00

MASKED RIDERS OF THE RANGE
Cartoon Art; nn 1952

nn - 20pgs; Magazine Enterprises reprints	£5.00

MASTER BUNNY
Brockhapton Press; 1951-1954

Master Bunny the Baker's Boy (1951) by Alison Winn & Molly Brett; 36pgs oblong	£0.75
Master Bunny at the Seaside (1952)	£0.75
Master Bunny Has a Birthday (1954)	£0.75

	N.MINT		N.MINT

MASTER COMICS
Miller; 1945-1958 (95 issues)
nn,nn,**49,55** (1945) 16pgs 2-tone gravure; Fawcett reprints — £10.00
nn (1946) 36pgs larger size — £6.00
50-140 (1950-1958) 28pgs — £3.50

MASTERMAN COMIC
Streamline; 1 Nov 1952-Aug 1953 (10 issues, mostly unnumbered)
1 28pgs; Masterman by Joe Colquhoun begins — £15.00
Dec 1952-Aug 1953 some incl. reprints from Will Rogers (Fox Publishing),
Real Clue Comics (Hillman) — £7.50

MATT BLACK
Willyprods; 1 1986-6 1987
1 Matt Black, Charcoal by Lionel Gracey-Whitman & Don Melia, black/gay superhero — £2.50
2,4-6 — £1.50
3 1st full size issue — £1.50

MATT SLADE GUNFIGHTER
Strato; 1-5 1957
1-5 68pgs; reprints from Kid Slade Gunfighter (Atlas), All Star Western (National Comics) — £5.00

MAUS
Penguin/Andre Deutsch; 1987, 1992
Maus (Penguin, 1987) 160pgs; art spiegelman story/art US reprints begin — £6.00
Maus II (Andre Deutsch, Mar 1992) 136pgs, hardcover — £14.00
Maus II (Penguin, Mar 1992) — £9.00

MAVERICK ANNUAL
World Distributors; 1961-1962
1961 text stories by Douglas Enefer — £5.00
1962 text stories by Douglas Enefer — £5.00

MAVERICK ANNUAL
Grandreams; 1981
1981 Based on TV series — £3.00

MAVERICK MARSHAL
Miller; 50-52 1959
50-52 28pgs; Charlton Comics reprints — £4.00

MAVERICK TELEVISION STORY BOOK
New Town; 1960-1962
1960-1962 — £4.00

MAX OVERLOAD
Dark Horse; 1 Mar 1994-2 Apr 1994
1 Lemmings by Hanson & Manley, Toejam & Earl by Caulfield & Phoenix, Chuck Rock by Ridout
& Lyttleton, Greendog by Carney & Hillyer all begin, all based on computer games — £1.00
2 — £0.75

MAXWELL THE MAGIC CAT
Acme; 1986-1987
Vol 1 newspaper strip reprints by Alan Moore begin — £2.00
Vol 2 — £2.00
Vol 3 includes illos. by Bolton, Emerson, Gibbons, Gibson, Leach, Talbot — £2.00
Vol 4 includes illos. by Bolland, Elliott, Lloyd, O'Neill, Ridgway, Shelto — £2.00
The Complete Litter 1-4 in cardboard folder — £8.00

MEK MEMOIRS
Kevin O'Neill; 1 1976
1 12pgs; Kevin O'Neill art — £2.00

MELLIFONT WESTERN
(Series of numbered western albums: W1 War-Path. W2 Stampede. W3 Gunsmoke. W4 Outlaws. W5
Apache. W6 Ranch. W7 Branded. W8 Bronco; see individual entries)

MELTDOWN
Marvel; 1 Aug 1991-5 Dec 1991
1 Akira, Nightbreed, Light & Darkness War, The Last American reprints begin — £1.50
2 Cholly & Flytrap reprints begin — £1.25
3-5 — £1.00

MEMORIES
Mandarin; nn Jan 1995
nn - Katsuhiro Otomo manga reprints — £9.00

MENG & ECKER
(See Lord Horror)
Savoy; 1 1989-present (9 to Jul 1995)
1 Meng & Ecker by David Britton & Kris Guido begin, copies siezed in Manchester by
James Anderton, police chief of Greater Manchester — £2.00
2-4 — £1.00
5 incl. transcripts of statements made to police — £1.50
6 incl. transcripts of statements made to police — £1.75
7 (Nov 1993) incl. various reprint reviews & features — £2.00
8 (Nov 1994) — £2.25
9 (Jul 1995) — £3.00

MERLIN AND EXCALIBUR IN QUEST OF THE KING
Marvel; nn Jul 1981
nn - American reprint — £1.00

MERRIDAY COMIC, THE
D. McKenzie; nn 1948
nn - 8pgs — £2.50

MERRY AND BRIGHT
Amalgamated Press; (1) 1 22nd Oct 1910-337 31st Mar 1917;
(2) 1 7th Apr 1917-928 19th Jan 1935 (joins Butterfly)
1 G.M.Payne, Tom Radford art — £45.00
2 — £15.00
3-5 — £12.00
6-337 incl. Bertie Brown, Julius Baker art — £8.00
1 (New Series) titled Merry & Bright the Favorite Comic — £12.00
2-928 incl. Allan Morley, Reg Parlett, Wally Robertson, George Wakefield, Roy Wilson,
Frank Minnitt, B.O.Wymer, C.H.Chapman, Vincent Daniel art — £6.00

MERRY COMIC, THE
Hamilton & Co.; nn 1947
nn - 16pgs; Bob Wilkin art — £3.00

MERRY COMICS
P.M. Productions; nn 1944
nn - 16pgs; Glyn Protheroe art — £3.00

MERRY-GO-ROUND
Martin & Reid; 1 Nov 1946-14 Oct 1949
1 H.E.Pease art — £4.00
2-8,10 incl. Mick Anglo art — £3.00
9,12-13 Frank Minnitt art — £3.00
11 Wally Robertson, Denis Gifford art — £3.00
14 tabloid size; Minnitt art — £3.00

MERRY GO ROUND
Swinnerton's; 1 Nov 1946
1 8pgs — £2.50

MERRY-GO-ROUND
J.B. Allen; 1 27th Sep 1949-4 18th Oct 1949 (joins Eagle)
1 Bill Holroyd, Edward Banger, Serge Drigin art — £6.00
2-4 — £4.00

MERRY-GO-ROUND COMIC
Foldes Modern Printing; nn 1947
nn - 12pgs; Bob Wilkin art — £4.00

MERRY MADCAP COMIC
Philmar; nn 1947
nn - 8pgs; Tony Speer, Ern Shaw art — £3.00

MERRY MAKER
John Matthews; 1 1946-10 1948
1 8pgs; H.E.Pease art — £3.00
2-10 — £2.50

MERRY MAKER COMIC, THE
Algar Printing Co./L.Burn; 1 1946-nn 1947 (11 issues, numbered to 8)
1 8pgs; Walter Booth art — £3.00
2-3 Stanley White, Basil Reynolds art — £3.00
4-8 larger size; incl. Reynolds art — £3.00
(9-11) (L.Burn) unnumbered, 9 Christmas number, 10 printed green/black, 11 printed red/blue — £2.50

MERRY MARVEL COMIC
Philmar; nn Jan 1947
nn - 8pgs; Tony Speer, Denis Gifford art — £4.00

MERRY MASCOT
John Matthew; 1-2 1947
1-2 8pgs; H.E.Pease art — £3.00

MERRY MAYPOLE COMIC
P.M. Productions; nn 1949
nn - 8pgs; Walter Bell, Frank Minnitt art — £3.00

MERRY MIDGET
Provincial Comics; 1 12th Sep 1931-20 23rd Jan 1932
1 Bert Hill art — £7.00
2-20 — £3.50

MERRY MINIATURES
Home Publicity; 1937-1939
Note: smallest comic known, 1.5x2.75"; undated, unnumbered giveaways released in three
formats a) 12pgs full colour, (b) 8pgs, (c) larger size 5x2.5", printed blue/orange.
Features characters from newspaper strips and comics including The Bruin Boys by
Herbert Foxwell, The Arkubs by J.F.Horrabin, Nipper by Brian White, Pip Squeak
& Wilfred by A.B.Payne and Popeye reprints by Seger. (each) — £6.00

MERRY MIRTHQUAKE COMIC, THE
Philmar; nn 1949
nn - 8pgs; Wally Robertson, Frank Minnitt art — £3.00

MERRY MOMENTS
George Newnes; 1 12th Apr 1919-194 23rd Dec 1922
1 8pgs tabloid — £25.00
2 — £10.00
3-5 — £7.50
2-194 — £5.00
CHRONOLOGY
*1921: given away as a supplement, The Children's Tit-Bits for 18 months. 18th Feb 1922: increased to
10pgs. 16th Dec 1922: reverts to 8pgs.*

MERRY MOMENTS
C.A. Ransom; 1 17th Sep 1928-20 20th Apr 1929
1 8pgs tabloid; reprints from The Golden Penny Comic begin — £25.00
2 — £10.00
3-5 — £7.50
2-28 — £5.00

MERRY MOMENTS
Martin & Reid; nn Feb 1946; 1-4 1948
nn - 8pgs; H.E. Pease art — £3.00
1-4 8pgs; incl. Frank Minnitt, Wally Robertson art — £2.50

MERRY PLAY
P.M. Productions; nn 1949
nn - 8pgs tabloid; Walter Bell, Frank Minnitt, Wally Robertson, Denis Gifford art — £3.50

MERRY PLAY COMIC
Philmar; nn Sep 1947
nn - 8pgs; Tony Speer, Walter Bell art — £2.50

MERRY TALES
Top Sellers; 1-4 1970 (becomes Pellephant and his Friends)
1-4 36pgs; foreign reprints from Pellephant — £0.50

MERRYMAKER, THE
National Sport Publications; nn 1947
nn - 12pgs — £2.00

METAL MEN ANNUAL
(see Brave & Bold Annual, Green Lantern Annual)
Thorpe & Porter; 1967
1967 bound together remaindered copies of selected DC comics incl. Metal Men #20, 25,
Superman #190, Batman #181, Tomahawk 108, Bob Hope #104 — £25.00

N.MINT   **N.MINT**

METEOR, THE
Children's Press; nn 1948

nn - 20pgs; Sam Fair, Alf Farningham art	£3.00

METEOR, THE
Paget Publications; 1-5 1948; 1 1948

1-5 8pgs; incl. Edward Banger art	£3.00
1 larger size	£4.00

MICK MARTIN
Martin & Reid; 1 1949

1 8pgs tabloid; Paddy Brennan art	£7.50

MICKEY MOUSE HOLIDAY SPECIAL
Willbank; 1936-1938 (3 issues)

1936 64pgs; Basil Reynolds, Reg Carter art	£50.00
1937-1938 Reg Perrott, Basil Reynolds art	£40.00

MICKEY MOUSE SPECIALS
IPC; May 1976-Jun 1980 (10 issues)

Fun Time Extra 1976,1977,1978,1979	£0.60
Holiday Special 1976,1977,1978	£0.60
Summer Special 1979,1980	£0.60
Fun Time Holiday Special 1980	£0.60

MICKEY MOUSE WEEKLY
Willbank/Odhams; (1) 8th Feb 1936-(920) 28th Dec 1957 (numbered inside only; splits into two comics, Zip and Walt Disney's Mickey Mouse)

1	£150.00
2	£100.00
3-5	£75.00
6-10	£50.00
11-47	£25.00
1937-1939 issues	£15.00
1940-1945 issues	£7.50
1946-1950 issues	£5.00
1951-1953 issues	£2.50
1954-1957 issues	£2.00

CHRONOLOGY
25 May 1940: page count reduced to 8. 5 Jul 1940: page size reduced. 13 Sep 1940: title shortened to Mickey Mouse, publication reduced to fortnightly. 11 Apr 1942: size reduced again. 25 Dec 1948: size enlarged. 3 Sep 1949: page count increased to 12. 4 Mar 1950: title retuned to Mickey Mouse Weekly, weeklypublication resumed. 21 Oct 1950: size increases. 1 Oct 1955: title changed to Walt Disney's Mickey's Weekly.

ARTISTS/FEATURES
Frank Bellamy in 25 Jul 1953-26 Jun 1954 (Monty Carstairs), plus occasional Walt Disney's Living World. Ron Embleton in various (Roger's Rangers, Strongbow the Mighty). James Holdaway (Davy Crockett). Reg Perrott in various (Road to Rome, White Cloud, Song of the Sword, Sir Roger de Coverlet, White King of Arabia). Tony Weare in various (Pride of the Circus, Billy Brave, Savage Splendour, Robin Alone).

MICKEY MOUSE ANNUAL
Dean & Son; 1931-1965

1931	£200.00
1932	£125.00
1933	£100.00
1934-1940	£75.00
1941-1943	£50.00
1946-1949	£25.00
1950-1959	£12.50
1960-1965	£7.50

MICKEY MOUSE XMAS SPECIAL
Willbank; nn 1939

nn - 72pgs, Basil Reynolds, Alan Philpott, reprint art	£75.00

MIDGET, THE
Provincial Comics; 1 5th Jun 1931-13 5th Sep 1931 (becomes The Merry Midget)

1 12pgs edition; Jack Long art	£5.00
1 8pgs edition	£5.00
2-13 12pgs	£3.50
2-13 8pgs	£2.50

Note: issued in two formats, 12pgs and 8pgs

MIDGET COMIC, THE
D.C. Thomson; 23rd Aug 1930-13th Sep 1930 (4 issues)

23 Aug-13 Sep 1930 32pgs pocket; Allan Morley, Chick Gordon art	£5.00

Note: giveaway with The Wizard

MIDGET COMIC, THE
D.C. Thomson; 21st Aug 1937

21 Aug 1937 36pgs pocket size; giveaway with Red Letter, Allan Morley art	£5.00

MIDGET COMIC, THE
R. & L. Locker; nn 1946

nn - 8pgs; R. Beaumont art	£3.00

MIDGET COMICS
P.M. Productions; nn 1944

nn - 8pgs; Glyn Protheroe art	£2.50

MIDNIGHT SURFER SPECIAL
(see also Strontium Dog Special)
Quality; 2 1986

2 2000AD reprints, Cam Kennedy art	£1.50

MIGHTY ATOM, THE
Denlee Publishing Co. (S.D.Frances); nn 1948

nn - 16pgs; Philip Mendoza art	£15.00

MIGHTY COMIC
Philipp Marx; nn 1945

nn - 16pgs; Glynn Protheroe art	£2.50

MIGHTY COMIC
(see All Favourites)
K.G. Murray Ltd; 1 late 1950s-41? early 1960s

1 rare 100pgs, squarebound begin; b/w reprints from National Periodical Publications incl. Tomahawk, Congo Bill, Wonder Woman, Mr. District Attorney, Robin Hood,	

Viking Prince (later issues features Justice League of America, Eclipso, Mark Merlin, Adam Strange among others); priced at 2 shillings   £75.00

2 rare	£50.00
3-5 very scarce	£40.00
6-10 scarce	£35.00
11-41? scarce	£30.00

Note: more issues thought to exist

MIGHTY COMIC ANNUAL
Gerald Swan; nn 1952

nn - rebound remainders of Swan comics in new cover	£6.00

MIGHTY MIDGET
Polystyle; 1 18th Sep 1976-2 25th Sep 1976

1 16pgs; Dr Who	£7.50
2 16pgs; Star Trek	£5.00

Note: published as supplements to TV Comic

MIGHTY THOR, THE
Marvel; 1 20th Apr 1983-39 11th Jan 1984; joins Spiderman

1 Thor reprints begin	£1.25
1 with free gift (red plastic spinner)	£3.00
2	£1.00
2 with free gift (Thor sticker)	£2.00
3,5-19	£0.75
4 John Higgins cover	£1.00
20 1st "Mighty Thor & Original X-Men"	£1.00
21-39	£0.75

MIGHTY WARRIORS ANNUAL
(World?); 1978

1979 Dr. Solar, Dagar, Magnus reprints from Gold Key	£5.00

MIGHTY WORLD OF MARVEL, THE
Marvel; 1 7th Oct 1972-329 17th Jan 1979 (becomes Marvel Comic)

1 Hulk, Fantastic Four, Amazing Spider-Man reprints begin	£6.00
1 with free gift (Green-skinned monster T-shirt transfer)	£12.00
2	£2.00
3	£1.50
4-18	£1.25
19 last Spider-Man	£1.25
20 Daredevil reprints begin	£1.25
21-45,47-48,50-66	£1.00
46 Avengers reprints begin	£1.00
49 X-Men reprints begin	£1.00
67 new look	£1.00
68-198	£0.75
199 1st "Mighty World of Marvel & Avengers"	£1.00
200-230,232-257	£0.75
231 1st "Mighty World of Marvel & Planet of the Apes"	£1.00
258 1st "Mighty World of Marvel & Fury"	£0.75
259-297,299-329	£0.60
298 1st "Mighty World of Marvel & Fantastic Four"	£0.75

MIGHTY WORLD OF MARVEL (2ND SERIES)
Marvel; 1 Jun 1983-17 Oct 1984 (joins Savage Sword of Conan)

1 X-Men (ends 6), Vision & Scarlet Witch (ends 4) reprints begin	£5.00
1 with free gift (X-Men Mighty World of Marvel sticker)	£7.50
2-4,6	£3.00
5 Miller Wolverine reprints begin (ends 8)	£3.00
7 1st "Mighty World of Marvel and Daredevils"; Captain Britain by Moore & Davis, Night Raven text by Jamie Delano begin, 1st Showcase	£6.00
8,10 12 Davis art	£3.50
9 Cloak and Dagger reprints begin (ends 12)	£3.00
13 X-Men and Micronauts reprints begin (ends 16), last Moore Captain Britain	£3.00
14,15 1st Davis script/art on Captain Britain	£3.00
16 last Captain Britain, Davis script/art	£2.50
17 Magik reprint, last issue	£1.25

MIGHTY WORLD OF MARVEL ANNUAL
Marvel; 1977-1979

1977 80pgs; reprints Hulk #179, FF #123,166, Man-Thing; colour	£4.50
1978 64pgs; Captain Marvel, Luke Cage reprints, Hulk featured; Daredevil cover by Brodsky/Adams; colour	£4.00
1979 reprints DD Ann #4, DD #140; colour	£3.50

MIGHTY WORLD OF MARVEL SUMMER SPECIAL
Marvel; nn Jun 1983

nn - 48pgs; US reprints of Thor and Hulk, b/w; Garry Leach painted cover and Thor centre-fold poster	£1.25

MIKE BARNETT MAN AGAINST CRIME
Miller; 50-54 1952

50 28pgs; Fawcett reprints	£5.00
51-54	£4.00

MIKE DONOVAN DETECTIVE COMIC
Arnold; 50 1951 (1 issue only)

50 Mike Donovan by Terry (Terrence Patrick)	£5.00

MIKE SHAYNE PRIVATE EYE
Top Sellers; 1962

1 68pgs; Dell reprints	£2.50

MINDBENDERS
(see Freddie's Last Dance, The Last Planet)
MSB Publishing; 1 Apr 1993

1 Pugh, Tiner, Bradbury, Wakelin art	£5.00

MINIATURE COMIC, THE
P.M. Productions; Aug 1944, 2 unnumbered issues

nn - 8pgs; Willie the Chimney Sweep	£2.00
nn 8pgs; Pop the Postman	£2.00

MINOTAUR'S TALE, THE
Victor Gollancz; nn Nov 1992

nn - graphic novel by Al Davison, hardback	£15.00

	N.MINT
nn - paperback	£10.00
MIRACLEMAN	
(see Eclipse Graphic Novels, Marvelman, Marvelman Special, Warrior)	
MIRACLE MAN	
Top Sellers; 1965, 13? issues	
1-13 68pgs; Spanish reprints. Some incl. Blackhawk reprints from US	£1.50
MIRROR MAN COMIC, THE	
Donald F. Peters; 21 1950, 1 issue	
21 20pgs; reprints from Mirror Man and Abbie & Slats	£3.00
MIRTH COMIC, THE	
Philmar; nn 1948	
nn - 8pgs; Jack Pamby art	£3.00
MISTY	
IPC; 4th Feb 1978-12th Jan 1979, 102 issues (joins Tammy)	
4 Feb 1978-12 Jan 1979	£0.35
MOBY DICK	
United Anglo-American; 1951, 2 editions	
nn - 28pgs, 6d; strip based on Herman Melville novel	£3.00
nn - 68pgs, 1/-; same strip with American reprint back-up strips	£4.00
MODERN COMICS	
Modern Fiction; 1 Oct 1949	
1 8pgs; Bob Monkhouse, Jock McCail art	£5.00
MODESTY BLAISE	
Star; 1978	
In the Beginning paperback format newspaper strip reprints by Peter O'Donnell & Jim Holdaway	£2.50
The Black Pearl and The Vikings	£2.00
MODESTY BLAISE	
Titan; 1985-Oct 1990	
The Gabriel Set-Up newspaper strip reprints by O'Donnell & Holdaway begin	£5.00
Mister Sun (Oct 1985)	£4.50
The Hell-Makers (Aug 1986)	£5.00
The War-Lords of Phoenix (Mar 1987) Enrique Romero Modesty Blaise begins	£5.00
Death of a Jester (Jul 1987)	£5.00
The Puppet Master (Oct 1987)	£5.00
The Iron God (Nov 1989)	£5.50
Uncle Happy (Oct 1990) Holdaway art	£5.50
MONOSHOCK	
Savoy; 1 1992	
1 36pgs; Guidio, Coulthart art	£1.50
MONSTER CLUB	
(see Halls of Horror)	
Chips/Pioneer Press; nn 1980	
nn - 32pgs; film promo, John Bolton art, scarce	£6.00
MONSTER COMIC	
Philipp Marx; nn 1945	
nn - 16pgs; Glynn Protheroe art	£2.50
MONSTER COMIC, THE	
C.A. Pearson; Jun-Nov 1939, 2 issues	
nn - 32pgs; issued for summer holiday	£4.00
nn - issued for Xmas; Hugh McNeill art	£4.00
MONSTER FUN COMIC	
IPC; 1 14 Jun 1975-29 Sep 1976 (joins Buster)	
No. 1 - 14 Jun 1975 Kid Kong by Robert Nixon	£1.50
No.1 with free gift (plate wobbler)	£3.00
21 Jun 1975-29 Sep 1976	£1.00
MONSTER FUN COMIC SUMMER SPECIAL	
IPC; nn 1976	
nn - 64pgs	£1.00
MONSTER MASSACRE	
Tundra (Atomeka); Jul-Aug 1993	
Monster Massacre (Jul 1993) Bisley, O'Neill, Braithwaite/Gibbons art	£5.00
Carnosaur Carnage (Aug 1993) Kev Walker, John McCrea art	£3.25
MONSTER MASSACRE	
Blackball Comics; 1 Apr 1994	
1 Bisley, O'Neill, Keith Giffen, James O'Barr art	£2.00
MONSTER OF FRANKENSTEIN	
Arnold Book Co.; 1 1953?-5? 1954	
1 Prize Publications reprints	£10.00
2-3	£6.00
4-5 cited in UK horror campaign	£15.00
MONSTER 1D COMIC, THE	
Fleetway Press/Amalgamated Press; 1 23rd Sep 1932-383 25th Jan 1930 (joins The Joker)	
1 Reg Carter art	£25.00
2	£10.00
3-5	£7.50
6-383 some incl. Felix the Cat reprints, Bert Wymer, Fred Atkins, Frank Minnitt,	
Bertie Brown, Roy Wilson art.	£5.00
CHRONOLOGY	
21 Jan 1928: 1st Amalgamated Press issue.	
MONSTER RUPERT ANNUAL	
Sampson Low; 1931-1934, 1948-1950	
1931 (Rupert and wolf)	£200.00
1932 (Rupert sitting on log)	£180.00
1933 (Rupert and bird)	£180.00
1934 (Rupert and young boy in storeroom)	£180.00
1948 (Rupert sitting on log) dustjacket	£35.00
1949 (Rupert and fox) dustjacket	£35.00
1950 (Rupert assisting young boy out of hole) dustjacket	£35.00
MONTE HALE WESTERN	
Miller; Sep 1950, 1 unnumbered issue; 50 Jun 1951-118 1959	
nn - 16pgs, 2-tone gravure; Fawcett reprints	£10.00
50-118 36pgs/24pgs; monthly series	£5.00

Mickey Mouse Weekly #1

Monster Fun Comic #1

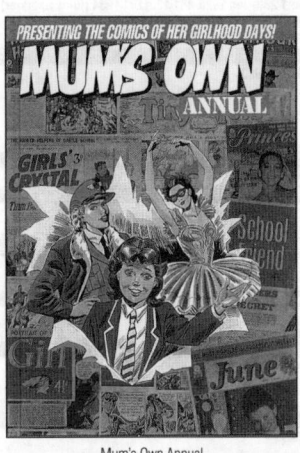

Mum's Own Annual

N.MINT | | N.MINT

MOON COMICS
A. Halle; nn 1948

nn - 8pgs; reprints from Comic Capers — £2.50

MOON COMIX
Birmingham Arts Lab; 1 1977-2 Nov 1977

1 32pgs; Hunt Emerson, David Noon art — £1.00

2 40pgs; Hunt Emerson, David Noon art — £1.00

MORNINGSTAR
Trident; 1 1990

Book One: **Black Dog** Nigel Kitching art — £1.25

MORT
Victor Gollancz; nn Sep 1994

nn - 96pgs; adapts Terry Pratchett novel, Graham Higgins art; hardcover — £13.00

nn - softcover of above — £8.00

MORTAL KOMBAT
Manga Publishing; 1 Sep 1995-present (4 to Dec 1995)

1 Based on Midway Manufacturing game; US comic reprints — £1.00

2-4 — £0.95

MOTION PICTURE COMICS
Miller; 50 Mar 1951-59 1952

50 36pgs; Code of the Silver Sage, Fawcett reprints based on movie — £7.50

51-59 later issues 24pgs — £5.00

MOTORMOUTH
(see Battletide, Killpower: The Early Years, Overkill) (see main American comics section)

MOVIE CLASSICS
World Distributors; 1 1955-88 1960

1 36pgs; Sir Walter Raleigh, Dell reprints — £12.00

2-88 — £6.00

MR DISTRICT ATTORNEY
Thorpe & Porter; 1-23 1953

1 68pgs; National Comics reprints based on TV series — £10.00

2-23 — £5.00

MR PUNCH
Victor Gollancz; nn Oct 1994

nn - 96pgs; by Neil Gaiman & Dave McKean; hardcover — £15.00

nn - softcover — £8.00

MRS WEBER'S DIARY
Fontana; nn 1982

nn - 68pgs oblong; reprints Posy Simmonds newspaper strip from the Guardian — £1.00

MUFFIN THE MULE
(see TV Comic)
Brockhampton; Jun 1952-Jul 1955

Muffin and His Friends (1952) Neville Main art — £2.50

Muffin on Holiday (1953) — £2.00

Muffin Makes Magic (1955) — £2.00

MUMMY, THE
Top Sellers; nn 1963

nn - 68pgs; Dell reprints — £2.00

MUM'S OWN ANNUAL
Fleetway; 1973

1973 — £1.50

Note: non-fiction look at British Girls' comics, but full of factual errors, mis-spelled artist's names etc.

MURDER BAG
C.A. Pearson (TV Picture Stories); 1 Apr 1959-3 Sep 1959

1 The Prison Break Murder by Franchi — £6.00

2-3 — £4.00

ARTISTS/FEATURES
1 The Prison Break Murder by Franchi. 2 Death of Big Foot. 3 The Too Tidy Murder by Cosmoartis.

MURMER
Penguin; nn Jun 1993

nn - 54pgs; European reprint by Jerry Kramsky & Lorenzo Mattotti — £9.00

MUSTANG GREY AND THE TEXAS RANGERS
(see Western Picture Library)

MY FAVOURITE
(previously Comic Life)
Amalgamated Press; 1 28th Jan 1928-351 13th Oct 1934 (joins Sparkler)

28 Jan 1928 George Wakefield, Bertie Brown, Albert Pease art — £35.00

4 Feb 1928-13 Oct 1934 incl. Jack Pamby art — £7.50

MYRA
Myra Hancock; 1 1982-9 1990

1 12pgs; Myra Hancock art begins, hand coloured cover — £1.50

2-3,6 — £0.50

4-5 more scarce — £0.75

7-9 2-colour covers — £1.00

MYS-TECH WARS
(see main American comics section)

MYSTERIES OF SCOTLAND YARD
Cartoon Art; 1 1955

1 28pgs; Magazine Enterprise (A.1 Series) reprints — £5.00

MYSTERIES OF THE UNEXPLORED
G.T. Ltd; nn 1959?

nn - card cover; Embleton, Light, Holdaway reprints — £10.00

MYSTERIES OF UNEXPLORED WORLDS
Miller; 1 1956

1 68pgs; Charlton reprints — £5.00

MYSTERY COMICS
T.V. Boardman; 7 1940-11 1941, 5 issues

7 36pgs; reprints from Smash Comics (Quality) — £6.00

8-11 20pgs — £3.50

MYSTERY IN SPACE
Miller; 1 1952-9 1954

1 28pgs; National Periodicals reprints — £12.50

2-9 — £6.00

MYSTERY IN SPACE
Strato Publications; 1 1954-13 1955

1 68pgs; National Periodicals reprints — £7.50

2-13 — £5.00

MYSTIC
Miller; 1 1961-66 1966

1 68pgs; incl. reprints from Atlas, Marvel, EC etc. — £5.00

2-66 — **£2**.50

N

NAPALM KISS
Birmingham Arts Lab; 1 Oct 1977

1 Mike Matthews art (1,000 copies) — £2.00

NASTY
One Off Comics; nn 1982

nn - 44pgs A5; John Watkiss art — £0.75

NASTY TALES
(see The Trials of Nasty Tales)
Bloom Publications; 1 Apr 1971-7 1972

1 Ogoth by Chris Welch begins — £3.00

2-7 — £2.00

Note: Nasty Tales was taken to court and tried for obscenity, but found Not Guilty

NATURE BOY
Miller; 1-2 1957

1-2 28pgs; Charlton reprints — £2.50

NAUSIATING MYSTERY COMIX
Nausiating Comix Group; 1 1971

1 28pgs; amateur comic, Peter Smith art — £0.75

NAVY PATROL
Streamline; 1 1955

1 68pgs; Key Publications reprints — £2.00

NAVY TASK FORCE
Streamline; 1 1955

1 28pgs; Stanmore Publications reprints — £2.00

NEAR MYTHS
Galaxy Media; 1 Sep 1978-5 Apr 1980

1 Luther Arkwright by Bryan Talbot, Tales From the Edge by Graham Manley begin — £6.00

2 Talbot art, Grant Morrison 1st appearence — £4.00

3 Gideon Stargrave by Grant Morrison begins, Talbot art — £4.00

4 Thiirania by Tony O'Donnell begins, Morrison, Talbot art — £4.00

5 Morrison, Talbot, Hunt Emerson art — £4.00

NECROSCOPE
Boxtree; nn Jul 1994

nn - reprints Malibu adaptation of Brian Lumley novel; Daerick Gross art — £8.00

NEMESIS
Titan (Best of 2000AD); 1984-Aug 1989, 1992

Book One O'Neill art — £5.00

Book Two O'Neill art — £5.00

Book Three Talbot art — £5.00

Book Four Talbot art — £5.00

Book Five Talbot art — £5.00

Book Six O'Neill, Talbot art — £5.00

Book Seven Hicklenton art — £5.00

Book Eight Roach art — £4.50

Book Nine Hicklenton art — £5.50

Nemesis the Beginning (1992) reprints Book One, Book Two — £9.00

NEMESIS THE WARLOCK
Eagle; 1 Sep 1984-7 Mar 1985

1 2000AD reprints, partly redrawn and resized by Kevin O'Neill — £1.50

2-7 — £1.25

NEMESIS POSTER PROG
Fleetway Editions; 1995

1 Poster with story — £1.00

NEW ADVENTURES OF BARBARELLA
Virgin; 1-4 1981

1-4 24pgs; reprints French strip — £2.00

NEW ADVENTURES OF CHARLIE CHAN
C.A. Pearson (TV Picture Stories); 1 Jun 1958-6 May 1959

1 68pgs pocket size — £5.00

2-6 — £3.00

ARTISTS/FEATURES
1 Three Men on a Raft. 2 Dateline Execution. 3 Death Of A Don. 4 The Sweater by Georgio Bellavitis. 5 No Future For Frederick. 6 The Noble Art of Murder.

NEW ADVENTURES OF DON JUAN, THE
Pett; 1 1948

1 20pgs; film adaptation by Norman Pett — £5.00

NEW AVENGERS ANNUAL
(see also Avengers Annual)
Brown Watson; 1977-1978

1977 features New Avengers (Steed, Gambit, Purdie), Bolton art — £4.00

1978 Bolton art — £3.25

NEW COMICS, THE
Philipp Marx; 1942, 2 unnumbered issues

nn - 8pgs tabloid; blue cover, Frank Jupo art — £4.00

nn - blue/green cover — £4.00

NEW FUNNIES
(see also Funnies Budget)
Gerald Swan; 1 Feb 1940-42 Jan 1951

1 68pgs; William Ward art — £15.00

	N.MINT
2-4 68pgs	£10.00
5-14 36pgs	£5.00
15 28pgs	£5.00
16-25 20pgs	£5.00
26-28 16pgs	£5.00
29-38 16pgs; format changes	£5.00
39-42 20pgs	£5.00
Specials:	
Spring, Autumn, Winter (1941) 52pgs	£8.00
Winter (1942) 44pgs	£8.00
Spring, Special (1943) 36pgs	£8.00
Winter (1944)	£8.00
Bumper New Funnies nn (Jun 1950, 36pgs) unsold issues bound in new cover	£10.00

NEW HOTSPUR, THE
(see The Hotspur)	

NEW JUNGLE COMICS
Cartoon Art; nn 1950	
nn - 36pgs; Dennis Reader art	£6.00

NEW STATESMEN
Fleetway; 1 1989-5 Jul 1990	
1,4 54pgs squarebound; Crisis reprints by Smith & Baikie begin	£1.75
2,5 Baikie, Phillips art	£1.75
3 Phillips, Fegrado art	£1.75
The Complete New Statesmen (Fleetway)	£8.00

NEW WORLDS COMIC
Cardal Publishing; 1 1947	
1 8pgs; Crewe Davies art	£4.00

NICK HAZARD
(see JRF Presents)	
Harrier; 1 Jan 1988	
1 Ron Turner art	£0.75

NIGHT FRUITS
Knockabout (Fanny); 1 1994	
1	£2.50

NIGHTMARE
Top Sellers; 1-? 1970s	
1 36pgs; US reprints	£1.00
2-?	£0.75

NIGHTMARE SUSPENSE PICTURE STORIES
M.V. Publications; 1 1966-14? 1967?	
1 68pgs pocket size; March of the Boneless One, foreign reprints	£1.00
2-14	£0.50

NIGHTRAVEN: THE COLLECTED STORIES
Marvel; nn 1990	
nn - Hulk Comic reprints by Jamie Delano, David Lloyd & John Bolton, newly coloured	£4.50

NIGHTRAVEN: HOUSE OF CARDS
Marvel; 1991, 1992	
nn - (1991) large pb format, by Jamie Delano & David Lloyd	£7.00
nn - (1992) prestige format, new Lloyd cover	£3.50
Note: heavily remaindered	

NIGHT VISION
Atomeka; nn 1993	
nn - by David Quinn & Hannibal King, John Bolton cover & poster	£2.50

NIPPER, THE
Brian White; nn Jun 1944	
nn - 20pgs pocket size; Nipper by Brian White	£8.00

NIPPER ANNUAL
Associated Newspapers; undated (1933)-1941 (1940)	
nd (1933) 132pgs; Nipper by Brian White reprints from Daily Mail	£12.00
1935-1939 incl. colour sections	£10.00
1940-1941 smaller size	£8.00

NIPPER CARTOONS: 100 OF THE BEST
B. & H. White; nn Oct 1946	
nn - 36pgs; Nipper reprints by Brian White	£8.00

NIPPER OMNIBUS OF COMIC STRIPS
B. & H. White; nn 1948	
nn - 100pgs; Nipper reprints by Brian White	£8.00

NODDY
Sampson Low; 1952-1953	
Noddy's Car Gets a Squeak stories by Enid Blyton, drawn by Harmsen Van Beek	£5.00
Noddy's Penny Wheel Car	£5.00
Noddy and the Witch's Wand	£5.00
Noddy and the Cuckoo's Nest	£5.00
Noddy Gets Captured	£5.00
Noddy Is Very Silly	£5.00
Noddy the Cry Baby	£5.00
Noddy Goes Dancing	£5.00
Noddy and the Snow House	£5.00

NODDY AND HIS FRIENDS
Hudvale; 9th Mar 1974-30th Apr 1975, 49 issues (joins Noddy Time)	
9 Mar 1974 features characters created by Enid Blyton	£1.00
16 Mar 1974-30 Apr 1975	£0.35

NO HIDING PLACE ANNUAL
World Distributors; 1966	
1966 "The Voice" (1st story)	£3.00

NOSEY PARKER'S HOLIDAY SPECIAL
D.C. Thomson; nn 2nd Jul 1938	
nn - giveaway with Rover, Allan Morley, Chick Gordon reprints	£4.00

NOSEY PARKER'S MIDGET COMIC
D.C. Thomson; nn 21st Dec 1935	
nn - giveaway with Rover, Allan Morley, Chick Gordon reprints	£4.00

	N.MINT
NO. 10	
Beaverbrook; nn 1973	
nn - 76pgs; reprints Peter Maddocks newspaper strip from Sunday Express	£1.00

NOT QUITE DEAD
Knockabout; 1 1994-2 1994	
1 Gilbert Shelton reprints begin	£2.00
2	£2.00

NOW I KNOW
IPCt; 1-26 1972	
1	£2.50
2-26	£1.00
Note: red binder available. A complete bound set would command a higher value.	

NURSE LINDA LARK
Top Sellers; 1 1965	
1 68pgs; Dell reprints	£2.00

NUTTY
D.C. Thomson; 1 16th Feb 1980-14th Sep 1985 (joins Dandy)	
No. 1 - 16 Feb 1980	£1.25
No. 1 with free gift (Space Dust powder sweet)	£3.00
No. 2 - 23 Feb 1980	£0.60
No. 2 with free gift (Zoomarang)	£1.25
No. 3 - 1 Mar 1980	£0.60
No. 3 with free gift (Whirlygig spinning balloon)	£1.25
8 Mar 1980-14 Sep 1985	£0.30

NYOKA THE JUNGLE GIRL
Miller; 1950, 1 unnumbered issue; 50 1951-117 1959	
nn - 16pgs, 2-tone gravure; Fawcett reprints	£8.00
50-117	£5.00

O

OFFICE HOURS (THE DAILY EXPRESS...CARTOONS)
Lane Publications; nn 1931	
nn - 68pgs; reprints newspaper strip by Batchelor	£3.00

OGOTH AND UGLY BOOT
H. Bunch (Cozmic); nn Dec 1973	
nn - 36pgs; Chris Welch art	£1.50

OH BOY! COMICS
(see also Wonderman)	
Paget Publications; 1 1948-24 1951	
1 8pgs; Tornado by Bob Monkhouse begins	£6.00
2-3, 6-7	£4.00
4-5 more common; 5. 1st Mick Anglo Tornado	£3.00
8-15, 21 12pgs	£4.00
16-20 16pgs	£4.00
nn (22) titled Oh Boy! and Wonderman; H. Stanley White Tornado	£4.00
23-24 Ron Embleton Tornado	£8.00

OH! WICKED WANDA
Penthouse; nn Jul 1976	
nn - Ron Embleton Penthouse reprints	£7.50

OINK!
IPC; nn Apr 1986	
nn - prototype issue containing material commissioned for the dummy issue two years earlier	
(Note: not the same issue given away free with 2000 AD several weeks later. That issue was #7)	£2.00
Preview Issue #7 with number/price blanked out. Presented free with various IPC weeklies.	
Cowpat County by Mark Rodgers and Davy Francis; Burp by Banx; Horace (Ugly Face)	
Watkins by Tony Husband; Tom Thug by Lew Stringer all begin	£1.00

OINK!
IPC/Fleetway; 1 3rd May 1986-68 Nov 1988	
No. 1 - 3 May 1986	£1.00
1 with free gift (flexidisc featuring Marc Riley and the Creepers)	£1.50
2	£0.75
3-7	£0.60
8 1st issue "officially" relocated away from the children's section of W.H. Smiths	
(no specific reason given)	£0.60
9-14, 17-24, 27, 29, 30	£0.50
15 Pete and hid Pimple by Lew Stringer; Psycho Gran by David Leach; Greedy Gorb by	
David Francis; Ham Dare by Stringer and Malcolm Douglas all begin	£0.50
16 Frank Sidebottom (by TV star of same name) begins	£0.50
25 parody of comic collectors	£0.50
26 cameo appearances of Robot Archie, Dan Dare, Grimly Feendish and others in Tom Thug strip	£0.50
28 occasional strips by Mike Higgs begin; Superman parody by Mark Rodgers and Ron Tiner	£0.50
31-40	£0.40
41 pull out 8pg Pete and his Pimple comic	£0.40
42, 43, 46-48, 50-61	£0.30
44 last fortnightly issue	£0.30
45 1st weekly issue; reduced from 32pgs to 24pgs	£0.30
49 The Superhero's Day Off by Lew Stringer and Dave Gibbons	£0.30
62 last weekly issue	£0.30
63 1st monthly issue	£0.50
64-67	£0.50
68 final issue; Tom Thug, Pete and His Pimple and Weedy Willy move over to Buster	£0.50

OINK! BOOK
IPC/Fleetway; 1988, 1989	
1988 softcover, 80pgs, rare; W.H. Smith refused to stock it (no specific reason given);	
The Truth About Santa by Lew Stringer and Kev O'Neil	£5.00
1989 softcover, 64pgs	£2.50

OINK! COMPUTER COMIC
IPC; nn 1987	
nn - 16pgs, given away free with CRASH computer magazine featuring characters	
promoting Oink! computer game	£0.25

	N.MINT
OINK! HOLIDAY SPECIAL	
IPC/Fleetway; 1987-1990	
1987 The Game is Greed by Mark Rodgers and Kev O'Neill	£1.50
1988, 1989	£1.00
1990	£0.75
OINK! SMOKEBUSTERS SPECIAL	
IPC; nn 1987	
nn - rare; anti-smoking comic featuring regular characters given away to schools	£1.00
OINK! WINTER SPECIAL	
Fleetway; nn 1989	
nn - softcover, 64pgs	£1.00
OKAY COMIC	
International Publications/ D.R. Burnside; Jan 1947-Apr 1949, 4 unnumbered issues	
nn - (International) 20pgs; John Turner art	£3.00
nn - 16pgs; John Turner art	£3.00
nn - 8pgs; John Turner, Bob Monkhouse art	£3.00
nn - 8pgs tabloid; Paddy Brennan, Denis Gifford art	£5.00
OKAY COMICS WEEKLY	
T.V. Boardman; Vol 1:1 16th Oct 1937-Vol 2:7 26th Feb 1938, 20 issues	
Vol 1:1 reprints of American strips incl. Terry & the Pirates, Tailspin Tommy,	
Joe Palooka, Mutt & Jeff, etc.; Eisner cover	£20.00
Vol 1:2 Eisner cover	£18.00
Vol 1:3-13	£6.00
Vol 2:1-7	£4.00
OKLAHOMA KID	
L. Miller; 1 1957	
1 28pgs; Ajax reprints	£4.00
ON THE LINE	
Kaye & Ward; nn 1969	
nn - 116pgs; George Stokes reprints from Evening News	£1.50
100 JACKLIN GOLFSTRIPS	
Beaverbrook Newspapers; nn 1972	
nn - 88pgs; Larry Horak newspaper strip reprints from Daily Express	£0.75
OOJAH SKETCH, THE	
London Publishing Co.; 8th Oct 1921-23rd Nov 1929, 422 issues	
8 Oct 1921 4pgs; weekly Saturday supplement to the Daily Sketch, titled The Oojah's	
Papers; Uncle Oojah by Thomas Maybank begins	£25.00
15 Oct 1921-22 Apr 1922 4pgs; title becomes The Oojah Sketch	£8.00
29 Apr-15 Jul 1922 reduced to 3pgs	£6.00
22 Jul 1922-23 Nov 1929 reduced to 2pgs, incl. J. Millar Watt art	£4.00
OOR WULLIE	
D.C. Thomson; 1941-present (bi-annual)	
1941 (large pic of Wullie sitting on bucket) Dudley D. Watkins art begins	£300.00
1943 (Wullie stood next to bucket, hands in pockets, satchel over shoulder)	£250.00
1949 (head/shoulders shot of Wullie against red background)	£100.00
1951 (16 different facial expressions)	£75.00
1953 (12 frames featuring Wullie in dunces cap, etc)	£75.00
1955 (Wullie reading copy of "Oor Wullie" with same pic on cover)	£40.00
1957 (Snowman of Wullie sitting on a bucket, cabin in background)	£40.00
1959 (Wullie with paint and brush behind wall with body painted on it)	£25.00
1961 (Wullie eating breakfast made to look like face)	£25.00
1963 (Wullie walking by wall casting policeman shaped shadow)	£20.00
1965 (Wullie on knees polishing bucket)	£20.00
1967-1971 (copyright dated, i.e. cy1966 for 1967)	£10.00
1973-1979	£5.00
1981-1989	£2.50
1991, 1993	£2.50
OOR WULLIE SUMMER FUN SPECIAL	
D.C. Thomson; Jun 1980-present	
1980 36pgs	£2.00
1981-present	£1.00
OPIUM	
Knockabout (Crack); nn 1986	
nn - Daniel Torres European reprints	£5.00
OPTIMIST	
Comic Collective; 1 1976	
1 16pgs tabloid; adult material	£1.00
ORANGE HAND	
Orange Hand; nn 1974	
nn - 6pgs, giveaway, features British original Batman story	£5.00
OREGON TRAIL	
Stafford Pemberton; 1979	
1979 Based on TV series	£3.00
ORIGINAL X-MEN	
Marvel; 1 27th Apr 83-17 23rd May 83 (joins The Mighty Thor)	
1 X-Men reprints from X-Men #1	£2.00
2-17 X-Men reprints	£1.50
ORPHEUS	
Steve Moore; 1 Mar 1971-2 Spr 1973 (continuation of Aspect)	
1 52pgs; Barry Smith, Steve Parkhouse art	£2.00
2 Parkhouse art	£1.00
O.S.S.	
(see TV Photo Stories)	
C.A. Pearson (TV Picture Stories); 1 Jun 1958-9 Nov 1959	
1 68pgs pocket size	£5.00
2-9	£3.00
ARTISTS/FEATURES	
1 Operation Flint Axe. 2 Operation Fracture. 3 Operation Pay Day. 4 Operation Tulip. 5 Operation Sweet	
Talk. 6 Operation Big House. 7 Operation Orange Blossom. 8 Operation Dagger. 9 Operation Love Birds.	
OTHER WORLDS ALBUM	
G.T. Ltd; nn 1959	
nn - card cover	£6.00

	N.MINT
OUT-AND-OUT SMASHER COMIC, THE	
P.J. Press; nn 1947	
nn - 8pgs; H.Cornell, R.Plummer art	£3.00
OUTER LIMITS ANNUAL, THE	
World Distributors; 1966-1967	
1966 scarce, Dell reprints; rocket cover	£10.00
1967 scarce, Dell reprints	£7.50
OUT OF THIS WORLD	
Strato Publications/ Thorpe & Porter; 1 Oct 1951-22 1953	
1 68pgs; reprints various US strips	£25.00
2	£12.50
3	£7.50
4-5	£5.00
6-22 incl. Captain Midnight, Captain Video, etc.	£3.00
OUT OF THIS WORLD	
Alan Class; nn 1960s ; 1 196?- ; 1 197?-	
nn - 68pgs; Charlton reprints	£20.00
1-?	£12.50
1-? 52pgs; Class series	£2.00
OUTER SPACE	
Miller; 1-? 1958	
1-? 68pgs; Charlton reprints	£3.00
OUTER SPACE	
G.T. Ltd; nn 1959?	
nn - card cover	£6.00
OUTER SPACE	
Alan Class; 1-9 1961	
1 68pgs; Charlton reprints	£2.50
2-9	£1.50
OUTLAWS	
(see Blue Bolt Series)	
Streamline; 1955	
nn - 68pgs; various censored reprints, incl. Hoot Gibson (Fox), Kid Colt Outlaw (Marvel), etc.	£6.00
OUTLAWS OF THE WEST	
Miller; 1 1958-7? 195?	
1-7 28pgs; Charlton reprints	£2.50
OUTLAWS PICTURE AND STORY ALBUM	
Mellifont; W4 1950s	
W4 96pgs	£3.00
OUTLAWS WESTERN STORIES	
Streamline; 1-2 1954	
1-2 28pgs; US reprints	£2.50
OUTPOST ADVENTURE COMIC, THE	
Martin & Reid; 1 1950	
1 16pgs; Mick Anglo art	£4.00
OUTRAGEOUS TALES FROM THE OLD TESTAMENT	
Knockabout (Crack); nn Nov 1987	
nn - Moore, Gaiman scripts; Gibbons script & art, Bolland, McKean, Emerson art	£5.00
OVERKILL	
(see Black Axe, Death's Head II (limited, ongoing), Digitek, Hell's Angel, Knights of Pendragon,	
Motormouth, Super Soldiers, Warheads)	
Marvel UK; 1 24th Apr 1992-52 24th Aug 1994	
1 32pgs; Hell's Angel by Bernie Jaye & Geoff Senior/Cam Smith, Warheads by Nick Vince	
& Gary Erskine, Knights of Pendragon by Dan Abnett/John Tomlinson & Phil	
Gascoine/Adolfo Buylla, Motormouth by Graham Marks & Gary Frank/Cam Smith	£0.55
2-11	£0.55
12 Death's Head II (mini-series) reprints begin	£0.60
13-14, 17-20 Death's Head II	£0.60
15-16 Death's Head II, Gary Erskine art	£0.60
21	£0.60
22 Death's Head II (ongoing) reprints begin, Liam Sharp art	£0.60
22-29, 31 Death's Head II, Sharp art	£0.60
30 Black Axe, Super Soldiers reprints begin, Liam Sharp art	£0.60
32-42 Death's Head II	£0.60
43 first monthly; Dark Guard, Wild Thing begin	£1.00
44-52	£1.00
Note: Early issues also published as a separate title by Marvel with additional pages for American market.	
From around issue 12 the full stories were published.	

P

	N.MINT
PAGET...COMIC, THE	
(see Paget's Tupney)	
Paget Publications; various one-off issues; 8pgs/12pgs, priced 2d	
The Paget Pageant Comic (1948) 8pgs; Banger, Anglo art	£3.50
The Paget Pep Comic (1948) Banger art	£3.50
The Paget Play Comic (1948) Banger art	£3.50
The Paget Pleasure Comic (1948) Banger art	£3.50
The Paget Plus Comic (1948) Banger, Anglo art	£3.50
The Paget Popular Comic (1948) Banger, Anglo art	£3.50
Paget's Gusto (1948) Anglo, Banger art	£3.50
Paget's Snips (1948) Anglo, Banger art	£3.50
Paget's Spree Comic (1948) Anglo, Banger art	£3.50
Paget's Zest (1948) Anglo, Banger art	£3.50
The Paget Prince of Comics (1949) 12pgs; Banger, Anglo, Robertson art, 1st enlarged issue	£4.00
The Paget Acme Comic (1949) Wally Robertson, E.Banger art	£3.50
The Paget Action Comic (1949) Banger art	£3.50
The Paget Bags-o'-Fun Comic (1949) Banger, Robertson art	£3.50
Paget Balloon (1949) Banger, Robertson art	£3.50
The Paget Budget-o'-Fun Comic (1949) Banger, Robertson art	£3.50
The Paget Fun Comic (1949) Banger, Robertson art	£3.50

	N.MINT
The Paget Parade Comic (1949) Banger, Anglo art	£3.50
The Paget Picnic Comic (1949) Banger art, Anglo reprint	£3.50
The Paget Pinnacle Comic (1949) Banger art, Anglo reprints	£3.50
Paget's Ace Comic (1949) Robertson, Banger art	£3.50
Paget's Happy Laughs (1949) Banger art	£3.50
Paget's Jolly Laughs (1949) Banger art	£3.50
Paget's Merry Laughs (1949) Banger, Robertson art	£3.50
PAGET'S…COMIC	
Paget Publications; various one-off titles; larger size, 8pgs/12pgs, priced 3d	
The Paget Pukka Comic (1948) 8pgs; Banger art	£3.50
Paget's Slam Comic (1948) Banger art	£3.50
Paget's Slick Comic (1948) Banger art	£3.50
Paget's Snappy Comic (1948) Banger art	£3.50
Paget's Sparkle Comic (1948) Banger art	£3.50
Paget's Sure-Fire Comic (1948) Banger art	£3.50
The Paget Prize Comic (Mar 1949) Banger art	£3.50
Paget's Super! (Mar 1949) Banger art	£3.50
Paget's Daily Comic (1949) 12pgs; Robertson art, 1st enlarged issue	£4.00
Paget's Dapper Comic (1949) Robertson art	£3.50
PAGET'S BUMPER TOTS' COMIC	
Paget Publications; nn 1950	
nn - 8pgs tabloid; Mick Anglo art	£3.50
PAGET'S FUNNY CUTS COMIC	
Paget Publications; 1-nn 1949, 8 issues, 1-4 numbered	
1-4 12pgs; Robertson art in all	£3.50
(5) Paget's Happy Funny Cuts Comic	£3.50
(6) Paget's Heady Funny Cuts Comic	£3.50
(7) Paget's Hearty Funny Cuts Comic	£3.50
(8) Paget's Hello Funny Cuts Comic	£3.50
PAGET'S SUPER DUPER COMIC	
Paget Publications; nn 1950	
nn - 16pgs; Banger, Minnitt art	£3.50
PAGET'S TUPNEY	
Paget Publications; 1-nn 1949, 10 issues, 1-2 numbered	
1-2 12pgs; Banger art in most	£4.00
(3) Paget Demon Tupney	£3.50
(4) Paget Dazzle Tupney	£3.50
(5) Paget Dashing Tupney	£3.50
(6) Paget Dandy Tupney	£3.50
(7) Paget Daddle Tupney	£3.50
(8) Paget Diamond Tupney	£3.50
(9) Paget Debonair Tupney	£3.50
(10) Paget Dependable Tupney	£3.50
PANCHO VILLA WESTERN COMIC	
Miller; 1 1954-63 1959	
1 Pancho Villa by Colin Andrew begins	£5.00
2-63	£2.50
PANDA COMICS	
(see Tom Puss Comics)	
B.B. Ltd; 701 1949	
701 16pgs; reprints Dutch strips by Marten Toonder, incl. Tom Puss	£20.00
PANGO	
Mundial Press; 50? 1953-85? 1956	
50? 28pgs; reprints French strip	£2.50
51-85	£1.25
PANTO PLAYTIME	
Hotspur Publishing Co.; nn 1948	
nn - 8pgs; Alan Fraser art	£2.50
PANTO PRANKS	
Hotspur Publishing Co.; nn 1949	
nn - 8pgs; Denis Gifford art	£3.00
PARAMOUNT COMIC	
R. & L. Locker; nn Feb 1945	
nn - 8pgs; C.Compton art	£4.00
PATSY'S CHRISTMAS REFLECTIONS	
Daily Mirror; nn Oct 1948	
nn - oblong; reprints Jack Dunkley strip from Daily Mirror	£3.00
PAUL TEMPLE ANNUAL	
R. & L. Locker; 1948	
1948	£8.00
PAUL TEMPLE LIBRARY	
Micron/G.M.Smith; 1 Mar 1964-10 Jul 1964	
1 68pgs pocket size; The Magpie Mystery by John McNamara; reprints newspaper strip from Evening News	£7.50
2-10	£3.50
P.C. 49	
Hawk (Eagle Classics); nn 1990	
nn - reprints Alan Stranks & John Worsley strip from Eagle	£5.00
P.C. 49 ANNUALS	
Juvenile/Preview/Dakers; 1951-1955	
P.C. 49 (Juvenile, 1951)	£10.00
On Duty With P.C. 49 (Juvenile, 1952)	£10.00
On the Beat with P.C. 49 (Juvenile, Sep 1953) text stories, Worsley illus.	£10.00
Eagle Strip Cartoon Book No.1 (Preview, Oct 1953) Eagle Worsley reprints	£10.00
Eagle Strip Cartoon Book No.2 (Preview, Sep 1954) Eagle Wosley reprints	£10.00
P.C. 49 Annual 1955 (Dakers, Aug 1955) text stories, Worsley illus.	£10.00
Note: All annuals except strip books issued in dust jackets. Price halved if dust jacket missing	
PECOS BILL	
Westworld Publications; 1 Sep 1951-Vol 8:7 1959, 91? issues	
1 36pgs; reprints French strip (Editions Mondiales)	£2.50
2-Vol 8:7	£1.25

New Triumph #772

Playbox #1

Pow #1

	N.MINT
PECOS BILL	
Top Sellers; 1 1971-?? 1973	
1-? 36pgs; French reprints	£1.25
PECOS BILL PICTURE LIBRARY	
Famepress; 1 1962-28? 1964	
1 68pgs pocket size; French reprints	£1.50
2-28	£0.75
PELICAN FUNNIES, THE	
National Sport Publications; nn 1948	
nn – 12pgs	£1.50
PENELOPE	
(see Lady Penelope)	
PENELOPE ANNUAL	
(previously Lady Penelope Annual)	
Century 21/IPC; 1969-1971	
1969	£7.50
1971-1972	£1.50
PENNY COMIC, THE	
P.M. Productions; nn 1946	
nn – 8pgs 3x3.5" size	£4.00
PENNY COMICS OF THE THIRTIES	
New English Library (Collectors Comics 1); 1975	
– facsimile of Merry Midget 1, Sparkler 20, Rattler 105, Target 53 in wrapround cover	£4.00
PERFECT CRIME	
Pemberton; 1-2 1951	
1-2 36pgs; Cross Publications reprints	£6.00
PERISHERS/THE PERISHERS OMNIBUS	
(see also Here Come the Perishers)	
Mirror; 1963-present	
Meet The Perishers (1963) oblong; reprints Maurice Dodd & Dennis Collins newspaper strip from the Daily Mirror	£20.00
The Perishers Strike Again (1965)	£15.00
The Perishers Back Britain (1968)	£6.00
Playtime with the Perishers (1968)	£6.00
Flat Out with the Perishers (1969)	£5.00
The Perishers Pop Up Again (1969)	£5.00
The Perishers Do Their Thing (1970)	£4.00
The Perishers 8-14 (1970)-(1973)	£3.00
15 (1973) Strips reprinted in sequential order hereon	£2.50
16-20 (1974-1978)	£1.50
21-22 (1978-1979) reprints from Scottish Sunday Mirror	£1.50
23-27 (1979-1981)	£1.50
The Perishers Omnibus all unnumbered (28)-(30)	£2.50
The Perishers Omnibus Maurice Dodd art, unnumbered (31)-(35)	£2.50
The Perishers Omnibus 1 (1974) reprints from books 1-4	£3.00
The Perishers Omnibus 2 (1975) reprints from books 5-7	£3.00
The Perishers Omnibus 3 (1976) reprints from books 8-10	£3.00
The Perishers Spectacolour (Mirror, 1979)	£5.00
The Perishers Rather Big For Its Size Storybook (Mirror, 1979)	£8.00
The Perishers Rather Big Little Books (Wellington, Marlon, Masie, Boot, 1979) small hardback (each)	£2.50
The Tale of a Tail (1981)	£2.00
PERISHERS ANNUAL, THE	
World Distributors; 1979-1980	
1979-1980	£2.50
PERSUADERS HOLIDAY SPECIAL	
Polystyle; nn May 1972	
nn – 48pgs	£4.00
PETE MANGAN OF THE SPACE PATROL	
Miller; 50 Jul 1953-55 Dec 1953	
50 28pgs; Pete Mangan begins	£10.00
51-55	£4.00
PETER PANK	
Knockabout (Crack); nn 1990	
nn – unexpurgated version of Peter Pank by Max european reprints	£5.50
PETER PAUL AND PERCY	
Faber & Faber; 1942-1945	
The Amazing Adventures of Peter Paul and Percy (Nov 1942) 68pgs; by Morley Adams, C.H. Chapman reprints from Farmer & Stockbreeder	£3.00
The Pranks of Peter Paul and Percy (Jan 1945) 50pgs; Chapman reprints	£2.00
PETS PLAYTIME COMIC	
Philmar; nn 1949	
nn – 8pgs; Walter Bell, Frank Minnitt, Tom Kerr art	£3.00
PETTS ANNUAL	
(see Jane)	
PHANTOM, THE	
(see The Phantom World Adventure Library, TV Tornado)	
Miller; 1 1959-18 1961	
1 68pgs; reprints American newspaper strip by Lee Falk	£5.00
PHANTOM, THE	
Wolf Publishing; 1 Jul 1992-11 May 1993	
1 32pgs; reprints Swedish strip by Tierres & Felmang	£1.00
2-11	£1.00
PHANTOM RANGER COMICS, THE	
World Distributors; 1-18 1955	
1 28pgs; reprints Australian strip published by Frew Publications, Sydney	£5.00
2-18	£3.00
PHANTOM WORLD ADVENTURE LIBRARY, THE	
(see The Phantom, TV Tornado)	
World Distributors; 1 Jan 1967-8 Aug 1967	
1 68pgs pocket size; The Deadly Catch, reprints Gold Key/King strips	£6.00
2-8 reprints	£4.00

	N.MINT
PHILBERT DESANEX 100, 000TH DREAM	
Hassel Free Press; nn 1979	
nn – 52pgs; US underground reprints	£3.00
PICTURE CLASSICS	
Watts; 1 1980	
1 King Solomon's Mines by C.L. Doughty, reprints from Look and Learn	£2.50
PICTURE EPICS	
Gerald Swan; 1 Oct 1952-4 Nov 1952	
1-4 each	£10.00
ARTISTS/FEATURES	
1 Back From the Dead by William McCail. 2 Old Hooky Buccaneer by William McCail. 3 Space Conquerors by William McCail. 4 Ah Wong versus the Cobra by John McCail.	
PICTURE PRANKS COMIC	
Martin & Reid; nn 1944	
nn – 8pgs	£2.50
PICTURE-SHOW	
Juvenile Productions; 6700-6701 1940s	
6700 Picture-Show of Robin Hood, 16pgs	£4.00
6701 Picture-Show of Robinson Crusoe	£4.00
PICTURE STORIES OF WORLD WAR TWO	
C.A. Pearson; 1 Aug 1960-56 1962?	
1-56 68pgs pocket size	£0.75
PICTURE STORY POCKET WESTERN	
World Distributors; 1 1958-24 1959?	
1 68pgs pocket size; US reprints	£5.00
2-24 incl. Maverick, Durango Kid US reprints	£3.00
PICTURE STORY READERS	
John Murray; 1-8 1956	
1-8	£4.00
FEATURES	
1 Coral Island. 2 Lorna Doone. 3 Treasure Island. 4 Kidnapped. 5 The Lost World. 6 Vice Versa. 7 Marco Polo's Amazing Adventures. 8 The Invisible Man.	
Note: all 32pgs oblong; reprints from The Children's Newspaper	
PICTURE STRIP BOOK	
Collins; Mar 1955	
Oliver Twist 16pgs	£2.00
Prince the Pony	£2.00
Jungle Giants	£2.00
PIGMY COMIC, THE	
P.M. Productions; nn 1944	
nn – 8pgs; Reg Carter art	£3.00
PILLAR BOX COMIC, THE	
Reynard Press; nn 1947	
nn – 8pgs; Tom Cottrell art	£3.00
PILOT, THE	
Amalgamated Press; 1 5th Oct 1935-131 2nd Apr 1938 (joins Wild West Weekly)	
1 24pgs	£40.00
2	£12.50
3-5	£6.00
6-131	£3.00
FEATURES	
Story paper which incl. some strips by John Jukes, Frank Minnitt, Jos Walker, Steve Chapman, etc. Some issues incl. Tarzan US newspaper reprints.	
PINWHEEL, THE	
McKenzie, Vincent; nn 1948	
nn – 8pgs; A.R.G. art	£3.00
PIONEER WESTERN COMIC, THE	
Wyndham House; 1-2 1950	
1-2 16pgs; Mick Anglo art, based on Timpo Toys characters	£2.50
PIP AND SQUEAK	
Daily Mirror; 15th Oct 1921-23rd May 1925 (continued as one page of main paper)	
15 Oct 1921 4pgs, supplement to Daily Mirror, features Pip Squeak & Wilfred by AustinPayne	£25.00
22 Oct 1921-18 Mar 1922	£10.00
25 Mar-1 Jul 1922 reduced to 3pgs	£5.00
8 Jul 1922-23 May 1925 reduced to 2pgs	£3.00
PIP POP COMIC	
Philmar; nn 1949	
nn – 8pgs tabloid; Frank Minnitt, Wally Robertson art	£3.00
PIPPIN	
TV Publications/Polystyle; 24th Sep 1966-5th Jul 1975, 459? issues	
24 Sep 1966 The Pogles by Bill Mevin, Woodentops, Camberwick Green by Betty Larom, Jimmy by Neville Main, The Musical Box by Fred Robinson begin	£1.50
1 Oct 1966-5 Jul 1975 later issues (1974-75) incl. Alfred Bestell Rupert reprints	£0.45
PIRATES COMICS	
Streamline; nn 1951-nn 1952, unnumbered issues	
nn – 68pgs; reprints from various US comics incl. Hillman. Some issues titled Pirates Adventure Comics	each 6.00
PLANET, THE	
J.B. Allen; 1 Mar 1949-2 Apr 1949 (becomes The Children's Rocket Book)	
1-2 Jack Pamby, Bill Holroyd, David Williams art	£5.00
PLANET COMICS	
Cartoon Art Productions; 1950	
nn – 28pgs; Fiction House reprints	£6.00
PLANET COMICS	
R. & L. Locker; 1-5 1951	
1-2 68pgs; Fiction House reprints, cited in UK horror campaign	£15.00
3-5	£6.00
PLANET OF THE APES	
Marvel; 1 26th Oct 1974-123 23rd Feb 1977, 123 numbered issues	
(joins Mighty World of Marvel)	
1 Planet of the Apes film adaptation reprints begin	£1.50

	N.MINT
1 with free gift (colour Apes poster)	£3.00
2 Planet of the Apes adaptation, Ka-Zor back-up begins (later back-ups incl. Gulliver Jones, Dr. Doom, Warlock, etc)	£1.25
3-11 Planet of the Apes adaptation	£1.00
12-34	£1.00
35-46 Beneath the Planet of the Apes adaptation	£1.00
47-48	£0.75
50-62 Escape from the Planet of the Apes adaptation	£0.75
63-74 Conquest of the Planet of the Apes adaptation	£0.60
75-87	£0.50
88 1st "Planet of the Apes & Dracula Lives", Spider-Man appears	£1.00
89-107	£0.50
108-123 Battle for the Planet of the Apes (cont. in Mighty World of Marvel)	£0.50

Note: some later stories reprint other titles with ape heads drawn on

PLANET OF THE APES
Brown & Watson; 1975

1975 strips, text and photo features based on the TV series	£3.50

PLANET STORIES
Atlas; 1 Jun 1961-?

1-? 28pgs; Fiction House reprints	£6.00

PLASTIC MAN
Popular; 2 Mar 1951-(various numbers)

2 36pgs; Quality reprints	£12.00
5, 60	£10.00

PLAYBOX, THE
Harmsworth/Amalgamated Press; 29th Oct 1898-?

29 Oct 1898 4pgs; supplement to Home Chat, Arthur White art	£20.00
5 Nov-17 Dec 1898, 31 Dec 1898 printed on white paper	£15.00
24 Dec 1898 1st Xmas double number	£20.00
1899 issues printed on green paper hereon	£12.50
1900-1903	£10.00
1904-? incl. Julius Stafford Baker art	£10.00

PLAYBOX, THE (2ND SERIES)
(titled The Monthly Playbox/The Playbox)
Amalgamated Press; Nov 1904-May 1910 (67 unnumbered issues; becomes Playbox (3rd Series)

Nov 1904-Apr 1905 titled The Monthly Playbox; 8pgs; supplement to The World & his Wife; Mrs. Hippo's Kindergarten (Tiger Tim) by Julius Stafford Baker	£30.00
May 1905 become The Playbox; 16pgs	£20.00
Jun-Dec 1905	£15.00
1906-1910 issues	£7.50

PLAYBOX (3RD SERIES)
Amalgamated Press; May 1910-Apr 1914

May 1910 8pgs; supplement to The New Children's Encyclopedia; Mrs. Hippo's Boys (Tiger Tim) by Julius Stafford Baker	£15.00
Jun-Dec 1910	£6.00
1911-1913 issues	£3.00

Note: New Children's Encyclopedia varies in title: October 1910 (#9) becomes Children's Magazine, March 1911 (#14) becomes Children's Encyclopedia Magazine, May 1911 (#16) becomes Children's Magazine, April 1914 (#51) becomes My Children's Magazine, at which time Playbox became integrated into the main body of the magazine. My Magazine continued until November 1933 (#285) during which time The Playbox as a title was restored (June 1929).

PLAYBOX, THE (4TH SERIES)
Amalgamated Press; 1 14th Feb 1925-1279 11th Jun 1955 (joins Jack & Jill)

1 12pgs, tabloid; Mrs Hippo's Boarding School by Herbert Foxwell	£35.00
1 with free gift (coloured baloon)	£100.00
2	£15.00
1925-1929 issues	£10.00
1930-1939 issues	£7.50
4 Nov 1939 becomes 24pgs, half-tabloid	£5.00
1939-1946	£4.00
1947-1951 8pgs, tabloid	£3.00
1952-1955	£1.50

CHRONOLOGY
1941: publication drops to fortnightly. 2 Feb 1952: resumes weekly publication.

PLAYBOX ANNUAL
Amalgamated Press; 1909-1940

1909 scarce	£50.00
1910	£25.00
1911-1920	£15.00
1921-1930	£10.00
1931-1940	£5.00

PLAYHOUR
Amalgamated Press/Fleetway/IPC; 21st May 1955-?

16 Oct 1954 titled Playhour Pictures; Prince the Wonder Dog by Sep Scott, Hugh McNeil, Philip Mendoza art begins	£7.50
23 Oct 1954	£4.00
30 Oct 1954-14 May 1955	£2.00
21 May 1955 1st Playhour; Basil Reynolds, Mendoza art	£1.50
28 May 1955-1959	£0.75
1960-1970	£0.40
1971-1990	£0.25

CHRONOLOGY
15 Mar 1957: 1st "Playhour & Chicks Own". 31 Jan 1959: 1st "Playhour & Tiny Tots". 11 Apr 1964: 1st "Playhour & Harold Hare". 2 Mar 1968: 1st "Playhour & TV Toyland". 1 Feb 1969: 1st "Playhour & Robin". 22 Sep 1973: 1st "Playhour & Hey Diddle Diddle". 17 May 1975: 1st "Playhour & Bonnie". 13 Mar 1982: 1st Playhour & Fun To Do". 6 Aug 1983: 1st "Playhour & Chips Comic".

ARTISTS/FEATURES
Artists incl. Jesus Blasco (various fairy tales). Ron Embleton (Tales of the Arabian Nights). Hugh McNeill (Peter Puppet, Sonny & Sally, Bunny Cuddles). Philip Mendoza (The Seven Dwarfs, Children of the Forest, Katie Countrymouse, etc). Basil Reynolds (Peter Puppet). Sep E. Scott (Prince the Wonder Dog).

	N.MINT
PLAYHOUR PICTURES	
(see Playhour)	

PLUG
(see The Bash Street Kids in The Beano)
1 24th Sep 1977-75 25th Feb 1978 (joins Beezer)

No. 1 - 24 Sep 1977	£1.00
No. 1 with free gift (Screamin' Demon balloon)	£2.00
1 Oct 1977-25 Feb 1978	£0.40

POCKET CHILLER LIBRARY
Top Sellers; 1-? 1971

1 68pgs pocket size; The Body, Italian reprints	£1.00
2-?	£0.50

POCKET COMIC
P.M. Productions; nn 1944

nn - 8pgs; Reg Carter art	£3.00

POCKET DETECTIVE LIBRARY
Top Sellers; 1-? 1971

1 68pgs pocket size; The Big Snatch, foreign reprints	£1.00
2-?	£0.50

POCKET ROMANCE LIBRARY
Top Sellers; 1-? 1971

1 68pgs pocket size; foreign reprints	£1.00
2-?	£0.35

POCKET WAR LIBRARY
Top Sellers; 1-? 1971

1 68pgs pocket size; A Man's Honour, Spanish reprints	£1.00
2-?	£0.50

POCKET WESTERN LIBRARY
Top Sellers; 1-? 1971

1 68pgs pocket size; The Lost Expedition, foreign reprints	£1.00
2-?	£0.50

POINT BLANK
John Brown/Acme; 1 May 1989-2 Jul 1989

1 Dieter Lumpen by Pellejero & Zentner, Marvin by Milazzo & Berardi foreign reprints begin	£1.25
2	£1.00

POLICE COMIC
Archer Press (King Comic Series); 1-6 1953

1-6 68pgs; Quality reprints	£8.00

POP PICTURE LIBRARY
Micron; 1 1965-?

1 68pgs pocket size	£2.00
2-?	£1.00

POP SHOTS
John W. Fisher; nn 1946

nn - 8pgs; W. Forshaw art	£3.00

POPEYE
Pembertons; 1 1950-19 1951

1-19 28pgs; Dell reprints, Bud Sagendorf art	£8.00

POPEYE
World Distributors; 1-7 1957

1-7 28pgs; Western Printing reprints, Bud Sagendorf art	£7.50

POPEYE
Miller; 1 1959-30 1963

1-30 28pgs; reprints American newspaper strip by Bela Zaboly	£5.00

POPEYE
Hawk Books; nn 1995

nn - 128pgs, hardcover; edited by Mike Higgs	£15.00

POW!
Odhams; 1 21st Jan 1967-86 7th Sep 1968 (joins Smash!)

1 Spider-Man (from Spider-Man #1), Nick Fury Agent of Shield (from Strange Tales #135), reprints begin, The Python by Borrell, Jack Magic, Dolls of St. Dominics, The Group, Dare-a-Day Davy by Ken Reid begin	£20.00
1 with free gift (Spider-Matic Gun and ammo)	£40.00
2	£7.50
2 with free gift (iron-on Spider-Man transfer)	£15.00
3-9	£2.50
10, 34, 35 no The Python	£1.50
11 no Jack Magic	£1.50
12-16	£1.50
17 last Jack Magic	£1.50
18 The Cloak by Mike Higgs begins	£1.50
19-33, 36-42, 45-51	£1.50
43 last The Python	£1.50
44 Experiment X by Ed Feito begins	£1.50
52 Fantastic Four (from FF27) reprints begin, last Nick Fury, The Group	£1.75
53 1st "Pow! and Wham!"; Two Faces of Janus by Ayhan, George's Germs by Cyril Price begin	£1.75
54-68, 70-86	£1.25
69 last Experiment X	£1.25

POW! ANNUAL
Odhams; 1968-1972 (joins Wham! Annual)

1968 reprints both stories from Amazing Spiderman #1 and 1st Nick Fury from Strange Tales #135	£6.00
1969	£5.50
1970-1972	£4.50

POWER COMIC
Martin & Reid; nn 1950

nn - 8pgs; Mick Anglo art	£4.00

PRAIRIE GUNS
(see Action Series)

PRAIRIE! WESTERN
Scion; 1 Jan 1952-nn 1952 (3 issues)

1 24pgs; Ron Embleton art	£8.00
2-nn 20pgs; Ron Embleton art, Norman Light art in 2	£8.00

N.MINT | N.MINT

PRANG COMIC
Hotspur Publishing Co.; nn 1948
nn - 8pgs £3.00

PREDATOR
(see also Aliens, Batman vs Predator)
Titan
Predator (1990) Dark Horse reprints £7.50
Predator: Big Game (1992) Dark Horse reprints, Evan Dorkin art £7.50
Predator: Cold War (Feb 1995) Dark Horse reprints, Ron Randall art £9.00

PREMIER, THE
Paget Publications; 1-7 1948
1-7 8pgs; some incl. Mick Anglo art £3.00

PRINCE COMIC, THE
Ensign Publishing; 1-2 1947
1-2 8pgs; W. Forshaw art £3.00

PRINCESS
Amalgamated Press/Fleetway; 30th Jan 1960-16th Sep 1967, 346 issues (becomes Princess Tina)
30 Jan 1960 Lorna Doone by H.M. Brock, Nikola the Polish Refugee by Guido Buzzelli begin £2.00
6 Feb 1960-16 Sep 1967 £0.50
ARTISTS/FEATURES
Artists incl. H.M. Brock, Tom Kerr, Hugh McNeill, Eric Parker, John Ryan, Sep E. Scott.

PRINCESS PICTURE LIBRARY
Fleetway; 1 Jul 1961-120 Jun 1966 (joins June and Schoolfriend Picture Library)
1 68pgs pocket size; Sue Day, Detective £1.00
2-120 £0.50

PRINCESS TINA
(combination of Princess and Tina)
IPC Magazines; 23rd Sep 1967-1973 (joins Pink)
23 Sep 1967 Barbie the Model Girl, Space Girls by Keith Watson, Jackie & the Wild Boys by Alberto Giolitti, Jane Bond by Michael Hubbard £2.00
30 Sep 1967-1973 some incl. Hugh McNeill, Alberto Salinas art £0.40

PRIVATE EYE PICTURE LIBRARY
C.A. Pearson; 1 1963-?
1 68pgs pocket size; The Rats of Paris £1.00
2-? £0.75

PRIVATE LIVES ROMANCES
Miller; 1-9 1959
1-9 68pgs; Standard Publications reprints from Popular Romances £2.50

PRIZE COMICS WESTERN
Streamline/United Anglo-American; 1950, 9+ issues
nn - 28pgs; Prize reprints £3.00
nn - 36pgs £3.00
3-9 £2.50

PRO JUNIOR
(no imprint); nn 1972
nn - 24pgs; reprints American underground comic, Robert Crumb, S. Clay Wilson art £2.50

PROJECT SWORD
City; 1968
1968 larger size; annual for planned TV series which never appeared £12.50

PROTECTORS ANNUAL
Polystyle; 1974
1974 £6.00

PSSST!
Never/Artpool; 1 Jan 1982-10 Oct 1982
1 Paul Johnson, Bob Wakelin art £2.00
2 Bryan Talbot Luther Arkwright begins, Rob Moran art £3.50
3 Talbot, John Higgins art £2.00
4 Talbot, Angus McKie art £2.00
5 Talbot, Moran art £2.00
6 Talbot art, Temptation by Glenn Dakin begins £2.00
7 Talbot, David Jackson, Mike Matthews art £2.00
8 Talbot, McKie, Johnson art £2.00
9 Talbot, McKie art £2.00
10 Talbot, Higgins, Johnson, McKie art £2.00
Note: each issue included a free poster which if intact will command up to 25% higher price

PSYCHO
Top Sellers; 1972?-
1 36pgs; Skywald reprints £1.00
2-? £0.75

PUB DOG
Daily Express; nn Jun 1984
nn - reprints Daily Express newspaper strip by Graham Allen £2.00

PUBLIC ENEMIES
R. & L. Locker; 1-8 1949
1-8 58pgs; D.S. Publishing reprints, cited in SOTI £12.00

PUCK
Harmsworth/ Amalgamated Press; 1 30th Jul 1904-1867 11th May 1940 (joins Sunbeam)
1 £50.00
2 £30.00
3-10 £20.00
11 1st Puck Junior section £25.00
1904-1910 £12.00
1911-1919 £10.00
1920-1940 incl. Rob the Rover by Walter Booth from 15th May 1920 £6.00
ARTISTS/FEATURES
Artists incl. Alex Akerbladh, Julius Baker, Bertie Brown, Herbert Foxwell, G.M. Payne, Tom Radford, Tom Wilkinson, Jack B. Yeats in early issues. Walter Booth, Vincent Daniel, Reg Perrott, Fred Robinson, Roy Wilson, Bert O. Wymer art in 1920-40 period.

PUCK ANNUAL
Amalgamated Press; 1921-1941
1921 scarce £40.00

1922 £25.00
1923-1929 £17.50
1930-1935 £15.00
1936-1941 £10.00

PUPPETOONS (GEORGE PAL'S...)
Miller; 1-2 1951
1-2 32pgs; Fawcett reprints £3.00

PUNCH AND JUDY COMIC
Martin & Reid; nn 1949
nn - 8pgs; Frank Minnitt, Denis Gifford art £3.00

PUNISHER AUTUMN SPECIAL, THE
Marvel; Oct 1992
1992 36pgs; reprints from Punisher Summer Special 1, Mark Texiera art £1.00

PURPLE HOOD
John Spencer; 1-2 1967?
1-2 Michael Jay art £3.00

Q

QUESTPROBE
Marvel; 1 Jun 1984
1 US reprint, based on computer game £0.75

QUICK TRIGGER WESTERN
Miller; 1-8? 1956
1-8 28pgs; Atlas/Marvel reprints £3.00

R

RACE FOR THE MOON
Alan Class; nn 1959
nn - 68pgs; Harvey reprints £5.00

RACE FOR THE MOON
Strato Publications/Top Sellers; 1 1959?-23 1960
1 68pgs; various reprints from Harvey, National Periodicals, A.C.G. etc. £12.50
2 £7.50
3-5 £6.00
6-23 £2.50

RACE INTO SPACE
Alan Class; 1 1961
1 68pgs; US reprints £6.00

RADAR THE MAN FROM THE UNKNOWN
Famepress Publishers; 1-16 1962
1-16 68pgs; Italian reprints £2.00

RADIANT COMICS
P.M. Productions; nn Dec 1943
nn - 16pgs; Frank Jupo art £3.00

RADIO FUN
Amalgamated Press; 1 15th Oct 1938-nn 18th Feb 1961, 1167 issues, mostly numbered (joins Buster)
1 George the Jolly Geegee by Roy Wilson, Flanagan & Allen by Alex Akerbladh begin £300.00
2 £150.00
3-5 £100.00
6-11 £80.00
12-53 £50.00
54-64 £40.00
1941-1945 £25.00
1946-1950 £10.00
1951-1955 £5.00
1956-1959 £3.00
1960-1961 £2.50
CHRONOLOGY
19 Sep 1953: 1st "Radio Fun & Wonder". 22 Aug 1959: title becomes Radio Fun and Adventures.
ARTISTS/FEATURES
Artists incl. Bertie Brown, George Heath (The Falcon, etc.), John Jukes, Hugh McNeill (Jack O'Justice), Roy Wilson. Superman newspaper strip reprints 1959-60.

RADIO FUN ANNUAL
Amalgamated Press; 1940-1960
1940 scarce £150.00
1941 scarce £100.00
1942-1944 £60.00
1945-1947 £45.00
1948-1949 £30.00
1950-1955 £15.00
1956-1960 £7.50

RAIDERS OF THE LOST ARK
Marvel; 1981
1981 reprints film adaptation £2.50

RAINBOW, THE
Amalgamated Press; 1 14th Feb 1914-1898 28th Apr 1956 (joins Tiny Tots)
1 Tiger Tim & the Bruin Boys by Julius Baker begins £75.00
1914 issues £20.00
1915 issues £15.00
1916-1920 £10.00
1921-1939 £8.00
1940-1945 £6.00
1946-1956 £4.00
Note: a facsimile of issue 168 was reprinted in 1972 as part of Six Comics of World War One (qv). It can be easily identified as the dot-to-dot on page 3 of the copy from which the facsimile was made had been roughly completed.

N.MINT

RAINBOW ANNUAL
Amalgamated Press; 1924-1957

1924 scarce	£75.00
1925	£50.00
1926-1930	£30.00
1931-1939	£20.00
1940-1949 scarce	£25.00
1950-1957	£15.00

RAMAR OF THE JUNGLE
Miller; 1-4 1959

1-4 28pgs; Charlton reprints	£4.00

RAMPAGE
Marvel; 1 19th Oct 1977-77 31st May 1978 (continued as Rampage Monthly)

1 The Defenders and Nova (origin) reprints begin	£1.50
1 with free gift (plastic Concorde model)	£3.00
2 Nova origin concluded	£1.25
2 with free gift (plastic Stratocruiser)	£2.50
3-5 complete Defenders stories begin	£1.00
6-77	£0.60

RAMPAGE MONTHLY/MAGAZINE
(previously Rampage)
Marvel; 1 Jul 1978-54 Dec 1982 (joins Marvel Super Heroes)

1 Hulk, X-Men, Dr. Strange reprints begin	£2.00
2-5	£1.50
6-27, 29-39, 42-54	£1.25
28 1st new look issue; John Byrne's X-Men reprints, Thing team-ups and Luke Cage reprints all begin	£1.50
40 Timesmasher by Paul Neary & Mick Austin begins	£1.55
41 The Origin of the Crusader by Alan Davis	£2.50

RANCH PICTURE AND STORY ALBUM
Mellifont; W6 1950s

W6 96pgs	£3.00

RANCHER, THE
Martin & Reid; 1 1949

1 16pgs; Paddy Brennan art	£6.00

RANGE BUSTERS
United Anglo-American; nn 1951

nn - 28pgs; Fox Features reprints	£3.00

RANGELAND WESTERN
Martin & Reid; nn 1949

nn - 8pgs; John McCail, Mick Anglo art	£3.00

RANGER
Fleetway; 18th Sep 1965-18th Jun 1966 (40 unnumbered issues, joins Look and Learn)

No. 1 - 18 Sep 1965 Rise and Fall of the Trigan Empire by Mike Butterworth & Don Lawrence, Rob Riley by Jesus Blasco begin	£7.50
No.1 with free gift (Space chart)	£15.00
25 Sep 1965	£4.50
2 Oct 1965-18 Jun 1966	£3.00

RANGER WESTERN COMIC, THE
Donald F. Peters; Vol 2:1 1955-Vol 3:5 1956

Vol 2:1 28pgs; Texas Rangers by Douglas Reay begins	£5.00
Vol 2:2-Vol 3:5 incl. Lone Wolf Skiner by John Wheeler	£3.00

RANGERS COMICS
Cartoon Art; nn 1950

nn - 20pgs; Fiction House reprints	£4.00

RANGERS COMICS
Thorpe & Porter; 1 1952-?

1 28pgs; Fiction House reprints	£4.00
2-?	£3.00

RANMA 1/2
Boxtree; Dec 1994

Volume 1 Rumiko Takahashi manga reprints begin	£6.00
Volume 2	£6.00

RAPID REFLEXES
Knockabout (Crack); Mar 1990

nn - 80pgs; Hunt Emerson art	£6.00

RATTLER
Target Publications; 1 19th Aug 1933-269 15th Oct 1938 (becomes Rattler & Chuckler)

1 12pgs; Bert Hill, Harry Banger art	£20.00
2-60 12pgs on pink paper	£6.00
61-221 8pgs on pink paper	£4.00
222-269 8pgs on blue paper	£4.00

RATTLER AND CHUCKLER
(previously two papers)
Target Publications; 1 22nd Oct 1938-25 8th Apr 1939 (joins Tip Top)

1 12pgs white; mostly reprints from other Target publications	£15.00
2-22 12pgs printed on green paper except 8 (blue)	£4.00
23-25 8pgs	£4.00

RAW PURPLE
Beyond the Edge; nn 1977

nn - 52pgs; Antonio Ghuru art (adult)	£1.00

RAY REAGAN
Modern Fiction; 1 Apr 1949

1 Ray Reagan by Ron Embleton	£15.00

RAZZLE DAZZLE
Cartoon Art; 1 1946-2 1947

1 8pgs; G.F. Christie art	£4.00
2 Christie, Dennis Reader art	£3.00

R.D.H. COMIX
R.D.Harwood; nn Sep 1971

nn - Brian Bolland art	£10.00

Radio Fun #1000

Rampage #1

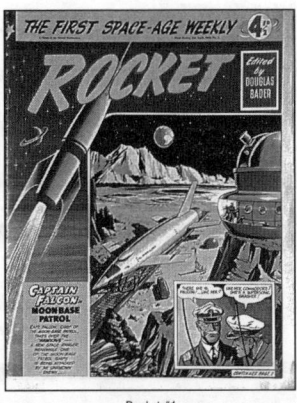

Rocket #1

	N.MINT		N.MINT
REAL CLUE CRIME STORIES		**RETURN TO MELNIBONE, THE**	
Streamline/United Anglo-American; 1-2 1951		Unicorn Bookshop; nn 1973	
1-2 36pgs; Hillman Periodicals reprints	£4.00	nn - Philip Druillet adaptation of Michael Moorcock	£8.00
REAL LIFE STORIES		**REVERBSTORM**	
Cartoon Art; 1 1955?		(see Lord Horror)	
1 Magazine Enterprises reprints	£4.00	**REVOLVER**	
REAL WESTERN HERO		(see Dare)	
Arnold Book Co.; 70 1949, 1 issue (continued as Western Hero)		Fleetway; 1 Jul 1990-7 Jan 1991 (joins Crisis)	
70 32pgs; Fawcett reprints	£3.00	**1** Purple Days by Charles Shaar Murray & Floyd Hughes, Dare by Grant Morrison &	
REALITY ADVERTISER		Rian Hughes, Happenstance & Kismet by Paul Neary & Steve Parkhouse, Rogan	
Eddie Campbell; nn Jul 1982)		Gosh by Pete Milligan & Brendan McCarthy, Dire Streets by Julie Hollings begin	£2.00
nn - Eddie Campbell art including hand-drawn cover, Harwood, Elliott art	£1.00	**2, 5**	£1.65
RED ARROW COMICS		**3** Fabry art	£1.65
Cartoon Art; nn 1948		**4** Al Davison, Pleece art, no Dire Streets	£1.65
nn	£3.00	**6** Rogan Gosh ends	£1.65
RED COMET INTERPLANETARY ADVENTURES		**7** Sean Phillips, McCarthy art	£1.65
Atlas; 1 1961-? 1962		**Horror Special** (1990) Gaiman script, Bolton, Pleece, Simpson art	£2.50
1 28pgs; Fiction House reprints from Planet Comics	£5.00	**Romance Special** (Mar 1991) Bolland cover, Phillips, Fabry, D'Israeli art	£2.00
RED DAGGER		**REX ALLEN**	
D.C. Thomson; 1 Oct 1979-30 Jun 1984		World Distributors; 1 Apr 1953-16 1954	
1 Twisty	£1.50	**1** 36pgs; Western Publishing reprints	£7.50
2, 4-8, 10-11, 15-16, 18, 20-30	£1.00	**2-16** later issues 28pgs	£5.00
3, 14 Morgyn the Mighty	£1.00	**RICHARD SHAFFER CODENAME SCORPIO**	
9, 13, 17 Denis Mcloughlin art	£1.00	Quasar; 1 1975	
12, 19 Braddock	£1.00	**1** 68pgs pocket size; Sounds of Silence by Trev Goring/Garry Leach	£4.00
RED DWARF SMEGAZINE		**RIDER, THE**	
Fleetway Editions; 1 Mar 1992-14 Apr 1993; Vol 2:1 May 1993-9 Jan 1994		Miller; 1-2 1957	
1 40pgs; based on TV series, Alan Burrows art	£7.50	**1-2** 28pgs; Ajax Publications reprints	£3.00
2	£5.00	**RIDERS OF THE RANGE (CHARLES CHILTON'S WESTERN ANNUAL...)**	
3-5	£4.00	Juvenile Productions; 1951-Nov 1955	
6-10	£3.00	**Riders of the Range** (1951) Pat Williams art	£5.00
11-14	£2.00	**Second Round-Up with the Riders of the Range** (1952)	£5.00
Vol 2:1 48pgs; new look	£3.50	**Charles Chilton's Western Annual Riders of the Range** (1953)	£5.00
2-8	£2.00	**Charles Chilton's Western Annual Riders of the Range** (1954)	£5.00
9 64-page special	£2.25	**Charles Chilton's Riders of the Range Annual 1956** (1955)	£5.00
RED FLASH COMIC		**RIDERS OF THE RANGE/RIDERS OF THE RANGE ANNUAL**	
Philmar/ P.M. Productions; nn 1948-2 1949		Hulton/Longacre; nn Sep 1956-Sep 1961	
nn - 16pgs; Ray Spede, the Rocket Man begins	£6.00	nn Frank Humphris cover, Roland Davis art	£5.00
2 Frank Minnitt art	£5.00	**2** Harry Bishop art	£5.00
REDFOX		**3-4** Desmond Walduck art	£5.00
(see The Book of Redfox)		**1961** first dated on cover, Desmond Walduck art	£10.00
Harrier/Valkyrie; 1 Jan 1986-20 Jun 1989		**1962** Desmond Walduck art	£10.00
1 Fox art begins	£5.00	**RIDERS OF THE RANGE**	
1 second printing	£1.00	Hawk (Eagle Classics); nn 1990	
2 scarce	£4.50	nn - Jack Scott, Frank Humphris strips reprinted from Eagle	£2.50
3	£2.00	**RIDERS OF THE RANGE STRIP BOOK**	
4	£1.50	Juvenile Productions; 1954	
5	£0.85	**Jeff Arnold in The Bozeman Trail** 46pgs; Pat Williams art	£25.00
6-11, 16 Fox/Harwood art	£0.75	**RIME OF THE ANCIENT MARINER**	
12-13, 15 Fox/O'Donnell art	£0.75	Knockabout (Crack); nn 1990	
14 Meadows/O'Donnell art	£0.75	nn - Hunt Emerson art	£6.00
17-19	£0.60	**RIN TIN TIN**	
20 partly by Gaiman & SMS (5pgs)	£1.50	World Distributors; 1 1955-13 1956	
RED HAWK		**1-13** 28pgs; Dell reprints based on TV series	£3.50
Cartoon Art; 1 1953		**RIN TIN TIN**	
1 28pgs; Magazine Enterprises reprints	£4.00	Top Sellers; 1 1972-? 1974	
RED MASK		**1** 36pgs; foreign reprints	£2.00
(see Action Series)		**2-?**	£1.50
RED RANGER, THE		**RINGO KID WESTERN**	
Modern Fiction; nn Apr 1949		Miller; 1 1955-17 1956	
nn - 8pgs; R. Beaumont art	£4.00	**1-17** 28pgs; Atlas reprints	£3.50
RED RYDER COMICS		**RIP CARSON**	
World Distributors; 1 1954-60 1959		Cartoon Art; 1 1950	
1 36pgs; Dell reprints	£5.00	**1** 16pgs; Fiction House reprints	£4.00
2-56 28pgs	£3.00	**RIP CARSON**	
57-60 68pgs	£4.00	United Anglo-American; nn 1951	
REDSKIN		nn - 28pgs; Fiction House reprints	£4.00
Streamline; 1-2 1950s		**RIP KIRBY**	
1-2 28pgs; censored Youthful Magazines reprints	£2.50	Associated Newspapers; 1948-1956 (5 titles)	
RED SPOT COMIC, THE		**The Menace of the Mangler** 16pgs; Alex Raymond newspaper reprints begin	£5.00
Martin & Reid; nn 1944		**Poison and Paradise** 52pgs	£5.00
nn - 8pgs; Bob Wilkin art	£3.00	**Moray's Last Gamble** 52pgs	£3.50
REEL COMICS		**The Man Who Stole A Million** 44pgs	£3.50
R. & L. Locker; nn Oct 1944		**The Beaumont Case/The Faraday Murder** 84pgs	£3.50
nn - 16pgs; William Dwyer art	£4.00	**RIPPING COMIC, THE**	
REFLECTIONS FOR CHILDREN		J.T. Comics; nn 1948-2 Nov 1948	
Mirror Features; nn 1947		nn - 8pgs; John Turner, Bob Monkhouse art	£4.00
nn - 52pgs; Pip Squeak & Wilfred by A.B. Payne	£8.00	**2** Turner, Monkhouse, Denis Gifford art	£3.50
REGAL COMIC		**ROAD MANIAX**	
Miller; nn 1950s		Fleetway Editions; 1 Oct 1995-present (3 to Dec 1995)	
nn - 28pgs; Fawcett reprints from Bill Boyd, etc	£3.00	**1** Based on Mattel toy; Jon Haward, Barrie Mitchell art	£1.00
REN AND STIMPY		**2-3**	£0.75
Marvel; 1 1994-16 1996		**ROAD OF COURAGE, THE**	
1 reprints US strips based on TV show	£1.00	Dragon's Dream; nn 1981	
2-16	£0.35	nn - Eagle reprints by Frank Hampson, softcover	£8.00
REN AND STIMPY SHOW, THE		nn - hardcover	£12.00
Titan		**ROARING WESTERN**	
Pick of the Litter	£7.00	Streamline; 1 1952	
Tastes Like Chicken	£7.00	**1** 28pgs; American reprints	£2.50
RETURN OF THE JEDI		**ROBIN**	
(see Star Wars)		Hulton/Longacre/IPC Magazines; Vol 1:1 28th Mar 1953-Vol 16:4 25th Jan 1969, 820	
		issues (joins Playhour)	

	N.MINT
Vol 1:1 Andy Pandy, Simon & Sally by Mike Noble, Flowerpot Men all begin	£10.00
Vols 1-2	£2.00
Vols 3-7	£1.50
Vols 8-16	£1.00
ROBIN ANNUAL	
Hulton/Longacre/IPC; 1954-1976	
1954	£7.50
1955-1959	£6.00
1960-1065	£4.00
1966-1969	£2.00
1970-1976	£1.50
ROBIN SPECIAL	
Fleetway Editions; Spring 1992	
Spr 1992 US reprints, Green Arrow reprints by Alan Moore	£1.50
ROBIN HOOD	
World Distributors; 1-4 1955	
1-4 28pgs; American reprints	£5.00
ROBIN HOOD	
(some issues titled Robin Hood Tales)	
Miller; 1 1957-34 1959	
1 Colin Andrew art	£5.00
2-34 some issues repinted from Charlton Comics, National Comics, others British originals	£2.50
ROBIN HOOD AND HIS MERRY MEN	
Streamline; 1956, 2 unnumbered issues	
nn - 28pgs; Charlton reprints	£2.50
nn - 52pgs	£3.00
ROBIN HOOD ANNUAL	
(see also The Adventures of Robin Hood Annual)	
Amalgamated Press; 1957-1960	
1957	£10.00
1958-1960	£10.00
ROBOCOP MOVIE SPECIAL	
Marvel; nn Mar 1988	
nn - movie adaptation	£0.75
ROBO HUNTER	
(see Sam Slade, Robo Hunter)	
Titan (Best of 2000AD); 1982-Mar 1985	
Book One 2000AD reprints by Ian Gibson begin	£3.50
Book Two	£4.50
Book Three	£4.00
Book Four	£4.00
ROBO HUNTER	
Eagle; 1 Apr 1984-5 Dec 1985	
1 2000AD reprints by Ian Gibson	£1.25
2-5	£1.00
ROBOT REBELLION	
Streamline; 1 1951	
1 28pgs; American reprints	£8.00
RO-BUSTERS	
Titan (Best of 2000AD); 1983	
Book One	£4.50
Book Two	£4.00
ROCK 'N' ROLL MADNESS FUNNIES	
H. Bunch (Cozmic); 1 Jun 1973-2 Mar 1974	
1 Chris Welch, Dave Gibbons, Edward Barker art	£3.50
2 Dave Gibbons, J.J. Petagno, Edward Barker art	£3.50
ROCKET	
Target Publications; 1 26th Oct 1935-157 22nd Oct 1938 (becomes Target & Rocket)	
1 8pgs on pink paper; Bert Hill art	£30.00
2-6 8pgs on pink paper; Bert Hill art	£10.00
7-93 8pgs on blue paper	£5.00
94-108 12pgs on blue paper	£5.00
109-157 pink paper, reverts to 8pgs with 110	£4.00
ROCKET	
News of the World/Eric Bemrose; 1 21st Apr 1956-32 24th Nov 1956	
(joins Express Weekly)	
1 Captain Falcon by Frank Black, Seabed Citadel by Ley Kenyon begin, Flash Gordon, Johnny Hazard, Brick Bradford US reprints begin	£25.00
2	£12.50
3	£7.50
4-10	£5.00
11-31	£3.00
32 last issue, includes pages introducing stories from Express Weekly	£3.00
ROCKET COMIC, THE	
Hotspur Publishing Co.; nn 1948	
nn - 8pgs	£4.00
ROCKET COMIC, THE	
P.M. Productions; nn-2 1949	
nn - 16pgs; Atom the Mighty Boy begins, Minnitt art	£4.00
2 Minnitt art	£3.00
ROCKETS - A WAY OF LIFE	
Assorted Images Ltd.; nn Apr 1988	
nn - 48pgs in cardboard slipcase, incl. 8pg mini-comic insert Jones Has Been Dismembered; Steve Appleby art	£1.50
ROCKETSHIP X	
United Anglo-American; nn 1951	
nn - 28pgs; Fox Features reprints	£6.00
ROCKY LANE WESTERN	
Miller; nn, 1950?; 50 Jun 1950-139 1959, 90 issues	
nn - 12pgs gravure; Fawcett reprints	£10.00
50 monthly publication	£7.50
51-139	£5.00

	N.MINT
ROCKY MOUNTAIN KING WESTERN COMIC	
Miller; 1 1955-65 1959	
1 Rocky Mountain King by Tom Barling begins (later by Colin Andrew)	£5.00
2-65	£2.50
ROD CAMERON WESTERN	
Miller; various issues 1950-1960	
1 (1950) 32pgs gravure; Fawcett reprints	£8.00
8 (1950?) 32pgs gravure, larger size	£5.00
50-64 (Oct 1951-1953) 24pgs	£3.00
1-? (1960) 68pgs; incl. reprints from Bob Steele, Young Eagle etc.	£2.50
ROGUE TROOPER	
Titan (Best of 2000AD); 1984-Apr 1988	
Book One Gibbons, Wilson art	£4.50
Book Two Gibbons, Wilson, Kennedy art	£4.50
Book Three Wilson, Ewins art	£5.00
Book Four	£5.00
Book Five	£5.00
Book Six	£5.00
Rogue Trooper's Future Wars	£5.50
ROGUE TROOPER ANNUAL	
Fleetway; 1991	
1991 Dillon, Hicklenton art, features new Rogue Trooper	£4.00
ROGUE TROOPER POSTER PROG	
Fleetway Editions; 1994	
1 Poster with story	£1.00
ROM SUMMER SPECIAL	
Marvel; 1982	
1982 48pgs; US reprints; centre-fold poster is often missing	£1.00
ROMEO BROWN (DAILY STRIPS)	
(see also Garth/ Romeo Brown)	
John Dakin; 2 1979, 6 Oct 1960	
2 The Arabian Knight by Peter O'Donnell & James Holdaway; A5 size	£1.50
6 Where There's A Will; A4 size	£1.50
ROMEO TUBBS	
United Anglo-American; nn 1951	
nn - 28pgs; Fox Features reprints	£3.00
ROOKIE COP	
Miller; 1 1956-?	
1-? 28pgs; Charlton reprints	£3.00
ROSE OF BAGDAD, THE	
Gaywood Press; nn 1952	
nn - 36pgs; adapts Italian cartoon film, Sandro Angiolini art	£2.00
ROUNDUP BUDGET OF FUN AND ADVENTURE, THE	
Children's Press; nn 1948	
nn - 20pgs; William McCail, Sam Fair art	£3.00
ROVER, THE	
D.C. Thomson; 1 4th Mar 1922-1855 31st Dec 1961	
(becomes Rover and Adventure)	
1 very scarce; story paper with only a few comic strips	£100.00
2 scarce	£50.00
3	£30.00
1922 issues	£20.00
1923-1930 issues	£15.00
1931-1940 issues	£10.00
1941-1950 issues	£7.50
1951-1955 issues	£5.00
1956-1959 issues	£3.00
1960-1969 issues	£2.00
1970-1973 issues	£1.50
CHRONOLOGY	
21 Jan 1961: 1st "Rover & Adventure". 23rd Nov 1963: 1st "Rover & Wizard".	
ROVER AND ADVENTURE, THE	
D.C. Thomson; 1 21st Jan 1961-626 13th Jan 1973 (joins Wizard)	
1 story paper	£12.50
2	£5.00
3-5	£2.50
1961 issues	£2.00
1962-1969 issues	£1.00
1970-1973 issues	£0.50
ROVER BOOK FOR BOYS, THE	
D.C. Thomson; 1926-1959	
(1926) (Boy in cross-country race jumping stream)	£50.00
(1927) (Cowboy mounting a bucking bronco)	£35.00
(1928) (Two boys in blazers driving an open-top car carrying camping gear)	£30.00
(1929) (Two boys in white shirts riding camels in desert)	£25.00
(1930) (Young man pulling two friends along road in a rickshaw)	£25.00
(1931) (Motor boat towing skiing boys)	£20.00
(1932) (Two boy hikers and dog trying to hitch a lift from a farmer)	£20.00
(1933) (Man on motor cycle trying to lassoo a galloping zebra)	£20.00
(1934) (Two naval men, one holding a rabbit)	£20.00
(1935) (Two naval men laughing at two chinamen - one in a barber's chair has been shorn)	£20.00
(1936) (Two boys in tropical gear watch a dinosaur)	£17.50
(1937) (A cowboy playing football bursts the ball on his spur)	£17.50
(1938) (A cowboy with his tooth tied with rope while another holding the other end rides off on horseback)	£17.50
(1939) (Two lumberjacks joust whilst riding a log on a river)	£17.50
(1940) (Mountie riding a moose jumps over snow-covered cliff to avoid wolves)	£17.50
(1941) (Lumberjack riding a log down a chute being passed by a man on skis)	£15.00
(1942) (Two men in tropical gear playing darts surprised as a spear hits the bullseye of the target)	£15.00
(1950) (Blacksmith repairing robot with a screwdriver) scarce	£20.00
(1956) (Globe in centre of cover with characters in stars at each corner)	£12.50
(1957) (Five horizontal divisions, five pictures, top pic of a plane)	£10.00

	N.MINT
(1958) (Five horizontal divisions, four pictures, top pic of an indian firing an arrow)	£10.00
(1959) (Airliner crossing over mountains, someone firing arrows at eagles below) scarce	£15.00
Note: no editions published for 1943-49, 1951-55.	
ROVER MIDGET COMIC, THE	
D.C. Thomson; nn 11th Feb 1933	
nn - 32pgs giveaway with The Rover; Dudley Watkins, Allan Morley art	£4.00
ROVER SUMMER FUN BOOK, THE	
D.C. Thomson; nn 6th Jun 1936	
nn - 8pgs giveaway with The Rover; Dudley Watkins, Allan Morley art	£4.00
ROY CARSON	
Boardman; nn 1948-36 Feb 1951 (8 issues, some numbered)	
nn (1) Smashing the Crime Wave With Roy Carson	£8.00
nn (3) RC Meets Cheetah, Queen of Spies	£8.00
nn (5) RC Strikes Again	£8.00
nn (7) RC Versus the Marquis	£8.00
13 RC and the Cornish Smugglers	£8.00
23 RC and the Case of the Educated Ape	£8.00
34 RC and the Return of Annette	£8.00
36 RC and the Boxing Racketeers	£8.00
Note: Denis McLoughlin art in all	
ROY CARSON ALBUM	
Moring; nn c1956	
nn - Denis McLoughlin reprints (5, 34, 7, 36, 52, 46)	£15.00
ROY CARSON COMIC	
Popular/ Alexander Moring; 46 Jan 1953, 54 1954; nn 1954	
46, 54 28pgs; McLoughlin art	£8.00
nn (Moring) 68pgs; McLoughlin reprints	£6.00
ROY OF THE ROVERS	
IPC/Fleetway; 25th Sep 1976-20 Mar 1993, 853 unnumbered issues	
25 Sep 1976 Roy of the Rovers by David Sque continued from Tiger	£1.00
2 Oct 1976-19 Nov 1983, 3 Dec 1983-30 Mar 1985	£0.25
26 Nov 1983 Goalkeeper! by John Stokes begins	£0.25
6 Apr 1985 Hotshot Hamish & Mighty Mouse by Sciaffino begins	£0.25
13 Apr 1985-10 May 1986, 24 May 1986-26 Jan 1989	£0.20
17 May 1986 Billy's Boots by John Gillatt begins	£0.20
4 Feb 1989 1st "Roy of the Rovers & Hot Shot!"	£0.20
11 Feb 1989-20 Mar 1993	£0.20
Note: 3 Apr 1982 issue undated on cover	
ROY OF THE ROVERS	
Fleetway; 1 Sep 1993-19 Mar 1995	
1 monthly; Roy of the Rovers, Tales From the Dug-Out by Warren & Gary Pleece begin, Roy, Look Out for Lefty reprints begin	£1.15
2-19	£0.75
ROY OF THE ROVERS	
Ravette Books; Mar 1993	
Melchester Magic 48pgs; reprints	£3.00
Eastern Promise	£3.00
ROY OF THE ROVERS ANNUAL	
Amalgamated Press/Fleetway/IPC; 1958-1990s	
1958	£20.00
1959	£15.00
1960-1965	£10.00
1966-1969	£6.00
1970-1979	£3.00
1980s/1990s	£2.00
ROY OF THE ROVERS COLLECTION, THE	
Today; 1 Aug 1987	
1 96pgs; reprints Roy of the Rovers by Kim Raymond from Today newspaper	£1.50
ROY ROGERS ANNUAL	
World Distributors; 1952-1966?	
1952 Dell reprints; original text stories	£5.00
1953 adapts stories from films	£6.00
1954-1966	£4.00
ROY ROGERS COMICS	
Pemberton/World Distributors; 1 Apr 1951-100 1959	
1 36pgs; Dell reprints	£10.00
2 b/w art	£7.50
3-15 b/w art	£5.00
16-18 2-colour art	£4.00
19-94 4-colour art; 57-84 titled Roy Rogers and Trigger	£4.00
95-100 68pgs	£4.00
ROY ROGERS' TRIGGER	
Pemberton/World Distributors; 1 1952-14 1953	
1-14 28pgs; Dell reprints	£3.00
RUPERT	
The Adventures of Rupert the Little Lost Bear (Nelson, 1921)	£400.00
The Little Bear and the Fairy Child (Nelson, 1922)	£350.00
Margot the Midget and Little Bear's Christmas (Nelson, 1922)	£350.00
The Little Bear and the Ogres (Nelson, 1922)	£350.00
RUPERT BOOKS	
Oldbourne Book Co.; 1960 (2 titles)	
Rupert and the Pink Letter	£20.00
Rupert and Dickory Dock	£20.00
RUPERT ACTIVITY BOOK	
Oldbourne Book Co.; 1959 (2 issues)	
1-2	£60.00
RUPERT ADVENTURE BOOK	
Beaverbrook Newspapers; 1-2 1975	
1 Rupert in Mysterland 32pgs; reprints	£3.50
2 Rupert at Rocky Bay	£3.50
RUPERT ADVENTURE SERIES	
Express; 1 Sep 1948-50 Jun 1963	

	N.MINT
1 Rupert & Snuffy; reprints begin	£50.00
2 reprints	£25.00
3-5 reprints	£20.00
6-25 reprints	£15.00
25-39 new material	£25.00
40-45 new material, more scarce	£45.00
46-48 new material, more scarce	£55.00
49 new marterial, scarce	£80.00
50 new material, scarce	£90.00
RUPERT AND HIS WONDERFUL BOOTS	
Sampson Low; nn Aug 1946	
nn - scarce, boot-shaped book	£125.00
RUPERT ANNUAL	
(see Monster Rupert Annual)	
Express; 1936-1994	
1936 full title The New Adventures of Rupert; red cloth boards and red spine; price 2/6; cover shows Rupert sitting down eating; very scarce with dustjacket	£1600.00
Note: Only 15-20 known copies exist with dustjacket, all in poor to fine condition with prices at auction rising to £2000 for top condition	
1936 without dustjacket	£350.00
1937 full title More Adventures of Rupert; cover shows Rupert and friends on a stone-arch bridge, Rupert waving a stick	£250.00
1938 full title The New Rupert Book; cover shows Rupert and friends up a tree, Rupert is waving	£200.00
1939 full title The Adventures of Rupert; cover shows Rupert and friends chasing a monkey who is flying a kite	£200.00
1940 1st in colour; full title Rupert's Adventure Book; price 3/-; cover shows Rupert scribbling with a pencil/crayon, looking over shoulder	£300.00
1941 full title The Rupert Book; price 3/6; cover shows Rupert in foreground waving and holding a paddle, Algy in background in boat	£275.00
1942 1st soft cover; full title More Adventures of Rupert; cover shows Rupert and friends sitting on battlements of castle waving; very scarce	£400.00
1943 full title More Rupert Adventures; Rupert holding a lantern reaching for a butterfly while his friends watch	£225.00
1944 full title Rupert in More Adventures; Rupert waving from the branches of a tree with his friends. Tiger Lily is bottom left	£175.00
1945	£150.00
1946	£85.00
1947-1949 last soft cover	£75.00
1950-1956	£50.00
1957-1959	£45.00
1960-1966 magic painting not done	£75.00
1960-1966 magic painting done	£25.00
1967-1968 magic painting not done	£40.00
1967-1968 magic painting done	£18.00
1969-1980	£5.00
1981-1984	£4.00
1985 Anniversary issue	£5.00
1986-1990	£4.00
1991-1994	£3.00
Facsimile 1936 (Hawk)	£25.00
Facsimile 1937-1938 (Hawk)	£20.00
Facsimile 1939-42 (Hawk)	£12.00
Facsimile 1943 (Hawk, 1995)	£18.00
RUPERT COLOUR LIBRARY	
Purnell; nn 1976	
nn	£2.00
RUPERT CUT-OUT AND STORY BOOK	
Sampson Low; 1949-1953	
Rupert and Edward and the Circus (1949)	£100.00
Rupert and the Snowman (1950)	£150.00
Rupert	£60.00
The Monster Rupert (1950) 200 cut-outs	£50.00
The Monster Rupert (1953) revised reprint of above, 120 cut-outs	£30.00
Note: Cut-outs must be intact	
RUPERT FORTNIGHTLY	
Celebrity Publications; 1 18th Oct 1989-20 20th Oct 1990	
1	£1.50
2-20	£1.00
RUPERT HOLIDAY SPECIAL	
Polystyle; 1979-1981	
1979 48pgs; Alfred Bestell reprints begin	£1.50
1980-1981	£1.00
RUPERT SUMMER SPECIAL	
Marvel; nn May 1983	
nn - 52pgs; reprints	£1.00
RUPERT LITTLE BEAR	
Sampson Low, 1925-1927, 6 volumes	
1-6 Mary Tourtel art	£300.00
RUPERT LITTLE BEAR LIBRARY	
Sampson Low; 1928-1937, 46 volumes	
1 Rupert and the Enchanted Princess (1928)	£25.00
2 Rupert and the Black Dwarf (1928)	£25.00
3 Rupert and his Pet Monkey (1928)	£25.00
4 Rupert and his friend Margot (1928)	£25.00
5 Rupert in the Wood of Mystery (1929)	£25.00
6 Further Adventures of Rupert (1929)	£25.00
7 Rupert and the Three Robbers (1929)	£25.00
8 Rupert, the Knight and the Lady, and Ropert and the Wise Goat's Birthday Cake	£25.00
9 Rupert and the Circus Clown (1929)	£25.00
10 Rupert and the Magic Hat (1929)	£25.00
11 Rupert and the Little Prince (1930)	£25.00
12 Rupert and King Pippin (1930)	£25.00

	N.MINT
13 Rupert and the Wilful Prince (1930)	£25.00
14 Rupert's Mysterious Flight (1930)	£25.00
15 Rupert In Trouble Again, and Rupert and the Fancy Dress Party (1930)	£25.00
16 Rupert and the Wooden Soldiers, and Rupert's Christmas Adventure (1930)	£25.00
17 Rupert and the Old Man of the Sea (1931)	£25.00
18 Rupert and Algy at Hawthorne Farm (1931)	£25.00
19 Rupert and the Magic Whistle (1931)	£25.00
20 Rupert Gets Stolen (1931)	£25.00
21 Rupert and the Wonderful Boots (1931)	£25.00
22 Rupert and the Christmas Fairies and Rupert and Bill Badger's Picnic Party	**£25.00**
23 Rupert and his Pet Monkey Again, and Beppo Back with Rupert (1932)	£25.00
24 Rupert and the Robber Wolf (1932)	£25.00
25 Rupert's Latest Adventure (1932)	£25.00
26 Rupert and Prince Humpty Dumpty (1932)	£25.00
27 Rupert's Holiday Adventure, Rupert's Message to Father Christmas,	
and Rupert's New Year's Eve Party (1932)	£25.00
28 Rupert's Christmas Tree, and Rupert's Picnic Party (1932)	£25.00
29 Rupert, the Witch and Tabitha (1933)	£25.00
30 Rupert Goes Hiking (1933)	£25.00
31 Rupert and Willy Wispe (1933)	£25.00
32 Rupert, Margot and the Bandits, and Rupert at School (1933)	£25.00
33 Rupert and the Magic Toy Man (1933)	£25.00
34 Rupert and Bill Keep Shop, and Rupert's Christmas Thrills (1933)	£25.00
35 Rupert Rupert and Algernon, and Rupert and the White Dove (1934)	£25.00
36 Rupert and Beppo Again (1934)	£25.00
37 Rupert and Dapple (1934)	£25.00
38 Rupert and Bill's Aeroplane Adventure (1934)	£25.00
39 Rupert and the Magician's Umbrella (1934)	£25.00
40 Rupert and Bill and the Pirates (1935)	£25.00
41 Rupert at the Seaside, and Rpert and Bingo (1935)	£25.00
42 Rupert Gets Captured, and Rupert and the Snow Babe's Christmas	
Adventures (1935)	£25.00
43 Rupert, The Manikin and the Black Knight (1935)	£25.00
44 Rupert and the Greedy Princess (1935)	£25.00
45 Rupert and Bill's Seaside Holiday, and Rupert and the Twins'	
Birthday Cake (1946)	£25.00
46 Rupert and Edward and the Circus, and Rupert and the Snowman (1936)	£25.00

Note: These 46 titles were re-issued many times, priced variously at 6d, 9d, 1/- and 1/3, and are generally in the £10-20 range. 18 titles were re-issued in 1970s under the same title, and are usually priced £3-5.

RUPERT LITTLE BEAR'S ADVENTURES
Sampson Low, 1924-1925, 3 volumes

1-3 Mary Tourtel art	£300.00

RUPERT STORY BOOK
Sampson Low; 1938-1940

The Rupert Story Book (1938) Mary Tourtel art	£150.00
Rupert Little Bear - More Stories (1939)	£150.00
Rupert Again (1940)	£150.00

RUPERT TV PLAYBOOKS
Stanfield; 1975

Rupert Goes to the Moon 16pgs	£2.00
Rupert and the Blue Mist	£2.00
Rupert the Postman	£2.00
Rupert and the Magician's Hat	£2.00

RUPERT TV STORYBOOKS
Stanfield; 1-6 1978

1-6 28pgs; Mick Wells art	£1.00

RUPERT WEEKLY
Marvel; 1 20th Oct 1982-100 15th Sep 1984

1	£3.00
2-5	£1.50
2-100	£1.00

RUPERT'S FAMOUS YELLOW LIBRARY
Sampson Low Marston; 1949

Rupert and his Friend Margo 20pgs; Mary Tourtel Daily Express reprints	£45.00
Rupert the Knight and the Lady	£45.00

S

SABRE ROMANTIC STORIES IN PICTURES
Sabre; 1 1971-?

1 68pgs pocket size; Spanish reprints	£1.00
2-?	£0.35

SABRE THRILLER PICTURE LIBRARY
Sabre; 1 1971-?

1 68pgs pocket size; Night of the Vulture, Spanish reprints	£1.00
2-?	£0.50

SABRE WAR PICTURE LIBRARY
Sabre; 1 1971-?

1 68pgs pocket size; The Unseen Enemy, Spanish reprints	£1.00
2-?	£0.50

SABRE WESTERN STORIES IN PICTURES
Sabre; 1 1971-?

1 68pgs pocket size; Time to Fight, Spanish reprints	£1.00
2-?	£0.50

SABRETOOTH
Boxtree; Mar 1995

Death Hunt (1995) reprints Marvel mini-series by Larry Hama & Mark Texeira	£7.00

SABU
United Anglo-American; 1-4 1951

1-4 28pgs; Fox Features reprints, based on Sabu the Elephant Boy film character	£2.50

Shiver 'n Shake #1

Smash #1

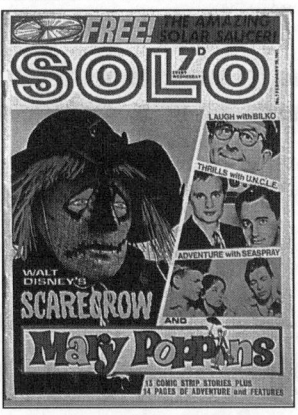
Solo #1

	N.MINT
SAD SACK	
Top Sellers; 1 1973-?	
1-? 36pgs; Harvey reprints	£1.50
SAGA OF THE MAN ELF, THE	
Trident Comics; 1 Aug 1989-5 1990	
1 Man Elf by Guy Lawley & Steve Whitaker begins; uses characters by Moorcock	£1.25
2	£1.10
3-5 Richard Western art	£1.10
SAINT, THE	
Top Sellers; 1-5 1966	
1-5 68pgs; American reprints based on Leslie Charteris character	£4.00
SAINT ANNUAL	
World Distributors/Stafford; 1968-1970, 1979-1980	
1968-1970 Roger Moore	£5.00
1979, 1980 titled Return of the Saint Annual, Ian Ogilvy	£2.00
SAINT ANNUAL, THE	
PBS; 1973	
1973 Roger Moore	£3.00
SAINT DETECTIVE CASES, THE	
Thorpe & Porter; 1 Oct 1951-4? 1952	
1 68pgs; Avon reprints	£7.50
2-4	£5.00
SAINT TELEVISION STORY BOOK, THE	
PBS; 1971	
1971	£3.50
SAM BRONX AND THE ROBOTS	
Acme/Eclipse (Atomic Comic Series 2); Feb 1990	
- hardback; Serge Clerc art	£2.50
SAM HILL PRIVATE EYE COMICS	
Thorpe & Porter; 1-5 1952	
1-5 68pgs; Closeup Inc. reprints	£2.50
SAMSON	
Miller; 1-3 1955	
1-3 28pgs; Ajax/Farrell Publications reprints	£3.00
SAMSON AND DELILAH	
Streamline; nn 1950	
nn - 28pgs; Fox Features reprints	£2.00
SANDMAN	
Titan; Jun 1990-present	
Preludes and Nocturnes (Oct 1991) reprints Sandman 1-8	£10.00
The Doll's House (Jun 1990) reprints Sandman 8-16	£9.00
Dream Country (Jul 1992) reprints Sandman 17-20	£7.00
Season of Mists (Sep 1992) reprints Sandman 21-28	£9.00
A Game of You (Sep 1993) reprints Sandman 32-37	£9.00
Fables and Reflections (Jan 1994) reprints Sandman 29-31, 38-40, 50, Special 1	£12.50
Brief Lives (Jan 1995) reprints Sandman 41-49	£12.50
World's End (Jun 1995) reprints Sandman 51-56	£12.50
SAVAGE ACTION	
Marvel; 1 Nov 1979-15 Jan 1982	
1 Punisher, Dominic Fortune, Moon Knight reprints begin, Night Raven text stories by Maxwell Grant (Alan McKenzie) begin	£1.50
2-15	£1.25
SAVAGE SWORD OF CONAN	
Marvel; 1 8th Mar 1975-18 5th Jul 1975 (joins The Avengers)	
1 Conan by Barry Smith, King Kull reprints begin	£5.00
2	£2.50
3-18	£1.25
SAVAGE SWORD OF CONAN	
Marvel; 1 Nov 1977-93 Jul 1985	
1 52pgs; Conan reprints by Thomas & Buscema/Alcala begin	£3.00
2-12, 14-84	£1.50
13 new cover format; 1st Red Sonja reprint	£2.00
85-93 "Savage Sword of Conan and Mighty World of Marvel"; Night Raven text stories by Jamie Delano	£1.50
ARTISTS	
Artists on Conan reprints include Neal Adams, John Buscema, Gil Kane, etc.	
SAVIOUR	
Trident Comics; 1 Dec 1989-5 1990	
1 Saviour by Mark Millar & Daniel Vallely begins	£1.50
2-5 Nigel Kitching art	£1.00
Saviour 128pgs; trade paperback; collects 1-5	£4.00
SCAVENGERS	
(see Spellbinders)	
SCHOOL FRIEND	
Amalgamated Press; 1 20th May 1950-766 23rd Jan 1965 (joins June)	
1 Silent Three at St. Kit's by Evelyn Flinders, Gay Cavalier by W. Bryce-Hamilton, Jill Crusoe by Roland Davies, Terry Brant by C.L. Doughty all begin	£50.00
2	£25.00
3-5	£7.50
6-10	£4.00
11-766	£2.00
SCHOOL FRIEND PICTURE LIBRARY	
Amalgamated Press; 1 Feb 1962-88 Sep 1965 (joins June and Schoolfriend Picture Library)	
1 68pgs; Tracy's Fabulous Fur	£3.00
2-88	£1.25
SCHOOLGIRL	
Gerald Swan; 1 1951	
1 36pgs; John McCail art, Archie reprints from US	£2.50
SCHOOLGIRLS' OWN ANNUAL	
Amalgamated Press; 1923-1942	
1923 scarce	£30.00
1924	£20.00

	N.MINT
1925-1929	£15.00
1930-1939	£10.00
1940-1942	£7.50
SCHOOLGIRLS' PICTURE LIBRARY	
Amalgamated Press; 1 Jul 1957-327 Sep 1965 (joins June and Schoolfriend Picture Library)	
1 68pgs pocket; Leader of the Secret Avengers	£3.00
2-327	£1.25
ARTISTS/FEATURES	
Silent Three in 58, 87, 120, 159.	
SCIENCE SERVICE	
Acme/Eclipse (Atomic Comic Series 1); 1989	
- hardcover; Rian Hughes art	£2.50
SCOOP	
D.C. Thomson; 1 21st Jan 1978-194 3rd Oct 1981	
1	£1.25
2-194	£0.50
SCOOP WESTERN, THE	
Martin & Reid; 1 1950	
1 16pgs; Mick Anglo, John McCail, Wally Robertson art	£5.00
SCOOPS COMIC	
Hotspur Publishing; nn 1948	
nn - 8pgs	£2.50
SCORCHER	
I.P.C. Magazines; 10th Jan 1970-26th Jun 1971, 70? issues (becomes Scorcher and Score)	
10 Jan 1970 Royal's Rangers by Leslie Branton, Sub by Ken Reid, Billy's Boots, Paxton's Powerhouse by Barrie Mitchell all begin	£2.00
17 Jan 1970-26 Jun 1971	£0.75
SCORCHER AND SCORE	
(previously two separate comics)	
I.P.C. Magazines; 3rd Jul 1971-5th Oct 1974, 167? issues (joins Tiger)	
3 Jul 1971 Jack of United, Jimmy of City, Billy's Boots, Manager Matt by Ken Reid all begin	£1.50
10 Jul 1971-5 Oct 1974	£0.50
SCORCHY	
Gold Star; 1 1972	
1 68pgs; American reprints, adult	£1.00
SCORE 'N' ROAR	
I.P.C. Magazines; 19th Sep 1970-26th Jun 1971, 41 issues (becomes Scorcher and Score)	
19 Sep 1970 Jack of United, Jimmy of City, Peter the Cat all begin	£1.00
26 Sep 1970-26 Jun 1971	£0.50
SCOTLAND YARD	
Famepress; 1 Nov 1965-?	
1 68pgs pocket size; An Innocent Crook, Italian reprints	£1.00
2-?	£0.50
SCREAM!	
I.P.C. Magazines; 1 24th Mar 1984-15 30th Jun 1984 (joins Eagle)	
1 Monster by Alan Moore & Heinzl (only Moore issue), The Thirteenth Floor by Ian Holland (Wagner/Grant) & Ortiz begin	£1.50
1 with free gift (plastic vampire fangs)	£3.00
2-3, 5-6, 8-15	£0.40
4 Cam Kennedy art	£0.75
7 Brendan McCarthy art	£0.75
SEA DEVIL, THE	
Scion; 1 Feb 1952	
1 20pgs; Terrence Patrick art	£4.00
SEA HERO	
Scion; nn 1952	
nn - 24pgs; King-Ganteaume art	£4.00
SEASIDE COMIC	
C.A. Pearson; Jun 1930-Jun 1939, 10 issues	
1930 12pgs; Walter Bell art	£8.00
1931, 1933-1934 A.W. Browne art	£8.00
1932	£8.00
1935-1939 Ray Bailey art in most	£8.00
SECOND CITY	
Harrier; 1 Nov 1986-4 May 1987	
1 Phil Elliot art begins	£1.00
2-4	£0.80
SECRET AGENT	
Fleetway (A Fleetway Super Library); 1 Jan 1967-26 Jan 1968	
1 132pgs; Johnny Nero (in all odd numbers)	£2.50
2 Code Name - Barracuda (in all even numbers)	£2.50
3-26	£2.00
ARTISTS/FEATURES	
1 Meet Johnny Nero by Paulo Montecchi. 2 Code Name - Barracuda. 3 The Devil's Secret. 4 Call For Barracuda. 5 Assassin's Anonymous by Estaquio Segrelles. 6 The Evil Ones. 7 Trail of Terror by Paulo Montecchi. 8 The Death Merchants. 9 The Murder Corporation by Paulo Montecchi. 10 Payment in Death. 11 Fatal Formula. 12 The Vanishing Astronaut by O.A. Novelle. 13 The Master Minds by Leo Duranona. 14 The Underground Jungle. 15 The Double Agent by Eustaquio Segrelles. 16 The Devil's Ransom by Antonio Raviola. 17 Traitor's Trail. 18 Crime Buster. 19 The Evil Shadow. 20 Operation Flashpoint. 21 The Mind Machine by M.S. 22 The Phantom Captain. 23 Trouble in Turkey by O.A. Novelle. 24 The Destroyers. 25 The Shadow of the Samurai. 26 Treacherous Trail.	
SECRET AGENT PICTURE LIBRARY	
C.A. Pearson; 1 1961-? 1962?	
1 68pgs pocket size	£2.50
2-?	£1.75
SECRET AGENT PICTURE LIBRARY HOLIDAY SPECIAL	
Fleetway; 1967-1970	
1967 224pgs pocket size; John Steel reprints from Thriller Picture Library, Luis Bermejo art	£2.00
1968 Spy 13 reprints from Thriller Picture Library	£2.00
1969-1970 1969 incl. Alberto Breccia art	£2.00

	N.MINT
SECRET AGENT X9	
(see Action Series)	
SECRET MISSIONS	
Streamline; nn 1951	
nn - 28pgs; Fox Features reprints	£4.00
SECRET SERVICE	
Streamline; nn 1951	
nn - 28pgs; US reprints	£4.00
SECRET SERVICE PICTURE LIBRARY	
M.V. Features; 1 Jun 1965-18? 1966	
1 68pgs pocket size; The Defector	£2.00
2-18	£1.50
SECRET SERVICE SERIES	
(see The Jet Plane Raiders, The Wreckers, The Crime Syndicate, The Forgers, Smuggler's Creek, Atomic Spy Ring)	
SECRET WARS	
(title varies: Secret Wars/Secret Wars Featuring Zoids/Secret Wars II)	
Marvel; 1 27th Apr 1985-80 10th Jan 1987	
1 32pgs; Secret Wars reprints begin	£1.50
1 with free gift (Secret Wars rub-down transfers)	£3.00
2	£1.25
2 with free gift (Captain America sticker) poster centrefold	£2.50
3	£1.00
3 with free gift (Dr. Doom sticker)	£2.00
4-18	£0.75
19 24pgs; Zoids toy tie-in strip by Ian Rimmer & Kev Hopgood begins	£0.75
20-34 features Zoids	£0.75
35-80 titled Secret Wars II	£0.60
SECRET WARS	
Marvel/Grandreams; 1986	
1986 reprints Secret Wars #1, Marvel Team-Up #7	£2.00
SECRET WARS WINTER SPECIAL	
Marvel; nn Oct 1985	
nn - reprints	£1.25
SECRET WARS II SPECIAL	
Marvel; nn Mar 1986	
nn - reprints	£1.00
SECRETS OF LOVE	
Gerald Swan; 1 1954-?	
1 Star reprints	£2.50
2-?	£1.25
SECRETS OF THE UNKNOWN	
Alan Class; 1 Oct 1962-249 Mar 1989	
1 68pgs; reprints from Atlas, Marvel, Charlton, A.C.G. etc; very scarce	£20.00
2 scarce	£10.00
3-5	£6.00
6-10	£4.00
11-50	£2.50
51-200	£1.50
201-249	£1.25
SENORITA RIO	
Cartoon Art; 1 1950	
1 16pgs; Fiction House reprints	£3.00
SERGEANT O'BRIEN	
S.N.P.I.; 50 Feb 1952-91 1954, 42 issues	
50 24pgs; reprints French strip by Jean Pape	£2.50
51-91	£1.50
SERGEANT PAT OF RADIO PATROL	
Modern Fiction; nn 1948	
nn - 16pgs; reprints American newspaper strip by Eddie Sullivan & Charlie Schmidt	£5.00
SERGEANT PRESTON OF THE YUKON	
World Distributors; 1 1953-16 1954	
1 28pgs; Western Publishing Co. reprints	£3.50
2-16	£2.00
SERIOUS COMICS	
H. Bunch (Cosmic Comics); 1 1975	
1 36pgs; William Rankin art, adult	£1.00
SEVEN AGES OF WOMAN	
Knockabout (Crack); nn Jun 1990	
nn - Kate Charlesworth, Melinda Gebbie, Julie Hollings, Carol Swain art	£6.00
SEVEN DEADLY SINS	
Knockabout (Crack); nn May 1989	
nn - Moore, Gaiman, Gibbons scripts, Emerson, Talbot art	£5.50
77 SUNSET STRIP COMIC ALBUM	
World Distributors; (1 cy1963?)	
1 98pgs softcover; Dell reprints	£10.00
SEX WARRIOR	
Apocalypse; nn Nov 1991	
nn - Toxicl reprints by Will Simpson	£1.50
Note: Sex Warrior later published in US by Dark Horse	
SEXY TALES	
Top Sellers; nn-3 1974	
nn, 2-3 132pgs pocket size; adult Italian reprints	£1.00
SHADOW, THE	
Boxtree; nn 1994	
nn - reprints Dark Horse movie adaptation, Michael Wm Kaluta art	£7.00
SHADOWMEN, THE	
Trident; 1 May 1990-2 1990	
1 28pgs; by Mark Millar & Andrew Hope/Ben Dilworth	£1.00
2	£0.85
SHADOW RIDERS	
Marvel; 1 Jun 1993-4 Sep 1993	

	N.MINT
1 Ross Dearsley art, guest stars Cable; embossed cover	£1.75
2 guest stars Ghost Rider	£1.50
3-4 guest stars Cable	£1.20
SHADOW'S EDGE, THE	
(see Legends of Larian)	
SHARP-SHOOTER WESTERN ALBUM	
G.T. Ltd; nn 1959?	
nn - card cover; McLoughlin Buffalo Bill (41, 43, 49), Norman Light reprints	£15.00
SHERIFF, THE	
Screen Stories; 1 Sep 1948-4 1949 (becomes The Sheriff and Elmo's Own)	
1-2 8pgs; western films adapted into strips, Dennis Gifford art	£5.00
3 tabloid size, Gifford art	£3.00
4 photo	£3.00
SHERIFF AND ELMO'S OWN, THE	
Screen Stories Publications; 1 15th Jul 1949-5 1950 (dated to 2, Sep 1949)	
1 8pgs tabloid; fumetti adaptations of western films, Elmo's Own comic insert	£3.50
2-3 Elmo's Own insert, Mick Anglo art	£3.00
4-5 full colour cover, Elmo's Own integrated into magazine	£3.00
SHERIFF OF COCHISE	
C.A. Pearson (TV Picture Stories); 1 Jun 1959-3 Sep 1959	
1 68pgs pocket size	£5.00
2-3	£3.00
ARTISTS/FEATURES	
1 The Kingdom by Cosmoartis. 2 The Safe Men. 3 The Holdup.	
SHERIFF OF TOMBSTONE	
Miller; 50-55 1959	
50-55 28pgs; Charlton reprints	£2.50
SHERLOCK HOLMES	
(see also Super Detective Library)	
Collins Lions; 1991	
The Speckled Band/The Blue Carbuncle Conan Doyle adaptations by Tim Quinn & George Sears	£3.50
The Hound of the Baskervilles	£3.50
SHERLOCK HOLMES	
Tundra; Feb 1993	
The Curious Case of the Vanishing Villain 36pgs; by Rennie & Phoenix	£3.00
SHIVER AND SHAKE	
(see Frankie Stein's Mini-Monster Comic Book)	
I.P.C. Magazines; 10th Mar 1973-5th Oct 1974, 83 issues	
No. 1 - 10 Mar 1973 Frankie Stein by Robert Nixon, Scream Inn by Brian Walker begin	£3.00
No.1 with free gift (1 of 4 practical jokes)	£6.00
17 Mar 1973	£1.50
24 Mar 1973-5 Oct 1974	£0.75
ARTISTS/FEATURES	
Leo Baxendale (Sweeny Toddler reprints). Ken Reid (Creepy Creations). Ron Turner (Malice in Wonderland).	
SHOCK	
Portman; 1 Oct 1979-4 Jan 1980	
1-4 52pgs; US reprints	£1.25
SHOCKWAVE	
London Editions; 1 (2 Mar 1991)-4 (16 May 1991)	
1 Animal Man (to 2), Hellblazer, Black Orchid reprints begin	£1.25
2	£1.00
3-4 Catwoman Year One reprints begin	£1.00
SHOOTING STAR COMIC	
Scion; nn 1948	
nn - 8pgs; Serge Drigin art	£4.00
SHOTS FROM THE FILMS	
(see Film Shots)	
D. McKenzie; nn 1948	
nn - 8pgs; fumetti adaptations of films	£4.00
SHOWBOAT COMIC, THE	
Pictorial Art; nn Sep 1948	
nn - 8pgs; Bob Wilkin art	£3.00
SIDESHOW COMICS	
Pan Graphics; 1 1988-v2:8 1991?	
1 Talbot/Welch reprint, Heart of Gold begins	£1.00
2-v2:8	£0.75
SIGNAL TO NOISE	
Victor Gollancz; nn Jul 1992	
nn - graphic novel by Neil Gaiman & Dave McKean, hardback	£15.00
nn - paperback	£10.00
SILVER KID WESTERN	
Streamline; 1955, 2 unnumbered issues	
nn - 28pgs; Stanmor Publications reprints	£2.00
nn - 68pgs	£3.00
SILVER KING, THE	
P.M. Productions; nn Apr 1946	
nn - 8pgs printed on silver paper; Denis Gifford art	£2.50
SILVER SPARKS COMIC	
Philipp Marx; nn 1946	
nn - 8pgs printed on one side silver/one side beige paper	£2.50
SILVER STAR FUN COMIC, THE	
P.M. Productions; nn Apr 1946	
nn - 8pgs printed on silver paper; Denis Gifford art	£2.50
SILVER SURFER WINTER SPECIAL	
Marvel; nn Nov 1982	
nn - 52pgs; reprints	£1.25
SIMPSONS, THE	
Titan	
Simpsons Comics Extravaganza	£6.00

	N.MINT
SINBAD AND THE EYE OF THE TIGER	
General Books; nn 1977	
nn - 32pgs; film adaptation by Ian Gibson	£1.25
SIN CITY	
H. Bunch; 1 Nov 1973	
1 Dave Gibbons art	£2.50
SIN CITY	
Titan Books	
Sin City (Jan 1993) Frank Miller art/story	£8.00
A Dame to Kill For (Jan 1995) Miller art/story	£9.00
The Big Fat Kill (Dec 1995) Miller art/story; hardcover	£17.00
SINGBAD THE SAILOR	
Children's Press; nn 1948	
nn - 20pgs; Sam Fair, Alf Farningham art	£2.50
SINISTER LEGENDS	
Savoy; nn May 1988	
nn - 112pgs; Kris Guido art	£5.00
SINISTER TALES	
Alan Class; 1 Jan 1964-227 Jan 1989	
1 68pgs; reprints from Atlas, Marvel, etc.; very scarce	£10.00
2 scarce	£7.50
3-5	£5.00
6-10	£3.00
11-200	£1.50
201-227	£1.25
SIX COMICS OF WORLD WAR ONE	
Peter Way (Great Newspapers Reprinted No.2); 1972	
- facsimiles of Lot-O-Fun 4 Nov 1914, Picture Fun 26 Dec 1914, Comic Life 31 Jul 1915, Funny Wonder 7 Aug 1915, Rainbow 28 Apr 1917, Illustrated Chips 21 Dec 1918 in wraparound cover	£2.50
SIX-GUN HEROES	
Miller; 1 Sep 1950-? 1950?; 50 Jul 1951-114 1959	
1-? 28pgs; Fawcett reprints	£7.50
50-114 36pgs/28pgs	£5.00
SIX-GUN HEROES WESTERN COMIC ANNUAL	
Miller; 1961	
1961 96pgs, softcover; Gabby Hayes, Lash LaRue reprints	£7.50
SIX-GUN WESTERN	
Miller; 1-9 1957	
1-9 28pgs; Atlas reprints	£2.50
SKIDMARKS	
Tundra Publishing UK; 1 Jun 1992-3 Sep 1992	
1 reprints Bic by Ed Hillyer	£3.00
2-3 reprints	£2.00
SKIN	
Tundra Publishing UK; nn Aug 1992	
nn - graphic novel by Pete Milligan, Brendan McCarthy & Carol Swain	£4.00
SKIN DEEP	
Penguin; nn Jan 1993	
nn - by Charles Burns	£9.00
SKIPPER, THE	
D.C. Thomson; 1 6th Sep 1930-543 1st Feb 1941	
1 scarce	£50.00
2	£25.00
3	£20.00
1930 issues	£15.00
1931-1935 issues	£10.00
1936-1941 issues	£7.50
SKIPPER BOOK FOR BOYS, THE	
D.C. Thomson; 1932-1948	
1932 scarce	£50.00
1933	£25.00
1934-1939	£20.00
1940	£15.00
1941-1948	£12.50
SKIPPER MIDGET COMIC, THE	
D.C. Thomson; nn 10th Nov 1934	
nn - 32pgs giveaway with The Skipper; Dudley Watkins, Allan Morley art	£5.00
SKIZZ	
Titan; nn Mar 1989	
nn - 2000AD reprints by Alan Moore & Jim Baikie	£7.00
SKIZZ II: ALIEN CULTURES	
Mandarin (2000AD Books); nn Sep 1993	
nn - 2000AD reprints, Baikie story & art	£6.00
SKY HERO COMIC	
Scion; nn 1952	
nn - 24pgs; King-Ganteaume art	£4.00
SKY HIGH COMIC	
P.M. Productions; nn 1949	
nn - 16pgs; Colin Merritt art	£4.00
SKYLINE COMIC	
Scion; 1 Jan 1952	
1 20pgs; King-Ganteaume art	£4.00
SKY POLICE COMICS	
Cartoon Art; nn 1949	
nn - 20pgs; Fiction House reprints	£4.00
SKY SHERIFF	
Pemberton; v1:1 1951	
Vol 1:1 36pgs; D.S. Publishing Co. reprints of Breeze Lawson, Sky Sheriff	£3.00
SLAINE	
Titan (Best of 2000AD); 1985-1987, 1990	
Book One	£4.50
Slaine Gaming Book	£4.50

	N.MINT
Slaine the King Fabry art	£4.50
Slaine the King Special Edition (1990)	£6.00
The Collected Slaine (Sep 1993)	£9.00
SLAINE THE HORNED GOD	
Fleetway/Mandarin (2000AD Books); 1 Nov 1989-3 Mar 1991; Sep 1993	
Volume 1 (1989) Pat Mills & Simon Bisley reprints from 2000AD	£4.50
Volume 2 (1990) Slaine reprints	£4.50
Volume 3 (1991) Slaine reprints	£4.50
Slaine the Horned God (Mandarin, 1993) hardcover	£17.00
Slaine the Horned God (Mandarin, 1993) softcover	£13.00
SLAM BANG COMICS	
Miller; 1-8 1954	
1-8 28pgs; Fawcett reprints	£4.00
SLEEZE BROTHERS, THE	
Marvel; 1 Aug 1989-6 Jan 1990	
1 Sleeze Brothers by John Carnell & Andy Lanning/Stephen Baskerville begins	£0.75
2-6	£0.60
Sleeze Brothers File (1990) reprints	£8.50
SLICK FUN	
Gerald Swan; 1 Jun 1940-19 1945 (becomes Coloured Slick Fun)	
1 36pgs; William Ward art	£12.00
2-10 36pgs	£6.00
11-12 28pgs	£6.00
13-19 20pgs	£6.00
Specials:	
Spring, Winter (1942)	£10.00
SLY SINISTER SCURVY ADVENTURES OF CAPTAIN REILLY-FFOULL, THE	
Mirror Features; nn 1940s	
nn - 36pgs; reprints Just Jake newspaper strip by Bernard Graddon from Daily Mirror	£6.00
SMALL KILLING, A	
Victor Gollancz; nn Sep 1991	
nn - (hardback) Alan Moore & Oscar Zarate	£15.00
nn - (paperback)	£9.00
SMASH!	
Odhams/IPC; 1 5th Feb 1966-3rd Apr 1971 (257 issues, numbered to 162)	
1 Bad Penny, The Nervs, The Swotts & the Blotts, Grimley Feendish - all by Leo Baxendale, Space Jinx by Brian Lewis, Queen of the Seas by Ken Reid begin	£30.00
1 with free gift (Big Bang Gun)	£50.00
2	£7.50
3-8, 10-14, 17-19	£3.00
9 Legend Testers by Jordi Bernet, Moon Madness by Lewis begin	£3.00
15 It's the Rubberman begins	£3.00
16 Hulk (from Hulk 2) reprints begin	£3.00
20 Batman Sunday newspaper reprints begin	£3.00
21-26, 28-35	£3.00
27 Fantastic Four (from FF1) reprints begin	£4.00
36 Avengers (from Avengers 4) reprints begin (ends 38)	£4.00
37 no Hulk	£3.00
38 British original Hulk strip (one-off), scarce	£10.00
39-75, 77-136	£1.50
76 Daredevil (from DD 2) reprints begin	£1.50
137 1st "Smash! and Pow!"; Spider-Man (from Spider-Man 34) reprints begin, The Cloak by Mike Higgs begins	£1.50
138-143, 145-162	£1.25
144 1st "Smash! and Pow! Incorporating Fantastic"; Thor (from Thor 140) reprints begin	£1.50
15th Mar '69 1st IPC issue, new look; Cursitor Doom by Eric Bradbury begins	£2.00
as above with free gift (Secret Codemaster card)	£4.00
22nd Mar '69-26th Apr '69, 10th May 69-3rd Apr '71	£1.00
3rd May '69 Eric the Viking by Don Lawrence (reprints Karl the Viking from Lion) begin	£1.00
SMASH! ANNUAL	
Odhams/Fleetway; 1967-1976	
1967	£6.00
1968-1970	£4.50
1971 softcover	£3.50
1972-1976	£2.00
SMASH COMICS	
T.V. Boardman; 7 1940-11 1941, 5 issues	
7-11 36pgs/20pgs; Quality reprints	£6.00
SMASH! HOLIDAY SPECIAL	
IPC; 1969-1970	
1969	£4.50
1970	£3.50
SMASHER COMIC	
CAS Ltd; nn 1947	
nn - 8pgs; Bob Wilkin art	£3.00
SMASHER COMICS	
Tongard Trading Co.; 1 1947	
1 8pgs; Bob Monkhouse, Bryan Berry art	£4.00
SMILEY BURNETTE WESTERN	
Miller; 1-4 1950	
1-4 28pgs; Fawcett reprints	£5.00
SMOKING GUNS WESTERN	
Scion; nn 1952	
nn - 24pgs; Ron Embleton, Norman Light art	£8.00
SMUGGLER'S CREEK	
(see Secret Service Series)	
Hotspur Publishing; 5 1949	
5 8pgs; Bob Wilkins art	£3.00
SNOOZY THE SEA LION	
Brockhampton Press; 1959-1960	
Snoozy the Sea Lion (1959) 36pgs oblong; by Dorothy Smith & Woolf Goldberg	£1.00
Snoozy Dives In (1960)	£1.00

N.MINT

SNOW WHITE
Top Sellers; nn 1974
nn - 132pgs pocket size; adult Italian reprints £1.00
SOLDIER COMICS
Miller; 1-6 1952
1-6 28pgs; Fawcett reprints £1.50
SOLO
City; 1 18th Feb 1967-31 16th Sep 1967 (joins TV Tornado)
1 very scarce; Sgt. Bilko by Tom Kerr, Man From UNCLE by Paul Trevillion begin £30.00
1 with free gift (Solar Saucer) £60.00
2 scarce £15.00
3-5 £10.00
6-18 £7.50
19 Mark of the Mysterons by Don Harley, Project SWORD begin £10.00
20-31 very scarce £7.50
FEATURES
All issues contain Walt Disney based strips (reprinted from Gold Key).
SOLTHENIS, THE
The Rogues' Gallery; 1 Sep 1987
1 Richard Piers Rayner script & art £2.00
SOMETIME STORIES
Hourglass Comics; 1 May 1977
1 32pgs; McCarthy/Ewins art £4.00
SONIC THE COMIC
Fleetway Editions; 1 29th May 1993-present (67 to 22nd Dec 1995)
1 Sonic the Hedgehog by Alan McKenzie & Anthony Williams begins, John Howard, Mike White art £0.75
2-57 £0.50
58 (18th Aug 1995) 1st New Look £0.95
59-67 £0.50
SOUTH WALES ECHO AND EXPRESS CHILDREN'S SUPPLEMENT
South Wales Echo & Express; 27th May 1933-8th Jun 1935
27 May 1933 4pgs supplement; Stanley White, Reg Perrott, Basil Reynolds art £10.00
3 Jun 1933-8 Jun 1935 £5.00
Note: title becomes The Children's South Wales Echo and Express in 1933, Boys and Girls South Wales Echo in 1934
SPACE ACE
Atlas; 1 Aug 1960-32 Mar 1963
1 Ron Turner art £12.00
2-13 Ron Turner art £8.00
14-32 £1.50
SPACE ADVENTURES
Miller; 1-? 1950s
1 68pgs pocket size; The Unknown Element, Charlton reprint £4.00
2-? £3.00
SPACE ADVENTURES
Miller; 50 1953-?
50-? 28pgs; Charlton reprints £4.00
SPACE ADVENTURES PRESENTS SPACE TRIP TO THE MOON
Alan Class; 1 1961
1 68pgs; Charlton reprints £8.00
SPACE AND ADVENTURE COMICS
Miller; 1-2 1961
1-2 Space Troopers begins, Jonathan Wild, Pancho Villa reprints £4.00
SPACE COMICS
Arnold Book Co.; 50 May 1953-81 May 1954
50 Captain Valiant by Mick Anglo begins £10.00
51-54 monthly issues £8.00
55-81 weekly issues, from 28 Nov 1953 £6.00
SPACE COMICS OMNIBUS
Arnold Book Co.; nn 1954
nn - Space Comics 55-60 rebound in new cover £10.00
SPACE COMMANDER KERRY
Miller; 50 Aug 1953-55 Jan 1954
50 Space Commander Kerry by Mick Anglo begins £10.00
51-55 £8.00
SPACE COMMANDO COMICS
Miller; 50 Sep 1953-59 May 1954
50 Space Commander Kerry, Sparky Malone by Mick Anglo begin £10.00
51-59 £8.00
SPACE DOG
Andre Deutsch; nn Oct 1993
nn - 64pgs; Space Dog by Hendrik Dorgathen £7.00
SPACE FAMILY ROBINSON ANNUAL
World Distributors; 1967
1967 sub-titled Lost in Space!; Melvyn Powell and John Leeder art £12.00
SPACEHAWKS
(see Blue Bolt series)
SPACE HERO COMIC
Scion; nn-2 1952
nn - 24pgs; Norman Light, Roger Davis art £8.00
2 24pgs; King-Ganteaume art £4.00
SPACEMAN
Gould-Light; 1 1953-15 1954
1 28pgs; Ron Embleton, Norman Light art begins £25.00
2-15 £15.00
SPACEMAN COMIC ALBUM
World Distributors; 1 1965
1 64pgs, Dell reprints in colour £4.00
SPACEMAN COMICS
Cartoon Art; nn 1950
nn - 28pgs; Fiction House reprints from Planet Comics £6.00

Sparky #1

Superadventure Comic #97

Superboy Double Double Comics

	N.MINT
SPACE 1999 ANNUAL	
World Distributors/World & Whitman; 1975-1979	
1975	£6.00
1976-1978	£5.00
1979 more scarce	£7.50
SPACE PATROL	
Young World; 12 Jun 1964, 24 Dec 1964 (2 issues)	
12, 24 Space Patrol by R. Paul Hoye, based on TV series	£6.00
Note: part of Super Mag series	
SPACE PICTURE LIBRARY HOLIDAY SPECIAL	
IPC; 1977-1981 (5 issues)	
1977-1979 192pgs pocket size; Kurt Caesar Jet Ace Logan reprints	£1.50
1980-1981 Ron Turner Rick Random/Jet Ace Logan reprints	£1.50
SPACE PRECINCT	
Manga Publishing; 1 31st Oct 1995-6 Mar 1996	
1 Based on Gerry Anderson TV series; John Erasmus art	£1.25
2-3 Erasmus, David Hine art	£1.25
4-6	£1.00
SPACE PRECINCT	
Manga Publishing; 1 Dec 1995	
Vol.1 48pgs; reprints story from Space Precinct, Erasmus art	£5.00
SPACE PRECINCT ANNUAL	
Granddreams; 1995	
1995	£5.00
SPACE SQUADRON	
Streamline; 1-2 1951	
1-2 28pgs; Atlas reprints	£6.00
SPACE TRAVELLERS	
Donald F. Peters; 1-10 1950s	
1-10 28pgs; reprints American newspaper strip Twin Earths	£4.00
SPACEWAYS COMIC	
(see Swift Morgan Space Comic)	
SPACEWAYS COMIC ANNUALL	
Moring; 1953-1955	
1953-1954 Denis McLoughlin reprints 52, 50, 54, 30	£10.00
1955 titled The New Spaceways Comic Annual No.1	£8.00
Note: all have McLoughlin Swift Morgan, Roy Carson reprints	
SPARK MAN	
Donald F. Peters; 19 1950	
19 20pgs gravure; reprints American strip	£5.00
SPARKLER	
Provincial Comics; 1 12th Sep 1931-20 23rd Jan 1932	
1	£25.00
2-20 Bert Hill, Reg Carter art	£7.50
SPARKLER	
(previously My Favourite)	
Amalgamated Press; 1 20th Oct 1934-251 5th Aug 1939 (joins Crackers)	
1 Bertie Brown, Percy Cocking, Frank Minnitt art	£40.00
2	£15.00
3-5	£7.50
6-50	£5.00
51-251	£4.00
SPARKLER ANNUAL	
Amalgamated Press; 1936-1940	
1936 scarce	£35.00
1937	£20.00
1938-1940	£10.00
SPARKLER COMIC BOOK SERIES	
Donald F. Peters; 1 1948-16 1949 (becomes Comics on Parade)	
1 United Features reprints	£5.00
2-16	£3.00
SPARKLER COMICS	
Miller; 1 Feb 1948	
1 United Features reprints	£3.00
SPARKLET COMIC	
Philmar/P.M. Productions; 1-2 1948	
1 8pgs; Arthur Martin, Frank Minnitt art	£3.00
2 Reg Parlett, Minnitt, Wally Robertson, Denis Gifford art	£3.00
SPARKLING COMIC	
International Fiction; 1 1945, in three different editions	
(a) 12pgs; John Turner art, incl. reprint of Super Science Thrills	£4.00
(b) 8pgs printed black/red	£3.00
(c) 8pgs printed b/w	£3.00
SPARKLING COMIC, THE	
Phillip Marx; nn 1945	
nn - 16pgs; Reg Carter art	£3.00
SPARKS	
James Henderson; 1 21st Mar 1914-198 29th Dec 1917 (joins The Big Comic, later Sparks and The Big Comic, and Sparks (new series))	
1 12pgs; Louis Briault, Walter Booth art	£70.00
2-5	£25.00
6-50	£15.00
51-198	£10.00
CHRONOLOGY	
1915: black/red printing. 1916: drops to 8pgs. 1917: returns to black printing.	
SPARKS (NEW SERIES)	
(previously Sparks and The Big Comic)	
James Henderson/Amalgamated Press; 277 3rd May 1919-327 17th Apr 1920 (51 issues, becomes Little Sparks)	
277 Walter Booth art	£30.00
278-280	£10.00
281-327 Amalgamated Press from 20 Mar 1920	£5.00

	N.MINT
SPARKS AND THE BIG COMIC	
(previously The Big Comic and Sparks)	
James Henderson; 247 5th Oct 1918-276 26th Apr 1919 (30 issues, becomes Sparks)	
247 Walter Booth art	£25.00
248-276 some incl. Allan Morley art	£5.00
SPARKY	
D.C. Thomson; 1 23rd Jan 1965-16th Jul 1977 (652 issues, joins Topper)	
1 Keyhole Kate by George Drysdale, Wee Tusky by Jack Monk, Hungry Horace by George Drysdale, Sparky by Ron Spencer all begin	£25.00
1 with free gift (The Flying Snorter balloon)	£50.00
2	£5.00
3-5	£2.50
20 Feb 1965-25 Jan 1970, 8 Feb 1970-16 Jul 1977	£1.00
1 Feb 1970 I Spy by Les Barton begins	£1.00
SPARKY BOOK, THE	
(amalgamates with Topper Book)	
D.C. Thomson; 1968-1980	
1968	£5.00
1969-1970	£3.50
1971-1980	£2.50
SPARKY WATTS	
United Anglo-American; 1949, 2 unnumbered issues	
nn-nn 36pgs; Columbia Publications reprints	£3.00
SPECIES	
Boxtree; nn Dec 1995	
nn - Dark Horse reprints based on movie; John Bolton cover	£9.00
SPECTACULAR COLOUR COMIC	
Scion; 1 Aug 1951-2 Sep 1951	
1-2 24pgs; King-Ganteaume art	£4.00
SPECTACULAR CRIMES	
Streamline; 1-2 1951	
1-2 28pgs; Fox Features reprints	£4.00
SPECTACULAR FEATURES	
Streamline; 1 1951	
1 28pgs; Fox Features reprints	£4.00
SPECTRE STORIES	
John Spencer; 1-6 1967?	
1-6 some incl. adapted Ron Embleton Bill Merrill reprints	£2.00
SPEED	
IPC; 23rd Feb 1980-25th Oct 1980 (31 issues, numbered to 3; joins Tiger)	
1 Journey to the Stars by Ron Turner, Baker's Half Dozen by Mike Western begin	£1.00
1 with free gift (red plastic Spinner)	£2.00
2	£0.40
2 with free gift (Super Speed Slide of Facts and Figures)	£1.00
3	£0.30
3 with free gift (fold-out Speed Games)	£0.75
16 Mar-16 Aug 1980	£0.25
23 Aug 1980 Winner by Ron Turner begins	£0.25
30 Aug-25 Oct 1980	£0.25
Note: no issues dated 24 May-21 Jun 1980	
SPEED ANNUAL	
IPC; 1981-1982	
1981-1982	£2.00
SPEED & POWER, THE BOOK OF	
(see Look & Learn Book of..) IPC; 1975	
1975 slightly oversized	£2.50
SPEED GALE COMICS	
Cartoon Arts; nn 1947	
nn - 16pgs; reprints stories from other Cartoon Arts comics	£4.00
SPEED KINGS COMIC	
Mans World; 12 Nov 1953-17 Apr 1964 (6 issues)	
12 Masked Marvel, Jim the Fish Boy begin	£5.00
13-17	£3.00
Note: part of Mans World Comic Library series	
SPELLBINDERS/SCAVENGERS	
Quality; 1 Dec 1986-25 1989	
1-6 52pgs; Slaine, Amadeus Wolf (Cursitor Doom from Smash!), Nemesis reprints begin	£1.25
7-12	£1.00
13 titled Spellbinders featuring Scavengers	£1.00
14-25 titled Scavengers	£1.00
SPELLBOUND	
Miller; 1 1961-66 1966	
1 68pgs; Atlas reprints	£5.00
2-5	£3.00
6-66	£2.50
SPELLBOUND ALBUM	
L. Miller; nn 1964	
nn - 64pgs; Atlas reprints, scarce	£10.00
SPELLBOUND MAGAZINE	
Cartoon Art; nn 1952	
nn - 68pgs; Magazine Enterprises reprints, cited in UK horror campaign	£6.00
SPIDER-MAN	
Boxtree; Dec 1994	
The Return of the Sinister Six (Dec 1994) Erik Larsen reprints	£10.00
Revenge of the Sinister Six (Mar 1995) Erik Larsen reprints	£9.00
SPIDER-MAN AND HULK OMNIBUS	
Marvel/Grandreams; 1983	
1983 128pgs; reprints Peter Parker Ann #2, Hulk 127, 129, 183	£3.00
SPIDER-MAN ANNUAL	
World Distributors/Marvel-Grandreams/Marvel; 1974-1986, 1990-1992	
1975 80pgs; reprints ASP #129-131 (Punisher), TTA #57	£6.00

	N.MINT		N.MINT

1976 reprints Spider-Man #1, ASM #8, Team-Up #20 — £6.00
1977 reprints Spider-Man Giant Size #3-4 (Doc Savage/Punisher) — £5.00
1978 reprints Amazing Spider-Man Annual #5, Amazing Spiderman #11 — £4.00
1979 reprints Amazing Spider-Man Annual #4 — £3.00
cover year 1979 1st Grandreams; reprints ASM #165-166 — £3.00
cy1980 Marvel/Grandreams; reprints Peter Parker #20-21 — £3.00
cy1981 white cover; reprints SM #48-49 — £3.00
cy1982 blue/photo insert cover; reprints Peter Parker Ann #4 — £3.00
cy1983 Death of Gwen Stacey, Green Goblin from Amazing Spider-Man #121-122 — £3.00
cy1984 reprints ASM 226-227 — £3.00
cy1985 orange b/g cover; reprints ASM #3, Team-Up #106 — £3.00
cy1986 reprints ASM 269-270 — £3.00
1990 reprints ASM #204-305; McFarlane art — £3.00
1991 reprints ASM 260-261 — £2.50
1992 reprints Marvel Fanfare #47 — £2.50

SPIDER-MAN COMICS WEEKLY
Marvel; 1 17th Feb 1973-666 14th Dec 1985
1 Spider-Man, The Mighty Thor (origin) reprints begin — £5.00
1 with free gift (Spider-Man mask) — £10.00
2 — £3.50
3-5 — £2.50
6-49 — £1.25
50 The Invincible Iron Man reprints begin — £1.25
51-157 — £1.00
158 1st titled "Super Spider-Man with the Super-Heroes", 1st landscape issue; X-Men reprints begin £0.75
159-161, 163-198, 200-204, 206-228, 230, 255-299, 301-310, 312-333 — £0.75
162, 205 Frank Hampson centre-spread art — £2.50
199 1st titled "Super Spider-Man and the Titans"; The Avengers, Captain America reprints begin — £0.75
229 reverts to standard format — £0.75
231 1st titled "Super Spider-Man and Captain Britain"; original Captain Britain strip,
Fantastic Four reprints begin — £1.00
232-247 feature original Captain Britain strips — £1.00
248-253 feature reprint Captain Britain (from Marvel Team-Up #65-66) — £1.25
254 Captain America reprints begin — £0.75
300 Spiderman origin retold — £1.25
311 1st titled "Spider-Man Comic"; Nova, Sub-Mariner reprints begin — £0.75
334 1st titled "The Spectacular Spider-Man Weekly"; Daredevil reprints begin — £0.75
335-375, 377-449, 451-499, 501-528 — £0.60
376 1st titled "Spider-Man and Hulk Weekly"; Hulk reprints begin — £0.75
450 1st titled "Super Spider-Man TV Comic" — £0.60
500 Hulk reprints return — £0.60
529 Fantastic Four reprints return — £0.60
530-552, 554-606, 611-633 — £0.60
553 1st titled "Spider-Man and his Amazing Friends" — £0.60
607-610 feature original Spiderman strip by Mike Collins, Jerry Paris, Barry Kitson,
Mark Farmer in various combinations — £1.00
634 1st titled "Spider-Man Comic" — £0.50
635-651, 653-666 — £0.50
652 1st titled "Spidey Comic" — £0.50
ARTISTS/FEATURES
Some issues contained original British material including posters by Mick Austin in 500, John Higgins in 482.

SPIDER-MAN AND ZOIDS
Marvel; 1 3rd Mar 1986-51 16th Feb 1987
1 — £1.00
2-14, 16-51 — £0.50
15 incorporates Star Wars — £1.00
ARTISTS
Artists include Kev Hopgood, Steve Parkhouse, John Ridgway, Geoff Senior, Ron Smith, Steve Yeowell. Some scripts by Grant Morrison.

SPIDER-MAN POCKET BOOK
Marvel; 1 Mar 1980-28 Jul 1982
1 52pgs small size; US reprints — £1.00
2-8, 10-19, 21-28 — £0.75
9, 20 100pgs; double size Xmas numbers — £1.25
Note: the story from issue 28 was continued in The Daredevils (qv).

SPIDER-MAN SPECIALS
Marvel; May 1979-May 1987; 1992
Summer Special 1979 Spider-Man origin from Amazing Fantasy 15 — £2.50
Winter Special 1979, 1980, 1981, 1982, 1983, 1984, 1985 — £1.25
Summer Special 1980, 1981, 1982, 1983, 1984, 1985, 1986, 1987 — £1.25
Holiday Special 1992 30th Anniversary special, Marvel Comics Presents reprints — £1.25

SPIDERWOMAN
Marvel/Grandreams; 1983
1983 reprints Spiderwoman #21 — £2.50

SPIKE
D.C. Thomson; 1 22nd Jan 1983-67 28th Apr 1984 (joins Champ)
1 Iron Barr by Mike White, Starhawk by Mones begin — £2.00
1 with free gift (Super Swooper Glider) — £4.00
2 — £1.25
2 with free gift (Ten Tattoo transfers) — £3.00
3 — £1.00
3 with free gift (Screamin' Demon Whistle) — £2.00
4 — £0.80
4 with free gift (Ghostly Glow badge) — £1.50
5-67 — £0.50
ARTISTS
Alcatena in 52-62. Carlos Cruz in 27-41, 57-67.

SPIRAL CAGE, THE
Titan; nn 1990
nn - Al Davison art, expansion of earlier Renegade US edition — £6.00

SPIRIT
Boardman; 12, 17 1949

12, 17 12pgs gravure; Will Eisner reprints with covers by Denis McLoughlin — £10.00

SPORT KOMIC, THE
Merseyside Sporting News; nn 1948
nn - 8pgs; Charles Ross art — £3.00

SPORTING SAM
Express Books; nn 1979
nn - 132pgs oblong; Sunday Express reprints by Reg Wooton — £1.00

SPORTS PARADE
Mirror Features; nn 1947
nn - 28pgs; reprints Jon (W.E. Jones) newspaper strip from Sunday Pictorial — £2.50

SPRING COMIC, THE
C.A. Pearson; Mar 1932-Mar 1934, 3 issues
1932 Walter Bell art — £6.00
1933-1934 A.W. Browne — £6.00

SPYMASTER COMICS
Scion; 1 Jun 1951-3 Feb 1952
1-2 24pgs; King-Ganteaume art — £4.00
3 20pgs; King-Ganteaume art — £4.00

SPY SMASHER
Miller; 50 Jul 1953-53 1953, 4 issues
50-53 28pgs; Fawcett reprints — £5.00

SPY 13 PICTURE LIBRARY SUMMER SPECIAL
Fleetway Publications; nn May 1966
nn - 224pgs pocket size; Thriller Picture Library reprints, incl. Luis Bermejo art — £2.00

SQUIBS FUN COMIC
Martin & Reid; nn 1949
nn - 8pgs; Frank Minnitt, Mick Anglo art — £3.00

STAINLESS STEEL RAT
Eagle; 1 Oct 1985-6 Mar 1986
1 double size; 2000AD reprints by Ezquerra — £2.50
2-6 — £1.25

STAMPEDE PICTURE AND STORY ALBUM
Mellifont; W2 1950s
W2 96pgs — £1.50

STARBLAZER
D.C. Thomson; 1 Apr 1979-281 Jan 1991
1 The Omega Experiment by Keith Robson — £2.00
2 — £1.00
3-44, 46-50 — £0.40
45 1st Mikal Kayn by Grant Morrison & Alcatena — £0.40
51-199 — £0.35
200-281 — £0.30
ARTISTS/FEATURES
Alcatena in 7, 16, 24, 29, 31, 32, 36, 45, 47, 49, 54, 56, 59, 62, 64, 66, 75, 77, 81, 87, 88, 113, 122, 125, 127, 141, 144, 149, 154, 161, 162, 166, 167, 168, 170, 173, 175, 177, 179, 185, 187, 190, 196, 199, 200, 207, 213, 219, 224, 231, 240, 250, 260, 271, 274, 277. Casanovas, Jr. in 188, 191, 198, 218, 237, 251, 281. Cam Kennedy in 105. Mike McMahon art in 71. Saichann in 25, 42, 50, 53, 67, 80, 83, 94, 124, 130, 135, 145, 156. Grant Morrison script in 15, 28, 45, 86, 127, 167, 177, 209.

STARBURST ANNUAL
Marvel/Granddreams; 1981
1981 articles & features on science fiction — £2.50

STAR COMIC
Donald F. Peters; 1-2 1954
1-2 20pgs; James Bleach art — £3.00

STAR COMICS
P.M. Productions; nn Dec 1943
nn - 16pgs black/red; Frank Jupo art — £3.00
nn - (1945?) reprint in black/yellow — £3.00

STAR FLASH COMIC
P.M. Production; 1 Aug 1948-2 1948
1-2 Colin Merritt, Wally Robertson art — £5.00

STAR HEROES
Marvel; nn Oct 1979
nn - 52pgs; US reprints — £1.00

STAR HEROES POCKET BOOK
Marvel; 1 Mar 1980-13 May 1981; continued as X-Men Pocket Book
1 52pgs pocketbook; Battlestar Galactica, Micronauts reprints begin — £1.00
2-8 — £0.50
9 100pgs double issue — £1.00
10 X-Men origin story — £1.00
11-13 X-Men reprints — £0.75

STARLIGHT COMICS, THE
Bear Hudson; nn 1947
nn - 12pgs — £4.00

STARLORD
IPC; 1 13th May 1978-7th Oct 1978 (22 mostly unnumbered issues; joins 2000AD)
1 Planet of the Damned, Timequake by Ian Kennedy, Strontium Dog by Ezquerra,
Ro-Busters by Carlos Pino begin — £3.00
1 with free gift (Starlord badge) — £5.00
2 Mind Wars begins — £2.00
2 with free gift (Space Calculator) — £4.00
27 May 1978 Gibbons art — £1.50
3 Jun-15 Jul 1978, 29 Jul-5 Aug 1978 — £1.25
22 Jul 1978, 26 Aug 1978 no Strontium Dog — £1.25
12 Aug 1978 Holocaust begins — £1.25
2 Sep-7 Oct 1978 — £1.25
ARTISTS/FEATURES
Carlos Ezquerra in 13 May-15 Jul 1978, 29 Jul-16 Aug 1978, 30 Sep-7 Oct 1978 (Strontium Dog). Dave Gibbons in 27 May 1978 (Ro-Busters). Ian Gibson in 9-16 Sep 1978 (Strontium Dog). Ian Kennedy in 13 May 1978, 27 May 1978 (Timequake), 10-17 Jun 1978, 5-12 Aug 1978 (Ro-Busters). Brendan McCarthy in 2 Sep 1978 (Strontium Dog).

	N.MINT
STARLORD ANNUAL	
Fleetway; 1980-1982	
1980 Strontium Dog by Brendan McCarthy	£3.00
1981-1982	£2.50
STARLORD SUMMER SPECIAL	
IPC; Jul 1978	
1978 48pgs	£1.50
STAR MAIDENS ANNUAL	
Stafford Pemberton; 1978	
1978 scarce; based on tv series	£2.00
STAR PIRATE COMICS	
Cartoon Art; nn 1950	
nn - 20pgs; Fiction House reprints	£4.00
STAR-ROCKET	
Comyns/Alexander Moring; 1 1953-5 1953, nn 1956?	
1-5 28pgs; Ron Turner, Ron Embleton art	£10.00
nn (Moring) 68pgs, reprints	£8.00
STAR STREAMLINE COMIC	
Streamline; nn 1950s	
nn - 132pgs; US reprints	£3.00
STAR TREK	
(see Mighty Midget)	
STAR TREK/THE FINAL FRONTIER	
Trident/Phoenix; 1 Mar 1992-?	
1 DC reprints	£1.25
2-10	£1.00
11-20	£0.80
21-? unofficial magazine	£0.75
STAR TREK	
Titan; Sep 1992-present	
The Modala Imperative (Sep 1992) DC reprints begin	£9.00
Debt of Honour (Nov 1992) Adam Hughes art	£7.00
Who Killed Captain Kirk (Aug 1993)	£9.00
Tests of Courage (Oct 1994) reprints The Tabukan Syndrome (ST #35-40)	£10.00
Ashes of Eden (Jul 1995) co-written by William Shatner	£10.00
STAR TREK ANNUAL	
World Distributors; 1968-1976	
1968 scarce; Gold Key reprints begin	£12.50
cy1968/69 1st story "Invasion of the City Builders"	£7.50
cy1969/70 1st story "When Planets Collide"	£6.00
1972-1975 dated on cover	£5.00
1976-1977	£3.00
STAR TREK COMIC ALBUM	
World Distributors; 1974	
1974 scarce; reprints Gold Key comics in b/w, designed as colouring book	£7.50
STAR TREK MONTHLY	
Titan; 1 Mar 1995-present (10 to Dec 1995)	
1 magazine format; DC/Malibu ST:NG/DS9 crossover reprints begin	£2.00
2-10	£2.00
STAR TREK SPECIAL	
Polystyle/IPC/Marvel; 1975-1982	
Winter Special (Polystyle, 1975)	£2.50
Special (IPC, 1978)	£2.00
Summer Special (Marvel, 1979)	£2.00
Summer Special (Marvel, 1981)	£1.50
Winter Special (Marvel, 1982)	£1.50
STAR TREK: THE NEXT GENERATION	
Titan; Apr 1993-present	
The Star Lost (Apr 1993) DC reprints	£8.00
The Best of Star Trek: The Next Generation (Feb 1994)	£10.00
Beginnings (Aug 1995)	£9.00
STAR TREK: THE NEXT GENERATION/DEEP SPACE NINE	
Titan; Aug 1995	
Crossover (Aug 1995) DC/Malibu reprints	£8.00
STAR TREK: DEEP SPACE NINE	
Boxtree; Jul 1994-present	
Deep Space Nine (Jul 1994) Malibu reprints	£8.00
Emancipation and Beyond (Aug 1994)	£8.00
Hearts and Minds (Jun 1995)	£9.00
STAR WARS	
(title varies: Star Wars Weekly/ Star Wars: The Empire Strikes Back/ Star Wars: The Empire Strikes Back Monthly/ Star Wars: The Return of the Jedi)	
Marvel; 1 8th Feb 1978-171 Jul 1983; 1 22nd Jun 1983-155 31st May 1986 (joins Spider-Man and Zoids)	
1 28pgs; Star Wars movie adaptation begins	£5.00
1 with free gift (cut out Star Wars X-Wing fighter)	£10.00
2 Star Wars movie adaptation	£2.50
2 with free gift (cut out Star Wars T.I.E. fighter)	£5.00
3-12 Star Wars movie adaptation	£1.50
13 reprints by Roy Thomas & Howard Chaykin begin	£1.25
14, 16-44, 46-50	£1.25
15 Starlord reprints by Claremont & Byrne begin	£1.25
45 Warlock reprints begin	£1.25
51 The Micronauts reprints begin	£1.00
52-72, 74-88, 90-117	£1.00
73 The Guardians of the Galaxy reprints begin	£1.00
89 Deathlok reprints begin	£1.00
118 (29 May 1980) becomes Star Wars: The Empire Strikes Back, movie reprints begin	£1.25
119-134 Empire Strikes Back reprints	£1.00
135 No movie reprint, Killraven reprints begin	£1.00
136-138 movie reprints	£1.00
139 (23 Oct 1980) last weekly issue	£1.00

	N.MINT
140 (Nov 1980) becomes monthly	£1.25
141-150, 152, 157-158, 160-170	£1.25
151 "The Pandora Effect" by Alan Moore & Adolfo Buylla	£2.50
153 "Dark Knights Deviltry" by Steve Moore & Alan Davis	£2.50
154, 155, 159 Alan Moore back-ups	£2.50
156 Alan Moore & Alan Davis backup	£2.50
171 (Jul 1983) last monthly issue	£1.00
1 (22 Jun 1983) becomes Star Wars: Return of the Jedi	£1.25
2-5	£1.00
6-155	£0.75
STAR WARS	
Dark Horse; 1 Oct 1992-10 Jul 1993	
1 Star Wars: Dark Empire by Veitch & Kennedy, Indiana Jones reprints begin	£1.75
2-6 Dark Empire reprints	£1.50
7 Tales of the Jedi, Classic Star Wars reprints begin	£1.50
8-10	£1.50
STAR WARS	
Boxtree	
Dark Empire (Jul 1994) Dark Horse reprints; Cam Kennedy art	£10.00
Tales of the Jedi (Jan 1995) Dark Horse reprints; David Roach art	£10.00
A New Hope (Apr 1995) reprints movie adaptation	£8.00
The Empire Stikes Back (Apr 1995) reprints movie adaptation	£8.00
Return of the Jedi (Apr 1995) reprints movie adaptation	£8.00
Droids (Jul 1995) Dark Horse reprints	£9.00
Dark Lords of Sith Book 1 (Jul 1995) Dark Horse reprints	£11.00
Classic Star Wars Book 1	£11.00
Classic Star Wars Book 2 (Nov 1995)	£11.00
Classic Star Wars Book 3 (Nov 1995)	£11.00
STAR WARS ANNUAL	
Brown Watson; 1978	
1978 reprints Marvel film adaptaion in colour & b/w	£4.00
STAR WARS ANNUALS	
Marvel/Granddreams; 1980, 1984	
Star Wars: The Empire Strikes Back (1980) reprints Marvel film adaptation	£2.50
Star Wars: Return of the Jedi (1984) reprints Marvel film adaptation	£2.50
Star Wars Special Edition reprints both of the above in one collected edition produced exclusively for BHS	£5.00
STAR WARS SPECIALS	
Marvel; May 1983-Jun 1985	
Summer Special 1983 Alan Moore, Steve Moore script reprints, Alan Davis, John Stokes art reprints	£1.50
Winter Special 1983, 1984	£1.25
Summer Special 1984, 1985	£1.25
STARK TERROR	
Portman; 1 Oct 1979-4 Jan 1980	
1-4 Stanley Publications reprints	£1.00
STARRY SPANGLES COMIC	
Philmar; nn 1948	
nn - 8pgs; Walter Bell, C. Montford, Frank Minnitt, Wally Robertson art	£3.00
STARTLING DETECTIVE	
Streamline; 1 1951	
1 28pgs; Fox Features reprints	£4.00
STARTLING TERROR TALES	
Arnold Book Co.; 1 1954?	
1 68pgs; Star Publications reprints, cited in UK horror campaign	£15.00
STEEL CLAW	
Quality; 1 Dec 1986-4 Mar 1987	
1-3 Jesus Blasco reprints from Valiant with new framing sequence begin	£1.00
4 52pgs	£1.00
STEVE SAMPSON	
Sports Cartoons/Miller; 1 Jun 1953-40 1955	
1 Steve Sampson by Nat Brand begins	£4.00
2-17	£2.50
18 incorporates Captain Vigour, Dick Hercules, Super-sonic; weekly	£2.50
19-40	£2.50
STINGRAY	
Ravette; 1992	
Battle Stations (1992) TV Century 21 reprints by Embleton	£4.00
Stand By For Action (1992)	£4.00
STINGRAY ANNUAL	
City/Fleetway; 1965-1966, 1992-1993	
1965	£15.00
1966	£10.00
1993-1994	£4.50
STINGRAY MONTHLY	
(see Stingray: The Comic)	
STINGRAY SUMMER SPECIAL	
Polystyle; Jun 1983	
1983 48pgs, reprints, Brian Lewis, Rab Hamilton art	£2.00
STINGRAY TELEVISION STORY BOOK	
PBS; 1965	
1965	£15.00
STINGRAY: THE COMIC/STINGRAY MONTHLY	
Fleetway; 1 10th Oct 1992-24 18 Oct 1993; v2:1 Oct 1993-8 May 1994 (joins Thunderbirds)	
1 Stingray reprints from TV Century 21 by Ron Embleton	£1.00
2-3, 5-8	£0.75
4 1st original stories	£1.00
9-24	£0.75
v2:1 monthly	£1.00
v2:2-8	£0.75
STIRRING WESTERN	
Streamline; 1-12 1950s	
1-12	£3.00

N.MINT

STONE DE CROZE	
Guernsey Evening Press and Star	
Stone de Croze (1975) reprints newspaper strip by Alan Guppy	£3.00
Stone de Croze Vol.2 (1979)	£2.50
STORIES OF BILLY THE BEE	
Beaverbrook; nn 1960s	
nn - 68pgs; reprints Harry Smith newspaper strip from Evening Standard	£1.50
STORM	
BEAP/Oberon; Aug 1982	
The Deep World Don Lawrence Dutch reprints	£4.00
STORM	
Titan; Oct 1987-Jan 1989	
The Last Fighter (Oct 1987) Don Lawrence Dutch reprints begin	£3.00
The Pirates of Pendarve (Jan 1989)	£4.00
STORMBRINGER	
Savoy Books; nn 1980	
nn - 32pgs; James Cawthorn art, based on Michael Moorcock novel	£4.00
STORMWATCHER	
Acme Press/Eclipse; 1 Apr 1989-4 Dec 1989	
1 Stormwatcher by Alan Cowsill/Ian Abbinnett & Andrew Currie begins	£1.25
2-4	£1.00
STRAIGHT ARROW	
Compix/Cartoon Art; 1 1952-20 195?	
1 24pgs; Magazine Enterprises reprints	£3.00
STRANGE EMBRACE	
Atomeka; 1 Apr 1993-4 1993	
1 David Hine art & story	£2.50
2-4	£2.00
STRANGE HAVEN	
Abiogenesis Press; 1 Jun 1995-present	
1 Gary Spencer Millidge story & art begins	£1.50
2	£1.50
STRANGE STORIES	
John Spencer; 1-6 1967?	
1-6 some incl. adapted Ron Embleton Bill Merrill reprints	£1.50
STRANGE SUSPENSE STORIES	
G.T. Ltd; nn 1959?	
nn - card cover	£12.00
STRANGE WORLDS	
Thorpe & Porter; 1 Oct 1951-200?	
1 68pgs; Avon reprints; scarce	£25.00
2	£12.50
3-5	£6.00
6-10	£3.00
11-100	£2.00
101-200	£1.25
STRANGE WORLDS	
Man's World; 12 Nov 1953-17 1954	
12 Hal Starr by Sydney Jordan begins	£3.00
13-17	£2.00
Note: part of Mans World Comic Library series	
STRAY DOGS	
CM Comics; 1 Feb 1994	
1 Chris Morgan script & art	£1.50
STREAMLINE COMICS	
Cardal Publishing; 1-4 1947	
1 20pgs; Streamline by Denis Gifford	£3.00
2-3 Denis Gifford art	£2.50
4 Bryan Berry art	£2.50
STREAMLINE PICTORIAL ROMANCE	
Streamline; 1-7 1950s	
1 28pgs; He Dared Her, US reprints	£1.50
2-7	£1.00
STREET COMIX	
Arts Lab Press; 1 1976-5 1978	
1 12pgs, giveaway	£1.00
2, 4-5 Emerson art	£1.00
3 titled Streetquomix	£1.00
STREETFIGHTER II	
Manga Publishing; 1 Sep 1995-present (15 to date)	
1 Masaomi Kanzaki reprints begin	£1.00
2-8, 11-15	£1.00
9-10 Streetfighter II movie adaptation	£1.00
STREETFIGHTER II	
Boxtree; Apr-Jul 1995	
Book 1 (Apr 1995) Masaomi Kanzaki reprints	£8.00
Book 2 (Jul 1995)	£9.00
STRIP	
(see The Chronicles of Genghis Grimtoad, Storm)	
Marvel; 1 17th Feb 1990-20 10th November 1990	
1 Marshal Law reprints by Mills & O'Neill, Genghis Grimtoad by Wagner/Grant & Gibson, Man From Cancer by Dakin & Elliott begin	£1.25
2 Storm reprints by Martin Lodewijk & Don Lawrence begin (to 7)	£1.00
3-5, 7	£1.00
6 badly printed issue, lower distribution	£1.25
6 special complimentary reissue (yellow cover)	£0.75
8 Thorgal reprints by Rosinski & Van Hamme begin (ends 13)	£1.00
9 Free reissue of 6	£1.00
9 without reissue	£0.50
10-11, 15	£1.00
12 last Marshal Law, McCrea art	£1.00
13 Death's Head by Furman & Senior begins (ends 15)	£1.00

Super-Heroes Monthly #1

Superman's Supacomic #3

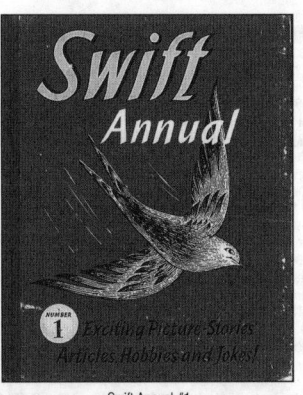

Swift Annual #1

	N.MINT
14 Storm: The Labyrinth of Death begins	£1.00
16 The Punisher reprints begin	£1.00
17-20 Punisher reprints; 18. Bisley cover	£1.00
STRIP COMICS	
Fairylite; nn 1944	
nn – 16pgs; Bob Wilkin art	£3.00
STRONTIUM DOG	
Eagle; 1 Dec 1985-4 Mar 1986	
1-4 2000AD reprints by Ezquerra	£1.25
STRONTIUM DOG	
Titan (Best of 2000AD); nn 1985	
nn – Ezquerra reprints	£5.00
STRONTIUM DOG SPECIAL	
Quality; 1 1986 (numbering continued by Midnight Surfer Special)	
1 2000AD reprints by Ezquerra	£1.25
ST. SWITHIN'S DAY	
Trident Comics; nn Apr 1990	
nn – Trident reprints by Grant Morrison & Paul Grist, newly coloured	£3.00
STUPENDOUS SERIES	
(see Fantastic Series)	
SUDDENLY AT TWO O'CLOCK IN THE MORNING	
Last Minute Productions; nn Jul 1974	
nn – Bolland art, very rare (50 copies)	£35.00
SUGARVIRUS	
Atomeka; nn 1993	
nn – 48pgs; by Warren Ellis & Martin Chaplin/Garry Marshall, John Bolton cover & poster	£2.50
SUMMER COMIC, THE	
C.A. Pearson; 1932, 1936-1938 (4 issues, see also Summer Holiday Comic)	
1932, 1936 12pgs; A.W. Browne	£6.00
1937-1938 incl. Ray Bailey art	£6.00
SUMMER HOLIDAY COMIC, THE	
C.A. Pearson; nn Jun 1935	
nn – 12pgs; G. Larkman art	£6.00
SUN	
(titled Fitness and Sun/Sun/Sun Comic)	
J.B. Allen/Amalgamated; 1 11th Nov 1947-17th Oct 1959 (551 issues, numbered to 537; joins Tiger)	
1	£25.00
2	£10.00
3-5	£5.00
6, 8-40	£3.00
7 (3 Feb 1948) Voyage to Venus by R.W. Plummer begins	£3.50
41 (24 May 1949) 1st Amalgamated Press issue	£6.00
42-53, 55-73, 75-105	£6.00
54 (26 Nov 1949) Young Joey by Hugh McNeill begins	£6.00
106 (18 Feb 1950) Highway Days (Dick Turpin) by McNeill begins	£5.00
107-283	£4.00
284 (16 Aug 1952) Billy the Kid by Geoff Campion begins	£4.00
285-360	£3.00
361 (7 Jan 1956) Battler Britton by Campion begins	£3.00
362-17 Oct 1959	£2.50
Note: one un-numbered/undated issue appeared between 27 Jun-15 Aug 1959.	
SUNBEAM, THE	
(previously Little Sparks)	
Amalgamated Press; 1 7th Oct 1922-173 23rd Jan 1926 (becomes The Sunbeam - new series)	
1 Walter Booth, Louis Briault art	£35.00
2	£12.50
3-5	£7.50
6-173	£5.00
SUNBEAM, THE	
Amalgamated Press; 1 30th Jan 1926-747 25th May 1940 (joins Tiny Tots)	
1 12pgs tabloid; Fred Crompton art	£30.00
2	£10.00
3-731 incl. Julius Baker, Don Newhouse, Bertie Brown art	£5.00
732-747 16pgs, smaller size; incorporates Puck from 746	£4.00
SUNDANCE WESTERN	
World Distributors; 50 1970-?	
50 68pgs pocket size; Spanish reprints	£2.00
51-?	£1.25
SUNDAY EXTRA	
Sunday Citizen; 6th Jun 1965-10th Jul 1967, 110 issues (continued in reduced format)	
6 Jun 1965 4pgs supplement on green paper; Gordon Hogg, Sally Artz, Graham Allen, Frank Langford art	£2.00
13 Jun-14 Nov 1965 green paper	£1.50
21 Nov 1965-10 Jul 1967 white paper; incl. John Burns, Frank Bellamy art	£1.00
SUNDAY POST FUN SECTION	
D.C. Thomson; 8th Mar 1936-present	
8 Mar 1936 8pgs supplement; Oor Wullie, The Broons by Dudley Watkins, Allan Morley Chick Gordon art	£40.00
15 Mar 1936-2 Jun 1940 8pgs	£8.00
9 Jun 1940-6 Apr 1941 6pgs	£6.00
13 Apr 1941-22 Apr 1942 4pgs	£5.00
29 Apr 1942-mid 1949 2pgs	£4.00
mid 1949-24 Aug 1969 4pgs	£1.50
31 Aug 1969-present	£0.50
FEATURES/ARTISTS	
Allan Morley reprints in 8 Mar 1936-15 Feb 1976, new strips 1941-58. Dudley D. Watkins Oor Wullie, The Broons in 8 Mar 1936-24 Aug 1969, reprints in 31 Aug 1969-2 Sep 1974, Watkins The Happy Tramps reprints in 1937. Oor Wullie by Tom Lavery 15 Sep 1974-29 Jun 1980, 5 Oct 1980-6 Jun 1982, Peter Davidson 6 Jul-28 Sep 1980, John Dolland 13 Jun 1982 to present. The Broons by Tom Lavery 29 Sep 1974-2 Mar 1980, Peter Davidson 9 Mar 1980-21 Oct 1984, John Dolland 28 Oct 1984 to present. 22 Feb	

	N.MINT
1976 to 25 Sep 1977 issues featured reprints from Dandy (Desperate Dan), Beano (Lord Snooty), etc.	
SUNNY COMIC	
International Publications; nn 1945	
nn – 8pgs; John Turner art	£3.00
SUNNY COMIC	
P.M. Productions; nn 1945	
nn – 16pgs; Reg Carter art	£3.00
SUNNY FUN COMIC	
Philmar; nn 1948	
nn – 8pgs; Wally Robertson art	£3.00
SUNNY SANDS	
C.A. Pearson; nnJun 1939	
nn – 12pgs; Norman Ward art	£6.00
SUNNYTIMES COMIC	
Rayburn Productions; 1 1948	
1 D. Lovern West, Bob Wilkin art	£3.00
SUNRISE	
Harrier; 1 Feb 1987-2 May 1987	
1 Abraxas by Grant Morrison & Tony O'Donnell begins	£1.00
2	£0.75
SUNSHINE	
Target Publications; 1 16th Jul 1938-39 8th Apr 1939 (joins Jingles)	
1 8pgs tabloid; Harry Banger, Bert Hill art	£25.00
2-15 8pgs; white paper to 6, yellow paper 7-16	£7.50
16-39 12pgs; pink paper from 17	£5.00
SUNSHINE PICTURE STORY BOOK, THE	
(no imprint); nn 1944	
nn – 14pgs oblong; Fred Robinson art	£3.00
SUPER ADVENTURE	
Alex White; 1 Jan 1968-36 Jun 1969	
1 68pgs pocket size; Bitter Bargain, foreign reprints	£1.50
2-36	£0.50
SUPERADVENTURE ANNUAL	
Atlas/Top Sellers Ltd; 1958-1972?	
1958-59 160pgs incl. Batman, Tommy Tomorrow, Congo Bill, Wyoming Kid, Aquaman	£35.00
1959-60 160pgs; 22 DC reprints incl. Johnny Quick, Congo Bill, Aquaman, Daniel Boone, Tommy Tomorrow	£25.00
1960-61 (Space Ranger cover) 100pgs incl. Tommy Tomorrow, Congo Bill, Aquaman, Roy Raymond	£17.50
1961-62 (Flash cover) 160pgs; incl. Flash, Aquaman, Tommy Tomorrow, Congo Bill	£20.00
1962-63 100pgs; incl. Jimmy Olsen, Superboy, Aquaman, Flash, Tommy Tomorrow	£15.00
1963-64 100pgs; incl. Aquaman, Flash, Tommy Tomorrow, Jimmy Olsen	£15.00
1964-65 62pgs incl. Flash, Jimmy Olsen, Tommy Tomorrow, Aquaman	£15.00
1967 28pgs incl. Flash, Tommy Tomorrow, Green Arrow, Jimmy Olsen; recoloured	£15.00
1968, 1969	£10.00
1970 titles Superadventure Bumper Book; scarce, features Batman, Superman, Supergirl, Superboy, Legion of Super-Heroes; colour	£15.00
1971, 1972 Top Sellers issues; no date on cover/inside (1972 issue has Superman being blasted by a flying saucer)	£8.00
SUPER ADVENTURE COMIC	
Atlas; 1 1950?-120? 1959?	
1 very rare; b/w reprints of Superboy and Aquaman from late 1940s (later issues have Superman and Batman reprints); new line drawn covers	£120.00
2 very rare	£70.00
3-5 rare	£35.00
6-10 scarce	£25.00
11-50	£15.00
51-120?	£10.00
Note: issues #1-4 called Adventure Comics starring Superboy. A second series to at least 59 issues was published in the late 1960s/early 1970s with the cover emblem Planet Comics. Mostly featured Justice League and Green Lantern reprints in black & white.	
SUPER ADVENTURES	
John Matthew; 1 1946	
1 8pgs	£3.00
SUPER ALBUM, THE	
Alexander Moring; nn 1956?	
nn – hardback; McLoughlin cover and illustrations	£8.00
SUPERBOY ANNUAL	
Atlas; 1953-1967?	
1953-54 192pgs; 17 reprints	£50.00
1954/55	£30.00
1955/56, 1956/57	£25.00
1957/58 titled Superboy Adventure Book; 17 stories, plus Rex the Wonder Dog reprints	£25.00
1958-59 18 reprints, plus Rex reprints	£20.00
1959-60 18 reprints, incl. Adventure #247, plus Rex	£20.00
1960-61 16 reprints, plus Rex, Detective Chimp	£17.50
1961-62 19 reprints, plus Rex, Detective Chimp	£15.00
1962-63 120pgs; 12 reprints, incl. Adventure #267, plus Rex	£15.00
1963/64-1964/65	£15.00
1965-66 96pgs; 8 reprints, plus Rex	£10.00
1967 11 stories, plus Detective Chimp	£10.00
SUPERBOY DOUBLE DOUBLE COMICS	
Thorpe & Porter?; 1 1967	
1 bound-together remaindered copies of selected DC comics incl. Superboy #132, #135 and Green Lantern #53	£2.50
SUPER-BUMPER COMIC, THE	
Valentine & Sons; nn 1948	
nn – 16pgs; Nat Brand, George Blow, Alf Farningham, Sam Fair art	£3.00
SUPERCAR ANNUAL	
Collins; 1961-1963	
1961 entitled Mike Mercury in Supercar	£35.00
1962-1963	£25.00

	N.MINT

SUPERCAR (A LITTLE GOLDEN BOOK)
Golden Press; 1962
1962 scarce, by G.Sherman | £15.00

SUPERCOLOURED COMIC ANNUAL, THE
Boardman; nn Nov 1949-1951 Oct 1951
nn, 1951 returned Boardman comics (Roy Carson, Swift Morgan, Buffalo Bill)
bound in hardcovers; McLoughlin art | £12.00
1950 contains Swift Morgan and the Knights of the Round Table, new McLoughlin art | £15.00

SUPER COMIC STRIPS
Martin & Reid; 1 1949
1 8pgs; Wally Robertson, Frank Minnitt, Denis Gifford art | £4.00

SUPER COMICS
P.M. Productions; 1 Dec 1943
1 16pgs; Frank Jupo art | £3.00
nn (1946) reprint, larger size | £3.00

SUPER D.C.
Top Sellers; 1 Jun 1969-14 Jul 1970
1 scarce, 40pgs; Superman, Batman, Superboy, Jimmy Olsen, Lois Lane reprints | £15.00
1 with free gift (Batman poster, wristwatch calendar, Superman Magic Disc) | £30.00
2 scarce | £7.00
3-5 | £4.00
6-14 | £3.00

SUPER D.C. BUMPER BOOK
Top Sellers; 1970
1970 1960s DC reprints, Superman, Batman, plus 3 new text stories | £10.00

SUPER DETECTIVE LIBRARY
Amalgamated; 1 Mar 1953-188 Dec 1960
1 Meet the Saint (reprints American newspaper strip) | £50.00
2 | £30.00
3-5 | £22.50
6-50 | £15.00
51-100 | £10.00
101-150 | £7.50
151-188 | £5.00
ARTISTS/FEATURES
Rick Random by Bill Lacey in 37, 48, 75, by Ron Turner in 44, 49, 64, 66, 70, 79, 83, 90, 97, 101, 111, 115, 123, 127, 129, 133, 137, 143, 153, 163, by others in 53, 91, 105, 139. Rip Kirby by Alex Raymond American newspaper reprints in 120, 122, 124, 126, 128, 130, 132, 134, 136, 138, 140, 142, 144, 146, 148, 150, 152, 154. Buck Ryan by Jack Monk British newspaper reprints in 156, 158, 159, 162, 164, 166, 168, 170, 174, 176, 180, 182, 184, 186. The Saint by John Spranger American newspaper reprints in 1, 5, 11, 33, 59, UK originals in 15, 28, 38. Alberto Breccia in 172. Ron Embleton in 58, 72. Ron Turner in 55, 109, 169, 177, 183, 188, see also Rick Random above.

SUPER-DUPER COMICS
Cartoon Art; 1 1946-20 1950
1 8pgs; titled The Superduper Comic | £4.00
2 8pgs tabloid; titled It's Super-Duper; Crimebusting Incognito begins | £4.00
3 8pgs tabloid; titled It's Super-Duper; Powerman by Dennis Reader | £5.00
3 alternative edition, same format but featuring Crimebusting Incognito | £4.00
4 16pgs; Dennis Reader art | £5.00
5 36pgs; titled Super-Duper; Power Girl by Reader | £5.00
5 (6) titled It's Super-Duper; Reader, Paddy Brennan art | £6.00
7 titled It's Super-Duper Comics Annual Bumper Edition 1948 | £4.00
8 titled Super-Duper Annual Bumper Edition 1948 | £4.00
9-10 titled Super-Duper Boy's Magazine | £3.00
11-13 titled It's Super-Duper (Comics); 13 incl. Paddy Brennan art | £6.00
14-16, 18 titled It's Super Duper Comic; reduced to 20pgs hereon | £2.50
17 titled It's Super Duper Comic Annual | £2.50
19 68pgs; incl. Fiction House reprints | £2.50
20 36pgs | £2.50
nn (1948) 16pgs; Dennis Reader art | £5.00

SUPER FUNNIES
T.V. Boardman; 29 1940-33 1941, 5 issues
29 36pgs; Quality reprints from Feature Comics | £6.00
30-33 20pgs | £4.00

SUPER HERO FUN AND GAMES
Marvel; 1 Mar 1979-18 Aug 1980
1-18 puzzles and games featuring Marvel characters | £0.75
Note: worth less if any puzzles or games begun or defaced

SUPER HERO FUN AND GAMES WINTER SPECIAL
Marvel; Winter 1979
Winter 1979 | £0.75

SUPER-HEROES, THE
Marvel; 1 8th Mar 1975-50 14th Feb 1976 (joins Spider-Man)
1 Silver Surfer, X-Men reprints begin, both from #1 | £2.00
1 with free gift (Silver Surfer poster) | £3.50
2 Silver Surfer, X-Men origin reprints | £1.50
3-22, 24-30 Silver Surfer reprints | £1.25
23 Doc Savage reprints begin | £1.25
31 The Cats reprints begin | £1.00
32-40, 42-44, 46-48, 50 | £1.00
41 The Scarecrow reprints begin | £1.00
45 The Thing reprints begin | £1.00
49 Black Knight reprints begin | £1.00

SUPERHEROES ANNUAL (MARVEL PRESENTS THE...)
(see also Marvel Superheroes Annual) Brown Watson; 1978
1978 reprints Thor #231, ASM #155, Silver Surfer | £5.00

SUPERHEROES ANNUAL, THE
London Editions; 1982-1984
1982 reprints Detective #327, JLA #70, Superman, Batman; Bolland pin-up | £5.00
1983 reprints JLA #138, Atom, Batman; new Wonder Woman text story by Kelvin Gosnell; Talbot end-papers | £4.00
1984 reprints JLA #202, Superman, Atom, Batman; Moore/Talbot text story; Talbot end-papers | £4.00

	N.MINT

SUPER HEROES MONTHLY
Egmont/London Editions; v1:1 Sep 1980-v2:7 Apr 1982 (19 issues)
Vol 1:1 52pgs; Superman, Batman, Wonder Woman reprints | £5.00
Vol 1:2 Superman origin from Action Comics #1, Leach cover | £3.00
Vol 1:3 reprints Batman #251 Joker by Neal Adams | £3.00
Vol 1:4 reprints Detective #400 Man-Bat by Adams | £2.50
Vol 1:5-6 Adams Batman reprints | £2.00
Vol 1:7 Superman II movie, Superman #76 (Batman/Superman) | £2.00
Vol 1:8 Flash origin from Showcase #4, Adams Batman reprint | £5.00
Vol 1:9 Marshal Rogers Batman reprint | £2.00
Vol 1:10 Captain Cold and The Huntress origins | £2.00
Vol 1:11 Silver age Hawkman origin from Brave & Bold #34, Talbot cover | £4.00
Vol 1:12 Adams Batman, Kubert Hawkman | £2.00
Vol 2:1 Flash from Showcase #13 | £3.00
Vol 2:2 Solomon Grundy origin, Swamp Thing | £2.00
Vol 2:3 Frank Miller Batman reprint, Talbot cover | £2.50
Vol 2:4 Kubert Hawkman from Brave & Bold #35, Talbot cover | £2.50
Vol 2:5-7 incl. Kubert Hawkman | £2.00

SUPER HORSE
(see Blue Bolt series)

SUPER JOLLY ROGER
(previously Jolly Chuckles) Martin & Reid; 12 1949
12 8pgs tabloid; Bob Monkhouse, Frank Minnitt art | £4.00

SUPER MAG
Young World; 1 Jan 1964-28? 1965?
1 36pgs; Flight of White Stallion, Gold Key reprints | £3.50
2-28 mostly Gold Key reprints, incl. Mickey Mouse, etc. | £1.50
Note: mostly reprints of Gold Key comics with two original British series'. See Space Patrol and The Terrible Ten. Super Mag title dropped at 20 but numbering continued

SUPERMAG COMIC
D.C. Thomson; 1 Oct 1986
1 Dennis & Gnasher in The Long Way Home, Nick Kelly | £1.25

SUPERMAG FOR BOYS
D.C. Thomson; 1 Oct 1986
1 Tracker in Death Run, The Feud | £1.25

SUPERMAG FOR GIRLS
D.C. Thomson; 1 Oct 1986
1 Where Is Wendy?, Three's A Crowd | £1.00

SUPERMAN
Atlas; 1 1950?-137? 1962?
1 very rare; b/w reprints from Superman and Action Comics plus Green Arrow and Johnny Quick alternating | £150.00
2 very rare | £80.00
3-5 very scarce | £35.00
6-10 scarce | £25.00
11-50 | £15.00
51-100 | £12.50
101-137? | £10.00

SUPERMAN
Titan; Dec 1992-present
The Death of Superman (Dec 1992) 168pgs; reprints Doomsday storyline | £3.50
World Without Superman (1993) reprints Funeral For A Friend | £5.00
The Return of Superman (Nov 1993) 480pgs; reprints Reign of the Supermen | £9.00
Time and Time Again (Sep 1994) reprints var issues from 1991 | £5.00
The Man of Steel (Feb 1995) reprints John Byrne Superman 1-6 | £6.00
Kal (Feb 1995) Elseworlds gn by Dave Gibbons & Jose Luis Garcia-Lopez | £4.00

SUPERMAN
Health Education Council; 1 Feb 1981-2 Oct 1982
1 (AS26) 8pgs; anti-smoking promo | £0.60
2 (AS30) 8pgs; anti-smoking promo | £0.50

SUPERMAN/THE ADVENTURES OF SUPERMAN
London Editions/Fleetway Editions; 1 16th Jun 1988-57 Mar 1993; New series; 1 Apr 1993-15 Jan 1994 (joins Batman)
1 US reprints begin; fortnightly publication | £1.00
2-19 | £0.60
20-34 monthly publication | £0.80
35-57 bi-monthly publication | £0.85
1-15 New series; fortnightly, later monthly | £1.00

SUPERMAN AND BATMAN ANNUAL
Brown Watson; 1974-1978
1974 1960s/70s DC reprints; colour | £5.00
1975-1976 1970s DC reprints; colour | £4.00
1977-1978 1970s DC reprints; part colour; Bolton illus | £5.00

SUPERMAN AND SPIDER-MAN
Marvel; nn 1982
nn - 68pgs; US reprints | £1.50

SUPERMAN ANNUAL/SUPERMAN OFFICIAL ANNUAL
Atlas/Top Sellers/Fleetway; Oct 1951-present
1951 Entitled Superman Bumper Edition; 192pgs; very rare; reprints US strips in b/w incl. origin and strips from circa 1947-48 Superman, Action, Worlds Finest comics; cover from Superman #53 (origin story) | £120.00
Note: Printed in Australia and published by K.G. Murray for distribution by Atlas; collects first six Australian issues (Jul-Dec 1950).
1952 1st entitled Superman Annual; 16 stories from 1947-50 Superman, Action comics; cover from Action Comics #137 | £60.00
1953-54 1st to use split year on title page; 16 stories from 1947-49 Superman, Action, Worlds Finest comics | £40.00
1954-55 14 Superman stories, 2 Batman stories | £30.00
1955-56 1st Superman Adventure Book; 1st cardboard spine; incl. 4 Captain Comet stories by Murphy Anderson | £25.00
1956-57 17 stories, 14 feat. Superman's Pal Jimmy Olsen by Curt Swan | £25.00
1957-58 160pgs; 5/6 price | £20.00

	N.MINT		N.MINT
1958-59 160pgs; 6/- price; reverts to Annual; incl. Vigilante by Dan Barry	£20.00	**SUPER WESTERN COMICS**	
1959-60 to 1960-1 incl. Green Arrow	£20.00	**Streamline; 1-2 1951**	
1961-62 incl. Jimmy Olsen, Lois Lane, Green Arrow, art by Jack Kirby	£15.00	**1** 28pgs; Youthful reprints	£5.00
1962-63 1st partly in full colour; smaller size; 7/6 price; features Green Arrow and Speedy	£13.50	**2** 68pgs	£3.50
1963-64 3 stories in colour	£12.50	**SUREFIRE COMIC**	
1964-65 reverts to larger size	£12.50	**Philmar/P.M. Productions; 1-2 1949**	
1965-66 (1966)	£10.00	**1-2** 16pgs; Frank Minnitt, Walter Robertson art	£3.00
1967 96pgs; 7 stories, 4 in colour	£9.00	**SURPRISE COMIC**	
1968 96pgs; 10 stories, 4 in colour; reprints Superman #146 "The Story of Superman's Life"	£9.00	**Paget Publications; nn-5 1948**	
1969 Top Sellers; (red cover) incl. Superman, Superman/Batman	£8.00	**nn** - 8pgs; Harry Banger art	£3.00
1970 Top Sellers; (yellow cover) titled Superman Giant Bumper Book incl. Superman, Superman/Batman	£8.00	**2-5**	£2.50
1971-1978	£6.00	**SUSIE OF THE SUNDAY DESPATCH**	
1979 Superman Official Annual; Egmont; 64pgs; 1960s/70s DC reprints; colour	£4.00	**Associated Newspapers; no date (1956?)**	
1980 64pgs; 1970s DC reprints; colour	£3.00	- 84pgs; newspaper reprints by Norman Pett	£15.00
1981 London Editions; 64pgs; 1970s DC reprints; Kev O'Neill cover; colour	£3.00	**SUSPENSE MAGAZINE**	
1982 64pgs; DC reprints; colour; Steve Dillon end-papers	£3.00	**Cartoon Art; 1 1952**	
1983 reprints DC Presents #27-29; Bolland cover, Gibbons end-papers	£4.00	**1** 28pgs; Magazine Enterprises reprints	£3.00
1984 reprints DC Presents, Jim Starlin art; Talbot cover	£3.50	**SUSPENSE PICTURE LIBRARY HOLIDAY SPECIAL**	
1985 1970s/80s DC reprints; Alan Moore & Delano text stories	£3.50	**I.P.C. Magazine; May 1977-May 1981**	
1986 1970/80s DC reprints; G. Morrison & P. Milligan text stories	£3.00	**1977** 196pgs; Action Picture Library reprints	£1.50
1987-present	£3.00	**1978-1981** 1980 incl. Luis Bermejo art	£1.00
SUPERMAN ANNUAL		**SUSPENSE STORIES**	
Brown & Watson; 1 1972		**Alan Class; 1 May 1963-241 Mar 1989**	
1 1970s DC reprints, plus text stories	£6.00	**1** 68pgs; Atlas reprints; very rare	£25.00
SUPERMAN POCKETBOOK		**2** very rare	£15.00
Egmont/Methuen; 1 Apr 1978-?		**3-5** rare	£10.00
1 100pgs; DC reprints	£2.00	**6-20** scarce	£5.00
2-?	£1.00	**21-50**	£2.50
SUPERMAN SPECTACULAR		**51-200**	£1.50
London Editions; nn Mar 1982		**201-241**	£1.25
nn - 52pgs; Superman reprints incl. Superman Red/Superman Blue	£1.50	**SUTTONS, THE**	
SUPERMAN STORY BOOK ANNUAL		**Ark Comics; nn 1988**	
World Distributors; 1967-1969		**nn** - reprint's newspaper strip by Phil Elliott	£1.50
1967 (Superman and flaming spaceship) 14 text stories	£12.00	**Note:** unsold copies were re-released in March 1994	
1968 (Superman 5 panel cover) 13 text stories	£10.00	**SUZIE AND JONNIE (THE LAID BACK ADVENTURES OF...)**	
1969 (Superman/Jimmy Olsen/Beppo cover) 11 text stories	£8.00	**Antonio Ghuru; nn 1981**	
SUPERMAN'S SUPACOMIC		**nn** - 52pgs; Ghuru art, adult material	£1.00
(see All Favourites, Five-Score Comic Monthly, Century Comics, Hundred Comic Monthly)		**SWEETMEATS**	
K.G. Murray Ltd; 1 1958-56? mid 1960s		**Atomeka; nn Mar 1993**	
1 rare 100pgs, squarebound begin; b/w reprints from National Periodical Publications incl.		**nn** - by Steve Tanner & Pete Venters; Bolton cover & poster	£2.50
Superman, Superboy, Jimmy Olsen, Lois Lane, Batman (later issues feature Supergirl		**SWELL COMIC**	
and The Legion of Super-Heroes); priced at 2 shillings	£100.00	**P.M. Productions; 1 1948-2 1949**	
2 rare	£60.00	**1** 8pgs; George Parlett, Frank Minnitt art	£2.50
3-5 very scarce	£45.00	**2** larger size; George Parlett, John McCail art	£2.50
6-10 scarce	£40.00	**SWIFT**	
11-56? scarce	£35.00	**Hulton/Longacre; v1:1 20th Mar 1954-v10:9 2nd Mar 1963 (462 issues; joins Eagle)**	
Note: more issues thought to exist		**Vol 1:1** Tarna the Jungle Boy by Harry Bishop, Nicky Nobody, Tom Tex,	
SUPER MOUSE		Paul English by Georgio Bellavitis	£20.00
Alan Class; 1 1950s		**2**	£10.00
1 68pgs; Charlton reprints	£5.00	**3-5**	£5.00
SUPER PICTURE SPECIAL		**6-29, 31-41**	£2.50
IPC; nn Jul 1969		**30** Swiss Family Robinson	£2.50
nn - 448pgs; picture library reprints incl. Turner Rick Random	£6.00	**Vol 2:**1-30, 32, 34-53	£2.00
SUPER SCIENCE THRILLS		**31** King Arthur and his Knights by Frank Bellamy begins	£2.00
(see also Sunny Comic)		**33** Cliff McCoy by James Holdaway begins	£2.00
International Fiction; nn 1945		**Vol 3:**1-12, 14-18, 20-52	£2.00
nn - 8pgs; A.R.G. art	£3.00	**13** Red Rider by James Holdaway begins	£2.00
SUPER SMASHER COMIC		**19** Robin Hood by Frank Bellamy	£2.00
Co-Ordination Press & Publicity; nn 1947		**Vol 4:**1-33	£2.00
nn - 8pgs; reprints Dutch newspaper strips Dockey Dare, Detective and Bim, both by Piet van Elk	£4.00	**34-50, 52**	£1.50
SUPER SOLDIERS		**51** Dixon of Dock Green begins	£1.50
(see main American comics section)		**Vol 5:**1-52	£1.25
SUPER-SONIC THE SUPER COMIC		**Vol 6:**1-34	£1.25
(continues numbering of The Football Comic, joins Steve Samson)		**35** 1st "Swift and Zip"; Wells Fargo by Don Lawrence begins	£1.25
Mans World; 12 Dec 1953-17 May 1954		**36-45**	£1.25
12 Thor Steele, The Invaders begin	£4.00	**Vol 7:**1-53	£1.25
13-17	£2.50	**Vol 8:**1-40 Pony Express by Don Lawrence	£1.25
SUPER SPIDER-MAN		**41-52**	£1.00
(see Spiderman Comics Weekly)		**Vol 9:**1-52	£1.00
SUPER STAR		**Vol 10:**1-9	£1.00
Berkeley Thomson/Fordwych; 1-4 1949		*ARTISTS/FEATURES*	
1 8pgs tabloid; Frank Minnitt, Chick Henderson, Bob Monkhouse art	£4.00	*Frank Hampson (covers) v8:29, v9:2.*	
2-4 2-3 incl. Wally Robertson, Bob Monkhouse art	£4.00	**SWIFT ANNUAL**	
SUPER STREAMLINE COMICS		**Hulton/Longacre; 1955-1963**	
Streamline; nn 1952?		**1955** blue cover	£12.50
nn - 132pgs; reprints US strip, Masterman by Joe Colquhoun	£8.00	**1956**	£7.50
SUPER SUMMER HOLIDAY ANNUAL		**1957-1959**	£5.00
Atlas; 1 early 1960s		**1960-1963** Don Lawrence art	£3.00
1 very scarce 64pgs, black and white reprints featuring Batman, Viking Prince,		**SWIFT ARROW**	
Superman and Lois Lane, Davy Crockett	£40.00	**Miller; 1 1957-4?**	
SUPER THRILL ALBUM		**1** 28pgs; Ajax reprints	£4.00
G.T. Ltd; nn 1959?		**2-4**	£2.00
nn - card cover; McLoughlin cover	£10.00	**SWIFT MORGAN**	
SUPERTHRILLER/SUPER THRILLER COMIC		**Boardman; nn 1948-38 Apr 1951 (7 issues)**	
(previously The Thriller)		**nn** (2) SM in the Lost World	£10.00
Foldes/World Distributors; 5 1948-33 195? (becomes Western Super Thriller)		**nn** (4) SM and the Ancient Romans	£10.00
5 12pgs; Rex Hart art	£7.50	**nn** (6) SM and the Ancient Egyptians	£10.00
nn (6) 20pgs; C. Purvis art	£5.00	**9** SM and the Feathered Serpent	£10.00
7-33 incl. James Bleach, Terrence Patrick, John Compare art	£3.00	**16** SM in Atlantis	£10.00
SUPERTHRILLER ANNUAL		**30** SM and the Flying Saucers	£10.00
World Distributors; Aug 1957		**38** SM and the Greek Wars	£10.00
1957	£4.00	**Note:** all have Denis McLoughlin art	

N.MINT

SWIFT MORGAN SPACE COMIC
Popular; 50 Mar 1953, 52 Nov 1953
50 McLoughlin art — £15.00
52 titled Swift Morgan Spaceways Comic, McLoughlin art — £15.00

SWIFTSURE
Harrier; 1 May 1985-16 Sep 1987
1 Lieut. Fl'tf, Dandy in the Underworld, Ram Assassin, Rock Solid, Codename Andromeda all begin — £0.75
2-3, 6 — £0.60
4-5 Fl'tf by Mike Collins — £0.60
7 combines with Conqueror — £0.60
8, 11-13 Fl'tf by Steve Yeowell — £0.60
9 Redfox origin story by Fox — £0.80
10, 14-16 — £0.60

SWORD OF FREEDOM
C.A. Pearson (TV Picture Stories); 1 Feb 1959-4 Jun 1959
1 Vendetta — £5.00
2-4 — £3.00
ARTISTS/FEATURES
1 Vendetta. 2 Adriana. 3 Violetta. 4 The Assassin.

SWORDS OF HEAVEN, FLOWERS OF HELL
Star; nn 1979
nn - 72pgs; Heavy Metal reprints — £1.50

T

T-MAN FIGHTER OF CRIME
Archer Press (King Comic Series); 1-6 1953
1-6 68pgs; Quality reprints — £6.00

TALES FROM THE CRYPT
Arnold Book Co.; 1-2 1952
1-2 68pgs; E.C. reprints, cited in UK horror campaign — £15.00

TALES FROM THE FRIDGE
H. Bunch (Cozmic); nn Mar 1974
nn - 36pgs; Kitchen Sink reprints — £2.00

TALES FROM THE TRIGAN EMPIRE
(see also Look and Learn Book of The Trigan Empire, The Trigan Empire)
Hawk Books; nn 1989
nn - hardcover; Trigan Empire by Don Lawrence reprints — £18.00

TALES OF ACTION
Alan Class; 1-2 1960s
1 68pgs; reprints Sgt. Fury #1 — £6.00
2 — £2.00

TALES OF DREAD ALBUM
G.T. Ltd; nn Jan 1959
nn - card cover — £6.00

TALES OF SKITTLE-SHARPERS AND THIMBLE-RIGGERS
To Yield Press, 1 1991-3 1992
1 24pgs; Thieves by Sam Peck & Chris Hogg begins — £1.50
2-3 — £1.50

TALES OF TERROR
Portman; 1 Sep 1978-?
1 68pgs; Marvel reprints — £1.50
2-? — £0.75

TALES OF TERROR PICTURE LIBRARY
Famepress; 1 1966-?
1 68pgs pocket size; Terror of Living Pulp, Italian reprints — £1.00
2-? — £0.50

TALES OF THE GOLD MONKEY ANNUAL
Grandreams; 1982
1982 scarce, based on US TV series — £3.00

TALES OF THE MYSTERIOUS TRAVELLOR
G.T. Ltd; nn 1959?
nn - card cover — £6.00

TALES OF THE SUPERNATURAL
Alan Class; 1 1960s
1 68pgs; US reprints — £5.00

TALES OF THE UNDERWORLD
Alan Class; 1-5 1960
1 68pgs; Charlton reprints — £5.00
2-5 — £3.50

TALKING TURKEY
Galaxy; v1:1 Oct 1991-v2:5 May 1992
Vol 1:1 Hunt Emerson, Graham Higgins art begins, Shelton reprints begin — £1.25
Vol 1:2-3 — £1.00
Vol 2:1-5 — £1.00

TAMMY
IPC; 6th Feb 1971-23rd Jun 1984 (joins Girl)
1 — £2.00
13 Feb 1971-23 Jun 1984 some incl. Jim Baikie art — £0.35

TANK GIRL
Penguin; 1990, 1995
Tank Girl (Aug 1990) Martin & Hewlett reprints from Deadline — £6.00
Tank Girl (Jan 1995) new colour edition of above — £9.00
Tank Girl 2 (Apr 1995) Deadline reprints in colour — £9.00
Tank Girl: The Movie (May 1995) Graphic novelisation by Pete Milligan &
Andy Pritchett, Bolton cover — £6.00

TANK GIRL
Manga Publishing; 1 Jul 1995-8 Feb 1995
1 68pgs; Tank Girl: The Odyssey reprints, Fireball, Booga by Philip Bond — £2.20
2-8 — £2.00

Terrific #1

Thunder #1

Tiger #1

	N.MINT

TAPPING THE VEIN
Titan; 1 Sep 1990-2 Oct 1990

1 reprints Eclipse prestige format adaptations of Clive Barker stories, Scott Hampton, P. Craig Russell art, John Bolton cover	£4.50
2 Klaus Janson, John Bolton art, Scott Hampton cover	£4.50

TARGET
Target Publications; 1 15th Jun 1935-176 22nd Oct 1938
(joins Target and Rocket)

1 8pgs on green paper; Bert Hill, Harry Banger art	£35.00
2 8pgs	£10.00
3-5 8pgs	£7.50
6-112, 131-176 8pgs	£5.00
113-130 12pgs	£5.00

TARGET AND ROCKET
(previously two separate comics)
Target Publications; 1 29th Oct 1938-24 8th Apr 1939 (joins The Jolly Comic)

1 12pgs on pink paper; Harry Banger, Bert Hill art	£30.00
2	£10.00
3-5	£5.00
6-19 12pgs, on yellow paper from 7	£4.00
20-24 8pgs	£4.00

TARGET COMICS
Miller; 1-6 1952

1-6 28pgs; Star Publications reprints	£2.00

TARZAN ADVENTURES
Westworld; Tarzan: The Grand Adventure Comic v1:1 15th Sep 1951-v2:36 3rd Apr 1953 (59 issues); Tarzan Adventures v3:1 8th Apr 1953-v9:32 26th Dec 1959 (342 issues)

Vol 1:1 Tarzan reprints begins (by Foster, Hogarth, etc.)	£15.00
2-23? published fortnightly	£7.50
Vol 2:1-36 (1 Aug 1952-3 Apr 1953) published weekly	£4.00
Vol 3:1-52 becomes Tarzan Adventures	£3.00
Vol 4:1-52 incl. James Bleach, Wally Robertson art	£3.00
Vol 5:1-50	£3.00
Vol 6:1-52	£3.00
Vol 7:1-52 1st edited by Michael Moorcock, incl. James Cawthorn art	£3.00
Vol 8:1-52 incl. Luis Bermejo, Lopez Espi art	£3.00
Vol 9:1-32 incl. Kimo Budesca art	£2.50
Note: began as a British edition of a French magazine which reprinted Tarzan from the American newspaper strip. Later issues had numerous filler text stories including tales by Moorcock which will command a higher price than other issues.	

TARZAN ANNUAL
World Distributors/Brown & Watson; 1965-1969, 1977

1965 Gold Key reprints	£3.00
1966-1969 Gold Key reprints	£2.50
1977 Brown & Watson issue; reprints with some text	£2.50

TARZAN COMIC
Donald F. Peters; v1:1 1950-v2:15 Oct 1951

Vol 1:1-4 68pgs; reprints Tarzan newspaper strip	£5.00
Vol 2:1-15 36pgs	£4.00

TARZAN OF THE APES
Top Sellers; 1 1970-? 1971

1-? 36pgs; Western Publishing reprints; monthly	£1.50

TARZAN OF THE APES
Top Sellers; nn 1972

nn - 260pgs pocketbook; Dell/Gold Key reprints	£1.00

TARZAN OF THE APES
Top Sellers; 1 1971-100 1975

1 36pgs; Western Publishing reprints; fortnightly	£1.50
2-100	£0.75

TARZAN SPECIAL
Byblos; May 1978-Nov 1981

Summer Special 1978 68pgs; US reprints	£1.00
Summer Special 1979-1981 52pgs	£0.75
Autumn Special 1979-1980	£0.75
Winter Special 1979-1981	£0.75
Spring Special 1980	£0.75

TARZAN OF THE APES SPECIAL SUPER ADVENTURE
Williams; 1-2 1972

1-2 52pgs; Dell reprints	£1.00

TARZAN: THE GRAND ADVENTURE COMIC
(see Tarzan Adventures)

TARZAN WEEKLY
Byblos; 11th Jun 1977-?

No.1 - 11 Jun 1977 Tarzan reprints, also incl. Ramon Sola/Ian Gibson art	£1.50
No.1 with free gift (Super Survival Kit Bag)	£3.00
No.2 - 18 Jun 1977 with centre-fold poster (sometimes missing)	£0.75
25 Jun 1977-?	£0.50

TARZAN WORLD ADVENTURE LIBRARY
World Disributors; 1 May 1967-4 Aug 1967

1 68pgs pocket size; Men of the Deep, Western Publishing reprints	£3.00
2-4	£2.00

TEDDY TAIL
A. & C. Black; 1915-1926

Adventures of Teddy Tail (1915) 36pgs; Charles Folkard reprints from Daily Mail	£20.00
Teddy Tail in Nursery Rhyme Land (1915)	£15.00
Teddy Tail in Fairyland (1916)	£15.00
Teddy Tail in Historyland (1917)	£15.00
Teddy Tail's Fairy Tale (1919)	£15.00
Teddy Tail at the Seaside (1920)	£12.00
Teddy Tail's Fairy Tale and In Babyland (1921)	£12.00
Teddy Tail's Alphabet (1921)	£10.00
Teddy Tail in Toyland (1922)	£10.00

	N.MINT
Teddy Tail's Adventures in the A.B. Sea (1926)	£8.00

TEDDY TAIL ANNUAL
Associated Newspapers; 1934-1962

1934 scarce	£40.00
1935-1936	£25.00
1937-1939	£15.00
1940-1942	£10.00
1949-1950	£10.00
1951-1955	£7.50
1956-1959	£5.00
1960-1962	£4.00
Note: No annuals published 1943-48.	

TEDDY TAIL SERIES
Associated Newspapers; 1950-1952

Teddy Tail and the Magic Drink 16pgs; Arthur Potts reprints from Daily Mail	£4.00
Teddy Tail and the Pearl Thief	£3.00
Teddy Tail Goes West	£3.00
The Willow Pattern Story	£3.00
Teddy Tail and the Cave Men 24pgs	£3.00
Teddy Tail and the Gnomes 16pgs	£2.50

TELEVISION FAVOURITES COMIC
World Distributors; 1 Jan 1958-18 1959

1 28pgs; Dell reprints	£10.00
2-17	£4.00
18 68pgs	£5.00

TELL ME WHY
Fleetway; 1 31st Aug 1968-82 21st Nov 1970 (joins World of Wonder)

1 24pgs; junior Look and Learn	£2.00
2-82	£0.60

TELL ME WHY ANNUAL
Fleetway; 1970-1973

1970-1973	£2.00

10-4 ACTION
C.B. News; 1 Nov 1981-6 May 1982

1 52pgs	£1.00
2-6	£0.40

TERMINATOR, THE
Trident/ Dark Horse; 1 Oct 1991-17 Feb 1993

1 Dark Horse reprints begin	£1.50
2-12	£1.00
13 1st Dark Horse issue	£1.50
14 52pgs; RoboCop vs Terminator reprints begin	£1.50
15-17 RoboCop vs Terminator	£1.50

TERMINATOR
Titan; 1991?

Terminator: Tempest Now Comics reprints	£7.50

TERRAHAWKS ANNUAL
World; 1983-1984

1983, 1984 based on Gerry Anderson series	£3.00

TERRIBLE TEN, THE
Young World; 11 Jun 1964, 23 Dec 1964

11, 23 based on TV series	£4.00
Note: part of Super Mag series	

TERRIFIC
Odhams; 1 15th Apr 1967-43 3rd Feb 1968

1 Sub-Mariner (from Tales to Astonish #70), Avengers (from Avengers #6), Dr. Strange (from Strange Tales #115) reprints begin	£5.00
1 with free gift (iron-on Iron Man transfer)	£10.00
2	£2.50
2 with free gift (Iron Man missile launcher)	£5.00
3 Living Dolls begins	£1.25
4-22, 24-43	£1.00
23 Giant Man (from Tales to Astonish #49) reprints begin	£1.00

TERRIFIC ANNUAL
Odhams; 1969

1969	£4.50

TEX AUSTIN
Miller; 1-3 1959

1-3 68pgs pocket size; US reprints	£2.00

TEX RITTER WESTERN
Miller; 50 1951-99 1959, 49 issues

50 36pgs; Fawcett reprints	£10.00
51-99 28pgs	£5.00

TEX WILLER
Top Sellers; 1 1971-?

1 128pgs pocket size; Italian reprints	£1.50
2-?	£0.50

TEXAN, THE
Pemberton; 1-8 1951

1-8 32pgs; St. John Publishing reprints	£2.00

TEXAS KID COMICS
Thorpe & Porter; 1-2 1952

1-2 68pgs; Atlas reprints	£4.00

TEXAS RANGERS IN ACTION
Miller; 1-16 1959

1-16 28pgs; Charlton reprints	£3.00

THELWELL ANNUAL
World Distributors; 1980

1980 collection of strips and articles/features on Norman Thelwell	£1.50

THEO DRAKE DETECTIVE
Miller; 1 1959-?

1- reprints Nero Wolfe newspaper strip	£2.00

	N.MINT
THEY CALL ME PUSSPUSS	
Knockabout; nn 1994	
nn – Hunt Emerson art	£2.00
THING IS BIG BEN, THE	
Marvel; 1 28th Mar 84-18 19th Jul 84 (joins Spider-Man)	
1 The Thing, Iron Man, Captain America reprints begin	£1.00
2-13, 15-18	£0.25
14 John Higgins cover	£0.25
THING IS BIG BEN SUMMER SPECIAL, THE	
Marvel; 1984	
1984 52pgs; reprints The Thing, X-Men	£1.25
THIRD WORLD WAR	
Fleetway-Quality; 1 Sep 1990-6 1991	
1 32pgs; Crisis reprints by Mills & Ezquerra begin	£1.50
2-6	£1.25
THREE CHEERS COMIC	
Lewis-King Publications; nn 1946	
nn – 8pgs	£2.50
3-D DOLLY	
United Anglo-American; 1 1953	
1 36pgs; Harvey reprints, 3-D	£5.00
THREE DIMENSION COMICS	
Monthly Magazines; 1-2 1953	
1-2 36pgs; St. John Publishing reprints, 3-D	£5.00
3-STAR ADVENTURES, THE	
R. Turvey/B.C.M. Demob; 1947, 2 unnumbered issues	
nn – 12pgs; Rex Hart art	£4.00
nn - Hart art	£4.00
THREE WESTERNERS	
Cartoon Art; 1-4 1951	
1-4 20pgs; US reprints	£3.00
THRILL COMICS	
Gerald Swan; 1 Apr 1940-35 1950 (joins Girls' Fun)	
1 36pgs; William McCail, William Ward, John McCail art	£8.00
2-11 36pgs	£5.00
12 28pgs	£5.00
13-21 20pgs	£5.00
22-24 16pgs	£5.00
25-35 16pgs, format changed	£5.00
Specials:	
Summer (1941) 52pgs	£8.00
Spring (1942) 36pgs	£8.00
Special (1943) 28pgs	£8.00
THRILLER	
World Distributors; 1 1970-?	
1 68pgs pocket size; Spanish reprints	£1.00
2-?	£0.50
THRILLER, THE	
Foldes; 1 1946-4 1947 (becomes Superthriller)	
1-3 12pgs; Bob Wilkin art	£4.00
4 titled The Thriller Adventure Comic	£4.00
THRILLER COMICS/THRILLER PICTURE LIBRARY	
Amalgamated/Fleetway; 1 Nov 1951-450 May 1963	
1 The Three Musketeers by W. Bryce-Hamilton **(prices vary widely on this issue)**	£250.00
1 facsimile	£5.00
2 Dick Turpin, Derek Eyles, Stephen Chapman, Colin Merritt art	£125.00
3 Treasure Island by Michael Hubbard	£75.00
4-5	£50.00
6-10	£25.00
11-30	£20.00
Note: the first 30 or so issues are very scarce and virtually all copies from the series suffer from rusty staples, the earlier copies that much more pronounced. Copies that are completely flat and free from rust could command up to 25% more	
31-50	£15.00
51-100	£10.00
101-162, 164-200	£7.50
163 becomes Thriller Picture Library	£7.50
201-300	£5.00
301-450	£4.00
ARTISTS	
Alberto Breccia in 348, 376. Jesus Blasco in 143, 262, 291, 299. H.M. Brock in 22, 25, 47, 81, 102, 109, 189. C.L. Doughty in 37, 44, 85, 92, 94, 101, 121, 137, 141, 153, 177, 178, 185, 192, 199, 214, 223. Derek Eyles in 2, 4, 110, 139, 159, 175. Hugh McNeill in 117, 239, 247. J. Miller-Watt in 145, 183. Eric Parker in 14, 18, 38, 43, 67, 79, 89, 180, 188, 208, 335. Alberto Salinas in 445. Sep E. Scott in 13, 28, 31, 41, 53, 73, 116, 118, 134, 156. Ron Turner in 418, 442.	
THRILLING HERO	
Mans World; 16-19 1953	
16 Channel Incident, Raiders of Space by Nat Brand	£2.00
17-19	£2.00
Note: part of Mans World Comic Library series	
THRILLS	
R.C. Pate; nn 1945	
nn – 8pgs; Frank Jupo art	£3.00
THRILLS AND FUN COMIC	
Martin & Reid; nn 1944	
nn – 8pgs	£4.00
THRRP!	
Knockabout (Crack); nn 1987	
nn – Leo Baxendale	£5.00
THUNDA KING OF THE CONGO	
(see Action Series)	

	N.MINT
THUNDER	
IPC; 17th Oct 1970-13th Mar 1971 (22 unnumbered issues; joins Lion)	
No. 1 - 17 Oct 1970 Fury's Family by Denis McLoughlin, Adam Eterno by Tom Kerr begin	£5.00
No. 1 with free gift (Jumping Kangaroo)	£10.00
24 Oct 1970-13 Mar 1971	£1.50
THUNDER ACTION	
Savoy Services; 1 Nov 1986-4 Feb 1987	
1 Thunder Agents reprints begin, Jonathan Shatter by Paul Johnson/Dave Hornsby begins	£0.75
2-4	£0.50
THUNDER ANNUAL	
IPC; 1972-1974	
1972	£2.50
1973 Denis McLoughlin art	£3.00
1974	£2.50
THUNDER COMICS	
Streamline; 1 1951	
1 28pgs; Fiction House reprints	£6.00
THUNDERBIRDS	
Ravette; Feb 1992-1992	
Thunderbirds to the Rescue 48pgs; Bellamy TV21 reprints	£4.00
Thunderbirds in Space Bellamy reprints	£4.00
Danger Zone Bellamy reprints	£4.00
Lift Off Bellamy reprints	£4.00
In Action Bellamy reprints	£4.00
Shockwave Bellamy reprints	£4.00
THUNDERBIRDS ANNUAL	
(see also The Official Thunderbirds Annual, below)	
City/Century 21/Purnell; 1966-1968, 1971-1972	
1966	£25.00
1967	£15.00
1968	£12.50
1971	£6.00
1972 (Purnell) more scarce, Ron Turner art	£8.50
Note: for 1969 see Captain Scarlet and Thunderbirds Annual	
THUNDERBIRDS ANNUAL, THE OFFICIAL	
Grandreams; 1992, 1993	
1992	£4.50
1993	£4.75
THUNDERBIRDS ARE GO	
(Alan Fennell); 1 13th May 1995-present (13 issues to Dec 1995)	
1 TV 21, Lady Penelope reprints	£1.00
2-13	£0.75
THUNDERBIRDS EXTRA	
City; Mar 1966	
1966 Ron Turner, Brian Lewis art	£30.00
THUNDERBIRDS HOLIDAY SPECIAL	
Fleetway Editions; Apr 1992-Apr 1993	
1992 48pgs; Frank Bellamy, Don Harley reprints	£1.50
1993 48pgs; Frank Bellamy, Don Lawrence reprints	£1.35
THUNDERBIRDS SPECIAL	
Polystyle; 1971, 1982-1984	
1971 titled Gerry Anderson's Thunderbirds; reprints TV21 Spring Extra: Thunderbirds	£6.00
1982 reprints from Annuals, Ron Turner art	£1.50
1983 reprints from Countdown Don Harley, Frank Langford art	£1.50
1984 reprints	£1.25
THUNDERBIRDS TELEVISION STORYBOOK	
PBS; 1966	
1966	£15.00
THUNDERBIRDS THE COMIC/THE NEW THUNDERBIRDS COMIC	
Fleetway; 1 19th Oct 1991-Apr 1995 (83 to Dec 1994)	
1 Frank Bellamy Thunderbirds reprints from TV21 begin	£2.00
2-8	£1.50
9 Lady Penelope reprints by Eric Eden begin	£1.00
10-14	£0.75
15-34	£0.70
35 Fireball XL5 reprints by Graham Coton begin	£0.75
36-47	£0.75
48 John Cooper Thunderbirds reprints from TV21 & Joe 90 begin	£0.75
49-56, 59-66	£0.75
57-58 Frank Hampson Lady Penelope reprints from TV21	£0.85
67 1st retitled "The New Thunderbirds featuring Captain Scarlet and Stingray"	£0.85
68-79	£1.00
80 Joe 90, Agent 21 both begin	£1.15
81-83	£1.15
Thunderbirds Poster Magazine 1-9 (Feb 1992-1993) 1, 3, 5 incl. 7pg strip	£0.95
Thunderbirds The Collection (Mar 1992) collects 1-3	£2.00
THUNDERBIRDS 2086	
Grandreams; 1983	
1983 based on Japanese TV series	£3.00
THUNDERCATS	
Marvel; 1 16th Mar 1989-129 12th Jan 1991	
1 Thundercats begins, based on TV cartoon series	£0.50
2-129	£0.25
TIC TAC TOE COMICS	
Pemberton; 1 1951	
1 28pgs; reprints Canadian comic published by Derby Publishing Co.	£3.00
TIGER	
Amalgamated/Fleetway/IPC; 1 11th Sep 1954-30th Mar 1985	
(1555 issues, numbered to 245; joins Eagle)	
1 Roy of the Rovers by "Stewart Colwyn" (Frank Pepper) & Joe Colquhoun begins	£60.00
2	£30.00
3-5	£15.00

	N.MINT
6-10	£12.50
11-50	£7.50
51-77, 85-100	£4.00
78-84 jointly numbered issue dated 3 Mar-14 Apr 1956	£4.00
101-14 Oct 1959	£3.00
21 Oct 1959 1st "Tiger and Comet"; Jet Ace Logan by Pepper & John Gillatt begins	£3.50
21 Oct 1959 with free gift (two football team photos)	£7.00
[Note: Issues dated from 28 Oct 1959-5 Dec 1959 also came with free gift of two football team photos]	£5.00
28 Oct 1959-24 Mar 1962	£2.50
31 Mar 1962 Johnny Cougar by Geoff Campion begins	£2.00
7 Apr 1962-2 May 1964, 16 May 1964-8 May 1965	£2.00
9 May 1964 Casey and the Champ by Joe Colquhoun begins	£2.00
15 May 1965 1st "Tiger and Hurricane"; Val Venture by Jesus Blasco begins	£1.50
22 May 1965-2 Apr 1966, 16 Apr 1966-10 Jun 1967, 24 Jun 1967-29 Mar 1969	£1.50
9 Apr 1966 Robot Builders by Carlos Cruz begins (later by Ron Turner)	£1.50
17 Jun 1967 Saber, King of the Jungle by Colquhoun begins (later by McLoughlin)	£1.50
14 Oct 1967 Peg-Leg's Flying Penguins by Colquhoun begins	£1.50
5 Apr 1969 1st "Tiger and Jag"	£1.00
12 Apr 1969-25 Oct 1980	£0.75
1 Nov 1980 1st "Tiger and Speed"; Death Wish by Vano, Topps on Two Wheels by Mike Western begin	£0.50
8 Nov 1980-30 Mar 1985	£0.50
Note: two un-numbered/undated issues appeared between 27th Jun-22nd Aug '59, fortnightly schedule Mar-Apr '74.	

TIGER ANNUAL
Amalgamated/Fleetway; 1957-1987

	N.MINT
1957	£10.00
1958-1959	£6.00
1960-1964	£5.00
1965 Don Lawrence art	£6.00
1966-1969	£4.00
1970-1980	£3.00
1981-1987	£2.00

TIGER GIRL
Cartoon Art; nn 1950

	N.MINT
nn - 16pgs; Fiction House reprints	£4.00

TIGER HOLIDAY SPECIAL
I.P.C. Magazines; Jun 1971-?

	N.MINT
1971-1973 96pgs	£3.00
1974-1975 80pgs	£2.00
1976-? 64pgs	£1.00

TIGER SPORTS LIBRARY
Fleetway; 1 Jul 1961-12 Dec 1961

	N.MINT
1 68pgs; Come on Carford by Alfredo Marculeta	£4.00
2-12 Carford on all odd numbers, Bradmere in all even numbers	£3.00

ARTISTS/FEATURES
1 Come On Carford by Alfredo Marculeta. 2 Shoot, Cannon! by Fred T. Holmes. 3 Danger Mark. 4 Bird on the Wing by Loredano Ugolini. 5 Private 'Jankers' - Inside Right by Josep Marti. 6 The Unknown Quantity by Giorgio Trevisan. 7 Hit and Run. 8 The Luck of the Bounce by Fred T. Holmes. 9 The Big Deal. 10 Heads...You Lose. 11 Rush-Tactics by Josep Marti. 12 Clash of Giants. Note: 13 and 14 advertised but thought not to have appeared

TIGER TIM'S ANNUAL
Amalgamated Press; 1922-1957

	N.MINT
1922 scarce	£60.00
1923	£35.00
1924-1925	£25.00
1926-1930	£20.00
1931-1935	£17.50
1936-1940	£15.00
1941-1949	£12.50
1950-1957	£10.00

TIGER TIM'S TALES
Amalgamated Press; 1 1st Jun 1919-28 24th Jan 1920 (becomes Tiger Tim's Weekly)

	N.MINT
1-6 monthly issues; Herbert Foxwell art	£35.00
7-28 (29 Aug 1919-24 Jan 1920) weekly issues	£10.00

TIGER TIM'S WEEKLY
Amalgamated Press; (1) 1 31st Jan 1920-94 12th Nov 1921; (2) 1 19th Nov 1921-965 18th May 1940 (joins The Rainbow)

	N.MINT
1 Herbert Foxwell, Fred Crompton, A.B. Payne art	£30.00
2	£12.50
3-5	£10.00
6-94	£8.00
1 New series; Tiger Tim & the Bruin Boys by Foxwell	£10.00
2-965	£4.00

TIM HOLT
Cartoon Art; 1-4 1952

	N.MINT
1-4 32pgs; Magazine Enterprises reprints	£4.00

TIM HOLT
United Anglo-American; 1-4 1953

	N.MINT
1-4 32pgs; Magazine Enterprises reprints	£3.00

TIM HOLT
World Distributors; 1 1953-24 1954

	N.MINT
1 28pgs; Magazine Enterprises reprints	£4.00
2-24 incl. reprints from Ghost Rider (Atlas), Red Hawk (ME), etc.	£2.50

TIM TYLER
(see Action series)

TINA
Fleetway Publications; 25th Feb 1967-16th Sep 1967, 30 issues (becomes Princess Tina)

	N.MINT
25 Feb 1967 Jane Bond by Michael Hubbard, Space Girls by Keith Watson begin	£1.00
4 Mar-16 Sep 1967 incl. Carlos Roume, Hugh McNeill art	£0.35

TINTIN
Methuen; 1958-1985

	N.MINT
The Crab With the Golden Claws (1958) Herge (Georges Remi) art in all	£20.00
King Ottokar's Sceptre (1958)	£15.00
The Secret of the Unicorn (1959)	£12.50
Red Rackham's Treasure (1959)	£10.00
Destination Moon (1959)	£10.00
Explorers on the Moon (1959)	£10.00
The Calculus Affair (1960)	£8.00
The Red Sea Sharks (1960)	£8.00
The Shooting Star (1961)	£8.00
The Seven Crystal Balls (1962)	£5.00
Prisoners of the Sun (1962)	£5.00
Tintin in Tibet (1962)	£8.00
The Castafiore Emerald (1963)	£8.00
Tintin and the Golden Fleece (1965) film adaptation	£10.00
The Black Island (1966)	£10.00
Tintin and the Blue Oranges (1967) film adaptation	£8.00
Flight 714 (1968)	£5.00
Cigars of the Pharaoh (1971)	£5.00
The Land of Black Gold (1972)	£5.00
Tintin and the Lake of Sharks (1973) film adaptation	£8.00
The Broken Ear (1975)	£5.00
Tintin and the Picaros (1976)	£4.00
Tintin in America (1978)	£4.00
The Blue Lotus (1983)	£4.00
The Making of Tintin I (1983)	£8.00
The Making of Tintin II (1985)	£8.00
Tintin in the Land of the Soviets (Les Edition du Petit Vingtieme, 1989)	£9.00

TINY COMIC
P.M. Productions; nn 1945

	N.MINT
nn - 8pgs on brown card; Reg Carter art	£3.00

TINY TOTS
Amalgamated Press; 1 22nd Oct 1927-1334 24th Jan 1959 (joins Playhour)

	N.MINT
1 12pgs tabloid; Fred Crompton, Terry Wakefield, Bertie Brown art	£35.00
1927 issues	£10.00
1928 issues	£7.50
1929-1938 issues	£5.00
1938-1949 issues	£3.00
1950-1955 issues	£2.00
1956-1959 issues	£1.50

CHRONOLOGY
1 Jun 1940: 1st "Tiny Tots & Sunbeam". 25 May 1940: frequency dropped to fortnightly. 26 Oct 1951: weekly publication resumed. 5 May 1956: 1st "Tiny Tots & Rainbow", drops text in favour of all-pictures. 27 Sep 1956: 1st full colour gravure issue.

TIP TOP
Amalgamated Press; 1 21st Apr 1934-727 29th May 1954 (joins TV Fun)

	N.MINT
1 8pgs tabloid; Terry Wakefield, George Parlett art	£35.00
1934 issues	£12.50
1935 issues	£10.00
1934-1938 issues	£8.00
1939-1949 issues	£5.00
1950-1954 issues	£3.00

CHRONOLOGY
6 Jan 1940: 1st full colour cover. 25 May 1940: 1st "Tip Top & Butterfly". 15 Jun 1940: frequency dropped to fortnightly. 25 Oct 1952: resumes weekly publication.

TIP TOP COMICS
Miller; 1 Dec 1940-2 Jan 1941 (becomes Comic on Parade)

	N.MINT
1-2 32pgs; United Features reprints	£4.00

TITANS
Marvel; 1 25th Oct 1975-58 24th Nov 1976 (joins Super Spider-Man)

	N.MINT
1 36pgs oblong; Captain America, Sub-Mariner, Inhumans, Nick Fury, Captain Marvel reprints begin	£1.25
2	£1.00
3-10	£0.75
11-12 Emergency issues, page count/price down, no glossy cover	£0.75
13 X-Men reprints begin	£0.75
14-25, 27-30, 32-52, 54-58	£0.75
26 X-Men origin story reprints	£0.75
31 Ghost Rider reprints begin	£0.75
53 Avengers reprints begin	£0.75

TITANS ANNUAL, THE
World Distributors; 1977-1978

	N.MINT
1977 reprints Submariner #72, X-Men #40, 42, 57, plus Captain America	£5.00
1978 reprints FF Ann #6, plus Black Widow	£3.00

TITANS POCKET BOOK
Marvel; 1 25th Sep 1980-13 12th Nov 1981

	N.MINT
1 52pgs pocketbook; Thor, Captain America, Iron Man origins begin; Tales of Suspense #40 reprinted; b/w	£1.00
2	£1.00
3 100pgs double issue	£1.25
4-13	£0.60

TITBITS SCIENCE FICTION COMIC
C.A. Pearson; Oct 1953-Mar 1954, 6 unnumbered issues

	N.MINT
Planet X1, The Giants of the Second World by Ron Turner	£20.00
The Terror of Titan, The Planetoid Plague by Turner	£20.00
Captain Diamond & the Space Pirates by Turner, The Space Crusader by Norman Light	£20.00
The Scourge of the Carbon Belt by Turner, War on Saourian by Holdaway	£20.00
The Dome of Survival, The Inner World by Turner, Escape From Varl by James Holdaway	£20.00
The Deimos Deadline, The Ninth Moon by Turner, Captain Diamond by George Ratcliffe	£20.00
Note: A seventh issue was prepared, containing a Turner story entitled The Diamonds of Death, but did not appear in the UK. The artwork later appeared in a French album.	

TITBITS WILD WEST COMICS
C.A. Pearson; Oct 1953-Mar 1954, 6 unnumbered issues

	N.MINT
Lobo Kid Lobo Kid by Norman Light, Curly Bill by George Radcliffe begin	£8.00

	N.MINT
Stagecoach Wreckers Light art	£8.00
Curly Bill & the Black Hood Light art	£8.00
Curly Bill & the Rival Railroads Light art	£8.00
Arizona Kid Arizona Kid by Norman Light begins	£8.00
Buffalo Bill Rides the Vengeance Trail Light art	£8.00
Note: A seventh issue was prepared, but did not appear in the UK. The artwork later appeared in French magazines.	
TOM AND JERRY	
Thorpe & Porter; 1 Jan 1953-4 1953	
1-4 36pgs; Dell reprints	£2.00
TOM AND JERRY SPECIALS	
World/Polystyle; May 1973-Jul 1984	
Summer Special 1973-1974 32pgs	£0.70
Holiday Special 1975-1984 48pgs	£0.60
Winter Special 1976-1979 48pgs	£0.50
TOM AND JERRY WEEKLY	
Spotlight Publications; 13th Oct 1973-3rd Aug 1974, 43 issues (joins TV Comic)	
13 Oct 1973 24pgs; Dell reprints	£1.00
20 Oct 1973-3 Aug 1974	£0.35
TOM CORBETT SPACE CADET	
World Distributors; 1 Apr 1953-9 Dec 1953	
1 36pgs; Dell reprints	£4.00
2-9	£2.50
TOM MIX WESTERN COMICS	
Miller; (1) 3 unnumbered issues; (2) 50 Apr 1951-134 1959	
nn - 16pgs 2-tone gravure; Fawcett reprints	£10.00
nn - 68pgs gravure	£7.50
nn - larger format 2-tone gravure	£7.50
50-134 28pgs	£5.00
TOM PUSS COMICS	
(see also Panda Comics)	
B.B. Ltd (Birn Bros); 700 1949	
700 16pgs; reprints Dutch newspaper strips by Marten Toonder	£30.00
TOMAHAWK	
Strato; 1 1954-40 1957	
1 68pgs; National Periodicals reprints	£4.00
2-40	£3.00
TONS O' FUN COMIC	
Philmar; nn 1948	
nn - 16pgs; Ern Shaw art	£3.00
TONTO	
World Distributors; 1 1953-32 1955	
1 28pgs; Dell reprints	£5.00
2-32	£2.50
TONY TRENT COMICS	
Streamline; nn 1951	
nn - 28pgs; Columbia Publications reprints	£3.00
TOP-HOLE COMICS	
P.M. Productions; nn Dec 1943	
nn - 16pgs; Frank Jupo art	£3.00
TOP MARK ADVENTURES	
Foldes Modern Printing; 1 1947	
1 12pgs; Rex Hart art	£4.00
TOP-NOTCH COMIC	
Apex Publicity; nn Sep 1947	
nn - Stanley White, John Jukes art	£5.00
TOP-NOTCH COMIC, THE	
Saward & Co.; nn 1945?	
nn - 16pgs; Bob Wilkin art	£3.00
TOPICAL FUNNIES	
(see also Funnies Budget)	
Gerald Swan; 1 Apr 1940-36 Jan 1951	
1 36pgs; Edward Banger, William Ward art	£8.00
2-12 36pgs	£5.00
13-23 20pgs	£5.00
24 16pgs	£5.00
25-34 16pgs; format changed	£5.00
35-36 20pgs	£5.00
Specials:	
Spring, Autumn, Winter (1941) 52 pgs	£8.00
Summer (1942) 36pgs	£8.00
Special (1943) 36pgs	£8.00
Double (1946)	£8.00
TOPIX	
Grafton; 1-4 1940s	
1-4 28pgs; Catechetical Guild reprints	£2.00
TOPPER	
D.C. Thomson; 1 7th Feb 1953-1963 15th Sep 1990 (joins The Beezer and Topper)	
1 tabloid size	£100.00
1 with free gift (The Big Crack Bang)	£150.00
2	£35.00
3	£15.00
1953-1955 issues	£7.50
1956-1959 issues	£5.00
1960-1965 issues	£3.00
1966-1969 issues	£1.50
1970-1979 issues	£0.75
1980-1990 issues	£0.50
CHRONOLOGY	

1 Micky the Monkey by Dudley Watkins, The Fighting Frasers by Bill Holroyd, Beryl the Peril by David Law, Flip McCoy by Paddy Brennan all begin, Treasure Island by Watkins reprints (from People's Journal) begin. 31 (3 Sep 1953) Kidnapped by Watkins reprints begin. 55 (20 Feb 1954) Robinson Crusoe by

Topper #1

TV Comic Annual 1954

TV Land #1

	N.MINT
Watkins reprints begin. 95 (7 Nov 1954) King Solomon's Mines by Watkins begins. 140 (8 Oct 1955) Allan Quatermain by Watkins begins. 251 (23 Nov 1957) Oliver Twist by Watkins reprints begin. 1145 (11 Jan 1975) 1st "Topper and Buzz". 1277 (23 Jul 1977) 1st "Topper and Sparky". 1440 1st small size	
ARTISTS/FEATURES	
Paddy Brennan in 1-80, 124-158, 193-282, 342-363, 471-489, 574-779, 868-901, 979-1152, 1153-1175, 1202, 1529-1631. David Law in 1-912. Allan Morley in 2-227. Dudley D. Watkins in 1-873.	

TOPPER BOOK

D.C. Thomson; 1955-present

	N.MINT
1955 landscape format begins (5 strips of 25 characters, last is panda)	£70.00
1956 (Dartboard design, logo in centre, characters in middle band)	£37.50
1957 (25 squares, each with character or object)	£32.50
1958 (20 diagonal diamond divisions each with different character)	£30.00
1959 (Captain Bungle holds rifle with monkey sitting on barrel aiming catapault)	£30.00
1960 (Logo diagonally down from left to right with various heads)	£17.50
1961 (Figaro and horse laughing whilst reading Topper Book)	£15.00
1962 (Character heads with their names, Beryl the Peril top right)	£12.50
1963 (Julius Cheeser sits in deck chair on box surrounded by drawing pins)	£12.50
1964 (Foxy with gun in back held by chicken)	£12.50
1965 (2 frames, Figaro holding up cowboy, cowboy lighting firework)	£12.50
1966 (4 frames, Tom Cat and Julius Cheeser and a fire-cracker)	£10.00
1967-1968 regular annual format begins, cover dated	£10.00
1969-1970	£7.50
1971-1980	£5.00
1981-1985 titled Topper and Sparky Book	£3.50
1986-1996	£3.00

TOPPER PICTURE BOOK

D.C. Thomson; nn Apr 1954

	N.MINT
- scarce	£75.00

TOPPER SUMMER SPECIAL

D.C. Thomson; 1983-May 1992

	N.MINT
1983-1985	£2.50
1986-1989	£1.50
1990-1992	£1.00

TOP SECRET PICTURE LIBRARY

IPC; 1 Jul 1974-40 Feb 1976

	N.MINT
1 68pgs pocket size; Wings of Death by Jorge Moliterni	£1.00
2-40	£0.50

ARTISTS/FEATURES

All issues feature John Havoc except 25, 26, 29, 30 which feature Jason Wilde. 1 Wings of Death by Jorge Moliterni. 2 Operation Scorpion by Enrique Breccia. 3 Takeover by Enrique Breccia. 4 The 50th Kill by Enrique Breccia. 5 Reign of Terror by Jorge Moliterni. 6 Menace Mountain by Enrique Breccia. 7 Hunt the Devil by Jorge Moliterni. 8 The Golden Crusader by P. Martinez. 9 The Death Rehersal by Jorge Moliterni. 10 Blood on his Hands by P. Martinez. 11 Living Target by Jorge Moliterni. 12 Tightrope. 13 Artist in Crime by Jorge Moliterni. 14 Dark Mountain. 15 The Deadly Deep. 16 Frame-Up. 17 Blood Sport by Jorge Moliterni. 18 The Wild Ones. 19 Hunted! 20 Dead on Time. 21 The Last Frontier. 22 See Naples and Die! 23 One Second to Doom. 24 Danger Road. 25 Secret Enemy by Ron Turner. 26 The Victim. 27 Point of No Return. 28 Iron Hand. 29 The Smoke Job. 30 Dice With Death. 31 The Hit-Man. 32 Too Many Crooks. 33 Follow My Leader by Juan Zanotto. 34 File X. 35 The Viking Horde. 36 Shadow of Fear. 37 Assassin. 38 High Risk. 39 Too Hot to Handle. 40 Target-Q.

TOP SPOT

Amalgamated/Fleetway; 25th Oct 1958-16th Jan 1960 (58 issues; joins Film Fun)

	N.MINT
25 Oct 1958	£10.00
1 Nov 1958-16 Jan 1960	£2.00

TOP THREE

Famepress; 1 1961-124 1966

	N.MINT
1 68pgs pocket size; Italian reprints	£1.00
2-124	£0.50

TORCHY GIFTBOOK

Daily Mirror; nn 1960-1964

	N.MINT
nn - undated (1960) features Gerry Anderson's Torchy by Roberta Leigh	£15.00
1961-1964 stories by Roberta Leigh	£10.00

TORNADO

IPC; 1 24th Mar 1979-22 18th Aug 1979 (joins 2000AD)

	N.MINT
1 Victor Drago by Mike Dorey, Mind of Wolfie Smith by Vano, Angry Planet by Belardinelli, The Tale of Benkie by Steve Moore & Musquera, Captain Klepp by Kev O'Neill begin	£3.00
2, 5-7, 9-22	£1.00
3 Storm by Musquera begins	£1.00
4 Blackhawk by Alfonso Azpiri begins	£1.00
8 Cam Kennedy Storm begins	£1.00
Note: many issues have photos of Dave Gibbons dressed as editor Big E. He looks fab!	

TORNADO ANNUAL

Fleetway; 1979-1980

	N.MINT
1979-1980	£2.00

TORNADO SUMMER SPECIAL

IPC; Jun 1979

	N.MINT
1979 64pgs	£1.00

TORRID

Gold Star; 1 Oct 1979-12 1982

	N.MINT
1-12 52pgs; foreign reprints, adult material	£1.00

TOTAL CARNAGE

Dark Horse; 1 Apr 1993-10 Jan 1994

	N.MINT
1 Batman vs Predator, Army of Darkness, The Mask, Grendel: War Child reprints begin	£1.50
2-8, 10	£1.50
9 Aliens/Predator: Deadliest of the Species by Claremont & Gulacy reprints begin	£1.50

TOTEM PICTURE LIBRARY IN COLOUR

Famepress; 1 1961-102 1967

	N.MINT
1 68pgs pocket size; Italian reprints	£1.00
2-102	£0.50

TOXIC!

(see Accident Man, Bogie Man, Makabre, Marshal Law, Sex Warrior)

Apocalypse Ltd.; 1 28 Mar 1991-31 4th Oct 1991

	N.MINT
1 Marshal Law by Mills & O'Neill, Accident Man by Mills/Skinner & Martin Emond, Mutomaniac by Mills & McMahon all begin, Bisley art	£1.00
2 Bogie Man by Wagner/Grant & Cam Kennedy begins	£1.00
3-6, 8, 10 10 incl. Arthur Ranson art	£1.00
7 Makabre by Grant & Alcatena begins	£1.00
9 Sex Warrior by Will Simpson begins	£1.00
11 Bogie Man by Wagner/Grant & Robin Smith begins	£1.00
12 Psycho-Killer begins	£1.00
13 Coffin begins	£1.00
14, 16-24, 26-29, 31	£1.00
15 Dinner Ladies From Hell begins	£1.00
25 Detritus Rex, T-Bone begins	£1.00
30 The Road to Hell by Colin McNeil begins	£1.00

TRAMPS IN THE KINGDOM

Hodder & Stoughton; nn 1979

	N.MINT
nn - 124pgs; Roland Fiddy reprints from Daily Express	£1.00

TRANSFORMERS

Marvel; 1 20th Sep 1984-332 1991

	N.MINT
1 all American reprints	£1.00
2-8 US reprints	£0.60
9-10 1st original British strip by Parkhouse & Ridgway	£1.00
11-12 Mike Collins art	£0.75
13-112, 114-152, 154-332	£0.30
113 1st Deaths Head	£4.00
153 incorporates Action Force	£0.30

ARTISTS

Artists include Mike Collins, Barry Kitson, John Ridgway, Geoff Senior, Will Simpson, Ron Smith in 82, John Stokes, etc.

TRANSFORMERS

Fleetway; 1 1994-4 (Dec 1994)

	N.MINT
1-4	£0.50

TREASURE COMIC

Martin & Reid; nn 1949

	N.MINT
nn - Harry Banger, Frank Minnitt art	£3.00

TRIALS OF NASTY TALES, THE

(see Nasty Tales)

H. Bunch; nn Feb 1973

	N.MINT
nn - 36pgs; Dave Gibbons, Edward Barker, Chris Welch art	£3.00

TRIDENT

(see St. Swithin's Day)

Trident Comics; 1 Aug 1989-8 1990

	N.MINT
1 50pgs; Light Brigade by Neil Gaiman & Nigel Kitching, Bacchus by Eddie Campbell, St. Swithin's Day by Grant Morrison & Paul Grist, Dom Zombi by Dominic Regan all begin	£2.00
2-4 Grant Morrison script, Campbell art	£1.75
5 Campbell art	£2.25
6 Light Brigade by Rob Moran, Campbell art	£2.25
7 Phil Elliott art, 1st Shadows by Vincent Danks/Steve Pini	£2.25
8	£2.25

TRIFFIK!

Communications Innovations; 1 29th Feb 1992-12 14 May 1992

	N.MINT
1 28pgs; Lew Stringer art	£0.75
2-12	£0.25

TRIGAN EMPIRE, THE

(see also Look and Learn Book of the Trigan Empire, Tales of the Trigan Empire)

Hamlyn; nn 1978

	N.MINT
nn - 192pgs hardback; reprints Trigan Empire by Don Lawrence from Ranger/Look & Learn	£8.00

TRIGGER

(see Roy Rogers' Trigger)

TRIGGER WESTERN ALBUM

G.T. Ltd; nn 1959?

	N.MINT
nn - card cover; McLoughlin Buffalo Bill (35, 45) reprints	£8.00

TRIPLE TERROR, THE

Donald F. Peters; 20 1949

	N.MINT
20 20pgs; reprints United Features strips from Tip Top Comics	£3.00

TRIUMPH

Amalgamated Press; 1 18th Oct 1924-814 25th May 1940 (joins The Champion)

	N.MINT
1 story paper for boys, no strips	£25.00
2-767 story paper	£3.00
768-814 incl. Superman reprints, Nat Brand, Stanley White art	£5.00
Note: there were 21 issues with the Superman strip, 4 of which had Superman on the cover and one of these was based on Action Comics #1. A set of these sold in 1994 for **£1,500**	

TRIUMPH ANNUAL

Amalgamated Press; 1937-1941

	N.MINT
1937 scarce; cover shows giant robot about to club two explorers	£40.00
1938	£25.00
1939-1941	£20.00

TROMBONE

Knockabout; 1 Mar 1990

	N.MINT
1 Emerson, Edika, Ouin, Maester, Carali, Reiser, Juba art	£1.95

TROUBLED SOULS

(see also For A Few Troubles More)

Fleetway; nn Feb 1990

	N.MINT
nn - 96pgs trade paperback; Crisis reprints by Garth Ennis & John McCrea	£6.50

TRUE COMPLETE MYSTERY

Streamline; nn 1950

	N.MINT
nn - 28pgs; Atlas reprints	£3.00

TRUE FAITH

Fleetway; nn Oct 1990

	N.MINT
nn - trade paperback; Crisis reprints by Garth Ennis & Warren Pleece, withdrawn by publishers in Dec 1990	£6.00

TRUE LIFE ADVENTURES

Mans World; 12 Nov 1953-17 Apr 1954

	N.MINT
12 Buried Alive, Kansi the Wolfboy begin	£2.00
13-17	£2.00

	N.MINT
Note: part of Mans World Comic Library series	
TRUE LIFE SECRETS	
Miller; 1-20 1952	
1-20 28pgs; Charlton reprints	£2.00
TRUE LIFE SPORTS	
Sports Cartoons; 1 Jun 1953	
1 28pgs	£2.50
TRUE LOVE CONFESSIONS	
Trent (Archer Press); 1-12 1953	
1-12 68pgs; US reprints	£2.00
TRUE LOVE CONFESSIONS	
Cartoon Art; 1 1954	
1 68pgs; Premier reprints	£2.00
TRUE LOVE ROMANCES	
Trent (Archer Press); 1-12 1953	
1-12 68pgs; US reprints	£2.00
TRUE MYSTERY	
Streamline; nn 1953	
nn - 28pgs; Fox Features reprints	£4.00
TRUE POLICE COMICS	
Cartoon Art; 1 1950	
1 36pgs; Gerald Quinn, Paddy Brennan art, cited in UK horror campaign	£15.00
TRUE SECRETS	
Miller; 1 1955-?	
1 28pgs; Atlas reprints	£2.50
2-?	£1.25
TRUE 3-D	
United Anglo-American; 1 1954	
1 28pgs; Harvey Publications reprints in 3-D	£10.00
TRUE TO LIFE ROMANCES	
Gerald Swan; 1 1954-16 1955	
1-16 Star Publications reprints	£1.50
TRUE WAR	
IPC Magazines; 1 Jun 1978-3 Aug 1978	
1 40pgs; Keith Watson art	£1.00
2-3 Ian Kennedy art	£0.75
TRUE WAR EXPERIENCES	
United Anglo-American; 1 1953	
1 28pgs; Harvey Publications reprints	£3.00
TRUE WESTERN	
Thorpe & Porter; nn 1950s	
nn - 36pgs; Marvel reprints	£2.00
TRUELY AMAZING LOVE STORIES	
Antonio Ghura; nn 1977	
nn - 52pgs; Ghura art, adult material	£1.00
TV ACTION	
(previously Countdown)	
Polystyle; 59 1st Apr 1972-132 25th Aug 1973 (joins TV Comic)	
59 Dr. Who by Gerry Haylock, The Persuaders by Harry Lindfield, Thunderbirds by Don Harley, Stingray reprints by Ron Embleton continued, Tightrope by Stanley Houghton, UFO, Hawaii Five-O by Leslie Branton, Countdown by John Burns begin	£15.00
60	£7.00
61 last original Thunderbirds, Stingray reprints	£4.00
62 1st original Stingray by Harley	£3.50
63 Embleton Captain Scarlet reprints begin	£3.50
64-69	£3.50
70 last Captain Scarlet (returns 78-82)	£3.50
71 last Bellamy Thunderbirds reprint, last Stingray, 1st Burns UFO	£3.50
72 1st Noble Fireball XL5 reprint	£3.50
73-76	£3.50
77 last Thunderbirds	£3.50
78-82	£3.00
83 1st Noble Zero X reprint	£3.00
84-87	£3.00
88 Mission Impossible by Burns begins	£2.50
89-100	£2.50
101 1st "Big Story"	£2.50
102 Dad's Army by Peter Ford begins	£2.50
103 Alias Smith and Jones by Colin Andrews begins	£2.50
104 The Protectors by Jose Ortiz begins	£2.50
105 Cannon by Martin Asbury begins	£2.50
106-132	£2.00
TV ACTION & COUNTDOWN HOLIDAY SPECIAL	
Polystyle; 1972	
1972 48pgs	£6.00
TV ACTION ANNUAL	
Polystyle; 1973-1974	
1973, 1974	£6.00
TV ACTION HOLIDAY SPECIAL	
Polystyle; Mar 1973	
1973 48pgs; features UFO, Dr. Who, The Protectors, Mission Impossible and The Persuaders; Martin Asbury art	£3.50
TV CENTURY 21	
City; 1 23rd Jan 1965-242 20th Sep 1969 (joins TV 21 and Joe 90)	
1 Burke's Law by Pat Williams, Fireball XL5 by Graham Coton, Stingray by Ron Embleton, Lady Penelope by Eric Eden, The Daleks by Terry Nation & Richard Jennings begin	£135.00
Note: interior coupon often clipped. Beware!	
1 with free gift (Secret Decoder)	£175.00
2	£50.00
3 Dalek cover	£60.00
4	£25.00
5	£17.50

	N.MINT
6 1st Mike Noble Fireball XL5	£12.50
7-10	£8.00
11-20	£7.50
21 Secret Agent 21 by Rab Hamilton begins	£7.50
22-39, 44-49	£6.00
40-43 Frank Hampson Fireball XL5	£7.00
50-51 1st Ron Turner Daleks	£5.00
52 Get Smart, The Munsters by Trevillion, Thunderbirds by Frank Bellamy	£4.00
53-70	£4.00
71 last Ron Embleton Stingray (Gerry Embleton art from 72)	£4.00
72, 74-89, 91-92	£4.00
73 The Investigator by Don Harley begins	£4.00
90 Catch or Kill by John Burns begins	£4.00
93-98 Don Harley Thunderbirds art	£4.00
99-100, 106-108, 110-131	£4.00
101-104 Thunderbirds Are Go photo story from movie. 104 last Daleks	£4.00
105 Zero X by Noble begins	£4.00
109 1st Don Lawrence Fireball XL5	£4.00
132 Front Page by John Burns begins	£3.00
133-140, 142-153, 155-167, 169-184	£3.00
141 Captain Scarlet by Ron Embleton begins	£3.00
154 title becomes TV21	£3.00
168 Project Sword text stories by Angus Allen begin	£3.00
185-186, 192-193, 210 Frank Bellamy Capt. Scarlet covers	£3.00
187-189, 191, 194-199	£2.50
190 1st "TV 21 and TV Tornado"; Tarzan, The Saint begin	£2.50
200-209, 211-242 later issues more scarce	£3.50
ARTISTS	
Frank Bellamy in 52-92, 99-242. John Burns in 90-114, 119-154. Ron Embleton in 1-57, 62-71, 141-157. Frank Hampson in 40-43. Don Lawrence in 109-140. Mike Noble in 6-39, 44-86, 90-100, 105-130, 135-154, 158-166, 172-179, 182-184, 187-189, 194-241. Ron Turner in 50-51, 59-104. Keith Watson in 167-169, 180-181, 190-191, 199-200, 205-206. Mike Western in 7.	
TV CENTURY 21 ANNUAL	
City/Fleetway; 1965-1973	
1965	£22.50
1966	£15.00
1967	£12.50
1968-1969 becomes TV 21 Annual	£7.50
1970-1973 no Gerry Anderson material	£2.50
TV CENTURY 21 INTERNATIONAL EXTRA	
City; 1965	
1965 48pgs; scarce, (Stingray cover), Ron Turner art	£32.50
TV CENTURY 21 STINGRAY SPECIAL	
City; 1965	
1965 48pgs; Ron Turner, Ron Embleton art	£27.50
1965 with free gift (WASP and Stingray badges)	£50.00
TV CENTURY 21 SUMMER EXTRA	
City; 1965-May 1966	
1965 48pgs; Lady Penelope by Hampson, Ron Embleton art	£27.50
1965 with free gift (Cosmic Capers Kit)	£50.00
1966 Don Harley art	£22.50
TV COMEDY SCENE	
ITV Publications; nn 1976	
nn - 52pgs; Harry North art	£1.00
TV COMIC	
News of the World/Beaverbrook/TV/Polystyle; 1 9th Nov 1951-1697 29th Jun 1984	
1 Muffin the Mule by Neville Main, Tom Puss (Dutch reprints) by Marten Toonder, Prince Valiant (US reprints) by Hal Foster begin	£60.00
2	£25.00
3-5	£12.50
6-15	£10.00
16-25	£5.00
26-50	£3.00
51-200	£2.00
201-438, 440-482	£1.50
439 Four Feather Falls by Main begins	£1.50
483 Supercar by H. Watts begins	£4.00
484-507, 509-564, 566-673	£3.00
508 Range Rider by Ron Embleton begins	£3.00
565 Fireball XL5 by Main begins	£4.00
674-719 Dr Who by Main (later by Bill Mevin, John Canning)	£3.00
720 The Avengers by Pat Williams begins, Dr. Who	£3.00
721-999 Dr Who	£3.00
1000-1132	£1.75
1133-1291 Dr Who returns by Gerry Haylock (later by Martin Asbury, Canning)	£1.50
1292 title becomes "Mighty TV Comic", 1st tabloid format, Dr Who	£1.50
1293-1385 tabloid format, Dr Who	£1.00
1386-1392 Dr Who reprints, redrawn as Tom Baker	£1.00
1393 1st "TV Comic incorporating Target", standard format, Dr. Who reprints	£1.00
1395-1430 Dr. Who reprints	£1.00
1431-1697	£0.50
TV COMIC ANNUAL	
News of the World/Beaverbrook/TV Publications/Polystyle; 1954-1985?	
1954 scarce	£35.00
1955	£17.50
1956-1959	£10.00
1960-1963	£7.50
1964 (TV) Fireball XL5, Supercar, Range Rider	£12.00
1965 (TV) Fireball XL5, Supercar	£10.00
1966 Troughton Dr Who by Neville Main	£8.00
1967 Avengers (Diana Rigg) strip, Dr Who by John Canning	£7.00
1968 Troughton Dr Who & Daleks by Pat Williams, Adam Adamant text story	£8.50

	N.MINT
1969 (Polystyle) Troughton Dr Who, Skippy text story	£6.00
1970-1971 Pertwee Dr Who, Avengers (Tara King) text stories	£3.25
1972, 1974	£3.00
1973 Avengers (Tara King)	£4.00
1975-1977 Tom Baker Dr Who	£2.50
1978 Tom Baker Dr Who	£2.25
copyright year 1978 titled New Mighty TV Comic Annual; Tom Baker Dr Who	£2.25
cy1979-cy1980 incl. Dr Who	£1.50
cy1981-cy1984	£1.25

TV COMIC HOLIDAY SPECIAL
TV/Polystyle; Jun 1963-Apr 1984

	N.MINT
1963	£5.00
1964	£3.00
1965 Troughton Dr Who by Neville Main	£5.00
1966-1970 Dr Who	£2.50
1971-1973	£1.00
1974-1978 Dr Who	£1.50
1979-1984	£0.75

TV COMIC SUMMER SPECIAL
TV; 1962 (becomes TV Comic Holiday Special)

	N.MINT
1962 48pgs; reprints	£4.00

TV CRIMEBUSTERS
TV; nn 1962

nn - hardback, scarce features Dangerman, Avengers (Steed and David Keel), Persuaders, Dixon of Dock Green, Four Just Men, Charlie Chan; all are a mixture of artwork and photographs	£25.00

TV EXPRESS
(previously Express Weekly)
TV; 286 23rd Apr 1960-375 6th Jan 1962 (90 issues, joins TV Comic)

286 Battleground by Embleton, Wulf the Briton by Embleton	
287	£3.00
288-305, 307-331, 333-346, 348-375	£2.50
306 Biggles by Embleton begins	£2.50
332 Col. Pinto by Embleton begins	£2.50
347 Danger Man text stories begin	£2.50
ARTISTS	
Ron Embleton in 286-371.	

TV EXPRESS ANNUAL
(previously Express Annual)
TV; 1961-1962

1961 Wulf the Briton by Embleton	£5.00
1962 Biggles by Embleton	£6.00

TV FAN
(see TV Fun)

TV FEATURES
Mick Anglo; 1 Nov 1960-8 Jun 1961

1-8 28pgs; Miller reprints	£3.00

TV FUN/TV FAN
Amalgamated/Fleetway; 1 19th Sep 1953-333 30th Jan 1960 (joins Valentine)

1 Arthur Askey by Arthur Martin, The House with Red Shutters by George Heath begin	£25.00
2	£12.50
3-5	£7.50
6-15	£5.00
16-50	£3.00
51-150	£2.50
151-312	£2.00
313 title becomes TV Fan	£1.75
314-333	£1.75
ARTISTS	
George Heath art in most issues (The House with Red Shutters, I Vow Vengeance, Our 'Tec Teaser, Cal Conway's Son, The Under-Sea Pirates, Roar with the Lyons, A Texan in the Big City, Family Theatre).	

TV FUN ANNUAL
Amalgamated; 1957-1960

1957	£6.00
1958-1960	£5.00

TV HEROES
Miller; 1 Jul 1958-26 Aug 1960

1 Robin Hood, Last of the Mohicans, Wyatt Earp begin	£5.00
2-7	£3.00
8 1st Mick Anglo edited issue	£3.00
9-25	£2.00
26 Don Lawrence reprints	£3.00
Note: Although subtitled "Your Favourite TV Stars and Others in Action" a disclaimer noted that "there is no connection between this magazine and the transmission of any television programme" (!)	

TV LAND
TV; 1 1st Jan 1960-68 16th Jan 1962 (joins TV Comic)

1 Gerry Anderson's Twizzle, Yogi Bear, Larry the Lamb by Neville Main	£15.00
1 with free gift (cardboard colour TV show)	£30.00
2	£6.00
3-5	£2.50
6-68	£1.25

TV PHOTO STORIES
C.A. Pearson; 1 Jan 1960-6 Mar 1960

1, 5 OSS	£5.00
2, 6 William Tell	£5.00
3 Dial 999	£5.00
4 Buccaneers	£5.00
Note: all photo-strips	

TV PICTURE STORIES
(C.A. Pearson; inter-related series of digest sized comics, numbered as a series on cover to 12, inside from 13. Each series was also numbered independently. See Adventures of Robin Hood, The Buccaneers, Dixon of Dock Green, Emergency Ward 10, Hawkeye and the Last of the Mohicans, Highway Patrol, Murder Bag, New Adventures of Charlie Chan, O.S.S., Sheriff of Cochise, Sword of Freedom, William Tell.)

TV TORNADO
City; 1 14th Jan 1967-88 14th Sep 1968 (joins TV 21)

1 Voyage to the Bottom of the Sea by Mick Anglo, Tarzan by Harry Bishop, Bonanza, Gold key reprints (Phantom, Flash Gordon, Lone Ranger), Batman, Superman begin	£30.00
1 with free gift (Bat Parachute)	£60.00
2	£15.00
2 with free gift (TV Tornado Magic Cards)	£30.00
3	£7.50
4-6, 8-14, 16-35	£5.00
7 Green Hornet, Magnus Robot Fighter reprints begin	£5.00
15 The Saint by Bishop begins	£5.00
36 Mysterons begin	£5.00
37 1st "TV Tornado & Solo"	£5.00
38-47, 49-57, 60-63, 65-88	£4.00
48 The Prisoner cover	£20.00
58 2pgs Troughton Dr.Who photo feature	£20.00
58 with free gift (blue plastic boomerang)	£40.00
59 Troughton/Ice Warriors cover	£20.00
64 Patrick MacNee Avengers cover	£25.00

TV TORNADO ANNUAL
City; 1967-1970

1967 96pgs; Tarzan, UNCLE, Green Hornet, Bonanza, Magnus strips	£5.50
1968 Phantom, UNCLE, Tarzan, Saint, Magnus strips, MacNee photo	£4.50
1969 Magnus, UNCLE, Lone Ranger, Tarzan, Saint strips	£3.50
1970 Lone Ranger, Tarzan, Saint strips	£3.50

TV TOYLAND
Fleetway Publications; 28th May 1966-23rd Feb 1968 (92 issues, joins Playhour)

28 May 1966 Champion the Wonder Horse, Leslie Crowther by Leslie Branton, Magic Roundabout, Rolf Harris by Philip Mendoza all start	£2.00
4 Jun 1966-23 Feb 1968	£0.35

TV 21
(see TV Century 21)

TV 21 & JOE 90
City/IPC; 1 27th Sep 1969-105 25th Sep 1971 (joins Valiant)

1 Tarzan by Don Lawrence, The Saint by Alcazar/Pino, Star Trek by Harry Lindfield, Joe 90 by Michael Strand, Thunderbirds by Frank Bellamy begin	£15.00
1 with free gift (Soccer Stars Portraits)	£30.00
2	£7.50
3	£6.00
4 last Bellamy Thunderbirds	£5.00
5-35, 37	£2.50
36 Last Joe 90	£2.50
38 last Thunderbirds, no further Gerry Anderson material	£2.50
39-57, 62-105	£1.50
58-61 Ron Turner Star Trek art	£1.50
ARTISTS/FEATURES	
Frank Bellamy in 1-4. Don Lawrence in 1-6,8-24,39-40,43-46,48,51. Mike Noble in 33-57. Ron Turner in 58-61.	

TV 21 SPRING EXTRA: THUNDERBIRDS
City; Mar 1967

1967 48pgs; Ron Turner, Brian Lewis, Don Harley art	£20.00

24 PAGES FILLED WITH JUST A COLLECTION OF AMERICAN UNDERGROUND COMICS
(no imprint); nn 1972?

nn - 28pgs; Robert Crumb, Gilbert Shelton underground reprints	£4.00

TWILIGHT ZONE ANNUAL
World Distributors; 1965

1965 scarce, Dell reprints in colour	£5.00

TWILIGHT ZONE COMIC ALBUM
World Distributors; 1 1964

1 scarce 64pgs, b/w Dell reprints	£4.00

TWIZZLE ADVENTURE STORIES
Birn Brothers; 1958, 1960

1958 stories by Roberta Leigh	£12.50
1960 entitled More Twizzle Adventure Stories, stories by Roberta Leigh	£10.00

TWIZZLE STORY BOOK
Birn Brothers; 1960

1960	£10.00

TWO FISTED TALES
Cartoon Art; 1 1951

1 28pgs; E.C. reprints	£6.00

TWO GUN KID
World Distributors; 1 1950-?

1 - 36pgs; Atlas reprints	£3.00

TWO GUN KID
Miller; 1 1955-38 1959?

1 28pgs; Atlas reprints	£4.00
2-38	£2.00

TWO GUN WESTERN
United Anglo-American; 1 1951-9? 195?

1 28pgs; Atlas reprints	£3.00
2-9	£2.00

TWO GUN WESTERN
Arnold Book Co.; 1 1952

1 28pgs; Atlas reprints	£4.00

2000AD
(See A.B.C. Warriors, Alan Moore's Shocking Futures, Alan Moore's Twisted Times, America, Anderson Psi Division, Bad Company, Best of 2000AD, Chopper, Complete Judge Dredd, Halo Jones, Judge Anderson, Judge Dredd, Killing Time, Midnight Surfer Special, Nemesis, Robo Hunter, Ro-Busters, Rogue Trooper, Slaine, Spellbinders, Strontium Dog, The VC's, Zenith)

IPC/Fleetway; 1 26th Feb 1977-present

1 Invasion by Blasco, Flesh by Boix, Mach 1 by Enio (ends 64, not in 47-51), Harlem Heroes by Gibbons begin; revived Dan Dare by Belardinelli begins (ends 23)	£50.00
1 with free gift (space spinner)	£70.00

N.MINT

Note: an authenticated sale of a Near Mint copy with free gift for **£150** occurred in 1995.
For some reason the sellotape that normally attaches the space spinner was not
used and therefore the front cover was undamaged

2 1st Judge Dredd by McMahon	£60.00
2 with free gift (bionic stickers)	£80.00
3 McMahon Dredd	£20.00
3 with free gift (survival manual)	£30.00
4 McMahon Dredd	£12.50
5 1st Ezquerra Dredd	£10.00
6-7 McMahon Dredd	£7.50
8 1st Belardinelli Dredd	£7.00
9 1st Turner Dredd, Robot Wars begin	£7.00
10	£7.00
11, 12, 15	£6.00
13 intro Walter the Wobot	£6.00
14 1st Gibson Dredd	£6.00
16-17 Robot Wars end	£5.00
18, 21-23	£4.50
19 Flesh ends, 1st John Cooper Dredd	£4.50
20 intro Max Normal	£4.50
24 O'Neill art	£4.00
25 1st Tharg's Future Shocks	£4.00
26-27 last Harlem Heroes	£4.00
28 Gibbons Dare begins	£4.00
29-32, 34-35	£3.50
33 Ewins/McCarthy art	£3.50
36 1st story credits; Inferno by Belardinelli begins (ends 75)	£3.50
37-39	£3.50
40 Bill Ward Dredd	£2.75
41 1st Bolland Dredd	£5.00
42-46, 48-49	£3.00
47 Bolland art	£3.50
50 Bolland art, Walter the Wobot by Gibson begins (ends 61)	£3.50
51 Bolland art, Invasion ends	£3.00
52 1st Bolland Walter the Wobot, Dredd, Future shock also by Bolland	£3.25
53-59 Bolland art	£3.00
60 Bolland art, 1st Lewis Dan Dare	£2.50
61 Bolland art, Cursed Earth begins (ends 85)	£2.50
62-64, 66 Bolland art	£2.50
65 Bolland art, Mach Zero begins (ends 75)	£2.50
67-70 Bolland art	£2.50
71 Burger Wars; Ant Wars begins (ends 85)	£5.00
72 scarce, Burger Wars	£5.00
73-75 scarce	£4.50
76 scarce, Robo-Hunter by Gibson begins (ends 85)	£4.00
77-78 scarce, Jolly Green Giant, Bolland art	£6.00
79-80 Goring/Garry Leach art Dan Dare begins	£1.75
81-82 Bolland, Leach art	£2.00
83 Leach art	£1.75
84 Gibbons/Leach art, 1st Walter the Wobot by McCarthy (ends 85)	£1.75
85 Gibson Dare ends (returns 100)	£1.75
86 1st "2000AD and Starlord"; Bolland art, Day The Law Died (Judge Caligula) (ends 108), Strontium Dog by Ezquerra (ends 94), Flesh II by Belardinelli (ends 99), Ro-Busters by Gibbons (ends 115, not in 102) all begin	£1.75
87, 98 Bolland art	£2.00
88 1st McCarthy/Ewins Dredd, O'Neill art	£1.75
89-91, 96-97, 99	£1.50
92-93 Ewins art	£1.50
94-95 Bolland/Leach art	£2.00
100 Robo-Hunter returns (ends 112), Dan Dare returns (ends 126)	£2.00
101-102 Bolland art	£2.00
103 Leach, O'Neill art	£1.30
104 Strontium Dog returns (ends 118), O'Neill art, 1st Ron Smith Dredd	£1.25
105-108, 111-112, 114-118, 121, 123-126	£1.25
109 no Dredd	£1.25
110 Bolland art	£1.45
113 1st Rick Random by S.Moore and Turner (ends 118)	£1.25
119 ABC Warriors by O'Neill (ends 139), Disaster 1990 by Carlos Pino (ends 139) begin	£1.25
120, 122 Bolland art	£1.45
127 1st "2000AD and Tornado"; Blackhawk by Belardinelli (ends 161, not in 129), Mind of Wolfie Smith by Gibson (to 145), Captain Klep by O'Neill all begin, Bolland art	£1.75
128-137, 139, 144	£1.25
138, 145 Leach, McMahon art	£1.40
140 Stainless Steel Rat by Ezquerra (ends 151), VC's by McMahon (ends 175, not in 144, 166-167, 170) begin	£1.20
141, 148 Leach art	£1.20
142-143, 146-147 Cam Kennedy art	£1.20
149 Bolland Judge Death begins (ends 151), intro Judge Anderson, Leach art	£2.50
150-151 Bolland art	£2.50
152 Kennedy art, Robo-Hunter returns (to 174), Fiends of the Eastern Front by Ezquerra begins (ends 161)	£1.20
153, 157-160, 163-164 Kennedy art	£1.20
154, 165, 168 Leach art	£1.20
155 Leach art, no Dredd	£1.20
156 Bolland art, Judge Child begins (ends 181)	£2.00
161 Leach, McMahon art	£1.20
162 Bolland, Kennedy art, Mach Zero begins (ends 165), Wolfie Smith (ends 177) returns	£2.00
166 Stainless Steel Rat Saves the World by Ezquerra begins (ends 177)	£1.20
167 1st Nemesis (Terror Tube) by O'Neill	£1.75
169, 171, 174-177	£1.20
170 more scarce, Moore script, McMahon art	£1.40
172-173, 182 Bolland art	£1.50

TV 21 #1

2000 AD #1

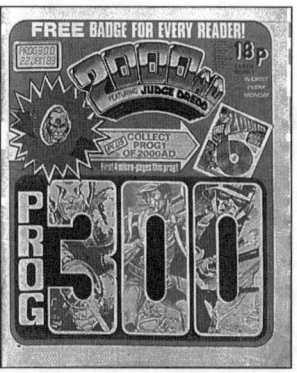

2000 AD #300

	N.MINT
178 Mean Arena by John Richardson (to 187, not in 181), Meltdown Man by Belardinelli (ends 227), Dash Decent by O'Neill (ends 198, not in 180), Nemesis (Killer Watt) by O'Neill (to 179) all begin, Strontium Dog returns (to 233, not in 198-199, 207-209)	£1.20
178 with free badge	£2.00
179-181, 183-188, 190-196	£1.10
189 Moore script	£1.20
197 Mean Arena returns (to 202), Bolland cover	£1.10
198-199, 201-204, 208, 210-213, 216, 220-221, 223	£1.10
200	£1.75
205 1st Dillon Dredd, Leach art	£1.10
206-207 Unamerican Graffiti (intro Chopper) by Ron Smith	£1.75
209 Moore script, 1st Colin Wilson Dredd	£1.20
214, 217 Moore script	£1.20
215 Leach art	£1.10
218, 229-230 Wilson art	£1.10
219 Moore script, Leach, Wilson art	£1.20
222 Nemesis Book 1 by O'Neill begins (ends 244, not in 234-237), Wilson art	£1.20
224 Bolland Judge Death Lives begins (ends 228)	£3.00
225 Bolland, Wilson art	£3.00
226 Bolland, Leach art	£3.00
227 Bolland art	£3.00
228 Bolland art, Rogue Trooper by Gibbons begins (to 392, not in 244-245, 259, 263-264, 302, 356-357, 365)	£3.00
231, 233, 239, 241-243	£1.10
232 more scarce, Ace Trucking Co by Belardinelli begins (to 293, not in 237-238, 286, 287)	£1.40
234, 237 Moore scripts	£1.20
235 more scarce	£1.40
236 McMahon Block Mania begins (ends 244)	£1.10
238, 240 scarce, Moore script	£1.20
244 Bolland art	£1.50
245 Moore script, Ezquerra Apocalypse War begins (ends 267)	£1.20
246 Moore script, Nemesis Book 2 by Redondo begins (ends 257)	£1.20
247, 249, 251-254, 268 Moore scripts	£1.20
248, 250, 255-256, 258	£1.10
257 Moore script, Talbot art	£1.20
259 Robo-Hunter returns (to 288, not in 273-274)	£1.10
260-264, 266, 274-277	£1.10
265, 267, 269 Moore script, Gibbons art	£1.20
270-272, 278, 282 Moore scripts	£1.20
273, 279-281, 283-286 Moore scripts	£1.20
287 Harry Twenty by Alan Davis begins (ends 307)	£1.20
288-290, 293-297, 301-307 Davis art	£1.20
291, 298-299 Moore script, Davis art	£1.20
292 Davis art, Robo-Hunter returns (to 334, not in 308-311)	£1.20
300 Davis art	£2.00
300 with free badge	£3.00
308 Skizz by Moore and Jim Baikie begins (ends 330)	£1.40
309-316, 318-321, 323-329, 331-332 Moore scripts	£1.20
317 1st D.R. and Quinch by Moore and Davis (in Future Shock)	£1.75
322 Moore script, Davis art	£1.20
330 Moore script, Slaine by Angie Mills begins (to 367)	£1.20
333, 334, 336-349	£1.10
335 1st McMahon Slaine, Nemesis Book 3 by O'Neill begins (ends 349), Strontium Dog returns (to 385, not in 346-349, 360-362)	£1.50
350 D.R. and Quinch by Moore and Davis return (to 367, not in 360-362)	£1.75
351-359 Moore script, Davis, McMahon art	£1.20
360-363, 368-375, 386	£1.10
364-367 Moore script, Davis art	£1.20
376 Halo Jones Book 1 by Moore and Gibson begins (ends 385)	£1.40
377 Moore script, Dredd Angel by Smith begins (ends 383)	£1.40
378 Moore script, Ace Trucking Co returns (to 400, not in 391)	£1.40
379-385 Moore script	£1.40
387 Nemesis Book 4 by O'Neill begins (ends 406)	£1.10
388 O'Neill art	£1.10
389-392, 394-399 Talbot Nemesis	£1.20
393 Talbot art, City of the Dammed begins (ends 406), Stainless Steel Rat for President by Ezquerra begins (ends 404)	£1.20
400 Talbot art	£2.00
401 Talbot art, Rogue Trooper returns (ends 432)	£1.00
402-404 Talbot Nemesis	£1.00
405 Moore script, Halo Jones Book 2 begins (ends 415), Talbot art	£1.50
406 Moore script, Talbot art	£1.50
407-410, 413-415 Moore script	£1.50
411 Moore script, Slaine returns by Fabry (to 434, not in 429-430)	£1.50
412 Moore script, Fabry art	£1.50
416 Anderson Psi Division by Brett Ewins (to 427), Strontium Dog returns (to 434)	£1.10
417-418, 423, 425-426 more scarce	£1.25
419, 427 Fabry art, scarce	£1.40
420-421 Fabry art	£1.40
422	£1.10
424 Midnight Surfer by Kennedy begins (ends 430)	£1.25
428 Fabry art, Ace Trucking Co returns (to 433)	£1.40
429-430, 432-434	£1.10
431 Fabry/Talbot art	£1.40
435 Nemesis Book 5 by Talbot begins (ends 445), Robo-Hunter returns (to 443)	£1.00
436-442 Talbot art	£1.00
443 Talbot art, last Robo-Hunter	£1.00
444 Talbot art, Rogue Trooper returns (to 449)	£1.00
445 Talbot art, Strontium Dog returns (to 587, not in 468, 500-504, 530-531, 537-539, 554-559, 574-577)	£1.00
446, 449-450	£1.00
447 Slaine by Fabry returns (to 461)	£1.25

	N.MINT
448 Fabry art	£1.25
451 Moore scripts, Halo Jones Book 3 begins (ends 466), Ace Trucking Co returns (ends 498, not in 473-474)	£1.40
452-455, 457-458, 460-463, 465-466	£1.40
456 1st Higgins Dredd	£1.40
459 Talbot art	£1.40
464 1st Kitson Dredd	£1.40
467	£0.95
468 Bad City Blues by Robin Smith (ends 477), Sooner or Later by McCarthy/Riot (to 499) begin, Judge Anderson returns (to 478)	£0.95
469-473, 476-481	£0.95
474-475 O'Neill art	£0.95
482 Nemesis Book by Talbot 6 begins (ends 504, not in 488-499)	£0.95
483 Metalzoic by O'Neill begins (ends 492) see DC Graphic Novell	£0.95
484 Fists of Stan Lee by Kitson (intro Deathfist)	£0.95
485-491, 494, 496-499	£0.95
492 Leach art	£0.95
493 Slaine returns by Collins/Farmer (to 508)	£0.95
495 Rogue Trooper returns (to 499)	£0.95
500 scarce, wraparound glossy cover; Bad Company by Ewins/McCarthy begins (to 519), Tharg's Head Revisited by Mills/Moore, Gibbons, McMahon, Kennedy, Gibson, O'Neill	£4.00
501-503 Fabry, Talbot art	£1.10
504 Fabry, O'Neill art	£1.10
505-508, 517-519 Fabry art	£1.10
509, 511-512, 514-516	£0.90
510 1st The Dead by Pete Milligan and Belardinelli (ends 579)	£0.90
513 Leach The Comeback (Jaxon Prince)	£1.00
520 scarce, 10th Birthday issue, 1st new look; Rogue Trooper by Dillon (to 531), Anderson by Kitson (to 532) return, Torquemada the God by O'Neill begins (ends 524)	£1.75
521-524 O'Neill art	£0.90
525 D.R. and Quinch agony page by Delano & Davis/Farmer begins (ends 534, not in 531)	£0.90
526-534	£0.90
535 Zenith Book 1 by Morrison & Yeowell begins (ends 550)	£0.95
536, 540 scarce	£0.95
537-539	£0.90
541 limited distribution	£1.00
542 limited distribution, Freaks by Milligan & Higgins begins (ends 547)	£1.00
543 limited distribution but more scarce	£1.25
544, 549-553, 556-557	£0.90
545 scarce, Dredd in Oz begins (ends 570)	£0.90
546 Nemesis Book 8 by John Hicklenton begins (ends 557)	£0.90
547, 554 scarce	£0.95
548 scarce, Bad Co returns (to 557)	£0.90
555 scarce, ABC Warriors return by Simon Bisley (to 566)	£0.95
558 Zenith "Interlude" begins (ends 559), Nemesis Book 8 by David Roach begins (ends 566)	£0.95
559, 562, 566	£0.95
560, 561, 563-565 scarce	£1.00
567-570, 572, 574-575	£0.90
571 Summer Magic by John Ridgway begins (ends 577)	£0.90
573 ABC Warriors returns (end 581)	£0.90
576 Bad Co returns (ends 585)	£0.90
577 Fabry art	£0.90
578-581	£0.90
582 Slaine by Fabry	£1.00
583-584, 587-588	£0.85
585 Davis/Farmer Dredd	£0.85
586 Nemesis Book 9 by Hicklenton begins (ends 593)	£0.85
589 new look/format; Slaine by Fabry returns (to 591), Zenith Book 2 begins (ends 606), Rogue Trooper returns	£0.85
590-591 Fabry art	£0.85
592-593, 595-597, 599	£0.85
594 Chopper by Colin Macneil begins	£0.85
598 Rogue Trooper returns (to 603)	£0.85
600 Fabry art, Strontium Dog returns (to 606)	£0.85
601 Bad Company (UKCAC story)	£0.80
602-604, 606, 608-611	£0.80
605 Nemesis Book 9 returns (to 608)	£0.80
607 Anderson returns (to 622, not in 610-611)	£0.80
612-613, 616-618, 620-623, 625	£0.80
614 Swifty's Return by Milligan & Hewlett (ends 617)	£0.80
615 Strontium Dog returns (to 621)	£0.80
619 Medivac 318 by Hilary Robinson & Nigel Dobbyn begins (to 624)	£0.80
624 Rogue Trooper returns (to 635, not in 631-632)	£0.80
626 Slaine The Horned God by Simon Bisley begins (to 635), Zenith Book 3 begins (to 634)	£2.25
627-629 Bisley art	£1.50
630-634 Bisley art	£1.50
635 Medivac returns (to 640), Anderson returns (to 647), Bisley art	£1.50
636 Strontium Dog returns (to 647, not in 642-644)	£0.80
637-649	£0.80
650 new look Rogue Trooper by Dave Gibbons & Will Simpson begins (to 653), Dead Man by Ridgway begins (to 662, continued in Judge Dredd), Slaine by Bisley returns (to 656), Zenith returns (to 662)	£1.25
651-653, 655-656 Bisley art	£1.00
654 Chopper returns (to 665), Bisley art	£1.00
657 Anderson returns (to 659)	£0.85
658-661, 665-666	£0.85
662 Slaine by Bisley returns (to 664), Tale of the Deadman (Dredd) begins	£1.00
663-664 Bisley art	£1.00
667 Rogue Trooper returns (to 671), Zenith returns (to 670)	£0.85
668 Dredd takes long walk	£0.85
669 Anderson returns (to 670)	£0.85
670, 673, 675-677, 679-681, 684-686	£0.85

	N.MINT
671 new look Harlem Heroes by Michael Fleisher & Steve Dillon/Kev Walker begins	
(to 705, not in 677-682, 700)	£0.85
672 Shadows by Pete Milligan & Richard Elson begins (ends 681)	£0.85
674 Necropolis (Dredd) begins (ends 699)	£0.85
678 Indigo Prime by John Smith & Chris Weston begins (to 682, not in 679)	£0.85
682 Strontium Dog returns by Colin Macneil (ends 687)	£0.85
683 Rogue Trooper returns (ends 687), Medivac returns (to 694)	£0.85
687 death of Johnny Alpha in Strontium Dog	£0.85
688 Slaine by Bisley returns (to 698)	£0.85
689-696, 698 Bisley art	£0.85
697 more scarce, Bisley art	£1.00
699	£0.85
700 Time Flies by Garth Ennis & Philip Bond (ends 711), Hewligan's Haircut by Milligan & Hewlett	
(ends 707) begin, Nemesis & Deadlock one-off, Anderson by Ranson returns (to 711)	£1.50
701	£1.25
702-711	£0.85
712 Anderson by Roach (to 717), Rogue Trooper both return	£0.85
713-717, 720-722	£0.85
718-719 Danzig's Inferno by John Smith & Sean Phillips	£0.85
723 Robo-Hunter by Casanovas (to 734), Nemesis and Deadlock by Carl Critchlow (ends	
729), Bix Barton (to 728) return, Tao de Moto begins (ends 749), free Mega-Scan (poster)	£0.90
724-725 free Mega-Scan by Bisley (Slaine, 724), Gibson (Halo Jones, 725)	£0.85
726-729, 731-734, 736, 738-739, 741-743, 745-749	£0.85
730 Rogue Trooper returns (to 741), Mean Machine by Richard Dolan begins (ends 736)	£0.85
735 Killing Time by John Smith & Chris Weston (to 744)	£0.85
737 Bix Barton returns (to 741)	£0.85
740 Fabry Dredd	£0.85
744 Revere by John Smith & Simon Harrison (to 749)	£0.85
750 Democracy storyline in Dredd begins (to 756), Sam Slade returns (to 759), Strontium Dogs by	
Steve Pugh (ends 761), ABC Warriors by Kevin Walker (to 757), free data-chips (cards)	£1.25
751-752 free data-chips	£1.00
753-757, 759-761, 763-766	£0.80
758 Anderson by Roach returns (ends 763)	£0.80
762 Durham Red by Ezquerra begins (ends 773)	£0.80
767 Skizz by Jim Baikie returns	£0.80
768-769, 771-779	£0.80
770 Finn by Mills & Jim Elston begins (to 779)	£0.80
780 ABC Warriors by Walker returns (to 784), Rogue Trooper returns (to 791),	
The Button Man by Wagner & Ranson begins (ends 791)	£0.80
781-785, 788-790	£0.80
786 Judgement Day (Judge Dredd Megazine X-over) begins (ends 799)	£0.80
787 ABC Warriors by Walker returns (to 790)	£0.80
791 Zenith returns (to 808)	£0.80
792 Sam Slade returns (to 802)	£0.80
793-799	£0.80
800 Flesh: Legend of Shamana begins (to 808), The Night Walker (Luke Kirby) begins (to 812)	£1.25
801-806, 808	£0.80
807 Finn returns (to 816)	£0.80
809 Revere returns (to 814)	£0.80
810-814 John Burns Dredd, Sam Slade returns 813 (to 816)	£0.80
815 Brigand Doom returns (to 818)	£0.80
816	£0.80
817 John McCrea Dredd, Strontium Dogs returns (to 824), Flesh returns (to 825)	£0.80
818 Higgins Dredd	£0.80
819 MacNeil Dredd, Sam Slade returns (to 822)	£0.80
820, 822-827	£0.80
821 Kelly's Eye by McKenzie & Ewins begins (to 830)	£0.80
828 Bad Company returns (to 837), Firekind by Smith & Paul Marshal begins (ends 840)	£0.80
829-833, 835-841	£0.80
834 Purgatory by Millar & Ezquerra begins (ends 841)	£0.80
842 Dredd: Inferno by Morrison & Ezquerra to 853), Big Dave by Morrison/Millar &	
Parkhouse, Slaughterbowl by Smith & Peart, Really & Truly by Morrison & Hughes,	
Maniac 5 by Millar & Yeowell all begin (all end 849)	£0.80
843-849, 851	£0.80
850 Strontium Dogs, Rogue Trooper, Luke Kirby by Ridgway, Slaine by Staples return	
(all end 851)	£0.80
852 Mean Arena by McKenzie & Williams (ends ???) begins, Tyranny Rex by Smith &	
Buckingham (to 859), Sam Slade by Hogan & Hughes (to 854), Slaine: Demon	
Killer by Mills & Fabry (to 859) return	£1.25
853-854, 856-858 Fabry art	£0.90
855 Strontium Dogs returns (to 866)	£0.80
859 Judge Dredd: Book of the Dead by Morrison/Millar & Power begins (to 866)	£0.80
860, 862-866, 868, 874-877	£0.80
861 Cannon Fodder by Mark Millar & Chris Weston begins (ends 867)	£0.80
867 Soul Gun Warrior by Shaky 2000 (to 872), Mother Earth by Bernie Jaye & Paul	
Neary/Cliff Robertson (ends 872), Revere Book III by Smith & Harrison begin (to 872)	£0.80
869 Big Dave returns (to 874)	£0.80
873 Luke Kirby (to 877), Tyranny Rex, Rogue Trooper return, Dinosty by Mills & Clint Langley begins	£0.80
878 The Grudge-Father by Millar & Jim McCarthy (to 883)	£0.80
879-883, 886-888	£0.80
884 John Higgins Dredd, Luke Kirby returns	£0.80
885 Bradley returns	£0.80
889 Slaine by Dermot Power (to 896), Rogue Trooper (to 891) return, Mambo by	
David Hine begins (to 896)	£0.75
890, 892-895, 898-899	£0.75
891 Mark Harrison Dredd (to 894), story continued in Megazine 57	£0.75
896 Rogue Trooper returns (to 899)	£0.75
897 Strontium Dogs, Brigand Doom return (both to 899)	£0.75
900 28pg Dredd/Rogue Trooper x-over	£0.85
901 Dredd: Judge Death the True Story by Wagner & Gibson (to 902); Durham Red by	
Mark Harrison, Rogue Trooper, Bradley, Nemesis return (all to 903)	£0.80
902, 905-907, 909-911, 913-917, 921-923, 925-927, 929-931	£0.80

	N.MINT
903 John Burns Dredd	£0.80
904 Dredd: Wilderlands by Wagner & Ezquerra begins (to 914, Megazine x-over; ep 13	
by Mick Austin); Big Dave (to 907), ABC Warriors by Walker (to 911), Sam Slade	
(to 911) all return; Button Man II by Wagner & Ranson begins (ends 919)	£0.80
908 Red Razors by Millar & Nigel Dobbyn begins (ends 917)	£0.80
912 Skizz III by Jim Baikie begins (ends 927), Bix Barton returns (to 917)	£0.80
918 The Corps by Ennis & Paul Marshall begins (ends 923)	£0.80
919 John Burns Dredd, McNeil pencils on The Corps begin	£0.80
920 52pgs; 18pg Dredd by Ross Dearsley & Dermot Power, Soul Gun Assassin by	
Shaky Kane (ends 925), Burns art	£0.80
924 Finn by Mills/Skinner & Liam Sharp returns (to 927); originally painted for Crisis)	£0.80
928 Star Trek cover; Dredd: Crusade by Millar/Morrison & Austin begins (ends 937), Rogue Trooper	
(to 931), Finn by Mills/Skinner & Paul Staples (to 937), Harlem Heroes (to 939) return	£0.80
932 Brigand Doom returns (to 936)	£0.80
933-935, 938-939, 941-945, 947, 949	£0.80
936 Paul Johnson art	£0.80
937 Rogue Trooper, Strontium Dogs return (both to 939)	£0.80
940 New Look, Stallone cover; Mambo by Hine (to 947), Stontium Dogs by Harrison	
(to 947), Finn by Staples (to 949), The Grudge-Father (to 945) all return	£0.80
946 Rogue Trooper returns (to 949)	£0.80
948 Tracer by Dave Stone & Paul Peart begins (ends 949)	£0.80
950 New Look, 44pgs; Dredd x 2 begins (incl. The Return of Rico by Mills & Johnson),	
Rogue Troopers by Charlie Adlard, Slaine by Greg Staples (to 956) return	£1.00
951 Vector 13 begins	£1.00
952	£1.00
953 Chris Foss Dredd & cover; Janus: Psi Division by Morrison/Maggie Knight & Paul Johnson	£1.00
954 Foss cover; John Burns Dredd; Luke Kirby returns (to 963)	£1.00
955 Foss cover; Higgins Dredd	£1.00
956 Maniac 5 by Steve Yeowell returns (to 963)	£1.00
957 Strontium Dogs by Harrison one-off	£1.00
958 Slaine by Clint Langley returns (to 963)	£1.00
959 John Burns Dredd	£1.00
960 Durham Red by Harrison returns (to 963); Dredd: Hammerstein by Mills/Skinner	
& Jason Brashill begins (to 963), Burns Dredd	£1.00
961-963 Burns Dredd, Harrison art	£1.00
964 Rogue Trooper, Chopper by John Higgins, ABC Warriors by Kev Walker return, PARAsites begins	£1.00
965-967	£1.00
968 Steve Yeowell Dredd	£1.00
969, 971-972, 974, 977-979	£1.00
970 Dredd; The Pit by Wagner/Ezquerra begins	£1.00
973 Flesh returns by White/Abnett/Erskine (to 979)	£1.00
975 Darkness Visible by Abadzis & Ridgway begins (to 979)	£1.00
976 Venus Blue Genes begins	£1.00
980 Janus Psi by Millar and Paul Johnson begins	£1.00

Note: issues 1-35 were uncredited, the main artists were as follows: Dan Dare: Massimo Belardinelli in 1-23, Dave Gibbons in 28-35; Flesh by Juan Boix, Ramon Sola 1-19; Harlem Heroes by Gibbons in 1-27; Judge Dredd by Belardinelli in 8, John Cooper in 19, Carlos Ezquerra in 5, 10, Ian Gibson in 14, 17, 22, 25, 27, 29, 31, 33, 35, Mike McMahon in 2-4, 6-7, 12, 15, 18, 20, 23-24, 26, 28, 30, 32, 34, Ron Turner in 9, 11, 13, 16, 21; various Kevin O'Neill art in 24, 28; Brian Bolland covers on 11, 13, 19, 20, 23, 27, 30.

ARTISTS/FEATURES

Mick Austin in 612-613, 625-626, 629, 635, 639, 717, 746, 832-834, 840. Jim Baikie in 308-330, 369, 546, 569-573, 626, 658, 767-775, 912-927. Massimo Belardinelli in 1-24, 36-75, 86-97, 116, 127-128, 130-131, 134-142, 145-161, 178-227, 232-236, 244-285, 288-293, 296-297, 306-312, 314, 331-334, 337-344, 360-367, 370, 374-375, 378-390, 392-393, 396-400, 407, 424, 428-433, 437-447, 451-472, 475-483, 485-498, 510-519, 525-538, 551, 554, 556-558, 563, 565, 569, 570, 572, 591, 607, 616-617, 641-646, 670, 672, 760. Simon Bisley in 555-558, 563-566, 577-581, 626-635, 650-656, 662-664, 688-698. Jesus Blasco in 1-3. Brian Bolland in 41, 47, 50-61, 65, 67-70, 77-78, 81-82, 86-87, 94-95, 98, 101, 102, 110, 120, 122-123, 127, 149-151, 156, 162, 172-173, 182, 224-228, 244. Philip Bond in 700-711. John Burns in 738, 754-756, 762-765, 810-814, 903, 919-920, 954. Mike Collins in 372, 493-499, 529-530, 539, 637 (script only in 509, 544, 554, 611, 636, 638). Carl Critchlow in 700, 723-729, 748. 800-808, 817-825, 829. Dave D'Antiques in 518, 524, 603, 608, 625, 632, 643, 664, 706-711, 717-722, 764-769, 771-773, 815-818. Alan Davis in 287-307, 317, 322, 350-359, 363-367, 509, 525-530, 532-534, 585. Steve Dillon in 189-190, 200, 205, 219-223, 242-243, 305-307, 322-328, 353, 374-375, 379-380, 393, 397-399, 404-405, 409, 442-443, 450, 479, 495-499, 505, 511-512, 520-531, 535-539, 561, 566-572, 574-575, 578, 582-584, 589, 598-600, (601 inks), 602-603, 609-610, 702-705 (624-630, 633-635, 671-676, 683-690, 691-703, 783-785 pencils). Gary Erskine in 741. Brett Ewins (often with Brendan McCarthy)in 37-38, 53-54, 88, 92-93, 96, 105, 113-115, 124, 161, 175, 206, 216, 260-261, 273-274, 286, 290-292, 299-301, 311-315, 323-326, 335-340, 359-363, 390-392, 500-519, 521, 523-524, 548-557, 576-585, 601, 750-759, 821-831, 841. Carlos Ezquerra in 5, 10, 34, 86-94, 102, 104-118, 140-162, 166-197, 200-206, 210-221, 224-233, 245-267, 269-272, 275-277, 281-288, 291-294, 296-297, 304, 308-314, 319-321, 331-345, 350-359, 363-385, 393-404, 416-434, 438-439, 445-467, 469-499, 505-529, 532-536, 544-553, 560-573, 638, 640, 651-655, 657-659, 669-699, 711-715, 719-720, 733-735, 762-773, 788-791, 794-797, 799, 815, 842-854, 867-871. Glenn Fabry in 411-412, 419-421, 427-428, 431, 447-448, 458-460, 500-508, 577, 579, 582, 589-591, 577, 600, 740, 852-858. Dave Gibbons art in 1-60, 64-78, 84-87, 91, 98-107, 109-126, 130-131, 157, 176, 181, 183-184, 196, 228-232, 234, 239-240, 249-250, 265, 267, 269, 310, 500. Script in 650-653, 667-671, 683-687. Ian Gibson in 14, 17, 22, 25, 27, 29, 31, 33, 35-36, 38, 42, 45-46, 48-51, 53-56, 76-84, 100-112, 116, 119-120, 127-130, 152-174, 188, 190-191, 195, 198-199, 201, 203-204, 208-209, 214, 220-223, 239-243, 259-272, 275-281, 283-288, 292-307, 312-442, 451-466, 468-469, 476, 496-498, 500, 521, 578-581, 780-782, 901-902. Simon Harrison in 522, 532-533, 539, 544-545, 552, 564, 592, 568, 580-583, 600-606, 615-621, 636-641, 645-647, 660-661, 666, 670, 682, 744-749, 795-799, 809-814, 885. Jamie Hewlett in 614-617, 700-707. John Hicklenton in 488, 515, 546-557, 586-593, 605-608. John Higgins in 108, 176, 202, 217, 241, 247-248, 252-253, 256, 272, 278, 289-290, 298, 309, 327, 434, 436, 456, 460, 471, 480, 494-495, 504, 531-533, 542-547, 564-565, 620-621, 650, 818, 884. Rian Hughes in 774-779, 842-849, 852-854. Cam Kennedy in 142-143, 146-153, 156-160, 163-164, 169, 265, 271, 278-284, 286-288, 293, 298, 304-310, 316-322, 327-332, 342-347, 350-355, 358-364, 366-377, 381-392, 401-406, 416-418, 424-429, 435, 437, 440-441, 451-455, 458, 461-463, 466-467, 477-479, 500, 507-510, 514, 521, 643-645, 718. Barry Kitson in 437, 440, 464-465, 473, 475, 481-482, 484, 491, 493, 501, 506, 520-531, 540-541, 557, 566-568, 587, 629-630. Garry Leach in 58, 94-95, 103, 138, 141, 145, 148, 154-155, 161-162, 165, 168, 205, 215, 219, 492, 513, 520, 547-550. Brendan McCarthy (often with Brett Ewins) in 37-38, 54, 84-85, 88, 93, 105, 120, 127-128, 146, 166, 369-392, 468-501, 519, 549, 551-552, 558-560, 614. John McCrea in 817. Mike McMahon in 2-4, 6-7, 12, 15, 18, 20, 23-24, 26, 28, 30, 32, 34, 37, 39, 43-44, 58-64, 66-68, 70-76, 79-80, 83, 85, 89-91, 96-97, 99-100, 105-108, 113-115, 121-122, 125-126, 129, 132-133, 137-140, 144-145, 147, 160-161, 163, 166, 170-171,

	N.MINT		N.MINT

176-178, 183-185, 193-196, 236-237, 245, 335-336, 345-359, 500. *Colin MacNeil in 508-509, 526, 540-543, 578-579, 594-597, 608-611, 627-628, 636, 654-665, 736, 819. Paul Marshall in 625, 627, 638, 647, 649, 657, 671, 828-840, 856-859. Kevin O'Neill in 24, 28, 36, 41-49, 88, 90, 103-104, 111-112, 119, 123, 127-128, 167, 178-179, 181-198, 222-233, 238-240, 243-244, 335-349, 387-388, 430, 474-475, 483-492, 500, 520-524. Sean Phillips in 718-719, 800-803. Dermot Power in 722, 746-748, 760, 837-839, 859-866. Arthur Ranson in 635-644, 700-711, 720, 742, 780-791, 904-919. John Ridgway in 377, 491, 525-526, 571-577, 588-591, 597, 605-606, 650-662, 708-716, 723-730, 800-812, 850-851. David Roach in 529-530, 539, 558-566, 614-622, 645-647, 669-670, 712-717, 758-763. Liam Sharp in 531, 534, 542-544, 575-576, 592-594, 599, 6632-634, 642, 924-927. William Simpson in 525, 535, 555-556, 561-563, 583-584, 586, 595-598, 603-604, 612, 623-625, 629-631, 637-643, 650-653, 662-665, 667-671, 683-687. Greg Staples in 761, 776-779, 806-807, 824-825, 830, 839, 850-851. Joe Staton in 133. Bryan Talbot in 257, 389-406, 431, 435-445, 459, 482-487, 500-504. Kevin Walker in 594, 596, 599, 610, 612, 614, (624-630), 633-635, 671-676, 683-692, 696-699, 701-702 inks), 703, (704 pencils). Colin Wilson in 209-210, 218-219, 229-230, 236-238, 241, 246-248, 251-253, 257-277, 285, 289. Steve Yeowell in 535-550, 558-559, 589-606, 626-634, 650-662, 667, 710, 716, 791-808, 842-849.*

2000AD ACTION SPECIAL
Fleetway Editions; Apr 1992
1992 new stories featuring classic Fleetway characters incl. Steel Claw by Sean Phillips, Cursitor Doom by Jim Baikie, Kelly's Eye by Brett Ewins, Mytek the Mighty by Shaky Kane, The Spider by John Higgins/David Hine, Doctor Sin by John Burns ... £2.00

2000AD ANNUAL/YEARBOOK
Fleetway; 1977-1995
1978 Dredd by McMahon, O'Neill art	£10.00
1979 Dredd by McCarthy, Ewins art	£8.00
1980 Dredd by David Jackson	£7.50
1981 Dredd by Ewins	£4.00
1982 Dredd by Bolland, Moore script	£4.50
1983 Dredd by "Emberton" (Gibson), Moore script, O'Neill art	£3.50
1984 Moore script, Gibson art	£3.50
1985 Dredd by Gibson, Moore script	£3.50
1986 Dredd by Gibson, Cam Kennedy art	£3.25
1987 Dredd by Talbot, Romero art	£3.25
1988 Dredd by McCarthy/Riot/Ewins, O'Neill art	£3.75
1989 Dredd by Higgins, Steve Parkhouse art	£3.00
1990 Dredd by Hopgood, Morrison script	£3.50
1991 Dredd, John Smith text story	£3.50
1992 becomes 2000AD Yearbook, Dredd by Kennedy, Glen Fabry Slaine	£5.00
1993 by Ewins, Ezquerra, Phillips art	£6.00
1994 by Burns, Staples, Hughes, Marshall, Parkhouse art	£6.00
1995 Dredd by Baikie	£4.00

Note: no yearbook published at Christmas 1995 for 1996

2000AD SCI-FI SPECIAL
(previously 2000AD Summer Special Supercomic)
IPC; nn May 1978-present
1978 Dredd by "Subliminal Kid" (McCarthy), Leach, O'Neill art, Ron Turner Rick Random reprint	£6.00
1979 Dredd by Ewins, Leach art	£4.50
1980 Dredd by Dillon, Moore script	£4.00
1981 Dredd by Colin Wilson, Nemesis by O'Neill	£3.50
1982 Dredd by Casanovas, Blackhawk by Joe Staton	£3.25
1983 Dredd by John Byrne	£2.75
1984 Dredd by Cliff Robinson, Ewins art	£2.50
1985 Dredd by Cam Kennedy, D.R. and Quinch by Moore and Davis, McCarthy art	£2.25
1986 Dredd by Dillon Fabry art	£2.25
1987 Dredd by Collins/Farmer	£1.75
1988 Dredd by Phil Elliott	£1.50
1989 no Dredd, Judge Corey by Mick Austin	£1.25
1990 Dredd reprint by Cam Kennedy, Bix Barton by Milligan & Jim McCarthy	£1.25
1991 Dredd by Dermot Power, D'Antiques art	£1.25
1992 Ridgway, Ewins, Phillips art	£1.50
16 first numbered; D'Antiques, Hine, Beeston/MacNeil art	£1.50
17 Dredd by Peter Doherty	£1.50
18 Dredd by Paul Peart; Dredd movie feature	£1.75

2000AD SUMMER SPECIAL SUPERCOMIC
IPC; nn Jun 1977 (continues as 2000AD Sci-Fi Special)
nn - scarce, Dredd by Kevin O'Neill	£9.00

2000AD MONTHLY
Eagle/Quality; 1 Apr 1985-6 Sep 1985
1-4	£1.00
5, 6 Quality issues	£0.90

2000AD PRESENTS/2000AD SHOWCASE
Quality/Fleetway-Quality; 1 Apr 1986-54 Nov 1990
1	£1.25
2-24	£0.80
25-26 becomes 2000AD Showcase	£0.75
27/28 jointly numbered issue	£0.75
29/30 jointly numbered issue; Zenith begins	£0.75
31-45 features Zenith	£0.75
46-54	£0.75

2000AD WINTER SPECIAL
Fleetway; 1 1988-present
1 Zenith by Morrison & Carmona, Dredd by Vanyo, Strontium Dog, Judge Anderson by Gibson, Rogue Trooper by Moore reprint	£2.50
2 Dredd by Arthur Ranson, Rogue Trooper by Steve Dillon & Chris Weston	£2.25
3 Dredd by Brett Ewins, Milligan, Smith scripts, Ezquerra art, Bisley cover	£2.25
4 Dredd by Greg Staples, Walker, Weston art	£2.25
5 Dredd by Paul Marshall, Morrison script, Ezquerra, MacNeil art	£2.35
Alternity (1995) alternative worlds, incl. Judge Dredd, medieval Dredd	£2.75

TWIN HEARTS
(see Heart to Heart, Magic Moment Romances) **K.G. Murray Ltd; 1 1958?-?**
1 very rare 100pgs, squarebound begin; b/w romance reprints from National Periodical Publications; priced at one shilling	£75.00
2-?	£40.00

Note: very little information available at time of going to press

U

UFO ANNUAL
Polystyle; 1970
1971	£8.00

UNCANNY TALES
Alan Class; 1 May 1963-?
1 68pgs; various reprints from Atlas, Marval, Fawcett, etc.; scarce	£12.00
2-?	£2.50

UNCENSORED LOVE
Alan Class; 1 1960s
1 68pgs; US reprints	£3.50

UNDERCOVER
Famepress; 1 1964-96? 1969?
1 68pgs pocket size	£1.00
2-96	£0.50

UNDERCOVER GIRL
United Anglo-American; nn 1951
nn - 36pgs; Magazine Enterprises reprints	£3.00

UNDERWORLD
R. & L. Locker; 1 1951
1 36pgs; D.S. Publishing reprints	£6.00

UNSEEN
Cartoon Art; 1 1955?
1 Standard Comics reprints	£3.00

UNUSUAL TALES
Alexander Moring; 1 1959
1 36pgs; Charlton reprints	£4.00

UNUSUAL TALES
Alan Class; 1 196?-?
1 68pgs; Charlton reprints	£12.00
2-?	£3.00

V

V FOR VENDETTA
Titan; nn 1990
nn - reprints V For Vendetta 1-10 by Alan Moore & David Lloyd	£10.00

VALIANT
Fleetway/IPC: 6th Oct 1962-16th Oct 1976 (713 unnumbered issues, joins Battle)
No.1 - 6 Oct 1962 Captain Hurricane, Steel Claw by Ken Bulmer & Jesus Blasco, To Glory We Steer by Parker, Jack O'Justice (Dick Turpin reprints from Sun) begin	£25.00
No.1 with free gift (League Ladders & Pocket Rocket)	£50.00
13 Oct 1962	£10.00
20 Oct 1962	£5.00
27 Oct 1962-16 Feb 1963	£3.50
23 Feb 1963 1st "Valiant and also Knockout"; Kelly's Eye by Lopez	£3.50
2 Mar 1963-21 Mar 1964	£2.50
28 Mar 1964 Wild Wonders by Tom Tully & Mike Western begins	£2.50
4 Apr 1964-17 Sep 1964	£2.00
24 Sep 1964 Mytek the Mighty by Bradbury begins	£2.50
1st Oct 1964-1st Oct 1966	£2.00
8 Oct 1966 House of Dolmann by Bradbury begins, 1st Bill Lacey Mytek	£2.00
15 Oct 1966-6 Jan 1968, 20 Jan 1968-24 Feb 1968	£1.50
13 Jan 1968 Sexton Blake (from TV series) by Eric Dadswell begins	£1.25
2 Mar 1968 Raven on the Wing by Solano Lopez begins	£1.25
9 Mar 1968-9 May 1970, 30 May 1970-3 Apr 1971	£1.00
16 May 1970 last Steel Claw	£1.00
23 May 1970 Slave of the Screamer by Tully & Blasco begins	£1.00
10 Apr 1971 1st "Valiant and Smash!"	£1.00
17 Apr 1971-29 May 1971, 12 Jun 1971-25 Sep 1971	£0.85
5 Jun 1971 Return of the Claw begins	£0.85
2 Oct 1971 1st "Valiant and TV21"; Star Trek by John Stokes begins	£1.50
9 Oct 1971-22 Dec 1973, 5 Jan 1974-18 May 1974	£1.25
29 Dec 1973 last Star Trek	£1.25
18 May 1974 last Kelly's Eye, Raven, Wild Wonders	£0.75
25 May 1974 1st "Valiant and Lion"	£0.75
1 Jun 1974-13 Dec 1975, 27 Dec 1975-3 Apr 1976, 17 Apr 1976-16 Oct 1976	£0.50
20 Dec 1975 Death Wish (some by Ian Gibson), One-Eyed Jack by John Cooper begin	£0.40
10 Apr 1976 1st "Valiant and Vulcan" (features Vulcan mini-comic)	£0.40

ARTISTS/FEATURES
Jesus Blasco in 6 Oct 1962-13 Apr 1968, 2 May 1970 (Steel Claw), 23 May 1970-3 Apr 1971 (Slave of the Screamer), 5 Jun 1971-27 Oct 1973 (Return of the Claw).
Note: jointly dated issue 6/13 Jun 1970, no issues dated 21 Nov 1970-30 Jan 1971, 19 Jan 1974, 2 Feb 1974, 16 Feb 1974, 6 Jul-27 Jul 1974.

VALIANT ANNUAL
Fleetway; 1964-1984
1964	£12.50
1965 Blasco art	£10.00
1966 Blasco art	£7.50
1967-1969	£5.00
1970-1979	£3.00
1980-1984	£2.00

VALIANT BOOK OF...
Fleetway; 1967, 1968, 1971, 1972, 1975
Pirates (1967) oversize	£5.00
TV's Sexton Blake 1969	£12.50
Conquest of the Air 1972	£2.50

	N.MINT
Sports 1973	£2.50
Magic and Mystery 1976	£5.00
Weapons and War 1976	£2.50
VALIANT PICTURE LIBRARY	
Fleetway; 1 Jun 1963-144 May 1969	
1 60pgs pocket size; War Eagle by Ferdinando Tacconi (reprint from Comet)	£3.00
2-5 incl. reprints from Thriller Picture Library	£2.00
6-49 incl. reprints from Thriller Picture Library	£1.50
50-144 mostly reprints from Air Ace, Battle, War picture libraries	£1.00
ARTISTS	
Luis Bermejo. Robert Forrest. Solano Lopez. Hugh McNeill in 9.	
VALIANT SPACE SPECIAL	
Fleetway; 1967-1968	
1967 incl. Steel Claw; softcover	£7.50
1968 incl. Steel Claw, softcover, scarce	£10.00
VALIANT STORY OF THE WEST	
Fleetway; 1-2 Apr 1966	
1 Westward Ho!	£3.00
2 The Far Frontier	£3.00
Note: Reprints Italian series Storia Del West by Gino D'Antonio & Renato Polese	
VALIANT SUMMER SPECIAL	
Fleetway/I.P.C. Magazines; 1966-1980	
1966 96pgs	£10.00
1967-1969 96pgs	£7.50
1970-1973 96pgs	£5.00
1974-1976 80pgs	£4.00
1977-1980 64pgs	£2.50
VALOUR	
Marvel; 1 5th Nov 1980-19 11th Mar 1981 (joins Future Tense)	
1 32pgs; Conan, Dr. Strange, Devil Dinosaur, Tales of Asgard reprints begin; slightly larger size than following issues	£1.25
1 with free gift (Devil Dinosaur jigsaw piece)	£2.50
2-3	£0.75
2-3 with free gifts (Devil Dinosaur jigsaw piece)	£1.50
2-19	£0.45
VALOUR WINTER SPECIAL	
Marvel; nn Nov 1980	
nn - 64pgs; Thor and Dr Strange reprints in b/w, colour centre-fold poster and pin-ups	£1.25
VAMPIRELLA	
I.P.C. Magazines; 1 Feb 1975-4 May 1975	
1 48pgs; Warren reprints	£10.00
2-4 48pgs; Warren reprints	£7.50
VAMPS	
Titan Books; nn Nov 1995	
nn - 144pgs; reprints Vertigo series by Lee & Simpson	£9.00
VAULT OF HORROR	
Arnold Book Co.; 1 1954	
1 68pgs; E.C. reprints, cited in UK horror campaign	£15.00
VC'S, THE	
Titan (Best of 2000AD); 1987	
Book One	£4.50
Book Two	£5.00
VELOCITY	
Warren & Garry Pleece; 1 1988-5?	
1-5 all material by Warren & Garry Pleece	£1.50
VENDETTA IN GOTHAM	
(see Judgement on Gotham)	
Fleetway/Mandarin; nn 1993, 1995	
nn - (Nov 1993) by Wagner/Grant & Cam Kennedy, DC reprint, Mignola cover; magazine format	£3.00
nn - (Mandarin, May 1995) softcover	£6.00
VENTURE COMIC	
P.M. Productions; nn 1948	
nn - 16pgs; George Parlett, Frank Minnitt art	£3.00
VIC FLINT	
Miller; 1 1955	
1 28pgs; US newspaper strip reprints	£2.50
VIC TORRY AND HIS FLYING SAUCER	
Miller; 1 1950	
1 32pgs; Fawcett reprints	£5.00
VICTOR	
D.C. Thomson; 1 25th Feb 1961-1657 21st November 1992	
1 I Flew With Braddock by Keith Shone begins	£20.00
1 with free gift (Super Squirt Ring)	£40.00
2 H.K. Rodd The Wonder Man begins	£10.00
2 with free gift (Sportsman's Wallet and team photos of Man. Utd and Wolves)	£20.00
3-5	£5.00
6-10	£2.25
11-57, 59-70, 72-108	£1.00
58 The Smasher by F.A. Philpott begins	£1.00
71 The Tough of the Tracks by Peter Sutherland begins	£1.00
109 Morgyn the Mighty by Ted Kearon begins	£0.60
110-624	£0.50
625 Cadman by Mike Dorey begins	£0.50
626-660, 662-1115, 1117-1657	£0.30
661 The Hammer Man by Ted Rawlings begins	£0.30
1116 The Rule of Rogat by Alcatena begins	£0.30
ARTISTS	
Alcatena in 1116-1131, 1211-1226, 1284-1299, 1338-1359, 1456-1472, 1485-1494, 1570-1588, 1611-1618, 1632-1635, 1653-1657.	
VICTOR BOOK FOR BOYS	
D.C. Thomson; 1964-1992	
(1964) (some commandos leaving a boat at St. Nazaire)	£15.00

Valiant #1

Valiant Space Special 1967

Victor #1

	N.MINT
(1965) (two canoes each with two commandos)	£10.00
1966-1969 first dated	£5.00
1970-1975	£3.00
1976-1992	£2.00

VICTOR FOR BOYS SUMMER SPECIAL
D.C. Thomson; 1967-1992

1967 32pgs; dinosaur cover	£3.00
1968-1970	£1.50
1971-1975	£0.75
1975-1992	£0.50

VICTORY FUNNIES
Fulton Publishing Co.; nn Nov 1944

nn - 8pgs; Bob Wilkin art	£3.00

VIEW FROM THE VOID
H. Bunch (Cozmic); nn Aug 1973

nn - 20 pgs; Trev Goring art	£1.00

VIOLENT CASES
Escape; nn Oct 1987

nn - Neil Gaiman & Dave McKean	£5.00
nn - (Titan, Jul 1991) colour edition	£5.00

VIZ COMIC
Viz Comics/John Brown; 1 Dec 1979-present (75 to Dec 1995/Jan 1996)

1 12pgs, rare (150 copies)	£100.00
2 16pgs, rare	£65.00
3 scarce	£45.00
4 scarce	£30.00
5-9 scarce	£20.00
10-15	£8.00
16-19	£6.00
20-24	£4.00
25-31	£2.50
32-39	£2.00
40-45	£1.50
46-59	£1.00
60-75	£1.25
Best of Viz 1-4 (Nov 1983), 20pgs	£10.00
Viz Monster Sex Remix (May 1985), best of 5-6	£7.50
Viz Big Hard One hardback, best of 1-12	£5.50
Viz Big Hard One softback	£5.00
Viz Big Hard One Number Two hardback, best of 13-18	£6.00
Viz Big Pink Stiff One (1988) hardback, best of 19-25	£6.00
Viz The Dog's Bollocks (1989) hardback, best of 26-31	£6.00
Viz Book of Crap Jokes hardback (small)	£4.00
The Spunky Parts (1990) hardback, best of 32-37	£7.00
Billy the Fish Football Yearbook (1990)	£3.50
Pathetic Sharks Bumper Special (Jun 1991)	£3.00
The Sausage Sandwich (1991) hardback, best of 38-42	£7.00
The Fish Supper (1992) hardback, best of 43-47	£7.00
Bumper Book of Absolute Shite For Older Boys and Girls (1993) hardback	£6.00
The Porky Chopper (1993) hardback, best of 48-52	£7.00
The Big Bell End (1995) hardback, best of 58-62	£8.00

VIZ HOLIDAY SPECIAL
John Brown; Jul 1988

1988 softback	£4.00

VOLTRON ANNUAL
World; 1987

1987 Japanese anime robot	£2.00

VOODOO
Miller; 1-8 1961

1-8 68pgs; Atlas reprints	£5.00

VOYAGE TO THE BOTTOM OF THE SEA ANNUAL
World Distributors; 1965-1966

1965	£10.00
1966	£7.50

VOYEUSE - WOMEN VIEW SEX
Knockabout (Fanny 2); 1991

2 32pgs; Rachael Ball, Julie Hollings, Corinne Pearlman, Carol Swain art	£2.50

VULCAN
IPC; 1st Mar 1975-20th Sep 1975 (30 unnumbered issues)

1 Mar 1975 Mytek the Mighty by Bradbury, The Spider by Reg Bunn, Saber, King of the Jungle by Colquhoun, The Trigan Empire by Don Lawrence, The Steel Claw by Jesus Blasco, Kelly's Eye by Solano Lopez, Robot Archie by Bert Bus reprints all begin	£4.00
8 Mar-19 Apr, 3 May-20 Sep 1975	£2.00
26 Apr 1975 McLoughlin Saber reprints begin	£2.00

VULCAN (NATIONAL EDITION)
IPC: 27th Sep 1975-3rd Apr 1976 (28 unnumbered issues, joins Valiant)

27 Sep 1975 reprints continue from Scottish edition	£1.50
4 Oct 1975-17 Jan 1976, 7 Feb-3 Apr 1976	£1.00
24 Jan 1976 Ron Embleton Trigon Empire reprints	£1.00

VULCAN ANNUAL
Fleetway; 1977

1977 softback, Don Lawrence reprints	£6.00

VULCAN HOLIDAY SPECIAL
IPC; Jun 1976

1976 64pgs; McLoughlin, Blasco reprints	£3.50

VULCAN MINI-COMIC
IPC; nn 10th Apr 1976-24th Apr 1976 (3 unnumbered issues, supplement to Valiant)

nn - severely edited reprints	£0.25

W

WAGONS, ROLL! WESTERN
G.T. Ltd; nn 1959?

nn - card cover	£5.00

WAGS
Joshua B. Powers/TV Boardman; 1 1st Jan 1937-88 4th Nov 1938

1-15 32pgs; American Sunday newspaper reprints	£40.00
16-30 28pgs from 17; incl. original strips, Bob Kane, Will Eisner art	£25.00
32-88 TV Boardman issues; incl. Eisner, Mort Meskin Sheena art	£12.00
Special	£15.00

Note: Published in America for export to UK, but carries British imprint from 32. Issue 31 is misnumbered 32, and 32 is given the number 32A. Continues publication in Australia.

WALLENSTEIN THE MONSTER
Top Sellers; 1 1974

1 132pgs pocket size; Italian adult reprints	£1.00

WALT DISNEY SERIES
World Distributors; 1 1956-52 1957

1 36pgs; Dell reprints	£4.00
2	£2.50
3-52	£2.00

FEATURES

Chip 'n' Dale in 12, 20, 31, 38, 50. Donald Duck in 2, 6, 10.14.17, 28, 32, 37, 47. Goofy in 3, 7, 11, 15, 18, 36. Jiminy Cricket in 16. Lady & the Tramp in 4, 8. Mickey Mouse in 1, 5, 9, 13, 21, 27, 35, 40, 51. Pluto in 19, 49. Scamp in 24, 25, 34, 45. Uncle Scrooge in 22, 52.

WALT DISNEY'S MICKEY MOUSE
Walt Disney Productions; 1 4th Jan 1958-56 19th Jan 1959 (becomes Walt Disney's Weekly)

1 12pgs gravure; features Disney characters	£4.00
2	£2.50
3-56	£2.00

WALT DISNEY'S PICTURE TREASURY
I.P.C. Magazines; 1972-1976

Snow White 32pgs	£0.50
Robin Hood	£0.50
Peter Pan	£0.50
Lady and the Tramp 48pgs	£0.50
Jungle Book	£0.50

WALT DISNEY'S UNCLE REMUS AND HIS TALES OF BRER RABBIT
Collins; nn 1947

nn - 16pgs; Dell reprints adapting Song of the South	£3.00

WALT DISNEY'S WEEKLY
Walt Disney Productions; 1 26th Jan 1959-118 24th Apr 1961 (joins Harold Hare's Own Paper)

1 16pgs gravure; features Disney features	£3.00
2-118	£1.50

WAMBI JUNGLE BOY
R. & L. Locker; 1 1951

1 68pgs; Fiction House reprints	£5.00

WANTED COMICS
Arnold Book Co.; 1950, 3 un-numbered issues

nn - 12pgs gravure; Orbit Publications reprints	£4.00
nn - 12pgs letterpress	£3.00
nn - 36pgs	£3.00

WAR
Miller; 1 1961-11 1962

1 68pgs; Atlas War Comics reprints begin	£2.50
2-11 52pgs	£2.00

WAR AT SEA
Miller; 1 1958-?

1 28pgs; Charlton reprints	£2.00

WAR AT SEA PICTURE LIBRARY
Fleetway Publications; 1 Feb 1962-36 Jul 1963

1 68pgs pocket size; Devil's Cargo by Farrugia	£3.00
2-36	£1.50

ARTISTS/FEATURES

1 Devil's Cargo by Farrugia. 2 Killer Fish by Gino D'Antonio. 3 The Nelso Touch by Jose Ortiz. 4 Escort by Gino D'Antonio. 5 Engage the Enemy by Farrugia. 6 The Long Haul by Juan Zanotto. 7 I Vow Vengeance by Gino D'Antonio. 8 Leatherneck by Victor de la Fuente. 9 Down Ramps. 10 Man of War. 11 Repel Borders by Roberto Diso. 12 Torpedo Run by Jorge Macabich. 13 The Navy Way by Aldoma Puig. 14 Ram - and Wreck by John Gillatt. 15 Crash Dive by Roberto Diso. 16 Destroyer by Farrugia. 17 To Strike Unseen. 18 Q-Ship. 19 Close Quarters by Solano Lopez. 20 Mosquito Navy. 21 The Thunder of Guns by Nevio Zeccara. 22 False Colours by Jesus Blasco. 23 Clear for Action by Renzo Calegari. 24 Flight Deck by Solano Lopez. 25 The Blind Eye by Giorgio Trevisan. 26 Ship-o-the-Line by Farrugia. 27 Errand of Mercy. 28 Sea Devil by John Gillatt. 29 Storm Centre. 30 The Savage Deep by Farrugia. 31 Fire All Guns. 32 Shock Wave. 33 Hazard Below by Jorge Moliterni. 34 Battle Stations by Hugo Pratt. 35 Wolf Pack. 36 Colours Flying.

WAR COMICS
Gerald Swan; 1 Apr 1940-20 Dec 1943 (joins Kiddyfun)

1 36pgs; William Ward art	£8.00
2-11 36pgs	£5.00
12 28pgs	£5.00
13-20 20pgs	£5.00
Specials:	
Summer, Winter (1941)	£8.00
Summer (1942)	£8.00
Spring, Special (1943)	£8.00

WAR COMICS
Streamline; 1951, 3 unnumbered issues

nn-nn 28pgs; Atlas reprints	£3.00
nn - 68pgs	£3.50

WAR HERO
World Distributors; 50 1970-?

	N.MINT		N.MINT

50 68pgs pocket size	£1.00
51-?	£0.50

WAR-PATH! PICTURE AND STORY ALBUM

Mellifont; W1 1950s	
W1 96pgs	£3.00

WAR PICTURE LIBRARY

Amalgamated/Fleetway/IPC; 1 Sep 1958-2103 Dec 1984

1 60pgs pocket size; Fight Back to Dunkirk by Nevio Zeccara	£15.00
2	£10.00
3-5	£7.50
6-20	£5.00
21-50	£2.50
51-571	£1.00
572-2103 68pgs; mostly reprints	£0.75

ARTISTS/FEATURES

1 Fight Back to Dunkirk by Nevio Zeccara. 2 Wings of Victory (2 stories) by Nevio Zeccara. 3 Action Stations by Renzo Calegari. 4 The Gallant Few by Renzo Calegari. 5 The Ship That Ran Away by Renzo Calegari. 6 For Valour (3 stories) by Nevio Zeccara, Reg Bunn. 7 The Red Devils by Gino D'Antonio. 8 Wings Over the Navy by Fred T. Holmes. 9 Bombs Away by Renzo Calegari. 10 Up Periscope by Nevio Zeccara. 11 Tracy of Tobruk by Renzo Calegari. 12 Course For Danger by Fred T. Holmes. Artists include Gino D'Antonio. Victor de la Fuente. Fernando Fernandez. Ian Kennedy. Solano Lopez. Hugo Pratt in 25, 40, 50, 58, 62, 91, 92, 133, 791, 992, 1102. Ferdinando Tacconi. Ron Turner in 1047, 1147, 1206, 1218, 1231, 1243, 1291, 1338, 1362, 1399, 1764, 1797, 1805, 1809, 1950, 1962, 1980, 2010, 2058.

WAR PICTURE LIBRARY HOLIDAY SPECIAL

I.P.C. Magazines; Jul 1963-?

1963 224pgs	£3.00
1964-1969	£2.00
1970-present	£1.25

WARHEADS

(see Overkill) (see main American comics section)

WARHEADS: BLACK DAWN

(see main American comics section)

WARLORD

D.C. Thomson; 1 28th Sep 1974-627 27th Sep 1986 (joins Victor)

1 Union Jack Jackson by Carlos Cruz, Bomber Braddock, Code-Name Warlord, Young Wolf begin	£1.50
1 with free gift (8 golden replica medals)	£3.00
2-5	£0.75
6-17, 19-120, 122-219	£0.50
18 Drake of E-Boat Alley by Ron Smith begins	£0.50
121 Killer Kane by Colin Andrew begins	£0.50
220 1st "Warlord and Bullet"; Fireball begins	£0.30
221-450, 452-627	£0.30
451 Sabor's Army by Alcatena begins	£0.30

ARTISTS

Alcatena in 451-466. Belardinelli in 403, 479, 482, 484, 486, 492, 500, 503. Denis McLoughlin in 248-257, 267-299, 353-363. Ron Smith in 3, 10, 17-36, 75 (some stories reprinted later).

WARLORD BOOK FOR BOYS

D.C. Thomson; 1976-1984

1976	£3.00
1977-1980	£2.50
1981-1984	£2.00

WARLORD PETER FLINT SPECIAL

D.C. Thomson; nn 1976

nn - 32pgs tabloid	£0.75

WARLORD SUMMER SPECIAL

D.C. Thomson; 1975-?

1975 32pgs tabloid	£1.25
1976-1980 32pgs	£0.75
1981-? 36pgs	£0.50

WARPATH/INDIANS ON THE WARPATH

Streamline; 1955, 3 issues?

nn - 28pgs; St John Publishing reprints	£3.00
nn - 68pgs; incl. Jimmy Durante (Magazine Enterprises) reprints	£3.00
3	£3.00

WARRIOR

Derek G. Skinn/Penwith Publications; 1 1974-6 1975

1 Wrath of the Gods, Kelpie the Boy Wizard both by John Burns, Erik the Viking by Don Lawrence, Heros the Spartan by Frank Bellamy, Olac the Gladiator by Don Lawrence, Black Axe by Tom Kerr, all reprints	£2.50
2 Thong by Steve Parkhouse begins	£1.25
3-4	£1.25
5 Horatius, the Hero of Rome by Del Castillo begins, McKie art	£1.25
6 Swordspell by Booth & Jackson begins (continued in Fantasy Advertiser)	£1.25

WARRIOR

Quality; 1 Mar 1982-26 Feb 1985

1 1st modern Marvelman (later Miracleman) by Alan Moore & Garry Leach, Laser Eraser and Pressbutton by Pedro Henry (Steve Moore) & Steve Dillon, V For Vendetta by Alan Moore & Dave Lloyd, Spiral Path by Parkhouse, Legend of Prester John by S. Moore & Bolton, Father Shandor reprints by Steve Moore & Bolton begin, 2pg by Gibbons	£4.00
2 Madman by Paul Neary begins	£3.00
3 1st Zirk by Henry and Bolland	£3.00
4 52pgs; "Summer Special", Marvelman by A. Moore, Dillon, Neary & Davis, Golden Amazon by Lloyd, Pressbutton origin by Henry & David Jackson	£3.00
5 new Shandor series by S. Moore & Jackson begins, 1st Neary & Austin Madman	£3.00
6 1st Davis/Leach Marvelman, Gibbons reprint	£2.50
7 last Madman (story incomplete)	£3.00
8 1st Davis Marvelman, Hunt Emerson art	£2.50
9-10 Warpsmith by Moore & Leach	£2.50
11 Laser Eraser ends	£2.50
12 last Spiral Path, Bojeffries Saga by Moore & Parkhouse begins, Young Marvelman by Moore & Ridgway	£2.50
13 Bojeffries ends, Zirk by Henry & Leach	£2.50

14 Twilight World by S.Moore & Jim Baikie begins, Ektryn by Henry & Cam Kennedy	£2.00
15 Laser Eraser returns (one issue only, story unfinished)	£2.00
16 Laser Eraser reprint from Sounds	£2.00
17 no Marvelman, V, Shandor	£2.00
18 Parkhouse, Asbury reprints from Halls of Horror	£2.00
19 Bojeffries returns (ends 20), Big Ben by Skinn & William Simpson begins, no Marvelman	£1.50
20 V filler by Lloyd & Tony Weare	£2.00
21 Marvelman ends (unfinished) under threat of legal action from Marvel Comics, 1st Davis Laser Eraser/Pressbutton	£2.00
22 1st Bogey European reprint by Segura & Sanchez, no Shandor, Laser Eraser	£1.50
23 1st John Ridgway Shandor	£1.50
24 no Bogey	£1.50
25 Ektryn by Kennedy, Shandor by John Stokes; Laser Eraser ends	£2.00
26 Garry Leach Zirk; scarce	£2.50

ARTISTS

Horacio Altuna in 25-26. Martin Asbury in 18. Jim Baikie in 14-17. Brian Bolland in 3. John Bolton in 1-3. Alan Davis 4, 8-11, 13-16, 18, 20-21, 24-25 (pencils 6-7). Steve Dillon in 1-11, 15. Hunt Emerson in 8. Dave Gibbons in 1, 6. David Jackson in 4-10, 13-21. Cam Kennedy in 14, 25. Garry Leach in 1-3, 5, 9-10, 13, 26 (inks 6-7). David Lloyd in 1-16, 18-26. Steve Parkhouse in 1-2, 4-8, 12-13, 18-20 (pencils 3, 9-12). John Ridgway in 12-13, 17, 22-24, 26 (inks 9-12). William Simpson in 19-24 (pencils 25-26). Alan Moore script in 1-21, 23-26. Grant Morrison script in 26. Steve Moore script in 1-13, 17-18.

WARRIOR WOMEN

Marvel; nn Jun 1980

nn - 52pgs; US reprints	£1.00

WATCHMEN

Titan; nn 1988

nn - reprints Watchmen #1-12 by Alan Moore & Dave Gibbons	£11.00

WEE CHUMS COMIC

Philmar; nn 1949

nn - 8pgs; Bob Wilkin art	£3.00

WEEKEND MAIL COMIC

Associated Newspapers; 13th Jan 1955-20th Oct 1955 (continued as single page)

13 Jan 1955 4pgs supplement to Weekend Mail; Mandrake, Vic Flint, Casey Ruggles US newspaper reprints, Perils of Love by Blasco reprints, Tom Kerr art	£2.00
20 Jan-16 Jun 1955	£1.50
23 Jun-20 Oct 1955 reduced to 2pgs	£1.00

WEIRD PLANETS

Alan Class; 1 1962-21 1963

1 68pgs; various reprints from Atlas, Charlton , A.C.G., etc	£12.50
2-5	£6.00
6-10	£4.00
11-21	£2.50

WEIRD SCIENCE ILLUSTORIES

Cartoon Art; 1 1956?

1 52pgs pocketbook; Magazine Enterprises reprints, incl. text story reprint by Philip K. Dick	£8.00

WEIRD WORLDS

Thorpe & Porter; 1 Mar 1953-?

1 68pgs; Atlas reprints	£12.50
2-5	£5.00
6-20	£2.50
21-?	£1.50

WEREWOLF

Marvel; nn Oct 1981

nn - 52pgs; US reprints	£1.00

WES SLADE

Express; nn 1979

nn - 68pgs pocket size; reprints George Stokes newspaper strip from Sunday Express	£3.00

WESTERN ADVENTURE LIBRARY

Micron/G.W.Smith; 1 Feb 1963-?

1 68pgs pocket size; Secret Witness	£2.00
2-?	£1.00

WESTERN BUMPER ALBUM

Top Sellers; 1-3? 1972

1-3? rebound remainders of Bonanza, Gunsmoke, Lone Ranger (each)	£2.00

WESTERN CLASSICS

World Distributors; 1 Feb 1958-40?

1 36pgs; Gunsmoke, Dell reprints	£5.00
2-40 incl. various western reprints	£3.00

WESTERN CLASSICS

Top Sellers; 1 1972

1 36pgs; Dell reprints	£2.00
2-?	£0.75

WESTERN DAYS

Scion; nn 1952

nn - 24pgs; King-Ganteaume art	£4.00

WESTERN FIGHTERS

Cartoon Arts; 1-2 1951

1-2 28pgs; Hillman reprints	£3.00

WESTERN FIGHTERS

Streamline; nn 1951-4 1954

nn - 36pgs; Hillman reprints	£5.00
nn - 32pgs	£4.00
nn - 28pgs	£4.00

WESTERN FUN COMIC

Gerald Swan; 8 1953-13 1954 (previously Western War Comic)

8-13	£5.00

WESTERN GUNFIGHTERS SPECIALS

Marvel; Jun 1980-Oct 1981

Summer Special 1980 Bellamy cover, Barry Smith, Kirby, Williamson reprints	£1.25
Summer Special 1981	£1.00
Winter Special 1981	£0.75

	N.MINT
WESTERN HERO	
Miller; 50 Sep 1950-149 1949, 100 issues (became Heroes of the West)	
50 28pgs; Fawcett reprints	£5.00
51-149	£3.00
WESTERN KID	
Miller; 1-12 1955	
1 28pgs; Atlas reprints	£4.00
2-12	£2.00
WESTERN KILLERS	
Streamline; 1950s	
nn 6d cover price	£5.00
nn 1/- cover price	£4.00
WESTERN OUTLAWS	
Miller; 1-2 1954	
1-2 28pgs; Marvel reprints	£4.00
WESTERN OUTLAWS	
Gerald Swan; 1-8 1954	
1 36pgs; US reprints	£3.00
2-8	£2.00
WESTERN OUTLAWS	
Streamline; 1-nn 1955	
1-2, nn 28pgs; reprints from Prize Westerns (Prize), Red Hawk (ME)	£3.00
WESTERN PICTURE LIBRARY	
C.A. Pearson; 1 Sep 1958-? (82+ issues)	
1 68pgs pocket size; Mustang Gray & the Texas Rangers	£3.00
2-10	£2.00
11-82	£1.00
WESTERN PICTURE LIBRARY	
G.M. Smith; 501 Jan 1979-828 Jun 1985	
501 68pgs pocket size	£1.00
502-828	£0.50
WESTERN ROUGH RIDERS	
Streamline; 1955, 2 unnumbered issues	
nn - 28pgs; Stanmor Publications reprints	£5.00
nn - 68pgs	£5.00
WESTERN ROUND-UP ANNUAL	
World Distributors; 1955-Aug 1958	
1955	£5.00
(1956) Gene Autry, Roy Rogers, Johnny Mack Brown, Dale Evans; Dell reprints	£5.00
1957 Gene Autry, Roy Rogers, Range Rider; Dell reprints	£5.00
1958 Wells Fargo, Wagon Train, Range Rider; Dell reprints	£5.00
WESTERN ROUNDUP ANNUAL	
World Distributors; 1 Jan 1955-39 1958	
1 28pgs; Dell reprints	£5.00
2-39	£3.00
WESTERN STAR PICTURE LIBRARY	
MV Features; 1 May 1965-?	
1 68pgs pocket size; Showdown, foreign reprints	£2.00
2-?	£1.00
WESTERN STARS COMIC	
Miller; 1 1952-17 1958	
1 68pgs; Fawcett reprints, incl. Ken Maynard, Hopalong Cassidy, Tom Mix, etc.	£10.00
2-17	£5.00
WESTERN SUPER THRILLER COMICS	
World Distributors; 34 1957-82 195? (previously Super Thriller)	
34-82 incl. James Bleach, Terrence Patrick, Gerry Embleton art	£5.00
WESTERN TALES	
World Distributors; 1 1955	
1 28pgs; Harvey Publications reprints	£5.00
WESTERN TALES	
United Anglo-American; 1-2 1956	
1-2 28pgs; Harvey Publications reprints	£4.00
WESTERN TALES	
Brugeditor; 1 1962-?	
1 68pgs pocket size; Spanish reprints	£1.50
2-?	£0.75
WESTERN THRILLER	
Streamline; 1 1955	
1 68pgs; various reprints from Prize Publications, Fiction House	£5.00
WESTERN THRILLERS	
Streamline; 1 1950	
1 28pgs; Fox Features reprints	£4.00
WESTERN TRAIL PICTURE LIBRARY	
Famepress; 1 Jan 1966-?	
1 68pgs pocket size; foreign reprints	£1.50
2-?	£0.75
WESTERN TRAILS	
Streamline; nn 1950s	
nn	£4.00
WESTERN TRAILS	
Miller; 1-5 1957	
1-5 28pgs; Atlas reprints	£3.00
WESTERN WAR COMIC	
Gerald Swan; 1 Jun 1949-5 Nov 1950 (becomes New Series)	
1 20pgs	£5.00
2-5	£4.00
WESTERN WAR COMIC (NEW SERIES)	
Swan; 1 1952-7 1953 (becomes Western Fun Comic)	
1-4, 7 36pgs	£3.00
5, 6 Ron Embleton art	£3.50
WESTWORLD FOURSOME COMIC	
Westworld Publications; 1-14 1950s	

	N.MINT
1 68pgs; reprints four issues of French (?) strip per issue	£4.00
2-14	£2.00
WHACKY RODEO	
Transatlantic Press/Funnibook Co.; 1947-Jul 1947, 2 unnumbered issues	
nn - 8pgs; Dennis Reader art	£4.00
nn - Denis Gifford art	£4.00
WHAM!	
Odhams; 1 20th Jun 1964-187 13th Jan 1968 (joins Pow!)	
1 General Nitt, The Tiddlers, Eagle Eye, Biff, Pest of The West, George's Germs	
(all by Baxendale), Kelpie the Boy Wizard by Ken Mennell & John Burns begin	£25.00
1 with free gift (Wham! Gun)	£50.00
2	£12.50
3	£7.50
4 Frankie Stein by Ken Reid begins	£6.00
5-10	£5.00
11-36	£4.00
37 Johnny Straight by Don Lawrence (Wells Fargo reprints from Zip) begin	£3.00
38-50	£3.00
51-111	£2.00
112 Fantastic Four reprints begin	£2.00
113-187	£1.50
WHAM! ANNUAL	
Odhams; 1966-1974	
1966	£7.50
1967-1969	£5.00
1970-1972	£3.00
1973-1974 titled Wham! and Pow! Annual	£2.50
WHEELS	
Byblos; nn Jun 1978; 1 Oct 1978-?	
nn (Preview) 52pgs; foreign reprints	£1.00
1-? 52pgs	£0.50
WHITE RIDER	
(see Blue Bolt series)	
WHITE TRASH	
Tundra (Atomeka); 1 Sep 1992-4 Jun 1993	
1 1st edition, 200 copies; Blast reprints by Gordon Rennie & Martin Emond	£5.00
1 2nd edition, revised lyrics	£3.00
2-4	£3.00
Note: first edition of first issue was pulped when Elvis Presley Estate objected to Presley lyrics being used, only 200 copies bound.	
WHIZ COMICS	
Miller; (1) nn 1945; (2) 60-76; (3) 50 Jun 1950-130 1959	
nn 16pgs gravure; Fawcett reprints	£15.00
60-70 16pgs gravure	£7.50
71-76 16pgs letterpress	£5.00
50-70 28pgs large gravure	£5.00
71-130 28pgs	£3.00
WHIZZBANG COMIC	
Philmar; 1 1948	
1 16pgs; Frank Jupo art	£3.00
WHIZZER AND CHIPS	
(see Best of Whizzer and Chips)	
I.P.C. Magazines/Fleetway Publications; 18th Oct 1969-27th Oct 1990	
(1038 issue, joins Buster)	
No.1 - 18 Oct 1969 Mike Lacey, Terry Bave, Graham Allen, Mike Higgs art,	
Space Accident by Ron Turner begins	£3.00
No.1 with free gift (12 super stickers)	£6.00
25 Oct 1969	£1.50
1 Nov-27 Dec 1969	£0.75
1970-1974 issues incl. Leo Baxendale, Ron Turner art	£0.50
1975-1990 issues	£0.35
CHRONOLOGY	
30 Jun 1973: 1st "Whizzer and Chips & Knockout". 22 Apr 1978: 1st "Whizzer and Chips & Krazy". 6 Apr 1985: 1st "Whizzer and Chips & Whoopee!".	
ARTISTS	
Ron Turner in 18 Oct 1969-23 Jun 1973, 19 Jun 1974-22 May 1976.	
WHIZZER AND CHIPS ANNUAL	
I.P.C./Fleetway; 1970-1992?	
1971	£3.50
1972-1979	£3.00
1980-1989	£2.50
1990-1992?	£2.00
WHIZZER AND CHIPS HOLIDAY SPECIAL	
I.P.C. Magazines/Fleetway Publications; 1970-1991?	
1970 96pgs	£3.50
1971-1972 96pgs	£1.25
1973-1975 80pgs	£0.60
1976-1991 64pgs	£0.50
WHIZZER AND CHIPS WINTER SPECIAL	
I.P.C.; 1992	
1992 glossy covers	£2.25
WHIZZER COMICS	
Cartoon Art; 1 Jun 1947-5 1948	
1 12pgs; Dennis Reader art	£4.00
2-4 16pgs; Reader art	£4.00
5 36pgs; Paddy Brennan, Reader art	£4.00
WHOOPEE!	
I.P.C. Magazines; 9th Mar 1974-30th Mar 1985 (joins Whizzer and Chips)	
9 Mar 1974 Brian Walker, Terry Bave, Sid Burgon art	£1.00
16 Mar 1974-9 Feb 1980	£0.40
16 Feb 1980-30 Mar 1985	£0.25

	N.MINT
CHRONOLOGY	
12 Oct 1974: 1st "Whoopee & Shiver and Shake". 9 Feb 1980: 1st "Whoopee & Cheeky". 2 Jul 1983: 1st "Whoopee & Wow".	
WHOOPEE COMIC	
Philmar; 1 1949	
1 16pgs; reprints from Super, Cheery, and Jolly Giant	£3.00
WHOOPEE FRANKIE STEIN SUMMER SPECIAL	
IPC; May 1977	
1977 80pgs	£1.50
WHOPPING COMIC	
International Publications; nn 1945	
nn - 8pgs; A.R.G., Denis Gifford art	£3.00
WILBUR COMICS	
Gerald Swan; 1 1950-?	
1 36pgs; Archie reprints	£2.50
2-?	£1.50
WILD BILL ELLIOTT COMICS	
World Distributors; 1 1954-18 1955	
1 28pgs; Dell reprints	£5.00
2-18	£3.00
WILD BILL HICKOK AND JINGLES	
Miller; 1 1959-16 1960	
1 28pgs; Dell reprints based on TV series	£5.00
2-16	£3.00
WILD BILL HICKOK COMICS	
Thorpe & Porter; 1 Dec 1952-14 1954	
1 68pgs; Avon Periodicals reprints from Wild Bill Hickok Comics, and Jesse James Comic	£4.00
2-14	£3.00
WILD BILL PECOS THE WESTERNER	
Pemberton; 1 1953-63 1958	
1 36pgs; Wanted Comics reprints	£2.50
2-63	£1.50
WILDCARD	
CM Comics; 1 Jan 1994	
1 Wildcard by Chris Morgan & Kelvin Cox	£1.60
WILD FRONTIER	
Miller; 1 1955-? 1956	
1 28pgs; Charlton reprints	£2.50
2-?	£1.50
WILD PALMS	
Arrow; nn Nov 1993	
nn - 72pgs; by Bruce Wagner & Julian Allen, reprints from Details	£8.00
Note: reprints strip which formed the basis for Oliver Stone TV series	
WILD THING	
(see main American comics section)	
WILD WEST COMIC ANNUAL	
World Distributors; 1952-1960?	
1952 John Wayne, Buffalo Bill, etc; Western Publishing reprints	£4.00
1953 Wild Bill Pecos, Lobo the Wolf Boy, Black Diamond reprints	£4.00
1954-1960	£4.00
WILD WEST PICTURE LIBRARY	
Fleetway; 1 May 1966-114 Jan 1971	
1 60pgs pocket size; Gun Rule	£3.00
2-92	£1.50
93-114 68pgs	£1.00
ARTISTS/FEATURES	
1 Gun Rule. 2 Twisted Trails by Robert Forrest. 3 Call of the Wild. 4 Death in Ambush. 5 Outlaw Gold. 6 Cattle Drive. Many issues reprint Kit Carson, Buck Jones, etc stories from Cowboy Comics with the lead character's name changed; artists include Jesus Blasco in 66, 73, 76, 78, 86, 100. Carlos V. Roume. Jose Luis Salinas in 109.	
WILD WEST PICTURE LIBRARY HOLIDAY SPECIAL	
I.P.C. Magazines/ Fleetway Publications; 1973-?	
1973 192pgs; reprints	£1.50
1974-	£1.00
WILD WEST PICTURE STORIES	
C.A. Pearson; 1 May 1960-?	
1 68pgs pocket size	£1.00
2-?	£0.75
WILD WESTERN	
Streamline; 1 1951	
1 28pgs; reprints from Prize Western (Prize)	£4.00
WILD WESTERN	
Miller; 1-9 1955	
1 28pgs; Atlas/Marvel reprints	£5.00
2-9	£4.00
WILFREDS ANNUAL	
Amalgamated; 1924-1939	
1924 scarce	£35.00
1925	£25.00
1926-1930	£17.50
1931-1935	£15.00
1936-1939	£12.50
WILL ROGERS WESTERN COMIC	
United Anglo-American; 1950, 2 unnumbered issues	
nn-nn 28pgs; Fox Features reprints	£5.00
WILLIAM TELL	
(see TV Photo Stories)	
C.A. Pearson (TV Picture Stories); 1 Feb 1959-3 Jun 1959	
1 68pgs pocket size; The Assassins	£5.00
2-3	£3.00
ARTISTS/FEATURES	
1 The Assassins. 2 The Bear. 3 The Prisoner.	

Wham #1

Whizzer & Chips #1

Wizard (2nd) #1

	N.MINT		N.MINT
WILLY THE KID BOOK, THE		**WONDER DUCK**	
Duckworth; nn 1976-1978		**United Anglo-American; 1 1950**	
nn - Leo Baxendale art begins	£5.00	**1** 28pgs; Marvel reprints	£2.50
Book 2	£5.00	**WONDER HEROES**	
Book 3	£5.00	**Sunburst Publications; 1 1981-2 1984**	
WINDJAMMER, THE		**1** 12pgs; Adam Sword	£1.50
Martin & Reid; nn 1950		**2** 24pgs; John Cooper, Harold Johns art	£1.00
nn - 16pgs; Mick Anglo, Bob Wilkin art	£3.00	**WONDER STORY COMIC**	
WINGS COMICS		**Newton Wickham; nn 1944**	
Cartoon Art; nn 1950		nn - 16pgs; Alf Farningham, John Turner art	£3.00
nn - Fiction House reprints	£4.00	**WONDERMAN**	
WINGS COMICS		(see Oh Boy! Comics, Wonderman)	
Streamline; 1951, 2 unnumbered issues		**Paget; 1 1948-24 1951**	
nn-nn 28pgs; Fiction House reprints	£4.00	**1** 8pgs; Wonderman by Mick Anglo begins	£7.50
WINGS COMICS		**2-3, 5-7** 4 more common	£5.00
Trent; 1-3 1953?		4 more common	£3.00
1-3 68pgs; Fiction House reprints	£3.50	**8-15, 21, 23-24** 12pgs	£4.00
WINNER COMIC, THE		**16-20** 16pgs	£4.00
H. Jeffrey/ D.R. Burnside; Jun 1947-Jul 1948, 2 unnumbered issues		nn (22) titled Oh Boy! and Wonderman; H. Stanley White Tornado	£4.00
nn - 16pgs; John Turner, Bob Monkhouse, Denis Gifford art	£4.00	**WONDERMAN**	
nn - Turner, Gifford, Frank Minnitt art	£3.00	**Alex White; 1 Jan 1967-26? 1968**	
WIZARD, THE		**1** 68pgs pocket size; Italian reprints	£1.00
D.C. Thomson; 1 23rd Sep 1922-1970 16th Nov 1963 (joins Rover)		**2-26**	£0.50
1 very scarce	£75.00	**WONDER WOMAN**	
2 scarce	£50.00	**Titan; Apr 1995**	
3-5	£30.00	**The Contest** DC reprints by William Messner-Loebs & Mike Deodato	£6.00
1922 issues	£25.00	**WONDER WOMAN OFFICIAL ANNUAL**	
1923 issues	£20.00	**Egmont/London Editions; 1980-1982**	
1924-1930 issues	£15.00	**1980** Egmont; DC reprints; Brian Bolland end-papers	£3.00
1931-1935 issues	£10.00	**1981** Egmont; DC reprints; Brian Bolland cover, Garry Leach end-papers	£3.00
1936-1940 issues	£7.50	**1982** London Editions; DC reprints	£2.00
1941-1950 issues	£5.00	**WORLD ADVENTURE LIBRARY SERIES**	
1951-1955 issues	£4.00	(see Bonanza, Flash Gordon, The Man From U.N.C.L.E., Mandrake the Magician, The Phantom, Tarzan.	
1956-1959 issues	£3.00	Note: Batman World Adventure Library and Superman World Adventure Library contain text stories, not	
1960-1963 issues	£2.00	comic strips)	
WIZARD		**WORLD FUN**	
D.C. Thomson; 1 14th Feb 1970-24th Jun 1978		**Martin & Reid; nn 1948**	
(435 issues, numbered to 153; joins Victor)		nn - Harry Banger, Frank Minnitt art	£3.00
1 Soldiers of the Jet Age by Martin Asbury begins	£3.00	**WORLD ILLUSTRATED**	
1 with free gift (Sure-Shot Shooter)	£6.00	**Thorpe & Porter; 1 1953-34 1963**	
2-5	£1.00	**1** 52pgs; Flight (US #8), Gilberton reprints from The World Around Us, new cover	£15.00
6-13 Jan 1974, 27 Jan-13 Jul 1974	£0.75	**2** Pirates (7)	£10.00
20 Jan 1974 1st "Wizard and Rover"	£0.75	**3** Horses (3)	£7.50
20 Jul 1974 The Wriggling Wrecker by Dave Gibbons begins	£1.25	**4** Prehistoric Animals (15)	£8.00
27 Jul 1974-24 Jun 1978 incl. some Gibbons, Bolland art	£0.30	**5** Space (5)	£7.00
ARTISTS/FEATURES		**6** Dogs (1)	£7.00
Martin Asbury (Soldiers of the Jet Age 1-23, 41-54, The Crimson Claw 26-34, The River Raiders 56-70,		**7** The F.B.I. (6)	£7.00
The Secret War of Deep 16 134-146, Big River Bill 2 Oct 1976-22 Jan 1971). Brian Bolland (The Box 25		**8** The Crusades (16)	£7.00
Sep 1976). Paddy Brennan (Longlegs the Desert Wild Boy 19 May-17 Nov 1973 reprint, King Solomon's		**9** Scientists (18)	£7.00
Mines 23 Feb-17 Aug 1974, reprint). Carlos Ezquerra (Chained to His Sword 25 Sep 1976-1 Jan 1977,		**10** French Revolution (14)	£8.00
The Wrong Face of Fear 19 Nov 1977). Dave Gibbons (The Wriggling Wrecker 20 Jul-21 Dec 1974, Year		**11** The Jungle (19)	£8.00
of the Shark Men 24 Apr-10 Jul 1976, The Deathless Army 14 Aug 1976, The Last Torpedo 28 Aug 1976,		**12** Communications (20)	£7.00
The Flying Tripehound 18 Dec 1976-12 Feb 1977, Cat and Mouse 13 Aug-15 Oct 1977, 3 Dec 1977, 17		**13** Ghosts (24)	£7.00
Dec-24 Dec 1977). Denis McLoughlin (Power the Danger Ranger 18 May-20 Jul 1974, Terror of the Tall		**14** Great Explorers (23)	£7.00
Tower 28 Sep 1974-25 Jan 1975, Black Jaguar 25 Jan 1975, It's Only Zeke 1 Feb-29 Mar 1975, Sign of		**15** Magic (25)	£8.00
the Shark 14 Jun-25 Oct 1975, The Frozen Man 29 Nov 1975-17 Apr 1976, Frankie and Johnnie 16 Oct		**16** High Adventure (27)	£7.00
1976-1 Jan 1977, etc).		**17** Whaling (28)	£7.00
WIZARD BOOK FOR BOYS, THE		**18** The Vikings (29)	£7.00
D.C. Thomson; Autumn 1935-Autumn 1941, Aut 1948		**19** Underwater Adventure (30)	£7.00
(1936) scarce	£75.00	**20** Hunting (31) new cover	£9.00
(1937)	£35.00	**21** Gold and Glory (32) new cover	£9.00
(1938)	£25.00	**22** Spies (35)	£7.00
(1939)	£20.00	**23** Fishing (34)	£7.00
(1940)	£15.00	**24** Famous Teens (33)	£7.00
(1941)	£15.00	**25** Fight for Life (36)	£7.00
(1942)	£15.00	**26** Day of Fury (new) mostly US art	£25.00
(1949)	£12.50	**27** Boating (22)	£7.00
Note: no annuals issued for 1943-1948		**28** The Sea (new) mostly US art	£15.00
WIZARD HOLIDAY BOOK		**29** Great Escapes (new)	£15.00
D.C. Thomson; Autumn 1937-Autumn 1938		**30** Life/Planets (new) mostly US art	£15.00
(1938) scarce, softcover (seaside scene)	£50.00	**31** North West Passage (new)	£15.00
(1939) scarce, softcover (railway scene)	£40.00	**32** Golden Horde (new)	£15.00
WIZARD MIDGET COMIC		**33** The Cossacks (new) mostly US art	£15.00
D.C. Thomson; nn 11th Sep 1954		**34** Disasters (new)	£20.00
nn - 32pgs giveaway with Wizard; incl. The Truth About Wilson, Limpalong Leslie	£3.00	**Note:** Follows European series	
WOLF IN SHADOW		**WORLD OF SPACE**	
Legend; nn Sep 1994		**PR; nn 1960s**	
nn - 96pgs; adapts David Gemmell novel, Fangorn art	£10.00	nn - 24pgs; text stories plus strip The Green Moon all illus. by Ron Embleton	£5.00
WONDER		**WORLD OF WONDER**	
(previously The Funny Wonder)		**IPC; 1 28 Mar 1970-?**	
Amalgamated; 1444 30th May 1942-1760 12th Sep 1953 (317 issues, joins Radio Fun)		**1**	£3.00
1444 8pgs; Pitch & Toss by Roy Wilson, Charlie Chaplin by Bertie Brown continue	£15.00	**1** with free gift (Great Explorers wall chart)	£6.00
1445-1450	£5.00	**2-?**	£1.00
1451-1717	£3.00	**WORLD WITHOUT SUPERMAN**	
1718 1st 12pgs; Into Strange Lands by Ron Embleton begins	£3.00	(see Superman)	
1719-1760	£2.50	**WORLD'S FINEST**	
ARTISTS/FEATURES		**Titan; nn Jan 1993**	
Ron Embleton in various (The Black Dagger, Into Strange Lands).		nn - reprints World's Finest #1-3 by Dave Gibbons, Rude/Kesel art	£9.00
WONDER BOY		**WOW!**	
Miller; 1-3 1955		**I.P.C.; 5th Jun 1982-25th Jun 1983 (joins Whoopee!)**	
1-3 28pgs; Atlas reprints	£5.00	**No.1 - 5 Jun 1982**	£1.25
		No.1 with free gift	£2.50

	N.MINT
No.2 - 12 Jun 1982	£1.00
No.2 with free gift (rubber spider)	£2.00
19 Jun 1982-25 Jun 1983	£0.75
WOW COMICS	
Miller; 1943-1950, various numbers	
nn - 68pgs 2-colour gravure; Fawcett reprints	£8.00
nn - 16pgs gravure	£6.00
30, 42, 44, 45, 49, 55 (12 issues in all) 16pgs 2-colour gravure	£5.00
WRECKERS, THE	
(see Secret Service series)	
Hotspur Publishing Co.; 2 1948	
2 8pgs; Bob Wilkin art	£3.00
WYATT EARP	
Miller; 1 1957-44 1960	
1 28pgs; Charlton reprints	£5.00
2-44	£3.00

X

	N.MINT
X-FILES, THE	
Manga Publishing; 1 Jun 1995-present (7 to Dec 1995)	
1 Topps Comics reprints begin, Adlard art	£20.00
1 with free gift (badge)	£25.00
2	£10.00
3	£7.50
4-5	£3.50
6	£2.00
7 free Book of the Unexplained supplement	£1.50
8-10	£1.50
X-FILES	
Manga Publishing; Nov 1995-present	
Firebird (Nov 1995) 148pgs; reprints X-Files 1-6	£10.00
Project Aquarius (July 1996)	£10.00
XMAS COMIC	
Crayburn Neil; nn 1947	
nn - 36pgs; Walter Booth, Basil Reynolds, Stanley White art	£3.00
X-MEN	
Boxtree; Jun 1994-present	
Wolverine (Jun 1994) Chris Claremont & Frank Miller reprints	£7.00
X-Men & Ghost Rider: Brood Trouble in the Big Easy (Jun 1994)	£5.25
God Loves, Man Kills (Dec 1994) Chris Claremont & Brent Anderson reprints	£6.00
Gambit (Aug 1995) Howard Mackie, Lee Weeks, Klaus Janson reprints	£8.00
The Adventures of Cyclops and Phoenix (Dec 1995) Scott Lobdell & Gene Ha	£9.00
X-MEN COLLECTOR'S EDITION	
Grandreams; 1981-1982	
1981 red cover; Uncanny X-Men #56, 58, Neal Adams art; colour	£3.50
1982 yellow cover; reprints Uncanny X-Men #61-63, Neal Adams art; colour	£3.00
X-MEN POCKET BOOK	
(previously Star Heroes Pocket Book)	
Marvel; 14 Jun 1981-28 Aug 1982	
14-19, 21-28 52pgs, small size; X-Men reprints	£0.50
20 100pgs; double size Xmas number	£1.00
X-MEN, THE ORIGINAL	
Marvel; 1 27th Apr 1983-17 23rd May 1983	
1 reprints begin from X-Men #1; colour	£2.00
1 with free gift (red/yellow or red/blue plastic gun)	£4.00
2-3	£1.25
2-3 with free gift (X-Men stickers)	£3.00
4-17	£1.00
X-MEN WINTER SPECIAL	
Marvel; Oct 1981-Nov 1982	
1981-1982 52pgs; reprints	£1.25
XPRESSO SPECIAL, THE	
Fleetway; 1 May 1991-2 1991	
1 68pgs; European reprints by Prado, Nabara, Mattotti; Phillips art	£2.00
2 new & reprint material by Prado, Bolton, Bolland, Darrow, Crumb, Bernet, Talbot	£2.25

Y

	N.MINT
YOUNG BRIDES	
Arnold Book Co.; 1-10 1952	
1-10 68pgs; Prize Publications reprints	£3.00
YOUNG BRIDES	
Strato; 1 1953-38 1955	
1 68pgs; Prize Publications reprints	£2.00
2-38	£1.50
YOUNG DEATH	
Mandarin (2000AD Books); nn Sep 1992	
nn - Judge Dredd Megazine reprints, Peter Doherty art	£7.00
YOUNG EAGLE	
Arnold Book Co./ Miller; (1) 1 1951-5 1952; (2) 50 1955-58 1956	
1-5 (Arnold) 24pgs; Fawcett reprints	£5.00
50-58 (Miller) 28pgs	£3.00
YOUNG KING COLE	
(see Blue Bolt series)	
YOUNG KING COLE DETECTIVE TALES	
Miller; 1-2 1959	
1-2 Star Publications reprints	£4.00
YOUNG LOVE	
Arnold Book Co.; 1-10 1952	

	N.MINT
1-10 68pgs; Prize Publications reprints	£4.00
YOUNG LOVE	
Strato; 1 1953-34 1955	
1-34 68pgs; Prize Publications reprints	£4.00
YOUNG LOVERS	
Famepress; 1 1960-136 1966	
1 68pgs pocket size; Italian reprints	£1.00
2-136	£0.50
YOUNG LOVERS' LIBRARY	
C.A. Pearson; 1 1958-?	
1 68pgs pocket size	£1.25
2-?	£0.75
YOUNG MARVELMAN	
Miller; 25 3rd Feb 1954-370 Feb 1963 (346 issues)	
25 Young Marvelman by George Parlett begins	£12.50
26, 28-36, 38-50	£5.00
27 1st James Bleach Y. Marvelman	£5.00
37 1st Marvelman/Y. Marvelman team-up	£5.00
51-100	£3.50
101-335	£2.75
336-370 monthly issues, mostly reprints	£2.50
YOUNG MARVELMAN ANNUAL	
(see Marvelman Jr. Annual)	
Miller: 1954-1961	
1954 scarce, softcover, (Y.Marvelman shaking hands with alien)	£40.00
1955 scarce, softcover, (Y.Marvelman and Dagger)	£35.00
1956 hardcover, slightly smaller format begins	£25.00
1957-1960	£15.00
1961 card cover, becomes "Young Marvelman Adventures"; Young Marvelman appears with Cap. Marvel Jr.'s cape	£12.50
YOUNG ROMANCE	
Strato; 1 1953-33 1955	
1 68pgs; Prize Publications reprints	£2.00
2-33	£1.25
YOUR FAVOURITE FUNNIES	
Valentine & Sons; nn 1948	
nn - 16pgs; Sam Fair, Alf Farningham art	£3.00

Z

	N.MINT
Z-CARS ANNUAL	
World Distributors; 1963-1966	
1963 stories/features by Ian Kennedy Martin based on TV series	£5.00
1964-1966 mostly stories by Ian Kennedy Martin	£4.00
ZANE GREY'S KING OF THE ROYAL MOUNTED	
(see King of the Royal Mounted)	
ZANE GREY'S STORIES OF THE WEST	
World Distributors; 1 1953-31 1955	
1 36pgs; Dell reprints	£5.00
2-31	£3.00
ZAZA THE MYSTIC	
Miller; 1 1956-?	
1 28pgs; Charlton reprints	£5.00
2-?	£3.00
ZENITH	
Titan (Best of 2000AD); Apr 1988-Aug 1990	
Book One	£5.00
Book Two	£5.00
Book Three	£5.00
Book Four	£5.95
Book Five	£5.50
ZIP	
Odhams; 4th Jan 1958-3rd Oct 1959 (85 unnumbered issues; joins Swift)	
No. 1 - 4 Jan 1958 Strongbow the Mighty by Ron Embleton, Wells Fargo by Don Lawrence begin	£10.00
No. 1 with free gift (Thunderclap Banger)	£20.00
11 Jan 1958	£5.00
18 Jan 1958-8 Mar 1958	£2.50
15 Mar 1958 1st Gerry Embleton Strongbow	£2.50
22 Mar-1 Nov 1958	£2.00
8 Nov 1958 last Strongbow	£2.00
15 Nov 1958 Nigel Tawney by Redvers Blake, Captain Morgan by Colin Andrew begin	£1.50
22 Nov 1958-27 Jun 1959, 22 Aug-3 Oct 1959	£1.50
Note: no issues were published dated 4 Jul-15 Aug 1959	
ZIP-BANG COMIC	
W. Forshaw/ Ensign Publishing Co.; 1 1946-2 1947	
1 8pgs; W. Forshaw art	£3.00
2 W. Forshaw, Charles Ross art	£3.00
ZIP COMIC	
W. Forshaw; nn 1946	
nn - W. Forshaw art	£3.00
ZIP COMIC	
P.M. Productions; nn 1948	
nn - 16pgs; Colin Merritt, Alan Philpott, Frank Minnitt art	£4.00
ZIP COMICS	
H. Bunch (Cozmic); 1 May 1973	
1 Dave Gibbons art	£2.00
ZIPPER-RIPPER COMIC	
(see Zippy Comics)	
Funnibook Co.; nn 1946	
nn - 8pgs	£2.50

Advertisers Index
& Advertisements

ADVERTISERS INDEX

As a free service to all our advertisers, below is a list of shops and publishers, publications and services. As a collector it is important to shop around and compare so don't be afraid of trying new retailers or services to the ones you are already using.
And you might try the American advertisers who often have a different range of comics.

A2
ACME TOO
36 Chapel Market,
Islington,
London N1
(0171) 278 5444

A6
ADVENTURELAND INC
309 Railton Road,
Herne Hill,
London SE24 0JN
Phone/fax: (0171) 346 0020

ADVENTURES INTO COMICS
(See Adventureland)

A5
ALTERED IMAGES
3 Eagle Star House,
299-301 High Street,
Sutton,
Surrey SM1 1LG
(0181) 770 3815
Fax: (01372) 720753

A20
ARCHIVE COLLECTIONS
328 High Street,
Orpington,
Kent BR6 0NQ
(01689) 824489

A14
AVALON COMICS & COLLECTIBLES
P.O. Box 821
Medford MA 02155
USA
(617) 391 5614

A3
AVALON COMICS & ENTERTAINMENT
143 Lavender Hill,
Battersea,
London SW11 5QJ
(0171) 924 3609
Fax: (0171) 801 9152

A21
BLUE SILVER
32 Northfield Avenue,
London W13 9RL
(0181) 840 9446

A7
BOOK & COMIC EXCHANGE
14 Pembridge Road,
London W11
(0171) 229 8420

A18
CALAMITY COMICS
160 Station Road,
Harrow,
Middlesex HA1 2RH
(0181) 427 3831

90 Queen's Road,
The Broadway,
Watford,
Herts WD1 2LA
(01923) 249293

A25
CASSON BECKMAN
Hobson House,
155 Gower Street,
London WC1E 6BJ
(0171) 387 2888
Fax: (0171) 388 0600

A25
PURPLE HAZE
38 Eastlake Walk,
Drake Circus Shopping Centre,
Plymouth,
Devon PL1 1BX
(01752) 254136

A20
SHEFFIELD SPACE CENTRE
33 The Wicker,
Sheffield S3 8HS
(01742) 758905

A30 &
INSIDE BACK COVER
SILVER ACRE COMICS
(Mail Order only)
The Studio Cottage,
Edern,
Pwllheli,
Gwynedd LL53 6JD
Phone/fax: (01758) 720532.
Phone before faxing.

A20
THEY WALK AMONG US
32 Union Court,
Sheen Road,
Richmond,
Surrey TW9 1AA
Phone/fax: (0181) 948 8476

COLOUR SECTION
TITAN BOOKS
42-44 Dolben Street
London SE1 0UP
Enquiries:
(0171) 620 0200
Fax: (0171) 620 0032

Trade Orders UK (Diamond):
(0171) 538 8300
Fax: (0171) 987 6744

Mail Order UK:
(01536) 763 631
Fax: (01536) 760 306

A22
TROPIC COMICS
313 S. State Road 7,
Florida FL 33317
USA
(001) 954 587 8878
Fax: (001) 954 587 0409

A21
VAULT COMICS
PO Box 257,
South Norwood,
London SE25 6JN
Tel/fax: (0181) 771 8278

A1
WHATEVER COMICS
2 Burgate Lane,
Canterbury ,
Kent CT1 2HH
(01227) 453226

5 Middle Row,
High Street,
Maidstone,
Kent ME14 1TF
(01622) 681041

A23
WONDERWORLD
143 Gloucester Road,
Bishopston,
Bristol BS7 8BA
(0117) 9244655

133 St. Mary Street,
Southampton SO14 1NX
(01703) 634658

(Mail Order only)
1 Landowne Crescent,
Bournemouth BH1 1RU
(01202) 293045

INSIDE FRONT COVER
WORLD'S FINEST COMICS
PO Box 340,
Castle Rock
WA 98611
USA
(001) 274 9163
Fax: (001) 274 2270

36 Chapel Market, Islington, N1
Telephone : 0171-278-5444
Administration : 0171-608-3333

(1 mile from the West End)
(2 minutes walk from Angel tube,
Northern Line)

Current Marvel, DC, Image, Dark Horse &
Other American Imports, British Comics,
2000AD, Manga, Books & Graphic
Novels, Role-Playing Games, Role-Playing
props and miniatures, Independent
comics, Anime Japanese Videos, Star
Trek/Star Wars/X-Files/Babylon 5 and
other videos, Models, Posters, Movie and
Comic Trading Cards, Game cards (Magic,
Kult etc.), T-Shirts, Posters, Badges,
Bags, Boards, Boxes and more back
issues than you can shake a stick at !

Open 7 days a week !

Regular writing, artwork and model painting
competitions, prize draws, special events
and guest signings !

Sign up for our computerised standing order service,
or use our comprehensive mail order service.

Mon-Thur	10.00 - 18.30
Fri-Sat	10.00 - 18.30
Sun	10.00 - 17.00

Move (müv) A change of house or place of sojourn. (1853)

Expand (ekspæ·nd) Spread out, unfold, open-out, develop (1560)

Altered Images (a-lterd i-magz). Offering a wide range of comics, film and TV books and magazines and graphic novels in a NEW shop (1996)

Altered Images
3 Eagle Star House
299-301 High Street
Sutton
Surrey SM1 1LG
Tel: 0181 770 3815
Fax: o1372 720753

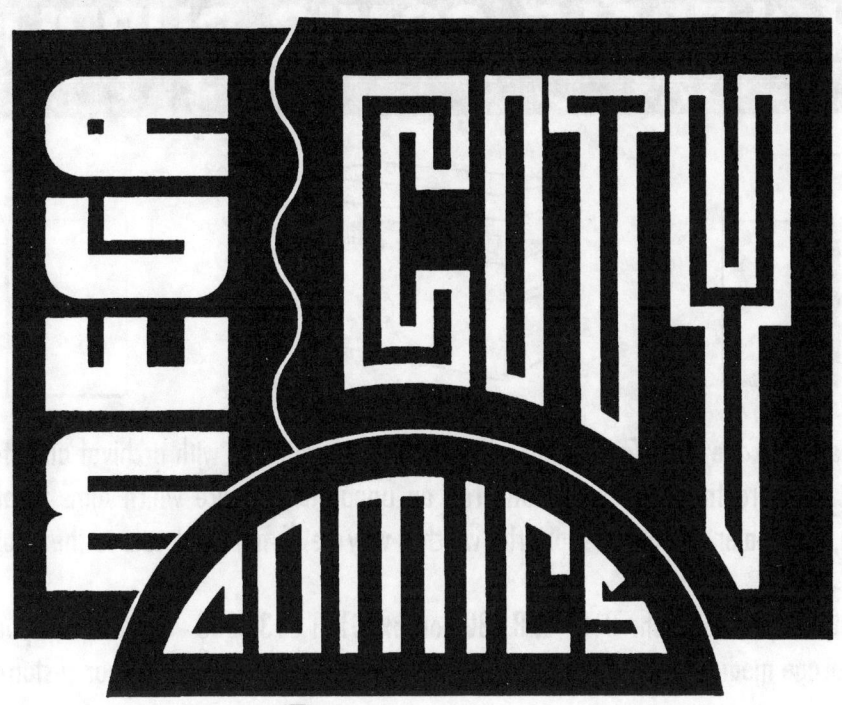

250 000 COMICS IN STOCK

NEW IMPORTS EVERY
WEEK - FAST

GRAPHIC NOVELS,
T-SHIRTS,
COMIC BAGS,
& BOXES

'LONDON'S BEST BACK
ISSUE SELECTION'
- EVENING STANDARD

SF, FANTASY & HORROR
PAPERBACKS

TRUE CRIME,
PARANORMAL,
BIZARRE & DEVIANT

RE:SEARCH,
AMOK, BETTY PAGE,
SKIN TWO

CULT FILM, FX,
EXPLOITATION MAGS

SHOP 'TILL YOU DROP AT EUROPE'S PREMIER COMIC SHOP
■ *FAST, EFFICIENT WORLDWIDE MAIL ORDER SERVICE* ■
■ *UK'S No.1 STANDING ORDER SERVICE SINCE 1982* ■

MEGA-CITY COMICS
18 INVERNESS STREET ■ CAMDEN TOWN ■ LONDON NW1 7HJ
OPEN 7 DAYS A WEEK ■ TEL: (0171) 485 9320

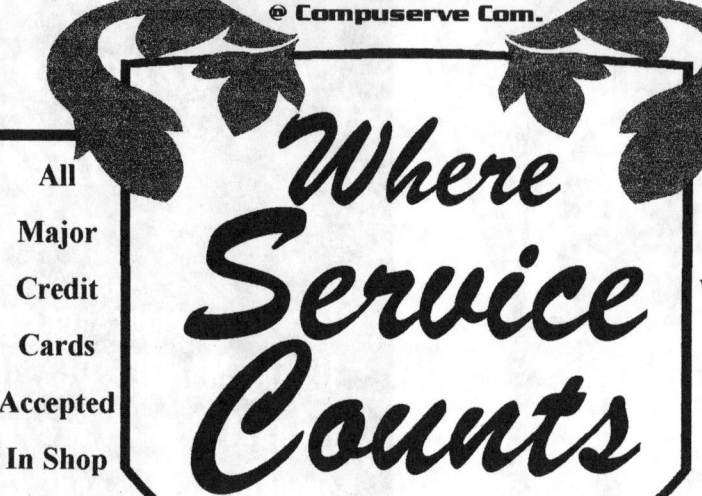

The best selection of American Comics anywhere in the U.K. And at the very best prices.

Mighty world of Comicana

DC Action Comics 5
Scarce
FN-- 32 (5.0) $7,000

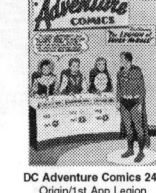
DC Adventure Comics 247
Origin/1st App Legion
VFN 55 (3.5) $4,000

DC All Star Comics 3
Origin/1st App J.S.A.
FN/VFN 50 (3.5) $25,000

DC All Winners Comics 1
Angel & Black Marvel App.
VFN 60 (4.5) $8,000

MVL Amazing Fantasy 15
Origin/1st App Spider-Man
VFN++ 68 (3.5) $20,000

FWCT America's Greatest 1
Mile High
NM+ 85 (2.0) $8,000

DC Batman 1
1st App Joker / Near Wht Pgs
VG/FN 30 (3.3) $22,000

DC Batman 3
3rd App Catwoman
VFN++ 68 (3.3) $11,000

DC Batman 5
1st App Batmobile
NM 80 (3.3) $8,000

FWCT Bulletman 3
Mile High / White Pages
NM/M 90 (3.0) $3,000

TIM Captain America 3
Murphy Anderson/Schomburg-C
FN+ 45 (5.5) $5,500

TIM Captain America 4
Murphy Anderson/Schomburg-C
FN+ 45 (5.5) $3,750

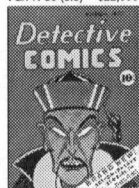
DC Detective Comics 1
(Scarce) / Fu-Manchu-C
M aFN 35 (5.0) $35,000

DC Detective Comics 33
Origin Batman
G/VG 15 (6.0) $4,950

DC Detective Comics 38
Origin/1st App Robin
L aVG/FN 25 (4.5) $6,750

MVL Fantastic Four 1
White Mountain Copy/White Pgs
NM+ 85 (3.0) $60,000

TIM Human Torch 2 (#1)
(#1) Intro/Origin Toro
VG+ 25 (5.0) $5,500

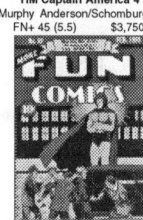
DC More Fun Comics 52
Mod. Restored by S.Ciccone
M aVFN 60 (4.0) $19,500

DC More Fun Comics 53
Origin Spectre Part 2
FN/VFN 50 (4.5) $19,500

DC More Fun Comics 101
Origin/1st App Superboy
VFN 60 (3.5) $10,500

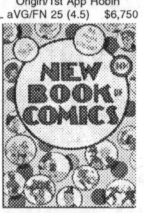
DC New Book Of Comics 2
Mile High / White Pages
NM 80 (2.0) $18,000

DC New York World's Fair 1940
Superman,Batman & Robin-C
VFN 60 (4.5) $9,000

FOX Phantom Lady 17
Ovst. Copy/Classic Bondage-C
VFN+ 65 (3.5) $5,750

DC Sensation Comics 2
Etta Candy Begins
VF/NM 70 (3.5) $5,500

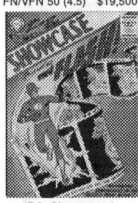
DC Showcase 4
Origin/1st App SA Flash
NM 80 (4.0) $40,000

DC Showcase 14
Mohawk Valley/4th App SA Flash
VFN 60 (5.5) $4,250

DC Superman 1
Moderate Restored
M aVG/FN 30 (6.5) $20,000

DC Superman 3
2nd Story-R From Action 5
VFN 55 (5.0) $6,000

CONT Suspense Comics 12
L.B. Cole Cover
FN+ 45 (4.5) $1,500

DC Woner Woman 17
Mile High / White Pages
M 94 (1.0) $2,750

PACIFIC COMIC EXCHANGE, INC.
WANTED!

SELLERS: The following comics and others are wanted by collectors trading on the Pacific Comic Exchange. Please contact The Exchange if you would like to *consign* these or other books at full market value. All books should be graded according to CGSA standards.

CGSA	M	NM/M	NM	VFN/NM	VFN	FN/VFN	FN	VG/FN	VG	G/VG	G	Fr	Pr
	100-91	90	88,85,80,75	70	65,60,55	50	45,40,35	30	25,20	15	10	6	3
0	1	2	2.5	3	3.3	4	5	6	6.5	7	7.5	8	8.5	9	9.5	10

Wanted immediately in all grades

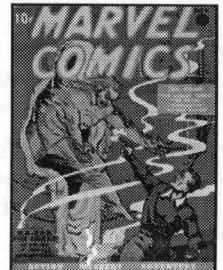

Action Comics 1   Detective Comics 27   Marvel Comics 1

	G 10	VG 20	FN 40	VFN 60	NM 80	NM/M 90
Action Comics 1	$25,000	$50,000	$80,000	$130,000	$260,000	$450,000
Detective Comics 27	$22,000	$45,000	$75,000	$115,000	$225,000	$375,000
Marvel Comics 1	$15,000	$25,000	$45,000	$65,000	$130,000	$260,000

Wanted Immediately in VFN 60 - NM/M 90

	VFN 60	NM 80	NM/M 90		VFN 60	NM 80	NM/M 90
Action Comics 1	$130,000	$260,000	$450,000	Green Lantern 1 (SA)	$1,800	$4,000	$7,500
Adventure Comics 40	$30,000	$60,000	$100,000	Green Lantern 1 (GA)	$15,000	$30,000	$60,000
Adventure Comics 210	$2,000	$5,000	$7,500	Incredible Hulk 1	$5,000	$12,000	$25,000
Adventure Comics 247	$2,500	$6,000	$10,000	Jimmy Olsen 1	$3,500	$10,000	$15,000
All Star Comics 3	$30,000	$60,000	$120,000	Journey Into Mystery 83	$2,500	$6,000	$12,000
All Star Comics 8	$25,000	$50,000	$75,000	Justice League 1	$2,000	$5,500	$10,000
All-American Comics 16	$50,000	$100,000	$175,000	Lois Lane 1	$2,000	$4,500	$8,500
Amazing Fantasy 15	---------	$25,000	$50,000	Marvel Comics 1	$65,000	$130,000	$260,000
Amazing Spider-Man 1	---------	$20,000	$35,000	More Fun Comics 52	$50,000	$100,000	$150,000
Batman 1	$40,000	$80,000	$130,000	More Fun Comics 55	$10,000	$20,000	$40,000
Batman 100	$1,200	$3,000	$6,000	Sensation Comics 1	$13,000	$25,000	$50,000
Captain America 1	$35,000	$70,000	$110,000	Showcase 4	$18,000	$35,000	$70,000
Detective Comics 1	$75,000	$150,000	$225,000	Showcase 22	$3,000	$8,000	$12,000
Detective Comics 27	$115,000	$225,000	$375,000	Sub-Mariner Comics 1	$12,000	$25,000	$50,000
Detective Comics 33	$25,000	$50,000	$100,000	Superman 1	$75,000	$125,000	$250,000
Detective Comics 38	$25,000	$50,000	$100,000	Superman 100	$1,500	$3,500	$6,000
Fantastic Four 1	---------	$20,000	$40,000	Suspense Comics 3	$7,000	$14,000	$21,000
Flash Comics 1	$40,000	$80,000	$140,000	Wonder Woman 1	$12,000	$30,000	$60,000
Flash Comics 104	$5,000	$10,000	$20,000	X-Men 1	---------	$6,000	$12,000

Pacific Comic Exchange, Inc.
See our World Wide Web page at *http://www.pcei.com/*

Corporate Office:
337 S. Robertson Blvd. Suite 203, Beverly Hills, CA 90211
Tel:{USA} 0101 (310) 836-7234 (PCEI)

Shipping Address:
P.O. Box 34849 Los Angeles, CA 90034
Fax: {USA} 0101 (310) 836-7127

BACK ISSUES!

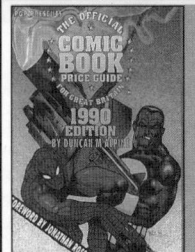

N⁰ 2 (1990)

Simon Bisley cover featuring Spiderman and the Punisher! Interior pin-ups by Ewins & Lloyd, Kitson and Ridgeway; first typeset Guide in the new familiar format. The days when Iron Man #55 was £4.00 and New Mutants #87 wasn't even out yet! £6.95
Special signed and hand-stamped edition £7.95

N⁰ 3 (1991)

Dave Gibbons cover featuring Judge Dredd and Dan Dare. New features include the famous First Appearance Index and Artist Gallery featuring Philips & Kane, Higgins & Hughes. £7.95
Special signed and hand-stamped edition £8.95
Signed and numbered Limited Edition. Only 250 of these were produced and some very low numbers (25-100) have been kept back for a first come, first served basis £9.95
Numbers #1–#10 also available . . . . please enquire

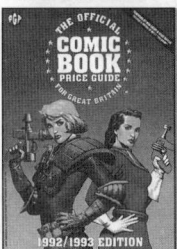

N⁰ 4 (1992)

Sean Philips cover featuring the "girlfriends" of Dredd and Dare— Judge Anderson and Dr. Jocelyn Peabody! Special colour section for the first time and many new features £8.95
Signed by author and cover artist £9.95
Special signed and hand-stamped edition £9.95
Signed and numbered Limited Edition. Only 50 of these were produced, signed by the author and cover artist £10.95
Numbers #1–#5 available. . . . . please enquire

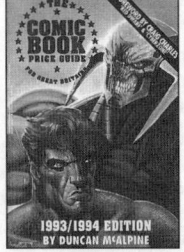

N⁰ 5 (1993)

Liam Sharpe cover featuring the unlikely team-up of Death's Head (a robot) and Magnus Robot Fighter £9.95
Signed by author and cover artist £10.95
Special signed and hand-stamped edition £10.95
Signed and numbered Limited Edition. Only 50 of these were produced, signed by the author and cover artist £11.95
Numbers #1–#5 available. . . . . please enquire

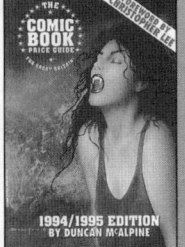

N⁰ 6 (1994)

John Bolton cover featuring a specially created character called "Liliana", one in a long line of vampiresses from the depths of the artist's imagination. £10.95
Signed by author and cover artist £11.95
Special signed and hand-stamped edition £11.95
Signed and numbered Limited Edition. Only 50 of these were produced, signed by the author and cover artist £12.95
Numbers #1–#5 available . . . . please enquire

FORBIDDEN PLANET

THE MIGHTIEST HEROES OF ANY UNIVERSE

MAIL ORDER SPECIALISTS
Send S.A.E for Advance Comics List

Forbidden Planet Mail Order,
71-75 New Oxford Street, London, WC1A 1DG Tel: 0171 497 2150

BRISTOL
30 Penn Street
01179 298692

CARDIFF
5 Duke Street
01222 228 885

CROYDON
175 North End
0181 688 7190

LONDON
71-75
New Oxford Street
0171 836 4179

EDINBURGH
3 Teviot Place
0131 225 8613

LIVERPOOL
92 Bold Street
0151 707 1491

NEWCASTLE
59 Grainger Street
0191 261 9173

CAMBRIDGE
60 Burleigh Street
01223 301666

COVENTRY
31 Cross Cheaping
01203 229672

DUBLIN
36 Dawson Street
01 671 0688

GLASGOW
168 Buchanan Street
0141 331 1215

LIMERICH
9/10 Patrick Street
061 411 488

NOTTINGHAM
129 Middle walk
01159 584 706

<u>Just</u> the <u>Facts</u>:

<u>Fact 1</u>: Absolutely no other comic dealer buys more Golden Age and Silver Age comics than we do.

Although the pages of Comic Buyers' Guide are filled with other dealers offering to pay "top dollar", **The Fact Is** that Metropolis spends more money on quality comic book collections, year in and year out, than any other dealer in the country. **The Fact Is** in 1995 we have spent over $2 million on collectibles. We have the funds and the expertise to back up our words. If you have books to sell, call us at: **00-1-212-260-4147**. If you know of any comic book or movie poster collections, call us today for a generous finder's fee. **All calls will be kept strictly confidential.**

<u>Fact 2</u>: Absolutely no other comic dealer sells more Golden and Silver Age books than we do.

We simply have the best stock of Golden and Silver Age comic books in the world. The thousands of collectors familiar with our strict grading standards and excellent service can attest to this. Chances are, if you want it, we have it.

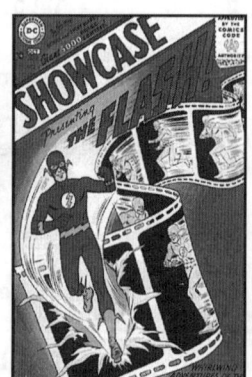

COLLECTIBLES

**873 Broadway
Suite 201
New York NY 10003
U.S.A.
Phone: 00-1-212-260-4147
Fax: 00-1-212-260-4304**

PRICE GUIDE PRODUCTIONS
Presents
TM & ©
HEROIC SOLUTIONS

SUPER METHOD TO CATALOGUE COMICS!

Heroic Solutions is the company that produced the database computer system for Price Guide Productions. Now in conjuntion with Price Guide Productions, we are able to bring the same tool to manage a personal comic collection. Also with the available guide add-ons, the system will be able to establish how much any collection of comics and any missing comics are actually worth.

FEATURES

- Complete inventory of titles listed in the current Price Guide.
- Comprehensive wants list system.
- Display Screens in similar formats to Price Guide.
- Hot Keys to enable fast access.
- Imports system for monitoring new comics purchased weekly.
- Database filters to display specific information (Eg. Sci-Fi titles).
- Various reports and the facility to export data to a text file.
- Customisable to tailor individual needs.
- Super VGA Mode for a full display of information.
- Windows 95, NT and 3x Versions available.
- Minimum requirements 386PC, 4MB RAM, 30MB Disk Space

INVENTORY COMPUTER PROGRAM

£24.95

ADD - ONS

Marvel Guide £9.95, DC Guide £9.95, INDIES Guide £9.95
Purchase all three guides and only pay for two!
PURCHASE THE INVENTORY PROGRAM AND ALL
THREE ADD-ONS FOR ONLY £39.95.

Please send a cheque or postal order (UK Currency only) made payable to Heroic Solutions. Clearly specify what combination of programs you require and which version. Postage for all UK orders is free (Foreign customers please add £5.00).	Send to: Heroic Solutions PO BOX 150 Enfield EN3 6HS ENGLAND

E-MAIL : 100414,3217 COMPUSERVE.COM